# International
# WHO'S WHO in

**2006**

# Classical
# MUSIC

# International WHO'S WHO in

# Classical
# MUSIC

## 2006

22nd Edition

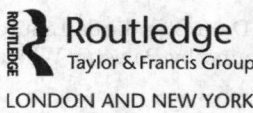

**Routledge**
Taylor & Francis Group

LONDON AND NEW YORK

First published 1935

ISBN-10: 1-85743-368-8
ISBN-13: 978-1-85743-368-5
ISSN: 1740-0155

**Series Editor:** Robert J. Elster
**Associate Editor:** Alison Neale
**Assistant Editor:** Huw Williams
**Freelance Editorial Team:** Annabella Gabb, Neil Higgins
**Online Producer:** Andreas Gosling
**Administrative Assistant:** Charley McCartney

Typeset by Data Standards Limited, Frome
Printed and bound by Polestar Wheatons, Exeter

# FOREWORD

The 22nd edition of the INTERNATIONAL WHO'S WHO IN CLASSICAL MUSIC provides biographical information on over 8,000 prominent people in the fields of classical and light classical music, including composers, instrumentalists, conductors, singers, arrangers, writers and managers. The biographies include information on career, education, repertoire, compositions, recordings, publications and, where available, personal and contact details.

For each edition, entrants are given the opportunity to make necessary amendments and additions to their biographies. Supplementary research is done by the editorial department in order to ensure that the book is as up to date as possible on publication.

In addition to the biographical information, the directory section provides appendices of orchestras, opera companies, festivals, music organizations, major competitions and awards, music libraries and music conservatoires. The introduction contains a list of abbreviations and international telephone codes. The names of entrants whose death has been reported over the past year are included in the obituary.

Readers are referred to the book's companion title in The Europa Biographical Reference Series, the INTERNATIONAL WHO'S WHO IN POPULAR MUSIC, for a comprehensive collection of information on the most famous and influential people in the popular music industry.

The assistance of the individuals and organizations included in this publication in providing up-to-date material is invaluable, and the editors would like to take this opportunity to express their appreciation.

March 2006

# ALPHABETIZATION KEY

The list of names is alphabetical, with the entrants listed under surnames. If part of an entrant's surname is in parentheses, indicating that this name is not usually used, this will be ignored for the purposes of the alphabetical listing.

If an entrant's name is spelt in a variety of ways, a cross reference is provided. An entrant who is known by a pseudonym or by an abbreviation of their name is either listed under this name or a cross reference is provided. Multiple pseudonyms are cross referenced where considered necessary.

All names beginning Mc or Mac are treated as Mac, e.g. McDevitt before MacDonald.

Names with Arabic prefixes are normally listed after the prefix, except when requested otherwise by the entrant.

In the case of surnames beginning with De, Des, Du, van or von the entries are normally found under the prefix.

Names beginning St are listed as if they began Saint, e.g. St Germain before Salamun.

# CONTENTS

# ABBREVIATIONS

| | | | |
|---|---|---|---|
| AA | Associate in Arts | BSE | Bachelor of Science in Engineering (USA) |
| AB | Alberta; Bachelor of Arts | BSFA | British Science Fiction Association |
| ABC | Australian Broadcasting Corporation; Australian | BTh | Bachelor of Theology |
| | Broadcasting Commission | BTI | British Theatre Institute |
| AC | Companion of the Order of Australia | | |
| ACA | American Composers' Alliance | c. | circa; child, children |
| Acad. | Academy | CA | California |
| ACLS | American Council of Learned Societies | CAMI | Columbia Artists Management International |
| ACT | Australian Capital Territory | CBC | Canadian Broadcasting Corporation |
| Admin. | Administrator, Administrative | CBE | Commander of (the Order of) the British Empire |
| AFofM | American Federation of Musicians | CBS | Columbia Broadcasting System |
| AFTRA | American Federation of Television and Radio Artists | CBSO | City of Birmingham Symphony Orchestra |
| AG | Aktiengesellschaft (Joint Stock Company) | CCMA | Canadian Country Music Association |
| AGMA | American Guild of Musical Artists | CD | compact disc |
| AIDS | acquired immunodeficiency syndrome | CD-ROM | compact disc read-only memory |
| AK | Alaska | CEO | Chief Executive Officer |
| aka | also known as | Chair. | Chairman, Chairwoman, Chairperson |
| AL | Alabama | Cia | Companhia |
| ALCS | Authors' Lending and Copyright Society | Cía | Compañía |
| AM | Member of the Order of Australia; Master of Arts; amplitude | Cie | Compagnie |
| | modulation | circ. | circulation |
| AO | Officer of the Order of Australia | CMA | Country Music Association |
| Apdo | Apartado (Post Box) | CMG | Companion of (the Order of) St Michael and St George |
| approx. | approximately | CNRS | Centre National de la Recherche Scientifique |
| APRA | Australian Performing Rights Association | c/o | care of |
| Apt | Apartment | Co. | Company; County |
| apto | apartamento | CO | Colorado; Chamber Orchestra |
| A & R | Artists and Repertoire | Col. | Colonia, Colima (hill) |
| AR | Arkansas | Coll. | College |
| ARCA | Associate of the Royal College of Art | Comm. | Commission |
| ARCM | Associate of the Royal College of Music | Commdr | Commandeur |
| ARCO | Associate of the Royal College of Organists | COO | Chief Operating Officer |
| ARCS | Associate of the Royal College of Science | Corpn | Corporation |
| ASCAP | American Society of Composers, Authors and Publishers | CP | Case Postale; Caixa Postal; Casella Postale (Post Box) |
| Asscn | Association | Cres. | Crescent |
| Assoc. | Associate | CRNCM | Companion, Royal Northern College of Music |
| Asst | Assistant | Ct | Court |
| ATD | Art Teacher's Diploma | CT | Connecticut |
| Aug. | August | Cttee | Committee |
| autobiog. | autobiography | CUNY | City University of New York |
| Avda | Avenida (Avenue) | CVO | Commander of the Royal Victorian Order |
| AZ | Arizona | CWA | (British) Crime Writers' Association |
| | | | |
| b. | born | d. | daughter(s) |
| BA | Bachelor of Arts | DBE | Dame Commander of (the Order of) the British Empire |
| BAC&S | British Academy of Composers and Songwriters | DC | District of Columbia; Distrito Central |
| BAFTA | British Academy of Film and Television Arts | DD | Doctor of Divinity |
| BArch | Bachelor of Architecture | Dd'ES | Diplôme d'études supérieures |
| BASCA | British Association of Songwriters, Composers and Authors | DE | Delaware |
| | (now BAC&S) | Dec. | December |
| BBC | British Broadcasting Corporation | DEd | Doctor of Education |
| BC | British Columbia | Dept | Department |
| BCL | Bachelor of Civil Law | D. ès L. | Docteur ès Lettres |
| BD | Bachelor of Divinity | D. ès Sc. | Docteur ès Sciences |
| Bd | Board | devt | development |
| Bdwy | Broadway | DF | Distrito Federal |
| BE | Bachelor of Engineering; Bachelor of Education | DFA | Doctor of Fine Arts; Diploma of Fine Arts |
| BEd | Bachelor of Education | DHL | Doctor of Hebrew Literature |
| BEng | Bachelor of Engineering | DipEd | Diploma in Education |
| BFA | Bachelor in Fine Arts | DipTh | Diploma in Theology |
| BFI | British Film Institute | Dir | Director |
| biog. | biography | DJ | disc jockey |
| BJ | Bachelor of Journalism | DJur | Doctor of Law |
| Bldg | Building | DLitt | Doctor of Letters |
| BLitt | Bachelor of Letters | DM | Doctor of Music |
| BLS | Bachelor in Library Science | DMA | Doctor of Musical Arts |
| Blvd | Boulevard | DME | Doctor of Musical Education |
| BM | Bachelor of Music; Bachelor of Medicine | DMEd | Doctor of Musical Education |
| BME | Bachelor of Music Education | DMus | Doctor of Music |
| BMEd | Bachelor of Music Education | DMusEd | Doctor of Music Education |
| BMI | Broadcast Music Inc | DN | Distrito Nacional |
| BMus | Bachelor of Music | DPhil | Doctor of Philosophy |
| BP | Boîte postale (Post Box) | dpto | departamento |
| BPhil | Bachelor of Philosophy | Dr(a) | Doctor(a) |
| bros | brothers | DSc | Doctor of Science |
| BS | Bachelor of Science; Bachelor of Surgery | DSocSci | Doctor of Social Science |
| BSc | Bachelor of Science | DTh | Doctor of Theology |

# ABBREVIATIONS

| | | | | |
|---|---|---|---|---|
| DVD | digital versatile disc | | km | kilometre(s) |
| | | | KS | Kansas |
| E | East(ern) | | KY | Kentucky |
| EC | European Community | | | |
| Ed. | Editor | | LA | Louisiana |
| Edif. | Edificio (Building) | | LAMDA | London Academy of Music and Dramatic Art |
| edn | edition | | LCM | London College of Music |
| e.g. | exempli gratia (for example) | | LEA | Local Education Authority |
| EMI | Electrical and Musical Industries | | L. ès L. | Licencié ès Lettres |
| ENO | English National Opera | | L. ès Sc. | Licencié ès Sciences |
| EP | extended-play (record) | | LHD | Doctor of Humane Letters |
| esq. | esquina (corner) | | Lic. en Let. | Licenciado en Letras |
| etc. | et cetera | | LLB | Bachelor of Laws |
| EU | European Union | | LLD | Doctor of Laws |
| eV | eingetragener Verein | | LL.L | Licentiate of Laws |
| Exec. | Executive | | LLM | Master of Laws |
| | | | LP | long-playing (record) |
| f. | founded | | LPO | London Philharmonic Orchestra |
| Feb. | February | | LRCP | Licenciate, Royal College of Physicians, London |
| FGCM | Fellow of the Guild of Church Musicians | | LRSM | Licenciate, Royal Schools of Music |
| FGSM | Fellow of the Guildhall School of Music and Drama | | LSE | London School of Economics and Political Science |
| FL | Florida | | LSO | London Symphony Orchestra |
| FLS | Fellow of the Linnaean Society | | Lt | Lieutenant |
| FM | frequency modulation | | LTCL | Licenciate of Trinity College of Music, London |
| FMA | Florida Music Association | | Ltd | Limited |
| fmr(ly) | former(ly) | | LW | long wave |
| FRAM | Fellow of the Royal Academy of Music | | LWT | London Weekend Television |
| FRCM | Fellow of the Royal College of Music | | | |
| FRCO | Fellow of the Royal College of Organists | | m. | married |
| FRGS | Fellow of the Royal Geographical Society | | MA | Massachusetts; Master of Arts |
| FRHistS | Fellow of the Royal Historical Society | | Man. | Manager; Managing |
| FRS | Fellow of the Royal Society | | MAT | Master of Arts and Teaching |
| FRSA | Fellow of the Royal Society of Arts | | MB | Manitoba |
| FRSL | Fellow of the Royal Society of Literature | | MBA | Master of Business Administration |
| | | | MBE | Member of (the Order of) the British Empire |
| GA | Georgia | | MC | master of ceremonies |
| Gen. | General | | MD | Maryland; Music Director |
| GmbH | Gesellschaft mit beschränkter Haftung (Limited Liability Company) | | MDiv | Master in Divinity |
| | | | ME | Maine |
| GMT | Greenwich Mean Time | | MEd | Master in Education |
| Gov. | Governor | | mem. | member |
| GP | General Practitioner | | MEngSc | Master of Engineering |
| GPO | General Post Office | | Met | Metropolitan Opera House, New York |
| GRSM | Graduate of the Royal School of Music | | MFA | Master of Fine Arts |
| GSMD | Guildhall School of Music and Drama, London (formerly GSM) | | MHRA | Modern Humanities Research Association |
| | | | MHz | megahertz (megacycles) |
| | | | MI | Michigan |
| hc | honoris causa | | MIDI | Musical Instrument Digital Interface |
| HHD | Doctor of Humanities | | mil. | military |
| HI | Hawaii | | MIT | Massachusetts Institute of Technology |
| HIV | human immunodeficiency virus | | MLA | Modern Language Association |
| HM | His (or Her) Majesty | | MLitt | Master of Letters; Master of Literature |
| HMV | His Master's Voice | | MLS | Master in Library Science |
| Hon. | Honorary; Honourable | | MM | Master of Music |
| Hons | Honours | | MME | Master of Music Education |
| HRH | His (or Her) Royal Highness | | MMEd | Master of Music Education |
| HS | Heraldry Society | | MMus | Master of Music |
| | | | MN | Minnesota |
| IA | Iowa | | MO | Missouri |
| IBA | Independent Broadcasting Authority | | MOBO | Music of Black Origin |
| ID | Idaho | | MP | Member of Parliament |
| i.e. | id est (that is to say) | | MPh | Master of Philosophy (USA) |
| IL | Illinois | | MPhil | Master of Philosophy |
| IMC | International Music Council | | MRCS | Member, Royal College of Surgeons of England |
| IMMIE | Indian Music Excellence (award) | | MS | Mississippi; Master of Science; manuscript |
| IN | Indiana | | MSA | Memphis Songwriters' Association |
| Inc. | Incorporated | | MSc | Master of Science |
| incl. | including | | MSO | Melbourne Symphony Orchestra |
| Inst. | Institute | | MT | Montana |
| int. | international | | Mt | Mount |
| IPC | Institute of Professional Critics | | MTh | Master of Theology |
| IRCAM | Institut de Recherche et Coordination Acoustique/Musique | | MTV | Music Television |
| ISCM | International Society for Contemporary Music | | MusB | Bachelor of Music |
| ISM | Incorporated Society of Musicians | | MusD | Doctor of Music |
| ITA | Independent Television Authority | | MusDoc | Doctor of Music |
| ITN | Independent Television News | | MusM | Master of Music |
| ITV | Independent Television | | MVO | Member of the Royal Victorian Order |
| | | | MW | medium wave |
| Jan. | January | | MWA | Mystery Writers of America |
| JD | Doctor of Jurisprudence | | | |
| JP | Justice of the Peace | | N | North(ern) |
| Jr | Junior | | NABOB | National Association of Black Owned Broadcasters |
| jt | joint | | NARAS | National Academy of Recording Arts and Sciences |
| | | | NAS | National Academy of Songwriters |
| KBE | Knight Commander, Order of the British Empire | | nat. | national |
| KCVO | Knight Commander of the Royal Victorian Order | | NB | New Brunswick |

# ABBREVIATIONS

| | | | |
|---|---|---|---|
| NBC | National Broadcasting Company | Rep. | Republic |
| NC | North Carolina | retd | retired |
| ND | North Dakota | rev. edn | revised edition |
| NDD | National Diploma in Design | RFH | Royal Festival Hall, London |
| NE | Nebraska; North-east(ern) | RGS | Royal Geographical Society |
| NEA | National Endowment for the Arts | RI | Rhode Island |
| NEH | National Endowment for the Humanities | RIAS | Radio im Amerikanischen Sektor |
| NF | Newfoundland | RLPO | Royal Liverpool Philharmonic Orchestra |
| NFSPS | National Federation of State Poetry Societies | RMA | Royal Musical Association |
| NH | New Hampshire | RMCM | Royal Manchester College of Music |
| NHK | Nippon Hoso Kyokai (Japanese broadcasting system) | RNCM | Royal Northern College of Music, Manchester |
| NJ | New Jersey | RNLI | Royal National Life-boat Institution |
| NL | Newfoundland and Labrador | RO | Radio Orchestra |
| NM | New Mexico | ROC | Rock Out Censorship |
| NME | New Musical Express | ROH | Royal Opera House, Covent Garden |
| no. | number | rpm | revolutions per minute |
| Nov. | November | RPO | Royal Philharmonic Orchestra |
| nr | near | RSA | Royal Society of Arts |
| NRK | Norsk Rikskringkasting (Norwegian broadcasting system) | RSAMD | Royal Scottish Academy of Music and Drama |
| NS | Nova Scotia | RSC | Royal Shakespeare Company |
| NSAI | Nashville Songwriters' Association International | RSL | Royal Society of Literature |
| NSW | New South Wales | RSNO | Royal Scottish National Orchestra (formerly SNO) |
| NT | Northwest Territories; Northern Territory | RSO | Radio Symphony Orchestra |
| NU | Nunavut Territory | RSPB | Royal Society for Protection of Birds |
| NUJ | National Union of Journalists | RTÉ | Radio Telefís Éireann |
| NV | Nevada | RTF | Radiodiffusion-Télévision Française |
| NW | North-west(ern) | RTS | Royal Television Society |
| NY | New York (State) | | |
| NYPO | New York Philharmonic Orchestra | S | South(ern); San |
| NYSO | New York Symphony Orchestra | s. | son(s) |
| NZSA | New Zealand Society of Authors | SA | Société Anonyme, Sociedad Anónima (Limited Company); South Australia |
| OBE | Officer of (the Order of) the British Empire | SACEM | Société d'Auteurs, Compositeurs et Editeurs de Musique |
| Oct. | October | SAG | Screen Actors' Guild |
| Of. | Oficina (Office) | SC | South Carolina |
| OH | Ohio | SD | South Dakota |
| OK | Oklahoma | SE | South-east(ern) |
| ON | Ontario | Sec. | Secretary |
| ONZ | Order of New Zealand | Sept. | September |
| ONZM | Officer, New Zealand Order of Merit | SFWA | Science Fiction and Fantasy Writers of America |
| OR | Oregon | SGA | Songwriters' Guild of America |
| org. | organization | SK | Saskatchewan |
| ORTF | Office de Radiodiffusion-Télévision Française | SL | Sociedad Limitada |
| OST | original soundtrack | SO | Symphony Orchestra |
| OUP | Oxford University Press | SOAS | School of Oriental and African Studies |
| | | SOCAN | Society of Composers, Authors and Music Publishers of Canada |
| p. | page | SOSA | State Opera of South Australia |
| PA | Pennsylvania | SPNM | Society for the Promotion of New Music |
| PBS | Public Broadcasting Service | Sr | Senior |
| PE | Prince Edward Island | St | Saint |
| PEN | Poets, Playwrights, Essayists, Editors and Novelists (Club) | Sta | Santa |
| PETA | People for the Ethical Treatment of Animals | STB | Bachelor of Sacred Theology |
| PF | Postfach (Post Box) | STD | Doctor of Sacred Theology |
| PGCE | Post Graduate Certificate of Education | Ste | Sainte |
| PhB | Bachelor of Philosophy | STL | Reader or Professor of Sacred Theology |
| PhD | Doctor of Philosophy | STM | Master of Sacred Theology |
| PhL | Licenciate of Philosophy | str | strasse |
| Pl. | Place | SUNY | State University of New York |
| PLC | Public Limited Company | SVSA | South West Virginia Songwriters' Association |
| PMB | Private Mail Bag | SW | South-west(ern); short wave |
| pnr | partner | | |
| PO | Philharmonic Orchestra | | |
| PO Box | Post Office Box | TCL | Trinity College of Music, London |
| Pres. | President | TLS | Times Literary Supplement |
| PR(O) | Public Relations (Officer) | TN | Tennessee |
| Prod. | Producer | trans. | translated; translation; translator |
| Prof. | Professor | Treas. | Treasurer |
| promo | promotional | TV | television |
| PRS | Performing Right Society | TX | Texas |
| pt. | part | | |
| Pty | Proprietary | u. | utca (street) |
| Publ.(s) | Publication(s) | UCLA | University of California at Los Angeles |
| | | UHF | ultra-high frequency |
| QC | Québec | UK | United Kingdom (of Great Britain and Northern Ireland) |
| QEH | Queen Elizabeth Hall, London | ul. | ulitsa (street) |
| Qld | Queensland | UN | United Nations |
| QSO | Queen's Service Order; Queensland Symphony Orchestra | UNESCO | United Nations Educational, Scientific and Cultural Organization |
| q.v. | quod vide (to which refer) | UNICEF | United Nations Children's Fund |
| RADA | Royal Academy of Dramatic Art | Univ. | University |
| RAH | Royal Albert Hall, London | Urb. | Urbanización (urban district) |
| RAI | Radio Audizioni Italiane | US(A) | United States (of America) |
| RAM | Royal Academy of Music | USSR | Union of Soviet Socialist Republics |
| R&B | Rhythm and Blues | UT | Utah |
| RCM | Royal College of Music | | |
| RCO | Royal College of Organists | VA | Virginia |

# ABBREVIATIONS

| | | | |
|---|---|---|---|
| VC | Victoria Cross | WA | Western Australia; Washington (State) |
| VHF | very high frequency | WCMD | Welsh College of Music and Drama, Cardiff |
| VI | (US) Virgin Islands | WI | Wisconsin |
| Vic. | Victoria | WNO | Welsh National Opera |
| Vol.(s) | Volume(s) | WV | West Virginia |
| VSO | Victoria State Opera | WY | Wyoming |
| VT | Vermont | | |
| | | | |
| W | West(ern) | YT | Yukon Territory |

# INTERNATIONAL TELEPHONE CODES

To make international calls to telephone and fax numbers listed in the book, dial the international code of the country from which you are calling, followed by the appropriate code for the country you wish to call (listed below), followed by the area code (if applicable) and telephone or fax number listed in the entry.

| | Country code | + or − GMT* |
|---|---|---|
| Afghanistan | 93 | +4½ |
| Albania | 355 | +1 |
| Algeria | 213 | +1 |
| Andorra | 376 | +1 |
| Angola | 244 | +1 |
| Antigua and Barbuda | 1 268 | −4 |
| Argentina | 54 | −3 |
| Armenia | 374 | +4 |
| Australia | 61 | +8 to +10 |
| Australian External Territories: | | |
|     Australian Antarctic Territory | 672 | +3 to +10 |
|     Christmas Island | 61 | +7 |
|     Cocos (Keeling) Islands | 61 | +6½ |
|     Norfolk Island | 672 | +11½ |
| Austria | 43 | +1 |
| Azerbaijan | 994 | +5 |
| The Bahamas | 1 242 | −5 |
| Bahrain | 973 | +3 |
| Bangladesh | 880 | +6 |
| Barbados | 1 246 | −4 |
| Belarus | 375 | +2 |
| Belgium | 32 | +1 |
| Belize | 501 | −6 |
| Benin | 229 | +1 |
| Bhutan | 975 | +6 |
| Bolivia | 591 | −4 |
| Bosnia and Herzegovina | 387 | +1 |
| Botswana | 267 | +2 |
| Brazil | 55 | −3 to −4 |
| Brunei | 673 | +8 |
| Bulgaria | 359 | +2 |
| Burkina Faso | 226 | 0 |
| Burundi | 257 | +2 |
| Cambodia | 855 | +7 |
| Cameroon | 237 | +1 |
| Canada | 1 | −3 to −8 |
| Cape Verde | 238 | −1 |
| The Central African Republic | 236 | +1 |
| Chad | 235 | +1 |
| Chile | 56 | −4 |
| China, People's Republic | 86 | +8 |
| Special Administrative Regions: | | |
|     Hong Kong | 852 | +8 |
|     Macao | 853 | +8 |
| China (Taiwan) | 886 | +8 |
| Colombia | 57 | −5 |
| The Comoros | 269 | +3 |
| Congo, Democratic Republic | 243 | +1 |
| Congo, Republic | 242 | +1 |
| Costa Rica | 506 | −6 |
| Côte d'Ivoire | 225 | 0 |
| Croatia | 385 | +1 |
| Cuba | 53 | −5 |
| Cyprus | 357 | +2 |
| 'Turkish Republic of Northern Cyprus' | 90 392 | +2 |
| Czech Republic | 420 | +1 |
| Denmark | 45 | +1 |
| Danish External Territories: | | |
|     Faroe Islands | 298 | 0 |
|     Greenland | 299 | −1 to −4 |
| Djibouti | 253 | +3 |
| Dominica | 1 767 | −4 |
| Dominican Republic | 1 809 | −4 |
| Ecuador | 593 | −5 |

| | Country code | + or − GMT* |
|---|---|---|
| Egypt | 20 | +2 |
| El Salvador | 503 | −6 |
| Equatorial Guinea | 240 | +1 |
| Eritrea | 291 | +3 |
| Estonia | 372 | +2 |
| Ethiopia | 251 | +3 |
| Fiji | 679 | +12 |
| Finland | 358 | +2 |
| Finnish External Territory: | | |
|     Åland Islands | 358 | +2 |
| France | 33 | +1 |
| French Overseas Departments: | | |
|     French Guiana | 594 | −3 |
|     Guadeloupe | 590 | −4 |
|     Martinique | 596 | −4 |
|     Réunion | 262 | +4 |
| French Overseas Collectivité Départementale: | | |
|     Mayotte | 269 | +3 |
| Overseas Collectivité Territoriale: | | |
|     Saint Pierre and Miquelon | 508 | −3 |
| French Overseas Territories: | | |
|     French Polynesia | 689 | −9 to −10 |
|     Wallis and Futuna Islands | 681 | +12 |
| French Overseas Country: | | |
|     New Caledonia | 687 | +11 |
| Gabon | 241 | +1 |
| Gambia | 220 | 0 |
| Georgia | 995 | +4 |
| Germany | 49 | +1 |
| Ghana | 233 | 0 |
| Greece | 30 | +2 |
| Grenada | 1 473 | −4 |
| Guatemala | 502 | −6 |
| Guinea | 224 | 0 |
| Guinea-Bissau | 245 | 0 |
| Guyana | 592 | −4 |
| Haiti | 509 | −5 |
| Honduras | 504 | −6 |
| Hungary | 36 | +1 |
| Iceland | 354 | 0 |
| India | 91 | +5½ |
| Indonesia | 62 | +7 to +9 |
| Iran | 98 | +3½ |
| Iraq | 964 | +3 |
| Ireland | 353 | 0 |
| Israel | 972 | +2 |
| Italy | 39 | +1 |
| Jamaica | 1 876 | −5 |
| Japan | 81 | +9 |
| Jordan | 962 | +2 |
| Kazakhstan | 7 | +6 |
| Kenya | 254 | +3 |
| Kiribati | 686 | +12 to +13 |
| Korea, Democratic People's Republic (North Korea) | 850 | +9 |
| Korea, Republic (South Korea) | 82 | +9 |
| Kuwait | 965 | +3 |
| Kyrgyzstan | 996 | +5 |
| Laos | 856 | +7 |
| Latvia | 371 | +2 |
| Lebanon | 961 | +2 |
| Lesotho | 266 | +2 |
| Liberia | 231 | 0 |
| Libya | 218 | +1 |

# INTERNATIONAL TELEPHONE CODES

| | Country code | + or – GMT* |
|---|---|---|
| Liechtenstein | 423 | +1 |
| Lithuania | 370 | +2 |
| Luxembourg | 352 | +1 |
| Macedonia, former Yugoslav republic | 389 | +1 |
| Madagascar | 261 | +3 |
| Malawi | 265 | +2 |
| Malaysia | 60 | +8 |
| Maldives | 960 | +5 |
| Mali | 223 | 0 |
| Malta | 356 | +1 |
| Marshall Islands | 692 | +12 |
| Mauritania | 222 | 0 |
| Mauritius | 230 | +4 |
| Mexico | 52 | –6 to –7 |
| Micronesia, Federated States | 691 | +10 to +11 |
| Moldova | 373 | +2 |
| Monaco | 377 | +1 |
| Mongolia | 976 | +7 to +9 |
| Morocco | 212 | 0 |
| Mozambique | 258 | +2 |
| Myanmar | 95 | $+6\frac{1}{2}$ |
| Namibia | 264 | +2 |
| Nauru | 674 | +12 |
| Nepal | 977 | $+5\frac{3}{4}$ |
| Netherlands | 31 | +1 |
| Netherlands Dependencies: | | |
|     Aruba | 297 | –4 |
|     Netherlands Antilles | 599 | –4 |
| New Zealand | 64 | +12 |
| New Zealand's Dependent and Associated Territories: | | |
|     Tokelan | 690 | –10 |
|     Cook Islands | 682 | –10 |
|     Niue | 683 | –11 |
| Nicaragua | 505 | –6 |
| Niger | 227 | +1 |
| Nigeria | 234 | +1 |
| Norway | 47 | +1 |
| Norwegian External Territory: | | |
|     Svalbard | 47 | +1 |
| Oman | 968 | +4 |
| Pakistan | 92 | +5 |
| Palau | 680 | +9 |
| Palestinian Autonomous Areas | 970 | +2 |
| Panama | 507 | –5 |
| Papua New Guinea | 675 | +10 |
| Paraguay | 595 | –4 |
| Peru | 51 | –5 |
| The Philippines | 63 | +8 |
| Poland | 48 | +1 |
| Portugal | 351 | 0 |
| Qatar | 974 | +3 |
| Romania | 40 | +2 |
| Russian Federation | 7 | +2 to +12 |
| Rwanda | 250 | +2 |
| Saint Christopher and Nevis | 1 869 | –4 |
| Saint Lucia | 1 758 | –4 |
| Saint Vincent and the Grenadines | 1 784 | –4 |
| Samoa | 685 | –11 |
| San Marino | 378 | +1 |
| São Tomé and Príncipe | 239 | 0 |
| Saudi Arabia | 966 | +3 |
| Senegal | 221 | 0 |
| Serbia and Montenegro | 381 | +1 |
| Seychelles | 248 | +4 |
| Sierra Leone | 232 | 0 |
| Singapore | 65 | +8 |
| Slovakia | 421 | +1 |
| Slovenia | 386 | +1 |
| Solomon Islands | 677 | +11 |
| Somalia | 252 | +3 |
| South Africa | 27 | +2 |
| Spain | 34 | +1 |
| Sri Lanka | 94 | +6 |
| Sudan | 249 | +2 |
| Suriname | 597 | –3 |
| Swaziland | 268 | +2 |
| Sweden | 46 | +1 |
| Switzerland | 41 | +1 |
| Syria | 963 | +2 |
| Tajikistan | 992 | +5 |
| Tanzania | 255 | +3 |
| Thailand | 66 | +7 |
| Timor-Leste | 670 | +9 |
| Togo | 228 | 0 |
| Tonga | 676 | +13 |
| Trinidad and Tobago | 1 868 | –4 |
| Tunisia | 216 | +1 |
| Turkey | 90 | +2 |
| Turkmenistan | 993 | +5 |
| Tuvalu | 688 | +12 |
| Uganda | 256 | +3 |
| Ukraine | 380 | +2 |
| United Arab Emirates | 971 | +4 |
| United Kingdom | 44 | 0 |
|     United Kingdom Crown Dependencies | 44 | 0 |
| United Kingdom Overseas Territories: | | |
|     Anguilla | 1 264 | –4 |
|     Ascension Island | 247 | 0 |
|     Bermuda | 1 441 | –4 |
|     British Virgin Islands | 1 284 | –4 |
|     Cayman Islands | 1 345 | –5 |
|     Diego Garcia (British Indian Ocean Territory) | 246 | +5 |
|     Falkland Islands | 500 | –4 |
|     Gibraltar | 350 | +1 |
|     Montserrat | 1 664 | –4 |
|     Pitcairn Islands | 872 | –8 |
|     Saint Helena | 290 | 0 |
|     Tristan da Cunha | 2 897 | 0 |
|     Turks and Caicos Islands | 1 649 | –5 |
| United States of America | 1 | –5 to –10 |
| United States Commonwealth Territories: | | |
|     Northern Mariana Islands | 1 670 | +10 |
|     Puerto Rico | 1 787 | –4 |
| United States External Territories: | | |
|     American Samoa | 1 684 | –11 |
|     Guam | 1 671 | +10 |
|     United States Virgin Islands | 1 340 | –4 |
| Uruguay | 598 | –3 |
| Uzbekistan | 998 | +5 |
| Vanuatu | 678 | +11 |
| Vatican City | 39 | +1 |
| Venezuela | 58 | –4 |
| Viet Nam | 84 | +7 |
| Yemen | 967 | +3 |
| Zambia | 260 | +2 |
| Zimbabwe | 263 | +2 |

* The times listed compare the standard (winter) times in the various countries. Some countries adopt Summer (Daylight Saving) Time— i.e. +1 hour—for part of the year.

# OBITUARY

| | | | |
|---|---|---|---|
| BERINI, Bianca | 14 July 2004 | LINN, Robert T. | 28 October 1999 |
| BERMAN, Lazar | 6 February 2005 | LYMPANY, Dame Moura | 28 March 2005 |
| BERTINI, Gary | 17 March 2005 | MANNINO, Franco | 1 February 2005 |
| BOSCHKOVA, Nelly | February 2004 | METTERNICH, Josef | 21 February 2005 |
| BRAININ, Norbert | 10 April 2005 | MOOG, Robert Arthur | 21 August 2005 |
| BREDEMEYER, Reiner | 5 December 1995 | NILSSON, Birgit | 1 January 2006 |
| BRONHILL, June | 24 January 2005 | PALM, Siegfried | 6 June 2005 |
| CAMPORA, Giuseppe | 5 December 2004 | PETROVA, Elena | 7 April 2002 |
| CAPPUCCILLI, Piero | 12 July 2005 | PILBERY, Joseph | 5 April 2003 |
| COHEN, Isidore Leonard | 23 June 2005 | READ, Gardner | 10 November 2005 |
| COMISSIONA, Sergiu | 5 March 2005 | REECE, Arley | 22 October 2005 |
| COOKE, Arnold Atkinson | 13 August 2005 | ROCHBERG, George | 29 May 2005 |
| CRICHTON, Ronald | 15 November 2005 | RUDZIŃSKI, Witold | 29 February 2004 |
| DAVIES, Albert Meredith | 9 March 2005 | SADIE, Stanley John | 21 March 2005 |
| DIAMOND, David Leo | 13 June 2005 | SÁNDOR, György | 9 December 2005 |
| DIMITROVA, Ghena | 11 June 2005 | SCHERMERHORN, Kenneth DeWitt | 18 April 2005 |
| DOW, Dorothy | 26 February 2005 | SCHLESINGER, John Richard | 25 July 2003 |
| EHRLING, Sixten | 13 February 2005 | SCHMID, Patric (James) | 6 November 2005 |
| FARNON, Robert (Joseph) | 22 April 2005 | SCHRÖDER-FEINEN, Ursula | 9 February 2005 |
| FREEDMAN, Harry | 16 September 2005 | SHTOKOLOV, Boris | 6 January 2005 |
| GIULINI, Carlo Maria | 14 June 2005 | SOKOL, Ivan | 2 August 2005 |
| GULIN, Angeles | 2002 | SPIESS, Ludovico | 28 January 2006 |
| HALE, Una | 4 March 2005 | STRAESSER, Joep | – |
| HOKANSON, Leonard Ray | 21 March 2003 | THOMPSON, Arthur | 21 August 2004 |
| HYDE, Miriam Beatrice | 11 January 2005 | UPPMAN, Theodor | 17 March 2005 |
| JAMES, (Richard) Ifor | 23 December 2004 | VAN DER WALT, Deon | 29 November 2005 |
| JOHANNESEN, Grant | 27 March 2005 | VIOTTI, Marcello | 15 February 2005 |
| KAKUSKA, Thomas | 4 July 2005 | WEBSTER, Beveridge | 30 June 1999 |
| KING, James | 20 November 2005 | WENZINGER, August | 1996 |
| LIDL, Vaclav | 8 August 2004 | ZABLOCKI, Jerzy | 31 January 1991 |

# Biographies

# A

**AADLAND, Eivind;** Norwegian violinist; b. 19 Sept. 1956, Bergen. *Education:* Norwegian State Music Acad., Oslo with Camilla Wicks, Int. Menuhin Music Acad., Switzerland with Alberto Lysy and Yehudi Menuhin, master-classes with Sándor Végh. *Career:* fmrly concertmaster, Bergen Philharmonic Orchestra; Music Dir, European Community Chamber Orchestra 1988–; has appeared in major halls and festivals world-wide, including Musikverein, Vienna, Concertgebouw, Amsterdam, Salle Pleyel, Paris and Gewandhaus, Leipzig. *Recordings:* 12 albums. *Address:* Arupsgate 10, 0192 Oslo, Norway.

**AAQUIST, Svend;** Danish composer, conductor and computer programmer; b. 1948. *Education:* Univ. of Copenhagen, Royal Danish Acad. of Music, Copenhagen; int. courses with teachers, including Elisabeth Klein, Arne Hammelboe, Michel Tabachnik. *Career:* debut 1969; conductor for numerous choirs, chamber ensembles and orchestras 1969–; High School teacher 1969–75; Teacher of Conducting, Royal Danish Acad. of Music and State Acad. of Music at Esbjerg; numerous workshops and seminars for musical and conducting courses; Chief Conductor and Artistic Dir, Esbjerg Symphony Orchestra; Artistic Adviser, Esbjerg Ensemble 1984–; appeared in many concerts, festivals, radio and television recordings, in Denmark and abroad; concerts given with many orchestras, including Odense Symphony Orchestra; concert tours with West German Chamber Orchestra, Ensemble Modern 1981, 1982, 1984; mem., LUT and LYT (co-founder), Danish State Music Council, Nordic Composers' Council (pres. 1973–74), Soc. for Publication of Danish Music (bd mem. 1974–84), Danish Composers' Soc. (chair. 1973–74), DUT Danish ISCM (chair. 1980–84). *Compositions include:* Pentagram 1969, Salut-Salut 1970, Ke-Tjak 1973, Unite 1974, Sinfonia Sisyphus 1976, Malinche 1979, Sun 1983, Hymn With Dances 1985, cello solo The Lilac Shall Bloom 1976, Tai Yang 1986, High Voltage Rag 1991, Le Malade Imaginaire 1994, Babylon 1996. *Address:* Bruserup Strand 9, 4873 Væggerløse, Denmark. *Telephone:* 54-16-70-00 (office); 54-17-82-20 (home). *E-mail:* aa@ajourdata.dk (office); svend@aaquist.com (home).

**ABAJAN, Maria;** singer (soprano); b. 1950, Eriwan, Armenia. *Education:* studied at Eriwan and Tchaikovsky Conservatory in Moscow; further studies at Los Angeles. *Career:* moved to USA in 1977; successful at singing competitions in New York, San Francisco, Italy and Mexico; appeared in Europe, 1985–, notably as Turandot in Liège, Abigaille in Nabucco, (Brussels, 1987) and Aida in Zürich; has sung Leonora in Trovatore and Elisabeth de Valois at Hamburg, Tosca and Amelia in Ballo in Maschera in Essen; appeared as Tosca with Scottish Opera, Glasgow, in 1990; Vienna Staatsoper, 1991–92, as Tosca and the Forza Leonora; season 1993 as Abigaille at Bregenz, and Giorgetta at Madrid; sang Santuzza in Cavalleria Rusticana at the Berlin Staatsoper and Nice, 1997, 1999. *Address:* c/o Scottish Opera, 39 Elmbank Crescent, Glasgow G2 4PT, Scotland.

**ABBADO, Claudio;** Italian conductor; *Chief Conductor and Music Director, Lucerne Festival Orchestra;* b. 26 June 1933, Milan; one c. *Education:* Giuseppe Verdi Conservatory, Milan and Acad. of Music, Vienna with Hans Swarowsky. *Career:* debut La Scala, Milan in concert celebrating tercentenary of A. Scarlatti 1960 conducted opening of La Scala season 1967; Music Dir Teatro alla Scala, Milan 1968–86, Vienna Philharmonic Orchestra 1972–, London Symphony Orchestra 1979–88, Vienna State Opera 1986–91; Principal Conductor Chamber Orchestra of Europe 1981; Principal Guest Conductor Chicago Symphony Orchestra 1982–85; Gen. Music Dir City of Vienna 1987–; Music Dir and Principal Conductor Berlin Philharmonic Orchestra 1989–2002; Artistic Dir Salzburg Easter Festival 1994; Chief Conductor and Music Dir Lucerne Festival Orchestra 2001–; f. European Community Youth Orchestra 1978, La Filharmonica della Scala 1982, Gustav Mahler Jugendorchester, Vienna 1986, Wien Modern (Modern Vienna) Contemporary Art Festival 1988, Vienna Int. Competition for Composers 1991, Encounters in Berlin (Chamber Music Festival) 1992; has conducted on tours world-wide, with numerous orchestras; guest conductor Rome 2005, Tokyo 2006, Carnegie Hall 2007. *Publications:* Musica sopra Berlino (Nonino Award 1999) 1998, Suite Concertante from the Ballet Hawaii 2000, La Casa del Suoni (juvenile). *Honours:* Dr hc (Aberdeen) 1986, (Ferrara) 1990, (Cambridge) 1994; Mozart Medal (Vienna) 1973, Gold Medal, Int. Gustav Mahler Gesellschaft (Vienna) 1985, Amadeus (Ferrara) 1996, award from the Presidency of the Council of Ministers 1997, Athena-Giovani e Cultura Award (Univ. of Milan) 1999, Conductor of the Year, Opernwelt Review 2000, Oscar della Lirica 2001, Praemium Imperiale 2003, MIDEM Classical Lifetime Achievement Award 2005; Grand Cross, Order of Merit (Italy) 1984, Officier, Légion d'Honneur, Bundesverdienstkreuz (Germany) 1992, Ehrenring, City of Vienna 1994. *Current Management:* Askonas Holt Ltd, Lonsdale Chambers, 27 Chancery Lane, London, WC2A 1PF, England. *Telephone:* (20) 7400-1700. *Fax:* (20) 7400-1799. *E-mail:* info@askonasholt.co.uk. *Website:* www .askonasholt.co.uk.

**ABBADO, Marcello,** DipMus; Italian composer; b. 7 Oct. 1926, Milan. *Education:* Milan Conservatory. *Career:* soloist and conductor in Europe, America, Africa, Asia 1944–; performed all Debussy and all piano concertos of Mozart; Prof. of Piano at Conservatories of Cagliari, Venice and Milan, and of Composition at Parma and Bologna 1950; Dir, Liceo Musicale, Piacenza 1958, Rossini Conservatory, Pesaro 1966, Verdi Conservatory, Milan 1972–96; founder, Symphony Orchestra Verdi, Milan 1993; jury mem., int. competitions

of chamber music, composition, conducting, piano, violin, voice and others world-wide; mem. Admin. Council, Teatro alla Scala 1973–96; mem. Fondazione Curci (Naples), Fondazione Puccini (Lucca). *Compositions include:* ballet: Scena Senza Storia, Hawaii 2000, Suite Concertante from the Ballet Hawaii 2000; orchestral: Concerto for Orchestra, Hommage à Debussy, Costruzioni for five Small Orchestras, Variazioni sopra un tema di Mozart, Risonanze for two pianos and chamber orchestra, La strage degli innocenti for vocal soloists, choir and orchestra, seven Ricercari and six Intermezzi for violin and orchestra, Quadruplo Concerto for piano, violin, viola, cello and orchestra 1970, Double Concerto for violin, piano and double chamber orchestra, L'Idea fissa for violin 'scordato' and percussion orchestra 1994, Ottavo Ricercare for violin and orchestra 1997, Concerto for flute and orchestra 2002, Ten Songs of Sicily for voice, violin and orchestra, Velicianie Aleksandr Nevsky for violin and choir, The Bells of Moscow for violin and percussion 1998, Lento e Rondo for violin and percussions, Musica Celeste for violin and orchestra, 15 Poesie T'ang for voice and four instruments, Ciapo for voice and nine instruments, Three Quatuor, Duo for violin and cello, Fantasia No. 1 for 12 instruments, Fantasia No. 2 for four instruments and 31 percussion, Capriccio su un tema di Paganini for violin and piano, Chaconne for solo violin, Riverberazioni for wind instruments and piano, Divertimento for 4 winds and piano, Concertante for piano and instrument, Sonata for flute, Incastri No. 1 and No. 2 for winds, Lamento for the Mother's Death for clavichord, Variazioni sopra un minuetto di Bach for piano, Aus dem Klavier for piano, Responsorio for choir and organ, Sarà Sara for guitar, Ostinato on a Rhythmic Motif from the Overture to Il Signor Bruschino by Rossini, for piano, string orchestra and percussions 1994, Nuova Costruzione for Wind Octet 2002, Australia, for violin, didgeridoo and percussions 2002, Asif Saleem Nasreen No. 1 and No. 2 for violin, alto, cello and string orchestra 2002, Six Ninne Nanne for solo voice, Vocalizzo on Ma se mi toccano, from Rossini's Il Barbiere di Siviglia, for voice and piano, Desprez; Entre Paris et la France, Fijetto dei corni, for choir 1999, Harmonic Variations for orchestra on Mozart's Marche Funèbre del Signor Maestro Contrapunto, DV 453a 2000, Costruzione for 12 cellos 2001, Risonanza magnetica for piano and percussion orchestra 2003, Music for Jean Cocteau's La voix humaine 2003, Concerto for harp and strings orchestra 2003, Il buio negli occhi (scenic action) 2003. *Address:* Viale Monza 9, 20125 Milan, Italy.

**ABBADO, Roberto;** conductor; b. 1954, Milan, Italy. *Education:* Pesaro and Milan Conservatories, studied with Franco Ferrara in Rome and at Teatro La Fenice, Venice. *Career:* debut with Orchestra of Accademia Santa Cecilia 1977; operatic debut with a new production of Simon Boccanegra at Macerata 1978; festival appearances at Edinburgh 1982, Israel 1984, Lille and Munich 1989; Chief Conductor, Munich Radio Orchestra 1991; engagements with Staatskapelle Dresden, Bamberg Symphony, Orchestre National de France, RAI Turin, The Orchestra of St Luke's in New York, Maggio Musicale Fiorentino Orchestra; opera engagements at La Scala with world premieres of Flavio Testi's Il Sosia and Riccardo III and a new production of Don Pasquale; Vienna State Opera with a new production of La Cenerentola; Bayerische Staatsoper, Munich, with a new production of La Traviata 1993, and Adriana Lecouvreur, Manon Lescaut, Don Pasquale; conducted La Forza del Destino at San Francisco 1993; appeared at Rome, Florence, Bologna, Venice, Berlin Deutsche Oper, Zürich, Barcelona and Tokyo with Teatro Comunale Bologna 1993; conducted Adriana Lecouvreur at the Metropolitan, New York 1994; Opéra Bastille debut in Lucia di Lammermoor 1995; Houston Grand Opera debut in Norma 1996; Aida at the 1997 Munich Festival; Le Comte Ory at Florence 1998. *Recordings include:* Bellini's I Capuleti e i Montecchi 1998. *Honours:* Deutsche Phono Akademi Echo Klassic Deutscher Schallplatten-preis (for recording of Rossini's Tancredi) 1997. *Current Management:* M. L. Falcone Public Relations, 155 W 68th Street, New York, NY 10023, USA. *Fax:* (212) 787-9638 (office).

**ABBOTT, Jocelyn,** ARCT, BMus, LRAM, DipRAM, ARAM; Concert Pianist; b. 15 Sept. 1954, Toronto, Canada. *Education:* Victoria Conservatory of Music, Victoria BC; Royal Conservatory of Music, Toronto; Univ. of Victoria; Royal Academy of Music, London. *Career:* concerts and recordings as soloist and accompanist, and since 1992 as part of ensemble The Abbott O'Gorman Piano Duo with Laura O'Gorman, including commissioning transcriptions and arranging orchestral repertoire; mem. Incorporated Society of Musicians. *Recordings:* Ravel à quatre mains, 1994; Classical Jazz à quatre mains, 1999. *Publications:* contrib. to Pianist Magazine. *Honours:* Associate of the Royal Academy of Music, 1987; 'Steinway Artist' Status, 1996. *Address:* Cubitt Music Management, 40 Cubitt Terrace, London, SW4 6AR, England (office). *Telephone:* (777) 1725002 (office). *Fax:* (20) 7720–8660 (office). *E-mail:* rjordan@cubittmusic.co.uk (office). *Website:* www.cubittmusic.co.uk (office).

**ABDRASAKOV, Askar;** Singer (bass); b. 1960, Ufa, Urals, Russia. *Education:* Ufa Conservatoire and with Irina Arkipova in Moscow. *Career:* soloist with the Bashkirian Opera from 1990, as Sobakin (The Tsar's Bride), Konchak in Prince Igor, Gremin, Zuniga, Sparafucile and Rossini's Don Basilio; recital with Arkhipova at the Wigmore Hall, 1994 and Rimsky's Invisible City of Kitezh at the Bregenz Festival, 1995; in recital at the Châtelet, Paris, the Bonze in Stravinsky's Nightingale under Pierre Boulez in Paris and London, Rimsky's Tsar Saltan at Florence and the Grand Inquisitor in Don Carlos at

Bologna, 1996–98; concerts include the Verdi Requiem, Puccini Messa di Gloria; Russian and French songs and Lieder. *Honours:* prizewinner at the 1991 Glinka Competition; winner, Chaliapin Bass Competition at Kazan, 1994; Grand Prix, Maria Callas Competition in Athens, 1995. *Current Management:* Askonas Holt Ltd, Lonsdale Chambers, 27 Chancery Lane, London, WC2A 1PF, England. *Telephone:* (20) 7400-1700. *Fax:* (20) 7400-1799. *E-mail:* info@askonasholt.co.uk. *Website:* www.askonasholt.co.uk.

**ABE, Keiko Kimura;** Japanese marimba player and composer; b. 18 April 1937, Tokyo. *Education:* studied xylophone with Eiichi Asabuki, Tokyo Gakugei Univ. composition with Shosuke Ariga and Toshio Kashiwagi, percussion with Masao Imamura and Yusuke Oyake. *Career:* joined Tokyo Marimba Group 1962; Lecturer, Tōhō Gakuen Coll. of Music, Tokyo 1969–88; annual recital tours of Europe, N America and Asia from 1981; Yamaha released standard five-octave marimba based on her ideas 1984; Prof., Tōhō Gakuen Coll. of Music, Tokyo 1988–; Visiting Prof., Utrecht Conservatoire. *Compositions:* Variations on Japanese Children's Songs, Mi-Chi, Ancient Vase, Wind in the Bamboo Grove, Memories of the Seashore, Prism, Little Windows, Frogs, Wind Sketch, Tambourin Paraphrase, Voice of Matsuri Drums, Itsuki Fantasy for Six Mallets, Ban-ka, Piacer d'amor, Alone, Kazak Lullaby, Marimba d'amore, Dream of the Cherry Blossoms, Prism Rhapsody II. *Recordings include:* Keiko Abe: Art of Marimba. *Address:* c/o Tōhō Gakuen Coll. of Music, 1-41-1 Wakaba-chô, Chôfu-shi, 182–0003 Tokyo, Japan (office).

**ABEL, Yves;** conductor; b. 1963, Canada. *Education:* Univ. of Toronto, Royal Conservatory, Mannes Coll. of Music, Tanglewood Music Center with Leonard Bernstein, Seiji Ozawa, Gunther Herbig and Roger Norrington. *Career:* conducted La Traviata at New York City Opera, televised on Live from Lincoln Center series; La Cenerentola with Seattle Opera; La Belle Hélène, with Opera Theatre of St Louis; Roméo et Juliette with Florida Grand Opera; Herold's Zampa at 1993 Wexford Festival and Wagner's Das Liebesverbot at 1994 Festival, also conducting Brahms' Ein Deutsches Requiem; Rigoletto with Opera Lyra Ottawa; Massenet's Werther at Skylight Opera; Dido and Aeneas at Canada's Elora Festival, broadcast nationwide on CBC Radio; Madama Butterfly with Opera Theater of Connecticut; Music Dir, L'Opéra Français de New York, with performances at Lincoln Center and Alice Tully Hall, conducting Offenbach's Barbe-Bleue, Médée by Cherubini and Le Comte Ory by Rossini; recently acclaimed debuts include Don Carlos with Opera North, Le Comte Ory with Glyndebourne Festival Opera, Hamlet with San Francisco Opera, L'Elisir d'amore with Royal Danish Opera, Rossini Opera Festival and performances of Faust with Paris Opéra; debut at Lyric Opera of Chicago with L'Elisir d'amore, Seattle Opera for Forza del Destino, Netherlands Opera for Barbiere and a revival of Les Dialogues des Carmélites, the Royal Danish Opera for Verdi, the WNO for Leonore 2000, and Bilbao Opera for Barbiere di Siviglia; third season at Metropolitan Opera with Carmen, with Domingo and Denyce Graves; Lyric Opera in Chicago for Barbiere 2001; season 2002–03 with the Metropolitan Opera (Carmen) and the Netherlands Opera, as well as new productions with the Santa Fe Opera (Così fan tutte), the Dallas Opera (Ermione), the Deutsche Oper Berlin (Don Pasquale) and the Teatro Comunale di Bologna (Iphigénie en Tauride); Prin. Guest Conductor Deutsche Oper, Berlin 2005–. *Current Management:* Askonas Holt Ltd, Lonsdale Chambers, 27 Chancery Lane, London, WC2A 1PF, England. *Telephone:* (20) 7400-1700. *Fax:* (20) 7400-1799. *E-mail:* info@askonasholt.co.uk. *Website:* www.askonasholt.co.uk.

**ABELL, David;** Conductor; b. 1965, USA. *Education:* Yale University and Juilliard School, New York; Further study with Leonard Bernstein and Nadia Boulanger. *Career:* Many appearances in USA and Europe with leading orchestras; London resident from 1996; Concerts with City of Birmingham Symphony Orchestra, Royal Philharmonic, Royal Scottish National Orchestra, and BBC Concert Orchestra; Rossini's La Gazza Ladra with Opera North, Madama Butterfly and Carmen at the Royal Albert Hall; US engagements with New York City Opera, Washington and Michigan Operas, Seattle and Alabama Symphonies; Italian debut 1999, with Rigoletto at the Lugio Musicale Trapanese; Season 2001 with the Brighton Philharmonic, BBC Concert Orchestra at the Covent Garden Festival, Sinfonia Viva, Ulster Orchestra, and Hong Kong Philharmonic; Conducted Rodgers & Hammerstein's Oklahoma! at the London Proms, 2002. *Current Management:* IMG Artists, Lovell House, 616 Chiswick High Road, London W4 5RV, England.

**ABENIUS, Folke;** Swedish producer and professor; b. 8 Oct. 1933, Stockholm; m., one s. one d. *Education:* Royal Univ. Coll. of Music, Stockholm; Opera Producing, Germany. *Career:* Debut: Royal Court Theatre, Drottwingholm; Producer, Malmo City Theatre, 1960–67; Producer, Royal Opera House, Stockholm, 1967–71, 1984–91; Artistic Leader, Opera House, Goteborg, 1971–77; Gen. Man., Royal Opera House, Stockholm, 1978–84; Prof., Univ. Coll. of Opera, Stockholm 1991–2001; Guest Producer, Copenhagen, Oslo, Helsinki, Hamburg, Kiel, Braunschweig; mem, Royal Acad. of Music, Stockholm. *Productions include:* Ring des Nibelungen, Der Rosenkavalier, Ariadne, Lohengrin, La Traviata, Otello, I Vespri Siciliani, Elektra, Fidelio, Die Zauberflöte, Marriage of Figaro. *Honours:* Litteris et Artibus. *Address:* Karlavagen 83, 114 59 Stockholm, Sweden.

**ABESHOUSE, Warren;** Australian composer; b. 8 May 1952, Sydney, NSW. *Education:* State Conservatoire, NSW. *Career:* ABC Radio and Television 1975–87; Office Man. 1994–. *Compositions include:* Five Bagatelles for Piano, 1972; Two Piano Sonatas, 1975, 1986; Psalm 70 for Chorus and Organ, 1975; Four Characteristic Pieces for Clarinet, 1976; Two Bagatelles for Cello, 1976;

Lemmata, Essay for Orchestra, 1977; On Love for Tenor and Piano, 1980; Shadow Darkly for Oboe and Strings, 1990; The Christopher Sonatina for Piano, 1991; Womblemov for Horn, Cello and Timpani, 1993; Lament for Piano, 1993. *Honours:* First Prize, Original work for solo instrument, City of Sydney Eisteddfod, 1990. *Address:* c/o APRA, 1A Eden Street, Crows Nest, NSW 2065, Australia.

**ABLINGER-SPERRHACKE, Wolfgang;** Austrian singer (tenor); b. 1967, Zell am See. *Education:* studied in Vienna with Gerhard Kahry. *Career:* first became mem. of Landestheater, Linz, then joined Basel Opera and Gärtnerplatz, Munich; debut at Opéra Nat. de Paris 1997, subsequently sang there Goro/Madama Butterfly (also Theatre Olympics, Japan), Monostatos, Dr Blind/Die Fledermaus, 1st Jew/Salome, premiere of Phillippe Manoury's K; other engagements have included Vašek, Reverend Horace Adams/Peter Grimes and Monostatos at Glyndebourne Festival, Spoletta/Tosca and Valzacchi/Der Rosenkavalier (La Monnaie), Dr Cajus/Falstaff (Aix, Madrid, Champs-Elysées), Mime/Das Rheingold (Dresden), Mime/Siegfried (Toulouse, Madrid), Regista/Un re in ascolto (Frankfurt), Pedrillo/Die Entführung aus dem Serail (La Conma), Trimalchio/Madema's Satyricon (Nancy); has worked with many conductors including Jordan, Conlon, Bychkov, Steinberg, Pappano and López Cobos; has appeared widely in concert, including recently Concertgebouw, Sao Paulo (Mahler's Lied von der Erde), Melbourne (Gurrelieder/Schönberg.); future engagements include Strasbourg (Aegisth/Elektra, Loge/Rheingold), Nancy (Hauptmaxm/Wozzeck), Madrid (Pedrillo). *Recordings:* DVD: Falstaff, Die Fledermaus. *Current Management:* Intermusica Artists Management Ltd, 16 Duncan Terrace, London, N1 8BZ, England. *Telephone:* (20) 7278 5455. *Fax:* (20) 7278 8434. *E-mail:* mail@intermusica.co.uk. *Website:* www.intermusica.co.uk.

**ABRAHAMSEN, Hans;** Composer; b. 23 Dec. 1952, Copenhagen, Denmark. *Education:* Studied horn, theory, and music history at Royal Danish Conservatory, Copenhagen, 1969–71; Composition with Pelle Gudmundsen-Holmgreen and Per Norgard at Jutland Academy of Music, Århus. *Compositions:* Orchestral: Foam, 1970; Symphony in C, 1972; Symphony No. 1, 1974; Stratifications, 1973–75; Nach und Trompeten, 1981; Marchenbilder for 14 players, 1984; Cello Concerto, 1987; Chamber: Fantasy Pieces After Hans Jorgen Nielsen for Flute, Horn, Cello and Piano, 1969, revised, 1976; October for Piano Left Hand, 1969, revised 1976; Round And In Between for Brass Quintet, 1972; 2 Woodwind Quintets: No. 1, Landscapes, 1972, No. 2, Walden, 1978; Nocturnes for Flute and Piano, 1972; Flowersongs for 3 Flutes, 1973; Scraps for Cello and Piano, 1973; 2 String Quartets: No. 1, 1973, No. 2, 1991, 10 Preludes, 1973, No. 2, 1981; Flush for Saxophone, 1974, revised, 1979; Double for Flute and Guitar, 1975; Winternacht for 7 instruments, 1976–79; Canzone for Accordion, 1978; Geduldspiel for 10 instruments, 1980; 6 Pieces for Violin, Horn and Piano, 1984; 10 Studies for Piano, 1983–87; Herbst for Tenor, Flute, Guitar and Cello, 1970–72, revised, 1977; Universe Birds for 10 Sopranos, 1973; Songs of Denmark for Soprano and 5 Instruments, 1974, revised 1976; Aria for Soprano and 4 Instruments, 1979; Autumn Song for Soprano and Ensemble, 1992. *Address:* c/o CODA, PO Box 2154, 1016, Copenhagen K, Denmark.

**ABRAMSKY, Jennifer,** CBE, BA; British radio producer and editor; *Director, BBC Radio and Music;* b. 7 Oct. 1946, d. of Chimen Abramsky and the late Miriam Abramsky (née Nirenstein); m. Alasdair D. MacDuff Liddell 1976; one s. one d. *Education:* Holland Park School and Univ. of East Anglia. *Career:* joined BBC Radio as Programme Operations Asst 1969, Producer, The World at One 1973, Ed. PM 1978–81, Producer Radio Four Budget Programmes 1979–86, The World at One 1981–86, Ed. Today programme 1986–87, News and Current Affairs Radio 1987–93, est. Radio Four News FM 1991, Controller BBC Radio Five Live 1993–96, Dir Continuous News Services, BBC (including Radio Five Live, BBC News 24, BBC World, BBC News Online, Ceefax) 1996–98, Dir BBC Radio 1998–2000, BBC Radio and Music 2000–; mem. Econ. and Social Research Council 1992–96, Editorial Bd British Journalism Review 1993–; Vice-Chair. Digital Radio Devt Bureau 2002–; Dir Hampstead Theatre 2003–; mem. Bd of Govs BFI 2000–; News Int. Visiting Prof. of Broadcast Media, Exeter Coll., Oxford 2002; Radio Acad. Fellowship 1998. *Honours:* Hon. Prof. Thames Valley Univ. 1994; Hon. RAM 2002; Hon. MA (Salford) 1997; Woman of Distinction, Jewish Care 1990, Sony Radio Acad. Award 1995. *Address:* BBC, Room 2811, Broadcasting House, Portland Place, London, W1A 1AA, England. *Telephone:* (20) 7765-4561 (office).

**ACEL, Ervin;** Music Director and Conductor; b. 3 June 1935, Timisoara, Romania; 1 s. *Education:* Choral conducting, C Porumbescu Conservatory, Bucharest, 1953–58; Orchestral conducting, Cluj-Napoca Conservatory, Romania, 1958–60; Orchestral conducting; Masterclass. *Career:* Debut: Botosani Symphonic Orchestra, 1963; Conductor, Botosani State Philharmonic Orchestra, Romania, 1960–63; Principal Conductor, 1963–91, Director, 1984–91, Oradea Philharmonic Orchestra, Romania; Music Director, Szeged Symphony Orchestra, Hungary, 1991–99; Toured throughout Europe, USA, Japan, Mexico, Brazil, Taiwan, Singapore; Worked with numerous operas including Dresden Staatsoper, Grand Opera Dublin, various Romanian operas, Szeged Opera and Szeged Festival Opera; Professor in Conducting of Internationale Musik Seminar in Vienna, Austria, 1996; Guest Professor, Conducting Class, Universität für Musik und darstellende Kunst, Vienna, 1997. *Recordings:* Over 35 albums including J. Haydn Harpsichord concertos, Bach Harpsichord concertos, Mozart flute concertos, Mozart violin concertos, Schubert symphonies, Tchaikovsky string serenade, Mahler Kindertotenlieder, Kabalevsky symphonies, Flute concertos by Ibert and Nielsen. *Honours:*

Cultural Order, Romania, 1978; Sebetia Ter, Italy, 1998. *Address:* 9725 Köszegszerdahely, Hegyi u. 15, Hungary.

**ACHIM, Erzsébet;** Organist; b. 6 Nov. 1954, Gyula, Hungary; m. Miklós Thaisz, 21 Oct 1978, 2 s. *Education:* Bartók Béla Konzervatórium; Faculty of Choir-Leading, Faculty of Organ, Ferenc Liszt Academy of Music, Budapest. *Career:* Played piece by Bartók for Hungarian Radio, age 5; Performs at organ concerts and concerts with orchestra, also as soloist and with choirs; Teaches church music; Several interviews and concerts broadcast by Hungarian radio and television; mem, Hungarian Church Music Society. *Recordings:* Several of chamber music, 1990–96; Handel, 6 Organ Concertos op 4, 1994; Glocken und Orgeln in Selm, 1999. *Contributions:* Articles in Magyar Nemzet, other Hungarian dailies, Uj Magyarország, Der Landbote, Switzerland, Südwest Presse, Germany, BBC Music Magazine. *Honours:* Extra Prize for Interpretation of Hungarian Composers, Ferenc Liszt International Musical Competition, 1978. *Address:* Apor Vilmos tér 3, 1124 Budapest, Hungary.

**ACHUCCARO, Joaquin;** Concert Pianist; b. 1 Nov. 1936, Bilbao, Spain. *Education:* Accademia Chigiana and with Walter Gieseking. *Career:* Many solo and concert performances world-wide from 1959, including appearances with the Berlin and New York Philharmonic, London Symphony and Philharmonia Orchestras, Orchestre National de France and Warsaw National Orchestra; Has also featured as soloist-conductor with chamber orchestras in the United Kingdom, Italy, Germany and Spain; from 1989 teacher at Southern Methodist University, Dallas; BBC recitals on tour, 1997. *Recordings include:* albums of Granados, Falla, Schubert, Ravel, Debussy and Brahms. *Honours:* Winner, 1959 Liverpool International Competition. *Current Management:* Olivia Ma Artists' Management, 65 Campden Street, London W8 7EL, England.

**ACKER, Dieter;** composer and teacher; b. 3 Nov. 1940, Sibiu-Hermannstadt, Romania. *Education:* studied piano, organ, theory with Fr Xav Dressler in Sibiu, composition with Sigismund Todutá at Cluj Conservatory. *Career:* Teacher of Theory and Composition, Cluj Conservatory, 1964–69; Teacher, Robert Schumann Conservatory, Düsseldorf, 1969–72; Teacher of Theory and Composition, 1972–76, Professor of Composition, 1976–, Munich Hochschule für Musik. *Compositions include:* Symphony No. 1, 1977–78; Eichendorff-Sonata for clarinet and piano, 1983; Mörike-Sonata for cello and piano, 1978; Bassoon Concerto, 1979–80; Violin Concerto No. 1, 1981; Piano Concerto, 1984; Piano Trio No. 2, 1984; String Trio No. 3, 1987; String Quartet No. 5, 1990–95; Music for Two Horns and Strings, 1991; Piano Trio No. 3, 1992; Symphony No. 3, 1992; Sinfonia Breve for brass, 1993; Notturno, for string orchestra, 1994; Violin Concerto No. 2, 1994–95; Sonata for two pianos, 1993; Sonata for Piano No. 2, 1993; Trinklieder for vocal quartet and piano, 1994; Sonata for Bassoon and Piano, 1996; Vocal music; Organ Music. *Recordings include:* Nachtstücke for two flutes; Piano Trio Stigmen; Rilke Sonate for violin and piano. *Honours:* Prag 1996 Prize for String Quartet No. 1; Johann-Wenzel-Stamitz-Prize, Stuttgart, 1970; Lions Club International Prize for String Quartet No. 4, Düsseldorf, 1973; Prix Henriette Renié for Music for Strings and Harp, Paris, 1988; Johann-Wenzel-Stamitz-Prize, Mannheim, 1990. *Address:* Kleiststrasse 12, 85521 Munich-Ottobrunn, Germany.

**ACKERT, Stephen,** DMus; American musician; b. 13 May 1944. *Education:* Univ. of Wisconsin, Madison Northwestern Univ., Evanston, IL. *Career:* resident keyboard artist and Music Dir of resident orchestra, Nat. Iranian Radio and Television Network, Tehran 1974–78; Dir of Music St Margaret's Episcopal Church, Washington, DC 1979–86; music program specialist, Nat. Gallery of Art, Washington, DC 1986–2004; Head of Music Dept, Nat. Gallery of Art 2004–; concert organist; teacher of applied organ; host of weekly classical music broadcasts on WOBC, Oberlin, OH and the Nat. Iranian Radio and Television Network, Tehran. *Publications:* articles in The American Organist. *Honours:* Fulbright Scholarship, Robert F. Smith Research Fellowship, Nat. Federation of Music Clubs Award, Alumnus of the Year Award, Oberlin Coll. 2002. *Address:* National Gallery of Art, Washington, DC 20565, USA (office). *Telephone:* (202) 842 6075 (office). *Fax:* (202) 842 2407 (office). *E-mail:* S-Ackert@nga.gov (office). *Website:* www.nga.gov (office).

**ACOSTA, Adolovna P.;** Concert Pianist, Music Teacher and Music Director; b. 3 Feb. 1946, Manila, Philippines. *Education:* Graduate Studies, Ethnomusicology, Wesleyan University, Connecticut, 1968–69; Teacher's Diploma, 1965, BM, Piano, 1966, MM, 1968, University of the Philippines; MS, Piano, The Juilliard School, 1971. *Career:* Solo recitals in New York including Carnegie Recital Hall, Alice Tully Hall, Merkin Concert Hall; Solo recitals in Wigmore Hall and Purcell Hall, London; Sunderland Art Gallery, Wolverhampton Art Gallery, England; Salle Cortot, Paris; Copenhagen and Stockholm; Solo recitals in Cultural Centre of the Philippines and Abelardo Hall, University of the Philippines; Soloist, four times, with the University of the Philippines Symphony Orchestra; Radio performances in Sweden, Philippines and the USA; Recitals in Philippine Consulates and Embassies; Jury Member, East and West Artists International Auditions, 1971, New York Chopin Competition, 1984; Former faculty mem., The Juilliard School Pre-College Division and New York University. *Recordings:* Andalucia and Danzas Afro Cubanas of Ernesto Lecuona; Piano Music of Carl Nielsen for Musical Heritage Society. *Address:* 310 Riverside Drive, Apt 313, New York, NY 10025, USA.

**ACS, Janos;** Conductor; b. 23 March 1952, Hungary; Divorced, 1 s., 2 d. *Education:* Diplomas in Flute, Pianoforte and Composition from Bela Bartók Institute, F. Liszt Academy, Budapest; Organ Diploma from Verdi Con-

servatorio, Milan. *Career:* debut, Fidelio at Teatro Carlo Felice, Genoa in 1979; Idomeneo at Opera di Roma, Tancredi at La Fenice, Falstaff, I Capuleti, Amico Fritz at Arena di Verona, Offenbach at Comunale di Firenze, La Bohème at Frankfurt, Symphonic Programmes in Tokyo, Manon, Pagliacci, La Traviata, and Otello in Denver, Carmen, Il Trovatore, and Tristan und Isolde in Pretoria, Faust in Hong Kong, and Luciano Pavarotti recital in Budapest; One of Pavarotti's conductors; Principal Conductor, Pact Theater, Pretoria, 1983–88; Principal Conductor at Opera Colorado in Denver, USA, 1985–91; mem, Co-Director, Franz Liszt Society of Germany. *Recordings:* Bellini Overtures; Donizetti Overtures; I Puritani; Carmen, video of Pact Theater in Pretoria; Respighi's Gli Uccelli, Trittico Botticelliano. *Honours:* Respighi Memorial Concert and Prize, 1985. *Address:* Via Carducci, 38, 2100 Milan, Italy.

**ADAM, Theo;** German singer (bass-baritone); b. 1 Aug. 1926, Dresden; s. of Johannes Adam and Lisbeth Adam (née Dernstorf); m. Eleonore Matthes 1949; one s. one d. *Education:* Gymnasium and Conservatory. *Career:* engagements with Dresden State Opera 1949, Bayreuth Festival 1952–80, Salzburg Festival 1969, 1970, 1980–89, 1992, 1995; mem. Deutsche Staatsoper, Berlin 1953–; has appeared with Vienna and Munich State Operas since 1967; Pres. of Curatorium Oper, Dresden 1985–; sang at Semper Opera House, Dresden 1985; staged Graun's Cesare e Cleopatra, Berlin State Opera 1992; performed at Royal Festival Hall, London 1994, Berlin Staatsoper 1997; numerous recordings; Österreichischer Kammersänger, Bayerischer Kammersänger. *Publications:* Seht, hier ist Tinte, Feder, Papier 1980, Die 100 Rolle, Wie schön ist doch die Musik 1996. *Honours:* Nat. Prize (First Class) of GDR. *Current Management:* Opéra et Concert, 7 rue de Clichy, 75009 Paris, France. *Telephone:* 1-42-96-18-18. *Fax:* 1-42-96-18-00. *E-mail:* agence@opera-concert.com. *Website:* www.opera-concert.com. *Address:* Schillerstrasse 14, 01326 Dresden, Germany. *Telephone:* (351) 2683997.

**ADAMIS, Mihalis;** composer and choral director; b. 19 May 1929, Piraeus, Greece; m. Pany Carella 1973; two s. *Education:* Athens University, Piraeus Conservatory, Hellenicon Conservatory, Brandeis University, Boston, USA. *Career:* founder and Director of Hellenic Royal Palace Boys Choir, 1950–67 and Athens Chamber Chorus, 1958–61; Taught Byzantine Music, directed choir, Greek Orthodox College of Theology, Boston, USA, 1961–63; Founder of first electronic music studio in Athens, Greece in 1968; Head of Music Department, Choir Director, Pierce College, Athens, 1968–; Many festival commissions including: Hellenic Weeks of Contemporary Music, 1967–72, English Bach Festival, 1971, 1973; World-wide performances of works include: ONCE Festival, USA, 1962, Barcelona, 1973, Leicester, 1976, Greek Month in London, 1975, 1989, Art Weeks throughout Europe, Middle and Far East; Many international radio and television broadcasts; Toured Europe and the Americas with ballet piece, Genesis, 1973; President, Supreme Council for Music, Ministry of Culture, 1993. *Compositions include:* Epallelon for Orchestra; Anakyklesis; Hirmos for voices; Kratema; Vision of God for mixed chorus and orchestra, 1997; Who is as Great as God? for women's chorus, 1999; Melos for alto saxophone, 2000. *Recordings:* Genesis; Apocalypsis; Minyrismos; Metallic Sculptures; Byzantine Passion; Psalmic Ode. *Address:* Gravias 43, 15342 Ayia Paraskevi, Athens, Greece.

**ADAMO, Mark,** BMus; American opera composer and critic; b. 1962, Philadelphia. *Education:* New York Univ., Catholic Univ. of America. *Career:* first opera Little Women premiered Houston Grand Opera 1998, performances include New York City Opera, Opera Omaha, Lyric Opera Cleveland; second opera Lysistrata, or, The Nude Goddess premiered Houston Grand Opera 2005; composer-in-residence New York City Opera 1999–; Master Artist Atlantic Center for the Performing Arts 2003; debut as stage dir, Lyric Opera Cleveland (Little Women) 2004. *Compositions:* opera: Little Women 1998, Lysistrata, or, The Nude Goddess 2005; orchestral: Late Victorians for singer, speaker, soloists and orchestra 1995, Alcott Portraits 1999, Harp Concerto; choral: Avow (miniature chamber opera) 1999, No.10/Supreme Virtue 1999, QWERTYUIOP 1999, Cantate Domino 1999–2000, Canticle 1999–2000, The Poet Speaks of Praising for men's chorus and piano, Pied Beauty for unaccompanied SATB chorus, Three Appalachian Folk Tunes for soprano and unaccompanied SATB chorus. *Publications:* John Corigliano: A Monograph 2000; has annotated programmes for Stagebill, the Freer Gallery of Art, BMG Classics; criticism and interviews in publs, including The Washington Post, Stagebill, Opera News, The Star-Ledger, The New Grove Dictionary of Music and Musicians. *Honours:* Paulette Goddard Remarque Scholarship for outstanding undergraduate achievement in playwriting, Theodore Pressler Prize for outstanding undergraduate achievement in composing. *Current Management:* c/o G. Schirmer Music Publishers, 257 Park Avenue S, 20th Floor, New York, NY 10010, USA. *Telephone:* (212) 254-2013. *Fax:* (212) 254-2100. *E-mail:* schirmer@schirmer.com. *Website:* www.schirmer.com.

**ADAMS, Byron,** BM, MM, DMA; composer, conductor, writer and teacher; b. 9 March 1955, Atlanta, Georgia, USA. *Education:* Jacksonville University, University of Southern California, Cornell University. *Career:* Composer-in-Residence, Music Center, University of the South, 1979–84; Guest Composer, 26th Warsaw Autumn Festival, 1983, and San Francisco Conservatory, 1986; Lecturer, Cornell University, New York City, 1985–87; Assistant Professor, Associate Professor, University of California at Riverside. *Compositions:* Quintet for piano and strings, 1979; Concerto for trumpet and string orchestra, 1983; Sonata for trumpet and piano, 1983; Concerto for violin and orchestra, 1984; Go Lovely Rose for male chorus, 1984; Missa brevis, 1988;

Three Epitaphs, 1988. *Recordings:* Nightingales, 1979; Serenata aestiva, 1986; contrib. to The Instrumentalist; Musical Quarterly; Notes. *Address:* Department of Music, University of California at Riverside, Riverside, CA 92521, USA.

**ADAMS, David,** BA; composer, conductor and librettist; b. 19 April 1949, Box Hill, Victoria, Australia. *Education:* Canberra School of Music. *Career:* Lowther Hall Anglican Girls Grammar School, 1977–81; Scotch College, 1978–83; Melbourne College of Advanced Education, 1985–87; Commissions from Sydney Dance Company, Australian Musicians Guild and the British Musical Society, 1987. *Compositions include:* Memories of the Future for guitar and harpsichord, 1979; Strangers, ballet, for string quartet, oboe, horn and percussion, 1981; being divinely for soprano, percussion and strings, 1983; Variations for oboe and guitar, 1983; In Memoriam, for soprano and ensemble, 1984; Fan Fare for chorus, orchestra, soprano and viola, 1985; Time Locked in his Tower, music theatre for flutes, guitar and percussion, 1987; In My Craft of Sullen Art for soprano and viola, 1994; Lunar aspects, song cycle for soprano and guitar, 1996. *Honours:* Winner, Australian Composition Sections at Geelong Eisteddfod, also Bandigo Eisteddfod, 1981–83. *Address:* c/o APRA, 1A Eden Street, Crows Nest, NSW 2065, Australia.

**ADAMS, John Coolidge;** American composer and conductor; b. 15 Feb. 1947, Worcester, MA. *Education:* Harvard Univ. *Career:* appearances as clarinettist and conductor; Head, Composition Dept, San Francisco Conservatory of Music 1971–81; Adviser on new music, San Francisco Symphony Orchestra 1978–82, Composer-in-Residence 1982–85; conducted Nixon in China at 1988 Edinburgh Festival; Creative Adviser, St Paul Chamber Orchestra, MN 1988–89; The Death of Klinghoffer premiered at Brussels, Lyon and Vienna 1991 (London premiere at Barbican Hall 2002); I Was Looking at the Ceiling performed at Berkeley, New York, Paris, Edinburgh and Hamburg 1995. *Compositions include:* opera: Nixon in China 1987, The Death of Klinghoffer 1991, I Was Looking at the Ceiling and Then I Saw the Sky 1995; orchestral works: Shaker Loops 1978, Common Tones in Simple Time 1979, Harmonium 1980, Grand Pianola Music 1981–82, Harmonielehre 1984–85, The Chairman Dances 1985, Short Ride in a Fast Machine 1986, Tromba Lontana 1986, Fearful Symmetries 1988, The Wound-Dresser 1989, Eros Piano 1989, El Dorado 1991, Violin Concerto 1993, Gnarly Buttons 1996; chamber and ensemble works: Christian Zeal and Activity 1973, China Gates 1977, Phrygian Gates 1977, Chamber Symphony 1992, John's Book of Alleged Dances 1994, Road Movies 1995, Naïve and Sentimental Music 1998, El Niño 2000, Guide to Strange Places 2001, On the Transmigration of Souls (Pulitzer Prize for Music 2003, Grammy Awards for Best Classical Album, Best Orchestral Performance, Best Classical Contemporary Composition 2005, Classical BRIT Award for Contemporary Music 2005) 2002, Doctor Atomic 2005. *Honours:* Guggenheim Fellowship 1982, Fellow BAC&S 2005; Grawemeyer Award for Music Composition 1995. *Current Management:* Boosey & Hawkes Ltd, 295 Regent Street, London, W1R 8JH, England.

**ADAMS, (Harrison) Leslie,** PhD; American composer and teacher; b. 30 Dec. 1932, Cleveland, OH. *Education:* Glenville High School, Oberlin Coll. Conservatory of Music, OH, Calif. State Univ. at Long Beach, Ohio State Univ. *Career:* piano accompanist for ballet and dance companies in New York, numerous performances of his compositions 1957–62; Assoc. Musical Dir, Karamu House, Cleveland, OH 1964–65, composer-in-residence 1979–80; Musical Dir, Kaleidoscope Players, Raton, NM 1967–68; composer-in-residence, Cuyahoga Community Coll., Cleveland 1980, Cleveland Music School Settlement 1981–82; founder and Pres., Accord Assocs. Inc. 1980–86, Exec. Vice-Pres. and composer-in-residence 1986–92; Exec. Vice-Pres. and composer-in-residence, Creative Arts Inc. 1997–; teacher, Soehl Jr High School, Linden, NJ 1962–63, secondary schools in Raton, NM 1966–67; Asst Prof. of Music, Fla A&M Univ., Tallahassee 1968; Assoc. Prof. of Music, Dir of the Univ. Choir, Dir of Choral Clinics, Univ. of Kan., Lawrence 1970–78; mem. advisory council, Musical Arts Assocn (Cleveland Orchestra) 1982; mem. American Choral Dirs' Assocn, American Guild of Organists. *Compositions:* Hark, to the Shouting Wind! 1951, I Hear A Voice 1951, Night 1951, The Constant Lover 1951, Break, Break, Break 1951, Teach Me, O Lord (from Psalm 119) 1951, Turn Away Mine Eyes 1951, Four Pieces for piano 1951, Pastorale for violin and piano 1952, Asperges Me for chorus 1952, Two Vachel Lindsay Songs 1952–53, Of Man's First Disobedience (from Paradise Lost) 1953, On the Sea 1953, Seven Amen Chorale Responses 1953, Intermezzo for violin and piano 1953, Theme and Variations in A-flat Major (or Variations on a Serious Theme) 1953, A Kiss in Xanadu (ballet) 1954, The Congo 1955, Romance for orchestra 1960, Five Songs on Texts by Edna St Vincent Millay (or Five Millay Songs) 1960, Six Songs (on Texts by African-American Poets) 1961, A White Road 1961, Sonata for violin and piano 1961, Three Preludes for piano 1961, Sonata for horn and piano 1961, Contrasts for piano 1961, Concerto for piano and orchestra (or CitiScape) 1964, All the Way Home 1965, Madrigal for chorus 1969, Love Song for chorus 1969, Hosanna to the Son of David for chorus 1969, Psalm 121 for chorus 1969, Under the Greenwood Tree for chorus 1969, Psalm 23 for chorus 1970, There Was an Old Man for chorus 1970, Vocalise for chorus 1973, Man's Presence: A Song of Ecology for chorus 1975, Trombone Quartet 1975, Sonata for cello and piano 1975, Etude in G Minor 1977, Prelude and Fugue for organ 1979, Ode to Life for orchestra 1979, Dunbar Songs (or Three Songs on Texts of Paul Laurence Dunbar) 1981, Christmas Lullaby 1983, Night Song for flute and harp 1983, Symphony No. 1 1983, The Righteous Man: A Cantata to the Memory of Dr Martin Luther King Jr (or Cantata No. 1) 1985, Blake (opera) 1986, The Wider View 1988, Hymn to

Freedom 1989, Love Expressions 1990, Love Memory 1990, What Love Brings 1991, A Christmas Wish for chorus 1991, Offering of Love for organ 1991, Amazing Grace 1992, Song of the Innkeeper's Children 1992, Song to Baby Jesus 1992, Christmas Lullaby for orchestra with chorus 1993, Song of Thanks 1993, Love Request 1993, Lullaby Eternal 1993, Anniversary Song 1993, Flying 1993, Midas, Poor Midas 1994, From a Hotel Room 1994, Daybirth 1994, Western Adventure for orchestra 1994, Hymn to All Nations for chorus 1997. *Publications:* contrib. articles The Mahlerian Mystique 1969, The Problems of Composing Choral Music for High School Use 1973. *Honours:* Nat. Asscn of Negro Women Inc. Composition Competition, New York 1963, Nat. Educ. Defense Act Fellowship 1969–70, Christian Arts Inc. Nat. Award for Original Composition for Choral Ensemble, New York 1974, Nat. Endowment for the Arts Award 1979, Rockefeller Foundation Study and Conference Center, Bellagio Italy 1979, Yaddo Artists Colony, Saratoga Springs NY 1980, 1984, Cleveland Foundation Fellow 1980, Jennings Foundation Fellow 1981, 'Meet The Artist' Cleveland Ohio Public Schools. *Current Management:* Creative Arts Inc., 9409 Kempton Avenue, Cleveland, OH 44108, USA. *Fax:* (216) 451-5159 (office). *E-mail:* CreativeArtsInc@webtv .net (office).

**ADAMS-BARBARO, Jennifer;** Singer (Soprano); b. 22 March 1953, London, England. *Education:* Guildhall School of Music and Drama. *Career:* Opera debut aged 15, Juliet in Gounod's Romeo and Juliet; Operatic roles, Gretel, Galatea, Euridice, Dido, Micaela, Naiad and Turandot; Star singer on Friday Night is Music Night, 1985; Glyndebourne Festival Opera; Mozart Requiem, Swansea Festival, Jane Glover, 1991. *Recordings:* Numerous BBC solo recordings including Rossini Petite Messe, Verdi Four Sacred Pieces with BBC Symphony Orchestra; Promenade concert; Video, Bartók Five Village Scenes with Pierre Boulez, Concertgebouw, Amsterdam. *Honours:* World Finalist in Luciano Pavarotti Prize, 1985; AGSM. *Address:* 68 Bellingham Road, Catford, London SE6 2PT, England.

**ADÈS, Thomas Joseph Edmund,** MA, MPhil; British composer, pianist and conductor; *Artistic Director, Aldeburgh Festival*; b. 1 March 1971, London; s. of Timothy Adès and Dawn Adès. *Education:* Univ. Coll. School, Guildhall School of Music, King's Coll., Cambridge, St John's Coll., Cambridge. *Career:* solo recitalist with the Composers' Ensemble 1992; PLG Young Concert Artists Platform concert at the Purcell Room 1993; Composer in Assoc., Hallé Orchestra 1993–95; Lecturer, Univ. of Manchester 1993–94; Fellow Commoner in Creative Arts, Trinity Coll., Cambridge 1995–97; Benjamin Britten Prof. of Music, RAM 1997–99; Musical Dir Birmingham Contemporary Music Group 1998–2000; Artistic Dir Aldeburgh Festival 1999–; conducted the BBC Symphony Orchestra at the BBC Proms, London 2002. *Compositions:* Five Eliot Landscapes 1990, Chamber Symphony 1990, Catch 1991, Darkness Visible 1992, Under Hamelin Hill 1992, Fool's Rhymes 1992, Still Sorrowing 1993, Life Story 1993, Living Toys 1993, ... but all shall be well 1993, Sonata da Caccia 1994, The Origin of the Harp 1994, Arcadiana 1994, Powder Her Face 1995, Traced Overhead 1995–96, These Premises are Alarmed 1996, Asyla 1997, Concerto Conciso 1997–98, America (A Prophecy) 1999, January Writ 1999, Piano Quintet 2000, Brahms 2001, The Tempest (Olivier Award for outstanding achievement in opera 2005, Royal Philharmonic Soc. award for large-scale composition 2005) 2004. *Television includes:* Music for the 21st Century: Thomas Adès (Channel 4), Powder her Face (Channel 4). *Honours:* Lutine Prize, GSM 1986, winner Paris Rostrum, for best piece by composer under 30 1994, Royal Philharmonic Prize 1997, Elise L. Stoeger Prize 1996, Royal Philharmonic Soc. Award for Large-scale Composition 1997, 2005, Salzburg Easter Festival Prize 1999, Ernst von Siemens Prize 1999, Grawemeyer Prize 2000, Hindemith Prize 2001, ISCM Young Composers Award 2002. *Address:* c/o Faber Music Ltd, 3 Queen Square, London, WC1N 3AU, England (office). *Telephone:* (20) 7833-7911 (office). *Fax:* (20) 7833-7939 (office). *E-mail:* sally.cavender@fabermusic.com (office). *Website:* www .fabermusic.com (office).

**ADEY, Christopher,** FRAM, FRCM, FRWCMD; British conductor; *Chief Conductor and Artistic Director, Royal Oman Symphony Orchestra*; b. 19 Feb. 1943, London; m. Catherine Cave 1965 (divorced 1980); one s. *Education:* Royal Acad. of Music, London. *Career:* violinist with Hallé Orchestra 1963–65, London Philharmonic Orchestra 1967–71; Assoc. Conductor, BBC Scottish Symphony Orchestra 1973–76, Ulster Orchestra 1981–83; Conductor and Prof. Royal Coll. of Music (RCM) 1979–92, Dir of Orchestral Studies, RCM Jr Dept 1973–84; Principal Conductor, Nat. Youth Orchestra of Wales 1996–2002; Chief Conductor and Artistic Dir, Royal Oman Symphony Orchestra 2001–; freelance conductor appearing as guest conductor with major orchestras in UK, Europe and South Africa; Cycle of the complete Martinu symphonies for BBC 1975. *Publication:* Orchestral Performance: A Guide for Conductors and Players 1998. *Honours:* Commemorative Medal of Czechoslovakian Govt 1986. *Address:* c/o Richard Haigh, Performing Arts, 6 Windmill Street, London, W1P 1HF (office); 137 Anson Road, Willesden Green, London, NW2 4AH, England.

**ADKINS, Cecil Dale;** Musicologist; b. 30 Jan. 1932, Red Oak, Iowa, USA. *Education:* BFA, University of Omaha, 1953; MM, University of South Dakota, 1959; PhD, University of Iowa, 1963. *Career:* Assistant Conductor and Arranger, Fourth Armoured Division Band, Fort Hood, Texas, 1954–55; Director of Instrumental Music, Paullina, IA, 1955–60; Graduate Assistant, University of Iowa, 1960–63; Instructor, Music department, Mount Mercy College, Cedar Rapids, IA, 1960–63; Professor of Music, University of North Texas, Denton, 1963–, Regents Professor, 1988–, Chairman, International

Musicological Society's Center for Musicological Works in Progress, 1969–; President, American Musical Instrument Society, 1987–91; mem, American Musicological Society; International Musicological Society; American Musical Instrument Society; Dansk Selskab for Musikforskning. *Publications:* Editor, Doctoral Dissertations in Musicology, 5th edition, 1971, 7th edition, 1984, with A Dickinson, 8th edition, 1989; The A flat y'Berg Positive Organ: Basle, Historical Museum 1927–28, Description and Technical Drawing, 1979; A Trumpet by Any Other Name: A History of the Trumpet Marine, with A Dickinson, 1987; Four Historical Trumpet Marines, Description and Technical Drawings, 1987; Doctoral Dissertations in Musicology, Second Series No. 1, 1990, No. 2, 1996. *Contributions:* articles in many journals and reference works. *Honours:* Francis Densmore Prize for best Journal Article on Instruments, American Musical Instrument Society, 1992; Curt Sachs Award, American Musical Instrument Society, 1999. *Address:* c/o College of Music, University of North Texas, Denton, TX 76203, USA.

**ADLER, Samuel Hans**, BM, MA; composer, conductor and music teacher; *Composition Faculty Member, Juilliard School of Music;* b. 4 March 1928, Mannheim, Germany; m. 1st Carol Ellen Stalker (divorced 1988); two d.; m. 2nd Emily Freeman Brown 1992. *Education:* Boston Univ., Harvard Univ., studied composition with Herbert Fromm, Hugo Norden, Walter Piston, Randall Thompson, Paul Hindemith and Aaron Copland, musicology with Karl Geiringer, conducting with Serge Koussevitzky at Berkshire Music Centre, Tanglewood. *Career:* founder and first conductor, 7th Army Symphony Orchestra 1952; Dir of Music, Temple Emanu-El, Dallas 1953–66; conductor, Dallas Lyric Theatre 1955–57; Prof. of Composition, North Texas State Univ., Denton 1957–66; Prof. of Composition 1966–95, Prof. Emeritus 1966–95, Chair Composition Dept 1973–95, Eastman School of Music, Rochester, NY; guest conductor, symphony orchestras and opera cos. worldwide; guest lecturer in USA and other countries; teacher of composition, Juilliard School of Music, New York, Composition Faculty mem. 1997–; mem. professional organizations. *Compositions include:* operas: The Outcasts of Poker Flat 1959, The Wrester 1970, The Lodge of Shadows 1973; orchestral works include: six symphonies 1953–85, Rhapsody for violin and orchestra 1961, Elegy for string orchestra 1962, Requiescat in Pace in memory of President John F. Kennedy 1963, Concerto for orchestra 1971, Sinfonietta 1971, Flute Concerto 1977, Piano Concerto No. 1 1983, Time in Tempest Everywhere for orchestra 1993, Guitar Concerto 1994, Cello Concerto 1995, Piano Concerto No. 2 1996; chamber music includes: eight string quartets 1945, 1950, 1953, revised 1964, 1963, 1969, 1975, 1981, 1990, organ pieces. *Publications include:* Anthology for the Teaching of Choral Conducting 1971, Sight Singing 1979, The Study of Orchestration 1982; contrib. to numerous journals. *Honours:* several hon. degrees; American Acad. and Inst. of Arts and Letters Music Award, ASCAP Aaron Copland Award for Lifetime Achievement 2003. *Address:* 9412 Sheffield Road, Perrysburg OH 43551, USA. *Telephone:* (419) 666-9519 (home). *Fax:* (419) 666-6417 (home).

**ADNI, Daniel;** Israeli/British concert pianist; b. 6 Dec. 1951, Haifa. *Education:* High Schools in Haifa and Tel-Aviv, Conservatoire of Music in Paris. *Career:* first recital in Haifa 1963; professional debut, London 1970; New York debut 1976; has played at most musical centres in the world including UK, Germany, Israel, USA, Japan, South Africa, Switzerland, Norway, Netherlands, Romania, Australia, New Zealand, Finland, Austria; has taught masterclasses including at Dartington Summer School (UK); made over 20 records for EMI-His Master's Voice. *Honours:* First Prize, Paris Conservatoire, First Prize, Young Concert Artists' Auditions, New York. *Address:* c/o 64A Menelik Road, London, NW2 3RH, England. *Telephone:* (20) 7794-4076. *Fax:* (20) 7794-4076. *E-mail:* danieladni@waitrose.com (home).

**ADOLPHE, Bruce;** American composer; *Artistic Advisor and Education Advisor, Chamber Music Society of Lincoln Center;* b. 31 May 1955, New York City. *Education:* Juilliard School, New York. *Career:* taught at New York Univ. Tisch School 1983, Yale Univ. 1984–85; Composer-in-Residence, 92nd Street Y School Concert Series 1988–90, Santa Fe Chamber Music Festival 1989, La Jolla SummerFest 1998–2001, 2003, 2005, Music from Angel Fire 1984, 1995 and many other festivals; Artistic Advisor and Educ. Advisor, Chamber Music Soc. of Lincoln Center, New York 1992–; Creative Dir PollyRhythm Productions; his operas have been performed in Boston and New York; comms from Orpheus Chamber Orchestra, Chamber Music Soc. of Lincoln Center, Itzhak Perlman, Beaux Arts Trio, Chamber Orchestra of Philadelphia, Brentano String Quartet, Metropolitan Opera Guild, Chicago Chamber Musicians, Chicago Humanities Festival, and many others. *Compositions include:* The Tell-Tale Heart (one-act opera after Edgar Allan Poe) 1982, Mikhoels The Wise (opera in two acts) 1982, The False Messiah (opera in two acts) 1983, The Amazing Adventure of Alvin Allegretto (one-act comic children's opera) 1994, Oceanophony (for chamber ensemble and actors, poems by Kate Light) 2004, Red Dogs and Pink Skies: A Musical Celebration of Paul Gauguin 2003, Time Flies (for chamber orchestra) 2004, What Dreams May Come? (for chamber orchestra) 2005, Violin Concerto 2005, Songs of Life and Love: to Poems by Persian, Arab, Israeli, and American Women (for mezzo-soprano and piano) 2005. *Recordings:* many recordings with PollyRhythm Productions, Telarc, Naxos, Delos, Koch, CRI and Summit. *Publications:* The Mind's Ear 1990, What To Listen For In The World 1996, Of Mozart, Parrots, and Cherry Blossoms in the Wind: A Composer Explores Mysteries of the Musical Mind 1999. *Address:* Chamber Music Society of Lincoln Center, 70 Lincoln Center Plaza, 10th Floor, New York, NY 10024, USA (office).

*Telephone:* (212) 875-5775 (office). *Website:* www.chambermusicsociety.org (office); www.pollyrhythm.com (office).

**ADORJÁN, András;** flautist; b. 26 Sept. 1944, Budapest, Hungary. *Education:* Dentist Diploma, Copenhagen, 1968; Musical Studies with Jean-Pierre Rampal and Aurèle Nicolet. *Career:* principal with the orchestra of the Royal Opera, Stockholm, 1970–72, Gurzenich Orchestra, Cologne, 1972–73, Sudwestfunk Baden-Baden, 1973–74 and Bavarian Radio Symphony Orchestra, 1974–88; Teacher at the Nice Summer Academy from 1971–1985; Professor at the Musikhochschule at Cologne, Germany from 1987 and the Musikhochschule München from 1996; Gave the 1981 premiere of Ground, concerto for Flute and Orchestra by Sven-Erik Werner; Dedication of Moz-Art à la Mozart by Alfred Schnittke, 1990; Concerto for Flute and Harp by Edison Denisov, 1995. *Recordings:* over 90 including the first complete recording of all 14 flute concertos by François Devienne. *Address:* Musikhochschule München, Arcisstr 12, 80333 Munich, Germany.

**AFANASSIEV, Valery;** pianist; b. 1947, Moscow, Russia. *Education:* Moscow Conservatory with Emil Gilels. *Career:* debut in Moscow, 1962; performances throughout Eastern Europe after winning 1969 Bach Competition at Leipzig; settled in Brussels, 1974, Versailles thereafter; chamber musician with violinist Gidon Kremer; concerts throughout Europe, Japan and USA; performs in own plays as actor and pianist, has done these one-man shows in several countries and in four languages. *Recordings:* Bach, Beethoven, Brahms, Mozart and Schubert with major recording companies including most recently Das Wohltemperierte Klavier Complete Vols I and II, by J. S. Bach, 1997; Sonatas D 958, D 959, D960 by Schubert, 1997; Diabelli Variations and Chopin's Nocturnes. *Publications:* four novels (in French), two plays inspired by Mussorgsky's Pictures at an Exhibition and Schumann's Kreisleriana. *Honours:* winner Queen Elisabeth of the Belgians Competition, Brussels 1972. *Address:* 1 square de Furstenberg, 78150 Le Chesnay, France.

**AFANASYEVA, Veronika;** violinist; b. 1960, Moscow, Russia. *Education:* Central Music School, Moscow. *Career:* co-founder of Quartet Veronique in 1989; many concerts in Russia notably in the Russian Chamber Music Series and 150th birthday celebrations for Tchaikovsky in 1990; masterclasses at Aldeburgh Festival in 1991; concert tour of the United Kingdom 1992–93; repertoire includes works by Beethoven, Brahms, Tchaikovsky, Bartók, Shostakovich and Schnittke. *Recordings include:* Schnittke's 3rd Quartet. *Honours:* with Quartet Veronique: Winner, All-Union String Quartet Competition at St Petersburg, 1990–91, 3rd Place, International Shostakovich Competition at St Petersburg, 1991. *Address:* c/o Sonata (Quartet Veronique), 11 Northgate Street, Glasgow G20 7AA, Scotland.

**AGACHE, Alexandru;** Singer (Baritone); b. 16 Aug. 1955, Cluj, Romania. *Education:* Studied in Cluj. *Career:* Debut: As Silvano in Ballo in Maschera, Cluj, 1979; Has sung Sharpless, Don Giovanni, Malatesta and Verdi's Posa, Luna, Nabucco and Germont at Cluj; Further appearances in Dresden, Budapest and Ankara; Sang Don Giovanni at Livorno and Toulon, 1987, Renato at Covent Garden followed by Enrico Ashton in Lucia di Lammermoor and Simon Boccanegra in a new production of Verdi's opera in 1991; La Scala debut as Belcore in L'Elisir d'amore, 1988; Marquis di Posa in Hamburg, 1988 and La Fenice, Venice, in 1992; Sang Renato in Ballo in Maschera in Zürich and Düsseldorf, 1989, Marcello in La Bohème at Lyon Opéra in 1991 and Renato at Opéra Bastille in Paris in 1992; Sang Amonasro at Covent Garden, 1994, returning 1997 and 2002 for Simon Boccanegra; Met debut as Boccanegra, 1999. *Recordings include:* Golem The Rebel by Nicolas Bretan; Video of Covent Garden performance of Simon Boccanegra under Solti. *Current Management:* Stage Door, Via Marconi 71, 40122 Bologna, Italy. *Telephone:* (51) 19984750. *Fax:* (51) 19984779. *E-mail:* info@stagedoor.it. *Website:* www.stagedoor.it.

**AGAZHANOV, Artyomovich;** Composer and Pianist; b. 3 Feb. 1958, Moscow, Russia. *Education:* piano and composition at Moscow Central Music School, 1965–76; further study at Moscow State Tchaikovsky Conservatoire. *Career:* teacher at Moscow Central Music School 1983–; concert appearances as composer and pianist in Russia, Bulgaria, Italy, Germany, including festivals: Moscow autumne 1986, 1987, 1989 and 1994, Moscow Stars 1989, and International Music Festival 1988; mem. Union of Russian Composers. *Compositions include:* Pax in terra for orchestra, 1983; On Beauty, Sorrow, Laughter and Grieving (cantata no. 2), for high soprano and large orchestra, texts by Issa Kobayashi, Matsuo Basho, Ihara Saikaku, 1983; Gloria (cantata no. 3) for soprano, mezzo-soprano, tenor, baritone, mixed chorus, large orchestra, tape ad libitum, 1984; Way of the Poet (cantata no. 4), for tenor, mixed chorus, large orchestra, text by Mikhail Lermontov, 1989; Kolobrod, music for film, 1990; Incite the City to Rebellion, music for film, 1992; Confessing Sinner (cantata no. 5), for mezzo-soprano, tenor, tenor/baritone, bass, large orchestra, tape ad libitum, 2000; Farewell in June, music for film, 2003. *Recordings:* Vision for Violin and Piano, 1988; Sonata for Violoncello and Piano, 1989; Gust, overture for Orchestra, 1989; From 3 till 6 for Piano, 1989; Variations on Theme by Chopin for Piano, 1992; 6 Japanese Hokku for Soprano and Piano, 1993; Way of the Poet (cantata no. 4), vocal symphony poem for Tenor, Mixed Choir and Full Orchestra, 1994; Without trace, vocal cycle for contralto and piano, 1999. *Publications:* Without Colouring The Truth 1993. *Honours:* All Union Competition of Young Composers 1981. *Address:* Brusov 8–10 Apt 55, Moscow 103009, Russia. *E-mail:* aaartem_@mtu-net.ru.

**AGHOVA, Livia;** Singer (Soprano); b. 1961, Slovakia, Czechoslovakia. *Education:* Studied in Bratislava. *Career:* Sang in opera at Bratislava, 1983–88; Mozart's Susanna, Donna Elvira and Pamina, Mimi, Micaela and Marguerite in Faust; National Theatre, Prague, 1988–; Marenka Marzellina and Martinů's Julietta; Berlin Staatsoper as Antonia in Hoffmann; Munich Staatsoper as Xenia in Dvořák's Dimitri; As Donna Elvira, Savonlinna Festival, 1991; Liu in Turandot, Houston, 1994; Puccini's Lauretta, Prague, 1996; Other roles include Jenůfa, Strauss's Sophie, Gounod's Juliette and Nedda in Pagliacci; Concerts include Beethoven's Ninth and Dvořák's St Ludmilla and The Spectre's Bride; Sang Janáček's Vixen at Venice, 1999. *Recordings:* Dimitri, Supraphon; Janáček's Osud, Orfeo; Glagolitic Mass. *Address:* c/o Music International, 13 Ardilaun Road, London N5 2QR, England.

**AGLER, David;** conductor; *Artistic Director, Wexford Opera Festival. Career:* fmr Prin. Conductor Australian Opera; fmr Resident Conductor San Francisco Opera; fmr Prin. Guest Conductor Oper der Stadt Köln; fmr Music Dir Syracuse Opera, Vancouver Opera; fmr Artistic Dir Opera Festival of New Jersey, Artistic Dir Wexford Opera Festival 2005–; fmr admin. Spoleto Festival; has conducted operas with Wexford Opera, Santa Fe Opera, Seattle Opera, Pittsburgh Opera, Opera Co. of Philadelphia, Opera Theater of St Louis, Edmonton Opera, New York City Opera, Calgary Opera, Manitoba Opera, L'Opera de Montreal, Opera Pacific, Banff Festival Orchestra, Western Australia Opera, Netherlands Opera, Teatro Comunale Rossini, Lugo; has conducted concerts with San Francisco Symphony, Minnesota Orchestra, Sydney Symphony Orchestra, Winnipeg Symphony, Warsaw Philharmonic, Nat. Arts Center Orchestra Ottawa, CBC Vancouver, Netherlands Radio Symphony, Netherlands Chamber Orchestra, Charlotte Symphony Orchestra, San Francisco Chamber Symphony Kitchener-Waterloo Symphony; Visiting Lecturer Banff Centre 2004. *Recordings:* Ned Rorem, Miss Julie 2005. *Current Management:* Pinnacle Arts Management, Thierschstrasse 11, Munich 80538, Germany. *Telephone:* (89) 3408630 (office). *Fax:* (89) 34086310 (office). *Website:* www.pinnaclearts.com (office). *Address:* c/o Wexford Festival Opera, Theatre Royal, High Street, Wexford, Ireland (office). *E-mail:* artisticdirector@wexfordopera.com. *Website:* www.wexfordopera.com.

**AGNEW, Paul;** Singer (tenor); b. 1964, Glasgow, Scotland. *Education:* Chorister at St Chad's Cathedral, Birmingham; Lay-Clerkships at Birmingham and Lichfield Cathedrals; Choral Scholar at Magdalen College, Oxford. *Career:* Tours with the Consort of Musicke to Germany, Switzerland, Netherlands, Italy, Spain, Austria, Sweden and Australia; Handel songs in the National Gallery, London with the Parley of Instruments; Promenade Concerts debut in 1989 in The Judgement of Paris; Has sung the Evangelist in the St Matthew Passion for the London Handel Orchestra; South Bank debut at the Purcell Room celebrating the centenary of Ivor Gurney's birth; Engaged for the St John Passion with the Schola Cantorum of Basle and for Les Noces in Zürich; Tour of the USA with the Festival of Voices directed by Paul Hillier; Sang in Monteverdi Madrigals with the Consort of Musicke at Promenade Concerts in 1993; Palais Garnier, Paris, 1996, as Rameau's Hippolyte; Sang with New London Consort at the Purcell Room, London, 1997; Season 1999 with Charpentier's Extremum Dei Judicum and Lalande's Dies Irae at the London Prom concerts; Sang in Rameau's Platée at the Palais Garnier; Season 2000 in Rameau's La Guirlande at Cologne and Acis and Galatea at the Salzburg Easter Festival. *Recordings include:* Monteverdi Madrigals. *Current Management:* Harrison/Parrott Ltd, 12 Penzance Place, London, W11 4PA, England. *Telephone:* (20) 7229 9166. *Fax:* (20) 7221 5042. *E-mail:* info@harrisonparrott.co.uk. *Website:* www.harrisonparrott.com.

**AGOPOV, Vladimir;** composer; b. 23 Nov. 1953, Voroshilovgrad, USSR; m. 1977; two s. one d. *Education:* Moscow Conservatoire. *Career:* debut in diploma concert, Moscow 1977; mem. Society of Finnish Composers. *Compositions:* Music for Chamber Orchestra, 1982; Ergo for violin and piano, 1985; Tres viae, Concerto for Cello and Orchestra, op 10; 1987; Decimetto, 1997. *Recordings:* Sonata for clarinet and piano, 1991; Concerto for cello and orchestra, 1992; Siciliana, 1992. *Honours:* Competition in Kouvola, Finland, 1982; Sibelius Violin Competition for Composers, 1985. *Address:* Limingantie 24, 00520 Helsinki, Finland.

**AGUERA, Luc-Marie;** Violinist; b. 1960, France. *Education:* Paris Conservatoire with Jean-Claude Pennetier and with members of the Amadeus and Alban Berg Quartets. *Career:* Member of the Ysaÿe String Quartet from 1985; Many concert performances in France, Europe, America and the Far East; Festival engagements at Salzburg, Tivoli, Bergen, Lockenhaus, Barcelona and Stresa; Many appearances in Italy notably playing the Haydn Quartets of Mozart; Tours of Japan and USA in 1990 and 1992. *Recordings:* Mozart Quartet K421 and Quintet K516; Ravel, Debussy and Mendelssohn Quartets. *Honours:* Grand Prix Evian International String Quartet Competition, 1988; Special Prizes for Best Performances of a Mozart Quartet, the Debussy Quartet and a contemporary work; 2nd Prize, Portsmouth International String Quartet Competition, 1988. *Current Management:* Artist Management International Ltd, 12–13 Richmond Buildings, Dean Street, London W1V 5AF, England.

**AHLIN, Sven Åke;** Swedish composer; b. 6 April 1951, Sundsvall; m. Emma Rosendal 1989; two s. one d. *Education:* Royal Coll. of Music, Stockholm, Indiana Univ., USA. *Career:* debut, Stockholm 1977; numerous performances of his choir music and chamber music in Sweden, including trombone concerto with Christian Lindberg as soloist in Jönköping; broadcasts include four first

performances by the Swedish Radio Choir, and piano concerto with Mats Widlund as soloist; performances abroad in Norway, Iceland, Russia, France, Spain, Hungary and the Netherlands; mem. Soc. of Swedish Composers. *Compositions:* Al Fresco, piano concerto; Narratives, trombone concerto; Across for orchestra; Ritual for Huitzilopochtli; Choral music including Dream of Elysium; Clashing Worlds; I have a dream; Concertos: Al fresco (piano); Narratives (trombone); Turning Points (String Quartet No. 2), 1997; Concerto for vihuela and string orchestra, 1998; Skuggan av ett regn (The shadow of a rain) for mezzo-soprano and chamber ensemble; numerous pieces of chamber music. *Address:* Ålstorp, Mossehus, 312 94 Laholm, Sweden. *Telephone:* (430) 61027. *Fax:* (430) 63018. *E-mail:* stringendo@rixtele.com.

**AHLSTEDT, Douglas;** Singer (Tenor); b. 16 March 1945, Jamestown, NY, USA. *Education:* Studied at State University, New York and Eastman School, Rochester. *Career:* Debut: As Ramiro in La Cenerentola, Western Opera Theater, San Francisco, 1971; Sang at Metropolitan Opera from season 1974–75, with debut as Italian Singer in Rosenkavalier, then as Fenton in Falstaff; Member of Deutsche Oper Düsseldorf, 1975–84, and guest appearances in Vienna, Hamburg, Zürich and Karlsruhe; Returned to New York in 1983 and sang Iopas in Les Troyens, Almaviva in Barbiere di Siviglia and Debussy's Pelléas, 1988; Salzburg Festival as Alfinoma in the Henze-Monteverdi Il Ritorno d'Ulisse, 1985; Teatro San Carlo in Naples as Orestes in Ermione by Rossini, 1988; Other engagements in Dallas, Philadelphia and Santiago as Don Ottavio, Genoa, Avignon and Rome as Idreno in Semiramide, 1982; Other roles include Tamino, Jacquino in Fidelio, Narcisio in Turco in Italia, the Fox in Cunning Little Vixen and Peter Quint in The Turn of the Screw; Sang Dorvil in La Scala di Seta in Stuttgart, 1991; Zürich Opera as Flamand in Capriccio, 1992. *Recordings include:* Video of Il Ritorno d'Ulisse, Salzburg, 1985. *Address:* c/o Staatstheater Stuttgart, Oberer Schlossgarten 6, 7000 Stuttgart, Germany.

**AHNSJO, Claes Haakon;** singer (tenor); b. 1 Aug. 1942, Stockholm, Sweden; m. Helena Jungwirth. *Education:* studied in Stockholm with Erik Saeden, Aksel Schiotz and Max Lorenz. *Career:* debut at Royal Opera Stockholm in 1969 as Tamino; sang in Stockholm until 1973, then with the Munich Opera notably in operas by Mozart and Rossini; Drottningholm Opera from 1969; Bayreuth Festival, 1973; Kennedy Music Center, NY, 1974 in Die Jahreszeiten by Haydn; guest appearances in Frankfurt, Cologne, Tokyo, Hamburg, Stuttgart and Nancy; Concert tours of Italy and Spain; Sang at Munich in 1985 as the Painter in Lulu, and in the premiere of Le Roi Bérenger by Sutermeister; Sang at Berlin in 1987 as Ramiro in La Cenerentola by Rossini; Sang Wolfgang Capito in Mathis der Maler and the Abbé in Adriana Lecouvreur, 1989; Munich Festival in premiere of Penderecki's Ubu Rex in 1991; Season 1997–98 in Monteverdi's Poppea and as Melot in Tristan und Isolde; Director of the Stockholm Royal Opera, from 1999/2000. *Recordings:* Bastien und Bastienne; Orlando Paladino, La Vera Costanza and L'Infedeltà Delusa by Haydn; Betulia Liberata by Mozart; Die Lustigen Weiber von Windsor; Bruckner's Te Deum. *Address:* c/o Bayerische Staatsoper, Pf 745, 8000 Munich 1, Germany.

**AHO, Kalevi;** composer, teacher and writer on music; b. 9 March 1949, Forssa, Finland. *Education:* Sibelius Academy, Helsinki, Staatliche Hochschule für Musik und Darstellende Kunst, Berlin with Einojuhani Rautavaara, Boris Blacher. *Career:* Lecturer on Music, University of Helsinki, 1974–88; Professor of Composition, Sibelius Academy, Helsinki, 1988–93; Composer-in-Residence, Sinfonia Lahti, Finland, 1992–; freelance artist in Helsinki, 1993–. *Compositions include:* Works for the stage: Avain (The Key), dramatic monologue for baritone and chamber orchestra, 1977–78; Hyönteisedämää (Insect Life), comic opera, 1985–87; Ennen kuin me kaikki olemme hukkuneet (Before We Are All Drowned), opera, 1995–99; Salaisuuksien kirja (The Book of Secrets), opera for soloists, choir and orchestra, 1998; Orchestral works: Symphonies Nos 1–11, 1969–1998, Concertos and chamber symphonies; Pergamon, for four instrumental groups, voices and organ, 1990; Hiljaisuus, for orchestra, 1982; Tristia, fantasy for wind orchestra, 1999; Chamber Music: Quintets and Quartets include: Quintet for flute, oboe, violin, viola and cello, 1977; Quintet for alto saxophone, bassoon, viola, cello and double bass; Sonata for oboe and piano, 1985; Sonatine for two pianos, 1997; Ballade, for flute, bassoon, cello and piano, 1999; Solo instruments: Sonata for violin, 1973; In memoriam for organ, 1980; Piano Sonata, 1980; Sonata No. 2 for accordion, mustat linnet (Black Birds), 1990; Solo III for flute, 1991–92; Solo IV for Cello, 1997; Solo V for bassoon, 1999; Solo VI for double bass, 1999; Clarinet Quintet, 1999; Vocal works: Lasimaalaus (Stained Glass), for female choir, 1975; Kiinalaisia lauluja (Chinese Songs) soprano and orchestra, 1997; Kolme Bertrandin monologia (Three Monologues of Bertrand), baritone and orchestra, 1999; Orchestrations and arrangements: Modest Mussorgsky: Songs and Dances of Death, 1984; Uuno Klami, Whirls (illustrations of the ballet act, 1988) Erik Tulindberg, string quartets; Sibelius, Karelia, reconstruction, 1997. *Recordings:* complete works recorded. *Publications include:* Finnish Music and the Kalevala, 1985; Finnish Music, co-author, 1996; Art and Reality, 1997. *Honours:* Leonie Sonning Prize, Copenhagen, 1974; Award of City of Hamburg, 1982; Henrik Steffens Prize, 1990; Flisaka '96 Prize, Toruń, Poland, 1996; Award, Stiftung Kulturfonds, Berlin, 1998; Pro Finlandia, 1999. *Address:* Taivaiskalliontie 15, 00600 Helsinki, Finland.

**AHRENS, Hans-Georg;** Singer (bass baritone); b. 1947, Hitzacker an der Elbe, Germany. *Education:* Berlin Musikhochschule. *Career:* Sang at Mainz Opera, 1973–75, Augsburg, Kassel and Kiel; Ludwigsburg Festival, 1978 as Leporello and Figaro, 1989; As Gauguin in Rautavaara's Vincent, Kiel Opera,

1991; Sang Don Alfonso, Wiesbaden Festival, 1992 and the Doctor in Wozzeck, Brunswick, 1996; Season 1997 at Kiel in the stage premiere of The Magic Fountain by Delius, Hagen in Götterdämmerung, 2000. Other roles include Wagner's King Henry, Marke and Gurnemanz, Gianni Schicchi, Dulcamara and Schigolch in Lulu; Concerts in music by Bach. *Recordings:* Don Giovanni, Electrola; Così fan tutte, Harmonia Mundi. *Address:* Bühnen der Landeshaupstadt Kiel, Rathausplatz 4, 24103 Kiel, Germany.

**AIKIN, Laura;** Singer (soprano); b. 1965, Buffalo, USA. *Education:* Studied at Buffalo, New York and Indiana University; Vocal studies with Reri Grist in Munich. *Career:* Appearances at the Staatsoper Berlin and elsewhere in Europe as Amenaide in Tancredi (Zürich), 1996, the Queen of Night, Adele and Gretel; Deutsche Oper Berlin debut as Madame Herz in Mozart's Schauspieldirektor; Schwetzingen Festival in L'Opera Seria by Florian Gassmann, under René Jacobs; Salzburg Festival recital with Maurizio Pollini, in Schubert's Hirt auf den Felsen, 1995; Strauss's Zerbinetta at the Vienna Staatsoper and a Jonathan Miller production of Ariadne auf Naxos at Florence, 1997; Il trionfo del Tempo by Handel at the Styriate Festival with Nicolas Harnoncourt and Concentus Musicus, 1997; Appearances in Berlin as Lulu and Silvia in Haydn's L'Isola disabitata; Further concerts include Schoenberg's oratorio Die Jakobsleiter under Michael Gielen, Beethoven's Christus am Ölberg with Daniel Barenboim in Jerusalem and Chicago, and Pierre Boulez 70th birthday celebrations at Carnegie Hall; Met debut as the Queen of Night; Madeleine in Le Postillon de Lonjumeau at the Berlin Staatsoper, 1998; Numerous appearances with The Ensemble Intercontemporain including: Salzburg, Edinburgh and Schleswig Holstein Festivals; Handel's Alcina at the Beaune Festival with Les Arts Florissants and William Christie; Ariadne at the Chicago Lyric; Suite from Prometeo by Luigi Nono with Claudio Abbado and the Berlin Philharmonic at Carnegie Hall, 1999; Season 1999–2000 engaged for Fidelio and Ariadne at La Scala, for Lulu at Zürich, Ariadne at Munich and Die schweigsame Frau at Vienna; Sang Lulu for Netherlands Opera, 2001. *Honours:* Winner, Lake Constance International Competition; Deutsche Akademische Austauschdienst Scholar, Munich, 1990–92. *Current Management:* Ingpen & Williams Ltd, 7 St George's Court, 131 Putney Bridge Road, London, SW15 2PA, England. *Telephone:* (20) 8874-3222. *Fax:* (20) 8877-3113. *E-mail:* info@ingpen.co.uk.

**AIMARD, Pierre-Laurent;** French pianist; b. 1957, Lyon; m. Irina Kataeva; two c. *Education:* Paris Conservatory, studied with Yvonne Loriod and Maria Curcio in Paris. *Career:* winner of the Olivier Messiaen Int. Competition 1973; invited by Pierre Boulez to be a founding mem. of Ensemble Intercontemporain 1977; has performed worldwide under conductors, including Boulez, Seiji Ozawa, Zubin Metha, Charles Dutoit, André Previn, Andrew Davis, Sir Simon Rattle, David Robertson, Esa-Pekka Salonen, Edo de Waart; US debut with Chicago Symphony Orchestra 1977; Carnegie Hall debut 2001; has performed with orchestras, including Boston SO, San Francisco Symphony, Toronto Symphony, London Philharmonia, Royal Concertgebouw, Orchestre de Paris, Orchestre Nat. de France; has featured at festivals, including Tanglewood, Salzburg, Berlin, Vienna, Edin., Köln Triennale, Holland, Paris Autumn; regular collaborations with composers, including Ligeti, Boulez and Stockhausen; artist-in-residence, Salle de Concerts Duchesse Josephine-Charlotte, Luxembourg 2005–06; contrib. to TV series on 20th-century composers (Arte TV). *Recordings:* György Ligeti Edition 3, Works for Piano 1997, György Ligeti, Project Vol. One (Melodien for Orchestra, Chamber Concerto, Piano Concerto, Mysteries of the Macabre), Boulez Conducts Ligeti (Piano Concerto), Olivier Messiaen, Vingt Regards sur l'Enfant-Jésus 2000, Olivier Messiaen, Turangalîla Symphony, Pierre-Laurent Aimard at Carnegie Hall 2002, Beethoven, Piano Concertos Nos 1–5 2003, Debussy, Images-Études 2003, Dvorák, The Golden Spinning Wheel 2004, Beethoven, Triple Concerto, Rondo in B flat, Choral Fantasy 2004, Ravel, Gaspard de la nuit/Carter, Night Fantasies 2005, Charles Ives, Three Quarter-Tone Pieces. *Honours:* Royal Philharmonic Soc. Award for Best Instrumentalist 2005. *Current Management:* c/o Lydia Connolly, HarrisonParrott Ltd, 12 Penzance Place, London, W11 4PA, England. *Telephone:* (20) 7229-9166. *Fax:* (20) 7221-5042. *E-mail:* lydia.connolly@harrisonparrott.co.uk. *Website:* www.harrisonparrott.co.uk.

**AINSLEY, John Mark;** British singer (tenor); b. 9 July 1953, Crewe; s. of John Alwyn Ainsley and Dorothy Sylvia Ainsley (née Anderson). *Education:* Royal Grammar School, Worcester, Madgalen Coll., Oxford. *Career:* debut in Stravinsky's Mass, Royal Festival Hall 1984; many concert performances from 1985 with Taverner Consort, New London Consort and London Baroque; appearances in Mozart Masses at The Vienna Konzerthaus with Heinz Holliger, Handel's Saul at Götingen with John Eliot Gardiner, the Mozart Requiem under Yehudi Menuhin at Gstaad and Pulcinella at the Barbican under Jeffrey Tate; other concerts with the Ulster Orchestra and the Bournemouth Sinfonietta; debut in USA at Lincoln Center in Bach's B Minor Mass with Christopher Hogwood 1990; opera debut at the Innsbruck Festival in Scarlatti's Gli Equivoci nel Sembiante, at the ENO in the Return of Ulysses 1989; title role in Méhul's Joseph for Dutch Radio, Handel's Acis in Stuttgart and Solomon for Radio France under Leopold Hager; has sung Mozart's Tamino for Opera Northern Ireland and Ferrando for Glyndebourne Touring Opera; sang Ferrando at Glyndebourne 1992, Don Ottavio 1994, Haydn's The Seasons with the London Classical Players, BBC Proms Concerts, London 1993, Stravinsky concert under Andrew Davis at Royal Festival Hall 1997, Monteverdi's Orfeo for the Munich Festival 1999, Jupiter in Semele for ENO 1999, Bach's St Matthew Passion at the BBC Proms 2002. *Recordings include:* Handel's Nisi Dominus under Simon Preston, Purcell's Odes with Trevor

Pinnock, Mozart's C Minor Mass with Christopher Hogwood, Great Baroque Arias with the King's Consort, Acis and Galatea, Saul. *Honours:* Grammy Award for Best Opera Recording 1995. *Address:* c/o Askonas Holt, Lonsdale Chambers, 27 Chancery Lane, London, WC2A 1PF, England (office). *Telephone:* (20) 7400-1700. *Fax:* (20) 7400-1799. *E-mail:* info@askonasholt.co.uk. *Website:* www.askonasholt.co.uk.

**AITKEN, Hugh,** MS; composer and teacher; b. 7 Sept. 1924, NY, USA. *Education:* Juilliard School with Wagenaar, Persichetti and Ward. *Career:* taught privately and at the Juilliard Preparatory Division, 1950–65; Faculty, Juilliard School, 1960–70; Professor, William Paterson College, 1970–. *Compositions:* Stage: Felipe, opera, Fables, chamber opera, and dance scores; Other: 3 Violin Concertos, 1984, 1988, Oratorio, The Revelation of St John The Divine, 1953–90, 10 Solo Cantatas, In Praise Of Ockeghem for Strings, Rameau Remembered for Flute and Chamber Orchestra, Happy Birthday, overture; Opus 95 Revisited for String Quartet, unaccompanied works for various instruments, Duo for Cello and Piano, Trios for 11 Players, Quintet for Oboe and String Quartet. *Recordings include:* Piano Fantasy and two Cantatas. *Honours:* National Academy of Arts and Letters, 1988; several NEA grants. *Address:* Music Department, William Paterson College of New Jersey, Wayne, NJ 07470, USA.

**AITKEN, Robert Morris;** Flautist, Teacher and Composer; b. 28 Aug. 1939, Kentville, Nova Scotia, Canada; m. Marion I Ross. *Education:* Studied flute as child in Pennsylvania, later with Nicholas Fiore, Royal Conservatory of Music, Toronto, 1955–59; Composition with Barbara Pentland, University of British Columbia, and with John Weinzweig; Electronic music with Myron Schaeffer; Flute with various teachers, 1964–65; MMus, University of Toronto, 1964. *Career:* Principal Flautist with Vancouver Symphony Orchestra, 1958–59, Stratford Festival Orchestra, Ontario, 1962–64; Soloist with orchestras and chamber music player with many tours abroad; Artistic Director of Music Today, Shaw Festival, Niagara-on-the-Lake, 1970–72, and New Music Concerts, Toronto, 1971–; Advanced studies in music programme, 1985–89; Professor of Flute, Staatliche Hochschule für Musik, Freiburg im Breisgau, 1988–. *Compositions include:* Rhapsody for Orchestra, 1961; Music for Flute and Electronic Tape, 1963; Concerto for 12 Solo Instruments, 1964; Kebyar for Flute, Clarinet, 2 Double Basses, Percussion and Tape, 1971; Shadows III, Nira for Solo Violin, Flute, Oboe, Viola, Double Bass, Piano and Harpsichord, 1974–88; Icicle for Flute, 1977; Folia for Woodwind Quintet, 1980; Berceuse for Flute and Orchestra, 1992; My Song, for 2 flutes, 1994. *Recordings:* Various compositions recorded; Many albums as soloist and chamber music artist. *Address:* 14 Maxwell Avenue, Toronto, ON, M5P 2B5, Canada.

**AJMONE-MARSAN, Guido;** Orchestral Conductor; b. 24 March 1947, Turin, Italy; m. Helle Winkelhorn 1971. *Education:* BMus, Conducting and Clarinet, Eastman School of Music, New York, USA, 1968; studied with F. Ferrara at Conservatory of St Cecilia, Rome, Italy, 1968–71. *Career:* Chief Conductor of the Gelders Orchestra, Arnhem, Netherlands, 1982–86; Music Adviser and Principal Conductor of the Orchestra of Illinois at Chicago, USA, 1982–87; Music Director of Opera House, Essen, Germany, 1986–90; Guest Conductor for many international orchestras and opera houses including: Jerusalem Symphony, Philharmonia, London Symphony, Covent Garden Opera, NHK Japan, Welsh National Opera, Spoleto Festival, La Scala Orchestra, Metropolitan Opera and English National Opera, New York City Opera, Teatro Colón, Buenos Aires, Opera of Santiago, Chile; Scottish Opera; mem, Royal Philharmonic Society. *Recordings:* Many for Radio broadcast with radio orchestras in Czechoslovakia, the United Kingdom, Germany, Japan, Australia, Netherlands, Denmark, Italy and France. *Honours:* Many Prizes, Cantelli Competition, Milan, 1969, Mitropoulos, NY, 1970, Winner, Rupert Foundation Conducting Competition, with one year assistantship to London Symphony, 1973, Winner, G Solti Competition, Chicago, 1973; The Deane Sherman Performing Arts Award, MD, USA, 1992. *Address:* 57 Wood Vale, London, N10 3DL, England. *E-mail:* marsan@vale57.fsnet.co.uk.

**AKIMOV, Yevgeny;** singer (tenor); b. 1970, St Petersburg, Russia. *Education:* St Petersburg Conservatoire. *Career:* Kirov Opera at the Mariinsky Theatre from 1996; roles have included Rossini's Almaviva, Froh in Das Rheingold, the Fisherman in Stravinsky's Nightingale and the Indian Merchant in Rimsky-Korsakov's Sadko; Sang the Simpleton in Boris Godunov with the Kirov at Covent Garden, 1997 and appeared in Parsifal at the Royal Albert Hall, 1999; Other roles include Cassio in Otello and Antonio in Prokofiev's Betrothal in a Monastery; Appearances with the Kirov Opera at the Royal Opera House, London, 2000; Mussorgsky's Boris Godunov at the London Proms, 2002. *Honours:* prizewinner Int. Pechkovsky Singing Competition 1994. *Address:* c/o Kirov Opera, Mariinsky Theatre, Mariinsky Square, St Petersburg, Russia.

**AKIYAMA, Kazuyoshi;** Conductor; b. 2 Jan. 1941, Tokyo, Japan. *Education:* Studied conducting with Hideo Saito, Toho School of Music, Tokyo. *Career:* Debut: Tokyo Symphony Orchestra, 1964; Music Director of the Tokyo Symphony Orchestra, 1964; Conductor, Japanese Orchestras; Music Director, American Symphony Orchestra, New York, 1973–78; Resident Conductor and Music Director, Vancouver Symphony Orchestra, BC, 1972–85; Music Director, Syracuse Symphony Orchestra, NY, 1985–. *Address:* c/o Syracuse Symphony Orchestra, 411 Montgomery Street, Syracuse, NY 13202, USA.

**AKOKA, Gérard;** Conductor; b. 2 Nov. 1949, Paris, France. *Education:* Studied at the Paris Conservatoire, at the Accademia di Santa Cecilia and with Jean Martinon, Igor Markevitch, Sergiu Celibidache and Franco

Ferrara. *Career:* Former assistant to Daniel Barenboim and Leonard Bernstein; Assistant to Boulez at Orchestre de Paris (1977) and musical director of the Lorraine Philharmonic, 1983–84; Recent engagements in Taiwan and elsewhere in the Far East. *Address:* c/o Taipei City Symphony Orchestra, 25 Pa Teh Road, Sec 3, Taipei 10560, Taiwan.

**AKOS, Francis (Ferenc),** DipMusEd; violinist and conductor; b. 30 March 1922, Budapest, Hungary; m. Phyllis Malvin Sommers 1981; two d. by previous marriage. *Education:* Franz Liszt Acad. of Music, Budapest. *Career:* debut, Mozart Concerto in D No. 4 for violin and orchestra, Budapest 1938; Concertmaster, Budapest Concert Orchestra 1945–46, Royal Opera and Philharmonic Soc. of Budapest 1947–48, Gothenburg (Sweden) Symphony Orchestra 1948–50, Municipal Opera (now Deutsche Oper), Berlin 1950–54, Minneapolis Symphony Orchestra 1954–55; Asst Concertmaster, Chicago Symphony Orchestra 1955–2004, Concertmaster Emeritus 1997–; also performed at Salzburg Festival, Scandinavian Festival in Helsinki, Prades Festival, and Berlin, Bergen and Vienna Festivals; founder and Conductor, The Chicago Strings chamber orchestra 1961–; founder and Conductor, The Highland Park strings 1979–. *Honours:* first prize Reményi Competition, Budapest 1939, first prize Hubay Competition, Budapest 1939. *Address:* 1310 Maple Avenue # 3B, Evanston, IL 60201, USA (home). *Telephone:* (847) 866-8832 (home). *E-mail:* violaki310@yahoo.com (home).

**ALAGNA, Roberto;** French singer (tenor); b. 7 June 1963, Clichy-sous-Bois; m. 1st (deceased); m. 2nd Angela Gheorghiu (q.v.) 1996. *Education:* studied in Paris, France and Italy. *Career:* debut as Alfredo in La Traviata, Glyndebourne Touring Opera at Plymouth 1988; Met, New York debut as Rodolfo 1996; appearances world-wide at Covent Garden, London, Monte Carlo, Vienna Staatsoper, Théâtre du Châtelet, Paris, La Scala, Milan, Chicago and at the New York Met; repertoire includes Rodolfo (La Bohème), Edgard (Lucia di Lammermoor), Rigoletto, L'Elisir d'Amore, Roméo, Don Carlos, Roberto Devereux, Duke of Mantua, Don Carlos, Alfredo, L'Amico Fritz, La Rondine, Faust. *Recordings include:* Duets and Arias (with Angela Gheorghiu), La Bohème 1996, Don Carlos 1996, La Rondine 1997. *Honours:* winner Pavarotti Competition 1988, Personalité Musicale de l'Année 1994, Laurence Olivier Award for Outstanding Achievement in Opera 1995, Victor Award for Best Singer 1997; Chevalier, Ordre des Arts et des Lettres. *Current Management:* Theateragentur Dr Germinal Hilbert, Maximilianstrasse 22, 80539 Munich, Germany. *Telephone:* (89) 290 7470. *Fax:* (89) 290 74790. *E-mail:* agentur@hilbert.de. *Website:* www.hilbert.de; www.alagna.com.

**ALAIMO, Simone;** Italian singer (bass-baritone); b. 3 Feb. 1950, Villabate, Palermo; m. Vittorio Mazzoni, 1988; one s. one d. *Education:* Univ. of Palermo, Scuola di Perfezionamento Teatro alla Scala, Milan with Giovani Lirici. *Career:* debut in Don Pasquale at Pavia 1977; appearances at La Scala, Teatro dell Opera, Rome, Teatro Comunale, Florence, Teatro San Carlo, Naples, Chicago, San Francisco, Dallas, Vienna, Monaco, Paris, Madrid, Barcelona, Lisbon and Marseilles; radio and television broadcasts in Luisa Miller, Cavalleria Rusticana and Zaira; sang Mustafà in L'Italiana in Algeri at San Francisco 1992, followed by Dulcamara, Rossini's Don Basilio at Genoa 1992; New York Met from 1995, as Mozart's Figaro and Rossini's Basilio; Faraone in Mosè in Egitto at Covent Garden 1994; Rossini's Basilio at Genoa 1998; first modern production of Donizetti's Alahor in Granata, Seville 1998; appeared in film of Il Barbiere di Siviglia; Mustafà for New Israeli Opera 2000; season 2003 as Rossini's Don Magnifico at Covent Garden. *Honours:* Lions Prize 1977, Voce Verdiane di Busseto Int. Competition 1978, Beniamino Gigli di Macerata Int. Competition 1978, Maria Callas Int. Competition 1980. *Recordings:* La Cenerentola, Don Giovanni, Il Turco in Italia, Maria Stuarda, I Masnadieri, L'Ebreo, Torquato Tasso, L'Esule di Roma, Convenienze Teatrali, Barbiere di Siviglia. *Current Management:* All'Opera Artists Management, Viale Giuseppe Mazzini 41, 00195 Rome, Italy; Columbia Artists Management, 1790 Broadway, New York NY 10019-1412, USA (office). *Telephone:* (6) 3215772 (Italy); (212) 841-9500 (USA). *Fax:* (6) 3215252 (Italy); (212) 841-9744 (USA). *E-mail:* info@allopera.net; info@cami.com. *Website:* www.allopera.net; www.cami.com. *Address:* Via Pacevecchia, Parc Conim, 82100 Benevento, Italy.

**ALAIN, Marie-Claire;** French organist; b. 10 Aug. 1926, Saint-Germain-en-Laye; d. of Albert Alain and Magdeleine Alain (née Alberty); m. Jacques Gommier 1950; one s. one d. *Education:* Institut Notre Dame, Saint-Germain-en-Laye, Conservatoire Nat. Supérieur de Musique, Paris. *Career:* organ teacher, Conservatoire de Musique de Paris; Lecturer, Summer Acad. for organists, Haarlem, Netherlands 1956–72; organ teacher, Conservatoire de Musique de Rueil-Malmaison 1978–94; numerous concerts world-wide 1955–; lecturer at numerous univs throughout world; expert on organology to Minister of Culture, Commission des Orgues des Monuments Historiques 1965–2002. *Recordings:* over 250 records, including complete works of J. Alain, C.P.E. Bach, J.S. Bach, C. Balbastre, G. Böhm, N. Bruhns, D. Buxtehude, L.N. Clérambault, F. Couperin, L.C. Daquin, C. Franck, N. de Grigny, J.A. Guilain, G.F. Handel, J. Haydn, F. Mendelssohn, A. Vivaldi. *Publication:* Notes critiques sur l'œuvre d'orgue de Jehan Alain 2001. *Honours:* Commdr, Légion d'honneur, Commdr, Ordre du Mérite, Commdr, Ordre des Arts et des Lettres; Hon. DHumLitt (Colorado State Univ.); Hon. DMus (Southern Methodist Univ., Dallas, Boston Conservatory); Dr hc (Acad. Sibelius, Helsinki); numerous prizes for recordings and performances, including Buxtehudepreis (Lübeck, Germany), Prix Léonie Sonning (Copenhagen, Denmark), Prix Franz Liszt (Budapest) 1987. *Address:* 4 rue Victor Hugo, 78230 Le Pecq, France. *Telephone:* 1-30-87-08-65. *Fax:* 1-30-61-43-61.

**ALARIE, Pierrette Marguerite,** CC; Canadian singer (soprano) and teacher; b. 9 Nov. 1921, Montréal; m. Léopold Simoneau 1946; two d. *Education:* studied voice and acting with Jeanne Maubourg and Albert Roberval, voice with Salvator Issaurel, Curtis Inst. of Music, Philadelphia with Elisabeth Schumann. *Career:* operatic debut at Montréal 1943; Metropolitan Opera debut as Oscar in Un Ballo in Maschera 1945; European debut in Paris 1949; sang in opera, concert and recital in leading N American and European music centres; retired from operatic stage in 1966, with farewell appearance as soloist in Handel's Messiah with Montréal Symphony Orchestra 1970; moved to California, USA 1972, as stage dir of numerous small opera cos; moved to Victoria, BC 1978 with the Festival Concert Soc. summer music programme; established Canada Opera Piccola 1978–88. *Recordings:* numerous including album of Mozart arias. *Honours:* Dr hc (McGill Univ.) 1994; winner Metropolitan Opera Auditions of the Air 1945, Grand Prix du Disque 1961, Gov. Gen.'s Performing Arts Award 2003.

**ALBANESE, Licia;** Italian fmr singer (soprano); b. 22 July 1913, Bari; m. Joseph Gimma, 7 April 1945. *Education:* Studied voice with Emanuel De Rosa, Bari and Giuseppina Baldassare-Tedeschi, Milan. *Career:* operatic debut as Butterfly, Teatro Lirico, Milan, 1934; formal operatic debut, New York as Cio-Cio San, 1940 and sang there until 1966 (286 performances in 17 roles); appeared in concerts; taught singing; roles included Butterfly, Violetta, Zerlina, Desdemona, Susanna, Manon, Tosca, Gounod's Marguerite, Mimi. *Recordings:* NBC radio broadcasts under Toscanini. *Honours:* Order of Merit of Italy; Lady Grand Cross of the Equestrian Order of the Holy Sepulchre. *Address:* Nathan Hale Drive, Wilson Point South, Norwalk, CT 06854, USA.

**ALBERGA, Eleanor;** composer; b. 30 Sept. 1949, Kingston, Jamaica. *Education:* Studied at the Royal Academy of Music, London, from 1970. *Career:* Has performed with an African dance company and played piano for the London Contemporary Dance Theatre. *Compositions:* Mobile I for orchestra, 1983; Jamaican Medley for piano, 1983; Clouds for piano quintet, 1984; Ice Flow for piano, 1985; Stone Dream for prepared piano and tape, 1986; Suite for piano 4 hands, 1986; Mobile II for ensemble, 1986; Whose Own for prepared piano and sound processor, 1988; Sun Warrior for orchestra, 1990; Dancing with the Shadows for ensemble, 1991; Jupiter's Fairground for orchestra, 1991; Snow White and the Seven Dwarfs, for narrators and orchestra, 1994; 2 String Quartets, 1993, 1994; The Wild Blue Yonder for piano and violin, 1995; Under Light Manners, for saxophones and ensemble, 1997; Only a Wish Away, for piano, 1997. *Address:* 166 Bethnal Green Road, London E2 6 DL, England.

**ALBERMAN, David,** MA, LRAM; violinist; b. 1959, London, England. *Education:* Merton College, Oxford; studied with Mary Long, Emanuel Hurwitz, Sheila Nelson, Vera Kantrovich, Igor Ozim in Cologne. *Career:* Leader of the National Youth Orchestra of Great Britain, 1977; Has performed with the London Mozart Players, Royal Philharmonic Orchestra, London Symphony, Associate Member, 1983–85, and the Academy of St Martin-in-the-Fields; Former leader of the Chamber Orchestra of Europe; Has performed music by Lutoslawski, Penderecki, Osborne and Bainbridge with such groups as the Ballet Rambert and Divertimenti; Member, Arditti Quartet, 1986–94; Many performances at festivals across Europe and North America; Resident string tutor at the Darmstadt Fereinkurse for New Music from 1986; Music in camera programme for BBC television, 1987; Cycle of Schoenberg's Quartets at the Purcell Room, London, November 1988; recital in the Russian Spring Series at South Bank, May 1991; Performed in all the quartets of Berg, Webern and Schoenberg at Antwerp, Cologne, Frankfurt, London and Paris, 1991–93; Took part in the premieres of quartets by Bose, No. 3, 1989; Bussotti, 1988; John Cage, Music for 4, 1988, 4, 1989; Ferneyhough Nos 3 and 4; Gubaidulina, No. 3, 1987; Harvey, No. 2; Kagel, No. 3, 1987; Nancarrow, No. 3, 1988; Pousseur, No. 2, 1989; Rihm, Nos 6 and 8; Xenakis, Akea, Piano Quintet, 1986, Tetora, 1991, Isang Yun, Flute Quintet, 1987; Premiere of Nono's Hay que caminar sonando for violin duo, with Irvine Arditti, Violin, 1989. *Recordings include:* Elliott Carter's Quartets; Quartets by Ferneyhough. *Address:* 14 Fairmead Road, London N19 4DF, England.

**ALBERT, Donnie Ray;** Singer (Bass-baritone); b. 1950, Louisiana, USA. *Career:* Sang Gershwin's Porgy at Houston (1976) and sang there regularly until 1990; Guest appearances at the New York City Opera (Scarpia, 1978), Washington Opera (Amonasro, 1990), Boston, San Francisco and elsewhere in the USA; Appearances in Berlin and Florence as Porgy; Other roles include Carlos in Ernani, Monterone, Nabucco, Iago, Jack Rance, Jochanaan, Escamillo, Varlaam, and the title role in Gruenberg's Emperor Jones; Season 1996 as Wagner's Dutchman at Cologne and Hidraot in Gluck's Armide at La Scala; Villains in Hoffmann at Cologne, 1998; Season 1999–2000 as Macbeth at Cologne, Amonasro at Cincinnati and Gershwin's Porgy at Munich; Concert engagements in New York, Los Angeles and Chicago. *Current Management:* Pinnacle Arts: Miller Division, 889 Ninth Avenue, 2nd Floor, New York 10019, USA. *Telephone:* (212)397-7911. *Fax:* (212) 397-7920. *E-mail:* jmiller@pinnaclearts.com. *Website:* www.pinnaclearts.com. *Address:* c/o Houston Grand Opera, 510 Preston Avenue, Houston, TX 77002, USA. *Website:* www.donnierayalbert.com.

**ALBERT, Marian;** singer (tenor); b. 1961, Poznań, Poland. *Education:* studied at Lubin, Poznan and the Salzburg Mozarteum. *Career:* choir and orchestra director in Poland, 1982–87; Sang Fenton, Vladimir in Price Igor, Lensky, Tamino, Narciso in Il Turco in Italia and Amenofi in Rossini's Mosè, Poznan Opera, 1988–; Guest at Brussels as Tamino and Wagner's Froh;

Antwerp as Cavaradossi and Berne as Belmonte; Belmonte, Strauss's Brighella and Giannetto in La Gazza Ladra, Theater am Gärtnerplatz, Munich, 1992; Cadi in Der Barbier von Bagdad by Cornelius, Frankfurt, 1994; Appearances at Salzburg Mozartwochen and Prague Spring Festivals. *Address:* Theater am Gärtnerplatz 3, 8000 Munich 5, Germany.

**ALBERT, Thomas;** conductor and director; b. 1950, Germany. *Career:* violinist with La Petite Bande and the Musikalische Compagney; founded Fiori Musicale, 1978, for the performances of Baroque music; Founded, Forum Alte Musik, 1982; Bremen Academy of Early Music, 1986; Teacher, Hamburg Academy of Music and Strasbourg Conservatoire; Professor, Bremen Academy of Music, 1989; Artistic Director, Bremen Music Festival, 1989. *Recordings:* Bach Cantatas 56 and 82; Keiser's Masagniello Furioso; Lubeck Cantatas. *Address:* c/o Bremen Academy of Music, Bremen, Germany.

**ALBERT, Werner Andreas;** conductor; b. 1935, Weinheim, Germany. *Education:* Mannheim Hochschule für Musik, Heidelberg University; studied conducting with Herbert von Karajan and Hans Rosbaud. *Career:* Chief Conductor of the North West German Philharmonic, Gulbenkian Orchestra, Lisbon, Nuremberg Symphony Orchestra, Queensland Symphony Orchestra, Queensland Philharmonic Orchestra, Australian and the Bavarian Youth Orchestra; Senior Lecturer at Nuremberg Conservatorium; Professor of Queensland University; President, Siegfried Wagner Society. *Recordings include:* Oboe Concertos by Leclair, Haydn and Dittersdorf; Beethoven's 9th Symphony; Rossini's Petite Messe Solennelle; Cello Concertos by Sutermeister; Mozart's Clarinet Concerto and Horn Concerto K447; Puccini's Messa di Gloria. *Honours:* First Prize, German Recording Industry, 1994; American Menza Award, 1994; Music Prize, Bavarian Academy of Fine Arts, 1998. *Address:* Rankestrasse 19, 90461 Nürnberg, Germany.

**ALBERY, Tim;** British theatre and opera director; b. 20 May 1952, *Plays directed include:* War Crimes 1981, Secret Gardens 1983, Venice Preserv'd 1983, Hedda Gabler 1984, The Princess of Cleves 1985, Mary Stuart 1988, As You Like It 1989, Berenice 1990, Wallenstein 1993, Macbeth 1996, Attempts on Her Life 1997, Nathan the Wise 2004. *Operas directed include:* (for ENO) Billy Budd 1988, Beatrice and Benedict 1990, Peter Grimes 1991, Lohengrin 1993, From the House of the Dead 1997, La Bohème 2000, War and Peace 2001; (for Opera North) The Midsummer Marriage 1985, The Trojans 1986, La Finta Giardiniera 1989, Don Giovanni 1991, Don Carlos 1992, Luisa Miller 1995 Così fan Tutte 1997, Katya Kabanova 1999, Cosi Fan Tutte 2004, One Touch of Venus 2004; (for Welsh Nat. Opera) The Trojans 1987, Nabucco 1995; (for Scottish Opera) The Midsummer Marriage 1988, The Trojans 1990, Fidelio 1994, The Ring Cycle 2003; (for Australian Opera) The Marriage of Figaro 1992; (for Netherlands Opera) Benvenuto Cellini 1991, La Wally 1993, Beatrice and Benedict 2001; (for Bayerische Staatsoper) Peter Grimes 1993, Simon Boccanegra 1995, Ariadne Auf Naxos 1996; (for Batignano Festival, Italy) The Turn of the Screw 1983; (for Bregenz Festival, Austria) La Wally 1990; (for Royal Opera House) Cherubin 1994; (for Metropolitan Opera, New York) Midsummer Night's Dream 1996, The Merry Widow 2000; (for Minnesota Opera) Passion 2004. *Address:* c/o Harriet Cruickshank, Cruickshank Cazenove, 97 Old South Lambeth Road, London, SW8 1XU, England.

**ALBIN, Roger;** conductor and cellist; b. 30 Sept. 1920, Beausoleil, France. *Education:* studied with Umberto Benedetti at Monte Carlo, Paris Conservatoire with Henri Busser, Milhaud and Olivier Messiaen. *Career:* played cello at Monte Carlo, The Paris Opéra and at the Société des Concerts du Conservatoire; Duo partnership with pianist Claude Helffer, 1949–57; Studied further with Roger Desormière, Carl Schuricht and Hans Rosbaud, and conducted from 1957 with chorus at the Opéra Comique, Paris; Musical Director at Nancy, 1960–61, Toulouse, 1961–66 and French Radio Orchestra at Strasbourg, 1966–75; Cellist with the French National Orchestra, 1978–81, also a member of the orchestra's String Sextet; Professor of Chamber Music at the Strasbourg Conservatory, 1981–87. *Recordings:* as cellist: Prokofiev's Concerto and Ravel's Trio; Fauré's Fantasie and the Fantasie for Piano and Orchestra by Debussy; Ibert's Diane Poitiers. *Honours:* Premier Prix in cello class at the Paris Conservatoire, 1936.

**ALBRECHT, Georg-Alexander;** conductor; b. 15 Feb. 1935, Bremen, Germany. *Education:* studied violin, piano and composition. *Career:* debut as conductor 1949; Chief Conductor at the Bremen Opera 1958–61, Hannover Opera from 1961; Guest Conductor with the Dresden Staatskapelle, the Berlin Philharmonic and other German orchestras; Professor at the Hannover Conservatory. Repertory includes the 1st Symphony of Wolfgang Rihm (premiere, 1984). *Address:* c/o Hochschule für Musik Hannover, Emmichplatz 1, 3000 Hannover 1, Germany.

**ALBRECHT, Gerd;** conductor; b. 19 July 1935, Essen, Germany. *Education:* studied conducting with Wilhelm Bruckner-Ruggenerg, Hamburg Hochschule für Musik and musicology at the Universities of Kiel and Hamburg. *Career:* Repetiteur and Conductor, Wurttemberg State Theater, Stuttgart, 1958–61; First Conductor, Mainz, 1961–63; Generalmusikdirektor, Lubeck, 1963–66 and Kassel, 1966–72; Chief Conductor, Deutsche Oper, West Berlin, 1972–79 and Tonhalle Orchestra, Zürich, 1975–80; Guest Conductor with Vienna State Opera, 1976–; Conducted the premieres of Henze's Telemanniana in Berlin in 1967, Fortner's Elisabeth Tudor in Berlin in 1972, Henze's Barcarola in Zürich in 1980 and Reimann's Troades at Munich in 1986; Guest appearances with various European and North American opera companies and orchestras; Conductor, Der fliegende Holländer at Covent Garden in 1986; Chief Conductor, Hamburg State Opera and Philharmonic State Orchestra,

1988–; Conducted Schreker's Der Schatzgräber at Hamburg, 1989–90 followed by Idomeneo and Tannhäuser; Conducted Tchaikovsky's Maid of Orleans at the 1990 Munich Festival, with Waltraud Meier; Chief Conductor of the Czech Philharmonic Orchestra, 1992–94; Hamburg State Opera from 1995; Season 1992 with Dvořák's Dimitri at Munich, Reimann's Troades at Frankfurt and Tannhäuser at Barcelona; Premiere of Schnittke's Historia von D Johann Fausten at Hamburg, 1995; Gurlitt's Wozzeck at Florence, 1998. *Recordings include:* Der Schatzgräber. *Honours:* Winner, Besançon, 1957; Conducting Conpetitions, Hilversum, 1958. *Address:* c/o Hamburg State Opera, Postfach 302448, 2000 Hamburg 36, Germany.

**ALBRECHT, Theodore John;** Orchestra Conductor and Musicologist; b. 24 Sept. 1945, Jamestown, NY, USA; m. Carol Padgham 1976. *Education:* BME, St Mary's Univ. 1967, MM 1969, PhD 1975, North Texas State Univ. *Career:* Asst Prof., Appalachian State Univ. 1975–76; Conductor, German Orchestra of Cleveland 1977–80; Music Dir, Northland Symphony Orchestra, Kansas City, MO 1980–87; Prof., Park Coll. 1980–92; Music Dir, Philharmonia of Greater Kansas City 1987–92; Prof., Kent State Univ., Kent, OH 1992–; notable performances include US premieres of Bruckner Dialog by Gottfried von Einem 1982, Symphony in C, op 46 by Hans Pfitzner 1983, Ludi Leopoldini by Gottfried von Einem 1984; first American conductor to conduct all nine Dvořák symphonies; world premiere of Song of the Prairie by Timothy Corrao 1987. *Publications:* Dika Newlin, Friend and Mentor: A Birthday Anthology (ed.) 1973; translation of Felix Weingartner's On the Performance of the Symphonies of Mozart 1985, translations of Felix Weingartner's Schubert and Schumann 1986, Thayer, Salieri, Rival of Mozart (ed.) 1989, Letters to Beethoven and Other Correspondence, three vols 1996, Beethoven im Gespräch 2002. *Honours:* Deems Taylor Award, ASCAP 1997. *Address:* 1635 Chadwick Drive, Kent, OH 44240, USA. *E-mail:* talbrech@kent.edu.

**ALCANTARA, Theo;** Conductor; b. 16 April 1941, Cuenca, Spain; m. Susan Alcantara. *Education:* Madrid Conservatory and Salzburg Mozarteum. *Career:* Conductor, Frankfurt am Main, 1964–66; Director of orchestras, University of Michigan, Ann Arbor, 1968–73; Music Director, Grand Rapids Symphony Orchestra, MI, 1973–78; Music Director, Phoenix Symphony Orchestra, 1978–89; Artistic Director, Music Academy of the West, Santa Barbara, CA, 1981–84; Principal Conductor, Pittsburgh Opera, 1987–; Conducted Elektra at Pittsburgh, 1989. *Honours:* Silver Medal, Mitropoulos Competition, 1966. *Current Management:* ICM Artists Ltd, 40 West 57th Street, New York, NY 10019, USA.

**ALDEN, David;** Stage Director; b. 16 Sept. 1949, New York City, USA. *Career:* Has directed the premieres of Stephen Burton's The Duchess of Malfi, Wolf Trap, 1978, Pasatieri's Washington Square and Conrad Susa's Don Perlimpin at San Francisco, Fidelio and Wozzeck at the Metropolitan Opera, and Rigoletto, Wozzeck and Mahagonny for Scottish Opera; Productions of The Rake's Progress for Netherlands Opera and at the Israel Festival, Werther at Nancy and the US premiere of Judith by Siegfried Matthus at Sante Fe in 1990; English National Opera with Mazeppa, Simon Boccanegra, A Masked Ball and double bill of Oedipus Rex and Duke Bluebeard's Castle in 1991; Staged Tristan and Isolde for ENO, 1996; Affiliations with opera at the Academy, New York, with La Calisto and New Israel Opera with Les Contes d'Hoffmann, La Bohème and the world premiere of Noam Sheriff's The Sorrows of Job; Monteverdi's Poppea for the Bavarian State Opera, 1997; Engaged for Handel's Ariodante at Houston, 2001. *Address:* c/o English National Opera, St Martin's Lane, London WC2 4ES, England.

**ALDULESCU, Radu;** Italian concert cellist; b. 17 Sept. 1922, Piteasca-Pasarea, Romania. *Education:* began to study cello aged 6; Bucharest Conservatory. *Career:* debut, soloist with Bucharest Radio Symphony Orchestra, 1941; soloist with the Georges Enescu Philharmonic, Bucharest, 1945–46 and with all the important Philharmonic Orchestras in Europe, South America and South Africa; Asst to Gaspar Cassado, 1964–, and formed string trio, Trio d'Archi di Roma, with Salvatore Accardo and A. Luigi Bianchi, 1972; chamber recitals with Carlo Zecchi; performed at many international festivals including Berlin, Rome, Barcelona, Prague, Salzburg, Granada, Copenhagen, Hannover, Gstaad, San Salvador; regularly participated in chamber music concerts with Yehudi Menuhin, Sándor Végh, Wolfgang Schneiderhan, Alberto Lysy, Salvatore Accordo, Rostropovich, Yo-Yo Ma and many others; teacher at many conservatories including Basle, Maastricht, Conservatoire Européen de Musique, Paris, International Menuhin Acad., Gstaad; Centre d'estudis musicals, Barcelona; masterclasses in Rome, Berlin, Paris, Geneva, Buenos Aires, Nantes, Weimar, Freiburg, Prussia Cove (Cornwall), Assisi, Taormina, Santiago de Compostela and Granada; mem., Philharmonic Acad. of Bologna, Acad. Tiberina, Rome. *Recordings include:* Beethoven Sonatas (two vols); Concertos and Recitals (six vols); historical recordings series. *Honours:* Harriet Cohen International Music Award, Best Cellist of the Year, London, 1967; Cavaliere Ufficiale dell'Ordine al Merito della Republica Italiana awarded by the President and Government of Italy, 1972; Saggitario d'Oro and Gonfalone d'Oro, Italy. *Address:* 30 avenue Malaussána 2è dr, 06000 Nice, France.

**ALEKSASHKIN, Sergei;** Russian singer (bass-baritone); b. 1954, Saratov. *Education:* Saratov Conservatory, studied at La Scala. *Career:* mem., Kirov Opera from 1984, including tours; roles include in Don Giovanni, Mephistopheles, Sarastro, Sobakin in The Tsar's Bride, Ivan Susanin, Glinka's Ruslan and Farlaf, Kutuzov in War and Peace, Rimsky's Ivan the Terrible, Gremin in Eugene Onegin, Boris Godunov, Prince Igor, The Damnation of Faust, Philip

II in Don Carlos, Rossini's Basilio, King Henry in Lohengrin, Rachmaninov's Miserly Knight, Balducci in Benvenuto Cellini, the General in The Gambler by Prokofiev; concerts include Shostakovich's 13th Symphony with the Chicago Symphony Orchestra 1995, Mussorgsky's Songs and Dances of Death (UK debut with the BBC Philharmonic Orchestra) 1996, Shostakovich's 14th Symphony at the Vienna Konzerthaus, Bach's B Minor Mass, Mozart's Requiem, Beethoven's Choral Symphony and the Verdi Requiem. *Current Management:* Askonas Holt Ltd, Lonsdale Chambers, 27 Chancery Lane, London, WC2A 1PF, England. *Telephone:* (20) 7400-1700. *Fax:* (20) 7400-1799. *E-mail:* info@askonasholt.co.uk. *Website:* www.askonasholt.co.uk.

**ALER, David;** singer (baritone); b. 26 April 1959, Stockholm, Sweden. *Education:* studied in Gothenburg with Jacqueline Delman, further studies with Geoffrey Parsons, Janet Baker, Kim Borg and Galina Vishnevskaya. *Career:* sang at Landestheater Coburg and in Sweden, 1988–, as Don Giovanni, Guglielmo and Tarquinius in The Rape of Lucretia; Appeared in Vadstena and Reykjavík, 1988–89 in the premiere production of Someone I Have Seen by Karolina Eriksdottir; Stora Theater in Gothenburg as Schaunard in La Bohème, 1989; Drottningholm Festival 1996, as Allworthy in Tom Jones by Philidor; Salzburg Festival 1998, as Frère Massée in St François d'Assise; Concert engagements in Stockholm with Drottningholm Baroque Ensemble and Chapelle Royale of Versailles. *Address:* c/o M & M Lyric Artists, 140 Battersea Park Road, London SW11 5NY, England.

**ALER, John;** Singer (Tenor); b. 4 Oct. 1949, Baltimore, MD, USA. *Education:* Bachelor and Master degrees in Voice Performance, School of Music, Catholic University of America, 1972; Juilliard School of Music, American Opera Center and Opera Training Department, 1972–75; Studied with Oren Brown and Martin Isepp. *Career:* Has sung in opera, oratorio and recitals in USA, Canada, the United Kingdom and most of Europe; Many appearances including Tanglewood, Glyndebourne and Aix-en-Provence Festivals, Salzburg Festival, La Scala and London Proms; Has sung with major national and international orchestras; Vienna Staatsoper debut 1982; Toured Japan with Royal Opera, Covent Garden, 1986; Toured Taiwan with Ludwigsburg Festival Chorus and Orchestra, 1987; Sang Eumolpus in Stravinsky's Persephone at Promenade Concerts, London, 1993. *Recordings include:* Handel's Messiah, 1986; Bizet's Les Pêcheurs des Perles, 1989; Songs and Duos of Saint-Saëns, with John Ostendorf and John van Buskirk, 1989; Enesco's Oedipe; Semele, with Kathleen Battle, 1990; Title role in Gazzaniga's Don Giovanni; Orfeo, 1990; Stravinsky works with London Sinfonietta, 1990; Rossini's Songs of My Old Age, 1991; Handel's Joshua, 1991; Gounod's Mors et Vita with Orchestre du Capitole de Toulouse under Michel Plasson, 1992; Dvořák's Stabat Mater with New Jersey Symphony, 1994; Merry Widow, Glyndebourne company in concert, 1994; Songs We Forgot to Remember, 1996. *Honours:* Grammy Award for Best Classical Vocal Soloist for Berlioz Requiem, 1985; Featured on 2 Grammy winning albums, Best Classical Album for Bartók–Cantata Profana and Best Opera Recording for Handel–Semele, 1994. *Current Management:* c/o Mary Lynn Fixler, Herbert Barrett Management, 266 W 37th Street, New York, NY 10018, USA. *Telephone:* (212) 245-3530. *Fax:* (212) 397-5860. *Website:* www.herbertbarrett.com.

**ALESSANDRINI, Rinaldo;** Italian conductor and harpsichordist; b. Rome. *Career:* leading interpreter of Italian early music; founder and Music Dir Concerto Italiano ensemble; numerous worldwide performances with Concerto Italiano, including London, Edin., Vienna, Barcelona, Paris, Köln, Milan, Buenos Aires, Rio de Janeiro, New York, Tokyo, Pergolesi's Missa Romana in Rome, Handel's Theodora in Spain, St Olav Festival, Trondheim, and int. tours of Monteverdi's Il Combattimento di Tancredi e Clorinda, Handel's Il Trionfo del Tempo e del Disinganno; has conducted Teatro del Maggio Musicale Fiorentino, Orchestre Nat. Bordeaux Aquitaine, Orchestra Regionale Toscana, Scottish Chamber Orchestra, Northern Sinfonia, Detroit Symphony, Orchestra of the Age of Enlightenment, Freiburger Barockorchester; has conducted operas, including Handel's Semele at Spoleto Festival, Jommelli's L'isla Disabitata for Rome Opera, Monteverdi's L'Incoronazione di Poppea and Mozart's Le Nozze di Figaro for WNO, Handel's Amadigi at Teatro di San Carlo di Napoli, Handel's Alcina for Liceu Barcelona, Handel's Giulio Cesare for Oslo Opera. *Recordings include:* with Concerto Italiano: Vivaldi's Vespri per l'Assunzione di Mari Vergine, L'Olympiade, Le Quattro Stagioni, Concerti Ripieni, La Senna Festeggiante, Concerti per Archi, Monteverdi's Musica Sacra/Le Passioni dell' Anima, Vespro della Beata Vergine, Secondo libro de' Madrigali, Quinto libro de' Madrigali, Domenico Scarlatti, Stabat mater a dieci voci, Marenzio, Madrigali, libro II, Pergolesi/Scarlatti, Stabat Mater, Bach, The Art of Fugue, Harpsichord Concertos; other: Dietrich Buxtehude, Harpsichord Pieces, Bach, A la Maniera Italiana, Georg Boehm, Suites and Partitas, Bernardo Pasquini, Sonate per Gravicembalo, Bach Brandenburg Concertos 2005. *Honours:* Chevalier, Ordre des Arts et des Lettres 2003; Preis der deutschen Schallplattenkritik, Gramophone Award 1994, Prix de la Nouvelle Académie du disque, Cini Foundation Premio internationale del disco Antonio Vivaldi, Prix de l'Académie Charles Cros, Premio Abbiati. *Current Management:* c/o Maxine Robertson, Van Walsum Management Ltd, 4 Addison Bridge Place, London, W14 8XP, England. *Telephone:* (20) 7371-4343. *Fax:* (20) 7371-4344. *E-mail:* mrobertson@ vanwalsum.com. *Website:* www.vanwalsum.co.uk.

**ALEXANDER, Haim;** composer; b. 9 Aug. 1915, Berlin, Germany; m. 1941; two s. *Education:* Sternsches Conservatory, Berlin, Palestine Conservatory and Academy of Music, studied in Freiburg, Germany. *Career:* teacher of piano and theory, 1945–; Associate Professor, Composition and Theory, Head,

Department of Theoretical Subjects, Rubin Academy of Music, Jerusalem, 1971–82; Associate Professor, 1972–76, Full Professorship, 1976–, Theoretical Subjects, Department of Musicology, University of Tel-Aviv; Retired 1982, but continuing part-time work. *Compositions include:* Miscellaneous works for piano, 2 pianos, chamber music, pieces based on Oriental Folklore, choral music, songs for voice and piano, works for orchestra; My Blue Piano, Lyrics by Else Lasker-Schüler, for 8 women's voices and percussion, 1990; Piano Sonata, 1994; Late Love for chamber orchestra, 1997; The West-Eastern Bridge, for organ solo, 1998; Two Ballads Recollected, for string quartet, 1998. *Publications:* Improvisation am Klavier 1986; contrib. to Encyclopaedia Hebraica. *Honours:* Golden Feather Prize for Lifetime Achievement from ACUM, 1996; The Israel Prime Minister's Prize for his life achievements, 2001. *Address:* 55 Tschernichowsky Street, 92587 Jerusalem, Israel.

**ALEXANDER, Leni;** composer; b. 8 June 1924, Breslau, Germany; m. Ernst Bodenhöfer 1941 (divorced); two s. one d. *Education:* Real-Gymnasium Hamburg, University of Chile, studied piano, cello, composition with Fre Focke, Conservatoire de Paris with Olivier Messiaen and composition studies with René Leibowitz. *Career:* moved to Chile 1939; public concerts of symphonique works in: Santiago de Chile, Buenos Aires, Paris, Rome, New York, Cologne (Chamber Music), Venice, Toulouse, Tokyo and Stuttgart; film Music, ballet music in Santiago; special broadcast commission, San Francisco. *Compositions include:* Cuarteto para Cuerdas, 1957; Cantata From Death to Morning; Equinoccio; ... ils se sont perdus dans l'espace etoile..., 1975; Aulicio II, 1985; Time and Consummation; Tessimenti; Adras; Par Quoi? A Quoi? Pour Quoi?; Maramoh; Los Disparates; Sous le quotidien, decelez l'inexplicable;... Est-ce donc si doux cette vie?... Ballet Music: Soon we shall be one, 1959, Les trois visages de la lune, 1966, Un medecin de campagne, Schigan for Organ, 1989, Dishona for Voice, Saxophone and 3 Percussions, 1988. *Publications:* contrib. to Music and Psychoanalysis; Alban Berg; The Music Which Freud Never Heard; Psychoanalytic Variations about a theme by Gustav Mahler. *Address:* c/o Beatrice Bodenhofer, Arzobispo Casanova, 24 Bellavista, Santiago de Chile, Chile.

**ALEXANDER, Roberta;** Singer (Soprano); b. 3 March 1949, Lynchburg, VA, USA. *Education:* Studied at the University of Michigan and with Herman Woltman at the Royal Conservatory, The Hague. *Career:* European debut as Rossini's Fanny, La Cambiale di Matrimonio, Netherlands Opera in 1975; Sang Pamina at Houston in 1980 and Strauss's Daphne at Santa Fe in 1981; Covent Garden debut as Mimi in La Bohème; Metropolitan debut in 1983 as Zerlina and returned to New York as Jenůfa, Mimi, Vitellia, Countess and Gershwin's Bess; Sang at Netherlands Opera as Vitellia, Fiordiligi and Violetta, Vienna State Opera as Donna Elvira, Jenůfa, and Hamburg State Opera as Elettra in Idomeneo, Donna Elvira and Countess; Glyndebourne debut in 1989 as Jenůfa; Sang Mozart's Vitellia at Zürich in 1989 and Elettra, Idomeneo, at the Hamburg Staatsoper in 1990; Sang Vitellia at Glyndebourne 1995; Donna Elvira at Fort Lauderdale, 1997; Concert appearances include Strauss Four Last Songs with Los Angeles Philharmonic under Previn, and San Francisco Symphony, Mahler No. 4 with Boston Symphony under Ozawa, Concertgebouw under Haitink, Cleveland under Ashkenazy, and Mahler No. 8 at the Salzburg Festival under Maazel; Concerts with Concentus Musicus Wien under Harnoncourt; Engaged for premiere of Angels in America, by Peter Eötvös, Paris Châtelet, 2004. *Recordings:* Mahler No. 4; Porgy and Bess excerpts; St John Passion; Giulio Cesare excerpts; Don Giovanni; Telemann Cantatas; Songs by Ives, Strauss, Mozart, Bernstein, Barber and Puccini; Goldschmidt's Beatrice Cenci and Der gewaltige Hahnrei. *Current Management:* Alferink Artists Management Amsterdam BV, Herengracht 340, 1016 CG Amsterdam, Netherlands. *Telephone:* 20 664 31 51. *Fax:* 20 675 24 26. *E-mail:* info@alferink.org. *Website:* www.alferink.org.

**ALEXANDRA, Liana;** Romanian composer; *Professor, National University of Music;* b. 27 May 1947, Bucharest; m. Serban Nichifor. *Education:* studied at Bucharest Univ. of Music, at Weimar and Darmstadt, Germany and in USA. *Career:* Prof., Doctor in Musicology teaching Orchestration, Musical Analysis and Composition, Univ. of Music, Bucharest 1971–. *Compositions:* over 100 works include seven symphonies, six concertos for different instruments and orchestra, three operas, one ballet, biblical cantata (Voice-Decalog) Jerusalem, 60 chamber works, choral music. *Recordings:* radio broadcasts and album recordings in Romania, Israel, USA, Netherlands, Belgium, Denmark, Germany, Italy, Spain, Australia, Austria. *Publications:* contrib. to books and articles published in Romania, Germany and Israel. *Honours:* Order of Cultural Merit (Second Class), Romania 2004; Gaudeamus Prize (Netherlands) 1979, 1980, Magadine Prize 1982, Bee-Sheva (Israel) 1986, Mannheim-Bedock Prize 1989, UNNA Prize (Dortmund) 1991, Int. Commendation of Success (USA) 2000, The 20th Century (USA) 2000, Int. Personality of the Year (UK) 2001, Researcher of the Year, American Biographical Inst. 2001, Woman of the Year, American Biographical Inst. 2002, Prize for Electroacoustic Composition (France) 2003, 2004, Int. Peace Prize, United Cultural Convention 2003. *Address:* Str. Rosia Montana Nr 4, Bloc 05, Scara 4, Apt 165, 060955 Bucharest, Romania (home). *Telephone:* (21) 772-30-29 (home). *E-mail:* lianaalexandra@pcnet.ro (home). *Website:* romania -on-line.net/whoswho/AlexandraLiana.htm (home).

**ALEXEEV, Dmitri Konstantinovich;** Russian pianist; b. 10 Aug. 1947, Moscow; s. of Konstantin Alekseyev and Gertrude Bolotina; m. Tatiana Sarkisova 1970; one d. *Education:* Moscow Conservatoire. *Career:* studied under Dmitri Bashkirov; performs regularly in Russia, in UK and throughout Europe and USA and has toured Japan, Australia etc.; has performed with

London Philharmonic Orchestra, London Symphony Orchestra, City of Birmingham Symphony Orchestra, the Royal Philharmonic Orchestra, St Petersburg Philharmonic Orchestra, Berlin Philharmonic, Chicago Symphony Orchestra, Philadelphia Orchestra, Royal Concertgebouw Orchestra of Amsterdam, Israel Philharmonic and the Munich Bavarian Radio Orchestra; worked with Ashkenazy, Boulez, Semyon Bychkov, Dorati, Giulini, Jansons, Muti, Kent Nagano, Rozhdestvensky, Salonen, Klaus Tennstedt, Michael Tilson Thomas, Sian Edwards, Valery Gergiev, Andrew Litton and Yuri Temirkanov; recordings include works by Bach, Brahms, Chopin, Grieg, Liszt, Medtner, Prokofiev, Rachmaninov, Schumann, Shostakovich and Scriabin. *Honours:* prizewinner Int. Tchaikovsky Competition, Moscow 1974, 5th Leeds Int. Piano Competition 1975 and other int. competitions; received Edison Award, Netherlands. *Address:* c/o IMG Artists, Lovell House, 616 Chiswick High Road, London, W4 5RX, England. *Telephone:* (20) 8233-5800.

**ALEXEYEV, Anya;** Concert Pianist; b. 1970, Moscow, Russia. *Education:* Studied with Dmitri Bashkirov at the Moscow Conservatoire and at the Royal College of Music, with Irina Zaritskaya, 1990–. *Career:* Frequent appearances in Russia and at the major London venues: Barbican Centre, South Bank and St John's Smith Square; Wigmore Hall recital, 1994; Tour of South America 1993 and with the Lithuanian Symphony Orchestra on tour to the United Kingdom, in Concerto No. 2 by Shostakovich; Rachmaninov 2 and Beethoven 4 with the Philharmonia in South Africa; Season 1994–95 with recitals in Ireland and at Festivals in Belgium, Spain, France and Finland; Schumann's Concerto with the Bournemouth Symphony Orchestra, the Grieg Concerto with the Royal Scottish National Orchestra, the United Kingdom tour with the Moscow State Orchestra and recitals at the Bath and Brighton Festivals; the United Kingdom tour with the Russian Symphony Orchestra, 2001; Past engagements have included performances with orchestras including the Philharmonia, BBC Philharmonic, London Mozart Players, Deutschland Radio, Vienna Chamber, National Symphony, Quebec Symphony and St Petersburg Philharmonic with Yuri Temirkanov; also solo recitals at major venues and festivals throughout Europe, regular appearances at the Wigmore Hall in London and appearances with various groups in the United Kingdom, Austria, Sweden and Finland. *Honours:* Winner, Newport International Piano Competition, 1991. *Current Management:* Harrison/Parrott Ltd, 12 Penzance Place, London, W11 4PA, England. *Telephone:* (20) 7229 9166. *Fax:* (20) 7221 5042. *Website:* www.harrisonparrott.com.

**ALEXEYEV, Valery;** Singer (Baritone); b. 1954, Novosibirsk, Siberia. *Education:* Studied in Novosibirsk and Milan. *Career:* Sang with the Kirov Opera, St Petersburg, 1984 in Prokofiev's War and Peace, The Enchantress by Tchaikovsky and the baritone leads in Prince Igor, Eugene Onegin and Boris Godunov; As Tomsky in The Queen of Spades, Vienna Staatsoper, 1996; As Ruprecht in Prokofiev's Fiery Angel, Covent Garden, 1992; Iago in Otello, Barcelona, 1992; Boris in Lady Macbeth, Frankfurt, 1993; Sang Nabucco, Bregenz Festival, 1993 and Rangoni in Boris Godunov, Salzburg, 1994; Sang Escamillo at Verona, 1995; Eugene Onegin, Zürich, 1996; Season 2000–01 as Giancotto in Francesca da Rimini at Buenos Aires, Iago for the Berlin Staatsoper and Count Luna at the New York Met; Other roles include Scarpia, Verdi's Miller, Santiago; Don Giovanni, Rigoletto, Mazeppa, Posa in Don Carlos and Valentin in Faust. *Recordings:* Otello. *Current Management:* Pinnacle Arts: Dietsch Division, Thierschstrasse 11/5 OG, 80802 Munich, Germany. *Telephone:* (89) 34086300. *Fax:* (89) 34086310. *E-mail:* jdietsch@pinnaclearts.com. *Website:* www.pinnaclearts.com. *Address:* c/o Kirov Opera, 1 Theatre Square, St Petersburg, Russia.

**ALGIERI, Stefano;** singer (tenor); b. 1959, USA. *Career:* sang at Bielefeld Opera, 1984–86; Verdi's Riccardo, Essen, 1986–87; As Turiddu, New York City Opera, 1986 and Radames at Costa Mesa Opera, 1988; Boris in Katya Kabanova, Amsterdam, Paris and Berlin; 1998–99 season as Don Carlos, Toronto; Don José, New Orleans; Andrea Chénier, Strasbourg; Sang Verdi's Alvaro and Pollione in Norma, Scottish Opera, 1990 and 1993 and Laca in Jenůfa, Bonn, 1994; Other roles include Puccini's Des Grieux, Dublin, 1991; Manrico, Lisbon. *Address:* c/o Scottish Opera, 39 Elmbank Crescent, Glasgow G2 4PT, Scotland.

**ALI-ZADEH, Franghiz;** composer and pianist; b. 29 May 1947, Baku, Azerbaijan, Russia. *Education:* Baku Conservatory. *Career:* teacher at the Baku Conservatory from 1977. *Compositions include:* The Legend about White Horseman, rock opera, 1985; Piano concerto, 1972; Symphony, 1976; Concerto for chamber orchestra, 1986; Songs about the Motherland, oratorio, 1978; Ode for chorus and orchestra, 1980; 2 piano sonatas, 1970, 1990; String Quartet, 1974, and other chamber music; Crossings for chamber ensemble, 1992; Songs; Empty Cradle, ballet, 1993; String Quartets Nos 3 and 4, 1995, 1998; Journey to the Immortal for baritone, chorus and ensemble, 1995–99. *Address:* c/o RAO, Bolchaia Bronnai 6a, Moscow 103670, Russia.

**ALIBERTI, Lucia;** Singer (Soprano); b. 1957, Messina, Sicily, Italy. *Education:* Studied at the Messina Conservatory. *Career:* Debut: Teatro Sperimentale, Spoleto in 1978 as Amina in La Sonnambula; Spoleto Festival in 1979 as Amina, Wexford Festival in 1979 in Crispino e la Comare by the brothers Ricci; Returned in 1980 in Un Giorno di Regno and in 1983 as Linda di Chamounix; Sang at Piccola Scala Milan in 1980 as Elisa in Il Re Pastore by Mozart, then in Handel's Ariodante; Glyndebourne Festival in 1980 as Nannetta and also at La Scala Milan in 1981; Sang at the Teatro Bellini Catania in 1982 as Elvira in I Puritani and Olympia in Les Contes d'Hoffmann; Deutsche Oper Berlin and Munich Opera in 1983 as Lucia and

Gilda; Cologne and Zürich in 1985 and 1986 as Violetta; Sang title role in Rossini's La Donna del Lago followed by Norma at Catania in 1990; Sang Violetta at Hamburg, 1993; Norma at Buenos Aires, 1995; Lucia di Lammermoor at La Scala, 1997; Season 2001 as Imogene in Bellini's Il Pirata at Catania and as Donizetti's Anna Bolena at the Deutsche Oper, Berlin. *Recordings include:* La Buona Figliuola by Piccinni; L'Arte del Bel Canto. *Address:* Oper der Stadt Bonn, Am Boselagerhof 1, 5300 Bonn, Germany. *Website:* www.lucia-aliberti.com.

**ALIEV, Eldar;** Singer (Bass); b. 1968, Baku, Russia. *Education:* Baku Conservatory, and with Anatoly Eusev. *Career:* Debut: Sarastro in Die Zauberflöte, conducted by Peter Maag, Treviso, 1994; Appearances at the Wexford Festival, in Giordano's Siberia, in Verdi's Attila at Genoa, as Sparafucile in Rigoletto at Lausanne, and Debussy's Arkel at Bologna; Commendatore in Don Giovanni at the Berlin State Opera, and Opéra Bastille, Paris, 2001; Further roles include Puccini's Colline, Ferrando in Il trovatore, Philip II (Don Carlo), Baldassare in La Favorita and Oroveso in Norma; Sang Capiello in I Capuleti e i Montecchi at Covent Garden, 2001; Concert repertoire includes Beethoven's 9th and Shostakovich's 13th Symphonies, and the Verdi and Mozart Requiems; Engaged as Banquo in Macbeth at the Opéra Bastille and as Timur in Turandot for Netherlands Opera. *Current Management:* Stage Door, Via Marconi 71, 40122 Bologna, Italy. *Telephone:* (51) 19984750. *Fax:* (51) 19984779. *E-mail:* info@stagedoor.it. *Website:* www.stagedoor.it. *Address:* Opéra Bastille, 120 rue de Lyon, 75012 Paris, France.

**ALLDIS, John,** ARCO, MA, FGSM; conductor; b. 10 Aug. 1929, London, England; m. Ursula Mason 1960; two s. *Education:* Felsted School, choral scholar King's College, Cambridge. *Career:* founder and Conductor, John Alldis Choir, 1962–; Professor, Guildhall School of Music, 1966–77; Founder and Conductor, London Symphony Chorus, 1966–69; Conductor of London Philharmonic Choir, 1969–82; Conductor of Danish Radio Choir, 1972–77; Musical Director, Groupe Vocal de France, 1978–83; Fellow, Westminster Choir College, Princeton, NJ, USA 1978. *Recordings:* Over 50 various recordings with John Alldis Choir, of contemporary music and opera; Beethoven's Missa Solemnis (Klemperer), Elgar's The Dream of Gerontius (Boult), Berlioz's Grande Messe des Morts, (Colin Davis) and L'Enfance du Christ, Ives Symphony No. 4, (Serebrier), Mozart's Die Entführung, (Davis), Puccini's Turandot, (Mehta), Tchaikovsky's Eugene Onegin, (Solti) and Vivaldi's Sacred Choral Works, Negri. *Honours:* Chevalier, Ordre des Arts et des Lettres 1984. *Address:* 3 Wool Road, Wimbledon, London SW20 0HN, England.

**ALLEN, Betty;** American singer (mezzo-soprano); b. Campbell, OH; d. of James Corr and Dora Catherine (née Michael) Allen; m. Ritten Edward Lee III 1953; two s. two d. *Education:* Wilberforce Univ., OH and Hartford School of Music. *Career:* opera debut Teatro Colón, Buenos Aires, Argentina 1964; has appeared with San Francisco Opera, Bellas Artes Opera, Mexico, Oslo Opera, Houston Opera, Montreal Opera, Canada, The Hague Opera and at numerous festivals including Marlboro, Helsinki, Saratoga, Caramoor Music, Cincinnati May and Tanglewood Festivals; appearances with major symphony orchestras on concert tours of USA, Europe, N Africa, Caribbean, Canada, S America and Asia; teacher, Teatro Colón 1985–86, Curtis Inst. of Music 1987–; Exec. Dir Harlem School of the Arts 1979, now also Artistic Dir; recordings for London, Vox, Decca, Deutsche Grammophon, Columbia, RCA and Odeon-Pathé; numerous radio and TV appearances in USA, Canada, Mexico, UK, Germany, Sweden; mem. Bd Dirs Arts Alliance, Karl Weigl Foundation, Diller-Quaile School of Music, US Comm. for UNICEF, Manhattan School of Music, Theatre Devt Fund, Children's Storefront, Chamber Music Soc. of Lincoln Center, New York Housing Authority, Exec. Cttee Carnegie Hall, Nat. Foundation for Advancement in the Arts; Rep. USA to Cultural Olympics, Mexico; John Hay Whitney Fellow 1953–54. *Honours:* numerous hon. degrees; Marian Anderson Award 1953–54, Man. Award, Nat. Music League 1953, Best Singer of Season (Critics' Circle) Argentina and Chile 1959, Uruguay 1961, Duke Ellington Memorial Award, 52nd St American Festival 1989, Bowery Award, Bowery Bank 1989, Harlem School of the Arts Award, Harlem School and Isaac Stern 1990, St Thomas Church Award, St Thomas Catholic Church 1990, Men's Day Celebration Award, St Paul's Church 1990, Martell House of Seagram Award, Avery Fisher Hall 1990. *Address:* Harlem School of the Arts, 645 St Nicholas Avenue, New York, NY 10030, USA.

**ALLEN, Giselle;** Singer (soprano); b. 1970, Belfast, N Ireland. *Education:* University of Wales; Guildhall School. *Career:* Roles included Janáček's Fox, Britten's Helena and Suor Angelica, GSMD, London; Walton's Cressida, Ischia; Musetta and Tatiana for Clonter Opera; Svatava in Sarka by Fibich, Wexford; Massenet's Iris, Holland Park; Helena at Singapore; Massenet's Salomé at Dublin, 2000; Concerts include Messiah, Albert Hall with David Willcocks; The Vaughan Williams Serenade with Simon Rattle and recitals in Northern Ireland, 1998–99 season. *Honours:* Guildhall and Ricordi Singing Prizes, GSMD. *Current Management:* Hazard Chase, 25 City Road, Cambridge, CB1 1DP, England. *Telephone:* (1223) 312400. *Fax:* (1223) 460827. *Website:* www.hazardchase.co.uk. *Address:* Music International, 13 Ardilaun Road, London N5 2AR, England.

**ALLEN, Paschal;** singer (baritone); b. 1960, Armagh, Northern Ireland. *Education:* studied in Belfast and at Guildhall School, London, with Norman Walker. *Career:* appearances at the Wexford and Glyndebourne Festivals, with English National Opera and for Dublin Grand Opera; Repertoire includes Leporello, Bartolo, Colline in La Bohème, Kecal (The Bartered Bride), Figaro and Sarastro; frequent tours with the English Opera Group; Concerts at the Edinburgh and Aldeburgh Festivals; Broadcasts for BBC and Radio Telefis Eireann; engagements for the Royal Opera, Covent Garden, include English stage premiere of Hindemith's Mathis der Maler, directed by Peter Sellars, 1995. *Address:* c/o Royal Opera House (Contracts), Covent Garden, London WC2E 9DD, England.

**ALLEN, Sir Thomas Boaz,** Kt, FRCM; British singer (baritone); b. 10 Sept. 1944, Seaham Harbour, Co. Durham; s. of Thomas Boaz Allen and Florence Allen; m. 1st Margaret Holley 1968 (divorced 1986); one s.; m. 2nd Jeannie Gordon Lascelles 1988; one step-s. one step-d. *Education:* Robert Richardson Grammar School, Ryhope, Royal Coll. of Music, London. *Career:* prin. baritone, Welsh Nat. Opera 1969–72, Royal Opera House, Covent Garden 1972–78; freelance opera singer 1978–, singing at Glyndebourne Opera 1973, ENO, London Coliseum 1986, La Scala 1987, Chicago Lyric Opera 1990, Royal Albert Hall 2000, London Proms 2002, Royal Opera House, Covent Garden 2003, Metropolitan Opera, New York 2005; Prince Consort Prof. Royal Coll. of Music 1994; Hambro Visiting Prof. of Opera Univ. of Oxford 2000–01, currently Fellow Jesus Coll.; Pres. British Youth Opera 2000–. *Art Exhibitions:* Chelsea Festival 2001, Salisbury Playhouse 2001. *Performances include:* Die Zauberflöte 1973, Le Nozze di Figaro 1974, Così fan Tutte 1975, Don Giovanni 1977, The Cunning Little Vixen 1977 and Simon Boccanegra, Billy Budd, La Bohème, L'Elisir d'Amore, Faust, Albert Herring, Die Fledermaus, La Traviata, A Midsummer Night's Dream, Die Meistersinger von Nürnberg; as producer Albert Herring 2002. *Film:* Mrs Henderson Presents 2005. *Publication:* Foreign Parts: A Singer's Journal 1993. *Honours:* Hon. Fellow RAM, Univ. of Sunderland; Hon. MA (Newcastle) 1984, Hon. DMus (Durham) 1988, Hon. DMus (Birmingham) 2004; Queen's Prize 1967, Gulbenkian Fellow 1968, Royal Philharmonic Soc. BBC Radio 3 Listeners' Award 2004. *Current Management:* Askonas Holt Ltd, Lonsdale Chambers, 27 Chancery Lane, London, WC2A 1PF, England. *Telephone:* (20) 7400-1700. *Fax:* (20) 7400-1799. *E-mail:* info@askonasholt.co.uk. *Website:* www.askonasholt.co.uk.

**ALLIK, Kristi;** composer and teacher; b. 6 Feb. 1952, Toronto, Ontario, Canada. *Education:* Toronto University, Princeton, and University of Southern California. *Career:* teacher at Queen's University, Kingston, Ontario, from 1988; Co-founder of electronic music studio at Queen's. *Compositions include:* Loom Sword River, opera, 1982; Of all the People for voices and ensemble, 1983, Skyharp, sound sculpture, 1991; Multi-media works with electronics Electronic Zen Garden (1983), Rondeau (1985), Comatose (1986), Rhythm and Culture (1986), Till Rust do us Part (1988), Vitamin B-52 (1989); Piano trio, 1979; Lend me your Harp for chorus and chamber orchestra, 1981; Zone Two for ensemble, 1984; Rohan for cello and chamber orchestra, 1988; Trio for clarinet, piano and low voice, 1989; Three Textures for strings, 1992; Illustrated Earth for orchestra, 1993; Nel mezzo del camina for soprano, guitar and tape, 1995. *Address:* c/o Queen's University, School of Music, Kingston, Ontario K7L 3N6, Canada.

**ALLIOT-LUGAZ, Colette;** singer (soprano); b. 20 July 1947, Notre-Dame-de-Bellecombe, France. *Education:* studied at Bonneville with Magda Fonay-Besson in Geneva and at the Opera Studio Paris with Rene Koster and Vera Rozsa; further study at the Lyon Conservatoire. *Career:* has sung widely in France and elsewhere as Mozart's Pamina, Cherubino and Zerlina; Engagements as Messager's Véronique, Rosina and Weber's Aennchen and in operas by Monteverdi, Haydn and Rameau; Has often appeared as Debussy's Mélisande notably at the Lyon Opéra in 1980; Festival performances at Aix and Glyndebourne and at the Paris Opéra and the Théâtre de la Monnaie, Brussels; Modern repertory includes La Passion de Gilles by Boesmans, creation 1983, and Berio's Opera; Sang Ascanius in Les Troyens at the opening of the Opéra Bastille, Paris in 1990; Appeared as Lully's Alceste at the Théâtre des Champs-Elysées, 1992; Season 1992–93 as Gluck's Alceste at Montpellier and Siebel in Faust at the Paris Opéra; Sang in Les Troyens by Berlioz with the Toulouse Orchestra under the direction of Michel Plasson at Toulouse and Athens, 1994; During 1995 gave many concerts with the Orchestra des Pays de Savoie; Sang a concert version of Pulcinella by Stravinsky at the Salle Pleyel, 1996, and the Brahms Requiem at Lyon, 1997; Season 1997–98 sang with the Cantate des Alpes in many concerts of traditional alpine songs throughout the Rhône-Alpes region. *Recordings include:* Pelléas et Mélisande, conducted by Charles Dutoit; Fragoletto in Les Brigands by Offenbach; Campra's Tancrède; Video of Pelléas et Mélisande, from Lyon (Arthaus). *Honours:* The Nadia and Lili Boulanger Prize, Académie des Beaux-Arts, Paris, 1993. *Address:* Les Frasses, 73590 Notre Dame de Bellecombe, France.

**ALLISON, John,** BMus, PhD, ARCO; British editor and critic; *Editor, Opera;* b. 20 May 1965, Cape Town, S Africa; s. of David Allison and Adele Allison; m. Nicole Galgut. *Education:* Univ. of Cape Town. *Career:* fmr organist at Cape Town Cathedral; music critic for The Times; Ed. Opera magazine 2000–. *Publications:* Edward Elgar: Sacred Music 1994, Mitchell Beazley Pocket Guide to Opera 1998; contrib. to Opera News, BBC Music Magazine, Classic FM Magazine, Financial Times, London Evening Standard, The Observer, The Australian, New Grove Dictionary of Music and Musicians, The New Penguin Opera Guide, Music and Words—Essays in Honour of Andrew Porter. *Address:* Opera Magazine, 36 Black Lion Lane, London, W6 9BE, England (office). *E-mail:* editor@operamag.clara.co.uk (office). *Website:* www.opera.co.uk (office).

**ALLISTER, Jean Maria,** LRAM, FRAM, FGSM; singer and teacher; b. 26 Feb. 1932, Northern Ireland; m. 1st Edgar Fleet 1955; one s.; m. 2nd René Atkinson 1974. *Education:* Royal Acad. of Music, London. *Career:* debut, Royal Albert Hall, London 1954; many oratorio and recital performances, England and abroad 1954–80; Henry Wood Promenade Concerts 1959–70; premiere, In Terra Pax 1960; Three Choirs Festivals 1961–77; appeared in L'Italiana in Algeri, Camden Festival 1961; Sadler's Wells Opera debut 1962; sang at Glyndebourne 1962–70; British premiere, Henze's Novae de Infinito Laudes, Leeds 1965; Alexander Nevsky, Festival Hall 1968; L'Ormindo, Munich 1969; Covent Garden debut as Page in Salome 1970; Scipio, Handel Opera Soc., Herrenhausen and Drottningholm 1970; premiere, John Gardner's The Visitors 1972; Delius's Koanga, Sadler's Wells Opera 1972; British premiere, F. Martin's Requiem 1975; final appearances before retiring from public performance, Jenůfa, Opera North 1980. *Recordings:* Stravinsky Mass (L'Oiseau Lyre) conducted by C. Davis, Pirates of Penzance, Ruddigore (D'Oyly Carte), Gilbert and Sullivan Selection, Koanga, Cavalli L'Ormindo, The Mikado (Sadler's Wells Orchestra), Gilbert and Sullivan Spectacular (various, London Concert Orchestra), Malcolm Arnold The Composer/The Conductor: A 75th Birthday Tribute (Song of Simeon), Dido and Aeneas (Purcell conducted by Britten with the English Opera Group Orchestra, reissue) 1999. *Publications:* Sing Solo Soprano (ed.) 1985. *Honours:* Minnie Hauk Prize 1953, Fellow Emeritus GSM. *Address:* Little Paddock, Elm Crescent, Charlbury, Oxfordshire OX7 3PZ, England.

**ALLMAN, Robert;** singer (baritone); b. 8 June 1927, Melbourne, Australia. *Education:* Melbourne Conservatory with Horace Stevens, studied with Marjorie Smith in Sydney and with Dominique Modesti in Paris. *Career:* sang with the Victoria National Opera Company, 1952, and Royal Opera House, Covent Garden in 1956 as Escamillo; Guest appearances at Sadler's Wells and at Berlin Staatsoper, Hamburg as Iago, Frankfurt, Munich and Cologne until 1967; Appearances in Australia from 1960 as Rigoletto, Jochanaan in Salome, Macbeth, Escamillo, Scarpia, Belcore and Valentine; Sang Don Giovanni, Iago and Nabucco, 1970–71, with the Elizabethan Opera Company; Further guest engagements at Stuttgart, Düsseldorf, Kassel, Zürich and Strasbourg as Macbeth and Simon Boccanegra; Glyndebourne Festival in 1979 as Pizarro; Member of the Australian Opera at Sydney from 1971; Sang Amonasro in Aida at Brisbane in 1988; Many concert performances notably in Messiah. *Address:* c/o Lyric Opera of Queensland, PO Box 677, South Brisbane, Queensland 4101, Australia.

**ALLWOOD, Ralph,** BA; teacher; b. 30 April 1950, Walton-on-Thames, England. *Education:* Tiffin School, Durham Univ., Univ. of Cambridge. *Career:* Precentor and Dir of Music, Eton Coll. 1985–; founded and directs the five annual Eton Choral Courses; Dir Rodolfus Choir; Dir Windsor and Eton Choral Society; adjudicator for Sainsbury's Choir of the Year and the Llangollen International Eisteddfod; choral advisor for Novello and Co. Ltd. *Recordings:* Music from Eton 1986, I will lift up mine eyes 1986, A Sequence for the Ascension 1992, Mater Ora Filium 1993, Music from Eton Choirbook 1994, Grier: Twelve Anthems 1995, Among the leaves so Green 1996, Choral evensong from Eton College 1997, Welsh Songs, Hymns and Anthems 1997, Parry: Songs of Farwell 1998, Eberlin: Sacred Choral Music 1999, Christmas Music from Eton College 2000, By Special Arrangement 2002, A Christmas Collection 2003, Musica Etonensis 2004, Abendlied 2004, Thomas Tallis: Latin Motets and Anthems 2005, A Celebration of Christmas 2005, A Bach Christmas 2005. *Honours:* Hon. FRSCM 2002, Hon. ARAM 2003. *Address:* Eton College, Eton, Berkshire SL4 6EW, England (office). *Telephone:* (1753) 671169 (office). *Fax:* (1753) 671170 (office). *E-mail:* r.allwood@etoncollege.org.uk (office). *Website:* www.etoncollege.com (office).

**ALMERARES, Paula;** Singer (Soprano); b. 1970, Argentina. *Education:* Studied in Buenos Aires. *Career:* Debut: Soloist in Mahler's 4th Symphony, La Plata, 1990; Stage debut as Mimi, La Plata, 1990; Early roles were Musetta, Micaela and Donizetti's Norina; Sang in Roméo et Juliette, Don Pasquale, La Bohème and Falstaff, Teatro Colón Buenos Aires, 1992; Offenbach's Antonia with Alfredo Kraus, 1993; Gounod's Juliette, 1996; Premiere of Mario Peruso's Guayaquil, 1993; Zarzuelas with Placido Domingo, Teatro Avenida, Buenos Aires, 1994; Gluck's Euridice, Venice, 1995; Sang at Trieste, 1996 as Adina in L'Elisir d'amore; Adina at Washington and Euridice at Naples, 1998 season; La Traviata, Il Barbiere, L'Elisir d'amore, Pittsburgh Opera; In Italy, La Sonnambula, I Puritani, Il Corsaro, La Traviata, L'Elisir d'amore and Massenet's Manon; Sang Massenet's Manon at Genoa, 1999. *Recordings:* Giulietta e Romeo (N Vaccai) first recording. *Honours:* Best Soprano, Belvedere Competition, Vienna, 1993; Winner of Traviata 2000 Competition, Pittsburgh, 1994. *Current Management:* Columbia Artists Management, 1790 Broadway, New York, NY 10019-1412, USA. *Telephone:* (212) 841-9500. *Fax:* (212) 841-9744. *E-mail:* info@cami.com. *Website:* www.cami.com.

**ALONSO, Odon;** conductor; b. 28 Feb. 1925, La Baneza, Leon, Spain. *Education:* Madrid Conservatoire and in Siena and Vienna. *Career:* Choral Director of the Madrid Soloists, 1952, specializing in Music of the Spanish Renaissance and Baroque; Conducted the Spanish National Orchestra, 1952–56, Madrid Philharmonic, 1956–58; Directed the Zarzuela Theatre at Madrid, 1956–57; Conducted the Spanish Radio and Television Orchestra from 1968; Guest engagements at the Vienna Volksoper, New York City Opera, Teatro Liceo Barcelona and the Madrid Opera. *Recordings include:* Guitar Concertos by Vivaldi and Rodrigo, with Narciso Ypes; Turina's Rapsodia Sinfonica.

**ALONSO-CRESPO, Eduardo,** MFA; composer and conductor; b. 18 March 1956, Tucuman, Argentina. *Education:* National University of Tucuman, Carnegie Mellon University, Pittsburgh. *Career:* Professor of Piano, School of Musical Arts, National University of Tucuman; debut conducting: Carnegie Mellon Philharmonic in Ginastera, USA, 1987; Tucuman Symphony in Alonso-Crespo, Mozart, Brahms, Argentina, 1988; Assistant Conductor, Pittsburgh Civic Orchestra, 1988–90; Associate Conductor, Carnegie Mellon Philharmonic, 1989–91; Music Director, Tucuman Symphony Orchestra and Carnegie Mellon Contemporary Ensemble, 1989–; Orquesta de Tucuman, seasons 1991, 1992; Carnegie Mellon Wind Ensemble, 1991–92; Conductor-in-Residence, Carnegie Mellon University, 1991–92; guest conducting, Argentina, USA. *Compositions include:* Gorbachev, Two-Act Opera; Juana, La Loca, One-Act Opera; Putzi, One-Act Opera; Medea, Ballet, for Chorus and Orchestra; Piano Concerto No. 1, Commentaries on Three Waltzes by Alberdi; Two Stories of Birds for Orchestra; Sinfonietta for String Orchestra. *Address:* Marcos Paz 250, Tucuman 4000, Argentina.

**ALPERIN, Yoram;** cellist; b. 1945, Romania. *Education:* Rubin Academy of Music, Tel-Aviv with Uzi Wiezel. *Career:* member and solo appearances with Israel Philharmonic, 1971–; Co-founded Jerusalem String Trio, 1977, giving many concerts, Israel and Europe, 1981–; Repertoire includes String Trios by Beethoven, Dohnányi, Mozart, Reger, Schubert and Taneyev, Piano Quartets by Beethoven, Brahms, Dvořák, Mozart and Schumann; Concerts with Radu Lupu and Daniel Adni. *Address:* c/o Ariën Arts & Music, de Boeystraat 6, 2018 Antwerp, Belgium.

**ALSOP, Marin,** MusM; American violinist and conductor; *Principal Conductor, Bournemouth Symphony Orchestra;* b. 16 Oct. 1956, Manhattan, NY; d. of LaMar Alsop and Ruth Alsop. *Education:* began piano studies aged two, violin studies aged five; Juilliard Pre-Coll., Yale Univ. and Juilliard School of Music. *Career:* freelance violinist with New York Symphony Orchestra, Mostly Mozart, New York Chamber Symphony, American Composers Orchestra, several Broadway shows 1976–79; began conducting studies with Carl Bamberger 1979, Harold Farberman 1985; f. String Fever (14-piece swing band) 1981; founder and Dir Concordia Orchestra 1984–; debut with London Symphony Orchestra 1988; Assoc. Conductor Richmond Symphony 1988; studied with Leonard Bernstein, Seiji Ozawa and Gustav Meier, Tanglewood Music Center 1989; Music Dir Eugene Symphony, OR 1989–96, Conductor Laureate 1996–; Music Dir Long Island Philharmonic 1990–96; debut with Philadelphia Orchestra and Los Angeles Philharmonic 1990; Music Dir Cabrillo Music Festival 1992–; Music Dir Colorado Symphony, Denver 1993–; debut Schleswig Holstein Music Festival 1993; Creative Conductor Chair. St Louis Symphony Orchestra 1996–98; Prin. Guest Conductor, Royal Scottish Nat. Symphony 1999–; Prin. Guest Conductor, City of London Sinfonia 1999–; Prin. Conductor Bournemouth Symphony Orchestra (first woman to lead UK symphony orchestra) 2001–(07); debut with ENO 2003; teacher, Nat. Orchestral Inst. 1991–, Oberlin Coll. 1998, Interlochen Center for the Arts 1998, Curtis Inst. 1998; apptd Music Dir Baltimore Symphony Orchestra (first woman to head a major US orchestra) (2007–10). *Recordings include:* Fever Pitch, Fanfares for the Uncommon Woman, Saint-Saens, Blue Monday, Victory Stride, Fiddle Concerto for Violin and Orchestra, Gorgon, Music of Edward Collins, Too Hot to Handel, Barber Vols I–IV, Passion Wheels, Tchaikovsky Symphony No. 4, Bernstein Chichester Psalms. *Honours:* Leonard Bernstein Conducting Fellow, Tanglewood Music Festival 1988, 1989, MacArthur Fellow 2005; Hon. DLitt (Gonzaga Univ.) 1995; Stokowski Conducting Competition 1988, Koussevitzky Conducting Prize 1989, ASCAP Award for Adventuresome Programming of Contemporary Music 1991, Univ. of Colorado Distinguished Service Award 1997, State of Colorado Gov.'s Award for Excellence in the Arts 1998, Royal Philharmonic Soc. Conducting Award 2003, Gramophone Artist of the Year 2003, Classical BRIT Award for Female Artist of the Year 2005. *Current Management:* 21C Media Group Inc., 30 W 63rd Street, Suite 15S, New York, NY 10023, USA. *Telephone:* (212) 842-0080. *Fax:* (212) 842-0034. *E-mail:* info@21cmediagroup.com. *Address:* c/o Bournemouth Symphony Orchestra, 2 Seldown Lane, Poole, BH15 1UF, England (office). *E-mail:* MarinAlsop@aol .com (office). *Website:* www.marinalsop.com (office).

**ALSTED, Birgitte;** composer and violinist; b. 15 June 1942, Odense, Denmark. *Education:* Royal Danish Academy of Music, Music Academy, Warsaw, Poland; composition seminars with Per Norgard, Copenhagen. *Career:* performer of new music in, Det unge Tonekunstnerselskab; Kvinder i Musik; Danmarks Radio, Television Acting Musician, Experimental Theatre; Teacher, Compositions performed in DUT, Radio, Television, KIM, Paris, Rome, New York, Mexico City, Berlin, Stockholm, London; Commissions, Contemporary Dance Theatre, London, Nordiske Forum 88, Danmarks Radio; mem, Dansk Komponistforening; Kvinder i Musik; Det Unge Tonekunstnerselskab. *Compositions include:* Klumpe, 1972; Stykke 2, 1973; 12 toner i Zoo, 1973; Smedierne i Granada, 1976; Strygekvartet i CD, 1977; Konkurrence, 1979; Haiku-Sange, 1979; Solen og jeg, 1981; Gentagne Gange, 1980; Solen på Moddingen, 1982; Phasing Moon Facing Changing, 1983; Antigone, 1983; Kaere Allesammen, 1984; På Afstand af Bolgen, 1984–85; Om Natten, 1985; Skiftetid, 1985; Kindleins Schlaflied, 1986; Frokost i det Gronne, 1985; Nostalgisk Extranummer, 1985; Extra Nostalgisk no. 2, 1986; Espressione Emotionale, 1987; Fatsy, 1987; Dromme-spil, 1988; Opbrud, 1988; Vakst, 1989; Lyst, 1990; 2 sange til Doden, 1990; Episoder til Thomas, 1991; Havet ved Forår, 1991; Karen's Å, 1992; Unoder, 1992; Natterdag, 1992; Berceuse Neptunoise, 1993; Spring I, 1994; Stelle, 1995; Sorgsang, 1995; Hojsang, 1995;

She Cinderella, opera, 1996; Church Bells for orchestra, 1996; Lament for baritone and piano, 1996; Very Sure, electro-acoustic, 1997. *Recordings:* Antigone; Frokost i det Gronne; Vakst; Natterdag; To Sange til Doden; Sorgsang. *Honours:* Komponistforemingens Jubilaeumslegat, 1985; Gustav Enna's Mindelegat, 1988; Several grants, Art Foundation of Danish State, including 3 years, 1980–83. *Address:* Dansk Komponistforening, Grabrodretorv 16, 1154 Copenhagen K, Denmark.

**ALTENBURGER, Christian;** violinist; b. 5 Sept. 1957, Heidelberg, Germany. *Education:* Vienna Academy of Music, Juilliard School, New York, studied violin with father and Dorothy DeLay. *Career:* debut in 1964; formal debut in recital, Musikverein, Vienna, 1976; soloist with various major orchestras in Europe and the USA; With Bruno Canino played the Sonata by Strauss, Schoenberg's Fantasy and Bartók's 2nd Sonata, Salzburg Festival, 1990.

**ALTMEYER, Jeannine;** singer (soprano); b. 2 May 1948, La Habra, CA, USA. *Education:* studied with Martial Singher and Lotte Lehmann in Santa Barbara, California; attended the Salzburg Mozarteum. *Career:* operatic debut as the Heavenly Voice in Don Carlos, Metropolitan Opera, New York, 25 September 1971; Appeared with the Chicago Lyric Opera, 1972, in Salzburg, 1973 and at Bayreuth, 1979; Member of the Wurttemberg State Theatre, Stuttgart, 1975–79; Then sang throughout Europe, achieving success as a Wagnerian; Roles: Elsa, Eva, Sieglinde, Isolde, Elisabeth, Gutrune and Brünnhilde; Sang Isolde at Bayreuth, 1986; Paris Opéra and Los Angeles, 1987 as Chrysothemis, Isolde; Brünnhilde in Götterdämmerung at the Zürich Opera, 1989; Sang Leonore at La Scala, 1990; Turin 1991, as Goldmark's Queen of Sheba; Sang Brünnhilde in Götterdämmerung for Netherlands Opera, 1998; Elektra at Aachen, 1999. *Recordings:* Sang Brünnhilde in The Ring under Janowski; Video and DVD of Die Walküre, in production from Bayreuth. *Address:* c/o Theateragentur Dr Germinal Hilbert, Maximilianstrasse 22, 8000 Munich 22, Germany.

**ALTMEYER, Theodor Daniel;** Singer (tenor); b. 16 March 1931, Eschweiler, Aachen, Germany. *Education:* Studied in Cologne with Clemens Glettenberg, 1953–56. *Career:* Sang at the Städtische Oper Berlin, 1955–60, notably in the 1958 premiere of Diary of a Madman by Searle; Sang at Hannover from 1960, in operas by Rossini, Lortzing and Mozart, and as Pfitzner's Palestrina; Sang in Stuttgart from 1958; Vienna from 1969; Many concert appearances, often as the Evangelist in the Passions of Bach; Guest engagements in France, Austria, Italy, Belgium, England, Switzerland and Netherlands; Festivals of Venice, Lucerne, Montreux, Ansbach, Vienna, Florence and Naples; Professor at the Hannover Musikhochschule from 1974. *Recordings:* St Matthew and St John Passions of Bach, Dettinger Te Deum by Handel, Beethoven and Haydn Masses, Bach Cantatas; Evangelist in the St Luke Passion by Telemann and the St John Passion by Schütz; Schütz St Matthew Passion. *Address:* Hochschule für Musik und Theater Hannover, Emmichplatz 1, 3 Hannover, Germany.

**ALVA, Luigi;** singer (tenor); b. 10 April 1927, Lima, Peru. *Education:* studied with Rosa Morales in Lima and with Emilio Ghiradini and Ettore Campogalliani in Milan. *Career:* debut singing at Lima in the Zarzuela Luisa Fernanda, 1949; Beppe in Pagliacci, 1950; Sang Paolino in Cimarosa's Il matrimonio segreto at La Scala, 1955; Salzburg Festival, 1957–58, as Fenton in Falstaff and Ferrando in Così fan tutte; Sang Rossini's Almaviva more than 300 times, starting at La Scala, 1956; Returned to Milan in 1958 for the local premiere of Janáček's The Cunning Little Vixen and world premieres of Una domanda di matrimonio by Luciano Chailly and Malipiero's La donna e mobile; appeared in Holland Festival in 1959 in Il mondo della luna by Haydn and made his Covent Garden debut in 1960; Glyndebourne Festival, 1961–62, as Nemorino in L'Elisir d'amore; Aix-en-Provence from 1960, Vienna Staatsoper from 1961; Metropolitan Opera, 1964–76 as Ernesto in Don Pasquale, Almaviva, Lindoro in L'Italiana in Algeri and Mozart's Tamino; Other appearances in Hamburg, Berlin, Moscow, Edinburgh, Stockholm, Lisbon, Venice, Florence and Mexico City; Artistic Director of Prolirica in Lima from 1982; Retired as singer, 1989. *Recordings include:* Il Barbiere di Siviglia, Il matrimonio segreto and Falstaff (Columbia); La Cenerentola (Deutsche Grammophon); Handel's Alcina, L'Italiana in Algeri and Mozart's Il re pastore (Decca); Haydn's L'Isola disabitata (Philips); Alfonso and Estrella by Schubert (Melodram). *Address:* La Scala Opera, Via Drammatici 21, 20121 Milan, Italy.

**ALVARES, Eduardo;** singer (tenor); b. 10 June 1947, Rio de Janeiro, Brazil. *Career:* started career in Europe, (debut as Don José) Linz, Frankfurt, Vienna and Stuttgart, returned to Brazil and then sang Des Grieux (Manon Lescaut) at Metropolitan, and Netherlands Opera (also Dick Johnson in Fanciulla del West), Manrico in Il Trovatore for Opera North and Calaf in Turandot for Scottish Opera; English National Opera as Radames in Aida, 1985 and Cavaradossi, 1987; Teatro Municipal Rio de Janeiro, 1987–88, as Don José and Bacchus; Other roles include Alfredo, Gabriele Adorno, Don Carlos, Faust, Werther and Alva in Lulu; Wexford Festival, 1983–84, in Hans Heiling and The Kiss. *Address:* c/o English National Opera, London Coliseum, St Martin's Lane, London WC2N 4ES, England.

**ALVAREZ, Carlos;** Spanish singer (baritone); b. 1963, Málaga. *Education:* Málaga Conservatory. *Career:* sang Morales in Carmen with Luis Lima and gave concert with him at the Teatro Arriaga in Bilbao; further appearances at the Teatro La Zarzuela, Madrid, Teatro Colón Buenos Aires, Vienna Staatsoper, La Scala Milan and Royal Opera, Covent Garden; operas have included Eugene Onegin (at Madrid), La Bohème, Il Barbiere di Siviglia (Zürich), La Traviata and Fedora (London), Don Carlos (Mannheim) and Madama Butterfly (Milan); frequent appearances with Plácido Domingo, including Il Guarany by Gomes at Bonn and concerts in Tokyo, Berlin, Madrid and Seville; Les Troyens with the London Symphony at the Barbican Hall under Colin Davis 1993; guest engagements in New York, Geneva and Washington; Posa in Don Carlos at Salzburg 1998; Don Giovanni at the Vienna Theater an der Wien 1999; season 2000–01 as Germont at Zürich, Don Carlo in Ernani at Madrid and Posa in Don Carlos at the Vienna Staatsoper; Rigoletto at Covent Garden 2002. *Honours:* Opera Actual magazine Award for best baritone 2005. *Current Management:* ICM Artists, 4–6 Soho Square, London, W1D 3PZ, England. *Telephone:* (20) 7432-0800. *E-mail:* classical@icmtalent.com. *Website:* .icmtalent.com.

**ÁLVAREZ, Marcelo;** Argentine singer (tenor); b. 1963, Cordóba. *Career:* debut in Bellini's La Sonnambula at Teatro la Fenice, Venice 1995; operatic roles include: The Duke in Rigoletto, Trieste, London 1996, Toulouse 1997, Verona 1997, Buenos Aires 1997, Brussels 1998, Metropolitan Opera New York 1999, Tokyo 2000, London 2001, Paris 2001, Macerata 2002, Barcelona 2004; Alfredo in La Traviata, Hamburg, Genoa, Venice, Vienna, Paris, The Met 1998, Royal Albert Hall, London 1998, Berlin 1999–2000, Fiorentino 1999–2000, Bavaria 2002; the title role in Massenet's Werther Genoa, Toulouse 1999–2000, Trieste 2002, London 2004, Vienna 2005; The Italian Tenor in Der Rosenkavalier at The Met 2000–01; Tonio in La Fille du Regiment, Bilbao 1997; Arturo in I Puritani, Bologna 1997; Fenton in Falstaff, Berlin 1998; Edgardo in Lucia di Lammermoor, Toulouse 1997–98, Naples 2001–02, Paris 2002, Japan 2002–03, Chicago 2004; Des Grieux in Massenet's Manon, Genoa 1997–98, Paris 2000–01, Naples 2001–02; the title role in Gounod's Faust, Munich 1999–2000; the title role in Tales of Hoffman, Covent Garden, London 2000–01; Gennaro in Lucrezia Borga, Teatro alla Scala, Milan 2002–03; Rodolfo in La Bohème at La Scala 2002–03, Paris 2003, Verona 2005; Rodolfo in Luisa Miller, London 2003; Riccardo in Un Ballo di Maschera at Covent Garden 2005, Zürich 2005. *Recordings:* Bel Canto 1998, Marcelo Alvarez sings Gardel 2000, French Tenor Arias 2002, Duetto (with Salvatore Licitra) 2003, Jules Massenet's Manon 2003, The Tenor's Passion 2004. *Honours:* Echo Klassik Singer of the Year Award, Germany 2002, L'Opera magazine Tenor of the Year Award, Italy 2003. *Current Management:* Zemsky/Green Artists Management, 730 Fifth Avenue, Suite 1802, New York, NY 10019, USA. *Telephone:* (212) 300-8003. *Fax:* (212) 300-8001. *E-mail:* zgartists@aol.com. *Website:* www.zemskygreen.com; www.marceloalvarez.com.

**ALVES DA SILVA, Luiz;** singer (countertenor); b. 1961, Brazil. *Career:* sang with various European vocal groups, including the Clemencic Consort, Vienna, Hesperion XX, Instituzioni Harmoniche di Bologne, Capella Real of Barcelona and Ensemble Turicum; Zürich Opera Studio 1990; Achilles in Handel's Deidamia; Vienna Konzerthaus, 1990 as Mozart's Ascanio; Sang at Ulm and Zürich in Ligeti's Le Grand Macabre and Britten's Oberon at Biel; Baroque and contemporary works on stage and the concert platform. *Recordings:* GG Brunetti's Stabat Mater. *Address:* c/o Opernhaus Zürich, Falkenstrasse 1, 8008 Zürich, Switzerland.

**ALWYN, Kenneth,** ARAM, FRAM; conductor; b. 28 July 1928, Croydon, England; m. Mary Law; two d. *Education:* Royal Schools of Music, London. *Career:* debut, London; Conductor, Royal Choral Union, New Zealand; Sadler's Wells Theatre Ballet; Royal Ballet, Royal Opera House, Covent Garden; BBC Staff Conductor; Principal Conductor, Yomiuri Nippon Symphony Orchestra, Tokyo; Musical Dir, Philomusica; radio and television presenter; mem. Incorporated Soc. of Musicians, BBC Central Music Advisory Cttee. *Compositions:* various concert, radio and television commissions. *Recordings:* major recordings with leading orchestras; conductor of first stereophonic recordings by Decca with London Symphony Orchestra 1958, Tchaikovsky's 1812 Overture; complete recording, Hiawatha, with Bryn Terfel and Welsh National Opera 1991. *Honours:* Mann's Prize for Conducting 1951, Gramophone Award for Best Film Music 1998. *Address:* Horelands, West Chiltington Lane, West Sussex RH14 9EA, England.

**ÅM, Magnar;** composer; b. 9 April 1952, Trondheim, Norway. *Education:* Bergen Conservatory, studied in Lidholm, Stockholm. *Compositions include:* Prayer for soprano, chorus and string orchestra, 1972; Song for brass and percussion, 1974; Dance for harp, guitar and harpsichord, 1977; Octet, 1977; Point Zero for soprano, alto, chorus, children's chorus and amateur orchestra, 1979; 2 alternative versions; Ajar, double-bass concerto, 1981; A Cage-bird's Dream, multimedia piece, 1981; Inconceivable Father for Child Soprano, children's chorus, bass clarinet, timpani, double bass and organ, 1982; My Planet, My Soul, symphony, 1982; Piano pieces; Like a Leaf on the River, for guitar, 1983; Omen, for violin, horn, piano, 1983; Conqilia for violin, horn, piano, recitor, 1984; Right Through All This, for orchestra, 1985; Freetonal Conversations, for violin, cello and piano, 1986; Hovering depths for double bass, 1986; A Miracle and a Tear, for mixed chorus, 1987; If We Lift As One, for orchestra, 1988; Tonebath, experience room, 1989; And Let the Boat Slip Quietly Out, for orchestra, 1989;… And Life, an oratorio, 1990; Quiet Ruby, for choir, 1992; Glimpses of an Embrace, for trumpet, horn and mountain echoes, 1994; Among Mirrors, for violin, cello and piano, 1995; Be Quiet, My Heart, for orchestra, 1995; The Silver Cord for string quartet, 1996; On the Wings of the Ka-bird, for choir, 1996; The Wondering and the Wonder, for orchestra and dolphins, 1996; You Are Loved, for soprano, choir (SSA), two horns and harp, 1997; But in the Middle of the Whirl, for Hardanger-fiddle,

cello and piano, 1998; Wandering Heaven, for alto voice and string sextet, 1998; 5 Paradoxes, for organ, 1999; Tree of Tenderness (an oratorio), 1999; Aching Hard, Aching Soft for solo violin, 2000; Here In the Resurrection for string quartet and recitor, 2001; Lonely/Embraced for bassoon and orchestra, 2003. *Recordings:* Hovering Depths; Study on a Norwegian Hymn; Point Zero; Like a Leaf on the River; The Silver Cord; Gratia; The Light in your Chest; You Are Loved; Wandering Heaven; Va Bene; Octet–in nude. *Address:* Vevendelvegen 46, 6100 Volda, Norway. *E-mail:* magnar.am@online.no. *Website:* www.magnaram.com.

**AMACHER, Maryanne,** BFA; American composer and multi-media artist; b. 25 Feb. 1942, Kates, PA. *Education:* University of Pennsylvania with George Rochberg, Univs of Pennsylvania and Illinois, studied with Karlheinz Stockhausen. *Career:* taught in the Experimental Music Studio at the School of Engineering, University of Illinois, 1964–66; Creative Associate at the Center of Creative and Performing Arts, State University, New York, 1966–67; Fellow at the Massachusetts Institute of Technology, 1972–76; Fellow at Radcliffe College, Harvard, 1978–79; Sound experiments with John Cage and Merce Cunningham; Has initiated various projects with natural sound experiments in the local environemnt. *Compositions include:* City Links, performed in New York, Buffalo, Paris and Chicago, 1967–79; Lecture on the Weather, collaboration with Cage, 1975; Remainder, dance music for Merce Cunningham, for Tape and Electronics, 1976; Mixed Media works include Sound-Joined Rooms, 1980–82; Close Up; Intelligent Life, 1982; Music for the Webern Car; Mini-Sound Series, 1985–; Petra for 2 pianos, 1991. *Honours:* Multi-Media Award from New York State Council of Arts, 1978–79; Composition Award from the National Endowment of the Arts, 1978–79; Beard Arts Fund, 1980. *Address:* ASCAP, ASCAP Building, 1 Lincoln Plaza, New York, NY 10023, USA.

**AMADUCCI, Bruno;** conductor; b. 5 Jan. 1935, Viganello-Lugano, Switzerland. *Education:* Conservatorio Giuseppe Verdi, Milan, Italy; Ecole normale de Musique, Paris, France. *Career:* first concert, Mozart Requiem, Swiss Radio Montenceri, 1951; first public concert with Alfred Cortot and Orchestra, Pomeriggi Musicali, Milan, 1951; former Conductor, Metropolitan Opera, Vienna State Opera, Vienna Symphony Orchestra, Paris Opéra, Deutsche Oper, Berlin; Member of Jury, Concorso Voci Verdiane, Busseto, Italy and Concours Internationale, Geneva. *Publications:* L'Amfiparnaso de Orazio Vecchi par rapport au développement de l'expression du langage musicale, 1951; La Musica nella Svizzera Italiana e La Presenzadella Radio-Orchestra, 1973; The Puccini Dynasty, 1973. *Address:* Casella Postale, Lugano, 6901, Switzerland.

**AMARA, Lucine;** American singer (soprano); b. 1 March 1925, Hartford, CT; d. of George and Adrine (née Kazanjian) Armaganian. *Career:* debut at Hollywood Bowl, LA 1948; soloist, San Francisco Symphony 1949–50; performances with Metropolitan Opera, New York, New Orleans Opera, LA, Hartford Opera, CT, Pittsburgh Opera, PA, St Louis Opera, MO, Stockholm Opera, St Petersburg Opera, FL, Venezuela Philharmonic Orchestra and at Glyndebourne and Edinburgh Festivals, UK; opera and concert tours of fmr USSR 1965, Philippines 1968, France 1966, Mexico 1966, Hong Kong and People's Repub. of China 1983, Yugoslavia 1988; numerous TV and radio performances; First Prize Atwater-Ken Radio Auditions 1948; Acad. of Vocal Arts Hall of Fame. *Operas include:* Aida, Turandot, Tosca, Un Ballo in Maschera. *Recordings include:* Beethoven's Symphony No. 9, I Pagliacci, La Bohème, Verdi's Requiem. *Address:* Metropolitan Opera, New York, NY 10023, USA.

**AMBACHE, Diana Bella,** BA, ARAM, LRAM; British pianist, orchestra director, musicologist, academic and broadcaster; *Musical Director, Ambache Chamber Orchestra;* b. 18 June 1948, Kent, England; m. Jeremy Polmear 1982. *Education:* Royal Acad. of Music, Univ. of Sheffield. *Career:* debut, Purcell Room 1979; founder and Musical Dir, Mozart Chamber Orchestra 1977–83; founder and Musical Dir, Ambache Chamber Orchestra 1984–; int. touring to 33 countries on five continents 1977–; first performances of Complete Version in Modern Times of Mozart, Rondo in D, K386 1980; Dussek Piano Concerto in G Minor Opus 49 1981; Fantasy for Piano by Francis Shaw 1982; 44 premieres of works by female composers of the last 250 years, including G. Tailleferre, Clara Schumann, Fanny Mendelssohn, Kozeluch, Benda, Amy Beach, Helen Hopekirk, Luise Le Beau and others; Lecturer for Martin Randall Travel; broadcasts for BBC World Service, BBC Radio 4, BBC Radio 3, Classic FM; Artistic Dir, Women of Note 1995–97. *Recordings include:* ten of Mozart's piano concertos and chamber music by Mozart, Beethoven, Louise Farrenc, Amy Beach and Ottorino Respighi, Sweet Melancholy: 20th Century oboe and piano English collection, Old Masters, New Mistresses (concert series) 2002–04. *Publications:* Marie Grandval, Deux Pieces (ed.) 2001, Hélène Liebmann, Grand Trio in A, Op 11 (ed.) 2002. *Honours:* Gold Medal Associated Bd 1966, scholarship to Royal Acad. of Music 1967; exhibition from Univ. of Sheffield 1970. *Address:* 9 Beversbrook Road, London N19 4QG, England (office). *Telephone:* (20) 7263-4027 (office). *E-mail:* diana@ambache.co.uk (office). *Website:* www.ambache.co.uk; www.womenofnote.co.uk.

**AMIRKHANIAN, Charles Benjamin;** Composer; b. 19 Jan. 1945, Fresno, California, USA. *Education:* BA, English Literature, California State University, Fresno, 1967; MA, Interdisciplinary Creative Arts, San Francisco State University, 1969; MFA, Mills College, Oakland, California, 1980; Studied electronic music and sound recording techniques with David Behrman, Robert Ashley and Paul de Marinis. *Career:* Composer-in-Residence, Ann Halprin's Dancers Workshop Company, 1968–69; Music Director, KPFA Radio, Berkeley, California, 1969–; Lecturer, San Francisco State University, 1977–80. *Compositions:* Live-Performance: Canticle No. 1 for Percussion Quartet, 1963; Canticle No. 2 for Flute and Timpani, 1963; Canticle No. 3 for Percussion Trio, 1966; Canticle No. 4 for Percussion Quartet, 1966; Ode to Gravity, Theatre Piece, 1967; Spoilt Music, Theatre Piece, 1979; Text-Sound (Tape): Oratora Konkurso Rezulto: Autoro de la Jara (Portrait of Lou Harrison), 1970; Each'll, 1971; If In Is, 1971; Sound Nutrition, 1972; Heavy Aspirations (Portrait of Nicolas Slonimsky), 1973; Seatbelt Seatbelt, 1973; She She and She, 1974; Mahogany Ballpark, 1976; Dutiful Ducks, 1977; Audience, 1978; Dreams Freud Dreamed, 1979; Hypothetical Moments (in the Intellectual Life of Southern California), 1981; Dog of Stravinsky, 1982; The Real Perpetuum Mobile, 1984. *Address:* c/o ASCAP, ASCAP Building, 1 Lincoln Plaza, New York, NY 10023, USA.

**AMORETTI, Ruben;** singer (tenor); b. 1968, Burgos, Spain. *Education:* Studied in Berne; Bloomington, Indiana. *Career:* Sang Rossini's Almaviva at Bilbao, Zürich, Stuttgart and Porto, 1995; Scarlatti's Il Trionfo del onore and Massenet's Le Portrait de Manon, Geneva Opera; Sang Flamino in L'amore dei tre re by Montemezzi, Vienna, 1996; concert repertory includes Bach, Magnificat, Mendelssohn's Elijah, Rossini's Petite Messe, Berlioz Te Deum and Puccini's Messa di Gloria. *Recordings:* songs by Falla, Verdi, Bellini and Respighi, Gallo. *Address:* c/o Opernhaus Zürich, Falkenstrasse 1, 8008 Zürich, Switzerland.

**AMOYAL, Pierre Alain Wilfred;** French violinist; b. 22 June 1949, Paris; s. of Dr Wilfred Amoyal and Vera Amoyal (née Popravka); m. 2nd Leslie Chabot 1988. *Education:* Cours d'Etat, Vanves, Conservatoire Nat. Supérieur de Musique, Paris, Univ. of Southern Calif., USA. *Career:* studied with Jascha Heifetz; invited by Sir Georg Solti to perform Berg's violin concerto with Orchestre de Paris 1971; invited by Pierre Boulez to perform Schoenberg's Concerto with Orchestre de Paris 1977; Prof. of Violin, Conservatoire Nat. Supérieur de Musique, Paris 1977–88; Lausanne Conservatory 1987–; numerous performances throughout world with orchestras including Royal Philharmonic, New Philarmonia, l'Orchestre Nat. de France, Residentie-Orkest, The Hague; First Prize, Conservatoire de Versailles 1960, Conservatoire Nat. Supérieur de Musique, Paris 1962, for chamber music, Conservatoire Nat. Supérieur de Musique. *Recordings include:* Symphonie espagnole (Lalo), Violin Concerto (Mendelssohn), Concertos Nos 1 and 2 and Two Sonatas (Prokofiev), Tartini's concertos, Third Concerto, Havanaise and Rondo Capriccioso (Saint-Saëns), Concerto No. 1 (Bruch), Concerto (Glazunov), Sonatas (Fauré), Horn Trio (Brahms), Concertos (Mozart), Concerto (Sibelius), Concerto (Tchaikovsky), Sonatas (Brahms), Concerto (Schoenberg). *Honours:* Chevalier, Ordre des Arts et des Lettres; Prix Ginette Neveu; Prix Paganini; Prix Enesco 1970; Grand Prix du Disque 1974, 1977. *Address:* c/o Jacques Thelen, 15 avenue Montaigne, 75008 Paris, France.

**AMRAM, David Werner,** BA, MusD, LLD; American composer, conductor and musician; b. 17 Nov. 1930, Philadelphia, PA; m. Loralee Ecobelli; one s. two d. *Education:* Oberlin Conservatory of Music, Manhattan School of Music, George Washington Univ., Moravian Coll., PA, Muhlenberg Coll., Univ. of Hartford, St Lawrence Univ. *Career:* pioneer of the French horn in jazz and Latin music during the late 1940s; world tours as a jazz player, multi-instrumentalist, folklorist, composer and conductor; Dir of Music, New York Shakespeare Festival 1956–67, Lincoln Center Theater 1963–65; Dir of Music for Young People's Concerts and Parks Concerts, Brooklyn Philharmonic 1971–98; fmr Leo Block Chair of Arts and Humanities, Univ. of Denver; work commissioned to celebrate the opening of the Jefferson Wing of the Library of Congress 1995; guest conductor annually with 14 orchestras, including Montreal, Toronto, Grant Park and Milwaukee Orchestras; mem. BMI. *Compositions include:* Ode to Lof Buckley for orchestra, The Final Ingredient (opera), 12th Night (opera), A Little Rebellion: Thomas Jefferson for narrator and orchestra, American Dance Suite, Trombone Alone 1996, Kokopelli: A Symphony in Three Movements 1997, Giants of the Night (flute concerto for James Galway) 2000. *Compositions for film and television:* Pull My Daisy 1958, The Turn of the Screw (TV series episode 'Startime') 1959, Cry Vengeance! (TV film) 1961, The Young Savages 1961, Splendor in the Grass 1961, The Manchurian Candidate 1962, The Arrangement 1969, Medea (TV film) 1983, Pigeon Feathers (TV film) 1987, The Beat Generation: An American Dream 1987, Frog Crossing 1996, The Source 1999. *Publications:* Vibrations: The Musical Times of David Amram 1968, At Home Around the World. *Honours:* Obie Award. *Current Management:* Ed Keane Associates, 32 St Edward Road, Boston, MA 02128, USA. *Telephone:* (617) 567-6300. *Fax:* (617) 569-5949. *E-mail:* info@edkeane.com. *Website:* www.edkeane.com; www .fmp.com/amram.

**AMSELLEM, Norah;** Singer (Soprano); b. 1970, Paris, France. *Education:* Studied in New York; Participant in Met's Young Artist Development Program. *Career:* Debut: Micaela at the Metropolitan Opera, 1995; Concert debut at Alice Tully Hall, New York; Opera appearances as Micaela at the Opéra Bastille, Paris, and Lyon; Liu at the Met and Mozart's Countess at the 1997 Glyndebourne Festival; Season 1997–98 as Micaela at the Met, under James Levine and with Placido Domingo, Liu in debut at the San Francisco Opera; Norina (Don Pasquale) and Gounod's Juliette at the Grand Théâtre, Bordeaux; Manon of Massenet at La Scala, Milan, and in Toulouse and Bordeaux; Micaela in Monte Carlo and Japan. *Current Management:* Columbia Artists Management, 1790 Broadway, New York NY 10019-1412,

USA. *Telephone:* (212) 841-9500. *Fax:* (212) 841-9744. *E-mail:* info@cami.com. *Website:* www.cami.com. *Address:* c/o Metropolitan Opera, Lincoln Center, New York, NY 10023, USA.

**AMY, Gilbert;** Conductor, Music Educator and Composer; b. 29 Aug. 1936, Paris, France. *Education:* Studied piano with Loriod and composition with Milhaud and Messiaen at the Paris Conservatory, attended Boulez's courses in new music at Darmstadt. *Career:* Commenced conducting 1962; Director, Domaine Musical, Paris, 1967–73; Founder-Conductor, Nouvel Orchestre Philharmonique de Radio France, Paris, 1976–81; Taught analysis and composition, Yale University, 1982; Director, Lyon Conservatory, 1984–. *Compositions:* Orchestral: Mouvements, 1958; Diaphonies, 1962; Antiphonies for 2 orchestras, 1964; Triade, 1965; Chant, 1968–69, revised 1980; Refrains, 1972; Orchestrale, 1985; Chamber: Piano Sonata, 1957–60; Epigrammes for piano, 1961; Inventions for ensemble, 1959–61; Alpha-Beth for wind sextet, 1963–64; Cycle for percussion sextet; 7 Bagatelles for organ, 1975; Quasi scherzando for cello, 1981; 2 String Quartets, 1992, 1995; Cantata breve for soprano and 3 instruments, 1957; D'un Espace deploye for soprano, 2 pianos and 2 orchestral groups, 1973; Strophe for soprano and orchestra, 1965–77; Une saison en enfer for soprano, piano, percussion and tape; Messe for soloists, chorus and orchestra, 1982–3; Ecrits sur toiles for reciter and small ensemble, 1983; Posaunen for four trombones, 1986; Choros for soloists, chorus and orchestra, 1989; Trois Scènes, for orchestra, 1995; Le Premier Cercle, opera in 4 acts premiered Lyon, 1999. *Address:* c/o Conservatoire National superieur de Musique de Lyon, 3 Quai Chauveau, 69009 Lyon, France.

**AN, Chengbi-Seungpil,** BA; Composer; b. 25 July 1967, China. *Education:* CNSM Paris, Shanghai Conservatory of Music. *Career:* debut as pianist, aged 7; Lecturer, Department of Composition, Shanghai Conservatory of Music 1993–94; teaching asst, Department of Composition, Shanghai Conservatory of Music 1991–93; Yanbian Korean Arts Troupe of Jilin, Beijing Chinese Arts Troupe 1984–86. *Compositions:* Hyun-Oh, 1998; Ressac, 1997; Electronic Music, 1996; Scintillations, 1996; Nong-mou, 1995; Symphony Movements, 1994; Ru, 1993; A Work, 1993; Lu, 1992; The Light of the Universe, 1992; Symphony Fantasy, 1991; Lou Shi Ming, 1990; Symphony Overture, 1990; Works, 1989; Mingwu, 1988; Ten Variations in Eight Notes, 1988; Sanjo, 1987; A Work, 1987; Arirang Suite, 1986; Unaccompanied Pieces, 1986; Parting, 1985; Piano Suite, 1985; Piano Piece, 1985. *Address:* 7 etg app 75, 2 rue des Cites, 93300 Aurervilliers, France.

**ANANIASHVILI, Nina Gedevanovna;** Georgian/Russian ballet dancer; *Artistic Director, Tbilisi Zakharia Paliashvili Opera and Ballet State Academic Theatre;* b. 28 March 1963, Tbilisi, Georgia; d. of Gedevan Ananiashvili and Lia Gogolashvili; m. Gregory Vashadze 1988. *Education:* State Choreographic Schools of Georgia and Bolshoi Theatre, Moscow. *Career:* Prima Ballerina, Bolshoi Ballet 1981–, Prin., American Ballet Theater (ABT) 1993–; has performed on tour world-wide with New York City Ballet, Royal Ballet, Royal Danish Ballet, Kirov Ballet, Royal Swedish Ballet, Ballet de Monte Carlo, The Munich Ballet and others; Artistic Dir Tbilisi Zakharia Paliashvili Opera and Ballet State Academic Theatre 2005–. *Dance:* over 100 roles including Giselle, Odette/Odile (Swan Lake), Aurora (Sleeping Beauty), Raimonda, Juliet (Romeo and Juliet), Nikya (La Bayadère), Kitri (Don Quixote). *Honours:* numerous awards include Grand Prix Int. Ballet Competition, Jackson 1986, People's Artist Repub. of Georgia and of Russia, State Prize of Russia 1992, State Prize of Georgia 1993, Order for Outstanding Service to Fatherland (Russia) 2000, Dance Magazine Award for Outstanding Achievements, USA 2002. *Address:* Frunzenskaya nab. 46, Apt. 79, 119270 Moscow, Russia. *Fax:* (32) 98-32-54. *E-mail:* ballet@comtv.ru (home). *Website:* www.ananiashvili.com (office).

**ANASTASSOV, Orlin;** Bulgarian singer (bass); b. 1976, Rousse, Bulgaria. *Education:* studied in Sofia with Nicola Ghiuselev. *Career:* debut singing Ramfis in Aida on tour to Germany with Ruse Opera; sang Rossini's Don Basilio at La Scala, Milan 1999; appearances in Faust, Aida, and La Sonnambula at Madrid, Berlin, Washington, and Munich; concerts with Colin Davis and the London Symphony Orchestra; season 2000–01 as Bellini's Oroveso at Rome, Sparafucile in Rigoletto at Hamburg and Verdi Requiem in Paris, Monte Carlo and Amsterdam; Ramfis in Vienna, Verona and Berlin; sang Federico Barbarossa in Verdi's La Battaglia in concert, with the Royal Opera at the Festival Hall, London 2000. *Current Management:* Ernesto Palacio Artists Management, Via Donizetti 11, 24050 Lurano (BG), Italy. *Telephone:* (35) 800623. *Fax:* (35) 4877812. *E-mail:* ernestopalacio@tiscali.it. *Website:* www.ernestopalacio.com. *Address:* c/o London Symphony Orchestra (contracts), Barbican Centre, Silk Street, London EC2Y 8DS, England.

**ANDERSEN, Bo;** composer, organist and musicologist; b. 10 Nov. 1963, Denmark. *Education:* University of Copenhagen; studied composition with Ib Nørholm, music theory with Yngve Trede and orchestration with Erik Norby, Royal Danish Academy of Music, Copenhagen, Royal Academy, Copenhagen. *Career:* numerous performances of most of his works, many commissions from ensembles and soloists; mem, Danish Composer's Association; Society for Publication of Danish Music. *Compositions:* Main Works: Vier Stücke im alten Stil, (String Quartet, No. 1), 1989 (revised 2001); Pezzo Concertante, 4 accordions and 2 percussionists, 1991, Pensieri notturni No. 1 for 3 woodwinds (former Serenade), flute, clarinet and bassoon, 1991 (revised, 1998); Moments Musicaux for 2 accordions, 1999 (revised 2001); Three Flowersongs for soprano and piano, 2000–01, texts by Kirsten Ahlemann; A Fantasia for the

Viol for solo cello, 1999; Invocation for solo flute, 1993 (revised 2001); Dream Calls for trumpet, percussion and orchestra; Concerto for trombone and orchestra. *Honours:* Astrid and Aksel Agerby Memorial Grant, 1993; several grants from the Danish State Arts Foundation. *Address:* c/o S E Mielche, Frederiksberg Allé 78 1.mf, 1820 Frederiksberg C, Denmark.

**ANDERSEN, Karsten;** conductor and violinist; b. 16 Feb. 1920, Kristiania (now Oslo), Norway. *Education:* studied in Norway and Italy. *Career:* Music Director, Stavanger Symphony Orchestra, 1945–65; Bergen Symphony Orchestra, 1965–85; Iceland Symphony Orchestra, 1973–80; Guest Conductor of Orchestras in Europe and the USA. *Recordings:* For Composers Recording Inc: Norskkultturrads Klassikerserie; Philips, including Svendsen's Concertos for Violin and Cello and Egge's Symphony No. 1.

**ANDERSEN, Stig Fogh;** Danish singer (tenor); b. 24 Feb. 1950, Horsholm; m. Tina Kiberg. *Education:* Music High School of Århus, Royal Acad. of Music, Copenhagen. *Career:* sang at Århus from 1978 and made debut at Royal Opera Copenhagen 1980, as Macduff in Macbeth; mem., Royal Opera Ensemble 1980–; many appearances in Copenhagen and elsewhere as guest, singing Tamino 1985, Sergei in Shostakovich's Lady Macbeth 1990, Don José 1992, Leander in Maskarade, Don Carlos, Lensky, Otello and Florestan; sang Siegfried at Århus 1994; Cardinal Albrecht in Mathis der Maler at Covent Garden 1995; Siegfried in The Ring at the Albert Hall and in Birmingham for the Royal Opera 1998; Meistersinger and Tannhäuser, Munich 1999; Siegfried in The Ring, Metropolitan Opera House, New York 2000; Tristan in Houston 2000; Parsifal at Covent Garden 2001; season 2000–01 as Herman in The Queen of Spades at Copenhagen, Siegfried at Mannheim and Geneva, and Tannhäuser at the Deutsche Oper Berlin; title role in production of Siegfried at Munich 2002; appeared in Siegfried and Die Walküre 2005. *Recordings:* Franz Schmidt's Das Buch mit sieben Siegeln, Mussorgsky's Boris Godunov (conducted by Dimitri Kitajenko), Weyse's The Sleep Potion, Nørgaard's Siddhartha. *Honours:* Ridder Af Danebrog, 1 Grad 2000. *Current Management:* Caecilia Lyric Department, Rennweg 15, 8001 Zürich, Switzerland. *Telephone:* (44) 2213388. *Fax:* (44) 2117182. *E-mail:* caecilia@caecilia-lyric.ch. *Website:* www.caecilia.ch. *Address:* c/o Det Kongelige Teater, Ekvipagemestervej 10, 1438 Copenhagen K, Denmark. *Website:* www.kgl-teater.dk.

**ANDERSEN, Terje;** Singer (tenor); b. 1970, Oslo, Norway. *Education:* Guildhall School and National Opera Studio, London; Milan with Franco Corelli. *Career:* Early roles in The Rape of Lucretia, The Carmelites and L'Enfant et les Sortilèges; Engagements at Oslo, as Tamino, and Macduff at Stuttgart; English National Opera as Nemorino, and Glyndebourne Festival as Gabriele Adorno; Alfredo in La Traviata on tour with Welsh National Opera; Froh in Das Rheingold and Mozart's Tamino for Münster Opera; Season 2001–2002 as Rodolfo and Pinkerton for the Royal Opera Stockholm, Cavaradossi in Tosca at Koblenz and Macduff for Singapore Lyric Opera; Concerts include the Verdi, Dvořák and Mozart Requiems, Elijah, Mors et Vita by Gounod and Bach's Christmas Oratorio. *Current Management:* Athole Still International Management, Forresters Hall, 25–27 Westow Street, London, SE19 3RY, England. *Telephone:* (20) 8771-5271. *Fax:* (20) 8768-6600. *Website:* www.atholestill.com.

**ANDERSON, Avril;** composer; b. 10 June 1953, Southsea, Hampshire, England. *Education:* Royal College of Music with Humphrey Searle and John Lambert, New England Conservatory, studied with David del Tredici in New York and with Jonathan Harvey at Sussex University. *Career:* Co-artistic Director of the contemporary music group Sounds Positive, 1987; Composer-in-Residence, The Young Place, London Contemporary Dance School; PRS Composer in Education 1996–97; Adjunct Professor, University of Notre Dame, London Programme. *Compositions:* Mono-staus for 3 clarinets, 1975; Où allons nous? for soprano and orchestra, 1976; Edward II, opera in 1 act, 1978; Black Eyes in an Orange Sky for soprano and piano, 1979; Private Energy for soprano and ensemble, 1983; Dynamics of Matter for piano, 1989; Winds of Change, 1989; Beating the System, 1993; Repetitive Strain for organ, 1995; Deadwood, 1996; Sephardic Songs, 1996; Dead on Time for ensemble, 1998; Nature's Voice, dance score, 1998; Rest Assured, 1999. *Recordings:* Deadwood; Sephardic Songs; Rest Assured. *Honours:* Cobbett Prize; Sullivan and Farrar Prize. *Address:* 28 Cavendish Avenue, London N3 3QN, England.

**ANDERSON, Barry;** Singer (Baritone); b. 1959, Australia. *Education:* Studied in Vienna and Milan. *Career:* Appearances at Naples as Verdi's Renato; At Catania as Rigoletto; At Cagliari as Count Luna; As Puccini's Sharpless and as Michonnet in Adriana Lecouvreur, Trieste, 1989; Bergamo Opera as Warney in Donizetti's Elisabetta al Castello di Kenilworth; Dresden Staatsoper as Macbeth and Munich Opera as Sharpless; As Macbeth, Simon Boccanegra and Rigoletto, Cologne Opera, 1991–94; Season 1993: As Mozart's Bartolo at the Deutsche Oper, Berlin; Ezio in Verdi's Attila at Buenos Aires; Other repertory includes Verdi's Il Corsaro, at Nîmes; Sang Mascagni's Gianni Rantzau, Livorno, 1991; Sang Germont at Jesi, 2000; Valentin in Gounod's Faust at Cachiari, 1996; Don Carlo in Verdi's Ernani at Montpellier, 1999; Michele in Il Tabarro by Puccini at Sydney Opera House, 2001; Gianni Schicchi by Puccini at Nantes, 2002. *Recordings:* Elizabetta Al Castello Di Kenilworth, Donizetti; I Rantzau, Mascagni; L'Arlesiana, Cilea; Zanà, Leoncavallo. *Current Management:* c/o Jennifer Eddy Artists, Suite 11, The Clivedon, 596 St Kilda Road, Melbourne, Victoria 3004, Australia. *Telephone:* (39) 5252700. *Fax:* (39) 5295410. *E-mail:* info@jeam.com.au; barry.tone.anderson@sii.it.

**ANDERSON, Beth,** BA, MA, MFA; American composer and musician (piano); b. 3 Jan. 1950, Lexington, KY; m. Elliotte Rusty Harold. *Education:* Univ. of California at Davis with Larry Austin and John Cage, Mills Coll., Oakland with Terry Riley and Robert Ashley. *Career:* founder Ear Magazine, New York 1975; solo performer as vocalist and piano accompanist at dance studios; Nat. Endowment for the Arts grant, Nat. Public Radio Satellite Program Development Fund grant; mem. New York Women Composers, Int. Alliance of Women in Music, Poets and Writers. *Compositions include:* April Swale for viola and harpsichord, August Swale for woodwind quintet, Belgian Tango, Brass Swale for brass quintet, Elizabeth Rex: Or The Well Bred Mother Goes To Camp (musical), Flute Swale for harpsichord, German Swale for tape, Guitar Swale for guitar duet, January Swale for string quartet, Joan (oratorio), March Swale for string quartet, May Swale for viola solo, Minnesota Swale for orchestra, Mourning Dove Swale for string orchestra, Net Work, New Mexico Swale for chamber ensemble, Nirvana Manor (musical), Pennyroyal Swale for string quartet, Queen Christina (opera), Revel for orchestra, Rhode Island Swale for harpsichord, Riot Rot (text-sound piece), Rosemary Swale for string quartet, Saturday/Sunday Swale for brass quintet, September Swale for mandolin and guitar, Soap Tuning (musical), The Fat Opera (musical), Three Swales for string orchestra, Trio: Dream In 'D'. *Publications:* Beauty is Revolution, The Internet for Women in Music. *Current Management:* Jeffrey James Arts Consulting, 316 Pacific Street, Massapequa Park, NY 11762, USA.

**ANDERSON, David Maxwell;** Singer (Tenor); b. 1964, Scotland. *Education:* Studied at the Glasgow Academy and Queen's College, Cambridge; Royal College of Music from 1986, National Opera Studio, 1989. *Career:* Debut: Rinuccio in Gianni Schicchi for Opera North, 1990; Has sung Rinuccio for English National Opera; Rodolfo in La Bohème for Scottish Opera and Glyndebourne Touring Opera, Pinkerton in Madama Butterfly for Opera North, the Duke of Mantua in Rigoletto for Opera North and the Teatro di Pisa, Alfredo in La Traviata for the Teatro di Pisa and Opera North; Other roles include Ŝteva in Jenůfa (English National Opera) and Oronte in I Lombardi (Opera North); Engaged as Anatole in Samuel Barber's Vanessa at Monte Carlo, 2001; Concert engagements include the Verdi Requiem (David Willcocks), Vaughan Williams Serenade to Music (Vernon Handley), Bruckner Te Deum (Alexander Gibson and John Eliot Gardiner), and the Rossini Stabat Mater (Rafael Frühbeck de Burgos). *Address:* Helen Sykes Artists' Management, 100 Felsham Road, Putney, London, SW15 1DQ, England. *Telephone:* (20) 8780-0060. *Fax:* (20) 8780-8772. *E-mail:* helen@helensykesartists.co.uk. *Website:* www.helensykesartists.co.uk. *Address:* 26 Aberdare Gardens, London NW6 3QA, England. *Website:* http://www.davidmaxwellanderson.com.

**ANDERSON, Julian,** BMus; British composer; b. 1967, London, England. *Education:* Royal Coll. of Music, London, studied with Tristan Murail in Paris, Alexander Goehr at Cambridge and with Oliver Knussen, attended Dartington Int. Summer School, Britten-Pears School, Tanglewood. *Career:* freelance composer, with performances at the 1996 Int. Rostrum of Composers (Paris), at the Brighton, Huddersfield Contemporary Music and Cambridge Elgar Festivals; further performances at the 1995 Ars Musica Festival, Brussels, London Proms, Tanglewood and 1996 Warsaw Festival; Visiting Prof. of Composition, RCM; composer-in-focus to the London PO 2002–03, Artistic Dir of their 'Music of Today' series 2004–; Cleveland Orchestra Daniel Lewis Young Composer Fellow 2005–07. *Compositions include:* Diptych two movements for orchestra 1991–95, Khorovod for 15 players 1994, The Bearded Lady for oboe, clarinet and piano 1994, The Colour of Pomegranates for alto flute and piano 1994, Scherzo with Trains for four clarinets 1989–93, Tiramisu for ten players 1994–95, I'm Nobody Who Are You for tenor, violin and piano 1995, Three Parts off the Ground for 13 players 1995, Piano Etudes Nos 1 and 2 1995–96, The Crazed Moon for orchestra 1995–96, Past Hymns for 15 solo strings 1996, Poetry Nearing Silence divertimento for seven instruments 1997, The Stations of the Sun 1998, Towards Poetry (extended ballet version of Poetry Nearing Silence) 1998, Alhambra Fantasy for 16 players 2000, The Bird Sings with its Feathers ballet for chamber orchestra 2001, Shir Hashirim for soprano and chamber orchestra 2001, Imagin'd Corners for orchestra 2002, Symphony (Composer Award for orchestral work) 2004. *Honours:* Royal Philharmonic Society Prize for young composers 1992. *Address:* Faber Music Limited, 3 Queen Square, London, WC1N 3AU, England.

**ANDERSON, June,** BA; American singer (soprano) and concert and oratorio vocalist; b. 30 Dec. 1952, Boston. *Education:* Yale Univ. *Career:* performances at Metropolitan, New York, New York City Opera, Milwaukee Florentine Opera, San Diego Opera, Seattle Opera, Royal Opera, London, La Scala, Milan. *Roles include:* Queen of the Night in The Magic Flute, New York City Opera 1978, title role in Lucia di Lammermoor, Milwaukee Florentine Opera 1982 and Chicago 1990, Gulnara in Il Corsaro, San Diego Opera Verdi Festival 1982, I Puritani, Edmonton Opera 1982–83, title role in Semiramide, Rome Opera 1982–83 and Metropolitan Opera 1990, Rosina in The Barber of Seville, Seattle Opera and Teatro Massimo 1982–83, Cunigonde in Candide 1989, Metropolitan Opera debut as Gilda in Rigoletto 1989, title role in Luisa Miller, La Fenice, Venice 2006; concert and oratorio vocalist: Chicago Pops Orchestra, Handel Festival Kennedy Center, Denver Symphony, St Louis Symphony, Cincinnati Symphony, Maracaibo (Venezuela) Symphony. *Current Management:* Askonas Holt, Lonsdale Chambers, 27 Chancery Lane, London, WC2A 1PF, England. *Telephone:* (20) 7400-1700. *Fax:* (20) 7400-1799. *E-mail:* info@

askonasholt.co.uk. *Website:* www.askonasholt.co.uk; www.june-anderson .com.

**ANDERSON, Laurie P.,** MFA; American performance artist, musician (keyboards, violin) and writer; b. 5 June 1947, Wayne, IL; d. of Arthur T. Anderson and Mary Louise (née Rowland) Anderson. *Education:* Columbia Univ., Barnard Coll. *Career:* instructor in Art History, City Coll., CUNY 1973–75; freelance critic Art News, Art Forum; composer and performer multi-media exhbns; Artist-in-Residence, ZBS Media 1974, NASA 2005–. *Exhibitions include:* solo shows: Barnard Coll. 1970, Harold Rivkin Gallery, Washington 1973, Artists' Space, New York 1974, Holly Solomon Gallery, New York 1977, 1980–81, Museum of Modern Art 1978, Queen's Museum, New York 1984, Barbican, London 2002; numerous group exhbns 1972–. *Other projects:* New York Social Life, Voices From The Beyond, Talk Normal, Natural History, Happiness 2002. *Film performances:* Carmen, Personal Service Announcements, Beautiful Red Dress, Talk Normal, Alive From Off Center, What You Mean We?, Language Is A Virus, This Is The Picture, Sharkey's Day, Dear Reader, Home of the Brave (writer, dir, performer) 1986, Puppet Motel (CD-ROM) 1995. *Recordings include:* O Superman 1981, Big Science 1982, United States 1983, Mister Heartbreak 1984, Strange Angels 1989, Bright Red 1994, The Ugly One With The Jewels And Other Stories 1995, Live At Town Hall, New York City 2002; film scores: Home Of The Brave 1986, Swimming To Cambodia, Monster In A Box. *Publications:* The Package 1971, October 1972, Transportation, Transportation 1973, The Rose and the Stone 1974, Notebook 1976, Artifacts at the End of a Decade 1981, Typisch Frac 1981, United States 1984, Empty Places: A Performance 1989, Laurie Anderson's Postcard Book 1990, Stories from the Nerve Bible 1993. *Honours:* Guggenheim Fellow 1983, Dr hc (Art Inst. of Chicago), (Philadelphia Coll. of the Arts). *Current Management:* Primary Talent International, Fifth Floor, 2–12 Pentonville Road, London, N1 9PL, England. *Telephone:* (20) 7833-8998. *Fax:* (20) 7833-5992.

**ANDERSON, Lorna;** British singer (soprano); b. 1962, Glasgow, Scotland. *Education:* Royal Scottish Acad. of Music (with Patricia MacMahon); Royal Coll. of Music, London. *Career:* concerts with Bach Choir, English Concert under Trevor Pinnock, and Scottish Chamber Orchestra; tour of Spain and Poland and appearances at Kings Lynn, City of London, Brighton, Edinburgh and Aldeburgh Festivals; sang with London Baroque under Charles Medlam, with the London Mozart Players under Andrew Parrott and the Bournemouth Sinfonietta under Roger Norrington 1988; Promenade Concert debut 1988; further concerts with London Classical Players, Orchestra of the Age of Enlightenment, Scottish Nat. Orchestra, Florilegium, The King's Consort, BBC Scottish Symphony Orchestra; sang Innocenza in first modern revival of Marazzoli's La Vita Humana, Scottish Early Music Consort, Glasgow 1990; The Fairy Queen with the Sixteen, Queen Elizabeth Hall 1990; Les Noces with Pierre Boulez and Ensemble Intercontemporain 1990, 1992; Morgana in Alcina, Halle Handel Festival and Innsbruck Festival 1992; Mozart Mass in C minor with the Scottish Chamber Orchestra under Charles Mackerras 1992; sang in Bach's St John Passion, Royal Festival Hall, London 1997; opera: Clorinda in Il Combattimento di Tancredi e Clorinda, Netherlands Opera 1991, 1993, Pulcheria in Handel's Riccardo Primo, Göttingen 1996; title role in Theodora, Glyndebourne Touring Opera 1997. *Recordings include:* The Fairy Queen with Harry Christophers/The Sixteen, Linley Shakespeare Ode with The Parley of Instruments; Hyperion Complete Schubert; Hyperion Complete Britten Folksongs; Complete Scottish Folksong arrangements by Joseph Haydn with Haydn Trio Eisenstadt for Joan Records; Hyperion: L'Allegro (Handel), The King's Consort; Semper Amor with Apollo Chamber Players for London Independent Records; Messiah with David Willcocks and Mormon Tabernacle Choir. *Honours:* First Prize in Peter Pears and Royal Overseas League Competition 1984, Purcell-Britten Prize for Concert Singers, Aldeburgh 1986. *Current Management:* Andrew Rosner, Allied Artists, 42 Montpelier Square, London, SW7 1JZ, England. *Telephone:* (20) 7589-6243. *Fax:* (20) 7581-5269. *E-mail:* info@alliedartists.co.uk. *Website:* www .alliedartists.co.uk.

**ANDERSON, (Leonard) Mark,** BMus, LRAM, PPRNCM; pianist; b. 8 Oct. 1963, Eureka, CA, USA. *Education:* San Jose State University, Royal Northern College of Music, Manchester. *Career:* debut New York, 1988; San Francisco, 1988; Tokyo, 1992; Toronto, 1993; London, 1994; Zürich, 1994; Alice Tully Hall, New York, 1994; Performances at major venues world-wide with leading orchestras and conductors. *Recordings:* Various solo piano works of Liszt, Brahms and Schumann; Brahms First Piano Concerto with the Hungarian State Symphony Orchestra, Adam Fischer conducting; Liszt Recital, 1996; Brahms Variations, op 118 and 119, 1997; Live solo concert of works by Copland and Gershwin, 1999. *Contributions:* Piano Quarterly; Keyboard Stylist. *Honours:* Winner, Leeds Pianoforte Competition, 1993; 1st Prize, William Kapell International Piano Competition, Washington DC, 1994. *Address:* 253 Tomas Way, Pleasanton, CA 94566, USA.

**ANDERSON, Nicholas Maurice William,** MA; Musician, Writer and Producer; b. 29 March 1941, Exeter, Devon; m.; one d. *Education:* Westminster School, London, New Coll., Oxford, Univ. Coll., Durham. *Career:* Editorial Man., Decca Record Co Ltd 1968–71; music producer, BBC Radio 3 1971–91; music consultant to Warner Music 1991–97, 2002–; freelance record producer to Harmonia Mundi, Virgin Classics, Chandos Record Co; Dir, Collegium Musicum 90. *Recordings as producer:* over 50 albums for Collegium Musicum 90. *Publications:* Baroque Music from Monteverdi to Handel 1994; contributions to A Companion to the Concerto 1988, Cambridge Guide to the Arts in Britain 1991, Oxford Composer Companions: J. S. Bach 2000, New Grove Dictionary of Music and Musicians, Collins Classical Music Encyclopedia 2000. *Address:* The Old Bank House, Nether Stowey, TA5 1NG, England. *Telephone:* (1278) 733747 (home). *Fax:* (1278) 732840 (home). *E-mail:* nicholas.anderson@btinternet.com (home).

**ANDERSON, Robert David,** MA, FSA; conductor, writer and editor; b. 20 Aug. 1927, Shillong, Assam, India. *Education:* Gonville and Caius Coll., Cambridge. *Career:* Asst Ed., Record News 1954–56; Asst Master and Dir of Music, Gordonstoun School 1956–62; Conductor, Moray Choral Union; Asst Conductor, Spoleto Festival 1962; Conductor, St Bartholomew's Hospital Choral Soc. 1965–90; Extra-Mural Lecturer, Univ. of London 1966–77; Assoc. Ed., The Musical Times 1967–85; critic, The Times 1967–72; Visiting Lecturer, City Univ. 1983–92; Co-ordinating Ed., Elgar Complete Edition 1983–2003; Hon. Prof. of History, State Univ. of Rostov-on-Don 2002; mem. Egypt Exploration Soc. (hon. sec. 1971–82), Royal Musical Asscn. *Publications:* Egyptian Antiquities in the British Museum III: Musical Instruments 1976, Wagner 1980, Egypt in 1800 (jt ed.) 1988, Wagner, in Heritage of Music III 1989, Elgar in Manuscript 1990, Elgar 1993, Music and Dance in Pharaonic Egypt in Civilisations of the Ancient Near East IV 1995, Elgar and Chivalry 2002, Baalbek, Heliopolis and Rome 2004. *Honours:* Hon. DMus (City Univ.) 1985, Hon. DHist (Russian State Univ. for Humanities, Moscow) 2000; Liveryman Worshipful Co. of Musicians 1977. *Address:* 54 Hornton Street, London, W8 4NT, England.

**ANDERSON, (Evelyn) Ruth;** composer and flautist; b. 21 May 1928, Kalispell, Montana, USA. *Education:* University of Washington, Columbia and Princeton Univs with Earl Kim and Ussachevsky; further studies with Nadia Boulanger, Darius Milhaud and Jean-Pierre Rampal. *Career:* Flautist with the Totenberg Instrumental Ensemble, the Portland and Seattle Symphony Orchestras and the Boston Pops Orchestra during the 1950s; Orchestrator for NBC Television and Broadway shows; Teacher of Composition and Electronic Music at Hunter College, New York, from 1966. *Compositions include:* The Pregnant Dream, 1968; DUMP, Collage, 1970; 3 Studies, 1970; State of the Union Message, Collage, 1973; Conversations, 1974; Dress Rehearsal, 1976; I Come Out of your Sleep, 1979; Mixed Media: Centering, Dance, for 4 performers and live electronics, 1979; Sound Sculptures: Sound Environment, 1975; Time and Tempo, 1984. *Recordings include:* 1750 Arch, 1977; Opus One, 1981; CRI, 1997, 1998; XI, 1998. *Honours:* Five MacDowell Colony Fellowships, 1957–73; Fulbright Scholarships, 1958, 1959; Martha Baird Rockefeller Fund; Alice M Ditson Fund. *Address:* c/o ASCAP, ASCAP Building, 1 Lincoln Plaza, New York, NY 10023, USA.

**ANDERSON, Sylvia;** singer (mezzo-soprano); b. 1938, Denver, Colorado, USA; m. Matthias Kuntzsch. *Education:* Eastman School with Anna Kaskas, Cologne Musikhochschule with Ellen Bosenius. *Career:* debut in Cologne 1962, as Fyodor in Boris Godunov; sang in the Hamburg Staatsoper, 1965–69, notably as Ophelia in the 1968 premiere of Searle's Hamlet; Bayreuth Festival, 1970–71; Salzburg Festival, 1973, in the premiere of De Temporum fine Comoedia by Orff; Guest appearances in Zürich, Stuttgart, Frankfurt, Düsseldorf, Brussels, Barcelona, Trieste and Amsterdam; Bayreuth 1970–71, as Schwertleite, Magdalena and Flosshilde; US engagements at the Metropolitan and New York City Operas, and in San Francisco, Washington and Santa Fe; Repertoire included Operas by Gluck, Purcell, Rossini, Verdi, Wagner and modern composers; Many concert appearances. *Recordings:* Schubert Masses; De Temporum fine Comoedia.

**ANDERSON, Thomas Jefferson, Jr;** Composer and Music Educator; b. 17 Aug. 1928, Coatesville, Pennsylvania, USA; m., 3 c. *Education:* BMus, West Virginia State College, 1950; MEd, Pennsylvania State University, 1951; Studied Composition with Scott Huston, Cincinnati Conservatory of Music, 1954; PhD, University of Iowa, 1958; With Philip Bezanson and Richard Hervig; With Darius Milhaud, Aspen School of Music, 1964. *Career:* Teacher, Instrumental Music, High Point, North Carolina Public Schools, 1951–54; Instructor, West Virginia State College, Institute, West Virginia, 1955–56; Professor of Music, Chairman of Music Department, Langston (Oklahoma) University, 1958–63; Professor of Music, Tennessee State University, Nashville, 1963–69; Orchestrated first complete performance of Treemonisha by Scott Joplin, 1972; Composer-in-Residence, Atlanta, Georgia, 1971–72; Professor of Music, Chairman, Music Department 1972–80, Chair, Austin Fletcher Professor of Music 1976–90, Emeritus 1990, Tufts University, Medford, Massachusetts; Doctor of Music, Honoris Causa, Bridgewater State College, 1991; Scholar-in-Residence, The Rockefeller Foundation, Study and Conference Centre, Bellagio, Italy, 1984, 1994; fellowship, John Simon Guggenheim Foundation, 1988; Fellow, National Humanities Centre, Research Triangle Park, North Carolina, 1996–97. *Compositions include:* Stage, The Shell Fairy, operetta, 1976–77; Re-Creation for 3 Speakers, Dancer and 6 Instruments, 1978; Spirituals, for orchestra, jazz quartet, chorus, children's choir, tenor and narrator, 1979; Soldier Boy, Soldier, opera, 1982; Walker, chamber opera with words by Derek Walcott, 1992; Orchestral, Introduction and Allegro, 1959; Classical Symphony, 1961; 6 Pieces for Clarinet and Chamber Orchestra, 1962; Symphony in 3 Movements, 1964; Songs of Illumination, song cycle, 1990; Whatever Happened to the Big Bands, 1991; Bahia, Bahia, for chamber orchestra, 1991; Spirit Songs commissioned by Yo-Yo Ma, for cello and piano, 1993; Here in the Flesh, hymn, 1993; 7 Cabaret Songs, for jazz singer, 1994; Flute, viola, cello and piano, Broke Baroque for violin and piano, 1996; Shouts, 1997; Huh? What did you say? for solo clarinet, string trio and solo violin, 1998; Boogie Woogie Fantasy for solo piano, 1999; Game Play for flute, viola, cello, harp, 2002; Slavery Documents for chorus, orchestra, soloists, 2002. *Recordings:* Chamber Symphony: London Philharmonic Orchestra, James Dixon conductor; Variations on a Theme by M B Tolson; Contemporary Chamber Ensemble, Arthur Weisberg conductor; Squares: Baltimore Symphony Orchestra, Paul Freeman conductor; Intermezzi, Videmus, Vivian Taylor, Artistic Director. *Honours:* Honorary DMA, College of the Holy Cross, 1983 and St Augustine's College, 1996; Honorary DM, West Virginia State College, 1984 and Bridgewater State College, 1991; Honorary DFA Northwestern University, 2002. *Address:* 111 Cameron Glen Drive, Chapel Hill, NC 27516, USA.

**ANDERSON, Valdine;** Singer (soprano); b. 1965, Canada. *Career:* Appearances with Edmonton Opera as Mozart's Blonde and Pamina, and with Vancouver Opera as Micaela; Contemporary repertory includes Lutoslawski's Chatefleurs et Chantefables (composer conducting), Michael Torke's Book of Proverbs, Gorecki's Symphony of Sorrowful Songs (Vancouver Symphony Orchestra) and the Maid in Powder Her Face by Thomas Adés (premiere, at the Cheltenham Festival); Varèse Offrandes with the BBC Scottish Symphony Orchestra, Berg's Altenberhlieder, Benjamin's A Mind of Winter, Kurtag's The Sayings of Peter Bornemisza; Season 1997 with Carmina Burana (Edmonton Symphony Orchestra), Messiah in Winnipeg and a Maxwell Davies premiere with Vancouver New Music; Other repertory includes Britten's Spring Symphony (Aldeburgh, 1995); Beethoven's Ninth (Toronto Symphony Orchestra) and Ein Deutsches Requiem; Sang Suzel in the premiere of Dr Ox's Experiment by Bryars, ENO, 1998; Oliver Knussen's Where the Wild Things Are and Higglety, Pigglety, Pop! at the London Proms, 2002. *Current Management:* Ingpen & Williams Ltd, 7 St George's Court, 131 Putney Bridge Road, London, SW15 2PA, England. *Telephone:* (20) 8874-3222. *Fax:* (20) 8877-3113. *E-mail:* info@ingpen.co.uk.

**ANDERSON-JAQUEST, Tommie Crowell,** BMus, MA, MMus, DMus, PhD; American singer (soprano), academic and musician (piano); *Principal Lecturer, Regents Business School;* b. 22 Feb. 1941; m. Gordon N. Jaquest 1993. *Career:* various professional solo recitals, concerts and operatic appearances, USA; has sung with the Chicago Lyric Opera and San Francisco Opera; major roles include Lady Billows (Albert Herring), Countess (Marriage of Figaro), title role in Suor Angelica, Nedda (Pagliacci), Magda (The Consul), Pamina (The Magic Flute), title role in Medea, Antonia (Tales of Hoffmann), Marschallin (Der Rosenkavalier); econ. analyst, Int. Coffee Org., London; Principal Lecturer and Academic Leader, Regent's Business School, London; writing and lecturing in the fields of music, int. relations; mem. American Guild of Musical Artists, Incorporated Soc. of Musicians (UK), Royal Inst. of Int. Affairs (UK), Higher Educ. Acad. (UK). *Address:* Regents Business School, Regents' College, Regents' Park, London, NW1 4NS, England (office); 29 Little Meadow, Loughton, Milton Keynes, Bucks. MK5 8EH, England (home). *Telephone:* (20) 7487-7676 (office); (1908) 240988 (home). *Fax:* (20) 7487-7602 (office); (1908) 240988 (home). *E-mail:* Andersot@regents.ac.uk (office); tscanderson@msn.com (home). *Website:* www.regents.ac.uk (office).

**ANDERSSON, Anders;** singer (tenor); b. 1954, Sweden. *Education:* Stockholm Music High School and Ave Opera Studio of the Royal Opera. *Career:* debut as Erland in Singoalla by de Frumerie, also at Savonlinna, Stockholm, 1989; sang Gunnar in Den Fredlose by Inger Wikstrom at Ulriksdal, 1989; as Gudmund in Stenhammar's Gildet pa Solhaug at Norrlands operan, 1990; title role in a revival of J G Naumann's Gustaf Wasa, Stockholm, 1992; sang Samson, and the Emperor in Turandot, Folkoperan, Stockholm, 1993; concert appearances and teaching engagements. *Recording:* Gustaf Wasa. *Address:* c/o Kungliga Teatern, PO Box 16094, 10322 Stockholm, Sweden.

**ANDERSSON, B. Tommy;** conductor and composer; b. 26 July 1964, Borås, Sweden. *Education:* Royal College of Music, Stockholm. *Career:* debut in Le nozze di Figaro, Södra Teatern, Stockholm, 1992; recurrent engagements with opera houses in Stockholm, Göteborg, Malmö, Umeå, Vadstena and Karlstad, including Die Geisterinsel (Reichardt), 1992; Fidelio (Beethoven), 1997; Il Prigioniero (Dallapiccola), 1997; Un ballo in maschera (Verdi), 1998; Wozzeck (Berg), 1999; Orlando (Handel), 2000; The Cunning Little Vixen (Janáček), 2000; Macbeth (Sandström), 2001; Lulu (Berg), 2002; recurrent concert engagements with all big orchestras and most chamber orchestras in Sweden; guest conducting in Germany, the United Kingdom, Switzerland, Netherlands, Finland, Denmark, Norway, Iceland, Uruguay, Czechoslovakia, Romania and Hungary; first performance of more than 120 works, including 11 operas; Artistic Director of KammarensembleN, an ensemble for contemporary music 1994–99; Principal Conductor of Stockholm Symphonic Wind Ensemble 1998–, Prof. of Orchestral Studies, Gothenburg Univ. School of Music 2003–; Fellow Royal Swedish Academy of Music; mem. Swedish Composers' Asscn, Swedish Section of ISCM, Swedish Conductors' Asscn. *Compositions:* Concerto for piano, winds and percussion 1984, Stabat Mater 1985, Te Deum 1987, Impromptu for clarinet and vibraphone 1987, Sonata for percussion and piano 1987, Conflicts for percussion ensemble 1988, Intrada for winds and percussion 1989, A Bed of Roses for percussion ensemble 1989, Concerto for horn and orchestra 1993, Dark Shadows for recorder and marimba 1990, Apollo, Concerto for percussion solo and orchestra 1995, Antique for male voice and piano 1999, Satyricon for large orchestra 2000, Sonnet XVIII for mixed choir a cappella 2002, Games for Gito for wind quintet 2002, Reflections, Concerto for soprano saxophone and orchestra 2003. *Recordings include:* music by Atterberg, Hallén, Hallström, Nysteom and Auber, several recordings of Swedish contemporary music with a.o. Swedish

Radio Symphony Orchestra, Royal Stockholm Philharmonic Orchestra and KammarensembleN. *Honours:* Swedish Royal Academy Scholarships 1990, 1993, Crusell Award for Young Conductors 1993, Sten Frykberg Award 1994, Crystal Prize for Interpretation of Contemporary Music 1995, Swedish Composers' Asscn Interpreters Prize 1998. *Address:* Jungfrugatan 45, 114 44 Stockholm, Sweden. *E-mail:* bta@chello.se.

**ANDERSSON, Laila;** singer (soprano); b. 30 March 1941, Losen, Blekinge, Sweden; m. Ulf Palme 1984. *Education:* studied with Sylvia Mang-Borenberg, Ragnar Hulten, and Hjordis Schymberg in Stockholm. *Career:* Royal Opera Stockholm from 1964, as Susanna, Leonore (Il Trovatore), Mathilde (Guillaume Tell), Madama Butterfly, Jenůfa and Sophie; Sang in the premieres of Herr von Hancken by Blomdahl 1965 and Granskibbutzen by Karkoff, 1975; Sang the title role in Berg's Lulu, 1977; Frequent visits to the Drottningholm Festival from 1967 (Gustaf Adolf och Ebba Brahe by the Abbé Vogler, 1973); Guest engagements at the Edinburgh Festival 1974, Copenhagen, Wiesbaden, Helsinki and Oslo; Sang Tosca at Stockholm, Grenoble and Bonn, 1977, Salome at the Metropolitan (debut, 1981), Gelsenkirchen, Vienna, Rio de Janeiro, Berlin and Montreal, 1985; Sang Brünnhilde at Århus, Denmark, 1987; Fidelio at Washington and Montreal, 1988; Sang Tiresias in the premiere of Backanterna by Daniel Börtz, 1992; as Elektra, Stockholm Opera, 1993; Stockholm 1994, in the premiere of Schederin's Lolita; Member of the Nya Bjorling Vocal Quartet; Chairman, Theatre Order, 750 Sisters; Member of Royal Swedish Academy of Music. *Honours:* Singer of the Royal Court, 1985; Litteris et Artibus, 1992. *Address:* Köpmantorget 10, 111 31 Stockholm, Sweden.

**ANDERSZEWSKI, Piotr;** Polish pianist; b. 4 April 1969, Warsaw. *Education:* Conservatories of Lyon and Strasbourg, Univ. of Southern California in Los Angeles, Chopin Acad., Warsaw. *Career:* recitals in Poland, USA and France; Wigmore Hall, London debut 1991; further British engagements include the Harrogate Festival 1991 and concerts with the Royal Liverpool Philharmonic and Hallé Orchestras; Festival Hall debut with the London Philharmonic conducted by Franz Welser-Möst; recordings for Polish radio and television; European recital tour 1992; regular duo pnr with violinist, Viktoria Mullova 1992–93 season; Edinburgh Festival debut in recital 1994; concert performances with City of Birmingham Symphony Orchestra 1994, Ulster Orchestra 1995, Lahti Symphony 1994, Nat. Symphony Orchestra of Ireland 1995; performances in season 2004–05 included recitals at the Berlin Philharmonie, Théâtre des Champs-Élysées, QEH, Zankel Hall, New York and Concertgebouw, Amsterdam; season 2005–06 recitals in Japan, tour with LSO, appearances with the symphony orchestras of Chicago, Boston, Atlanta and Houston. *Recordings include:* Prokofiev Sonata for Violin and Piano No. 1 Op 80 (recital with Viktoria Mullova), Debussy Sonata for Violin and Piano, Janáček Sonata for Violin and Piano, Brahms Sonatas for Piano and Violin, Bach, Beethoven and Webern solo, Bach keyboard works, Beethoven's Diabelli Variations (Diapason d'or, Choc du Monde de la Musique, France) 2000, Mozart piano concerti, Bach's Partitas 1, 3 and 6, Solo pieces by Szymanowski 2005. *Honours:* Int. Piano Foundation Scholarship to IPF on Lake Como, Italy 1994–95; Szymanowski Prize 1999, Royal Philharmonic Soc. Best Instrumentalist Award 2001, Gilmore Artist 2002–06. *Current Management:* c/o Jilly Clarke, Askonas Holt Ltd, Lonsdale Chambers, 27 Chancery Lane, London, WC2A 1PF, England. *Telephone:* (20) 7400-1700. *Fax:* (20) 7400-1799. *E-mail:* jilly.clarke@askonasholt.co.uk. *Website:* www.askonasholt.co.uk; www .anderszewski.net.

**ANDONIAN, Andrea;** singer (mezzo-soprano); b. 1950, Colorado, USA. *Education:* Florida and Ohio Universities, Operastudio in Cologne. *Career:* sang at Cologne Offenbach Theatre, 1977–78; engaged at Krefeld-Monchengladbach, 1978–85; has sung with Deutsche Oper Berlin, 1986–; guest appearances, Germany and elsewhere, in repertory including Cherubino, Dorabella, Ramiro in Mozart's Finta Giardiniera, Idamante in Idomeneo and Annio in La Clemenza di Tito; Humperdinck's Hansel, Siebel in Faust, the Prince in Massenet's Cendrillon, and Britten's Lucretia and Hermia; Sang Urbain in Les Huguenots with Deutsche Oper, 1987, and at Covent Garden, 1991; Paris Opéra-Comique, 1992, in Rossini's L'Occasione fa il Ladro, La Scala di Seta, La Cambiale di Matrimonio and Il Signor Bruschino; Mrs Sedley in Peter Grimes at Cologne, 1994; Season 1999–2000 at Cologne, as Annina in La Traviata, Wellgunde in Götterdämmerung, Larina in Eugene Onegin and Sycorax in Spohr's Faust. *Recordings include:* Schumann's Requiem. *Address:* Deutsche Oper Berlin, Richard Wagnerstrasse 10, 1000 Berlin 10, Germany.

**ANDRADE, Levine;** violist; b. 1954, Bombay, India. *Education:* studied violin at the Yehudi Menuhin School with Robert Mastres; studied with Menuhin and Nadia Boulanger; viola studies with Patrick Ireland; Royal Academy of Music with Frederick Grinke, Max Gilbert, Sidney Griller and Colin Hampton. *Career:* co-founded the Arditti String Quartet, 1974 and member until 1989; Frequent concerts with the London Symphony Orchestra, Royal Philharmonic, Academy of St Martin-in-the-Fields, the London Sinfonietta and the London Mozart Players; Guest Professor at the Royal Academy of Music; Many concerts with the Arditti Quartet in Europe and North America; Festival engagements at Aldeburgh, Bath, BBC Proms, Berlin, Budapest, Paris, Venice Biennale, Vienna and Warsaw; Music in Camera programme, BBC television, 1987; Series of seven recitals for Radio 3, 1987; Played in all Schoenberg's quartets in a single recital, Queen Elizabeth Hall, London, November, 1988; Took part in the premieres of quartets by Georges Aperghis, 1985; Berio, Divertimento for Trio, 1987; Bose, No. 3, 1989;

Britten, Quartettino, 1983; Gavin Bryars, 1985; Bussotti, 1988; John Cage, Music for 4, 1988; Davies, 1983; Ferneyhough, Numbers 2 and 3; Gubaidulina No. 3, 1987; Harvey, Numbers 1 and 2; Hindemith Quartet 1915, 1986; Kagel, 1987; Nancarrow, No. 3, 1988; Ohana, No. 2, 1982; Pousseur, No. 2, 1989; Premiered quartets by Michael Finnissy, Michael Nyman and Tim Souster. *Recordings include:* Henze's Five String Quartets. *Honours:* Deutsche Schallplattenpreis for Henze Quartets, 1987. *Address:* 80 Whellock Road, London W4 1DJ, England.

**ANDRADE, Rosario;** singer (soprano); b. 6 April 1951, Veracruz, Mexico. *Education:* studied in Veracruz and Accademia di Santa Cecilia, Rome. *Career:* debut as Madama Butterfly, Mexico City, 1974; sang at Glyndebourne Festival as Donna Elvira in Don Giovanni, 1977–78; Many guest appearances in Europe and North America, Brussels, 1978, Lyon (in Cavalli's La Calisto), 1979, Warsaw, 1981–82, Connecticut, 1987, Pittsburgh and Mississippi Opera Company, 1988; Metropolitan Opera debut, 1982, as Antonia in Les Contes d'Hoffmann, returning as Manon, 1986; Other roles include Mimi, Micaela, Marguerite, Donna Anna, Aida and Maddalena in Andrea Chénier; Concert repertory includes Marguerite in La Damnation de Faust. *Address:* c/o Metropolitan Opera, Lincoln Center, New York, NY 10023, USA.

**ANDRASOVAN, Tibor;** conductor and composer; b. 3 April 1917, Slovenska, Lupca, Czechoslovakia; m. 1st Ivanka Dimitrová 1948; one s. two d.; m. 2nd Mária Kutejová 1973. *Education:* Pedagogic University, Bratislava Conservatory with E. Suchon and A. Moyses, Master School of Music, Prague. *Career:* Professor, 1941; Conductor since 1945; Repetiteur, Slovak National Theatre, 1946–57; Artistic Director, Slovak Folk Artistic Ensemble, 1955–58, 1969–74. *Compositions:* Stage: Gelo the Joker, 1957; The Quadrille, Operetta, 1960; The White Disease, Music Drama, 1967; The Gamekeeper's Wife, Opera, 1973–74; The King of Fools, Musical, 1982; Ballets: Orpheus and Euridice, 1948; The Song of Peace, 1949; The Festival of Solstice, 1985; Orchestral: Little Goral, Overture, 1961; Concerto for Cembalo and Strings, 1977; Chamber: String Quartet, Folklorica, 1976; Partita Romantica for Piano, 1983; Tokajik, Cantata for Soprano, Chorus and Orchestra, 1975; The Echoes of the Uprising Mountains, Song Cycle for Narrator, Soprano, Tenor and Piano, 1979; The Recruit Songs, Song Cycle, 1973; The Pines Whispered, Song Cycle for Soprano and Piano, 1976; The Woman and Muse, Song Cycle for Bass-Baritone and Piano, 1978; Also Incidental Music, Film Scores and Music for Folk Ensembles. *Publications:* Tonal System of Slovak Music 1996. *Address:* c/o SOZA, Bratislava 3, 821 08 Bratislava, Slovakia.

**ANDRASSY, Gabor;** singer (bass); b. 1951, Transylvania, Romania. *Career:* sang at the Berne Opera, 1979–81, then at Krefeld, 1981–87; Karlsruhe, 1988–90, with guest appearances at Geneva, Théâtre des Champs-Elysées Paris, as Fafner in The Ring and at Seattle (1989) as Wagner's Daland; Has performed widely in France as King Marke at Nantes, Hunding and Hagen at Nice, and Fafner, Boris Godunov and Ivan Khovansky at Strasbourg, 1991–92; Seattle Opera in The Ring and as Rocco in Fidelio; Other roles include the Commendatore in Don Giovanni, Boris Godunov and King Philip, King Henry and Grand Inquisitor; Season 1995–96, as Walter in Luisa Miller at Strasbourg and Capitan in the premiere of Florencia en las Amazonas by Daniel Cátan at Houston; Sang in Der Freischütz at Seattle, 1999, and Sarastro in Die Zauberflöte; Season 2000–01 as Dansker in Billy Budd, at Seattle and Los Angeles. *Current Management:* Merle Hubbard Management, 133 West 71st Street, Apt 8a, New York, NY 10023, USA.

**ANDRÉ, Martin;** Conductor; b. 10 Dec. 1960, West Wickham, England. *Education:* Studied at the Yehudi Menuhin School, the Royal College of Music and Cambridge University. *Career:* Played with the National Youth Orchestra as Percussionist from 1970; Founded the Mozart Chamber Ensemble at Cambridge and was appointed conductor of the University Orchestra and Chorus, and the University Chamber Orchestra; Conducted his edition of Purcell's King Arthur at Cambridge and the Minack Theatre, Cornwall, 1982; Has worked with the Welsh National Orchestra from 1982, leading Aida, Jenůfa, Ernani, Rigoletto, Madama Butterfly, Un Ballo in Maschera, Eugene Onegin and Il Barbiere di Siviglia; Vancouver Opera from season 1986–87 with Janáček's From the House of the Dead and Cunning Little Vixen, Ariadne auf Naxos, La Traviata and La Bohème; Seattle Opera 1987, Carmen; London concert debut January 1987, with the English Chamber Orchestra at the Barbican; Further concerts with the Scottish Chamber Orchestra and the Northern Sinfonia; Scottish Opera from 1989, The Merry Widow and La Clemenza di Tito; Conducted The Love of Three Oranges at the English National Opera, 1990, and at Teatro São-Carlos, Lisbon, 1991; Madama Butterfly for Opera North; World premiere, The Bacchae by John Buller for ENO, 1992; Music Director, English Touring Opera, 1993; Recent notable debuts include Verdi's Un Ballo in Maschera at the Royal Opera House Covent Garden; Conducted the United Kingdom premiere of Matthus' Cornet Christoph Rilke's Song of Love and Death for Glyndebourne Touring Opera; The Makropulos Case for GTO in 1997; Engagements with the New Israeli Opera include conducting Don Pasquale and Love for Three Oranges; The Magic Flute for Opera Northern Ireland, 1998. *Current Management:* Ingpen & Williams Ltd, 7 St George's Court, 131 Putney Bridge Road, London, SW15 2PA, England.

**ANDRÉ, Maurice;** French trumpeter; b. 21 May 1933, Alès, Gard; s. of Marcel André and Fabienne Volpélière; m. Lilianne Arnoult 1956; four c. *Education:* Conservatoire nat. supérieur de musique, Paris. *Career:* apprenticed as coal miner before formal music studies; won Prix d'honneur for trumpet; joined Paris Radio Orchestra; subsequently First Trumpet, Lamoureur Orchestra and other orchestras; played in jazz groups and chamber orchestras; now soloist with world's leading orchestras; specialises in baroque and contemporary music; Prof. of Trumpet, Paris Conservatoire 1967–; has made about 260 recordings, including 30 trumpet concertos. *Honours:* first prize Geneva Int. Competition 1955, Munich Int. Competition 1963, Schallplattenpreis, Berlin 1970, Victoire de la musique 1987; Chevalier, Légion d'honneur, Commdr, Ordre des Arts et des Lettres. *Current Management:* c/o Harry Lapp Organisation, 9 avenue de la Liberté, 67000 Strasbourg, France. *Address:* Presles-en-Brie, 77220 Tournan-en-Brie, France (home).

**ANDREAE, Marc Edouard;** Conductor; b. 8 Nov. 1939, Zürich, Switzerland. *Education:* Zürich Conservatory; University of Zürich; Study with Nadia Boulanger in Paris, with Franco Ferrara in Rome. *Career:* Chief Conductor, Broadcasting Orchestra of Italian Switzerland, Lugano, 1991; Regular Guest, numerous European, US and Japanese symphony orchestras and at festivals, Paris, Berlin, Lucerne, Vienna, Salzburg, Ascona, Brescia; Numerous concerts and operas for television including Eurovision; Music and Artistic Director of the Angelicum in Milan, Italy, 1990–93; mem, Swiss Music Edition (past president). *Recordings:* With NDR Hamburg, Hamburg Philharmonic Orchestra, Munich Philharmonic, Cologne Radio Symphony Orchestra, Bamberg Symphony, National Orchestra of France, NHK Symphony Orchestra, Tokyo. *Publications:* Music of Weber, Rossini, Donizetti, Schumann, Lortzing, Tchaikovsky and Liszt. *Honours:* 1st Prize, Swiss National Competition, 1966; 2 Grand Prix, Italian Record Critics, 1974; LP Techno Distinction, Tokyo, 1975. *Address:* Via Moretto 6, 6924 Sorengo, Switzerland. *E-mail:* marc.andreae@bluewin.ch.

**ANDREESCU, Horia;** conductor; b. 18 Oct. 1946, Brasov, Romania. *Education:* Brasov School of Music, Bucharest Conservatoire, studied with Hans Swarowsky in Vienna and Sergiu Celibidache in Munich. *Career:* Chief Conductor of Ploiesti Philharmonic, 1974–87; Permanent Guest Conductor, Mecklenburgische Staatskapelle Schwerin, 1979–90; Permanent Guest Conductor, Radio Symphony Orchestra, Berlin, 1981–91; Permanent Guest Conductor, Dresden Philharmonia, 1983–91; Joint Artistic Director of the George Enescu Philharmonic at Bucharest, 1987–; Professor, Academy of Music, 1988–90; Conductor, Virtuosi of Bucharest Chamber Orchestra; Conductor, Bucharest George Enescu Philharmonic Orchestra; Chief Conductor and General Music Director, Bucharest National Radio Orchestra, 1992–. *Recordings include:* The first complete orchestral work of George Enescu; Recorded for Radio Bucharest, Radio East Berlin (Haydn, Brahms, Wagner, Stravinsky, Hindemith, Prokofiev), Radio Leipzig (Bartók), BBC (Haydn, Mozart, Beethoven, Tchaikovsky), Radio Madrid, Radio Copenhagen and Radio Suisse Romande. *Honours:* prizewinner at Geneva and Copenhagen Competitions. *Address:* c/o Radio Romania, Directia Formatilor Muzicale, Str General Berthelot 62–68, Bucharest, Romania.

**ANDREEV, Andrei;** violinist; b. 1950, Crimea, USSR. *Career:* co-founded Rachmaninov Quartet under auspices of Sochi State Philharmonic Society, Crimea, 1974; Many concerts in former Soviet Union; From season 1975–76 tours to Switzerland, Austria, Bulgaria, Norway and Germany; Participation in Shostakovich Chamber Music Festival, Vilnius, 1976 and festivals in Moscow and St Petersburg; Repertoire includes works by Haydn, Mozart, Beethoven, Bartók, Brahms, Schnittke, Shostakovich, Boris Tchaikovsky, Chalayev and Meyerovich. *Honours:* with Rachmaninov Quartet: Prizewinner at First All-Union Borodin String Quartet Competition, 1987. *Address:* 11 North Park Street, Glasgow, G20 7AA, Scotland.

**ANDREW, Jon;** singer (tenor); b. 1936, New Zealand. *Education:* studied in Auckland. *Career:* debut as Don José in Carmen, Auckland, 1982; sang with Sadler's Wells Opera, 1963–68, as Ricardo, Radames, Don José, and Agrippa in the British premiere of The Fiery Angel (New Opera Company); Sang in Germany, 1969–, notably in Karlsruhe, Mannheim and Düsseldorf in Wagner roles including Siegmund in Die Walküre; Glyndebourne Festival as the Italian Singer in Rosenkavalier, 1965; Covent Garden, 1967 and 1974, as Froh in Das Rheingold and Dimitri in Boris Godunov; Further appearances with Welsh National Opera, Handel Opera Society, 1967, and at San Diego as Siegmund and Otello, 1975–76; Also sang Siegmund at Madrid, Berlin Staatsoper, and with English National Opera, 1975; Wexford Festival as Pedro in Tiefland, 1978; Further engagements at La Scala, Milan, and Nice and Santiago, 1981; Other roles have included Turiddu, Erik in Fliegende Holländer, Max in Der Freischütz, Laca in Jenůfa, and Bob Boles in Peter Grimes. *Address:* c/o English National Opera, St Martin's Lane, London WC2 4ES, England.

**ANDREW, Sarah;** bassoonist; b. 1975, England. *Education:* Royal College of Music with Martin Gatt, studied in Vienna. *Career:* co-founded Aurora Ensemble 1997, with wide range of wind quintet repertory, including commissioned works performed throughout Britain; Venues include ORF studios, Vienna, Purcell Room (London), Cheltenham and English Music Festivals, South Bank Centre Rimsky-Korsakov Festival and International Akademia Prag-Wien-Budapest; BBC Radio 3 Young Artists' Forum Series; education project Sounds Exciting (2000) and performance visits to educational establishments; Schubert's Octet at the National Gallery London 2001 with Piros Ensemble (founded 2000). *Honours:* Prizewinner, Music d'Ensemble Competition, Paris 2001. *Address:* c/o Royal College of Music, Prince Consort Road, London, SW7 2BS, England.

**ANDREYEV, Kostyantyn;** Ukrainian singer (tenor); b. Odessa. *Career:* performed at Ten Tenors Gala, RFH, London 2004; opera roles include Manek in Foerester's Eva, Wexford Festival 2004, title role in Jules Massenet's Werther, Turin 2005, Giosta Berling in I cavalieri di Ekebu, Catania 2006, Puccini's La Bohème, Jerez 2006; recitals, London 2005. *Recordings:* Josef Bohuslav Foerester, Eva 2005. *Current Management:* Atelier Musicale, Via Caselle 76, San Lazzaro di Savena, 40068, Italy. *Telephone:* (51) 19-98-44-44. *Fax:* (51) 19-98-44-20. *E-mail:* info@ateliermusicale.com. *Website:* www.ateliermusicale.com.

**ANDRIESSEN, Louis;** Composer; b. 6 June 1939, Utrecht, Netherlands. *Education:* studied with his father, Hendrik Andriessen, with Kees van Baaren, Royal Conservatory of Music, The Hague 1957–62, with Luciano Berio, Milan 1962–63. *Career:* Trilogy of the Last Day received the United Kingdom premiere at the 1999 London Prom concerts; Passion—The Music of Louis Andriessen, concert series at South Bank Centre, London 2002. *Compositions:* Stage: Reconstructie, Opera, 1968–69, in collaboration with 4 colleagues; Matthew Passion, 1976; Orpheus, 1977; George Sand, 1980; Orchestral: What it's Like for live Electronic Improvisers and 52 Strings, 1970; Uproar for 16 Winds, 6 Percussionists and Electronic Instruments, 1970; The 9 Symphonies of Beethoven for Promenade Orchestra and Ice Cream Bell, 1970; Symphony for Open Strings, 1978; Velocity, 1983; De Stijl, 1985; Chamber: Flute Sonata, 1956; Percosse for Flute, Trumpet, Bassoon and Percussion, 1958; A Flower Song I for Violin, 1963, II for Oboe, 1963; and III for Cello, 1964; Double for Clarinet and Piano, 1965; Souvenirs d'enfance for Piano and Tape, 1966; The Persistence for Piano and Winds, 1972; Felicitatie for 3 Trumpets, 1979; Disco for Violin and Piano, 1982; Overture to Orpheus for Harpsichord, 1982; Piano Pieces; Nocturne for Soprano and Chamber Orchestra, 1959; Il Principe for 2 Choirs, Winds, Piano and Bass Guitar, 1974; The State for 4 Women's Voices and 27 Instruments, 1972–76; Mausoleum for 2 Baritones and Chamber Ensemble, 1979, revised 1981; Time for Choir and Orchestra, 1981; Madrigal Concerto for Choir, 1984; 3 Dancing on the Bones for children's voices and ensemble, 1997; Collaboration with Peter Greenaway in 1991 television series Not Mozart: M is for Man, Music, Mozart; Rosa, a horse drama, 1994; Trilogy of the Last Day for orchestra, 1998; Writing to Vermeer, music theatre, 1999. *Address:* Boosey & Hawkes Music Publishers, 295 Regent Street, London, W1, England.

**ANDSNES, Leif Ove;** Norwegian pianist; b. 7 April 1970, Stavanger. *Education:* Bergen Music Conservatory. *Career:* debut, Oslo 1987; British debut with Oslo Philharmonic, Edinburgh Festival 1989; US debut with Cleveland Orchestra under Neeme Järvi 1990; recitals in London, Berlin, Vienna, Amsterdam, New York (Carnegie Hall); performs with Orchestre Nat. de France, Berlin Philharmonic, Chicago Symphony, BBC Symphony, London Symphony, LA Philharmonic, Japan Philharmonic, New York Philharmonic; soloist, Last Night of the Proms 2002; Co-Artistic Dir Risør Music Festival; recorded works of Brahms, Chopin, Grieg, Janacek, Liszt, Schumann. *Recordings:* Rachmaninov Piano Concertos 1 & 2 2005. *Honours:* Commdr Royal Norwegian Order of St Olav 2002; First Prize, Hindemith Competition, Frankfurt am Main and prizewinner at other int. competitions, Levin Prize (Bergen) 1988, Norwegian Music Critics' Prize 1988, Grieg Prize (Bergen) 1990, Dorothy B. Chandler Performing Arts Award, Los Angeles 1992, Gilmore Prize 1997, Instrumentalist Award, Royal Philharmonic Soc. 2000, Gramophone Award (Best Concerto Recording) 2000, (Best Instrumental Recording) 2002. *Current Management:* c/o Kathryn Enticott, IMG Artists, Lovell House, 616 Chiswick High Road, London, W4 5RX, England. *Telephone:* (20) 8233-5800. *Fax:* (20) 8233-5801. *Website:* www.andsnes.com.

**ANGAS, Richard;** British singer (bass); b. 1942, Surrey. *Education:* Studied in Vienna and London. *Career:* Debut: With Scottish Opera as Fafner in The Ring; Appearances with the Welsh National Opera and at Covent Garden; Performances in Germany as King Mark and King Henry, Baron Ochs, Osmin, Rocco and Mephistopheles; Engagements throughout Europe, Israel, Australia and South America in Oratorio and Recital; English National Opera as Monteverdi's Seneca and Pluto, Basilio in Il Barbiere di Siviglia, Pimen (Boris Godunov), Daland (The Flying Dutchman) and Jupiter (Orpheus in the Underworld); The Mikado, 1990, and Bartolo in Figaro; The Doctor in a new production of Wozzeck, 1990; Has sung in the world premiere of Birtwistle's The Mask of Orpheus, 1986, and the British premiere of The Making of the Representative for Planet 8 by Philip Glass, 1988; Sang in The Love for Three Oranges with Opera North, Leeds; Debut in Paris, Opéra Garnier, as Pontius Pilate in Höller's Master and Margarita, 1991; Debut in USA as Rocco in Fidelio, 1994; Tosca and The Mikado for ENO, 1994; Mulhouse, 1996, as the Commandant in From the House of the Dead; Season 1998 with Pistol in Falstaff at Garsington and Sarastro at Belfast; Season 1999–2000 as Waldner in Arabella for Opera North, Aga in Martinu's Greek Passion at Bregenz (repeated at Covent Garden) and the High Priest in Nabucco for ENO; Cunning Little Vixen, Opera North and Barcelona 2004; Love for Three Oranges (Netherlands), Julietta (Opera North, Ravenna and Prague), Curlew River (Trento and Pisa), Peter Grimes (Zürich) 2005. *Address:* c/o Musichall Ltd, Vicarage Way, Ringmer, East Sussex, BN8 5LA, England. *Telephone:* (1273) 814240. *Fax:* (1273) 813637. *E-mail:* info@musichall.uk.com. *Website:* www.musichall.uk.com.

**ANGEL, Marie;** Singer (Soprano); b. 30 July 1953, Pinnaroo, South Australia; m. David Freeman. *Career:* Has sung with Opera Factory London and Opera Factory Zürich in Così fan tutte (Fiordiligi, also televised); The Knot Garden (Denise); Birtwistle's Punch and Judy (Pretty Polly); Aventures by Ligeti; Mahagonny Songspiel; Gluck's Iphigenia operas (title role); Donna Anna and Mozart's Countess Fiordiligi, 1991, all 3 televised; Other roles include Euridice in Monteverdi's Orfeo and Hecate and the Oracle of the Dead in the premiere of The Mask of Orpheus, 1986 for the English National Opera; Mozart's Queen of Night for Welsh National Opera; Musetta for Opera North; Sang Berio's Recital at South Bank and Jo-Ann for Glyndebourne Touring Opera in Tippett's New Year; Created the role of Morgana Le Fay in the premiere of Birtwistle's Gawain at Covent Garden, May 1991; Sang Monteverdi's Poppea in a new production by Opera Factory, 1992; Has also sung Donna Anna for Victoria State Opera and appeared with Houston Grand Opera and at the New York City Opera; Created the role of Esmerelda in Rosa, the opera by Peter Greenaway and Louis Andriessen at the Music Theatre, Amsterdam, 1994; Sang Hecate in The Mask of Orpheus at the Festival Hall, London, 1996 (recorded); English National Opera 1996, as Countess de la Roche in Zimmermann's Die Soldaten, and at Basle, 1998–99; Kagel's Aus Deutschland, Dichterin and Kammersängerin, Basle and Holland Festivals, 1997; In Satyricon by Maderna, sang Fortunata for Basle and toured to Venice, 1998; Sang title role in Die Lustige Witwe at Basle Theatre, 1999. *Recordings:* Gawain, 1994; Andriessen's Rosa, recorded and filmed, 1998; Prospero's Books, P. Greenaway, recorded and filmed (Nyman), 1989; Hannover, Europera 5, John Cage, 2001/2002; Nyman's Facing Goya, Spanish Tour, recorded 2002. *Current Management:* Allied Artists Agency, 42 Montpelier Square, London, SW7 1JZ, England. *Telephone:* (20) 7589-6243. *Fax:* (20) 7581-5269. *E-mail:* info@alliedartists.co.uk. *Website:* www.alliedartists.co.uk.

**ANGEL, Ryland;** Singer (Countertenor); b. 22 Nov. 1966, England. *Education:* Vocal studies with David Mason in London and Gerald Lesne. *Career:* Appearances in Handel's Amadigi at the Karlsruhe Festival, 1996–97, Purcell's Dido and Aeneas, Blow's Venus and Adonis with René Jacobs at De Vlaamse Opera; Peri's Euridice with Opera Normandie, the medieval Play of Daniel in New York and a staged production of Caldara's oratorio La Santissima Annunziata with Le Parlement de Musique at the Louvre, Paris; Settings of Orfeo by Monteverdi and Gluck with English National Opera and English Touring Opera, Purcell Fairy Queen with the English Bach Festival and for ENO, 1998; Further concerts with La Chapelle Royale, Le Concert Spirituel and Les Jeunes Solistes; Festival appearances at Lucerne, BBC Proms, Athens, Lufthansa Baroque Festival (London) and Venice International Contemporary Music Festival; Solo recitals in Paris; Sang Zephyrus in Mozart's Apollo et Hyacinthus, Britten Theatre, London, 1998; Further engagements include: Bertarido in Handel's Rodelinda with Il Combattimento in Amsterdam, and a concert tour with La Fenice; Season 1999–2000 with the title role in Handel's Radamisto at St Louis Festival and Non Erat Bonus by Brixi with Musiktheater Transparant. *Current Management:* Robert Gilder & Co., 91 Great Russell Street, London, WC1B 3PS, England. *Telephone:* (20) 7580-7758. *E-mail:* rgilder@robert-gilder.com. *Address:* 39 Rue de Rivoli, 75004 Paris, France.

**ANGELICH, Nicholas;** American pianist; b. 1970, Cincinnati, OH. *Education:* Conservatoire Nat. Superieur de Musique, Paris, France with Aldo Ciccolini, Yvonne Loriod and Michel Beroff, numerous masterclasses. *Career:* resident pianist of the Fondation Internationale per il Pianoforte, Cadenabia, Italy 1996; performed at the Fourth Annual Miami Int. Piano Festival of Discovery 2001. *Recordings:* Rachmaninov: Etudes–Tableaux, Brahms: Sonates pour alto et piano (with Laurent Verney), Ravel: Miroirs, Gaspard de la nuit, La Valse, Liszt: Les Années de pèlerinage, Brahms: Piano Trios (with Renaud and Gautier Capuçon), Brahms Violin Sonatas (with Renaud Capuçon) 2005. *Honours:* Second Prize R. Casadesus Int. Competition, Cleveland 1989, Fifth Prize Tokyo Int. Competition, First Prize Gina Bachauer Int. Competition 1994, Second Prize Umberto Micheli Competition 1997. *Address:* c/o Virgin Classics, EMI Group plc, 27 Wrights Lane, London, W8 5SW, England.

**ANGELO, Mariana;** singer (soprano); b. 1954, Sofia, Bulgaria. *Education:* Conservatoire of Sofia. *Career:* sang at the Komische Oper Berlin, 1978–84; Berne Opera, 1984–86; Has appeared at the Nationaltheater Mannheim, 1987–, and has sung as guest at Dresden, Karlsruhe, Sofia, Graz, Nancy, Paris, Ghent and Antwerp; Lausanne Opera, 1989, as Liu in Turandot; Other roles include Verdi's Leonora (Il Trovatore and La Forza del Destino), Amelia Grimaldi, Aida, Violetta and Desdemona; Puccini's Mimi, Manon Lescaut and Madama Butterfly; Nedda, Tatiana and Mathilde in Guillaume Tell; Sang Aida at the Berlin Staatsoper, 1991. *Address:* c/o Music International, 13 Ardilaun Road, London N5 2QR, England.

**ANGERER, Paul;** Austrian conductor, composer and instrumentalist; b. 16 May 1927, Vienna; s. of Otto Angerer and Elisabeth Angerer; m. Anita Rosser 1952; two s. two d. *Education:* Hochschule für Musik und darstellende Kunst, Vienna. *Career:* viola player, Vienna Symphony 1947, leading solo viola player 1953–57; viola player, Tonhalle Zürich 1948; Suisse Romande Orchestra, Geneva 1949; Dir and Chief Conductor, Chamber Orch. of Wiener Konzerthausgesellschaft 1956–63; composer and conductor, Burgtheater, Vienna and Salzburg and Bregenz festivals 1960–; Perm. Guest Conductor, Orchestra Sinfonica di Bolzano e Trento "Haydn" 1964–90; First Conductor, Bonn City Theatre 1964–66; Music Dir Ulm Theatre 1966–68; Chief of Opera, Salzburger Landestheater 1967–72; Dir SW German Chamber Orch., Pforzheim 1971–82; Prof. Hochschule, Vienna 1983–92; Moderator ORF 1984–2001; Radio Stephansdorn 2001; Leader of Concilium Musicum. *Works include:* orchestral pieces, chamber works, viola and piano concertos, a dramatic cantata, television opera, works for organ, harp, viola, harpsichord, etc.; numerous recordings both as soloist and conductor. *Publications:* Und s'ist elles noch wehr! Briefe eines Eipeldaners Mozart auf Reisen. Reisebriefe Leopold Mozarts aus Wren 1762–1773. *Honours:* several prizes including Austrian State Prize 1956, Theodor Körner Prize 1958, Vienna Cultural Prize 1983, Cultural Prize of Lower Austria 1987; Nestroy-Ring, City of Vienna 1998; Austrian Order of Honour for Sciences and Arts Class 1. *Address:* Esteplatz 3/26, 1030 Vienna, Austria. *Telephone:* (1) 714 12 71. *Fax:* (1) 714 12 71. *E-mail:* PaulAngerer@concilium.at (home).

**ANGERMÜLLER, Rudolph Kurt;** German/Austrian Music Editor and Music Librarian; *General Secretary, International Mozarteum Foundation*; b. 2 Sept. 1940, Bielefeld, Germany; m. Hannelore Johannböke, one s., one d. *Education:* MA; PhD 1970; Graduate, Försterling Conservatory of Music, Bielefeld. *Career:* Assistant, Musicology Institute, University of Salzburg; Chief Editor, New Mozart Edition, and Librarian, International Mozarteum Foundation, 1972–; Chief of Research Department International Mozarteum Foundation, 1981–; General Secretary, International Mozarteum Foundation, 1988; Professor, 1993; mem, International Musicological Society; Society for Music Research; Austrian Musicological Society. *Publications:* Untersuchungen zur Geschichte des Carmen-Stoffes, 1967; Antonio Salieri, Sein Leben und seine weltichen Werke unter besonderer Berücksichtigung seiner grossen Opern, 3 Vols, 1971, 1972, 1974; W A Mozarts Musikalische Umwelt in Paris, 1778, Eine Dokumentation, 1982; Mozart's Operas, 1988; Ich johannes chrisostomus Amadeus Wolfgangus Sigismundus Mozart, 1991; Mozarts Reisen in Italien, 1994; Franz Xaver Wolfgang Mozart, Reisetagebuch 1819–1821, 1994; Mozart auf der Reise nach Prag, Dresden, Leipzig und Berlin, 1995; Geistliche Werke von Antonio Salieri in der Hofkapelle in Wien, 1996; Francesco Benucci: Mozarts erster Figaro und Guglielmo, 1998; Pariser Don Juan: Rezensionen 1805–1806, 1998; Antonio Salieri: Dokumente seines Lebens, 2000. *Contributions:* Bulletin of the International Mozarteum Foundation; Mozart-Jahrbuch; Haydn-Jahrbuch; Die Musikforschung; Österreichische Musikzeitschrift; Wiener Figaro; Musical Times; Deutsches Jahrbuch für Musikwissenschaft; Numerous other professional journals and books. *Honours:* Socio Accademia degli Agiati Rovereto, 1995; Socio d'onore R Accademia Filarmonica di Bologna, 1997; Stella d'oro al valor mozartiano, 2001. *Address:* 92A Moosstrasse, 5020 Salzburg, Austria. *Telephone:* 826735 (office).

**ANGUS, David Anthony;** British conductor; b. 2 Feb. 1955, Reading, England; m.; one d. *Education:* Surrey Univ., Leeds Univ., Royal Northern Coll. of Music. *Career:* debut as Chorister at King's College, Cambridge; Chorus Master and Staff Conductor, Glyndebourne 1989–95; conducted most major orchestras in the UK, including London Philharmonic Orchestra; many performances at Glyndebourne; appears regularly in Italy; Principal Conductor, Symphony Orchestra of Flanders; broadcasts with BBC Orchestra and BBC Singers; conductor British opera premieres, Brighton Festival; appeared in Denmark, Norway, Finland, Austria, Belgium and France; specialises in Mozart, romantic and 20th Century opera. *Recordings:* Britten's Curlew River, modern British choral and orchestral works with London Philharmonic Orchestra. *Honours:* three Ricordi prizes for opera conducting 1985–87, finalist Leeds Conductors' Competition 1988. *Current Management:* Patrick Garvey Management, Cedar House, 10 Rutland Street, Filey, North Yorkshire YO14 9JB, England. *Website:* www.patrickgarvey.com.

**ANHALT, Istvan,** OC; Canadian composer, writer and educator; *Professor Emeritus, Queen's University*; b. 12 April 1919, Budapest, Hungary. *Education:* Royal Hungarian Acad. of Music, Conservatoire National de Musique de Paris, France, composition with Zoltán Kodály and Nadia Boulanger, conducting with Louis Fourestier, piano with Soulima Stravinsky. *Career:* appointed as a Lady Davis Fellow and Asst Prof. to Faculty of Music, McGill Univ., Montréal, Canada 1949, later Assoc. and full Prof.; carried out experimentation and compositional work at electronic music laboratory of National Research Council of Canada, Ottawa, Columbia-Princeton Electronic Music Centre and Bell Telephone Laboratories; installed electronic music studio and appointed dir; mem. of the senate, McGill Univ. 1968; appointed Visiting Slee Prof., New York State Univ. at Buffalo 1969; Head of Music, Queen's Univ., Kingston, ON 1971–81, Emeritus Prof. 1984–. *Compositions include:* dramatic works: Arc en Ciel 1951, Cycle of 4 musico-dramatic (operatic) works: La Tourangelle: A Musical Tableau 1975, Winthrop: A Musical Pageant 1983, Traces (Tikkun): A Pluri-drama for solo lyric baritone and orchestra 1995, Millennial Mall (Lady Diotima's Walk): A Voice-Drama for the Imagination for solo lyric soprano, choir and orchestra 1998; orchestral: Interludium 1950, Symphony No. 1 1958, Symphony of Modules, Symphony No. 2 1967, Simulacrum 1987, Sparkskraps 1988, Sonance Resonance (Welche Töne?) 1989, Twilight Fire (Baucis' and Philemon's Feast) 2001, The Tents of Abraham (A Mirage-Midrash) 2003; chorus: The Bell-Man 1954, revised 1980, Three Songs of Love 1951, revised 1998, Three Songs of Death 1954, Journey of the Magi 1951, Thisness a duo-drama for mezzo-soprano and pianist 1986, Cento for choir with tape; chamber music: Funeral Music, for chamber ensemble 1951, Trio for violin, cello and piano 1953, Sonata for violin and piano 1954, Sonata for piano 1951, Fantasia for piano 1954, Electronic Tape: Electronic Composition Nos 1–4 1959–62, Foci for soprano and chamber orchestra with tape, Doors. . . Shadows (Glenn Gould in Memory) String Quartet 1992. *Recordings include:* Cento, Fantasia for Piano, Foci, Sonata for Violin and Piano, Trio for violin, cello and piano. *Publications:* Alternative Voices, Essays on Contemporary Vocal and Choral Composition

1984, Istvan Anhalt Pathways and Memory (eds Robin Elliott and Gordon E. Smith) 2001, numerous other publications and papers. *Honours:* DMus hc (McGill Univ.) 1982, Hon. LLD (Queen's Univ.) 1992, personal papers and manuscripts held in the Music Division, National Library of Canada, Ottawa, ON. *Address:* 274 Johnson Street, Kingston, ON K7L 1Y4, Canada (home).

**ANIEVAS, Agustin;** pianist and teacher; b. 11 June 1934, New York, USA. *Education:* Juilliard School of Music, New York with Steuermann, Samaroff and Marcus. *Career:* formal debut as soloist with the Little Orchestra Society, New York, 1952; later toured North and South America, Australia and the Far East; Professor of Piano, Brooklyn College of the City University of New York, 1974–. *Recordings:* For Angel-EMI and Seraphim, notably of music by Bartók, Prokofiev, Rachmaninov, Chopin and Liszt. *Honours:* Concert Artists Guild Award, 1959; First Prize, Dimitri Mitropoulos Competition, 1961. *Address:* c/o Music Department, Brooklyn College of the City University of New York, Brooklyn, NY 11210, USA.

**ANISIMOV, Alexander;** Singer (bass); b. 1960, Krasnoyarsk, Russia. *Education:* Studied with Ekaterina Yofel in Krasnoyarsk. *Career:* Joined the Bolshoi Theatre Moscow and sang major roles in Glinka's Ivan Susanin and Tchaikovsky's Iolanta; Season 1992 as the Grand Inquisitor in Don Carlos at La Scala and the Old Prisoner in Lady Macbeth of the Mtsensk District at the Opéra Bastille, Paris; Prince Gremin in Eugene Onegin, at the Théâtre du Châtelet; Season 1993–94 as the Commendatore at La Scala, Sparafucile, in Rigoletto at the Berlin Staatsoper and the Glagolitic Mass with the London Philharmonic; US debut at the New York Met in Lady Macbeth and also at the Bastille; Season 1994–95 as Il Bonzo in Madama Butterfly at the Bastille; Season 1995–96 as Lodovico in Otello, Sparafucile and Commendatore in Don Giovanni at the Met, King Dodon in The Golden Cockerel at Nice, the Verdi Requiem in Tel-Aviv and Oroveso in Norma at the Carnegie Hall; Season 1996–97 as Timur in Turandot at Chicago and the Metropolitan Opera House, New York and Pimen in Boris Godunov at Frankfurt; Season 1997–98 Boris in Boris Godunov with Milwaukee Symphony Orchestra, Ramphis in Aida at Dallas, Pimen in Boris Godunov at Frankfurt and concerts at the Colmar International Festival; Season 1998–99 as Oroveso in Norma with the Canadian Opera Company, King Rene in Iolanthe in Toronto, Verdi's Requiem with Madrid Philharmonic Orchestra and Antwerp Opera, Tom in Un Ballo in Maschera at San Diego; Inquisitor in Don Carlo at Palm Beach; Season 1999–2000 with Basilio in Il Barbiere at Las Palmas and in Don Carlo at Barcelona; Further engagements include: Lady Macbeth of Mtsensk at the Dresden Staatsoper, Boris Godunov at Seattle, Fiesco in Simon Boccanegra in Nancy. *Recordings include:* Russian Church Music; Don Carlos; Eugene Onegin. *Honours:* Prizewinner, Glinka Competition, 1987; Prizewinner Tchaikovsky Competition, 1990. *Current Management:* Italartist Austroconcert Kulturmanagement GmbH, Gluckgasse 1, 1010 Vienna, Austria. *Telephone:* (1) 5132657. *Fax:* (1) 5126154. *E-mail:* austroconcert@ia-ac.com. *Website:* www.ia-ac.com.

**ANISIMOVA, Tanya;** cellist; b. 15 Feb. 1966, Grozny, Russia; m. Victor Taratuta 1989. *Education:* Central Music School, Moscow, 1975–84; Studied Cello with Natalia Shakhovskaya, Igor Gavrysh, Galina Kozolupov, graduated with honours, 1984–89; Assistantship, Cello, String Quartet, Graduate School, Moscow Conservatory, 1989–90; Studied with George Neikrug, Artist's Diploma, Boston University, 1990–92; Graduate Studies with Aldo Parisot, Yale University School of Music, 1992–. *Career:* Solo Recitals, Russia, Massachusetts, Virginia, Washington DC, and Soloist with Orchestras, Young Performers Series, Moscow, Minsk, Gorky, Ulianovsk, Lugansk and local Philharmonic Orchestras, Russia, and Central Massachusetts Symphony, USA, 1985–91; With Glazunov String Quartet, Russia, Poland, Greece, Japan, Germany; Artist-in-Residence, Banff Music Festival, 1993. *Recordings:* Moscow State Radio, 1987; With Glazunov String Quartet, Athens Radio, Greece, 1989; WBGH Public Radio, Boston, Massachusetts, 1991; WCUW Radio, Worcester, Massachusetts, 1992. *Publications:* contrib. to magazines, reviews, journals. *Honours:* 1st Prize, Concertino Praha International Competition, Prague, 1981; 1st Prize, All-Union String Quartet Competition, Voronezh, Russia, 1987. *Address:* c/o Aldo Parisot, Yale University, School of Music, PO Box 2104A, Yale Station, New Haven, CT 06520, USA.

**ANISSIMOV, Alexander;** Russian conductor; b. 1947. *Education:* St Petersburg Conservatory and Moscow Conservatory. *Career:* Principal Conductor, Bolshoi Theatre, Belarus 1980; f. and conductor, Nat. Youth Orchestra of Belarus; Principal Guest Conductor, Radio Telefís Éireann (RTÉ) Nat. Symphony Orchestra, Dublin 1995–98; Principal Conductor 1998–2001, Conductor Emeritus 2001–; regular guest conductor with Nat. Youth Orchestra of Ireland; Principal Conductor, Belorussian State Philharmonic 1996, Nat. Philharmonic Orchestra of Belarus 2001, Opera Rostov-on-the-Don, Russia 2003; he has conducted world-wide, including the Bolshoi Theatre (Moscow), Kirov Opera (St Petersburg), Opéra Bastille (Paris), Staatsoper Hamburg, Komische Oper Berlin, State Opera of South Australia, Norske Opera (Oslo), North Holland Sinfonia, Concertgebouw (Amsterdam), Opera Ireland, Teatro del Liceo (Barcelona), Teatro Colón (Buenos Aires), San Francisco Opera, Houston Grand Opera, La Fenice (Venice), Florence Opera; Hon. Pres. Wagner Soc. of Ireland 2002–. *Recordings:* Beethoven Symphony No. 9 in D minor, Alexander Konstantinovich Glazunov Orchestral Works Vol. 1 (Raymonda, Op. 57), Vol. 5 (Symphonies Nos 2 & 7 "Pastoral"), Vol. 7 (Symphonies Nos 1 "Slavyanskaya" & 4), Vol. 8 (The Seasons, Op. 67, Op. 52, Op. 81), Vol. 12 (Symphonies Nos 3 & 9), Vol. 13 (Symphony No. 6, Op. 58 Symphonic Poem "The Forest", Op. 19), Vol. 15 (Symphonies Nos 5 & 8),

Rachmaninov Symphony No. 1 and Op. 13 Caprice Bohémien and Op. 12, Rachmaninov Symphony No. 2, Rachmaninov Symphony No. 3 and Op. 44 Mélodie in E Polichinelle, Rachmaninov The Bells Op. 35, Mahler Symphony No. 2 "The Resurrection", Anton Rubinstein The Demon, Tchaikovsky Symphony No. 5 and Concerto No. 1, Classical Favourites Vols 1 and 2, Vivat Opera Live 1999. *Honours:* Hon. DMus (Nat. Univ. of Ireland) 2001. *Current Management:* Askonas Holt Ltd, Lonsdale Chambers, 27 Chancery Lane, London, WC2A 1PF, England. *Telephone:* (20) 7400-1700. *Fax:* (20) 7400-1799. *E-mail:* info@askonasholt.co.uk. *Website:* www.askonasholt.co.uk. *Address:* c/o RTÉ National Symphony Orchestra, Radio Telefís Éireann, Donnybrook, Dublin 4, Ireland. *Website:* www.alexanderanissimov.com.

**ANNEAR, Gwynneth;** singer (soprano, mezzo-soprano); b. 1939, Tailenbend, South Australia. *Education:* University of Adelaide, Royal College of Music, London. *Career:* debut, sang in Amahl and the Night Visitors while at the Royal College of Music, 1964; Sang the title role in Anna Bolena by Donizetti at the 1965 Glyndebourne Festival; Tour of Italy with Italian Company, 1968, in Fidelio and Così fan tutte; Has sung at the Camden Festival and with opera companies in Australia; Frequent broadcasts and concert engagements; Glyndebourne Festival 1970 and 1973, First Lady in Die Zauberflöte.*Address:* c/o Australian Opera, Sydney Opera House, Sydney, NSW, Australia.

**ANRAKU, Mariko,** BM, MM; harpist; b. 7 March 1970, Japan. *Education:* Juilliard School, New York, Royal Conservatory of Music, Toronto, Canada. *Career:* debut as soloist with Toronto Symphony; recitals, Weill Recital Hall, Carnegie Hall, New York; Jordan Hall, Boston; LA County Museum; Opéra-Comique, Paris; Casals and Kioi Halls, Tokyo; Soloist, Many orchestras; Spoleto Festival, Italy; Newport Festival; Festival of the Sound; Takefu Festival, Tanglewood; Banff Festival; Harpist, Metropolitan Opera Orchestra. *Recordings:* Mariko Anraku harp recital I and II, 1997 and 1998. *Honours:* 3rd prize and the Pearl Chertok prize, The International Harp Contest, Israel, 1992; 1st prize, The 1st Harp contest, Japan, 1989; Pro Musicis International Award, 1993. *Address:* c/o The Metropolitan Opera Orchestra, Lincoln Center, NY, NY 10023, USA.

**ANSELL, Gillian;** Violist; b. 1968, Auckland, New Zealand. *Education:* Studied at Royal College of Music, London, and with Igor Ozim and the Amadeus Quartet in Cologne. *Career:* Played with Kent Opera Orchestra, Chamber Orchestra of Europe and Philharmonia, 1984–; Co-Founded New Zealand String Quartet, under auspices of Music Federation of New Zealand, 1987; Debut Concert, Wellington, May 1988; Concerts at Tanglewood School, USA, Banff International Competition, Canada; Performances with Lindsay Quartet at International Festival of the Arts, Wellington, 1990; Soloist with New Zealand Symphony Orchestra; Artist-in-Residence, Victoria University, Wellington; Tour to Australia for Musica Viva Australia, 1990; New Zealand tours, 1992; Concerts in New York, 1993. *Current Management:* Ingpen & Williams Ltd, 7 St George's Court, 131 Putney Bridge Road, London, SW15 2PA, England.

**ANTHONY, Charles;** Singer (Tenor); b. 15 July 1929, New Orleans, Louisiana, USA. *Education:* Studied voice with Dorothy Hulse at Loyola University; Continued training with Riccardo Picozzi and Giuseppe Ruisi in Italy. *Career:* Won Metropolitan Opera Auditions of the Air, 1952; Metropolitan debut 1954, as Missail in Boris Godunov; Later sang Ernesto in Don Pasquale, Almaviva in Il Barbiere di Siviglia, David in Die Meistersinger and Nemorino in L'Elisir d'amore; Has sung nearly 2000 performances with Metropolitan company; Also sang as guest in Dallas, Santa Fe and Boston; Sang Eisslinger in a new production of Die Meistersinger at the Metropolitan, 1993. *Address:* c/o Metropolitan Opera House, Lincoln Center, New York, NY 10023, USA. *Website:* www.charlesanthony.com.

**ANTHONY, Susan B.;** American singer (soprano); b. 1959, Michigan. *Education:* Zürich Opera Studio. *Career:* appearances in opera throughout Europe from 1985; Berlin Staatsoper from 1991 as the Trovatore Leonora, Ines in L'Africaine; Elena in Vespri Siciliani and Eva in Die Meistersinger, 1994; sang Strauss's Daphne, 1991, and Leonore in Fidelio, 1996, Rome Opera; Bregenz, 1995; season 1995–96 as Tatiana at Cologne and Elsa in Lohengrin at the Vienna Staatsoper; Geneviève in Chausson's Roi Arthus at Bregenz and Cologne and Freia in Das Rheingold at La Scala and Hamburg; season 1997 in Fidelio at Buenos Aires; season 1998 as Leonore in Paris, Marie in Wozzeck at Montpellier; sang Maria in Strauss's Friedenstag at Dresden; Senta in Tokyo and Fidelio in Vienna; season 1999 as Elsa in Paris and Vienna; Ariadne and Empress in Frau ohne Schatten in Dresden; Liebe der Danaë in Munich and Marie in Wozzeck at Cologne; season 2000 with Salome in Bologna, Ariadne at La Scala and Frau ohne Schatten in Dresden; Die Frau ohne Schatten at Vienna Staatsoper, Barcelona; world premiere of 'K' by Phillipe Manouri, Bastille Opéra; Brünnhilde (Siegfried) at Grand Théâtre, Geneva; Elektra at Santa Fe Opera; season 2002–04 in Paris as the Empress in Strauss's Frau and also in Vienna and Dresden and new productions in the Deutsche Oper, Berlin, Washington, Rome, Barcelona and two in Tokyo; Senta in Madrid, with Barenboim 2003. *Recordings:* Ernest Chausson's Le Roi Artus, Zemlinsky's Der Traumgörge, Arte Nova Voices (with Slovak Radio Symphony Orchestra, Bratislava). *Honours:* Opernwelt Singer of the Year 1995–96, 1997–98. *Current Management:* Laifer Artists Management, 410 W 24th Street, Suite 2i, New York, NY 10011-1369, USA. *Telephone:* (212) 929-7429. *Fax:* (212) 633-2628. *E-mail:* laiferart@aol.com. *Website:* www.laiferart .com; www.susan-anthony.com.

**ANTINORI, Nazzareno;** singer (tenor); b. 1950, Anzio, Italy. *Education:* Accademia di Santa Cecilia, Rome. *Career:* sang Pinkerton, Rome Opera, 1979, repeated at Verona Arena, 1983; Appearances at Naples, Trieste, Macerata and Palermo; Sang Forresto in Atilla by Verdi, La Scala, Milan, 1991; other roles have included Verdi's Ismaele, Alfredo, Malcolm and Don Carlos, Cavaradossi, Maurizio in Adriana Lecouvreur and Števa in Jenůfa; Cavaradossi at Macerata, 1995; Season 1998 as Ismaele at Rome and Verona. *Recordings:* Tosca and Madama Butterfly. *Honours:* winner Maria Callas Competition 1980. *Address:* c/o Rome Opera, Piazza B Gigli 8, 00184 Rome, Italy.

**ANTOINE, Bernadetta;** singer (soprano); b. 8 March 1940, Nancy, France. *Education:* Conservatories of Nancy and Paris. *Career:* debut at Theatre Region Parisienne 1967, as Musetta; has sung at the Grand Opéra and the Opéra-Comique, Paris and in Lyon, Marseille, Toulouse, Rouen, Hamburg, Brussels, Lisbon and Geneva; ORTF, Radio France, in the 1972 premiere of Don Juan ou l'amour de la geometrie by Semenov; Strasbourg 1974, in the premiere of Les Liaisons Dangereuses by Prey; Repertoire includes works by Gluck, Mozart, Puccini, Berlioz, Debussy, Poulenc, Britten and Prokofiev; Many concert appearances; Member of the Saarbrücken Opera, 1985–86.

**ANTOKOLETZ, Elliott Maxim,** BA, MA, PhD; American musicologist and writer; *Professor of Musicology, University of Texas at Austin*; b. 3 Aug. 1942, Jersey City, NJ; m. Juana Canabal 1972; one s. *Education:* Juilliard School of Music, Hunter Coll., Graduate School and Univ. Center CUNY. *Career:* Lecturer and mem. of faculty string quartet, Queens Coll., CUNY 1973–76; Prof. of Musicology 1976–, Head Musicology Division 1992–94, Univ. of Texas at Austin; co-ed., Int. Journal of Musicology 1992–; mem. American Musicological Soc. *Publications:* The Music of Béla Bartók: A Study of Tonality and Progression in Twentieth-Century Music 1984, Béla Bartók: A Guide to Research 1988, Twentieth Century Music 1992, Bartók Perspectives (ed. with V. Fischer and B. Suchoff) 2000, Musical Symbolism in the Operas of Debussy and Bartók 2004; contrib. three chapters to The Bartók Companion, one chapter to Sibelius Studies; contrib. to scholarly books and professional journals. *Address:* c/o School of Music, University of Texas at Austin, Austin, TX 78712, USA.

**ANTONACCI, Anna-Caterina;** Italian singer (soprano); b. 5 April 1961, Ferrara. *Education:* Bologna Conservatory. *Career:* initial experience in Bologna Comunale Theatre Chorus; debut as Rosina, Arezzo 1986; subsequent roles include Flora in La traviata, Bologna, Dorliska in Torvaldo and Dorliska, Savona 1988, Elcia in Mosè in Egitto, Rome 1988 and London 1994, Horatia in Gli Orazi ed i Curiazi, Cimarosa, Rome 1989 and Lisbon, Elizabeth in Maria Stuarda, Bari 1989, Ninetta in La gazza ladra, Philadelphia 1989, and Zelmira, Rome 1989; sang Fiordiligi at Venice and Macerata, Adalgisa at Catania, Polyxena in Manfroce's Ecuba and the title role of Paisiello's Elfrida at Savona 1990; Anaide in Mosè, Bologna 1991, Semiramide Catania 1991, Elisabetta, regina d'Inghilterra, Naples 1991, title role of Ermione, Rome 1991, London 1992 (also Buenos Aires, San Francisco concert performance and Glyndebourne for two seasons), Elena in La donna del lago, Amsterdam 1992; other roles at this time include Mayr's La rosa bianca e la rosa rossa at Bergamo, Polissena in Manfroce's Ecuba; sang Donna Elvira in Ferrara, Gluck's Alceste in Vienna and Berlin and Gluck's Armide at La Scala; an Adalgisa in Catania 1990, which she later sang at San Francisco and in Naples 1995; sang Monteverdi's Poppea in Bologna, Milan and Buenos Aires, the title role in Gluck's Armide at La Scala 1996, and Angelina in La Cenerentola, Toronto 1996; season 1999 included Fiordiligi at Naples, Rodelinda at Glyndebourne, Donna Elvira at Vienna and Ravenna, and Gluck's Armide and Paisiello's Nina at La Scala; season 2001–02, sang Dido at Florence, Marchesa del Poggia in Un giorno di regno at Bologna, and Elisabetta in a concert performance of Maria Stuarda in Edinburgh; recent roles include Agrippina at the Barbican 2003, Cassandra in Les Troyens at the Chatelet Theatre 2003, Carmen for Glyndebourne 2004, Cherubini's Medea at the Chatelet in 2005, Alceste in Salzburg Festival 2005, Nerone in L' incoranazione di Poppea in Cremona, Como, Ferrara, Pavia, Ravenna 2005–06, Poppea in L' incoronazione di Poppea, Munich 2006, Vitellia in La clemenza di Tito, Geneva 2006; concerts/recitals Luxembourg and Wigmore Hall, London 2006. *Recordings include:* Paisiello's Elfrida, Mayr's La Rosa Bianca e La Rosa Rossa, Polissena in Manfroce's Ecuba, Fiordiligi in Così fan tutte, Ermione, Puccini's Messa di Gloria, Stravinsky's Pulcinella, Pergolesi's Stabat Mater. *Honours:* won Verdi Competition, Busseto 1987, Pavarotti Competition, Philadelphia 1988, Maria Callas Competition 1988. *Current Management:* Askonas Holt Ltd, Lonsdale Chambers, 27 Chancery Lane, London, WC2A 1PF, England. *Telephone:* (20) 7400-1700. *Fax:* (20) 7400-1799. *E-mail:* info@askonasholt.co.uk (office). *Website:* www.askonasholt.co.uk.

**ANTONIOU, Theodore;** composer, conductor and teacher; b. 10 Feb. 1935, Athens, Greece. *Education:* National Conservatory, Athens, studied composition with Yannis Papaioannou, Hellenic Conservatory, composition and conducting with Gunter Bialas, Munich Hochschule für Musik, attended the Darmstadt Summer Courses. *Career:* active as a Conductor with various contemporary music groups; Teacher of Composition and Orchestration, Stanford University, 1969–70, University of Utah, 1970, Philadelphia Music Academy 1970–75, Berkshire Music Center, Tanglewood, 1975, University of Pennsylvania, 1978, Boston University, 1979–. *Compositions:* Stage Periander, opera, 1977–79; Ballets, Bacchae, 1980, and The Magic World, 1984; Music Theatre pieces, including The Imaginary Cosmos, ballet, 1984; Bacchae, opera, 1992; Monodrama for actor and ensemble, 1992; Oedipus at

Colonus, opera, 1998; Mixed media scores; Incidental music to various dramas; Film Scores; Orchestral, Concerto for clarinet, trumpet, violin and orchestra, 1959; Antithese, 1962; Piano Concertino, 1962; Jeux for cello and strings, 1963; Micrographies, 1964; Violin Concerto, 1965; Kinesis ABCD for 2 string orchestras, 1966; Threnos for wind ensemble, piano, percussion and double bass, 1972; Double Concerto for percussion and orchestra, 1977; The GBYSO Music, 1982; Various Choral Works, Solo Vocal Pieces and Chamber Music with Tape including Ode for soprano and ensemble, 1992. *Recordings:* as conductor of his own works and of works by other contemporary composers. *Honours:* many commissions and awards. *Address:* c/o Music Department, Boston University, Boston, MA 02215, USA.

**ANTONIOZZO, Alfonso;** Singer (Bass-Baritone); b. 1963, Italy. *Education:* Studied with Sesto Bruscantini. *Career:* Sang at the Montepulciano Festival from 1986, Florence and Torre del Festival, 1987, Bologna, 1988; Has appeared widely in Italy in Turandot (as Ping), Rossini's L'occasione fa il ladro, Adina and Il Barbiere di Siviglia; San Francisco; as Taddeo in L'Italiana in Algeri; Other roles include Pistol in Falstaff, Bizet's Don Procopio, Schaunard in La Bohème and Patroclus in Paer's Achille; Season 1995–96 as Mustafà in Rossini's Adina at Rome and Don Magnifico at Monte Carlo, San Francisco and Dallas 1996, as Leporello. *Recordings include:* Don Procopio and Cimarosa's I traci amanti (Bongiovanni). *Current Management:* Columbia Artists Management, 1790 Broadway, New York, NY 10019-1412, USA. *Telephone:* (212) 841-9500. *Fax:* (212) 841-9744. *E-mail:* info@cami.com. *Website:* www.cami.com. *Current Management:* Atelier Musicale, Via Caselle 76, San Lazzaro di Savena 40068, Italy. *Telephone:* (51) 19984444. *Fax:* (51) 19984420. *E-mail:* info@ateliermusicale.com. *Website:* www.ateliermusicale.com. *Address:* c/o PG & PM, 7 Whitehorse Close, Royal Mile, Edinburgh, EH8 8BU, Scotland.

**ANTONSEN, Ole Edvard;** Trumpeter; b. 25 April 1962, Ringsaker, Norway. *Education:* Studied with Harry Kvaebek at the Norwegian State Academy of Music, Diploma 1982. *Career:* Played with the Oslo Philharmonic 1982–90; Solo career from 1990; Concerto appearances with Atlanta Symphony, Dresdner Philharmonie, Stuttgart Chamber Orchestra. I Fiamminghi Chamber Orchestra, Wurtembergisches Kammerorchester, Swedish Radio Symphony Orchestra, Oslo and Bergen Philharmonic Orchestras in Sweden, Kioi Sinfonietta, Tokyo, Israel Chamber Orchestra, Orchestre de la Suisse Romande, Leipzig Radio Orchestra, Prague Symphony, London Festival Orchestra, Royal Swedish Chamber Orchestra and Cantilena (Scotland); Tour of 15 different countries 1989, including Russia and Brazil; Season 1990 with Paris debut (Oslo Philharmonic) and engagements in Spain, USA (New York and Washington recitals), West Germany and Switzerland; Plays jazz and contemporary music as well as the standard classics; 1995–96 included a recital debut with Wayne Marshall at the Royal Festival Hall, London; Appearances for the Istanbul International, City of London and Bermuda Festivals, concerts in Germany, Switzerland, Scandinavia and Austria and a 6th tour of Japan; 1997 included a return to the Schleswig-Holstein Festival, a tour with Dmitri Sitkovetsky and the New European String Orchestra and engagements in Europe, North America and the Far East; Recital with the Norwegian Chamber Orchestra, conducted by Iona Brown; with Wayne Marshall and the ECO, 1992; Berlin Philharmonic Orchestra with M Jansons and M Rudy for EMI. *Recordings include:* Tour de Force, 1993; Trumpet and piano recital with Wolfgang Sawallisch in 1996. *Honours:* First prize at the 1987 CIEM-Competition in Geneva; Laureat of the 1989 UNESCO Competition in Bratislava; Norwegian Grammy; Arets, Spillemann, for his Norwegian recording, Tour de Force, 1992.

**ANTUNES, Jorge,** PhD; university professor, composer, conductor and violinist; b. 23 April 1942, Rio de Janeiro, Brazil; m. Mariuga Lisboa Antunes 1969; three s. *Education:* University of Brazil, Instituto Torcuato di Tella, Buenos Aires, Sorbonne, Univ. of Paris, France. *Career:* Prof. of Composition, Dir of Electronic Music Laboratory, Co-ordinator of Composition and Conducting, General Co-ordinator of Nucleus for Studies and Research in Sonology, Univ. of Brasilia; television and radio appearances; mem. Academia Brasileira de Música, Brazilian Society for Electroacoustic Music (pres. 2004). *Compositions:* Cromorfonetica, 1969; Tartinia MCMLXX, 1970; Para Nascer Aqui, 1970–71; Macroformobiles 1, 1972–73; Catastrophe Ultra-Violette, 1974; Plumbea Spes, 1976; Congadasein, 1978; Elégie Violette pour Monseigneur Romero, 1980; Qorpo-Santo, opera, 1983; Sinfonia das Diretas, 1984; Dramatic Polimaniquexixe, 1985; Modinha para Mindinha, 1986; Serie Meninos, for young violinist and tape, 1986–87; Amerika 500, 1992; Olga, opera, 1993; Rimbaudiannisia MCMXCV, for children's choir, lights, masks and orchestra, 1994; Ballade Dure, electro-acoustic music, 1995; La beauté indiscrète d'une note violette, 1995; Cantata dos Dez Povos, 1999; Sinfonia em cinco movimentos, 2000; Eloquens, 2003; Toccata Irisée, 2004. *Recordings include:* Jorge Antunes–Musica Eletronica, 1975; Jorge Antunes Com A Orquestra Sinfonica Brasileira, 1978; No Se Mata La Justicia–Jorge Antunes, 1982; Musica Eletronica 70s, Vol. I, 1994; Musica Eletronica 70s, Vol. II, 1995; Musica Eletronica 90s Vol.III, 1997; Savage Songs, early Brazilian electronic music by Jorge Antunes, Pogus, NY, 2001. *Publications:* Sobre a correspondência entre os s. e as cores 1982, Notaçao na música contemporânea 1989, Uma Poética Musical brasileira e revolucionária 2002, Sons Novos para o piano, a harpa eo violão 2004. *Honours:* first prize Premio Angelicum di Milano 1971, Premio Vitae, Brazil 1991, Premio APAC 1992, Prix Musica Criativa 1994, Cidadão Honorário de Brasília 2002; Chevalier, Ordre des Arts et des Lettres 2002. *Address:* Universidade de Brasilia, Departamento de Música, 70910-970 Brasilia, DF, Brazil. *Fax:* (55) 61-368-1797. *E-mail:* antunes@unb.br. *Website:* www.americasnet.com.br/antunes.

**ANTUNES DE OLIVEIRA, Glacy,** MMus, PhD; concert pianist; b. 15 Oct. 1943, Goiania, Goias, Brazil. *Education:* Conservatory of Music at the Federal Univ. of Goias, Nat. School of Music at the Federal Univ. of Rio de Janeiro, Inst. of Arts at the Federal Univ. of Goias, postgraduate work in Rio de Janeiro and USA. *Career:* has worked under Professor José Kliass, São Paulo, and at Brigham Young University, Utah; Recitals, Solo and Chamber Music, all over Brazil, North and South America, Germany, Switzerland, Austria; Founder, Director, Musika Centro de Estudos, Goiania; President, National Piano Competition, Co-ordinator, Postgraduate Diploma Course in Music, Institute of Arts, Federal University. *Recordings:* three as soloist with Orquestra de Camara de Blumenau. *Address:* Rua 19 No. 32 S Oeste, Goiania, Goias 740001-970, Brazil.

**ANZAGHI, Davide;** composer and teacher; b. 29 Nov. 1936, Milan, Italy. *Education:* Milan Conservatory, studied composition with E. Pozzoli, A. Maggioni, G. Ghedini and F. Donatoni. *Career:* Teacher of Composition, Milan Conservatory; mem, President of Novurgia (Associazione Italiana per l'Arte, lo Spettacolo, la Cultura, Oggi). *Compositions:* Orchestral: Limbale, 1973; Ausa, 1973; Egophonie, 1974; Aur'ore for chorus and orchestra, 1975–76; Ermosonio, 1978; Anco, 1987; First Piano Concerto, 1987–88; Second Piano Concerto, 1990–91; Concerto Breve for clarinet and strings, 1990–91; Concerto for violin and orchestra, 1992; Third Piano Concerto 1993; Archindò for violin and strings, 1998; Chamber: Limine for string trio, 1971; In-Chiostro for 2 violins and viola, 1975, revised 1982; Alena for 10 wind instruments, 1976; Remota for 7 players, 1977; Alia for bass clarinet and piano, 1980; Oiseau Triste for piccolo and piano, 1980; Soavodia for clarinet and piano, 1980; Eco for cello and piano, 1980; Onirama for soprano and piano, 1980; Tornelli for oboe and piano, 1981; Labia for string quartet, 1982; Ricrio for brass octet, 1982; Soliludio for flute, clarinet, violin, cello and piano, 1982; Mitofania for flute, clarinet, violin, cello, piano and percussion, 1982; For Four for string quartet, 1983; Airy for clarinet, 1983; Halpith for flute, 1984; Elan for 9 instruments, 1984; Pri-ter for string quartet, 1985; Queen That for wind quintet, 1985; Apogeo for 5 instruments, 1987; Tremes for viola and piano, 1988; Viol-Once-All, 3 Pieces for cello, 1988; Settimino for clarinet, horn, bassoon, piano, violin, viola and cello, 1992; Invenzione, Schizzo, Variazioni for guitar, 1994; Elea for violin and piano, 1994; Riturgia for two recitant voices, chorus and orchestra, 1994; Chitattro and Repetita for 4 guitars, 1995; Phantasus for cello and piano, 1995; Ludus for ensemble, 1995; Musica per 3 for violin, cello and piano, 1996; Declinava un'estate inquieta, for recitant, piano and percussion, 1996; D'Ance for accordion; In nomine Filii, Oratorio for recitant, chorus, soprano and ensemble, 1997; Chifla, for flute and guitar, 1997; Il Labirinto di Sangue for recitant, 2 pianos and 2 percussion, 1998; Rondò per Pia for sax soprano, 1999; Piano Pieces: Segni, 1968–70; Ritografia, 1971; Revenants, 1981; Segni e Suoni, 1983; Due Intermezzi, 1983; Due Improvvisi, 1985; Variazioni, 1991; Sèpalo for 4 hands; Marcia Funebre con Variazioni, 1997; Notturni d'Averno, 1999. *Address:* Via Previati 37, 20149 Milan, Italy.

**APKALNA, Iveta;** Latvian organist; b. 1976, Rezekne (Lettland). *Education:* Vitols Latvian Acad. of Music, London Guildhall School for Music and Drama (scholarship), Conservatory of Stuttgart. *Career:* official organist during the visit of Pope John Paul II to Latvia 1993; regular organ and piano performances with Latvian Chamber Orchestra and Rezekne Symphony Orchestra; has toured extensively in Europe. *Recordings:* Orgel 2003, Touchdown in Riga, Himmel und Hoelle (Heaven and Hell) 2004 (ECHO Klassik Instrumentalist of the Year Award, Germany 2005), Plays the Organ of Parish Church St Martin in Wangen. *Honours:* third prize Lahti Int. Organ Competition, Finland 1997, first prize N London Piano School Competition 1998, third prize Int. M.K. Ciurlionis Organ Competition, Lithuania 1999, Royal Bank Calgary Int. Organ Festival and Competition Bach Ancillary Prize 2002.

**APONTE-LEDÉE, Rafael,** DipMus; composer and teacher; b. 15 Oct. 1938, Guayama, Puerto Rico. *Education:* Madrid Conservatory with Cristobal Halffter, Latin American Inst. of Higher Musical Studies with Alberto Ginastera, Di Tella Inst., Buenos Aires. *Career:* teacher of theory and composition, University of Puerto Rico, 1968–73, and the Puerto Rico Conservatory of Music, 1968–; promoter of avant-garde music festivals; mem, Musical Director of Latin American Foundation for Contemporary Music. *Compositions include:* Orchestral: Elejia, 1965, revised, 1967, Impulsos, in memoriam Julia de Burgos, 1967, Dos Cuentos Para Orquesta, 1987, Canción De Albada Y Epitafio, 1991; Orchestra and Soloist: Cantata, 1988; Chamber Orchestra: A Flor De Piel with 2 singers; Chamber Opera: El Paseo de Buster Keaton; Solo Instruments: Tres Bagatelas for Guitar, Tema Y Seis Diferencias for Piano; Chamber: Dialogantes for Flute and Viola, 1965; Piano pieces, many other works for various instruments, tape; Canción de Albada for orchestra, 1991. *Recordings:* Musica de Cámara, 1976; La Canción De Arte Puertorriquena with Margarita Castro, 1989; La Musica De Rafael Aponte Ledée. *Publications:* Tema y seis diferencias; Sombras, Zona de Carga y Descarga; La Ventana Abierta. *Honours:* ASCAP 1989, 1990, 1991. *Address:* c/o Conservatorio de Musica de Puerto Rico, Apdo 41227, Minillas Station, Santurce, 00940 Puerto Rico.

**APPEL, Andrew;** harpsichordist; b. 8 June 1951, New York, NY, USA. *Education:* Duke University, Juilliard School. *Career:* debut at Carnegie Recital Hall, 1977; solo recitals in Europe and USA; Director of Four Nations

Ensemble; Festival participation at Spoleto, Aston Magna; Teacher at Temple University, Juilliard, Princeton; Mostly Mozart; mem, American Musical Society; Early Music America; South Eastern Historical Keyboard Society. *Recordings:* Bach, Works for Harpsichord, 1983; Couperin, Works for Harpsichord, 1989; JB Bach-Bridge, 1987; Couperin, 1991. *Publications:* Gaspard Le Roux – Complete Works, 1989. *Honours:* 1st Prize, Erwin Bodkey Competition, 1977. *Address:* 39 Plaza Street, Brooklyn, NY 11217, USA.

**APPELGREN, Curt;** Singer (bass baritone); b. 1945, Sweden. *Career:* Began as a violinist and later made his debut as a singer at the Drottningholm Court Theatre as Dulcamara in L'Elisir d'amore; Sang Pogner in Götz Friedrich's production of Die Meistersinger at the Royal Opera in Stockholm; Other Swedish roles include Cimarosa's Maestro di Capella, Jokanaan in Salome and Leporello in Don Giovanni; Sang Oxenstierna in the premiere of Christina by Hans Gefors, 1986; Perugia Festival in Spontini's La Vestale; Sung at Glyndebourne as Rocco and Bottom, and in Peter Hall's productions of Fidelio and A Midsummer Night's Dream; Sang Bottom at the Hong Kong Festival and Rossini's Basilio at Glyndebourne; Appearances with the London Choral Society and the London Philharmonic Orchestra at the Festival Hall; Sang Johann in a revival of Vogler's Gustaf Adolf och Ebba Braha at Drottningholm, 1990; King Mark in Tristan und Isolde at the Festival Hall, London, 1993; Glyndebourne 1995, as Publio in La Clemenza di Tito; Oroveso in Norma at Stockholm, 1997. *Current Management:* Askonas Holt Ltd, Lonsdale Chambers, 27 Chancery Lane, London, WC2A 1PF, England. *Telephone:* (20) 7400-1700. *Fax:* (20) 7400-1799. *E-mail:* info@askonasholt.co.uk. *Website:* www.askonasholt.co.uk.

**ARAD, Atar;** violist; b. 1943, Israel. *Career:* member of the Cleveland Quartet, 1980–87; Regular tours of USA, Canada, Europe, Japan, South America and the Middle East; Faculty of Indiana University, Bloomington; Concerts in Paris, Lyon, London, Bonn, Prague, Brussels and Houston; Appeared at Salzburg, Edinburgh, Aspen, Mostly Mozart and Lucerne festivals; In addition to standard repertory performs works by John Harbison, Samuel Adler, Christopher Rouse, Toru Takemitsu and Solo Sonata for Viola by Atar Arad. *Recordings:* Repertoire from Mozart to Ravel; Recordings in collaboration with Cleveland Quartet, Emanuel Ax and Yo-Yo Ma. *Address:* 1657 Bellemeade Avenue, Bloomington, IN 47401, USA.

**ARAGALL GARRIGA, Giacomo Jaime;** Spanish singer (tenor); b. 6 June 1939, Barcelona; s. of Ramon Aragall and Paola Garriga; m. Luisa Aragall 1964; three s. *Education:* with Jaume Francisco Puig, Barcelona and Vladimiro Badiali, Milan. *Career:* winner int. competition, Busseto; debut at Teatro La Fenice de Venezia, Palermo, Metropolitan, New York 1968; has sung in more than 100 opera productions at Gran Teatre del Liceu. *Performances include:* El Amico Fritz, La Bohème (La Scala, Milan), Madame Butterfly, La Favorita, La Traviata, Faust, Tosca, etc. *Honours:* numerous prizes include Peseta de Oro and Medalla de Plata for appearing at 1992 Olympics, Barcelona, Medalla de Oro de Bellas Artes 1992, etc. *Current Management:* 2wise Artist Management, Ronda Sant Pere 29 2°- 3ª, 08010 Barcelona, Spain. *Telephone:* (93) 3041168; 630 021 281 (mobile). *E-mail:* miguelpons@2wiseartist.com. *Website:* www.2wiseartist.com.

**ARAIZA ANDRADE, Francisco José;** Mexican singer (tenor) and teacher; *Professor,* Stuttgart Musikhochschule; b. 4 Oct. 1950, Mexico City; s. of José Araiza and Guadalupe Andrade; m. 1st Vivian Jaffray (divorced); one s. one d.; m. 2nd Ethery Inasaridse; one s. one d. *Education:* Univ. of Mexico City and Nat. School of Music, Mexico City and Munich Acads of Music. *Career:* first engagement as lyric tenor in Karlsruhe, FRG 1974; debut as Ferrando in Così fan Tutte 1975; debut at Zurich Opera House with Almaviva 1976, perm. mem. 1978–; has become one of the leading tenors world-wide, performing at all the major opera houses, as well as recitals accompanied by piano or orchestra; Kammersänger, Vienna State Opera 1988; has participated in festivals of Salzburg (debut under von Karajan 1980), Hohenems, Bayreuth, Edinburgh, Pesaro, Verona, Aix-en-Provence, Orange, Garmisch; Prof., Stuttgart Musikhochscule 2003–. *Recordings include:* The Magic Flute, Faust, Das Lied von der Erde, Die schöne Müllerin, Don Giovanni, Idomeneo, Rossini's Messa di Gloria, 200 Jahre La Fenice, Die Winterreise, La Bohème, Berlioz' Requiem. *Films include:* videos: Don Giovanni, Die Schöpfung, Liederabend Tokio, Die Zauberflöte, Mozart Gala Verona 1 & 2. *Television includes:* Melodien aum Muttertag 2000, Gala der Europahilfe 2000, Kein Schöner Land 2000, Zauber der Musik mit André Rieu 2002, Sternstuden der Musik 2003. *Honours:* Deutscher Schallplattenpreis, Orphée d'Or, Mozart Medal, Univ. of Mexico City, Otello d'Oro, Goldener Merkur, Best Performer's Award, Munich 1996. *Current Management:* Kunstler Management, M Kursidem, Tal 28, 80331 Munich, Germany. *Telephone:* (89) 29161661 (office). *Fax:* (89) 29161667 (office). *E-mail:* faraiza@aol.com. *Website:* www.francisco -araiza.ch. *Current Management:* Opern-Agentur und Artists' Mgt Lewin, Tal 28, 80331 Munich, Germany. *Telephone:* (89) 29161661/62. *Fax:* (89) 29161667. *E-mail:* kursidem@opern-agentur.com. *Website:* www.opern -agentur.de.

**ARASON, Jon Runar;** singer (tenor); b. 29 March 1962, Iceland. *Education:* studied in Iceland with Magnus Johnsson, in Sweden with Harald Ek. *Career:* debut as Rodolfo, La Bohème, at Århus, Denmark, 1995; Sang roles of Pinkerton in Madama Butterfly and First Jew in Salome, Gothenburg Opera, 1996–97; Duke in Rigoletto, Oslo Opera, 1996–97; Pinkerton, 1997–98; Rodolfo, La Bohème; Worked at operas in both Reykjavík and Gothenburg as chorus member; Mozart's Magic Flute; Roderigo in Otello; Borsa, Rigoletto;

Bardolfo, Falstaff; Beppe, Donizetti's Rita; Swan, Orff's Carmina Burana; Tenor, Rossini's Stabat Mater. *Address:* c/o Oslo Arts Management AS, Den Gamle Logen, Grev Wedels Plass 2, 0151 Oslo 1, Norway.

**ARAYA, Graciela;** singer (mezzo-soprano); b. 16 May 1958, Santiago, Chile. *Education:* studied in Santiago and São Paulo. *Career:* debut, as Maddalena in Rigoletto, Santiago, 1981; Sang in South America until 1985; Sang in Germany in Weise von Liebe und Tod by Matthus, Deutsche Oper Berlin, 1985; and as Cherubino, Hansel, Cenerentola, Britten's Lucretia and Sesto in Handel's Giulio Cesare, 1989, Deutsche Oper am Rhein from 1986; Guest appearances as Massenet's Charlotte, Stuttgart; As Octavian and Rosina, Aachen; and as Carmen, Bremen; Season 1994–95: as Enriquetta in I Puritani, Vienna Staatsoper in premiere of Schnittke's Gesualdo; US debut as Carmen, Costa Mesa, 1995; Mignon by Thomas at the Vienna Volksoper, 1996; Season 1998 as Maddalena at Antwerp and Amastre in Serse, Geneva; Charlotte, Venice; Season 2000–01 as Countess Geschwitz in Lulu at Vienna, Clairon in Capriccio at Amsterdam, and Maddalena in Rigoletto at Antwerp. *Current Management:* Robert Gilder & Co., Enterprise House, 59–65 Upper Ground, London, SE1 9PQ, England. *Telephone:* (20) 7928-9008. *Fax:* (20) 7928-9755. *E-mail:* rgilder@robert-gilder.com. *Current Management:* Opera Vladarski, Döblinger Hauptstraße 57/18, 1190 Vienna, Austria. *Telephone:* (1) 3686960/61. *Fax:* (1) 3686962. *E-mail:* opera.vladarski@utanet.at.

**ARCHER, Neill;** Singer (tenor); b. 31 Aug. 1961, Northampton, England. *Education:* Studied at the University of East Anglia and the Brevard Music Centre in North Carolina. *Career:* Concert engagements with the London Philharmonic, BBC Symphony, English Baroque Soloists and the Junge Deutsche Philharmonie; Promenade Concerts debut in 1983 with Babylon The Great is Fallen, by Alexander Goehr; Festival Hall debut in Mozart's Requiem followed by Schoenberg's Moses und Aron under John Pritchard; Sang in Bach's St John Passion at the Accademia di Santa Cecilia in Rome, the St Matthew Passion in Stavanger and Schumann's Das Paradies und die Peri at Paris Opéra; Season 1987–88 with Tamino for Kent Opera, Ferrando for Scottish Opera and Don Ottavio with Welsh National Opera; Teatro Regio Turin in 1988 in Testi's Riccardo III; Returned to Italy as Andres in Wozzeck at Parma; Buxton Festival in 1988 as Ubaldo in Haydn's Armida followed by Carmina Burana at the Edinburgh Festival; Sang Ferrando in Così fan tutte for Opera Factory, also televised; Season 1989–90 included Almaviva in Oslo and for Opera North; Sang at English National Opera and Covent Garden in 1991 as Tamino and Jacquino; Sang Pylade in Iphigénie en Tauride at Basle in 1991; Season 1991–92 included Don Ottavio in New Zealand and Pelléas with WNO in a Pierre Boulez/Peter Stein presentation of Debussy's opera; Sang the Steersman in a new production of Der fliegende Holländer at Covent Garden in 1992; Season 1994 as Tamino for ENO and Almaviva at Garsington; Opera North 1996, as Achille in Gluck's Iphigenie en Aulide and 1998 as Jenik; Retired from stage 1999 and became Anglican priest.

**ARCHIBALD, Ann;** Singer (Soprano); b. 1967, Scotland. *Education:* Studied at the Royal Scottish Academy of Music and Drama with Elizabeth Izatt. *Career:* Concert debut with the City of Glasgow Philharmonic at Glasgow Royal Concert Hall; Concert repertory includes Carmina Burana, Handel and Bach Cantatas (Göttingen Festival), Beethoven's Ninth (with the Royal Scottish National Orchestra) and Mahler's 4th Symphony; Opera debut 1992, as Papagena with Scottish Opera; Further appearances as Second Niece in Peter Grimes, Mozart's Barbarina and Mrs Honor in Tom Jones by Philidor (Drottningholm Festival, 1995); Season 1995–96 as Musetta and the Sandman in Hansel and Gretel for Scottish Opera, and in Monteverdi's Orfeo for English National Opera; Sang the role of Fish in Broken Strings in a Param Vir double bill for Scottish Opera, 1998 and Exultate Jubilate with the Scottish Chamber Orchestra. *Recordings:* Carmina Burana with the Royal Philharmonic Orchestra. *Honours:* Numerous prizes with the Royal Scottish Academy. *Current Management:* Askonas Holt Ltd, Lonsdale Chambers, 27 Chancery Lane, London, WC2A 1PF, England. *Telephone:* (20) 7400-1700. *Fax:* (20) 7400-1799. *E-mail:* info@askonasholt.co.uk. *Website:* www.askonasholt.co.uk.

**ARDAM, Elzbieta;** singer (mezzo-soprano); b. 22 Sept. 1959, Kielczewo, Poland; m. Udo Gefe 1991; one s. *Education:* Conservatory of Poznan. *Career:* debut, Santuzza, 1983; Reigen, World Premier at Brussels, 1983, Orfeo, La Scala di Milan, Emelia in Otello, Chicago Symphony and New York Carnegie Hall; Brussels from 1987, as Gluck's Orpheus, Ottone in Poppea, Anna in Les Troyens and Donna Elvira; Frankfurt 1995 as Waltraute and Third Norn; Season 2000–01 as Gaea in Strauss's Daphne at Karlsruhe, Monteverdi's Ottone and Federica in Luisa Miller for Frankfurt Opera; mem, Teatr Wieki, Poznan, 1982–87. *Recordings:* Janáček Diary; Boesmans Reigen. *Honours:* Silver Medal, Geneva, 1981; Tchaikovsky Bronze Medal, Moscow, 1982; R Vinas Bronze Medal, Barcelona, 1984. *Address:* Gartenstrasse 38, 60596 Frankfurt, Germany.

**ARDEN-GRIFFITH, Paul,** GRSM, ARMCM; British singer (tenor); b. 18 Jan. 1952, Stockport, England. *Education:* Royal Manchester Coll. of Music, Cantica Voice Studio, London. *Career:* debut as Puck in Benjamin Britten's Midsummer Night's Dream, Sadler's Wells Theatre, London 1973; other performances include Franz Lehar's The Merry Widow, Henze's We Come to the River, Britten's Paul Bunyan, Carlisle Floyd's Of Mice and Men, Carl Orff's Carmina Burana, Prokofiev's The Duenna, Count Almaviva in Barber of Seville, Puccini's Il Tabarro, Rossini's Count Ory, La Traviata, Mozart's Die Zauberflöte, Phantom of the Opera, The Legendary Lanza, Babes in the Wood, Sunset Boulevard, That Old Minstrel Magic; concerts and cabarets include

London Dorchester Hotel, Hyde Park Intercontinental, Picadilly Theatre, The Belfry Club, Savoy Hotel, Tramshed, Theatre Royal Drury Lane, The Limelight Club, Royal Artillery House; world-wide concert tours, festival appearances, masterclasses and lecture tours of UK music colls and arts faculties; founder mem. Arts Council Opera 80, the United Kingdom Touring Co.; Pres. Barezzi Theatre School; recent performances include Strauss' Die Fledermaus with WNO 2001, Puccini's La Bohème with Somerset Opera 2003, Sondheim's Sweeney Todd at Covent Garden 2003–04; Strauss' Die Fledermaus with Opera Holland Park, London 2004. *Recordings:* The Song Is You 1986, Phantom Of The Opera (original cast recording) 1987, An Evening With Alan Jay Lerner 1987, Minstrel Magic (cast soundtrack) 1993, A Minstrel On Broadway 1994, Encore! 1995, The Classic Collection 1995, Accolade! 1996. *Honours:* Gwilym Gwalchmai Jones Scholarship for Singing 1974. *Current Management:* Ken Spencer Personal Management, 138 Sandy Hill Road, London, SE18 7BA, England. *Telephone:* (20) 8854-2558. *Fax:* (20) 8854-2558.

**ARDITTI, Irvine;** Violinist; b. 8 Feb. 1953, London, England; m. Jenny Whitelegg, 3 s. *Education:* Royal Academy of Music with Clarence Myerscough and Manoug Parikian, 1969–74. *Career:* Concert Violinist; Co-Founder, Leader, Arditti String Quartet with many 20th Century performances worldwide, 1974–; Co-leader, London Symphony Orchestra, 1976–80; Engagements, major festivals in cities throughout Europe including Aldeburgh, Bath, BBC Proms, Berlin, Budapest, Paris, Venice Biennale, Vienna, Warsaw and USA; Resident String Tutor, Darmstadt Ferienkurse for New Music, 1982–; BBC television Music in Camera, Radio 3 series of 7 recitals, 1987; All Schoenberg's quartets in single recital, Queen Elizabeth Hall, London, November, 1988; Solo appearances in Turin, Brussels, Berlin, Belgian and Turin Radio Symphony Orchestras, London Sinfonietta, Spectrum and Ensemble Cologne; World Premiere, solo works by various composers including J Dillon, J Harvey and Xenakis; With Arditti Quartet has given complete quartets of Berg, Webern and Schoenberg and numerous other composers; Promenade concert debut with United Kingdom premiere of L Francesconi's Rita Neurali in 1993. *Recordings:* Complete Kurtag Quartets, Lachenmann, Dutilleux, and Nono; Rihm, Harvey Quartets; La Lontanza for violin and tape. *Publications:* Premiere of New Work for Violin and Orchestra by Liebermann, 1994. *Honours:* Gold Medal, Worshipful Society of Musicians, 1994; Chamber Music Award, Royal Philharmonic Society. *Address:* c/o Lorraine Lyons, 12 Chatteris Avenue, Harold Hill, Romford, Essex RM3 8JX, England.

**ARDOVA, Asya;** pianist, publisher, musicologist, translator and music teacher; b. 11 Oct. 1972, St Petersburg, Russia. *Education:* Music College at St Petersburg Conservatoire, St Petersburg Pedagogical University. *Career:* debut with Shostakovich Preludes and Fugues, St Petersburg, 1996; Concerts in St Petersburg and elsewhere in Russia; Festivals include Musical Spring, St Petersburg, 1998–2000; Congress of Composers, 2000; International Children's Festival, St Petersburg, 2001. *Publications include:* Monographs on Arkhidimandritov, Firtich; Translation from Russian into English and publication of: Vivaldi 'The Seasons' (poems), J. S. Bach Six Flute Sonatas (preface and commentaries); S. Slonimsky 'The Visions of Ioann Grozny' (libretto and commentaries); B. Tischenko 'Letters of D. D. Shostakovich to B. Tischenko', 2000. *Honours:* Diploma of the St Petersburg Pedagogical University, 1999; Secretary of the Association of Modern Music (AMM). *Address:* Belgradskaya St 44-1-44, St Petersburg, Russia.

**ARENS, Rolf-Dieter;** pianist; b. 16 Feb. 1945, Zinnwald, Germany. *Education:* Leipzig Musikhochschule. *Career:* many appearances in Germany and elsewhere in Europe as soloist and chamber musician; soloist with the Berlin Symphony Orchestra, from 1986; teacher at the Leipzig Hochschule from 1970, Franz Liszt Hochschule, Weimar, 1976. *Honours:* Prizewinner at the Budapest International Competition, 1966, Bach International at Leipzig, 1968, Long-Thibaud Competition at Paris, 1971. *Address:* c/o Hochschule für Musik Franz Liszt, Platz der Demokratie 2–3, 5300 Weimar, Germany.

**AREVALO, Octavio;** Singer (tenor); b. 1963, Mexico City, Mexico. *Education:* Studied at the Verdi Conservatoire, Milan, 1984–85; Further study with Ernst Haefliger and James King in Munich. *Career:* Concert appearances in Switzerland, in Bach's Christmas Oratorio and Mozart's C Minor Mass; Stage debut as Paolino in Il Matrimonio Segreto at the Gärtnerplatz Theatre, Munich, 1989; Sang Tamino at Mexico City, 1990; Stadttheater Lucerne, as Mozart's Belmonte, Tamino and Don Ottavio, Nemorino, Rodolfo and Pinkerton, 1991–; Vienna Staatsoper debut as Nemorino, 1992; Season 1994–95 as Rinuccio in Gianni Schicchi at the Komische Oper Berlin, Ferrando (Così fan tutte) at Mexico City, Verdi's Fenton in Madrid and Polyceute in Donizetti's Les Martyrs at Nancy; Season 1996–97 in Le Roi Arthus by Chausson at the Bregenz Festival, Orombello in Beatrice di Tenda at the Deutsche Oper Berlin and Leicester in Maria Stuarda at the Herkulessahl, Munich; Further concert repertory includes Dvořák's Stabat Mater (in Zürich), the Verdi Requiem (Moscow) and Bruckner's Te Deum (Madrid, 1997). *Recordings include:* Rossini's Il Signor Bruschino and Semiramide. *Current Management:* Opéra et Concert, 7 rue de Clichy, 75009 Paris, France. *Telephone:* (1) 42961818. *Fax:* (1) 42961800. *E-mail:* agence@opera-concert.com. *Website:* www.opera-concert.com.

**ARGENTA, Nancy;** singer (soprano); b. 17 Jan. 1957, Nelson, BC, Canada. *Education:* Univ. of Western Ont., studied singing in Germany and with Peter Pears, Gerard Souzay, Vera Rozsa. *Career:* appearances at the Vienna and Schwetzingen Festivals with London Baroque; sang in Scarlatti's La Giuditta in Italy, Mozart Mass in C minor with the English Chamber Orchestra, Handel's Messiah and Giulio Cesare in Canada; concerts with the Songmakers' Almanac; opera engagements as Susanna with WNO, Haydn's L'Infedelà Delusa in Paris, Brussels and Cologne, Astreia in Handel's Tamerlano at the Opéra de Lyon, La Chasseuresse in Rameau's Hippolyte et Aricie and Purcell's King Arthur at Aix-en-Provence; sang the title role in L'Incoronazione di Poppea, on South Bank, London; Purcell's Dido in Utrecht, Paris, Beaune and Saintes; further concerts in the Schoenberg Reluctant Revolutionary series on South Bank and Cupid in Venus and Adonis by Blow at the 1989 Promenade Concerts; sang Vespina in Haydn's L'Infedelà Delusa, Antwerp 1990; Rossanne in the N American premiere of Floridante, Toronto 1990; sang Clärchen's songs in Beethoven's Egmont at the Festival Hall 1991; Mozart's Requiem at the 1991 Proms, conducted by Roger Norrington; debut in 1996 at the Salzburg, Flanders and Budapest Festivals, singing Euridice in Gluck's Orfeo ed Euridice with Ivan Fischer and the Budapest Festival Orchestra; also performed with Tafelmusik in Toronto, the Nat. Arts Centre Ottawa, the Scottish Chamber Orchestra, Ensemble Baroque de Limoges, the Orchestra of the Age of Enlightenment, Acad. of Ancient Music and at the Ansbach, Halle and Spitalfields Festivals; Mahler's 2nd Symphony at the Festival Hall 1997; Mozart's Exultate Jubilate and Haydn's Nelson Mass at the 1999 London Proms. *Recordings include:* Handel's Solomon and the Magnificat by Bach, Bach B Minor Mass, St John Passion and Christmas Oratorio, Monteverdi's Orfeo, Handel's Tamerlano, Barbarina in Le nozze di Figaro, Mozart's Requiem and Don Giovanni, Bach Solo Cantatas, Handel's Saul. *Current Management:* Askonas Holt Ltd, Lonsdale Chambers, 27 Chancery Lane, London, WC2A 1PF, England. *Telephone:* (20) 7400-1700 (office). *Fax:* (20) 7400-1799 (office). *E-mail:* info@askonasholt.co.uk (office). *Website:* www.askonasholt.co.uk (office). *Current Management:* Konzertagentur Erika Esslinger, Spittlerstrasse 6, 70190 Stuttgart, Germany. *Telephone:* (711) 283276. *Fax:* (711) 261421. *E-mail:* esslinger@konzertagentur.de. *Website:* www.konzertagentur.de.

**ARGENTO, Dominick,** BA, PhD; composer and teacher; b. 27 Oct. 1927, York, PA. *Education:* Peabody Conservatory of Music, Baltimore with Nicolas Nabokov and Hugo Weisgall, Florence Conservatory with Pietro Scarpini and Luigi Dallapiccola, Eastman School of Music with Bernard Rogers, Howard Hanson and Alan Hovhaness. *Career:* teacher of theory and composition, 1958–, Regents Professor, 1979–, University of Minnesota; European premiere of the Dream of Valentino at Kassel, 1999; Compositions include: Operas: The Boor, 1957, Christopher Sly, 1962–63, The Shoemaker's Holiday, 1967, The Voyage of Edgar Allan Poe, 1975–76, Casanova's Homecoming, 1980–84; The Aspern Papers, 1988; The Dream of Valentino, 1993; Monodramas: A Water Bird Talk, 1974; Ballets: The Resurrection Of Don Juan, 1955, Incidental music to plays; Orchestral: Ode To The West Wind, concerto for Soprano and Orchestra, 1956, Bravo Mozart!, 1969, In Praise Of Music, 1977, Le Tombeau d'Edgar Poe, 1985; Chamber: Divertimento for Piano and Strings, 1954; Songs About Spring for Soprano and Piano or Chamber Orchestra, 1954, The Revelation Of St John The Divine for Tenor, Men's Voices, Brass and Percussion, 1966, Letters From Composers for Tenor and Guitar, 1968, To Be Sung Upon The Water, song cycle for High Voice, Clarinet and Piano, 1972, From The Diary Of Virginia Woolf, song cycle for Mezzo-Soprano and Piano, 1974, I Hate And I Love, song cycle for Chorus and Percussion, 1981, Te Deum for Chorus and Orchestra, 1987; Spirituals and Swedish Chorales, 1994; Walden Pond for chorus, 3 cellos and harp, 1996; A Few Words About Chekhov for mezzo-soprano, baritone and piano, 1996; mem, Institute of Arts and Letters, 1980. *Honours:* Fulbright Fellowship, 1951–52; Guggenheim Fellowships, 1957, 1964; Pulitzer Prize in Music, 1975; numerous commissions; honorary doctorates. *Address:* c/o Boosey & Hawkes Ltd, 295 Regent Street, London W1R 8JH, England.

**ARGERICH, Martha;** Argentine pianist; b. 5 June 1941, Buenos Aires. *Education:* studied with V. Scaramuzzo, Friedrich Gulda, Nikita Magaloff, Madeleine Lipatti and Arturo Benedetto Michaelangeli. *Career:* debut Buenos Aires 1949; London debut 1964; soloist with world's leading orchestras; with Chamber Orchestra of Europe, Barbican Hall, London 1991; Schumann Concerto, BBC London Proms 2000. *Honours:* Officier, Ordre des Arts et des Lettres 1996, Accademica di Santa Cecilia di Roma 1997; First Prize Busoni Contest and Geneva Int. Music Competition 1957, Int. Chopin Competition, Warsaw 1965, Praemium Imperiale Award 2005. *Current Management:* Jacques Thelen Agence Artistique, 15 Avenue Montaigne, 75008 Paris, France.

**ARGIRIS, Spiros;** conductor; b. 24 Aug. 1948, Athens, Greece. *Education:* studied piano with Alfons Kontarsky, conducting with Hans Swarowsky; studied with Nadia Boulanger in Paris. *Career:* conducted at opera houses in Berlin, Hamburg, Cologne and elsewhere in Germany; Has led concerts at the Venice Biennale and at the Maggio Musicale, Florence; Musical Director of the Festival of Two Worlds, Spoleto-Charleston, 1986; Conducted Salome in 1989; Musical Director of the Trieste Opera, 1987, leading The Queen of Spades in 1988 and Il Barbiere di Siviglia and Parsifal in 1989; Conducted Elektra at the Teatro Nuovo, Spoleto, 1990; Parsifal and Le nozze di Figaro at Charleston; Modern repertoire includes Henze's El Rey de Harlem, premiere 1980, and Hans Jurgen von Bose's Die Nacht aus Blei, premiere 1981; Appointed Musical Director of the Opera and Orchestre Philharmonique at Nice, 1988. *Address:* Orchestre Philharmonique de Nice, Opera de Nice, Rue Saint Francois de Paule, 06300 Nice, France.

**ARHO, Anneli;** composer; b. 12 April 1951, Helsinki, Finland. *Education:* Sibelius Academy, Helsinki, studied with Klaus Huber and Brian Ferneyhough at Freiburg. *Career:* Teacher at the Sibelius Academy from 1979. *Compositions:* Minos for harpsichord, 1978; Answer for mezzo, horn and string quartet, 1978; Once upon a Time for wind quintet, 1979; Par comparison for 3 cellos, 1981; Les temps emboîtés for 3 cellos, 1987. *Address:* c/o Sibelius Academy of Music, Töölönkatu 28, 00260 Helsinki, Finland.

**ARISTO, Giorgio;** singer (tenor); b. 28 Dec. 1950, New York, NY, USA. *Education:* Manhattan School of Music, studied in Milan and Zürich. *Career:* sang at Passau, 1979–81, as the Duke in Rigoletto, Rodolfo in La Bohème and Rossini's Count Almaviva; Engaged in Essen, 1981–83, Hannover, 1983–; Guest appearances in Düsseldorf as Don José, Vienna as Massenet's Werther, Munich in The Bartered Bride and Copenhagen as Cavaradossi; Season 1988–89 as Calaf in Nantes and Andrea Chénier in Toulon and Liège; Other roles include Alfredo and Turiddu; Munich Opera from 1992, as Cavaradossi and Manrico; Many concert appearances. *Address:* c/o Bayerische Staatsoper, Max-Joseph-Platz, 80539 Munich, Germany.

**ARKADIEV, Mikhail;** pianist and composer; b. 1958, Moscow, Russia. *Education:* Tchaikovsky Conservatoire, Moscow, Gnessin Institute. *Career:* solo performances throughout Russia and recital accompanist to baritone Dmitri Hvorostovsky, 1990–; tours to Europe, America, East Asia and the Pacific Music Festival; Solo debut in Berlin, 1990; Chair of the Piano Department at the Academy of Choral Art in Moscow. *Compositions include:* Mass for Choir And Organ; Vocal and chamber works. *Publications include:* The Temporal Structures of New European Music; An Essay in Phenomenological Study, 1992.

**ARKHIPOVA, Irina Konstantinovna;** Russian singer (mezzo-soprano); b. 2 Jan. 1925, Moscow; d. of Vetoschkin Konstantin and Galda Evdokija; m. Piavkò Vladislav; one s. *Career:* attended vocal classes with Nadezda Malysheva at Inst. of Architecture, Moscow, from which graduated, 1948; entered Moscow Conservatoire 1959 (pupil of L. Savransky); stage début as soloist (Lubasha) of Tsar's Bridge with Sverdlovsk Opera and Carmen with Bolshoi Theatre, 1956, leading soloist –1958; mem. CPSU 1963–91; mem. USSR Supreme Soviet 1962–66; People's Deputy 1989–91; Prof. at Moscow Conservatoire 1982–; Pres. Int. Union of Musicians, Irina Arkhipova Foundation; opera performances and song recitals since 1956 at Milan, Vienna, Paris, London and in USA; performs Russian, French and Italian repertoire, roles include Carmen, Amneris in Aida, Hélène in War and Peace, Eboli in Don Carlos; mem. Acad. of Creative Endeavours 1991, Int. Acad. of Sciences 1994. *Publications:* My Muses 1992, Music of Life 1997. *Honours:* People's Artist of USSR 1966; Lenin Prize 1978; Hero of Socialist Labour 1984, People's Artist of Kyrgyzstan 1993, State Prize 1997. *Address:* Bryusov per. 2/14, Apt. 27, 103009 Moscow, Russia. *Telephone:* (095) 229-60-29 (office); (095) 229-43-07 (home). *Website:* members.xoom.com/almatadema/Singers/arkhipova.html.

**ARMENGUARD, Jean-Pierre;** pianist; b. 17 June 1943, Clermont-Ferrand, France. *Education:* Ecole Normale, Sorbonne, Univ. of Paris, and studied with Jacques Février. *Career:* has performed throughout France and elsewhere in Europe in a wide repertory, including 20th century music; founded the Sainte-Baume music festival and co-founded (1970) a trio with clarinet and piano; French cultural ambassador to Sweden (1982–85) and to Greece (1985–88). *Publications include:* History of Music from the time of Beethoven.

**ARMILATO, Fabio;** Singer (Tenor); b. 1963, Genoa, Italy. *Education:* Paganini Conservatoire and the Academia Virgiliana, Mantua. *Career:* Debut: Teatro Pergolesi di Jesi, 1986, as Licinio in La Vestale; Appearances at La Scala and throughout Italy as Faust in Mefistofele, Alfredo, Edgardo, Turiddu, Pinkerton and Gabriele Adorno; Vlaamse Opera Antwerp as Don Carlos, Rodolfo, Des Grieux and Cavaradossi; North American debut at the New York City Opera as Don José; Metropolitan Opera as Radames, Gabriele, Turiddu, Manrico and Loris in Fedora; San Francisco Opera from 1994, as Manrico and Radames, (1997); Further engagements with the Houston Opera as Pinkerton, at Pittsburgh as Don José, Buenos Aires as Andrea Chénier and in Paris as Cavaradossi (also at Antwerp, 1996); Sang Radames at Verona and the New York Met, Faust at Buenos Aires, 1999; Season 2000–01 as Puccini's Ramirez at Nice, Andrea Chénier for the Vienna Staatsoper (returned as Don Carlos), and as Manrico for Washington Opera. *Honours:* Winner, 1986 Tito Schipa Competition. *Current Management:* Opéra et Concert, 7 rue de Clichy, 75009 Paris, France. *Telephone:* 1-42-96-18-18. *Fax:* 1-42-96-18-00. *E-mail:* agence@opera-concert.com. *Website:* www.opera-concert.com. *Current Management:* Atelier Musicale, Via Caselle 76, San Lazzaro di Savena 40068, Italy. *Telephone:* (51) 19984444. *Fax:* (51) 19984420. *E-mail:* info@ateliermusicale.com. *Website:* www.ateliermusicale.com.

**ARMITSTEAD, Melanie;** Singer (Soprano); b. 1957, England. *Education:* Studied at Guildhall School of Music. *Career:* Debut: Frasquita and Micaela in Carmen for Scottish Opera; Appearances with Kent Opera, 1987–, as Venus in Rameau's Pygmalion, First Lady in The Magic Flute, and Minerva in The Return of Ulysses; Scottish Opera debut as Titania in Eugene Onegin in 1988 returning as Fiordigili; English National Opera and Opera North debuts in 1990 as Nicoletta in The Love for Three Oranges and Mélisande in Ariane et Barbe-Bleue; Returned to Leeds as Xenia in Boris Godunov in 1992; Created the Niece in Fenelon's Le Chevalier Imaginaire, Théâtre du Châtelet, Paris, 1992; Concert performances with Liverpool Philharmonic, the Halle and Royal Philharmonic; Season 1989–90 included Vivaldi's Gloria with English

Chamber Orchestra, Messiah with Tokyo Philharmonic, St John Passion in Netherlands, and Bach's Magnificat at the Barbican Hall; Recitalist at the Wigmore Hall (Debut 1987), Purcell Room and Queen Elizabeth Hall; Appearances with the pianist Julian Drake and oboist Nicholas Daniel. *Current Management:* Robert Gilder & Company, 91 Great Russell Street, London WC1B 3PS, England. *Telephone:* (20) 7580-7758. *E-mail:* rgilder@robert-gilder.com. *Address:* c/o Opera North, The Grand Theatre, 46 New Briggate, Leeds, Yorkshire LS1 6NU, England.

**ARMSTRONG, Craig;** British composer; b. 1959, Shettleston, Scotland. *Education:* Royal Acad. of Music. *Career:* resident student composer, London Contemporary Dance Theatre 1980; music and dance specialist, Strathclyde Council 1982; founder of performance music, theatre and dance group 1988; fmr mem., Hipsway, The Big Dish, The Kindness of Strangers, Texas; worked with Björk, Evan Dando, Massive Attack, Madonna, McAlmont, Luciano Pavarotti, Tina Turner, U2. *Compositions for film:* Daddy's Gone 1994, Close 1995, Fridge 1995, A Good Day for the Bad Guys 1995, Romeo and Juliet (Ivor Novello Award, Anthony Asquith Award, BAFTA Award) 1996, Orphans 1997, Best Laid Plans 1998, Plunkett & Macleane 1998, One Day in September (documentary) 1999, The Bone Collector (ASCAP Award) 1999, Moulin Rouge! (Golden Globe for Best Original Music 2001, IF Award 2001) 2000, Kiss of the Dragon 2001, The Quiet American 2002, Love Actually 2003, The Clearing 2004, Ray 2004, Fever Pitch 2005, Must Love Dogs 2005; contrib. music to Mission Impossible, Goldeneye, Batman Forever. *Compositions for television:* Encounters (BBC2) 1991, Tartan Shorts (STV) 1994, London Bridge (Carlton) 1995. *Other compositions:* 7 Stations 1985, String Quartet 1988, Crow 1988, Losing Alec 1988 score to Macbeth (Tron Theatre) 1993, score to The Broken Heart (RSC, Barbican) 1994, If Time Must Pass 1999, When Morning Turns To Light 2000, My Grandmother's Love Letters 2000, Visconti 2001. *Recordings include:* albums: Hope (with others) 1993, The Space Between Us 1998, As If To Nothing 2002, Piano Works 2004. *Honours:* GLAA Young Jazz Musician of the Year 1980, World Soundtrack Award for Discovery of the Year 2001, American Film Inst. Award for Composer of the Year 2001. *Current Management:* c/o ie:music Ltd, Greenwood House, 4/7 Salisbury Court, London, EC4 8BT, England. *E-mail:* info@iemusic.co.uk. *Website:* www.iemusic.co.uk; www.craigarmstrong.com.

**ARMSTRONG, Karan;** Singer (soprano); b. 14 Dec. 1941, Horne, Montana, USA; m. Götz Friedrich (died 2000). *Education:* Studied in Minnesota with Thelma Halverson, California with Lotte Lehmann and Fritz Zweig. *Career:* Debut: Metropolitan Opera in 1969 in Hansel and Gretel; Appearances with opera companies in Houston, Seattle, Cincinnati and Portland; Roles include Donizetti's Norina, Puccini's Butterfly, Verdi's Alice Ford and Wagner's Eva; Sang at New York City Opera, 1975–78 as Minnie, Tosca, Concepcion and the Queen of Shemakha; European debut at Strasbourg in 1976 as Salomé; Guest appearances in Munich, Frankfurt, Geneva, Oslo and Vienna; Bayreuth debut in 1979 as Elsa; World premiere performances in Von Einem's Jesu Hochzeit, Vienna in 1980, Sinopoli's Lou Salomé at Munich in 1981 and Berio's Un Re in Ascolto at Salzburg in 1984; Covent Garden in 1981 as Lulu in the first British performance of the 3 act version of Berg's opera; Other roles include Berg's Marie and the Woman in Schoenberg's Erwartung; Sang Katerina Izmailova at Berlin in 1988 and Emilia Marty and Regina in Mathis der Maler, 1990; Wiesbaden Festival in 1989 as Katya Kabanova, Alice Ford at Los Angeles in 1990 followed by Leonore; Sang Wagner's Sieglinde and Gutrune at Covent Garden in 1991, Janáček's Emilia Marty at Los Angeles in 1992, and Megara in the premiere of Desdemona und Ihre Schwestern by Siegfried Matthus at Schwetzingen Festival in 1992; Concert appearances in the Four Last Songs of Strauss, Zemlinsky's Lyric Symphony and the Bruchstücke from Wozzeck; Sang Schoenberg's Woman at the Deutsche Oper Berlin, 1994; Jocasta in Enescu's Oedipe at Berlin, 1996; Floyd's Susannah in 1997; Sang Brünnhilde in Götterdämmerung at Helsinki, 1998; Season 2000-01 as the Marschallin and Wagner's Venus at the Deutsche Oper Berlin, Weill's Begbick at Genoa. *Recordings include:* Elsa in Lohengrin from Bayreuth. *Current Management:* Boris Orlob Management, Jägerstrasse 70, 10117 Berlin, Germany. *Telephone:* (30) 20450839. *Fax:* (30) 20450849. *E-mail:* info@orlob.net. *Website:* www.orlob.net. *Current Management:* Aria's di Novella Partacini & Alexandra Plaickner, Via Josef Weingartner 4, 39022 Lagundo, Italy. *Telephone:* (473) 200200. *Fax:* (473) 222424. *E-mail:* info@arias.it. *Website:* www.arias.it.

**ARMSTRONG, Sir Richard,** Kt, CBE; British conductor; b. 1 July 1943, Leicester, England. *Education:* Univ. of Cambridge. *Career:* mem. of music staff, Royal Opera, Covent Garden 1966–68; Music Dir, WNO 1973–86; Covent Garden debut in 1982 with Billy Budd, returning for Andrea Chénier, Un Ballo in Maschera and Don Carlos 1989; conducted Elektra, Die Frau ohne Schatten, Wozzeck, operas by Janáček, The Midsummer Marriage and Peter Grimes; led the WNO in The Ring at Covent Garden 1986; guest engagements with Netherlands Opera in Elektra, Komische Oper Berlin in Peter Grimes, Frankfurt in Der fliegende Holländer, with new productions of Elektra and Ariadne auf Naxos and at Geneva in Don Carlos; conducted the premiere of John Metcalf's Tornrak for WNO 1990, followed by Otello and House of the Dead; Music Dir, Scottish Opera 1993–2005 (adviser 2005–07); conducted Moses und Aron and La Voix Humaine at the 1992 Edinburgh Festival, Werther at Toulouse 1997; British stage premiere of Magic Fountain by Delius, Scottish Opera 1999; new production of Parsifal 2000; Wagner's Ring Cycle 2003. *Honours:* Royal Philharmonic Soc. opera award 2004. *Current Management:* Ingpen & Williams Ltd, 7 St George's Court, 131 Putney Bridge

Road, London, SW15 2PA, England. *Telephone:* (20) 8874-3222. *Fax:* (20) 8877-3113.

**ARMSTRONG, Sheila Ann,** FRAM; British opera and concert singer (soprano); b. 13 Aug. 1942, Ashington, England; d. of William R. Armstrong and Janet Armstrong; m. David E. Cooper 1980 (divorced 1999). *Education:* Hirst Park Girls' School, Ashington, Northumberland and Royal Acad. of Music. *Career:* sang Despina in Così fan tutte at Sadler's Wells 1965, Belinda in Dido and Aeneas, Glyndebourne 1966, Mozart's Pamina and Zerlina and Fiorila in Rossini's Il Turco in Italia, Glyndebourne; sang in the premiere of John McCabe's Notturni ed Alba at Three Choirs Festival 1970; New York debut with New York Philharmonic 1971; sang with Los Angeles Philharmonic under Mehta; Covent Garden debut as Marzelline in Fidelio 1969; sang Donizetti's Norina and Mozart's Donna Elvira for Scottish Nat. Opera; concert engagements included Messiah at the Concertgebouw, tour of the Far East with the Bach Choir, Britten's Spring Symphony, Strauss' Four Last Songs with Royal Philharmonic, Elgar's Oratorios and the Sea Symphony by Vaughan Williams; Pres. Kathleen Ferrier Soc., trustee Kathleen Ferrier Award; Fellow Hatfield Coll., Univ. of Durham 1992; mem. Royal Philharmonic Soc. *Recordings include:* Samson, Dido and Aeneas, Mozart's Requiem, Carmina Burana, Elgar's Apostles, The Pilgrim's Progress, Cantatas by Bach, Haydn's Stabat Mater, Beethoven's Ninth Symphony, Mahler's 2nd and 4th. *Honours:* Hon. MA (Newcastle); Hon. DMus (Durham) 1991; Mozart Prize 1965, Kathleen Ferrier Memorial Award 1965. *Address:* Harvesters, Tilford Road, Hindhead, Surrey, GU26 6SQ, England.

**ARNAULD, Serge;** Swiss composer and scholar; b. 16 Nov. 1944, Geneva; m. Christiane Wirz 1965; three s. one d. *Education:* Maîtrise, Philosophy with Professor Vladimir Jankélévitch, Sorbonne, Paris, 1973; Studied composition with Darius Milhaud, Marcel Landowski, Adrienne Clostre and Louis Saguer. *Career:* Radio: Swiss selection for Paul Gilson Prize and Prix Italia with Pugilat, 1979, and mini-opera, Masculin-Singulier, 1987; Films: Jean-Luc Godard's Sauve qui Peut (La Vie) et Passion, participated as actor; Musicology: Les Manuscrits de Carpentras, 1979, Scènes de la Vie Judéo-Comtadine, 1980; Founder and Artistic Director for International Music Festival from the Academies of Rome, 1984–88; Collaborateur à la dramaturgie au Grand Théâtre de Genève, 1989–2001; mem. Institut Suisse, Rome 1983. *Compositions:* Le jeu de la Tarasque, ballet-pantomime, 1985; L'Esprit de Genève, directed by Jean-Louis Martinoty, 1986, to commemorate the 450th anniversary of the Reformation in Geneva; Opéra sans le sou: Le double et sa doublure, cabaret songs (with Louis Saguer, 1990); Guillaume Tell, mythe jacobin, to commemorate the bicentenary of the French Revolution and for the 700th anniversary of the Swiss Confederation, 1991; 3 Lettres, ballet dissocié, 1993; Signes des Temps, 1997; Opéra Imaginaire (La Vie à deux), 1999; Dramaturge du spectacle musical, Le Petit Prince, music by Richard Cocciante, performed at Casino de Paris, Oct 2002. *Recordings:* Cantates Ambivalentes; Requiem de Pâques; L'Amour. *Publications:* La Cotonalité and Le Système Hexacordal, Paris, 1968–69; Le Chalet dans tous ses états (la construction de l'imaginaire helvétique), 1999–2000; Genève-Oser paraître: Mentalités, goûts et moeurs du regard du théâtre 2004. *Address:* 6 rue de la Mairie, 1207 Geneva, Switzerland.

**ARNELL, Richard Anthony Sayer;** British composer and conductor; b. 15 Sept. 1917, London; s. of the late Richard Sayer Arnell and Helène Marie Scherf; m. Joan Heycock 1992; three d. from previous marriages. *Education:* Mall School, University Coll. School and Royal Coll. of Music. *Career:* Music consultant, BBC North American Service 1943–46; Lecturer, Trinity Coll. of Music, London 1948–87; Lecturer, Royal Ballet School 1958–59; Ed. 'The Composer' 1961–64; Visiting Lecturer (Fulbright exchange), Bowdoin Coll., Maine, USA 1967–68; Visiting Prof., Hofstra Univ., NY 1968–70; Music Dir and mem. Bd London Int. Film School 1975–89; Chair. Composers' Guild of GB 1974–75, 1977–79 (Vice-Pres. 1992–), Young Musicians' Symphony Orch. Soc. 1973–75, 1977–79, Saxmundham Music and Arts 1993–96 (Pres. 1996–); Music Dir Ram Filming Ltd 1980–91; Dir A plus A Ltd 1984–89; Chair. London Int. Film School Trust 1981–87; Founder, Chair. Friends of London Int. Film School 1982–87, Vice-Pres. 1987–; Founder, Chair. Friends of Trinity Coll. of Music Jr Dept 1986–87, Vice-Pres. 1987–; Founder, Chair. Tadcaster Civic Soc. Music and Arts 1988–91; Hon. Fellow, Trinity Coll. of Music, London 1950–. *Compositions include:* opera: Love in Transit 1953, Moonflowers 1958, Boudicca, Queen of East England 2002; ballet scores: Punch and the Child 1947, Harlequin in April 1951, the Great Detective 1953, The Angels 1957, Giselle (re-orchestrated) 1965; film scores: The Land 1941, The Third Secret 1963, The Visit 1964, The Man Outside 1966, Topsail Schooner 1966, Bequest for a Village 1969, Second Best 1972, Stained Glass 1973, Wires Over the Border 1974, Black Panther 1977, Antagonist 1980, Dilemma 1981, Toulouse Lautrec 1984, Light of the World 1988; other works: Symphonic Portrait, Lord Byron, for Sir Thomas Beecham 1953, Landscapes and Figures 1956, Petrified Princess, puppet operetta for BBC 1959; Robert Flaherty, Impression for Radio Eireann 1960, Musica Pacifica for Edward Benjamin 1963, Festival Flourish for Salvation Army 1965, Piano Concerto for Royal Philharmonic Orchestra (RPO) 1967, Overture, Food of Love, for Portland Symphony Orchestra 1968, My Ladye Greene Sleeves, for Hofstra Univ. 1968, Nocturne 1968, I Think of All Soft Limbs 1971, Astronaut One 1973, Life Boat Voluntary, for Royal Nat. Lifeboat Inst. 1974, Call, for London Philharmonic Orchestra 1980, RVW's Almanac 1984, Six Lawrence Poems 1985, Ode to Beecham, for RPO 1986, Con Amore for Cantamus Girls Choir 1988, Xanadu for Harlow Choral Soc. 1993, Symphonic Statement for Nelson

Mandela 1999, "B" Queen Boudicca 2002; also six symphonies, two violin concertos, harpsichord concerto, two piano concertos, six string quartets, two quintets, organ works, music for string orchestra, wind ensembles, brass ensembles, song cycles and electronic music. *Plays:* libretti: Moonflowers 1958, The Madrigal Murders 1995. *Honours:* Composer of the Year 1966 (Music Teachers' Asscn Award); Tadcaster Town Council Merit Award 1991. *Address:* Benhall Lodge, Benhall, Suffolk, IP17 1JD, England. *Telephone:* (1728) 602014. *Fax:* (1728) 603256 (office).

**ARNESTAD, Finn Oluf Bjerke;** Composer and Music Critic; b. 23 Sept. 1915, Oslo, Norway. *Education:* Studied violin and piano at Oslo, composition with Bjarne Brustad, African and Oriental Folk Music in Paris, 1952. *Career:* Music Critic in Oslo. *Compositions:* Orchestral: Constellation, 1948, Conversation for Piano and Orchestra, 1950, Meditation, 1952, INRI, 2 suites from a symphonic mystery play, 1952–55, Violin Concerto, 1957, Aria Appassionata, 1962, Cavatina Cambiata, 1965, Overture, 1970, Toccata, 1972, Arabesque, 1975, Piano Concerto, 1976, Mouvement Concertant for Double Bass and Orchestra, 1978; Chamber: String Quartet, 1947, Sextet for Flute, Clarinet, Bassoon, Violin, Cello and Piano, 1959, Quintet for Flute and Strings, 1962, Suite In Old Dance Rhythms for Flute, Oboe, Harpsichord and Strings, 1966, Trombone Sonata, 1971, Solo Violin Sonata, 1980, Solo Double Bass Sonata, 1980, Piano Music; Several vocal works.

**ARNET, Marie;** Singer (soprano); b. 1970, Solna, Sweden. *Education:* Royal Academies, Stockholm and London; London Opera Studio. *Career:* Anne Trulove, in The Rake's Progress and Mozart's Sandrina and Barbarina for RAM; Adelaide in Handel's Lotario for the London Handel Society; Susanna for Clonter Opera, Rossini's Berta for British Youth Opera, and in Burning Mirrors, for ENO Studio; Recitals and Oratorios in Sweden, Qatar, Brussels, Aix-en-Provence and Sicily; Barbarina in Le nozze di Figaro at the Glyndebourne Festival 2001; Studies with Alison Pearce at the National Opera Studio; Concert repertoire includes Bach's St John Passion, Mahler's Symphony no. 2 and 4, Brahms, Fauré and Mozart Requiems, Rossini's Petite Messe Solonelle, Pergolesi's Stabat Mater, Haydn's Nelson Mass and The Creation, Bruckner's Te Deum and television appearances in Madrid in performances of Child of Our Time, Berlioz's L'enfance du Christ at the Three Choirs Festival and Mozart's Requiem with Paul McCreesh and the Gabrieli Consort; Engagements include Barbarina in Le Nozze di Figaro at Glyndebourne, Diana in Iphigénie en Aulide at Glyndebourne, Sophie in Der Rosenkavalier at Opera North (debut) and Pamina in Die Zauberflöte for Scottish Opera; Debut as Ilia in Idomeneo at the Glyndebourne Festival under Sir Simon Rattle. *Current Management:* Hazard Chase, 25 City Road, Cambridge CB1 1DP, England. *Telephone:* (1223) 312400. *Fax:* (1223) 460827. *Website:* www.hazardchase.co.uk. *Address:* c/o National Opera Studio, Morley College, 61 Westminster Bridge Road, London, SE1 7XT, England.

**ARNOLD, David Charles;** American opera and concert singer (baritone); b. 1949, Atlanta, GA. *Career:* debut, Metropolitan Opera as Enrico in Lucia; ENO as Escamillo in Carmen; New York City Opera as Zurga in Les Pêcheurs de Perles; Escamillo in Carmen, Komische Oper Berlin; performances of many world premieres, including John Harbison's Full Moon in March and his Winter's Tale, David Diamond's Ninth Symphony for Baritone and Orchestra, Leonard Bernstein conducting at Carnegie Hall, Charles Fussell's Specimen Days, James Ynaut's Such Was the War; two guest appearances at the White House singing Berlioz's L'Enfance du Christ and performance of American song repertoire; performances of Amonasro in Aida with Opera Company of Boston, L'Opéra de Montréal and Opera Omaha and Le nozze di Figaro with L'Opéra de Québec; performances with most leading orchestras, including The Boston Symphony for six seasons, St Louis Symphony, Atlanta Symphony, American Symphony Orchestra, San Francisco Symphony, Chicago Symphony, Buffalo Philharmonic, Singapore Symphony Orchestra, The Spoleto Festivals, Philadelphia Orchestra and the Israel Philharmonic. *Recordings:* Schoenberg's Gurrelieder, Boston Symphony; Harbison's Full Moon in March; Judith Lang's Zaimont's Magic World; Mendelssohn's Walpurgisnacht; Beethoven's 9th Symphony; Mozart's Requiem; Haydn's Lord Nelson Mass; Cherubini's Médée; Elijah; Bach's St Matthew Passion; Scott McLean's Scripture Songs; Moravec's Songs of Love and War. *Current Management:* William Knight, Grant House, 309 Wood Street, Burlington, NJ 08016, USA.

**ARNOLD, Sir Malcolm Henry,** Kt, CBE, FRCM, FRNCM; British composer and musician; b. 21 Oct. 1921, Northampton; s. of William Arnold and Annie Arnold; m. 1st Sheila Nicholson 1942; one s. one d.; m. 2nd Isobel Gray 1963 (died 1992); one s. *Education:* Royal Coll. of Music, London. *Career:* Prin. Trumpet, London Philharmonic Orchestra 1942–44 and 1946–48; served army 1944–46; full-time composer and conductor 1948–; Hon. mem. Royal Northern Coll. of Music 1997; Hon. RAM 1983; Bard of the Cornish Gorsedd 1969; Freeman City of London 1950. *Works include:* films: more than 100 film scores including St Trinians series, Hobson's Choice, Whistle down the Wind, Heroes of Telemark; symphonies: No. 1 1949, No. 2 1953, No. 3 1957, No. 4 1960, No. 5 1961, No. 6 1967, No. 7 1973, No. 8 1978, No. 9 1986, Symphony for Brass Instruments 1979; overtures: Beckus the Dandipratt 1943, Tam O'Shanter 1955, Peterloo 1967; other compositions: 18 concertos, 5 ballets, 2 one-act operas, 2 string quartets, 2 brass quintets and vocal, choral and chamber music. *Film:* Malcolm Arnold: Journey into the Unknown (dir Tony Palmer) 2004. *Honours:* Hon. Freeman Borough of Northampton 1989; Hon. DMus (Exeter) 1969, (Durham) 1982, (Leicester) 1984, (Trinity Coll. London) 1991; Dr hc (Miami, Ohio) 1990; Ivor Novello Award for music for Inn of Sixth

Happiness 1952, Oscar for music for film Bridge on the River Kwai 1957, Ivor Novello Award for Outstanding Services to British Music 1986, Wavendon All Music Composer of the Year 1987, BAFTA Fellowship 2001, Inc. Soc. of Musicians, Distinguished Musician Award 2004. *Address:* Malcolm Arnold Society, 6 Walton Street, Barnsley, South Yorkshire (office); Music Unites, 26 Springfields, Attleborough, Norfolk, NR17 2PA, England. *Telephone:* (1226) 284116 (Society) (office); (1953) 455420 (Music Unites). *Fax:* (1953) 455420 (Music Unites). *E-mail:* musicunites@btopenworld.com. *Website:* www.malcolmarnold.co.uk.

**ARONICA, Roberto;** Singer (Tenor); b. 1968, Italy. *Education:* Studied with Carlo Bergonzi. *Career:* Appearances as Rodolfo, Turin, 1992; As Donizetti's Edgardo at Macerata as Alfredo, at Treviso, 1995; Guest engagements as the Duke of Mantua, Santiago, 1992; As Alfredo, Welsh National Opera; As Rodolfo and Alfredo, San Francisco, 1993 and 1995; Further appearances as Rodolfo at La Scala, 1996; As Rodolfo, Opéra Bastille, Paris and Tel-Aviv, 1998; Season 2000–01 as Alfredo at the New York Met and the Duke of Mantua at Chicago. *Current Management:* Iberkonzert, C/ Rodríguez Arias 23 - 6° - Dt.10, 48011 Bilbao, Spain. *Telephone:* (94) 4104746. *Fax:* (94) 4218582. *Website:* www.iberkonzert.com/artistas.html. *Current Management:* Columbia Artists Management, 1790 Broadway, New York NY 10019-1412, USA. *Telephone:* (212) 841-9500. *Fax:* (212) 841-9744. . *Website:* www.cami.com. *Address:* c/o San Francisco Opera, Van Ness Avenue, San Francisco, CA 94102, USA.

**ARONOFF, Josef,** MBC, AGSM, LRAM; violinist, violist and conductor; b. 13 June 1932, Budapest, Hungary; m. Astrid Gray; three s. one d. *Education:* Franz Liszt Academy of Music, Budapest, Guildhall School of Music, London. *Career:* radio and television broadcasts, Hungary, Austria, the United Kingdom, Portugal, France, Germany, USA, Hong Kong, Australia; Professor, Royal Manchester College of Music, England, 1965–70; Head of String Department, Queensland Conservatorium of Music, Australia, 1970–75; Musical Director, Conservatorium Chamber Orchestra, 1970–75; Musical Director, Artemon Ensemble and Orchestra, 1971–; Concertmaster, Director of Instrumental Studies, Darling Downs Institute of Advanced Education, 1975–77; Conductor, Allegri Players, 1975–77; Senior Lecturer, Adelaide College of Arts, 1977–79; Musical Director, South-Western Symphony Orchestra, 1977–79; Professor, Guildhall School of Music and Drama, England, 1979–88; Professor, Birmingham School of Music, 1979–88; Senior Examiner, Australian Music Examination Board, 1988–. *Recordings:* Viola Concerto 1989 by C Reichard-Gross; Memories of Sunny Days for Violin and Orchestra by C Reichard-Gross, with Hungarian Northern Symphony Orchestra, soloist Josef Aronoff (viola/violin), conductor Laszlo Kovacs. *Address:* 40 Isabella Street, Tarragindi, Brisbane, Queensland 4121, Australia.

**ARP, Klaus;** conductor and composer; b. 2 April 1950, Soltau, Germany. *Education:* Staatliche Hochschule für Musik, Hamburg. *Career:* debut at the Hamburgische Staatsoper, 1979; Pianist, Hamburgische Staatsoper, 1975; Conductor, Hamburg Youth Orchestra, 1979; First Kapellmeister Opera Theater, Koblenz, 1981; Chief Conductor, Radio Orchestra, Sudwestfunk, Baden-Baden 1987–95; Artistic Director, Villa Musica, Mainz, 1992–; Professor of Conducting, Staatliche Hochschule für Musik, Heidelberg-Mannheim, 1993–. *Compositions:* Odysseus auf Ogygia, opera, world premiere, Koblenz, 1979. *Recordings include:* Faust, opera by Louis Spohr, 1989; Adolphe Adam, Le Postillion de Lonjumeau; Stravinsky, Le Chant du Rossignol. *Address:* Schillerstr 60, 67071 Ludwigshafen, Germany.

**ARROYO, Martina,** BA; American singer (soprano) and professor of music; *Distinguished Professor, School of Music, Indiana University;* b. 1936, New York; d. of Demetrio and Lucille (née Washington) Arroyo. *Education:* City Univ. of New York, Hunter Coll. and Metropolitan Opera, New York. *Career:* Visiting Prof., Louisiana State Univ., Baton Rouge; debut Carnegie Hall (New York) 1958; Leading Soprano, Metropolitan Opera, New York; appearances at all major US Opera Houses and La Scala, Milan, Italy, Munich Staatsoper and Berlin Deutsche Oper, Germany, Rome Opera, Vienna State Opera, Royal Opera House, Covent Garden, London, Teatro Colon, Argentina and Edinburgh, Tanglewood, Vienna, Berlin and Helsinki Festivals; has performed with all major orchestras in USA and Europe; recordings for London, Philips, EMI, RCA, Angel and Columbia; currently Distinguished Prof. of Voice, Indiana Univ. School of Music; fmr mem. Nat. Endowment of the Arts, Washington, DC; Fellow, American Acad. of Arts and Sciences 2002–; Trustee Carnegie Hall, New York. *Recordings:* more than 50 recordings. *Honours:* Outstanding Alumna, Hunter Coll., Dr hc (Hunter Coll.) Amici di Verdi Medal 2002. *Address:* School of Music, Indiana University, Bloomington, IN 47405, USA (office). *Telephone:* (812) 855-8127 (office). *E-mail:* marroyo@indiana.edu (office); martinaarroyo@aol.com (home). *Website:* www.music.indiana.edu (office); www.martinaarroyofoundation.org.

**ARTAUD, Pierre-Yves;** flautist; b. 13 July 1946, Paris, France. *Education:* Paris Conservatoire. *Career:* played the piccolo in the Orchestre Philharmonique, Ile-de-France, 1964–68, and flute with the Orchestra Laetitia Musica, 1971; directed contemporary flute studies at Sainte-Baume, 1973–80; Visiting Professor at Pecs and Csingrad in Hungary from 1978; Responsible for instrumental research at IRCAM, Paris, Electronic Music Studio, 1981; Professor at Darmstadt, 1982; Performer in recital groups including Arcadie, quartet of flutes, 1964, Da Camera, wind quintet, 1970–72, and the Albert Roussel Quintet, 1973–74; Collaboration with harpist Sylvie Beltrando and

harpsichordist Pierre Bouyer; Has premiered works by Brian Ferneyhough, Betsy Jolas, Tristan Murail, Franco Donatoni, Maurice Ohana and André Boucourechliev; Professor of Chamber Music at Paris Conservatoire from 1985 and of Flute from 1987. *Publications:* La Flute 1987. *Honours:* 1st Prize at the Conservatoire, 1969 and 1970; Medal Of Arts, Sciences and Letters, 1978; Grand Prix of French Contemporary Music Interpretation, 1982; Prix de l'Academie du Disque Français, 1984; Prix Charles Inos, 1985. *Address:* 209 Avenue Jean Jaurès, 75079 Paris, France.

**ARTETA, Ainhoa;** Singer (Soprano); b. 1966, Spain. *Career:* Appearances at North American opera houses from 1990, including Tarrytown, NY as Ah-Joe in Leoni's L'Oracolo; Other roles have included Violetta, Gilda and Liu in Turandot; Sang Micaela in Carmen for Scottish Opera, 1992; As Olga in Fedora, and Mimi; Leila in Les Pêcheurs de perles, Seattle, 1994; Magda in La Rondine, Bonn; Mimi for Netherlands Opera; Zarzuela performances with Placido Domingo, Hamburg, 1996; Season 1998: As Magda at Washington; Violetta at Cincinnati. *Recordings:* Dona Francesquita by Vives. *Honours:* Metropolitan Auditions and Placido Domingo Competition, 1993; Sang Musetta in La Bohème at the New York Met, 2000. *Current Management:* Iberkonzert, C/ Rodríguez Arias 23 - 6° - Dt.10, 48011 Bilbao, Spain. *Telephone:* (94) 4104746. *Fax:* (94) 4218582. *Website:* www.iberkonzert.com/artistas.html. *Current Management:* Zemsky/Green Artists Management, 730 Fifth Avenue, Suite 1802, New York, NY 10019, USA. *Telephone:* (212) 300-8003. *Fax:* 2(12) 300-8001. *E-mail:* zgartists@aol.com. *Website:* www.zemskygreen.com. *Address:* c/o Washington Opera, John F Kennedy Center, Washington DC 20566, USA.

**ARTYOMOV, Vyacheslav;** composer; b. 29 June 1940, Moscow, Russia. *Education:* Moscow Conservatory, studied composition with Pirumov and Sidelnikov. *Compositions:* Piano Concerto, 1961; 2 Clarinet Sonatas, 1966, 1971; Variations, Nestling Antsali for Flute and Piano, 1974; Capriccio For New Year's Eve for Soprano, Saxophone, Baritone Saxophone and Vibraphone, 1975; Totem for Percussion Group, 1976; A Symphony Of Elegies, 1977; Way To Olympus for Orchestra, 1984; In Memoriam, symphony for Violin Solo and Orchestra, 1968–84; Tristia for Orchestra, 1983; Invocations for Soprano and Percussion Group, 1981; Moonlight Dreams, cantata, for Soprano (mezzo-soprano), Alto Flute, Cello and Piano, 1982; Hymns Of Sudden Wafts for Ensemble, 1985; Gurian Hymns for 3 Violins and Orchestra, 1986; Requiem for Soloists, 2 Choirs and Orchestra, 1988; Sola Fide (By Faith Alone), ballet, 1987; Ave Maria for soprano and chorus, 1989; Hymns of Fiery Torches for ensemble, 1994; Various works for different instruments. *Address:* c/o RAO, Bolchaia Bronnai 6-1, Moscow 103670, Russia.

**ARTZT, Alice Josephine,** BA; American classical guitarist, writer and teacher; b. 16 March 1943, Philadelphia, PA; d. of Harriett Green Artzt and Maurice G. Artzt; m. Bruce B. Lawton, Jr. *Education:* Columbia Univ. and studied composition with Darius Milhaud and guitar with Julian Bream, Ida Presti and Alexandre Lagoya. *Career:* taught guitar at Mannes Coll. of Music, New York 1966–69, Trenton State Univ. 1977–80; world-wide tours as soloist 1969–; f. Alice Artzt Guitar Trio (with M. Rutscho and R. Burley) 1989; toured in duo with R. Burley; fmr mem. Bd of Dirs Guitar Foundation of America (Chair. 1986–89). *Recordings include:* Bach and His Friends, Guitar Music by Fernando Sor, Guitar Music by Francisco Tarrega, 20th Century Guitar Music, English Guitar Music, The Music of Manuel Ponce, The Glory of the Guitar, Virtuoso Romantic Guitar, Musical Tributes, Variations, Passacaglias and Chaconnes, American Music of the Stage and Screen, Alice Artzt Classic Guitar, Alice Artzt Plays Original Works. *Publications:* The Art of Practicing, The International GFA Guitarists' Cookbook (ed.), Rythmic Mastery 1997; numerous articles in guitar and music periodicals. *Honours:* several Critics' Choice Awards. *Address:* 51 Hawthorne Avenue, Princeton, NJ 08540, USA. *Telephone:* (609) 921-6629. *Fax:* (609) 924-0091. *E-mail:* guitartzt@aol.com (home).

**ARUHN, Britt Marie;** Singer (soprano); b. 11 Nov. 1943, Motala, Sweden. *Education:* Stockholm Acad. of Music. *Career:* debut, Stockholm in Les Contes d'Hoffmann, 1974; has sung at Stockholm and the Drottningholm Festival as Norina, Zerbinetta, Gilda, Violetta, Mélisande, Susanna, Rosina, Musetta, Mimi, Marguerite, Nedda, Sophie, Gepopo and Adina; Staatsoper Dresden as Gilda and Sophie, 1976; Covent Garden as Zerbinetta, 1978; Wiener Staatsoper as Gilda, 1978, Sophie, 1980; Paris as Gepopo in Der Grosse Makaber and Zdenka, 1981; Hamburg Staatsoper as Olympia, 1981, Musetta, 1982; Brussels as La Fée in Cendrillon, La Comtesse in Le Conte d'Ory and Musetta, 1983, Mélisande and Susanna, 1984, Adèle, 1985, Sandrina in La Finta Giardiniera (and at Drottningholm), 1987; La Scala as Lucio Cinna in Lucio Silla, 1984; Drottningholm as Sandrina, 1987 and in Luigi Rossi's Orfeo, 1997; Helsinki as Violetta, 1988; Oslo as Violetta, 1991. *Recordings include:* Brahms' Ein Deutsches Requiem; Strauss' Vier Letzte Lieder. *Film:* First Lady in The Magic Flute, 1974. *Honours:* Royal Court Singer, 1998. *Address:* Kungliga Operan, PO Box 16094, 10322 Stockholm (office); Fornborgsgrand 12A, 16858 Bromma, Sweden (home). *Fax:* (8) 374320 (home). *E-mail:* bmaruhn@hem.utfors.se (home).

**ARVIDSSON, Bjorn;** Singer (Tenor); b. 1965, Stockholm. *Education:* Studied singing, Sundsgarden, Malmo; Guildhall School of Music and Drama with Laura Sarti, 1992. *Career:* Sang Bernini Opera: Nemorino, Wexford Festival; Title role, Robinson Crusoe, British Youth Opera; Travelling Opera; Appearances in Holland Park, Don Ottavio and Beppe; Rodolfo for Kentish Opera; Liverpool Playhouse; Toured with Pavilion Opera as Tamino; The

Count of Luxembourg, D'Oyly Carte; Liberto in Poppea for Welsh National Opera; Appeared in Antwerp; Opera Project; Tour of Ireland with Co-opera; Alfredo at the Théâtre de Caen; Regular appearances in concert and oratorio; 1999 International Festival, Aix en Provence, Academie Européene de Musique; Toured France, Italy and Switzerland. *Recordings:* Several roles in The Coronation of Poppea, Welsh National Opera for BBC. *Current Management:* Theateragentur Heidi Schäfer, Glauburgstraße 83, 60318 Frankfurt am Main, Germany. *Telephone:* (69) 283347; 1712884544 (mobile). *E-mail:* hs@santuzza.de. *Address:* 58 Alexandra Park Road, London N10 2AD, England.

**ASAWA, Brian;** American singer (countertenor); b. 1966. *Education:* studied in New York. *Career:* season 1995 as Britten's Oberon with the London Symphony Orchestra, Endimione in La Calisto at Brussels, Arsamenes in Handel's Xerxes at the Cologne Opera and a Wigmore Hall recital with Melvyn Tan; season 1996–97 in Handel's Semele at the Berlin Staatsoper, Monteverdi's Orfeo in Amsterdam and Lyon and Orlofsky in Die Fledermaus for San Francisco Opera; Seattle and Göttingen debuts as Arsamenes, Opéra Bastille and Covent Garden debuts as Tolomeo in Giulio Cesare; season 1997–98 in Mozart's Mitridate for Lyon Opéra and Monteverdi's Nero for Australian Opera, and Dallas Opera debut in Handel's Ariodante; Handel's Admeto in Australia and at Montpellier 1998; recitals at Lincoln Center, the Geneva Opera, Sydney Festival and on tour to Japan; season 2000–01 as Farnace in Mozart's Mitridate at the Paris Châtelet, Handel's Tolomeo in Sydney, Baba the Turk in The Rake's Progress for San Francisco Opera and Britten's Oberon at Naples. *Recordings include:* A Midsummer Night's Dream, Arsamenes in Handel's Serse and Farnace in Mozart's Mitridate, solo recitals, The Dark is My Delight, A Midsummer Night's Dream, Vocalise. *Honours:* winner Metropolitan Opera Auditions 1991, Richard Tucker Foundation grant 1993, prizewinner Placido Domingo Operalia Competition 1994. *Current Management:* Askonas Holt Ltd, Lonsdale Chambers, 27 Chancery Lane, London, WC2A 1PF, England. *Telephone:* (20) 7400-1700. *Fax:* (20) 7400-1799. *E-mail:* info@askonasholt.co.uk. *Website:* www .askonasholt.co.uk. *Current Management:* Mirshak Artists Management, 15 West 28th Street, Penthouse B, New York City, NY 10001, USA. *Telephone:* (917) 282-0687. *Fax:* (718) 784-0143. *E-mail:* Robert@MirshakArtists.com. *Website:* www.mirshakartists.com.

**ASAZUMA, Fumiki,** BMus; Japanese professor of viola, conductor and viola d'amore player; b. 23 Aug. 1931, Tokyo; m. Michiko Nagamatsu 1957; one s. two d. *Education:* Tokyo National University of Fine Arts and Music, Vienna Academy. *Career:* violist, NHK Symphony Orchestra, Tokyo, 1956–62; Professor of Viola, Tokyo National University of Fine Arts and Music, 1962–; Director and Conductor, Tokio Akademiker Ensemble (Kammerorchester) Tokyo, 1968–; Many television and radio appearances, NHK and especially on FM-Tokyo, 1968–85; President, Japan Viola Research Society; The Dolmetsch Foundation; Japan Musicology Society; Nippon Conductors Association; Rotary Club. *Recordings:* with Tokio Akademiker Ensemble: 3 Divertimentos by Mozart, 1972, Stamitz, Bach, Mozart, 1975, Flute Concertos by Vivaldi with Christian Larde, 1975, Mozart with Christian Larde and Marie Claire Jamet, 1977, Doppler, Fauré, Gluck, Kreisler, Genin, with Paula Robison, 1984. *Publications:* Translator, The Interpretation of the Music of the XVII and XVIII Centuries by Arnold Dolmetsch, 1966. *Address:* 13-17 Hachiyama, Shibuya-ku, Tokyo 150, Japan.

**ASBURY, Stefan;** British conductor; b. 2 July 1965, Dudley, West Midlands. *Education:* Univ. of Oxford, Royal Coll. of Music with Oliver Knussen, Tanglewood Music Centre. *Career:* engagements with SWR Stuttgart, SWR Sinfonieorchester Baden-Baden & Freiburg, WDR Cologne, NDR Hamburg, NDR Hannover, Deutschland Radio, RIAS Kammerchor, Århus Symphony, Norwegian Radio Orchestra, Royal Scottish Nat. Orchestra and contemporary ensembles, including Ensemble Modern, musikFabrik, Asko Ensemble, London Sinfonietta, Klangforum Wien, Ensemble Intercontemporain; festival appearances include Berlin Festival, Wien Modern, Ultima Festival, Venice Biennale; opera includes premiere of Rob Zuidam's Freeze at Munich Biennale, Birtwistle's Punch & Judy and Chagas Rosa's Melodias Estranhas with Remix Ensemble, Weir's The Blond Eckbert with NDR Hannover, premieres of Staud's Berenice at Munich Biennale and Berlin Festival 2004, and van Vlijmen's Thyeste at La Monnaie. *Recordings:* Harvey, One Evening with Ensemble Intercontemporain (Monde de la Musique Award), Grisey 'Les Espaces Acoustiques' with orchestra of WDR Cologne and Asko Ensemble, Works by Ursuk Chin with Ensemble Intercontemporain. *Honours:* Leonard Bernstein Fellowship, Tanglewood 1990, Conducting Prize, Munich Biennale 1994. *Current Management:* Harrison Parrott Ltd, 12 Penzance Place, London, W11 4PA, England. *Telephone:* (20) 7229 9166. *Fax:* (20) 7221 5042. *E-mail:* nicole.rochman@harrisonparrott.co.uk. *Website:* www .harrisonparrott.com.

**ASCHENBACH, Hans;** Singer (Tenor); b. 1965, Idaho, USA (Swedish and German parents). *Education:* Studied in Idaho and with Neville Marriner. *Career:* Engagements at the New Orleans Opera, Lyric Opera of Queensland, New York Metropolitan, English National Opera and Connecticut Opera; Sang Schoenberg's Aron with the Leipzig Opera and in concert with the Philharmonic Orchestra at the Festival Hall, London, 1996; Other roles include Alwa in Lulu, Nuremberg Opera, 1996; Season 2000–01 as Lohengrin at Weimar and Tannhäuser at Schwerin; Concerts at Carnegie Hall and throughout Europe. *Current Management:* Agentur Sigrid Rostock, Eugen-Schönhaar-Straße 1, 10407 Berlin, Germany. *Telephone:* (30) 4257514. *Fax:*

(30) 4239136. *E-mail:* sigridrostock@web.de. *Address:* c/o Stadtische Buhnen Nurnberg, Richard Wagner Platz 2-10, 8500 Nurnberg 70, Germany.

**ASGEIRSSON, Jón Gunnar;** Icelandic music educator; b. 11 Oct. 1928, Isafjördur; m. Elisabet Thorgeirsdottir 1955; two s. one d. *Education:* Reykjavík Music School, Royal Scottish Academy of Music, Glasgow. *Career:* music teacher at elementary school, Hafnarfjördur 1958–62; music teacher 1962–81, Lecturer 1981–94, Prof. 1994–98, College of Education; music critic for Morgunbladid 1970–; mem. Société de Compositeurs d'Islande, Tónskáldafélag Islands. *Compositions:* Orchestral: Folklore Rhapsody; Lilja, symphonic poem; A Poem of Seven Strings; Blindisleikur, ballet suite; Three Concertos, for Cello and Orchestra, for Horn and Orchestra, for Clarinet and Orchestra; Ancient Dances Suite; Chamber music: Woodwinds Octet; 2 Woodwind Quintets; Folkloric Quintet for Piano and String Quartet; Four Movements for Solo Guitar; String Quartet, 2000; Ten Icelandic Folk Songs for solo guitar, 2000; Choral works and songs; Numerous arrangements of Icelandic folksongs and dances; Operas: Thrymskvida, based on mythological poem; Galdra-Loftur, based on a play by Johann Sigurjónsson. *Recordings:* For Icelandic Broadcasting Service; Ten Icelandic Folk Songs, 1999; Galdia Loftw (opera); Svarfálfa dans (Dance of the Black Elves). *Honours:* 1st Prize in Opera Competition, Icelandic National Theatre, 1974. *Address:* Flókagata 56, 105 Reykjavik, Iceland.

**ASHE, Rosemary Elizabeth,** LRAM, ARAM; British singer (soprano); b. 1953, England; m. Roderick Jones. *Education:* Royal Acad., London Opera Centre. *Career:* sang in the premiere of Tavener's Thérèse at Covent Garden 1979, for ENO has sung Papagena, Esmeralda (Bartered Bride), Fiakermilli (Arabella), Venus (Orpheus in the Underworld) and ZouZou (La Belle Vivette); other roles include the Queen of Night and Julie Laverne (Showboat) for Opera North, Despina (Così fan tutte) and Lucy Lockitt (The Beggar's Opera) on BBC television; Frasquita (Earl's Court and Japan), Josephine (HMS Pinafore) at City Center New York, Musetta, for Opera Northern Ireland, Offenbach's Hélène at Sadler's Wells and Clorinda in La Cenerentola at the Garsington Festival, Dinah in Trouble in Tahiti for Musiktheater Transparant in Antwerp; season 1994–95 as Shakespeare's Hermia at Barbados and in Brand's Maschinist Hopkins in Amsterdam; performed in Coward's After the Ball at the Covent Garden Festival 1999; many appearances in musicals; created role of Carlotta in Andrew Lloyd Webber's The Phantom of the Opera; created role of Felicia Gabriel in The Witches of Eastwick at the Theatre Royal, Drury Lane, London 2000–01 and also at the Princess Theatre, Melbourne 2002; Madame Thenardier in Les Miserables 2002–03; Miss Andrew in Mary Poppins, Prince Edward Theatre, London 2004–. *Recordings:* original cast recordings of The Phantom of the Opera, The Boyfriend, Bitter Sweet, Kismet, Oliver!, The Student Prince, The Killer Soprano. *Current Management:* Hilary Gagan Associates, 187 Drury Lane, London, WC2B 5QD, England. *Telephone:* (20) 7404-8794 (office). *Fax:* (20) 7430-1869 (office). *Website:* hilary@hgassoc.freeserve.co.uk (office). *E-mail:* rosie@rosemaryashe .com. *Website:* www.rosemaryashe.com.

**ASHER, Nadine;** singer (contralto); b. 1957, Chicago, Illinois, USA. *Education:* Indiana University and Juilliard, New York. *Career:* sang at first in concert, then opera engagement at Kiel from 1984; Guest appearances at Heidelberg, Munster and Lucerne, as Bostania in Cornelius's Barbier von Bagdad; Zürich Opera from 1987, as Wagner's Flosshilde and Grimgerde, Edwige in Guillaume Tell and Ulrica (Ballo in maschera); Zürich 1996 in the premiere of Schlafes Bruder by H Willi. *Address:* c/o Opernhaus Zürich, Falkenstrasse 1, 8008 Zürich, Switzerland.

**ASHKENASI, Shmuel;** American violinist; b. 11 Jan. 1940, Tel-Aviv, Israel; m. Mihaela Ionescu Ashkenasi; two s. *Education:* Curtis Inst. of Music, Philadelphia. *Career:* concert violinist since 1962; First Violinist, Vermeer String Quartet; Prof. of Music, Univ. of Northern Illinois 1969–. *Honours:* First Prize, Merryweather Post Contest, Washington, DC 1958, Finalist, Queen Elizabeth Competition, Brussels 1959, Second Prize, Tchaikovsky Competition, Moscow 1962. *Address:* Caecilia, 5 Place de la Fustene, 1204 Geneva, Switzerland.

**ASHKENAZY, Dimitri;** clarinettist; b. 1969, New York, USA. *Education:* Lucerne Conservatory with Giambattista Sisini. *Career:* concerts 1992–93 at the Hollywood Bowl and with the Royal Philharmonic in London (Mozart's Concerto); first tour of Japan 1993, followed by Maxwell Davies's Strathclyde Concerto No. 4 with the composer conducting; 1994 premiere of Marco Tutino's concerto at La Scala; collaborations with Barbara Bonney 1995, 1997, 1998, 2003 and Krzysztof Penderecki 1997, 1998, 1999; season 1996–97 with the premiere of Filippo del Corno's Concerto and concerts in Japan with the European Soloists Ensemble; tours with Sinfonia Varsovia in Spain and Poland playing Penderecki's concerto with the composer conducting 1998–99, and collaboration with Edita Gruberova 1999; appearance at Casals Festival, Puerto Rico 2000; tours of Japan 2000, 2002, including duo recitals with Vovka Ashkenazy and appearance with Gary Bertini at Suntory Hall, Tokyo; appearances in S Africa with KwaZulu-Natal Philharmonic 2002–03, with Brodsky Quartet 1999–2004; duo recitals with Vladimir Ashkenazy in Germany and Austria 2003; world premiere of Maxwell Davies's Clarinet Quintet, Hymn to Artemis Locheia with The Brodsky Quartet at the Lucerne Festival 2004; Berlin debut with the Rundfunk-Sinfonie-Orch. Berlin, Konzerthaus 2004. *Recordings include:* Rossini Variations in C; Richard Strauss Duet-Concertino; Stravinsky Ebony Concerto; Stravinsky Chamber Music; Françaix Clarinet Concerto; Finzi, Copland, Bozza Clarinet Concertos;

Blacher Clarinet Concerto. *Current Management:* Harrison/Parrott Ltd, 12 Penzance Place, London, W11 4PA, England. *Telephone:* (20) 7229 9166. *Fax:* (20) 7221 5042. *Website:* www.harrisonparrott.com. *E-mail:* dasliedvondererde@bluemail.ch (home).

**ASHKENAZY, Vladimir;** Icelandic (b. Russian) concert pianist and conductor; *Music Director, NHK Symphony, Tokyo;* b. 6 July 1937, Gorky, USSR; s. of David Ashkenazy and Evstolia Ashkenazy (née Plotnova); m. Thorunn Sofia Johannsdóttir 1961; two s. three d. *Education:* Cen. Music School, Moscow and Moscow Conservatoire. *Career:* Second Prize, Int. Chopin Competition, Warsaw 1955; Gold Medal, Queen Elizabeth Int. Piano Competition, Brussels 1956; Jt Winner (with John Ogdon) Int. Tchaikovsky Piano Competition, Moscow 1962; Prin. Guest Conductor, Philharmonia 1982–83; Music Dir Royal Philharmonic Orchestra 1987–94; Deutsches Symphonie-Orchester Berlin (fmrly Berlin Radio Symphony) 1989–99; Chief Conductor Czech Philharmonic Orchestra 1998–2003; Music Dir EUYO (European Union Youth Orchestra) 2002–; Music Dir NHK Symphony, Tokyo 2003–; concerts world-wide; many recordings; apptd Artist Laureate, Royal Liverpool Philharmonic Orchestra during Liverpool's tenure as European City of Culture 2008. *Publication:* Beyond Frontiers (with Jasper Parrott) 1985. *Honours:* Hon. RAM; Icelandic Order of the Falcon; Hon. DMus (Nottingham) 1995. *Current Management:* Harrison/Parrott Ltd, 12 Penzance Place, London, W11 4PA, England. *Telephone:* (20) 7229 9166. *Fax:* (20) 7221 5042. *Website:* www.harrisonparrott.com. *Address:* Savinka, Käppelistr. 15, 6045 Meggen, Switzerland.

**ASHKENAZY, Vovka;** pianist; b. 1961, Moscow, Russia; m. Ariane Haering. *Education:* early piano studies in Iceland with Rögnvaldur Sigurjonsson, Royal Northern College of Music. *Career:* debut, Barbican Hall, London 1983 in Tchaikovsky 1st Piano Concerto with London Symphony Orchestra; Concerts in Germany, Italy, Netherlands, France and Canada; Appearances with most London orchestras in concertos by Brahms, Schumann, Grieg, Tchaikovsky and Rachmaninov; US debut with Los Angeles Philharmonic, at Hollywood Bowl; Recital tour of Israel and tours of Australia and Japan; Appearances in many countries including: Austria, Australia, Belgium, Canada, Denmark, France, Greece, Guatemala, Germany, Netherlands, Iceland, Italy, Ireland, Japan, Malta, Norway, New Zealand, Finland, Russia, Israel, Switzerland and Spain. *Recordings:* Arensky and Tchaikovsky Piano Trios; Bartók Sonata for Two Pianos and Percussion. *Current Management:* c/o Jens Gunnar Becker, Grünstrasse 13, 58313 Herdecke, Germany.

**ASHLEY, Robert Reynolds;** Composer; b. 28 March 1930, Ann Arbor, MI, USA. *Education:* Studied theory at University of Michigan, Ann Arbor, BMus in 1952, Piano and composition at Manhattan School of Music, NY, MMus in 1952; Postgraduate studies in acoustics and composition at University of Michigan, 1957–60. *Career:* Active with Milton Cohen's Space Theater, 1957–64, the ONCE Festivals and ONCE Group, 1959–69, and the Sonic Arts Union, 1966–76; Toured with these groups in the US and Europe; Director, Center for Contemporary Music, Mills College, Oakland, CA, 1969–81. *Compositions include:* Operas: That Morning Thing, 1967, Atlanta (Acts of God), 1982; Television operas Now Eleanor's Idea (1993), Foreign Experiences (1994), The Immortality Songs (1994–98), Balseros (1997); Various electronic music theatre pieces including Heat, 1961, Public Opinion Descends Upon The Demonstrators, 1961, Kittyhawk: An Antigravity Piece, 1964, Night Train, 1965, The Trial Of Anne Opie Wehrer And Unknown Accomplices For Crimes Against Humanity, 1968, Fancy Free, 1970, It's There, 1970; Films; Video Operas: Music With Roots In The Aether, 1976, Title Withdrawn, 1976, The Lessons, 1981, Atlanta Strategy, 1984; Commission from Florida Grand Opera for opera on the Cuban 'Rafters', 1997; Instrumental pieces including Fives for 2 Pianos, 2 Percussion and String Quintet, 1962, In Memoriam... Kit Carson, opera, 1963, Odalisque, 1985, Superior Seven, 1988; Piano pieces. *Address:* 10 Beach Street, New York, NY 10013, USA.

**ASHMAN, David;** Singer (baritone); b. 1965, England. *Education:* Royal Academy of Music, London. *Career:* Debut: Sang Belcore in L'Elisir d'amore for Gemini Opera; Appearances as Falke in Die Fledermaus for London City Opera, Ajax in La Belle Hélène for New Sadler's Wells Opera and title role in the premiere of The Plumber's Gift by David Blake for English National Opera, 1989; The Speaker in Die Zauberflöte, Rossini's Bartolo, Mozart's Figaro and Malatesta in Don Pasquale for the London Opera Players; Season 1994 with Glydebourne Touring Opera, including appearances in Il Barbiere di Siviglia. *Honours:* Andrew Sykes Award, Van Smit Prize and Peter Moores Foundation Scholarship, RAM.

**ASHMAN, Mike;** British opera director and administrator; *Artistic Director, Opera Zuid;* b. 16 April 1950, Hertford, Herts. *Career:* Assoc. Producer for Royal Coll. of Music Opera School, London 1989–98; Artistic Dir Opera Zuid, Maastrict, Netherlands 2000–04; has directed for Royal Opera House, Covent Garden, Welsh Nat. Opera, Scottish Opera Go-Round, Opera Holland Park, Opera Ireland and Banff Centre, Alberta; has made performing translations of The Bartered Bride and Weill's Der Jasager. *Recent productions:* for Opera Zuid: Dutch premiere of Death in Venice 2001, Jenufa 2003, Un Ballo in Maschera 2003, Der fliegende Hollander 2004; for Cincinnati Opera: Le Nozze di Figaro 2002; for Royal Danish Opera: L'Elisir d'Amore 1999; for Den Norske Opera: Der fliegende Hollander 1999, Der Ring des Nibelungen 1993–97; French premieres of Cox and Box and Trial by Jury, Musee d'Orsay, Paris 1999. *Publications:* contributes regular articles on operatic subjects (espe-

cially Wagner) to books, journals, newspapers and record booklets. *Address:* 22 Little Brook Road, Roydon, Essex, CM19 5LR, England.

**ASHWORTH, Valerie Grace;** Pianist; b. 12 Sept. 1956, Sale, Cheshire, England; m. Vincent Pirillo, 2 d. *Education:* Chetham's School of Music, Manchester, 1969–75; Studied with Kendall Taylor at Royal College of Music, London, 1975–79; Masterclasses in solo repertoire with William Glock, Albert Ferber, Rudolf Firkusny, Hochschule für Musik, Vienna, 1979–81; ARCM, Piano Performer, 1971; LLRAM, Piano Performer, 1974; ARCM, Teacher's Diploma, 1977. *Career:* Debut: Radio debut, Young Artists, 1969; Soloist, chamber musician and accompanist in England, France, Switzerland, Italy, Denmark, Germany, Japan, Hungary and Austria; Television debut on John Amis Music On Two, 1972 and Austrian television debut in 1982; American debut at Carnegie Hall in 1989; Official accompanist including Jacqueline du Pré masterclasses, England, 1979, Summer Academy, Nice, France, 1980, Irwin Gage in Zürich, 1984–86, Carinthia Summer 1984 and Summer Academy at Salzburg in 1991; Teaching Contract: Coach, String Department, 1982–87, Vocal Department, 1987–89, Hochschule für Musik at Vienna; Taught piano at University of Osnabruck, 1989–93. *Current Management:* Wilhelm Hansen, Denmark.

**ASIKAINEN, Matti Tapio;** Pianist and Composer; b. 25 June 1957, Hankasalmi, Finland. *Education:* MA, Musicology, University of Jyväskylä, Finland, 1996; Pianist Diploma, Sibelius Academy, Helsinki, 1985; MA, Piano Department, Moniuszko Academy of Music, Gdańsk, Poland, 1991. *Career:* debut, Concert Hall of Sibelius Academy, Helsinki, 1974; recordings for Finnish Broadcasting Company, 1971–; appearances on Finnish, Lithuanian and Polish television; solo recitals also in Russia and Italy, including Incontri di Serra Maiori Festival; participant, Probaltica Festival of Chamber Music, Poland; soloist, Symphony Orchestras of Polish Philharmonia; mem. Int. Rachmaninoff Soc., England, Chopin Soc. of Finland, Asscn of Finnish Piano Teachers. *Publications:* contributions to music magazines and reviews. *Honours:* Vienna Musikseminar Int. Piano Competition, 1985; Knight Cross of Merit, Order of Merit (Polish President's award), 2002. *Address:* Pyynpolku 5, 40900 Säynätsalo, Finland. *Telephone:* (14) 378-2827. *Fax:* (14) 260-1331.

**ASKER, Björn;** Swedish singer (baritone); b. 23 Sept. 1941, Stockholm. *Education:* Royal Music Acad., Stockholm, studied with Tito Gobbi in Rome. *Career:* many appearances at Royal Opera, Stockholm from 1969, including the premiere of Werle's Tintomara 1973 and as Don Giovanni, Macbeth, Rossini's Figaro, Telramund, Wotan, Kurwenal, Alberich and Simon Boccanegra; guest appearances at Helsinki, Tel-Aviv and the Drottningholm Festival; sang Renato in Un Ballo in Maschera at Stockholm 1986; Lionel in Tchaikovsky's Maid of Orleans, Rigoletto and Wagner's Dutchman; Amfortas in Mexico and USA; many concert and recital dates; Swedish Court Singer 1983.

**ASTI, Eugene;** Pianist; b. 1962, USA. *Education:* Mannes College of Music, Fontainbleau, France; Guildhall School, London. *Career:* appearances at the Aldeburgh, Arundel and Cheltenham Festivals; accompanist for Margaret Price throughout Europe and recitals with Felicity Lott; Wigmore Hall debut with Elizabeth Connell; further recitals with Alison Buchanan, Susan Gritton, Nancy Argenta and Rebecca Evans; Schubert's Winterreise with Stephen Varcoe; Brahms and Mendelssohn recital series in London and Bristol 1997; Strauss/Poulenc recital series, London 1999; Schumann series, London 2003; recitals at Lincoln Center and Weill Recital Hall, New York; Musikverein, Vienna; regular appearances with Sophie Daneman and Stephan Loges; broadcasts on BBC Radio 3. *Recordings:* Songs by Felix and Fanny Mendelssohn; Clara Schumann; Eric Coates. *Honours:* Ferdinand Rauter Award (Richard Tauber Competition) for piano accompaniment; Megan Foster Award (Maggie Teyte Competition) for piano accompaniment. *Current Management:* Harlequin Artist Agency, 203 Fidlas Road, Cardiff CF4 5NA, Wales.

**ASTON, Peter George,** DPhil, GBSM, FTCL, FCI, ARCM, FRSCM, FRSA; British composer, conductor and academic; *Emeritus Professor of Music, University of East Anglia;* b. 5 Oct. 1938, Birmingham, England; m. Elaine Veronica Neale 1960; one s. *Education:* Birmingham School of Music, Univ. of York. *Career:* Lecturer in Music, Univ. of York 1964–72, Sr Lecturer 1972–74; Prof. and Head of Music, School of Fine Arts and Music, Univ. of East Anglia, Norwich 1974–98, Professorial Fellow 1998–2001, Emer. Prof. of Music 2001–, Dean 1981–84; Dir, The Tudor Consort 1959–65; Conductor, English Baroque Ensemble 1967–70, Aldeburgh Festival Singers 1974–88; Principal Guest Conductor, Sacramento Bach Festival, USA 1993–99; Incontri Corali, Italy 1996, Schola Cantorum Gedanensis, Poland 1999; Series Ed., UEA Recordings 1979–98, Peter Aston Editorial Library 2000; jt and founder Artistic Dir, Norwich Festival of Contemporary Church Music 1981–; Lay Canon, Norwich Cathedral 2002–; Chair., Eastern Arts Asscn Music Panel 1976–81; Chair., Norfolk Asscn for the Advancement of Music 1990–93, Pres. 1993–98; Guild of Church Musicians Academic Bd 1996–; Royal School of Church Music Norfolk and Norwich Area Cttee 1998–2006. *Compositions:* chamber music, opera, Church music, numerous choral and orchestral works, including I Am the True Vine for chorus and organ 1999, editions of Baroque music, including complete works of George Jeffreys. *Recordings:* Mellers' Life Cycle; Jeffreys' Anthems and Devotional Songs; Choral music by Holst and Britten; Numerous choral and orchestral works. *Publications:* The Music of York Minster 1972, Sound and Silence (co-author) 1970, Music Theory in Practice (three vols) 1992–93. *Honours:* Hon. RCM 1991, FGCM 1995. *Address:* 9

Bourne Close, Long Stratton, Norwich NR15 2RW, England. *Telephone:* (1508) 530644 (home).

**ATANASIU, George;** cellist and conductor; b. 15 Nov. 1958, Galati, Romania; two s. *Education:* Bucharest Academy of Music with Serafim Antropov, Petre Lefterescu, Uzi Wiesel and Laszlo Meszo, Bayreuth Youth Festival, Weimar International Music Seminar, Hitzaker Chamber Music Academy. *Career:* debut as soloist with Galati Youth Orchestra, Golterman cello concerto, aged 13; Cello Professor, Rowan University of New Jersey and Conductor of PYPO Orchestra and Enescu Piano Trio, 1988–; appeared as soloist or in recitals on radio and television in Romania, USA, Germany, Italy, Spain, Switzerland, Hungary, Austria, the United Kingdom and Venezuela; Performed at Bayreuth Youth Festival, Weimar International Music Seminar, Hitzaker Chamber Music Academy, Carmel Bach Festival, California and George Enescu International Festival, Bucharest; Principal cellist of the Garden State Philharmonic, 1988–90; South Jersey Symphony Orchestra, 1990–94; mem, American String Teacher Association. *Recordings:* George Enescu Trio in A minor no. 2. *Honours:* winner of Romania National Competition, cello, 1975, 1983; Chamber music, 1979; Bronze medal at International Chamber Music Competition, Florence, 1983. *Address:* 505 Bloomfield Avenue, Drexel Hill, PA 19026, USA.

**ATHERTON, David,** OBE, MA, LRAM, LTCL, LGSM; British conductor; *Conductor Laureate, Hong Kong Philharmonic Orchestra;* b. 3 Jan. 1944, Blackpool; s. of Robert Atherton and Lavinia Atherton; m. Ann Gianetta Drake 1970; one s. two d. *Education:* Univ. of Cambridge. *Career:* Répétiteur, Royal Opera House, Covent Garden 1967–68; Resident Conductor, Royal Opera House 1968–79; Artistic Dir and Conductor, London Stravinsky Festival 1979–82, Ravel/Varèse Festival 1983–84; debut La Scala, Milan 1976, San Francisco Opera 1978, Metropolitan Opera, New York 1984; youngest-ever conductor at Henry Wood Promenade Concerts, London 1968; debut Royal Festival Hall, London 1969; has conducted performances in Europe, Middle East, Far East, Australasia, N America 1970–; Music Dir and Prin. Conductor San Diego Symphony Orchestra 1980–87; Prin. Conductor and Artistic Adviser Royal Liverpool Philharmonic Orchestra 1980–83, Prin. Guest Conductor 1983–86; Prin. Guest Conductor BBC Symphony Orchestra 1985–89; Music Dir and Prin. Conductor Hong Kong Philharmonic Orchestra 1989–2000, Conductor Laureate 2000–; Artistic Dir Mainly Mozart Festival, Southern Calif. 1989–, London Sinfonietta 1967–73, 1989–91 (Founder 1967); Prin. Guest Conductor BBC Nat. Orchestra of Wales 1994–97; Co-Founder, Pres. and Artistic Dir Global Music Network 1998–; Licentiate, Trinity Coll. of Music, Guildhall School of Music and Drama. *Publications:* The Complete Instrumental and Chamber Music of Arnold Schoenberg and Roberto Gerhard (ed.) 1973, Pandora and Don Quixote Suites by Roberto Gerhard (ed.) 1973; contrib. to The Musical Companion 1978, The New Grove Dictionary 1981. *Honours:* Conductor of the Year Award, Composers' Guild of GB 1971, Edison Award 1973, Grand Prix du Disque Award 1977, Koussevitzky Award 1981, Int. Record Critics' Award 1982, Prix Caecilia 1982. *Current Management:* Askonas Holt Ltd, Lonsdale Chambers, 27 Chancery Lane, London, WC2A 1PF, England. *Telephone:* (20) 7400-1700. *Fax:* (20) 7400-1799. *E-mail:* info@ askonasholt.co.uk. *Website:* www.askonasholt.co.uk.

**ATHERTON, Diane;** singer (soprano); b. 1970, Yorkshire, England. *Education:* Guildhall School, London. *Career:* appearances in Mendelssohn's Midsummer Night's Dream, as Eva in Joseph Tal's The Garden and Carmina Burana by Orff, all at the Queen Elizabeth Hall, London; Britten's Aminta in Mozart's Il re Pastore at Aldeburgh; Opera Holland Park as Musetta, and as Mozart's Zerlina, Pamina and Susanna; British tour in Strauss Gala, conducted by Christopher Warren-Green; Handel's Messiah for HTV, Wales; Sang Pythia in the British premiere of Oresteia by Xenakis, for the English Bach Festival, Linbury Studio, Covent Garden, 2000. *Recordings include:* Purcell's Fairy Queen. *Address:* c/o English Bach Festival, Linbury Theatre, Royal Opera, Covent Garden, London WC2, England.

**ATHERTON, Joan,** GRSM, ARCM; British violinist; b. 6 April 1948, Blackpool, England; two d. *Education:* Royal Coll. of Music, London. *Career:* freelance violinist, solo, chamber and orchestral player; principal with London Sinfonietta 1970–; mem. Inc. Soc. of Musicians, Musicians' Union. *Honours:* Tagore Gold Medal 1970. *Address:* 12 Addison Way, London, NW11 6AJ, England (office). *Telephone:* (20) 8455-0658 (office).

**ATHERTON, Michael,** MA; Australian composer, musician and writer; *Director of Research, College of Arts, University of Western Sydney;* b. 17 Feb. 1950, Liverpool, England. *Education:* Univ. of New South Wales, Univ. of Sydney, Univ. of New England, USA. *Career:* Artist-in-Residence, Australian Museum 1993; Foundation Prof. of Music, Univ. of Western Sydney 1993–, Chair of Contemporary Arts 1999–, currently Dir of Research, Coll. of Arts; performer of classical, early music, folk and Asia Pacific instruments in various groups internationally; serves on State and Commonwealth Ministerial Cttees for the Arts. *Compositions include:* The Mahogany Ship for choir, strings and percussion 1993; Exhortation for double choir and percussion 1996; Namatjira for choir 1995; Songs for Imberombera for choir, strings and percussion 1997; Theme for Children's Hospital, Australian Broadcasting Corporation Television 1997; I Saw Eternity for double SATB choir 1999; Score for the feature film Dogwatch 1999, Kamawrah for orchestra 2001. *Recordings:* Ankh (CD of ancient Egyptian music) 1998, Abundance 2003, Melismos (CD of ancient Greek music) 2004. *Honours:* Centenary Medal for Services to Society (Music). *Address:* Locked Bag 1797, University of Western

Sydney, Penrith, 5th DC, NSW 1797 (office); 10/1 Kiara Close, North Sydney, NSW 2060, Australia (home). *Telephone:* (2) 9772-6306 (office). *Fax:* (2) 9772-6737 (office). *E-mail:* m.atherton@uws.edu.au (office).

**ATKINSON, Ann,** BEd, LRAM; Welsh singer (mezzo-soprano); b. 24 Aug. 1965, Corwen, Clwyd; m. Kevin John Sharp. *Education:* Univ. of Wales, Royal Acad. of Music with Kenneth Bowen, studied with Ryland Davies. *Career:* performed with Britain's leading opera cos, including Scottish Opera, Glyndebourne Festival and Touring Opera, Wexford Festival Opera; operatic roles include Carmen for Garden Opera, Azucena and Ines (Il Trovatore) for Scottish Opera, Niklausse (Tales of Hoffmann), Larina and Filipyevna (Eugene Onegin), Annina (La Traviata) for Glyndebourne, Maddalena (Rigoletto), Marcellina (Le Nozze di Figaro); also sang Mamma Lucia (Cavalleria Rusticana) in Ho Chi Minh City; created roles of Mrs Baines in Andrew Gant's The Basement Room and Ann Clwyd, MP in world premiere of Alun Hoddinott's opera Tower for Opera Box; numerous concert performances include Verdi's Requiem, Beethoven's 9th Symphony, Brahms' Alto Rhapsody, Mozart's Requiem, Mendelssohn's Elijah (QEH), Handel's Messiah; conductor of two male voice choirs, Cor Meibion Bro Glyndwr and Cor Meibion Froncysyllte. *Honours:* winner Nat. Eisteddfod of Wales, Llangollen Int. Eisteddfod. *Address:* Glaslwyn, Mill Street, Corwen, Denbighshire LL21 0AU, Wales (home). *Telephone:* (1490) 412735 (home). *E-mail:* annatkinson@ntlworld.com (home).

**ATKINSON, Lynton;** British singer (tenor); b. 11 Oct. 1962, London, England. *Education:* studied in Cambridge with George Guest, London with David Mason and Gita Denise. *Career:* concert appearances in festivals at Innsbruck, Utrecht, Malta, Brighton and Edinburgh; Sang at cathedrals of Canterbury, Wells, Durham and Birmingham, at King's College Cambridge and the Sheldonian Theatre in Oxford; Has sung in Bach's St John Passion on tour to Spain, the St Matthew Passion in Bad Homburg and L'Incoronazione di Poppea at the Spitalfields Festival; Vienna in 1989 with Handel's Susanna under Martin Haselbrock; Sang Alfredo in a production of La Traviata in Mauritius; Handel's Belshazzar with Concerto Köln in Germany and Italy; Sang at Edinburgh Festival and in Poland with the City of London Sinfonia under Richard Hickox; Covent Garden, 1990–91 as First Prisoner in Fidelio and Ywain in the world premiere of Birtwistle's Gawain; Sang at Buxton Festival and Spitalfields in 1991 in Il Sogno di Scipione by Mozart and Acis and Galatea; Season 1992 as Nathaniel in Hoffmann and Zefirino in Il Viaggio a Reims at Covent Garden. *Recordings include:* L'Incoronazione di Poppea; Video of Covent Garden Fidelio as First Prisoner. *Honours:* Prizewinner, Alfredo Kraus International Singing Competition, Las Palmas, 1990. *Current Management:* Robert Gilder & Company, 91 Great Russell Street, London, WC1B 3PS, England. *Telephone:* (20) 7580-7758. *E-mail:* rgilder@robert -gilder.com.

**ATLANTOV, Vladimir Andreevich;** Russian singer (tenor); b. 19 Feb. 1933, Leningrad. *Education:* Leningrad Conservatory (pupil of Natalya Bolotina). *Career:* mem. CPSU 1966–88; joined Leningrad Kirov 1963; further study, La Scala, Milan 1963–65; won Tchaikovsky Competition 1966 and Int. Contest for Young Singers, Sofia 1967; soloist with Moscow Bolshoi Theatre 1968–88, with Vienna State Opera 1987–, Kammersänger 1987; major roles include German in The Queen of Spades, José in Carmen, Otello, Cavaradossi in Tosca; many tours and recordings. *Honours:* RSFSR People's Artist 1972, USSR People's Artist 1976. *Address:* c/o Wiener Staatsoper, Opernring 2, 1015 Vienna, Austria. *Fax:* (1) 51444-2330.

**ATLAS, Allan Warren;** Musicologist; b. 19 Feb. 1943, New York, USA. *Education:* BA, Hunter College of the City University of New York, 1964; MA, 1966, PhD, 1971, New York University. *Career:* Faculty, Brooklyn College, 1971–; Visiting Professor, New York University, 1971, 1984, 1986; Executive Officer, PhD and DMA Programs in Music, Director, Center for the Study of Free-Reed Instruments, Graduate School, City University of New York. *Publications:* The Cappella Giulia Chansonnier: Rome, Biblioteca Apostolica Vaticana, CG XIII. 27, 2 vols, 1975–76; Music at the Aragonese Court of Naples, 1985; The Wheatstone English Concertina in Victorian England, 1996; Renaissance Music, 1998; Anthology of Renaissance Music, 1998. *Contributions:* Articles in the New Grove Dictionary of Music and Musicians and in various journals. *Address:* 945 Cedar Lane, Woodmere, NY 11598, USA.

**ATTROT, Ingrid;** Singer (Soprano); b. 1961, Canada. *Education:* Graduated, University of Toronto's Opera School, 1985; Britten-Pears School at Aldeburgh; National Opera Studio, 1986–87. *Career:* Has appeared as Mozart's Countess and Donna Anna and Meg Page in Sir John In Love by Vaughan Williams, Ibert's Angélique and Respighi's Maria Egiziaca; Sang Madeline in Debussy's Fall of the House of Usher at Elizabeth Hall, 1989; Wigmore Hall and Purcell Room recitals in 1989; Handel's Ode to St Cecilia with Charles Dutoit and the Montreal Symphony; Bach's B minor Mass in Montreal; Vivaldi's Gloria in Ottawa and New York under Trevor Pinnock; Mendelssohn's Midsummer Night's Dream under Neville Marriner at the Festival Hall; Season 1989–90 with Carmina Burana and the Petite Messe Solennelle; Szymanowski recital at the Purcell Room; Handel's Floridante in Canada and California; Stravinsky's Les Noces in Antwerp and Elgar's The Kingdom; Tour of Russia with English National Opera productions of Macbeth and The Turn of the Screw; Season 1992 as Mathilde in Guillaume Tell for Haddo House Opera and the Governess in The Turn of the Screw for Pimlico Opera; Sang Donna Anna at Belfast, 1994. *Honours:* Winner, Eckhardt-Gramatte Competition for Contemporary Music, Canada; Awards from

Canada Council, University of Toronto, the Canadian Aldeburgh Foundation and the Friends of Covent Garden. *Current Management:* Ariën Arts & Music Management, De Boeystraat 6, 2018 Antwerp, Belgium. *Telephone:* (3) 285-96-80. *Fax:* (3) 230-35-23. *E-mail:* arien@pandora.be. *Address:* Juggs Cottage, Forebridge, Little Bedwyn, Marlborough, Wiltshire SN8 3JS, England.

**ATZMON, Moshe;** Israeli conductor; b. 30 July 1931, Budapest, Hungary; m. 1954; two d. *Education:* Tel-Aviv Acad. of Music, Guildhall School of Music, London. *Career:* left Hungary for Israel 1944; played the horn professionally in various orchestras for several years; has conducted in Israel, England, Australia, Germany, Sweden, Norway, Switzerland, Spain, Finland, Italy, Austria, Turkey and USA; Chief Conductor, Sydney Symphony Orchestra 1969–71; Chief Conductor, North German Symphony Orchestra 1972; Musical Dir Basel Symphony Orchestra 1972–86; Chief Conductor Tokyo Metropolitan Orchestra 1979–83, Nagoya Symphony Orchestra 1987–92; Musical Dir Dortmund Opera House and Philharmonic Orchestra 1991–. *Honours:* second prize Dimitri Mitropoulos Competition for Conductors, New York 1963, Leonard Bernstein Prize 1963, First Prize, Int. Conductors Competition, Liverpool, England 1964. *Address:* PMG, Top Floor, 59 Lansdowne Place, Hove, East Sussex, BN3 1FL, England (office).

**AUBERSON, Jean Marie;** conductor; b. 2 May 1920, Chavorney, Vaud, Switzerland. *Education:* Lausanne Conservatory; studied conducting with Van Kampen at Siena and with Gunther Wand in Cologne. *Career:* played violin with the Lausanne Chamber Orchestra, 1943–46, and Suisse Romande Orchestra, 1946–49; Conducted the Lausanne Chamber Orchestra, then the Radio Beromunster Orchestra at Zürich, the Suisse Romande Orchestra and the Zürich Tonhalle; Ballet evenings at the Geneva Opera and the Hamburg Staatsoper; Further career with Orchestra of Radio Basle and of Ville de Saint-Gall; Conducted the premieres of the ballet Paris by Henri Sauguet in 1964, Ginastera's Piano Concerto in 1977 and La Folie de Tristan by Schibler in 1980. *Recordings include:* Mozart C minor Mass with the Vienna Philharmonic; Handel's Organ Concertos with Lionel Rogg and the Geneva Baroque Orchestra; Tchaikovsky's Violin Concerto with Tibor Varga; Oboe Concertos by CPE Bach, Marcello and Bellini, with Heinz Holliger. *Address:* c/o Grand Théâtre de Genève, 11 Boulevard du Théâtre, 1211 Geneva 11, Switzerland.

**AUDI, Pierre;** Stage Director; b. 1957, Beirut, Lebanon. *Education:* Exeter College, Oxford, 1975–78. *Career:* Founded the Almeida Theatre, Islington, London, 1979; Director of theatre and annual contemporary music festival until 1989; Artistic Director of Netherlands Opera from 1988, productions include Schoenberg's Die Glückliche Hand, Feldman's Neither and Monteverdi's Il Ritorno d'Ulisse, part of a complete cycle and Wagner's Ring, concluding in 1998; Directed stage works by Wolfgang Rihm, Michael Finnissy (The Undivine Comedy) and John Casken (Golem) for the Almeida Theatre; Opera North 1990 with the British stage premiere of Verdi's Jerusalem; Produced Birtwistle's Punch and Judy for Netherlands Opera in 1993; Staged premiere of Henze's Venus and Adonis at Munich, 1997, Rameau's Zoroastre at Drottningholm 2005. *Honours:* Lesley Boosey Award, 1990. *Current Management:* Ingpen & Williams Ltd, 7 St George's Court, 131 Putney Bridge Road, London, SW15 2PA, England.

**AUGUIN, Philippe;** French conductor; *General Music Director, Nuremberg State Theatre;* b. 1962. *Education:* studied in Vienna and Florence. *Career:* musical asst to Herbert von Karajan 1986–; associated with Georg Solti at the Salzburg Festival; La Scala Milan, with Don Giovanni, La Damnation de Faust, Die Zauberflöte and Figaro from 1993; Covent Garden with La Traviata and Un Ballo in Maschera 1994; Music Dir, Braunschweig Opera, leading Tristan und Isolde, Parsifal, Salome, Pelléas et Mélisande and Wozzeck 1994; Mahler and Schoenberg cycles with Czech and Royal Philharmonics, Dresden State Orchestra and Orchestre Nat. de France; fmrly Prin. Conductor, Staatstheater Stuttgart, with Tannhäuser, Elektra, Lohengrin, Rosenkavalier and Ariadne; Otello at the Hamburg Staatsoper, Der fliegende Holländer at Leipzig and La Sonnambula at Cologne; Salzburg Festival 1991–; with Fidelio 1996; season 1996–97 with Figaro at La Scala, Tannhäuser for Australian Opera, Le Roi Arthus in Cologne and concerts with the Royal Scottish Nat.; Gen. Music Dir, Nuremberg State Theatre 1998–; La Forza del Destino at La Scala 1999. *Current Management:* Askonas Holt Ltd, Lonsdale Chambers, 27 Chancery Lane, London, WC2A 1PF, England. *Telephone:* (20) 7400-1700. *Fax:* (20) 7400-1799. *E-mail:* info@askonasholt.co.uk. *Website:* www.askonasholt.co.uk. *Address:* Staatstheater Nürnberg, Richard-Wagner Platz 2-10, 90443 Nürnberg, Germany. *Website:* www.staatstheater -nuernberg.de.

**AUSTBÖ, Hakon;** pianist; b. 22 Oct. 1948, Kongsberg, Norway. *Education:* studied in Norway and at the Paris Conservatoire and Ecole Normale de Musique, Juilliard School, New York, USA, Staatliche Hochschule für Musik, Munich, Germany, private studies in London. *Career:* played with Bergen Philharmonic Orchestra, 1963; first Oslo recital, 1964; concert and solo engagements throughout Scandinavia and Europe; piano duo with Marina Horak, and chamber concerts with Trio du Nord until 1985; numerous radio and television performances; Professor at the University of Utrecht from 1979. *Honours:* winner Messiaen Competition, Royan 1971, prizewinner Scriabin Competition, Oslo 1972, Ravel Competition, Paris 1975. *Address:* c/o Utrechts Conservatorium, Mariaplaats 28, 3511 LL Utrecht, Netherlands.

**AUSTIN, Larry Don;** Composer and Music Educator; b. 12 Sept. 1930, Duncan, Oklahoma, USA; m. Edna Navarro 1953, 2 s., 3 d. *Education:* BME, 1951, MM, 1952, University of North Texas, Denton; Studied with Darius Milhaud, Mills College, Oakland, CA, 1955; Seymour Shifrin and Andrew Imbrie, University of California, Berkeley, 1955–58; Computer music workshops, Stanford University, 1969; Massachusetts Institute of Technology, 1978. *Career:* Professor, 1958–72, Director of University's bands, 1958–72, Co-director, New Music Ensemble, 1963–68, University of California, Davis; Publisher and Owner, Source and Composer/Performer Edition, 1966–; University of South Florida, Tampa, 1972–78, University of North Texas, 1978–. *Compositions include:* Woodwind Quintet, 1949; Mass for Chorus and Orchestra, 1955–58; Quartet Three, electronic music on tape, 1971; Quadrants, 1–11; Catalogo Sonoro-Narcisso for Viola and Tape, 1978; Protoforms, hybrid musics for 3 Sopranos and Computer, 1980; Euphonia: A Tale Of The Future, opera, 1982; Sonata Concertante for Pianist and Computer, 1983–84; Violet's Invention for Piano, 1988; A Universe Of Symphony: The Earth, Life Pulse And Heavens, 1974–93; Accidents Two: Sound Projections for Piano with Computer Music, 1992; Electro-acoustic music, including Variations... Beyond Pierrot, 1995; Shin-Edo: CityscapeSet, 1996; BluesAx, 1996; Djuro's Tree, 1997; Taragato, 1998; Singing! For baritone and tape, 1998. *Publications:* Learning to Compose: Modes, Materials and Models of Musical Invention, with Thomas Clark, 1988. *Contributions:* Articles in various publications. *Honours:* numerous grants, commissions and awards. *Address:* 2109 Woodbrook, Denton, TX 76205, USA.

**AUSTIN-PHILIPS, Eric,** BMus; composer and conductor; b. 12 Oct. 1947, Melbourne, Victoria, Australia. *Education:* University of Melbourne, studied composition with John McCabe and conducting with Roger Norrington. *Career:* Faculty Member, The University High School, 1972–; Conductor, Music Critic. *Compositions include:* Portraits of my Friends and Others, for flute, oboe, clarinet, bassoon and piano, 1971; Nirthanjali for mandolin and orchestra, 1973; Into the Air for piano, 1976; Macavity: The Mystery Cat, for choir, 1981; Comfits and Joys for soprano, choir and strings, 1982; The Black Swan, for choir, 1984; Sinfonietta No. 2 for plectra ensemble, 1986; Commissions from the British Music Society (1972), Melbourne Mandolin Orchestra and The Melbourne Chronicle (1982). *Honours:* Dorian Le Gallienne Prize, 1972. *Address:* c/o APRA, 1A Eden Street, Crows Nest, NSW 2065, Australia.

**AUVINEN, Ritva;** singer (soprano); b. 1945, Finland. *Education:* Sibelius Academy, Helsinki, studied with Gina Cigna in Rome and Peter Klein in Vienna. *Career:* Debut: Helsinki concert, 1965; Many appearances with the Finnish National Opera from 1965, notably as Riita in the premiere of Kokkonen's The Last Temptations, 1975, also at the New York Met, 1983; Other roles include Renata in Prokofiev's The Fiery Angel, 1985; Strauss's Ariadne, 1986; Janáček's Emilia Marty, 1988; Lady Macbeth at the Savonlinna Festival, 1993; Guest engagements at St Petersburg, Zürich and Stockholm, with concerts and recitals in New York, London, Vienna and Salzburg; Sang Ms Lovett in Sondheim's Sweeney Todd at Helsinki 1997–98; Premiere of Tapio Tuomela's Mother and Daughter at Helsinki (concert) 1999. *Address:* Finnish National Opera, PO Box 176, Helsingkatu 58, 00251 Helsinki, Finland.

**AVDEYEVA, Larisa Ivanova;** Singer (mezzo-soprano); b. 21 June 1925, Moscow, Russia; m. Evgeny Svetlanov. *Education:* Stanislavsky Opera Studio. *Career:* Sang at the Stanislavsky Music Theatre, Moscow from 1947 as Offenbach's La Périchole, Susuki in Madama Butterfly and in Khrennikov's Into The Storm and Molchanov's The Stone Flower; Bolshoi Theatre in Moscow from 1952 as Olga in Eugene Onegin, Marina in Boris Godunov, Lehl in The Snow Maiden by Rimsky-Korsakov, Konchakovna in Prince Igor, Akhrosimova in Prokofiev's War and Peace, Carmen, and the Sorceress in the opera by Tchaikovsky; Has toured as opera and concert singer in Canada, Europe, USA and the Far East. *Honours:* People's Artist of RSFSR, 1964. *Address:* c/o Bolshoi Theatre, Pr Marxa 8-2, 103009 Moscow, Russia.

**AVELING, Valda,** OBE; harpsichordist; b. 16 May 1920, Sydney, Australia. *Education:* New South Wales Conservatorium of Music. *Career:* debut at Town Hall, Sydney, with Malcolm Sargent, 1938; appearances with all leading orchestras and at all Music Festivals in the United Kingdom; Frequent concert and record collaboration with Richard Bonynge and Joan Sutherland; Numerous recitals as Duo with Evelyn Barbirolli (oboe); Numerous tours of Europe, Canada and Far East including tour of Germany as joint soloist with Yehudi Menuhin; Performances at Rome Harpsichord Festival, Italy, 1971, 1972; Four visits to Australia for Australian Broadcasting Commission, latest 1976; Recital, University of Indiana, USA, 1976. *Recordings include:* Scarlatti Sonatas for harpsichord, for EMI, 1976; Chio Mi Scordi di Te, Mozart; Harpsichord Pieces, Thomas Morley; The Collection of Historic Instruments at the Victoria and Albert Museum, London; Music for Four Harpsichords; Harpsichord Continuo. *Honours:* Honorary FTCL. *Address:* 15 Priory Road, London NW6 4NN, England.

**AVNI, Tzvi Jacob;** Israeli composer and professor of music; *Professor of Music Theory and Composition, Rubin Academy, Jerusalem;* b. 7 Sept. 1927, Saarbrucken, Germany (living in Israel since 1935); m. Hanna Avni, 26 Aug 1979, 1 s., 1 d. *Education:* Diploma in Theory and Composition, Israel Music Acad., Tel-Aviv, 1958; Further studies in USA, 1962–64. *Career:* Dir, AMLI Central Music Library, Tel-Aviv, 1961–75; Prof. of Music Theory and Composition Rubin Academy, Jerusalem 1971–, Dir, Electronic Music Studio, 1977–1995; NE Univ., Boston, 1993–94; Queens Coll., New York, 1994–95; Jury Chair. Arthur Ribinstein Int. Piano Competition 1989, 1992; mem, Israel

Composers League, Chair. 1978–80; Chair., Israel Jeunesses Musicales. *Compositions include:* Two String Quartets, Wind Quintet, Five Pantomimes for 8 Players; Works for choir, various electronic pieces, works for ballet, art films and radio plays; Vitrage for Harp Solo, 1990; Desert Scenes, symphony in 3 movements, 1990; Three Lyric Songs on P Celan Poems for Mezzo Soprano, English Horn and Harp, 1990; Fagotti Fugati for 2 Bassoons, 1991; Variations on a Sephardic Tune for Recorder Ensemble, 1992; Haleluyah for Mixed Choir, 1993; Triptych for Piano, 1994; The Three Legged Monster, musical legend, for Narrator, Piano and Small Orchestra with text by Hanna Avni, 1994; Anthropomorphic Landscapes, No. 1 Flute Solo, No. 2 Oboe Solo, No. 3 Clarinet Solo; Songs and Melodies, for mixed choir, in memory of Itzhak Rabin, 1996–97; Pray for the Peace of Jerusalem for symphony orchestra, 1997; Se Questo é un Uomo, five songs for soprano and orchestra on poems by Primo Levi, 1998; The Ship of Hours, four orchestral sketches on paintings by M Ardon, 1999; Apropos Klee, four pieces for choir and instruments on Paul Klee Paintings, 2000; Bassoon Concerto, 2001. *Recordings include:* Love Under a Different Sun, Chamber-Vocal Works; Program Music 1980 with Israel Philharmonic and Mehta; Piano Sonata No. 1; String Quartet No. 1 (Summer Strings), Israeli String Quartet; 5 Variations for Mr 'K', for percussion; Epitaph (sonata No. 2) for Piano, 1998. *Publications include:* An Orchestra is Born; Gittit, Israel (Ed.) 1966–80. *Contributions:* Dictionary of 20th Century Music; Music in Israel. *Honours:* Israel Prime-Minister's Prize for life achievements, 1998; Saarland (Germany) State Prize for life achievement, 1998; Israel State Prize in Music, 2001. *Address:* 54 Bourla Street, Tel-Aviv 69364, Israel. *Telephone:* (2) 6759911 (office); (3) 6991105 (home). *Fax:* (2) 6527713 (office); (3) 6993937 (home). *E-mail:* avniador@netvision.net.il (home). *Website:* www.tzvi-avni.com (home).

**AVSHALOMOV, Jacob David;** American conductor (retd) and composer; b. 28 March 1919, Tsingtao, China. *Education:* Studied with his father, Aaron Avshalomov in Shanghai, with Ernst Toch in Los Angeles, 1938, at Reed College in Portland, Oregon, 1939–41 and with Bernard Rogers at Eastman School of Music, Rochester, New York, 1941–43. *Career:* Teacher, 1947–54, Conductor of Chorus and Orchestra, Columbia University; US premieres, Bruckner Mass in D, Handel's Triumph of Time and Truth, Tippett's A Child of Our Time; Conductor of Portland Junior Symphony Orchestra, 1954–78 and Portland Youth Philharmonic, 1978–94. *Compositions include:* The Taking of T'ung Kuan for orchestra, 1943, revised, 1953; Sinfonietta, 1946 (Naumberg Recording Award 1955); Evocations for clarinet and chamber orchestra, 1947; Sonatine for viola and piano, 1947; Prophecy for cantor, chorus and organ, 1948; How Long, O Lord, cantata, 1948–49; Tom O'Bedlam for chorus, 1953 (NewYork Music Critics' Circle Award 1954); Psalm 100 for chorus and wind instruments, 1956; Inscriptions at the City of Brass for female narrator, chorus and orchestra, 1956; Phases of the Great Land for orchestra, 1959; Symphony: The Oregon, 1959–61, Revised Jubilee version 1999; City Upon The Hill for narrator, chorus, orchestra and liberty bell, 1965; The Thirteen Clocks for two storytellers and orchestra, 1973; Raptures for orchestra, 1975; Quodlibet Montagna for brass sextet, 1975; Praises from the Corners of the Earth for chorus and orchestra, 1976; Songs for Alyce, 1976; The Most Triumphant Bird, chorus, piano and viola concertante, text Emily Dickinson, 1986; Glorious The Assembled Fires for chorus and orchestra, 1990; Songs in Season for chorus, CB and piano, 1993; Songs from the Goliards, chorus and cello, 1994; His Fluid Aria for chorus and bass clarinet, 1995; Doris Songs for mezzo and guitar, 1997; Seasons' Greetings for full orchestra, 1997. *Recordings:* Collections of contemporary American music; Phases of the Great Land Cantata: How Long O Lord; Taking of T'ung Kuan Prophecy; Open Sesame; Praises from the Corners of the Earth, Raptures for Orchestra, Symphony of Songs; Three Generations Avshalomov; 24 songs; Fabled Cities; Music for Virtuoso Chorus and Virtuosolo Instruments; recorded Aaron Avshalomov's orchestral works with Moscow Symphony Orchestra 1997. *Publications:* The Concerts Reviewed, 65 Years of the Portland Youth Philharmonic, 1989; Avshalomovs' Winding Way (biography of father, Aaron, and Jacob), 2001. *Honours:* Guggenheim Fellowship 1952; Gov.'s Arts Award 1981. *Address:* 2741 SW Fairview Boulevard, Portland, OR 97201, USA (home). *Telephone:* (503) 227-6919 (also fax) (home). *E-mail:* javshalomov@yahoo.com (home). *Website:* www.composers.com/avshalomov (home).

**AWAD, Emil,** BM, PhD; Mexican composer, conductor and educator; b. 2 Aug. 1963. *Education:* Manhattan School of Music, Harvard Univ. *Career:* Artistic Dir, Dudley Orchestra, Harvard 1989–94; Ensemble de las Rosas 1994–96, Fin de Siglo en Xalapa 1998–; Guest Conductor, Manhattan Contemporary Ensemble, Harvard Contemporary Ensemble, Orquesta de Cámara de Bellas Artes; Artistic Dir for over 100 premieres in Mexico 1994–, including works by Babbitt, Carter, Davidovsky, Kim and Martino; Chair. Composition Dept, Conservatorio de las Rosas 1994–98; Dir of Graduate Studies, Prof., Music Dept, Universidad Veracruzana 1999–. *Compositions include:* Duo for violin and piano, Guitar Quartet, Woodwind Trio, Pashkat (for women's chorus, harp and string orchestra), Zazil for orchestra, Piedras Sueltas (text by Octavio Paz) for flute, violin, viola, cello, piano, soprano. *Recordings:* Artificios, Cuarteto Manuel M. Ponce 2002. *Publications:* La Parte del Oyente, Ciencia con Arte. *Honours:* Harvard grant, Manhattan School of Music Merit Scholarship, Juilliard School of Music Composition Prize, Fellow and composer-in-residence, Universidad Veracruzana 1998–99. *Address:* c/o Facultad de Música, Universidad Veracruzana, Barragán No. 32, Xaiapa, Veracruz CP 91000, Mexico.

**AX, Emanuel,** BA; pianist; b. 8 June 1949, Lvov, Poland; m. Yoko Nozaki 1974; one s. one d. *Education:* Columbia University, NY, USA, Juilliard School of Music. *Career:* concert pianist, 1974–; appearances in USA and abroad; Performances with major orchestras including the New York Philharmonic, Philadelphia Orchestra, Chicago Symphony Orchestra, Los Angeles Philharmonic Orchestra, Cleveland Orchestra, Concertgebouw Orchestra, NHK Symphony and London Philharmonic; Played Beethoven's 2nd Concerto with London Philharmonic at the Festival Hall in 1991, and Brahms 1st Concerto at Promenade Concerts in 1991; Mozart's D minor Concerto at the 1994 Proms; World premieres of concertos by John Adams with the Cleveland Orchestra, 1997, Christopher Rouse (New York Philharmonic, 1999), Bright Sheng (Boston Symphony, 2000); All-Beethoven concerto cycles with New York Philharmonic at Lincoln Center Festival, 1999, and Cleveland Orchestra, 2001; Mozart K482 at London Proms 2000; Schoenberg concerto at Salzburg Festival, 2000; Beethoven's Concerto No. 4 in G Major at the London Proms, 2002; mem, Advisory Board, Palm Beach Festival; Chopin Society. *Recordings:* With Philadelphia Orchestra, Chicago Symphony, Cleveland Quartet and Guarneri Quartet; Brahms Concerto (Boston Symphony/Haitink); Adams Concerto (Cleveland Orchestra); Chamber music with Yo-Yo Ma, Isaac Stern, Jaime Laredo; Duos with Yo-Yo Ma. *Honours:* 1st Prize, Arthur Rubenstein International Piano Master Competition, 1974; Record of the Year Award, Stereo Review, 1977; 1 of 5 Best Records of the Year Award, Time Magazine, 1977; Avery Fisher Award, 1979. *Current Management:* ICM Artists Ltd, 40 W 57th Street, New York, NY 10019, USA.

**AXERLIS, Stella;** singer (soprano); b. 5 March 1944, Alexandria, Greece. *Education:* University of Melbourne, Australia. *Career:* debut, Hagen, Germany, in 1968 as Aida; sang at the Deutsche Oper am Rhein, Düsseldorf, 1970–85 as Leonore, Elisabeth de Valois, Lady Macbeth, Senta, Venus, Sieglinde, Gutrune, Tatiana, Marina, the Marschallin, Jenůfa, Santuzza and Madama Butterfly; guest appearances in Hamburg, Cologne, Kassel, Amsterdam, Paris, Sydney and Covent Garden in London; Zürich Opera in 1986 as the Kostelnicka in Jenůfa; Sang Ortrud in Lohengrin at Sydney, 1987. *Address:* Deutsche Oper am Rhein, Heinrich Heine Allee, Düsseldorf, Germany.

**AYDIN, Özgür;** pianist; b. 4 June 1972, Boulder, Colorado, USA. *Education:* Ankara Conservatory, Royal College of Music, London, Hannover Musikhochschule. *Career:* appeared at the 1994 Salzburg Festival and the 1995 Schleswig-Holstein Music Festival; Concerts broadcast by Classic FM, London, 1993, ABC Sydney, 1996, North German Radio, 1997; Played Brahms' first piano concerto with the Bavarian Radio Symphony Orchestra, Herkules-Saal München, live broadcast by Bavarian Radio and television, 1997; Appeared at the International Istanbul Music Festival and the Rheingau Music Festival in 1998; Concerts broadcast by Deutschland Radio Berlin and North German Radio, 1998. *Honours:* Winner of the 46th International Music Competition of the ARD, Munich, 1997; Nippon Music Award, Tokyo, 1997. *Address:* Roscherstrasse 3, 30161 Hannover, Germany.

**AYKAL, Gurer;** music director and conductor; b. 1942, Turkey; m. (deceased); three s. *Education:* Ankara State Conservatory, Guildhall School of Music, London, Accademia Santa Cecilia, Pontifical Inst. of Sacred Music with Dominico Bartolucci, studied with Andre Previn and George Hurst in London. *Career:* resident conductor under direction of Franco Ferrera, Accademia Santa Cecilia 1973; apptd permanent conductor of Presidential Symphony Orchestra, Turkey; founder, Ankara Chamber Orchestra; toured Russia as conductor of Moscow State Symphony Orchestra 1984; toured South America and Caribbean Islands as conductor of English Chamber Orchestra; Music Dir and conductor, Lubbock Symphony Orchestra, TX 1987–93; conducted Istanbul Symphony Orchestra 1989; principal guest conductor of Amsterdam Concertgebouw Chamber Orchestra 1989; Music Dir and conductor, El Paso Symphony Orchestra, TX 1992–. *Recordings:* works with London Philharmonic Orchestra. *Honours:* Turkish Government State Artist 1981. *Address:* El Paso Symphony Orchestra, 10 Civic Center Plaza, El Paso, TX 79901, USA.

**AYLDON, John;** singer (bass-baritone); b. 1950, London. *Career:* appearances with D'Oyly Carte Opera, until 1982, with tours to North America, Austrialia and New Zealand; Engagements from 1982 with Canadian Opera; New Sadler's Wells, Welsh National, Dublin Grand Opera and at the Wexford Festival; Roles include Geronimo in Il Matrimonio Segreto, Don Pasquale, Sacristan in Tosca, Frank in Die Fledermaus and Schaunard in La Bohème, Concian in Wolf-Ferrari's I Quattro Rusteghi, Otec in Smetana's The Kiss and Pooh-Bah in The Mikado. *Address:* Music International, 13 Ardilaun Road, London N5 2QR, England.

**AYRTON, Norman Walter;** British theatre and opera director; b. 25 Sept. 1924, London, England. *Education:* Old Vic Theatre School, London with Michael Saint Denis. *Career:* war service, RNVR 1939–45; mem., Old Vic Co. 1949, Festival Season 1951; repertory at Farnham and Oxford 1949–50; staff mem., Old Vic Theatre School 1949–52; opened own teaching studio 1952; began dramatic coaching for Royal Opera House, Covent Garden 1953; Asst Prin. 1954–66, Prin. 1966–72, London Acad. of Music and Dramatic Art; taught at Shakespeare Festival, Stratford, Ont., Canada and Royal Shakespeare Theatre, England 1959–62; Dir, Artaxerxes for Handel Opera Soc., Camden Festival 1963, La Traviata at Covent Garden 1963, Manon at Covent Garden 1964, Sutherland-Williamson Grand Opera Season, Australia 1965, Britten's Midsummer Night's Dream, Sydney 1973, Lakmé for Australian

Opera 1976, Der Rosenkavalier for Australian Opera Centre 1983; guest dir for many int. productions 1973–84; Faculty, Juilliard School of Music, New York 1974–85; Stage Dir, American Opera Center 1979–85, Vancouver Opera 1975–83, Melbourne Theatre Co. 1974–, Hartford Stage Co. and American Stage Festival 1978–, Spoleto Festival, USA 1984, Vassar Coll., New York 1990–, Utah Shakespeare Festival 1994, Cornell Univ., New York 1995, 1998 and Sarah Lawrence Coll., New York 1994, 1997, 2001; Dir of Opera, Royal Acad. of Music 1986–90; Dean, British American Drama Acad. 1986–98, Fla State Univ. 1997–. *Honours:* Hon. RAM 1989. *Address:* c/o British American Drama Academy, 14 Gloucester Gate, London, NW1 4HG, England (office); 40a Birchington Road, London, NW6 4LJ, England (home). *Telephone:* (20) 7487-0730 (office); (20) 7328-6056 (home). *Fax:* (20) 7487-0731 (office).

**AZARMI, Nassrin;** singer (soprano); b. 5 Jan. 1949, Brujderd, Iran. *Education:* studied in Tehran and Cologne. *Career:* debut as Mozart's Despina, Tehran, 1967; sang at the Vienna Volksoper, 1968–69; Linz, 1969–71; Deutsche Oper am Rhein, Düsseldorf from 1971 as Mozart's Queen of Night, Pamina, Susanna and Constanze, Adina in L'Elisir d'amore, Offenbach's Olympia, Rossini's Elvira; Guest appearances include Berg's Lulu at Antwerp, 1982; In Die Zauberflöte at Salzburg, 1990; Sang Musetta at Düsseldorf, 1993; Further roles have included Nicolai's Frau Fluth, Gilda, Micaela, Strauss's Aminta and Nannetta in Falstaff; Concert and oratorio engagements. *Address:* c/o Deutsche Oper am Rhein, Heinrich Heine Allee 16a, 40213 Düsseldorf, Germany.

**AZEVEDO, (António) Sérgio Arede Torrado Marques;** Portuguese composer; b. 23 Aug. 1968, Coimbra. *Education:* Academia de Amadores de Música, Escola Superior de Música, Lisbon. *Career:* teacher at Escola Superior de Música; ed. for Portuguese Nat. Radio. *Compositions include:* Coral I 1991, Tranquilo 1997, Retábulo de Brecht (music theatre) 1998, Festa 1998, Concerto for two pianos and chamber orchestra 1999–2000. *Publications:* 1958–1998: Forty Years of Contemporary Music in Portugal, World New Music Magazine 1998, A invenção dos sons 1998. *Address:* R. João de Barros, lote 21, 1 Esq. Alapraia, São João do Estoril, 2765 Estoril, Portugal. *Telephone:* 9 6339 7727. *Fax:* 2 1466 5042. *E-mail:* sergio.aze@sapo.pt.

**AZMAIPARASHVILI, Zaza;** Georgian conductor; *Music Director, Tbilisi Zakharia Paliashvili Opera and Ballet State Academic Theatre. Career:* has conducted Tchaikovsky Symphony Orchestra, Moscow, St Petersburg Academic Philharmonic Orchestra; Music Dir Tbilisi Zakharia Paliashvili Opera and Ballet State Academic Theatre 2005–. *Honours:* second prize Int. Prokoviev Conducting Competition 1996. *Address:* Tbilisi Zakharia Paliashvili Opera and Ballet State Academic Theatre, 25 Rustaveli Avenue, Tbilisi, Georgia (office). *E-mail:* opera@acces.sanet.ge (office).

**AZZOLINI, Sergio;** Italian bassoonist; b. 15 Jan. 1967, Bolzano. *Education:* Claudio Monteverdi Conservatory of Music with Romano Santi, Bolzano, and Hanover Musikhochschule with Klaus Thunemann. *Career:* principal solo bassoon, European Community Youth Orchestra; Prof., Stuttgart Musikhochschule 1989–98; Prof., Basle State Acad. of Music 1998–; directs his own ensemble, Il Proteo; mem., Ma'alot Quintetts, Sabine Meyer Bläserensemble, Maurice Bourgue Trio, and several early music groups; under contract to EMI for future chamber music recordings. *Honours:* first prizes in int. competitions at Ancona, Prague, Belgrade, Martigny, Bonn, first prize C.M. von Weber competition, Munich. *Address:* Caroline Martin Musique, 126 rue Vieille du Temple, 75003 Paris, France (office). *Website:* www.caroline-martin-musique.com (office).

# B

**BABBITT, Milton Byron,** DMus, MFA; American composer; b. 10 May 1916, Philadelphia; s. of Albert E Babbitt and Sarah Potamkin; m. Sylvia Miller 1939; one d. *Education:* New York and Princeton Univs. *Career:* Music Faculty, Princeton Univ. 1938–, Math. Faculty 1943–45, Bicentennial Preceptor 1953–56, Prof. of Music 1966–84, Prof. Emer. 1984–; Dir Columbia-Princeton Electronic Music Center; mem. Faculty, Juilliard School 1971–; Fromm Prof., Harvard Univ. 1988; Guggenheim Fellow 1960–61; MacArthur Fellow 1986–91; mem. American Acad. of Arts and Sciences, American Acad. of Arts and Letters. *Works include:* Music for the Mass 1940, Composition for Four Instruments 1948, Woodwind Quartet 1953, All Set 1957, Vision and Prayer 1961, Philomel 1964, Tableaux 1972, Reflections 1975, Solo Requiem 1977, Paraphrases 1979, Ars Combinatoria 1981, Melismata 1982, The Head of the Bed 1982, Canonic Form 1983, Piano Concerto 1985, Transfigured Notes 1986, The Joy of More Sextets 1986, Whirled Series 1987, Consortini 1989, Emblems 1989, Soli e Duettini 1989–90, Play It Again Sam 1989, Envoi 1990, Preludes, Interludes and Postlude 1991. *Publication:* The Function of Set Structure in the Twelve Tone System 1946. *Honours:* Hon. D.Mus. (Glasgow); Hon. DFA (Northwestern Univ.); American Acad. of Arts and Letters Award 1959; Gold Medal, Brandeis Univ. 1970; Pulitzer Prize 1982, Schoenberg Inst. Award 1988, William Schuman Award 1992. *Address:* 222 Western Way, Princeton, NJ 08540-5306, USA.

**BABINGTON, Amanda-Louise,** BMus, MusM; British musician and musicologist; b. 12 Oct. 1979, Oxford. *Education:* Univ. of Manchester. *Career:* Leeds Baroque Orchestra 2000–; Contemporary Baroque (ensemble) 2001–; Britten Pears Orchestra, Handel, Richard Egarr 2002, Charpentier, Emmanuelle Haim 2003, Bach, Richard Egarr 2003, Mozart and Handel, Paul McCreesh and Richard Egarr 2004; Academie D'Ambronay, Handel's Athalia, Paul McCreesh 2003; Les Talens Lyrique, Handel 2004; mem. Musicians' Union. *Recordings:* Wagner Prelude to Die MeisterSinger, Ravel Daphnis et Chloé, National Youth Orchestra of Scotland, Takho Yuasa 1999, Tragédiennes 2005, Aristeo 2006. *Publications:* Handel's Solo Sonatas, Early Music Performer Issue II March 2003. *Honours:* Scottish Arts Trust 2003, 2002, 2001, SRP Walter Bergmann Memorial Fund 2001, The Robert Nicol Trust 2001, Proctor Gregg Travel Award 2001, 2000, 1999. *Address:* 9 Patterson Avenue, Chorlton, Manchester, M21 9NB, England (home). *Telephone:* (161) 881-1672 (home). *E-mail:* ababington@hotmail.com (home).

**BABYKIN, Anatol;** singer (bass); b. 29 Sept. 1944, Tscheljabinsk, Russia. *Education:* Astrakhan Conservatory. *Career:* member of the Bolshoi Opera at Moscow from 1976; Roles have included King René (Iolanthe), Gremin (Eugene Onegin), Leporello in The Stone Guest by Dargomyzhsky and Don Alfonso (Così fan tutte); Sang with the Bolshoi at the Edinburgh Festival in 1991, operas by Tchaikovsky and Rimsky-Korsakov. *Address:* c/o Bolshoi Opera, 103009 Moscow, Russia.

**BACELLI, Monica;** singer (mezzo-soprano); b. 1960, Italy. *Career:* debut as Mozart's Dorabella, Spoleto Festival, 1987; sang Zerlina at Rome, 1990; Cecilio in Mozart's Lucio Silla, San Francisco, 1991; Appearances as Cherubino, Salzburg Festival, 1992; Covent Garden Vienna State Opera and Rossini Festival, Pesaro; Roles include Rosina, Nicklausse, Ravel's Child and Mozart's Idamante, Idomeneo; Season 1998 with Cherubino, Rome; Sang Ascanio in Benvenuto Cellini in concert, at the Barbican, London, 1999; Season 1999–2000: Premiere of Berio's Cronaca del Luogo, Salzburg; Rossini's Isabella for Netherlands Opera; Ottavia in Poppea at Florence and Bellini's Romeo at Catania; Berio's Outis at La Scala and the Châtelet, Paris; Season 2001 in Handel's Tamerlano at Halle. *Recordings:* La Finta giardiniera, Teldec; Le nozze di Figaro. *Address:* c/o Netherlands Opera, Waterlooplein 22, 1011 Amsterdam, Netherlands.

**BACH, Andreas;** pianist; b. 29 July 1968, Dennbach, Germany. *Education:* studied with Prof. Karl-Heinz Kammerlung, Hannover. *Career:* debut with Alte Oper, Frankfurt in 1984; appearance in Eurovision Competition, 1984; first tour to USA with debuts at New York, San Francisco and Washington DC, 1987 and to Japan, 1988; several further tours to USA and appearances in France, England, Switzerland, Italy and Portugal. *Recordings:* Schumann Op 6, Op 7, 1989; Beethoven Op 7, Op 31 No. 2, Op 126, Novalis, 1990. *Honours:* winner, several Youth Competitions, 1975–84; Bernhard Sprengel Prize for Music, 1985; Kulturpreis von Rheinland-Pfalz, 1990. *Address:* c/o Concerto Winderstein, Leopoldstrasse 25, 80802, Munich, Germany.

**BACH, Jan Morris,** BMus, MMus, DMA; American composer and fmr educator; b. 11 Dec. 1937, Forrest, IL; m. Dalia Zakaras 1971; two d. *Education:* Univ. of Illinois, Urbana-Champaign. *Career:* asst first horn, US Army Band 1962–65; instructor in music, Univ. of Tampa, FL 1965–66; Prof. of Music, Northern Illinois Univ., Dekalb 1966–98, Distinguished Research Prof. Emer. 1998–; Presidential Research Prof., Northern Illinois Univ. 1982–86; mem. American Soc. of Composers, Authors and Publishers, BMI. *Compositions include:* Four Two-Bit Contraptions, 1967; Skizzen, 1967; Burgundy Variations, 1968; Woodwork, 1970; Eisteddfod, 1972; The System, 1973; Piano Concerto, 1975; The Eve of St Agnes, for antiphonal wind ensemble, 1976; Praetorius Suite, 1977; Canon and Caccia, for five French horns, 1977; Happy Prince, 1978; Quintet for Tuba and Strings, 1978; Gala Fanfare, 1979; The Student from

Salamanca, 1979; Rounds and Dances, 1980; Sprint, 1982; French Suite, for unaccompanied horn, 1982; Horn Concerto, 1983; Dompes and Jompes, 1986; Harp Concerto, 1986; Concerto for Trumpet and Wind Ensemble, 1987; Concerto, for Euphonium and Orchestra, 1990; Anachronisms, for string quartet. 1991; People of Note, 1993; Concerto for Steel Pan and Orchestra, 1994; The Last Flower, 1995; Foliations, 1995; Concertino for Bassoon and Strings, 1996; Pilgrimage, 1997; Variations on a theme of Brahms, 1997; Choral: Hair Today, 1977; Dear God, 1998; In the Hands of the Tongue, 1999; The Duel, 2000; Songs of the Streetwise, 2000. *Recordings include:* Laudes for Brass Quintet; Skizzen for Woodwind Quintet; Four Two-Bit Contraptions; Eisteddfod, 1972; My Very First Solo, 1973; Praetorius Suite, 1976; Concert Variations, for Euphonium and Piano, 1977; Fanfare and Fugue for Five Trumpets, 1979; Rounds and Dances, 1980; Triptych, for Brass Quintet, 1989; Steel Pan Concerto, 1994; The Duel, 2000; Horn Concerto 2005, Gala Fanfare 2005, French Suite 2005, Helix 2005. *Honours:* Award for Excellence in Undergraduate Education, Northern Illinois Univ. 1978. *Address:* PO Box 403, Wasco, IL 60183, USA. *E-mail:* janbach@janbach.com. *Website:* www.janbach.com.

**BACH, Mecthild;** singer (soprano); b. 1970, Limburg an der Lehn, Germany. *Education:* Frankfurt Musikhochschule with Elsa Calveti; Hartmut Holl and Michael Schneider, Studio for Early Music; Vera Rozsa and Laura Sarti in London. *Career:* Darmstadt Staatstheater and the opera studio of the Deutsche Oper am Rhein, Düsseldorf, Heidelberg Opera, 1991–96; Stage and concert appearances with conductors Frieder Bernius, Reinhard Goebel, Michael Schneider and Sigiswald Kuijken. *Recordings:* Flavio in Jommelli's Il Vologeso, Orfeo; Jommelli's Didone Abbandonata as Selene, Orfeo; Gristostomo in Telemann's Don Quichotte; Durante's Lamentations; Monteverdi's Vespers; Mendelssohn's Lobesgesang; Handel's Acis and Galatea and Ode for St Cecilia's Day; Mozart Masses. *Address:* c/o Heidelberg Opera, Friedrickstrasse 5, 69117 Heidelberg, Germany.

**BACHLER, Klaus;** Austrian artistic director; *Director, Vienna Burgtheater;* b. 1951. *Education:* Max Reinhardt Seminar, Vienna. *Career:* trained as an actor in Vienna; made his acting debut at the Landestheater Salzburg, spent several years acting in theatres in Germany; apptd Artistic Dir State Drama Theatre, Berlin 1987; Prod. Taller Europe Festival, Paris 1990; Intendant Vienna Festival 1991–96; Dir Volksoper, Vienna 1996–99; Dir Burgtheater, Vienna 1999–(2008); (Intendant Bayerische Staatsoper 2008–). *Address:* Burgtheater, Dr Karl-Lueger-Ring 2, Vienna 1010, Austria (office). *Telephone:* (1) 51444-4140 (office). *Fax:* (1) 51444-4143 (office). *Website:* www.burgtheater.at.

**BACHLUND, Gary;** Singer (Tenor); b. 1958, New York, NY, USA. *Education:* Studied in New York. *Career:* Sang Parsifal at Carnegie Hall and appeared in operas by Mussorgsky, Wagner (Das Rheingold) and Gounod (Roméo et Juliette) at the Metropolitan Opera; Sang Strauss's Bacchus with Minnesota Opera; Florestan for Boston Opera and Don José for Scottish Opera at Glasgow (European debut, 1986); Other roles include Agrippa in The Fiery Angel, Jimmy in Mahagonny and Aegisthus in Elektra (all at Los Angeles); Ennée in Les Troyens at the Opéra Bastille, Paris, 1990 and Wagner's Erik at Cologne (1992); Sang Tristan at Milwaukee, 1993 (also at Brunswick, 1996); Santiago 1993, as Don José; Kaiserslautern, 1995, Tannhäuser; Season 2000 as Tristan at Honolulu and Dmitri in Boris Godunov at Kassel. *Current Management:* Peter Seyfferth Artists Management, Avenue de la Concorde 385, 06190 Roquebrune Cap Martin, France. *Telephone:* 4-93-35-01-05. *Fax:* 4-93-35-02-17. *E-mail:* peter@seyfferth.de. *Website:* www.seyfferth.de. *Address:* c/o Musicaglotz, 11 rue le Verrier, F–75006, Paris, France.

**BACHMANN, Rhonda;** singer (soprano); b. 24 Oct. 1952, Chicago, IL, USA; m. Arthur Hammond 1986 (deceased) 1991. *Education:* Conservatoire National Superieur de Musique de Paris. *Career:* Chicago Opera Theatre, 1979–80; Opéra de Lyon, 1981; Opéra de Wallonie, Belgium, 1982; Opéra du Rhin, Strasbourg 1981–84; Théâtre du Palais Royal, Paris, 1981; Concerts include, Radio France 1980; 1989–1993 Marie Antoinette Bicentennial, Naantali Festival, Finland, 1981; Salle Gaveau, Paris, 1981; Royal Opera House, Friends of Covent Garden Christmas Gala, 1985; Institut Français London, 1986; Pavillon Dauphine, Paris, 1986; Many recitals and chamber music concerts in Paris, Germany, Italy, including the music of Vivaldi, Bach, Handel, Mozart, Schubert, Spohr, Brahms, Schoenberg, Ravel and Dowland; Appearances on television, New York, Paris, Marseilles; Acted in 3 films, 1974–76; Leading role, Harriet Smithson, The Life of Berlioz, 1981; Toured extensively with recital in 18th Century Costume as Queen Marie Antoinette, Songs for the Queen, Songs for the Revolution, 7 programmes, 175 performances of which 73 in the Grand Trianon, Versailles, 1988–2000; Tours to America, England, Scotland, Ireland, Bulgaria, Austria with Peter Gellhorn, piano; 13 recital programmes, Malibran and Viardot (bel canto repertoire), The Romantic Nightingale (Lieder) and From Times of War (20th century up to 1948), tours to Italy, France, Austria and the United Kingdom, Covent Garden Festival, 55 performances, with Peter Gellhorn, piano, 1992–2001. *Recordings:* Cassettine: Quand tu étais petit, Lieder in French translation by Mozart, Schubert and Brahms with Noel Lee, piano; Video: Queen Marie Antoinette and the Kindling Fire, with Peter Gellhorn, piano,

2000. *Address:* 7 Norfolk House, Courtlands, Sheen Road, Richmond, Surrey TW10 5AT, England.

**BACK, Andrée;** singer (soprano); b. 1950, England. *Education:* Royal College of Music. *Career:* has sung in oratorios, recitals and symphony concerts with appearances in most major European and American cities; Frequent engagements in Switzerland, Norway, Austria, Belgium and the Netherlands (Radio Symphony Orchestra, Rotterdam); Has sung in Carmina Burana at Liège, Siegen and Edinburgh, Berlioz's La Mort de Cléopâtre with Berlin Symphony Orchestra, Mozart's Requiem and Coronation Mass in Marienstatt with the Bonn Bach Choir, and Mozart Concert Arias with the Schwabische Symphony Orchestra; Sang in Mahler's 4th Symphony at Cheltenham Festival and in A Child of Our Time at Bury St Edmunds, Telemann Cantatas in Hamburg and Haydn's Berenice and Strauss's Four Last Songs with the Billings Symphony Orchestra, 1989; Other concert repertoire includes Bach's Mass in B minor, Magnificat, Passions and Christmas Oratorio, Beethoven's Missa Solemnis, Mass in C and Choral Symphony, Requiems by Brahms, Fauré, Britten and Verdi, Handel's Messiah, Judas Maccabaeus, Jephtha, Joshua, Acis and Galatea, Hercules, Israel in Egypt, Samson, Saul and Chandos Anthems, Janáček's Glagolitic Mass, Mahler's 2nd and 8th Symphonies, Rückert Lieder, Schubert's Salve Regina, Masses, Vivaldi's Gloria and Magnificat, Wagner's Wesendonck Lieder. *Address:* Mancroft Towers, Oulton Broad, Lowestoft, Suffolk NR32 3PS, England.

**BACQUIER, Gabriel;** French singer (baritone); b. 17 May 1924, Béziers; s. of Augustin Bacquier and Fernande Severac; m. 1st Simone Teisseire 1943; one s.; m. 2nd Mauricette Bénard 1958; one s. *Education:* Paris Conservatoire. *Career:* debut at Théâtre Royal de la Monnaie, Brussels 1953; joined Opéra de Paris 1956; debut at Carnegie Hall 1960, Metropolitan Opera, New York 1961; has appeared at the Vienna State Opera, Covent Garden, La Scala, Opéra de Paris and most leading opera houses; repertoire includes Otello, Don Giovanni, Pelléas et Mélisande, Damnation de Faust, Tosca, Falstaff; several recordings. *Films include:* La Grande Récré, Falstaff. *Honours:* Prix nat. du disque français 1964; Chevalier, Légion d'honneur; Officier, Ordre nat. du Mérite; Commdr des Arts et des Lettres; Médaille de Vermeil, Paris, Victoires de la Musique 1985. *Address:* c/o OIA, 16 avenue Franklin D. Roosevelt, 75008 Paris, France (home).

**BACRI, Nicolas;** French composer; b. 23 Nov. 1961, Paris. *Education:* Paris Conservatoire, Acad. de France in Rome. *Career:* Head of Chamber Music Dept, Radio France 1987–91; composer-in-residence, Casa de Velasquez, Spain 1991–93, Orchestre de Picardie 1996–98, CNR de Bayonne 2001. *Compositions include:* Quatuor à cordes 1980, Concerto pour violon 1982–83, Symphonie No. 1 1983–84, Concerto pour violoncelle 1985–87, Fleur et le miroir magique (conte lyrique for children) 1996–97, Symphonie No. 6 1998, Concerto da camera pour clarinette 1999, Concerto pour trompette No. 2 2000. *Recordings include:* Concerto pour violoncelle Folia, Requiem, Tre canti e finale, Etcetera, Concerto pour trompette, Verany Arion. *Honours:* first prize for composition, Paris Conservatoire 1983, Grand Prix Académie du Disque 1993, Lauréat de la Fondation d'entreprise Natexis 1993–96. *Address:* c/o Peer Musikverlag, Muhlenkamp 45, 22303 Hamburg, Germany (office). *Website:* www.peermusic-classical.de.

**BACULEWSKI, Krzysztof Jan;** Composer; b. 26 Dec. 1950, Warsaw, Poland; m. Agnieszka Dmowska, 20 Dec 1979. *Education:* MA, Academy of Music, Warsaw, 1974; Postgraduate Studies, Conservatoire National Supérieur de Musique, Paris, 1976–77; PhD, Warsaw University, 1982. *Career:* Debut: Warsaw, 1975; Many Compositions Performed at Warsaw Autumn International Festival of Contemporary Music and Abroad, including USA, France, Germany, Finland, Hungary, South America; Professor, Music Academy, Warsaw, 1998–; mem, Polish Composers Union; ISCM; Society of Authors ZAiKS. *Compositions:* Vivace e Cantilena for Chamber Ensemble, 1975; Epitaphium for Orchestra, 1973; Ground for Orchestra, 1981; Concerto for Orchestra, 1983; A Walking Shadow for Orchestra, 1990; Antitheton I, for Piano Trio, 1989; Antitheton II, for Baroque instruments, 1996. *Recordings:* Sonata for Percussion, Rilke-Lieder for Choir a Cappella, Nox Ultima, Motet for Choir a Cappella, The Profane Anthem to Anne, text by John Donne, a Cantata; Chansons Romanesques et Frivoles for voice and baroque instruments, 1998; Sonata Canonica for two violins, 1998. *Contributions:* Ruch Muzyczny; Studio. *Publications:* Polish Musical Output, 1945–1984, 1987; Vol. X (Contemporary Music), The History of Polish Music, 1996. *Honours:* Many Prizes at Polish Competitions. *Address:* ul Ludwika Hirszfelda 8m 42, 02-776 Warsaw, Poland.

**BADER, Hans-Dieter;** singer (tenor); b. 16 Feb. 1938, Stuttgart, Germany. *Education:* studied with Rudolf Gehrung and in Stuttgart. *Career:* debut at Stuttgart Staatsoper in 1960 as Arturo in Lucia di Lammermoor; Sang at Brunswick, Karlsruhe, Essen, Kassel and Mannheim; appeared in Hannover, 1965–84 as Rodolfo in La Bohème, Faust at Nuremberg, Hamburg, Düsseldorf, Strasbourg and Vienna Volksoper; Other roles include Ferrando in Così fan tutte and the Duke of Mantua; Season 1995–96, as Herod in Salome and Tiresias in Orff's Antigonae at Hannover; Strauss's Emperor at Kiel; Season 2000–01 as Shuisky in Boris Godunov and Aegisthus in Elektra, at Hannover. *Recordings include:* Reger's Requiem, Sly by Wolf-Ferrari; Strauss's Feuersnot. *Address:* Staatstheater Hannover, Opernhaus, Opernplatz 1, 30159 Hannover, Germany.

**BADIAN, Maya;** Composer and Musicologist; b. 18 April 1945, Bucharest, Romania; m. Lucian Munteanu, 1 s. (died 1989). *Education:* MMus, Composition, Music Academy of Bucharest, Bucharest; DMus, Composition, Montreal University, Montreal, Canada. *Career:* Debut: Symphonic Movement, Romania in 1968; Musical Director for RTV, Bucharest, 1968–72; Professor of Composition and Keyboard, Bucharest, 1972–87; Settled in Montreal, Canada since 1987; Teacher at the Montreal University since 1990; Musicology writings; Lecturer at international contemporary music festivals and congress in Europe and Canada; Concerts in Europe, USA and Canada; Member of various international juries. *Compositions:* Over 50 works including: Symphonic: Holocaust–In Memoriam, symphony; Concertante music: Concertos for Piano, for Violin, for Guitar, for Cello, for Marimba and Vibraphone for Clarinet and Saxophone for 4 Timpani (To Mircea Badian); Children's World for orchestra, 1997; Vocal-Orchestral works: Canada 125–Cantata Profana, Towards The Pinnacle, poem for Soprano; Chamber: Concerto for Horn and Percussion, Solos, duos, trios and other chamber ensembles. *Recordings:* Maya Badian, Romania, 1977; Towards The Pinnacle, Canada, 1994. *Publications:* All compositions published in Lucian Badian Editions, Canada. *Contributions:* Various musical periodicals; RTV interviews. *Honours:* All her archival documents and manuscripts are deposited at the Manuscript Collection, Music Division, National Library of Canada, Ottawa. *Address:* No. 2001, 1140 Fisher Avenue, Ottawa, Ontario K1Z 8M5, Canada.

**BADINSKI, Nikolai,** DipMus; composer, violinist and pedagogue; b. 19 Dec. 1937, Sofia, Bulgaria. *Education:* Academy of Music, Sofia, masterclass in composition, Acad. of Arts, East Berlin, scholarships for masterclasses, Accademia Musicale, Siena, Italy. *Career:* active as composer, university teacher in Berlin, Sofia, Halle; concert violinist; concertmaster; special adviser for music education, String Quartet; active in the Darmstadt Int. Courses for New Music 1974–78; Guest Professor, Universities of Stockholm and Copenhagen; Assistant to Max Deutsch, Sorbonne and Ecole Normale de Musique, Paris, 1982; Scholar of the French Government, Paris 1985–86; Composer-in-Residence Djerassi Foundation and Fulbright Scholar, Calif. 1987; appearances at various festivals; numerous performances, radio and television broadcaster; mem. European Academy of Arts, Sciences and Humanities (Paris). *Compositions:* numerous compositions including 3 Symphonies, Several Concertos for instruments and orchestra; Widerspiegelungen der Weisheit for S, B, choir and orchestra, Ballets, Music for Orchestra, Chamber Music; 3 Espressioni for soprano and tape, 1981; Cantico di S Francesco for baritone and tape, 1981–82; Vocal, Organ Music; Electroacoustic Music; Schwebndes Berliner Märchen, Traumvisionen, Dostoevsky Reflections, Homage to Kafka, Rotation (in Memory of a Cosmonaut), Phoenixe, Sevtopolis; Water Music, 1980; Musik mit Papier; Luftmusik, 1980–81; Musicvisual Correspondence P, 1980–82; Six Capricci for baritone and piano, 1991; Seven Memorial Stones, In memoriam of the Holocaust Victims–A Requiem (F. G. Lorca); Die trunkene Fledermaus for orchestra. *Address:* Fröaufstr 3, 12161 Berlin, Germany.

**BADURA-SKODA, Eva;** Musicologist; b. 15 Jan. 1929, Munich, Germany; m. Paul Badura-Skoda, 4 c. *Education:* Universities of Heidelberg, Vienna and Innsbruck; PhD, 1953; Hochschule für Musik, Vienna. *Career:* Freelance Lecturer and Writer, until 1962; Summer School Lecturer, Mozarteum Salzburg; Professor, University of Wisconsin, 1964–74; Guest Professor, University of Boston, 1976; Queen's University, Kingston, Canada, 1979; McGill University, Montreal, Canada, 1981–82, Winter-term; Universitat Goettingen, 1982–83; mem, International Musicological Society; Haydn Institute, Cologne; Zentralinstitut für Mozart-Forschung des Mozarteums, Salzburg. *Publications:* Mozart Interpretation, 1957; Interpreting Mozart on the Keyboard, 1961; Mozart's C Minor Piano Concerto, 1971; An Unknown Singspiel by Joseph Haydn, 1972; Schubert Studies, 1982; Internationaler Joseph Haydn Kongress Wien 1982 Congress Report, Henle Verlag Munich, 1985; Aspects of Performance Practice, 1994. *Contributions:* Musical Journals; New Grove Dictionary of Music and Musicians, 1980; More than 100 scholarly articles on History of Viennese Classical Music and History of the Fortepiano. *Honours:* Austrian Decoration: Honorary Cross Litteris et Artibus; 3 University Grants. *Address:* Zuckerkandlgasse 14, 1190 Vienna, Austria.

**BADURA-SKODA, Paul;** Austrian pianist; b. 6 Oct. 1927, s. of Ludwig Badura and Margarete Badura (née Winter); m. Eva Badura-Skoda (née Halfar); two s. two d. *Education:* Realgymnasium courses in conducting and piano, Konservatorium der Stadt Wien and Edwin Fischer's Master Class in Lucerne. *Career:* regular concerts since 1948; tours all over the world as soloist and with leading orchestras; conductor of chamber orchestra 1960–; yearly master classes fmrly in Edin., Salzburg and Vienna Festival 1958–63; Artist in Residence, Univ. of Wisconsin, master classes in Madison, Wis. 1966–71; recorded over 200 L.P. records and CDs including complete Beethoven and Schubert sonatas. *Compositions:* Mass in D, Cadenzas to Piano and Violin Concertos by Mozart and Haydn, completion of 5 unfinished Piano Sonatas by Schubert 1976 and of unfinished Larghetto and Allegro for 2 Pianos by Mozart, Elegy for Piano 1980, Sonatine Romantique for Violin and Piano 1994. *Publications:* Interpreting Mozart on the Keyboard (with Eva Badura-Skoda), Die Klaviersonaten von Beethoven (with Jörg Demus) 1970, Interpreting Bach at the Keyboard 1993; Editions of Schubert, Mozart, Chopin; numerous articles. *Honours:* First Prize Austrian Music Competition 1947, Austrian Cross of Honour for Science and Arts (1st Order) 1976, Bösendorfer-Ring 1978, Chevalier, Legion d'honneur 1992. *Address:* c/o Hochschule für Musik und darstellende Kunst, Lothringerstrasse 18, 1037 Vienna, Austria (office); c/o 3116 Live Oak Street, Dallas, TX 75204, USA.

**BAEK, Kwang-hoon;** South Korean singer (baritone) and choir conductor; b. 29 April 1954, Soon-chun City; m. Park Kyung-nyum 1987; one s. *Education:* Kyung-Hee University, Seoul; postgraduate studies of singing and choir conducting, Music University, Wuppertal, Germany. *Career:* debut as Scarpia in Tosca at National Theatre, Seoul; freelance singer and choir conductor; Schubert's Winterreise, KBS Broadcasting Station, 1989; has sung main parts in Tosca, La Traviata, Pagliacci, Le nozze di Figaro, Cavalleria Rusticana, Noye's Fludde, Madama Butterfly, Un Ballo in Maschera in Korea and Slovakia; mem, Schubert Association, Seoul; Opera Association, Seoul; Deutscher Liederverein, Germany. *Recordings:* Winterreise; Hymns Solo; Conductor, The Creation by Haydn. *Address:* 101 Ho, 1428-7, Seocho-Dong, Seocho-Ku, Seoul, Republic of Korea.

**BAERG, Theodore;** Singer (Baritone); b. 19 Dec. 1952, Toronto, Canada. *Career:* Debut: Canadian Opera Company, 1978, as Monterone in Rigoletto; Sang in the Canadian premiere of Tchaikovsky's The Maid of Orleans (1980) and in Lulu, The Merry Widow and Die Zauberflöte (Papageno); Other roles include Mozart's Count (Hamilton Opera, 1984), Rossini's Figaro (Vancouver) and Ramiro in L'Heure Espagnole (Glyndebourne, 1988); Guested as Marcello in La Bohème at San Diego (1990) and Papageno at Washington (1991); Toronto, 1992, in the premiere of Mario and the Magician by Harry Somers. *Current Management:* Wolf Artists Management, 250 West 99th Street 2A, New York, NY 10025, USA. *Telephone:* (212) 531-1514. *Fax:* (212) 531-1610. *E-mail:* wolfartists@wolfartists.com. *Website:* www.wolfartists.com. *Address:* c/o Canadian Opera Company, 227 Front Street East, Toronto, Ontario M5A 1E8, Canada.

**BAEVA, Vera;** composer and pianist; b. 18 March 1930, Burgas, Bulgaria. *Education:* Sofia State Acad. *Career:* conducted the chorus of Radio Sofia, from 1954; Lecturer at the Sofia State Academy from 1986; Teacher of chamber music at the Open Society Foundation, 1993. *Compositions:* Five Impressions for piano, 1973; Four Songs, 1975; 2 Preludes for cello, 1984; Nostalgichno for chamber ensemble, 1986; Sonata for piano 4 hands, 1988; Butterfly for female voices and ensemble, 1989; Tristezza for violin, 1990; Dance around the Fire of the God Tangra for male voices and ensemble, 1991. *Address:* c/o Union of Bulgarian Composers, rue IV Vazov, 1000 Sofia, Bulgaria.

**BAGINSKI, Zbigniew,** MA; composer and teacher; b. 19 Jan. 1949, Stettin, Poland; m. Alicja 1988; two d. *Education:* High School of Music, Warsaw. *Career:* many performances of compositions in Germany, the United Kingdom, Denmark, Sweden, USA, USSR, Netherlands, Hungary, Cuba; Assistant Professor, 1978–88, Associate Professor 1988–; Vice-Dean, Faculty of Composition, Conducting and Music Theory, 1987–90, Academy of Music Frederic Chopin, Warsaw; mem, Polish Composers Union, Vice-President of Warsaw Branch, 1985–89, General Secreaty, 1989. *Compositions:* Sinfonia Notturna, 1984; Concerto for Harpsichord and Orchestra, 1985; Oh, Sweet Baroque Suite for String Orchestra, 1985; Symphony in Seven Scenes, 1988; String Quartet No. 3, 1992; Mass for chorus, 1995; Little Elegiac Symphony, 1995; Piano Concerto, 1995; Violin Concerto, 1996; Canons, Scherzos and Epigrams, 1987; Nocturne-Berceusee, 1989; Trio with Coda, 1983; Piano Quartet, 1990; Refrain for 2 Pianos, 1975; Acho for Organ, 1974; Expeditions on the Other Side, 1973. *Address:* ul Schillera 8m5, 00-248 Warsaw, Poland.

**BAGLIONI, Bruna;** Singer (mezzo-soprano); b. 8 April 1947, Frascati, Italy. *Education:* studied with Gina Maria Rebori and Walter Cataldi-Tassoni in Rome. *Career:* debut, Festival Dei Due Mondi, Spoleto in Boris Godunov 1970, soon afterwards sang La Favorita in Bologna with Luciano Pararotti; has sung at major theatres including La Favorita, Norma, Un Ballo In Maschera, Cavalleria Rusticana at La Scala, Milan; La Fenice, Venice; San Carlo, Naples; Trieste; Rome; Bologna; Palermo; Torino; Arena of Verona for 21 years; Eboli in Don Carlos at Covent Garden, London; Metropolitan, New York; Tokyo; Berlin; Munich; Hamburg; Paris; Vienna; Particularly identified with the role of Verdi's Amneris; Major tours include: Norma in Moscow with La Scala Milan; Dalila in Samson and Dalila with the Met of New York and with Covent Garden in Korea and Japan; Repertoire includes Verdi: Amneris in Aida, Azucena in Il Trovatore, Ulrica in Un Ballo in Maschera, Eboli in Don Carlos, Preziosilla in La Forza del Destino, Fenena in Nabucco and Messa da Requiem; Laura in La Gioconda of Ponchielli, Charlotte in Werther by Massenet; Leonore in Donizetti's la Favorite; Fedora; Dalila in Samson et Dalila; Santuzza in Cavalleria Rusticana; Giovanna Seymour in Anna Bolena; Carmen; Principessa of Bouillon in Adrian Lecouvreur; Adalgisa in Norma. *Recordings include:* videos: Don Carlos at Covent Garden; Nabucco at Arena of Verona; Aida in Luxor; albums: Norma with La Scala in Moscow; Luisa Muiller at La Scala, Milan; La Favorita in Bern. *Address:* Vicolo Manara 9, 00044 Frascati, Rome, Italy.

**BAGRATUNI, Suren;** Cellist; b. 17 March 1963, Yerevan, Armenia. *Education:* Yerevan State Komitas Conservatory; Moscow State Tchaikovsky Conservatory; New England Conservatory, Boston; Central Music School (Yerevan). *Career:* Debut: Solo in Yerevan, 1976; With an orchestra in Yerevan, 1978; Solo recitals in Grand Hall, Moscow Conservatory; Carnegie (Weill), New York; Jordan and Symphony Halls, Boston; Gasteig-Munchen; Gaveau-Paris; Alice Tully; Merkin, New York; Tonhalle, St Gallen, Switzerland; Professor, Michigan State University; Concertos and recitals throughout the world; mem, Nobilis Trio. *Recordings:* Solo Cello and Two Cellos, 1995; Shostakovich, Prokoviev–Sonatas, 1997; Trios by Beethoven (Op 1, No. 3)

Brahms (Op 8), Tchaikovsky, Rachmaninov, 1997; Babajanian, Trio, 1997; Short Pieces for cello and piano, 1997; Shostakovich and Prokofiev Cello Sonatas (Great Russian Cello Sonatas, Ongaku), 1998; Rachmaninov, Debussy-Sonatas; Stravinsky Suite Italienne, 2001. *Honours:* First Prize, Armenia National, 1980; First Prize, Trancaucasus, 1981; Winner, USSR National, 1981; Silver Medal, Tchaikovsky, 1986; First Prize, Vittorio Gui, 1988. *Current Management:* Boston Classical Artists. *Address:* 1291 Sebewaing Road, Okemos, MI 48864-3450, USA. *E-mail:* bagratuni@yahoo.com.

**BAHK, Jehi;** Austrian violinist; b. 26 June 1971, Vienna. *Education:* Vienna Acad. for Music and Performing Arts. *Career:* debut, Konzerthaus, Vienna 1995; founding mem. and leader, Hugo Wolf Quartet 1993–; Salzburg Mozarteum, Schubertiade Feldkirch, Carinthian Summer 1996; Munich Herkules-Saal, Nurnberg Kaiserburg, Prague, Rudolfinum 1997; Edinburgh Festival, Carnegie Hall, New York 1998; Musikverein Vienna, Cité de la musique Paris, Palais des Beaux-Arts Brussels, Philharmonie Cologne 1999; Wigmore Hall London, Philharmonie Berlin 2000; Tonhalle Zürich 2003; Amsterdam Concertgebouw, Birmingham Symphony Hall, Megaron Athens; Prof. of Violin, German School of Music, Weimar 2005–, Kangnam Univ., Republic of Korea 2005–. *Publications:* Hugo Wolf, Italian Songbook (vol. two, arrangement for string quartet and voice) 2003. *Honours:* first prize Int. Competition for String Quartets, Cremona, Italy 1995. *Current Management:* Till Dönch Künstlermanagement, Rögergasse 24–26/G2, 1090 Vienna, Austria. *Telephone:* (1) 470-80-83. *Fax:* (1) 479-69-71. *E-mail:* cora@doench .at. *Website:* www.doench.at. *Address:* Schützengasse 13/12, 1030 Vienna, Austria (office). *Website:* www.jehibahk.com.

**BAILES, Anthony James;** lutenist; b. 18 June 1947, Bristol, England; m. Anne Van Royen. *Education:* Bulmershe Coll. of Further Education, studied with Michael Watson in Bristol, Diana Poulton in London, Gusta Goldschmidt in Amsterdam, Eugen M. Dombois (Schola Cantorum Basiliensis). *Career:* debut, Purcell Room 1971; solo concerts and tours throughout Europe and Scandinavia; many recordings both solo and in ensemble; Prof. of Lute; hon. mem. Lute Soc., Svenska Gitarr Och Luta Sallskapet. *Recordings include:* Pieces de Luth, Lauten Galanterie, A Musical Banquet, Airs de Cour, Lautenmusik der Habsbergische Lande. *Publications:* An Introduction to 17th-Century Lute Music 1983, Lessons for the Lute (with A. Van Royen) 1983, 32 Easy Pieces for Baroque Lute 1984; contrib. articles to various journals and magazines. *Honours:* Edison Klassiek 1977. *Address:* Hollenweg 3A, 4144 Arlesheim, Switzerland.

**BAILEY, Judith Margaret;** composer and conductor; b. 18 July 1941, Camborne, Cornwall, England. *Education:* Royal Academy of Music. *Career:* conductor and composer from 1971; mem, BASCA; BASBWE; COMA; Cornish Music Guild; Portsmouth District Composers Alliance. *Compositions:* Trencrom, symphonic poem, 1978; 2 symphonies, 1981, 1982; Seascape for women's chorus, woodwind trio and orchestra, 1985; Penwith, overture, 1986; Fiesta for orchestra, 1988; Concerto for clarinet and strings, 1988; Havas for orchestra, 1991; Joplinesque for wind band; Festive Concert Piece for wind band; Chamber music. *Address:* c/o British Music Information Centre, 10 Stratford Place, London W1N 9AE, England.

**BAILEY, Norman Stanley,** CBE, BMus; British singer (bass-baritone); b. 23 March 1933, Birmingham; s. of the late Stanley Ernest and Agnes Train Bailey (née Gale); m. 1st Doreen Evelyn Simpson 1957 (divorced 1983); two s. one d.; m. 2nd Kristine Ciesinski 1985. *Education:* East Barnet Grammar School, England, Boksburg High School, South Africa, Prince Edward School, Rhodesia, Rhodes Univ., South Africa, Akad. für Musik und Darstellende Kunst, Vienna. *Career:* engaged full time at Linz Landestheater, Austria 1960–63, Wuppertaler Bühnen 1963–64, Deutsche Oper am Rhein, Düsseldorf and Duisburg 1964–67; Prin. Baritone English Nat. Opera, Sadler's Wells 1967–71; freelance 1971–; debut at La Scala, Milan 1967, Royal Opera House, Covent Garden 1969, Bayreuth Festival 1969, Paris Opera 1973, Vienna State Opera 1976, Metropolitan Opera, New York 1976; appearances Paris Opera, Edin. Festival, Hamburg State Opera, Munich State Opera; Prof. of Voice, Royal Coll. of Music, London 1990–. *Major recordings and TV films include:* Der fliegende Holländer, Die Meistersinger von Nürnberg, King Priam, Der Ring des Nibelungen, Macbeth, La Traviata, Falstaff. *Honours:* Hon. RAM 1981; Hon. DMus (Rhodes) 1986; Sir Charles Santley Memorial Prize 1977. *Address:* PO Box 655, Victor, ID 83455, USA. *Telephone:* (208) 787-2580 (office). *Fax:* (208) 787-2588 (office). *E-mail:* nbnsbailey@aol.com (office).

**BAILEY, Simon,** RNCM; British singer (bass baritone); *House Soloist, Frankfurt Opera;* b. 1972, Lincoln; m. Anna Ryberg. *Education:* Royal Northern College of Music and Clare College, Cambridge; Academy of Teatra alla Scala, Milan. *Career:* Appearances at La Scala in supporting roles in La Bohème, Carmélites, Wozzeck, Peter Grimes and Ariadne auf Naxos; Season 2001–02 with Jeffrey Tate, James Conlon and Riccardo Muti; Roles in Turandot and Verdi's Un giorno de regno; Premieres of Tatiana by Corghi, and in Figaro at Rouen; Season 2002–03 at Frankfurt Opera in Salome, Hercules by Handel, Der Schatzgräber by Schreker, Berio's Un re in ascolto, Manon and Verdi's Jérusalem; Papageno in Die Zauberflöte and Dulcamara in L'elisir d'amore; debut as Bartolo (Barber of Seville) La Scala, Milan 2005. *Recordings:* various including Stainer Crucifixion with Clare Coll. Choir. *Honours:* First Prize Concorso Int. di Musica Sacra 2004. *Current Management:* Hazard Chase, Norman House, Cambridge Place, Cambridge CB2 1NS, England. *Telephone:* (1223) 312400. *Fax:* (1223) 460827. *Website:* www .hazardchase.co.uk.

**BAILLIE, Alexander;** Concert Cellist; b. 6 Jan. 1956, Stockport, Lancashire, England. *Education:* Studied with Jacqueline du Pré, at the Royal College of Music and with André Navarra in Vienna. *Career:* Many performances with leading British Orchestras; Concerts in Europe and North America include the first Canadian performance of Penderecki's 2nd Concerto; Tour of the United Kingdom with the Budapest String Orchestra, 1991, followed by tour of the Far East; Promenade Concert appearances include the Concerto by Colin Matthews, 1984, Henze's Sieben Liebeslieder, Takemitsu's Orion and Pleiades 1989, Schumann Concerto, 1990 and the Delius Concerto, 1993; Has premiered works by Lutoslawski (Grave), Schnittke (Sonata for Cello and Piano), Gordon Crosse (Wave-Songs) and Takemitsu (Orion and Pleiades); Principal Guest Artist with the East of England Orchestra; Concerts with the Villiers Piano Quartet; Recital debut at the Kennedy Center in Washington, 1992; Season 1993 with US Concerto debut, Boston Philharmonic, and visits to the Edinburgh and Harrogate Festivals; Recital of unaccompanied works at the Wigmore Hall, London, 1997; Professor at the Royal Academy of Music. *Recordings include:* Tippett Triple Concerto with Ernst Kovacic and Gerard Causse; Concertos by Elgar, Colin Matthews and Bernard Stevens; Frank Bridge's Oration, the Britten Cello Suites and Sonata; Sonatas by Rachmaninov, Shostakovich, Prokofiev and Schnittke. *Honours:* Prizewinner in competitions at Budapest (Casals) and Munich (ARD). *Current Management:* TransArt (UK) Ltd, Cedar House, 10 Rutland Street, Filey, YO14 9JB, North Yorkshire, England. *Telephone:* (1723) 515819. *Fax:* (1723) 514678. *E-mail:* transartuk@transartuk.com. *Website:* www.transartuk.com.

**BAILLIE, Peter;** singer (tenor); b. 29 Nov. 1933, Hastings, New Zealand. *Education:* studied in Australia and New Zealand. *Career:* sang with New Zealand Opera and the Elizabethan Opera Trust at Sydney, from 1963; roles included Tamino, Ferrando, Jacquino (Fidelio) and Gounod's Faust; member of the Vienna Volksoper, 1967–88, in such character roles as Mozart's Bartolo and Monostatos, Albert Herring and Nando in Tiefland; also appeared in The Bartered Bride, From the House of the Dead and Zemlinsky's Kleider machen Leute; Glyndebourne debut, 1968, as Hervey in Anna Bolena, Wexford, 1968 (Mozart's Titus) and Salzburg, 1971 (first modern revival of Mozart's Mitridate); other roles include Ernesto in Don Pasquale, Malcolm in Macbeth and Svatopluk Cech in The Excursions of Mr Brouček; sang Mozart's Basilio for Wellington City Opera, 1995. *Address:* c/o Volksoper, Währingerstrasse 78, 1090 Vienna, Austria.

**BAINBRIDGE, Elizabeth;** British singer (mezzo-soprano); b. 28 March 1936, Lancashire, England. *Education:* Guildhall School with Norman Walker. *Career:* debut, Glyndebourne 1963 in Die Zauberflöte; sang in British premiere of Rossini's La Pietra del Paragone, London 1963; mem., Covent Garden Opera from 1965, in Butterfly (Suzuki), The Midsummer Marriage, Götterdämmeruug (Norn); Falstaff (Mistress Quickly), Les Troyens, Un Ballo in Maschera (Arvidson), Troilus and Cressida and Lulu, Erda, (Rheingold, Siegfried), Amelia, Otello, Jenůfa (Grandmother), Onegin (Nurse), Aida (Amneris); tours to La Scala, Milan 1976; Far East, 1979; Los Angeles; Athens Festival; guest appearances with ENO, Scottish Opera, WNO; US debut, Chicago, 1977 in Peter Grimes; Buenos Aires debut, 1979; Israel, Jenůfa, 1993, 1995; Covent Garden, First Maid in Elektra, Innkeeper's Wife in The Cunning Little Vixen, 1990; Peter Grimes, Dublin Grand Opera Society; Widow Sweeney in The Rising of the Moon, Wexford Festival; sang the Hostess in the Covent Garden premiere of Prokofiev's The Fiery Angel, 1992; Grandmother Burjya in Jenůfa at Geneva, 2001. *Recordings include:* Dido and Aeneas, Sorceress; Sir John in Love, Mistress Ford; The Rape of Lucretia, Bianca; Peter Grimes, Auntie; Cendrillon, Dorothée; Filipyevna in Eugene Onegin for EMI; Troilus and Cressida; Midsummer Marriage. *Address:* Buckleys, Forestside, Rowlands Castle, Hants PO9 6ED, England.

**BAINBRIDGE, Simon Jeremy;** composer and conductor; b. 30 Aug. 1952, London, England; m. Lynda Richardson 1980; one d. *Education:* Central Tutorial School for Young Musicians (now Purcell School), Highgate School, Royal College of Music, studied composition with John Lambert at the Berkshire Music Center, Tanglewood, Massachusetts, USA with Gunther Schuller. *Career:* freelance composer 1972–; his music performed extensively in the United Kingdom, USA, Europe, Australia; has worked as conductor with BBC Symphony Orchestra, BBC Scottish Symphony Orchestra, Bournemouth Symphony Orchestra, London Sinfonietta, Northern Sinfonia, Nash Ensemble, Composers' Ensemble, Capricorn and Divertimenti; teaches composition at Royal College of Music and Guildhall School of Music and Drama; mem. exec. cttees, Society for the Promotion of New Music, International Society for Contemporary Music, Association of Professional Composers. *Compositions include:* Wind Quintet; String Quartet; String Sextet; Clarinet Quintet; Works for small and large Chamber Ensembles, with and without voice; Choral Music; Works for large orchestra; Dance Score for Rambert Dance Company; Music for 2 Madame Tussaud Exhibitions, London and Amsterdam; Double Concerto for oboe, clarinet and chamber orchestra, 1990; Clarinet Quintet, 1993; Henry's Mobile for viol consort, 1995; Landscape and Memory for horn and ensemble, 1995; 4 Primo Levi Settings for mezzo-soprano, clarinet, viola and piano, 1996; 'Tis Time I Think for soprano and string quartet, 1996; Eicha for mezzo-soprano, chorus and wind ensemble, 1997; Chant for 12 amplified voices and ensemble, 1998; Three Pieces for orchestra, 1998; Guitar Concerto, 1998; Towards the Bridge for large ensemble, 1999; Dances for Moon Animals for guitar, 1999; Scherzi for orchestra, 2000; Voices, for bassoon and 12 strings, 2001. *Recordings:* Music of Simon Bainbridge: Fantasia for Double Orchestra–BBC Symphony Orches-

tra/Composer, Viola Concerto–London Sinfonietta/Michael Tilson Thomas-Walter Trampler Viola, Concertante in moto perpetuo-Composers' Ensemble/composer-Nicholas Daniel oboe. *Honours:* Margaret Lee Crofts Fellowship, USA, 1973; Leonard Bernstein Fellowship, USA, 1974; Forman Fellowship, 1976; USA-UK Bicentennial Fellowship, 1978; Published by United Music Publishers, Novello-Music Sales. *Address:* 38 Constantine Road, London NW3 2NG, England.

**BAIOCCHI, Regina Harris,** BA; American composer and musician; b. 16 July 1956, Chicago, IL. *Education:* Richards Vocational High School, Chicago, Paul Laurence Dunbar Vocational High School, Roosevelt Univ., Ill. Inst. of Tech., Inst. of Design, Chicago, New York Univ., DePaul Univ. *Career:* began composing aged ten; Orchestral Suite performed at Detroit Symphony Orchestra/Unisys Corpn Symposium 1992; composer-in-residence, Mostly Music Inc. 1992; guest composer, Wayne State Univ., Detroit 1993–94; guest composer/public relations lecturer, Northeastern Ill. Univ., Chicago 1993–94; guest composer, Columbia Coll., Chicago 1995, Northwestern Univ., Evanston 1996; composer, Musical Dir, Steppenwolf Theatre, Chicago 1997. *Compositions:* Equipoise by Intersection for piano 1978, Realizations for strings 1978, Chasé 1979, Who Will Claim The Baby? for chorus 1984, Send Your Gifts for chorus 1984, Father We Thank You for chorus 1986, Zora Neale Hurston Songs 1989, Psalm 138 for chorus 1990, We Real Cool for jazz ensemble 1990, Miles Per Hour (Jazz Sonatina) for trumpet 1990, Autumn Night for flute 1991, Crystal Stair for vocal ensemble 1991, Foster Pet 1991, Langston Hughes Songs 1991, Orchestral Suite 1991–92, Sketches for piano trio 1992, Shadows 1992, A Few Black Voices 1992, Teddy Bear Suite for orchestra 1992, Legacy 1992, Bwana's Libation 1992, QFX 1993, Much in Common for vocal ensemble 1993, Nobody's Child for chorus 1993, Mason Room 1993, Three Pieces for Greg 1994, Deborah for percussion 1994, Liszten, My Husband is Not a Hat for piano 1994, After the Rain 1994, Friday Night 1995, Darryl's Rose 1995, Gbeldahoven: No One's Child (opera) 1996, African Hands for orchestra with soloists 1997, Skins for percussion 1997, Dreamhoppers 1997, Nikki Giovanni 1997, Muse for orchestra 1997, Message to My Muse 1997, Dream Weaver 1997. *Honours:* City of Chicago Dept of Cultural Affairs CAAP grant 1992–94, 1996, AT&T grant 1994, Nat. Endowment for the Arts/Randolph Street Gallery Regional Artist Program grant 1995, Chicago Music Asscn Award 1995, ASCAP Special Awards grants 1996, 1997, Art Inst. of Chicago and the Lila Wallace/Reader's Digest Fund Award 1997. *Address:* PO Box 450, Chicago, IL 60690-0450, USA (office).

**BAIRD, Janice;** Singer (soprano); b. 1960, New York, USA. *Education:* Studied with Astrid Varnay and Birgit Nilsson; City University of New York. *Career:* Sang as mezzo-soprano throughout the USA; Dramatic soprano roles in opera throughout Germany from 1991; Season 1998 at Chemnitz as Elektra, Leonore, and Brünnhilde; Leonore at the Deutsche Oper Berlin, 1999, and Brünnhilde in Der Ring an einem Abend; Salome at the Vienna Staatsoper and the Berlin Staatsoper; Season 1999–2000 as Brünnhilde at Gothenburg and Geneva; Season 2000–2001 in The Ring at Catania, Salome in Berlin and Turandot at the Opéra du Rhin, Strasbourg. *Current Management:* Athole Still International Management, Forresters Hall, 25–27 Westow Street, London, SE19 3RY, England. *Telephone:* (20) 8771-5271. *Fax:* (20) 8768-6600. *Website:* www.atholestill.com.

**BAIRD, Julianne;** singer (soprano); b. 10 Dec. 1952, Stateville, NC, USA. *Education:* Eastman School with Masako Ono Toribara, Stanford University, studied with Walter Berry and Harnoncourt, and at Salzburg Mozarteum. *Career:* sang in New York with Waverly Consort and Concert Royal; Stage debut in Handel's Il Pastor Fido; Later appearances at Santa Fe, Washington DC, Philadelphia and Los Angeles in operas by Gluck, Mozart, Purcell, Charpentier and Gagliano; Concert engagements in sacred music by Bach and French Baroque music; Sang in Dido and Aeneas with Academy of Ancient Music at the Barbican Hall, London, 1992; teacher at Rutgers University. *Recordings include:* Handel's Imeneo, Acis and Galatea, Joshua and Siroe; Cantatas by Bach, Telemann and Clerambault; Bach's Magnificat and B Minor Mass; J C Bach's Amadis de Gaule; La Serva Padrona by Pergolesi and Monteverdi's Orfeo; Handel's Faramondo (Vox, 1996). *Publications:* contrib. to journals, such as Continuo and Early Music. *Address:* c/o Washington Opera, John F Kennedy Center for the Performing Arts, Washington DC 20566, USA.

**BAKELS, Kees;** Dutch conductor; b. 14 Jan. 1945, Amsterdam. *Education:* Amsterdam Conservatory, Accademia Chigiana, Siena with Franco Ferrara and Bruno Rigacci, studied with Kiril Kondrashin. *Career:* tours to England, Belgium, Spain and the USA; has led all the major Dutch orchestras and has guested with the Warsaw Philharmonic, BBC Philharmonic, BBC Nat. Orchestra of Wales, San Diego, Québec and Oregon Symphony Orchestras, New Belgian Chamber Orchestra, Ulster Orchestra, Scottish Chamber, Bournemouth Sinfonietta, Royal Liverpool Philharmonic; appeared with the Nat. Youth Orchestra at the Promenade Concerts 1985; Chief Guest Conductor, Bournemouth Symphony and Prin. Conductor, Netherlands Radio Symphony Orchestra; has worked with the soloists Yehudi Menuhin, Claudio Arrau, Pierre Fournier, Paul Tortelier, David Oistrakh and Ruggiero Ricci; appearances with Netherlands Opera in Nabucco, Ariadne auf Naxos, Carmen, Lucia di Lammermoor, Idomeneo and I Puritani; San Diego Opera, Oberto and Madama Butterfly; Vancouver Opera, Carmen, Così fan tutte, Le nozze di Figaro and Die Zauberflöte; conducted the Lyon Opéra in Cinderella (also on tour to Poland); WNO with Die Zauberflöte, La Bohème and Carmen; at ENO has led Aida and Fidelio; conducted Carmen at San Diego 1992; Prin. Conductor and Artistic Adviser, Malaysian Philharmonic Orchestra

1997–2005; season 2005–06 performances with Tapiola Sinfonietta, Quebec SO, Netherlands SO, Bern SO, Ensemble Orchestral de Paris. *Recordings:* Vaughan Williams Symphonies with the Bournemouth Symphony; Complete Nielsen Concerti with the Bournemouth Symphony Orchestra. *Current Management:* IMG Artists, Lovell House, 616 Chiswick High Road, London, W4 5RX, England.

**BAKER, Alice,** BA, MA; singer (mezzo-soprano); b. 27 March 1961, Detroit, MI, USA. *Education:* Oakland University, California State University, Los Angeles, apprenticeships with Lyric Opera of Chicago and San Diego Opera. *Career:* debut in USA, Opera, in alternating productions of Otello with Plácido Domingo and Madama Butterfly with Leona Mitchell, Los Angeles, 1986; European debut as Carmen opposite José Carreras at Teatro dell'Opera di Roma, 1987; In Europe has appeared in Rome as Giulio Cesare, 1998; Carmen, 1987; Isabella, 1987; L'Italiana in Algeri, 1987; Siebel, Faust, 1988; Suzuki, Madama Butterfly, 1990; Stabat Mater, 1989; In Turin as Elisabeth I in Maria Stuarda, 1999; As the Old Lady, Candide, 1997; In Venice, Leonora, La Favorita, 1988; Concert in Debussy's La Damoiselle Elue, 1989; In concert in smaller cities, Santa Margherita, Verdi Requiem, 1998 and Beethoven's 9th Symphony, 1997; Verona, in recital, 1989; Rome, in recital, 1996; Mantua, La Forza del Destino, 1999; United Kingdom debut with Wexford Festival Opera, 1988, as Carlotta in Elisa e Claudio; On tour to London at Queen Elizabeth Hall; In Germany as Rosina in Il Barbiere di Siviglia at Frankfurt Opera, 1988, 1989, 1990; Brahms Alto Rhapsody, 1992; In Spain in title role of La Cenerentola, Teatro Liceu, Barcelona, 1992; In Norway in concert with Stavanger Symphony, Mozart Grand Mass in C Minor, 1989; In Slovenia at International Festival Ljubljana, Verdi Requiem, 1998; Carmen, 2000; In USA and Canada: return engagements in Los Angeles to sing the title role in Cenerentola, 1988; Revivals of Otello, 1989; Hermia in A Midsummer Night's Dream, 1988; The Mother Superior in The Fiery Angel, 1989; Vancouver Opera debut, Suzuki in Madama Butterfly, 1995; Edmonton Opera as Cornelia in Giulio Cesare, 1994; Amneris in Aida for Greenville Opera, 1988; Parsifal, Carnegie Hall, New York, 1986; Lyric Opera of Chicago debut as Peep-Bo in Peter Sellers' The Mikado, 1983; St Louis Symphony, Mahler Third, 1988, return appearances for Otello, 1989; Pittsburgh Symphony debut in Rossini's Stabat Mater, 1989; Festival Internazionale Valentiniano, Rieti, Italy, Rossini's Stabat Mater with Moscow State Orchestra, 2000; Manzoni Requiem of Verdi, 2001; Recital tour in USA of songs by American and British composers and by Bizet, 2001. *E-mail:* info@cmi-arts.com. *Website:* digilander.iol.it/cmi.

**BAKER, Claude;** Composer; b. 12 April 1948, Lenoir, North Carolina, USA. *Education:* Eastman School, Rochester. *Career:* Professor, University of Louisville, 1976–88; Indiana University School of Music, Bloomington, from 1988; Composer in Residence, St Louis Symphony Orchestra, 1991–99. *Compositions:* Canzonet for solo tuba, 1972; Elegy for Solo Violin, 1979; Divertissement for clarinet, violin, cello and piano, 1980; Omaggi e Fantasie for tuba and piano, 1981, revised 1987; The Glass Bead Game for orchestra, 1982; Omaggi e Fantasie for double bass and piano, 1984; 4 Nachtszenen for harp, 1985, revised 1990; Fantasy Variations for string quartet, 1986; Tableaux Funèbres for piano and string quartet, 1988, revised 2003; Three Pieces for 5 timpani, 5 roto-toms and wind ensemble, 1990; Shadows for orchestra 1990; Awaking the Winds for orchestra, 1993, for chamber orchestra, 1994; Whispers and Echoes for orchestra, 1995; Into the Sun, for mezzo-soprano and orchestra, 1996; Flights of Passage for piano, 1998; Sleepers Awake for mezzo-soprano, percussion and strings, 1998; The Mystic Trumpeter for orchestra, 1999; Symphony No.1, 2000; Aus Schwanengesang for orchestra, 2001; Three Fantasy Pieces for viola and percussion, 2002. *Honours:* ASCAP Serious Music Awards, annually 1976–; George Eastman Prize, 1985; Eastman-Leonard Prize, 1988; Acad. Award in Music, American Acad. of Arts and Letters, 2002Fellowships: John Simon Guggenheim Memorial Foundation, 2001; Koussevitzky Music Foundation, 2002; Bogliasco Foundation, 2002. *Address:* School of Music, Indiana University, Bloomington, IN 47405, USA. *Telephone:* (812) 855-7423. *E-mail:* bakerwc@indiana.edu.

**BAKER, Gregg;** singer (baritone); b. 7 Dec. 1955, Chicago, Illinois, USA. *Education:* Northwestern University, studied with Andrew Smith. *Career:* Sang on Broadway in musicals; Metropolitan Opera debut, as Crown in Porgy and Bess, 1985, appearing later as Escamillo and the High Priest in Samson and Delilah; Has also sung Crown at Glyndebourne, 1985, and in Helsinki and Tulsa; Concert performance of Porgy and Bess at the Queen Elizabeth Hall, London, 1989; Other roles include Ford in Falstaff, Count Almaviva and Marcello in La Bohème; Old Vic Theatre, London in Carmen Jones, 1991; Sang Crown in Porgy and Bess at Covent Garden, London and Savonlinna Festival, Finland, 1992; Caesaerea 1993 as Amonasro; Jokanaan at Philadelphia and Detroit, 1995–96; Jokanaan in Salome at Vancouver 1997; Italian debut as Escamillo, at the 1996 Verona Festival; Season 2000 as Amonasro at Houston, Scarpia at Philadelphia, and Escamillo at Naples. *Recordings include:* Porgy and Bess. *Current Management:* Pinnacle Arts Management Inc., 889 Ninth Avenue, Second Floor, New York, NY 10019, USA. *Telephone:* (212) 397-7915. *Fax:* (212) 397-7920. *Website:* pinnaclearts.com.

**BAKER, Israel;** violinist; b. 11 Feb. 1921, Chicago, IL, USA. *Education:* studied with Adolf Pick, Chicago Conservatory, Louis Persinger at Juilliard

School of Music in New York, Jacques Gordon and Bronislaw Huberman. *Career:* soloist with various orchestras; concertmaster; many chamber music appearances including 2nd violinist, Heifetz-Piatigorsky Chamber Concerts; Often heard in Schoenberg's Concerto and Berg's Chamber Concerto; Member of Pacific Art Trio; Professor of Music at Scripps College, Claremont, CA. *Recordings:* various as soloist and chamber music player, including works by Ives, Antheil, Kubik and Stravinsky. *Address:* c/o Scripps College, Claremont, California, USA.

**BAKER, Dame Janet (Abbott),** CH, DBE, FRSA; British singer (mezzo-soprano); b. 21 Aug. 1933, Hatfield, Yorks.; d. of Robert Abbott Baker and May Baker (née Pollard); m. James Keith Shelley 1957. *Education:* York Coll. for Girls and Wintringham School, Grimsby. *Career:* Pres. London Sinfonia 1986–; Chancellor Univ. of York 1991–; Trustee Foundation for Sport and the Arts 1991–; Hon. Fellow, St Anne's Coll., Oxford 1975, Downing Coll., Cambridge 1985. *Publication:* Full Circle (autobiog.) 1982. *Honours:* Hon. DMus (Birmingham) 1968, (Leicester) 1974, (London) 1974, (Hull) 1975, (Oxford) 1975, (Leeds) 1980, (Lancaster) 1983, (York) 1984, (Cambridge) 1984; Hon. LLD (Aberdeen) 1980; Hon. DLitt (Bradford) 1983; Daily Mail Kathleen Ferrier Memorial Prize 1956, Queen's Prize, Royal Coll. of Music 1959, Shakespeare Prize, Hamburg 1971, Grand Prix, French Nat. Acad. of Lyric Recordings 1975, Leonie Sonning Prize (Denmark) 1979; Gold Medal of Royal Philharmonic Soc. 1990; Commdr des Arts et des Lettres. *Address:* TransArt (UK) Ltd, Cedar House, 10 Rutland Street, Filey, North Yorkshire YO14 9JB, England. *Telephone:* (1723) 515819. *Fax:* (1723) 514678. *E-mail:* transartuk@transartuk.com. *Website:* www.transartuk.com.

**BAKER, Mark;** Singer (Tenor); b. 1953, Tulsa, Oklahoma, USA. *Education:* Bachelor of Music, 1984, Masters Degree in Counselling, 1986, Indiana University. *Career:* Metropolitan Opera from 1986, as Paris in Roméo et Juliette (debut role), Narraboth in Salome, Froh in Das Rheingold and Melot in Tristan und Isolde; Glimmerglass Opera, 1987, as Lensky in Eugene Onegin, Santa Fe, 1988 (Erik in Fliegende Holländer), Glyndebourne Touring Opera, 1990, as Florestan; Sang Steva in Jenůfa and Ferrando in Così fan tutte at 1989 Glyndebourne Festival; Nantes, 1991, as Monteverdi's Ulisse, Théâtre du Châtelet, Paris, 1992 and Met, 1997, as the Drum Major in Wozzeck; Season 1995–96 as Siegmund at Santiago and Vladimir in Prince Igor at San Francisco; Laca in Jenůfa at Santiago, 1998; Engaged as Samson in Samson et Dalila and Tom in The Great Gatsby at the Met (world premiere, 1999–2000) and Siegmund in Die Walküre at San Francisco Opera; Season 2000–01 as the Drum Major in Wozzeck at Dallas and Samson for Cleveland Opera. *Recordings include:* Jenůfa, from Glyndebourne (Virgin Classics). *Honours:* Winner in the Metropolitan Opera National, 1986. *Current Management:* Munro Artist's Management, 786 Dartmouth Street, South Dartmouth, MA 02748, USA. *Telephone:* (508) 993-9011. *Fax:* (508) 993-9044. *E-mail:* Operamom@aol.com. *Address:* c/o Metropolitan Opera, Lincoln Plaza, New York, NY 10023, USA.

**BAKER, Michael Conway;** Canadian composer and lecturer; b. 13 March 1937, West Palm Beach, FL, USA; m. Penny Anne Baker. *Education:* BMus, Univ. of British Columbia, 1966; MA, Western Washington State Coll., 1972. *Career:* film and concert composer; over almost 25 years has taught and developed music programmes for children of all ages, adult education and univ. students; taught two courses at Univ. of British Columbia as well as one extension course at Simon Fraser Univ.; Composer-in-Residence for Vancouver School Board; now retired; mem., ALCM. *Compositions include:* Counterplay for viola and strings, 1971; Concerto for flute and strings, 1974; Sonata for piano, 1974; Concerto for piano and orchestra, 1976; Symphony No. 1, Highland, 1977; Washington Square, 60-minute ballet for orchestra, 1978; Evocations for flute, quartet and orchestra, 1982; Seven Wonders: A Song Cycle for soprano and piano, 1983; Chanson Joyeuse for orchestra, 1987; Intermezzo for flute and harp, 1988; Through the Lions' Gate: Tone Poems for orchestra, 1989; Capriccio for clarinet and orchestra, 1991; Cinderella—Frozen in Time, 90-minute ice ballet, 1993; Century Symphony (no. 2), 1994; Summit Concerto for trumpet and orchestra, 1995; Vancouver Variations, 1996; His Fanfare to Expo '86 opened the proceedings in Vancouver. *Recordings:* 116 concert works and 180 film projects. *Honours:* Juno, Best Classical Composition, 1991; Order of British Columbia, 1997. *Address:* 2440 Treetop Lane, North Vancouver, BC V7H 2K5, Canada.

**BAKER, Richard Douglas James,** OBE, MA; British broadcaster and author; b. 15 June 1925, s. of Albert Baker and Jane I. Baker; m. Margaret C. Martin 1961; two s. *Education:* Kilburn Grammar School and Peterhouse, Cambridge. *Career:* Royal Navy 1943–46; actor 1948; teacher 1949; BBC Third Programme announcer 1950–53; BBC TV newsreader 1954–82; commentator for State Occasion Outside Broadcasts 1967–70; TV introductions to Promenade concerts 1960–95; panellist, Face the Music (BBC 2) 1966–79; presenter, Omnibus (BBC TV) 1983; presenter of various shows on BBC Radio including Start the Week 1970–87, These You Have Loved 1972–77, Baker's Dozen 1978–87, Mainly for Pleasure 1986–92, Comparing Notes 1987–95; presenter, Classic Countdown for Classic FM radio 1995–97, Sound Stories Radio 3 1998–2000, Melodies for You 1999–2003, Your Hundred Best Tunes 2003–; mem. Broadcasting Standards Council 1988–93. *Publications:* Here is the News (broadcasts) 1966, The Terror of Tobermory 1972, The Magic of Music 1975, Dry Ginger 1977, Richard Baker's Music Guide 1979, Mozart 1982, London, A Theme with Variations 1989, Richard Baker's Companion to Music 1993, Franz Schubert 1997. *Honours:* Hon. Fellow, London Coll. of Music; Hon. FRCM; Hon. mem. Royal Liverpool Philharmonic Soc.; Hon. LLD

(Strathclyde) 1979, (Aberdeen) 1983; TV Newscaster of the Year (Radio Industries Club), 1972, 1974, 1979, BBC Radio Personality of the Year (Variety Club of GB) 1984, Sony Gold Award for Radio 1996. *Address:* c/o Stephannie Williams Artists, 9 Central Chambers, Wood Street, Stratford upon Avon, CV37 6JQ, England. *Telephone:* (1789) 266272.

**BAKER, Simon;** Singer (Countertenor); b. 1973, Edinburgh, Scotland. *Education:* Edinburgh Academy and Christ's Hospital; Royal College of Music, with Ashley Stafford. *Career:* Sang Handel's Ottone, and Claudio in the modern premiere of Silla at the 23rd London Handel Festival, 2000; Arsamenes in Xerxes for British Youth Opera at the Queen Elizabeth Hall, Messiah in Dublin and London and Canticles by Britten for the Spitalfields Winter Festival; Season 2001 with Flavio for the London Handel Festival, St Matthew Passion at Wells Cathedral, St John Passion at Christ's Hospital and Fileno in Handel's Clori, Tirsi e Fileno for the Covent Garden Festival; other roles include Nero in Monteverdi's Poppea. *Recordings:* Silla, by Handel conducted by Denys Darlow. *Honours:* Featured Artist, Great British Hopes, London Times 2000. *Address:* c/o Royal College of Music, Prince Consort Road, London, SW7 2BS, England. *Website:* www.countertenor.co.uk.

**BAKHCHIEV, Alexander,** MA; pianist; b. 27 July 1930, Moscow, USSR; m. Elena Sorokina 1962; one d. *Education:* Moscow Conservatory. *Career:* debut in solo programme, Liszt, Beethoven Hall, Bolshoi Theatre, Moscow, 1954; State television and radio, over 35 years; Solo, with orchestra, in chamber music ensembles, with singers; Regular duo with wife; Played with orchestras conducted by Rozhdestvensky. Svetlanov, Kondrashin, Chaikin, with V Popov (bassoon), A Korneyev (flute), others; Performed, France, 1954; Chamber music concerts, 1970s; Many educational television and radio series; Concerts all over USSR, including Moscow State Conservatory and with St Petersburg Philharmonic; Duets, Soviet and British modern music, England, 1989; International festivals including Mozart Festival, Tokyo, 1991; Teaching Chamber Ensemble, Moscow State Conservatory, 1990–; 8 programmes, all Schubert piano duets (with wife); Piano duo festivals, Novosibirsk, Ekaterinburg, 1993–95; Piano Duet lecture series for teachers and students, Russia; Music dedicated to him and wife by Boyarsky, Lubovksy, Fried, Moore; Gubaidulina's concerto Introitus written for him. *Recordings include:* solo recordings include Haydn, Liszt, Bach, Handel, Rubinstein, Arensky, Liadov, Lyapunov, Mussorgsky, Borodin; Ensembles: All sonatas, flute, harpsichord, Bach, Handel; Vivaldi (with A Korneyev); With Valery Popov: Masterpieces of Baroque; Czechoslovakian music, bassoon, piano; Series: Early Mozart, solo, ensembles; Duets with wife: Schubert, all Mozart, Rachmaninov, Russian Salon Piano Music; Music of France; Albums: Music of Old Vienna; J. S. Bach, his family and pupils. *Address:* 4-32 Koshkin str, Moscow 115409, Russia.

**BAKKE, Ruth;** composer and organist; b. 2 Aug. 1947, Bergen, Norway. *Education:* Bergen Conservatory, Oslo University, studied in the USA. *Career:* organist at the Storetveit Church, Bergen from 1973. *Compositions:* Organ sonata, 1970; Colour Clouds for orchestra, 1972; Rumus for chamber orchestra, 1976; Bonn for organ, soprano and guitar, 1976; Trollsuite for string quartet, 1981; Into the Light for violin and organ, 1982; Meditation for horn and organ, 1986; Nonsense for solo voice, 1990; Sphaerae for organ, 1992; Suite ACD for Renaissance instruments, 1992; Psalm 2000 for organ and tuba, 1993. *Address:* c/o TONO, 4 Galleri Oslo, Toyenbekken 21, Postboks 9171, Gronland, 0134 Oslo 1, Norway.

**BAKST, Lawrence;** singer (tenor); b. 1955, Washington, DC, USA. *Education:* studied in America and Europe. *Career:* sang Radames with Opera Delaware and Kentucky Operas; Verdi's Don Carlos at several Italian centres; Macduff in New Jersey, Barcelona and Marseilles; Gabriele Adorno, Riccardo, Manrico, Canio, Calaf and Faust in Mefistofeles; Appearances at the New York City Opera, Zagreb, Wexford, Detmold, Wuppertal and the Opera Forum in Holland; Season 1990–91 as Faust, Cavaradossi and Edgar (Lucia di Lammermoor) in Wuppertal; Bob Boles in Peter Grimes at Marseilles and Pylade in Iphigénie en Tauride at the Opéra de Bastille, Paris; Sang Pylade with the Tanztheater of Wuppertal at Rome, 1992; Sang Puccini's Calaf at Kiel, 1995; Pylade in Iphigénie en Tauride at Rio de Janeiro, 1997. *Honours:* Winner, Metropolitan Opera National Council Auditions Competition; Premier Grand Prix and Best Tenor Award in the Vinas Competition, Barcelona; Concours International de Chant, Toulouse; 1st Prize, G B Viotti Competition, Vercelli. *Address:* c/o Music International, 13 Ardilaun Road, London N5 2QR, England.

**BALADA, Leonardo;** composer and professor; b. 22 Sept. 1933, Barcelona, Spain; m. 1st; one s.; m. 2nd Joan Winer 1979. *Education:* Barcelona Conservatory, New York Coll. of Music, Juilliard School of Music, Mannes Coll. of Music, studied with Copland, Tansman, Persichetti, Markevitch. *Career:* teacher, United Nations International School 1963–70; Faculty 1970–75, Prof. 1975–90, Univ. Prof. 1990–, Carnegie-Mellon Univ. *Compositions include:* Opera: Christopher Columbus, 1987, premiered in 1989, Barcelona Opera, with José Carreras and Monserrat Caballé singing leading roles; Orchestral: Piano Concerto, 1964, Guitar Concerto, 1965, Guernica, 1966, Bandoneon Concerto, 1970, Steel Symphony, 1972, Ponce de Leon for narrator and orchestra, 1973, Homage to Casals and Sarasate, 1975, Sardana, 1979, Quasi un Pasodoble, premiered with New York Philharmonic, 1981, Alegrias for flute and string orchestra, 1988, Symphony No. 4, premiered by the Lausanne Chamber Orchestra, 1992, Music for oboe and orchestra, Lorin Maazel and the Pittsburgh Symphony Orchestra, 1993, Shadows, Cincinnati Symphony Orchestra, 1995, Morning Music, premiered by Julius Baker flute,

and Carnegie Mellon Philharmonic, 1995; Concierto Magico, for guitar and orchestra, 1997, premiered by guitarist Angel Romero and the Cincinnati Symphony Orchestra, 1998; No-Res, revised, 1997; Cantata, with Barcelona Symphony Orchestra and National Chorus of Spain, 1997; Folk Dreams for orchestra, 1998, premiere National Orchestra of Ireland; Concerto for Piano and Orchestra No. 3, 1999, premiere Berlin Radio Symphony Orchestra; Passacaglia for orchestra, 2000; Music for Flute and Orchestra, 2000. *Recordings include:* Steel Symphony with Pittsburgh Symphony Orchestra under Lorin Maazel; Torquemada, cantata; Concerto for Piano, Winds and Percussion; Music for Oboe and Orchestra; Maria Sabina, Cantata with Louisville Orchestra; Divertimentos for string orchestra. *Honours:* Nat. Composition Prize of Catalonia, Barcelona 1993. *Address:* c/o Music Associates of America, 224 King Street, Engelwood, NJ 07631, USA.

**BALASHOV, Oleg;** singer (tenor); b. 1968, Moscow, Russia. *Education:* Moscow Conservatoire. *Career:* sang with Moscow Municipal Theatre New Opera from 1998; Young Singers' Academy of the Mariinsky Theatre, St Petersburg, 1999–; Roles with the Kirov Opera and elsewhere have included Andrei in Mazeppa, Vaudémont in Tchaikovsky's Iolanta, Kuragin in War and Peace by Prokofiev, and Verdi's Alfredo; Further engagements as Mozart in Rimsky-Korsakov's Mozart and Salieri, Lukov in Rimsky's The Tsar's Bride, Sinodal in The Demon by Rubinstein and Grigory in Boris Godunov; Appearances with the Kirov Opera in summer season at Covent Garden 2000 as Prince Anatol Kuragin in War and Peace. *Address:* c/o Kirov Opera, Mariinsky Theatre, Mariinsky Square, St Petersburg, Russia.

**BALASSA, Sándor;** Hungarian composer; b. 20 Jan. 1935, Budapest; s. of János Balassa and Eszter Bora; m. Marianna Orosz 1994; one s. one d. *Education:* Budapest Conservatory and Music Acad. of Budapest. *Career:* began career as a mechanic; entered Budapest Conservatory at age 17; studied composition under Endre Szervánszky at Budapest Music Acad., obtained diploma 1965; Music Dir Hungarian Radio 1964–80; Teacher of Instrumentation, Music. Acad. Budapest 1981. *Compositions include:* vocal: Eight Songs from Street Rottenbiller 1957, Two Songs to Poems by Dezső Kosztolányi 1957, Two Songs to Poems by Attila József 1958, Five Choruses (for children's choir) 1967, Legenda 1967, Antinomia 1968, Summer Night (for female choir) 1968, Requiem for Lajos Kassák 1969, Cantata Y 1970, Motetta 1973, Tresses 1979, Kyrie for female choir 1981, Madaras énekek (for children's choir) 1984, The Third Planet, opera-cantata 1986, Bánatomtól szabadulnék (for female choir) 1988, Oldott kéve for mixed choir 1992, Kelet népe for children's choir 1992, Damjanich's prayer for mixed choir 1993, Chant of Orphans 1995, Capriccio for Female Choir 1996, Spring Song, Autumn Song (for female choir) 1997, Woodcutter (for male choir) 1998, Moon-gesang and Sun-anthem (for male choir) 1998, Winter cantata (for children's chorus and string orchestra) 1999, Legend of Christmas (for female choir) 1999; opera: Az ajtón kivül (The Man Outside) 1976, Karl and Anna 1992, Földindulás 2001; instrumental: Dimensioni 1966, Quartetto per percussioni 1969, Xenia 1970, Tabulae 1972, The Last Shepherd 1978, Quintet for Brass 1979, The Flowers of Hajta 1984, Divertimento for two cimbaloms 1992, Sonatina for harp 1993, Little Garland (trio for flute, viola and harp) 1994, Five Brothers (piano) 1994, Jánosnapi muzsika (solo violin) 1994, Vonósnégyes (string quartet) 1995, Bells of Nyirbátor (for twelve brass instruments) 1996, Sonatina for Piano 1996, Preludes and Fantasia for Organ 1996, Duets (for flute and harp) 1998, Pastoral and Rondo (for violin and horn) 1998; orchestral: Violin Concerto 1965, Lupercalia 1971, Iris 1972, Chant of Glarus 1978, The Island of Everlasting Youth 1979, Calls and Cries 1980, A Daydreamer's Diary 1983, Three Phantasias 1984, Little Grape and Little Fish 1987, Tündér Ilona 1992, Prince Csaba for string orchestra 1993, Bölcske Concerto for string orchestra 1993, Dances of Mucsa 1994, Sons of the Sun 1995, Four Portraits 1996, Number 301 Parcel 1997, Pécs Concerto 1998, Hungarian Coronation Music 1998, Hun's Valley (Val d'Anniviers) 1999, Double Concerto for oboe, horn and string orchestra 2000, Eight Movements for two clarinets 2001, Secrets of Heart (cantata) 2002, Fantasy for harp and string orchestra 2002, Flowers of October for orchestra 2003, Songs from the Street Sümegvár, Duets (for two violins), Gödöllő Concerto (for guitar orchestra), Excursion to the Sun Mountain (for string orchestra), Sonatina II (for piano), Three songs to poems by Albert Wass, Xenia II (nonetto), To Speak to the Stork (for mixed choir). *Honours:* Erkel Prize 1972, Critics' Prize (Hungarian Radio) 1972, 1974, Listeners' Prize (Hungarian Radio) 1976, Distinction for Best Work of the Year, Paris Int. Tribune of Composers 1972, Merited Artist of the Hungarian People's Repub. 1978, Kossuth Prize 1983, Bartók-Pásztory Prize 1988, 1999. *Address:* str. 18 Sümegvár, 1118 Budapest, Hungary. *Telephone:* (1) 319-7049.

**BALATSCH, Norbert;** Chorus Master; b. 10 March 1928, Vienna, Austria. *Education:* Studied at the Vienna Music Academy; Private studies in cello and piano. *Career:* Sang with the Vienna Boys' Choir as a child, then directed after graduation; Directed the Vienna Mens' Chorus, then from 1952 the chorus of the Vienna Staatsoper (Chorus Master 1978–84); Director of the Bayreuth Festival Chorus from 1972 together with the Philharmonic Chorus, London (1974–79); Chorus of Accademia di Santa Cecilia, Rome from 1984; Has directed sacred works by Mozart, Haydn and others at the chapel of the Viennese Court; Led the chorus in Der fliegende Holländer at Bayreuth, 1990; Nikikai Chorus Group of Tokyo in Lohengrin, 1997. *Address:* Festspielhaus, 8580 Bayreuth, Germany.

**BALDWIN, Dalton;** Pianist; b. 19 Dec. 1931, Summit, New Jersey, USA. *Education:* Juilliard School of Music, New York; BM, Oberlin College Conservatory of Music; Studies with Nadia Boulanger, Madeleine Lipatti,

Paris; Special coaching from Sibelius, Barber, Poulenc, et al. *Career:* Toured extensively as Accompanist including: Gerard Souzay, Elly Ameling, Marilyn Horne and Jessye Norman; Took part with Souzay in the premiere of Rorem's War Scenes, 1969. *Recordings:* Numerous recordings including the complete songs of Fauré, Debussy, Ravel and Poulenc. *Address:* c/o Columbia Artists Management, 165 West 57th Street, NY 10019, USA.

**BALKIND, Jonathan (Paul Brenner);** British impresario and civil servant; b. 6 July 1946, Los Angeles, CA. *Education:* Cambridge Univ., Architectural Association, London. *Career:* historic buildings inspector, GLC/English Heritage with special responsibility for Spitalfields 1974–88; bd mem. and adviser, Endymion Ensemble 1980–; Gen. and Artistic Dir, Opera London 1988–; Grant Assessor, Arts Council England, Arts Councils of Scotland and Northern Ireland, Nat. Heritage Lottery Fund and Community Fund 1996–2000; Dir, Songbird Films (Music and Arts); Artistic Adviser, City of London Sinfonia 1988–91; Chair., Collegium Music '90; founder and Dir, Spitalfields Festival 1976–82; Festivals of Handel 1977, Early Music 1978, English Music 1979, Young Mozart 1980; produced Mozart Lucio Silla, last performances by Janet Baker of Dido and Aeneas and many other concerts and first performances; produced operas for stage in Spitalfields and other festivals, Barbican, South Bank and Sadler's Wells, including Gluck's Armide 1982 (Spitalfields), broadcast BBC, Handel's Alcina, restaged in Los Angeles, Monteverdi's L'Incoronazione di Poppea, and Britten's A Midsummer Night's Dream (all recorded); produced extensive music theatre with Endymion Ensemble, including Birtwistle's Punch and Judy with Opera Factory; Dir operas by Gluck, Mozart and Mussorgsky; Music Adviser TV films, Janet Baker – Full Circle (BBC) 1982, Jessye Norman – Singer (BBC)1986, dance documentaries (Channel 4), Beethoven in Love (BBC); Sr Administrator, UN Peacekeeping Dept. *Publications:* contrib. to various publications, notes for concerts by Endymion Ensemble and City of London Sinfonia; ed., festival and opera programmes. *Address:* 45 Chalcot Road, London, NW1 8LS, England.

**BALKWILL, Bryan Havell,** FRAM; British conductor; b. 2 July 1922, London, England; m. Susan Elizabeth Roberts 1949; one s. one d. *Education:* Royal Academy of Music. *Career:* debut, New London Opera Co. 1947; Conductor, New London Opera 1947–49; Glyndebourne, Wexford Festivals, 1950–64; Sadler's Wells, English National Opera, Royal Opera House, Covent Garden, 1959–65; toured USSR with the English Opera Group, conducting Albert Herring and A Midsummer Night's Dream with Covent Garden in Lisbon; gave premiere of Bennett's A Penny for a Song at Sadler's Wells, London 1967; Musical Dir, Welsh National Opera 1963–67; freelance, opera and concerts in the UK, Europe, USA and Canada; Prof. of Conducting, Indiana Univ., USA 1977–92; life mem. Royal Philharmonic Society. *Recordings:* Madama Butterfly Highlights, Sadler's Wells Opera; Recital with Geraint Evans and Suisse Romande Orchestra. *Address:* 8 The Green, Wimbledon Common, London SW19 5AZ, England.

**BALL, Christopher,** ARAM, LRAM, ARNCM; British composer, conductor and professor; b. 7 July 1936, Leeds. *Education:* Royal Academy of Music, Royal Northern College of Music, Guildhall School of Music. *Career:* debut as Dir, Praetorius Consort, Wigmore Hall 1971; conductor, BBC Philharmonic, BBC Scottish Symphony Orchestra, Ulster Orchestra, City of Birmingham Symphony Orchestra, Vancouver Symphony Orchestra, Royal Opera House Covent Garden Orchestra, Bavarian Opera Orchestra, Maggio Musicale Orchestra of Florence; mem Performing Right Soc., RAM Club, Composers' Guild. *Compositions:* Recorder Concerto, The Piper of Dreams; Oboe concerto; Flute concerto; Orchestral dances; Dance contrasts for full orchestra; wind quintet, Scenes from a comedy; Pagan Piper; Pan Overheard; On a Summer Day; Celtic Moods; Adderbury in Spring; The Coming of Summer; Autumn Landscape; Christmas at the Rookery. *Recordings:* Dances From Terpsichore; German And Polish Dances; The Dancing School Of Lambrangi; Orchéso-graphie; Music By Holborne; Recordings by London Baroque Trio; The Praetorius Consort; Joyful Noyse. *Honours:* Gold medal for orchestral playing; John Solomon wind prize; Ricordi conducting prize. *Address:* 122 Wigmore Street, London W1U 3RX, England.

**BALL, Michael,** DMus, ARCM; British composer; b. 10 Nov. 1946, Manchester, England. *Education:* Royal Coll. of Music. *Career:* compositions covering most areas, including six commissions from the BBC; main publr, Novello; mem. British Acad. of Composers and Songwriters, Incorporated Soc. of Musicians, Soc. for the Promotion of New Music. *Compositions include:* Sainte Marye Virgine 1979, Resurrection Symphonies 1982, Frontier! 1984, A Hymne to God my God 1984, Omaggio 1986, Danses vitales: Danses macabres 1987, Nocturns 1990, Chaucer's Tunes 1993, Saxophone Concerto 1994, Whitsun Wakes 1997, Euphonium Concerto 2002, ...all the flowers of the mountain... 2004. *Honours:* RCM Octavia Travelling Scholarship. *Address:* 31 Sefton, Rochestown Avenue, Dun Laoghaire, Co. Dublin, Ireland (home). *E-mail:* michaelball@iol.ie.

**BALLARD, Louis;** Composer; b. 6 July 1931, Devil's Promenade, Oklahoma, USA. *Education:* Studied at Oklahoma and Tulsa Universities; MM, 1962; Further study with Milhaud, Bela Rozsa, Castelnuovo-Tedesco and Carlos Surinach. *Career:* Programme Director, Bureau of Indian Affairs, Washington, District of Columbia, 1979–. *Compositions include:* Koshare, ballet on Indian themes, 1966; The God will Hear, cantata, 1966; Four Moons, ballet, 1967; Ritmo Indio for wind instruments, 1968; Dialogue Differgutia, oratorio with orchestra and soloists; Katcin Dances for cello and piano, 1970; Desert Trilog for winds, strings and percussion, 1971; Cacega Ayuwipi for percussion ensemble, 1973; Devil's Promenade for orchestra, 1973; Incident at Wounded Knee for orchestra, 1974; Thus Spake Abraham, cantata, 1976; City of Fire for piano; City of Silver, piano; City of Light, piano; Companion of Talking God for orchestra, 1982; Fantasy Aborigine III for orchestra, 1984; Fantasy Aborigine No. 5, 1986, No. 6 'Niagara', 1991; The Maid of the Mist and the Thunder-beings, dance, 1991; The Lonely Sentinel for ensemble, 1993; Feast Day, sketch for orchestra, 1994; The Fire Moon, string quartet, 1997. *Publications include:* My Music Reaches to the Sky, 1973; Music of North American Indians, 1974. *Address:* c/o ASCAP, ASCAP Building, 1 Lincoln Plaza, New York, NY 10023, USA.

**BALLEYS, Brigitte;** singer (mezzo-soprano); b. 18 June 1959, Martigny, Wallis, Switzerland. *Education:* Bern Conservatory with Jakob Stämpfli, studied with Elisabeth Schwarzkopf. *Career:* sang in concert from 1982, notably in sacred music by Bach, the Brahms Alto Rhapsody, Masses by Mozart, Haydn, Schubert, Bruckner, Dvořák and Rossini; Schumann and Mahler Lieder; appearances in Switzerland, Germany, Austria, Italy, France, Portugal, Spain, South America, USA, Czechoslovakia; festival engagements at Zürich, Lucerne, Florence and Siena; recitalist in songs by de Falla, Shostakovich, Schoeck and Wolf-Ferrari, as well as French chansons and German songs; sang in opera at Freiburg 1985, with guest appearances at Zürich, Geneva, Avignon, Schwetzingen, Lausanne, and Montpellier; Vienna Staatsoper 1987, as Cherubino conducted by Leinsdorf; sang Octavian in Bern, Montpellier, Toulouse 1990; season 1992 as Fragoletto in Offenbach's Les Brigands at Amsterdam and Ramiro in Jean-Claude Malgoire's Vivaldi pastiche Montezuma at Monte Carlo; sang Nerone in Monteverdi's Poppea at Amsterdam 1996; other roles include Jocasta in Oedipus Rex (at Palermo), Gluck's Orpheus, Ottavia in Coronation of Poppea, Charlotte in Werther by Massenet, Meg Page and Orlofsky, Mrs Montgomery in L'Héritière by Damasé (at Marseilles); Geneviève in Debussy's Pelléas at the Paris Opéra-Comique 1998 and at La Scala, Milan 2004; season 1999 sang Sesto in Giulio Cesare by Handel at Montpellier and the title role in Didon by Henri Desmarest at Beaune, Versailles and Metz; sang Isadora in Le Foy by Marcel Landowski at Montpellier 2000; sang in Nerone at BAM Festival, Brooklyn, NY 2002; teacher at Lausanne Conservatoire 2001–. *Recordings include:* La Demoiselle Elue by Debussy and Janáček's Diary of One who Disappeared; Mendelssohn's St Paul and Die Zauberflöte, as Second Lady; Zelenka's Requiem; Leguerney, Melodies; Martucci, Canzone de Ricordi; Respighi, Il Tramonto; Les Nuits d'Été by Berlioz; Schumann, Lieder; Honegger, Judith; Frank Martin, In Terra Pax; Ernest Bloch's 4 chants d'automne; Frank Martin's Der Cornet; Löffler's Melodies; Chants du Japon. *Honours:* first prize Benson and Hedges in London 1983, Special Prize for Lied. *Address:* Bächtoldstrasse 1, 8044 Zürich; Chemin des Planches 19, 1008 Prilly, Switzerland. *Telephone:* (21) 634-4877.

**BALLISTA, Antonio;** Pianist; b. 30 March 1936, Milan, Italy. *Education:* Studied piano and composition Milan Conservatory, graduated 1955. *Career:* Toured widely as a soloist, also many duo recitals with the pianist Bruno Canino; Took part in the premieres of Rapsodia (1984), by Davidee Anzaghi, Concerto for two pieces by Berio (1973), Tableaux Vivants (1964), by Berio, Fogliod'album (1969), by Bussotti, Couplets (1979) by Castiglioni, B.A.C.H. (1970) and Piano Concerto (1976), by Aldo Clementi, Estratto (1969), by Donatoni and De La Nuit, 1971, by Sciarrino; Professor at Giuseppe Verdi Conservatory from 1964. *Recordings:* Several recordings of contemporary works. *Address:* c/o Ingrassia, Via San Zanobi 7, 1–50018 Scandicci (Fi), Italy.

**BALOGH, Endre;** Violinist; b. 1954, Los Angeles, California, USA. *Education:* Attended Yehudi Menuhin's School, England, at age 9; Violin studies with Joseph Piastro, Manuel Compinsky and Mehli Mehta. *Career:* Debut: New York Town Hall, 1971; Played 1st concerto with orchestra at age 6; Recital, Los Angeles, at age 15; 1st European tour including concerts in Berlin and London, 1973; Performed in Austria, Netherlands and Italy; Recital for BBC, London, and on-the-air, Amsterdam; Appearances with various orchestras including Los Angeles Philharmonic and Washington, Seattle, Honolulu and other Symphony Orchestras; Numerous recitals in key US cities; Performed with Berlin Philharmonic, Rotterdam Philharmonic, Frankfurt Symphony, Tonhalle Orchestra of Zürich, Basel Symphony; As soloist with orchestra under conductors Zubin Mehta, Lawrence Foster, Henry Lewis, Vladimir Golschmann, Milton Katims, Hirouko Iwaki, Edo de Waart; Numerous appearances with American Youth Symphony, under Mehli Mehta; Played many benefits for State of Israel, United Nations, Philosophical Research Society and others; Violinist, Pacific Trio, throughout USA and Canada. *Recordings:* Pacific Trio, 1990; Brahms C major and Shostakovich E major trios. *Address:* c/o UCLA, Music Faculty, 405 Hilgard Ave, Los Angeles, CA 90024, USA.

**BALSACH, Llorenç;** composer and music theorist; b. 16 April 1953, Sabadell, Barcelona, Spain; m. Sedes Garcia-Cascon 1991. *Education:* University of Barcelona, Sabadell and Barcelona Conservatories of Music, composition with Josep Soler. *Career:* freelance composer, 1976–; commissions, Baden-Baden Südwestfunk Orchestra, 1979, Associació Catalana de Compositors, 1983, 1991, CDMC, Barcelona City Council, 1991, Vallès Symphony Orchestra, 1991, Spanish Ministry of Culture, 1992, Radio Nacional de España, 1993, 1994, film Entreacte, 1985, and stage works; Creator, pioneer music software in GADIN Company, 1983–87; Editor, LA MA DE GUIDO Music Publishing House editions, 1986–; Consultant, Phonos, Pompeu Fabra University, 1994–. *Compositions include:* Orchestral: Gran Copa especial, 1979; Poema Promiscu, 1981; Visions grotesques, 1992; Quatre dibuìxos per a guitarra i cordes, 1994; Chamber: De Caldetes a Moià, 1978; Suite Gàstrica, 1979; Rondó, 1983; Musica-Màgica, 1992; Trìo per a cordes, 1992; Tres converses for 10 instruments, 1997; Música groga, 1980; Sìs cançons breus, 1982; Olis d'olimpia, 1991. *Address:* Les Planes 37, 08201 Sabadell, Barcelona, Spain.

**BALSADONNA, Renato;** Italian conductor and repetiteur; b. 1966, Venice; one s. *Education:* Milan Conservatoire. *Career:* chorus repetiteur and Asst Chorus Master, Opéra de Basle 1993; Asst Chorus Master, La Monnaie, Brussels 1995, Dir of Chorus 1997; Asst Dir, Bayreuth Festival Chorus 1999; Chorus Dir, Royal Opera House, Covent Garden 2004. *Address:* c/o Royal Opera House, Covent Garden, London, WC2E 9DD, England (office).

**BALSLEV, Lisbeth;** Singer (soprano); b. 21 Feb. 1945, Abenraa, Denmark. *Education:* Vestjysk Conservatory in Esbjerg, Denmark; Royal Opera School, Copenhagen. *Career:* Debut: Copenhagen, 1976, as Jaroslavna in Prince Igor; Sang Mozart's Fiordiligi, Leonora in Il Trovatore and Wagner's Senta in Copenhagen; Bern Opera, 1977, as Electra in Idomeneo; Bayreuth from 1978, as Senta in Der fliegende Holländer; Hamburg Opera debut, 1979, as Elsa in Lohengrin; Munich Staatsoper, 1979, in the title role of Iphigénie en Tauride by Gluck; Guest appearances in Dresden, Amsterdam, Berlin, Stuttgart, Cologne and Frankfurt; La Scala, Milan, 1987, as Salome; Lisbon and Berne, 1987, Senta and Elisabeth; Turin and Florence, 1988, as Wagner's Isolde; Leonore in Fidelio with Cologne Opera, Hong Kong, 1989; Isolde in a concert performance of Tristan und Isolde with Jutland Opera, Edinburgh Festival, 1990; Agave in The Bassarids at Düsseldorf, 1991; Nice, 1993 and Montpellier, 1996, as Isolde; Debut as Elektra at Århus, 1998. *Recordings include:* Senta in Der fliegende Holländer from Bayreuth. *Current Management:* Ingpen & Williams Ltd, 7 St George's Court, 131 Putney Bridge Road, London, SW15 2PA, England.

**BALSOM, Alison;** British trumpeter; b. Herts. *Education:* GSMD, Paris Conservatoire, studied with Håkan Hardenberger. *Career:* performances include BBC Proms, Barbican Mostly Mozart Festival, Bamberg Symphony with Mikko Franck, Stuttgart Radio Symphony with Sir Roger Norrington, Munich Chamber Orchestra with Christoph Poppen, London Chamber Orchestra, Belgian Nat. Orchestra, Milwaukee Symphony Orchestra, BBC Symphony, BBC Nat. Orchestra of Wales; Joby Talbot's Trumpet Concerto commissioned for her by Munich Chamber Orchestra and Liverpool Philharmonic; mem. BBC Radio 3 New Generation Artists scheme. *Recording:* Trumpet and Organ Recital 2002. *Honours:* Maurice André Int. Trumpet Competition Most Beautiful Sound Award, Paris 2000. *Current Management:* c/o Matt Fretton, HarrisonParrott Ltd, 12 Penzance Place, London, W11 4PA, England. *Telephone:* (20) 7313-3511 (office). *Fax:* (20) 7221-5042 (office). *E-mail:* matt.fretton@harrisonparrott.co.uk (office). *Website:* www.harrisonparrott.co.uk (office).

**BALTHROP, Carmen (Arlen);** Singer (Soprano); b. 14 May 1948, Washington DC, USA. *Education:* Studied at the University of Maryland, College Park and the Catholic University of America. *Career:* Debut: Washington DC in 1973 as Virtue in L'Incoronazione di Poppea, and as Minerva in the US premiere of Il Ritorno d'Ulisse, 1974; Sang the title role in Scott Joplin's Treemonisha at Houston Opera in 1975; In 1977 sang in Cavalli's L'Egisto at Wolf Trap and made her Metropolitan debut as Pamina; Sang at New York City Opera in 1978 as Roggiero in Rossini's Tancredi; Innsbruck Early Music Festival in 1980 as Monteverdi's Poppea, in the edition by Alan Curtis; Sang Poppea at Spoleto in 1979 and Santa Fe in 1986; Sang in Venice as Gluck's Euridice and Poppea in Handel's Agrippina, 1982–83; Michigan Opera Theater as Treemonisha and Pamina, 1982–84; Sang Gretel at Milwaukee, 1995; Created the title role in Vanqui by Leslie Burrs for Opera Columbus 1999. *Recordings include:* Treemonisha. *Honours:* Winner, Metropolitan Opera Auditions, 1975. *Current Management:* Dorothy Cone Artists Representatives, 150 West 55th Street, New York, NY 10019, USA. *Telephone:* (212) 765-7412. *Fax:* (212) 765-7443. *E-mail:* dcone@ix.netcom.com. *Website:* www.dorothyconeartistrep.com. *Address:* c/o Santa Fe Opera, PO Box 2408, Santa Fe, NM 878504, USA.

**BALTSA, Agnes;** Greek singer (mezzo-soprano); b. Lefkas. *Education:* Acad. of Music, Athens and in Munich (Maria Callas Scholarship). *Career:* opera debut as Cherubino, Frankfurt 1968; debut at Vienna State Opera (Octavian) 1970, Salzburg Festival 1970, La Scala, Milan (Dorabella) 1976, Paris Opera and Covent Garden, London (Cherubino) 1976, Metropolitan Opera, New York (Octavian) 1980; mem. Deutsche Oper Berlin 1973–; performs at all maj. opera houses in world and has given concerts in Europe, USA and Japan with Karajan, Böhm, Bernstein, Muti, etc.; Österreichische Kammersängerin 1980; has made about 30 operatic recordings. *Honours:* Deutscher Schallplattenpreis 1983, Prix Prestige Lyrique (French Ministry of Culture) 1984. *Address:* c/o Management Rita Schültz, Rütistr 52, 8044 Zurich-Gockhausen, Switzerland.

**BALUN, Frantisek;** Singer (Baritone); b. 13 Sept. 1948, Chminianska Nová Ves, Czechoslovakia; m. Melánia Balúnová, 3 s., 1 d. *Education:* The State Conservatory in Brno, Czech Republic (with Professor Richard Novák). *Career:* Debut: Theater of the Jonás Záborsky, Presov, 1968; Slovak National Theatre, Bratislava 1972–77; The State Theatre, Kosice, 1977–; Tchaikovsky's Iolanta; Ravel, The Spanish Hour; Sang Nabucco in Paris, 1994; Sang in Germany: Bettelstudent, 1996, Carmen, 1997; Sang in Austria: Nabucco, Carmen, 1997; In Czech Republic: Il Trovatore, Madama Butterfly; Opera and operetta arias; Folk songs for Slovak Radio; mem, Ján Cikker Foundation.

*Honours:* Prize of the Musical Fund for Tosca (Scarpia), Il Trovatore (Luna); Annual Prize of the Musical Fund and the Ministry of Culture for the performance of Mr Scrooge by Ján Cikker. *Current Management:* Opera Director, East Slovak State Theatre, Kosice. *Address:* Dvorkinova 6, 040 22 Kosice, Slovakia.

**BALZANI, Vincenzo;** Concert Pianist; b. 1965, Milan, Italy. *Education:* Studied at the Giuseppe Verdi Conservatory in Milan with Alberto Mozzati. *Career:* Debut: Has performed in public from age 14; Italian engagements at La Fenice Venice, the Comunale of Bologna, the Verdi Theatre in Trieste and the Academia Filarmonica Romana; Further appearances in France, Germany and Spain; London recital debut at the Purcell Room in 1989 playing Scarlatti Sonatas, Brahms Paganini Variations, Gaspard de la Nuit, Chopin Etudes Op 10 and Liszt Rigoletto Paraphrase. *Recordings include:* Music by Liszt, Mozart and Hummel; Chopin Etudes Op 10. *Honours:* Liszt Prize at the Maria Canals Competition in Barcelona.

**BAMBERGER, David,** BA; American opera director and producer; b. 14 Oct. 1940, Albany, NY; m. Carola Beral; one s. *Education:* Yale University School of Drama, Université de Paris, France, Swarthmore College. *Career:* Stage Director/Producer: The Barber of Seville, The Magic Flute, Der Rosenkavalier, New York City Opera; Rigoletto, Lucia di Lammermoor, National Opera, Santiago, Chile; Madama Butterfly, Don Pasquale, Cincinnati Opera; Don Pasquale, Pittsburgh Opera; The Flying Dutchman, Harford Opera Company; Producer/Director, Don Giovanni, Four Saints in Three Acts, Madama Butterfly, Così fan tutte; The Gondoliers, Die Fledermaus, Menotti's Tamu-Tamu (1st production after world premiere), Oberlin Music Theatre, Ohio; General Director, Cleveland Opera, 1976–, 50 productions including La Traviata, La Bohème, Daughter of the Regiment, Tosca, Aida, Faust, Falstaff, The Medium, The Secret Marriage, The Merry Widow, Holy Blood and Crescent Moon (world premiere); Artistic Director, Toledo (Ohio) Opera, 1983–85, staged Faust, Don Pasquale, Aida, Barber of Seville. *Address:* 1422 Euclid Avenue, Cleveland, OH 44115, USA.

**BAMERT, Matthias;** Swiss conductor and composer; *Principal Conductor and Artistic Adviser, Malaysian Philharmonic Orchestra*; b. 5 July 1942, Ersigen; m. Susan Exline 1969; one s. one d. *Education:* studied in Bern and Paris, studied composition with Jean Rivier and Pierre Boulez. *Career:* asst conductor to Leopold Stokowski 1970–71; Resident Conductor Cleveland Orchestra 1971–78; Music Dir Swiss Radio Orchestra, Basel 1977–83; Prin. Guest Conductor Scottish Nat. Orchestra 1985–90; Dir Musica Nova Festival, Glasgow 1985–90; Lucerne Festival 1992–98; Music Dir London Mozart Players 1993–2000; has appeared with Orchestre de Paris, Rotterdam Philharmonic, Cleveland Orchestra, Pittsburgh Symphony, Montreal Symphony, Royal Philharmonic Orchestra, London, London Philharmonic Orchestra, BBC Philharmonic, City of Birmingham Symphony Orchestra and at BBC Promenade Concerts, London; has toured worldwide; Prin. Conductor and Artistic Adviser Malaysian Philharmonic Orchestra 2005–. *Compositions:* Concertino for English horn, string orchestra and piano 1966, Septuria Lunaris for orchestra 1970, Rheology for string orchestra 1970, Mantrajana for orchestra 1971, Once Upon an Orchestra for narrator, 12 dancers and orchestra 1975, Ol-Okun for string orchestra 1976, Keepsake for orchestra 1979, Circus Parade for narrator and orchestra 1979. *Honours:* George Szell Memorial Award 1971. *Address:* Malaysian Philharmonic Orchestra, Dewan Filharmonik PETRONAS, Level Two, Tower Two, PETRONAS Twin Towers, Kuala Lumpur City Centre, 50088 Kuala Lumpur, Malaysia. *Website:* www.malaysianphilharmonic.com.

**BAMPTON, Rose E.,** BMus, LHD; American concert and opera singer (soprano); b. 28 Nov. 1909, Cleveland, OH; m. Wilfred Pelletier. *Education:* Curtis Institute of Music, Philadelphia, Drake University, Iowa. *Career:* debut, Metropolitan Opera, New York City, 1932, as Laura in La Gioconda; Metropolitan Opera, New York, 1932–50, notably as Leonora (Il Trovatore), Sieglinde, Kundry and Donna Anna; Covent Garden, London, England, 1937; As Amneris, Teatro Colón, Buenos Aires, Argentina, 1945–50; Sang Daphne in the first South American performance of the Opera by Strauss, 1948; Chicago Opera, San Francisco Opera; Voice faculty, Manhattan School of Music, 1962–82, Juilliard School of Music, 1974–. *Recordings:* Gurrelieder, Stokowski; Fidelio, Toscanini; Operatic Arias, Wilfred Pelletier. *Honours:* Hon. LHD (Holart and William Smith Colls, Geneva and New York) 1978. *Address:* 322 E 57th Street, New York, NY 10022, USA.

**BANDITELLI, Gloria;** Singer (Mezzo-Soprano); b. 1954, Italy. *Career:* Sang first in Sacchini's Fra Donato, for RAI, Naples; Siena, 1980, in Cavalieri's La Rappresentazione; Teatro Vale Rome, 1982, in Gagliano's Dafne, Innsbruck Festival, 1983, as Cesti's Tito, followed by Handel's Rodrigo, Medea in Cavalli's Giasone, Teodota in Handel's Flavio and Amastris in Serse; Bologna, 1984 and 1991, in Gluck's Armide and as Maria in Mosè in Egitto; La Scala, Milan, 1988, in Jommelli's Fetonte, Utrecht Festival, 1988, in Giasone and Montpellier, 1989, as Gluck's Orpheus; Concerts include Mozart's Requiem in Vienna, on 200th anniversary of his death; Sang the Messenger in Monteverdi's Orfeo at Palermo, 1996; Monteverdi's Penelope at Palermo 1998; Season 2000–01 in Monteverdi's Orfeo and Poppea at Beaune, and in Dido and Aeneas at Florence. *Recordings include:* Le Cinesi by Gluck (Harmonia Mundi), Pergolesi's Adriano in Siria (Bongiovanni) and Penelope in Monteverdi's Ulisse (Nuova Era). *Current Management:* Atelier Musicale, Via Caselle 76, San Lazzaro di Savena 40068, Italy. *Telephone:* (51) 19984444. *Fax:* (51) 19984420. *E-mail:* info@ateliermusicale.com. *Website:* www

.ateliermusicale.com. *Address:* c/o Teatro Massimo di Palermo, Via R. Wagner 2, 90139 Palermo, Italy.

**BANFIELD, William (Bill) Cedric,** BMus, MA, DMA; American composer, academic and musician (guitar); b. 24 March 1961, Detroit, MI. *Education:* Cass Tech. High School, New England Conservatory of Music, Boston, Tufts Univ., Medford, Boston Univ., Univ. of Mich. – Ann Arbor. *Career:* mem. Detroit bands, including Cool Breeze and The Sapphire from age 12; f. Bill Banfield Quintet 1980; founder and operator, B Magic Operations, Boston 1984–88; guest guitar soloist with Detroit Metropolitan Orchestra 1984, 1989; conductor, La Chorale des Martyrs de L'Ouganda (Senegalese Choir and Orchestra) 1988; f. Undine Smith Moore Collection, Ind. Univ. 1993; teacher public schools, Boston 1980–86; Musical Dir, Days in the Arts Program, Tanglewood Music Festival, Tanglewood, MA 1984–88; Minister of Educ., Union United Church, Boston 1984–88; Program Co-ordinator, Boston Theological Inst. 1985–88; founder and Dir, Young Artists Devt Inc., Boston 1985–88, Boston Music Community Center 1986–88; guitar instructor, Univ. of Mich. – Ann Arbor 1988–89, jazz instructor 1988–90; private instructor in composition, arranging and guitar pedagogy 1988–92; instructor, Hartford Biblical Studies Inst., Detroit, MI 1989–92; Asst Prof., Dept of Afro-American Studies, Ind. Univ. – Bloomington 1992–97; Prof. of Music, Ind. Univ./Purdue Univ., Indianapolis 1992–97; Dir and composer-in-residence, Soul Revue/Black Popular Arts Ensemble, Afro-American Arts Inst., Ind. Univ. 1992–97; witness series, composer-in-residence, Plymouth Music Series, Minneapolis, MN 1993–95; visiting artist and scholar at numerous insts., including Univ. of Mich. – Ann Arbor 1994, Carleton Coll. 1995, St Augustine Coll. 1995, Tufts Univ. 1995, Univ. of Mass – Amherst 1995, Univ. of Minneapolis 1995, Butler Univ. 1996, Duke Univ. 1996, Univ. of Akron 1996; W. E. B. Dubois Fellow, Harvard Univ. 2001; Endowed Chair Humanities and Fine Arts, Univ. of St Thomas, St Paul 1997–, currently Dir American Cultural Studies Program and Assoc. Prof.; mem. of: American Guild of Organists, Nat. Advisory Council, ASCAP, Coll. Music Soc., Minn. Composers' Forum, Nat. Asscn of Negro Musicians. *Compositions include:* for solo instruments: Warmly Embraced for piano 1980, A Stroll in Lydian for piano 1981, Reversed Roles for piano 1981, One Segment Samba for piano 1981, Belshazzar for guitar 1981, Hanaha for guitar 1981, A Little Look At Me for piano 1982, I V bVIII 5b7 b7 for piano 1982, Karla for guitar 1982, Song for Earl for guitar 1983, Song for Mic for guitar 1983, Gibbit for oboe 1985, Fantasy for piano 1987, Mead 28 for piano 1989, Waggussyduke for piano 1989, Suite for Richard for trumpet 1990, Two Tall Tales for bassoon 1992; for small instrumental ensembles: Derwin E.: Six Minutes for String Quartet No. 1 1983, Susan: String Quartet No. 2 1985, El Dia de Derber: Wedding Suite for string quartet and piano 1985, Bobby's Theme 1985, Brass Belly 1988, Spirituals 1988, Zola 1988, Cone Tone: String Quartet No. 3 1989, Four Persons 1991, For Bass Wrapped in Pita Pocket with Ketchup, Mayo and a Dash of Hot Mustard 1991, Can We All Get Along? 1992, Dance Like The Wind for woodwind 1995; for jazz ensemble: The Dream Suite 1980, Carla 1983, Straightline 1983, A Friend's Advice 1984, Just A Note From Sam 1988, Her Embrace 1990, Last Night She Had a Really Good Dream 1992, Blues for Anne 1992, Lisa 1993, Magdalene 1993, Rachel 1993, Derry Alan 1993, Brooke 1993, And What Would You Like to Hear Little Lady? 1994, TIM (Time in Motion) 1995, She Made It Crystal Clear 1995, Song for George 1996, Three Late Night Discussions 1996, Bill's Blue 1996, Brookes Way 1997, A Prayer 1997; for concert band: Concerto for Wind Symphony 1995, The Seed: Fanfare for Wind Symphony 1998; for full orchestra: Fantasy for Orchestra on Themes from Shakespeare 1989, Symphony No. 1: Brevities of Experience 1990, Dreams Realized/Nightmare Resolved 1992, Symphony No. 5: Five Shades of a Woman in Black 1993, Four Songs for Five American Voices: Symphony No. 6 1993, Essay for orchestra 1995; for orchestra with soloists: Marsheila 1982, Baroque Suite for guitar and string orchestra 1987, Susej Moments for guitar and string orchestra 1987, Three Movements and Themes on Shakespeare 1988, Jenny Festival for guitar and orchestra 1989, Moods and Colors concerto for trombone and orchestra 1991, You Can Tell the World 1992, Delancey Street 1994, Symphony No. 7: Reveries, A Summer's Circle 1997; for orchestra with chorus: Guide Us Through the Years 1988, Visions: Symphonic Songs for orchestra and double chorus 1988, Job's Song: Symphony No. 3 1992, Life Suite 1995; vocal: Pleasing Thought 1979, I'm Won 1984, Are You Thinking About Me? 1984, Baby You 1984, All I Gotta Do 1984, Unmistakable You 1985, Steadfast Love: Psalm 118 for chorus 1986, Harp Song 1989, Summer Lies 1989, The Prophetess 1989, Steadfast Love: Psalm 138 for chorus 1989, I Love You My Life 1990, Momma Why?: Questions of a Young American (opera) 1991, Spiritual Songs 1991, Desire: Langston Living Amongst the Poets Unknown 1992, The Prophetess II 1992, Eyes (musical) 1995, Luyala (opera) 1997, Fisherman's Dock (opera) 1997. *Publications:* Musical Landscapes in Color: Conversations with Black American Composers 2003; contrib. numerous articles. *Honours:* Chrysler Corpn Scholarship, Youth of Understanding 1978, Boston Foundation Artist Award 1987, winner Savannah Symphony American Symphony Orchestra League nat. search for black talent 1994, McKnight Foundation Composers-in-Residence Fellowship from the American Composers Forum, Carleton Coll., Univ. of St Thomas 1995–96, Detroit Symphony/UNISYS Award 1995. *Address:* Department of American Cultural Studies, University of St Thomas, Loras 105, South Campus, Mail #BEC9, 2115 Summit Avenue, St Paul, MN 55105, USA (office). *Telephone:* (651) 962-5893 (office). *E-mail:* wcbanfield@stthomas.edu (office). *Website:* www.stthomas.edu/acs (office).

**BANFIELD, Stephen David,** BA, DPhil, FRSA, FRCO; British academic and writer; *Stanley Hugh Badock Professor of Music, University of Bristol;* b. 15 July 1951, Dulwich, London, England. *Education:* Clare Coll., Cambridge, Harvard Univ., St John's Coll., Oxford. *Career:* Lecturer 1978–88, Sr Lecturer 1988–92, Univ. of Keele; Elgar Prof. of Music 1992–2003, Head School of Performance Studies 1992–97, and Dept of Music 1996–98, Univ. of Birmingham; Visiting Prof. of Musicology, Univ. of Minnesota 1998; Stanley Hugh Badock Prof. of Music, Univ. of Bristol 2003–; mem. American Musicological Soc., Royal Musical Asscn, Soc. for American Music, Kurt Weill Foundation. *Publications:* Sensibility and English Song 1985, Sondheim's Broadway Musicals 1993, The Blackwell History of Music in Britain, Vol. VI: The Twentieth Century (ed.) 1995, Gerald Finzi 1997; contrib. to scholarly books and journals. *Honours:* First Kurt Weill Prize, USA, Irving Lowens Award, USA 1995. *Address:* c/o Department of Music, Victoria Rooms, Queens Road, Bristol, BS8 1SA, England.

**BANKS, Barry;** British singer (tenor); b. 1960, Stoke-on-Trent, England. *Education:* Royal Northern Coll. of Music with Josef Ward. *Career:* Covent Garden debut as Beppe in Pagliacci 1989; other roles and appearances include Rossini's Almaviva, Fenton, the Novice in Billy Budd, Mozart's Basilio, Arturo in Lucia di Lammermoor, Iopas in Les Troyens, Griffiths/Mozart pastiche The Jewel Box, Pedrillo in Die Entführung, Il Signor Bruschino, Peri's Euridice, Tamino, Mozart's Mitridate, Gianetto in The Thieving Magpie, Tom Rakewell, Edgardo, Candide, Lucio Silla, Argirio in Tancredi, Britten's Flute, Nemorino, Belfiore in Il Viaggio a Reims, Don Ottavio, Brighella in Ariadne auf Naxos. *Honours:* Peter Moores Foundation Scholarship 1983. *Current Management:* Harrison/Parrott Ltd, 12 Penzance Place, London, W11 4PA, England. *Telephone:* (20) 7229 9166. *Fax:* (20) 7221 5042. *Website:* www.harrisonparrott.com.

**BANNATYNE-SCOTT, Brian;** Singer (bass); b. 4 Nov. 1955, Edinburgh, Scotland; m. Frances Stewart Leaf 1979, 1 s., 1 d. *Education:* St Andrew's University; Guildhall School of Music; Further study with Norman Bailey. *Career:* Debuts at La Fenice Venice, 1981, and the Rome Opera, 1982; Scottish Opera from 1982, as Colline, Don Fernando (Fidelio), Nourabad (The Pearl Fishers) and the Speaker in The Magic Flute; English National Opera from 1987 as Monterone (Rigoletto), Pogner and the Commendatore (1991); Varlaam (Boris Godunov), Opera North and BBC Prom, 1992; Banquo, ENO, 1993; Sang Fafner and Hagen in the City of Birmingham Touring Opera version of The Ring; Tour of Europe as Cold Genius in Purcell's King Arthur; Salzburg Festival debut, 1991, as Polyphemus in Acis and Galatea; Bermuda Festival, 1991, as Don Alfonso in Così fan tutte; Concert engagements with leading British orchestras; Has sung Christus in the St John Passion settings of Bach and Arvo Pärt (in Italy, Germany and Japan); Stravinsky's Les Noces with London Sinfonietta and Simon Rattle, 1993; Aldeburgh masterclasses with Galina Vishnevskaya (also televised) and recital at 1990 Prom Concert; Appearances: The Trojans, London Symphony Orchestra, 1993, 1994; Swallow in Peter Grimes, Nantes; Bastille Opéra, Tosca; Gurrelieder, City of Birmingham Symphony Orchestra; Flanders Festival, Handel's Chandos Anthems; Liège, Der Kaiser von Atlantis; 1995: Bartolo in Figaro, Bermuda Festival; Sarastro in Magic Flute, Nantes; Purcell's King Arthur in Europe and Buenos Aires; Sang Araspe in Handel's Tolomeo at Halle, 1996. *Recordings include:* King Arthur; Poppea; Dioclesian and Timon of Athens; The Wreckers; A Midsummer Night's Dream; Tolomeo. *Current Management:* Musicmakers International Artists Representation, Tailor House, 63–65 High Street, Whitwell, Hertfordshire SG4 8AH, England. *Telephone:* (1438) 871708. *Fax:* (1438) 871777. *E-mail:* musicmakers@compuserve.com. *Website:* www.operauk.com.

**BANSE, Juliane;** Singer (soprano); b. 10 July 1969, Tettnang, Wurttemberg, Germany. *Education:* Trained as ballet dancer in Zürich; Vocal Studies in Zürich and with Brigitte Fassbaender and Daphne Evangelatos in Munich. *Career:* Debut: Sang Pamina in Harry Kupfer's production of Die Zauberflöte at Komische Oper Berlin, 1989; Engagements at Komische Oper as Ilia and Susanna, 1991–92; Pamina in Stuttgart and Brussels; Sophie in Rosenkavalier at Landestheater Salzburg and Zerlina at Glyndebourne, 1994, 1995; Sophie, Susanna, Pamina and Zdenka; Contract with Vienna State Opera, 1993–; Concert repertoire includes all major oratorio repertoire; European concert performances with Orchestre de Bastille, Paris, Mahler's 4th Symphony with Vienna Philharmonic Orchestra under Claudio Abbado; Many Lieder recitals throughout Europe; US debut in 1995 in St Louis and Indianapolis; Sang in Henze's Raft of the Medusa at the Festival Hall, London, 1997; Season 1998 as Musetta at Cologne and Manon at the Deutsche Oper, Berlin; Mahler's 4th Symphony with Cleveland and Philadelphia Orchestra; Mahler's 2nd Symphony with the Vienna Philharmonic and Simon Rattle at the 1999 London Prom Concerts; Created the title role in Holliger's Schneewittchen, Zürich, 1998; Season 2000 as Pamina at the ·ienna Staatsoper, and soloist in the premiere of Lukas Passion by Wolfgang Rihm (Stuttgart). *Recordings include:* Lieder by Schoeck; Bach's Christmas Oratorio with the Windsbacher Knabenchor; Berg's Lulu Suite and Altenberg Lieder with Vienna Philharmonic Orchestra, Claudio Abbado; Mendelssohn's Paulus with H Rilling; Video of Don Giovanni, Glyndebourne 1995 (Warner). *Honours:* Winner, Kulturforum Competition, Munich, 1989; Schubert Award, Vienna, 1993. *Current Management:* Organisation Internationale Artistique (Bettina Brentano), 16 Avenue Franklin D. Roosevelt, 75008 Paris, France. *Telephone:* 1-42-25-58-34. *Fax:* 1-42-25-64-97. *E-mail:* oia@oia-poilve.com. *Website:* www.oia-poilve.com. *Current Management:* Walter Beloch Artists

Management, Via Melzi d'Eril 26, 20154 Milan, Italy. *Telephone:* (2) 33101922. *Fax:* (2) 3313643. *E-mail:* lirica@walterbeloch.com. *Website:* www .walterbeloch.com. *Current Management:* Colbert Artists Management, 111 West 57th Street, New York, NY 10019, USA. *Telephone:* (212) 757-0782. *Fax:* (212) 541-5179. *E-mail:* nycolbert@colbertartists.com. *Website:* www .colbertartists.com.

**BAPTISTE, Eric;** French radio executive; *Director-General, International Confederation of Societies of Authors and Composers. Education:* École nationale d'administration. *Career:* Gen. Man., Radio France Int. 1990–95; Vice-Pres., Radio Néo; Dir-Gen., Int. Confed. of Socs of Authors and Composers (CISAC) 1998–; chair. of govt think tank on digital convergence. *Publications:* Rapport sur les relations entre les diffuseurs télévisuels et les producteurs cinématographiques et audiovisuals 1989, L'infosphère: straté-gies des medias et role de l'État 2000. *Address:* c/o CISAC, 20–26 blvd du Parc, 92200 Neuilly-sur-Seine, France. *Telephone:* 1-55-62-08-50. *Fax:* 1-55-62-08-60. *E-mail:* cisac@cisac.org. *Website:* www.cisac.org.

**BÄR, Olaf;** singer (baritone); b. 19 Dec. 1957, Dresden, Germany. *Education:* studied in Dresden. *Career:* sang in Dresden Kreuzchor 1966–75; prin. mem., Dresden State Opera –1991; British debut 1983, at Wigmore Hall; returned summer 1985; Covent Garden debut 1985, as Harlekin in Ariadne auf Naxos; Aix-en-Provence Festival 1986, in Ariadne; Die Zauberflöte at La Scala; Glyndebourne Festival 1987, as the Count in Capriccio; Aix 1988, as Guglielmo in Così fan tutte, conducted by Jeffrey Tate; concert performances in Europe and USA; US debut 1987, as Christus in the St Matthew Passion with the Chicago Symphony Orchestra conducted by Solti; tours of Australia 1989, 1993, Japan 1989, 1992; created roles in premieres of operas by Matthus 1985, and Mayer 1989; at Covent Garden Opera sang Papageno 1991; Glyndebourne as Don Giovanni 1991; sang in Britten's War Requiem; Oliver in Capriccio, Opernhaus Zürich 1992; Marcello in La Bohème, Staatsoper Dresden 1992; Count in Le nozze di Figaro, Netherlands Opera Amsterdam 1993; operatic debut, USA as Papageno, Chicago 1996; sang in Schubert's Alfonso und Estrella at the Vienna Festival 1997; Mozart's Count at Rome and Wolfram in Tannhäuser by Wagner at Dresden 1998; new production of Ariadne auf Naxos at Dresden 1999, Die Fledermaus at the Vienna Festival 1999; sang Froila in Schubert's Alfonso und Estrella at Zürich 2001; Die Fledermaus, Salzburg 2001; Spielman in Königshinder, Naples 2002, Der Ring des Nibelungen, Bayreuth 2002–04; Die Tote Stadt, Zürich 2003; Die Zauberflöte, Paris 2005. *Recordings:* Schumann Dichterliebe Op 48 and Liederkreis Op 39, Kerner-Lieder Op 35 and Liederkreis Op 24, Schubert Die schöne Müllerin, Winterreise and Schwanengesang, Wolf Mörike Lieder, Brahms Lieder, Beethoven Lieder, Mozart Arien, Bach Christmas Oratorio (with John Eliot Gardiner and the Monteverdi Choir), Christus in the St Matthew-Passion, St Matthew-Passion, St John-Passion, Fauré and Duruflé Requiems, Papageno in Mozart's Die Zauberflöte, Adam in Haydn's Creation and Harlekin in Strauss's Ariadne auf Naxos, Hugo Wolf: Italienisches Liederbuch (with Dawn Upshaw), Spanisches Liederbuch (with Ann-Sophie von Otter), Kurwenal in Tristan und Isolde. *Honours:* Robert-Schumann Preis der Stadt Zwickau 1998. *Current Management:* c/o Shirley Thomson, IMG Artists Vocal Division, Lovell House, 616 Chiswick High Road, London, W4 5RX, England.

**BARAB, Seymour;** Composer and Cellist; b. 9 Jan. 1921, Chicago, Illinois, USA. *Education:* Studied the cello with Gregor Piatigorsky and Edmund Kurtz. *Career:* Performed first as church organist in Chicago; Played the cello in symphony orchestras of Indianapolis, Cleveland, Portland and San Francisco, 1940–60; Assisted in the organisation of the Composers Quartet and the New York Pro Musica; Has taught at Rutgers, the State University of New Jersey and the New England Conservatory. *Compositions include:* Operas: Chanticleer, after Chaucer, Aspen, 1956; A Game of Chance, Illinois, 1957; Little Red Riding Hood, New York, 1962; The Toy Shop, New York, 1978; A Piece of String, Colorado, 1985; The Maker of Illusion, New York, 1985; Song settings of A Child's Garden of Verses and Songs of Perfect Propriety. *Address:* c/o ASCAP, ASCAP Building, 1 Lincoln Plaza, New York, NY 10023, USA.

**BARABAS, Sari;** Singer (Soprano); b. 14 March 1914, Budapest, Hungary; m. Franz Klarwein (1914–91). *Education:* Studied in Budapest. *Career:* Debut: Budapest in 1939 as Gilda in Rigoletto; Member of the Hamburg Staatsoper from 1949; Sang in San Francisco in 1950 as the Queen of Night and Glyndebourne, 1953–57 as Constanze in Die Entführung, Adèle in Le Comte Ory and Zerbinetta in Ariadne auf Naxos; Florence Maggio Musicale in 1955; Guest appearances in Germany and Austria in operettas; Sang in London in 1969 in The Great Waltz. *Recordings include:* Le Comte Ory from the Glyndebourne Festival, 1956; Excerpts from works by Johann Strauss, Gasparone, Telefunken.

**BARAN, Peter;** Cellist; b. 16 March 1950, Bratislava, Czechoslovakia; m. Beata Baranova, 15 Aug 1975, 2 s. *Education:* Music School, Bratislava, 1956–65; Conservatory, Bratislava, 1965–72; Hochschule für Musik und Darstellende Kunst, Vienna, 1979–83. *Career:* Debut: Haydn's Cello Concerto in D major, 1972; Slovak Philharmonic Orchestra, 1972–; Suchon Quartet, 1973–77; Bratislava Chamber Harmony, 1973–80; Capella Istropolitana Chamber Orchestra, 1982–89; Bratislava String Trio, 1985–; Kontrapunkte, ensemble of 20th century music, Vienna, 1988–; Concertmaster, Slovak Philharmonic Orchestra, 1989–; Soloist and Member, Orchestra Ensemble Kanazawa, Japan, 1992–; Major performances, solo: Concerto for 2 Celli (Handel) with Slovak Philharmonic Orchestra, 1984; Symphonia Concertante

(Haydn) with Slovak Chamber Orchestra, 1985; Cello Concerto op 33 (Saint-Saëns) with Slovak Philharmonic Orchestra, 1985; Concerto for String Trio and Orchestra (C Stamitz), 1987; Quatuor pour la fin du temps (Messiaen) at BHS Festival, 1987; Brahms Double Concerto and Sonata da Camera and Orchestra (Martinů), both with Slovak Philharmonic Orchestra, 1993; Don Quixote with Slovak Philharmonic, 1997; Cellist, Kyoto Symphony Orchestra; Slovak and Austrian Radio performances: 'Hunt' Quartet (Mozart); Cello Concerto in C major (Haydn); For television: Sonata in F major, op 99 (Brahms); String Trio Serenade (Dohnányi); Divertimento (Mozart); Trio in G major (Hummel); Little Trio (A Moyzes); Ernest Bloch, Schelomo, Hebraic Rhapsody for Violoncello and orchestra; mem, Slovak Music Union; Musicians' Union, Japan. *Recordings:* Vivaldi: Cello Concerto in A minor, Concerto in G minor for 2 celli; Beethoven: Septet, op 20; String Trio in G major by Hummel; Clarinet Quartet E flat, J N Hummel and Concerto for string trio and orchestra, C Stamitz; Concerto No. 1 G Major by C Stamitz. *Address:* Medena 35, 81102 Bratislava, Slovakia.

**BARANOWSKI, Marcin;** Violinist and Professor; b. 30 Nov. 1961, Poznań, Poland; m. Monika Rosenkiewicz 2000. *Education:* Academy of Music, Poznań, Poland 1985. *Career:* debut, State Philharmonic Orchestra, Poznan 1984; Karol Szymanowski Violin Concerto; mem. of Amadeus Chamber Orchestra 1981–; concerts all over the world; over 20 recordings; television and radio appearances; Polish String Quartet, 1994; Leader of the second violin, Amadeus Chamber Orchestra, 1995; Prof., Paderewski Academy of Music. *Recordings:* Amadeus Chamber Orchestra, 1989 and 1993. *Honours:* Third Prize, International Chamber Music Competition, Łódź, Poland, 1983; Award of Ministry of Culture, 1992. *Current Management:* Warsaw Artistic Management. *Address:* ul Rozana, 5A/2, 61577 Poznań, Poland. *E-mail:* marcin.b@inetia.pl.

**BARANTSCHIK, Alexander;** Violinist; b. 1953, Leningrad, USSR. *Education:* Studied at the Leningrad Conservatory, 1960–72, with Professor Waiman, 1972–77. *Career:* Gave concerts in Russia, then emigrated, 1979, becoming leader of the Bamberg Symphony Orchestra; Leader of the Radio Philharmonic Orchestra of the Netherlands, 1982; Solo engagements with leading orchestras in Germany, Netherlands, the United Kingdom and Hungary; Appearances in Russia with the Kazan Symphony and the Leningrad Philharmonic; Performed the Sibelius Concerto with the London Symphony in Spain, 1987, Prokofiev's 1st in the USA and London, 1989–90; Leader of the London Symphony Orchestra from 1989, played the Tchai-kovsky Concerto with the orchestra, Mar 1991, Bach on tour to the USA, Aug 1991; Brahms Double Concerto at the Barbican, 1997. *Honours:* Winner, International Violin Competition at Sion, 1980. *Address:* c/o London Symphony Orchestra, Barbican Centre, London EC 2Y 8 DS, England.

**BARBACINI, Paolo;** singer (tenor); b. 20 Nov. 1946, Reggio Emilia, Italy. *Career:* has sung throughout Italy in operas by Mozart and Rossini, notably Don Giovanni, Il Re Pastore, Cenerentola, Il Turco in Italia, Adina and Aureliano in Palmira; La Scala Milan from 1980, in Falstaff and Figaro and on tour to Tokyo and Sofia; Has sung in La Pietra del Paragone for the Israel Festival, Il Turco in Italia in Aix and Rossini's Elisabetta in Turin and on tour to the USA; Modern repertory includes Manzoni's Doctor Faustus (premiere, at La Scala, 1985), Wozzeck, Orff's Catulli Carmina and the premiere of Bussotti's L'Ispirazione (Florence, 1988); Sang Pang in Turandot at Macerata, 1996 and Bologna, 1997; Season 2000–01 as the Doctor in Penderecki's Devils of Loudun at Turin and as Bardolph in Falstaff at La Scala.

**BARBAUX, Christine;** Singer (Soprano); b. 1955, Saint-Mande, France. *Education:* Studied at Paris Conservatory. *Career:* Debut: Strasbourg, as Despina, 1977; Sang Barbarina in Le nozze di Figaro in Paris, 1978, Vienna and Salzburg under Karajan; Further engagements in Geneva in The Love of Three Oranges, 1984; Théâtre de la Monnaie, Brussels, as Servilia in La Clemenza di Tito and Sophie in Rosenkavalier, 1982, 1986, Aix-en-Provence as Sophie, Amsterdam and Norina, 1988, Salzburg Festival as Servilia, 1988; Other roles include Ophelia in Hamlet by Thomas, Gilda, and Blanche Force in Les Dialogues des Carmélites; Sang Alice Ford in Falstaff at Bonn, 1991; Sang Contesse Fedora in Donizetti's Gli Esiliati di Siberia at Montpellier, 1999. *Recordings include:* Werther and Pelléas et Mélisande; Fauré's Pénélope; Le nozze di Figaro. *Address:* c/o Opéra de Montpellier, 11 Blvd. Victor Hugo, 34967 Montpellier, Cédex, France.

**BARBER, Graham David,** BA, MMus, FRCO, ARNCM; British organist, harpsichordist and pianist; *Professor of Perfomance Studies, University of Leeds;* b. 30 Dec. 1948, London; m. Dianne Mackay 1990; one d. *Education:* University of East Anglia, Royal Northern College of Music. *Career:* debut, Royal Festival Hall, London 1978; int. concert organist; frequent BBC radio broadcasts as organist, mainly featuring German Baroque music and Max Reger; Lecturer in Music, Univ. of Leeds 1981–; Chorus Master, Leeds Philharmonic Soc. 1983–92; Curator, Historic Schulze Organ, St Bartholo-mew's Church, Armley 1986–; Chorus Master, Sheffield Philharmonic Chorus 1987–97; Tutor in Organ Studies, Royal Northern Coll. of Music 1995–; Prof. of Performance Studies, Univ. of Leeds 1998–; adviser, bd mem. Percy Whitlock Trust; mem. Incorporated Soc. of Musicians, BIOS, ABC, Karg Elert Soc. (pres. 1998), Incorporated Asscn of Organists. *Recordings include:* Johann Gottfried Walther Organ Works (Reid Concert Hall, Edinburgh), Franz Schmidt: Organ Works, English Romantic at Truro Cathedral, Bach Neumeister Chorales and Early Organ Works Vol. 1, Vol. 2, Organ Music from Salisbury Cathedral, The Sandtner Organ at Villingen Münster, The Klais

Organ at Altenberg Dom, Complete Organ Works of Percy Whitlock (three vols). *Publications:* contrib. to Musical Times 1984, Cambridge Companion to the Organ 1998. *Honours:* Limpus and F. J. Reed Prizes. *Address:* 16 Vernon Road, Harrogate, HG2 8DE, England. *E-mail:* g.d.barber@leeds.ac.uk.

**BARBER, Kimberley;** singer (mezzo-soprano); b. 1961, Canada. *Career:* debut singing Hansel in Hansel and Gretel for Calgary Opera 1985; has sung widely in Canada and in Europe in travesti roles by Mozart, Rossini and Strauss; also sings Massenet's Cendrillon, Nicklausse in Les Contes d'Hoffmann and Lazuli in L'Etoile; Frankfurt Opera from 1989, as the Composer, Hermia, Ramiro (La finta giardiniera), Dorabella, Cherubino and Rosina; sang Pauline in The Gambler for ENO and has appeared in concert with the Chicago, Toronto and Cincinnati Symphonies; New York and Wigmore Hall concert debuts 1994. *Current Management:* Dean Artists Management, 204 St George Street, Toronto, ON M5R 2N5, Canada. *Telephone:* (416) 969-7300. *Fax:* (416) 969-7969. *E-mail:* deanarts@interlog.com. *Website:* www.deanartists.com; www.barber.de.

**BARBIROLLI, Lady Evelyn,** OBE, MA, DMus, FTCL, RNCM; British oboist (retd), adjudicator and lecturer; b. (Evelyn Rothwell), 24 Jan. 1911, Wallingford, England; m. Sir John Barbirolli CH 1939. *Education:* Royal Coll. of Music, London. *Career:* played with Scottish, London Symphony, Glyndebourne Festival Opera Orchestras 1932–39; soloist and chamber music player later; mem. Incorporated Soc. of Musicians (fmr pres.). *Compositions:* many arrangements and editions for oboe. *Recordings:* Concertos by Haydn, Mozart, Corelli, Handel, Pergolesi, Cimarosa, Albinoni, Marcello. *Publications:* Oboe Technique 1953, The Oboist's Companion (three vols), A Tune for Oboe, A Book of Scales for The Oboe; contrib. many articles for various magazines. *Honours:* Hon. DMus (Durham), Hon. MA (Leeds);Hon. FRCM, RAM, RCM, FRNCM, RTCL. *Address:* 15a Buckland Crescent, London, NW3 5DH, England. *Telephone:* (20) 7586-2464.

**BARBIZET, Pierre;** French pianist; b. 20 Sept. 1922, Arica, Chile. *Education:* Paris Conservatoire. *Career:* many performances as soloist and chamber musician, notably with violinist Christian Ferras; frequent performances of Chabrier, and Dir of Marseilles Conservatory, 1963–. *Recordings include:* complete Beethoven violin sonatas, with Christian Ferras. *Honours:* prizewinner, Long-Thibaud Competition. *Address:* Conservatoire National de Marseille, 2 Place Carli, 13001 Marseille, France.

**BARBONI YANS, Geneviève,** PhD; stage designer and costume designer; b. 26 Dec. 1947, Montegnée, Belgium. *Education:* Univ. of Liège, Belgium, Univ. of Reims, France. *Career:* debut as opera producer, at Opera House, Liège, Belgium; broadcast: introductions to concerts, RTB, Liège, 1969; staging (set, costumes): Walloon Gala, Li Voyèdje di Tchaudfontaine, opera by J.-N. Hamal, Liège, 1970; Ravel, ballet gala, Grand Théâtre, Nancy, 1975; staging for television and radio: Evolution of the Opera in Emilia-Romagna, RAI Bologna, 1982; Man., Centro Canto Cesenatico, specialised services for the education, re-education and improvement of the speaking and singing voice, 1991–; transcriptions of operas: Cavalli's L'Hipermestra, Stradella's La Circe; mem., Voice Foundation, Philadelphia, Italian Society of Phonatricians and Logopedists. *Recordings:* Li Voyèdje di Tchaudfontaine (video), 1970. *Publications:* Un opéra de Francesco Cavalli, pour la cour de Florence: L'Hipermestra, 1979; Contributo alla storia della gestione degli spettacoli nel Ducato Estense dal 1650 al 1790, 1994; contrib. to magazines and journals in Italy. *Address:* Via Viola 13, 47042 Cesenatico, Italy.

**BARCE, Ramon;** Composer; b. 16 March 1928, Madrid, Spain; m. Elena Martin, 22 June 1984. *Education:* Conservatory of Madrid, 1950–54; PhD, 1956. *Career:* Foundation Member, Group Nueva Musica, 1958; Foundation Member, Group Zaj, 1964; Foundation Member, Group Sonda, 1967; Editor, contemporary music magazine 'Sonda', 1967–74; Musical Critic, newspaper 'Ya', 1971–78; Foundation Member Asociacion de Compositores Sinfonicos Espanoles and First President, 1976–88; mem, Asociacion de Compositores Sinfonicos Espanoles;Sociedad Espanola de Musicologia; Sociedad General de Autores y Editores. *Compositions:* six Symphonies 1975, 1982, 1983, 1984, 1995, 1998; Concert for Piano, 1974; Nine Conciertos de Lizara, 1973–88; Forty Eight Preludios for Piano, 1973–83; Ten String Quartets, 1958–94; Coral hablado, 1966; Melodramas Oleada and Hacia manana hacia hoy, 1982, 1987; Nuevas polifonias I–II, 1971, 1985; Parabola, 1963 and Travesia 1979 for brass quintet. *Recordings:* Canada-Trio 1970 and 1993; Twenty Four Preludios, 1987; Obertura fonética, 1977, 1979 and 1994; Siala, 1973; Estudio de valores for piano, 1992; Sonata No. 3 for violin and piano, 1990; Sintesis de Siala, 1993; Musica funebre, 1979, 1994; Tango para Yvar, 1995. *Publications:* Fronteras de la musica, 1985; Tiempo de tinieblas y algunas sonrisas, 1992; Boccherini en Madrid, 1992; Translations of Harmonielehre of Schoenberg 1974, Alois Haba 1984 and Schenker 1990. *Contributions:* 12 advertencias para una sociologia de la musica in Coloquio Artes 72, Lisbon 1987; La vanguardia y yo in Revista Musical Catalana 59, Barcelona, 1989. *Honours:* National Prize of Music, 1973; Prize of Comunidad de Madrid, 1991; Medalla de Oro al m érito en las Bellas Artes, 1996. *Address:* Valdevarnes 35, 28039 Madrid, Spain.

**BARCELLONA, Daniela;** Italian singer (mezzo-soprano); b. 1973, Trieste. *Education:* studied in Trieste. *Career:* early appearances at Spoleto, Florence, Bordeaux, Rome, Wexford Festival and Geneva; season 1998–99 as Orsini in Lucrezia Borgia at La Scala, Arsace in Semiramide at Genoa and Isabella (L' Italiana in Algeri) at Verona; Rome Opera as Rossini's Rosina and in La Fiamma by Respighi; further engagements as Vivaldi's Bajazet at Istanbul, as

Rossini's Tancredi Pesaro and Jane Seymour in Anna Bolena at Naples; concerts include the Verdi Requiem (in Dresden, Rome, Berlin and elsewhere), Roméo et Juliette by Berlioz (Barbican Hall, London 2000), Beethoven's Missa Solemnis at the Concertgebouw and Rossini's Stabat Mater; New York Met debut 2001, in a Verdi Gala, returning for Bellini's Norma; Ginevra di Scozia by Mayr at Trieste, Malcolm in La Donna del Lago at Pesaro; season 2002 as Romeo in Bellini's Capuleti et i Montecchi in Paris and Isabella in Rome. *Recordings include:* La Fedeltà Premiata by Haydn, Verdi Requiem. *Honours:* Opera Actual magazine Premio de la Mejor Mezzo-Soprano 2005. *Current Management:* Ernesto Palacio Artist Management, Via Donizetti 11, Lurano (BG), Italy. *Telephone:* 035 800623. *Fax:* 035 4877812. *E-mail:* ernestopalacio@tiscali.it. *Website:* www.ernestopalacio.com.

**BARCLAY, Yvonne;** singer (soprano); b. 1965, Ayrshire, Scotland. *Education:* Royal Scottish Acad., Glasgow and Nat. Opera Studio, London. *Career:* appearances with the Royal Opera, Covent Garden, as Frasquita in Carmen, Mozart's Barbarina and Papagena, Priestess in Aida and Javotte in Manon; English Bach Festival as Belinda in Dido and Aeneas, Gluck's Euridice and in The Fairy Queen 2001; ENO as Lucia in The Rape of Lucretia, Echo in Ariadne auf Naxos, Sandman in Hansel and Gretel and Euridice in Monteverdi's Orfeo; Opera North as Eurydice in Orpheus in the Underworld; Glyndebourne Touring Opera as Blondchen in Die Entführung and Mélisande in Pelléas et Mélisande; for Scottish Opera roles in Die Zauberflöte, Hansel and Gretel, L'Egisto by Cavalli and Death in Venice; Emmie in Albert Herring for Glyndebourne and Far East tour as Norina in Don Pasquale; further roles include Blondchen and Gretel at the Leipzig Opera and First Niece in Peter Grimes at the Paris Châtelet, and in Lisbon and Bremen; frequent concert appearances and broadcasts. *Recordings:* HMS Pinafore (as Josephine, for D'Oyly Carte Opera), Peter Grimes (as First Niece) (Grammy Award). *Current Management:* Music International, 13 Ardilaun Road, London, N5 2QR, England.

**BARCZA, Peter;** Singer (Baritone); b. 23 June 1949, Stockholm, Sweden. *Education:* Graduated Toronto University, 1971. *Career:* Sang with Canadian Touring Opera, 1972–73, notably as Guglielmo (Così fan tutte), Papageno, Enrico (Lucia di Lammermoor), Marcello and Germont; Guest appearances at Memphis (1981), New Orleans (from 1985), Seattle and the New York City Opera (from 1990); European appearances include Monteverdi's Ulisse at Bad Hersfeld; Other roles include Rossini's Figaro, Malatesta (Don Pasquale), Luna, Ping (Turandot), Valentin (Faust), and Rangoni in Boris Godunov. *Address:* c/o New York City Opera, Lincoln Center, New York, NY 10023, USA. *Website:* www.peterbarcza.com.

**BARDON, Patricia;** Singer (mezzo-soprano); b. 1964, Ireland. *Career:* Operatic engagements include Arsace in Semiramide at La Fenice, Venice; Carmen, Hamburg Staatsoper and Welsh National Opera; Penelope in Il Ritorno d'Ulisse at the Maggio Musicale Florence; Orlando in New York, Paris and Lyon; Smeaton in Anna Bolena at San Francisco; Amastris in Xerxes at the Munich Staatsoper; Juno in Sémele at Innsbruck; 3rd Lady in Die Zauberflöte at Verona and roles in Rigoletto, Mosè in Egitto, Guillaume Tell and Mefistofele for Royal Opera at Barbican Hall; Concert engagements have taken her to USA, Canada, Japan and all major European Centres including La Scala, La Monnaie, (Brussels), BBC Proms London, Edinburgh, Aix en Provence and Montreux Festivals, Concertgebouw, Amsterdam and Schauspielhaus, Berlin; Season 2000–01 as Erda in The Rhinegold, for ENO, and Ursule in Béatrice et Bénédict for Netherlands Opera. *Recordings include:* Orlando, Elijah, Olga in Eugene Onegin and Giovanna in Rigoletto. *Honours:* Prizewinner, Cardiff Singer of the World Competition. *Current Management:* Ingpen & Williams Ltd, 7 St George's Court, 131 Putney Bridge Road, London, SW15 2PA, England.

**BARENBOIM, Daniel,** FRCM; Israeli pianist and conductor; b. 16 Nov. 1942, Buenos Aires, Argentina; s. of Prof. Enrique and Aida (née Schuster) Barenboim; m. 1st Jacqueline du Pré 1967 (died 1987); m. 2nd Elena Bashkirova 1988; two s. *Career:* studied piano with his father and other musical subjects with Nadia Boulanger, Edwin Fischer and Igor Markevitch; début in Buenos Aires at age of seven; played Bach D Minor Concerto with orchestra at Salzburg Mozarteum at age of nine; has played in Europe regularly 1954–; yearly tours of USA 1957–; has toured Japan, Australia and S America; has played with or conducted London Philharmonic, Philharmonia Orchestra, London Symphony Orchestra, Royal Philharmonic, Chicago Symphony Orchestra, New York Philharmonic, Philadelphia Orchestra, Israel Philharmonic, Vienna Philharmonic, Berlin Philharmonic; frequently tours with English Chamber Orchestra and with them records for EMI (projects include complete Mozart Piano Concertos and late Symphonies); other recording projects include complete Beethoven Sonatas and Beethoven Concertos (with New Philharmonia Orchestra conducted by Klemperer); has appeared in series of master classes on BBC Television; presented Festival of Summer Music on South Bank, London 1968, 1969; leading role in Brighton Festival 1967–69; appears regularly at Edinburgh Festival; conductor, Edinburgh Festival Opera 1973; Musical Dir Orchestre de Paris 1975–89, Chicago Symphony Orchestra 1991–; Musical and Artistic Dir Deutsche Staatsoper, Berlin 1992; Hon. DMus (Manchester) 1997. *Publication:* A Life in Music (jtly) 1991, Parallels and Paradoxes (with Edward W. Said) 2003. *Honours:* Beethoven Medal 1958; Paderewski Medal 1963; Beethoven Soc. Medal 1982; Prix de la Tolérance, Protestant Acad. of Tutzing 2002, Wolf Foundation Prize in Arts, 2004. *Address:* c/o Daniel Barenboim Secretariat, 29 rue de la Coulouvrenière, 1204 Geneva, Switzerland.

**BARGIELSKI, Zbigniew,** PhD; Austrian (b. Polish) composer; *Professor and Head of Department of Composition and Theory of Music, Bydgoszcz Academy of Music*; b. 21 Jan. 1937, Lomza, Poland. *Education:* studies in piano at Lublin Conservatory, Warsaw Conservatory with Szeligowski, Music Acad., Katowice with Boleslaw Szabelski; composition studies with Nadia Boulanger in Paris and at Graz. *Career:* music critic and journalist; Pres. Young Polish Composers 1967–70; Sec. Polish Composers Asscn, Warsaw 1967–70; premiere of opera In a Small Country House (The Little Haunted Manor) at Warsaw Grand Theatre 1984; mem. Polish Composer's Asscn, Österreichischer Komponistenbund; Prof. and Head of Dept of Composition and Theory of Music, Bydgoszcz Acad. of Music, Poland 2002–; compositions have been performed throughout Europe, in USA, Australia and South America and at int. festivals for contemporary music including Warsaw-Autumn, Muzicki Biennale Zagreb, Festival de Paris, Steirischer Herbst, Graz, Austria, Leningrad Spring, Encontros Gulbenkian, Lisbon, Helsinki Festival, Tsumari Triennale, Festival de Strasbourg, World Music Festival, and others. *Compositions include:* Danton, or Some Scenes from the History of the Great French Revolution (opera) 1968–69, The Little Prince (musical tale) 1970, Alice in Wonderland (youth opera) 1972, Phantoms do not Lie (comic opera) 1981, Parades for orchestra 1965, Percussion Concerto 1975, Espace étrapé for orchestra 1973, Violin Concerto 1975, Ballads for wind and percussion 1976, String Quartet No. 1 1976, String Quartet No. 2 ('Primaverile') 1980, String Quartet No. 3 ('Still Life with a Scream') 1985, In Nobody's Land (oratorio) 1989, Requiem for orchestra 1991–92, Trigonalia for guitar, accordion, percussion and chamber orchestra 1994, String Quartet No. 4 ('Le temps ardent') 1994, Fountain of hope for alto saxophone and marimba 1995, Dance on the Verge of Light for chamber ensemble 1995, A la recherche du son perdu for flute 1996, Landscape of remembrance for violin, cello and piano 1996, A la espagnola for guitar 1996, Hierofania for five percussionists 1996, Forgotten – Regained for violin 1996, Slapstick for chamber orchestra 1997, Tango for chamber ensemble 1997, Shrine for an Anonymous Victim, (computer musiic) 1999, Light Cross (computer music) 2000, Towards Organic Geometry (computer music) 2001, String Quartet No. 5 ('Le temps qui n'est plus) 2001, Music for Children for piano 2001–02, Le cristal flamboyant for harpsichord and tape 2002, Jeux à trois for three accordions 2003. *Recordings:* works by Zbigniew Bargielski 1996. *Publications:* Sacrum in der Musik 1996. *Honours:* Order 'Merit for Polish Culture' 1990; Officer's Cross, Order of Polonia Restituta 1995; First Prize, Young Polish Composers Competition (Warsaw) 1965, Arthur Malawski Composer's Competition Award, Kraków 1976, UNESCO Int. Composer's Rostrum Award, Paris 1981, 1995, Austrian Govt Grant of the German Academic Exchange Service 1985, First Prize, Int Composers Competition 1986, Anton Benya Prize (Vienna) 2000, Polish Composers' Union Prize (Warsaw) 2001. *Address:* c/o Society of Authors ZAiKS, 2 Hipoteczna Street, 00 092 Warsaw, Poland (office). *Telephone:* (52) 321-11-42 (office). *E-mail:* sekr@amuz.bydgoszcz.pl (office). *Website:* www .amuz.bydgoszcz.pl (office); www.bargielski.com (home).

**BARHAM, Edmund;** singer (tenor); b. 22 March 1950, Beckenham, England. *Education:* Trinity Coll. of Music, London and London Opera Centre. *Career:* sang leading lyric roles in Wuppertal, then became mem. of the co. of the Theater am Gärtnerplatz, Munich; many appearances at leading German opera houses; ENO from 1985, as Jenik in The Bartered Bride, Turiddu, Narroboth in Salome, Pinkerton, Cavaradossi, Gabriele Adorno, and Vakula in the first British production of Rimsky-Korsakov's Christmas Eve; engagements with Opera North as Don José, Boris in Katya Kabanova and Dimitri in Boris Godunov; sang in the Gounod Grande Messe Solennelle for BBC television; sang Alfredo, ENO 1990, and Macduff in a new production of Macbeth (also on tour to USSR); sang Manrico at St Gallen 1991; Don Carlos, ENO 1992; overseas appearances include The Rise and Fall of Mahagonny and Adriana Lecouvreur in Switzerland, Howard Blake's Benedictus in Norway, and Don José at the Bregenz Festival; sang Otello for the Victoria State Opera 1993; Manrico in Il Trovatore for Opera North 1994; Don José for WNO 1997; sang Otello at Halle 2000. *Recordings:* First Armed Man in Die Zauberflöte, 18th Century English Songs for orchestra and chorus, Rossini's Petite Messe Solennelle.

**BARK, Jan;** Composer; b. 19 April 1934, Harnosand, Sweden. *Education:* Studied in Stockholm with Larsson, Blomdahl and Ligeti; Further study in Far East. *Career:* Worked at Tape Music Center, San Francisco, and with Swedish Broadcasting Service; Co-Founder, Culture Quartet (4 trombones) with Folk Rabe. *Compositions include:* Piano Sonata, 1957; 2 string quartets, 1959, 1962; Metakronismer for orchestra, 1960; Lamento for ensemble, 1962; Boca Chica for chamber ensemble, 1962; Pyknos for orchestra, 1962; Missa Bassa for small orchestra with 7 conductors, 1964; Nota for mixed chorus, 1964; Bar, electronic music; Light Music for chorus a cappella, 1968; Lyndon Bunk Johnson, 1968; Irk-Ork for chamber ensemble, 1970; Mumma in memoria for chamber ensemble, 1974; Utspel for band, 1978; Malumma for tuba and band, 1984; Concerto for orchestra, 1985; Beacon for 4 trombones, 1996; Theatre and film music. *Address:* c/o STIM, Sandhamnsgatan 79, PO Box 27372, 102 54 Stockholm, Sweden.

**BARKAUSKAS, Vytautas (Pranas Marius);** composer and academic; b. 25 March 1931, Kaunas, Lithuania; m. 1st Elena Tverijonaite 1954; m. 2nd Tiina Vabrit 1984; m. 3rd Svetlana Cherniavska 1991; one s. one d. *Education:* Lithuanian State Conservatory, Vilnius. *Career:* accompanist, Vilnius Coll. of Music 1954–58; Instructor, House of the People's Creative Work of the Republic 1958–61; Prof. of Theory, Composition, Lithuanian State Acad. of Music, Vilnius 1961–; mem. Union of Composers, Lithuania. *Compositions include:* six symphonies, 1962, 1971, 1979, 1984, 1986, 2001; Intimate Composition for oboe and 12 string 1968, Three Aspects for symphony orchestra 1969, Contrast Music for flute, cello and percussion 1969, Gloria Urbi for organ 1972, Prelude and Fugue for chorus 1974, Legend About Love (opera) 1975, Salute Your Land oratorio-mystery 1976, Sonatas for violin and piano, No. 1 Sonata subita 1976, No. 2 Dialogue 1978, No. 3 1984, Open Window for mezzo-soprano and five instruments 1978, Rondo capriccioso 1981, Concerto for viola and chamber orchestra 1981, The Sun (symphonic picture) 1983, Duo Sonata for violin, viola 1984, Sonata for two pianos and three performers 1984, Sextet 1985, Cantus Amores (cantata) 1986, Sonata for double bass and piano 1987, Hope (oratorio) 1988, The Second Legend of Ciurlionis for piano 1988, Credo for organ 1989, Concerto for piano and orchestra 1992, Konzertstück für Orchester No. 1 1992, Concert Suite for cello, piano 1993, Reminiscence for harpsichord 1993, Intimate Music, op 100 for flute, percussion 1993, Divertimento for piano six hands 1993, The Third Legend of Ciurtionis for piano 1993, Inspiration for organ 1994, Konzertstück No. 2 für Orchester 1994, Trio a deux for violin, viola, cello 1995, Allegro Brillante for two pianos 1996, Modus vivendi for violin, cello and piano 1996, Scherzo for violin and chamber orchestra 1996, Duo for guitar and piano 1997, Toccamento No. 2 for viola solo, violin, cello and piano 1998, Here and Now for symphonic orchestra 1998, Symphony No. 6 2001, Jeux concerto for violin and symphony orchestra 2002–03, Agnus Dei for mixed choir and organ 2003, Summer 2004, Mido 2004, Duo concertante for violin and symphony orchestra 2004, Lune a l'Aube d'Ete for coloratura soprano and eight cellos 2004, Silhouette for violin solo 2004, Opus 126 in E for string orchestra 2005. *Recordings:* Ars vivendi 1992, Cavalli 1993, Proud Sound 1995, Lithuanian New Music series 1997, Ondine 1997, Triton 2002, AVIE 2005. *Honours:* Médaille d'Honneur de Saint-Nazaire, France 2002, Lithuanian Nation Prize for Art 2003. *Address:* Saltiniu Street 11/15 b. 44, Vilnius 03214, Lithuania. *Telephone:* (5) 2162813. *Fax:* (5) 2162813. *E-mail:* svetvyt@takas.lt.

**BARKER, Cheryl;** Australian singer (soprano); b. 22 April 1960, Sydney; m. Peter Coleman-Wright. *Education:* studied with Joan Hammond. *Career:* appearances as the Governess in The Turn of the Screw, Princess in Rusalka, Oksana in Rimsky's Christmas Eve, with ENO 1989–; sang Cherubino and Marzelline, Glyndebourne Touring Opera 1989; sang Mozart's Annio, Tatiana in Eugene Onegin and Adina, L'Elisir d'amore, Scottish Opera 1991–94; sang Tatiana at Sydney 1994; Violetta at Auckland 1995; season 1996 in The Midsummer Marriage at Covent Garden and as Suor Angelica at Antwerp; season 1997–98 as Butterfly for Opera Australia, Falla's Salud at Brussels, Liu in Turandot and Butterfly for ENO; season 2000–01 as Butterfly and Suor Angelica at ENO and Donna Elvira for Australian Opera; title role in Tosca for ENO 2002; Salome for ENO 2005. *Recordings include:* La Bohème. *Current Management:* Artists Management Zürich, Rütistrasse 52, 8044 Zürich-Gockhausen, Switzerland. *Telephone:* (44) 821 89 57. *Fax:* (44) 821 01 27. *E-mail:* schuetz@artistsman.com. *Website:* www.artistsman.com; www .cherylbarker.be.

**BARKER, Noelle,** OBE, MA, FGSM; singing teacher; b. 28 Dec. 1928, Aberdeen, Scotland; m. Christopher Peake; three c. *Education:* Aberdeen University, Dartington Hall; Amsterdam Conservatory, Munich Academy, studied with Hans Hotter. *Career:* debut, Royal Festival Hall, London; oratorio, Lieder and contemporary music with leading choral societies and ensembles; appearances with Three Choirs and at various festivals; sang with the English Opera Group, London Sinfonietta and Dreamtiger Ensemble; broadcasts on BBC and European stations; Prof., Guildhall School of Music and Drama, Royal Acad., London and Conservatoire National, Paris; private teaching in London and Paris; masterclasses world-wide and jury mem. of various int. competitions; Dir, British Youth Opera; co-ed., Pathodia Sacra e Profana; ed., The Junior Recitalist. *Recordings:* complete solo vocal works of Messiaen, Jazz Songs. *Honours:* Hon. RAM 1999. *E-mail:* noellebarker@onetel.com. *Address:* Brontë Cottage, 89 South End Road, London NW3 2RJ, England (home). *Telephone:* (20) 7794-3615 (home).

**BARKER, Paul (Alan);** Composer; b. 1 July 1956, Cambridge, England; m. (1) Christine Susan Barker, 3 Sept 1977, divorced 1991, (2) Maria Huesca, 23 May 1992. *Education:* Guildhall School of Music, 1974–78; GGSM 1st Class; MMus, Durham University, 1983–85. *Career:* Visiting Lecturer, City University, 1978–83; Musical Director of Dancers Anonymous, 1979–86; Associate Lecturer, Kingsway-Princeton College, 1984–90; Artistic Director of Modern Music Theatre Troupe, 1985–94; Composer in Residence, West Sussex, 1991–93; Composer in Association, London Mozart Players, 1993–; Lecturer, Hertfordshire University, 1997–; mem, Executive Committee, APC; Honorary Associate Member, OMTF; PCS Committee of ISM. *Compositions include:* Operas: The Marriages Between Zones 3, 4 and 5, The Place, 1985, Phantastes, Camden Festival 1986, The Pillow Song, 1988, La Malinche, 1989, Albergo Empedocle, 1990, Dirty Tricks, 1997, at London International Opera Festival and Prologue at Festival del Centro Historico, Mexico City, 1992; 10 Contemporary dance scores for European companies; Orchestral works include Fantasy on Four Notes, 1978; Instrumental ensemble, vocal, choral and chamber works; Music for Theatre; Children's Operas and educational music; Three Songs for Sylvia, commissioned by London Festival Orchestra, Bristol Cathedral, 1994; Concerto for 8, for London Mozart Players, Henley Festival, 1995; Concerto for Violin and Orchestra for Tasmin Little and London Mozart Players 1996. *Recordings:* Barbican Fanfare, 1979; The Pied Piper of Hamelin, 1980. *Honours:* Royal Philharmonia Society Prize for Composition, 1978. *Current Management:* Modern Music Theatre Troupe. *Address:* Flat 3, 33 Hopton Road, London SW16 2EH, England.

**BARKIN, Elaine R(adoff),** BA, MFA, PhD; American composer, professor of music and writer on music; b. 15 Dec. 1932, New York, NY; m. George J Barkin 1957; three s. *Education:* Queens Coll., Brandeis Univ., Berlin Hochschule für Musik; Studied with Karol Rathaus, Irving Fine, Boris Blacher, Arthur Berger and Harold Shapero. *Career:* Asst to Co-Ed., Perspectives of New Music, 1963–85; Lecturer in Music, Queens Coll., 1964–70, Sarah Lawrence Coll. 1969–70; Asst, later Assoc. Prof. of Music Theory, Univ. of Michigan, 1970–74; Visiting Asst Prof., Princeton Univ. 1974; Assoc. Prof. of Composition and Theory, UCLA 1974–77, Prof. 1977–97; Guest Lecturer at various colls and univs. *Compositions:* String Quartet, 1969; Sound Play for violin, 1974; String Trio, 1976; Plein Chant, alto flute, 1977; Ebb Tide, 2 vibraphones 1977;… the Supple Suitor… for soprano and 5 players, 1978; De Amore, chamber mini-opera, 1980; Impromptu for violin, cello and piano, 1981; Media Speak, theatre piece, 1981; At the Piano, piano, 1982; For String Quartet, 1982; Quilt Piece, graphic score for 7 instruments, 1984; On the Way to Becoming, for 4-track Tape Collage, 1985; Demeter and Persephone for violin, tape, chamber ensemble and dancers, 1986; 3 Rhapsodies, flutes and clarinet, 1986; Encore for Javanese Gamelan Ensemble, 1988; Out of the Air for Basset Horn and Tape, 1988; To Whom It May Concern, 4-track Tape Collage, Reader, 1989; Legong Dreams, Oboe, 1990 (and since 1980 many improvised group and duo sessions on tape); Gamélange, harp and mixed gamelan band, 1992; Five Tape Collages (CD) 1993; For My Friends' Pleasure, for soprano and harp, 1993; Touching All Bases, electric bass, percussion, Balinese gamelan, 1996; Music for Soloists and Small Ensembles 1974–1993 (CD) 1999; Poem for winds and percussion, 1999; Song for Sarah, violin, 2001; Ballade, violincello, 2002; Tambellan Suite, mallet percussion, 2004; Instrumental and Vocal Music 1977–99 (CD), 2004. *Publications:* An Anthology, music, text and graphics, 1997; Audible Traces: gender, identity, music (co-Ed.) 2000. *Honours:* Fulbright Award, 1957; NEA Awards, 1975, 1979; Rockefeller Foundation, 1980; Meet the Composer, 1994. *Address:* Department of Music, 405 Hilgard Avenue, University of California, Los Angeles, CA 90095, USA.

**BARKL, Michael Laurence Gordon,** BMus, DipEd, MMus, PhD, FTCL; Australian composer; *Head Teacher of Music, Illawarra Institute of Technology*; b. 9 Aug. 1958, Sydney, NSW; m. Sharyn Lee 1986; one d. *Education:* New South Wales State Conservatorium of Music, Trinity Coll. of Music, London, Univ. of New England, Sydney Coll. of Advanced Education, Deakin Univ. *Career:* tutor, Univ. of New England 1982; Head Teacher of Music, Illawarra Inst. of Technology 1987–; commissions from Seymour Group, Synergy, Elision, Duo Contemporain, Manly Art Gallery and Orange City Council. *Compositions include:* The Time, The Time for choir 1981, Voce di Testa and Voce di Petto for orchestra 1981–82, Chroma for harpsichord 1981, Drumming for piano 1983, Psychonaut for chorus 1983, Iambus for wind quintet and strings 1983, Cabaret for orchestra 1985, Expressive and Ferocious for string quartet 1985, Backyard Swing for concert band 1986, Blues for clarinet and marimba 1986, Rondo for chamber orchestra 1988, Disco for percussion quartet 1989, Smoky for harpsichord 1997. *Honours:* Segnalata, Valentino Bucchi competition for Composition, Italy 1981. *Address:* 119 Combermere Street, Goulburn, NSW 2580, Australia.

**BARLEY, Matthew;** Concert Cellist; b. 1965, England. *Education:* Guildhall School, London; Moscow Conservatoire. *Career:* debut, Shostakovich First Concerto with London SO at Barbican Hall; guest principal with the LSO, London Philharmonic Orchestra, Philharmonia, RPO, London Sinfonietta; solo and chamber music engagements in North America, Asia, Australasia and throughout Europe; concertos with London Sinfonietta, Orchestra Internazionale d'Italia, Royal Scottish National Orchestra, Brno Symphony Orchestra, Athens Camerata, Hong Kong Sinfonietta, New Zealand Symphony Orchestra; festival appearances at Taranaki, New Zealand, WOMAD, Lucerne, Prague Autumn, Dijon, Koshigaya, Harrogate, Norwich, Dartington, Chester, Salisbury, City of London, Cheltenham; premieres of works by John Woolrich, Carl Vine, Peter Wiegold, Fraser Trainer, Detlev Glanert, Dave Maric, Deirdre Gribben; non-classical collaboration with Viktoria Mullova, Amjad Ali Khan, Julian Joseph, Django Bates and others; founder of performance and education group, Between the Notes, 1997. *Recordings include:* Through the Looking Glass, The Silver Swan, Strings Attached. *Current Management:* Askonas Holt Ltd, Lonsdale Chambers, 27 Chancery Lane, London, WC2A 1PF, England. *Telephone:* (20) 7400-1700. *Fax:* (20) 7400-1799. *E-mail:* info@askonasholt.co.uk. *Website:* www.askonasholt.co.uk; www.matthewbarley.com; www.betweenthenotes.co.uk.

**BARLOW, Clara;** Singer (Soprano); b. 28 July 1928, Brooklyn, New York, USA. *Education:* Studied with Cecile Jacobson in New York. *Career:* Debut: Berne Opera 1962, as Venus in Tannhäuser; Sang at Oberhausen, 1963–65, Kiel 1965–66; Komische Oper Berlin 1967, as Donna Anna; Engaged at Wiesbaden 1967–69, Zürich 1969–70; Guest appearances at the Spoleto Festival (as Isolde, 1968), San Diego (1969) and the Metropolitan Opera (as Leonore, 1970); Returned to New York 1974, as Isolde; Deutsche Oper Berlin 1970, Vienna Staatsoper 1973; Sang Fata Morgana in The Love of Three Oranges at La Scala 1974; Appearances as Brünnhilde at Seattle (1970–72 and 1976) and Dallas (1981); Scottish Opera 1973, as Isolde; Further appearances at Dresden, Stuttgart, Hamburg, Munich, Chicago (1976–77), Houston, Copenhagen, Toronto, Budapest and Mexico City; Stadttheater Bremen 1985–86, as Elektra and Leonore; Other roles have included the

Dyer's Wife (Die Frau ohne Schatten), Agathe, Senta, Elsa, Elisabeth, Ariadne, Salome, Aida, Elisabeth de Valois, Jenůfa, Marina (Boris Godunov) and Giulietta in Les Contes d'Hoffmann. *Address:* c/o Bremer Theater, Postfach 101046, 2800 Bremen, Germany.

**BARLOW, Stephen;** Conductor; b. 30 June 1954, Seven Kings, Essex; m. Joanna Lumley. *Education:* Studied in Canterbury, at Trinity College, Cambridge, and Guildhall School of Music. *Career:* Founded New London Chamber Group, based at the Riverside Studios, Hammersmith; Guest conductor of opera at the Guildhall School, notably Falstaff and Maw's The Rising of the Moon; Glyndebourne Festival and Tour, 1979–85, leading Die schweigsame Frau, Der Rosenkavalier, Arabella, Oliver Knussen double bill, Così fan tutte, Gluck's Orfeo, The Rake's Progress and Love of Three Oranges; For English National Opera has conducted The Flying Dutchman, Carmen, Abduction from the Seraglio, The Damnation of Faust, La Cenerentola, L'italiana in Algeri, Barber of Seville; Scottish Opera from 1983, with Hansel and Gretel, The Bartered Bride, Intermezzo; Conducted Opera 80 from its inception, Musical Director from 1987, leading Marriage of Figaro, A Masked Ball, The Rake's Progress, The Merry Widow, 1989–90; Covent Garden debut, 1989, with Turandot, returning for Die Zauberflöte in 1991; San Francisco Opera, 1990, Capriccio; Has also worked for Opera North and Vancouver Opera; Australian debut, Melbourne, in Die Zauberflöte, 1991; Conducted Faust for Opera Northern Ireland, 1992; Conducted Capriccio in Catania, Marriage of Figaro at Garsington, Carmen in Adelaide; Madama Butterfly at Auckland, 1994 and in Belfast, 1997; Season 1998 with Falstaff at Garsington; Concert engagements with the English Chamber Orchestra, City of London Sinfonia, London Sinfonietta, City of Birmingham Symphony, Royal Liverpool Philharmonic, Scottish Chamber Orchestra, BBC Scottish and Bournemouth Sinfonietta; Concerts in Spain, Netherlands, Germany; BBC National Orchestra of Wales, Radio Philharmonic Orchestra, Hilversum; New Zealand, Vancouver, Melbourne and Detroit Symphony Orchestras, BBC Philharmonic; Artistic Director, Opera Northern Ireland, 1996–98; Music Director Queensland Philharmonic Orchestra, 1996–98. *Honours:* Fellow, Royal College of Organists, 1972; Fellow, Guildhall School of Music and Drama, 1985. *Current Management:* Musichall. *Address:* c/o Musichall, Vicarage Way, Ringmer, East Sussex BN8 5 LA, England.

**BARNARD, Keith,** AMus; British composer, poet and teacher; b. 26 Oct. 1950, London, England. *Education:* Trinity Coll. of Music, London; studied composition with Arnold Cooke; Int. Writers' Asscn, Int. Poets' Acad., Madras, India. *Career:* teacher of piano, music theory and composition 1972–; numerous concerts and recitals of his own compositions; conductor, multicultural concert; mem. Performing Right Asscn, Musicians' Union, New Age Music Asscn. *Compositions include:* Healing 1–4 for Piano, Colour Harmonies for Keyboard Synthesizer, Healing Rays of Emerald-Blue for 5 Flutes, The Golden Temple of Wisdom for 4 Flutes, Angelic Nocturne for Piano. *Publications:* Outer World Poems 1982, The Sacred Cup 1982, The Legend of Bran 1982, The Legend of Fonn 1983, The Adventures of Fionn Mac Chumail 1984, Heroes and Rituals 1984, Dreams of Wisdom 1986, Visions 1988, Perspectives 1989, Dream Soul 1990, Kingdoms 1991; contrib. to East-West Voices, Rising Stars, Samvedana-Creative Bulletin, Poet International, Souvenir Tribute to Professor Saidhana, Canopy, Indian Literary Journal. *Address:* 115 San Jose Avenue, Santa Cruz, CA 96060, USA.

**BARNARD, Trevor John,** ARAM, ARCM, GradMIMIT, LPIBA; pianist and academic; b. 3 Jan. 1938, London, England; m. Helen Richmond 1974. *Education:* Royal Academy of Music, Royal College of Music, Inst. of Musical Instrument Technology, studied with Herbert Fryer, Harold Craxton. *Career:* pianist-in-residence, Boston Univ. Radio 1967–71; Faculty, New England Conservatory, Boston, MA 1968–72; piano tutor, Monash Univ., Australia 1972–74; Lecturer in Music, Melbourne Coll. of Advanced Education 1974–88; Lecturer in Music, Univ. of Melbourne and examiner, Australian Music Examinations Board 1989–2003; many appearances as pianist, BBC and ABC television; Music-in-the-Round Chamber Music Festivals; many orchestras, music socs; mem. Australian Musicians' Guild (hon. sec. 1982–93), Camberwell Music Soc. (pres. 1990–2000, hon. life mem. 2000–). *Recordings:* An Introduction to Piano Music; Bliss Piano Concerto; J. S. Bach transcriptions and piano music from Australia; Busoni 24 preludes; Bliss Sonata; Blue Wrens, piano music from Australia. *Recordings for television and film:* Schumann and Bliss concerti, Mozart, Concerto Rondo (K382). *Publications:* Pedalling and Other Reflections on Piano Teaching, 1991; A Guide to the Study of Solo Piano Repertoire at Tertiary Level, 1996; contrib. to Clavier (journal), 1998–2002; Australia Music Teacher (magazine) 1992–. *Honours:* Full Scholarship Royal Coll. of Music 1955. *Address:* 10 Grosvenor Road, Glen Iris, Vic. 3146, Australia.

**BARNEA, Sever (Aurelian);** Romanian singer (baritone); *First Soloist, Baritone, National Opera, Bucharest*; b. 1 July 1960, Bucharest; one s. *Education:* piano principal study, Lyceum of Art, singing principal study, Universitatea de Muzica, int. music classes, Weimar. *Career:* First Perm. Baritone, Romanian Nat. Opera Bucharest, 1989; Mozart, Papageno in The Magic Flute; Figaro in Le nozze di Figaro; title role in Don Giovanni; Donizetti, Dr Malatesta in Don Pasquale and Dulcamara in L'Elisir d'amore; Verdi, Amonasro in Aida; Iago in Otello; title role in Falstaff; Gounod, Mephisto in Faust; Rossini, Mustafa in Italiana in Algeri; Bartolo in Il Barbiere di Siviglia; Basilio in La Cenerentola, Saint-Saëns, The Grand Priest of Dagon in Samson and Delilah; Ponchielli, Barnaba in Gioconda; Gomes in C Gomes, Don Gil de Tarragona in Maria Tudor; Puccini, Marcello in La

Bohème; Madama Butterfly; Scarpia in Tosca; Ping in Turandot; Bizet, Escamillo in Carmen; Tchaikovsky, title role in Eugene Onegin; Wagner, Holländer in Der fliegende Holländer; Georges Enescu, title role in Oedipe; Pascal Bentoiu, Laertes in Hamlet; Nicolae Bretan, title role in Golem; Bach; Haydn; Fauré; Carl Orff. *Recordings:* Romanian national radio and television, Bulgaria; BBC; Participated in several festivals at Georges Enescu International Festival, Romania; Temps Musicaux, Ramatuelle Festival Anvers sur Oise, France; Medway Arts Festival, 1995; Athens Festival; Toured Austria, Belgium, France, Spain, Bulgaria, Germany, Greece, Switzerland, Netherlands, United Kingdom, Italy, Hungary, Poland, Japan, Albania, Moldova, Macedonia. *Honours:* Performanta in Spectacolul de Opera Award, Actualitatie Musicale 2000, Meritul Cultural in Grad Cavaler Presidential Award 2004. *Address:* Str. Compozitorilor 1 Mai, 32 B1 F8, Sc B apt 24 Sector VI, Cod 61634 Bucharest, Romania. *Telephone:* (21) 7252429; (745) 074023. *Fax:* (21) 3120505. *E-mail:* severbarnea@pcnet.ro. *Website:* www.geocities.com/severbarnea.

**BARNES, Gerald Linton,** FRCO, GRSM, ARAM, ARCM; British musician; b. 6 June 1935, Hampstead, England; s. of William Leslie Barnes and Constance Grace Linnington; m. Rachel Mary Townsend. *Education:* Kilburn Grammar School, Hertford Coll., Oxford, Royal Acad. of Music. *Career:* Organist, Bloomsbury Central Church 1956–81; St Columba's Pont Street 1988–; Prof., examiner London Coll. of Music 1965–; Lecturer City Literary Inst. 1971–; conductor, Elysian Choir 1975–, Wembley Philharmonic Soc. 1981, Thiman Orchestra of London 1985–; appeared as organist on television, radio and at cathedrals, univs and major concert halls in England, Europe and USA; mem. Savage Club, Royal Soc. of Musicians. *Compositions:* hymn tunes and anthems. *Recordings:* various organ recordings. *Publications:* contrib. to Musical Times, Musical Opinion and choral and musical journals. *Honours:* Hon. FLCM 1985. *Address:* 35 Dollis Avenue, London, N3 1BY, England (home). *Telephone:* (20) 8346-6637 (home).

**BAROVÁ, Anna;** Singer (mezzo-soprano); b. 1932, Plzeň, Czechoslovakia. *Education:* Prague Acad. *Career:* sang at the Leipzig Opera, 1959–69, notably in the 1961 German premiere of Prokofiev's War and Peace, as Sonia; guested widely in former E Germany; sang at the Janáček Opera, Brno, 1969–92; roles included Dorabella, Rosina, Carmen, Ulrica, Suzuki, Olga; concert repertory includes Beethoven's Ninth, the Verdi, Mozart and Dvořák Requiems, Dvořák's Stabat, and vocal recitals; Prof., Janáček Acad. of Performing Arts, Brno, 1990–. *Recordings include:* The Devil and Kate by Dvořák, Eva by Foerster, Jenůfa by Janáček. *Address:* Kotlanova 1c, 628 00 Brno, Czech Republic.

**BARRELL, David;** Singer (Baritone); b. 1962, England. *Education:* London University and the Royal Academy of Music; Opera Center at the Juilliard School, New York. *Career:* Sang Gounod's Ourrais (Mireille) and Don Giovanni at Juilliard; Appearances at the Spoleto Festivals (Italy and USA) 1986; Wexford Festival 1987 and Britten's Demetrius at the Bloomsbury Festival; Welsh National Opera as Ottokar in Der Freischütz, The Speaker in Die Zauberflöte, Don Carlos (Ernani) and Germont; Season 1992–93 as Rossini's Figaro and Alfonso in La Favorita, with WNO at Covent Garden; Sang 'I' in the British premiere production of Schnittke's Life with an Idiot (English National Opera, 1994); Šiškon in House of the Dead in Nice; Wolfram in Tannhäuser for Chelsea Opera Group and Thaos in Iphigénie en Tauride at the 1996 Edinburgh Festival; Season 1996–97 with Germont for Opera Northern Ireland, Major Haudy in Zimmermann's Die Soldaten for ENO, Puccini's Marcello, The Forester in The Cunning Little Vixen and Balstrode in Peter Grimes, for Scottish Opera; Mandryka in Arabella at Glyndebourne Festival; Concerts include: The Brahms Requiem, Carmina Burana, Elijah and Elgar's The Kingdom; Premiere of Tippett's Tempest Suite, season 1995–96; Season 1997–98 as Josquin Desprez in Pfitzner's Palestrina at the Metropolitan, New York, Thaos in Iphigénie en Tauride at Rio de Janeiro, Tokyo and Madrid, and Redburn in Billy Budd for ENO. *Honours:* Winner, New York Oratorio Society International Soloist Competition, Carnegie Hall; Associate of Royal Academy of Music. *Address:* Allied Artists, 42 Montpelier Square, London SW7 1JZ, England. *Website:* www.davidbarrell.com.

**BARRERA, Giulia;** Singer (Soprano); b. 28 April 1942, Brooklyn, New York, USA. *Education:* Studied in New York with Dick Marzollo. *Career:* Debut: New York City Opera, 1963, as Aida; Sang in Baltimore, New Orleans, Pittsburgh, Washington and Seattle; Member of New York City Opera: Roles included Verdi's Amelia and Leonora (Il Trovatore), Santuzza, Don Giovanni, Sieglinde in Die Walküre, Tosca, Manon Lescaut, Venus in Tannhäuser and Monteverdi's Euridice; Guest appearances in Copenhagen, Rome, Parma, Cardiff, Montreal and Nuremberg. *Recordings include:* The Mother in Dallapiccola's Il Prigioniero.

**BARRETT, Richard;** British composer and classical guitarist; b. 7 Nov. 1959, Swansea, Wales. *Education:* studied with Peter Wiegold and in Darmstadt. *Career:* teacher, Darmstadt, 1986 and 1988; Co-director, Ensemble Expose. *Compositions:* Essay in Radiance for ensemble, 1983; Principia for baritone and piano, 1984; Cogitum for mezzo and ensemble, 1985; Illuminer le temps for ensemble, 1986; Ne Songe plus a fuir for amplified cello, 1986; Temptation for ensemble, 1986; Alba for bassoon and electronics, 1987; Recticule for violin, 1988; The Unthinkable for electronics and tape, 1989; Dark Ages for cello, 1990; Another Heavenly Day for ensemble, 1990; Lieder vom wasser for soprano and ensemble; Basalt for trombone, 1991; Praha for cello, 1991; Negatives for guitar and ensemble, 1992; Knospend–gespaltner

for clarinet, 1993; Vanity for orchestra, 1994; Trawl for 5 players, 1994–97; Von Hinter dem Schmerz for amplified cello, 1992–97; Opening of the Mouth for 2 female voices, instruments, tapes and live electronics, 1992–97; Stress for string quartet, 1995–97; Unter Wasser, opera for mezzo-soprano and 13 instruments, 1995–98. *Address:* c/o British Music Information Centre, 19 Stratford Place, London W1N 9AE, England.

**BARRIÈRE, Jean-Baptiste (Marie);** Composer and Director of Musical Research; b. 2 Jan. 1958, Paris, France; m. Kaija Saariaho, 26 May 1984. *Education:* Licence, Mathematical Logic, 1980, DEA Philosophy, 1981, Doctorate in Philosophy, 1987, University of Paris I, Panthéon Sorbonne. *Career:* Member of the Synthesizer Ensemble of the Centre Européen pour la Recherche Musicale, Metz, 1976–77; Researcher, Composer, 1981–84, Director of Musical Research, 1984–97, Institut de Recherche et de Co-ordination Acoustique Musique, Paris; mem, Collectif pour la Recherche en Information Musicale. *Compositions:* Pandémonium: Ville Ouverte, 1975; Pandémonium: Non, Jamais l'Esperance, 1976; Sophistic Variations, 1980; Chreode I, 1983; Collisions, 1984; Epigénèse, 1986; Hybris, 1987; World Skin, 1997; Cellitude, 1998; Time Dusts, 1998. *Recordings:* Pandémonium: Ville Ouverte, 1977; Pandémonium: Non, Jamais l'Esperance, 1978. *Publications:* Le Timbre: Métaphores pour la Composition, 1987–88; Actes du Symposium Systèmes Personnels et Informatique Musicale, 1987. *Contributions:* Chreode I: A Path to a New Music with the Computer, for Contemporary Music Review No. 1, 984; Mutations de l'Escriture, Mutations du Matériau, for Inharmoniques No. 1, 1987. *Honours:* Digital Music Prize in the Electro-Acoustic Music Competition, Bourges, France, 1983; Prix Ars Electronica, Linz, 1998. *Address:* c/o Centre de la Musique Contemporain, Cité de la Musique, 16 Place de la Fontaine, F–75019 Paris, France.

**BARRON, Bebe;** Composer; b. 16 June 1927, Minneapolis, Minnesota, USA. *Education:* Studied at the Universities of Minnesota and Mexico and in New York with Riegger and Cowell. *Career:* With husband Louis Barron (1920–89) co-founded electro-acoustic music studio in New York, 1949; Secretary of the Society for Electro-Acoustic Music from 1985. *Compositions:* With Louis Barron, Dramatic Legend, 1955; Ballet, 1958; Heavenly Menagerie, 1952; For an Electronic Nervous System, 1954; Music of Tomorrow, 1960; Spaceboy, 1971; The Circe Circuit, 1982; Elegy for a Dying Planet, 1982; Film scores, including Forbidden Planet, 1956, and Cannabis, 1975. *Address:* c/o ASCAP, ASCAP House, 1 Lincoln Plaza, New York, NY 10023, USA.

**BARROSO, Sergio;** Composer and Synthesist; b. 4 March 1946, Havana, Cuba. *Education:* Composition; Piano; Organ; Theory; National Conservatory, Havana, 1950–66; Postgraduate, Prague Superior Academy of Music; Orchestral Conducting, University of Havana; Computer Music, CCRMA, Stanford University, USA. *Career:* Professor; Composition; Institute of Arts, Havana; Performances include: Monte Carlo Theatre, 1972; Warsaw Autumn Festivals, 1972, 1985; Budapest Opera, 1976; Teatro de la Zarzuela, Madrid, 1976; MET-Lincoln Center, New York, 1977–78; San Francisco Opera, 1977; Bratislava Philharmonic Hall, 1979; ISCM Festival, Belgium, 1980, Oslo, 1990; IRCMA, Paris, 1980; Array, Toronto, 1981; Utrecht Conservatorium, Netherlands, 1982; Manuel de Falla Festival, Granada, 1985; Wired Society, Toronto, 1986; ACREQ, Montreal, 1987; Museo Tamayo, Mexico City, 1988; National Arts Centre, Ottawa, 1988; South Bank Centre, London, 1989; Toronto New Music Concerts, 1990; Sub-Tropics Festival, Miami, 1991; LIEM, Centro Reina Sofia, Madrid, 1991; ICMC, Montreal, 1991; New Music Across America, Seattle, 1992; Others. *Compositions:* 2 ballets; Plásmasis, 1970; La Casa de Bernarda Alba, 1975; Oboe Concerto, 1968; Yantra IV flute, tape, 1982; Ireme, voice, percussion, tape, 1985; En Febrero Mueren las Flores, violin, tape, 1987; Tablao, guitar, tape, 1991; Concerto for violin and orchestra, 1992; Synthesizers: Soledad, 1987; Canzone, 1988; La Fiesta, synthesizers, tape, 1989; La Fiesta Grande, synthesizers, orchestra, 1990; Cronicas de Ultrasueño, oboe, synthesizers, 1992; Sonatada, 1992; Concerto for viola and orchestra, 1996; Viola Desnuda, viola solo, 1997; La Noche, viola, bass clarinet and tape, 1997; Sandunga, viola or clarinet and tape, 1998; Cuartetas, viola, bass clarinet, piano and tape, 1999; Callejero, bass clarinet and tape, 1999; Pregones, cello and tape, 2000. *Recordings:* Digital Keyboard Music, 1988; Cronicas, 1995; Concerto for viola and Concerto for violin, 1998; Charangas Delirantes, solo and electronic works, 1998; Viola Desnuda, 2000. *Address:* IREME EMS, 7938, 122 A Street, Surrey, British Columbia, V3W 3T3, Canada.

**BARRUECO, Manuel;** American classical guitarist; b. 16 Dec. 1952, Santiago de Cuba, Cuba. *Education:* Eŝteban Salas Conservatory, Santiago de Cuba and the Peabody Conservatory, MD, USA. *Career:* debut, New York 1974; many concert appearances as soloist; faculty mem., Peabody Conservatory; assisted in the creation of a faculty for guitar at the Manhattan School of Music; gave the US premiere of Takemitsu's guitar concerto 1985. *Recordings include:* Rodrigo (with Placido Domingo), Bach Sonatas, Albeniz, Turina (solo). *Honours:* Concert Artists' Guild Award 1974. *Current Management:* M. B. General Management, PO Box 4466, Timonium, MD 21094-4466, USA. *Website:* www.barrueco.com.

**BARRY, Gerald;** Irish composer; b. 28 April 1952, Clarecastle. *Education:* studied in Cologne with Stockhausen and Kagel, studied organ with Piet Kee in Amsterdam. *Compositions include:* Chevaux de frise for orchestra (performed at the Proms 1988), The Intelligence Park (opera, ICA commission, first performed at the 1990 Almeida Festival), The Triumph of Beauty and Deceit (Channel 4 TV commission 1992), The Conquest of Ireland (vocal and orchestral work, BBC Symphony Orchestra commission), String Quartet 1994, The Ring for chorus and orchestra 1995, Quintet 1995, Octet 1995, Piano Quintet No. 2 1996, The Road for orchestra 1997, The Bitter Tears of Petra Von Kant (based on the play and film by Rainer Werner Fassbinder, first performed at ENO) 2005. *Recordings:* Piano and Chamber music (with Noriko Kawai on piano and the Nua Nos ensemble). *Publications:* contrib. The Intelligence Park (in Contemporary Music Review) Vol. 5, Irish Wit (in The Musical Times) Sept. 1993, Bob's Your Uncle (in The Musical Times) April 1995. *Address:* c/o Oxford University Press, Great Clarendon Street, Oxford, OX2 6DP, England. *Website:* www.oup.co.uk/music/repprom/barry.

**BARRY, John,** OBE; British composer; b. (Jonathan Barry Prendergast), 3 Nov. 1933, York. *Career:* formed group The John Barry Seven 1957–62; stage musical, Billy 1974; composer of film scores 1959–; Fellow BAFTA 2005–. *Compositions for film:* Beat Girl 1959, Drumbeat 1959, Never Let Go 1960, Girl on a Roof 1961, The Amorous Prawn 1962, Stringbeat 1961, Man in The Middle 1962, Dr No 1962, The L-Shaped Room 1962, It's All Happening 1963, Zulu 1963, From Russia with Love 1963, A Jolly Bad Fellow 1964, Séance on a Wet Afternoon 1964, Goldfinger 1964, Boy on a Bicycle 1965, The Party's Over 1965, Mister Moses 1965, Four in the Morning 1965, The Knack 1965, The Ipcress File 1965, King Rat 1965, Passion Flower Hotel 1965, Thunderball 1965, Dutchman 1966, The Chase 1966, Born Free (Acad. Awards for Best Original Song, Best Original Score 1967) 1966, The Wrong Box 1966, The Quiller Memorandum 1966, You Only Live Twice 1967, The Whisperers 1967, Boom 1968, Petulia 1968, Deadfall 1968, The Lion in Winter 1968, Midnight Cowboy (Acad. Award for Best Original Score) 1969, On Her Majesty's Secret Service 1969, Monte Walsh 1970, Mary Queen of Scots 1971, The Last Valley 1971, They Might Be Giants 1971, Walkabout 1971, Lolita My Love 1971, Alice's Adventures in Wonderland 1971, Diamonds Are Forever 1971, Follow Me! 1972, Bang Bang 1972, A Doll's House 1973, The Tamarind Seed 1974, The Dove 1974, The Man with the Golden Gun 1974, The Day of the Locust 1975, Robin and Marian 1976, King Kong 1976, The White Buffalo 1977, The Deep 1977, First Love 1977, The Betsy 1978, Game of Death 1978, Starcrash 1979, Hanover Street 1979, Moonraker 1979, The Black Hole 1979, Somewhere in Time 1980, Night Games 1980, Inside Moves 1980, Raise the Titanic 1980, Touched by Love 1980, The Legend of the Lone Ranger 1981, Body Heat 1983, Hammett 1982, Frances 1982, Murder by Phone 1982, The Golden Seal 1983, High Road to China 1983, Octopussy 1983, Mike's Murder 1984, Until September 1984, The Cotton Club 1984, A View To A Kill 1985, Jagged Edge 1985, Out of Africa (Acad. Award for Best Original Score, Golden Globe for Best Original Score) 1985, A Killing Affair 1986, Howard the Duck 1986, Peggy Sue Got Married 1986, Hearts of Fire 1987, The Living Daylights 1987, Masquerade 1988, Dances with Wolves (Acad. Award for Best Original Score) 1990, Chaplin 1992, Indecent Proposal 1993, Ruby Cairo 1993, My Life 1993, The Specialist 1994, Cry, the Beloved Country 1995, The Scarlet Letter 1995, Across the Sea of Time 1995, Swept from the Sea 1997, Mercury Rising 1998, Playing by Heart 1998, Beyondness of Things 1999, A Song of Africa 2000, The Last Valley 2001, Enigma 2001. *Composition for television:* Drumbeat (series) 1959, Juke Box Jury (series theme) 1959, Discs a Go-Go (series theme) 1961, Impromptu (series) 1964, The Newcomers (series theme) 1965, Vendetta (series theme) 1966, The Persuaders (series theme) 1971, The Adventurer (series theme) 1972, Great Mysteries (series theme) 1973, The Glass Menagerie (film) 1973, Love Among the Ruins (film) 1975, Eleanor and Franklin (film) 1976, The War Between the Tates (film) 1977, Young Joe, the Forgotten Kennedy (film) 1977, The Gathering (film) 1977, The Corn is Green (film) 1979, Willa (film) 1979, The Witness (film) 1992. *Recordings include:* albums: Elizabeth Taylor in London 1963, Sophia Loren in Rome 1965, Eternal Echoes 2001. *Current Management:* c/o J. H. Cohn LLP, 1212 Avenue of the Americas, 24th Floor, New York, NY 10036, USA. *Telephone:* (212) 826-6000 (office). *Fax:* (212) 421-2583 (office).

**BARSHAI, Rudolf Borisovich;** Russian/British conductor; b. 28 Sept. 1924, Labinskaya, Krasnodar Territory; s. of Boris and Maria Barshai. *Education:* Moscow Conservatoire. *Career:* performed in chamber ensembles with Shostakovich, Richter, Oistrakh, Rostropovich; Founder and Artistic Dir Moscow Chamber Orchestra 1956–77; Prin. Conductor and Artistic Adviser, Bournemouth Symphony Orchestra 1982–96; Guest Conductor Orchestre Nat. de France; numerous tours abroad; author of orchestrations and arrangements for chamber orchestra of old and contemporary music. *Honours:* Hon. DMus (Southampton). *Current Management:* Askonas Holt Ltd, Lonsdale Chambers, 27 Chancery Lane, London, WC2A 1PF, England. *Telephone:* (20) 7400-1700. *Fax:* (20) 7400-1799. *E-mail:* info@askonasholt.co.uk. *Website:* www.askonasholt.co.uk. *Address:* Homberg Str. 6, 4433 Ramlinsburg, Switzerland. *Telephone:* (61) 931-12-84. *Fax:* (61) 931-35-64.

**BARSTOW, Dame Josephine Clare,** DBE, BA; British singer; b. 27 Sept. 1940, Sheffield; d. of Harold Barstow and Clara Barstow; m. 1st Terry Hands 1964 (divorced 1968); m. 2nd Ande Anderson 1969 (died 1996). *Education:* Birmingham Univ. *Career:* taught English in London area for two years; debut in operatic profession with Opera for All 1964; for short time co. mem. Welsh Nat. Opera, then ENO; now freelance singer in all nat. opera houses in UK and in Paris, Vienna, Salzburg, Zürich, Geneva, Turin, Florence, Cologne, Munich, Berlin, USSR, Chicago, San Francisco, New York, Houston and many other American opera houses. *Chief roles:* Violetta (Traviata), Leonora (Forza del Destino), Elisabeth (Don Carlos), Lady Macbeth, Leonore (Fidelio), Sieglinde, Arabella, Salome, Chrysothemis, Amelia, The Marschallin, Tosca, Mimi, Minnie, Manon Lescaut, Emilia Marty, Jenůfa, Katya Kabanova,

Medea, Renata (The Fiery Angel), Katerina Ismailova, Kostelnicka (Jenůfa), Marie (Wozzeck), Gloriana, Lady Billows (Albert Herring); world premières of Tippett, Henze and Penderecki. *Film:* Owen Wingrave 2001. *Recordings include:* Verdi Recital Record with ENO Orchestra and Mark Elder, Amelia with Herbert von Karajan, Anna Maurant in Street Scene, Kate in Kiss Me Kate, Four Finales, Gloriana, Albert Herring. *Honours:* Hon. DMus (Birmingham, Kingston, Sheffield Hallam); Fidelio Medal. *Address:* c/o Askonas Holt, Lonsdale Chambers, 27 Chancery Lane, London, WC2A 1PF, England. *Telephone:* (20) 7400-1700.

**BÁRTA, Aleš;** Czech organist; b. 30 Aug. 1960, Rychnov; m. 1984; one s. *Education:* Brno Conservatoire, Acad. of Music, Prague. *Career:* debut with Prague Symphony Orchestra, Prague Spring Festival 1984; tours of Denmark 1979, Austria 1983, Hungary 1984, 1985, Turkey 1985, Germany 1986, 1990, France 1987, Russia 1988; US debut at concert of Czech music, New York 1990; also Japan, China, Hong Kong, Finland, Switzerland, Spain; festival appearances include recitals at Prague Spring Festival 1984, 1988 and 1991, Avignon Festival 1987, Istanbul Festival 1985, Leipzig Festival 1986; debut with Prague Radio Symphony Orchestra, Berlin Festival 1987, also Tokyo, Yokohama, Sapporo, Passau, Linz and Zürich festivals; concerts with Czech Philharmonic Orchestra and Czech Radio Symphony Orchestra; Czech Radio soloist 1995–. *Recordings:* Organ recital of Bach, Reger and Flosman 1986, Organ recital of Bach 1991, Organ recital live recording of Bach, Reger, Sokola 1992, Organ Works of Mozart, Complete Organ Works of J. S. Bach, Russian Organ Music, Organ Illusion, Reger Organ Works, The Best of German Organ Music, Liszt Organ Works, Gems of French Organ Music, Czech Organ Music across the Centuries. *Honours:* first prize Anton Bruckner Int. Organ Competition, Linz 1982, first prize Czech Organists Competition 1984, first prize Prague Spring Int. Organ Competition 1984, Supraphon Gold Disc (for Bach's Organ Works recording) 1993, Japanese Critics Prize 1995. *Current Management:* Arco Diva Management, 12 000 Prague 2, Czech Republic. *Telephone:* 224 238 673 (office). *Fax:* 224 238 619 (office). *E-mail:* arcodiva@ arcodiva.cz (office). *Website:* www.arcodiva.cz/barta (office). *Address:* Nuselska 6, 14 000 Prague 4, Czech Republic (home). *Telephone:* 241 741 097 (home). *E-mail:* barta.ales@tiscali.cz (home).

**BÁRTA, Jiri;** Czech composer; b. 19 June 1935, Sumice; m. Jindra Bartova 1964; one d. *Education:* conservatoire; Janáček Acad. of Music and Dramatic Arts, Brno, Czechoslovakia. *Career:* debut, Concerto for Orchestra 1962; music theory teacher, Conservatory, Brno 1968–; mem. Asscn of Composers and Music Publicists, Camerata Brno. *Compositions:* Lyric Variations for Violin and Piano, Melancholy and Defiance for Violin, Cello and Piano, Concerto da Camera per Pianoforte ed Archi, Reliefs for Orchestra, Music for Strings: In Memoriam Miloslav Istvan, Chitra Chamber Opera, Concerto for Viola and Orchestra, Concertino for Piano, Harpsichord and Chamber Orchestra. *Recordings:* Camerata Brno Live I (two Impromptus for Piano), Camerata Brno Live II (Drink from the Vine), Czech Radio. *Honours:* Prizes, Union of Czech Composers 1986, Czech Musical Fund 1990, 1991. *Address:* Solnicni 5-9, 602 00 Brno, Czech Republic.

**BARTA, Michael (Mihaly);** Violinist and University Professor; b. 6 Feb. 1954, Budapest, Hungary; m. Irene Barta, 3 May 1980, 1 s. *Education:* Béla Bartók Conservatory, 1964–69; F Liszt Academy, Budapest, 1969–75; Postgraduate study with Arthur Grumiaux, –1975. *Career:* Concerts, Wigmore Hall, London, Tokyo, Frankfurt, Carnegie Recital Hall, New York, Detroit Art Institute, Austria; Radio: Radio France, Scottish BBC, Radio Bremen, Berlin, Hungarian Radio, WDR Köln, PBS USA; Concerts in Sofia Conservatory, La Valetta (Malta), Budapest (Franz Liszt Academy); Hungarian Television, PBS-USA; Malta, Bulgaria, Latvia, Spain. *Recordings:* Goldmark Suite for Violin and Piano; Prokofiev: Sonata for Two Violins; Numerous recordings for major labels and national and international radio stations. *Honours:* 2nd Prize, Joseph Szigeti International Competition, Budapest, 1973; Gold Medal, Belgian Eugene Ysaÿe Society, 1973; Special Prize, finals, Tchaikovsky International Competition, Moscow, 1974. *Address:* 45 Twin Creeks Lane, Murphysboro, IL 62966, USA.

**BARTELINK, Bernard G. M.;** Organist and Composer; b. 24 Nov. 1929, Enschede, Netherlands; m. Rina Stolwyk 1955, 2 s. *Education:* Diploma, Composition, 1955, Prix d'excellence, organ, 1954, Amsterdam Conservatory. *Career:* Recitals in major concert halls and cathedrals in the United Kingdom, Europe and USA; Radio appearances in many countries; Professor of organ at Sweelinck Conservatory, Amsterdam until 1989; Organist at St Bavo Cathedral, Haarlem, –1999. *Compositions:* The Beatitudes for voice and organ; Works for organ, choir and chamber music, commissioned by Dutch Government, City of Amsterdam. *Recordings:* Several solo albums. *Honours:* First prize, International Organ Improvisation Contest, Haarlem, 1961; Knight in the Papal Order of St Sylvester; Silver Medal of the Academic Society, Arts, Sciences and Letters, Paris; Officer in the Order of Oranje-Nassau. *Address:* Leeghwaterstraat 14, 2012 GD Haarlem, Netherlands.

**BARTH, Ned;** Singer (Baritone); b. 1963, Syracuse, New York. *Education:* Studied at Princeton and the Manhattan School of Music. *Career:* Debut: Berne, 1987 as Mozart's Count; Sang Mandryka in Arabella, Wolfram in Tannhäuser, Donizetti's Enrico, Germont, Nabucco and Napoleon in Prokofiev's War and Peace, Karlsruhe Opera, 1989–92; Guest appearances as Verdi's Don Carlo, Marseilles; Paolo, Dresden, Marcello, 1994; Cologne, Iago, 1996; As Wolfram, Flanders Opera at Antwerp; Season 1998: as Scarpia at Cologne; Season 1999 as Scarpia at Cologne, Posa for the Komische Oper

Berlin and Jokanaan in Salome for Glimmerglass Opera; Other roles include Riccardo in I Puritani, Eugene Onegin, Verdi's Renato and Ford, Don Giovanni and Belcore; Concerts include Schubert's Winterreise, Carmina Burana, Mahler's Wunderhorn Lieder, Cologne, 1996, and works by Bach and Stravinsky. *Current Management:* Peter Seyfferth Artists Management, Avenue de la Concorde 385, 06190 Roquebrune Cap Martin, France. *Telephone:* 4-93-35-01-05. *Fax:* 4-93-35-02-17. *E-mail:* peter@seyfferth.de. *Website:* www.seyfferth.de. *Address:* c/o Oper der Stadt Köln, Offenbachplatz, Pf 18024, 50505 Cologne, Germany.

**BARTHA, Clarry;** Singer (soprano); b. 1958, Sweden. *Education:* Studied at the Accedamia di Santa Cecilia, Rome, with Maria Teresa Pediconi and George Favaretto; Further study with Vera Rozsa in London. *Career:* Debut: Donna Anna at Drottningholm, Sweden, 1981; Has sung Donna Anna in Catania, at the Montepulciano Festival and at Brighton Festival with the Drottningholm Company; At Marseilles has sung Lisa in The Queen of Spades, Fiordiligi and Margherita in Mefistofele; Basle Opera as Agathe, Tatiana in Eugene Onegin and Mozart's Countess; Performances of Gluck's La Danza at Bologna, season 1986–87; Frankfurt Opera, 1987–88 as Iphigénie en Tauride, Desdemona and Fiordiligi; She sang Mozart's Countess at Rome in 1989; Sang Katya Kabanova at Basle, 1991; Season 1995–96 as Katya at Düsseldorf and Leipzig, Chrysothemis at Nice; Sang Tosca at Bonn, 2000; Concert commitments at the Prague Spring, Palermo and Ravello Festivals; Has sung with the Italian Radio, RAI, in Rome, Naples and Milan; Accademia di Santa Cecilia in Rome and the Maggio Musicale in Florence; Mozart's Vespers and Mendelssohn's Elijah in Stockholm; Tour of Israel with Gary Bertini. *Honours:* Prizewinner at the Beniamino Gigli and Vincenzo Bellini competitions. *Current Management:* Ingpen & Williams Ltd, 7 St George's Court, 131 Putney Bridge Road, London, SW15 2PA, England.

**BARTKIEWICZ, Urszula;** Harpsichordist; b. 28 Jan. 1952, Bielsko-Biała, Poland; m. Jerzy Kozub, 13 Sept 1987, 1 s. *Education:* Certificate of Maturity, 1971; Studies at the Academy of Music in Kraków headed by Kryzsztof Penderecki, 1971–75; Graduation with distinction; Studies at Conservatoire National de Bobigny, Paris, 1976–77; Harpsichord Class of Huguette Dreyfus; International Master Courses: with Zuzana Ruzickova, Rafael Puyana and Kenneth Gilbert; Doctor's Thesis in Musicology at Polish Academy of Sciences in preparation. *Career:* Numerous concerts in Poland, e.g. International Festivals, Warsaw Autumn; Wratislavia Cantans; Lancut Chamber Festival; Concerts in France, Czechoslovakia, Germany, Russia, Switzerland, Belgium, Austria, the United Kingdom and USA; Co-operation with the Polish National Philharmony, Jerzy Maksymiuk's Polish Chamber Orchestra; Several appearances on television and radio in Poland and USA; Masterclass and recital for students of Wayne State University, Department of Music, Detroit, Jan 1988. *Recordings:* Regular recordings for Polish Radio 1975–90; International and Polish harpsichord music from XVI–XX centuries, solo and chamber music; Records with Polish National Philharmony and Jerzy Maksymiuk's Polish Chamber Orchestra, basso continuo. *Address:* ul Bacha 10m 301, 02-743, Warsaw, Poland.

**BARTLETT, Clifford Alfred James;** British musicologist and writer on music; b. 15 Aug. 1939, London, England; m. Elaine King 1975; one s. one d. *Education:* Dulwich Coll., Magdalene Coll., Cambridge. *Career:* Deputy Music Librarian, BBC, 1970–82; Keyboard Player for Ars Nova, 1969–75; Freelance Writer and Publisher, 1983–; Dir, Early Music Centre Festival, 1987–88; Chair., Eastern Early Music Forum, Nat. Early Music Assocn. *Publications:* Under his own imprint, King's Music, has published editions of a large quantity of music, especially opera, by Monteverdi, Purcell, Handel and other baroque composers; Also edited Handel's Messiah, Coronation Anthems and other works for Oxford University Press; contrib. monthly surveys in Early Music News, 1977–94; Editor, chief writer and publisher of Early Music Review, 1994–; Editor, Brio, 1974–85; contrib. of numerous programme notes for major record companies and festivals. *Address:* Redcroft, Banks End, Wyton, Huntingdon, Cambridgeshire PE28 2AA, England. *E-mail:* clifford .bartlett@btopenworld.com.

**BARTO, Tzimon;** Pianist and Conductor; b. 1963, Florida, USA. *Education:* Studied piano and Conducting, Juilliard School. *Career:* Composed first opera aged 8; Began conducting at 14; Performer, Spoleto Festival, 1985; Numerous performances, major European capitals, USA and Japan; Salzburg Easter Festival, 1989; Salzburg Summer Festival, 1989; Many major festivals. *Recordings:* Prokofiev's Piano Concerto No.3; Ravel's Concerto in G Major; Chopin-Liszt-Schumann recital programme; Bartók's piano concerto No.2; Rachmaninov's Piano concerto No.3; Chopin piano concerto No. 2; Liszt piano concerto No. 2, Royal Philharmonic Orchestra. *Address:* Monckebergallee 41, 30453 Hannover, Germany.

**BARTOLETTI, Bruno;** Conductor; b. 10 June 1926, Sesto Fiorentino, Italy; m. Rosanna Bartoletti, 2 c. *Education:* Studied flute at Cherubini Conservatory, Florence; Received training in piano and composition. *Career:* Debut: Conducting, Dec 1953, with Rigoletto; Symphonic debut, Maggio Musicale Fiorentino, 1954, resident conductor, 1957–64; US Debut, Lyric Opera of Chicago, 1956; Played flute in orchestra of the Teatro Comunale, Florence; Assistant conductor from 1949, working with Rodzinski, Mitropoulos, Gui and Serafin; Led the premieres of Rocca's Antiche iscrizioni, 1955, and Malipiero's Il figluol prodigo and Venere prigioniera, 1957, at Florence; Mortari's La scuola delle mogli, 1959, at La Scala and Ginastera's Don Rodrigo at the Teatro Colón Buenos Aires, 1964; Italian premieres of Egk's Der Revisor and

The Nose by Shostakovich; Conducted Italian opera at The Royal Opera, Copenhagen, 1957–60; Artistic Director, 1965–69, Co-artistic Director, 1975–, Rome Opera; Artistic adviser 1986–87; Artistic Director, Teatro Comunale Florence, 1987–92, conducted Madama Butterfly and I Puritani in Florence, 1988–89; Lyric Opera, Chicago 1988–89 with La Traviata and Tancredi; Guest conductor with many opera houses in Europe, USA and South America; Grand Théâtre Geneva, 1991, Peter Grimes; Conducted I Quattro Rusteghi at Geneva, 1992; Norma at Genoa, 1994; Conducted Simon Boccanegra at Rome, 1996; Season 1998 with Wolf-Ferrari's Il Campiello at Bologna and Macbeth at Genoa. *Recordings:* Il Barbiere di Siviglia; Vivaldi's Gloria and Credo, Deutsche Grammophon; Manon Lescaut; Un Ballo in Maschera. *Address:* c/o Chicago Lyric Opera, 20 North Wacker Drive, Chicago, IL 60606, USA.

**BARTOLI, Cecilia;** Italian singer (coloratura mezzo-soprano) and recitalist; b. 4 June 1966, Rome; d. of Pietro Angelo Bartoli and Silvana Bazzoni. *Education:* Accademia di Santa Cecilia, Rome. *Career:* professional career began with TV appearance aged 19; US debut in recital at Mostly Mozart Festival, New York 1990; Paris debut as Cherubino in The Marriage of Figaro, Opéra de Paris Bastille 1990–91 season; debut, La Scala, Milan in Rossini's Le Comte Ory 1990–91 season; appeared as Dorabella in Così fan tutte, Maggio Musicale, Florence 1991; debut with Montreal Symphony Orchestra and Philadelphia Orchestra 1990–91 season; recitals in collaboration with pianist András Schiff since 1990; appeared in Marriage of Figaro and Così fan tutte conducted by Daniel Barenboim in Chicago Feb. 1992; debut at Salzburg Festival 1992; appeared in recital at Rossini bicentenary celebration at Lincoln Center, New York 1992; has appeared with many leading conductors including the late Herbert von Karajan, Claudio Abbado, Riccardo Chailly, Myung-Whun Chung, William Christie, Charles Dutoit, Adam Fischer, Nikolaus Harnoncourt, Christophher Hogwood, James Levine, Sir Neville Marriner, Zubin Mehta, Riccardo Muti, Giuseppe Sinopoli and the late Sir George Solti; particularly associated with the operas of Mozart and Rossini; highlights of the 2000–01 season included Cenerentola in Munich, Così fan tutte and Don Giovanni in Zurich, concert performances of Haydn's Orfeo with Hogwood in Birmingham, Amsterdam, Bremen and Paris, orchestral appearances with Harnoncourt and the Berlin Philharmonic in Berlin, Barenboim and the Chicago Symphony in Chicago and New York, Boulez and the London Symphony Orchestra in London and Amsterdam, Chailly and the Concertgebouw Orchestra in Amsterdam, all-Vivaldi concerts with the Giardino Armonico in Merano, Zurich, Paris, Lindau, Liechtenstein, New York, Vancouver, Los Angeles and San Francisco, baroque music concerts with the Akademie für Alte Musik in Oslo, Goteborg, Stockholm, Helsinki and Vienna. *Recordings include:* albums: Rossini Arias, Rossini Songs, Mozart Arias, Rossini Heroines, Chants d'amour, If You Love Me 1992, Mozart Portraits 1995, An Italian Songbook 1997, Cecilia Bartoli – Live Vivaldi Album 1999, Cecilia & Bryn, Il Turco in Italia, Mitridate, Rinaldo, Armida in Italy, The Salieri Album, The Vivaldi Album, Gluck Italian Arias, Opera proibita 2005. *Honours:* Chevalier, Ordre des Arts et des Lettres; two Grammy Awards for Best Classical Vocal Album 1994, Deutsche Schallplatten Preis, La Stella d'Oro, Italy, Caecilia Award, Belgium, Diapason d'Or, France, Best Opera Recording of the Year for La Cenerentola, Japan, Classical BRIT Award for Female Artist of the Year 2004; hon. mem. RAM 2005. *Current Management:* MusicArt Management AG, PO Box 123, 8702 Zollikon-Zurich, Switzerland.

**BARTOLI, Sandro Ivo;** concert pianist; b. 10 Feb. 1970, Pisa, Italy. *Education:* Florence State Conservatory, 1991; RAM, London, 1993; studied privately with Shura Cherkassky, London, 1994. *Career:* debut, Mozart's Concerto K 271 at The Imperial Theatre, San Remo, 1991; perfomed Respighi Toccata for piano and orchestra, BYCO (BBC recording debut); Bach Double Concertos with Alex Kelly at the Basilica di San Giovanni, Lucca, 1993; Mozart Concertos K 413, 414, and 415 at St John's, Smith Square, London, 1995; PBS live broadcast debut, Seeger Auditorium, Johnson City, TN, USA, 1995; Beethoven Concerto No. 5 at St James's, Piccadilly, London (BBC live recording), 1996; recitalist at Centre Georges Pompidou, Paris, 1996; performed Mozart concertos at Livorno Festival, 1997; Rachmaninov's Paganini Rhapsody at the Bridgewater Hall, Manchester, 1999; recitalist at Warwick and Leamington Festival, 1999; Troldhallen, Bergen, 2000; Nybrokayen Music Acad., 2000; Brighton Festival, England, 2000; Aix-en-Provence (radio broadcast), 2000; Ogier and Le Masurier International Piano Festival, Jersey, Channel Islands, 2000; Fairfield Hall, London, 2001; performed Beethoven Concerto No. 5, Nordhausen, Germany, 2001; Shostakovich Concerto No. 1, Stockholm, 2001; performed at the Festival d'Avignon, France, 2001; recitalist, Teatro Carignano, Turin, Italy, 2002; Opera Holland Park, London, 2002; performed Rachmaninov Concerto No. 3, London, 2003; founded, directed and performed at Opera Etcetera, London, 2002. *Recordings:* Malipiero: Piano Music, 1995; Fugitives–Works by Casella, Grainger and Pabst, 1997; Casella: Piano Music, 1998; Opera Etcetera, 2003; Encores, 2003. *Honours:* Mary Elizabeth B'Stard Scholarship 1991–92; Royal Acad. Foundation Scholarship 1991–92; Gina Rosso Prize for Outstanding Work in the Arts, Lyric Club Renato Bruson, Turin, 2002. *Current Management:* Musikarte, Calle Palma 14, 07330 Consell, Islas Baleares, Spain.

**BARTOLINI, Lando;** Opera Singer (tenor); b. 11 April 1937, Casale di Prato, Florence, Italy; m. Deanna Mungai 1966, 2 d. *Education:* 5-year scholarship to Academy of Vocal Arts, Philadelphia, USA, 1968–73; Vocal instruction with Nicola Moscona; graduated, 1973. *Career:* debut, Iris of Mascagni at the Gran Liceo of Barcelona, Oct 1973; American debut in Cavalleria Rusticana, New

York City Opera, 1976; Appeared at special events including: Concert with Philadelphia Orchestra; New Production of Ernani with Chicago Lyric; Manon Lescaut with Vienna State Opera in Tokyo; Simon Boccanegra at Festival d'Orange; New Production of Turandot at Munich State Opera; Turandot with La Scala, Milan; In Seoul during Olympic Games; Has sung in many other major venues around the world including La Scala, Arena di Verona, Paris Opéra, Metropolitan Opera, Covent Garden, Vienna, Budapest, Buenos Aires, Santiago del Chile, South Africa, Canada, Lisbon, Boston and Cleveland with Metropolitan Opera; Wide repertoire includes: Aida, Tosca, La Bohème, Il Trovatore, Don Carlo, Macbeth, Forza del Destino, Il Tabarro, Mephistopheles and Rigoletto; Sang Manrico in Il Trovatore at the Orange Festival, 1992; Radames for Opera Pacific, 1994; Sang Des Grieux in Manon Lescaut at Torre del Lago, 1996; Season 1996 as Radames at the Vienna Staatsoper and Verdi's Alvaro at Antwerp; Andrea Chénier at Monte Carlo, 1998; Season 1999-2000 as Radames at Florence and Puccini's Des Grieux at Catania. *Recordings:* I Cavalieri di Ekebu, with director Gianandrea Gavazzeni; Hungaroton, 1992; Respighi's La Semirama, 1st recording; Hungaroton, 1991 Solo Tenor Arias; Turandot Last Duet Alfano original, first time on record, 1990. *Publications:* La Follia Di New York, 1989; Orpheus Berlin, 1990; Das Opern Glas Germany, 1990; Opera News New York, 1991-93. *Current Management:* ICM Artists, New York. *Address:* Via Bargo 12, 50047 Casale di Prato, Florence, Italy.

**BÄRTSCHI, Werner;** Swiss pianist and composer; b. 1 Jan. 1950, Zürich, Switzerland; m.; two c. *Education:* Volksschule and Gymnasium Zürich; studied as pianist, composer and conductor in Zürich and Basel. *Career:* concerts in 35 countries on five continents; festival appearances include Yehudi Menuhin-Festival, Gstaad, Lucerne Festival, Zürcher Festspiele, Festival international de piano de la Roque d'Anthéron, Salzburger Festspiele; television appearances in various countries; film actor in Justiz, by Geissendörfer; initiation and realization of the Satie-Saison, 1980-81, and the Ives-Zyklus, 1985-86, both in Zürich; premiered works by John Cage, Klaus Huber, Wilhelm Killmeyer, Terry Riley, Dieter Schnebel, Wladimir Vogel and others; Pres., Music Committee of City of Zürich, 1990-92; Artistic Adviser of 1991 June Festival in Zürich; Artistic Dir of various concert series in Switzerland; performances of his own compositions in over 30 countries; several broadcasts and recordings; mem. Schweizerischer Tonkünstlerverein, Schweizerischer Musikpädagogischer Verband, Komponistensekretariat Zürich. *Compositions:* over 30 works of orchestral music, chamber music, vocal music, piano music; several transcriptions: Rossini, Fauré, Schoeck, Schnebel. *Recordings:* over 30 recordings, including music of over 40 composers; music for 10 films for Swiss television. *Publications:* Die unvermeidliche Musik des John Cage, 1969; Musik der Entfremdung – entfremdete Musik, 1981-82; Ratio und Intuition in der Musik, Kunst und Wissenschaft, 1984; Italian translation, 1989, Zu meinem Klavierstück in Trauer und Prunk, 1989; Leistung und Plausch im Musikunterricht, 1989; German editions of selected writings by Erik Satie, 1980 and Charles Ives, 1985; Music Editions of works by Zdenek Fibich, 1988, and Wladimir Vogel, 1989. *Honours:* Grand Prize, Académie du disque française, 1983. *Address:* Zolliker Strasse 97, 8702 Zollikon, Switzerland. *Telephone:* (52) 6204646 (home). *E-mail:* baertschi.w@rezital.ch (home).

**BARTZ, Ingrid;** Singer (Mezzo-Soprano); b. 20 March 1964, Aachen, Germany. *Education:* Studied in Cologne and Berne with Juliette Bise-Delnon, Edith Mathis and Brigitte Fassbaender. *Career:* Sang at Aachen Opera, from 1982, including Britten's Hermia; Opera-studio at Düsseldorf Opera, with Hänsel, 1986-87; Karlsruhe Opera, as Cherubino, Octavian, the Composer in Ariadne auf Naxos, Suzuki, Flora, Rosina, Mignon and Sesto in Handel's Giulio Cesare, from 1988; Guest appearances include major roles at Düsseldorf, Liège, Luxembourg, Strasbourg, Zürich, Lucerne, Frankfurt, Mannheim, Essen, Vienna; Concert engagements with most German radio and television stations and abroad; Bonn Opera, 1993-, including several premieres and debuts: Nicklausse, Zerlina, Orlofsky, Fenena, from 1993; Bavarian State Opera Munich: since 1999, guest appearances; Season 1999-2000 as Suzuki in Butterfly at the Eutin Festival, Wellgunde in Götterdämmerung at Bonn and Ludmila in The Bartered Bride for the Munich Staatsoper. *Recordings include:* Lieder by Mahler (Rückert and Wunderhorn Lieder), Brahms (Zigeunerlieder) and Wagner (Wesendoncklieder); Die Walküre, from Munich, 2002 (CD and DVD). *Address:* c/o NWB Apollon & Hermes, PR-Arts-Media Services Production, Im Flögerhof 12, 53819 Neunkirchen, Cologne, Germany. *Website:* www.culture-universal.com/bartz/bartz.html.

**BARYLLI, Walter;** Violinist; b. 16 June 1921, Vienna, Austria. *Education:* Vienna Hochschule; Violin study with F von Reuter, Munich. *Career:* Debut: Munich, 1936; Concert tours throughout Europe and overseas; Member, Vienna State Opera Orchestra and Vienna Philharmonic, 1938-; Formerly, leader of both orchestras; Leader Barylli Quartet, 1945-; Professor of Violin, Vienna Conservatory, 1969-. *Honours:* Kreisler Prize (twice won). *Address:* Rennweg 4-14, 1030 Vienna, Austria.

**BARZUN, Jacques Martin,** AB, PhD, FRSA, FRSL; American writer and academic; *Professor Emeritus, Columbia University*; b. 30 Nov. 1907, Créteil, France; s. of Henri Martin and Anna-Rose Barzun; m. 1st Mariana Lowell 1936 (died 1979); two s. one d.; m. 2nd Marguerite Lee Davenport 1980. *Education:* Lycée Janson de Sailly and Columbia Univ. *Career:* Instructor in History, Columbia Univ. 1929, Asst Prof. 1938, Assoc. Prof. 1942, Prof. 1945, Dean of Graduate Faculties 1955-58, Dean of Faculties and Provost 1958-67,

Seth Low Prof. 1960-67, Univ. Prof. 1967-75; Prof. Emer. 1975-; Literary Adviser, Scribner's 1975-93; fmr Dir Council for Basic Educ., New York Soc. Library, Open Court Publications Inc., Peabody Inst.; mem. Advisory Council, Univ. Coll. at Buckingham, Editorial Bd Encyclopedia Britannica 1979-; mem. Acad. Delphinale (Grenoble), American Acad. of Arts and Letters (Pres. 1972-75, 1977-78), American Historical Asscn, Royal Soc. of Arts, American Arbitration Asscn, American Philosophical Soc., Royal Soc. of Literature, American Acad. of Arts and Sciences; Extraordinary Fellow, Churchill Coll., Cambridge 1961. *Publications:* The French Race: Theories of its Origins and their Social and Political Implications Prior to the Revolution 1932, Race: A Study in Modern Superstition 1937, Of Human Freedom 1939, Darwin, Marx, Wagner: Critique of a Heritage 1941, Romanticism and the Modern Ego (revised edn as Classic, Romantic, and Modern) 1943, Introduction to Naval History (with Paul H. Beik, George Crothers and E. O. Golob) 1944, Teacher in America 1945, Berlioz and the Romantic Century 1950, God's Country and Mine: A Declaration of Love Spiced with a Few Harsh Words 1954, Music in American Life 1956, The Energies of Art: Studies of Authors, Classic and Modern 1956, The Modern Researcher (with Henry F. Graff) 1957, Lincoln the Literary Genius 1959, The House of Intellect 1959, Science, the Glorious Entertainment 1964, The American University: How it Runs, Where it is Going 1968, On Writing, Editing and Publishing: Essays Explicative and Horatory 1971, A Catalogue of Crime (with Wendell Hertig Taylor) 1971, The Use and Abuse of Art 1974, Clio and the Doctors: Psycho-History, Quanto-History and History 1974, Simple and Direct: A Rhetoric for Writers 1975, Critical Questions 1982, A Stroll with William James 1983, A Word or Two Before You Go 1986, The Culture We Deserve 1989, Begin Here: On Teaching and Learning 1990, An Essay on French Verse for Readers of English Poetry 1991, From Dawn to Decadence: 500 Years of Western Cultural Life 2000, A Jacques Barzun Reader 2001; editor: Pleasures of Music 1950, The Selected Letters of Lord Byron 1953, New Letters of Berlioz (also trans.) 1954, The Selected Writings of John Jay Chapman 1957, Modern American Usage; translator: Diderot: Rameau's Nephew 1952, Flaubert's Dictionary of Accepted Ideas 1954, Evenings with the Orchestra 1956, Courteline: A Rule is a Rule 1960, Beaumarchais: The Marriage of Figaro 1961; contrib. of articles to various scholarly and non-scholarly periodicals and journals. *Honours:* Chevalier de la Légion d'honneur, Presidential Medal of Freedom 2004; Gold Medal for Criticism, American Acad. of Arts and Letters. *Address:* 18 Wolfeton Way, San Antonio, TX 78218, USA.

**BASELT, Franz (Bernhard);** Professor of Musicology; b. 13 Sept. 1934, Halle, Saale, Germany; m. Elfried Kalisch, 3 Oct 1962, 1 s., 1 d. *Education:* Abitur, 1953; Hochschule für Musik Halle; Martin-Luther-Universität Halle, Dipl phil, 1958; Dr Phil, 1963; Dr sc phil, 1975. *Career:* Freeland, 1958-59; Assistant Professor, 1959-76; Professor of Musicology, 1977-82; Full Professor of Musicology, 1983; Chief Editor, Hallische Händel-Ausgabe, 1989; University Halle-Wittenburg; President, Georg-Friedrich-Händel-Gesellschaft, 1991; Editor, Händel-Jahrbuch, 1991. *Publications:* Händel-Handbuch vol. I–III, 1978-86; G. F. Händel, Leipzig, 1988; Editions of operas by G. P. Telemann, C. W. Gluck, G. F. Händel, 1967, 1969, 1970, 1988; Editions of Händel's Oreste, Kassel 1991; Telemann's Don Quixote, Madison, 1991. *Contributions:* Händel-Jahrbuch; Musical Times; Veroff der Intern; Händel-Akademie Karlsruhe; Music and Letters. *Address:* Reilstrasse 83, 04020, Halle, Saale, Germany.

**BASHFORD, Christina,** BA, MMus, PhD, CertTHE; Musicologist and Lecturer; b. 20 Dec. 1961, Penryn, Cornwall; m. John Wagstaff. *Education:* King's Coll. London, Wadham Coll., Oxford. *Career:* Man. Ed., New Grove Dictionary of Opera 1988-92; Lecturer then Senior Lecturer, Oxford Brookes Univ. 1994-; mem. Royal Musical Asscn, British Asscn of Victorian Studies. *Publications:* Music and British Culture 1785-1914: Essays in Honour of Cyril Ehrlich (ed. with Leanne Langley) 2000; contrib. to The New Grove Dictionary of Music and Musicians 2001. *Honours:* Jack Westrup Prize (Music and Letters) 1991. *Address:* Oxford Brookes University, Headington, Oxford, OX3 0BP, England (office). *Telephone:* (1865) 484985 (office). *E-mail:* cmbashford@brookes.ac.uk (office).

**BASHMET, Yuri Abramovich;** Russian violist and conductor; b. 24 Jan. 1953, Rostov-on-Don; m. Natalia Bashmet; one d. *Education:* Moscow State Conservatory. *Career:* concerts since 1975; gave recitals and played with maj. orchestras of Europe, America and Asia; played in chamber ensembles with Sviatoslav Richter, Vladimir Spivakov, Victor Tretyakov and others; restored chamber repertoire for viola, commissioned and was first performer of music by contemporary composers, including concertos by Alfred Schnittke, Giya Kancheli, Aleksander Tchaikovsky; first viola player to give solo recitals at leading concert halls including Tchaikovsky Hall, Moscow, Concertgebouw, Amsterdam, La Scala, Milan, Suntory Hall, Tokyo; Founder and Artistic Dir Chamber Orchestra Soloists of Moscow 1989-; Artistic Dir and Chief Conductor Young Russian Symphony Orchestra 2002-; f. Yuri Bashmet Int. Competition for Young Viola Players 1994-; Artistic Dir Dec. Nights Festival, Moscow 1998-; Founder and Artistic Dir Elba Music Festival 1998-; f. Yu. Bashmet Viola Competition, Moscow 1999-; f. Int. Foundation to award Shostakovich Prize annually. *Honours:* prize winner of int. competitions in Budapest 1975, Munich 1976; People's Artist of Russia 1986, State Prize of Russia 1993, Sonning Prize (Denmark) 1995. *Current Management:* ICM Artists Ltd, 40 West 57th Street, New York, NY 10019, USA. *Telephone:* (095) 561-66-96. *Address:* Briyusov per. 7, Apt. 16, 103009 Moscow, Russia (home). *Telephone:* (095) 229-73-25 (home).

**BASS, Alexandra,** ARCM, GRSM, PGCE; British musician (flautist); *Music Director, Alibas*; b. 15 Dec. 1962, Funtington, W. Sussex; m. Sebastian Toke-Nichols; one d. *Education:* Royal Coll. of Music, 1980–84; Homerton Coll., Cambridge, 1984–85; Conservatoire Hector Berlioz and Ecole Normale, Paris, 1986–87; Guildhall School of Music and Drama 1999–2000. *Career:* led 1986 expedition to Peru and Bolivia to study the indigenous music of the Indians; orchestral player in BBC Symphony Orchestra, London Philharmonic Orchestra, Royal Philharmonic Orchestra, Liverpool Philharmonic, Hallé, and the orchestra of the Royal Opera House, Covent Garden; soloist and chamber music player; f. and Music Dir, Alibas mem. Incorporated Society of Musicians, Musicians' Union. *Recordings:* Humoreske (Alibas flute and guitar duo), 2005. *Honours:* Chamber Music Prize, Royal Coll. of Music, 1980; Prix Supérieur, Hector Berlioz Conservatoire, Paris, 1987. *Current Management:* Alibas, Briar House, 6 The Green, Blakesley, Towcester, Northants NN12 8RD, England. *Telephone:* (1327) 861151 (home). *Fax:* (1327) 861151 (home). *E-mail:* alex@alibas.fsnet.co.uk (home). *Website:* www.alibas.co.uk (home).

**BASSETT, Leslie Raymond,** BA, MMus, AMusD; composer; b. 22 Jan. 1923, Hanford, CA, USA; m. Anita Denniston 1949; two s. one d. *Education:* Fresno State College (now California State University, Fresno), University of Michigan, Ecole Normale de Musique, Paris, studied with Ross Lee Finney, Nadia Boulanger, Arthur Honegger, Roberto Gerhard. *Career:* Henry Russel Lecturer, Univ. of Michigan 1984; Albert A. Stanley Distinguished Univ. Prof. of Music Emeritus; mem. American Acad. of Arts and Letters. *Compositions:* Variations for Orchestra; Echoes from an Invisible World, orchestra; Concerto for Orchestra, 1991; From a Source Evolving, orchestra; Concerto Lirico, trombone and orchestra; Fantasy for Clarinet and Wind Ensemble; Sounds, Shapes and Symbols, band; Colors and Contours, band; Thoughts that Sing, Breathe and Burn for orchestra, 1995; Trio-Inventions for 3 cellos, 1996; Sextet for Piano and Strings; Fourth String Quartet, 1978; Arias for Clarinet and Piano; Dialogues for Oboe and Piano; Narratives for Guitar Quartet. *Honours:* Pulitzer Prize for Variations for orchestra, 1966; Rome Prize, American Academy in Rome, 1961–63; Koussevitsky Foundation Commissions, 1971, 1990; Guggenheim Fellow, 1973, 1980; Naumberg Recording Award, 1974; Distinguished Artist Award, State of Michigan, 1981. *Address:* 1618 Harbal Drive, Ann Arbor, MI 48105, USA.

**BASTIAN, Hanns;** Singer (Tenor); b. 30 Jan. 1928, Pforzheim, Germany. *Education:* Studied in Karlsruhe with Karl Hartlieb and in Coburg and Pforzheim. *Career:* Sang first in Pforzheim, 1946–53, then at Coburg; Engaged at Basel Opera, 1955–80, notably in premiere of Titus Feuerfuchs by Sutermeister, 1966, and in buffo and character roles; Guest appearances in Zürich, Berne, Darmstadt and Bregenz. Other roles included Florestan, Mozart's Pedrillo and Monostatos, David in Die Meistersinger, and many parts in operetta. *Address:* c/o Theater Basel, Theaterstrasse 7, 4010 Basel, Switzerland.

**BATCHVAROVA, Vania (Petrova);** Bulgarian opera director; *Associate Professor and Opera Stage Director, Cukurova University, State Conservatory, Adana, Turkey*; b. 22 May 1950, Pleven; m. Rusko Russkov 1985. *Education:* Studied Piano, Music High School, Russe, Bulgaria, 1965–69; Music Theory and Pedagogy, Bulgarian Academy of Music, Sofia, 1970–72; Musicology, Martin Luther University, Halle/Saale, Germany, 1972–73; Masters Degree, Opera and Stage Direction, Masters in Music (Piano), Hochschule für Musik 'Hanns Eisler', Berlin, Germany, 1973–78; Teatro alia Scata di Milano (Italy), 1986; St Petersburg (Russia), Simeon Ilitch Lapirov, 1989; Graduate courses in Effective Management, Managing Customer and Client Relations and Accounting for Managers from The Open University, UK, 1993–96; Computer Courses, Voice Pedagogy Courses, Music Semiotic Courses at NBU, Bulgaria, 1992–97. *Career:* Stage Director, Russe Opera House, 1979–82; Associate Professor, Opera Stage Directing and Opera Singing, Bulgarian Academy of Music, Sofia, 1982–97; Dean, Music and Performing Arts Department, New Bulgarian University, Sofia, Associate Professor, Opera Stage Directing and Opera Singing, 1992–98; Principal Stage Director, Plovdiv Opera House, 1996–97; Associate Professor, Cukurova University, State Conservatory, Turkey, 1998–; Directed works include Wagner's Götterdämmerung, Leipzig, 1976; Mussorgsky's Boris Godunov, Russe, 1979; Verdi's Falstaff, Sofia Opera House; Productions and directed works include: Dvořák, Rusalka, Plauen, Germany, 1978; Donizetti, L'Elisir d'amore, Stara Zagora, 1983; Puccini, Madama Butterfly, Sliven, 1986; Verdi, Nabucco, Burgas, 1987; Otto Nicolai's Die Lustige Weiber, Bulgaria, Moldova, Russia, 1989; Donizetti, Lucia di Lammermoor, Russe, 1995; Mozart, Le nozze di Figaro, New Bulgarian University, 1995; Verdi, Il Trovatore, Rigoletto, Nabucco, Plovdiv, Bulgaria, Seville, Spain and Palma de Mallorca, Menorca, 1996, etc.; Established Music Department in NBU and first education programme for opera stage directors in Bulgaria; Performances of children's musicals; performances for students in voice and opera education, Bulgaria (Academy of Music, NBU), Turkey (Cukurova University), guest in Vilnius, Lithuania and Moscow, Russian Fed.; Member of the organizing committee and of the jury of the following competitions in Bulgaria: Sv. Obretenov National Competition for singers and players; International Competition for Young Talented Musicians; G.Zl. Cherkin Natsonal Competition for Singers; Participated in International Festival for the Young 'Euroart2004' in Bulgaria; Participated in and submitted papers to numerous symposia and international conferences in art, music education and semiotics; Workshops; Television opera productions; Piano and chamber concerts; Numerous radio programmes about opera. *Publications:* Libretto, Bulgarian Roses, musical for children; The Golden

Donkey by Apulej, opera; Books: Educating the Singing Actor 1995; A View of Mozart's Philosophy through His Operas, 1997; Requiem for Dried Up Rivers, essays, 1998; The Dramaturgy of Opera, 1999; Contributions: Numerous articles in newspapers and magazines. *Address:* C.U. State Conservatory, 01330 Balcali/Adana, Turkey (office). *Telephone:* (322) 3386264 (office); (322) 2279886 (home); (532) 3011590 (office). *Fax:* (322) 3386265 (office). *E-mail:* vania@cu.edu.tr (office). *Website:* www.cu.edu.tr (office).

**BATE, Jennifer Lucy,** BA, FRCO, FRSA, LRAM, ARCM; British organist; b. 11 Nov. 1944, London; d. of Horace Alfred Bate and Dorothy Marjorie Bate. *Education:* Univ. of Bristol. *Career:* Shaw Librarian, LSE 1966–69; full-time concert career 1969–; has performed world-wide; has organized several teaching programmes; collaboration with Olivier Messiaen 1975–92; designed portable pipe organ with N. P. Mander Ltd 1984 and a prototype computer organ 1987; gives masterclasses world-wide and lectures on a wide range of musical subjects; mem. Inc. Soc. of Music; British Music Soc., vice-pres., Royal Philharmonic Soc., Royal Soc. *Compositions:* Toccata on a Theme of Martin Shaw, Introduction and Variations on an Old French Carol, Four Reflections, Homage to 1685: Four Studies, The Spinning Wheel, Lament, An English Canon, Variations on a Gregorian Theme. *Recordings:* Complete Works of Messiaen, Complete Works of Franck, An English Choice, Virtuoso French Organ Music, Panufnik: Metasinfonia, Vivaldi Double and Triple Concertos, Jennifer Bate and Friends, Jennifer Plays Vierne, From Stanley to Wesley on period instruments, Reflections: the organ music of Jennifer Bate. *Television:* South Bank Show on Messiaen, La Nativité du Seigneur (Channel 4). *Publications:* Grove's Dictionary of Music and Musicians, Organist's Review. *Honours:* hon. Italian citizenship for services to music 1996; F. J. Read Prize, Royal Coll. of Organists, Young Musician 1972, voted Personnalité de l'Année, France 1989, one of the Women of the Year, UK 1990–97, Grand Prix du Disque (Messiaen), Diapason d'Or, Prix de Répertoire, France, Preis der deutschen Schallplattenkritik, Germany and MRA Award for 18th century series From Stanley to Wesley. *Current Management:* PVA Management Ltd, Hallow Park, Worcester, WR2 6PG, England. *Address:* c/o PA Mrs Helen Harris, 35 Collingwood Avenue, Muswell Hill, London, N10 3EH, England. *Telephone:* (20) 8883-3811. *Fax:* (20) 8444-3695. *E-mail:* jenniferbate@classical-artists.com (home). *Website:* www.classical-artists.com/jbate (home).

**BATES, Lucy;** Singer (Soprano); b. 1973, Beverly, Yorkshire. *Education:* Royal Northern College of Music, with Sandra Dugdale; Masterclasses with Evelyn Tubb, Nigel Douglas and Robin Bowman. *Career:* Roles with RNCM included Mozart's Papagena and Blondchen, Ophelia, Catherine in La jolie Fille de Perth, Barena in Jenůfa and Sandrina in La finta giardiniera; Yum-Yum in The Mikado and Frasquita for Phoenix Opera, Rossini's Elvira for the Accademia Rossiniana, and Belinda in Dido and Aeneas; Glyndebourne Festival debut 2000, as Barbarina in Le nozze di Figaro. *Honours:* Peter Moores Foundation Scholar; Finalist, Frederic Cox Award Competition, 2000. *Address:* c/o Glyndebourne Festival Centre, Glyndebourne, Lewes, Sussex BN8 5UU, England.

**BATIASHVILI, Elisabeth;** Georgian violinist; b. 1979. *Education:* Munich Musikhochschule with Ana Chumachenco, studied with Mark Lubotsky in Hamburg. *Career:* appearances in Mozart's Sinfonia Concertante K364, with Colin Davis, at Ravinia with the Chicago SO, recitals at the Wigmore Hall and Châtelet, Paris, and with the Cleveland Orchestra at the Blossom Festival; London Proms debut 2000; further engagements with the City of Birmingham SO, Orchestre de Paris, Melbourne SO, NHK Symphony (Tokyo), Los Angeles PO, Philadelphia Orchestra and St Petersburg PO; played Prokofiev's First Concerto with the CBSO at the London Proms 2002; debut with the Berlin Philharmonic Orchestra 2004; with New York Philharmonic 2005; chamber musician with Pierre-Laurent Aimard, Till Fellner, Alban Gerhardt and Steven Osborne. *Recordings include:* Brahms, Schubert and Bach recital, Brahms Double Concerto with Alban Gerhardt. *Honours:* prizewinner Sibelius Competition, Helsinki 1995, Leonard Bernstein Award in Schleswig Holstein 2003. *Current Management:* Harrison/Parrott Ltd, 12 Penzance Place, London, W11 4PA, England. *Telephone:* (20) 7229 9166. *Fax:* (20) 7221 5042. *Website:* www.harrisonparrott.com.

**BATIZ, Enrique;** Pianist and Conductor; b. 4 May 1942, Mexico City, Mexico; m. 1965, divorced 1982, 1 s., 1 d. *Education:* Bachelor's Degree, Mexico University Centre, 1959; Southern Methodist University, Dallas, USA, 1960–62; Juilliard School of Music, New York, studied piano with Adele Marcus; Conducting with Jorge Mester, 1963–66; Postgraduate work, Warsaw Conservatory. *Career:* Debut: Mexico City, 1969; Founder-Conductor, Orquesta Sinfónica del Estado de México, 1971–73, 1990–; Appointed Guest Conductor, Royal Philharmonic Orchestra, London, England, 1984–; Guest Conductor with 150 orchestras world-wide; Conductor, Royal Philharmonic Orchestra tour in Mexico, 1988; mem, IAPA; Club de Clubes; Club Cambridge, Mexico City. *Compositions:* Es Tiempo de Paz, symphonic poem, 1976. *Recordings include:* Over 150 recordings including 41 with the Royal Philharmonic, 29 with the Orquesta Sinfónica del Estado de México and 19 with the Mexico City Philharmonic Orchestra. *Contributions:* Joaquin Rodrigo, His Life, in Epoca, 1993. *Current Management:* Mrs C A Ross, 6 Petersfield Crescent, Coulsdon, Surrey CR5 2JQ, England. *Address:* Plaza Fray Andres de Castro, Edif. 'C', Primer Piso, Toluca, Estado de Mexico CP 5000, Mexico.

**BATJER, Margaret;** Violinist; b. 17 Feb. 1959, San Angelo, TX, USA; m. Joel McNeely, 14 April 1985. *Education:* Interlochen Academy; Studied with Ivan

Galamian and David Cerone at Curtis Institute of Music. *Career:* Debut: Solo appearance in Violin Concerto by Menotti with Chicago Symphony, aged 15; Appeared as Soloist with Philadelphia Orchestra at Academy of Music, with Dallas and Seattle Symphonies in Mendelssohn's Concerto at the St Louis Symphony; Chamber Orchestra of Europe; Prague Chamber Orchestra; Berlin Symphony Orchestra; New York String Orchestra at Carnegie Hall; Radio Telefis Dublin, with Prokofiev's 2nd Concerto; Concerts at the Marlboro Music Festival, Vermont and US tour with Music of Marlboro Ensemble; Tour of Germany, 1984. *Recordings:* Bach Concerto for Two Violins with Salvatore Accardo and the Chamber Orchestra of Europe; Mozart Concertone with Salvatore Accardo and the Prague Chamber Orchestra; Verdi and Borodin String Quartets, Mozart Complete Viola Quintets. *Honours:* Winner, G B Dealey Competition, Dallas, 1979. *Current Management:* Del Rosenfield Associates, 714 Ladd Road, Bronx, NY 10471, USA. *Address:* 5971 Lubao Ave, Woodland Hills, CA 91367, USA.

**BATTEL, Giovanni (Umberto);** Pianist; b. 11 Dec. 1956, Portoguaro, Venice, Italy; m. Mariangela Zamper, 15 June 1985. *Education:* Liceo in Classical Studies, 1975; Conservatory Tartini, Trieste, 1977; National Music Academy St Cecilia, Rome, 1984; Degree in Musicology, Bologna University. *Career:* S Remo Theatre, 1980; RAI Radio 3, 1981; Stresa Festival, 1981; With symphony orchestra, Auditorium RAI Rome, 1982; RAI 1, 1982, 1983, 1984; Alghero Festival, 1983; Mater Festival, 1983; Trondheim Symphony Orchestra, 1983; With Scarlatti Orchestra, Auditorium RAI Naples, 1983; Trieste Theatre, 1985; Auditorium Cagliari, 1985; Musik Halle Hamburg, 1986; Lubeck, Bonn, 1986; Athens, Salonika, Greece, 1986; San Francisco, Los Angeles, USA; Paris, Nantes, Lille, France, 1987; Todi Festival, 1988; London, 1988; Director, Conservatory of Music 'Benedetto Marcello' in Venice; Artistic Director of piano competitions and of musical associations. *Recordings:* Miroirs and Valses Nobles et Sentimentales, Ravel; Busoni's Piano Concerto; E. Wolf-Ferrari, Piano Trios Op. 5 and Op. 7. *Honours:* 1st prize, national competitions: La Spezia, 1975; Trieste, 1978; Taranto, 1979; Albenga, 1979; International competition: 2nd prize, Vercelli, 1978; 2nd prize, Seregno, 1979; 4th prize, Bolzano, 1980; 1st prize, Enna, 1982. *Address:* Via Baratta Vecchia 253, 31022 Preganziol, Treviso, Italy.

**BATTERHAM, Andrew (Bruce);** Composer and Musician; b. 22 July 1968, Melbourne, Australia; m., 1 s., 2 d. *Education:* Bachelor of music, composition, University of Melbourne. *Career:* National Music Camp, Sydney, 1987, 1988; Australian Composers Orchestral Forum, 1997; Queensland Philharmonic, 1995; Perihelion, 1997; Tasmanian Symphony, 1997; Eliseon, 1988; Melbourne Symphony, 1999; Australian Chamber Orchestra, 1999; Melbourne Symphony, 2000, 2002; Member, Australian Performing Right Association; Musicians and Arrangers Guild of Australia; Melbourne Composer's League; Australian Music Centre, Sydney. *Compositions:* Thugine Legend; Cortege; Symphony No. 1, Off The Leash; Chiaroscuro; Organ Sonata; Maniacs and Broken Glass; Drum and Bass; The End of All Journeys, 2000. *Recordings include:* Melbourne Composers' League, 2000. *Honours:* Quantas Youth Award, 1994; Corbould Composition competition winner, 1995; Shortlisted for Albert H Maggs Award (Commendation), 1999. *Address:* 26 Rosslyn Street, Blackburn, Melbourne, Australia, 3130.

**BATTLE, Kathleen Deanna,** MMus; American singer (soprano); b. 13 Aug. 1948, Portsmouth, OH; d. of Ollie Layne Battle and Grady Battle. *Education:* Coll.-Conservatory of Music, Univ. of Cincinnati. *Career:* professional début in Brahms Requiem, Cincinnati May Festival, then Spoleto Festival, Italy 1972; début Metropolitan Opera, New York as shepherd in Wagner's Tannhäuser 1977; regular guest with orchestras of New York, Chicago, Boston, Philadelphia, Cleveland, LA, San Francisco, Vienna, Paris and Berlin, at Salzburg, Tanglewood and other festivals and at the maj. opera houses including Metropolitan, New York, Covent Garden, London, Paris and Vienna; appearances in 1985/86 season included Sophie in Der Rosenkavalier and Susanna in Figaro, Metropolitan New York, US première parts of Messiaen's St Francis of Assisi with Boston Symphony Orchestra and recitals USA and in Toronto, Paris, Vienna and Florence; appearances in 1986/87 season included Zerbinetta in Ariadne auf Naxos and Adina in L'Elisir d'amore, Metropolitan New York and recitals in Japan, London, Salzburg and Vienna; planned recordings include Fauré Requiem. *Recordings include:* Brahms Requiem and Songs, Mozart Requiem, Don Giovanni, Seraglio and concert arias, Verdi's Un Ballo in Maschera and Berg's Lulu Suite; New Year's Eve Gala, Vienna. *Honours:* Dr hc (Cincinnati and Westminster Choir Coll., Princeton), Grammy Award 1987, 1988. *Current Management:* Columbia Artist Management Inc., 165 West 57th Street, New York, NY 10019, USA.

**BATURIN, Sergei;** Violinist; b. 1952, Moscow, Russia. *Education:* Studied at Moscow Conservatoire with Fjodor Druzhinin. *Career:* Co-founded Amistad Quartet, 1973, changed named to Tchaikovsky Quartet in 1994; Many concerts in former Soviet Union and Russia, with repertoire including works by Haydn, Mozart, Beethoven, Schubert, Brahms, Tchaikovsky, Borodin, Prokofiev, Shostakovich, Bartók, Bucci, Golovin and Tikhomirov; recent concert tours to Mexico, Italy and Germany; Series in commemoration of Tchaikovsky in Moscow. *Recordings:* Recitals for US-Russian company Arts and Electronics; By Tchaikovsky Quartet. *Honours:* With Amistad Quartet: Prizewinner at Béla Bartók Festival, 1976 and Bucchi Competition, Rome, 1990. *Current Management:* Sonata, Glasgow, Scotland. *Address:* 11 North Park Street, Glasgow G20 7AA, Scotland.

**BAUDO, Serge;** French conductor; *Musical Director, Orchestre Symphonique de Prague (F.O.K.);* b. 16 July 1927, Marseille; s. of Etienne Baudo and Geneviève Tortelier; m. Madeleine Reties 1947; one s. one d. *Education:* Conservatoire nat. supérieur de musique, Paris. *Career:* Music Dir Radio Nice 1957–59; Conductor Paris Opera Orchestra 1962–66; titular Conductor and Orchestral Dir a.i. Orchestre de Paris 1968–70; Music Dir Opéra de Lyon 1969–71, Orchestre Nat. de Lyon 1971–87; Musical Dir Orchestre Symphonique de Prague (FOK) 2001–; has conducted many of world's leading orchestras; Founder Berlioz Festival, Lyon 1979–89. *Films:* music for Le Monde sans Soleil 1964. *Honours:* Chevalier, Ordre nat. du Mérite; Officier des Arts et des Lettres, Officier, Légion d'honneur; numerous prix du disque and other awards. *Address:* Les Hauts du Ferra, 2901 Chemin Charré, 13600 Ceyreste, France (home); Matthias Vogt, 1714 Stockton Street, Suite 300, San Francisco, CA 94133-2930, USA. *Telephone:* (415) 788-8073 (US). *Fax:* 4-42-71-86-47 (home); (530) 684-5535 (US). *E-mail:* matthias.vogt@usa.net (office).

**BAUER, Hartmut;** Singer (Bass); b. 1939, Kassel, Germany. *Education:* Studied at the Frankfurt Musikhochschule. *Career:* Sang at Augsburg Opera, 1965–68, Coburg, 1968–70, Wuppertal from 1970–90, notably as Creon in the 1972 German premiere of Milhaud's Médée; Bayreuth Festival, 1973–75, as Fafner and Hans Schwarz; Other appearances as Ariodeno in Cavalli's L'Ormindo, Mozart's Bartolo and Commendatore, Ramphis (Aida), Colline (La Bohème), Pimen, Schigolch (Lulu) and Cornelius' Abu Hassan; Guest at Cologne, Frankfurt, Barcelona and Hannover; Sang in the premiere of V D Kirchner's Erinys, Wuppertal, 1990; Gurnemanz in Parsifal, 1994; Season 1999 as Rocco in Fidelio at Eutin, Sarastro and Baron Ochs at Gelsenkirchen. *Address:* c/o Musiktheater im Revier, Kennedyplatz, pf 101854, 4650 Gelsenkirchen, Germany.

**BAULD, Alison (Margaret);** Composer; b. 7 May 1944, Sydney, New South Wales, Australia; m. Nicholas Evans, 4 April 1978, 1 s., 1 d. *Education:* Diploma, National Institute of Dramatic Art, Sydney; BMus, Sydney University; Composition Studies with Elisabeth Lutyens and Hans Keller; DPhil, York University, 1974; Studied Piano with Sverjensky, New South Wales Conservatorium. *Career:* Professional Actress, Shakespeare and Australian Television; Finalist, Radcliffe Competition, 1973; Musical Director, Laban Centre for Dance, Goldsmiths' College, University of London, 1975–78; Composer-in-Residence, New South Wales Conservatory, Sydney, 1978; Teaches part-time for University of Delaware, Hollins College and Pepperdine University, London; Works performed and broadcast, London, also Aldeburgh, York and Edinburgh Festivals, several European countries, Australia; mem. Association of Professional Composers; Musician's Union. *Compositions include:* On the Afternoon of the Pigsty for speaker and ensemble, 1971; Humpty Dumpty for tenor, flute and guitar, 1972; In a Dead Brown Land, music theatre, 1972; Mad Moll for solo soprano, 1973; Dear Emily, for soprano and harp, 1973; One Pearl for soprano and string quartet, 1973; Concert for piano and tape, 1974; Exiles, music theatre, 1974; Van Diemen's Land for choir, 1976; One Pearl II for soprano, flute and strings, 1976; I Loved Miss Watson for soprano, piano and tape, 1977; Banquo's Buried for soprano and piano, 1982; Richard III for voice and string quartet, 1985; Monody for solo flute, 1985; Copy Cats for violin and piano, 1985; Once Upon a Time, music theatre, 1986; Nell, Ballad opera, 1988; My Own Island for clarinet and piano, 1989; Farewell Already for string quartet, 1993; In Memoriam Uncle Ken for baritone and piano, 1997; Shakespeare Songs. *Recordings include:* Banquo's Buried; Farewell Already, string quartet and soprano. *Publications:* Play Your Way, piano and composition tutor, 1993; Shakespeare Songs for soprano and piano; Novel, Mozart's Sisters, 1997. *Honours:* Gold Medal, Piano, New South Wales, 1959; Paris Rostrum, composition, 1973. *Address:* 7 Suffolk Road, Barnes, London SW13, England.

**BAUMANN, Ludwig;** Singer (Baritone); b. 9 Nov. 1950, Rosenheim, Germany. *Education:* Studied in Munich, USA and Italy. *Career:* Sang bass roles at the Munich State Opera, 1970–72 including the premiere of Sim Tjong by Isang Yun; Baritone at the Coburg Opera, 1972–79 with many concerts elsewhere; Theater am Gärtnerplatz, Munich, 1979–85; Cologne Opera from 1985 with guest appearances at Lausanne, Valentin in Faust, 1986; Paris Châtelet, Gluck's Oreste, 1988; Turin, Hamlet by Thomas; Sang Kurnewal in Tristan, at Marseilles, 1992; Wolfram in Tannhäuser at Naples, 1998; Other roles include Rameau's Thesée, Opéra Comique, Paris; Rossini's Figaro at Nancy; Mozart's Papageno and Guglielmo. *Recordings:* La Bohème; Strauss's Daphne. *Address:* c/o Teatro San Carlo di Napoli, Via San Carlo, 80132 Naples, Italy.

**BAUMEL, Herbert,** DipMus; American violinist, conductor and composer; b. 30 Sept. 1919, New York, NY; m. 1st Rachael Bail 1949 (divorced 1970); one s. two d. (one deceased); m. 2nd Joan Patricia French 1971. *Education:* Mannes School of Music, Curtis Inst. of Music, Santa Cecilia, Accademia Chigiana, Rome and Siena, studied violin with Louis Persinger, Nathan Milstein. *Career:* violinist, Concertmaster, conductor of orchestras, chamber groups, Broadway shows, jazz ensembles, ballets, operas, worldwide 1939–; violin soloist, Samuel Barber Violin Concerto, Curtis Symphony, Philadelphia Orchestra 1939–40; New York City Ballet, Fort Wayne Philharmonic, WQXR Orchestra, Radio Italiana, Radio Nacional Venezuela 1945–; first violin, Philadelphia Orchestra 1942–45; mem., Baumel-Booth Duo 1968–, Baumel-Booth-Smith Trio 1969–72; violinist and story teller 1969–; Concertmaster, Philadelphia, New York City and San Carlo Operas, Orquesta Sinfonica Venezuela, Broadway musicals including Fiorello 1959, She Loves Me 1963, Fiddler on the Roof 1964, A Little Night Music 1973; Presidential

Gala Orchestra, Washington, DC and New York 1961–65; Conductor, Fort Wayne Civic and Corvallis Symphonies, Chamber Music Assocs Orchestra, Alessandro Scarlatti Orchestra (Naples), Oregon State Univ. Chamber Players 1945–; commentator on All Things Considered (Nat. Public Radio) 1999–. *Recordings include:* Selections from Fiddler on the Roof 2000. *Address:* Baumel Associates, 86 Rosedale Road, Yonkers, NY 10710, USA.

**BAVERSTAM, Asa;** Singer (Soprano); b. 1958, Sweden. *Education:* Studied at the Conservatory of Jutland in Århus, Denmark and at the Royal Opera Academy, Copenhagen. *Career:* Debut: Royal Opera in Copenhagen, 1990, as Despina; Has performed Susanna and Sophie in Der Rosenkavalier with the Opera Academy; Sang in the premiere of Life is a Bed of Roses by Arne Melinas, 1989; Theater Basel from 1990 as Xenia in Boris Godunov, Adina; Zerlina (1992); Has sung in masses and oratorios by Bach, Haydn, Handel, Mozart and Schubert in Denmark and Sweden; Concerts with the baroque orchestra La Stravaganza and as a member of the renaissance quartet Ensemble Charneyron; Season 2000 in Die schweigsame Frau, by Strauss, at Århus. *Honours:* Fourth round, Cardiff Singer of the World Competition, 1989. *Current Management:* Tivoli Artists Management, 3 Vesterbrogade, POB 233, 1630 Copenhagen, Denmark. *Telephone:* 33-75-04-00. *Fax:* 33-75-03-75. *E-mail:* artistsmanagement@tivoli.dk. *Website:* www.tam.dk.

**BAVICCHI, John (Alexander);** Composer, Conductor and Teacher; b. 25 April 1922, Boston, Massachusetts, USA. *Education:* Studied Business Engineering and Administration, Massachusetts Institute of Technology, 1940–42; Civil Engineering, Newark College of Engineering, 1942–43; Cornell University, 1943; BM, New England Conservatory of Music, 1952; Studied composition with Carl McKinley, Francis Judd Cooke, Harvard University Graduate School, 1952–55; Theory with Archibald T Davison; Composition with Walter Piston; Musicology with Otto Gombosi. *Career:* Many teaching positions including: South End Music School, 1950–64; Boston Center for Adult Education, 1952–55; Cape Cod Conservatory of Music, 1956–58; Cambridge Center for Adult Education, 1960–73; Professor, Composition, Berklee College of Music, 1964–; Various conducting positions including: American Festival Ballet Company, 1962–65; Arlington Philharmonic Orchestra, 1968–82. *Compositions:* Orchestral: Concerto for clarinet and string orchestra, 1954; Suite No. 1, 1955; A Concert Overture, 1957; Fantasy for harp and chamber orchestra, 1959; Concertante for oboe, bassoon and string orchestra, 1961; Fantasia on Korean Folk Tunes, 1966; Caroline's Dance, 1974–75; Mont Blanc, overture, 1976–77; Music for small orchestra, 1981; Fusions for trombone and orchestra, 1984–85; Pyramid, 1986; Canto I for string orchestra, 1987; Songs of Remembrance, 1990; Quintet for Clarinet and String Quartet, 1995; Band: Summer Incident, 1959; Suite No. 2, 1961; Festival Symphony, 1965; JDC March, 1967; Spring Festival Overture, 1968; Suite No. 3, 1969; Concertante No. 2, 1972–75; Band of the Year, 1975; Symphony No. 2, 1975–77; Fantasy, 1979; Concord Bridge, 1982–83; Concerto for clarinet and wind ensemble, 1984; Large Ensemble: Suite No. 2 for clarinet ensemble, 1961; Fireworks, 1962; Music for mallets and percussion, 1967; Ceremonial Music, 1978–82; Concerto for 2 pianos and percussion, 1985; Concerto for Tuba and concert Band, 1988; Chamber Music; Piano Pieces; Organ Music; Choruses; Solo Songs. *Honours:* Award, National Institute of Arts and Letters, 1959; Featured composer, Cardiff Festival, Wales, 1981. *Address:* 26 Hartford Street, Newton, MA 02461, USA.

**BAVOUZET, Jean-Efflam;** concert pianist; b. 1962, France. *Education:* Paris Conservatoire with Pierre Sancan; masterclasses with Paul Badura-Skoda, Nikita Magaloff, Menahem Pressler, György Sandor. *Career:* Recitals in major concert halls world-wide, including the Kennedy Center, Lincoln Center, Kaufmann Hall, New York and the Salle Gaveau, Paris; Tours of Japan and USA; British engagements from 1987; Has appeared as concerto soloist with such conductors as Marek Janowski, Andrew Litton, Jorge Meste and Michel Plasson; Engagements in Germany, Netherlands, Japan, France and USA; Ravel's Left Hand Concerto with the Solingen Philharmonica and the Bournemouth Symphony, 1991; Has performed with many leading international orchestras including Gurzenich Orchestra of Cologne, Bournemouth Symphony, Hallé Orchestra, Manchester, Weimar Staatskapelle, Hong Kong Philharmonic, Calgary Philharmonic, Utah Symphony, Hungarian National Philharmonic and Symphony Nat. de Belgique; Debut with the Boston Symphony Orchestra under Ingo Metzmacher, 2002; Berliner Sinfonie Orchester under Jean-Claude Casadesus and Orchestre de Paris under Pierre Boulez; Season 2004–05 Appearances with London Symphony Orchestra; Concerto repertoire includes all the concerti of Bartók, Beethoven and Prokofiev, complete solo piano works of Ravel and Schumann. *Recordings:* Haydn 4 Sonatas and Fantaisie; Ravel's complete solo works for piano, MDG; Haydn and Schumann recitals for Harmonic Records; Debussy Etudes and an all-Chopin CD for Pony Canyon Classics. *Contributions:* Interview with Zoltan Kocsis for Le Monde de la Musique. *Honours:* Finalist at the 1987 Leeds International Competition; Prizewinner at the Young Concert Artists Competition, 1986, USA; Tomassoni-Beethoven Cologne, 1986; Special Jury Prize, Santander, Spain; Guilde Française des Artistes Solistes; First Prize, Paris Conservatoire, for Piano and Chamber Music; Chamber Music Prize, 1989; 'Choc' Award from Le Monde de la musique for Ravel complete solo works for piano and Haydn recordings; Diapason d'or for Ravel complete solo works for piano. *Current Management:* Robert Gilder & Co., Enterprise House, 59–65 Upper Ground, London, SE1 9PQ, England. *Telephone:* (20) 7928-9008. *Fax:* (20) 7928-9755. *E-mail:* rgilder@robert-gilder.com.

**BAWDEN, Rupert;** Composer, Conductor and Violinist; b. 1958, London. *Education:* Studied at Cambridge University with Robin Holloway. *Career:* Debut: Conductor at the 1986 Aldeburgh Festival; Plays violin and viola with various ensembles, including London Sinfonietta and the English Concert; Performances of works by Birtwistle, Goehr, Harvey, Weir and Hoyland, including several world premieres; Television recordings of works by Gruber, Holloway and Kagel; Michael Nyman's The Man who Mistook his Wife for a Hat for BBC radio; Engagements with the Bath, King's Lynn and London International Opera Festivals; BBC Symphony and Scottish Chamber Orchestra; Works have been performed in USA, Australia, Far East, the United Kingdom and France; 1989 performances by the London Sinfonietta and at the Promenade Concerts; Ballet commission from Munich Biennale 1990. *Compositions:* Railings for flute and piano 1980; Three-part Motet for soprano, mezzo, baritone and orchestra 1980; Passamezzo di Battaglia for oboe, horn and harpsichord, 1984; Sunless for ensemble 1984; Seven Songs from the House of Sand for brass quintet 1985; Le Livre de Fauvel for soprano, mezzo and ensemble 1986; The Angel and the Ship of Souls for 19 players 1983–87; Souvenirs de Fauvel for 2 pianos 1987; Dramatic Cantata on the Legend of Apollo and Daphne for violin, cello and 13 players 1989; Ultima Scena, Commissioned by Henry Wood Promenade Concerts 1989; Ballet Le Livre de Fauvel 1990. *Address:* c/o BMI, 79 Harley House, Marylebone Road, London, NW1, England.

**BAX, Alessio;** Italian pianist; b. 1977, Bari; m. Lucille Chung. *Education:* Bari Conservatory, Chigiana Acad., Siena, Southern Methodist Univ., Dallas with Joaquin Achucarro. *Career:* recitals throughout Europe, USA and Asia; concerts with London Philharmonic, City of Birmingham Symphony, Royal Liverpool Philharmonic, Royal Scottish Symphony Orchestra, Dallas Symphony, Houston Symphony, NHK Symphony, Tokyo Symphony, New Japan Philharmonic; tours of Japan (Suntory and Kioi Hall), Italy, Germany, UK, USA, Israel, Spain; worked with Sir Simon Rattle, Vernon Handley, Petr Altrichter, Owain Arwel Hughes, Sergiu Commissiona, Dmitry Sitkovetsky, Ken-ichiro Kobayashi; festivals include London Int. Piano Series, Bath, Harrogate, Ruhr Klavier Festivals, Beethoven Fest Bonn, Mecklenburg and the Snape Maltings Proms in Aldeburgh. *Recordings include:* Baroque Reflections, Piano and Organ music by Marcel Dupré, Brahms D minor Concerto with New Japan Philharmonic, Ligeti Two piano and four hands music with Lucille Chung, Beethoven Third Concerto with Hamamatsu SO. *Honours:* winner Hamamatsu Int. Piano Competition 1977, Leeds Int. Pianoforte Competition 2000. *Address:* c/o Warner Classics, 46 Kensington Court, London, W8 5DA, England. *Telephone:* (20) 7938-5632. *Fax:* (20) 7368-4903. *E-mail:* lucy.bright@warnerclassics.com. *Website:* www.alessiobax.com; www.warnerclassics.com.

**BAYLEY, Clive;** Singer, Bass; b. 15 Nov. 1960, Manchester, England; m. Paula Bradley, 15 July 1989. *Education:* Studied at the Royal Northern College of Music and at the National Opera Studio. *Career:* Debut: With Opera North; Sang in The Rape of Lucretia, Il Barbiere di Siviglia and as Claggart in Billy Budd, while at the RNCM; Professional debut as Schwarz in Die Meistersinger for Opera North, followed by the King in Aida, Colline in La Bohème, Don Basilio, Banquo, Bartolo in Le nozze di Figaro and in British premiere of Verdi's Jerusalem; English National Opera debut 1987, as Pietro in Simon Boccanegra, followed by appearances in Billy Budd, Un ballo in Maschera, Don Giovanni, Doctor Faust and The Return of Ulysses; Netherlands Opera 1989, as Trufaldino in Ariadne auf Naxos; December 1989 in a concert performance of Bernstein's Candide, conducted by the composer; Sang in the premiere of Birtwistle's Gawain at Covent Garden, May 1991; Concert repertory includes the Verdi Requiem, Elgar's Dream of Gerontius and Apostles, the Brahms Requiem, Handel's Messiah, Israel in Egypt, the Choral Symphony, Rossini's Petite Messe Solennelle and Christus in the St Matthew Passion; Roles at ROH with parts in Fidelio, The Fiery Angel, Die Meistersinger, Colline in La Bohème; Further roles at Opera North include: Sparafucile, The Monk in Don Carlos and Raleigh in Gloriana; Sang Ferrando in Il Trovatore for Opera North, 1994; Mozart's Figaro for Opera North, 1996; Season 1998 as Kecal in The Bartered Bride and Verdi's Grand Inquisitor for the Royal Opera; Season 2000–01 as Debussy's Arkel for ENO, Alvise in La Gioconda for Opera North, Drago in Schumann's Genoveva at Garsington, and as Britten's Collatinus at Lausanne; Weber's Euryanthe at the London Proms, 2002. *Recordings:* Candide, DGG. *Honours:* Curtis Gold Medal for Singing; The Robin Kay Memorial Prize for Opera, RNCM. *Current Management:* Tom Graham, IMG Artists. *Address:* c/o IMG Artists, Lovell House, 616 Chiswick High Road, London W4 5RX, England.

**BAYO, Maria;** Singer (Soprano); b. 1964, Navarra, Spain. *Career:* Won prizes at the Francisco Vines and Maria Callas Competitions and has appeared from 1998 at Lucerne (Lucia di Lammermoor) and St Gallen (Amina in La Sonnambula); Sang Susanna at Madrid and Marseille (1990), Micaela at Monte Carlo (1991) and Musetta in La Bohème (debut role at La Scala, 1991); Season 1991/92 as Susanna at the Opéra Bastille, Paris, Norina in Don Pasquale at Hamburg, Amenaide in Tancredi at Schwetzingen and Rosina at Strasbourg; Season 1993–94 as Zerlina at Buenos Aires and Ensoleillad in Massenet's Chérubin at Covent Garden; Cavalli's Calisto at Brussels (1993); Berlin Staatsoper (1996) and Lyon Opéra (1999); Cherubino at Salzburg, 1998; Sang Liu in Turandot at the reopening of the Liceu Theatre, Barcelona, 1999; Season 2000–01 as Susanna at Salzburg, Manon at Madrid and Bizet's Leila for Marseilles Opera. Concert repertory includes Rossini's Stabat Mater and Mahler's 2nd Symphony. *Current Management:* Opéra et Concert, 7 rue de Clichy, 75009 Paris, France. *Telephone:* 1-42-96-18-18. *Fax:* 1-42-96-18-00. *E-mail:* agence@opera-concert.com. *Website:* www.opera-concert.com. *Current Management:* Hilbert Artists Management, Maximilianstrasse 22, 80539 Munich, Germany. *Telephone:* (89) 2907470. *Fax:* (89) 29074790. *E-mail:* agentur@hilbert.de. *Website:* www.hilbert.de; www.mariabayo.net.

**BAZOLA, François;** singer (bass); b. 1965, Paris, France. *Education:* Paris Conservatoire with William Christie. *Career:* has sung with Les Arts Florissants in Lully's Atys (in Paris and New York), Rameau's Les Indes Galantes and Castor et Pollux, Purcell's Fairy Queen (Aix-en-Provence) and Charpentier's Le malade imaginaire; Sang Arcas in Médée by Charpentier in Paris, Lisbon and New York (1993) and Pan in King Arthur by Purcell (Paris and London, 1995); Assistant to William Christie with the choir of Les Arts Florissants, from 1994. *Address:* c/o Les Arts Florsissants, 10 rue de Florence, 75008 Paris, France.

**BEACH, David (Williams);** Professor of Music Theory and Administrator; b. 5 Sept. 1938, Hartford, CT, USA; m. Marcia Francesca Salemme, 20 June 1964, 1 s., 1 d. *Education:* BA, Brown University, 1961; MMus, 1964; PhD, 1974, Yale University. *Career:* Academic; Assistant Professor, Yale University, 1964–71; Assistant Professor, Brooklyn College, City University of New York, 1971–72; Associate Professor, 1974–85; Chairman, Theory Department, 1981–90, 1995–96; Professor, 1985–, Eastman School of Music; Chairman, Theory Department, 1981–90; University Dean of Graduate Studies, University of Rochester, 1991–1995; Professor and Dean, Faculty of Music, University of Toronto, 1996–; mem, Society for Music Theory, Executive Board, 1984–87; Chairman, Publications Committee, 1979–84; American Musicological Society. *Publications:* The Art of Strict Musical Composition by J P Kirnberger, translated by D Beach and J Thym with introduction and explanatory notes by Beach, 1982; Aspects of Schenkerian Theory, Editor, 1983; Music Theory in Concept and Practice, co-editor, 1997. *Contributions:* Acta Musicologia; Music Analysis; Journal of Music Theory; Music Theory Spectrum; Theory and Practice; Journal of Musicological Research; Integral; Journal of Music Theory Pedagogy. *Honours:* Deems Taylor Award ASCAP, 1983. *Address:* Faculty of Music, University of Toronto, 80 Queens Park, Toronto, Ontario M5S 2C5, Canada.

**BEALE, Matthew;** Singer (tenor); b. 1975, England. *Education:* Choral Scholar, New Coll., Oxford; Royal Coll. of Music, with Margaret Kingsley. *Career:* choral singing with the Tallis Scholars, The Sixteen and The Gabrieli Consort; Carmina Burana with the Liverpool Philharmonic Orchestra, Messiah at Worcester Cathedral and Bach's B Minor Mass at St John's Smith Square, 2000; opera roles include Mozart's Ferrando, Cimarosa's Paolino, Sir Philip and Narrator in Britten's Owen Wingrave and Sellem in The Rake's Progess; title role in the premiere of Francis Grier's St Francis of Assisi; Ugone in Flavio from the London Handel Festival, 2001; recitals in Japan, England and Wales; On Wenlock Edge by Vaughan Williams at St John's Smith Square, London, 2001. *Honours:* Sybil Tutton Award, RCM. *Current Management:* Caroline Phillips Management, The Old Brushworks, Pickwick Road, Corsham, Wiltshire, SN13 9BX, England. *Telephone:* (1249) 716716. *Fax:* (1249) 716717. *E-mail:* cphillips@caroline-phillips.co.uk. *Website:* www.caroline-phillips.co.uk/beale. *Address:* c/o Royal College of Music, Prince Consort Road, London SW7 2BS, England.

**BEAMISH, Sally;** British composer and violist; b. 26 Aug. 1956, London; d. of Anthony Beamish and Ursula Snow-Beamish; m. Robert Irvine 1988; two d. one s. *Education:* Royal Northern Coll. of Music (Manchester) and Staatliche Hochschule für Musik (Detmold, Germany). *Career:* Viola player, Raphael Ensemble, Acad. of St Martin-in-the-Fields, London Sinfonietta, Lontano 1979–1990; Composer 1990–; Composer-in-Residence Swedish Chamber Orchestra 1998–2002, Scottish Chamber Orchestra 1998–2002; performed première of her Viola Concerto at BBC Henry Wood Promenade Concert, London 1995; comms from the City of Reykjavík, BBC TV, English Nat. Opera, Brighton Festival, etc. *Compositions include:* Tuscan Lullaby 1989, Symphony 1992, Violin Concerto 1994, Viola Concerto 1995, Piano Sonata 1996, Knotgrass Elegy (BBC Proms comm.) 2001, Monster (opera) 2002. *Recordings include:* River (Cello, Viola and Oboe Concertos), Sun on Stone (Saxophone Concertos). *Honours:* Dr hc (Glasgow) 2001; Paul Hamlyn Award for Outstanding Achievement in Composition 1993, Creative Scotland Award 2000. *Address:* Scottish Music Information Centre, 1 Bowmont Gardens, Glasgow G12 9LR, Scotland. *Telephone:* (141) 334-6393. *Fax:* (141) 337-1161.

**BEARDSLEE, Bethany;** Singer (Soprano); b. 25 Dec. 1927, Lansing, Michigan, USA; m. (1) Jacques-Louis Monod, (2) Godfrey Winham, 1956. *Education:* Michigan State University; Juilliard School. *Career:* Debut: New York, 1949; Concerts with Jacques-Louis Monod, giving the US premieres of works by Berg, Stravinsky, Webern, Krenek and Schoenberg; Concerts of Medieval and Renaissance music with the New York Pro Musica, 1957–60; Commissioned and performed Babbitt's Philomel 1964; Performed Schoenberg's Pierrot Lunaire with members of the Cleveland Orchestra 1972; Taught at Westminster Choir College from 1976; Partnership with pianist Richard Goode 1981; Professor of singing at University of Texas, Austin, 1981–82; Brooklyn College, City University of New York, from 1983. *Recordings:* Pierrot Lunaire, conducted by Robert Craft; Works by Babbitt, George Perle, Mel Powell, Bach, Haydn and Pergolesi. *Honours:* Laurel Leaf from American Composers Alliance, 1962; Ford Foundation Grant 1964; Honorary Doctorate, Princeton University, 1977.

**BEARE, Charles,** OBE; British musical instrument restorer; *Chairman, J. & A. Beare Ltd*. *Career:* currently Chair. and Dir musical instrument restorer, J. & A. Beare Ltd. *Publication:* Antonio Stradivari: The Cremona Exhibition of 1987 1994. *Address:* J. & A. Beare Ltd, 30 Queen Anne Street, London, W1G 8HX, England. *Telephone:* (20) 7307-9666. *Fax:* (20) 7307-9651. *E-mail:* violins@beares.com. *Website:* www.beares.com.

**BEAT, Janet Eveline,** BMus, MA; composer; b. 17 Dec. 1937, Streetly, Staffordshire, England. *Education:* Birmingham Univ. *Career:* freelance horn player, 1962–65; Lecturer in Music, Madeley College of Education, 1965–67; Lecturer in Music, Worcester College of Education, 1967–71; Lecturer, Royal Scottish Academy of Music and Drama, 1972–96; Lecturer, Music Department (part-time), University of Glasgow, 1996–2002; mem. BACS. *Compositions include:* Brass: Hunting Horns are Memories, 1977; Fireworks in Steel, 1987; Chard Fanfare, 1992; Bold As Brass!, 1996; Vision Nocturne, 2003; Keyboard: Pentad, 1969; Piangam, 1978–79; Sonata No. 1, 1985–87; Cross Currents and Reflections, 1981–82; Alexa's Comet, 1984; Capriccios Vol 1, 1999–2002; Fanfare for Haydn, 2000; Dynamism, 2000; Sunsets and Lakes, 2003; Orchestra: Synchronism, 1977; Strings: Le Tombeau de Claude, 1973; The Leaves of My Brain, 1974; Circe, 1974; After Reading 'Lessons of War', 1977; 'Vincent' Sonata, 1979–80; A Willow Swept By Rain, 1982; Arabesque, 1985; Cat's Cradle for the Nemuri Neko, 1991; Convergencies, 1992; Scherzo Notturno, 1992; Joie de Vivre, 1994; Equinox Rituals, 1996; Violin Sonata No. 2, 1997; Concealed Imaginings, 1998; String Quartet No. 1, 1992–99; Violin Sonata No. 3, 1999; Summer Poem No. V, 1970; The Fiery Sunflower, 1972; Landscapes, 1976–77; Premiers Désirs, 1978; Mitylene Mosaics, 1983–84; Nomoi Aulodiki, 1984; Sylvia Myrtea, 1985; Aztec Myth, 1987; Aspara Music 1, 1994; Gedenkstück fur Kaethe, 2003; Woodwind: Apollo and Marysas, 1972–73; Inventions for Woodwind, 1974; Seascape With Clouds, 1978; Mitylene Mosaics, 1983–84; Two Caprices, 1998; Nomoi Aulodiki, 1984; En Plein Air, 2000–01; Electronic: Aztec Myth, 1987; A Springtime Pillow Book, 1990; Beating Around the Bush, 1990; Not Necessarily: As She Opened Her Eyes, 1990; Lydian Mix, 1990; Mandala, 1990; Memories of Java, 1990; The Song of The Silkie, 1991; Fêtes Pour Claude, 1992; Der Regenpalast, 1993; Strings: Mexican Night of the Dead, 2001; Harmony Opposites, 2002; Encounter, 2002; The Dream Magus, 2002. *Honours:* G. D. Cunningham Award, 1963; Honorary Research Fellow, Glasgow University, 1999. *Address:* The Scottish Music Centre, 1 Bowmont Gardens, Glasgow G12 9LR, Scotland. *E-mail:* info@scottishmusiccentre.com. *Website:* www.scottishmusiccentre.com/janet_beat.

**BEATH, Betty,** DipMus; Australian composer and pianist; b. 19 Nov. 1932, Bundaberg, Qld. *Education:* Queensland and New South Wales Conservatories. *Career:* lecturer and accompanist, Queensland Conservatory 1967–98. *Compositions include:* Strange Adventures of Marco Polo, 1 act opera, 1972; Francis, 1 act opera 1974; Songs from the Beasts' Choir for soprano and piano, 1978; Poems from the Chinese for soprano, clarinet, cello and percussion, 1979; Piccolo Victory, 1982; Black on White for piano left hand, 1983; Points in a Journey for soprano, flute and piano, 1987; Abigail and the Mythical Beast, music theatre, 1985; River Songs for soprano and piano, 1992; Lagu Lagu Manis for cello and piano, 1994; Asmaranda for orchestra, 1994; Journeys: An Indonesian Triptych for chamber orchestra, 1994; Indonesian Diptych, 1994; Golden Hours for chamber orchestra, 1995; Dreams and Visions, 1996; From a Quiet Place, 1997; Encounters for violin and cello, 1999; Lament for Kosovo, 1999; A Garland for St Francis for soprano, string quartet, flute, clarinet and percussion, 2002; Many national broadcasts include interview and performance of works to mark the 70th birthday, ABC Classic FM, 1996; Commissions from the Queensland Opera, 1973, Philharmonic, 1995 and Australian Broadcasting Corporation, 2002; Towards the Psalms (song cycle) 2004. *Recordings:* Indonesian Diptych on Music from Six Continents, 1995; Lagu Lagu Manis, Music from Six Continents, 1996; Dreams and Visions, 1997; River Songs, 1998; Lament for Kosovo, Music from Six Continents, 2001; Woman's Song, Music from Six Continents, 2001; From a Quiet Place, 2003. *Honours:* Perform/4MBS Award 2000.

**BEAUCHAMP, Michael John;** British opera director, theatre director and teacher; b. 2 June 1949, London, England. *Education:* University College, Durham, Glyndebourne Opera. *Career:* Staff Producer, Sadler's Wells and English National Opera, 1973–75; Resident Producer, Australian Opera, 1975–80; Freelance, 1980–; Productions: Happy End, Adelaide; Simon Boccanegra; HMS Pinafore; La Bohème; Australian Opera; La Bohème, National Opera of New Zealand and Glyndebourne Touring Opera; Rake's Progress, Brisbane and Sydney; Rigoletto, Perth, Western Australia and Melbourne; Lucia di Lammermoor, Tancredi, Wexford; The Happy Prince, Dunstan and The Devil, Morley Opera; Director, gala premieres for Australian Bicentennial, New South Wales Directorate; Teaching posts in Australia and England. *Address:* 40A Regents Park Road, London NW1 7SX, England.

**BEAUDRY, Jacques,** BA; Canadian symphony and opera conductor; b. 10 Oct. 1929, Sorel, QC; m. Pauline Bonneville. *Education:* Univ. of Montréal, Royal Conservatory of Music, Brussels, Belgium, studied with René Defossez, Paul Van Kempen, Willem Van Otterloo. *Career:* Prof. of Orchestral Conducting, Univ. of Montréal; toured Europe as conductor with Montréal Symphony, Opéra Comique, Paris Opéra House, and New York Metropolitan Opera; radio broadcasts in Canada, Belgium, Netherlands, Italy, Czechoslovakia, Norway, Luxembourg and France; concerts in Russia, Poland, Guatemala, Switzerland, Greece, Monaco and USA; television appearances in Canada and France. *Honours:* Gold Medal of Quebec, Lieutenant Governor's Award 1958. *Current Management:* Beaudry Concerts, 235 Sherbrooke O P2, Montréal, QC H2X 1X8, Canada. *Telephone:* (514) 287-9435 (office).

**BEAUMONT, Adrian,** BA, MMus, DMus, ARCM .; Composer and Lecturer; b. 1 June 1937, Huddersfield, England; m. Janet Price 1963. *Education:* Univ. of Wales, Cardiff; composition with Nadia Boulanger (Fontainebleau). *Career:* appointed to staff of Music Department of University of Bristol, 1961; subsequently Reader in Composition until 2002; founder-conductor Bristol Bach Choir 1967–78. *Compositions:* include 3 Symphonies; Now Burns the Bright Redeeming Fire; Oboe Concerto; Summer Ecstasies; 2 string quartets; A Glimmer of Unshapen Dawn; Cello Sonata; three song cycles. *Publications:* Expectation and Interpretation in the Reception of New Music in Thomas (ed), Composition, Performance, Reception. *Address:* 73 Kings Drive, Bishopston, Bristol, BS7 8JQ, England (home). *Telephone:* (117) 9248456 (home).

**BECCARIA, Bruno;** Singer (Tenor); b. 4 July 1957, Rome, Italy. *Career:* Debut: Bologna, 1986, as Edgardo in Lucia di Lammermoor; Sang at La Scala, Milan, 1986–87, as Ismaele and Pinkerton; Philadelphia Opera, 1986 and 1988, Vienna Staatsoper from 1987, New York Metropolitan debut, 1987, as Rodolfo; Verona Arena from 1988, as Enzo in La Gioconda, Radames and Turiddu; Teatro La Fenice Venice, 1990, as Ernani; Other roles include Gabriele Adorno (Catania, 1992), Andrea Chénier (San Francisco Opera), Faust, Don Carlos, and Maurizio in Adriana Lecouvreur. *Recordings include:* Beethoven's Mass in C (Decca). *Address:* c/o Metropolitan Opera, Lincoln Center, New York, NY 10023, USA.

**BECERRA, Gustavo;** Composer; b. 26 Aug. 1925, Temuco, Chile. *Education:* Studied at Santiago Conservatory, with Pedro Allende and with Domingo Santa Cruz. *Career:* Cultural Attaché to Chilean Embassy in Bonn, 1968–70; Freelance composer. *Compositions:* La Muerte de Don Rodrigo, opera, 1958; Three Symphonies, 1955, 1958, 1960; La Araucuna and Lord Cochrane, oratorios, 1965, 1967; Violin Concerto, 1950; Flute Concerto, 1957; Concerto for piano with oboe, clarinet, bassoon and strings, 1970; Three Violin Sonatas; Viola Sonata; Three Cello Sonatas; Sonata for double bass and piano; Choral music. *Honours:* Premio Nacional de Arte, 1971. *Address:* Kurt Schumacher Str. 11, 26131 Oldenburg, Germany.

**BECHLY, Daniela;** singer (soprano); b. 1960, Hamburg, Germany; m.; three c. *Education:* Hamburg Hochschule für Musik. *Career:* debut, Vienna Kammeroper 1984; Wexford Festival 1986, as Humperdinck's Goose Girl in Königskinder; sang at Brunswick Opera 1983; appeared with the Krefeld-Mönchengladbach co. 1985–87; soloist at the Deutsche Oper Berlin 1987– ; sang Susanna, Zerlina, Aennchen, Pamina, Anna in Die Lustige Weiber von Windsor, Gretel, Sandrina in La Finta Giardiniera, Elvira in Don Giovanni (Bern 1991); Malwina in Der Vampyr by Marschner (Wexford 1992) and Haydn's L'Incontro Improvviso; Rhinemaiden, Covent Garden 1997; Cherubino, Deutsche Oper am Rhein, Düsseldorf, and Agathe at the Opera Festival at Zwingenberg, Germany 1998; recital, Women and Music, Villa Musica, Germany 1999; collaboration with Trio Kaivos on Shostakovich Op. 127 and Haydn-Beethoven Folksongs arrangements; Margerite in Faust, Opera South 2005; concert repertoire includes all major oratorio works, Mozart concert arias, Strauss four last songs; Mahler Lieder eines fahrenden Gesellen; Wagner Wesendonck; engagements in Ireland, Denmark, Norway, France, Italy, Austria. *Recordings:* Blumenmädchen in Parsifal recording under Barenboim, Ronnefeld Song Cycles 2000. *Honours:* first prize Hamburg Singing Contest 1980, finalist Vienna Belvedere Competition 1984, second prize Bordeaux Festival Int. de Jeunes Solistes. *Current Management:* Music International, 13 Ardilaun Road, London, N5 2QR, England. *Telephone:* (1206) 271291. *E-mail:* danielabechly@tiscali.co.uk.

**BECHT, Hermann;** Singer (baritone); b. 19 March 1939, Karlsruhe, Germany. *Education:* Studied with E. Wolf-Dengel in Karlsruhe and with Josef Greindl. *Career:* Sang at Brunswick and Wiesbaden; Deutsche Oper am Rhein, Düsseldorf, from 1974; Roles include Strauss's Mandryka, Falstaff, Amfortas and Pfitzner's Borromeo; Bayreuth Festival from 1979, as Alberich and Kurwenal; Covent Garden Opera in The Ring; Sang Alberich at the Festival Hall, London in a concert performance of Das Rheingold; Guest appearances in New York, Stuttgart, Vienna and Staatsoper Munich (1986, in the premiere of V D Kirchner's Belshazzar); Waldner in Arabella, Teatro Liceo Barcelona, 1989; Sang Kurwenal at Nantes, 1989 and Alberich in Das Rheingold, Bonn, 1990; Sang in the premiere production of Mayer's Sansibar, Schwetzingen, 1994; Schigolch in Lulu at Dusseldorf, 2000. *Recordings:* Alberich in Ring cycle from Bayreuth. *Current Management:* Ingpen & Williams Ltd, 7 St George's Court, 131 Putney Bridge Road, London, SW15 2PA, England.

**BECK, Jeremy;** Composer; b. 15 Jan. 1960, Painesville, Ohio. *Education:* DMA, Yale University; MA Duke University; BSc, Mannes College of Music; Dagbe Drumming Institute, Ghana. *Career:* Debut: Carnegie Recital Hall, 1987; Associate Professor, University of Northern Iowa; Guest Lecturer in American Music, St Petersburg Conservatory, Russia; University of West Bohemia. *Compositions:* Death of a Little Girl with Doves, for soprano and orchestra, 1998; Laughter in Jericho, chamber opera, 1997; 3 sonatas for cello and piano, 1981, 1988, 1997; 3 string quartets, 1987, 1990 and 1994. *Recordings:* Four Pieces, 1995; Kopeyia for percussion ensemble, 1995; Songs Without Words, for flute and harp, 1997; Sonata No. 1, 1983; Toccata for piano solo, 1988. *Contributions:* Elliott Carter's Tonal Practice in the Rose Family,

Essays in American Music Vol. II. *Address:* 2103 Walnut Street, Cedar Falls, IA 50613, USA.

**BECKER, Andreas;** Singer (Bass-baritone); b. 13 May 1940, Berlin. *Education:* Berlin Conservatory. *Career:* Debut: As Landgrave in Tannhäuser, Osnabruck, 1966; Repertoire of about 350 roles, opera, operetta and musicals; Appearances throughout Germany from 1966, notably at Krefeld, Bielefeld and Essen; Dortmund Opera from 1972, with guest appearances at Munich and elsewhere; Other roles have included Pizarro and Rocco in Fidelio, Wagner's Marke, Hunding and Fasolt, Verdi's Zaccaria and King Philip; Mozart's Osmin and Sarastro, Ochs (Rosenkavalier) and Alfonso, with further engagements at Munich, Hamburg, Paris, Netherlands and the Far East; Sang Mordred in Le Roi Arthus by Chausson at Dortmund, 1996; Doolittle in My Fair Lady and also appeared in The Merry Widow; Teacher, Dortmund Hochschule; Season 2000–01 at Dortmund as Kecal in The Bartered Bride and in the premiere of Wallenbeg by Erkki-Sven Tüür. *Address:* c/o Stadtische Buhnen Dortmund, Kuhstrasse 12, 4600 Dortmund, Germany.

**BECKER, Günther (Hugo);** Composer and Music Educator; b. 1 April 1924, Forbach, Baden, Germany. *Education:* Studied conducting with Gerhard Nestler, Badische Hochschule für Musik, Karlsruhe, 1946–49; Composition with Wolfgang Fortner, 1948–56; Choral conducting with Kurt Thomas, 1953–55; North West German Academy of Music, Detmold. *Career:* Music Teacher, Greek National School Anavryta, Athens, 1956–58; Music Adviser, Goethe Institute, Athens, 1957–68; Music Teacher, German Dörpfeld Gymnasium, Athens, 1957–68; Founded, Mega-Hertz, live electronic music group, Germany, 1969; Teacher, International Summer Courses for New Music, Darmstadt, 1967, 1968, 1970; Lecturer, Musikhochschule Rheinland, Robert Schumann Institute, Düsseldorf, 1973–74; Professor of Composition and Live Electronics, Hochschule für Musik, Düsseldorf, 1974–89; mem, International Society for Contemporary Music, President German Section, 1971–74. *Compositions:* Orchestral: Nachtund Traumgesänge for Chorus and Orchestra, 1964; Stabil-instabil, 1965; Correspondances I for Clarinet and Chamber Orchestra, 1966; Griechische Tanzsuite, 1967; Caprices concertants, 1968; Transformationen for Orchestra, Live Electronic Ensemble and Tape, 1970; Attitude, 1972–73; Konzert for Electronic Modulated Oboe and Orchestra, 1973–74; Ihre Bosheit wird die ganze Erde zu einer Wüste machen, sacred concerto for Speaker, Alto, Chorus, Organ, Instrumental Ensemble and Tape, 1978; Magnum Mysterium-Zeugenaussagen zur Auferstehung, scenic oratorio, 1979–80; Psychogramme for Trombone, Accordion and Percussion, 1993; Pieces for various instruments and electronics; 3 String Quartets, 1963, 1967, 1988; Befindlichkeiten for saxophone, cello and piano, 1997. *Address:* Arminiusstraße 41, 33175 Bad Lippspringe, Germany.

**BECKER, Heinz,** PhD; German musicologist and music educator; b. 26 June 1922, Berlin. *Education:* Berlin Hochschule für Musik, Humboldt Univ., Berlin. *Career:* Asst Lecturer, Inst. of Musicology 1956–66, Habilitation 1961, Univ. of Hamburg; Prof. of Musicology, Ruhr-Univ., Bochum 1966–87; mem. Gesellschaft für Musikforschung 1951– . *Publications:* Klarinettenkonzerte des 18. Jahrhunderts 1957, Der Fall Heine-Meyerbeer 1958, Giacomo Meyerbeer: Briefwechsel und Tagebücher (ed., four vols) 1960–85, Geschichte der Instrumentation 1964, Beitrage zur Geschichte der Musikkritik 1965, Studien zur Entwicklungsgeschichte der antiken und mittelalterlichen Rohrblattinstrumente 1966, Beiträge zur Geschichte der Oper 1969, Die Couleur locale in der Oper des 19 Jahrhunderts 1976, Giacomo Meyerbeer in Selbstzeugnissen und Bilddokumenten 1980, Giacomo Meyerbeer: Ein Leben in Briefen (with G. Becker) 1983, Giacomo Meyerbeer. Weltbürger der Musik, Ausstellungskatalog zum 200 Geburtstag Meyerbeers (with Gudrun Becker), Im Auftrag de Staatsbibl. BLN, Preußischer Kulturbesitz 1991, The 19th-century Legacy, Heritage of Music 1989, Johannes Brahms 1993; contrib. articles to various music journals and other publications. *Honours:* Festschrift published in honour of 60th birthday 1982, G. Meyerbeer–Musik als Welterfahrung, Festschrift in honour of 70th birthday (ed Sieghart Döhring and Jürgen Schläder) 1992. *Address:* Wohnstift Augustinum, App 1242, Sterleyer Str 44, 23879 Mölln, Germany.

**BECKER, Rolf;** Singer (Bass); b. 1935, Germany. *Career:* Sang with Cologne Opera, 1959–62, Hannover, 1962–92; Roles have included Mozart's Sarastro and Commendatore, Rocco, Daland, Fafner, Hunding, Gurnemanz, and Mephistopheles; Has also sung such modern repertory as Wesener in Die Soldaten by Zimmermann and buffo roles, including Basilio, Osmin, Kecal and Bartolo; Concert engagements in Spain, France and Italy. *Address:* c/o Niedersachsische Staatstheater, Opernhaus, Opernplatz 1, W-3000 Hannover 1, Germany.

**BECKWITH, Daniel;** Conductor; b. 1954, Chicago, USA. *Education:* Studied at Westminster Choir College, Princeton. *Career:* Opera Conductor; Recent engagements with Il Matrimonio Segreto, Falstaff, Die Entführung aus dem Serail and Il Barbiere di Siviglia at Wolf Trap, Così fan tutte for the Lyric Opera of Chicago, Grétry's Zemire et Azor at Houston; Giulio Cesare, The Rape of Lucretia and Turandot at Edmonton; The Coronation of Poppea and Mozart's Il Re Pastore for Canadian Opera; Lucia di Lammermoor in Cincinatti; Other appearances include Don Giovanni at the Metropolitan (1995, 1997), Figaro at Vancouver and Il Barbiere di Siviglia in Florida; L'Italiana in Algeri for Cleveland Opera; Season 1997 with Theodora at the Glyndebourne Festival, L'Elisir d'amore at Fort Worth, Handel's Xerxes in Seattle and Rinaldo for the Geneva Opera; The Crucible and The Magic Flute at Washington DC; Il Barbiere di Siviglia at Opera North, England, 1998; Further performances of Orphée et Eurydice in Utah; Platée (Rameau) New York City Opera; The Magic Flute, Seattle; Don Giovanni, San Francisco; Artistic Director of the Lake George Summer Opera Festival, 1999. *Address:* IMG Artists, 7th Avenue, 3rd Floor, New York, NY 10019, USA.

**BECKWITH, John,** BMus, MMus; Canadian composer, teacher, writer and pianist; b. 9 March 1927, Victoria, BC. *Education:* Univ. of Toronto, Royal Conservatory of Music, Toronto with Alberto Guerrero, studied composition with Nadia Boulanger in Paris. *Career:* Public Relations Dir, Royal Conservatory of Music, Toronto 1948–50; staff writer for radio music continuity, Canadian Broadcasting Corporation, Toronto 1953–55; freelance radio programmer and writer 1955–70; reviewer and columnist, Toronto Daily Star 1959–62, 1963–65; part-time special lecturer, Univ. of Toronto 1952–53, Lecturer 1954–60; Asst Prof. 1960–66; Assoc. Prof. 1966–70, Dean 1970–77, Prof. 1977–90; Dir, Inst. for Canadian Music 1984–90. *Compositions:* 4 songs to poems of e e cummings, 1950; Fall Scene and Fair Dance, 1956; Night Blooming Cereus, 1958; Concerto Fantasy, 1960; Flower Variations and Wheels, 1962; Jonah, 1963; The Trumpets of Summer 1964; Sharon Fragments, 1966; Circle, with Tangents, 1967; Canada Dash, Canada Dot, 1967; Gas!, 1969; Taking a Stand, 1972; All the Bees and All the Keys, 1973; Musical Chairs, 1973; Quartet, 1977; The Shivaree, 1978; Keyboard Practice, 1979; 3 Motets on Swan's China, 1981; Sonatina in 2 movements, 1981; A Little Organ Concert, 1981; Mating Time, 1981; 6 Songs to poems by E. E. Cummings, 1982; A Concert of Myths, 1983; Études, 1983; Arctic Dances, 1984; Harp of David, 1985; Crazy to Kill, 1988; Peregrine, 1989; Round and Round, 1992; Taptoo!, 1994; Eureka, 1996; Basic Music, 1998; Lady Wisdom, 2000; A New Pibroch, 2002. *Recordings:* Harp of David; Quartet; Keyboard Practice; Études; Arctic Dances; Sharon Fragments; Circle, with Tangents; 3 Motets on Swan's China; Stacey; Round and Round; A Concert of Myths; Synthetic Trios; The Trumpets of Summer. *Publications:* Gen. Ed., Canadian Composers Series, 1975–91; Canadian Consultant, The New Grove, London, 1980; Ed. or Co-ed., The Modern Composer and His World, 1961; Contemporary Canadian Composers, 1975; The Canadian Musical Heritage, Vol. 5, 1986, Vol. 18, 1995; Musical Canada, 1987; Author, Music Papers, 1997. *Honours:* five hon. doctorates, Member of the Order of Canada 1987. *Address:* 121 Howland Avenue, Toronto, M5R 3B4, Canada.

**BECZALA, Piotr;** Polish singer (tenor); b. 1968, Czechowice-Dziedzice. *Education:* Studied at the Katowice Music Acad. and in Weimar, Kraków and Villecrose; Sena Jurinac has been among his teachers. *Career:* Sang at the Linz and Salzburg Landestheater, as Mozart's Ferrando and Tamino, Gaston in Krenek's Schwergewicht, Cassio, Werther and Belmonte, 1992–98; Zürich Opera debut as Rinuccio in Gianni Schicchi (company member from 1998), 1996; Further appearances as Alfredo, Lensky and Don Ottavio at Linz and as Alfred in Fledermaus; Concerts include Bruckner's Te Deum with the Vienna Philharmonic under Giulini and Schubert's E flat Mass under Muti; Further engagements at the Vienna Musikverein, and in Milan, Leipzig and Dresden; Théâtre de la Monnaie, Brussels, as Rinuccio, 1997; Season 2000–01 as the Duke of Mantua for Zürich Opera, and the Shepherd in Szymanowski's King Roger, at Amsterdam; debut performances at Scala, Milan, Munich State Opera and New York Metropolitan Opera 2006; returning to Salzburg Festival, Zürich, Lisbon, Frankfurt, Bilbao, Covent Garden 2006. *Address:* c/o Franz Hainl Artists' Management, POB 17, 1043 Vienna, Austria. *Telephone:* (1) 5864536 (office). *Fax:* (1) 5855551 (office). *E-mail:* office@hainzl.net (office). *Website:* www.beczala.com.

**BEDFORD, David,** ARAM, FTCL; British composer; b. 4 Aug. 1937, London; s. of L. H. Bedford and L. F. K. Duff; m. 1st M. Parsonage 1958 (divorced); two d.; m. 2nd S. Pilgrim 1969 (divorced); two d.; m. 3rd Allison Powell 1994; one s. two d. *Education:* Lancing Coll. and Royal Acad. of Music. *Career:* teacher of Music, Whitefield School, Hendon, London 1966–69, Queen's Coll., Harley Street, London 1969–80; Assoc. Visiting Composer, Gordonstoun School 1980–81; Youth Music Dir English Sinfonia 1986–93, Composer in Asscn English Sinfonia 1993–; Patron Barnet Schools Music Asscn 1987; since 1980 freelance composer and arranger; Deputy Chair. Performing Right Soc. 1999, Chair. 2002; Licentiate of Trinity Coll. of Music. *Compositions:* Music for Albion Moonlight 1965, Star Clusters 1971, The Golden Wine 1974, Star's End 1974, The Rime of the Ancient Mariner 1978, The Death of Baldur 1979, Sun Paints Rainbows 1982, Symphony No. 1 1983, Symphony No. 2 1985, some music for film The Killing Fields 1984, Absolute Beginners 1985, The Mission 1986, Into Thy Wondrous House 1986, Ma non Sempere 1987, Gere Curam Mei Nobis (for Katherine) 1987, A Charm of Blessings 1996, String Quartet No. 2 1998, Oboe Concerto 1999, The Sultan's Turret 1999, The City and the Stars 2001, Like a Strand of Scarlet 2002. *Address:* 12 Oakwood Road, Bristol, BS9 4NR, England. *Telephone:* (117) 962-4202. *E-mail:* dvbmus@aol.com (office). *Website:* www.jeffgower.com/bedford.html (office).

**BEDFORD, Steuart John Rudolf,** BA, FRCO, FRAM; British conductor; b. 31 July 1939, London; s. of L. H. Bedford and Lesley Bedford (née Duff); m. 1st Norma Burrowes (q.v.) 1969 (divorced 1980); m. 2nd Celia Harding 1980; two d. *Education:* Lancing Coll., Sussex, Univ. of Oxford, Royal Acad. of Music. *Career:* operatic training as repetiteur, Asst Conductor, Glyndebourne Festival 1965–67; English Opera Group (later English Music Theatre), Aldeburgh and London 1967–73; Co-Artistic Dir, English Musical Theatre 1976–80, Artistic Dir English Sinfonia 1981–90, Artistic Dir (also Exec. Artistic Dir) Aldeburgh Festival 1987–98; freelance conductor, numerous performances with ENO, Welsh Nat. Opera, Metropolitan Opera, New York

(operas include Death in Venice, The Marriage of Figaro), Royal Danish Opera; also at Royal Opera House, Covent Garden (operas include Owen Wingrave, Death in Venice, Così fan tutte) Santa Fe Opera, Teatro Colón, Buenos Aires, Lyon etc.; conductor for Orchestre Philharmonique de Montpellier, Mahler Chamber Orchestra, Southern Sinfonia; recordings include Death in Venice, Phaedra, Beggar's Opera, Collins Britten series. *Honours:* Medal of the Worshipful Co. of Musicians. *Address:* 76 Cromwell Avenue, London, N6 5HQ (home); c/o Harrison-Parrott Ltd, 12 Penzance Place, London, W11 4PA, England (office).

**BEECROFT, Norma Marian;** Canadian composer; b. 11 April 1934, Oshawa, Ont.; d. of Julian and Eleanor (née Norton) Beecroft. *Education:* Toronto Royal Conservatory of Music, Berks. Music Centre, Acad. of St Cecilia, Rome and in Germany and UK. *Career:* freelance commentator on modern music 1969–; Dir Workshops, York Univ., Ont. 1984–87; numerous TV and radio appearances; producer programmes on TV and radio, including programmes on Murray Adaskin 1993 and Violet Archer 1994; mem. Composers', Authors' and Publishers' Asscn of Canada; numerous comms. *Compositions include:* Tre Pezzi Brevi 1961, From Dreams of Brass 1964, Elegy and Two Went to Sleep 1967, Undersea Fantasy 1967, The Living Flame of Love 1967, Three Impressions From Sweetgrass 1973, Piece for Bob 1975, Consequences for Five 1977, Quaprice 1980, Cantorum Vitae 1981, Troissants 1982, Macbeth (score) 1983, Midsummer Night's Dream (score) 1984, Jeu de Bach 1985, Images 1987, The Dissipation of Purely Sound 1988, Accordion Play 1988, Hemispherics 1990, Evocations: Images of Canada 1991, Amplified String Quartet 1991–92, Esprit Eternel 1994, Face à Face 1994. *Honours:* Dr hc (York) 1996; Armstrong Award for Excellence in FM Broadcasting, Victor M Lynch–Staunton Award 1978–79, 1989–90. *Address:* 1866 Glendale Drive, Pickering, Ontario, L1V 1V5, Canada.

**BEER, Birgit;** Singer (Soprano); b. 1962, Lubeck, Germany. *Education:* Lubeck Musikhochschule. *Career:* Debut: Sang Tebaldo in Don Carlos at Augsburg; Sang at Saarbrucken, 1984–85; Lucerne, 1985–87; Vienna Volksoper, 1987–90; Further study with Renate Holm and Hanna Ludwig in Vienna; Theater am Gärtnerplatz, 1990–92 as Mozart's Blondchen, Offenbach's Olympia, Zerbinetta, and Adele in Die Fledermaus; Guest appearances at the Vienna Staatsoper, in Verona and Berlin and as Papagena at La Scala, Milan; Deutsche Oper Berlin as Rosina and Salzburg, 1994, as Frasquita in Carmen; Bonn Opera from 1992, as Puccini's Lauretta and Lisetta; Season 1996 as Papagena at Bonn and Marzelline in Fidelio at Liège; Sang Musetta at Essen, 1999. *Current Management:* Opera Vladarski, Döblinger Hauptstraße 57/18, 1190 Vienna, Austria. *Telephone:* 1 368 69 60/61. *Fax:* 1 368 69 62. *E-mail:* opera.vladarski@utanet.at. *Address:* c/o Oper der Stadt Bonn, Am Boeselagerhof 1, Pf 2440, 3111 Bonn, Germany.

**BEESLEY, Mark;** Singer (bass); b. 1961, Harrogate, Yorkshire, England. *Education:* Studied at Sussex University (MSc) and with Dennis Wicks and Laura Sarti. *Career:* Appearances with New Sussex Opera, the City of Birmingham Touring Opera, Opera North, Opera 80 and at the Batignano Festival; Member of the Royal Opera Covent Garden, 1989–, in Idomeneo (Voice of Neptune), Arabella, Fidelio, Capriccio, Samson et Dalila, Turandot (Timor), La Bohème (Colline), I Capuleti, Otello (Lodovico), and La Damnation de Faust (Brander, 1993); Other engagements in Poppea at the City of London Festival, Tosca (Angelotti) in Hong Kong and Midsummer Night's Dream (Theseus) at Aix-en-Provence; Sang in La Traviata and Don Carlos at Covent Garden, 1996; Concert repertoire includes the Verdi Requiem (at Seville) and Beethoven's Ninth (Brussels Philharmonic); Season 1999 with Schumann's Scenes from Faust at the London Prom concerts; Sang Sparafucile in Rigoletto for ENO, 1999; Season 2000–01 as Sarastro and Rossini's Basilio for ENO, and Drago in Schumann's Genoveva at Garsington. *Current Management:* Athole Still International Management, Forresters Hall, 25–27 Westow Street, London, SE19 3RY, England. *Telephone:* (20) 8771-5271. *Fax:* (20) 8768-6600. *Website:* www.atholestill.com.

**BEESON, Jack Hamilton,** BMus, MMus; composer, educator and writer; b. 15 July 1921, Muncie, Indiana, USA; m. Nora Beate Sigerist; one s. (deceased) one d. *Education:* Eastman School of Music, University of Rochester, Columbia University, studied privately with Béla Bartók. *Career:* debut ss actor in own opera, My Heart's in the Highlands, NET 1970. *Compositions:* over 60 published including: Jonah; Hello Out There; The Sweet Bye and Bye; Lizzie Borden; My Heart's in the Highlands; Captain Jinks of The Horse Marines; Dr Heidegger's Fountain of Youth; Cyrano; Sorry, Wrong Number, Practice in the Art of Elocution (operas); Symphony No. 1 in A. *Publications:* contrib. to journals and Grove's Dictionary (sixth edn). *Honours:* Hon. DMus (Columbia Univ.) 2002. *Address:* 404 Riverside Drive, New York, NY 10025, USA.

**BEGG, Heather,** OBE, DCNZM; singer (mezzo-soprano); b. 1 Dec. 1932, Nelson, New Zealand; d. of William James Begg and Johanna Swanson Begg (née Coghill). *Education:* Nat. School of Opera, London, vocal studies with Dame Sister Mary Leo and Gertrude Narev in Auckland, Marianne Mathy in Sydney, Florence Wiese-Norberg in London. *Career:* debut in Auckland, New Zealand 1954, as Azucena in Il Trovatore; Nat. Opera of Australia 1954–56; J. C. Williamson's Italian Opera, Australia 1955; Carl Rosa Opera, London 1960; resident, Sadler's Wells Opera, London 1961–64; New Zealand Opera 1964–67; ENO guest artist 1968–72; Royal Opera, Covent Garden guest artist 1959–99, resident 1972–76; resident, Opera Australia 1976–97, guest artist 1997–; guest artist in Edinburgh, London, Salzburg and Orange

Festivals, Strasbourg, Bordeaux, Milan, Vancouver, Chicago, San Francisco, San Diego, Singapore, Barcelona and Australasia; concert artist and recitalist for radio and TV in the UK, New Zealand and Australia; operatic repertoire of over 100 principal mezzo-soprano roles, including Madame Armfeldt in Sondheim's A Little Night Music, with Canterbury Opera, New Zealand 2004. *Recordings include:* Les Troyens; La Traviata; I Lombardi; La Sonnambula; Mefistofele; I Puritani; The Little Sweep; Die Fledermaus; Films of Die Fledermaus; Adriana Lecouvreur; Dialogues of the Carmelites; La fille du Régiment; The Mikado; Voss; Gipsy Princess; Patience; Le nozze di Figaro. *Honours:* Sydney Sun Aria winner 1955, New Zealand Govt Music Bursary 1956, Countess of Munster Scholarship 1959, Distinguished Companion of the New Zealand Order of Merit 2000. *Address:* c/o Opera Australia, 480 Elizabeth Street, Surry Hills, Sydney, NSW 2010, Australia (office). *Telephone:* (2) 9699-3184 (office). *Fax:* (2) 9699-3184 (office). *E-mail:* enquiries@opera-australia .org (office).

**BEGGS, Patricia K.;** American opera administrator; *General Director and CEO, Cincinnati Opera. Career:* joined Cincinnati Opera as Dir of Marketing 1984, Man. Dir 1997–2004, Gen. Dir and CEO 2004–; bd mem. and treas. OPERA America; bd mem. Downtown Cincinnati Inc. *Address:* Cincinnati Opera, Music Hall, 1243 Elm Street, Cincinnati, OH 45202, USA (office). *Telephone:* (513) 768-5500 (office). *Fax:* (513) 768-5552 (office). *E-mail:* info@ cincinnatiopera.org (office). *Website:* www.cincinnatiopera.org.

**BEGLARIAN, Eve;** Composer and Record Producer; b. 22 July 1958, Ann Arbor, Michigan, USA. *Education:* BA, Princeton University; MA, Columbia University. *Career:* Music performed at Washington Ballet, Kennedy Center, May 1991; Anthony de Hare, Kennedy Center, May 1990; New York New Music Ensemble, June 1988; Dinosaur Annex, Boston, 1989, 1990; Monday Evening Concerts, Los Angeles, 1990, 1991; Weill Recital Hall, April 1987. *Compositions:* Eloise (Electric Cello and Tape); The Beginning of Terror (Electronic Tape); Making Sense of It (flute, cello, violin, violoncello, pianoforte, percussion, tape); Miranda's Kiss (Piano solo); A Big Enough Umbrella (Viola, Tape); Elf Again for ensemble, 1998; Father/Daughter Dance, electro-acoustic, 1998; Non-Jew, 2 speakers, 1998. *Recordings:* Space 1986; Needful Things—Stephen King Audio Book, 1991; Born Dancin'/Eloise, 1991. *Publications:* Mikrokosmos, Bartók, corrected edition 1989.

**BEGLARIAN, Grant;** Composer and Consultant; b. 1 Dec. 1927, Tbilisi, Georgia, Russia; m. Joyce Ellyn Heeney, 2 Sept 1950, 1 s., 1 d. *Education:* BM, Composition, 1950, MM, Composition, 1961, DMA, 1958, University of Michigan, Ann Arbor, USA; Berkshire Music Center with Aaron Copland, 1960. *Career:* Director, Contemporary Music Project, The Ford Foundation, New York and Washington, 1960–69; Dean, Professor of Music, School of Performing Arts, University of Southern California, Los Angeles, 1969–82; President of National Foundation for Advancement in the Arts, Miami, 1982–91; Consultant in the Arts and Education, 1991–; International Coordinator, Think Quest, Amrenk, New York; mem. ASCAP; International Council of Fine Arts Deans. *Compositions include:* Duets for Violins, 1955; First Portrait for Band, 1959; Sinfonia for Orchestra, 1961; A Short Suite for String Orchestra, 1968; Fables, Foibles and Fancies for Narrator and Cellist, 1971; Diversions for Viola, Cello and Orchestra, 1972; To Manitou for Soprano and Orchestra, 1976; Partita for Orchestra, 1986. *Publications:* Film-Video as an Artistic Discipline, editor, 1978; The Arts in Shaping the American Experience, 1979; The Professional Education and Career Entry of Artists, 1982. *Honours:* George Gershwin Prize, 1959; Ysaye Medal, 1973; Distinguished Service Award, Music Teachers National Association, 1991. *Address:* 141 River Road, Scarborough, NY 10510, USA.

**BEGLEY, Kim;** Singer (Tenor); b. 23 June 1952, Wirral, Cheshire, England. *Education:* Guildhall School of Music, 1980–82; National Opera Studio, 1982–83. *Career:* Royal Opera House Covent Garden from 1983 as Andres in Wozzeck; Lysander in A Midsummer Night's Dream; The Prince in Zemlinsky's Florentine Tragedy; Achilles in King Priam and Froh in Das Rheingold; Other appearances include Boris in Katya Kabanova, Pellegrin in Tippett's New Year and Laca in Jenůfa for Glyndebourne Festival; Dancing Master in Ariadne and Male Chorus in Rape of Lucretia for ENO; Shuisky in Boris Godunov, Fritz in the British premiere of Der Ferne Klang, 1992, and Lohengrin and Alfred, Die Fledermaus in Frankfurt; Narraboth at the 1993 Salzburg Festival; Sang in Pfitzner's Palestrina at Covent Garden, Drum Major in Wozzeck at La Scala and Der Freischütz in Berlin, 1997; Sang Captain Vere in Billy Budd at the Opéra de La Bastille and Max in Der Freischütz at La Scala, 1998; Season 1999–2000 as Parsifal for ENO and Peter Grimes for Netherlands Opera; Wagner's Erik at Covent Garden, 2000; Season 2000–01 as Loge in Das Rheingold at Bayreuth and Florestan at Glyndebourne; Mendelssohn's Elijah at the London Proms, 2002; Drum Major in new production of Wozzeck at Covent Garden, 2003; Concert appearances include Die Fledermaus, Alfred, with André Previn at the Royal Philharmonic Orchestra; Elgar's Dream of Gerontius with the Philharmonia under Vernon Handley, Tippett's New Year with the London Philharmonic Orchestra and Janáček's From the House of the Dead with the BBC Symphony Orchestra. *Recordings include:* Florestan in Leonore with John Eliot Gardiner; Mephistopheles in Dr Faustus with Kent Nagano. *Current Management:* IMG Artists Europe, Lovell House, 616 Chiswick High Road, London W4 5RX, England. *Telephone:* (20) 8233-5800. *Fax:* (20) 8233-5801. *E-mail:* artistseurope@imgworld.com. *Website:* www.imgartists.com. *Current Management:* Aria's di Novella Partacini & Alexandra Plaickner, Via Josef

Weingartner 4, 39022 Lagundo, Italy. *Telephone:* (473) 200200. *Fax:* (473) 222424. *E-mail:* info@arias.it. *Website:* www.arias.it.

**BEHAGUE, Gerard (Henri);** Musicologist; b. 2 Nov. 1937, Montpellier, France. *Education:* Studied Piano and Composition at the National School of Music, University of Brazil, and at the Brazilian Conservatory of Music, Rio de Janeiro; Studied further at the Institute de Musicologie at the University of Paris, with Chailley; Musicology with Gilbert Chase at Tulane University, PhD 1966. *Career:* Joined faculty of University of Illinois and was appointed Professor of Music at the University of Texas, 1974; Associate Editor of the Yearbook for Inter-American Musical Research, 1969–75; Editor, Music Section of the Handbook of Latin American Studies, 1970–74; Editor of Ethnomusicology, 1974–78, and Latin American Music Review, from 1980; Editorial Adviser and major contributor to the New Grove Dictionary of Music and Musicians, 1970–80. *Publications include:* The Beginnings of Musical Nationalism in Brazil (Detroit 1971); Music in Latin America: An Introduction, 1977; Heitor Villa-Lobos: The Search for Brazil's Musical Soul, 1994. *Address:* c/o New Grove Dictionary, 25 Ecclestone Place, Victoria, London WC1, England.

**BEHLE, Renate;** Austrian singer (mezzo-soprano); *Professor, Hochschule für Musik und Theater, Hamburg*; b. Graz. *Education:* University and Music Academy of Graz. *Career:* Sang as mezzo-soprano at Gelsenkirchen, 1979–82; Hanover State Opera, 1982–97, as Minnie, Mozart's Elettra, Leonore in Fidelio, Sieglinde, Tosca, the Marschallin and Ariadne; Other Strauss roles include the Dyer's Wife in Die Frau ohne Schatten, 1993–, and Chrysothemis (at Barcelona, 1997); Guest engagements at Hamburg, Cologne, La Scala Milan (as Salome) and Los Angeles (Isolde, 1997); 20th Century repertory includes Agave in Henze's Bassarids, Shostakovich's Katarina and Montezuma in Rihm's Die Eroberung vom Mexico, all at Hamburg; Katya Kabanova; New productions of Fidelio and Die Walküre at Stuttgart; Tristan und Isolde in Houston; Sieglinde and Senta in Hamburg; Dyer's Wife, Salome, Leonore and Isolde in Dresden and all three Brünnhildes in Cologne. Concerts include the Dvořák Requiem, the Shostakovich 14th Symphony in Leipzig and Beethoven's Ninth in Granada, 1997; Zemlinsky's Lyrische Sinfonie in Amsterdam and Munich; Mahler's Symphony No. 8 on tour with Michael Gielen and the Südwestfunk-Sinfonieorchester; Guest Visit to Carnegie Hall, New York with Bernd Alois Zimmermann's Requiem for a Young Poet; Fidelio in Valencia; Siegfried with the Bamberg Symphony Orchestra and Schoenberg's Gurrelieder at the Ravinia Festival; Further engagements include Die Walküre in Austin, Texas, and Die Frau ohne Schatten in Essen; Sang the Götterdämmerung Brünnhilde at Bonn 2000; Orfrud, Klytemänstra in Hamburg and Dresden 2005; Schönberg's Erwartung in Montreal and Glasgow 2005; Herodias in Cologne 2005; Prof., Hochschule für Musik und Theater, Hamburg 2000–. *Recordings include:* Zemlinsky's Der Kreidekreis and Spohr's Jessonda, Die Enberung o. Mexico (W. Ruhm, Penthesilea), Fidelio/Walküre DVD, Stuttgart. *Honours:* Kammersängerin Staatsoper Hannover 1987. *Current Management:* c/o Haydn Rawstron Ltd, 36 Station Road, London, SE20 7BQ, England. *Website:* www.haydn-rawstron.com; www .renate-behle.de.

**BEHNKE, Anna-Katharina;** Austrian singer (soprano); b. 1964, Wuppertal, Germany; d. of Georg Nowak; m.; one d. *Education:* Munich Musikhochschule. *Career:* debut, Vienna Kammeroper as Mozart's Susanna 1986; wide repertoire includes roles as Aida, Desdemona, Elisabeth in Tannhäuser, Chrysothemis, Lulu (Basle 1994, Karlsruhe 1995, debut at Opéra Bastille, Paris 1998), Shostakovich's Lady Macbeth (Karlsruhe 1996), Marschallin (Munich 1996), Bartók's Judith (Halle 1996–2000), Lucia di Lammermoor (Nat. Theatre, Prague 1998), Korngold's Violanta (Bergen 1998), Die Frau in Schoenberg's Erwartung (BBC Wales 1999), Gutrune and Senta (Trieste 2001), the Arabella (Paris 2002), Beethoven's Leonore (Kassel, Mainz, Graz, Wiesbaden and Antwerp 2002), Elsa in Lohengrin (Essen 2002) Marietta (Braunschweig 2003), Janáček's Fox in Cunning Little Vixen (La Scala, Milan 2003), Emila Marty in The Makropoulos Case (Braunschweig 2004), Salome (Bologna, Nuremberg, Hanover, Mannheim, Düsseldorf, La Scala, Milan debut 2002, Tokyo 2004), Senta (Moscow debut 2004, Rome debut 2004). *Current Management:* Herwald Artists Management, Strasse des Roten Kreuzes 64, 76228 Karlsruhe, Germany. *E-mail:* info@herwald-artists.com. *Website:* www.herwald-artists.com.

**BEHR, Randall;** Conductor and Pianist; b. 1958, USA. *Career:* Conducted Peter Hall's production of Salome at Los Angeles Music Center, 1989; Has returned to Los Angeles for La Traviata, Tosca (with Maria Ewing and Placido Domingo) and Peter Hall's production of Die Zauberflöte, 1993; Other repertory includes the Oliver Knussen double bill, Orfeo ed Euridice, Nixon in China, Così fan tutte, Die Frau ohne Schatten, La Bohème and Vivaldi's Orlando Furioso; Music Director of Long Beach Opera, California; Peter Brook's La Tragédie de Carmen on Broadway; Conducted La Traviata at the Liceu, Barcelona, 1992; Die Walküre in Valencia and Tancredi at Bilbao, with Marilyn Horne; Vienna Staatsoper debut, 1993–94, Madama Butterfly; Hansel and Gretel at Toronto, 1998; Appearance as pianist with Maria Ewing at Covent Garden and at the Teatro Comunale Florence, Théâtre du Châtelet Paris, the Vienna Konzerthaus and the Opéra de Lyon.

**BEHRENS, Hildegard;** German singer (soprano); b. 1937, Oldenburg; m. Seth Schneidmann. *Education:* Freiburg Music Conservatory. *Career:* opera debut, Freiburg 1971; resident mem. Deutsche Oper am Rhein, Düsseldorf; has appeared with Frankfurt Opera, Teatro Nacional de San Carlo, Lisbon,

Vienna State Opera, Metropolitan Opera, New York; soloist, Chicago Symphony Orchestra 1984; appeared in Jenufa, Salzburg Festival 2001. *Current Management:* Herbert H. Breslin Inc., W 57th Street, New York, NY 10019, USA.

**BEHRMAN, David;** Composer; b. 16 Aug. 1937, Salzburg, Austria. *Education:* Studied privately in New York with Wallingford Riegger and at Princeton with Walter Piston; European studies with Henri Pousseur and Karlheinz Stockhausen. *Career:* From 1966 toured widely in the US with the Sonic Arts Union, giving performances of electronic music; Associated with John Cage, David Tudor and Gordon Mumma at the Merce Cunningham Dance Company, 1970–76; Formerly Artist-in-Residence at Mills College, Oakland, serving as Co-Director of the Center for Contemporary Music. *Compositions include:* Players with Curtains, 1966; Wave Train, 1966; Runthrough, 1967; For Nearly an Hour, 1968; A New Team Takes Over, 1969; Pools of Phase-locked Loops, 1972; Cloud Music, 1974–79; Figure in a Clearing, 1977; On the Other Ocean, 1977; Touch Tones, 1979; Indoor Geyser, 1979–81; Singing Stick, 1981; She's Wild, 1981; Sound Fountain, 1982; 6-Circle, 1984; Orchestral Construction Set, 1984; Interspecies Smalltalk, 1984; Installation for La Villett, 1985. *Recordings include:* Many albums of experimental music. *Address:* c/o ASCAP, ASCAP Building, 1 Lincoln Plaza, New York, NY 10023, USA.

**BEILMAN, Douglas;** Violinist; b. 1965, Kansas, USA. *Education:* Studied at Juilliard and the New England Conservatory, with Dorothy DeLay. *Career:* Co-founded the Sierra Quartet and performed at the Olympic Music Festival; Co-founded the New Zealand String Quartet, 1987, under the auspices of the Music Federation of New Zealand; Debut concert in Wellington, May 1988; Concerts at the Tanglewood School in USA, Banff International Competition in Canada and performances with the Lindsay Quartet at the 1990 International Festival of the Arts, Wellington; Soloist with New Zealand Symphony Orchestra and Artist-in-Residence at Victoria University, Wellington; Tour to Australia, 1990, for Musica Viva Australia; Tours of New Zealand, 1992, and concerts in New York, 1993. *Current Management:* Ingpen & Williams Ltd, 7 St George's Court, 131 Putney Bridge Road, London, SW15 2PA, England.

**BEKKU, Sadao;** Composer; b. 24 May 1922, Tokyo, Japan. *Education:* studied with Milhaud, Rivier and Messiaen at the Paris Conservatoire, 1951–54. *Career:* teacher in Tokyo; mem. Japanese branch of International Society for Contemporary Music (pres. 1968–73). *Compositions include:* Operas: A Story of Three Women, Tokyo, 1965; Prince Arima, Tokyo, 1967; Aoi-no-ue, Tokyo, 1981; Two Japanese Suites, 1955, 1958; String Quartet, 1955; Two Prayers for Orchestra, 1956; Symphonies for Strings, 1959; Piano Sonatina, 1965; Kaleidoscope for Piano, 1966; Violin Sonata, 1967; Violin Concerto, 1969; Three Paraphrases for Piano, 1968; Sonata in Classical Style for Piano, 1969; Viola Concerto, 1972; Piano Concerto, 1981; 5 Symphonies, 1962, 1977, 1984, 1991, 1999; Cello Concerto, 1997. *Recordings:* works by Sadao Bekku: Symphony No. 3, Spring; Symphony No. 4, The Summer 1945; Symphony No. 5, piano concerto, violin concerto, cello concerto. *Publications include:* The Occult in Music 1972. *Address:* 8-4-18-503 Shimorenjaku, Mitakashi, Tokyo, Japan.

**BELAMARIC, Miro;** Composer and Conductor; b. 9 Feb. 1935, Sibenik, Dalmatia. *Education:* Studied with Milan Horvat and Stjepan Sulek at the Zagreb Academy of Music; Lovro von Matacic in Salzburg; Sergiu Celibidache in Siena. *Career:* Conductor of the Symphony Orchestra of Zagreb Radio from 1959; Chief Conductor of the Komedija Theatre and from 1978 Chief Conductor of Zagreb Opera; Assistant to Karajan at Salzburg Festival, 1965–68, to Karl Böhm, 1975–77. *Compositions include:* Operas: The Love of Don Perlimplin, Zagreb, 1975; Don Juan–ein Rebell für alle Zeiten, 1983. *Honours:* Winner, Vienna State Opera Competition for Don Juan, 1983. *Address:* c/o Vienna Staatsoper, Opernring 2, 1010 Vienna, Austria.

**BELCOURT, Emile;** Singer (Tenor); b. 1934, Saskatchewan, Canada. *Education:* Academy of Music, Vienna; Paris with Pierre Bernac and Germaine Lubin. *Career:* Early opera appearances in Germany and France; Paris Opéra Comique as Pelléas; Sang in Debussy's opera for Scottish Opera, 1962; Covent Garden 1963, as Gonzalez in L'Heure Espagnole; Sadler's Wells/English National Opera from 1963, in Die Fledermaus, Orpheus in the Underworld, Bluebeard, The Violins of St Jacques, Patience, Salome and Lucky Peter's Journey, Loge in The Ring; Sang in premieres of Bennett's A Penny for a Song, 1967; Hamilton's The Royal Hunt of the Sun, 1977; Blake's Toussaint l'ouverture, 1977; Lead in stage musicals Man of La Mancha and Kiss me Kate; Canadian Opera debut in Heloise and Abelard, 1973; San Francisco, 1982, as Herod in Salome; Sang in the Covent Garden premiere of Berg's Lulu, 1981. *Recordings include:* Loge in The Ring Cycle, conducted by Reginald Goodall. *Address:* c/o English National Opera, London Coliseum, St Martin's Lane, London WC2N 4ES, England.

**BELKIN, Boris;** Belgian violinist; b. 26 Jan. 1948, Sverdlovsk, USSR. *Education:* violin studies aged six, Central Music School, Moscow, Moscow Conservatory with Yankelevitz and Andrievsky. *Career:* public appearances from 1955; emigrated 1974; debut in West, 1974 with Zubin Mehta and the Israel Philharmonic; orchestras with which he has appeared include Berlin Philharmonic, Concertgebouw, Israel Philharmonic, Los Angeles Philharmonic, Philadelphia, Cleveland; Season 1987–88, Pittsburgh, Royal Philharmonic and Tokyo Philharmonic Orchestras; conductors include Muti, Bernstein, Maazel, Haitink, Mehta, Ashkenazy and Steinberg. *Recordings:* Paganini

Concerto No. 1 with the Israel Philharmonic; Tchaikovsky and Sibelius Concertos with the Philharmonia Orchestra; Prokofiev's Concertos with the Zürich Tonhalle Orchestra; Brahms Concerto with the London Symphony; Glazunov and Shostakovich Concerto No. 1 with the Royal Philharmonic; Brahms Sonatas with Dalberto. *Honours:* winner Soviet National Competition for Violinists 1972. *Current Management:* Terry Harrison Artists Management, The Orchard, Market Street, Charlbury, Oxfordshire OX7 3PJ, England. *Telephone:* (1608) 810330. *Fax:* (1608) 811331. *E-mail:* artists@terryharrison.force9.co.uk.

**BELL, Christopher,** BMus, MMus; British conductor; *Chorus Director, Grant Park Music Festival, Chicago*; b. 1961, Belfast, Northern Ireland. *Career:* Assoc. Conductor BBC Scottish Symphony Orchestra 1989–91; Chorusmaster Royal Scottish Nat. Orchestra 1989–2002; Artistic Dir Edinburgh Royal Choral Union 1993–94; Principal Guest Conductor State Orchestra of Victoria, Australia 1997–99; Founder and Music Dir Ulster Youth Choir 1999–2004; Chorus Dir Grant Park Music Festival, Chicago USA, Belfast Philharmonic Choir; Chorusmaster of RSNO Jr Chorus; Artistic Dir and Founder Nat. Youth Choir of Scotland and Children's Classic Concerts; conducted Royal Philharmonic, London Philharmonic, Ulster, Scottish Chamber, City of London Sinfonia, London Concert, RTE Nat. Symphony and Bournemouth Symphony Orchestras; overseas has worked with Duisburg Symphony Orchestra, Basel Symphony Orchestra, Dutch Radio Symphony, Brabants Orkest, Orquesta Filharmonica de Gran Canaria, Noord Nederlands Orkest, Philharmonie of Essen, New Zealand, Melbourne and Perth Symphony Orchestras;. *Honours:* Scotsman of the Year Award for Creative Talent 2001, Charles Grove Prize for his contrib. to cultural life in Scotland and rest of UK 2003. *Current Management:* Robert Gilder & Co., Enterprise House, 59–65 Upper Ground, London, SE1 9PQ, England. *Telephone:* (20) 7928-9008. *Fax:* (20) 7928-9755. *E-mail:* rgilder@robert-gilder.com.

**BELL, Donald (Munro);** Professor and Baritone; b. 19 June 1934, Burnaby, British Columbia, Canada. *Education:* Royal College of Music, 1953–55; Berlin, Private and in the Stadtische Oper Studio; Papers presented at: Phenomenon of Singing, Memorial University NFLD, Using Digital Technology in a Voice Lesson, 1997; XIV International Congress of Phonetic Sciences, co-author Dr Michael Dobrovolsky, Acoustic Characteristics of Vibrato Onset in Singing, San Francisco, 1999. *Career:* Debut: Wigmore Hall, 1958; Bayreuth, 1958, The Nightwatchman in Meistersinger, 1959–1960; the Herald in Lohengrin, the Steersman in Tristan and Isolde; CBC, BBC, NOS Holland, WDR, Nord Deutsche Rundfunk, Germany; Appeared at Luzern Festival with Thomas Beecham, 1959, Glyndebourne in 1963 as the Speaker in Die Zauberflöte; Grand Théâtre, Geneva, London Royal Festival Hall, Royal Albert Hall, by invitation at the opening of Lincoln Center, New York and Carnegie Hall with the Philadelphia Orchestra and many other venues; mem, Rotary Club; NATS. *Honours:* Recipient of various honours and awards. *Address:* University of Calgary, Department of Music, 2500 University Drive NW, Calgary, Alberta T2N 1N4, Canada.

**BELL, Donaldson;** Singer (Bass); b. 1958, Ayrshire, Scotland. *Education:* Royal Scottish Academy, Glasgow. *Career:* Company principal with the Royal Opera from 1978; Appearances in such operas as Werther, La fanciulla del West, Die Entführung, Der Rosenkavalier, Die Meistersinger (Night-Watchman), Die Zauberflöte, La Traviata, and Death in Venice; Royal Opera House education workshops; Oratorio and recital engagements in Britain and abroad. *Address:* c/o Royal Opera House (contracts), Covent Garden, London, WC2, England. *Telephone:* (20) 7240 1200. *Fax:* (20) 7212 9502.

**BELL, Elizabeth,** BA, BS; Composer; b. 1 Dec. 1928, Cincinnati, OH, USA; m. 1st Frank D. Drake 1953, three s.; m. 2nd Robert E. Friou 1983. *Education:* Wellesley Coll., Wellesley, MA, Juilliard School of Music, New York; studied with Peter Mennin, Vittorio Giannini, Paul Alan Levi. *Career:* performances throughout USA, also Russia, Ukraine, Bulgaria, Armenia, Japan, Australia, Canada, South America; four retrospective concerts in Ithaca, NY 1973, Cincinnati 1985, New York 1991, 1998, 2003; Music critic for Ithaca Journal, 1971–1975, now independent; radio and television interviews; mem., founder and officer, now Dir, New York Women Composers; mem. of the Board of Governors, American Composers' Alliance. *Compositions include:* Variations and Interludes for piano, 1952; String Quartet, 1957; Songs of Here and Forever, 1970; Fantasy-Sonata for cello and piano, 1971; Symphony No. 1, 1971; 2nd Sonata for piano, 1972; Soliloquy for solo cello, 1980; Loss-Songs for soprano and piano, 1983; Perne in a Gyre for clarinet, violin, cello and piano, 1984; Duovarios for 2 pianos, 1987; Millennium for soprano, clarinet and piano, 1988; Spectra for 11 instruments, 1989; Night Music for piano, 1990; River Fantasy for flute and string trio, 1991; Andromeda for piano, string orchestra and percussion, 1993; Les Neiges d'Antan, Sonata for violin and piano, 1998. *Recordings:* 2nd Sonata; Perne in a Gyre; Millennium; Andromeda; Night Music; Variations and Interludes; The Music of Elizabeth Bell (includes Andromeda, String Quartet, Perne in a Gyre, Symphony No. 1); Snows of Yesteryear (includes Spectra, Songs of Here and Forever, Duovarios, Les Neiges d'Antan); CDs on Classic Masters, North/South Records, Vienna Modern Masters, Master Musicians Collective. *Honours:* first prize, Utah Composers' Competition 1986, Grand Prize 1996; Delius Prize 1994; awards from Meet-The-Composer and New York Council for the Arts. *Current Management:* American Composers' Alliance. *Address:* 21 Beech Lane, Tarrytown, NY 10591-3001, USA. *Telephone:* (914) 631-4361. *Fax:* (914) 631-6444. *E-mail:* ebelfri@earthlink.net.

**BELL, Emma;** British singer (soprano); b. 1970, Leamington Spa, England; m. Finnur Bjarnason; one s. *Education:* Royal Acad., London with Joy Mammer. *Career:* sang Handel's Radamisto and Salustia (Alessandro Severo) and Lia in Debussy's L'Enfant Prodigue at the RAM; Handel's Rodelinda for the Glyndebourne Tour 1998, and at the Festival 1999; season 1999–2000 with Mozart's Exsultate Jubilate K165 at the QEH and Elvira in Don Giovanni for Opera North; sang Handel's Rodelinda at the Royal Festival Hall 2002; mem. of co., Komische Oper, Berlin 2002–05, singing Mimi in La Bohème, the Countess in Marriage of Figaro; sang Vitellia in La Clemenza di Tito for ENO 2005; Covent Garden debut as Leonore in Nielsen's Maskarade 2005. *Recordings:* Emma Bell 2004, Handel Arias (with Richard Egarr and the Scottish Chamber Orchestra) 2005. *Honours:* Yamaha Music Foundation of Europe Scholarship, RAM Dove Prize, Kathleen Ferrier Award 1988, Borletti-Buitoni Trust grant 2003. *Current Management:* Askonas Holt Ltd, Lonsdale Chambers, 27 Chancery Lane, London, WC2A 1PF, England. *Telephone:* (20) 7400-1700. *Fax:* (20) 7400-1799. *E-mail:* info@askonasholt.co.uk. *Website:* www.askonasholt.co.uk.

**BELL, Joshua;** American violinist; b. 9 Dec. 1967, Indiana. *Career:* youngest guest soloist at a Philadelphia Orchestra Subscription concert 1982; European tour with St Louis Symphony 1985; German tour with Indianapolis Symphony 1987; European tour with Dallas Symphony 1997; European tours with Nat. Symphony Orchestra 2002, Minnesota Orchestra 2003; guest soloist with numerous orchestras in USA, Canada, Europe; has also appeared in USA and Europe as a recitalist; played premiere of violin concerto by Nicholas Maw, written for him, with Philharmonia Orchestra 1993; Visiting Prof. at RAM, London. *Recordings:* Mendelssohn and Bruch concertos with the Academy of St Martin-in-the-Fields and Sir Neville Marriner, Tchaikovsky and Wieniawski concertos with the Cleveland Orchestra and Vladimir Ashkenazy, recital album of Brahms, Paganini, Sarasate and Wieniawski with Samuel Sanders, Lalo Symphonie Espagnole and Saint-Saëns Concerto with Montreal Symphony Orchestra and Charles Dutoit, Franck, Fauré and Débussy, Chausson Concerto for violin, piano and string quartet with Thibaudet and Isserlis, Poème with Royal Philharmonic Orchestra and Andrew Litton, Mozart Concertos Nos 3 and 5 with the English Chamber Orchestra and Peter Maag, Prokofiev violin concertos with Montréal Symphony Orchestra and Charles Dutoit, Barber and Walton concertos and Bloch Baal Shem with Baltimore Symphony Orchestra and David Zinman, recital disc with Olli Mustonen, Gershwin Fantasy with London Symphony Orchestra and John Williams, Short Trip Home with Edgar Meyer, The Red Violin film soundtrack with Philharmonia Orchestra, Sibelius Goldmark Concertos with Los Angeles Philharmonic Orchestra and Esa-Pekka Salonen, Maw Concerto for violin with London Philharmonic Orchestra and Roger Norrington, Bernstein Serenade and West Side Story Suite with Philharmonia Orchestra and David Zinman, Beethoven and Mendelssohn concertos with Camerata Salzburg and Sir Roger Norrington, Irish film soundtrack, Tchaikovsky Violin Concerto 2005. *Honours:* Gramophone Award for Best Concerto Recording 1998 (for Barber Concerto), Mercury Music Award 2000, Acad. Award – Best Soundtrack for Red Violin, Grammy Award 2001. *Current Management:* IMG Artists, Lovell House, 616 Chiswick High Road, London, W4 5RX, England. *Telephone:* (20) 7957-5800. *Fax:* (20) 7957-5801. *E-mail:* artistseurope@imgartists.com. *Website:* www.imgartists.com.

**BELLING, Susan;** Opera Singer (Soprano); b. 3 May 1943, Bronx, NY, USA. *Education:* Chatham Square Music School, 1958–60; Kathryn Long School, 1965–67; Metropolitan Opera Studio, 1964–67; Manhattan School of Music, 1960–63. *Career:* Masterclasses and workshops at Stanford University, California, 1978, University of Houston, 1978, and Manhattan School of Music, 1984; Faculty, New School of Social Research, 1986–; Over 100 American and world premieres; Sang title role in Reimann's Melusine for Santa Fe Opera, and Kirchner's Lily with New York City Opera; Performance of Arnold Schoenberg's Second Quartet with Erich Leinsdorf and the Boston Symphony; Sang Belinda in Dido and Aeneas for Metropolitan Opera's premiere season of the Forum Opera, Lincoln Center; Performed on numerous occasions with conductor James Levine in such roles as Zerlina in Don Giovanni at Hollywood Bowl, Papagena in Magic Flute with Cleveland Concert Associates, as soprano soloist in A Midsummer Night's Dream and the Mahler Fourth Symphony with the Chicago Symphony, and with Atlanta Symphony in The Marriage of Figaro; Debut in Europe, Baroque Festival of Venetian Music, Castelfranco, Veneto and Teatro Olimpico, Italy, 1977; Numerous other performances include Haydn's Lord Nelson Mass with Minnesota Orchestra, Neville Marriner conducting, and Pamina in The Magic Flute. *Address:* c/o Allied Artists Bureau, Michael Leavitt, 195 Steamboat Road, Great Neck, NY 11024, USA.

**BELLO, Vincenzo;** Singer (Tenor); b. 1950, Mogliano, Treviso, Italy. *Career:* Debut: Manrico in Il Trovatore, Treviso, 1975; Appearances throughout Italy from 1975 and at Barcelona and Munich; Sang Manrico at Verona and the Metropolitan, New York, 1978; Festival engagements at Macerata as Alfredo, (1978); Orange as Verdi's Macduff and at Florence as Ismaele in Nabucco, 1977; Sang Donizetti's Edgardo and Rodolfo in La Bohème at Brescia, Ruggero in La Rondine at Venice; Venice and Trieste, 1990–91 as Edgardo, Rodolfo in Luisa Miller and Arturo in Bellini's La Straniera; Further appearances at Covent Garden, as Verdi's Riccardo, 1988 and at Lisbon, in Roberto Devereux. *Honours:* Winner, Toti dal Monte Competition, 1975. *Address:* c/o Teatro Comunale, Riva Novembre 1, 34121 Trieste, Italy.

**BELLU, Cristina;** Cellist; b. 7 Feb. 1968; m. James A Holzwarth, 29 Feb 1992. *Education:* Diploma, Violoncello, 1991; Chicago Musical College, Roosevelt University, 1994. *Career:* Member, Civic Orchestra of Chicago. Appearances with Orchestra da Camera Fiorentina, Orchestra Lirico-Sinfonica del Teatro del Giglio di Lucca, University of Chicago Symphony Orchestra; Chicago Chamber Orchestra; Orchestra del Maggio Musicale Fiorentino; Numerous performances world-wide; Co-founder, Operacion Tango group; Professor of Violoncello, Ecole Nationale de Musique, Mulhouse, France. *Recordings:* Operacion Tango en Concert, 1999. *Address:* 11 Avenue Marechal Foch, 68100 Mulhouse, France.

**BELLUCCI, Giacomo;** Composer; b. 20 Jan. 1928, Recanati, Italy. *Education:* Classical Studies Certificate, Lyceum; Studied at Rossini's Conservatory, Pesaro, with Giorgi and Rome's S Cecilia with Margola and Mortari; Diploma in Composition, 1961; Conducting with Ferrara. *Career:* Conductor of orchestra and choir (also in lyric stage and Polyphony), performing in Italy and abroad (Europe and USA); Founder and Director of Recanati's Gigli Music Institute, 1977–82; Professor at Rossini's Conservatory, Pesaro, 1965–98; Principal of various Italian conservatories, 1982–90. *Recordings:* RAI; ORF; Suisse Romande. *Compositions:* Coreographie (Ballet); Il Punto (opera ballet); 3 symphonies; 3 overtures; 3 suites; 16 concertos for solo instrument and orchestra; 16 string quartets; 7 trios; 5 oratorios; 2 psalms; other orchestral compositions; many chamber works for various instruments, voice, organ, and sacred music. *Publications:* Many articles, texts and essays on music, critical notes to concertos for dailies and periodicals. *Address:* 5 via Zanucchi, 61100 Pesaro, Italy.

**BELLUGI, Piero;** Italian conductor; *Musical Director, Teatro Massimo;* b. 14 July 1924, Florence; s. of Mario Bellugi and Giulia Favilli; m. Ursula Herzberger 1954 (divorced); five c. *Education:* Conservatorio Cherubini, Florence, Accad. Chigiana, Siena, Akad. des Mozarteums, Salzburg and Tanglewood, Mass., USA. *Career:* Musical Dir Oakland (Calif.) and Portland (Ore.) Symphony Orchs. 1955–61; Perm. Conductor, Radio Symphony Orchestras, Turin 1967; Prof. courses for orchestral players and conductor, Italian Youth Orchestra 1981–; Guest Conductor, La Scala, Milan (début 1961), Vienna State Opera, Rome Opera, Aix-en-Provence Festival, Berlin Radio, Paris, Rome S. Cecilia, Chicago, San Francisco Operas, etc; Musical Dir Teatro Massimo, Palermo. *Honours:* Hon. mem. Nat. Acad. Luigi Cherubini of Music, Letters and Arts. *Address:* Via della Montagnola, 50027 Strada in Chianti, Florence, Italy. *Telephone:* (55) 858556. *Fax:* (55) 858556. *E-mail:* pierobellugi@tin.it (home).

**BĚLOHLÁVEK, Jiří;** Czech musician and conductor; *Chief Conductor, BBC Symphony Orchestra;* b. 24 Feb. 1946, Prague; m. Anna Fejérová 1971; two d. *Education:* Acad. of Performing Arts, Prague with Sergiu Celibidache. *Career:* Conductor Orchestra Puellarum Pragensis (chamber orchestra), Prague 1967–72; Asst Conductor Czech Philharmonic Orchestra 1970–71; Conductor Brno State Philharmonic Orchestra 1971–77; Chief Conductor Prague Symphony Orchestra 1977–90; Conductor Czech Philharmonic Orchestra 1981–90, Prin. Conductor and Music Dir 1990–92; Conductor Int. Philharmonic Youth Orchestra, Prague 1987–; founder and Music Dir Prague Philharmonia 1994–; Principal Guest Conductor BBC Symphony Orchestra 1995–2000, Chief Conductor 2006–; Prof. Acad. of Music, Prague 1995–; Principal Guest Conductor Nat. Theatre Prague 1998; guest appearances with numerous orchestras, including USSR State Symphony Orchestra, BBC Philharmonic, BBC Nat. Orchestra of Wales, Scottish Nat. Orchestra, Royal Liverpool Philharmonic, City of Birmingham Symphony, Berlin Philharmonic, Vienna Symphony Orchestra, Leipzig Gewandhaus, Stockholm Philharmonic, Bavarian Radio Orchestra, Dresden Philharmonic, Deutsche Kammerphilharmonie, Tonhalle (Zürich) Orchestra, New York Philharmonic, Boston Symphony Orchestra, St Louis Orchestra, Washington Nat. Orchestra, Toronto Symphony Orchestra, NHK Philharmonic (Tokyo). *Honours:* Supraphon Prize 1977, Artist of Merit 1986, Supraphon Golden Disc 1986, 1987, 1994, 1999, Diapason d'Or 1992, Barclay Theatre Award 2000, Medal for Merit, Prague 2001. *Address:* c/o BBC Symphony Orchestra, BBC Maida Vale Studios, Delaware Road, London, W9 2LG, England (office). *Telephone:* (20) 7765-2956 (office). *Fax:* (20) 7286-3251 (office). *E-mail:* bbcso@bbc.co.uk (office). jiri.belohlavek@bon.cz (home). *Website:* www.bbc.co.uk/orchestras/symphonyorchestra (office).

**BELSKAYA, Nina;** Violist; b. 1960, Moscow, Russia. *Education:* Studied at Moscow Conservatoire with Professor Strakhovos. *Career:* Member of the Prokofiev Quartet, founded at the Moscow Festival of World Youth and the International Quartet Competition at Budapest; Many concerts in the former Soviet Union and on tour to Czechoslovakia, Germany, Austria, USA, Canada, Spain, Japan and Italy; Repertoire includes works by Haydn, Mozart, Beethoven, Schubert, Debussy, Ravel, Tchaikovsky, Bartók and Shostakovich. *Current Management:* Sonata, Glasgow, Scotland. *Address:* 11 North Park Street. Glasgow G20 7AA, Scotland.

**BELTON, Ian;** Violinist; b. 1959, England. *Education:* Studied at the Royal Northern College of Music; Diplomas, BMus, Manchester University; GRNCM; PPRNCM. *Career:* Founder member of the Brodsky String Quartet; Resident at Cambridge University for 4 years and later residencies at Dartington International Summer School, Devon; Concert engagements include the Shostakovich Quartets at the Queen Elizabeth Hall in London and performances at the Ludwigsburg and Schleswig-Holstein Festivals; New York debut at the Metropolitan Museum; Tours of Italy, North America,

Australia, Poland, Czechoslovakia, Istanbul and Japan; Complete quartets of Schoenberg for the BBC; French concerts include Théâtre du Châtelet, Paris; Concert in Amsterdam and performances at Berlin Festival, Carnegie Hall; Tour of Australia in 1993. *Recordings include:* Quartets of Elgar and Delius; Schubert A minor and Beethoven Op 74; Complete Quartets of Shostakovich; Borodin Quartet No. 2; Tchaikovsky Quartet No. 3; Collaboration with Elvis Costello entitled Juliet Letters. *Address:* c/o Brodsky Quartet, 21–22 Old Steine, Brighton BN1 1EG, England.

**BELTRAN, Tito;** Chilean singer (tenor); b. 1969. *Education:* Gothenburg Acad. and with Vera Rosza and Robin Stapleton, London. *Career:* roles include Nemorino, Ernesto, Edgardo, Rodolfo, Ruggero (La Rondine), Pinkerton, Rinuccio Italian Tenor (Der Rosenkavalier), Duca, Macduff, Ismaele, Alfredo, Tybalt, Tebaldo; has sung at Covent Garden (debut Rodolfo 1995), Opera North, Vienna (debut Nemorino 1997), Hamburg, Ludwigsfaafen, Bayerische Staatsoper Munich, Deutsche Oper Berlin, Leipzig, Mannheim, Opera Bastille (debut Der Rosenkavalier 2002), Toulouse, Bordeaux, La Scala (debut Der Rosenkavalier 2003), Genoa, Teatro Regio Torino, Parma, Arena di Verona, Roma, Lucca, Cosenza, Fenno, Monte Carlo, Geneva, Zurich, Gothenburg, Copenhagen, Norske Opera Oslo, Iceland, Menorca, Santiago Chile, Rio de Janeiro, Michigan (USA debut Rodolfo 1996), San Francisco, Orlando, Pittsburgh, Portland, New Nat. Theatre, Tokyo; numerous world-wide concerts and TV appearances; lives in Sweden. *Recordings:* four solo CD s for Suva Screen Classics: Tito, Romantica, A Tenor At The Movies, Amazing Grace; Celemin in La Dolores by Tomas Bretón (with Placido Domingo) for Decca. *Television:* sang Tybalt in Iambic Productions film of Romeo et Juliette (with Roberto Alagna and Angela Gheorghiu) (Channel 4) 2004. *Honours:* finalist, Cardiff Singer of the World Competition 1993, Opera Now Artist of the Year 1999. *Current Management:* c/o Penelope Marland Artists Management, 10 Roseneath Road, London, SW11 6AH, England. *Telephone:* (20) 7223-7319. *Fax:* (20) 7771-0675. *E-mail:* Penelope@marlandartists.fsnet.co .uk. *Website:* www.titobeltran.com.

**BELYAEV, Yevegeni;** Violinist; b. 1950, Crimea, Russia. *Career:* Co-Founder, Rachmaninov Quartet, 1974, under auspices of the Sochi State Philharmonic Society, Crimea; Many concerts in the former Soviet Union and from 1975–76 tours to Switzerland, Austria, Bulgaria, Norway and Germany; Participation in the 1976 Shostakovich Chamber Music Festival at Vilnius and in festivals in Moscow and St Petersburg; Repertoire has included works by Haydn, Mozart, Beethoven, Bartók, Schnittke, Shostakovich, Boris Tchaikovsky, Chalayev and Meyerovich. *Honours:* With the Rachmaninov Quartet: Prizewinner, First All-Union Borodin String Quartet Competition, 1987. *Current Management:* Sonata, Glasgow, Scotland. *Address:* 11 North Park Street, Glasgow G20 7AA, Scotland.

**BEN-OR, Nelly;** pianist and teacher; *Professor, Piano Department, Guildhall School of Music and Drama;* b. Warsaw, Poland. *Education:* Music High School Poland, Music Acad., Israel. *Career:* in Israel: awarded first prize in Mozart Competition; solo recitals, chamber music broadcasts; soloist with Radio Orchestra; in England: recitals in London, including Queen Elizabeth Hall, Wigmore Hall, St John's, Smith Square, for BBC and throughout the UK; recitals, broadcasts and masterclasses worldwide; teacher of the Alexander Technique 1963–; specialist in application of the Alexander Technique to piano playing; Prof. in Piano Dept, Guildhall School of Music and Drama 1975–; mem. Incorporated Soc. of Musicians, European Piano Teachers' Asscn (UK founder cttee mem.), Soc. of Teachers of the Alexander Technique. *Recordings:* Piano Variations (various composers), Beethoven Complete Bagatelles, Beethoven Piano Quartet op 16 (with Jerusalem String Trio), Chopin Dances, Debussy (Complete Images), Schubert Impromptus D899 and D935, Dvorak/Fibch Piano Quartets (with Jerusalem String Trio), Bach Toccata in D, Chopin (Mazurkas), Kinghorn piano sonata, Mazurkas from Poland and Mexico (Chopin, Szymanowski and Ponce). *Publications:* contrib. articles to various professional publications, including publications on the application of the Alexander Technique to piano playing. *Address:* c/o Roger Clynes, 23 Rofant Road, Northwood, Middlesex HA6 3BD, England (office). *Telephone:* (1923) 822268 (office). *Fax:* (1923) 822268 (office). *E-mail:* roger.clynes@virgin.net (office). *Website:* www .pianocourseswithalexandertechnique.com (office).

**BEN-YOHANAN, Asher;** Israeli composer and music educator; b. 22 May 1929, Kavala, Greece; m. Shoshana Zwibel; one s. one d. *Education:* studied oboe and piano; composition studies with Paul Ben-Haim, Israel, Aaron Copland, USA and Luigi Nono, Italy; studies with Gustave Reese and Jan La Rue, New York Univ.; MMus, Univ. of Michigan. *Career:* compositions performed in Israel, Europe, South America and Hong Kong; Head of Music Dept and Teacher of Theory, Thelma Yellin Music and Arts School, Tel-Aviv, Israel, 1966–87; Prof. of Music, Bar-Ilan Univ. 1973–96; mem. Israel Composers' League, Chair. 1989–92. *Compositions include:* Two Movements for Orchestra, 1959; String Quartet, 1962–64; Music for Orchestra, 1967; Chamber Music for 6, 1968; Quartetto Concertato, 1969; Mosaic, 1971; Concerto for String Orchestra, 1973; Four Summer Songs, 1974; Impressions for Piano, 1976; Soliloquy for Violin, 1977; Desert Winds for Flute, 1979; Three Songs without Titles, 1983; Episode for Trombone, 1984; Woodwind Quintet, 1985; Divertimento for Brass Trio, 1988–89; Hidden Feelings for Harp, 1990; Meditations for chamber orchestra, 1992, and other works. *Recordings include:* A Composer's Profile 2005. *Publications:* Music in Israel, A Short Survey 1975, Music Notation 1983. *Honours:* Morse Fellowship in Composi-

tion, Univ. of Cincinnati, USA 1971. *Address:* 4 Bloch Street, Tel-Aviv 64161, Israel (home).

**BENACKOVA, Gabriela;** Singer (Soprano); b. 25 March 1944, Bratislava, Czechoslovakia. *Education:* Bratislava Academy with Janko Blaho and Tatiana Kiesakova. *Career:* Debut: Prague National Theatre, 1970 as Natasha in War and Peace; Returned as Mimi, Marenka in The Bartered Bride, Jenůfa and Libuše in Smetana's opera, 1983; Appeared at Covent Garden in 1979 as Tatiana in Eugene Onegin, Cologne Opera in 1983 as Maddalena in Andrea Chénier, Vienna Staatsoper, 1985 as Marguerite in a new production of Faust directed by Ken Russell, San Francisco in 1986 as Jenůfa, Vienna Staatsoper in 1987 as Rusalka; Sang Desdemona at Stuttgart in 1990, Leonore at 1990 Salzburg Festival, Katya Kabanova at the Metropolitan in 1991; Season 1992 as Fidelio at Covent Garden; Sang Maddalena in Andrea Chénier at Zürich, 1994; Sang Wagner's Senta at Hamburg, 1996; Jenůfa at Zürich, 1998; Sang Desdemona at the New York Met, 1991, and Janáček's Emilia Marty at Brno, 2001. *Recordings:* Janáček's Jenůfa and The Cunning Little Vixen; The Bartered Bride; Libuše; Rusalka (Supraphon); Soloist in Janáček's Glagolitic Mass; Dvořák's Requiem. *Honours:* Prizewinner, Janáček Competition, Luhacovice in 1962; Winner, Dvořák Competition, Karlovy Vary in 1963; Czech National Artist in 1985. *Current Management:* Askonas Holt Ltd, Lonsdale Chambers, 27 Chancery Lane, London, WC2A 1PF, England. *Telephone:* (20) 7400-1700. *Fax:* (20) 7400-1799. *E-mail:* info@askonasholt.co .uk. *Website:* www.askonasholt.co.uk.

**BENARY, Barbara;** Composer and Gamelan Performer; b. 7 April 1946, Bay Shore, NY, USA. *Education:* BA, 1968, Sarah Lawrence College; PhD in Ethnomusicology, Wesleyan University, 1973. *Career:* Has played the violin and has performed on various stringed instruments of India, China and Bulgaria; In 1974 formed the Gamelan Son of Lion, an ensemble of Javanese instruments; Assistant Professor at Livingstone College, Rutgers University, New Jersey, 1973–80. *Compositions include:* Music Theatre: Three Sisters Who Are Not Sisters, 1967, The Only Jealousy Of Emer, 1970, The Interior Castle, 1973, The Gauntlet, 1976, Sanguine, 1976, The Tempest, 1981; Gamelan: Convergence, 1975, Braid, 1975, No Friends In An Auction, 1976, In Time Enough, 1978, Sleeping Braid, 1978, The Zen Story, 1979, In Scroll Of Leaves, 1980, Moon Cat Chant, 1980, Singing Braid, 1980, Solkattu, 1980, Sun Square, 1980, Exchanges, 1981, Hot-Rolled Steel, 1984; Dance Scores: Night Thunks, 1980, A New Pantheon, 1981, Engineering, 1981. *Address:* c/o American Music Center, 30 West 26th Street, Suite 1001, New York, NY 10010-2011, USA.

**BENDER, Madeline;** Singer (Soprano); b. 1970, USA. *Education:* Manhattan School of Music Opera Theater, Santa Fe Opera Apprentice Program. *Career:* Appearances as Ippolito in Traetta's Ippolito e Aricia at Montpellier, Mimi for Opera Birmingham, Ismene in Mitridate and Gluck's Eurydice at the Paris Châtelet; Tigrane in Handel's Radamisto at St Louis, Micaela in Carmen and Pannotchka in Rimsky's May Night for Sarasota Opera; Sister in Weill's Der Protangonist with the BBC Symphony Orchestra; Further concerts with the Cincinnati, Toronto, Detroit, National and St Louis Symphonies; Glyndebourne Festival debut as Helena in A Midsummer Night's Dream, 2001; Violetta for Opera Birmingham, 2001–2002. *Recordings include:* Babes in Toyland by Herbert. *Current Management:* Neil Funkhouser Artists Management, 105 Arden Street #5G, New York, NY 10040-1119, USA. *Telephone:* (212) 304-3796. *Fax:* (212) 304-4507. *E-mail:* neil@ funkhouserartists.com. *Website:* www.funkhouserartists.com. *Address:* c/o Glyndebourne Festival Opera, Glyndebourne, Lewes, Sussex, BN8 5UU, England.

**BENEDETTI, Nicola;** Scottish violinist; b. 1987, West Kilbride. *Education:* Yehudi Menuhin School, studies with Maciej Rakowski. *Career:* led the Nat. Children's Orchestra of Scotland aged eight; has performed at venues including Royal Festival Hall, QEH, St Martin-in-the-Fields, Wigmore Hall, Purcell Rooms, Glasgow Royal Concert Hall, Usher Hall, Glastonbury Classical Festival; performed with Scottish Symphony Orchestra at Scottish Proms, Glamis Castle 2004; invited to perform at opening of Scottish Parl. 2004; Carnegie Hall debut with Eos Orchestra of New York 2005. *Recordings:* Szymanowski, Violin Concerto No. 1 (with LSO and Daniel Harding) 2005. *Current Management:* c/o Vicky Corley-Smith, IMG Artists, Lovell House, 616 Chiswick High Road, London, W4 5RX, England. *Telephone:* (20) 7957-5800 (office). *Fax:* (20) 7957-5801 (office). *E-mail:* artistseurope@imgartists.com (office). *Website:* www.imgartists.com (office).

**BENEDICT, Roger;** Violist; b. 1962, England. *Education:* Studied with Patrick Ireland and Eli Goren at the Royal Northern College of Music. *Career:* Principal violist of the Philharmonia Orchestra and soloist in Strauss's Don Quixote at the Edinburgh Festival and Festival Hall, London; Vaughan Williams Flos Campi with the New London Orchestra and premiere of Michael Berkeley's Concerto, with Philharmonia Orchestra, 1994; Also plays concerto works by Mozart, Bartók, Walton and Berlioz with Philharmonia, Royal Philharmonic, Ulster Orchestra; Member of the Bell'Arte Ensemble with performances at Symphony Hall, Birmingham; Performed with Wanderer Trio, Hagai Shaham and Noriko Ogawa at the Bastad Festival in Sweden; Al Bustan Festival, Beirut with flautist Patrick Gallois and harpist Fabrice Pierre, 1998; On leaving the Philharmonia became regular principal of English Chamber Orchestra; Appointed Prof. at the Royal Northern Collage of Music, 1998; International engagements include performances in South Africa, Scandinavia, the Middle East and Japan; In 2002 moved to Australia,

Principal viola in the Sydney Symphony Orchestra; Artistic Director of James Fairfax Young Artists Program; Senior Lecturer at Sydney Conservatorium; solo tours of Japan, 2002; soloist with S.S.O. and other Australian Orchestras. *Address:* 9 Alison Street, Roseville, NSW, 2069, Australia. *Telephone:* (2) 9880–7005. *E-mail:* rogerbenedict@dodo.com.au.

**BENELLI, Ugo;** Italian singer (tenor); b. 20 Jan. 1935, Genoa; m. Angela Maria Patrone; one s. one d. *Education:* Scuola di Perfezionamento del Teatro alla Scala with Giulio Confalonieri. *Career:* debut, Piccola Scala 1960; festival appearances include Wexford, Glyndebourne, Salzburg, Vienna, Edinburgh, Aix-en-Provence, Wiesbaden and Rossini Opera Festival Pesaro; roles include Rossini's Almaviva, Lindoro, Don Ramiro, Bellini's Elvino, Donizetti's Nemorino, Ernesto and Tonio, Bizet's Nadir, Massenet's Des Grieux and Werther, Weber/Mahler's Die drei Pintos, Conte Riccardo (I Quattro Rusteghi), Contino Belfiore and Don Anchise (La Finta Giardiniera), Basilio (Le Nozze di Figaro), Hauk (The Makropulos Case), Hans Styx (Orphée aux Enfers) Jack O'Brien (Mahagonny), Falsacappa (Les Brigands di Offenbach), Truffaldino (L'Amour des trois oranges), Ernesto (Don Pasquale). *Recordings include:* Il Barbiere di Siviglia, La Cenerentola, Mozart's Requiem, I Pagliacci, Don Pasquale, La figlia del Reggimento, Il Cappello di Paglia di Firenze, L'Aio nell'imbarazzo, Elisabeth d'Inghilterra, Rossini's Messa di Gloria, La Spinalba, Le Nozze di Figaro, I'Italiana in Algeri, La Riconoscenza, Linda di Chamounix, La Buona Fígliola, Il Mondo della Luna, Il Dixit, Il Barone di Rocca Antica, La Finta Giardiniera, Il Giovedi Grasso, Il Crociato in Egitto, L'Innocenza Giustificata, La Rita, Il Campiello. *Honours:* La Cara Vella d'Oro, Genoa 1959, Ausgezeichnet mit der Tz-Rose, Munich 1972, Il Palco Scenico d'Oro 1979, Premio Regionale le Ligure 1983, La Margherita d'Oro, Santa Margherita Ligure 2001, Premio Melvin Jones Fellow 2001. *Address:* Viale Nazario Sauro, 6A Int. 4, 16145 Genoa, Italy. *Telephone:* (010) 311381 (home). *Fax:* (010) 311381 (home). *E-mail:* ugo.benelli@libero.it (home). *Website:* www .ugobenelli.com (home).

**BENEŠ, Jiří,** PhD; viola player and musicologist; b. 24 Sept. 1928, Komárno, Czechoslovakia; m. 1st; one s.; m. 2nd Zdenka Bubeníčkova; one d. *Education:* Univ. of Brno, Conservatory of Brno, Janáček Acad. of Musical Arts. *Career:* debut as viola player, Brno 1952; State Philharmonic Orchestra, Brno 1951–69; Moravian Quartet 1965–92; Dramaturg 1992–, including Brno Int. Music Festival (Moravian Autumn) 1993–; appearances on radio and television with Moravian Quartet, Czechoslovakia, Germany, Sweden, Italy; tours of most European countries; teacher, Janáček Acad. 1968–74, Conservatory of Brno 1969–82, Masaryk Univ. 2003–; mem. Czech Musical (Janáček) Soc. *Publications:* contrib. to professional journals, radio programme notes, record sleeve notes. *Honours:* Italian Quartet Prize 1965, Janáček Medal 1978, Prize, Novecento Musicale Europeo, Naples 1988, Czech Music Council Award 2002. *Address:* Filipova 19, 63500 Brno, Czech Republic. *Telephone:* (546) 220204. *E-mail:* benesova@mujbox.cz.

**BENESTAD, Finn;** Music Educator and Musicologist; b. 30 Oct. 1929, Kristiansand, Norway. *Education:* violin lessons with Ernst Glaser, 1947–50; music courses at Univ. of Oslo; MA, 1953; PhD, 1961. *Career:* teacher, 1950–59; music critic, 1953–61; Prof. of Musicology at Univ. of Trondheim, 1961–64, Univ. of Oslo, 1965–98; Chair., Collected Works of Grieg. *Publications:* Johannes Haarklou: mannen og verket, 1961; Waldemar Thrane: en pioner i norsk musikkliv, 1961; Musikklaere, 1963, 5th edition, 1977; Musikkhistorisk oversikt, 1965, 3rd edition, 1976; Editor, Norsk musikk: Studier i Norge, vol. 6, 1968; Editor, Skolens visebok, 1972; Co-author, Edvard Grieg: Mennesket og kunstneren, 1980, English edition as Edvard Grieg: The Man and The Artist, 1988; Co-author, Johan Svendsen: Mennesket og kunstneren, 1990 and Edvard Grieg, Chamber Music, 1993; Edvard Grieg: Brev til Frants Beyer 1872–1907 (co-editor with Bjarne Kortsen), 1993; Edvard Grieg: Dagböker (Diaries) 1865, 1866, 1905, 1906, 1907, editor, 1993; Edvard Grieg: Briefwechsel mit dem Musikverlag C F Peters 1863–1907 (co-editor with Hella Brock), 1997; Edvard Grieg und Julius Röntgen. Briefwechsel 1883–1907 (co-editor with Hanna de Vries Stavland), 1997; Edvard Grieg: Brev i utvalg 1862–1907, vols I–II, 1998; Edvard Grieg: Letters to Colleagues and Friends, 2000; Edvard Grieg: Diaries, Articles, Speeches (co-editor with W. H. Halverson), 2001. *Contributions:* articles in various journals and other publications. *Honours:* Fulbright Scholar, Univ. of California, Los Angeles, 1968–69; elected mem., Norwegian Acad. of Sciences and Letters, 1979; Royal Danish Acad. of Sciences and Letters, 1991; Academia Europaea, 1992. *Address:* Agder allé 4A, 4631 Kristiansand, Norway.

**BENGL, Volker;** Singer (Tenor); b. 19 July 1960, Ludwigshafen, Germany. *Education:* Mannheim-Heidelberg Musikhochschule in Munich. *Career:* Staatstheater am Gartnerplatz, Munich; Guest, Vienna, Berlin, Wiesbaden; Sang at Saarbrucken from 1985; Dresden Semperoper; Guest appearances in Essen, Brunswick, Karlsruhe and Heidelberg; Sang Jenik in The Bartered Bride at Kaiserslautern, 1990; Other roles include Max in Der Freischütz, Tamino, Belfiore in La Finta Giardiniera, Don José, Pinkerton and parts in operetta; As concert singer appeared in New York, 1989, Berlin (Bruckner F minor Mass and Te Deum) and elsewhere in Europe; Other Repertoire includes Bach Christmas Oratorio and Dvořák Requiem; Sang Wilhelm Meister in Mignon at the Munich Gärtnerplaztheater, 2000. *Compositions:* Wiegenlied, words and music, 1997. *Recordings include:* Vorhang auf; Schön is die Welt. *Address:* Marschalls h-6, 80802 Munich, Germany.

**BENGTSSON, Erling Blondal;** Cellist; b. 1932, Copenhagen, Denmark; m. Merete Bengtsson 1958, two s. *Education:* Studied with Piatigorsky at Curtis Institute, USA. *Career:* Debut: First public concert at age 4; First concerto with orchestra at age 10; Professor of Cello, Curtis Institute, USA, the Royal Danish Conservatory, Copenhagen; the Swedish Radio's Music Academy, Stockholm and the State Academy in Cologne; Professor at the School of Music, University of Michigan, Ann Arbor, USA, 1990–; Masterclasses at Aldeburgh in England, Switzerland, Scandinavia and USA. Played with most of the world's leading orchestras with such conductors as Monteux, Sargent, Lutoslawski, Pritchard, Dorati, Groves, Ehrling, Berglund, Temirkanov and Yansons; Scandinavian first performances of cello-concertos by Britten, Barber, Khatchaturian, Delius, Lutoslawski and Walton. *Recordings:* Over 50 albums; Complete standard repertoire for cello and orchestra; Many contemporary concertos dedicated to him; Beethoven and Brahms Sonatas; Bach Suites for Solo Cello; Rachmaninov and Shostakovich sonata; Kodály Solo-sonata; Reger suites; Sonatas by Barber, Debussy, Prokofiev, 2001. *Contributions:* Edited Bach and Reger Solo Cello Suites for the Internet publishing company .SheetMusicNow.com. *Honours:* Honours and awards include: Knight, first class, of the order of Dannebrog, Denmark; Grand Knight of the order of the Falcon, Iceland; The English Hyam Morrison Gold Medal for cello; The title "Chevalier du Violoncelle" by Indiana University; Award of Distinction, The RNCM Manchester International Cello Festival, 2001. *Current Management:* Tivoli Artists, Copenhagen. *Address:* 1217 Westmoorland, Ypsilanti, MI 48197, USA. *Website:* www.erlingbb.com.

**BENGUEREL, Xavier;** Spanish composer; b. 9 Feb. 1931, Barcelona. *Education:* studied in Santiago and Barcelona with Cristobal Taltabull. *Career:* represented Spain at ISCM Festival 1960. *Compositions include:* two violin sonatas 1953, 1959, String Quartet 1955, Concerto for piano and strings 1955, Cantata d'Amic i Amat 1959, Concerto for two flutes and strings 1961, Sinfonia Continua 1962, Successions for wind quartet 1960, Duo for clarinet and piano 1963, Nocturno for soprano, chorus and orchestra 1963, Violin Concerto 1965, Sinfonia per a un Festival 1966, Sinfonia for small orchestra 1967, Paraules de cada día for voice and chamber orchestra 1967, Musica for three percussionists 1967, Sinfonia for large orchestra 1969, Dialogue Orchestrale 1969, Musica Riservata for strings 1969, Crescendo for Organ 1970, Organ Concerto 1971, Arbor (cantata) 1972, Verses for guitar 1973, Destructio for orchestra 1973, Capriccio Stravagante for ensemble 1974, Thesis for chamber group, Concerto for percussion and orchestra 1976, Spleen (opera) 1984, Libre Vermell 1988 7 Faules de La Fontaine 1995, Dos Poemas de Charles Baudelaire for baritone and orchestra 1999, Dalí (opera) 1999, Concerto for piano and orchestra 2004. *Honours:* Composition Prize of the Barcelona Juventudes Musicales 1955, Luigi Dallapicola Award 1977. *Address:* c/o SGAE, Fernando VI 4, Apdo 484, 28080 Madrid 4, Spain. *Fax:* (93) 309 2294 (home).

**BENHAM, Hugh Raymond,** BA, PhD, ARCO; teacher, examiner and organist; b. 14 Dec. 1943, Westbury, England; m.; one d. *Education:* Univ. of Southampton. *Career:* teacher 1968–97; examiner 1980–92, 1996–; organist 1965–; mem. Royal Musical Asscn, Incorporated Soc. of Musicians. *Publications:* Latin Church Music in England c.1460–1575, John Taverner (complete edition, Early English Church Music), John Taverner: his Life and Music, Listening Tests for students; contrib. to Music & Letters, The Musical Times, The Music Review, Early Music, Plainsong and Medieval Music, Music Teacher, Classroom Music, New Grove Dictionary of Music and Musicians 2001, Oxford Dictionary of Nat. Biography 2004. *Address:* 11 North End Close, Chandler's Ford, Eastleigh, Hants SO53 3HY, England (home). *E-mail:* hugh .benham@talk21.com (home).

**BENINI, Maurizio;** Italian conductor; b. 1968. *Education:* Bologna Conservatory. *Career:* Principal Conductor, Philharmonic Orchestra, Teatro Communale, Bologna, 1984; opera debut at Bologna with Rossini's Il Signor Bruschino; Don Carlo and Rossini's Donna del Lago at La Scala, Milan; La Scala di Seta at Pesaro; engagements in Paris at the Opéra Bastille and Palais Garnier; Principal Conductor, Wexford Festival Opera, 1995–97, with Pacini's Saffo, Donizetti's Parisina, 1996; Mercadante's Elena da Feltre, 1997; New York Met debut, 1998, L'Elisir d'amore; Royal Opera debut, 1999, with Un giorno di regno, Festival Hall; other repertory includes Rossini's Zelmira, Lyon and Paris; Nabucco and Don Pasquale; 1999–2000 season: La Traviata, Deutsche Oper Berlin, La Sonnambula at La Scala and Faust at Opéra Bastille; season 2002–03 at Covent Garden, with La Sonnambula and Madama Butterfly. *Recordings:* Elena da Feltre. *Current Management:* Stage Door, Via Marconi 71, 40122 Bologna, Italy. *Telephone:* (051) 19 98 47 50. *Fax:* (051) 19 98 47 79. *E-mail:* info@stagedoor.it. *Website:* www.stagedoor.it.

**BENJAMIN, George William John,** FRCM; British composer, conductor, pianist and teacher; b. 31 Jan. 1960, London; s. of William Benjamin and Susan Benjamin (née Bendon). *Education:* Westminster School, Paris Conservatoire, King's Coll., Cambridge, Institut de recherche et coordination acoustique/musique, Paris. *Career:* first London orchestral performance, BBC Proms 1980; Prince Consort Prof. of Composition, RCM 1984–2001; Henry Purcell Prof. of Composition, King's Coll. London 2001–; has conducted widely in GB, Europe, USA, Australia and Far East; Prin. Guest Artist, Hallé Orchestra 1993–96; operatic conducting debut Pelléas et Mélisande, La Monnaie, Brussels 1999; Carte Blanche at Opéra Bastille, Paris 1992; founding Artistic Dir Wet Ink Festival, San Francisco Symphony Orchestra 1992, Meltdown Festival, South Bank 1993; Featured Composer, 75th Salzburg Festival 1995, Tanglewood Festival 1999, 2000, 2003, Deutsches Symphonie Orchester 2004–05, Strasbourg Musica Festival 2005, Spanish Nat. Orchestra 2005; London Symphony Orchestra Retrospective 'By George',

Barbican, London 2002–03; Artistic Consultant BBC Sounding the Century 1996–99; mem. Bavarian Acad. of Fine Arts 2000. *Publications:* orchestral works: Ringed by the Flat Horizon 1980, A Mind of Winter 1981, At First Light 1982, Jubilation 1985, Antara 1987, Sudden Time 1993, Three Inventions for Chamber Orchestra 1995, Sometime Voices 1996, Palimpsests 2002, Dance Figures 2004; chamber music: Piano Sonata 1978, Octet 1978, Flight 1979, Sortilèges 1981, Three Studies for Piano 1985, Upon Silence 1990, Viola, Viola 1997, Shadowlines (for solo piano) 2001, Three Miniatures for violin 2001, Piano Figures 2004. *Honours:* Hon. RAM; Chevalier, Ordre des Arts et des Lettres 1996; Lili Boulanger Award, USA 1985, Koussevitzky Int. Record Award 1987, Grand Prix du Disque de l'Académie Charles Cros 1987, Gramophone Contemporary Award 1990, Edison Award 1998, Schönberg Prize, Deutsche Sinfonie Berlin 2002; Royal Philharmonic Soc. Award 2003, 2004. *Address:* c/o Faber Music, 3 Queen Square, London, WC1N 3AU, England. *Telephone:* (20) 7833-7910. *Fax:* (20) 7833-7939. *E-mail:* promotion@ fabermusic.com (office). *Website:* www.fabermusic.co.uk.

**BENNETT, Elinor,** OBE, LLB; Welsh harpist; *Artistic Director, William Mathias Music Centre*; b. 17 April 1943, Llanidloes, Wales; m. Dafydd Wigley 1967; three s. (two deceased) one d. *Education:* University College of Wales, Royal Academy of Music, London. *Career:* debut, Wigmore Hall, London; freelance harpist with London Symphony Orchestra, Philharmonia, English Chamber Orchestra, 1967–71; soloist and recitalist, BBC Radio 3; HTV, A Day in the Life of Elinor Bennett; BBC, At Home (Richard Baker); chamber music player; dir of festivals; dedicatee of many new works by contemporary composers, including Alun Hoddinott, Malcolm Williamson and John Metcalf; Artistic Dir, William Mathias Music Centre 2002–. *Recordings:* Two Harps; With Harp and Voice; The Harp of Wales; Portrait of the Harp, 1988; Nimbus: Images and Impressions, with Judith Hall (flute); Lorelt: Sea of Glass, 1994; Nimbus: Mathias, Santa Fe Suite and other 20th century classics, 1995; Sain: Harps and Songs, Portrait of the Harp, The Harp of Wales, Two Harps; Victorian Harp Music; John Thomas: 24 Welsh Melodies–The Complete Collection, 1998. *Publications:* Living Harp, Living Harp II 1998, John Thomas' Harp Duets 2000. *Honours:* Hon. Fellowships Univ. of Wales Aberystwyth, Cardiff Univ., Royal Welsh Coll. of Music and Drama. *Address:* Hen Efail, Bontnewydd, Caernarfon, Gwynedd LL54 7YH, Wales. *Telephone:* (1286) 830010. *E-mail:* elinor@elinorbennett.com. *Website:* www .elinorbennett.com.

**BENNETT, Sir Richard Rodney,** Kt, CBE, FRAM; British composer; b. 29 March 1936, Broadstairs, Kent; s. of H. Rodney Bennett and Joan Esther Bennett. *Education:* Leighton Park School, Reading, Royal Acad. of Music, London and under Pierre Boulez, Paris. *Career:* commissioned to write two operas by Sadler's Wells 1962; Prof. of Composition, RAM 1963–65, Visiting Prof. 1995–; Vice-Pres. RCM 1983–; mem. Gen. Council, Performing Right Soc. 1975–. *Compositions:* The Approaches of Sleep 1959, Journal, Calendar, Winter Music 1960, The Ledge, Suite Française, Oboe Sonata 1961, Nocturnes, London Pastoral, Fantasy 1962, Aubade, Jazz Calendar, String Quartet No. 4, Five Studies 1964, The Mines of Sulphur (opera) 1964, Symphony No. 1 1965, A Penny for a Song (opera) 1966, Epithalamion 1966, Symphony No. 2 1967, Wind Quintet, Piano Concerto 1968, Victory (opera) 1969, All the King's Men (children's opera) 1969, Jazz Pastoral 1969, Oboe Concerto 1970, Guitar Concerto 1971, Viola Concerto 1973, Commedia I–IV 1972–73, Spells (choral) 1975, Serenade for Youth Orchestra 1977, Isadora (ballet) 1981, Dream Songs 1986, Marimba Concerto 1988, Diversions 1989, Concerto for Stan Getz 1990, Partita 1995, Reflections on a 16th-Century Tune 1999, Seven Country Dances 2000, The Glory and the Dream 2000, Reflections on a Scottish Folksong 2006. *Film music:* Indiscreet, Devil's Disciple, Blind Date, The Mark, Only Two Can Play, Wrong Arm of the Law, Heavens Above, Billy Liar, One Way Pendulum, The Nanny, The Witches, Far from the Madding Crowd, Billion Dollar Brain, The Buttercup Chain, Secret Ceremony, Figures in a Landscape, Nicholas and Alexandra, Lady Caroline Lamb, Voices, Murder on the Orient Express, Equus, Sherlock Holmes in New York, L'Imprecateur, The Brinks Job, Yanks, Return of the Soldier, Four Weddings and a Funeral, Swann. *Television music includes:* Hereward the Wake, The Christians, The Ebony Tower, Poor Little Rich Girl, Gormenghast. *Recordings include:* When Lights Are Low (with Claire Martin) 2005. *Honours:* Arnold Bax Soc. Prize for Commonwealth Composers 1964; Anthony Asquith Memorial Award for Murder on the Orient Express film music, Soc. of Film and TV Awards 1974. *Current Management:* c/o Alice Gribbin, Clarion/ Seven Muses, 47 Whitehall Park, London, N19 3TW, England. *Website:* www .c7m.co.uk.

**BENNETT, William;** Flautist; b. 7 Feb. 1936, London. *Education:* Guildhall School London, with Geoffrey Gilbert; Paris with Jean-Pierre Rampal, and with Marcel Moyse. *Career:* Former Principal Flautist with the London Symphony and Royal Philharmonic Orchestra, English Chamber Orchestra and Academy of St Martin-in-the-Fields; Many appearances as soloist in Britain and abroad in concerto repertory, including works dedicated to him by William Matthias and Richard Rodney Bennett; Contributed to world-wide development of flute manufacture tuned to William Bennett Scale; Teacher at Royal Academy, London, and transcriber of various works for flute. *Recordings:* Many albums in solo and chamber music repertory including works by Bach and Mozart. *Honours:* O.B.E., 1995. *Address:* c/o Royal Academy of Music, Marylebone Road, London, NW1 5HT, England.

**BENNETT, Zon,** BMus, MMus; Musicologist and Composer; b. 10 Aug. 1961, New York, NY, USA; m. Clare; two s. *Education:* Univ. of Michigan, USA,

Univ. of Edinburgh, Univ. of Oxford. *Career:* Reader in Music, Durham Univ. 2000–; Senior Lecturer in Music, Hull Univ. 1994–2000; Tutor in Music, Univ. of Oxford 1990–94; Gen. Ed., Nineteenth-Century Music Review 2002–, Music in Nineteenth-Century Britain (book series) 1997–; mem. American Musicological Soc., Coll. Music Soc., Royal Musical Asscn. *Compositions:* Litany of the Sea for Orchestra 2000, Gothic Fragment 2000, Military Fanfare 1998, Communion Service 1995, Matins Responsary for Woman's Choir 1994. *Recordings:* The Gentlemen of St John's College Choir 1990. *Publications:* Music and Metaphor in Nineteenth-Century British Musicology 2000, The English Plainchant Revival 1992; contrib. to numerous publications and journals from 1989, including Nineteenth-Century British Music Studies, Music & Letters, Music & Liturgy, The Hymn Tune Index (ed. Nicholas Temperley), The Shorter Oxford Book of Carols, Early Music, New Dictionary of National Biography, The New Grove Dictionary of Music (second edn), Irish Musical Studies. *Honours:* Arts and Humanities Research Board Research Leave Grant 2003, Louise Dyer Award, Musica Britannica Trust 1992, Overseas Research Student Awards, CVCP 1990, 1991, Univ. of Hull Research Leave Award 1999. *Address:* University of Durham School of Music, Palace Green, Durham, DH1 3RL, England (office). *Telephone:* (191) 3343156 (office). *E-mail:* bennett.zon@durham.ac.uk (office). *Website:* www.dur.ac.uk/music (office).

**BENNINGSEN, Lillian;** Singer, (Contralto); b. 17 July 1924, Vienna, Austria. *Education:* Studied in Vienna with Anna Bahr-Mildenburg. *Career:* Debut: Salzburg Landestheater, 1948; Sang with Cologne Opera, 1950–52; Munich Staatsoper from 1951; As Eboli in Don Carlos, Fricka, Carmen, Amneris, Octavian and Dorabella; Marcellina in Le nozze di Figaro; Covent Garden, 1953 in the British premiere of Strauss's Die Liebe der Danaë, with the Munich Company; Salzburg Festival, 1955, in the premiere of Egk's Irische Legende; Schwetzingen Festival, 1961, in the premiere of Henze's Elegie für junge Liebende; Munich 1969 in the premiere of Aucassin and Nicolette by Bialas; Widely heard in recital and concert. *Recordings:* Le nozze di Figaro; Magdalene in Die Meistersinger conducted by Keilberth; Ariadne auf Naxos; Die tote Stadt by Korngold.

**BENOIT, Jean-Christophe;** Singer, (Bass-Baritone); b. 18 March 1925, Paris, France. *Education:* Studied at the Paris Conservatoire. *Career:* Sang in the French provinces, then at the Paris Opéra and Opéra-Comique; Guest appearances in Geneva for the premieres of Monsieur de Pourceaugnac by Martin, 1963; Milhaud's La Mère Coupable, 1966; Aix-en-Province Festival, 1954–57; Salzburg Festival, 1956; La Scala Milan, 1958; Further engagements at the Holland Festival, Monte Carlo and Brussels; Best known as Mozart's Guglielmo and Antonio; Rossini's Basilio; Raimbaud in Le Comte Ory; Somarone in Béatrice et Bénédict; Boniface in Le Jongleur de Notre Dame; Torquemada in L'Heure Espagnole; Brussels 1983, in the premiere of Le Passion de Giles by Philippe Boesmans; Professor of Singing at the Paris Conservatoire. *Recordings:* Carmen; Platée; Lakmé; Les Contes d'Hoffmann and Il Barbiere di Siviglia; Les Indes Galantes; Paer's Le Maître de Chapelle. *Address:* c/o Conservatoire National de Musique, 14 Rue de Madrid, 75008 Paris, France.

**BENSON, Clifford (George);** Concert Pianist; b. 17 Nov. 1946, Grays, Essex, England; m. 1 Sept 1973, 2 d. *Education:* ARCM Performance Diploma, 1964; Studied Piano with Lamar Crowson and Cyril Smith, Royal College of Music, London; Private Studies with George Malcolm, 1964–69; Studied Composition with Herbert Howells. *Career:* Debut: Royal Festival Hall, London, 1970; Performed Recordings and Broadcasts, BBC Radio 3, 1969–; Soloist, Royal Albert Hall Promenade Concerts, 1975; Travelled extensively playing at many major music festivals; Numerous recitals, solo and chamber music, also concertos; Duos with Thea King, William Bennett and Levon Chilingirian; mem. Incorporated Society of Musicians; Royal College of Music Union. *Compositions:* 3 Pieces for piano, 1983; Mozart Goes to Town (piano duet), 1985. *Recordings:* CRD; Deutsche Grammophon; CBS; Hyperion. *Honours:* Chopin Sonata Prize, Royal College of Music, 1966; Tagore Gold Medal, Royal College of Music, 1969; BBC Beethoven Duo Competition, 1969, Munich International Duo Competition, 1971 (with violinist Levon Chilingirian); Martin Musical Scholarship, NPO, 1968. *Address:* 76 Quarry Hill Road, Tonbridge, Kent TN 9 2PE, England.

**BENSON, Joan;** Clavichord Player, Fortepiano Player and Lecturer; b. 1935, St Paul, MN, USA. *Education:* MMus, Univ. of Illinois; protégée of Edwin Fischer, Switzerland; studies in clavichord music with Fritz Neumeyer, Germany, Santiago Kastner, Portugal; advanced study in Vienna, Paris, Italy and Germany. *Career:* concerts, lectures, appearances in festivals; television and radio appearances throughout USA, Europe, Near and Far East; Lecturer in Music, Stanford Univ., 1970–76; Asst Prof. of Music, 1976–82, Adjunct Prof., 1982–87, Univ. of Oregon. *Recordings:* Music by Kuhnau and C. P. E. Bach, 1988; Haydn and Pasquini, Boston Museum of Fine Arts clavichords, 1982; C. P. E. Bach on clavichord and fortepiano, 1972; Music for Clavichord, 1962. *Publications:* Haydn and the Clavichord, 1982; The Clavichord in 20th Century America, 1992; Bach and the Clavier, 1996. *Contributions:* articles: Haydn and the Clavichord, Vienna, 1982; Gulbenkian Society, Portugal; The Clavichord in 20th Century America, 1989; American Liszt Society Journal; Edwin Fischer, 1985; Clavier Magazine, Bach and the Clavier, 1990;. *Honours:* Performer's award, Univ. of Indiana; Kate Neal Award for Performance. *Current Management:* Marla Lowen. *Address:* 2795 Central Boulevard, Eugene, OR 97403, USA.

**BENT, Ian (David);** University Teacher; b. 1 Jan. 1938, Birmingham, England; m. Caroline Coverdale, 27 Aug 1979, 2 s., 1 d. *Education:* ARCO, 1958; St John's College, Cambridge, 1958–65; BA, 1st Class, Music Tripos, 1961; BMus, 1962; MA, 1965; PhD, 1969. *Career:* Lecturer in Music, King's College, University of London, 1965–75; Senior Consulting Editor, The New Grove Dictionary of Music, 1970–80; Professor of Music, University of Nottingham, 1975–87; Visiting Professor, Harvard University, USA, 1982–83; Visiting Professor, Columbia University, 1986–87; Professor, Columbia University, 1987–; mem, American Musicological Society; Royal Musical Association; Society for Music Theory; International Musicological Society. *Publications:* The Early History of the English Chapel Royal, 1066–1327, 1969; Source Materials and the Interpretation of Music; A Memorial Volume to Thurston Dart, 1981; Analysis, 1987; Music Analysis in the Nineteenth Century, 2 vols, 1994; Music Theory in the Age of Romanticism, ed., 1996. *Contributions:* Journal of the American Musicological Society; Music Analysis; Musical Times; Music and Letters; Proceedings of the Royal Musical Association; Theoria; General Editor, Cambridge Studies in Music Theory and Analysis. *Address:* Columbia University, New York, NY 10027, USA.

**BENT, Margaret Hilda,** PhD; British musicologist; b. 23 Dec. 1940, St Albans, England; m. Ian Bent. *Education:* Girton Coll., Cambridge. *Career:* taught at Cambridge, King's Coll. London 1965–75, Goldsmiths' Coll. from 1972; teacher, Brandeis Univ. 1975–81; Princeton from 1981; researched Old Hall MS under Thurston Dart at Cambridge, published study with Andrew Hughes; Pres., American Musicological Soc. 1983. *Publications:* The Old Hall Manuscript in the Corpus Mensurabilis Musicae series, XLVI 1969–73, Dunstable, London 1981; contrib. articles on John Dunstable, Notation, Old Hall MS, Leonel Power and Square in the New Grove Dictionary of Music and Musicians 1980; Rossini's Il Turco in Italia (ed. for the Critical Edition) 1988, The Grammar of Early Music: Preconditions for Analysis (ed.) 1998. *Address:* All Souls College, Oxford, OX1 4AL, England. *E-mail:* margaret.bent@all-souls.oxford.ac.uk.

**BENTLEY, Andrew;** Composer and Computer Music Researcher; b. 30 June 1952, Fleetwood, England; m. Anna-Kaarina Kiviniemi, 9th Aug 1975, 2 s. *Education:* BA, Honours; DPhil, Composition, University of York, England. *Career:* Designer; Electronic Music Studio; Finnish Radio Experimental Studio, 1976–84; Teacher, Sibelius Academy, Helsinki, 1981–82; Studio Director, Helsinki University, 1982–84; Lecturer, Salford College of Technology, 1985–86; Director, Composers Desktop Project, York, 1986–; Leverhulme Computer Music Fellow, University of Nottingham, 1987–. *Compositions include:* Bowing, 1979; Portrait, 1979; Modulo, 1979; Contact with Bronze, 1979; Zoologic, 1980; Winter Winters, 1980; Aerial Views, 1981; Time for Change, 1981; Divertimento, 1983; Small Print, 1983. *Contributions:* Electronic Music for Schools, 1984; Professional Journals. *Honours:* Bourges International EAM Competition, 1979; Luigi Russolo Competition, 1979. *Address:* Leankatu 4 B 13, Helsinki 00240, Finland.

**BENZA, Georgina;** singer (soprano); b. 1959, Russia (of Hungarian parentage). *Education:* studied in Kiev and Budapest and in Munich with Wilma Lipp. *Career:* has sung at the Munich Staatsoper from 1983, in such roles as Adina, Lauretta, Sophie, Pamina and Fiordiligi; more recent repertory includes Violetta, Tosca, Tatiana, Suor Angelica, Madama Butterfly, Marguerite and Aida; guest engagements in Berlin (Deutsche Oper and Staatsoper), Frankfurt, Copenhagen, Leipzig, Bonn, Dresden and Barcelona; Bielefeld Opera as Tosca and Amelia in Un Ballo in Maschera; sang Abigaille in Nabucco at Saarbrücken, 1999. *Honours:* winner Mozart Prizes in Vienna and Salzburg.

**BENZI, Roberto;** Italian/French conductor; b. 12 Dec. 1937, Marseille; s. of Giuseppe Benzi and Maria Pastorino; m. Jane Rhodes 1966. *Career:* studied conducting with Andre Cluytens; debut as conductor, France 1948; tours in Europe and S America 1949–52; opera conducting debut 1954; conducted Carmen, Paris Opera 1959; guest conductor Europe, Japan, Israel, Mexico, Canada, USA, S Africa and main music festivals; Music Dir Bordeaux-Aquitaine Orchestra 1973–87, Arnhem Philharmonic 1989–98, Dutch Nat. Youth Orchestra 1991–96. *Publications:* orchestrations of Brahms op. 23 Schumann Variations 1970, Brahms op. 24 Variations and Fugue on a theme by Handel 1973, Rossini Prélude, Thème et Variations 1978, Erik Satie Je te veux, valse 1987. *Honours:* Chevalier, Légion d'honneur, Ordre Nat. du Mérite, Ordre des Palmes Académiques, Order of Orange-Nassau. *Address:* 12 Villa Ste-Foy, 92200 Neuilly-sur-Seine, France (home). *Telephone:* 1-46-24-27-85 (home). *Fax:* 1-46-24-55-73 (home).

**BERBIÉ, Jane;** Singer (Mezzo-Soprano); b. 6 May 1934, Villefranche-de-Lauragais, Toulouse, France. *Education:* Studied at the Toulouse Conservatory. *Career:* After debut in 1958, sang at La Scala 1960, in L'Enfant et les Sortilèges, Glyndebourne Festival, 1969–71, 1983–84, as Despina in Così fan tutte; London Coliseum in the British premiere (concert) of Roussel's Padmavati, Aix-en-Provence, 1969–70; Salzburg Festival, 1974, as Marcellina in Le nozze di Figaro; Paris Opéra from 1975, as Zerlina and in Das Rheingold and Jenůfa; Guest appearances in Tokyo, Munich, London, Cologne and Milan, Rosina in Il Barbiere di Siviglia; Other roles include Concepcion in L'Heure Espagnole, Orsini in Lucrezia Borgia, Cherubino and Ascanio in Benvenuto Cellini; Salzburg Festival, 1988 as Mozart's Marcellina; Sang Annina in Der Rosenkavalier at the Théâtre des Champs Elysées, Paris, 1989; Teatro San Carlos, Lisbon, as the Marquise in La Fille du Régiment, 1989.

*Recordings:* Benvenuto Cellini, conducted by Colin Davis; Così fan tutte; L'Enfant et les Sortilèges; Il Turco in Italia; Massenet's Cendrillon. *Honours:* Grand Prix; Toulouse Conservatory. *Address:* c/o Théâtre des Champs Elysées, 15 Avenue Montaigne, 75008, Paris, France.

**BERCZELLY, Istvan;** Singer (Baritone); b. 9 Sept. 1939, Budapest, Hungary. *Education:* Studied in Budapest. *Career:* Debut: Debrecen, 1967, as Don Giovanni; Sang at Debrecen until 1970; Budapest National Theatre from 1970, notably as Verdi's Renato, Basilio in La Fiamma by Respighi, Valentin (Faust), Bellini's Capulet, Wagner's Gunther, and the title role in Samson by Szokolay; Budapest, 1987, in the premiere of Szokolay's Ecce Homo; Premier of A Man from Venice by Ferenc Farkas, 1991; Sang Wagner's Hagen at Budapest, 1998. *Address:* c/o Hungarian State Opera, Nepoztarsasag utja 22, 1061 Budapest, Hungary.

**BERDULLAS DEL RIO, Jorge;** Composer; b. 20 Aug. 1960, Villagarcia de Arosa, Pontevedra, Spain. *Education:* conservatories in La Coruña, Santiago and Madrid; graduated as music teacher. *Career:* conducted choirs; became state music teacher/player 1985; founded contemporary music group, Talea 1986; founder mem., Galician Asscn of Composers 1987. *Compositions include:* El Paso, Op. 15a and 15b, for 6 and 12 percussionists and 2 conductors 1969, Biomecánicas (Letania para el día de los derechos del hombre), Op. 17, for piano and bass voice 1990, Proum (Homenaje a El Lissitzky) String Quartet No. 2, Op. 19 1991, Alogón (El dominio del caos), Op. 20, for string orchestra and 4 mixed voices 1991, Las estructuras del caos, Op. 23, methodology for a science of movement and simultaneous tempos in music 1995–96, Res Facta (Bajo el impulso de neoriel), Op. 24, for 5 orchestral groups (voice and instruments) situated in different places, and 5 conductors temporised by computer 1998–2000, El Apocalipsis según San Juan, Op. 25, for 12 orchestral groups (vocals and instruments) in different places, 12 speakers and 12 conductors 2001–. *Address:* Calle Rua Agriña No. 16 bajo derecha, 15705 Santiago de Compostela, Spain. *Telephone:* (981) 557225.

**BERENS, Barbara;** Singer (Soprano); b. 25 April 1966, St Ingbert, Germany. *Education:* Studied with Erika Köth and Josef Metternich, and in London with Vera Rozsa. *Career:* Sang with the Deutsche Oper am Rhein at Düsseldorf from 1988, notably as Susanna, Fiordigili, Pamina, Elvira in I Puritani, Liu and Hanna Glawari; Guest engagements in Cologne (as Gretel), Saarbrucken (Mme Cortese in Il Viaggio a Reims) and elsewhere in Germany; Also a noted recitalist. *Address:* c/o Deutsche Oper am Rhein, Heinrich Heine-Allee 16a, W-4000 Düsseldorf, Germany.

**BERESFORD, Hugh;** singer (baritone, tenor); b. 17 Dec. 1925, Birkenhead, England. *Education:* Royal Northern College of Music, Manchester, Vienna Music Academy; studied with Dino Borgioli and Alfred Piccaver. *Career:* debut, Linz, 1953, as Wolfram in Tannhäuser; Sang at Deutsche Oper am Rhein, Düsseldorf, from 1960; Sang in Graz, Augsburg and Wuppertal; Guest appearances at Covent Garden, Vienna, Munich, Stuttgart, Cologne, Brussels and Paris; Holland Festival, 1963, 1966; Venice, 1966, as Mandryka in Arabella; Sang further as Rigoletto, Posa in Don Carlos and Don Giovanni; Later career as tenor with Otello and Florestan at the Vienna Staatsoper, 1973; Tannhäuser at Bayreuth, 1972–73; Cologne Opera, 1981 as Florestan, and Erik in Der fliegende Holländer. *Address:* c/o Oper der Stadt Köln, Offenbachplatz, 5000 Cologne, Germany.

**BEREZOVSKY, Boris Vadimovich;** Russian pianist; b. 4 Jan. 1969, Moscow; m. 1989. *Education:* Moscow Conservatoire. *Career:* London début Wigmore Hall 1988; appeared with Soviet Festival Orchestra, London 1990; recitals in New York, Washington, London, Amsterdam, Salzburg, Moscow, Leningrad, Tokyo, Osaka, etc.; appearances with orchestras including Philharmonia, New York Philharmonic, Philadelphia Orchestra, NDR Hamburg and Danish Nat. Radio Symphony Orchestra. *Recordings:* Chopin Godowsky Etudes 2005. *Honours:* winner Prize of Hope competition, City of Ufa 1985, Gold Medal Int. Tchaikovsky Piano Competition, Moscow 1990. *Current Management:* IMG Artists, Lovell House, 616 Chiswick High Road, London, W4 5RX, England. *Telephone:* (20) 8233-5800; (095) 241-74-87 (Moscow).

**BERG, Nathan;** Singer (Baritone); b. 1968, Saskatchewan, Canada. *Education:* Augustana University, Alberta; University of Western Ontario; Maitrise Nationale de Versailles; Guildhall School with Vera Rozsa. *Career:* Debut: Recital at Wigmore Hall, London; Sang Thésée in Rameau's Hippolyte, Peter Quince, Dr Falke and Eustachio in Donizetti's L'Assedio di Calais at the Guildhall School; Has sung professionally as Guglielmo, Masetto, Leporello, Figaro (Mozart), Schuanard, Thésée; Various recordings and appearances with Abbado, Dohnányi, Salinnen, Shaw, Tilson Thomas; Leppard and William Christie among others. Various oratorio and recital work; Sang Abramane in Rameau's Zoroastre at Brooklyn Academy and on tour to Europe, 1998; Season 2000–01 in Handel's Theodora at the Salzburg Easter Festival, Masetto at Glyndebourne and Leporello for ENO. *Honours:* Prizewinner, Peter Pears, Kathleen Ferrier, Walter Gruner and Royal Overseas League Competitions. *Current Management:* IMG Artists, Lovell House, 616 Chiswick High Road, London W4 5RX, England. *Telephone:* (20) 8233-5800. *Fax:* (20) 8233-5801. *E-mail:* artistseurope@imgworld.com. *Website:* www.imgartists.com.

**BERGAMIN, Peter;** Conductor; b. 1965, Canada. *Career:* Appearances with the Toronto Symphony, Israel Chamber Orchestra, Royal Liverpool Philharmonic Orchestra, Scottish National Orchestra and Winnipeg Symphony:

Music Director of the Vienna Taschenoper, 1994–97, with Maxwell Davies' Resurrection in Vienna and at Glasgow Mayfest. Further engagements with the Opéra National de Lyon, North Hungarian Symphony Orchestra and the King's Singers, London; Repertoire includes Mozart, Mahler, Beethoven, Wagner, Strauss and contemporary music. *Address:* c/o IMG Artists, Lovell House, 626 Chiswick High Road, London W4 5RX England.

**BERGANZA, Teresa;** Spanish singer (mezzo-soprano); b. 16 March 1935, Madrid; d. of Guillermo Berganza and Ascensión Berganza; m. 1st Felix Lavilla 1957; one s. two d; m. 2nd José Rifa 1986. *Career:* début in Aix-en-Provence 1957, in England, Glyndebourne 1958; has sung at La Scala, Milan, Opera Rome, Metropolitan, New York, Chicago Opera House, San Francisco Opera, Covent Garden, etc.; has appeared at festivals in Edinburgh, Holland, Glyndebourne; concerts in France, Belgium, Holland, Italy, Germany, Spain, Austria, Portugal, Scandinavia, Israel, Mexico, Buenos Aires, USA, Canada, etc.; appeared as Rosina in Il Barbiere di Siviglia, Covent Garden 1967; sung Carmen, at opening ceremony of Expo 92, Seville, also at opening ceremonies Barcelona Olympics 1992, mem. Real Academia de Bellas Artes de San Fernando, Spanish Royal Acad. of Arts 1994. *Film:* Don Giovanni. *Publication:* Flor de Soledad y Silencio 1984. *Honours:* Premio Lucrezia Arana, Premio Extraordinario del Conservatorio de Madrid, Grande Cruz, Isabel la Católica, Harriet Cohen Award, Int. Critic Award 1988; Commdr, Ordre des Arts et des Lettres, Grand Prix de Disque (six times), Grand Prix Rossini. *Address:* c/o Askonas Holt, 19A Air Street, London, W1, England (office); La Rossiniana, Archanda 5, P.O. Box 137, 28200 San Lorenzo del Escorial, Madrid, Spain. *Telephone:* (1) 8960941 (Madrid). *Fax:* (1) 8960816 (Madrid).

**BERGASA, Carlos;** Singer (Baritone); b. 1966, Spain. *Career:* Many engagements at opera houses in Spain and elsewhere in Europe, notably in Donizetti's La Favorita, Mozart's Così fan tutte (as Guglielmo) and Gounod's Faust (as Valentin); Also sings the Mörike-Lieder by Wolf; Contestant at the 1995 Cardiff Singer of the World Competition. *Address:* Fernan Gonzales 17, Madrid 28009, Spain.

**BERGE, Sigurd;** Composer; b. 1 July 1929, Vinstra, Norway. *Education:* Studied with Thorleif Eken at the Oslo Conservatory, also with Finn Mortensen, Course in Electronic Music, Stockholm, Utrecht. *Career:* First amanuensis in music at High School, Oslo; Tutor, Sagene College of Education, from 1959; Chairman, Norwegian composers Union, 1985–88. *Compositions:* Episode for violin, piano, 1958; Pezzo orchestrale, 1958; Tamburo piccolo for strings, percussion, 1961; Sinus for string and percussion, 1961; Chroma for Orchestra, 1963, A for Orchestra, 1965, B for Orchestra, 1966; Yang-Guan for wind quintet, 1967; Ballet for 2 dancers, percussion, 1968, 1970; Horncall, 1972; Between Mirrors for violin, chamber orchestra, 1977; Juvenes, amateur string orchestra, 1977; Music for Orchestra, 1978; Gudbrandsdalsspelet, music drama, 1980; Wind Ballet, 1981; Music for 4 horns, 1984; Horn Trio, 1987; Springar; Chorale for brass quintet, 1990; Horn Solo, 2000; Electronic pieces. *Recordings include:* Raga for Oboe and Orchestra, 1990; Springar; Chorale; Episode; Chroma; Flauto Solo; Horncall; Yang-Guan. *Publications include:* Viser og Blues, Books 1 and 2, 1999; Lydforming, 1999. *Address:* Norwegian Music Information Centre, Tollbugata 28, N–0157 Oslo, Norway.

**BERGEL, Erich;** Romanian conductor; b. 1 June 1930, Rosenau. *Education:* Sibiu and Cluj Conservatories, studied in Cluj with Ciolan. *Career:* debut, Houston Symphony Orchestra, USA 1975; flute, Sibiu Philharmonic Orchestra 1945–48; conductor, Oradea Philharmonic 1955–59, Cluj Philharmonic 1959–72; Music Dir, Nordwestdeutsche Philharmonie 1972–74; Principal Guest Conductor, Houston Symphony Orchestra 1979–81; fmr Dir, BBC Nat. Orchestra of Wales, Cardiff; Professor of Conducting, Berlin Hochschule für Musik. *Publications include:* Bach's Art of Fugue, vol. 1 1979. *Address:* c/o Hochschule für Musik 'Hanns Eisler' Berlin, Wilhelmstraße 53, 10117 Berlin, Germany.

**BERGEN, Beverly;** Singer (Soprano and Mezzo-Soprano); b. 1950, New Zealand. *Education:* Studied at London Opera Centre. *Career:* Has appeared as guest artist at the Deutsche Oper Berlin, also in Hamburg, Düsseldorf and elsewhere in Germany; Sang in premiere of Maderna's Hyperion at Brussels; Operatic roles include Constanze, Jenůfa, Strauss's Countess, Katherina in Lady Macbeth of Mtsensk, Senta, Luisa Miller, Violetta, Musetta and Lucia di Lammermoor; Has performed throughout Australia in Messiah, Beethoven's Ninth and Das klagende Lied by Mahler; Other repertoire includes Mozart's Requiem, The Trojans, Bruckner's Te Deum, with the Sydney Symphony Orchestra and Judas Maccabaeus with St Hedwig's Cathedral Choir, Berlin; Changed to mezzo-soprano repertoire, 1989, appeared as Amneris in Aida; Engagements with Opera Factory, London.

**BERGER, Roman;** Composer; b. 9 Aug. 1930, Cieszyn, Poland; m. Ruth Strbova, 6 July 1968. *Education:* Academy of Musical Arts, Katowice, 1949–52; Academy of Musical Arts Bratislava, 1952–56, 1960–65. *Career:* Professor of Piano, Conservatoire, Bratislava, 1955–66; Fellow, television sound laboratory, 1966–67; Secretary, Union of Slovak composers, 1967–69; Lecturer on theory of composition, contemporary music and electronic music, Academy of musical arts, Bratislava, 1969–71, 1983–85; Contracted to Musicological Institute of the Slovak Academy of Sciences, 1977–91. *Compositions:* Transformations, 4 symphonic pieces, 1965; Memento for orchestra, 1974; Epitaph to Copernicus for electronics, 1973; De Profundis for bass, cello and electronics, 1980; Exodus 4 pieces for organ, 1982, 1997. *Publications:* Music and Truth, essays, 1997–87; Theory Wrongly Present,

1989; Velvet Revolution and Music, 1990; Permanent Conflict between Art and power, 1992; The Structure and Meaning of Heritage, 1996. *Address:* Bazovského 11/17, SR 841 01, Bratislava, Slovakia.

**BERGER-TUNA, Helmut;** Singer (bass); b. 7 May 1942, Vienna, Austria. *Education:* Hochschule für Musik und darstellende Kunst, Vienna, and with Franz Schuch-Tovini. *Career:* debut, first engagement with Kammeroper Wien; mem. Landestheater Linz 1969–72, Opernhaus-Graz 1972–77, Staatsoper Stuttgart (Germany) 1977–; 60 roles include Omin, Leporello, Sarastro, Rocco, van Bett, Falstaff (Nicolai), Kecal, Daland, Hunding, Fafner, Fasolt, Pogner, König Heinrich, Landgraf, Kaspar, Ramphis, Sparafucile, Baculus, Plumkett, Magnifico, Bartolo (Barbier), Don Pasquale, Baron Ochs (performed more than 100 times); operetta includes Ollendorf, Zsupan, Baron Webs, Frank); guest engagements in Staatsoper Hamburg, Berlin, Munich, Vienna, Teatro alla Scala, Deutsche Oper Berlin, Komische Oper Berlin, Opera House Zürich, Grande Opéra Paris, Royal Opera House Covent Garden London, Dresden, Düsseldorf, Cologne, Frankfurt, Barcelona, Lisbon, Madrid, Amsterdam, Oslo, Royal Opera House Copenhagen, Santa Cecilia Rome, Musikverein Vienna, Bruckner Haus Linz, Teatro la Fenice, Music Center Los Angeles, Seattle Opera; sang at the Salzburg Festival 1981, in the premiere of Cerha's Baal; other festivals include Bregenz and Mörbisch (Austria), Bergen (Norway). *Recordings:* Zar und Zimmermann; Die schweigsame Frau; Baal, K. A. Hartmann's Simplicius Simplissimus; Meistersinger von Nürnberg, Die Zigeunerbaron, Wolf's Der Corregidor, La faciulla des west, R. Schumann's Faust-Szenen. *Television:* appearances in Zar und Zimmermann, Martha, Der Vögelhandler, Der Zigeunerbaron. *Honours:* Kammersänger des Landes Baden-Württemberg 1985. *Address:* c/o Opéra et Concert, 1 rue Volney, 75002 Paris, France.

**BERGLUND, Ingela;** Singer (Soprano); b. 1959, Sweden. *Education:* Studied viola at Stockholm College of Music, 1974–79; State Opera School, Stockholm, 1985–88, with Kerstin Meyer and Elisabeth Söderström. *Career:* Debut: Royal Opera Stockholm, 1988, as Donna Anna; Member of Royal Stockholm Philharmonic Orchestra, 1979–84; Sang Mozart's Countess and the Woman in La Voix Humaine at Stockholm, 1988; Salzburg Landestheater, 1989–92 as Donna Anna, Musetta, Tatiana, Fiordiligi and Hanna Glawari in Die Lustige Witwe; Beatrice in Boccaccio by Suppé at Royal Opera, Stockholm; Guest appearances at Semper Opera, Dresden, and in Austria, USA, Spain and Japan. *Recordings:* Radio and television in Sweden. *Current Management:* IM Audio and Music AB, Stockholm. *Address:* Asogatan 67 VI, 118 28 Stockholm, Sweden.

**BERGLUND, Paavo Allan Engelbert;** Finnish conductor; b. 14 April 1929, Helsinki; s. of Hjalmar Berglund and Siiri (Loiri) Berglund; m. Kirsti Kivekäs 1958; one s. two d. *Education:* Sibelius Acad., Helsinki. *Career:* violinist, Finnish Radio Symphony Orchestra 1949–56, Conductor 1956–62, Prin. Conductor 1962–71; Prin. Conductor Bournemouth Symphony Orchestra 1972–79, Helsinki Philharmonic Orchestra 1975–79; Prin. Conductor Royal Stockholm Philharmonic Orchestra 1987–91, Royal Danish Orchestra 1993–96, London Philharmonic 1997. *Recordings:* complete Sibelius symphonies including first recording of Kullervo Symphony 1971–77, Má Vlast (Smetana), Shostakovich Symphonies Nos. 5, 6, 7, 10, 11, many other recordings. *Publication:* A Comparative Study of the Printed Score and the Manuscript of the Seventh Symphony of Sibelius 1970. *Honours:* State Award for Music 1972; Hon. OBE. *Address:* Munkkiniemenranta 41, 00330 Helsinki 33, Finland.

**BERGMAN, Erik (Valdemar);** Finnish composer; b. 24 Nov. 1911, Nykarleby; m. 1st Solveig von Schoultz 1961 (died 1996); m. 2nd Christina Indrenius-Zalewski 2000. *Education:* Literature and Aesthetics, Musicology, Univе. of Helsinki, 1931–33; Composition Diploma, Sibelius Academy, Helsinki, 1939; Studied Composition in Berlin with Heinz Tiessen and in Switzerland with Wladimir Vogel. *Career:* Debut: Helsinki, 1940; Conductor, Helsinki Univ. Chorus, 1950–69; Prof. of Composition, Sibelius Acad, Helsinki, 1963–76; Concerts in Washington DC and New York, 1981, 1991, Paris, 1967, London, 1967, 1986, Leningrad, 1989, St Petersburg, 1992, Stockholm, 1993; Berlin, The Singing Tree, opera, 1999; Works performed at several int. festivals; mem., Acad. of Finland 1982. *Compositions:* The Singing Tree, opera (1995); The Journey, ballet, 1998–99; Works for orchestra, concertos for soloists and orchestra, works for soloists, choir and orchestra, works for solo instruments, chamber music. *Recordings:* The Singing Tree; Concerto for violin and orchestra; Birds in the Morning, flute and orchestra; Concerto for Chamber Orchestra, 1997; Chamber works, works for piano, guitar, choral and vocal works; The Maestro and his Orchestra, for violin and chamber orchestra, 1996; Musica Concertante for string quartet, 1997; Concerto for violoncello and strings, 1998; Meditation and Emotion for orchestra, 2001; Fantasia for trumpet and orchestra, 2002. *Honours:* Pro Finlandia Medal, Sibelius Int. Prize, 1965; DPhil, hc, 1978, 1982; Royal Swedish Acad. of Music; Hon. Mem., Soc. of Finnish Composers; Cmmdr, Order of the White Rose of Finland; Cmmdr, Order of the Lion of Finland; The State's Music Prize, 1989; The Nordic Council Music Prize, 1994; Finland Prize, 1997. *Address:* Berggatan 22 C 52, 00100 Helsinki, Finland.

**BERGONZI, Carlo;** Italian singer (tenor); b. 13 July 1924, Busseto, Parma; m. Adele; two c. *Education:* Parma Conservatory. *Career:* début (baritone) as Figaro (Il Barbiere di Siviglia) at Lecce 1948; début as tenor in title role of Andrea Chénier, Teatro Petruzzelli, Bari 1951; subsequently appeared at various Italian opera houses including La Scala, Milan; US début in Il Tabarro and Cavalleria Rusticana, Lyric Opera, Chicago 1955; appeared at Metropolitan Opera, New York in Aïda (as Radames) and Il Trovatore (as Manrico) 1955–56; appeared at all the maj. opera houses in Europe and also in USA and S America; retd 1994 with occasional appearances thereafter; currently a vocal coach. *Current Management:* Askonas Holt Ltd, Lonsdale Chambers, 27 Chancery Lane, London, WC2A 1PF, England.

**BERKELEY, Michael Fitzhardinge,** FRAM, FRWCMD; British composer; b. 29 May 1948, London; s. of the late Sir Lennox Berkeley and of Elizabeth Freda Berkeley (née Bernstein); m. Deborah Jane Coltman-Rogers 1979; one d. *Education:* Westminster Cathedral Choir School, The Oratory School, Royal Acad. of Music. *Career:* writer on music and arts for the Observer, Vogue and The Listener 1970–75; presents music programmes (including Proms) for BBC TV 1975–; BBC Radio 3 announcer 1974–79; Dir Britten-Pears Foundation 1996–; mem. Exec. Cttee Asscn of Professional Composers 1982–84, Cen. Music Advisory Cttee, BBC 1986–90; Music Panel Adviser to Arts Council 1986–90; Visiting Prof. Huddersfield Univ. (fmrly Polytechnic) 1991–94; Artistic Dir Cheltenham Int. Festival 1995–2005; Co-Dir Spitalfields Festival 1994–97; Dir Royal Opera House, Covent Garden 1996–2000 (mem. 1994–98, Chair. Opera Bd 1998); Chair. Bd of Govs Royal Ballet 2003–; Composer-in-Asscn BBC Nat. Orchestra of Wales, Welsh Coll. of Music and Drama 2002–; has also composed music for film, TV and radio. *Major works include:* Meditations for Strings, Oboe Concerto, Fantasia Concertante, Gregorian Variations (orchestra), For The Savage Messiah (piano quintet), Or Shall We Die? (oratorio to text by Ian McEwan), 4 String quartets, Piano Trio, Songs of Awakening Love, Entertaining Master Punch, Clarinet Concerto, Speaking Silence, Baa Baa Black Sheep (opera), Jane Eyre (opera) 2000, Viola Concerto, Catch Me If You Can (chamber), Dark Sleep (keyboard), Tristessa (orchestra), The Garden of Earthly Delights (orchestra). *Publication:* The Music Pack 1994; numerous articles in newspapers and magazines. *Honours:* The Guinness Prize for Composition 1977, Silver Medal, Worshipful Co. of Musicians 2003. *Address:* c/o Oxford University Press, 70 Baker Street, London, W1U 7DN, England (office). *Telephone:* (20) 7616-5900 (office). *Website:* www.oup.co.uk/music/repprom/berkeley/ (office).

**BERKES, Kalman;** Clarinettist; b. 1952, Budapest, Hungary. *Education:* Studied music from the age of 4; Béla Bartók Conservatory, 1966–70; Ferenc Liszt Academy of Music, 1977. *Career:* Principal Clarinettist, Budapest State Opera Orchestra and Budapest Philharmonic, 1972; Budapest Chamber Ensemble and Jeunesses Musicales Wind Quintet, 1973; Extensive Guest Performances throughout Europe including: Austria, France, Germany, Netherlands, Italy and Switzerland; Played Trios by Beethoven, Brahms and Zemlinsky at St John's, London, 1997. *Recordings:* Has made a number of records including Bartók's Contrasts. *Honours:* Silver Medal, Geneva International Musical Competition, 1972. *Address:* Franz Liszt Academy of Music, PO Box 206, Liszt Ferenctér 8, H–1391 Budapest VI, Hungary.

**BERKOWITZ, Paul;** Concert Pianist; b. 1 Oct. 1948, Montreal, Canada. *Education:* McGill University and Curtis Institute with Serkin and Horszowski. *Career:* Debut: London, 1973 (resident in London, 1973–93, Santa Barbara, California, 1993–); New York Solo Debut, Alice Tully Hall, 1978; Recitalist, Wigmore and Queen Elizabeth Halls, London; Tivoli, Copenhagen and throughout Europe and North America; Soloist with major orchestras in the United Kingdom and North America; Festival engagements in Belgium, Denmark, England, France, Italy, Scotland and Spain; Frequent solo radio broadcasts and recitals for BBC and CBC; Barcelona Festival with the Endellion Quartet and the Albion Ensemble; Beethoven duets with Richard Goode at the Wigmore Hall, 1990–91; Appearances with the BBC Scottish Symphony and English Sinfonia; Professor, Guildhall School, 1975–93; Professor, University of California, Santa Barbara, 1993–; Masterclasses at McGill University, University of British Columbia, Queens University, Royal Conservatory of Music, Toronto, in Canada and Yehudi Menuhin School and elsewhere in the United Kingdom, France and Barcelona; Repertoire includes sonatas and other major works by Schubert, Beethoven, Brahms, Mozart, Schumann, Chopin and Bartók; The Brahms Handel Variations and Klavierstücke op 76 and opp 116-119 and Schumann's Kreisleriana and C major Fantasy. *Recordings include:* Complete Sonatas of Schubert (7 vols); Schumann's Kreisleriana and Davidsbündlertänze, Brahms Piano Pieces Opp 116-118. *Honours:* Fellow of the Guildhall School of Music, 1988; Canada Council Grants, 1989–91; BBC Record Review and BBC Magazine First Choice Award for recording of Schumann's Kreisleriana, 1993. *Address:* Department of Music, University of California, Santa Barbara, CA 93106-6070, USA.

**BERL, Christine;** Composer; b. 22 July 1943, New York City, USA; 2 s. *Education:* BS in Piano, Mannes College of Music, 1961–64; MA in Composition, Queen's College, 1968–70. *Career:* Performances by Emanuel Ax in Highland Park, Ravinia, 1988; Commissioned by Peter Serkin for 1989–90, The Chamber Music Society of Lincoln Center for their 20th Anniversary Season with Frederica von Stade as guest artist, 1989, Cornell University Chorus, 1989; Concert devoted to Berl's works on Distinguished Artists Series of 92nd Street Y, 1990; Commissioned work for 2 pianos for Peter Serkin and Emmanuel Ax; Other participants: Patricia Spence, Matt Haimovitz, Richard Stoltzman, Richard Goode, Andre-Michel Schub, 1994; World premiere by French violinist Pierre Amoyal and Jeremy Menuhin of Masmoudi, a violin sonata commissioned by Radio France; New York premiere of Masmoudi at Merkin Concert Hall, 1994. *Compositions:* Elegy for Piano Solo, 1974; Three Pieces for Chamber Ensemble, 1975; Ab La

Dolchor for Soprano, Female Chorus and Orchestra, 1979; Sonata for Piano, 1986–87; Dark Summer for Mezzo Soprano, Piano and String Trio; The Lord of the Dance, for Peter Serkin; The Violent Bear It Away for Orchestra, 1988; Cantilena for Cello and Piano, for Matt Haimovitz; Masmoudi for violin and piano, 1991. *Recordings:* Three Pieces for Chamber Ensemble, 1975, with Arthur Weisburg and members of the Contemporary Chamber Ensemble and Speculum Musicae, Ursula Oppens, Piano; Elegy, The Lord of The Dance; Piano Sonata by Edipan. *Address:* c/o ASCAP, ACAP Building, One Lincoln Plaza, New York, NY 10023, USA.

**BERMAN, Boris,** BA, MA; concert pianist and professor of piano; b. 3 April 1948, Moscow, Russia; m. Zina Tabachnikova 1975; one s. one d. *Education:* Moscow Tchaikovsky Conservatory. *Career:* debut in Moscow 1965; performances in over 30 countries, appeared with Concertgebouw, Philharmonia, Royal Scottish, Detroit, Minnesota, Houston, Atlanta, Toronto, Israel Philharmonic, Moscow Philharmonic, St Petersburg Philharmonic and many others; festivals include Bergen, Ravinia, Israel, Marlboro; numerous radio and television appearances around the world; former Prof. of Piano, Tel-Aviv University, Indiana University, Boston University, Yale School of Music; Music Dir, Music Spectrum concert series, Tel-Aviv 1975–84; Music Dir, Yale Music Spectrum, USA 1984–97; Dir, Summer Piano Institute at Yale 1990–92; Dir, International Summer Piano Institute, Hong Kong 1995–97; juror at various national, international piano competitions. *Recordings:* all solo piano works by Prokofiev in 9 vols, Stravinsky Concerto with Orchestre de la Suisse Romande, N Järvi, Prokofiev Concertos 1, 4, 5 with Concertgebouw Orchestra, N Järvi, Shostakovich, Scriabin all Sonatas in 2 vols; recitals or works by Debussy, Stravinsky, Shostakovich, Schnittke, Cage; numerous chamber recordings. *Honours:* Edison Classic Award, Netherlands 1990. *Current Management:* Askonas Holt Ltd, Lonsdale Chambers, 27 Chancery Lane, London, WC2A 1PF, England. *Telephone:* (20) 7400-1700. *Fax:* (20) 7400-1799. *E-mail:* info@askonasholt.co.uk. *Website:* www.askonasholt.co.uk. *Address:* Yale School of Music, PO Box 208246, New Haven, CT 06520, USA.

**BERN, Jeni;** Singer (soprano); b. 1973, Glasgow, Scotland. *Education:* Royal Scottish Academy; Royal College of Music, London. *Career:* Debut: Covent Garden Company 1998, as Mozart's Barbarina; Mozart's Susanna for English Touring Opera; Deidamia, and Sigismondo in Arminio for the London Handel Festival; Atalanta in Serse for the Early Opera Company; Dalinda in Ariodante for the Covent Garden Festival and Donizetti's Adina at Cambridge; Cristina in The Makropulos Case for Scottish Opera Go Round, Purcell's Belinda for Israel Chamber Orchestra and Jano in Jenůfa at Glyndebourne, 2000; Other roles include Britten's Titania, Janáček's Vixen and Narcissa in Haydn's Philemon and Baucis; Concerts include Messiah in Switzerland, Bruckner's Te Deum, a British tour with Vivaldi by Candlelight and the premiere of Michael Torke's Book of Proverbs, Flowermaiden in Parsifal with the Royal Opera in concert. *Honours:* Countess of Munster Award. *Current Management:* Musicmakers International Artists Representation, Tailor House, 63–65 High Street, Whitwell, Hertfordshire SG4 8AH, England. *Telephone:* (1438) 871708. *Fax:* (1438) 871777. *E-mail:* musicmakers@compuserve.com. *Website:* www.operauk.com. *Address:* c/o Glyndebourne Festival Opera, Glyndebourne, Lewes, Sussex, BN8 5UU, England.

**BERNARD, André;** Conductor and Trumpeter; b. 6 April 1946, Gap, France. *Education:* Diplome Superieur of Conducting, Paris; 1st Place for Trumpet, Paris Superior Conservatory; Laureat International Trumpet Competition, Geneva, Switzerland, 1968; Studied German romantic repertory with Carlo Maria Giulini and Italian opera with Bruno Bartoletti, Siena, Italy. *Career:* Guest Conductor for many international orchestras including London Philharmonic, London Symphony Orchestra, and Mozarteum Salzburg; Opera conducting in Strasbourg, Lille, Siena, Geneva; Television appearances in France, Germany and Japan; Radio appearances in USA, Canada, Japan, Germany, Italy and France; Solo appearances including Salzburg Festival, Berlin Philharmonie, Carnegie Hall and Lincoln Center in New York, Paris, Tokyo, London, Rome, Prague, Madrid, Venice, and Washington; Appearances with world's leading orchestras; 31 Concerts on tour conducting Philharmonia Hungarica, including Carnegie Hall and Los Angeles, 1986; Contract for concert series in London, tours in France and Italy and recordings with New Symphony Orchestra of London and London Chamber Orchestra, 1982–87. *Recordings:* 20 with Academy of St Martin-in-the-Fields, English Chamber Orchestra, and Ensemble Instrumental de France. *Current Management:* Columbia Artists Management, NY, USA. *Address:* 19 Rue Joliot Curie, 93100 Montreuil, Paris, France.

**BERNARD, Annabelle;** Singer (Soprano); b. 11 Oct. 1934, New Orleans, Louisiana, USA. *Education:* Studies, Xavier University, New Orleans; The New England Conservatory. *Career:* Debut: Sang Susanna in Le nozze di Figaro, conducted by Boris Goldovsky, 1958; Appeared as Butterfly in Stuttgart, 1959; Lieder recitals with Hermann Reutter; Vienna Staatsoper debut as Aida, conducted by Karajan; Sang at the Deutsche Oper Berlin from 1962, debut as Aida; Salzburg Festival, 1973, as Electra in Idomeneo, conducted by Karl Böhm; Visits with the Deutsche Oper to Japan as Fiordiligi and in The Ring, 1987; Washington Opera, 1986, as Fiordiligi; New Orleans Opera as Maddalena in Andrea Chénier; Sang in the stage premiere of Mussorgsky's Salammbô at San Carlo, Naples; Modern repertory includes the premieres on Montezuma by Sessions, 1964 and Dallapiccola's Ulisse, 1968; Concert appearances with the Cleveland Orchestra conducted by Lorin Maazel at Carnegie Hall, the Berlin Philharmonic Orchestra. *Honours:*

Berliner Kammersängerin, 1970; MD, Honoris Causa, Xavier University, 1976. *Address:* c/o Deutsche Oper Berlin, Richard Wagnerstrasse 10, 1000 Berlin, Germany.

**BERNARDI, Mario;** Conductor and Pianist; b. 20 Aug. 1930, Kirkland Lake, Ontario, Canada; m. Mona Kelly, 12 May 1962, 1 d. *Education:* Diplomas in Piano; Organ; Composition, B Marcello Conservatory, Venice, 1947; Piano with Lubka Kolessa, Toronto. *Career:* Sadler's Wells Opera, 1963–69, with many performances of operas by Verdi; San Francisco Opera 1967, 1968, 1982; New York City Opera, 1970–86; Metropolitan Opera, 1984; Several major orchestras including Chicago, Pittsburgh, San Francisco, Toronto, Montreal, BBC; 13 years with National Arts Centre Orchestra, Ottawa, 1969–82, giving many premieres of works by Canadian Composers; Music Director, Calgary Philharmonic; Season 1987–88, with Cendrillon at Washington and Don Giovanni at Montreal; Conducted Lucia di Lammermoor at Washington 1989; Gave the Verdi Requiem at the 1988 Olympic Arts Festival; Conducted Fidelio at Toronto, 1991; Massenet's Chérubin at Covent Garden, 1994; Les Pêcheurs de Perles at Chicago, 1998; mem, Savage Club, London; Ranchmen's Club, Calgary. *Recordings:* Numerous recordings for EMI; RCA; CBC with Sadler's Wells Company; National Arts Centre Orchestra, Toronto, Vancouver Symphonies, CBC Radio Orchestra. *Recordings include:* Hansel and Gretel, with Sadler's Wells Company; Mozart Symphony K551 and Concerto K219, with Steven Staryk; Haydn arias and symphony No. 85; Brahms Serenade Op 11. *Honours:* Companion of the Order of Canada; Several honorary doctorates. *Current Management:* Columbia Artists Management, New York. *Address:* 248 Warren Road, Toronto, Ontario M4V 2S8, Canada.

**BERNARDINI, Alfredo;** Oboist; b. 30 Oct. 1961, Rome, Italy; 2 s., 1 d. *Education:* Studies, Royal Conservatory, The Hague, Netherlands, 1982–; Soloist diploma, 1987; Diploma, University of Oxford, 1985. *Career:* Performs with major European ensembles such as Hesperion XX, Les Arts Florissants, La Petite Bande, Capella Coloniensis, Amsterdam Baroque Orchestra, Collegio Strumentale Italiano, La Grande Ecurie, Concerto Armonico Budapest and Concerto Italiano. *Recordings:* With EMI, D&GM, Astrée and Bongiovanni. *Contributions:* Articles to Il Flauto Dolce; Early Music; Journal of the American Musical Instruments Society. *Address:* Via Sebenico 2, 00198 Roma, Italy.

**BERNAS, Richard;** conductor; b. 21 April 1950, New York, USA; m. 1st Deirdre Busenberg (divorced); m. 2nd Beatrice Harper; two s. *Career:* debut, as pianist, Kent University 1966, as conductor, London, England 1976; Warsaw Autumn Festival, 1977; Vienna Festival, 1984; Opéra de Lyon and Paris Opéra, 1985; London Sinfonietta, England, 1986; Edinburgh Festival, Scotland, 1986; The Royal Helsinki Philharmonic, 1988; Royal Ballet, Covent Garden, BBC Symphony Orchestra, 1989; Holland Festival, 1989; Aldeburgh Festival Opera, Suffolk, England, 1990; English National Opera, London, 1990; Netherlands Opera, Amsterdam and The Hague, 1991; Ars Musica Festival, Brussels, 1991; Orchestre National de Belgique, Brussels, 1993; Netherlands Radio Symphony Orchestra, 1994; Opéra de Bastille, 1995; Musique Oblique, Paris, 1995; Conductor, Saltarello Choir, 1976–80; Conductor, Music Projects, London, 1978–; Conductor in Residence, Sussex University, 1979–82. *Recordings:* Factory Classics; Virgin Classics; Continum; NMC; Decca-Argo. *Current Management:* Robert Gilder & Co., Enterprise House, 59–65 Upper Ground, London, SE1 9PQ, England. *Telephone:* (20) 7928-9008. *Fax:* (20) 7928-9755. *E-mail:* rgilder@robert-gilder.com. *Address:* 73 Avenue Gardens, London, W3 8HB, England.

**BERNASCONI, Silvano;** Pianist and Composer; b. 16 Oct. 1950, Chiasso, Switzerland; m. Irene Cairoli Alessandra, 20 June 1984, 1 s. *Education:* Conservatoire de Lausanne; Piano with Francesto Zaza; Composition with Andor Kovach; Electronic music with Rainer Bosch; Conservatorio Santa Cecilia in Rome; Composition with Vieri Tosatti, Gregorian song with Domenico Bartolucci; Organ with Ferdinando Germani; Electronic music with Franco Evangelisti. *Career:* Debut: Rome, 1974; Pianist and composer, 1980–85; Executions of music commissioned by Musica Ticinensis, 1982 and Television; mem, Association of Swiss Musicians; European Composers Union. *Compositions:* Sounds and Crystals for two Vibraphones, 1982; Psallite, four lines for organ, 1974; Tourbillon, for violin and orchestra, 1993. *Recordings:* Sounds and Crystals, transparencies for two vibraphones and piano; Sounds Am Bach, for piano played by the composer. *Publications:* Didactics compositions in the European year of Music, 1985; Contributor to Musica & Teatro magazine. *Honours:* Invitation by UNCM to found a European Composers Union, 1991. *Address:* Casa Am Bach, 6803 Famignolo-Lugana, Switzerland.

**BERNASEK, Vaclav;** Czech violoncellist; b. 29 Oct. 1944, Kladno, Czechoslovakia; m. Milka Berskova1968; one d. *Education:* Acad. of Music, Prague. *Career:* Debut: Principal Cello, Prague Symphony Orchestra; Founder, Mem., Kocian Quartet, 1972–; Teacher, Docent, Chamber Music, Acad. of Music, Prague; mem., Czech Music Soc. *Recordings:* Bruckner, String Quartet in F major; Schubert, String Quintet in C major; Dvořák, String Quartets No. 10, 12, 13, 14; Mozart, String Quartets Nos 14–23; Brahms, String Sextets Op. 18 and Op. 36, with members of Smetana Quartet; Haydn, String Quartets op 20; Fibich, String Quartets; Tchaikovsky, Sextet; Schulhoff, Quartets and duo for Violin and Cello. *Honours:* Grand Prix du Disque; Academie Charles Cros; Diapason d'Or. *Address:* Kadnerova 312, 16400 Prague, Czech Republic. *Telephone:* (603) 802129 (home). *E-mail:* bernasek@h.amu.cz (office). *Website:* www.concerts-prague.cz/kocian.

**BERNATHOVA, Eva,** DipArt; British concert pianist and academic; *Senior Lecturer, Trinity College of Music;* b. 4 Dec. 1922, Budapest, Hungary; m. Joseph Bernath 1947. *Education:* Gymnasium, Budapest, Franz Liszt Acad. of Music, Budapest. *Career:* debut, Prague 1948; has toured in Europe, USA, Canada, Far East, India, Japan, Australia and New Zealand; soloist with many world famous orchestras, including Berlin Philharmonic, Czech Philharmonic, Orchestre de la Suisse Romande, Royal Philharmonic Orchestra, Gewandhaus Orchestra; Sr Lecturer, Trinity Coll. of Music, London. *Recordings include:* Solo works by J. H. Vorišek, Franz Liszt, M. Balakirev, J. Suk, Mozart; Janáček's Concertino for Piano and Chamber Orchestra, Martinů's Concertino for Piano and Orchestra; Franck's Symphonic Variations; Ravel's Concerto in G; Bartók's Concerto No. 3; Chamber Music: Dvořák's Piano Quintet in A, Brahms' Piano Quintet in F minor, Franck's Piano Quintet in F minor, Shostakovich's Piano Quintet in G minor, Martinů's Piano Quintet. *Honours:* Grand Prix du Disque Français, Paris (for Janacek piano solo works), Grand Prix du Disque Acad. Charles Cros, Paris (for Franck's Piano Quintet with the Janáček Quartet). *Address:* 8 Purley Avenue, London, NW2 1SJ, England. *Telephone:* (20) 8452-3936 (home).

**BERNEDE, Jean-Claude;** Conductor and Violinist; b. 19 Sept. 1935, Angers, France. *Education:* Studied at the Paris Conservatoire with Pierre Dervaux and Igor Markevitch. *Career:* Soloist with the Ensemble de Musique Contemporain from 1958; Founded the Bernede string quartet, 1965, and was director of the Chamber Orchestra of Rouen, 1973–82; Artistic advisor of the Concerts Lamoureux from 1977 and director of the Rennes City Orchestra, 1981–85; Chief conductor of the Concerts Lamoureux from 1983 and professor of chamber music at the Paris Conservatoire, 1984. *Address:* c/o Association des Concerts Lamoureux, 252 Rue du Faubourg St Honoré, 75008 Paris, France.

**BERNET, Dietfried;** conductor; *Musical Director, Tiroler Landestheater, Innsbruck;* b. 14 May 1940, Vienna, Austria; m. Johanna Lonsky. *Education:* Academy of Music and Performing Arts, Vienna with Hans Swarowsky and Dimitri Mitropoulos. *Career:* debut in orchestral concerts in Austria; conducted at major opera houses and guested with leading orchestras since 1962; Permanent Conductor at both Austrian State Opera Houses, 1964–; General Director of Music, City of Mainz and Conductor, Vienna State and Volksoper; Musical Dir Tiroler Landestheater, Innsbruck 2005–; Appearances with the Vienna and Chicago Symphonies, London Philharmonic and Philharmonia; RAI Orchestras in Italy, Berlin Philharmonic, Munich Radio and Philharmonia Hungarica; Festival engagements at Salzburg, Vienna, Spoleto, Glyndebourne, Budapest and Turin; repertoire includes works by Brahms, Bruckner, Mahler, Wagner, Verdi, Puccini and composers of the 20th century; Season 1991–92 with Die Meistersinger at Marseille, Don Giovanni at the Mozart Festival Schoenbrunn, Vienna; 1992–93 with Les Contes d'Hoffmann and Der Freischütz at the Volksoper; Idomeneo at Pretoria; 1994 concerts at Teatro Colón, Buenos Aires; Clemenza di Tito at Marseille; 1995 Tannhäuser at Copenhagen; Pearl Fishers at Leeds, with Opera North; Guest with Royal Danish Opera at Covent Garden with The Love of Three Oranges; Verdi Requiem with Royal Philharmonic Orchestra at Royal Albert Hall; Meistersinger at Torino; Chief Guest Conductor of the Royal Danish Opera, 1995–2000; 1996, Entführung at Geneva; House of the Dead, at Strasbourg; Arabella at Glyndebourne Festival; Don Giovanni at Covent Garden; 1997, Boris at Torino; Così fan tutte at Covent Garden (BBC live transmission); Mahler 3rd Symphony and Arabella at Copenhagen; Berlioz's Romeo and Juliette with Théâtre de la Monnaie, Brussels; Merry Widow with Royal Opera, London, 1998; Has also conducted opera at Munich, Hamburg, Cologne, Stuttgart, Naples, Barcelona, Venice, Palermo and Trieste; Conducted Martinů's Julietta at Bregenz, 2002. *Honours:* winner Int. Conductor's Competition, Liverpool 1962, granted title of Professor by the Austrian State President for merits for the republic of Austria 1995. *Address:* Tiroler Landestheater, Rennweg 2, 6020 Innsbruck, Austria (office). *Telephone:* (512) 52074. *Fax:* (512) 52074333. *E-mail:* tiroler@landestheater.at. *Website:* www.landestheater.at.

**BERNHEIMER, Martin;** Music Critic; b. 28 Sept. 1936, Munich, Germany; m. (1) Lucinda Pearson, 30 Sept 1961, divorced 1989, 1 s., 3 d.; (2) Linda Winer, 27 Sept 1993. *Education:* BMus, 1958–59; MA, New York University, 1961; Studied musicology with Gustave Reese. *Career:* Teacher, New York University, 1959–62; Contributing critic, New York Herald Tribune, 1959–62; Contributing Editor, Musical Courier, 1961–64; Temporary Music Critic, New York Post, 1961–65; Assistant to the music editor, Saturday Review, 1962–65; Managing editor, Philharmonic Hall Programme, New York, 1962–65; New York correspondent 1962–65, Los Angeles Correspondent 1965–97; Opera; Music Editor and Chief Music Critic, Los Angeles Times, 1965–96; Teacher, University of Southern California, Los Angeles, 1966–71; University of California at Los Angeles, 1969–75; California Institute of the Arts, 1975–82; California State University, Northridge, 1978–81; New York Music Critic for the Financial Times of London and guest Critic on Newsday, 1996–; Music Critic for New York Sidewalk (Microsoft), 1997–; Lecturer, Metropolitan Opera Guild, 1997–; mem, Pulitzer Prize Music Jury, 1984, 1986, 1989. *Contributions:* Articles in New Grove Dictionary of Music and Musicians; Articles and reviews in various journals; Liner notes for recordings; New Grove Dictionary of American Music; New Grove Dictionary of Opera; Regular panellist, moderator, essayist on Metropolitan Opera Broadcasts; Frequent guest on CBC broadcasts. *Honours:* Winner of Pulitzer Prize in Criticism, 1981.

**BERNIUS, Frieder;** Conductor; b. 1945, Ludwigshafen, Germany. *Education:* Studied in Stuttgart and Tubingen. *Career:* Founder, Stuttgart Chamber Choir, 1968; Regular appearances with the Stuttgart Baroque and Chamber Orchestras and German Chamber Philharmonic, Bremen; Suisse Romande Orchestra; Prague Philharmonic; Founder, International Festival of Early Music, Stuttgart, 1987; Professor, Mannheim Musikhochschule; Conductor, Haydn's Orfeo, London; Jommelli's Il Vologeso, Stuttgart, 1993; Demofoonte, Rome; Schwetzingen, 1995; Dresden Semperoper, Hasse's Olimpiade and Artemisia; Operas by Rameau including Hippolyte et Aricie at Bad Urach. *Recordings:* Il Vologeso. *Address:* c/o Kammerorchester Stuttgart, Heumadener Strasse 23, 7302 Ostfidern, Germany.

**BERNSTEIN, Lawrence F.;** Musicologist and University Professor; b. 25 March 1939, New York, NY, USA. *Education:* BS, Hofstra University, 1960; PhD, New York University, 1969. *Career:* Instructor, 1965–66; Assistant Professor, 1966–70; Music and Humanities, University of Chicago; Associate Professor 1970–81; Chairman Department of Music, 1972–73, 1974–77; Professor of Music, 1981–, University of Pennsylvania; Visiting Lecturer, Columbia University, Graduate School of Arts and Sciences, 1979; Visiting Associate Professor, Princeton University, 1980; Visiting Professor, Rutgers University, 1982–83; Supervising Editor, Masters and Monuments of the Renaissance, 1970–; Editor-in-Chief, Journal of the American Musicological Society, 1975–77. *Publications:* Ihan Gero; Madrigali italiani et canzoni francese a due voci, with James Haar, 1980; La Couronne et fleur des chansons a troys, 1984; The French Secular Chanson in the Sixteenth Century. *Contributions:* Articles in New Grove Dictionary of Music and Musicians, 1980; Articles and reviews in journals and other publications. *Address:* c/o Department of Music, University of Pennsylvania, 201 S 34th Street, Philadelphia, PA 19104-6313, USA.

**BÉROFF, Michel;** Pianist; b. 9 May 1950, Epinal, France. *Education:* Conservatories of Nancy and Paris, with Yvonne Loriod. *Career:* Debut: Paris, 1966; Has appeared on television and at Festivals in Portugal and Iran, 1967, also at Royal and Oxford Bach Festivals; Has lectured and given recitals and concerts in various European and South American countries; Appearances with the London Symphony Orchestra, Concerts Colonne, Orchestre de Paris, New York Philharmonic and BBC Symphony Orchestras; Toured Japan and South Africa. *Recordings include:* Prokofiev's Visions Fugitives; Messiaen's Quatuor pour la fin du Temps and Vingt Regards sur L'Enfant Jésus; Debussy's Préludes, Estampes and Pour le Piano; Music by Bartók, Stravinsky and Mozart. *Honours:* First Prize, Nancy Conservatory, 1962, 1963; First Prize, Paris Conservatory, 1966; First Prize, Olivier Messiaen Competition, Royan. *Address:* 114 rue de Dames, Paris 17, France.

**BERONESI, Debora;** Singer (Mezzo-soprano); b. 1965, Rome, Italy. *Education:* Accademia di Santa Cecilia, Rome. *Career:* Debut: Spoleto, 1988 as Eboli in Don Carlos; Appearances at Macerata and Treviso as Dorabella, Rossini's Isabella at Trieste and Meg Page in Falstaff at Enschede; Isaura in Rossini's Tancredi at Bologna; Palermo, 1993 in the premiere of Alice by Testoni; Salzburg Festival, 1993–94 as the Messenger in Monteverdi's Orfeo; Nero in Monteverdi's Poppea at La Scala, Milan and Antwerp; Frankfurt Opera, 1995 as Cecilio in Lucio Silla by Mozart and Idamante in Idomeneo; Sang Purcell's Dido at the 2001 Maggio Musicale, Florence. *Honours:* Winner, A Belli Competition, Spoleto, 1988. *Address:* c/o Frankfurt Opera, Untermainanlege 11, 6000 Frankfurt am Main, Germany.

**BERRY, John;** musician (clarinet) and opera director; *Artistic Director, ENO. Career:* fmr freelance clarinettist; established music coll., Sounds Alive, for young musicians in northern England; Casting Dir, ENO 1995, Dir of Opera Programming 2003–, also Artistic Dir 2005–; he has also acted as artistic consultant to numerous organizations, including the BBC, Channel 4, the Hallé Orchestra and the Royal Coll. of Music; f. Brereton Int. Music Symposium summer programme. *Address:* English National Opera, London Coliseum, St Martin's Lane, Trafalgar Square, London, WC2, England (office). *Website:* www.eno.org.

**BERTHOLD, Beatrice;** Concert Pianist; b. 11 Sept. 1964, Wiesbaden, Germany. *Education:* Academies of Music, Vienna and Cologne; Academy of Music, Detmold. *Career:* Debut: Wiesbaden National Theatre, 1978 (C. M. von Weber, konzertstück); Television debut on ZDF/Eurovision, presented by singer Annelise Rothenberger (Liszt, piano concerto No. 2); Solo Recitals and Concerts with Renowned Orchestras in Europe: Lucerne Music Festival, Berlin (Philharmonie), Hamburg (Musikhalle), Cologne (Philharmonie), London, 1983–; US debut at the German American Piano Festival in Atlanta, 1995; Several Concert Tours to South America: Porto Alegre, (Teatro da Ospa), Caracas, (Teatro Teresa Careno) 1996–; Television and radio appearances with Beethoven Piano Concerto No. 5; Rachmaninov Piano Sonata No. 1 and 2; Granados, Goyescas; Brahms, Fantasias op 116; Rhapsodies op 78; Scriabin, Fantasia op 28; Villa-Lobos, Ciclo Brasilieiro. *Recordings:* The Young Rachmaninov, 1990; Tchaikovsky/Rachmaninov/Scriabin: Early Piano Works, 1992; Granados: Goyescas + El Pelele, 1992; Hommage au Piano, 1994. *Current Management:* Konzertagentur Jens Gunnar Becker. *Address:* Grunstrasse 13, 58313 Herdecke, Germany.

**BERTI, Marco;** Singer (Tenor); b. 1961, Turin, Italy. *Education:* Studied at the Verdi Conservatory in Milan. *Career:* Sang widely in Italy as Jim in Mahagonny by Weill; Sang Pinkerton in Consenza, 1990, and Don Ottavio at Macerata, 1991; Frankfurt, 1991, as Guevara in a concert performance of Franchetti's Cristoforo Colombo; Strasbourg, 1992, as Alfredo; St Gallen,

1993, as Roberto Devereux; Season 1994–95 as Rodolfo and in Verdi's Stiffelio at La Scala; Season 1999–2000 as Foresto in Attila at Karlsruhe, Ismaele in Nabucco at the Deutsche Oper Berlin and Macduff at the Vienna Staatsoper; Riccardo (Ballo in Maschera) at the Bregenz Festival and Don José at Copenhagen; Sang Foresto at Montpellier, and made Covent Garden debut 2002, as Gabriele Adorno; Pinkerton, 2003. *Recordings include:* Cristoforo Colombo (Koch); Don Giovanni (Koch); Manon Lescaut (Sony). *Current Management:* IMG Artists, Lovell House, 616 Chiswick High Road, London W4 5RX, England. *Telephone:* (20) 8233-5800. *Fax:* (20) 8233-5801. *E-mail:* artistseurope@imgworld.com. *Website:* www.imgartists.com. *Current Management:* IMG Artists Paris – Vocal Division, 44 rue Blanche, 75009 Paris, France. *Telephone:* 1-44-31-00-10. *Fax:* 1-44-31-44-01. *E-mail:* artistsparis@imgartists.com. *Website:* www.imgartists.com. *Address:* c/o Opéra du Rhin, 19 Place Broglie, 67008 Strasbourg, France.

**BERTIN, Pascal;** Singer (countertenor); b. 1970, France. *Education:* Paris Conservatoire with William Christie. *Career:* Children's Choir of Paris, from age 11, with tours throughout the world; founder, Indigo, vocal jazz group, 1995; many concert and opera appearances with conductors Marc Minkowski, Christophe Rousset, John Eliot Gardiner, Sigiswald Kuijken and Philippe Herreweghe. *Recordings:* Oronte, Handel's Riccardo Primo; Caldara's Conversione di Clovedeo; The Three Countertenors and Pathways of Baroque Music–Cathedrals and Chapels; Orlando in Handel's Amadigi. *Honours:* First prize, Baroque vocal music, Paris Conservatoire. *Address:* c/o Harmonia Mundi UK, 45 Vyner Street, London, E2 9DQ, England. *Telephone:* (20) 8709-9525. *Fax:* (20) 8709-9501.

**BERTOLINO, Mario (Ercole);** Singer (Bass-Baritone); b. 10 Sept. 1934, Palermo, Italy. *Education:* Studied in Palermo and with Mario Basiola in Milan; Giuseppe Danise in New York. *Career:* Debut: Teatro Nuovo Milan, 1955; Marcello in La Bohème; Sang at La Scala, in Rome, Palermo, Munich, Lyon and Mexico City; Moved to Forest Hills, NY, sang widely in the US at Boston, Cincinnati, Pittsburgh, San Antonio, Washington and New York City Opera; Roles have included Verdi's Amonasro, Renato, Macbeth, Iago, Germont and Luna; Donizetti's Dulcamara, Don Pasquale and Enrico; Gerard in Andrea Chénier; Puccini's Sharpless and Lescaut; Iago in Otello; Connecticut Opera 1987–88 as Don Pasquale and Dulcamara; Rome 1989, as Mozart's Bartolo; Also sang in concert.

**BERTOLO, Aldo;** Singer (Tenor); b. 22 Oct. 1949, Turin, Italy. *Career:* Debut: Sang Mozart's Ferrando at Susa, 1978; Many appearances in Italy; South America; Europe, in the lyric repertoire; Among his best roles are Donizetti's Edgardo, Tonie and Ernesto; Pylades, in Piccinni's Iphigénie en Tauride; Rossini's Lindoro, Adalbert in Adelaide di Borgogna and Don Ottavio; Season 1985 sang Arturo in I Puritani at Martina Franca; Ramiro in La Cenerentola, in Santiago; At Valle d'Itria 1986, sang Thoas in the first modern revival of Traetta's Ifigenia in Tauride; Elvino in La Sonnambula at Piacenza, 1986; Teatro Carlo Felice, Genoa 1988, as Narciso in L'Italiana in Algeri; Other roles include the Fisherman in Guillaume Tell, Lorenzo in Fra Diavolo and Verdi's Alfredo; Season 1991, as Ernesto at Pisa and Narciso at Trieste. *Address:* c/o Teatro Carlo Felice, 16100 Genoa, Italy.

**BESA, Alexander;** Czech violist; b. 28 Feb. 1971, Havana, Cuba; m.; one d. *Education:* Music School, Znojmo, Czech Republic, State Conservatory, Brno, Int. Menuhin Music Acad., Switzerland, Music Akademie Basel. *Career:* debut, Mozart Sinfonia Concertante K 364 with Moravian Chamber Orchestra, Brno 1990; appeared as viola soloist with Camerata Bern, Kurphälzisches Kammerorchester, Camerata Lysy, Basle Symphony and Radio Orchestra, Janáček Philharmonic, Ostrava, B. Martinů Philharmonic, Zlin, Lucerne Symphony Orchestra, State Philharmonic, Kosice; principal violist, Lucerne Symphony Orchestra and Camerata Bern. *Recordings:* A Lysy, Camerata Lysy, Mendelssohn 1992; T. Zehetmair, Camerata Bern – Vivaldi 1995; H. Holliger, Camerata Bern, Bach 1996; Ensemble Tiramisu, Quintets by Brahms and Herzogenberg, Octets by Mendelssohn and Gade 1996; Viola Recital 1997; Music for Viola and Piano (Recording of the Year) 1999; M. Bruch: Double Concerto for clarinet, viola and orchestra (Recording of the Year 2002) 2000; Alessandro Rolla: Sonatas for viola and bass 2001. *Honours:* winner Beethoven Int. Viola Competition, Czech Republic 1994, winner H. Schaeuble Viola Competition, Lausanne 1995, L. Tertis Viola Competition Morris Maddrell Prize, Isle of Man 1997. *Current Management:* Central European Music Agency, Kapucínské nám. 308/14, 602 00 Brno, Czech Republic. *Telephone:* (542) 213 053. *Fax:* (542) 213 056. *E-mail:* agency@cema-music.com. *Website:* www.cema-music.com.

**BESRODNY, Igor;** Conductor and Violinist; b. 7 May 1930, Tbilisi, Russia. *Education:* Graduated Moscow Conservatoire, 1955. *Career:* Many appearances in Russia and elsewhere from 1948, after winning the Prague International Competition; Teacher at the Moscow Conservatoire from 1957 (professor, 1972); Debut as conductor, 1970, directing the Moscow Chamber Orchestra, 1977–83; Premiered the first Concerto by Kabalevsky, 1948. *Address:* c/o Moscow Conservatoire, ul Gertzena 13, 103009 Moscow, Russia.

**BEST, Jonathan;** Singer (Bass); b. 1958, Kent, England. *Career:* Debut: Sang Sarastro with Welsh National Opera, 1983; Many leading roles in the bass repertory, with Welsh National Opera, Scottish Opera, Dublin Grand Opera, Kent Opera and Opera North; Appearances at Covent Garden in Die Meistersinger, Otello, Don Carlos and King Arthur (as Grimbauld, with Les Arts Florissants, 1995); Season 1994–95 in The Rake's Progress at Salzburg, in The Queen of Spades at Glyndebourne and The Fairy Queen for English

National Opera; Other roles include Don Alfonso in Così fan tutte (Opera North, 1997); Sang Trulove in The Rake's Progress for Welsh National Opera, 1996; Season 1998 with Cassandro in Mozart's Finta Semplice at Garsington and Garibaldo in Rodelinda for GTO at Glyndebourne; Season 1999–2000 as Leporello and Britten's Bottom for Opera North; St Magnus Festival 2000 in the premiere of Mr. Emmett takes a Walk, by Peter Maxwell Davies. *Current Management:* Musichall Ltd, Vicarage Way, Ringmer, East Sussex BN8 5LA, England. *Telephone:* (1273) 814240. *Fax:* (1273) 813637. *E-mail:* info@musichall.uk.com. *Website:* www.musichall.uk.com.

**BEST, Matthew,** MA; singer (bass-baritone) and conductor; b. 6 Feb. 1957, Farnborough, Kent, England; m. Rosalind Mayes 1983. *Education:* King's Coll., Cambridge, National Opera Studio, studied with Otakar Kraus, Robert Lloyd and Patrick McGuigan. *Career:* debut, Seneca in The Coronation of Poppea, Cambridge University Opera Society, 1978; Principal Bass, Royal Opera, 1980–86; regular guest artist with WNO, Opera North, Netherlands Opera, Scottish Opera, ENO; extensive concert career; Founder and Dir of the Corydon Singers 1973–, Corydon Orchestra 1991–; Principal Conductor of the Hanover Band 1998–99; has also worked frequently, as guest conductor, with English Chamber Orchestra, London Mozart Players, City of London Sinfonia, plus appearances with English Northern Philharmonia, Manchester Camerata, RTE Concert Orchestra, Royal Seville Symphony Orchestra; BBC National Orchestra of Wales; recent opera appearances (as singer) include Pizarro (Beethoven, Leonore) at the 1996 Salzburg Festival, BBC Proms, Lincoln Center Festival, New York, The Flying Dutchman, Jochanaan (Salome), King Mark (Tristan & Isolde) and Kutuzov (War and Peace) for ENO, Kurwenal (Tristan und Isolde), Amfortas (Parsifal) and Scarpia (Tosca) for Scottish Opera; sang Wotan in Das Rheingold (concert) for ENO 2001; Wotan in Das Rheingold and Die Walküre for Scottish Opera at the Edinburgh Festival 2000–01; Scarpia (Tosca) for Florida Grand Opera; sang the Wanderer in Siegfried at the 2002 Edinburgh Festival; complete Ring cycles (as Wotan) at the 2003 Festival. *Compositions:* Alice, opera, work performed Aldeburgh Festival 1979. *Recordings:* As singer: include, Beethoven, Leonore; Elgar, The Dream of Gerontius; Britten, Peter Grimes; Billy Budd; Berlioz, L'Enfance du Christ; Verdi, Don Carlo (video); Vaughan Williams, Sir John in Love; As conductor: include Bruckner, Te Deum and Masses; Berlioz L'Enfance du Christ; Beethoven Mass in C and Emperor Cantatas; Fauré Requiem; Duruflé, Requiem; Vaughan Williams, Hugh the Drover; Rachmaninov Vespers; Works by Vaughan Williams, Britten, Finzi, Tchaikovsky, Mendelssohn, Simpson and others, all with Corydon Singers, Corydon Orchestra, English Chamber Orchestra, City of London Sinfonia. *Honours:* SE Arts Association; Friends of Covent Garden, Bursary, 1980; Decca-Kathleen Ferrier Prize, 1982. *Current Management:* IMG Artists, Lovell House, 616 Chiswick High Road, London, W4 5RX, England. *Telephone:* (20) 8233-5800. *Fax:* (20) 8233-5801. *E-mail:* artistseurope@imgworld.com. *Website:* www.imgartists.com.

**BEST, Roger;** Violist and College Professor; b. 28 Sept. 1938, Liverpool, England; m. Bronwen Naish, 5 c. *Education:* Royal Manchester College of Music. *Career:* Debut: Manchester 1955; With Hallé Orchestra, 1958–60; Principal Viola, Northern Sinfonia Orchestra, 1961–73; Gave world premieres of viola concertos by Malcolm Arnold, 1972 and Richard Rodney Bennett, 1973; Professor, Royal College of Music. *Honours:* Open Scholarship, RMCM, 1955; Hiles Gold Medal, 1958; Barber Trust Scholarship to Birmingham University, 1960. *Address:* 9 Granard Road, Wandsworth Common, London SW12, England.

**BESUTTI, Paola;** Musicologist; b. 18 April 1960, Mantua, Italy; m. Roberto Giuliani 1992. *Education:* Musicological studies at Parma University; Pianoforte at Conservatory of Music in Mantua. *Career:* Professor at Pesaro Conservatory of Music; Member of editorial staff of Rivista Italiana di Musicologia; Professor, Researcher, Institute of Musicology of Parma University, 1990–; mem, American Musicological Society; International Musicological Society; Società Italiana di Educazione Musicale; Società Italiana di Musicologia. *Recordings:* Collaborated with Parrott, Vartolo, Savall, Gini; BBC, RAI, Radio France, RSI. *Publications include:* La corte musicale di Ferdinando Carlo Gonzaga, Mantova Areari, 1989; Hildegard von Bingen, Ordo Virtutum, Sa musique et s. idée de théatre, in Actes de la Société Internationale pour l'étude du théatre médiéval, Barcelona, Institut del Teatro, 1997; Ave maris stella: la tradizione mantovana nuovamente posta in musica da Monteverdi in Claudio Monteverdi, Studi e prospettive, Firenze, Olschki, 1997; Tasso contra Guarini: una Rappresentazione con intermedi degli Intrichi d'amore (1606) in Torquato Tasso e la cultura estense, Firenze, Olschki, 1997; La figura professionale del cantante d'opera: Quaderni storici, XXXII n 2 agosto, 1997; Giostre e tornei a Mantova Parma e Piacenza fra Cinque e Seicento in Musica e tornei nel Seicento Italiano, Lucca, LIM. *Contributions:* Music reviews and publications including: Atlas Mondiale du Baroque, Dizionario degli Editori Musicali Italiani, The New Grove, The New Grove Dictionary of Opera. *Address:* Piazzale Vittorio Veneto 1, 46100 Mantova, Italy.

**BEUDERT, Mark;** Singer (Tenor); b. 4 June 1961, New York. *Education:* Studied at Columbia University and Michigan University. *Career:* Sang at Santo Domingo Opera from 1983; Grand Rapids Opera, 1985; At Philadelphia and the New York City Opera; Washington, 1986, as Pedrillo in Die Entfuhrung; Queensland State Opera at Brisbane as Pinkerton and Faust, 1987, 1991; Season 1988–89 as Candide by Bernstein for Scottish Opera and the Old Vic Theatre, London; Sam Kaplan in Weill's Street Scene for English

National Opera. *Honours:* Winner, Pavarotti Competition at Philadelphia, 1985. *Address:* c/o New York City Opera, Lincoln Center, New York NY 10023, USA.

**BEURON, Yann;** Singer (Tenor); b. 1970, France. *Education:* Paris Conservatoire with Anna Maria Bondi. *Career:* Appearances as Belmonte, Strasbourg; Fernando at Bordeaux and in Rossini's Cenerentola at the Ascoli Festival; In Rameau's Hippolyte et Aricie, Paris Palais Garnier, Geneva, Opéra in Offenbach's Orphée, 1997; Concerts include the Evangelist in Bach's Passions; Soloist, Berlioz Te Deum. *Recordings:* Le Chevalier Danois, Gluck's Armide. *Current Management:* IMG Artists, Lovell House, 616 Chiswick High Road, London W4 5RX, England. *Telephone:* (20) 8233-5800. *Fax:* (20) 8233-5801. *E-mail:* artistseurope@imgworld.com. *Website:* www.imgartists.com. *Current Management:* IMG Artists Paris – Vocal Division, 44 rue Blanche, 75009 Paris, France. *Telephone:* 1-44-31-00-10. *Fax:* 1-44-31-44-01. *E-mail:* artistsparis@imgartists.com. *Website:* www.imgartists.com. *Address:* c/o Geneva Opéra, 11 Boulevard du Théâtre, 1211 Geneva 11, Switzerland.

**BEVAN, Maurice (Guy Smalman);** Singer; b. 10 March 1921, London, England; m. Anne Alderson, 1 d. *Education:* Magdalen College, Oxford; BMus Cantuar, 1990; FTCL; ARCM, Hon. FGCM. *Career:* Vicar Choral, St Paul's Cathedral, 1949–89; Founder Member, The Deller Consort; Oratorio and Recitals, BBC; Soloist in the United Kingdom, Europe, USA, Israel and South America. *Recordings include:* Purcell's Fairy Queen; Handel's Acis and Galatea. *Publications:* Editions of English vocal music of the 17th and 18th Centuries. *Contributions:* Journal of the American Musicological Society; Die Musik in Geschichte und Gegenwart; Grove's Dictionary of Music and Musicians. *Address:* 45 Court Way, Twickenham, Middlesex TW2 7 SA, England.

**BEYER, Frank Michael;** German composer and professor of composition; b. 8 March 1928, Berlin; s. of Oskar Beyer and Margarete (née Löwenfeld) Beyer; m. Sigrid Uhle 1950; one s. one d. *Education:* Berliner Kirchenmusikschule, Staatliche Hochschule für Musik (HDK), piano training in Leipzig. *Career:* began career in church music; Scholarship, Cité Internationale des Arts Paris 1968; Docent Berliner Kirchenmusikschule 1953–62; with Hochschule für Musik Berlin, Prof. of Composition 1968–; initiated range of 'musica nova sacra' 1970–85; promoter Inst. für Neue Musik 1990; Supervisory mem. of Gema 1973–83; Exec. mem. German Music Bds 1978–82; mem. Akad. der Künste Berlin 1979–, Dir of Music Div. 1986–; mem. Bayerische Akad. der Schönen Künste 1981–. *Compositions:* orchestral and chamber music, organ and solo piano works, music for TV films. *Honours:* Kunstpreis Berlin for Young Generation 1957, Bernhard-Sprengel Prize 1962, Prix Jeunesse Musicale 1967. *Address:* Akademie der Künste, Hanseatenweg 10, 10557 Berlin (office); Söhtstrasse 6, 12203 Berlin, Germany. *Telephone:* (30) 8338051.

**BEZDUZ, Soner Bülen;** Singer (tenor); b. 1970, Turkey. *Education:* Music Academy of Gazi University, Ankara; European Opera Centre, Manchester. *Career:* Debut: Mozart's Lucio Silla on tour with the European Opera Centre, 1999; State Opera of Mersin as Rodolfo in La Bohème, Edgardo (Lucia di Lammermoor) and the Duke of Mantua; Verdi's Alfredo at the Aspendos Festival; Cassio in Otello and roles in Benvenuto Cellini and Les Troyens in concert performances under Colin Davis; Season 2000–2001 as Alfredo in Nancy and Rennes, and Fenton in Falstaff for Opera de Lausanne. *Honours:* Prizewinner, Concours International de Chant de Paris, 1999. *Current Management:* Athole Still International Management, Forresters Hall, 25–27 Westow Street, London, SE19 3RY, England. *Telephone:* (20) 8771-5271. *Fax:* (20) 8768-6600. *Website:* www.atholestill.com.

**BEZNOSIUK, Pavlo Roman;** Irish/Ukranian violinist; b. 4 July 1960, London, England. *Education:* Guildhall School of Music and Drama. *Career:* Leader of Parley of Instruments 1984–7; founded Beethoven String Trio of London 1992; solo debut at Proms 1993; soloist and concertmaster with period-instrument orchestras, including The Acad. of Ancient Music, Amsterdam Baroque Orchestra, Orchestra of the Age of Enlightenment and the Hanover Band; Prof. of Baroque Violin, Koninklijk Conservatorium, The Hague. *Recordings include:* Bach Brandenburg Concertos with the New London Consort, Vivaldi's Op. 6 Concertos with Academy of Ancient Music, Schubert Octet with Hausmusik, Biber's Rosary Sonatas. *Address:* 170 Bow Common Lane, London, E3 4HH, England.

**BEZUYEN, Arnold;** singer (tenor); b. 1965, Netherlands. *Education:* Int. Opera Centrum Nederland, Alkmaar. *Career:* debut as Rodolfo in La Bohème, at Alkmaar; sang at Augsburg and Bremen as Turiddu, Pinkerton, Alfredo in La Traviata, Ismael in Nabucco and Aegisthus in Elektra; Bayreuth Festival as Loge, and in Parsifal and Lohengrin; La Scala Milan in Die Frau ohne Schatten, under Giuseppe Sinopoli; season 2001–02 as the Berlioz Faust at Bremen, Shuisky in Boris Godunov at Kassel Wagner's Vogelgesang for Netherlands Opera and Beethoven's Florestan for Nationale Reis-opera; other roles include Cassio in Otello, Idomeneo and Don José. *Recordings include:* Das Rheingold, conducted by Gustav Kuhn (Arte Nova). *Current Management:* Hilbert Artists Management, Maximilianstrasse 22, 80539 Munich, Germany. *Telephone:* (89) 290747-0 (office). *Fax:* (89) 290747-90 (office). *E-mail:* agentur@hilbert.de (office). *Website:* www.hilbert.de.

**BEZZUBENKOV, Gennady;** Singer (Bass); b. 1955, St Petersburg, Russia. *Education:* Graduated St Petersburg Conservatoire 1979. *Career:* Appearances in opera throughout Russia; Kirov Opera from 1989; Roles have included Glinka's Ivan Susannin, Khan Konchak in Prince Igor, Gremin in Eugene Onegin, Pimen, Varlaam and Ivan Khovansky; Further engagements as Wagner's Gurnemanz and King Henry, Verdi's Grand Inquisitor and Mozart's Bartolo, and in London concert performances of The Legend of the Invisible City of Kitezh (Barbican Hall, 1994), Katerina Izmailova by Shostakovich and Parsifal (Royal Albert Hall, 1999); Sang Kutuzov in War and Peace and Dosifei in Khovanshchina with the Kirov Opera at Covent Garden, 2000; Sang Banquo at St Petersburg and the premiere of Gubaidulina's St John Passion, at Stuttgart, 2000; St John Passion at the London Proms, 2002. *Recordings include:* War and Peace, The Gambler, The Maid of Pskov, Sadko and Ruslan and Lyudmila (Phillips Classics). *Address:* c/o Kirov Opera, Mariinsky Theatre, Mariinsky Square, St Petersburg, Russia.

**BIANCHI, Lino;** Musicologist and Composer; b. 14 May 1920, Vedano Olona, Vasese, Italy; m. Gabriella Limentani. *Education:* Diploma in Composition, G Rossini Conservatory, Pesaro, 1945. *Career:* Artistic Director, Centro Oratorio Musicale, Rome, 1949–63; Edition de Santis, Rome, 1960–; GP da Palestrina Foundation, 1973–; Numerous broadcasts on Palestrina, Carissimi and other early composers; Italian radio and television, 1952–. *Compositions:* Il Principe Felice, one-act opera; Uruel, three-act dramatic commentary. *Recordings:* As conductor, works by Carissimi, Stradella, A Scarlatti and D Scarlatti. *Publications:* Editions of complete works of G Carissimi and GP de Palestrina; Complete oratorios of A Scarlatti, 1964–; A Stradella, 1969; Musical encyclopedias and journals. *Address:* Circonvallazione Clodia 82, 00195 Rome, Italy.

**BIANCONI, Lorenzo Gennaro,** PhD; Swiss/Italian musicologist; *Professor of Musical Dramaturgy, University of Bologna*; b. 14 Jan. 1946, Muralto, Switzerland; m. Giuseppina La Face 1979; two s. *Education:* Univ. of Heidelberg, Germany, studied music theory with Luciano Sgrizzi in Lugano, Switzerland. *Career:* collaborator, Répertoire International des Sources Musicales, Italy 1969–70; mem., German Inst., Venice 1974–76; guest asst. German Historical Inst., Rome 1976; guest Prof., Princeton Univ., USA 1977; Prof. of Musical Dramaturgy, Univ. of Bologna, Italy 1977–; Prof. of the History of Music, Siena Univ., Arezzo, Italy 1980–83; Co-Ed., Rivista Italiana di Musicologia 1973–79; Ed., Acta Musicologica 1987–91; Head of Programme Cttee, 14th Int. Musicological Congress, Bologna 1987; Co-Ed., Musica e Storia 1993–; Co-Ed., Il Saggiatore Musicale 1994–; Ed., Historiae Musicae Cultores 1999–; Head of Music Dept, Bologna Univ., Italy 1998–2001; hon. mem. Accademia Filarmonica, Bologna; corresponding mem., American Musicological Soc. *Publications:* B. Marcello, Sonates pour clavecin (ed. with Luciano Sgrizzi) 1971, P. M. Marsolo, Madrigali a 4 voci (1614) 1973, A Il Verso, Madrigali a 3 e a 5 voci (1605–19) 1978, Il Seicento 1982, La Drammaturgia Musicale 1986, Storia dell'Opera Italiana 1987, I Libretti Italiani di G. F. Händel (with G. La Face) 1992, Il Teatro d'Opera in Italia 1993, G. Frescobaldi, Madrigali a 5 voci (with M. Privitera) 1996, Guida al percorso museale (Museo della Musica, Bologna) 2004. *Honours:* Dent Medal of the Royal Musical Asscn 1983, Premio Imola per la Critica 1994. *Address:* Dipartimento di Musica e Spettacolo, Università di Bologna, via Barberia 4, 40123, Bologna (office); via A. Frank 17, 40068 San Lazzaro di Savena, Bologna, Italy (home). *Telephone:* 051 2092156 (office). *Fax:* 051 2001 (office). *E-mail:* lorenzo.bianconi@unibo.it (office).

**BIANCONI, Philippe;** Concert Pianist; b. 1960, France. *Career:* Many appearances in concerto repertory and recitals; Carnegie Hall debut recital 1987, followed by engagements with the orchestras of Cleveland, Los Angeles, Atlanta, Dallas, Pittsburgh and Montreal; BBC London Proms debut with the Orchestre de Paris and Semyon Bychkov; Other conductors include Lorin Maazel, Georges Prêtre, Jeffrey Tate, Kurt Masur, Edo de Waart and Christoph von Dohnányi; European recitals in London, Berlin, Vienna, Milan and Amsterdam; Chamber concerts with the Sine Nomine Quartet, Janos Starker and Gary Hoffman; Season 2000–01 with concerts in Budapest, Paris, Rome, Montreal, Mexico City; Rachmaninov 2nd Concerto at Palais Garnier, Paris; Recital debut at the Berlin Philharmonie, 2002; Season 2001–02: Concerts in Paris, New York, Reykjavik, Santiago do Chile, Tours in the USA, Germany and Spain, including with Berlin Philharmonic Orchestra. *Recordings include:* Ravel, Schubert and Schumann (Lyrinx); Brahms Piano Quintet (Clavos); Shostakovich and Prokofiev Cello Sonatas (Le Chant du Monde). *Honours:* Silver Medal, Seventh Van Cliburn International Competition. *Address:* c/o Musicaglotz, 11 rue Le Verrier, 75006 Paris, France.

**BIBBY, Gillian;** Composer; b. 31 Aug. 1945, Lower Hutt, New Zealand. *Education:* Studied at the University of Otago and at Victoria University with Douglas Lilburn; Further study in Berlin and Cologne, with Aloys Kontarsky, Kagel and Stockhausen. *Career:* Teacher in New Zealand, and editor of Canzona, 1982–84. *Compositions include:* Lest you be my enemy, ballet, 1976; Synthesis for tape, 1977; In Memoriam for 8 voices, organ and percussion, 1979; Marama Music, music-theatre, 1978; 11 Characters in Search of a Composer, for military band and percussion. *Address:* c/o New Zealand Music Centre, PO Box 10042, Level 13, Brandon Street, Wellington, New Zealand.

**BICCIRE, Patrizia;** Singer (Soprano); b. 1973, Porto San Giorgio, Italy. *Education:* Conservatorio Rossini and Accademia Rossiniana in Pesaro. *Career:* Debut: Rossini Festival at Pesaro 1992, as Protagonist in La Scala di Seta; Many appearances throughout Italy in bel canto and Mozart repertory; Glyndebourne Festival debut 2000, as Elvira in Don Giovanni; Season 2000–2001 as Nannetta in Falstaff at La Monnaie, Brussels, and

Susanna in Le nozze di Figaro at Glyndebourne; Il turco in Italia at Grand Théâtre, Geneva. *Recordings include:* Albums for EMI Classics. *Current Management:* IMG Artists, Lovell House, 616 Chiswick High Road, London W4 5RX, England. *Telephone:* (20) 8233-5800. *Fax:* (20) 8233-5801. *E-mail:* artistseurope@imgworld.com. *Website:* www.imgartists.com. *Current Management:* IMG Artists Paris – Vocal Division, 44 rue Blanche, 75009 Paris, France. *Telephone:* 1-44-31-00-10. *Fax:* 1-44-31-44-01. *E-mail:* artistsparis@imgartists.com. *Website:* www.imgartists.com. *Address:* c/o Glyndebourne Festival Opera, Glyndebourne, Lewes, Sussex BN8 5UU, England.

**BICKERS, Helen;** Singer (Soprano); b. 1959, Atlanta, Georgia, USA. *Career:* Sang at Bremerhaven Opera from 1986 as Amelia, Ballo in Maschera; Agathe in Der Freischütz, Vitellia in La Clemenza di Tito, Aida, Butterfly and Donizetti's Anna Bolena; Freiburg 1989–93 as Leonora in Il Trovatore; Elettra in Idomeneo, Ariadne, the Marschallin in Rosenkavalier and Janáček's Jenůfa; Dessau, 1993–95, as Anna Bolena and Lucrezia in I Due Foscari by Verdi; Guest appearances in London, Washington as Maria Stuarda; Düsseldorf, as Elisabeth in Don Carlos; Season 1995–96 as Amelia at the Deutsche Oper Berlin and Gioconda at Bremen; Season 2001–02 as Strauss's Ariadne and Chrysothemis, at Hannover. *Address:* c/o Staatstheater Hannover, Opernplatz 1, D-30159 Hannover, Germany.

**BICKERSTAFF, Robert;** Australian singer (baritone) and voice teacher; b. 26 July 1932, Sydney; m. Ann Howard. *Education:* New South Wales Conservatorium with Lyndon Jones, Melbourne Conservatorium with Henry Portnoj, Paris with Dominique Modesti. *Career:* debut, Marseilles 1962, as Thoas in Iphigénie en Tauride; Sang in Nice, Bordeaux and Marseille; Principal Baritone Sadler's Wells and English National Opera, 1964–70; Roles included: Amonasro, Escamillo, Macbeth, Boccanegra, Scarpia, Wotan, Mozart's Count and Eugene Onegin; Guest appearances with Pittsburgh Opera, Welsh National Opera and at Covent Garden; Over 60 roles in Opera; Other roles included Wagner's Dutchman, Ezio in Attila, Luna, Renato in Un Ballo in Maschera, Enrico in Lucia di Lammermoor and Massenet's Hérode; Boris in Lady Macbeth of Mtsensk by Shostakovich, Adelaide Festival; Oratorio and recital performances; Appearances on BBC radio and television; Previously Professor of singing at the Royal Academy in Music; London and Tutor of Singing at King's College, Cambridge. *Recordings:* La Juive, Raritas; Private Collection; Society of Musicians, London. *Honours:* Hon. ARAM. *Address:* 8 William Street, North Sydney, 2060, Australia.

**BICKET, Harry;** Conductor and Harpsichordist; b. 1960, Liverpool, England. *Education:* Royal College of Music and Oxford University. *Career:* Organist and harpsichordist with Academy of Ancient Music, The English Concert, Monteverdi Orchestra, Philharmonia and City of Birmingham Symphony Orchestra; Now Opera and Concert Conductor; Conducted Monteverdi's Orfeo and Combattimento di Tancredi e Clorinda and Handel's Ariodante, for English National Opera; Other productions include Gluck's Orfeo for Scottish Opera, Magic Flute for Opera North, The Return of Ulysses at Buxton Festival and for Opera North, and Werther for English Touring Opera; Conducted Storace's No Song, No Supper with BBC Scottish Symphony Orchestra; Conducted many British orchestras including Bournemouth Sinfonietta, City of London Sinfonia and Ulster Orchestra; Conducted Theodora at Glyndebourne, 1996; Season 1997–98 included Figaro at New York City Opera, Giulio Cesare for Australian Opera; Season 1998–99 with Rodelinda on Glyndebourne Tour, Orfeo with Royal Danish Opera and Semele with ENO; Further engagements include new opera productions for New York City Opera with Clemenza di Tito and Rinaldo, Bavarian State Opera with Rinaldo, and Opera North with Radamisto; in 2001–02 conducted Giulio Cesare with Los Angeles Opera, La Clemenza di Tito for WNO and Xerxes for ENO; Season 2002–03 included Messiah with WNO and Royal Liverpool Philharmonic Orchestra, Mathew Passion Rotterdam Philharmonic and Haydn Symphonies with Danish Radio Sinfonietta; Opera productions included Theodora for Glyndebourne Festival Opera, Tamerlano for Spoleto (USA) and debut with Chigaco Lyric Opera conducting Partnenope; Television work includes My Night with Handel for Channel 4, 1996. *Recordings:* Susan Graham and Orchestra of the Age of Enlightenment; David Daniels and OAE. *Current Management:* Askonas Holt Ltd, Lonsdale Chambers, 27 Chancery Lane, London, WC2A 1PF, England. *Telephone:* (20) 7400-1700. *Fax:* (20) 7400-1799. *E-mail:* info@askonasholt.co.uk. *Website:* www.askonasholt.co.uk.

**BICKLEY, Susan;** Singer (Mezzo-Soprano); b. 27 May 1955, Liverpool, England. *Education:* City University, London, and the Guildhall School of Music. *Career:* Debut: As Proserpina in Monteverdi's Orfeo, at Florence; Opera roles include Baba the Turk and Ulrica for Opera 80, Mozart's Marcellina and Elvira, Janáček's Kabanicha and Kostelnicka for the Glyndebourne Tour; Britten's Florence Pike, Hippolyta and Mrs Sedley at the Glyndebourne Festival; Dorabella and Andromache in King Priam for English National Opera, Feodor in Boris Godunov at Covent Garden; Further engagements as Kabanicha and a Flowermaiden at the Opéra Bastille (1997), Octavian at the Hong Kong Festival and Herodias in Salome at San Francisco; Concerts include Ligeti's Requiem at the 1994 Salzburg Festival and the Missa Solemnis on tour with Les Arts Florissants to Vienna and in France, 1995; Season 1995–96 with El Amor Brujo in Rome and Stravinsky's Faun and Shepherdess in Hong Kong; Further concerts with the London Symphony, Philharmonia, London Philharmonic Orchestra, London Sinfonietta, London Classical Players and Allegri and Brodsky Quartets; Season 1996–97 included Messiah with the Hallé Orchestra, Stravinsky with the BBC Symphony Orchestra and Das Lied von der Erde with the BBC National Orchestra of

Wales; Premiere by a British company of Henze's The Prince of Homburg, 1996; Handel's Admeto at Beaune, 1998; Sang in the premiere of Louis Andriessen's Writing to Vermeer, Amsterdam 1999; Season 2000–01 as the Ghost in the premiere production of Birtwistle's The Last Supper, Berlin Staatsoper and Glyndebourne Touring Opera; Kostelnička in Jenůfa at Glyndebourne and in the premiere of David Sawer's From Morning to Midnight, for ENO; London Proms, 2002. *Recordings include:* Socrate by Satie, Monteverdi's Il Ballo delle Ingrate, Dido and Aeneas, and The Fairy Queen (EMI); Other labels include Hyperion, Nimbus and DGG. *Current Management:* Intermusica Artists Management Ltd, 16 Duncan Terrace, London N1 8BZ, England. *Telephone:* 20 7278 5455. *Fax:* 20 7278 8434. *E-mail:* mail@intermusica.co.uk. *Website:* www.intermusica.co.uk.

**BIDDINGTON, Eric Wilhelm,** BA, BSc, BMus, MA; New Zealand composer; b. 19 Oct. 1953, Timaru; m. Elizabeth Ann Biddington 1989. *Education:* Univ. of Canterbury, Christchurch. *Career:* debut, Christchurch Arts Centre, Christchurch; Major recitals of chamber music, Christchurch, 1985–97, Lower Hutt, 1988, Hamilton, 1989; Premiere performance of Concerto for Two Violins and String Orchestra at Tempe, Arizona, USA, 1989; mem. APRA. *Compositions:* Mainly chamber music and some orchestral works, including Suite for Violin and Piano, 1985; Three Pieces for Cello and Piano, 1986; Scherzetto, for Clarinet and Piano, 1986; Autumn Music for Viola and Piano, 1987; Flute Concerto, 1987; Music for Friends for piano trio, 1988; Suite for Oboe and Piano, 1989; Two Dances for Alto Saxophone and Piano, 1989; Four Piano Preludes, 1990; Three Bagatelles for Flute and Piano, 1990; Haere Ra– A Song for 2-part Treble Voices and Piano; Flute Concerto, 1991; Introduction for Clarinet and Piano, 1993; Concertos for Oboe, Alto Saxophone, Two Violins; Sinfonietta; Overtures; Sonatinas for Violin and Pianoforte, Tenor Saxophone and Piano, Oboe and Piano, Clarinet and Piano, Treble Recorder and Piano, Flute and Piano, Trumpet and Piano; Beauty and The Beast, ballet, 1994; Divertimento for Orchestra, 1996. *Recordings:* The Chamber Music of Eric Biddington; Music for Friends; Southern Melodies; Tunes and Airs, Chamber music by Eric Biddington; Flute Concerto and Chamber Music. *Publications:* 46 publs of chamber music, 10 with Nota Bene Music, 36 others; Pastorale for Clarinet and Piano, 1994; Introduction and Allegro for Alto Saxophone and Piano, 1994; Two Amourettes for Oboe and Piano, 1995. *Honours:* Award, Composers Association of New Zealand Trust Fund, 1989. *Address:* 27 Torrens Road, Hillmorton, Christchurch 2, New Zealand. *E-mail:* ebiddington@actrix.co.nz (home).

**BIEITO, Calixto;** Spanish opera and theatre director; b. 2 Nov. 1963, Miranda de Ebro, Catalonia; m. Roser Carni; one s. *Education:* Univ. of Barcelona, Drama School of Tarragona, Theatre Inst. of Barcelona. *Career:* opera productions include La Verbena de la Paloma (Zarzuela) at Edinburgh Festival 1997, Un Ballo in Maschera for ENO 2000, for Gran Teatre del Liceu, Barcelona 2001, Don Giovanni for ENO 2001, Così fan tutte for WNO 2002, Die Dreigroschenoper, Bobigny, Paris 2003, Il Trovatore at Staatsoper Hanover, Die Entführung aus dem Serail at Komische Oper, Berlin 2004, Il Trovatore at Edinburgh Festival 2004. *Honours:* Premio Ercillo for Life is a Dream 2000, Irish Times best director award for Barbaric Comedies, Glasgow Herald outstanding artist award 2003. *Address:* c/o Teatro Romea de Barcelona, Calle Hospital 51, Barcelona, Spain (office).

**BIEITO, Calixto;** Spanish opera and theatre director; *Artistic Director, Teatre Romea, Barcelona*; b. 1963, Miranda de Ebro. *Career:* noted for his controversial interpretations of classic operas; operas directed include La Verbena de la Paloma, Edin. 1997, Pierrot Lunaire, Barcelona 1998, Il Mondo Della Luna, Maastricht 1999, Carmen, Festival Peralada 1999, Così fan tutte, Welsh Nat. Opera 2000, Un Ballo in Maschera, Barcelona 2001, ENO 2002, Don Giovanni, ENO 2001, 2004, Threepenny Opera, Barcelona 2002, The Abduction from the Seraglio, Berlin 2003, Il Trovatore, Edin. 2004, Die Fledermaus and La Bohème, Welsh Nat. Opera, Madama Butterfly, Berlin 2005, Woyzeck, Barcelona 2005; theatre works include Ramón del Valle-Inclán's Comédias Bárbaras, Edin. 2000, Macbeth, Edin. 2001, Hamlet, Edin. 2003, Dublin Theatre Festival 2005; Artistic Dir Teatre Romea, Barcelona 2000–. *Address:* c/o Teatre Romea, 51 Carrer de l'Hospital, Barcelona, Spain (office). *Telephone:* (98) 3181431 (office); (98) 3015504. *Website:* www.teatral.net (office).

**BIEL, Ann-Christin;** Singer (Soprano); b. 1958, Sweden. *Education:* Studied at the Royal Music Academy, Stockholm with Birgit Sternberg and with Daniel Ferro, in New York. *Career:* Debut: Drottningholm 1981, as Cherubino; Has appeared at the Summer festival at Drottningholm, Stockholm, as Pamina 1982, 1989; Fiordiligi, 1984–85; Ilia, 1986, 1991; Susanna 1987; Serpetta in La Finta Giardiniera, 1988, 1990; Royal Opera Stockholm 1985, L'arbore di Diana by Martín y Soler; 1986 as Oscar in Un Ballo in Maschera; Sang Konstanze in the Berne, 1986, world premiere of Armin Schibler's Mozart und der graue Bote, Mozart's last days; Toured as Micaela in the Peter Brook version of Carmen, Paris, Hamburg, New York and Tokyo, 1982–86; Théâtre des Champs-Elysées, Paris 1986, as Barbarina in Le nozze di Figaro; Sang Julie in the world premiere of Miss Julie at Stockholm 1990; (music by Margareta Hallin, the part of Julie written for Ms Biel); Sang Gluck's Orpheus at Drottningholm, 1992; Concert appearances in Stockholm, New York, Paris, Amsterdam, Parma, Verona, Milan and Copenhagen: repertoire includes Bach's Passions, Die Schöpfung, Mozart's Vespers and Requiem, Monteverdi's Vespers and Ein Deutsches Requiem. *Recordings:* Videos of Mozart operas from Drottningholm, directed by Goran Järvefelt, conducted by Arnold Östman. *Address:* Drottningholms Slottstheater, PO Box 27050, 102 51 Stockholm, Sweden.

**BIELAWA, Herbert;** Composer; b. 3 Feb. 1930, Chicago, Illinois, USA. *Education:* BM; MM; BA at University of Illinois; DMA, University of Southern California; Studied with Gordon Binkerd, Burrill Phillips, Ingolf Dahl, Halsey Stevens, Ellis Kohs. *Career:* Professor of Music and Director of Electronic Music Studio at San Francisco State University from 1966–91; Now retired. *Compositions:* A Bird in the Bush, Chamber Opera 1962; Spectrum for band and tape, 1965; Divergents, for orchestra, 1969; A Dickinson Album for choir, synthesized sound; piano; guitar, 1972; Dreams, for SSAA chorus, 1984; Rants, for SATB and violin, 1988; Song Cycles, The Snake and Other Creatures and Stone settings, song cycles, for soprano and piano, 1991; Quodlibet SF42569 for organ and tape, 1981; Duo for violin and harpsichord, 1984; Ants for soprano, violin and piano 1985; Through Thick and Thin, for flute, clarinet, viola and piano, 1991; Undertones, for organ, 1980; Monophonies, for organ, 1979; Organ Booklet for organ, 1992; Pentarcs, for piano, 1982; Expressions, for piano, 1992; Pipes and Brass for organ and brass quintet, 1997; Blurts for flute, clarinet and piano, 1997; Cyber for violin and cello, 1998; Feedback for organ and orchestra, 1999; Piano Concerto, 1999; Seque a Quattro for flute, clarinet, violin and cello, 1999; Earth, for flute, clarinet, violin, cello and piano, 2000. *Recordings include:* Pipe Organ Adventures. *Address:* 38 Sunset Drive, Kensington, CA 94707, USA.

**BIERHANZL, Petr;** Czech classical guitarist; b. 27 July 1952, Prague; m. Jana Bierhanzlova 1977; one s. *Education:* Conservatory of Prague, Czech Republic. *Career:* debut in Prague, 1975; Member, Guitar duo with Jana Bierhanzlova; Czech Republic, 1975–97; Poland, 1986, 1990, 1994; Germany, 1995, 1997, 1998; Lithuania, 1997; Radio: Poland, 1990; Czech Republic, 1992, 1993, 1995, 1996, 1997; Television: German television, 1978; Czech television, 1992, 1993, 1994, 1996, 1997; Repertoire includes: J Dowland's Lachrimae Pavan, Welcome Home, A Michna's Czech Lute, J. S. Bach's Preludes and fugues, Scarlatti's Sonata K 380, A Vivaldi's Concerto op 3 No. 6, A Soler's Sonatas, W A Mozart's Divertimento KV 439 b, F Sor's L'Encouragement op 34, F Carulli's Duo op 34 No. 2, E Granados' Danzas Espanolas; I Albeniz's Granada, Sevilla, A Dvořák's Sonatina op 100, Educational activity: Professor at the Jezek Conservatory of Prague, 1980–; Intergram, Prague; Lithuania, 2001; Spain, 2002. *Recordings:* The European Guitar Duets (Czech Guitar Duo), Scarlatti, Carulli, Sor and Truhlar (the first Czech recording of a guitar duo) 1992; English Renaissance Music (Czech Guitar Duo), Dowland, Byrd, Johnson and Bull; Czech Guitar Duo Plays Flamenco, 2001. *Address:* V Sareckem Udoli 2, 160 00 Prague 6, Czech Republic.

**BILGRAM, Hedwig;** Organist and Harpsichordist; b. 31 March 1933, Memmingen, Germany. *Education:* Studied with Karl Richter and Friedrich Wührer. *Career:* Teacher at the Munich Hochschule für Musik from 1961, Professor, 1964–; Many performances under Karl Richter in Munich and elsewhere, in the Baroque repertoire; Appeared also with trumpeter Maurice André; Premieres of works by André Jolivet, Henri Tomasi and Harald Genzmer. *Address:* c/o Hochschule für Musik, Areisstr 12, 8000 Munich 2, Germany.

**BILINSKA, Jolanta;** Musicologist; b. 1 March 1951, Rzeszów, Poland. *Education:* Diploma with Honours, Musicology Department, Jagiellonian University, Kraków, 1976. *Career:* Secretary of the Warsaw International Festival of Contemporary Music, 1979–95; Director of Polish Radio Music Recording Department. *Publications:* Opery Mozarta na scenach polskich w latach 1783-1830 (Mozart's Operas on Polish Stages from 1783–1830); Musikbiliothek und Musikleben am Hof der Fuerstin Izabella Lubomirska in Lancut 1791–1816, Musik des Ostens, Bd 11, 1989; Recepcja dziel Mozarta w Polsce 1783–1830 (Reception of Mozart's Works in Poland 1783–1830), 1991, German edition, 1992. *Contributions:* Ruch Muzyczny, a bi-weekly music magazine; Polish Music, quarterly. *Address:* Osowska 23m 5, 04 312 Warsaw, Poland.

**BILSON, Malcolm;** Concert Pianist; b. 24 Oct. 1935, Los Angeles, CA, USA; m. Elizabeth Jármay 1961; two d. *Education:* BA, Bard Coll. 1957; Vienna State Acad., Reifezeugnis 1959; Ecole Normale de Musique, Paris, Licence Libre 1960; DMA, Univ. of Illinois, 1968. *Career:* Asst Prof., Cornell Univ. 1968, Assoc. Prof. 1970, Prof. 1975, Frederick J. Whiton Prof. of Music, 1990; specialises in repertoire of Viennese Classical School on period fortepianos; toured extensively in North America, Europe, the Far East and Oceania as soloist, chamber musician and soloist with orchestras, including the English Baroque Soloists, the Acad. of Ancient Music, Tafelmusik, Concerto Köln, Philharmonia Baroque and numerous modern-instrument orchestras; workshops and masterclasses world-wide, including the Sibelius Acad., Helsinki, Liszt Acad., Budapest, Kunitachi Coll., Tokyo, Griffith Conservatory, Brisbane, Jerusalem Music Centre, Scottish Acad. of Music and Dance, Glasgow, Royal Coll. of Music, London; Adjunct Prof., Eastman School of Music 1992–; mem. American Acad. of Arts and Sciences. *Recordings:* Complete Mozart Concertos for fortepiano and orchestra, with John Eliot Gardiner and the English Baroque Soloists; complete Mozart piano-violin sonatas with Sergui Luca; complete Mozart solo piano Sonatas; complete Beethoven piano sonatas (with other players), Claves; complete Beethoven cello-piano sonatas with Anner Bijlsma; complete Schubert piano sonatas (including unfinished works); Schubert 4-hand piano works with Robert Levin. *Honours:* Hon. doctorate, Bard Coll., 1991. *Address:* c/o Department of Music, Lincoln Hall, Cornell University, Ithaca, NY 14853, USA.

**BIMBERG, Siegfried Wolfgang,** BA, PhD, Dr paed habil, DrSc phil; German musicologist, psychologist, composer and conductor; b. 5 May 1927, Halle, Saale; m. Ortrud Rummler 1953; one s. *Education:* Martin Luther Univ., Halle. *Career:* debut at Martin Luther Univ., Halle; Lecturer of Musicology, Halle Univ. 1952–1956; Lecturer in Musicology, Humboldt Univ., Berlin 1956–62; Ordinary Prof. of Musicology and Music Education 1964–92; Head of Dept for Musikdidatik, Martin Luther Univ., Halle-Wittenberg 1962–90; Conductor and Leader, Chamber Choir, Halle Univ. Hallenser Madrigalisten 1963–80; concert tours throughout Europe; records, radio and television; mem. Freie deutsche Akademie der Künste und Wissenschaften, Bonn, Landesverband Sachsen-Anhalt, Deutscher Komponisten, Verband deutscher Schulmusiker. *Compositions include:* The Singing Horse (opera) 1961, Eulenspiegels Brautfahrt 1987; cantatas: Die Rosen schlafen nicht 1990, Jonas und der Wal 1996, Ohne Natur vergeht unser Leben 1997, Vom Wind getragen 1997, Mit Degen und Fagott 1998, Verba nulla pretio emuntur 1998, Zwischen Nil und Ninive, Sonne, Mond und Sterne 2000, Schildbürger 2005. *Recordings:* own compositions (choir works), interpretation of own works and works of other composers. *Publications include:* Einfuehrung in die Musikpsychologie 1957, Vom Singen zum Musikverstehen 1957, Methodischdidaktische Grundlagen der Musikerziehung 1968, Handbuch der Musikaesthetik (ed. and author) 1979, Kontrast als musikaesthetische Kategorie 1981, Handbuch der Chorleitung (ed. and author) 1981, Lieder lernen-Lieder singen 1981, Ferruccio Busoni: Von der Macht der Toene (ed.) 1983, Musik-Erleben-Lernen 1995, Nachhall 1 and 2 1996, Musikwissenschaft und Musikpädagogik Perspektiven für das 21 Jahrhundert (with Guido Bimberg) 1997, Lieder von Wende zur Wende – das deutsche Gemeinschaftslied im 20 Jahrhundert 1998. *Address:* Ernestusstrasse 24, 06114 Halle, Germany. *Telephone:* (45) 5232554 (home).

**BINGHAM, Judith,** FRNCM, ARAM; British composer; *Associate Composer, BBC Singers;* b. 21 June 1952, Nottingham, England; m. Andrew Petrow 1985. *Education:* Royal Acad. of Music, London, studied with Hans Keller. *Career:* commissions from Peter Pears, King's Singers, BBC Singers, Songmakers' Almanac, Omega Guitar Quartet, New London Consort, television and radio scores; singing debut at Proms 1984 in Strauss's Deutsche Motette; appearances with Taverner Consort, Combattimento; Assoc. Composer, BBC Singers 2006–; mem. ISM. *Compositions:* Cocaine Lil for soprano and piano 1975, A Divine Image for harpsichord 1976, Chopin for piano 1979, A Falling Figure for baritone, clarinet, piano 1979, Mercutio for baritone, piano 1980, Iago for bass-baritone, piano 1980, Clouded Windows for mezzo, piano 1980, The Ruin 1981, A Midsummer Night's Dream for mezzo, piano 1981, Into the Wilderness for organ 1982, Pictured Within for piano 1982, Ferrara for tenor, piano 1982, A Hymn Before Sunrise in the Vale of Chamounix for 24 singers 1982, Cradle Song of the Blessed Virgin 1983, Mass Setting, Sterna Paradisaea for singers and organ 1984, A Winter Walk at Noon for 27 solo voices 1984, Just Before Dawn 1986, Chartres for orchestra 1987, Dove Cottage by Moonlight for two pianos 1989, The Ghost of Combermere Abbey for chorus 1993, Beyond Redemption for orchestra 1995, The Temple at Karnak for orchestra 1996, The Mysteries of Adad (children's theatre) 1996, The American Icons for wind band 1997, The Snow Descends for brass ensemble, Passaggio concerto for bassoon 1998, The Shooting Star concerto for trumpet 1999, Walzerspiele for orchestra 1999, Water Lilies for chorus 1999, Shelley Dreams for violin and piano 1999, The Christmas Truce (British Composer Award for choral work) 2004, Missa brevis: The Road to Emmaeus (British Composer Award for liturgical work) 2004, Down and Out 2004, Edington Canticles 2005, A Formal Order 2005, Ghost Towns of the American West 2005, The Shepheardes Calender 2006. *Honours:* Principal's Prize for Composition 1971, BBC Young Composer 1976, Barlow Prize, USA 2005. *Address:* Maecenas Music, 5 Bushey Close, Old Barn Lane, Kenley, Surrey CR8 5AU, England. *Telephone:* (20) 660-4766 (office). *E-mail:* maecenascontemp@aol.com (office). *Website:* www.maecenasmusic.com.

**BINI, Carlo;** Singer (Tenor); b. 1947, Naples, Italy. *Education:* Studied at the Naples Conservatory. *Career:* Debut: Teatro San Carlo Naples, 1969, as Pinkerton; Sang in Italy and at the Deutsche Oper Berlin; State Opera Houses of Munich and Stuttgart; Hamburg Staatsoper, 1974, as Alfredo in La Traviata and Rodolfo; Sang further in Brussels, Paris, Marseille, Rio de Janeiro and New York City Opera; Metropolitan Opera, 1982, as Enzo in La Gioconda; La Scala, 1984, in I Lombardi; Sang Arrigo in I Vespri siciliani at Santiago, 1990; Avito in Montemezzi's L'amore dei tre re at Palermo, 1990; Other roles include, Rodolfo in Luisa Miller, Don Carlos, Gabriele Adorno, Don José, Laca in Jenůfa and Tchaikovsky's Vakula. *Recordings:* Verdi Requiem; Eine Nacht in Venedig; Video of I Lombardi. *Address:* c/o Teatro Massimo, 90100, Palermo, Italy.

**BINNS, Malcolm,** ARCM; British concert pianist; b. 29 Jan. 1936, Nottingham; s. of Douglas Priestley Binns and May Walker. *Education:* Bradford Grammar School, Royal Coll. of Music. *Career:* soloist with the major British orchestras 1960–; toured with Scottish Nat. Orchestra and Limbourg Orchestra 1987–88; regular performer at the Promenade Concerts 1962–; more than 30 recordings, including Balakirev Piano Concertos 1 and 2 and Rimsky-Korsakov Piano Concerto (English Northern Philharmonia) 1992; concerts at Aldeburgh, Leeds, Three Choirs and Canterbury Festivals; performances are regularly broadcast on BBC. *Honours:* Chappell Medal 1956, Medal of Worshipful Co. of Musicians 1956. *Address:* 233 Court Road, Orpington, Kent BR6 9BY, England. *Telephone:* (1689) 831056.

**BIONDI, Fabio;** Italian violinist and conductor; b. 15 March 1961, Palermo. *Education:* studied with Salvatore Cicero and Mauro lo Guercio. *Career:* concerto debut with the Italian Radio Symphony Orchestra aged 12; formed Stendhal Quartet 1981; worked with Hesperion XX, Les Musiciens du Louvre, Musica Antiqua of Vienna, the Camerata di Lugano and the orchestra of the Due Dimensioni festival, Parma; founder ensemble, Europa Galante 1990; works as soloist and guest conductor with orchestras including the Santa Cecilia in Rome, Rotterdam Chamber Orchestra, the Opera of Halle, Zurich Chamber Orchestra, the Norwegian Chamber Orchestra, Orchestre Nationale de Montpellier, Orquesta Ciudad de Granada; Conductor, New York Collegium; directed European Union Baroque Orchestra 2002. *Recordings include:* Italian Violin Sonatas (Veracini, Locatelli, Mascitti, Geminiani, Tartini), J. S. Bach Arias and Cantatas with Ian Bostridge, Vivaldi's L'Estro armonico, String Quintets by Boccherini, Vivaldi's violin concertos Il cimento dell'armonia e dell'inventione (including The Four Seasons), Vivaldi Stabat mater, Scarlatti Concerti and Sinfonie. *Honours:* (with Europa Galante) Académie Charles Cros, Diapason d'Or de l'Année, Prix RTL and Grand Prix du Discophile. *Current Management:* Satirino Classical Music Agency, 59 rue Orfila, 75020 Paris, France. *E-mail:* ianmalkin@satirino.fr (office). *Website:* www.satirino.fr (office).

**BIRET, Idil;** Turkish pianist; b. 1941, Ankara; d. of Münir and Leman Biret; m. Sefik Büyükyüksel 1976. *Education:* Paris Conservatoire. *Career:* debut 1957; has given concerts throughout the world with major orchestras including Boston Symphony Orchestra, USA, Leningrad Philharmonic, Russian Fed., Leipzig Gewandhaus, Germany, London Symphony, UK, Tokyo Philharmonic, Japan, Sydney Symphony, Australia, Dresden Staatskapelle, Germany; has performed with major conductors and at int. festivals including Montréal, Canada, Athens, Berlin, Dubrovnik, Croatia, Istanbul (performance with Yehudi Menuhin) etc.; mem. jury Queen Elisabeth Competition, Belgium, Van Cliburn Competition, USA, Busoni, Italy; Lily Boulanger Memorial Fund, Boston 1954, 1964. *Recordings:* Over 70 recordings including Beethoven, Liszt, Brahms, Chopin, Rachmaninov, Boulez, Ligeti and Stravinsky. *Honours:* Harriet Cohen/Dinu Lipatti Gold Medal, London 1959, State Artist of Turkey 1973, Polish Artistical Merit 1974, Grand Prix du Disque Chopin, Poland 1995, Golden Diapason Award, France 1995; Chevalier de l'Ordre Nat. du Mérite 1976. *Address:* 526 ave Louise, 1050 Brussels, Belgium; 255 Moda cad, Kadiköy, Istanbul, Turkey. *Fax:* (2) 648-40-17 (Belgium). *E-mail:* Sefik.Buyukyuksel.dc.67@aya.yale.edu. *Website:* www.idilbiret.de.

**BIRKELAND, Oystein;** Cellist; b. 1958, Norway. *Education:* Norwegian State Academy of Music; Studied in Basel with Heinrich Schiff, in London with William Pleeth and Ralph Kirshbaum. *Career:* Has worked with Frans Helmersson, Arto Noras, Erling Blondal Bengtsson and Jacqueline du Pré; Member, 1982–, Principal Cellist, 1985–, Norwegian Chamber Orchestra; Performances as soloist, Norway, the United Kingdom, Germany, Switzerland, in concertos by Haydn, Boccherini, Vivaldi and others; Has played with Oslo Philharmonic, Trondheim Symphony Orchestra and Norwegian Radio Orchestra; Recent debut with Academy of St Martin-in-the-Fields, playing the Haydn Concerto in C major in Oslo, Helsinki and Stockholm; Recent festival appearances include Bergen International Music Festival, the Contemporary Music Festivals Platform, London, and Schleswig Holstein Music Festival; Plays a cello by Francesco Ruggiere (Cremona, 1680). *Recordings:* For BBC with pianist Joanna McGregor; With pianist Havard Gimse; 3 Russian sonatas with Ian Brown. *Current Management:* Diana Walters Artists Management, England. *Address:* c/o Diana Walters Artists Management, Ivy Cottage, 3 Main Street, Keyham, Leicestershire LE7 9JQ, England.

**BIRKS, Ronald;** British violinist; b. 1945, England. *Education:* Royal Manchester Coll. of Music with Béla Katona, Walter Jorysz and Alexander Moskovsky. *Career:* mem., Lindsay String Quartet 1971–, later The Lindsays; regular tours of Europe, the UK, USA; quartet-in-residence Univ. of Sheffield 1972–78, Univ. of Manchester 1978; premiered the 4th Quartet of Tippett at the Bath Festival 1979, commissioned Tippett's 5th Quartet 1992; Chamber Music Festival established at Sheffield 1984; resident ensemble Music in the Round Festival, Sheffield –2005; plays Campo Selice Stradivarius of 1694. *Recordings:* Complete Cycles of Bartók, Tippett and Beethoven quartets, Mozart Quintets, Haydn Quartets Live from the Wigmore Hall, Second Series of Beethoven Quartets, All Haydn Quartets from Op. 20 onwards. *Honours:* Dr hc (Univs of Keele, Manchester, Leicester, Sheffield (two) and Sheffield Hallam); Gramophone Chamber Award for late Beethoven quartets 1984, Classic FM Gramophone Special Achievement Award 2005.

**BIRTWISTLE, Sir Harrison,** Kt, CH; British composer; b. 1934, Accrington, Lancs.; m. Sheila Birtwistle 1958; three s. *Education:* Royal Manchester Coll. of Music and Royal Acad. of Music, London. *Career:* Dir of Music, Cranborne Chase School 1962–65; Visiting Fellow Princeton Univ. (Harkness Int. Fellowship) 1966; Cornell visiting Prof. of Music, Swarthmore Coll., Pa 1973–74; Slee Visiting Prof., New York State Univ., Buffalo, NY 1975; Assoc. Dir Nat. Theatre 1975–88; Composer-in-Residence London Philharmonic Orchestra 1993–98; Henry Purcell Prof. of Composition King's Coll., London Univ. 1994–2001; Visiting Prof., Univ. of Ala at Tuscaloosa 2001–02; Hon. Fellow Royal Northern Coll. of Music 1990; Dir of Contemporary Music, RAM 1996–2001; works have been widely performed at the major festivals in Europe including the Venice Biennale, the Int. Soc. of Contemporary Music Festivals in Vienna and Copenhagen, the Warsaw Autumn Festival and at Aldeburgh, Cheltenham and Edinburgh; formed, with Sir Peter Maxwell

Davies, The Pierrot Players. *Operatic and dramatic works:* The Mark of the Goat (cantata) 1965, Punch and Judy (one-act opera) 1966, The Visions of Francesco Petrarca (sonnets for baritone and orchestra) 1966, Monodrama for soprano, speaker, ensemble 1967, Down by the Greenwood Side (dramatic pastoral) 1969, The Mask of Orpheus 1973, Ballet, Frames, Pulses and Interruptions 1977, Bow Down 1977, Yan Tan Tethera 1983, Gawain 1988, The Second Mrs Kong 1992, The Last Supper 1999. *Orchestral works:* Chorales for Orchestra 1962, Three Movements with Fanfares 1964, Nomos 1968, An Imaginary Landscape 1971, The Triumph of Time 1970, Grimethorpe Aria for Brass Band 1973, Melencolia I 1976, Silbury Air for small orchestra 1977, Still Movement for 13 solo strings 1984, Earth Dances 1985, Endless Parade for trumpet, vibraphone, strings 1987, Ritual Fragment 1990, Antiphonies for piano and orchestra 1992, The Cry of Anubis for tuba and orchestra 1994, Panic 1995, Night's Black Bird (British Composer Award British Acad. of Composers and Songwriters 2005). *Choral works and narration:* Monody for Corpus Christi for soprano and ensemble 1959, A Description of the Passing Year for chorus 1963, Entr'actes and Sappho Fragments for soprano and ensemble 1964, Carmen Paschale for chorus and organ 1965, Ring a Dumb Clarion for soprano, clarinet, percussion 1965, Cantata for soprano and ensemble 1969, Nenia on the Death of Orpheus for soprano and ensemble 1970, The Fields of Sorrow for 2 sopranos, chorus, ensemble 1971, Meridian for mezzo, chorus, ensemble 1970, Epilogue: Full Fathom Five for baritone and ensemble 1972, agm. for 16 solo voices and 3 instruments 1979, On the Sheer Threshold of the Night for 4 solo voices and 12-part chorus 1980, White and Light for soprano and ensemble 1989, Four Poems by Jaan Kaplinski for soprano and ensemble 1991, The Woman and the Hare, for soprano, reciter and ensemble 1999, Ring Dance of the Nazarene (British Composer Award British Acad. of Composers and Songwriters 2005). *Instrumental works:* Refrains and Choruses for wind quintet 1957, The World is Discovered for ensemble 1960, Tragoedia for ensemble 1965, Three Lessons in a Frame 1967, Chorales from a Toyshop 1967, Verses for Ensembles 1969, Ut heremita solus, arr of Ockeghem 1969, Hoquetus David, arr of Machaut 1969, Medusa for ensemble 1970, Chronometer for 8-track tape 1971, For O For O the Hobby Horse is Forgot for 6 percussion 1976, Carmen Arcadiae Mechanicae Perpetuum for ensemble 1977, Pulse Sampler 1980, Clarinet Quintet 1980, Secret Theatre 1984, Words Overheard 1985, Fanfare for Will 1987, Salford Toccata for brass band and bass drum 1988, Nine Movements for string quartet 1991, An Uninterrupted Endless Melody for oboe and piano 1991, Five Distances for five instruments 1992, Tenebrae for soprano and ensemble 1992, Night for soprano and ensemble 1992, Movement for string quartet 1992, Slow Frieze for piano and 13 instruments 1996, Pulse, Shadows 1997, Harrison's Clocks for piano 1998, The Silk House Tattoo for 2 trumpets and percussion 1998, Three Niedecker Verses for soprano and cello 1998, Exody 1998, The Axe Manual 2000, The Shadow of Night 2001, Theseus Game 2002, The Io Passion 2004, Night's Black Bird 2004, The Story of 10 2004. *Theatre:* music for Hamlet, Nat. Theatre 1975, The Oresteia, Nat. Theatre 1986, The Bacchae, Nat. Theatre 2002. *Honours:* Chevalier des Arts et Lettres; Siemens Prize 1995; Grawemeyer Award (Univ. of Louisville, Ky) 1987. *Current Management:* Allied Artists Agency, 42 Montpelier Square, London, SW7 1JZ, England.

**BISATT, Susan;** Singer (Soprano); b. 1963, England. *Career:* Frequent festival engagements, including Almeida Contemporary Opera (Isabelle Rimbaud in The Man Who Strides the Wind by Kevin Volans) and Edinburgh (Salome in the opera by Strauss); Roles with Opera Restor'd in Britain and Abroad, in Dido and Aeneas, The Death of Dido (Pepusch) and Pyramus and Thisbe (Lampe); Other appearances with Opera North (as Papagena) and elsewhere as Violetta, Donna Elvira, Lucia di Lammermoor, Gilda, Norina and the soprano leads in Les Contes d'Hoffmann; Gluck's Eurydice, Mozart's Countess, and Rosina; Tours of the United Kingdom, Ireland and Finland with Opera Circus; Opera workshops with Opera North, Compact Opera, Théâtre de Complicité and the David Glass Ensemble; Television includes: The Singing Voice, for Channel 4. *Recordings include:* English Baroque Opera (Hyperion); Scenes from operas by Charles Dibdin; Purcell Songs (Naxos). *Address:* c/o C&M Craig Services Ltd, 3 Kersley Street, London SW11 4 PR, England.

**BISCARDI, Chester,** BA, MA, MM, MMA, DMA; American composer and teacher; b. 19 Oct. 1948, Kenosha, WI. *Education:* Univ. of Wisconsin, Madison, Universita di Bologna, Conservatorio di Musica G. B. Martini, Yale Univ. School of Music. *Career:* teacher, Univ. of Wisconsin 1970–74, Yale Univ. 1975–76; teacher in music faculty, Sarah Lawrence Coll., Bronxville, NY 1977–, Dir of Music Program, 1st William Schuman Chair in Music; Visiting Artist, American Acad. in Rome 1987. *Compositions include:* Tartini 1972, Tenzone 1975, They Had Ceased to Talk 1975, Trio 1976, At the Still Point 1977, Mestiere 1979, Trasumanar 1980, Di Vivere 1981, Piano Concerto 1983, Incitation to Desire (Tango) 1984–93, Tight-Rope (chamber opera) 1985, Piano Sonata 1986, Traverso for flute and piano 1987, Companion Piece (for Morton Feldman) 1989–91, Netori 1990, The Gift of Life for soprano and piano 1990–93, Music for an Occasion for brass, piano and percussion 1992, Nel giardinetto della villa for piano four hands 1994, Resisting Stillness for two guitars 1996, Modern Love Songs 1997–2002, Prayers of Steel 1998, Recovering 2000, In Time's Unfolding 2000, Piano Quintet 2004, The Viola had Suddenly Become a Voice 2005. *Recordings include:* Piano Sonata, Mestiere, Trasumanar, Traverso, The Gift of Life, Companion Piece, Incitation to Desire (tango), Tenzone, At the Still Point, Resisting Stillness, Nel giardinetto della villa, In Time's Unfolding, Baby Song of the Four Winds,

Recovering, Guru. *Honours:* American Acad. and Inst. of Arts and Letters Charles E. Ives Scholarship 1975–76, American Acad. in Rome Prize 1976–77, John Simon Guggenheim Memorial Foundation Fellowship in Music Composition 1979–80, Nat. Endowment for the Arts Composer/Librettist Fellowship grants 1977–78, 1980–81, MacDowell Colony Fellowships 1981, (Norlin Foundation Fellowship in Honor of Aaron Copland) 1984, 1992, 1993, 1994–95, (Frances and William Schuman Fellowship) 1998, 2000, 2004, Djerassi Foundation Music/Composition Fellowship (Ridge Vineyards) 1989, Japan Foundation Professional Fellowship 1989–90, NY Foundation for the Arts Fellowships in Music Composition 1990, 1998, Rockefeller Foundation Bellagio Study and Conference Center Fellowship, Villa Serbelloni, Lago di Como, Italy 1993, Univ. of Wis. Alumni Asscn Distinguished Alumni Award 1997, Bogliasco Foundation Liguria Study Center for the Arts and Humanities Fellowship, Villa Orbiana, Bogliasco, Italy 1999, 2005, Harvard Comm. Fromm Music Foundation 1999–2002, Copland House Aaron Copland Award 2001. *Address:* Music Program, Sarah Lawrence College, One Meadway, Bronxville, NY 10708-5888 (office); 380 Riverside Drive, 4C, New York, NY 10025-1819, USA (home). *Telephone:* (914) 395-2334 (office); (212) 665-3349 (home). *Fax:* (914) 395-2507 (office). *E-mail:* biscardi@slc.edu (office). *Website:* www.chesterbiscardi.com.

**BISCHOF, Rainer,** PhD; Composer; b. 20 June 1947, Vienna, Austria. *Education:* Univ. of Vienna, studied composition privately with Hans Apostel. *Compositions:* Sonatine for Clarinet, 1969; Sonatine for Horn, 1970; Duo for Flute and Clarinet, 1970; Theme and 7 variations for Oboe and Cello, 1970; Quartet for Flute, Oboe, Horn and Bassoon, 1971; Grave for Violin and Piano, 1970–71; Deduction for Strings, 1973–74; Characteristic Differences for Violin and Piano, 1974; In Memoriam Memoriae, song cycle for Mezzo-soprano, Speaker, Vibraphone, Celesta, Bass, Clarinet and Cello, 1975–77; Orchesterstücke, 1976–82; Flute Concerto, 1978–79; Studies from the Flute Concerto for solo flute, 1978; Concerto for Violin, Cello and Orchestra, 1979–80; Variations for Organ, 1981; Viola Tricolor, 32 variations for Viola, 1982; Music for 6 Recorders, 1982–83; String Sextet, 1990; Studie in PP, 1991; Das Donauergeschenk, chamber opera, 1991; Quasi una fuga for orchestra, 1995; Sinfonia, 1995; Gesänge zur Kunst for chorus, 1996; Auf der Suche nach... for piano, 1996; Totentanz for orchestra, 1999; Der narrische Uhu, concerto for violin, 2001; Requiem fur Errol, 2003. *Address:* AKM, 111 Baumstr 8–10, 1031 Vienna, Austria.

**BISPO, Antonio (Alexandre);** Musicologist; b. 17 March 1949, São Paulo, Brazil (resident in Germany, 1974). *Education:* Diploma, Architecture, University of São Paulo, 1972; Licence Music Education, Institute Musical de São Paulo, 1972; Diploma in Composition and Directing, 1973; Postgraduate studies in Music Theory, 1975; PhD, 1979, Doctor. habil. 1997. *Career:* Director, Conservatorio Jardim America, São Paulo, 1971–72; Lecturer, Ethnomusicology and Aesthetics of Music, 1972–74; Researcher, Institut für Hymnologische und Musikethnologische Studien Maria Laach, Germany, 1979–; Councillor, Pontifical Association of Church Music, 1979–85; Director, Musikschule der Stadt Leichlingen, Germany, 1981–84; Director, Institut für Studien der Musikkultur des portugiesischen Sprachraumes e.V., 1989–; Lecturer, Musikwissenschaftliches Institut, University of Cologne; 1997–; Lecturer, Musikwissenschaftliches Seminar, University of Bonn, 2002–; Chairman, Ethnomusicology Section, Institute of Hymn and Ethnomusicology Studies, 1984–; President, Akademie Brasil-Europa. *Publications:* Numerous works, including, Die katholische Kirchenmusik in der Provinz São Paulo, 1979; Collectanea Musicae Sacrae Brasiliensis, 1981; Grundlagen christlicher Musikkultur in der aussereuropäischen Welt der Neuzeit, 1989; Leben und Werk von Martin Braunwieser, 1991–92; Christliche Volkstraditionen und Synkretismus in Brasilien, 1989–90; Die Musikkulturen der Indianer Brasiliens, 1994–95; Christliche Musikanthropologie, 1999; Die Musikkulturen der Indianer Brasiliens II, 1999; Brasil/Europa & Musicologia, 1999, 2000; Die Musikkulturen der Indianer Brasiliens III, 2000; Brasil-Europa 500 Jahre: Musik und Visionen 2000; Die Musikkulturen der Indianer Brasiliens IV, 2002. *Honours:* National Order of Bandeirentos; Award of the Academia Paulistznade de Historia; Honour, Brazil Association of Folklore. *Address:* Theodor-Heuss-Ring 14, 50668 Cologne 1, Nordrhein-Westphalen, Germany. *E-mail:* bispo@netcologne.de.

**BISSON, Yves;** Singer (Baritone); b. 31 May 1936, Mostaganem, Algeria. *Education:* Studied at Paris Conservatoire with Renee Gilly-Musy and Louis Noguera. *Career:* Sung at the Paris Opéra, and the Opéra-Comique, notably in Manon, Faust, Platée, La Bohème, Werther, Roméo et Juliette, and Les Pêcheurs de Perles (all televised); Festival engagements at Aix-en-Provence as Rodolphe in Les Fêtes Vénitiennes by Campra, Avignon, Carpentras and Orange; Has sung in France, New York, Washington, Amsterdam, Brussels, Covent Garden London, Lisbon, Geneva, Zürich, Barcelona, Madrid, Vienna, Naples and Russia; Other roles include Lescaut in Auber's Manon Lescaut, Escamillo, Nilakantha in Lakmé, Mercutio, Sander in Zémire et Azor by Grétry, Massenet's Lescaut, Albert and Caoudal in Sapho, Mozart's Figaro and Masetto, Rangoni in Boris Godunov, Puccini's Marcello, Schaunard, Sharpless and Lescaut, Rameau's Oromases in Zoroastre and Citheron in Platée, Verdi's Posa, Germont and Ford; Sang François in Le Chemineau by Leroux at Marseilles, 1996. *Address:* c/o Opéra de Marseille, 2 Rue Molière, 1321 Marseille, Cédex 01, France.

**BISWAS, Anup (Kumar);** Composer and Concert Cellist; b. 1957, West Bengal, India. *Education:* Studied in India with Rev T Mathieson, at Royal College of Music; Further study with Pierre Fournier in Geneva, and

Jacqueline du Pré in London. *Career:* Concerts throughout the United Kingdom, including St James and Lambeth Palaces; Elizabeth and Wigmore Halls; Grays Inn and Riverside Studios; Festival engagements at Cleveland; Belfast; Greenwich; Hereford; Masterclasses at the Dartington Summer School and concerts in Germany, Finland and Norway; JS Bach Tercentenary concerts in cathedrals and churches in the United Kingdom, featuring the suites for unaccompanied cello; Artistic Director of the Dante Alighieri Orchestra, from 1989; Royal Albert Hall, 1992, performing Celebration from his own ballet Ten Guineas under the Banyan Tree; Purcell Room Concert, 1993, playing Beethoven, Shostakovich, Walton and Brahms. *Compositions:* Music for Theatre Taliesin, Wales, 1986 production of Tristan and Essylt, featured by BBC Wales. *Address:* East West Arts Ltd, 93b Cambridge Gardens, London W10 6JE, England.

**BJARNASON, Finnur;** Singer (tenor); b. 1975, Reykjavík, Iceland. *Education:* Guildhall School and National Opera Studio, London. *Career:* debut, Male Chorus in the Rape of Lucretia for Icelandic Opera; sang Don Ottavio for Glyndebourne Touring Opera, 2000; appearances in Messiah throughout Britain and Beethoven's Ninth with the Icelandic Symphony Orchestra; recitals at St George's, Bristol, for the BBC and Wigmore Hall with Graham Johnson; Season 2001–2002 with Tebaldo in I Capuleti e i Montecchi for Grange Park Opera, Tamino with Icelandic Opera, and Don Ottavio at the 2002 Glyndebourne Festival. *Current Management:* Hazard Chase, Norman House, Cambridge Place, Cambridge CB2 1NS, England. *Telephone:* (1223) 312400. *Fax:* (1223) 460827. *Website:* www.hazardchase.co.uk.

**BJERNO, Majken;** Singer (Soprano); b. 29 May 1963, Århus, Denmark. *Education:* Studied in Copenhagen. *Career:* Debut: Opera Studio Copenhagen, 1989, as Pamina; Royal Opera Copenhagen from 1989 as Offenbach's Antonia, Mozart's Countess, Micaela, Mimi, Fiordiligi in Così fan tutte, Leonora in Nielsen's Maskarade and Mihail in Saul and David; Guest appearances at the Jutland Opera, Århus as Gutrune in Götterdämmerung and Mimi; Concert engagements in Bach's Passions; Beethoven's Ninth and Missa Solemnis; Requiems by Fauré, Brahms and Dvořák; Handel's Saul and Messiah; Masses by Mozart and Carmina Burana; Also sang recitals. *Recordings:* Mahler's 8th Symphony. *Address:* Tivoli Artists Management, 3 Vesterbrogade, POB 233, 1630 Copenhagen, Denmark. *Telephone:* 33-75-04-00. *Fax:* 33-75-03-75. *E-mail:* artistsmanagement@tivoli.dk. *Website:* www.tam.dk.

**BJONER, Ingrid;** opera and concert singer (soprano); b. 8 Nov. 1927, Kraakstad, Norway. *Education:* University of Oslo, Conservatory of Music, Oslo with Gudrun Boellemose, Hochschule für Musik, Frankfurt with Paul Lohmann; further study with Ellen Repp in New York. *Career:* Sang Third Norn and Gutrune in Norwegian radio recording of Götterdämmerung, 1956; Stage Debut, Oslo, 1957, as Donna Anna; Drottningholm Opera, 1957, as Handel's Rodelinda; Member, Wuppertal Opera, Germany, 1957–59; Deutsche Oper am Rhein Düsseldorf, 1959–61; Bayreuth Festival 1960, as Freia, Helmvige and Gutrune; Sang with Bayerische Staatsoper Munich from 1961, notably as the Empress in Die Frau ohne Schatten (1963) and as Isolde, in the centenary production of Tristan and Isolde, 1965; Metropolitan Opera debut 1961, as Elsa in Lohengrin; Covent Garden from 1967, as Senta, Sieglinde and Leonore (Fidelio); Salzburg Festival, 1969–1970, Leonore; Sang the Duchess of Parma in the US premiere of Doktor Faust by Busoni, Carnegie Hall, 1974; Oslo and Copenhagen, 1985–86, as Elektra; Further appearances at La Scala, Vienna, Hollywood Bowl, Hamburg, Deutsche Oper Berlin, Cologne Opera, Warsaw and Vancouver; Season 1986–87 sang Isolde at Bayreuth and the Kostelnicka in Jenůfa at Karlsruhe; Staatsoper Munich 1988, as the Dyer's Wife in Die Frau ohne Schatten; Oslo Opera, 1989, Senta; The Dyer's Wife at Karlsruhe, 1990; Concert appearances world-wide, often in the songs of Grieg; Professor at Royal Academy of Music, Copenhagen, 1991–; Professor at Royal Academy of Music, Oslo, 1992–. *Recordings include:* Götterdämmerung, Decca; Die Frau ohne Schatten, DGG; Wagner's Wesendonck Lieder; Songs by Sibelius. *Honours:* Order of St Olav, Norway, 1964; Bavarian Order of Merit. *Address:* Gregers Grams vei 33, 0382 Oslo 3, Norway.

**BJORLIN, Ulf;** Composer and Conductor; b. 21 May 1933, Stockholm, Sweden. *Education:* Studied with Igor Markevitch in Salzburg and Nadia Boulanger in Paris. *Career:* Director of Royal Dramatic Theatre, Stockholm, 1963–68; Freelance Composer; Conductor of leading orchestras in Sweden and elsewhere in Scandanavia. *Compositions:* Pinocchio, children's musical, 1966; Ekon for orchestra, 1967; In Five Years, opera for actors and chamber ensemble, 1967; Epitaph for Lars Gorling, for orchestra, 1967; Of Melancholy, choreographic oratoria, 1970–; The Bit Theatre, opera, 1972; The Ballad of Kasper Rosenrod, opera, 1972; Karlekin till Belisa, radio opera, 1981; Wind Quintet, 1983; Tillfalle gor Tiufven, opera buffa, 1983; Den Frammande Kvinnan, opera, 1984. *Address:* c/o STIM, Sandhamnsgatan 79, PO Box 27372, 102 54 Stockholm, Sweden.

**BJORNSSON, Sigurd;** Singer (Tenor); b. 19 March 1932, Hafnarfjordur, Iceland. *Education:* Studied with Gerhard Husch in Munich. *Career:* Debut: Stuttgart, 1962, as Arturo in Lucia di Lammermoor; Sang at Stuttgart until 1968, Kassel, 1968–72, Graz, 1972–75, and Theater am Gärtnerplatz Munich until 1977; Among his best roles were Mozart's Belmonte, Ferrando and Tamino, Lionel in Martha, Nicolai's Fenton, Wagner's Froh and Steuermann, Bellini's Riccardo and Rinuccio in Gianni Schicchi; Guest appearances at the Deutsche Oper Berlin, Munich, Hamburg, the Vienna Volksoper and the

Bregenz and Schwetzingen Festivals. *Address:* c/o Staatstheater am Gärtnerplatz, Gärtnerplatz 3, W-8000 Munich 5, Germany.

**BLACK, Jeffrey;** Singer (Baritone); b. 6 Sept. 1962, Brisbane, Australia. *Career:* Debut: European, Harlekin in Ariadne auf Naxos at Monte Carlo, 1986; Sang with Australian Opera from 1985 as Mercutio, Schaunard, Papageno, Dr Falke, Dandini, Rossini's Figaro and Ottone in Poppea; Glyndebourne Festival, from 1986, as Sid in Albert Herring, Demetrius and the Count in Figaro and Capriccio; Covent Garden appearances as well as engagements at Los Angeles as Guglielmo and Marcello, 1993, Opéra Bastille in Paris, Puccini's Lescaut, Geneva Opéra, Fieramosca in Benvenuto Cellini, San Francisco, Rossini's Figaro; Lyric Opera of Chicago and 1993 Salzburg Festival as Guglielmo, Teatro Colón, (Buenos Aires) as Dandini, Don Giovanni in Antwerp, Count (Le nozze di Figaro) in Washington, Figaro (Barbiere) at the Met, New York and in Munich, Valentin (Faust) in Geneva and Eugene Onegin at San Diego; Returned to Australia to appear with Lyric Opera of Queensland and Victoria State Opera, Melbourne; Sang Britten's Demetrius for New Israeli Opera, 1994; Mozart's Count at the Metropolitan, and Onegin at Sydney, Australia, 1997; Tannhäuser at Sydney and Posa in Don Carlos for Opera North, 1998; Don Carlo in Australia in 1999; Concerts include tour of Australia with Geoffrey Parsons and the ABC Orchestras, Carmina Burana with the London Philharmonic and Christus in the St Matthew Passion under Franz Welser-Möst; Kiri Te Kanawa International Tour, 1999. *Recordings include:* Carmina Burana; Songs of the Wayfarer, Mahler. *Address:* Jenifer Eddy Artists' Management, Suite 11, 596 St Kilda Road, Melbourne, VIC 3004, Australia. *Telephone:* (3) 9525-2700. *Fax:* (3) 9529-5410. *E-mail:* info@jeam.com.au.

**BLACK, Leo,** BMus, MA; British writer, broadcaster, translator and pianist; b. 28 July 1932, London, England; m. Felicity Vincent. *Education:* Univ. of Oxford. *Career:* music publisher, Universal Edition, Vienna, London 1956–60; music programmes, BBC radio 1960–88, Producer 1960–71, Chief Producer 1971–82, Exec. Producer 1982–88; concerts as a song-accompanist; lecture-recital on Schubert's Arpeggione Sonata, with cellist Felicity Vincent. *Publications:* Franz Schubert: Music and Belief, 2003; translations; contrib. to Über die Aufnahme der Musik Franz Schmidts, 1986; Franz Schmidt und das musikalische Hören, 1992; The Music of Hugh Wood; Heimito von Doderer, An English View, 1996; five major bicentenary articles on Schubert 1997, Schubert durch die Brille 2001; articles to Musical Times, The Listener, Opera Quarterly, Books and Bookmen. *Address:* 112 Chetwynd Road, London, NW5 1DH, England (home). *Telephone:* (20) 7485-1211. *E-mail:* leo.black@btinternet.com.

**BLACK, Lynton;** Singer (Bass-Baritone); b. 1960, England. *Education:* Studied at the Royal Academy of Music. *Career:* Debut: High Priest in Handel's Teseo, Covent Garden; Appearances with English Touring Opera, English Bach Festival, Garsington Festival Opera and Grange Park Opera; Principal Bass, D'Oyly Carte Opera, 1994–98; Debut at Salzburg Festival in Monteverdi's Orfeo, 1993; Debut at Paris Opéra as Notar in Der Rosenkavalier, 1996; Debut at Basle Opera as Achille in Handel's Giulio Cesare, 1998; Debut at Aix-en-Provence Festival as Achilles in La Belle Hélène, 1999; Debut at La Monnaie, Brussels, as Lesbo in Handel's Agrippina, 2000; Debut at Barcelona Opera as Achille in Giulio Cesare, 2001; Debut at Glyndebourne as Bartolo in Le nozze di Figaro, 2001; Other roles include Commendatore in Don Giovanni, Budd in Albert Herring, Don Alfonso in Così fan tutte, Frank in Die Fledermaus, Dick Deadeye in HMS Pinafore, The Mikado, Sultan in Haydn's L'Incontro Improvviso, Antonio in Le nozze di Figaro (Salzburg, 1995, 1996, 1998; Paris Opéra, 1999), Sciarrone in Tosca (La Monnaie, Brussels, 2000), Sagristano in Tosca (Paris, 2000), Hobson in Peter Grimes (Paris, 2001); mem, Equity; Savage Club; Sketch Club; Loophole Club; Curzon Club; President of D'Oyly Carte Dining Club; debut at Munich staatsoper as Father Trulove in The Rake's Progress 2002; other roles include BassI Israel in Egypt, Cadmus & Somnus in Handel's Semele. *Recordings:* Die Fledermaus (Frank); Rose of Persia (Gaoler). *Honours:* LRAM, 1981; DipRAM, 1983; ARAM, 1995. *Address:* 3 Temple Fortune Lane, London NW11 7UB, England. *E-mail:* lyntonbass@aol.com. *Website:* LyntonBlack.com.

**BLACK, Neil,** OBE, BA; British oboist; *Professor of Oboe, Guildhall School of Music and Drama. Education:* Univ. of Oxford. *Career:* fmr mem. Nat. Youth Orchestra of Great Britain; fmr prin. oboist LPO, Acad. of St Martin-in-the-Fields, English Chamber Orchestra; numerous int. tours and festivals; currently Prof. GSMD; Musical Dir Kirckman Concert Soc. *Recordings include:* with the Acad. of St Martin-in-the-Fields: Vivaldi: L'estro armonico 1994, Vivaldi: The Four Seasons 2000, Mozart: Clarinet and Oboe Concertos 2000; with the English Chamber Orchestra: Delius/Vaughan Williams/Walton: Orchestral Works 1993, Haydn: The London Concert 2004; other: Baroque Concerto in England, with Thames Chamber Orchestra, Mozart/Strauss/Weber, Wind Concertos with Philadelphia Orchestra. *Honours:* Hon. Fellow RAM . *Address:* Guildhall School of Music and Drama, Silk Street, Barbican, London, EC2Y 8DT, England (office). *E-mail:* music@gsmd.ac.uk (office). *Website:* www.gsmd.ac.uk (office).

**BLACK, Virginia;** Harpsichordist; b. 1950, England; m. Howard Davis. 2 s. *Career:* London concerts in the Wigmore Hall, Purcell Room and Queen Elizabeth Hall; Appearances at major festivals in the United Kingdom and Europe including the Prague Spring Festival; Recordings for the BBC and the Westdeutsche Rundfunk; Television performance of Bach's 5th Brandenburg Concerto, with the English Chamber Orchestra; Tours to Europe, the USA,

Australia and New Zealand; Concerts with Howard Davis, violin; Other repertoire includes: Sonatas by Soler and Scarlatti; Bach's Chromatic Fantasy and Fugue, Concertos in E and C Minor, Fantasie and Fugue in A minor, Toccata in D and Partitas, Bach's Goldberg Variations; Pieces by Rameau, Dandrieu, Duphly and Forqueray; Falla's Harpsichord Concerto; Professor of Harpsichord at the Royal Academy of Music and Postgraduate Tutor since 1999; Chair of Postgraduate Diploma Studies at Royal Academy of Music from 2002. *Recordings:* 17 albums of harpsichord music including The Essential Harpsichord. *Honours:* Dip RAM, 1964; FRAM, 1988–89; Soler Sonatas, Critic's Choice in Gramophone, 1988; Goldberg Variations, Critic's Choice in Classic CD, 1991. *Address:* 123 Sheering Road, Old Harlow, Essex CM 17 0 JP, England.

**BLACK, William (David);** Concert Pianist; b. 23 Feb. 1952, Dallas, TX, USA. *Education:* BM, Oberlin College, 1974; MM 1976, DMA 1979, The Juilliard School. *Career:* Debut: New York, 1977; London, England, 1979; Solo and orchestral engagements across the USA, Canada, England, France, Netherlands, Belgium, Germany, Iceland, Japan, China and Italy; Television appearances in the USA and numerous USA and European radio broadcasts including world-wide broadcasts of the Voice of America; Bohemians, New York Musicians Club; European Piano Teachers' Association. *Recordings:* Works of David Diamond; World premiere recording of the original version of the 4th Piano Concerto of Sergei Rachmaninov; Hunter Johnson Piano Sonata; Gershwin, Rhapsody in Blue. *Contributions:* Keyboard Classics. *Honours:* Pi Kappa Lambda, 1974; Concert Artists Guild Award; Morris Loeb Award, The Juilliard School; Solo Recitalist Grant, National Endowment for The Arts, 1991.

**BLACKBURN, Bonnie J.,** MA, PhD, FBA; musicologist; b. 15 July 1939, Albany, NY, USA; m. 1st Edward E. Lowinsky 1971 (died 1985); m. 2nd Leofranc Holford-Strevens 1990. *Education:* Wellesley Coll., Univ. of Chicago. *Career:* Research Asst, Dept of Music, Univ. of Chicago 1963–76, Visiting Assoc. Prof. 1986; Lecturer, School of Music, Northwestern Univ., 1987; Visiting Assoc. Prof., State Univ. of New York, Buffalo, 1989–90; Gen. Ed., Monuments of Renaissance Music, 1993–; mem. American Musicological Soc., Royal Musical Assocn, Int. Musicological Soc., Koninklijke Vereniging voor Nederlandse Muziekgeschiedenis, Plainsong and Mediaeval Music Soc., Renaissance Soc. of America, Soc. for Renaissance Studies, Società Italiana di Musicologia. *Publications:* Music for Treviso Cathedral in the Late Sixteenth Century: A Reconstruction of the Lost Manuscripts 29 and 30, 1987; Josquin des Prez: Proceedings of The International Josquin Festival-Conference, 1976, ed with E Lowinsky; ed Johannis Lupi Opera omnia, 3 vols, 1980–89; ed, Music in the Culture of the Renaissance and Other Essays by Edward E Lowinsky, 1989; Ed. with E Lowinsky and C A Miller, A Correspondence of Renaissance Musicians, 1991; The Oxford Companion to the Year (with Leofranc Holford-Strevens), 1999; Composition, Printing and Performance: Studies in Renaissance Music, 2000; Ed., with Reinhard Strohm, Music as Concept and Practice in the Late Middle Ages (New Oxford History of Music, 3, 2nd Edn, Part 1), 2001. *Contributions:* Musical Quarterly; Journal of The American Musicological Society; Musica Disciplina; Early Music History; The New Grove Dictionary of Music and Musicians; Early Music; Studi Musicali; Journal of Musicology; Die Musik in Geschichte und Gegenwart; Journal of the Royal Musical Association; Oxford Dictionary of National Biography. *Honours:* John Simon Guggenheim Memorial Foundation Fellowship, 1988–89. *Address:* 67 St Bernard's Road, Oxford OX2 6EJ, England. *E-mail:* bonnie.blackburn@wolfson.ox.ac.uk (office).

**BLACKBURN, Olivia;** Singer (Soprano); b. 1960, London, England. *Education:* Studied at Trinity College, London, and at the Pears-Britten School. *Career:* Regular concert on South Bank, London, in Die Schöpfung by Haydn, Vivaldi's Magnificat and Handel's Jephtha; German Requiem by Brahms at the Barbican with the Philharmonia and the St Matthew Passion with the Steinitz Bach Players; European performances in the Bach B Minor Mass, Haydn's Paukenmesse (Missa in tempore belli), Messiah and the Mozart Requiem; Opera debut in The Poisoned Kiss by Vaughan Williams at the Bloomsbury Theatre; Wexford Festival, 1987; With Cologne Opera has sung Naiad in Ariadne auf Naxos, Siebel in Faust, Sandrina (La Finta Giardiniera), Helena in A Midsummer Night's Dream and Pamina; Song recitals in Paris, Dublin, London, and Cambridge; Appearances with the Songmakers' Almanac in London and at the Nottingham and Buxton Festivals; Season 1989–90 in Ode to the West Wind by Arnell, Aci in Handel's Aci, Galatea e Polifemo with London Baroque at the Beaune Festival and Mendelssohn's Lobgesang conducted by Richard Hickox; Mozart's C Minor Mass in Scotland and in France with Malgoire and Portugal with Brüggen conducting; Covent Garden debut, 1992, as a Young Nun in The Fiery Angel; Television recording of Handel's Roman Vespers in Vienna. *Recordings include:* Bach B Minor Mass. *Address:* c/o Ron Gonsalves Management, 10 Dagnan Road, London SW12 9LQ, England.

**BLACKHAM, Joyce;** Singer (Soprano); b. 1 Jan. 1934, Rotherham, Yorkshire, England; m. Peter Glossop (divorced). *Education:* Studied at the Guildhall School of Music with Joseph Hislop. *Career:* Debut: Sadler's Wells Opera 1955, as Olga in Eugene Onegin; Covent Garden debut as Esmeralda in The Bartered Bride; Best known as Carmen, also sang Dorabella, Mimi, Norina, Rosina and roles in operettas by Offenbach, Johann Strauss and Lehar; Guest appearances Berlin, New York and New Zealand; With Welsh National Opera sang Rosina, Amneris and Cherubino; Sang Maddalena in Rigoletto at Covent Garden, 1974.

**BLACKWELL, Harolyn;** American singer (soprano); b. 1955, Washington, DC. *Education:* Catholic Univ. of America, studied with Carlo Bergonzi and Renata Tebaldi in Italy. *Career:* has sung Jemmy in Guillaume Tell at the San Antonio Festival, Papagena in Cleveland, Oscar in Hamburg, Gilda with the Miami Opera, Sister Constance in Dialogues des Carmélites for Canadian Opera and Clara in Porgy and Bess at the Glyndebourne Festival 1986; symphonic engagements with the Nat. Symphony, St Louis Philharmonic, Cincinnati Symphony, Minnesota Orchestra and Buffalo Philharmonic; Carnegie Hall as Xanthe in Die Liebe der Danaë by Strauss; recitals in Buffalo, Denver, Dallas and New York (debut 1987); season 1986–87 with debuts at Chicago as Oscar (Un Ballo in Maschera) and at the Metropolitan as Pousette in Manon; Xenia in Boris Godunov, conducted by James Conlon; season 1987–88 with concert performance of Porgy and Bess under Simon Rattle, Nannetta in Falstaff at Nice and the Princess in L'Enfant et les Sortilèges at Glyndebourne; season 1988–89 included Schubert's A-flat Mass in Detroit, Barbarina and Sophie (Werther) at the Met, Olga in Giordano's Fedora at Carnegie Hall and Zdenka (Arabella) at Glyndebourne; season 1989–90 with Adele at the Met and Marie (La Fille du Régiment) in Seattle; Blondchen in Die Entführung at Aix-en-Provence; season 1990–91 highlights were Oscar at the Met, Mahler's 4th Symphony in Florida and Charleston, Bach and Handel with the New York Chamber Symphony, Mozart's Le nozze di Figaro (Susanna) in Toronto; Mozart's Zerlina at San Francisco 1991; La Fille du Regiment at the Met 1992–93; sang Lakmé and Lucia di Lammermoor at Seattle 2000; Norina in Don Pasquale with Seattle Opera 2003. *Recordings include:* Porgy and Bess, Blackwell sings Bernstein, Strange Hurt, Brahms: Ein deutsches Requiem, Candide, All Through the Night, Sondheim: A Celebration at Carnegie Hall. *Honours:* Hon. DHL (Siena Coll.), Hon. DMus (George Washington Univ.). *Current Management:* Columbia Artists Management LLC, 165 W 57th Street, New York, NY 10019-2276, USA. *Telephone:* (212) 841-9500. *Fax:* (212) 841-9744. *E-mail:* info@cami.com. *Website:* www .cami.com.

**BLACKWOOD, Easley;** Composer, Pianist and Music Educator; b. 21 April 1933, Indianapolis, Indiana, USA. *Education:* Received piano training in Indianapolis; Studied composition, Berkshire Music Center, Tanglewood, Massachusetts, summers, 1948, 1949 (with Messiaen), 1950, with Heiden, Indiana University School of Music, Bloomington; With Hindemith, Yale University, MA, 1954, and with Boulanger in Paris, 1954–56. *Career:* Appeared as soloist with the Indianapolis Symphony Orchestra, 1947; Concerts throughout North American and Europe; Faculty member, 1958–68, Professor, 1968–, University of Chicago; Retired, 1997. *Compositions:* Orchestral: Symphony No. 1, 1954–55, No. 2, 1960, No. 3, 1964, No. 4, 1977, No. 5, 1992; Chamber Symphony, 1954; Clarinet Concerto, 1964; Symphonic Fantasy, 1965; Oboe Concerto, 1965; Violin Concerto, 1967; Flute Concerto, 1968; Piano Concerto, 1970; Chamber: Viola Sonata, 1953; 2 string quartets, 1957, 1959; Concerto for 5 instruments, 1959; 2 violin sonatas, 1960, 1973; Fantasy for Cello and Piano, 1960; Pastorale and Variations for Wind Quintet, 1961; Sonata for Flute and Harpsichord, 1962; Fantasy for Flute, Clarinet and Piano, 1965; Symphonic Episode for Organ, 1966; Piano Trio, 1967; 12 Microtonal Etudes for Synthesizer, 1982; Piano pieces; Un voyage à Cythère for soprano and winds, 1966; 4 Letter Scenes from Gulliver's Last Voyage for mezzo-soprano, baritone and tape, 1972; Sonatina for Piccolo Clarinet and Piano, 1994; Sonata for Piano, 1996; Two Nocturnes for piano, 1996. *Recordings:* Piano works of Casella, Szymanowski; Ives, Copland, Prokofiev, Stravinsky, Berg, Nielsen and Alain. *Publications:* The Structure of Recognizable Diatonic Tunings, 1986. *Honours:* Fulbright Scholarship, 1954–56; 1st Prize, Koussevitzky Music Foundation, 1958; Creative Arts Award, Brandeis University, 1968; Several commissions. *Current Management:* Magna Carta Management, 3359 Kelly Lane SW, Roanoke, VA 24018, USA. *Address:* 5300 S Shore Drive #44, Chicago, IL 60615, USA.

**BLADIN, Christer;** Singer (Tenor); b. 1947, Stockholm, Sweden. *Education:* Studied in Freiburg and Stockholm. *Career:* Sang at the Freiburg Opera, 1972–76, Berne, 1976–78, Darmstadt, 1978–84, and at the Bonn Opera from 1986; Guest appearances at Perugia (Salieri's Les Danaides, 1984, Haydn's Orfeo, 1985) and Aix-en-Provence (Rossini's Armida, 1988); Other roles include Froh in Das Rheingold (Barcelona, 1986), Mozart's Belmonte and Tamino, Admète in Lully's Alceste and Ernesto in Don Pasquale; Has also appeared at La Scala, Milan, Nantes, Ghent and Marseille; Montpellier 1993–94, in operas by Philippe Hersant and René Koering. *Address:* c/o Oper der Stadt Bonn, Am Boeselagerhof 1, W-5300 Bonn, Germany.

**BLÁHA, Ivo;** Czech composer and teacher; b. 14 March 1936, Litomyšl. *Education:* pupil of Ridky and Sommer, graduated 1958, postgraduate studies with Hlobil, 1965–70, Prague Acad. of Music; training in electronic music from Kabelac and Herzog, Plzeň Radio. *Career:* teacher, Prague Acad. of Music, 1964–; Docent, Film and TV Faculty, 1967–, Prof. 1999–, Head, Dept of Sound Design, FAMU; mem. Asscn of Czech Composers, Prague. *Compositions:* four string quartets: 1957, 1966, 1983, 'Curriculum vitae' 2000, Concerto for orchestra 1957, 3 Movements for violin and piano 1961, Spring Plays for wind quintet 1962, Concerto for percussion and orchestra 1964, Solitude, sonata for solo violin 1965, Music for wind quintet 1965, 3 Toccata Studies for piano 1967, Violin Concerto 1968, Duetto facile per violini 1970, Music to Pictures of a Friend for flute, oboe and clarinet 1971, Cello Sonata 1972, 2 Inventions for solo flute 1974, Duo for bass clarinet and piano 1975, Cet amour for speaker, wood instruments and tape 1975, Rays for piano 1976, Per archi: Sinfonia 1977, The Violin for violin solo 1979, Hymn for organ 1980, Sonata transparenta for flute and piano 1982, Moravian Lullabies: Musical pictures on folk songs, for soprano, flute and piano 1982, Something for Ear: 3 children's choirs with piano 1983, Zoolessons I for guitar 1984, II 1987, Vaults for organ 1986, Funny Things with Four Strings: 5 miniatures for 2–3 violins or violin ensemble 1986, Imaginations for violin and piano 1988, Sonata introspecta for viola 1989, Joy to Everyone, Christmas Cantata for children's choir and instrumental ensemble 1997, To Ancient Strings for children's choir a cappella 1998, Quasi Sonata for Harpsichord 1998, Welcome Spring! Little Cantata for choir of younger children and instruments 1998, Macrocosmos for piano 1998, Bergamasca: Symphonic Scherzo 2000, Soliloquy with Marimba for marimba and player's voice 2001, Living Water: songs for choir of younger children and piano 2001, 1 Plus Minus 1: musical scene for flautist-woman and violinist-man 2001, Hádes: ancient picture for contrabassoon and piano 2002, Ornaments for piano and orchestra 2003, Satyr's Circles for clarinet solo 2003, Missing Bow (Senza arco) for viola quartet 2004, Bear's Songs for children's choir and piano 2004, Quadrille: dance fantasy for viola foursome 2004. *Recordings:* 3rd and 4th String Quartets, Spring Plays for wind quintet, Solitude, sonata for solo violin, 3 Toccata Studies for piano, Violin Concerto, Duetto facile per violini, Cello Sonata, 2 Inventions for solo flute, Duo for bass clarinet and piano, Cet amour for speaker, wood instruments and tape, Rays for piano, Per archi: Sinfonia, The Violin for violin solo, Hymn for organ, Something for Ear: 3 children's choirs with piano, Zoolessons I for guitar, II, Vaults for organ, Imaginations for violin and piano, Sonata introspecta for viola, Joy to Everyone, Christmas Cantata for children's choir and instrumental ensemble, To Ancient Strings for children's choir a cappella, Quasi Sonata for Harpsichord, Macrocosmos for piano, Bergamasca: Symphonic Scherzo, Hádes: ancient picture for contrabassoon and piano, Ornaments for piano and orchestra, Satyr's Circles for clarinet solo. *Publication:* Sound Dramaturgy of Audio-visual Work 1995. *Honours:* Front position, Int. Rostrum of Composers, UNESCO 1991; Annual Prize of CHF Prague 1993. *Address:* FAMU, Smetanovo nábr. 2, 110 00 Prague 1, Czech Republic (office); Jablonecká 418, 190 00 Prague, Czech Republic. *E-mail:* ivoblaha@seznam.cz (home). *Website:* www.famu.cz (office); members.sibeliusmusic.com/ivoblaha (home).

**BLAHOVA, Eva;** University Professor and Singer; b. 1 Dec. 1944, Skalica, Czechoslovakia; Divorced, 1 s., 1 d. *Education:* Music Academy, Bratislava, Slovakia, 1962–68; Music Academy, Vienna, Austria, 1968–71; Masterclass, Professor D Ferro and Erik Werba. *Career:* Debut: Slovak Philharmony, 1965; Sang in Concert Festivals: Music Festival, Bratislava, Slovakia; Kraków; Easter Festival, Poland; The Prague Spring Festival, Czech Republic; Carinthian Summer Festival, Ossiach, Austria; Ottawa, Montreal, Canada; Parma, Trento, Italy; Chartres, France; Vienna, Austria; Washington DC, New Jersey, USA; Hyundai Arts Center, Korea; Tokyo, Osaka, Japan; Professor of Singing, Music Academy, Bratislava, 1969–, European Music Foundation, 1992–98; Masterclasses in Netherlands and Czech Republic. *Recordings:* Nine German Arias, 1979; Haydn, Mozart, Beethoven Concert Arias, 1983; Romantic Songs, 1997. *Contributions:* Music Life; Slovak Reviews. *Address:* Lermontovova 16, 81105 Bratislava, Slovakia.

**BLAHUSIAKOVA, Magdalena;** Singer (Soprano); b. 1947, Czechoslovakia. *Education:* Studied in Sofia and Bratislava. *Career:* Member of the Brno Opera, 1969–82, notably as Santuzza, Aida, Donna Anna and Donna Elvira, Fiordiligi, Tatiana and Amelia (Simon Boccanegra and Un Ballo in Maschera); Guest appearances in Barcelona (1980), Genoa (as Jenůfa), and Lausanne (Rusalka); Sang Santuzza in Cuba (1987) and Yaroslavna in Prince Igor with the Slovak National Opera at Edinburgh, 1991; Concert engagements in The Spectre's Bride by Dvořák, Vienna, 1984, the Requiems of Dvořák and Mozart and Beethoven's Ninth; Concert tour of the USA, 1985. *Address:* c/o Janáček Opera, Dvořákoáva 11, 65770 Brno, Czech Republic.

**BLAIR, James;** Conductor; b. 1940, Stirling, Scotland. *Education:* Studied at Trinity College, London, and with Adrian Boult; Won Ricordi Conducting Prize and an Italian Government Scholarship to study with Franco Ferrara in Siena and Venice. *Career:* Artistic Director and Principal Conductor, Young Musicians' Symphony Orchestra, 1971–; Many performances of Mahler, Messiaen and Strauss; Engagements with all leading British orchestras and works with Opera North, Dublin Grand Opera and Athens Opera; US debut, 1984, with the Delaware Symphony; Later conducted Colorado Springs and Kansas City Symphony Orchestras; Many Young Musicians' Symphony Orchestra concerts given on BBC, including Mahler's 8th Symphony. *Recordings:* Late Romantic repertory.

**BLAKE, David,** BA, MA; composer; b. 2 Sept. 1936, London, England; m. Rita Muir 1960; two s. one d. *Education:* Gonville and Caius Coll., Cambridge, Deutsche Akademie der Künste, Berlin, Germany. *Career:* Lecturer in Music 1964–71, Senior Lecturer 1971–76, Prof. of Music 1976–2001, Univ. of York, retired 2001. *Compositions include:* Variations for Piano, 1960; Three Choruses to Poems of Robert Frost, 1964; What is the Cause for Chorus; Fulke Greville, 1967; Nonet for Wind, 1971; Violin Concerto, BBC Proms, 1976; Toussaint, libretto Anthony Ward, premiere London Coliseum, 1977, opera in 3 acts, 1974–77; Clarinet Quintet, 1980; Scherzi ed Intermezzi for Orchestra, 1984; Seasonal Variants for 7 Players, 1985; Pastoral Paraphrase for Bassoon and Small Orchestra, 1988; The Plumber's Gift, libretto John Birtwhistle, premiere, London Coliseum, 1989; A Little More Night Music, for Saxophone Quartet, 1990; Mill Music for Brass Band, 1990; Cello Concerto, 1992; Three Ritsos Choruses, 1992; The Griffin's Tale for Baritone and Orchestra, text by John Birtwhistle, 1994; The Fabulous Adventures of Alexander the Great, for soloists, chorus and orchestra of young people, text by John Birtwhistle, 1996; Scoring a Century, an entertainment, text by Keith Warner, 1999; The Shades of Love for bass baritone and small orchestra, poems by C. P. Cavafy, 2000; String Quartet No. 4, 2003, Rings of Jade for medium voice and orchestra (text by Ho Chi Minh, trans. by Birtwhistle). *Recordings:* Violin Concerto In Praise of Krishna, Variations for Piano, The Almanack. *Publications:* Hanns Eisler: A Miscellany 1995. *Address:* Mill Gill, Askrigg, Nr Leyburn, North Yorkshire DL8 3HR, England (home). *Telephone:* (1969) 650364 (home). *E-mail:* david.blake9@btopenworld.com (home).

**BLAKE, Howard;** Composer; b. 28 Oct. 1938, London, England. *Education:* Royal Academy of Music with Harold Craxton and Howard Ferguson. *Career:* Pianist, conductor, orchestrator and composer, London, 1960–70; From 1971 freelance composer; Benedictus performed at Manchester, Llandaff and St Alban's Cathedrals, Perth and Three Choirs Festivals, by the Bach Choir in London (1988) and with the Philharmonia RFH, 1989; Barbican concerts for children; Director of Performing Right Society and Executive Director, 1978–87; Visiting Professor of Composition at Royal Academy of Music, 1992; mem, MU; APC; Incorporated Society of Musicians; Garrick Club; Groucho Club. *Compositions:* The Station, comic opera, 1987; Orchestral: Toccata, 1976; The Annunciation (ballet); Concert Dances, 1984; Clarinet Concerto, 1984; Diversions for cello and orchestra, 1985; Three Sussex Songs, 1973; Two Songs of the Nativity, 1976; The Sor·; of St Francis, 1976; A Toccata of Galuppi's for baritone and harpsichord, 1978; Benedictus, dramatic oratorio, 1979; The Snowman for narrator, boy soprano and orchestra, 1982; Festival Mass for double choir a capella, 1987; Shakespeare Songs for tenor and string quartet, 1987; Instrumental: Piano Quartet, 1974; The Up and Down Man, children's suite, 1974; Penillion for violin and harp, 1975; Eight Character Pieces for piano, 1976; Dances for 2 pianos, 1976; Prelude for solo viola, 1979; Sinfonietta for 10 brass, 1981; Piano Concerto, Philharmonia commission to celebrate 30th birthday of HRH Princess of Wales, 1991; Violin Concerto, world premiere; Leeds City Council commission for their Centenary; The Snowman, ballet, 1993; Charter for Peace, commissioned for UN 50th Anniversary, 1995; A Midsummer Night's Dream, commissioned by RSC, 1996; Eva, ballet, 1996; The Bear, 1998; Stabat Mater, for soprano, narrators, chorus and orchestra, 2001; Also many scores for films, theatre, ballet. *Recordings:* Diversions for cello and orchestra, Toccata, 1991; Snowman; Benedictus; Clarinet and Piano Concertos; Granpa; Violin Concertos, The Snowman Ballet, A Midsummer Night's Dream. *Publications:* Many. *Honours:* Fellow, Royal Academy of Music, 1989; O.B.E., services to music, 1994. *Address:* Studio Flat 6, 18 Kensington Court Place, London W8 5BJ, England.

**BLAKE, Rockwell (Robert);** Singer (Tenor); b. 10 Jan. 1951, Plattsburgh, NY, USA; m. Deborah Jeanne Bourlier, 25 Aug 1973. *Education:* Studied voice with Renata Booth in high school; State University of New York, Fredonia; Catholic University of America, Washington DC. *Career:* Soloist: US Navy Band; Washington DC, Opera, 1976; Hamburg State Opera, 1977–79; Vienna State Opera, 1978; New York City Opera, 1979–81; Metropolitan Opera, New York, 1981–83, 1986, 1988, as Lindoro in L'Italiana in Algeri, Almaviva, Don Ottavio and Arturo in I Puritani; Chicago Lyric Opera, 1983, 1987; Rossini Opera Festival, Pesaro, 1983–85, 1987–88; San Francisco Opera, 1984; Paris Opéra, 1985; Naples San Carlo, 1985–88; Opéra-Comique, Paris, 1987; Bavarian State Opera, Munich, 1987; Rome Opera, 1988–89; Sang James V in La Donna del Lago at Bonn, 1990; Arturo in I Puritani at Barcelona, 1990; Tonio (La Fille du Régiment) at Santiago; Concert performance of Meyerbeer's Il Crociato in Egitto at the 1990 Montpellier Festival; Rossini cantatas at Martina Franca; Title role in Il Pirata at Lausanne, 1992; Season 1992 as Rossini's Almaviva at Genoa, Selim in Rossini's Adina at Rome, James V in La Donna del Lago at La Scala, Mozart's Ferrando at Dallas; Almaviva at the 1992 Caracalla Festival; Sang in Semiramide at the 1994 Pesaro Festival; Aix Festival 1996, as Jupiter in the French premiere of Handel's Semele; Ramiro in Cenerentola at Hamburg, 1998; Sang Oronte in Alcina at the Paris Palais Garnier and Lyric Opera of Chicago, 1999; Season 2000–01 as Libenskof in Il Viaggio a Reims at La Coruña, and as Idreno in Semiramide at Liège; Various concert engagements. *Recordings:* The Rossini Tenor; The Mozart Tenor; Encore Rossini; Alina la Regina di Golconda; Il Barbiere di Siviglia; Video of Rossini's Barber from the Metropolitan. *Honours:* First winner, Richard Tucker Award, 1978; National Opera Institute Grantee, 1975, 1976; Honorary DMus, State Orchestra. *Current Management:* IMG Artists, Lovell House, 616 Chiswick High Road, London W4 5RX, England. *Telephone:* (20) 8233-5800. *Fax:* (20) 8233-5801. *E-mail:* artistseurope@imgworld.com. *Website:* www.imgartists.com. *Current Management:* IMG Artists Paris – Vocal Division, 44 rue Blanche, 75009 Paris, France. *Telephone:* 1-44-31-00-10. *Fax:* 1-44-31-44-01. *E-mail:* artistsparis@imgartists.com. *Website:* www.imgartists.com. *Current Management:* Thea Dispeker Inc., 59 East 54th Street, Suite 81, New York, NY 10022, USA. *Telephone:* (212) 421-7676. *Fax:* (212) 935-3279. *E-mail:* info@dispeker.com. *Website:* www.dispeker.com.

**BLANC, Ernest (Marius Victor);** Singer (Baritone); b. 1 Nov. 1923, Sanary-sur-Mer, France; m. Eliane Guiraud. *Education:* Studied at the Toulon Conservatory, 1946–49. *Career:* Debut: Marseille, 1950, as Tonio in Pagliacci; Paris Opéra from 1954, debut as Rigoletto; Sang in Paris until 1976, in operas by Puccini, Wagner, Offenbach and Verdi; Bayreuth Festival, 1958–59, as Telramund; La Scala Milan, 1960; Glyndebourne, 1960, as Don Giovanni and as Riccardo in I Puritani; Guest appearances in Naples, New York, Barcelona, Lisbon, Tel-Aviv, Florence and Amsterdam. Season 1986–87 as Des Grieux (père) at Nancy and Germont at Marseille. *Recordings:* Faust, Carmen, Iphigénie en Tauride, Les Contes d'Hoffmann, Les Pêcheurs de Perles.

**BLANC, Jonny;** Singer (Tenor); b. 10 July 1939, Lessebo, Sweden. *Education:* Studied at the Stockholm Conservatory with Kathe Sundstrom and with Clemens Kaiser-Breme in Essen. *Career:* Sang as baritone, 1962–67; Tenor debut, Stockholm, 1967, as Dmitri in Boris Godunov; Sang in the premieres of operas by Braein and Werle and as Florestan, Siegmund, Eisenstein in Die Fledermaus, Don Carlos, Don José, Cavaradossi and Riccardo in Un Ballo in Maschera; Sang in a revival of the Abbé Vogler's Gustaf Adolf och Ebba Brahe at Drottningholm, 1973; Sang Števa in the Stockholm Opera production of Jenůfa at the Edinburgh Festival, 1974; Guest appearances with Scottish Opera and in Malmö, Oslo, Frankfurt, Copenhagen, Miami, Lisbon and Helsinki; Well-known as concert singer; Artistic Manager, Malmö City Theatre, 1986; Opera Manager, Royal Opera Stockholm, 1991–; Principal, University College of Opera, Stockholm, 1994. *Address:* Dag Hammarskjölds väg 24, 11527 Stockholm, Sweden.

**BLANCK, Kirsten;** Singer (Soprano); b. 1965, Neumünster, Holstein, Germany. *Education:* Studied in Hamburg with Judith Beckmann and in Kiel and Lubeck. *Career:* Debut: Saarbrucken, 1986; Sang at the Lubeck and Kiel Operas from 1990, notably as Mozart's Queen of Night, and in Dresden, Berlin, Stuttgart and Frankfurt; Other roles include Donna Anna (Kiel, 1991), Gilda (Hanover, 1993), Sophie in Der Rosenkavalier, Zerbinetta, and Lulu; Season 1992–93 at Kiel as Violetta and Donna Clara in Zemlinsky's Der Zwerg; Aminta in Die schweigsame Frau at Dresden, 1998; Season 2000–01 as Zerbinetta at La Scala, The Queen of Night at Dresden, Sophie in Der Rosenkavalier for San Francisco Opera and Constanze at Chemnitz; Many concert appearances. *Current Management:* Aria's di Novella Partacini & Alexandra Plaickner, Via Josef Weingartner 4, 39022 Lagundo, ItalyEmail: Phone: +39 Fax: +39. *Telephone:* (473) 200200. *Fax:* (473) 222424. *E-mail:* info@arias.it. *Website:* www.arias.it.

**BLANCKE-BIGGS, Elizabeth;** American singer (soprano); b. 1965. *Career:* appearances as Madama Butterfly and Liu in Turandot for Opera Grand Rapids, Nedda in Pagliacci for El Paso opera and the Trovatore Leonora for Augusta Opera; Micaela for Opera Colorado, Mimi at the Virginia Opera and Norma for the Di Capo Opera Theatre; European engagements as Donizetti's Maria Stuarda at Turin and in Honegger's Le Roi David at Nice; other concerts include Beethoven's Ninth and Die Walküre in New Zealand; Fauré's Requiem, Mozart's C Minor Mass and Beethoven's Mass in C; sang Mozart's Countess at the Aotea Centre, Auckland; season 2001–02 as Violetta for the Metropolitan Opera and Tosca for New York City Opera. *Current Management:* Robert Lombardo Associates, 61 W 62nd Street, Suite 6F, New York, NY 10023, USA. *Telephone:* (212) 586-4453. *Fax:* (212) 581-5771. *E-mail:* lewis@rlombardo.com. *Website:* www.rlombardo.com.

**BLAND, Edward (Ed);** American composer and musician (clarinet, baritone saxophone); b. 25 July 1926, Chicago, IL. *Education:* DuSable High School, Englewood High School and Sherwood School of Music, Chicago, Wilson Jr Coll., Chicago, Univ. of Chicago, American Conservatory of Music, Chicago. *Career:* clarinettist and baritone saxophonist, US Navy band, Treasure Island, San Francisco 1945–46; composer and arranger for numerous artists, including Maya Angelou, George Benson, Country Joe & The Fish, Dizzy Gillespie, Lionel Hampton, King Harvest, Richie Havens, Al Hirt; Head of A&R, Exec. Prod. and Prod., Vanguard Records 1974–78; composer-in-residence, Bennington Coll., VT 1980–84; visiting lecturer at numerous colls and univs; Presidential Commissionaire, Comm. for the White House Record Library 1979–81; mem. American Composer Alliance, BMI, Nat. Acad. of Recording, Arts and Sciences (New York Chapter, bd of governors 1979–80), American Fed. of Musicians Local 47, American Music Center. *Compositions include:* Trio No. 1 1944, Fragment for Piano 1948, Fragment for string quartet 1949, Trio No. 2 1950, Trio No. 3 1950, String Quartet No. 2 1951, Cello/Tympani 1953, Fragment for Cello 1953, For Clarinet 1953, Sketches Set One 1957, Sketches Set Two 1958, If You Grin You Are In 1963, Moonshot 1964, Toe Jam 1968, Chicken Scratch 1969, Fly Vines 1969, Juicy Lucy 1969, A Gritty Nitty 1975, Loose and Juicy 1975, Skunk Juice 1975, Eddie A 1976, Aldon B 1976, Mushroom Alley 1977, For Bassoon 1979, Piece for Chamber Orchestra 1979, For Violin 1980, For Flute 1980, Brass Quintet 1981, Woodwind Quintet No. 1 (The Jazz Quintet) 1981, Primal Counterpoint 1981, Partita for strings 1982, Piano Trio 1982, Magnetic Variations 1982, White Satin (dance) 1983, Dear Vera (dance) 1984, Arion's Song (Woodwind Quintet No. 2 or Sketches Set Six) 1986, Concerto for electric violin and chamber orchestra 1986, Romantic Synergy 1987, Sketches Set Seven for piano 1987, Atalanta's Challenge 1988, Passacaglia in Blue 1988, Romantic Soul 1989, Paean for an Endangered Planet 1989, Let Peace Be Free for orchestra 1991, New World Order 1991, Rambunctious Serenade for orchestra 1992, Classical Soul for piano 1992, Clarinet Trio 1992, Grand Slam for orchestra 1993, For Viola and Four Others 1993, Feeling Good (dance) 1994, For Flute No. 2 1994, For Flute No. 3 1994, For Oboe 1994, For Bass Clarinet 1994, For Trumpet 1994, Assassins of the Soul (opera) 1997; for jazz ensemble: Greasy Greens 1966, Grits and Gravy 1966, King Cool 1967, Chicken Giblets 1968, Guava Jelly 1968, Blue Cuchifrito 1969, Casabah Melon 1969, Clabber Biscuits 1969, The Fly Fox 1969, Pot Licka 1969, Rutabaga Pie 1969, Stomped and Wasted 1969, Turkey Fan 1969, Turnip Tops 1969, Bobby A 1975, Stefanie 1975, Keep it Greasy 1976, Old King Tut 1976, Philomene 1976, Sun in Pieces 1976, Azure Blue 1977, Digital Display 1977, Dirty Dude 1977, Get To That 1977, Gettin' Down 1977, Moody Magic 1977, Party Man 1977, Slew Foot 1977, Soul Mama

1977, Soul Time 1977, Sweet Stuff 1977, Love Theme 1990, Radio Theme 1990, Walter's Theme 1990. *Film scores:* To Live Together 1950, Reflections 1957, The Cool World 1964, Ganja and Hess 1973, A Soldier's Story 1984, A Raisin in the Sun 1988. *Television scores:* J.T. 1971, The House of Dies Drear 1985. *Address:* c/o Osmund Music Inc., PO Box 451112, Los Angeles, CA 90045-9998, USA.

**BLANK, Allan;** Composer; b. 27 Dec. 1925, New York, NY, USA. *Education:* High School of Music and Art in New York; Juilliard, 1946–47, Washington Square College; MA, University of Minnesota, 1950; University of Iowa. *Career:* Violinist, Pittsburgh Symphony Orchestra, 1950–52; Teacher, Western Illinois University, 1966–68, Patterson State College, 1968–70, Lehmann College, 1970–77, and Virginia Commonwealth University at Richmond, 1978–; Music Director of the Richmond Community Orchestra, 1986–89. *Compositions include:* Operas Aria da Capo, 1960; Excitement at the Circus, children's opera, Patterson, 1969; The Magic Bonbons, 1983; The Noise, Richmond, 1986; Incidental music for Othello, 1983, and Measure for Measure, 1984; 5 String Quartets, 1958, 1981, 1989, 1998 (2); Concert Piece for band, 1963; Music for Orchestra, 1967; Wind Quintet, 1970; An American Medley, 1976; Music for Tubas, 1977; Divertimento for tuba and band, 1979; Kreutzer March for band, 1981; Concertino for bassoon and strings, 1984; Concert for 5 players, 1986; Concertino for string orchestra, 1987; Forked Paths, suite of 11 miniatures for trumpet, 1988; Overture for a Happy Occasion, 1986; Polymorphics, 1988; Concerto for clarinet and string orchestra, 1990; Songs from the Holocaust, 1996; Concerto for Violin and Orchestra, 1995; Concerto for Contrabass and String Orchestra, 1996; Songs; Concerto for piano and orchestra, 2001; Lines for Solo Contrabassoon, 2001; Three Tableaux for small orchestra, 2001; Concerto for Bassoon and Small Orchestra, 2002; Music for Multiply Violins, 2003; Becoming for Clarinet, Cello and Piano, 2003; Ensemble for Brass Quintet, 2003. *Honours:* George Eastman Competition, 1983; National Endowment for the Arts, 1983; Virginia Music Teachers Association Commission, 1979, 1988, 1991. *Address:* 2920 Archdale Road, Richmond, VA 23235, USA.

**BLANKENBURG, Heinz (Horst);** Singer (Baritone) and Stage Director; b. 15 Oct. 1931, New York, NY, USA; m. (1) 2 s., 1 d., (2) Gayle Cameron-McComb, 14 Dec 1986. *Education:* Local universities, Los Angeles. *Career:* Debut: San Francisco Opera, 1955; Leading baritone, Glyndebourne Festival Opera, 1957–70, roles there included Mozart's Papageno and Figaro, Rossini's Raimbaud and Busoni's Arlecchino; Hamburg State Opera, 1959–73, San Francisco Opera, 1955–66; As Beckmesser, Schaunard, Fra Melitone (Forza del Destino) and Paolo in Simon Boccanegra; Sang with the Hamburg Staatsoper in the British premiere of Die Frau ohne Schatten, Sadler's Wells Theatre, 1966; Guest baritone with opera companies of Munich, Berlin, Vienna, Paris, Frankfurt, Metropolitan, Amsterdam, Rome, Brussels, Lausanne, Basle, Strasbourg, Naples, Venice, New Zealand, St Louis, Portland, Vancouver (1978); Seattle, Los Angeles; Faculty, University of California, Los Angeles and California State University, Los Angeles. *Recordings:* Discs, 2 labels; Television and radio recordings for BBC, RAI and ZDF. *Honours:* Kammersänger, Hamburg State Opera, 1966; Maori Welcome, New Zealand, 1971; Honorary Doctor of Performing Arts, California State University, Los Angeles, 1977, University of California, Los Angeles, 1986; Maori Welcome, New Zealand, 1971. *Address:* Opera Theatre, California State University, 5151 State University Drive, Los Angeles, CA 90032, USA.

**BLANKENHEIM, Toni;** Singer (Bass-baritone); b. 12 Dec. 1921, Cologne, Germany. *Education:* Studied with Paul Lohmann in Frankfurt and with Res Fischer in Stuttgart. *Career:* Debut: Frankfurt, 1947, as Mozart's Figaro; Sang at Frankfurt until 1950, then at Hamburg; Bayreuth Festival, 1954–59, as Kothner, Klingsor and Donner; Darmstadt, 1965–68; Stuttgart from 1968; Sang at Hamburg in the premieres of operas by Mihalovici, Martinů, Henze, Krenek, Von Einem, Goehr, Searle, Kelemen and Constant; Performances of works by Berg, Stravinsky, Liebermann and other modern composers; Sang Schigolch at the Paris Opéra in the 1979 premiere of Berg's Lulu (3 act version); Guest appearances in Vienna, Berlin, Munich, Milan, Paris, Mexico City, San Francisco and New York; Sang in the first local performance of The Birthday by Kalevi, at Hamburg, 1982; Many concert appearances. *Recordings:* Bastien et Bastienne by Mozart; Lulu; Donner in Das Rheingold, Bayreuth, 1957; Klingsor in Parsifal, Bayreuth, 1956.

**BLANKENSHIP, Rebecca;** American singer (soprano); b. 24 March 1954, New York; d. of William Blankenship. *Education:* Studied voice in New York with Judith Oas. *Career:* Sang two seasons at Ulm as a Mezzo Soprano; Sang Ariadne at Berlin Staatsoper, 1986; Appeared in Basle 1986–88 as Mozart's Elettra and First Lady, Leonora in Il Trovatore, Katharina in Lady Macbeth of Mtsensk; Season 1988–90: Martha, in Tiefland in Berlin and Vienna Volksoper, Leonore in Fidelio in Stuttgart and with Opera Forum in Netherlands, Elsa in Liège and Senta at Bregenz Festival; Marie in Wozzeck with Vienna Staatsoper, 1990–92; Regular appearances in Vienna, 1991–; Other roles include Female Chorus, in The Rape of Lucretia, Agathe in Der Freischütz, Hanna Glawari in Die Lustige Witwe; Sang Sieglinde (San Francisco Opera) 1990, (Wiener Staatsoper), 1991, Marie in Wozzeck (La Fenice, Venice) 1992, Lady Macbeth of Mtsensk, Katarina (Wiener Volksoper) 1992, Erwartung by Schoenberg (Canadian Opera at Toronto, and Edinburgh Festival) 1993, Erwartung (Le Grand Théâtre, Geneva) 1995, Erwartung (Graz Opera) 2001, Kostelnicka in Jenufa (Graz Opera) 2003. *Theatre and film:* The Seven Streams of the River Ota (Lyttelton, Nat. Theatre, London) 1996, Kindertotenlieder 1999, Le Polygraph 2001. *Address:* Music International, 13 Ardilaun Road, London N5 2QR, England. *E-mail:* reblank@ mindspring.com (home).

**BLANZAT, Anne-Marie Eliane;** French singer (soprano); b. 24 Nov. 1944, Neuilly-sur-Seine; d. of Marius and Paulette (née Delaveau) Blanzat; m. Jacques Plas 1965; one s. *Education:* Maîtrise de Radio-France. *Career:* began singing career in child operatic rôles aged 13; int. career performing at operas, concerts and festivals including Aix-en-Provence, Glyndebourne and Gulbenkian Festivals, Opéra de Bruxelles, Paris, Geneva, Lyons, Strasbourg, Naples, Palermo, Turin, Lisbon etc. *Operas include:* Pelleas et Mélisande, Carmen, Le Nozze di Figaro, Falstaff, Les dialogues des Carmélites, Les contes d'Hoffmann, Béatrice et Bénédicte, Les pêcheurs de perles, Les liaisons dangereuses, Manon, Le Consul, La dame de pique, La Voix Humaine. *Videos:* Pelleas et Mélisande 1982, Les dialogues des Carmélites 1982, Manon 1984. *Honours:* Chevalier des Arts et Lettres 1984; Oscar for Best Lyric Singer in France 1974. *Address:* 2 square Servan, 75011 Paris, France. *Telephone:* (1) 48-05-37-36.

**BLASI, Angela Maria;** American singer (soprano); b. 16 Aug. 1956, Brooklyn, NY. *Education:* Loyola Univ., Los Angeles. *Career:* ensemble mem., Hessen State Theater, Wiesbaden 1982–85; Bavarian State Opera, Munich 1985–88; debut as Pamina at Salzburg Festival, Covent Garden, La Scala Milan; guest appearances in European opera houses, including Hamburg, Berlin, Vienna, Zürich, Florence; appeared as Liu in Turandot in the Forbidden City, Beijing with Zubin Mehta 1998; Marguerite in Faust, Munich 2000; New York Met debut as Pamina 2000; Ellen Orford in Peter Grimes, Montpellier, France 2001; Conception in L'Heure Espagnole, Brussels, Belgium 2001; Nedda in Pagliacci, Brussels Monnaie 2002; La Bohème at the Met 2003; Agathe in Der Freischutz, Montpellier 2003. *Film:* Comencini's film of La Bohème (Musetta) 1987. *Recordings:* Mozart's Requiem and Mahler's 4th Symphony. *Honours:* Bavarian Kammersängerin 1994, Munich Merkur Prize, People's Choice Award for Interpretation of Marguerite in Faust at the Bavarian State Opera. *Current Management:* Robert Lombardo Associates, 61 W 62nd Street, Suite 6F, New York, NY 10023, USA. *Telephone:* (212) 586-4453. *Fax:* (212) 581-5771. *E-mail:* lewis@ rlombardo.com. *Website:* www.rlombardo.com. *Address:* c/o Bayerische Staatsoper, Max-Joseph Platz, 80539 Munich, Germany. *Telephone:* (171) 3558875 (office). *Website:* www.angelamariablasi.com.

**BLASIUS, Martin;** Singer (Bass); b. 5 June 1956, Schwelm, Westphalen, Germany. *Education:* Studied at the Folkwang-Musikhochschule, Essen. *Career:* Sang at first in concert, notably for Austrian and Italian Radio, at the Bach-Woche Ansbach, the Göttingen Handel Festival and at the Frankurt Festival; Opera debut as Dulcamara, Gelsenkirchen, 1983; Moved to Hannover in 1987 and Düsseldorf in 1989; Guest appearances in opera and concerts throughout Germany; Appeared in a new production of Henze's The Bassarids, Duisburg, 1991 and sang the Grand Inquisitor in Don Carlos at Düsseldorf; Gärtnerplatztheater Munich 1992, as Mussorgsky's Ivan Khovansky; Bielefeld 1988, as Orth in Weill's Burgschaft; Season 1999–2000 as Wagner's Hunding at Münster, and Fafner in Siegfried. *Recordings include:* Der Traumgörge by Zemlinsky; Saint-Saëns's Christmas Oratorio; Golgotha by Martin; Kreutzer's Das Nachtlager von Granada. *Address:* c/o Deutsche Oper am Rhein, Heinrich Heine Allee 16, 4000 Düsseldorf, Germany.

**BLATNÝ, Pavel;** Czech composer, conductor, musician (piano) and musicologist; b. 14 Sept. 1931, Brno; m. Danuse Spirková 1982; one s. one d. *Education:* Brno Conservatory, Univ. of Brno, Berklee Coll. of Music, Boston, USA. *Career:* more than 2,000 recitals of piano music, often in a third-stream mode, mixing jazz and classical techniques; conductor of many concerts in the former Czechoslovakia; Chief of the Music Division, Czech television 1971–92; Prof., Janácek Acad. of Musical Arts, Brno 1979–90; Pres., Club of Moravian Composers. *Compositions include:* Music for Piano and Orchestra 1955, Concerto for Orchestra 1956, Concerto for Jazz Orchestra 1962–64, Twelfth Night (based on Shakespeare's play) 1975, Forest Tales: The Well and Little House (television opera for children) 1975, The Willow Tree (cantata with orchestra) 1980, The Bells, symphonic movement 1981, Christmas Eve (cantata with orchestra) 1982, The Midday Witch (cantata with orchestra) 1982, Two Movements for Brasses 1982, Hommage à Gustav Mahler for orchestra 1982, Per organo e big band 1983, Prologue for mixed choir and jazz orchestra 1984, Ring a Ring o' Roses, for solo piano 1984, Signals for Jazz Orchestra 1985, Confrontation (written with his son, Marek Blatny) for rock group and symphony orchestra 1995, Play Rock, Play New Music (written with his son, Marek Blatny) 1997, Meditation 1999, Symphony Erbenia'da 2003; other music for wind instruments, for piano. *Recordings:* Pavel Blatny – Jazz in Modo Classico, 1980. *Honours:* Leoš Janácek Prize 1984, Anfiteatro d'Argento, Naples, Italy 1989, Lifetime Achievement Award, Brno 2000. *Address:* Absolonova 35, 62400 Brno, Czech Republic (home). *Telephone:* (5) 4122-3062.

**BLATTERT, Susanne;** Singer (Mezzo-soprano); b. 1966, Freiburg, Germany. *Education:* Studied in Hamburg with Judith Beckman. *Career:* Sang at Gelsenkirchen Musiktheater, 1990–93; Essen Opera from 1993; Further appearances at Hamburg, Cologne, the Bregenz Festival and in Budapest; Roles have included Mozart's Zerlina, Cherubino and Dorabella, Rossini's Rosina, Tancredi and Cenerentola; Essen, 1996 as Sesto in La Clemenza di Tito; Season 1997–98 as Wellgunde in Das Rheingold at Bonn; Season 2000–01 at Bonn as Dorabella, Wellgunde, and Micha in a staged version of Handel's Saul. *Honours:* Prizewinner, Concours International de Chant,

Toulouse, 1992. *Current Management:* Alferink Artists Management, Herengracht 340, 1016 CG Amsterdam, Netherlands. *Telephone:* (20) 6643151. *Fax:* (20) 6752426. *E-mail:* info@alferink.org. *Website:* www.alferink.org. *Address:* c/o Oper der Stadt Bonn, Am Boeselagenhof 1, Pf 2440, 5311 Bonn, Germany.

**BLAUSTEIN, Susan (Morton);** Composer; b. 22 March 1953, Palo Alto, California, USA. *Education:* Studied with Pousseur in Liège, and at Yale with Jacob Druckman and Betsy Jolas. *Career:* Former Junior Fellow at Harvard University; Assistant professor at Columbia University, New York, 1985–90. *Compositions include:* Commedia for 8 players, 1980; To Orpheus, 4 sonnets, 1982; String Quartet, 1982; Sextet, 1983; Concerto for cello and chamber orchestra, 1984; Song of Songs for mezzo, tenor and orchestra, 1985. *Honours:* Commissions from the Koussevitsky and Fromm Foundations. *Address:* c/o ASCAP, ASCAP House, 1 Lincoln Plaza, New York, NY 10023, USA.

**BLAZE, Robin;** British singer (countertenor) and academic; *Professor of Vocal Studies, Royal College of Music;* b. 1971, England; m.; one s. *Education:* Magdalen Coll., Oxford, Royal Coll. of Music. *Career:* regular solo engagements in Europe, USA, S America and Asia with the King's Consort, the Acad. of Ancient Music, Bach Collegium Japan, Collegium Vocale, Gent, The English Concert, The Gabrieli Consort, Orchestra of the Age of Enlightenment, RIAS Kammerchor, Amsterdam Bach Orchestra, and The Sixteen; soloist with Nat. Symphony Orchestra Washington, St Paul Chamber Orchestra, BBC Philharmonic, BBC Nat. Orchestra of Wales, Hallé Orchestra, La Chapelle Royale, Scottish Chamber Orchestra, and Tafelmusik; appearances at festivals, including Edinburgh, BBC Proms, Bremen, Barossa, Boston, Schwetsingen, Istanbul, Potsdam, Leipzig, Flanders, Melbourne, Ambronay and Beaune; opera performances include Bertarido in Rodelinda (Glyndebourne Touring Opera and at the Göttingen Handel Festival), Anfinomo in Il Ritorno d'Ulisse in Patria (Teatro Sao Carlos, Lisbon), Arsamenes in Xerxes (ENO), Athamas in Semele (Royal Opera House, Covent Garden) 2003; chamber music concerts with Concordia, Fretwork, Sonnerie, Palladian Ensemble; recitals at the Wigmore Hall, BBC Radio 3, in Karlsruhe, Innsbruck, Göttingen, Halle and many UK festivals; Prof. of Vocal Studies, Royal Coll. of Music. *Recordings:* over 40 albums, including Bach Cantata Cycle with Bach Collegium Japan and recitals with lute player, Elizabeth Kenny. *Current Management:* Caroline Phillips Management, The Old Brushworks, 56 Pickwick Road, Corsham, Wiltshire SN13 9BX, England. *Telephone:* (1249) 716716. *Fax:* (1249) 716717. *E-mail:* cphillips@caroline -phillips.co.uk. *Website:* www.caroline-phillips.co.uk/blaze.

**BLEGEN, Judith;** American singer (soprano); b. Lexington, KY; d. of Dr Halward Martin Blegen and Dorothy Mae (Anderson) Blegen; m. 1st Peter Singher 1967 (divorced 1975); one s.; m. 2nd Raymond Gniewek 1977. *Education:* Curtis Inst. of Music, Philadelphia, Pa, Music Acad. of the West, Santa Barbara, Calif. *Career:* leading soprano, Nuremberg Opera, FRG 1965–68, Staatsoper, Vienna, Austria 1968–70, Metropolitan Opera, New York 1970–; Vienna roles include Zerbinetta (Ariadne auf Naxos), Rosina (The Barber of Seville), Aennchen (Der Freischutz), Norina (Don Pasquale); numerous performances at Metropolitan include Marzelline (Fidelio), Sophie (Werther), Mélisande (Pelléas et Mélisande), Sophie (Der Rosenkavalier), Adina (L'Elisir d'amore), Juliette (Roméo et Juliette), Susanna (The Marriage of Figaro); other appearances include Susanna (The Marriage of Figaro), San Francisco, title role in Manon, Tulsa Opera, Gilda (Rigoletto), Chicago, Despina (Così fan tutte), Covent Garden, Blondchen (The Abduction from the Seraglio), Salzburg Festival, Mélisande (Pelléas et Mélisande), Spoleto Festival, Susanna (The Marriage of Figaro), Edinburgh Festival, Sophie, Paris Opera; Fulbright Scholarship. *Recordings include:* La Bohème (Puccini), Carmina Burana (Orff), Symphony No. 4 (Mahler), Harmonienmesse (Haydn), The Marriage of Figaro (Mozart), A Midsummer Night's Dream (Mendelssohn), Nelson Mass (Haydn), Gloria (Poulenc), Peer Gynt Suite (Grieg), Lieder recital (Richard Strauss and Hugo Wolf), baroque music recital. *Honours:* Grammy Awards. *Address:* c/o Thea Dispeker, 59 East 54th Street, New York, NY 10022, USA.

**BLINKHOF, Jan;** Singer (Tenor); b. 10 July 1940, Leiden, Netherlands. *Education:* Studied in Amsterdam, with Joseph Metternich in Cologne and with Luigi Ricci in Rome. *Career:* Debut: With Netherlands Opera, 1971, as Arturo in Lucia di Lammermoor; Holland Festival, 1971, in the premiere of Spinoza by Ton de Kruyf; Amsterdam, 1974, in the premiere of Dorian Gray by Kox; Geneva Opera, 1985, as Tristan; Nice, 1986, as Herman in The Queen of Spades; Sang Laca in Jenůfa at the Zürich Opera, 1986; Other roles include Ismaele in Nabucco; Boris in Katya Kabanova, and roles in Wozzeck, The Rape of Lucretia, The Gambler by Prokofiev and Henze's Der Junge Lord; Sang Tristan at Nice, 1986–87, Laca at Covent Garden, 1988; Deutsche Oper Berlin, 1988, as Sergei in Lady Macbeth of the Mtsensk District; Sang Boris in Katya Kabanova at Geneva and Florence, 1989; Albert Gregor in The Makropulos Case at Berlin, 1990, followed by Sergei in Hamburg and Laca (Jenůfa) at Barcelona; Season 1994 as Florestan at Lisbon and Sergei at Florence; Season 1996 as Luca in From the House of the Dead at Nice and Florestan in Fidelio at Rome; Laca at Hamburg, 1998; Calaf at Barcelona, 1999; Sang the Drum Major in Wozzeck at the Vienna Staatsoper (2000), Janáček's Laca and Shuisky in Boris Godunov at Hamburg. *Address:* c/o Deutsche Oper Berlin, Richard Wagnerstrasse 10, 1000 Berlin, Germany.

**BLOCH, Augustyn;** Composer; b. 13 Aug. 1929, Grudziądz, Poland. *Education:* Studied composition with Tadeusz Szeligowski and organ with

Felik Raczkowski at Warsaw Conservatory. m. Halina Lukomska. *Career:* Music Consultant to the Polish Radio Theatre from 1954; mem, Polish Composers Union. *Compositions include:* Opera: Jephtha's Daughter, 1968; Children's Opera-Pantomime: Sleeping Princess, 1974; Musical: Tale of The Violin Soul, 1978; Ballet: Voci, 1967, Gilgamesh, 1968, The Looking Glass, 1975; Orchestral: Meditations for Soprano, Organ and Percussion, 1961, Dialogues for Violin and Orchestra, 1963, Enfiando for Orchestra, 1970, A Poem About Warsaw for Narrator, Chorus and Orchestra, 1974, Oratorio for Organ, Strings and Percussion, 1982, Abide with Us, Lord, for Orchestra, 1986, Exaltabo Te for Mixed Choir, 1988, Ostra Brama Litany for Choir and Orchestra, 1989, Trio for Violin, violoncello and Piano, 1992, Upwards for Orchestra, 1993, Scared Out, song for Baritone, Viola, Cello and Piano to a text by Else Lasker-Schüler; Die Verscheuchte for baritone, viola, cello and piano, 1995; Hac festa die for chorus, organ, period instruments and orchestra, 1996. *Recordings:* Bloch Plays Bloch; Thou Shalt Not Kill; Chamber Music. *Honours:* Cavalier's and Officer's Cross of The Rebirth of Poland, 1969 and 1979; Polish Composers Union Prize, 1981; Brighton Festival Prize, 1989. *Address:* Wybieg 14, 00 788 Warsaw, Poland.

**BLOCHWITZ, Hans Peter;** Singer (Tenor); b. 28 Sept. 1949, Garmisch-Partenkirchen, Germany. *Education:* Studied at Darmstadt, Mainz and Frankfurt. *Career:* Sang at first in concert, notably as the Evangelist in the St Matthew Passion and in Lieder recitals (Die schöne Müllerin by Schubert); Opera debut Frankfurt 1984, as Lensky; Sang in the Scala-staged version of the St Matthew Passion at San Marco, Milan, 1985; Théâtre de la Monnaie, Brussels, and Geneva 1986, as Don Ottavio and Lensky; Guest appearances in Hamburg, Amsterdam and London (Ferrando in Così fan tutte, 1989); Aix-en-Provence Festival 1987–89, as Belmonte and Ferrando; Sang Idamante in Idomeneo at San Francisco, 1989; Don Ottavio at the Metropolitan Opera, 1990; Sang in the Choral Symphony at the 1993 Prom Concerts, London; Wilhelm in Henze's Der Junge Lord, Munich, 1995; Flamand in Capriccio at Dresden, 1996; Title role in Il ritorno d'Ulisse in Patria, Athens, 1997; Mozart's Titus at Glyndebourne, 1999; Teaches at Musikhochschule, Bern. *Recordings include:* Bach St Matthew Passion; Bach Christmas Oratorio; Bach B-Minor Mass; Mozart Requiem; Mozart Die Zauberflöte; Mozart Don Giovanni; Mozart Così fan tutte; Mozart La Finta Semplice; Mozart C-Minor Mass; Mozart Coronation Mass; Beethoven Missa Solemnis; Beethoven Fidelio; Handel Theodora; Handel Messiah; Haydn Schöpfung; Mendelssohn Lobgesang Symphony; Mendelssohn St Paul; Schubert and Die schöne Magelone by Brahms. *Current Management:* Alferink Artists Management, Herengracht 340, 1016 CG Amsterdam, Netherlands. *Telephone:* (20) 6643151. *Fax:* (20) 6752426. *E-mail:* info@alferink.org. *Website:* www .alferink.org.

**BLOMSTEDT, Herbert Thorson;** Swedish conductor; *Music Director, Leipzig Gewandhaus Orchestra;* b. 11 July 1927, Springfield, Mass, USA; s. of Adolphe Blomstedt and Alida Armintha Thorson; m. Waltraud Regina Peterson 1955 (died 2003); four d. *Education:* Royal Acad. of Music, Stockholm, Uppsala Univ., Mozarteum, Salzburg, Austria, Schola Cantorum, Basel, Switzerland, Juilliard School, New York, USA, Tanglewood, Mass. *Career:* Music Dir, Norrköping Symphony Orchestra 1954–61; Prof. of Conducting, Swedish Royal Acad. of Music 1961–70; Perm. Conductor, Oslo Philharmonic 1962–68; Music Dir of Danish Radio Symphony Orchestra 1967–77, of Dresden Staatskapelle Orchestra 1975–85, of Swedish Radio Symphony Orchestra 1977–82; Music Dir and Conductor, San Francisco Symphony Orchestra 1985–95, Conductor Laureate 1995–; Music Dir NDR Symphony Orchestra, Hamburg 1996–98, Leipzig Gewandhaus Orchestra 1998–2005; mem. Royal Acad. of Music, Stockholm 1965;. *Publications:* Till Kennedomen om Johann Christian Bachs Symfonies 1951, Lars-Erik Larsson och Lars Convertinor (co-author) 1957, Berwald: Sinfonie Siuguliers 1965. *Honours:* Hon. Conductor NHK Symphony, Tokyo 1985; Kt Royal Order of the North Star (Sweden); Kt Royal Order of Dannebrog (Denmark); Grosses Verdienstkreuz der Bundesrepublik Deutschland 2003; Hon. DMus (Andrews); Hon. PhD (Gothenburg) 1999; Dr hc (Southwestern-Adventist Univ., TX) 1993; Jenny Lind Scholarship, Swedish Royal Acad. of Music, Litteris et Artibus, Gold Medal (Sweden), Deutscher Schallplattenpreis 1978, Golden Reward Prize, Tokyo 1984, Grand Prix du Disque 1989, Gramophone Award, London 1990, Record Acad. of Japan Award 1991, Ditson Award for Distinguished Services to American Music, Columbia Univ., New York 1992, Grammy Awards 1993, 1996, Schallplattenpreis der Deutschen Musikkritik 1994, Ehrenpräsident der Stiftung Musikforschung Zentralschweiz 2001, Anton-Bruckner-Preis der Betil-Östbo-Bruckner-Stiftung, Linz 2001, Haederpris, Carl Nielsen Soc., Denmark 2002. *Address:* c/o Kuenstlep Sekretariat am Gasteig, Rosenheimer Strasse 52, 81669 Munich, Germany (office). *Telephone:* (89) 444-8879-0 (office). *Fax:* (89) 444-9522 (office).

**BLOOMFIELD, Arthur John,** BA; American music critic and food writer; b. 3 Jan. 1931, San Francisco, CA; m. Anne E. Buenger 1956; one s. two d. *Education:* Stanford Univ. *Publications:* Fifty Years of the San Francisco Opera, 1972; The San Francisco Opera 1922–78, 1978; Arthur Bloomfield's Restaurant Book, 1987; Sunday Evenings with Pierre Monteux, 1997; The Gastronomical Tourist, 2002; music critic for San Francisco Examiner, 1965–79; San Francisco correspondent for Opera, 1964–89; program notes, Music and Arts records, 1996–. *Address:* 2229 Webster Street, San Francisco, CA 94115, USA.

**BLOOMFIELD, Theodore (Robert);** Conductor; b. 14 June 1923, Cleveland, Ohio, USA. *Education:* Studied conducting with Maurice Kessler, piano

training, BM, 1944, Oberlin College Conservatory of Music; Conducting with Edgar Schenkman, Juilliard Graduate School, New York; Piano with Claudio Arrau; Conducting with Pierre Monteux. *Career:* Debut: New York Little Symphony Orchestra, 1945; Apprentice conductor to George Szell and Cleveland Orchestra, 1946–47; Conductor, Cleveland Little Symphony Orchestra, Cleveland Civic Opera Workshop, 1947–52; Music Director, Portland (Oregon) Symphony Orchestra, 1955–59, Rochester (New York) Philharmonic Orchestra, 1959–63; First Conductor, Hamburg State Opera, 1964–66; General Music Director, Frankfurt am Main, 1966–68; Chief Conductor, (West) Berlin Symphony Orchestra, 1975–82. *Recordings:* For several labels. *Address:* c/o Das Sinfonie Orchester Berlin, Kurfurstendamm 225, 1000 Berlin, Germany.

**BLUMENTHAL, Daniel;** American pianist; b. 23 Sept. 1952, Landstuhl, Germany. *Education:* University of Michigan and at Juilliard, New York, 1975–77. *Career:* many performances in Europe and elsewhere in the solo and chamber repertory, notably French and American music; with the Piano Trio of La Monnaie, Brussels, premiered the G minor Trio of Debussy, 1985; other partners include Pierre Amoyal, Barry Tuckwell and the Orlando Quartet; Prof. of Piano, Flemish Conservatory, Brussels, 1985–. *Current Management:* Helen Jennings Concert Agency, 2 Hereford House, Links Road, London, W3 0HX, England.

**BLUNT, Marcus,** BMus; British composer and teacher; b. 31 Dec. 1947, Birmingham; m. Maureen Ann Marsh 1988. *Education:* Univ. Coll. of Wales. *Career:* compositions performed in at least 10 countries and on BBC Radio 3 and Classic FM; woodwind teacher 1976–; mem. British Acad. of Composers and Songwriters, Performing Rights Soc., Inc. Soc. of Musicians. *Compositions:* Symphony, The Rings of Saturn for Orchestra, Piano Concerto, Once in a Western Island... for violin and orchestra, Concerto Pastorale for oboe d'amore and strings, Aspects of Saturn for strings, Capricorn for 12 winds, Venice Suite for brass ensemble, The Throstle-Nest in Spring for octet, Cerulean for wind quintet, two string quartets, A Celebration of Brahms and Joachim for piano trio, Lorenzo the Much Travel'd Clown for bassoon and piano, The Life Force for piano. *Address:* Craigs Cottage, Lochmaben, Lockerbie, Dumfriesshire, DG11 1RW, Scotland. *E-mail:* marcusblunt@ argonet.co.uk. *Website:* www.scottishmusiccentre.com/marcus_blunt.

**BLYTH, Alan,** MA; British music critic and editor; b. 27 July 1929, London, England; m. Ursula Zumloh. *Education:* Univ. of Oxford. *Career:* critic, The Times 1963–76; Assoc. Ed., Opera 1967–84; Music Ed., Encyclopaedia Britannica 1971–76; critic, Daily Telegraph 1976–89; mem. Critics' Circle, Garrick Club. *Publications:* The Enjoyment of Opera 1969, Colin Davis: A Short Biography 1972, Opera on Record (ed.) 1979, Remembering Britten 1980, Wagner's Ring: An Introduction 1980, Opera on Record 2 (ed.) 1983, Opera on Record 3 (ed.) 1984, Song on Record (ed.) Vol. 1 1986, Vol. 2 1988, Choral Music on Record 1990, Opera on CD 1992, Opera on Video 1995; contrib. entries on singers to New Grove Dictionary 1980, 2000; contrib. to Gramophone, BBC. *Address:* 22 Shilling Street, Lavenham, Suffolk CO10 9RH, England.

**BLYTHE, Stephanie;** Singer (Mezzo-soprano); b. 1970, Mongaup Valley, New York. *Education:* Crane School of Music, Potsdam, New York. *Career:* Metropolitan Opera from 1994 in Parsifal, as Mistress Quickly in Falstaff, Baba the Turk in The Rake's Progress and Cornelia in Handel's Giulio Cesare, 1999; Mascagni's Mama Lucia on tour to Japan, 1997; Lincoln Center recital debut, 1997; Season 1999–2000 as Mistress Quickly at the Opéra Bastille, Paris, Fricka in The Ring for Seattle Opera, Carmen with Tulsa Opera and Rossini's Isabella at Philadelphia; Concerts include Mahler 8 with the San Francisco Symphony Orchestra, 1999; Beethoven 9 with the Boston Symphony Orchestra; Schumann's Scenes from Faust in Paris; Messiah with the Minnesota and Florida Orchestras, 1999–2000; Covent Garden debut 2003, as Mistress Quickly in Falstaff, followed by Ino in Semele. *Honours:* Richard Tucker Career Grants, 1995–96. *Current Management:* International Creative Management, 4-6 Soho Square, London W1D 3PZ. *Telephone:* (20) 7432-0800. *E-mail:* classical@icmtalent.com. *Website:* www.icmtalent.com. *Current Management:* International Creative Management, 40 West 57th Street, New York, NY 10019, USA. *Telephone:* (212) 556-5600. *E-mail:* classical@icmtalent.com. *Website:* www.icmtalent.com.

**BO, Sonia;** Composer; b. 27 March 1960, Lecco, Italy. *Education:* Graduated, Milan Conservatory, 1985, and studied further with Donatoni in Rome. *Career:* Teacher of composition at the Piacenza Conservatory. *Compositions:* Concerto for chamber orchestra, 1984; Come un'allegoria for soprano and ensemble, 1986; D'Iride for ensemble, 1988; Polittico, five songs with ensemble, 1992. *Honours:* Winner, 1985 Guido d'Arezzo International Competition. *Address:* c/o SIAE, Via della Letteratura n 30, 00101 Rome, Italy.

**BOATWRIGHT, McHenry;** Singer (Bass-Baritone); b. 29 Feb. 1928, Tennille, GA, USA. *Education:* Studied at the New England Conservatory; BM, 1950–54. *Career:* Debut: Jordan Hall, Boston, 1956; New York Town Hall debut in 1958; New England Opera Theater, 1958 as Arkel in Pelléas et Mélisande; Concert appearances with Charles Munch, Leonard Bernstein and other leading conductors; Sang with the Hamburg Staatsoper in contemporary works, notably in the 1966 premiere of Schuller's The Visitation at the Metropolitan Opera, 1967; Concert tour of the Far East and Europe in 1966; Sang at the funeral of Duke Ellington, 1974; Well known in Negro Spirituals. *Recordings:* La Damnation de Faust; Porgy and Bess. *Honours:* Marian

Anderson Award, 1953, 1954; Winner, Arthur Fielder Voice Contest; Winner, National Federation of Music Clubs Competition, 1957.

**BOBESCO, Lola;** Violinist; b. 9 Aug. 1921, Craiova, Romania. *Education:* Studied with her father, Professor Aurel Bobescu. *Career:* Many solo appearances from 1934, appearing with such conductors as Kempe, Klemperer, Böhm and Ansermet; Chamber musician, and until 1979 leader of the Eugene Ysaÿe string orchestra; Professor at the Brussels Conservatoire. *Honours:* Prizewinner at the 1937 Eugene Ysaÿe Competition. *Address:* Conservatoire de Musique, 30 Rue de la Régence, Brussels, Belgium.

**BOCELLI, Andrea;** Italian singer (tenor); b. 22 Sept. 1958, Lajatico, Pisa; m. Enrica Bocelli; two c. *Career:* fmr lawyer. *Recordings include:* albums: various music: Bocelli 1995, Romanza 1997, Sogno 1999, Cieli di Toscana 2001, MW 2006; opera: Viaggio Italiano 1995, Aria 1998, Sacred Arias 1999, Verdi 2000, La Bohème 2000, Verdi Requiem 2001, Sentimento (Classical BRIT Award for Best Album 2003) 2002, Tosca 2003, Aria: The Opera Album 2005. *Current Management:* MT Opera and Blues Production and Management, via Irnerio 16, 40126 Bologna, Italy. *E-mail:* mtorped@tin.it. *Website:* www.andreabocelli.org.

**BOCHKOVA, Irina;** Violinist; b. 2 Nov. 1938, Moscow, Russia. *Education:* Studied in Kazan and at the Moscow Conservatoire, 1957–62. *Career:* Many appearances in Russia and Europe from 1962, notably as chamber music partner with Vladimir Krainev (piano) and Natalia Gutman (cello); Teacher at the Moscow Conservatory from 1978. *Honours:* Silver Medal, 1962 Tchaikovsky Competition, Moscow; Winner, 1963 Long-Thibaud Competition, Moscow. *Address:* c/o Moscow Conservatory, ul Gertzena 13, 103009 Moscow, Russia.

**BODE, Hannelore;** Singer (soprano); b. 2 Aug. 1941, Berlin, Germany; m. Heinz Feldhofl. *Education:* Studied with Ria Schmitz-Gohr in Berlin, at the Salzburg Mozarteum, Fred Husler, Lugano, and Karl-Heinz Jarius, Frankfurt. *Career:* Sang in Bonn from 1964; Basle, 1967–68; Deutsche Oper am Rhein, Düsseldorf, from 1968, notably as Weber's Agathe, Wagner's Elsa, Eva, Elisabeth and Sieglinde; Kammersängerin, Nationaltheater, Mannheim, 1971–; Appearances in London, Buenos Aires, Washington, Vienna, Munich, Berlin; Bayreuth, 1969–80, as Elsa, Eva and in The Ring; Sang at Mannheim 1996, in Hannas Traum by Harold Weiss and 1998 as Leocadia Begbick in Weill's Mahagonny. *Recordings:* Parsifal; Die Meistersinger conducted by Solti; Die Meistersinger, conducted by Varviso; Trionfo d'Afrodite by Orff. *Address:* c/o Nationaltheater Mannheim, Goethestrasse, 68161 Mannheim, Germany.

**BODER, Michael;** German conductor. *Education:* Hochschule für Musik, Hamburg. *Career:* asst to and student of Riccardo Muti and Zubin Metha, Florence 1980–84; worked with Michael Gielen, Frankfurt Opera 1984–88; Music Dir and Chief Conductor Basle Opera 1989–93; conducts regularly at Vienna State Opera, Munich State Opera, Berlin State Opera, San Francisco Opera; world premieres include Penderecki's Ubu Rex in Munich, Reimann's Das Schloss in Berlin, Trojahn's Was Ihr Wollt in Munich, Peter Turrini and Friedrich Cerha's Der Reise vom Steinfeld in Vienna 2002, Reimann's Finite Infinity at Zürich Tonhalle; conducted Alban Berg's Wozzeck, Vienna 1995, San Francisco 1999, Berg's Lulu in Vienna 2000, 2005, Munich 2004, Schönberg's Die Jakobsleiter, Vienna 2000, Puccini's Gianni Schicchi, Vienna 2000, Richard Strauss's Elektra in Vienna 2001, Wagner's Ring Cycle, San Francisco 1999, Wagner's Der Fliegende Holländer, San Francisco 2003, Enescu's Oedipe, Vienna 2005, Bucharest 2005, Ligeti's Le Grand Macabre, San Francisco 2005, Richard Strauss's Die Frau ohne Schatten in Dresden 2005, Beethoven's Fidelio, Tokyo 2005, Isang Yun's Bara, Berlin 2005; has also conducted concerts with Hamburg Philharmonic, Vienna Radio SO, Leipzig Gewandhaus, Oslo Philharmonic, New Hong Kong SO, Tokyo PO. *Address:* c/o Wiener Staatsoper, Openring 2, Vienna 1010, Austria (office).

**BODIN, Lars-Gunnar;** Swedish composer; b. 15 July 1935, Stockholm, Sweden. *Education:* studied with Lennart Wenstrom, visited Darmstadt. *Career:* composer-in-residence, Mills College, Oakland 1972 and Dartmouth College 1990; teacher, Stockholm College of Music 1972–76; Dir of the Electronic Music Studio, Stockholm 1979–89; collaboration with Bengt Emil Johnson in text-sound compositions; mem. Royal Swedish Academy of Music 1978–89. *Compositions include:* Dance pieces, Place of Plays, 1967, and... from one point to any other point, 1968; Music for brass instruments, 1960; Arioso for ensemble, 1962; Semi-Kolon: Dag Knutson in Memoriam for horn and ensemble, 1962; Calendar Music for piano, 1964; My World in Your World for organ and tape, 1966; Primary Structures for bassoon and tape, 1976; Enbart for Kerstin for mezzo and tape, 1979; Anima for soprano, flute and tape, 1984; Diskus for wind quintet and tape, 1987; Electronic: Winter Events, 1967; Toccata, 1969; Traces I and II, 1970–71; Memoires d'un temps avant la destruction, 1982; For Jon II Retrospective Episodes, 1986; Wonder-Void, 1990; Divertimento for Dalle, 1991; Best Wishes from the Lilac Grove, 1994; Bobb—The Life Manager, 1997; Jenseits von Licht und Dunkel, 2000; Lipton's Adventures, 2002; Text-sound pieces. *Recordings:* En Face, 1990; The Pioneers, 1992. *Honours:* Rosenberg Prize, 1984; The Stockholm City Award, 1986; Atterberg Award, 2004. *Address:* Helgalunden 17, 11858 Stockholm, Sweden. *Telephone:* (8) 642-52-44 (home). *E-mail:* bodin.l-g@swipnet.se (home).

**BODLEY, Seoirse;** Composer; b. 4 April 1933, Dublin, Ireland. *Education:* Studied at the Royal Irish Academy and in Stuttgart with Johann Nepomuk

David. *Career:* Associate Professor of Music at University College, Dublin. *Compositions:* 5 symphonies, 1959, 1980, 1981, 1990, 1991; 2 chamber symphonies, 1964, 1982; Piano concerto, 1996; Sinfonietta, 1998; Violin sonata, 1957; Scintillae for 2 harps, 1968; Two String quartets, 1969, 1992; Choruses and incidental music; Pax bellumque for soprano and ensemble, 1997; News from Donabate for piano, 1999. *Address:* c/o University College, Faculty of Music, Dublin, Ireland.

**BODOROVA, Sylvie;** Composer; b. 31 Dec. 1954, Ceske Budejovice, Czech Republic; m. Jiri Stilec, 10 Aug 1984. *Education:* Studied in Brno, Bratislava and Prague; Further study with Franco Donatoni in Siena. *Career:* Performances of works in London, Dresden and at the Prague Spring Festival; Teaching in CCM Cincinnati, Ohio, 1995–96; Quattro, Prague. *Compositions include:* Passion Plays for viola and orchestra, 1982; Pontem video for organ, percussion and strings, 1983; Canzoni for Guitar and Strings, 1985; Messagio, violin concerto, 1989; Magikon for oboe and strings, 1990; Panamody for flute and strings, 1992; Vocal and instrumental music, including Una volta prima vera, violin sonata, 1992; Dona Nobis Lucem, 1995; Concerto dei Fiori, 1996; Terezin Ghetto Requiem, 1997; Concierto de Estio, 1999; Saturnalia, 1999; Shofarot-String Quartet, 2000; Juda Maccabeus, 2002; Mysterium druidum for harp and strings 2003. *Recordings:* Prague Guitar Concertos; Pontem Video; Terezin Ghetto Requiem; Concierto de Estío; Juda Maccabeus. *Address:* Lidická 990, 253 01 Hostivice, Czech Republic. *E-mail:* jistilec@arcodiva.cz. *Website:* www.bodorova.cz.

**BODY, Jack;** Composer and Ethnomusicologist; b. 7 Oct. 1944, Te Aroha, New Zealand. *Education:* University of Auckland. *Career:* Taught at Indonesian Music Academy, 1976–77, and at Victoria University, Wellington, from 1980. *Compositions include:* Orchestra: Melodies, 1983, Little Elegies, 1985, Pulse, 1995, Carmen Dances, 2002; Piano: Four Stabiles, 1968, Five Melodies, 1982, Three Rhythmics (duet), 1986, Sarajevo, 1996; Choir: Carol to St Stephen, 1975, Five Lullabies, 1988; Voice: Love Sonnets of Michelangelo for soprano and mezzo-soprano, 1982; String Quartet; Three Transcriptions, 1987, Arum Manis (with tape), 1991, Campur Sari (with Javanese musician), 1996, Saetas, 2002; Electro-acoustic: Musik dari Jalan (Music from the Streets), 1975; Musik Anak-anak (Children's Music), 1978, Fanfares, 1981, Jangkrik Genggong, 1985, Vox Humana, 1991; Ensemble: Turtle Time, 1968, The Caves of Ellora, 1979, Interior (with tape), 1987, The Garden, 1996; Homage to the Blues, 2004; Opera: Alley, 1997. *Recordings:* Composer Portrait: Jack Body; Sacred and Profane; Pulse. *Publications include:* Editor, Waiteata Music Press, 1980–; Recordings of traditional music of Indonesia and China. *Honours:* Officer, NZ Order of Merit 2002; Winner, Bourges Competition for Electronic Music 1976, Laureate, NZ Arts Foundation 2004. *Address:* c/o School of Music, Victoria University of Wellington, PO Box 600, Wellington, New Zealand. *Telephone:* (4) 463-5853 (office). *Fax:* (4) 463-5157 (office). *E-mail:* jack.body@vuw.ac.nz.

**BOE, Alfred;** Singer (tenor); b. 1974, Fleetwood, Lancashire. *Education:* Royal College of Music and National Opera Studio, London; Vilar Young Artists' Programme, Covent Garden, 2001. *Career:* Performances with D'Oyly Carte Company from 1994; Concerts include Verdi Requiem, Rossini Petite Messe and Stabat Mater, Puccini Messa di Gloria and Elijah; Season 1999–2000 as Ernesto for Scottish Opera-Go-Round and Rodolfo for Glyndebourne Touring Opera; Season 2001–2002 engagements as Roderigo in Otello at La Monnaie, Brussels, Ferrando for Grange Park Opera, First Night of London Proms (2001) and Albert Herring at the 2002 Glyndebourne Festival. *Honours:* Prizewinner, Lyric Tenor of World Competition, Munich; Winner, John McCormack Golden Voice, Athlone, 1998. *Current Management:* Askonas Holt Ltd, Lonsdale Chambers, 27 Chancery Lane, London, WC2A 1PF, England. *Telephone:* (20) 7400-1700. *Fax:* (20) 7400-1799. *E-mail:* info@askonasholt.co.uk. *Website:* www.askonasholt.co.uk.

**BOEHMER, Konrad;** composer; b. 24 May 1941, Berlin, Germany. *Education:* Cologne Univ. *Career:* scientific asst, Utrecht Institute of Sonology 1966–68; fmr music ed., Vrij Nederland; teacher, Royal Conservatory, The Hague 1971; Dir, The Hague Inst. of Sociology 1993. *Compositions include:* Dr Faustus, Paris Opéra, 1985; Woutertje Pieterse, Stadsschouwburg Rotterdam, 1988 (premiere); Kronos protos for ensemble, 1995; Un monde abandonée des facteurs for 4 mezzos, 1996; Logos Protos (electronic) 2000; Circe et Circenses for five sopranos and pianos 2001. *Publication:* Schoenberg and Kandinsky, a historic encounter (ed.) 1994. *Honours:* Rolf-Liebermann Opera Prize (Hamburg) 1983. *Address:* Royal Conservatory of Music and Drama, Juliana van Stolberglaan 1, 2595 CA The Hague, Netherlands (office). *Telephone:* (70) 315-1466 (office). *E-mail:* boehmer@koncon.nl (office). *Website:* www.koncon.nl (office).

**BOESCH, Christian;** Singer (Baritone); b. 27 July 1941, Vienna, Austria. *Education:* Studied at the Vienna Hochschule für Musik. *Career:* Debut: Berne in 1966; Sang in Saarbrucken, Lucerne and Kiel; Joined Vienna Volksoper in 1975; Sang at Salzburg Festival in 1978 as Papageno in Die Zauberflöte, Metropolitan Opera from 1979 as Papageno, Masetto and Wozzeck, and as Papageno at the Théatre des Champs Elysées, Paris in 1987; Often heard in modern repertoire; Sang in Wolf-Ferrari's La Donne Curiose at the Cuvilliés Theatre in Munich, 1989; Sang Wozzeck at Buenos Aires in 1989. *Recordings:* Die Zauberflöte; Il Prigioniero by Dallapiccola; Haydn's Die Feuersbrunst. *Address:* c/o Volksoper, Wahringerstrasse 78, A 1090 Vienna, Austria.

**BOESE, Ursula;** Singer (Mezzo-Soprano); b. 27 July 1928, Hamburg, Germany. *Education:* Studied at the Musikhochschule, Hamburg. *Career:* Began career as concert soloist; Bayreuth Festival, 1958–65, in Parsifal and Der Ring des Nibelungen; Hamburg Opera from 1960, notably in Handel's Giulio Cesare, with Joan Sutherland, 1969; San Francisco, 1968, in Oedipus Rex; Guest appearances in Milan, Rome, Buenos Aires, London, Paris and New York; Opera roles have included Gluck's Orpheus, Handel's Cornelia, Dalila, Gaea in Daphne, Jocasta, Verdi's Ulrica and Azucena and Wagner's Fricka, Erda, Waltraute and Magdalene; Schwetzingen Festival 1982, in the premiere of Udo Zimmermann's Die wundersame Schustersfrau; Often sang Bach in concert. *Recordings:* Christmas Oratorio by Bach; Der Evangelimann by Kienzi; Salome and Lulu; Parsifal and The Devils of Loudun. *Honours:* Kammersängerin, 1969. *Address:* c/o Hamburgische Staatsoper, Grosse-Theaterstrasse 34, 20354 Hamburg, Germany.

**BOESMANS, Phillipe;** Belgian composer; b. 17 May 1936, Tongeren. *Education:* Liège Conservatory with Froidebise and Pousseur. *Career:* Music Prod., Belgian radio from 1961; worked at Liège electronic music studios, Centre de Recherches Musicales de Wallonie from 1971; pianist with the Ensemble Musique Nouvelle. *Compositions include:* Etude I for piano 1963, Sonance for two pianos 1964, Sonance II for three pianos 1967, Impromptu for 23 instruments 1965, Correlations for clarinet and two instrumental groups 1967, Explosives for harp and 10 instrumentalists 1968, Verticles for orchestra 1969, Blocage for voice, chorus and chamber ensemble 1970, Upon La, Mi for voice, amplified horn and instrumental group 1970, Fanfare for two pianos 1971, Fanfare II for organ 1972, Intervalles I for orchestra 1972, Intervalles II for orchestra 1973, Intervalles III for voice and orchestra 1974, Sur MI for two pianos, electric organ, crotale and tam-tam 1974, Multiples for two pianos and orchestra 1974, Element-Extensions for piano and chamber orchestra 1976, Doublures for harp, piano, percussion and four instrumental groups 1976, Attitudes musical spectacle for voice, two pianos, synthesizer and percussion 1977, Piano Concerto 1978, Violin Concerto 1979, Concerto for violin and orchestra 1980, Conversions for orchestra 1980, La Passion de Gilles (opera) 1983, Ricercar for organ 1983, Extases II 1985, String Quartet I 1988, Surfing for alto solo and instrumental ensemble 1989, Daydreams for marimba 1991, Love and Dance Tunes for baritone and piano (after Shakespeare) 1993, Reigen (opera) 1993, Summer Dreams for string quartet 1994, Smiles for two percussions 1995, Ornamented Zone for alto clarinet, piano and cello 1996, Wintermärchen (opera after Shakespeare) 1999, Julie (opera) 2005. *Honours:* Italia Prize 1971. *Current Management:* Pelléas Artists, Avenue de la Liberté 36/4, 1081 Brussels, Belgium. *Telephone:* (2) 241 59 88. *Fax:* (2) 241 59 88. *Website:* www.pelleas-artists.com.

**BOETTCHER, Wolfgang;** Cellist; b. 1940, Berlin, Germany. *Education:* Hochschule der Kunste, Berlin. *Career:* Soloist, Berlin Philharmonic until 1976; Co-founder, Brandis String Quartet, 1976, with chamber music appearances in Munich, Hamburg, Milan, Paris, London and Tokyo including concerts with the Wiener Singverein and the Berlin Philharmonic; Festival engagements at Salzburg, Lucerne, Vienna, Florence, Tours, Bergen and Edinburgh; Co-premiered Helmut Eder's Clarinet Quintet, 1984, the 3rd Quartet of Gottfried von Einem, 1981, and the 3rd Quartet of Giselher Klebe, 1983; Founding member of the Philharmonische Solisten, Berlin; Concerto appearances with such conductors as Celibidache, Fischer-Dieskau, Lutoslawski, Karajan and Menuhin; Professor at the Hochschule der Kunste, Berlin. *Recordings include:* Albums in the standard repertoire from 1978, recent releases include quartets by Beethoven, Weill, Schulhoff and Hindemith and the String Quintet by Schubert. *Honours:* Prizewinner, International ARD Competition in Munich. *Address:* c/o Konzert-Direktion Hans Adler (Brandis Quartet), Auguste-Viktoria-Strasse 64, D–14199 Berlin, Germany.

**BOEYKENS, Walter;** Clarinettist; b. 6 Jan. 1938, Bornem, Belgium. *Education:* Studied at the Brussels Conservatoire. *Career:* From 1964 soloist with the Belgian Radio Symphony and has appeared with many other leading orchestras throughout Europe; Chamber engagements with the Amadeus, Grumiaux and Via Nova Quartets; Premiered Domains by Boulez and works by Philippe Boesmans and Marcel Poot; From 1969 Teacher at Conservatories in Anvers and Utrecht. *Address:* c/o Utrecht Conservatorium, Mariaplaats 28, 3511 LL Utrecht, Netherlands.

**BOGACHEV, Vladimir;** Singer (Tenor); b. 1960, Moscow, Russia; Many appearances at the Bolshoi, Moscow and in Europe as Radames, Cavaradossi, Don José, Dmitri in Boris Godunov and Otello; Lensky in Eugene Onegin and Herman in the Queen of Spades, Montreal, 1990; Season 1993 with Otello at Orlando, Florida, Radames in Liège and Don Carlos in Portland; sang in Tchaikovsky's Iolanta at Dresden, staged by Peter Ustinov; Sang Aeneas in Les Troyens with the London Symphony Orchestra under Colin Davis at the Barbican Hall, London, 1993, repeated at La Scala, 1996; Season 1996 as Otello in Amsterdam, Calaf at the Macerata Festival and in Khovanshchina at Brussels; Many appearances on Russian broadcasting services; Sang Otello for the Royal Opera at the Albert Hall and Calaf at Dallas, 1997–98. *Address:* c/o Dallas Opera, The Centrum, 3102 Oak Lawn Avenue, Suite 450, LB–130, Dallas, TX 75219, USA.

**BOGACHEVA, Irina;** Singer (Mezzo-Soprano); b. 1940, Russia. *Career:* Appearances with the Kirov Opera, St Petersburg, from 1963 as Verdi's Amneris, Azucena, Ulrica and Eboli; Marina in Boris Godunov, Hélène in War and Peace, Konchakovna in Prince Igor, Lyubava in Sadko and Clarice in The Love for Three Oranges; Further engagements as Carmen, Dalila, Charlotte in Werther, Naina in Ruslan and Lyudmilla, Grandmother in The Gambler and the Sorceress in The Fiery Angel; Guest appearances at the Opéra Bastille, Paris, New York Met and La Scala, Milan; Sang the Kirov in Summer season at Covent Garden, 2000. *Honours:* Honoured Artist of Russia. *Address:* c/o Kirov Opera, Mariinsky Theatre, Mariinsky Square, St Petersburg, Russia.

**BOGART, John-Paul;** Singer (Bass); b. 17 Sept. 1952, USA. *Education:* Studied at Princeton, Yale and the Juilliard School. *Career:* Sang as child in production of Die Zauberflöte at the Metropolitan Opera; Sang at Santa Fe, Miami and Philadelphia; Dallas Opera as First Nazarene in Salome; La Scala Milan as Basilio in Il Barbiere di Siviglia; Vienna Staatsoper as Ramphis, Sarastro, Raimondo, Sparafucile and Colline; Basle Opera, 1984–85 as Mozart's Figaro and as La Roche in Capriccio; Paris Opéra Comique in 1985 in The Stone Guest by Dargomyzhsky; Théâtre Châtelet, Paris, in I Masnadieri by Verdi; Chicago Lyric Opera as Masetto in Don Giovanni; Baltimore Opera as Gremin in Eugene Onegin; Sang in the premiere of Célestine by Maurice Ohana at the Paris Opéra in 1988; Milwaukee in 1989 as Gounod's Mephistopheles; Lodovico in Otello at Lisbon in 1989; Bonn Opera 1994, as Alonso in Il Guarany by Gomes; Also heard as concert singer. *Recordings:* Zuniga in Carmen; Turandot; Chichester Psalms; L'Esule di Roma by Donizetti.

**BOGATSCHOVA, Irina;** Singer (Mezzo-Soprano); b. 2 March 1939, Leningrad, Russia. *Education:* Studied at the Leningrad Conservatory. *Career:* Sang at the Kirov Theatre, Leningrad, from 1965, and guested at the Bolshoi, Moscow, and abroad as Marina (Boris Godunov) and in Prokofiev's War and Peace (San Francisco, 1991); Sang the Countess in The Queen of Spades at Hamburg (1990), La Scala, Théâtre des Champs Elysées, Paris, Barbican Hall (1999) and elsewhere; Sang Saburova in Rimsky's The Tsar's Bride at San Francisco, 2000. *Recordings:* Several issues on Melodiya. *Address:* c/o Kirov Theatre, St Petersburg, Russia.

**BOGIANCKINO, Massimo,** PhD; Italian opera director; b. 10 Nov. 1922, Rome; s. of Edoardo T. Bogianckino and Fiorangela Liberi; m. Judith Matthias 1950. *Education:* Conservatory of Music and Acad. Santa Cecilia, Rome and Univ. of Rome. *Career:* fmr musicologist and concert pianist; Dir Enciclopedia dello Spettacolo 1957–62; Dir Accademia Filarmonica, Rome 1960–63; Dir Teatro dell' Opera, Rome 1963–68; Artistic Dir Festival of Two Worlds, Spoleto 1968–71; Dir of Concert Programs, Accad. Santa Cecilia, Rome 1970–71; Artistic Dir La Scala, Milan 1971–74; Gen. Man. Teatro Comunale, Florence 1974–82; Admin. Gen. Paris Opera 1982–85; apptd Mayor of Florence 1985. *Publications:* L'arte clavicembalistica di D. Scarlatti 1956 (English version 1968), Aspetti del teatro musicale in Italia e in Francia nell' età Barocca 1968, Le canzonette e i madrigali di V. Cossa 1981. *Honours:* Grosses Bundesverdienstkreuz (FRG). *Address:* c/o Palazzo Vecchio, 50122 Florence, Italy (office).

**BOGUSLAVSKI, Igor;** Russian violist, viola d'amore player and professor of viola; *Professor of Viola, Russian Gnesin Academy of Music;* b. 18 July 1940, Moscow; m. Anna Litvinenko 1969; one d. (died 2003). *Education:* Gnesin Academy of Music and Moscow Tchaikovsky Conservatory with V. Borissovski. *Career:* debut as viola soloist with Symphony Orchestra, conducted by Y. Aranovich, Moscow Conservatory; Appearances with BSO on Russian radio and television playing concertos by Hindemith including viola d'amore chamber music, Bartók and Berlioz; Prin. viola soloist, Bolshoi Theatre Orchestra, 1977–; Prof., Russian Gnesin Acad. of Music 1977–; Only active soloist to give concerts on viola d'amore; Played with numerous conductors including Rozhdestvensky, Blazhkov, Fedosseev, Lazarev and Simonov, Aranovich and Dudarova; Repertory includes Bach, Purcell, Vivaldi, Mozart, Paganini, Brahms, Glinka, Schumann, Bartók, Tchaikovsky, Britten, Hindemith, Martinů, Milhaud, Shostakovich, Prokofiev, Schnittke, Denisov; Several works specially composed for him; Viola teacher, giving masterclasses and participating in festivals in France, Taiwan, USA and Japan; has given world premieres of concertos for viola and orchestra by A. Holminov, A. Baltin, S. Kallosc, J. Butzko, Y. Grinstein and V. Bibik; also premieres of Paganini's Sonata for viola and strings in C major (new version for orchestra); Martini's Plaisir d'amore for viola d'amore and strings; Shostakovitch's Viola Sonata (version for viola and strings by P. Lando); Stravinsky's Russian Song for viola and strings; Grinstein's Concerto in Retro Style for viola and strings; Performed in Tchaikovsky Conservatory Great Concert Hall and Russian Composers' Union Concert Hall, both in Moscow. mem, Viola d'Amore Soc. of America; Jury Member, Tchaikovsky Competition, Moscow, competitions in Geneva, Munich, Markneukirchen; mem. UN Acad. of Information. *Recordings:* Hindemith, Kammermusik No. 5, Der Schwanendreher, for viola and orchestra; Strauss, Don Quixote; Brahms, Two Sonatas for Viola and Piano; J C Bach, Viola Concerto; Paganini, Sonata for Grand Viola and Strings; Graupner, Concerto for Viola d'Amore, viola and strings; Glinka, Sonata for Viola and Piano; Denisov, Variations on a Choral Theme by J. S. Bach; Three Pictures by Paul Klee, for viola and instrumental ensemble; Schnittke, Suite in the Old Style for viola d'amore, harpsichord and percussion; Igor Boguslavski plays the viola and viola d'amore with Bolshoi String Orchestra, conducted by Pavel Lando; Suslin Sonata for viola and cimbalo; Over 60 recordings on discs, CD and from radio. *Publications:* Alfred Shnittke, Suite in the Old Style, Ed. of score for viola d'amore solo, cembalo, companelli, vibratono, campane and marimba 2004, Sir A. Bliss, Viola Sonata, N. Paganini, Viola Sonata (with cadenza by Boguslavski), B. Martini, Viola

Sonata, K. M. Weber, Andanta, Rondo. *Honours:* Honoured Art Worker of Russia. *Address:* Build 2, Apt 5, 30 Studencheskaya Street, Moscow 121165, Russia. *Telephone:* (95) 2492776 (also fax) (home). *E-mail:* ibogusla@df.ru (home).

**BOHAC, Josef;** Composer; b. 25 March 1929, Vienna, Austria. *Education:* Pupil of Petrzelka, Janáček Academy of Music, Brno, 1951–56. *Career:* Director, Panton publishing concern, 1968–71; Head, Department of Music Broadcasts, Czech Television; Secretary, Union of Czech Composers, 1979–; Rumcajs, 1985. *Compositions:* Operas: The Wooing, 1967; The Eyes, 1973; Goya, 1971–76; Golden Wedding, 1981; Hidden Tears, 1994; Orchestral: Symphonic Overture, 1964; Fragment, 1969; Elegy for Cello and Chamber Orchestra, 1969; Dramatic Suite for Strings and Kettledrums, 1969–70; Blue and White, suite, 1970; February Overture, 1973; Piano Concerto, 1974; Concerto for Violin and Chamber Orchestra, 1978; Concertino Pastorale for 2 Horns and Orchestra, 1978; Concerto for Orchestra, 1983; Dramatic Variants for Viola and Orchestra, 1983; Alfresco, violin concerto, 1996; Partita Concertante, 1997; Capriccio Sinfonico, 1997; Chamber: String Trio, 1965; Sonetti per Sonatori for Flute, Bass Clarinet, Harpsichord, Piano and Percussion, 1974; Sonata Giovane for Piano, 1983; My Lute Resounds, monodrama for Tenor, Soprano and Nonet or Piano, 1971; 2 cantatas, 1976, 1979; Sonata Lirica for Soprano, Strings and Vibraphone, 1982; Vokální Poéma for chorus and ensemble, 1987. *Address:* c/o OSA, Cs Armady 20, 160–56 Praha, 6–Bubenec, Czech Republic.

**BOHAN, Edmund,** MA; Singer (tenor) and Writer; b. 5 Oct. 1935, Christchurch, New Zealand; m. Gillian Margaret Neason 1968; one s. one d. *Education:* Canterbury Univ., New Zealand; singing with Godfrey Stirling, Sydney, Eric Green and Gustave Sacher London. *Career:* oratorio debut 1956, opera debut 1962, New Zealand; repertoire of over 170 operas and major works including opera, oratorio, concerts in England, Europe, Australasia and Brazil; opera, English Opera Group, Dublin Grand Opera, London Chamber Opera, State Opera of South Australia, Canterbury Opera New Zealand; Wexford Festival, New Zealand International Festival of the Arts, Aldeburgh Festival, Norwich Triennial, Adelaide Festival; National Opera of Wellington, New Zealand; television includes Australian Broadcasting, BBC Proms, ABC, and New Zealand Radio; film, Barber of Seville; venues include Royal Festival Hall, Queen Elizabeth Hall and other major halls with Royal Philharmonic Orchestra, London Concert, BBC Concert and Ulster Orchestras; oratorio soloist with British, Australian and New Zealand Choral Societies. *Recordings:* A Gilbert and Sullivan Spectacular; When Song is Sweet; Sweet and Low; Gilbert and Sullivan with Band and Voice; The Olympians (Bliss) Intaglo. *Publications include:* biogs: Edward Stafford – New Zealand's First Statesman; Blest Madman – FitzGerald of Canterbury; To Be A Hero Sir George Grey); history: The Story So Far – A Short Illustrated History of New Zealand; 7 novels including A Present for the Czar; The Irish Yankee; The Matter of Parihaka; The Dancing Man; The Opawa Affair. *Address:* 5 Vincent Place, Opawa, Christchurch, New Zealand.

**BÖHM, Ludwig;** German music archivist, writer and editor; b. 5 July 1947, Munich. *Education:* Univs of Munich and Würzburg. *Career:* secondary school teacher of English, French and Spanish, Munich 1981–83; founder, Theobald Böhm Archives 1980, Theobald Böhm Soc. 1990; organizer commemorative concerts 1981 1994, 2006, and first Int. Theobald Böhm Competition for Flute and Alto Flute, Munich 2006. *Publications:* Complete Musical Works for Flute by Theobald Böhm (ed., 15 vols) 2005, Commemorative Publication on the Occasion of Böhm's 200th Birthday 2005, Letters to and Articles about Böhm concerning Flute Construction (ed.) 2005, Letters to and Articles about Böhm not concerning Flute Construction (ed.) 2005, Catalogue of the Concerts by and with Böhm 2005, Catalogue of the Musical Works of Böhm 2005, Catalogue of the Still Existing Flutes of Böhm 2005, Commemorative Writing on the Occasion of the 125th Anniversary of Böhm's Death 2005, Complete Letters and Articles by Böhm (ed.) 2005, Five Publications on Flute Construction by Böhm (ed.) 2005, Biographies of Böhm by Karl von Schafhäutl, Marie Böhm and Karl Böhm (ed.) 2005. *Address:* Asamstrasse 6, 82166 Gräfelfing, Germany.

**BOHMAN, Gunnel;** Singer (Soprano); b. 4 March 1959, Stockholm, Sweden. *Education:* Studied at the Opera School, Stockholm. *Career:* Engaged by Lorin Maazel for the Vienna Staatsoper; Sang at the Mannheim Opera as Pamina, Fiordiligi and Marenka in The Bartered Bride; Sang Pamina at the Bregenz Festival and appeared further in Vienna, Zürich, Houston and Hamburg as Mozart's Countess, Agathe, Micaela, Mimi and Lola; Sang in the Jussi Björling Memorial Concert in Stockholm, 1985, with Birgit Nilsson, Elisabeth Söderström, Nicolai Gedda and Robert Merrill; Bregenz Festival, 1985–86, as Pamina, Vienna Volksoper from 1987 (as Fiordiligi), Staatsoper from 1988; Zürich and Parma, 1987, as Smetana's Marenka and Gluck's Euridice; Glyndebourne Festival, 1989, as the Countess in Figaro (also at the Albert Hall); Sang Elisabeth in Tannhäuser at the 1996 Savonlinna Festival; Luisa Miller and Hanna Glawari at Frankfurt, 1996; Weber's Agathe, 1998; Sang Jenůfa for Flanders Opera 1999; Season 2000–01 as Luisa Miller, and the Daughter in Hindemith's Cardillac, at Frankfurt; Concert repertoire includes Bach's Passions, B minor Mass and Christmas Oratorio; Ein Deutsches Requiem and Requiems of Mozart and Dvořák; Haydn Die Schöpfung and Die Jahreszeiten; Strauss Vier Letzte Lieder and Wagner Wesendonck Lieder. *Honours:* Jenny Lind Fellowship, 1978. *Current Management:* Svenska Konsertbyrån AB, Jungfrugatan 45, 11444 Stockholm, Sweden. *Telephone:*

(8) 665-8088. *Fax:* (8) 665-8066. *E-mail:* info@svenskakonsertbyran.se. *Website:* www.svenskakonsertbyran.se.

**BOISSEAU, Pierrick;** Singer (Baritone); b. 1970, France. *Education:* Conservatoire National de Région de Versailles; Royal College of Music with Ryland Davies. *Career:* Sang with Paris Opéra Boys Choir as a child; Les Chantres de la Chapelle, Centre for Baroque Music at Versailles, under Jean-Claude Malgoire, Christophe Rousset and Ton Koopman; Oratorio soloist in Paris, Athens, Morocco, USA and Malta; Handel's Julius Caesar and Alcindoro in La Bohème, with the Centre de Formation Lyrique de l'Opéra Bastille; Season 2000–2001 in the St John Passion at St John's Smith Square, under Peter Schreier, and Lotario in Flavio, with the London Handel Festival. *Honours:* Lavoisier Scholarship and Audrey Sacher RCM Scholarship. *Current Management:* Agence Artistique Internationale Veronique Valray, 19 rue du Couvent, 33520 Bruges, Belgium. *Telephone:* (5) 5628-3075; (6) 0807-4132 (mobile). *Fax:* (5) 5628-3075. *E-mail:* veroniquevalray@free.fr. *Website:* www.agenceartistiqueveroniquevalray.com. *Address:* c/o Royal College of Music, Prince Consort Road, London SW7 2 BS, England.

**BOISSY, Nathalie;** Singer (Soprano); b. 1963, Beaune, Côte d'Or, France. *Education:* Studied at Colmar, Strasbourg, Paris and the Oberlin Conservatory, USA. *Career:* Sang at the Linz Opera from 1988, as Frau Fluth (Nicolai), Marzelline, the Countess in Roméo et Juliette, Mimi, Romilda in Xerxes, Micaela, Leila in Les Pêcheurs de Perles and the Infantin in Der Zwerg by Zemlinsky; Sang Micaela at Bregenz (1991) and in Mendelssohn's Elijah at Linz, 1991; Donna Anna at the Munich Gärtnerplatztheater, 1999. *Address:* c/o Landestheater, Promenade 39, 4010 Linz, Austria.

**BOKES, Vladimir;** Composer; b. 11 Jan. 1946, Bratislava, Slovakia; m. Klara Olejárová 1970; two s. one d. *Education:* Secondary Music School, Konzervatorium 1960–65; Acad. of Music, Vysoka skola muzickych umeni, Bratislava 1965–70. *Career:* teacher in Conservatory, Bratislava, 1971–75; Asst, Acad. of Music, Bratislava 1975, Docent 1988, Prof. 1993; mem. Union of Slovak Composers (pres. 1995–99), Slovak section of Int. Soc. for Contemporary Music, International Festival of Contemporary Music Melos-Ethos Bratislava (pres. 1993–97). *Compositions:* Symphony No. 1, 1970, No. 2, 1978, No. 3, 1980, No. 4, 1982, No. 5, 1987; Piano Concerto No. 1, 1976, No. 2, 1984; String Quartet No. 1, 1970, No. 2, 1974, No. 3, 1982; Wind Quintet No. 1, 1971, No. 2, 1975, No. 3, 1982; Piano Sonata No. 1, 1973, No. 2, 1979, No. 3, 1980, No. 4, 1985; Vocal cycles, Sposob ticha, The way of silence, 1977, and Na svoj sposob, In its own way. 1978; Music for Organ and Wind Instruments, 1986; Preludes and Fugues for pPiano, 1989; Missa Posoniensis for 4 soli, choir, organ and orchestra, 1991; Variations on a Theme from Jan Egry for 8 wind instruments, 1995; Commedia dell'arte, aria for tenor and piano, 1995; Divertimento for 4 wind instruments, 2001. *Recordings:* Variations on a Theme from Haydn for Piano, 1975; 1st Piano Concerto, 1978; 3rd Symphony, 1989; Sonata for Viola and Piano, 1993; Cadenza II, 2000; Music for Piano (Preludes and Fugues, Sonata No. 2 an No. 4), 2001; Inquieto for Clarinet and Piano, 2003. *Contributions:* to Hudobny zivot, Bratislava: Biennale Zagreb, 1977; Communicativity in Music, 1988; Music of Defiance (interview), 1990; to Slovenska hudba, Bratislava: Cantate Domino Canticum Sacrum, 1991; Interview with Vladimir Bokes, 2001. *Address:* Svoradova 5, 811 03 Bratislava, Slovakia.

**BOLCOM, William;** Composer; b. 26 May 1938, Seattle, Washington, USA; m. (1) Fay Levine, divorced 1967, (2) Katherine Agee Ling, divorced 1969, (3) Joan Morris, 28 Nov 1975. *Education:* BA, University of Washington, 1958; MA, Mills College, 1961; Paris Conservatoire de Musique, 1959–61, 1964–65; DMusArt, Stanford University, 1964; Piano studies with Berthe Poncy Jacobson; Composition studies with John Verrall, Leland Smith, Darius Milhaud, George Rochberg. *Career:* Acting Assistant Professor of Music, University of Washington, 1965–66; Lecturer, Assistant Professor of Music, Queen's College, City University of New York, 1966–68; Visiting Critic in Music Theatre Drama School, Yale University, 1968–69; Composer in Residence, New York University, School of the Arts, 1969–71; Assistant Professor, 1973, Associate Professor, 1977, Professor, 1983–, Ross Lee Finney Distinguished Professor of Composition, 1993–, School of Music, University of Michigan; Board, American Music Center; Charles Ives Society; American Composers' Alliance. *Compositions include:* 4 Violin Sonatas, 1956–94; 6 Symphonies, 1957–97; Concertos for piano, 1975–76, violin, 1983, clarinet, 1990; 10 String Quartets, 1950–88; 12 New Etudes for piano, 1977–86; Sonata for Cello and Piano, 1989; Casino Paradise, musical, 1990; McTeague, opera, 1992; A View from the Bridge, opera, 1999; Songs of Innocence and of Experience, 1956–82; Many more chamber, choral and orchestral works including Suite for violin and cello, 1997. *Publications:* Reminiscing with Sissle and Blake, 1973. *Contributions:* Grove's Dictionary; Contributing Editor, Annals of Scholarship. *Honours:* Kurt Weill Award for Composition, 1963; Guggenheim Foundation Fellow; Rockefeller Foundation Awards; NEA Grants; Pulitzer Prize for Music, 1988; American Academy of Arts and Letters, 1993; Henry Russel Lectureship, 1997. *Current Management:* ICM Artists, 40 W 57th St New York, NY 10019, USA. *Address:* 3080 Whitmore Lake Road, Ann Arbor, MI 48105, USA.

**BOLDYREV, Vladimir;** Baritone; b. 1955, Ukraine. *Education:* Studied at the Kharkov Institute of Arts. *Career:* Principal at the Kharkov Opera from 1985, notably as Don Giovanni, Germont, Rossini's Figaro, Escamilo, Eugene Onegin, Yeletsky, Silvio and Samson; Further opera and recital engagements in the USA, Germany, France and Italy; Repertoire includes songs by

Rachmaninov, Glinka and Tchaikovsky, and Lieder by Mahler, Schubert and Schumann. *Honours:* Prizewinner at the 1987 All-Union Glinka Song Competition. *Address:* Sonata Ltd, 11 North Park Street, Glasgow G20 7AA, Scotland.

**BOLGAN, Marina;** Singer (Soprano); b. 20 March 1957, Mestre, Venice, Italy. *Education:* Studied at Conservatories in Venice, Siena and Rome. *Career:* Debut: Sang Rosina in various Italian cities, 1981; Sang Nannetta in Falstaff at the Teatro della Zarzuela, Madrid, 1982, and Gilda at Toulouse! Adina in L'Elisir d'amore, Venice, 1984; Bellini's Elvira at the Bregenz Festival, 1985; Paisiello's Nina at Catania; Annetta in Crispino e la comare by the brothers Ricci at Teatro La Fenice, Venice, and Théâtre des Champs Elysées, Paris; Elvira and Lucia, Zürich Opera, 1987, 1989; at the Hamburg Staatsoper, sang Adina and elsewhere in Donizetti's La Romanziera and Betly; Further appearances at Bologna, Verona and the Vienna Staatsoper (Lucia, 1988); Sang Selinda in Vivaldi's Farnace at the Valle d'Istria Festival, Martina Franca, 1991; Gnese in Wolf-Ferrari's Il Campiello at Trieste (1991) and Mascagni's Lodoletta at Mantua, 1994.

**BOLKVADZE, Eliso;** Pianist; b. 2 Jan. 1967, Tbilisi, Georgia. *Education:* Special School of Music, Tbilisi, 1972–84; Conservatoire Superieur in Tbilisi, 1984–89; Worked with Michel Sogny in Austria, 1989–92. *Career:* Debut: Concert Hall, Tbilisi; Herkules Saal, Munich; Alt Opera, Frankfurt; Auditorium Louvre, Salles Pleyel and Gaveau, Paris; Pasadena Hall, Los Angeles; Concert Hall, Chicago; Teatro Mauzoni, Milan; Schubert Hall, Vienna. *Recordings:* 4 albums recorded with orchestra in Tbilisi, 1994–96; Saint Petersburg, 2 albums at Villa Schindler, Austria. *Honours:* International piano competitions: 1st prize, Lisbon Vianna de Motta, 1987; Van Cliburn competition, 1989; 3rd prize, Dublin, 1987. *Current Management:* Michel Sogny. *Address:* Villa Schindler, Obermarktstrasse 45, 6410 Telfs, Tirol, Austria.

**BOLLIGER, Phillip John;** Australian composer and classical guitarist; b. 2 May 1963, Sydney, NSW. *Education:* Vienna Hochschule, University of Sydney, studied in Siena and Basle, and with Peter Sculthorpe. *Career:* freelance guitarist and private teacher; composer of film music 1991–. *Compositions include:* Inventions for guitar, 1986; The Birds of My Gully for flute, 1988; Sailing Song for piano, 1990; Four Greek Dances for two guitars, 1990; Romance for flute and orchestra, 1990; Three Preludes for guitar, 1992; Benedictus Balaenarum for trombone and piano, 1993; Requiem Chernobyl for choir and orchestra, 1993; Zagorsk for string quartet and piano, 1993; Monsoon for flute, 1997. *Honours:* First Prize, City of Sydney Eisteddfod, 1987; First Prize, Warringah Eisteddfod, 1992. *Address:* c/o APRA, 1A Eden Street, Crows Nest, NSW 2065, Australia.

**BOLOGNESI, Mario;** Singer (Bass-baritone); b. 1957, Rome, Italy. *Career:* Sang Apollo in Gagliano's Dafne, London, 1981; Season 1983–84: in Gli Orazi e i Curiazi by Cimarosa at Savona and in Gluck's Alceste at Bologna; Further early repertory includes Albinoni's Il nascimento dell' Aurora, Venice, 1984; Jommelli's La Schiava liberata, Naples; Agenore in Mozart's Il re Pastore, Rome, 1989; Season 1989 in the premiere of Manzoni's Doktor Faust at La Scala and Rossini's Basilio at Glyndebourne; Season 1994–95 in Rossini's Maometo II at La Scala, Bardolph at Navarra and as Lucarno in Poppea by Monteverdi; Season 1997–98: As Pasqua in Wolf–Ferrari's Il Campiello at Bologna and Spoletta in Tosca at the Verona Arena; Season 2000–01 at La Scala and Palermo, in Adriana Lecouvreur and Tosca. *Address:* c/o Teatro Comunale di Bologna, Largo Respighi 1, 40126 Bologna, Italy.

**BOLTON, Ivor;** British conductor; b. 17 May 1958, Lancashire, England. *Education:* Clare Coll., Royal Coll. of Music, Nat. Opera Studio. *Career:* conductor, Schola Cantorum of Oxford, Glyndebourne 1982–92; Conductor, Gluck's Orfeo, Glyndebourne 1989, has led Il Barbiere di Siviglia, Die Zauberflöte, The Rake's Progress and La Bohème for the Touring Co.; Music Dir, Glyndebourne Touring Opera, La Clemenza di Tito 1993–94; founded St James Baroque Players 1984, and directs annual Lufthansa Festival of Baroque Music at St James, Piccadilly; Music Dir, English Touring Opera 1990–93, leading Don Giovanni, Figaro, Lucia di Lammermoor, Così fan tutte, Die Zauberflöte, La Cenerentola and Carmen; Così fan tutte at the Aldeburgh Festival; ENO debut, with Xerxes 1992; La Gazza Ladra for Opera North and Monteverdi's Poppea in Bologna 1993; season 1997 with Giulio Cesare, Serse and Poppea at the Munich Festival; Chief Conductor, Scottish Chamber Orchestra from 1994, regular concerts with the London Mozart Players, English Chamber Orchestra, Scottish Symphony, Bournemouth Sinfonietta and BBC Symphony; Die Entführung at Geneva 2000; Handel's Saul and Rodelinda for the Bayerische Staatsoper 2003. *Recordings include:* Bach's concertos for Harpsichord, Purcell's Dido and Aeneas, Brahms and Mendelssohn Violin Concertos, Vivaldi's Stabat Mater, Handel's Ariodante (from Munich) 2000. *Current Management:* Ingpen & Williams Ltd, 7 St George's Court, 131 Putney Bridge Road, London, SW15 2PA, England.

**BONALDI, Clara;** Violinist; b. 9 March 1937, Dombasle-sur-Mourthe, France. *Education:* Studied at the Paris Conservatoire (first prize for violin, 1955). *Career:* Many appearances at major festivals in France and elsewhere in Europe; Has edited for performance the sonatas of Francoeur and Tartini and partnered harpsichordist Luciano Scrizzi (pianist Noel Lee from 1980). *Honours:* Prizewinner at the 1955 Long-Thibaud Competition and at the 1963 Munich International (as piano duettist). *Address:* c/o Noel Lee, 4 Villa Laugier, 75017 Paris, France.

**BONAZZI, Elaine;** Singer (Mezzo-Soprano); b. 1936, Endicott, New York, USA. *Education:* Studied at the Eastman School of Music, Rochester, and at Hunter College, New York. *Career:* Santa Fe Opera from 1959, notably as Meg Page in Falstaff and in the 1961 US premiere of Hindemith's Neues vom Tage; Appearances in Cincinnati, Houston, Dallas, Pittsburgh, Mexico City, Vancouver and New York (City Opera); Caramoor Festival New York in Semele, 1969; Often heard in operas by Rossini and in contemporary music; sang the Marquise in La Fille du Régiment at St Louis, 1990; Sang Linfea in La Calisto for Glimmerglass Opera, 1996; Many engagements as concert singer; Taught at Peabody Conservatory, Baltimore; mem, American Academy of Teachers of Singing; National Association of Teachers of Singing. *Recordings:* La Pietra del Paragone by Rossini; Le Rossignol by Stravinsky. Honours Sullivan Foundation Grant, 1960; Concert Artists Guild Award, 1960; Eastman Alumni Award, 1972; Directors Recognition Award, Peabody Academy, 1989. *Address:* c/o Opera Theater of St Louis, PO Box 13148, St Louis, MO 63119, USA.

**BONCOMPAGNI, Elio;** Conductor; b. 8 May 1933, Arezzo, Italy. *Education:* Violin and Composition, Florence and Padua; Conducting in Perugia and Hilversum. *Career:* Debut: Bologna, 1962, Don Carlos; Conductor at opera houses in Europe, including Théâtre de la Monnaie, Brussels, from 1974; British debut, 1983, Cherubini's Médée at the Barbican Hall, London; Un Ballo in Maschera for Opera Montreal, 1990; conducted José Carreras concert at the Scottish Exhibition Centre, Glasgow, 1991. *Honours:* Prize, Italian Radio International Competition, 1961, and Mitropoulos Competition, New York, 1967. *Address:* c/o Opéra de Montreal, 1157 Rue Sainte Catherine E, Montreal, Quebec H2L 2G8, Canada.

**BOND, Graham;** British conductor; b. 20 March 1948, Blackburn, Lancashire. *Education:* Piano, trombone and cello, Royal College of Music, London; Accademia Chigiana, Siena. *Career:* Repetiteur, London Opera Centre, 1969–70; Conductor, London Festival Ballet, 1970–1975; Principal Conductor, London Festival Ballet, 1975–80; Music Director, London Festival Ballet, 1980–94; Many British, European and other world tours, 1970–79; Theatres and orchestras in France, Spain, Italy, Germany, China, Yugoslavia, Greece, Venezuela and Turkey; Two extensive tours of Australia and two long seasons in Paris with Nureyev, 1975 and 1977; Guest performances, 1978–81, Royal Theatre, Copenhagen; Stuttgart Ballet Company; Capetown Ballet Company; Conducting staff, Royal Coll. of Music, London 1984; Series of concerts, St John's Smith Square, 1984–95; Monte Carlo Opera, 1984; Tivoli Symphony Orchestra, Copenhagen, 1985; Stanislavsky Theatre, Moscow, 1987; Turin Opera; Granada Festival; Guest Conductor, Hong Kong Philharmonic Orchestra, Hong Kong Festival, 1987; Also Champs Elysées Theatre, Paris, and the Teatro Massimo, Sicily; Deutsche Oper, Berlin, 1990; Guest Conductor, Bolshoi Ballet, during tour of England, 1991; Guest engagement, Durban, South Africa, 1992; Opera House, Budapest; Guest Conductor, Sofia Opera Orchestra, Athens Festival, 1993; Palacio de Bellas Artes, Mexico City, 1993; Appointed Chief Ballet Conductor, Royal Danish Ballet, Royal Theatre, Copenhagen, 1994–; Guest performances in 1994 in Prague, Bratislava, Sicily and Orange County, USA; Conductor, Peter Maxwell Davies's Caroline Mathilde ballet, Royal Opera House, London, 1995; The Love of Three Oranges, Royal Theatre, Copenhagen and Bergen Festival, 1996; Guest Conductor, Dutch National and Netherlands Dance Companies, 1996–97; Deutsche Oper, Berlin, 1997–98; Conductor, Peter Grimes, Royal Theatre, Copenhagen, 1997; Guest Conductor, London Royal Ballet, 1998 and Far East tour, 1999; Guest, Teatro Real, Madrid, 1998; The Magic Flute and Madama Butterfly, Royal Danish Opera, 1998; Guest Conductor, Royal Opera, London 2000–05 including tours to Bolshoi and Maryinsky Theatres; Guest Conductor, Royal Opera, Stockholm 2004–05. *Honours:* Worshipful Company of Musicians Medal, 1969; Hon RCM, 1994. *Address:* 8 Calverley Park Crescent, Tunbridge Wells, Kent TN1 2NB, England.

**BOND, Timothy M.;** Concert Organist and Lecturer; b. 21 July 1948, Mullion, Cornwall, England. *Education:* BMus, FRCO, ARCM, Royal College of Music, London, England. *Career:* Debut: Westminster Cathedral, 1974; British Premiere, Schoenberg's Sonata Fragment, 1974; Premieres at Henry Wood Proms of: Ligeti–Two Studies, 1976; Schoenberg-Variations on a Recitative, 1979; Messiaen-L'Ascension, 1981; Schoenberg Festival, Royal Festival Hall, 1989; Appearances at Festivals including: Aldeburgh, Huddersfield, Southampton, City of London, Normandy; For television: Ceremonies and Rituals, broadcast of Messiaen's L'Ascension; Many broadcasts of Modern Organ Music including: Schoenberg, Messiaen, Stockhausen, Berio, Pousseur, Goehr; British Premiere of original version of Schoenberg's Variations on a Recitative, 1974; Commission and Premieres of works specially written: Uccelli by John Lambert, 1992; Echo Toccata by John Lambert, 1993; The Grass is Sleeping by Avril Anderson, 1979; Concerto for Organ and Orchestra: Crossing The Great Water, by David Sutton-Anderson, 1992; Lecturer, Royal College of Music, London. *Recordings:* Messiaen: L'Ascension; Quatre Méditations Symphoniques. *Contributions:* Musical Times, 1978. *Honours:* SPNM Young Artists and Twentieth Century Music, 1975. *Address:* Spreekenhorst, 27321 Bahlum, Germany.

**BOND, Victoria Ellen,** DMus; American composer and conductor; b. 6 May 1945, Los Angeles, Calif.; d. of Philip and Jane Bond; m. Stephan Peskin 1974. *Education:* Univ. of Southern Calif. and Juilliard School of Music. *Career:* Musical Dir New Amsterdam Symphony Orchestra, New York 1978–80, Pittsburgh Youth Symphony Orchestra 1978–80, Bel Canto Opera, New York 1983–86, Roanoke Symphony Orchestra 1986–95, Empire State Youth

Orchestra 1988–90; Artistic Dir Opera Roanoke 1989–95, Bel Canto Opera 1986–88, Harrisburg Opera, Pennsylvania 1998–; Artistic Adviser Wuhan Symphony, China 1997–; Guest Conductor with numerous orchestras including Colorado Philharmonic, Houston Symphony, Buffalo Philharmonic, Pittsburgh Symphony, Anchorage Symphony, Hudson Valley Philharmonic, RTE Symphony, Dublin, Albany Symphony, Des Moines Symphony, Virginia Symphony, Shanghai Symphony; mem. Music Panel, New York State Council of Arts 1987–; Bd of Dirs American Music Center 1987–, Conductors Guild; mem. American Soc. of Composers, Authors and Publishers (ASCAP), American Fed. of Musicians, American Symphony Orchestra League. *Commissions include:* Molly Manybloom 1990, Hot Air 1990, Dreams of Flying 1990, Goodbye My Fancy 1992. *Recordings include:* Live from Shanghai, Victoria Bond: Compositions. *Honours:* Dr hc (Hollins Coll., Roanoke Coll. l) 1995; numerous awards from ASCAP 1975–, Victor Hubert Award 1977, named Exxon Arts Endowment Conductor 1978–80, Virginia Woman of the Year 1990. *Address:* American International Artists, 315 E 62nd Street, New York, NY 10021 (office); 256 W 10th Street, 3B, New York, NY 10014, USA (home). *Telephone:* (212) 715-0470 (office); (212) 691-6858 (home). *Fax:* (212) 715-0461 (office); (212) 627-4258 (home). *E-mail:* Bond006@ concentric.net.

**BONDARENKO, Alexander;** Violinist; b. 1950, Crimea, Russia. *Career:* Co-Founder, Rachmaninov Quartet, 1974, under the auspices of the Sochi State Philharmonic Society, Crimea; Concerts in the former Soviet Union and from 1975–76 tours to Switzerland, Austria, Bulgaria, Norway and Germany; Participant in 1976 Shostakovich Chamber Music Festival at Vilnius, and in festivals in Moscow and St Petersburg; repertoire has included works by Haydn, Mozart, Beethoven, Bartók, Schnittke, Shostakovich, Boris Tchaikovsky, Chalayev and Meyerovich. *Honours:* Prize, First All-Union Borodin String Quartet Competititon with the Rachmaninov Quartet, 1987. *Current Management:* Sonata, Glasgow, Scotland. *Address:* 11 North Park Street, Glasgow G20 7AA, Scotland.

**BONDE-HANSEN, Henriette;** Singer (Soprano); b. 3 Sept. 1963, Funen, Denmark. *Education:* Opera School of Copenhagen Opera until 1991. *Career:* Appearances with Jutland and Royal Copenhagen Operas as Susanna and Barbarina in Figaro, Musetta, and Adele in Die Fledermaus; Season 1994–95 with Jutland and Oslo Operas as Woodbird in Siegfried; Opéra du Rhin Strasbourg and at Brussels in Mozart's Zaide, 1995; Season 1996 as Sophie in Der Rosenkavalier at Stuttgart and Mozart's C Minor Mass with the Academy of St Martin's on tour to Germany; Season 1999–2000 as Adina at Toronto, Gounod's Juliette at Strasbourg, Marzelline in Fidelio at La Coruña (concert); Other concert repertory includes Bach St John Passion; Haydn's Seasons; Brahms' Requiem; Poulenc's Gloria. *Recordings:* Mahler's 8th Symphony. *Current Management:* Alferink Artists Management, Herengracht 340, 1016 CG Amsterdam, Netherlands. *Telephone:* (20) 6643151. *Fax:* (20) 6752426. *E-mail:* info@alferink.org. *Website:* www.alferink.org. *Address:* c/o The Royal Opera, Copenhagen, Denmark.

**BONELL, Carlos Antonio;** British musician, teacher, guitarist and composer; b. 23 July 1949, London; s. of Carlos Bonell and Ana Bravo; m. Pinuccia Rossetti 1975; two s. *Education:* William Ellis School, Highgate and Royal Coll. of Music, under John Williams (q.v.). *Career:* solo début as solo guitarist, Wigmore Hall, London 1971; concerto début with Royal Philharmonic Orchestra 1975; American début, Avery Fisher Hall, New York 1978; concert appearances with all the prin. British orchestras; appearances with John Williams (q.v.), Teresa Berganza (q.v.), Pinchas Zukerman (q.v.) 1975–; formed Carlos Bonell Ensemble 1983; Prof. Royal Coll. of Music 1972–, London Coll. of Music 1983–. *Recordings include:* Guitar Music of Spain 1975, Guitar Music of the Baroque 1976, Showpieces 1981, Rodrigo Concerto 1981, Paganini Trios and Quartets 1983, Twentieth Century Music for Guitar 1987, Once Upon a Time, with Xer-Wai (violin) 1992, Walton Bagatelles and Anon in Love 1993, Britten Folksongs (with Philip Langridge) 1994, The Sea in Spring 1997, The Private Collection 1998, Kinkachoo I Love You (Millennium Guitar, The First 1000 Years) 2000, Trinity Coll. Grade pieces 2003, Carlos Bonell plays Gordon Mizzi 2003, Guitar Classics 2004. *Publications:* 20 First Pieces 1982, Tarrega: Fantasia on "La Traviata", 3 Spanish Folk Songs, Purcell: Music from the Fairy Queen, Fantasy for 3 Guitars 1995, Technique Builder 1997, Millennium Guitar, The First 1000 Years 2000. *Honours:* Hon. ARCM. *Address:* Bravo Music International, PO Box 19060, London, N7 0ZD (office). *Fax:* (20) 7689-9964. *E-mail:* carlos@ carlosbonell.com (home). *Website:* www.carlosbonell.com (home).

**BONETTI, Antoni (Robert);** Violinist and Conductor; b. 6 Nov. 1952, London, England; m. Ruth Back, 16 Mar 1974, 3 s. *Education:* AMusA, DSCM, New South Wales Conservatorium, 1973; ARCM, 1978. *Career:* Violinist, Principal 2nd Violin, 1968–72, Australian Youth Orchestra; Tour to Japan, 1970, South East Asia, 1974; Freelance Violinist, London, 1975–76, appearing with Royal Philharmonic Orchestra, New Philharmonia Orchestra, London Mozart Players; Concertmaster, Norrlands Opera Orchestra, Sweden, 1976–77; Stockholm Ensemble, 1977–78; Conductor, Musik Sällskap, Umeå, 1978; Baroque Violin with Gammerith Consort, Austria, 1978; Member of Kurpfalzisches Kammerorchester, 1979–81; Concertmaster, Queensland Theatre Orchestra, 1981–84; Lecturer, Queensland Conservatorium of Music, 1982–92; Head of Orchestral Studies, St Peter's Lutheran College, 1985–; Conductor, Baroque Orchestra of Brisbane, Brisbane Christian Chamber Orchestra, 1986–89, Concert Society Orchestra, 1987–90; Extensive tours with Divertimento Bonetti ensemble throughout Europe; Various conducting engagements with Redcliffe City Choir, Cleveland Symphony Orchestra, Ipswich Youth Orchestra, 1989; Director and Founder, Brisbane Sinfonia, 1990–; Adjudicator, various Eisteddfods. *Compositions:* Jacaranda for orchestra, 1992. *Honours:* Fellowship, Australian Council for the Arts, 1974.

**BONFATTI, Gregory;** Singer (Tenor); b. 1964, Italy. *Career:* Debut: Don Ramiro in La Cenerentola at Spoleto, 1991; Many appearances throughout Italy and elsewhere in Europe in the bel canto repertory; Ravenna Festival as Paolino in Cimarosa's Il Matrimonio Segreto, Tebaldo (I Capuleti e i Montecchi) and Lindoro in L'Italiana in Algeri; Festival della Valle d'Itria, Macerata, as Don Rodrigo in Mercadante's Caritea, regina di Spagna; Pubblio in Pacini's L'Ultimo Giorno di Pompei, 1996; Monte Carlo Opera 1996 in Pagliacci, with Leo Nucci and Placido Domingo. *Recordings include:* Caritea, regina di Spagna, and L'Ultimo Giorno di Pompei (Dynamic). *Honours:* Winner, Singing Competition of Teatro Belle, Spoleto, 1991. *Address:* c/o Teatro Arena Sferisterio, Piazza Mazzini 10, 62100 Macerata, Italy.

**BONIG, Andrea;** Singer (Mezzo-soprano); b. 1959, Bamberg, Germany. *Education:* Studied with Donald Grobe in Berlin and in Basle and Frankfurt. *Career:* Many concert engagements in Germany and elsewhere, including Liszt's Legend of St Elizabeth with the Bamberg Symphony Orchestra; Donizetti's Requiem with the Berlin Philharmonic; Teatro Liceo Barcelona, 1990 as Dryad in Ariadne auf Naxos; Rossweise in Die Walküre in Valencia and Bonn, 1991–92; Berlin Staatsoper from 1996, including Flosshilde in Das Rheingold; Season 1997–98 with Hippolyta in A Midsummer Night's Dream at the Vienna Volksoper; Further concert repertory includes Beethoven's Ninth and Saint-Saëns's Christmas Oratorio. *Current Management:* Opern-Agentur und Artists' Mgt Lewin, Mag. Tamara Herzl Wasagasse 12/1/3, 1090 Vienna, Austria. *Telephone:* (1) 3106096. *Fax:* (1) 3106094. *E-mail:* herzl@opern -agentur.com. *Website:* www.opern-agentur.de. *Address:* c/o Volksoper, Wahringerstrasse 78, 1090 Vienna, Austria.

**BÓNIS, Ferenc,** DMus; Hungarian musicologist; *President, Ferenc Erkel Society;* b. 17 May 1932, Miskolc; s. of Jószef Bónis and Ilona Kelemen; m. Terézia Csajbók. *Education:* Ferenc Liszt Academy of Music, Budapest. *Career:* Music Producer, Hungarian Radio, 1950–70; Scientific Collaborator, Musicological Institute of Hungarian Academy of Sciences, 1961–73; Professor, Musicological Faculty, Ferenc Liszt Academy of Music, 1972–86; Editor, Magyar Zenetudomány (Hungarian Musicology), 1959–; Editor, Magyar Zenetörténeti Tanulmányok (Studies on History of Hungarian Music), 1968–; Editor, Complete Edition of B Szabolcsi's Works, 1977–; Leader, Music Department for Children and Youth, Hungarian Radio, 1970–94; Leading Music Producer, Hungarian Radio, 1994–96; mem, Gesellschaft für Musikforschung; President, Hungarian Kodály Society 1993; President, Ferenc Erkel Society 1989–. *Recordings:* Editor, Early Hungarian Chamber Music; Works by P Wranitzky and L Mozart; Béla Bartók–As We Saw Him (recollections); Zoltán Kodály–As We Saw Him (recollections). *Publications include:* Mosonyi Mihály, 1960; G Mahler und F Erkel, 1960; Béla Bartók, His Life in Pictures and Documents, 1980; Zoltán Kodály, A Hungarian Master of Neoclassicism, 1982; Tizenhárom találkozás Ferencsik Jánossal (Meeting J Ferencsik), 1984; International Kodály Conference (with E Szönyi and L Vikár), 1986; Kodály Zoltán Psalmus Hungaricusa, commented facsimile edition, 1987; Harmincháром óra ifjabb Bartók Bélával (33 hours with B Bartók Jr), 1991; Hódolat Bartóknak és Kodálynak (Devotion to Bartók and Kodály), 1992; Bartók-Lengyel, A csodálatos mandarin, 1993; Himnusz (Hungarian National Anthem), facsimile edition, 1994; Igy láttuk Kodályt (3rd enlarged edition), 1994; Igy láttuk Bartókot (2nd enlarged edition), 1995; A Himnusz születése és másfél százada (The Birth of the Hungarian National Anthem and its 150 Years), 1995; Das leidende Volk und die unterdrückte Nation auf der ungarischen Opernbühne, 1995; Ein städtisches Fest und die Idee der Vereinigung: Budapest 1923, 1996; Brahms und die ungarische Musik, 1996; Heldentum und Sehnsucht nach Freiheit. Zur Frage Beethoven und die ungarische Musik, 1998; The Dance Suite of Béla Bartók, facsimile edition, 1998; Szabolcsi, Kodály and the Bach-theory of Reverend Werker, 1999; From Mozart to Bartók, 2000; In Memoriam Ferenc Farkas, 2001; Die Ungarn im Finale der Symphonie No. 4 von Brahms, 2001; Üzenetek a XX. századból (Messages from the 20th Century), 2002; Mihály Mosonyi, 2002; Bartók-Lengyel, The Miraculous Mandarin, 2002; Gondolatok Bartók zenekari Concertójáról (On Bartók's Concerto for Orchestra), 2004; A Budapesti Filharmóniai Társaság százötven esztendeje (150 Years of the Budapest Philharmonic Society), 2005. *Honours:* Ferenc Erkel Prize, 1973; Officer's Cross of Order of the Hungarian Republic, 1992; Honorary Freeman of F. Erkel's native town Gyula, 1999; Doctor of the Hungarian Acad. of Sciences, 2003. *Address:* Belgrád rakpart 27.I.5, Budapest 1056, Hungary (office). *Telephone:* (1) 337-9975 (office). *Fax:* (1) 337-9975 (office).

**BONNEMA, Albert;** Singer (Tenor); b. 18 April 1953, Trummarum, Netherlands. *Education:* Sweelinck Conservatory, Amsterdam and with Nicolai Gedda. *Career:* Sang in operettas by Lehar and Offenbach at Amsterdam and Enschede; Guest appearances in Berlin, Salzburg and Klagenfurt (Cassio in Otello, 1989); Lensky in Eugene Onegin at Berne; Giovanni in Mona Lisa by Schillings at Kiel and Walther in Die Meistersinger at Amsterdam, 1995; Števa in Jenůfa at Dresden, 1996; Season 1997–98 as Lohengrin at Tokyo and Števa at Hamburg; Season 2000–01 at Dresden as Števa in Jenůfa, Wagner's Erik and Apollo in Strauss's Daphne; Florestan at the Komische Oper Berlin, the Götterdämmerung Siegfried at Stuttgart, and Dmitri in Boris Godunov at Hamburg;Modern repertory includes Goldschmidt's Der gewaltige Hahnrei and Judith by Siegfried Matthus, both at Berne; Frequent concert appearances. *Current Management:* Artists Management Zürich, Rütistrasse 52, 8044 Zürich-Gockhausen, Switzerland. *Telephone:* (44) 8218957. *Fax:* (44) 8210127. *E-mail:* schuetz@artistsman.com. *Website:* www.artistsman.com. *Address:* c/o Netherlands Opera, Waterlooplein 22, 1011 Amsterdam, Netherlands.

**BONNER, Tessa;** British singer (soprano); b. 1955, England. *Education:* Leeds Univ., Guildhall School of Music. *Career:* Solo singer and consort member of such groups as the Tallis Scholars, the New London Consort, the Lute Group, Gabrieli Consort, Taverner Consort and the Early Opera Project; Frequent appearances with Musica Secreta, notably at the Early Music Centre Festival, the Lufthansa Festival of Baroque Music, and at the National Gallery; Early Music Network Tour of Britain, Nov 1991, with programme Filiae Jerusalem (sacred music for women's voices by Monteverdi, Carissimi, Cavalli, Viadna, Grandi and Marco da Gagliano); Other repertoire includes works by Marenzio, Luzzaschi, Wert, Luigi Rossi and the women composers Francesca Caccini and Barbara Strozzi; Participation in lecture-recitals and workshops on performance practice and ornamentation. *Address:* c/o Hyperion Records Limited, PO Box 25, London, SE9 1AX, England.

**BONNER, Yvette,** Dip. RAM, ARAM; British opera singer (soprano). *Education:* Arts Education School, London, 1984–90; Royal Acad. of Music, 1995–98; postgraduate vocal course, graduated Dip-RAM for performance. *Career:* debut as Yniold in Pelléas and Mélisande, for ENO; performances include Jennie Hildebrand in Street Scene with Houston Grand Opera, 1994; Flora in Turn of the Screw for WNO 1995; Shepherd Boy in Tannhäuser for Opera North, 1997; Semele in Die Liebe der Danaë, 1999; First Maid in Die Agyptische Helena; Debut for Royal Opera (in concert) as Hermione in Strauss's Die Agyptische Helena, 1998; Esmeralda in The Bartered Bride, 1999; Flora in The Turn of the Screw for WNO, 2000; Season 2001–02, premiere of Alice in Wonderland, title role, for Nederlandse Opera; Esmeralda in The Bartered Bride for Royal Opera, Covent Garden; Genevieve in Siruis on Earth for Almeida Opera; El Trujaman in El Retablo De Maese Pedro, London Proms, 2002; Vixen in The Cunning Little Vixen, Aix en Provence Festival and tour 2002–03, Susanna and Barbarina in The Marriage of Figaro, Savoy Opera 2004, Esmeralda in The Bartered Bride, Royal Opera 2005, Gretel in Hansel and Gretel, Cork Opera 2005, Rusalka, Ilford Festival 2005, Sophie in Werther, Rome Opera 2006; concert work includes Les Illuminations, The Acad. of St Martin in the Fields, Carmina Burana, The Symphony Hall, Birmingham, Bach Magnificat and Vivaldi Gloria for The English Chamber Orchestra, Haydn's Nelson Mass at St John's, Smith Square. *Recordings:* Weill's Street Scene (Joan), with ENO, 1989; Emmie in Albert Herring, 1996; Die Liebe der Danae; The Marriage of Figaro 2004; The Bartered Bridge 2005. *Honours:* Blyth-Buesst Operatic Prize, 1998; Emmy Destinn Award for Young Singers, for Czech opera and song, 2000. *Current Management:* Helen Sykes Artists Management, 100 Felsham Road, Putney, London SW15 1DQ, England. *Website:* www.yvettebonner.co.uk.

**BONNEY, Barbara;** American singer (soprano); b. 14 April 1956, Montclair, NJ; d. of Alfred Bonney III and Janet Gates; m. 1st Håkan Hagegård 1989; m. 2nd Maurice Whittaker. *Education:* Univ. of New Hampshire and Mozarteum, Salzburg. *Career:* maj. appearances include: Der Rosenkavalier, Covent Garden 1984, Metropolitan Opera, New York 1990, Die Zauberflöte, La Scala 1985, Falstaff, Metropolitan Opera 1990, The Marriage of Figaro, Covent Garden 1995, Zurich Opera, Metropolitan Opera 1998, 1999, Les Boréades, Salzburg Festival 1999, Idomeneo, San Francisco 1999; noted especially for Mozart and Strauss interpretations; appeared regularly as recitalist accompanied by Geoffrey Parsons. *Recordings include:* works by Schönberg, Haydn, R. Strauss, Donizetti, Mozart, Mendelssohn, Wolf etc. *Address:* c/o IMG, 616 Chiswick High Road, London, W4 5RX, England. *Telephone:* (20) 8233-5800. *Fax:* (20) 8233-5801.

**BONYNGE, Richard,** AO, CBE; Australian conductor; b. 29 Sept. 1930, Sydney, NSW; s. of C. A. Bonynge; m. Dame Joan Sutherland (q.v.) 1954; one s. *Education:* NSW Conservatorium of Music, Royal Coll. of Music. *Career:* trained as a pianist; debut as conductor with Santa Cecilia Orchestra, Rome 1962; conducted first opera Faust, Vancouver 1963; Musical Dir Sutherland/Williamson Grand Opera Co., Australia 1965; Artistic Dir Vancouver Opera 1974–77; Musical Dir Australian Opera 1976–86; has conducted La Sonnambula, La Traviata, Faust, Eugene Onegin, L'Elisir d'amore, Orfeo, Semiramide, Giulio Cesare, Lucia di Lammermoor, Norma, Orfeo and The Tales of Hoffmann; has revived many operas not in the repertoire, including Les Huguenots, La Fille du Régiment, Maria Stuarda, Lucrezia Borgia and Thérèse. *Videos include:* Les Huguenots, La Fille du Régiment, The Merry Widow, Norma, Die Fledermaus and The Magic Flute. *Recordings include:* opera: Alcina, La Sonnambula, Norma, Beatrice di Tenda, I Puritani, Faust, Semiramide, Lakmé, La Fille du Régiment, Messiah, Don Giovanni, Les Huguenots, L'Elisir d'amore, Lucia di Lammermoor, Rigoletto, Les Contes d'Hoffmann, Thérèse, Le Toréador, The Land of Smiles and Giuditta, Lucrezia Borgia, Maria Stuarda, Giulio Cesare, Merry Widow, L'Oracolo, Esclarmonde, Le Roi de Lahore, Suor Angelica, Die Fledermaus, Hamlet, I Masnadieri, La Traviata, Il Trovatore; ballet: Le Diable à Quatre, Giselle, Marco Spada, La Péri, Les Sylphides, Coppélia, Sylvia, Le Carillon, La Cigale, Le Papillon, La Boutique Fantastique, Aschenbrödel, The Nutcracker, Sleeping Beauty, Swan Lake. *Publication:* The Joan Sutherland Album (with Dame Joan Sutherland) 1986. *Honours:* Commdr, Ordre des Arts et des Lettres 1989. *Current Management:* Ingpen & Williams Ltd, 7 St George's Court, 131 Putney Bridge Road, London, SW15 2PA, England.

**BOOGAARTS, Jan;** Dutch university lecturer, choir director, organist and composer; b. 10 May 1934, Helmond; m. Dorine Sniedt 1964; two s. one d. *Education:* Conservatory of Tilburg, Royal Conservatory, The Hague, Institute of Musicology, University of Utrecht. *Career:* radio recordings for BBC, various Dutch Radio stations, Sud Deutscher Rundfunk, ORTF, France, Culture France, Radio DDR, Radio Warsaw, Poland, Belgian Radio; Television: NOS KRO (Holland Festival), Warsaw Poland; Docent Choir Direction, Royal Conservatory, The Hague; Lecturer at University Utrecht; Visiting Professorships throughout Europe and America. *Recordings:* 30 including Plainsong, Holy Week, Ordo Missae Instauratus Concilii Vaticani II, Vespers, Compline; Missa Ambrosiana, Famous Hymni and Sequentiae; Renaissance Music: Madrigals and Chansons with texts by Petrach and Ronsard; Works of R White, Josquin, Lassus, Isaak, Senfl and others. *Publications:* Inleiding tot het Gregoriaans 1985; contrib. many articles to period Festschrift and small publications, magazines and journals. *Address:* Havezate Die Magerhorst, Ploenstraat 48, Duiven, 6921 PN, Gelderland, Netherlands.

**BOONE, Charles;** Composer; b. 21 June 1939, Cleveland, Ohio, USA. *Education:* Pupil of Karl Schiske, Vienna Academy of Music, 1960–61; Received private instruction from Ernst Krenek and Adolph Weiss, Los Angeles, 1961–62; Studied theory at the University of Southern California, Los Angeles, BM, 1963 and composition at San Francisco State College, MA 1968. *Career:* Chairman, San Francisco Composers' Forum; Co-ordinator, Mills College Performing Group and Tape Music Center; Composer-in-Residence, Berlin, under the sponsorship of the Deutscher Akademischer Austauchdienst, 1975–77; Writer and Lecturer on contemporary music. *Compositions:* 3 Motets for Chorus, 1962–65; Oblique Formation for Flute and Piano, 1965; Starfish for Flute, Clarinet, 2 Percussions, 2 Violins and Piano, 1966; A Cool Glow of Radiation for Flute and Tape, 1966; The Edge of the Land for Orchestra, 1968; Not Now for Clarinet, 1969; Zephyrus for Oboe and Piano, 1970; Vermilion for Oboe, 1970; Quartet for Clarinet, Violin, Cello and Piano, 1970; Chinese Texts for Soprano and Orchestra, 1971; First Landscape for Orchestra, 1971; Vocalise for Soprano, 1972; Second Landscape for Chamber Orchestra, 1973, also for Orchestra, 1979; String Piece for String Orchestra, 1978; Streaming for Flute, 1979; Little Flute Pieces, 1979; Springtime for Oboe, 1980; Winter's End for Soprano, Countertenor, Viola da Gamba, and Harpsichord, 1980; Slant for Percussion, 1980; The Watts Tower for 1 Percussion, 1981; Trace for Flute and 10 Instruments, 1981–83; Solar One for Flute and Trumpet, 1985; The Timberline and Other Pieces for Carillon, 1987; Morphosis for 6 Percussion, 1997. *Honours:* National Endowment for the Arts Grants, 1968, 1975, 1983; Commissions. *Address:* 37003 Gravstark Street, Houston, TX 77006, USA.

**BOOTH, Claire,** BA; British singer (soprano). *Education:* Univ. of Oxford, ENO Studio Baylis Programme, Guildhall School of Music and Drama; Nat. Opera Studio, London and pvt study with Rudolf Piernay. *Career:* operatic roles include Susanna in Le Nozze di Figaro, Hero in Beatrice et Benedict, Romilda in Xerxes, Female Chorus in The Rape of Lucretia, title roles in La Didone and Orfeo, Woman II in Harrison Birtwistle's The Io Passion (world premiere, Aldeburgh Festival 2004), British Dancing Girl in The Death of Klinghoffer with Scottish Opera 2005, second Niece in Peter Grimes with Opera North; concert performances include Schonberg's Pierrot Lunaire 2003 and Birtwistle's Nenia on the Death of Orpheus 2004, at Lucerne Int. Festival, Birtwistle's The Second Mrs Kong with the BBC SO, various works of Sir Peter Maxwell Davies with London Sinfonietta at the QEH 2005; has also appeared at Purcell Room, Barbican Centre and Wigmore Hall in London, Settembre Musica Festival in Turin, Helix Centre in Dublin, concerts with BBC Scottish SO, Ensemble InterContemporain, Endymion Ensemble; oratorio performances include L'Allegro, with the King's Consort at Théâtre des Champs-Elysées, Paris, Mozart's Mass in C Minor and Requiem and Handel's Israel in Egypt with Britten Sinfonia, also Haydn's Nelson Mass and the Bach Passions in London. *Honours:* Sybil Tutton Award 2003, 2004, Worshipful Co. of Musicians Silver Medal. *Current Management:* Allied Artists, 42 Montpelier Square, London, SW7 1JZ, England. *Telephone:* (20) 7589-6243 (office). *Fax:* (20) 7581-5269 (office). *Website:* www.alliedartists.co.uk (office).

**BOOTH, Juliet;** Singer (Soprano); b. 1961, London, England; m. William Symington, 1 June 1996. *Education:* Studied at Bristol University and the Guildhall School of Music. *Career:* Opera North from 1987, Frasquita (debut role), Ninetta in The Love for Three Oranges, Xenia in Boris Godunov; Pusette in Manon, Arminda in La Finta Giardiniera, Norina in Don Pasquale and Lauretta; Has also sung Mélisande at Aldeburgh, Virtu and Valletto in Opera London's L'Incoronazione di Poppea and Mozart's Countess for Welsh National Opera; Aix-en-Provence, 1991, as Helena in A Midsummer Night's Dream; Concert appearances at the South Bank and the Barbican, in France, Belgium and Singapore; Handel's Solomon in Berlin and Carmina Burana at the Edinburgh Festival under Neeme Järvi; Television appearances include Dennis O'Neill and Friends on BBC 2; Season 1990–91 with The Kingdom (Elgar), Haydn's Nelson Mass and Creation, Salieri's Prima la Musica with the City of London Sinfonia; Concert arias with the English Chamber Orchestra; Messiah; Gilda in Rigoletto, Opera North, 1992; Countess in Figaro, Glyndebourne Touring Opera, 1992; Morgana in Alcina, Covent Garden debut, 1992; Musetta and Mimi in La Bohème, Opera North, 1993; Alexina in Le Roi malgré Lui, 1994. *Recordings include:* L'Incoronazione di Poppea conducted by Richard Hickox (Virgin Classics); Bruckner Mass in F, Hyperion, 1992. *Honours:* Gold Medal for Singers, Schubert Prize for Lieder and the Ricordi Opera Prize, at the Guildhall School. *Current Management:* IMG Artists Europe. *Address:* c/o Opera North, Grand Theatre, 46 New Briggate, Leeds, Yorkshire, LS1 6NU, England.

**BOOTH, Philip;** Singer (Bass); b. 6 May 1942, Washington, DC, USA. *Education:* Sang with US Army Chorus, then studied further at the Eastman School of Music, with Julius Huehn, and with Todd Duncan in Washington. *Career:* Kennedy Center, Washington, 1971, in Ariodante; Many appearances as concert singer; Engagements at the opera houses of San Diego, Houston and San Francisco; Metropolitan Opera from 1973, as Pimen in Boris Godunov, Ramphis, Fasolt and Fafner in Der Ring des Nibelungen, Basilio and Osmin; Sang in the US premiere of Mascagni's Le Maschere, with Westchester Opera, 1989. *Address:* c/o Metropolitan Opera, Lincoln Center, New York, NY 10023, USA.

**BOOTH-JONES, Christopher,** ARAM; British singer (baritone); b. 4 Oct. 1943, Somerset; m. Leonora, two s., one step-s., three step-d. *Education:* Dover Coll. ., Royal Acad. of Music, London. *Career:* toured with Welsh Nat. Opera (WNO) for All as Mozart's Figaro and Rossini's Bartolo, 1972–73; WNO, Figaro in Mozart's Marriage and Bohème; Glyndebourne Festival and Touring Opera; Phoenix Opera; English Music Theatre; London Musical Theatre Co. Narrator in Brecht's Caucasian/Chalk circle, Newcastle Festival; ENO from 1982 in Roméo et Juliette, Patience, Così fan tutte, Pagliacci, La Bohème, War and Peace, Osud, Akhnaten and Xerxes; sang Claudio in a new production of Beatrice and Benedict, 1990; Mr Astley in a revival of The Gambler; English Music Theatre in Tom Jones, La Cenerentola and The Threepenny Opera; Die Zauberflöte; Opera North in Der Freischütz, A Midsummer Night's Dream, Beatrice and Benedict and Danilo in The Merry Widow; Kent Opera as Monostatos in Die Zauberflöte; Season 1992 with ENO in the premiere of Bakxai by John Buller and as the Music Master in Ariadne auf Naxos; Demetrius in A Midsummer Night's Dream, Count in The Marriage of Figaro and Schaunard in La Bohème, 1996; Season 1998 as Ford in Falstaff and Puccini's Sharpless for ENO; Germont Père in La Traviata, 1997, 1998, 1999; Sang Melot in Tristan und Isolde, Carmen and Die Frau Ohne Schatten (Strauss) for the Royal Opera in London, 2000. *Recordings:* Julius Caesar and Pacific Overtures; Tosca; Videos of The Gondoliers, Princess Ida, Rusalka, Xerxes, Billy Budd, Carmen, Great Things: 20th Century English Song. *Current Management:* Helen Sykes Artists Management, 100 Felsham Road, Putney, London SW15 1DQ, England.

**BOOTHBY, Richard;** British viola da gamba player and cellist; b. 1955, England. *Career:* Member of the Purcell Quartet, debut concert at St John's Smith Square, London, 1984; Extensive tours and broadcasts in France, Belgium, Netherlands, Germany, Austria, Switzerland, Italy and Spain; Tours of the USA and Japan, 1991–92; British appearances include 4 Purcell concerts at the Wigmore Hall, 1987, later broadcast on Radio 3; Repertoire includes music on the La Folia theme by Vivaldi, Corelli, C P E Bach, Marais, A Scarlatti, Vitali and Geminiani; Instrumental works and songs by Purcell, music by Matthew Locke, John Blow and Fantasias and Airs by William Lawes; 17th century virtuoso Italian music by Marini, Buonamente, Gabrieli, Fontana, Stradella and Lonati; J. S. Bach and his forerunners: Biber, Scheidt, Schenk, Reinken and Buxtehude; Member of Fretwork, debut concert at the Wigmore Hall, 1986; Appearances in the Renaissance and Baroque repertoire in Sweden, Austria, Belgium, Netherlands, France and Italy; Tour of Soviet Union, Sept 1989, Japan, June 1991; Gave George Benjamin's Upon Silence at the Queen Elizabeth Hall, 1990; Wigmore Hall concerts, 1990–91, with music by Lawes, Purcell, Locke and Byrd; Other repertory includes In nomines and Fantasias by Tallis and Parsons, dance music by Holborne and Dowland (including Lachrimae), London Cries by Gibbons and Dering, Resurrection Story and Seven Last Words by Schütz. *Recordings include:* With the Purcell Quartet: On the La Folia theme; Purcell Sonatas for 2 violins, viola da gamba and continuo; Sonatas by Vivaldi and Corelli; Series of 10 recordings with Fretwork. *Address:* Wigmore Hall (Contracts), Wigmore Street, London W1, England.

**BOOZER, Brenda (Lynn);** Singer (Mezzo-soprano); b. 25 Jan. 1948, Atlanta, Georgia, USA; m. Robert Martin Klein, 29 April 1973. *Education:* BA, Florida State University, Tallahassee, 1970; Postgraduate studies, Juilliard School, New York, 1974–77. *Career:* Chicago Lyric Opera, 1978; Festival of Two Worlds, Spoleto, Italy, 1978, 1979; Greater Miami Opera, 1979; Houston Grand Opera, 1979; Metropolitan Opera, New York, 1979–83, 1985, as Hansel, Meg Page, the Composer (Ariadne auf Naxos), Octavian and Orlofsky; Netherlands Opera, Amsterdam, 1981; Paris Opéra, 1982–83; Falstaff, at Covent Garden, 1983; Spoleto Festival, 1989, as Nicklausse in Les Contes d'Hoffmann; Concerts; Television appearances. *Honours:* Recording of Falstaff with the Los Angeles Philharmonic was nominated for a Grammy Award in 1984. *Address:* c/o Columbia Artists Management Inc, 165 West 57th Street, New York, NY 10019, USA.

**BORDAS, Ricard;** Singer (Countertenor); b. 1965 Barcelona, Spain. *Education:* Studied with Charles Brett at the Royal Academy of Music. *Career:* Proms debut in the St Matthew Passion under Joshua Rifkin, 1994; Carmina Burana at La Scala and the Granada Festival and Bach's Magnificat at the Barbican, London; London Handel Festival as Siroe and in Alexander's Feast; Ottone in Handel's Agrippina for Midsummer Opera and Scarlatti's Mitridate at the Schwetzingen Festival, 1996; Jonathan Miller's staged St Matthew Passion, tour of Dido and Aeneas in Mexico and Monteverdi's Poppea with Netherlands Opera; Season 1996–97 as Selino in Cesti's L'Argia at

Innsbruck, the Monteverdi Vespers in Ripon Cathedral and Handel's Israel in Egypt at Bristol; Sang Valentiniono in Handel's Ezio at Halle, 1998. Music Director of Camerata Hispanica in London and the Group Vocal Odarum in Barcelona; Guest teacher at major London colleges. *Honours:* Shinn Fellowship, at the RAM.

**BORETZ, Benjamin (Aaron);** Composer, Music Theorist, Teacher and Writer on Music; b. 3 Oct. 1934, New York, NY, USA. *Education:* Piano and cello study; Training, conducting from Julius Rudel, harpsichord from Erwin Bodky; BA, Brooklyn College, 1954; Manhattan School of Music, New York; MFA, Brandeis University, 1957; Aspen Music School; University of California, Los Angeles; MFA, 1960, PhD, 1970, Princeton University; Composition teachers included Irving Fine, Harold Shapero, Arthur Berger, Darius Milhaud, Lukas Foss, Roger Sessions. *Career:* Consultant, Writer, Fromm Music Foundation, 1960–70; Founding Co-Editor, 1961–64, Editor, 1964–84, 1993–95, Perspectives of New Music; Music Critic, The Nation, 1962–70; Teacher, including New York University, 1964–69, Columbia University, 1969–72, Bard College, 1973–; Distinguished Visiting Professor, University of California, Los Angeles, 1991; Visiting Professor, University of California, Santa Barbara, 1991; Invited, Interdisciplinary Conference, Calgary, 1991; Co-Editor, The Open Space magazines, 1998–. *Compositions include:* Concerto grosso, string orchestra, 1956; Violin concerto, 1956; Divertimento, 5 instruments, 1957; String Quartet, 1958; Group Variations I, orchestra, 1967, II, computer, 1971; Liebeslied, piano, 1974;... my chart shines high where the blue milk's upset..., piano, 1978; Passage for Roger Sessions, piano, 1979; Language, as a Music, 6 Marginal Pretexts for Composition, speaker, piano, prerecorded tape, 1980; Soliloquy I, piano, 1981; Soundscore works; Scores for Composing series, 1991–93; Music/Consciousness/Gender sound/video, 1995; Echoic/Anechoic, piano, 1997; Black/Noise I, II, III, (video and computer sound) 1997–98; Camille, video piece, 1997; UN (-) for orchestra, 1999. *Recordings include:* An Experiment in Reading, 1981; One (exercise) 8 piano solo sound sessions, Open Space, 1992; Open Space, 1993. *Publications include:* Edited with Edward T Cone: Perspectives on Schoenberg and Stravinsky, 1968, 2nd edition, 1972; Perspectives on American Composers, 1971; Perspectives on Contemporary Music Theory, 1972; Perspectives on Notation and Performance, 1976; If I am a Musical Thinker, 1981; Language as a Music, 1985; Music Columns from the Nation, 1962–1968, 1989 Open Space, 1991; Meta-variations: Studies on the Foundations of Musical Thought, 1994. *Contributions:* Professional magazines and journals. *Address:* 29 Sycamore Drive, Red Hook, NY 12571, USA.

**BOREYKO, Andrey;** Conductor, Composer and Teacher; b. 22 July 1957, St Petersburg, Russia; m. Julia Wolk 1990; one d. *Education:* conducting and composition with Elisabeta Kudriavzeva and Alexander Dimitriev, Rimski-Korsakov Conservatory. *Career:* debut as conductor, aged 20; founder, Dir, Res Facta early music group, Leningrad 1977, Barocco Consort, Leningrad 1984; Conductor, St Petersburg Theatre of Music 1985–86; Prin. Conductor, State Symphony Orchestra of Ulyanovsk, Russia, and Chamber Music Theatre 1987–89; Gen. Music Dir, Ural Philharmonic Orchestra, Yekaterinenburg 1990–92; Artistic Dir, Chief Conductor, Poznan Philharmonic Orchestra, Poland 1992–95; Prin. Assoc. Conductor, Russian Nat. Orchestra 1998–2001; Chief Conductor, Gen. Music Dir Jenaer Philharmonie, Prin. Guest Conductor Vancouver Symphony, 1998–2003; Music Dir, Winnipeg Symphony Orchestra 2001–02; Chief Conductor, Hamburger Symphoniker, First Guest Conductor, SWR Radio Symphony Orchestra, Stuttgart, 2004–05; int. guest performances and concerts with Deutsches Symphonie-Orchester Berlin, Gewandhausorchester Leipzig, Württembergisches Staatsorchester Stuttgart, SWR Radio Symphony Orchestra Stuttgart, Bamberger Symphoniker, NDR Symphony Orchestra Hamburg, Hamburger Symphoniker, Radio Symphony Orchestra Berlin, Radio Symphony Orchestra Frankfurt, Nationaltheater Orchester Mannheim, Dresdner Philharmonie, Symphony Orchestra of the MDR Leipzig, Cologne Gürzenich Orchester, Beethoven Orchester Bonn, Orchestre de la Suisse Romande, Basle Symphony Orchestra, Stockholm Royal Philharmonic, Malmö Symphony, Bergen Philharmonic, Trondheim Symphony Orchestra, Royal Flanders Philharmonic Orchestra, Belgian Nat. Orchestra, Philharmonia Orchestra, BBC Symphony Orchestra London, St Petersburg Symphony Orchestra, Prague Symphony Orchestra FOK, Orchestra del Maggio Musicale Fiorentino, Danish Nat. Orchestra, Oslo Philharmonic, Warsaw Philharmonic Orchestra, Polish Nat. Radio Orchestra, Symphony Orchestras of Montréal, Toronto, Detroit, San Diego, Sydney, Melbourne, Brisbane, Adelaide, Chamber Orchestra of the Kremerata Baltica, Amsterdam Sinfonietta, Royal Concertgebouw Orchestra Amsterdam, Berliner Philharmoniker, Chicago Symphony Orchestra, Münchner Philharmoniker, and others; guest at festivals in the Netherlands, Germany, Austria, Switzerland, Belgium, Italy, France and the USA; repertoire puts particular emphasis on contemporary Russian composers, including Sofia Gubaidulina, Gija Kantsheli, Valentin Silvestrov, Alexander Raskatov and Leonid Desyatnikov; engagements in 2004–06 include conducting the Chicago Symphony Orchestra, the Münchner Philharmoniker, the Pittsburgh Symphony Orchestra, the Vienna Radio Symphony Orchestra and the Gulbenkian Orchestra Lisbon, tours of the USA with the Czech Philharmonic, and of Germany with the Junge Deutsche Philharmonie, and the gala concert of the 70th anniversary of the Jenaer Philharmonie. *Recordings:* Silvestrov, Monadia, Sinfonie No. 4, 1992; Silvestrov, Sinfonie No. 5, 1992; A Ginastera, Ballettmusik, Philharmonie Poznan, 1993; Takemitsu, Nostalgie für Violine und Orchester, 1998. *Recordings:* Pärt's Da pacem Donime (with SWR Stuttgart RSO) 2005. *Honours:* hon. conductor, Jenaer Philharmonie, best concert programme from Deutscher Musikverleger-Verband 1999–2000, 2001–02, 2002–03. *Current Management:* Monica Ott, Berliner Konzertagentur, Dramburger Str. 46, 12683 Berlin, Germany. *Telephone:* 5144858. *Fax:* 5142659. *E-mail:* BerlinKonzert.ott@t-online.de. *Website:* www .BerlinKonzert-ott.de.

**BORG, Matti;** Composer and Opera Singer (Baritone); b. 1956 Copenhagen, Denmark; Gitta-Maria Sjoberg, 1 July 1989, 1 s. *Education:* Theory of Music, University of Copenhagen, 1975–78; Diploma in Composition, 1983, Diploma in Solo Singing, 1987, Royal Conservatory of Denmark. *Career:* Debut: Copenhagen, 1987; Appeared as soloist in concerts in Scandinavia and on television and radio; Opera debut in Sweden, Norrlandsoperan; Works performed in Sweden, Norway, Denmark, Belgium, Spain and Canada; mem, Danish Composers' Society. *Compositions:* Choral works, chamber music and songs, music for theatre, musicals; Symboise for mixed choir and solo instruments, 1979; Thirteen ways of looking at a blackbird, trio for soprano, flute and piano, 1981; Recollection, string quartet, 1983; Musicals: What are we dreaming of, 1986; Irene and her men, 1991; Fabliau, for female voice and 12 celli, 1995; Poems by Mörike, for mixed choir, 1997. *Address:* Obdams Allé 24, DK 2300 Copenhagen S, Denmark.

**BORGIR, Tharald;** Musicologist (Keyboard); b. 27 Dec. 1929, Gjerpen, Norway; m. 5 Sept 1951, 3 s., 1 d. *Education:* Music Conservatory, Oslo, 1951; MM, Yale University, USA, 1960; PhD, University of California, Berkeley, 1971. *Career:* Debut: Piano, Oslo, 1957; Teaching, 1967–93, Professor, 1987–, Chair, 1987–92, Oregon State University, Corvallis, USA; Numerous appearances on piano, harpsichord, fortepiano; mem, Greenberg Award Committee, American Musicology Society; College Music Society; Early Music America. *Publications:* The Performance of the Basso Continuo in Italian Baroque Music, 1987, paperback, 1988. *Address:* Department of Music, Oregon State University, Corvallis, OR 97331, USA.

**BORISENKO, Vera;** Singer (Mezzo-Soprano); b. 16 Jan. 1918, Goel, Russia. *Education:* Studied in Gomel and at the Minsk Conservatory; Further study in Kiev with Evtushenko and in Moscow and Sverdlovsk. *Career:* Sang at Sverdlovsk, 1941–45, Kiev, 1945–46, Bolshoi Theatre, Moscow, 1946–65, notably as Lyubava in Sadko, Lyubasha in The Tsar's Bride and Bonny Spring in The Snow Maiden; Other roles included Marfa in Khovanshchina and Carmen; Guest with the Bolshoi in Paris 1969, as Larina in Eugene Onegin; Gave concert performances from the 1960s. *Recordings include:* The Snow Maiden, Prince Igor, Dargomyzhsky's Rusalka, Tchaikovsky's The Enchantress, Rimsky's May Night, Carmen (title role) and Rigoletto (Maddalena). *Address:* c/o Bolshoi Theatre, Pr Marxa 8/2, 103009 Moscow, Russia.

**BORISOVA, Rosa;** Cellist; b. 1960, Moscow, Russia. *Education:* Central Music School, Moscow. *Career:* Co-Founder, Quartet Veronique, 1989; Concerts in Russia, including Russian Chamber Music Series and the 150th birthday celebrations for Tchaikovsky, 1990; Masterclasses at the Aldeburgh Festival, 1991; Concert tour of the United Kingdom in season, 1992–93; Repertoire includes works by Beethoven, Brahms, Tchaikovsky, Bartók, Shostakovich and Schnittke; Resident Quartet, Milwaukee University, USA, 1993–94. *Recordings include:* Schnittke's 3rd Quartet. *Honours:* With the Quartet Veronique: Winner, All-Union String Quartet Competition in St Petersburg, 1990–91; Third Place, 1991 International Shostakovich Competition at St Petersburg; Participated in Evian and London Quartet Competitions, 1994. *Current Management:* Sonata, Glasgow, Scotland. *Address:* 11 North Park Street, Glasgow G20 7AA, Scotland.

**BORK, Robert;** Singer (Baritone); b. 1959, Chicago, Illinois, USA. *Education:* Studied at Wheaton College, Illinois and at the Cologne Opera Studio. *Career:* Sang at Cologne from 1987, notably as Hummel in Reimann's Gespensterso-nate, as Tarquinius in The Rape of Lucretia, Papageno, Belcore, Escamillo, Tsar Peter (Lortzing) and Schaunard in La Bohème; Dörfling in Der Prinz von Homburg by Henze, Cologne, 1992; Sang Donner in Das Rheingold at Toulouse and Redburn in Billy Budd at the Vienna Staatsoper, 2001; Concerts include The Raft of the Medusa by Henze, Bach's B Minor Mass and St Matthew Passion, Ein Deutsches Requiem and Mahler's 8th. *Current Management:* Robert Gilder & Company, 91 Great Russell Street, London, WC1B 3PS, England. *Telephone:* (20) 7580-7758. *E-mail:* rgilder@robert -gilder.com. *Current Management:* Boris Orlob Management, Jägerstrasse 70, 10117 Berlin, Germany. *Telephone:* (30) 20450839. *Fax:* (30) 20450849. *E-mail:* info@orlob.net. *Website:* www.orlob.net. *Address:* c/o Oper der Stadt Köln, Offenbachplatz, W-5000 Cologne 1, Germany.

**BORKH, Inge;** Swiss singer (soprano); b. 26 May 1921. *Education:* Drama School, Vienna and Vienna Acad. *Career:* theatre performances (dancing, piano) in Vienna and Milan, then in Switzerland in German version of The Consul (Menotti); Int. career 1951–, Bayreuth, Paris, Vienna, Edin. Festival; first visit to USA 1953; World Première of Irische Legende (Egk) 1955; appeared as Salome and Elektra, Carnegie Hall, New York 1958; Metropolitan Opera, New York 1958; appeared at opening of Nationaltheater, Munich, in Die Frau ohne Schatten 1963. *Publication:* Ich komm vom Theater nicht los (autobiog.). *Honours:* Bavarian Court Singer 1963; Grand Prix du Disque for Elektra, Antigone (Orff) and Schönberg's Gurrelieder; Reinhard Ring Award 1973. *Address:* Florentinerstrasse 20, Apt 2018, 70619 Stuttgart, Germany. *Telephone:* 47022018. *Fax:* 47022018 (home).

**BORKOWSKI, Marian;** Teacher and Composer; b. 17 Aug. 1934, Pabianice, Poland. *Education:* MA, Academy of Music, Warsaw, 1959–65; MM, Warsaw

University, 1959–66; Postgraduate studies with Nadia Boulanger and Olivier Messiaen, Paris Conservatory; Musicology with Jacques Chailley and Barry S Brook, Paris University; Philosophy with Jean Hyppolite and Jules Vuillemin, Sorbonne and Collège de France, 1966–68; Master's courses: International Courses of New Music, Darmstadt, 1972, 1974; Accademia Musicale Chigiana, Siena, 1973, 1975, studied with Franco Donatoni, Diploma with distinction, 1975. *Career:* Assistant Lecturer and Senior Assistant Lecturer, Department of Composition, 1967–71, Assistant Professor of Composition, 1971–76, Associate Professor, 1976–, Vice-Dean, Faculty of Composition, Conducting and Music Theory, 1975–78, Vice-Rector, 1978–81, 1987–, Artistic Director, Laboratory of New Music, 1985–, Chopin Academy of Music, Warsaw; Concert, radio and television performances; Performances at numerous international festivals. *Compositions include:* Spectra, 1980; Dynamics, 1981; Mater mea for mixed choir a cappella, to words by Krzysztof K Baczynski, 1982; Apasionate, 1983, Avante, 1984; Concerto, 1985–86; Pax in terra I, 1987, II, 1988. *Recordings:* Numerous. *Contributions:* Numerous critiques in magazines and newspapers. *Address:* ul Galczynskiego 5m 17, 00-362 Warsaw, Poland.

**BORNEMANN, Barbara;** Singer (Mezzo-Soprano); b. 8 March 1955, Dingelstadt, Germany. *Education:* Studied in Weimar and at the Hanns Eisler Musikhochschule Berlin, with Hannelore Kuhse. *Career:* Debut: Halberstadt, 1978, as Olga in Eugene Onegin; Sang at Halberstadt until 1981, at Schwerin, 1981–86; Member of the Berlin Staatsoper from 1986; Further appearances in Dresden, Leipzig Czechoslovakia, Poland and Japan; Bayreuth Festival, 1990 as Mary in Der fliegende Holländer; Geneviève in Pelléas et Mélisande in Berlin, 1991; Sang Gaea in Strauss's Daphne (concert performance) Rome, 1991; Other roles include Mozart's Marcellina, Verdi's Ulrica and Mistress Quickly, Wagner's Magdalene and Fricka; Season 1994–95 as Cimarosa's Fidalma in Berlin and in Lulu at Salzburg; House-keeper in Die schweigsame Frau at Dresden, 1998; Concert repertoire includes Bach's Christmas Oratorio and St John Passion, the Mozart and Verdi Requiems, Mendelssohn's Elijah and St Paul, Mahler's Kindertotenlie-der. *Current Management:* Musiespaña, Calle José Marañón 10, 28010 Madrid, Spain. *Telephone:* (91) 5913290. *Fax:* (91) 5913291. *E-mail:* horan@ musiespana.com. *Address:* c/o Deutsche Staatsoper Berlin, Unter den Linden 7, 1087 Berlin, Germany.

**BÖRNER, Klaus;** German pianist, conductor, composer and academic; b. 22 June 1929, Senftenberg; m. Helga Kibat 1958; one s. one d. *Education:* Weimar Acad. of Music, Lausanne Conservatoire de Musique, masterclasses with Alfred Cortot, Edwin Fischer, Wilhelm Kempff. *Career:* debut, Weimar, Mozart Piano Concerto E flat major K482, conductor Carl Ferrand 1950; concerts as Pianist, 70 countries, solo recitals or with orchestra, Berlin, Düsseldorf, Bamberg, Lima, Guatemala, elsewhere; chamber music with Melos String Quartet, Michael Goldstein, others; festivals include Berlin, Madrid, Bad Hersfeld, New Zealand; radio, television; taught, Düsseldorf Conservatory 1956–69; founder, Acting Dir, Int. Music Summer Camp, Sylt 1959–89; Prof., Mainz Univ. 1969–97; guest prof., Hong Kong, Japan, Indonesia, New Zealand; juror, nat. and int. competitions. *Compositions:* Trio for horn, violin, piano 1961, three Lieder for soprano, piano 1990, Fantasie über eine Phantasie, Hommage à Mozart for piano four hands 1993, Quartet for four bassoons 1997. *Recordings:* Handel Chaconne G, J. S. Bach Partita E minor, Haydn Sonatas, C minor, C# minor, Beethoven Sonatas, A major op 2,2, G major op 31,1, Schumann Papillons op 2, Kreisleriana op 16. *Publications:* Klavierschulen für den Aufangsunterricht – Eine vergleichende Analyse 1978, Chance und Dilemma des Urtextes 1982, Piano Duet Repertoire 2005. *Honours:* Prize for Young solists, Weimar 1950, scholarship of German Industry 1953, winner Int. piano competitions in Barcelona 1956, Milan/Monza 1967, selected for Konzerte junger Künstler (German Art Council) 1959, hon. mem. Jeunesses Musicales, German section 1990. *Address:* Nibelungenstr 38, 41462 Neuss, Germany.

**BORODINA, Olga Vladimirovna;** Russian singer (mezzo-soprano); b. 29 July 1963, Leningrad; d. of Vladimir Nikolaevich and Galina Fedorovna Borodin; three s. *Education:* Leningrad Conservatory (student of Irina Bogacheva). *Career:* soloist of Kirov (now Mariinsky) Theatre of Opera and Ballet 1987–; debut as Delilah (Samson and Delilah) at Royal Opera House, Convent Gardent with Placido Domingo 1992; leading roles in operas Khovanshchina (Marfa), Prince Igor (Konchakovna), Queen of Spades (Poline), Sadko (Lubava), Boris Godunov (Marina Mnichek), La Cenerentola (Cinderella), Carmen (Carmen), Amneris (Aida), Eboli (Don Carlos), Delilah (Samson and Delilah), Isabella (The Italian Girl in Algiers); regular performances in all major opera houses as well as recitals and concerts around the world. *Honours:* winner of First Prizes: All-Union Glinka Competition 1987, Int. Rosa Poncell Competition (New York) 1987, Int. Francisco Vignas Competition (Barcelona) 1989. *Current Management:* c/o NFBM Ltd, 28 Smalley Close, London, N16 7LE, England. *Telephone:* (20) 7254-9606 (office). *Fax:* (20) 7254-9606 (office). *E-mail:* Nicola-Fee@nfbm.com (office). *Website:* www.nfbm.com (office).

**BORODINA, Tatiana;** Singer; b. 1972, Perm, Russia. *Education:* graduated Perm Musical Coll. and St Petersburg Conservatoire, 1999. *Career:* Young Singers' Acad. of the Mariinsky Theatre, St Petersburg, 1998; repertoire has included Tchaikovsky's Tatiana and Iolanta, Marguerite in Faust, Mimi, Maria in Mazeppa and Wagner's Elsa and Freia; sang Elsa at Baden-Baden, 1999, Maria and Kupara in Rimsky-Korsakov's The Snow Maiden with the Kirov Opera at Covent Garden, 2000. *Honours:* prizewinner, New Voices of the West Competition, Rome 1997; prizewinner, International Rimsky-Korsakov Competition, St Petersburg. *Address:* c/o Kirov Opera, Mariinsky Theatre, Mariinsky Square, St Petersburg, Russia.

**BOROWSKA, Joanna;** Singer (Soprano); b. 1956, Warsaw, Poland. *Education:* Studied in Warsaw, and at the Opera Studio of Vienna Staatsoper, 1980–82. *Career:* Debut: Romilda in Serse and Micaela in Carmen at Warsaw, 1980; Member of Vienna Staatsoper from 1982, notably as Marenka in The Bartered Bride and as Mozart's Fiordiligi, Susanna and Marzelline, Gluck's Iphigénie en Aulide, (1987), Mimi, 1988, and Marguerite in Faust; Further engagements at Klagenfurt (Countess in Figaro), Bregenz (in Zeller's Der Vogelhändler, 1984), Barcelona and Covent Garden, London, Marenka at Bonn, 1991. *Recordings include:* Emma, in Khovanshchina, Vienna Staatsoper, 1989, and Maidservant in Elektra, conducted by Abbado. *Address:* c/o Oper der Stadt Bonn, Am Boselagerhof 1, 5300 Bonn, Germany.

**BOROWSKI, Daniel;** Singer (Bass); b. 1968, Lodz, Poland. *Education:* Chopin Academy of Music, Warsaw, with Teresa Zylis-Gara. *Career:* Roles at Warsaw and Poznan Operas have included the King in Aida, and in Penderecki's Ubu Rex, Ferrando in Il Trovatore and Rossini's Bartolo; Further engagements as the Commendatore at Strasbourg and Schwetzingen, the Monk in Don Carlos at the Amsterdam Concertgebouw, Colline in La Bohème at Frankfurt and Massimiliano in I Masnadieri for the Royal Opera in concert; Season 1998–99 with Pietro in Simon Boccanegra at Glyndebourne and Water Sprite in Rusalka for Vara Radio; Concerts include Bach's Christmas Oratorio, Messiah, and Mozart and Verdi Requiems. *Recordings include:* Die Zauberflöte. *Current Management:* Konzertdirektion Hans Ulrich Schmid UK, 4 Addison Bridge Place, London W14 8XP, England. *Telephone:* (20) 7602-3648. *Fax:* (20) 7371-4344. *E-mail:* kds_uk@kdschmid.co.uk. *Website:* www.kdschmid.de. *Current Management:* Aria's di Novella Partacini & Alexandra Plaickner, Via Josef Weingartner 4, 39022 Lagundo, Italy. *Telephone:* (473) 200200. *Fax:* (473) 222424. *E-mail:* info@arias.it. *Website:* www.arias.it. *Current Management:* Zemsky/Green Artists Management, 730 Fifth Avenue, Suite 1802, New York, NY 10019, USA. *Telephone:* (212) 300-8003. *Fax:* (212) 300-8001. *E-mail:* zgartists@aol.com. *Website:* www .zemskygreen.com. *Address:* c/o National Theatre, Warsaw, Place Teatraing 1, 00–950 Warsaw, Poland.

**BORRIS, Kaja;** Singer (Mezzo-Soprano); b. 8 Jan. 1948, Den Haag, Netherlands. *Education:* Studied in Cologne and at the Opera Studio of the Deutsche Oper Berlin. *Career:* Member of the Deutsche Oper Berlin from 1973, singing Verdi's Mistress Quickly and Ulrica, Annina in Rosenkavalier, Azucena and Emilia (Othello), Geneviève in Pelléas et Mélisande, 1984, and Marthe in Faust, 1988; Appeared in the premiere of Reimann's Gespenstersonate, 1984; Salzburg Easter Festival, 1982–83, as Mary in Fliegende Holländer; Further engagements at Munich, Hamburg, Vienna and Schwetzingen and in the concert hall; Sang the Sphinx in Enescu's Oedipe at the Deutsche Oper, 1996, and La Cieca in La Gioconda 1998; Season 2000–01 in Strauss's Die Aegyptische Helena (concert) and Mistress Quickly in Falstaff. *Recordings include:* Der fliegende Holländer; Feuersnot by Strauss; Die Lustige Witwe; Der Corregidor by Wolf; Schmidt's Notre Dame and Midwife in Zemlinsky's Der Kreidekreis. *Address:* c/o Deutsche Oper Berlin, Richard Wagnerstrasse 10, 1000 Berlin 10, Germany.

**BORROFF, Edith;** Composer and Musicologist; b. 2 Aug. 1925, New York, NY, USA. *Education:* Studied at the Oberlin Conservatory and the American Conservatory of Music in Chicago; PhD, University of Michigan, 1958. *Career:* Teacher at Milwaukee Downer College, 1950–54, Hillsdale College, Michigan, 1958–62, University of Wisconsin, 1962–66, Eastern Michigan University, 1966–72, and the State University of New York at Binghamton, 1973–92. *Compositions include:* String Trio, 1943; Clarinet Quintet, 1948; Sonata for cello and piano, 1949; Spring over Brooklyn, musical, 1954; IONS for flute and piano, 1968; The Sun and the Wind, musical fable, 1976; Game Pieces for woodwind quintet, 1980; Concerto for marimba and small orchestra, 1981; The Elements, sonata for violin and cello, 1987; Music for piano and organ; Choral music; Songs. *Recordings include:* Passacaglia (organ), 1946; Sonata for Horn and Piano, 1954; Publications include: Elisabeth Jacquet de la Guerre, 1966; The Music of the Baroque, 1970; Music in Europe and the USA, A History, 1971, 1989; Music in Perspective, 1976; Three American Composers, 1987; Music Melting Round: A History of Music in the United States, 1995. *Address:* 65 Forest at Duke Drive, Durham, NC 27705, USA.

**BORST, Danielle;** Singer (Soprano); b. 27 Jan. 1946, Geneva, Switzerland; m. Philippe Huttenlocher. *Education:* Studied at Geneva Conservatoire and with Juliette Bisse and Philippe Huttenlocher. *Career:* Former member of the Ensemble Vocale de Lausanne, under Michel Corboz; Opera appearances in Geneva, Lausanne, Biel-Solothurn, Aix-en-Provence, Montpellier and Vienna (Staatsoper); Paris Opéra, 1988, as Eurydice in Orphée aux Enfers; Mezières, 1988, as Gluck's Euridice; Sang Urbain in Les Huguenots at Montpellier, 1990; Hero in Béatrice et Bénédict at Toulouse, Pamina at Monte Carlo and Vitellia in Gluck's La Clemenza di Tito at Lausanne, 1991; Other roles include Mozart's Despina, Susanna, Sandrina and Illia, Gounod's Juliette, Dalinda (Ariodante), Rameau's Aricie, Micaela and Aennchen in Der Freischütz; Sang Mitrena in Vivaldi's Montezuma, at Monte Carlo 1992; Gounod's Mireille at Lausanne, 1994; Sang Rosalinde at Lyon, 1995–96; Concerts include: Haydn's Schöpfung and Jahreszeiten, Berlioz L'Enfant du Christ, Honegger's Roi David, Passions and Oratorios by Bach, works by Monteverdi, Pergolesi, Handel and Mahler. *Recordings include:* Fauré's Pénélope, Armide by Lully,

Monteverdi's Orfeo, Dido and Aeneas; Iphigénie en Tauride; Title role in L'Incoronazione di Poppea, conducted by René Jacobs. *Address:* c/o Opera de Lausanne, PO Box 3972, 1002 Lausanne, Switzerland.

**BORST, Martina;** Singer (Mezzo-Soprano); b. 13 Jan. 1957, Aachen, Germany. *Education:* Studied with Elsa Cavelti in Frankfurt and with Carla Castellani in Milan. *Career:* Sang at the National Theater Mannheim, from 1981, notably as Annius in La Clemenza di Tito, Cherubino, Dorabella, Rosina, Cenerentola, Orpheus and the Composer in Ariadne auf Naxos; Ludwigsburg Festival, 1982, 1984 as Annius and as Juno in Semele; Vienna Volksoper 1987, as Dorabella; Bregenz Festival, 1988 as Nicklausse in Les Contes d'Hoffmann; Liège and Nantes, 1989 as Bersi in Andrea Chénier; Sang Octavian at Hanover, 1990; Schwetzingen Festival, 1995 as Timante in Demofoonte by Jommelli; Sang Countess Geschwitz in Lulu at Mainz, 1999; Many concert hall appearances, including Mahler's Kindertotenlieder. *Recordings:* Così fan tutte, Harmonia Mundi.

**BÖRTZ, Daniel;** Composer; b. 8 Aug. 1943, Osby, Sweden. *Education:* Studied with Hilding Rosenberg, with Blomdahl and Lidholm at the Stockholm Music High School; Electronic Music, University of Utrecht. *Career:* Debut: Voces for orchestra, Concert Hall, Stockholm, 1968; Freelance Composer, 1968–; Opera Backanterna performed at the Royal Opera, Stockholm in production by Ingmar Bergman, 1991; Member, 1989–, President, 1998–2003, Royal Swedish Academy of Music. *Compositions include:* 2 string quartets, 1971, 1987; 10 Sinfonias, 1973–92; Concerto Grosso No. 2 for wind band, 1981; Violin Concerto, 1985; Oboe Concerto, 1986; 3 Cello concertos, 1981, 1985, 1996; Parodos for orchestra, 1987; Intermezzo for orchestra, 1989–90; Backanterna opera after Euripides, 1991; Songs about Death, for soprano and orchestra. 1992–94; Ballad for alto guitar, 1992–94; Strindberg Suite for orchestra, 1993–94; Variations and Intermezzi for strings, 1994; Sonata for piano, 1994; Songs and dances, trumpet concerto, 1994–95; Songs and Shadows, Violin concerto No. 2, 1995–96; Marie Antoinette, opera, 1996–97; Songs and Light, clarinet concerto, 1998; A Joker's Tales, recorder concerto, 1999–2000; Piano Trio, 2000; Songs, piano concerto, 2000–01; His Name was Orestes, oratorio, 2001–02. *Recordings include:* Parodos Symphonies Nos 1 and 7, Strindberg Suite with Stockholm Royal Philharmonic Orchestra and Gennady Rozhdestvensky; Symphony No. 6, chamber and choir works, with Stockholm Royal Philharmonic Orchestra, Hugh Wolff, Eric Ericson chamber choir; The Bacchae opera; Oboe Concerto; Marie Antoinette, opera; Songs and Dances, trumpet concerto; Sonata for Piano; A Joker's Tales; His Name was Orestes, oratorio. *Honours:* Christ Johnson Music Prize, Stockholm, 1987; International Rostrum of Composers, Paris, 1989; Litteris et Artibus, Stockholm, 1995. *Address:* c/o Carl Gehrmans, Box 6005, 10231 Stockholm, Sweden.

**BORUP-JORGENSEN, Alex;** Composer; b. 22 Nov. 1924, Hjorring, Denmark. *Education:* Studied Piano with Rachlew and Orchestration with Schierbeck and Jersild, Royal Conservatory, Copenhagen, 1946–51; Darmstadt, 1959, 1962. *Career:* Piano Teacher, Else Printz Music School, Copenhagen, 1950–64, then privately. *Compositions:* Partita viola, 1954; Improvisations quartet, 1955; Music for percussion and Viola, 1956; Duino Elegies by Rilke for mezzo, flute, violencello, 1956; Mikroorangisma Quartet, 1956; Sommasvit, string orchestra, 1957; Several songs with piano or other instruments, 1957–60; Sonatina, 2 violins, 1958; Winter Pieces, piano, 1961; Cantata, Rilke Herbsttag, alto, 7 instruments, 1963; Many songs for mezzo and piano, also for several voices, mostly Rilke and Th. Storm; Schlusztuck, Rilke, choir, 5 instruments, 1964; 5 String Quartets, 1950–65; Nordic Summer Pastoral small orchestra, 1964; Torso quartet and tape, 1965; Wintereleige, Holderlin, 3 voices, 9 instruments; Marin Orchestra, 1970; Mirrors; Soprano; Marimba; Guitar, 1974; Works for speaking choir, 1971–72; Tagebuch im Winter, flute, quartet, 1974; Praembula, guitar, 1976; Morceaux, guitar, 1974; Deja vu, concerto for guitar and string orchestra, 1983; Coast of sirens, 7 instruments and multivoice, tape, 1985; Thalatta, Piano, 1988; Raindrop Interludes for piano, 1994; Several works for recorder instruments, solo or with harpsichord. *Address:* Fredsholmvej 11, DK 3460 Birkerod, Denmark.

**BOSABALIAN, Luisa;** Singer (Soprano); b. 24 March 1936, Marseille, France. *Education:* Studied in Beirut, Milan, with Vittorio Ruffo. *Career:* Debut: Théâtre de la Monnaie, Brussels, as Micaela, 1964; Sang at Brussels as Mimi, Donna Anna, Donna Elvira, Desdemona, Giulietta and Antonia in Les Contes d'Hoffmann; Concert appearances at Edinburgh and the Holland Festival, conducted by Giulini; Metropolitan Opera, 1966, as Jenůfa; Guest appearances in London, Düsseldorf, Frankfurt, Rome, Moscow, Oslo, Milan and Vienna; Strasbourg 1974, in Les Indes Galantes by Rameau; Concert appearances in contemporary works; Music by Bach; Gave Lieder recital in Stuttgart, 1988; Concerts for Armenian relief at Munich, 1988–89; Sang at the Hamburg Staatsoper, 1965–73.

**BOSQUET, Thierry;** stage designer and costume designer; b. 1932, Belgium. *Education:* National School of Architecture, Art and Design, Brussels. *Career:* from 1959 sets and costumes for more than 70 operas and ballets at the Théâtre Royale de la Monnaie, Brussels; Many other stagings in France, Italy, Switzerland, Germany, Canada, South America and Australia; Rigoletto and Otello in Liège, La Belle Hélène for Canadian Opera; New York City Opera with Werther, Die Zauberflöte and La Traviata; San Francisco Opera from 1980, with costumes for Aida, Carmen, Fledermaus and Capriccio; Realisations of original designs and costumes for Ruslan and Lyudmila (1995), Der Rosenkavalier (original Alfred Roller designs) and Tosca (San Francisco premiere, 1932); Pelléas et Mélisande at San Francisco, 1997. *Address:* c/o San Francisco Opera, War Memorial House, Van Ness Avenue, San Francisco, CA 94102, USA.

**BOSTOCK, (Nigel) Douglas,** BMus, MMus; conductor; b. 11 June 1955, Northwich, Cheshire, England. *Education:* Northern School of Music, University of Sheffield; private lessons with Adrian Boult, London; conducting masterclass with Prof. Dr Francis Travis; Freiburg Hochschule für Musik, Germany. *Career:* Musikdirektor, Konstanz, Germany, 1979–93; Regular Guest Conductor, Southwest German Philharmonic; Principal Conductor and Music Director, Karlovy Vary Symphony Orchestra, Czech Republic, 1991–98; Principal Guest Conductor, Chamber Philharmonic of Bohemia, 1991–; Permanent Guest Conductor, Munich Symphony Orchestra, 1997–; Music Director, Tokyo Kosei Wind Orchestra, 1999–; Principal Conductor, Aargau Symphony Orchestra Switzerland, 2001–; Guest conducting appearances with major orchestras throughout Europe, America and Japan; Conducted for television and radio; Guest artist at many international music festivals. *Recordings:* Dvořák, Fibich, Smetana, Novak, Mozart, Brahms, Bellini, other composers; Series of rare French music, 3 vols; Albums in Czech Republic, the United Kingdom with Royal Philharmonic, Germany, Japan, baroque music in Italy, Germany, Japan; Nielsen symphonies and other orchestral works with Royal Liverpool Philharmonic, 6+ vols; British Symphonic Collection with various orchestras: Bax, Delius, Vaughan Williams, Elgar, Holst, Butterworth, Arnold Gregson, McCabe, Hoddinott etc, 9+ vols. *Publications:* Hans Pfitzner: The Last Romantic, 1979. *Current Management:* Hazard Chase Ltd, Norman House, Cambridge Place, Cambridge, CB2 1NS, England. *Telephone:* (1223) 312400. *Fax:* (1223) 460827. *Website:* www.hazardchase.co .uk. *Address:* Seestrasse 68, 78479 Reichenau, Germany.

**BOSTRIDGE, Ian Charles,** CBE, MA, DPhil; British singer (tenor); b. 1965, London; s. of the late Leslie John Bostridge and of Lilian Winifred (née Clark); m. Lucasta Miller 1992; one s. *Education:* Westminster School, Univs of Oxford and Cambridge. *Career:* debut recital performance in Wigmore Hall, London 1993; operatic debut in Edin. Festival 1994; has since performed at Carnegie Hall and Lincoln Center, New York, Salzburg Festival, Théâtre du Châtelet, Philharmonie, Berlin etc.; annual lieder recitals Munich Opera Festival. *Television:* Winterreise (Channel 4) 1997, Britten Serenade (BBC) 1999, The South Bank Show (ITV) 2000, Janacek documentary (BBC 4) 2004. *Opera:* A Midsummer Night's Dream, Edin. Festival 1994, The Magic Flute, ENO 1996, The Turn of the Screw, Royal Opera House 1997, 2002, The Bartered Bride, Sadler's Wells 1998, L'incoronazione di Poppea, Munich Festival 1998, The Diary of One Who Vanished, Munich and New York 1999, The Rake's Progress, Munich Festival 2002, Don Giovanni, Royal Opera House, Covent Garden 2003, Ades and The Tempest, Covent Garden 2004, The Rape of Lucretia, Munich 2004. *Recordings include:* Britten 2005. *Publication:* Witchcraft and its Transformations 1650–1750 1997. *Honours:* Hon. Fellow Corpus Christi Coll., Oxford; Hon. DMus (St Andrews); awards include Gramophone Solo Vocal Awards 1996, 1998, Time Out Classical Music Award 1999, Edison Award 1999, 2002, Grammy Award (opera) 1999, Critics' Choice Classical Brit Award (for The English Songbook) 2000, Preis der Deutschen Schallplattenkritik 2001, Acad. Charles Cros, Grand Prix du Disque 2001. *Current Management:* Askonas Holt Ltd, Lonsdale Chambers, 27 Chancery Lane, London, WC2A 1PF, England.

**BOTES, Christine;** singer (mezzo-soprano); b. 1964, Kingston upon Thames, England. *Education:* with Frederic Cox at the Royal Northern College of Music and at the National Opera Studio. *Career:* Sang with Glyndebourne Chorus then with the RSC in The Tempest; Appearances with Scottish Opera as Iolanthe and Second Lady in The Magic Flute; Opera Factory as Diana in La Calisto, Thea in Knot Garden and Dorabella, also televised; Mozart roles include Cherubino at Sadler's Wells, Donna Elvira in the Netherlands and Belgium; With English National Opera has sung as Hansel on tour to Russia in 1990 and as the Fox in The Cunning Little Vixen, 1991; For ENO sang Cherubino in The Marriage of Figaro, 1991; Sang in the Mikado, 1991, Proserpina in Orfeo, 1992, Minerva in Return of Ulysses in 1992; Concert engagements with the Royal Philharmonic in Elgar's Sea Pictures and the London Sinfonietta, City of London Sinfonia and The Hanover Band; Bach's B Minor Mass in France and Poland and Messiah with the Orchestre de Liège and the City of Birmingham Choir; Concerts in Cologne and Lisbon with the Ensemble Modern of Frankfurt; Sang Herodias in Stradella's San Giovanni Battista, Batignano, 1996. *Current Management:* Robert Gilder & Co., Enterprise House, 59–65 Upper Ground, London, SE1 9PQ, England. *Telephone:* (20) 7928-9008. *Fax:* (20) 7928-9755. *E-mail:* rgilder@robert -gilder.com.

**BOTHA, Johan;** singer (tenor); b. 1965, Rustenberg, South Africa. *Education:* studied in Pretoria. *Career:* sang at Pretoria from 1988, in the premiere of Hofmeyer's The Fall of the House of Usher and other works; Europe from 1990 (concerts in Warsaw and Moscow); Kaiserslautern 1991, as Gustavus in Un Ballo in Maschera, Dortmund Opera as the Prince in The Love for Three Oranges; other roles include Max (Der Freischütz), Florestan (at Bonn), Pinkerton, Cassio (Otello), Pedro in Tiefland and Theo in Rautavaara's Vincent; Royal Opera, Covent Garden 1995 as Rodolfo; sang Turiddu at Bonn and Pinkerton at La Scala 1996; season 1998 as Verdi's Arrigo at the Vienna Staatsoper; season 2000–01 as Radames at Los Angeles and the Emperor in Die Frau ohne Schatten at Dresden. *Honours:* Kammersänger 2003. *Address:* c/o Stadtische Buhnen, Kuhstrasse 12, 4600 Dortmund, Germany.

**BOTT, Catherine;** Singer (Soprano); b. 11 Sept. 1952, Leamington Spa, England. *Career:* Many appearances with leading early music ensembles, notably the New London Consort; Appearances at major concert halls in Europe, Latin America and USSR; British engagements include Early Music Network Tours; Festival concerts at Bath, Edinburgh and City of London; Mediaeval Christmas Extravaganza on the South Bank and concerts for the South Bank's 21st anniversary; Season 1988–89 with visits to Israel, Spain, Netherlands and Italy; French debut as Salome in Stradella's San Giovanni Battista at Versailles; Solo recitals at Flanders and Utrecht Festivals, Sadler's Wells Theatre and the King's Singers Summer Festival at the Barbican; Promenade Concert, London, 1990, with The Bonfire of the Vanities (Medici Wedding Celebration of 1539); Season 1991 with concerts and recordings in France, recitals in Netherlands and Belgium and tour of Japan; Sang Mozart's Zaide at Queen Elizabeth Hall, 1991; Purcell's Dido at the Barbican, 1992; Sang in Michael Nyman concert on South Bank, 1996; Oswald von Wolkenstein concert, 1997. *Recordings include:* Monteverdi Vespers and Orfeo; Virtuoso Italian vocal music: de Rore, Rasi, Cavalieri, Luzzaschi, G and F Caccini, Gagliano, Marini, Rossi, Frescobaldi, Monteverdi, Barnardi and Carissimi (Il Lamento di Maria Stuarda); Cantigas de Amigo by Martin Codax and Cantigas di Santa Maria, anon (all with the New London Consort); Vaughan Williams Sinfonia Antarctica, with the London Symphony Orchestra; English canzonets and Scottish songs, with Melvyn Tan; English restoration theatre music: mad songs by Purcell and by Eccles and Weldon; Walton film music, with the Academy of St Martin-in-the-Fields. *Current Management:* Clarion/Seven Muses, 47 Whitehall Park, London, N19 3TW, England. *Telephone:* (20) 7272-4413/5125/8448. *Fax:* (20) 7281-9687. *E-mail:* admin@c7m.co.uk. *Website:* www.c7m.co.uk.

**BOTTI, Patrick;** Conductor; b. 27 July 1954, Marseille, France; m. Catherine Fuller, 2 d. *Education:* Conservatoire National Supérieur de Musique, Paris; École Normale de Musique, Paris; Université de Paris, Sorbonne, Paris; New England Conservatory of Music, Boston, USA; Boston University, Boston; Conservatoire National de Marseille; Université de Droit et Sciences Politiques, Aix en Provence. *Career:* Debut: As a pianist, Palais des Festivals, Cannes, France, 1967; As a conductor, Marseille, 1974; Conducted in France, England, Italy, Canada, USA; Music Director, Concilium Musicum of Paris, 1977–82; Artistic Adviser and Principal Guest Conductor, Concilium Musicum of Paris, 1982–; Music Director, Conductor, French Symphony of Boston, since season 1984–85; Artistic Director, Conductor, New Hampshire Philharmonic Orchestra, since season 1993–94; Principal Guest Conductor, Central Massachusetts Symphony Orchestra, since season 1993–94; As Guest Conductor appearances included Colorado Springs Symphony Orchestra, Boston Philharmonic, New Hampshire Philharmonic Orchestra. *Address:* Conductor's Cooperative Management, 1208 Massachusetts Avenue, Suite #8, Cambridge, MA 02139, USA.

**BOTTOMLEY, Sally Ann;** Concert Pianist and Educator; b. 18 May 1959, Yorkshire, England. *Education:* Chetham's School of Music; Royal Northern College of Music, PPRNCM. *Career:* Debut: Concert debut with City of Birmingham Symphony, 1980; London recital debut, Purcell Room, 1981; Appearances with Royal Philharmonic, London Symphony, City of Birmingham, Hallé, Royal Liverpool Philharmonic Orchestra, Scottish National; Conductors include, Skrowaczewski, Järvi, Groves, Downes, Litton, Tortelier; Two Piano Partnerships with John Gough; Lecturer, Huddersfield University and Chetham's School of Music; Several television appearances and advertisements and radio performances. *Address:* c/o Chetham's School of Music, Long Millgate, Manchester, M3 1 SB, England.

**BOTTONE, Bonaventura,** FRAM; singer (tenor); b. 19 Sept. 1950, England. *Education:* Royal Acad. of Music with Bruce Boyce. *Career:* debut at Covent Garden, as Italian Singer in Der Rosenkavalier, conducted by Haitink; Returned in Capriccio by Strauss; US debut as Pedrillo in Die Entführung, at Houston Opera; Has sung with English National Opera as David in Die Meistersinger, the Duke of Mantua, Beppe, Nanki Poo in Jonathan Miller's production of The Mikado, Sam Kaplan in Weill's Street Scene, Truffaldino in the Love for Three Oranges, 1989 and Alfredo in La Traviata, 1990; Scottish Opera, 1989, as Governor General in Candide and Loge in Das Rheingold; Sang the Italian Tenor in Capriccio at Glyndebourne, 1990; Season 1992, as Verdi's Fenton at the London Coliseum and Conte di Libenskof in Il Viaggio a Reims at Covent Garden; Sang the Berlioz Faust with ENO, 1997; Season 1998, as Doctor Ox in the premiere of Gavin Bryar's opera and Rodolfo in La Bohème for ENO, debut at Santiago, Chile with Alfred in Die Fledermaus, and Italian Singer in Capriccio at Glyndebourne and the Metropolitan Opera; Frequent broadcaster in a wide range of BBC programmes; Sang in the Berlioz Te Deum, Royal Festival Hall, 2000; Season 2001 in Caruso and Mario Lanza tributes in Manchester and Dublin; Verdi's Riccardo for Atlanta Opera; Pinkerton at Santiago and Beethoven's Ninth in Germany; Season 2002–03 with Verdi's Duke in Milwaukee and roles with Chicago Lyric and Met Operas. *Recordings:* The Mikado; Orpheus in the Underworld. *Current Management:* Stafford Law, Candleway, Broad Street, Sutton Valence, Kent ME17 3AT, England. *Website:* www.stafford-law.com.

**BOUCHARD, Antoine,** BA, LTh; Canadian organist and professor of organ; *Professor Emeritus, Faculty of Music, Laval University;* b. 22 March 1932, St Philippe-de-Neri, Quebec. *Education:* Laval Univ., Quebec. *Career:* concerts and festivals, Quebec City, Montreal, Paris, France; concerts in Canada and USA; radio performances, CBC and ORTF; series of concerts on 20 European historical organs, Radio Canada; Organ Prof. and Dir School of Music, Laval

Univ., Quebec 1977–80, Prof. Emer. 1999–. *Compositions:* Prelude and In Paradisum, for organ, in Le Tombeau de Henri Gagnon. *Recordings:* Music by Dandrieu and Buxtehude, Noels français du 18e Siècle, Bach and Pachelbel, Anthologie de l'organiste, Vols I, II, III, The Early Pipe Organs of Quebec, Vols II, IV, VII, The 18 Chorals, by J. S. Bach, Oeuvres de Gaston Litaize, L'Orgue Français classique en Nouvelle-France, 7 historical organs of north-western Germany, Nicolas Lebegue, Complete Pachelbel organ works. *Publications:* L'Organiste (three vols) 1982, Quelques réflexions sur le jeu de l'orgue 2003. *Contributions:* The Organ Yearbook, Netherlands, L'Orgue, Paris, Musicanada, L'Encyclopédie de la musique au Canada. Bulletin des Amis de l'Orgue. *Address:* 908 rue du Belvédère, St-Nicolas-Est, Quebec G7A 3V3, Canada. *E-mail:* antoinebou@videotron.ca.

**BOUE, Georgi;** Singer (Soprano); b. 16 Oct. 1918, Toulouse, France; m. Roger Bourdin, deceased 1973. *Education:* Studied at the Toulouse Conservatory, in Paris with Henri Büsser and Reynaldo Hahn. *Career:* Debut: Toulouse, 1935, as Urbain in Les Huguenots. Mireille in the opera by Gounod; Sang at Toulouse as Siebel in Faust, Hilda in Reyer's Sigurd, Mathilde in Guillaume Tell and Bizet's Micaela; Paris Opéra-Comique from 1938; Paris Opéra from 1942, notably in Les Indes Galantes by Rameau, 1953; Guest appearances in Arles, Brussels, Nice, Barcelona, Germany, Mexico City and Italy; La Scala Milan as Debussy's Mélisande; Tour of Russia as Tatiana in Eugene Onegin and Madama Butterfly; Théâtre de la Monnaie Brussels, 1960, in La Belle Hélène; Die Lustige Witwe; Appeared as Malibran in the film by Sacha Guitry. *Recordings:* Thais, Urania; Faust conducted by Beecham; Les Contes d'Hoffmann; L'Aiglon; Founded the Centre Lyrique Populaire de France, Paris, 1966.

**BOUGHTON, William Paul;** Conductor; b. 18 Dec. 1948, Birmingham, England; m. Susan Ann Cullis 1981. *Education:* Guildhall School of Music, London; Prague Acad.; AGSM. *Career:* founder, Dir, English String Orchestra; Principal Conductor, English Symphony Orchestra and Jyvaskyla Sinfonia, Finland 1986–93; Artistic Dir, Malvern Festival 1983–88; guest conductor with Philharmonia, Royal Philharmonic Orchestra, London Philharmonic Orchestra and London Symphony Orchestra; mem. Royal Overseas League. *Recordings include:* first recordings of Finzi's Love's Labours Lost and Parry's 1st Symphony and Death to Life. *Honours:* Jyvaskyla City Award; Hon. DLitt; Hon. Assoc., Janáček Acad. *Address:* c/o Eleanor Hope, 9 Southwood Hall, Wood Lane, London, N6 5UF, England.

**BOUKOV, Yuri;** French pianist; b. 1 May 1923, Sofia, Bulgaria. *Education:* studied in Bulgaria and at the Paris Conservatoire. *Career:* debut, Sofia, 1938; many appearances throughout Europe in post-war period, with tour to China, 1956; often heard in the sonatas of Prokofiev and premiered works by Menotti and Wissmer.

**BOULEYN, Kathryn;** Singer (Soprano); b. 3 May 1947, Maga Vita, Maryland, USA. *Education:* Studied at Indiana University and the Curtis Institute. *Career:* Debut: San Diego, 1978, as Nannetta in Falstaff; Miami, 1978, as Desdemona; New York City Opera from 1979; Spoleto Festival at Charleston in Haydn's La Vera Costanza, St Louis, 1981, in the US premiere of Fennimore and Gerda by Delius (as Fennimore); European debut, 1981, as Janáček's Fox (The Cunning Little Vixen) with Netherlands Opera; Other appearances as Gutrune at San Francisco (1985), Mozart's Countess at San Diego (1986), Tatiana in Eugene Onegin for Welsh National Opera (1988), Vitellia in La Clemenza di Tito (Scottish Opera), Donna Elvira, Elisabeth de Valois, Mimi, Manon Lescaut, Micaela and Venus in Tannhäuser; Seattle 1991 as Mozart's Countess. *Address:* c/o New York City Opera, Lincoln Center, New York, NY 10023, USA.

**BOULEZ, Pierre;** French composer and conductor; b. 26 March 1925, Montbrison; s. of Léon Boulez and Marcelle Calabre. *Education:* Paris Conservatoire. *Career:* studied with Messiaen, Vaurabourg-Honegger and Leibowitz; Dir of Music to Jean-Louis Barrault theatre co. 1948; aided by Barrault and Madeleine Renaud Barrault he founded the Concert Marigny which later became the Domaine Musical, Paris; Prin. Guest Conductor Cleveland Symphony Orchestra 1968; Prin. Conductor BBC Symphony Orchestra 1971–75; Musical Dir New York Philharmonic 1971–77; Dir Inst. de Recherches et de Coordination Acoustique/Musique (IRCAM) 1975–91, Hon. Dir 1992–; Founder and Pres. Ensemble Intercontinental 1977–98; Prof. Collège de France 1976–95; Prin. Guest Conductor Chicago Symphony Orchestra 1995–; conducted the centenary production of Wagner's Ring, Bayreuth 1976. *Works:* First Piano Sonata 1946, Sonatina for Flute and Piano 1946, Le Visage nuptial (5 poems of René Char for 2 solo voices, female choir and orch.) 1946–50, Second Piano Sonata 1948, Le Soleil des eaux (2 poems of René Char for voice and orch.) 1948, Livre pour Quatuor (string quartet) 1949, Le Marteau sans maître (cantata for voice and instruments to texts by René Char, also ballet 1965) 1955, Structures (2 pianos) 1964, Third Piano Sonata 1957–58, Improvisations sur Mallarmé (soprano and chamber ensemble) 1958, Doubles (orch.) 1958, Poésie pour pouvoir (orch.) 1958, Tombeau (soprano and orch.) 1959, Pli selon Pli 1958–62, Figures–Doubles–Prismes 1964/74, Eclat and Eclat/Multiples 1965, Domaines 1968–69, cummings ist der dichter 1970, explosante-fixe for 8 solo instruments 1973, Rituel 1974, Messagesquisse 1977, Notations 1979, Répons 1981–86, Dérive 1984, Dialogue de l'ombre double 1984, Mémorial 1985, le Visage nuptial 1989,. . . explosante-fixe . . . for Midi-flute, 2 solo flutes, ensemble and electronics 1993, Anthèmes 2 1997, sur Incises 1998, Notations VII 1999, Dérive 2 2001. *Publications:* Penser la musique aujourd'hui 1966, Relevés

d'apprenti (essays) 1967, Par volonté et par hasard 1975, Points de repère 1981, Le pays fertile: Paul Klee 1989, Orientations: Collected Writings 1986. *Honours:* Hon. Conductor Staatskapelle Berlin 2005, Fellow British Acad. of Composers and Songwriters 2005; Hon. CBE; Dr hc (Cambridge) 1980, (Bâle) 1980, (Los Angeles) 1984, (Oxford) 1987, (Brussels) 1988; Prize of the Siemens Foundation 1979, Praemium Imperiale, Japan Art Asscn 1989, Polar Music Prize, Sweden 1996, Wolf Foundation Prize in Arts 2000, Grawemeyer Award 2001. *Address:* IRCAM, 1 place Igor Stravinsky, 75004 Paris, France; Postfach 100022, 76481 Baden-Baden, Germany.

**BOULIN, Sophie;** Singer (Soprano) and Composer; b. 1960, France. *Education:* Paris Conservatoire; Paris Opéra Studio. *Career:* Contemporary music concerts with Vinko Globokar, Diego Masson and Claude Prey; Baroque music with René Jacobs, Gustav Leonhardt, Jean-Claude Malgoire, Sigiswald Kuijken, William Christie and Philippe Herreweghe; Opera appearances in France and Germany, notably in productions by Herbert Wernicke of Monteverdi's Poppea, Gluck's Echo et Narcisse and Graun's Montezuma. *Compositions:* Le leçon de musique dans un parc, premiered under William Christie, 1982; Tou azimuts, given at Hamburg, Paris and Munich. *Recordings:* Echo in Echo et Narcisse; Rossane in Handel's Alessandro; Cantatas by Jacquet de la Guerre. *Address:* c/o SACEM, 225 Avenue Charles de Gaulle, 92521 Neuilly sur Seine, Cédex, France.

**BOULTON, Timothy;** British violist; b. 14 July 1960. *Career:* mem., Domus Piano Quartet, 1985–95, Raphael Ensemble, 1991–98, Vellinger String Quartet, 1998–2002; Prof. of Viola, Guildhall School of Music and Drama; Head of Strings, Junior Guildhall; founder of MusicWorks (Chamber Courses), running residential courses for teenagers; many international chamber music tours. *Recordings:* many recordings with the aforementioned groups. *Honours:* Gramophone Chamber Music Award, 1996. *E-mail:* tboulton@eurobell.co.uk.

**BOUMAN, Hendrik;** Harpsichordist, Fortepianist, Conductor and Professor; b. 29 Sept. 1951, Dordrecht, Netherlands; one s. *Education:* teaching certificate, 1977, Harpsichord solo performance diploma, 1978, Sweelinck Conservatorium, Amsterdam. *Career:* debut, conducting, Basilica of Notre Dame, Montréal, Canada, premiere of Tu me cherches by Alain Pierard; Mass for orchestra; several hundred Choristers; International Year of Youth, 1985; harpsichordist of Musica Antiqua Köln, 1976–83; extensive tours throughout Europe; festivals in Berlin, London, Netherlands, Flanders, Besancon, Festival de Paris; world tours of South America, 1980, North America, 1981, Asia, including India and Japan, 1982; regular radio recordings for all major European stations; founder, Dir, Ensemble Les Nations de Montréal, 1986; Prof., Univ. of Laval, Québec, 1987, Concordia Univ., 1985–; masterclasses and lectures, 1979–; mem., CAPAC. *Compositions:* several transcripts for harpsichord duo. *Publications:* Basso Continuo realisations for Marais; Sonnerie; Maresienne; Mancini; Recorder Concerto; Figured Bass and Harpsichord Improvisation. *Honours:* Diapason d'Or, 1982, for Giles; Diapason d'Or, 1982 for Monteverdi; Deutscher Schallplattenpreis, 1982; Early Music Award, 1982.

**BOURGEOIS, Derek,** MA, DMus; British director of music; b. 16 Oct. 1941, Kingston on Thames, England; m. Jean Berry 1965. *Education:* Magdalene College, Cambridge, Royal College of Music. *Career:* Lecturer in Music, Bristol University, 1971–84; Director of Music, National Youth Orchestra of Great Britain, 1984–93; Founder, National Youth Chamber Orchestra of Great Britain, 1989–93; Director of Music, St Paul's Girls' School, London, 1994–2002; mem, Vice-President of Composers Guild of Great Britain, Chairman, 1980–83. *Compositions include:* 206 works, including 20 symphonies; Concertos for double bass, clarinet, trombone (2), tuba, organ, euphonium, 3 trombones, percussion, trumpet and bass trombone, tenor horn, saxophone; 4 Concertos for Brass Band; 6 Symphonies for Wind Orchestra; Symphonic Fantasy: The Globe; 8 works for chorus and orchestra; 2 operas. *Recordings:* many of his original compositions. *Address:* La Tramuntana, Calle Orquidea No. 24 - Betlem, 07579 Arta, Mallorca, Balearics (home). *Telephone:* 971 589236 (home). *E-mail:* tramuntana@infoarta.com (home). *Website:* www.tramuntana.infoarta.com (home).

**BOURGUE, Daniel;** Horn Player; b. 12 Jan. 1937, Avignon, France. *Education:* Avignon Conservatoire and Paris Conservatoire. *Career:* soloist and chamber musician; concerts with the Musica wind quintet, 1961–67; horn soloist, Garde Republicaine Orchestra, 1963; at Concerts Pasadeloup, 1964; Opéra-Comique, 1967; Orchestre National de France; The Ensemble Inter-contemporain; Ensemble Orchestral de Paris; Nouvel Orchestre Philharmonique; first horn soloist Paris Opéra Orchestra, 1964–89; mem., Paris Octet 1965–82; performed in Europe, Scandinavia, Africa, USA, Latin America, Canada, Japan; has premiered works by Messiaen (Appel Interstellaire), Francaix (Divertimento), Xenakis (Anaktoria, 1965), Pousseur, Jolas, Ballif, Constant and Delerue (Concerto); teaches at Versailles Conservatoire; lectures, masterclasses in France, Belgium, Germany, Italy, Bulgaria, USA, Canada, Spain, Japan; organizes training sessions with the Spanish National Youth Orchestra three times a year 1987–; Dir, Editions Billaudot's Florilège Collection; Pres., Asscn Nat. des Cornistes Français. *Recordings:* music by Mozart, Handel, Rossini, Telemann, Haydn, Strauss, Saint-Saëns, Stamitz, Hoffmeister, Dukas, Chabrier, Corrette, Bréval, d'Indy, Gounod and others. *Publications:* five-volume teaching work Techni-cor (publr); Parlons du cor. *Address:* c/o Valmalè, 7 rue Hoche, 92300 Levallois Perret, Paris, France.

*Address:* 12 rue Erik Satie, 94440 Santeny, France (home). *Telephone:* 1-43-86-04-61 (home). *E-mail:* danbourg@tele2.fr (home).

**BOURGUE, Maurice;** French oboist and conductor; b. 6 Nov. 1939, Avignon. *Education:* Paris Conservatoire. *Career:* principal oboist, Basle Orchestra 1964–67, Orchestre de Paris 1967–79; solo appearances with the Israel CO, I Solisti Veneti, I Musici, Lucerne Festival Strings and all the major French orchestras; British debut at the Wigmore Hall 1979; engagements with the ECO, Chamber Orchestra of Europe, Royal Philharmonic, and the London Symphony Orchestra under Abbado; premieres include Chemins IV by Berio 1974, Les Citations by Dutilleux 1991, and Messiaen's Concert à Quatre 1994; founder, Ensemble à Vent Maurice Bourgue 1972; has conducted the Oslo Philharmonic Orchestra, Ensemble Orchestral de Paris, Israel CO and Orchestras in Lyon, Montpellier, Nancy and the Auvergne; tour of the UK with the Bournemouth Sinfonietta 1995; currently Prof., Conservatoire Nat. Supérieur de Musique et de Danse de Paris, and Conservatoire de Musique de Geneve; mem. Int. Double Reed Soc. *Honours:* winner Competitions at Birmingham 1985, Prague 1968, Budapest 1970. *Address:* Conservatoire National Supérieur de Musique et de Danse de Paris, 209 avenue Jean Jaurès, 75019 Paris, France.

**BOUSKOVA, Jana;** Czech harpist; b. 27 Sept. 1970, Prague; m. Jiri Kubita 1993; one s. *Education:* Prague Conservatory, Ostrava University, Indiana University, studied with Libuse Vachalova, Susann McDonald. *Career:* Concert Harpist, solo, chamber, concerts in USA, Japan, Germany, France, Italy, Spain, Greece, Canada, Czech Republic, Slovakia, Netherlands, Switzerland; Recital at Lincoln Center, 1993; Concert at the Berliner Philharmony Hall; International Music Festivals; Many recordings for television and radio; Teacher at the Prague Conservatory Concerts at the World Harp Congresses (Vienna, Paris, Copenhagen, Seattle, Prague); Concerts with Patrick Gallois, Mstislav Rostropovich; Artistic Chairman for the Seventh World Harp Congress in Prague, 1999. *Recordings:* Harp Recital (Scarlatti, Bach, Tournier, etc); Harp Recital (J L Dussek); Harp Recital (J F Fischer); Harp Concertos (Handel, Krumpholz, Boieldieu); Harp Concertos (J Ch Bach); Harp Concertos (J K Krumpholz Nos 1–6); Harp Recital (Bach, Fischer); Harp-Violin (Kreutzer-Nocturnos); Harp-Flute (Spohr, Ravel); Jana Bouskova Plays Virtuoso Encores (Chopin, Liszt, Falla); Solos for Harp (Ravel and Debussy); Harp Concertos (Dittersdorf, Wagenseil, Albrechtsberger). *Honours:* 1st Prize, Gold Medal, USA International Harp Competion, 1992; 2nd Prize, 11th International Harp Contest, Israel, 1992; 1st Prize, Grand Prix Concours International de Musique de Chambre de Paris, 1998; 1st Prize, TIM Torneo Internazionale di Musica, 1999; Harpa Award, 1999. *Address:* Oddechová 398, 15531 Prague 5, Lipence-Kazín, Czech Republic. *E-mail:* jana@bouskova.cz. *Website:* www.bouskova.cz.

**BOVINO, Maria;** Singer (Soprano); b. 1960, England. *Education:* Studied at Sheffield University and the Guildhall School of Music and Drama. *Career:* Debut: At King's College in London, as Bella in Schubert's Die Verschworenen; Sang Fiorella in Offenbach's Les Brigands with the Intermezzi Ensemble; Opera 80 from 1982 as Adele in Die Fledermaus, Despina in Così fan tutte and Elvira in L'Italiana in Algeri; Season 1984–85 as Emmie in Albert Herring at Glyndebourne and Titania in A Midsummer Night's Dream for Glyndebourne Tour; Sang First Boy in The Magic Flute for English National Opera in 1986 followed by the Queen of Night in 1988; With Scottish Opera from 1987 as Blondchen in Die Entführung and Papagena; English Bach Festival in Gluck's Orfeo and Dido and Aeneas in London, Granada and Athens; Covent Garden debut in 1989 in Albert Herring; Performances with Travelling Opera in season 1990–91 as Mimi and Gilda; Also sings Gilbert and Sullivan with the London Savoyards; Sang Susanna with Crystal Clear Productions in 1991; Sang Gilda with English Touring Opera, 1996; Queen of Night for Mid Wales Opera, 1998. *Address:* c/o Mid Wales Opera, 5 Llandaff Road, Cardiff, CF11 9NF, Wales.

**BOWATER, Helen;** Composer; b. 16 Nov. 1952, Wellington, New Zealand. *Education:* Studied with Gwyneth Brown and at Victoria University, Wellington. *Career:* Resident composer at Nelson School of Music, 1992; Mozart Fellow at University of Otago, 1993. *Compositions include:* Black Rain for soprano and cello, 1985; Songs of Mourning for baritone and string quartet, 1989; Stay Awake Ananda for 5 percussionists, 1990; The Bodhi Tree, string quartet, 1991; Witch's Mine for tape, 1991; Magma for orchestra, 1992. *Address:* c/o New Zealand Music Centre, PO Box 10042, Level 13, Brandon Street, Wellington, New Zealand.

**BOWEN, Geraint Robert Lewis,** BA, MA, MusB, FRCO; conductor and organist; *Organist and Director of Music, Hereford Cathedral;* b. 11 Jan. 1963, London, England; m. Lucy Dennis 1987; two s. *Education:* Univ. of Cambridge, Trinity College, Dublin, studied with Christopher Herrick, John Scott and Stephen Cleobury. *Career:* Organ Scholar, Jesus College, Cambridge, 1982–85; Television and radio broadcasts as organ accompanist and conductor, 1984–; Assistant Organist at Hampstead Parish Church, St Clement Danes Church, 1985–86, St Patrick's Cathedral, Dublin, 1986–89 and Hereford Cathedral, 1989–94; Assistant Conductor and Accompanist, Hereford Choral Society, 1989–94; Festival Organist at Hereford Three Choirs Festival, 1991, 1994; Appearances as conductor and recitalist in the United Kingdom, Ireland, USA and Australia; Organist and Master of the Choristers at St David's Cathedral, Wales, 1995–2001; Artistic Director, St David's Cathedral Festival, 1995–2001; Founder and Conductor, St David's Cathedral Festival Chorus, 1996–2001; Director of choral workshops in USA, 1997–;

Organist and Director of Music, Hereford Cathedral, 2001–; Conductor, Hereford Choral Society, 2001–; Conductor at the Three Choirs Festival, 2002–; orchestras include Philharmonia, RPO, Bournemouth Symphony Orchestra. *Recordings:* Aeternae laudis lilium; The Psalms of David, vol. 1; Te Deum and Jubilate, vol. 3; The Sound of St David's. *Honours:* Selected for Gramophone Magazine's Critics' Choice, 1985. *Address:* 7 College Cloisters, The Close, Hereford, HR1 2NG, England.

**BOWEN, John;** Singer (tenor); b. 1968, England. *Education:* Royal College of Music. *Career:* appearances with Bath and Wessex Opera, Garsington Festival, City of Birmingham Touring Opera and Opera Factory Zürich; roles include Ugone in Flavio and Pan in La Calisto; concerts with the English Chamber Orchestra, Royal Liverpool Philharmonic Orchestra, London Mozart Players, and The King's Consort in The Indian Queen and Judas Maccabaeus; sang in the premiere of Tavener's Apocalypse at the London Proms in 1994 and tour of Bach's B minor Mass with René Jacobs; sang Soliman in Mozart's Zaide at the 1996 Covent Garden Festival. *Recordings include:* Rachmaninov's Vespers; Messiah; Monteverdi's Vespers. *Current Management:* Caroline Phillips Management, The Old Brushworks, Pickwick Road, Corsham, Wiltshire, SN13 9BX, England. *Telephone:* (1249) 716716. *Fax:* (1249) 716717. *E-mail:* cphillips@caroline-phillips.co.uk. *Website:* www.caroline-phillips.co.uk/bowen.

**BOWEN, Kenneth (John);** Singer (Tenor), Conductor, Teacher and Adjudicator; b. 3 Aug. 1932, Llanelli, Wales; m. Angela Mary Bowen, 31 Mar 1959, 2 s. *Education:* BA, University of Wales; MA, BMus, St John's College, Cambridge; Institute of Education, University of London. *Career:* Debut: Tom Rakewell, New Opera Company, Sadler's Wells, 1957; Flying Officer, Education Branch, RAF, 1958–60; Professor of Singing, 1967–, Head of Vocal Studies, 1987–91, RAM; Conductor of London Welsh Chorale, 1983–, and London Welsh Festival Chorus; Former concert and operatic tenor, retired in 1988; Appeared at Promenade Concerts, Aldeburgh, Bath, Swansea, Llandaff and Fishguard Festivals, throughout Europe, Israel, North America and the Far East; Performed at Royal Opera House, ENO, WNO, Glyndebourne Touring Opera, English Opera Group, English Music Theatre, Kent Opera, and Handel Opera Society; Frequent broadcasts, numerous first performances and many recordings. *Honours:* Prizes in Geneva, 's-Hertogenbosch, Liverpool and Munich International Competition (1st) and Queens Prize; Honorary RAM, John Edwards Memorial Award, GPWM. *Address:* 61 Queen's Crescent, London NW5 3QG, England.

**BOWERS, Evan;** Singer (tenor); b. 1960, New York, USA. *Career:* Sang Alfredo and Gounod's Tybalt for Texas Opera Theatre, Ernesto in San Francisco and for the Metropolitan Opera Guild; Ferrando and the Duke of Mantua for Israeli Vocal Arts Institute; European debut 1992, as Don Ottavio for the Wiener Kammeroper; Engagement with the Nuremberg Opera as Tamino, Oberon, Leopold in La Juive, Andres in Wozzeck and Rossini's Almaviva; Guest as Fenton at Innsbruck and Nemorino at the Salzburg Landestheater; Leipzig Opera from 1994, as Rodolfo, Lensky and Don Ottavio; Graz Opera debut as Tamino; Season 1996–97 as Beethoven's Jacquino, Don Ottavio at the Schönbrunn Festival and Gratiano in The Merchant of Venice for Portland Opera; Concerts include: The Missa Solemnis, Haydn's Creation and Seasons, Requiems of Verdi and Mozart; Venues include: France, Germany and the USA. *Current Management:* Athole Still International Management, Forresters Hall, 25–27 Westow Street, London, SE19 3RY, England. *Telephone:* (20) 8771-5271. *Fax:* (20) 8768-6600. *Website:* www.atholestill.com.

**BOWERS-BROADBENT, Christopher Joseph,** FRAM; British organist and composer; *Organist and Choirmaster of Gray's Inn and Organist of the West London Synagogue;* b. 13 Jan. 1945, Hemel Hempstead; s. of Henry W. Bowers-Broadbent and Doris E Mizen; m. Deirdre Cape 1970; one s. one d. *Education:* King's Coll. Cambridge, Berkhamsted School and Royal Acad. of Music. *Career:* Organist and Choirmaster of St Pancras Parish Church 1965–88; Organist of West London Synagogue 1973–; Organist and Choirmaster of Gray's Inn 1983–; debut organ recital, Camden Festival 1966; Prof. of Organ, Royal Acad. of Music 1976–92; Recordings include: Trivium, O Domina Nostra, Meditations Sur, Mattins Music, Duets and Canons. *Operas include:* The Pied Piper 1972, The Seacock Bane 1979, The Last Man 1983–2000. *Honours:* Three Choirs Festival Composers' Competition Prize 1978. *Address:* 94 Colney Hatch Lane, Muswell Hill, London, N10 1EA, England. *Telephone:* (20) 8883-1933. *Fax:* (20) 8883-8434; (20) 8888-8434 (home). *E-mail:* chris@christopherbowers-broadbent.com (home). *Website:* christopherbowers-broadbent.com (home).

**BOWLES, Edmund Addison,** BA, PhD; American fmr musicologist and timpanist; b. 24 March 1925, Cambridge, MA; m. Marianne von Recklinghausen; one s. one d. *Education:* Swarthmore College, Yale University, Berkshire Music Center, Tanglewood, MA. *Career:* instructor in humanities, Mass. Institute if Technology 1951–55; Publicity Staff, Bell Telephone Laboratories, 1955–59 Senior Program Adminstrator, IBM Corporation, 1959–88; Consultant, Music Division, Library of Congress, 1955–; mem. American Musical Instrument Society; American Musicological Society, Fellowship of Makers and Researchers of Musical Instruments; The Galpin Society; Medieval Academy of America. *Publications:* Computers in Humanistic Research: Readings and Perspectives, 1967; Musikleben des 15. Jahrhunderts, 1976; Musical Performance in The Late Middle Ages 1983; Musical Ensembles in Festival Books: An Iconographical and Documentary

Survey, 1989; The Timpani: A History in Pictures and Documents, 2002; contrib. to various professional journals; Dictionary of the Middle Ages; Encyclopaedia Britannica; Garland Encyclopedia of Percussion; Several New Grove dictionaries; The New Harvard Dictionary of Music. *Honours:* Bessaraboff Prize, 1991 and Curt Sachs Award, 1997, American Musical Instrument Society. *Address:* 3210 Valley Lane, Falls Church, VA 22044, USA (home).

**BOWLES, Garrett H.;** Music Librarian; b. 3 Feb. 1938, San Francisco, CA, USA; 1 s., 1 d. *Education:* BA, Music, University of California, Davis, 1960; MA, Music Composition, San Jose State University, 1962; MLS, University of California, Berkeley, 1965; PhD, Musicology, Stanford University, 1978. *Career:* Head Music Cataloguer, Stanford University, 1965–79; Head Music Librarian, 1979–, Assistant Adjunct Professor of Music, 1980–, University of California, San Diego; Visiting Lecturer at University of Exeter, England, 1983. *Compositions include:* Festklang for Ernst Krenek, in Perspectives of New Music, 1985. *Recordings:* Handel's Messiah, 1984. *Publications:* Directory, Music Library Automation Projects, 1973, 1979; Ernst Krenek, Bio-bibliography, 1989; Editor, Ernst Krenek Newsletter, 1990–. *Contributions:* Journal of Association for Recorded Sound Collectors; Notes; Forte Artis Musicae. *Address:* Music Library 0175-Q, University of California at San Diego, 9500 Gilman Drive, La Jolla, CA 92093-0175, USA.

**BOWMAN, James Thomas,** CBE, DipEd, MA; British singer (countertenor); b. 6 Nov. 1941, Oxford, England. *Education:* Cathedral Choir School, Kings School, Ely, Cambridgeshire, New Coll., Oxford. *Career:* sang with English Opera Group 1967–, with debut as Britten's Oberon; sang with Early Music Consort 1967–76; operatic performances include Sadler's Wells Opera 1970–, Glyndebourne Festival Opera 1970–, Opéra Comique, Paris 1979–, Geneva 1983, Dallas and San Francisco Operas, USA; operatic roles include Endymion in La Calisto, The Priest in Taverner in the world premiere at Covent Garden 1972, Apollo in Death in Venice, Astron in The Ice Break 1977 premiere; title roles include Handel's Giulio Cesare, Tamerlano, Scipione; appearances include La Scala, Milan 1988 as Jommelli's Fetonte, ENO 1989 as Amphinomus in The Return of Ulysses, Promenade Concerts 1991 in Purcell's Ode for St Cecilia's Day; sang Britten's Oberon at Aix-en-Provence 1992, Barak in Handel's Deborah 1993 Prom Concerts, London; other roles include Goffredo in Rinaldo, Lidio in Cavalli's Egisto, Ruggiero in Vivaldi's Orlando; sang Herod in Fux's La Fede Sacrilega in Vienna and Monteverdi's Ottone in Poppea at the Spitalfields Festival, London; Bach's St John Passion at St John's, London 1997; Daniel in Handel's Belshazzar 1996 Göttingen Festival; sang Britten's Oberon at the Barbican 1998; title role in Handel's Silla, Royal Coll. of Music 2000. *Recordings:* oratorio, Mediaeval and Renaissance vocal music. *Honours:* Hon. DMus (Univ. of Newcastle upon Tyne) 1996;Hon. Fellow New Coll., Oxford. *Address:* c/o Hyperion Records Limited, PO Box 25, London, SE9 1AX, England.

**BOWYER, Kevin John;** British organist; b. 9 Jan. 1961, Essex, England; m. Ursula Steiner 1981; two s. two d. *Education:* Royal Acad. of Music with Douglas Hawkridge and Christopher Bowers-Broadbent, studied with David Sanger. *Career:* debut, Royal Festival Hall 1984; concerts throughout Europe and N America, specializing in unusual and contemporary repertoire; performances of Kaikhosru Sorabji's Organ Symphony in London 1987, Århus 1988 and Linz 1992; broadcasts for BBC Radio 3 include works by Ligeti, Hugh Wood, Malcolm Williamson, Berio, Henze, Brian Ferneyhough, Charles Camilleri, Niccolo Castiglioni; numerous broadcasts for other networks. *Recordings:* A Late Twentieth Century Edwardian Bach Recital, Alkan Organ Works, Brahms Complete Organ Works, Reubke's 94th Psalm Sonata, Schumann's 6 Fugues on Bach, Organ Works by Dupré, Langlais, Hindemith, Pepping, Arnold Schoenberg, Complete Organ Works of J. S. Bach, Messiaen Organ Works (two vols), Sorabji Organ Symphony No. 1, works by Busoni, Ronald Stevenson, Alistair Hinton. *Publications:* contrib. articles on Sorabji to The Organ and Organists Review. *Honours:* Countess of Munster Musical Trust grant, first prize St Albans Int. Organ Festival 1983, first prize int. organ festivals in Dublin, Paisley, Odense and Calgary 1990. *Address:* 2 Kingston Barn College, Kingston Farm, Chesterton, Leamington Spa CV33 9LH, England. *E-mail:* kevinbowyer@cwcom.net.

**BOYD, Anne (Elizabeth);** Composer, University Music Teacher and Music Critic; b. 10 April 1946, Sydney, Australia; 1 d. *Education:* BA, 1st Class Honours, University of Sydney; DPhil, University of York; NSW Conservatorium of Music; Composition Teachers: Peter Sculthorpe, Wilfrid Mellers, Bernard Rands. *Career:* Debut: Adelaide Festival of Arts, 1966; Festival performances include: Adelaide in 1966, 1968, and 1976; Opening Season Festival of Sydney Opera House, 1973; Appearances at Edinburgh Windsor Festival, 1974, Aldeburgh Festival, 1980, Hong Kong Arts Festival, 1985, ISCM Festival, Hong Kong, 1986, 'Donne in Musica', Fiuggi, Italy, 1999 and Vale of Glamorgan Festival, Wales, 2001; Lecturer in Music, University of Sussex, 1972–77; Founding Head and Reader, Department of Music at University of Hong Kong, 1981–90; First Australian and first woman to be appointed Professor of Music at the University of Sydney, 1990–. *Compositions include:* Angklung, meditations for solo piano, 1974; Book of the Bells, for piano, 1980; String Quartets Nos 1 and 2; The Voice Of The Phoenix for solo piano, guitar, harp, harpsichord and full orchestra; As It Leaves The Bell for piano, 2 harps and 4 percussion; Goldfish Through Summer Rain, for flute and piano, 1979; Red Sun, Chill Wind, for flute and piano, 1980; Cloudy Mountain for flute and piano, 1981; Bali Moods No. 1 for flute and piano, 1987; Black Sun for orchestra, 1989; String Quartet No. 3, 1991; Grathwai, for orchestra, 1993;

Ullaru Mourns, for cello, 1996; '. . . at the rising of the sun. . . ', for orchestra, 2001; Choral: As I Crossed a Bridge of Dreams, 1975; The Little Mermaid, children's opera, 1978; The Death of Captain Cook, oratorio, 1978; Coal River, choral symphony, 1979; The Beginning of the Day, children's opera, 1979; The Last of His Tribe, 1980; Revelations of Divine Love, 1995; Dreams for the Earth, youth cantata, 1998; A Vision: Jesus Reassures His Mother, for vocal soloists, 1999; Song cycles for voice and chamber ensemble: My Name is Tian, 1979; Cycle of Love, 1981; Meditations on a Chinese Character, 1996; Last Songs of the Kamikaze, 1997. *Recordings include:* Meditations on a Chinese Character, 1997; Crossing a Bridge of Dreams, 1998. *Contributions:* Founding Managing Editor, Music Now; Musical Times; Miscellanea Musicologica; Australian Journal of Music Education. *Honours:* AM in the Order of Australia, 1996; Hon. Doctor of the Univ. of York, 2003. *Address:* c/o Department of Music, University of Sydney, Sydney, NSW 2006, Australia.

**BOYD, Douglas;** British oboist; b. 1 March 1959, Glasgow, Scotland. *Education:* Royal Acad. with Janet Craxton, studied with Maurice Bourgue in Paris. *Career:* solo engagements in works by Strauss and Mozart, in Europe, The Far East and USA; conductors have included Abbado, Berglund, Menuhin, Alexander Schneider and Michael Tilson Thomas; co-founder, Chamber Orchestra of Europe as principal oboist and leading mem. of the wind soloists; played in the Lutoslawski Concerto for oboe and harp, Glasgow 1991; world premiere of Sally Beamish's Oboe Concerto, written for him, at the QEH, London 1993; during 1993–94 season performed with the Basle Radio Symphony Orchestra under Rudolph Barshai, Nat. Arts Centre Orchestra of Ottawa under Nicholas McGegan, Hong Kong Philharmonic under David Atherton, BBC Scottish Symphony Orchestra under Alun Francis, and Budapest String Soloists; has also appeared at the Bath and Boxgrove Festivals and Glasgow's Mayfest; concertos with various orchestras and tours of the USA with Jeffrey Kahane and the Ridge Ensemble; invitations to the Perth, Vancouver and Prague Autumn Festivals; made first tour of Japan 1997; chamber music with Andras Schiff 1999; developing conducting career, performances include Scottish Chamber Orchestra, Manchester Camerata, Hong Kong Philharmonic, New Arts Philharmonic Orchestra, Pretoria, Orchestra Nat. de Lyon, France, Upsalla Chamber Orchestra, Sweden. *Recordings:* Bach Concertos with Salvatore Accardo, Beethoven Music for Wind Instruments, Dvořák Serenade in D minor, Haydn Sinfonia Concertante, Vivaldi and Strauss Concertos, Mozart Concerto, Concertante K297b, Quartet K370, Serenades in E flat and C minor, Serenade (Gran partita), K361, Schumann recital (with Maria João Pires). *Current Management:* Frank Salomon Associates, 201 W 54th Street, Suite 1C, New York, NY 10019, USA.

**BOYD, James;** Violist; b. 1960, England. *Education:* Studied at the Yehudi Menuhin School, Guildhall School of Music and the Menuhin Academy in Gstaad. *Career:* Debut: South Bank, London premiere of Robert Simpson's 13th Quartet; BBC Radio 3 debut in 1991; Frequent tours with the Rafael Ensemble; Co-founder of Vellinger String Quartet in 1990; Participated in masterclasses with the Borodin Quartet at the Pears-Britten School, 1991; Concerts at the Ferrara Music Festival in Italy; Season 1992–93 concerts in London, Glasgow, Cambridge, Davos Festival, Switzerland and the Crickdale Festival in Wiltshire; Played at Wigmore Hall with works by Haydn, Gubaidulina and Beethoven, and at Purcell Room with Haydn's Seven Last Words. *Recordings include:* Elgar's Quartet and Quintet, with Piers Lane. *Honours:* Joint Winner of the Bernard Shore Viola Prize, 1988. *Address:* Vellinger String Quartet, c/o Georgina Ivor Associates, 66 Alderbrook Road, London SW12 8 AB, England.

**BOYDE, Andreas;** German pianist; b. 13 Nov. 1967, Oschatz. *Education:* Spezialschule and Musikhochschule, Dresden, Guildhall School of Music and Drama, London, masterclasses at Musikfestwochen Luzern. *Career:* debut with Berlin Symphony Orchestra 1989; concerts with Dresden Philharmonic Orchestra 1992, 1996; recital, Munich Philharmonic Hall, Gasteig 1992; Festival La Roque d'Antheron, France 1993; concert, Zürich Tonhalle with Zürich Chamber Orchestra 1994; concerts with Freiburg Philharmonic Orchestra 1994, 1997, 1999; Dresden State Orchestra 1994, 1995; recitalist in Schumann Cycle, Düsseldorf 1995; South American debut, recital in Teatro Municipal Santiago, Chile 1996; concert, Munich Herkulessaal, with Munich Symphony 1997; concert tour with Northwest German Philharmonic Orchestra 1997; recital, Munich Prinzregenten Theatre 1997; concert tour with Odessa Philharmonic Orchestra, including Cologne Philharmonic Hall and Stuttgart Liederhalle 1997; recital, Dresdner Musikfestspiele 1998; gave European premiere of piano concerto, Four Parables by Schoenfield with Dresdner Sinfoniker 1998; concerts with Hallè Philharmonic 1999, 2004; Schumann recital tour including own reconstruction of Schubert Variations in New York, Germany, London Wigmore Hall 2000; world premiere of piano concerto by John Pickard with Dresdner Sinfoniker 2000; concerts with Konzertsaal KKL Lucerne with Lucerne Symphony Orchestra 2000; concerts with Bamberger Symphoniker 2000, 2001; concert tour with Nat. Symphony Orchestra of Ukraine in the UK 2001; concert with Bournemouth Symphony Orchestra 2001; frequent broadcasts with most German radio stations and the BBC. *Recordings include:* Schumann, Tchaikovsky, Mussorgsky, Ravel, Dvořák, Schoenfield, Brahms and Rachmaninov. *Publications:* Robert Schumann, Variationen über ein Thema von Schubert, reconstructed score by Andreas Boyde 2000. *Current Management:* Künstlersekretariat A. Schoerke, Grazer Strasse 30, 30519 Hanover, Germany.

**BOYKAN, Martin,** BA, MM; American composer; *Irving G. Fine Professor of Music, Brandeis University*; b. 12 April 1931, New York; m. Susan Schwalb 1983. *Education:* Berkshire Music Center, Tanglewood, Univ. of Zürich, Harvard Univ., Yale Univ. *Career:* composer-in-residence, Composer's Conference, Wellesley 1987, Warebrook Festival 1998, Abravanel Distinguished Composer, Salt Lake City 2001; Visiting Prof. of Composition, Columbia Univ. 1988–89, New York Univ. 1993, 1999–2000; currently Irving G. Fine Prof. of Music, Brandeis Univ. *Compositions:* Psalm 126, 1965; String Quartets Nos 1, 1967, 2, 1972, 3, 1988; Concerto for 13 Players, 1971; Piano Trio, 1976; Elegy for soprano and 6 instruments, 1982; Epithalamion, 1985; Shalom Rav, 1987; Fantasy-Sonata for piano, 1987; Symphony No. 1, 1989; Piano sonata No. 2, Nocturne for cello, piano and percussion; Eclogue for 5 instruments, 1991; Echoes of Petrarch, for flute, clarinet and piano, 1992; Voyages for Soprano and piano, 1992; Sonata for cello and piano, 1992; Sea-Gardens for soprano and piano, 1993; Impromptu for violin solo, 1993; Three Psalms for soprano and piano, 1993; Pastorale for piano, 1993; Sonata for violin and piano, 1994; Maariv Settings for chorus and organ, 1995; City of Gold for flute solo, 1996; String Quartet No. 4, 1996; 3 Shakespeare's Songs for Women's Chorus, 1996; Piano Trio No. 2, 1997; Psalm 121, for soprano and string quartet, 1997; Usurpations for piano solo, 1997; Sonata for violin solo, 1998; Flume for clarinet and piano, 1999; Romanza for flute and piano, 1999; A Packet for Susan, 5 songs for voice and piano, 2000; Motet–Al Mishkavi for mezzo-soprano and consort of viols, 2001; Songlines for flute, clarinet, violin, cello; Concerto for violin and orchestra 2003; Second Chances, songs for mezzo-soprano and piano 2005. *Recordings:* String Quartets Nos 1 and 2; Elegy and Epithalamion; String Quartet No. 4; Piano Trio No. 2; City of Gold; Echoes of Petrarch; Sonata for violin and piano; Sonata for solo violin; A Packet for Susan; Flume. *Publications:* Quartets, Nos 1, 3, 4, 1987; Fantasy-Sonata, 1992; Piano Sonata No. 2, 1995; Sonata for cello; Echoes of Petrarch; Impromptu for violin solo; Sonata for violin and piano; City of Gold; Psalm 126; String Quartet No. 2; Piano Trio No. 1; Sonata for Solo Violin, 2000, Usurpations for Piano, 2004, Piano Trio No. 2; Silence and Slow Time: Studies in Musical Narrative, 2004. *Honours:* Rockefeller Award 1974, Fromm Foundation Commission Award 1976, National Endowment for the Arts Grant 1983, winner National Competition of International Society for Contemporary Music 1984, Guggenheim Fellowship 1984, Serge Koussevitzky Music Foundation Grant 1985, American Acad. and National Inst. of Arts and Letters Awards 1986, 1988, Sr Fulbright Lecturer Bar-Ilan Univ. (Israel) 1994. *Address:* Brandeis University, Waltham, MA 02454 (office); 10 Winsor Avenue, Watertown, MA 02472, USA (home). *Telephone:* (781) 736-3337 (office); (617) 926-0188 (home). *E-mail:* boykan@brandeis.edu (office).

**BOYLAN, Orla;** Irish singer (soprano); b. Sept. 1971, Dublin. *Education:* studied in Dublin and Milan, Italy, masterclasses with Leyla Gencer, Robert Kettleson and Renata Scotto). *Career:* concerts include Mozart's Requiem, Coronation Mass and Mass in C minor, Weill's Street Scenes, Orff's Carmina Burana, Messiah, Verdi's Requiem and Rossini's Petite Messe, premiere of Barry's Bitter Tears of Petra von Kant; RTE production of Mendelssohn's A Midsummer Night's Dream and Strauss's Four Last Songs with the Wexford Symphonia; song recitals at the Salle Cortot, Paris, and throughout Ireland; season 1996–97 with Mozart's Fiordiligi in Milan, the C Minor Mass in Liverpool and Dublin and concerts with the RTE Concert Orchestra; season 1997–98, leading roles in Falstaff, Turn of the Screw, Nozze di Figaro, Eugene Onegin; Sang Celia in Mozart's Lucio Silla, Opera for Europe 1998; appearances in The Rape of Lucretia and The Valkyrie; title role in Die Liebe der Danae, Jenůfa at Glyndebourne Opera. *Honours:* winner Veronica Dunne Bursary 1995, prize winner European Operatic Singing Competition, La Scala 1996, Belvedere Int. Singing Competition Graz and Klagenfurt special prizes, Vienna 1996, Austrian Theatre Ibla Grand Prize. *Current Management:* Harrison/Parrott Ltd, 12 Penzance Place, London, W11 4PA, England. *Telephone:* (20) 7229 9166 (office). *Fax:* (20) 7221 5042 (office). *Website:* www.harrisonparrott.com (office).

**BOYLAN, Patricia;** Singer (Mezzo-Soprano); b. 1945, London, England. *Education:* Trinity College of Music; National Opera School; London Opera Centre. *Career:* English Opera Group with tours in Britten's operas under the composer to Russia; Appearances with Scottish Opera in Peter Grimes and Die Walküre, concerts and oratorios throughout the United Kingdom, including the Aldeburgh and Edinburgh Festivals; After raising her family returned to the concert hall in such works as Beethoven's Ninth and Mass in C, Mozart's C minor Mass and Requiem, the Verdi Requiem and Mahler's Kindertotenlieder; Sang in El Amor Brujo at the Manuel de Falla Festival in Seville; Operatic appearances as Larina in Eugene Onegin in Lisbon, Azucena in Madrid, Orpheus, Carmen and Amneris at Malaga; Sang Clytemnestra in Elektra for Welsh National Opera in 1992 and Auntie in Peter Grimes for Scottish Opera, 1993; Witch in Hansel and Gretel at Belfast, 1998. *Address:* c/o Opera Northern Ireland, 35 Talbot Street, Belfast, Northern Ireland, BT1 2LD.

**BOZARTH, George S.;** Historical Musicologist; b. 28 Feb. 1947, Trenton, New Jersey, USA. *Education:* MFA 1973, PhD 1978, Princeton University. *Career:* Professor of Music, University of Washington; Executive Director of the American Brahms Society; Director of Brahms Archive, Seattle, WA; Director of International Brahms Conference, Washington DC, 1983; Performer on historical pianos of late 18th through mid-19th centuries; Member of The Classical Consort; Co-Artistic Director of Gallery Concerts in Seattle. *Publications:* Editions: Johannes Brahms, Orgelwerke, The Organ

Works, Munich, G Henle, 1988, J. S. Bach, Cantata, Ach Gott vom Himmel sieh darein, BWV2, Neue Bach Ausgabe, 1/16, 1981, 1984; The Brahms-Keller Correspondence, 1996; Facsimile editions of Brahms' manuscripts; Editor of Brahms Studies: Analytical and Historical Perspectives, 1990. *Contributions:* Numerous articles on Brahms' Lieder and Duets, the genesis and chronology of Brahms' works, Brahms' piano sonatas and First Piano Concerto, editorial problems and questions of authenticity, Brahms' piano and piano music; performance practice in Brahms' late chamber music. *Address:* School of Music, Box 353450, University of Washington, Seattle, WA 98195-3450, USA. *E-mail:* brahms@u.washington.edu.

**BOZIC, Darijan;** Composer; b. 29 April 1933, Slavonski Brod, Yugoslavia. *Education:* Composition and Conducting, Ljubljana Academy of Music, 1958, 1961; Further study in London and Paris. *Career:* Conductor and Director of Studies, Slovene Opera, 1968–70; Conductor and Artistic Director, Slovenia Philharmonic, 1970–74; Professor, University of Ljubljana, 1980–94, University of Maribor, 1988–95; Director of SNG Opera, Ljubljana, 1995. *Compositions include:* Stage Works: La Bohème, 57, Opera, 1958; La Putain Respecteuse, Opera after Sartre, 1960; Iago, Happening for 8 performers and tape after Shakespeare, 1968; Ares-Eros Musical Drama after Aristophanes, 1970; Lysistrata 75, Operatic Farce after Aristophanes; Kralj Lear, Music Drama after Shakespeare, 1985; Telmah, Music Drama after Shakespeare; Bolt's A Man for All Seasons, 1990; 2 Symphonies, 1965, 1994; Concerto for Two, 1994; Piece of Music for Gerry Mulligan, for 5 saxophones and computer, 1996. *Address:* c/o Slovensko Narodno Gledaslisce, Zupanciceva 1, 61000 Ljubljana, Slovenia.

**BRABBINS, Martyn;** British conductor; *Artistic Director, Cheltenham International Festival of Music*; b. 1959, England. *Education:* Goldsmiths' Coll., London and Leningrad Conservatoire with Ilya Musin. *Career:* from 1988 appearances with most leading chamber and symphony orchestras in the UK, including all the BBC Orchestras (BBC Scottish at the 1997 Edinburgh Festival); further festival engagements at Lichfield (Philharmonia Orchestra), Windsor, Cheltenham, Bath, Aldeburgh, Three Choirs and St Magnus Proms, annually since 1993; guest with the St Petersburg Philharmonic Orchestra, North German Radio Symphony Orchestra and Orchestra of Gran Canaria; tour with Australia Youth Orchestra 1995; tour of Russia with Sinfonia 21 1996, Contemporary Music Network tour of the UK 1997; opera includes Don Giovanni at the Kirov, Magic Flute for ENO, Schreker's Der ferne klang for Opera North, From Morning to Midnight for ENO and Alice in Wonderland for Netherlands Opera; Assoc. Principal Conductor BBC Scottish Symphony Orchestra, Principal Conductor of Sinfonia 21 and Conducting Consultant at the Royal Scottish Acad.; premiere recording of Die Kathrin by Korngold with BBC Concert Orchestra 1997; season 1999 with Elgar's Enigma Variations at the London Prom concerts; conducted the BBC Symphony Chorus, the BBC Scottish Symphony Orchestra and Sinfonia 21 at the London Proms 2002; founder and Dir, Orkney Conducting Course (annual event) 2003–, coinciding with the St Magnus Festival; Artistic Dir, Cheltenham Int. Festival of Music 2005–. *Honours:* winner Leeds Conductors' Competition 1988. *Current Management:* Allied Artists, 42 Montpelier Square, London, SW7 1JZ, England.

**BRABEC, Lubomir;** Czech classical guitarist; b. 21 May 1953, Plzeň. *Education:* Conservatoire Plzeň, Conservatoire Prague, Royal Academy of Music, Early Music Centre. *Career:* regular appearances with Prague Orchestras; Has performed throughout Europe, USSR, North and Latin America; Many television and radio appearances, including two one-hour television recitals; mem. SAI. *Recordings:* Baroque Music: Bach, Handel, Weiss, Jelinek; Spanish Music: Torroba, Falla, Albeniz; Turina, Rodrigo; A Vivaldi–Guitar Concertos with Prague Chamber Orchestra and with Violist L Maly and Guitarist M Myslivecek; Arrangements: Satie, Falla, Prokofiev; Transformation II–Bach, Janáček, Mussorgsky, Marcello; Lubomir Brabec Live at Prague Spring Festival–Dowland, Bach, Villa-Lobos; Viola and Guitar, Italian Music with Lubomir Maly. *Honours:* Title, Laureate of the Concours International de Guitare, Paris, 1974; H Villa-Lobos Medal, 1987, from Brazilian Government. *Current Management:* Pragokoncert, Maltezske nam 1, 11813 Prague 1, Czech Republic.

**BRACANIN, Philip Keith,** MA, PhD; Australian composer; *Professor and Head, School of Music, University of Queensland*; b. 26 May 1942, Kalgoorlie, Western Australia. *Education:* Univ. of Western Australia. *Career:* Faculty, Univ. of Queensland 1970–, Prof. and Head, School of Music 1997–; comms from Univ. of Queensland and Queensland Symphony Orchestra. *Compositions include:* With and Without for small orchestra 1975, Trombone Concerto 1976, Selections from the Omar Khayyam for choir and strings 1979, Heterophony for orchestra 1979, Rondellus for string orchestra 1980, Because We Have No Time, song cycle for low voice and orchestra 1981, Clarinet Concerto 1985, Concerto for Orchestra 1985, Throw Me a Heaven Around a Child, for baritone and chamber orchestra 1986, Concerto for Orchestra No. 2 1987, Dance Poem for chamber orchestra 1990, Guitar Concerto 1991, Symphony No. 2 for soprano, SATB choir and symphony orchestra 1995, Symphony No. 3 1995, Eternal Images for soprano, clarinet, horn and piano 1998, Windmills of Time for string orchestra 2000, Blackwoodriver Suite for guitar quintet 2001, Clocktower for orchestra 2002, Blackwood River Concerto for guitar and marimba/vibraphone 2002, Shades of Autumn, concerto for oboe and chamber orchestra 2003. *Recordings:* Guitar Concerto, Clarinet Concerto, Violin Concerto, Symphony No. 2, Symphony No. 3, Dance Gundah Concerto for Didjeridu and Orchestra, Under Yaarandoo for Didjeridu, Guitar and

Orchestra. *Publications:* Symphony No. 2, 1998, Symphony No. 3, 1998. *Honours:* Australasian Performing Right Assoc Award 1995. *Address:* c/o School of Music, University of Queensland, St Lucia, Queensland 4072 (office); 50/12 Bryce Street, St Lucia, Queensland 4067, Australia (home). *Telephone:* (7) 3365-3502 (office); (7) 3371-9889 (home). *Fax:* (7) 3365-4488 (office). *E-mail:* p.bracanin@uq.edu.au (office). *Website:* www.uq.edu.au/music (office); www .bracanin.com (home).

**BRACEFIELD, Hilary Maxwell,** MA, DipMus, DipTchg, LTCL; music lecturer and critic; b. 30 June 1938, Briggs, Dunedin, New Zealand. *Education:* Univ. of Otago. *Career:* teacher Bayfield High School, Dunedin; Lecturer Worcester Coll. of Education; Sr Lecturer and Head of Dept Univ. of Ulster; currently part-time lecturer Univ. of Ulster and Open Univ.; mem. Incorporated Soc. of Musicians, Royal Musical Assoc (Vice-Chair), Int. Federation of Univ. Women. *Publications:* Contact Journal of Contemporary Music (part ed.), contrib. to Music and Musicians, Musical Times, Radio Times, BBC Radio; academic articles. *Honours:* Blair Trust Travelling Fellowship 1970–73; M.Univ ( Open Univ.) 1999. *Address:* 103 Monkstown Road, Newtownabbey, County Antrim, BT37 0LG, Northern Ireland (home). *Telephone:* (28) 9086-9044 (home). *Fax:* (28) 9086-9044 (home). *E-mail:* HM.Bracefield@ulster.ac.uk (office).

**BRACHT, Roland;** Singer (Bass); b. 1952, Munich. *Education:* Studied at the Munich Musikhochschule; Studied at the Munich Music College, under Professor Blaschke. *Career:* Debut at the National Theatre in Verdi's Don Carlos; Sang at the Munich Opera Studio from 1971; Member of the Stuttgart Opera from 1973, notably as the Commendatore, in the production of Don Giovanni which reopened the Staatsoper, 1984; Ludwigsburg, 1978 as Masetto; Schwetzingen Festival, 1983, in the premiere of The English Cat by Henze; San Francisco, 1985 in Der Ring des Nibelungen; Debut in the War Memorial Opera House in San Francisco, June 1985; Debut at the Metropolitan Opera as King Heinrich, 1986; Sang Pogner in Die Meister-singer at the opening of the new Essen Opera, 1988; King Heinrich at Pretoria, 1989; Sang Colline in La Bohème at Stuttgart, 1991 and Mustafà in L'Italiana in Algeri, 1996; Season 1998 as Mozart's Osmin, and Rocco in Fidelio; Season 2000–01 at Stuttgart as Wagner's Hagen and Philip II in Don Carlos. *Recordings:* Don Giovanni; Die Entführung; Das Rheingold; Die Zauberflöte; Oedipus Rex; Alceste by Gluck; Die Feen by Wagner; Video of Der Freischütz. *Current Management:* Robert Gilder & Company, 91 Great Russell Street, London, WC1B 3PS, England. *Telephone:* (20) 7580-7758. *E-mail:* rgilder@robert-gilder.com. *Current Management:* Opera Vladarski, Döblinger Hauptstraße 57/18, 1190 Vienna, Austria. *Telephone:* (1) 368-6960/ 61. *Fax:* (1) 368-6962. *E-mail:* opera.vladarski@utanet.at. *Address:* c/o Staatstheater Stuttgart, Oberer Schlossgarten 6, 7000 Stuttgart, Germany.

**BRADBURY, Colin;** Clarinettist; b. 1935, England. *Education:* Studied at the Royal College of Music with Frederick Thurston, graduating in 1956. *Career:* Principal Clarinettist of the BBC Symphony, 1968–93; Performances of Concertos by Mozart, Weber, and Nielsen at the London Prom Concerts and director of the RCM Wind Ensemble; Duo partnership with pianist, Oliver Davies from 1978 with performances and recordings of Italian operatic fantasias, sonatas by Reger, Victorian music and The Art of The Clarinettist; Tutor with the National Youth Orchestra of Great Britain. *Address:* Manygate Management, 13 Cotswold Mews, 30 Battersea Square, London SW11 3 RA, England.

**BRADLEY, Gwendolyn;** Soprano; b. 12 Dec. 1952, New York City, USA. *Education:* North Carolina School of the Arts, Winston-Salem, North Carolina; Curtis Institute of Music, Philadelphia; Academy of Vocal Arts, Philadelphia. *Career:* Debut: Nannetta, Falstaff, Lake George Opera, New York, 1976; Metropolitan Opera debut, Nightingale, L'Enfant et les Sortilèges, 1981; Appearing as Blondchen, Gilda and Offenbach's Olympia; European debut, Corfu Festival, Greece, 1981; Guest appearances with opera companies in Cleveland, Philadelphia, Central City, Amsterdam, Glyndebourne, Ham-burg, Berlin, Monte Carlo, Nice; Sang Rodelinda with Netherlands Opera, 1983–84 (also Sophie in Der Rosenkavalier); Paris Opéra 1986, Zerbinetta; Appeared as the Fiakermilli in Arabella at the 1987 Glyndebourne Festival; Deutsche Oper Berlin, 1989, as Musetta; Sang Gilda at the Wiesbaden Festival, 1990, with the company of the Deutsche Oper; Sang the Heavenly Voice in Don Carlos at the Deutsche Oper, 1992; Mozart's Blonde at Los Angeles, 1995; Season 1995–96 with Oscar and Nannetta at the Berlin Staatsoper; Pamina at Los Angeles, 1998; Deutsche Oper Berlin 2000, as Verdi's Oscar and Gilda; Many engagements as soloist with leading USA orchestras; Recitals. *Address:* c/o Columbia Artists Management Inc, 165 West 57th Street, New York, NY 10019, USA.

**BRADSHAW, Claire;** Singer (mezzo-soprano); b. 1970, Hull, England; m. Craig Ogden. *Education:* Royal Northern Coll. of Music, and with Barbara Robotham, David Pallard. *Career:* appearances, 1994– with Scottish Opera-Go-Round and Scottish Opera as Maddalena, Cherubino, Hansel and Dryad, and concert performances as Carmen for WNO; Spoleto Festival with Richard Hickox and in Vaughan Williams's The Poisoned Kiss with Hickox and the London Symphony Orchestra; concerts throughout the north of England at King's Coll., Cambridge (Messiah), with the Hallé Orchestra and in Western Australia and Provence; with Suzuki in concert (Royal Liverpool Philharmo-nic Orchestra) and recitals throughout the UK and Australia, 1997; sang Suzuki for WNO, 1998; Season 1999 included Lisetta in Il Mondo della Luna, 2nd Lady for WNO and a tour of South Africa with her husband, Australian

classical guitarist Craig Ogden, in recital and appearing with major orchestras; sang St Matthew Passion with Aalborg Symphony Orchestra, Copenhagen; Mercédès with WNO, 2000; Varvara in Katya Kabanova with WNO, 2001. *Honours:* Webster Booth/ESSO Award; James Gulliver Prize, Scotland. *Current Management:* Harlequin Agency Limited, 203 Fidlas Road, Cardiff, CF14 5NA, England.

**BRADSHAW, Murray Charles,** MMus, PhD; academic; b. 25 Sept. 1930, Illinois, USA; m.; two s. one d. *Education:* American Conservatory of Music, University of Chicago. *Career:* Prof. of Musicology; mem. International and American Musicological Socs, American Guild of Organists. *Compositions:* several organ compositions in The Organists Companion. *Publications:* The Origin of the Toccata, 1972; The Falsobordone, 1978; Francesco Severi, 1981; Girolamo Diruta Il Transilvano, 1984; Giovanni Luca Conforti, 1985; Gabriele Fattorini, 1986; Emilio de'Cavalieri, 1990; Giovanni Luca Conforti: Breve et facile, 1999; contrib. to Journal of Musicology; Performance Practice Review; The Music Quarterly; The Music Review; Studi Musicali; Musica Antiqua; Musica Disciplina; Tijdschrift. *Honours:* American Philosophical Soc. award 1987. *Address:* Department of Musicology, UCLA, Los Angeles, CA 90024, USA.

**BRADSHAW, Richard James,** BA; British conductor; *General Director, Canadian Opera Company;* b. 26 April 1944, Rugby, England; m. Diana Hepburne-Scott 1977; one s. one d. *Education:* Univ. of London, studied conducting with Sir Adrian Boult, Calouste Gulbenkian Fellowship to work with Royal Liverpool Philharmonic under Sir Charles Groves. *Career:* f. and Artistic Dir, New London Ensemble; Chorus Dir, Glyndebourne Festival 1975–77; resident conductor, San Francisco Opera 1977–89; Chief Conductor, Head of Music Canadian Opera Co. 1989–94, Artistic Dir 1994–98, Gen. Dir 1998–. *Recordings:* Canadian Broadcasting Corporation; Conductor: Rarities by Rossini and Verdi, plus chorus; French and Italian Arias, with Richard Margison; Soirée Française, with Michael Schade and Russell Braun; Recordings of Brahms, Bruckner, Verdi; Serata Italiana with Michael Schade and Russell Braun; Don Giovanni: Leporello's Revenge (Rhombus Media film soundtrack) with Dmitri Hvorostovsky. *Honours:* Order of Ontario, Canada 2005; Hon. DJur (Toronto) 2003; Opera Canada Award for Opera Builder 2003. *Address:* c/o Canadian Opera Company, 227 Front Street East, Toronto, ON M5A 1E8, Canada. *Website:* www.coc.ca.

**BRAEM, Thuering L. M.;** Conductor and Composer; b. 10 April 1944, Basel, Switzerland. *Education:* Basel University; Heidelberg University; Piano Diploma, degree in Conducting, Academy of Music, Basel; MA, Composition, University of California, Berkeley; Studied Conducting, Curtis Institute of Music, Philadelphia. *Career:* Director, Music School, Basel, 1973–87; Director, Lucerne Conservatory, 1987–; Music Director, Radio-Choir, Basel and Junge Philharmonie Zentralschweiz; President, Jeunesses Musicales, Switzerland, 1984–90; Principal Guest Conductor, Bohemian Chamber Philharmony, Pardubic, and others. *Compositions:* Lettres de Cezanne; Alleluja for Voice; Ara for Flute Ensemble (all Nepomuk-Verlag, AARAU); Chamber Music, Choral Music; Ombra for Violin, viola and String Orchestra, 1991; Torrenieri for Horn and Strings, 1992; Concerto for Piano Trio and Orchestra, 1992. *Recordings:* Children's Songs of the American Indians; Fauré's Requiem; Music for cello and Orchestra by Martinů, Fauré, Dvořák and Tchaikovsky; Panton, Orchestral Music with Young Philharmonic of Central Switzerland. *Publications:* Musik und Raum, Basel, 1986; Series, Information und Versuche, 1975–90, 20 Issues; Bewahren and Oeffnen, Aarau, 1992; Research and Development in Future Institutions of Higher Learning in Music, 1997. *Contributions:* Articles in newspapers and journals. *Honours:* Edwin Fischer Prize, 1992. *Address:* Lerchenstr 56, 4059 Basel, Switzerland.

**BRAITHWAITE, Nicholas Paul Dallon,** FRAM; musician and conductor; b. 26 Aug. 1939, London, England; m. Gillian Agnes Haggarty 1985; one s. one d. *Education:* Royal Academy of Music; Festival Masterclasses in Bayreuth and with Hans Swarowsky, Vienna. *Career:* Chief Conductor, Adelaide Symphony Orchestra, 1987–91; Principal Guest Conductor, 1977–84, Principal Con-ductor, 1984–91, Manchester Camerata; Chief Conductor, Tasmanian Symphony Orchestra; Permanent Guest Conductor, Norwegian State Radio Orchestra; Associate Conductor to Constantin Silvestri with Bournemouth Symphony Orchestra; Frequent Guest Conductor for all major orchestras in the United Kingdom; Toured Japan and Korea as Associate Conductor to Georg Solti with London Philharmonic Orchestra; Appearances with ORTF Orchestra, Paris; Oslo Philharmonic; Bergen Harmonien Symphony Orches-tra; Odense Symphony Orchestra; New Zealand Symphony Orchestra; Melbourne Symphony Orchestra; Sydney Symphony Orchestra; Danish Radio Orchestra; Bergen Festival; Symphony Nova Scotia, Halifax; Musical Director and Chief Conductor, Stora Teater Opera and Ballet Companies, Gothenberg, 1981–84; Musical Director, Glyndebourne Touring Opera, 1976–80; Associate Principal Conductor, English National Opera Company, 1970–74; Dean of Music, Victorian College of the Arts, 1988–91; Conducted Tosca at Elder Park, Adelaide, 1990; Francesca da Rimini for Chelsea Opera Group, 1994; Fledermaus for Scottish Opera, 1997; mem. ISM; MU. *Address:* Taringa Park, Mount Barker Road, Mahndorf, South Australia 5245.

**BRAMALL, Anthony;** Conductor; b. 6 March 1957, England; m. Elisabeth Werres. *Education:* Singing, Guildhall School of Music and Drama, London; postgraduate advanced conducting course. *Career:* Musical Dir, Southend Symphony Orchestra, Musical Dir, Southend Symphony Chorus, 1979–81; Asst to the Music Dir, Municipal Opera Pforzheim, Germany, 1981–85; House

Conductor and Head of Music Staff, Municipal Opera Augsburg, 1985–89; Guest Conductor, Southwest German Chamber Orchestra, Vienna Chamber Orchestra, State Opera Brunswick, State Opera Darmstadt; Conductor, RIAS Radio Symphony Orchestra, and debut in the Berlin Philharmonie, 1988; Senior House Conductor, Coburg Opera, 1989; Senior House Conductor, State Opera Hanover, and Guest Conductor with the NDR Radio Symphony Orchestra, 1990–95; debut, Semper Opera, Dresden, 1992; Music Dir, Opera Krefeld and Principal Conductor, Niederrhein Symphony, 1995–2002; Music Dir and Principal Conductor, Badisches Staatstheater, Karlsruhe, 2002–; recent productions: La Bohème, La Cenerentola, La Clemenza di Tito (Dresden), Elektra, Turandot, Der Rosenkavalier, Madama Butterfly, Parsifal, Falstaff, Flying Dutchman, Figaro, Otello, Tosca, Wozzeck. *Recordings:* albums with Slovak Philharmonic and the Slovak Radio Symphony Orchestra; radio broadcasts with RIAS Berlin, NDR Hanover and WDR Cologne. *Honours:* Special Prize for 20th Century Music, Third International Hans Swarowsky Conducting Competition.

**BRANDIS, Thomas;** Violinist; b. 1935, Hamburg, Germany. *Education:* Studied with Eva Hauptmann at the Musikhochschule Hamburg, 1952–57 and with Max Rostal in London. *Career:* Leader, Berlin Philharmonic Orchestra, 1962–63; Co-Founder, Brandis Quartet, 1976; Many Chamber engagements in Europe and Tokyo, with the Wiener Singverein and the Berlin Philharmonic; Festival appearances at Salzburg, Florence, Vienna, Edinburgh, Tours and Bergen; Has co-premiered the Clarinet Quintet by Helmut Eder, 1984, and the 3rd Quartets of Gottfried von Einem and Giselher Klebe, 1981, 1983; Solo Concerto work under such conductors as Karajan, Böhm, Solti, Abbado, Schmidt-Isserstedt, Keilberth, Jochum, Tennstedt, and Albrecht. *Recordings:* As soloist: Albums with Karajan and Böhm; With the Brandis Quartet: Complete quartets of Schubert and Beethoven with other repertoire for the EMI/Electrola, Teldec, Orfeo, Nimbus and Harmonia Mundi labels. *Honours:* Prize, German Hochschulen Competition, 1946; International ARD Competition in Munich, 1947. *Address:* c/o Konzert-Direktion Hans Adler (Brandis Quartet), Auguste-Viktoria-Strasse 64, D–14199 Berlin, Germany.

**BRANDSTETTER, John;** Singer (Baritone); b. 2 Oct. 1949, Wayne, Nebraska, USA. *Education:* Studied at the University of Nebraska and with Richard Hughes in New York. *Career:* Debut: Minnesota Opera, 1976, as Ben in Conrad Susa's Black River; Sang at Minneapolis in the premiere of Argento's The Voyage of Edgar Allan Poe, 1976; Has also sung in the premieres of Bernstein's, A Quiet Place, 1983, repeated in Vienna, 1986, as Josuke in Miki's Joruri, St Louis, 1985, and in The Balcony by Di Domenica, Boston, 1990; Season 1986–87 appeared as Enrico (Lucia di Lammermoor) at Seattle, Silvio (Pagliacci) in Detroit and as the Beast in the US premiere of Stephen Oliver's Beauty and the Beast, at St Louis; Sang Egberto in Verdi's Stiffelio at Sarasota, 1990, and the High Priest in Alceste at the Chicago Lyric Opera; Other roles include Mozart's Almaviva and Papageno, Figaro, Germont and Falke; Has also appeared at Düsseldorf, the City Opera New York, Miami and Philadelphia.

**BRANDT, Anthony;** Composer; b. 23 June 1961, New York City; m., 1 s., 1 d. *Education:* Harvard University, BA, 1983; California Institute of the Arts, 1987. *Career:* Assistant Professor of Composition, Rice University, 1998–; Visiting Lecturership, Harvard University, 1993–97; Tufts University, 1996; MIT, 1997. *Compositions:* Septet-à-tête for seven players, 1993; String quartet, 1994; Hidden Motives for two pianos, 1996; Octopiece for eight players, 1996; Songs for soprano and string quartet, 1997; Turbulent Tones for orchestra, 1998; Breathing Room for soprano and string orchestra, 1998; Piéce de Résistance for three trombones, piano and percussion, 1998; Creeley Songs for soprano and piano, 1999; Roman à Clef for cello and piano, 2000; Crucible of the Millennium, documentary film score, 2001; Four Shadowings - String Quartet No.2, 2001–02; Express for orchestra, 2002; Handful for piano, 2002. *Contributions:* Editor-in-Chief, Soundout Digital Press. *Honours:* Fellow, MacDowell Colony, 1996 and 1998; Composer in Residence, International Music Festival of Morelia, Mexico, 1996; Fellow, Tanglewood Music Center, 1994; Fellow, Wellesley Composers, 1993. *Address:* 5206 Cheena Drive, Houston, TX 77096, USA.

**BRANDUS, Nicolae,** PhD; Romanian composer, pianist and musicologist; *Professor, National University of Music, Bucharest*; b. 16 April 1935, Bucharest; m. 1st Maria Cecilia Ostrowska 1969; m. 2nd Ioana Jeronim 1982; two s., one d. *Education:* Nat. Univ. of Music, Bucharest, Cluj-Napoca Acad. of Music. *Career:* debut: pianist, George Enescu Philharmony of Bucharest 1955, piano soloist 1958–75; concert performances in Romania and abroad; soloist, Ploiesti Philharmonic Orchestra 1959–69; Prof., Nat. Univ. of Music, Bucharest 1968–81, 1992–; Ed. Muzica Review, Bucharest 1981–; compositions printed, recorded, played and broadcast on radio and TV in Bucharest and abroad; mem. Romanian Composers' and Musicologists' Union, SACEM, Paris; Pres. Romanian Section, Int. Soc. of Contemporary Music 1992–2002; Visiting Composer and Lecturer in Europe, Asia and USA. *Compositions:* ed and recorded: Pieces for piano 1966, 1984, 7 Psalms 1969, 1981, Mamsell Hus 1977, 2002, Dialo(va)gos, concerto for piano and orchestra 1988–2002: ed: 8 Madrigals for choir a capella 1968, Sonata for 2 pianos 1978, The Betrothal (opera) 1981, Languir me fais 1986, Rhythmodia 1989, Oratorio on texts of the Gospel of Thomas 1996, Melopedia and Fuga for piano 1998, Ostinato for piano solo 2004. *Recordings include:* Vagues 1990, Kitsch-N 1984, Antifonia 1986, With the Gipsy Girls (opera) 1988, Dance in Rhythms, Ak-Sak 1998, European Parody 2001, Oratorio on texts of the Gospel of Thomas 2001,

Phtora I – Durations 2001, 2nd Concerto for piano and orchestra 2002, Tabulatures 2002, Soliloque I 2004, Soliloque IV (Reverberations) 2004, Cnatus Firmus 2004, Match-Monodie and Polyphonie 2004. *Publications:* Interrelations (musical studies) 1984; numerous contribs to magazines and journals. *Honours:* Order of Cultural Merit (Bucharest) 1968, Officer 2004; Prize, Romanian Composers and Musicologists Union 1974, 2002, George Enescu Prize, Romanian Acad. 1977, prizes from Romanian radio and TV 1975, 1977. *Address:* Str. Dr Felix 101, Bl. 19 Sc. A Apt 42, 011036 Bucharest, Romania (home). *Telephone:* (21) 6507409 (home). *E-mail:* nbrandus@b.astral .ro (home). *Website:* www.cimec.ro/muzica/Pers/branduseng.htm (home).

**BRANSCOMBE, Peter John,** MA, PhD; British lecturer (retd) and musicologist; *Emeritus Professor, University of St Andrews*; b. 7 Dec. 1929, Sittingbourne, Kent, England; m. Marina Elizabeth Riley 1967; two s. one d. *Education:* Dulwich Coll., London, Worcester Coll., Oxford, Bedford Coll., London. *Career:* appearances on BBC radio and television, Austrian radio, Scottish television; Lecturer in German 1959–69, Sr Lecturer 1970–79, Prof. of Austrian Studies 1979–, Emeritus Prof. 1996, Univ. of St Andrews; Gov., Royal Scottish Acad. of Music 1967–73; mem. Scottish Early Music Consort (advisory cttee 1981–89), Royal Musical Asscn, MHRA, Int. Nestroy Soc., Internationales Franz Schubert Institut, Schubert Inst. (UK), Haydn Soc. of Great Britain, W. H. Auden Soc., Scottish Arts Council (music cttee 1974–81, council 1976–79), Conference of Univ. Teachers of German in Scotland (chair. 1983–85). *Publications:* Mozart and his World in Contemporary Pictures (trans.) 1961, Mozart: A Documentary Biography (co-trans.) 1965, Schubert Studies: Problems of Style and Chronology (co-ed.) 1982, Mozart: Die Zauberflöte 1991, Johann Nestroy Sämtliche Werke (ed.) Vols 35 1998, 36 2000, 37 2001, 38 1996; contrib. some 120 articles to New Grove Dictionary of Music and Musicians 1980, 2001, some 120 articles to New Grove Dictionary of Opera 1992, contrib. to various professional journals. *Address:* 32 North Street, St Andrews, Fife KY16 9AQ, Scotland.

**BRANT, Henry (Dreyfus);** Composer; b. 15 Sept. 1913, Montreal, Quebec, Canada. *Education:* Studied at McGill Conservatorium, Montreal, 1926–29, the Institute of Musical Art and The Juilliard School in New York, 1932–34; Private study with Wallingford Riegger, Aaron Copland, George Antheil and Fritz Mahler. *Career:* Worked for Radio, Films, Jazz Groups and Ballets as Composer, Conductor and Arranger; Commercial music in Hollywood and Europe; Teacher at Columbia University, 1945–52, The Juilliard School, 1947–54 and Bennington College, 1957–80; Performer on Wind and Percussion Instruments; Music has employed spatial separation with variously contrasted instrumental and vocal groups. *Compositions include:* Antiphony I for 5 Orchestral Groups, 1953, revised 1968; Ceremony, Triple Concerto for violin, oboe and cello with voices, 1954; Labyrinth I (strings) and II for winds, 1955; The Grand Universal Circus, spatial opera, 1956; Conclave for Mezzo, Baritone and Instrumental ensemble, 1955; On the Nature of Things, for chamber orchestra, 1956; The Children's Hour for Voices, Brass, Organ and Percussion, 1958; Atlantis, Antiphonal Symphony, 1960; Violin Concerto with Lights, 1961; Fire in Cities, for 2 choirs and 2 instrumental ensembles, 1961; Odyssey–Why Not? for 2 Flutes and 4 small orchestral groups, 1965; Verticals Ascending for 2 wind ensembles, 1967; Windjammer for 5 Wind Instruments, 1969; An American Requiem, for wind orchestra, 1973; Divinity: Dialogues in the Form of Secret Portraits, spatial chamber music, 1973; Six Grand Pianos Bash Plus Friends, 1974; Solomon's Gardens for Voices, 24 Handbells and 3 Instruments. 1974; Homage to Ives, for baritone and orchestral groups, 1975; American Commencement for 2 Brass and percussion groups; Antiphonal Responses, for 3 bassoons and orchestra, 1978; Cerberus, for double bass and piccolo, 1978; The $1,000,000 Confessions for 2 Trumpets and 3 Trombones, 1978; Trinity of Spheres for 3 orchestral groups, 1978; Orbits for 80 Trombones, Soprano and Organ, 1979; The Glass Pyramid, spatial fantasy, 1980; Inside Track, spatial piano concerto, 1980; The Secret Calendar, spatial chronicle, 1980; Horizontals Extending, for 2 wind ensembles and jazz drummer, 1982; Desert Forests for orchestral groups, 1983; Litany of Tides for Solo Violin, 2 orchestras and 4 Voices, 1983; Meteor Farm, spatial oratorio, 1983; Fire under Water, multiple improvisations, 1983; Burning Brant on the Amstel, mobile spatial aquatic spectacle, 1984; Western Springs for 2 orchestras, 2 choruses and 2 jazz combos, 1984; More recent compositions include: Pathways to Security, ambulant spatial cantata, 1990; Prisons of the Mind, spatial symphony for 8 orchestral groups, 1990; Skull and Bones, spatial oratorio, 1991; Hidden Hemisphere, spatial assembly for 4 concert bands, 1992; Fourscore, 4 spatial string quartet including tenor-cello, 1993; Homeless People, spatial string quartet with percussion inside piano, 1993; Trajectory, spatial cantata with silent film, 1994; Dormant Craters, for spatial percussion orchestra, 1995; Plowshares and Swords, total symphonic orchestral environment in 74 individual parts, 1995; Jericho for 16 trumpets and drums, 1996; Festive Eighty for concert band, 1997. *Address:* 1607 Chino Street, Santa Barbara, CA 93101-4757, USA.

**BRAUCHLI, Bernard;** clavichord player; b. 5 May 1944, Lausanne, Switzerland. *Education:* piano studies in Lausanne and Vienna, 1963–69; studied musicology at the New England Conservatory with Julia Sutton; researched Iberian keyboard music at Lisbon, 1977. *Career:* debut, Fribourg, Switzerland, 1972; US debut at Marlboro Coll., Vermont, 1973; numerous tours of Europe and North America with keyboard works of the 16th–18th Centuries, including works by Portuguese and Spanish composers; has given summer courses in Austria and Spain, 1978–82; Lecturer at the Boston Museum of Fine Arts, 1978–83; Prof. of Clavichord at the New England

Conservatory 1983–92; founder and pres. of the Festival Musica Antica a Magnano; mem. of programme cttee, Festival International de l'Orgue Ancien de Valère; hon. life mem. Midwestern Historical Keyboard Society; mem. Het Clavichord, Netherlands. *Recordings include:* The Renaissance Clavichord; 18th Century Portuguese Keyboard Music; 18th Century Music for Two Keyboard Instruments; Keyboard Works of Carl Philip Emmanuel Bach. *Publications include:* The Clavichord (Nicholas Bessarabof Prize 1999), 1998; contributions to many professional journals. *Honours:* Julius Adams Stratton Prize for Cultural Achievement 1983. *Address:* Associazione Musica Antica a Magnano, via Roma 43, 13887 Magnano, Italy (office); 19a ave des Cerisiers, 1009 Pully, Switzerland (home). *Telephone:* (015) 679260 (office); (21) 728-5976 (home). *Fax:* (015) 679260 (office); (21) 728-7056 (home). *E-mail:* mam@bmm.it (office); bbrauchl@worldcom.ch (home). *Website:* www.mam.biella.com (office); www.bernardbrauchli.ch (home).

**BRAUN, Lioba;** Singer (Mezzo-Soprano); b. 1963, Germany. *Education:* Studied with Charlotte Lehmann. *Career:* Appearances in opera at Karlsruhe, 1987–89; Vienna Volksoper, 1989–90; Vienna Staatsoper 1992–93, notably in The Ring, conducted by Dohnányi; Mannheim Opera from 1993, as Wagner's Fricka, Venus and Brangaene; Countess Geschwitz in Lulu, Dalila, Carmen and Azucena; Bayreuth Festival as Brangaene in Tristan and Isolde, conducted by Barenboim; Further engagements at La Scala (The Ring, from 1994), Dresden, Zürich, Rome (Waltraute in Götterdämmerung) and Tokyo (season 1999–2000); Kundry in Parsifal at Mannheim, 2000, and Mahler's 8th Symphony in Berlin; Other concerts at Leipzig, Amsterdam, Munich and Rome (Gurrelieder by Schoenberg); Season 2001–02 in Das Rheingold at the Vienna State, the Brahms Alto Rhapsodie in Dresden, Mahler's 3rd in Munich and Waltraute at Bayreuth, Brangaene at Barcelona, 2002; Festival appearances include the Semperoper of Dresden, Opera Leipzig, the Opera House of Zurich, the State Theatre Stuttgart, in Genova, in Rome and La Scala, performing with the Munich Philharmonic, the Viennese and the Bamberg Symphony Orchestras, the Leipzig Gewandhaus Orchestra, the Concertgebouw Amsterdam and the conductors Blomstedt, Barenboim, Abbado, Maazel, Herreweghe, Levine, Muti, Sawallisch, Stein and Sinopoli. *Address:* c/o Theateragentur Dr G. Hilbert, Maximilianstr. 22, 80539 Munich, Germany. *E-mail:* schmidt@hilbert.de. *Website:* www.hilbert.de.

**BRAUN, Russell;** Singer (Baritone); b. 1968, Frankfurt, Germany. *Education:* Studied in Frankfurt and Toronto. *Career:* Appearances with Canadian Opera as Mozart's Guglielmo and Papagaeno, Rossini's Figaro and in concert performances of Henri VIII by Saint-Saëns and Massenet's Cendrillon; New York City Opera 1992, as Morales in Carmen, Pacific Opera 1993 as Britten's Demetrius; Concerts include Messiah in Montreal, Belshazzar's Feast with the Hartford Symphony Orchestra and at Salzburg in Mozart concert arias; Season 1995–96 as Mozart's Count in Monte Carlo and at the Paris Opéra-Comique; Sang Borilée in Rameau's Les Boréades at the 1999 London Prom concerts; Season 2000–01 as Chorèbe in Les Troyens at Salzburg and Billy Budd in Toronto. *Current Management:* IMG Artists, Lovell House, 616 Chiswick High Road, London W4 5RX, England. *Telephone:* (20) 8233-5800. *Fax:* (20) 8233-5801. *E-mail:* artistseurope@imgworld.com. *Website:* www.imgartists.com. *Current Management:* Organisation Internationale Artistique (Bettina Brentano), 16 Avenue Franklin D. Roosevelt, 75008 Paris, France. *Telephone:* 1-42-25-58-34. *Fax:* 1-42-25-64-97. *E-mail:* oia@oia-poilve.com. *Website:* www.oia-poilve.com. *Current Management:* Columbia Artists Management, 1790 Broadway, New York, NY 10019-1412, USA. *Telephone:* (212) 841-9500. *Fax:* (212) 841-9744. *E-mail:* info@cami.com. *Website:* www.cami.com. *Address:* c/o Poilvé, 16 Avenue Franklin D. Roosevelt, F–75008 Paris, France.

**BRAUTIGAM, Ronald;** Pianist; b. 1 Oct. 1954, Haarlemmermeer, Netherlands; m. Mary Elizabeth Jane Cooper, 14 Dec 1995. *Education:* Sweelinck Conservatory, Amsterdam; RAM, London; Rudolf Serkin, USA. *Career:* Debut: Concertgebouw Amsterdam, 1979; Appearances with all major orchestras in the Netherlands; Foreign engagements include Oslo Philharmonic Orchestra, Bavarian Radio Symphony Orchestra Munich, English Chamber Orchestra; Salzburg Festival debut, 1992, with the Concertgebouw Orchestra under Frans Brüggen; mem, Ronald Stevenson Society, Edinburgh; Frank Martin Society, Netherlands. *Recordings:* Shostakovich, Concerto No. 1 (Concertgebouw Orchestra/Chailly, Decca); Hindemith, 2nd Kammermusik (Concertgebouw Orchestra/Chailly, Decca); Mendelssohn, piano concertos (Nieuw Sinfonietta Amsterdam, Markiz); Complete Piano Sonatas of W.A. Mozart and J. Haydn on fortepiano (Bis). *Honours:* Dutch Music Prize, 1984. *Current Management:* Marianne Brinks. *Address:* c/o Marianne Brinks, O.Z. Voorburgwal 72, 1012 GE Amsterdam Netherlands.

**BRAY, Roger,** MA, DPhil; British university teacher; *Professor of Music, Lancaster University*; b. 29 March 1944, Sheffield, England; m. Juliet Brown; one s. one d. *Education:* King's Coll. Choir School, Cambridge, King Edward's School, Birmingham, Magdalen Coll., Oxford. *Career:* Lecturer Univ. of Victoria, Canada 1968–70, Asst Prof. 1970; Lecturer in Music Manchester Univ. 1970–79; Prof. of Music Lancaster Univ. 1979–; mem. Royal Musical Asscn. *Publications:* Blackwell History of Music in Britain II, The Sixteenth Century (ed.), Robert Fayrfax, complete works I and II (ed.), Early English Church Music 43 and 45 (ed.); contrib. to Music and Letters, Early Music, Musica Disciplina, Proceedings of the Royal Musical Association, RMA Research Chronicle, Journal of Plainsong and Medieval Music Society. *Address:* Department of Music, Lancaster University, Lancaster, LA1 4YW, England (office). *E-mail:* r.bray@lancaster.ac.uk (office).

**BRAZDA, Josef;** Czech horn player; b. 12 March 1939, Babice u Rosic, Brno; m. Vlasta Brázdová 1974; 2 d. *Education:* private artistic school, Brno, State Conservatoire, Brno, Janáček Acad. of Musical Arts, Brno. *Career:* debut: State Philharmonic Orchestra, Brno; Prague Academic Wind Quintet; Prague Chamber Orchestra; Musici d' Praga-Chamber Orchestra; Haydn Sinfonietta Vienna; Solo concertos and sonatas; horn instructor. *Compositions:* Instructive Compositions for 2, 3, 4 Horns. *Recordings:* Richard Strauss, Horn Concerto No. 2; Paul Hindemith, Horn Concerto; Franz Danzi, Horn Concerto E Major; Paul Hindemith, both Sonatas; Joseph Haydn, Horn Concerto D Major, Hob VII; Joseph Haydn, Divertimenti, Baritone Octets, with Haydn Sinfonietta Vienna. *Honours:* 2nd Prize, IX Int. Musikwettbewerb, Munich 1960, 1st Prize, XV Int. Prague Spring Festival 1962. *Address:* Roklanska 1095, 25101 Ricany u, Prague, Czech Republic.

**BREAM, Julian,** CBE, FRCM, FRNCM; British classical guitarist and lutenist; b. 15 July 1933, London; s. of Henry G. Bream; m. 1st Margaret Williamson; one adopted s.; m. 2nd Isobel Sanchez 1980 (divorced). *Education:* Royal Coll. of Music. *Career:* began professional career Cheltenham 1947, London debut, Wigmore Hall 1950; has made many transcriptions for guitar of Romantic and Baroque works; commissioned new works from Britten, Walton, Henze and Arnold; tours throughout the world, giving recitals as soloist and with the Julian Bream Consort (f. 1960); many recitals with Sir Peter Pears and Robert Tear, and as guitar duo with John Williams; 60th Birthday Concert, Wigmore Hall, London 1993. *Honours:* Hon. DUniv (Surrey) 1968, Hon. DMus (Leeds) 1984; Villa-Lobos Gold Medal 1976, numerous recording awards. *Current Management:* Hazard Chase, Norman House, Cambridge Place, Cambridge, CB2 1NS, England. *Telephone:* (1223) 312400. *Fax:* (1223) 460827. *Website:* www.hazardchase.co.uk.

**BRECKNOCK, John;** Singer (Tenor); b. 29 Nov. 1937, Long Eaton, Derbyshire, England. *Education:* Birmingham Music School with Frederic Sharp and Dennis Dowling. *Career:* Debut: Alfred in Die Fledermaus, Sadler's Wells, London, 1967; Later repertoire includes Rossini's Almaviva and Comte Ory, Mozart's Belmonte and Ottavio and Verdi's Duke of Mantua; With the English National Opera at the London Coliseum sang in the British stage premieres of Prokofiev's War and Peace, 1972, and Henze's The Bassarids, 1974, and in the world premiere of Gordon Crosse's The Story of Vasco, 1974; Covent Garden debut 1974, as Fenton in Falstaff; Glyndebourne debut 1971; Has sung at the Metropolitan Opera and toured Canada in 1973; At the Teatro Regio Parma, 1985, sang Almaviva in Il Barbiere di Siviglia; Season 1985–86 sang Rossini roles in Paris. *Recordings include:* Alfredo in an English language Traviata, opposite Valerie Masterson. *Address:* c/o Teatro Regio Parma, Via Garibaldi 16, 43100 Parma, Italy.

**BREEDT, Michele;** Singer (Mezzo-soprano); b. 1962, Johannesburg, South Africa. *Education:* Studied at Cape Town University. *Career:* Debut: Mozart's Cherubino in Cape Town; Performances in Cologne, Brunswick and Oldenburg as Adalgisa in Norma, Zerlina in Don Giovanni, Meg Page in Falstaff; Tchaikovsky's Pauline and Bellini's Romeo; Other roles include Emilia in Otello by Rossini; Verdi's Flora; Hansel, and Lola in Cavalleria Rusticana; Idamante in Idomeneo for Pretoria Opera; Season 1997–98 as Diana in Cavalli's Calisto for the Vienna Kammeroper and as Nicklausse in Les Contes d'Hoffmann at Cape Town; Many concert engagements in South Africa; Season 2000–01 as Magdalena at Bayreuth, Charlotte at Innsbruck and Nicklausse for the Vienna Staatsoper. *Address:* Opera of the Cape, PO Box 4107, Cape Town 8000, South Africa.

**BREHM, Alvin;** composer, conductor and double bass player; b. 8 Feb. 1925, New York, USA. *Education:* Juilliard with Zimmermann and Giannini; Columbia University, MA with Wallingford Riegger. *Career:* Played double bass with the Pittsburgh Symphony Orchestra, 1950–51; The Contemporary Chamber Ensemble, 1969–73; The Group for Contemporary Music, 1971–73; The Philomusica Chamber Music Society, 1973–83; The Chamber Music Society of Lincoln Center, 1984–89; Conductor of Contemporary Music from 1947; Founder-Conductor of the Composers' Theater Orchestra, 1967; Teacher, State University of Stony Brook, 1968–75; Manhattan School of Music, 1969–75; and SUNY at Purchase from 1982; Dean of Purchase, State University of New York Music Division, 1982–92; Head of Composition, Purchase, 1992–; Member of Fulbright Composition Panel, 1992–95. *Compositions include:* Divertimento for Trumpet, Horn and Trombone, 1962; Dialogues for Bassoon and Percussion, 1964; Brass Quintet, 1967; Cello Sonata, 1974; Concertino for Violin and Strings, 1975; Quarks for flute, Bassoon, String Quartet and Piano, 1976; Sextet for Piano and Strings, 1976; Piano Concerto, 1977; Double Bass Concerto, 1982; Tuba Concerto, 1982; Sextet for Woodwind Quintet and Piano, 1984; Children's Games for Flute, Clarinet, String Trio and Piano, 1985; Cialles for Russian Town, piano, 1993; Metamorphy, European Tour, piano; Lament for the Victims of AIDS for string quartet, 1996. *Recordings:* Cycle of Songs to Poems of Lorca, for soprano and 10 instruments; Quintet for Brass; Bassoon Quartet; 3 works for piano. *Contributions:* Clavier magazine, cover articles; American Record Guide, reviews. *Honours:* Grants: Naumburg Foundation, NEA, New York State Arts Council.

**BRELL, Mario;** German fmr singer (tenor); b. 1936, Hamburg. *Education:* studied at Hamburg. *Career:* sang operetta at Hof 1963–65, Lucerne 1965–67, Oldenburg 1967–71, Krefeld 1971–73, Gelsenkirchen 1973–82; sang such repertory as Lohengrin, Parsifal, Zemlinsky's Zwerg, Hoffmann in Les Contes d'Hoffmann; mem., Deutsche Oper am Rhein, Düsseldorf from 1982, singing

Diomedes in Penthesilea by Schoeck 1986; guest appearances in Zürich, Frankfurt, Karlsruhe, Milan, Barcelona and Berlin (both Die Fledermaus), Cologne, Hamburg and Bilbao (all Lohengrin), Gothenburg (Hoffman's Erzählungen), Wiesbaden (premiere of Kirchner's Belshazar 1986), Antwerp (Ariadne auf Naxos), Barcelona (Fledermaus), Amsterdam (Busoni's Mephisto and in Alexander von Zemlinsky's Kreidekreis); Bielefeld as Bacchus in Ariadne auf Naxos 1990; other roles include the Count in Schreker's Irrelohe and Max in Der Freischütz; sang the major in Einem's Besuch der alten Dame, Gelsenkirchen 1991; Dortmund as Siegfried 1995; broadcasts include Dessau's Lukullus, Smetana's The Kiss, Nestroy's Tannhäuser-Parodie, Mahagonny. *Recordings include:* Der Zar lässt sich photographieren by Weill, Tannhäuser-Parodie by Nestroy. *Address:* c/o Deutsche Oper am Rhein, Heinrich-Heine Allee 16, 40213 Düsseldorf (office); Siegener Str. 29, 47533 Kleve, Germany (home).

**BREM, Peter;** Violinist; b. 1948, Munich, Germany. *Education:* Graduate, Richard Strauss Conservatory, Munich, 1970. *Career:* Berlin Philharmonic Orchestra, 1970–76; Co-Founder, Brandis String Quartet, 1976, with concerts in Tokyo, London, Hamburg, Munich, Paris and Milan and engagements with the Wiener Singverein and the Berlin Philharmonic; Festival appearances at Salzburg, Edinburgh, Lucerne, Tours, Bergen, Florence and Vienna; Has Co-Premiered the 3rd Quartets of Gottfried von Einem and Giselher Klebe, 1981, 1983, and the Clarinet Quintet of Helmut Eder, 1984; Solo concerts with such orchestras as the Radio-Sinfonieorchester Berlin. *Recordings include:* Albums in the standard repertoire from 1978 with the EMI/Electrola, Teldec, Orfeo and Harmonia Mundi labels; Recent releases of Beethoven, Weill, Schulhoff and Hindemith and the Schubert String Quintet with Nimbus. *Honours:* Prizewinner at the Deutsche Hochschulewettbewerb. *Address:* c/o Konzert-Direktion Hans Adler (Brandis Quartet), Auguste-Viktoria-Strasse 64, D–14199 Berlin, Germany.

**BREMERT, Ingeborg;** Singer (Soprano); b. 1930, Germany. *Career:* Sang at Pforzheim, 1953–55, Zürich Opera, 1955–57; Member of the Munich Opera, 1960–67; Schwetzingen Festival, 1961, as Elizabeth in the premiere of Henze's Elegy for Young Lovers; Many guest appearances as Mozart's Arminda (La finta giardiniera) and Cherubino, Eva, the Composer (Ariadne auf Naxos), Isabella in Krenek's Karl V and Regina in Mathis der Maler by Hindemith. *Address:* c/o Bayerische Staatsoper, Max Joseph-Platz, W-8000 Munich 1, Germany.

**BRENDEL, Alfred;** Austrian pianist and writer; b. 5 Jan. 1931, Wiesenberg; s. of Ing. Albert and Ida (née Wieltschnig) Brendel; m. 1st Iris Heymann-Gonzala 1960 (divorced 1972); one d.; m. 2nd Irene Semler 1975; one s. two d. *Career:* studied piano under Sofija Deželić (Zagreb), Ludovika v. Kaan (Graz), Edwin Fischer (Lucerne), Paul Baumgartner (Basel), Edward Steuermann (Salzburg); studied composition under A. Michl (Graz) and harmony under Franjo Dugan (Zagreb); first piano recital Musikverein Graz 1948; concert tours through Europe, Latin America, North America 1963–; Australia 1963, 1966, 1969, 1976; has appeared at many music festivals, including Salzburg 1960–, Vienna, Edinburgh, Aldeburgh, Athens, Granada, Puerto Rico, London Proms and has performed with most of the major orchestras of Europe and USA, etc.; numerous recordings, including complete piano works of Beethoven, Schubert's piano works 1822–28; mem. Acad. of Arts and Sciences (USA). *Recordings:* extensive repertoire; Beethoven's Complete Piano Works, Beethoven Sonatas, Beethoven Concertos (with Vienna Philharmonic Orchestra and Simon Rattle) 1998. *Publications:* essays on music and musicians in Phono, Fono Forum, Österreichische Musikzeitschrift, Music and Musicians, Hi-Fi Stereophonie, New York Review of Books, Die Zeit, Frankfurter Allgemeine Zeitung, Musical Thoughts and Afterthoughts 1976, Nachdenken über Musik 1977, Music Sounded Out (essays) 1990, Musik beim Wort genommen 1992, Fingerzeig 1996, Störendes Lachen während des Jaworts 1997, One Finger Too Many 1998, Kleine Teufel 1999, Collected Essays on Music 2000, Alfred Brendel on Music 2001, Augerechnet Ich 2001 (English edn The Veil of Order: In Conversation with Martin Meyer 2002), Spiegelbild und Schwarzer Spuk (poems) 2003, Cursing Bagels (poems) 2004. *Honours:* Hon. RAM; Hon. RCM; Hon. Fellow, Exeter Coll. Oxford 1987; Commdr des Arts et des Lettres 1985, Hon. KBE 1989, Ordre pour le Mérite (Germany) 1991; Hon. DMus (London) 1978, (Oxford) 1983, (Warwick) 1991, (Yale) 1992, (Exeter) 1998, (Southampton) 2002, Hon. DLitt (Sussex) 1981, Dr hc (Cologne) 1995; Premio Città de Bolzano, Concorso Busoni 1949, Grand Prix du Disque 1965, Edison Prize (five times 1973–87), Grand Prix des Disquaires de France 1975, Deutscher Schallplattenpreis (four times 1976–84, 1992), Wiener Flötenuhr (six times 1976–87), Gramophone Award (six times 1977–83), Japanese Record Acad. Award (five times 1977–84, with Scottish Symphony Orchestra/Sir Charles Mackerras 2002), Japanese Grand Prix 1978, Franz Liszt Prize (four times 1979–83), Frankfurt Music Prize 1984, Diapason D'Or Award 1992, Heidsieck Award for Writing on Music 1990, Hans von Bülow-Medaille, Kameradschaft der Berliner Philharmoniker e. V., 1992, Cannes Classical Award 1998, Ehrenmitgliedschaft der Wiener Philharmoniker 1998, Léonie Sonnings Musikpris, Denmark 2002, Ernst von Siemens Musikpreis 2004. *Current Management:* Ingpen & Williams, 7 St George's Court, 131 Putney Bridge Road, London, SW15 2PA, England. *Telephone:* (20) 8874-3222. *Fax:* (20) 8877-3113.

**BRENDEL, Wolfgang;** German singer (baritone); b. 20 Oct. 1947, Munich. *Education:* studied in Munich. *Career:* sang Don Giovanni in Kaiserslautern, 1970, then became a member of the Bayerische Staatsoper Munich; Roles include Papageno, Germont and Pelléas; Guest appearances in Hamburg,

Düsseldorf, and Karlsruhe; Metropolitan Opera debut 1975, as Mozart's Count; Sang Verdi's Miller with the Chicago Lyric Opera, 1983; Bayreuth Festival, 1985, as Wolfram in Tannhäuser; Covent Garden debut 1985, as Luna in Il Trovatore; Eugene Onegin and Donizetti's Enrico, 1988; Metropolitan Opera and Bayreuth Festival, 1989, as Germont and Wolfram; Teatro, San Carlos, Lisbon, 1989, as Amfortas; Chicago 1990, as Eugene Onegin; Other roles include Puccini's Marcello and Strauss's Mandryka; Season 1991–92 as Amfortas in Parsifal at La Scala and as Count Luna at Munich; Sang Verdi's Renato, 1994; Wagner's Dutchman at the Deutsche Oper Berlin, 1997; Sang the Count in Capriccio at the New York Met, 1998; Season 2000–01 as Amfortas and the Dutchman at the Deutsche Oper, Berlin, Strauss's Mandryka at Zürich and Munich, Barak in Die Frau ohne Schatten at Essen. *Recordings:* Die Lustigen Weiber von Windsor, Paer's Leonora and Der Freischütz (Decca); Die Zauberflöte, La Bohème and Zar und Zimmermann (HMV); Ein Deutsches Requiem (Deutsche Grammophon); DVD of Die Meistersinger, Deutsche Oper 1995 (Arthaus). *Address:* c/o Ingpen & Williams Ltd, 7 St George's Court, 131 Putney Bridge Road, London, SW15 2PA, England.

**BRENER, Uri;** Composer; b. 17 July 1974, Moscow; m. Ingrid Klüger, 19 Dec 1995, 1 s. *Education:* Central Special Music School, 1981–89; Gnessin College, Moscow, 1989–91; Robert Schumann Hochschule, Düsseldorf, 1991, 1994–96; Köln Hochschule, 1992–94; Sweelinck Conservatory, Amsterdam. *Career:* Concerts in Russia, Germany and Israel; Music to a short film; Form, Farbe und Licht, Fantasia for cello and piano, Reverie for piano, broadcast by Israeli classical music radio channel, 1998; Performances by the leading Israeli modern music performers as well as soloists; GEMA, 1996–; Israel Composer's League, 1997–. *Compositions:* Pieces for piano solo, Triptych, 1991; Aquarelles, 1990–97; Form, Farbe und Licht, 1995; Au debut et a la Fin, 1996; Aphorismes, 1997; Pieces for solo clarinet, Marimba, Cello, three vocal pieces, 1993; Sacrifice for soprano, violin and piano, 1990; Pieces for tuba, cello, clarinet and violin with piano; Chamber ensembles including string quartet, 1990; Wind quintet, 1991; Preludium, Fantasia and Fuga for 9 players, 1993; Three ballet scenes for 6 players, 1996; On The Other Side of Sound, 1998; Quartet for oboe, horn, cello and piano, 1998. *Recordings:* String quartet, 1997; Form, Farbe und Licht, 1998. *Publications:* IMC. *Honours:* Extraordinary Talented Composer, Special Committee of the Israeli Government, 1998. *Address:* Or Hachaim 1549/2, 87300 Ofakim, Israel.

**BRENET, Thérèse;** French fmr composer; b. 22 Oct. 1935, Paris; d. of Gen. François Brenet and Marguerite Warnier. *Education:* Paris Conservatoire. *Career:* Prof., Paris Conservatoire from 1970. *Compositions include:* La nuit de Maldoror for female voice, piano and cello 1963, Pantomime for flute 1974, Lyre d'etoiles for string trio with recitative 1979, Cristaux for Celtic harp and mandolin 1982, Odi et Amo for violin and orchestra 1992, Chimeres for mandolin and orchestra 1993, Le Retour de Quetzalcoatl for cello and orchestra 1994, Moires for six ondes martenots and strings 1985, Incandescence for baritone, saxophone and piano 1986, Vibration for Celtic harp and strings 1984, Oceanides for piano left hand 1986, Plus souple que l'eau for ondes martenot and percussion 1986, Au vent d'ouest for piano 2000. *Honours:* Premier Grand Prix de Rome 1965, Hon. Prof. Conservatoire Nat. Superieur de Paris. *Address:* c/o SACEM, 225 avenue Charles de Gaulle, 92521 Neuilly sur Seine Cédex, France (office).

**BRENNEIS, Gerd;** Singer (Tenor); b. 3 Jan. 1936, Nienhegen, Mecklenburg, Germany. *Career:* Debut: Essen, 1960, as Curzio in Figaro; Sang at Augsburg from 1965 as Verdi's Manrico and Gabriele Adorno, Idomeneo, Andrea Chénier, Lensky and Dmitri (Boris Godunov) and in operas by Wagner; Bayreuth Festival, 1973–74, as Walther and Siegmund; Deutsche Oper Berlin from 1974 as Wagner's Parsifal, Lohengrin and Tannhäuser, Strauss's Bacchus and the Emperor in Die Frau ohne Schatten; Huon in Oberon, 1986; Metropolitan Opera, 1976, as Walther; Has sung Tristan at Pretoria, South Africa, 1985, in Tokyo with the company of the Vienna Staatsoper, 1986, and Turin, 1987; Has also sung in Munich, Cologne, Florence and Milan; New York, 1976–81, as the Emperor; Nice Opera, 1988, as Siegfried; Television appearances include the title role in Wagner's Parsifal, with the Wiesbaden Opera; Deutsche Oper 1994, as Wagner's Erik. *Address:* Deutsche Oper Berlin, Richard Wagnerstrasse 10, 1000 Berlin, Germany.

**BRESNICK, Martin;** Composer; b. 13 Nov. 1946, New York, USA; 1 d. *Education:* BA in Music Composition, Hartt School of Music, University of Hartford, 1967; MA, 1968 and DMA, 1972 in Music Composition, Stanford University; Akademie für Musik, Vienna, Austria, 1969–70. *Compositions:* Trio for 2 Trumpets and Percussion, 1966; Introit, 1969; Ocean of Storms, 1970; Intermezzi, 1971; Musica, 1972; B's Garlands, 1973; Wir Weben, Wir Weben, 1978; Conspiracies, 1979; Der Signal, 1982; High Art, 1983; String Quartet No. 2 Bucephalus; One, 1986; Lady Neil's Dumpe, 1987; Trio, 1988; Pontousuc, 1989; Musica Povera, Nos 1–12, 1991–1999; String Quartet No. 3, 1992; Cadillac Desert, 1996; GRACE, concerto for 2 marimbas and orchestra, 2000; Songs of the House People, 1999; For the Sexes: The Gates of Paradise, solo piano and DVD, 2001; My Twentieth Century, chamber music, 2002. *Recordings:* B's Garlands; Conspiracies; 3 Intermezzi; String Quartet No. 2 Bucephalus; Wir Weben, Wir Weben; Lady Neil's Dumpe; Piano Trio; Just Time. *Publications:* How Music Works. *Contributions:* Mosaic; Yale Journal of Music Theory. *Honours:* Charles Ives Living Award, American Academy of Arts and Letters. *Address:* Yale School of Music, PO Box 208246, New Haven, CT 06520, USA.

**BRESNIG, Ulla;** Singer (Mezzo-Soprano); b. 1939, Germany. *Education:* Studied at the Graz Conservatory. *Career:* Sang at the St Gallen Opera, 1964–65, Trier, 1967–69, and Kiel from 1969 (notably in the German premiere of Milhaud's La Mère Coupable); Hanover Opera, 1969–76; Among her best roles have been Mozart's Marcellina, Erda, the Countess in Lortzing's Der Wildschütz, Octavian, Verdi's Fenena and Azucena, and Orzse in Kodály's Háry Janos; Many concert appearances.

**BRESS, Hyman;** Violinist; b. 30 June 1931, Cap, Canada. *Education:* Studied at the Curtis Institute and with Heifetz at Tanglewood. *Career:* Soloist with the Montreal Symphony, 1956–60, and has given many concertos and solo engagements in North America and Europe; Bach's D Minor partita at the Wigmore Hall, London; Premiered the Virtuose Musik by Blacher, 1968. *Recordings include:* Solo violin works by Ysaÿe. *Publications include:* An Introduction to Modern Music.

**BRETT, Charles,** MA; British singer (countertenor); b. 27 Oct. 1941, Maidenhead, Berkshire, England; m. 1st Brigid Barstow 1973 (divorced); one s. one d.; m. 2nd Cecile Bourasset 1999. *Education:* King's Coll., Cambridge. *Career:* leading performer with early and Baroque music ensembles led by Munrow, Harnoncourt, Leonhardt, Hogwood, Gardiner, Herreweghe and Malgoire; recent engagements in USA, France, Switzerland, Germany, Spain and Norway; Handel's Theodora, in Oslo; Israel in Egypt in Geneva; Bach's Christmas Oratorio in Versailles; Bach's St John Passion in Cambridge and London; B Minor Mass with Collegium Vocale Gent at Lourdes, Paris and Lyon; many concerts with Le Grande Ecurie et la Chambre du Roy, conducted by Malgoire; opera debut 1984, in Angelica Vincitrice di Alcina by Fux, at Graz; Handel's Semele at Ludwigsburg; tour of France with La Clemenza di Tito by Gluck; Aachen Opera 1987, as Oberon; founder and Dir, Amaryllis Consort (vocal group specializing in Renaissance repertoire); Prof., Royal Acad. of Music; masterclass in Canada, Belgium, Germany, Spain, Mexico, France; as conductor, performances of works by various composers in France; Dido and Aeneas for Cervantino Festival, Mexico 1995; Visiting Prof., Toulouse Conservatoire; mem. ISM. *Recordings:* Handel's Dixit Dominus, Rinaldo, Messiah, The Triumph of Time and Truth, Bach's B Minor Mass, Lambert's Leçons des Ténèbres, Mozart Masses, Bach's Cantatas, Burgon's Canciones de Alma, Italian and English madrigals with Amaryllis Consort, Vivaldi's Nisi Dominus and Stabat Mater, Blow's Ode on the Death of Mr Henry Purcell. *Honours:* Hon. RAM 1991. *Address:* c/o Royal Academy of Music, Marylebone Road, London, NW1 5HT, England.

**BRETT, Kathleen;** Singer (Soprano); b. 4 Sept. 1962, Campbell River, Canada. *Career:* Appearances with the Canada Opera Ensemble and elsewhere in Canada as Susanna, Bizet's Leila (Manitoba Opera), Adina (Calgary Opera) and Pamina (Edmonton Opera); European debut as Dorinda in Handel's Orlando at Antwerp, followed by Mozart's Barbarina at Covent Garden, Susanna at Monte Carlo and Amor in Gluck's Orphée et Euridice with L'Opera Française in New York; Other repertory includes Kristina in The Makropulos Case (San Francisco), Drusilla in Monteverdi's Poppea (Dallas Opera), Despina (Vancouver Opera), Zerlina, and Amarilli in Handel's Pastor Fido (at Toronto); Concerts include Messiah at Montreal, the Fauré Requiem with the Vancouver Symphony Orchestra, and A Midsummer Night's Dream by Mendelssohn; Season 1997–98 with Sophie in Der Rosenkavalier at Seattle, Pamina at Dallas, Nannetta in Falstaff at Los Angeles, Mozart's Servilia at Antwerp and Iris in Semele for Opera Pacific. *Honours:* Best Canadian Singer at the 1991 International Mozart Competition; Sullivan Award winner; Canadian Council Career Development Grant. *Address:* c/o Seattle Opera Association, PO Box 9248, Seattle, WA 98109, USA.

**BREUL, Elisabeth;** Singer (Soprano); b. 25 Aug. 1936, Gera, Germany. *Education:* Studied at the Musikhochschule of Gera and Dresden. *Career:* Debut: Gera 1958, as Donna Anna; Member of the Dresden Opera from 1960; Guest appearances in Berlin, Brussels, Brno, Łódź, Budapest, Genoa and Wiesbaden and music centres in Russia, France, Romania and Spain; Other roles include Tatiana in Eugene Onegin, Natasha in War and Peace, Marguerite, Tosca, Agathe, and Mozart's Countess and Susanna; Many appearances in the concert hall, in music by Bach and Handel; Teacher at the Musikhochschule of Dresden and Leipzig. *Honours:* Winner, Schumann Competition, Zwickau, 1973.

**BREVIG, Per A.,** BA, DMus; Norwegian conductor and fmr trombonist; *Music Director, East Texas Symphony Orchestra*; b. 7 Sept. 1936, Halden; m. Berit Brevig 1959; two s. two d. *Education:* Juilliard School; conducting studies Bergen, Norway 1963, 1964, Norrkoping, Sweden 1963, 1965, Hilversum, Netherlands 1964, The Juilliard School, New York, USA 1966–68, Leopold Stokowski Symposium for Young Conductors, New York 1966–68. *Career:* debut as soloist with Bergen Philharmonic Orchestra, 1961; principal trombonist, Detroit Symphony Orchestra 1966, Bergen Philharmonic Orchestra, Norway 1957–65, American Symphony Orchestra, New York 1966–70, Metropolitan Opera Orchestra, New York 1968–94; Music Dir and Conductor, Empire State Opera Company, New York 1990–; Conductor, Island Lyric Opera, New York 1993–2000; Music Dir, East Texas Symphony Orchestra; faculty mem., The Juilliard School, Manhattan School of Music, Mannes Coll. of Music, New York; Aspen Music Festival, Colorado; int. guest conductor for opera and symphonies; commissions and dedications include Roger Smith, Sonata for Trombone and Piano 1965, Alcides Lanza, Acufenos for Trombone and Four Instruments 1966, Egil Hovland, Concerto for Trombone and Orchestra, Noel Da Costa, Four Preludes for Trombone and Piano 1973,

Vincent Persichetti, Parable for Solo Trombone 1978, Robert Starer, Serenade for Trombone, Vibraphone and Strings 1982, Paul Turok, Canzona Concertante No. 2 1982, Walter Ross, Trombone Concerto No. 2 for Trombone and Orchestra 1984, Melvyn Broiles, The Great Northern Posaune for Trombone and Brass Ensemble 1989, Arne Nordheim, Return of the Snark for Trombone and Electronic Tape 1989; Guest conducts orchestras worldwide; Music Director of East Texas Symphony Orchestra 2002–; founder and Pres. of the Edvard Grieg Society Inc., New York; mem. advisory boards of Medical Problems of Performing Artists and Musikphysiologie und Musik Medizin. *Publications include:* Avant Garde Techniques in solo Trombone Music, Problems of Notation and Execution, 1974; Losing One's Lip and Other Problems of Embouchure, 1990; Edvard Grieg and the Edvard Grieg Society, 1993; Medical Problems of Musicians, 1995. *Honours:* Koussevitsky Fellowship, Henry B Cabot Award, 3 Naumburg Fellowships, Neill Humfeld Award for excellence in teaching, Royal Medal of St Olav, presented by Norwegian King Olav V in recognition of his efforts on behalf of Norwegian music and culture in the USA 1990.

**BREVIK, Tor;** Composer, Conductor and Music Critic; b. 22 Jan. 1932, Oslo, Norway. *Education:* Studied violin, viola and theory, Oslo Conservatory; Also Sweden. *Career:* Founded Youth Chamber Orchestra, Oslo, 1958; mem, The Society of Norwegian Composers. *Compositions:* Opera, Da kongen kom til Spilliputt, 1973; Adagio and Fugue for Strings, 1958; Overture, 1958; Serenade for Strings, 1959; Chaconne for Orchestra, 1960; Concertino for Clarinet and Strings, 1961; Music for Violin, 1963; Canto Elegiaco for Orchestra, 1964; Contrasts, chamber ballet, 1964; Elegy for Soprano, Viola, Double bass and Percussion, 1964; Divertimento for wind quintet, 1964; Adagio Religioso for Horn, 1967; String de Quartet, 1967; Concertino for Strings, 1967; Music for 4 strings, 1968; Intrada for orchestra, 1969; Romance for Violin and Orchestra or Piano, 1972; Andante Cantabile for Violin and Strings, 1975; Septet, 1976; Fantasy for Flute, 1979; Light of Peace, Christmas play for children, 1980; Viola Concerto, 1982; Sinfonietta, 1989; Choral music; Songs; Sinfonia Brevik, 1991; The Singing Raft, cantata for soprano, mixed chorus, children's chorus and strings, 1992; Music for Orchestra, 1993; Serenade for 10 Winds, 1994; On Request!, music for band, 1994. *Recordings:* String Quartet, Divertimento for Wind Quintet; Septet and Elegy for Soprano. *Address:* Nebbaveien 53, NB 1433 Vinterbro, Norway.

**BREWER, Aline;** Harpist; b. 14 Sept. 1963, Shropshire, England. *Education:* Royal College of Music with Marisa Robles. *Career:* Debut: Wigmore Hall, 1990; Principal Harp with the Royal Philharmonic Orchestra; Former member of the European Community Orchestra and the Britten-Pears Orchestra; Solo appearances with the London Mozart Players, Primavera and the Britten-Pears Orchestra; Duo recitals with flautist Jennifer Stinton; Member of the Britten-Pears Ensemble, with performances throughout the United Kingdom and the USA. *Recordings include:* Romantic music for Flute and Harp; Mozart's Concerto K299, with Jennifer Stinton and the Philharmonia Orchestra. *Honours:* Joint Winner, South East Arts Young Artists Platform. *Address:* c/o Owen White Management, 14 Nightingale Lane, London N8 7QU, England.

**BREWER, Bruce;** Singer (Tenor); b. 12 Oct. 1941, San Antonio, Texas, USA; m. Joyce Castle. *Education:* Studied with Josephine Lucchese at University of Texas, Austin, and with Richard Bonynge in New York and London; Further study with Nadia Boulanger and Rosalyn Tureck. *Career:* Sang as first in concert, notably in Baroque and early music; Opera debut San Antonio 1970, as Don Ottavio; Camden Festival, London, in Donizetti's Torquato Tasso, 1974; Sang at Opera Houses in Boston, San Francisco, Berlin, Paris, Toulouse, Spoleto and London, Covent Garden 1979; Aix-en-Provence Festival in revival of music by Campra; La Scala Milan 1980, in L'Enfance de Christ by Berlioz; Rossini's Le Comte Ory, 1991; Often heard in Bach and Mozart; Sang Lord Puff in Henze's English Cat in Paris, and in the premieres of Ballif's Dracula and Denisov's L'écume des jours; Paris Opéra, 1988, in the premiere of La Célestine by Maurice Ohana; Sang Fatty in Weill's Mahagonny at the Maggio Musicale, Florence, 1990; Truffaldino in Busoni's Turandot at Lyon, 1992. *Recordings:* Les Indes Galantes by Rameau; Rameau's Platée and Les Paladins; Messiaen's St François d'Assise; Rameau's Zoroastre; Boulevard Solitude by Henze; Beethoven's 9th Symphony; Berlioz's works for Soloists and Chorus; Les Nuits d'été; Gretry's L'Amant Jaloux; Liszt's Complete Songs for Tenor; Lully's Alceste; Offenbach's Orphée aux Enfers. *Address:* 1 rue du Courier, 53250 Couptrain, France.

**BREWER, Christine;** Singer (soprano); b. 1960, USA. *Education:* Studies in the USA with Birgit Nilsson. *Career:* Appearances with the Opera Theatre of St Louis as Ellen Orford in Peter Grimes, Ariadne, Donna Anna (also for Vancouver Opera, 1994); Sang Sifare in Mozart's Mitridate at the 1992 Mostly Mozart Festival in New York, Lady Billows in Albert Herring at San Diego and Vitellia in La Clemenza di Tito; Concert engagements include Szymanowski's Stabat Mater in Cleveland, the Vaughan Williams Benedicte in Louisville and Poulenc's Stabat Mater with the Leipzig Gewandhaus Orchestra; Beethoven's Ninth Symphony at Columbus and the Missa Solemnis at Washington DC and San Diego; Mendelssohn's Elijah with the Houston and Honolulu Symphonies; Recent engagements include the Mozart and Dvořák Requiems in Toronto, the Janáček Glagolitic Mass in Atlanta and at the Mann Music Center with the Philadelphia Orchestra under Charles Dutoit; Gretchen in Schumann's Faust at the Caramoor Festival; Donna Anna at Covent Garden, 1996; Strauss's Ariadne at Santa Fe, 1999; Schoenberg's Gurrelieder and Mahler's Symphony of a Thousand, at the London Proms,

2002; Sang in Le Roi Arthus by Chausson at the 2002 Edinburgh Festival; Sang Isolde in concert with the BBC SO, 2002–03. *Honours:* Winner, Metropolitan Opera National Council Auditions, 1989. *Current Management:* Askonas Holt Ltd, Lonsdale Chambers, 27 Chancery Lane, London, WC2A 1PF, England. *Telephone:* (20) 7400-1700. *Fax:* (20) 7400-1799. *E-mail:* info@ askonasholt.co.uk. *Website:* www.askonasholt.co.uk.

**BRIDEOAKE, Peter;** Composer; b. 23 April 1945, Adelaide, South Australia. *Education:* MMus, Adelaide University, 1971; Study with Richard Meale, 1969–71. *Career:* Faculty Member, Elder Conservatory, 1975–; Commissions from the Australian Chamber Orchestra, Seymour Group and Victoria String Quartet. *Compositions include:* Composition for Winds, 1971; Music for Flute and Percussionists, 1972; Gedatsu for guitar, 1972; Chiaroscuro, 1978; String Quartet, 1980; Interplay for 2 clarinets and harp, 1981; Imagery for string orchestra, 1981; Shifting Reflections for chamber ensemble, 1982; Canto for Clarinet Alone, 1987; A Poet's Lament for soprano and piano, 1988. *Honours:* John Bishop Memorial Prize, 1976. *Address:* c/o APRA, 1A Eden Street, Crows Nest, NSW 2065, Australia.

**BRIDGES, Althea;** Singer (Soprano); b. 11 Jan. 1936, Sydney, Australia. *Education:* Studied at the Sydney Conservatory. *Career:* Member of the Australian Opera Company, 1961–64; Sang in Europe from 1964, at first in Austria (Graz); Vienna, Theater an der Wien, in the premiere of Hauer's Die schwarze Spinne, 1966; Stuttgart, 1968, in the premiere of Orff's Prometheus; Landestheater Linz, 1971–83; Sang Tosca at Frankfurt and Donna Anna at the Glyndebourne Festival; Bari, Italy, as Ortrud in Lohengrin; Other roles include Strauss's Elektra and Marschallin, Marguerite in Faust and Azucena in Il Trovatore; Sang in the premiere of Michael Kohlhaas by Karl Kögler at Linz, 1989; Season 2000 at Linz as Baba the Turk in The Rake's Progress and Auntie in Peter Grimes. *Address:* c/o Landestheater, Promenade 39, 4010 Linz, Austria.

**BRIGER, Alexander;** Conductor; b. 1965, Australia. *Education:* Sydney Conservatorium; Richard Strauss-Konservatorium, Munich. *Career:* Assistant to Charles Mackerras at Edinburgh Festival including Fidelio and Figaro; Engagements with Opera Australia in Jenůfa, Madama Butterfly and Il Barbiere di Siviglia; Conducted Eclat/Multiples by Boulez and works by Birtwistle with Ensemble Intercontemporain; Season 2001–2002 with the Birmingham Contemporary Music Ensemble, Danish Radio Sinfonietta, Sydney SO and Scottish Chamber Orchestra; The Cunning Little Vixen at the Aix-en-Provence Festival, 2002; 2002–03 with the Hanover Band, Philharmonic, LPO, and Swedish Radio Symphony Orchestra, BCMG; forthcoming operqa includes productions for Opera Australia, Royal Opera House and Glyndebourne; 2004 symphonic debuts include Deutschland Radio, Berlin & Frankfurt Radio, Orchestre de Paris. *Honours:* Winner International Workshop/Competition for Conductors, Czech Republic. *Current Management:* Askonas Holt Ltd, Lonsdale Chambers, 27 Chancery Lane, London, WC2A 1PF, England. *Telephone:* (20) 7400-1700. *Fax:* (20) 7400-1799. *E-mail:* info@askonasholt.co.uk. *Website:* www.askonasholt.co.uk.

**BRIGGS, Sarah (Beth);** British concert pianist; b. 1972; m. 19 Nov 1994. *Education:* Studied with Denis Matthews at Newcastle, with John Lill, and Chamber Music with Bruno Giuranna at Blonay, Switzerland. *Career:* Debut: Fairfield Hall, Beethoven's 2nd Piano Concerto with New Symphony Orchestra; Many recitals and concerto performances throughout England and Scotland, Germany, Switzerland, Austria, France and USA; Int. radio and TV recordings; Chester Summer Festival, 1989, with world premiere of posthumous pieces by Benjamin Britten; London concerto debut at the Barbican, 1989, playing Mozart K453; Also plays Mozart's 20 other original concertos; Further engagements with the Royal Liverpool Philharmonic, Northern Sinfonia, English Chamber Orchestra, Royal Philharmonic, Northern Chamber Orchestra; Ulster Orchestra, Scottish Chamber Orchestra, Manchester Camerata and the London Soloists Chamber Orchestra; US debut, July 1991, in the San Francisco Stern Grove Festival with the Midsummer Mozart Festival Orchestra, conducted by George Cleve; Further visits to USA for concertos and recitals; Returned to Midsummer Mozart Festival, 1993; Queen Elizabeth Hall debut, 1992, performing 2 Mozart piano concertos with Manchester Camerata; Chamber music concerts including recent series at the Royal Coll. of Music, Manchester; Season 1997–98 included further concerts, Midsummer Mozart Festival, San Francisco, debuts with the Hallé and BBC Concert Orchestra; Formed Trio Melzi with leader and prin. cellist of Manchester Camerata, 1999; Trio debut at Bridgewater Hall, Manchester, 2000; Trio featured on BBC Radio 3 and BBC 2; Vienna Chamber Orchestra Dec. 2001. *Honours:* 1st Prize, Surrey Young Pianist of the Year Competition; 3rd Prize, BBC Young Musician of the Year, 1984; 1st Prize, Yorkshire Television Young Musicians' Awards, 1987; Hindemith Scholarship, 1987; Joint Winner, International Mozart Competition, Salzburg, 1988 (leading to engagement with Austrian Radio Symphony under Michael Gielen). *Address:* 86 The Green, Acomb, Yorks YO26 5LS, England. *E-mail:* enquiries@sarahbethbriggs.co.uk. *Website:* www.sarahbethbriggs.co.uk.

**BRIGHT, Colin (Michael);** Composer and Music Lecturer; b. 28 June 1949, Sydney, New South Wales. *Education:* Studied with Mary Egan, Linden Sands, Christopher Nicols and Ton de Leeuw (composition, 1982). *Career:* Lecturer for High School Music Teachers, from 1987; Commissions from Synergy, Seymour Group, Southern Crossings and Sydney Symphony Orchestra. *Compositions include:* Percussion Quartet, 1980; Earth Spirit for

orchestra, 1982; The Dreamtime for baritone and ensemble, 1982; Earth, Wind and Fire for saxophone quartet, 1982; Long Reef for string quintet and wind quintet, 1984; Midnight Tulips song cycle for soprano and large ensemble, 1985; The Sinking of the Rainbow Warrior, 1 act opera; Tulipstick Talk for percussion, 1985; Red Earth for 6 players, 1985; Music for contrabass octet and didjeridoo, 1986; Sun is God, string quartet, 1989; The Journey, opera, 1991; The Butcher's Apron for four percussion, 1991; Young Tree Green: Double Bass Concerto, 1993; War and Peace, vocal sextet, 1994; The Sinking of the Rainbow Warrior, one-act opera, 1994; Oceania, orchestral suite, 1999; The Wild Boys, 1997. *Honours:* 1 Act Opera Award, Australian Music Centre, 1986; Australian Music Centre, Best Composition, 1997. *Address:* c/o APRA, 1A Eden Street, Crows Nest, NSW 2065, Australia.

**BRILIOTH, Helge;** Singer (Tenor); b. 7 May 1931, Lund, Sweden. *Education:* Studied at the Royal Academy and the Opera School in Stockholm; Academia di Santa Cecilia, Rome; Mozarteum Salzburg. *Career:* In 1960 at Drottningholm sang the Baritone role of Bartolo in Paisiello's Il Barbiere di Siviglia; Bielefeld, 1962–64; Tenor debut as Don José, Stockholm, 1966; Bayreuth, 1969–75 as Siegmund and Tristan; Salzburg Easter Festival 1970 as Siegfried, under Karajan; Covent Garden 1970–, as Siegmund, Siegfried, Tristan and Parsifal; Metropolitan Opera debut 1971, as Parsifal; Glyndebourne 1971, as Bacchus in Ariadne auf Naxos; Drottningholm 1972, in the title role of Cavalli's Scipione Affricano; At the Royal Opera Stockholm, 1975 sang the Emperor in the Swedish premiere of Die Frau ohne Schatten; Sang at Stockholm in the 1986 premiere of Christina by Hans Gefors. *Recordings include:* Siegfried in Götterdämmerung. *Address:* Birger Jarlsgatan 79, 11356 Stockholm, Sweden.

**BRILOVA, Elena;** Singer (soprano); b. 9 Feb. 1961, Moscow, Russia. *Education:* Graduate, Moscow Conservatoire, 1986. *Career:* Sang in Concert, 1986–88; Bolshoi Opera Moscow from 1988 as the Queen of Shemakha, Antonida (A Life for the Tsar), Traviata, Rosina and other leading roles; Concert appearances as Constanze, Sophie, Oscar, Norina, Lucia, Amina and Leila (Les Pêcheurs de perles); Further engagements as the Queen of Night at Cologne and Vienna, Gilda in Oslo and Vienna; Palmide in Il Crociato in Egitto at the 1991 Ludwigsburg Festival; British debut, 1992, as the Queen of Shemakha with the London Symphony Orchestra; Season 1993 as Gilda at the Bergen Festival and in concert performances of Rigoletto at Tel-Aviv, conducted by Zubin Mehta; Concert engagements at Brussels and Frankfurt and with such conductors as Bashmet, Simonov, Rostropovich, Rozhdestvensky and Svetlanov; Sang in Berio's Outis at the Théâtre du Châtelet, 1999, and as Rossini's Elvira at Dusseldorf, 2001. *Current Management:* Athole Still International Management, Forresters Hall, 25–27 Westow Street, London, SE19 3RY, England. *Telephone:* (20) 8771-5271. *Fax:* (20) 8768-6600. *Website:* www.atholestill.com.

**BRINKMANN, Bodo;** Singer (Baritone); b. 7 Dec. 1942, Binder, Brunswick, Germany. *Education:* Studied at the Berlin Musikhochschule with Karl-Heinz Lohmann. *Career:* Debut: Kaiserslautern, 1971; Member of the National Theatre Mannheim from 1974; Staatsoper Hamburg in Lohengrin; Munich Staatsoper, notably as Escamillo, 1984, and in the 1986 premiere of Reimann's Troades; Guest appearances in Berlin, Paris and Strasbourg; Deutsche Oper am Rhein 1987, as Telramund; Munich Olympia Hall, 1987, as Prince Igor; Bayreuth Festival 1987–92, Kurwenal, Donner and Gunther; Sang Jochanaan in Salome at Barcelona, 1989; Cologne Opera 1990, as Wotan in Die Walküre; Düsseldorf 1995–96, as Wolfram and Wotan; Season 2000–01 as the Wanderer in Siegfried at Münster and Meiningen. *Recordings include:* Video of The Ring from Bayreuth. *Address:* c/o Oper der Stadt Köln, Offenbachplatz, 5000 Cologne, Germany.

**BRIZZI, Aldo;** Conductor and Composer; b. 7 June 1960, Alessandria, Italy. *Education:* Bologna University; Milan Conservatorio. *Career:* Debut: 1st appearance as Conductor, 1978; Conducted concerts in Europe, Israel, USA, Central and South America; Principal performances with Berlin Philharmonic Chamber Ensemble, The Cluj Philharmonic Orchestra; Santa Cecilia Chamber Orchestra of Rome, The Haydn Orchestra of Bolzano; Musical Conductor of the Ensemble of Ferienkurse, Darmstadt; Permanent Conductor of E M Ferrari Orchestra, Alessandria and Akabthos Ensemble. *Compositions:* Works performed by numerous European orchestras, ensembles and soloists including, Ecyo, Danish Radio Orchestra, Montepulciano Festival Orchestra, New Philharmonic Orchestra of Paris, Ens de Cuivres et Percussion de l'Intercontemporain; Works broadcast by 21 European Radio Stations, 2 USA and Israeli State Radio. *Recordings:* Salabert conducting the Arditti String Quartet Consort; Electrecord conducting the Bacau Symphony Orchestra; Edipan with Composition of A Brizzi. *Publications:* Proposte Musicali, 1980; La Musica, Le Idée, Le Cose, 1981. *Contributions:* numerous magazines. *Honours:* Venezia Opera Prima, 1981; Stipendiendpreis, Darmstadt, 1984; Young Generation in Europe, Venice, Paris, Cologne, 1985; Franco Evangelisti, Rome, 1986; Young Composers' Forum, Cologne, 1989; Artistic Director of Scelsi Foundation, Rome. *Address:* Via Boves 6, 15100 Alessandria, Italy.

**BRKANOVIC, Zeljko;** composer, conductor and academic; b. 20 Dec. 1937, Zagreb, Croatia; m. Ivanka Brkanovic 1964; one s. one d. *Education:* Zagreb Music Academy, Skopje Music Academy, Academia Chigiana Siena, Italy, High School Stuttgart, Germany. *Career:* debut with first string quartet in Zagreb, 1974; Conductor, Croatian National Theatre Opera, Split and Zagreb, 1963–69; Musical Editor on radio and television, 1969–80; Professor, Music Academy Zagreb, 1980–; mem. Croatian Composers' Soc. *Compositions:*

Nomos, Suite for Strings, Ricercari, Two Symphonies; Concerto for Violin; Concerto for Piano and Orchestra (Josip Slavenski Award, 1983); Concerto for Violin, Violoncello and Orchestra; Lyrical Concerto for Piano and Orchestra; Concerto for Percussion and 3 Clarinets (Ministry of Culture Award, 1997); Concert Rondo for Piano, Wind and Brass Orchestra; also chamber, piano and organ music. *Recordings:* Tonal Sonata, 1977; Divertimento For Strings, 1977; Concerto for Piano and Orchestra, 1981; Concerto for Violin, 1983; Antependium, 1989; Second Symphony, 1991; Figures, 1995; Song Book, 1996; Author CDs, 1996 and 2002. *Publications:* Professor Dr E. Karkoschka, Stuttgart, 1991; Bulletin/Croatian Composers' Society, 1992; contrib. to Schweinfurtische Nachrichten, Vjesnik Zagreb, Vecernji list Zagreb, Slobodna Dalmacija Split, Piano Journal No. 49 London, p 46, 1992, Cantus Zagreb, 2003; Frankfurter Allgemeine Zeitung, 2003. *Honours:* Vladimir Nazor Concert Award 2003. *Address:* Zagreb Music Academy, Trg kralja Tomislava 18, 10000 Zagreb, Croatia. *Fax:* (1) 4922260. *E-mail:* ivanka.brkanovic@inet.hr.

**BROAD, Daniel;** Singer (Baritone); b. 1967, England. *Education:* Chetham's School, Manchester; Royal Northern College of Music, with Robert Alderson. *Career:* Glyndebourne Chorus from 1996; Keeper of the Madhouse in The Rake's Progress at the Festival, 2000; Sang Rossini's Figaro at Aix and for Castleward Opera, Yamadori in Butterfly for Clonter Opera, Marcello at Holland Park and Sid in Albert Herring at the Perth Festival; Further engagements in Béatrice and Bénédict for European Opera Union and Eugene Onegin in Baden Baden and Paris; Other roles include Mozart's Count, Tarquinius in The Rape of Lucretia and Ping in Turandot. *Recordings include:* Anthony in Sweeney Todd, for Opera North. *Honours:* Peter Moores Foundation Scholar. *Address:* c/o Glyndebourne Festival Opera, Glyndebourne, Lewes, Sussex BN8 5UU, England.

**BROADBENT, Graeme;** Singer (bass); b. 1962, Halifax, England. *Education:* Royal Coll. of Music with Lyndon Van der Pump; Moscow Conservatoire with Evgeny Nesterenko. *Career:* performed in recital and oratorio throughout the UK and abroad, appearing at all the major London concert halls and at the Proms; repertoire encompasses 81 operatic roles and 47 oratorio and concert works, ranging from Monteverdi's Vespers to Schoenberg's Serenade Op 24; debut with Royal Opera, Covent Garden in Salome in 1997; sang in Palestrina at the Metropolitan Opera House on the Royal Opera's tour to New York; appeared with Royal Opera every season since; performed roles with ENO, Opera North and Scottish Opera; performed Judge/Hotel Manager/Duke in Powder her Face by Adès at the Aldeburgh and Almeida Festivals and Channel 4 television, Rossini's Stabat Mater with the Royal Liverpool Philharmonic Orchestra, Verdi's Requiem, at the Queen Elizabeth Hall, The Dream of Gerontius in Gloucester Cathedral; Beethoven's 9th Symphony at the Barbican; joined Royal Opera, Covent Garden as Principal Bass, 1999; roles for the Royal Opera include Nightwatchman in Meistersinger, Colline in La Bohème, Dr Grenvil in La Traviata, Angelotti in Tosca, Timur in Turandot, King Marke in Tristan, Leone in Atilla, Capellio in I Capuleti and King of Egypt in Aida; Glyndebourne Festival debut as Commendatore in 2000. *Current Management:* Askonas Holt Ltd, Lonsdale Chambers, 27 Chancery Lane, London, WC2A 1PF, England. *Telephone:* (20) 7400-1700. *Fax:* (20) 7400-1799. *E-mail:* info@askonasholt.co.uk. *Website:* www.askonasholt.co.uk.

**BROADSTOCK, Brenton (Thomas);** Composer; b. 12 Dec. 1952, Melbourne, Victoria, Australia; m., 3 c. *Education:* BA, Monash University, 1975. MMus, Memphis State University, USA; Diploma in Composition, University of Sydney; Composition with Peter Sculthorpe; AMusTCL, Trinity College of Music; DMus, University of Melbourne. *Career:* Tutor in Music, 1982–84; Senior Tutor in Music, 1984–87, Senior Lecturer in Music, 1989, then Associate Professor, Faculty of Music, University of Melbourne; Inaugural Composer-in-Residence, Melbourne Symphony Orchestra, 1988; Performances: Melbourne Summer Music Festival, 1985; Stroud Festival, England, 1985; Adelaide Festival, 1986; Spoleto Festival, Melbourne, 1986; Nova Festival, Brisbane, 1987; Music Today Festival, Tokyo, 1988; International Society for Contemporary Music World Days, Hong Kong, 1988, Oslo, 1990. *Compositions:* Symphony No. 3; 4 String Quartets; The Mountain for orchestra; Tuba Concerto; Piano Concerto; Battlements for orchestra; Woodwind Quartet; Aureole 104 for flute and piano; Solo Bass Clarinet; Oboe and Piano; Solo Piano; Beast from Air for trombone and percussion; Many works for brass band; Symphony No. 1, 1988; Symphony No. 2, 1989; Bright Tracks, soprano and string trio, 1994; Celebration for chamber ensemble, 1995; Saxophone Concertino, 1995; Dancing on a Volcano for orchestra, 1996; Catch the Joy, overture, 1998; I Touched Your Glistening Tears for oboe and piano trio, 1998. *Recordings:* Many works performed, recorded and broadcast by ABC; Fahrenheit 451, opera, 1992. *Honours:* Paul Lowin Prize, 1994. *Current Management:* G Schirmer, Australia. *Address:* 20 Simmons Street, Box Hill North, Victoria 3129, Australia.

**BROADWAY, Kenneth;** Duo Pianist; b. 1950, USA. *Education:* Studied at the Cleveland Institute of Music with Vronsky and Babin. *Career:* Formed Piano Duo partnership with Ralph Markham and has given many recitals and concerts in North America and Europe; BBC debut recital, 1979 and further broadcasts on CBC television, Radio France Musique, the Bavarian Radio and Radio Hilversum in Netherlands; Stravinsky's Three Dances from Petrushka at the Théâtre des Champs Elysées, Paris, 1984; Season 1987–88 included 40 North American recitals, concert with the Vancouver Symphony and New York debut on WQXR Radio; Season 1988–89 included the Concertos for Two Pianos by Mozart and Bruch in Canada and a recital tour of England and

Germany; Recent performances of the Bartók Sonata for Two Pianos and Percussion, with Evelyn Glennie and a 1990–91 tour of North America, Europe and the Far East; Festival appearances include Newport USA 1988. *Recordings include:* Duos by Anton Rubinstein; Vaughan Williams Concerto for Two Pianos; Bartók Sonata for Two Pianos and Percussion. *Honours:* Young Artist of the Year, Musical America Magazine, 1989 (with Ralph Markham).

**BROCHELER, John;** Singer (Baritone); b. 21 Feb. 1945, Vaals, Limbourg, Netherlands. *Education:* Studied with Leo Ketelaars in Maastrict and with Pierre Bernac in Paris. *Career:* Sang at first in concert, notably in the Bach Passions, the Choral Symphony and the Brahms Requiem; Berlin Festival in the premieres of Die Erprobung de Petrus Hebraicus by Henri Pousseur, 1974 and Mare Nostrum by Kagel, 1975; San Diego Opera as Sharpless in Madama Butterfly, Ford in Falstaff, and in the 1979 premiere of Menotti's La Loca, with Beverly Sills; Netherlands Opera as Germont, Don Giovanni and Marcello, and in Donizetti's Maria Stuarda with Joan Sutherland; Frankfurt Opera 1983, as Amfortas in Parsifal; Glyndebourne 1984, as Mandryka in Arabella; Los Angeles Opera as Nabucco; La Scala Milan 1985, as Jochanaan in Salome and Golaud in Pelléas et Mélisande; Stuttgart 1985, in Henze's König Hirsch; Other appearances in New York and Paris, Vienna 1988 Goulaud in Pelléas et Mélisande, Bonn 1989; Wolfram, Tannhäuser, Munich 1989; Mathis der Maler, Hindemith; Sang Orestes in Elektra at Barcelona, 1990; Hindemith's Mathis and Von Einem's Danton at the 1990 Munich Festival; Sang Barak in Die Frau ohne Schatten for Netherlands Opera, 1992; Wozzeck, Stuttgart, 1993; Simon Boccanegra, Frankfurt, 1993; Wanderer in Siegfried, 1994; Dr Schön in Lulu, Salzburger Festspiele, 1995 and at the Berlin Staatsoper, 1997; Sang the Wanderer at Amsterdam, 1998; Season 1999–2000 as Dr Schön in Lulu at Salzburg and Amfortas in Munich; Hans Sachs at Covent Garden, 2002. *Recordings:* Dichterliebe; Handel's Dettinger Te Deum and Judas Maccabaeus; Kindertotenlieder, Mahler; Des Knaben Wunderhorn (Mahler); Lucrezia Borgia; Das Paradies und Die Peri. *Address:* c/o Bayerische Staatsoper, Postfach 745, 8000 Munich 1, Germany.

**BROCK, Hannes;** Singer (Tenor); b. 1 Nov. 1952, Stuttgart. *Education:* Studied in Berlin and Wuppertal. *Career:* Berlin Theater des Westens, 1978–79; Bach's St Matthew Passion with the Berlin Philharmonic, 1981; Sang at Opera at Hagen, Essen and Dortmund, 1981–95; Eutin Festival, 1986 in The Bartered Bride and Zeller's Der Vogelhändler; St Gallen Opera from 1995, with guest appearances at Mannheim, Düsseldorf, Dresden and Hamburg; Dortmund Opera 2001, in Wallenberg by Erkki-Sven Tüür, and as Monostatos; Roles have included Mozart's Tamino, Mime in Das Rheingold, Handel's Xerxes, Shuisky in Boris Godunov and Beppe in Pagliacci; Modern repertory includes the Captain in Wozzeck, Tom Rakewell, Steva in Jenůfa and Weill's Jim Mahoney. *Address:* c/o Stadttheater St Gallen, Museumstrasse 24, 9000 St Gallen, Switzerland.

**BRODARD, Michael;** Singer (Bass-Baritone); b. 1 April 1946, Fribourg, Switzerland. *Education:* Fribourg Conservatoire, 1965–74. *Career:* Concert Singer in France and Switzerland; Opera engagements at Geneva, Lausanne, Lucerne, Nancy and Metz; Further concerts at Brussels, Marseille, Frankfurt, Barcelona, Lisbon, Buenos Aires, Madrid and Warsaw; Repertoire ranges from Baroque to Modern Works. *Recordings include:* L'Enfant et les Sortilèges, Pelléas et Mélisande, Bach's Christmas Oratorio, Haydn's St Theresa Mass, Madrigals and Vespers by Monteverdi, Schubert's E-flat Mass and Vivaldi's Psalm 110; Stravinsky's Renard and Les Noces, Masses by Mozart. *Address:* Conservatoire de Musique, 228–A rue Pierre Aeby, CH – 1700 Fribourg, Switzerland.

**BRODERICK, Kathleen;** Singer (Soprano); b. 1958, Vancouver, Canada. *Education:* Studied in Montreal, St Louis and New York. *Career:* Sang at Kaiserslautern, 1984–88; Saarbrucken, 1988–91; Berne 1990 as Dvořák's Rusalka; Other roles have included Mozart's Fiordiligi, Pamina, Countess Almaviva; Agathe in Der Freischütz, Violetta, Jenny in Mahagonny; Virginia Opera, Salome, 1993; Minnesota Opera as Turandot, 1994; Hamilton Opera, Canada, as Amelia in Un Ballo in Maschera, 1996; Orlando Opera, USA as Leonora in Il Trovatore, 1997; Season 1998 with Turandot for Florida Grand Opera, Turandot and Milada in Dalibor for Scottish Opera and Turandot for Flanders Opera at Antwerp; Long Beach Opera as Judith in Bluebeard's Castle, 1999; Lady Macbeth in the Scottish Opera Macbeth at the Edinburgh Festival, 1999; Turandot, Senta/Flying Dutchman, Elektra/title role at Nationaltheater Mannheim, 2000–03; Season 2000–01 as Lady Macbeth at Edinburgh, Bregenz, Vienna and Berlin (Deutsche Oper); Abigaille/Nabucco at Semperoper Dresden, 2001; Brünnhilde in English National Opera's Ring cycle (Valkyrie/Siegfried/Twilight of the Gods), 2002–05; Frequent concert appearances. *Address:* c/o Artists Management Zürich, Rutistrasse 52, 8044 Zürich-Gockhausen, Switzerland.

**BROITMANN, Ruben;** Singer (Tenor); b. 1959, Mexico City. *Education:* Mexico City and Juilliard, American Opera Center. *Career:* Early roles included Mozart's Ferrando and Don Ottavio; Rinuccio in Gianni Schicchi; Tour of Germany, Italy and Japan with the Peter Brook Carmen; Aix-en-Provence, 1987, as Pedrillo in Die Entführung; Guest appearances at Montevideo, Nancy, Puerto Rico and Frankfurt; Season 1992–93 as Alfredo at Graz, Don José at Freiburg and Ismaele in Nabucco at the Bregenz Festival; Vienna Staatsoper from 1993; Vienna Volksoper as Laertes in Hamlet, 1995; Raffaele in Verdi's Stiffelio, 1996; Sang Werther at Mannheim, 2001; Sings a varied concert repertoire. *Address:* c/o Vienna Staatsoper, Opernring 2, 1010 Vienna, Austria.

**BROKAW, James Albert, II;** Historical Musicologist; b. 4 Feb. 1951, Princeton, New Jersey, USA; m. Mollie Sandock, 27 June 1984. *Education:* BA, German Literature, Kenyon College, 1973; Studies in Music History and Theory, Baldwin Wallace Conservatory, 1977–78; PhD, Musicology, University of Chicago, 1986. *Career:* Assistant Professor of Music, Northeastern Illinois University, 1989–; Lecturer in Music, Chicago State University, 1986–; Lecturer in Music, University of Chicago Open Programme, 1987–; Advisory Board Member, Riemenschneider Bach Institute, 1982–86; Judge, Mu Phi Epsilon Music History Competition, 1988. *Publications:* The Genesis of the Prelude in C Major, in Bach Studies, Cambridge University Press, 1989; Techniques of Expansion in the Preludes and Fugues of Johann Sebastian Bach, dissertation; Programme Notes: The Chicago Symphony Orchestra/ Performances for Peace, 1984–88; Music of the Baroque, 1984, 1987. *Contributions:* Reviews of scholarly editions of keyboard music of J. S. Bach, C P E Bach and Louis Couperin, in Notes, 1985, 1986, 1989; Recent Research on the Genesis and Sources of Bach's Well-Tempered Klavier, II, in Bach: The Quarterly Journal of the Riemenschneider Bach Institute, 1985. *Address:* Box 125 Ogden Dunes, Portage, IN 46368, USA.

**BROKMEIER, Willi;** Singer (Tenor); b. 8 April 1928, Bochum, Germany. *Education:* Studied in Mainz. *Career:* Debut: Stadttheater Mainz, 1952; Appearances in lighter operatic roles at the Deutsche Oper am Rhein Düsseldorf; Many engagements in operetta, notably at the Theater am Gärtnerplatz, Munich, and elsewhere in Germany; Cologne Opera, 1965, in the premiere of Zimmermann's Die Soldaten; Munich Festival, 1973, as Pedrillo in Die Entführung. *Recordings:* Gräfin Mariza; Lehar's Lustige Witwe and Land des Lächelns; Die Kluge by Orff; Korngold's Die Tote Stadt (RCA); Feuersnot by Strauss (Acanta).

**BRONDER, Peter;** Singer (Tenor); b. 22 Oct. 1953, Herefordshire, England. *Education:* Studied at the Royal Academy of Music with Joy Mammen and at the National Opera Studio. *Career:* Principal Tenor with the Welsh National Opera from 1986–90; Covent Garden debut as Arturo in Lucia di Lammermoor in 1986, also Major Domo in Der Rosenkavilier; Youth in Die Frau ohne Schlatten, 1992; First Jew in Salome, 1995; Sang Kudryash in Katya Kabanova in 1989 and Andres in Wozzeck in 1990 with the English National Opera; Shepherd in Oedipus Rex, 1991; Almaviva in 1992–93; Alfred in Die Fledermaus and Italian Tenor in Der Rosenkavalier, 1993; Further appearances include: Netherlands Opera as Ernesto, 1989 and the Prince in Les Brigands, 1992; Glyndebourne Festival, 1990; For Welsh National Opera performances in New York, 1989, Milan, 1989 and Tokyo, 1990; Debut at the Bavarian State Opera, Munich, as Mazal in The Adventures of Mr Brouček, also Narraboth, 1994; Invitations for Pedrillo in Die Entführung at Covent Garden, also Istanbul; Sang Pylades in Gluck's Iphigenia auf Tauris, Edinburgh, 1996; Alexander in Il Re Pastore for Opera North, 1998; Season 2000 as Mime for Longborough Festival, Loge at Edinburgh and in Dallapicolla's Il Prigioniero for ENO; Concert appearances in London, Paris, Vienna, Lisbon and for the Australian Broadcasting Company, Perth. *Recordings include:* Kiri Te Kanawa recital, Turco in Italia (Phonogram); Adriana Lecouvreur (Decca); Osud, Beethoven 9 (EMI); La Traviata, Ballo in Maschera (Teldec). *Honours:* Associate, Royal Academy of Music, 1989. *Current Management:* Allied Artists, London. *Address:* c/o Allied Artists, 42 Montpelier Square, London SW7 1JZ, England.

**BRONFMAN, Yefim;** Russian pianist; b. 10 April 1958, Tashkent. *Education:* Juilliard School of Music, New York, USA, Curtis Inst., Philadelphia, studied with Rudolf Serkin and Arie Vardi. *Career:* debut, Israel Philharmonic with Kostalanetz 1974; soloist with Montreal Symphony Orchestra, Philadelphia, Los Angeles Philharmonic, New York Philharmonic, Minnesota Orchestra, Mostly Mozart Orchestra, English Chamber Orchestra, St Louis Symphony Orchestra, Scottish Chamber Orchestra, Vancouver Symphony Orchestra, Pittsburgh Symphony Orchestra, London Philharmonia, St Paul Chamber Orchestra, Houston Symphony Orchestra, Toronto Symphony Orchestra, Goteborg Symphony Orchestra, Royal Philharmonic, San Francisco Symphony Orchestra, Berlin Philharmonic, Chicago Symphony Orchestra, Baltimore Symphony Orchestra, Rotterdam Philharmonic, Bournemouth Symphony Orchestra, Cleveland Orchestra, Nat. Symphony Orchestra, Rochester Philharmonic, Jerusalem Symphony Orchestra, Winnipeg Symphony Orchestra, Richmond Symphony Orchestra, New Jersey Symphony. *Recordings:* all Fauré; Prokofiev Violin Sonatas with Shlomo Mintz; Musical Heritage, Brahms Sonata in F minor and Scherzo Op 4; Mozart Sonatas for violin and piano with Robert Mann; Prokofiev Piano Sonatas 7 and 8; Mussorgsky, Pictures at an Exhibition, Stravinsky, 3 scenes from Petrushka; Rachmaninov: Piano Concertos 2 and 3, with Esa-Pekka Salonen and Philharmonia Orchestra, 1992; Prokofiev: Piano Concertos 1, 3 and 5, with Zubin Mehta and Israel Philharmonic, 1993. *Honours:* American-Israeli Cultural Foundation Scholarship 1974, Avery Fisher Prize 1991. *Current Management:* ICM New York, 40 W 57th Street, New York, NY 10019, USA. *Telephone:* (212) 556-5600. *Website:* www.icmtalent.com.

**BRONK, Stephen;** Singer (Bass-baritone); b. 1958, Hyannis, MA, USA. *Education:* Studied at the Aachen Musikhochschule. *Career:* Debut: Justifiar in Kienzl's Evangelimann, Bregenz, 1984; Appearances in opera at Bremerhaven and Saarbrucken; Bonn Opera from 1993 as Mozart's Osmin, Figaro, Alfonso and Speaker in Die Zauberflöte; Grand Inquisitor in Don Carlos and King in Aida; Sang Pizarro in Fidelio at Bonn, 1995, and in Janáček's From the House of the Dead at Strasbourg, 1996; Other roles include Fasolt, Alberich and Hunding in The Ring; Concerts include Beethoven's Ninth at Bonn, 1994; Sang Pizarro in Fidelio and Don Alfonso at Dusseldorf, 1999–2000. *Address:* Bonn Opera, Am Boeselagerhof 1, Pf 2440, 5311 Bonn, Germany.

**BROOK, Peter Stephen Paul,** CH, CBE, MA; British theatre director, film director and writer; *Director, Bouffes du Nord Theatre, Paris;* b. 21 March 1925, s. of Simon Brook; m. Natasha Parry 1951; one s. one d. *Education:* Westminster and Gresham's Schools and Magdalen Coll., Oxford. *Career:* joined RSC 1962; Producer, Co-Dir Royal Shakespeare Theatre; f. Centre for Theatre Research, Paris 1970, opened Théâtre des Bouffes du Nord, Paris 1974; Dir Int. Centre for Theatre Creations. *Films include:* The Beggar's Opera 1952, Moderato Cantabile 1959, Lord of the Flies 1963, Marat/Sade 1967, Tell Me Lies 1967, King Lear 1969, Meetings With Remarkable Men 1976–77, La Tragédie de Carmen 1983, The Mahabharata 1989, The Tragedy of Hamlet 2002. *Productions include:* Dr. Faustus 1943, Pygmalion, King John, Lady from the Sea 1945, Romeo and Juliet (at Stratford) 1947, Dir of Productions at Covent Garden Opera 1949–50, Faust (at Metropolitan Opera, New York) 1953, The Dark is Light Enough (London) 1954, House of Flowers (New York) 1954, Cat on a Hot Tin Roof (Paris) 1956, Eugene Onegin (New York) 1958, View from the Bridge (Paris) 1958, The Fighting Cock (New York) 1959, Irma la Douce 1960, King Lear 1963, The Physicists (New York) 1964, The Marat/Sade (New York) 1965, Oedipus (Seneca) 1968, A Midsummer Night's Dream 1970, The Conference of the Birds 1973, Timon of Athens (Paris) 1974, The Ik (Paris) 1975, (London) 1976, (USA) 1976, Ubu (Paris) 1977, Meetings with Remarkable Men (film, also dir screenplay) 1977, Antony and Cleopatra (Stratford and London) 1978, Measure for Measure (Paris) 1978, Conference of the Birds, L'os (Festival Avignon and Paris) 1979, (New York) 1980, The Cherry Orchard (Paris) 1981, (New York) 1988, (Moscow) 1989, La Tragédie de Carmen (opera) (Paris) 1981, (film) 1983, Le Mahabharata (Avignon and Paris) 1985, (World tour) 1988, Woza Albert! (Paris) 1989, The Mahabharata (film) 1989, La Tempête (Paris) 1990, Impressions de Pelléas (opera) 1992, L'Homme Qui (Paris) 1993, 1997, The Man Who 1994, Oh! Les Beaux Jours (Lausanne) 1995, (Paris) 1996, Don Giovanni (opera) 1998, Je suis un phénomène (Paris) 1998, Le Costume (Paris) 1999, The Tragedy of Hamlet (Paris) 2000, Far Away (Paris) 2002, La Tragédie d'Hamlet (Paris) 2002, La Mort de Krishna (Paris) 2002, Ta Main Dans La Mienne (Paris) 2003, Tierno Bokar (Paris) 2004, Le Grand Inquisiteur (Paris) 2004. *Publications:* The Empty Space 1968, The Shifting Point: Forty years of theatrical exploration 1946–87, 1987, There Are No Secrets 1993 (appeared in USA as The Open Door: Thoughts on Acting and the Theatre), Threads of Time (autobiog.) 1998, Evoking Shakespeare 1999. *Honours:* Officier des Arts et Lettres; Officier Légion d'honneur; Praemium Imperiale; Hon. DLitt (Birmingham), (Strathclyde) 1990; Freiherr von Stein Foundation, Shakespeare Award 1973, Wexner Prize (Ohio State Univ.) 1991, Onassis Int. Award 1993, Times Award 1994, Dan David Prize, 2005. *Address:* Théâtre des Bouffes du Nord, 37 bis boulevard de La Chapelle, 75010 Paris, France (office). *E-mail:* cict@wanadoo.fr (office).

**BROOKS, Darla;** Singer (Soprano); b. 1957, West Virginia, USA. *Education:* Studied in the USA and at Graz. *Career:* Sang throughout the USA in opera and concert, notably in Chicago and Cincinnati; European debut with Lucerne Opera 1985, followed by engagements at Würzburg and Cologne; Roles have included Norina in Don Pasquale, Blondchen, Zerlina, Zerbinetta, Adele in Die Fledermaus and Adina in L'Elisir d'amore (at the Deutsche Oper Berlin); Other venues include the Teatro Liceu Barcelona, and the State Operas of Munich and Vienna; Schwetzingen Festival 1995 in Salieri's Falstaff. *Address:* c/o Deutsche Oper, Richard Wagner Strasse 10, D–10585 Berlin, Germany.

**BROPHY, Gerard;** composer; b. 7 Jan. 1953, Sydney, Australia. *Education:* masterclasses with Turibio Santos, 1976; Composition seminar, Mauricio Kagel, Basel, Switzerland; Studied with Richard Toop, NSW State Conservatorium of Music, 1981; Studied with Franco Donatoni, Italy; Graduated, Accademia Nazionale de Santa Cecilia, Rome, 1983; Composition course, Accademia Chigiana di Siena, 1983. *Career:* Composer in Residence, Musica Viva Australia, 1983; Australian Chamber Orchestra, 1986; Queensland Conservatorium of Music, 1987; Pittsburgh New Music Ensemble, 1988; Queensland Conservatorium of Music, 1989. *Compositions include:* Orchestral Works: Orfeo, 1982; Le Reveil de L'Ange, 1987; Matho, 1987; Ensemble Works: Lace, 1985; Mercurio, 1985; Spur, 1988; Head, 1988; Séraphita, 1988; Forbidden Colours, 1988; Frisson, 1989; Vocal Works: Flesh, 1987; Shiver, 1989; Instrumental Works: Chiarissima, 1987; Pink Chair Light Green Violet Violent FLASH, 1990; Vorrei Baciarti, for baritone and chamber ensemble, 1991; Tweak, for piccolo, 1991; Pluck It!, for solo guitar, 1992; Twist, for solo clarinet, 1993; Recent works include: Tudo Liquido, for wind and percussion, 1994; Colour Red... Your Mouth... Heart, for orchestra, 1994; Es, for solo flute, 1994; Bisoux, for english horn and bass clarinet, 1994; Umbigada, Obrigado!, for percussion quartet, 1995; Trip, for wind ensemble, 1996; Coil, 1996; Crimson Songs, for soprano and ensemble, 1997; Samba Mauve, 1997; Merge–a memoir of the senses for percussion quartet, large orchestra and sound design, commissioned by the Melbourne Symphony Orchestra, 1998; Hot Metallic Blues, for electric bass and ensemble, 1999; Ru B fogo, for ensemble, 1999; Birds of Paradise, for guitar orchestra, 1999; Body Map, for ensemble, 1999; Yo Yai Pakebi, Man Mai Yapobi, for African percussion and large orchestra, 1999; Heavy Metal Boyhood, for ensemble, 2000; Pink Edges, for six voices, 2000; Abraco, for solo piano, 2000; Sheer Nylon Dances, for violin, cello and piano, 2001; ...Vision Fugitive, for violin, cello and piano, 2001; Danses Veloutées, for solo viola and orchestra, 2001; ...Danse de l'Extase, for orchestra, 2001; Chorinho Pra Ela, for bass clarinet, 2002; Berceuse, for SATB motet, 2002; Pas de Deux, for clarinet and cello, 2002; Concerto in Blue, for guitar and orchestra, 2002; Trance Ripples, for solo marimba, 2002; Topolo-NRG, for baritone sax, double bass and piano, 2002; mFm, for soprano/baritone sax, bass guitar, marimba and piano, 2002; Chi's Cakewalk, for solo bass clarinet, 2002; Songo, for percussion quintet, 2002; Mantras, for orchestra, 2003; Brisbane Drumming, for percussion, 2003; Choro Pra Linos, for wind quintet, 2003; Phobia, for music theatre performers, 2003; Maracatu, for orchestra 2003; Songs of the North, for soprano and ensemble, 2004; Cancao, for wind quintet, 2004; Frevo, for wind quintet, 2004. *Recordings include:* Hydra, Synergy Percussion; Nadja, Sydney Symphony Orchestra; Shiver, Elision; Head, Het Trio; Nymphe-Echo Morphologique, Laura Chislett; November Snow, Music Box; Forbidden Colours, Queensland Symphony Orchestra; Angelicon, Lisa Moore; Breathless, Laura Chislett; Twist (Philippa Robinson, Floyd Williams, Roslyn Dunlop); Bisous (Barry Davis and Floyd Williams, Philippa Robinson, Roslyn Dunlop, Deborah de Graaff); Pluck It! (Ken Murray, Peter Constant); We Bop (Duo Contemporain, Margery Smith and Daryl Pratt); Charm, Marshall McGuire, Geoffrey Collins and Patricia Pollett; NRG, Henri Bok; Obsidian, Ex Novo Ensemble; Birds of Paradise, Guitarstrophy; Glove, six_new music ensemble; Crimson Songs, Perihelion; Pearl licks, pearl rub, pearl dub, Two Complete Lunatics; the Room of the Saints, Patricia Pollett and Daryl Pratt; Chorinho pra Ela, Henri Bok. *Honours:* Numerous grants and fellowships including: Composer Fellowship, Australia Council Music Board, 1982, 1983; Italian Government Scholarship. *Address:* 26 Nott Street, Red Hill, Qld 4059, Australia. *E-mail:* g.brophy@griffith.edu.au.

**BROS, José;** Singer (tenor); b. 1965, Barcelona, Spain. *Education:* Barcelona Conservatory. *Career:* debut, Carmina Burana at Palma, 1987; many performances in leading roles at major opera houses, 1992–; Duke of Mantua at Palma and Nadir in Les Pêcheurs de Perles, followed by Percy in Anna Bolena, at Barcelona; leads in La Favorita at Las Palmas, Falstaff and I Capuleti at Lisbon, Lucia di Lammermoor at Zürich, Don Pasquale and Così fan tutte at Bilbao and L'Elisir d'amore (Nemorino, Covent Garden, 1997); further recent engagements at Hamburg, Vienna, Rome, Naples, Munich, Florence (Edgardo, under Zubin Mehta, at the Maggio Musicale), Bologna and Marseille; Nemorino at Barcelona and Madrid; Edgardo at Barcelona and Donizetti's Roberto Devereux at Hamburg (concert), 2000; recitals and concerts throughout Europe and in London. *Current Management:* Miguel Lerin, La Rambla 54, 2°, 1a, 08002 Barcelona, Spain.

**BROSTER, Eileen;** Pianist; b. 23 June 1935, London, England; m. R Chaplin, 6 May 1972, 1 s. *Education:* Studied with Frank Merrick and Cyril Smith at The Royal College of Music. *Career:* Debut: Wigmore Hall; Performed on BBC radio and television; Appeared in all South Bank Halls; Toured extensively as soloist in recitals and concerti; Performances at Wigmore Hall; mem, Incorporated Society of Musicians; EPTA. *Address:* 199 Beehive Lane, Gants Hill, Ilford, Essex, England.

**BROTT, Alexander,** OC, OQ, LicMus, DMus, LLD; Canadian musical director, conductor and professor of music; b. 14 March 1915, Montréal; m. Lotte Goetzel 1933 (died 1997); two s. *Education:* McGill Univ., Quebec Acad. of Music, Juilliard School of Music, NY, Chicago Univ., Queen's Univ. *Career:* Prof. and conductor-in-residence, McGill Univ. 1939–; Concertmaster and Asst Conductor, Montréal Symphony Orchestra; founder and fmr Musical Dir, McGill Chamber Orchestra; fmr conductor Jeunes Virtuoses, conductor of Montréal Pops Concerts; Conductor and Musical Dir, Kingston Symphony Orchestra and Kingston Pops Concerts; mem. The Lapitsky Foundation. *Compositions:* 18 Symphonies (13 commissioned), 25 solo and chamber music (12 commissioned), eight vocal works (five commissioned) 1938–71, songs and orchestrations (11 commissioned) 1971–78. *Recordings include:* many with McGill Chamber Orchestra including own compositions and works by Mozart, Haydn, Schubert and Bach; Alexander Brott's Compositions 1994. *Honours:* Hon. Fellow RSA, London 1960, Knight of Malta Order of St John of Jerusalem 1985, elected 'Great Montrealer' 1994. *Address:* 5459 Earnscliffe Avenue, Montréal, QC H3X 2P8, Canada (office). *Telephone:* (514) 487-4221 (office). *Fax:* (514) 486-4580 (office). *E-mail:* alexbrott@hotmail.com.

**BROTT, Boris;** Conductor; b. 14 March 1944, Montreal, Quebec, Canada; m. Ardyth Webster, 2 s., 1 d. *Education:* Conservatoire de Musique, Montreal; McGill University, Montreal; Studied conducting with Pierre Monteux, Igor Markevitch, Leonard Bernstein, Alexander Brott. *Career:* Debut: As violinist with Montreal Symphony, 1949; Founder, Conductor, Philharmonic Youth Orchestra, Montreal, 1959–61; Assistant Conductor: Toronto Symphony Orchestra, 1963–65; New York Philharmonic, 1968–69; Music Director: Northern Sinfonia Orchestra, England, 1964–69; Royal Ballet, Covent Garden, 1966–68, including the Covent Garden premiere of Stravinsky's The Soldier's Tale; Lakehead University, Thunder Bay, Ontario, 1967–72; Regina Symphony, 1970–73; Conductor, Music Director: Hamilton Philharmonic Orchestra, 1969–90; Ontario Place Pops Orchestra, 1983–91; Chief Conductor: BBC National Orchestra of Wales, 1972–77; CBC Symphony, 1976–83; President, Great Music Canada, 1977–; Artistic Director, Stratford Summer Music Festival, Ontario, 1982–84; Conductor, McGill Orchestra, Montreal, Quebec, 1989–; Artistic Director, Brott Music Festivals, Hamilton,

Ontario, 1988–95; Conductor and MD, New West Symphony, Los Angeles, 1995–; Conductor and Music Director, Ventura Symphony, Ventura, California, 1990–95; Guest Conductor, All British orchestras, all major Canadian orchestras, USA, Korea, Japan, Germany, France, Sweden, Israel, Mexico, El Salvador, Italy, Denmark; Principal Guest Conductor and Music Adviser, Symphony Nova Scotia, 1981–; Co-conductor of McGill Chamber Orchestra, 1989; Music Director of the New West Symphony, California, 1992; Guest Conductor, Sadler's Wells Opera, Canadian Opera Company, Edmonton Opera; Writer, Host, Conductor, over 100 television programmes, the United Kingdom, USA, Canada; Appeared in film and radio; Conducted for Pope John Paul II at the Vatican, 2000. *Recordings:* Numerous for CBC, Sceptre-Mace, Mercury, including suites from operas by Handel; Dvořák's Serenade op 44; Symphonies by Richter, Holzbauer and Cannabich; Sibelius Pelléas; Ravel Le Tombeau de Couperin. *Address:* 301 Bay Street South, Hamilton, Ontario L8P 3JZ, Canada.

**BROTT, Denis;** Cellist; b. 9 Sept. 1950, Quebec, Canada; m. 27 Aug 1976, 1 s, 3 d. *Education:* Studied with Gregor Piatigorsky, University of Southern California, USA. *Career:* Festivals include Marlboro, Aspen, Hampden-Sydney, Orford and Sitka; Artistic Director, Festival of the Sound, Ontario, 1991; Faculty of the Music Academy of the West, Santa Barbara, 1993 and 1994 summer season, performing chamber music at festivals in Hampden-Sydney, Virginia and Sitka Alaska; Jury member, Evian International String Quartet Competition in France, also recitalist, chamber artist and soloist with orchestra; Professor of Cello and Chamber Music at Conservatoire de Musique de Montreal, Canada; In 1995 established a two-week Festival de Musique de Chambre de Montréal, a celebration of chamber music in the Chateau de Belvedere atop Mont Royal; On jury for the 1993 Evian International String Quartet Competition in France and the 1996 Munich String Quartet Competition; One of 3 invited guest lecturers for the Piatigorsky Seminar for Cellists, University of Southern California in Los Angeles, 1997. *Recordings include:* 20 chamber music works including the complete string quartets of Beethoven with the Orford String Quartet and Homage to Piatigorsky; Works of his father, Alexander Brott, featuring Arabesque for Cello and Orchestra, 1993. *Publications include:* Article, Schelome: The Message of King Solomon, Violoncello Society and Canadian Jewish News Viewpoints, 1993. *Current Management:* Davis Joachim, Les Concerts Davis Joachim Inc, 201 Brock Avenue North, Montreal, Quebec H4X 2G1, Canada. *Address:* 201 Brock Avenue North, Montreal, Quebec H4X 2G1, Canada.

**BROUWER, Leovigildo (Leo);** Cuban composer, conductor and classical guitarist; b. 1 March 1939, Havana. *Education:* studied with Isaac Nicola, Peyrellade Conservatoire, Havana, Juilliard School, New York, USA with Stefan Wolpe and Vincent Persichetti, Hartt Coll. with Isadore Freed. *Career:* debut 1956; Dir Music Dept, Instituto Cubano 1960; teacher, Nat. Conservatory, Havana 1961–67, Dir experimental dept of Cuban film music from 1967; created the Experimentación de Sonidos (with Silvio Rodriguez and Pablo Milanes) 1968; many tours as guitar soloist; guitar competition founded in his honour, Japan 1984; fmr conductor, Orquesta de Cuba; co-founder, Orchestra de Córdoba, Spain 1992. *Compositions for film:* Historias de la revolución 1960, Papeles son papeles 1966, La Muerte de un burócrata 1966, Hanoi, martes 13 1967, Las Aventuras de Juan Quin Quin 1967, Memorias del subdesarrollo 1968, La Primera carga al machete 1969, La Bataille des dix millions 1971, Un Día de noviembre 1972, Una Pelea cubana contra los demonios 1972, Ustedes tienen la palabra 1973, El Extraño caso de Rachel K 1973, El Hombre de Maisinicú 1973, Ranchador 1975, La Cantata de Chile 1975, El Otro Francisco 1975, La Última cena 1976, Destino manifiesto 1977, Son o no son 1978, El Recurso del método 1978, No hay sábado sin sol 1979, Los Sobrevivientes 1979, La Viuda de Montiel 1979, Una y otra vez 1982, Cecilia 1982, Alsino y el cóndor 1982, Tiempo de amar 1983, Los Refugiados de la cueva del muerto 1983, Amada 1983, La Rosa de los vientos 1983, Hasta cierto punto 1983, La Segunda hora de Esteban Zayas 1984, Jíbaro 1984, Tiempo de morir 1985, Visa USA 1986, Como agua para chocolate 1992, Mátame mucho 1998, Ficción sin ficción 2002. *Compositions include:* Sonograms for prepared piano 1963, Tropos for orchestra 1967, Hexahedron for six players 1969, Flute Concerto 1972, Homenaje a Lenin for electronics, five guitar concertos 1972–92, Doble Concierto for violin, guitar and orchestra 1995, Lamento for Rafael Orozco for clarinet and strings 1996, many smaller pieces for guitar. *Address:* c/o Chester Music and Novello & Co., 8–9 Frith Street, London, W1D 3JB, England.

**BROWN, Christopher (Roland),** MA; British composer; b. 17 June 1943, Tunbridge Wells, Kent; m. 1st Anne Smillie 1969; one s. one d.; m. 2nd Fiona Caithness 1985; one s. *Education:* Westminster Abbey Choir School, 1952–57; Dean Close School, Cheltenham, 1957–62; King's College, Cambridge, 1962–65; Royal Acad. of Music, London, 1965–67; Hochschule für Musik, Berlin, Germany, 1967–68. *Career:* Freelance Composer, 1968–; Mem., Professorial Staff, Royal Acad. of Music, 1969–; Conductor, Huntingdonshire Philharmonic, 1976–91, 1994–95; Composer-in-Residence, Nene Coll., Northampton, 1986–88; Conductor, Dorset Bach Cantata Club, 1988–; Conductor, New Cambridge Singers, 1997–. *Compositions:* Regularly performed worldwide including: Triptych; The Sun: Rising; Organ Concerto; Festive Prelude; Festival Variations; 4 Operas; 2 String Quartets; Chamber Music for 5 instruments; Images; Ruscelli d'oro; La Légende de L'Etoile; Choral works include: David; A Hymn to the Holy Innocents; Three Medieval Lyrics; Magnificat; Chauntecleer; The Vision of Saul; The Snows of Winter; Hodie Salvator Apparuit; Tres Canti Sacri; Landscapes; The Circling Year;

Numerous songs, carols, church music; Mass for 4 voices, 1991; Christmas Cantata, 1992; The Ship of Fools, 1992; Star Song I, 1994; Summer Winds, 1995; Star Song III, 1996; Brown the Bear, 1997; Star Song IV, 1999; Invocation, 1999; To the Hills, 2000; Dance Variants, 2001; Like a Child, 2002; Star Song V, 2005. *Recordings include:* Laudate Dominum, Dean Close School Choir; Laudate Dominum, Canterbury Cathedral Choir; 'Tis Christmas Time, Huntingdonshire Philharmonic and Canticum; Seascape, British Chamber Choir and Brass Unlimited. *Publications:* Numerous. *Honours:* FRAM 1993. *Address:* Halefield Lodge, Oundle Road, Woodnewton, Peterborough, PE8 5EG England. *Telephone:* (1832) 274226. *E-mail:* cb@cbmusic.freeserve.co.uk.

**BROWN, David;** Professor of Musicology, University Teacher, Writer on Music and Broadcaster; b. 8 July 1929, Gravesend, Kent, England; m. Elizabeth Valentine, 24 Dec 1953, 2 d. *Education:* Sheffield University, 1947–52, BA 1950, BMus 1951, DipEd 1952, MA 1960; PhD, Southampton University, 1971; LTCL. *Career:* Schoolmaster, 1954–59; Music Librarian, London University, 1959–62; Lecturer in Music, 1962–, Professor of Musicology, 1983–89, Southampton University; mem, Royal Musical Association; Royal Society of Arts; Member of Editorial Committee of Musica Britannica. *Publications:* Thomas Weelkes, 1969; Mikhail Glinka, 1973; John Wilbye, 1974; Tchaikovsky, 4 vols, vol. 1 1840–74, 1978, vol. 2 1874–78, 1982, vol. 3 1878–85, 1986 and vol. 4 1885–93, 1991; Tchaikovsky Remembered, 1993; Musorgsky, 2003. *Contributions:* Music and Letters; Musical Times; Music Review; Monthly Musical Record; Listener; Survey; etc. *Honours:* Derek Allen Prize of The British Academy, for Tchaikovsky vol. 2, 1982; Yorkshire Post Music Book Award, for Tchaikovsky vol. 4, 1991. *Address:* Braishfield Lodge West, Braishfield, Romsey, Hampshire SO51 0PS, England. *E-mail:* dandebrown@blwest.fsnet.co.uk.

**BROWN, Donna;** Singer (soprano); b. 15 Feb. 1955, Renfrew, ON, Canada. *Education:* studied with Edith Mathis in Salzburg. *Career:* opera debut in Paris as Michaela in Peter Brook's Tragedie de Carmen; has sung Pamina in Die Zauberflöte, Sophie in Der Rosenkavalier, Almirena in Rinaldo, Gilda in Rigoletto, Nanetta in Falstaff, Rosina in Il barbiere di Siviglia, Servillia in La Clemenza di Tito, Morgana in Alcina, and Michaela in Carmen; also appeared as Chimène in world premiere of Debussy's unfinished opera Rodrigue et Chimène; season 2003–04 concert tour and recording of Noel Coward and Ivor Novello songs, appearances with London Philharmonic, National Arts Centre Orchestra, San Francisco Symphony. *Recordings include:* Rodrigue et Chimène, Brahms' Requiem, Die Schöpfung, Lieder by Fanny Mendelssohn, Debussy Mélodies de jeunesse. *Address:* c/o Opéra et Concerts, 1 rue Volnay, 75002, Paris, France. *E-mail:* c.verset@opera-concert.com.

**BROWN, Ian;** Pianist and Conductor; b. 1955, England. *Career:* Originally began as a bassoonist, then became Pianist-in-Residence, Southampton University; Concerto soloist with many leading British orchestras including BBC Symphony Orchestra, BBC National Orchestra of Wales, Bournemouth Symphony Orchestra, performing in major European and Scandinavian countries, the Middle East, North and South America, Singapore, Hong Kong and Japan; Pianist with Nash Ensemble from 1978, playing in the annual Wigmore series and at all major British festivals; Has appeared in duo with Mstislav Rostropovich, Henryk Szeryng, Ruggiero Ricci, Elisabeth Söderström, Felicity Lott, Ralph Kirshbaum, György Pauk, James Galway and others; Soloist in Messiaen's Oiseaux Exotiques at the Proms; Toured Germany with BBC Philharmonic Orchestra in concerts celebrating Hans Werner Henze's 60th birthday; Recent appearances as conductor with Northern Sinfonia, the City of London Sinfonia, Scottish Chamber Orchestra and Bournemouth Symphony Orchestra and Sinfonietta; London conducting debut at the Barbican (Mahler's Resurrection Symphony with the Salomon Orchestra and London Choral Society). *Recordings:* Extensive recordings of chamber music from Haydn to the present day, with the Nash Ensemble. *Current Management:* Diana Walters Artists Management, England. *Address:* c/o Diana Walters Artists Management, Ivy Cottage, 3 Main Street, Keyham, Leicestershire LE7 9JQ, England.

**BROWN, John;** Violinist; b. 1943, Yorkshire, England. *Education:* Royal Manchester College of Music, with Endre Wolf and György Pauk, and at Salzburg Mozarteum. *Career:* Co-leader, 1968, Leader, 1973, London Symphony Orchestra; Leader of the Orchestra of the Royal Opera House, Covent Garden, 1976–96; Solo appearances with the BBC Scottish, BBC Symphony and London Symphony Orchestras; Plays a Stradivarius violin. *Honours:* Prizewinner of the BBC Violin Competition, 1966; O.B.E., 1987. *Address:* c/o London Symphony Orchestra, Barbican Centre, Silk Street, London, EC 2Y 8 DS, England.

**BROWN, Justin;** British conductor; *Music Director, Alabama Symphony Orchestra*; b. 1962, England. *Education:* Trinity College, Cambridge, and at Tanglewood with Rozhdestvensky, Ozawa and Bernstein. *Career:* appearances with the London Symphony Orchestra, Royal Philharmonic Orchestra, BBC Symphony Orchestra and Scottish Symphony Orchestra, Royal Liverpool Philharmonic Orchestra, Bournemouth Symphony Orchestra, Ulster Orchestra, Orchestre National du Capitole de Toulouse, Gothenburg Symphony Orchestra, Dresden Philharmonic Orchestra, Oslo Philharmonic, Sydney Symphony Orchestra St Petersburg Philharmonic Orchestra, Melbourne Symphony Orchestra and Orchestra Internazionale d'Italia; engagements with English National Opera, Scottish Opera and at the Maggio Musicale, Santa Fe, Lisbon, Stuttgart, Strasbourg and La Monnaie (Brussels) opera houses; season 1996–97 with debut at Norwegian and Nantes Opera; as

pianist, chamber music recitals in UK and Scandinavia, concertos (Beethoven, Mozart, Bach) directed from the keyboard UK, Malmö Symphony Orchestra, Israel Sinfonietta; Music Dir Alabama Symphony Orchestra 2006–. *Recordings:* Bernstein, Candide, Scottish Opera; Tavener, The Protecting Veil, Wallfisch R. Philharmonic Orchestra;,Koch, Orchestral Works, Odense Symphony Orchestra. *Honours:* Winner, London Mozart Players Best Young Conductor, 1990. *Address:* c/o IMG Artists, Lovell House, 616 Chiswick High Road, London W4 5RX, England.

**BROWN, Paul;** Stage Designer; b. 1960, Vale of Glamorgan, Wales. *Education:* Studied with Margaret Harris. *Career:* Designs for Monteverdi's Poppea at Bologna, Philidor's Tom Jones and Grétry's Zémire et Azor at Drottningholm; Royal Opera, Covent Garden with Mitridate, The Midsummer Marriage, I Masnadieri and Falstaff (2000); Lulu and Pelléas et Mélisande at Glyndebourne; Parsifal at the Opéra Bastille, Paris; Don Carlos for Opera Australia and Fidelio for English National Opera; Metropolitan Opera, New York, with Schoenberg's Moses und Aron and Lady Macbeth by Shostakovich; Designs for Purcell's King Arthur for the Châtelet, Paris, and Covent Garden, 1995; Season 2000–01 with Peter Grimes at the Bastille. *Address:* c/o Glyndebourne Festival Opera, Glyndebourne, Lewes, Sussex BN8 5UU, England.

**BROWN, Rachel;** Flautist and Recorder player; b. 1962, USA. *Education:* Royal Northern College of Music. *Career:* Principal Flautist with the King's Consort, the Hanover Band, Academy of Ancient Music and the Brandenburg Consort: Concerto performances on tour in Japan, Europe and America; Former Professor at RNCM, Manchester; Guildhall School, London and Royal College of Music, 2000–; Performances with the London Handel Festival 2001. *Recordings include:* Concertos by Vivaldi, Quantz, Handel, Telemann, JS and JC Bach; Sonatas by Schubert and Boehm (Chandos); Concertos by Quantz and CPE Bach (Hyperion). *Honours:* Winner, American National Flute Competition, 1984. *Address:* c/o Royal College of Music, Prince Consort Road, London SW7, England.

**BROWNE, Sandra;** Singer (Mezzo-Soprano); b. 27 July 1947, Point Fortin, Trinidad, West Indies. *Education:* BA Modern Languages, Vassar College, USA; Brussels Conservatory with Mina Bolotine; Royal Manchester College of Music with Frederic Cox. *Career:* Debut: With Welsh National Opera in Nabucco, 1972; Sang in the premiere of Alun Hoddinott's The Beach of Falsea, 1974; Kent Opera as Monteverdi's Poppea, English National Opera from 1974, as Octavian, Rosina, Monteverdi's Poppea, Dido and Carmen; Guest appearances in Toulouse, Marseille, Nancy and Florence as Carmen; Verona 1978, in a revival of Vivaldi's Orlando Furioso; La Scala Milan 1981 in Ariodante; Aix-en-Provence 1983, in Mozart's Mitridate; Other engagements in Pergolesi's Adriano in Siria (Florence), Dido and Aeneas (New York City Opera), Salome (Welsh National Opera), Radamisto and Ottone (Handel Opera Society); Concerts with most leading British orchestras, and in Norway, Portugal, France, Italy, Latin America and Australia; Regular Prom concert appearances. *Recordings:* Offenbach, Robinson Crusoe; Songs by Barber and Copland; Songs by Falla, Rodrigo, Granados and Montsalvatge; Rossini, Mosè in Egitto (Philips); Albinoni, Il Nascimento dell'Aurora (Erato); Vivaldi, Serenata a tre, Mio Cor Povero Cor (Erato). *Honours:* Kathleen Ferrier Memorial Scholarship 1971; RMCM Gold Medal for Voice 1972; Nominated for Laurence Olivier Award, 1991. *Address:* New Zealand Cottages, Barnham, Thetford, Norfolk IP24 2PL, England.

**BROWNER, Alison;** Singer (Mezzo-soprano); b. 22 Sept. 1958, Dublin, Ireland; m. Wilhelm Gries, 1 s., 1 d. *Education:* BA, Trinity College, Dublin; School of Music, Dublin; Private Studies, Hans Hotter, Munich. *Career:* Debut: Ludwigsburger Schloss Festspiele; National Theatre, Mannheim; Appeared at Bayreuth, Stuttgart, Zürich, Brussels, Antwerp, Covent Garden, Wexford Opera Festival, Staatsoper Berlin; Roles include La Cenerentola, Rosina (Barbiere), Cherubino, Hansel, Sesto, Idamante; Season 1995 as Rosina at Santiago and Cherubino at Antwerp; Season 1997–98 appeared at Melbourne and Brisbane Festivals; Extensive tour of Netherlands with St Matthew Passion and Sigiswald Kuikjen; Appeared at Madrid Opera, 1999; Engaged to tour in Poland and the Czech Republic with St John Passion also concert performances in Ireland of Messiah and Beethoven's Missa Solemnis, 2000. *Recordings:* Oberto (Verdi) Christmas Oratorio, B Minor Mass, St Matthew Passion (Bach), Hugo Wolf Orchestral Songs with Choir; Lo Speziale (Haydn opera); Mahler 4th Symphony; Konradin Kreutzer 'Faust'. *Current Management:* Music International. *Address:* Römer 9-11, 65549 Limburg, Germany.

**BROWNRIDGE, Angela (Mary);** Concert Pianist; b. 14 Oct. 1944, North Humberside, England; m. Arthur Johnson, 12 Oct 1968. 1 s. *Education:* Piano Scholar, Edinburgh University; Private study with Dorothy Hesse, Guido Agosti and Maria Curcio. *Career:* Debut: Wigmore Hall, London, 1970; Appearances in major London concert halls and with major orchestras in England and Abroad; Regular Broadcaster with Radio 3 and stations worldwide; Extensive recital tours in England, America, Canada, Far East and Europe; mem, Incorporated Society of Musicians; Musicians Union; EPTA; Beethoven Piano Society of Europe; Liszt Society. *Compositions:* Piano pieces, aged 7. *Recordings:* Solo piano repertoire by Camilleri, Satie, Barber Tchaikovsky, Scriabin, Schumann, Gershwin and Liszt; First ever completed collections of solo works by Barber, and Gershwin, Barber and Satie voted Records of the Month; Concertos with Royal Philharmonic, London Symphony and Hallé Orchestras. *Honours:* Scholarship to Edinburgh University, 1963;

Tovey Prize for Performance, 1965; Frazer Scholarship, 1966; Vaughan Williams Trust Fund, 1972; Arts Council Award, 1972. *Current Management:* ManyGate Management, 13 Cotswold Mews, 30 Battersea Square, London SW11 3 RA. *Address:* 118 Audley Road, Hendon, London NW4 3HG, England.

**BROZAK, Daniel;** Composer, Theoretician and Violinist; b. 13 April 1947, Písek, Czechoslovakia. *Education:* Prague Conservatory; Royal Conservatory in the Hague; Institute for Sonology at Utrecht State University. *Career:* Debut: In Prague with own works for solo violin, 1973; Leader of Prague Chamber Studio until 1969; Musica Intuitiva until 1975; Theoretical research in the field of 12 tone harmony, 1975–84; Electronic and computer music, 1975–94; mem, IG-Komponisten Salzburg; SEAH Prague; SPNMS; SNH 39815; Artistic Initiative-EKVNM. *Compositions:* Les Voiles, 1977; Slunovrat, 1978; Equinox, 1978; The Seasons, 1981; Concerto da Chiesa, 1984; Diseased Society, 1988; Requiem, 1991. *Recordings:* Fresky, 1974; Rigorosum, 1975; Ave, 1978; In Manus Tuas, 1987; In A, 1988; In The Middle of Nowhere, 1988–90; Poetische Stunde, 1989; Dopisy Olze, 1990; Zbytecná Hudba, 1992; Necas Trhovcu, 1994; Katolické Radovánky, 1996; Privat Sky, 1997. *Publications:* Interval Keys, 1977; Structural Harmony, 1988; Pathology of Music, 1991; Zkazena Sul, 1997; Liturgie Zbabelych, 1998. *Contributions:* Interval Keys and Structural Harmony (with D Pandula) in Accademia Cristiana, Roma, Studie 110-11, 1987. *Honours:* Wieniawski Composition Competition (Sonata for solo violin, op 52), 1980. *Current Management:* Donemus, Amsterdam, Netherlands. *Address:* Paulus Potterstraat 16, 1071 CZ, Amsterdam, Netherlands.

**BRUA, Claire;** French singer (soprano); b. 1970. *Education:* Nice Conservatoire with Albert Lance, Paris Conservatoire with Rachel Yakar, Gundula Janowitz and William Christie. *Career:* many performances in France and abroad with such conductors of Baroque music as René Jacobs and Jean-Claude Malgoire; appearances with William Christie and Les Arts Florissants include Purcell's Dido, in Paris and Rome; repertory includes Handel, Mozart and Rossini, and recitals of French song; Rinaldo in Jommelli's Armida abandonata at Beaune 1994; Cavalli's Dido at the Paris Opéra Comique 1998; sang Pulcheria in Handel's Riccardo Primo, with Les Talents Lyriques under Christophe Rousset, Fontevraud 1995; Mozart roles, Dorabella in Così fan tutte, Cherubino in Le nozze di Figaro, Zerlina in Don Giovanni, Annio in La Clemenza di Tito, Zweite Dame in Die Zauberflöte. *Recordings include:* Riccardo Primo. *Current Management:* Agence Artistique Thérèse Cédelle, Boulevard Malesherbes 78, 75008 Paris, France. *Telephone:* (1) 49-53-00-02. *Fax:* (1) 45-63-70-23.

**BRUBAKER, Robert;** Singer (Tenor); b. 1963, USA. *Career:* Sang Henri in Verdi's Vespri Siciliani at Carnegie Hall, New York, 1990; Canadian Opera at Toronto as Cassio in Otello; Season 1993 as Cavaradossi at Seattle and in the title role of Zemlinsky's Der Zwerg at the Spoleto Festival (USA and Italy) and Rome; Sang Pinkerton at Detroit (1994) and Rodolfo at Montreal, 1995; British debut for ENO 1991 as Weill's Jim Mahoney and Don José (returned 1999-2000, as Peter Grimes and as Mao in Nixon in China by John Adams); Washington Opera 1994 in the premiere of Argento's The Dream of Argento; Season 2000-01 as Pierre in War and Peace at the Opéra Bastille and Grimes at Aldeburgh; New York Met as Mephistopheles in Busoni's Faust and Albert Gregor in The Makropoulas Case; Covent Garden debut as Bacchus in Ariadne auf Naxos, 2002; Season 2002–03 in Boris Godunov at the Bastille, Schreker's Der Schatzgräber at Frankfurt and Peter Grimes at Toronto; Siegmund in Madrid, 2003. *Address:* IMG-Paris, 54 Ave Marceau, F–75008 Paris, France.

**BRUCE, Margaret,** ARCM; Canadian/British pianist; b. 28 June 1943, Vancouver, British Columbia, Canada; m. The Hon. H. L. T. Lumley-Savile 1972; three s. (triplets). *Education:* Scholar Toronto Conservatory of Music, Royal College of Music, London. *Career:* debut, Wigmore Hall, 1968; Performances at Wigmore Hall, 1968, 1979; Purcell Room, 1970, 1975, 1978, 1980, 1983; Barbican, 1983, 1985; Royal Concert Huddersfield, 1982; Italian debut, 1983; Tours: Czechoslovakia, 1968, 1981, Canada, 1984, 1987, 1989; Originator, new concert series at St John's, Smith Square, London, Canadians and Classics, 1986, 1988, 1989, 1990; Many other concerts at St John's, including solo and duet; With Royal Philharmonic Orchestra, Barbican, 1985; Bulgarian debut, 1992; Chomé Piano Trio debut, Barbican; Many concerts and recordings to follow, 1993; Bruce-Colwell Duo, Edinburgh Festival debut, 1994; Bruce/Lyttleton Duo recitals of poetry and piano solos, concerts USA, Canada, Italy, the United Kingdom, 1999; concerts Bermuda, Italy, Hebden Bridge Arts Festival 2004; works have been written for her by Herbert Howells, Lennox Berkeley, Jean Coulthard, Antonin Tucapsky. *Compositions:* CBC Recordings, Canada, 1969, 1982, 1984. *Recordings:* Premiere recording of Dvořák's From the Bohemian Forest, Op 68, with Peter Gellhorn; Solo recording, 1983; Divertimenti: 3 concerti written for her; Mozart Concerti K414 and K449, 2001. *Honours:* Royal College of Music, 1962; Sir James Caird Scholarship, 1966. *Address:* Via dei Pandolfini 27, 50122 Florence, Italy (office); Walshaw, Hebden Bridge, West Yorkshire HX7 7AX, England (home). *Telephone:* (777) 327-8477 (office); (1422) 842275 (home). *E-mail:* mls@ musician.org (office); margaretbruce333@aol.com (home).

**BRUCE, Neely;** Composer, Pianist and Conductor; b. 21 Jan. 1944, Memphis, Tennessee, USA. *Education:* Studied Piano with Roy McAllister, University of Alabama; Piano and Composition with Soulima Stravinsky and Ben Johnston, University of Illinois. *Career:* Teacher, Wesleyan University, 1974–, and Conductor, American Music/Theater Group; Piano performances of much

American music including premieres of works by Cage, Duckworth, Farwell, Brant; New York debut, 1968, at the Electric Circus; European debut, Warsaw, 1972, in songs by Ives; Directed scenes from American operas at Holland Festival, 1982; Member, Editorial Committee, New World Records, 1974–79; Chairman, New England Sacred Harp Singing, 1976, 1979, 1982; Senior Research Fellow, Institute for Studies in American Music, Brooklyn College, 1980. *Compositions include:* Pyramus and Thisbe, chamber opera, 1965; The Trials of Psyche, opera, 1971; Concerto for violin and chamber orchestra, 1974; Americana, or, A New Tale of the Genii, opera, 1983; The Blades O' Blue Grass Songbook, solo voices, piano, 1984–95; Atmo-Rag, chamber orchestra, 1987; Santa Ynez Waltz, chamber orchestra, 1990; Orion Rising, First Album for orchestra, 1991; Barnum's Band, large wind ensemble, 1992; Tanglewood, oratorio, 1993; Trio for Bands, 3 rock bands, 1994; Hugomotion, oratorio on texts of Hugo Grotius, 1995; Hansel and Gretel, opera, 1998; Instrumental, chamber, choral and vocal works. *Recordings:* Eight Ghosts, The Dream of the Other Dreamers, The Plague: A Commentary on the Work of the Fourth Horseman, composed for Electric Phoenix vocal quartet with electronics, 1992; Perfumes and Meaning, Illinois Contemporary Chamber Singers with William Brooks, conductor, 1992; Stanzas for Shep and Nancy, Linda Hirst, mezzo-soprano, composer at piano, 1992; For Tom Howell, John Fonville, flautist, 1992. *Current Management:* Jonathan Wentworth Associates, Mt Vernon, New York, USA. *Address:* 440 Chamberlain Road, Middleton, CT 06457, USA.

**BRUCE-PAYNE, Sally;** Singer (Mezzo-soprano); b. 1968, London. *Education:* Royal College of Music and with Felicity Palmer. *Career:* Concerts have included Bach's Choice of Hercules at the Göttingen Festival, the B Minor Mass on tour to Japan and Korea, English Baroque Soloists; Messiah with the Bach Choir and Bach Cantatas in the USA; Season 1998–99: With the St Matthew Passion on tour in Europe, Eryxene in Handel's Poro at Halle and Monteverdi's Ottavia in Japan; European tour of Messiah; Ottone in Handel's Agrippina at St John's Smith Square, Duruflé's Requiem at The Three Choirs Festival and Verdi Requiem with the Philharmonia conducted by David Willcocks; Works regularly with major British orchestras including Royal Liverpool Philharmonic Orchestra, Philharmonia, Bournemouth Symphony Orchestra and Scottish Chamber Orchestra; Season 2001–02 included title role in Offenbach's Dick Whittington at the City of London Festival, Elijah with the Philharmonia conducted by Wolfgang Sawallisch, Partenope at the Royal Opera House Linbury Theatre and the Buxton Festival and Messiah at the Lyon Festival. *Recordings:* Schubert's Mass in A flat and Haydn's Theresien and Nelson Masses conducted by John Eliot Gardiner; Vivaldi's operas Ottone in Villa, Tito Manlio and Giustino; Copland's In the Beginning. *Honours:* English Song Prize at the RCM; Muriel Kistner Prize. *Address:* c/o IMG Artists, Lovell House, 616 Chiswick High Road, London W4 5RX, England.

**BRUDERHANS, Zdenek,** MMus; Flautist and University Reader; b. 29 July 1934, Prague, Czechoslovakia; m. Eva Holubarova 1962; one s. one d. *Education:* Baccalaureate, Akademicke Gymnasium, Prague; Distinction Diploma, Prague Conservatorium of Music; Prague Acad. of Music. *Career:* Debut: Prague, 1957; Asst Prin. Flautist, Prague Nat. Theatre, 1955–59; Prin. Flautist, Prague Radio Symphony Orchestra, 1960–68; Represented Czechoslovakia at M.I.D.E.M in Cannes, France, 1968; Flute Prof., Sweden, 1969–73; Lecturer, Adelaide Univ., South Australia, later Sr Lecturer, Reader, Dean of Music, 1987–88, 1973–97; Flute Soloist in 18 European countries, USA, Australia and Asia on radio; Recitals, concertos and in Festivals. *Recordings:* 16 recordings including recitals of works by Bach, Mozart, Haydn, Hindemith, Martinů, Messiaen, Berio, Debussy, Varèse, Ravel, Feld and Telemann; Zdenek Bruderhans Almanacs; Sonatas by Martinů, Feld, Prokofiev; 3 Flute Anthologies. *Publications:* Music, Tectonics and Flute Playing, 1997. *Contributions:* Miscellania Musicologica; The Instrumentalist; Pan and the Flute. *Honours:* Grand Prize, Int. Competition of Wind Instruments, Prague Spring Festival, 1959. *Address:* 2 McLaughlan Avenue, Brighton 5048, Australia. *Telephone:* (8) 8298-3099 (also fax) (home). *E-mail:* flute@senet.com .au. *Website:* www.senet.com.au/~flute.

**BRUEGGEN, Frans;** Dutch conductor and musicologist; b. 30 Oct. 1934, Amsterdam. *Education:* Musieklyceum, Amsterdam and Univ. of Amsterdam; studied recorder with Kees Otten. *Career:* many engagements as performer and conductor, in early and modern music; Played original 18th century flutes and recorders or copies; Member of avant-garde ensembles, including SourCream; Has commissioned many works (Berio's Gesti, 1966); Erasmus Professor of late Baroque music at Harvard University, 1972–73; Regent's Professor, University of California, Berkeley, 1974; Professor of recorder and early 18th century music at the Royal Conservatory, The Hague; Frequent concerts with cellist Anner Bylsma and harpsichordist Gustav Leonhardt; From 1981 has conducted symphonic music; Founder and Conductor of the Orchestra of the Eighteenth Century (concerts with the orchestra and Malcolm Bilson for the Mozart Bicentenary, 1991); Conducted Idomeneo for Netherlands Opera, 1991; Principal Guest Conductor of the Orchestra of the Age of Enlightenment from 1992, leading it at the 1993 Promenade Concerts in Haydn's London and Beethoven's Ninth Symphonies; Gluck's Orfeo at Lyon, 1998. *Recordings include:* Mozart's Piano Concertos K466 and K491 (John Gibbons), Symphony K550 and Beethoven's 1st Symphony; Haydn Symphonies Nos 90 and 93; Rameau Suites from Dardanus and Les Boréades; Vivaldi Flute Concertos. *Publications:* various editions of early music. *Current Management:* Askonas Holt Ltd, Lonsdale Chambers, 27 Chancery Lane,

London, WC2A 1PF, England. *Telephone:* (20) 7400-1700. *Fax:* (20) 7400-1799. *E-mail:* info@askonasholt.co.uk. *Website:* www.askonasholt.co.uk.

**BRUHN, Siglind;** Concert Pianist and Music Analyst; b. 11 Oct. 1951, Hamburg, Germany; m. Gerhold Becker, 20 Aug 1985. *Education:* MM, Piano Performance, Piano Pedagogy, Musikhochschule Hamburg and Stuttgart; MA, Romance Literature, Philosophy, University of Munich; Masterclasses with Wladimir Horzowski, Hans Leygraf, Nikita Magaloff; DrPhil, Music Analysis, Musikhochschule and University of Vienna, 1985. *Career:* Debut: 1965; Head of Community Music School, Munich, 1978–82; Head, Institute for Musical Interpretation, 1982–87; Director, Pianists' Academy, Ansbach, 1984–87; Director of Studies, University of Hong Kong, 1987–94; Guest Professor, Beijing Central Conservatory of Music, 1990; Visiting Scholar, University of Michigan, Ann Arbor, 1993–97; Permanent Research Associate, Institute for Humanities, University of Michigan, 1997–; Performances in all major West German cities, Zürich, London, Paris, Lisbon, Venice, Athens, Beirut, Rio de Janeiro, Quito, Johannesburg, Cape Town, Hong Kong, Manila, Beijing, Shanghai, Melbourne, Adelaide, Washington DC; Television and radio appearances on most German stations and for British, French, Swiss, Italian, Lebanese, South African, and Australian broadcasting corporations. *Recordings:* Ravel, Moussorgsky, 1984; Dvořák, 1986; Hindemith, duo sonatas, 1997; Hindemith, piano solo, 1997. *Publications:* Analysis and Interpretation in J. S. Bach's Well-Tempered Klavier, 1993; Musikalische Symbolik in Olivier Messiaens Weihnachtsvignetten, 1997; Images and Ideas in Modern French Piano Music, 1997; Alban Berg's Music as Encrypted Speech, editor, 1997; The Temptation of Paul Hindemith: Mathis der Maler as a Spiritual Testimony, 1998; Messiaen's Language of Mystical Love, editor, 1998; Signs in Musical Hermeneutics, editor, 1998; Musical Ekphrasis: Composers Responding to Poetry and Painting, forthcoming; Musical Ekphrasis in Rilke's Marien-Leben, forthcoming. *Contributions:* Scholarly journals, handbooks and collections in Europe, Asia and USA. *Address:* 1308 Broadway, Ann Arbor, MI 48105, USA.

**BRUK, Fridrich;** Composer; b. 18 Sept. 1937, Kharkov, Ukraine; m. Nadezhda Bruk 1959; one s. *Education:* Silver Medal, Kharkov Music Coll. of the Kharkov Conservatory 1956; diploma in composition, Conservatory Rimsky-Korsakov, Leningrad 1961. *Career:* debut, The Forty First (opera based on Boris Lavrenev's story) 1961; composer of opera, orchestral works and chamber music, music for theatre and film, popular songs; teaches pedagogue in various Finnish musical institutes; mem. Soc. of Finnish Composers, Finnish Composers' Copyright Bureau, Guild of Light Music Composers and Authors, Soc. of Russian Composers. *Compositions:* String quartet No.1 1983; music for children: Spring 1982, Snowdrop 1983, Sleigh Bells 1984, Summer 1985, Golden Autumn 1988, Winter 1988; Sunflecks, suite for orchestra 1987, Five duets for clarinet (B) and violoncello or bassoon 1983, Lyrical images, suite for piano 1985, Variations for piano on the Karelian song Strawberry 1985, Concert Variations on the old Kalevala song, for violoncello and piano 1985, The Steppe, suite for woodwind quartet, As Lace Against the Night, 7 songs for 3-voice choir 1986, Sonata for Cantele 1986, String quartet No.2 1987, Concertino for 2 violins and string orchestra or piano 1987, Sonata for 2 violins 1988, Sonata for violoncello 1989; Sonata for 2 trumpets 1989; music for television films 1988, 1989, Sonata for viola 1990, Sonata for clarinet (B) 1991, Sonata for piano 1994, Seven dialogues for oboe and viola 1995, Trio for clarinet (B), viola and violoncello 1996, Symphony No. 1 for orchestra and trombone solo 1998, Symphony No. 2 for orchestra and piano 1999, The Wander Singer, oratorio for baritone, soprano, mixed choir and orchestra (poetry by Oiva Paloheimo) 2000, Artist Chagall, Symphony No. 3 for orchestra and tenor 2000, Sounds of Spring, poem for orchestra 2000, Carelia, Symphony No. 4 for soprano, bass, drums, piano, harp and string orchestra (poetry from Kalevala and Eino Leino) 2001, Musik für Quartett 2001, The Hand of God, Christmas oratorio for narrator, soloists, children's choir and instrumental ensemble 2002, Sonata for Piano No. 2 2002, Symphony No. 5 for Orchestra 2002, Birds of Passage, Symphony No. 6 for baritone and orchestra (poetry by Viljo Kajava) 2001–03, The Cat's House (opera for children, libretto by Samuel Marshak) 2003. *Recordings:* Compositions by Fridrich Bruk 1993, Lyrical Images 1994, From Kalevala 1994, The Snowdrop 1996, Dialogues 1996, Artist Chagall, Symphony No. 3 for orchestra and tenor 2002, The Hand of God 2003, The Sunshine 2004. *Honours:* Cross of Merit of the Order of the Lion of Finland 1988, various Finnish grants and scholarships. *Address:* Papinkatu 18 A 41, Tampere, 33200 Suomi, Finland. *Telephone:* (3) 2144040. *Fax:* (3) 2144040.

**BRUMAIRE, Jacqueline;** Singer (Soprano); b. 5 Nov. 1921, Herbley, France. *Education:* Studied at the Paris Conservatoire. *Career:* Debut: Paris Opéra-Comique, 1946, as The Countess in Le Nozze di Figaro; Sang in Paris as Mimi in La Bohème, Micaela, Manon, Antonia in Les Contes d'Hoffmann and Fiordiligi; Opéra-Comique 1951, in the premiere of Madame Bovary by Bondeville; Paris Opéra 1962, as Donna Elvira in Don Giovanni; Visited Peking 1981, to sing Carmen. *Recordings:* Opera arias, Philips; Milhaud's Les malheurs d'Orphée and Le Pauvre Matelot; Le Roi d'Yvetot by Ibert.

**BRUMBY, Colin (James);** Composer, Lecturer and Conductor; b. 18 June 1933, Melbourne, Victoria, Australia. *Education:* BMus, 1957; DMus, 1972; Conservatorium of Music, University of Melbourne. *Career:* Lecturer in Music, Kelvin Grove Teachers College, 1960–62; Head of Music Department, Greenford Grammar School, Middlesex, 1962–64; Lecturer in Music, 1964–65; Senior Lecturer, 1966–75; Associate Professor of Music, 1976–98; University of Queensland; mem, Australian Performing Right Association. *Compositions:*

Flute Concerto; The Phoenix and the Turtle; Festival Overture on Australian Themes; Charlie Bubbles Book of Hours; Three Italian Songs for High Voice and String Quartet; Violin Concerto 1 and 2; Piano Concerto; South Bank Overture; Symphony No. 1 (The Sun); The Vision and The Gap (Cantata); Bassoon Concerto; Bassoon Sonata; Clarinet Sonatina; Flute Sonatina; Haydn Down Under (Bassoon Quintet); Victimae Paschali (SATB and Strings); Stabat Mater (Cantata); Piano Quartet; Christmas Bells, 1986; A Service of Rounds, 1985; Four Australian Christmas Carols, 1986; Operas: Fire on the Wind; Summer Carol; The Heretic, 1998–99; Borromeo Suite for flute and guitar; Viola Concerto, Tre aspetti di Roma; Trumpet Concerto; Clarinet Concerto, 1988; Canti pisani, 1989. *Publications:* Missa Canonica, 1991; Harlequinade, 1987; Of a Rose, a Lovely Rose, 1994; Organ Concerto, 1994; Cello Concerto, 1995; Toccata for Organ, 1995. *Honours:* Advance Australia Award (Music), 1981. *Current Management:* Australia Music Centre, PO Box N690 Grosvenor Place, Sydney, NSW 2000, Australia. *Address:* 9 Teague Street, Indooroopilly, Queensland 4068, Australia.

**BRUMMELSTROETE, Wilke;** Singer (mezzo-soprano); b. 1968, Netherlands. *Education:* Royal Academy, Hague; Britten-Pears School and Mozarteum, Salzburg. *Career:* Debut: Purcell's Dido, 1991; Netherlands Opera 1992, in Monteverdi's Poppea; Fortuna and Anfinomo in Monteverdi's Ulisse at Brussels, Vienna, Berlin and South Africa; Turno in Bononcini's Il Trionfo di Camilla at Utrecht, 1997: Teseo in Handel's Arianna at Göttingen 1999; Juno and Ino in Semele at San Francisco, 2000; Other roles include Andronico in Handel's Tamerlano, Carmen, and Clothilde in Norma; Concerts include Beethoven's Ninth in Lisbon, Mozart's Requiem in Japan and C minor Mass in Florence; Messiah in Vienna, Bach's Magnificat at the Barbican and Cantatas at the Queen Elizabeth Hall; Elgar's The Kingdom in Buenos Aires, Aldeburgh and Sydney; Season 2001–2002 with Ruggiero in Alcina at Göttingen, Dido with the Irish Chamber Orchestra and concert tour with Israel Camerata. *Current Management:* Askonas Holt Ltd, Lonsdale Chambers, 27 Chancery Lane, London, WC2A 1PF, England. *Telephone:* (20) 7400-1700. *Fax:* (20) 7400-1799. *E-mail:* info@askonasholt.co.uk. *Website:* www.askonasholt.co.uk.

**BRUNNER, Eduard;** Clarinettist; b. 14 July 1939, Basle, Switzerland. *Education:* Studied in Basle and Paris. *Career:* Chamber musician in Germany and Switzerland, from 1959; Soloist with the Bavarian Radio Symphony Orchestra, from 1963; Collaborations with such musicians as violinist Gidon Kremer (at Lockenhaus), Heinz Holliger (oboe) and Aurèle Nicolet (flute); Has premiered works by Francaix and Isang Yun (Concerto, 1982, Quintet, 1984). *Address:* c/o Rundfunkorchester des Bayerischen Rundfunks, Rundfunkplatz: 1, W-8000 Munich 2, Germany.

**BRUNNER, Evelyn;** Singer (Soprano); b. 17 Dec. 1949, Lausanne, Switzerland. *Education:* Studied at the Lausanne Conservatory with Paul Sandoz, in Milan and with Herbert Graf in Geneva. *Career:* Sang with the Ensemble Vocal de Lausanne under Michael Corboz and with the Orchestre de Chambre de Lausanne under Victor Desrazens; Appearances at the Grand Théâtre de Genève as Micaela in Carmen, Marguerite in Faust and Cimarosa's Il Matrimonio Segreto, 1971; Sang Mozart's Countess at the Paris Opéra and in Hamburg and Berlin; Opéra du Rhin, Strasbourg, as Elsa in Lohengrin, 1986; Engagements at opera houses in Lyon, Toulouse, Avignon and Nantes; Other roles include Mozart's Fiordiligi and Donna Anna, Liu in Turandot and Verdi's Elisabeth de Valois and Violetta; Many concerts with the Collegium Academicum de Genève. *Recordings:* Rossini's Il Signor Bruschino, conducted by Robert Dunand.

**BRUNNER, Heidi;** Singer (Mezzo-soprano); b. 1965, Rothenburg, Switzerland. *Education:* Studied in Lucerne, Zürich and Basle. *Career:* Debut: Biel Opera, 1989 as Rossini's Cenerentola; Appearances at Biel as Isabella in L'Italiana in Algeri, Mozart's Zerlina and Dorabella; Ottavia in Poppea and Baba the Turk in The Rake's Progress; Guest appearances in Orontea by Cesti in Basle and Innsbruck; Landstheater Dessau fron 1993, as Giovanna in Anna Bolena and Pisaro in Verdi's Due Foscari; Komische Oper Berlin, 1995 as Cenerentola and Massenet's Charlotte; Berlin Staatsoper, 1996 as Roggiero in Rossini's Tancredi; season 1998 as Messenger and Proserpina in Monteverdi's Orfeo at the Vienna Festival; Sang Gounod's Siebel at Munich, 2000. *Address:* c/o Bayerische Staatsoper, Max-Joseph-Platz, D–80539 Munich, Germany.

**BRUNNER, Richard;** Singer (Tenor); b. 1953, Ohio, USA. *Education:* Studied at the Opera School of Toronto and the Academy of Vocal Arts in Pittsburgh. *Career:* Sang Ramiro in Cenerentola with Philadelphia Opera (1978), Mime in Das Rheingold (Cincinnati and Dallas, 1981–82), Steva in Jenůfa at the Spoleto Festival, Florestan with Scottish Opera (1991) and roles such as Elemer (Arabella), Narraboth (Salome) and Cassio (Otello) at the Vienna Staatsoper; Denver Opera, 1992, as Walther von Stolzing; Other roles include Melot, Sellem (The Rake's Progress) and Eisenstein in Die Fledermaus; Bayreuth Festival 1994–96, as Wagner's Froh; Sang Narraboth in Salome at San Diego, 1998; Season 1999–2000 as Strauss's Emperor and Janáček's Albert Gregor at Darmstadt, Sam in Carlisle Floyd's Susannah for Washington Opera. *Address:* c/o Opera Colorado, 695 South Colorado Boulevard, Suite 20, Denver, CA 80222, USA.

**BRUNO, Joanna (Mary);** Singer (Soprano); b. 1944, Orange, New Jersey, USA. *Education:* Studied with Katherine Eastment in New Jersey, at the Juilliard School with Jennie Tourel and with Luigi Ricci in Rome. *Career:* Debut: Spoleto Festival 1969, in The Medium by Menotti; Sang in Santa Fe, Houston, Chicago, Fort Worth, City Opera, New York notably in the 1971 premiere of Menotti's The Most Important Man; European engagements in

Trieste, Paris, Amsterdam and for Scottish Opera; Other roles include Mozart's Despina, Susanna and Pamina; Anne Trulove in The Rake's Progress, Micaela, Verdi's Nannetta; Puccini's Butterfly, Musetta and Mimi.

**BRUSA, Elisabetta (Olga Laura);** Italian Composer and Professor; *Professor of Composition and Orchestration, Conservatorio of Milan;* b. 3 April 1954, Milan, Italy; m. Gilberto Serembe, 3 May 1997. *Education:* Diploma, Composition, Conservatorio of Milan with Bruno Bettinelli and Azio Corghi, 1980; Further studies with Hans Keller, London. *Career:* Debut: First Composition performed, Piccola Scala, 1982; Television programme on Young Italian Composers, 1983; Various commissions, performances; Radio and television broadcasts in Italy, England, USA, Canada, Australia, Russia, France, Ukraine, Germany, Austria, Switzerland, Korea, and Albania with Orchestras such as the BBC Philharmonic, BBC Scottish Symphony Orchestra, CBC Vancouver Orchestra, St Petersburg Symphony Orchestra, National Symphony Orchestra of Ukraine, Philharmonisches Orchestra des Theatres Altenburg-Gera, Virtuosi of Toronto; Boris Brott Festival Orchestra, Radio and Television Symphony Orchestra of Tirana, London Chamber Symphony, New England Philharmonic, Tanglewood Music Center Orchestra, Alea III Ensemble, Contemporary Music Forum of Washington DC; Women's Philharmonic of San Francisco; Professor, Composition at: Conservatorio of Vicenza, 1980–82; Conservatorio of Mantova, 1982–84; Conservatorio of Brescia, 1984–85; Conservatorio of Milan, 1985–. *Compositions include:* Belsize String Quartet, 1981; Fables for chamber orchestra, 1983; Marcia Funebre for piano, 1984; Suite Concertante for orchestra, 1986; Sonata for piano, 1986; Nittemero Symphony for chamber orchestra, 1988; Symphony No. 1 for large orchestra, 1990; Sonata Rapsodica for violin and piano, 1991; La Triade for large orchestra, 1992; Firelights for large orchestra, 1993; Requiescat for mezzo-soprano and large orchestra, 1995; Fanfare for large orchestra, 1996; Adagio for string orchestra, 1996; Wedding Song for large orchestra, 1997; Florestan for large orchestra, 1997; Messidor for orchestra, 1998; Symphony No. 2 for large orchestra; Merlin, for large orchestra 2004. *Recordings:* Orchestral Works Vols. 1 and 2. *Honours:* 1st Prize Washington International Competition, 1982; Fellowship, Tanglewood Music Center, 1983; Fulbright Bursary, 1983; Fellowship, MacDowell Colony, 1988, 1989, 1990. *E-mail:* elisabetta.brusa@tiscali.it (office). *Website:* www.elisabettabrusa.it.

**BRUSON, Renato;** Singer (Baritone); b. 13 Jan. 1936, Este, Italy. *Education:* Studied in Padua, Italy. *Career:* Debut: Spoleto Festival, 1961; Has appeared at all major Italian Opera Houses including La Scala, Milan, Debut 1972; Specialising in Verdi and Donizetti operas in Attila, La Traviata, La Favorita and Lucia di Lammermoor; Other opera houses include Vienna, Hamburg, Berlin, Paris, Brussels etc; Covent Garden debut 1976, as Renato in Un Ballo in Maschera; Appearances in USA include Chicago, New York Metropolitan Opera and San Francisco; Debut as Enrico at the Metropolitan, 1969; Has sung at the Verona Arena 1975–76, 1978–82, 1985; Los Angeles and Covent Garden, 1982, as Falstaff; Also at Parma, 1986; Munich, 1985, as Macbeth; Sang Iago at La Scala, 1987; Don Giovanni at the Deutsche Oper Berlin, 1988; Carnegie Hall, New York, 1990, as Montfort in Les Vêpres Siciliennes; Sang Carlos in Ernani at Parma, 1990, Germont at Turin, Carlos at La Fenice, Venice; Sang Enrico in Lucia di Lammermoor at La Scala, 1992, Germont at the 1992 Macerata Festival and at Covent Garden, 1995; Sang Macbeth at Monte Carlo, 1997; Germont at the 1999 Orange festival; Falstaff at Macerata, 1998; Season 2000–01 at the Vienna Staatsoper as Don Carlo in Ernani, and Iago. *Recordings:* Luisa Miller; Falstaff; Samson and Delilah etc. Films and television include Don Carlos, La Scala and Luisa Miller, Covent Garden. *Address:* Teatro Alla Scala, Via Filodrammatici 2, Milano, Italy.

**BRUYNEL, Ton;** Composer; b. 26 Jan. 1934, Utrecht, Netherlands. *Education:* Piano at Utrecht Conservatory. *Career:* Associated with Electronic Music Studio, University of Utrecht; Established own electronic music studio in 1957. *Compositions include:* Mostly with soundtracks; Resonance l, ballet, 1960–62; Reflexes for Birma Drum, 1961; Relief for Organ, 1964; Mobile, 1965; Milieu, 1965–66; Mekaniek for Wind Quintet, 1967; Decor, ballet, 1967; Signs for Wind Quintet and Video Projection, 1969; Intra 1 for Bass Clarinet, 1971; Elegy for Female Voices, 1972; Looking Ears for Bass Clarinet and Grand Piano, 1972; Soft Song for Oboe, 1975; Dialogue for Bass Clarinet, 1976; Translucent ll for String Orchestra, 1978; From the Tripod for Loudspeakers, Women and Listeners, 1981; John's Lullaby for Chorus and Tape, 1985; Continuation for Chorus and Tape, 1985; Adieu petit Prince for Voice, 1983; Denk Mal das Denkmal for Man's Voice, 1984; Chicharras text, 1986; Toccare for Clavicembalo, 1987; Ascolta for Chorus and Soloist, 1989; Nocturnos en Pedraza for Flute and Soundtrack, 1988; Kolom for Organ, 1987; Non Sono un Cello for Tenor and Bass Baritone; La Dernière pavane for Small Mixed Choir, 1989; La Cadulta for Tenor Bass Baritone; Tropico for Tenor Bass Baritone, 1990; Dust for Small Organ, 1991; Tarde for Cello, 1992; Le Jardin for Alto Flute, Harpsichord and Woman's Voice, 1992; Ball'alla luce for strings, tape and percussion, 1997. *Address:* Fen Have 13, 7983 KD, Wapse Diever, Netherlands.

**BRUZDOWICZ-TITTEL, Joanna,** MA; French/Polish composer and music critic; b. 17 May 1943, Warsaw, Poland; d. of Konstanty Bruzdowicz and Countess Maria Wilczek; m. Jürgen Tittel; three s. *Education:* Warsaw Conservatory, studied piano with Irena Protasewicz and Wanda Losakiewicz, composition with Kazimierz Sikorski, Nadia Boulanger, Olivier Messiaen, Pierre Schaeffer in Paris. *Career:* Groupe de Recherches Musicales, French radio and television, Paris; Groupe International de Musique Electroacous-

tique de Paris; IPEM; Electronic studios, Univ. of Ghent, Belgian radio and television; founder, Jeunesses Musicales, Poland; founder and Pres., Frédéric Chopin and Karol Szymanowski Soc., Belgium; Vice-Pres., Int. Federation of Chopin Socs; music criticism; advocate of contemporary music; mem. SACD, SACEM (France), Soc. of Authors, ZAiKS, ZKP, Poland. *Film scores:* Bobo la tête 1980, Tante Blandine (TV) 1983, Sans toit ni loi 1985, Kung-Fu master 1987, Le Jupon rouge 1987, Jacquot de Nantes 1991, Un air si pur... 1997, Les Glaneurs et la glaneuse 2000, Les Glaneurs et la glaneuse... deux ans après 2002. *Compositions include:* operas: In der Strafkolonie, or La Colonie Pénitentiaire 1972, Les Troyennes 1973, The Gates of Paradise 1987, Tides and Waves (opera, musical) 1992; ballet: Le Petit Prince 1976; orchestral: Piano Concerto 1974, Symphony 1975, Violin Concerto 1975, Aquae Sextiae for winds 1978, Double Bass Concerto 1982, Four Seasons' Greetings (four concertos for violin, piano, flute, marimba, string orchestra) 1989, The Cry of the Phoenix for cello and symphony orchestra 1994; chamber: Trio dei Due Mondi for violin, cello, piano 1980, Dum Spiro Spero for flute and tape 1981, Para y contra for double bass and tape 1981, Trio per Trio for flute, violin, harpsichord 1982, Dreams and Drums for percussion 1982, Oracle for bassoon and tape 1982, Aurora Borealis for harp and organ 1988, String Quartet No. 1: La Vita 1983, No. 2: Cantus Aeternus with speaker 1988, Spring in America (violin-piano sonata) 1994; cantata: Urbi et Orbi for tenor, children's choir, two trumpets, two trombones, organ 1985, The Cry of the Phoenix cello concerto 1994, Song of Hope and Love for cello and piano 1997, The World (five songs for soprano and piano, poetry by Czeslaw Milosz) 1995–96, 16 Pictures of a Salvador Dalí Exhibition for piano 2004; piano pieces;, organ music, electronic and electro-acoustic pieces. *Honours:* hon. mem. Donne in Musica, Italy; Officer of Polonia Restituta, Poland 2001. *Address:* Mas Terrats, 66400 Taillet, France. *Telephone:* (4) 68 87 48 59. *E-mail:* tibruz@wanadoo.fr.

**BRYAN, John Howard,** BA, BPhil; musician (early instruments) and academic; *Principal Lecturer in Music, University of Huddersfield;* b. 24 Feb. 1952, Ilford, Essex, England; one s. two d. *Education:* University of York. *Career:* debut, 1973; Co-Director, Landini Consort; Director, Rose Consort of Viols; Artistic Adviser, York Early Music Festival; Principal Lecturer, University of Huddersfield; Also plays with Consort of Musicke and Musica Antiqua of London; mem. North East Early Music Forum; National Early Music Association. *Recordings:* Nowell, Landini Consort; Songs and Dances of Fourteenth Century Italy, Landini Consort; The Play of Daniel, Landini Consort and Pro Cantione Antiqua; Elizabethan Christmas Anthems, Rose Consort of Viols; Dowland, Lachrimae, Rose Consort of Viols; Born is the Babe, Ah, dear Heart, Rose Consort of Viols; John Jenkins, Consort Music, Rose Consort of Viols; William Byrd, Consort music, songs and anthems, Rose Consort of Viols; Orlando Gibbons, Consort music, songs and anthems, Rose Consort of Viols; John Dowland, Dances and lute Songs, Purcell, Fantasias and in Nomines, Rose Consort of Viols; Elizabethan Consort Music, Rose Consort; Alfonso Farrebosco I & II Consort Music, Rose Consort; John Ward Consort Music, Rose Consort; A Songbook for Isabella, Musica Antiqua of London; Music for Henry VIII's Six Wives, Musica Antiqua of London. *Contributions:* Music in Education; Compendium of Contemporary Musical Knowledge, 1992. *Address:* 28 Wentworth Road, Scarcroft Hill, York YO24 1DG, England. *E-mail:* j.h.bryan@hud.ac.uk.

**BRYARS, Gavin,** BA; British composer and professor of music; *Associate Research Fellow, Dartington College of Arts;* b. 16 Jan. 1943, Goole, Yorkshire; s. of Walter Joseph Bryars and Miriam Eleanor Bryars; m. 1st Angela Margaret Bigley 1971 (divorced 1993); two d.; m. 2nd Anna Tchernakova 1999; one s. one step d. *Education:* Goole Grammar School, Sheffield Univ., Northern School of Music and pvt composition study with Cyril Ramsey, George Linstead and Benjamin Johnston. *Career:* freelance double bassist 1963–66; Lecturer in Liberal Studies, Northampton Coll. of Technology 1966–67; freelance composer/performer 1968–70; Lecturer in Music, Portsmouth Polytechnic 1969–70; Sr Lecturer, School of Fine Art, Leicester Polytechnic 1970–78, Sr Lecturer and Head of Music, School of Performing Arts 1978–85; Prof. of Music, De Montfort Univ. 1985–96; currently Assoc. Research Fellow Dartington Coll. of Arts; collaborations with artists, including Aphex Twin, John Cage, Brian Eno, Tom Waits; mem. Collège de Pataphysique, France 1974–; Ed. Experimental Music Catalogue 1972–81; British Rep. Int. Soc. for Contemporary Music Festival 1977; Visiting Prof. Univ. of Herts.; Arts Council Comms 1970, 1980, 1982, Bursary 1982. *Films:* Sea and Stars (Nat. Film Bd of Canada) 2003. *Radio:* I Send You This Cadmium Rec (BBC Radio 3, with John Berger and John Christie) 2002, Egil's Last Days (BBC Radio 3) 2004. *Television:* Last Summer (CBC TV, Dir Anna Tchernakova) 2000. *Compositions include:* The Sinking of the Titanic 1969, Jesus' Blood Never Failed Me Yet 1971, Out of Zaleski's Gazebo 1977, The Vespertine Park 1980, Medea (opera with Robert Wilson) 1982, My First Homage for two pianos 1978, Effarene 1984, String Quartet No. 1 1985, Pico's Flight 1986, By the Vaar for double bass and ensemble 1987, The Invention of Tradition 1988, Glorious Hill 1988, Cadman Requiem 1989, String Quartet No. 2 1990, Four Elements (dance piece) 1990, The Black River for soprano and organ 1991, The White Lodge 1991, The War in Heaven for chorus and orchestra 1993, Epilogue from 'Wonderlawn' for four players 1994, Three Elegies for Nine Clarinets 1994, The North Shore for solo viola and small orchestra 1994, After Handel's Vesper 1995, Cello Concerto 1995, The Adnan Songbook 1996, Doctor Ox's Experiment (opera) 1997, String Quartet No. 3 1998, The Porazzi Fragment for strings 1998, Biped (ballet) 1999, First Book of Madrigals 2000, Violin Concerto 2000, G (opera) 2001, Second Book of Madrigals 2001, Double Bass Concerto 2002, Book of Laude 2003, Writings on

Water (ballet) 2003, Third Book of Madrigals 2003, Eight Irish Madrigals 2004, New York (percussion concerto) 2004, From Egil's Saga 2004. *Publications:* contrib. to Music and Musicians, Studio International, Art and Artists, Contact,The Guardian. *Address:* c/o Schott and Co. Ltd, 48 Great Marlborough Street, London, W1F 7BB, England (office). *Telephone:* (20) 7494-1487 (office). *Fax:* (20) 7287-1529 (office). *E-mail:* questions@gavinbryars.com (office). *Website:* www.gavinbryars.com (office).

**BRYDON, Roderick;** Conductor; b. 8 Jan. 1939, Edinburgh, Scotland. *Education:* Daniel Stewart's College, Edinburgh; BMus Edinburgh University; Chigiana Academy, Siena. *Career:* Debut: Covent Garden, 1984, with A Midsummer Night's Dream; Close association with Sadler's Wells Opera and Scottish Opera in operas by Janáček (From the House of the Dead), Stravinsky, Mozart, Puccini, Debussy and Cavalli, (L'Egisto); Formerly General Music Director Lucerne Opera, conducting Carmen, Don Giovanni, Albert Herring and Fidelio; Musical Director of Berne Opera, 1988–90, leading A Village Romeo and Juliet, Capriccio and Peter Grimes; Guest engagements in Hannover, Copenhagen, Karlsruhe (Handel's Alcina); Bordeaux, (Così fan tutte) and Geneva (Death in Venice, The Rake's Progress and La Clemenza di Tito); Mozart's Mitridate and Rossini's Otello in Venice; Death in Venice at the 1983 Edinburgh Festival; La Traviata; The Rake's Progress with Opera North; Artistic Director of the Scottish Chamber Orchestra for the first 9 years of its existence including concerts at the Aix and Edinburgh Festivals; Promenade Concerts, 1982; Further concerts in Munich, Paris and Venice; Conducted Parsifal at the City Theatre Berne, 1989; Concert performances of The Cunning Little Vixen, 1990; Conducted Albert Herring at Los Angeles, 1992, followed by A Midsummer Night's Dream; The Rake's Progress, at the 1992 Aldeburgh Festival; Lucia di Lammermoor at Sydney, 1996; Catán's Florencia en el Amazones at Los Angeles, 1997; Handel's Serse at Geneva, 1998. *Address:* c/o Music International, 13 Ardilaun Road, London N5 2QR, England.

**BRYN-JULSON, Phyllis;** Singer (Soprano); b. 5 Feb. 1945, Bowdon, North Dakota, USA. *Education:* Studied singing at the Berkshire Music Center and at Syracuse University. *Career:* Debut: With the Boston Symphony in Berg's Lulu Suite, 1966; Has given performances of works by George Crumb, David Del Tredici, Lukas Foss, Ligeti, Berg, Webern and Schoenberg (Pierrot Lunaire); Appearances at the Berlin, Edinburgh, Lucerne and Aldeburgh Festivals; British debut 1975, in Pli selon Pli by Boulez, conducted by the composer; Boulez 60th birthday celebrations at Baden-Baden 1985; Orchestras with whom she has appeared include the New York Philharmonic, the Boston Symphony, Chicago Symphony, Berlin Philharmonic under Abbado; First operatic role as Malinche in Montezuma by Roger Sessions, US premiere, Boston 1976; Sang in Stravinsky's Nightingale and Ravel's L'Enfant et les Sortilèges at Covent Garden, season 1986–87; Tours of Australia, New Zealand, USSR and Japan with Boulez; Ensemble Intercontemporain; Tours of the US with the Los Angeles Philharmonic and of Europe with the BBC Symphony; Gave master classes at the Moscow Conservatoire in 1987 and took part in the 80th birthday celebrations for Olivier Messiaen and Elliott Carter, 1988; Sang in Carter's A Mirror on Which to Dwell, at London's Queen Elizabeth Hall, Feb 1991; Schoenberg's Erwartung at the Festival Hall, 1991; Premiered Marrying the Hangman (one-woman chamber opera) by Ron Caltabiano in New York and San Francisco; Staged and televised opera Il Prigioniero by Dallapiccola in Tokyo, with Charles Dutoit conducting. *Recordings include:* A Mirror on which to Dwell; Le Visage Nuptial and Le Soleil des Eaux by Boulez, Erato; Il Prigioniero by Dallapiccola, Salonen, Swedish Radio Symphony; Erwartung by Schoenberg, Simon Rattle, City of Birmingham Symphony Orchestra; Schumann's Frauenliebe und Leben, with Leon Fleisher, piano. *Honours:* Distinguished Alumni Award, Syracuse University; Amphion Foundation Award. *Current Management:* Howard Stokar Management. *Address:* c/o Howard Stokar Management, 870 West End Avenue New York, NY 10025-4948, USA. *E-mail:* hstokar@stokar.com.

**BRYSON, Roger;** Singer (Bass); b. 1944, London, England. *Education:* Guildhall School, London; London Opera Centre with Walther Gruner and Otakar Kraus. *Career:* Glyndebourne Festival and Touring Opera from 1978 as Neptune in Il Ritorno d'Ulisse, Quince and Bottom in A Midsummer Night's Dream, Osmin in Die Entführung, Rocco in Fidelio and Leporello in Don Giovanni; Kent Opera in Rigoletto, Die Zauberflöte and Don Giovanni; English National Opera in the British premiere of Ligeti's Le Grand Macabre, 1982; Opera North in Die Meistersinger, Werther, La Fanciulla del West and Love of Three Oranges; Scottish Opera as Schigolch in Lulu and Don Alfonso in Così fan tutte; Sang at Nancy in the French premiere of Tippett's King Priam and on television in the Midsummer Marriage, 1989; As Alvise in La Gioconda for the Chelsea Opera Group, Mephistopheles in Faust for New Sussex Opera, 1989, Swallow in Peter Grimes, Don Pasquale for Opera North, Bartered Bride for New Tel-Aviv Opera; Sang in concert performances of Ligeti's Le Grand Macabre at the Festival Hall, 1989, Don Pasquale for Opera North, 1990, Premieres of Europeras 3 and 4 by John Cage at the 1990 Almeida Festival, London; Sang Quince in A Midsummer Night's Dream, Sadler's Wells, Dikoi in Katya Kabanova for Glyndebourne Touring Opera, 1992, Flint in Billy Budd, 1992, Claggart in Billy Budd for Opéra de Nancy, 1993, Don Basilio in Barber of Seville for Opera Northern Ireland, Calandro in L'Incontro Improvviso by Haydn, for Garsington Festival, and Don Alfonso in Così fan tutte for ENO. *Address:* c/o Music International, 13 Ardilaun Road, Highbury, London, N5 2QR, England.

**BUCHAN, Cynthia;** Singer (mezzo-soprano); b. 1948, Edinburgh, Scotland. *Education:* Royal Scottish Academy of Music, 1968–72. *Career:* Debut: Edinburgh 1968 in Monteverdi's Il Ballo delle Ingrate; Has appeared widely in the United Kingdom and Europe as Mozart's Cherubino and Dorabella, Massenet's Charlotte, Rossini's Rosina, Verdi's Preziosilla, Tchaikovsky's Olga and as Carmen; In 1987 sang in L'Enfant et les Sortilèges at Glyndebourne, Carmen for Opera North and Mistress Quickly in Peter Stein's production of Falstaff for the Welsh National Opera; Guest appearances in Madrid, Munich, Paris as Rosina, Frankfurt as Babette in Henze's English Cat, Adelaide, Hamburg as Miranda in Cavalli's L'Ormindo and Amsterdam as Varvara in Katya Kabanova; Glyndebourne 1989 as Hermia in A Midsummer Night's Dream; Sang Despina in Così fan tutte for New Israeli Opera, 1994; Maddalena in Rigoletto for WNO, 1997; Concert appearances in London, Munich, Paris and Lyon; Conductors include Gielen, Andrew Davis, Rattle, Ivan Fischer, Knussen, Del Mar, Bernstein and Bertini. *Recordings include:* Video of Bersi in Andrea Chénier, at Covent Garden in 1985.

**BUCHANAN, Alison;** Singer (Soprano); b. 1969, England. *Education:* Studied at the Guildhall School of Music and the Curtis Institute, Philadelphia. *Career:* Appearances as Clara in Porgy and Bess at the Barbican, in Messiah at Chichester Cathedral, Mozart's Requiem and Bach's Christmas Oratorio at Chelmsford Cathedral and Strauss's Four Last Songs at Curtis Hall; Debut with the San Francisco Opera with Western Opera Theatre as Mozart's Countess; Season 1995–96 at San Francisco as Mimi, Juliana in Argento's The Aspern Papers, and Micaela; Season 1996–97 with Porgy and Bess excerpts in Bruges and Paris and appearances in Elektra, Death in Venice and Rigoletto at San Francisco; Other roles include Rosalinde, Mathilde in Guillaume Tell, Helena in A Midsummer Night's Dream and Madame Cortese in Il Viaggio a Reims; Sang Giunone in Cesti's Il Pomo d'Oro at Batignano, 1998. *Honours:* First Prize, Washington International Competition, 1995; Pavarotti Competition in Philadelphia, 1995. *Address:* c/o San Francisco Opera, Van Ness Avenue, San Francisco, CA, USA.

**BUCHANAN, Dorothy (Quita);** Composer; b. 28 Sept. 1945, Christchurch, New Zealand. *Education:* Graduated, University of Canterbury, 1967. *Career:* Founded music workshops at Christchurch, 1973; Music educationalist from 1977; Composer-in-Residence at New Zealand Film Archives, Wellington, 1984. *Compositions include:* Five Vignettes of Women for flute and female chorus, 1987, and other vocal music; Sinfonietta in 5 Movements, 1989; Due concertante for violin, cello and orchestra, 1991; Music for stage and screen; The Layers of Time for cello, women's voices and orchestra, 1995; Chamber music, including Echoes and Reflections for clarinet, guitar, violin and cello, 1993. *Address:* c/o SOUNZ, PO Box 10 042 Wellington, 39 Cambridge Terrace, Wellington, New Zealand.

**BUCHANAN, Isobel Wilson;** British singer (soprano); b. 15 March 1954, Glasgow; d. of Stewart Buchanan and Mary Buchanan; m. Jonathan Stephen Geoffrey King (actor Jonathan Hyde) 1980; two d. *Education:* Cumbernauld Comprehensive High School and Royal Scottish Acad. of Music and Drama. *Career:* professional début in Sydney, Australia with Richard Bonynge and Joan Sutherland 1976–78; British début, Glyndebourne 1978; US and German début 1979; Vienna Staatsoper début 1979; ENO début 1985, Paris Opera début 1986; now freelance artist working with all major opera cos and orchestras. *Recordings:* Beethoven's Ninth Symphony, Werther, Mozart Arias and Duets. *Current Management:* Marks Management Ltd, 14 New Burlington Street, London, W1X 1FF, England.

**BUCHBINDER, Rudolf;** Pianist; b. 11 Feb. 1946, Leitmeritz, Austria. *Education:* Studied piano with Bruno Seidlhofer. *Career:* Extensive repertoire of concert pieces, both classical and modern; Has performed works rarely played including The Diabelli Variations, a collection from 50 Austrian composers; Has performed a cycle of all 32 Beethoven Sonatas; Performances in many major cities in Europe, USA, South America, Australia and Japan; Regular guest at major music festivals; Has played with all important leading conductors. *Recordings:* The Diabelli Variations; Collection of Joseph Haydn piano works; Over 80 recordings. *Honours:* Grand Prix du Disque, for Haydn's piano works. *Current Management:* Astrid Schoerke. *Address:* c/o Monckebergallee 41, 30453 Hannover, Germany.

**BUCHLA, Donald Frederick;** Composer, Performer and Electronic Instrument Designer; b. 17 April 1937, Southgate, CA, USA. *Education:* BA, Physics, Univ. of California at Berkeley, 1961. *Career:* installed first Buchla synthesizer, San Francisco Tape Music Center, 1966; Founder of Buchla Assocs, Berkeley, 1966; designed and manufactured various electronic instruments; designed electronic music studios including Royal Academy of Music, Stockholm, and IRCAM, Paris; Co-Founder, Electric Weasel Ensemble, 1975; Co-Dir, Artists Research Collective, Berkeley, 1978–. *Compositions:* various pieces with electronic instruments including Cicada Music for some 2,500 Cicadas, 1963; 5 Video Mirrors for Audience of 1 or More, 1966; Anagnorisis for 1 Performer and 1 Voice, 1970; Harmonic Pendulum for Buchla Series 200 Synthesizer, 1972; Garden for 3 Performers and 1 Dancer, 1975; Keyboard Encounter for 2 Pianos, 1976; Q for 14 Instruments, 1979; Silicon Cello for Amplified Cello, 1979; Consensus Conduction for Buchla Series 300 Synthesizer and Audience, 1981. *Honours:* Guggenheim Fellowship, 1978; National Endowment for the Arts Grant, 1981. *Address:* c/o Buchla and Associates, PO Box 10205, Berkeley, CA 94709, USA. *Website:* www.buchla.com.

**BUCHNER, Eberhard;** Singer (Tenor); b. 6 Nov. 1939, Dresden, Germany. *Education:* Studied at the Carl Maria Von Weber-Musikhochschule, Dresden, 1959–64. *Career:* Debut: Schwerin in 1964 as Tamino; Staatsoper Dresden from 1966, and Staatsoper Berlin from 1968, notably in operas by Strauss, Mozart and Wagner; Sang Schubert's Die schöne m üllerin, in Vienna, 1972; Appeared at the Vatican in 1973 in a concert conducted by Bernstein; Sang at Metropolitan Opera in 1974, Covent Garden in 1975, Hamburg Staatsoper in 1983 in a revival of Armadis de Gaule by JC Bach, Théâtre de la Monnaie in Brussels, and Salzburg Festival in 1985 and 1990 as Flamand in Capriccio, and Royal Opera Copenhagen in 1986 as Wagner's Lohengrin; Sang Adolar in Euryanthe at the Berlin Staatsoper, 1986; La Scala Milan in 1988 as Erik in Der fliegende Holländer and sang Lohengrin at Lisbon in 1990; Sang Dionysus in The Bassarids at Hamburg, 1994 and as Der Alte in the premiere of Schnittke's Historia von D Johann Fausten, 1995. *Recordings:* Die schweigsame Frau by Strauss; Froh in Das Rheingold; Bach Cantatas; Bach's B minor Mass; Sacred Music by Mozart; Beethoven's 9th Symphony.

**BUCHT, Gunnar,** PhD; Swedish composer and writer; b. 5 Aug. 1927, Stocksund; m. Bergljot Krohn 1958. *Education:* studied composition with Karl Birger-Blomdahl, Carl Orff, Goffredo Petrassi, Max Deutsch, piano with Yngve Flyckt. *Career:* debut as composer and pianist 1949; Chair., Soc. of Swedish Composers 1963–69; teacher, Stockholm Univ. 1965–69; Vice-Pres., Int. Soc. for Contemporary Music 1969–72; cultural attaché to the Swedish Embassy at Bonn 1970–73; Prof. of Composition, Royal Coll. of Music 1975–85, Dir 1987–93; mem. Royal Acad. of Music. *Compositions include:* 12 symphonies 1952–97, two cello concertos 1955–90, three string quartets 1951, 1959, 1997, String Quintet 1950, Sonata for piano and percussion 1955, La fine della diaspora for tenor, chorus and orchestra (Quasimodo) 1957, The Pretenders (opera, after Ibsen) 1966, Symphonie pour la musique libérée for tape 1969, Lutheran Mass 1973, Journées oubliées 1975, Au delá 1977, Violin Concerto 1978, The Big Bang – and After 1979, Georgica 1980, En Clairobscur for chamber orchestra 1981, One Day I Went Out Into The World novel for orchestra 1983–84, Blad från mitt gulsippeänge for clarinet and piano 1985, Fresques mobiles 1986, Unter Vollem Einsatz for organ and five percussionists 1987, Tönend bewegte Formen for orchestra 1987, Piano Concerto 1994, Coup sur Coup for percussion 1995, Concerto de Marle for viola and orchestra 1996, Movements in Space for orchestra 1996, Panta Rei for soli, chorus and orchestra 1998–99, Alienus' Dream for orchestra 1999, Partita for two violins 2001, Den starkare (Strindberg) monodram for mezzo-soprano and orchestra 2001, Superstrings for orchestra 2002, Tre per due for two violins 2002. *Recordings:* Symphony 7, Violin Concerto, Piano Concerto, Georgica, Cantata, Quatre pièces pour le pianiste, Coup sur Coup, Sections of One Day I Went Out Into the World, Odysseia (Kazantzakis) half-scenic oratorio for soli, chorus and orchestra, part one 2000–03, The Infinite Melody for orchestra 2004. *Publications:* Electronic Music in Sweden 1977, Europe in Music 1996, Född på Krigsstigen (autobiog.) 1997, Rum, rörelse, tid 1999, Pythagoras' String 2005; contrib. to Swedish Journal of Musicology, Nordic Journal of Aesthetics. *Honours:* Royal Medal Litteris et artibus, Royal Acad. of Music För tonkonstensfrämjande. *Address:* Burge Hablingbo, 62011 Havdhem, Sweden (home); Rådmansgatan 74, 11360 Stockholm, Sweden. *Telephone:* (08) 736 60 31 (home). *E-mail:* gb.bucht@telia.com (home).

**BUCK, Peter;** cellist; b. 18 May 1937, Stuttgart, Germany. *Education:* Stuttgart Conservatory with Ludwig Hoelscher. *Career:* former mem. of Karl Munchinger's Stuttgart Chamber Orchestra in Heilbronn; co-founder of Melos Quartet of Stuttgart, 1965; represented Germany at the Jeunesses Musicales in Paris, 1966; international concert tours from 1967; bicentenary concerts in the Beethoven Haus at Bonn in 1970; toured Russia, Eastern Europe, Africa, North and South America, The Far East and Australia; British concerts and festivals from 1974; cycle of Beethoven quartets at Edinburgh Festival, 1987; played at Wigmore Hall, St John's Smith Square and Bath Festival in 1990; associations with Rostropovich in the Schubert Quintet and the Cleveland Quartet in works by Spohr and Mendelssohn; teacher at the Stuttgart Musikhochschule. *Recordings include:* Complete Quartets of Beethoven, Schubert, Mozart and Brahms; Quintets by Boccherini with Narcisco Ypes, and by Mozart with Franz Beyer. *Honours:* with Melos Quartet, Grand Prix du Disque and Prix Caecilia, from Academie du Disque in Brussels. *Current Management:* Ingpen & Williams Ltd, 7 St George's Court, 131 Putney Bridge Road, London, SW15 2PA, England.

**BUCKEL, Ursula;** Singer (Soprano) and Teacher; b. 11 Feb. 1926, Lauscha, Germany. *Education:* Studied with Hans Hoefflin in Freiburg and with Ria Ginster in Zürich. *Career:* Sang in Bach's St John Passion at Kreuzlingen, Switzerland; Based in Geneva from 1954; Many performances of cantatas and Passions by Bach, notably at the Bach-Festwochen at Schaffhausen and Ansbach; Tours of Switzerland, England, Finland, Austria, France, Germany and Italy; Far East tour with the Deutsche Bach-Solisten under Helmut Winschermann; Further tours to Athens and to Israel; Performances of music by Frank Martin; Sang Mozart's Donna Anna, 1970; Teacher of Voice at the Geneva Conservatory from 1971. *Recordings:* Mendelssohn's Elijah; Bach Cantatas; Christmas Oratorio by Schütz; L'Incoronazione di Poppea by Monteverdi.

**BUCKLEY, Richard E(dward);** Conductor; b. 1 Sept. 1953, New York City, USA. *Education:* BM, North Carolina School of the Arts, Winston-Salem, 1973; MMus, Catholic University of America, Washington DC, 1974; Aspen School of Music, Colorado, 1974; Salzburg Mozarteum, 1977. *Career:* Assistant Conductor and Chorusmaster, Washington Opera Society, 1973–74; Assistant

to Music Director Seattle Opera, 1973–74; Assistant Associate, Resident, and Principal Guest Conductor at Seattle Symphony Orchestra, 1974–85; Music Director, Oakland Symphony Orchestra, California, 1983–86; Guest Conductor, New York Philharmonic Orchestra, Philadelphia Orchestra, Houston Symphony Orchestra, San Antonio Symphony Orchestra, Oregon Symphony Orchestra, Los Angeles Philharmonic Orchestra, Minnesota Orchestra, Indianapolis Symphony Orchestra, BBC Symphony Orchestra, Royal Philharmonic Orchestra, Royal Liverpool Philharmonic Orchestra, Chicago Lyric Opera, Los Angeles Opera, New York City Opera, Houston Grand Opera, Canadian Opera, Netherlands Opera, and Hamburg State Opera, Covent Garden, Paris Opéra Bastille, Berlin Deutsche Oper, Royal Opera, Copenhagen, Teatro Bellini, Teatro San Carlos, Lisbon; Recent operatic premieres include Paulus' The Postman Always Rings Twice with Miami Opera and The Woodlanders at St Louis; US premiere of Sallinen's The King Goes Forth to France, for Sante Fe Opera; Other projects include Les Contes d'Hoffmann with Los Angeles Music Center Opera, Aida at Chicago and Rossini's Il Viaggio a Reims at St Louis; Conducted Il Barbiere di Siviglia for Miami Opera in 1990, and Dvořák's The Devil and Kate at St Louis; Season 1996 with Butterfly at Los Angeles and Aida at Philadelphia. *Honours:* Prizewinner, Besançon Competition in 1979; Rupert Foundation Competition in 1982. *Current Management:* Herbert Barrett Management Inc, 1776 Broadway, New York, NY 10019, USA. *Address:* 500 N Guadalupe Street, Ste G-896, Santa Fe, NM 87501, USA.

**BUCQUET, Marie-Francoise;** Pianist; b. 28 Oct. 1937, Montvilliers, France. *Education:* Studied at the Vienna Music Academy, The Paris Conservatoire and with Wilhelm Kempff, Alfred Brendel and Leon Fleisher. *Career:* Debut: Marguerite Long School in 1948; Attended course by Eduard Steuermann at Salzburg to study music of Schoenberg and followed courses by Pierre Boulez at Basle; Sylvano Bussotti, Betsy Jolas and Iannis Xenakis have written for her; Performs works by Bach, Haydn, Stockhausen, Schoenberg and standard repertory music; Professor of Accompaniment and Piano Pedagogy at the Paris Conservatoire from 1986. *Address:* c/o Conservatoire de Paris, 209 Avenue Jean Jaurés, Paris 75019, France.

**BUCZYNSKI, Walter;** Composer and Pianist; b. 17 Dec. 1933, Toronto, Canada. *Education:* Studied Composition with Milhaud, 1956 and Nadia Boulanger, 1960–62 at Toronto Conservatory. *Career:* Teacher of Piano and Theory at Royal Conservatory of Toronto, 1962, and Theory at University of Toronto from 1970. *Compositions include:* Piano Trio, 1954; Suite for Wind Quintet, 1955; Divertimento for Violin, Cello, Clarinet and Bassoon, 1957; Children's operas Mr Rhinoceros And His Musicians, 1957 and, Do Re Mi, 1967; Squares In A Circle for Flute, Violin, Cello and Strings, 1967; Four Movements for Piano and Strings, 1969; Zeroing In, 5 pieces for various vocal and instrumental groups, 1971–72; Three Against Many for Flute, Clarinet, Bassoon and Orchestra, 1973; Concerto for Violin, Cello and Orchestra, 1975; Olympics '75 for Brass Quintet; From The Buczynski Book Of The Dead, chamber opera, 1975; Naked At The Opera, 1979; Piano Concerto, 1979; Piano Quintet, 1984; The August Collection, 27 preludes, 1987; Litanies for Accordion and Percussion, 1988; Songs and piano music. *Address:* SOCAN, 41 Valleybrook Drive, Don Mills, Ontario M3B 2S6, Canada.

**BUDAI, Livia;** Hungarian singer (mezzo-soprano); b. 23 June 1950, d. of Ferenc and Martha (née Koszegi) Budal; m. Julian Batky. *Education:* Ferenc Liszt Acad. of Music (Budapest). *Career:* mem. Artistic Staff Budapest State Opera 1973–75, Gelsenkirchen Music Theatre, Germany 1977–80, Munich State Opera, Germany 1980–83; appearances in Brussels, Royal Opera House (Covent Garden, London), Paris, Canada, Metropolitan Opera (New York), San Francisco (USA); mem. Bd of Dirs J. B. EM Services Inc., St Laurent, Montréal; numerous recordings and TV appearances; Ravel Prize 1974. *Current Management:* Ariën Arts & Music Management B.V.B.A., De Boeystraat 6, 2018 Antwerpen, Belgium. *Telephone:* (3) 285 96 80. *Fax:* (3) 230 35 23. *Website:* www.liviabudai.com.

**BUDD, Harold;** Composer; b. 24 May 1936, Los Angeles, CA, USA; m. Paula Katzman, 26 June 1960, 2 s. *Education:* Los Angeles City College, 1957–59; BA, San Fernando State College, 1963; MM, University of Southern California, 1966. *Career:* Composition Faculty, California Institute of the Arts, 1971–76. *Compositions:* The Pavilion Of Dreams, 1978; The Plateaux Of Mirror, with Brian Eno, 1980; The Serpent (In Quicksilver), 1981; The Pearl, with Brian Eno, 1984; Abandoned Cities, 1984; The Moon And The Melodies, with The Cocteau Twins, 1986; Lovely Thunder, 1986; The White Arcades; Walk into my Voice, 1996. *Honours:* National Endowment for The Arts, Composer Fellowship, 1974, 1979. *Current Management:* Opal Ltd. *Address:* c/o Opal Ltd, 330 Harrow Road, London W9 2HP, England.

**BUDDEN, Julian Medforth,** OBE, BA, BMus, MA, FBA; musicologist and writer; b. 9 April 1924, Hoylake, Cheshire, England. *Education:* Queen's Coll., Oxford, Royal Coll. of Music, London. *Career:* music library clerk, BBC radio 1951, Music Presentation Asst 1955, Prod. for Music Programmes 1955–70, Chief Prod. for Opera 1970–76, Music Organizer for External Services 1976–83; editorial cttee mem. Critical Edition of the Works of G. Verdi; Pres., Centro Studi Giacomo Puccini, Lucca. *Publications:* The Operas of Verdi (three vols) 1973, 1978, 1981, Verdi 1985, Puccini 2002; contrib. to professional journals, including Music and Letters, Musical Times, The Listener. *Honours:* Yorkshire Post Award for Best Book on Music 1979, Derek Allen Prize, British Acad. 1980, Premio Diego Fabbri 1989. *Address:* 94

Station Road, Finchley, London, N3 2SG, England; via Fratelli Bandiera 9, 50137 Florence, Italy.

**BUDIN, Jan;** Clarinettist; b. 20 May 1950, Prague, Czechoslovakia; m. Vlasta Budínová, 5 July 1973, 1 s., 1 d. *Education:* Academy of Arts, Prague. *Career:* Concert performances in European countries; Television performances in the Czech Republic, Poland, Germany, Sweden, Denmark. *Compositions:* Some compositions for various chamber ensembles. *Recordings:* František Vincenc Kramár–Quartet B flat major, Op 21, No. 1; Quartet E flat major, Op 21, No. 2; Quintet B flat major, Op 95–Jan Budín with Panocha Quartet; Johannes Brahms–Quintet B minor, Op 115–Jan Budín with Panocha Quartet; František Vincenc Kramar–Symphonia Concertante E flat major, Op 70; Julius Fucik: Chamber music for two clarinets and bassoon; More recordings (especially early Czech music for clarinet). *Contributions:* Editor-in-Chief of Musical Journal for Blind. *Honours:* First Prize in the International Competition of Blind Musicians, Prague, 1975. *Address:* 11 Dusní Street, 110 00 Prague 1, Czech Republic.

**BUFFLE, Christine;** Singer (Soprano); b. 1971, Switzerland. *Education:* Studied at Geneva Conservatoire; Guildhall School of Music and Drama, London; Opera Studio, Zürich. *Career:* Sang Ninetta in La Finta semplice and Doralice in Scarlatti's Trionfo dell' Onore, Geneva; Musetta, Naiad (Ariadne) Berlin Komische Opera; Coryphée, Gluck's Armide, Versailles; Queen of Night, Scottish Opera; Zürich Opera as Sicle in Cavalli's L'Ormindo, Papagena, High Priestess, Barbarina, Suor Angelica, Echo, Queen of Night and Donna Anna in Gazzaniga's Don Giovanni; Season 1999–2000 with Musetta and Naiad for the Komische Oper, Anna in Kurt Weill's Seven Deadly Sins in Geneva; Concerts include Handel's Samson and Haydn's The Seasons; Mozart's C Minor Mass and Requiem; Vivaldi's Gloria; Bach's Magnificat and St John Passion; Honegger's King David, Geneva, 2000. *Recordings:* Stravinsky's Les Noces and songs. *Address:* c/o Music International, 13 Ardilaun Road, London N5 2QR, England.

**BUFKENS, Roland;** Belgian singer (tenor) and academic; b. 26 April 1936, Ronse; m. Simone Deboelpaepe 1961; one d. *Education:* Brussels Conservatoire. *Career:* debut in Germany; German concerts specialising in Bach tradition and also the St John and St Matthew Passion; performances with several German orchestras conducted by Kurt Thomas, Karl Richter, Kurt Redel and Nikolaus Harnoncourt; Berlioz's Romeo and Juliet in a tour of Japan and later in Paris' Théâtre des Champs Elysées, both conducted by Lorin Maazel; other performances include Stravinsky's Mavra in the Concertgebouw of Amsterdam, Martin's Mystère de la Nativité at Madrid Teatro Real (all performances broadcast); Manuel de Falla's Vida Breve conducted by R. F. de Burgos in Palais des Beaux-Arts Bruxelles; participated several times in the Holland Festival, Biennale of Zagreb, Festival of Lourdes, Schwetzinger Festspiele, Festival van Vlaanderen; Prof., Brussels Conservatoire and Lemmens Inst., Leuven. *Recordings:* works by Schubert, Grétry, Gossec, Lully, Schütz, Bach, Dumont and Carl Orff, compositions by Belgian composers André Laporte and Willem Kersters. *Publications:* contrib. to Lemmensinstitute Adem, articles for Dutch Singers' Asscn ANZ. *Honours:* first prize Brussels Conservatoire 1959, Cecilia Prize for Zemire et Azor, F. M. Grétry, Belgium 1974; Chevalier, Ordre de la Couronne 1978. *Address:* 25 avenue Georges Leclerq, 1083 Brussels, Belgium. *Telephone:* (2) 425 3521 (home).

**BUGHICI, Dumitru;** Composer and Teacher; b. 14 Nov. 1921, Iasi, Romania. *Education:* Studied with Salmanov, Iasi Conservatory and with Schittke, Leningrad Conservatory, 1950–55. *Career:* Faculty, Bucharest Conservatory; Israel resident from 1985. *Compositions include:* Orchestral: Simfonie-Poem, 1961, No. 3, Ecouri De Jazz, 1965–66, Simfonia Bucegilor, 1978–79, Simfonie Lirico-Dramatica-In Memoriam for String Orchestra, 1984, Simfonia Aspiratillor, 1985; Sinfoniettas: Simfonieta Tinertii, 1958, Muzica De Concert, Simfonieta III, 1969; Filimon Sarbu, 1959, Poemul Bucuriei, 1962, Monumentul, 1964, Omagiu, 1967, Balada Concertana for Violin and Orchestra, 1969, Sinfonietta Da Camera, 1970, Cello Concerto, 1974, Trumpet Concerto, 1975, Jazz Concerto, 1982–83; Flute Concerto, 1985; Chamber: Suite for Violin and Piano, 1953, Scherzo for Cello and Piano, 1954, Fantasia for Trumpet and Piano, 1960, Violin Sonata, 1963, Fantasia Quartet, 1969, Six String Quartets, 1954–83, Fantasy for Xylophone and Double Bass, 1980; Flute Concerto, 1985; Bass Clarinet Concerto, 1986; Symphony of Gratitude, 1990; Piano Pieces. *Address:* Conservatorui de Muzica Ciprian Porumbescu, Str Stirbei Voda 33, 70732 Bucharest, Romania.

**BUJARSKI, Zbigniew;** Composer; b. 21 Aug. 1933, Muszyna, Poland. *Education:* Studied composition with Wiechowicz and conducting with Wodiczko at the Kracow State College of Music. *Compositions include:* Burning Bushes for Soprano and Chamber Ensemble, 1958; Triptych for String Orchestra and Percussion, 1959; Synchrony I for Soprano and Chamber Ensemble, 1959, II for Soprano, Chorus and Orchestra, 1960; Zones for Chamber Ensemble, 1961; Kinoth for Orchestra, 1963; Chamber Composition for Voice and Ensemble, 1963; Contraria for Orchestra, 1965; El Hombre for Vocal Soloists, Chorus and Orchestra, 1969–73; Musica Domestica for 18 Strings, 1977; Concert for Strings, 1979; Similis Greco, symphonic cycle, 1979–83; Quartet On The Advent, 1984; Quartet For The Resurrection, 1990; Pavane for the Distant One for strings, 1994; Lumen for orchestra, 1997; Five Songs for soprano and strings, 1997. *Address:* c/o Society of Authors ZAiKS, 2 Hipoteczna Street, 00 092 Warsaw, Poland. *Telephone:*

(4822) 828 17 05. *Fax:* (4822) 828 13 47. *E-mail:* sekretariat@zaiks.org.pl. *Website:* www.zaiks.org.pl.

**BUJEVSKY, Taras;** Composer; b. 23 June 1957, Kharkiv, Ukraine; m. Jekaterina Tarakanova, 8 June 1991.one s. one d. *Education:* Composer, 1989; Postgraduate Course, Moscow State Conservatoire, 1991. *Career:* Musical Editor, Russian television, 1993–98; Lecturer, Russian Theatre Academy, 1995–97; His music is frequently heard on Russian radio and television, including 7 large broadcasts devoted to his life and music, 1991–99 mem. Moscow Composers Union, Russian Union of Cinematography. *Compositions:* Symphony, 1989; Repercussions of the Light for string orchestra, 1992; Foreshortenings, chamber symphony for percussion, trumpet, two pianos and mechanical devices, 1993; Post Scriptum for symphony orchestra, 1994; Breathing of Stillness for chamber orchestra, 1995; Eisenstein-Line, Suite for symphony orchestra, 1997; Music for Chamber Ensembles and Solo Instruments includes: Sensus Sonoris for flute and percussion, 1990; Silver Voices for four trumpets, 1991; Pathes of Phonosphere for clarinet; Voice of Loneliness for tenor saxophone, 1993; Mosaics, Suite for grand piano, 1994; Ciao Antonio for flute, oboe, violin, cello, harpsichord and tape; Für Isabella for sextet, 1995; Quartet for oboe, clarinet, bassoon and piano, 1996; Agnus Dei for mixed choir a capella, 1998; Electronic music, music for 30 films and television performances: Participant in international festivals: Moscow Autumn 1990–2003; 5 Capitals, Kiev, 1993; Festival of Contemporary Russian Music in Helsingborg, Sweden, 1994; Festival of Electronic Music, Synthesis-95, Bourges, France;Omen for symphony orchestra, 2000; Aria.ru-monoopera for actress, piano and tape, 2000; Music of Sovok for prepared dustpan and tape, 2000; Largo ricitare for violin and tape, 2001; Dolente cantabile for oboe d'amore, 2002; Das Kolophonium for 12 cellos, 2002; Choirs on poems by K. Vojtyla, 2003; Music for computer's games. *Publications:* Music for S Eisenstein's film The General Line, score for symphony orchestra, 1997; Repercations of the Light, score for string orchestra, 2003; Mosaics, Suite for grand piano, 2004; Collected verses, 2003; Essay About Death but more about Life, 2003. *Honours:* Russian TV TEFI, 1999. *Address:* Novoslobodskaja Str 67/69, Apt 113, Moscow 127055, Russia. *E-mail:* buyevsky@mtu-net.ru.

**BUKOWSKI, Miroslaw Andrzej;** Composer and Conductor; b. 5 Jan. 1936, Warsaw, Poland; m. Hanna Burzynska, 20 Aug 1966, 1 d. *Education:* MA, Composition, Academy of Music, Poznan, 1959; MA, Conducting, Academy of Music at Gdansk and Poznan, 1963. *Career:* Debut: Polish Students' Music Festival in Poznan, 1957; Assistant, 1963–67, Lecturer, 1967–80, Assistant Professor, 1980–88, Professor, 1988–, Academy of Music, Poznan; Conductor, Wielkopolska Symphony Orchestra, 1971–75; Professor, Pedagogical College in Zielena Gora, 1984–; mem, Association of Polish Composers, Society of Authors ZAiKS. *Compositions include:* Requiem for Solo Voices, Mixed Choir and Orchestra, based on Akhmatova's poem; Pastourelle, Interferences for Symphony Orchestra; Concerto for Cello and Orchestra; Ostinato and Mobile for Percussion Ensemble; Swinging Concerto; Symphonic Allegro for Symphony Orchestra; 4 Piano Sonatas; Sonatina for Piano; Expression for Piano; Three Sleepy Poems for Mixed Choir; 2 Cycles of Songs, Znikomosc, Stances. *Address:* Osiedle Pod Lipami 5-182, 61-632 Poznań, Poland.

**BULCHEVA, Zlata;** Singer (Mezzo-Soprano); b. 1970, St Petersburg, Russia. *Education:* Graduated St Petersburg Conservatoire 1995. *Career:* Appearances with the Kirov Opera from 1996, notably as Olga in Eugene Onegin, Konchakovna (Prince Igor), Carmen, Cherubino, and Erda in Das Rheingold; Further engagements as Ratmir (Ruslan and Lyudmila), Nezhata (Sadko), Frasya in Prokofiev's Semyon Kotko and Fyodor in Boris Godunov; Concerts include Mahler 2nd and 3rd Symphonies; Sang with the Kirov Opera at Covent Garden, 2000. *Recordings include:* Boris Godunov. *Honours:* Prizewinner, Young Opera Singer's International Vocal, St Petersburg, 1996, International Rimsky-Korsakov Competition, 1998, and International Tchaikovsky, Moscow, 1999. *Address:* c/o Kirov Opera, Mariinsky Theatre, Mariinsky Square, St Petersburg, Russia.

**BULJUBASIC, Mileva;** Singer (Soprano); b. 17 Aug. 1937, Sarajevo, Yugoslavia. *Education:* Studied in Sarajevo, Italy and Austria. *Career:* Featured as Concert Artist since 1960; Stage career from 1970, with guest appearances in Italy, Germany, England, Russia, Japan and Czechoslovakia; Member of the Deutsche Oper am Rhein, Düsseldorf, from 1979; Sang at Seattle in 1975; Roles have included Butterfly, Mimi, Marenka in The Bartered Bride, Rusalka, Beethoven's Leonore and Verdi's Amelia in Ballo in Maschera and Leonora in Il Trovatore; Season 1992 as Butterfly at Hannover and Tosca at Düsseldorf. *Honours:* Prize for Interpretation; Modern Yugoslavian Musik Prize; Prix des Concours, Madama Butterfly, Japan, 1973. *Address:* Sertoriusring 7, 55126 Mainz, Germany.

**BULJUBASIC, Sead;** Singer (tenor) and Professor of Opera Singing; b. 10 Oct. 1942, Cazin, Bosnia; m. Mileva Buljubasic, 17 Feb. 1973. *Education:* BA, Italian Language and Literature; Musical Faculty of Art and Magisterium-Belgrade Conservatorio Giuseppe Verdi Milano; Mozarteum Salzburg. *Career:* Debut: National Theatre Opera Stage Belgrade, Eugene Onegin, Lenski; Opera Houses: Yugoslavia, Romania, Austria, Germany, USA; RTV Belgrade, RTV Sarajevo, until 1988, Duke of Mantua, Manrico, Alfred Germont, Rodolfo, Cavaradossi, Pinkerton, Calaf, Count Almaviva, Radames, Werther, Don José, Jenik, Prince (Rusalka), Lenski, Turiddu, Bluebeard, Faust, Edgardo. Recordings. Television and radio, Sarajevo, Belgrade, opera arias and songs; Concert Repertoire Songs: Schumann, Schubert, Strauss, Debussy, De Falla,

Turina, Tchaikovsky, Rachmaninov. *Address:* Sertorius Ring 7, 55126 Mainz, Germany.

**BULL, Edvard (Hagerup);** Composer; b. 10 June 1922, Bergen, Norway; m. Anna Kvarme, 1955, 2 d. *Education:* Examination, Oslo University, 1944; Organ Diploma, Oslo Conservatory, 1947; Studied organ, composition and piano with Sandvold, Irgens Jensen, Brustad, Riefling and Wester; Pupil of Charles Koechlin, 1947–49; Composition with Darius Milhaud and Jean Rivier; Analysis with Olivier Messiaen; Diploma and Prize for Musical Composition, Conservatoire National Superieur de Musique, Paris, France, 1948–53; Pupil of Boris Blacher and Josef Rufer at Hochschule für Musik, Berlin, 1958–60. *Career:* Debut: Philharmonic Orchestra, Paris; Formerly Teacher of Theory, Oslo Klaverakademi and Oslo Musikkonservatorium; Performances in over 30 countries; Many commissions from French radio and television, Ministry of Culture, Quatuor Instrumental de Paris, Ensemble Moderne de Paris, Trio Daraux de Paris, Trio de France, Quatuor des Clarinettes de Belgique, Norske Blåse-Kvintett. *Compositions include:* 5 Symphonies, 1955–72; 6 Concertos; Le Soldat De Plomb, ballet, 1949; Portrait Münchhausen, ballet, 1961; Le Jeu Du Feu, one-act opera, 1974; Lamentation Pour Un Cygne Maudit, Hommage A Israel, opera, 1972–77; Chamber, instrumental and vocal works. *Recordings include:* Sonata Cantabile Op 35, 1988; 1Re Concerto pour Trompette et Orchestre Op 9, 1992; Trois Mouvements Symphoniques Op 16, 1992; Trois Bucoliques Op 14, 1992; Ad Ususm Amicorum Op 20, 1997; 6 Epigrammes Op 36, 1997; Rhapsody in Rag for trumpet and orchestra, 1998. *Address:* c/o TONO, 4 Galleri Oslo, Toyenbekken 21, Postboks 9171, Gronland, O134 Oslo 1, Norway.

**BULLOCK, Susan,** BMus, FRAM; British singer (soprano); b. 9 Dec. 1958, Cheshire. *Education:* Royal Holloway Coll., Univ. of London, Royal Acad. of Music and Nat. Opera Studio, London. *Career:* roles with ENO have included Donna Anna, Marguerite (Faust), Alice Ford, Butterfly, Ellen Orford, Princess Natalie (Henze's Prince of Homburg) 1996, Desdemona and Isolde; Glyndebourne debut as Jenůfa 1996, followed by Katya Kabanova and Lisa (Queen of Spades); guest appearances with New Israeli Opera and Flanders Opera (in Tippett's King Priam); American debut as Butterfly at Portland and title role in British premiere of Die Aegyptische Helena by Strauss at Garsington 1996; other important roles include Wagner's Isolde for Opera North, Oper Frankfurt, Rouen, Dusseldorf and Verona, Bninnhilde (Die Walküre) and Siegfried in Tokyo, and Gotterdammerung in Tokyo and at Perth Festival, Els (Schreker's Der Schatzgraber) Oper, Frankfurt, R. Strauss's Elektra in Brussels, Frankfurt, Dresden, Lady Macbeth (Bloch's Macbeth) in Vienna, Magda Sorel (Menotti's The Consul), Spoleto Festival, Italy and Teatro Colon, Buenos Aires, Argentina, Female Chorus (Britten's Lucretia), Mtinchen, Seville, Trittico in Charleston, and Tosca at Royal Albert Hall and debut Wigmore Hall recital; concerts include Berlioz's La Mort de Cleopatre with BBC Philharmonic Orchestra, Mahler's 4th Symphony with Royal Liverpool Philharmonic, Beethoven's Missa Solemnis with Les Arts Florissants, Salome with Hong Kong Philharmonic Orchestra, and Messiaen's Poèmes pour Mi at the Proms 2004. *Recordings include:* Hindemith's Sancta Susanna, Menotti's The Consul and Britten's Albert Herring. *Honours:* Hon. Fellow, Royal Holloway Coll. 2004. *Current Management:* HarrisonParrott, 12 Penzance Place, London, W11 4PA, England. *Telephone:* (20) 7229-9166. *Fax:* (20) 7221-5042. *Website:* www.harrisonparrott.com.

**BULYCHEV-OKSER, Michael;** Pianist and Composer; b. 17 Feb. 1981, Moscow, Russia. *Education:* Moscow Central Music School for Gifted Children, Moscow State Conservatoire, 1988–96; Piano and Composition, Moscow State Conservatoire, 1990–96; Piano and Composition, Manhattan School of Music, 1996–98, Piano, College Division, 1998–. *Career:* Debut: Piano and Composition debut, Rachmaninov Recital Hall, Moscow Conservatoire, 1993; Tour, with group of Russian musicians, to Greece, Egypt, Israel and Turkey, 1993; Moved to USA, 1996; Performed in 33 different piano recitals; Scholarship, Summer Composition Program, La Schola Cantorum, Paris, France, 1998; Debut on New York radio on Robert Sherman's Young Artists Showcase series Soloist, Manhattan Philharmonic Orchestra, 1998; Spring Music Program concert, Oyster Bay, Long Island, New York, 1999; Solo Piano Recital, Italian Culture Centre of Long Island, 1999; Young Musicians Concert at Weill Recital Hall at Carnegie Hall, New York, 1999. *Compositions:* Sea Landscape; Near Ancient Jerusalem Walls; Kizi–the dying sacred place; Clouds are over Trinity-St Sergey Monastery; The Areadna's Thread, theme and variations; Lullaby for Violin and Piano; Prelude in C Major for Violin and Piano; Sonate in D Major for Cello and Piano; Old Moscow Houses, to words by Marina Zvetaeva. *Recordings:* Solo Piano Recital, 1996; Solo Original Composition Concert, 1997; Robert Sherman's Young Artist Showcase performance, 1998; Young Musicians Concert, 1999. *Address:* 499 East 8 Street, Apt 2C, Brooklyn, NY 11218, USA.

**BULYCHEVA, Zlata;** Singer (Mezzo-soprano); b. 1970, Russia. *Education:* Graduated St Petersburg Conservatory, 1995. *Career:* Appearances with the Kirov Opera from 1996, as Carmen, Olga, Fyodor in Boris Godunov, Cherubino, Konchakovna in Prince Igor and Ratmir in Ruslan and Lyudmilla; Froysa in Prokofiev's Semyon Kotko, Nezhata in Rimsky's Sadko, Polina (The Queen of Spades) and Erda in Das Rheingold; Mezzo roles in operas by Verdi, and Maria Bolkonskaya in War and Peace; Sang with the Kirov on tour to Covent Garden, London, 2001. Concerts include: Mahler's 2nd and 3rd Symphonies. *Recordings include:* Boris Godunov. *Honours:* Prizewinner, International Rimsky-Korsakov Vocal competition, St Petersburg, 1993 and

International Tchaikovsky, Moscow, 1994. *Address:* c/o Kirov Opera, Mariinsky Theatre, 1 Theatre Square, St Petersburg, Russia.

**BUMBRY, Grace;** American singer (soprano, mezzo-soprano); b. 4 Jan. 1937, St Louis, MO; d. of Benjamin Bumbry and Melzia Bumbry. *Education:* Boston and Northwestern Univs, Music Acad. of the West. *Career:* début, Paris Opera as Amneris in Aida March 1960; Basel Opera 1960–63; Carmen with Paris Opera and toured Japan; Royal Opera, Brussels; Die Schwarze Venus, Tannhäuser, Bayreuth Festival 1961 and 1962; Vienna State Opera 1963; Covent Garden 1963, 1968, 1969, 1976, 1978; Salzburg Festival 1964; Metropolitan Opera 1965–79; La Scala 1964–79, Chicago Lyric 1962–78; Porgy and Bess, New York Metropolitan Opera 1985. *Honours:* Hon. Citizen of Baltimore, LA, Philadelphia, St Louis; Commdr des Arts et Lettres 1996, Kammersängerin 2003; Hon. DH (Univ. of St Louis), (Rust Coll.); Hon. DMus (Rockhurst Coll.); Richard Wagner Medal 1963, Grammy Award 1979, Royal Opera House Medal 1988, Puccini Award 1990. *Current Management:* J.F. Mastroianni Associates, 161 West 61st Street, New York, NY 10032, USA.

**BUNDSCHUH, Dieter;** Singer (Tenor); b. 10 May 1940, Würzburg, Germany. *Career:* Sang in opera in Germany from 1965, Staadttheater Würzburg; Vienna Staatsoper, 1984–87 as Strauss's Matteo and Flamand; Belmonte in Die Entführung and Alfred in Die Fledermaus, Wiesbaden, 1981 in the premiere of Das Kalte Herz, by Kirchner; Guest appearances throughout Germany including Arnold in Guillaume Tell at Mannheim, 1987; Premiere of Hans Zender's Don Quichotte at Stuttgart, 1993; Sang Dr Caius in Falstaff at Bonn, 1989; Other roles include Zemlinsky's Zwerg, Vere in Billy Budd and the Captain in Wozzeck; Many concert and broadcast engagements. *Address:* c/o Bonn Opera, Am Boeselagerhof 1, Pf 2440, 5311 Bonn, Germany.

**BUNDSCHUH, Eva-Maria;** Singer (Soprano); b. 16 Oct. 1941, Brunswick, Germany. *Education:* Studied in Chemnitz and Leipzig. *Career:* Debut: Bernburg 1967, as Humperdinck's Hansel; Sang at Chemnitz, 1969–74, Potsdam, 1974–77; Associated with the Staatsoper Berlin from 1976, the Komische Oper from 1981; Sang first as mezzo, as Dorabella, Carmen and Eboli then soprano repertory from 1978; Olympia and Antonia in Les Contes d'Hoffmann, Wagner's Eva and Freia, Violetta, Musetta and Donna Anna; Recent Berlin Staatsoper roles have included the title part in the premiere of Judith by Siegfried Matthus, 1985, Jenůfa, 1986, and Isolde, 1988; Komische Oper, 1987–88, as Donna Anna and Salome; Bayreuth Festival, 1988, as Gutrune; Further engagements at Amsterdam (Shostakovich's Lady Macbeth, 1994), Salzburg, Wiesbaden, Bucharest and Moscow; Sang Chrysothemis in a new production of Elektra for Welsh National Opera, 1992; Elektra in a new production at Netherlands Opera, 1996; Gutrune in Götterdämmerung for Netherlands Opera, 1998. *Address:* c/o Welsh National Opera (Contracts), John Street, Cardiff, Wales CF1 4SP.

**BUNNING, Christine;** Singer (Soprano); b. 1960, Luton, England. *Education:* Guildhall School and with Irmgard Seefried, Vienna. *Career:* Appearances as Verdi's Lady Macbeth, Covent Garden and Edinburgh; Glyndebourne Festival in The Electrification of the Soviet Union (Nigel Osbourne), Katya Kabanova, and Berlioz's Hero for Opera North; Violetta, Mimi, Marenka in The Bartered Bride and Tosca for Welsh National Opera; Chelsea Opera Group in The Olympians by Bliss, as Chabrier's Gwendoline and as Elena in Mefistofele; Other roles include Suor Angelica; Donna Elvira for Opera Factory; Verdi's Abigaille; Medora, Il Corsaro; Amelia, Ballo in Maschera; Rosalinde, Die Fledermaus; English National Opera as Miss Jessel, Turn of the Screw and in Don Carlos, Street Scene and Trittico; Lady Macbeth for Opera Zuid, 1999; Florinda in Schubert's Fierrabras at the Buxton Festival, 2000. *Address:* Music International, 13 Ardilaun Road, London N5 2QR, England.

**BUNTEN, Wolfgang;** Singer (Tenor); b. 1968, Munich, Germany. *Education:* Studied in Munich at the Opera Studio in Bavarian State Opera. *Career:* Appearances with the Tolzer Knabenchor as a child; Sang widely in concerts and oratorios with appearances in France, Spain and Germany; Stage debut as Arturo in Lucia di Lammermoor at Munich; Innsbruck, 1992–94 as Fenton in Falstaff, Tom Rakewell, Nemorino and Rodolfo; Mozart's Tamino at Vienna, 1994; Stuttgart, Zürich, 1995 and Brussels, 1996; Season 1995–96, as Rodolfo at Basle; In Stravinsky's Rossignol at the Festival Hall, London; Percy in Anna Bolena at Bologna; US debut as Števa in Jenůfa, Cincinnati, 1998; Season 1999–2000 at Cologne, as Alfredo, Rinuccio in Gianni Schicchi and Froh in Das Rheingold. *Address:* c/o Opernhaus Zürich, Falkenstrasse 1, 8008 Zürich, Switzerland.

**BURA, Corina,** DMusicol; Romanian violinist and professor of music; *Professor, National University of Music;* b. 15 Feb. 1948, Cluj. *Education:* Lyceum Emil Racovitza, Cluj, Music Lyceum, Cluj, Conservatory of Music, Bucharest. *Career:* debut, soloist with The Philharmonia, Cluj 1967; recitals and concerts with orchestras in Romania; recitals in Germany; TV appearances; radio recordings of Bach, Handel, Telemann, Corelli, Pergolesi, Rameau, Tchaikovsky, Paganini, Szymanowski, Bartók and Romanian music; Prof., Nat. Univ. of Music, Bucharest; mem. Professorial Asscn of the Conservatory of Bucharest, Mihail Yora Foundation, Deutsche Gesellschaft für Musikphysiologie und Musikermedizin. *Recordings:* two albums of Handel music. *Publications:* The 20th Century Violin Concerto 2002; studies about modern music and aesthetics published in the Conservatory's publications; perm. column in Morning Star Literature Review 2001–. *Honours:* Diploma of Chief Promotion, The Music Lyceum 1965, 1966, 1967, Diploma of Chief

Promotion, The Conservatory of Bucharest 1972. *Address:* Str. Ecaterina Teodoroiu No. 17, 010971 Bucharest, Romania. *Telephone:* (21) 6502721.

**BURCHINAL, Frederick;** singer (baritone); b. 7 Dec. 1948, Wichita, KS, USA. *Education:* Emporia State University, Juilliard School. *Career:* worked with the Metropolitan Opera Studio and made European debut in Floyd's of Mice and Men, at Amsterdam, 1976; Sang Scrooge in the 1979 premiere of Musgrave's A Christmas Carol, Virginia Opera; New York City Opera, State Theater, 1978–88; Metropolitan Opera from 1988 as Macbeth and Rigoletto; Other US appearances for the San Francisco Opera, Miami, Houston, New Orleans and San Diego Opera; Deutsche Oper am Rhein, Düsseldorf, from 1988; Title role in Simon Boccanegra with the Cologne Opera in 1990; Has also sung in London, Zürich, Berlin and Frankfurt; Other roles include Rossini's Figaro, Iago, Jack Rance, Tonio, Di Luna, Scarpia, Falstaff and Nick Shadow; Sang Posa in Don Carlos at Düsseldorf in 1991; Boccanegra at the Opéra Bastille, Paris, 1994; Sang Scarpia at Palermo, 2001.

**BURCHULADZE, Paata;** Singer (bass); b. 12 Feb. 1951, Tbilisi, Russia. *Education:* Studied at the Tbilisi Conservatory. *Career:* Debut: Tbilisi in 1975 as Mephistopheles in Faust; Sang in Russia and Milan; Studied further in Italy and began international career after winning competitions, 1981–82; Roles include Basilio in Il Barbiere di Siviglia, Leporello, King Rene in Iolantha, Gremin in Eugene Onegin and Boris Godunov; Guest appearances at the Bolshoi in Moscow; British debut in 1983 at the Lichfield Festival, in The Dream of Gerontius by Elgar; Covent Garden debut in 1984 as Ramfis in Aida; Salzburg Festival appearances as the Commendatore in Don Giovanni under Karajan; Sang Rossini's Basilio at the Metropolitan in 1989, and Khan Konchak in a new production of Prince Igor at Covent Garden in 1990; Sang Boris Godunov in a revival of Mussorgsky's opera, 1991, the Inquisitor in Prokofiev's The Fiery Angel in 1992; Sang King Philip in Don Carlos at Santiago, 1994; Sang Zaccaria in Nabucco at the Verona Arena and Konchak in Prince Igor at San Francisco in 1996; Walter in Luisa Miller for the Royal Opera at Edinburgh, 1998; Season 2000–01 at the Grand Inquisitor in Don Carlos at Washington, Boris Godunov at Hamburg, and Ramphis in Aida for San Francisco Opera. *Recordings include:* Scenes from operas by Mussorgsky and Verdi; Don Giovanni; Fiesco in Simon Boccanegra; Sparafucile in Rigoletto; Ramfis in Aida; Samson et Dalila. *Current Management:* Askonas Holt Ltd, Lonsdale Chambers, 27 Chancery Lane, London, WC2A 1PF, England. *Telephone:* (20) 7400-1700. *Fax:* (20) 7400-1799. *E-mail:* info@askonasholt.co.uk. *Website:* www.askonasholt.co.uk.

**BURDEN, William;** Singer (tenor); b. 1965, Florida, USA. *Education:* Studied at Indiana University. *Career:* Appearances with the San Francisco Opera as Belmonte, Count Lerma in Don Carlos and the title role in Bernstein's Candide; European debut as Rodolfo for Opera North (returned as Tamino); Further appearances as Rossini's Almaviva with Opera Northern Ireland, Janek in The Makropulos Case at San Francisco, Ali (L'Incontro Improvviso by Haydn) at Nice, Ramiro (Cenerentola) in South Africa and Ubalo in Haydn's Armida, at St Louis; Season 1995–96 with New York Met debut as Janek, and Tybalt in Roméo et Juliette; Mozart's La Finta Giardiniera for Glimmerglass Opera; Season 1997–98 as Tom Rakewell at Genoa, Tamino for Florida Opera, Ali in Bourdeaux and Cimarosa's Il Matrimonio Segreto in Lausanne; Sang Tybalt at the Met, 1998; Concert repertoire from Bach to Bernstein, with Messiah under William Christie. *Current Management:* Askonas Holt Ltd, Lonsdale Chambers, 27 Chancery Lane, London, WC2A 1PF, England. *Telephone:* (20) 7400-1700. *Fax:* (20) 7400-1799. *E-mail:* info@askonasholt.co.uk. *Website:* www.askonasholt.co.uk.

**BUREAU, Karen;** Singer (Soprano); b. 3 Feb. 1951, Glen Ellyn, Illinois, USA. *Education:* Opera School of the New York Metropolitan, 1981–84. *Career:* Debut: New York Met, 1982 as Lady in Waiting in Macbeth; Sang at Hannover Opera from 1985; As Leonore in Fidelio, Rezia in Oberon; Wagner's Senta, Freia, Elsa and Elisabeth; Leonora in La forza del Destino, Maddalena, Andrea Chenier, and Andromache in Troades by Reimann, 1987; Seattle Opera from 1986 as Gutrune and Elisabeth in Tannhäuer; Deutsche Oper Berlin, 1991 as Leonore; Brünnhilde in Wagner's Ring at Hannover; Wiesbaden and Flagstaff, Arizona Opera, 1996 and 1998; Other roles include Lady Macbeth, Heidelberg, 1995; Aida and the Dyer's Wife in Die Frau ohne Schatten, season 1997–98 at Kiel Opera; Elettra in Idomeneo; Donna Anna, Weber's Rezia and Euryanthe, Wagner's Eva and Isolde; Sang Abigaille in Nabucco at Hannover, 1999.

**BURGANGER, Judith,** MM; American concert pianist and academic; *Professor and Artist-in-Residence, School of the Arts, Florida Atlantic University;* b. 1939, Buffalo, NY; m.; three d. *Education:* State Conservatory of Music, Stuttgart, Germany. *Career:* debut solo recital, Buffalo; orchestral, with Amherst Symphony; early performances 1946–60 as soloist with Buffalo Philharmonic, Toronto Symphony, Nat. Symphony (Washington, DC), Marlboro Festival (Vermont); later performances 1960– as soloist with symphony orchestras throughout USA, Germany, Austria, Netherlands, Scandinavia, Italy, Switzerland, Thomas, Conlon, Akiyama; int. guest performances, solo recitals and chamber music; Artist Teacher, Cleveland Inst. of Music; Assoc. Prof., Artist-in-Residence, Texas Technical Atlantic Univ.; Artist Teacher, Carnegie Mellon Univ.; Assoc. Prof., Florida Atlantic Univ. 1980, Prof. 1984–; Dir of Conservatory Music, Coll. of Liberal Arts, School of the Arts, Coll. of Arts, Florida Atlantic Univ., currently Prof. and Artist-in-Residence 1983– (developed and implemented a certificate in piano performance and pedagogy for the univ.); created an annual Brahms Festival 1983, performing all chamber music compositions and works for four hands at one piano and songs include masterpieces from Friends of Brahms; founder, FAU Chamber Soloists 1987, ensemble performing subscription series throughout Florida and works for all combinations of instruments and voice; collaborative artist with string quartets, including Cleveland, Emerson, Ridge, Shanghai, Lark, Cavani Alexander, Ciompi and Miami. *Recording:* Burganger and Leonid Treer, The Art of Four Hands at One Piano 1997. *Honours:* first prize ARD Int. Piano Competition, Munich, Germany, first prize Merriweather Post Nat. Competition, Washington, DC, Bronze Medal Geneva Int. Piano Competition, Switzerland, Deutscher Industrie Preis grant. *Address:* School of the Arts, College of Arts, Florida Atlantic University, 777 Glades Road, Boca Raton, FL 33431, USA (office). *Telephone:* (561) 297 3329 (office). *Fax:* (561) 297 2944 (office). *E-mail:* burgang@fau.edu (office).

**BURGE, John,** MMus, DMA, ARCT; Canadian composer; b. (David Byson), 2 Jan. 1961, Dryden, ON. *Education:* Royal Conservatory of Music, Toronto, Univ. of Toronto and Univ. of British Columbia. *Career:* Assoc. Prof. of Composition and Theory, Queen's Univ., Kingston, ON 1987–; Pres. Canadian League of Composers 1998–. *Compositions include:* Mass for Prisoners of Conscience 1989, Thank You God 1992, Divinum mysterium 1995, Symphony No. 1 1997. *Address:* Queen's University School of Music, Harrison-LeCaine Hall, Room 204, 39 Queen's Crescent, Kingston, ON K7L 3N6, Canada (office). *E-mail:* burgej@post.queensu.ca (office). *Website:* www.queensu.ca/music (office).

**BURGER, Ernst Manfred;** German pianist and writer on music; b. 26 March 1937, Munich; m. Dorothea Maillinger 1972; one s. *Education:* Liberal Arts High School, Staatliche Hochschule für Musik, Munich, Künstlerische Staatsprüfung, Pädagogische Staatsprüfung. *Career:* writer on music and researcher on Chopin and Liszt. *Publications:* Franz Liszt, A Chronicle of His Life in Pictures and Documents, Munich, 1986, Paris, 1988, New York, 1989; Frédéric Chopin, A Chronicle of His Life in Pictures and Documents, Munich, 1990; Carl Tausig, Bonn, 1990; Robert Schumann, A Chronicle of His Life in Pictures and Documents, Mainz, 1998; Franz Liszt in Contemporary Photography, Munich, 2003; contrib. to Die Musik in Geschichte und Gegenwart (MGG) and Süddeutsche Zeitung; Music Journals; Articles about Jazz; Commentaries for recorded music. *Honours:* Grand Prix de Littérature Musicale, 1988; Ordre du Mérite en faveur de la culture polonaise, 1991; Robert Schumann Prize, Zwickau, 1999; Deutscher Musikeditions Prize for his book on Robert Schumann, 1999. *Address:* Erhardtstrasse 6, 80469 Munich, Germany.

**BURGESS, Brio,** BA; American composer, dramatist, poet and jazz singer; b. 27 April 1943, San Francisco, CA. *Education:* Russell Sage Coll. *Career:* various clerical positions at Federal, state, city and county agencies 1972–; performances in Saratoga Springs, NY, San Francisco, San Mateo, CA, Albany, NY, and Troy, NY, of music and words (original works) in various formats; presentation of Street Kids on Radio WRPI, NY and Play with Music, 1992, Radio Free America Broadcast. *Compositions:* Suite for Picasso; Escape, ballet, for Piano, Harp, Feet and Chains; Girl on a Ball, Children's Dance and Toys, piano tunes; Sound Dreams, piano music; Space Visions, including The Painter's Song; Hippy Children's Concentration Camp Blues, for Piano, Harp and Words; Tin Angel Blues, 1990; Purple Hood Suite, 1991–92. *Recordings:* Clear, 1978; Briomindsound, 1979; Ulysses Dog No. 9, 1980; Gathered Hear, 1980; Still, 1981; Ringade, 1982; Grate, 1982; Ether, 1982; Zen Meditations, 1987. *Publications:* poems in Poetalk Publications and BAPC Anthologies, 1989–95; Outlaw Blues, eight song-poems, 1992; Poem in Open Mic: The Albany Anthology, 1994; Street Kids and Other Plays, four opera-musical libretto, 1995. *Current Management:* Gail G. Tolley, 5 Cuyler Street, Albany, NY 12202, USA. *Address:* c/o ASCAP, ASCAP Building 1 Lincoln Plaza, New York, NY 10023, USA.

**BURGESS, Grayston;** Conductor and Countertenor; b. 7 April 1932, Cheriton, Kent, England; m. Katherine Mary Bryan, 3 d. *Education:* MA, King's College, Cambridge. *Career:* Sang with Westminster Abbey Choir, 1955–69; Sang Oberon in Britten's A Midsummer Night's Dream at Covent Garden; Dowland television programme; Performances with Handel Opera Society and the Henry Wood Promenade Concerts; Numerous radio broadcasts; Founder and Director of The Purcell Consort of Voices, 1963; Debut as Conductor at the 1963 Aldeburgh Festival; Concerts and recordings with the Purcell Instrumental Ensemble, the Elizabeth Consort of Voices, Musica Reservata, the London Sackbut Ensemble, the Philip Jones Brass Ensemble and the Jaye Consort of Voices. *Recordings include:* Josquin's Deploration sur la Mort de Johannes Ockeghem; Dunstable's Laudi; Ockeghem's Vive le Roy and Ave Maria; Machaut's La Messe de Notre Dame; William Byrd's Church Music; Richard Davy's St Matthew Passion; Music by Schütz, Schein and Scheidt; Doulce Memoire; 16th Century French Chansons; English Madrigals from the Reign of Queen Elizabeth; English Secular Music of the Late Renaissance; The Eton Choir Book; The Triumphs of Oriana; High Renaissance Music in England.

**BURGESS, Sally,** ARCM; British singer (mezzo-soprano); b. 9 Oct. 1953, Durban, South Africa; d. of Douglas Burgess and Edna Rushton (née Sharman); m. Neal Thornton 1988; one s. *Education:* Royal Coll. of Music. *Career:* joined ENO 1977–; Covent Garden debut as Siebel in Faust 1983; one-woman show, Sally Burgess' Women (Lyric Hammersmith) 1997; performances at all major opera houses and festivals; roles include Zerlina (Don Giovanni), the Composer (Ariadne), Carmen, Sextus (Julius Caesar), Orlofsky

(Die Fledermaus), Minerva (The Return of Ulysses), Fricka (Die Walküre), Amneris (Aida), Judith (Duke Bluebeard's Castle), Dalila, Widow Begbick (Mahagonny), Herodias (Salome), Isabella (The Voyage), Dulcinée (Don Quixote), Ottavia (Poppea), Eboli (Don Carlos), Kabanica (Katya Kabanova), Mère Marie (The Carmelites), Margareta (Genoveva), Baba The Turk (The Rake's Progress), Azucena, Polinesso (Ariodante), Fortunata (Satyricon), Hanna Glawin (Merry Widow), Mrs Thatcher as Public Opinion (David Pountney's production of Orpheus in the Underworld), Tigrana (Edgar), Julie La Verne (Show Boat), and roles in The Love of Three Oranges, Wagner's Ring Cycle, Cavalli's Eritrea, On The Town; concert appearances include Elgar's Dream of Gerontius, Verdi's Requiem, Songs of the Auvergne by Canteloube, premiere of Twice Through the Heart by Mark-Anthony Turnage, premiere of Paul McCartney and Carl Davis' Liverpool Oratorio. *Current Management:* AOR Management, PMB 221, 6910 Roosevelt Way NE, Seattle, WA 98103, USA. *Telephone:* (206) 729-6160. *Fax:* (206) 985-8499. *E-mail:* jennyrose@aormanagementuk.com. *Website:* www.aormanagementuk.com.

**BURGON, Geoffrey;** British composer and conductor; b. 15 July 1941, Hambledon; s. of Alan Wybert Burgon and Ada Vera Isom; m. 1st Janice Garwood 1963 (divorced); one s. one d.; m. 2nd Jacqueline Krofchak 1992; one s. *Education:* Pewley School, Guildford, Guildhall School of Music. *Career:* freelance trumpeter/composer 1964–71; conductor 1964–; full-time composer 1971–. *Compositions include (dramatic works):* Epitaph for Sir Walter Raleigh 1968, Joan of Arc 1970, The Fall of Lucifer 1977, Orpheus 1982, Hard Times (opera) 1990; (*orchestral and solo music*): Concerto for String Orchestra 1963, Gending 1968, Alleluia Nativitas 1970, Paradise Dances (Brass Band) 1994, City Adventures 1997, Singapore Vtns 1997, Fantasia on REX 1997, A Different Dawn 1999; (*with voices*): Acquainted with Night 1965, Think on Dredful Domesday 1969, Canciones del Alma 1975, Requiem 1976, Magnificat and Nunc dimittis 1979, The World Again 1983, Revelations 1984, Title Divine 1986, A Vision 1990, Trumpet concerto 1992, First Was the World 1993, Music's Empire 1993, Merciless Beauty 1997; (*ballet music*): The Golden Fish 1964, The Calm 1974, Running Figures/Goldberg's Dream 1975, Songs, Lamentations and Praises 1979, Mass 1984, Prometheus 1988; (*chamber music*): Four Guitars 1977, Six Studies 1980, Waiting (for solo pianoforte) 1993, Almost Peace 1995, The Wanderer 1998, Recitativo 1998, Dancers in a Landscape 1999; (*with voices*): Hymn to Venus 1966, Five Sonnets of John Donne 1967, Worldës Blissë 1971, Two Love Songs, Lunar Beauty 1986, Nearing the Upper Air 1988, Heavenly Things 2000; (*choral music*): Three Elegies 1964, Short Mass 1965, Golden Eternity 1970, The Fire of Heaven 1973, Dos Coros 1975, A God and Yet a Man 1984, Prayer to St Richard 1989, Songs of the Creation 1989, The Song of the Creatures 1989, Five Love Songs, The First World War 1991, Christ's Love 2000, Magic Words 2000, Three Mysteries 2003; (*music for children*): Divertimento 1964, Five Studies 1965, Now Welcome Summer 1966, Beginnings 1969; (*film music*): Life of Brian 1979, Dogs of War 1980, Turtle Diary 1985, Robin Hood 1991, When Trumpets Fade 1998; (*TV music*): Dr Who 1975, Tinker Tailor Soldier Spy (Ivor Novello Award 1980) 1979, Brideshead Revisited (Ivor Novello Award 1981) 1981, Testament of Youth 1979, How Many Miles to Babylon 1981, Bewitched 1983, The Death of the Heart 1985, Happy Valley 1987, The Old Wives Tale 1988, Sophia and Constance 1988, The Chronicles of Narnia 1988–90, Children of the North 1990, A Foreign Field 1992, Martin Chuzzlewit 1994, Silent Witness 1995, Turning World 1996, Cider with Rosie 1998, Longitude (BAFTA Award 2001) 2000, Labyrinth 2001, The Forsyte Saga (BAFTA Award) 2002, Island at War 2004. *Honours:* Gold Disc 1986. *Address:* c/o Chester Music, 8–9 Frith Street, London, W1D 3JB, England. *Telephone:* (20) 7434-0066. *Fax:* (20) 7287-6329. *E-mail:* burgon@argonet.co.uk (home).

**BURMESTER, Pedro;** Pianist; b. 9 Oct. 1963, Oporto, Portugal. *Education:* Oporto Musical Conservatory; Private studies with Helena Costa, Sequeria Costa, Leon Fleisher and Dmitri Paperno; Teaching, Oporto High School of Music. *Career:* Debut: 1972; Solo recitalist; Guest Soloist with orchestras in Portugal, Spain, Austria, France, Germany, Italy and USA; Television appearances in Portugal; Various musical festivals in Portugal and Macao; Radio appearances in Portugal and the USA. *Honours:* 1st Prize, 9th International Vianna da Mota Piano Competition, Lisbon, 1983; Jury Discretionary Award, 8th Van Cliburn International Piano Competition, Fort Worth. *Current Management:* Liliane Weinstadt, Bureau de Concerts, 59 avenue de Busleyden, 1020 Brussels, Belgium. *Telephone:* (2) 263-6565 (office). *Fax:* (2) 263-6566. *E-mail:* info@concerts-weinstadt.com. *Website:* www.concerts-weinstadt.com.

**BURNETT, Yvonne;** Singer (Mezzo-Soprano); b. 1965, Aberdeen, Scotland. *Education:* Royal Scottish Academy, Guildhall School and National Opera Studio. *Career:* Debut: Bianca in Les Brigands by Offenbach for Netherlands Opera; Sang Flosshilde in Das Rheingold at Nantes, Puccini's Suzuki and Olga in Eugene Onegin for Welsh National Opera; Lady Essex in Britten's Gloriana for Opera North; Appearances as Olga for Glyndebourne Touring Opera, 1994. *Honours:* Mary Garden International Prize; Sir James Caird Scholarship; Countess of Munster Scholarship. *Address:* c/o Glyndebourne Touring Opera, Glyndebourne, Lewes, Sussex BN8 5UU, England.

**BURNSIDE, Iain;** Pianist; b. 1950, Glasgow, Scotland. *Education:* Studied in Oxford, London and Warsaw. *Career:* Recital accompanist to Margaret Price, Victoria de Los Angeles, Sarah Walker, Nancy Argenta, Thomas Allen and Stephen Varcoe; Chamber Music performances with the Brodsky and Delmé Quartets, Douglas Boyd and Shmuel Ashkenasi; Appearances at the major British festivals and recitals in Europe, USA, Canada and Japan; Devised

song series for Schoenberg, The Reluctant Revolutionary concert series on South Bank, London, 1988–89; Further contributions to the French Revolution Festival and Hermann Prey's Schubertiade, 1989; Artistic Director of series of vocal and chamber concerts at St John's Smith Square, London, 1989–; Recitals featuring Karol Szymanowski on South Bank. *Recordings include:* Gurney's Ludlow and Teme with Adrian Thompson and the Delmé Quartet. *Address:* c/o Ron Gonsalves, 10 Dagnan Road, London SW12 9LQ, England.

**BURRELL, Diana;** British composer; *Artistic Director, Spitalfields Festival;* b. 1948, Norwich. *Education:* Cambridge Univ. *Career:* began career as a teacher, later a freelance viola player; first gained recognition as a composer with Missa Sancte Endeliente for soloists, chorus and orchestra 1980; currently Lecturer Guildhall School of Music and Drama London; Artistic Dir Spitalfields Festival, London 2006–. *Compositions:* orchestral: Praeludium 1983, Archangel 1987, Landscape 1988, Landscape with Procession 1988, Scene with Birds 1989, Resurrection 1992, Das Meer so gross und weit ist da wimmelts ohne Zahlgrosse kleine Tiere 1992, Anima 1993, Viola Concerto 1994, Enchaînements 1994, Symphonies of Flocks, Herds and Shoals 1995, Dunkelhvide Månestråler 1996, Clarinet Concerto 1996, Ring 1996, Flute Concerto 1997, The Four Temperaments 2003, Temper 2004; choral: Missa Sancte Endeliente 1980, Come and See the Christ-child 1982, Io Evoe! 1984, Creator of the Stars of Night 1989, Lights and Shadows 1989, You Spotted Snakes 1991, Night Songs 1991, Christo Paremus Cantica 1993, Come Holy Ghost, our Souls Inspire 1993, Benedicam Dominum 1996, Magnificat & Nunc Dimittis 1996, Michael's Mass 1997, Ave Verum Corpus 1998, The St Pancras Evening Canticles 2005, And So the Night Became 2005; for ensemble: Io! 1984, Concertante 1985, Angelus 1986, Untitled Composition 1988, Shadow 1988, Wind Quintet 1990, Barrow 1991, Invocation for Justice 1992, Gulls and Angels 1993, Confession 1996, Gate 1997, Bronze 1998, Earth 1998, Ritual Sentences 1999, Double Image 1999, Athletes 2000, Gold 2001, King Shall Bright Ring Give in Hall 2003; solo and duo: Arched Forms with Bells for organ 1990, Bright Herald of the Morning for clarinet and piano 1992, Tachograph for baritone and piano 1993, Festival for organ 2001, North Star for trumpet and organ 2002, Longtemps ce fut l'eté for soprano and piano 2004, Terce for accordion and piano 2005; opera: The Albatross 1987. *Address:* c/o United Music Publishers Ltd, 33 Lea Road, Waltham Abbey, Essex EN9 1ES, England (office). *E-mail:* info@ump.co.uk (office). *Website:* www.ump.co.uk.

**BURROUGHS, Bruce (Douglas);** Singer (Operatic Baritone), Pedagogue and Writer; b. 12 Nov. 1944, Hagerstown, Maryland, USA. *Education:* AB, English Literature, University of California, Los Angeles, 1966; MM, Voice and Vocal Pedagogy, New England Conservatory of Music, 1971. *Career:* Debut: Papageno, in Magic Flute, Los Angeles Guild Opera, 1965; Metropolitan Opera debut in Einstein on the Beach, 1976; More than 40 roles including title roles of Monteverdi's Orfeo, Mozart's Don Giovanni, Busoni's Arlecchino, Menotti's Bishop of Brindisi; Editor-in-Chief, The Opera Quarterly; Music Critic, Los Angeles Times; mem, American Guild of Musical Artists. *Recordings:* Several. *Publications:* Author of biographical essays in International Dictionary of Opera, 1996; Author, Metropolitan Opera Guide to Opera on Video, 1997; Contributor, Collier's Encyclopaedia, 1998. *Contributions:* Articles, features and reviews to Music Journal and Opera News. *Honours:* Deems Taylor Award, American Society of Composers, Authors and Publishers, 1991. *Address:* 14832 Hart Street, Van Nuys, CA 91405, USA.

**BURROWES, Norma Elizabeth,** BA, FRAM; British singer (soprano); b. Bangor, Co. Down; d. of Henry Burrowes and Caroline Burrowes; m. 1st Steuart Bedford (q.v.) 1969 (divorced 1980); m. 2nd Emile Belcourt 1987; one s. one d. *Education:* Queen's Univ., Belfast, Royal Acad. of Music. *Career:* début with Glyndebourne Touring Opera singing Zerlina in Don Giovanni 1969, début with Royal Opera House, Fiakermili in Arabella 1976; sings regularly with Glyndebourne Opera, Scottish Opera, Aldeburgh Festival, English Nat. Opera, Welsh Nat. Opera and others; abroad: Salzburg, Paris, Munich, Aix-en-Provence, Avignon, Ottawa, Montreal, New York, Vienna, Chicago, Buenos Aires; has sung with all the prin. London orchestras and on BBC radio and TV; numerous recordings. *Roles include:* Blöndchen in The Abduction from the Seraglio, Oscar (Ballo in Maschera), Despina (Così Fan Tutte), Woodbird (Siegfried), Sophie (Der Rosenkavalier), Cunning Little Vixen, Manon (Massenet), Titania (Midsummer Night's Dream), Nanetta (Falstaff), Gilda (Rigoletto), Marie (Daughter of the Regiment), Juliet (Romeo and Juliet), Adina (Elisir d'Amore), Susanna (Nozze di Figaro), Lauretta (Gianni Schicchi). *Honours:* Hon. DMus (Queen's Univ., Belfast) 1979; Order of Worshipful Co. of Musicians.

**BURROWS, Donald (Donwald) James,** BA, CertEd, MA, PhD; British academic, conductor, organist and harpsichordist; *Professor of Music, Open University;* b. 28 Dec. 1945, London, England; m. Marilyn Jones 1971; three s. *Education:* Trinity Hall, Cambridge and Open Univ. *Career:* Dir of Music, John Mason School, Abingdon 1970–81; Lecturer in Music, Open Univ. 1982–89; Sr Lecturer in Music 1989–95; Prof. of Music 1995–, Head of Music Dept 1991–2002; Conductor, Abingdon and District Music Soc. 1972–83; Conductor, Oxford Holiday Orchestra 1978–; organist and choirmaster, St Nicholas Church, Abingdon 1972–82; Master of the Music, St Botolph's, Aspley Guise 1985–95; contributor to BBC Radio 4, BBC 2 television; mem., Redaktionskollegium, Hallische Händel-Ausgabe 1984–; founder-mem., Handel Inst. 1985–, Chair. of Trustees and Council 1998–; mem., Vorstand, Georg Friedrich Händel-Gesellschaft 1987–, Vice-President 1999–; mem. Advisory

Bd, Maryland Handel Festival, USA 1988–2001; mem. British Library Advisory Cttee for the Arts, Humanities and Social Sciences 2000–02; mem. Royal Musical Asscn, Royal Coll. of Organists. *Publications:* Handel: 'Messiah' 1991, A Catalogue of Handel's Musical Autographs 1994, Handel 1995, The Cambridge Companion to Handel (writer and ed.) 1997, Music and Theatre in Handel's World: The Papers of James Harris 1732–1780 2002, Handel and the English Chapel Royal 2005; editor: Handel's Alexander's Feast, The Anthem on the Peace, Foundling Hospital Anthem, Violin Sonatas, Messiah, As Pants the Hart, Songs for Soprano and Continuo, Belshazzar, Imeneo, Elgar pieces for violin and piano, Handel and the English Chapel Royal 2005; insert notes for recordings, including Handel's Water Music, Anthems, Utrecht Te Deum, Ode for St Cecilia's Day, Israel in Egypt, Organ Concertos and Messiah; contrib. to The Musical Times, Music and Letters, Early Music, Göttinger Händel-Beiträge. *Honours:* British Acad. research grants 1979, 2004; Vincent H. Duckles Award 1996, Händelpreis der Stadt Halle 2000. *Address:* 126 High Street, Cranfield, Bedford MK43 0DG, England (office). *Telephone:* (1908) 653280 (office). *Fax:* (1908) 653750 (office).

**BURROWS, Stuart;** Singer (tenor); b. 7 Feb. 1933, Pontypridd, Wales; m. Enid Lewis; one s. one d. *Education:* Trinity Coll., Carmarthen. *Career:* sang in concerts at first; stage debut with WNO in 1963 as Ismaele in Nabucco; Don Ottavio in Don Giovanni, Jenek in Bartered Bride, Ernesto in Don Pasquale, Rodolfo in Bohème; Athens in 1965 as Oedipus Rex with Stravinsky; Covent Garden from 1967 as Beppe in Pagliacci, Tamino in Magic Flute, Ottavio in Don Giovanni, Fenton in Falstaff, Elvino in La Sonnambula, Lensky in Onegin, Ernesto in Don Pasquale, Alfredo in Don Pasquale, Pinkerton in Butterfly, Alfredo in Traviata, Idomeneo, Titus in La Clemenza di Tito, Faust; US from 1967 as Tamino, Lensky, Pinkerton, Ottavio, Des Grieux; Vienna Staatsoper in 1970 as Tamino and Ottavio, Faust, Pinkerton, Salzburg Festival from 1970 in Mozart Roles; Metropolitan Opera from 1971 as Ottavio, Tamino, Pinkerton, Faust, Alfredo and Belmonte; Paris Opéra, 1975 Ottavio, Belmonte; appearances at Aix-en-Provence and Orange Festivals, and at Hamburg, Geneva, Houston, (Des Grieux), Santa Fe, (Tamino, Alfredo) and Boston; sang Mozart's Titus at Brussels, 1982 and Covent Garden, 1989; Mozart's Basilio at Aix, 1991; many concert appearances notably in music by Bach and Handel; BBC television films of Faust, La Bohème and Rigoletto; had own television series for eight years entitled Stuart Burrows Sings, also radio programmes; in demand as an adjudicator and singing teacher and for masterclasses. *Recordings:* Maria Stuarda by Donizetti; Die Zauberflöte; Beethoven's 9th Symphony; Eugene Onegin; La Clemenza di Tito; Don Giovanni; Die Entführung; many ballad recordings. *Honours:* Blue Riband, National Eisteddfod of Wales 1959; hon. doctorates, Carmarthen 1989, Univ. of Wales, Aberystwyth 1992; fellowships from Aberystwyth and Cardiff Univs and Trinity Coll., Carmarthen. *Address:* 29 Blackwater Grove, Fordingbridge SP6 3AD, England. *E-mail:* meryl@nicholls.f9.co.uk (office). *Website:* www .stuartburrows.f9.co.uk (office).

**BURT, Francis,** ARAM; British composer and academic; b. 28 April 1926, London, England; m. Lina Burt. *Education:* Royal Acad. of Music, Hochschule für Musik, Berlin. *Career:* Prof. of Composition, Hochschule für Musik und darstellende Kunst, Vienna 1973–93. *Compositions include:* Iambics for orchestra, Volpone (opera), Espressione Orchestrale, Der Golem (ballet), Fantasmagoria for orchestra, Barnstable (opera), Unter der blanken Hacke des Monds for baritone and orchestra, Und Gott der Herr sprach for solo voices, two choruses and orchestra, Morgana for orchestra, Echoes for nine players, Hommage à Jean-Henri Fabre for five players 1994, two string quartets 1952, 1991, Blind Visions for oboe and small orchestra 1995, Bavarian Gentians for chamber chorus and six players. *Recordings:* Francis Burt: Unter der blanken, Hacke des Monds, Echoes, Morgana, Der Golem, Und Gott der Herr Sprach for solo voices, two choruses and orchestra, EXXJ, Hommage à Jean-Henri Fabre for five players, Francis Burt zum 75 Geburstag (String Quartets 1 and 2). *Honours:* Mendelssohn Scholarship 1954, Körner Prize 1973, Austrian Federal Ministry of Education and Art Würdigungspreis für Musik 1978, City of Vienna Prize for Music 1981, Grosses Silbernes Ehrenzeichen für Verdienste um die Republik Österreich 1992. *Address:* Mayerhofgasse 12/20, 1040 Vienna, Austria (home).

**BURT, Michael;** Singer (Bass baritone); b. 1943, Farnham, Surrey, England. *Education:* Studied with Richard Federicks in New York. *Career:* Debut: Caracas, 1977, as Monterone and Sparafucile in the same performance of Rigoletto; Concert soloist in North America, including Bach's Christmas Oratorio and B minor Mass at Carnegie Hall; Covent Garden, London, 1979, as Second Armed Man in Die Zauberflöte; Further appearances at Frankfurt as Pizarro in Fidelio and at New Orleans as King Henry in Lohengrin; Zaccaria and the Hoffmann villains at Hannover, 1986–87; King Philip in Don Carlos and Wotan in Der Ring des Nibelungen at Graz, 1988; Adolfo in Schubert's Alfonso und Estrella, 1991; Sang Wagner's Dutchman at Montpellier, 1992, Jochanaan in Salome at Barcelona, 1991; Nuremberg 1995–96 as Gurnemanz, Orestes and Wotan; Aachen 1996, as Boris Godunov; Sang Wagner's Daland at Koblenz, 1999, and the Commendatore in Don Giovanni, 2000. *Address:* c/o Vereinigte Buhnen, Kaiser Josef Platz 10, 8010 Graz, Austria.

**BURT, Robert;** Singer (Tenor); b. 22 May 1962, England. *Education:* Graduated from the Guildhall School in 1989. *Career:* Appearances with Opera 80 as Monostatos and Don Ottavio, Dancing Master in Ariadne auf Naxos directed by Jonathan Miller with Chelsea Opera Group as Kleontes in Daphne and Mid-Wales Opera as Goro in Butterfly; Sang Don Jerome in the British premiere of Prokofiev's The Duenna, at the Guildhall School under Rostropovich, 1991; Glyndebourne Festival debut in 1992 as Tchaplitsky in The Queen of Spades, repeated at the Promenade Concerts, London; Sang Don Curzio in Figaro with Glyndebourne Touring Opera in 1992 and Janáček's From The House of the Dead, at the Barbican Hall, 1993; Young Servant in Elektra at opening night of BBC Proms, 1993; Recitals and oratorios include Carmina Burana at Snape, Vaughan Williams' Serenade to Music at the Barbican, and the Easter Oratorio by Bach and Mozart's Requiem in Munich; Festival engagements at Bath, Sully-sur-Loire and Dijon; Sang Iro in Monteverdi's Ulisse at Aix-en-Provence, 2000. *Address:* 8 Baranscraig Avenue, Brighton, Sussex BN1 8RE, England.

**BURT, Warren Arnold,** MA; American composer; b. 10 Oct. 1949, Baltimore, MD. *Education:* Univ. of California at San Diego, studied with Robert Erickson and Kenneth Gaburo. *Career:* Australian Centre for Arts and Technology 1994; resident, Mills Coll., Oakland 1995, Univ. of Illinois, Urbana-Champaign 2001–02, Univ. of Wollongong 2004–; multimedia artist, writer; Australia Council Composer's Fellowship 1998–2000. *Compositions include:* (many with visuals and electronics) Nighthawk 1973–76, Aardvarks IV 1975, Moods 1978–79, The Wanderer: Pocket Calculator Music II 1983, Woodwind Quintet 1985, Meditations 1986, Voice, Tuning Fork and Accordion 1986, Samples III 1987, String Quartet No. 4 1987, Chaotic Research Music 1990, Some Kind of Seasoning 1990–91, Dense Room 1994, Music for Microtonal Piano Sounds 1992–98, Diversity 1998, Playing in Traffic 2000–01, The Wilson Installations 2002–04. *Recordings include:* Aardvarks V 1978, Song Dawn Chords 1981, Four Pieces for Synthesizer 1981, Almond Bread Harmonies II 1985, Chaotic Research Music 1989–90, Three Inverse Genera 1990, Parts of Speech 1992, 39 Dissonant Etudes 1996, Miss Furr and Miss Skeene 1998, Diversity (multimedia theatre) 1998. *Publications:* Music Talks, 24 pamphlets written or edited for Council of Adult Education, Melbourne 1982–85, Writings from a Scarlet Aardvark – 15 Essays on Music and Art, Critical Vices: The Myths of Post-Modern Theory (with Nicholas Zurbrugg) 1999, Art Performance Media (31 interviews by Nicholas Zurbrugg) 2004. *Honours:* Djerassi Residents' Program Sounds Australian Award 1998. *Address:* PO Box U-27, Wollongong, NSW 2500, Australia (office). *E-mail:* waburt@melbourne.dialix.com.au (office). *Website:* www.emf.org/subscribers/ burt.html.

**BURTON, Amy;** Singer (Soprano); b. 14 May 1958, USA. *Career:* Théâtre des Champs Elysées, Paris, as Woglinde and Woodbird in The Ring, 1987, also at Nice; Season 1988 as Adele in Die Fledermaus for Scottish Opera; As Douglas Moore's Baby Doe, for Colorado Opera at Central City; Sang Juliette at Zürich, 1990 and Nannetta in Falstaff at New Orleans; Sophie in Werther at Cincinnati, 1993; Season 1997–98, in Handel's Serse for New York City Opera and Ford's Wife in Falstaff for Glimmerglass Opera; Sang John Musto's Dove Sta Amore with Scottish Chamber Orchestra, 2000; Other roles include Luisa in The Duenna by Prokofiev; Governess in The Turn of the Screw, 2000; La Folie in Rameau's Platée, 2000; Concepcion in L'Heure Espagnole for New York City Opera, 2000; Liù in Turandot for Pittsburgh Opera, 2001. *Recordings:* Ernst Bacon Songs, 2001. *Address:* New York City Opera, Lincoln Center, New York, NY 10023, USA.

**BURTON, Humphrey McGuire,** CBE, BA (Cantab); British writer, academic and broadcaster; b. 25 March 1931, Trowbridge, England; two s. three d. *Education:* Univ. of Cambridge. *Career:* Head of Music and Arts, BBC Television 1965–67, 1975–81; Ed., presenter, Aquarius (ITV) 1970–75; presenter of concerts, opera and ballet (BBC) 1975–94; presenter, Young Musician of the Year 1978–94; Chair., EBU TV Music working party 1976–86; Artistic Dir, Barbican Centre 1988–90; Dir, Tender is the North, Festival of Scandinavian Arts, Barbican Centre 1992; television dir 1999–2002, including Flight at Glyndebourne (Channel 4), Falstaff (BBC 2), The Return of Ulysses (Aix/DVD) 2002; broadcaster, Artist in Focus (BBC Radio 3), Walton and Menuhin series (Classic FM), Ada Vincent in Brixton (BBC4); conducted the Verdi Requiem at the Royal Albert Hall 2001; mem. RPS. *Recordings:* Mozart Harpsichord Duet K19d (with Erik Smith). *Publications:* Leonard Bernstein (biog.) 1994, Menuhin (biog.) 2000, Walton – The Romantic Loner 2002. *Honours:* Hon. FCSD; Hon. Fellow, Fitzwilliam Coll., Cambridge. *Address:* 13 Linden Road, Aldeburgh, Suffolk IP15 5JQ, England. *Telephone:* (1728) 452548. *E-mail:* humphreyburton@suffolkonline.net.

**BURTON, Stephen;** Composer; b. 24 Feb. 1943, Whittier, California, USA. *Education:* Studied at the Oberlin Conservatory, 1960–62 Salzburg Mozarteum, 1962–65; Further study with Hans Werner Henze, 1966–67; Peabody Conservatory, 1972–73. *Career:* Director of the Munich Kammerspiel, 1963–64; Teacher, Heritage Chair in Music, George Mason University, Fairfax, VA, 1974–; Heritage Chair in Music, (endowed Chair for life), 1996–. *Compositions include:* Concerto Da Camera, 1963; Ode To A Nightingale for Soprano and Ensemble, 1963; Symphony No. 1, 1968; No Trifling With Love, opera, 1970; Stravinskiana for Flute and Orchestra, 1972; Dithyramb, 1972; 6 Hebrew Melodies, after Byron, 1973; String Quartet, 1974; Piano Trio, 1975; Songs Of The Tulpehocken for Tenor and Orchestra, 1976; Six Songs for Voice and 13 Instruments, 1977; Ballet Finisterre, 1977; The Duchess Of Malfi, opera after Webster, 1978; Symphony No. 2, after Sylvia Plath poems, for Mezzo, Baritone and Orchestra, 1979; Variations On A Theme Of Mahler for Chamber Orchestra, 1982; Violin Concerto, 1983; Aimee, opera, 1983; I Have A Dream, cantata for Narrator, Soprano and Orchestra, 1987; An American Triptych, 3 one-act operas after Crane's Maggie, Hawthorne's Dr Heidegger's Experiment and Melville's Benito Cereno,

1989; From Noon to Starry Night for chorus and chamber orchestra, 1989; Burning Babe, cantata, 1999; Brotherhood, Music Theatre, with Peter Burton, 1992; Restored film scores (with Gillian Anderson): Ben Hur, 1997, Passion of St Joan, 1998, Ten Commandments, 1998, Robin Hood, 1999. *Recordings:* Symphony No. 2 Ariel; Songs of the Tulpehocken. *Publications:* Orchestration, 1980. *Honours:* 30 major commissions and prizes. *Address:* GMU, 4400 University Drive, Fairfax, VA 22030, 4444, USA.

**BURY, Alison (Margaret);** Violinist; b. 20 Jan. 1954, Woking, England. *Education:* Studied with Sylvia Rosenberg and Frances Baines at the RCM, London; Sándor Végh and Nikolaus Harnoncourt, Salzburg, 1976–77. *Career:* Appearances with the Vienna Concentus Musicus, Academy of Ancient Music (1975–90), Taverner Players (1976–92), Amsterdam Baroque Orchestra, under Ton Koopman (1980–86) and the English Baroque Soloists under John Eliot Gardiner (leader from 1983); Leader of the Orchestra of the Age of Enlightenment, 1986–; Teacher and Director of the Baroque Orchestra, Royal College of Music, London; Chamber recitals with the Chandos Baroque Players, 1981–89, L'Ecole d'Orphée, 1982–89 and Geminiani Trio, 1983–90. *Recordings include:* Vivaldi's Four Seasons, with the Academy of Ancient Music and with the Taverner Players; Bach Double Concerto with Monica Huggett, and Elizabeth Wallfisch. *Address:* c/o Royal College of Music, Prince Consort Road, London SW7, England.

**BURY, Grzegorz (Piotr Michal);** Composer; b. 17 Nov. 1961, Katowice, Poland. *Education:* K Szymanowski Academy of Music, Katowice, Theory of Music, 1981–86, Composition, 1986–89, MA in Art, 1990. *Career:* Debut: Festival of Fascinating Music in Katowice, 1983. *Compositions include:* Solo instruments: Suite for Flute, Lament Songs (Treny) for Piano, Sonata With Air-Hammer for Piano, Little Prince, suite, for Piano, Echo, Clouds And Mountains for Piano: Pieces for solo instrument and piano: Walo, lullaby, for Viola and Piano, Gabeag, folk dance, for Violin and Piano, Polonaise, Golliwogs' War, Largo Cantabile e Finale for Bassoon and Piano, Sheheresade for Oboe and Piano; Symphonic: Crux, from texts from The Bible, for Boy Soprano, Tenor, Bass, Reciter, Mixed Choir and Orchestra, Concerto for Piano and Orchestra, Symphony for Jazz Band or Soloist improvising and Symphonic Orchestra, Missa Pro Defunctis, Requiem, for Voices, Choir and Orchestra; Chamber Music: Imitations for Flute, Oboe, Bassoon and Percussion, Oberek for Brass Quintet, In The Circus for 2 Pianos, Songs On The Lapse of Time for Bass/Baritone/Oboe and Percussion, Classic Quartet for String, Black And White for 2 String Orchestras, Happy Sorrow for 5 Musicians, Rhapsody, in suite form, for Percussion, Piano and Percussion Group, Variations for Violin and Cello, Dialogues for Viola and Bassoon, Trio for Clarinet, Bassoon and Piano, Alarm for Voice, Dock and Chamber Ensemble, Elegia for Voice and Piano, 1993. *Address:* 40-866 ul Piastow 7-3, Osiedle 1000 Iecia, Katowice, Poland.

**BUSCHING, Rainer;** Singer (Bass); b. 1943, Halle/Saale, Germany. *Education:* Studied at the Felix Mendelssohn Bartholdy Academy of Music, Leipzig; Examination as opera and concert singer, 1972. *Career:* Guest appearances in Germany then engaged at Landestheater Dessau, 1973–85; Member of the Soloist ensemble at Dresden Staatsoper from 1985 notably as Wagner's Daland, Landgrave and King Henry, Verdi's Zaccaria, Ramphis and Padre Guardiano, Mozart's Sarastro and Commendatore, Weber's Lysiart and Kaspar, Basilio in Il Barbiere di Siviglia, Handel's Giulio Cesare and Gremin in Eugene Onegin; Guest appearances in Italy, Netherlands, Austria, Poland, Brazil and Russia; Sang Sarastro at Lubeck, 1992, at the reopening of the Chemnitz Opera; Season 2000 at the Semper Oper Dresden, as Sarastro and the Minister in Fidelio; Concert repertory includes St John and Matthew Passions by Bach, Messiah, Die Schöpfung and Jahreszeiten by Haydn, and Schubert's Winterreise. *Address:* c/o Dresden Staatsoper, 01069 Dresden, Germany.

**BUSSE, Barry;** Singer (Tenor); b. 18 Aug. 1946, Gloversville, NY, USA. *Education:* Studied at Oberlin College and the Manhattan School of Music. *Career:* Has sung as tenor from 1977 in Carlisle Floyd's Of Mice and Men at Houston; Created Bothwell in Musgrave's Mary, Queen of Scots for Virginia Opera in 1977 and repeated the role at the New York City Opera in 1980; Sang at Santa Fe in 1979 as Alwa in the US premiere of the 3 act version of Lulu; European debut in 1982 as Don José for Netherlands Opera; Further appearances in Toulouse, San Francisco, Santa Fe and Miami; Seattle Opera in 1985 as Siegmund in Die Walküre; Sang Tichon in Katya Kabanova at Florence in 1988 and at Geneva in 1989; Sang Mephistopheles and Agrippa in Prokofiev's Fiery Angel at the Holland Festival in 1990; Other roles include Florestan, Cavardossi, Canio, Parsifal at Toulouse in 1987, Peter Grimes, Narraboth, Apollo in Daphne, Pollione and Massenet's Des Grieux; Created the title role in Nosferatu by Randolph Peters, Toronto, 1995; Sang Louis Sullivan in Daron Hagen's The Shining Bow, Chicago, 1998. *Recordings include:* Mary Queen of Scots. *Address:* c/o Seattle Opera Association, PO Box 9248, Seattle, WA 98109, USA.

**BUSSI, Francesco;** Musician and Musicologist; b. 14 Sept. 1926, Piacenza, Italy; m. Maria Villa, 20 July 1957, 1 s., 1 d. *Education:* Laurea in Lettere Classiche, 1948; Diploma di Pianoforte, 1949; Diploma di Paleografia Musicale, 1953; Diploma di Musica Corale, 1955. *Career:* Docente di Storia ed Estetica Musicale al Conservatorio di Parma, 1955–59; Docente di Storia ed Estetica Musicale al Conservatorio di Piacenza e Bibliotecario, 1959–; mem, SIDM; AIBM; AMS; Membro Effettivo della Deputazione di Storia Patria per le Province Parmensi; Socio Onorario del Rotary Club Piacenza-Farnese,

1993–. *Recordings:* Francesco Cavalli, Missa Pro Defunctis (Requiem) a 8 Voci, con il responsorio Libera me, Domine a 5 Voci, 1985; Gasparo Villani, Gratiarum Actiones a 20 Voci, 1993. *Publications:* Antifonario-Graduale di S Antonino in Piacenza; Umanità e Arte di G Parabosco; Catalogo dell' Archivio Musicale del Duomo di Piacenza; La Musica Sacra di F Cavalli in rapporto a Monteverdi; Storia, Tradizione e Arte nel Requiem di Cavalli; L'Opera Veneziana dalla Morte di Monteverdi alla Fine del '600; Tutti I Lieder di Johannes Brahms, 1999. *Contributions:* Jone di Chio; Il Cantore Spagnolo Pedro Valenzuela; Le 'Toscanelle' di Gabriele Villani; La Musica Strumentale di J Brahms; Tutti i lieder di J Brahms; Altro Cavalli Sacro Restituito; New Grove Dictionary of Music and Musicians; New Grove Dictionary of Opera; MGG; DEUMM and many others; Moderna Edizione Critica di Pezzi di Girolamo Parabosco, del Requiem di Cavalli, delle Toscanelle e delle Gratiarum Actiones a 20 Voci, 1993, delle Composizioni Sacre di G. Allevi detto Piacenza;, di Altri Pezzi Sacri e dei 3 Vesperi di Cavalli; Edizione Italiana dei Voll 2, 4 and 5 della New Oxford History of Music; Storia di Piacenza, 1980, 1984, 1997. *Honours:* S Antonino d'oro, 1990; Premio internazionale L Illica, 1991–; Piacentino Benemerito, 1998. *Address:* Strada Guastafredda, 45-29100 Piacenza, Italy.

**BUSSOTTI, Sylvano;** Composer, Painter, Film Director and Stage Designer; b. 1 Oct. 1931, Florence, Italy. *Education:* Florence Conservatory, 1940–45, with Dallapiccola, Maglioni and Lupi; Private composition studies, 1949–56; Studied with Deutsch in Paris; Darmstadt courses with Cage; USA, 1964–65 on Rockefeller Foundation Grant. *Career:* Appearances at music festivals from 1958; Co-Founder of the exhibition Musica e Segno, seen in Europe and USA, 1962; Exhibited his own paintings in Italy, US, Japan, France and Germany; Director and Designer of stage works including his own; Professor of Music Drama at the L'Aquila Academy of Fine Arts Scuola di Musica di Fiesole, 1971–74; Director of the Teatro La Fenice, Venice, 1975; Director, The Puccini Festival, Torre del Lago, 1981–1985; Bussotti opera-ballet, Scuola Spettacolo, 1984–92; Designs and Production for La Bohème, Turandot, Trittico La Fanciulla del West (Puccini); Aida, Ballo in Maschera, Un giorno di regno, Rigoletto (Verdi); Ulisse (Dallapiccola); Otello, Barbiere (Rossini); Carmen (Bizet); Cavalleria Rusticana (Mascagni); Pagliacci (Leoncavallo) and La Gioconda, Genoa and Florence. *Compositions include:* Stage: Tema-Variazioni, Geographie Francaise, 1956, Raramente, mystery play, 1971, Bergkristall, ballet, 1974, Nottetempo, lyric drama, 1976, Le Racine, 1980, Fedra, lyric tragedy, 1988; L'Ispirazione, 1988; Satiresca, 1993, Tieste, 1993; Quartettino di Miniature, 1996; Concert: El Carbonero for 5 Voices, 1957, Breve for Ondes Martenot, 1958, Sette Fogli, 1959, Phrase A Trois for String Trio, 1960, Torso for Solo Voices and Orchestra, 1960–63, Rara for Guitar and String Trio, 1964–67, Julio Organum Julii for Speaker and Organ, 1968, I Semi Di Gramsci for String Quartet and Orchestra, 1962–71, Novelletta for Piano, 1962–73, Opus Cygne for Orchestra, 1979; Concerto a L'Aquila for piano and 9 instruments, 1986; Furioso, for mezzo and orchestra, 1994; Lingue Ignote for voices and chamber orchestra, 1994; Madrelingua, 1994; Modello for violin and orchestra, 1998. *Honours:* First Prize, Italian Section ISCM, 1965, 1972; DAAD, Berlin, 1972; Commandeur l'Ordre des Arts et des Lettres. *Address:* Via di Colle Marta 1, 2, 00030 Genazzano (RM), Italy.

**BUSTERUD, James;** Singer (Baritone); b. 1957, USA. *Career:* Sang Dandini in La Cenerentola at Philadelphia, 1986; Season 1987 as Malatesta in Don Pasquale and Mercutio in Roméo et Juliette at Washington; Santa Fe Opera as Sharpless in Butterfly, in Strauss's Friedenstag and Feuersnot; American premiere of Judith Weir's A Night at the Chinese Opera, 1989; Sang Don Ferdinand in Gerhard's The Duenna, Wexford, 1989; In Turandot for Miami Opera; Glimmerglass Opera, 1994 as Robert in Tchaikovsky's Iolanta and Portland Opera, 1996; As Bassiano in Le Marchand de Venise by Reynaldo Hahn. *Recordings:* Schaunard in La Bohème. *Address:* c/o Portland Opera Assn Inc, 1516 South West Alder Street, Portland OR 97205, USA.

**BUSWELL, James Oliver, IV;** Violinist, Conductor and Teacher; b. 4 Dec. 1946, Fort Wayne, IN, USA. *Education:* BA, Harvard College, 1970; Studied violin with Ivan Galamian at Juilliard School of Music, NY. *Career:* Debut: Violinist, St Louis in 1963; New York recital debut at Philharmonic Hall in 1967; Soloist with various orchestras, recitalist and chamber music player; Appearances as conductor; Visiting Professor at University of Arizona, Tucson, 1972–73; Teacher, Indiana University School of Music, Bloomington, 1974–86, and New England Conservatory of Music, Boston, 1986–; Former Member, Buswell Parnas Luvisi Trio; Television host for Stations of Bach on PBS Television. *Address:* c/o New England Conservatory of Music, 290 Huntington Avenue, Boston, MA 02115, USA.

**BUTLER, Mark;** Canadian/British violinist and chamber music coach; b. 5 Feb. 1949. *Education:* Royal Coll. of Music with Leonard Hirsch. *Career:* co-leader, Ulster Orchestra, 1970–71; BBC debut in 1971, London debut in 1972; solo recitals in the UK and Canada; Second Violinist of the Chilingirian Quartet, 1971–92; resident, Quartet of Liverpool Univ., 1973–76, Sussex Univ., 1978–92, and Royal Coll. of Music, 1986–92; annual series of concerts at the Queen Elizabeth Hall and Wigmore Hall; performances at the Edinburgh, Bath and Aldeburgh Festivals, Munich Herkulessaal, Amsterdam Concertgebouw, Zürich Tonhalle, Vienna Konzerthaus, and Stockholm Konserthuset; New York debut, 1976; tours of USA, Canada, Australia, New Zealand, South America and the Far East; represented the UK at the New York International Festival Quartet Series; television and radio appearances throughout Europe on national public radio in USA, and the BBC; mem., Acad. of St Martin-in-the-Fields, 1995–. *Recordings:* The Ten Great Mozart Quartets; Late Schubert

Quartets; Debussy and Ravel Quartets; Elgar Quartet and Piano Quintet; Schubert Cello Quintet and Octet; Mozart Clarinet Quintet; Complete Quartets of Bartók and Dvořák; Bartók Piano Quintet. *Address:* c/o Academy of St Martin-in-the-Fields, Raine House, Raine Street, London, E1 9RG, England.

**BUTLER, Martin,** BMus, PPRNCM, MFA, FRNCM; British composer and professor of music; b. 1 March 1960, Hampshire, England. *Education:* Winchester School of Art, University of Manchester, Royal Northern College of Music, Princeton University, USA. *Compositions include:* From an Antique Land for ensemble, 1982; Concertino for chamber orchestra, 1983; Dance Fragments for ensemble, 1984; Cavalcade for orchestra, 1985; Tin Pan Ballet, 1986, arranged as Ballet con Salsa, 1987; Bluegrass Variations for violin, 1987; Piano Piano for 2 pianos and tape, 1988; Graffiti for tape, 1989; Jazz Machines for ensemble, 1990; O Rio, for full orchestra, 1990; Chaconne, for solo oboe, 1991; Down Hollow Winds, for wind quintet, 1991; Going with the Grain, for solo marimba and ensemble, 1992; On the Rocks, for solo piano, 1992; Still Breathing, for wind orchestra, 1992; Craig's Progress, opera, 1994; A Better Place, opera, 1999; Suzanne's River Song, for violin and piano, 1999. *Recordings:* Tin Pan Ballet; O Rio. *Publications:* Craig's Progress, 1994. *Address:* Repertoire Promotion Department, Oxford University Press, 70 Baker Street, London, W1U 7DN, England. *E-mail:* repertoire.promotion.uk@ oup.com.

**BUTT, John,** MA, PhD, FRCO (CHM), FRSE, ADCM; Musician, Musicologist and University Professor; b. 17 Nov. 1960, Solihull, England; m. Sally; three s. one d. *Education:* Solihull School; King's College, Univ. of Cambridge. *Career:* Organ Scholar, King's College, Cambridge, 1979–82; Lecturer, University of Aberdeen, 1986–87; Research Fellow, Magdalene College, Cambridge, 1987–89; Professor of Music and University Organist, University of California, Berkeley, 1989–97; Lecturer, Univ. of Cambridge, Fellow of King's College, 1997–2001; Gardiner Professor of Music, University of Glasgow, 2001–; mem. Royal Society of Edinburgh, Royal Musical Association, Royal College of Organists, American Musicological Society. *Recordings:* 11 organ and harpsichord recordings for Harmonia Mundi; Telemann: Fantasies, 1999; Bach: Organ Toccatas, 2000; Elgar: Organ Works, 2002. *Publications include:* Cambridge Companion to Bach, 1997; Playing with History, 2002. *Honours:* W. H. Scheide Prize of the American Bach Society, 1991; Dent Medal, 2003. *Address:* University of Glasgow, 14 University Gardens, Glasgow, G12 8QQ, Scotland (office). *Telephone:* (141) 3304571 (office). *Fax:* (141) 3303518 (office). *E-mail:* j.butt@music.gla.ac.uk (office). *Website:* www.gla.ac.uk/department/ music (office).

**BUTTERFIELD, Adrian,** ARCM, MA; British violinist and viola d'amore player; *Professor, Royal College of Music;* b. 1965, England; s. of Kenneth and Ruth Butterfield; m. Rachel Brown; one d. *Education:* chorister at St Paul's Cathedral, London, St Paul's School, Barnes, Trinity Coll., Cambridge, Royal Coll. of Music. *Career:* many appearances as soloist and dir with modern and period-instrument ensembles; concert master and assoc. dir of the London Handel Orchestra (London Handel and Tilford Bach Festivals); engagements with the Brandenburg Consort, Parley of Instruments and Stuttgart Baroque Orchestra (Mozart's Concertante, K364); soloist in Bach's Concerto for two violins, with performances from Telemann to Mendelssohn, for BBC and on tour in Europe; founder, London Handel Players, with concert at St George's Hanover Square 2000; Concerto Accademico by Vaughan Williams, Three Choirs Festival 2001; freelance violinist; Prof., Royal Coll. of Music 2003–. *Recordings include:* String Quartets by Boccherini and Donizetti, Violin Sonatas by C. P. E. Bach, Handel Trio Sonatas Op. 5 2005. *Address:* c/o Royal College of Music, Prince Consort Road, London, SW7, England (office).

**BUTTERLEY, Nigel (Henry);** Composer and Pianist; b. 13 May 1935, Sydney, Australia. *Compositions include:* Chamber Music: String Quartets No. 1, 1965, No. 2, 1974, No. 3, 1979, No. 4, 1995; Trio for Clarinet, Cello and Piano, 1979; Forest I for Viola and Piano, 1990; The Wind Stirs Gently, for flute and cello, 1992; Forest II, for trumpet and piano, 1993; Radiophonic: Watershore, 1978; Piano: Uttering Joyous Leaves, 1981; Lawrence Hargrave Flying Alone, 1981; Il Gubbo, 1987; Vocal: The True Samaritan, 1958; First Day Covers (with Barry Humphries), 1973; Sometimes with One I Love, 1976; The Owl, 1983; There came a Wind like a Bugle, Emily Dickinson, 1987; The Woven Light for Soprano and Orchestra, Kathleen Raine, 1994; Spring's Ending, Du Fu, 1997; Spell of Creation for choir, soloists and orchestra, 2000; Paradise Unseen for 6 solo voices, 2001; Orchestral: Meditations of Thomas Traherne, 1968; Violin Concerto, 1970; Fire in the Heavens, 1973; Symphony, 1980; Goldengrove, 1982; In Passing, 1982; From Sorrowing Earth, 1991; Poverty, 1992. Opera: Lawrence Hargrave Flying Alone, 1988. *Recordings:* Violin Concerto; Meditations of Thomas Traherne; Goldengrove; From Sorrowing Earth; The Owl; Laudes; Letter from Hardy's Bay; Uttering Joyous Leaves; String Quartet No. 3; The True Samaritan; There came a Wind like a Bugle. *Honours:* Italia Prize for In the head the fire, 1966; Member of Order of Australia, 1991; Lowin Prize for Spell of Creation, 2001. *Current Management:* Tall Poppies Management, PO Box 373, Glebe, NSW 2037, Australia. *Address:* 57 Temple Street, Stanmore, NSW 2048, Australia. *E-mail:* nigelbut@bigpond.net.au.

**BUTTERWORTH, Arthur Eckersley,** MBE; British composer and conductor; b. 4 Aug. 1923, Manchester; m.; two d. *Education:* Royal Manchester Coll. of Music. *Career:* trumpeter, Scottish Nat. Orchestra 1949–55, Hallé Orchestra 1955–62; Conductor, Huddersfield Philharmonic Orchestra

1962–93; guest conductor with various orchestras 1965–. *Compositions:* Violin Concerto, Viola Concerto, Cello Concerto, Symphony No. 1 1957, Symphony No. 2 1965, Symphony No. 3 1979, Piano Trio 1983, Symphony No. 4 1986, String Quartet 1998, Organ Sonata 1999, Mist on the Marshes for soprano, piano and double bass 1999, Haworth Moor choral suite 2000, Guitar Concerto 2000, Symphony No. 5 2002, concertos for organ, bassoon and trumpet, various large-scale and shorter orchestral works, symphonic works for brass band, chamber music. *Recordings include:* Symphony No. 1 (Munich Symphony Orchestra) 1998, Romanza for Horn and Orchestra (CBC Orchestra) 1998, The Path Across the Moors (Royal Ballet Sinfonia) 1999, Summer Music (Bassoon Concerto, Royal Ballet Sinfonia) 2001. *Address:* c/o Comus Edition, Heirs House Lane, Colne, Lancashire BB8 7TA, England (office); Pohjola, Dales Avenue, Embsay, Skipton, North Yorkshire BD23 6PE, England. *Telephone:* (1282) 864985 (office); (1756) 792968 (home). *Fax:* (1282) 860770 (office). *E-mail:* sales@comusic.demon.co.uk (office). *Website:* www .comusic.demon.co.uk.

**BUTTERWORTH, (David) Neil,** BA, MA; British fmr composer, conductor, writer and broadcaster; b. 4 Sept. 1934, London; m. Anne Mary Barnes 1960; three d. *Education:* Univ. of London, Guildhall School of Music, London, Univ. of Nottingham. *Career:* Lecturer, Kingston Coll. of Technology 1960–68; Head of Music Dept, Napier Coll., Edinburgh 1968–87; conductor Edinburgh Schools Choir 1968–72, Glasgow Orchestral Soc. 1975–83, 1989–2002, Edinburgh Chamber Orchestra 1983–85; music critic, Times Educational Supplement 1993–97; Winston Churchill Travelling Fellowship 1975; mem. Incorporated Soc. of Musicians, PRS, Scottish Soc. of Composers. *Compositions include:* two horn concertos, Overture Budapest, A Scott Cantata, Dunblane, In Memory of Auschwitz, Partita, Dances for Dalkeith, Count Dracula (opera), many songs and instrumental works. *Publications:* Haydn 1970, 400 Aural Training Exercises 1970, A Musical Quiz Book 1974, Dvořák 1978, A Dictionary of American Composers 1983, Aaron Copland 1984, 20th Century Sight-singing Exercises 1984, Sight-singing Exercises from the Masters 1984, Vaughan Williams 1989, Neglected Music 1991, The American Symphony 1998; contrib. to periodicals, including Classic CD, Classical Music, Musical Opinion, The Scotsman, The Herald. *Honours:* Hon. FLCM; Guildhall School of Music and Drama Conducting Prize 1961. *Address:* The Lodge, 42 E High Street, Greenlaw, Berwickshire, TD10 6UF, Scotland. *Telephone:* (1361) 840408 (home).

**BUWALDA, Sytse;** Dutch singer (countertenor); b. 28 Sept. 1965, Zuiderwoude. *Education:* Sweelinck Conservatoire, Amsterdam. *Career:* regular appearances in baroque and classical opera; roles in 20th Century operas; solo ensemble; worked with some of the world's best known conductors and directors; performs theatre shows; performed at Festivals throughout Europe and Japan; extensive oratorio and concert repertoire from the Renaissance to the present. *Recordings include:* most Bach Cantatas, compilation albums of arias and songs by various composers, work with ensembles. *Address:* Laan Nieuwer Amstel 34, 1182 JT Amstelveen, Netherlands.

**BYBEE, Luretta;** Singer (mezzo-contralto); b. 1965, Midland, Texas, USA. *Career:* Has sung widely in the USA and Europe as Isabella (Cologne and Dublin), Cherubino, Falliero in the US premiere of Rossini's Bianca e Falliero, Meg Page, Farnaces in Mozart's Mitridate at Wexford, Orlofsky, Nicklausse and Maddalena (New Orleans); Season 1993–94 as Dalila with Indianapolis Opera; Recent engagements as Carmen for Dayton Opera (following earlier appearances in Peter Brook's La Tragédie de Carmen), Amneris, Laura (La Gioconda), Venus and Waltraute; Concerts include the Verdi Requiem at Carnegie Hall, Messiah in Texas and the Mozart Requiem at Anchorage, Alaska. *Current Management:* Athole Still International Management, Forresters Hall, 25–27 Westow Street, London, SE19 3RY, England. *Telephone:* (20) 8771-5271. *Fax:* (20) 8768-6600. *Website:* www.atholestill.com.

**BYCHKOV, Semyon;** Russian-born conductor; b. 1952, Leningrad; brother of Yakov Kreizberg. *Education:* Leningrad Conservatory (pupil of Musin). *Career:* invited to conduct Leningrad Philharmonic Orchestra; left. USSR 1975; debut with Concertgebouw, Amsterdam and Berlin Philharmonic 1984–85; toured Germany with Berlin Philharmonic 1985; Music Dir Grand Rapid Symphony Orchestra 1980, Buffalo Philharmonic Orchestra 1986–87, Orchestre de Paris 1989–98, Semperoper, Dresden 1999–2003; conducted Czech Philharmonic 1989–90; Prin. Guest Conductor Maggio Musicale Fiorentino 1992–. *Recordings:* R. Strauss's Daphne (with Cologne Radio Chorus and Symphony Orchestra) 2005, Elektra (with Chorus and Symphony Orchestra of Westdeutscher Rundfunk, Cologne) 2005. *Honours:* Franco Abbiati Prize 1996. *Current Management:* IMG Artists (UK) Inc., Media House, 3 Burlington Lane, Chiswick, London, W4 2TH, England.

**BYERS, David;** Composer; b. 26 Jan. 1947, Belfast, Northern Ireland. *Education:* Studied at Queen's University Belfast, 1965–67, and at the Royal Academy, London, 1968–71; Further study with Henri Pousseur in Liège, 1972–73. *Career:* Producer for BBC Northern Ireland, 1977–. *Compositions include:* Woyzeck, incidental music, 1986; Polyphony for ensemble, 1975; Dodecaphony, for two organs, 1980; At the Still Point of the Turning World, for string quartet, 1981; Caliban's Masque, for Wind Band, 1982; A Planxty for the Dancer, for orchestra, 1983; The Wren's Blether, for voices and ensemble, 1984; The Moon is Our Breathing for narrator and ensemble, 1985; Columba and the Crane, for tuba and tape, 1985; The Deer's Horn, for oboe and cello, 1988; The Journey of the Magi, for string quartet, 1990; Out of the Night, for orchestra, 1991; Medea, incidental music, 1991; Toccata: la morte d'Orfeo for

Orchestra, 1996; Epigrams for piano, 1998. *Address:* c/o British Music Information Centre, 11 Stratford Place, London W1, England.

**BYERS, Reginald;** Singer (Tenor); b. 5 Dec. 1934, Sydney, Australia. *Education:* Sydney Conservatory and in Austria. *Career:* Debut: As Cavaradossi with Australian Opera at Sydney; Guest appearances in New York City Opera and with Scottish Opera in Glasgow; Many engagements with opera companies in Australia; Other roles have included Verdi's Radames, Ismaele in Nabucco, Gabriele Adorno, Riccardo, Alfredo and Don Carlos, Faust, Turiddu, Rodolfo, Dick Johnson, Calaf, Števa in Jenůfa and Bacchus in Ariadne auf Naxos; After retirement from stage, gave concerts and taught in Sydney. *Address:* c/o Sydney Opera House, Sydney, New South Wales, Australia.

**BYLES, Edward;** Singer (Tenor); b. 1935, Ebbw Vale, Wales. *Career:* Debut: Glyndebourne 1957, as Brighella in Ariadne auf Naxos; Toured with Opera For All and sang with major companies including Royal Opera and in Europe, Russia, Australia and Ireland; Joined English National Opera in 1974 with roles including Monostatos, Mime, Missail in Boris Godunov and Vitek in The Makropulos Case; Has sung in Tosca, War and Peace, Madama Butterfly, Orpheus in the Underworld and Pacific Overtures; In 1988 took part in the first British performance of Rimsky-Korsakov's Christmas Eve; Season 1992 with English National Opera as the Broomstick-maker in Königskinder and Trabuco in The Force of Destiny; Spoletta in Tosca for ENO, 1994. *Address:* c/o English National Opera, London Coliseum, St Martin's Lane, London WC2N 4ES, England.

**BYLSMA, Anner;** Cellist and Teacher; b. 17 Feb. 1934, The Hague, Netherlands. *Education:* Studied with Carel Boomkamp, Royal Conservatory of Music, The Hague. *Career:* Principal Cellist, Concertgebouw Orchestra, Amsterdam, 1962–68; Toured throughout the world as Soloist with orchestras; Recitalist and Chamber-music player; British debut, Wigmore Hall, 1963; Many trio appearances with Frans Brueggen and Gustav Leonhardt; Teacher, Royal Conservatory of Music, The Hague; Sweelinck Conservatory, Amsterdam; Erasmus Scholar, Harvard University, 1982; Played Cello Suites by Bach, BBC Lunchtime Concert, 1992. *Recordings:* Numerous recordings including Angel-EMI; Das Alte Werk; Decca London; Harmonia Mundi; Philips; Pro Arte; RCA; Teldec; Telefunken. *Honours:* Winner, Pablo Casals Competition, Mexico City, 1959; Prix d'excellence, Royal Conservatory of Music, 1957. *Address:* c/o Byers Schwalbe & Associates Inc, One Fifth Avenue, New York, NY 10003, USA.

**BYRNE, Connell;** Singer (Tenor); b. 1936, Australia. *Education:* Studied in Australia, Italy and London. *Career:* Sang in such small London companies as Group Eight and Philiopera Circle, from 1961; Member of the Brunswick Opera, 1963–64, Mannheim Opera from 1965; Appearances at Graz and Berne from 1969 and at Bremen until 1980; Member of the Deutsche Oper am Rhein at Dusseldorf, 1976–82; Guest appearances at Sadler's Wells, London, 1968, as Walther in The Mastersingers, at Barcelona (Aegisthus, 1970), Turin (Tristan, 1976), the Vienna Staatsoper (Laca and Cavaradossi) and Dublin; Other roles include Erik, Lohengrin, Rienzi, Tannhäuser, Parsifal, Bacchus, Don Carlos and Don José. *Address:* c/o Deutsche Oper am Rhein, Heinrich-Heine-Allee 16a, D–40213 Dusseldorf, Germany.

**BYRNE, Desmond;** Singer (Bass-baritone); b. 1965, Montreal, Canada. *Education:* McGill University, Montreal, 1989. *Career:* Season 1989–90 as Leporello at Aldeburgh, under Steuart Bedford, Silvano (Un Ballo in Maschera) at Montreal and Melisso in Alcina at Vancouver; Season 1991–92 with Leporello at Seattle, Ravel/Poulenc double bill at the Paris Châtelet, The Dream of Gerontius with the Orchestre National de France, Masetto in Vancouver and Monterone (Rigoletto) at the Opéra Bastille; Further engagements in Lucia di Lammermoor at Tours, Massenet's Panurge in St Etienne and Gounod's Romeo in Toulouse (1993–1994). Sang in Gluck's Armide at Hamburg (1996), as Mozart's Figaro in Dublin and Massenet's Sancho Panza in Nantes (1997); Britten's Bottom in Strasbourg (1998), Créon in Enescu's Oedipe, in Paris and Bucharest, and Thoas in Iphigénie en Tauride at Nantes (1999); Season 2000–01 with Rangoni in Boris Godunov, and Balstrode in Peter Grimes at Tours. *Address:* c/o Musicglotz, 11 rue Le Verrier, 75006 Paris, France.

**BYRNE, Elizabeth;** Singer (Soprano); b. 1965, Lancashire, England. *Education:* Royal Northern College of Music and National Opera Studio, London. *Career:* Appearances with English National Opera as Oksana in the British premiere of Rimsky's Christmas Eve (1988), Amelia (A Masked Ball) and Madama Butterfly; Tosca, Bianca in Macmillan's Ines de Castro and

Brünnhilde in Die Walküre (2001) for Scottish Opera; Aida for Welsh National Opera and Turandot for Mid-Wales Opera; Engagements with Lyric Opera Chicago as Tosca, Wagner's Gutrune, and Elena/Margherita in Mefistofele; Season 2000/2001 as Salome for Glimmerglass Opera, The Duchess of Parma in Busoni's Faust at the Met and Puccini's Minnie for Austin Lyric Opera; Sang Brünnhilde in Siegfried for Scottish Opera, 2002. *Address:* c/o Scottish Opera, 39 Elmbank Crescent, Glasgow, G2 4PT, Scotland.

**BYRNE, Peter,** ARCM, BMus, MMus; British musicologist, academic and director of music; b. 21 Nov. 1932, Grimsby; m. Anne J. Lavery; one s. two d. *Education:* Nat. Youth Orchestra of GB, Royal Coll. of Music, Goldsmiths Coll., London. *Career:* Dir of Music, Cardinal Wiseman School, Ealing 1959–64, Salvatorian Coll., Harrow 1965–79, Wimbledon Coll., Merton 1979–84; Prin. Lecturer, Goldsmiths Coll., London 1979–87; Academic Prof., Royal Mil. School of Music, London 1986–94; Organist and Choirmaster, Holy Ghost and St Stephen, Shepherds Bush 1960–63, St Benedict's Abbey, Ealing 1963–68; Musical Dir, Cecilians Operatic Soc., Ealing 1969–74; mem. Inst. of Advanced Musical Studies, King's Coll., London 1974–87; mem. Royal Musical Asscn. *Compositions:* Christopher Marlowe (opera) 1972. *Publications:* edn of seven works of Marc-Antoine Charpentier: H394 In Honorem Caeciliae Valeriani et Tiburtii canticum, H397 Caecilia virgo et martyr octo voc[ibus], H413 Caecilia virgo et martyr [I], H415 Caecilia virgo et martyr [II], H415a Prologue de la Ste Caecile après l'ouverture[:] Harmonia coelestis, H240 Motet: O sacrum [convivium] p[ou]r trois religieuses, H491 Dances from Medée [string orchestra]; Les Puys de musique d'Évreux. *Address:* Westgate House, Westgate, Louth, LN11 9YQ, England (home). *Telephone:* (1507) 354388/215 (home).

**BYRNES, Garrett;** Composer; b. 30 Dec. 1971, Bad Kreuznach, Rheinland-Pfalz, Germany. *Education:* Bachelor of Music, Composition, Boston Conservatory, 1995; Master of Music, Composition, Peabody Conservatory of Music, 1999; DMA, Indiana University, in progress. *Compositions include:* Orchestral Music: Concertino for Two Cellos and String Orchestra, 1994; Concerto for Cello and Orchestra, 1997; Nordic Realms (Chamber Symphony No. 1), 1998; Episodes for String Orchestra, 1998; Flames of Imbolc, 1999; Dearg Gaelach for orchestra, 2000; Nor'easter: Study for Orchestra, 2001; Chamber Music: Wraps, music for ballet for oboe, 2 clarinets and string quartet, 1994; Impressions of the Ocean, for flute, violin and piano, 1995; Introduction and Scherzo for violin and cello, 1997; Three Pieces for flute and guitar, 1999; Visions in Twilight for solo harp, 2000; Vocal Music: Sketch of the Peternera, song cycle for soprano and guitar, text by Lorca, 1995; Two Poems of Robert Frost, for flute, soprano, vibraphone and cello, 1998; Twilight Night, for treble voice and piano, text by Christina Rossetti, 1999; Solo Instrumental Music: Three Pieces for Solo Flute, 1993; Sonata for solo violoncello, 1993; Sonata for Violin Solo, 1994; Nanna's Lament for solo viola, 1999; Piano Music: Fantasy for Piano, 1994; Piano Sonata, 1995; Suite for Piano, 1995; Miniature Pictures, 1996. *Address:* 3188 Braeside Drive, Bloomington, IN 47408, USA.

**BYRNES-HARRIS, Aleicia;** Singer (Soprano); b. 1950, Toronto, Ontario, Canada. *Education:* Studied in California, at Aspen and the San Diego Opera Studio. *Career:* Sang at first in San Diego and Los Angeles as Santuzza, Magda in The Consul and Mme Lidoine in The Carmelites; European engagements from 1981, notably at Oldenburg, Wiesbaden, Nürnberg and Hamburg as Butterfly, Desdemona, Marie in Wozzeck, Irene in Rienzi, Amelia in Ballo in Maschera, Leonore, the Dyer's Wife, Kundry and Isolde; Tosca, Senta, Elektra (Elektra), Ariadne, Rosalinde; Appeared at Zürich and Munich National Theatre; Title role in Aida by Verdi, Los Angeles Music Center Opera; Die Sängerin in Reigen by Boesmans, Vienna Modern Music Festival. *Address:* Zimmerstr. 12, 10969 Berlin, Germany.

**BYRON, Michael,** BA; composer; b. 7 Sept. 1953, Chicago, IL, USA. *Education:* California Institute of the Arts with Mario Guarneri, Thomas Stevens and Joe Higgins; York University, ON. *Career:* active on behalf of other US composers; works in collaboration with the performance art group, Maple Sugar. *Compositions include:* Song Of The Lifting Up Of The Head for Piano, 1972; Starfields for Piano 4 Hands, 1974; Morning Glory for Percussion, 1975; Marimbas, 1976; A Living Room At The Bottom Of A Lake for Orchestra, 1977; Music for 1 Piano, 1978; Three Mirrors for Percussion Ensemble, 1979; Music Of Steady Light; 158 Pieces for Strings, 1979–82; Tidal for Ensemble, 1981; Double String Quartet, 1984. *Honours:* Grants from York University, the Ontario Arts Council, The National Endowment for The Arts and The New York State Council of The Arts.

# C

**CABALLÉ, Montserrat;** Spanish singer (soprano); b. Barcelona; m. Bernabé Marti (tenor) 1964; one s. one d. *Education:* Conservatorio del Liceo. *Career:* studied under Eugenia Kemeny, Conchita Badia and Maestro Annovazi; début as Mimi (La Bohème), State Opera of Basel; N American début in Manon, Mexico City 1964; U.S. début in Lucrezia Borgia, Carnegie Hall 1965; appeared at Glyndebourne Festival as the Marschallin in Der Rosenkavalier and as the Countess in The Marriage of Figaro 1965; début at Metropolitan Opera as Marguerite (Faust) Dec. 1965; now appears frequently at the Metropolitan Opera and numerous other opera houses throughout the USA; has performed in most of the leading opera houses of Europe including Gran Teatro del Liceo, Barcelona, La Scala, Milan, Vienna State Opera, Paris and Rome Operas, Bayerische Staatsoper (Munich), etc. and also at Teatro Colón, Buenos Aires; repertoire of over forty roles. *Recordings include:* Lucrezia Borgia, La Traviata, Salomé, Aida. *Honours:* Most Excellent and Illustrious Doña and Cross of Isabella the Catholic, numerous hon. degrees, awards and medals, including Commdr des Arts et des Lettres 1986.

**CABELL, Nicole;** American singer (soprano); b. 17 Oct. 1977, Panorama City, CA. *Career:* mem. Chicago Lyric Opera Center for American Artists 2002–05; roles performed at Chicago Lyric include the Rooster and Jay in The Cunning Little Vixen, Barbarina in Le Nozze di Figaro, Isabel in The Pirates of Penzance, Crobyle in Thaïs; concert appearances include Mahler's Symphony No. 2 with the Oregon Symphony, Mahler's Symphony No. 4 with the Florida Orchestra, Barbarina at the Ravinia Festival under Daniel Barenboim, Sir Michael Tippett's A Child of Our Time with the Chicago Symphony Orchestra, conducted by Sir Andrew Davis 2005, and Brahms' Deutsches Requiem with Antonio Pappano at the Accademia di Santa Cecilia, Rome 2005. *Honours:* BBC Cardiff Singer of the World 2005. *Current Management:* c/o Michael Benchetrit, Columbia Artists' Management, 1790 Broadway, New York, NY 10019-1412, USA. *Telephone:* (212) 841-9559 (office). *Fax:* (212) 841-9687 (office). *Website:* www.cami.com (office).

**CABLE, Margaret;** Singer (Mezzo-Soprano); b. 1950, England. *Career:* Appearances in Europe, Scandinavia, Israel and the USA; Festival engagements at the Bath and Three Choirs Festivals; Promenade Concerts in London; Performances in Baroque repertoire with ensembles, using original instruments, including Bach's St Matthew Passion under Andrew Parrott and Messiah at the 1985 Lucerne Festival under Christopher Hogwood; Broadcasts include Handel's Belshazzar, Tippett's A Child of Our Time, works by orchestra by Arthur Bliss and Robin Holloway; Stage roles with Kent Opera included Mrs Grose in The Turn of The Screw, Dorabella, and Marcellina in Le nozze di Figaro, also at the 1986 Vienna International Festival; Sang Juno in Handel's Semele at York Early Music Festival in 1991; Sang in Bach's St John Passion at the Festival Hall, London, 1997. *Recordings include:* Haydn Masses with the Academy of Ancient Music; Madrigals directed by Peter Pears; Works by Mozart and Scarlatti directed by George Guest; Glazunov Songs and Lux Aeterna by William Mathias, with the Bach Choir; Handel's Carmelite Vespers and Messiah with Andrew Parrott and The Taverner Players.

**CACHEMAILLE, Gilles;** Singer (bass-baritone); b. 25 Nov. 1951, Orbe, Switzerland. *Education:* Lausanne Conservatoire. *Career:* concert hall appearances 1978–, at the Aix and Salzburg Festivals, at Paris, Lyon, Buenos Aires, Madrid, Strasbourg, Lisbon and Tokyo; repertoire has included the Passions of Bach, L'Enfance du Christ by Berlioz, Franck's Les Béatitudes, Haydn's Schöpfung and Jahreszeiten, works by Monteverdi and songs by Duparc, Poulenc, Schubert and Strauss; debut as mem. of the Lyon Opéra in the stage premiere of Rameau's Les Boréades at Aix, 1982; Lausanne Opéra as Guglielmo, Simone in La Finta Semplice, Mozart's Figaro and Papageno, and Belcore in L'Elisir d'amore, 1988; Mézières in 1988 at Gluck's Orpheus, Leporello at the Hamburg Staatsoper in 1987 and Vienna in 1989; sang in Martinů's Les Trois Souhaits at Lyon, 1990, and Leporello at Houston, 1991; sang Don Giovanni at Glyndebourne, 1994; Merlin in Chausson's Le Roi Arthus, at the Bregenz Festival, 1996; Leporello at Aix-en-Provence, 1998; sang Leporello at Toronto, Figaro (Mozart) at Barcelona and Don Alfonso for Opéra Lyon, 2000–01. *Recordings include:* L'Enfance du Christ; Chausson's Le Roi Arthus; Iphigénie en Aulide; Les Boréades; Gluck's La Rencontre Imprévue; Dominic in Arabella; Golaud in Pelléas et Mélisande; Guglielmo in Così fan tutte under Harnoncourt; Claudio in Béatrice et Bénédict. *Current Management:* Balmer & Dixon Management AG, Kreuzstrasse 82, 8032 Zürich, Switzerland. *Telephone:* (43) 244-8644. *Fax:* (43) 244-8649. *Website:* www.badix.ch.

**CADDY, Ian Graham,** LRAM, ARCM, ARAM; British singer (bass baritone); b. 1 March 1947, Southampton, England; m. Kathryn Dorothy Ash 1979 (divorced 1994); one s. two d. *Education:* Royal Acad. of Music. *Career:* debut in London 1974; sang with Opera For All, Kent Opera, New Opera Co., Phoenix Opera, Glyndebourne, Scottish Opera, WNO, Royal Opera Covent Garden, ENO, Houston Grand Opera, Nantes Opera, Vancouver Opera, Teatro la Fenice; opera, oratorio, festivals and recitals throughout the UK and in Austria, Brazil, Canada, at Wexford and Versailles Festivals, in Denmark, Ireland, France, Germany, Hong Kong, Iceland, Netherlands, Spain, USA and Yugoslavia; edited, published, performed and broadcast works by J. S. Mayr and Donizetti; staging dir of baroque opera in strict period style; numerous TV

and radio broadcasts world-wide; runs own publishing title, Caddy Publishing; co-founder The Mayr-Donizetti Collaboration 1985–. *Recordings include:* L'Amor Coniugale by Mayr, Jigs, Reels and Songs of the Bottle by Holbrooke, Vivaldi's Dixit Dominus, Rameau's Princesse de Navarre and Nais, Schoeck's Notturno, Wallace's Maritana. *Video recordings:* Macbeth, The Beggar's Opera, La Fanciulla del West, Intermezzo, Sullivan's The Rose of Persia, Berners's Le Carosse du Saint-Sacrement. *Current Management:* Concert Directory International, Lyndhurst, Denton Road, Ben Rhydding, LS29 8QR, England; Music International, 13 Ardilaun Road, London, N5 2QR, England. *Address:* Convent Lodge, Andover Down, Hampshire SP11 6LR, England.

**CADOL, Christine;** Singer (Mezzo-Soprano); b. 1956, France. *Education:* Studied at the Paris Conservatoire, where she won a prize for her interpretation of Carmen. *Career:* Debut: 1978; Appearances from 1978 as Dalila at Nantes, Britten's Lucretia at Rouen, Anita in La Navarraise by Massenet at Marseilles, and Suzuki in Madama Butterfly; Further guest engagements at Liège, Limoges and Saint-Cere; Other roles include Meg Page, Waltraute and Marguerite in La Damnation de Faust; Many concert appearances. *Address:* 164 Avenue de la Capelette, 13010 Marseille, France.

**CADUFF, Sylvia;** Conductor and Professor of Conducting and Orchestral Studies; b. 7 Jan. 1937, Chur, Switzerland. *Education:* Studied at the Conservatoire of Lucerne; Further studies with Karajan at the Berlin Conservatory and with Kubelik, Matacic and Van Otterloo. *Career:* Debut: With the Tonhalle Orchestra, Zürich; Guest Conductor in all the European countries, USA, Japan, South Korea; Appearances with New York Philharmonic, Munich and Berlin Philharmonics, Radio Orchestra Berlin, Royal Philharmonic London; Assistant to Bernstein at the New York Philharmonic, 1966–67; As Music Director in Solingen, 1977–86, was first woman to be appointed Music Director in Europe; Taught conducting at the Berne Conservatory, 1972–77; mem, Swiss Musicians Association; Swiss Conductors Union. *Honours:* 1st Prize, Mitropoulos Competition, New York, 1966. *Address:* Belleriverstrasse 29, 6006 Lucerne, Switzerland.

**CAETANI, Oleg;** Swiss conductor; *Chief Conductor and Artistic Director, Melbourne Symphony Orchestra;* b. 1956, Lausanne; s. of Igor Markevitch. *Education:* studied with Nadia Boulanger, Franco Ferrara in Rome, Kyrill Kondrashin in Moscow and Ilia Mussin in Leningrad. *Career:* Asst to Otmar Suitner, Staatsoper Berlin 1981–84; Deutsche Nationaltheater Weimar 1984–87; Kapellmeister, Städtische Buhnen Frankfurt am Main; Music Dir, Wiesbaden 1992–95, leading the Ring, Tristan und Isolde, La Forza del Destino, Otello, Rimsky's Invisible City of Kitezh and Bluebeard's Castle; guest engagements with Semiramide in Vienna, Les Vêpres Siciliennes in Nice, Lucia di Lammermoor and Tosca at Trieste and Verdi's Falstaff at Stuttgart 1996–97; Zürich Opera with Rigoletto, The Nutcracker, La Bohème and Norma; led Tchaikovsky's Maid of Orleans at Strasbourg 1998; concert repertory includes music by Beethoven, Schubert, Schumann and Shostakovich, with soloists such as Martha Argerich, Viktoria Mullova, Shlomo Mintz and the late Sviatoslav Richter; Music Dir, Chemnitz 1996–2001; Chief Conductor Designate, Melbourne Symphony Orchestra 2003–04, Chief Conductor and Artistic Dir 2005–. *Honours:* winner RAI Competition in Turin 1979, prizewinner Herbert von Karajan Competition 1982. *Address:* Melbourne Symphony Orchestra, GPO Box 9994, Melbourne, VIC 3001, Australia. *E-mail:* olegcaetani@hotmail.com. *Website:* www.olegcaetani.com.

**CAFORIO, Armando;** Singer (Bass); b. 1956, Civitavecchia, Italy. *Education:* Studied in Alessandria and the USA. *Career:* Debut: Genoa, 1982, as Count Rodolfo in La Sonnambula; Florence, 1983, as Colline in La Bohème, Turin and Martina Franca from 1984; Guest appearances, 1984–85, in Dublin, Geneva, 1987; Torre del Lago and Maggio Musicale Festivals from 1987; Savona, 1990, in L'Ebreo by Apollini; Verona 1993, as Rodolfo in Catalani's Loreley; Other roles include Rossini's Don Magnifico and Basilio, the Grand Inquisitor, and Loredano in Verdi's Due Foscari; Sang Geronte in Manon Lescaut at Catania and Zaccaria in Nabucco at the Verona Arena, 2000. *Address:* c/o Teatro Comunale, Via Solferino 15, 50123 Florence, Italy.

**CAHILL, Teresa Mary,** LRAM, AGSM; British singer (soprano); b. 30 July 1944, Maidenhead, Berks.; d. of Henry D. Cahill and Florence Cahill (née Dallimore); m. John Anthony Kiernander 1971 (divorced 1978); partner Dr Robert Saxton. *Education:* Notre Dame High School, Southwark, Guildhall School of Music and Drama and London Opera Centre. *Career:* debut at Glyndebourne 1969, Covent Garden 1970, La Scala, Milan 1976, Philadelphia Opera 1981; Prof. Trinity Coll. of Music, London; specializes in works of Mozart, Strauss, Mahler, Elgar and Tippett; has given concerts with all the London orchestras, Boston Symphony Orchestra, Chicago Symphony Orchestra, Berlin, Vienna and Bath Festivals and throughout Europe, USA and the Far East; masterclasses, Dartington Festival 1984, 1986, Univ. of Oxford 1995–96, Peabody Inst. Baltimore 1999; Artistic Adviser Nat. Mozart Competition 1997–; Adjudicator Live Music Now 1988– (Musical Adviser 2000–); Gov. Royal Soc. of Music 2000–04; masterclasses, 's-Hertogenbosch 1988, 2000, RAM 2002, Bowdoin Coll., Maine 2004. *Recordings include:* works by Elgar, Strauss, Mahler, Mozart, Rachmaninov, Saxton and Lutyens. *Publications:* contrib. to 'Divas in their Own Words', compiled by Andrew Palmer. *Honours:* Worshipful Company of Musicians Silver Medal 1966, John

Christie Award 1970. *Address:* 65 Leyland Road, London, SE12 8DW, England. *Telephone:* (020) 8852-0847 (home). *E-mail:* tesssitura@btopenworld.com (office).

**CAHOVA, Monika;** Singer (Soprano); b. 20 June 1966, Prague, Czechoslovakia. *Education:* The State Conservatory, Prague. *Career:* Debut: Sang Inez in Il Trovatore at the National Theatre, Prague, 1988; Many appearances at the Opera Theatre Liberec and also sings in the National Theatre of Prague; Roles in opera include: Marenka in Smetana's The Bartered Bride; Blazenka in The Secret; Vendulka in The Kiss; Titka in Dalibor; Dvořák's Rusalka, Terinka and Julie in Jakobin; Elisabeth de Valois in Don Carlo, Leonora in Il Trovatore, and Amelia in Simon Boccanegra; Mimi in La Bohème, and Tosca; Gioconda in La Gioconda; Marguerite in Faust; Micaela and Carmen in Carmen; Giulietta in Les Contes d'Hoffman and Hélène in La Belle Hélène; Donna Elvira in Don Giovanni and the Countess; Lisa in Tchaikovsky's Queen of Spades; Marica in Kalman's Die Gräfin Maritza; Liza in Das Land des Lächelns and Hana in Die Lustige Witwe; Also sang in Britten's War Requiem at the Summer Festival in Olomouc at Zagreb in The Days of Czech Opera, sang Dvořák's Rusalka and Marenka; Sang Donna Elvira with the National Theatre of Brno in Italy; Also appeared at the Teatro dell'Aquila, Fermo Teatro di Cita, Salerno; Dvořák's Stabat Mater at the Summer Festival in Marianskelazne; Sang Mozart's Requiem in Belgium and the Third Lady in Die Zauberflöte in Germany and in Tokyo; Regular guest appearances in Germany. *Address:* Nadrazni 7/294, Prague 5, Smichov 15000, Czech Republic.

**CAILLARD, Jean-Philippe;** Choral Director; b. 31 July 1924, Paris, France. *Career:* Formed first vocal ensemble, 1944, for the performance of then little heard Renaissance music; Recorded many albums, 1955–70, beginning with Josquin's Missa Pange Lingua; Associations with such conductors as Jean-François Paillard and Louis Frémaux in the performance of French Baroque music; Pedagogic and educational activities from 1951, and has researched early music performance. *Address:* c/o 23 Rue de Marly, 7860 Etang la ville, France.

**CAINE, Rebecca;** singer (soprano); b. 1962, Toronto, Canada. *Education:* Guildhall School of Music, London. *Career:* North American debut in 1991 as Lulu for Canadian Opera, returning as Despina, Micaela and Pamina; Further appearances with New Sadler's Wells Opera, Handel Opera Society, Glyndebourne and Tulsa Opera; Created L A Lola in Mason's Playing Away with Opera North in 1994 (Munich and Leeds), and returned to Leeds in 1995 as Thomas' Ophelia; Opera Lyra Ottawa as Gilda and English National Opera as Pamina in 1995; Opéra de Nice in 1995 as Balkis in Haydn's L'Incontro Improvviso; Sang Violetta at Belfast, 1996; Season 1996–97 included Musetta and Susanna for English National Opera, Bernstein's Cunegonde for the BBC; sang Martinů's Julietta for English National Opera, 1997–98; sang Janáček's Vixen at Spoleto and Mozart's Aminta for Opera North, 1998; Fotis in the world premiere of The Golden Ass for Canadian Opera, 1999. *Honours:* Dora Mavor Moore Award 1998.

**CAIRE, Patrice;** Organist; b. 17 June 1949, Lyon, France. *Education:* Baccalaureate, 1968; Faculty of Law; Lyon Conservatory; Conservatoire National Superieur de Musique, Paris; Licence de Concert, Ecole Normale de Musique, Paris, 1975. *Career:* Organist, Sainte Croix Church, Lyon, 1973–83; Organist, St Bonaventure Sanctuary, Lyon, 1983–; Keeper, Grandes Orgues de l'Auditorium Maurice Ravel, Lyon, 1980–; Commissioner, International Improvisation Competition, 1982–83; Teacher, Conservatoire National Superieur de Musique, Lyon, 1979–; Recitals in, France, Germany, England, Scotland, Switzerland, Sweden, Spain, Italy, Belgium, USA and Canada; Concert performances: Radio France; France Musique; France Culture; Radio Cando; Radio Suisse Romande; Spanish Radio Television; Sweden Radio; With orchestra under S Baudo, E Krivine, S Skrowaczewski, J Nelson and E Tchakarov; mem, Founder; Artistic Director, Les Grandes Orgues de l'Auditorium Maurice Ravel, Lyon. *Recordings:* 2 recitals; Ch M Widor, Symphony No. 6; A Guilmant, Sonata No. 1 REM; 6 Pieces; Brass; Organ; Percussion; Busser; Litaize; Dupré; Vierne: Gigout, REM; N J Lemmens; Fanfare; Priere; Sonatas No. 1, 2, 3, REM; Lemmens, Lefebure Wely, REM; C Franck et l'orgue du Trocadero, REM; L Vierne, Finales of 6 Symphonies; Ch M Widor, Symphonies No. 4, 5,; Ch M Widor, Symphonies, No. 1 2; L Boellmann, Work for Grand Organ; C Franck, 12 Pieces for Grand Organ; Les Maitres du Trocadero; Guilmant; Widor; Lemmens; Franck; Dubois; Gigout; Saint-Saëns. *Current Management:* North America; Ph Truckenbrod, PO Box 69, West Hartford, CT 06107, USA. *Address:* 73 Rue Pierre Corneille 69006, Lyon, France.

**CAIRNS, Christine;** Singer (Mezzo-Soprano); b. 11 Feb. 1959, Ayrshire, Scotland. *Education:* Royal Scottish Academy of Music and Drama, Glasgow; Further study with Neilson Taylor. *Career:* Concerts with André Previn and the Los Angeles Philharmonic 1985; Prokofiev's Alexander Nevsky in Los Angeles and with the Cleveland and Philadelphia Orchestras; Royal Philharmonic Orchestra 1988, in Mahler's Kindertotenlieder; Tour of the US with Mahler's 4th Symphony; Festival Hall London, 1988, in Schoenberg's Songs Op 22; Promenade Concerts London, 1989, in Mozart's Coronation Mass, returned 1990; Guest appearances throughout the British Isles, Athens, Basle, Tokyo, Berlin, San Francisco and Dortmund; Touring throughout Spain; Guest engagements in Paris, Madrid, Rome, Zürich, Singapore and Rio de Janeiro; Staged performances of Monteverdi's Orfeo in Valencia; Concerts with Ashkenazy in Berlin and London, 1990; Mahler with

Simon Rattle and Yuri Temirkanov in LA, 1991; Season 1996–97 with Beethoven's Mass in C at the Bath Mozart Festival and Elijah with the Ulster Orchestra. *Recordings:* Mendelssohn's Midsummer Night's Dream, Previn, Vienna Philharmonic; Prokofiev's Alexander Nevsky, Previn, LA Philharmonic; Die Erste Walpurgisnacht, Dohnányi, Cleveland Orchestra. *Current Management:* Carroll Artist Management. *Address:* c/o Carroll Artist Management, 11 Palmerston Place, Edinburgh EH1L 5 AF, Scotland.

**CAIRNS, David Adam,** CBE, MA; British journalist and musicologist; b. 8 June 1926, Loughton, Essex; s. of Sir Hugh William Bell Cairns and Barbara Cairns (née Smith); m. Rosemary Goodwin 1959; three s. *Education:* Winchester Coll., Oxford, Princeton Univ. Graduate Coll., USA. *Career:* Library Clerk, House of Commons 1951–53; critic, Record News 1954–56; mem. editorial staff, Times Educational Supplement 1955–58; music critic, Spectator 1958–63, Evening Standard 1958–63; asst music critic, Financial Times 1963–67; music critic, New Statesman 1967–70; mem. staff, Philips Records, London 1968–70, Classic Programme Co-ordinator 1970–73; asst music critic, Sunday Times 1975–84, music critic 1985–92; Leverhulme Research Fellow 1972–74; Distinguished Visiting Prof., Univ. of California, Davis 1985; Distinguished Visiting Scholar, Getty Center for the History of Art and Humanities 1992; Visiting Resident Fellow, Merton Coll., Oxford 1993. *Publications:* The Memoirs of Hector Berlioz (ed. and trans.) 1969, Responses: Musical Essays and Reviews (co-author) 1973, The Magic Flute (ENO Opera Guide) 1980, Falstaff (ENO Opera Guide) 1982, Berlioz: The Making of an Artist 1803–1832 1989, Berlioz: Servitude and Greatness 1832–1869 (Whitbread Biog. of the Year 2000, Samuel Johnson Non-Fiction Prize 2000) 1999, Mozart and his Operas 2006; contrib. to articles on Beethoven and Berlioz, in Viking Opera Guide 1993. *Honours:* Officier, Ordre des Arts et des Lettres 1991; Hon. DLitt (Southampton) 2001; British Acad. Derek Allen Memorial Prize 1990, Royal Philharmonic Soc. Award 1990, 1999, Yorkshire Post Prize 1990. *Address:* 49 Amerland Road, London, SW18 1QA, England. *Telephone:* (20) 8870-4931.

**CAIRNS, Janice;** singer (soprano); b. 1955, Ashington, Northumberland, England. *Education:* Royal Scottish Academy with John Hauxvell, and with Tito Gobbi in Rome. *Career:* debut as Verdi's Desdemona at the Thessaloniki Festival, directed by Gobbi; London debut as Odabella in Attila, for University College Opera; Appearances with Kent Opera as Alice Ford and Donna Anna; Manon Lescaut and Leonora in La Forza del Destino for Chelsea Opera Group; With English National Opera has sung Musetta, Ariadne, Eva, Maria in Mazeppa, Lisa, Maria Boccanegra, Tosca and Amelia; Scottish Opera as Rezia in Oberon, Leonara (Il Trovatore), Aida and Madama Butterfly; For Opera North has sung Aida, Leonore and Helen in the British stage premiere of Verdi's Jerusalem, 1989; Italian debut with Scottish Opera at La Fenice, Venice, as Rezia; Concert engagements include the Verdi Requiem with the London Symphony Orchestra, Odabella at the Concertgebouw, Rachmaninov's The Bells at the Proms and Britten's War Requiem at the Norwich Festival; English National Opera, 1992, as Anna in Street Scene and as Ariadne; Sang Turandot for Welsh National Opera, 1994; Tosca for English National Opera, 1996; Season 1997 with Korngold's Violanta for Opera North and at the London Proms; Foreign Princess in Rusalka for ENO, 1998.

**CAIRNS, Tom;** British stage director and stage designer; b. 1950, England. *Career:* designed and directed premiere production of Birtwistle's Second Mrs Kong, for Glyndebourne Touring Opera at Glyndebourne, 1994; Other engagements include Tippett's King Priam for Opera North and Flanders Opera, La Bohème at Stuttgart, Don Giovanni for Scottish Opera and Un Ballo in Maschera at Munich; Stage Designs for Mozart's Apollo and Hyacinth at Batignano, Don Giovanni for Opera 80, The Midsummer Marriage, La Finta Giardiniera and Gianni Schicchi for Opera North; The Trojans for Scottish Opera, WNO and Opera North (also seen at Covent Garden): Billy Budd and Beatrice and Benedict for English National Opera; Samson et Dalila at the Bregenz Festival and Benvenuto Cellini by Berlioz for Netherlands Opera. *Address:* c/o Glyndebourne Touring Opera, Glyndebourne, Lewes, Sussex BN8 5UU, England.

**CALDWELL, John Anthony,** BMus, MA, DPhil, FRCO; British lecturer, writer and composer; *Professor of Music, University of Oxford*; b. 6 July 1938, Bromborough, England; m. Janet; one s. one d. *Education:* Birkenhead School, Liverpool Matthay School of Music, Univ. of Oxford. *Career:* Asst Lecturer in Music, Bristol Univ. 1963–66; Lecturer in Music, Univ. of Oxford 1966–, Prof. 1999–; Fellow of Jesus Coll., Oxford 1999–: mem. Royal Musical Asscn, Plainsong and Mediaeval Music Soc. (mem. of council), Soc. for the Promotion of New Music. *Compositions:* Paschale mysterium trilogy: Good Friday 1998, The Word 2001, Pascha nostrum 2002; Divertimento for Orchestra 1999, The Story of Orpheus 2004. *Publications:* English Keyboard Music Before the Nineteenth Century 1973, Medieval Music 1978, Editing Early Music 1985, The Oxford History of English Music (two vols) 1991, 1999; contrib. to Early Music, Music and Letters, The New Grove Dictionary of Music and Musicians 1980, 2002, Early English Church Music (gen. ed.). *Address:* Faculty of Music, St Aldate's, Oxford, OX1 1DB, England (office). *Telephone:* (1865) 276131 (office). *Fax:* (1865) 276128 (office). *E-mail:* john.caldwell@music.ox.ac.uk (office).

**CALDWELL, Sarah;** Conductor; b. 6 March 1924, Maryville, USA; Opera Impresario; Opera Director. *Education:* University of Arkansas; Hendrix College; Violin with Richard Burgin, New England Conservatory of Music; Viola with Georges Fourel; Apprenticeship with Boris Goldovsky. *Career:*

Assistant to Boris Goldovsky, Opera Dept, New England Conservatory of Music; Director, Boston University Opera Workshop, 1952–60; Founder; Director, Opera Group, Boston, 1958, which became Opera Company of Boston, 1965; Conducted or Produced the US Premieres of Prokofiev's War and Peace, Nono's Intolleranza, Schoewberg's Moses and Aron and Montezuma by Roger Sessions; Producer of the original versions of Boris Godunov and Don Carlos; Guest Conductor, Various orchestras including New York Philharmonic, Pittsburgh Symphony, Boston Symphony and Indianapolis Symphony. *Honours:* 1st Woman to appear as a Conductor with the Metropolitan Opera, New York, 1976, La Traviata. *Address:* c/o Opera Company of Boston, PO Box 50, Boston, MA 02112, USA.

**CALLAND, Deborah;** trumpeter. *Education:* RAM. *Career:* recitals in France, Germany, Denmark, Finland, Iceland, USA, as well as venues throughout the UK; has performed with Singapore Symphony Orchestra, Virtuosi di Kuhmo (Finland), Britten Sinfonia; world premiere performances include Einojuhani Rautavaara's Hymnus 1999, Jonathan Dove's Moonlight Revels 2002, Robin Holloway's Canzona and Toccata 2003, all at the Hampstead and Highgate Festival, London; also Huw Watkins' Three Orations, Cheltenham Festival 2003, Sally Beamish's Juno, Chelsea Festival 2005; has also played commissioned pieces by Rhian Samuel, Diana Burrell, Bent Lorentzen, John Hawkins, Hugh Wood; performed Judith Weir's Ettrick Banks and Hugh Wood's Cantilena and Fugue, St John's, Smith Square, London 2005; selected trumpet pieces for syllabus, TCL 2004. *Publications:* Top Brass, Onstage Brass, Trumpet Allsorts; contribs as critic to BBC Music Magazine.

**CALLEJA, Joseph;** Maltese singer (tenor); b. 1978. *Career:* studies with Paul Asciak; made professional debut as Macduff in Macbeth, Malta 1997; opera roles include Rodolfo in La Bohème (Toronto, Bregenz Festival, Frankfurt Opera, Dresden Semperoper), The Duke in Rigoletto (Covent Garden, Welsh Nat. Opera, Deutsche Oper Berlin, Rotterdam, Zürich Opera, Vienna State Opera, Copenhagen), Almaviva in Il Barbiere di Siviglia (Washington Opera, Liege), Rinuccio in Gianni Schicchi (Spoleto Festival), Edgardo in Lucia di Lammermoor (Minn. Opera), Leicester in Maria Stuarda (Stockholm, Parma), Alfredo in La Traviata (Opera Nat. du Rhin, Covent Garden), Fenton in Falstaff (Torino), Edoardo di Sanval in Un Giorno di Regno (Bologna), Ernesto in Don Pasquale (Brussels), Don Ottavio in Don Giovanni (Regenburg Festival, Teatre Principal Majorca), Lind in Azio Corghi's Isabella (world premiere, Rossini Opera Festival, Pesaro), Roméo in Roméo et Juliette (Frankfurt), Elvino in La Sonnambula (Vienna State Opera, Zürich Opera), Arturo in I Puritani (Vienna State Opera, Deutsche Oper Berlin), Nemorino in L'Elisir d'Amore (Liceu Barcelona); concert appearances include Hampton Court Festival, Faenol Festival, Sejong Cultural Centre in Seoul, Republic of Korea, Salzburg Festival. *Recordings:* Tenor Arias (Gramophone Magazine Ed.'s Choice) 2003, The Golden Voice 2005. *Honours:* prizewinner Belvedere Hans Gabor competition 1997, winner Caruso Competition, Milan 1998, prizewinner Placido Domingo's Operalia 1999. *Current Management:* c/o Jeffrey D. Vanderdeen, IMG Artists Europe, Lovell House, 616 Chiswick High Road, London, W4 5RX, England. *Telephone:* (20) 7957-5800 (office). *Fax:* (20) 7957-5801 (office). *E-mail:* jvanderdeen@imgartists.com (office). *Website:* www.imgartists.com (office).

**CALLEO, Riccardo;** Singer (Tenor); b. 1947, Endicot, New York, USA. *Education:* Studies at Yale, the Verdi Conservatory in Milan and at the Curtis Institute; Further study with Ken Neate in Stuttgart. *Career:* Sang at Bonn Opera, 1974–77, Innsbruck, 1977–79, and at the New York City Opera from 1979; Guest engagements at Cincinnati, Washington (Edgardo, 1983), Houston, Miami, Baltimore and Portland; Nantes Opera, 1989, Dorset Opera, 1991, as Boito's Faust; Other roles include Manrico, Turiddu, Radames, Rodolfo, Nemorino, Percy in Anna Bolena, the Duke of Mantua and Riccardo (Gustavus). *Address:* c/o New York City Opera, Lincoln Center, New York, NY 10023, USA.

**CALLIGARIS, Sergio;** Argentine composer, pianist and professor of piano; b. 1941, Rosario. *Career:* concerts in Europe, the Americas, Asia and South Africa 1954–; Chair of Piano, Cleveland Inst. of Music, OH, USA and California State Univ., Los Angeles 1969; teacher at conservatories in Italy from 1974; Art Dir American Acad. of the Arts in Europe; jury member of nat. and int. piano competitions in Italy and abroad; musical profile as composer and pianist, Società Aquilana dei Concerti, 40th Anniversary Concert Cycle 1986; works performed on television internationally. *Compositions include:* published and recorded works: 24 Studi 1978, 1979, 1980, Il Quaderno Pianistico di Renzo, for piano 1978, Tre Madrigali 1979, Published works: Scherzo 1957, Sonata Op. 9, for cello and piano 1978, Passacaglia 1983, Due Danze Concertanti 1986, Suite op. 21 for three pianos 1985, Suite Op. 28 for solo cello 1992, Suite da Requiem Op. 17a, for violin, horn and piano 1983, Scene Coreografiche Op. 30 for 2 Pianos (or Piano 4-Hands) and String Orchestra 1994, Sonata Fantasia Op. 31 for Trumpet and Piano 1994, and Op. 32 for Solo Piano 1994, Preludio, Corale e Finale Op. 33 for Accordion 1994, Clarinet Quartet No. 1 Op. 34 1995, String Quartet No. 2 Op. 35 1995, Toccata, Adagio and Fugue Op. 36, for string orchestra 1995, Double Concerto Op. 37, for piano, violin and string orchestra 1996, Sonata Op. 38, for clarinet and piano, Sonata Op. 39, for viola and piano, Sonata Op. 40, for violin and piano 1997, Double Concerto Op. 41, for two pianos and orchestra, 2000, Ave Verum Op. 42 for choir and piano, 2000, Ave Verum Op. 42a, for solo piano, 2000, Suite Op. 43, for two pianos and four drums, 2002, Preludio e Toccata Op. 44, for solo piano, 2002, Il Giorno, Suite for youth Op. 45, for chorus, piano, or

organ, violin or flute and percussion; recorded works: Ave Maria 1978, Symphonic Dances Op. 26, for large orchestra 1990, Seconda Suite di Danze Sinfoniche Op. 27 for Large Orchestra 1990, Concerto for Piano and Orchestra Op. 29 1992. *Recordings include:* Concerts for Union Europeènne Radiodiffusion 1977, 1985, 1987, 1994, 1999, 2001, 2003, Sergio Calligaris, recital; album dedicated to him of works by Chopin, Rachmaninov, Vitalini and Calligaris 1993, Piano Concerto Op. 29, Second Suite of Symphonic Dances Op. 27 and Sonata Fantasia for piano Op. 32 1996, Clarinet Quartet No. 1 Op. 34 1999, Double Concerto Op. 37 for violin 1999, Piano and String Orchestra for the Union Europeenne Radio Diffusion 1999, Shorts for Spot and Film, contemporary classical music by Sergio Calligaris. *Contributions:* CD Classica 1995, 1999, Piano Time 1996, 2002, Musica 1996, 2001, Amadeus 1997, Il Giornale della Musica 1997, Suonare News 1999, Inarcassa 2003, Terza Pagina 2004. *Honours:* Int. Musician of the Year, Int. Biographical Centre, Cambridge, UK 2004. *Address:* Viale Libia 76, 00199 Rome, Italy. *Website:* calligaris.carisch.it.

**CALM, Birgit;** Singer (Mezzo-soprano); b. 1959, Lubeck, Germany. *Education:* Studied in Lubeck and Hamburg. *Career:* Sang first at the Kiel Opera, then Osnabruck, 1984–85; Appearances at the Bayerische Staatsoper from 1984 have included Humperdinck's Hansel, Alkmene in Die Liebe der Danaë and Carlotta in Die schweigsame Frau; Guest appearances in concert and opera in Germany and abroad; Sang Rossweise and Flosshilde in The Ring at the Salle Pleyel, Paris, 1992. *Recordings:* Sacred music by Dittersdorf, Harmonia Mundi; Third Maid in Elektra, conducted by Sawallisch. *Address:* c/o Bayerische Staatsoper, Postfach 100148, 8000 Munich 1, Germany.

**CAMANI, Adrianna;** Singer (Mezzo-Soprano); b. 27 March 1936, Padua, Italy. *Education:* Studied at the Padua Conservatory with Sara Sforni Corti. *Career:* Debut: Naples 1968, as the Nurse in L'Incoronazione di Poppea; Has sung widely in Italy, notably in Genoa, Turin, Trieste, Venice and Naples; Sang in the Scala premiere of Dallapiccola's Ulisse; Major roles included La Cieca in La Gioconda, Ulrica in Un Ballo in Maschera, Eboli in Don Carlos and parts in Madama Butterfly, Andrea Chénier, Francesca da Rimini and Il Quattro Rusteghi. *Address:* c/o Conservatorio Statale di Musica Cesare Pollini, Via Eremitani 6, I–35121 Padua, Italy.

**CAMBRELING, Sylvain;** French conductor; b. 2 July 1948, Amiens. *Career:* conducting debut with Orchestre de Lyon 1975; Prin. Guest Conductor, Ensemble Intercontemporain, Paris 1976; subsequent appearances in Paris with Orchestre de Paris, Nat. Orchestra of France and Ensemble Intercontemporain; has worked regularly at Paris Opéra since conducting Chéreau's production of Les Contes d'Hoffmann; Glyndebourne Opera debut (The Barber of Seville) 1981; Music. Dir Nat. Opera, Théâtre Royal de la Monnaie, Brussels 1981–; debut at La Scala (Lucio Silla) 1984, Metropolitan Opera, New York (Romeo et Juliette) 1986; has also appeared at Salzburg, Aix-en-Provence and Bregenz festivals; has worked in UK with Halle and Royal Liverpool Philharmonic orchestras, in Germany with Berlin Philharmonic, Berlin Radio Symphony and other orchestras and in USA. *Address:* c/o Frankfurt Opera, Staedtische Buehnen, 60275 Frankfurt am Main, Germany.

**CAMDEN, Anthony,** FGSM, ARCM; British oboist; b. 26 April 1938, London, England; s. of Archie Camden and Jan Kerrison;; m. 1st Diane (divorced), one s. one d.; m. 2nd Lilly, one d. *Education:* Royal Coll. of Music, London. *Career:* founder mem., London Virtuosi 1972–; Prin. oboe, London Symphony Orchestra 1973–88; Chair. of Bd of Dirs, London Symphony Orchestra 1975–87; Prof., Dir and Provost of Queensland Conservatorium of Music 1988–93, (Griffith Univ.); Dean of Music, Hong Kong Acad. of Performing Arts 1993–2003, Fellow 2004–. *Recordings:* 36 concertos recorded in London since 1995, including Bach Concerto for Violin and Oboe, with Yehudi Menuhin, 16 Albinoni Oboe Concertos for Naxos with London Virtuosi, Grace Williams Oboe Concerto London Symphony Orchestra, Mozart Oboe Quartet, Telemann Concerto for Flute and Oboe, with James Galway, Complete Handel Oboe Concertos, Italian Oboe Concertos, Vols 1 and 2, The Art of the Oboe, The Mozart Oboe Concerto, The Art of Anthony Camden. *Honours:* Hon. Prof., Shanghai Conservatory, China. *Current Management:* Baron & Weingartner KEG, International Artists Management, Bösendorferstrasse 4/12, 1010 Vienna, Austria. *Telephone:* (1) 489-61-54. *Fax:* (1) 489-61-54-44. *E-mail:* schwemle@baronartists.com. *Website:* www.baronartists.com. *Address:* Unit 9, River Gallery, 6, Merthyr Road, New Farm, Brisbane, Queensland, 4005, Australia (home). *Telephone:* (7) 3358-2368 (home). *Fax:* (7) 3358-6503 (home). *E-mail:* anthony@anthonycamden.com (home). *Website:* www.anthonycamden.com (home).

**CAMERON, Fiona Mary,** FRAM; British pianist; b. 4 March 1931, London, England; m. Derek Simpson 1954 (divorced); two s. one d. *Education:* Royal Acad. of Music, London with Harold Craxton, studied in Paris with Yvonne Léfebure. *Career:* debut on piano with Derek Simpson, cello, Recital Room, RFH 1953; broadcasts with Derek Simpson, cello 1955–62, and Carl Pini, violin 1962–64; concerts at music clubs and Wigmore Hall until 1971, including Purcell Room with Diana Cummings, violin 1968; piano teacher, Royal Acad. of Music 1974–86, Royal Ballet School 1963–86; Head of Piano, St Paul's Girls' School, London 1987–92; mem. Incorporated Soc. of Musicians, Royal Soc. of Musicians. *Recordings:* Mendelssohn Sonata in D major for cello and piano (with Derek Simpson). *Address:* Cremona, 19 Willowhayne Avenue, East Preston, Littlehampton, West Sussex BN16 1PE, England. *Telephone:* (1903) 784629. *Fax:* (1903) 784629. *E-mail:* fiona@cameron41.fsnet.co.uk.

**CAMILLERI, Charles,** MusBac; British/Maltese composer; b. 7 Sept. 1931, Malta; s. of Carmel Camilleri and Josephine Quinton; m. Doris Vella 1957; one s. one d. *Education:* Lyceum High School and Toronto Univ., Canada. *Career:* composer, teacher, lecturer, conductor in Malta –1949, Australia 1949–53, UK 1954–57, Toronto, conductor with CBC, Toronto 1958–63, London 1964–; apptd Dir Inst. of Mediterranean Music Foundation of Int. Studies, UNESCO 1987; Prof. of Music, Univ. of Malta 1990; comm. by UNESCO Songs of Infant Species for soprano and piano 1987; commissioned by Aga Khan Foundation: Mimar for piano, vibraphone and gongs 1987; visits to many countries in Far East, Europe and N America 1949–. *Publications:* over 80, including Missa Mundi 1968, 2nd Piano Concerto 1969, Piano Trio 1970, String Quartet 1973, Cosmic Visions 1974, Five Books on Improvisation 1983, 3rd Piano Concerto 1985, Interchangeable Galaxies, Diaphanion 1987, The Elements (ballet), Music of the Mediterranean 1987, Compostella (opera in two Acts) 1988, City of Brass 1989, Cello Concerto 1989, Ombras 1990. *Honours:* many Arts Council Awards. *Address:* 24 Orchard Avenue, Finchley, London, N3 3NL, England. *Telephone:* (20) 8349 1728.

**CAMILLETTI, Simonetta;** Italian classical guitarist; b. 10 Feb. 1962, Civitavecchia, Rome. *Education:* Univ. La Sapienza, Rome, Conservatory A. Casella, L'Aquila, Music Acad., Chigiana, Siena. *Career:* winner selection, Castel Sant'Angelo's Friends, Rome 1987; performed for Radiotelevisione Italiana 1987–89, for Swiss television 1999; Prof. of Guitar, State Conservatory of Music 2003–. *Compositions:* Songs for voice and guitar: Eagles Fly; This Evening; Beethoven's Street, Look at the Sky; Bagatella; Aria; composed melodies to accompany poems. *Recordings:* Guitar Has a Soul. *Publications:* Oltre l'Azzurro (fiction), Attimi... (poems); articles in Heitor Villa Lobos and The Guitar; Editor, AFM Accord for Music; contributions to a biographical dictionary of Italians. *Honours:* Prize Bereshit International 1999. *Address:* Viale Eroi di Rodi 228, 00128 Rome, Italy.

**CAMPANELLA, Bruno;** Conductor; b. 6 Jan. 1943, Bari, Italy. *Education:* Studied Conducting with Piero Bellugi, Hans Swarowsky and Thomas Schippers; Composition with Dallapiccola. *Career:* Debut: Spoleto Festival, 1967; From 1971, has conducted 19th Century Italian opera at La Scala Milan, elsewhere in Italy and in Europe and North America; Conducted Rossini's Le Comte Ory at Montreal 1989; Don Pasquale at Covent Garden; Piccinni's La Cecchina at the 1990 Martina Franca Festival; Conducted L'Italiana in Algeri at the Teatro Regio Turin, 1992; 1992 at La Scala, Le Comte Ory and Fra Diavolo; Direttore stabile, Teatro Regio, Turin, 1992–; Conducted La Fille du Régiment in San Francisco and La Cenerentola in Florence 1993; Returned to Covent Garden for Cenerentola in 1994 and Houston in 1995; Season 1996–97 at Vienna State Opera with Linda di Chamounix by Donizetti, Don Pasquale and L'Italiana in Algeri; Rota's Italian Straw Hat at La Scala and La Cenerentola, L'Italiana in Algeri and I Capuleti e i Montecchi at the Paris Opéra, 1998; I Capuleti at Covent Garden, 2001. *Recordings:* Il Barbiere di Siviglia; La Fille du Régiment; DGG recording of bel canto arias with Kathleen Battle. *Address:* c/o Royal Opera House (Contracts), Covent Garden, London WC2E 9 DD, England.

**CAMPBELL, David,** GRSM, ARCM, LRAM; clarinettist; b. 15 April 1953, Hemel Hempstead, Hertfordshire, England; m. 1981; one s. *Education:* Barton Peveril, Hampshire, Royal College of Music. *Career:* debut at Wigmore Hall, April 1975; Solo clarinettist, recitalist and chamber music; Has played in 40 countries; Concertos with Royal Philharmonic Orchestra, English Chamber Orchestra, City of London Sinfonia, London Mozart Players, BBC Concert and BBC Scottish; BBC National Orchestra of Wales, BBC Philharmonic, Bournemouth Sinfonietta, Quebec Symphony, Bilbao Symphony and San Sebastian Symphony; Professor and Head of Woodwind, London College of Music; mem, Incorporated Society of Musicians; Clarinet and Saxophone Society. *Recordings:* Mozart Clarinet Concerto with City of London Sinfonia under Hickox on Pickwick; Steptoe Quintet and Complete Chamber Music for Clarinet by Brahms on Phoenix; Ravel Introduction and Allegro, Virgin Classics; Beethoven and Brahms Trios on Pickwick; Schubert Octet; Messiaen Quartet for the End of Time, Collins. *Publications:* Regular contributor to Allegro magazine. *Honours:* Mozart Memorial Prize, 1976; Martin Musical Scholarship, 1976. *Current Management:* c/o Janet Hughes, 76 Cross Oak Road, Berkhamsted, Hertfordshire HP4 3HZ, England. *Address:* 83 Woodwarde Road, Dulwich, London SE22 8UL, England.

**CAMPBELL, Ian David,** BA; Opera Director and Stage Director; b. 21 Dec. 1945, Brisbane, Qld, Australia; m. Ann Spira 1985; two s. *Education:* voice studies with Godfrey Stirling, Sydney 1964–72; Univ. of Sydney. *Career:* debut, Australian Opera, Sydney 1967; principal tenor, Australian Opera 1967–74; Senior Music Officer, Australia Council 1974–76; Gen. Man., State Opera of South Australia 1976–82; Asst Artistic Administrator, Metropolitan Opera, New York 1982–83; Gen. Dir, San Diego Opera, CA 1983–; Producer and Host, At The Opera 1985–97, San Diego Opera Radio Program 1985–97, both on Radio KFSD-FM, San Diego; new series of San Diego Opera radio programme on X-BACH-AM 1997–2001; At the Opera on KPBS-FM 2002–; masterclasses, Music Acad. of the West, Santa Barbara, CA 1991–96; Stage Dir, La Bohème 1981, Les contes d'Hoffmann 1982, State Opera of South Australia; Cavalleria Rusticana/Pagliacci, Santa Barbara Grand Opera 1999; Falstaff 1999, Il Trovatore 2000, Tosca 2002 at San Diego Opera; Fellow, Australian Institute of Management; mem. Kona Kai Club, San Diego, Opera America (board mem. 1985–93, 1997–2001, chair. 2001–), San Diego Convention and Visitors' Bureau (board mem. 1997–2001). *Recordings:* War and Peace (television, opening of Sydney Opera House) 1973. *Honours:* Peri Award for services to California opera 1983, San Diego Press Club Headliner of Year 1991, Father of the Year, San Diego 1997, First Place for a Radio Series, Best of Show (Radio) for At the Opera with Ian Campbell 2003. *Address:* 18th Floor, Civic Center Plaza, 1200 Third Avenue, San Diego, CA 92101-4112, USA.

**CAMPBELL, James (Kenneth);** Clarinettist; b. 10 Aug. 1949, Leduc, Alberta, Canada. *Education:* Studied at Toronto University and with Yona Ettlinger in Paris. *Career:* CBS studio performances with Glenn Gould; Many appearances as concert soloist, including the Copland Concerto under the composer, 1978–79. Engagements with Allegri; Amadeus (until 1987) and Guarneri quartets, notably in Quintets by Mozart and Brahms; Quintets written for him by André Prevost and Ezra Laderman; Recitals with pianist John York, Toronto University 1978–87. Professor at Indiana University, 1987–. *Recordings include:* Duos with Glenn Gould and John York. *Honours:* Winner, CBC Talent Festival and Jeunesses Musicales, Belgrade, 1971. *Address:* Music Faculty, Indiana University, Bloomington, IN 47405, USA.

**CAMPBELL, Margaret;** British writer and lecturer on music; b. London, England; m. Richard Barrington Beare; two s. one d. *Education:* art scholarship, London. *Career:* talks and interviews on BBC radio; Cleveland Radio; Voice of America; USA; CBC Canada; BBC and Southern Television; Lectures at Cornell; Oberlin; Indiana; Oklahoma and Southern Methodist Universities; Manhattan School of Music, New York; Rice University; University of Texas at Austin; University of Southern California, USA; Cambridge, Guildford and Bath Universities; Guildhall School of Music and Drama; Purcell School, England; Festivals at Bergen and Utrecht, Netherlands; Editor, Journal of British Music Therapy, 1974–90; Member of Jury, International Cello Competition at Spring Festival, Prague, Czech Republic, 1994; Lectures at the Conservatoire and University of Sofia, Bulgaria, 1996; Member of Council (ESTA), 1996; Lectures at Sibelius Academy of Music, Helsinki, Finland, 1998; mem. Society of Authors; Royal Society of Literature; Royal Society of Arts; English Speaking Union; European String Teachers Association. *Publications:* Dolmetsch: The Man and His Work, London and USA, 1975; The Great Violinists, London and USA, 1981, Germany, 1982, Japan, 1983, and China, 1999; The Great Cellists, London 1988, Japan, 1996, China, 1999; Henry Purcell: Glory of His Age, London 1993; Married to Music, a biography of Julian Lloyd-Webber, 2001. *Contributions:* The New Grove Dictionary of Music and Musicians, 1980, 2000; The Independent; The Strad; The Cambridge Companion to the Cello, 1999; Collins Encyclopaedia of Classical Music, 2000; The Great Violinists and The Great Cellists, 2nd edition, 2004. *Honours:* Winston Churchill Memorial Travelling Fellowship, 1971; Fellow of the Royal Society of Arts, 1991. *Address:* 71 Shrublands Avenue, Berkhamsted, Hertfordshire HP4 3JG, England.

**CAMPBELL, Richard;** Violin Player; b. 1960, England. *Career:* Member of Fretwork, first London concert at the Wigmore Hall, London, July, 1986; Appearances in the Renaissance and Baroque repertoire in Sweden, France, Belgium, Netherlands, Germany, Austria, Switzerland and Italy; Radio broadcasts in Sweden, Netherlands, Germany and Austria; Televised concert on ZDF, Mainz, Tour of Soviet Union Sept 1989; Japan June 1991; Festival engagements in the United Kingdom; Repertory includes in Nomines and Fantasias by Tallis, Parsons and Byrd; Dance music by Holborne and Dowland, including Lachrimae; Six-part consorts by Gibbons and William Lawes; Songs and instrumental works by Purcell; Collaborations with vocal group Red Byrd in verse anthems by Byrd and Tomkins, London Cries by Gibbons and Dering; Resurrection Story and Seven Last Words by Schütz; Gave George Benjamin's Upon Silence at the Queen Elizabeth Hall, Oct 1990; Wigmore Hall concerts 1990–91 with music by Lawes, Purcell, Locke, Dowland and Byrd. *Recordings:* Heart's Ease, late Tudor and Early Stuart; Armada, Courts of Philip II and Elizabeth I; Night's Black Bird, Dowland and Byrd; Cries and Fancies, Fantasias, In Nomines and The Cries of London; Go Nightly Cares, Consort songs, dances and In Nomines by Byrd and Dowland; All on Virgin Classics Veritas label. *Address:* c/o Virgin Classics Ltd, 64 Baker Street, London W1M 1DJ, England.

**CAMPBELL-WHITE, Martin Andrew,** FRSA; British business executive; *Joint Chief Executive Officer, Askonas Holt Limited;* b. 11 July 1943, s. of late John Vernon Campbell-White and Hilda Doris Ash; m. Margaret Mary Miles 1969; three s. *Education:* Dean Close School, Cheltenham, St John's Coll., Oxford, Univ. of Strasbourg, France. *Career:* with Thomas Skinner & Co. Ltd (Publrs) 1964–66, Ibbs & Tillett Ltd (Concert Agents) 1966–72, Dir 1969–72, Harold Holt Ltd (Concert Agents), subsequently Askonas Holt Ltd 1972–, Dir 1973–, Deputy Chair. 1989–92, Chief Exec. 1992–98, Jt Chief Exec. 1998–; Chair. British Asscn of Concert Agents 1978–81; Council mem. London Sinfonietta 1973–86; Dir Chamber Orchestras of Europe 1983–93; Asst Dir Festival of German Arts 1987; Founding Dir Japan Festival 1991; mem. Bd Première Ensemble 1991–, Riverside Studios 1998–; Trustee Abbado Trust for Young Musicians 1987–, Salzburg Festival Trust 1996–. *Honours:* Sebetia Ter prize for Culture, Naples, Italy 1999. *Address:* Askonas Holt Ltd, Lonsdale Chambers, 27 Chancery Lane, London, WC2A 1PF, England (office). *Telephone:* (20) 7400-1700 (office). *Fax:* (20) 7400-1799 (office). *E-mail:* martin.campbell-white@askonasholt.co.uk (office).

**CAMPION, Joanna;** Singer (mezzo-soprano); b. 1968, England. *Education:* Choral Scholar, Trinity College, Cambridge, England; Royal College of Music, Guildhall School, Britten Pears School and the National Opera Studio. *Career:* Debut: Ursula in Beatrice et Benedict, for Cambridge Operatic Society; Other roles include title part in Prokofiev's The Duenna, Mrs Page in The Merry Wives of Windsor, Britten's Hermia for Singapore Lyric Opera, and Carmen (British Youth Opera, 1992); Baba the Turk in The Rake's Progress at Glyndebourne, Cenerentola and Hansel for Welsh National Opera and Rosina for English Touring Opera; Sang the Mother in Menotti's Amahl and the Night Visitors at the Spoleto Festival, later released on film directed by Menotti; Season 1998–99, engaged as Feodor in Boris Godunov for Welsh National Opera, Annina in Der Rosenkavalier for Scottish Opera and Sabina in Respighi's La Fiamma at the Wexford Festival; Concerts include Messiah on tour with Les Arts Florissants (1994), Mozart's C minor Mass at St Martin in the Fields, Bach's Passions at St John's Smith Square, Dream of Gerontius, Elijah and the Verdi Requiem at the Royal Albert Hall; Mahler Lieder, Elgar Sea Pictures and the Brahms Alto Rhapsody; Birthday celebrations for Yehudi Menuhin at Buckingham Palace, 1996. Current Management: Athole Still International Management, Forresters Hall, 25–27 Westow Street, London, SE19 3RY, England. Telephone: (20) 8771-5271. Fax: (20) 8768-6600. Website: www.atholestill.com.

**CAMPO, Régis,** BPhil; French composer; b. 6 June 1968, Marseilles; m. Kanako Abe 1997. Education: Aix-en-Provence, Marseilles Conservatory with Danielle Sainte-Croix,Georges Boeuf, Nice Conservatory with Jacques Charpentier, Conservatoire National Supérieur de Paris with Gérard Grisey, studied composition with Edison Denisov and Henri Dutilleux. Career: works have been commissioned by numerous international bodies and often played in many festivals or concert seasons world-wide by ensembles such as Nieuw Ensemble, Ensemble Intercontemporain, 2e2m, Orchestre national d'Ile de France. Compositions include: Fabel, for piano and ensemble, 1994; Commedia, for 19 musicians, 1995; Anima, for 6 musicians, 1996; Violin Concerto, 1997; Phantasmagoria, for orchestra, 1997; Les Jeux de Rabelais, 1998; Le Livre de Sonates for organ, 1997–99; Piano Concerto, 1998–99; Nova, for 12 voices, choir and large ensemble, 1998–99; Livre de fantaisies for cello, 1999; Faërie, for orchestra, 2000–01; First Book for Piano, 2000–02; Symphony No. 1 for orchestra, 2002–03. Recordings: numerous recordings and monographies. Honours: Gaudeamus Prize, 1996; First Prize, Special Young Composer Prize and Prix du Public of 3rd Dutilleux Competition, 1996; Dugardin Prize, SACEM, 1999; Pierre Cardin Prize, Institut de France, 1999; Residency, Villa Medici, Rome, 1999–2001. Address: c/o Les éditions Henry Lemoine, 41 rue Bayen, 75017 Paris, France.

**CAMPOS, Anisia;** Concert Pianist and Pedagogue; b. 1940, Brazil; m. Remus Tzincoca. Education: Graduate, Ecole Normale de Musique de Paris and Mozarteum Academy of Music, Salzburg, Austria; Studied with Alfred Cortot, Reine Gianoli and Claudio Arrau. Career: Recitals in Brazil, Portugal, Romania, France, Germany, England, Canada and Austria; Soloist with many orchestras including: Brazilian Symphony Orchestra in Rio de Janeiro, Brazil, the Bucharest George Enescu Philharmonic, Radio Television Orchestra in Bucharest, Cluj Philharmonic and Timisoara Philharmonic; Gave the first performance of Enescu's Sonata No. 1 in many cities; Collaborated with Remus Tzincoca in the discovery and reconstruction of the original version, in Romanian language, of Bartók's Cantata Profana, 1980s; Full Professor for Piano and Head of Clavier Section (Piano, Organ, Harpsichord), Conservatoire de Musique of Montreal (State Conservatory); Professor for Interpretation, Ecole Supérieure de Musique, Vincent d'Indy, Montreal, and University of Ottawa for several years; Held summer courses at the Orford Arts Centre; mem, Co-Founder, President, Canadian Enescu Foundation; Jury Member, Ecole Normale de Musique de Paris, France. Address: 632 Avenue Hervé-Beaudry, Laval, Quebec H7E 2X6, Canada.

**CANARINA, John (Baptiste);** Conductor; b. 19 May 1934, New York, USA. Education: BS, 1957; MS, 1958, Juilliard School; Conducting with Pierre Monteux and Jean Morel, Piano with Arthur Lloyd and Double Bass with Frederick Zimmermann. Career: Conductor, 7th US Army Symphony Orchestra, 1959–60; Assistant conductor, New York Philharmonic, 1961–62; Music Director, Jacksonville Symphony Orchestra, Florida, 1962–69; Director of Orchestral Activities, Drake University, 1973–; Guest Conductor: Royal Philharmonic; Philharmonia Orchestra; Bournemouth Symphony; BBC National Orchestra of Wales and BBC Scottish Symphony; Belgian Radio Orchestra; Slovak Radio Symphony Bratislava. Publications: Contributor to Tempo, High Fidelity, Opus and Keynote. Address: 3663 Grand Avenue, Apt 903, Des Moines, IA 50312, USA.

**CANAT DE CHIZY, Edith;** Composer; b. 26 March 1950, Lyon, France. Education: Studied with Maurice Ohana and Ivo Malec at the Paris Conservatoire, 1978–84. Career: Director of a conservatory in Paris from 1986. Compositions include: String sextet, 1982; Luceat for 10 solo violins, 1983; Livre d'heures for solo voices and ensemble, 1984; Yell for orchestra, 1985; Kyoran for ensemble, 1987; De noche for orchestra, 1991; Hallel for string trio, 1991; Siloël for strings, 1992; Canciones for 12 solo voices, 1992; Tombeau de Gilles de Rais, oratorio, 1993; Moïra, concerto for cello and orchestra, 1998. Recordings: Yell Hallel Canciones de Noche, 1994; Tombeau de Gilles de Rais, 1995; Exultet Siloël Moïra, 1999. Honours: Prix de la Tribune Internationale des Compositeurs, 1990. Address: c/o SACEM, 225 avenue Charles de Gaulle, 92521 Neuilly sur Seine Cédex, France.

**CANIHAC, Jean-Pierre;** Cornet Player; b. 16 April 1947, Toulouse, France; m. Michele Chauzy, 17 Aug 1968, 1 s., 1 d. Education: Baccalaureate, 1966; Conservatoire de Toulouse; Conservatoire de Versailles; Conservatoire National Superieur de Musique, Paris. Career: Founder, Saqueboutiers de Toulouse; Professor, CNR, Toulouse; Professor, Conservatoire National Superieur de Musique, Lyon; Member of Hesperion XX, La Grande Ecurie et la Chambre du Roi, La Chapelle Royale, Clemencic Consort. Recordings: L'Art de Cornet, Arion; Schütz, Symphoniae Sacrae, Erato; 7 Last Words of Christ, H Mundi; Siècle d'or à Venise, Adda; Six Marian Vespers of Monteverdi, Malgoire; and other music conducted by Parrott, Herreweghe and Corboz. Contributions: Brass Bulletin; Blue Brass. Honours: 1st Prize, Conservatoire de Toulouse, 1966; 1st prize, Conservatoire de Versailles, 1968; 1st prize Conservatoire National Superieur, Paris, 1970. Address: 8 rue Maran, 31400 Toulouse, France.

**CANIN, Stuart V.;** Violinist and Educator; b. 5 April 1926, New York City, USA; m. Virginia Yarkin, 8 June 1952, 2 s. Education: Juilliard School of Music, 1946–49. Career: Professor, Violin, State University of Iowa, 1953–60; Oberlin Conservatory of Music, 1960–66; Concertmaster, Chamber Symphony of Philadelphia, 1966–68; Concertmaster, San Francisco Symphony, 1970–80; Concertmaster, San Francisco Opera, 1969–72; Artist Faculty, Aspen Colorado Music Festival, 1960–63; Artist Faculty, Music Academy of the West, Santa Barbara, 1983–; Senior Visiting Lecturer, University of California, Santa Barbara, 1983–; Concertmaster, Casals Festival, San Juan, Puerto Rico, 1974–75, Mostly Mozart Festival, New York City, 1980. Honours: 1st Prize, Paganini International Violin competition, Genoa, 1959; Fulbright Professor to Freiburg, Germany Staatliche Hochschule für Musik, 1956–57. Address: 1302 Holmby Avenue, Los Angeles, CA 90024, USA.

**CANINO, Bruno;** Pianist and Composer; b. 30 Dec. 1935, Naples, Italy. Education: Studied at the Milan Conservatory with Calace and Bettinelli. Career: Piano Duo partner from 1953 with Antonio Ballista; Career as soloist from 1956, notably in works by Bussotti, Donatoni and Castiglioni; Professor of Music at the Milan Conservatory from 1961; Played in premieres of Rapsodia, by Davide Anzaghi, 1984; Played Ode by Castiglioni, 1966, Tableaux Vivants by Bussotti, 1964, Concerto for 2 Pianos and Orchestra by Berio, 1973; Member of the Trio di Milano; Accompanist to instrumentalists and singers including Cathy Berberian until 1983; Appearances with András Schiff include Schubert and Janáček Festival, London, 1995. Compositions include: Chamber and Instrumental Music. Honours: Prizes at Piano Competitions of Bolzano and Darmstadt, 1956–60. Address: Conservatorio Giuseppe Verdi, Via Conservatorio 12, 20122 Milan, Italy.

**CANN, Antoinette,** DipRCM; British pianist; b. 27 Sept. 1963, England; twin sister of Claire Cann. Education: studied piano with Phyllis Sellick at the Royal Coll. of Music, and with Anton Kuerti, Jean Paul Sevilla and Gilbert Kalish at the Banff School of Fine Arts. Career: duo piano player with twin sister; first major concert aged 13; many appearances in Europe, Canada, USA, New Zealand, Japan and the Middle East; extensive tours of the UK, including concerts at the Royal Festival Hall, Barbican Hall, Fairfield Halls, London, St David's Hall Cardiff, Glasgow Royal Concert Hall; concertos with the London Philharmonic, Royal Philharmonic, BBC Concert, London Mozart Players, English Sinfonia, Wren Orchestra, Glasgow Philharmonic; television engagements in the UK, Japan, USA, New Zealand; world premieres of Terry Winter Owens' Homage to Corelli and Pianophoria No. 3; Carey Blyton's Cinque Ports; Michael Elliott's Geminae and Berceuse pour Deux; Timothy Blinko's two-piano concerto with English Sinfonia and Philip Ellis, 2003; South Bank premiere of the Max Bruch concerto for two pianos and orchestra, Royal Festival Hall. Recordings: albums: Gemini; La Danse; Rhapsody; Reflections; Fantasy; Complete Piano Duet Works of Carey Blyton. Honours: Gramophone Critic's Choice; Penguin Rosette Award; Classic FM Critic's Choice; Sound Sense Award; PLG Series; Countess of Munster Trust Awards; RCM President's Rose Bowl. Current Management: Appassionata, 5 Engleric, Chrishall, Royston Herts SG8 8QZ, England. Telephone: (1763) 261535. E-mail: twopianos@canntwins.com (home). Website: www.canntwins.com (home).

**CANN, Claire,** DipRCM; British pianist; b. 27 Sept. 1963, England; twin sister of Antoinette Cann. Education: studied piano with Phyllis Sellick at the Royal Coll. of Music, and with Anton Kuerti, Jean Paul Sevilla and Gilbert Kalish at the Banff School of Fine Arts. Career: duo piano player with twin sister; first major concert aged 13; many appearances in Europe, Canada, USA, New Zealand, Japan and the Middle East; extensive tours of the UK, including concerts at the Royal Festival Hall, Barbican Hall, Fairfield Halls, London, St David's Hall Cardiff, Glasgow Royal Concert Hall; concertos with the London Philharmonic, Royal Philharmonic, BBC Concert, London Mozart Players, English Sinfonia, Wren Orchestra, Glasgow Philharmonic; television engagements in the UK, Japan, USA, New Zealand; world premieres of Terry Winter Owens' Homage to Corelli and Pianophoria No. 3; Carey Blyton's Cinque Ports; Michael Elliott's Geminae and Berceuse pour Deux; Timothy Blinko's two-piano concerto with English Sinfonia and Philip Ellis, 2003; South Bank premiere of the Max Bruch concerto for two pianos and orchestra, Royal Festival Hall;. Recordings: albums: Gemini; La Danse; Rhapsody; Reflections; Fantasy; Complete Piano Duet Works of Carey Blyton. Honours: Gramophone Critic's Choice; Penguin Rosette Award; Classic FM Critic's Choice; Sound Sense Award; PLG Series; Countess of Munster Trust Awards; RCM President's Rose Bowl. Current Management: Appassionata, 5 Engleric, Chrishall, Royston, Herts SG8 8QZ, England. Telephone: (1763) 261535. E-mail: twopianos@canntwins.com (home). Website: www.canntwins.com (home).

**CANNAN, Phyllis;** Singer (Soprano); b. 22 Aug. 1947, Paisley, Scotland. *Career:* Sang as soprano with most major companies in the United Kingdom; Soprano repertoire from 1983; First Major role in Vivaldi's Griselda, Buxton Festival 1983; Sang Gluck's Alceste at the Queen Elizabeth Hall; Kostelnicka in Jenůfa and Katerina in The Greek Passion for Welsh National Opera; Santuzza, Tosca, Rusalka and Goneril, in the British premiere of Reimann's Lear, for English National Opera; Appearances in Der Rosenkavalier and King Priam at Covent Garden; Senta in Der fliegende Holländer at the 1987 Hong Kong Festival; Gerhilde in Die Walküre at the 1989 Promenade Concerts; Concert engagements include Britten's War Requiem in Belgium; Sang the Overseer in Elektra at the First Night of the 1993 London Proms. *Address:* c/o English National Opera, St Martin's Lane, London, WC2, England.

**CANNE MEIJER, Cora;** Singer (Mezzo-Soprano), Coach and Voice Teacher; b. 11 Aug. 1929, Amsterdam, Netherlands. *Education:* Amsterdam Conservatory with Jan Keizer and Re Koster; Studied further with Noemie Perugia in Paris and Alfred Jerger in Vienna. *Career:* Debut: With Netherlands Opera, Amsterdam, 1951; Glyndebourne, 1956, as Cherubino and in Die Zauberflöte and Cenerentola; Salzburg, 1959, in Haydn's Il Mondo della Luna; Zürich Opera, 1960–62; Regular appearances at the Holland Festival; Has sang at many major opera houses including, Vienna, Frankfurt, Brussels, Munich and Hamburg; Performed over 65 roles including: Dorabella, Isolier, Rosina, Isabella, Octavian, Marina in Boris Godunov and Carmen; Sang in world premiere of Milhaud's La Mère Coupable, Geneva, 1966; Was also widely in demand as Lied, concert and oratorio singer, repertory including works by Stravinsky and Berlioz, Bach's St Matthew Passion, Verdi's Requiem; Appeared on television as Carmen and Rosina; For over 20 years has taught at Amsterdam Sweelinck Conservatorium and giving master classes at home and abroad; Produced and Directed open air production of Mozart's Zauberflöte, summer 1989; Frequent Jury Member, International vocal competitions. *Recordings:* Les Noces by Stravinsky; Der Tag des Gerichts by Telemann; Comte Ory from Glyndebourne; Spanish Folksongs; French and Spanish Songs; Diary of One who Disappeared by Janáček. *Address:* Weteringstraat 48, 1017 SP Amsterdam, Netherlands.

**CANNON, Philip;** Composer; b. 21 Dec. 1929, Paris, France; m. Jacqueline Laidlaw, 1950, 1 d. *Education:* Dartington Hall Devon; Royal College of Music, London. *Career:* Lecturer in Music, Sydney University, 1958–60; Professor of Composition, Royal College of Music, 1960–95; mem, RMA; RPS; ISM; NFMS; PRS; MCPS. *Compositions:* 3 Operas, 2 Symphonies, including Son of Man commissioned by the BBC to mark the United Kingdom's entry to the EC; Choral works, Lord of Light, large scale requiem; Chamber Music, all broadcast and performed internationally; Piano quintet, 1998; Millennium Symphony, 1999. *Recordings:* Commissions: BBC; RF; BBC television; Three Choirs Festival; Gulbenkian Foundation; Chromatica USA; Phillip Cannon's Music performed by the Medici String Quartet, 1997. *Publications:* Biographical and critical articles in various magazines. *Honours:* Grand Prix; Critics Prize, Paris, 1965; FRCM, 1970; Te Deum, Commissioned by and dedicated to HM The Queen, 1975; Bard of Gorsedd Vernow, 1997. *Address:* Elmdale Cottage, Marsh, Aylesbury, Bucks., HP17 8SP, England.

**CANONICI, Corrado;** double bassist; b. 26 March 1961, Ancona, Italy. *Education:* Rossini Conservatory, Pesaro, double bass masterclasses with Franco Petracchi and Gary Karr, composition masterclasses with Hans Werner Henze and Brian Ferneyhough. *Career:* recitals in Italy, the United Kingdom, Ireland, USA, Luxembourg, Portugal, Spain, Switzerland, Sweden, Germany, Romania, Netherlands; Chamber music with Ensemble Modern, Music Projects/London, others; Appearances, Italian Radio, Romanian Television, German Radio, French Radio, Spanish Radio, USA Radio in Los Angeles; Masterclasses, New York University, Harvard University, Boston University, universities in Los Angeles and Manhattan School of Music, New York, Dartington International Summer Music courses; Double bass version of solo work by Stockhausen dedicated to Canonici and premiered in London, 4 Oct 1997; Artistic Director, Musica 2000 Festival, Italy; mem, Musicians Union. *Recordings:* Contrabass, including world premiere recording of Luciano Berio's solo bass piece, 1995; Cassandra, as a duo with clarinettist Roger Heaton, 1998; Sonage, as a duo with the former Mingus' trumpeter Jack Walrath, 2000. *Publications:* contrib. to New Notes magazine 1997, Double Bassist Magazine 1998. *Honours:* Xenakis Award, Paris, 1992; Darmstadt Award, 1992; International New Music Consortium Award, 1993, 1997, 1999; Performer in Residence, New York University, 1996. *Address:* World Concert Management, Unit 282, 95 Wilton Road, London, SW1V 1BZ, England.

**CANONICI, Luca;** Singer (Tenor); b. 22 June 1960, Montevarchi, Arezzo, Tuscany, Italy. *Education:* Studied in Rome with Tito Gobbi and at Pesaro. *Career:* Debut: Teatro Sociale Mantua, 1988, as the Duke of Mantua; Sang the Duke in Rome, 1986; Appearances in various Italian theatres, including Bologna and Florence, notably in the Italian premiere of Monteverdi's Ulisse in the version by Henze; Appeared as Rodolfo in the 1987 film version of La Bohème; Other roles include Nemorino and Ernesto, Fernando in Donizetti's Il Furioso all' isola di San Domingo; Frederico in L'Arlesiana; Almaviva and Werther; Bergamo 1990, in Mayr's La rosa bianca a la rosa rossa; Season 1991 as Fenton in Falstaff at Bonn; Pilade in Rossini's Ermione at Rome; Leading role in La Cambiale di Matrimonio at the Pesaro Festival; Sang Max in Leoncavallo's La Reginetta della Rosa, Palermo, 1992; Idreno in Semiramide at Zürich and Tonio in La Fille du Régiment at Rome; Season 1996 in the premiere of Berio's Outis at La Scala, as Bellini's Tebaldo at Genoa and Wolf-

Ferrari's Filepeto at Parma; Sang Mascagni's Fritz at Naples, 1998; Season 1999–2000 as Conte Potioski in Donizetti's Gli Esilati di Siberia, at Montpellier, and Nemorino at the Vienna Staatsoper. *Address:* c/o Teatro dell'Opera, Piazza B Gigli 8, 00184, Rome, Italy.

**CANTELO, April;** Singer (Soprano), Singing Coach, Teacher and Adjudicator; b. 2 April 1928, Purbrook, Hampshire, England. *Education:* Studied at London with Julian Kimbell and at Dartington with Imogen Holst. *Career:* Debut: Sang Barbarina in Figaro and Echo in Ariadne auf Naxos with the Glyndebourne Company at Edinburgh, 1950; Glyndebourne Festivals, 1953, 1963, as Blondchen and Marzelline; English Opera Group, 1960–70, notably as Helena in the premiere of A Midsummer Night's Dream and as Emmeline in Purcell's King Arthur; At Sadler's Wells Theatre, 1962–66, sang in the premieres of Williamson's Our Man in Havana and The Violins of St Jacques; British premieres of Henze's Boulevard Solitude and Weill's Aufstieg und Fall der Stadt Mahagonny; Also created roles in Williamson's The Happy Prince, 1965, and Julius Cesar Jones, 1966; Directed Purcell's The Fairy Queen in New Zealand, 1972; made frequent broadcasts and concert appearances; mem, Equity; ISM; AOTOS. *Recordings:* The Indian Queen; Albert Herring and The Little Sweep; Béatrice et Bénédict; 18th Century Shakespeare Songs; Berlioz' Irelande; Haydn Masses with St John's College Choir, Cambridge. *Address:* 1 The Coalyard, All Saints Lane, Sutton Courtenay, Oxon OX14 4 AG, England.

**CANTINI, Lorenza;** Stage Director; b. Italy; m. *Education:* Accademia d'Arte Drammatica, Milan. *Career:* staged Boris Godunov, Florence 1993; Producer, I Due Foscari, Seoul, Leyle und Medjumn, Montepulciano 1993, Orfeo... Cantando Tolse, Favola di Orfeo 1994, L'Elisir d'Amore 1995, Gli Zoccoli in Villa 1996, Passione Secondo Giovanni 1997, La Forza del Destino, Athens, Il Campanello, Bologna 1998, La Serva Padrona, Florence, La Prova di un Opera Seria, Rome 1999; I Lombardi alla prima Crociata, Cremona 2001, La Serva Padrona, Florence 2001; Assoc. Producer at La Scala with work in Milan and on tour including Capuleti e i Montecchi, Covent Garden 2001, Adriana Lecouvrer, Moscow 2002. *Recordings:* La Forza del Destino 1997, La Serva Padrona 1999, I Lombardi alla Prima Crociata 2001. *Address:* c/o Fondazione Teatro La Scala, Via dell'Innovazione, 20100 Milan, Italy. *Telephone:* (2) 887-9326. *E-mail:* brianrichardearl@tiscali.it.

**CANTRELL, Derrick (Edward);** Cathedral Organist; b. 2 June 1926, Sheffield, England; m. Nancy Georgina Bland, 4 c. *Education:* MA; BMus, Oxford University; FRCO. *Career:* Organist, Manchester Cathedral, 1962–77; Lecturer, Royal Northern College of Music. *Recordings:* Manchester Cathedral Organ. *Honours:* Recipient of Sawyer and Limpus Prizes, Royal College of Organists. *Address:* 36 Parsonage Road, Manchester M20 9 PQ, England.

**CAPOBIANCO, Tito;** stage director, producer, set and lighting designer and educator; b. 28 Aug. 1931, La Plata, Argentina; m. Elena Denda; two s. *Career:* Producer and Technical Director, 1964, Producing Director, Technical Director and Set Designer, 1958, Teatro Colón, Buenos Aires; Artistic Director of Santiago Opera Festival; Stage Director of National Ballet of Chile; Professor of Acting and Interpretation at University of Chile, 1956; Stage Director and Lighting Designer of SODRE National Ballet and Opera; Stage Director of SODRE, Montevideo, Uruguay 1957; Artistic Director of Teatro Argentino; Producing Director and Stage Director of National Drama Company of Buenos Aires, 1959; Artistic Director, Cincinnati Opera and Summer Festival; Director of Opera Productions throughout the USA, 1961–65; Producer and Director, International Opera Festival, Mexico City, 1963–65; Founder and General Director of American Opera Centre, Juilliard School of Music, NY 1968–71; Created Opera Department of College of Performing Arts, Philadelphia, 1972; Artistic Director, 1975; General Director 1977; Created Verdi Festival 1978; Young American Conductor's Programme 1980; San Diego Opera; Vice-President and General Director, Pittsburgh Opera, 1983; Professor, Opera Department, Yale University 1983. *Compositions:* Libretto of Zapata. *Publications:* The Merry Widow, Franz Lehar, Translation. *Honours:* Cavaliere della Republica, Italy, 1979; Officier dans l'Ordre des Arts et Lettres, France, 1984; Doctor of Music, Duquesne University, 1988; Doctor of Letters, Indiana University of Pennsylvania, 1988; Doctor of Humane Letters, La Roche College, 1989. *Address:* Pittsburgh Opera, 711 Penn Avenue, Pittsburgh, PA 15222, USA.

**CAPOIANU, Dumitru;** Composer; b. 19 Oct. 1929, Bucharest, Romania. *Education:* Studied at the Bucharest Conservatory 1941–53. *Career:* Manager of the George Enescu Philharmonic Orchestra, 1959–73. *Compositions:* Wind Quintet, 1950; Viola Sonata, 1952; 2 Suites for orchestra, 1953, 1954; 2 String Quartets, 1954, 1959; Divertissement for string orchestra and 2 clarinets, 1956; Violin concerto 1957; Cosmos 60, ballet scene 1960; Cinematographic Variations for Orchestra, 1965; Steel, ballet 1965; String Trio 1968; Curte domneasca, The Princely Courtyard, spectacle of sound and light, 1969; Moto perpetuo for violin and orchestra, 1972; Chemari 77 for orchestra; Muzica de ambianta for orchestra 1980; Valses ignobles et sentimentales du tout for mezzo and strings, 1986; Three musicals, Dragostei Printesei, 1982, Censareasa 1984, and Tested Love, 1995; The Phoenix Bird for orchestra, 1994; Les verités de Dracula, suite for orchestra, 1995; Choral Music. *Address:* c/o UCMR-ADA, Calea Victoriei 141, Sector 1, Bucharest, Romania. *Telephone:* 21 212 7966. *Fax:* 21 210 7211. *E-mail:* ucmr@itcnet.ro.

**CAPOLONGO, Paul;** French conductor; b. 17 March 1940, Algiers, Algeria. *Education:* Algiers and Paris Conservatories. *Career:* Dir, Quito Symphony, 1963–67, Quito Conservatory, 1963–66; Asst to Leonard Bernstein at the New York Philharmonic, 1967–68; Conductor of Rhine Symphony Orchestra at

Mulhouse, 1975–85. *Honours:* Mitropoulos Competition winner, 1967. *Address:* c/o Orchestre Symphonique du Rhin-Mulhouse, 38 Passage du Théâtre, 68100 Mulhouse, France.

**CAPPELLETTI, Andrea;** Violinist; b. 21 May 1961, Italy. *Education:* Diploma cum laude, Naples Conservatory, Parallel course, Liceo Linguistico. *Career:* 1st Violin, ECYO, 1977; Debut, Israel, 1984; Debut, RFH, 1986; Queen Elizabeth Hall, 1988; Regular appearances with leading orchestras, Italy; France; Germany; Scandinavia; Regular appearances in Europe; Australia; USA; Appointed Art Director, United Nations Concerts for the Disabled, 1990. *Recordings:* Exclusive contract, Koch International with 5 Mozart violin concertos, Italian Baroque Concerti, Respighi Concerti and Tartini sonatas for violin solo; For UNICEF Haydn Concerti. *Honours:* Vittorio Veneto, 1975; Kiefer Balitzel, 1977–78; Fordergemeinschaft, 1986. *Current Management:* Robert Kirp Corporation. *Address:* Via della Ripa 77, 50075 Montespertoli, Ripa F1, Italy.

**CAPRIOLI, Alberto;** Composer, Conductor and Musicologist; b. 16 Nov. 1956, Bologna, Italy. *Education:* Studied Composition with F Margola, C Togni (Parma Conservatory), B Schaeffer (Salzburg Mozarteum); Conducting with O Suitner, Vienna Academy of Music; Humanities with E Raimondi, C Ginzburg; U Eco (Bologna Univ.). *Career:* Guest Conductor, several European orchestras and new music festivals; Prof., Bologna Conservatory of Music; mem., Bd of Dirs, Italian Soc. for Comparative Literature, Florence; Centro Interdisciplinare Studi Romantici, Univ. of Bologna. *Compositions:* Frammenti dal diario, piano, 1974; Abendlied, soprano and orchestra, 1977; Sonata in memorian Alban Berg, piano, 1982; Sonetti di Shakespeare, child reciter and 10 instruments, 1983; Trio, piano, violin and cello, 1984; Del celeste confine, string quartet, 1985; Serenata per Francesca, 6 players, 1985; A la dolce ombra, piano trio, 1985; Dialogue, solo contrabass and 2 string quartets, 1986; Per lo dolce silentio de la notte, piano and computer music tape, 1987; Due Notturni d'oblio, 10 players, 1988; Symphoniae I, II, III, violin, 1988–89; Il vostro pianto aurora o luna, 5 players, 1989; Intermedio I, flute and computer music tape, 1989; Vor dem singenden Odem, quintet, 1990; Kyrie per Dino Campana, soloists, choir and 29 instruments, 1991; John Cage Variations, quintet, 1991; A quinze ans, cello, 1992; Anges, G-flute, viola and harp; Folâtre (Notturno di rosa), 2 guitars, 1993; L'ascesa degli angeli ribelli, reciter and 13 players, 1994; Dittico baciato, choir and orchestra, 1994; Elegia per Carlo Michelstaedter, oboe and 13 instruments, 1998; Canto, orchestra and reciter, 1998; Era, alto-saxophone and brass quintet, 1999; Fiori d'ombra, strings, 2001; Verweile... (danza notturna), reciter and 5 instruments, 2001; Gilles, violin and live electronics, 2002; Stelle assenti, chamber orchestra 2004. *Recordings:* five albums. *Publications include:* L'Italia nell'Europa Romantica, 1993; Luigi Nonos, A Carlo Scarpa, 1997; Pierre Boulez musicien-écrivain, 1998; La profezia del sacro in Hector Berlioz, 2000; Poesia romantica in Musica, 2004, 2005. *Contributions:* Comparatistica, 1998–99; Shakespeare Yearbook, 1994; Musica-Realtà, 1998; Giacomo Leopardi e la nuova musica, 1999. *Address:* D Guglielmini 7, 40137 Bologna, Italy. *E-mail:* alberto .caprioli@inwind.it. *Website:* www.cdmc.asso.fr/html/compositeurs/bio/a_c/ caprioli.htm; www.lingue.unibo.it/romanticismo/membri/caprioli/caprioli .htm.

**CAPRONI, Bruno;** Singer (Baritone); b. 1960, England. *Education:* Studied at the Royal Northern College of Music and the National Opera Studio. *Career:* Sang in Menotti's The Consul, Madama Butterfly and Rigoletto while in college; Appearances with Opera Northern Ireland, Dublin Grand Opera, Wexford and Glyndebourne festivals; Royal Opera House Covent Garden from 1988 in Madama Butterfly, Don Carlos, Rigoletto, Der Freischütz, Otello, Die Meistersinger and Turandot; Sang Ezio in Verdi's Attila in a concert performance conducted by Edward Downes; Other roles include Marcello in La Bohème; Belcore; Ottokar in Der Freischütz; Verdi's Germont, Posa and Amonasro; Sang Schaunard in La Bohème at Covent Garden, 1996; Season 1998 as Ottokar in Der Freischütz, and Marcello at Cologne; Season 2000–01 as Nabucco for ENO, Rigoletto at Antwerp, Posa for the Vienna Staatsoper and Renato (Ballo in Maschera) at La Scala. *Honours:* Vaughan Williams; Frederick Cox award, 1987; Ricordi Prize for Opera 1988. *Address:* c/o Cologne Opera, Offenbachplatz, Pf. 180241, D–50505 Cologne, Germany.

**CARBY, Catherine;** Singer (Soprano); b. 1973, Australia. *Education:* Canberra School of Music, Australian National University; Royal College of Music, London. *Career:* Appearances with Victoria State Opera, Queensland and Opera Australia. Roles have included Rosina, Mercédès (Carmen), Mallika in Lakmé and Jano in Jenůfa; English National Opera in 1999, as Kate in Madama Butterfly; Jerwood Young Singers Program, 2000; Season 2000–01 as Britten's Lucretia for British Youth Opera, title role in Muzio Scevola and Vitige in Flavio for the London Handel Festival. *Honours:* Winner, ABC Young Performer of the Year Awards, 1996; STA Australian National Aria Competition; Tait Memorial Trust Scholarships, RCM; Finalist, Kathleen Ferrier and Richard Tauber Awards. *Address:* c/o Royal College of Music, Prince Consort Road, London SW7, England.

**CARD, June;** Singer (Soprano); b. 10 April 1942, Dunkirk, New York, USA. *Education:* Studied at Mannes College, New York. *Career:* Sang on Broadway from 1959, with New York City Opera from 1963; European engagements at Munich, two titles of Kammersängerin from Frankfurt and Munich; Gartnerplatztheater, from 1967; Member of the Frankfurt Opera 1969–; Appearances in Hamburg, London, Paris, Barcelona, Vienna, Cologne, Met New York, San Carlo (Naples); Over 140 roles, including Violetta, Jenůfa,

Madama Butterfly, Minnie in La Fanciulla del West and Countess in Die Soldaten by Zimmermann; Has sung Janáček's Vixen, Katya and Emilia Marty, Magda in La Rondine, and roles in Schreker's Die Gezeichneten, Henze's Der Junge Lord and Bassarids and The Rake's Progress; Sieglinde and Katerina Izmailova; Frankfurt, 1988 in Poulenc's La Voix Humaine; Holland Festival in The Oresteia by Milhaud; Produced La Clemenza di Tito at Giessen, 1988; Fidelio, in France; Sang the Mother in Die Wände Adriana Hölsky at Frankfurt, 2000; Professor for Opera and Voice, University of Illinois, 1999–; Produced Mozart's Figaro and Così fan tutte, Weill's Street Scene. *Recordings:* Traviata, Gezeichneten. *Current Management:* Agentur Haase, 80802 Munich, Martiussti 3, Germany. *Address:* Arabellastrasse 5-1411, 81925 Munich, Germany.

**CARDEN, Joan Maralyn,** AO, OBE; Australian opera and concert singer; b. 9 Oct. 1937, Richmond, Vic.; d. of late Frank Carden and of Margaret Carden (née Cooke); m. William Coyne 1962 (divorced 1980); two d. *Education:* schools in Melbourne, language studies in London, Trinity Coll. of Music, London and London Opera Centre, voice studies with Thea Phillips and Henry Portnoj, Melbourne and Vida Harford, London. *Career:* debut, world premiere of Malcolm Williamson's Our Man in Havana, Sadler's Wells, 1963; joined Australian Opera (Opera Australia) 1971–; Royal Nat. Opera, Covent Garden as Gilda (Rigoletto) 1974; Glyndebourne as Anna (Don Giovanni) 1977; Scottish Opera as Constanze 1977; US debut at Houston as Amenaide (Tancredi) 1977, Metropolitan Opera Tour as Anna (Don Giovanni) 1978, Kennedy Center 1980, Miami Opera 1981; Singapore Festival 1983; Adelaide Festival 1984; other appearances include Victoria State Opera, Lyric Opera of Queensland, State Opera of South Australia; major roles include most Mozart heroines, Liu (Turandot), Marguerite (Faust), Gilda (Rigoletto), 4 heroines (Contes d'Hoffmann), Natasha (War and Peace), Tatyana (Onegin), Lakme, Leonora (Forza del Destino/Il Trovatore), Violetta (La Traviata), Alice (Falstaff), Mimi, Musetta (La Bohème), Madama Butterfly, Eva (Die Meistersinger), Feldmarschallin (Der Rosenkavalier), Elisabetta (Maria Stuarda), Medee, Tosca, Mother Abbess (Sound of Music); performs regularly in concert with SSO, MSO and QSO, and for Australian Broadcasting Corpn; concert repertoire includes Mozart Masses, concert arias, choral works, 4 Letzte Lieder (R. Strauss), works by Australian composers including Moya Henderson, Peter Sculthorpe. *Recordings:* Joan Carden Sings Mozart, Great Opera Heroines: Joan Carden. *Honours:* Dame Joan Hammond Award for Outstanding Service to Opera in Australia 1987, Australian Government Creative Fellowship 1993, DUniv (Swinburne Univ. of Technology, Melbourne) 2000. *Address:* Opera Australia, PO Box 291, Strawberry Hills, NSW 2012, Australia. *Website:* www.opera-australia.org.au.

**CARDY, Patrick Robert Thomas,** BMus, MMA, DMus; Canadian composer and professor of music; b. 22 Aug. 1953, Toronto, ON. *Education:* University of Western Ontario, McGill University. *Career:* Professor, School for Studies in Art and Culture, Carleton University, Ottawa, 1977–; performances in Canada, USA and Europe. *Compositions include:* Golden Days, Silver Nights, 1977; Vox Humana, 1977; Jig, 1984; Mirages, 1984; Outremer: The Land Beyond the Sea, 1985; Mimesis, 1987; Qilakitsoq: The Sky Hangs Low, 1988; Tango!, 1989; Tombeau, 1989; The Little Mermaid, 1990; Avalon, 1991; Serenade, 1992; Chaconne, 1992; Autumn, 1992; 'Dulce et decorum est...', 1993; Danses folles et amoureuses, 1993; Et in Arcadia ega, 1994; Fhir a Bhata: The Boatman, 1994; Silver and Shadow, 1994; Te Deum, 1995; Dreams of the Sidhe, 1995; La Folia, 1996; Sans Souci, 1996; Bonavista, 1997; The Return of the Hero, 1997; '...and in the night the gentle earth is falling into morning...', 1998; Kalenda Maya, 1999; Zodiac Dances, 2000: Trabadores, 2000; Rhythm in Your Rubbish, 2001. *Recordings include:* Virelai; Éclat; Tango!; Tombeau; Dances Folles et Amoureuses; Sans Souci; Liesel, Suse, Ilze and Gerda; Jig; Numerous on major labels. *Address:* 29 Morgan's Grant Way, Kanata, ON K2K 2G2, Canada.

**CARELLA, Giuliano;** Conductor; b. 1956, Milan, Italy. *Education:* Studied with Franco Ferrara at Siena. *Career:* Conductor of opera performances throughout Europe from 1986; Engagements at Verona, Munich and Hamburg Staatsoperas; Bologna, Salle Gaveau, Paris, Barcelona and Buenos Aires; L'Italiana in Algeri for the Bayerische Staatsoper; Festival of Martina Franca, with operas by Mercadante, and L'Ultimo Giorno di Pompei, by Pacini, 1996; La Morte di Didone at the Rossini Festival Pesaro, and the premiere of Lorenco Ferrero's La Nascite di Orfeo, at the Verona Teatro Filarmonico. *Recordings include:* Ernani; La Sonnambula by Bellini; Il Giuramento and Caritea regina di Spagna by Mercadante (Dynamic); L'Ultimo Giorno di Pompei (Dynamic). *Address:* c/o Accademia Chigiana, Via di Citta 69, 53100 Siena, Italy.

**CAREWE, John (Maurice Foxall);** Conductor; b. 24 Jan. 1933, Derby, England; 2 d. *Education:* Guildhall School of Music and Drama, London; Conservatoire National, Paris. *Career:* Founded Music Today, New Music Ensemble, 1958; Principal Conductor, BBC National Orchestra of Wales, 1966–71; Musical Director, Principal Conductor, Brighton Philharmonic Society, 1974–87; Principal Conductor, Fires of London, 1980–94; General Music Director of the Opera and the Robert Schumann Philharmonic, Chemnitz, 1993–96. *Recordings:* Stravinsky, Histoire du Soldat; Milhaud, Création du Monde; Bennett, Calendar; Maxwell Davies, Leopardi Fragments; Bedford, Music for Albion Moonlight; Debussy, Ibéria; Falla, Interlude and Dance, La Vida Breve; Bridge, Enter Spring and Oration; Colin Matthews, Landscape and Cello Concerto; Muller-Siemens, Under Neon Light I; Leyendecker, Cello Concerto; Debussy, Pelléas et Mélisande; Dvořák,

Symphony No. 8; Brahms, Tragic Overture. *Honours:* Bablock Prize, 1960. *Current Management:* Jürgen Erlebach, Hamburg. *Address:* c/o Jürgen Erlebach, Grillparzerstrasse 24, 22085 Hamburg 76, Germany.

**CAREY, Thomas;** Singer (Baritone); b. 29 Dec. 1931, Bennetsville, Connecticut, USA. *Education:* Studied at the Henry Street Music School, New York, and with Rose Bampton; Further study at the Stuttgart Musikhochschule and with Hans Hotter. *Career:* Debut: Netherlands Opera, Amsterdam, as Germont, 1964; Sang in Lisbon, Nice, Paris, Stockholm, Basle, Zagreb, Venice and Belgrade; Guest singer at the State Operas of Munich, Hamburg, Stuttgart and Berlin; Covent Garden, 1970, as Mel in the premiere of Tippett's The Knot Garden; US engagements in Boston, Memphis and New Orleans; Many concert appearances; Teacher of Voice at the University of Oklahoma, Norman. *Recordings include:* The Knot Garden. *Address:* c/o University of Oklahoma, Catlett Music Center, Norman, OK 73019, USA.

**CARIAGA, Marvellee;** Singer (Mezzo-soprano); b. 11 Aug. 1942, California, USA. *Education:* Studied at California State University. *Career:* Sang with San Diego Opera from 1971; Fricka in performances of Der Ring des Nibelungen for Seattle Opera, 1975–81; Guest appearances at Vancouver, 1975–78, San Francisco, 1981, and Pittsburgh, Portland and Los Angeles, 1987–88; Rio de Janeiro, 1979, as Santuzza; Netherlands Opera, 1979 and 1982; Other roles have included Wagner's Venus, Ortrud, Waltraute, Brünnhilde (Siegfried), Isolde and Magdalene; Donna Anna, Amelia (Ballo in Maschera), Herodias and Kostelnicka in Jenůfa; Colorado, 1986, in the premiere of Pasatieri's The Three Sisters; Los Angeles Music Center Opera, 1991, as Mrs Grose in The Turn of the Screw; Mrs Herring at the Dorothy Chandler Pavilion, Los Angeles, 1992. *Recordings include:* The Three Sisters. *Address:* Los Angeles Music Center Opera, 135 North Grand Avenue, Los Angeles, CA 90012, USA.

**CARIDIS, Miltiades;** Greek/Austrian conductor; b. 9 May 1923, Danzig; s. of Xenophon Caridis and Barbara Fuchs-Caridis; m. Sonja Caridis 1945; one d. *Education:* Kreuzschule, Dresden, Dörpfeldt Gymnasium, Athens and Musikhochschule, Vienna. *Career:* Opernhaus, Graz 1948–59; Opernhaus, Cologne 1959–62; Philharmonia Hungarica 1960–67; Staatsoper, Vienna 1962–69; Radio Symphony Orchestra, Copenhagen 1962–70; Oslo Philharmonic Soc. 1969–75; Duisburger Sinfoniker, Duisburg 1975–81; Tonkünstler-Orchester, Vienna 1979–85; Artistic and Music Dir Athens Radio Symphony Orchestra 1995–. *Address:* Himmelhofgasse 10, 1130 Vienna, Austria. *Telephone:* 8779233. *Fax:* 8779233.

**CARL, Eugene (Gene) Marion, Jr;** Composer and Pianist; b. 8 Nov. 1953, Los Angeles, California, USA. *Education:* BA cum laude, Pomona College, USA, 1971–75; Freiburg im Breisgau, Germany, 1974; Institute for Sonology, Utrecht State University, Netherlands, 1975–76; Prize for Composition, Royal Conservatory, The Hague, 1976–81; Piano studies with John Ritter, 1971–74, Geoffrey Madge, 1976–81, master classes with Padolsky, Voorhies, Kontarsky; Composition with Karl Kohn, 1971–75, Konrad Lechner, 1974, Jan van Vlymen and Jan Boerman, 1976–81, master classes, Darmstadt, 1976. *Career:* Debut: Beethoven Piano Concerto No. 1, with Sepulveda Orchestra, 1968; Composition teaching; (Co-)Producer for special projects; Synthesizer programming and performance De Materie, L. Andriessen and Robert Wilson; Gene Carl band tours, 1995–96, 1996–97, 2000–01; Resident at the Djerassi Foundation near San Francisco, 1999. *Compositions include:* Scratch, violin solo, 1985; Gagarin for double orchestra, mixed choir, 2 solo voices, children's choir, synthesizers, tape, 1986–99; Leonardo, Leonardo for violin, electric guitar, tuba, drum kit, synthesizers, tape, voice, 1986; Hommage à Tarkovski for 2 saxophones, violin, synthesizers, percussion, tape, 1987; Claremont Concerto for B-flat clarinet, piano and string quartet, 1987; Roscoe Boulevard for 2 saxophones (doubling bass clarinet and clarinet) and ensemble, 1988; Pink Chinese Restaurants, a cantata for mezzo and 8 instruments, 1990; Laika for solo synthesiser, 1993; Nocturne for tuba, string trio and synthesizer, 1996; Tree of Time for 7 pianos, 1996; Below Paradise for 8 instruments, 1996; Wyoming Elegy, cantata for baritone and 8 instruments (in memoriam Matthew Shepard), 1998–2000. *Recordings:* 2 albums as member of Hoketus Ensemble; Pianist with 5 UUs; Motor Totemist Guild; Balans, with Hoketus. *Contributions:* Co-editor, Ed., 1976–78, Journal of the Schoenberg Institute; Key Notes, Amsterdam; Cage's Sonatas and Interludes, catalogue, Antiqua Musica, Municiple Museum, The Hague, 1989. *Honours:* Djerassi Resident Artist Program, 1999. *Address:* c/o Donemus, Paulus Potterstraat 14, 1071 CZ Amsterdam, Netherlands.

**CARL, Jeffrey;** Singer (Baritone); b. 1961, Canada. *Education:* BMus, Hons, Voice Performance, McGill University; Diploma, University of Toronto, with Louis Quilico, at Siena and the Britten-Pears School. *Career:* Nick Shadow in Stravinsky's The Rake's Progress, Vancouver Opera; Ford in Falstaff at the Aldeburgh Festival; Verdi's Germont, di Luna, Macbeth; Puccini's Sharpless, Marcello, Scarpia; Tchaikovsky's Onegin, Mozart's Don Giovanni, Guglielmo; Donizetti's Enrico; Bellini's Riccardo, Gounod's Valentin, Thomas' Hamlet, Bizet's Escamillo as well as Henry VIII (Saint-Saëns), Genoveva (Schumann), Brandenburgers in Bohemia (Smetana) and Gershwin's Blue Monday, Italian debut in 1997; Concerts include: standard repertoire under David Willcocks with the Montreal Symphony, Simon Rattle with the Royal Liverpool Philharmonic and Michael Tippett: Messiah, Carmina Burana, Verdi's Requiem, Beethoven's Ninth, Bach Passions, The Creation, Belshazzar's Feast; Further engagements include: La Gioconda in Toronto, Carmen in Portugal, Child of Our Time in Singapore, Mascagni's Iris in Italy, Ballo in

Maschera in Italy, Falstaff (Ford) in London, Mahler Eighth and Scarpia in Verona. *Recordings:* Weill's Firebrand of Florence with Thomas Hampson; La Bohème (Alagna, Ramey, Vaduva, Pappano conducting); The Czarevich with Hadley/Gustafson and Giuditta with Hadley/Riedel conducted by Richard Bonynge; Further recordings include: Caterina Cornaro, Donizetti, with Richard Bonynge. *Address:* c/o Franco Silvestri, Via Marconi 2, 37011 Bardolina, Italy.

**CARLOS, Wendy,** AB, MA; American synthesist, recording engineer and composer; b. (Walter Carlos), 14 Nov. 1939, Pawtucket, RI. *Education:* Brown Univ., Columbia Univ. *Career:* worked as a recording engineer, associating with Robert Moog in the development of the Moog Synthesizer 1964; pioneer in utilising the resources of the synthesizer; collaboration with Larry Fast in the development of a digital process of soundtrack restoration and surround stereo conversion, Digi-Surround Stereo Sound 1992–95; has delivered papers at New York Univ., Audio Engineering Soc. Digital Audio Conference, Dolby New York City Surround Sound demonstration and panel, and at other music/audio conferences; mem. Audio Engineering Soc., Soc. of Motion Picture and Television Engineers, Nat. Acad. of Recording Arts and Sciences. *Compositions include:* Noah (opera) 1964. *Recordings include:* albums as Walter Carlos: Switched-on Bach (three Grammy Awards) 1968, The Well-Tempered Synthesizer 1969, Timesteps 1971, Sonic Seasonings 1972, A Clockwork Orange (soundtrack) 1972, Pompous Circumstances 1974, Switched-on Bach II 1974, By Request 1975; albums as Wendy Carlos: Switched-on Brandenburgs 1979, The Shining (soundtrack) 1980, Tron (soundtrack) 1982, Digital Moonscapes 1984, Beauty In the Beast 1986, Land of the Midnight Sun 1986, Secrets of Synthesis 1987, Peter and the Wolf (with Al Yankovic) 1988, Woundings (soundtrack) 1998, Switched-On Bach 2000 1992, Tales of Heaven and Hell 1998, Switched-On Boxed Set 1999. *Address:* c/o Audio Engineering Society Inc., International Headquarters, 60 E 42nd Street, Room 2520, New York, NY 10165-2520, USA. *E-mail:* email@wendycarlos.com. *Website:* www .wendycarlos.com.

**CARLSEN, Toril;** Singer (Soprano); b. 1954, Oslo, Norway. *Education:* Studied in Oslo and Budapest. *Career:* Appearances at the National Theatre, Oslo, from 1979, notably as Fiordiligi, Pamina, Adina, Micaela and Zdenka; Guest at the Berlin Staatsoper from 1989 (Mélisande, 1991); Many concert appearances. *Recordings include:* Peer Gynt by Grieg (Unicorn). *Address:* c/o Den Norske Opera, PO Box 8800, Youngstorget, 0028 Oslo, Norway.

**CARLSON, Claudine;** Singer (Mezzo-soprano); b. 26 Feb. 1950, Mulhouse, France. *Education:* Vocal training in California; Pupil of Gertrude Gruenberg, Jennie Tourel and Esther Andreas, Manhattan School of Music, New York. *Career:* Numerous appearances as soloist with major orchestras, including Boston Symphony, Detroit Symphony, New York Philharmonic, Minnesota Philharmonic, Los Angeles Philharmonic, St Louis Symphony, National Symphony, London Symphony Orchestra, Orchestre de Paris, Israel Philharmonic; Many festival appearances; Recitalist world-wide. *Recordings:* Various labels. *Honours:* 1st Prize, National Federation of Music Clubs Singing Competition; Martha Baird Rockefeller Award. *Address:* c/o ICM Artists Ltd, 40 West 57th Street, New York, NY 10019, USA.

**CARLSON, Lenus (Jesse);** Singer (Baritone) and Teacher; b. 11 Feb. 1945, Jamestown, North Dakota, USA; m. Linda Kay Jones, 20 Aug 1972. *Education:* BA, 1967; Postgraduate studies with Oren Brown, Juilliard School, 1970–73. *Career:* Apprentice Artist, Central City (Colorado) Opera, 1965–66; Debut as Demetrius, Midsummer Night's Dream, Minnesota Opera, 1968; Sang with opera companies in Dallas, 1972–73, San Antonio, 1973, Boston, 1973, Washington DC, 1973, New York (Metropolitan Opera, debut as Berlioz's Aeneas, 23 Feb 1973), Amsterdam, 1974, others; British debut, Scottish Opera, Edinburgh Festival, 1975; Covent Garden debut, London, as Valentin, 1976; Sang at the Deutsche Oper Berlin as Paul in Die tote Stadt by Korngold, 1983; Nevers in Les Huguenots, 1987, Arcesias in Die toten Augen by d'Albert, 1987; Premiere of Oedipus by Wolfgang Rihm, 1988; Sang the Acrobat in Lulu at the Festival Hall, London, 1994; Creon in Enescu's Oedipe at the Deutsche Oper, 1996 and Klingsor in Parsifal, 1998; Season 1999–2000 at the Deutsche Oper as the Speaker in Die Zauberflöte, Strauss's Faninal and Kothner in Die Meistersinger; Various concert engagements; Teacher, Voice, Minneapolis, 1965–70, New York, 1970–. *Address:* c/o Columbia Artists Management Inc, 165 West 57th Street, New York, NY 10019, USA.

**CARLYLE, Joan Hildred;** British singer (soprano) and teacher; b. 6 April 1931, d. of the late Edgar J. Carlyle and Margaret M. Carlyle; m.; two d. *Education:* Howell's School, Denbigh, N Wales; studied singing with Madame Bertha Nichlass Kempner. *Career:* Prin. Lyric Soprano, Covent Garden 1955; has sung at La Scala Milan, Staatsoper Vienna, Munich, Berlin, Teatro Colón Buenos Aires, San Carlo Naples, Monet Monte Carlo, Nico Milan, Cape Town, Brussels, Geneva, Zurich, Amsterdam, Boston, New York; teaches privately and also in London 2003; gives masterclasses, promotes young singers and judges prestigious competitions. *Major roles sung in UK include:* Oscar, Un Ballo in Maschera 1957–58, Sophie, Der Rosenkavalier 1958–59, Nedda, Pagliacci (Zeffirelli production) 1959, Mimi, La Bohème 1960, Titania, Midsummer Night's Dream, Britten (Gielgud production) 1960, Pamina, Magic Flute 1962, 1966, Countess, Marriage of Figaro 1963, Zdenka, Arabella (Hartman Production) 1964, Suor Angelica 1965, Desdemona, Othello 1965, Arabella 1967, Marschallin, Der Rosenkavalier 1968, Jenifer, Midsummer Marriage 1969, Donna Anna, Don Giovanni 1970, Reiza, Oberon 1970,

Adrianna Lecouvreur 1970, Russalka, Elisabetta, Don Carlos 1975. *Major roles sung abroad include:* Oscar, Nedda, Mimi, Pamina, Zdenka, Micaela, Donna Anna, Arabella, Elisabetta and Desdemona. *Recordings include:* Von Karajan's production of Pagliacci as Nedda, Midsummer Marriage as Jenifer, Medea, Pagliacci from Buenos Aires, Mavra, Purcell Anthology, Voice from the Old House (1/11) 2002, (12/29), (30/42) 2003, Complete versions of Otello, Arabella, Suor Angelica, Highlights from La Bohème 2003, complete versions of Arabella and Adriana Lecouvreur, Rusalka, Oberon, Benevuto Cellini 2004. *Address:* Laundry Cottage, Hanmer, SY13 3DQ, Clywdd, Wales. *Telephone:* (1948) 830265. *E-mail:* joan@joancarlyle.co.uk (home). *Website:* www .joancarlyle.co.uk (home).

**CARMICHAEL, John Russell;** Composer; b. 5 Oct. 1930, Melbourne, Victoria, Australia. *Education:* Mus Dip (Hons), University of Melbourne, 1951; Paris Conservatoire, 1954; Study with Arthur Benjamin 1955–57 and Anthony Milner, 1957–60; Commission from Friends of the Victorian Opera, 1995. *Compositions include:* Concierto Folklorico, for piano and strings, 1970; Trumpet Concerto, 1975; Fantasy Concerto for flute and orchestra, 1982; Lyric Concerto for cornet and piano, 1982; A Country Flair for clarinet and orchestra, 1989; Fêtes Champêtres for clarinet, 1989; Monotony for 2 pianos, 1990; When Will the Sun for soprano and piano, 1990; Bravura Waltzes for 2 pianos, 1990; Saxophone Concerto, 1990; Dark Scenarios for 2 pianos, 1994; From the Dark Side for piano, 1995. *Address:* c/o APRA, 1A Eden Street, Crows Nest, NSW 2065, Australia.

**CARR, Colin (Michael);** Cellist; b. 25 Oct. 1957, Liverpool, England. *Education:* Yehudi Menuhin School, 1966–74; Associate (Honours), Royal College of Music, 1972. *Career:* Soloist throughout Europe, North America, Australia and Far East with major orchestras including: The Royal Philharmonic Orchestra, Concertgebouw Orchestra, BBC Symphony, Philharmonic, Chicago Symphony, National Symphony Washington, English Chamber Orchestra, Scottish Chamber Orchestra, CBSO, Philadelphia Orchestra, Montreal Symphony; Recitals, London, Amsterdam, Paris, New York, Washington, Boston, Los Angeles, television and radio recordings, throughout both continents; Faculty Member, New England Conservatory, Boston, USA, 1983–89; Royal Academy of Music 1998–; State University of New York Story Brook, 2002–. *Recordings:* Sonatas by Debussy and Franck; Elegie, Romance and Papillon by Fauré; Complete Schubert works for Piano Trio; Complete Mendelssohn works for Piano Trio; Complete Brahms Trios with Golub, Kaplan, Carr Trio; Bach Solo Cello Suites; Brahms Sonatas. *Address:* c/o Caroline Baird Artists, 9 Onslow Gardens, London, N10 3JT, England.

**CARR-BOYD, Ann;** Composer; b. 13 July 1938, Sydney, New South Wales, Australia. *Education:* Studied at the University of Sydney (MA, 1963) and in London with Fricker and Goehr. *Career:* Teacher at the University of Sydney, 1967–73. *Compositions include:* Symphony, 1964; 2 string quartets, 1964, 1966; Vocal music, including Home Thoughts from Abroad for mezzo and ensemble, 1987; Instrumental pieces, including Dance Suite for woodwind quintet, 1984, and Theme and Variations for organ, 1989. *Address:* c/o APRA, 1A Eden Street, Crows Nest, New South Wales 2065, Australia.

**CARRERAS, José;** Spanish singer (tenor); b. 5 Dec. 1947, Barcelona; s. of José Carreras and Antonia Carreras; m. Ana Elisa Carreras; one s. one d. *Career:* opera debut as Gennaro in Lucrezia Borgia, Liceo Opera House, Barcelona 1970–71 season; appeared in La Bohème, Un Ballo in Maschera and I Lombardi alla Prima Crociata at Teatro Regio, Parma, Italy 1972; US debut as Pinkerton in Madame Butterfly with New York City Opera 1972; debut Metropolitan Opera as Cavaradossi 1974; debut La Scala as Riccardo in Un Ballo in Maschera 1975; has appeared at major opera houses and festivals including Teatro Colón, Buenos Aires, Covent Garden, London, Vienna Staatsoper, Easter Festival and Summer Festival, Salzburg, Lyric Opera of Chicago; recordings include Un Ballo in Maschera, La Battaglia di Legnano, Il Corsaro, Un Giorno di Regno, I Due Foscari, Simone Boccanegra, Macbeth, Don Carlos, Tosca, Thais, Aida, Cavalleria Rusticana, Pagliacci, Lucia di Lammermoor, Turandot, Elisabetta, regina d'Inghilterra, Otello (Rossini); Pres. José Carreras Int. Leukaemia Foundation 1988–. *Films include:* La Bohème, I Lombardi, Andrea Chenier, Turandot, Carmen, Don Carlos, La Forza del Destino, Fedora, Jerusalem, My Life. *Publication:* Singing from the Soul 1991. *Honours:* Hon. mem. RAM 1990; Grammy Award 1991, Sir Lawrence Olivier Award 1993, Gold Medal of City of Barcelona, ABC Schweizer Music Award 1996; Commdr des Arts et Lettres, Chevalier Légion d'honneur and numerous other awards and prizes. *Address:* c/o José Carreras International Leukaemia Foundation, Muntaner, Barcelona (office); c/o Opera Caballé, via Augusta 59, Barcelona (office); c/o FIJC, Muntaner 383, 2°, 08021 Barcelona, Spain. *Telephone:* (93) 4145566 (office). *Fax:* (93) 2010588 (office). *E-mail:* fundacio@fcarreras.es. *Website:* www.fcarreras.es (office).

**CARRINGTON, Simon (Robert);** Musician, Bass Player and Music Director; b. 23 Oct. 1942, Salisbury, Wiltshire, England; m. Hilary Stott, 2 Aug 1969. 1 s., 1 d. *Education:* Christ Church Cathedral Choir School, Oxford; The King's School, Canterbury; King's College, Cambridge; New College, Oxford; MA (Cantab); Teaching Certificate (Oxon); Choral Scholar, King's College, Cambridge. *Career:* Co-Founder and Director of the King's Singers, 1968–93 with 3,000 performances world-wide and numerous concerts, radio and television appearances; Freelance Double Bass Player with all major British symphony and chamber orchestras; Since 1994 Professor, Artist in Residence and Director of Choral Activities at the University of Kansas;

Monteverdi Vespers, 1994; Britten War Requiem, Tallis 40 part Motet, Tribute to Henry Purcell, 1995; Walton Belshazzar's Feast, Ligeti Lux Aeterna, Josquin Missa Gaudeamus, 1996; Mendelssohn Elijah (staged as an opera), Music from the time of the Mexican Viceroys, Bach Motets, 1997; Director of the Graduate Degree Programs in Choral Directing; Freelance Choral Workshop Director and Choral Competition Judge in the United Kingdom, USA, France, Germany, Netherlands and Hungary; Choral Conductor world-wide including Carnegie Hall performances, 1996 and 1997. *Compositions:* Numerous arrangements for The King's Singers. *Recordings:* Numerous with various labels internationally, 1971–93 including madrigals, motets, folk songs from five centuries. *Publications:* The King's Singers–A Self Portrait, 1981; Video: The Art of The King's Singers. *Address:* Department of Music and Dance, 332 Murphy Hall, University of Kansas, Lawrence, KS 66044, USA.

**CARROLI, Silvano;** singer (baritone); b. 22 Feb. 1939, Venice, Italy. *Education:* Opera School of La Fenice, Venice. *Career:* debut in Venice 1964, as Marcello in La Bohème; Sang widely in Italy and toured North America with the company of La Scala, 1976; Verona Arena from 1973, in Samson et Dalila, as Ezio in Attila (1985), Renato in Un Ballo in Maschera (1986) and as Amonasro (2000); Washington Opera 1977–78, as Cavaradossi; London, Covent Garden, as Iago and in La Fanciulla del West; Chicago Lyric Opera 1978; Brussels 1980, in a revival of Donizetti's Il Duca d'Alba; Barcelona 1983, as Escamillo; Paris Opéra 1984, as Nabucco and in Verdi's Jérusalem; Further appearances at the Metropolitan Opera and at the Deutsche Oper Berlin; Amonasro, Luxor, Egypt, 1987; Season 1988–89, Barnaba, Alfio at Verona, Michele in Il Tabarro at Florence, Puccini's Jack Rance at Caracalla Festival, Rome; Iago, Covent Garden, 1990; Scarpia, Arena di Verona; Season 1992, as Gerard in Andrea Chénier at Turin, Scarpia at Covent Garden, Amonasro at the Festival di Caracalla; Sang Scarpia at Hanover, 1994 and at Verona, 1998. *Recordings include:* Video of I Lombardi (Topaz).

**CARROLL, Joan;** Singer (Soprano); b. 27 July 1932, Philadelphia, USA. *Education:* Studied in America, then with Margarethe von Winterfeldt in Berlin. *Career:* Debut: New York Opera Company 1957, as Zerbinetta; Appearances in North America and in Havana; Santa Fe 1963, as Lulu (US premiere of Berg's opera); European engagements in Belgium, France, Denmark, Switzerland and Netherlands; Sang Lulu in Hamburg, Munich and Zürich during the 1960s; Member of the Deutsche Oper am Rhein, Düsseldorf, from 1967; Sang Mozart's Constanze, Donna Anna and Queen of Night, as well as modern repertory, in Hanover, Berlin, Stuttgart, Cologne and Nuremberg. *Recordings include:* Works by Gorecki and Stravinsky.

**CARRON, Elizabeth;** Singer (Soprano); b. 12 Feb. 1933, New York, NY, USA. *Education:* Studied in New York. *Career:* Debut: New York City Opera, 1957, as Madama Butterfly; Sang in New York until 1977 and made guest appearances in Cincinnati, Chicago, Pittsburgh, San Francisco and New Orleans; Dallas, 1958, as Dirce in Cherubini's Médée, opposite Maria Callas; Edinburgh Festival, 1984, with the Washington Opera; Other roles have included Mozart's Constanze, Susanna and Zerlina, Violetta, Micaela, Mimi and Liu, Norina, Strauss's Salome and Daphne, Aithra in Die Ägyptische Helena and Birdie in Regina by Blitzstein. *Recordings include:* Regina. *Address:* c/o Washington Opera, Kennedy Center for the Performing Arts, Washington, DC 30566, USA.

**CARSEN, Robert;** stage director; b. 23 June 1954, Toronto, Canada. *Education:* Upper Canada College, York University, Toronto, Bristol Old Vic Theatre School. *Career:* Assistant Dir, Glyndebourne Festival Opera, 1982–85; Production of Boito's Mefistofele seen at Geneva 1988 and at San Francisco, Chicago, Houston, Washington and Metropolitan Operas, 1989–99; Aix-en-Provence Festival from 1991–96, with A Midsummer Night's Dream, Handel's Orlando, Die Zauberflöte, Semele (French premiere); Salome in Lyon; Bellini's La Straniera for Wexford, A Village Romeo and Juliet for Opera North, Mozart's Finta Semplice and Finta Giardiniera for the Camden Festival, London, and Cendrillon for Welsh National Opera; Metropolitan Opera debut with Eugene Onegin, European premiere of Blitzstein's Regina for Scottish Opera; Lucia di Lammermoor at Zürich and Munich, Katya Kabanova in Canada and Figaro for Bordeaux, Paris, Israel and Barcelona, 1997; seven-part Puccini cycle for the Flemish Opera, 1990–96; Otello, Falstaff and Macbeth in Cologne, Die Frau ohne Schatten and Verdi's Jérusalem in Vienna; Alcina, Lohengrin, Nabucco, Capuleti e i Montecchi and Manon Lescaut at the Opéra Bastille, Paris; Carmelites in Amsterdam, Semele at English National Opera and Antwerp; Tales of Hoffmann for the Paris Opéra, The Ring in Cologne, Jenůfa and Cunning Little Vixen in Antwerp, Dialogues of the Carmelites at La Scala; Capriccio for Paris Opera, Rosenkavalier at Salzburg, La Traviata at Teatro La Fenice, Venice, 2004; Elektra for Tokyo Opera Nomuri with Seiji Ozawa, Manon Lescaut at the Vienna Staatsoper and Il Trovatore in Bregenz 2005. *Honours:* Carl Ebert Award for directing, 1982; French Critics Prize, 1992; Chevalier des Arts et des Lettres, 1996; Grand Prix de la Presse Musicale Internationale, 1996. *Address:* Judy Daish Associates Ltd, 2 St Charles Place, London, W10 6EG, England.

**CARSON, Clarice;** Singer (Soprano); b. 23 Dec. 1936, Montreal, Canada. *Education:* Studied with Pauline Donalda and Jacqueline Richard in Montreal, with Julia Drobner in New York. *Career:* Debut: Montreal Opera 1962, in Menotti's Amahl and the Night Visitors; Many guest engagements in North America; New York City Opera 1965, as Mozart's Countess;

Metropolitan Touring Opera 1967; European engagements in Barcelona, Rouen, Amsterdam and with Scottish Opera, Glasgow, 1969; Schwetzingen 1976, as Paer's Leonora; Other roles include Cassandre in Les Troyens; Mozart's Donna Anna, and Constanze; Verdi's Desdemona, Violetta, Aida, Elisabeth, Amelia and Leonora (Il Trovatore); Puccini's Tosca, Mimi, Liu, Butterfly and Musetta; Marguerite in Faust and the title role in Salome; Many concert performances. *Recordings include:* Leonora by Paer (MRF).

**CARTER, Barbara;** American singer (soprano); b. 1947, Columbus, OH. *Education:* Capital University, University of Toronto with Louis Quilico, Musical Academy of the West with Martial Singher. *Career:* sang Violetta and Musetta with the Canadian Opera Co. on tour of the USA and Canada; European debut with the Essen Opera, then appeared as Queen of Night in Die Zauberflöte with the Covent Garden Opera on tour to the Far East; further appearances in Berlin, Munich, Buenos Aires, Paris, Vienna, Amsterdam, La Scala, Milan, Venice, Barcelona, New York, Ottawa and Bregenz; roles have included Lucia, Gilda, Marie in La Fille du Régiment, Zerbinetta, Sophie, Constanze, Zerlina, Rosina, Elvira in Puritani, Amenaide in Tancredi, Olympia, Nannetta and Gretel; season 1990–91 as Constanze in Amsterdam and the Italian Singer in Capriccio at the Vienna Staatsoper; concert appearances in works by Bach, Mozart, Haydn, Handel, Brahms, Orff, Schubert and Charpentier; Mahler's Symphonies 2, 4 and 8; engagements with Giuseppe Sinopoli leading the Czech Philharmonic, the Philharmonia (London) on tour in Japan, the Accademia di Santa Cecilia in Rome and the Deutsche Oper Berlin (Fiakermilli in Arabella); recital repertoire includes German Lieder and songs in Russian, French, English, Spanish, Italian and Portuguese. *Honours:* Capital Univ. Life Achievement Award, Columbus 1996. *Address:* Bruckerstrasse 7, 82284 Grafrath, Germany. *E-mail:* barbara .carter@soprano.de (home). *Website:* www.soprano.de.

**CARTER, Elliott,** AB, AM; American composer; b. 11 Dec. 1908, New York; s. of Elliott Carter and Florence Carter (née Chambers); m. Helen Frost-Jones 1939 (died 2003); one s. *Education:* Harvard Univ., Ecole Normale de Musique, Paris. *Career:* Musical Dir Ballet Caravan 1937–39; critic, Modern Music 1937–42; tutor, St John's Coll., Annapolis 1939–41; teacher of composition, Peabody Conservatory 1946–48, Columbia Univ. 1948–50, Queen's Coll. (New York) 1955–56; Prof. of Music, Yale Univ. 1960–61; Prof., Dept of Composition, Juilliard School, New York 1966–82; Andrew White Prof.-at-Large, Cornell Univ. 1967; mem. Bd of Trustees, American Acad., Rome; mem. Int. Soc. for Contemporary Music, Dir 1946–52, Pres. American Section 1952, Nat. Inst. of Arts and Letters; mem. American Acad. of Arts and Sciences. *Works include:* orchestral: Symphony No. 1 1942, Variations for Orchestra 1955, Double Concerto (New York Critics' Circle Award 1961) 1961, Piano Concerto 1965, Concerto for Orchestra 1969, Symphony of Three Orchestras 1977, Oboe Concerto 1987, 3 Occasions for Orchestra 1989, Violin Concerto 1990, Clarinet Concerto 1996, Symphonia 1998, Asko Concerto 2000, Cello Concerto 2001, Boston Concerto 2002; chamber music: Quartet for Four Saxophones (American Composers' Alliance Prize 1943), Elegy 1943, Sonata for Cello and Piano, Woodwind Quintet 1948, Sonata for Flute, Oboe, Cello and Harpsichord 1952, Brass Quintet 1974, five String Quartets (Pulitzer Prize for Second String Quartet, for Third String Quartet 1973) 1951–93, Triple Duo 1982, Penthode 1985, Oboe Quartet for Heinz Holliger 2001; vocal music: A Mirror on Which to Dwell 1975, In Sleep In Thunder 1983, Of Rewaking 1992; choral music: The Defense of Corinth 1949; instrumental music: Piano Sonata 1946, Night Fantasies for piano 1980, A Six-letter Letter for English Horn; stage works: Pocahontas 1939, The Minotaur 1947, What Next? (opera) 1999, and numerous others. *Honours:* Commdr des Arts et Lettres; hon. degrees from Swarthmore Coll. and Princeton Univ. 1969, Univs of Harvard, Yale and Boston 1970, Univ. of Cambridge, UK 1983; First Prize, Liège Int. Music Competition 1953, Prix de Rome 1953, Sibelius Medal, Harriet Cohen Foundation 1960, Ernst Von Siemens Prize, Munich 1981, Gold Medal, Nat. Inst. of Arts and Letters 1971, Handel Medallion of New York 1978, awarded Nat. Medal of Art by Pres. Reagan 1985, Gold Medal, Royal Philharmonic Soc. 1996. *Address:* c/o Boosey & Hawkes Inc., 35 East 21st Street, New York, NY 10010, USA.

**CARTER, Peter (John Burnett);** Violinist; b. 30 Jan. 1935, Durban, South Africa; m. Sally Mackay, 20 Dec 1974, 1 s., 1 d. *Education:* Royal College of Music, London, 1952–55; Conservatoire Royale de Musique, Brussels, 1955–58; ARCM; LRCM; MMus Honoris Causa, University of Hull, 1987. *Career:* 2nd Violin, Dartington String Quartet, 1958–68; Director, Music, Natal Performing Arts Council, 1968–69; 1st Violin, Delmé String Quartet, Member ECO, 1969–74; Senior Lecturer, Cape Town, 1974–77; 1st Violin, Allegri String Quartet, Allegri Robles Ensemble, 1977, Melos Ensemble, 1984; mem, Incorporated Society of Musicians. *Recordings:* Complete Schubert Quartets, 1979–81; Brahms Quartets; Beethoven Quartets and Quintets; Ravel Septet; Stolen Gems, James Campbell, 1986; Leader Bath International Ensemble, 1988; Brahms Clarinet Quintet (James Campbell); Piano Quintet (Rian de Waal), 1992 CALA; Lombardini Sirman 6 Quartets, 1994; Bruch and Brahms 2 Viola Quintets, 1995; Schubert, Newbould, 1996; Haydn Op 33 No. 3, 1996; Ravel, 1996; Haydn, Shostakovich No. 3, 1996; Schubert, Newbould, Stravinsky, Mozart Clarinet quintet, 1997; Beethoven op 131, Britten No. 3, 1998; Romberg and Brandts Buys Quintets (with William Bennett, flute). *Honours:* Doctor of Music, Nottingham University, 1994; Doctor of Music, Southampton University, 1995; FRSA. *Current Management:* Biranda. *Address:* 35 Gartmoor Gardens, London SW19 6NX, England. *E-mail:* allegri@appleonline.net.

**CARTER, Roland M.,** MA; American composer and teacher; b. 4 May 1942, Chattanooga, TN. *Education:* Howard High School, Hampton Univ. VT, New York Univ., Catholic Univ. of America, Washington, DC, Aspen Choral Inst., CO. *Career:* Asst Dir, accompanist and arranger, Crusader Male Chorus of Hampton 1962–79, Dir 1980–89; Asst Dir, Choir Dirs and Organists Guild of the Hampton Univ. Ministers Conference 1963–79, Dir 1980–89; Dir, Peninsula Youth Symphony, Hampton 1974–80; founder and Chief Exec., Mar-Vel Publishers, Chattanooga 1978–; accompanist and coach for Marilyn Thompson 1982–; Dir, Chattanooga Choral Soc. for the Preservation of Negro Spirituals 1989–; Dir of Music, First Baptist Church, Chattanooga 1992; teacher Summer Music Inst. for High School Students, Hampton Univ. 1964–69, Dir 1966–69; Dir of Choral Music, Hampton Univ. 1965–88, Chair 1986–89; Music Dept Faculty, Univ. Tenn. Chattanooga 1989–, Dept Head 1989–95. *Compositions include:* A Hampton Portrait: Prologue 1968, Hold Fast to Dreams 1978, You Must Have That True Religion 1982, No Room in the Inn 1988, Psalm 23 1988, Anniversary Hymn 1988, How Beautiful Are the Feet 1989, I Dream A World 1994. *Honours:* Hampton Univ. Lindback Award for Distinguished Teaching 1982, Coll. of Arts and Sciences, Univ. of Tenn. at Chattanooga Excellence in Service Award 1992; MacLellan Foundation Fellowship, Chattanooga 1965–66, Nat. Asscn of Negro Musicians Distinguished Musician Award 1974, Musician of the Year (Eastern Region) 1981, Black Music Caucus of MENC Nat. Award 1994. *Address:* PO Box 6082, Chattanooga, TN 37401, USA (office). *Telephone:* (423) 267-0704 (office). *Fax:* (423) 267-4505 (office).

**CARTER, Ronald;** singer (tenor); b. 1961, Texas, USA. *Career:* sang first as baritone then appeared as Don José with New Rochelle Opera, Manrico for Long Island Opera and Canio for the Metro Lyric Opera of New Jersey; Has appeared with Augsburg Opera as Tichon (Katya Kabanova), Strauss's Emperor (1993), Turiddu and Cavaradossi; Guest appearances as Bacchus at Kaiserslautern and in Basle and Hanover; Sang Florestan at Krefeld, 2000. *Honours:* Awards from the Jugend in Wien competition, the Pavarotti Competition and the Liederkranz Foundation.

**CARTERI, Rosanna;** Singer (Soprano); b. 14 Dec. 1930, Verona, Italy. *Education:* Studied with Cuisnati and Nino Ederle. *Career:* Debut: Rome 1949, as Elsa in Lohengrin; La Scala debut 1951, in La Buona Figliuola by Piccinni; Sang in many concerts, notably in Donizetti's Requiem and in the premiere of Pizzetti's Ifigenia (Italian Radio 1950); Salzburg Festival 1952, as Desdemona, conducted by Furtwängler; Florence 1953, as Natasha in the premiere of Prokofiev's War and Peace; San Francisco 1954, as Mimi; Chicago Lyric Opera 1955, as Marguerite in Faust; Verona Arena 1958–59; Covent Garden 1960, Mimi; Sang in the premiere of Pizzetti's Calzare d'Argento, Milan 1961; Premiere, Gilbert Bécaud's Opera d'Aran, Théâtre des Champs-Elysées, Paris, 1962. *Recordings include:* La Traviata (RCA); Falstaff, Guillaume Tell, Suor Angelica, La Bohème (Cetra); Solo in the Brahms Requiem, conducted by Bruno Walter.

**CARVER, Anthony Frederick,** BMus, PhD; University Teacher; b. 16 Nov. 1947, Brighton, England; m.; two s. one d. *Education:* Westlain Grammar School, Brighton and Birmingham Univ. *Career:* Lecturer in Music, Queen's Univ., Belfast 1973, Senior Lecturer 1974–; mem. Royal Musical Assn, Asscn of Univ. Teachers. *Publications:* Cori Spezzati (two vols), Irish Church Praise (co-ed.), contrib. to ACTA Musicologica: Proceedings of the Royal Musical Association, Early Music. *Address:* School of Music, Queen's University, Belfast, BT7 1NN, Northern Ireland (office). *Telephone:* (28) 9097-5208 (office). *Fax:* (28) 9097-5053 (office). *E-mail:* a.carver@qus.ac.uk (office).

**CARY, Tristram Ogilvie,** AM, BA, MA, AMusTCL, LMusTCL; composer, writer and teacher; b. 14 May 1925, Oxford, England; m. Doris E. Jukes 1951 (divorced 1978); two s. one d. *Education:* Christ Church, Oxford, service in Royal Navy, Trinity Coll. of Music. *Career:* debut at Wigmore Hall, London 1949; composing from age 14; record shop asst 1951–54; first electronic music studio 1952; self-employed as composer, teacher, writer, computer music consultant 1955–; music for concerts, films, radio, television, theatre, musical directories; founder of an electronic studio, Royal Coll. of Music 1967; Sr Lecturer, Univ. of Adelaide 1974, Reader, Dean of Music 1982. *Compositions:* 345, Narcissus, Trios, Sonata for Guitar Alone, Three Threes and One Make Ten, Arrangement of Bach's 6-part Ricercar, Continuum, Contours and Densities at First Hill, Peccata Mundi, Divertimento, The Songs Inside; Romantic Interiors, Steam Music, Two Songs from the Piae Cantiones, Nonet, Soft Walls, I Am Here, Family Conference, Seeds, Trellises, Strands, String Quartet II, Sevens, The Dancing Girls, Black White and Rose, Strange Places, Earth Holds Songs, Messages 1993, Inside Stories 1993, The Impossible Piano 1994, Suite–The Ladykillers 1996, Dublin Square for orchestra 1997, Through Glass 1998, Scenes From a Life 2000, Songs for the Adelaid Baroque 2004. *Recordings include:* Computer and orchestral music; many radio, film, television score recordings; Quatermass and the Pit, the Film Music of Tristram Cary Vol. 1; The Ladykillers; Suite (music from Ealing Films); Soundings, electro-acoustic works, 1955–1996, 1999; The Hammer Quatermass Film Music Collection, 2000; Blood from the Mummy's Tomb, 2002; Devils' Planets – the Music of Tristram Cary for Dr Who, 2003. *Publications:* Illustrated Compendium of Musical Technology (aka Dictionary of Musical Technology) 1992; contrib. to Musical Times, Composer, The Electronic Music Review, The Guardian, Opera Australia, The Australian. *Honours:* Hon. RCM 1972. *Address:* 30 Fowlers Road, Glen Osmond, SA 5064, Australia.

**CASA-DEBELJEVIC, Lisa Della;** Swiss singer (soprano); b. 2 Feb. 1919, Burgdorf, Bern; d. of Dr Francesco Roberto Della Casa and Margareta Della Casa (née Müller). *Education:* Berne Conservatoire. *Career:* début at Zürich Opera House 1943; mem. Vienna State Opera Co. 1947–, New York Metropolitan Opera Co. 1953–; has appeared at Festivals at Salzburg 1947, 1948, 1950, 1953–58, Glyndebourne 1951, Bayreuth, Edin. 1952, Zürich, Lucerne, Munich 1951–58; has also appeared in London, Berlin, Paris, Milan, San Francisco and in South America, etc.; apptd Austrian State Kammersängerin. *Address:* Schloss Gottlieben, Thurgau, Switzerland.

**CASADESUS, Jean Claude;** French conductor; *Director, Lille National Orchestra;* b. (Jean Claude Probst), 7 Dec. 1935, Paris; s. of Lucien Probst and Gisèle Casadesus; m. Anne Sevestre; two s. one d. *Education:* Paris Nat. Conservatoire and Ecole Normale, Paris. *Career:* solo timpanist, Concert Colonne 1959–68; percussion soloist, Domaine Musical (with Boulez); Conductor, Paris Opéra 1969–71; Co-Dir Orchestre Pays de Loire 1971–76; Founder and Dir Lille Nat. Orchestra 1976–; appears as guest conductor with leading orchestras in UK, USA, France, Germany, Norway, Russia, Czech Repub., int. music festivals etc.; Gen. Sec. Conseil Supérieur de la Musique; Pres. Musique Nouvelle en Liberté. *Recordings include:* works by Dutilleux (1st Symphony), Berlioz, Mahler, Bizet, Stravinsky, Mozart, Beethoven, Ravel, Debussy, Poulenc, Groupe des Six, Prokofiev, Dukas, Massenet, Milhaud, Honneger, Mussorgsky, Franck. *Publications:* Le plus court chemin d'un coeur à un autre 1998, Stock (ed.). *Honours:* Commdr Légion d'honneur; Commdr Ordre nat. du Mérite; Commdr des Arts et des Lettres; Chevalier Ordre des Palmes académiques; Commdr Order of Orange Nassau (Netherlands); Officer Order of Crown (Belgium); Grand Prix de la SACEM and several other prizes and awards for recordings. *Address:* Orchestre National de Lille, 30 place Mendès-France, BP 119, 59027 Lille Cedex (office); 23 blvd de la Liberté, 59800 Lille (home); 2 rue de Steinkerque, 75018 Paris, France (home). *Telephone:* 3-20-12-82-40 (office). *Fax:* 3-20-40-22-89 (home); 3-20-78-29-10 (office). *E-mail:* casajc@wanadoo.fr (home).

**CASAPIETRA, Celestina;** Singer (Soprano); b. 23 Aug. 1938, Genoa, Italy; m. Herbort Kegel (deceased 1990). *Education:* Studied at the Milan Conservatory with Gina Cigna. *Career:* Debut: Teatro Nuovo, Milan, 1961, in Mese Mariano by Giordano; Sang in Genoa, San Remo, Pisa, Venice and Lyons; Sang at the Staatsoper Berlin from 1985, notably as Elsa, Constanze, Donna Anna, Agathe, Mimi, Micaela, Tatiana in Eugene Onegin and the title role in Daphne by Strauss; Salzburg Mozartwochen, 1984, as Vitellia in La Clemenza di Tito; Las Palmas, 1986, as Elisabeth in Tannhäuser; Guest engagements in London, Moscow, Helsinki, Copenhagen, Vienna and Prague; Zemlinsky's Der Kreidekreis, Hamburg, 1983, Amsterdam, 1989; Season 1994 as Tosca at Genoa and Ariadne at Lyon. *Recordings include:* Fiordiligi in Così fan tutte; Mozart's Masses; Orff's Trionfi. *Address:* c/o Deutsche Staatsoper, Unter den Linden 7, 1086 Berlin, Germany.

**CASCIOLI, Gianluca;** Italian concert pianist, conductor and composer; b. 1979, Turin. *Education:* began piano studies 1986; entered the Accademia Musicale in Imola, 1991; composition classes at the Verdi Conservatory, Turin. *Career:* many recital appearances throughout Italy specialising in classical and contemporary repertory, 1994–; Engagements with Orchestra della Scala, Orpheus Chamber Orchestra, Gustav Mahler Orchestra, Berliner Sinfonie-Orchestre, Orchestra Nazionale della RAI, Orchestra Sinfonica di Santa Cecilia, Orchester des Mozarteum, Salzburg; has worked with the conductors Claudio Abbado, Peter Rundel, Myung-Whun Chung, Daniele Gatti, Yuri Temirkanov, Roberto Abbado, Riccardo Muti, Daniel Harding, Lorin Maazel, Valery Gergiev and Mstislav Rostropovich; Concerts in Munich, Vienna, Berlin, Salzburg, Hanover, Frankfurt, Bremen, Hamburg, Paris, Barcelona, Lisbon, Athens, Tokyo, Beijing; Further engagements in Paris and Athens and in International Piano Series at the Queen Elizabeth Hall, London; named Star of the Year at Munich. *Recordings include:* Scarlatti; Beethoven; Debussy; Prokofiev; Boulez, Ligeti, Webern and Schoenberg, 1996, Beethoven variations for solo piano 1999, Schumann Phantasie for piano and orchestra 2002, Chopin 4 Scherzi 2005. *Compositions include:* Variations for piano 2001, Quintetto per pianoforte e archi 2002, Sonatina per pianoforte 2004. *Honours:* First prize, Umberto Micheli International Piano Competition, Milan, 1994. *Current Management:* Ibercamera, Gran Via 636 1o 2a, 08007 Barcelona, Spain. *Website:* www.gianlucacascioli.com.

**CASELLA, Elena;** Conductor; b. 28 Jan. 1966, Milan, Italy; 1 d. *Education:* Diploma in Piano; Diploma in Composition; Diploma in Conducting, Milano Conservatorio di Musica G Verdi; Masterclasses in conducting with Ervin Acél, Italy and Hungary, Julius Kalmar, Vienna, Gustav Kuhn, Italy, Myung-Whun Chung, Italy. *Career:* Debut: Sala Verdi, Conservatorio in Milan with Orchestra Pomeriggi Musicali, Milan, 1994; Teacher of Orchestral Training, Hungary, 1995; Assistant of Gustav Kuhn, 1994–97; Numerous concerts with many orchestras including A Toscanini, Parma; Pomeriggi Musicali, Milan; Szegend Symphony, Hungary; Novi Musici, Naples; Serenade Ensemble, Trieste; Assistant of Ervin Acél in Wiener Musikseminar, 1998–. *Compositions:* Eos I and II, for solo guitar. *Honours:* Premio Internazionale, Sebetiater, for Music, Naples, 1997. *Address:* 26 Via Mose Bianchi, 20148 Milano, Italy.

**CASHIAN, Philip John,** DMus; British composer; b. 17 Jan. 1963, Manchester. *Education:* Univ. of Cardiff, Guildhall School of Music and Drama. *Career:* Northern Arts fellow-in-composition, Univ. of Durham 1993–96; Visiting Lecturer in Composition, Bath Spa Univ. 1997; composer-in-residence, Goldsmiths Coll., London 1999; co-founder and Dir, Oxford Festival of Contemporary Music. *Compositions include:* String Quartet 1988, Nightmaze 1991, Dark Inventions 1992, Chamber Concerto 1995, A Sea of Tales 1998, Night Journeys 1998, The Devil's Box 1999, Music for the Night Sky 1999, Tableaux 2003, Spitbite 2004, Three Pieces 2004. *Recordings:* String Quartet No. 1 (Bingham Quartet, NMC), Music for the Night Sky (Schubert Ensemble, NMC), Dark Inventions (BCMG, Asbury, NMC). *Honours:* Britten Prize 1991. *Address:* c/o British Music Information Centre, Lincoln House, 75 Westminster Bridge Road, London, SE1 7HS, England (office). *Website:* www.bmic.co.uk.

**CASHMORE, John;** British singer (baritone); b. 1960, Birmingham, England. *Education:* Birmingham School of Music and the National Opera Studio, London. *Career:* debut singing Guglielmo with Birmingham Music Theatre; opera engagements with English National Opera, Scottish Opera-Go-Round, Wexford Festival, Batignano and the New D'Oyly Carte Opera Company; Guglielmo for Opera Forum in Netherlands, 1991, Figaro in a British tour of Mozart's opera, Marullo in Rigoletto for ENO, 1992, and roles from 1992 at Aachen including Lortzing's Zar and Don Giovanni; Opera galas at the Albert Hall, Festival Hall and in Glasgow; Oratorio engagements include Carmina Burana in Birmingham and Glasgow, Monteverdi Vespers at Coventry Cathedral and Victory's Ultima Rerum in Dublin. *Current Management:* Rudolf W. Vanderhuck, Untere Donnerbergstraße 80, 52222 Stolberg, Germany. *Telephone:* (2402) 863020. *Fax:* (2402) 28136. *E-mail:* vanderhuck@t-online.de. *Website:* www.john-cashmore-entertainment.com.

**CASKEL, Christoph;** Percussionist; b. 12 Jan. 1932, Greifswald, Germany. *Education:* Studied in Cologne, 1949–55. *Career:* Many performances of modern music at Darmstadt and elsewhere, notably with the brothers Kontarsky in Bartók's Sonata for two Pianos and Percussion; Collaborations with Stockhausen (premiere of Zyklus, 1959, and Kontakte), Mauricio Kagel and keyboard player Franz-Peter Goebels; Has performed with the Capella Coloniensis and given courses at Darmstadt and Cologne. *Address:* c/o Hochschule für Musik Rheinland, Dagoberstrasse 38, 5000 Cologne 1, Germany.

**CASKEN, John;** Composer; b. 15 July 1949, Barnsley, Yorkshire, England. *Education:* Birmingham University with Peter Dickinson and John Joubert, 1967–71; Warsaw Academy of Music (Polish Government Scholarship) with Andrzej Dobrowolski and consultations with Witold Lutoslawski, 1971–72. *Career:* Lecturer, Birmingham University, 1973–79; Research Fellow, Huddersfield Polytechnic, 1979–81; Lecturer, Durham University, 1981–92; Professor of Music at Manchester University, 1992–; Featured Composer, Bath Festival, 1980; Musica Nova, Glasgow, 1984; Huddersfield Contemporary Music Festival, 1986 and 1991; Southampton International New Music Week, 1989; Almeida Festival, 1989; Music Today, Tokyo, 1990. *Compositions include:* Orchestral: Tableaux des Trois Ages, 1977; Orion over Farne, 1984; Maharal Dreaming, 1989; Darting the Skiff for strings, 1993; Sortilège, 1996; Concertos: Masque for oboe, 1982; Erin for double bass, 1983; Cello Concerto, 1991; Violin Concerto, 1995; Distant Variations, concerto grosso for saxophone quartet and wind orchestra, 1997; Apriès un silence for violin and small orchestra/large ensemble, orchestration of work for violin and piano, 1998; Ensemble: Music for the Crabbing Sun for 4 players, 1974; Amarantos for 9 players, 1978; Firewhirl for soprano and 7 players, 1980; String Quartet No. 1, 1982; Clarion Sea for brass quintet, 1985; Vaganza for large ensemble, 1985; Piano Quartet, 1990; String Quartet No. 2, 1994; Infanta Marina for cor anglais and 6 players, 1994; Instrumental: Thymehaze for treble recorder and piano, 1976; Salamandra for 2 pianos, 1986; A Spring Cadenza for solo cello, 1994; Apriès un silence for violin and piano, 1998; Choral: To Fields We Do Not Know, 1984; Three Choral Pieces, 1990–93; La Orana, Gaugin for soprano and piano, 1978; Sharp Thorne for 4 solo voices, 1992; Still Mine for baritone and orchestra, 1992; Opera: Golem, 1986–88; God's Liar, opera after Tolstoy, 2000. *Honours:* First Britten Award for Composition, 1990; Gramophone Award, for Best Contemporary Recording, 1990; Northern Electric Performing Arts Award, 1990; Fondation Prince Pierre de Monaco Composition Prize, 1993; Northern Sinfonia Composer in Association, 1991–; Fellowship, Royal Northern College of Music, Manchester, 1996. *Current Management:* Schott Music Publishers. *Address:* 48 Great Marlborough Street, London W1V 2BN, England. *Website:* www.schott-music.com.

**CASOLLA, Giovanna;** Singer (soprano); b. 1944, Italy. *Education:* Conservatorio di San Pietro, Naples. *Career:* debut, Lisbon 1977, as Eboli in Don Carlos; sang at Turin 1978, 1982, Trieste 1979, Buenos Aires 1980, Detroit 1981; San Diego 1982, in the American premiere of Zandonai's Giulietta e Romeo; Metropolitan Opera 1984, as Zandonai's Francesca da Rimini, returned 1986, as Eboli; La Scala Milan 1983 and 1986, as Giorgetta in Il Tabarro; Verona Arena 1986 and 1988, as Maddalena in Andrea Chénier and La Gioconda; Caracalla Festival 1987, 1989, as Tosca; further guest appearances at Vienna and Miami 1988, Deutsche Oper Berlin 1989, Tosca, Stuttgart and Venice Eboli 1991; La Scala and Florence 1991, as Minnie in La Fanciulla del West and Santuzza; Puccini Festival, Torre del Lago 1991, as Giorgetta; other roles include Fedora, Amelia (Ballo in Maschera), Adriana Lecouvreur, Manon Lescaut, Silvana in Respighi's La Fiamma, Bartók's Judith, Maria in Tchaikovsky's Mazeppa and Elena Makropoulos; sang Santuzza at Florence 1996, and Gioconda 1998, Turandot at Barcelona 1999; season 2000 as Tosca at La Scala and Leonora (La Forza del Destino) at the Verona Arena; many concert appearances.

**CASONI, Bianca-Maria;** Singer (Mezzo-Soprano); b. 1 March 1932, Milan, Italy. *Education:* Studied at the Milan Conservatory with Bruna Jona and Mercedes Llopart. *Career:* Debut: Milan 1956, as Mercédès in Carmen; Sang widely in Italy after winning La Scala Competition; Salzburg 1960, as Giacinta in La Finta Semplice, 1960; Glyndebourne 1965, as Cherubino; Concert performance of Bellini's La Straniera, New York, 1969; Appearances at Covent Garden and the Festivals of Aix and Edinburgh; Monte Carlo, Geneva, Barcelona, Philadelphia and the Metropolitan Opera; Turin 1975, in the Italian premiere of Die drei Pintos, Mahler/Weber; Berlin Staatsoper 1981, as Cinderella. *Recordings include:* Mozart's Coronation Mass; La Straniera; Preziosilla in La Forza del Destino (EMI). *Address:* c/o Deutsche Staatsoper, Under den Linden 7, 1086 Berlin, Germany.

**CASSELLO, Kathleen;** Singer (Soprano); b. 1958, Wilmington, Delaware, USA. *Education:* Dan Pressley, Delaware; Wilma Lipp, Salzburg; Sesto Bruscantini, Italy. *Career:* European debut as Queen of Night in Hamburg, 1985; More than 200 Queen of Night performances since in Hamburg, 1986–88, Deutsche Oper and Staatsoper, Berlin, 1986–89, Moscow, 1987, Zürich, Geneva and Salzburg, 1988, Stuttgart, 1990; Staatstheater Karlsruhe Ensemble, 1987–89; Lucia in Karlsruhe, 1989–92, São Paulo, 1989, Marseille, San Sebastian and Zürich, 1990, Malaga, 1992, Treviso, Rome and Palermo, 1993; Traviata in Karlsruhe, 1987–92, Oviedo, 1991, Toulouse, 1992, Festival Orange and Rome, 1993, Tokyo, 1994, and Geneva; Elvira in Puritani at Marseille, 1991, Malaga, 1993; Gilda in Rigoletto at Marseille, 1992, Mexico City and Nice, 1993, La Scala with Riccardo Muti, 1994; Konstanze in Entführung in St Gallen, 1986–87, Vienna, 1988, Karlsruhe, 1989, Zürich, 1990, Munich National Theater, 1992, Avignon, 1993, Marseille and Hamburg, 1994–; Other roles include: Manon at the Met, 1990; Thaïs at Marseille, 1991; Pamina at Barcelona, 1991; Musetta at the Arena di Verona, 1992; Vitellia in La Clemenza di Tito in Toulouse, 1992, Athens, 1994; Amina in La Sonnambula at Messina, 1993; Elettra in Idomeneo at Venice, 1993; Giulietta in I Capuleti e i Montecchi at Parma, 1994; Amina at Rome, 1996; Season 2000 as Constanze and Donna Anna at Dresden, Donizetti's Maria di Rohan at Aachen. *Address:* c/o Mondial, 17 rue Brey, F–75017 Paris, France.

**CASSIDY, Paul;** Violist; b. 1959, Ireland. *Education:* Studied at the Royal College of Music, University of California at Los Angeles and Detmold, Germany. *Career:* Founder member of the Brodsky Quartet (name derives from violinist Adolph Brodsky, Principal of the Royal Manchester College of Music, 1895–1929); Resident at Cambridge University for 4 years and later residencies at the Dartington International Summer School, Devon; Concert engagements include the Shostakovich quartets at the Queen Elizabeth Hall, London, and performances at the Ludwigsburg and Schleswig-Holstein Festivals; New York debut at the Metropolitan Museum; Further tours of Italy, North America, Australia, Poland, Czechoslovakia and Japan; Complete quartets of Schoenberg for the BBC, 1992; French concerts include visit to the Théâtre du Châtelet, Paris. *Recordings include:* Quartets of Elgar and Delius; Schubert A minor and also Schubert D minor and Crumb, Black Angels; Beethoven Op 74; Complete quartets of Shostakovich. *Address:* c/o PRO Musicis (Brodsky Quartet), Ringstrasse 6, CH –6300 Zug, Switzerland.

**CASSINELLI, Riccardo;** Singer (Tenor); b. 27 Feb. 1936, Buenos Aires, Argentina. *Education:* Opera School of the Teatro Colón, Buenos Aires. *Career:* Debut: Berne, 1968, as Amenofi in Rossini's Mosè in Egitto; Appearances at Geneva and Toulouse Operas; Théâtre des Champs Elysées, Paris, as Ferrando in Così fan tutte, Nicolai's Fenton, and Nemorino; Glyndebourne Festival, 1973, 1976; Opéra de Lyon, 1979 in Cavalli's Ercole Amante; Leading tenor at Buenos Aires until 1990; Salzburg Festival, 1986 as Mozart's Basilio; Geneva, 1987 in the premiere of Le Forêt by Liebermann; Festival engagements at Montpellier, Beziéres, Mozart's Monostatos, 1991, and Lausanne, Dr Caius in Falstaff, 1995; Nice Opéra, 1996 in From the House of the Dead by Janáček; Season 1998 as Brighella in Ariadne auf Naxos at Toulouse; Sang Malatestino in Zandonai's Francesca da Rimini at Buenos Aires, 2000. *Address:* c/o Toulouse Opera, Théâtre du Capitole, Place du Capitole, 31000 Toulouse, France.

**CASSIS, Alessandro;** Singer (Baritone); b. 1949, Italy. *Career:* Debut: Florence, 1971, in Un Ballo in Maschera; Sang in the Maggio Musicale, Florence, 1974, in La Fanciulla del West; Piccola Scala Milan in La Favola d'Orfeo by Casella; Sang Germont at Turin, 1977, Amonasro at the Verona Arena, 1982; La Scala Milan, 1983, as Michele in Il Tabarro, Sharpless in Butterfly, 1985; Returned to Verona in 1986 and 1988, as Gérard (Andrea Chénier) and Barnaba (La Gioconda); Further appearances at Naples, Genoa, Geneva, Palermo, Trieste and Lisbon; Baths of Caracalla, Rome, 1991, as Amonasro; Other roles include Carlo in La Forza del Destino and Verdi's Luna, Rigoletto and Renato; High Priest in Samson et Dalila; Sang Nabucco at Brescia, 1994 and Alfonso in La Favorita at Bergamo, 1995. *Recordings include:* I Lutuani by Ponchielli; Nerone by Boito. *Address:* c/o Teatro Donizetti, Piazza Cavour 4 I–24100 Bergamo, Italy.

**CASSUTO, Alvaro (Leon);** Conductor and Composer; b. 17 Nov. 1938, Oporto, Portugal. *Education:* Studied violin and piano as a child; Studied composition with Arthur Santos and Lopes Graca; Courses with Ligeti, Messiaen and Stockhausen, Darmstadt, summers 1960 and 1961; Studied conducting with Karajan, Pedro de Freitas Branco, Lisbon, and with Ferrara in Hilversum; PhD, Law, University of Lisbon, 1964; MA, Conducting, Vienna Academy of Music, 1965. *Career:* Assistant Conductor, Gulbenkian Orchestra, Lisbon, 1965–68; Little Orchestra, New York, 1968–70; Permanent Con-

ductor, 1970–75, Music Director, 1975–89, National Radio Orchestra, Lisbon; Lecturer, 1974–75, Professor in Music, 1975–79, Conductor, Symphony Orchestra, University of California, Irvine; Music Director, Rhode Island Philharmonic Orchestra, Providence, 1979–85; National Orchestra Association, New York, 1981–87; Nova Filarmonia Portuguesa, 1988–93; Orquestra Sinfonica Portuguesa, 1993, Israel Raanana Symphony Orchestra, 2001. *Compositions:* In the Name of Peace, opera, 1971; Orchestral: Sinfonia breve No. 1, 1959, No. 2, 1960; Variations, 1961; Permutations for 2 orchestras, 1962; Concertino for piano and orchestra, 1965; Cro(mo-no)fonia for 20 strings, 1967; Canticum in Tenebris for soloists, chorus and orchestra, 1968; Evocations, 1969; Circle, 1971; To Love and Peace, symphonic poem, 1973; Homage to My People, suite for band, 1977; Return to the Future, 1985; The Four Seasons for piano and orchestra, 1986; Chamber: String Sextet, 1962; Song of Loneliness for 12 performers, 1972. *Recordings:* Various. *Honours:* Koussevitzky Prize, Tanglewood, Massachusetts, 1969. *Address:* Quinta do Mogo, Malveira Da Serra, 2750 Cascais, Portugal.

**CASTEL, Nico;** Singer (Tenor) and Educator; b. 1 Aug. 1931, Lisbon, Portugal. *Education:* Studied in Caracas, Milan, Frankfurt and the USA. *Career:* Debut: Santa Fe, 1958, as Fenton in Falstaff; New York City Opera, 1965, in The Fiery Angel by Prokofiev; Celebrated 30 years as Principal Artist, 1970–, Metropolitan Opera: Le nozze di Figaro; Hänsel und Gretel; Ariadne auf Naxos; Boris Godunov; Guillot, in the Sills recording of Manon; Appearances in Lisbon, Florence, Tel-Aviv, Caracas, Graz, Dresden, Frankfurt and the USA; Parallel career as diction and multi-lingual phonetics teacher and coach for singers at the Metropolitan, the Juilliard School, The Mannes College of Music and the International Institute of Vocal Arts in Israel, France and China; Staff Diction Coach, Santa Fe Opera, 2001–. *Recordings include:* La Bohème; Manon, Contes d'Hoffmann. *Publications:* The Nico Castel Ladino Song Book, 1983; A Singers' Manual of Spanish Lyric Diction, 1994; The Complete Puccini, Verdi and Mozart, Belcanto, Verismo French Opera Libretti, phoneticized and fully translated word by word, 1994. *Address:* 214 West 92nd Street, Apt 77E, New York City, NY 10025, USA.

**CASTLE, Joyce;** Singer (Mezzo-soprano); b. 17 Jan. 1944, Beaumont, Texas, USA. *Education:* Studied at the University of Kansas, the Eastman School and in New York. *Career:* Debut: San Francisco 1970, as Siebel in Faust; Debut, Metropolitan Opera, 1985; Die Fledermaus, Eugene Onegin; Puccini, Trittico; Wagner's Ring Cycle; Boris Godunov; Debut, New York City Opera, 1983, Ballad of Baby Doe, Sweeney Todd, Rake's Progress, Casanova; Regularly sang with Santa Fe Opera, Seattle Opera, Houston, Dallas, Washington, Montreal; Created role of Nazimova in Argento's Valentino, 1994, Kennedy Center; 1st performance of Bernstein's Arias and Barcarolles with Bernstein at the Piano; World premiere of Weisgall's Esther, 1993, New York City; Turin 1996 as Madame de la Haltière in Massenet's Cendrillon; Season 2000–01 as Orlovsky at Chicago, Herodias (Salome) in Antwerp and Augusta Tabor in The Ballad of Baby Doe for New York City Opera. *Recordings:* Candide, Old Lady, New York City Opera Recording; Grammy Winner, Sondheim Book of the Month Recording; Vocal Music of Stefan Wolpe; Vocal Music of Joseph Fennimore. *Current Management:* Janice Mayer & Associates. *Address:* 201 W 57th Street, New York, NY 10019, USA.

**CASTRO, Carlos José;** Costa Rican composer; b. 25 Jan. 1963, San José. *Education:* Castella Conservatory and Univ. of Costa Rica. *Career:* mem., Contemporary Music Centre, San José 1985–; teacher of music, Nat. Univ. School of Dance. *Compositions:* Gobierno de alcoba (comic opera after play by Samuel Rovinsky), Mambrú se fue a la guerra (after play by Mario Vargas Llosa) 1992, La chunga 1995. *Honours:* Aquileo J. Echevarría Nat. Music Prize. *Address:* c/o Universidad Nacional, Centro de Arte, Segundo Piso, Heredia, Costa Rica (office).

**CASTRO-ALBERTY, Margarita;** Singer (Soprano); b. 18 Oct. 1947, San Juan, Puerto Rico. *Education:* Studied at the Pablo Casals Conservatory, Puerto Rico, the Accademia di Santa Cecilia, Rome, and at Juilliard, New York. *Career:* Debut: Santiago, 1978, as Amelia in Un Ballo in Maschera; Sang at the Teatro Colón, Buenos Aires, 1979–80; European debut, 1980, in La Vida Breve by Falla; Carnegie Hall, 1981, as Lucrezia in I Due Foscari; Metropolitan debut, 1982, as Amelia; Festival d'Orange, 1983, as Aida; Guest engagements in Venice, Berlin, Vienna, Nancy, Rome and Toronto; Other roles include Donna Anna, Amelia Grimaldi, Nedda, Butterfly, Lucrezia Borgia, Elisabeth de Valois and the Trovatore Leonora; Sang at Marseilles, 1987. *Address:* c/o Opéra de Marseille, 2 Rue Molière, 13231 Marseille Cédex 01, France.

**CASTRONOVO, Charles;** American singer (tenor); b. Queens, NY. *Education:* California State Univ., Fullerton. *Career:* resident artist, Los Angeles Opera 1997–99, with debut as First Priest in Die Zauberflöte 1998, followed by nine other roles, including Baron Rouvel in Fedora, Parpignol in La Bohème, Remendado in Carmen, Reverend Perris in The Crucible, and Don Basilio in Le nozze di Figaro; European debut in Rossini Stabat Mater, Cologne 1999; sang Tamino in Die Zauberflöte in San Francisco Opera Center's Merola Opera Program; joined Metropolitan Opera Linderman Young Artists Development Program, debut as Beppe in Pagliacci 1999; Don Ottavio in Don Giovanni for Boston Lyric Opera 2000; sang Camille in The Merry Widow for Los Angeles Opera 2001; Ferrando in Così fan tutte at Santa Fe 2003, ROH Covent Garden 2004; sang Germont in La Traviata at ROH, Nadir in The Pearl Fishers for San Francisco Opera 2005. *Recordings:* Beppe in Pagliacci 2000, Rossini Stabat Mater (Opus 111). *Current Management:* c/o Judith

Salpeter, Columbia Artists Management Ltd, 28 Cheverton Road, London, N19 3AY, England. *E-mail:* info@cami.com (office).

**CASULA, Maria;** Singer (Soprano); b. 1939, Cagliari, Sardinia, Italy. *Education:* Studied in Rome and Venice. *Career:* Sang with I Virtuosi di Roma, in concert; Vienna Staasoper, 1967, as Vitellia in La Clemenza di Tito; Glyndebourne, 1969, Despina; Rome, 1978, in the Italian premiere of The Beggar's Opera, arranged by Britten; Cagliari, 1987, in Guillaume Tell. *Recordings include:* Il Barbiere di Siviglia, La Clemenza di Tito, Le nozze di Figaro, Leonora by Paer. *Address:* c/o Teatro Lirico, Viale Regina Margherita 6, 09100 Cagliari, Italy.

**CATANI, Cesare;** Singer (Tenor); b. 1970, Ascoli, Italy. *Education:* Studied at the Bergamo Conservatory. *Career:* Debut: Kochkarev in The Marriage by Mussorgsky, St Petersburg; Appearances in Moise et Pharaon at the Pesaro Rossini Festival, as Edoardo in Verdi's Un Giorno di regno at Parma and as Tebaldo in Bellini's I Capuleti e i Montecchi at Reggio Emilia; Wexford Festival, 1997 as Ubaldo in Mercadante's Elena da Feltre; Season 1998 as the Doge in Rossini's Otello at Pesaro and as Rodolfo in La Bohème at Toscana; Season 1999 sang Arrigo in Verdi's La battaglia di Legnano at Parma, Piacenza and Modena; Hindemith's Cardillac, as Il cavaliere, in Genova; Alfredo in La Traviata in Macerata and Gabriele Adorno in Verdi's Simon Boccanegra at Toscana; Concerts include Rossini's Petite Messe Solennelle, Salzburg and Rome; Mozart's Requiem, Turin. *Recordings:* Rossini Petite Messe; Elena da Feltre. *Address:* c/o Rossini Opera Festival, Via Rossini 37, 61100 Pesaro, Italy.

**CATHCART, Allen;** Singer (Tenor); b. 2 Aug. 1938, Baltimore, Maryland, USA. *Education:* Studied at the University of California and with Boris Goldovsky in New York. *Career:* Debut: Metropolitan Opera Studio, 1961, as Guglielmo in Così fan tutte; European engagements in Brussels, Rome, Zürich, Cologne, Stuttgart and Kiel; Welsh National Opera in Cardiff; Paris Opéra-Comique, in The Stone Guest by Dargomyzhsky, 1985; Paris Opéra as The Drum Major in Wozzeck; Other roles include Don José, Florestan, Cavaradossi, the Emperor in Die Frau ohne Schatten, Laca in Jenůfa and parts in operas by Wagner. *Recordings include:* Jason in Mayr's Medea in Corinto.

**CATLING, Ashley;** Singer (Tenor); b. 1975, England. *Education:* Guildhall School, with William McAlpine, and National Opera Studio, London. *Career:* Appearances in Friend of the People (premiere) by David Horne for Scottish Opera, Fenton and Ferrando for London Opera Players; Male Chorus in The Rape of Lucretia for The Other Theatre Company, Nemorino, and Steve Reich's video opera Three Tales on European and US tours; Concerts include St Matthew Passion at Westminster Cathedral and Carissimi's Jephté at St John's Smith Square; Season 2001–2002 as Ferrando and Fenton in Guernsey, and Rossini's Petite Messe; Other roles include Sellem in The Rake's Progress, and Simon in Birtwistle's The Last Supper. *Address:* c/o National Opera Studio, Morley College, 61 Westminster Bridge Road, London, SE1 7XT, England.

**CAUDLE, Mark;** British bass violinist, bass violist and cellist; b. 1950, England. *Career:* Member of The Parley of Instruments; Frequent tours in the United Kingdom and abroad, including the British Early Music Network; Performances in Spain, France, Germany, Netherlands, Poland and Czechoslovakia; US debut in New York, 1988; Many concerts with first modern performances of early music in new editions by Peter Holman; Numerous broadcasts on Radio 3 and elsewhere; Repertoire includes Renaissance Violin Consort Music (Christmas music by Michael Praetorius and Peter Philips, music for Prince Charles I by Orlando Gibbons and Thomas Lupo); Baroque Consort Music by Monteverdi, Matthew Locke (anthems, motets and ceremonial music), Purcell (ayres for theatre), Georg Muffat (Armonico Tributo sonatas, 1682), Heinrich Biber (Sonate tam aris, quam aulis servientes, 1676), Vivaldi (sonatas and concertos for lute and mandolin, concertos for recorders) and J. S. Bach (Hunt cantata No. 208), with Crispian Steele-Perkins, trumpet, and Emma Kirkby, soprano, among others.

**CAUSSE, Gérard;** Violist; b. 26 June 1948, Toulouse, France. *Education:* Studied in Toulouse and at the Paris Conservatoire. *Career:* Violist of the Via Nova Quartet, 1989–71, Parrenin Quartet, 1972–80; Member of the Ensemble Intercontemporain from 1976; Professor at the Boulogne Conservatoire, 1980, Lyon, 1982, Paris, 1987; Chamber musician from 1982, notably with the Ivaldi Quartet; Season 2002–03 artistic director of the Toulouse National Chamber Orchestra, as conductor and as soloist; Concerto appearances include Radio France's Orchestre National, the Suisse Romande, Lille National Orchestra (Casadesus), Montpellier Philharmonic (Levi), Malaysia Philharmonic (Baakels), Luxembourg PO (Krivine) and Sao Paulo SO; Plays a Gasparo da Salo (1560); Professor at the Reina Sofia school in Madrid. *Address:* c/o Conservatoire National, 14 Rue de Madrid, 75008 Paris, France.

**CAUSTON, Richard,** BA, MA, ARCM (PG); British composer; *Fellow Commoner in the Creative Arts, Trinity College, Cambridge;* b. 12 March 1971, Whitechapel, London. *Education:* ILEA Centre for Young Musicians, London, Univ. of York, Royal Coll. of Music, Civica Scuola di Musica, Milan. *Career:* compositions written for performers such as BBC Symphony Orchestra, City of Birmingham Symphony Orchestra, London Sinfonietta and Evelyn Glennie; founded and runs the Royal Coll. of Music Gamelan programme; Fellow Commoner in the Creative Arts, Trinity Coll., Cambridge 2003–; mem. Soc. for the Promotion of New Music. *Compositions:* Non mi comporto male for piano 1993, The Peristence of Memory for chamber ensemble 1995, two pieces for clarinet duet 1995, Notturno for chamber ensemble 1998, rev. 2001, Millennium Scene for large orchestra 1998, rev. 2001, Concerto for solo percussion and gamelan 2001, Seven States of Rain for violin and piano (British Composer Award for Best Solo/Duo 2004) 2002, Between Two Waves of the Sea for orchestra with sampler 2004, La Terra Impareggiabile song cycle for baritone and piano 2005. *Publications:* contrib. to Tempo: Berio's Visage and the Theatre of Electroacoustic Music, The Guardian: Music of the Spheres, article on Concerto for solo percussion and gamelan, The Guardian: The God of Small Things, article on Jeremy Dale Roberts 2004. *Honours:* Fast Forward composition prize 1995, first prize of the Third International 'Nuove Sincronie' Composition Competition 1996, Mendelssohn Scholarship 1997, SPNM George Butterworth Award 1997, honourable mention in Large-scale Composition category of the Royal Philharmonic Soc. Awards 2000. *Current Management:* Oxford University Press, Repertoire Promotion Department, 70 Baker Street, London, W1U 7DN, England. *Telephone:* (20) 7616-5900 (office). *Fax:* (20) 7616-5901 (office). *E-mail:* repertoire.promotion@oup.co.uk (office). *Website:* www.oup.co.uk/music.repprom/causton (office).

**CAVA, Carlo;** Singer (Bass); b. 16 Aug. 1928, Ascoli Piceno, Italy. *Education:* Studied in Rome. *Career:* Debut: Spoleto, 1955, in L'Italiana in Algeri; Netherlands Opera, Amsterdam, 1959; Glyndebourne, 1961–65, as Seneca in L'Incoronazione di Poppea, as Sarastro, Bartolo in Le nozze di Figaro, Basilio in Il Barbiere di Siviglia and Henry VIII in Anna Bolena; La Scala, 1973, as Boris Godunov; Appearances in Cairo, Amsterdam, Brussels, Frankfurt, Vienna, Munich, Berlin and Paris. *Recordings include:* Oroveso in Norma; Zaccaria in Nabucco; L'Incoronazione di Poppea; Il Barbiere di Siviglia; Linda di Chamounix. *Address:* c/o Teatro alla Scala, Via Filodrammatici 2, 21021 Milan, Italy.

**CAVALLIER, Nicolas;** singer (bass); b. 1964, France. *Education:* Royal Academy of Music and National Opera Studio, with Elisabeth Söderström and with Iris dell'Acqua. *Career:* debut, Nancy Opera, 1987, as Cascanda in The Merry Widow; Sang Achilles in Giulio Cesare conducted by Trevor Pinnock at the Royal Academy of Music; Season 1988–89 in Massenet's Thaïs for Chelsea Opera Group and roles in Les Malheurs d'Orphée (Milhaud), Renard (Stravinsky) and Geneviève de Brabant (Satie) at the Queen Elizabeth Hall; Season 1989–90 with Glass's Fall of the House of Usher in Wales, Henze's The English Cat in Berlin, Messiah with the Bournemouth Sinfonietta and John Metcalf's Tornrak at the Banff Centre in Canada; Sarastro in Die Zauberflöte at Glyndebourne; Sang Don Fernando (Fidelio) for the Glyndebourne Tour, 1990, Zuniga for Welsh National Opera and in Alcione by Marais for Les Arts Florissants in Paris; Masetto for Nancy Opéra; Other roles include Don Giovanni, Narbal in Les Troyens, Don Quichotte, Sparafucile and Mozart's Bartolo and Osmin; Season 1991–92 as Masetto at Nancy, Raleigh in Roberto Devereux at Monte Carlo and Celeus in Lully's Atys with Les Arts Florissants; 1992–93 in Hamlet by Thomas at Monte Carlo, Leporello at Metz and Mr Flint in Billy Budd at Nancy; Loredano in I Due Foscari by Verdi for Scottish Opera at the 1993 Edinburgh Festival; Sang Félix in Donizetti's Les Martyrs at Nancy, 1996; Sang Lord Sydney in Il Viaggio a Reims at Liège, 2000; Concert repertoire includes the Verdi and Mozart Requiems, A Child of our Time, Monteverdi Vespers and Die Schöpfung. *Honours:* Anne Lloyd Exhibition, Helen Eames Prize, Paton Award and Ricordi Award, Royal Academy of Music. *Current Management:* Robert Gilder & Co., Enterprise House, 59–65 Upper Ground, London, SE1 9PQ, England. *Telephone:* (20) 7928-9008. *Fax:* (20) 7928-9755. *E-mail:* rgilder@robert-gilder.com.

**CAVE, Penelope,** ARAM, GRSM, LRAM; harpsichordist; b. 17 April 1951, Guildford, Surrey, England; m. Michael Heale 1974; one s. one d. *Education:* Purcell School, Royal Acad. of Music, lessons and masterclasses with Kenneth Gilbert, Colin Tilney, Ton Koopman and Gustav Leonhardt. *Career:* debut, Wigmore Hall 1980; solo recitals at major festivals in England and abroad; played at Purcell Room and Wigmore Hall and for BBC Radio 3, Belgian Radio and Classic FM; solo recitals at Edinburgh and Ryedale Summer Music Festivals 1995; regular tutor of harpsichord courses, masterclasses and workshops in England and abroad; mem. Incorporated Soc. of Musicians. *Recordings:* with the Camerata of London, Garth Hewitt and the Feinstein Ensemble; From Lisbon to Madrid (solo CD). *Publications:* contrib. to Harpsichord Fortepiano magazine, Music Teacher, Consort. *Honours:* Raymond Russell prize, winner Nat. Harpsichord Competition, Southport. *Address:* Betteridge House, 2 St Omer Ridge, Guildford, Surrey GU1 2DD, England. *E-mail:* penelope.cave@ntlworld.com. *Website:* www.impulse-music .co.uk/cave.htm.

**CAVINA, Claudio;** Italian singer (countertenor); *Artistic Director, La Venexiana.* *Education:* Schola Cantorum Basiliensis with Kurt Widmer, studied with Candace Smith, Cristina Miatello. *Career:* founder La Venexiana vocal ensemble 1995–, serves as Artistic Dir; the ensemble has performed at MusikVerein Golden Hall, Vienna, De Singel, Antwerp, Brugge Festival, Howard Mayer Brown Int. Early Music Series, Chicago, and in Barcelona, Brussels, Utrecht, Strasbourg, Amiens, San Sebastián, Mexico City, Tokyo, New York, Bogotà, San Francisco, Tucson, San Diego, Seattle; solo appearances include La Fenice, Venice, La Scala, Milan, Verona Arena, Concertgebouw, Amsterdam; collaborations with vocal ensembles, including Huelgas Ensemble, La Colombina, Al Ayre Espanol, Clemencic Consort, Elyma Ensemble; gives masterclasses at Belluno Int. Course, Italy, Tsuru Early Music Course, Japan. *Recordings:* Scarlatti, Cantatas and Duets 1994, Marcello, La Stravaganza – Arias & Duets 1999, Aliotti, Il Sansone 2002, De

Vitae Fugacitate 2002; with La Venexiana: Sigismondo d'India, Il Terzo Libro de Madrigali 1997, Claudio Monteverdi, Settimo Libro dei Madrigali 1998, Luzzasco Luzzaschi, Quinto Libro de' Madrigali 1999, Luca Marenzio, Il Nono Libro de Madrigali 1999, Sigismondo d'India, Libro Primo de Madrigali 2000, Gesualdo da Venosa, Il Quarto Libro di Madrigali 2001, Marenzio, Il Sesto Libro de Madrigali 2001, Monteverdi, Il Terzo Libro di Madrigali 2001, Giaches de Wert, La Gerusalemme Liberata 2002, Monteverdi, Secondo Libro dei Madrigali 2004, Monteverdi, Madrigals Book 6 2005. *Honours:* with La Venexiana: Premio Cini 1999, Prix Cecilia 1999, Gramophone Award 2000, Cannes Classical Award 2001, Grand Prix du Disque 2004. *Address:* c/o Glossa Music SL, Timoteo Padrós 31, San Lorenzo de El Escorial 28200, Spain (office). *E-mail:* info@glossamusic.com (office).

**CAZURRA, Anna;** Composer and Musicologist; b. 1940, Barcelona; m., 1 s., 1 d. *Education:* Studied with Josep Soler, Barcelona Conservatoire; Doctorate, The Universitat Autonoma de Barcelona. *Career:* Researcher, Universitat Autonoma, Barcelona; Researcher, Centre for 18th Century musical studies, University of Wales, College of Cardiff; Universitat Pompeu Fabra, Barcelona; Collaborations with Musical Associations and groups. *Compositions:* Poema Para Quinteto de Metal, for brass quintet; Cuatro Evolaciones, for piano; Postales de Viaje, for piano; String Quartets; El Grito, for soprano, flute, guitar and cello; Trio, for violin, cello and piano; Psalmus, for soprano and orchestra. *Recordings:* Poema Para Quintets de Metal, by 2111 Gothic quintet; El Grito. *Publications:* Introduccio a la Historia de la Musica, 1999; Les Obertures de Josep Doran, 1995; El Compositor Inestre de Capella Joan Rossell, doctoral thesis, 1993. *Contributions:* Some articles for the New Grove Dictionary, Diccionario de la Musica Espanola, Encyclopedia Catalana de la Musica. *Address:* Paseo Maragall, 315–317 Escalera A Entresvelo B, 08032 Barcelona, Spain.

**CECCARINI, Giancarlo;** Singer (Baritone); b. 19 July 1951, Pisa, Italy. *Education:* Studied in Pisa and Rome. *Career:* Debut: Spoleto 1975, as Belcore in L'Elisir d'amore; Has appeared widely in Italy as Marcello (La Bohème), Cimarosa's Maestro di Capella and Osmano in L'Ormindo by Cavalli (Venice 1976); Performances of Monteverdi's Combattimento at Terni, Bologna, Zürich, Mantua, Cremona and Frankfurt, 1980. *Recordings:* On Swiss Radio from 1977, including La Gazetta by Rossini; At Genoa has sung Podestà in Docteur Miracle by Bizet, and Gianni Schicchi; San Remo, 1982, as Nabucco; Ping in Turandot at Helsinki, 1991; Records include I Pazzi per Progresso by Donizetti (UORC); Turandot (Nuova Era). *Address:* c/o Teatro La Fenice, Campo S Fantin 1965, 30124 Venice, Italy.

**CECCATO, Aldo;** Italian director of music and conductor; b. 18 Feb. 1934, Milan; m. Eliana de Sabata; two s. *Education:* Milan Conservatory, Hochschule für Musik Berlin. *Career:* Musical Dir Detroit Symphony 1973–77, Hamburg Philharmonic 1974–82; Chief Conductor Hannover Radio Orchestra 1985–, Bergen Symphony 1985–; guest conductor to all major symphony orchestras and opera houses in four continents. *Music:* numerous recordings. *Honours:* Hon. DMus (Eastern Michigan Univ.). *Address:* c/o Rundfunkorchester Hannover, Rudolf von Bennigsen Ulfer 22, 3000 Hannover, Germany (office); Chaunt da Crusch, 7524 Zuoz, Switzerland.

**CECCHELE, Gianfranco;** Singer (Tenor); b. 25 June 1940, Galliera Veneta, Italy. *Education:* Studied with Marcello del Monaco in Treviso. *Career:* Sang at Catania from 1964; Many appearances on the major Italian stages; Guest appearances in London, Paris, Barcelona, Hamburg, Munich, Nice, Chicago, Philadelphia and Montreal; Carnegie Hall New York 1968, as Zamoro in a concert performance of Verdi's Alzira; Best known in operas by Puccini and Verdi; Verona between 1967 and 1984; Rio de Janeiro, 1988, as Radames; Mercadante's La Vestale at Split, 1987; Season 1993–94 as Walter in Catalani's Loreley (Teatro Filarmonico) and Calaf at Viterbo. *Recordings include:* Aroldo by Verdi; Loreley by Catalani; Alzira; Title role in Rienzi by Wagner, Decio in Mercadante's La Vestale, Bongiovanni. *Address:* c/o Arena di Verona, Piazza Bra 28, 1-3 7121 Verona, Italy.

**CECCHI, Gabriella;** Composer; b. 3 Nov. 1944, Ricco del Golfo, La Spezia, Italy. *Education:* Studied at the Lucca Institute, Genoa Conservatory, 1974–77, in Siena with Franco Donatoni and in Sargiano-Arezzo with Brian Ferneyhough. *Career:* Performances of her music throughout Italy and elsewhere in Europe. *Compositions include:* Kite for chamber orchestra, 1981; In proiezione for orchestra, 1986; Riverberi for violin and harpsichord, 1988; Parvula for 10 flutes, 1990; Il gallo rosso, small chamber opera, 1992; Doppel atmung for 4 recorders and percussion, 1993; Grig Bian Ner, ballet, for piano, saxophone and percussion, 1994; Joueurs, for flute, clarinet, violin, cello, sax and double bass, 1995;... In un Mare..., for soprano, clarinet and piano, 1996. *Address:* via del Sempione 2, 19122 La Spezia, Italy.

**CEELY, Robert Paige;** American composer; b. 17 Jan. 1930, Torrington, Connecticut; m. Jonatha Kropp, 13 Jan 1962. *Education:* BMus, New England Conservatory, Boston, MA; MA, Mills College, CA; Graduate study at Princeton University, NJ; Major composition teachers include Darius Milhaud, Leon Kirchner, Roger Sessions and Milton Babbitt. *Career:* Faculty of Composition, Director of Electronic Music at New England Conservatory of Music, Boston, 1967. *Compositions:* String Trio, 1953; Woodwind Quintet, 1954; Composition for 10 Instruments, 1963; Stratti for Magnetic Tape, 1963; Elegia for Magnetic Tape, 1964; Vonce for Magnetic Tape, 1967; Modules for 7 Instruments, 1968; Logs for 2 Double Basses, 1968; Hymn for Cello and Bass, 1969; Beyond the Ghost Spectrum, ballet, 1969; Mitsyn for Computer-Generated Tape, 1971; Slide Music for 4 Trombones, 1974; Rituals for 40 Flutes, 1978; Frames for Computer-Generated Tape, 1978; Lullaby for Trombone and Soprano, 1979; Flee, Floret, Florens for 15 Solo Voices, 1979; Piano Piece, 1980; Bottom Dogs for 4 Double Basses, 1981; Roundels for Large Wind Ensemble and Tape, 1981; Piano Variations, 1982; Totems for Oboe and Tape, 1982; Dialogue for Solo Flute, 1983; Giostra for Oboe and Tape, 1984; Minute Rag for Solo Piano, 1985; Pitch Dark for Jazz Ensemble, 1985; Synoecy for Clarinet and Tape, 1986; Timeshares for Percussion Ensemble, 1988; Special K Variations for Piano, 1989; Post hoc, ergo propter hoc for Solo Bass Clarinet, 1989; Harlequin for Solo Double Bass and Tape, 1990; Hypallage for Solo Trumpet and Tape, 1990; Asyndeton for Piano and Tape, 1993; Opera from Fernando Arrabal's The Automobile Graveyard, 1994; Group Sax, for five saxophones, 1996; Music for Ten, 1996; Enchanted Cycles, for computer-generated tape, 1996; Auros, for five instruments, 1997; Wieman's treibt, for bass clarinet and tape, 1997; Gymel, for two oboes, 1998; Triple Double for oboe, English horn, bassoon and tape, 1998; Mutual Implications for tape, 1999; Extensions for solo piano, 2000; Five Contemplative Pieces for chorus, 2000; Canons for alto flute, clarinet and bassoon, 2001; Seven etudes for piano, 2002; Three Satires for Orchestra, 2002, Carol for mixed chorus and solo trumpet 2003, Three Songs for Baritone and Piano 2003, Three pieces for String Quartet 2004, Whitman (5 songs for Soprano and Piano) 2005. *Publications:* A Composer's View of MITSYN 1971, A Composer's Letter to Perspectives of New Music 1972, Electronic Music Resource Book 1979, Compositional Limitation of Current Electronic Music Synthesizers 1980. *Honours:* Harvard Univ. Project Zero Lectureship 1971, Northeastern Univ. Artist in Residence 1976; Hobart Coll. Sesquicentennial Award 1972, Cine Golden Eagle Awards for film sound for Incendio and Bleve 1977, Massachusetts Council Grant 1979, Nat. Endowment for the Arts Grant 1986, Brookline Council for the Arts Grant 1986, Margaret Fairbank Jory Grant 1994. *Address:* 33 Elm Street, Brookline, MA, USA (home). *Telephone:* (617) 731-3785 (home). *E-mail:* ceelyinfo@ceelymusic.com (home). *Website:* www.Ceely music.com (home).

**CEGOLEA, Gabriela;** Singer, (Soprano); b. 1950, Moldova, USSR. *Education:* Studied in Bucharest and at the Benedetto Marcello Conservatory, Venice; Sang at the Taormina Festival, then studied further at the School of the Royal Opera, Stockholm. *Career:* Debut: Stockholm, 1977, as Tosca; Appearances as Tosca at Oslo and as Manon at Venice; La Scala Milan with Placido Domingo, conducted by Georges Prêtre; Further engagements in New York, Berlin, Stuttgart, San Francisco, Naples and Rome; Tours of Australia, Brazil and South Korea; Liège, 1989, as Maddalena in Andrea Chénier.

**CELLI, Joseph;** American Composer and Oboist; b. 19 March 1944, Bridgeport, Connecticut, USA. *Education:* BME, Hartt College of Music, Hartford, Connecticut, USA, 1962–65; MM (major in oboe performance/composition), Northwestern University, Chicago, 1970–72; Performance Seminar (2 summers), Oberlin Conservatory, Ohio, Private oboe/English horn study with Ray Still (Chicago Symphony) Albert Goltzer (New York Philharmonic), Wayne Rapier (Boston Symphony Orchestra) John Mack (Cleveland Symphony Orchestra), 1970 and 1971; Fulbright Scholar, Korean Traditional Performing Arts Center, Seoul, Korea, 1991–93. *Career:* Composer, videomaker, performer throughout Europe, Asia, North and South America, 1972–; Gave US premieres of Stockhausen's Spiral and Solo for oboe; Executive Director, Real Art Ways (contemporary arts center), Hartford, Connecticut, 1975–86; CEO/Executive Director, New Music America Miami Festival, Florida, 1987–89; Director of Cultural Programs, Miami-Dade Community College, Miami, Florida, 1989–90; Director, OO DISCS Inc Recording company (contemporary American music), 1991–; Founder/Director, Korean Performing Arts Institute, New York/Seoul, 1993–; Exec. Dir, Founder, Int. Performing Arts; Founder, multicultural Black Rock Art Center. *Compositions include:* World Soundprint: Asia for radio (with Jin Hi Kim), 1993; Pink Pelvis: Music For Dance for double reeds, Korean ajeng and Brazilian percussion, 1994; Sunny's piece: Music For Dance with double reeds, Komungo, percussion, 1994; Quintet: for Kayagum, Wx-7 and three kalimba, 1995. *Address:* Black Rock Art Center, 2838 Fairfield Avenue, Bridgeport, CT 06605 (office); 261 Groovers Avenue, Black Rock, CT 06605-3452, USA (home). *Telephone:* (203) 367-7917 (office); (203) 367-9061 (home). *Fax:* (203) 333-0603 (office). *E-mail:* oodiscs@connix.com (office). *Website:* www .InternationalPerformingArts.com (office).

**CEMORE, Alan;** Singer (Baritone); b. 1958, Wisconsin, USA; m. Dr Ursula Baumgartner. *Education:* BM, Vocal Performance, University of Northern Iowa, 1981; MMus, Indiana University, 1985; Hochschule für Musik, Frankfurt, 1981–82; Studied Voice with Margaret Harshaw and David Smalley. *Career:* Leading Baritone at the Wiesbaden Opera, 1986–88, Basel Opera, 1988–90, Graz Opera 1990–97, Bremen Theatre, 1998–; Spoleto Festival, 1984 in Die lustige Witwe, 1985, in La Fanciulla del West; Sang Tom in Henze's English Cat at Frankfurt (1986), at Turin and at the 1987 Edinburgh Festival; Wexford as Biagio in Gazzaniga's Don Giovanni and Pantalone in Busoni's Turandot, 1988; Radio and television appearances in Europe, Asia and USA; Over 50 opera roles in the USA and Europe; mem, Pi Kappa Lambda, Rotary International. *Recordings include:* Die grossmuetige Tomyris by Keiser; Oh wie verfuehrerisch, operatic selections from television show Happy Birthday George Gershwin!. *Honours:* Prizewinner, ARD International Music Competition, Munich, 1984; Rotary International Graduate Fellowship, 1981; Cole Porter Memorial Fellowship Winner, 1984. *Address:* Richard Wagner Str. 29, 28209 Bremen, Germany.

**CEPICKY, Leos;** Musician; b. 21 Aug. 1965, Pardubice, Czechoslovakia; m. Katerina Kus, 28 April 1985, 1 s., 1 d. *Education:* Prague Academy of Arts. *Career:* Debut: Prague Spring Quartet Competition, 1988; Member, Wihan Quartet, Music Festivals in England, Austria, Germany, France, Italy, Belgium, Spain, Portugal, Singapore, USA, Japan, Rome and on Radio France. *Recordings:* Supraphon (Suk, Dvořák, Janáček); Haydn op 64, op 71; Mozart K168, K458, K465; Dvořák, Smetana 1; Janáček 1 and 2; Ravel and Britten 2; Beethoven op 59 1, 2, 3, op 14; Dvořák op 51 and op 106. *Contributions:* The Strad. *Honours:* Prize, Prague Spring Competition, 1988; Prize, London International String Quartet Competition. *Current Management:* Pragoart Music. *Address:* Archaeologicka 1884, 15000 Prague 5, Czech Republic.

**CERAR, Maja;** Violinist; b. 27 May 1972, Zürich, Switzerland. *Education:* Concert Diploma, Conservatory of Winterthur, 1995, studied with Aida Stucki-Piraccini; Student of Dorothy DeLay, New York; MA, Musicology, 1998, Doctoral studies in progress, Columbia University, New York. *Career:* Debut: Performed Mozart Violin Concerto K 218 with Symphony Orchestra of Zürich, Jiri Malat conducting, Zürich Tonhalle, 1991; Soloist with renowned conductors and orchestras, Europe; Collaboration with composers such as G Kurtag and B Furrer; Numerous premieres of contemporary music, USA, Europe; Lead roles in theatre and multimedia productions; Classical recital tours, Europe and USA, including Dame Myra Hess Memorial Concert Series, Chicago; Featured, news and portrait shows, Switzerland and Slovenia, and in film at Young Artists in Concert Festival, Davos; Member, Editorial Board, Musicology, 1998–. *Recordings:* Recollections, Sonata by U Krek, dedicated to her, 1996; Sonatas by Beethoven, Schubert, Brahms, with pianist Gérard Wyss, 1997; Violin Concerto by Samuel Barber, 2000. *Honours:* Supported by Swiss Study Foundation for Outstanding University Students, 1992–; Migros Foundation Study Grant Award, 1995–97; Fellowship, Columbia University, 1999. *Address:* 514 West 114th Street, Apt 23, New York, NY 10025, USA.

**CERHA, Friedrich;** Composer; b. 17 Feb. 1926, Vienna, Austria. *Education:* Studied at the Vienna Academy, 1946–51, with Vasa Prihoda (violin) and Alfred Uhl (composition) and at the university; DPhil. *Career:* With Kurt Schwertsik co-founded ensemble Die Reihe, 1958, with performances of contemporary music and works by the Second Viennese School; Completion of Act III of Alban Berg's Lulu performed at the Paris Opéra, 1979; Opera Baal premiered at the 1981 Salzburg Festival; Der Rattenfänger at Graz, 1987; British premiere of Cello Concerto at 1999 Prom concerts, London. *Compositions:* Espressioni fondamentali for orchestra, 1957; Relazioni fragili for harpsichord and chamber orchestra, 1956–57; Fasce for orchestra, 1959; Spiegel I–VII, 1960–61; Netzwerk, musical theatre, 1962–80, premiered Wiener Festwochen, 1981; Exercises for baritone and chamber ensemble, 1962–67; Langegger Nachtmusik I and II for orchestra, 1969, 1970, III, 1991; Double Concerto for violin, cello and orchestra, 1975; Baal-Gesänge for Baritone and orchestra, 1981; Keintate I, 1981–83, II, 1984–85, for voice and 11 instruments; Requiem für Hollensteiner for baritone, choir and orchestra, 1982–83; Eine Art Chansons for voice and 3 instruments, 1985–86; Phantasiestück for cello and orchestra, 1989; String-Quartett I, 1989, II, 1990, III, 1992; Impulse for orchestra, 1992–93; Concerto for viola and orchestra, 1993; Concertino for violin, accordion and ensemble, 1994; Requiem for choir and orchestra, 1994, completed 2003; Saxophon-Quartett, 1995; Acht Sätze nach Hölderlin-Fragmenten für Streichsextett, 1995; Jahr lang ins Ungewisse hinab für Ensemble, 1995–96; Concerto for Cello and Orchestra, 1996–97; Lichtenberg-Splitter, for baritone and ensemble, 1997; Der Riese vom Steinfeld, opera (libretto by Peter Turrini), 1999; Im Namen der Liebe for baritone and orchestra, 2000, premiered Staatsopen Wien, 2002; Hymnus for orchestra, 2000–01. *Recordings:* Spiegel I–VII; Baal; I Keintate, Eine letzte Art Chansons; String-Quartets 1–3; Acht Sätze nach Hölderlin-Fragmenten für Streichsextett; 12 CD Box From early works to the present, ORF Edition Zeitton 180. *Address:* Kupelwiesergasse 14, 1130 Vienna, Austria.

**CERMÁKOVÁ, Vera;** Czech composer, pianist and music teacher; b. 17 March 1961, Prague, Czechoslovakia; m. Josef Cermak 1984; one s. *Education:* Prague Conservatoire, Piano studies with Alena Polakova, 1977–83; Studied Composition with Oldrich Semerak, 1986–92. *Career:* teaches Piano and Composition at music school in Kladno; Interpretation of piano compositions; performs at festivals of classical and contemporary music; mem. Asscn of Composers, Prague; Ateliero90; Music Studio N. *Compositions:* Free cycle for 3 String Quartets The Play of Lights, 1993; Fragments Nos 1–4 for Symphonic Orchestra, 1993; Seven Preludes for Guitar Solo, 1994; Three Bagatelles for Saxophone Quartet, 1996; Metamorphosis for Violoncello and Piano, 1997. *Recordings:* Prelude and Rhythmic Fantasia; Piano Solo, 1992; Fantasia (piano solo), 1993; Ostinato, Melodic No. 2 (piano solo), 1995; Kaleidoskop (piano solo), 1996; Seclusion of Clarinet solo, 1997; Reliefs for Chamber Orchestra, 1999; String Quartet No. 4, 2000; Genesis for Saxophone Quartet, 2000, Reflections and Meditations for Soprano, Tenor and Chamber Orchestra 2001, Solo for Soprano Saxophone 2002, Solo for Alto Saxophone 2002, Solo for Tenor Saxophone 2002, Solo for Baritone Saxophone 2002, The Spectrum for String Orchestra 2004. *Honours:* Musica Iuvenis, Prague, 1997. *Address:* Karla Tomana 824, 27204 Kladno; Karla Tomana 824, 27204 Kladno, Czech Republic (home). *Telephone:* (312) 26-74-31 (home).

**CERNY, Florian;** Singer (Baritone); b. 4 Oct. 1946, Bavaria, Germany. *Education:* Studied in Australia, Vienna and Munich. *Career:* Solo debut with the Israel National Opera; Principal baritone of the Kiel Opera and has sung in Hamburg, Düsseldorf, Hanover and elsewhere in Europe; Geneva Opera as

Biterolf in Tannhäuser; Season 1984–85 as Alfio and Tonio (Cav and Pag) with Opera North and Mozart's Figaro with English National Opera; Bayerische Staatsoper Munich 1986–, as Bretigny in Manon, Caliph in Der Barbier von Bagdad, Schaunard, and Dominic in Arabella; Other roles include Wagner's Dutchman and Kothner, Riccardo (I Puritani), Iago and Don Carlos (La Forza del Destino); Sang Wagner's Telramund at Leipzig, 1992; Season 1995–96 as Jochanaan at Dessau and Pizarro at Sydney; Sang Wotan in Das Rheingold at Braunschweig, 1999. *Address:* Music International, 13 Ardilaun Road, London N5 2QR, England.

**CERNY, Pavel;** Organist; b. 9 Oct. 1970, Prague, Czechoslovakia. *Education:* Academy of Music. *Career:* Live television recording, 1994; Several Czech radio recordings of historic Organ; Set of Historical Organ Recordings for the Dutch Radio (KRO) and Production; Prague Philharmony (Recital, 1995); Chartres, Padova, Verona (Recitals, 1996); Vienna, 1994; Salzburg, 1994. *Recordings:* Romantic Organ Repertoire for Four Hands and Four Legs, with Martin Rost (Germany), 1997; Jiri Ropek, Composer and Organist. *Publications:* Cooperation to International Organ Dictionary, Belgium. *Contributions:* Studies of significant Prague Organs, Hetorgel, 1997. *Honours:* 1st Prize, Opava (National), 1990; 1st Prize, Ljublja, 1992; 1st Prize, Prague, 1994. *Address:* Noutonice 10, 252 64 Velké Prilepy, Czech Republic.

**CERQUETTI, Anita;** Singer (Soprano); b. 13 March 1931, Montecorsaro-Macerata, Italy. *Education:* Studied at the Liceo Morlacchi in Perugia. *Career:* Debut: Spoleto 1951, as Aida; Sang Aida and the Trovatore Leonora at Verona, 1953; Chicago Lyric Opera, 1955–56, debut as Amelia in Un Ballo in Maschera; New York 1957, in Paride ed Elena by Gluck; Milan 1958 as Abigaille in Nabucco; Other roles include Norma, La Gioconda and Elena in I Vespri Siciliani. *Recordings:* La Gioconda (Decca); Reiza in Oberon; Mathilde in Guillaume Tell; Elvira in Verdi's Ernani; Zoraima in Les Abencérages by Cherubini (Cetra). *Address:* c/o Accademia Nazionale di Santa Cecilia, Vocal Faculty, Via Vittoria 6, I–00187 Rome, Italy.

**CERVENA, Sona;** Singer (Mezzo-Soprano); b. 9 Sept. 1925, Prague, Czechoslovakia. *Education:* Studied with Robert Rosner and Lydia Wegener in Prague. *Career:* Janáček Opera Brno, 1952–58, Staatsoper Berlin, 1958–61, Deutsche Oper Berlin, 1962–64, Opera Frankfurt, 1964–90; Title, Kammer-saengerin Berlin and Frankfurt; Guest appearances, Prague, Vienna, Amsterdam, Brussels, Geneva, London, Milano, Paris, Barcelona, Lisbon, San Francisco, Los Angeles, Chicago; Festivals, Bayreuth 1960–66, Salzburg 1961, Glyndebourne 1963–64 as Clairon in Capriccio, Edinburgh 1966–78; Season 1987–88 at Frankfurt in Jenůfa and Schreker's Die ferne Klang. *Address:* Thalia Theater, Alstertor, 20095 Hamburg, Germany.

**CERVENKA, Jan;** Conductor; b. 1940, London, England. *Education:* Studied at the Royal College of Music and the Berlin Hochschule. *Career:* Assistant and Conductor at the Munster and Wiesbaden opera houses then returned to England to conduct Britten's Noye's Fludde; Guest with the BBC orchestras, in Venezuela with Nielsen's 4th Symphony, Netherlands, Bulgaria and Romania; Further concerts at the Albert and Festival Halls, London; Music Director of Worthing Borough Council from 1979; Guest Conductor with the Belgian Radio Symphony Orchestra and Choir from 1986. *Address:* c/o Orchestre Symphonique de la RTBF, Place Eugène Flagey 18, B–1050 Brussels, Belgium.

**CERVETTI, Sergio;** Composer and Teacher; b. 9 Nov. 1940, Dolores, Uruguay. *Education:* E Krenek and S Grove, Peabody Conservatory of Music, Baltimore, USA, 1963–67. *Career:* Composer in Residence, German Artists' Programme, West Berlin, 1969; Faculty, Tisch School of the Arts, New York University, 1970–; mem, Broadcast Music Inc. *Compositions:* String Trio, 1963; Piano Sonata, 1964; 5 Sequences for flute, horn, cello, electric guitar, piano, percussion, 1966; Orbitas, orchestra, 1967; El Carro de Heno, 1967; Zinctum, 1968; Peripetia, 1970; Plexus, 1971; Madrigal III, 1976; 4 Fragments of Isadora, 1979; Enclosed Time for electronics, 1985; Night Trippers, 1986; Leyenda, for soprano and orchestra, 1991; 4 string quartets, 1968, 1972, 1990, 1992; Concerto for harpsichord and 11 instruments, 1992; The Triumph of Death (song cycle for piano and soprano). *Recordings:* Compositions recorded on Composers' Recordings Inc and Periodic Music Inc; Candombe Alberada and Hard Rock for harpsichord, 1993; Candombe II for orchestra, 1998; Film Music, Segments of The Hay Wain used in Oliver Stone Natural Born Killers, 1994. *Honours:* Many commissions; Grants for NEA, New York State Council for the Arts, and Meet the Composer. *Address:* 212 East Court Street, Doylestown, PA 18901, USA.

**CHABRUN, Daniel;** Conductor; b. 26 Jan. 1925, Mayenne, France. *Education:* Graduated Paris Conservatoire, 1954. *Career:* Many performances of modern music in France and elsewhere; Anton Webern festival with the ensemble Ars Nova, 1965, and premiere of Claude Prey's opera Jonas, 1966; Has also given works by Maurice Ohana, Lutoslawski, Xenakis, Barraud and Denisov; French premiere of Purcell's Indian Queen, 1966; Directed the orchestra of the Paris Conservatoire from 1972; Professor at the Montreal Conservatoire, 1975; Inspector with the French Ministry of Culture, 1980. *Address:* c/o Université de Montreal, Faculty of Music, 2900 Boulevard Edouard Montpetit, Montreal, Quebec H3C 3J7, Canada.

**CHACHAVA, Vazha;** Pianist and Accompanist; b. 20 April 1933, Tbilisi, Georgia. *Education:* Graduate, 24th Male School, Tbilisi, 1951; Study, Ruslaveli Theatre College, Tbilisi, 1953–57; Graduate, Central Music School, Tbilisi, 1952; Studies, Saradzhishvili Tbilisi Conservatory, 1958–62. *Career:*

Debut: Solo Concert, Tbilisi Conservatory, 1952; Concerts and Recitals with E Obraztsova, I Archipova, V Chernov, V Lukiyanets in many Countries of Europe, America and Asia, Among them Recitals in La Scala, Lisbon, Maryinsky Theatre and Many Famous Concert Halls; Many Russian film, television and radio broadcasts and appearances. *Recordings:* Melodia; R Schumann, Romances, E Obraztsova, 1979; Tchaikovsky, Romances, E Obraztsova, 1979; G Rossini Petite Messe Solennelle, 1981; Lieder von Komitas with Hasmik Papian, 1996. *Publications:* Gerald Moore–Singer and Accompanist, 1987; Chamber-Vocal Music, Tchaikovsky Romances, 1988; G Sviridov Romances, Accompanist's Notes, 1995. *Address:* Bolshoi Nicolopescovsky per 3-16, Moscow 121002, Russia.

**CHAILLY, Riccardo;** Italian conductor; *Music Director, Giuseppe Verdi Symphony Orchestra;* b. 20 Feb. 1953, Milan; s. of the late Luciano Chailly and of Anna Marie Motta; m. Gabriella Terragni 1987; two s. *Education:* Giuseppe Verdi and Perugia Conservatories and with Franco Caracciolo and Franco Ferrara. *Career:* Asst to Claudio Abbado, La Scala, Milan 1972–74; debut as Conductor with Chicago Opera 1974; debut, La Scala 1978, Covent Garden (operatic debut) 1979; concert debut with London Symphony Orchestra and Edin. Festival 1979; American concert debut, Los Angeles Philharmonic, CA 1980; Metropolitan Opera debut 1982; Prin. Guest Conductor, London Philharmonic Orchestra 1982–85; Chief Conductor Radio Symphony Orchestra, Berlin 1982–89; Vienna State Opera debut 1983; appearances Salzburg Festival 1984, 1985, 1986; Japan debut with Royal Philharmonic Orchestra 1984; New York Philharmonic Orchestra debut 1984; Music Dir Bologna Orchestra, Teatro Comunale 1986–93; Chief Conductor Royal Concertgebouw Orchestra, Amsterdam 1988–2004, Conductor Emeritus 2004–; Principal Conductor and Music Dir Giuseppe Verdi Symphony Orchestra, Milan 1999–; Chief Conductor-elect Leipzig Gewandhaus; Music Dir-elect Leipzig Opera; Hon. mem. Royal Acad. of Music, London. *Honours:* Gramophone Award Artist of the Year 1998, Diapason d'Or Artist of the Year 1999; Grand' Ufficiale della Repubblica Italiana, Knight of Order of Netherlands Lion 1998, Cavaliere di Gran Croce (Italy) 1998, Abrogino d'Oro, Comune Milano (Italy). *Address:* c/o Royal Concertgebouw Orchestra, Jacob Obrechtstraat 51, 1071 KJ Amsterdam, Netherlands. *Website:* www.concertgebouworkest.nl (office).

**CHAITKIN, David;** Composer; b. 16 May 1938, New York City, USA; m. Carol McCauley, 23 July 1960, 1 s. *Education:* BA, Pomona College, 1959; MA, University of California at Berkeley, 1965; Studied with Luigi Dallapiccola, Seymour Shifrin, Max Deutsch, Andrew Imbrie and Karl Kohn. *Career:* Early experience as a jazz pianist; Composed music for film, The Game; Commissions from Philadelphia Composers' Forum, Sylvan Winds, New Hampshire Music Festival, Da Capo Chamber Players/New York State Council on the Arts, Quintet of the Americas/Chamber Music America; Gordon Gottlieb; Pomona College, in honour of its Centennial; Anders Paulsson/Gotland (Sweden) Chamber Music Festival, Francesco Trio/Koussevitzky Music Foundation; Professor of Music, Reed College, 1968–69; New York University, 1969–76. *Compositions:* Symphony; Summersong, for 23 wind instruments; Etudes for piano; Concerto for flute and strings; Seasons Such as These for mixed chorus a cappella; Serenade for 7 players; Scattering Dark and Bright, duo for piano and percussion; Quintet, mixed chamber ensemble; Pacific Images, for chamber orchestra; Music in Five Parts, for septet; Nocturne for woodwind quintet; Impromptu for piano; Song Cycle for soprano and piano; Three Dances for piano; Rhapsody for cello and piano; Aria, for soprano saxophone and strings; Trio for violin, cello and piano. *Recordings:* Etudes for piano, David Burge pianist; Serenade, New York New Music Ensemble, Black; Seasons Such as These, Cantata Singers, Harbison; Summersong, for 23 wind instruments, Sylvan Winds, Weisberg; Scattering Dark and Bright. *Publications:* Etudes for piano; Summersong; Nocturne; Impromptu for piano; Quintet; Prelude and Dance, Piano Solo. *Honours:* National Endowment for the Arts, 1981; Guggenheim Fellowship, 1985; American Academy of Arts and Letters, 1980, 1994. *Current Management:* Music Publishing Services, 236 West 26th Street, Suite 11-S, New York, NY 10001, USA. *Address:* 160 West 87th Street, New York, NY 10024, USA.

**CHAKRABARTY, Kaushiki;** Indian singer; b. 1980, Kolkata; d. of Pandit Ajoy and Chandna Chakrabarty. *Education:* Sangeet Research Acad., Shrutinandan School of Music, studied with Gnan Prakash Ghosh and her father. *Career:* performs khayal and thumri forms of Hindustani music; has performed in USA, Canada and Europe; performed QEH, London 2005; contributed to film soundtrack, Deepa Mehta's Water. *Recordings:* albums: Footsteps 1998, Journey Begins 2002, Pure 2004. *Honours:* BBC World Music Award for Asia/Pacific 2005. *Address:* c/o Sense World Music, 93 Belgrave Road, Leicester, LE4 6AS, England (office). *E-mail:* info@senseworldmusic .com (office).

**CHALKER, Margaret;** Singer (Soprano); b. 1958, Waterloo, New York, USA. *Education:* BME, Studied at Baldwin-Wallace College in Ohio; MM, Syracuse University. *Career:* Mostly Mozart Festival New York as Sifare in Mitridate and Giunia in Lucio Silla; Houston Opera as Pamina; Deutsche Oper am Rhein, Düsseldorf, from 1985, as Oscar (Ballo in Maschera), Gilda, Celia (Haydn's La Fedelta Premiata) and Lauretta in Gianni Schicchi; Zürich Opera from 1987, as Pamina, Gilda, Jemmy in Guillaume Tell, Sophie (Rosenkavalier) and Janáček's Vixen; Other roles include Mozart's Countess and Donna Anna, Micaela, Antonia in Les Contes d'Hoffmann and Helen in Gluck's Paride ed Elena; Season 1996 as Puccini's Lauretta at Zürich, Ariadne at Meiningen and the Marschallin in Prague; Season 1999 at Zürich as Viclinda in I Lombardi and Freia in Das Rheingold; Many concert appearances, notably in

works by Bach and Composers of the 20th Century. *Address:* c/o Opernhaus Zürich, Falkenstrasse 1, 8008 Zürich, Switzerland.

**CHALLENGER, Robert;** singer (tenor); b. 1967, South Yorkshire, England. *Education:* Guildhall School of Music, studied with with Martin Isepp, Suzanne Danco and Hugues Cuenod at Aldeburgh. *Career:* concert appearances as the Evangelist in Bach's Passions, Handel's Messiah and Alexander's Feast; Mozart Requiem and C Minor Mass; Haydn Creation and Mass in Time of War; Britten Rejoice in the Lamb and Cantata Accademica; other concert repertory includes music by Palestrina, Byrd, Cage and Feldman; operatic roles include Beppe in Pagliacci, Brack Weaver in Weill's Down in the Valley and parts in La Jolie Fille de Perth, and Rossini's Il Viaggio a Reims, Covent Garden, 1992. *Honours:* Winner, Young Songmakers' Almanac Competition (recital at St John's Smith Square); Gramophone Prize for recording of Chamber Music, 1992.

**CHALLIS, Philip;** Pianist; b. 11 Aug. 1929, Huddersfield, Yorkshire, England; m. Mary J White, 19 Nov 1955. *Education:* Huddersfield College; Royal Manchester College of Music, studies with Herbert Fryer, Marguérite Long, Joszef Gat and Ilona Kabos. *Career:* Debut: BBC, London, 1943; Many broadcasts and television appearances in England, America and Canada; Innumerable concert tours in England, America and Canada, Europe, Scandinavia and the Far East; mem, Incorporated Society of Musicians, Chairman of Brighton Centre, 1983–86. *Recordings:* Mephisto Music, Liszt; Liszt-Beethoven, Piano Transcriptions; Sonatas of John Field; Selected Piano works, Moscheles; Second Piano Concerto, Josef Holbrooke. *Honours:* Fellow, Royal Manchester College of Music, 1972. *Address:* Balaton, 97 Alinora Crescent, West Worthing, Sussex BN12 4 HH, England.

**CHALMERS, Penelope;** singer (soprano); b. 5 Oct. 1946, Worcester, England. *Education:* Bristol University. *Career:* has sung such roles as the Marschallin (Der Rosenkavalier), Leonora (Trovatore), Turandot and Tosca with fringe opera companies; Title role in the British premiere of Bruch's Lorelei for University College Opera, Fiordiligi for Pavilion Opera and Rezia in Weber's Oberon at Haddo House, Scotland; London debut at the Prom concerts in Lambert's Rio Grande; Recent appearances as the Dyer's Wife in Die Frau ohne Schatten at Geneva, Helmwige and Ortlinde in Die Walküre at Covent Garden and Emilia Marty in The Makropulos Case at Hagen, Germany; Donna Anna and Lady Billows in Albert Herring for Opera 80, season 1991–92; Judith in Bluebeard's Castle, at the English National Opera, 1993; Sang title role in Salome with Scottish Opera; National Television debut as prima donna in BBC production of Stendhal's Le Rouge et le Noir, 1993. *Current Management:* Robert Gilder & Company, 91 Great Russell Street, London, WC1B 3PS, England. *Telephone:* (20) 7580-7758. *E-mail:* rgilder@ robert-gilder.com.

**CHAMBERS, Becky;** Violist; b. 1975, England. *Education:* Royal College of Music, with Simon Rowland-Jones and Chillingirian Quartet. *Career:* Co-founded Tavec String Quartet at RCM, 1999; Performances given at London's National Gallery (Schubert's Octet, 2001), St Martin-in-the-Fields, Serpentine Gallery (BBC Proms) and Queen Elizabeth Hall; Music Society concerts throughout Britain and workshops and educational projects; Festival engagements at Lower Wye Valley Chamber Music Festival, 2000–2001; Association with the Piros Ensemble from 2000, giving large scale popular chamber works. *Honours:* Helen Just String Quartet Prize; Rio Tinto Ensemble Prize and NETA Music Prize, Bristol. *Address:* c/o Royal College of Music, Prince Consort Road, London, SW7 2 BS, England.

**CHAMPNEY, Wendy;** Violist; b. 23 Feb. 1958, USA. *Education:* Studied at Indiana University, the International Menuhin Academy in Gstaad. *Career:* Co-Founder and Violist of the Carmina Quartet, 1984; Appearances from 1987 in Europe, Israel, USA and Japan; Regular concerts at the Wigmore Hall from Oct 1987; Concerts at the South Bank Centre, London, Amsterdam Concertgebouw, the Kleine Philharmonie in Berlin, Konzertverein Vienna; Four engagements in Paris 1990–91, seven in London; Tours in Australasia, USA, Japan; Concerts at the Hohenems, Graz, Hong Kong, Montreux, Schleswig-Holstein, Bath, Lucerne and Prague Spring Festivals; Collaborations with Dietrich Fischer-Dieskau, Olaf Bär and Mitsuko Uchida. *Recordings:* Albums for Ex Libris, Bayer, Claves and Denon (from 1991). *Honours:* Joint winner (with members of Carmina Quartet) Paolo Borciani String Quartet Competition in Reggio Emilia, Italy, 1987. *Address:* c/o Intermusica Artists' Management, 16 Duncan Terrace, London N1 8BZ, England.

**CHANCE, Michael;** British singer (countertenor); b. 7 March 1955, Penn, Buckinghamshire, England. *Education:* King's Coll., Cambridge. *Career:* appearances with the English Chamber Orchestra, Acad. of Ancient Music, English Concert, Orchestra of St John's, Smith Square, and the Bournemouth Sinfonietta; Handel's Messiah at the Alice Tully and Avery Fisher Halls New York; concerts with John Eliot Gardiner and the Monteverdi Choir in New York and at the Göttingen and Aix-en-Provence Festivals; operatic roles include Apollo in Cavalli's Jason, Buxton Festival 1983; Andronico in Handel's Tamerlano, Lyon Opéra 1985; Otho in Handel's Agrippina, Bath Festival, Ottone in Monteverdi's L'Incoronazione di Poppea and the Military Governor in the world premiere of Judith Weir's A Night at the Chinese Opera, Kent Opera; Britten's Oberon and Voice of Apollo with Glyndebourne Opera; Paris Opéra debut 1988, as Ptolomeo in Handel's Giulio Cesare; season 1992 as Amphinomous in Monteverdi's Ulisse for ENO, Julius Caesar for Scottish Opera and Britten's Apollo at Glyndebourne; sang in the premiere of Birtwistle's Second Mrs Kong 1994; concerts include Bach cantatas at the

Promenade Concerts, London, Messiah at King's Coll., Cambridge, Royal Albert Hall and in Edinburgh; Handel's Theodora at the Paris Opéra 1987; Israel in Egypt in Stuttgart and at La Scala, Milan; Jephtha in London and Göttingen; Bach's St Matthew Passion in Spain and London, B Minor Mass with the Manchester Camerata; world premiere of Bennett's Ophelia 1988; Apollo in Death in Venice with Glyndebourne Touring Opera at Norwich 1989; The Fairy Queen with The Sixteen, Queen Elizabeth Hall 1990; Promenade Concerts, London, Britten's Cantata Misericordium, Mozart's Credo Mass 1991; sang the title role in Gluck's Orpheus for ENO 1997; season 1998 as Monteverdi's Ottone for WNO; season 2000–01 as Gluck's Orpheus at Leipzig and soloist in the St Matthew Passion at La Scala; London Proms Chamber Music 2002. *Recordings:* Bach's St John Passion, Christmas Oratorio and St Matthew Passion, Handel's Messiah, Jephtha, Cavalli's Giasone, Bacco and other roles in The Death of Orpheus by Stefano Landi, Handel's Tamerlano, Orfeo settings by Monteverdi and Gluck. *Current Management:* Ingpen & Williams Ltd, 7 St George's Court, 131 Putney Bridge Road, London, SW15 2PA, England.

**CHANCE, Nancy (Laird);** Composer; b. 19 March 1931, Cincinnati, Ohio, USA; m. 7 Sept 1950, divorced, 3 s. *Education:* Magna cum laude, The Foxcroft School, 1945–49; Bryn Mawr College, 1949–50; Columbia University, part-time, 1959–68; Piano with William R Smith and Lilias McKinnon; Theory and Composition with Otto Luening and Vladimir Ussachevsky; Sundance Institute Film Composer Fellow, 1988. *Career:* Performances of her works by Philadelphia Orchestra, St Louis Symphony, The Jupiter Symphony, The American Composers Orchestra, The League ISCM, The Group for Contemporary Music, The New Music Consort, Da Capo Chamber Players, Relache, Continuum, The Goldman Memorial Band and numerous others; World premiere of Planasthai with the Cleveland Chamber Symphony. *Compositions:* Odysseus, solo voice, percussion and orchestra; String Quartet No. 1; Liturgy for orchestra; Elegy for string orchestra; Woodwind Quintet; Domine, Dominus: Motet for double chorus acapella; Duos III for violin and cello; Exultation and Lament for alto saxophone and timpani; Ritual Sounds, for brass quintet and percussion; Daysongs for alto flute and percussion; 3 Rilke Songs for soprano, flute, English horn and cello; In Paradisum, solo voice, mixed chorus, orchestra; Rhapsodia For Marimba Quartet; Ceremonial for Percussion Quartet; Planasthai, chamber orchestra, piano and percussion, 1992. *Recordings:* Daysongs, Ritual Sounds, Duos III and Lament. *Honours:* Winner: ASCAP Rudolph Missim Prize for Orchestral Compositions, 1982, 1984; NEA Composer Fellowships, 1981, 1983. *Address:* PO Box 96, Austerlitz, New York, NY 12017, USA.

**CHANG, Sarah;** Violinist; b. 10 Dec. 1980, Philadelphia, USA. *Education:* The Juilliard School. *Career:* Debut: New York Philharmonic, 1990; Live from Lincoln Center, New York Philharmonic; Berlin Philharmonic; Carnegie Hall, Montreal Symphony. Repertoire includes Tchaikovsky Concerto; Sibelius Concerto; Mendelssohn Concerto; Paganini Concerto no. 1; Vieuxtemps Concerto; Sibelius Concerto with the CBSO at the 1999 London Prom concerts; Also plays Bartók's Second Concerto (BBC, 1999). *Recordings:* Paganini First Concerto with the Philadelphia Orchestra and Sawallisch; Lalo Symphonie Espagnole with the Royal Concertgebouw; Sibelius and Mendelssohn Concertos under Dutoit; Berlin Philharmonic, Jansons, Simply Sarah. *Contributions:* New York Times; Washington Post; The Times; Life; People; The Strad; Strings. *Honours:* Gramophone, Young Artist of the Year, 1993; German Echo Schallplattenpreis, 1993; International Classical Music Award, Newcomer of the Year, 1994. *Current Management:* ICM Artists. *Address:* c/o IMG Artists, Lovell House, 616 Chiswick High Road, London, W4 5RX, England.

**CHAPIN, Schuyler Garrison;** American musical impresario; b. 13 Feb. 1923, New York; s. of L. H. Paul Chapin and Leila H. Burden; m. 1st Elizabeth Steinway 1947 (died 1993); four s.; m. 2nd Catia Zoullas Mortimer 1995. *Education:* Longy School of Music. *Career:* Spot Sales, NBC Television, New York 1947–50; Gen. Man. Tex and Jinx McCrary Enterprises, New York 1950–53; Booking Dir Judson O'Neill and Judd Div., Columbia Artists Man. 1953–59; CBS Dir Masterworks, Columbia Records Div. 1959–62, Vice-Pres. Creative Services 1962–63; Vice-Pres. Programming, Lincoln Center for the Performing Arts Inc. 1964–69; Exec. Producer, Amberson Productions 1969–72; Gen. Man. Metropolitan Opera Asscn Inc. 1972–75; Dean of Faculty of Arts, Columbia Univ., New York 1976–87, Dean Emer. 1987–; Vice-Pres. Worldwide Concert & Artists Activities, Steinway & Sons 1990–92; Commr of Cultural Affairs for City of New York 1994–2002; Special Consultant, Carnegie Hall Corpn 1976–79, trustee and mem. artistic cttee; Trustee, Naumburg Foundation 1962–; Bagby Music Lovers Foundation 1959–2002, mem. Bd of Dirs, Amberson Group Inc. 1972–; mem. The Century Asscn, The Knickerbocker Club; Chair. Exec. Cttee Franklin and Eleanor Roosevelt Inst. 1983–; Curtis Inst. of Music 1986–, Lincoln Center Theatre 1985. *Publications:* Musical Chairs, A Life in the Arts 1977, Leonard Bernstein: Notes from a Friend 1992, Sopranos, Mezzos, Tenors, Basses and Other Friends 1995. *Honours:* Hon. LHD (New York Univ. and Hobart-William Smith Colls.) 1974, (Hofstra Coll.) 1999; Hon. LittD (Emerson Coll.) 1976, Hon. DMus (Mannes Coll., New York) 1990, (Curtis Inst. of Music) 2000; Air Medal 1945; NY State Conspicuous Service Cross 1951; Christopher Award 1972, Emmy Awards 1972, 1976, 1980; Chevalier, Légion d'honneur 2002. *Address:* 655 Park Avenue, New York, NY 10021, USA (home). *Telephone:* (212) 734-5553 (home). *Fax:* (212) 628-8631 (home).

**CHAPMAN, Janice;** Singer (Soprano) and Teacher; b. 10 Jan. 1938, Adelaide, Australia. *Education:* Studied at the University of Adelaide and at the Royal College of Music in London and the London Opera Centre. *Career:* Sang leading roles with Sadler's Wells/English National Opera, Welsh and Scottish Operas and in many European houses; Toured Russia with the English Opera Group under Benjamin Britten and worked with the composer on the roles of Miss Jessel and Mrs Grose in The Turn of the Screw; Sang Mrs Julian in the stage premiere of Owen Wingrave at Covent Garden 1973; Other Britten roles have been Ellen Orford and Lady Billows, and she has sung in operas by Mozart, Wagner, Verdi and Puccini; Concert engagements with leading orchestras; Sang with her trio The Alexandra Ensemble at the Women's Music Festival at Beersheba in Israel, 1986; Appeared as Mrs Grose for New Israel Opera, 1990, conducted by Roderick Brydon; Professor of Voice at the London College of Music.

**CHAPPLE, Brian,** GRSM, ARAM, LRAM; British composer; b. 24 March 1945, London, England. *Education:* Royal Acad. of Music, London. *Career:* commissions and premieres from London Sinfonietta, London Mozart Players, New London Orchestra, BBC Singers, St Paul's Cathedral, Dartington Festival, Highgate Choral Soc., Finchley Children's Music Group and others; mem. Performing Right Soc. *Compositions include:* Scherzos for four pianos 1970, Trees Revisited 1970, Praeludiana 1971, Green and Pleasant 1973, In Ecclesiis 1976, Piano Concerto 1977, Cantica 1978, Venus Fly Trap 1979, Little Symphony 1982, Lamentations of Jeremiah 1984, Piano Sonata 1986, Magnificat 1986, In Memoriam 1989, Berkeley Tribute 1989, Frink Tribute 1990, Requies 1991, Missa Brevis 1991, Three Motets 1992, Songs of Innocence 1993, Ebony and Ivory 1995, The St Paul's Service 1996, A Bit of a Blow 1996, Tribute for Jo Klein 1997, Songs of Experience 1998, Klein Tribute Quartet 1998, Burlesque 2000, The Cloud-Capped Towers 2000, Viola Suite 2004, Tribute for J.M.C. 2004, Ecce Lignum Crucis, Passiontide at St Paul's; anthems, canticles, children's songs, piano music, instrumental music. *Honours:* BBC Monarchy 1000 Prize 1973, UNESCO Int. Rostrum of Composers 1976. *Address:* Music Sales Ltd, 8–9 Frith Street, London, W1D 3JB, England (office). *Telephone:* (20) 7434-0066 (office). *Fax:* (20) 7287-6329 (office). *E-mail:* promotion@musicsales.co.uk (office).

**CHAPPUIS, Vincent;** Composer; b. 26 Feb. 1960, Switzerland. *Education:* School of Music, Freiburg; Music Certificate, Lausanne; Composition sessions, France. *Career:* Numerous international festivals of contemporary music, mainly in Romania; Radio broadcast with Radio Canada, Quebec; Radio Belgium; France music and Swiss Espace 2; TU with Tele Europe Nova in Romania; mem, Founder and member of the Composers' Association Ici et Maintenant; Member of the Swiss Association of Musicians; Member of Forum Ircam, Paris. *Compositions:* Symphonie for big orchestra, 1991; Sinfonietta for chamber orchestra, 1992; Procession electro-acoustic piece, 1993; Dilemme trio for violin, double bass and piano, 1994; Fusions for 2 pianos and percussion, 1995; Quatuor for string quartet, 1996; Fusions II for piano and chamber orchestra, 1997; Rituels for piano, percussion and clarinet, 1998; Symphonie No. 2 for large orchestra and choir, 2001; Quatuor No. 2 for string quartet, 2002. *Recordings:* Quatuor; Trio Dilemme; Trio Rituels. *Honours:* Honorary member of the Percussion Ensemble of Cluj, Romania. *Address:* Rue Liotard 35, 1202 Geneva, Switzerland.

**CHAPUIS, Gérard;** Singer (Bass); b. 21 Oct. 1931, Lyon, France. *Education:* Studied at the Lyon Conservatory. *Career:* Sang with the Lyon Opéra, 1954–56, Paris Opéra, 1956–73; Among his best roles have been the Minister in Fidelio, Sparafucile, Ramphis, Raimondo (Lucia di Lammermoor), Pistol, Hector in Les Troyens, Sarastro (Die Zauberflöte), Commendatore (Don Giovanni), Osmin (Die Entführung), and in Un ballo in Maschera and Barbiere di Siviglia; Other appearances at the Paris Opéra-Comique; President, des Voix d'Or; President, Scene Française. *Honours:* Concours de Voix d'Or 1st Prize Caruso, 1956. *Address:* 5 rue Lyautey, 75016 Paris, France.

**CHARBONNEAU, Pierre;** Singer (Bass); b. 14 June 1949, Montreal, Canada. *Career:* Sang first in Canada, notably at Vancouver from 1974, and then with Canadian Opera at Toronto from 1978; Opéra de Montreal from 1983; Guest appearances with Washington Opera (1976), Opéra de Lyon from 1988; Sang Jupiter in Orphée aux Enfers at the Paris Opéra (1988), Don Pasquale at Rio de Janeiro, 1989; Carnegie Hall, 1991, in Boieldieu's La Dame Blanche; Other roles include Masetto, Sparafucile, Rocco, Raimondo, Hunding, Arkel and Timur in Turandot. *Address:* c/o L'Opéra de Montréal, 260 de Maisonneuve Boulevard West, Montréal, Québec H2X 1Y9, Canada.

**CHARD, Geoffrey;** Singer (Baritone); b. 9 Aug. 1930, Sydney, Australia. *Education:* Studied at the New South Wales Conservatory. *Career:* Debut: Sydney 1951, in Carmen; Moved to England and became a member of the English National Opera; Other appearances with Welsh National Opera and the Glyndebourne and Edinburgh Festivals; Aldeburgh Festival 1967, 1968, in the premieres of Berkeley's The Castaway and Birtwistle's Punch and Judy; London Coliseum 1973–83, in the British premiere of Penederecki's The Devils of Loudun; Ginastera's Bomarzo and Ligeti's Le Grand Macabre; Roles in operas by Gluck, Mozart, Wagner, Britten, Orff, Menotti, Shostakovich, Janáček and contemporary British composers; Many engagements as concert singer; Sang Bartolo in Il Barbiere di Siviglia for Victoria State Opera, 1989; Germont in Traviata for the Ballarat Opera Festival, 1992, Balstrode (Peter Grimes) and Pizarro at Sydney; Tonio in Pagliacci at Sydney, 1996. *Address:* Victoria State Opera, 370 Nicholson Street, Fitzroy, VIC 3065, Australia.

**CHARLTON, David;** Musicologist; b. 20 June 1946, London, England. *Education:* BA, Nottingham University, 1967; Cambridge; PhD, 1974. *Career:* Lecturer, 1970, Reader, 1991, University of East Anglia; Reader, then Professor, Royal Holloway, University of London, 1995–. *Publications:* Many articles and reference works on French opera in the New Grove Dictionary of Music and the New Grove Dictionary of Opera; Grétry and the Growth of Opéra-Comique, 1986; French Opera 1730–1830: Meaning and Media, 2000; Editorial: ETA Hoffmann's Musical Writings, 1989; Hector Berlioz, Choral Works with Orchestra, 1993; Michel Sedaine 1719–1797: Theatre, Opera, Art, 2000; The Cambridge Companion to Grand Opera, 2003. *Address:* Department of Music, Royal Holloway, Egham, Surrey TW20 0EX, England. *E-mail:* D.Charlton@rhul.ac.uk.

**CHARNOCK, Helen;** Singer (Soprano); b. 1958, England. *Education:* Studied at the University of East Anglia, BA with Honours in Music and at Guildhall School with Laura Sarti. *Career:* Many performances with Opera Factory and London Sinfonietta, including the world premieres of Hell's Angels by Nigel Osborne and Birtwistle's Yan Tan Tethera, 1986; Sang in Weill's Mahagonny Songspiel, Ligeti's Aventures, Nouvelles Aventures and the British premiere of Reimann's Ghost Sonata; Workshops and performances in many venues with the London Sinfonietta's Education Programme, including Holloway Prison and the Huddersfield Contemporary Music Festival; Australian debut in 1986 as Clytemnestra in Iphigénie en Tauride; Sang in the premiere of Greek by Mark-Anthony Turnage at 1988 Munich Biennale, repeated at Edinburgh Festival in 1988 and English National Opera 1990; Has sung Britten's Governess and Mrs Coyle at Aldeburgh Festival and has appeared elsewhere as Semele, First Lady, Pamina, Micaela, Butterfly, Titania, Gretel, Adele, Despina and Musetta; Television appearances in works by Birtwistle, Ligeti and Turnage. *Recordings:* Greek by Turnage, 1993. *Honours:* The English Singers and Speakers Prize; 2 Royal Society of Arts Awards; Incorporated Society of Musicians Young Artists Award; Ian Fleming Bursary. *Address:* 21 Glengall Road, London SE15 6 NJ, England.

**CHARTERIS, Richard,** BA, MA, PhD, FAHA, FRHistS; musicologist, writer and editor; *Professor in Historical Musicology, University of Sydney;* b. 24 June 1948, Chatham Islands, New Zealand. *Education:* Victoria Univ., Wellington, Univ. of Canterbury, UK, Univ. of London, UK. *Career:* Australian Research Council Chief Investigator, Music Dept, Univ. of Sydney 1981–90; Australian Research Council Sr Research Fellow (Reader) 1991–94, Prof. in Historical Musicology, Music Dept, Univ. of Sydney 1995–. *Publications include:* more than 150 books and editions devoted to the music of Johann Christian Bach, Giovanni Bassano, John Coprario, Alfonso Ferrabosco the Elder, Domenico Maria Ferrabosco, Andrea and Giovanni Gabrieli, Adam Gumpelzhaimer, Hans Leo Hassler, Thomas Lupo, Claudio Monteverdi and others, and mostly in the series Corpus Mensurabilis Musicae, Musica Britannica, Recent Researches in the Music of the Baroque Era, Boethius Editions, Fretwork Editions, King's Music Editions, Baroque and Classical Music Series; and books on composers, music and early sources in the series Boethius Editions, Thematic Catalogues Series, Musicological Studies and Documents and Altro Polo. *Honours:* Sr Scholar 1970–71, Mary Duncan Scholar 1975, Louise Dyer Award Royal Musical Asscn 1975, Australian Acad. of Humanities Travelling Fellow 1979–80, Top Award Australian Hi Fi FM Classical Music Section 1988, Australian Centenary Medal 2003. *Address:* Music Department, University of Sydney, Sydney, NSW 2006, Australia.

**CHASE, Roger;** Concert Violist; b. 1958, London, England. *Education:* Studied at Royal College of Music with Bernard Shore and in Canada with Steven Staryk. *Career:* Debut: Solo with the English Chamber Orchestra, 1979; Performances internationally from 1976 with such ensembles as the London Sinfonietta, the Esterhazy Baryton Trio and the Nash Ensemble; Concerts with the chamber ensemble Hausmusik, featuring works by Mendelssohn, Schubert and Hummel; Modern repertoire includes a concerto by Richard Harvey, premiere at the Exeter Festival, 1991; Toured the USA with Hanover Band, 1992 playing Mozart's Sinfonia Concertante; Professor at the Guildhall School of Music and Drama. *Recordings include:* Works by Mendelssohn, Mozart's Concertante and Britten's Lachrymae. *Current Management:* Owen/White Management. *Address:* c/o Owen/White Management, 14 Nightingale Lane, London N8 7QU, England.

**CHASLIN, Frédéric;** Conductor and Pianist; b. 1963, Paris, France; pnr. Nancy Gustafson. *Career:* Assistant to Daniel Barenboim at the Orchestre de Paris 1987–89 and to Pierre Boulez at Ensemble Intercontemporain, 1989–91; Music Director of Rouen Opera and Symphonie 1991–94; Guest with the Orchestre National de France, from 1993, Orchestre de Paris (1994), Vienna Symphony Orchestra (1993–95), RAI Milan and orchestras of Nice, Marseilles, Lyon, Düsseldorf, Stuttgart and Toho Gakuen in Tokyo; Permanent Guest at the Bregenz Festival, 1993–, with Nabucco and Fidelio; Season 1994–95 with Lakmé at the Paris Opéra-Comique, followed by Der Ring des Nibelungen at Hanover; UK concert debut as guest with Manchester Hallé Orchestra, 1996; Season 1997–98 with Carmen and Manon at the Paris Opéra Bastille, Samson et Dalila for Scottish Opera; Season 1998 with La Favorita at Rome and La Traviata for New Israeli Opera; Concerts in Israel include Le Marteau sans Maître by Boulez; Chief conductor Jerusalem Symphony Orchestra 1999–2002; Tales of Hoffmann at Oper Leipzig 2001–02; Berlioz: Damnation de Faust for Opera North, 2003; La Traviata in Munich, 2003; Concerts with Royal Scottish National Orchestra devoted to Richard Strauss, with Nancy Gustafson, 2003. *Address:* Allied Artists, 42 Montpelier Square, London SW7 1JZ, England.

**CHATEAUNEUF, Paula;** British/American lutenist and early guitar player; b. 1958, USA. *Education:* Univ. of Connecticut, New England Conservatory, with Patrick O'Brien in New York; Fulbright Scholar, Guildhall School of Music, London with Nigel North. *Career:* moved to London, 1982; appearances with many early music ensembles, including the New London Consort, Orchestra of the Age of Enlightenment, English Concert, Sinfonye and the Gabrieli Consort; has worked extensively as soloist and continuo player, particularly in Baroque opera; involved in groups and projects devoted to improvisation and early dance music; tours of Europe, Australia and the Americas as soloist and ensemble player, performing at major festivals and recording for radio and TV; Tutor, Univ. of Birmingham Centre for Early Music Performance and Research. *Recordings include:* video, music for San Rocco, with the Gabrieli Consort; To the Unknown Goddess: A Portrait of Barbara Strozzi. *Address:* 170 Bow Common Lane, London, E3 4HH, England.

**CHAUSSON, Carlos;** Spanish singer (bass-baritone); b. 17 March 1950, Zaragoza. *Education:* studied in Madrid and at the Univ. of Michigan. *Career:* debut, San Diego 1977, as Masetto; appearances at Boston, Miami, New York City Opera and Mexico City (as Bartolo in Il Barbiere di Siviglia); sang at Madrid from 1983, Barcelona from 1985; Vienna Staatsoper from 1986, as Paolo in Simon Boccanegra, and Don Alvaro in Il Viaggio a Reims, conducted by Abbado; Vienna Konzerthaus in Les Danaides by Salieri; Parma 1987, as Falstaff, Bologna 1988–89, as Michonnet in Adriana Lecouvreur, Pantaleone in Le Maschere by Mascagni and Sharpless in Butterfly; Barcelona 1989, in the premiere of Cristobal Colón by Balades; returned 1990 as Paolo; Modena 1990, as Geronte in Manon Lescaut; sang Mozart's Figaro at Madrid, Masetto at the 1990 Vienna Festival; Grand Théâtre de Genève 1991 as Paolo; Madrid 1992 as Bartolo in the new production of Il Barbiere di Siviglia conducted by Alberto Zedda; sang Don Magnifico in Cenerentola at the Palais Garnier, Paris 1996; Giorgio in Paisiello's Nina at Zürich, and John Plake in Wolf-Ferrari's Sly 1998; season 2000–01 as Don Alfonso for Zürich Opera, Fra Melitone (La Forza del Destino) and in La Cenerentola at Madrid. *Current Management:* Caecilia Lyric Department, Rennweg 15, 8001 Zurich, Switzerland. *Telephone:* (1) 221-33-88. *Fax:* (1) 211-71-82. *Website:* www.caecilia.ch.

**CHAUVET, Guy;** Singer (Tenor); b. 2 Oct. 1933, Montlucon, Tarbes, France. *Education:* Studied with Bernard Baillour in Tarbes. *Career:* After winning prizes at Cannes, Toulouse and Paris, sang at the Paris Opéra 1959, as Tamino, returned as Faust, Cavaradossi, Florestan, Aeneas in Les Troyens and Jason in Médée; Holland Festival and Buenos Aires, 1961; Covent Garden debut as Cavaradossi, 1963; London Coliseum, 1969, in a concert performance of Roussel's Padmavati; Verona Arena 1971, as Radames; Has sung Parsifal in Brussels, Lohengrin in Berlin and Samson in Geneva; Vienna Staatsoper as Aeneas and Otello; Further appearances in New York, Metropolitan, as John of Leyden, Le Prophète, 1979; Monte Carlo, Lisbon and Dublin; Rio de Janeiro, Don José, 1981; San Francisco, Samson, 1983; Retired as singer 1985 and taught at Tarbes and Paris (Conservatoire). *Recordings:* Highlights from Werther and Hérodiade by Massenet; Scenes from Les Troyens; Sigurd by Reyer. *Address:* c/o San Francisco Opera, War Memorial Opera House, San Francisco, CA 94102, USA.

**CHEDEL, Arlette;** Singer (Contralto); b. 25 May 1933, Neuchâtel, Switzerland. *Education:* Studied in Neuchâtel and at the Vienna Musikakademie with Erik Werba. *Career:* Concert appearances in works by Schütz, Handel, Bach, Kodály, Frank Martin and Honegger; Radio Lausanne 1974, in the premiere of Trois Visions Espagnoles by Gerber; Montreux Festival, 1986, in Folie de Tristan by Schibler; Guest engagements in Vienna, Prague, Berlin, Rome and Besançon; Opera roles included Wagner's Erda, Magdalene and Mary, Mozart's Marcellina, Catherine in Jeanne d'Arc au Bûcher, the Nurse in Boris Godunov and Geneviève in Pelléas et Mélisande. *Recordings include:* L'Enfant et les Sortilèges and Les Noces by Stravinsky (Erato). *Address:* c/o Grand Théâtre de Genève, 11 Blvd du Théâtre, 1211, Genève 11, Switzerland.

**CHEEK, John;** Singer (Bass-Baritone); b. 17 Aug. 1948, Greenville, South Carolina, USA. *Education:* Studied at the North Carolina School of Arts and at the Accademia Chigiana in Siena with Gino Bechi. *Career:* Sang at the Festivals of Ravinia and Tanglewood and elsewhere in the USA, notably in music by Mozart; Metropolitan Opera debut 1977, as the Doctor in Pelléas et Mélisande: later appeared as Pimen, Ferrando in Il Trovatore, Klingsor, Panthée in Les Troyens, Monterone and Figaro; New York City Opera 1986, as Mephistopheles in Faust; Other roles include Wurm in Luisa Miller; Attila, New York, 1988; Padre Guardiano, Toronto; Metropolitan, La Bohème, 1989; Ramphis in Aida, Cincinnati Opera, 1990; Sang Don Pasquale at Cincinnati, 1996; Sang the Berlioz Mephistopheles at Helsinki, 2000; Television appearances and concerts. *Recordings include:* Tosca; Haydn Creation, Stravinsky The Rake's Progress, as Nick Shadow; Messiah; César Franck, Les Béatitudes (Satan), Hänssler. *Honours:* Doctor of Music (Honorary), 1985; North Carolina Prize, 1987. *Current Management:* Thea Dispeker Artist Representative, 59 E 54th Street, New York, NY 10022, USA. *Address:* Thea Dispeker Artist Representative, 59 E 54th St, New York, NY 10022, USA.

**CHEN, Leland;** Concert Violinist; b. 8 July 1965, Taiwan. *Career:* won the Yehudi Menuhin International Competition and made London concerto debut with the London Philharmonia at the Barbican; further concerts with the London Philharmonic Orchestra and London Symphony Orchestra; tour of North America in 1985 with the Royal Philharmonic Orchestra; Royal Concert London in 1986 playing the Bach Double Concerto with Yehudi Menuhin; tours of Poland and the Netherlands and a 60-city recital tour of the USA;

played Vivaldi's Four Seasons at Kennedy Center, Washington DC, televised by CBS; performances at Gstaad and Schleswig-Holstein festivals; performed throughout Europe with the Netherlands Philharmonic, Polish Chamber Orchestra, Warsaw Sinfonia and Chamber Orchestra of Europe; repertoire includes works by Bartók, Beethoven, Elgar, Mozart, Mendelssohn, Sibelius and Tchaikovsky. *Current Management:* Upbeat Classical Management, PO Box 479, Uxbridge, UB8 2ZH, England. *Telephone:* (1895) 259441. *Fax:* (1895) 259341. *E-mail:* info@upbeatclassical.co.uk. *Website:* www.upbeatclassical.co.uk.

**CHEN, Pi-Hsien;** Pianist; b. 1950, Taiwan. *Education:* Studied in Taiwan and at the Cologne Musikhochschule, Diploma 1970; further studies with Hans Leygraf and master classes with Wilhelm Kempff, Tatiana Nikolayeva and Geza Anda. *Career:* From 1972 has given performances in London (BBC Proms, South Bank, Barbican), Amsterdam, Zürich, Berlin, Munich, Barcelona and Tokyo; Festival appearances at Huddersfield, Lucerne, Schwetzingen, Hong Kong and Osaka; Orchestras include London Symphony, BBC Symphony, Royal Concertgebouw, Radio orchestras in Austria and Germany, the Züricher Kammerorchester, Tonhalle Orchestra and the Collegium Musicum Zürich; Conductors include Colin Davis, Bernard Haitink, Jean Martinon, the late Ferdinand Leitner, Bernhard Klee, Marek Janowski, the late Paul Sacher, Horst Stein and Peter Eötvös; Repertory ranges from Scarlatti to Boulez; Piano Duo performances with Pierre-Laurent Aimard. *Honours:* Prizewinner, Concours Reine Elisabeth, 1972, Belgium; First Prize, Competition of the Rundfunkanstalten Munich, 1972. *Current Management:* Ingpen & Williams Ltd, 7 St George's Court, 131 Putney Bridge Road, London, SW15 2PA, England.

**CHEN, Shih-hui,** DMusA; Taiwanese composer; b. 6 Sept. 1962, Taibei. *Education:* Nat. Acad. of Arts. *Career:* resident in USA 1982–; currently Asst Prof. of Composition and Theory, Shepherd School of Music, Rice Univ. *Compositions include:* String Quartet No. 1 1979, String Quartet No. 2 1987, Water Ink 1988, Mime 1988, 66 Times 1992, Moments 1995, Little Dragonflies 1996, String Quartet No. 3 1998, Fu (Ambush) I 1998, Fu II 1999, 'i' 2001, Jian (Gold) 2002, Twice Removed 2000–02, Shui 2003, Furl 2004, String Quartet No. 4 2004. *Honours:* American Acad. in Rome Prize 1999, Guggenheim Fellowship 2000, Barlow Commission 2001. *Address:* c/o Shepherd School of Music, MS 532, Rice University, PO Box 1892, Houston, TX 77251-1892, USA (office). *Telephone:* (713) 348-3742 (office). *Website:* www.ruf.rice.edu (office).

**CHEN, Xieyang;** Chinese conductor; b. 4 May 1939, Shanghai; s. of Chen Dieyi and Liang Peiqiong; m. Wang Jianying 1973. *Education:* Music High School, Shanghai Conservatory. *Career:* Conductor, Shanghai Ballet 1965–84; studied with Prof. Otto Mueller, Yale Univ., USA 1981–82; Conductor, Aspen Music Festival, Group for Contemporary Music, New York, Brooklyn Philharmonia, Honolulu Symphony, Philippines State Orchestra, Hong Kong Philharmonic, Shanghai Symphony Orchestra, Cen. Philharmonic, Beijing 1981–83, Symphony Orchestra of Vilnius, Kaunas, Novosibirsk, USSR 1985, Tokyo Symphony Orchestra 1986, Orchestre Regional de Cannes 2003; Music Dir Shanghai Symphony Orchestra; has made recording for Kuklos CBE, France 1983; Dir China Musicians' Asscn; Pres. Shanghai Symphonic Music Lovers' Soc. *Honours:* Excellent Conducting Prize, Shanghai Music Festival 1986. *Address:* Shanghai Symphony Orchestra, 105 Hunan Road, Shanghai 200031, People's Republic of China. *Telephone:* 64333752 (office); 64672915 (home). *Fax:* 64333752 (office). *E-mail:* shso105@sh163.net (office).

**CHEN, Yi;** Composer and Violinist; b. 4 April 1953, Guangzhou, China; m. 1983. *Education:* BA, 1983, MA, 1986, Central Conservatory of Music, Beijing; DMA, 1993, Columbia University, NY, USA. *Career:* Concert Mistress, Beijing Opera Troupe Orchestra, 1970–78; Composer in Residence, The Women's Philharmonic, Chanticleer, San Francisco, 1993–96; Member of Composition Faculty, Peabody Conservatory, Johns Hopkins University, 1996–98; Cravens Millsap Missouri Distinguished Professor in Composition, University of Missouri, Kansas City Conservatory, 1998–. *Compositions:* Works performed and broadcast in Europe, USA and China, 1984–; Duo Ye No. 2, orchestra; Symphony No. 1; Xian Shi for viola and orchestra; Sprout for string orchestra, 3 Poems from Sung Dynasty for chorus; Woodwind Quintet; Near Distance, sextet for chamber ensemble; As in a Dream for soprano, violin and cello; Overture No. 1 and No. 2 for Chinese orchestra; Piano Concerto; Symphony No. 2; Sparkle for chamber ensemble, 1992; Song in Winter, two versions, 1993; Ge Xu (Antiphony) for orchestra, 1994; The Linear for orchestra, 1994; Shuo for string orchestra, 1994; Set of Chinese Folksongs for mixed choir or school choir and strings, 1994; Tang Poems Cantata, 1995; Chinese Myths Cantata, 1996; Qi for chamber ensemble, 1997; Golden Flute for flute and orchestra, 1997; Spring Dreams for mixed chorus, 1997; Fiddle Suite for erhu (Chinese fiddle) and string orchestra or full orchestra; Romance and Dance for string orchestra, 1997; Momentum for orchestra; Sound of the Five for cello and string quartet; Feng for woodwind quintet; Percussion Concerto for percussion and orchestra; Eleanor's Gift for cello and orchestra, 1998; Baban for piano solo; Chinese Poems for girls' chorus; Dunhuang Fantasy for organ and wind ensemble; Spring Festival for children's wind ensemble, 1999; Chinese Folk Dance Suite for violin and orchestra, 2001; Ba Yin for saxophone quartet and string orchestra, 2001; Chinese Mountain Songs for women's choir, 2001; Bright Moonlight for soprano and piano, 2001; Know You How Many Petals Falling for mixed choir, 2001; Ning for violin, cello and pipa, 2001; To the New Millennium for mixed choir, 2001; Wu Yu for chamber ensemble, 2002;... as like a raging fire... for chamber ensemble, 2002; Burning for string quartet, 2002; Singing in the Mountain for piano; Tu for full

orchestra, 2002; At the Kansas City Chinese New Year Concert for string quartet; Chinese Fables for erhu, pipa, cello, percussion, 2002; Ballad, Dance and Fantasy for cello and full orchestra, 2003; Caramoor's Summer for chamber orchestra, 2003; Landscape for mixed choir, 2003; The West Lake for mixed choir, 2003; Two Chinese Folk Songs for mixed choir, 2003; Symphony No.3 for full orchestra, 2003. *Honours:* Ives Living Award (2001–04) from American Academy of Arts and Letters. *Address:* Theodore Presser Co, 4550 Warwick Blvd, Apt 1114, Kansas City, MO 64111, USA. *E-mail:* chenyi@aol.com. *Website:* www.presser.com/composers/chen.html.

**CHEN, Zuohuang,** MM, DMA; Chinese conductor; *Music Director, OFUNAM, Mexico City and Shanghai Philharmonic Orchestra*; b. 2 April 1947, Shanghai; s. of Chen Ru Hui and Li He Zhen; m. Zaiyi Wang 1969; one c. *Education:* Cen. Conservatory of Beijing, Univ. of Michigan, USA. *Career:* Musical Dir China Film Philharmonic 1974–76; Assoc. Prof., Univ. of Kansas, USA 1985–87; Prin. Conductor Cen. Philharmonic Orchestra of China 1987–96; Music Dir/Conductor Wichita Symphony Orchestra 1990; Music Dir/Conductor Rhode Island Philharmonic Orchestra 1992–96; Artistic Dir, Conductor China Nat. Symphony Orchestra 1996–2000; Music Dir OFUNAM of Mexico 2002–; Music Dir Shanghai Philharmonic Orchestra 2004–; Guest Conductor in over 20 countries with Zürich Tonhalle Orchestra, Vancouver Symphony Orchestra, Hungary Philharmonic Orchestra and State Symphony, Gulbenkian Orchestra, Iceland Symphony Orchestra, Tanglewood Music Festival Orchestra, Colorado Symphony Orchestra, Pacific Symphony Orchestra, Virginia Symphony Orchestra, Alabama Symphony Orchestra, Russian Philharmonic Orchestra, Haifa Symphony, Slovak Radio Symphony Orchestra, Hong Kong Philharmonic Orchestra, Singapore Symphony Orchestra, Pusan Philharmonic Orchestra, Mexico Nat. Symphony Orchestra and Mexico City Philharmonic Orchestra, Taipei Symphony Orchestra; numerous recordings.

**CHÉREAU, Patrice;** French film, theatre and opera director; b. 2 Nov. 1944, s. of Jean-Baptiste Chéreau and Marguerite Pélicier. *Education:* Lycée Louis-le-Grand and Faculté de Lettres, Paris. *Career:* Co-Dir Théâtre nat. populaire (TNP) 1972–81; Dir Théâtre des Amandiers, Nanterre 1982–90. *Theatre productions include:* L'Intervention 1964, L'Affaire de la rue de Lourcine 1966, Les Soldats 1967, La Révolte au Marché noir 1968, Don Juan, Richard II, Splendeur et Mort de Joaquin Murieta 1970, La Finta Serva 1971, Lulu 1972, Massacre à Paris 1972, La Dispute 1973, Lear 1975, Peer Gynt 1981, Les Paravents 1983, Combats de Nègre et de Chiens 1983, La Fausse suivante 1985, Quai Ouest 1986, Dans la solitude des champs de coton 1987, 1995, Hamlet 1988, Le Retour au désert 1988, Le Temps et la Chambre 1991. *Opera productions:* L'Italiana in Algeri 1969, The Tales of Hoffmann 1974, Der Ring des Nibelungen (Bayreuth 1976–80), Lulu 1979, Lucio Silla 1984, Wozzeck 1992, Don Giovanni (Salzburg 1994–96). *Films include:* La Chair de l'Orchidée 1974, Judith Therpauve 1978, L'Homme blessé 1984, Hôtel de France 1987, Le Temps et la Chambre 1993, Queen Margot 1994, Those Who Love Me Can Take The Train 1998 (César Award for Best Dir), Intimacy 2001 (Golden Bear, Berlin Film Festival). *Honours:* Chevalier, Légion d'honneur; Officier des Arts et Lettres; numerous prizes. *Address:* c/o Artmédia, 10 avenue Georges V, 75008 Paris, France.

**CHERICI, Paolo;** Italian lute teacher; b. 26 March 1952, Naples. *Education:* Milan Conservatoire and Schola Cantorum of Basel. *Career:* concerts of Renaissance and Baroque music as lute soloist and in ensemble in Italy and abroad; appearances on radio and television in Italy and Switzerland; lute teacher at summer courses in Vicenza, Monza, Moneglia, Venice, Rocchetta Nevina, Trieste, Mercogliano; founder of the lute class at Milan Conservatoire; mem. The Lute Society, England, The Lute Society of America. *Recordings:* Collaborations with several recordings with music from the Renaissance to Baroque period. *Publications:* A Piccinini, Toccata per 2 liuti, 1977; J. S. Bach, Opere complete per liuto, 1980; A Vivaldi, Concerto per liuto e archi in D major, 1981; contrib. articles and reviews to Il Fronimo. *Honours:* Società Italiana del Liuto. *Address:* Via Ciro Menotti 7, 20129 Milan, Italy.

**CHERNEY, Brian;** Canadian composer and educator; *Professor, Faculty of Music, McGill University, Montreal*; b. 4 Sept. 1942, Canada; m. Rochelle Terri Soren 1969; one s. one d. *Education:* BMus, 1964, MMus, 1967, PhD, Musicology, 1974, University of Toronto; ARCT Piano, 1961; Studied composition with Samuel Dolin and John Weinzweig. *Career:* Professor, Faculty of Music, McGill University, Montreal, 1972–; mem, Canadian League of Composers; Associate Composer, Canadian Music Center. *Compositions:* Chamber Concerto for viola and 10 players, 1974; String Trio, 1976; Dans le crépuscule du souvenir for piano, 1977–80; Adieux for orchestra, 1980; River of Fire for harp and oboe d'amore, 1983; In the Stillness of the Seventh Autumn for piano, 1983; Into the Distant Stillness for orchestra, 1984; String Quartet No. 3, 1985; In Stillness Ascending for viola and piano, 1986; Illuminations for string orchestra, 1987; Shekhinah for solo viola, 1988; Oboe Concerto, 1989; Transfiguration for orchestra, 1990; Et j'entends la nuit qui chante dans les cloches, for piano and orchestra, 1990; Apparitions, for cello and 14 musicians, 1991; Doppelganger for 2 flutes, 1991; In the Stillness of September 1942 for English horn and 9 solo strings, 1992; Like Ghosts from an Enchanter Fleeing, for cello and piano, 1993; Die klingende Zeit, for flute and chamber ensemble, 1993–94, String Quartet No. 4 1994, Et la solitude dérive au fil des fleuves, for orchestra, 1995; Tombeau, for piano, 1996; Echoes in the Memory for clarinet, cello and piano 1997, Entendre marcher un ange, for flute and percussion 1998, String Quartet No. 5 2000, La princesse lointaine, for harp, English horn and orchestra 2001, Tenebrae, for a cappella choir

2002, Vers minuit, for orchestra 2002, Le miroir des anges, for chamber ensemble and 8 cellos 2003. *Recordings include:* Adieux; River of Fire: Into the Distant Stillness; Illuminations. *Publications:* Harry Somers, book, 1975; compositions published 1970–2004. *Honours:* First Place, String Trio, International Rostrum of Composers, 1979; Jules Léger Prize for New Chamber Music, 1985. *Address:* Faculty of Music, McGill University, 555 Sherbrooke Street West, Montreal, Québec H3A 1E3, Canada (office). *Telephone:* (514) 398-4535 (office).

**CHERNOMORTSEV, Victor;** Singer (Baritone); b. 1950, Krasnodar, Russia. *Education:* Graduated Tchaikovsky Conservatoire, Moscow, 1973. *Career:* Many appearances throughout Russia in opera and concert; Mariinsky Theatre, St Petersburg, from 1994 as Mazeppa, Rigoletto, Prince Igor, Nabucco Tomsky in The Queen of Spades, Amonasro, Count Luna, Scarpia, Alberich in Das Rheingold and Grasnoi in The Tsar's Bride by Rimsky-Korsakov; Tours with the Kirov Opera throughout Europe and to the New York Metropolitan; Other roles include Robert in Iolanta and the Chinese Inspector in Stravinsky's The Nightingale; Sang Matreyev in War and Peace with the Kirov Opera at Covent Garden 2000. *Honours:* Honoured Artist of Russia. *Address:* c/o Kirov Opera, Mariinsky Theatre, Mariinsky Square, St Petersburg, Russia.

**CHERNOUSHENKO, Vladislav;** Conductor; b. 14 Jan. 1936, Leningrad, Russia. *Education:* Studied at the Leningrad State Conservatoire. *Career:* Sang with the Boys Choir of the Glinka State Capella from 1944; Conducted the Karelia State Radio Orchestra, then the Leningrad Chamber Choir, 1962–74; Music Director of the Glinka State Capella, 1974–; Directed the premiere performance of Rachmaninov's complete Vespers, 1974; Re-established the Symphony Orchestra of the Glinka State Capella, 1988 and has toured with it to Germany, Netherlands, Switzerland, Ireland and France with a repertoire including Haydn, Shostakovich, Brahms, Bruckner, Schnittke and Mozart; Rector, Leningrad-St Petersburg State Conservatoire, 1979–. *Recordings include:* A wide repertoire. *Address:* c/o Sonata, 11 Northpark Street, Glasgow G20 7AA, Scotland.

**CHERNOV, Vladimir Kirillovich;** Russian baritone; b. 1956, Belorechensk; m. Olga Chernova; one s. *Education:* Moscow Conservatory (pupil of Georgy Seleznev and Hugo Titz). *Career:* winner of All-Union Glinka Competition, int. Competitions: Tchaikovsky (Moscow), Voci Virdiagni (Vercelli), M. Helin (Helsinki); soloist of Kirov (now Mariinsky) Theatre 1990–; début in USA 1988 (La Bohème, Boston), in UK 1990 (Forza del Destino, Glasgow); perm. soloist of Metropolitan Opera 1990–, Wiener Staatsoper 1991–; guest singer at La Scala, Chicago Lyric Opera, Mariinsky Opera, La Monnaie (Brussels) and other theatres of Europe and America; leading parts in operas Queen of Spades, Boris Godunov, Barber of Seville, La Traviata, Eugene Onegin, Don Carlos, War and Peace, The Masked Ball, Faust, Rigoletto, Falstaff; in concerts and recitals performs opera arias, song cycles of Mahler, Tchaikovsky, romances. *Address:* c/o Columbia Artists Management Inc., 165 West 57th Street, New York, NY 10019, USA. *Telephone:* (212) 799-8721.

**CHERNYKH, Pavel;** Singer (Baritone); b. 1960, Moscow, Russia. *Education:* Studied at Tchaikovsky Music School and with Yevgeny Nesterenko at the Moscow Conservatoire. *Career:* Debut: Stage Debut in season 1989–90 as Tchaikovsky's Onegin at the Bolshoi; Concerts and recordings with the Maly State Symphony, the St Petersburg Philharmonic and the Moscow Radio Orchestras, 1987–; Further performances as Silvio in Pagliacci, Robert in Tchaikovsky's Iolanta, Yeletsky in The Queen of Spades and Renato (Ballo in Maschera); Sang Onegin at the Paris Opéra Comique, 1987 and for the Vlaamse Opera in Antwerp, 1990; Stars of the Bolshoi Theatre concerts in Germany and Norway, 1990; Toured with the Bolshoi as Onegin to the USA, 1990 and sang at the Wolf Trap Theatre, Washington DC; Edinburgh Festival as Onegin, 1991; Sang Germont at St Petersburg, 1998. *Address:* c/o Sonata, 11 Northpark Street, Glasgow G20 7AA, Scotland.

**CHESWORTH, David (Anthony);** Composer and Sound Designer; b. 31 March 1958, Stoke, England. *Education:* BA (Hons), La Trobe University, 1979; National Young Composers School, 1986. *Career:* Sound Design School, 1987–92; Freelance Composer, 1993–; Commissions from Paris Autumn Festival, 1985; Melbourne Festival, 1990–91; Australian Broadcasting Corporation, 1993. *Compositions include:* Choral, for piano, 1982; Stories of Imitation and Corruption for orchestra and tape, 1986; Lacuna, chamber opera, 1992; Duet I for violin, cello and vibraphones, 1993; Exotica Suite for ensemble, 1993; The Soft Skin for cello, clarinet and piano, 1993; The Two Executioners, chamber opera, 1994; Focal Wall Soundscape, 1995; Cosmonart, opera commissioned by Opera Australia, 1997; Olympic Stadium Sound Environment, commissioned by the Olympic Co-ordination Authority, 1999. *Honours:* Prix Ars Electronica, Austria, 1993. *Address:* c/o APRA, 1A Eden Street, Crows Nest, NSW 2065, Australia.

**CHEW, Geoffrey (Alexander);** British university professor; b. 23 April 1940, South Africa; s. of James Alexander Chew and Florence Hilda Chew; m. Jennifer Comrie, 22 July 1967, 1 s., 2 d. *Education:* Royal Coll. of Music, 1958–61; Caius Coll., Cambridge 1961–64; BA, 1963; MusB, 1964; PhD, Manchester Univ., 1968. *Career:* Univ. Lecturer: Johannesburg, 1968–70; Aberdeen, 1970–77, Royal Holloway, Univ. of London, 1977–05; mem, Royal Musical Asscn, American Musicological Soc., Gesellschaft für Musikforschung, International Musicological Soc., Soc. for Music Theory. *Contributions:* Journal of The American Musicological Society; Music Analysis;

Musiktheorie; Cambridge Opera Journal. *Address:* Department of Music, Royal Holloway, University of London, Egham Hill, Egham, Surrey TW20 0EX (office); The Mount, Malt Hill, Egham, Surrey TW20 9PB, England (home). *Telephone:* (1784) 443537. *Fax:* (1784) 439441. *E-mail:* chew@sun.rhul .ac.uk.

**CHI, Jacob;** Music Director and Conductor; b. 9 Dec. 1952, Qingdao, Shandong, China; m. Lin Chang, 11 July 1987, 1 s. *Education:* BA, Music, magna cum laude, Siena Heights University, 1985; MM, Violin Performance, University of Michigan, 1987; DMA Orchestra Conducting, Michigan State University, 1996. *Career:* Conductor, Qingdao Opera, China, 1975–80; Music Director, Conductor, Pueblo Symphony, 1991–93, 1996–; Music Director, Conductor, Miami University Symphony Orchestra, 1993–97; Conductor, Colorado Music Festival, 1995–; Conductor, Echtenach International Music Festival, Luxembourg, 1996; mem, Conductors' Guild; American Symphony League; Music Teachers National Association. *Compositions:* Operetta, Apricot Field, 1976. *Recordings:* Festival International, Luxembourg; J C Bach Viola Concerto in C minor; Vivaldi, Four Seasons. *Honours:* First Prize, Fine Art Composition Contest, Shantung, China, 1976. *Address:* 516 W Golfwood Drive, Pueblo West, CO 81007, USA.

**CHIARA, Maria;** Italian singer (soprano); b. 24 Nov. 1939, Oderzo; m. Antonio Cassinelli. *Education:* Conservatorio Benedetto Marcello, Venice, with Maria Carbone. *Career:* début as Desdemona in Otello, Doge's Palace, Venice, 1965, then Rome Opera début 1965; frequent performances in Italy, including Turandot with Plácido Domingo, Verona 1969; débuts Germany and Austria 1970; début La Scala, Milan as Micaela, Carmen 1972; début Royal Opera House, Covent Garden, London, Turandot 1973; début Metropolitan Opera, New York in La Traviata and at Lyric Opera, Chicago in Manon Lescaut 1977; sings in all maj. opera houses of Europe, USA and S. America; opened 1985/86 season at La Scala in Aïda. *Recordings include:* Aïda, Madame Butterfly, Il Segreto di Susanna and a disc of operatic arias (Decca). *Address:* c/o S. A. Gorlinsky Ltd, 33 Dover Street, London, W1X 4NJ, England (office); Národni divaldo, Ostrovní 1, Prague 1, Nové Mesto, Czech Republic.

**CHIHARA, Paul (Seiko);** Composer; b. 9 July 1938, Seattle, Washington, USA. *Education:* Studied with Robert Palmer at Cornell University, with Nadia Boulanger in Paris, Ernst Pepping in Berlin and with Gunther Schuller at the Berkshire Music Center. *Career:* Teacher, University of California, Los Angeles, 1966; Associate Professor, UCLA until 1974; Founded and Directed the Twice Ensemble; Andrew Mellon Professor, California Institute of Technology, 1975; Teacher, California Institute of the Arts, 1976; Composer-in-Residence, San Francisco Ballet, 1980; Commissions from the Boston Symphony Orchestra and the Los Angeles Philharmonic. *Compositions include:* Magnificat for 6 female voices, 1965; Driftwood for string quartet, 1967; Branches for 2 bassoons and percussion, 1968; Forest Music for orchestra, 1970; Windsong for cello and orchestra, 1971; Grass for double bass and orchestra, 1972; Ceremony III for flute and orchestra, 1973; Shinju, ballet, 1975; Missa Carminum, 1975; The Beauty of the Rose is in its Passing for ensemble, 1976; String Quartet (Primavera), 1977; 2 Symphonies, 1975, 1980; Misletoe Bride, ballet, 1978; Concerto for string quartet and orchestra, 1980; Sinfonia Concertante for 9 instruments, 1980; The Tempest, ballet, 1980; Saxophone concerto, 1981; Sequoia for string quartet and tape, 1984; Shogun the Musical, 1990; Forever Escher for saxophone quartet and string quartet, 1995; Sonata for viola and piano, 1997; Minidoka for chorus, percussion and tape, 1998; Concerto for violin, clarinet and orchestra, 1999; Film and television scores; Arrangements for musicals. *Address:* c/o ASCAP, ASCAP Bulding, 1 Lincoln Plaza, NY 10023, USA.

**CHILCOTT, Robert (Bob) Lionel;** composer; b. 9 April 1955, Plymouth, Devon, England; m. Polly Ballard 1981; one s. three d. *Education:* Royal College of Music, London. *Career:* mem. SPNM; Royal Society of Musicians. *Compositions:* Singing by Numbers, 1995; Fragments From His Dish, 1995; City Songs, 1996; Organ Dances, 1996; Friends, 1997; The Elements, 1997. *Address:* c/o Oxford University Press, New Music Promotion, 70 Baker Street, London W1M 1DJ, England.

**CHILINGIRIAN, Levon,** OBE, FRCM, ARCM; British violinist; b. 28 May 1948, Nicosia, Cyprus; nephew of Manoug Parikian; m. Susan Paul Pattie 1983; one s. *Education:* Royal Coll. of Music (RCM), London. *Career:* f. Chilingirian string quartet 1971; has performed in N and S America, Africa, Australasia, Europe and Far East; Prof., RCM 1985; Musical Dir Camerata Roman of Sweden; BBC Beethoven Competition 1969, Munich Duo Competition (with Clifford Benson) 1971. *Recordings include:* ten Mozart quartets, last three Schubert quartets, Debussy and Ravel quartets, Schubert octet and quintet, six Bartok quartets and piano quintet, late and middle Dvořák quartets, Tippett Triple Concerto; music by Panufnik, Tavener, Pärt, Chausson, Grieg, Vierne, Hahn and Komitas (with Chilingirian Quartet). *Honours:* Hon. DMus (Sussex) 1992; Cobbett Medal 1995, Royal Philharmonic Soc. Chamber Music Award 1995. *Address:* 7 Hollingbourne Road, London, SE24 9NB, England. *Telephone:* (20) 7978-9104. *Fax:* (20) 7274-5764.

**CHIN, Unsuk;** South Korean composer; b. 1961, Seoul; m. Maris Gothoni; one s. *Education:* Nat. Univ. of Seoul, studied with György Ligeti in Hamburg. *Career:* work features both electronic and acoustic scores; work has been performed worldwide by Ensemble InterContemporain, Ensemble Modern, Kronos Quartet, London Sinfonietta, pianist Rolf Hinds, violinist Viviane Hagner; works in electronic studio of the Technische Univ., Berlin 1988–; composer-in-residence, Deutsches Symphonie Orchester, Berlin 2001–02.

*Compositions include:* Gestalten 1984, Troerrinnen 1986, Gradus ad infinitum 1989, Akrostichon-Wortspiel (Acrostic-Wordplay) for soprano and ensemble 1991–93, Santika Ekatala 1993, Fantaisie mécanique 1994, ParaMetaString 1996, Klavierkonzert 1996–97, Xi for ensemble and electronics (Bourges Electroacoustic Music Prize) 1998, Miroirs des temps 1999, six Piano Etudes 1999–2000, Kalà 2000, Violinkonzert (Grawemeyer Award for Music Composition 2004) 2001, Doppelkonzert 2002, snagS & Snarls 2003–04, Cantatrix Sopranica 2005. *Recordings:* Electroacoustic Music 1996, Orchestral Works 2005. *Address:* c/o Boosey and Hawkes MP Ltd, Aldwych House, 71–91 Aldwych, London, WC2B 4HN, England (office).

**CHINGARI, Marco;** Singer (Baritone); b. 1963, Rome. *Career:* Sang at Busseto, Italy, 1987–88 in Verdi's Il Corsaro and La Forza del Destino; Appearances at Rome Opera, 1989 in Mascagni's Il Piccolo Marat; Season 1991–92: As Mathieu in Andrea Chénier at Turin and Escamillo in Carmen at Palma; Season 1994–95: As Max in Betly by Donizetti in Bergamo and in Zandonai's Francesca da Rimini at Palermo; Other roles include Michonnet in Adriana Lecouvreur and Verdi's Duke of Mantua; Season 2000 as Tonio in Pagliacci at Bologna and Sharpless in Butterfly at Torre del Lago. *Recordings:* La Fanciulla del West; I Vespri Siciliani. *Honours:* Prizewinner, Voci Verdiane Competition, Busseto. *Address:* c/o Teatro Donizetti, Razza Cavour 14, 24100 Bergamo, Italy.

**CHISSELL, Joan Olive,** ARCM, GRSM; British musicologist; b. 22 May 1919, Cromer, Norfolk, England. *Education:* Royal Coll. of Music. *Career:* Lecturer in Music for Extra-Mural Depts, Univs of London and Oxford 1942–48; piano teacher, Jr Dept, Royal Coll. of Music 1943–53; Asst Music Critic, The Times 1948–79; regular broadcaster for BBC from 1943; reviewer for The Gramophone 1968–2003; jury mem., int. piano competitions including Milan, Leeds, Zwickau, Budapest, Dublin and Sydney, Australia; mem. Critics' Circle, Royal Coll. of Music Soc. *Publications:* Robert Schumann 1948, Chopin 1965, Schumann's Piano Music 1972, Brahms 1977, Clara Schumann: A Dedicated Spirit 1983; contrib. to A Companion to the Concerto 1988, Benjamin Britten (A Symposium), Chamber Music, The Concerto, numerous journals and magazines, including Radio Times and The Listener. *Honours:* Robert Schumann Prize, Zwickau 1991.

**CHITTY, Alison Jill,** OBE; British stage designer; b. 1960, England. *Education:* St Martin's School of Art, Central School of Art and Design, London. *Career:* designs for premiere production of Tippett's New Year, at Houston and Glyndebourne 1989–90, premieres of Birtwistle's Gawain 1991, Goehr's Arianna at Covent Garden, Jenůfa in Dallas, Billy Budd in Geneva, Paris, Los Angeles and London, Giulio Cesare and Der fliegende Holländer in Bordeaux, Khovanshchina for ENO, Turandot in Paris, Otello in Munich, Tristan und Isolde at Chicago and Seattle, Die Meistersinger in Copenhagen, Aida in Geneva, Dialogues des Carmélites for Santa Fe Opera, premiere production of Birtwistle's The Last Supper at Berlin and Glyndebourne 2000–01; Dir, Motley Theatre Design Course. *Address:* c/o Glyndebourne Festival Opera, Glyndebourne, Lewes, Sussex BN8 5UU, England.

**CHIUMMO, Umberto;** Singer (Bass, Baritone); b. 1970, Italy. *Education:* Pescara Conservatoire. *Career:* Engagements as Dulcamara at Parma, Enrico in Anna Bolena at Washington and Raimondo in Lucia di Lammermoor for Welsh National and New Israeli Operas; Gounod's Mefistofele at Como, Frère Laurent at the Opéra Comique, Fenicio in Rossini's Ermione at La Monnaie, Brussels, and Alidoro in Houston; Don Giovanni at Sassari, Leporello in Turin and Publio in La Clemenza di Tito for Welsh National Opera; Count in Le nozze di Figaro for Rome Opera, and Bartolo at La Scala, Milan; Ariodate in Xerxes at Monaco and Ircano in Ricciardo e Zoraide at the Rossini Opera Festival, Pesaro; Glyndebourne Tour 1994, 1996 as Rossini's Basilio and Mozart's Figaro; Garibaldo in Handel's Rodelinda at the Festival, 1998; Season 1998–99 as Raimondo in Toulouse, Leporello in Turin, and Ariodate for the Bayerische Staatsoper, Munich. *Address:* c/o Glyndebourne Festival Opera, Lewes, Sussex, BN5 5UU, England. *Telephone:* 01273 812321. *Fax:* 01273 812783.

**CHLITSIOS, George;** Conductor and Lecturer; b. 25 March 1969, Volos, Greece. *Education:* Studied Viola, Piano, Composition, Conducting, Epirotic Conservatory, Ioannina, Greece; Rotterdam Conservatorium and Royal (Koninklijk) Conservatorium, Hague, Netherlands; London College of Music; Thames Valley University. *Career:* Debut: Conductor, Tsakalof Youth Symphony Orchestra, 1989; Principal Conductor, Tsakalof Symphony Orchestra, 1993–97; Guest Conductor, LCM Symphony Orchestra, 1994; Guest Conductor, Athens State Orchestra, 1997; Principal Conductor, Epirus Opera House, Greece, 1997–; Music Director, Tsakalof Symphony Orchestra, 1997–; Concerts in Greece, France, England, Germany; Conducted many world premieres of symphonic works; Appearances in television and radio networks in Greece and abroad. *Honours:* Scholarship, Academy of Athens, 1993; Representative Conductor for Greece, VE-Day Celebrations, London, 1995; Medal, Mayor of Ioannina, Greece, 1995; Medal, Mayor of Kifisia, Greece, 1996. *Address:* c/o Tsakalof Symphony Orchestra, Platia G, Stavrou 5, 454 44 Ioannina, Greece.

**CHMURA, Gabriel;** Conductor; b. 7 May 1946, Wrocław, Poland; m. Mareile Chmura, 1 s., 1 d. *Education:* Diploma (Conducting), Vienna Academy of Music; Ecole Normale de Musique, Paris; MA, Piano and Composition, Tel-Aviv University. *Career:* Assistant to Karajan, 1971–73; Generalmusikdirektor, Aachen, 1974–82; Bochum Symphony Orchestra, 1982–87; Music Director-Designate, 1986–87, Principal Conductor, Music Director, 1987–90,

National Arts Centre Orchestra, Ottawa, Canada; Guest Conductor: Berlin Philharmonic Orchestra; Vienna Symphony Orchestra; London Symphony Orchestra; Orchestre Nationale de France, Paris; Tonhalle Orchester, Zürich; North German Radio Symphony Orchestra; Bavarian Radio Symphony Orchestra, Munich; South German Radio Symphony Orchestra, Stuttgart; New York Philharmonic Orchestra; Paris Opéra; Bavarian State Opera, Munich; Conducted Werther at Parma, 1990; Music Director, Ottawa and American orchestras, 1991–97. *Compositions:* Pièce pour piano, 1968; 3 Songs for soprano and piano; Text James Joyce. *Recordings include:* Mendelssohn Overtures with London Symphony Orchestra; Schubert, Lazarus; Haydn Symphonies 6, 7, 8 with National Arts Centre Orchestra, Canada. *Honours:* Gold Medal, Guido Cantelli Conducting Competition, Milan, 1971; 1st Prize, Herbert von Karajan Conducting Competition, Berlin, 1971; Prix Mondial du Disque de Montreux, 1983. *Current Management:* TransArt (UK) Ltd, Cedar House, 16 Rutland Street, Filey, YO14 9JB, North Yorkshire, England. *Telephone:* (1723) 515819. *Fax:* (1723) 514678. *E-mail:* transartuk@transartuk.com. *Website:* www.transartuk.com.

**CHODOS, Gabriel;** Pianist and Teacher; b. 7 Feb. 1939, White Plains, New York, USA. *Education:* BA, Philosophy, 1959, MA, Music, 1964, University of California, Los Angeles; Diploma in Piano, Akademie für Musik, Vienna, 1966. *Career:* Debut: Carnegie Recital, New York City, 1970; Appearances throughout USA; Numerous tours of Europe, Israel and Japan; Solo performances with Chicago Symphony Orchestra, Radio Philharmonic, Netherlands, Jerusalem Symphony Orchestra and Aspen Chamber Symphony; Masterclasses at Aspen Festival, Rutgers Summer Festival, Chautauqua Festival, Hochschule für Musik, Leipzig, Toho Conservatory, Kunitachi Music University, Osaka University of Arts and elsewhere throughout Japan. *Recordings:* Schubert's Sonata in B-flat major and smaller works; Encore Favourites; Bartók's Sonata; Bloch's Visions and Prophecies; Franck's Prélude, Aria et Final; Berlinsky's Sonata for Violin and Piano; Beethoven's Sonata op. 111; Schubert's Moments Musicaux, Schubert's Sonata in G major, Brahms Klavierstücke op.76. *Address:* 245 Waban Avenue, Waban, MA 02468, USA.

**CHOJNACKA, Elisabeth,** MA; French harpsichordist; b. 10 Sept. 1939, Warsaw, Poland; d. of Tadeusz Chojnacki and Edwarda Chojnacka; m. Georges Lesèvre 1966. *Education:* Warsaw Acad. of Music, Ecole Supérieure de Musique and with Aimée van de Wiele, Paris. *Career:* first recital of contemporary harpsichord, L'Arc, Paris 1971; interpreter of harpsichord works by many contemporary composers including Xenakis, Ligeti, Halffter, Donatoni, Ferrari, Bussotti, Górecki, Takemitsu etc.; many works for modern harpsichord written for her and dedicated to her; has created completely new repertoire for solo modern harpsichord, initiated repertoire combining harpsichord with organ, percussion, bandéon, orchestra; soloist with Orchestre de Paris, Cleveland and Minneapolis Orchestras 1974, Suisse Romande Orchestra 1979, Orchestre National de France 1981; Prof. of Contemporary Harpsichord, Mozarteum Acad. of Music, Salzburg 1995–; numerous tours in Europe, USA, Japan and Mexico; appearances at prin. festivals of contemporary music; master classes; collaborates with choreographer Lucinda Child 1991–; numerous recordings of classical and contemporary music. *Publications:* articles in La Revue Musicale. *Honours:* First Prize, Int. Harpsichord Competition, Vercelli, Italy 1968; Orphée Prize 1981, 2000, Grand Prix de la SACEM 1983; Chevalier Légion d'honneur, Officier des Arts et des Lettres, Croix d'Officier Ordre de Mérite pour la Pologne. *Address:* 17 rue Emile Dubois, 75014 Paris, France. *Telephone:* 1-45-89-52-82 (office); 1-45-82-52-82. *Fax:* 1-45-65-31-90 (office).

**CHOO, David Ik-sung,** BMus, MMus, DMusA; South Korean conductor; b. 10 Sept. 1962, Seoul. *Education:* California State University, Northridge, University of Southern California, Peabody Conservatory of Music, studied conducting with Frederik Prausnitz, violin with Manuel Compinsky, Miwako Watanabe and Kathleen Lenski, piano with Nobuko Fujimoto. *Career:* debut as Guest Conductor, Aspen Concert Orchestra, 1988; Central Philharmonic Orchestra of China, Beijing, 1991; Conductor: US Chamber (assistant) and Symphony Orchestras (guest); Washington Central Choir and Central Orchestra; Los Angeles Orchestra; The Central Philharmonic Orchestra of China (guest); The Savaria Symphony Orchestra (guest), Hungary, 1992; Ploisti Philharmonic Orchestra (guest), Romania, 1994; St Petersburg Congress Orchestra (Guest), Russia, 1995; Hradec Kralove Philharmonic (guest), Czech Republic, 1995; St Petersburg Hermitage Orchestra (guest), 1997; Seoul Philharmonic Orchestra (guest), 1998; Savannah Symphony Orchestra (guest), 1998; Music Director of Columbia Camerata Musica Chamber Orchestra and Chesapeake Youth Symphony Orchestra; Bavaria Symphony Orchestra. *Publications:* Doctoral Dissertation on Franco Leoni's L'Oracolo: A Study in Orientalism, 1998. *Honours:* Prizewinner, Nicolai Malko Conducting Competition, Copenhagen, 1992. *Address:* 4808 Circling Hunter Dr #203, Columbia, MD 21045, USA.

**CHOOKASIAN, Lili;** Singer (Mezzo-Soprano); b. 1 Aug. 1921, Chicago, Illinois, USA. *Education:* Studied with Philip Manuel in New York and with Rosa Ponselle in Baltimore. *Career:* Debut: Chicago Symphony Orchestra conducted by Bruno Walter in Mahler, 1957; Stage debut Little Rock 1959, as Adalgisa in Norma; New York debut 1962, in Prokofiev's Alexander Nevsky; Metropolitan Opera debut 1962, as La Cieca in La Gioconda; Returned as Wagner's Erda and in Suor Angelica, Pelléas et Mélisande, IL Tabarro and Falstaff; New York City Opera 1963, The Medium by Menotti; Appearances at Salzburg, Bayreuth (Erda 1965), Mexico City, Hamburg and Buenos Aires;

Created the Queen in Inès de Castro by Pasatieri (1976); Other roles include Amneris, Azucena, Mary in Der fliegende Holländer, Ulrica, and Madelon in Andrea Chénier; Concert engagements with major US orchestras. *Recordings:* Symphony No. 2 by Yardumian and Mahler's Das Lied von der Erde, with the Philadelphia Orchestra; Götterdämmerung; Mahler 2; Beethoven 9.

**CHORZEMPA, Daniel Walter,** PhD; American pianist, organist, musicologist and composer; b. 7 Dec. 1944, Minneapolis; s. of Martin Chorzempa Sr and Henrietta Reiswig. *Education:* Univ. of Minnesota. *Career:* fmr church organist; Organ Instructor, Univ. of Minn. 1962–65; Fulbright Scholar, Cologne 1965–66; extensive piano and organ recitals in Germany, Denmark, Italy and UK 1968–. *Recordings:* major works of Liszt for Philips. *Honours:* J. S. Bach Prize, Leipzig 1968. *Address:* 5000 Cologne 1, Grosse Budengasse 11, Germany. *Telephone:* 231271.

**CHOU, Wen-Chung;** American composer; *Director of Center, US-China Arts Exchange, Columbia University;* b. 29 July 1923, Chefoo (Yentai), China; m. Yi-An; two s. *Education:* New England Conservatory with Slonimsky, Columbia University with Otto Luening, studied with Edgar Varèse, Bohuslav Martinu. *Career:* teacher at several American univs; Prof. of Composition, Columbia Univ. 1964–91, Dir of Center, US-China Arts Exchange 1978–; Dir Fritz Reiner Center for Contemporary Music, School of the Arts 1984–91, Acting Dean 1987, Chair. Music Div. 1969–89; ed Varèse works, including Amériques 1972, Intégrales 1980, Octandre 1980, Dance for Burgess 1998; ed and completed Varèse works Nocturnal 1972, Tuning Up 1998; Rockefeller Foundation grant 1954; Guggenheim Fellowships 1955, 1956. *Compositions:* Landscapes for orchestra 1949, All in the Spring Wind for orchestra 1952–53, And The Fallen Petals for orchestra 1956, The Willows are New 1957, Soliloquy of a Bhiksuni for solo trumpet, brass and percussion ensemble 1958, Metaphors for wind orchestra 1961, Cursive for flute and piano 1963, Yü Ko for chamber ensemble 1965, Pien for piano, ten winds and percussion 1969, Yün for winds, two pianos and percussion 1969, Peking in the Mist for 11 players 1986, Echoes from the Gorge for percussion quartet 1989, Windswept Peaks for violin, cello, clarinet and piano 1990, Concerto for violoncello and orchestra 1992, Clouds for string quartet 1997, Streams for string quartet 2003. *Honours:* Hon. life mem. Asian Composers' League 1981, elected to the Inst. of the American Acad. 1982, Hon. Prof. of Musical Composition, Central Conservatory of Music, Beijing 2004; Gold Dragon Award for Writers and Artists, Hong Kong 1998; Officier, Ordre des Arts et des Lettres 2000. *Address:* Spiralis Music Trust, 188 Sullivan Street, New York, NY 10012, USA (office). *Telephone:* (212) 473-2661 (office). *Fax:* (212) 673-0724 (office). *E-mail:* cwc@spiralismusic.org (office). *Website:* www.chouwenchung .org (office).

**CHOWNING, John (MacLeod);** Composer and Teacher; b. 22 Aug. 1934, Salem, New Jersey, USA. *Education:* BM, Wittenberg University, Springfield, Ohio, 1959; Studied with Nadia Boulanger, Paris, 1959–62; PhD, Stanford University, 1966. *Career:* Teacher, 1966–, Director, Computer Music and Acoustics Project, 1966–74, Center for Computer Research in Music and Acoustics (CCRMA), 1975, Professor of Music, 1979, at Stanford University; Inventor of FM sound synthesis. *Compositions:* Pieces for computer-generated quadrophonic sound including: Sabelithe, 1971; Turenas, 1972; Stria, 1977; Phone, 1981. *Recordings:* Music with Computers, John Chowning. *Publications:* FM Theory and Applications, 1986. *Contributions:* The Simulation of Moving Sound Sources, 1972, The Synthesis of Complex Audio Spectra by Means of Frequency Modulation, 1973, both to Journal of the Audio Engineering Society. *Honours:* National Endowment for the Arts Grants; Commissions from Institut de Recherche et de Coordination Acoustique/ Musique; Fellow, American Academy of Arts and Sciences, 1988; Awarded the Hooker Chair by the School of Humanities and Sciences at Stanford, 1993; Diplôme d'Officier dans l'Ordre des Arts et Lettres 1995. *Address:* c/o Center for Computer Research in Music and Acoustics, Music Department, Stanford University, Stanford, CA 94305-8180, USA.

**CHRETIEN, Raphaël;** Cellist; b. 17 Feb. 1972, Paris, France. *Education:* National Superior Conservatory. *Career:* Played, Europe: Barbican Hall, 1993, Théâtre des Champs Elysées, 1994; Basel Symphonic Hall, 1995; USA: Marlboro Music Festival, 1994, 1995; Japan: Touring Major Halls, 1994; Appearances with Prague Television and Radio, Philharmonic Orchestra, Dvořák, 1994, Basel Symphony Orchestra, Lalo, 1995, Cannes Philharmonic Orchestra, Tchaikovsky, 1994; Cello Teacher, Bordeaux National Conservatory. *Recordings:* Piatti, Caprices for Solo Cello; Brahms Trio Op.114; H Duparc and G Ropartz, Sonatas. *Honours:* 1st Prize Cello and Chamber Music, National Superior Conservatory, Paris; Vienna, 1993, Prague, 1994, Trapani and Belgrade, 1995, International Cello Competitions. *Current Management:* European Artistic Management, Paris. *Address:* 15 rue Hermel, 75018 Paris, France.

**CHRIBKOVA, Irena,** MgA; Czech organist; b. 22 July 1959, Bohumin. *Education:* Kromeriz Conservatory, Prague Academy of Music, Conservatoire National de Rueil-Malmaison, Paris, international organ masterclasses in Rotterdam, Biarritz, Porrentruy. *Career:* debut, Prague, 1981; solo organ recitals at int. festivals: Olomouc, Paris, 1985; Brno, Ljubljana, 1987; Paris 1988; Piran, Slovakia, 1992; Warsaw, Poland, Auxerre and Bourges, France 1993; Hamburg, Germany 1994; Prague, Czech Republic, Wisla, Warsaw, Fromborg, Poland 1995; Swedish Premiere of Faust, for Organ and Reciter by Peter Eben, 1995; Slovenia Premiere of Faust and Four Biblical Dances by Peter Eben, Ljubljana 1995; Berlin, Traunstein, Germany, Monte Carlo,

Bourges, Prague, 1996; Berlin, Chartres, France, Serravalle Sesia, Italy, Hanover, Germany, 1997; TV broadcasts of concerts in Piran, 1992 and Warsaw, 1995; performed in Tokyo and Yokohama, Japan 2002; Czech Premiere of The Labyrinth of the World (organ and speaker) 2004; Dir, Int. Organ Festival, St James's Basilica, Prague; titular organist of St James's Basilica in Prague; mem. of juries at several int. organ competitions; Contrib. Organiste (periodical) 2002–. *Recordings:* Organs and Composing Organists of Prague St James's Basilica, 1996; Music of Paris Churches and Cathedrals, 2003. *Address:* Nádrazní 19, 150 00 Prague 5, Czech Republic. *Telephone:* (604) 20-84-90 (office). *E-mail:* auditeorganum@volny.cz (office); chribkova@ seznam.cz (home). *Website:* www.audileorganum.cz (office); www .irenachribkova.cz (home).

**CHRIST, Wolfram;** German violist; b. 17 Oct. 1955, Hachenburg. *Education:* studied at Freiburg. *Career:* prizewinner ARD competition, Munich 1976; numerous solo concertos with conductors such as Abbado, Metha, Karajan, Maazel, Ozawa, Kubelik with Berlin Philharmonic, Munich Philharmonic, Hamburg Philharmonic, Czech Philharmonic and other orchestras throughout the world; principal violist, Berlin Philharmonic Orchestra 1978–. *Recordings:* Bartók Viola Concerto, Ozawa, BPO; Berlioz Harold in Italy, Maazel, BPO; Hindemith Viola Concerto, Abbado, BPO; Mozart Sinfonia Concertante, Abbado, BPO; Plays regularly at international festivals as soloist and chamber musician. *Address:* c/o Stiftung Berliner Philharmoniker, Herbert-von-Karajan-Str. 1, 10785 Berlin, Germany. *Website:* www.berlin -philharmonic.com.

**CHRISTENSEN, Dieter;** Professor of Ethnomusicology; b. 17 April 1932, Berlin, Germany; m. Nerthus Karger; one s. one d. *Education:* cello, Berlin State Conservatory; PhD, musicology, Free Univ., Berlin 1957. *Career:* debut, RIAS Radio, Berlin, 1949; taught at Univ. of Berlin and Hamburg, then at Wesleyan Univ., City Univ. of New York, USA and Universidade Nova, Lisbon, Portugal; Prof. and Dir, Center for Ethnomusicology, Columbia Univ., New York; Co-Dir, UNESCO project The Universe of Music: A History, –1993; Ed., UNESCO Collection of Traditional Music, 1994–2002. *Recordings:* Lappish folk songs; Kurdish folk music; Yugoslav folk music; Traditional Arts of Oman, 1993; A Wedding in Sohar, Oman, 1993. *Publications include:* Die Musik der Kate und Sialum, 1957; Die Musik der Ellice-Inseln (with G. Koch), 1964; Hornbostel Opera Omnia (co-ed.), 1974; Der Ring des Tlalocan, 1977; Musical Traditions in Oman, 1993; Shauqi's Dictionary of Traditional Music in Oman, 1994. *Contributions:* German and international professional journals; book review ed., Journal of Society for Ethnomusicology; Ed., Yearbook for Traditional Music. *Address:* Department of Music, Columbia University, New York, NY 10027, USA.

**CHRISTENSEN, Jesper (Boje);** Danish harpsichordist, professor and musicologist; *Professor, Schola Cantorum, Basel;* b. 3 Dec. 1944, Copenhagen, Denmark; 1 d. *Education:* Diploma, Composition, Theory, Pianoforte, Royal Danish Academy of Music, 1971. *Career:* numerous concerts and masterclasses at most major festivals and centres of Ancient Music; Prof. Schola Cantorum, Basel 1988–; Visiting Prof. Conservatoire Supérieur de Musique, Lyon 1989–2000, Centre de Musique Ancienne, Geneva 1989–98, Hochschule für Musik, Würtzburg 1992–95, Kunstuniversitat Graz (Abteilung Alte Musik 2004–05, Univ. de Basilicata, Potenza 2005–; mem. jury, Festival van Vlaanderen, International Harpsichord Competition 1992–; Founder and Musical Director ensemble Arcomelo 1997; recognized world-leading authority on basso continuo; also specializing in performance practice including romantic interpretation as documented on earliest historical recordings. *Recordings:* J. Mattheson, 12 Sonatas, for traverso and harpsichord; A. Corelli op 5 Sonatas, for violin and basso continuo; Corelli op 6 Concerti Grossi; G. Muffat, Armonico Tributo; F. A. Bonporti, Invenzioni op 10, for violin and basso continuo; F. Geminiani, Six Sonatas for Violoncello and basso continuo; Timewave (world music, jazz, flamenco). *Publications:* Der Generalbass bei Bach und Händel 1985, Die Grundlagen des Generalbass-Spiels im 18 Jahrhundert 1992, French ed. 1994, English ed. 2002, Italian ed. 2003: 18th Century Continuo Playing, Generalbass, article in new MMG 1996, Zu einigen Heiligen Kühers des Generalbass-Spiels im 20 Jahrhundert 1995, Francesco Maria Veracini über das Dirigieren 2000. *Honours:* Carl Nielsen Prize, Copenhagen, 1971. *Address:* Schillerstrasse 29/13, A-8010 Graz, Austria.

**CHRISTENSEN, Mogens;** Composer and Assistant Professor; b. 7 April 1955, Laesoe, Denmark; m. Helle Kristensen. *Education:* Diploma in Music History and Music Theory, Royal Academy of Music, Århus, 1983; Teaching Certificate, Royal Academy of Music, Århus, 1983; Diploma in Composition, Royal Academy of Music, Århus, 1988; MMus, University of Århus, 1992; Soloist Diploma (PhD) in Composition, Royal Academy of Music, Copenhagen, 1993. *Career:* Debut: As a Composer, Denmark, 1982; His music has been performed in almost all European countries, in USA and South America. Being prizewinner at the UNESCO Composers International Rostrum, 1994, his piece Winter Light was broadcast all over the world; Composer-in-Residence (Copenhagen Philharmonic Orchestra); Teacher, Royal Academies of Music, Copenhagen and Århus, Academies of Music in Aalborg and Esbjerg and the Universities of Århus and Aalborg; Assistant Professor, Academy of Music, Esbjerg; mem, Danish Composers Society. *Compositions include:* Orchestral, Zurvan Akarana, 1986; Dreams within Dreams, 1st Violin Concerto, 1990; Las flores del mar de la muerte, 2nd Violin Concerto, 1993; Circulus Stellae, 1998; Crystalline Light, 1999; Chamber works, Orphian Fire Mountains, 1988; The Lost Poems of Princess Ateh, 1991; The Khazarian Mirrors, 1993; Vocal works, Hyperions Schicksalslied, 1982; Pessimisticum,

1993; Systema Naturae, chamber opera, 1998. *Recordings:* Mogens Christensen, Vocal and Chamber Music vol. I, 1991, vol. II, 1993, vol. III, 1995; Odriozola and Kristensen play Christensen and Odriozola (including Winter Light), 1995; 1994 Ensemble Nord (including The Lost Poems of Princess Ateh), 1992; Music for Solo Instruments, vol. I, 1998; Music for Recorder, 1999; Systema Naturae, 2001. *Publications:* Winter Light, 1994; 3 Works for Violin Solo, 1995. *Contributions:* Betrachtungen Über den Tonalitätsbegriff bei Edvard Grieg und Carl Nielsen (from Die Gratulanten kommen, 1993). *Honours:* Artist Prize of the County of Bergen, 1991; Artist Scholarship of the Danish State, 1993–95; Prizewinner, UNESCO Composers International Rostrum, 1994. *Address:* Stavnsholtvej 161, 3520 Farum, Denmark.

**CHRISTESEN, Robert;** Singer (Baritone); b. 15 Feb. 1943, Washington DC, USA. *Education:* Studied at the Manhattan School of Music and at Aspen School of Music with Aksel Schiotz and Jennie Tourel. *Career:* Debut: Henrik in Maskarade by Nielsen at St Paul, 1972; Sang with the Frankfurt and Dortmund Operas (1973–80) and appeared as guest Berlin (Komische Oper), Copenhagen, Budapest, Warsaw, Toulouse, Brno, Prague and in North and South America; Other roles have included Mozart's Count and Don Giovanni, Verdi's Ford, Germont and Luna, Eugene Onegin, Jochanaan, Rossini's Figaro, Kaspar in Der Freischütz and Lescaut in Henze's Boulevard Solitude.

**CHRISTIE, Sir George William Langham,** Kt, CH; British music administrator; b. 31 Dec. 1934, s. of John Christie, CH and Audrey Mildmay Christie; m. Patricia Mary Nicholson 1958; three s. one d. *Education:* Eton Coll. *Career:* Asst to Sec. of Calouste Gulbenkian Foundation 1957–62; Chair. Glyndebourne Productions 1956–99; mem. Arts Council of GB and Chair. Music Panel 1988–92; Founder Chair. of London Sinfonietta. *Honours:* Hon. mem. Guildhall School of Music and Drama 1991; DL; Hon. FRCM 1986; Hon. FRNCM 1986; Hon. DMus (Sussex) 1990, (Keele) 1993; Hon. DLitt (Exeter) 1994. *Address:* Old House, Moor Lane, Ringmer, E Sussex, BN8 5UR, England (home).

**CHRISTIE, Michael;** American conductor; *Music Director, Phoenix Symphony Orchestra;* b. 30 June 1974, New York. *Education:* Oberlin College Conservatory of Music. *Career:* Conducting engagements with the Los Angeles and Buffalo Philharmonics, the Lahti Symphony and the Helsinki and Tampere (Finland) Philharmonics, Royal Scottish National Orchestra; United Kingdom debut with the City of Birmingham Symphony Orchestra, 1996; Season 1997–98, Assistant to Franz Welser-Möst, Zürich Opera; Apprentice Conductor, Chicago Symphony Orchestra, 1995–96; Music Dir, Colorado Music Festival, 2000–; Chief Conductor, The Queensland Orchestra 2001–04; Music Dir Phoenix Symphony Orchestra 2005–; engagements with Swedish Radio Symphony; Netherlands Radio Symphony; Royal Liverpool Philharmonic; NDR Hannover; Czech Philharmonic; Orchestre Philharmonique de Luxembourg; DSO Berlin; Los Angeles Philharmonic; Dallas Symphony; Atlanta Symphony; Florida Philharmonic. *Honours:* Prize for Outstanding Potential at the First International Sibelius Conductors' Competition, Helsinki, 1995. *Current Management:* IMG Artists, 616 Chiswick High Road, London, W4 5RX, England. *Telephone:* (20) 8233-5800. *Fax:* (20) 8233-5801. *E-mail:* cdennes@imgworld.com; artistseurope@imgworld.com. *Website:* www.imgartists.com.

**CHRISTIE, Nan;** Singer (soprano); b. 6 March 1948, Irvine, Scotland. *Education:* Royal Scottish Academy of Music; London Opera Centre. *Career:* Repertoire with Scottish Opera includes Britten's Tytania, Rimsky's Queen of Shemakha, The Queen of Night and Zerbinetta in Ariadne auf Naxos; Tours to Portugal, Poland, Switzerland and Germany; Sang in Mozart's La Finta Giardiniera and the premiere of Oliver's Tom Jones, with English Music Theatre; Tytania with Opera North; Isotta in Die schweigsame Frau and Despina in Così fan tutte, at the Glyndebourne Festival; Zdenka in Arabella, the Queen of Night and Offenbach's Eurydice with English National Opera; European engagements with Netherlands Opera, Despina, Opéra de Nancy as Pamina; Zürich Opera in the Ponnelle production of Lucio Silla and Frankfurt Opera as Zerbinetta, Marie in Die Soldaten and Susanna; Scottish Opera, 1990 as Despina in a new production of Così fan tutte; Birdie Hubbard in the British premiere of Blitzstein's Regina, Glasgow, 1991; Concerts at the Hong Kong Festival, Hallé Orchestra, BBC Symphony and London Symphony Orchestra, Nash Ensemble and the London Sinfonietta; Television appearances in Mozart's Schauspieldirektor and Ravel's L'Enfant et les Sortilèges; Italian debut in Mitridate by Mozart, La Fenice, Venice, and the Queen of Night in The Magic Flute for ENO, 1992; Premiere of Jonathan Harvey's Inquest of Love, English National Opera, 1993; Sang Third Official in the premiere of The Doctor of Myddfai, by Peter Maxwell Davies, Cardiff, 1996. *Recordings:* Videos of Glyndebourne Festival Così fan tutte; The Gondoliers, The Sorcerer and Princess Ida. *Current Management:* Askonas Holt Ltd, Lonsdale Chambers, 27 Chancery Lane, London, WC2A 1PF, England. *Telephone:* (20) 7400-1700. *Fax:* (20) 7400-1799. *E-mail:* info@askonasholt.co.uk. *Website:* www.askonasholt.co.uk.

**CHRISTIE, Natalie;** Singer (soprano); b. (Natalie Abrahamson), 17 Jan. 1975, Melbourne, Australia. *Education:* Victorian Coll. of the Arts, Guildhall School of Music and Drama, London, with Rudolf Piernay. *Career:* opera, La Bohème, British Youth Opera 1998, Carmen, Clonter Opera 1998, The Carmelites, WNO 1999, Orphee et Eurydice 2000, Der Rosenkavalier 2000, Le Nozze di Figaro 2001, The Magic Flute 2001, Leonore 2001, Adele in Die Fledermaus 2002; St John Passion (soloist), ENO (debut) 2000; Le Nozze di Figaro, Opera Australia 2000; Zerlina in Don Giovanni, Royal Opera House (debut), London 2002; soloist for BBC Nat. Orchestra of Wales, BBC Concert Orchestra, Tasmanian Symphony Orchestra; Roles for WNO 2002–03 Adele in Die Fledermaus, Adina in The Elixir of Love, Zerlina in Don Giovanni and Susanna in Le Nozze di Figaro. *Honours:* 20th Century Aria prize, Veronica Dunn Singing Competition 1997, Australian Music Foundation Award 1998, Sir John Moores Award, WNO 2000, Finalist Cardiff Singer of the World 2001. *Current Management:* Peter Bloor, Askonas Holt Ltd, Lonsdale Chambers, 27 Chancery Lane, London, WC2A 1PF, England. *Telephone:* (20) 7400-1700. *Fax:* (20) 7400-1799. *E-mail:* info@askonasholt.co.uk. *Website:* www.askonasholt.co.uk.

**CHRISTIE, William Lincoln,** BA; French (b. American) harpsichordist, conductor and musicologist; b. 19 Dec. 1944, Buffalo, NY; s. of William Christie and Ida Jones. *Education:* Harvard Univ., Yale School of Music. *Career:* studied harpsichord with Ralph Kirkpatrick, Kenneth Gilbert and David Fuller; moved to France 1971; mem. Five Centuries Ensemble 1971–75, René Jacobs' Concerto vocale 1976–80; f. Les Arts Florissants vocal and instrumental ensemble 1979; Prof., Conservatoire Nat. Supérieur de Musique, Paris 1982–95; conducts many leading int. orchestras; recent career highlights include Handel's Theodora, Glyndebourne 1996, Handel's Semele, Aix-en-Provence Festival 1996, Rameau's Hippolyte et Aricie, Paris 1996/97, Lully's Thésée, Barbican, London 1998, Monteverdi's Il ritorno d'Ulisse in patria, Aix-en-Provence 2000; conducted the Berlin Philharmonie and led Le jardin des voix, new workshop for young singers, followed by European tour 2002; currently Pres. of the jury Concours de Chant Baroque de Chimay, Belgium. *Recordings:* numerous recordings including all works for harpsichord by Rameau, works by Monteverdi, Purcell, Handel, Couperin, Charpentier, Desmarest, Mozart, etc. *Honours:* Chevalier Légion d'honneur 1993, Officier des Arts et des Lettres, Prix Edison, Netherlands 1981, Grand prix du disque, Prix mondial de Montreux, Switzerland 1982, Gramophone Record of the Year, UK 1984, 1995, 1997, Deutscher Schallplattenpreis 1987, Grand prix de la Critique (best opera performance) 1987, Prix Opus, USA 1987, Prix int. de musique classique 1992, Prix Grand siècle Laurent Perrier 1997, Grammy Award for Handel's Acis and Galatea 2000, Grammy and Cannes Classical Awards for Alcina 2001; Hon. DMus (New York) 1999. *Address:* Les Arts Florissants, 2 rue Saint-Pétersbourg, 75008 Paris (office); 81 avenue Victor Hugo, 75116 Paris (home); Le Bâtiment, Thiré, 85210 Sainte-Hermine, France (home). *E-mail:* w.christie@wanadoo.fr. *Website:* www.arts-florissants.com.

**CHRISTIN, Judith;** Singer (Mezzo-Soprano); b. 15 Feb. 1948, Providence, Rhode Island, USA. *Education:* Studied at Indiana University. *Career:* Sang at first in concert, opera from 1980; Washington Opera from 1981 and at Santa Fe in the US premieres of Weir's A Night at the Chinese Opera, Penderecki's Schwarze Maske and Judith by Matthus; Los Angeles from 1983, San Diego, 1984, Philadelphia, 1986; New York Metropolitan from 1988, in Eugene Onegin, Faust, Die Zauberflöte, Luisa Miller and Le nozze di Figaro; European career from 1987 (Netherlands Opera); Roles have included Despina (Santa Fe, 1988–90), the Hostess in Boris Godunov, Suzuki in Butterfly and Carlotta in Die schweigsame Frau; Santa Fe 1996, as Suzuki and Baba the Turk in The Rake's Progress; Sang in the premiere of Carlisle Floyd's Cold Sassy Tree, Houston 2000. *Address:* c/o Metropolitan Opera, Lincoln Center, New York, NY 10023, USA.

**CHRISTOFF, Dimiter,** DrHabil; Bulgarian composer and academic; b. 2 Oct. 1933, Sofia. *Education:* State Music Acad., Sofia with M. Goleminov, study tours in Germany, USA, France, Netherlands. *Career:* teacher 1960–76, Prof. 1976–, State Music Acad.; Gen. Sec., Int. Music Council, UNESCO 1975–79; leader, Int. Composers' Workshop (a Bulgarian-Dutch initiative) 1977–; Ed.-in-Chief, Scientific Music Magazine, Bulgarian Musicology, Acad. of Sciences 1989–; publisher, Music, Yesterday, Today 1994; mem. Int. Soc. for Music Education, Bulgarian Composers' Union (vice-pres. 1972–85). *Compositions:* operas: The Game 1978, The Golden Fish Line 1984; orchestral: three piano concertos 1954, 1983, 1994, Sinfonietta for strings 1956, Poem 1957, three symphonies 1958, 1964, 1969, Overture 1961, Symphonic Episodes 1962, three violin concertos 1966, 1996, 1997, Chamber Suite for two piccolos, piano, percussion and strings 1966, Cello Concerto 1969, Concert Miniatures 1970, Overture with Fanfares 1974, Quasi una fantasia-gioco 1981, Game for cello and orchestra 1983, Perpetui mobili in pianissimi 1987, Groups Troupes 1988, Silent Adagio 1989, Cantilena Sopra due Toni 1990, Merry-go-round of the Suffering 1991, Collapse in the Silence 1992, Crash Down in the Mute 1992, Up High I Look for You 1993, It Streams It Runs Out 1994, I Rise in the Chaos 1995, I Set It Ajar, Peep In 1996, There High it Shines 1997, In for Millenniums Predicted 2000, Here is So Silent 2000, Vibrating, Burning 2004; chamber: Suite for brass quartet 1953, Two Dances for trumpet and piano 1960, Sonata for solo cello 1965, Concerto for three small drums and five instruments 1967, String Quartet 1970, Quartet for flute, viola, harp and harpsichord 1973, Give Me Solace 1983, piano ensemble music (duo, trio and quartet of piano players), Meditation of a Lonely Violoncello 1991, The Violoncello album dons the Right Hand of the Piano 1992, 18 piano sonatas, Blown Away from the Wind for string orchestra 1993, Await Your Pizzicatti 1994, Sad Silk Bows for violin and accompanying viola 1996, Eroica Variations for piano & strings 2002, Cool and Warm for strings 2002, 12 etudes for harp 2002–04; choruses and songs. *Publications:* Ideas about Fugue Composition in 'Well Tempered Klavier' by J. S. Bach 1968, Hypothesis about Counterpoint Structure 1970, Theoretical Foundations of the Melodic Structure Vols 1–3 1973, 1982, 1989, Composer & Public Awareness 1975. *Honours:* numerous nat. and int. awards including Int. Acad. for the Arts Award (France) 1999. *Address:* Mavrovets 7, 1415 Sofia-Dragalevtsi, Bulgaria. *Telephone:* 2-9672351.

**CHRISTOPHERS, Harry;** British conductor; *Conductor, The Sixteen Choir & The Symphony of Harmony and Invention;* b. 26 Dec. 1953, Goudhurst, Kent; m. Veronica Mary Hayward 2 June 1979; two s. two d. *Education:* Canterbury Cathedral Choir School (Head Chorister), King's School Canterbury; BA, Honours, Music, Magdalen College, Oxford (Academical Clerk). *Career:* f. The Sixteen 1977, The Orchestra of The Sixteen 1986 (newly named The Symphony of Harmony and Invention 1997), Coro (own record label); South Bank debut 1983; Salzburg Festival debut 1989; BBC Prom debut 1990; Lisbon Opera debut 1994; Musikverein, Vienna debut 1998; Concertgebouw, Amsterdam debut 1999; ENO debut 2000; orchestras conducted include BBC Philharmonic, Academy of St Martin-in-the-Fields, London Symphony Orchestra, Hallé Orchestra, Royal Liverpool Philharmonic, English Chamber Orchestra, Northern Sinfonia, City of London Sinfonia, BBC Nat. Orchestra of Wales, Scottish Chamber Orchestra, Avanti!, Tapiola Sinfonietta, Lahti Symphony Orchestra, Helsinki Philharmonic, Bergen Philharmonic; tours with The Sixteen Choir and The Symphony of Harmony and Invention throughout Europe, Scandinavia, Israel, Japan, Australia, USA, Brazil; conducted Messiah at Barbican Hall, London 1999, Handel's Samson at BBC London Proms 2002. *Recordings:* more than 90 recordings, including Taverner's Festal Masses, Vols I–IV 1984–93 and Missa Gloria Tibi Trinitas 1989, Monteverdi's Masses 1987 and Vespers 1988, Handel's Messiah (Grand Prix du Disque 1989) 1989, Chandos Anthems 1990, Alexander's Feast (Deutschen Schallplattenkritik 1992) 1992, Esther 1996, Samson 1997, Italian Cantatas 1998, Byrds's Mass a 5 1989 and Mass a 4 1990, Poulenc's Figure Humaine 1990, Bach's St John Passion 1990, Christmas Oratorio 1993, B Minor Mass 1994, Eton Choir Book vols I–V 1991–95, Sheppard's Sacred Music vols I–IV 1990–92, Teixeira's Te Deum (Diapason d'Or 1992) 1991, Britten's Choral Music 1992–93, Stravinsky's Symphony of Psalms (Diapason d'Or 1995) 1995, Messiaen's Cinq rechants 1996, Scarlatti's Stabat Mater 1997, Victoria's Sacred Music vols I–III 1997–99, Video: Handel's Messiah in Dublin 1992, Tallis: Spem in Alium 2004, Handel Arias: Heroes and Heroines (with Sarah Connolly) 2004, Renaissance (Best Ensemble Album of the Year, Classical BRIT Awards 2005) 2004. *Honours:* Gramophone Early Music Award 1992. *Current Management:* The Sixteen Ltd, New Marston Centre, 1A Jack Straw's Lane, Oxford, OX3 0DL, England. *Telephone:* (1865) 793999. *Fax:* (1865) 793274. *E-mail:* info@thesixteen.org.uk. *Website:* www.thesixteen.com.

**CHRISTOS, Marianna;** Singer (Soprano); b. 1950, Beaver Falls, Pennsylvania, USA. *Career:* Sang with the New York City Opera, 1975–79, debut as Liu in Turandot; Has appeared widely in the USA at Pittsburgh, Washington, St Louis, Houston, Los Angeles and San Francisco; Roles have included Mimi, Gilda, Adina in L'Elisir d'amore, Margharita in Mefistofele, Donna Anna, Donna Elvira, Micaela, and Antonia in Les Contes d'Hoffmann; New Orleans 1985, as Bizet's Leila. *Address:* c/o New York City Opera, Lincoln Center, New York, NY 10023, USA.

**CHRISTOU, Nicolas;** Singer (Bass-baritone); b. 1940, Alexandria. *Education:* Studied in Brussels. *Career:* Sang at Brussels, 1966–81 as Golaud in Pelléas et Mélisande, Philip II in Don Carlos and Wagner's Wotan; Gunther and Kothner; Guest appearances throughout Europe, notably at Liège as the Father in Louise, Grandier in The Devils of Loudun and Pizarro in Fidelio, 1991–95; Festival engagements at Aix-en-Provence, as the Speaker in Die Zauberflöte and at Wexford; Deutsche Oper am Rhein, Düsseldorf, from 1991; Bremen Opera, 1996 as Boris Godunov; Other roles have included Mozart's Figaro and Leporello, Rossini's Basilio; Wagner's Telramund, Pogner, Amfortas and Dutchman; Mandryka in Arabella and Ramphis in Aida; Sang Dr Schön in Lulu at Liège, 1999. *Address:* c/o Bremen Opera, Pf 101046, 2800 Bremen, Germany.

**CHU, Wang-Hua;** Composer and Pianist; b. 5 Sept. 1941, Jiangsu, China. *Education:* BMus, Central Conservatory, Peking, 1963; MMus, University of Melbourne, 1985. *Career:* Piano Department, Central Conservatory of Music, Beijing, China, 1963–82; Freelance composer and pianist in Australia, 1982–; mem, The Australian Music Centre. *Compositions include:* Seven Piano Preludes, and Three Piano Variations, 1961–80; The Yellow River Piano Concerto (co-composer), 1970; The Spring Mirrored the Moon for piano, 1972; Sinjiang Capriccio for piano, 1977; Piano Sonata, 1981; String Quartet, 1983; Ash Wednesday for orchestra, 1984; The Borderland Moon for soprano and ensemble, 1984; Concerto for Chamber Orchestra, 1984; The Bamboo for piano and orchestra, 1986; Drinking Alone by Moonlight for soprano and chamber ensemble, 1985; 30 Chinese Folk Songs for piano, 1979–86; Barcarolle for piano, 1979; Autumn Cry for orchestra, 1988; Symphony, 1988; Sinfonia for chamber orchestra, 1988; The Ancient Battlefield for percussion solo, 1989; Piano Concerto, 1989; Fantasia Symphony: The Silk Road, 1990; Eva, Beloved Mother, for piano, 1993; Air and Variations for choral, 1998. *Recordings:* The Yellow River Piano Concerto, co-composer, 1970, 1980, 1990; Piano Sonata, 1986; A number of piano works, 1980, 1990. *Publications:* The Yellow River Piano Concerto, co-composer, 1975. *Honours:* 1st Prize, Albert Magg's Composition Competition, Australia, 1987. *Address:* 20 Bruce Street, Toorak, Vic 3142, Australia.

**CHUCHROVA, Liubov;** Singer (Soprano); b. 1971, Vilnius, Lithuania. *Education:* Studied at Vilnius, 1985–89; Guildhall School, London. *Career:*

Sang Satirino in La Calisto and Maria in Krenek's Der Diktator at the GSM; Olga in Dargomyzhsky's Rusalka, 1997 Wexford Festival; Other roles include Anne Trulove, The Rake's Progress; Tatiana, Marguerite and Mozart's Vitellia, Vilnius Opera; Gorislava in Ruslan and Lyudmilla for Dorset Opera; Spoleto Festival, 1999; War and Peace; Concerts include Vivaldi's Gloria; Bruch's Das Lied von der Glocke; Rossini's Petite Messe at Tel-Aviv; Mozart's Requiem at the Barbican, London. *Honours:* Winner, Maggie Teyte Competition, GSM. *Address:* c/o Music International, 13 Ardilaun Road, London N5 2QR, England.

**CHUDOVA, Tatiana;** Composer; b. 16 June 1944, Moscow, Russia. *Education:* Studied at the Moscow Central Music School and Conservatory, notably with Khrennikov. *Career:* Teacher in Moscow from 1970. *Compositions include:* Operas: The Dead Princess and the Seven Heroes, 1967, and To the Village, to Grandfather, 1978; 3 Suites for orchestra of folk instruments, 1980–82; Symphonic trilogy, 1981–82, and Symphony No. 4, 1988; Choral, solo vocal and instrumental music, including 2 violin sonatas, 1974, 1987. *Address:* c/o RAO, Bolchaia Bronnai 6-1, Moscow 103670, Russia.

**CHUNG, David Yu Sum,** PhD, MPhil, LRSM, LTCL; Chinese university lecturer; *Assistant Professor and Performance Co-ordinator, Hong Kong Baptist University;* b. 10 April 1968, Hong Kong. *Education:* Guildhall School of Music and Drama, London; Univ. of Cambridge, Chinese Univ. of Hong Kong. *Career:* Asst Prof. and performance co-ordinator at Hong Kong Baptist Univ. 1998–; harpsichordist and musicologist, with performances in Europe, Asia and USA on a variety of historic and modern keyboard instruments; mem. British Clavichord Soc., Royal Musical Asscn, Southeastern Historical Keyboard Soc., American Musicological Soc. *Recordings:* Stylus Phantasticus Works for Harpsichord 2003; contrib. to articles in Early Music 2003, Piano Artistry 2003, Early Keyboard Journal 2001. *Publications:* Jean–Baptiste Lully: 27 Opera Pieces Transcribed for Keyboard in the 17th and 18th Centuries, 2004. *Honours:* Christopher Kite Award 1997, Pres.'s Award for Outstanding Performance 2001. *Address:* Dept of Music and Fine Arts Hong Kong Baptist University, Kowloon Tong, Hong Kong (office). *Telephone:* 3411-7871 (office). *Fax:* 3411-7870 (office). *E-mail:* dchung@hkbu.edu.hk (office). *Website:* www.hkbu.edu.hk (office).

**CHUNG, Kyung-wha;** South Korean violinist; b. 26 March 1948, Seoul; sister of Myung-whun Chung and Myung-wha Chung; m. Geoffrey Leggett 1984; two s. *Education:* Juilliard School, New York with Ivan Galamian. *Career:* started career in USA; European debut 1970; has played with maj. orchestras, including all London orchestras, Chicago, Boston and Pittsburgh Symphony Orchestra, New York, Cleveland, Philadelphia, Berlin, Israel and Vienna Philharmonics, Orchestre de Paris; has toured world; recordings for EMI; played at Salzburg Festival with London Symphony Orchestra 1973, Vienna Festival 1981, 1984, Edinburgh Festival 1981 and at eightieth birthday concert of Sir William Walton March 1982; with Hallé Orchestra, BBC Proms, London 1999. *Recordings:* Concertos by Bartók, Beethoven, Bruch, Mendelssohn, Stravinsky, Tchaikovsky, Vieuxtemps, Walton. *Honours:* winner of Leventritt Competition 1968. *Current Management:* Harrison Parrott Ltd, 12 Penzance Place, London, W11 4PA, England.

**CHUNG, Mia;** Concert Pianist and Assistant Professor of Music; b. 9 Oct. 1964, Madison, Wisconsin, USA. *Education:* BA magna cum laude, Harvard University, 1986; MM, Yale University, 1988; DMA, Juilliard School of Music, 1991. *Career:* Debut: Hall of the Americas, OAS Building, Washington DC, 1983; Assistant Professor of Music and Artist-in-Residence, Gordon College, 1991–; Appearances with Baltimore Symphony Orchestra, 1977, 1981; Performed with National Symphony Orchestra, 1983; Performed with National Gallery Orchestra, 1987; Performed with Fort Collins Symphony Orchestra, 1990; Performed with New Haven Symphony, 1989; Solo Recitals and Chamber Performances at OAS, Alice Tully Hall, National Gallery of Art, the Kennedy Center for Performing Arts, American Academy of Arts and Sciences and other venues; Records exclusively for Channel Classics Records. *Recordings:* Beethoven Bagatelles, Op 126 and Sonatas No. 16 in G major Op 31, No. 1 and No. 32 in C minor Op 111. *Honours:* First Prize in 1981 Johann Sebastian Bach International Competition in New York City, 1993. *Current Management:* Concert Artist Guild. *Address:* Fine Arts Department, Gordon College, Wenham, MA 01984, USA.

**CHUNG, Myung-wha;** South Korean cellist; b. 19 March 1944, Seoul; sister of Myung-whun Chung and Kyung-wha Chung. *Education:* Juilliard School with Leonard Rose, Univ. of Southern California masterclass with Gregor Piatigorsky. *Career:* debut with the Seoul Philharmonic before study in New York; has appeared widely in Europe and North America 1971–, notably in England, Italy, Denmark, Germany, Spain, Sweden, Netherlands, Belgium, France, Switzerland, Portugal, Israel and Mexico; festival appearances at Lucerne, Flanders, Spoleto, Palma de Majorca, Birmingham, Evian and Dijon; television programmes in the USA, England, Germany and Switzerland; plays a 1731 Stradivarius cello known as Braga; Goodwill Ambassador for UN Drug Control Programme 1992–; faculty mem., Mannes Coll. of Music, New York and Korean Nat. Inst. of Arts. *Recordings include:* Tchaikovsky Rococo Variations with the Los Angeles Philharmonic under Charles Dutoit, Ten Piano Trio Works with the Chung Trio. *Honours:* First Prize Geneva Int. Music Competition 1971, Nat. Order of Cultural Merit, Republic of Korea 1992. *Address:* 315 West 70th Street, Suite 5G, New York, NY 10023, USA.

**CHUNG, Myung-whun;** South Korean conductor and pianist; b. 22 Jan. 1953, Seoul; brother of Kyung-wha Chung and Myung-wha Chung. *Educa-*

*tion:* Mannes Coll. of Music and Juilliard School, New York, USA. *Career:* asst to Carlo Maria Giulini as Assoc. Conductor, Los Angeles Philharmonic 1978–81; moved to Europe 1981, conducting Berlin Philharmonic, Munich Philharmonic, Amsterdam Concertgebouw, Orchestre de Paris, major London orchestras; Music Dir and Principal Conductor Radio Orchestra of Saarbrücken 1984–89; in USA has conducted the New York Philharmonic, Nat. Symphony Washington, the Boston Symphony, the Cleveland and Chicago Orchestras, Metropolitan Opera, San Francisco Opera 1986–; Guest Conductor, Teatro Comunale, Florence 1987; Musical Dir Opéra de la Bastille, Paris 1989–94; Covent Garden debut, conducting Otello 1997; Music Dir and Principal Conductor Orchestra of the Nat. Acad. of Santa Cecilia, Rome 1997–2005; conducted the Swedish Radio Symphony Orchestra at the London Proms, playing Beethoven's Fourth Piano Concerto and Nielsen's Fifth 1999; Musical Dir Radio France Philharmonic Orchestra 2000–; f. and Musical Dir Philharmonic Orchestra of Asia. *Honours:* Second Prize Tchaikovsky Competition, Moscow 1974, Abbiati Prize (Italian critics) 1987, Victoires de la Musique Best Conductor, Best Lyrical Production, Best French Classical Recording 1995. *Current Management:* Askonas Holt Ltd, Lonsdale Chambers, 27 Chancery Lane, London, WC2A 1PF, England. *Telephone:* (20) 7400-1700. *Fax:* (20) 7400-1799. *E-mail:* info@askonasholt.co.uk. *Website:* www .askonasholt.co.uk.

**CHURCH, Francis;** Singer (Baritone); b. 1973, Liverpool, England. *Education:* Royal Scottish Academy, with Jeffrey Lawton, and National Opera Studio, London; Mozart and Britten roles with Thomas Allen at the Pears-Britten School. *Career:* Opera roles include Angelotti in Tosca, Benoit in La Bohème, Britten's Starveling and Sid, Guglielmo, and Sharpless in Madama Butterfly; Concerts include Elgar's Coronation Ode, Elijah by Mendelssohn, Messiah, A Child of our Time (Tippett) and Fauré's Requiem. *Honours:* Verdi Prize, National Mozart Competition and John Noble Competition, Scottish Opera. *Address:* c/o National Opera Studio, Morley College, 61 Westminster Bridge Road, London, SE1 7XT, England.

**CHURGIN, Bathia Dina;** American/Israeli musicologist; b. 9 Oct. 1928, New York, NY, USA. *Education:* BA, Hunter Coll., New York City, 1950; MA, Radcliffe Coll., 1952; PhD, Harvard Univ., 1963. *Career:* Instructor to Full Prof., Vassar Coll. 1952–57, 1959–71; Prof., Founding Head of Dept, Bar-Ilan Univ., Ramat Gan, Israel, 1970–84; Visiting Prof., Harvard Summer School, Northwestern Univ., Univ. of North Carolina, Chapel Hill, CUNY, Queens Coll. and Graduate Center, Indiana Univ., Tel-Aviv Univ., The Hebrew Univ., Jerusalem, Rubin Acad. of Music, Jerusalem; Prof. Emer., Bar-Ilan Univ. 1996–; Festschrift published in her honour, JM XVIII, 2001; mem., Israel Musicological Soc. (Chair. 1994–95); American Musicological Soc., Int. Musicological Soc. *Publications:* The Symphonies of G B Sammartini, vol. 1: The Early Symphonies, 1968; Thematic Catalogue of the Works of Giovanni Battista Sammartini, Orchestral and Vocal Music (with Newell Jenkins), 1976; A New Edition of Beethoven's Fourth Symphony 1978; Israel Studies in Musicology II (Ed.), 1980; G B Sammartini, Sonate a tre stromenti, A New Edition with Historical and Analytical Essays, 1981; G B Sammartini: Ten Symphonies, 1984; Israel Studies in Musicology VI (Ed.), 1996; Beethoven's Fourth Symphony (Ed.), 1998. *Contributions:* Professional Journals: Francesco Galeazzi's Description (1796) of Sonata Form, JAMS XXI, 1968; A New Edition of Beethoven's Fourth Symphony: Israel Sudies in Musicology Vol. I 1978, Beethoven and Mozart's Requiem: A New Connection, JM V, 1987; Beethoven's Sketches for his String Quintet, Op 29, LaRue Festschrift, 1990; Harmonic and Tonal Instability in the Second Key Area of Classic Sonata Form, Ratner Festschrift, 1992; Sammartini and Boccherini: Continuity and Change in the Italian Instrumental Tradition of the Classic Period, Chigiana XLIII, 1993; The Andante con moto in Beethoven's String Quartet op 130: The Final Version and Changes on the Autograph, JM XVI, 1998; Beethoven and the New Development. Theme in Sonata-Form Movements, JM XVI, 1998; Exploring the Eroica: Aspects of the New Critical Edition, Tyson Festschrift, 1998, Stormy Interlude: Sammartini's Middle Symphonies and Overtures in Minor in Giovanni Batista Sammartini and his Musical Environment 2004, Recycling Old Ideas in Beethoven's String Quartet Op. 132, Somfai Festschrift 2005. *Honours:* American Council of Learned Socs Fellowships 1964, 1986. *Address:* Department of Music, Bar-Ilan University, Ramat Gan, 52900 (office); Rehov Havazelet 6/3, Kirzon, 55454 Israel (home). *Telephone:* (3) 531-8405 (office); (3) 534-0205 (home). *Fax:* (3) 635-6281 (office). *E-mail:* churgin@mail.biu.ac.il (office).

**CHUSID, Martin;** American musicologist and professor; b. 19 Aug. 1925, Brooklyn, New York; m. Anita B Chusid, 1 s. *Education:* BA, 1950, MA, 1955, PhD, 1961, University of California, Berkeley. *Career:* Teaching Assistant, 1953–55, Associate, 1955–57, University of California, Berkeley; Instructor, 1959–62, Assistant Professor, 1962–63, University of Southern California, Los Angeles; Associate Professor, 1963–68, Professor, 1968–, Acting Chairman, Music Department, 1966–67, 1981, 1986–87, New York University; Chairman, Music Department, Washington Square College of Arts and Sciences, 1967–70; Associate Dean, Graduate School of Arts and Sciences, 1970–72; Director, American Institute for Verdi Studies, 1976–; Visiting Professor of Music: Boston University, 1975, University of British Columbia, 1979, Southern Methodist University, 1980, Princeton University, 1981, Brigham Young University, 1982; Principal Editor, Verdi Newsletter, 1981–96. *Publications:* Schubert's Unfinished Symphony: A Monograph and Edition, 2nd edition, 1971; A Catalog of Verdi's Operas, 1974; The Verdi Companion (with W Weaver), 1979; Editions of works by Schubert and Verdi; Verdi's

Middle Period, 1997; Schubert's Schwanengesang: Facsimiles and Reprint, 2000; A Companion to Schubert's Schwanengesang, 2000. *Contributions:* Articles on Verdi, Schubert, Mozart, Haydn, Dvořák, Performance Practice, to various publications including The Cambridge Companion to Schubert, 1997. *Honours:* Honorary Doctor of Humane Letters, Centre College of Kentucky, 1977. *Address:* Department of Music, New York University, Washington Square, New York, NY 10003 (office); 4 Washington Square Village, New York, NY 10012, USA (home). *Telephone:* (212) 998-8305 (office); (212) 228-6215 (home). *Fax:* (212) 995-4147 (office). *E-mail:* mc4@nyu.edu (office).

**CHYLINSKA, Teresa Wanda,** MA; Polish musicologist, music editor and writer on music; b. 20 June 1931, Wojciechowice; m. 1957 (divorced 1960); one s. *Education:* Jagiellonian Univ., Kraków. *Career:* Chief Dept of Polish Music, Polish Music Publications, Kraków 1954–89; Lecturer, Jagiellonian Univ. and Acad. of Music 1970s; Pres., The Karol Szymanowski Music Soc. 1979–80; mem. scientific bd The Chopin Soc., Warsaw 1982–88. *Publications include:* first critical edn of The Complete Works of Karol Szymanowski (26 vols), complete edn of Szymanowski's correspondence, Vol. 1 1982, Vol. 2 1994, Vol. 3 1997, Vol. 4 2002, Szymanowski's Literary Writings 1989, Szymanowski's Days at Zakopane (fourth edn) 1982, Szymanowski and his Music (popular monograph for young readers, third edn) 1990, Karol Szymanowski, His Life and Works (in English) 1993, K Szymanowski: Lottery for Husbands 1998; contrib. to New Grove Dictionary of Music and Musicians, Encyclopedia Muzyczna PWM, Pipers Enzyklopädie des Musik Theaters, Die Musik in Geschichte und Gegenwart. *Honours:* Jurzykowski Foundation Award, New York 1984, Polish Composers' Union Award 1996, Karol Szymanowski Foundation Award 1997, Noweksiazki Award 2002. *Address:* ul Boguslawskiego 10.13, 31-038 Kraków, Poland (home). *Telephone:* (12) 422-30-18 (home). *E-mail:* TChylinska@interia.pl (home).

**CIANNELLA, Giuliano;** Singer (Tenor); b. 25 Oct. 1943, Palermo, Italy. *Career:* Debut: La Scala 1976, as Cassio in Otello; Metropolitan Opera from 1979, as Don Carlos, Des Grieux in Manon Lescaut, Rodolfo, Pinkerton, Alfredo and Macduff; Guest engagements in San Francisco, as Don José 1984 and Munich, Don Carlos, 1985; Covent Garden debut 1986, as Manrico in Il Trovatore; Verona Arena, 1983, 1986 and 1988; Bregenz Festival 1987, as Ernani; Cologne Opera, 1988, as Don José and Puccini's Des Grieux; Riccardo in Ballo in Maschera, at Parma, 1989; Season 1990–91 at the Vienna Staatsoper, as Riccardo (Ballo) and Manrico. *Address:* c/o Teatro Regio, Via Garibaldi 16, 43100 Parma, Italy.

**CIARDI, Fabio Cifariello;** composer; b. 1960, Rome, Italy. *Education:* Accademia S Cecilia, Rome, University of Bologna; postgraduate studies with Giacomo Manzoni, Tristain Murail and Phillipe Manoury in Paris at IRCAM, Franco Donatoni at Accademia Nazionale di S Cecilia, Rome. *Career:* Composer in Residence, EMS, Stockholm, 1995; Collaboration with Psychology Department of Rome University on recognition of sonic events; Teacher of Composition, Conservatorium of Perugia; Member of Edison Studio, association of composers for production of computer music, Director, 1999–; mem. Interuniversity Centre for Research on Cognitive Processing. *Compositions include:* Tre Piccoli Paesaggi, for tape, 1999; Frans van Mieris, for actor and bassoon, on a text by Edoardo Sanguineti, 1999; Canto di Festa, for actor, flute, clarinet, piano, violin, viola, cello, on a text by Luciano Violante, 1999; Piccolo Cantico, for choir, 1999; Future commissions include a work for viola and tape; Work for oboe and orchestra concerto; Work for tape. *Address:* via Coste di Fontana Conte 30, 00067 Morlupo, Rome, Italy.

**CICCOLINI, Aldo;** Concert Pianist; b. 15 Aug. 1925, Naples, Italy. *Education:* Studied with Paolo Denza at the Naples Conservatory. *Career:* Debut: Naples 1942, in Chopin's F Minor Concerto; Professor at the Naples Conservatory from 1947; Moved to France 1949; Professor at the Paris Conservatoire 1971–89; US debut 1950, with the New York Philharmonic, playing Tchaikovsky's 1st Concerto; Many concerts with the world's leading orchestras; Recital programmes include music by Fauré, Ravel, Liszt and Debussy. *Recordings:* Liszt, Années de Pelèrinage and Harmonies Poetiques et Religieuses; Complete piano works of Satie; Concertos by Saint-Saëns; Piano Concerto in D by Alexis de Castillon, conducted by Georges Prêtre. *Honours:* Santa Cecilia Prize, Rome, 1948; Marguérite Long-Jacques Thibaud Prize, Paris, 1949. *Address:* c/o Conservatoire National Superieur de Musique, 14 Rue de Madrid, 75008 France.

**CICOGNA, Adriana;** Singer (Mezzo-soprano); b. 1955, Este, Italy. *Education:* Studied in Padua with Gina Cigna. *Career:* Engagements from 1983 throughout Italy including Pizzetti's Fedra at Palermo; Donizetti's Sancia di Castiglia at Bergamo and Maddalena in Rigoletto at Florence; La Scala, 1987 as Suzuki in Madama Butterfly, also at Torre del Lago, 1995; Other roles include Fidalma in Il Matrimonio Segreto; Smeton in Anna Bolena and appearances in operas by Monteverdi, Rossini (La Gazzetta) and Mozart; Season 1998 at the Teatro Pergolesi, Jesi, as Metalce in a revival of Pergolesi's Il Prigionier superbo. *Recordings:* Requiem by Pacini. *Address:* c/o Teatro Comunale G Pergolesi, Piazza della Repubblica, 60035 Jesi, Italy.

**CIESINSKI, Katherine;** Singer (Mezzo-Soprano); b. 13 Oct. 1950, Newark, Delaware, USA. *Education:* Studies with Margaret Harshaw at Curtis Institute, Philadelphia. *Career:* Sang in the US premiere of Berg's 3 act Lulu; European debut 1976 at Aix-en-Provence; Later sang in Asia, Israel and elsewhere in Europe; In 1988 sang in premiere of Argento's The Aspern Papers at Dallas and La Celestine by Maurice Ohana, Paris; Metropolitan Opera debut 1988, as Nicklausse in Les contes d'Hoffmann, returning as

Judith in Duke Bluebeard's Castle by Bartók; Other roles include Waltraute in Götterdämmerung, Strauss's Composer and Octavian, Brangaene in Tristan und Isolde, Britten's Lucretia, Laura in La Gioconda and Barber's Vanessa; Cassandre in Les Troyens for Scottish Opera and at Covent Garden; La Favorite, title role, in revival of original French version, 1991; Santa Fe 1998, as Herodias in Salome. *Recordings:* War and Peace by Prokofiev, Dukas' Ariane et Barbe Bleue; Sapho by Massenet; Pauline in The Queen of Spades.

**CIESINSKI, Kristine (Frances);** Singer (Soprano); b. 5 July 1952, Wilmington, DE, USA; m. Norman Bailey, 1985. *Education:* Temple University, 1970–71; University of Delaware, 1971–72; BA in Voice, Boston University, 1974. *Career:* New York concert debut as Soloist in Handel's Messiah, 1977; European operatic debut as Baroness Freimann in Der Wildschütz at Salzburg Landestheater, 1979, singing there until 1981; Member of Bremen State Opera, 1985–88; Guest appearances at Cincinnati Opera, Florentine Opera, Milwaukee in 1983 and 1987, Cleveland Opera, 1985, Scottish Opera, 1985 and 1989, Canadian Opera, 1986, Opera North, Leeds, 1986 and 1988, Augsburg Opera, 1986, Mexico City, 1986, Welsh National Opera, 1987 and 1989, Bregenz Festival, 1987, Zagreb National Opera, 1988, Wexford Festival, 1988, English National Opera, 1989–93, Munich State Opera, 1989, Baltimore Opera, 1989, Winnipeg Opera, 1989 and 1991, Frankfurt State Opera, 1990 and 1993, New Orleans Opera, 1992, Leipzig Opera, 1992, and La Scala Milan in 1992; Roles include: Medea, La Wally, Eva, Senta, Donna Anna, Tosca, Aida, Ariadne, Salome, Verdi's Lady Macbeth, Shostakovich's Lady Macbeth of Mtsensk, Erwartung, Judith from Bartók's Bluebeard, Berg's Marie, Beethoven's Leonora, Tchaikovsky's Tatiana and Salome, also many concert engagements in a repertory ranging from traditional works to contemporary scores; Sang Salome in a new production of Strauss's opera, ENO, 1996 and at Santa Fe, 1998; Season 1999–2000 as Wagner's Gutrune in San Francisco and Emilia Marty for Opera Zuid, Netherlands. *Recordings:* Several. *Honours:* Gold Medal, Geneva International Competition, 1977; 1st Prize, Salzburg International Competition, 1977. *Address:* c/o Trawick Artists Management Inc, 129 West 72nd Street, New York City, NY 10023-3239, USA.

**CIOFI, Patrizia;** Singer (Soprano); b. 1967, Casole d'Elsa, Siena, Italy. *Education:* Livorno Istituto Musicale; Siena and Fiesole, with Carlo Bergonzi, Alberto Zedda and Claudio Desderi. *Career:* Debut: Florence 1989, in Gino Negri's Giovanni Sebastiano; Appearances throughout Italy as Donna Anna, Gilda, Nannetta in Falstaff, Fulvia in Rossini's La Pietra del Paragone, and Violetta; Martina Franca 1994–96 as Amina in La Sonnambula, Dirce in Cherubini's Médée and Silvia in L'Americano by Niccolo Piccinni; Clorinda in La Cenerentola at Lima and Gilda at Savona and Palermo; Other venues include Parma, Trieste and Bologna; Concerts include Mozart's Mass in C minor; Covent Garden debut as Gilda, 2002. *Honours:* Winner, Giacomo Lauri Volpi Competition, 1998, and Ettore Bastianini Competition, Siena, 1991. *Address:* c/o Teatro Arena Sferisterio, Piazza Mazzini 10, 62100 Macerata, Italy.

**CIONI, Renato;** Singer (Tenor); b. 15 April 1929, Portoferraio, Elba. *Education:* Studied at the Florence Conservatory. *Career:* Debut: Spoleto 1956, as Edgardo in Lucia di Lammermoor; Italian television 1957, as Pinkerton; La Scala Milan from 1958; Spoleto 1959, in a revival of Donizetti's Il Duca d'Alba; Appearances in San Francisco and Chicago from 1961; Palermo 1963, in I Capuleti e i Montecchi by Bellini; Covent Garden 1964–65, as Cavaradossi, with Callas; The Duke of Mantua and Gabriele Adorno; Verona Arena 1966, as Cavaradossi; Engagements in Berlin, Prague, Paris, Berlin, Copenhagen, Buenos Aires, Bucharest and Edinburgh; Metropolitan Opera 1969–70; Sang Steva in Jenůfa at La Scala, 1974; Tours Opera 1979. *Recordings:* Rigoletto and Lucia di Lammermoor, with Joan Sutherland; Tosca, from Covent Garden.

**CIORMILA, Mariana;** Singer (Mezzo-Soprano); b. 1956, Romania. *Education:* Studied in Gelsenkirchen and sang there, 1982–84. *Career:* Appearances at Klagenfurt Opera, 1984–85, Houston Opera, 1986 (Marina in Boris Godunov), and Montpellier, 1987 (Orsini in Lucrezia Borgia); Has sung widely in Belgium as Adalgisa, Tancredi, Eboli and the Princess in Adriana Lecouvreur; Deutsche Oper Berlin, 1991, as Sextus in La Clemenza di Tito, Monte Carlo, 1992, as Dulcinée in Don Quichotte; Other roles include Dorabella, Isabella (Rossini) and Cenerentola; Deutsche Oper Berlin 1995–96, as Marina in Boris Godunov and the Countess in Andrea Chénier; Season 1997–98 in Clemenza di Tito, L'Italiana in Algeri, Enescu's Oedipe and La Gioconda (as Laura); Season 2000 at the Deutsche Oper as Fenena in Nabucco, Merope in Enescu's Oedipe and Mercedes in Carmen. *Address:* c/o Opéra de Monte Carlo, Place du Casino, Monte Carlo.

**CIUCIURA, Leoncjusz;** Polish composer; b. 22 July 1930, Grodzisk Mazowiecki; m. Sylwia Grelich 18 June 1967. *Education:* BA, Composition, Theory and Conducting, High School of Music, Warsaw, 1960. *Career:* Debut: Concert at High School of Music, Warsaw; Co-founder, Polish branch of Jeunesses Musicales movement, 1958–62; Founder, Editor, Carmina Academica Musical Publication; Editor, Musical Publication for Contemporary Music, 1989; Compositions performed world-wide, 1964–2005, including Festival ISCM World Music Days, International Festival of Music, Warsaw Autumn; Numerous international festivals of contemporary music worldwide; mem, Union of Polish Composers, Society of Authors ZAiKS. *Compositions:* Penetrations for Orchestral Groups, 4 Conductors and Composer, 1963; Emergenza for Choirs and Orchestra, 3 Conductors and Composer, 1963; In

progress from 1963, Spiral Form. *Publications:* Spirale I per uno, Spirale II per uno e piu, 1964–2005; Creatoria I, II, 1964–2005; Intarsio, I, II, 1964–2005; Rencontre, I, II, 1964–2005; Incidenti I, II, 1964–2005; In Infinitum I, II, 1964–2005 (all for optional instruments and accompaniment). *Honours:* Laureate Prize, Ministry of Culture and Art, 1960; Prize, Polish Composers Union Competition for Canti al Fresco, 1961; Prize at International Composers Competition (Prague) for Concertino da Camera, 1962; Polish Broadcast and Television Prize for Ornamenti, 1963. *Address:* Zwirki and Wigury 5, 05-825 Grodzisk Mazowiecki, Poland.

**CIULEI, Lenuta;** Violinist; b. 25 May 1958, Bucharest, Romania; m. 2 s. *Education:* Bucharest Music Academy, and in Germany, Belgium and USA; Study with Stephan Gheorghiu, André Gertler, Raphael Druian and Ruggiero Ricci. *Career:* Debut: Romanian Television broadcast, 1967; Played concerts with orchestras, recitals as solo violinist and was leader of chamber music ensembles in 35 countries throughout Europe, North and South America, Asia; Performed at the UN Palais, Geneva, Bartók Memorial House, Budapest, the Great Hall of the Tchaikovsky Conservatory, Moscow, the Lincoln Center's Alice Tully Hall and in Madrid for the Spanish Royal Family; Participated in many international festivals; Artistic Director Associate of Virtuosi de Caracas; Gives master classes at universities, international festivals and orchestras in the USA, Venezuela and Europe. *Honours:* First Prize, International Competitions; Pennsylvania Solo Recitalist Award; Order of Brazil for South American Music. *Current Management:* Gaiam International Arts Management. *Address:* PO Box 32239, Philadelphia, PA 19146, USA.

**CIURCA, Cleopatra;** Singer (Mezzo-Soprano); b. 1954, Romania. *Career:* Sang in Western Europe from 1981, notably at Reggio Emilio in Il Turco in Italia, at Dublin as Carmen, in Brussels as Eboli and at the Verona Arena as Laura in La Gioconda; New York Metropolitan from 1984, as Olga in Eugene Onegin, Marina, Maddalena and Eboli; Further engagements in San Francisco, Washington, Milan (Fenena in Nabucco), Paris and Detroit; Concert appearances include the Verdi Requiem in Vancouver (1986) and Adriana Lecouvreur (as the Princess) in London, 1987; Sang Carmen with Connecticut Opera, 1990. *Address:* c/o Metropolitan Opera, Lincoln Center, New York, NY 10023, USA.

**CIURDEA, Teodor;** Singer (Bass); b. 1957, Romania. *Education:* Studied in Bucharest. *Career:* Appearances at the National Opera, Bucharest from 1983; Sang Lothario in Mignon at the Wexford Festival, 1987; Prague State Opera, 1992; Vienna Staatsoper, 1987 as Mozart's Bartolo and Volksoper, 1991 as Achior in La Betulia Liberata by Mozart; Guest engagements at London, Basle and Bregenz; Sang Rossini's Basilio at Leipzig, 1993; Concerts and recitals in Vienna, Geneva and Paris. *Honours:* Prizewinner in competitions at Vienna, 1987. *Address:* c/o Leipzig Opernhaus, Augustusplatz 12, 1010 Leipzig.

**CLAASSEN, René;** Singer (Tenor); b. 1937, Helmond, Netherlands. *Education:* Amsterdam Conservatory, The Hague. *Career:* Debut: Maastricht, 1960; Sang at Bremerhaven from 1964, Kassel from 1968 as Wagner's Loge and Mime, Monostatos in Die Zauberflöte, Shuratov in From the House of The Dead, and the Villains in Les Contes d'Hoffmann; Appeared in Der Ring des Nibelungen, 1989 and sang Aschenbach in Death in Venice; Amsterdam 1986 in Zemlinsky's Der Kreidekreis and as Loge and Mime at Rotterdam, 1989; Sang Leonard in Nielsen's Maskarade at Kassel, 1994; Many concert appearances. *Address:* c/o Der Nederlandse Opera, Waterlooplein 22, 1011 PG Amsterdam, Netherlands.

**CLAPTON, Nicholas,** MA; British singer (counter-tenor); *Professor of Singing, Royal Academy of Music;* b. 1955, Worcester, England. *Education:* Magdalen Coll., Oxford and Univ. of London, studied with David Mason and Diane Forlano. *Career:* debut, Wigmore Hall, London 1984; Aldeburgh Festival 1985; London recital debut 1986, Purcell Room; numerous appearances throughout Europe and in the Far East; operatic roles for ENO, Opera North, Channel 4 television, Batignano, EBF, ranging from Monteverdi and Handel to world premieres (Barry, Lefanu, Benedict Mason); premieres of concert works by Helen Roe, Daryl Runswick, David Bedford, Simon Holt; many recitals (Purcell, Rossini, Romantic song, etc.) with Jennifer Partridge; currently Prof. of Singing, RAM; fmr Visiting Prof., Zeneakademia, Budapest; mem. ISM. *Recordings:* Purcell: Hail, Bright Cecilia, Duruflé: Requiem, Benedetto Marcello: Cantatas, Nicola Porpora: Cantatas. *Publication:* Moreschi: The Last Castrato (biog.) 2004. *Honours:* Hon. Dr of Liberal Arts (Liszt Ferenc Music Univ., Budapest) 2005; winner English Song Award 1987, winner Heart of England Int. Competition for Singers 1987, two prizes Concurso 'Francisco Viñas', Barcelona 1985. *Address:* c/o Royal Academy of Music, Marylebone Road, London, NW1 5HT, England. *E-mail:* contact@nicholasclapton.com. *Website:* www.nicholasclapton.com.

**CLARET, Lluis;** Cellist; b. 10 March 1951, Andorra; m. Anna Mora, 1 s. *Education:* Liceo Conservatory, Barcelona; Conservatoire European, Paris; Bloomington School of Music, USA; Teachers include Enric Casals; Radu Aldulescu; Eva Janzer; György Sebok. *Career:* Debut: Boccherini Cello Concerto, Barcelona, 1968; Soloist concerts with National Symphony of Washington and Moscow Philharmonic; Orchestra National de France; English Chamber Orchestra; Czech Philharmonic, under Rostropovich, Pierre Boulez, Vaclav Neumman, Witold Lutoslawski; Played at closing ceremony of Barcelona 92 Olympics; mem, Barcelona Trio. *Recordings:* Bach: Complete Suites for cello solo, Auvidis Valois, 1999; Schubert: Sonata Arpeggione for cello and piano, Harmonia Mundi, 1992; Chopin: Sonata for cello and piano;

Strauss: Sonata for cello and piano, Harmonia Mundi, 1991; Kodály: Sonata for cello, 1990; Schumann: Concerto for cello and orchestra, 1990; Haydn: Concerto No. 1 in C for cello and orchestra; Boccherini: Concerto No. 3 in G minor for cello and orchestra; Dvořák: Trio, Dumky, op. 90, Trio in F minor, 1992; Other works by Boulez, Mendelssohn and Ravel. *Honours:* First prize, Rostropovich Competition, 1977; Casals, 1978; Bologna Competition, 1975. *Current Management:* Carmen Netzel. *Address:* c/o Netzel, Pasaie Marimon, 10-4, 08021 Barcelona, Spain.

**CLAREY, Cynthia;** American singer (mezzo-soprano); b. 25 April 1949, Smithfield, Va, USA; m. Jake Gardner 1978 (divorced 2000), one s. *Education:* BMus, Howard Univ., Washington DC; Postgraduate Diploma, Juilliard School. *Career:* sang first with the Tri-Cities Opera Company; has sung in The Voice of Ariadne by Thea Musgrave with the New York City Opera; Boston Opera Company in the US premiere of Tippett's The Ice Break (1979) and The Makropulos Case (1986); Binghamton, New York, 1986, in the premiere of Chinchilla by Myron Fink; British debut at the Glyndebourne Festival, 1984, as Monteverdi's Ottavia, followed by Serena in Porgy and Bess (1986); Wexford Festival, 1985 and 1986, as Polinesso in Ariodante and Thomas's Mignon; has toured with Peter Brook's version of Carmen and appeared in the 1989–90 season in concert versions of Anna Bolena (Concertgebouw, as Jane Seymour), Weill's Lost in the Stars (Almeida Festival, London) and The Ice Break (as Hanna, at the Promenade Concerts, London); has also sung in operas by Cavalli, Mozart, Verdi, Puccini, Menotti and Offenbach; other roles include Monteverdi's Penelope, Cavalli's Diana (La Calisto), Handel's Rinaldo, Zerlina, Isoletta (La Straniera), Preziosilla, Dalila, Butterfly, Nicklausse and Octavian; sang Serena in the Covent Garden premiere of Porgy and Bess, 1992, and in Weill/Grosz Concert at the 1993 London Proms; three roles in Berg's Lulu at the Festival Hall, London, 1994; sang Gershwin's Bess at Cape Town, 1996; sang Kristina in The Makropulos Case at Aix-en-Provence, 2000; has sung with major orchestras including: Chicago Symphony, Boston Symphony, Oakland Symphony, New York Philharmonic, BBC Symphony, City of London Sinfonia, Hallé Orchestra and Dallas Symphony; numerous concert appearances. *Recordings include:* Porgy and Bess; Tippett's The Ice Break; Duffy's A Time for Remembrance, Afrika Songs, Will: Lost in the Stars, Turnage: Somedays. *Current Management:* Herbert H Breslin, 132 Leroy Street, Binghamton, NY 13905, USA. *Telephone:* (607) 723-2235 (also fax) (home). *E-mail:* cclarey@localnet.com (home).

**CLARK, Derek (John);** Conductor, Coach and Accompanist; b. 22 Aug. 1955, Glasgow, Scotland; m. Heather Fryer, 26 April 1980, 1 d. *Education:* Dumbarton Academy, 1967–72; Royal Scottish Academy of Music and Drama, 1972–76, Dip MusEd (hons), DipRSAM; University of Durham, BMus, hons 1st class, 1978; London Opera Centre, 1976–77. *Career:* Debut: Accompanist, Purcell Room, 1976; Conductor, Welsh National Opera, 1982; Staff Conductor, Welsh National Opera, 1976–97; Guest Conductor, Mid Wales Opera, 1989–92; Coach, Conductor, Welsh College of Music and Drama, 1992–97; Head of Music, Scottish Opera, 1997–; Guest Coach, RSAMD, 1998–; Conductor's repertoire includes: Tamerlano, Samson, Marriage of Figaro, Così fan tutte, Magic Flute, Die Entführung, La finta giardiniera, Lucia di Lammermoor, Don Pasquale, Count Ory, Beatrice and Benedict, Carmen, La Traviata, Rigoletto, La Bohème, Barber of Seville, Tosca, The Rake's Progress, Noye's Fludde and Maxwell Davies's Cinderella. *Compositions:* 3 One Act Operas for Young People: Hardlock House, 1988; The Witch of Mawddwy, 1993; The Forest Child, 1998 Songs, Choral Music and Arrangements. *Honours:* Worshipful Company of Musicians Silver Medal, 1976. *Address:* Dalmally, 96 East King Street, Helensburgh G84 7DT, Scotland.

**CLARK, Graham;** Singer (tenor); b. 10 Nov. 1941, Littleborough, Lancashire, England; m. Joan Clark 1979, 1 step-d. *Education:* MSc, Loughborough University, 1969–70; Studied with Bruce Boyce, London, Bologna, Mantova. *Career:* Debut: with Scottish Opera, 1975; English National Opera, 1978–85 (over 150 performances); Sang with Royal Opera, Covent Garden, Welsh National Opera and Opera North, United Kingdom; Extensive international career, appearing at the Metropolitan Opera in New York for 13 seasons, 1985–2002; Bayreuth Festival, 1981–92, 2001–02 (over 100 performances); Appearances in Paris, Vienna, Berlin, La Scala Milan, Salzburg Festival, Hamburg, Brussels, Madrid, Aix en Provence, Dallas, Bilbao, Catania, Matsumoto, Yokohama, Tokyo, Chicago, San Francisco, Munich, Zürich, Barcelona, Turin, Nice, Rome, Toronto, Amsterdam, Stockholm, Bonn, Tel-Aviv, Vancouver; Has also sung in concert with many of the world's leading orchestras and at the festivals of Lucerne, Edinburgh, Brussels, Berlin, Paris, Chicago, Rome, Amsterdam, Washington, Cologne, Copenhagen, London Proms; Recorded with Philips, Sony, BMG, Decca, EMI, Erato, Teldec, The Met and BBC; Appears on several videos, including Bayreuth performances of Die Meistersinger, Der Fliegende Holländer and 1992 Ring des Nibelungen, as well as the Met's Ghosts of Versailles; Has sung over 300 Wagner performances including over 200 performances of Der Ring des Nibelungen (Loge and Mime). *Honours:* Olivier Award, 1986, for his portrayal of Mephistopheles in Busoni's Doctor Faust; Hon. DLitt, Loughborough University, 1999; Sir Reginald Goodall Prize, London Wagner Society, 2001. *Current Management:* Ingpen & Williams Ltd, 7 St George's Court, 131 Putney Bridge Road, London, SW15 2PA, England. *E-mail:* gclarkgb@aol.com. *Website:* www.grahamclark.org.

**CLARK, J. Bunker;** Musicologist; b. 19 Oct. 1931, Detroit, Michigan, USA; m. Marilyn Jane Slawson, 3 Aug 1964. *Education:* BMus 1954, MMus 1957, PhD 1964, University of Michigan. *Career:* Instructor of Organ and Theory,

Stephens College, Columbia, Missouri, 1957–59; Lecturer in Music, University of California, Santa Barbara, 1964–65; Professor of Music History, University of Kansas, 1965–93; Emeritus, 1993–. *Publications:* Transposition in Seventeenth Century English Organ Accompaniments and the Transposing Organ, 1974; Editor, Anthology of Early American Keyboard Music, 1787–1830, 1977; Editor, Nathaniel Giles: Anthems, 1979; The Dawning of American Keyboard Music, 1988; Editor, American Keyboard Music through 1865, 1990; Series Editor, Bibliographies in American Music, 1975–84; Series Editor, Detroit Studies in Music Bibliography, 1985–; Series Editor, Detroit Monographs in Musicology/Studies in Music, 1990–. *Contributions:* American Organist; Choral Journal; Music and Letters; Musica Disciplina; Journal of the American Musicological Society; American Music. *Honours:* Citation for Distinguished Service, Sonneck Society, 1998. *Address:* 1618 Cypress Point Drive, Lawrence, KS 66047-1721, USA.

**CLARK, Richard J.;** Singer (baritone); b. 25 April 1943, Tucson, Arizona, USA. *Education:* Academy of Vocal Arts, Philadelphia, and Juilliard School, New York. *Career:* Debut: San Francisco, as Monterone in Rigoletto; Metropolitan Opera from 1981, as Verdi's Monterone and di Luna, Wagner's Amfortas and Kurwenal, Barnaba in La Gioconda, Michele in Il Tabarro and Gianciotto in Francesca da Rimini by Zandonai. *Address:* c/o Metropolitan Opera, Lincoln Center, New York, NY 10023, USA.

**CLARKE, Adrian;** Singer (baritone); b. 1953, Northampton, England. *Education:* Royal College of Music, London, and the London Opera Centre. *Career:* Appearances with Opera North in Die Fledermaus, The Mikado, Fanciulla del West, The Golden Cockerel, Faust and Carmen (as Escamillo); Don Ferdinand in the British stage premiere of Gerhard's The Duenna, 1994; Rossini's Barber for Scottish Opera and Dublin Grand Opera, Guglielmo and Taddeo in L'Italiana in Algeri for Opera 80; Nick Shadow in The Rake's Progress for New Sussex Opera; Contemporary music includes: Maxwell Davies's Martyrdom of St Magnus for Opera Factory, the premieres of Casken's Golem and Cage's Europera III (London, Berlin and Paris); Gerald Barry's Triumph of Beauty and Deceit for Channel 4 television, the British premiere of Mason's Playing Away (Opera North), Osborne's I am Goya and Rihm's Unsungen (Glasgow and Amsterdam); Season 1995–96 with Rossini's Barber for English Touring Opera, Rigoletto for Mid-Wales Opera and La Bohème for Glyndebourne Touring Opera; Season 2000 as Prince Afron in The Golden Cockerel at Bregenz and the title role in the premiere of Mr. Emmett Takes a Walk by Peter Maxwell Davies, at Kirkwall. *Current Management:* Musicmakers International Artists Representation, Tailor House, 63–65 High Street, Whitwell, Hertfordshire SG4 8AH, England. *Telephone:* (1438) 871708. *Fax:* (1438) 871777. *E-mail:* musicmakers@compuserve.com. *Website:* www .operauk.com.

**CLARKE, Karin;** Singer (Soprano); b. 1963, New York, USA. *Education:* Tri-Cities Opera, New York, and International Opera Studio, Zürich. *Career:* Appearances at the Trier Opera as Giulietta in Hoffmann, Marguerite, Mozart's Countess and Anne Trulove; Further engagements at Hagen, Saarbrucken, Munster and Bielefeld notably as Fiordiligi, Saffi (Zigeuner-baron) and Rosalinde in Die Fledermaus; Guest at Brussels, Ghent, Liège and Linz, with concert appearances in New York and throughout Germany; Other roles include Agathe, Lady (Hindemith's Cardillac), Elvira in Ernani, Marenka in The Bartered Bride and the Marschallin; Sang the title role in a revival of Zemlinsky's Sarema, Trier Opera 1996 (first production 20th century). *Recordings include:* Sarema (Koch International). *Address:* c/o Theater der Stadt Trier, Am Augustinerhof, 5500 Trier, Germany.

**CLARKE, Paul Charles;** Singer (Tenor); b. 1965, Liverpool, England. *Education:* Royal College of Music with Neil Mackie. *Career:* Many performances throughout the United Kingdom including concerts with Bournemouth Sinfonietta, London Ensemble and Scottish Chamber Orchestra; Duke in Rigoletto, Fenton, the High Priest, Idomeneo and Rodolfo with Welsh National Opera, 1990–93; Paris debut, 1991 as Fenton at Théâtre des Champs Elysées; recent engagements as Dmitri in Boris Godunov and Rodolfo for Opera North, Alfredo and Nemorino for Scottish Opera, 1993–94; Covent Garden debut, 1994–95; Cassio in Otello; Tybalt in Roméo et Juliette; Alfredo in La Traviata; USA debut with Seattle Opera singing the Duke in Rigoletto, 1995; Engaged as Faust with Welsh National Opera and Rodolfo at Royal Opera House, Covent Garden, 1996; Season 1997–98 as Verdi's Macduff at Monte Carlo, Gabriele Adorno for WNO and the Duke of Mantua for Scottish Opera; Roméo at the Met and Rodolfo at Seattle; Sang Alfredo at Cincinnati and Pinkerton for WNO, 1998; Season 2000–01 as Verdi's Gabriele Adorno at Wellington, the Duke of Mantua for Santa Fe Opera and Massenet's Des Grieux at Dallas. *Honours:* Peter Pears Scholarship and Kathleen Ferrier Memorial Prize. *Current Management:* Askonas Holt Ltd, Lonsdale Chambers, 27 Chancery Lane, London, WC2A 1PF, England. *Telephone:* (20) 7400-1700. *Fax:* (20) 7400-1799. *E-mail:* info@askonasholt.co.uk. *Website:* www .askonasholt.co.uk.

**CLARKE, Stephen (David Justin);** Conductor; b. 21 July 1964, Thame, Oxon, England; m. Helen Victoria Morrison, 1 s. *Education:* New College, Oxford, 1977–82; MA, Music, Honours, Hertford College, organ scholarship, Oxford University; ARCO; Diploma, Guildhall School of Music and Drama. *Career:* Conductor, Oxford Philharmonia, 1983–85; Founder, St Michael's Sinfonia, 1981; Conductor, Oxford University Opera Club, 1983–85; Conductor, Schola Cantorum of Oxford, 1985–87; Guest Conductor, Oxford Pro Musica, 1985; Guest Conductor, St Endellion Festival Orchestra, 1987;

Worked with Kent Opera, 1988, Geneva Grand Opera, 1988, Royal Scottish Academy of Music and Drama, 1988–89, British Youth Opera, 1988; Assistant Chorus Master, English National Opera, 1990; Head of Music, Scottish Opera, 1993. *Honours:* Ricordi Conducting Prize, 1985–86; Guildhall Diploma of Conducting, 1986. *Address:* 5 Crown Circus, Glasgow G12 9HB, Scotland.

**CLAUSEN, Jeanne;** Violinist; b. 16 Oct. 1944, Los Angeles, California, USA; m. John Cleveland, 2 July 1990, 1 d. *Education:* BA, Sarah Lawrence College, New York City; MMus, Cleveland Institute of Music, Ohio; Juilliard School of Music, New York City; Music Academy of the West, Santa Barbara, California; Meadowmount School of Music, New York City; Studied with Sascha Jacobsen, Dorothy DeLay, Donald Weilerstein, Sigiswald Kuijken and Ivan Galamian. *Career:* Founder and Leader of Ensemble La Cetra of Milan, Italy; Former Member of Amsterdam Baroque Orchestra, Netherlands, and California New Music Ensemble of Los Angeles; Performances on the Lira da Braccia; mem, International Lira Society. *Recordings:* Numerous. *Contributions:* Article on the Lira da Braccia. *Honours:* Coleman Chamber Music Auditions in Los Angeles, 1959, 1961; Scholarship, J M Kaplan Fund, New York, 1967. *Address:* c/o Amsterdam Baroque Orchestra, Meerweg 23, 1405 BC Bussum, Netherlands.

**CLAYTON, Beth;** Singer (Mezzo-soprano); b. 1970, Arkansas, USA. *Education:* Manhattan School of Music and with Mignon Dunn. *Career:* Sang Don Ramiro in La finta giardiniera at Washington, 1996; Cherubino at Caracas, Venezuela; Houston Opera in Roméo et Juliette and Virgil Thomson's Four Saints in Three Acts, also in New York and Edinburgh; Season 1998–99 with Cherubino and Nicklausse at Houston, Janáček's Fox at Toronto; Mère Marie in The Carmelites conducted by Seiji Ozawa and Mozart's Sesto in Israel; Season 1999–2000 with the premiere of Carlisle Floyd's Cold Sassy Tree at Houston and Carmen for Welsh National Opera; Concerts include Mahler's 8th Symphony with the Montreal Symphony Orchestra, 1999–2000; Messiah, Dallas Symphony Orchestra; A Midsummer Night's Dream; Sang in British premiere of Saariaho's L'amour de loin, Barbican Hall, 2002. *Address:* c/o Houston Grand Opera Association, 510 Preston Avenue, Houston, TX 77002, USA.

**CLAYTON, Laura;** Composer and Pianist; b. 8 Dec. 1943, Lexington, Kentucky, USA. *Education:* Studied with Milhaud at the Aspen School, Wuorinen at the New England Conservatory, and at the University of Michigan. *Compositions include:* Implosure for 2 dancers, slide and tape, 1977; Cree Songs for the Newborn for soprano and chamber orchestra, 1987; Panels for chamber ensemble, 1983; Sagarama for piano and orchestra, 1984; Clara's Sea for women's voices, 1988; Terra Lucida for orchestra, 1988. *Honours:* NEA awards and Guggenheim Fellowship. *Address:* c/o ASCAP, ASCAP House, 1 Lincoln Plaza, New York, NY 10023, USA.

**CLEGG, John;** British concert pianist; b. 7 Nov. 1928, London, England. *Education:* Jesus Coll., Cambridge, Royal Coll. of Music, studie piano with Herbert Fryer. *Career:* debut, Wigmore Hall, London 1951; has given recitals, concerts and broadcasts in most countries, with frequent tours of Africa, Middle East and Far East, and concerts in principal European centres; regular performer on BBC radio and television; pianist-in-residence, Lancaster Univ. 1981–93. *Recordings include:* Complete piano music by Alan Rawsthorne, 1996; Piano music of Milhaud, Koechlin, Ibert and Schmitt, 1998; Music by Chopin-Liszt; Poulenc and Adrian Self, 2000; Music by Fauré and Poulenc, 2002; Music by Howard Ferguson, William Mathias, Kenneth Leighton, 2002. *Honours:* Harriet Cohen Int. Award 1968. *Current Management:* J. Audrey Ellison, International Artists' Management, 135 Stevenage Road, Fulham, London, SW6 6PB, England. *Address:* Concord, 53 Marine Drive, Hest Bank, Lancaster, LA2 6EG, England (home). *Telephone:* (1524) 822357 (home). *E-mail:* jandjc@onetel.com (home).

**CLEIN, Natalie;** British cellist and composer; b. 1977, England. *Education:* Royal Coll. of Music, Musik Hochschule (Heinrich Schiff), Vienna. *Career:* debut, London Proms Concerts 1997 with Haydn's C major concerto; appearances with Royal Philharmonic, English Chamber, Philharmonia, London Philharmonic and City of Birmingham Orchestras; Elgar Concerto with LPO in Madrid and London; Lutoslawski Concerto with Hallé Orchestra; US concerto debut with the California SO, with further engagements at Verbier, Delft and Divonne Festivals, Schwartzenberg Schubertiade, Kronberg, Manchester Cello Festival, Spannungen, Barbican Mostly Mozart; chamber recitals at Wigmore Hall and Cheltenham and Bath Int. Festivals; Schumann Quintet with Martha Argerich; Dvořák Concerto at St Magnus Festival 2001; season 2000–01 with Royal Philharmonic Orchestra, BBC Nat. Orchestra of Wales and tour of UK, including Wigmore Hall recital; New Generation Artists concerts with BBC; recital debuts in Teatro Colón with Buenos Aires Philharmonic 2003, New York Lincoln Centre 2004. *Recordings:* Taverner (with the English Chamber Orchestra), Dvorat Sextet (with the Nash Ensemble), recital album of Brahms, Schubert (with Charles Owen, piano). *Honours:* BBC Young Musician of Year 1994, winner Eurovision Competition for Young Musicians, Warsaw 1994, Kronberg Akad. Ingrid zu Solms Cultur Preis 2003, Classical BRIT Award for Young British Classical Performer 2005. *Current Management:* Askonas Holt Ltd, Lonsdale Chambers, 27 Chancery Lane, London, WC2A 1PF, England. *Telephone:* (20) 7400-1700. *Fax:* (20) 7400-1799. *E-mail:* gaetan.ledivelec@askonasholt.co.uk. *Website:* www.askonasholt.co.uk.

**CLEMENCIC, René;** Austrian musician, composer, recorder player, harpsichordist and conductor and clavichord player; b. 27 Feb. 1928, Vienna; m. (1) 1 d., (2) Edda Rischka, 11 April 1968, 1 d. *Education:* PhD, University of Vienna, 1956; Old Music with J Mertin, Musical Theory with J Polnauer, Recorder with H U Staeps, L Höffer, V Winterfeld, W Nitschke, Harpsichord with Eta Harich-Schneider. *Career:* Clavichord player; Founder, Leader, early music ensemble Clemencic Consort, from 1968; Editor, mediaeval Carmina Burana; Baroque opera performances (1st modern including: Draghi's L'Eternita Soggetta al Tempo, Peri's Euridice, Leopold I's Il Lutto dell'Universo); Television play; Concerts world-wide; Soloist on the clavichord. *Compositions:* Maraviglia III and V; Sesostris II and III; Chronos II; Bicinia Nova; Music for Ariana Mnouchkine's film Molière; Musik zum Urfaust; Tolldrastische Szenen; Stufen; Musik zum Prinzen von Homburg; Missa Mundi; Unus Mundus; Requiem pro Vivis et Mortuis; Musica Hermetica; Drachenkampf; Strukturen Musica Instrumentalis; Revolution; Opus für Flöte und Streicher, 1991; Kabbala, 1992; Kammeroper, Der Berg, 1993; Apokalypsis, 1996; Klaviertrio Jeruschalajim, 1997; Emblemata, 1998; Reise nach Niniveh, 1999, Concerto per Archi 2000, Klavierduo 2000, Stabat Mater 2001, Der Schlüssel zum Paradies 2002, Klaviertrio Das Haus 2004. *Recordings:* Over 100 as soloist on recorder and with consort; Numerous flute solos; Josquin: Missa Hercules Dux Ferrariae, Musica Sacra; Monteverdi: Missa da Capella, Il Combattimento, Messa a 4 voci; Mediaeval Carmina Burana; Dufay: Missa Ave Regina Coelorum, Missa Sine Nomine, Missa Caput, Missa Ecce Ancilla; Obrecht: Missa Fortuna Desperata; Ockeghem: Requiem; Marcello: Sonate a Flauto; Biber: Fidicinium; Fux: Dafne in Lauro; Carvalho: Testoride; Vivaldi: L'Olimpiade; Pergolesi: Stabat Mater; René Clemencic: Le Combat du Dragon; Kabbala; Apokalypsis; Fux: Requiem; Historic Tablatures: Johannes von Lubin; Dunstable: Sacred Music; Ockeghem: Missa sine Nomine. *Publications:* Alte Musikinstrumente, 1968; Carmina Burana, 1979. *Honours:* Ehrenmedaille in Gold der Bundeshauptstadt Wien 1989, Vienna Music Prize 1997, Anima Mundi Prize Venice Biennale d'Arte Sacra 2004. *Address:* Reinerstrasse 26/7, 1030 Vienna, Austria (home). *Telephone:* (1) 712-53-41 (home). *Fax:* (1) 712-50-20 (home). *E-mail:* clemencic.consort.utanet.at (office). *Website:* www.clemencio.at (office).

**CLEMENTI, Aldo;** Composer; b. 25 May 1925, Catania, Italy. *Education:* Studied with Pietro Scarpini in Siena, at Catania and with Petrassi in Rome, 1952–54; Summer courses at Darmstadt, 1955–62. *Compositions:* Concertino in forma di variazioni, 1956; Tre Studi for chamber orchestra, 1957; 7 Scenes for chamber orchestra, 1961; Collage I–III, 1961–67; Informel I–III for various instrumental combinations, 1962–63; Variante A for chorus and orchestra and B for orchestra, 1964; Silben for female voice, clarinet, violin and 2 pianos, 1966; Concerto for wind orchestra and 2 pianos, 1967; Reticolo for string quartet, 1968; Concerto for piano and 7 instruments, 1970; Replica for harpsichord, 1972; Blitz, musical action for chamber ensemble, 1973; Sinfonia da camera, 1974; Concerto for piano, 24 instruments and carillons, 1975; Clessidra for 11 instruments, 1976; Reticolo for 12 strings, 1978; Collage Jesu meine Freude, action for 8 strings, 8 winds and tape, 1979; Es, rondeau in 1 act, produced at Teatro la Fenice, Venice, 1981; AEB for 17 instruments, 1983; Finale for 4 sopranos and orchestra, 1984; O du Selige for orchestra, 1985; Concerto for piano and 11 instruments, 1986; Romanza for piano and orchestra, 1991; Rapsodia for soprano, contralto and orchestra, 1994; Carillon, 1-act opera, 1996; Canone Perpetuo for 8 female voices and 9 instruments, 1996; Concerto for 2 harpsichords and strings, 1996; Passacaglia 2 for ensemble, 1997; Veni Creator for ensemble, 1997; Largo for strings, 1999; Von Himmel Hoch for 4 instruments, 1999. *Address:* SIAE (Sezione Musica), Viale della Letteratura n 30, 00144 Rome, Italy.

**CLEMENTS, Joy;** Singer (Soprano); b. 1931, Dayton, Ohio, USA. *Education:* Studied at University of Miami and in Philadelphia and New York. *Career:* Debut: Miami Opera 1956 as Musetta in La Bohème; Sang 1959–72 at New York City Opera and in Pittsburgh, Cincinnati, Baltimore, San Diego, Fort Worth, Hawaii; Appeared as Mary Warren in premiere of The Crucible by Robert Ward, New York, 1961; Appearances at Metropolitan from 1963; Guest engagements at Tel-Aviv 1963 and Brussels 1975; Other roles have included Mozart's Despina, Pamina and Susanna; Verdi's Violetta and Gilda, Gounod's Juliette, Manon, Martha, Gershwin's Bess; Many concert appearances. *Address:* c/o Metropolitan Opera, Lincoln Center, NY 10023, USA.

**CLEMMOW, Caroline Anne,** ARAM, LRAM, ARCM; British concert pianist; b. 10 Feb. 1959, London; m. Anthony Goldstone. *Education:* Walthamstow Hall School, Sevenoaks, Royal Acad. of Music, London. *Career:* leading piano duo with husband, Anthony Goldstone, appearing throughout British Isles and abroad, including USA; chamber music, including major tour of Russia, Ukraine; collaborations with percussionist Evelyn Glennie; occasional concerto soloist; mem. Incorporated Soc. of Musicians. *Recordings:* 28 piano duo recordings, seven chamber music recordings. *Address:* Walcot Old Hall, Alkborough, North Lincolnshire DN15 9JT, England (home). *E-mail:* carolineclemmow@aol.com (home).

**CLEOBURY, Nicholas Randall,** MA, FRCO; British conductor; b. 23 June 1950, Bromley, Kent; s. of John Cleobury and Brenda Cleobury; m. Heather Kay 1978; one s. one d. *Education:* King's School, Worcester and Worcester Coll., Oxford. *Career:* Asst organist, Chichester Cathedral 1971–72, Christ Church, Oxford 1972–76; conductor, Schola Cantorum of Oxford 1973–76; chorus master, Glyndebourne Festival Opera 1977–79; Asst Dir BBC Singers 1977–79; Prin. Opera Conductor, Royal Acad. of Music 1980–87; Guest Conductor, Zurich Opera House 1992–; Music Dir Oxford Bach Choir 1997–; Artistic Dir Aquarius 1983–92, Cambridge Symphony Soloists 1990–92,

Britten Sinfonia 1992–, Sounds New 1996–; Music Dir Broomhill 1990–94, Artistic Dir Cambridge Festival 1992, Mozart Ways Canterbury 2003–; Artistic Advisor Berkshire Choral Festival 2002–; has conducted worldwide from Australia to USA 1979–; numerous recordings. *Honours:* Hon. RAM 1985. *Address:* 20 Denbigh Street, London, SW1V 2ER (office); China Cottage, Church Lane, Petham, Canterbury, Kent, CT4 5RD, England (home). *Telephone:* 07831 148637 (office); (1227) 700584. *Fax:* (1227) 700827. *E-mail:* nicholascleobury@aol.com (home). *Website:* www.nicholascleobury.net.

**CLEOBURY, Stephen John,** MusB, MA, FRCM, FRCO; British conductor; b. 31 Dec. 1948, Bromley; s. of John Frank Cleobury and Brenda Julie Cleobury (née Randall). *Education:* King's School, Worcester and St John's Coll., Cambridge. *Career:* organist, St Matthew's, Northampton 1971–74; sub-organist, Westminster Abbey 1974–78; Master of Music, Westminster Cathedral 1979–82; Dir of Music, King's Coll. Cambridge 1982–; mem. Council, Royal School of Church Music 1982–; Pres. Inc. Asscn of Organists 1985–87, Cathedral Organists' Asscn 1988–90, Royal Coll. of Organists 1990–92 (Hon. Sec. 1981–90); Chief Conductor BBC Singers 1995–; recordings of solo organ works and directing choir of King's Coll. and BBC Singers. *Honours:* Hon. DMus (Anglia Polytechnic) 2001. *Address:* King's College, Cambridge, CB2 1ST, England. *Telephone:* (1223) 331224 (office). *Fax:* (1223) 331890 (office). *E-mail:* choir@kings.cam.ac.uk.

**CLEVE, George;** Conductor; b. 9 July 1936, Vienna, Austria. *Education:* Studied at Mannes College, New York, and with Pierre Monteux, George Szell, Franco Ferrara and Leonard Bernstein. *Career:* Debut: Salzburg Festival; Appearances with major American orchestras, including the New York Philharmonic and Symphony Orchestras of Chicago, Boston, Cleveland, Minnesota and San Francisco; Music Director of the San Jose Symphony and founder of the Midsummer Mozart Festival in San Francisco, 1974; Has conducted La Bohème, La Traviata, Le nozze di Figaro and Oedipus Rex; European engagements with the Northern Sinfonia, the Vienna Symphony Orchestra and the Orchestre National de France; Flanders Festival, 1990, Don Giovanni; Tour of Europe with the English Chamber Orchestra; Germany with the Stockholm Chamber Orchestra. *Honours:* Officier, Ordre des Arts et des Lettres, from the French Government; Silver Medal of Honour, City of Vienna. *Current Management:* Terry Harrison Artists Management, The Orchard, Market Street, Charlbury, Oxfordshire OX7 3PJ, England. *Telephone:* (1608) 810330. *Fax:* (1608) 811331. *E-mail:* artists@terryharrison .force9.co.uk. *Website:* www.terryharrison.force9.co.uk (office).

**CLIBURN, Van (Harvey Lavan, Jr);** American pianist; b. 12 July 1934, Shreveport; s. of Harvey Lavan and Rildia Bee Cliburn (née O'Bryan). *Career:* studied with mother and at Juilliard School; public appearances, Shreveport 1940; début, Houston Symphony Orchestra 1952, New York Philharmonic Orchestra 1954, 1958; concert pianist on tour in USA 1955–56, USSR 1958; appearances in Brussels, London, Amsterdam, Paris, etc. *Honours:* Hon. HHD (Baylor), MFA (Moscow Conservatory) 1989; Winner first Int. Tchaikovsky Piano Competition, Moscow 1958, Arturo Toscanini Award, Classical Music Broadcaster's Asscn 1998, Kennedy Center Honor 2001. *Address:* PO Box 470219, Fort Worth, TX 76147-0219 (office); Van Cliburn Foundation, 2525 Ridgmar Boulevard, Suite 307, Fort Worth, TX 76116-4583, USA (office).

**CLINGAN, Judith Ann,** AM, BA; Australian composer and conductor; *Director, Canberra Choral Society;* b. 19 Jan. 1945, Sydney, NSW; d. of Victor Lawrence and Marian Dorothy (née Tasker) Clingan; one d. *Education:* Univs of Sydney and New S Wales, Australian Nat. Univ. and Kodaly Inst. of Music Educ., Hungary. *Career:* composer for Kodaly Educ. Inst. 1986, ACT Bicentennial Year 1987, 1988; Founder and Dir Gaudeamus 1983–93; Creative Arts Fellow ANU 1989; Composer-in-Residence Gaudeamus and Young Music Soc. 1990; Composer Fellow 1991; Dir Voicebox Youth Opera S. Australia; Dir of Music Mt Barker Waldorf School, S Australia 1994–; Dir Canberra Choral Soc. 2004–, Wayfarers Australia (f. as Waldorf Wayfarers 1997), The Variables, Imagine Music Theatre Workshops; mem. numerous orgs. *Compositions include:* Francis 1986, Nganbra 1988, Terra Beata – Terra Infirma 1989, Kakadu 1990 (Sounds Australian Award 1991), The Birds' Noel 1990, Marco 1991, Songs of Solitude 1991, The Grandfather Clock 1992, Everyone Sang 2002, Sit, Jessica 2002, Spiritus Sanctus Australia 2002, Esperamus 2002, Seasons of the Soul 2002, The Tree of Life 2003, The Dancing Wombat 2004. *Recordings:* Choralations 2000, Short and Sweet 2001, Songs of the Tree of Life 2002. *Publications include:* The Complete Chorister 1971, So Good a Thing 1981, Music is for Everyone 1984, Songs of the Tree of Life I. Vol. I 1998, Vol. II 1996. *Address:* 11 Mirbelia Crescent, Rivett, ACT 2611, Australia. *Telephone:* (2) 6287 4132 (office); (2) 6287 3427 (home). *E-mail:* clingan@netspeed.com.au.

**CLOAD, Julia;** Pianist; b. 6 Oct. 1946, London, England. *Education:* Royal College of Music, London; Liszt Academy, Budapest, Hungary; Further studies with Maria Curcio and Hans Keller. *Career:* Debut: Wigmore Hall; Concerto performances with Royal Philharmonic Orchestra, London Philharmonic Orchestra, Hallé Orchestra, Royal Liverpool Philharmonic Orchestra, under conductors including Bernard Haitink, John Pritchard, Adrian Boult, James Loughran, Christopher Seaman; Recitals, at the Wigmore Hall, Queen Elizabeth Hall, BBC and Budapest Spring Festival; Concertos: Royal Festival Hall and Radio 3. *Recordings:* Haydn Piano Sonatas; Schumann Sonatas. *Address:* 1/6 Colville Houses, Talbot Road, London W11 1JB, England.

**CLOSE, Shirley;** Singer (Mezzo-soprano); b. 1962, Oklahoma, USA. *Education:* University of Southern California. *Career:* Sang at the Augusta Opera

from 1985; Amneris in Aida for Boston Opera; Mozart's Marcellina at Miami, 1988; Magdalena in Die Meistersinger at Nice, 1986; In Wagner's Ring at Orange, 1988; Cologne Opera, 1989–93 as Wagner's Fricka and Waltraute; Geneviève in Pelléas; Orlofsky in Die Fledermaus and Mary in Der fliegende Holländer; Guest appearances at Munich as Fenena in Nabucco; Bayreuth Festival, Waltraute, 1992 and the Deutsche Oper, Berlin; Sang Gluck's Alceste at Strasbourg, 1996. *Recordings:* Elektra; Die Walküre. *Address:* c/o Opéra du Rhin, 19 Place Broglie, 67008 Strasbourg Cédex, France.

**CLOSTRE, Adrienne;** Composer; b. 9 Oct. 1921, Thomery, France. *Education:* Studied at the Paris Conservatoire with Messiaen and Milhaud. *Compositions include:* Stage works: Nietzsche, 1975; Le secret, 1981; 5 scenes de la vie italienne, 1983; L'albatross, 1988; Annapurna, 1988: Melodramas: L'écriture du Dieu, 1991 and El Zaïr, 1992; Le Triomphe de la Vertu, 1995; Oboe concerto, 1970 and Concerto for flute, violin and chamber orchestra, 1972; Waves and Sun: Une lecture de Virginia Woolf, 1991; Le Zaire, sung melodrama, 1992. *Honours:* 1st Grand Prix de Rome, 1949; Grande Prix Musical Ville de Paris, 1955; Prix Florence Gould, 1976; Prix Musique de la SACD, 1987. *Address:* 15 Avenue Hoche, 75008 Paris, France.

**CLOZIER, Christian (Robert Adrien);** Composer and Director; b. 25 Aug. 1945, Compiègne, France; one d. *Education:* National Conservatory of Music, Paris; Practical School for Higher Studies, Paris. *Career:* Founder, Director, IMEB; Director, International Competition of Electro-acoustic Music, Bourges; Hon. President, International Confederation of Electro-acoustic Music (ICEM); Conceptor of Music Electro-acoustic Instruments. *Compositions include:* La Discordature; Opéra, A Vie; 22 août; Loin la Lune; Symphonie pour un enfant Seul; A la Prochaine, la Taupe; Quasars; Markarian 205; Par Pangloss Gymnopède; Le Bonheur, une idée neuve en Europe, Mon nom sous le soleil est France, le Temps scintille et le songs est savoir; Eleven spectacles multimedia;Démotique: De la grève, au loin; Clarissophone Ont été; Le père, le fils. *Recordings:* La Discordatura, Pathé Marconi; Lettre à une Demoiselle; Dichotomie, Pathé Marconi; Par Panglos Gymnopède; Le temps scintille et le songe est savoir; Le Clarissophone Symphonie pour un Enfant Seul, Edition IMED; Quasars, Le Chant du Monde. *Contributions:* Musique en Jeu No. 8, 1970; Faire 2–3, 1974; Faire 4–5, 1975; Poésie Sonore Internationale, Edition J.M. Place. *Address:* Institut International de Musique Electroacoustique, BP 39 Place Andre Malraux, 18000 Bourges, France. *E-mail:* administration@ime-bourges.org. *Website:* www.imeb.net.

**CLURMAN, Judith;** Conductor; b. 11 March 1953, Brooklyn, New York, USA; m., 1 s. *Education:* Oberlin College, 1971–73; BMus, 1977; MMus, Juilliard School of Music, 1978. *Career:* Founder, Director, New York Concert Singers, 1988–; Director of Choral Activities, The Juilliard School, 1989–; Project Youth Chorus, 1996–; New York Chamber Symphony Chorus, 1996–98; Judith Clurman Choral Workshop, 1998–; Performed with New York Philharmonic, Boston Symphony, Orchestra of St Luke's, American Composers Orchestra, Mostly Mozart, Classical Band, Lincoln Center's Great Performers series; Musical Director, 92nd Street Y's Music of the Jewish Spirit, 1998–2001; Director of Choral Activities, TodiMusicFest, 2001–; Conducted numerous premieres including music by Leonard Bernstein, William Bolcom, John Corigliano, Philip Glass, Aaron Jay Kernis, Libby Larsen, David Diamond, Stephen Paulus, Ned Rorem, Christopher Rouse, Ellen Taaffe Zwilich, Tania Leon, Paul Schoenfield and Robert Beaser; mem, Chorus America; American Choral Directors Association. *Recordings:* Divine Grandeur; The Mask; A Season's Promise. *Honours:* First Prize, ASCAP; Chorus America Award, with New York Concert Singers, 1992. *Address:* 75 East End Avenue 9L, New York, NY 10028, USA.

**CLUTTON, James Charles;** British opera and theatre producer; *Producer, Opera Holland Park;* b. 18 Jan. 1966, London. *Career:* Assoc. Prod., Bill Kenwright Ltd 1998–2000; Line Prod., UNICEF The Return Festival, Kosovo 1999; Prod., Opera Holland Park 2000–; productions include Weill and Brecht's Happy End, Herrmann and Harman's Romance Romance, Hardy's Far from the Madding Crowd. *Compositions:* Oscar (musical based on life of Oscar Wilde) 1995, Great Things (Thomas Hardy poem set to music) 1997. *Recording:* Oscar 1995. *Address:* Opera Holland Park, Central Library, Phillmore Walk, London, W8 7RX, England (office). *E-mail:* jamesclutton@ operahollandpark.com (office). *Website:* www.operahollandpark.com (office).

**COAD, Jonathan;** Singer (Baritone); b. 1958, Crayford, Kent, England. *Education:* Studied at the Royal College of Music, London, England. *Career:* Many concert appearances, including tours with the Groupe Vocale de France throughout Europe and North America; Concert soloist in England and France; Sang Pooh-Bah in The Mikado for D'Oyly Carte Opera, and in Bernstein's Candide at the Old Vic, 1989; Engagements with the Royal Opera, Covent Garden, in Death in Venice, The Fiery Angel, Jenůfa, Tosca, Arabella, and La Bohème; Rigoletto 1997, as Court Usher, and sang Cross in Paul Bunyan for the Royal Opera, 1997–98. *Recordings include:* Albums with Groupe Vocale de France. *Address:* c/o Royal Opera House (Contracts), Covent Garden, London WC2E 9 DD, England.

**COATES, Gloria;** Composer; b. 10 Oct. 1938, Wausau, Wisconsin, USA. *Education:* BMus, Composition, Voice; BA, Art, Theatre; MMus, Composition, Musicology; Studied with Otto Luening and Alexander Tcherepnin. *Career:* Freelance Composer, Munich, Germany, 1969–; Organiser of German-American Contemporary Music Series, Munich and Cologne, 1971–84; Demonstrated work in vocal multiphonics, International Summer Course for New Music, Darmstadt, 1972; Taught for University of Wisconsin International Programs, Munich, 1975–83, London, 1976. Compositions widely performed, Europe, USA, India, including Warsaw Autumn Festival, 1978, Musica Viva Series in Munich, East Berlin Festival, 1979, Montepulciano, Dartington, Geneva Festivals; Radio recordings include for BBC-London, Suisse Romande, RAI Rome, Radio Poland, German Radio stations, Radio Johannesburg, Sweden, USA; Additional broadcasts, China, Finland, Spain, Portugal, Brazil, Canada, Belgium, Netherlands; Invited lectures, Harvard University, 1981, Max Mueller Bhavans, India, 1982. *Compositions include:* Music on Open Strings, 1974; String Quartet, commissioned by Kronos Quartet; Orchestral piece for New Music American Festival, New York, 1989; Piece for harp, flute and viola for Dresden Festival; 11 Symphonies, 1973–99; 5 String Quartets, 1966–88. *Recordings:* Bielefelder Catalog, Music on Open Strings, String Quartets I, II, III and IV; Symphonies 1, 2, 4, 7, Time frozen, Homage to Van Gogh, Tones in Overtones. *Honours:* Music on Open Strings cited as 1 of 12 most important recorded works by living composer, International Koussevitzky Panel, 1986; Yaddo Grants; MacDowell Colony; UNESCO Grant, 1990. *Address:* Postfach 430363, 80733 Munich, Germany.

**COATES, Leon;** University Lecturer and Composer; b. 15 June 1937, Wolverhampton, England; m. 11 Sept 1976. *Education:* St John's College, Cambridge. *Career:* University Lecturer; Various radio appearances as pianist, harpsichordist, with Scottish Baroque Ensemble; Several broadcasts; Organist and Choirmaster, St Andrew's and St George's Church, Edinburgh; Lecturer, Edinburgh University, 1965–2002; mem, Scottish Society of Composers; Royal College of Organists; Guild of Professional Composers and Songwriters. *Compositions:* Song Cycle, North West Passage, 1994; Concertos for viola, 1979 and harpsichord, 1984; Music for Concert Band and Choir; Te Deum and Jubilate for choir and organ. *Recordings:* BBC Archive Recording of Music for 2 Harpsichords. *Publications:* Song Cycle North West Passage, 1994. *Contributions:* Tempo; Music in New Zealand; Short articles on relevant musical terms in The Oxford Composer Companions: J. S. Bach, 1999. *Address:* 35 Comely Bank Place, Edinburgh EH4 1ER, Scotland.

**COATES, Oliver;** British cellist; b. 19 May 1982, London, England. *Education:* Junior Academy of Music from 1992; Royal Academy of Music, studied with Colin Carr. *Career:* Debut at age 15 playing Haydn's C major Concerto at St John's Smith Square, 1999; Recitals and concertos in UK in Aldeburgh, Edinburgh and London, and across Europe and Asia including Japan, Holland, France and Norway: London Soloists' Chamber Orchestra Cello Festival, 2002; Paris Chopin Festival, 2003; Gala concert, Int. Cello Festival, Manchester 2004; Premieres of solo and chamber music by Elena Firsova, Stephane Altier, Dmitri Smirnov, Graham Williams; TV/radio: appearances on BBC1, Channel 5 and BBC Radio; mem., New Professionals Ensemble. *Honours:* Dame Ruth Railton chamber music prize at RAM; Winner, Douglas Cameron Cello Competition, May Mukle Cello Competition, Montefiore Prize, S&M Eyres Scholarship, Sir John Barbirolli Memorial Prize. *Address:* 169 Fordwych Road, London, NW2 3NG, England. *E-mail:* ollycoates@yahoo.com.

**COBBE, Hugh Michael Thomas,** OBE, MA, FSA; British musicologist and librarian; *Deputy Chairman, RVW Trust;* b. 20 Nov. 1942, Farnham, Surrey; m. Katherine Chichester 1982; two d. *Education:* St Columba's Coll., Dublin, Ireland, Trinity Coll., Dublin, Trinity Coll., Oxford. *Career:* Asst Keeper, Manuscript Dept, British Museum 1967–73 and British Library 1973–78; Head of Publications, British Library 1978–85, Head of Music Collections 1985–2001, Head of British Collections 2001–02; Deputy Chair. Ralph Vaughan Williams (RVW) Trust 2004–; mem. Royal Musical Asscn (Pres. 2002–), Gerald Coke Handel Foundation (Chair. 1996–). *Publications:* The Letters of Ralph Vaughan Williams; contrib. to Musical Times, Fontes Artis Musicae, New Grove Dictionary of Music and Musicians, Oxford Dictionary of National Biography. *Address:* Fox House, North End, Newbury, RG20 0AY, England *Telephone:* (1635) 253190 (home). *Fax:* (1635) 253191 (home). *E-mail:* hugh.cobbe@pop3.hiway.co.uk (home).

**COBURN, Pamela;** Singer (soprano); b. 29 March 1955, Dayton, OH, USA. *Education:* De Pauw University, Eastman School and Juilliard. *Career:* Has sung at Munich Staatsoper from 1982. Vienna from 1984; Maggio Musicale Florence 1988 as Ellen Orford in Peter Grimes; Los Angeles 1990 as Ilia in Idomeneo; Sang Saffi in Der Zigeunerbaron at Zürich and Alice Ford in Falstaff for Miami Opera 1991; Salzburg and Munich Festivals 1991, as Mozart's Countess; Sang Ellen Orford in a production of Peter Grimes by Tim Albery, Munich, 1991; Engaged for Giulio Cesare and Das Rheingold at the 1997 Munich Festival; Other roles include Fiordiligi; Rosalinde in Die Fledermaus and Lauretta in Gianni Schicchi; Sang Hanna Glawari at the Deutsche Oper Berlin, 2000. *Recordings:* Honegger's King David; Siebel in Faust, Mozart's L'Oca del Cairo; Marzelline in Fidelio; Zemlinsky's Traumgörge; First Lady in Die Zauberflöte; Flowermaiden in Parsifal conducted by Barenboim. *Honours:* Prizewinner at ARD Competition, Munich 1980; Metropolitan Auditions of the Air 1982. *Current Management:* Ingpen & Williams Ltd, 7 St George's Court, 131 Putney Bridge Road, London, SW15 2PA, England.

**COBURN, Robert James,** BMus, MA, PhD; American composer and educator; *Professor and Chair, Department of Music Composition and Theory, Conservatory of Music, University of the Pacific;* b. 29 Oct. 1949, Montebello, CA; m. Jeanne N. Ashby 1974; one s. *Education:* Univ. of California at Berkeley, Univ. of the Pacific, Univ. of Victoria, Canada. *Career:* composition commissions include Sun River Music Festival, San Francisco New Music Ensemble, Oregon Coast Music Festival, Sound-Art Environment Comm, City of Philadelphia Avenue of Arts 1995, Oregon Convention Centre (landscape), Henry Gallery, Seattle; performances include Festival of New Music, Roulette, New York, Forum '82 Int. Festival, New York, Electronic Music Plus Festival; mem. Int. Soc. for the Arts, Sciences and Technology, Computer Music Asscn; founding mem. World Forum for Acoustic Ecology. *Compositions:* Tranquil Turmoil Dreaming for computer and video, Patterns Luminous for shakuhachi and computer, Traces (Star Map l) for viola and computer sound, Staursahng electroacoustic music and images, Cantos for chamber orchestra, Bell Circles II permanent sound environment (Oregon Convention Center), Luminous Shadows for cello, piano, and percussion 1993, Songs of Solitude for chorus, Ellipse for solo flute, Shadowbox for clarinet 1994, Ad Vesperum for soprano and ten instruments. *Sound installations:* between... beyond (site-specific installation for four-channel sound and image boxes), 39 Bells (permanent sound installation, Avenue of the Arts, Philadelphia), Bell Circles II (permanent sound installation, Oregon Convention Center, Portland). *Publications:* Hearing is Believing: Visual Schemata in the Experience of Unfamiliar Music: Scientific Contributions to General Psychology (in Psicologia Generale, Musical Behavior and Cognition) 1999, Composing Space: The Integration of Music, Time and Space in Public Art (in Systems Research in the Arts Volume III) 2001, Composing Space: The Integration of Music, Time and Space in Multi-Dimensional Sound Installations (in Form, Space and Time, Australasian Computer Music Asscn) 2002; contrib. to Portland Review, Prologue; book and CD reviews for Leonardo, the Journal of the Int. Soc. for the Arts, Sciences and Technology, MIT Press 1993–. *Honours:* Oregon Artists Fellowship 1978, Eberhardt Research Fellowship 1995, Eberhardt Teacher/Scholar Award 1999. *Address:* Conservatory of Music, University of the Pacific, Stockton, CA 95211, USA (office). *Telephone:* (209) 946-2186 (office). *E-mail:* rcoburn@pacific.edu (office).

**COCCIANTE, Richard (Riccardo);** composer, singer, musician (piano) and arranger; b. Saigon, Viet Nam; m. Catherine Boutet; one s. *Career:* composer, solo artist 1972–; world-wide television, radio appearances; tour venues include Gran Teatro La Fenice, Venice 1988, Sporting Club, Monaco 1988, 1990, 1995, Teatro dell'opera Caracalla, Rome 1991, Vina del Mar Festival, Chile 1994, Olympia, Paris 1994, 1996, Zenith, Paris 1994, Taj Mahal, Atlantic City 1995, Teatro Sistina, Rome 1988, 1993, 1995, 1997, Théâtre St Denis, Montréal 1994, 1996, Stadsschouwberg, Amsterdam 1995, Vienna Rathaus 1997; collaborated with producers, including Paul Buckmaster, Humberto Gatica, Ennio Morricone, James Newton-Howard, Vangelis; participated in album World War II, interpreting Michelle with London Symphony Orchestra; concert, Christmas In Vienna (with Placido Domingo, Sarah Brightman and Helmut Lotti) 1997. *Compositions:* Notre Dame de Paris (musical, Felix Award for Album of the Year, Canada) 1998–99, 2000 (Hymne pour la ville de Lyon) commissioned by Raymonde Barre, Mayor of Lyon, to celebrate the new millennium, Le Petit Prince (musical) 2002. *Recordings include:* albums: (in Italian) Mu 1972, Poesia 1973, Anima 1974, L'alba 1975, Concerto per Margherita 1976, Riccardo Cicciante: A Mano A Mano 1978, ...E Io Canto 1979, Cervo a Primavera 1981, Cocciante (Celeste Nostalgia) 1982, Sincerità 1983, Il Mare dei Papaveri 1985, La Grande Avventura 1987, Se Stiamo Insieme 1991, Eventi e Mutamenti 1993, Un Uomo Felice 1994, Innamorato 1997; in French: Atlanti 1973, Quand un Amour 1974, Concerto pour Marguerite 1978, Je Chante 1979, Au Clair de tes Silences 1980, Vieille 1982, Sincérité 1983, L'Homme qui vole 1986, Empreinte 1993, L'Instant Présent 1995; 10 albums in Spanish; three albums in English; film soundtracks: Tandem 1987, Storia di una capinera 1994, Toy Story 1996, Astérix and Obélix contre César 1999; international hit singles: Bella Senz' Anima (Italy)/Bella Sin Alma (Spain, Latin America) 1973, Quand un Amour (France, Belgium, Canada) 1974, Margherita (Italy)/Marguerite (France, Belgium, Canada)/Margarita (Spain, Latin America) 1976–78, Coup de Soleil (France, Belgium) 1980, Cervo a Primavera (Italy)/Yo Renascere (Spain, Latin America) 1980, Sincéritié (France)/Sincerità (Italy, Holland)/Sinceridad (Spain, Latin America)/Sincerity (USA) 1983, Questione di Feeling (duet with Mina, Italy)/Question de Feeling (duet with Fabienne Thiebeault, France, Belgium, Canada)/Cuestion de Feeling (duet with Melissa, Spain, Latin America) 1985–86, Se Stiamo Insieme (Italy, Belgium, Holland, Brazil) 1991, Pour Elle (France)/Per Lei (Italy, Brazil)/I'd Fly (Italy, France, Belgium, Holland)/Por Ella (Latin America)/Voorbij (Holland) 1993–95, Il ricordo di un istante (Italy, France, Belgium, Canada, Holland), Belle, Le Temps des Cathédrales, Vivre (excerpts from musical Notre Dame de Paris, France, Belgium, Canada) 1998–99. *Honours:* Rose d'Or Award (Greece) 1981, Rino Gaetano Award (Italy) 1982, winner, San Remo Festival (Italy) 1991, Telegatto (Italy) 1991, Medaille de la Ville de Paris (France) 1998, Victoire de la Musique Awards (France) for Song of the Year 1999, for Show of the Year 1999, Grande ufficiale della Repubblica Italiana (Italy) 1999, World Music Award (Monaco) for Best-selling French Artist/Group 1999, Rolf Marbot Award (France) for Song of the Year 1999, Felix Awards (Canada) for Song of the Year 1999, for Show of the Year 1999, for Best-selling Album 1999, for Album of the Year 1999. *Address:* Boventoon BV, Information Office, 4 rue Chauveau Lagarde, 75008 Paris, France.

**COCHRAN, William;** Singer (Tenor); b. 23 June 1943, Columbus, Ohio, USA. *Education:* Studies with Martial Singher at the Curtis Institute, Philadelphia and with Lauritz Melchior and Lotte Lehmann in California. *Career:* Sang Wagner roles in San Francisco and Mexico; Many appearances in Europe from 1967, notably in Hamburg and Frankfurt, roles include Max in Der Freischütz, Jason in Médée, Otello, Herod in Salome and Dmitri in Boris Godunov; Concert with the New York Philharmonic 1971; Covent Garden debut 1974, as Laca in Jenůfa; San Francisco 1977, as Tichon in Katya Kabanova; Appearances in operas by Busoni, Janáček, Zimmermann, Shostakovich and Stravinsky (Tom Rakewell at Frankfurt 1983); Sang Bacchus in Ariadne auf Naxos at the Metropolitan Opera 1985; Deutsche Oper Berlin, 1989 Schreker's Die Gezeichneten; Season 1988–89 at Düsseldorf; Sang Siegfried in Paris and Brussels, 1991; Zimmermann's Die Soldaten at Strasbourg and Tichon (Katya Kabanova), Los Angeles; The Councillor in The Nose by Shostakovich, Frankfurt City Opera; Title role, Otello for Welsh National Opera, May 1990; Season 1992 as Samson at Amsterdam and Schoenberg's Aron (concert performance) at the Edinburgh Festival; Sang Aegisthus in Elektra at the First Night of the 1993 London Proms; Herod in Salome at San Francisco, 1997; Season 1998 with Aegisthus at Catania and Peter Grimes at Madrid; Season 2000–01 as Aegisthus in Elektra at Munich and Shuisky in Boris Godunov at Dusseldorf. *Recordings:* Mathis der Maler and Act I of Die Walküre; Doktor Faust by Busoni; Mahler's 8th Symphony. *Address:* c/o Welsh National Opera, John Street, Cardiff CF1 4SP, Wales.

**COCKER, Jonathan;** Stage Director; b. 1963, England. *Education:* Guildhall School of Music and Drama. *Career:* Productions of Purcell's Dido and Orfeo et Euridice for Jerusalem Studio Opera; Britten's Turn of the Screw for the Buxton Festival; Carmen and Orfeo for Northern Opera; Martinů's Comedy on the Bridge and Rimsky's Mozart and Salieri at the Ryedale Festival; Nielsen's Maskarade for the Opera North Tour, Purcell's Fairy Queen at festivals of Madrid, Athens and Valencia; Also for English Bach Festival at Linbury Theatre, Covent Garden, 2001; Further engagements with New Israel Opera, Opera North and Opera Studio; Musicals and Plays in the West End and on Tours to the United Kingdom and Europe.

**CODREANU-MIHALCEA, Claudia;** Singer (Mezzo-soprano); b. 1969, Romania. *Career:* Many concert and opera engagements in Romania and elsewhere in Europe; Repertory includes Mozart's Clemenza di Tito, Rossini's Cenerentola, and songs by Brahms and Mussorgsky; Contestant at the 1995 Cardiff Singer of the World Competition. *Address:* Bloc 3, SC 1, Apt 38, Sector 2, Str Doamna Ghieca nr 5, 72404 Bucharest, Romania.

**COELHO, Elaine;** Singer (soprano); b. 1950, Rio de Janeiro, Brazil. *Education:* Studied in Rio and Hanover. *Career:* Sang at Landestheater Detmold from 1974 as Verdi's Violetta and Nannetta, Mozart's Constanze, Zdenka in Arabella and Liu in Turandot; Stadttheater Bremen from 1976, as Norina in Don Pasquale, Mozart's Susanna, Euridice, Fiorilla in Il Turco in Italia and Lulu; Sang at Frankfurt am Main from 1984 and appeared as guest in Turin as Lulu; Further engagements at Aachen, the Vienna Volksoper and the Bregenz Festival, Giulietta in Les Contes d'Hoffmann, 1988; Sang Donna Anna in Don Giovanni at the Teatro Municipal, Rio de Janeiro, 1991; Vienna Volksoper 1992, as Abigaille in Nabucco; Season 1995–96 as Salomé in Hérodiade at the Vienna Staatsoper, Donna Elvira and Elettra in Idomeneo at the Munich Staatsoper; Season 2000–01 at the Vienna Staatsoper, as Elvira in Ernani and Offenbach's Giulietta.

**COELHO DE SOUZA, Rodolfo,** MA; Brazilian composer; b. 8 Aug. 1952, São Paulo. *Education:* University of São Paulo, University of Texas, Austin, USA. *Career:* Co-director, Santos and São Paulo New Music Festival, 1984–93; Director of Symposium at Winter Festival of Campos do Jordão, 1998–93; Chiarosuro premiered by the American Composers Orchestra, 1996. *Compositions:* Phantasiestück for string quartet, 1982; Carnavalia, for orchestra, 1983; Rébus, for piano, 1985; Galáxias for piano and orchestra, 1998; Diálogos for marimba and vibraphone, 1998; Oblique Rain, for ensemble, 1992; Luminosidades, for orchestra, 1993; Fractal Landscapes, for ensemble, 1993; Chiaroscuro, for piano, tape and two percussionists, 1995; Invariants, for wind quintet and piano, 1995; What Happens Beneath the City While Janis Sleeps, electro-acoustic, 1997. *Address:* c/o SBAT, Rua da Quintanda 194-1o, Caixa Postal no. 1503, Rio de Janeiro (GB), Brazil.

**COEN, Massimo;** Violinist and Composer; b. 11 March 1933, Rome, Italy; m. Mirella Thau, 2 s., 1 d. *Education:* Law Degree, Rome University; Violin Diploma, St Cecilia Conservatory, Rome; Private Study, Chamber Music and Violin. *Career:* Founder, Chamber Music Groups; I Solisti di Roma, 1961 and Quartetto Nuova Musica, 1963, giving concerts and radio performances throughout Europe; Tour of USA and Canada as soloist with Cameristica Italiana, 1969; Founder, Music School, Rome; Teacher, National Academy of Dance; Discoverer, Editor and Performer of numerous ancient Italian musical MSS; mem, Professional Associations and Councils. *Compositions:* Quartetto II, 4 Temperamenti, 1987; Divertimento I, flute and strings, 1988; Divertimento II, La Marsigliese, 1989; Violin-Concerto, Saudades de Rio, 1991; C'Era una Volta, 1979; Integrazioni, 1980; Dosilado, 1983; Nascite, 1983; Peav Suite, 1983; Didone, 1983; La Donna Senz'ombra, 1984; Il Rovescio della Medaglia, 1984; Sophitour, 1985; Introduzione e Valzer in Do, 1985; Quartetto per Archi No. 1, 1986; Quartetto per Archi No. 2, 1987; Concerto Grosso per Orchestra D'Archi, 1988; 2 Divertimenti, 1988–89; Fantasia Per Oboe e Quartetto D'Archi, 1993; 3 Liriche Per Soprano and Violin, 1994; Maternidade, As Palabras, A Obra per soprano e violino su poesie di M. L. Verdi, 1994; Crysolith D 12 per violino e fisarmonica, 1996; Lolly, per quartetto d'archi e danza, 1996; Le Opere e i Giorni per due violini, 1996; L'Anima Negli Occhi per violino e viola, 1996; O' Mazzamauriello per violino e violoncello, 1996; Tenores per sax soprano e quartetto d'archi, 1997; Mneme per soprano, sax

soprano e quartetto d'archi; Transcrizioni da Handel, Haydn, Mozart, Donizetti per voce e quartetto d'archi, 1998; Accelerazioni, Serpentine e Itaca per quartetto d'archi, 1999; Mediterraneo per violino, flauto, clarinetto e sassofono, 2000; Nascita di Afrodite for Violin, clarinet, Sax alto, dance, 2000; Cosi 'Fan Tutti for violin and actor; Accelerazioni II for violin, percussion and dance, 2001; Lo Sforzo Umano for violin, percussion, actor and dancers, 2002; Moby Dick for violin, bass clarinet, percussion and actor, 2003; Zampe, Zampette — Ninna Nanna for string quartet and Bell 2003; Kleines Quartettsatz for strings, 2003. *Recordings:* Baroque and Contemporary Music; Massimo Coen works Edipan Rome; Massimo Coen Live Portrait, 2002. *Contributions:* Mondo Operaio. *Honours:* Member, International Jury, Gaudeamus Foundation Competition, Rotterdam, 1976; 2002 Carsulae Award. *Address:* Via Ipponio 8, 00183 Rome, Italy.

**COERTSE, Mimi;** Singer (Soprano); b. 12 June 1932, Durban, South Africa. *Education:* Studied in Johannesburg and in Vienna, with Josef Witt. *Career:* Debut: With the Vienna Staatsoper in Naples, as a Flowermaiden in Parsifal, 1955; Basle 1956, as the Queen of Night; Tour of South Africa; Appearances at the Salzburg Festival as Constanze in Die Entführung, 1956; Glyndebourne Festival 1957, as Zerbinetta; Sang at the Vienna Staatsoper from 1957; Salzburg 1960, as the Queen of Night; Mahler's 8th Symphony; Guest Appearances in London, Cologne, Brussels, Frankfurt and Munich; Sang Mozart's Countess in Pretoria, South Africa, 1989. *Recordings:* Fiakermilli in Arabella.

**COGEN, Pierre;** French organist, composer and professor of music; b. 2 Oct. 1931, Paris, France; m. Michèle Vermesse, 5 July 1986. *Education:* Cathedral Music School for Children, 1944–51; Higher studies in Philosophy, Paris, 1957–59; Organ study with Jean Langlais, Schola Cantorum; Certificate of Competence as Professor of Organ at National Conservatories; CAPES, Music Education (Secondary). *Career:* Liturgical Organist, 1945–94; Director of Boys' Choir, 1952–65; Concert Organist, 1959–; Professor of Organ and Music Education, 1961–93; Assistant to Jean Langlais, Sainte Clotilde and Schola Cantorum, 1972–76; Organist, Basilique Sainte Clotilde, 1976–94. *Compositions include:* Pieces for Organ, published in Das neue Orgelbaum II, 1986; Pieces for Organ, in Pedals Only, 1988; Offrande, 1990; Nocturne, 1992; Deux Chorals, 1992; Cortège, 1996; Various unpublished works. *Recordings:* Organ works of Jean Langlais, 3 recordings; Sept Chorals-Poémes pour les Sept Paroles du Christ, de Charles Tournemire. *Publications:* Autour du grand-orgue du Basilique Sainte Clotilde, Les orgues d'Aquitaine. *Honours:* Recipient, prizes for organ and for composition, Président de la Fédération Francophone des Amis de l'Orgue F.F.A.O., 2003. *Address:* 12 rue Saint-Saëns, 75015 Paris, France. *E-mail:* pierre.cogen@wanadoo.fr (office).

**COGHILL, Harry MacLeod,** ARMCM; British opera and concert singer (bass); b. 14 April 1944, Edinburgh, Scotland; m. Anna Sweeny 1970; one s. one d. *Education:* Royal Manchester College of Music, studied singing with Frederick Cox, with Yvonne Rodd-Marling. *Career:* debut with English National Opera, as Seneca in Monteverdi's L'Incoronazione di Poppea, 1971; Concert tour of North America, 1965; Member of Glyndebourne Festival Chorus, 1970, 1971; Principal Bass, English National Opera, 1971–79; Created several roles in contemporary operas; Extensive repertoire in all periods of opera and oratorio; Freelance appearances with English Music Theatre, Handel Opera, Kent Opera, Opera 80 and other English companies, 1979–; Appearances in festivals at Aldeburgh, Belfast, Dortmund, Exeter, Munich, Vienna; Founder, A Song for Ockenden, concert series for The Ockenden Venture, in aid of refugee children, 1980; Lecturer in Singing, School of Music, University of Auckland, New Zealand, 1987. *Contributions:* Educational supplements. *Address:* Derryheen, Hook Heath Road, Woking, Surrey GU22 0LB, England.

**COGNET, André;** Singer (Bass-baritone); b. 1967, France. *Education:* Marseille Conservatoire; Studio of the Paris Opéra. *Career:* Sang Puccini's Schaunard at Toulouse, in Stravinsky's Pulcinella at the Théâtre des Champs Elyseés, Escamillo in Peter Brook's version of Carmen, baritone roles in Les Contes d'Hoffmann and Mozart's Figaro; Wexford Festival appearances as Gaveston in La Dame Blanche and Donizetti's L'Assedio de Calais; Further engagments as Zuniga in Carmen at Munich, Guglielmo at Karlsruhe, Hamlet at Rouen and Zurga for Opera North; Captain in Gulitt's Wozzeck at Rouen, 1997; Season 1997/98 with Les Noces by Stravsinsky under Marek Janowski, L'Enfance du Christ by Berlioz in Madrid, and the title role in Paisiello's Il Re Teodoro a Venezia, at the Teatro La Fenice; Verona Arena 1999 as Escamillo in Carmen; Season 2000–2001 as Puccini's Lescaut, with the Israel Philharmonic and Ravel's L'Enfant et les Sortilèges in Berlin; US debut as Gounod's Mephistopheles for Florida Grand Opera, 2002. *Address:* c/o Musicaglotz, 11 rue Le Verrier, 75006 Paris, France.

**COGRAM, John;** singer (tenor); b. 1967, Sussex, England. *Education:* Royal College of Music, National Opera Studio and with Janice Chapman; masterclasses with Birgit Nilsson and Luigi Alva. *Career:* Ulm Opera 1994–96, as M. Triquet in Eugene Onegin, Wenzel in The Bartered Bride, Steersman in Fliegende Hollander, Remendado (Carmen) and Bajazet in Handel's Tamerlano; Other roles include Alfredo in La Traviata at Clonter Farm, Pinkerton with English Festival Opera and Rodolfo with English Touring Opera; Oronte in Handel's Alcina in concert performances at Cologne; Basle Opera from 1996, as Pedrillo (Entführung) and Pang in Turandot; Recitals include: Die schöne Müllerin and Dichterliebe. *Honours:* Cuthbert Smith Award, RCM.

**COHEN, Arnaldo;** Concert Pianist; b. 22 April 1948, Rio de Janeiro, Brazil; 1 s., 2 step-c. *Education:* Engineering University of Rio de Janeiro; Graduate in Piano and Violin, School of Music, Federal University of Rio de Janeiro. *Career:* Debut: Royal Festival Hall, London, 1977; Appearances at Albert Hall, Barbican, Queen Elizabeth Hall and Wigmore Hall in London, La Scala in Milan, Concertgebouw in Amsterdam and Musikverein in Vienna; Performed in the Amadeus Piano Trio, 1988–92; Fellow of RNCM, Manchester, 1992–; Served on the Jury of the Busoni, Liszt and Chopin Competitions; Concerts under Menuhin, Tennstedt, Sanderling and Masur; Masterclasses in Europe, USA and South America; Currently teaching at the Royal Academy of Music, London. *Recordings:* Brasiliana, Three Centuries of Music from Brazil; Chopin 2nd Scherzo, 4th Ballade, Allegro de Concert, Largo and Bolero; Liszt B Minor Sonata, Dante Sonata, Scherzo and March. Schumann Fantasie op 17, Arabesque op 18, Brahms Handel variations; Liszt Sonata. *Recordings:* For television and radio, BBC, Dutch, German, Italian and others. *Honours:* 1st Prize, Beethoven Competition, 1970; 1st Prize, Busoni Piano Competition, Italy, 1972; Broadwood Fellow in Piano studies at Royal Northern College of Music, 1991; Appointed to the Broadwood Trust Fellowship, Royal Northern College of Music, 1992; Fellow, Royal Northern College of Music honoris causa, 2000. *Telephone:* (20) 7723 7787 (home). *E-mail:* arnalddocohen@ compuserve.com (home). *Current Management:* Arts Management Group, Mr William Capone, St James Building, 1133 Broadway, Suite 1025, New York, 10010, USA. *Fax:* (20) 7738 0909.

**COHEN, David;** Belgian concert cellist; b. 14 June 1980, Tournai. *Education:* Conservatoire Royal de Bruxelles, 1991–93; Yehudi Menuhin School, 1994–98; Guildhall School of Music and Drama, London, 1998–2002, with Oleg Kogan; Masterclasses with Rostropovich, Natalia Gutman, William Pleeth, Steven Isserlis, Bernard Greenhouse and Boris Pergamenschikov. *Career:* Played in Rostropovich's cello sextet at age 17 and tour in Germany with Saint-Petersburg Philharmonic Orchestra; Int. soloist from age 11 with Belgian, French, Swiss, UK and Polish orchestras including the Polish Philharmonic under Menuhin (Tchaikovsky's Pezzo Capriccioso) and Philharmonia Orchestra, Royal Festival Hall, London (Shostakovitch Concerto) under Sir Charles Mackerras; Youngest Ever Principal Cellist of the Philharmonia Orchestra, 2001. *Recordings:* Lalo Cello Concerto, with the Liège Philharmonic (Cyprès); Lutowslasky pieces with Forlane; Jeunes solistes francophones. *Honours:* numerous grants and awards including First Prize, Int. Music Competition, Wathrelos, France, 1995; 1st Grand Finalist, Audi Int. Competition, UK, 1995; Winner, Geneva Int. Cello Competition, Patrick F. Liechti Special Prize, 2000; Guildhall Gold Medal, 2002; Young Soloist of the Year, Community of French speaking Radios of the World (CRPLF), 2003; Radio Suisse Romande Award, Hattory Foundation, 2003. *Address:* c/o Philharmonia Orchestra, 1st Floor, 125 High Holborn, London, WC1V 6QA, England. *Telephone:* (20) 7274-6116 (home). *Fax:* (7887) 649026 (office). *Website:* www.davidcohen.be.

**COHEN, Joel,** MA; Conductor, Lutenist, Writer and Lecturer; *Director, Boston Camerata;* b. 23 May 1942, Providence, Rhode Island, USA. *Education:* Brown Univ., MA Harvard Univ.; studied theory and composition with Nadia Boulanger, Paris. *Career:* Dir Boston Camerata 1968–; guest conductor at various music festivals (Aix-en-Provence, Strasbourg, Tanglewood); Lecturer Early Music Performance at US and European univs and conservatories; specialist in Mediaeval, Renaissance and Baroque music. *Recordings:* with Boston Camerata and Cambridge Consort; Johnny Johnson by Weill, Cantigas de Santa Maria 1999. *Honours:* Grand Prix du Disque 1989. *Address:* c/o The Aaron Concert Management, 729 Boylston Street, Suite 206, Boston, MA 02116, USA.

**COHEN, Raymond;** Violinist; b. 27 July 1919, Manchester, England; m. 8 Mar 1953, 1 s., 1 d. *Education:* Fellow, Royal Manchester College of Music. *Career:* Debut: As a child; International soloist, having played with major orchestras in many parts of the world; Leader of many orchestras, including Royal Philharmonic Orchestra, 1959–65; Violinist, Cohen Trio; Soloist on BBC radio and television; mem, Incorporated Society of Musicians. *Recordings:* Violinist, Delius's Double Concerto, with Royal Philharmonic Orchestra; Soloist, Robert Farnon's Rhapsody; Saint-Saëns's Introduction and Rondo Capriccioso; Vivaldi's Concerto for 2 violins and orchestra. *Honours:* 1st Prizewinner, Carl Flesch International Competition, 1945; Honorary Member, Royal College of Music. *Address:* 6 Alvanley Gardens, London NW6 1 JD, England.

**COHEN, Robert;** British cellist, conductor and academic; *Professor of Advanced Cello Studies, Conservatorio della Svizzera Italiana di Lugano*; b. 15 June 1959, London; s. of Raymond Cohen and Anthya Rael; m. Rachel Smith 1987; four s. *Education:* Purcell School and Guildhall School of Music, cello studies with William Pleeth, André Navarra, Jacqueline du Pré and Mstislav Rostropovich. *Career:* started playing cello aged five; Royal Festival Hall debut (Boccherini Concerto), aged 12; London recital debut, Wigmore Hall, aged 17; Tanglewood Festival, USA 1978; recording debut (Elgar concerto) 1979; concerts USA, Europe and Eastern Europe 1979; since 1980, concerts world-wide with major orchestras and with conductors who include Muti, Abbado, Dorati, Sinopoli, Otaka, Mazur, Davis, Marriner and Rattle; Dir Charleston Manor Festival, E Sussex 1989–; regular int. radio broadcasts and many int. TV appearances; plays on the 'Ex-Roser' David Tecchler of Rome cello dated 1723; conductor, various chamber orchestras 1990–; symphony orchestras 1997–; Visiting Prof., RAM 1998–; Prof. of Advanced Cello Studies, Conservatorio della Svizzera Italiana di Lugano 2000–; Fellow

Purcell Scholl for Young Musicians 1992–. *Recordings include:* Elgar concerto (new Elgar concerto 1993), Dvořák concerto, Tchaikovsky Rococo Variations, Rodrigo Concierto en modo Galante, Beethoven Triple concerto, Grieg sonata, Franck sonata, Virtuoso Cello Music record, Dvořák Complete Piano trios with Cohen Trio, Schubert String Quintet with Amadeus Quartet, Complete Bach solo cello Suites, Howard Blake Diversions, Bliss Concerto 1992, Walton Concerto 1995, Britten Cello Suites 1997, Morton Feldman Concerto 1998, Britten Cello Symphony 1998, Sally Beamish Cello Concerto River 1999, HK Gruber Cello Concerto 2003. *Television:* Bach Sarabandes (BBC), Elgar Cello Concerto (BBC), Beamish Cello Concerto (BBC). *Honours:* Winner Young Concert Artists Int. Competition, New York 1978, Píatigorsky Prize, Tanglewood Festival 1978, Winner UNESCO Int. Competition, Czechoslovakia 1981. *Address:* True Music, 15 Birchwood Avenue, London, N10 3BE, England (office). *Telephone:* (20) 8444-1065 (office). *Fax:* (20) 8365-2563 (office). *E-mail:* info@true-music.com (office). *Website:* www.true-music.com (office); www .robertcohen.info (home).

**COHN, James (Myron);** Composer, Musicologist and Inventor; b. 12 Feb. 1928, Newark, New Jersey, USA; m. Eileen B Wions, 3 Sept 1979. *Education:* BS, 1949, MS, 1950, Juilliard School of Music; Postgraduate study in Electronic Music, Hunter College, New York; Study of Musical Composition with Roy Harris, Wayne Barlow and Bernard Wagenaar. *Career:* Musicologist, American Society of Composers, Authors and Publishers, 1954–84; Inventor of various patented control devices for electronic musical instruments; mem, American Federation of Musicians; American Society of Composers, Authors and Publishers; Songwriters' Guild of America. *Compositions include:* Published works: Symphonies Nos 3–8; A Song of the Waters; Variations on The Wayfaring Stranger; Variations on John Henry; The Little Circus; Sonata for Flute and Piano; Statues in the Park, choral; 2 Concertos for Clarinet and String Orchestra. *Recordings include:* Concerto da camera; Quintet for Winds; Little Overture; Sonatina for clarinet and piano; Sonata for flute and piano; Serenade for flute, violin and cello; Trio for piano, violin and cello; Mount Gretna Suite for chamber orchestra; Homage, Tone poem for orchestra; Concerto for piano and orchestra; Concerto for trumpet and strings; Concerto for concertina and strings; Evocations Concerto No. 2 for clarinet and strings; Concerto No. 1 for clarinet and strings; A song of the Waters, Tone poem for orchestra, (Variations on Shenandoah). Recordings for radio, television and films. *Contributions:* Book reviews to Library Journal. *Honours:* Queen Elisabeth of Belgium Prize for Symphony No. 2, 1953; AIDEM Prize for Symphony No. 4. *Address:* 38-62 240th Street, Little Neck, NY 11363, USA.

**COHRS, (Benjamin) Gunnar;** conductor, music researcher and publicist; b. 1965, Hameln, Germany. *Education:* Jugendmusikschule Hameln, 1972–85; Hochschule für Künste Bremen, 1989–94; University of Adelaide, 1994–95 (as DAAD Scholar); High Distinction Degrees in Conducting, Flute and Voice, 1994; Diploma in Musicology, 1996. *Career:* Conductor of the Jugendstreichorchester Hameln, 1985–90; Bremen String Orchestra, 1991–95; Several choirs; Conducting assistances and appearances; International conducting debut, Russian National Orchestra, Moscow, 2000; Japanese Debut: Royal Flanders Philharmonic, Tokyo, 2001; Principal Guest Conductor of the New Queen's Hall Orchestra, London, 2002; mem, Internationale Bruckner Gesellschaft Wien. *Compositions include:* Chamber Music: amour perdu for Piano, 1994, arranged for small orchestra, 1999. *Publications:* Bruckner, IX Symphony, Finale, (completed performing version), 1993; Frank Martin: Sonata da Chiesa, arranged for flute and strings, 1995; Bruckner, Studienband zum 2. Satz der IX Sinfonie, 1998: Bruckner Two discarded Trios for the IX Sinfonie, completed performing versions, 1998; Bruckner, IX Sinfonie, (new critical edition and report), 1999. *Contributions:* Radio Bremen; Fono Forum; Klassik Heute; BREMER-Die Stadtillustrierte; Weserkurier; Programme notes; CD booklets; essays; articles; papers at international conferences. *Current Management:* Arte Music, Bettina Braun-Angott, Maximilian-Wetzger-Str. 6, 80636, Munich. *Address:* Postfach 107507, 28075 Bremen, Germany. *E-mail:* artiumbremen@yahoo.de.

**COKER, Paul;** Pianist; b. 1959, London, England. *Education:* Began piano studies aged 5 and entered Yehudi Menuhin School, 1967, piano with Louis Kentner. *Career:* Won National Federation of Music Societies' Concert Award, 1978, and soon gave several London recitals, as well as concerts in France, Germany, Belgium, Netherlands, the USA, Canada and India; Further study at Tanglewood, USA, from 1980, winning the Jackson Master Award there; Has played with most leading British orchestras and with the Berlin Philharmonic; The Grieg Concerto with the Belgian National Symphony; Many recitals with Yehudi Menuhin in Europe, the USA, Far East and Australia.

**COKU, Alexandru;** Singer (Soprano); b. 1963, USA. *Education:* Studied with Margaret Harshaw at Indiana University. *Career:* Has sung in Europe from 1988, notably as Euridice to the Orpheus of Jochen Kowalski at Covent Garden and as Pamina at the rebuilt Frankfurt Opera, 1991; Further engagements as Pamina at Vienna, Munich and Düsseldorf; Amsterdam, 1992, as Ismene in Mozart's Mitridate; US appearances as Anne Trulove in The Rake's Progress at Chicago (1990) and Cecilio in Lucio Silla at San Francisco (1991); Season 1995–96 as Mozart's Elektra, Offenbach's Antonia and Constanze at Düsseldorf, Romilda in Handel's Xerxes at Cologne, 1998; Giulietta in Les Contes d'Hoffmann; Season 2000–01 as Mozart's Countess in Cologne, Ellen Orford at Nancy and Handel's Agrippina for Glimmerglass

Opera. *Address:* c/o Cologne Opera, Offenbachplatz, Pf. 180241, D–50505 Cologne, Germany.

**COLAIANNI, Domenico;** Singer (Baritone); b. 1964, Italy. *Education:* N. Piccinni Conservatory, Bari. *Career:* Early appearances as Mengotto in Piccinni's La Cecchina, Papageno and Schaunard in La Bohème; Enrico in Donizetti's Il Campanello and Slook in Rossini's La Cambiale at Bologna; Cimarosa's Maestro di Capella at Parma, Ping in Turandot at Lecce and Bizet's Don Procopio in Novara; Further engagements in Australia, in Paisiello's Il Barbiere di Siviglia, Rossini's Il Signor Bruschino in Tokyo and Osaka, and Donizetti's Olivio e Pasquale in Germany; Operas by Salieri, Vivaldi and Hasse in Budapest; Sang in the first modern performance of I Rantzau, by Mascagni, at Livorno; Festival of Martina Franca in Leo's Amor vuol sofferenza, and as Lisandro in Piccinni's L'Americano, 1996. *Recordings include:* L'Americano (Dynamic).

**COLBERT, Brendan;** Composer; b. 11 Sept. 1956, Ballarat, Victoria, Australia. *Education:* Studied with Brenton Broadstock, 1983–86 Riccardo Formosa 1986–88; National Orchestral Composers School, 1991, 1995. *Compositions include:* Passages for alto saxophone, electric guitar, piano and percussion, 1987; Murderers of Calm for ensemble, 1987; Agite II for mandolin, 1989; Fourplay for viola, cello, clarinet and piano, 1991; Agite I for flute, 1991; Parallaxis for ensemble, 1993; Agite II for piano, 1993–95; Mirror, Picture, Echo, Shadow, Dream for cello, flute, percussion and piano, 1994; Entfernt for string orchestra, 1994; Sphinx for ensemble, 1995; Sanctuary for orchestra, 1995. *Honours:* Warringah Eisteddfod Young Composers Competiton, 1985. *Address:* c/o APRA, 1A Eden Street, Crows Nest, NSW 2065, Australia.

**COLD, Ulrik;** Singer (Bass); b. 15 May 1939, Copenhagen, Denmark. *Education:* As Singer, privately educated in Copenhagen and Århus; Bachelor of Laws from Copenhagen University. *Career:* Sang in concert from 1963, then in opera in Copenhagen; Engaged at Kassel, 1969–71; Komische Oper Berlin, 1971, as Massenet's Don Quixote; Sang Sarastro in the Bergman film version of Die Zauberflöte; Intendant of the Royal Opera Copenhagen, 1975–77; Baroque repertory concerts in France, Germany, Netherlands, Switzerland and Scandinavia; Operatic roles include: Wagner's Marke, Landgraf and Gurnemanz; Verdi's Padre Guardiano and Zaccaria; Roles in works by Handel, Monteverdi and Rameau; US debut, San Francisco, as Sarastro, 1980; Alazim in Zaide, Wexford Festival, 1981; Sang at Teatro Comunale Bologna, 1987; The General in The Gambler by Prokofiev, English National Opera, 1991; Saul in a concert version of Nielsen's Saul and David, London, 1992. *Recordings:* Armide by Lully; Admeto by Handel; Rameau's Hippolyte et Aricie and Handel's Xerxes; L'Incoronazione di Poppea; St Matthew Passion by Bach; Ulrik Cold Sings Carl Nielsen; Schnittke's Faust Cantata. *Address:* c/o Allied Artists Agency, 42 Montpelier Square, London SW7 1JZ, England.

**COLDING-JORGENSEN, Henrik;** Composer, Organist, Pedagogue and Choir Leader; b. 21 March 1944, Riisskov, Denmark; m. (1) Birgit Nielsen, 1966–87, (2) Mette Bramso, 1992–99, 1 d. *Education:* Organist, 1966, Organ Pedagogue, Royal Danish Conservatory. *Career:* Organ teacher; Teacher of Musical Theory; Organist; Choir Leader; Producer of radio and television programmes; Composer; Chairman of Board, Holstebro Electronic Music Studio, 1977–85; Member, Musical Committee, Roskilde County, 1979–87; Member, Committee of Representatives of State Music Council, 1981–91; Member, Committee of Representatives of State Art Council, 1981–85; Member, Danish Arts Council, 1981–84; mem, Danish Composer Society, Board, 1981–91; Danish ISCM, Board until 1982; Danish Organist and Cantor Society, Board, 1992–95; Danish Choirleaders, 1996. *Compositions include:* Ave Maria, 1974; Balances, 1974; To Love Music, 1975; Victoria Through the Forest, 1975; Boast, 1980; Dein Schweigen, 1982; Recitativ and Fuga; An Die Nachgeborenen ll, 1984; Du Sollst Nicht, 1984; Sic Enim, 1985; Nuup Kangerlua, 1985; Partita, aria e minuetto, 1986; Le Alpi Nel Cuore, 1988; 2 Songs by Keats, 1988; Nunc Est, 1989; The Soul and The Butterfly, 1990; Babylon, 1991; As a Traveller, 1992; Krystal; Metamorfose for string quartet, 1993; Discourse with Time, 1996; Sourires, 1997; Four British Songs, 1997; Duo Viri in Vestibus Albis, 1999; Dolori, 2000; Elegie-Wiegenlied, 2000; Englens Händ, 2001; Primavere, 2002; Kyrie Agnus Dei, 2002. *Honours:* Various bursaries, prizes and commissions; Concours International de Composition Musicale Opera et Ballet, Geneva, 1985. *Address:* Kildehuset 3, 3.tv, 2670 Greve, Denmark. *E-mail:* mail@hc-j.dk. *Website:* www.hc-j.dk.

**COLE, Rosamund;** Singer (Soprano); b. 1968, England. *Education:* Royal Northern College of Music; National Opera Studio, London; Cologne Opera Studio. *Career:* Appearances with British Youth Opera, 1992 and 1993, as Susanna in Le nozze di Figaro and Ninetta in La Gazza Ladra; With Opera North in 1996 as Barbarina; At Cologne Opera, 1996–98, as Ännchen in Der Freischütz, Priestess in Aida, Johanna in Sondheim's Sweeney Todd, Barbarina, Despina, Zerlina and Gretel in Hänsel und Gretel; Darmstadt Staatstheater, 1998–2000, as Serpetta in La Finta Giardiniera, Hannchen in Der Vetter aus Dingsda, Frasquita in Carmen, Valencienne in Die Lustige Witwe and Gretel; Concert appearances include Wigmore Hall recital in 1994 and Flowermaiden in Parsifal with the Cologne Philharmonie with James Conlon. *Honours:* Countess of Munster Award; Sybil Tutton Prize; Wolfson Prize Grant. *Address:* Music International, 13 Ardilaun Road, London N5 2QR, England.

**COLE, Steve;** Singer (Tenor); b. 1954, USA. *Career:* Sang with Washington Opera from 1981, Aix-en-Provence (as Monostatos), 1982, and in Paris,

Avignon (Henze's Boulevard Solitude), and Nice; New York Metropolitan debut, 1987, as Brighella in Ariadne auf Naxos; San Francisco Opera from 1990; Other modern repertory includes the premieres of Medea by Gavin Bryars (Lyon, 1984) and La Noche Triste by Prodromidès (Nancy, 1989); Other buffo and character roles include Bardolph in Falstaff, Pong in Turandot and Sellem in The Rake's Progress; Sang John Styx in Orphée aux Enfers, Geneva, 1998; Season 1999–2000 as Monostatos in Barcelona and Osmin in Haydn's l'Incontro Improvviso at Eisenstadt. *Address:* c/o San Francisco Opera, War Memorial House, Van Ness Avenue, San Francisco, CA 94102, USA.

**COLE, Tobias;** Singer (Countertenor); b. 1969, Australia. *Education:* BMus (Hons) University of Sydney, 1993, ARCM, Royal College of Music, 1994. *Career:* Appearances included Medoro in Handel's Orlando for West Australian Opera, Eustazio in Rinaldo for Opera Australia and Ulisse in Deidamia for the London Handel Festival; Title role in Rinaldo for Abbey Opera; Other roles include Farnace in Mitridate and Handel's Julius Caesar; Oratorios include St Matthew Passion for City of Bath Bach Choir, Messiah for Queensland and Adelaide Symphonies, Bernstein's Chichester Psalms with the Sydney Phiharmonia and Handel's Brockes Passion for the London Handel Festival, 2000–2001; Sang in Purcell's Fairy Queen for the English Bach Festival at the Linbury Theatre, Covent Garden, 2001.

**COLE, Vinson;** Singer (Tenor); b. 21 Nov. 1950, Kansas City, Kansas, USA. *Education:* Studied at the Curtis Institute, Philadelphia. *Career:* Debut: Sang Werther in the opera by Massenet while still a student, 1975; Sang in the premiere of Jubilee by Ulysses Kay at Jackson, Mississippi, in 1976; European debut, 1976, with Welsh National Opera, as Belmonte in Die Entführung aus dem Serail; Later appearances in Stuttgart, Naples, Salzburg, Paris and Marseilles; St Louis, 1976–80, as Tamino and Rossini's Comte Ory; New York City Opera, 1981, as Fenton in Die lustigen Weiber von Windsor; Other roles include Gennaro in Lucrezia Borgia, Nadir in Les Pêcheurs de Perles, Lenski in Eugene Onegin, Gluck's Orfeo and Gounod's Faust; Sang in Mozart's Requiem under Georg Solti at Vienna, 1991; Sang Donizetti's Edgardo at Detroit, Ferrando at Seattle, 1992; Nadir in Les Pêcheurs de Perles in Seattle, 1994; Sang Jason in Cherubini's Medea, Athens 1995; Don Carlo in the French version of Verdi's opera, Brussels, 1996; Renaud in Gluck's Armide, to open the 1996–97 Season at La Scala; Season 1999–2000 as Mozart's Titus at Covent Garden (house debut); Season 2000–01 as Gerald in Lakmé at Seattle, the Berlioz Faust at Edinburgh and Cavaradossi in Sydney. *Address:* c/o Seattle Opera Association, PO Box 9248, Seattle, WA 98109, USA.

**COLEMAN, Tim;** British stage director; b. 30 Oct. 1949, Eastbourne, Sussex, England. *Education:* Univ. of Cambridge and Amsterdam Conservatory. *Career:* wrote incidental music for over 30 plays; Chief Dramaturg, Netherlands Opera 1986–90; freelance dir 1990–; debut as Dir with Opera Northern Ireland in Die Fledermaus 1990, returned for Le nozze di Figaro 1991 and Rigoletto 1992; US debut with The Beggar's Opera for the Manhattan School of Music; season 1991–92, Tosca for Minnesota Opera and Opera Omaha, Tamerlano for Dublin Opera Theatre, and The Merry Wives of Windsor for the Guildhall School of Music; season 1992–93, L'Italiana in Algeri for Dublin Grand Opera/Opera Ireland, Così fan tutte in Oklahoma City; season 1993–94, Rigoletto in Hong Kong, L'Isola disabitata in New York, Tosca in Indianapolis, Le nozze di Figaro for the Kirov Opera in the Mariinsky Theatre, St Petersburg; festivals of Mikkele, Finland, Schleswig-Holstein, Germany, and Beth Shean (Israel); season 1994–95; directed Romeo et Juliette in Shanghai 1995; Chief Dramaturg, Deutsche Oper am Rhein Duesseldorf/Duisburg 1996–99; Artistic Dir, opera of Oporto; Swiss debut with production of I Puritani for Ensemble Theater (Biel/Bienne) 2000, and Il Pirata 2002; other recent productions include Stiffelio at Theatre Argentina, La Plata, Madama Butterfly for Opera Holland Park and Cork Opera, La Traviata at Megaron Musiki, Thessaloniki, Die Fledermaus for Opera Cork, Il barbiere di Siviglia for Opera Holland Park, Lucia di Lammermoor for Mississippi Opera, Carousel for Opera Illinois, and Kiss Me Kate in Gelsenkirchen.

**COLEMAN-WRIGHT, Peter;** Singer (baritone); b. 1958, Australia; m. Cheryl Barker. *Education:* Studied in London with Otakar Kraus, Joan Hammond, Paul Hamburger and Geoffrey Parsons. *Career:* Has sung at Glyndebourne as Guglielmo, Demetrius, Dandini, Morales in Carmen and Sid in Albert Herring; English National Opera as Niels Lyhne in Fennimore and Gerda, Rossini's Barber, Schaunard, Billy Budd and Don Giovanni; Australian Opera as Mozart's Count; Covent Garden, Dandini, then Don Alvaro in Rossini's Il Viaggio a Reims and Papageno; Bordeaux Opera, Guglielmo, Masetto; Victoria State Opera, Wolfram, Papageno, Valentin in Faust; Further engagements with Netherlands Opera, the Fenice Venice and the Australian Opera; Grand Théâtre Genève; Other roles include Eisenstein and Falke in Die Fledermaus, Masetto, Rossini's Figaro, Wolfram in Tannhäuser, Zurga and the Soldier/Brother in Busoni's Doctor Faust; Lieder recitals at the South Bank, Covent Garden, Théâtre du Châtelet in Paris and the Aix and Spoleto Festivals; Brahms Requiem and Mahler Kindertotenlieder in Austria; Concerts in Netherlands, Spain, Germany, Finland, Iceland and for the Australian Broadcasting Commission; Premiere of Inquest of Love by Jonathan Harvey, English National Opera, 1993; Wigmore Recital, 1993; Bordeaux, Count Almaviva, 1993; Australian Opera, Don Giovanni, 1993; Staatsoper Munich, Don Giovanni; Masetto, Rossini's Figaro, Grande Théâtre Genève and Covent Garden in Eugene Onegin, ENO and Lyric Opera Queensland; Billy Budd, Covent Garden; Chorèbe in Les Troyens, Australian Opera; Sang Escamillo in Carmen at the Opéra Bastille, Paris, 1997; Sang in premiere production by a British company of Strauss's Die Liebe der Danaë, Garsington, 1999; Concerts with BBC Symphony including the British premiere of Hindemith's Mörder Hoffnung der Frauen; Season 2000–01 with The Prisoner (ENO), Don Giovanni (Vancouver) and Die Liebe der Danaë (New York). *Recordings include:* Oedipus Rex by Stravinsky, EMI; Mass of Life; Fennimore and Gerda by Delius; Saint Paul by Mendelssohn; Paul Bunyan, The Pilgrim's Progress. *Honours:* Glyndebourne Touring Prize. *Current Management:* Harrison/Parrott Ltd, 12 Penzance Place, London, W11 4PA, England. *Telephone:* (20) 7229 9166. *Fax:* (20) 7221 5042. *Website:* www .harrisonparrott.com.

**COLES, Samuel;** Flautist; b. 1964, England. *Education:* Studied with James Galway, at the Guildhall School of Music and at the Paris Conservatoire with Jean-Pierre Rampal. *Career:* Solo and chamber music performances in the United Kingdom and Europe in Holland Concertgebouw and The Hague, with the Bordeaux Symphony, the Monte Carlo Orchestra and the London Soloists Chamber Orchestra; Mozart Concerto K313 with the Orchestre de Paris at Rampal's Gala Concert, Paris; Chamber recitals with members of the European Community Youth Orchestra and duet partnership with harpist Isabelle Courret; Concerto engagements with Kenneth Montgomery, Aldo Ceccato and Alain Lombard; As orchestral player has performed under Simon Rattle, Claudio Abbado and Pierre Boulez. *Recordings include:* Mozart Concerti with the English Chamber Orchestra under Yehudi Menuhin. *Honours:* Premier Prix at the Paris Conservatoire, 1987; Winner, Scheveningen International Flute Competition, Netherlands, and National Flute Association Young Artists' Competition, San Diego, USA. *Address:* c/o Guildhall School of Music, Barbican, London, EC 2Y 8DT, England.

**COLETTI, Paul;** Concert Violist and Professor; b. 1959, Scotland. *Education:* Studied at Royal Scottish Academy, International Menuhin Academy, Banff Center and Juilliard School; Teachers included Alberto Lysy, Sándor Végh and Don McInnes. *Career:* Solo concerts at the Queen Elizabeth Hall, Geneva, Buenos Aires, Edinburgh, Assisi, Toulon and Harrogate Festivals; Recitals at Toronto, Chicago, Cincinnati, Belgrade and Los Angeles; NY debut recital in 1983; Member of the Menuhin Festival Piano Quartet; Chamber performances with Menuhin in Paris, London and Gstaad; Member of Chamber Society of Lincoln Center, NY; Further engagements with Camerata Lysy Ensemble and playing Bartók's Viola Concerto in Berlin; Former Professor of Viola and Chamber Music at Menuhin Academy; Former Head of Viola Department at Peabody Conservatory, Baltimore; Head of String Department at University of Washington, Seattle; Guest conducted the New Japan Philharmonic in Tokyo. *Compositions:* From My Heart, 1994; Viola Tango, 1994; Dream Ocean, 1995. *Recordings:* Chamber pieces by Mozart, Strauss and Mendelssohn; 20 albums recorded. *Current Management:* Tom Parker Artists. *Address:* c/o University of Washington, Music Department (Strings Faculty), Seattle, Washington, USA.

**COLGRASS, Michael (Charles);** Composer; b. 22 April 1932, Chicago, Illinois, USA; m. Ulla Damgaard, 25 Nov 1966, 1 s. *Education:* BMus, University of Illinois, 1956; Composition with Lukas Foss, Berkshire Music Center, Tanglewood, summers 1952, 1954; Darius Milhaud, Aspen, Colorado Music School, summer 1953; Wallingford Riegger, 1958–59, Ben Weber, 1959–62, New York. *Career:* Freelance solo percussionist, various New York groups, 1956–67. *Compositions include:* Stage: Virgil's Dream, music theatre, 1967; Nightingale Inc, comic opera, 1971; Something's Gonna Happen, children's musical, 1978; Orchestral: Auras, harp, orchestra, 1973; Concertmasters, 3 violins, orchestra, 1975; Letter from Mozart, 1976; Déjà vu, 4 percussionists, orchestra, 1977; Delta, violin, clarinet, percussion, orchestra, 1979; Memento, 2 pianos, orchestra, 1982; Demon, amplified piano, percussion, tape, radio, orchestra, 1984; Chaconne, viola, orchestra, 1984; The Schubert Birds, 1989; Snow Walker, Organ, orchestra, 1990; Arctic Dreams, symphonic band, 1991; Chamber: Wolf, cello, 1976; Flashback, 5 brass; Winds of Nagual: A Musical Fable, wind ensemble, 1985; Strangers, Variations, clarinet, viola, piano, 1986; Folklines, string quartet, 1987; Piano pieces; The Earth's a Baked Apple, chorus, orchestra, 1969; New People, mezzo-soprano, viola, piano, 1969; Image of Man, 4 solo voices, chorus, orchestra, 1974; Theatre of the Universe, solo voices, chorus, orchestra, 1975; Best Wishes USA, 4 solo voices, double chorus, 2 jazz bands, folk instruments, orchestra, 1976; Beautiful People, chorus, 1976; Mystery Flowers of Spring, 1978; Night of the Raccoon, 1979. *Recordings:* Chaconne; Variations for 4 Drums and Viola; The Earth's a Baked Apple; New People; Déjà vu; Light Spirit; As Quiet As; Fantasy Variations; Concertmasters; Night of the Raccoon; Three Brothers; Many others. *Contributions:* Articles to New York Times. *Honours:* Guggenheim Fellow, 1964, 1968; Rockefeller Grant, 1968; Ford Foundation Grant, 1972; Pulitzer Prize in Music, 1978; Emmy Awards, 1982, 1988; Jules Léger Chamber Music Prize. *Address:* 583 Palmerston Avenue, Toronto, Ontario M6G 2P6, Canada.

**COLIBAN, Sorin;** Singer (Bass); b. 1971, Romania. *Education:* Studied at the Bucharest Conservatory. *Career:* Debut: Bartók's Bluebeard at Bucharest, 1993; Season 1995–96 with Don Giovanni at Athens, Royal Opera debut as Alvaro in a concert performance of Verdi's Alzira, and the Monk in Don Carlos at the London Proms; Season 1996–97 included Colline at Royal Opera House, Covent Garden; In 1997 debut at San Francisco Opera as Mozart's Bartolo; Season 1998–99 Alidoro (La Cenerentola) at Palais Garnier; Capelio in I Capuleti e i Montecchi (Bastille-Paris) and Zuniga at Monte Carlo; 1999–2000 Capulet (Roméo et Juliette) at Covent Garden, Raimondo (Lucia) at San Francisco; Other roles include Procida (Les Vêpres Siciliennes) and Fiesco

(Simon Boccanegra). *Honours:* Winner of Don Giovanni Competition in Athens and national competitions in Romania. *Address:* c/o Theateragentur Erich Seitter, Opernring 8/13, 1010 Vienna, Austria.

**COLIN, Georges;** Composer; b. 15 June 1921, Schaerbeek, Brussels, Belgium; m. Albertine De Clerck, 17 Mar 1948, 2 s., 2 d. *Education:* Royal Conservatory of Music, Brussels; Harmony, 1943; Counterpoint, 1948; Fugue, 1949; History of Music, 1959. *Career:* Teacher, Athenee and Ecole Normale de Schaerbeek, 1976; Headmaster, Academy of Music, Anderlecht, 1976–81; mem, SABAM; CeBeDeM. *Compositions:* Symphonie breve for orchestra, 1950; Cinq Poèmes français de R M Rilke for voice and piano, 1952; Woodwind Quartet, 1955; Concertstuck La Folia, for contrebasse and orchestra, 1964; Cinq Croquis d'eleves, for piano, 1962; Sonatine for violin and piano, 1962; Sonate for flute and piano, 1965; La Porte de pierre, poem of André Doms, for baritone solo, mixed choir and orchestra, 1969; Phantasme for harp, 1977; Sequences for violin and piano, 1978; Pièces brèves for piano, 1996; Lithos, atmosphères pour 14 intruments, 1997; Never More, for cello, marimba and piano, 1999; Femme de Meuse–7 poèmes d'André Doms, for mezzo, flute and piano, 2000; Cinq Eclats D'"Illuminee"–poèmes d'André Doms, for soprano (or tenor), oboe, clarinet and cello, 2000; Five Short Pieces for string quartet, 2000; Never More, Cathie, 2nd version, for cello, marimba and piano, 2000; With Jeanne Colin: Le Tombeau d'André Jolivet for 2 pianos, 1975; Short Pieces for harps, 1976; Flute Quartet, 1976; Two Pieces for flute and harp, 1979; Cantate Pour Le Vif Des Temps, poems of André Doms, tryptique profane pour soprano and baritone solos, mixed choir and orchestra; Ryoan-Ji, 1986; Corps de feu, 1991. *Publications:* 9 Chants Populaire, Chants and Danses Populaires; Doucle France, flauto dolce; La Flute à bec alto (méthode en 3 vols). *Honours:* Médaille Commemorative de la Guerre, 1940–45; Prix de Composition de la Province de Brabant, 1964; Lettres à un jeune compositeur, 1996. *Address:* Haut du Village 40, 5600 Sautour, Philippeville, Belgium.

**COLLARD, Jean Philippe;** French pianist; b. 27 Jan. 1948, Mareuil-sur-Aÿ (Marne); s. of Michel Collard and Monique (Philipponnat) Collard; m. 2nd Ariane de Brion; one s., one d. and two s. from a previous marriage. *Education:* Conservatoire National de Musique de Paris. *Recordings include:* music by Bach, Brahms, Debussy, Fauré, Franck, Rachmaninov, Ravel, Saint-Saëns, Schubert, Chopin, Mozart. *Honours:* Chevalier des Arts et des Lettres, Chevalier Ordre nat. du Mérite; Chevalier Légion d'honneur 2003. *Current Management:* Angela Sulivan, Sullivan Sweetland, 28 Albion Street, London W2 2AX, England. *Telephone:* (20) 7262-0333. *E-mail:* pianojpc@aol.com (home).

**COLLIER, Gilman (Frederick);** Composer, Conductor, Pianist and Teacher; b. 14 April 1929, New York, NY, USA. *Education:* AB, Harvard University, 1951; Yale School of Music, 1950–51; Mannes Music School, 1951–53; Studied theory and composition with Walter Piston, Paul Hindemith, Bohuslav Martinů, conducting with Carl Bamberger, Leonard Bernstein and Pierre Monteux, piano privately with Nadia Reisenberg. *Career:* Music Director, Conductor, the Monmouth Symphony Orchestra, 1964–72; Faculty Member, New School for Social Research, New York City, 1953–60; Faculty Member, Westchester Conservatory of Music, White Plains, New York, 1954–74; Faculty Member, 1969, Assistant Director, 1975–95, Monmouth Conservatory of Music. *Compositions:* 3 piano sonatas and many shorter works for piano solo; Sonata for 1 piano, 4 hands; Duo sonatas for flute, oboe, English horn, clarinet, French horn, trumpet, violin, viola and cello with piano; String Quintet; Fantasy for double-reed ensemble; Trios for flute, violin, piano, violin, cello, piano and oboe, English horn and piano; 2 String Quartets; Piano quintet; 4 Chicago Psalms, SSAA; Concerto Grosso for string orchestra and piano; Almande Smedelyn and Divertimento for double reed ensemble; Two Song Cycles for voice and orchestra or piano; Sinfonietta for classical orchestra, 1997. *Address:* 65 Larchwood Avenue, Oakhurst, NJ 07755, USA.

**COLLINS, Anne,** ARCM, LRAM; British opera and concert singer (contralto); b. 29 Aug. 1943, Durham, England. *Education:* Royal College of Music, London. *Career:* debut as Governess in The Queen of Spades, SWO, Coliseum; English National Opera; Covent Garden; Welsh National Opera Company; Glyndebourne Festival; Scottish Opera; Grand Théâtre Genève; Canadian Opera Company; Théâtre de la Monnaie Brussels; Châtelet Paris; Opéra Bastille; Hamburg Staatsoper; La Scala Milan; Roles included Erda, Waltraute, Mrs Herring and Ulrica; Mistress Quickly, Florence Pike, Auntie, Mrs Sedley, Baba the Turk, Marcellina; Beroe and Akhrosimova in the British stage premieres of The Bassarids and War and Peace; Sosostris (Midsummer Marriage) and Anna in Les Troyens, (Covent Garden debut, 1977), Scottish Opera, Opera North; BBC Promenade Concerts; Recordings and song recitals; Concerts with major orchestras and choral societies in the United Kingdom and Europe; Toured Australia for ABC; Video films of Gilbert and Sullivan operas, Gondoliers, Mikado, Iolanthe, Patience and Princess Ida, 1983; Sang the Angel of Death in the premiere of MacMillan's Inès de Castro, Edinburgh, 1996. *Recordings:* Erda, Rhinegold and Siegfried (English National Opera, Goodall); Janáček Glagolitic Mass, Kempe; Vivaldi Cantatas; Elgar Coronation Ode; Third Lady in Die Zauberflöte; Mrs Peachum in Britten's version of The Beggar's Opera; Dame Carruthers in Yeomen of the Guard; Mrs Sedley in Peter Grimes; Mrs Herring in Albert Herring; Empress Persicaria in The Poisoned Kiss. *Current Management:* Askonas Holt Ltd, Lonsdale Chambers, 27 Chancery Lane, London, WC2A 1PF, England. *Telephone:* (20) 7400-1700. *Fax:* (20) 7400-1799. *E-mail:* info@askonasholt.co.uk. *Website:* www .askonasholt.co.uk.

**COLLINS, Kenneth;** Singer (Tenor); b. 21 Oct. 1935, Birmingham, England. *Education:* Studied with Charles Dean and Ettore Campogaliani. *Career:* Debut: Camden Festival 1970, as Marcello in the British premiere of Leoncavallo's La Bohème; Has sung with Welsh National Opera, Scottish Opera, Covent Garden, Aldeburgh Festival, English National Opera, Paris Opéra, NY City Opera, Colon/Buenos Aires, the Australian Opera, Strasbourg, Cologne, Granada, Valence, Madrid, Florence, Los Angeles; Repertoire includes Calaf, Manrico, Alvaro, Don Carlos, Radames, Gustavus, Dick Johnson, Andrea Chénier, Ernani and Cavaradossi; Season 1994–95 with Australian Opera as Canio and Ismaele (Nabucco); Cavaradossi, 1998. *Honours:* Awarded Australia Medal 1993 for services to opera. *Current Management:* Jenifer Eddy Artists' Management, 11/596 St Kilda Road, Melbourne 3004, Australia.

**COLLINS, Michael;** British clarinettist; b. 27 Jan. 1962, London, England. *Education:* began clarinet studies aged 10, Royal Coll. of Music with David Hamilton, further studies with Thea King. *Career:* Carnegie Hall debut 1984; BBC Promenade Concert debut 1984, with Thea Musgrave's Concerto; 1985 Proms season played the Copland Concerto and was soloist in Bernstein's Prelude, Fugue and Riffs; Prof., Royal Coll. of Music 1985; played the Finzi Concerto with the City of London Sinfonia 1987; performances of Weber's 2nd Concerto conducted by Stanislaw Skrowaczewski and Esa-Pekka Salonen; prin. clarinet, Philharmonia Orchestra 1988; associated with the Takacs Quartet, the Nash Ensemble and the pianists Noriko Ogawa and Kathryn Stott in chamber music; recital partnership with Mikhail Pletnev, piano; played Malcolm Arnold's 2nd Concerto at the Last Night of the Proms, London 1993; Stravinsky's Ebony Concerto at South Bank, London 1999; Messiaen's Quartet for the End of Time at the London Prom concerts 1999; performed premiere of 'Riffs and Refrains' by Mark-Anthony Turnage 2005. *Recordings:* Finzi's Concerto, Bernstein's Prelude, Fugue and Riffs and Stravinsky's Ebony Concerto, Quintets by Mozart and Brahms with the Nash Ensemble. *Honours:* BBC TV Young Musician of the Year, Frederick Thurston Prize, first prize Leeds Nat. Competition, Concert Artists' Guild of New York Amcon Award 1983. *Current Management:* Van Walsum Management Ltd, 4 Addison Bridge Place, London, W14 8XP, England. *Telephone:* (20) 7371-4343. *Fax:* (20) 7371-4344. *Website:* www.vanwalsum.co.uk.

**COLLINS, Michael (Augustus);** Conductor and Pianist; b. 16 Oct. 1948, Sydney, Australia; m. Lynette Kay Jennings, 24 Nov 1971, 2 s. *Education:* CBHS, St Mary's Cathedral, Sydney (Leaving Certificate, 1965); Performers and Teachers Diploma in Piano, New South Wales State Conservatorium of Music, 1965–68; Conducting Hochschule für Musik, Vienna, 1973–74. *Career:* Repetiteur and Conductor, Australian Opera, 1970–73; Repetiteur, Vienna Staatsoper, 1974–77; Repetiteur and Conductor, Württembergische Staatsoper, Stuttgart, 1977–79; Musical Director, Stuttgart Ballet, 1979–84; Conductor, Bayerische Staatsoper, Munich, 1984–90; 1 Kapellmeister Staatstheater Braunschweig, Guest Conductor, Deutsche Oper, Berlin, 1990. *Address:* c/o Deutsche Oper Berlin, Richard Wagnerstrasse 10, 1000 Berlin, Germany.

**COLLINS, Michael B.;** Professor of Musicology; b. 26 July 1930, Turlock, California, USA. *Education:* BA, 1957, MA, 1958, PhD, 1963, Stanford University. *Career:* Eastman School of Music, 1964–68; School of Music, University of North Texas, Denton, 1968–2001, retired; mem, American Musicological Society. *Publications:* Editor, Alessandro Scarlatti's Tigrane, 1983; Co-Editor, Opera and Vivaldi, 1984; Editor, Gioachino Rossini's Otello, 1994. *Contributions:* Dramatic Theory and the Italian Baroque Libretto, Cadential Structures and Accompanimental Practices in Eighteenth-Century Italian Recitative, Brazio Bracciolo's Orlando furioso: A History and Synopsis of the Libretto, in Opera and Vivaldi; The Performance of Sesquialtera and Hemiolia in the 16th century, 1964; The Performance of Triplets in the 17th and 18th Centuries, 1966, A Re-examination of Notes inégales, 1967, In Defence of the French Trill, 1973, The Literary Background of Bellini's I Capuleti e i Montecchi, 1982, in Journal of the American Musicological Society; A reconsideration of French Over-dotting, Music and Letters, 1969. *Honours:* Fulbright-Hays Grant for research in Italy, 1963–64. *Address:* College of Music, University of North Texas, Denton, TX 76203, USA. *E-mail:* mbc0019@unt.edu.

**COLLOT, Serge;** Violinist; b. 27 Sept. 1923, Paris, France. *Education:* Studied at the Paris Conservatoire, 1944–48 (composition with Arthur Honegger). *Career:* Co-founder and member of the Parrenin Quartet, 1944–57; French String Trio from 1960; Violist with the Domaine Musical Concerts, 1953–70, and premiered the Sequenza for viola by Berio; Teacher at the Paris Conservatoire from 1969 and violist with the orchestra of the Paris Opéra until 1986. *Address:* c/o Conservatoire National, 14 Rue de Madrid, 75008 Paris, France.

**COLOMBARA, Carlo;** Italian singer (bass); b. 1964, Bologna. *Career:* sang at Teatro Donizetti, Bergamo, 1985, in a Young Singers Concert; Teatro dell'Opera Rome as Silva in Ernani and Wurm in Luisa Miller; Creon in Oedipus Rex by Stravinsky at Venice, Banquo in Macbeth and Oroveso in Norma in Tokyo; Guest appearances at Vienna Staatsoper, Bolshoi Moscow, London, Berlin, Buenos Aires, Brussels and San Francisco; La Scala debut, 1989, as Procida in I Vespri Siciliani, and appeared in Moscow with the company of La Scala in Turandot and I Capuleti e i Montecchi; Verdi Requiem at Festival Hall, London, 1990; Sang Assur in Semiramide at Venice, 1990, Rodolfo in La Sonnambula; Engagements with such conductors as Giulini,

Colin Davis, Gianandrea Gavazzeni, Maazel, Sawallisch and Solti; Sang Raimondo in Lucia di Lammermoor at Munich, 1991, Padre Guardiano at Cremona and Colline at 1992 Verona Arena Festival; Attila in Verdi's opera at Macerata, 1996; Season 1996 as Verdi's Oberto, Oroveso at Houston and Enrico (Anna Bolena) at Bologna; Moor in I Masnadieri for the Royal Opera at Edinburgh, 1998; Season 2000–01 as Genoa as Verdi's Attila and Roger (Jérusalem), at Madrid, as Silva in Ernani, and at Zürich as King Philip in Don Carlos; Television appearances include Aida and Lucia di Lammermoor from La Scala. *Recordings:* Colline in La Bohème; Verdi Requiem; Handel's Rinaldo. *Honours:* winner G.B. Viotti International Competition, Vercelli 1985. *Current Management:* Angelo Gabrielli, Via Marconi 71, 40122 Bologna BO, Italy. *Telephone:* (051) 19984750. *Fax:* (051) 19984779. *E-mail:* info@stagedoor.it. *Website:* www.carlocolombara.com.

**COLONELLO, Attilio;** stage director and stage designer; b. 9 Nov. 1930, Milan, Italy. *Education:* studied architecture with Gio Ponti and Ernesto Rogers in Milan. *Career:* Designed Traviata for 1956 Florence Festival, Mefistofele at La Scala, 1958; Returned to Milan for Don Pasquale, 1965 and 1973, and the premiere of Pizzetti's Clitennestra, 1965; US debut at Dallas, 1962, Otello and L'Incoronazione di Poppea, 1963; Metropolitan Opera, New York, with designs for Lucia di Lammermoor, 1964, Luisa Miller, 1968, and Il Trovatore, 1969; Designs and productions at San Carlo, Naples, 1964–88, for Roberto Devereux, Adriana Lecouvreur, Samson et Dalila, Carmen, La Gioconda and I Puritani; Verona Arena, 1962–84, with Nabucco, Cavalleria Rusticana, La Bohème, Rigoletto, La Forza del Destino, Aida, Un Ballo in Maschera and I Lombardi; Teatro Margherita, Genoa, 1991, Andrea Chénier; Directed the Italian premiere of Rossini's Le Siège de Corinthe at Genoa, 1992, Turandot at 1992 Caracalla Festival.

**COLONNA, Monica;** Italian singer (soprano); b. 1970. *Career:* appearances as Donizetti's Adina, Modena, 1995 and as Mimi and Carolina in Il Matrimonio Segreto, Spoleto; Season 1996 in Rota's Notte di un nevrastenico at Cosenza; Cimarosa's Le astuzie femminili at Ferrara and Donizetti's Parisina, Wexford; Mercadante's Elena da Feltre, 1997 Wexford Festival; Donna Anna, Cologne and Aix, 1998; Sang Mercadante's Elena da Feltre at Lugo, 1999; season 2000–01 as Fiordiligi at Detroit, Donna Elvira for Scottish Opera and Britten's Lucretia at the Teatro Goldoni, Florence. *Recordings include:* Elena da Feltre. *Honours:* Winner, Modena Competition, 1995; Finalist, Lauri-Volpi Competition, 1993; Pavarotti Competition, 1995. *Current Management:* Ornella Cogliolo, Via del Babuino 76, 00187 Rome, Italy. *Telephone:* 6 3207627. *Fax:* 6 3207628. *E-mail:* cogliolo@cogliolo.it. *Website:* www.cogliolo.it.

**COLPOS, Mariana;** Singer (Soprano); b. 1965, Romania. *Education:* Bucharest Academy. *Career:* Appearances at Bucharest and throughout Europe as Tosca, Aida, Butterfly, Norma, Lucia di Lammermoor and Ariadne auf Naxos; Leonora in Il Trovatore, Marguerite, Donna Elvira, Elisabeth de Valois and Mimi; Season 1998 with Norma and Micaela on tour in the United Kingdom with the Moldovan Opera; Atelier Lyrique, Paris as Butterfly; Concerts include Mozart, Verdi and Britten's Requiems; Mahler 2nd, 4th and 8th symphonies; Beethoven's 9th; Radio and television appearances. *Address:* Music International, 13 Ardilaun Road, London N5 2QR, England.

**COLZANI, Anselmo;** Singer (Baritone); b. 28 March 1918, Budrio, Bologna, Italy. *Education:* Studied with Corrado Zambelli in Bologna. *Career:* Debut: Bologna, 1947, as the Herald in Lohengrin; Verona Arena from 1952; La Scala from 1954, notably in the stage premiere of Milhaud's David; US debut, 1956, as Count Luna at San Francisco; Metropolitan Opera debut, 1960, as Boccanegra; Returned to New York for 16 seasons in 201 performances, including Verdi's Falstaff and Amonasro, Puccini's Scarpia and Jack Rance, Gerard in Andrea Chénier and Ashton in Lucia di Lammermoor; Sang Amonasro for Houston Grand Opera, 1966. *Recordings:* La Gioconda; La Forza del Destino; Maria di Rohan by Donizetti; Iphigénie en Tauride, with Callas; Agnese di Hohenstaufen by Spontini, Florence, 1957; Zandonai's Francesca da Rimini. *Address:* c/o Metropolitan Opera, Lincoln Center, New York, NY 10023, USA.

**COMENCINI, Maurizio;** Singer (Tenor); b. 1958, Italy. *Education:* Studied at the Verona Conservatory and the Scala Opera Milan. *Career:* After winning prizes at the Toti del Monte and Maria Callas Competitions has sung widely in Italy, notably as Fenton in Falstaff at Parma (1986), in Monteverdi's Ulisse (Florence, 1987) and as Belfiore in Mozart's Finta Giardiniera (Alessandria, 1991); Further engagements at Palermo in Auber's Fra Diavolo, at Genoa in 1992 as Neocles in Rossini's Siège de Corinthe and at Lucca as Donizetti's Nemorino; Season 1994–95 as Nemorino and Elvino at Genoa, Rossini's Lindoro at Brescia and Almaviva at the Vienna Staatsoper; Many radio and other concert engagements. *Address:* c/o Teatro Comunale, Via 1 Frugoni 1516, 16121 Genoa, Italy.

**COMES, Liviu;** Composer, Musicologist and Professor; b. 13 Dec. 1918, Serel-Transylvania, Romania; m. 1st Valeria 1943; one s. one d.; m. 2nd Alice 1992. *Education:* Composition, Cluj-Napoca Acad. of Music, 1950. *Career:* Prof., Harmony, Counterpoint and Musical Forms, 1950–69, Pro-Rector, 1963–65, Rector, 1965–69, Cluj-Napoca Music Academy; Professor, Counterpoint, 1969–81, Pro-Rector, 1971–74, Bucharest Music Academy. *Compositions:* Sonatas for Piano, 1951; For Violin and Piano, 1954; For Clarinet and Piano, 1967; Wind Quintet, 1964; Wind Trio, 1981; A Song in Stone, oratorio, 1978; Salba for Orchestra, 1969; Maguri for Orchestra, 1986; Transylvanian Offer, cantata, 1987; Vocal and Choral music; String Quartet, 1989; Byzantine Mass,

1990; Sonatina for oboe and piano, 1992; Sonata for violin, 1995. *Publications:* The Melody of Palestrina, 1971, Italian translation, 1975; Treatise on Counterpoint, 1986; The World of Polyphony, 1984. *Contributions:* Articles and papers to Romanian Press. *Honours:* Order of Labour, 1965; Order of Cultural Merit, 1969; Prize of the Romanian Academy, 1974; Honorary Citizen of Cluj, 1994 and Bistritza, 1995; Doctor honoris causa, Cluj Music Academy, 1998. *Address:* Str Spatarului No. 42, 70241 Bucharest, Romania.

**COMMAND, Michele;** Singer (Soprano); b. 27 Nov. 1946, Caumont, France. *Education:* Studied at the Conservatories of Grenoble and Paris. *Career:* Debut: Lyon, 1967, as Musetta in La Bohème; Toulouse 1968, as Fiordiligi; Sang in Paris, at the Opéra and the Opéra-Comique, as Mozart's Donna Elvira and Fiordiligi, Gounod's Mireille, Mélisande and Portia in the premiere of Reynaldo Hahn's Le Marchand de Venise; Paris Palais des Sports 1989, as Micaela in Carmen; Sang Gounod's Sapho at Saint-Etienne, 1992 (Adriana Lecouvreur and Massenet's Chimène, 1994–95); Compiègne 1996, as Cherubini's Médée. *Recordings:* Pelléas et Mélisande; Ariane et Barbe-Bleue and Fauré's Pénélope; Don Quichotte by Massenet; Orphée aux Enfers by Offenbach, Siebel in Faust; Harawi by Messiaen.

**COMPARATO, Marina;** Singer (Mezzo-soprano); b. 1970, Perugia, Italy. *Education:* Florence Conservatory. *Career:* Appearances as Rossini's Rosina Sesto in La Clemenza di Tito, and Siebel in Faust at Spoleto; Teatro Comunale, Florence, as Isolier in Le Comte Ory, and roles in Elektra, Rimsky's The Tale of Tsar Salten, Orfeo ed Euridice and Les Troyens, 2001; Glyndebourne Festival debut 2000, as Cherubino; Further engagements as Annio in La Clemenza di Tito at Ferrara, La Cenerentola and Il Viaggio a Reims at Pesaro, Monteverdi's Ulisse in Athens and Boris Godunov at Rome; Flowermaiden in Parsifal at the Opéra Bastille, Paris; Concert engagements throughout Europe. *Recordings include:* Vivaldi's Juditha Triumphans (Opus 111). *Address:* Teatro Comunale, Via Solferino 15, 50123 Florence, Italy.

**CONANT, Robert (Scott);** Harpsichordist; b. 6 Jan. 1928, Passaic, New Jersey, USA; m. Nancy Lydia Jackson, 10 Oct 1959, 1 s., 1 d. *Education:* BA, Yale University, 1949; Juilliard School, 1949–50; MM, Yale School of Music, 1956; Piano with Sascha Gorodnitzki; Harpsichord with Ralph Kirkpatrick. *Career:* Debut: Town Hall, New York, 1953; Wigmore Hall, London, England, 1958; Major recital series and ensemble engagements in USA and Europe, 1956–; Chicago, Denver and Philadelphia Symphony Orchestras; Founded annual Festival of Baroque Music, now held in Saratoga Springs and Greenfield Center, New York, 1959–; Assistant Professor, Yale School of Music, 1961–66; Associate Professor, Professor, 1967–86, Professor Emeritus, 1986–, Chicago Musical College, Roosevelt University; Harpsichordist with: Viola da Gamba Trio of Basel; The Robert Conant Baroque Trio, with Terry King on baroque cello and Kenneth Goldsmith on baroque violin, 1986–; Nova/ Antiqua, with James Ketterer, percussion, and Brian Cassier on double bass, 1986–. *Recordings:* Solo on old harpsichords, Yale Collection of Musical Instruments, vol. 1; Robert Conant, Harpsichord, Foundation for Baroque Music; Ensemble performances on several labels. *Publications:* Twentieth Century Harpsichord Music: A Classified Catalog (with Frances Bedford), 1974. *Address:* 163 Wilton Road, Greenfield Center, NY 12833, USA.

**CONDO, Nucci;** Singer (Mezzo-soprano); b. 15 Jan. 1938, Trieste, Italy. *Education:* Studied in Rome. *Career:* Sang in Vivaldi's Juditha Triumphans at the Queen Elizabeth Hall, London, 1972; New York Kennedy Center, 1972; Glyndebourne Festival, 1972–79, in Le nozze di Figaro, Falstaff, Il Ritorno d'Ulisse and Der Rosenkavalier; Cologne, 1984, as Lucia in La Gazza Ladra; La Scala, 1985, in a revival of Rossi's Orfeo; Guest appearances with Netherlands Opera and at the Prague and Dubrovnik Festivals; Sang as Ida in Gemma di Vergy at the Teatro Donizetti, Bergamo, 1987; Sang Mozart's Marcellina at the Teatro La Fenice, Venice, 1991; Concert tours of Yugoslavia, Austria and the USA. *Recordings include:* La Gazza Ladra: Rossini's Otello; Il Ritorno d'Ulisse; Mefistofele by Boito; Video of Le nozze di Figaro, Glyndebourne, 1973. *Address:* c/o Teatro Donizetti, Piazza Cavour 14, 241 Bergamo, Italy.

**CONLON, James Joseph,** BMus; American conductor; *Music Director, Los Angeles Opera;* b. 18 March 1950, New York; s. of Joseph and Angeline Conlon; m. Jennifer Ringo; two d. *Education:* High School of Music and Art, New York and Juilliard School. *Career:* fmr faculty mem. Juilliard School of Music; since making debut with New York Philharmonic has conducted every major US orchestra and many leading European orchestras; Conductor New York Philharmonic Orchestra 1974–, Metropolitan Opera, New York 1976–; debut at Metropolitan Opera 1976, Covent Garden 1979, Paris Opera 1982, Lyric Opera of Chicago 1988, La Scala, Milan 1993, Kirov Opera 1994; Music Dir Cincinnati May Festival 1979–, Berlin Philharmonic Orchestra 1979, Rotterdam Philharmonic Orchestra 1983–91, Ravinia Festival 2005–; Musical Adviser to Dir Paris Opera 1995– (Prin. Conductor 1996–2004); conducted opening of Maggio Musicale, Florence 1985; Gen. Music Dir and Chief Conductor, Cologne Opera 1989–2002; Music Dir Los Angeles Opera 2006–; has conducted at major int. music festivals and with numerous leading orchestras. *Recordings:* numerous, of works by Mozart, Liszt, Poulenc etc. *Honours:* Officier, Ordre des Arts et des Lettres 1996; Grand Prix du Disque for recording of Poulenc Piano Concertos, Opera News Award 2005. *Current Management:* Shumen Associates, 120 W 58th Street, New York, NY 10019, USA.

**CONNELL, Elizabeth,** BMus; Irish singer (soprano); b. 22 Oct. 1946, Port Elizabeth, South Africa; d. of the late (Gordon) Raymond Connell and (Maud) Elizabeth Connell (née Scott). *Education:* Univ. of the Witwatersrand and Johannesburg Coll. of Educ., SA and London Opera Centre. *Career:* début at Wexford Festival, Ireland as Varvara in Katya Kabanova 1972; Australian Opera 1973–75; English Nat. Opera 1975–80; début Royal Opera House, Covent Garden, London as Viclinda in I Lombardi 1976; Ortrud in Lohengrin, Bayreuth Festival 1980; Electra in Idomeneo, Salzburg Festival 1984; début Metropolitan Opera, New York as Vitellia in La Clemenza di Tito 1985; début Vienna State Opera as Elisabeth in Tannhäuser 1985; début Glyndebourne, England as Electra in Idomeneo 1985; début La Scala, Milan as Ortrud in Lohengrin 1981; sang full range of dramatic mezzo repertoire until 1983 when moved into dramatic soprano field; sings worldwide, freelance in opera, oratorio, concert and recital work. *Honours:* Maggie Teyte Prize 1972. *Address:* c/o Connaught Artists' Management, 2 Molasses Row, Plantation Wharf, London, England (office).

**CONNELL, John;** singer (bass); b. 11 March 1956, Glasgow, Scotland. *Education:* Royal Northern College of Music, National Opera Studio. *Career:* debut with English National Opera; Roles at Royal Opera, Covent Garden: Titurel in Parsifal, the Monk in Don Carlos, Sparafucile in Rigoletto (1985) and as Ramphis in Aida; With English National Opera has sung the Commendatore, Colline, the Monk in Don Carlos, Ferrando in Trovatore, Leporello in The Stone Guest, Pogner, Basilio, Banquo and Sarastro; Televised appearances in Billy Budd and Lady Macbeth by Shostakovich; Season 1990–91 in new productions of Pelléas et Mélisande and Peter Grimes, as Arkel and Swallow; Sang Banquo at the Bolshoi, Moscow, and Kirov St Petersburg, 1990, on tour with English National Opera; Welsh National Opera, Sarastro in The Magic Flute and Silva in Ernani; Opera North in Salome, The Barber of Seville and La Bohème; Other engagements as Hunding in Spain and France; Concert engagements in the Verdi Requiem at The Barbican and as Pimen in Boris Godunov; Windsor Festival, 1987, as Fidelio; Season 1992 as Padre Guardiano in The Force of Destiny and as Sarastro for English National Opera; The Hermit in Der Freischütz, with the New York Philharmonic and in Peter Grimes with the London Symphony Orchestra and Rostropovich; Swallow in Peter Grimes at La Monnaie, Brussels and Don Basilio for Garsington Opera, 1994; Dansker in Billy Budd for Royal Opera House, Covent Garden, 1995; Don Fernando in Fidelio, ENO, 1996; Season 1997 with Mozart's Bartolo and Wagner's Daland for ENO; Count des Grieux in Manon, 1998. *Recordings include:* Elijah (Philips); Serenade to Music by Vaughan Williams (Hyperion). *Address:* c/o Hyperion Records Ltd, PO Box 25, London, SE9 1AX, England.

**CONNOLLY, Justin (Riveagh);** Composer; b. 11 Aug. 1933, London, England. *Education:* Royal College of Music with Peter Racine Fricker and Adrian Boult. *Career:* Harkness Fellowship, 1963–65, studying with Mel Powell; Taught at Yale University, 1963–66; Professor of Theory and Composition at the Royal College of Music from 1966–89; mem, Association of Professional Composers; Liveryman, Worshipful Company of Musicians. *Compositions include:* Sonatina in 5 Studies for Piano; Antiphonies for orchestra; Cinquepaces for brass quintet; Poems of Wallace Stevens I and II for soprano and instruments, 1967, 1970; Anima for violin and orchestra, 1974; Diaphony for organ and orchestra, 1977; Chamber music series with titles Obbligati, Triads and Tesserae, 1966–89; Ceilidh for 4 violins, 1976; Waka for mezzo-soprano and piano, 1981; Sestina A and B for ensemble, 1978; Verse and Prose for a cappella chorus Fourfold, from The Garden of Forking Paths for 2 pianos, 1983; Ennead (Night Thoughts) for piano, 1983; Spelt from Sibyl's Leaves for 6 solo voices and ensemble, 1989; Nocturnal, flutes with piano, percussion, double-bass, 1990; Cantata, soprano and piano, 1991; Symphony, 1991; Sapphic for soprano and 7 instruments, 1992; Gymel A for flute and clarinet, 1993; Gymel B for clarinet and cello, 1995; Studies from the Garden of Forking Paths for piano, 2000; Piano Trio, 2000. *Honours:* Collard Fellowship, The Musicians' Company, 1986. *Address:* c/o Novello & Co Ltd, Lower James Street, London W1, England.

**CONNOLLY, Sarah;** British singer (mezzo-soprano); b. 1963, County Durham, England; m. Carl Talbot 1998; one d. *Education:* Royal Coll. of Music and with David Mason and Gerald Martin Moore. *Career:* concert engagements include Mozart's Requiem under Neville Marriner, Bach's B Minor Mass with Philippe Herreweghe, at Berlin Philharmonia and Honegger's Jeanne d'Arc au Bûcher with the Royal Liverpool Philharmonic, Prom Concerts, London 1997; Wigmore Hall Recital debut with Julius Drake 1998; opera debut as Annina in Der Rosenkavalier for WNO 1994; further roles include the Messenger in Orfeo and the Fox in The Cunning Little Vixen (ENO), Charlotte in Massenet's Werther for English Touring Opera and the Musician in Manon Lescaut at the Glyndebourne Festival 1997; season 1997–98 for ENO as Handel's Xerxes, Meg in Verdi's Falstaff; Eduige in Rodelinda for Glyndebourne Touring Opera 1998; world premiere of Rime D'Amore by Matteo D'Amico conducted by Giuseppe Sinopoli in Rome 1998; Ariodante for New York City Opera 1999; Ruggiero in Handel's Alcina, ENO 1999; the roles of the Queen of Sheba and Second Woman with Ivor Bolton in Handel's Solomon for Maggio Musicale 1999; world premiere of Mark Anthony Turnage's The Silver Tassie, ENO 2000; sang Juno and Ino with San Francisco Opera in Handel's Semele, conducted by Charels Mackerras; role of Nerone in L'Incoronazione di Poppea at Maggio Musicale 2000; further concerts include Bach's St Matthew Passion with the Gabrieli Consort in Spain and with Herreweghe 1998; The Dream of Gerontius in Sydney and Mark Anthony Turnage's Twice Through the Heart, with Markus Stenz in Rome and London; Ravel's L'Heure espagnole at the London Proms 2002;

Carnegie Hall debut, Pergolesi Stabat Mater 2003; sang Dido in Dido and Aeneas at the Proms 2003; Annio in La Clemenza di Tito at the New York Met 2003–04; title role in Giulio Cesare at the Glyndebourne Festival 2005. *Recordings include:* Bach Cantatas with Philippe Herreweghe, Les Fêtes d'Hébé by Rameau with Les Arts Florissants and Juditha Triumphans, Vivaldi with the King's Consort. *Honours:* prizewinner opera section of the 's-Hertogenbosch Competition, Netherlands 1994, Gramophone Award for Baroque Opera 1998. *Current Management:* Askonas Holt Ltd, Lonsdale Chambers, 27 Chancery Lane, London, WC2A 1PF, England. *Telephone:* (20) 7400-1700. *Fax:* (20) 7400-1799. *E-mail:* info@askonasholt.co.uk. *Website:* www.askonasholt.co.uk.

**CONRAD, Barbara;** Singer (Mezzo-soprano); b. 11 Aug. 1945, Pittsburg, Texas, USA. *Education:* Studied at the University of Texas, Austin. *Career:* Metropolitan Opera from 1982, as Verdi's Preziosilla and Maddalena, Annina in Der Rosenkavalier and Maria in Porgy and Bess; European engagements at Frankfurt, Vienna, Brussels and Munich; Sang at Greater Miami Opera, 1989; Other roles include Wagner's Fricka and Verdi's Azucena and Eboli. *Recordings include:* Hamlet (Thomas) and Porgy and Bess. *Address:* c/o Bess Pruitt and Associates Inc, 819 East 168th Street, Bronx, NY 10459, USA.

**CONSOLI, Marc-Antonio;** Composer, Conductor and Editor; b. 19 May 1941, Italy. *Education:* BMus, 1966; MMus, 1967; DMA, 1976; Studied with Ernst Krenek, Gunther Schüller, George Crumb. *Career:* Commissioned by Fromm and Koussevitsky Foundations, the Royan in France, Steirischer Herbst of Austria (Festivals); Works performed at International Festivals including International Society for Contemporary Music in Helsinki, 1978, Belgium, 1981; New York Philharmonic and Los Angeles Philharmonic, mem, Broadcast Music Association; American Composers' Alliance. *Compositions include:* Sciuri Novi; Interactions I, II, III, IV, V, 1970–71; Isonic, 1971; Lux Aeterna, 1972; Profile, 1973; Music for Chambers, 1974; Sciuri Novi II, 1974; Canti Trinacriani, 1976; Memorie Pie, 1976; Tre Canzoni, 1976; Odefonia, 1976; Tre Fiori Musicali, 1987; Vuci Siculani, 1979; Naked Masks, 1980; Orpheus Meditation, 1981; The Last Unicorn, 1981; Afterimages, 1982; String Quartet, 1983; Ancient Greek Lyrics, 1985; Musiculi II, 1985–86; Reflections, 1986; Eyes of the Peacock, 1987; Cello Concerto, 1988; Greek Lyrics, 1988; String Quartet II, 1989; Arie Mutate, 1990; Musiculi IV, 1990, 1992; Musiculi III, 1992, 1994; Games for 2, 3 and 4, 1994, 1995; Cinque Canti, 1995; Varie Azioni, 1995; Di-ver-ti-mento, 1995; Collected Moments, 1996; Sciuri novi III, 1996; Pensieri Sospesi, 1997; Rounds and Relays, 1997; Varie Azioni II, 1998; Varie Azioni III, 1999. *Honours:* Guggenheim Memorial Fellowships, 1971, 1979; Fulbright Scholarship to Poland, 1972–74; National Endowment for the Arts Grants, 1976, 1979; Prize, Competition, Monaco. *Address:* c/o ASCAP, ASCAP Building, One Lincoln Plaza, New York, 10023, USA.

**CONSTABLE, John Robert,** FRAM; Piano Accompanist and Harpsichordist; b. 5 Oct. 1934, Sunbury-on-Thames, Middlesex, England; m. Katharine Ingham; two d. *Education:* studied with Harold Craxton, Royal Acad. of Music, London. *Career:* repetiteur, Royal Opera House, Covent Garden, London, 1960–72; principal keyboard player, London Sinfonietta, since its formation; principal harpsichordist, Acad. of St Martin-in-the-Fields, 1984–; Prof., Royal Coll. of Music, 1985–; mem. Incorporated Society of Music, Musicians' Union. *Recordings:* many with London Sinfonietta and Acad. of St Martin-in-the-Fields, playing harpsichord continuo for operas and as accompanist on recital records. *Address:* 13 Denbigh Terrace, London, W11 2QJ, England.

**CONSTANT, Marius;** Composer and Conductor; b. 7 Feb. 1925, Bucharest, Romania; 1 s. *Education:* Bucharest Conservatory of Music; National Conservatory of Music, Paris. *Career:* Musical Director, French Radio, 1952–; Musical Director, Roland Petit Ballet and Paris Opéra Ballet, 1973–78; Conductor, Ars Nova Ensemble; Regular guest conductor of leading orchestras in Europe, Canada, USA and Japan; Teaches composition at Stanford University, USA, and conducting at Hilversum, Netherlands. *Compositions:* Operas: Le Souper, 1969; Jeu de Sainte Agnés, 1974; La Tragédie de Carmen, (version of Bizet), 1981; Impressions de Pelléas (version of Debussy), 1992; Sade/Teresa (original), 1996; Oratorios, Des Droits de l'Homme, 1989, and Chants de Retour, 1995; Ballets: Cyrano de Bergérac, 1959; Eloge de la Folie, 1966; Paradis Perdu, 1967; Candide, 1970; Septentrion, 1975; Nana, 1976; L'Ange Bleu, 1985; Orchestral: 24 Preludes, 1959; Twilight Zone, signature tune, 1961; Turner; Chants de Maldoror, 1962; Chaconne et Marche Militaire, 1968; Candide for harpsichord and orchestra, 1971; Concerto Gli Elementi for trombone and orchestra, 1977; Symphony for Winds, 1978; Concertante for alto saxophone and orchestra, 1978; Nana-Symphony, 1980; 103 Régards dans l'Eau, 1981; Pelléas et Mélisande-Symphony, 1983; L'Inauguration de la Maison for wind band, 1985; Choruses and Interludes for French Horn and Orchestra, 1990; Hameenlinna: An Imaginary Landscape, for orchestra, 1991; Brevissima Symphony, 1992; Symphonie Concertante for 6 pianos and orchestra, 1994; Winds, 1968; 14 Stations for percussion and 6 instruments, 1970; Traits, Cadavre Exquis, aleatoric, 1971; Chamber music. *Recordings:* Music by Satie, Xenakis, Debussy, Varèse, Messiaen and Constant. *Honours:* 1st Prize for Composition, Paris Conservatory; Officier, Légion d'Honneur; Grand Officier, Ordre du Mérite; Prix Italia, 1952; Member of the Académie de Beaux-Arts, 1993. *Address:* 16 rue des Fosses St Jacques, 75005 Paris, France.

**CONSTANTIN, Rudolf;** Singer (Baritone); b. 16 Feb. 1935, Paris, France. *Education:* Studied in Paris and Zürich. *Career:* Sang at Rheydt, 1958–59,

Aachen, 1959–60, Berne, 1960–63, Graz, 1963–67, Cologne, 1967–69; Frankfurt am Main, 1969–83; Guest appearances at Dresden, Berlin, Amsterdam, Brussels, Vienna (Volksoper), Paris and Copenhagen; Sang Ruprecht in The Fiery Angel at Zürich, Gunther in Götterdämmerung at Covent Garden and the Villains in Les Contes d'Hoffmann at the Salzburg Festival; Other roles have included Mozart's Don Giovanni, Count and Guglielmo, Verdi's Amonasro, Luna, Germont, Nabucco, Simon Boccanegra, Rigoletto, Macbeth, Posa and Iago; Wagner's Telramund, Dutchman, Wolfram, Amfortas and Wotan (Die Walküre); Strauss's Orestes, Jochanaan, Mandryka and Faninal; Golaud in Pelléas et Mélisande and Mittenhofer in Elegy for Young Lovers by Henze; Further engagements at Geneva, Marseille, Monte Carlo, Prague and Edinburgh; Many concert appearances; Tchaikovsky Festival at Prague, 1993.

**CONSTANTINE, Andrew;** British conductor; b. 1964, England. *Education:* studied in Siena, at the Turin Opera and the St Petersburg Conservatoire. *Career:* engagements from 1991 with the London Philharmonic in Prokofiev's 5th Symphony, the Hallé and English Chamber Orchestras, the Royal Philharmonic Orchestra and London Mozart Players; Asst Conductor, ENO's Madama Butterfly and Principal Conductor, Sinfonia of Birmingham; further appearances with the St Petersburg and Sofia Philharmonics and the Komische Opera, Berlin; led Das Rheingold at Leicester 1998. *Honours:* winner Donatella Flick Conducting Competition, London 1991. *Current Management:* Patrick Garvey Management, Cedar House, 10 Rutland Street, Filey, North Yorkshire YO14 9JB, England. *Website:* www.patrickgarvey.com.

**CONSTANTINESCU, Dan;** Composer; b. 10 June 1931, Bucharest, Romania. *Education:* Composer's Diploma, Bucharest Conservatory of Music. *Career:* Debut: Jassy Philharmonic, 1957; Lecturer in Harmony and Composition, Bucharest Conservatory; mem, Romanian Composers' Union. *Compositions include:* Divertissement for string orchestra; Ballad for orchestra; Chamber Symphony; Symphony Concertante; Concerto for piano and string orchestra; Concerto for 2 pianos and small orchestra; 4 Sonatas for 2 instruments; Trio for violin, clarinet, piano and percussion; 5 Quartets; Symphony for string orchestra; Symphony for wind instruments; Concerto for harpsichord, harp and wind instruments; String sextet; Symphony for 32 voices; 5 cycles of piano music. *Recordings:* Piano part, various works. *Honours:* Georges Enescu Prize, Romanian Academy, 1968. *Address:* Strada Corneliu Botez 3, Bucharest 9, Romania.

**CONSTANTINESCU, Mihai;** Violinist and Professor; b. 22 Aug. 1926, Chisinau, Russia; m. Corina Bura 1981; one d. *Education:* Bachelorship, Matel Basarab High School, diploma, Conservatoire of Music, Bucharest. *Career:* debut, Radio Bucharest 1941; recital, Dalles Hall, Bucharest 1943; soloist, George Enescu Philharmonic, Bucharest; radio and television appearances; tours of Russia, Czechoslovakia, Korea, China, Germany, Viet Nam, Poland, Bulgaria, France, Belgium, Luxembourg, Hungary, Yugoslavia, Italy, Cuba, Spain, Venezuela, Chile, Argentina, Ecuador and elsewhere; Prof., Conservatoire of Music, Bucharest. *Compositions:* Cadenzas for Mozart's Third Concerto for violin and orchestra and Haydn's First Concerto for violin and orchestra. *Recordings:* works by Mozart, Beethoven, Pergolesi, Handel, Sabin Dragoi, Livui Comes, Wilhelm Berger (Romanian music), two Handel recordings, and Rameau 1986. *Address:* Str Ecaterina Teodoriou 17, 010971 Bucharest 1, Romania.

**CONTE, David;** Composer and Teacher; b. 20 Dec. 1955, Denver, Colorado, USA. *Education:* BM, Bowling Green State University, Ohio; MFA, DMA, Cornell University; Private study with Nadia Boulanger, 2 years. *Career:* Faculties, Cornell University, Colgate University, Interlochen Centre for the Arts, San Francisco Conservatory of Music; mem, ASCAP. *Compositions:* Invocation and Dance for male chorus and orchestra; Requiem Triptych (im memoriam Nadia Boulanger) for male chorus and orchestra; Piano Fantasy; The Masque of the Red Death; Ballet for orchestra; Of a Summer's Evening, guitar duo; The Dreamers; 2 act Chamber Opera; Pastorale and Toccata for organ; Piano Quintet; In Praise of Music, SATB and orchestra; Ave Maria; The Gift of the Magi, one-act chamber opera; Songs of Consolation, soprano and organ. *Honours:* Fulbright Scholarship, 1976; Meet the Composer Grant, 1983, 1986, 1987; Ralph Vaughan Williams Fellowship. *Current Management:* E C Schirmer Music Co, 138 Ipswich Street, Boston, MA 02215, USA. *Address:* San Francisco Conservatory of Music, 1201 Ortega Street, San Francisco, CA 94122, USA.

**CONTI, Nicoletta;** Orchestral Conductor and Teacher; b. 12 July 1957, Bologna, Italy. *Education:* Bologna Conservatory of Music; Milan Conservatory. *Career:* Debut: Liszt Academy, Budapest, 1984; Aspen Music Festival, 1984; Tanglewood Music Center, 1985; Appearances with Orchestra Sinfonica di Bari, Orchestra Regionale Toscana, Orchestra Simphonia Perusina, Orchestra Sinfonica Abrudiese, Orchestra Pro Musica Riminia, Danish Radio Orchestra; mem, American Symphony Orchestra League. *Honours:* Concorso da Camera Stresa, 1981; Malko Competition for Young Conductors, 1986. *Address:* Via Palestro 7, 40123 Bologna, Italy.

**CONTIGUGLIA, John and Richard (twins);** Pianist; b. 13 April 1937, Auburn, New York, USA. *Education:* Received advice from Percy Grainger; Studied with Jean Wilder and Bruce Simonds, Yale University; Dame Myra Hess, London. *Career:* Debut: Duo recital at age 6; Professional debut, London, 1962; Performed throughout the world as a virtuoso duo; Repertoire includes works from the past to contemporary scores; Special emphasis on the piano transcriptions of Liszt; Premiere of Liszt's Grosses Konzertstück über

Mendelssohns Lieder ohne Worte, Utrecht, 1986. *Recordings:* Several. *Honours:* Ditson Fellowship. *Address:* c/o ICM Artists Ltd, 40 West 57th Street, New York City, NY 10019, USA.

**CONVERY, Robert;** American composer; b. 4 Oct. 1954, Wichita, Kansas, USA. *Education:* Studied at Westminster Choir College, Curtis Institute and Juilliard, New York; David Diamond, Vincent Persichetti and Ned Rorem were among his teachers. *Career:* Resident Composer with Phillips Exeter Academy, 1988, 1991, Dickinson College, 1989–90, and the New York Concert Singers, 1991–93. *Compositions:* Pyramus and Thisbe, 2 scenes after Shakespeare, 1983; The Blanket, opera in one act 1988 (Charles E Ives Award), Songs of Children, cantata for choir, strings, piano, 1991; Clara, opera in five scenes 2004. *Honours:* Charles Miller-Alfredo Casella Award. *Address:* c/o ASCAP, ASCAP Building, 1 Lincoln Plaza, New York, NY 10023, USA. *E-mail:* robertconvery@earthlink.net (home).

**CONWELL, Julia;** Singer (Soprano); b. 1954, Philadelphia, Pennsylvania, USA; m. Giancarlo del Monaco. *Education:* Studied at Curtis Institute of Music and with Margaret Harshaw. *Career:* Sang in various US opera houses, notably as Musetta in La Bohème for Michigan Opera; European debut with Munich Staatsoper as Musetta; Further appearances as Nedda in Pagliacci, Liu in Turandot, Düsseldorf, 1982, and Oscar in Ballo in Maschera, Frankfurt, 1984; Sang Charpentier's Louise at Nice and Zerlina at Rome, 1984; Other roles have included Paolina in Poliuto by Donizetti, Rome, 1986; Gilda and Salome at Augsburg, 1988, and Diana in Iphigénie en Tauride, Deutsche Oper Berlin; Member of the Stuttgart Staatsoper from 1985. *Recordings:* Sandrina in La Finta Giardiniera; Euridice in Orfeo by Gluck; Works by Henze. *Address:* c/o Stuttgart Staatstheater, Oberer Schlossgarten 6, 7000 Stuttgart, Germany.

**CONYNGHAM, Barry (Ernest);** Composer; b. 27 Aug. 1944, Sydney, New South Wales, Australia. *Education:* MA, University of Sydney; Postdoctoral Studies Certificate, University of California, San Diego; D.Mus, University of Melbourne. *Career:* Part-time Lecturer, Tutor, University of New South Wales and National Institute of Dramatic Art, 1968–70; Senior Tutor, University of Western Australia, 1971; Postdoctoral post, University of California, San Diego, 1972–73; Visiting Fellow, Princeton University, 1973–74; Composer and Researcher in residence, University of Aix-Marseille, 1974–75; Lecturer, 1975–79, Senior Lecturer, 1979–84, Reader, 1984–89, University of Melbourne; Dean, Creative Arts, University of Wollongong, 1989–94; Vice-Chancellor, Southern Cross University, 1994–; Board, Playbox Theatre Company; Deputy Chair, Opera Australia, 1995–. *Compositions:* Crisis: Thoughts in a City, 1968; The Little Sherriff, 1969; Five Windows, 1969; Three, 1969; Five, 1970; Water…Footsteps…Time, 1970; Ice Carving, 1970; Edward John Eyre, 1971–73; Six, 1971; Playback, 1972; Without Gesture, 1973; From Voss, 1973; Snowflake, 1973; Ned, 1974–77; Mirror Images, 1975; Sky, 1977; Apology of Bony Anderson, 1978; Mirages, 1978; Bony Anderson, 1978; Concerto for double bass, 1979; Basho, 1980; Journeys, 1980; Viola, 1981; Imaginary Letters, 1981; Horizons: Concerto for orchestra; Southern Cross: Concerto for violin and piano, 1991; Dwellings, 1982; Fly, 1982–84; Voicings, 1983; Cello Concerto, 1984; Preview, 1984; Antipodes, 1984–85; The Oath of Bad Brown Bill, 1985; Generations, 1985; Recurrences, 1986; Vast I The Sea, II The Coast, III The Centre, IV The Cities, 1987; Glimpses, 1987; Bennelong, 1988; Matilda, 1988; Streams, 1988; Monuments: Piano Concerto, 1989; Waterways: Viola Concerto, 1990; Cloudlines: Harp Concerto, 1990; Decades for orchestra, 1993; Alterimages for koto and orchestra, 1994; Dawning, 1996; Nostalgia, 1997; Passing, 1998; Yearnings, 1999; String Quartet 2, 1999. *Recordings:* Many. *Publications:* Scores published by major publishers. *Honours:* 4 Fellowships: Churchill, 1970, Harkness, 1972–74, Australia Council, 1975, Fulbright Senior, 1982; Member, Order of Australia. *Address:* c/o Boosey and Hawkes, Locked Bag 188, Artarmon, NSW 1570, Australia.

**COOK, Brian (Robert) Rayner,** BA, ARCM (Hons); British singer (baritone); b. 17 May 1945, London; s. of Robert Cook and Gladys Soulby; m. Angela M. Romney 1974; one s. one d. *Education:* Univ. of Bristol, Royal Coll. of Music and privately with Alexander Young (vocal studies) and Helga Mott (repertoire). *Career:* church organist and choirmaster aged 15; major conducting debut (opera) 1966; professional singing debut 1967; has appeared as soloist in oratorio, recitals, music-theatre and opera throughout the UK, Europe, USA, Canada, S America, the Middle East, the Far East and N Africa and has broadcast frequently in UK, Europe and many other countries; has given first performances of various works written for him by distinguished composers; dir singers' workshops, jury mem. int. singing competitions and specialist adjudicator; Visiting Tutor in Vocal Studies and Postgraduate Examiner, Birmingham Conservatoire 1980–99; fmrly Tutor Welsh Coll. of Music and Drama, Cardiff; Specialist Univ. Music Assessor, Higher Educ. Funding Councils of England and Wales 1994–95. *Recordings include:* opera, oratorio and songs by Schütz, Charpentier, Adam, Fauré, Dvořák, Nielsen, Orff, Camilleri, Parry, Elgar, Delius, Butterworth, Vaughan Williams, Holst, Havergal Brian, Coates, Poston, Rubbra, Cruft, Walton, Ferguson and Williamson. *Television:* professional solo debut (BBC) 1970; has since appeared in televised concerts in many European countries in works ranging from Mozart's Requiem to Mahler's 8th Symphony. *Honours:* Kathleen Ferrier Memorial Scholarship 1969 and many other major singing prizes. *Address:* The Quavers, 53 Friars Avenue, Friern Barnet, London, N20 0XG, England. *Telephone:* (20) 8368-3010.

**COOK, Deborah;** American opera and concert singer (soprano) and cantor; b. 6 July 1948, Philadelphia, PA; m. Ronald Marlowe 1985; one s. *Education:* studied with Irene Williams. *Career:* debut, Operatic-Glyndebourne and Covent Garden; Glyndebourne Touring Opera, 1971, as Zerbinetta; 3 years principal soprano in Bremen, 2 years Munich National Theatre; Sang in Sydney, Melbourne, Barcelona, Edinburgh, Geneva, Rome, Paris, Los Angeles, San Francisco, Leipzig, East Berlin; Appeared at Covent Garden Opera House, Hamburg State Opera (from 1981), Deutsche Oper Berlin, Frankfurt Opera, Stuttgart Opera, Deutsche Oper am Rhein; Bonn Opera, 1984–85; Roles include Verdi's Gilda, Strauss's Zerbinetta, Donizetti's Lucia and Mozart's Queen of Night and Constanze; Created role of Rachel in Henze's We Come to the River, Covent Garden, 1976, and Angel of Bright Future in Rochberg's The Confidence Man; Sang Lucia di Lammermoor at the Buxton Festival, 1979. *Recordings:* Dinorah; Ariadne auf Naxos; L'Etoile du Nord. *Address:* c/o Opera Rara, 25 Compton Terrace, London N1 2UN, England.

**COOK, Edward;** Singer (Tenor); b. 30 June 1954, Oxnard, California. *Education:* Studied at New England Conservatory, Boston and at Bloomington; Further study with James King. *Career:* Sang Gianni Schicchi, Rossini's Figaro and other baritone roles; Froh in Das Rheingold at the Metropolitan; Miami Opera as Siegmund in Die Walküre, 1990; Further Wagner roles include Parsifal at Wuppertal and Schwerin, 1994–95; Siegfried at Essen, 1996; Siegmund and Siegfried at Karlsruhe, 1994–95; Further engagements at Rome and Turin as Gluck's Orestes and Festival Hall, London, as Florestan; Other roles include Idomeneo and Strauss's Bacchus. *Address:* c/o Karlsruhe Opera, Baumeisterstrasse 11, Pf1449, 7500 Karlsruhe, Germany.

**COOK, Jeff (Holland);** Music Director, Conductor and Composer; b. 21 Aug. 1940, Chicago, Illinois, USA; m. Kate Young, 12 May 1974, 1 d. *Education:* BM, Northwestern University, 1962; MA, Ohio State University, 1964; MM, New England Conservatory of Music, 1966; Studied with Pierre Boulez, John Barbirolli, Jean Fournet, Bruno Maderna, Herbert von Karajan, Erich Leinsdorf, Karlheinz Stockhausen, György Ligeti. *Career:* Music Director, Conductor, Wheeling Symphony Orchestra, 1973–85; Music Director, Conductor, Mansfield Symphony Orchestra, Ohio, 1976–; Associate Conductor, Pittsburgh Ballet Theatre, 1987–91; Conductor, Louisville Ballet, Kentucky, 1990–; Guest Conductor: Anchorage Symphony, Eastern Music Festival, Rhode Island Philharmonic, North Carolina Symphony, Orquesta Sinfonica Nacional (Santo Domingo), Ballet of Ljubljana (Slovenia); North Bay Music Festival (Ontario). *Compositions:* Euripides Electra, 1972. *Recordings:* Broadcasts on West Virginia Public Radio, Ohio Public Radio, Canadian Broadcasting Corporation. *Address:* 649 Robinwood Drive, Pittsburgh, PA 15216, USA.

**COOK, Terry;** Singer (Bass); b. 9 Feb. 1956, Plainville, Texas, USA. *Education:* Studied at Texas University. *Career:* Sang with the Chicago Lyric Opera from 1980, at Santa Fe (Festival) from 1982, and at the Metropolitan from 1983; Roles have included Dr Grenvil in Traviata, Ferrando, the King in Aida, Oroe in Semiramide and Gershwin's Porgy; Further engagements at Seattle (1985), Théâtre Châtelet, Paris (in Handel's Rinaldo), at the Grand Opéra Paris as Colline in La Bohème and the Opéra-Comique as the Speaker in Die Zauberflöte; Other roles include Achillas in Giulio Cesare, Raimondo in Lucia di Lammermoor and the Minister in Fidelio; Sang Oroe in Semiramide at Dallas, 1993; Sang Crown in Porgy and Bess at Munich, 2000; Many concert appearances. *Address:* c/o Metropolitan Opera, Lincoln Center, New York, NY 10023, USA.

**COOK-MacDONALD, Linda;** singer (soprano); b. 22 Sept. 1947, Twin Falls, Idaho, USA. *Education:* studied in Cincinnati and Mainz. *Career:* debut, Krefeld, 1971, as Fiordiligi; Sang at such German houses as Krefeld, Wuppertal, Essen and Darmstadt; US appearances at Memphis, Cincinnati, Pittsburgh and Portland; Sang in New York at City Opera; Roles have included Mozart's Constanze, Pamina, Queen of Night and Zerlina, Agathe, Alice Ford, Marguerite, Musetta and Zdenka; Modern repertoire has included Thalmar in Leben des Orest by Krenek and Philippe in Penderecki's The Devils of Loudun; Many concert appearances.

**COOKE, Mervyn John,** BA, MPhil, MA, PhD; British composer and musicologist; b. 29 Aug. 1963, Dover, Kent, England. *Education:* Royal Acad. of Music and King's Coll., Cambridge. *Career:* Research Fellow, Fitzwilliam Coll., Cambridge 1987–93; Lecturer in Music, Univ. of Nottingham 1993, Head of Music Dept 1998, Prof. of Music 2000–. *Compositions:* Symphonic Poem Messalina (BBC Concert Orchestra, Radio 3) 1979, Horn Sonata (BBC Radio 3) 1986, incidental scores for Cambridge Greek Plays 1983, 1989. *Publications:* Britten and the Gamelan (chapter in Death in Venice, ed. by Donald Mitchell) 1987, Britten: Billy Budd 1993, Britten: War Requiem 1996, The Chronicle of Jazz 1997, Britten and the Far East 1998, Jazz 1998, The Cambridge Companion to Benjamin Britten 1999, The Cambridge Companion to Jazz 2002, Letters from a Life: Selected Letters of Benjamin Britten Vol. 3 1946–51 (ed. with Philip Reed and Donald Mitchell) 2004; contrib. to Musical Times, Journal of Musicological Research, Journal of Royal Musical Assscn, Music and Letters, Journal of the American Musicological Soc., Music Analysis. *Address:* Department of Music, University of Nottingham, Nottingham, NG7 2RD, England.

**COOKE, Richard;** Conductor; b. 1958, England. *Education:* Chorister at St Paul's Cathedral; Choral scholar at King's College, Cambridge, under David Willcocks. *Career:* Conducted various University orchestras; Led the chamber ensemble in the War Requiem at the Festival Hall, 1984; Trained the London Philharmonic Choir in Mahler 8 and for The Kingdom by Elgar; Has conducted concerts at the Albert and Festival Halls and throughout South East England; Gothenburg Symphony Orchestra from 1989 in Belshazzar's Feast, the Glagolitic Mass, Dvořák 6 and the Sea Symphony by Vaughan Williams; Has also conducted the Brahms Requiem, A Child of our Time, Monteverdi's Vespers and St Nicolas in Sweden; Verdi Requiem at the Uppsala International Festival (1990) and in Boulogne and Canterbury; Conductor of the Chalmers Music Weeks in Sweden and Artistic Director of the St Columb Festival in Cornwall. *Recordings include:* Mahler 8th Symphony and The Kingdom, with the London Philharmonic Choir.

**COOP, Jane Austin;** Canadian concert pianist; *Professor and Head of Keyboard Division, School of Music, University of British Columbia*; b. 18 April 1950, Saint John, NB; m. George Laverock 22 Feb. 1984; one d. *Education:* Art diploma, 1971, BMus, Performance, 1972, University of Toronto; MM, Peabody Conservatory, Baltimore, 1974. *Career:* debut: St Lawrence Centre, Toronto, Canada; Wigmore Hall, London, England; Carnegie Recital Hall, New York, USA; soloist with all major Canadian orchestras; recitals and concerts in Canada, USA, England, France, Poland, Netherlands, Yugoslavia, Hungary, Czechoslovakia, Russia; major tours of Hong Kong, China, Japan; Prof. Head of Keyboard Div. School of Music Univ. of British Columbia. *Recordings:* The Romantic Piano; Beethoven–Eroica variations and Sonatas Op 109 and Op 111; Bach, English Suite No. 3 and Partita No. 5; Haydn, 4 Sonatas; Mozart, The Piano Quartets, with members of the Orford Quartet; Piano Pieces; Piano Variations (Schumann, Schubert, Brahms); Piano Concerti (Bartók, Prokofiev), Piano Concerti (Britten, Ireland, Finzi, Rawsthorne), Chamber Music (Brahms Horn Trio, Jenner Clarinet and Horn Trio), Chopin Nocturnes and Mazurkas, Chopin: the Late Works. *Honours:* Distinguished Univ. Scholar; 1st Prize, Washington International Piano Competition, 1975; Finalist, Munich International Competition, 1977; Killam Award for Career Excellence, 1989. *Current Management:* Andrew Kwan Artists Management, 1315 Lawrence Avenue East, Suite 515, Toronto, M3A 3R3, Canada. *Telephone:* (416) 445-4441. *Website:* www.skylark-music .com (home).

**COOPER, Anna;** Singer (Mezzo-soprano); b. 1965, England. *Education:* Studied at the Royal Academy of Music, and at La Fenice, Venice. *Career:* Many appearances with leading British opera companies, including Glyndebourne, English National Opera and English Opera Group; Roles have included parts in Albert Herring, Die Walküre, Die Zauberflöte, L'Italiana in Algeri and Dido and Aeneas; Appearances with the Royal Opera, Covent Garden, as Flora, Lola, the Madrigal Singer (Manon Lescaut), Kate Pinkerton, Grimgerde, Countess Ceprano (Rigoletto) and Annina; Glasa in Katya Kabanova, 1997; Further engagements in Brussels, Saarbrucken, Milan, Athens, Korea, Strasbourg, Japan and the USA. *Honours:* Winner, Kathleen Ferrier Award; Scholarship to La Fenice, Venice. *Address:* c/o Saarbrücken Opera, Schillerplatz, D–66111 Saarbrücken, Germany.

**COOPER, Barry Anthony Raymond,** MA, DPhil, FRCO; academic; b. 2 May 1949, Westcliff-on-Sea, Essex, England; m. Susan Catherine Baynes 1973; four c. *Education:* Univ. Coll., Oxford, studied organ with John Webster, composition with Kenneth Leighton. *Career:* Lecturer in Music, St Andrews Univ. 1973; Research Officer 1974, Lecturer in Music 1978, Sr Lecturer in Music 1989, Univ. of Aberdeen; Sr Lecturer in Music 1990, Reader in Music 2000, Prof. of Music 2003, Univ. of Manchester; mem. Royal Musical Asscn, Royal Coll. of Organists. *Compositions:* Oratorio, The Ascension; Song-Cycle, The Unasked Question; Wind Band, Mons Graupius; Choral, Organ and Chamber Music. *Publications include:* G. B. Sammartini, Concerto in G (Ed OUP) 1976; J. C. Schickhardt, Sonata in D (Ed OUP) 1978; Catalogue of Early Printed Music in Aberdeen Libraries, 1978; Englische Musiktheorie im 17 und 18 Jahrhundert (in Geschichte der Musiktheorie, Band 9, 1986); Beethoven's Symphony No. 10, First Movement (Realisation and Completion), Universal Edition, 1988; English Solo Keyboard Music of the Middle and Late Baroque, 1989; Beethoven and the Creative Process, 1990; L. van Beethoven, Three Bagatelles (Ed Novello), 1991; The Beethoven Compendium (Ed), 1991; Beethoven's Folksong Settings, 1994; J. Blow, Complete Organ Music (Ed Musica Britannica), 1996; D. F. Tovey, A Companion to Beethoven's Pianoforte Sonatas (Ed), 1999; Beethoven (Master Musicians), 2000. *Publications:* contrib. to Musical Times; Music and Letters; Music Review; RMA Research Chronicle; Proceedings/Journal of RMA; Recherches sur la Musique Française Classique; Early Music; Acta Musicologica; Beethoven Journal; BBC Music Magazine; Welsh Music History; Irish Musical Studies; Bulletin of the John Rylands University Library of Manchester; New Grove Dictionary of Music and Musicians, Ad Parnassum. *Honours:* Osgood Prize 1972, Halstead Scholarship 1972–74, RSE Research Fellow 1986–87. *Address:* Martin Harris Building (Music), University of Manchester, Coupland Street, Manchester M13 9PL, England.

**COOPER, Imogen;** British concert pianist; b. 28 Aug. 1949, London; d. of the late Martin Du Pré Cooper and of Mary Stewart; m. John Batten 1982. *Education:* Paris Conservatoire and in Vienna with Alfred Brendel. *Career:* TV début at Promenade Concerts, London 1975, has appeared regularly since then; first British pianist and first woman pianist in South Bank Piano series, Queen Elizabeth Hall, London; broadcasts regularly for BBC; performs with New York, Berlin, Vienna and LA Philharmonic orchestras and with Boston, London, Sydney, Melbourne and Concertgebouw Symphony orchestras; gives solo recitals worldwide. *Recordings include:* Schubert's Schwannengesang,

Winterreise, Die Schöne Mullerin and Schumann's Heine Lieder and Kerner Lieder (with Wolfgang Holzmair), Mozart's Concerto for two pianos K. 365 (with Alfred Brendel), Schubert four-hand piano music with Anne Queffélec and "The Last Six Years" of Schubert's piano music. *Honours:* Premier Prix, Paris Conservatoire 1967, Mozart Memorial Prize 1969; Hon. Mus.D. (Exon) 1999. *Current Management:* Van Walsum Management Ltd, 4 Addison Bridge Place, London, W14 8XP, England. *Telephone:* (20) 7371-4343. *Fax:* (20) 7371-4344. *Website:* www.vanwalsum.co.uk.

**COOPER, Kenneth;** American harpsichordist, pianist, musicologist, conductor and educator; *Director, Baroque Aria Ensemble, Manhattan School of Music*; b. 31 May 1941, New York City, USA; m. Josephine Mongiardo, 1 June 1969, 1 s. *Education:* High School of Music and Art, New York City; BA, 1962, MA, Graduate faculties, 1964, PhD, Graduate Faculties, 1971, Columbia Univ.; Harpsichord Study with Sylvia Marlowe, Mannes Coll. of Music. *Career:* Debut: Wigmore Hall, 1965; Alice Tully Hall, USA, 1973; Academic Instructor, Barnard Coll., 1965–71; Adjunct Assistant Prof., Brooklyn Coll., 1971–73; Prof. of Harpsichord, Director of Collegium, Mannes Coll., 1975–85; Visiting Specialist in Performance Practice, Montclair State Coll., 1977–92; Artist-in-Residence, Columbia Univ., 1983–; Graduate seminars in Baroque Performance Practice, Manhattan School of Music, 1984–; Director, Baroque Aria Ensemble, Manhattan School of Music 1984–, Chairman, Harpsichord Department 1984–; Graduate Workshops in Performance Practice, Peabody Conservatory of Music, 1987–90; Graduate workshops at New England Conservatory, 2001; Many residencies and guest appearances and lectures; Performance: Premieres of works by Seymour Barab, Noel Lee, Ferruccio Busoni, Paul Ben-Haim, Ernst Krenek, Victoria Bond and others; Dozens of modern day revivals; Guest appearances and festivals; Harpsichordist and Pianist, Grand Canyon Chamber Music Festival, 1985–; Director, Berkshire Bach Ensemble 1991–;. *Recordings:* Numerous including: soundtracks, Van Gogh Revisited; Every Eye Forms Its Own Beauty; Valmont; Louis Cat Orze; Bach: 6 Brandenburg Concerti; Gamba-Harpsichord Sonatas, with Yo-Yo Ma; Flute-Fortepiano Sonatas with Susan Rotholz; Silks and Rags; Mother Goose and More; Bach Goldberg Variations; Bach Sonatas for Violin and Fortepiano (with Ani Kavafian); Baroque Fireworks (with Frank Morelli); Should Auld Acquaintance Be Forgot. *Publications include:* Three Centuries of Music in Score, Bach: Two-Part Inventions (Music Publishers Assocn Award) 2004. *Contributions:* professional journals. *Address:* 425 Riverside Drive, New York, NY 10025, USA.

**COOPER, Lawrence;** Singer (Baritone); b. 14 Aug. 1946, Los Angeles, California, USA. *Education:* Studied at the San Fernando State College. *Career:* Sang with the San Francisco Opera from 1977 and at the City Opera New York from 1983; Wexford Festival, 1981, as George in Moore's Of Mice and Men, Houston Opera, 1982, as Wozzeck; Guest engagements in Los Angeles, Chicago (Lyric Opera), Seattle and Detroit (1988); Other roles include Ford in Falstaff, Marcello in La Bohème, Valentin (Faust) and Germont; Frequent concert appearances. *Address:* c/o New York City Opera, Lincoln Center, New York, NY 10023, USA.

**COOTE, Alice;** British singer (mezzo-soprano); b. 10 May 1968, Frodsham, Cheshire, England. *Education:* Guildhall School of Music and Drama, London, Royal Northern Coll. of Music and Nat. Opera Studio. *Career:* concerts include oratorio with London and Liverpool Philharmonic Orchestras, Bergen Philharmonic, London Mozart Players, appearances at the BBC Proms 1997, 2002, 2003, recitals at Cheltenham and Edinburgh Festivals, on BBC Radio 3, and at the Wigmore Hall, London; roles include Cherubino in Figaro, Dorabella in Così fan tutte, Penelope in The Return of Ulysses, Kate Pinkerton in Madama Butterfly, Suzy in La Rondine, the Page in Salome, Glycère in Cherubini's Anacréon ou l'amour fugitif, Fortuna and Valletto in Poppea, Hanna Kennedy in Mary Stuart; season 1998–99 included her debut at Opéra Bastille in Parsifal, the title role in Rape of Lucretia at Nantes, Tamyris in Il Re Pastore for Opera North, Ruggiero in Alcina at Stuttgart; season 2002–03 included Covent Garden debut as Dryade in Ariadne auf Naxos, Ruggiero in Alcina at San Francisco, Octavian in Der Rosenkavalier for ENO, Strauss' Composer in Chicago, Dido in Les Troyens for San Francisco Opera, Turnspit in Rusalka and Orlando at Covent Garden; Rinaldo at Göttingen, Der Komponist in Ariadne auf Naxos for WNO 2004. *Recordings include:* Vaughan Williams' Hugh the Drover 1994, Rossini's Ricciardo e Zoraide 1997, Great Operatic Arias 2002, Verdi's Falstaff 2002, Handel: The Choice of Hercules 2002, Songs 2003. *Honours:* Brigitte Fassbaender Award for Lieder Interpretation, Decca-Kathleen Ferrier Prize 1992. *Current Management:* IMG Artists, Lovell House, 616 Chiswick High Road, London, W4 5RX, England. *Telephone:* (20) 8233-5800. *Fax:* (20) 8233-5801. *E-mail:* smardo@imgworld.com. *Website:* www.imgartists.com.

**COPE, David (Howell);** Composer, Writer and Instrument Maker; b. 17 May 1941, San Francisco, California, USA. *Education:* Studied at Arizona State University and with Halsey Stevens, Ingolf Dahl and George Perle at the University of Southern California. *Career:* Teacher at Kansas State College, 1968–69, California Lutheran College, the Cleveland Institute, Miami University of Ohio and the University of California, Santa Cruz, from 1977; Editor of The Composer, 1969–81. *Compositions include:* Tragic Overture, 1960; 4 Piano Sonatas, 1960–67; 2 String Quartets, 1961, 1963; Variations for piano and wind, 1965; Contrasts for orchestra, 1966; Music for brass and strings, 1967; Iceberg Meadow for prepared piano, 1968; Streams for orchestra, 1973; Spirals for tuba and tape, 1973; Requiem for Bosque Redondo, 1974; Arena for cello and tape, 1974; Re-Birth for concert band,

1975; Rituals for cello, 1976; Vectors for 4 percussion, 1976; Tenor Saxophone Concerto, 1976; Threshold and Visions for orchestra, 1977; Glassworks for 2 pianos and tape, 1979; Piano Concerto, 1980; The Way for various instruments, 1981; Corridors of Light for various instruments, 1983; Afterlife for orchestra, 1983. *Address:* c/o ASCAP, ASCAP Building, 1 Lincoln Plaza, New York, NY 10023, USA.

**COPLEY, John Michael Harold;** Opera Director and Producer; b. 12 June 1933, Birmingham, England. *Education:* Sadler's Wells Ballet School; Diploma, honours in Theatre Design, Central School of Arts and Crafts, London. *Career:* Stage Manager: Opera and ballet companies, Sadler's Wells in Rosebery Avenue, 1953–56, musicals, plays and so on, London West End; Deputy Stage Manager, 1960–63, Assistant Resident Producer, 1963–65, Associate Resident Producer, 1966–72, Resident Producer, 1972–75, Principal Resident Producer, 1975–88, Covent Garden Opera Company, productions including: Suor Angelica, 1965, Così fan tutte, 1968, 1981, Le nozze di Figaro, 1971, Don Giovanni, 1973, Faust, 1974, Benvenuto Cellini, 1976, Ariadne auf Naxos, 1976, Maria Stuarda, Royal Silver Jubilee Gala, 1977, La Traviata, Lucrezia Borgia, 1980, Semele, 1982; Other productions include: Numerous operas, London Coliseum, Athens Festival, Netherlands Opera, Belgian National Opera, Wexford Festival, Dallas Civic Opera (US debut, 1972, Lucia di Lammermoor), Chicago Lyric Opera, Greek National Opera, Australian Opera, English Opera North, Scottish Opera, English Opera Group; Vancouver Opera; Ottawa Festival, San Francisco Opera, Metropolitan Opera (New York), Santa Fe Opera, La Bohème, 1990; Houston Grand Opera, Washington Opera, San Diego Opera, London West End; Dallas production of Hansel and Gretel seen at Los Angeles, 1992; Directed local premiere of Britten's A Midsummer Night's Dream, Houston, 1993; Season 1996 with La Rondine at St Louis and Madama Butterfly at Santa Fe; Appearances include: Apprentice, Britten's Peter Grimes, Covent Garden, 1950; Soloist, Bach's St John Passion, Bremen, Germany, 1965; Co-director with Patrick Garland, Fanfare for Europe Gala, Covent Garden, 1973. *Current Management:* Hazard Chase, Norman House, Cambridge Place, Cambridge CB2 1NS, England. *Telephone:* (1223) 312400. *Fax:* (1223) 460827. *Website:* www.hazardchase.co.uk. *Address:* 9D Thistle Grove, London SW10 9RR, England.

**CORAL, Giampaolo;** Composer; b. 22 Jan. 1944, Trieste. *Education:* Diploma at the Conservatory of Music B Marcello, Venice. *Career:* Founder and Art Director of International Contemporary Music Festival, Trieste Prima; Art Director of International Competition for musical composition, Prize Town of Trieste. *Compositions include:* Stage Works, Mr Hyde, opera in one act; Schwanengesang, chamber opera in one act; Favola, romantic pantomime in one act; Orchestral Works, Magnificat for soprano and orchestra, Amras for violin and orchestra, Kubin Zyklus for orchestra, Tout a coup et comme par jeu for flute and orchestra, Requiem for orchestra; Chamber music, Osservando Paul Klee for violin, cello, piano, Trakl Lieder for soprano and piano, Seconda Sonata for piano, Klavieralbum I–III, Raps I–XI for ensemble, Damonen und Nachtgesichte von A. Kubin for ensemble, Modulazioni for piano (four hands), Aloe for vocal ensemble and five brass. *Publications:* Editio Musica, Budapest; Suvini Zerboni, Milano; Sonzogno, Milano; Curci, Milano; Edipan, Roma; Dictionary: Riemann Musik Lexikon, Utet. *Address:* Via Ponchielli 3, 34122 Trieste, Italy.

**CORAZZA, Remy;** Singer (Tenor); b. 16 April 1933, Revin, Ardennes, France. *Education:* Studied at the Toulouse and Paris Conservatories. *Career:* Debut: Opéra-Comique, Paris, as Beppe in Pagliacci, 1959; Sang Gonzalve in L'Heure Espagnole at the Paris Opéra, 1960; Many performances in Paris and elsewhere in France as Pinkerton, Rodolfo, Hoffmann, Nadir and in Mozart roles; Opéra du Rhin, Strasbourg, from 1974, Salzburg from 1978, as Monostatos and the Hoffmann buffo roles; Professor at the Paris Conservatory, 1985; Glyndebourne debut, 1987, as Torquemada in L'Heure Espagnole; Nantes Opera 1990 in Le Pré aux clercs by Hérold and Le Roi l'a dit by Delibes. *Address:* c/o Conservatoire National, 14 Rue de Madrid, 75008 Paris, France.

**CORBELLI, Alessandro;** singer (baritone); b. 21 Sept. 1952, Turin, Italy. *Education:* studied with Giuseppe Valdengo. *Career:* debut in Bergamo, 1974, as Marcello in La Bohème; many appearances in the buffo repertory at opera houses in Italy, Vienna, Paris and Germany; Rossini roles include Pacuvio in La Pietra del Paragone (Picco Scala and Edinburgh, 1982), Dandini in La Cenerentola (Glyndebourne, 1985) and Gaudenzio in Il Signor Bruschino (Paris, 1986); Rome Opera, 1985–86, as Belcore (L'Elisir d'amore) and Marcello; Covent Garden debut, 1988, as Taddeo in L'Italiana in Algeri; Season 1989–90 in Pergolesi's Lo frate' nnamorato at La Scala, conducted by Muti, as Don Alfonso at the Salzburg Festival and as Germano in La Scala di Seta at Schwetzingen; Other roles include Papageno (Ravenna, 1986), Guglielmo, Escamillo, Malatesta and the Figaros of Mozart, Rossini and Paisiello; Fabrizio in Crispino e la Comare, Pantaleone in The Love of Three Oranges and Monteverdi's Ottone; Season 1992 as Belcore at Parma, Rossini's Martino and Gormano at Cologne, the Paris Opéra-Comique and the Schwetzingen Festival; Sang Leporello at Lausanne, 1996 and Alfonso at Covent Garden, 1997; Dandini in Cenerentola at Pesaro and Dulcarmara at Madrid, 1998; Season 2000–01 as Rossini's Dandini and Taddeo at the New York Met. Leporello at Glyndebourne and Belfiore in Verdi's Un giorno di regno, at Bologna; Dandini at Covent Garden, 2003. *Recordings include:* La Cenerentola, conducted by Abbado; L'Italiana in Algeri; Paisiello's Barbiere di Siviglia and La Buona Figliuola by Piccinni. *Current Management:* Patricia Greenan and Penelope Marland Associates, 7 Whitehorse Close, Royal Mile,

Edinburgh, EH8 8BU, Scotland. *Telephone:* (131) 557 5872. *Fax:* (131) 556 5825. *E-mail:* patricia@greenanartists.fsnet.co.uk.

**CORBETT, Sidney;** Composer; b. 26 April 1960, Chicago, Illinois, USA. *Education:* BA with high distinction in Music Composition, 1982, further studies, 1978–82, University of San Diego, California; Studied composition principally with Pauline Oliveros, Bernard Rands, Joji Yuasa, Jean-Charles François; MM, 1984, MMA, 1985, DMA, 1989, Yale School of Music; Principal composition teachers include Jacob Druckman and Martin Bresnick; Thesis on Metaphor Structures in Contemporary Music; DAAD Fellow and member of G Ligeti Seminar, Hamburg, Germany, 1985–87. *Career:* Compositions performed in USA and Europe, including radio broadcasts; Active as composer in Germany, 1985–. *Compositions:* Arien, violin solo, 1983; Pastel Nos 1 and 2, trombone quartet, 1984, 1988; Ghost Reveille for orchestra, 1984; For Pianos, for 4 pianos, 1984; Bass Animation for contrabass with 2 percussions, 1985; Arien IV: Solo Music for guitar, 1986; Kandinsky Romance for chamber ensemble, 1986; Cactus Flower for solo flute, 1988; Pianos' Dream, piano duo, 1989; Concerto for trombone and wind orchestra, 1989; Lieder aus der Dunkelkammer for soprano, harp and chamber orchestra, 1990; Symphony No. 1 Tympan, 1991–92; Hamlet Variations (in memoriam John Coltrane) for solo euphonium, 1992; Gloucester Epiphonies for chamber ensemble, 1993. *Address:* Vogelsangstrasse 55, 7000 Stuttgart 1, Germany.

**CORBOZ, Michel;** Conductor; b. 14 Feb. 1934, Marsens, Switzerland. *Education:* Studied at Ecole Normale in Fribourg. *Career:* Chorus Master at Notre-Dame in Lausanne from 1954, leading such works as the Fauré Requiem; Accompanied singers at the organ and worked at various Lausanne churches; Founded the Ensemble Vocal et Instrumental de Lausanne, 1961, giving notable performances of Monteverdi's Orfeo; Conductor of the choirs of the Gulbenkian Foundation in Lisbon from 1969, leading works by Bach, Monteverdi and Vivaldi; Conducted Monteverdi's Il Ritorno d'Ulisse at Mézières, 1989. *Recordings:* Monteverdi's Orfeo and Vespers, Bach's B minor Mass, Cavalli's Ercole Amante, Charpentier's David et Jonathas, works by Vivaldi and Giovanni Gabrieli. *Address:* c/o Conservatoire de Musique, 228-Arue Pierre Aeby, CH –1700 Fribourg, Switzerland.

**CORDERO, Roque,** BA; Panamanian composer, conductor and educator; b. 16 Aug. 1917, Panama City; m. Elizabeth L. Johnson 1947; three s. *Education:* Hamline Univ., studied composition with Ernst Krenek, conducting with Dimitri Mitropoulos, Stanley Chapple and Leon Barzin. *Career:* Dir and Prof., Nat. Inst. of Music, Panama 1950–64; conductor, Nat. Orchestra of Panama 1964–66; guest conductor in Colombia, Brazil, Chile, Argentina, Puerto Rico, USA, El Salvador and Guatemala; Prof. of Music and Asst Dir, Latin American Music Center, Indiana Univ., USA 1966–69; Prof. of Music, Illinois State Univ. 1972–. *Compositions:* over 20 published including Cinco Mensajes para Cuatro Amigos for guitar, 1983; Cantata for Peace for solo baritone, choir and orchestra, 1979; Fourth Symphony, Panamanian, 1986; Serenata, for flute, viola, clarinet and harp, 1987. *Recordings:* Violin Concerto and 8 Miniatures with Detroit Symphony; 2nd Symphony; Duo, 1954; Dodecaconcerto; Cinco Mensajes para Cuatro Amigos for Guitar; Sonatina Ritmica; Permutaciones 7; Quinteto; Four Messages for flutes and piano; 8 Miniatures (Chicago Sinfonietta); Second Symphony, The Louisville Orchestra. *Publications include:* Curso de Solfeo, Argentina 1963, Mexico 1975; The Music of Panama: Four Messages for flutes and piano, 1992; Fanfarria Jubilosa for orchestra, 1994; Duos for oboe and bassoon, 1996; Centennial Symphonic tribute for orchestra, 1997; contrib. to Buenos Aires Musical; Revista Musical Chilena; Journal of Inter-American Studies; Grove's Dictionary of Music. *Address:* Music Department, Illinois State University, Normal, IL 61790-5660, USA.

**CORDIER, David John,** MA; singer (countertenor); b. 1 May 1959, Rochester, Kent, England; m. Ursula Cordier 1990; one s. one d. *Education:* King's College, Cambridge, Royal College of Music, London. *Career:* debut at Wigmore Hall, 1989; Darmstadt (Lear by Reimann), 1990; Handel Opera, Göttingen; Halle and Karlsruhe Festivals; Recital Berlin Philharmonic, 1996; Opera in Amsterdam, Munich, Düsseldorf, Dresden; Innsbruck, Salzburg and Bern; Season 1998 with Ezio at the Halle Handel Festival and Bertarido in Rodelinda for GTO; sang Handel's Radamisto at Halle, 2000; Teacher at Hanns Eisler Hochschule in Berlin (countertenor). *Recordings include:* Bach Matthew Passion, conducted by Gustav Leonhardt; Solo recitals English song. *Address:* Lindlarer Str 98, 51491 Overath, Germany.

**CORGHI, Azio,** DipMus; Italian composer; b. 9 March 1937, Cirie, Turin. *Education:* Turin Conservatory, Milan Conservatory with Bruno Bettinelli. *Career:* freelance composer; teacher of composition, Conservatorio Giuseppe Verdi, Milan. *Compositions include:* Symbola 1971, Tactus 1974, Actus III (ballet) 1978, Gargantua (two-act opera, after Rabelais, Teatro Regio, Turin) 1984, Mazapegul (ballet) 1986, Blimunda (three-act opera, after Memoriale del Convento by José Saramago, Teatro Lirico, Milan) 1990, Divara (opera, after In nomine Dei by José Saramago, Städtische Bühnen Münster) 1993, Rinaldo (opera, after Rinaldo by Handel, Catania) 1997, Isabella (opera, after L'italiana in Algeri by Rossini, Pesaro) 1998, Tat'jana (opera, after Tat'jana Repina by Anton Chekhov, Milan) 2000, Dissoluto assoluto (opera) 2005. *Publications:* Critical edns of L'Italiana in Algeri and Tosca. *Address:* c/o Conservatorio Giuseppe Verdi, Via del Conservatorio 12, 20122 Milan, Italy.

**CORIGLIANO, John Paul;** Composer and Teacher; b. 16 Feb. 1938, New York, NY, USA. *Education:* BA, Columbia University, 1959; With Otto Luening, Vittorio Giannini, Manhattan School of Music; Privately with Paul

Creston; Honorary doctorates from Manhattan School of Music, 1992 and Ithaca College, 1995. *Career:* Music Programmer, WQXR-FM and WBAI-FM, New York, 1959–64; Associate Producer, Musical Programmes, CBS-TV, 1961–72; Music Director, Morris Theatre, New Jersey, 1962–64; Teacher of Composition: College of Church Musicians, Washington DC, 1968–71; Manhattan School of Music, 1971–; Lehman College, City University of New York, 1973–; Distinguished Professor, 1986–; Composer-in-Residence, Chicago Symphony Orchestra, 1987–89; Symphony No. 1 premiere, Boston Symphony, also New York Philharmonic, Chicago Symphony, Seattle Symphony; The Ghosts of Versailles premiere, Metropolitan Opera, 1991; Fanfares to Music, Cincinnati Symphony, 1995; mem, American Society of Composers, Authors and Publishers. *Compositions:* Kaleidoscope, 2 pianos, 1959; Sonata, violin, piano, 1963; Elegy, orchestra, 1965; The Cloisters, 4 songs, voice, piano, 1965, voice, orchestra, 1976; Christmas at the Cloisters, chorus, organ or piano, 1966; Tournaments Overture, 1966; Piano Concerto, 1968; Poem in October, tenor, 8 instruments, 1970, tenor, orchestra, 1976; The Naked Carmen, mixed-media opera, 1970; Creations, 2 scenes from Genesis, narrator, chamber orchestra, 1972; Gazebo Dances, band, 1973; Aria, oboe, strings, 1975; Oboe Concerto, 1975; Poem on His Birthday, 1976; Etude Fantasy, piano, 1976; Voyage, string orchestra, 1976, flute, string orchestra, 1983; Clarinet Concerto, 1977; Pied Piper Fantasy, Flute Concerto, 1981; 3 Hallucinations, 1981; Promenade Overture, 1981; Echoes of Forgotten Rites: Summer Fanfare, 1982; Fantasia on an Ostinato, piano, 1985, orchestra, 1986; Symphony No. 1, 1989–90; Opera, The Ghosts of Versailles, 1991; Phantasmagoria (on Themes from The Ghosts of Versailles), cello and piano, 1993; How Like Pellucid Statues, Daddy, 1994; Amen, for double a cappella chorus, 1994; String Quartet, 1996; Chiaroscuro, 1997; Fancy on a Bach Air, 1997; The Red Violin, Chaconne for violin and orchestra, 1998; Troubadours, variations for guitar and orchestra, 1999; Vocalise, 1999; A Dylan Thomas Trilogy, chorus, soloists and orchestra (1960–76; rev. 1999); The Mannheim Rocket, 2000; Phantasmagoria: Suite from The Ghosts of Versailles, orchestra, 2000; Symphony No. 2, 2000; Mr. Tambourine Man: Seven Poems of Bob Dylan, 2000; Incidental music for plays; Film scores. *Recordings:* Symphony No. 1, Chicago Symphony/Barenboim; Pied Piper Fantasy; Fantasia on an Ostinato; Of Rage and Remembrance–Symphony No. 1, 1996; String Quartet, 1996; Video of The Ghosts of Versailles (DGG); Phantasmagoria (The Fantasy Album). *Honours:* Guggenheim Fellow, 1968–69; NEA Grant, 1976; Award, 1990, Member, 1991, American Academy and Institute of Arts and Letters; L. Grawemeyer Award, 1991; Musical American Composer of the Year Winner, 1992; Grammy Award, Classical Album of the Year, 1996; Grammy Award, Composition of the Year, 1996; George Washington University Presidential Medal of Honor, 1996. *Current Management:* Jay K. Hoffman & Associates, 136 East 57th Street, New York, NY 10017, USA. *Address:* 365 West End Avenue, New York, NY 10024, USA.

**CORNWELL, Joseph;** Singer (tenor); b. 1959, England. *Education:* BA in Music, York University. *Career:* Sang originally with such early music groups as the Consort of Musicke and the Taverner Consort; Promenade Concert debut, 1982, in Monteverdi's Vespers under Andrew Parrott; Tours of Netherlands and France in the Bach Passions; Verdi's Requiem at the Albert Hall, conducted by David Willcocks; Bruckner's Te Deum at the Festival Hall; Appearances at the Paris, Bruges, Flanders, Three Choirs and Brighton Festivals; Conductors include Trevor Pinnock, Stephen Cleobury, Ton Koopman and Roger Norrington; Bach's B minor Mass with the London Bach Orchestra at the Barbican, Nov 1990; Has sung on ITV, Swiss television and BBC television; Opera roles include Fenton in Falstaff, Frederic in Mignon, Jove in The Return of Ulysses (Kent Opera) and parts in Mahagonny and Let's Make an Opera; Sang title role in Monteverdi's Orfeo for Oslo Summer Opera, conducted by Andrew Parrott, and in 1993 for Boston Early Music Festival; Also sang Lurcanio in Handel's Ariodante for St Gallen Opera, in Switzerland; Arretro in Peri's Euridice in Rouen, 1992–93; Sang in King Arthur with The Sixteen, Lisbon, 1996. *Recordings include:* Monteverdi Christmas Vespers; Handel's Messiah; Albums for several labels; Monteverdi Vespers with Parrott; Rossini's Petite Messe Sollenelle with Jos Van Immerseel. *Current Management:* Hazard Chase Ltd, Norman House, Cambridge Place, Cambridge, CB2 1NS, England. *Telephone:* (1223) 312400. *Fax:* (1223) 460827. *Website:* www.hazardchase.co.uk.

**CORP, Ronald;** British conductor and ecclesiastic; b. 4 Jan. 1951, Wells, Somerset, England. *Education:* MA (Oxon); Dip Theol (Southampton). *Career:* librarian, producer and presenter, BBC Radio 3, 1973–87; Founder Conductor, New London Orchestra, 1988 and New London Children's Choir, 1991; Musical Dir, The London Chorus Soc. and Conductor, Highgate Choral Soc.; broadcasts for BBC with BBC Singers, BBC Concert Orchestra, Ulster Orchestra, New London Orchestra and New London Children's Choir; Promenade Concert debut, 1990 with Britten's Noye's Fludde and further Proms with New London Orchestra in 1991, 1995, 1998, 1999 and with BBC Concert Orchestra, 1996 and 1997; Ordained Deacon in the Church of England 1998, Priest 1999–; mem. Asscn of British Choral Dirs (ABCD), Nat. Fed. of Music Socs (NFMS); Vice Pres. Sullivan Soc.; Trustee Musician's Benevolent Fund and Chair. of the Education Cttee. *Compositions:* And All the Trumpets Sounded, 1989; Laudamus, 1992; Four Elizabethan Lyrics, 1994; Jubilate Deo, 1995; Cornucopia, 1997; Piano Concerto, 1997; A New Song, 1999; Mass 'Christ Our Future', 2000; Mary's Song, 2001; Adonai Echad, 2001; Other choral works. *Recordings:* 18 albums with New London Orchestra, including British Light Music Classics I–IV, Kaleidoscope 2002, Dover Beach (BBC Singers Commission) 2003, Forever Child 2004; Poulenc,

Satie, Milhaud, Prokofiev and Virgil Thomson; Britten recording with New London Children's Choir;. *Publications:* The Choral Singer's Companion, 1987. *Address:* 76 Brent Street, London NW4 2ES, England. *Telephone:* (208) 202-8123. *Fax:* (208) 203-4134. *E-mail:* ronald.corp@btconnect.com. *Website:* www.ronaldcorp.com.

**CORSARO, Frank Andrew;** American theatre and opera director; *Artistic Director, Vocal Arts Department, Juilliard School;* b. 22 Dec. 1924, New York; s. of Joseph and Marie (née Quarino) Corsaro; m. Mary Cross Bonnie Lueders 1971; one s. *Education:* Yale Univ. *Career:* began career as actor 1948, appearing since in productions including Mrs. McThing, Broadway 1951; first film appearance in Rachel 1967; Dir of numerous plays including A Hatful of Rain, Broadway 1955–56, The Night of the Iguana 1961–62, Tremonisha 1975, 1600 Pennsylvania Avenue 1976, Cold Storage, Lyceum 1977–, Whoopee! 1979, Knockout 1979; directed and acted in numerous TV productions; one-man art show 1976; Dir numerous operas with New York City Opera 1958–, Washington Opera Soc. 1970–74, St Paul Opera 1971, Houston Grand Opera 1973–77, Assoc. Artistic Dir 1977–; Artistic Dir The Actors Studio 1988–; Drama Dir Juilliard Opera Centre 1989, Artistic Dir, Vocal Arts Dept, Juillard School 1988. *Theatre productions include:* La Traviata, Madame Butterfly, Faust, Manon Lescaut, A Village Romeo and Juliet, L'Incoronazione di Poppea, The Angel of Fire, Hugh the Drover, Rinaldo, Love for Three Oranges (Glyndebourne 1983), La Fanciulla del West (Deutsches Oper Berlin 1983), Rinaldo (Metropolitan Opera 1983), Fennimore and Gerda (Edinburgh Festival 1983), Where the Wild Things Are, Higgeldy, Piggeldy, Pop (Glyndebourne 1985), Alcina (Spitalfields 1985), (LA Opera Centre 1986), L'Enfant et les Sortilèges, L'Heure espagnole, Glyndebourne Festival 1987, Hansel and Gretel (Houston, Toronto, Zurich 1997–98), Kuhlhandel (Juilliard 1998). *Publications include:* L'histoire du soldat (adaptation), La Bohème (adaptation), A Piece of Blue Sky (play), Maverik 1978, Libretto: Before Breakfast (music by Thomas Pasatieri), Libretto: Heloise and Abelard (music by Steven Paulus), Kunma (novel). *Address:* 60 Lincoln Plaza, New York, New York, NY 10023 (office); 33 Riverside Drive, New York, NY 10023, USA (home). *Telephone:* (212) 799-5000 ext. 261 (office); (212) 874-1048. *Fax:* (212) 724-0263 (office).

**CORTE, Miguel;** Singer (Tenor); b. 1952, Mexico. *Education:* Studied in Monterrey and New York. *Career:* Debut: Metropolitan Opera, 1981, as Alfredo; Sang with Kentucky Opera as the Duke of Mantua, Rodolfo, Pinkerton, Fenton and Jacquino; European engagements as the Duke at Zürich (1984), Alfredo at Trieste (1985) and Werther in Mexico City (1985); Has also sung in Salzburg (Alfredo, 1983), San Francisco (as Pinkerton) and in the Verdi Requiem (at Seattle). *Address:* c/o Kentucky Opera, 631 South Fifth Street, Louisville, KY 40202, USA.

**CORTES, Gardar;** Conductor and Singer (tenor); b. 1950, Reykjavík, Iceland. *Education:* Studied at Royal Academy of Music and Trinity College of Music in London. *Career:* Has conducted choirs in Iceland and founded the Reykjavík Symphony Orchestra, 1985, leading it on a tour of Denmark; With Icelandic Opera has conducted Orpheus in the Underworld, Pagliacci and Die Fledermaus, Noye's Fludde at the International Festival in Reykjavík; Appearances as singer with Oslo Opera, Royal Swedish Opera, Seattle Opera, Windsor Festival, Opera North and Belfast Festival; Intendant of the Gothenburg Opera, Sweden; Roles have included Eisenstein, Tamino, Hoffmann, Radames, Cavaradossi, Florestan and Otello.

**CORTEZ, Luis Jaime;** Mexican composer and musicologist; b. 1963, Morelia, Michoacán. *Education:* Univ. of Mexico. *Career:* Dir, Centro Nacional de Investigación, Documentación e Información Musical 1987–1994; Dir, Conservatorio de las Roses, Morelia 1996–. *Compositions include:* Formas demasiado lejos 1985, Canto por un equinoccio 1989, Lluvias (Symphony No. 1) 1992, En blanco y negro (Symphony No. 2) 1995, Las tentaciones de San Antonio (opera) 1996. *Address:* Conservatorio de las Roses, Santiago Tapia No. 30, Col. Centro, Morelia, CP 58000, Mexico (office).

**CORTEZ, Viorica;** Singer (Mezzo-soprano); b. 22 Dec. 1935, Bucium, Romania; m. Emmanuel Bondeville, 1974 (deceased 1987). *Education:* Studied at the Iasi and Bucharest Conservatories. *Career:* Debut: Iasi Opera, 1960, as Dalila; Sang Dalila at Toulouse, 1965; Bucharest Opera, 1965–70; Covent Garden debut, 1968, as Carmen; Italian debut, 1969, as Amneris at Naples; La Scala Milan, 1970, as Dalila; US debut, Seattle Opera, 1971; Metropolitan Opera from 1971, as Carmen, Amneris, Giulietta in Les Contes d'Hoffmann, Adalgisa in Norma and Azucena; Chicago debut, 1973, in Maria Stuarda; Sang in the premiere of Bondeville's Antoine et Cléopatre, Rouen, 1974; Paris Opéra, 1980, in Bluebeard's Castle, Oedipus Rex and Boris Godunov; Sang La Cieca in La Gioconda at the Verona Arena and Barcelona, 1988; Gertrude in Hamlet, Turin, 1990, and the title role in the premiere of La Lupa by Marco Tutino at Livorno; Season 1992 as Ulrica at Genoa; Montpellier 1995, as Uta in Reyer's Sigurd; Sang Rosa in Cilea's L'Arlesiana at Montpellier, 1996; Season 2000–01 as the Marquise in La Fille du régiment at Strasbourg, and as Lia in Magnard's Bérénice at Marseilles. *Recordings:* Carmen; Aida; Il Trovatore; Verdi's Oberto; Donizetti's Requiem; Rigoletto; Video of Rigoletto. *Address:* c/o Opéra de Montpellier, 11 boulevard Victor Hugo, 34967 Montpellier, France.

**CORY, Eleanor;** Composer; b. 8 Sept. 1943, Englewood, NJ, USA. *Education:* Studied with Charles Wuorinen and others at Columbia University in New York. *Career:* Has taught at Yale University, Manhattan School of Music, and Sarah Lawrence College among others. *Compositions include:* Waking for soprano and ensemble, 1974; Octagons for ensemble, 1976; Tapestry for orchestra, 1982; String Quartet, 1985; Of Mere Being for chorus and brass quintet, 1987; Fantasy for flute, guitar and percussion, 1991; Canyons for chamber orchestra, 1991. *Address:* c/o ASCAP, ASCAP Building, 1 Lincoln Plaza, New York, NY 10023, USA.

**COSMA, Octavian (Lazar);** Musicologist, Professor and Doctor; b. 15 Feb. 1933, Treznea, Salaj, Romania; m. Elena, 15 Nov 1958, 1 s., 1 d. *Education:* Rimsky Korsakov Conservatory, St Petersburg, Russia, 1959. *Career:* Debut: Muzica, 1954; Councillor, Ministry of Culture and Education, 1959–63; Assistant Lecturer, Professor, Academy of Music, Bucharest, 1959–; Secretary, 1990, Vice President, 1992, Romanian Union of Composers and Musicologists; Editor-in-Chief of journal, Mizica, 1990; mem, Romanian Union of Composers; American Musicological Society. *Publications:* The Romanian Opera, 2 vols, 1962; Enescu's Oedipus, 1967; The Chronicle of Romanian Music, vols I 1973, II 1974, III 1975, IV 1976, V 1983, VI 1984, VII 1986, VIII 1988, IX 1991; The Universe of Romanian Music, 1995. *Contributions:* Various professional journals. *Honours:* Ciprian Porumbescu Prize, Romanian Academy, 1962; Prize, Romanian Union of Composers, 1968. *Current Management:* Conservatorul Ciprian Porumbescu, Bucharest. *Address:* Cotroceni 5–7, Bucharest 76528, Romania.

**COSMA, Viorel;** Musicologist and Professor; b. 30 March 1923, Timisoara, Romania; m. Coralia Cosma. *Education:* Municipal Conservatory, Timisoara; Academie of Music, Bucharest. *Career:* Debut: As conductor in 1944; Musicologist and Music Critic from 1946; Professor from 1950. *Publications:* Historiographic Works: Two Millenia of Music, in English, 1982, Musicological Exegeses, 1984; Lexicography: Romanian Musicians, Lexicon, 1970, Musicians of Romania (A-C), Lexicon, 1989; Monographs: Ion Vidu, 1956, Ciprian Porumbescu, 1957, Elena Teodorini, 1960, Nicolae Filimon, 1966, The George Enescu Philharmonic, 1968, The Madrigal Choir, 1971, Enescu Today, 1981, Dinu Lipatti, 1991; Epistolography: Bartók, 1955, Enescu, 2 vols, 1974 and 1981; Romanian Performers: Lexicon, 1996. *Honours:* Prize, Romanian Composers, 1970, 1972, 1978, 1983, 1988, 1991; Prize, Academy of Romania, 1971. *Address:* Str Luterana 3, Bucharest, Romania.

**COSSA, Dominic;** Singer (Baritone) and Teacher; b. 13 May 1935, Jessup, Pennsylvania, USA; m. Janet Edgerton, 26 Dec 1957, 1 s., 1 d. *Education:* BS, University of Scranton, 1959; MA, University of Detroit, 1961; LhD, University of Scranton; Detroit Institute of Musical Arts, Philadelphia Academy of Vocal Arts; Principal vocal teachers: Anthony Marlowe, Robert Weede and Armen Boyajian. *Career:* Debut: Operatic debut as Morales, Carmen, New York City Opera, 1961; Leading baritone roles, New York City Opera; Metropolitan Opera debut, New York, as Silvio in Pagliacci, 1970–76; Other Met roles were Masetto, Rossini's Figaro, Marcello and Puccini's Lescaut; Opéra du Rhin, Strasbourg, 1976; Sang M. Triquet in Eugene Onegin at Florence, 2000; Faculty Manhattan School of Music, New York; Chair, Voice/Opera, University of Maryland, College Park. *Recordings:* For Decca-London; New World Records; RCA-Victor including Achilles in Giulio Cesare, conducted by Julius Rudel. *Honours:* Inducted into Hall of Fame for great American Singers, Philadelphia Academy of Vocal Arts, 1993. *Address:* 845 Stonington Way, Arnold, MD 21012, USA.

**COSSOTI, Max-René;** Singer (Tenor); b. 1950, Italy. *Career:* Debut: Siena, 1973, in Gazzaniga's Don Giovanni; Genoa, 1974, Ernesto at Spoleto (1975) and Glyndebourne from 1976, as Fenton, Ferrando, Almaviva, Eurymachos in Monteverdi's Ulisse and Fileno in Haydn's La Fedeltà Premiata; Further engagements at Innsbruck, 1983, in Cesti's Il Tito; Lisbon, 1985, as the Prince in Cenerentola and Trieste, 1992, as Zemlinsky's Zwerg; Other roles include Elvino in La Sonnambula, Alfredo, Gerald in Lakmé, Werther, and Alfred in Die Fledermaus; Sang L'incredible in Andrea Chenier at Rome, 1996; Dagobert in Lehar's Eva at Naples, 1998; Sang Mozart's Basilio at Klagenfurt, 2001. *Recordings include:* Videos of Ulisse, Falstaff and Il Barbiere di Sivigila from Glyndebourne. *Address:* c/o Teatro Comunale G Verdi, Riva Novembre 1, 34121, Trieste, Italy.

**COSSOTTO, Fiorenza;** Singer (Mezzo-soprano); b. 22 April 1935, Crescentino, Italy; m. Ivo Vinco, 1958. *Education:* Turin Conservatory; Study with Ettore Campogalliani. *Career:* Debut: La Scala Milan, 1957, in the premiere of Poulenc's Les Dialogues des Carmélites; Returned to Milan until 1973, notably as Verdi's Eboli, Amneris and Azucena, and in La Favorite, Les Huguenots, Il Barbiere di Siviglia and Cavalleria Rusticana; Sang Jane Seymour in Anna Bolena at Wexford in 1958; Covent Garden debut, 1959, as Neris in Cherubini's Médée; Chicago Lyric Opera, 1964, in La Favorite; Metropolitan Opera debut, 1968, as Amneris, returning for Laura in La Gioconda, Adalgisa, Norma, Carmen and Mistress Quickly (Falstaff); Sang, Verona Arena, 1960–89, notably as Amneris, which she sang at the Metropolitan, 1989; Sang Dalila at Newark, New Jersey, 1989, the Princess in Adriana Lecouvreur, Rome; Sang Santuzza, Piacenza, 1990; Ulrica at Lisbon and Amneris at Buenos Aires; Sang Ulrica at Genoa, 1992. *Recordings:* Roles in Andrea Chénier, Norma, Madama Butterfly, La Sonnambula, Macbeth, Don Carlos, Cavalleria Rusticana, Médée and Il Trovatore. *Address:* c/o Teatro Comunale, Opera de Genova, Passo al Teatro 4, Italy.

**COSTA, Mary;** American opera singer; b. Knoxville, Tenn. *Education:* Los Angeles Conservatory of Music. *Career:* debut at Los Angeles Opera 1958, San Francisco Opera 1959, Metropolitan Opera (New York) 1964, Bolshoi (USSR, now Russian Fed.) 1970; performed at opening of J. F. Kennedy Center, Washington DC 1970; appearances at opera houses in UK, Canada, USSR,

Portugal; Vice-Pres. Hawaiian Fragrances 1972, California Inst. of the Arts; mem. Nat. Council on the Arts 2003–. *Operas include:* La Bohème 1959, La Traviata 1964, 1970, Candide 1971. *Films:* Marry Me Again 1953, The Big Caper 1957, Sleeping Beauty (voice of Sleeping Beauty), The Great Waltz 1972, Titus Andronicus 2000; BBC films of La Traviata, Faust, The Merry Widow. *Honours:* Los Angeles Woman of Year 1959; DAR Honour Medal 1974; Tennessee Hall of Fame Award 1987; Women of Achievement Award Nat. Women's Bd of Northwood Inst. (Palm Beach, Fla) 1991, Licia Albanese Puccini Foundation Lifetime Achievement Award 1999, Disney Legends Award 1999, Metropolitan Opera Guild Distinguished Verdi Performance Award 2001. *Address:* c/o California Artists Management, 564 Market Street, Suite 420, San Francisco, CA 94104-5412, USA. *Telephone:* (415) 362-2787 (office). *Fax:* (415) 362-2838 (office). *E-mail:* don@calartists.com (office). *Website:* www.calartists.com (office).

**COSTANZO, Giuseppe;** Singer (Tenor); b. 1958, Catania, Italy. *Career:* Debut: Bari, 1983, as Arturo in Lucia di Lammermoor; Macerata Festival, 1984, as Almaviva; Bergamo, 1984, as Ernani, Trieste and Tel-Aviv, 1985, as Pinkerton; La Scala debut, 1988, as Conte Alberto in L'Occasione fa il ladro; Cologne, 1991, as Gabriele Adorno in Simon Boccanegra; Other roles include Ernesto, Rinuccio in Gianni Schicchi, Edgardo, and Alfredo (Lisbon, 1987); Many concert engagements. *Address:* c/o Teatro Nacional San Carlos, Rua Serpo Panto no G, 1200 442 Lisbon, Portugal.

**COSTINESCU, Gheorghe,** PhD; composer, conductor, pianist, musicologist and educator; *Professor Emeritus, Lehman College, City University of New York;* b. 12 Dec. 1934, Bucharest, Romania; m. Silvelin von Scanzoni 1971. *Education:* Bucharest Conservatory, Darmstadt and Cologne, Juilliard School, Columbia Univ., studied composition with Mihail Jora in Romania, Luciano Berio in USA, studied with Nadia Boulanger, Karlheinz Stockhausen, Henry Pousseur, Mario Davidovsky and Chou Wen-chung, conducting with Harold Faberman, Maurice Peress and Dennis Russell Davies in USA and with Sergiu Celibidache in Germany. *Career:* debut as composer and pianist, Sonata for violin and piano at Shiraz-Persepolis Festival, Iran 1967; debut as conductor, The Washington premiere of Peter Maxwell Davis' Miss Donnithorn's Maggot at the Corcoran Gallery of Art 1979; Prof. Emeritus, Lehmann Coll., CUNY; premieres: Evolving Cycle of Two-Part Modal Inventions for piano, Romanian Broadcast 1964; Past Are The Years for tenor and vocal ensemble with Juilliard Chorus, Lincoln Center, New York 1970; Jubilus for soprano, trumpet and percussive body sounds, commissioned and broadcasted by Nat. Public Radio, USA 1981; premiere of stage work: The Musical Seminar at Tanglewood Festival 1982; German premiere at State Opera of Stuttgart 1989; British premiere with Paragon Opera Project at Royal Scottish Acad. of Music, Glasgow 1992; premiere of Pantomime for chamber orchestra at the Romanian Nat. Opera Bucharest 1998; premiere of Paragon 2000 for chamber orchestra, with the Paragon Ensemble of Scotland, Glasgow 2000, full orchestra version with the Concerto Orchestra, Bucharest 2001; first retrospective concert, The Ensemble Sospeso at Miller Theatre, New York 2002. *Recordings:* Composers Recordings Inc, USA; published works: Evolving Cycle for piano 1964, Song of the Rivers vocal symphonic work 1967, Sonata for violin and piano 1968. *Publications:* Treatise on Musical Phonology 1968; studies and articles on contemporary music, essays on comparative aesthetics. *Honours:* Romanian Acad. George Enescu Prize 1965, Juilliard School Alexandre Gretchaninoff Prize 1970, American Acad. and Inst. of Arts and Letters Music Award 1995, League of Composers/ISCM Competition Music Theater Prize 1986, New York Foundation for the Arts Fellowship Award 1988, NEA Producers and Composers grants 1986, 1989, Fulbright Scholar Award 1997–98. *Address:* 120 Riverside Drive, Apt 6E, New York, NY 10024, USA. *Telephone:* (212) 877-3494. *E-mail:* g.s.costinescu@rcn .com.

**COTRUBAŞ, Ileana;** Romanian singer (soprano); b. 9 June 1939, Galaţi; d. of Vasile Cotrubaş and Maria Cotrubaş; m. Manfred Ramin 1972. *Education:* Scoala Speciala de Musica, Conservatorul Ciprian Porumbescu, Bucharest. *Career:* lyric soprano range; leading soloist of children's radio chorus 1950; debut as Yniold in Pelléas et Mélisande at Bucharest Opera 1964; Frankfurt Opera 1968–70; Glyndebourne Festival 1968; Salzburg Festival 1969; Staatsoper Vienna 1969; Royal Opera House, Covent Garden 1971; Lyric Opera of Chicago 1973; Paris Opera 1974; La Scala, Milan 1975; Metropolitan Opera, New York 1977; operatic roles include Susanna, Pamina, Norina, Gilda, Traviata, Manon, Antonia, Tatyana, Mimi, Mélisande, Sophie; concerts with all major European orchestras; lieder recitals at Musikverein Vienna, Royal Opera House, Covent Garden, Carnegie Hall, New York, La Scala; retd from public singing 1990; master classes world-wide. *Recordings:* Bach Cantatas, Mozart Masses, Brahms Requiem, Mahler Symphonies 2, 8; complete operas including Le Nozze di Figaro, La finta giardiniera, Così fan tutte, Die Zauberflöte, Hänsel und Gretel, Calisto, Louise, L'Elisir d'amore, Les Pêcheurs de perles, La Traviata, Rigoletto, Alzira, Manon. *Publication:* Opernwahrheiten 1998. *Honours:* Hon. Citizen of Bucharest 1995; Grand Officer, Order of Sant'Iago da Espada (Portugal) 1990; First Prize, Int. Singing Competition, Hertogenbosch, Netherlands 1965, First Prize, Munich Radio Competition 1966; Austrian Kammersängerin 1981.

**COTTELI, Honorat;** Violinist; b. 4 Jan. 1941, Banska Bystrica, Czechoslovakia; m. 2 s., 2 d. *Education:* Conservatory of Music, Bratislava, Slovakia, 1955–60. *Career:* Debut: Diplom Concert, 1960; Radio Symphony Orchestra, Bratislava, 1959; Slovak Philharmonic Orchestra, 1960–67; Concert Master, State Opera Orchestra, Banska Bystrica, 1964; Concertmaster, Opera

Orchestra, Sankt Gallen, Switzerland, 1967–70; Conservatory of Music, Zürich, 1976; Opera Orchestra, Zürich, 1970; mem, Swiss Musicians Union. *Compositions:* Trio burlesco, 1994; Intrada for strings, 1989; Impressions for strings, 1993; Bagatellen for solo instruments, strings, 1991; Orchestino, concertino for grand orchestra, 1996; Capriccio for violin and piano, 1996; Preludi for violin and piano, 1995; Fantasticherie, 1995; Episodi, 1996; Fantasia gioccosa, 1997; Partita Slovacca, 1997; Brass Quintet, 1997; Musica per Contrabbassi, 1997; Swing Part for strings, 1995; Favole Slovacche, 1998; Suit per tre, 1998; Racconti di Faust, 1996; 5 songs for voice, 1996–98; Music of Stadent, 1987. *Honours:* Second prize, Composition Competition, Bratislava, Slovakia, 1996. *Address:* Poststrasse 29, CH 8957, Spreitenbach, Switzerland.

**COULAIS, Bruno;** French composer; b. 1960, Paris. *Compositions for film and TV:* Nuit féline 1978, México mágico 1979, Quidam (TV) 1984, Meurtres pour mémoire (TV) 1985, Bel ragazzo 1986, Lien de parenté 1986, Qui trop embrasse… 1986, La Femme secrète 1986, Les demoiselles de Concarneau (episode in TV series, L'Heure Simenon) 1987, Adieu Christine (TV series) 1989, Juliette en toutes lettres (TV series) 1989, Zanzibar 1989, Le Lien du sang (TV) 1990, Faut pas rêver (TV series) 2001, La Campagne de Cicéron 1990, Peinture fraîche 1991, Le Jour des rois 1991, Piège pour femme seule (TV) 1991, Ma soeur, mon amour 1992, Les Équilibristes 1992, Odyssée bidon (TV) 1992, Le Retour de Casanova 1992, Le Petit prince a dit 1992, Vieille canaille 1992, La Place du père (TV) 1992, Siméon 1992, Flight from Justice (TV) 1993, L'Instit (TV series) 1993, Le Juge est une femme (TV series) 1993, Le Fils du requin 1993, L'Ange et le génie - Correspondances Paris-Berlin 1994, Der Grüne Heinrich 1994, Cognacq-Jay (TV) 1994, Mort d'un gardien de la paix (TV) 1994, La Colline aux mille enfants (TV) 1994, Waati 1995, Le Blanc à lunettes (TV) 1995, Un si bel orage (TV) 1995, Des mots qui déchirent 1995, L'Enfant des rues (TV) 1995, La Rivière Espérance (mini TV series) 1995, Adultère, mode d'emploi 1995, Le Nid tombé de l'oiseau (TV) 1995, Embrasse-moi vite! (TV) 1995, Coeur de cible (TV) 1996, Sixième classique (TV) 1996, Microcosmos: Le peuple de l'herbe 1996, Une fille à papas (TV) 1996, L'Orange de Noël (TV) 1996, J'ai rendez-vous avec vous (TV) 1996, Vice vertu et vice versa (TV) 1996, Victor (TV) 1997, La Mère de nos enfants (TV) 1997, La Belle vie (mini TV series) 1997, Pardaillan (TV) 1997, La Famille Sapajou (TV) 1997, Jeunesse 1997, L'Amour dans le désordre (TV) 1997, Les Héritiers (TV) 1997, Combat de fauves 1997, Flammen im Paradies 1997, Le Dernier été (TV) 1997, Mireille et Vincent (TV) 1997, Deux flics (TV series) 1998, Don Juan 1998, Serial Lover 1998, Déjà mort 1998, Préférence 1998, Le Comte de Monte Cristo (mini TV series) 1998, L'Enfant des terres blondes (TV) 1998, Das Mädchen aus der Fremde 1999, Belle maman 1999, Véga (TV series) 1999, Himalaya - l'enfance d'un chef 1999, Balzac (TV) 1999, Un dérangement considérable 1999, La Débandade 1999, Épouse-moi 2000, Scènes de crimes 2000, Le Libertin 2000, Comme un aimant 2000, Jacqueline dans ma vitrine 2000, Les Fleurs d'Harrison 2000, Les Rivières pourpres 2000, Le Blanc et le rouge (TV) 2000, Zaïde, un petit air de vengeance (TV) 2001, Belphégor - Le fantôme du Louvre 2001, De l'amour 2001, Un aller simple 2001, Origine océan - 4 milliards d'années sous les mers 2001, Vidocq 2001, Le Peuple migrateur 2001, Les Ailes de la nature (TV) 2002, Les Tombales 2002, Drengen der ville gøre det umulige 2002, Toute une histoire 2003, Les Parents terribles (TV) 2003, Les Choristes 2004, Agents secrets 2004, Genesis 2004, Milady (TV) 2004, Brice de Nice 2005. *Other compositions include:* Mémoires d'un cabotin for nine pianos 1985. *Current Management:* Uzik, 80 rue du Faubourg St-Denis, 75010 Paris, France. *Telephone:* 1 40 26 75 33. *Fax:* 1 40 26 13 73. *Website:* www.uzik.com.

**COUROUPOS, Yorgos;** Composer; b. 1 Jan. 1942, Athens, Greece. *Education:* Studied the piano at Athens Conservatory, and composition with Messiaen in Paris, 1968–72. *Career:* Administrative posts at National Lyric Theatre, Athens; Director of Kalamata Municipal Conservatory from 1985. *Compositions:* Music theatre works, notably: Dieu le Veut, 1975; Grisélidis, 1977; Pylades, opera in 1 act with libretto by G Himonas after Sophocles and Euripides, performed at the Athens Concert Hall, 1992; Odyssey, ballet, 1995: The Runaways of the Chessboard, opera, 1998. *Address:* c/o AEPI, Fragoklisias and Samou Street 51, 151 25 Amarousio, Athens, Greece.

**COUROUX, Marc;** Pianist, Lecturer and Writer; b. 1970, Montreal, Canada. *Education:* Humanities and Mathematics; Studies with Louis-Philippe Pelletier, McGill University, 1989–94. *Career:* Repertory includes Night Fantasies by Elliott Carter, Euryali by Iannis Xenakis, 14 Etudes by György Ligeti, Other Works by Ambrosini, Cage, Donatoni, Lindberg, Messiaen, Nancarrow, Rzewski, Schoenberg, Stockhausen, Szymanowski and Tippett, along with Canadian Composers Brégent, Cherney, Gonneville, Tremblay and Vivier; Premieres of Envolée by Sean Ferguson and Variations by James Harley, 1994; Soloist, McGill Symphony Orchestra in the North American Premiere of Bengt Hambraeus' Concerto for Piano and Orchestra, 1995; Recital of Canadian and Belgian Works, ARS Musica Festival Brussels, 1995; Performed, Concerto for piano and orchestra by György Ligeti with CBC Vancouver Orchestra, 1996; Performed Piano Solo Pieces, Nouvel Ensemble Moderne, 1996; Artist-in-Residence, Banff Centre for the Arts, Princeton and Rutgers Universities, Domaine Forget Summer Course for New Music, St-Irénée, Quebec; Lecturer, Universities of New York, Stony Brook, and Buffalo. *Publications:* Several articles in professional journals. *Address:* c/o Latitude 45, Arts Promotion Inc, 109 St Joseph Blvd West, Montreal, Quebec H2T 2P7, Canada.

**COURTIS, Jean-Philippe;** Singer (Bass); b. 24 May 1951, France. *Education:* Studied at the Paris Conservatoire. *Career:* Sang first at the Paris Opéra (from 1980), then the Opéra-Comique (1983); Appearances at the Aix Festival in Werther, Semiramide, and Ariadne auf Naxos, and guest engagements throughout Europe as Henry VIII in Anna Bolena (Amsterdam, 1989), Don Giovanni (Strasbourg, 1990) and Arkel (Vienna Staatsoper, 1991); Sang Méphistophélès in Faust at the Paris Opéra, 1988, and appeared in the 1990 opening of the Opéra Bastille (Les Troyens); Other roles include the Commendatore in Don Giovanni, Don Quichotte, and Frère Bernard in Messiaen's St François d'Assise (premiere, 1983); Season 1994–95 as Falstaff in Le Songe d'une nuite d'été by Thomas, Creon in Cherubini's Médée at Martina Franca and Gounod's Frère Laurent at Houston; Isménor in Rameau's Dardanus at Lyon, 1998; Sang Somarone in Béatrice et Bénédict at Amsterdam, 2001; Many concert engagements. *Address:* c/o Opéra de la Bastille, 12 Rue de Lyon, 75012 Paris, France.

**COVELL, Roger David,** AM, PhD, FAHA; Australian professor of music, critic, composer and conductor; *Professor Emeritus, University of New South Wales;* b. 1 Feb. 1931, Sydney; s. of Harold Covell and Margaret Bardsley; m. 1st Sue Catling 1953 (divorced 1964); one s. one d.; m. 2nd Merle Berriman 1965 (divorced 1976); two s.; m. 3rd Patricia Brown 1976. *Education:* Brisbane High School and Univs of Queensland and NSW. *Career:* Chief Music Critic, The Sydney Morning Herald 1960–; Sr Lecturer and Head Dept of Music, Univ. of NSW 1966, Assoc. Prof. 1973, Prof. 1984, Head School of Music and Music Educ. 1993–96, Prof. Emer. 1998–; Artistic Dir Univ. of NSW Opera 1968; Co-Founder, Australia Ensemble 1980; mem. Australia Council 1977–83; Pres. Australian Soc. for Music Educ. 1978–81; Pres. Musicological Soc. of Australia 1983–84; Challender Memorial Lecture 1994; mem. Council, Australian Acad. of Humanities 1986–88. *Publications:* Australia's Music: Themes of a New Society 1967, Music in Australia: Needs and Prospects 1970, Folk Songs of Australia, Vol. 2 (with J. Meredith and P. Brown); ed. of baroque opera scores. *Honours:* Geraldine Pascall Prize for Music Criticism 1993. *Address:* 9 Kubya Street, Blackheath, NSW 2785, Australia (home). *Telephone:* 047-87 6182 (home).

**COVEY-CRUMP, Rogers;** Singer (Tenor); b. 1944, England. *Education:* Royal College of Music, London; BMus, London University. *Career:* Concert, broadcasting and commercial recording engagements as a solo artist and as a member of the Hilliard Ensemble, Gothic Voices, the Deller and Taverner Consorts and Singcircle (Stockhausen's Stimmung); Promenade Concerts, 1984–99, Purcell's Odes, Pärt's Miserere, Bach's St Matthew Passion; and premiere of MacMillan's Quickening; Performances of Bach, Haydn and Pärt in Finland and Estonia, 1985–96, Bach's St John Passion in Vancouver, 1997, Bach's Matthew passion in Stockholm for Swedish Radio with Tonu Kaljuste, 1997; Tours of the United Kingdom, 1988, 1992 and 1998, with Contemporary Music Network in Pärt's Passio, Miserere and Litany; Summer Schools with the Hilliard Ensemble in Lewes, Cambridge, Finland, Germany and Austria since 1984; Residencies in California and Pennsylvania 1988 and 1992; Lecturer and writer on aspects of vocal ensemble singing. *Recordings include:* Bach's B Minor Mass and St John Passion, Monteverdi's Vespers and Purcell with Andrew Parrott and the Taverner Players; Bach's St Matthew Passion with Roy Goodman and the choir of King's College, Cambridge; Bach's St Mark Passion with the European Union Baroque Orchestra; Pärt's Passio, Miserere and Litany; Lute Songs, with Paul O'Dette and with Jakob Lindberg; Hilliard Ensemble collaboration with Norwegian saxophonist, Jan Garbarek in the albums Officium and Mnemosyne. *Address:* 4 Garland Court, Victoria Street, St Albans, AL 1 3SY. *Website:* www.hazardchase.co.uk.

**COVIELLO, Roberto;** Italian singer (baritone); b. 1958. *Career:* debut in Naples, 1983; sang Guglielmo at Bari, 1984, and Paisiello's Figaro at the 1986 Spoleto Festival; La Scala Milan from 1987, as Don Giovanni and other major baritone roles; Pesaro Festival, 1988–89, in La Scala di Seta and La Gazza Ladra; other roles include Mozart's Figaro, Belcore, Malatesta, Valentin, Mercutio (Roméo et Juliette), Valentin and Ford in Falstaff; season 1990–91 in opera at Bonn, Santiago, Bergamo and Trieste.

**COWAN, Richard;** Singer (bass-baritone), Composer and Artistic Director; b. 24 Dec. 1957, Euclid, OH, USA. *Education:* degree in Vocal Performance and Composition, Indiana Univ. *Career:* debut, Chicago Lyric, 1983, in Lady Macbeth of the Mtsensk District by Shostakovich; has sung frequently in Chicago (Escamillo 1991, Anthony and Cleopatra 1991, Simon Boccanegra 1995, The Consul 1996) and guested in Los Angeles, Detroit, Toronto, Vancouver and numerous other locations world-wide; Maggio Musicale, Florence, 1985, as the Animal Tamer in Lulu, Aix Festival, 1986, as Masetto and Théâtre du Châtelet, Paris, 1988–89, in Der Freischütz and Fidelio; La Scala Milan debut, 1989, Metropolitan, New York from 1990, as Schaunard, Don Giovanni and Guglielmo; Bartók's Bluebeard at Geneva, 1995; sang in The Consul by Menotti in Chicago, 1996; best known as Don Giovanni (Avignon, Marseilles, Strasbourg, Santa Fe, Metropolitan Opera, Toronto, Rio de Janeiro, Detroit, St Etienne); founder, Artistic Dir Festival Lyrique de Belle Ile en Mer, Brittany 1998–. *Recordings:* Sharpless in Madama Butterfly (film and recording), 1994, Ravel's Brain, 2000. *Honours:* Grand Prize, Paris Int. Singing Contest 1986, George London Award 1986. *Address:* Chateau Fouquet, BP 80, Belle Ile en Mer, 56360, France.

**COWAN, Sigmund;** singer (baritone); b. 4 March 1948, New York, NY, USA. *Education:* University of Miami; University of Florida; New York Institute of Finance; Scholarship, Juilliard School; Fellowship, Manhattan School of Music. *Career:* Appearances: New York City Opera, Deutsche Oper am Rhein; Spoleto Festival, Kennedy Center, Miami Opera, Basel, Essen, Wiesbaden,

Vienna Festival, Berlin Staatstheater, Brussels, Amsterdam (Opera and Concertgebouw), Carnegie Hall, Mexico City, Dublin, and Calgary and Edmonton (Canada), Rotterdam (VARA television), Utrecht (Radio KRO), Amsterdam (VARA Radio), Italy (RAI), USA (NBC television), Austria (ORF television), Germany (3rd Channel); Sang with Rochester Philharmonic, National Symphony, Baltimore Symphony and at Flagstaff Festival; Appeared with National Orchestra, Mexico City, Canadian Opera, L'Opera de Montreal, Baltimore Opera; Television Live from Lincoln Center PBS Tonio in Pagliacci; Roles in Nabucco, Rigoletto, Macbeth, Il Trovatore, I Due Foscari, Un Ballo in Maschera, La Forza del Destino, La Traviata; Sang Rigoletto at Toronto, 1996; Engaged for debut in Marseille, France, as Germont in La Traviata, 2000. *Recordings include:* Die Gezeichneten with Edo de Waart. *Address:* c/o Dorothy Cone, 150 W 55th Street, New York, NY 10019, USA.

**COWIE, Edward;** Composer, Painter, Natural Scientist, Writer and Film-maker; b. 17 Aug. 1943, Birmingham, England; m. Heather Jean Johns, 1995, 2 d. by second marriage. *Education:* BEd, London University; BMus, D.Mus, Southampton University; PhD, Lancaster University. *Career:* Senior Lecturer, Lancaster University, 1973–83; Professor, Creative Arts, University of Wollongong, New South Wales, Australia, 1983–89; Granada Composer/Conductor, Royal Liverpool Philharmonic Orchestra, 1983–86; Professor, Creative Arts, James Cook University, Queensland, Australia, 1989–95; Professor and Director of Research, Dartington College of Arts, Devon, England, 1995–; Artist in Residence with the Royal Society for the Protection of Birds, 2002–2005; Associate Composer BBC Singers, 2002–2005; mem, British Ornithologists Union; Fellow, Royal Society of Arts. *Compositions include:* Commedia, opera, 1979; Concerto for Orchestra, 1982; 5 string quartets, 1974–95; Symphony (American), 1983; Choral Symphony, 1984; Ancient Voices 1 and 2, 1983, 1991; Cello Concerto; 1992; Water, Stone, Wood and Breath, for chorus and percussion, 1996; Between Two Waves for 12 voices, 1999; Oboe Concerto, 1999; From Moment to Moment for chamber orchestra, 2000. *Recordings:* many compositions recorded. *Publications:* Music published in London; 41 exhibitions as painter; Birds Talk, 2001. *Honours:* Many prizes won as composer. *Address:* c/o Dartington College of Arts, Totnes, Devon TQ9 6EJ, England. *Website:* www.edward-cowie.com; www.ump.co.uk/cowie.htm.

**COX, Jean;** Singer (Tenor); b. 16 Jan. 1922, Gadsen, Alabama, USA. *Education:* University of Alabama and the New England Conservatory; With Wally Kirsamer in Frankfurt, Luigi Ricci in Rome and Max Lorenz in Munich. *Career:* Debut: New England Opera Company, 1951, as Lensky in Eugene Onegin; Spoleto, 1954, as Rodolfo; Sang at Brunswick, 1955–59, Mannheim from 1959; Bayreuth Festival, 1956–75, as the Steersman, Erik, Lohengrin, Parsifal, Siegfried and Walther; Hamburg Staatsoper, 1958–73; Guest appearances in Berlin, Vienna, Munich, Stuttgart and Frankfurt; Bregenz Festival, 1961, in Fra Diavolo; Chicago Lyric Opera, 1964, 1970, 1973; Paris Opéra, 1971, as Siegmund; Covent Garden, 1975; Siegfried; Metropolitan Opera debut, 1976, as Walther; Further engagements in Lisbon, Stockholm, Geneva, Zürich, Mexico City, Houston and Pittsburgh; Other roles included Strauss's Herod and Bacchus; Alvaro in La Forza del Destino, Max in Der Freischütz and the Cardinal in Mathis der Maler by Hindemith; Siegfried and Walther von Stolzing, Bayreuth Festival, 1983–84; Sang Captain Vere in Billy Budd at Mannheim, 1989. *Recordings include:* Die Meistersinger; Jean Cox sings Wagner. *Address:* Nationaltheater, Postfach 102362, 6800 Mannheim, Germany.

**COXON, Richard;** Singer (Tenor); b. 25 Aug. 1968, Nottingham, England. *Education:* Royal Northern College of Music, with John Mitchinson. *Career:* Debut: Flavio in Norma for Scottish Opera, 1993; Further roles with Scottish Opera have included Narraboth in Salome, Jacquino, Nemorino, Alfred in Die Fledermaus, Barbarigo in Verdi's Due Foscari, Don Ottavio, Alfredo, and Jiri in The Jacobin by Dvořák; Guest appearances for Opera Northern Ireland, Opera Zuid in Maastricht, Glyndebourne Festival Opera, Nationale Reisoper Holland and English National Opera; Concerts include Mendelssohn's St Paul with the Scottish National Orchestra, Messiah with the Bergen Philharmonic Orchestra and engagements with the Hallé Orchestra, BBC Concert Orchestra, BBC Scottish Symphony Orchestra and London Pops Orchestra; Fenton in Falstaff and Young Convict in From the House of the Dead, Painter in Lulu and Nick in The Handmaid's Tale for English National Opera; Mr By-Ends in Pilgrim's Progress for Royal Opera, in concert; Brighella in Ariadne auf Naxos for Scottish Opera at the Edinburgh Festival and on tour; Edgardo in film version of Lucia di Lammermoor, directed by Don Boyd; Squeak in Billy Budd, Gastone in La Traviata for Royal Opera; Italian Tenor Der Rosenkavalier for Opera North and at the Spolete Festival, Italy; Kudjas in Katya Kabanova for Opera de Montreal, Florida Grand Opera and Scottish Opera. *Honours:* Webster Booth/Esso Award; Clonter Opera Prize; Ricordi Opera Prize. *Address:* c/o IMG Artists, Lovell House, 616 Chiswick High Road, London W4 5RX, England.

**CRAFT, Robert Lawson,** BA; American conductor and writer on music; b. 20 Oct. 1923, Kingston, NY. *Education:* Juilliard School of Music, New York, Berkshire Music Center, Tanglewood, studied conducting with Pierre Monteux. *Career:* conductor, Evenings-on-the-Roof and Monday Evening Concerts, Los Angeles 1950–68; asst to, later close assoc. of Igor Stravinsky 1948–71; numerous collaborations with Stravinsky; conducted first performances of various later works by Stravinsky; conducted works ranging from Monteverdi to Boulez; US premiere of Berg's Lulu (two-act version) Santa Fe 1963. *Recordings include:* works of Stravinsky, Webern and Schoenberg 1998.

*Publications:* Conversations with Igor Stravinsky 1959, Memories and Commentaries 1960, Expositions and Developments 1962, Dialogues and a Diary 1963, Themes and Episodes 1967, Retrospections and Conclusions 1969, Chronicle of a Friendship 1972, Prejudices in Disguise 1974, Stravinsky in Photographs and Documents (with Vera Stravinsky) 1976, Current Convictions: Views and Reviews 1977, Present Perspectives 1984, Stravinsky's Selected Correspondence (trans. and ed., two vols) 1982, 1984, Stravinsky: Glimpses of a Life 1992, The Moment of Existence: Music, Literature and the Arts 1996, An Improbable Life 2003; contrib. articles to various journals and other publications. *Address:* 1390 S Ocean Blvd, Pompano Beach, FL 33062, USA.

**CRAFTS, Edward (James);** Singer (Bass-Baritone); b. 11 Nov. 1946, New York, NY, USA. *Education:* Studied at Curtis Institute and Indiana University. *Career:* Has sung widely in the USA from 1982, notably at Houston Opera (as Dulcamara), St Louis and the City Opera New York (as Escamillo); Santa Fe, 1984, in the US premiere of Zemlinsky's Eine Florentinische Tragödie; La Scala Milan, 1984, in Bernstein's Trouble in Tahiti; Seattle, 1987, as Iago; New Jersey, 1983, in the US premiere of Wagner's Liebesverbot; Further appearances at La Scala, Covent Garden, Cleveland and Chicago; Other roles include Falstaff, Scarpia and Mephistopheles; Sang Wotan in The Ring for Arizona Opera at Flagstaff, 1996. *Address:* c/o New York City Opera, Lincoln Center, New York, NY 10023, USA.

**CRAGG, Elizabeth;** Singer (Soprano); b. 1970, England. *Education:* Royal Holloway College, London; Royal College of Music, with Elisabeth Robson. *Career:* Solo engagements in Messiah, at St John Smith's Square, Bach's B minor Mass in Singapore, St Matthew Passion with the English Concert and recital at the Victoria and Albert Museum, London; Season 2000–01 as Celia in the British premiere of Handel's Silla, and Orazio in Muzio Scevola, for the London Handel Festival; Choral Singer with The Sixteen, BBC Singers, The Choir of the Enlightenment and the English Concert Choir. *Recordings include:* Handel's Silla. *Honours:* Dorothy Silk Prize, RCM. *Address:* c/o Royal College of Music, Prince Consort Road, London SW7, England.

**CRAIG, Jon;** Singer (Tenor); b. 30 Oct. 1923, St Louis, Missouri, USA. *Education:* Studied in Washington, at Juilliard and with Paul Althouse. *Career:* Debut: Sang Pinkerton in 1948; Sang at New York City Opera, 1952–65, notably in the 1954 premiere of The Tender Land by Copland and in US premieres of Der Prozess, 1953, Der Revisor by Egk, 1960, and The Fiery Angel, 1965; Metropolitan Opera from 1953, San Francisco from 1957; Further engagements at Pittsburgh, Chicago, Philadelphia, Mexico City and New Orleans; Other roles have included the Duke of Mantua, Fenton and Alfredo by Verdi, Cavaradossi, Don José, Turiddu, Rodolfo, Erik in Der fliegende Holländer, Dimitri, Boris Godunov and Walton's Troilus; Fort Worth Opera 1970, in Die Fledermaus. *Recordings:* Highlights from Les Contes d'Hoffmann.

**CRAIG, Russell;** Stage Designer; b. 1948, New Zealand. *Education:* Studied in New Zealand and moved to London in 1974. *Career:* Designs for Scottish Opera with Savitri, Hedda Gabler, Rossini double bill, Oberon and L'Elisir d'amore, 1981–94, Welsh National Opera with Barber of Seville, Die Entführung, Ariadne and Le Comte Ory, 1986–91, and English National Opera with The Rape of Lucretia and Ariadne auf Naxos, 1983; Designs for Opera North include Così fan tutte, The Magic Flute, A Village Romeo and Juliet, Acis and Galatea, Showboat, and Oberto, 1983–94; La Bohème for Glyndebourne Touring Opera in 1991. *Address:* c/o Jeffrey Campbell, 11a Grey Stone Court, South Street, Eastbourne BN21 4LP, England.

**CRANE, Louise;** Singer (Mezzo-Soprano); b. 1965, England. *Education:* Studied at the Guildhall School of Music, 1982–86, and at the Royal Northern College of Music with Barbara Robotham. *Career:* Sang in Opera Factory's Don Giovanni and Dialogues des Carmélites for Opéra de Lyon; Further engagements as Third Lady and Mistress Quickly with English Touring Opera, in The Siege of Corinth and The Nightingale for Chelsea Opera Group, Stravinsky's Mother Goose at Aldeburgh and Mozart's Marcellina for European Chamber Opera; English National Opera debut, 1993 in the premiere of Harvey's Inquest of Love; Sang Rita in Zampa for Opera Omnibus, 1996; Concert engagements in Rossini's Stabat Mater, Messiah, Beethoven's Ninth and Missa Solemnis, The Dream of Gerontius and Das Lied von der Erde; Touring performances of Gilbert and Sullivan. *Address:* Helen Sykes Artists Management, 100 Felsham Road, Putney, London SW15 1DQ, England.

**CRASS, Franz;** Singer (Bass-baritone); b. 9 Dec. 1928, Wipperfurth, Germany. *Education:* Studied at the Cologne Musikhochschule with Clemens Glettenberg. *Career:* Debut: Krefeld, 1954, as the King in Aida; Sang at Hanover, 1956–62; Bayreuth Festival, 1959–73, as King Henry, the Dutchman, Fasolt, Wolfram, King Marke and Gurnemanz; La Scala, 1960, as Rocco and the Commendatore; Salzburg Festival as Sarastro; London, 1960, 1964, in the Missa Solemnis and Mozart's Requiem, conducted by Klemperer; From 1964 sang in Hamburg, Munich, Frankfurt and Vienna; With Hamburg Opera sang Barak in the British premiere of Die Frau ohne Schatten, Sadler's Wells Theatre, 1966; Other roles included Philip II, Nicolai's Falstaff, Duke Bluebeard and the Hermit in Der Freischütz (Frankfurt, 1980); Often heard in sacred music by Bach. *Recordings include:* Der fliegende Holländer; Lohengrin; Ein Deutsches Requiem; Die Zauberflöte; Fidelio; Parsifal; Giulio Cesare by Handel; Der Freischütz; Speaker, Second Armed Man and Second Priest in Die Zauberflöte, conducted by Klemperer, recording issued 1989.

*Address:* EMI Classics (Artists' Contracts), 30 Gloucester Place, London W1A 1ES, England.

**CRAWFORD, Bruce,** BS; American arts manager; *Chairman, Lincoln Center for the Performing Arts*; b. 16 March 1929, West Bridgewater, MA; m. Christine Crawford 1958. *Education:* Univ. of Pennsylvania. *Career:* entered advertising 1956; CEO, BBDO Int. 1977–; Pres., Batten, Barton, Durstine & Osborn 1978–; joined Bd of Metropolitan Opera 1976, serving on Exec. Cttee from 1977, Vice-Pres. 1981, Pres. 1984, Gen. Man. 1985–89; Chair. Lincoln Center 2002–05. *Address:* c/o Lincoln Center for the Performing Arts, 140 W 65th Street, New York, NY 10023, USA.

**CRAWFORD, John Charlton,** BMus, MMus, PhD; American composer and educator; b. 19 Jan. 1931, Philadelphia; m. Dorothy Lamb 1955; one s. one d. *Education:* Yale School of Music, Harvard Univ. *Career:* Instructor of Music, Amherst Coll. 1961–63; Asst Prof., Wellesley Coll. 1963–70; Assoc. Prof. of Music 1970–75, Prof. of Music 1975–94, Univ. of California, Riverside; mem. ASCAP, American Musicological Soc., American Music Center. *Compositions include:* Magnificat 1959, Ash Wednesday 1968, Three Shakespeare Songs 1970, Psalm 98 1971, Don Cristobal and Rosita 1979, Two Shakespeare Madrigals 1980, Prelude, Fugue and Meditation for String Quartet 1993, Concerto for viola and orchestra 1995. *Recordings:* String Quartet No. 2 (Sequoia Quartet) 1993. *Publications:* Arnold Schoenberg, Wassily Kandinsky: Letters, Pictures and Documents (translator and essayist) 1984, Expressionism in 20th Century Music (with Dorothy L. Crawford) 1993; contrib. to Musical Quarterly, Journal of Arnold Schoenberg Inst. *Honours:* Harvard Univ. Boott Prize in Choral Composition 1956, ASCAP Serious Music Award 1969–74, 1994–2004. *Address:* 203 Lexington Avenue, Cambridge, MA 02138, USA.

**CRAWFORD, Timothy (Terry);** Lutenist and Musicologist; b. 11 July 1948, Farnham, Surrey, England; m. Emilia de Grey, 18 April 1975, 2 s., 1 d. *Education:* University of Sussex, 1966–69; Royal College of Music, 1971–75; Arts Council Research Grant for Continental Travel, 1976. *Career:* Founder Member of early music ensembles Ars Nova and Parley of Instruments; Frequent appearances with English Baroque Soloists, London Philharmonic Orchestra; Assistant Editor, Early Music Magazine, 1984–85; Music Co-ordinator for Royal Academy of Arts; Research Fellow, King's College London, 1989–; Projects include: Electronic Corpus of Lute Music (ECOLM), Online Music Recognition and Searching (OMRAS); mem. Lute Society, Committee 1975–87; National Early Music Association, Committee 1985–86; RMA; Musicians' Union. *Recordings:* Orfeo (Conductor: J E Gardiner); Il Ritorno d'Ulisse (Conductor: R Leppard); Sacred Music of Monteverdi (with Parley of Instruments and Emma Kirkby, Ian Partridge and David Thomas). *Publications:* Editor: Lute Society Journal and The Lute, 1979–87; Silvius Leopold Weiss, The Moscow Manuscript, 1995; S. L. Weiss, Complete Works, The Dresden Manuscript, 2000. *Contributions:* Frequently to The Lute, Early Music, Chelys, Journal of the Lute Society of America. *Address:* 40 Albion Drive, Hackney, London E8 4LX, England.

**CREECH, Philip;** Singer (Tenor); b. 1 June 1950, Hempstead, New York, USA. *Education:* Studied at Northwestern University. *Career:* Sang with Chicago Symphony Chorus, 1973–75; Metropolitan Opera, debut 1979 as Beppe in Pagliacci; Other roles at the Metropolitan have been Mozart's Pedrillo, Edmondo in Manon Lescaut, Brighella in Ariadne auf Naxos, Hylas in Les Troyens and Rinuccio in Gianni Schicchi; Premiere of The Voyage by Philip Glass at the Met, 1996; Many concert appearances. *Recordings:* Carmina Burana. *Address:* c/o Metropolitan Opera, Lincoln Center, NY 10023, USA.

**CREED, Kay;** Singer, Voice Teacher, Opera Coach and Lecturer; b. 19 Aug. 1940, Oklahoma City, USA; m. Carveth Osterhaus, 5 Oct 1975, 1 d. *Education:* BMus, MPA, Oklahoma City University; Study in Munich, Germany, 1965. *Career:* Debut: New York City Opera, 1965; Created role of Fortuna in Don Rodrigo by Ginastera; Mrs Danton in Danton's Death; Opera roles include Carmen, Cenerentola, Dorabella, Hansel, Giulietta, Sextus in Julius Caesar, Ulrica, Urbain (Les Huguenots); Solo Performances with New York Philharmonic, Chicago Symphony, Philadelphia Orchestra, Carnegie Hall, Les Huguenots; Dallas Symphony, Naumberg Orchestra, Oklahoma City Symphony; Board of Directors, Cimarron Circuit Opera, 1985; Lecturer in Opera and Voice, Cantor Classes for Catholic Litugy; Founding Member, Oklahoma City Guild of Tulsa Opera; Founding Member, Oklahoma Opera and Musical Theater Company; Founding Director, Edmond Central Historical Opera. *Address:* 415 W Eubanks, Oklahoma City, OK 73118, USA.

**CREFFELD, Rosanna;** Singer (Mezzo-Soprano); b. 1945, England; m. Richard Angas. *Education:* Royal College of Music with Flora Nielsen; Paris with Pierre Bernac; Further study with Vera Rosza in London. *Career:* Debut: Glyndebourne 1969, as Second Lady in Die Zauberflöte; Glyndebourne Touring Opera 1969–70, as Dorabella, and as Olga in Eugene Onegin; Appearances at Aix-en-Provence, Amsterdam, Strasbourg, Lyon and Bremen; Scottish Opera Glasgow as Dorabella and Cherubino; Monteverdi's Orfeo with the English National Opera; Paris Opéra as Cherubino and as Lucretia in The Rape of Lucretia by Britten; Engagements in San Diego 1984, and Pittsburgh 1986; Lausanne 1986, in Honegger's Antigone. *Recordings include:* Matilde in Rossini's Elisabetta Regina d'Inghilterra (Philips). *Address:* c/o English National Opera, St Martin's Lane, London WC2N 4ES, England.

**CRESHEVSKY, Noah;** Composer; b. 31 Jan. 1945, Rochester, New York, USA. *Education:* Studied at the Eastman School, Rochester, 1950–61 and at the Juilliard School with Berio, 1966; Further study with Nadia Boulanger in Paris and with Virgil Thomson. *Career:* Teacher, Juilliard and Hunter College, New York; Brooklyn College from 1969; Visiting Professor, Princeton University, 1987–88 Director, centre for Computer Music, Brooklyn College, 1992–. *Compositions include:* Vier Lieder, stage piece, 1966; Three pieces in the Shape of a Square for 4 performers and tape, 1967; Monogenesis for voices, chamber orchestra and tape, 1968; Variations for 4 pianists and tape, 1969; Mirrors for dancers and tape, 1970; Circuit for tape, 1971; Broadcast, 1973; Chaconne for piano or harp, 1974; Guitar, 1975; In Other Words: Portrait of John Cage, 1976; Great Performances for any 2 instruments and tape, 1977; Great Performances, 1978; Portrait of Rudy Perez, 1978; Highway, 1979; Sonata, Nightscape and Celebration for tape, 1980–83; Strategic Defense Initiative, 1986; Electric String Quartet, 1988; Talea, 1991; Private Lives, 1993; Coup d'état; Gone Now, 1995; Who, 1995; Sha, 1996; Electric Fanfare, 1997. *Honours:* National Endowment of the Arts Grant, 1981. *Address:* c/o ASCAP, ASCAP Building, 1 Lincoln Plaza, NY 10023, USA.

**CRESPIN, Régine;** French singer (soprano); b. 23 Feb. 1927, Marseilles; d. of Henri and Marguerite Crespin (née Meirone). *Education:* Conservatoire Nat. d'Art Dramatique. *Career:* singer, Paris Opéra; has sung in prin. concert houses, Europe and America; Prof. of Music, Higher Nat. Conservatory of Music 1976–92. *Publication:* A la scène, à la ville (memoirs) 1997. *Honours:* Commdr Légion d'honneur; Grand Officier Ordre nat. du Mérite; Commdr Ordre des Arts et Lettres; Opera News Award 2005. *Address:* 3 avenue Frochot, 75009 Paris, France.

**CRESSWELL, Lyell Richard,** BMus, MMus, PhD; composer; b. 13 Oct. 1944, Wellington, New Zealand; m. Catherine Mawson 1972. *Education:* Victoria Univ. of Wellington, Univ. of Toronto, Canada, Aberdeen Univ. *Career:* music organizer, Chapter Arts Centre, Cardiff 1978–80; Forman Fellow in Composition, Edinburgh Univ. 1980–82; Cramb Fellow in Composition, Glasgow Univ. 1982–85; freelance composer 1985–; mem. British Acad. of Composers and Songwriters, Composers' Asscn of New Zealand. *Compositions:* Ylur, 1990–91; Voices of Ocean Winds; The Pumpkin Massacre; Il Suono di Enormi Distanze; A Modern Ecstasy; Cello Concerto; O!; Salm; Speak for Us, Great Sea; Passacagli; O Let the Fire Burn, Concerto for String Quartet and Orchestra (premiered 1997); Kaea, Trombone Concerto, 1997 (premiered, 1998); The Voice Inside, concerto for violin and soprano (premiered 2002); Of Smoke and Bickering Flame, concerto for Chamber Orchestra (premiered 2003); Shadows Without Sun (premiered 2003), Ara Kopikopiko (premiered 2005). *Honours:* Ian Whyte Award 1978, APRA Silver Scroll 1980, Creative Scotland Award 2001, Hon. DMus (Victoria Univ. of Wellington) 2002, Inaugural Elgar Bursary 2002. *Address:* 4 Leslie Place, Edinburgh EH4 1NQ, Scotland.

**CRIDER, Michele;** Singer (Soprano); b. 1963, Illinois, USA. *Career:* Debut: Leonora in Il Trovatore at Dortmund, 1989; Appearances from 1991 at La Scala, Covent Garden, Deutsche Oper Berlin and the State Operas of Hamburg, Vienna, Munich, Stuttgart and Wiesbaden; Further appearances at Florence, Zürich and Barcelona; Roles have included Aida, Luisa Miller, Butterfly, the Trovatore and Forza Leonoras, Odabella (Attila), Lucrezia (Due Foscari) and Amelia (Un Ballo in Maschera); US debut as Butterfly for San Diego, followed by Elisabeth in Don Carlos and the Trovatore Leonora at the Metropolitan; La Scala 1995 as Elena and Margherita in Mefistofele; Opéra Bastille, Paris as Madama Butterfly; Engaged as Aida for Netherlands Opera, 2000; Season 2000–01 as Verdi's Odabella at Genoa, the Trovatore Leonora at the New York Met and Aida at San Francisco; Concert engagements at Salzburg, Maggio Musicale Florence, Orange and Ravinia Festivals, Salle Pleyel Paris and London Barbican. *Recordings include:* Un Ballo in Maschera, under Carlo Rizzi; Elena and Margherita in Mefistofele, conducted by Muti; Verdi Requiem, under Richard Hickox. *Honours:* Finalist, 1988 Pavarotti Competition; Prizewinner, 1989 Geneva International Music Competition. *Address:* c/o Metropolitan Opera, Lincoln Center, New York, NY 10023, USA.

**CRILLY, David Robert,** DPhil, MA, LTCL, LLCM; British lecturer; b. 3 June 1959, Birkenhead. *Education:* City of Leeds Coll. of Music, Univ. of Southampton, Univ. of London RHBNC, Univ. of Oxford. *Career:* Sr Lecturer in Music, Dir of Research, composer and performer; Artistic Dir, annual Cambridge Shakespeare Festival. *Compositions:* In that quiet earth, for symphony orchestra, voice and narrator 2000, Leap of faith, for chamber orchestra and voices 2003. *Publications:* Is the application of the principles of semiology to music analysis founded upon a philosophical mistake?, in European Journal for Semiotic Studies 2002, Wiggenstein, Music Language – Games, The Open Space issue no. 2, Spring 2002, Elastic form and concrete structure: the analysis of improvised music, in Nikos Mastorakis ed. Mathematics and Computers in Modern Science 2002, Perception of Mathematical Structure and Architectural Design: Form and Forming in Music, in ISAMA 1999 International Society of the Arts, Mathematics and Architecture, The Problem of Form in Analytical Discussions, in Ideas and Production, a journal in the history of ideas Vol. XI. *Address:* Music Department, Anglia Polytecnic University, East Road, Cambridge, CB1 1PT, England (office); 6a Fair Street, Cambridge, CB1 1HA, England (home). *Telephone:* (1223) 363271 (office); (1223) 321984 (home). *E-mail:* d.crilly@apu.ac.uk (office); Bartok2571@msn.com (home). *Website:* www.apu.ac.uk/music (office).

**CRIST, Richard,** MM; American singer (bass) and vocal instructor; b. 21 Oct. 1947, Harrisburg, PA. *Education:* New England Conservatory, Boston. *Career:* debut in Berlioz's Les Troyens, Opera Company of Boston, 1972; Appearances with Opera Companies including: Santa Fe, Boston, Philadelphia, San Francisco, Memphis, Mobile, Orlando, Lake George and the Virginia and Goldovsky Opera Theatres; European debut with Opéra de Lyon in the French creation of Die Soldaten by Zimmermann (1982) under Ken Russell and Serge Baudo; Opera and Oratorio appearances throughout USA and with various orchestras; Canadian debut with Toronto Mendelssohn Choir, 1984; Operatic Repertoire of over 75 roles and nearly 100 Oratorio and Symphonic Works; Opera Performance of Tchaikovsky's The Queen of Spades, filmed for PBS television, Philadelphia, 1984; Debut in La Traviata, Metropolitan Opera, 1985; Sang in Semiramide, Fidelio, Meistersinger, Der Freischütz and Ballo in Maschera, Hamburg State Opera, 1985; Debut in Contes d'Hoffmann, San Diego Opera, 1985; Debut in Pelléas and Mélisande, Philadelphia Orchestra, 1986; Appearances in Henze's The English Cat, Alte Oper, Frankfurt, Germany and Turin, Italy, 1986; First Performance in USA of Mayr's Requiem, Alice Tully Hall 1986; Sang with the Company of the Bolshoi, Moscow, at Boston, 1988 in Shchedrin's Dead Souls; premiere of The Balcony by Di Domenica, Boston, 1990; other roles include Mozart's Leporello, Osmin, and Sarastro; Rocco in Fidelio, Gremin in Eugene Onegin and Samuel in Un Ballo in Maschera; Season 1991/2 in Gluck's La Rencontre Imprévue at Wexford, as Mozart's Bartolo in Dublin and in the Rossini Birthday Gala at the Barbican Hall; Svetlovsk Philharmonic Orchestra, 1993; mem, American Guild of Musical Artists. *Current Management:* Thea Safimm, Ludvig Brunner, 250 W 57th Street, New York, NY 10107, USA. *Address:* c/o New England Conservatory of Music, Vocal Faculty, 290 Huntington Avenue, Boston, MA 02115, USA.

**CROCKETT, Donald;** Composer, University Professor and Conductor; b. 18 Feb. 1951, Pasadena, California, USA; m. (1) divorced, 1 d., (2) Vicki Ray, 6 June 1988. *Education:* BM, 1974, MM, 1976, University of Southern California; PhD, University of California, Santa Barbara, 1981. *Career:* Conductor, USC Contemporary Music Ensemble; Guest Conductor with Monday Evening Concerts; Cleveland Chamber Symphony; Pittsburgh New Music Ensemble; Regional and national premieres of music by Lutoslawski, Davies, Musgrave, Gruber, Ruders, et al; Composer-in-Residence, Pasadena Chamber Orchestra (conductor Robert Duerr), 1984–87; Professor, University of Southern California; Composer-in-Residence, Los Angeles Chamber Orchestra (conductor Christof Perick), 1991–97; Conductor, Xtet (Los Angeles based new music ensemble). *Compositions:* Lyrikos (tenor and orchestra), 1979; The Pensive Traveller (high voice and piano), 1982; Vox in Rama (double chorus and orchestra), 1983; Melting Voices (orchestra), 1986; The 10th Muse (soprano and orchestra), 1986; Occhi dell'alma mia (high voice and guitar), 1977; Array for String Quartet, commissioned by the Kronos Quartet, 1988; Pilgrimage for piano solo, 1988; Still Life with Bell, 14 players, commissioned by the Los Angeles Philharmonic, 1989; Celestial Mechanics, oboe and string quartet, 1990; String Quartet No. 2, commissioned by the Stanford String Quartet, 1993; Roethke Preludes (orchestra), commissioned by the Los Angeles Chamber Orchestra, 1994; Island for concert band, 1998; The Falcon's Eye for solo guitar, 2000. *Recordings:* Melting Voices, orchestra, Orchestra of the Americas, Paul Freeman, conductor; Celestial Mechanics (oboe and string quartet), Los Angeles Chamber Orchestra; Array, String Quartet No. 2, to be sung on the water, Stanford String Quartet, 1998; Pilgrimage: Vicki Ray, Pianist, 1999. *Publications include:* Still Life with Bell, 14 players, Celestial Mechanics, oboe and string quartet; Roethke Preludes for orchestra; Island for concert band; The Falcon's Eye. *Address:* School of Music, University of Southern California, Los Angeles, CA 90089-0851, USA.

**CROFT, Richard;** Singer (Tenor); b. 1959, Cooperstown, New York, USA. *Career:* Sang Nemorino at Washington and Ramiro in La Cenerentola at St Louis, season 1986–87; European engagements include Mozart's Belfiore, Achille in Gluck's Iphigénie en Aulide and Belmonte at Drottningholm; Strasbourg and Nice, 1990–91, as Don Ottavio and Ferrando; Welsh National Opera, 1989, as Belmonte (repeated at the Metropolitan, 1991); Glyndebourne, 1991, Don Ottavio; Septimus in Handel's Theodora at Glyndebourne, 1996 and Tom Rakewell at Santa Fe; Season 1999 with Debussy's Pelléas at Glyndebourne and the London Prom concerts. *Recordings include:* Video of Die Entführung (Virgin). *Address:* c/o Metropolitan Opera, Lincoln Center, New York, NY 10023, USA.

**CROLL, Gerhard;** Musicologist; b. 25 May 1927, Düsseldorf, Germany. *Education:* Studied at University of Gottingen, doctorate 1954. *Career:* Assistant Lecturer, University of Munster, 1958; Chair of Musicology, Salzburg from 1966; President, International Gluck-Gesellschaft from 1987. *Publications:* Editions of Steffani's Tassilone and Die Entführung aus dem Serail; Gluck's Le Cinesi for the complete edition, 1958, (Editor-in-Chief from 1960) and Alceste 1988; Entries on Gluck and Weerbecke in The New Grove Dictionary of Music; Articles on Mozart discoveries Larghetto and Allegro in E-flat for two pianos and string quartet arrangement of a Bach fugue, K405; Gluck in Wien (1762), 1997; Rossini in Neapel, 1998; Member of Zentralinstitut für Mozart-Forschung and contributor to the Neue-Mozart-Ausgabe. *Address:* c/o New Grove Dictionary, 4 Porter's South, Crinian Street, London, N1 9XW, England.

**CRONIN, Stephen (John);** Composer; b. 2 Sept. 1960, Brisbane, Queensland, Australia. *Education:* PhD, University of Queensland, 1995; Studied with Colin Brumby, 1978–81. *Career:* Faculty Member, University of Queensland, 1984, Queensland Conservatory, 1986; Commissions from Seymour Group 1993, Synergy 1993; Australian Chamber Orchestra, 1995. *Compositions include:* In Moments Unseen for string quartet, 1984; Requiem, for chorus, percussion, 2 pianos and harp, 1985; Duo Concertante, for clarinet, viola and strings, 1986; The Drover's Wife for narrator and orchestra, 1987; Piano Concerto, 1989; The Snake Pit for ensemble, 1990; Eros and Agape for chamber ensemble, 1990; House Songs for tenor and ensemble, 1991; Eros Reclaimed, for ensemble, 1992; Carmina Pu for chorus, 1992; Cries and Whispers, for orchestra, 1993; Even Love can Wield a Stealthy Blade, for bass clarinet and percussion, 1993; Blow for wind octet, 1994; Kiss, for percussion quartet, 1994; Aprilès Nuages for string orchestra, 1995. *Honours:* Vienna Modern Masters Recording Project, 1992. *Address:* c/o APRA, 1A Eden Street, Crows Nest, NSW 2065, Australia.

**CROOK, Howard;** Singer (Tenor); b. 15 June 1947, New Jersey, USA. *Education:* Studied at State University, Illinois, and appeared at first in concert. *Career:* Sang at the Seattle Opera, then appeared as Pelléas and Belmonte at Amsterdam; Paris Opéra-Comique, 1987, as Lully's Atys, Aix-en-Provence, 1987, as Vulcan in Lully's Psyche; Schwetzingen, 1988, in Salieri's Tarare, Versailles, 1988, in Rameau's Pygmalion; Albert Hall, London, 1989, in Daniel Purcell's The Judgement of Paris; Sang in Cesti's Orontea at the 1990 Innsbruck Festival, Rameau's Castor et Pollux at Aix (1991) and Lully's Alceste at the Théâtre des Champs-Elysées, Paris; Sang with Les Musiciens du Louvre in Lully's Acis et Galatée at Beaune, 1996. *Recordings include:* St Matthew Passion and Messiah (DGG); Scylla et Glaucus (Erato); Bach Magnificat and Pygmalion (Harmonia Mundi). *Address:* c/o P.G. Alferink Artists BV, Apollolaan 181, NL–1077AT, Amsterdam, Netherlands.

**CROOK, Paul;** Singer (Tenor); b. 1943, Blackburn, England. *Education:* Studied in Geneva and London. *Career:* Appearances with Geneva Opera and English National Opera; Royal Opera, Covent Garden, from 1975 as Mozart's Monostatos, Mime in Der Ring des Nibelungen and Herod in Salome; Other roles in Ariadne auf Naxos, Falstaff, Hoffmann, Die Meistersinger, Tosca, Don Pasquale and Turandot; Guest appearances for Deutsche Oper Berlin and San Francisco Opera (as Mime) and in Naples, Warsaw, Paris and Buenos Aires. Tours of Japan and South Korea with the Royal Opera.; Sang Pfeifer in English Stage premiere of Hindemith's Mathis der Maler, Covent Garden 1995. *Recordings include:* Otello, Werther, La fanciulla del West and Les Contes d'Hoffmann. *Address:* c/o San Francisco Opera, War Memorial House, Van Ness Avenue, San Francisco, CA, USA.

**CROOM, James;** Singer (Tenor); b. 1960, North Carolina, USA. *Education:* Studied with James Schwabacher. *Career:* Appeared for two seasons as apprentice artist with Santa Fe Opera; Has sung twenty roles with Scottish Opera, the Glasgow Grand Opera (Calaf, 1990), Western Opera Theatre and San Francisco Opera; Appearances in Simon Boccanegra, Manon Lescaut, Die Zauberflöte (Monostatos) and Die Meistersinger for Scottish Opera; Other roles include Arbace (Idomeneo), Goro (Madama Butterfly) and Mephistopheles in Busoni's Doktor Faust. *Recordings include:* Video of L'Africaine, from San Francisco Opera. *Honours:* Regional finalist, Metropolitan Opera Auditions; Regional Winner, National Association of Teachers of Singing Competition. *Address:* c/o War Memorial Opera House, Van Ness Avenue, San Francisco, CA 94102, USA.

**CROPPER, Peter;** British violinist; *Artistic Director, Sheffield Music in the Round Festival*; b. 1945, England. *Education:* Royal Acad. of Music with Sidney Griller, Univ. of Keele, studied with Vilmos Tatrai in Budapest. *Career:* founder mem., Lindsay String Quartet 1971–; later The Lindsays; regular tours of Europe, England and the USA; quartet-in-residence Univ. of Sheffield 1972–78, Univ. of Manchester 1978; premiered the 4th Quartet of Tippett at the Bath Festival 1979, commissioned Tippett's 5th Quartet 1992; Chamber Music Festival established at Sheffield 1984; resident ensemble Music in the Round Festival, Sheffield –2005, Artistic Dir of the festival 2005–; plays Stradivarius from the Golden Period. *Recordings include:* Complete Cycles of Bartók, Tippett and Beethoven, Haydn Quartets Live from the Wigmore Hall. *Honours:* prizewinner (with mems of Lindsay String Quartet) Liège Int. Competition 1969, Gramophone Chamber Award for late Beethoven Quartets 1984. *Address:* c/o Music in the Round, 3 Tudor Square, Sheffield, S1 2LA, England.

**CROSS, Gregory;** singer (tenor); b. 1960, USA. *Career:* European debut, 1992, as Renaud in Gluck's Armide at Versailles, under Marc Minkowski; further appearances as Rossini's Almaviva for Opéra de Nancy, Ferrando at Strasbourg, Tamino for Greater Miami Opera, Lurcano in Ariodante for Welsh National Opera and in Messiah at San Francisco; Sang Iopas in Les Troyens under Colin Davis and Leukippos in Daphne under André Previn, both with the London Symphony Orchestra; Further concerts include Haydn's Seasons and Mozart's Requiem in Canada, and the Saint Matthew Passion and Mozart's C minor Mass at the Kennedy Center, Washington DC; sang Don Ottavio at Fort Lauderdale, 1997. *Recordings include:* Les Troyens, under Charles Dutoit.

**CROSSE, Gordon;** composer; b. 1 Dec. 1937, Bury, Lancashire, England. *Education:* Univ. of Oxford with Wellesz, Accademia di Santa Cecilia, Rome with Petrassi. *Career:* Tutor in Extra Mural Dept and in Music Dept, Univ. of Birmingham 1964–69; Fellow in Music, Univ. of Essex 1969–76; Visiting Prof. of Composition, Univ. of California 1977; freelance composer 1978–, with commissions from the BBC Symphony Orchestra, Royal Philharmonic

Orchestra, London Symphony Orchestra and Festivals of Aldeburgh, Cheltenham and Edinburgh; The Story of Vasco premiered at the London Coliseum. *Compositions:* Stage Purgatory, 1-act opera after Yeats, 1966; The Grace of Todd, comedy, 1969; Wheel of the World, entertainment on Chaucer's The Canterbury Tales, 1972; The Story of Vasco, opera in 3 acts, 1974; Potter Thompson, 1-act music drama, 1975; Orchestral: Elegy, 1959; Concerto da Camera, 1962; Symphony No. 1, 1964; Ceremony, 1966; 2 Violin Concertos, 1962, 1970; Some Marches on a Ground, 1970; Ariadne for oboe and ensemble, 1972; Symphony No. 2, 1975; Epiphany Variations, 1976; Wildboy, 1977; Thel for ensemble, 1978; Symphony for chamber orchestra, 1976; Dreamsongs, 1979; Cello Concerto, 1979; Array for trumpet and orchestra, 1986; Quiet, for wind band, 1987; Vocal: Changes for soprano, baritone, chorus and orchestra, 1965; The Covenant of the Rainbow for chorus and organ; For the Unfallen for tenor, horn and strings, 1963; Memories of Morning Night for mezzo and orchestra, 1971; The New World, poems by Ted Hughes for voice and piano, 1978; Harvest Songs for chorus and orchestra, 1980; Dreamcanon I, for chorus, 2 pianos and percussion, 1981; Sea Psalms for chorus, children's voices and orchestra, 1990; Chamber: String Quartet, 1980; Trio for Clarinet, 'Cello and Piano, 1981; Wave Songs for cello and piano, 1983; Piano Trio, 1986; Meet My Folks, 1964, Holly from the Bongs, 1974 (all for children). *Address:* Brants Cottage, Blackheath, Wenhaston, Halesworth, Suffolk IP19 9EX, England.

**CROSSLEY, Paul Christopher Richard,** CBE, MA; British concert pianist and music director; b. 17 May 1944, Dewsbury; s. of the late Frank Crossley and Myra Crossley (née Barrowcliffe). *Education:* Silcoates School, Wakefield, Mansfield Coll., Oxford. *Career:* has performed all over world as concert pianist; dedicatee and first performer of works by Tippett, Henze, Berio, Takemitsu, Adams, Lindberg, Salonen, Knussen, Benjamin; Artistic Dir London Sinfonietta 1988–94; 15 major films on twentieth-century composers. *Recordings include:* complete piano music of Franck, Fauré, Debussy, Ravel, Poulenc, Janacek, Tippett, Takemitsu; works for piano and orchestra by Franck, Messiaen, Takemitsu, Lutoslawski, Stravinksi, Adams. *Honours:* Hon. Fellow Mansfield Coll., Oxford 1991. *Current Management:* Connaught Artists Management, 2 Molasses Row, Plantation Wharf, London, SW11 3UX, England. *Telephone:* (20) 7738-0017 (office). *Fax:* (20) 7738-0909 (office). *E-mail:* classicalmusic@connaughtartists.com (office).

**CROSSMAN, (Wallace) Bruce,** BMus, MMus, MPhil; composer; b. 2 Nov. 1961, Auckland, New Zealand; m. Colleen Anne Guild 1986; one s. *Education:* Otago University, Dunedin, York University, England, 1990; Doctor of Creative Arts, University of Wollongong. *Career:* New Zealand Queen Elizabeth II Arts Council Grants, 1983–93; Composer-in-Residence, Nelson School of Music, New Zealand, 1987; Fellow in Composition, Pacific Composers Conference, Japan, 1990; Mozart Fellow, Otago University, New Zealand, 1992; Visiting Lecturer in Music, Waikato University, 1994; mem, Composers Association of New Zealand; Australian Music Centre. *Compositions:* Piece Number Two for orchestra, 1984; Pezzo Languendo for solo piano, 1984; Expression in Blue for violin and piano, 1988; Dual for two violins, 1988; Dialogue for Jerusalem for clarinet and piano, 1989; A Peace in Time for 2 pianos, 1989; City of Broken Dreams for orchestra, 1989; Timbres for guitar, 1991; Colour Resonances and Dance for orchestra, 1996; Rituals for soprano and string quartet, 1996. *Recordings:* Expression in Blue on A Violin and Piano Recital: Mark Menzies and Dan Poynton, The Waiteata Collection of New Zealand Music: Vol. I. *Honours:* Corbould Composition Competition Prize, 1996; Australian Post-graduate Award, 1996–99. *Address:* c/o Faculty of Creative Arts, University of Wollongong, Northfields Avenue, Wollongong, NSW 2522, Australia.

**CROW, Todd,** BA, MS; pianist and music professor; *Professor of Music, Vassar College;* b. 25 July 1945, Santa Barbara, CA, USA; m. Linda Goolsby 1967; one s. one d. *Education:* Univ. of California, Juilliard School, Music Acad. of the West. *Career:* debut in London, 1975; New York, 1981; London orchestral debut, London Philharmonic Orchestra, 1986; has given numerous concerts in USA, Europe and South America; Mount Desert Festival of Chamber Music, Maine; Maverick Concerts, Woodstock, New York, Music Mountain, Connecticut; radio appearances on BBC, National Public Radio and New York City Stations; Prof. of Music, Department of Music, Vassar College, Poughkeepsie, NY; New York orchestral debut with American Symphony Orchestra, 1992; additional festivals include: Casals Festival and Bard Music Festival; Music Director, Mount Desert Festival of Chamber Music, Maine; performances with St Luke's Chamber Ensemble. *Recordings:* Schubert Piano Sonatas; The Artistry of Todd Crow; Mozart Piano Concerto K467; Liszt E flat Piano Concerto; Berlioz/Liszt Symphonie Fantastique; Complete music for cello and piano by Mendelssohn (with Mark Shuman, cellist); Piano Works by Taneyev; Ernst Toch Piano Concerto No. 1; Haydn Piano Sonatas; Piano Works by Dohnányi. *Publications:* Bartók Studies 1976; contrib. to Journal of the American Liszt Society. *Honours:* Univ. of California Distinguished Alumni Award 1986. *Address:* Department of Music, Vassar College, Poughkeepsie, NY 12604, USA. *E-mail:* tocrow@vassar.edu.

**CROWN, David;** Singer (Bass Baritone); b. 1965, England. *Education:* Purcell School of Music; King's College, Cambridge; Masterclasses with Graham Johnson, and Roger Vignoles; Training as Baritone with David Pollard. *Career:* Early roles (as bass) included Don Giovanni, Leporello, Uberto in La Serva Padrona and Mefistofele; Companies included Broomhill Opera, Covent Garden and Batignano Festivals, and Pavillion Opera; Concerts as baritone include Messiah at Durham Cathedral, Elijah at Truro, Beethoven's Mass in C, Tippett's A Child of our Time and Fauré's Requiem; Season 2000 with Bach's Magnificat and Handel's Israel in Egypt with the

Whitehall Choir at St John's Smith Square. *Honours:* Wagner Society Bayreuth Bursary and National Federation of Music Societies Award, 1997. *Address:* c/o Whitehall Choir, St John's Smith Square, London, W1, England.

**CROWTHER, John Victor,** BA, MA, DipEd, PhD; university lecturer; b. 3 Sept. 1937, Todmorden, England; m. Valerie; one d. *Education:* Grammar School, Todmorden, Univ. Coll. Durham, Nottingham Univ. *Career:* music teacher at secondary schools in Leeds 1959–66; Lecturer/Principal Lecturer in Music Education at Loughborough Coll. of Education 1966–77; Dir of the Music Centre at Loughborough Univ. 1977–97; Ed. and Musical Dir of Cesti's opera 'Orontea' Vicenza 1969; public lectures and conference papers at Siena, Modena, Dublin, Durham, Edinburgh, Nottingham; mem. Royal Musical Asscn, Commissione Scientifica, Edizione Nazionale Dell' Opera Omnia Di Alessandro Stradella. *Publications:* The Oratorio in Modena 1992, The Oratorio in Bologna 1650–1730 1999, editions of 17th-century Italian oratorios by Vitali, Ferrari, Stradella, Freschi and Colonna, critical edition of Alessandro Stradella's oratorio 'La Susanna' Opera Omnia, Ser. III, Vol. I; contrib. to The Music Review, Music and Letters, Victorian Studies, Irish Musical Studies, Alessandro Stradella e Modena. *Address:* 21 Priory Road, Loughborough, Leicestershire, LE11 3PW, England (home). *Telephone:* (1509) 215533 (home).

**CROXFORD, Eileen;** Cellist; b. 21 March 1924, Leighton Buzzard, Bucks, England; m. David Parkhouse, (deceased 1989), 2 s. *Education:* Royal College of Music; Studied with Effie Richardson, Ivor James, Pablo Casals. *Career:* Debut: London, Wigmore Hall; BBC Promenade Concerts G Royal Albert Hall; Recitalist world-wide with husband, Concert Pianist, David Parkhouse; Concertos with leading orchestras; Trio with David Parkhouse and High Bean; Acclaimed in 1987 as world's longest standing Trio; Tours of East and West Europe, North and South America, Far East, Middle East, China and North Africa; Professor of Cello, Royal College of Music for 40 years; Founder, Member with David Parkhouse of Music Group of London. *Recordings:* Beethoven, Ghost and Archduke Trios, Irish Songs; Schubert, Trout Quintet; Trios by Bush, Mendelssohn and Ravel; Cello and piano sonatas by Dohnányi, Barber, Rachmaninov, Kodály, Debussy; Vaughan Williams, 2 Quartets, On Wenlock Edge, Studies on Folk Songs; Warlock, The Curlew; Lennox Berkeley, Sextet; Elgar, String Quartet. *Honours:* Alexander Prize, 1945; Queen's Prize, 1948; Boise Foundation Award, 1949; Fellow, Royal College of Music, 1983; Cobbett Medal of the Worshipful Co of Musicians for services to Chamber Music, 1991; Founder, Parkhouse Award, The International Chamber Music Award for Piano based groups in memory of David Parkhouse. *Address:* 11 Roehampton Court, Queens Ride, London SW13, England.

**CRUDELI, Marcella;** Concert Pianist, State Music Conservatory Director and Teacher; b. 16 April 1940, Gondar, Ethiopia; 1 s. *Education:* Language School; Mozarteum, Akademie für Musik, Salzburg, Austria; Hochschule, Akademie für Musik, Wien, Austria; State Conservatory G Verdi, Milan, Italy. *Career:* Debut: Rome, 1955; Over 2,000 concerts in 85 countries; Director, State Conservatory 'L. D'Annunzio' of Pescara; Teacher at the Ecole Normale de Musique de Paris 'Alfred Cortot' and at the Academia Pescarese. *Recordings include:* D Cimarosa, 62 Sonatas; B Galuppi, 12 Sonatas; R Schumann, Concerto A Minor, with Symphony Orchestra of Taipei; Glinka, variations on theme of Sonnambula, with Orchestra Rias of Berlin; Beethoven, Sonata Op 81; Mozart, Sonata K576; Schubert, Impromptus Op 90; E Grieg, Concerto A Minor, with Symphony Orchestera of Taipei. *Publications:* D Cimarosa, Revision of 62 Sonatas; B Galuppi, Revision of 12 Sonatas. *Honours:* Appointed by the President of the Republic 'Cavaliere al Merito Della Repubblico Italiana'. *Address:* Via Pierfranco Bonetti 90, 00128 Rome, Italy.

**CRUM, Alison,** BA, LTCL, LRAM, MTC (London); viol player and teacher; *Professor of Viol, Trinity College of Music;* b. 23 Nov. 1949, Derby, England; m. Roy Marks. *Education:* Shrewsbury High School for Girls, Univ. of Reading, Univ. of London, studied with Wieland Kuijken and Jordi Savall. *Career:* solo viol player, consort player and teacher, with numerous worldwide performances since 1975; Prof. of Viol, Trinity Coll. of Music 1987–; Visiting Specialist, W Dean Coll. 1987–; mem. Incorporated Soc. of Musicians, Musicians' Union, Viola da Gamba Soc. of Great Britain (pres. 1997–). *Recordings include:* over 80 with many British early music groups, notably with Rose Consort of Viols, Musica Antiqua of London; Consort of Musicke, Dowland Consort; four solo recordings of Bach, Marais, Rogniono, Dalla Casa. *Publications:* Play the Viol 1989, seven books of music for viols 1989–; contrib. to Chelys, Early Music Today. *Address:* 87 Olive Road, London, NW2 6UR, England (home). *Telephone:* (20) 8452-3254 (home). *Fax:* (20) 8452-3254 (home). *E-mail:* alison@alisoncrum.co.uk (home). *Website:* www.alisoncrum.co.uk.

**CRUMB, George,** BM, MM, DMA; American composer; *Annenberg Professor, University of Pennsylvania;* b. 24 Oct. 1929, Charleston, WV; s. of George Henry and Vivian Reed; m. Elizabeth Brown 1949; two s. one d. *Education:* Mason Coll. of Music, Univ. of Illinois, Univ. of Michigan, Hochschule für Musik (Berlin). *Career:* Prof., Univ. of Colorado 1959–63; Creative Assoc., State Univ. of New York at Buffalo 1963–64; Prof. of Composition, Univ. of Pa 1971–, Annenberg Prof. 1983–. *Compositions include:* Four Processionals for orchestra, Ancient Voices of Children, Black Angels for electric string quartet, Eleven Echoes of Autumn 1965, Songs, Drones and Refrains of Death, Vox Balaenae for three masked musicians 1971, Makrokosmos vols I–V 1972–79,

Music for a Summer Evening, Five Pieces for Piano, Night of the Four Moons, Night Music I, Echoes of Time and the River (Pulitzer Prize for Music) 1968, Four Nocturnes for violin and piano, Dream Sequence for violin, cello, piano and percussion 1976, Star-Child for soprano, children's chorus and orchestra 1977, Celestial Mechanics, Apparition, Whitman for soprano and piano 1979, A Little Suite for Christmas 1979, Gnomic Variations for piano 1981, Pastoral Drone for organ 1982, Processional for piano 1983, A Haunted Landscape for orchestra 1984, The Sleeper, An Idyll for the Misbegotten, Federico's Little Songs for Children for soprano, flute and percussion 1986, Zeitgeist for two amplified pianos 1987, Quest for guitar and ensemble 1990, Easter Dawning for carillon 1991, Mundus Canis for guitar and percussion 1998, Eine Kleine Mitternachtmusik 2002, Unto the Hills 2002, Otherworldly Resonances 2002. *Honours:* Koussevitsky Int. Recording Award 1971, UNESCO Int. Rostrum of Composers Award 1971, Prince Pierre de Monaco Prize 1989, Edward MacDowell Colony Medal, Peterborough 1995. *Address:* Music Building, University of Pennsylvania, PA 19104 (office); 240 Kirk Lane, Media, PA 19063, USA. *Telephone:* (215) 565-2438.

**CRUZ DE CASTRO, Carlos;** Composer, Professor and Production Manager; b. 23 Dec. 1941, Madrid, Spain. *Education:* Studied Law and Social Sciences at Universidad Central de Madrid; Studied music at Royal High Conservatory of Music, Madrid, composition with Gerardo Gombau and Francisco Calés, conducting with Enrique García Asensio and composition with Milko Kélemen at Hochschule Robert Schumann in Düsseldorf and with Gunther Becker and Antonio Janigro. *Career:* Participant at the VII Biennial in Paris, representing Spain with his pieces, Menaje for Non-Conventional Instruments and, Pente for Wind Quintet, 1971; Co-Founder with Mexican pianist and composer, Alicia Urreta of the Spanish-Mexican Festival of Contemporary Music, 1973; Took part in Premio Italia representing Spanish National Radio with his work, Mixtitlan in 1975 and at the Composers' International Tribune in Paris in 1979; With 6 other composers he established the Spanish Association of Symphonic Composers in 1976; Professor of Composition, Counterpoint, Chamber Music, Musical Forms and Aesthetics at the Conservatory at Albacete, 1983; Production Manager of Radio Clásica for Spanish National Radio; mem, Spanish Association of Symphonic Composers. *Compositions include:* Theatre: El Momento De Un Instante II, 1973–74; Ballet: Carta A Mi Hermana Salud, 1985; Instrumental: Imagenes De Infancia for piano; There And Back for guitar; Concerto for orchestra, 1984, Suite for guitar No. 1, 1993; Toccata Vieja En Tono Nuevo; 4 string quartets, 1968, 1975, 1994, 1998; Saxophone Concerto, 1997; Symphony 'Canarias', 1998; Barcarola for piano, 1999; La Sombra del Inquisitor, opera, 1999. *Recordings include:* Ida Y Vuelta; Concierto Para Guitarra Y Orquesta De Cuerda; Menaje; Morfologia Sonora No. 1. *Honours:* Music Prize by Mexican Union of Theatre and Music Chroniclers, 1977. *Address:* Clara Del Rey 46, 28002 Madrid, Spain.

**CRUZ-ROMO, Gilda;** Opera Singer (Soprano); b. 12 Feb. 1940, Guadalajara, Mexico. *Education:* Mexico City Conservatory, with Angel Esquivel. *Career:* Debut: Mexico City 1962, in Die Walküre; Metropolitan Opera from 1970 as Madama Butterfly, Puccini's Tosca, Manon and Suor Angelica; Verdi's Leonora (Trovatore and La Forza del Destino), Elisabeth de Valois, Aida, Amelia (Ballo in Maschera) and Violetta; Season 1972–73 at Covent Garden and La Scala Milan, as Aida; Appearances in Australia, South America and the Soviet Union and at the Vienna State Opera, Rome Opera, Paris Opéra, New York City Opera and Chicago Lyric Opera; Concert appearances in Canada, Mexico, USA, Japan, Israel and Soviet Union; Vienna Staatsoper, 1979 as Leonora in La Forza del Destino; New Jersey and Connecticut, 1988 as Donna Anna and Cherubini's Medea; Ars Musica Chorale and Orchestra, Englewood, New Jersey, as Santuzza and Matilda in the US premiere of Mascagni's Silvana, 1988–89. *Recordings include:* Rossini's Stabat Mater; Video of Aida at 1976 Orange Festival. *Honours:* 1st Prize, Metropolitan Opera National Award, 1970. *Address:* c/o Connecticut Grand Opera, 61 Atlantic SE, Stamford, CT 06901, USA.

**CSAPO, Gyula;** Composer; b. 26 Sept. 1955, Papa, Hungary; m. Eva Botai, 10 Oct 1980, 1 s. *Education:* Béla Bartók Conservatory; Diploma in Composition and Music Theory, Franz Liszt Academy of Music, Budapest, 1981; Institut pour la Recherche et Coordination Acoustique/Musique, Paris, 1982; PhD, Composition, State University of New York, Buffalo, 1989. *Career:* Member, New Music Studio, Budapest; Extensive concert performances, radio recordings and broadcasts with, or without the Studio in Budapest, Warsaw, Toruń (Poland), Vienna, Darmstadt, Milan, Rotterdam, London, Frankfurt am Main, Edmonton (Alberta, Canada), Buffalo, New York; Film music scores; Associated with Protean Forms Collective, New York City. *Compositions include:* Krapp's Last Tape, After Beckett, 1974–75; Tao Song, 1:1/2, 1974–77; Fanatritraritrana, 1977–81; Handshake After Shot, 1977; Hark, Edward..., 1979–81; Na'Conxypan, 1978–88; Phedre's Hymn to the Sun, 1981; Yagul, 1987; Infrared Notes, No.1 (Prismed Through Darkness), 1986–88; Remnants in White, tape, 1989; Choral in Perfect Time for keyboard and bass drum, 1993; Phèdre: une tragédie en musique, 1996–. *Address:* 182 Graham Avenue, Apt No. 3, Brooklyn, NY 11206, USA.

**CSENGERY, Adrienne;** singer (soprano); b. 3 Jan. 1946, Bavaria, Germany. *Education:* Bartók Conservatory, Budapest, Franz Liszt Acad. with Eva Kutrucz. *Career:* early engagements at the Budapest State Opera and in Monteverdi's Vespers, conducted by Lovro von Matacic; Engagements in Zagreb, Dubrovnik and Palermo; Marzelline in Fidelio at the 1974 Munich Festival; Hungarian State Opera Budapest as Marguerite, Lulu and Anne Trulove; Mozart roles at Munich; Susanna, Pamina, Fiordiligi and Zerlina;

Appearances at Hamburg, Bayreuth, Cologne, Amsterdam and Bern with Sawallisch, Pritchard, Haitink, Lopez-Cobos, Michael Gielen and Roderick Brydon; Glyndebourne Festival 1976–77 as Susanna and Zerlina, in productions directed by Peter Hall; Wigmore Hall recital 1980, with English Canzonettas by Haydn; Gave the world premiere of Kurtag's Messages of the Late Miss RV Troussova, with the Ensemble Intercontemporain conducted by Boulez, 1981; Later performances of the work in La Rochelle, Milan, Venice, Florence, Budapest, Bath, Edinburgh and London; Gave the British premiere of Kafka Fragments by Kurtag at the 1989 Almeida Festival, London. *Recordings include:* Wigmore Hall Recital 1980 (Hungaroton); Messages of the late RV Troussova (Erato). *Honours:* Gramophone Record Prize, 1983; Gramophone Contemporary Music Award, 1985.

**CUBAYNES, Jean-Jacques;** Singer (Bass-baritone); b. 14 Feb. 1950, Toulouse, France. *Education:* Studied at the Toulouse Conservatory and the Paris Opéra studio. *Career:* Sang at the Toulouse Opera from 1978, notably as Zuniga, Mephistopheles, Colline and Monterone; Paris Opéra debut 1987, as Publio in La Clemenza di Tito; Opéra Bastille as the Old Hebrew in Samson et Dalila, Samuel in Ballo in Maschera and Zuniga in Carmen, 1991–95; Artistic Director, The Festival Déodat de Severac, Toulouse, France, 1994–; Guest appearances throughout France and in Dublin, Perugia, Liège, Bonn, Karlsruhe, Regensburg and Seville; Other roles have included Don Giovanni in 1988, Lothario in Thomas's Mignon, 1989, Arkel in Pelléas et Mélisande, Gessler in Guillaume Tell, Sparafucile, Daland and Rodolfo in La Sonnambula; Bregenz Festival 1991, as Zuniga in Carmen; Sang Melcthal in Guillaume Tell at Liège, 1997 and Ramfis in Aida in 1998. *Recordings include:* Gounod's Mireille and Roussel's Padmavati. *Current Management:* Living Art Impresariat, 9 Boulevard Montmartre, 75002 Paris, France. *Address:* 40 Rue Alsace-Lorraine, 31000 Toulouse, France.

**CUBERLI, Lella (Alice),** BMus; American concert and opera singer (soprano); b. 29 Sept. 1945, Austin, TX; m. Luigi Cuberli 1972. *Education:* Southern Methodist University. *Career:* Debut: European Violetta in La Traviata in Hungary, 1975. Sagra Musicale Umbria in the oratorio La Betulia Liberata by Mozart, 1975; Spoleto Festival concerto da camera with music by Schubert and Beethoven, 1977; Debut at La Scala in Milan in Mozart's Abduction, 1978; Since then regular appearances in operas such as Mozart's Re Pastore, 1979, Handel's Ariodante, 1981 (Opera taken on tour by La Scala to the Edinburgh Festival, 1982), Mozart's Lucio Silla, 1984; Le nozze di Figaro, 1987 and Orfeo by Gluck, 1989; Debut at Festival Woche in Berlin with the Beethoven Missa Solemnis, conductor Herbert von Karajan, 1985, also performed in the Beethoven 9th, 1986, and the Brahms Requiem, 1987, again with Karajan conducting; 1986 debut at Salzburg Festival with Le nozze di Figaro (role of Countess) with James Levine conducting with repeats in 1987 and 1988; 1986 debut at the Mozart Festival in Paris again in Figaro with Daniel Barenboim conducting; 1987, new production of Traviata made especially for her at the Monnaie in Brussels; 1988 debut at Vienna Staatsoper in Viaggio a Reims, Claudio Abbado conducting; 1989 concert at Pesaro Opera, Festival of Beethoven's Schottische Lieder, Pianist Maurizio Pollini; Sang Mozart's Countess at Orchestra Hall, Chicago, 1992; Antonia in Les Contes d'Hoffmann at the Opéra Bastille, the Countess with the Royal Opera in Japan and at Florence, 1992; Sang Donna Anna at the 1996 Salzburg Festival. *Recordings include:* Beethoven, Missa Solemnis, Deutsche Grammophon (Karajan), 1985; Mozart, Da Ponte operas, Erato (Barenboim) Berlin Philharmonic, 1990. *Honours:* Franco Abbiati Italian Critics Award, 1981 and Premio Jorio, 1984; Le Grand Prix du Disque conferred by the Academy of France in Paris and Prix Rossini of Paris and the Maschera d'argento award in Campione d'Italia, 1986; Premio Paisiello in Taranto, Italy, 1987. *Address:* c/o Oldani, Viale Legioni Romane 26, 20147 Milan, Italy.

**CUCKSTON, Alan,** BMus, MA; British harpsichordist, pianist, conductor and lecturer; b. 2 July 1940, Horsforth, Yorkshire, England; m. Vivien Broadbent 1965; two s. three d. *Education:* Kings Coll., Cambridge. *Career:* debut, Wigmore Hall 1965; BBC recitalist 1964; solo concerts in Europe, the USA; keyboard accompanist with Acad. of St Martin in the Fields and Pro Cantione Antiqua; Conductor The Alan Cuckston Singers 1961–. *Recordings:* Solo Piano Music of Alan Rawsthorne, William Baines, Eugene Goossens, Edward German, John Field, Sterndale Bennett, Stanford, Corder; Solo Harpsichord Music of Burnett, Kinloch, Farnaby, Tallis, Byrd, Handel, Couperin, Rameau, harpsichord/lute duets and fortepiano/guitar duets with Stuart Willis in recitals and recordings; Conductor, English Northern Philharmonia in K. Leighton, M. Hurd, J. Gardner, Conductor City of Bradford Orchestra in Rawsthorne. *Publications:* chapters in William Walton – Music and Literature 1999, Arthur Bliss – Music and Literature 2002, Ronald Stevenson – Music and Literature 2005. *Address:* Turnham Hall, Cliffe, Selby, North Yorkshire YO8 6ED, England (home). *Telephone:* (1757) 638238 (office). *E-mail:* alancuckston@email.com (home).

**CUÉNOD, Hugues Adhémar;** Swiss singer (tenor); b. 26 June 1902, Corseaux-sur-Vevey. *Education:* Conservatories of Geneva and Basle, studied in Vienna. *Career:* debut, Paris 1928, in the French premiere of Krenek's Jonny spielt Auf; sang in Geneva 1930–33, Paris 1934–37; concert tour of N America with Nadia Boulanger 1937–39; Prof., Geneva Conservatory 1940–46; widely known in French songs and in early music; Lieder recitals with Clara Haskil; sang in the premiere of Honegger's Le Danse des Morts, Basle 1940; performances as the Evangelist in Bach's St Matthew Passion; created Sellem in The Rake's Progress, Venice 1951; Covent Garden 1954, as the Astrologer in The Golden Cockerel; Glyndebourne from 1954, notably as

Don Basilio, in Cavalli's L'Ormindo and La Calisto, and in Le nozze di Figaro (50th Anniversary Season 1984); Metropolitan Opera debut 1987, as the Emperor in Turandot; Geneva Opera 1989, as Monsieur Taupe in Capriccio. *Recordings:* St Matthew Passion, L'Enfant et les Sortilèges, Ariadne auf Naxos, Oedipus Rex, Les Contes d'Hoffmann, La Calisto, Le nozze di Figaro, Early Music.

**CULLAGH, Majella;** Irish singer (soprano); b. 1963, d. of Tom Cullagh and the late Mrs Cullagh. *Education:* Cork School of Music, Nat. Opera Studio, London. *Career:* appearances with the Royal Danish Opera as Donizetti's Adina, Adèle in Le Comte Ory with the Glyndebourne Tour, Isabella in Wagner's Das Liebesverbot at Wexford and Mozart's First Lady for Opera North; Melissa in Handel's Amadigi at the Covent Garden Festival and New York, and the title role in Medea by Gavin Bryars; concerts include Huit scènes de Faust by Berlioz in Venice, and engagements in the USA; season 2000–01 with Fiordiligi in the Canary Islands, Micaela in Carmen and Countess for Opera North, Donna Anna in Regensburg and Tatiana in Eugene Onegin for Grange Park Opera; Manon for Opera New Zealand; Ninetta in Lagazza Ladra and Arminda in La Finta Giardiniera for Opera North; Violetta in La Traviata and Musetta in La Bohème for Glyndebourne on tour; Nedda in I Pagliacci, Bérénice in L'Occasione Fa Il Ladro and Ghita in Der Zwerg for Opera North. *Recordings include:* Mendelssohn 2nd Symphony, Donizetti's Zoraida di Granata and Rossini's Bianca e Falliero, Don Giovanni, Donizetti's Pia de'Tolomei, Rossini's Elisabetta Regina d'Inghilterra and Mercadante's Zaira, The Thieving Magpie and The Magic Flute. *Current Management:* International Music Talents, 59 Quai de Valmy, 75010 Paris, France. *Telephone:* 1 40 40 94 75. *Fax:* 1 40 40 94 84. *E-mail:* sesto@wanadoo .fr. *Website:* www.majellacullagh.com.

**CULLELL MUNIESA, Rosa;** Spanish business executive; *Director-General, Gran Teatre del Liceu;* b. 14 March 1958, Barcelona; m.; two c. *Education:* Universidad Autónoma de Barcelona, IESE. *Career:* fmr journalist, working for Mundo Diario, the BBC, TVE-Catalonia and El País; Dir of Communication, La Caixa 1988, later Gen. Man., Exec. Vice-Pres. and Sr Exec. Vice-Pres. –2002, representing La Caixa on the bds of Panrico, Telesp (Telefónica de Sao Paulo) and Port Aventura 2002–; CEO Grup 62 2002–; Dir-Gen., Gran Teatre del Liceu 2005. *Address:* Gran Teatre del Liceu, La Rambla 51–59, 08002 Barcelona, Spain. *Website:* www.liceubarcelona.com.

**CULLEN, Bernadette;** Singer (Mezzo-soprano); b. 1949, Australia. *Career:* Appearances from 1981 with Australian Opera as Maffio Orsini in Lucrezia Borgia, Nicklausse and Giulietta in Hoffman, Cherubino in Figaro, Angelina in Cenerentola, Ottavia in Poppea, the Secretary in The Consul, Charlotte in Werther and Rosina in Il Barbiere di Siviglia; Further performances include Brangaene in a new production of Tristan, Sesto in Clemenza di Tito, Donna Elvira in Don Giovanni, also for Lyric Opera of Queensland; Eboli in Don Carlos and Adalgisa in Norma for Victoria State Opera; Vitellia in concert under Christopher Hogwood, Gala Concert with Joan Sutherland and Richard Bonynge in Perth, Dorabella at Hong Kong and British debut as Isolier in Le Comte Ory for Welsh National Opera; Sang Donna Elvira at the reopening of the Tyl Theatre, Prague, under Charles Mackerras, Leonara in La Favorita for WNO in Cardiff and at Covent Garden, Dido in Dido and Aeneas in Palermo (1994), Cassandre in La Prise de Troie for the Australian Opera, Brangaene in Tristan and Isolde for Scottish Opera; Venus in Tannhäuser at Sydney, 1998; Concert repertoire includes Mahler's 8th under Charles Dutoit; Rossini Stabat Mater and Petite messe Solennelle; Verdi Requiem in Sydney under Carlo Rizzi and with the Hallé Orchestra, Liverpool Oratorio under Carl Davis, Dream of Gerontius with the Ulster Orchestra and Beethoven's Ninth; Season 2000–01 as Eboli at Melbourne and Azucena at Sydney. *Recordings:* Pulcinella with the Australian Chamber Orchestra; The Bohemian Girl, conducted by Richard Bonynge. *Honours:* Vienna State Opera Award, Opera Foundation Australia, 1995. *Address:* c/o Braden Arts Management Ltd, Station House, 790 George Street, Sydney, NSW 2000, Australia.

**CULLIS, Rita;** Singer (Soprano); b. 25 Sept. 1952, Ellesmere Port, Cheshire, England. *Education:* Royal Manchester College of Music. *Career:* Joined the chorus Welsh National Opera, 1973; Principal on Contract, Welsh National Opera, 1976; Roles include Leila (Pearl Fishers), the Countess (Figaro), Tytania (Midsummer Night's Dream), Pamina (Magic Flute), Ellen (Peter Grimes), Donna Anna (Don Giovanni) and Lenio in Martinů's Greek Passion; Buxton Festival 1981, as Elisetta in Cimarosa's Il Matrimonio Segreto; Opera North 1985, as Jenifer in The Midsummer Marriage and as Christine in Strauss's Intermezzo; Season 1986–87 sang the Countess of Tel-Aviv Opera, Ariadne for Opera Northern Ireland and Donna Anna for her debut at the English National Opera, returned for The Fox in Janáček's Cunning Little Vixen; Concert engagements with RAI Milan, Hallé Orchestra, Ulster Radio, Royal Liverpool Philharmonic and the Bournemouth Symphony; Netherlands Opera, Freischütz, 1989–90; Other engagements as the Composer and Fiordiligi, English National Opera, the Fox in The Cunning Little Vixen, Scottish Opera, and the Countess and Donna Anna, debuts with the Canadian Opera Company and San Diego Opera, 1992; Season 1992–93 as the Composer in Ariadne for ENO and Covent Garden debut as Janáček's Fox; Sang Third Norn in Götterdämmerung at Covent Garden, 1995; Bach's St Matthew Passion at the Festival Hall, 1997; Season 1997–98 with Elisabeth in Tannhäuser for Opera North, Senta for ENO, Ellen Orford and Sieglinde for Royal Opera; Season 1999 as Hecuba in King Priam for ENO, Mozart's Countess at Hamburg and Creusa in the premiere of Param Vir's Ion, at

Aldeburgh. *Address:* c/o P.G. Alferink Artists BV, Apollolaan 181, NL–1077AT, Amsterdam, Netherlands.

**CULMER-SCHELLBACH, Lona;** Singer (Soprano); b. 4 Feb. 1954, Miami, Florida, USA. *Career:* Prizewinner at the 1985 Mozart Competition, Salzburg, and appeared in the 1986 premiere of Penderecki's Schwarze Maske, at Salzburg; Also sang the role of Europa in Die Liebe der Danaë at the Vienna Staatsoper and at Santa Fe, 1988; Sang in the premiere of Patmos by Wolfgang von Schweinitz at Munich (1990) and appeared at Kassel from 1989; Lady Macbeth by Shostakovich, 1996; Further appearances in Essen, Paris, Berlin and Dresden, as Marie in Wozzeck, Shostakovich's Lady Macbeth, Elsa, Donna Elvira and Ariadne; Season 2000–01 as Aida at Heidenheim, Marina in Boris Godunov and Tosca at Kassel, Santuzza for Frankfurt Opera; Frequent concert engagements. *Address:* c/o Staatstheater Kassel, Friedrichplatz 15, W-3500 Kassel, Germany.

**CULVER, (David) Andrew,** MM; composer and performer; b. 30 Aug. 1953, Morristown, NJ, USA. *Education:* composition with Bengt Hambaeus; McGill University. *Career:* Founder Member of SONDE, Canadian music design and performance group; Has worked at Yellow Springs Institute for Contemporary Studies, New Music Concerts Toronto, Staten Island Children's Museum, 1983 and the Children's Museum of Manhattan, 1989–91; Collaborations with John Cage 1981–92, including computer assistance with the premiere of Europeras 1 and 2 at the Frankfurt Schauspielhaus, 1987; Founder, Anarchic Harmony Foundation; mem, SOCAN. *Compositions:* Stage works Viti 1981; Music with Tensegrity Sound Source No. 5, 1983; Hard Lake Frozen Moon, 1989; Quasicrystals, sound sculpture, 1989; Ocean 1-95, 1994; From Zero (film), 1995; Architonic Space, 1996. *Address:* 127 Willowbrook Road, Clinton Corners, NY 12514, USA.

**CUMBERLAND, David;** Singer (Bass-baritone); b. 1945, Ohio, USA. *Education:* Studied at the Juilliard School, New York. *Career:* Debut: Sang Pizarro in a concert performance of Fidelio under Leonard Bernstein at Lincoln Center; Has appeared widely at German opera houses, notably in Frankfurt, Gelsenkirchen, Wiesbaden, Cologne, Leipzig and Freiburg; Repertoire has included Hans Sachs, the Landgrave in Tannhäuser, King Phillip in Don Carlo and the Dutchman; Has sung at the opera of Marseille and appeared in La Serva Padrona and Bastien and Bastienne at Clermont-Ferrand; Linz Opera in Der fliegende Holländer; US engagements at the Kentucky Opera, Philadelphia Opera; National Grand Opera and in Dallas; San Francisco and New York (City Opera); Spoleto Festival as Rodolfo in La Sonnambula; British debut with Opera North, 1988 as the Dutchman; Concert appearances at the Carnegie Hall, in Boston, at the Vienna Musikverein and in Santiago; Francesco Cenci in the world premiere of Beatrice Cenci, by Berthold Goldschmidt, 1994; Sang King Lycomedes in the world premiere of Wolfgang Andreas Schultz's Achill und der zehn Mädchen, Kassel, Germany, in 1997, Pogner in Die Meistersinger von Nürnberg at the reopening of the opera house in Magdeburg, Germany and sang Alberich in Wagner's Rheingold in Magdeburg and in further performances of Wagner's Ring in 1998. *Address:* Weinmarkt 5, CH 6004, Luzern, Switzerland.

**CUMMINGS, Claudia;** Opera Singer (Soprano); b. 12 Nov. 1941, Santa Barbara, California, USA; m. (1) H W Cummings, 12 June 1962, (2) Jack Aranson, 26 May 1973, 1 d. *Education:* BA, Vocal Performance, San Francisco University, 1963. *Career:* Debut: San Francisco Opera, 1971; San Francisco, New York City, Houston, Seattle, San Diego, Minnesota, Miami, Charlotte Opera Companies; Netherlands Opera; Stuttgart Opera premiere of Satyagraha by Philip Glass, 1980; Canadian Opera; Sang Countess de la Roche by B A Zimmermann, 1991 at New York City Opera; Other roles have included Violetta, Rosalinda, Lucia di Lammermoor, Lulu, Marguerite, 3 Heroines in the Tales of Hoffmann, Countess in The Marriage of Figaro. *Recordings:* Satyagraha, Philip Glass. *Address:* PO Box 4306, New Windsor, NY 12553, USA.

**CUMMINGS, Conrad,** BA, DMA; American composer, conductor and musician (keyboard); *composition faculty member, The Juilliard School;* b. 10 Feb. 1948, San Francisco, CA. *Education:* Yale Univ., State Univ. of New York, Stony Brook, Columbia Univ., Tanglewood, Computer Music Project, Stanford, IRCAM, Paris. *Career:* teacher Columbia-Princeton Electronic Music Center 1974–76; Electronic Music Co-ordinator, Brooklyn Coll. CUNY 1976–79; Assoc. Prof., Dir Music and Media Program, Oberlin Conservatory 1980–91; Vice-Pres., CFO Hyperspace Cowgirls (children's interactive media co.), New York 1995–2002; mem. composition faculty (evening div.), The Juilliard School 2003–; commissions from the Smithsonian Inst., Oberlin Coll., San Francisco Opera Center, Cleveland Chamber Orchestra, Canadian Brass, Opera Delaware, Brandywine Baroque, Avian Orchestra; panellist, Nat. Endowment for the Arts Opera Music-Theatre Div. 1993, 1994. *Compositions include:* Fragments from 'The Golden Gate' for mezzo soprano, tenor and piano 1985, I Wish They All Could Be... for instrumental octet 1986, Where I Live for soprano, baritone and baroque ensemble 1987, Positions 1956 for amplified voices and instruments 1988, Insertions for amplified voices and instruments 1988, Photo-Op opera 1992, Scenes from Tonkin for voices and chamber orchestra 1990, Dénouement for large orchestra 1992, There Is No Hope For Art for soprano, piano and double bass 1992, Tonkin (opera in three acts) 1993, Barnar Venet: Lignes (film score) 1995, 1996, Pierrette Bloch, Boucles (film score) 1997, 1998, Shakespeare in Love for soprano and baritone voices and baroque ensemble 2000, In Memorian Marge Laszlo for chamber ensemble 2004. *Honours:* MacDowell

Colony Fellowships 1981, 1986, Djerassi Foundation Fellowship 1985, grants from the Nat. Endowment for the Arts 1981, 1992, Martha Baird Rockefeller Fund 1980, Opera America 1992, The Rockefeller Foundation 1992. *Address:* 415 W 23rd Street, Apt 11–D, New York, NY 10019, USA (office). *Telephone:* (212) 741-1559 (office). *E-mail:* conrad@conradcummings.com (office). *Website:* www.conradcummings.com.

**CUMMINGS, Diana,** ARAM; Violinist; b. 27 April 1941, Amersham, Buckinghamshire, England; m. Luciano Jorios; two s. one d. *Education:* recital diploma, RAM. *Career:* debut, Wigmore Hall; has toured throughout the UK as soloist and chamber musician; numerous television and radio broadcasts; formerly leader of English Piano Quartet; mem., Cummings String Trio; with Trio gave Haydn's Op 53 No. 1, Martinů's trio and Beethoven's Op 9 No. 1, for the BBC 1991; mem. Musicians' Union, ISM. *Recordings include:* Complete String Trios of Beethoven. *Honours:* Prizewinner, International Paganini Competition, Genoa 1963, International Competition A, Curci, Naples 1967. *Address:* 2 Fairhazel Mansions, Fairhazel Gardens, London, NW6, England.

**CUMMINGS, Douglas,** FRAM; British cellist; b. 5 Oct. 1946, England; m. two s. *Education:* Univ. Coll. School, London, Univ. of Paris, RAM, Univ. of Southern Calif. *Career:* Principal Cellist, London Symphony Orchestra 1969–92; fmr Prof., RAM, Royal Welsh Coll. of Music and Drama. *Recordings:* two Bach Suites for unaccompanied cello, Swan Lake duet (with Ida Haendl on violin and the London Symphony Orchestra), Schubert Quintet in C (with the Lindsay Quartet), Trout Quintet, Schubert (with Dame Moira Lympani and Principals of LSO). *Address:* 7 Yerbury Road, London, N19 4RN, England. *Telephone:* (20) 7272-0750.

**CUMMINGS, Laurence;** Harpsichordist and Conductor; b. 1968, Sutton Coldfield, England. *Education:* Studied at Oxford University (Organ scholar at Christ Church) and the Royal College of Music. *Career:* Has performed with the Orchestra of the Age of Enlightenment, The Sixteen, The Gabrieli Consort; conducted Esther (1732), Alexander Balus, Agrippina for the London Handel Festival; Theodora for Glyndebourne on Tour; Ariodante for English Touring Opera, Autumn 2003; Future plans include La Spinalba, Casa da Musica, Porto; Semele English National Opera, Autumn 2004; Giulio Cesare, Glyndebourne Festival, 2005; Musical Director of London Handel Society 2002–; Musical Director Tilford Bach Society 2002–; Head of Historical Performance, Royal Academy of Music 1997–. *Recordings include:* Louis and Francois Couperin keyboard music. *Address:* 81 Chetwynd Road, Dartmouth Park, London NW5 1DA, England. *E-mail:* laurence@chetwynd.clara.co.uk.

**CUNNINGHAM, Thomas (Tom);** composer and conductor; b. 24 March 1946, Edinburgh, Scotland; m. Alison Hannah 1972; two d. *Education:* George Heriot's School, Edinburgh, Univ. of Edinburgh, Morley Coll., London. *Career:* Musical Dir, Brussels Gilbert & Sullivan Soc. 1978–82; Brussels Choral Soc. 1984–2002, Hot Air 2003, Con Spirito 2003–05; composer of choral music and editor of choral music; mem. Asscn of British Choral Dirs. *Compositions:* Merry Christmas Jazz, Esta Noche, Rock O my Soul, Sweet was the Song, The Good-bye Jazz. *Recordings:* Joseph Jongen: Mass op. 130, Christmas Concert 1988, Festive Joy 2000. *Publications:* Choral scores of Gustav Mahler: Symphony Nos 2 and 3, Jongen: Mass op. 130, Deus Abraham, Quid sum Miser, and Three Sacred Songs (ed.). *Address:* 7 Lauder Road, Edinburgh, EH9 2EW, Scotland. *Telephone:* (131) 667-8614. *E-mail:* europa@cflat.co.uk.

**CUPER, Philippe;** Clarinettist; b. 25 April 1957, Lille, France. *Education:* Studied at the Paris Conservatoire with Guy Deplus, Henri Druart, Guy Dangain, Jacques Lancelot and Gilbert Voisin and with Stanley Drucker at Juilliard, New York. *Career:* Soloist with the Concerts Lamoureux, 1978–87; Orchestra of the Paris Opéra from 1984; Many appearances as concert soloist and as chamber musician with the Paris Wind Octet, pianists Paul Badura-Skoda and Michel Dalberto and violinist Augustin Dumay. *Recordings:* 25 albums. *Contributions:* Clarinette magazine; International Clarinet Society magazine; Band Journal, Tokyo; Clarinet and Saxophone Society Magazine, London. *Honours:* Prizewinner, Munich International Competition, 1982, Geneva, 1979, and Prague, 1986; 1st Prize, Prague, 1986. *Address:* c/o Association des Concerts Lamoureux, 252 Rue du Faubourg St Honoré, 75008 Paris, France.

**CUPIDO, Alberto;** singer (tenor); b. 19 March 1948, Portofino, Italy. *Education:* Giuseppe Verdi Conservatory, Milan and at the Accademia Chigiana in Siena. *Career:* debut in Genoa 1977 as Pinkerton; Sang widely in Italy and in Strasbourg, Vienna and Frankfurt; Glyndebourne 1978 as Rodolfo; Munich Staatsoper 1982 as Faust; US debut San Francisco 1983; Florence 1983 as Rinuccio in Gianni Schicchi; La Scala debut 1984 as Edgardo in Lucia di Lammermoor; Returned 1986 as Orontes in I Lombardi; Wiesbaden 1986 in Giulietta e Romeo by Zandonai; Further appearances in Cologne, Hamburg, Berlin and Montreal; Other roles include Alfredo, Fenton, the Duke of Mantua, Fernando in La Favorita and Rodolfo in Luisa Miller; Sang Edgardo at Monte Carlo, 1987; Faust at Geneva, 1988; Teatro Comunale Florence, 1989; As Faust in Mefistofele, Rodolfo at Rome, 1990; Gabriele Adorno in a new production of Simon Boccanegra at Brussels, 1990; Debut at the Verona Arena as Cavaradossi; Season 1991–92 as Boito's Faust at the Lyric Opera Chicago and as Don Carlo at Verona; Season 1994–95 as Rodolfo and Don José at Verona, Reyer's Sigurd and Cavaradossi at Marseille and Graz, 1995; Enzo in La Gioconda at Berlin, 1993; Also heard in the concert hall; Season 2000–01 as Hoffmann in Vienna, Pollione in Norma at Florence

and Calaf at the Deutsche Oper Berlin. *Honours:* prizewinner at Competitions in Parma 1975, Busseto 1976.

**CURA, José;** Argentine singer (tenor); *President, Cuibar Productions S. L.;* b. 1962, Rosario, Santa Fe; m. Silvia Ibarra 1985; two s. one d. *Education:* Univ. of Rosario, School of Arts, Teatro Colon, Buenos Aires, vocal studies with Horacio Amauri in Argentina and Vittorio Terranova in Italy. *Career:* appearances at leading int. opera houses 1992–; Pres., Cuibar Productions SL. *Opera includes:* Makropoulos Affair, Le Villi, Fedora, Stiffelio, Iris, Samson et Dalila, Carmen, Cavalleria Rusticana, Norma, Tosca, La Gioconda, I Pagliacci, Otello, Aida; *Recordings include:* Le Villi, Iris, Argentine Songs, Puccini Arias, Samson et Dalila, Otello, I Pagliacci, Manon Lescaut. *Honours:* Chevalier, Lebanese Government; Premio Abbiatti, Italian Critics' Award, Premio Carrara, Cultura Millenaria 1997, XII Premio Internazionale di Arte e Cultura Cilea 1997. *Address:* JC International, Avda Machupichu 26, Apt 111, 28043 Madrid, Spain (office). *Telephone:* (91) 3000134 (office). *Fax:* (91) 7599577 (office). *E-mail:* contact@cuibar.com. *Website:* www.cuibar.com; www .josecura.com.

**CURLEY, Carlo;** Concert Organist; b. 24 Aug. 1952, USA. *Education:* North Carolina School for the Arts; Privately with Virgil Fox, Robert Elmore (Philadelphia), Arthur Poister (Syracuse University) and Sir George Thalben-Ball (Temple Church, London). *Career:* Organist-Choirmaster and Teacher of Music, Girard College, Philadelphia; Director of Music, Druids Hills Baptist Church, Atlanta, Georgia; Artist-in-Residence, Fountain Street Church, Grand Rapids, Michigan; Organist, Alexandra Palace, London; Performances and Masterclasses at National Music Camp, Interlochen, Michigan; Frequent appearances on radio and television in USA, England, Australia, Canada, Japan and Denmark; Organ Consultant and Designer. *Recordings:* The Emperor's Fanfare, Brightly Shining, Organ Fantasia, Organ Imperial, Bach Organ Favourites, Bach Great Organ Works; The World of Carlo Curley (all for Decca). *Honours:* Patron, Holbrook Music Society (the United Kingdom); Patron and Organ Consultant to the City of Melbourne. *Address:* c/o PVA Management Ltd, Hallow Park, Worcester WR2 6PG, England.

**CURNYN, Christian;** British conductor; *Founder and Music Director, Early Opera Company;* b. 1965, England. *Education:* York Univ., Guildhall School of Music and Drama, London. *Career:* founder and Music Dir, Early Opera Co. 1994–; productions of Purcell, M. A. Charpentier and Handel's Orlando, Queen Elizabeth Hall; Monteverdi Ballets for the York Early Music Festival, L'Orfeo and L'Incoronazione di Poppea; Charpentier's La Descente d'Orphée aux Enfers, for the Spitalfields Festival, and Médée; Handel's Rinaldo for the Guildhall School; Cesti's Il Pomo d'Oro and Handel's Aci, Galatea a Polifermo for the Batignano Festival, Italy. Season 2000–01 with Acis and Galatea and Purcell's Fairy Queen at the Wigmore Hall; Messiah in Tokyo and Handel's Partenope for the Covent Garden Festival. *Recording:* Partenope 2005. *Website:* www.earlyopera.com.

**CURPHEY, Margaret;** Singer (Soprano); b. 27 Feb. 1938, Douglas, Isle of Man. *Education:* Studied with John Carol Case in Birmingham and with David Galiver and Joan Cross in London. *Career:* Debut: Sadler's Wells Opera 1965, as Micaela in Carmen; Sang with Sadler's Wells/English National Opera in operas by Mozart, Wagner, Verdi and Puccini; Sang Eva in new production of The Mastersingers, conducted by Reginald Goodall, Sieglinde in The Valkyrie and Gutrune in The Twilight of the Gods; Camden Theatre 1967, in the British premiere of Mozart's Lucio Silla, Guest engagements in Sofia and elsewhere in Europe; Sang Brünnhilde at the London Coliseum, 1977; Brünnhilde at Santiago and Seattle 1978; Season 1981–82 as Rezia in Oberon for Opera North and Jaroslavna in Prince Igor; Many appearances as concert singer. *Recordings:* The Ring of the Nibelung, conducted by Reginald Goodall. *Honours:* Prizewinner at 1970 International Competition, Sofia. *Address:* c/o Opera North, Grand Theatre, 46 New Briggate, Leeds, Yorkshire, LS1 6NU, England.

**CURRAN, Alvin;** Composer and Performer; b. 13 Dec. 1938, Providence, Rhode Island, USA. *Education:* BA, Brown University, 1960; Studied composition with Ron Nelson (Brown) and Elliott Carter (Yale), Yale University, 1963. *Career:* Co-Founder, Musica Elettronica Viva Group, Rome, 1966; Solo performances in major festivals (new music), 1973–; Large-scale environmental works for chorus, orchestra, ship's horns and foghorns, 1980–; Milhaud Professor of Music Composition, Mills College, 1992–. *Compositions:* Songs and Views from the Magnetic Garden; Light Flowers, Dark Flowers; Canti Illuminati; For Cornelius; Maritime Rites, 1979–1992 (Music on Water); 1985 A Piece for Peace, 3 choruses, 3 speakers, 3 percussion, cello, violin, saxophone, 3 accordions, 1984; Electric Rags II, saxophone quartet, 1989; Notes from Underground/Floor Plan, sound installation, 1991; Animal Behaviour, solo performance live electronics, 1992; Schtyx, piano, violin, percussion, 1993; Inner Cities, 1994; The Twentieth Century, 1996; Endangered Species, 1996; Caged Notes, 1993–96; Erat Verbatim, 6 part sound work for radio, 1989–97; Pittura Fresca, violin concerto and small ensemble, 1997; Rose of Beans, double trio, 1998–99; Theme Park x 4, percussion quartet, 1998; Toto Donaueschingen, computer-generated sound installation in large Baroque Park, 1999. *Publications:* Maritime Rites, the book, 1984; Maritime Rites: The Lake, 1989; Music from the Centre of the Earth, 1994; Featured Composer in Musik Texte, 1994. *Honours:* National Endowment for the Arts Grants, 1977, 1983; Prix Italia for Radio Works, 1985–A Piece for Peace; DAAD Resident Composer in Berlin, 1986; Ars Acoustica International, 1989; Prix Italia (Special Award), 1988;

Fromm Foundation, 1998. *Address:* Mills College, Department of Music, Oakland, California 94613, USA.

**CURRY, Diane;** Singer (mezzo soprano); b. 26 Feb. 1942, Clifton Forge, Virginia, USA. *Career:* Sang at the City Opera, New York, from 1972, Spoleto Festival from 1975 and at Graz in 1977; Other European engagements at the Deutsche Oper Berlin (1984–88), Hamburg Staatsoper, Köln, Bonn, Brussels, Geneva, Marseille, Nice, Teatro di Bologna and Maggio Musicale di Firenze, Arena di Verona (Amneris); Teatro di Roma; Teatro La Fenice Venice and Théâtre du Châtelet, Paris; Returned to the USA at the Metropolitan, New York (Nurse in Die Frau ohne Schatten, 1990), San Francisco and Seattle, the Chicago Lyric Opera; Other roles include Ulrica, Azucena, Laura and Cieca in La Gioconda, Fricka, Waltraute, Brangaene, Herodias, Clytemnestra, Mère Marie in Dialogues des Carmelites; Additions to her repertoire in 1999 included: Erda in Das Rhinegold and Siegfried, the Old Prioress in Dialogues des Carmelites and La Principessa in Suor Angelica; Many concert appearances, notably the Mahler Symphonies and the Verdi Requiem; Recorded Verdi Requiem for Telarc. *Honours:* Grammy Award, Gramophone Award, 1988. *Address:* c/o Metropolitan Opera, Lincoln Center Plaza, New York, NY 10023, USA.

**CURTIN, Phyllis;** Singer (Soprano); b. 3 Dec. 1921, Clarksburg, West Virginia, USA. *Education:* BA, Wellesley College; Studied at Wellesley College with Olga Avierino; Opera study with Boris Goldovsky at New England Conservatory and Tanglewood. *Career:* Debut: With New England Opera Theater, 1946 as Countess in The Marriage of Figaro and Lady Billows in Albert Herring; Sang at New York City Opera from 1953, notably in Von Einem's Der Prozess, Salome and in the premieres of Floyd's Susannah and The Passion of Jonathan Wade; Also sang Cressida in Walton's Troilus and Cressida, Giannini's The Taming of The Shrew and Poulenc's Les Mamelles de Tirésias; Sante Fe in 1958 in premiere of Floyd's Wuthering Heights; Glyndebourne in 1959 as Donna Anna; Metropolitan Opera from 1961 as Fiordiligi, Rosalinde, Eva, Mozart's Countess, Violetta and Ellen Orford in Peter Grimes; New York concert performances of Pelléas et Mélisande, 1962; Guest appearances in Vienna, Buenos Aires, Frankfurt, Milan, Glasgow, Paris and Trieste; Other roles included: Salome and Alice Ford in Falstaff; Sang Rosine in the premiere of Milhaud's La Mère Coupable, Geneva, 1966; Ellen Orford at Edinburgh Festival, 1968; Retired from public singing in 1984; Teacher at Aspen School of Music and the Berkshire Music Center; Artist-in-Residence at Tanglewood, 1964–; Guest Teacher, Central Conservatory, Beijing, 1987 and Moscow Conservatory, 1989; Recitalist across USA, Canada, Australia, New Zealand and South America; Soloist with major orchestras of US and other countries; US premieres of Britten's War Requiem with Boston Symphony and Shostakovich's Symphony No. 14 with the Philadelphia Orchestra; Dean Emerita and Professor of Voice and Artistic Director at Opera Institute in Boston University School for the Arts; Head of Vocal Program at Tanglewood; mem, Formerly served on National Council of The Arts. *Honours:* Ambassador for The Arts by US Government. *Address:* 9 Seekonk Road, Great Barrington, MA 01230-1558, USA.

**CURTIS, Alan;** Harpsichordist, Conductor and Musicologist; b. 17 Nov. 1934, Mason, Michigan, USA. *Education:* BM, Michigan University, 1955; PhD, University of Illinois, 1963; Amsterdam with Gustav Leonhardt, 1957–59. *Career:* Joined Faculty of University of California at Berkeley, 1960; Professor, 1970–; Active as keyboard player and conductor in the USA and Europe; Productions of L'Incoronazione di Poppea, staged and designed by Filippo Sanjust, in Amsterdam, Brussels, Innsbruck, Spoleto and Venice; Handel's Ariodante at La Scala, 1980, Later productions in Innsbruck and Turin; Conducted Rameau's Dardanus at Basel, 1981; Il Sant'Alessio by Stefano Landi at Rome Opera, 1981; La Schiava Liberata by Jommelli for Netherlands Opera, 1982, and at the San Carlo, Naples, 1984; Cesti's Il Tito at Innsbruck, 1983, and Venice and Turin 1984; First production since 1707 of Handel's Rodrigo, Innsbruck, Madeira and Lisbon, 1984; Conducted a new production of Gluck's Armide, to open the restored Bibiena Theatre in Bologna, 1984; Gluck's Paride ed Elena at Vicenza, 1988; Conducted Cimarosa's Gli Orazi e i Curiazi at Rome, 1989, to mark the 200th anniversary of the French Revolution; Handel's Floridante with the Tafelmusik Baroque Orchestra at Toronto, 1990; Revival of Gli Orazi at Lisbon, 1990; Collector of early keyboard instruments by Martin Skowroneck. *Recordings:* Cavalli's Erismena, L'Incoronazione di Poppea, Handel's Admeto and Rodrigo, La Schiava Liberata, La Susanna by Stradella, Goldberg Variations by Bach, CPE Bach's Rondos nebst eine Fantasie for Fortepiano, Buova d'Antona by Traetta, Vivaldi's Montezuma 2006. *Publications:* Sweelinck's Keyboard Music: A Study of English Elements in Seventeenth Century Dutch Composition, 1969, 1972; Edition of Jommelli's La Schiava Liberata and L'Incoronazione di Poppea, Novello, 1990. *Current Management:* Music International, 13 Ardilaun Road, Highbury, London N5 2QR, England.

**CURTIS, Mark;** Singer (Tenor); b. 1958, Hertfordshire, England. *Education:* Studied at the Royal Northern College of Music and at the National Opera Studio; Italy with Maestro Campogalliani. *Career:* Appearances with Glyndebourne Touring Opera in Die Zauberflöte and as Fenton and Jacquino; At Covent Garden in Alceste, Pagliacci (Beppe), Manon Lescaut and Fidelio; Kent Opera as Don Ottavio and Monostatos and in King Priam and Carmen; With Opera North has sung The Steersman, Vasek, Stroh (Intermezzo), Don Basilio (Le nozze di Figaro) and Arv in the British premiere of Nielsen's Maskarade; English National Opera as Amenophis in Mosè, and Don Ottavio,

and in the world premiere of Birtwistle's The Mask of Orpheus, 1986; Other roles include Hylas in Les Troyens, the Madwoman in Curlew River and Nadir in Les Pêcheurs de Perles; Sang in the Mozart pasticcio The Jewel Box and King Priam (Hermes) for Opera North, 1991; Has also sung at Bath Abbey and the South Bank Halls and in Dublin, Brussels, Hanover, Berlin, Rome, Palermo, Seville, Hong Kong, Jerusalem, Helsinki and Edinburgh; Many concert appearances with English National Opera, Hilarion in Princess Ida and at Théâtre Royal de la Monnaie, Brussels, Der Soldat in world premiere of Philippe Boesmans's Reigen, 1993; English National Opera in King Priam (Hermes), 1995; Sang Goro in Butterfly for Opera North, 1996; Season 1997–98, sang M. Triquet in Eugene Onegin and Eumeus in The Return of Ulysses for Opera North; Nadir in The Pearl Fishers for English National Opera; Sang with Wiener Symphoniker in Vienna, Hamburg Philharmonic (L'Enfance du Christ), the Bamberg Symphoniker (Beethoven's 9th Symphony) and the Schwetzinger Festival (Beethoven's Missa Solemnis) under Roger Norrington; Sang Don Basilio in Le nozze di Figaro, Garsington Festival Opera, 1999; Goro in Opera Ireland's Madama Butterfly; Rev. Horace Adams in Tours production of Peter Grimes, France; Season 1999–2000 as Hermes in King Priam for ENO, Mozart's Basilio at Garsington and Goro in Butterfly at Dublin. *Recordings include:* Trabuco in La Forza del Destino and Yamadori in Madama Butterfly; Simpleton in Boris Godunov for Opera North conducted by Paul Daniel. *Address:* c/o Music International, 13 Ardilaun Road, Highbury, London N5 2QR, England.

**CURTIS-SMITH, Curtis;** Composer and Pianist; b. 9 Sept. 1941, Walla Walla, Washington, USA. *Education:* Studied at Northwest University, 1965; Composition with Bruno Maderna, Tanglewood, 1992. *Career:* Piano soloist and concerts, 1968–; Western Michigan University, 1968–. *Compositions:* 3 string quartets, 1964, 1965, 1980; Winter pieces for chamber orchestra, 1974; Belle du Jour for piano and orchestra, 1975; Music for handbells, 1977; Plays and Rimes for brass quintet, 1979; The Great American Symphony for orchestra, 1981; Songs and cantillations for guitar and orchestra, 1984; Float Wild Birds; Sleeping for orchestra, 1988; Gold Are My Flowers, cantata, 1992; African Laughter, sextet, 1994; Violin concerto, 1994. *Honours:* Koussevitsky prize, 1972. *Address:* c/o ASCAP, ASCAP Building, 1 Lincoln Plaza, New York, NY 10023, USA.

**CURTIS-VERNA, Mary;** Singer (Soprano); b. 9 May 1927, Salem, Massachusetts, USA. *Education:* Studied at Hollis College, Virginia and with Ettore Verna. *Career:* Debut: Teatro Lirico Milan, 1949 as Desdemona; Appearances in Vienna, Paris, Munich, Stuttgart and Florence; Returned to USA 1951 and sang in Philadelphia; San Francisco 1952, Aida and Donna Anna; New York City Opera 1954 as Donna Anna; La Scala Milan 1954 as Desdemona; Metropolitan Opera from 1957 as the Trovatore Leonora, Tosca, Amelia in Un Ballo in Maschera, Santuzza, Aida, Turandot, Elisabeth de Valois and Violetta; Sang Desdemona at Baltimore, 1969; Further engagements in Buenos Aires and at the Verona Arena. *Address:* c/o Metropolitan Opera, Lincoln Center, NY 10023, USA.

**CURZI, Cesare;** Singer (Tenor); b. 14 Oct. 1926, San Francisco, USA. *Education:* Studied privately. *Career:* Debut: San Francisco 1947 as Pinkerton; Sang in San Francisco and elsewhere in North America; Moved to Europe 1955 and appeared at opera houses in Kiel, Nuremberg and Frankfurt (Alfredo 1957); Salzburg Festival 1959, in Il Mondo della Luna by Haydn; Further engagements in Stuttgart, Hamburg, Berlin and Cologne; Maggio Musicale Florence, 1959 and 1973–74; Member of the Deutsche Oper am Rhein Düsseldorf from 1965 and sang at Nuremberg until 1986; Other roles included Rodolfo, Ferrando in Così fan tutte, Ernesto and the Duke of Mantua. *Recordings:* Rigoletto (Electrola); Eine Nacht in Venedig; Die Fledermaus. *Address:* c/o Deutsche Oper am Rhein, Heinrich-Heine Allee 16, 0-4000 Düsseldorf, Germany.

**CVEJIC, Biserka;** Singer (Mezzo-soprano); b. 5 Nov. 1923, Krilo-Jesenice, Split, Yugoslavia. *Education:* Studied at Belgrade Music Academy. *Career:* Debut: Belgrade Opera 1950, as Maddalena in Rigoletto; Sang at Belgrade 1954–60, notably as Charlotte in Werther and as Amneris on tour to Vienna 1959; Metropolitan Opera debut 1961, as Amneris; Vienna Staatsoper 1959–79, Zagreb Opera 1975–78; Further appearances at Covent Garden, Verona Arena, La Scala and Buenos Aires; Sang in Massenet's Marie-Magdalene at Paris, 1977; Other roles have included Eboli, Azucena, Carmen and Delilah; Retired 1990. *Recordings:* Eugene Onegin, The Queen of Spades, Prince Igor, Boris Godunov, The Snow Maiden; War and Peace; Zigeunerbaron. *Address:* c/o Vienna Staatsoper, Opernring 2, Vienna, Austria.

**CYNAN JONES, Eldrydd;** Welsh singer (soprano); b. 1965. *Career:* concerts and recitals throughout Europe, with opera in Wales and England; repertory includes Handel's Giulio Cesare, Turandot and Adriana Lecouvreur; also sings songs by Strauss and Duparc; contestant at the 1995 Cardiff Singer of the World Competition.

**CZAPO, Eva;** Singer (Soprano) and Teacher; b. Nov. 1944, Budapest, Hungary. *Education:* Studied at Bartók Conservatory, Budapest, in Basel and with Elsa Cavelti. *Career:* Sang with Trier Opera 1968–69; Guest appearances in concert and opera at Basel, Zürich, Lucca, 1981, Bologna and Spoleto 1981; Appearances at the Salzburg, Lausanne, Lucerne, Lugano, Schwetzingen, Helsinki and Granada festivals; Concert repertoire has included Bach's B minor Mass, Beethoven's Ninth, Messiah, Elijah and St Paul by Mendelssohn, Haydn's Schöpfung and Jahreszeiten, Mozart's Requiem and C minor Mass and works by Schoenberg, Nono, Dallapiccola,

Stravinsky, Szymanowski, Messiaen and Hindemith; Further engagements at Berlin, Hamburg, Munich, Milan, Rome, Turin, Parma and Lisbon; Voice Teacher at Basel and Founder of the Divertimento Vocale, Basel, 1987. *Recordings:* Bach Cantatas and Cavalieri's Rappresentazione di anima e di corpo; Schoenberg's Moses und Aron, conducted by Gielen; Schubert Masses; Davidde Penitente by Mozart and Carissimi's Dives malus. *Address:* c/o Musik-Akademie der Stadt Basel, Leonhardsstrasse 6, 4501 Basel, Switzerland.

**CZYZ, Henryk;** Conductor and Composer; b. 16 June 1923, Grudzjdz, Poland; m. Halina Buczacka. *Education:* Studied Law and Philosophy in Torun; Conducting and Composition at the Music High School, Poznan. *Career:* Conducting debut with Polish National Radio Orchestra, 1948; Art Director and Chief Conductor, Philharmonic Orchestra of Łódź, 1957–60 and 1974–80 and Kraków, 1964–68; Gave triple bill of works by Debussy, Honegger and Stravinsky at the Warsaw Opera in 1962; Conducted the premieres of Penderecki'sStLuke Passion (Munster 1966) and The Devils of Loudun (Hamburg 1969); US debut 1973, with the Minnesota Orchestra; Conducted the Düsseldorf Orchestra, 1971–74; Professor at Warsaw Academy, 1980–95. *Compositions:* Etude for orchestra, 1949; Symphonic Variations, 1952; Comic Opera, The Dog Lover's Dilemma, 1967; Ingrid Bartsch, musical, 1982. *Recordings include:* St Luke Passion, Dies Irae and other works by Penderecki, Szymanowski's 2nd Symphony and excerpts from King Roger; Schumann's Das Paradies und die Peri. *Publications:* Writer, 7 books edited, 1973–85; Editor, 3 biographical books, 1993, 1995. *Address:* Moliera 2-21, Warsaw 00076, Poland.

# D

**DA SILVA, Miguel;** Violist; b. 1960, France. *Education:* Studied at the Paris Conservatoire with Jean-Claude Pennetier and with members of the Amadeus and Alban Berg Quartets. *Career:* Member of the Ysaÿe String Quartet from 1984; Many concert performances in France, Europe, America and the Far East; Festival engagements at Salzburg, Tivoli (Copenhagen), Bergen, Lockenhaus, Barcelona and Stresa; Many appearances in Italy, notably with the 'Haydn' Quartets of Mozart; Tours of Japan and the USA 1990 and 1992. *Recordings:* Mozart Quartet K421 and Quintet K516 (Harmonia Mundi); Ravel, Debussy and Mendelssohn Quartets (Decca). *Honours:* Grand Prix Evian International String Quartet Competition, May 1988, special prizes for best performances of a Mozart quartet, the Debussy quartet and a contemporary work; 2nd Prize, Portsmouth International String Quartet Competition, 1988. *Address:* c/o 12/13 Richmond Buildings, Dean Street, London W1V 5 AF, England.

**D'ACCONE, Frank Anthony,** BMus, MMus, MA, PhD; musicologist and academic; b. 13 June 1931, Somerville, MA, USA. *Education:* Boston University, Harvard University; studied with Karl Geiringer, Gardner Read, Nino Pirrotta, A. Tillman Merritt and Walter Piston. *Career:* Assistant, Associate, Professor of Music, State University of New York, Buffalo, 1960–68; Visiting Professor, 1965–66, Professor of Music, 1968–, University of California, Los Angeles; Editor, Music of the Florentine Renaissance, Corpus Mensurabilis Musicae series XXXII, 1966–; mem. American Musicological Soc. *Publications:* Alessandro Scarlatti's Gli equivoci nel sembiante: The History of a Baroque Opera, 1985; The Civic Muse: Music and Musicians in Siena during the Middle Ages and the Renaissance, 1997; contrib. articles in many journals and publications including The New Grove Dictionary of Music and Musicians. *Honours:* Guggenheim Fellowship, 1980–81; International Galileo Galilei Prize of the Rotary Club of Italy, 1997. *Address:* c/o Music Department, University of California, Los Angeles, CA 90024, USA.

**DADÁK, Jaromír;** Composer and Conductor; b. 30 May 1930, Znojmo, Czechoslovakia; m. Ludmila Zapletalová; one s. three d. *Education:* Janáček Acad. of Art, Brno, 1956. *Career:* Conductor, Ostrava Radio Orchestra, 1960–63, Brno Radio Orchestra, 1953–90, Bratislava Radio Orchestra, 1982–91; Sec., Czechoslovak Composer Federation, 1967–69; Dir, Olomouc State Symphony Orchestra, 1969–71; mem., Society of Czech Composers (pres. 1993–98), Asscn of Music Artists and Scientists, Society of Czech Composers, Society for New Music, Přítomnost (founder mem.). *Compositions:* Orchestral: Never More for symphony orchestra, 1959; Concerto-Symphony for piano and symphony orchestra, 1959; Concertino for dulcimer and orchestra, 1965; Concerto for piano 4-hands and symphony orchestra, 1972; Concerto for alto (viola) and small orchestra, 1976; Sonata corta for string orchestra, 1977; Concerto for tuba and small orchestra, 1982; Four Scanty Honours for bassoon and string orchestra, 1991; Ludi for string quartet and symphony orchestra, 1991; Benedictum for symphony orchestra, 1996; Chamber music: Three studies for piano 4-hands and percussions, 1965; Partita for violin, clarinet and piano, 1965; Four concert studies for dulcimer, 1967; Per aspera ad astra for organ, 1971; Four miniatures for dulcimer, 1975; Musica gioccosa for violin, clarinet, violoncello and piano, 1980; Sonata for dulcimer, 1980; Concerto for alto (with piano), 1983; Sonata for violin and piano, 1989; Sonata for violoncello, 1992; Transformations for hautboy, clarinet, bassoon and piano, 1994; Sonata for piano, 1994; Double-sonata for violoncello and piano, 1995; Capriccio for piano, 1997; Ballad for piano, 1998; Small terzet for two for basclarinet and piano with percussions, 1998; Exclamatio ad astra for organ, 2000. *Publications:* Our Folk Song, 1991. *Honours:* National Prize, 1960; CMF Prize, Prague, 1972; Grand Prix Radio Bratislava, 1981. *Address:* Kubelíkova 43, 130 00, Prague 3, Czech Republic (home). *E-mail:* jdadak@scznam.cz (home).

**DAGGETT, Philip;** Singer (Tenor); b. 1962, Chesterfield, England. *Education:* Studied in Chesterfield and at Guildhall School of Music, 1985–. *Career:* Songman at York Minster, 1981–85; Concert appearances include Bach's Actus Tragicus in Paris and the St John Passion throughout Spain; Has sung in Mozart's C Minor Mass and Requiem; Mendelssohn's Lobgesang (Queen Elizabeth Hall debut) and Elijah; Britten's Cantata Misericordium and St Nicolas; Operatic roles include Paris in La Belle Hélène, Beppe in Pagliacci and Mozart's Ferrando; Premiere of Birtwistle's Gawain at Covent Garden, May 1991; Also sings Count Almaviva in Il Barbiere di Siviglia; Sang Tamino with Opera Lirica at the Holland Park Theatre, 1992; Premiere of Maxwell Davies's The Doctor of Myddfai, 1996; Sang Boyar in Boris Godunov for Welsh National Opera, 1998. *Recordings include:* The Fairy Queen with Harry Christophers and The Sixteen; A Festal Mass at the Imperial Court of Vienna and Charpentier's Vespers for the Feast of St Louis with the Yorkshire Baroque Soloists and Peter Seymour. *Address:* c/o Simply Singers, 23 Freke Road, London SW11 5PU, England.

**DAHL, Tracy;** Singer (Soprano); b. 1964, Winnipeg, Manitoba, Canada. *Education:* Studied with the Merola Opera Program. *Career:* Sang in the USA from 1986, notably as Offenbach's Eurydice at Houston, Olympia at Chicago (1987), Serpetta in La Finta Giardiniera at St Louis (1988) and Oscar in Ballo in Maschera at San Francisco (1990); Also appeared as Oscar at the New York Metropolitan, 1990, returning 1991 in the premiere of The Ghosts of Versailles by Corigliano (repeated, 1995); Toronto Opera, 1992, as Nannetta, Sophie in

Werther and Zerbinetta, 1995; Season 1999–2000 as Verdi's Oscar and as Lucia di Lammermoor, Servilia in La Clemenza di Tito at New York City Opera. *Address:* c/o Metropolitan Opera, Lincoln Center, New York, NY 10023, USA.

**DAHLBERG, Stefan;** Singer (Tenor); b. 3 May 1955, Sweden. *Education:* Studied at the State Academy of Music and the State College of Musical Drama in Stockholm. *Career:* Concerts and Broadcasts throughout Scandinavia; Operatic roles include Rustighello in Lucrezia Borgia by Donizetti, Tamino, Beppe, Count Almaviva, King Charles in The Maid of Orleans by Tchaikovsky and Sextus in Giulio Cesare; Royal Opera Stockholm as Tamino, Sextus, Ferrando and Don Ottavio; Drottningholm 1987, as Titus in La Clemenza di Tito; Visited Brighton with the Drottningholm Company, 1987; Season 1988–89 with concert performance of Haydn's Armida in Amsterdam; Grand Théâtre Geneva as Jacquino in Fidelio, conducted by Jeffrey Tate; Gounod's Faust at the Stockholm Opera; Concertgebouw Amsterdam, 1989, as Ubaldo in Rossini's Armida; Drottningholm, 1989, as Tamino; Sang Calaf in Busoni's Turandot at Lyon, 1992; Leading tenor role of Vicente Martin y Soler's Una Cosa Rara; Alfredo in Verdi's La Traviata, Stockholm Royal Opera, 1993; Haydn's Orlando at Drottningholm, 1994; Concert repertoire includes Suter's Der Abwesende Gott, Die Schöpfung by Haydn, Le Roi David by Honegger, Messiah, Puccini's Messa di Gloria and works by Thomas Jernefelt and Sven-David Sandström. *Recordings:* Videos of La Clemenza di Tito, Die Zauberflöte and Don Giovanni, from Drottningholm. *Address:* c/o Drottningholms Slottstheater, PO Box 27050, 10251 Stockholm, Sweden.

**DAIKEN, Melanie (Ruth);** Composer; b. 27 July 1945, London, England. *Education:* Studied at the Royal Academy and at the Paris Conservatoire with Loriod and Messiaen. *Career:* Deputy Head of Composition at the Royal Academy from 1986. *Compositions include:* Operas: Eusebius, 1968, and Mayakovsky and the Sun, Edinburgh, 1971; Viola Sonata, 1978; Attica for Orchestra, 1980; Requiem for Piano, 1983; Der Gärtner for 13 Solo Strings and Piano, 1988; Song settings of poems by Lorca, Beckett, Trakl and Baudelaire. *Address:* c/o PRS Ltd, 29–33 Berners Street, London W1P 4AA, England.

**DALAYMAN, Katarina;** Swedish singer (soprano); b. 1968. *Education:* Stockholm Royal Coll. of Music. *Career:* debut, Stockholm Royal Opera 1991, as Amelia in Simon Boccanegra; Stuttgart Opera from 1993, as Marie in Wozzeck, Desdemona, Eva in Die Meistersinger and Elisabeth in Tannhäuser 1997; further appearances as Mimi and Marietta in Die tote Stadt at Stockholm, Strauss's Ariadne at the Brussels Opera 1997, Marie at the Maggio Musicale, Florence 1998; season 1998–99 with Parisian debut at the Opéra Nat. as Marie; season 1999–2000 included Ariadne auf Naxos, Tannhäuser and The Queen of Spades in Munich, Dr Faustus at the Met and the Salzburg Festival, Bluebeard's Castle at the Royal Opera House, Covent Garden; concerts include Mahler's 8th Symphony with the London Symphony Orchestra, Sibelius's Kullervo Symphony, under Colin Davis, and Penderecki's Requiem, conducted by the composer; Wagnerian Gala Evening in San Diego and La Damnation de Faust with the Munich Philharmonic and James Levine 1999; appeared with the London Symphony Orchestra and Simon Rattle in concert performances of Ariadne auf Naxos 2000; season 2001–02 included Wozzeck at the Metropolitan Opera, New York and the Royal Opera House, Covent Garden; Brangäne (Tristan and Isolde) at the Met; Ariadne and Kundry (Parsifal) at the Paris Opéra Bastille; Die Walküre and Lady Macbeth at Covent Garden; Tannhäuser in Brussels; sang title role in Shostakovich's Lady Macbeth of Mtsensk at Covent Garden 2003–04; Pique Dame and Walküre at The Met 2004; Tosca in Stockholm 2004; Tannhauser in Munich 2004. *Current Management:* Artistsekratariat Ulf Törnqvist, Sankt Eriksgatan 100, 2 tr, 1133 31 Stockholm, Sweden.

**DALBAVIE, Marc-André;** French composer; b. 10 Feb. 1961, Neuilly-sur-Seine. *Education:* Conservatoire national supérieur de musique, Paris. *Career:* researcher, IRCAM 1985–90; worked in Berlin 1992–93, at the Medici Villa, Rome 1995–96; Prof. of Orchestration, Paris Conservatoire 1996–; composer-in-residence, Cleveland Orchestra. *Compositions include:* Les Miroirs transparents for orchestra 1985, Diadèmes for solo viola, electronics and instrumental ensemble 1986, Impressions, mouvements (oratorio) 1989, Logos cycle (including Instances 1991, Seuils 1991), Sextuor 1992–93, In Advance of the Broken Time... 1994, Concertino à une pèce du XVIIème siècle for Baroque orchestra 1994, Offertoire for male choir and orchestra 1995, Concerto pour violon 1995–96, Tactus for orchestra 1996, Non-Lieu for women's choir and instrumental ensemble 1997, Color for orchestra 2001, Palimpseste 2002. *Recordings:* Les Paradis mécaniques, Diadèmes and seuils, (Ensemble Intercontemporain, Boulez). *Address:* c/o Conservatoire National Supérieur de Musique, 209 avenue Jean Jaurès, 75019 Paris, France.

**DALBERG, Evelyn;** Singer (Mezzo-Soprano); b. 23 May 1939, Leipzig, Germany. *Education:* Studied with Parry Jones at Guildhall School of Music, Annelies Kupper in Munich and with her father, Frederick Dalberg, at Cape Town and Mannheim. *Career:* Debut: Koblenz 1964, as Venus in Tannhäuser; Sang at various provincial German Opera Houses and in South Africa, notably Cape Town and Johannesburg; Other roles have included Verdi's Ulrica, Amneris, Eboli and Mistress Quickly, Nancy in Martha, Giulietta in Les Contes d'Hoffmann, Judith in Bluebeard's Castle, the Witch in Hansel and

Gretel and Prince Orlofsky in Die Fledermaus. *Address:* c/o Johannesburg Operatic and Dramatic Society, PO Box 7010, Johannesburg 2000, Transvaal, South Africa.

**DALBERTO, Michel;** French pianist; b. 2 June 1955, Paris; s. of Jean Dalberto and Paulette Girard-Dalberto. *Education:* Lycée Claude Bernard, Lycée Racine, Conservatoire National Supérieur de Musique, Paris. *Career:* prin. teachers at Conservatoire: Vlado Perlemuter, Jean Hubeau; started professional career 1975; concerts in maj. musical centres and at int. festivals; Artistic Dir Festival des Arcs 1991–; Pres. of the Jury Clara Haskil Competition 1991–. *Recordings:* albums: Schubert Piano Music (complete recordings), French Mélodies (with Barbara Hendricks), Debussy Preludes, Mozart Concerti. *Honours:* Chevalier Ordre nat. du Mérite; Clara Haskil Prize 1975; First Prize Leeds Int. Pianoforte Competition 1978; Acad. Charles Cros Award 1980 and Acad. Disque Français Award 1984 for recordings; Diapason d'Or Award for Best Concerto Recording 1991. *Address:* c/o IMG Artists, Lovell House, 616 Chiswick High Road, London, W4 5RX, England. *E-mail:* knaish@imgworld.com (office).

**DALBY, Martin;** Composer; b. 25 April 1942, Aberdeen, Scotland. *Education:* Studied at the Royal College of Music from 1960, with Herbert Howells (composition) and Frederick Riddle (viola); Further study in Italy. *Career:* BBC Music Producer in London, 1965–71; Cramb Research Fellow in Composition at Glasgow University, 1972; Head of Music, BBC Scotland, 1972–93; Chairman Composers' Guild of Great Britain, 1995–98; mem, PRS; MCPS; ISM; British Academy of Composers and Songwriters. *Compositions:* Several compositions for cello, piano and string instruments 1965–79; More recent compositions include: Man Walking, octet for wind and strings, 1980; Antoinette Alone for mezzo and piano, 1980; Chamber Symphony, 1982; Nozze di Primavera for orchestra, 1984; A Plain Man's Hammer for symphonic wind ensemble, 1984; Piano Sonata No. 1, 1985; De Patre ex Filio octet for wind and strings, 1988; Piano Sonata No. 2, 1989; The Mary Bean for orchestra, 1991; Path for brass band, 1992; Sarabande for St Kevin, for organ, 1992, Butterfly Music for brass quintet, 1993; Variations for a Fair Maid of Perth for orchestra, 1993; Cantata: John Clare's Vision for soprano and strings, 1993; The White Maa for orchestra, 1994; String Quartet, 1995; Piano Sonata No. 3, 1998; A Wheen in Doric for symphony orchestra, 2000. *Honours:* Sony Gold Award for Best Classical Music Programme, 1993; BASCA Gold Badge Award, 1998. *Current Management:* Scottish Music Information Centre, Glasgow; Novello and Co, London. *Address:* 23 Muirpark Way, Drymen, Glasgow G63 0DX, Scotland.

**DALE, Clamma;** Singer (Soprano); b. 4 July 1948, Chester, Pennsylvania, USA. *Education:* BMus 1970, MS 1975, Juilliard School, New York; Studied Voice, Philadelphia Settlement Music School. *Career:* Debut: Operatic debut as Antonia, Les Contes d'Hoffman, New York City Opera, 1975; Sang with numerous Opera Companies; Toured as Concert Singer; Roles include: Pamina, Countess Almaviva, Nedda, Musetta, Gershwin's Bess at the Theater des Westens, Berlin, 1988; Deutsche Oper Berlin, 1989, as Liù in Turandot. *Recordings:* For Deutsche Grammophon; RCA. *Address:* c/o New York City Opera, Lincoln Center, New York, NY 10023, USA.

**DALE, Laurence;** Singer (Tenor); b. 10 Sept. 1957, Pyecombe, Sussex. *Education:* Studied at the Guildhall School of Music, 1976–80 and at the Mozarteum, Salzburg. *Career:* Debut: With English National Opera as Camille in The Merry Widow, 1981; Covent Garden debut 1982, as Second Noble in Lohengrin; Sang Don José in Peter Brook's La Tragédie de Carmen in Paris, 1981 and on Broadway, 1983; in 1983 sang Gounod's Romeo at Basle and Ramiro at Glyndebourne; Visited Los Angeles with the Royal Opera, 1984, singing Pong in Turandot; English National Opera 1983, as Monteverdi's Orfeo; For Welsh National Opera has sung Mozart's Ottavio and Ferrando and Eisenstein in Die Fledermaus; With Opera North as Mozart's Tamino and Belmonte and Jenik in The Bartered Bride; Further appearances in Lyon, Paris, Hamburg, Amsterdam, Aix, Geneva, Brussels (Tamino and Idomeneo) and Zürich; Other roles include Tchaikovsky's Lensky, Jacquino in Fidelio, Méhul's Joseph and Gonzalve in L'Heure Espagnole; Concert engagements include Mozart's C Minor Mass and Haydn's St Cecilia Mass with the London Philharmonic; Bach's Christmas Oratorio with the Los Angeles Philharmonic; Britten's Spring Symphony at the Festival Hall; The Dream of Gerontius and Liszt's Faust Symphony at the Brighton Festival; Messiah in Vienna, Stravinsky's Pulcinella and Rossini's Stabat Mater; Appearances on television in the United Kingdom and Europe; On 27 January 1991 sang Tamino in Die Zauberflöte at the Landestheater Salzburg, to inaugurate the Mozart Bicentenary; Season 1991/92 as Ferrando at Stuttgart and Belfiore in La Finta Giardiniera at the Salzburg Festival; Sang Don Ottavio at Genoa, 1993; Pelléas at Brussels, 1996; Season 1999 as Chevalier de la Force in Les Dialogues des Carmélites at the London Prom concerts; Season 1999–2000 as Monteverdi's Orfeo in Amsterdam and Chicago. *Recordings:* La Tragédie de Carmen; Videos of Princess Ida, Die Zauberflöte from Aix and Cenerentola from Glyndebourne; Mozart's C Minor Mass. *Address:* c/o Théâtre Royal de la Monnaie, 4 rue Leopold, B–1000 Brussels, Belgium.

**DALIS, Irene,** AB, MS, MA; American singer (mezzo-soprano) and professor of music; *General Director, Opera San Jose;* b. 8 Oct. 1925, San Jose, CA; m. George Loinaz 1957; one d. *Education:* San Jose State University, Columbia University Teachers' College, studied voice with Edyth Walker in New York, Paul Althouse, Otto Mueller in Milan, Italy. *Career:* debut with Berlin State Opera 1955; Metropolitan Opera, New York 1957; leading dramatic mezzo-soprano, Metropolitan Opera 1957–77 as Eboli, Amneris, Santuzza, Azucena, Lady Macbeth and Dalila, 22 roles in 232 performances; first US born Kundry to open Bayreuth Festival 1963; opened the Met opera season as Amneris in Aida 1963; premiered Dello Joio's Opera, Blood Moon 1961 and Henderson's Opera, Medea 1972; sang The Nurse in Die Frau ohne Schatten at Sadler's Wells Theatre 1966; Prof. of Music, San Jose State Univ. 1977–2004; founder and Gen. Dir, Opera San Jose 1984–. *Honours:* Fulbright Scholar 1951, Distinguished Service Award Columbia University 1961, Wagner Medallion 1963, Tower Award San Jose State University 1974, California Public Educators Hall of Fame 1985, Award of Merit People of the City of San Francisco, Honoured Citizen of San Jose 1986, Hon. DMus (Santa Clara Univ.) 1987, Hon. DFA (California State Univ.) 1999. *Address:* Opera San Jose, 2149 Paragon Drive, San Jose, CA 95131, USA (office). *Telephone:* (408) 437-4470 (office). *Fax:* (408) 437-4455 (office). *E-mail:* dalis@operasj.org (office). *Website:* www.operasj.org (office).

**DALLAPOZZA, Adolf;** Singer (Tenor); b. 14 April 1940, Bozen, Austria. *Education:* Studied with Elisabeth Rado in Vienna. *Career:* Sang in the chorus of the Vienna Volksoper while a student; Solo debut 1962, as Ernesto in Don Pasquale; Sang at the Volksoper until 1972, and guested in Munich, Hamburg, Milan, Brussels and Cologne; Bregenz Festival, 1972–84; Many roles in works by Mozart, Italian Opera and in Operas of the Baroque; Many appearances in Operettas; Wilhelm Meister in Mignon at the Vienna Volksoper, 1988; Season 1990 in Strauss's Intermezzo at Bologna and as Lensky at the Volksoper; Sang Dr Caius in Falstaff at the Volksoper, 2000. *Recordings:* Die Fledermaus, Der Vogelhändler; Idomeneo; Intermezzo; Fidelio; Die Meistersinger; Königskinder by Humperdinck. *Address:* c/o Volksoper, Währingerstrasse 78, 1090 Vienna, Austria.

**DALLEY, John;** Violinist; b. 1 June 1935, Madison, Wisconsin, USA. *Education:* Studied at Curtis Institute, Philadelphia, with Ivan Galamian. *Career:* Member of the Oberlin Quartet, formerly teacher at Oberlin Conservatory, Performed in Chamber Music with Rudolf Serkin at the Marlboro Festival and prompted by Alexander Schneider to co-found the Guarneri String Quartet, 1984; Many tours in America and Europe, notably appearances at the Spoleto Festival, 1965, to Paris with Arthur Rubinstein and London 1970, in the complete quartets of Beethoven; Noted for performances of the Viennese Classics, and works by Walton, Bartók and Stravinsky; Season 1987–88 included tour of Japan and concerts at St John's Smith Square and the Queen Elizabeth Hall, London; On faculty of the Curtis Institute, Philadelphia, and at the University of Maryland. *Recordings:* Mozart's Quartets dedicated to Haydn; Complete Quartets of Beethoven; With Arthur Rubinstein, Piano Quintets of Schumann, Dvořák and Brahms; Piano Quartets by Fauré and Brahms. *Honours:* Edison Award for Beethoven recordings 1971. *Current Management:* Ingpen & Williams Ltd, 7 St George's Court, 131 Putney Bridge Road, London, SW15 2PA, England.

**DALL'OLIO, Gabriella;** Harpist; b. 7 May 1965, Bologna, Italy. *Education:* Harp Studies, Conservatories of Bologna and Verona, with Anna Loro, Diploma with Honours, 1978–87; Graduated, honours, Liceo Scientifico, Bologna, 1984; Masterclasses with Pierre Jamet, Jacqueline Borot and Fabrice Pierre in Italy and France, 1986–90; Ecole Normale Supérieure de Paris with Fabrice Pierre (harp) and Michael Hentz (chamber music), Diplôme Supérieur de Harpe and Diplôme Supérieur de Musique de Chambre, 1988–90; Meisterklassdiplom, Hochschüle für Musik, Würzburg, 1993–94. *Career:* Recitals and solo appearances with orchestras and chamber music ensembles throughout Europe and The Middle East; Live recordings on radio and television in Europe; Contemporary music workshops; Appearances with several leading chamber ensembles including Kontraste and Holst Singers; Regular appearances as Guest Principal Harpist with numerous orchestras since 1987 including Chamber Orchestra of Europe, BBC Symphony and Concert Orchestras, Royal Opera House, Bavarian Radio Symphony, English Chamber Orchestra and numerous regional and festival orchestras; Worked under many leading conductors; Harp Teacher, Trinity College of Music, London. *Recordings include:* Tema y Variaciones by Joaquin Turina; Two Recitals for Harp with works including Rossini, Handel, Fauré, Bach, Britten, Ginastera, Hindemith, and Roussel; Donatoni; Jean Francaix; Wandering Winds, flute and harp works with Wissam Boustany; Chamber Music Works by Marek; Harp Concerto by Villa-Lobos. *Honours:* Victor Salvi Competition, Italy; Scholarships from French and German Governments; Prizes, National Competitions in Alessandria and Latina, Italy. *Address:* 16 Elspeth Road, Wembley, Middlesex, HA0 2BW. *Telephone:* (20) 8900-0593. *Fax:* (20) 8900-0593. *E-mail:* gabrielladallolio@hotmail.com.

**DALTON, Andrew;** Singer (Countertenor); b. 29 Sept. 1950, Melbourne, Australia. *Education:* Studied in Brisbane. *Career:* Debut: Sang at Vadstena, Sweden in Provenzale's La Stellidaura vendicata; Has sung in Baroque Opera at Venice, Innsbruck, Munich, Berne and Amsterdam; Appeared with Scottish Opera in Cavalli's Egisto and at the 1987 Buxton Festival as Fernando in Conti's Don Chisciotte in Sierra Morena; Season 1988–89 in Jommelli's Fetonte at La Scala, Milan, in Monteverdi's Ulisse with Opera de Lausanne at Mézières, and as Apollo in Death in Venice with Australian Opera at Sydney; Engagements in Germany and Switzerland as Britten's Oberon, and has sung in Monteverdi's Orfeo, Handel's Agrippina and Ariodante, and Jommelli's La Schiava Liberata; Sang in Purcell's Indian Queen at the Barossa Festival, Australia, 1995. *Address:* Australian Opera, Sydney Opera House, New South Wales, Australia.

**DAM-JENSEN, Inger;** Danish singer (soprano); b. 13 March 1964, Copenhagen; m. Morten Ernst Lassen. *Education:* Royal Danish Acad. of Music, Danish Opera School, studied with Kirsten Buhl Møller. *Career:* started career 1992, winner Cardiff Singer of the World Competition 1993; roles include Zdenka (Arabella), Ophelia (Hamlet), Norina (Don Pasquale), Sophie (Der Rosenkavalier), Adina (L'elisir d'amore), Susanna (Le Nozze di Figaro), Musetta (La Bohème), Gilda (Rigoletto), Cleopatra (Giulio Cesare), Despina (Così fan Tutte), Lisa (La Sonnambula), Blöndchen (Die Entführung aus dem Serail), Sifare (Mitridate); concert appearances with numerous orchestras, including Danish Radio Symphony, New York Philharmonic, Berlin Philharmonic, Czech Philharmonic and Gabrieli Consort; performed closing scene from Strauss' Daphne, London Proms 1999; has performed at Edin. Festival. *Recordings:* Mahler's Fourth Symphony, Grieg's Peer Gynt, Brahms' Ein Deutsches Requiem. *Current Management:* Harrison/Parrott Ltd, 12 Penzance Place, London, W11 4PA, England. *Telephone:* (20) 7229-9166. *Fax:* (20) 7221-5042. *Website:* www.harrisonparrott.com. *E-mail:* inger@danlassen.dk.

**DAMARATI, Luciano;** Composer, Conductor and Organist; b. 6 Feb. 1942, Lucca, Italy. *Education:* Diplomas: Piano, 1965; Composition, 1970; Organ, 1971; Orchestral Conducting, 1975; Studies: Organ with Alessandro Esposito and Fernando Germani; Orchestral Conducting with Franco Ferrara; Choral Conducting with Nino Antonellini; Musicology at Chigiana Academy of Music, Siena. *Career:* Many concerts as Organist and Orchestral Conductor; Broadcasts as Composer, Orchestra Conductor and Choir Conductor on Italian Radio and Television; mem, Italian Society of Musicology. *Compositions:* Impressioni (viola and piano), 1968; Fuga (organ), 1970; Preludio (organ), 1978; Immagini (piano), 1980; Contrasti (piano), 1980; Preghiera semplice (voice, choir and orchestra), 1986; I due fanciulli (voice and piano), 1986; Inno di lode a Dio (voice, choir of mixed voices, violin and organ), 1988; Le Ciaramelle (voice, violin and piano), 1988; La voce (voice, violin and piano), 1989; A Silvia (voice and piano), 1991; Mottettone (choir of mixed voices, 2 trumpets, trombone, tam-tam, kettledrums and organ), 1995. *Contributions:* La Provincia di Lucca, 1974; Actum Luce, 1980; Rivista di Archeologia Storia e Costume. *Honours:* 2nd Prize for Composition, Rodolfo del Corona, Leghorn. *Address:* Piazza S Francesco 14, 55100 Lucca, Italy.

**DAMASE, Jean-Michel;** Composer and Pianist; b. 27 Jan. 1928, Bordeaux, France. *Education:* Conservatoire National Superieur de Paris. *Career:* US debut 1954, as Pianist and Composer in a New York Concert. *Compositions:* Quintet for Flute, Harp and String Trio, 1947; Interludes for Orchestra, 1948; Rhapsody for Oboe and String Orchestra, 1948; Trio for Flute, Harp and Cello, 1949; Piano Concerto, 1950; Ballet La Croqueuse de Diamants, 1950; Violin Concerto, 1956; La Tendre Eleonore, Opéra-Bouffe, Marseilles, 1962; Colombe, Comedie Lyrique, Bordeaux, 1961; Eugene Le Mysterieux, Feuilleton Musical, Paris, 1964; Madame de Roman, Musical, Monte Carlo, 1970; Eurydice, Comédie Lyrique, Bordeaux, 1972; L'heritiere, Opera in 4 Acts after Washington Square by Henry James, Nancy, 1974; Quartet for Flute, Clarinet and Piano, 1992; Concerto for Flute and Orchestra, 1993; Variations, Mozart: for Piano and Orchestra, 1994; Four Facettes for flute and guitar, 1997. *Honours:* Prix de Rome, 1947. *Address:* c/o PRS Ltd, Member Registration, 29–33 Berners Street, London W1P 4AA, England.

**DAMIANI, Davide;** Singer (Baritone); b. 1966, Pesaro, Italy. *Career:* Recital, concert and opera appearances throughout Italy and Europe; Contestant at the 1995 Cardiff Singer of the World Competition; Repertory includes Le nozze di Figaro and Don Carlo, Lieder by Strauss and Schumann; Seasons 1995–99 as house-baritone at the Vienna State Opera; Welsh National Opera 1996, as Don Giovanni; Season 2000–01 as Don Giovanni at Toronto and Britten's Tarquinius at Florence. *Address:* c/o Miss Elin de Kat, Stage Door Management, Via Giardini 941/2, 41040 Saliceta San Giuliano (Modena), Italy.

**DAMISCH-KUSTERER, Sieglinde;** Singer (Soprano); b. 1951, Amsterdam, Netherlands. *Education:* Studied at the Salzburg Mozarteum and in Vienna with Hilde Konetzni. *Career:* Sang at the Vienna Staatsoper from 1979, Salzburg Festival, 1981 (Das Buch mit sieben Siegeln by Schmidt); Further engagements at Augsburg and elsewhere in Germany as Fiordiligi, Elisabeth de Valois, Tatiana, Jenůfa, Mimi and Pamina; Sang Jenůfa at Mönchengladbach, 1991; Frequent concert appearances. *Address:* c/o St ädtische Buhnen Augsburg, Kasernstrasse 4–6, Pf 111949, Augsburg, Germany.

**DAMONTE, Magali;** Singer (Mezzo-Soprano); b. 30 June 1960, Marseilles, France. *Education:* Studied in Marseilles. *Career:* Debut: Sang Zulma in L'Italiana in Algeri at Marseilles in 1978; Many appearances in France with operas by Rossini, Cimarosa and Gounod; Paris Opéra 1980, as Iphise in Rameau's Dardanus; Aix-en-Provence Festival from 1981, as Rosina, Cenerentola and Isaura in Tancredi; At the Opéra de Lyon has sung Aloès in L' Etoile (visit with the company to the Edinburgh Festival, 1985); Marseilles 1987, as Fidalma in Il Matrimonio Segreto; Théâtre des Champs Elysées, Paris 1989, as Hedwige in Guillaume Tell; Other Rossini roles include Isabella, Ragonde (Le Comte Ory) and Marie (Moise); Sang Carmen at Covent Garden, 1994, and at Vancouver, 1996. *Recordings:* L'Etoile, conducted by John Eliot Gardiner. *Address:* c/o Opéra de Lyon, 9 Quai Jean Moulin, 89001, France.

**DANBY, Graeme;** singer (bass); b. 1955, Durham, England. *Education:* Royal Academy of Music. *Career:* sang with Scottish Opera until 1995; Appearances with English National Opera in Salome, Boris Godunov, Semele, Rigoletto, Damnation of Faust (Brander), Figaro, Peter Grimes, Poppea and

Manon Lescaut; Further engagements with Mid Wales Opera in Aida and Garsington Opera in Le nozze di Figaro; Glyndebourne Tour in Die Entführung and Music Theatre Wales in The Rape of Lucretia and Birtwistle's Punch and Judy; Royal Opera debut 2001, as Marquis d'Obigny in La Traviata; Concerts include Will Todd's oratorio St Cuthbert, at Durham Cathedral, 2001. *Current Management:* Stafford Law, Candleway, Broad Street, Sutton Valence, Kent ME17 3AT, England. *Website:* www.stafford-law.com.

**DANCEANU, Liviu;** Romanian composer; *Professor of Composition, University of Music, Bucharest;* b. 19 July 1954; m. Rodica Danceanu 1976. *Education:* Acad. of Music C. Poroumbescu, Bucharest, composition with Stefan Niculescu. *Career:* debut, Academy of Music, C. Porumbescu, 1978; Concerts in Bucharest and other musical centres, London, Paris, Rotterdam, Turin, Munich, Warsaw, Prague, Moscow, New York, Salzburg, Vienna, Valencia, Porto, Geneva; Appearances on Romanian Radio and Television, BBC London, Radio France, Bayerisches Rundfunk, Suisse Romande, RAI Turin; Recordings with Electrecord Recording House, Bucharest; Leader and Conductor, The Workshop for Contemporary Music ARCHAEUS, 1985–; Prof. of Composition, History of Music and Music Aesthetic, Nat. Univ. of Music, Bucharest 1990–; Visiting Lecturer at the Academies of Music in Lyon, Munich, Alcoi, Cleveland, Munster, Carbondale, Chisinau, Moscow, Oldenburg, Turin and Dijon. *Compositions:* Les Heros, op 1, 1978; La Rocade De Janus, op 2, 1978; Allegorie, op 3, 1979; Sonate pour Basson, op 4, 1980; In Memoriam Lucian Blaga, op 5, 1981; Angulus Ridet, op 7, 1981; A Cache-Cache, op 8, No. 1, 1982; Steps to Melody, op 8, No. 2, 1982; Ossia, op 9, 1982; To Peace, op 10, 1982; Quasifuga, op 11, 1983; Quasiconcerto, op 12, 1983; Quasisymphonia (Symphony No. 1), op 13, 1983; Quasiricercare, op 14, 1984; 3 Chansons Infantiles, op 15, No. 1, 1984; 6 Stop-Cadres, op 15, No. 2, 1984; Quasipreludiu, op 16, 1984; Florilège, op 17, 1985; Protocantus, op 18, 1985; Quasipostludiu (Addenda), op 19, 1985; Glass Music, op 20, 1985; Quasitoccata, op 21, 1985; Rhymes for Archaeus, op 22, 1986; Quasiopera, op 38, 1986; Concerto for bassoon, op 49, 1989; Hexaphonic Melody, op 50, No. 1, 1988; The Great Union, op 50, No. 2, 1988; Trochos, op 51, 1989; L'Effetto Doppler, op 52, 1989; Quasisonata, op 53, 1989; Palimpseste de Couternon, op 54, 1954; Palimpseste 1 &2, op 55, 1990; Seven Days, op 56, 1992; Syntiphoniy, op 57, 1991; Concertino Sintoboe, op 58, 1991; Symphony No. 2, op 59, 1992; Saxas, op 60, 1992; Opus 61, 1993; Feast Music, op 62, 1993; Aliquote, op 63, 1994; Andamento, op 64, 1994; Game, op 65, 1994; Climax, op 66, 1995; Chinonic, op 67, 1995; Parallel Musics No. 1, op 68, 1995; Parallel Musics No. 2, op 69, 1996; Sega-Nomia, op 70, 1997; History 1, op 71, 1997; Bas-soon, op 72, 1997; Sifflet en Scène, op 73, 1997; L'Abîme de Pascal, op 74, 1998; History 2, op 75, 1998; Micro-Pseudo-Requiem, op 76, 1999; Domestic Music, op 77, 1999; History-Rhapsody, op 78, 1999; Opus 79, 2000; Opus 80, 2000; Tachycardia, op 81, 2000; Panta rei, op 82, 2001; Baclamo, op 83, 2001; Beverdillini, op 84, 2001; Dance by Dance, op 85, 2002; Superbia, op 86, 2002; Lili-Acul, op 87, 2002; One Day of D.G.'s Life, op 88, 2002; Ira, op 89, 2002; Prayer, op 90, 2002; Luxuria, op 91, 2003; Vocabule, op 92, 2003; Tachycardia Again, op 93, 2003; Pietas, op 94, 2003. *Publications:* Angulus ridet; Symphony No. 1; Symphony No. 2; Aliquote4; Quasipreludiu; Quasifuga; Quasipostludiu; Quasiopera; Books: Implosive Essays I, 1998; Introduction in the Epistemology of Music, 1999; Implosive Essays II, 2001 Book with Instruments, 2002; Book with Dances, 2002, Seasons of Music – An Elliptic and Didactic History of Music, 2003. *Honours:* Romanian Culture Order 2004; Studieen de Toulouse Prize, France 1986, ATM Prize 1987, ACIM Prize 1988, Union of Romanian Composers Prize 1988, 1990, 1994, 2000, 2003, Romanian Acad. Prize 1989, SOROS Prize 1997. *Address:* Calea Vacaresti No. 276, Bl 63, Apt 49, Sector 4, 040062 Bucharest, Romania. *E-mail:* liviud@itcnet.ro.

**DANCUO-PEHARDA, Mirjana;** Singer (Soprano); b. 16 Jan. 1929, Karlovac, Croatia; m. Zdenko Peharda. *Education:* Studied in Zagreb. *Career:* Debut: National Opera, Zagreb 1945, as Giannetta in L'Elisir d'amore; Sang Belgrade, Sofia, Brno and elsewhere in Eastern Europe; Guest appearances at Teatro Liceo Barcelona, The Vienna Volksoper, Den Norske Opera, Oslo, Stockholm and Gothenburg in Sweden; Herodias in Salome (Strauss); Other roles have included Mozart's Countess and Donna Anna, Verdi's Amneris, Amelia in Ballo in Maschera and Trovatore Leonora, La Gioconda, Margherita in Mefistofele, Yaroslavna in Prince Igor, Leonore in Fidelio, Marina in Boris Godunov, Wagner's Sieglinde and Elisabeth, the Marschallin in Der Rosenkavalier, Tosca and Desdemona; Kostelnicka in Jenůfa, Lady Billows in Albert Herring; Teacher at the Operatic High School in Oslo, 1994–; mem, Norwegian Opera Singers Association. *Honours:* Oslo City Culture Prize, 1978. *Address:* Jerikoveien 89B, 1052 Oslo, Norway.

**DANEL, Mark;** Violinist; b. 1965, England. *Education:* Studied in London and with Feodor Droujinin, violist of Russia's Beethoven Quartet. *Career:* Many concerts throughout the United Kingdom, notably at the Aldeburgh Festival with Quartet in Residence, Huddersfield, Andover and Middle Temple; Repertoire includes quartets by Shostakovich and Fauré and English works. *Honours:* As member of Danel Quartet: Prizewinner in competitions at Florence, St Petersburg, Evian and London, 1991–94. *Address:* c/o Irene Witmer Management, Liedesgracht 42, NL–1016 AM Amsterdam, Netherlands.

**DANEMAN, Sophie;** British singer (soprano); b. 1968, England; m. Simon Robson 2001; one s. *Education:* Guildhall School of Music and Drama. *Career:* works with Christie, Hogwood, Marriner, Lesne, Malgoire, Herreweghe, King, Daniel, Hickox, McGegan, Ivor Bolton, Kraemer and Rattle; has sung with

RIAS Kammerchor, Philharmonische Staatsorchester Halle, Freibourg Baroque Orchestra, Les Arts Florissants, Scottish Chamber Orchestra, Berlin Philharmonic and Orchestra of the Age of Enlightenment; regular appearances at the South Bank Centre, Wigmore Hall, Maggio Musicale Fiorentino, Lufthansa Festival of Baroque Music, Edinburgh, Belfast and Saintes Festivals; title role in Handel's Arianna in Creta at Göttingen 1999; Rameau's La Guirlande (concert) at Cologne, and in Handel's Theodora and Acis and Galatea, at Salzburg 2000, Eileen in Wonderful Town 2004; repertoire includes Despina, Susanna, Frasquita, Mélisande and Euridice; recitalist at Wigmore Hall, Queen Elizabeth Hall, Carnegie Hall, Concertgebouw, Vienna Concerthaus, Schwarzenberg. *Recordings include:* Handel's Rodelinda; Rameau's Grand Motets (Gramophone Award) and Castor and Pollux; Montéclaire's Jephté, Dido and Aeneas; Charpentier's Médée and La Descente D'Orphée, Mendelssohn and Schumann Lieder, Handel's Acis and Galatea (Gramophone Award), Handel's Theodora (title role), Giovanni Pergolesi's Marian Vespers; Jean-Baptiste Lully's Divertissement de Versailles, Noel Coward (with Ian Bostridge). *Address:* 29 Christchurch Road, London, SW14 7AQ, England. *Telephone:* (7710) 829-948 (home). *E-mail:* sophdane@dircon .co.uk (home).

**DANGAIN, Guy;** musician (clarinet); b. 12 July 1935, Sains-en-Gohelle, France; one d. *Education:* Conservatoire National Superieur de Musique, Paris, studied clarinet with Prof. Ulysse Deleclute, chamber music with Prof. Ferrand Oubradous. *Career:* clarinet soloist with National Orchestra of France 1963–93; Prof., Ecole Normale, Paris, Conservatoire National Superieur du Musique, Paris; Dir, International Festival, Haut Bugey. *Compositions:* over 50 collections of compositions. *Recordings:* Brahms Sonata; Debussy, Rhapsody; Rhapsody with National Orchestra of Martinon; Repertoire from young clarinettist H. Mundi; Creation du Monde, du Bernstein; Hommage à Louis Ca Huzoc; Guisganolerie: Hommage à Guisganol; Quinette et Two Songs. *Publications:* Prestige de la clarinette, 1987; A propos de la clarinette, 1991. *Honours:* Chevalier des Arts et des Lettres. *Address:* 14 Ruelle à Potier, 95590 Nerville la Forêt, France.

**D'ANGELO, Gianna;** Singer (Soprano); b. 18 Nov. 1929, Hartford, Conneticut, USA. *Education:* Studied at the Juilliard School, New York, and in Italy with Toti dal Monte. *Career:* Debut: Rome 1954, as Gilda; Glyndebourne 1955–56 and 1962, as Rosina, Clorinda in La Cenerentola and Zerbinetta in Ariadne auf Naxos; Brussels Opera 1956; Metropolitan Opera from 1961, as Gilda, Amina in La Sonnambula, Lucia di Lammermoor, Rosina and Zerbinetta; 8 Seasons with 36 Performances in 7 roles; Guest appearances in Milan, Paris and London. *Recordings:* Rigoletto; La Bohème; Il Barbiere di Siviglia; Les Contes d'Hoffmann. *Address:* c/o Metropolitan Opera, Lincoln Center, New York, NY 10023, USA.

**D'ANGELO, James,** BMus, MMus, PhD; American teacher, composer and pianist; b. 17 March 1939, Paterson, NJ; m. Georgina Joysmith 1970; two d. *Education:* Columbia Univ., New York Univ., Manhattan School of Music, studied with Gunther Schuller, William Russo, John Lewis (MJQ), Jan Gorbaty and Jean Catoire. *Career:* debut, Carnegie Recital Hall, New York 1966; Prof. of Music, CUNY 1970–86; Lecturer, Goldsmiths' Coll., London 1987–; workshop leader in the Psychology of Musical Performance and Therapeutic Voice Work 1992–; mem. advisory bd, Caduceus Journal 1993–; as composer, works performed at various colls in USA 1968–75, and at various London venues 1985–; song cycle debuted at Carnegie Recital Hall 1971; as pianist, London concerts of own music 1986–; featured composer, Planet Tree Music Festival London 1998, 2000; guest presenter at Findhorn Foundation, Scotland. *Compositions:* Tintinnabulations song cycle for soprano, Toccata for solo percussionist, Songs on poems by e e cummings, The Way of the Spiritual Warrior 1989, The Elements 1990, The Great Happiness 1991, Fool and Angel Entering a City 1993, Fools (three movement suite for flute and percussion) 1997, The Song of Solomon 1998, The Holy City 1998, Tenebrae Factae Sunt 2001, Pater Noster for baritone and string quartet 2003. *Recordings:* Fast Cats and Mysterious Cows (including Krishna Portraits) 1999, Suite of Ten Third Stream Songs 2004. *Publications:* Healing with the Voice 2000, The Healing Power of the Human Voice 2005; contrib. to International Dictionary of Opera, Hindemith Jahrbuch, Contemporary Music Review. *Address:* 33 Morpeth Street, Gloucester, Gloucestershire G41 4TN, England (home). *Telephone:* (1594) 517-333 (office). *E-mail:* healingvibes@soundspirit.co.uk (office); james .dangelo@lineone.net (home). *Website:* www.soundspirit.co.uk.

**DANIEL, Nicholas Jeremy Gordon,** FRAM, FGSM; British oboist, conductor and teacher; b. 9 Jan. 1962, Liss, Hampshire, England; m. Joy Farrall 1986; two s. *Education:* chorister Salisbury Cathedral School, Purcell School, London, Royal Acad. of Music. *Career:* debut, South Bank 1982; concerto and recital appearances at home and abroad; Proms debut 1990, four subsequent appearances; founder and Dir, Haffner Wind Ensemble 1990; Daniel-Drake Duo 1980–; regular broadcasts of wide repertoire; tours include USA, Japan, Australia, Scandinavia, Netherlands, Italy, Bulgaria, Spain, France, Switzerland, Germany, S America; performances with Brodky, Allegri, Brindisi, Vanbrugh, Lindsay String Quartets; Prof., Guildhall School of Music and Drama 1984–97; Prof. of Oboe, Bloomington, Indiana 1997–99; Prince Consort Prof. of Oboe, Royal Coll. of Music, London 1999–2002; Prof., Hochschule für Musik und Kunst, Trossingen, Germany 2004–; Artistic Dir, Osnabruck Kammermusiktage 2001–; founder mem. and Assoc. Artistic Dir, Britten Sinfonia 2002–; Artistic Dir, Leicester Symphony Orchestra 2001–; Leicester Int. Music Festival 2004; regional council mem., Arts Council England, East; Artistic Dir, Barbirolli Isle of Wight Int. Oboe Competition 2005. *Honours:*

BBC Young Musician of the Year 1980, Gillet Young Artists Prize, Graz 1984, Munich Competition 1986; Hon. Fellow Purcell School 1988. *Address:* Hedgerow House, 48 Station Road, Warboys, Cambridgeshire PE28 2TH, England. *E-mail:* SoloOboe@aol.com.

**DANIEL, Paul Wilson,** CBE; British conductor; b. 5 July 1958, Birmingham, England; m. Joan Rodgers (q.v.) 1988; two d. *Education:* sang in choir of Coventry Cathedral, King's Coll., Cambridge, Guildhall School of Music and Drama, London, studied with Franco Ferrara in Italy and with Adrian Boult and Edward Downes. *Career:* mem. music staff ENO, London 1982–87, Music Dir 1997–2005; Music Dir Opera Factory 1987–90, Opera North, Leeds 1990–97; Prin. Conductor English Northern Philharmonia 1990–97; has conducted all the maj. London orchestras and most of the regional UK orchestras and orchestras in USA, Germany, Netherlands, France and Australia. *Operas conducted include:* (ENO) The Mask of Orpheus, Akhnaten, Tosca, Rigoletto, Carmen, Figaro's Wedding, King Priam, Flying Dutchman, From the House of the Dead, Tales of Hoffman, Falstaff, Manon, Othello, Boris Godunov, La Traviata, The Carmelites, Nixon in China, The Silver Tassie, War and Peace, Lulu, The Trojans, Twilight of the Gods; (Opera North) Ariane et Barbe-Bleue, Attila, King Priam, Don Giovanni, Der Ferne Klang, Boris Godunov (also at BBC Proms 1992), Rigoletto, Don Carlos, Wozzeck, Gloriana, Baa Baa Black Sheep (world premiere), Playing Away, Il Trovatore, Pelléas et Mélisande, Jenůfa, Luisa Miller; (Royal Opera Covent Garden) Mitridate; has also conducted opera productions in Nancy, Munich, Brussels, Geneva. *Honours:* Olivier Award for Outstanding Achievement in Opera 1997, Gramophone Award for English Music Series 1999. *Address:* c/o Ingpen and Williams, 26 Wadham Road, London, SW15 2LR, England.

**DANIELS, Barbara;** Singer (soprano); b. 7 May 1946, Granville, OH, USA. *Education:* BA, Ohio State Univ., MA, Univ. of Cincinnati. *Career:* debut, West Palm Beach, FL, as Susanna 1973; sang in Europe from 1974, notably in Innsbruck as Violetta and Cologne as Alice Ford, Rosalinda, Mozart's Countess and Manon Lescaut; appeared in the Michael Hampe productions and films of Agrippina and Il Matrimonio Segreto; Covent Garden from 1978 as Musetta, Donna Elvira, Rosalinde and Alice Ford; Washington DC 1979, as Donizetti's Norina; San Francisco from 1980, as Zdenka in Arabella and as Violetta, Liu and Micaela; Zürich Opera as the Comtesse, in the Ponnelle production of Le Comte Ory; Metropolitan Opera from 1983, as Musetta, Violetta, Rosalinde, Marguerite and the title role in Les Mamelles de Tirésias; Musetta at Rome 1987; Teatro Regio Turin as Violetta 1988; Rosalinde in Fledermaus at the Metropolitan and Chicago 1990; Jenůfa at Innsbruck 1990; Minnie in La Fanciulla del West at the Metropolitan 1991; sang Senta at Cincinnati 1996; Alice Ford at Baltimore 1997; sang Puccini's Minnie at Nice 2000; concert appearances in Rossini's Mosè at Perugia, Boito's Mefistofele at the Zürich Tonhalle, Schumann's Scenes from Faust with the Berlin Philharmonic and the Missa Solemnis under Giulini at the Maggio Musicale Florence; Prof. of Voice, Salzburg Mozarteum and Innsbruck Conservatory. *Recordings include:* Scenes from Faust, La Bohème (conducted by Bernstein), Mad About Puccini, Fanciulla de West (video), Il Matrimonio Segreto (video), Agrippina (video). *Honours:* Dr hc, Cincinnati Univ. 1992. *Address:* c/o Opéra et Concert, 1 rue Volney, 75002, Paris, France.

**DANIELS, Charles;** Singer (tenor); b. 1960, Salisbury, England. *Education:* Choral Scholar at King's College, Cambridge; Royal College of Music, with Edward Brooks. *Career:* Many appearances in the UK, Europe, Canada and USA; Handel's La Resurrezione in Oslo; Saul in Göttingen; Solomon in Halle; L'Allegro at Handel's Church in London; Mendelssohn's Elijah and Puccini's Messa di Gloria under Michel Corboz; Bach St Matthew Passion for De Nederlandse Bach Vereniging; Christmas Oratorio in St Gallen, Lugano, Dublin; regular appearances at the BBC Promenade Concerts; Elgar's Dream of Gerontius; Luigi Nono's Canti di Vita e Amore (Edinburgh Festival); Britten's War Requiem (Canterbury Festival); Cavalieri's Anima e Corpo (Schwabische Gmund); Schubert Mass in E Flat with London Phiharmonic Orchestra; Handel's Esther in Hebrew and English in New York; Monteverdi's Orfeo and Purcell's King Arthur in Toronto; the premiere of Wojciech Kilar's Missa Pro Pace with the Warsaw Philharmonic. *Recordings include:* Handel Messiah and Schütz Christmas Story, with Paul MacCreesh; Bach's Easter Oratorio, with Andrew Parrott; Dowland songs, with David Miller; Senfl tenorlied, with Fretwork; Peachum in The Beggar's Opera; The Fairy Queen, under William Christie; many Purcell albums, with the King's Consort; Haydn's St Cecilia Mass; Charpentier Vêpres aux Jésuites, under Michel Corboz. *Honours:* Hubert Parry Prize at the GKN English Songs Awards, 1986. *Current Management:* Hazard Chase, Norman House, Cambridge Place, Cambridge CB2 1NS, England. *Telephone:* (1223) 312400. *Fax:* (1223) 460827. *E-mail:* info@hazardchase.co.uk. *Website:* www.hazardchase.co.uk.

**DANIELS, Claire;** Singer (Soprano); b. 1963, England. *Education:* Studied at the Royal Northern College of Music and in Paris with Janine Reiss. *Career:* Appearances include: Jennie Hildebrand in Street Scene; A Nymph, in Rusalka; Niece, in Peter Grimes for English National Opera; Amor, in Orfeo ed Euridice for Opera North; Zerlina for Kent Opera; Sang in Purcell's King Arthur at the Buxton Festival; Rossini's L'Occasions fa il ladro and L'Italiana in Algeri and Grétry's Le Huron; Vespina, in Haydn's L'Infedeltà Delusa for Garsington Opera; Nannetta, in Falstaff for Opera Zuid in Netherlands; Mozart's Susanna and Servilia and Adina in L'Elisir d'amore for Scottish Opera (1993); The Girl, in Nigel Osborne's Sarajevo, for Opera Factory; Serpetta in La finta giardiniera by Mozart for Klagenfurt Opera in Austria; Concert appearances throughout Germany and at Aix-en-Provence, Barcelona and Gothenberg; Mozart's Mass in C Minor with Charles Mackerras; Les Nuits d'Été at Perth Festival; Carmina Burana in Valencia; Sang in Peter Grimes with the London Symphony Orchestra under Rostropovich; Mozart's Exultate Jubilate for concert tour of Great Britain with the Stuttgart Philharmonic Orchestra. *Address:* c/o Marks Management, 14 New Burlington Street, London W1X 1FF, England.

**DANIELS, David;** American singer (countertenor); b. 12 March 1966, Spartanburg, SC. *Education:* Univ. of Michigan with George Shirley. *Career:* debut as Nero in L'Incoronazione di Poppea at the Glimmerglass Opera Festival 1994; Handel's Tamerlano at Glimmerglass 1995; followed by Arsamenes in Xerxes with the Boston Lyric Opera season 1995–96, in Israel in Egypt at the Vienna Musikverein, Messiah in Boston and Handel's Saul with the Philharmonia Baroque Orchestra; Salzburg Festival debut as Hamor in Handel's Jephtha 1996; sang Didymus in Theodora at the Glyndebourne Festival 1996; opened 1996–97 season with ENO as Oberon in A Midsummer Night's Dream; London and New York recital debuts at the Wigmore Hall and Lincoln Center 1996; sang in Monteverdi's Ulisse at Los Angeles Opera, as Sesto in Handel's Giulio Cesare for the Royal Opera, London 1997, the same role at the Metropolitan 1999; sang Handel's Rinaldo at the London Barbican 2000, at Bavarian State Opera 2001; other roles include Monteverdi's Nero (San Francisco 1998) and Arsace in Handel's Partenope (Glimmerglass 1998); sang Giulio Cesare at the Palais Garnier, Paris 2002. *Current Management:* Askonas Holt Ltd, Lonsdale Chambers, 27 Chancery Lane, London, WC2A 1PF, England. *Telephone:* (20) 7400-1700. *Fax:* (20) 7400-1799. *E-mail:* info@askonasholt.co.uk. *Website:* www.askonasholt.co.uk.

**DANILEVSKI, Alexander;** Composer and Lutenist; b. 4 Sept. 1957, St Petersburg, Russia; m. Emilia, 9 Sept 1990, 3 s., 2 d. *Education:* Composition, Leningrad Conservatoire, 1974–80; Lute, Scola Cantorum Basilensis, 1991–93. *Career:* Debut: The I Sonato for Violin, St Petersburg Philharmonic 1981 and Lute Recital; 90 Solo Recitals and Concerts throughout Russia; Festivals, Recitals and Concerts in Europe (early music); Founder, 'Syntagma' (ensemble of early music); Performances of Lauda, Antiphones, Sonata for Cello in Grand Festival des Musiques Slaves, Paris, 1996, 1997; More than 30 concerts of early music given by Syntagma; mem, American Lute Society. *Compositions:* Sonatas for Violin, Violoncello and Piano; Missa for Choir and Orchestra; Seven Words of Christ on the Cross; Strophes enfilees (nai kai); Concerto for Organ, Harpsichord and Piano; Quatuors 1-4, Chamber Music; Lauda, for voice and ensemble; Antiphones-I, for recorder quartet; Antiphones-II, for string quartet; Revelation, for cello, 1997; Sonatos 1–3 for piano; Concert and Night Music for 2 pianos; Seven Words for soprano and ensemble. *Recordings:* Guillaume Dufay and Music of His time, with Ensemble Pro Anima, St Petersburg; Medieval and Renaissance Music with the same; Johannes Ciaconia and His Time; Solo; Francesco da Milano, Fancies and Ricercars, St Petersburg. *Publications:* Works for Piano, 1997–98; 20 Russian Barocco Songs. *Address:* 30 Rue de la Marne, 57000 Metz, France.

**DANON, Oskar;** Conductor and Composer; b. 7 Feb. 1913, Sarajevo, Yugoslavia. *Education:* Studied at Prague Conservatory and University. *Career:* Conducted Opera and Concerts in Sarajevo from 1938; Director and Conductor of Belgrade Opera, 1945–60; Led performances of The Bartered Bride in Prague, then Prince Igor and Don Quichotte with the Belgrade Company on tour to Paris, 1958; Wiesbaden Festival, 1959; The Love for Three Oranges, Paris Opéra 1960, with Boris Godunov; Edinburgh Festival, 1962, leading Don Quichotte, Prince Igor and the British premieres of Prokofiev's The Gambler and The Love for Three Oranges; Prince Igor at the Chicago Lyric Opera, 1962; Further engagements with Tristan und Isolde at Barcelona, 1969, and Arabella at Amsterdam, 1970; Opened the restored National Theatre Belgrade, 1990 with The Prince of Zeta by Konjovic. *Recordings:* Prince Igor and A Life for the Tsar with the Belgrade Company. *Address:* National Theatre, Belgrade, Croatia.

**DANZ, Ingeborg;** Singer (Contralto); b. 1961, Witten, Germany. *Education:* Studied in Detmold. *Career:* Frequent appearances from 1987 as concert and oratorio singer; Tours of North and South America, USA, Japan, Russia and Europe, with Neville Marriner, Herreweghe, Harnoncourt and Helmuth Rilling; Season 1996 with Bach's St John Passion at the Amsterdam Concertgebouw and Handel's Jephtha with the Bamberg Symphony Orchestra at the Salzburg Festival; Other festival engagements at Stuttgart, Oregon, Ludwigsburg, Schwetzingen and Tanglewood; Recital tour with Juliane Banse and Thomas Quasthoff, 1997. *Recordings include:* Mozart Masses with Nikolaus Harnoncourt, St Matthew Passion with Helmuth Rilling. *Honours:* Scholarship from Richard Wagner Federation. *Address:* c/o Kunstler Sekretariat am Gasteig, Rosenheimerstrasse 52, 81669 Munich, Germany.

**DAO, Nguyen-Thien;** French (b. Vietnamese) composer; b. 16 Dec. 1940, Hanoi, Viet Nam; m. Hélène Latapie 1963. *Education:* Paris Conservatory with Olivier Messiaen. *Career:* debut at Festival de Royan 1969. *Compositions include:* The 19 for female voices and ensemble 1969, Nho for soprano, cello and five double basses 1970, Khoc To Nhu for mixed voices, Koskom for orchestra 1971, Bai tap ondes Martenot for piano 1974, Camatithu for six percussions 1974, Framic for bass flute 1974, Mau va hoa for orchestra 1974, Bao gio for two percussions and two pianos 1975, Mua for harpsichord 1976, A Mi K giao tranh for double bass 1976, Giai phong for orchestra and electro-acoustics 1977, Bay for percussions 1977, Mai Sau for violin and strings 1977, Phu Dong II, 4 for two percussions 1977, Noi Xa 2 ondes Martenot for electric guitar and percussion 1977, My-chau Trong-thuy for opera 1978, Hoang Hon

for soprano and orchestra 1979, Ecouter/Mourir for opera 1980, Concerto Ten Do Gu for percussion and orchestra 1980, Chuong gam song for organ 1981, Tuon Han for soprano and clarinet 1982, Than Mong for cello concerto 1982, Poussière d'empire for soprano, mixed voices and percussion 1983, Tay-Son for percussion 1984, L'Aube est une oeuvre for children's or female choir, string quartet and percussion 1984, Piano concerto 1984, Cimes murmerées for string trio 1985, La mer pétrifiée (opera) 1986, Tim Lua for piano 1987, Pliombre for bass clarinet 1987, Temps songe for seven percussionists (165 instruments) 1987, VV2 for bassoon 1987, Concerto Thien Thaï for violin and orchestra 1988, Concerto l'Envol for flute and strings 1988, Symphonie pour pouvoir for symphony orchestra and soprano 1989, Concerto 1989 for string sextet and orchestra 1989, 1789 l'aurore for string sextet, Voie-Concert for ensemble 1990, Quatuor à Cordes No. 1 1991, Les Enfants d'Izieu for opera-oratorio (Prix Gian Carlo Menotti for recording) 1991, Les Perseides 1992, Feuillets pour quatuor et perc 1994, Hoa-Tau 1995 for string orchestra 1995, Giao-Hoa Sinfonia for orchestra 1996, Khai-Nhac for orchestra 1997, Hon-Non-Nuoc for soloists, choir and orchestra 1998, Khai Minh Prelude for small orchestra 1999, Scherzovivo 1999, Song Hon for orchestra 2000, Arco Vivo for solo cello 2000, Kosmofonia for orchestra and choir 2000, Chuyen Coi for small orchestra 2001, Song Nhat Nguyen Concerto pour Monocorde for cello and orchestra 2002, Song Nhac Truong Chi (ballet) 2003, Quatre Lyriques de Ciel et de Terre (chamber opera) 2003, Song Than for orchestra, bass and choir 2004, Khoi Truong Chi monocorde vietnamien solo 2004, Khoi Song cithare vietnamien solo 2005. *Honours:* Chevalier, Ordre des Arts et des Lettres, Médaille de la Résistance (Viet Nam), Médaille de la Culture (Viet Nam); Prix Olivier Messiaen de Composition Musicale de la Fondation Erasme (Netherlands), Prix André Caplet de l'Académie des Beaux Arts. *Address:* 28 rue Madame, 75006 Paris, France (home). *Telephone:* 1 42 22 18 91 (home). *Fax:* 1 42 22 18 91 (home). *E-mail:* nguyenthien.dao@wanadoo.fr (home). *Website:* www.nguyenthiendao.com.

**DAOUD, Rageh,** BMus; Egyptian composer, musician (piano) and teacher; b. 23 Nov. 1954, Cairo. *Education:* Cairo Conservatoire, Vienna Acad. of Music. *Career:* composer 1978–; teacher and Research Asst, Cairo Conservatoire 1978–81, Assoc. Prof. of Composition 1988–; conductor, Hanager Center Chamber Orchestra, Egyptian Ministry of Culture 1993–. *Compositions include:* Egyptian Glimpse for orchestra 1978, Sonata for piano 1978, Lied for soprano and piano 1978, Four Pieces for string orchestra 1981, Fugue for string orchestra 1981, Fantasy for harp, cello and percussion 1982, Four Dances for string quartet 1982, Fantasy for woodwinds and string orchestra 1983, Lied for alto and piano 1984, Takassim for clarinet and orchestra 1984, Quartet for flute, oboe, clarinet and bassoon 1985, Quartet for woodwinds 1985, Der neue Ankommende lied for alto, bass clarinet and vibraphone 1986, Meditation for string orchestra 1986, Portrait No. 1 for string orchestra 1986, Trio for piano, violin and cello 1987, Three Pictures for oboe and piano 1987, Three Children's Pictures for two pianos 1987, Portrait No. 2 for string orchestra 1987, Rhapsody for string orchestra 1988, Nocturne for cello and piano 1989, Nocturne for piano 1989, Requiem for choir and orchestra 1990, Thirty Songs for children and small orchestra 1991, Suite for alto flute solo 1992, Suite for flute and piano 1992, Rhapsody for flute, violin and orchestra 1992, Passacaglia for lute, organ and string orchestra 1993. *Honours:* Ministry of Culture Artistic Creation Prize 1990, Alexandria Film Festival Prize 1991, Film Critics' Asscn Prize 1992. *Address:* Cairo Conservatoire, Avenue of the Pyramids, Giza, Egypt (office).

**DARA, Enzo;** Singer (Bass); b. 13 Oct. 1938, Mantua, Italy. *Education:* Studied with Bruno Sutti in Mantua. *Career:* Debut: Fano 1960, as Colline in La Bohème; Reggio Emilia 1966, as Dulcamara in L'Elisir d'amore; La Scala Milan debut 1970, as Bartolo in Il Barbiere di Siviglia; Sang Bartolo on his New York (1982) and Covent Garden (1985) debuts; Pesaro 1984, in a revival of Rossini's Il Viaggio a Reims; Guest appearances in Naples, Bologna, Moscow, Brussels, Venice, Palermo and Rome; Returned to Covent Garden 1987, as Dulcamara; Pesaro Festival, 1988, in Il Signor Bruschino; Don Pasquale at Venice, 1990; Teatro de la Zarzuela Madrid, 1990, in Il Turco in Italia; Sang Bartolo at the Verona Arena, 1996; Sang Geronio in Il Turco in Italia and Don Magnifico in Cenerentola at Buenos Aires and Munich, 2000. *Recordings:* Il Barbiere di Siviglia and Il Viaggio a Reims; L'Italiana in Algeri; La Buona Figliuola by Piccinni; Donzetti's L'ajo nell' imbarazzo; Il Turco in Italia.

**DARBELLAY, Jean Luc;** Swiss composer, conductor and clarinettist; b. 2 July 1946, Berne; m. Elsbeth Darbellay-Fahrer 1971; one s. one d. *Education:* Berne Univ., Berne Conservatory, studied composition with Theo Hirsbrunner, Cristobal Halffter, Dimitri Terzakis, Lucerne Conservatory with Edison Denisov and Klaus Huber, Foundation Ludus Ensemble Berne, studied conducting with Pierre Dervaux and Franco Ferrara. *Career:* concerts throughout Europe as conductor of various orchestras, including Ludus Ensemble, Landesjugendchor Niedersachsen and Quaderni Perugini di Musica Contemporanea, Ensemble Contrechamps, MDR Kammerphilharmonie, John Cage Festival, Perugia. *Compositions include:* Glanum 1981, Amphores 1983, C'est un peu d'eau qui nous separe 1989, Cello Concerto (Radio France recording in Paris with Ensemble Denosjours, dedicated to Siegfried Palm) 1989, Interférences 1991, Before Breakfast (film score) 1991, Pranam III (command of the Quaderni Perugini and Siegfried Palm) 1992, Cantus (command of the Altenburger Orgelkonzerte) 1993, Itinéraires (for St Petersburg Festival) 1994, Elégie 1994, Incanto horn concerto (Plauen) 1995, A la recherche (creation in Moscow), PRANAM IV cello concerto for Siegfried

Palm (in Halle), Ein Garten für Orpheus (Bauhaus Dessau) 1996, Écumes for string quartet 1996, Valàre for violin and piano 1997, Lumières 1998, Chant d'adieux 1998, Shadows for percussion ensemble 1999, Gestes-Effleurements for string trio 1999, Messages for piano 2000, Azur 2001, Oyama 2001, A Quattro for four horns and orchestra 2002, Alea concerto for violin 2003, Alani trio for violin, horn and piano 2003, Nocturne 2004, Delphes des trois fois 2004. *Recordings:* Leading the Sächsisches Kammerorchester Leipzig: Mozart Divertimento, K251, Violin Concerto, K218, Haydn's Horn Concerto No. 2 and Symphony No. 1, Mozart's Serenade in C minor, K388, Darbellay's Espaces, Sept Poèmes Romands and Wind Octet, Aube Imaginaire with Choeur Novantiqua Sion, Résonances with pieces for violoncello and horn (with Olivier Darbellay) 1997. *Address:* c/o Editors Editions Tre Media, Amalienstrasse 40, 76133 Karlsruhe, Germany (office); Englische Aulagen 6, 3005 Bern, Switzerland (home). *E-mail:* cordebasset@freesurf.ch (home). *Website:* www.jean-luc-darbellay.ch (home).

**D'ARCANGELO, Ildebrando;** Italian singer (bass-baritone); b. 1969, Pesaro. *Education:* studied with Maria Vittoria Romano and in Bologna. *Career:* engagements in La Bohème at Chicago, I Capuleti by Bellini at the Berlin Staatsoper, Rossini's Armida and Guillaume Tell at Pesaro and as Mozart's Masetto at the New York Met, Figaro at Salzburg, 1996; Don Giovanni in Bonn and Leporello at the Bayerische Staatsoper; Banquo in Macbeth at Bologna and Colline in La Bohème at Covent Garden 1996; season 1997-98 as Figaro in Rome, Paris and New York, Enrico in Lucia di Lammermoor at the Edinburgh Festival and Leporello in Vienna; Leporello at the Theater an der Wien 1999; sang Rossini's Mosè at Monte Carlo 2000; season 2002-03 in Le nozze di Figaro in Milan, Don Giovanni in Naples. *Recordings include:* Rigoletto and I Lombardi under James Levine; Otello under Myung Wha Chung; Semiramide; Le nozze di Figaro; Don Giovanni (as Leporello, under John Eliot Gardiner); Don Carlos; Lucia di Lammermoor (with Mackerras); Don Giovanni (with Abbado). *Honours:* winner Concorso Internazionale Toti dal Monte, Treviso, Premio della Critica Musicale 'Franco Abbiati' 2003. *Current Management:* Atelier Musicale, via Caselle 76, San Lazzaro di Savena, 40068, Italy. *Telephone:* (51) 1998-4444. *Fax:* (51) 1998-4420. *E-mail:* info@ateliermusicale.it. *Website:* www.ateliermusicale.it.

**DARLINGTON, Jonathan;** British conductor; *Music Director, Vancouver Opera;* b. 1962, England. *Career:* engagements with the Teatro San Carlo, Naples, Hamburg State Opera, Lausanne Opéra and Bordeaux Opera; Principal Guest Conductor, Deutsche Oper am Rhein, Düsseldorf, and concerts with the Orchestra Sinfonia di San Carlo and Swedish Chamber Orchestra; season 2001-02 with the Bochum Symphony, Orchestre Philharmonique de Strasbourg, Orchestre Nat. de L'Ile de France and China Philharmonic Orchestra at the Peking Music Festival; further opera work at the Théâtre des Champs Elysées, Paris, and Vancouver Opera; repertoire includes works by Mozart, Beethoven, Mendelssohn, Schubert and Brahms; choral repertoire includes the Bach Passions and B minor mass, Haydn's Creation, Requiems of Dvoràk and Mozart and the Glagolitic Mass by Janáček; Prin. Conductor, Vancouver Opera -2005, Music Dir 2005-. *Address:* c/o Vancouver Opera, 835 Cambie Street, Vancouver, BC V6B 2P4, Canada. *Website:* www.vancouveropera.ca.

**DARLINGTON, Stephen Mark,** MA, DMus, FRCO; British organist; *Organist and Tutor in Music, Christ Church, Oxford;* b. 21 Sept. 1952, Lapworth, Warwickshire, England; m. Moira Ellen Hill 1975; three d. *Education:* Christ Church, Oxford. *Career:* Asst Organist, Canterbury Cathedral 1974-78; Master of the Music, St Alban's Abbey 1978-85; Artistic Dir, Int. Organ Festival, St Albans 1979-85; Organist and Tutor in Music, Christ Church, Oxford 1985-; Choragus, Univ. of Oxford 1998-; Pres., Royal Coll. of Organists 1998-2000, currently council mem. *Recordings include:* Masses by Byrd, Esteves, Lassus, Martin, Palestrina, Poulenc, Taverner, Victoria; Choral works by Haydn, Mathias, Pygott, Tippett, Vaughan Williams, Vivaldi, Walton, Weelkes; Choral Works by Britten, Haydn, Janacek, Goodall; Masses by Aston and Ashwell. *Address:* Christ Church, Oxford, OX1 1DP, England. *Website:* www.chchchoir.org.

**DARLOW, Denys,** FRCM, FRCO, FLCM; British conductor, composer and teacher; b. 13 May 1921, London, England; m. Sophy Margaret Guillaume. *Career:* founder, Tilford Bach Festival 1952, London Handel Festival 1976, BBC Third Programme; Prom Concert; appearances in Sweden, Germany, Austria, Netherlands, Belgium, France, America, New Zealand; concerts and radio; fmr Prof. Royal Coll. of Music; conducted Handel's Alessandro Severo at the RCM 1997; Radamisto 1998; first modern performance of Silla 2000; 80th Birthday Concert with Handel's L'Allegro, St George's, London 2001; world premiere of staged performance Handel's Brockes Passion 2002; mem. Royal Soc. of Musicians. *Compositions include:* Te Deum, Stabat Mater, Requiem, Music for Holy Week, High Hills for soprano and six instruments. *Recordings:* The Triumph of Time and Truth; Oratorio, Handel; Aminta e Fillide; Cantata, Handel; Silla, Opera, Handel; Il Duello Amoroso, Cantata, Handel. *Address:* The Coach House, Drury Lane, Redmarley D'Abitot, Gloucestershire GL19 3JX, England. *Telephone:* (1531) 650616.

**d'ASCOLI, Bernard Jacques-Henri Marc;** French concert pianist; b. 18 Nov. 1958, Aubagne; one s. *Education:* Marseille Conservatoire. *Career:* became blind 1962; took up music 1970; youngest Baccalauréat matriculate of France 1974; first public appearances on both piano and organ 1974; elected as most talented French artist of the year (Megève) 1976; began int. professional career 1982, following débuts at maj. London concert halls with Royal

Philharmonic Orchestra and first recording; toured Australia with Chamber Orchestra of Europe 1983; début Amsterdam Concertgebouw 1984, USA, with Houston Symphony Orchestra 1985, Musikverein, Vienna 1986, Henry Wood Promenade Concerts, London 1986, Tokyo Casals Hall and Bunka Kaikan Hall 1988, with Boston Symphony Orchestra 1992; recordings of Chopin and Schumann (with Schidlof Quartet). *Honours:* first prize Int. Maria Casals competition, Barcelona 1979; prizewinner, Leipzig Bach competition and Warsaw Chopin competition 1980; 3rd prize, Leeds Int. piano competition 1981. *Current Management:* Van Walsum Management Ltd, 4 Addison Bridge Place, London, W14 8XP, England. *Telephone:* (20) 7371-4343. *Fax:* (20) 7371-4344. *Website:* www.vanwalsum.co.uk. *Address:* TransArt (UK) Ltd, Cedar House, 10 Rutland Street, Filey, YO14 9JB, North Yorkshire, England. *Telephone:* (1723) 515819. *Fax:* (1723) 514678. *E-mail:* transartuk@transartuk.com. *Website:* www.transartuk.com.

**DASZAK, John;** Singer (Tenor); b. 24 Feb. 1967, Ashton-under-Lyne, England. *Education:* Guildhall School, London, and the Royal Northern College of Music, with Robert Alderson. *Career:* Opera roles have included Števa in Jenůfa, Jack in Mahagonny and Pang in Turandot, for English National Opera; The Duke of Mantua and Mozart's Ferrando in Italy, Peter Grimes for English Touring Opera and Rustighello in Donizetti's Lucrezia Borgia at the Martina-Franca Festival; Concerts include Otumbo in Verdi's Alzira at Covent Garden, Don Ottavio for the Liverpool Mozart Orchestra, Britten's Serenade and Rossini's Petite Messe at the Buxton Festival; Verdi's Requiem at Chester Cathedral and the Manchester Free Trade Hall, Messiah in Blackburn Cathedral and St John's Smith Square, London; Season 1997-98 with Skuratov in From the House of the Dead and Dmitri in Boris Godunov for English National Opera; Peter Grimes and Dmitri for Welsh National Opera; Števa in Jenůfa, 1998; Roles in Mahagonny at Lausanne; Weber's Euryanthe at the London Proms, 2002. *Address:* c/o IMG Artists, Lovell House, 616 Chiswick High Road, London W4 5RX, England.

**DATYNER, Harry;** Pianist; b. 4 Feb. 1923, La Chaux-de-Fonds, Switzerland; m. Bluette Blum, 14 June 1954, 1 s. *Education:* Etudes Conservatoire National in Paris with Marguerite Long and later with Edwin Fischer. *Career:* Concerts in Europe, northern and southern Africa, North and South America; Soloist with orchestras: Suisse Romande, Lausanne, Montreal, Bucharest, Montevideo, Baden-Baden, Madrid, Bruxelles National, London Philharmonic, Prague, Barcelona, Paris; Masterclass, Conservatoire de Musique de Genève; Festival appearances at Montreux, Lausanne, Montevideo, Salzburg, Ascona, Prague, Espagne and Portugal; Member of Jury at International Competitions at Genève, Cologne, Athens, Berlin, Mallorca, Lisbon; Conductors: Ansermet, Prêtre, Dutoit, Sawallisch, Stein, Jordan, Matacic, Carvalho, Dervaux, Groves; Cours d'Interpretation: Suisse, Television Suisse, Espagne, Canada. *Honours:* 1st Prize a l'unanimite Concours d'éxecution musicale, Geneva; Prix de l'institut Neuchatelois, 1973. *Address:* 1245 Collonge-Bellerive, Switzerland.

**DATZ, Irene;** Singer (Soprano); b. 14 April 1963, Zhytomyr, Ukraine. *Education:* Studied at the Kiev State Conservatoire from 1980. *Career:* Sang with the Kiev State Radio Orchestra, 1985 and made her debut with Kiev National Opera in 1986, at first as Mezzo-Soprano; At Kiev and Bolshoi Operas has sung Donna Anna, Mimi, Tosca, Nedda, Cherubino, Marguerite, Marfa in The Tsar's Bride, and Iolanta; Tours of North America from 1991 with appearances at the Metropolitan Opera as Tatiana; Solo recitals in Chicago, Philadelphia, Illinois and Washington; Sang Wagner's Elsa at the Kiev Opera in 1994. *Address:* Sonata Ltd, 11 North Park Street, Glasgow G20 7AA, Scotland.

**DAUGHERTY, Michael;** Composer; b. 28 April 1954, Cedar Rapids, Iowa, USA. *Education:* Studied at North Texas State (BM) and the Manhattan School of Music (MA, 1976); Jacob Druckman, Roger Reynolds, Bernard Rands and Gil Evans at Yale University, DMA, 1986; Further study at IRCAM, Paris, 1979-80, and with Ligeti at the Hamburg Musikhochschule, 1982-84. *Career:* Faculty of Oberlin Conservatory, 1986-91; Full Professor of Composition, University of Michigan, Ann Arbor. *Compositions include:* Piano Plus, 1985; Snap-Blue Like an Orange for 16 players, 1987; Strut for string orchestra, 1989; Beat Boxer for string quartet and pre-recorded DAT tape, 1991; Firecracker for oboe and 6 players, 1991; Flamingo for chamber orchestra, 1991; Desi, Bizarro, and Niagara Falls for symphonic wind band, 1991-92; Sing Sing: J Edgar Hoover for string quartet and tape, 1992; Dead Elvis for bassoon and 6 players, 1993; Metropolis Symphony (premiered Carnegie Hall), 1988-93; Le Tombeau de Liberace, for piano and ensemble, 1994; Paul Robeson Told Me for string quartet and tape, 1994; Motown Metal for brass ensemble and percussion, 1994; Lounge Lizards for 2 pianos and 2 percussion, 1994; What's That Spell? for 2 amplified sopranos and 16 players, 1995; Jackie's Song, for cello, 1996; Jackie O, chamber opera in 2 acts (premiere Houston Opera), 1997; Route 66 for orchestra, 1998; Spaghetti Western for English horn and orchestra, 1998; Sunset Strip for chamber orchestra, 1999; UFO for percussion solo and orchestra, 1999; Hell's Angels for bassoon quartet and orchestra, 1999. *Recordings:* Numerous for major labels. *Address:* c/o Faber Music, 3 Queen Square, London WC1N 3AU, England.

**DAUSGAARD, Thomas;** Conductor; b. 1963, Denmark. *Education:* Studied in Scandinavia. *Career:* Assistant Conductor to Seiji Ozawa at the Boston Symphony Orchestra, 1993-96; Beethoven's Missa Solemnis with the Swedish Radio Symphony Orchestra and Chorus, 1993; Further concerts with the Danish National Radio Symphony Orchestra; Season 1996-97 with the Oslo,

St Petersburg and Royal Philharmonic Orchestras and the Montreal Symphony; Principal Guest Conductor with Danish Radio Symphony Orchestra from 1997 (tour of Germany, 2001); Conducted the Danish National Symphony Orchestra at the London Proms, 2002; Music Dir of the Swedish Chamber Orchestra, 1997–; Prin. Guest Conductor 2001–04, and Chief Conductor 2004– of the Danish National Symphony Orchestra; Guest conductor to the Bayerischer Rundfunk, Dresden Philharmonic, Frankfurt Radio Symphony and Leipzig Gewandhaus Orchestras in Germany and the Orchestre Philharmonique de Radio France in Paris; Recent engagements include conducting the Netherlands Philharmonic Orchestra, the RSB Berlin, the Stockholm and Oslo Philharmonic Orchestras, St Petersburg Philharmonic Orchestra, RAI Turin and La Scala Philharmonic Orchestras. *Recordings include:* Zemlinsky's Seejungfrau and Sinfonietta (Chandos); Beethoven Symphony Nos 1, 2, 4, 5 and 7 and Piano Concertos No 1, 2 and 3 and the Triple Concerto; Other comnposers include Berwald, Brahms, Grieg, Hamerik, Hartmann, Kunzen, Langgaard, Ligeti, Liszt, Mozart, Nørgård, Riisager, Sibelius, Sinding, Stenhammar, Svendson and Wiren. *Honours:* Music Critics' Circle Prize, Denmark, 1993; Prizewinner at International Competitions. *Address:* c/o IMG Artists, Lovell House, 616 Chiswick High Road, London W4 5RX, England.

**D'AVALOS, Francesco;** Teacher, Composer and Conductor; b. 11 April 1930, Naples, Italy. *Education:* Studied Classics at college, Naples; Philosophy, Naples University; Started Piano study with Vicenzo Vitale at age 12, then Composition with Renato Parodi; Diploma in Composition, San Pietro a Majella Conservatory, Naples; Accademia Chigiana, Siena, with Franco Ferrara and Sergiu Celibidache. *Career:* Debut: Concert as Conductor, RAI, Rome, 1964; Has appeared with Philharmonia Orchestra, London, 1987–; has taught at several Italian conservatories; Holds Chair of Fugue and Advanced Composition and Chair of Conducting, San Pietro a Majella Conservatory, Naples. *Compositions:* Hymne an die Nacht, 1958, conducted by H W Henze, Hessischer Rundfunk; Studio Sinfonico, 1982, conducted by d'Avalos, Lugano; Symphony for Orchestra and Soprano, premiered Norddeutscher Rundfunk, Hamburg; Qumran, study for orchestra, La Scala with Eliahu Inbal; Maria di Venosa-Gesualdo, musical drama in 2 acts, 1992; Die Stille Stadt for soprano, timpano and strings, 1994; Qumran, musical drama in 3 parts, 2001; Other orchestral works, works for voice, chamber music. *Recordings:* Over 30 including: Brahms, complete orchestral works; Martucci, complete orchestral works; Wagner, overtures; Bruckner, Symphony No. 7; Mendelssohn, complete orchestral works; Clementi, complete orchestral works; Maria di Venosa with Philharmonia Orchestra and Chorus, soloists, madrigalists, 1994. *Honours:* Premio Marzotto for Composition; Grand Prix International du Disque for Martucci's Symphonies, Académie Charles Cros, Paris, 1990; MRA Award for Raff's Symphony No. 3, Im Walde, 1993. *Address:* 50 via dei Mille, Naples, Italy.

**DAVENPORT, Glyn;** Singer (bass-baritone); b. 3 May 1948, Halifax, Yorkshire, England; m. Jane Keay 1972; two s. *Education:* Royal Coll. of Music, London, 1966–70; ARCM, viola, LRAM, singing; Staatliche Musikhochschule, Hamburg, Germany, 1970–73. *Career:* debut, Wigmore Hall, London, England, 1973; opera appearances with English Opera Group, English Music Theatre, Scottish Opera, Royal Opera House, Kent Opera, Wexford Festival Opera, Opera Factory, Zürich; recitals for BBC Radio 3, Songmakers' Almanac, British Council in Near and Middle East; oratorio in major London venues and BBC, Switzerland, Germany and Iceland. *Recordings:* The English Cat, Hans Werner Henze. *Honours:* winner, Kathleen Ferrier Memorial Competition, 1972. *Current Management:* Musicmakers International Artists Representation, Tailor House, 63–65 High Street, Whitwell, Hertfordshire SG4 8AH, England. *Telephone:* (1438) 871708. *Fax:* (1438) 871777. *E-mail:* musicmakers@compuserve.com. *Website:* www .operauk.com. *Address:* Wendover, Horsell Rise, Horsell, Woking, Surrey GU21 4BD, England. *E-mail:* glyndavenport@boltblue.com.

**DAVERNE, Gary Michiel,** ONZM, DipEd, FTCL, LRSM; New Zealand music director, composer, conductor and music producer; *Director of Music and Conductor, Auckland Symphony Orchestra;* b. 26 Jan. 1939, Auckland. *Education:* Auckland Univ., Auckland Teachers' Coll., Trinity Coll. of Music, London. *Career:* self-employed, int. conductor, composer, arranger, record prod. of over 40 albums; conductor and arranger of music for TV, film and radio; fmr teacher of economics and accountancy 1962–77; Composer in Schools 1978–79; Pres., Composers' Asscn, New Zealand 1979; Dir of Music and Conductor, Auckland Symphony Orchestra 1975–; Dir of Music, Waitangi Day celebrations; Music Dir, Military Searchlight Tattoo, New Plymouth 1997; Music Dir, premiere of Jewish oratorio, Hear! O Israel by Cormac O'Duffy to celebrate Israel's 50th nat. birthday; arranger and prod. credits include Sir Howard Morrison, Kylie Harris. *Compositions include:* over 100 pop songs, operettas, songs for children, three rock operas, concert accordion music, over 600 TV and radio jingles, film soundtracks; many symphonic works for orchestra (recorded by New Zealand SO), including Rhapsody for accordion and orchestra. *Address:* 48 Shelly Beach Road, Herne Bay, Auckland 1002, New Zealand. *E-mail:* daverne@ihug.co.nz. *Website:* www .aucklandsymphony.gen.nz.

**DAVID, Avram;** Composer, Teacher and Pianist; b. 30 June 1930, Boston, Massachusetts, USA; m. Leslie, 3 Dec 1977. *Education:* BA Music, 1955; MA Music, 1956; DMA Musical Composition, 1964; Boston University; Berkshire Music Center, Tanglewood, Summer 1948; Kranichsteiner Musikinstitut, Darmstadt, West Germany, Summer 1961 and 1966; Private Study of Piano and Philosophy of Performance and Composition with Margaret Chaloff and Composition with Francis Cooke, Harold Shapero, Karlheinz Stockhausen, Pierre Boulez. *Career:* Private Teaching, 1960–64; Chairman, Composition Department, Composer-in-Residence, Boston Conservatory of Music, 1964–73; Director, Avram David Studio, 1973–77; Director, Margaret Chaloff Studio, 1977–; Lecturer, Harvard University and New England Conservatory of Music; Appearances as solo pianist in concert and on television and radio. *Compositions:* Composer of 133 works including: 2 Orchestral Works including 1 Symphony; 21 works for Chamber Ensembles; 6 String Quartets; 2 Solo Violin Sonatas; 43 works for Solo Piano including 5 Sonatas; 24 works for Solo Winds; 8 Choral works. *Recordings:* Sonata for Horn Solo, Opus 101. *Address:* c/o ASCAP, ASCAP Building, One Lincoln Plaza, New York, NY 10023, USA.

**DAVIDOVICH, Bella;** American (b. USSR) pianist; b. 16 July 1928, Baku, Azerbaijan; m. Julian Sitkovetsky 1950 (died 1958); one s. *Education:* Moscow Conservatory. *Career:* studied with Konstantin Igumnov and Jakob Flier; First Prize, Chopin Competition, Warsaw 1949; soloist with Leningrad Philharmonic for 28 consecutive seasons; toured Europe; went to USA 1978; mem. faculty Juilliard School, NY 1983–; became US citizen 1984; has performed with world's leading conductors in USA, Europe and Japan; Prof., Juilliard School. *Honours:* Deserving Artist of the Soviet Union. *Address:* c/o Agnes Bruneau, 155 West 68th Street, No. 1010, New York, NY 10023, USA (office).

**DAVIDOVICI, Robert;** Violinist and Professor of Violin; b. 1 Oct. 1946, Sutu-Mare, Romania; m. Tamara Golan, 8 Mar 1973, 2 s., 2 d. *Education:* School of Music No. 1, Bucharest, 1958–62; Conservatorium of Music High School, Sydney, Australia, 1962–63; Performers and Teacher Diploma, 1st Class Honours, 1966; Juilliard School, New York, USA, 1967–73; Postgraduate Diploma, 1970. *Career:* Debut: Alice Tully Hall, New York, USA, 1972; mem, College Music Society; American String Teachers Association; Violin Society of America. *Recordings:* Recital with Steven DeGroote of works by Copland, Gunther Schuller, Walter Piston, Hugh Aitken and Paul Schonfield. *Honours:* 1st Prize, Carnegie Hall International American Music Competition, 1983; 1st Prize, Naumberg Competition, New York, 1972; Flaggler Award, 1973. *Current Management:* Shaw Concerts Incorporated.

**DAVIDOVSKY, Mario;** American composer and teacher; b. 4 March 1934, Buenos Aires, Argentina; m. Elaine Davidovsky. *Education:* received violin lessons in childhood; Studied composition and theory with Guillermo Graetzer, Buenos Aires; Studied with Theodore Fuchs, Erwin Leuchter and Ernesto Epstein; Completed training with Aaron Copland and Milton Babbitt, Berkshire Music Center, Tanglewood, 1958. *Career:* Associated with Columbia-Princeton Electronic Music Center, 1960–; Teacher, University of Michigan, 1964; Di Tella Institute, 1969–70; City College of the City University of New York, 1968–80; Columbia University, 1981–; Director, Columbia-Princeton Electronic Music centre, 1981–94; Professor of Music, Harvard University, 1994–; mem, Elected to Institute of American Academy of Arts and Letters, 1982. *Compositions include:* Synchronisms No. 1 for flute and electronics, 1963, No. 2 for flute, clarinet, violin, cello and electronics, 1964, No. 3 for cello and electronics, 1965, No. 4 for men's or mixed chorus and electronics, 1967, No. 5 for percussion ensemble and electronics, 1969, No. 6 for piano and electronics, 1970, No. 7 for orchestra and electronics, 1973, No. 8 for woodwind quintet and electronics, 1974; No. 9 for violin and electronics, 1988; No. 10 for guitar and electronics, 1992; Orchestral: Concertino for percussion and strings, 1954; Pianos, 1961; Divertimento for cello and orchestra, 1984; Concertante for string quartet and orchestra, 1990; Concertino for violin and chamber orchestra, 1995; Chamber: 4 String Quartets, 1954, 1958, 1976, 1980; Flashbacks for ensemble, 1995; Tape: Electronic Study No. 1, 1961, No. 2, 1962, No. 3, 1965. *Honours:* Guggenheim Fellowships, 1960, 1971; Rockefeller Fellowships, 1963, 1964; American Academy of Arts and Letters Award, 1965; Pulitzer prize in Music, 1971; Naumberg Award, 1972; Guggenheim Award, 1982; Various commissions. *Address:* Music Department, Harvard University, Cambridge, MA, USA.

**DAVIDSON, Cheyne;** Singer (Baritone); b. 1965, USA. *Education:* Studied at the Cleveland Institute of Music and the Manhattan School of Music. *Career:* Tour of Europe, Japan and Israel, as Escamillo in Peter Brook's version of Carmen, La Tragédie de Carmen; Zürich Opera as the Speaker in Die Zauberflöte, Massenet's Hérodiade, Marcello, David in L'Amico Fritz, Sharpless, and Ramiro in L'Heure Espagnole (1996); Guest appearances at Stuttgart as Sharpless and the Speaker, 1994; Escamillo at Hamburg; In Francesca da Rimini at the Bregenz Festival; Season 1996–97 as the Messenger in Robert Wilson's production of Oedipus Rex at the Paris Théâtre du Châtelet, and Schaunard in La Bohème at Zürich; Premieres include Ein Narrenparadies by Ofer Ben-Amot, at Vienna, and the song cycle with orchestra Vom Unvergänglichen by Franz Thurauer, at Bregenz; Season 2000 as Escamillo, Donner in Das Rheingold and Tomsky in The Queen of Spades at Zürich. *Address:* c/o Opernhaus Zürich, Falkenstrasse 1, 8008 Zürich, Switzerland.

**DAVIDSON, Joy;** Singer (Mezzo-Soprano); b. 18 Aug. 1940, Fort Collins, Colorado, USA. *Education:* Studied in Los Angeles, at Florida State University and with Daniel Harris. *Career:* Debut: Miami, 1965 as Rossini's Cenerentola; Sang at the opera houses of Dallas, Houston, New Orleans and San Francisco; Santa Fe 1969, in the US premiere of Penderecki's The Devils of Loudun; Appearances with the Welsh National Opera and at Lisbon, Sofia,

Vienna, Munich, Milan and Florence; Other roles include Carmen, Charlotte in Werther, Dalila, Verdi's Eboli and Preziosilla and Gluck's Orpheus; Also heard as concert Singer; Sang Baba the Turk in The Rake's Progress at the State Theatre, New York, 1984.

**DAVIDSON, Robert;** Composer; b. 17 Dec. 1965, Brisbane, Queensland, Australia. *Education:* BMus (Hons), University of Queensland, 1987; Further study with Terry Riley and LaMonte Young, 1995. *Career:* Freelance Composer; Performer in orchestra, including Queensland and Sydney Symphony Orchestras. *Compositions include:* Dodecahedron for string orchestra, 1985; Eight, for ensemble, 1986; Stained Glass for 2 violins, 2 cellos, 2 clarinets, 2 pianos, 1986; Zemar for piano, 1987; Sound Panels, for flute, string quartet and double bass, 1988; Triptych for orchestra, 1988; Tapestry, for viola, cello, clarinet and piano, 1989; Refrains, for double bass and piano, 1989; Adeney Cycle, for violin and viola, 1990; Strata for mixed ensemble, 1990; Variations and Episodes, for piano, 1990; Arch for 3 violins, 1992; Conversations, for viola, cello and clarinet, 1993; Mesh, for double bass and piano, 1993; Violin Concerto, 1994; Three Grounds, for ensemble, 1994; Chaconne for orchestra, 1994; Boombox Pieces for multiple cassette players, 1995. *Address:* c/o APRA, 1A Eden Street, Crows Nest, NSW 2065, Australia.

**DAVIDSON, Tina;** Composer and Pianist; b. 30 Dec. 1952, Stockholm, Sweden; m., 1 d. *Education:* BA, Piano and Composition, Bennington College, 1972–76; Composition Studies with Henry Brant, Vivian Fine, Louis Calabro. *Career:* Associate Director, RELACHE, The Ensemble for Contemporary Music, 1978–89; Piano Instructor, Drexel University, 1981–85; Residencies: Chamber Music Conference and Composers' Forum; Milay Colony for the Arts, October 1981; Yellow Springs Fellowship of the Arts, May 1982; Charles Ives Center, 1986; Composer-in-Residence, Orchestra Society of Philadelphia, 1992–94; Composer-in-Residence, Opera Delaware Symphony Orchestra and YWCA of Wilmington Delaware, 1994–97; Fleisher Art Memorial Composer in Residence, 1997–99. *Compositions include:* Inside And Out, piano and 2 players, 1974; Recollections of Darkness, string trio, 1975; Two Beasts From The Forest Of Imaginary Beings, narrator and orchestra, 1975, commissioned by Sage City Symphony, student commission, 1976; Five Songs from The Game of Silence, soprano and viola, 1976; Billy and Zelda, music theatre (8 singers, 1 actress, string quartet and percussion), 1977; Piano Concerto, piano and orchestra, 1981; Unicorn/Tapestry, mezzo-soprano, violoncello and tape, 1982; Other Echoes, 2 violins, 1982; Wait For The End Of Dreaming, 2 baritone saxophones, Double Bass, 1983–85; Shadow Grief, soprano (or alto saxophone), 1983; Day of Rage, and I Am The Last Witness, piano solo, 1984; Blood Memory: A Long Quiet After The Call, cello and orchestra, commissioned by Sage City Symphony, 1985; Bleached Thread Sister Thread, 1992; Fire on the Mountain, marimba, vibraphone and piano, 1993; They Come Dancing for full orchestra, 1994; Over Salt River, soprano, 1995; Star Fire, for youth orchestra, 1996; It Is My Heart Singing, string sextet, 1996; Of The Running Way, for clarinet (or alto saxophone) and piano, 1996; Lost Love Songs, for solo cello, 1997. *Recordings:* Cassatt, 1994; I Hear the Mermaids Singing, 1996. *Honours:* Pennsylvania Council Fellowship, 1983–96; PEN Fellowship, 1992–94. *Address:* 508 Woodland Terrace, Philadelphia, PA 19104, USA.

**DAVIES, Arthur;** singer (tenor); b. 11 April 1941, Wrexham, Wales. *Education:* Royal Northern College of Music. *Career:* has sung with Welsh National Opera as Nemorino, Albert Herring, Nadir in Les pêcheurs de Perles, Rodolfo, and Don José; Covent Garden debut 1976, in the world premiere of We Come to the River by Henze; has returned in Lucia di Lammermoor, and as Alfredo, the Italian Tenor in Der Rosenkavalier, Števa in Jenůfa, and Pinkerton; Scottish Opera at the Edinburgh Festival as the Fox in The Cunning Little Vixen, and David in Die Meistersinger; Appearances with English National Opera as the Duke of Mantua, Alfredo, the Gounod Faust, and Werther; Opera North as Jenik in The Bartered Bride, Pinkerton, Don José and Nadir; Foreign engagements in Chicago, Cincinnati, Connecticut, Ghent, Leipzig, Lisbon, New Orleans, Moscow, Santiago and New York (Metropolitan House with the ENO company); Sang Faust with ENO, Jan 1990; Gaston, British stage premiere of Verdi's Jérusalem, Opera North; Cavaradossi and Pinkerton for Scottish Opera; Cincinnati Opera, July 1990 as Faust; Edinburgh Festival, 1990 as Yannakos in The Greek Passion by Martinů; Sang Cavardossi for Opera Pacific at Costa Mesa, 1992; Don José at San Diego and the Duke of Mantua for ENO; Sang Verdi's Foresto at Buenos Aires, 1993; Samson at Metz, 1996; Concerts include the Verdi Requiem at the Festival Hall, London, conducted by Giulini. *Recordings:* Rigoletto (EMI; also on video); The Dream of Gerontius, with the London Symphony Orchestra (Chandos); Elijah; Rossini's Stabat Mater; The Kingdom of Elgar.

**DAVIES, David (Somerville);** Conductor and Artistic Director; b. 13 June 1954, Dunfermline, Scotland; m. Virginia Henson, 15 Sept 1986. *Education:* Royal Scottish Academy of Music, University of Edinburgh; Salzburg Mozarteum; Conservatoire National De Marseille. *Career:* Assistant Principal Flute, Scottish National Orchestra, 1975–80; Principal Flute, Scottish Opera, 1980–85; Freelance Conductor, 1985–, working with BBC Scottish Symphony Orchestra, Scottish Chamber Orchestra, Royal Scottish National Orchestra, Royal Liverpool Philharmonic Orchestra in England; l'Orchestre Philharmonique de Radio France, l'Opéra de Marseille, l'Orchestre Philharmonique de Marseille in France; Ensemble Caput in Iceland and the Stadtorchester Winterhur in Switzerland; Conductor and Artistic Director, Paragon Ensemble, Scotland, Paragon Opera Projects, Scotland, 1985–; Lecturer, Royal Scottish Academy of Music and Drama, 1991–. *Recordings:* Two vols of

world premiere recordings of Scottish Contemporary music, 1991 and 1993. *Address:* c/o Paragon Ensemble Ltd, 2 Port Dundas Place, Glasgow G2 3LB, Scotland.

**DAVIES, Dennis Russell;** Conductor and Pianist; b. 16 April 1944, Toledo, OH, USA. *Education:* BMus, 1966, MS, 1968, DMA, 1972, Juilliard School of Music, New York; Studied piano with Berenice B MacNab, Lonny Epstein and Sascha Gorodnitzki; Conducting with Jean Morel and Jorge Mester. *Career:* Teacher, Juilliard School of Music, 1968–71; Co-founder with Luciano Berio, Conductor, Juilliard Ensemble, 1968–74; Music Director, Norwalk (Conn) Symphony Orchestra, 1968–73; St Paul (Minn) Chamber Orchestra, 1972–80; Cabrillo (Calif) Music Festival, 1974–92; American Composers Orchestra, NY, 1977–; Generalmusikdirektor, Wurttemberg State Theatre, Stuttgart, 1980–87; Principal Conductor and Director of Classical Music Programming, Saratoga, NY, Performing Arts Center, 1985–88; Generalmusikdirektor, City Theatre and Beethoven Hall Orchestra, Bonn, 1987–95; Guest Conductor with various opera companies and orchestras in North America and Europe; Champion of Contemporary Music; Conducted premieres by: Luciano Berio, John Cage, Hans Werner Henze, Philip Glass (Akhnaten, 1984), Mauricio Kagel, William Bolcom, Joan Tower, Pauline Oliveros, Lou Harrison, Kurt Schwertsik; Conducted the premiere of William Bolcom's Songs of Innocence and Experience, Stuttgart, 1984; Music Director, Brooklyn Academy of Music, 1991–93; Principal Conductor, Brooklyn Philharmonic, 1991–95; Conducted the premiere of Manfred Trojhan's Enrico, Schwetzingen Festival, 1991; Chief Conductor: Stuttgart Chamber Orchestra, 1995–, Vienna Radio Symphony Orchestra from 1996; Led Thomson's Four Saints in Three Acts at the 1996 Lincoln Center Festival. Season 1998 with Lulu at the Opéra Bastille and Weill's Mahagonny at Salzburg; Chief Conductor, Linz Opera (Landstheater), Austria, 2002–; Chief conductor and Music Director, Bruckner Orchester Linz, 2002–. *Recordings:* Many for various labels including Philip Glass, Heroes Symphony, 1997. *Honours:* Alice M Ditson Award for Conductors, 1987. *Address:* c/o Columbia Artists Management Inc, 165 West 57th Street, New York, NY 10019, USA.

**DAVIES, Eirian,** BA; singer (soprano); b. 22 May 1954, Llangollen, Wales; one s. *Education:* University College of Wales at Aberystwyth, Royal Academy of Music, London. *Career:* debut, Vivaldi's Griselda, Buxton Festival, and Gounod's La Colombe, 1983; Welsh National Opera: Rhinemaiden, in Das Rheingold and Götterdämmerung; Gerhilde, in Die Walküre; Lisa in La Sonnambula; Aenchen in Der Freischütz; English National Opera: Pamina in The Magic Flute; Frasquita in Carmen; Orpheus in the Underworld; Opera North Mimi in La Bohème; Christine in Robert Saxton's Caritas (world premiere); Glyndebourne: world premiere of Nigel Osborne's Electrification of the Soviet Union; Garsington: Rezia in L'Incontro Improvviso, by Haydn; Music Theatre Wales: Dotty in world premiere of Hardy's Flowers; Edinburgh Festival: World premiere of Macmillan's Tourist Variations and Craig Armstrong's Anna; Semur en Auxois Festival; Mozart's Constanze; More recent performances include: Princess Natalie in Der Prinz von Homburg, in Cologne; Gepopo in Le Grand Macabre and Aventures et Nouvelles Aventures, by Ligeti in Zürich; World premiere of Kubo's Rashomon in Graz; Salzburg Festival debut, 1997, in Feldman's Neither, also Wien Moderne Festival in Rihm's Frau Stimme; Appearances on television for BBC and HTV, and for BBC Radio 3. *Recordings:* Le Grand Macabre; Caritas by Robert Saxton. *Honours:* Catherine and Lady Grace James Award; Winner, Francisco Vinas International Competition, Barcelona, 1984.

**DAVIES, Joan;** Singer (Mezzo-Soprano); b. 1940, Swansea, Wales. *Education:* Royal College of Music, London. *Career:* Sang with the Glyndebourne Chorus, then with Sadler's Wells until 1969, notably as Offenbach's Hélène and in the premiere of Bennett's A Penny for a Song, 1965; Debut with Welsh National Opera as Meg Page in Falstaff; Sang Meg Page at Covent Garden and appeared in La Traviata and the premiere of Henze's We Come to the River, 1976; Other engagements in Munich and Berlin and with Scottish Opera, Opera North, Pheonix Opera, Basilica Opera and Dublin Grand Opera; New Sadler's Wells Opera from 1983 in The Mikado, The Count of Luxembourg, The Merry Widow and works by Gilbert and Sullivan (also in New York); Appearances at the Wexford Festival in The Devil and Kate, and Gazzaniga's Don Giovanni (1987); Other roles include Mme Popova in Walton's The Bear (Lisbon), Auntie in Peter Grimes at the Royal Opera, Ghent, and Mozart's Marcellina in Bordeaux and Rouen; Television appearances as Meg Page, Marcellina and Mary in Der fliegende Holländer; Concert engagements with the Royal Liverpool Philharmonic and the Ulster Orchestra. *Address:* Music International, 13 Ardilaun Road, London N5 2QR, England.

**DAVIES, John Lloyd;** British stage director and designer; *Head of Opera Development, ROH2;* b. 1950, Wales. *Career:* new production and revivals for ENO, with Carmen, Rusalka, Carmen and Madama Butterfly; The Cunning Little Vixen and Les Troyens for Scottish Opera; Don Giovanni, Die Zauberflöte and Rigoletto for the Vienna Kammeroper; Wozzeck and Rimsky-Korsakov's May Night in London; Un Ballo in Maschera at Klagenfurt, Zar und Zimmermann at Aachen and Danton's Death by Einem at Brighton; Tosca in Malmö. Reimann's Das Schloss in Vienna; Albert Herring at Aldeburgh and Tchaikovsky's The Enchantress for New Sussex Opera; currently Dir of Productions, Musik Werkstatt Wien and New Sussex Opera; season 2001–02 with Les Contes d'Hoffmann in Nuremberg; Head of Opera Development, ROH2 programme 2005–. *Honours:* Josef Kainz Medal,

Austria. *Address:* ROH2, Royal Opera House, Bow Street, Covent Garden, London, WC2E 9DD, England.

**DAVIES, Menai;** Singer (Mezzo-soprano); b. 17 Nov. 1939, Wales. *Education:* Studied with Gwilym Gwalchmai Jones and Valetta Jacopi. *Career:* Taught music for 14 years; Engaged with Welsh National Opera 1974–86, in repertory from Monteverdi to Britten, to the premiere of Metcalf's The Journey (1981); Mamma Lucia in Cavalleria Rusticana, 1995; Glyndebourne Touring Opera from 1987 (debut in L'Enfant et les Sortilèges) and Festival from 1989, as Grandmother in Jenůfa, Auntie in Peter Grimes and Cleaner in The Makropulos Case (1995); Other appearances with Scottish Opera, English National Opera and Opera North's Gloria, H K Gruber; Britten's Mrs Herring at Rome and Reggio Emilia, Mrs Grose in Peter Grimes at Cologne, Schwetzingen and Dresden; Théâtre du Châtelet, Paris, in Jenůfa and in premieres of operas by Fenelon and Philippe Manoury; The Makropulos Case at Barcelona and New York; Ideally suited for older roles in modern works.

**DAVIES, Neal;** Singer (Baritone); b. 1965, Newport, Gwent, Wales. *Education:* Studied at King's College, London, The Royal Academy of Music and the International Opera Studio, Zürich. *Career:* Many roles at the Coburg Opera, Germany, including Papageno in a Brigitte Fassbaender production of Die Zauberflöte; Concerts at the Edinburgh Festival include Prokoviev's Hamlet, Janáček's Sarka, Schubert's Die Freunde von Salamanca, Leonore and Ninth Symphony by Beethoven, and the Scenes from Faust by Schumann, 1992–; Further opera includes Starveling in Midsummer Night's Dream with the London Symphony Orchestra, Handel's Radamisto at Marseilles and Orlando at the City of London Festival, La Bohème with the Oslo Philharmonic Orchestra and Masetto in Don Giovanni for Welsh National Opera; Season 1996–97 as Schaunard for WNO, in Stravinsky's Rossignol under Pierre Boulez for the BBC, Elijah with the Liverpool Philharmonic Orchestra and Messiah with the Gabrieli Consort under Paul McCreesh; Debut with the Royal Opera in Rameau's Platée (also at Edinburgh), 1997; Sang Mozart's Figaro and Handel's Achilla with the Royal Opera, 1998; Season 1999 with Nielsen's Springtime on Funen at the London Prom concerts; Revueltas's la noche de los mayas at the London Proms, 2002; Many recital engagements. *Recordings include:* A Midsummer Night's Dream; Classics; Elijah; Messiah; Henri Dutilleux Songs with orchestra; Vivaldi Cantatas with Robert King. *Honours:* Winner, Lieder Prize at the Cardiff Singer of the World Competition, 1991. *Current Management:* Askonas Holt Ltd, Lonsdale Chambers, 27 Chancery Lane, London, WC2A 1PF, England. *Telephone:* (20) 7400-1700. *Fax:* (20) 7400-1799. *E-mail:* info@askonasholt.co.uk. *Website:* www.askonasholt.co.uk.

**DAVIES, Noel;** conductor; b. 1945, London, England. *Education:* Royal College of Music, with Richard Austin and Adrian Boult. *Career:* Conducting Staff, Sadler's Wells Opera, then Resident Conductor, English National Opera, 1974–; Many performances of the standard repertory, including operas by Mozart, Verdi and Puccini; Collaborations with Janet Baker, Ann Murray, Thomas Allen, Rosalind Plowright and Felicity Lott; Guest Conductor with Rigoletto for the Bergen Festival, Giulio Cesare at Houston and Gloriana at the Metropolitan, New York; Xerxes, Giulio Cesare and Don Giovanni, 1997; Bavarian State Opera, Il Trovatore at Dublin and Giulio Cesare for the Covent Garden company at the Barbican, season 1997–98; Performing editions with Charles Mackerras of operas by Handel, including Xerxes for English National Opera.

**DAVIES, Sir Peter Maxwell,** Kt (see Maxwell Davies, Sir Peter)

**DAVIES, Ryland;** British singer (tenor); b. 9 Feb. 1943, Cwm Ebbw Vale, Monmouthshire (now Gwent); s. of Joan and Gethin Davies; m. 1st Anne Howells (q.v.) 1966 (divorced 1981); m. 2nd Deborah Jane Rees 1983; one d. *Education:* Royal Manchester Coll. of Music (Fellow 1971). *Career:* voice teacher Royal Northern Coll. of Music (RNCM) 1987–94, Royal Coll. of Music, London 1999–; Dir Opera Productions RNCM Mananan Festival, Clonter Opera Trust; début as Almaviva in The Barber of Seville, Welsh Nat. Opera 1964, subsequent appearances including Tamino in The Magic Flute 1974, Yenick in Bartered Bride 1989; Glyndebourne Festival Chorus 1964–66, taking parts including Belmonte in The Abduction from the Seraglio, Ferrando in Così fan tutte, Flamand in Capriccio, Lysander in A Midsummer Night's Dream, The Prince in Love of Three Oranges, Lensky in Eugene Onegin, Tichone in Katya Kabanova, Basilio/Curzio in Le nozze di Figaro, Auctioneer in The Rake's Progress; appearances with Scottish Opera as Ferrando and as Fenton in Falstaff, Tamino in The Magic Flute and as Nemorino in L'Elisir d'Amore; with Sadler's Wells Opera as Almaviva, Essex in Britten's Gloriana; with Royal Opera as Hylas in The Trojans, Don Ottavio in Don Giovanni, Ferrando, Cassio in Otello, Nemorino in L'Elisir d'Amore, Ernesto in Don Pasquale, Lysander in A Midsummer Night's Dream and Almaviva; with English Nat. Opera as Eisenstein in Die Fledermaus, Basilio in Le nozze di Figaro, Rev. H. Adams in Peter Grimes, Albazar in Turk in Italy, L'Aumonier in Dialogues des Carmélites, Gaudenzio in La Bohème; overseas appearances include Salzburg Festival, at San Francisco, Chicago, Paris, at Metropolitan Opera, New York, Hollywood Bowl, Paris Opera, Geneva, Brussels, Lyons, Amsterdam, Mannheim, Israel, Buenos Aires, Stuttgart, Nice, Nancy, Philadelphia, Berlin, Hamburg; returned to Covent Garden 1994, 2002, Welsh Nat. Opera 1994, New York Metropolitan Opera 1994, 1995, 2001, Glyndebourne 1997, New Israeli Opera 1997, Chicago Lyric Opera 1998, 2003, Santa Fe Opera 1998, 1999, New Israeli Opera 1998, Netherlands Opera 1998, 1999, 2002, English Nat. Opera 1999, Houston

Grand Opera 2002, Japan 2002, Florence 2002, Zauberflote/Monastatos Netherlands 2003, Covent Garden Monostatos 2003, Basilio, Chicago Lyric Opera 2003, Peter Grimes, London Symphony, Barbican and New York, Colin Davis 2004, A Midsummer Night's Dream, La Fenice, Venice 2004; Boise Mendelsohn Foundation Scholarship 1964; Fellow Welsh Coll. of Music and Drama 1996. *Recordings include:* The Abduction from the Seraglio, L'Amore dei Tre Re (Montemezzi), La Navarraise (Massenet), The Trojans, Saul, Così fan tutte, Thérèse (Massenet), Monteverdi Madrigals, Idomeneo, The Seasons (Haydn), Messiah, L'Oracolo (Leone), Judas Maccabaeus, Pulcinella, Il Matrimonio Segreto, Lucia di Lammamoor, Otello, Mozart's Requiem, C Minor Mass, Credo Mass, Coronation Mass, Messe Solonelle; Oedipus Rex (Shepherd), Il Trovatore (Ruiz), Don Carlo (Conte di Lerma), Le nozze di Figaro (Basilio/Curzio), Esclarmonde (Massenet). *Video films include:* Don Pasquale, A Midsummer Night's Dream, Die Entführung aus dem Serail, Love of Three Oranges, Trial by Jury, Katya Kabanova. *Television:* Merry Widow, Capriccio (BBC, Glyndebourne), A Goodly Manner for a Song (STV), On Wenlock Edge (BBC Wales, Glyndebourne), Dido and Aeneas (BBC, Glyndebourne), Mass in C Minor. *Achievements:* played rugby for Wales Schoolboys, 2 caps 1957–58, Wales Boys Clubs under-18s 1959–60. *Honours:* Hon. Fellow Royal Manchester Coll. of Music 1971 Ricordi Opera Prize, Royal Manchester Coll. of Music 1963, Imperial League of Opera Prize, Royal Manchester Coll. of Music 1963, First John Christie Award, Glyndebourne 1965. *Address:* c/o Hazard Chase Ltd, 25 City Road, Cambridge, CB1 1DP (office); "Elm Cottage", Loseberry Road, Claygate, Surrey, KT10 9DQ, England (home). *Telephone:* (20) 8233-5800 (office). *E-mail:* rylandtenore@hotmail.com (home).

**DAVIES, Wyn;** British conductor; *Director of Music, NBR New Zealand Opera;* b. 8 May 1952, Gowerton, Wales; m. Jane Baxendale 1975. *Education:* Christ Church, Oxford. *Career:* appearances in concert with BBC Nat. Orchestra of Wales, BBC Scottish Orchestra, Bournemouth Symphony Orchestra, English Chamber Orchestra, Scottish Chamber Orchestra, City of Birmingham Symphony Orchestra, Northern Chamber Orchestra, Orchestra of Opera North, Manchester Camerata, Halle, Northern Sinfonia, Auckland Philharmonia, Belgrade Philharmonic; guest conductor, Opera North, ENO, Scottish Opera, New Sadler's Wells Opera, WNO, Carl Rosa Opera, New Zealand Opera, Asst Conductor, Metropolitan Opera, New York, USA 1985–86; one-man cabaret show, Just Wyn; Dir of Music, NBR New Zealand Opera 2005–. *Current Management:* Performing Arts, 6 Windmill Street, London, W1P 1HF, England. *Address:* c/o The NBR New Zealand Opera, PO Box 6478, Wellesley Street, Auckland, New Zealand (office); Springmount, Lidgett's Lane, Rainow, Cheshire SK10 5TG, England (home). *Website:* www.nzopera.com.

**DAVIS, Sir Andrew,** Kt, CBE; British conductor; *Musical Director, Chicago Lyric Opera;* b. 1944; m. Gianna Rolandi 1989; one s. *Education:* Royal Coll. of Music, King's Coll., Cambridge. *Career:* studied conducting with Franco Ferrara, Rome; continuo player with Acad. of St Martin-in-the-Fields and English Chamber Orchestra; Festival Hall début conducting BBC Symphony Orchestra Nov. 1970; Asst Conductor Philharmonia Orchestra 1973–77, Prin. Guest Conductor Royal Liverpool Philharmonic Orchestra 1974–77; Music Dir Toronto Symphony 1975–88, Conductor Laureate 1988–; Musical Dir Glyndebourne Festival Opera 1988–2002; Chief Conductor BBC Symphony Orchestra 1989–2000, Conductor Laureate 2000–, tours with orchestra: Far East 1990, Europe 1992, Japan 1993, 1997, USA 1995, 1998, South America 2001, Far East and Australia 2002; Prin. Guest Conductor Royal Stockholm Philharmonic 1995–99; Musical Dir. Chicago Lyric Opera 2000–; has conducted London Philharmonic, London Symphony, Royal Philharmonic, Boston, Chicago, Cleveland, Los Angeles Philharmonic, New York Philharmonic, Pittsburg Symphony, Orchestre Nat. de France, Frankfurt Radio Orchestra, Royal Concertgebouw Orchestra, Tonhalle Orchestra, Stockholm Philharmonic Orchestra, Israel Philharmonic, Bavarian Radio Symphony and Berlin Philharmonic orchestras, London Sinfonietta, Dallas Symphony and Dresden Staatskapelle orchestras; has conducted at Glyndebourne Festival Opera, Covent Garden Opera, Metropolitan Opera, Washington, DC, Chicago Lyric Opera, Bavarian State Opera, Paris Opéra, La Scala, Milan, Sir Henry Wood Promenade Concerts, maj. British and European music festivals; tours of People's Republic of China 1978, Europe 1983 with Toronto Symphony Orchestra; recordings for CBS including Duruflé's Requiem (Grand Prix du Disque 1978), cycle of Dvořák symphonies and, for EMI, Tippett's The Mask of Time (won a Gramophone Record of the Year Award 1987, Grand Prix du Disque 1988); currently recording for Teldec Classics (has completed Vaughan Williams symphony cycle). *Address:* c/o Askonas Holt Ltd, Lonsdale Chambers, 27 Chancery Lane, London, WC2A 1PF, England. *Telephone:* (20) 7400-1700. *Fax:* (20) 7400-1799. *E-mail:* info@askonasholt.co.uk (office).

**DAVIS, Carl,** BA; American composer and conductor; *Principal Guest Conductor, Munich Symphony Orchestra;* b. 28 Oct. 1936, New York; s. of Isadore Davis and Sara Davis; m. Jean Boht 1971; two d. *Education:* New England Conservatory of Music, Bard Coll. *Career:* Asst Conductor, New York City Opera 1958; Assoc. Conductor, London Philharmonic Orchestra 1987–88; Prin. Conductor, Bournemouth Pops 1984–87; Prin. Guest Conductor Munich Symphony Orchestra 1990–; Artistic Dir and Conductor, Royal Liverpool Philharmonic Orchestra, Summer Pops 1993–2000; Guest Conductor Hallé Orchestra, Birmingham Symphony Orchestra, Scottish Symphony Orchestra. *Musical theatre:* Diversions (Obie Prize Best Review) 1958, Twists (Arts Theatre London) 1962, The Projector and Cranford (Theatre Royal Stratford

East), Pilgrim (Edinburgh Festival), The Wind in the Willows, Peace (Opera North), Alice in Wonderland (Hammersmith) 1987, The Vackees (Haymarket) 1987, The Mermaid. *Incidental music for theatre includes:* Prospect Theatre Co., Nat. Theatre, RSC. *Ballet:* A Simple Man 1987, Lipizzaner 1988, Liaisons Amoureuses (Northern Ballet Theatre) 1988, Madly, Badly, Sadly, Gladly, David and Goliath, Dances of Love and Death (London Contemporary Dance Theatre), The Picture of Dorian Gray (Sadler's Wells Royal Ballet), A Christmas Carol (Northern Theatre Ballet) 1992, The Savoy Suite (English Nat. Ballet) 1993, Alice in Wonderland (English Nat. Ballet) 1995, Aladdin (Scottish Ballet) 2000, Pride and Prejudice: First Impressions (Central Ballet School Tour) 2002. *Music for TV includes:* The Snow Goose 1971, The World at War (Emmy Award) 1972, The Naked Civil Servant 1975, Our Mutual Friend 1978, Hollywood 1980, Churchill: The Wilderness Years 1981, Silas Marner 1985, Hotel du Lac 1986, The Accountant (BAFTA Award) 1989, The Secret Life of Ian Fleming 1989, Separate but Equal 1991, The Royal Collection 1991, A Year in Provence 1992, Fame in the 20th Century: Clive James 1992, Ghengis Cohn 1993, Thatcher: The Downing Street Years 1993, Pride and Prejudice 1995, Oliver's Travels 1995, Eurocinema: The Other Hollywood 1995, Cold War 1998–99, Good Night Mr Tom 1998, The Great Gatsby 2000, The Queen's Nose, An Angel for May, Book of Eve 2003, Promoted to Glory 2003. *Operas for TV:* The Arrangement, Who Takes You to The Party?, Orpheus in the Underground, Peace. *Film music:* The Bofors Gun 1969, The French Lieutenant's Woman (BAFTA award) 1981, Champions 1984, The Girl in a Swing 1988, Rainbow 1988, Scandal 1988, Frankenstein Unbound 1989, The Raft of the Medusa 1991, The Trial 1992, Voyage 1993, Widow's Peak 1994, Topsy Turvy 2000; series of Thames Silents including Napoleon 1980, 2000, The Wind, The Big Parade, Greed, The General, Ben Hur, Intolerance, Safety Last, The Four Horsemen of the Apocalypse 1992, Wings 1993, Waterloo 1995, Phantom of the Opera 1996, 6 Mutuals (Chaplin Shorts) 2004. *Concert works:* Music for the Royal Wedding, Variations on a Bus Route, Overture on Australian Themes, Clarinet Concerto 1984, Lines on London Symphony 1984, Fantasy for Flute and Harpsichord 1985, The Searle Suite for Wind Ensemble, Fanfare for Jerusalem 1987, The Glenlivet Fireworks Music 1988, Norwegian Brass Music 1988, Variations for a Polish Beggar's Theme 1988, Pigeons Progress 1988, Jazz Age Fanfare 1989, Everest 1989, Landscapes 1990, The Town Fox (text by Carla Lane) 1990, A Duck's Diary 1990, Paul McCartney's Liverpool Oratorio (with Paul McCartney) 1991. *Recordings include:* Napoleon 1983, Christmas with Kiri (with Kiri Te Kanawa) 1986, Beautiful Dreamer (with Marylin Horne) 1986, The Silents 1987, Ben Hur 1989, A Simple Man 1989, The Town Fox and Other Musical Tales (text by Carla Lane) 1990, Paul McCartney's Liverpool Oratorio 1991, Leeds Castle Classics, Liverpool Pops at Home 1995. *Publications:* sheet music of television themes. *Honours:* Hon. Fellowship (Liverpool Univ.) 1992, Hon. Dr of Arts (Bard, New York) 1994, Hon. DMus (Liverpool) 2002; Special Achievement Award for Music for Television and Film 2003; Chevalier, Ordre des Arts et des Lettres 1983, Hon. CBE 2005. *Address:* c/o Paul Wing, 3 Deermead, Little Kings Hill, Great Missenden, Bucks., HP16 0EY (office); 8 Smith Street, London, SW3 4LL, England. *Telephone:* (1494) 890511; (20) 7730-9477. *Fax:* (20) 7930-9199 (office). *E-mail:* admin@threefoldmusic.co.uk (office). *Website:* www.carl-davis.com (office).

**DAVIS, Sir Colin Rex,** Kt, CBE, CH; British conductor and musician; *Principal Conductor, London Symphony Orchestra;* b. 25 Sept. 1927, Weybridge, Surrey; s. of Reginald George Davis and Lilian Colbran; m. 1st April Cantelo 1949 (dissolved 1964); one s. one d.; m. 2nd Ashraf Naini 1964; three s. two d. *Education:* Christ's Hospital and Royal Coll. of Music. *Career:* Asst Conductor, BBC Scottish Orchestra 1957–59; Conductor, Sadler's Wells Opera House 1959, Musical Dir 1961–65; Chief Conductor, BBC Symphony Orchestra 1967–71; Chief Guest Conductor 1971–75; Artistic Dir Bath Festival 1969; Musical Dir Royal Opera House, Covent Garden 1971–86; Prin. Guest Conductor, Boston Symphony Orchestra 1972–84; Prin. Guest Conductor, London Symphony Orchestra 1975–95, Prin. Conductor 1995– (2007, Pres. 2007–); Prin. Guest Conductor, New York Philharmonic Orchestra 1998–2003; Music Dir and Prin. Conductor, Bavarian State Radio Orchestra 1983–92; Hon. Conductor Dresden Staatskapelle 1990–. *Honours:* Hon. Freedom of the Worshipful Co. of Musicians 2005; Hon. DMus (Keele) 2002; (RAM) 2002, Dr hc (Sorbonne, Univ. of Paris) 2006; Grosser Deutscher Schallplattenpreis 1978, Grammy Award 'Opera Recording of the Year' 1980, Freedom of the City of London 1992, Royal Philharmonic Soc. Gold Medal 1995, Pipe Smoker of the Year 1995, Distinguished Musician Award (ISM) 1996, Grammy Award 'Best Orchestral Recording' 1997, Sibelius Birth Place Medal 1998, Grammy Awards 'Best Classical Album' and 'Best Opera Recording' (for Les Troyens) 2002, South Bank Show Award 2004; Commendatore of the Repub. of Italy 1976, Commdr.'s Cross of the Order of Merit, Fed. Repub. of Germany 1987, Commdr Ordre des Arts et des Lettres 1990, Order of the Lion of Finland (Commdr 1st Class) 1992, Bayerischen Verdienstorden 1993, Officier, Légion d'honneur 1999, Maximiliansorden (Bavaria) 2000. *Address:* c/o Alison Glaister, 39 Huntingdon Street, London, N1 1BP, England. *Telephone:* (20) 7609-5864. *Fax:* (20) 7609-5866. *E-mail:* aglaister@ rexx.demon.co.uk (office).

**DAVIS, Howard;** Musician; b. 9 April 1940, Wolverhampton, England; m. Virginia Black 1965; two s. *Education:* Royal Academy of Music. *Career:* Leader, Alberni String Quartet; World-wide tours with many broadcasts and television appearances; Professor, Royal Academy of Music, London. *Recordings:* Many including complete chamber music of Beethoven, Mozart, Schumann and complete quartets of Benjamin Britten. *Honours:* FRAM;

FRSAMD; FRSA. *Address:* The Garden Flat, 74 Harley Street, London, W1G 7HQ England. *Telephone:* (20) 7323 0559. *E-mail:* hwrddvs2@aol.com.

**DAVISLIM, Steve;** Singer (Tenor); b. 1967, Australia. *Education:* Studied with Joan Hammond and John Modenos. *Career:* Engaged with the Zürich Opera, as Rossini's Almaviva, the Narrator in The Rape of Lucretia and Ferrando in Così fan tutte; Further appearances at Hamburg and Berlin as Almaviva, at the Salzburg Festival in Concerts, First Prisoner under Solti, as Don Curzio (Figaro) under Harnoncourt and Athens as Don Ottavio, 1996, Ludwigsburg Festival as Tamino, 1998–; Fenton under Abbada in Ferrara and Berlin; Concerts include Liszt's Faust Symphony, Beethoven's Missa Solemnis (with Roger Norrington, in London) and Matthew Passion (Bach), with Riccardo Chailly; Concerts with orchestras such as Chicago Symphony, Tonhalle Orchestra, Zürich, Cleveland Symphony, Wiener Philharmoniker, San Francisco BBC Symphony, Camerata Bern. *Recordings include:* Beethoven's 9th, Schumann's Manfred, Broadway Songs; Masses of Johann Zach; Bertoni's Orfeo; Holliger's Schneewittchen, opera world premiere. *Honours:* Australia Arts Council Grant; Queen Elizabeth II Silver Jubilee Scholarship. *Address:* c/o Opernhaus Zürich, Falkenstrasse 1, 8008, Zürich, Switzerland.

**DAVITASHVILI, Shalva;** Composer; b. 1 Jan. 1934, Telavi, Georgia; m. Nino Zabukidze, 6 Nov 1959, 1 s., 1 d. *Education:* Tbilisi State Conservatoire. *Career:* Debut: The Tiger and the Young Man, symphonic poem, Tbilisi State Conservatoire, 1960; Director, music school, Akhalnalexi. 1966–68; Georgian television, 1968–70; Teacher at musical college, 1970–; Director, Polioshvili Museum, 1992–; mem, Georgian Union of Composers, 1980–96. *Compositions:* 2 symphonies; 3 symphonic poems; 2 ballets; 3 cantata; 5 concertos; 2 vocal-symphonic cycles; Choral works; Pieces for piano; Pieces for other instruments; Incidental music; Film scores; Songs. *Recordings:* 3 concertos for clarinet and orchestra; 9th April, symphonic poem; Vocal cycles; Parts of ballets; Sakartveloze, cantata; Songs. *Publications:* Concerto No. 1, 1972; Concerto No. 2, 1981; Concerto No. 3, 1988; 9th April, 1990; Symphony No. 2, 1992. *Contributions:* Vladimir Kremen, Premier of Zviadauri in Kutaisi, Sovijetski balet, 1987. *Honours:* Merited Artist of Georgia, 1982. *Address:* Gorgasali str 39, app 21, 380014 Tbilisi, Georgia.

**DAVY, Gloria;** Singer (Soprano) and Professor of Voice; b. 29 March 1937, Brooklyn, NY, USA. *Education:* Studied at the Juilliard School with Belle Julie Soudant and in Milan with Victor de Sabata. *Career:* Sang the Countess in the US premiere of Strauss's Capriccio (Juilliard) 1954; World tour in Porgy and Bess; Recital and oratorio appearances before returning to NY in concert performance of Anna Bolena, at the Metropolitan as Pamina, Aida, Nedda and Leonora in Il Trovatore from 1958; Sang in Vienna in Aida, Covent Garden debut, 1959–60, as Aida, Deutsche Oper Berlin from 1961 with Wieland Wagner and Karl Böhm, as Aida, Amelia, Butterfly, Fiordiligi, Donna Anna, Donna Elvira and Salome; Guest engagements 1963–69 in Hamburg, Munich, Geneva, Paris, Madrid, Brussels and London; Sang in the premiere of Henze's Nachtstücke und Arien, 1957, Stockhausen's Momente, 1972, Vortrag über Hu, 1974; Concert tours of Germany, Switzerland, Italy, and France, 1975–85; Debut recital at Wigmore Hall, London, 1983; Professor of Music in Voice at Indiana University School of Music, Bloomington, from 1985; Sang Berg's Sieben Frühe Lieder, Lulu and Der Wein, with the conductors Otmar Suitner and Kurt Masur, 1981–85; New Year's Eve in Milan, Dortmund, 1988–89; Other repertoire included Handel's Acis, Gluck's Iphigénie, Mozart's Countess and Pamina, Strauss's Daphne and Anaide in Mosè by Rossini, Bach St Matthew Passion, Beethoven Missa Solemnis, Handel's Deborah, Schoenberg Erwartung and Shostakovich 14th Symphony. *Recordings include:* Aida; Il Trovatore; Cavalleria Rusticana; Stockhausen's Momente; Zandonai's Conchita; Verdi's Requiem; Dido and Aeneas. *Address:* c/o Dortmund Opera, Kuhstrasse 12, 4600 Dortmund, Germany.

**DAWIDOFF, Mikhail;** Singer (Tenor); b. 1960, Russia. *Education:* Russian Academy of the Theatrical Arts, Moscow. *Career:* Many appearances with the Bolshoi Opera and elsewhere in Russia; Lucerne Opera as Don José, Pedro in Tiefland and Don Carlos; Radames and Vaudemont in Tchaikovsky's Iolanta at St Gallen; Further engagements as Cavaradossi for Palm Beach Opera, Manrico at Antwerp, Don Carlos in Netherlands and Calaf for Basle Opera; Bolshoi Opera as Alfredo, Lensky, Vladimir in Prince Igor and Verdi's Riccardo, Radames at the Deutsche Opera, Berlin, and Verona; Sang Des Grieux in Manon Lescaut at Glyndebourne, 1999. *Honours:* Prizewinner, 1994 Tchaikovsky Competition, Moscow. *Address:* c/o Glyndebourne Festival Opera, Lewes, Sussex BN8 5UU, England. *Telephone:* 01273 812321. *Fax:* 01273 812783.

**DAWKINS, Timothy;** Singer (Baritone); b. 1965, England. *Education:* Royal College of Music. *Career:* Appearances at Glyndebourne as Dominik in Arabella and Captain in Eugene Onegin; Leporello at the Batignano Festival, Italy, Mozart's Figaro in the South of France and Switzerland, and the Speaker in Die Zauberflöte on tour to USA; Budd in Albert Herring and Dr Bombasto in Busoni's Arlecchino at Aldeburgh; Colline in La Bohème for European Chamber Opera and roles in Goehr's Arianna; English Bach Festival in Dido and Aeneas, and in The Fairy Queen at the Linbury Theatre, Covent Garden, 2001; Further engagements with Scottish Opera, Opera North Wexford Festival Opera and Chelsea Opera Group. *Honours:* Erich Vietheer Memorial Award, Glyndebourne. *Address:* c/o English Bach Festival, Linbury Theatre, Royal Opera House, London WC2E 9 DD, England.

**DAWNEY, Michael William,** BA, MLitt, MPhil; British music journalist, editor, teacher and lecturer, pianist, organist, arranger and composer; b. 10

Aug. 1942, Romford, Essex, England. *Education:* Durham Univ., Lincoln Coll., Oxford with Edmund Rubbra and Egon Wellesz, Inst. of Dialect and Folk Life Studies, Leeds Univ., London Int. Film School with Richard Arnell, Bournemouth Univ. *Compositions:* A Carolan Suite for harpsichord or strings; Five Irish Dances for orchestra; A Christmas Greeting for choir; Now Welcome Summer for choir; Christmas Morn for choir and orchestra; The Cattery, song cycle; Echoes for brass; Lions in Heraldry for brass; The Punk's Delight for brass; An Easter Improvisation, Fantasia, Finale, Veni Emmanuel, In Paradisum, Prelude and Fugue, Adeste Fidelis, Veni Creator Spiritus, Fuga Spirituale for organ; Good King Wenceslas Lets His Hair Down; three songs for junior choir; many arrangements for organ of works by Saint-Saëns, Humperdinck, Purcell, Verdi, Fauré, Franck, others. *Recordings:* Hail Holy Queen, Hail Holy Queen (in film The House of Mortal Sin), Reap Me the Earth, Hymns for Celebration. *Publications:* folksong books for English Folk Dance and Song Society, Doon the Wagon Way 1973, The Iron Man 1974, The Ploughboy's Glory 1976; contrib. to Dictionary of Christian Biography 2001. *Honours:* jt first prize Cork Int. Choral Festival 1976, first prize Queen's Silver Jubilee Competition, Trent Park Music Centre 1977. *Address:* 29A West Road, Bournemouth, BH5 2AW, England.

**DAWSON, Anne;** Singer (Soprano); b. 9 Feb. 1959, Stoke, England. *Education:* Studied at the Royal Northern College of Music. *Career:* Sang Angelica in Handel's Orlando at the Bath Festival, 1978, Grenoble Festival, 1979; Recital tours throughout the United Kingdom; With Glyndebourne Touring Opera has sung Eurydice, Susanna and Micaela; Welsh National Opera as Gilda and Pamina; Marguerite, Gilda and the title role in The Cunning Little Vixen with English National Opera; Covent Garden debut in Don Carlos, 1988; Overseas engagements include Gilda in Frankfurt, the Vixen in Vancouver, and appearances with the Netherlands and Lausanne Operas; Sang Hero in Beatrice and Benedict, London Coliseum, 1990; Susanna for Welsh National Opera; Season 1992 as Ninetta in The Thieving Magpie for Opera North, Anne Trulove for Glyndebourne Touring Opera and Chloe in The Queen of Spades at the Festival; Mimi in La Bohème for GTO, 1995; Cecilio in Mozart's Lucio Silla for Garsington Opera, 1998; Sang Polly in The Beggar's Opera at Strasbourg, 2000; Concert repertoire includes Schubert's Fierrabras, at South Bank conducted by Jeffrey Tate, Carmina Burana, and Mozart's Exsultate Jubilate (Fishguard Festival). *Recordings include:* Songs by English composers. *Honours:* John Ireland Festival Centenary Competition and the Gerald Finzi Song Award Competition, 1981; Soprano prize at the 1981 International Singing Competition, 's-Hertogenbosch; Kathleen Ferrier Memorial Scholarship, 1982. *Address:* 50 Great Portland Street, London W1N 5AH, England.

**DAWSON, Lynne;** Singer (Soprano); b. 3 June 1956, York, England. *Education:* Studied at the Guildhall School of Music, London. *Career:* Appearances from 1985 with Trevor Pinnock and the English Concert; John Eliot Gardiner, the Monteverdi Choir and English Baroque Soloists and Christopher Hogwood and the Academy of Ancient Music; Further concerts with Barenboim, Davis, Rattle, Mackerras, Ashkenazy, and Giulini; Tours of Europe and the USA; Opera debut as the Countess with Kent Opera, 1986; Monteverdi's Orfeo at Florence, 1988; Festival engagements at Aldeburgh, Edinburgh, Salzburg, Bruges, Aix-en-Provence, Paris, Vienna and Promenade Concerts; Opera career includes Zdenka in Arabella at the Châtelet, Pamina, Berlin Staatsoper; Appearances as Fiordiligi at Naples, Constanze Brussels, Teresa in Benvenuto Cellini for Netherlands Opera, 1991; Other roles include, Xiphares in Mitridate (Châtelet, Paris, 1991), Amenaide in Rossini's Tancredi, Berlin Staatsoper, 1994; Shéhérezade at the 1995 London Proms; Sang Nitocris in Belshazzar at the 1996 Handel Festival, Göttingen; Opera North 1996 as Gluck's Iphigénie (en Aulide); Sang Libera Me from Verdi's Requiem at the funeral of Diana, Princess of Wales, 1997; Sang Dido in Dido and Aeneas at Vlaamse Opera, 1998; Engaged for premiere of Elliott Carter's opera What Next?, Berlin, 1999; Season 2000 at Lyon and Graz, in Handel's Hercules and Agrippina. *Recordings:* Over 60 including: Bach B Minor Mass, Monteverdi Orfeo, Purcell, Dido and Aeneas; Messiah; Mozart C Minor Mass; Purcell Timon of Athens and Dioclesian, Iphigénie en Aulide; Jephtha; Vespers by Mozart; Mozart's Requiem; Gluck's La Recontre Imprévue; Mozart's Elvira and Constanze, Beethoven 9, Midsummer Night's Dream, Acis and Galatea; Ginevra in Ariadonte; Norina in Don Pasquale; Zaide. *Address:* c/o IMG Artists, Lovell House, 616 Chiswick High Road, London W4 5RX, England.

**DAWSON, Ted,** BMus, BEd, MMA, PhD; Canadian composer and teacher; b. 28 April 1951, Victoria, BC. *Education:* Victoria School of Music, University of Victoria with Brian Cherney and Rudolf Komorous, McGill University with Bengt Hambraeus and Alcides Lanza, University of Toronto, State University of New York at Buffalo with Charles Wuorinen, Peter Otto, Jan Williams, Jeremy Noble and Martha Hyde. *Career:* Lecturer at Concordia University, 1974–78 and Vanier College in Montreal, 1978–80; Assistant Professor at Queen's University, Kingston, Ontario, 1987–88; Assistant Professor at Brock University, St Catherines, Ontario, 1988–90; Founder of the ComPoster Project to promote Canadian music through education; Artistic Director of Canadian Music Days Festival of Contemporary Canadian Music, held in Estonia, 1993; Organiser, The True North Festival, in Taiwan, 12 concerts of Canadian music and a major contemporary art exhibition, 1998. *Compositions:* Pentad for string quartet, 1971; Concerto Grosso 1 for tape with/without amplified viola, bassoon, trombone, and percussion, 1972–74; Chameleon for amplified flute, 1975; The Land of Nurr, 1975; The Clouds of Magellan for tape and slides, 1976–77; Binaries for 4 dancers, amplified piano and percussion,

1978–80; Joint Actions for solo female dancer and male double bass player, 1981; Phantasms for solo piano, 1986–87; Portraits in a Landscape for tape, 1988; Traces in Glass for orchestra, 1986–92; Symphony 1 for orchestra, 1992–94; Topographical Sonata for amplified piano and tape, 1992–96; Dragon Songs, for bass baritone voice and orchestra, 1995–98; Piano Concerto Wisteria, 2002, Ice Dreams for Wind Quintet 2004. *Recordings:* True North Festival in Taiwan, including Symphony 1 and Dragon Songs performed by the Taipei Symphony Orchestra conducted by Victor Feldbrill. *Publications:* Teacher's Guide to Canadian Music 1991. *Honours:* William St Clair Low Award for Chamber Music Composition 1972, Murray Adaskin Award 1974, SOCAN Prize for Orchestral Composition Winnipeg New Music Festival's Canadian Composers Competition 1995. *Address:* 3420 Bayview Avenue, Toronto M2M 3S3, Canada.

**DAYMOND, Karl;** singer (baritone); b. 1965, England. *Education:* Guildhall School with Thomas Hemsley, National Opera Studio. *Career:* appeared at Glyndebourne Festival, 1992; Sang Valentin for Opera Northern Ireland; Season 1993 as Schaunard for Welsh National Opera and Mountjoy in Gloriana for Opera North; Claudio in Beatrice and Benedict for WNO, Hamlet, Marcello, Papageno, Opera North; Dandini in Cenerentola at Garsington; For Vlaamse Opera in Il Trittico and Un Ballo in Maschera; Anthony in Sweeney Todd for Opera North and Hector in Antheil's Transatlantic for Minnesota Opera; Appeared as Purcell's Aeneas for BBC 2 television, 1995; Marcello in La Bohème for Opera North, 1996; Sang Paride in Cesti's Pomo d'Oro at Batignano, 1998; Season 1999 in Bernstein's Wonderful Town, at the BBC Prom concerts, London; Sang Kopernikus in the premiere of Rêves d'un Marco Polo by Claude Viviers for Netherlands Opera, 2000. *Recordings:* Méhul's Stratonice with Les Arts Florissants; Wonderful Town; Dido and Aeneas; Weir's A Night at the Chinese Opera, 1999. *Honours:* British Song Prize, 1987; Polonsky Foundation Award, 1989.

**DAZELEY, William;** Singer (Baritone); b. 1966, England. *Education:* Studied at Guildhall School, London. *Career:* Season 1990–91 as Onegin with British Youth Opera; Season 1991–92 as Schaunard with British Youth Opera and Don Giovanni for Opera North; British premiere of Schreker's Der Ferne Klang, 1992; Season 1992–93 with Opera North in Billy Budd and as Mozart's Count and Schaunard, also as Don Giovanni for English Touring Opera; Season 1993–94 as Mowgli in world premiere of Michael Berkeley's Baa Baa Black Sheep for Cheltenham Festival, also as Mowgli for Opera North, Harlekin for Broomhill and Papageno for Opera North; Season 1994–95 as Rossini's Figaro for Glyndebourne Touring Opera, as Demetrius for Teatro Regio, Turin, and as Pelléas for Opera North; Mozart's Count for GTO at Glyndebourne, 1996; Soldier in Busoni's Faust at Salzburg, 1999; Sang Mercutio in Gounod's Roméo et Juliette at Covent Garden, 2000; Sang Christ in the premiere of Birtwistle's The Last Supper, Berlin, 2000; London Proms, 2002. *Recordings include:* Billy Budd; Doktor Faust (Erato); La Bohème. *Honours:* Decca-Kathleen Ferrier Prize, 1989; Richard Tauber Prize; Winner, Walter Gruner International Lieder Competition, 1991. *Current Management:* Askonas Holt Ltd, Lonsdale Chambers, 27 Chancery Lane, London, WC2A 1PF, England. *Telephone:* (20) 7400-1700. *Fax:* (20) 7400-1799. *E-mail:* info@askonasholt.co.uk. *Website:* www.askonasholt.co.uk.

**DE BEENHOUWER, Jozef;** Belgian concert pianist; b. 26 March 1948, Brasschaat. *Education:* Univ. of Louvain, Chapelle Musicale Reine Elisabeth Argenteuil, Royal Flemish Conservatory, Antwerp. *Career:* concert pianist with orchestras and solo recitals; chamber music in Vienna (Musikverein, Konzerthaus with Vienna Symphony), Amsterdam (Concertgebouw), Lisbon (Foundation Gulbenkian), London, Berlin (Schauspielhaus), Dresden (Semper-Oper), Rheinisches Musikfest, Flanders Festival, Estival de Paris and in USA; Prof. of Piano, Royal Flemish Conservatory 1983–; Artistic Dir, Brussels Lunchtime Concerts 1990; jury mem. in various int. piano competitions. *Recordings include:* Schumann Op 12; Ravel's Gaspard de la Nuit, 1982; Peter Benoit's Contes et Ballades and Sonata, 1984; Joseph Ryelandt's Piano Works, 1986; Clara Schumann's Complete Piano Works, 1991; Robert Schumann's Op 16, 111 and 133, 1994; Robert Schumann's Dichterliebe with Robert Holl, 1994; Belgian Piano Music by P Benoit, L Mortelmans, J Jongen, M de Jong and V Legley, 1997; Cello Sonatas by A De Boeck and J L Nicodé (with M Van Staalen), 1998; Songs and piano music by Lod Mortelmans, 1999; Johannes Brahms, Klavierstücke, Op 76, 118 and 119, 2000; Ludwig Schuncke, Piano Sonata etc. 1986–2000; Hans Pfitzner, Klaviertrios (with Robert Schumann Trio), 2001; Peter Benoit: Liefdedrama – Uit Henriette's Album, 2002; Marinus de Jong: Piano Concerto no. 1, piano music, 2003; Songs by Wagner, Nystroem and De Boeck (with Nina Stemme) 2004; Robert Schumann: Carnaval, Waldszenen and Kinderszenen 2005. *Honours:* Robert Schumann Prize (Zwickau) 1993. *Address:* Frilinglei 45, 2930 Brasschaat, Belgium (office). *Telephone:* (3) 654-97-72 (home). *E-mail:* jozef.de.beenhouwer@pandora.be (home).

**DE CALUWE, Peter;** Dutch opera house director; *Artistic Director, Nederlandse Opera;* b. 1963, Dendermonde. *Career:* began career at Théâtre Royal de la Monnaie, Brussels; worked with Nederlandse Opera, Amsterdam from 1990, Artistic Dir –(2007); Dir-Gen. Théâtre Royal de la Monnaie (2007)–. *Address:* De Nederlandse Opera, Waterlooplein 22, 1011 PG Amsterdam, The Netherlands (office); Théâtre Royal de la Monnaie, Place de la Monnaie, Brussels 1000, Belgium (office). *Website:* www.dno.nl; www.lamonnaie.be.

**DE CANDIA, Roberto;** Singer (Baritone); b. 1968, Molfetta, Bari, Italy. *Education:* Studied singing with Sesto Bruscantini. *Career:* Debut: Sang in Puccini's Messa di Gloria (concert) at the Santa Cecilia, Rome, and in Massenet's Manon at Parma; Engagements as Gianni Schicchi at Turin; Marcello at the Verona Arena, Taddeo (L'Italiana in Algeri) and Masetto in Don Giovanni at the Salzburg Festival; Other roles include: Rossini's Figaro (Paris Opéra-Comique), Parmenione in L'Occasione fa il ladro (Pesaro) and Alcandro in Pacini's Saffo (Wexford Festival); La Scala, Milan, 1996–97, as Ubalde in Gluck's Armide and Poeta (Il Turco in Italia); Glyndebourne Festival 1997, as Lescaut in a new production of Manon Lescaut; Season 1997–98 as Massenet's Lescaut at the Metropolitan, Dandini and Belcore (L'Elisir d'amore); Season 1998–99 La Bohème; Gala Concert with Luciano Pavarotti at the Metropolitan Opera in New York; Sang in La Forza del Destino and Il Barbiere di Siviglia at La Scala; Season 2000–01 as Rossini's Dandini at Pesaro, Falstaff at Modena and Massenet's Lescaut at the Met. *Recordings:* Saffo; Mascagni's Messa di Gloria; Il turco in Italia with Riccardo Chailly; La Bohème with Riccardo Chailly. *Current Management:* Prima International Artists Management. *Address:* c/o Prima International Artists Management, Palazzo Zambeccari, Piazza de'Calderini 2/2, 40124 Bologna, Italy.

**DE CAROLIS, Natale;** Italian singer (bass-baritone); b. 25 July 1957, Anagni. *Education:* Pont Institute of Vatican State, studied with Renato Guelfi and Maria Vittoria Romano. *Career:* Debut: 1983; La Scala, Milan; Metropolitan Opera, New York; La Fenice, Venice; Maggio Musicale, Florence; Salzburg Festival; La Zarzuela, Madrid; Sydney Opera House; Rossini Opera Festival; Pesaro Teatro Comunale; Bologna Opera; Zürich Opera; Teatro Massimo, Palermo; Teatro Bellini, Catania; Buenos Aires; Paris; Macerata; S Carlo, Napoli and Bonn; Sang Don Parmenione in a Rossini double bill at Cologne and Schwetzingen, 1992; Count Robinson in Il Matrimonio Segreto at the 1992 Ravenna Festival; Vienna, Musikverein, Staatsoper, Konzerthaus; Frankfurt, Don Giovanni, Figaro, Guglielmo, Belcore; Rome, Teatro Dell'Opera; Hamburg, Berlin, Lausanne, Montpellier, Aix-en-Province, Lisbon, Touloun, Oviedo; Sang Donizetti's Belcore at Covent Garden, 1997; Season 1998 with Guglielmo for the Royal Opera London, and Fernando in Rossini's Gazza Ladra at Venice; Season 2000–01 as Don Giovanni at Glyndebourne and Don Alfonso at Detroit. *Recordings:* Signor Bruschino, Scala di Seta (Rossini); Don Giovanni (Mozart); Rinaldo (Handel); Mozart Recital; L'Occasione fa Il Ladro and L'Inganno Felice (Rossini); Le nozze di Figaro (Mozart); La Ninfa Pazza per Amore (Paisiello); Mozart Recital; Don Giovanni, Così fan tutte, Le nozze di Figaro, Highlights. *Honours:* Spoleto; Baroque Festival Viterbo; Toti Dal Monte (Treviso); Lauri Volpi.

**DE CASTRO-ROBINSON, Eve,** DMus; composer; b. 9 Nov. 1956, London, England. *Education:* University of Auckland. *Career:* Composer-in-Residence with the Auckland Philharmonic, 1991; Performances of her music with the Karlheinz Company in Auckland and with UNESCO in Paris. *Compositions include:* Stringencies for 11 solo strings, 1986; Peregrinations, piano concerto, 1987; Concerto for 3 clarinets, 1991; Instrumental pieces, including Tumbling Strains for violin and cello, 1992, and Tingling Strings for piano, 1993. *Address:* c/o New Zealand Music Centre, PO Box 10042, Level 13, Brandon Street, Wellington, New Zealand.

**DE CLARA, Roberto;** Conductor; b. Hamilton, Ontario, Canada; m. Anna Colangelo, 1 Oct 1983, 1 s. *Education:* BMus, Summa Cum Laude, McMaster University, Canada; Wiener Meisterkurse; Vienna Mozarteum; Salzburg Sommerakademie; Accademia Chigiana, Siena; Aspen Music School; University of Toronto; Royal Conservatory, Toronto. *Career:* Debut: Hamilton Philharmonic, 1981; Assistant Conductor, Opera Hamilton, 1979–84; Assistant Conductor, Hamilton Philharmonic, 1981–82; Music Director, Prince George Symphony, 1984–87; Music Director, York Symphony, 1990–; Israel Vocal Arts, Tel-Aviv, 1994–95; Musical Director, Oakville Symphony, 1997–; European Opera debut with Così fan tutte, National Theatre Prague, 1998; mem, American Federation of Musicians; Opera America. *Honours:* Heinz Unger Conducting Prize, Toronto, 1978; Canada Council Scholarships, 1979, 1980; Hans Haring Conducting Prize, Salzburg Mozarteum, 1984; Canada-Israel Cultural Foundation Grant, 1994. *Address:* 129 Sirente Drive, Hamilton, Ont L9A 5H5, Canada.

**DE FUSCO, Laura;** concert pianist; b. 1950, Catellammare di Stabia, Italy. *Education:* Studied at the Conservatorium San Pietro a Maiella in Naples. *Career:* Many concert appearances from 1966, notably in Europe, USA, South America and Japan; Orchestras have included the Detroit Symphony, Philadelphia, Orchestra National de Paris, Budapest Philharmonic, Santa Cecilia Rome, Moscow Symphony, Residentie Den Haag and the Yomiuri Nippon Symphony; Conductors have featured Muti, Mehta, Ceccato, Chailly, Inbal, Maag, De Burgos and Fedoseyev; Marlboro Festival concerts at the invitation of Rudolf Serkin; Debut with the BBC Philharmonic, Feb 1991.

**DE GRANDIS, Renato;** Composer; b. 24 Oct. 1927, Venice, Italy. *Education:* Studied Musicology and Composition with Malipiero in Venice; Masterclasses in Siena. *Career:* As Composer, has been concerned with dodecaphonic and aleatory techniques; Resident in Darmstadt, 1959–81, then Venice. *Compositions:* Unperformed Operas, La Fanciulla del Lago, Il Gave and Il Pastore, 1951–54; Il Cierco di Hyuga, 1959 (Staged Bonn, 1969); Gloria al Re, 1962 (Staged Kiel, 1967); Eduard und Kunigunde, Wiesbaden, 1971; Das Wahrhaftige ende des Don Giovanni, Bonn, 1973; Die Schule Der Kahlen,

Karlsruhe, 1976. *Honours:* Italian Radio Prize, 1945; National First Prize for Composition, 1953. *Address:* SIAE (Sezione Musica), Viale della Letteratura n.30, 00144 Roma (EUR), Italy.

**DE GREEVE, Gilbert-Jean;** Belgian concert pianist; b. 11 Nov. 1944, St Truiden. *Education:* Studied Piano with Eugene Traey, Royal Conservatory of Antwerp, Belgium, 1958–69; Performing major, with First Prizes in Piano and Chamber Music and a Diplome superieur for Chamber music; Composition major, with First Prizes in Music Theory, Harmony, Analysis, Counterpoint and Fugue; 1970 Peabody Institute of Music, Baltimore, Maryland, USA; Private studies with Rudolph Serkin, Eugene Ormandy and Leonard Pearlmann; 1972, Franz Liszt Academy of Budapest, Hungary. *Career:* Active world-wide as pianist 1970–; Director of the State Music Academy of Antwerp and Professor of the Royal Conservatory of Antwerp, 1970–; Working in a permanent duo with the Belgian soprano Martine De Craene, 1988–, repertoire of more than 14 hours music from Baroque until today, including 3 books of melodies by Gabriel Fauré; Lieder cycles by composers from Hungary and Canada have been dedicated to and world-created by the Duo. Concerts and Masterclasses in 5 continents; Major foreign tours: Canada, Australia, New Zealand, Africa, Finland, Netherlands, Antilles, Greece. *Compositions:* Chamber Music, a Lieder cycle of 36 Lieder on poems by James Joyce. *Recordings:* Belgian Radio and Television; CBC Canada; Hungarian Radio Budapest. *Address:* Anselmostraat 38, 2018 Antwerpen, Belgium.

**DE GROOTE, Philip;** Cellist; b. 25 Dec. 1949, South Africa. *Career:* Co-Founder and Cellist of the Chilingirian Quartet, 1971; Resident Quartet of Liverpool University, 1973–76; Resident Quartet of Sussex University, 1978–; Resident Quartet of Royal College of Music, 1986–; Annual Series of Concerts at the Queen Elizabeth Hall and Wigmore Hall; Performances at the Edinburgh, Bath, Aldeburgh Festivals; Munich Herkulessaal, Amsterdam Concertgebouw, Zürich Tonhalle, Vienna Konzerthaus, Stockholm Konserthuset; New York debut 1976; Annual coast-to-coast tours of the USA and Canada; Represented the United Kingdom at the New York International Festival quartet series; Tours of Australia, New Zealand, South America, the Far East; Television and Radio throughout Europe, National Public Radio in the USA, the BBC. *Recordings:* All Great Mozart Quartets; Late Schubert Quartets; Debussy and Ravel Quartets; Elgar Quartet and Piano Quintet; Schubert Cello Quintet and Octet; Mozart Clarinet Quintet; Complete Quartets of Bartók and Dvořák; Bartók Piano Quintet. *Address:* c/o Intermusica Artists Management, 16 Duncan Terrace, London N1 8BZ, England.

**DE JONG, Conrad (John);** Composer and Professor; b. 13 Jan. 1934, Hull, Iowa, USA. *Education:* BM, Music Education and Trumpet, North Texas State University, Denton, 1954; MM, Music Theory with B Heiden and Brass Instruments, Indiana University School of Music, 1959; T de Leeuw, Amsterdam, 1969. *Career:* Professor of Music, University of Wisconsin, River Falls, 1959–. *Compositions:* Prelude and Fugue for Brass Trio, 1958; 3 Studies for Brass Septet, 1960; Music for 2 Tubas, 1961; Essay for Brass Quintet, 1963; String Trio, 1964; Fun and Games for Any Woodwind, Brass or String Instrument(s) and Piano, 1966, revised 1970; Peace On Earth for Chorus and Organ, 1969; Aanraking (Contact) for Trombone, 1969; Hist Whist for Voice, Flute, Viola and Percussion, 1969; Grab Bag for Tuba Ensemble, 1970; The Silence of the Sky in My Eyes for 1/2 Track Stereo Tape, Musicians, Light and Optional Dance and Audience Participation, 1973; A Prayer for Chorus, Piano, Brass Wind Chimes and Optional Audience, 1975; Ring! My Chimes for Chimes, 1/2 Track Stereo Tape and Slides, 1977; 3 Short Variation Fanfares for Brass Quintet, 1980; La Dolorosa for English Horn, 1982. *Address:* c/o Music Department, University of Wisconsin at River Falls, River Falls, WI 54022, USA.

**DE KANEL, Vladimir;** Singer (Bass-baritone); b. 1940, Shanghai, China. *Career:* Debut: Colombia, 1962, as Rossini's Bartolo; Frankfurt Opera from 1969, as Mozart's Leporello, Don Alfonso and Papageno, Oroveso in Norma and Rossini's Basilio; Guest appearances throughout Germany and France; Schumann's Genoveva in Paris and Rameau's Castor et Pollux for Frankfurt Opera; Liège Opera, 1985–92, as Gounod's Mephistopheles and Rodolfo in La Sonnambula; Wagner's Daland at Rio de Janeiro, 1987; Frankfurt, 1996, as Wurm in Luisa Miller; Concerts of Russian songs.

**DE LA GRANGE, Henry-Louis;** French writer on music; b. 26 May 1924, Paris. *Education:* studied letters at Aix-en-Provence and the Sorbonne, Paris, Yale Univ. School of Music, studied piano with Yvonne Lefébure and harmony, counterpoint and analysis with Nadia Boulanger. *Career:* music critic for French and American publications; guest lecturer at Columbia, Stanford and Indiana Univs 1974–81, Geneva 1982, Leipzig, Juilliard, Univ. of California at Los Angeles 1985, Budapest 1987, Hamburg 1988, Oslo 1993, also Paris Conservatory, Kyoto, Hong-Kong, Wellington, Sydney, Canberra, Melbourne, Boulder, San Francisco 1998; taught a DEA Seminar at the Ecole Normale Supérieure, Paris; founded the Bibliothèque Musicale Gustav Mahler, Paris 1986; Hon. Pres. Médiathèque Musicale Mahler. *Publications include:* Gustav Mahler: Chronique d'une Vie, 3 vols, 1979–84; Vienne, Une Histoire musicale, 2 vols, 1990–91; Mahler, Vol. I, England and USA, 1973–74. Vols II and III, England and USA, 1995–2000. *Honours:* Chevalier, Légion d'honneur, Commandeur, Ordre du Mérite national, Commandeur, Ordre des Arts et des Lettres. *Address:* c/o Médiathèque Musicale Mahler, 11 bis, rue de Vézelay, 75008 Paris, France (office); 2B Chemin du Buchet, 1025 Saint-Sulpice, Switzerland (home). *Telephone:* 1 53 75 16 35 (office); (21) 691-0295 (home). *Fax:* 1 53 75 19 77 (office); (21) 691-5055 (home). *E-mail:* hlg@bluewin .ch. *Website:* www.mediathequemahler.org (office).

**DE LA MORA, Fernando;** Singer (Tenor); b. 1958, Mexico City. *Education:* Studied in Mexico City, New York, Tel-Aviv and at North Carolina University. *Career:* Debut: Sang Borsa in Rigoletto at Mexico City; Has appeared widely in Mexico as Pinkerton, Cavaradossi and Alfredo; San Francisco Opera, 1988–89, as Gounod's Romeo, and Rodolfo; Alfredo at Vienna Staatsoper and the Deutsche Oper Berlin 1989; Faust at Cologne and the Verdi Requiem on tour to Moscow with the ensemble of La Scala; Milan debut 1990, as Alfredo, which he sang also at the Santa Fe Festival, 1991; Barcelona 1992 as Nemorino; Season 1995–96 as Rodolfo at Buenos Aires and Werther for Miami Opera; Season 2000 as Don José at Miami, Rodolfo for Santa Fe Opera, Alfredo in Baltimore, Roberto Devereux for New York City Opera and Macduff at Montpellier. *Address:* c/o Opéra et Concert, 1 rue Volney, F–75002 Paris, France.

**DE LAET, Joris (Maurits);** Professor; b. 12 July 1947, Antwerp, Belgium; m. Maria Vervoort, 11 Aug 1774, 1 d. *Education:* Basic music theory at Academies of Antwerp; Autodidact in electronic and computer music and recording techniques, computer information and composition, first performances in International Cultural Centre, Antwerp, 1974. *Career:* Tape music composition, Parametric; Live electronics, video-art at festivals in Europe, Canada and Brazil; Many radio appearances since 1973; International seminars and lectures; Concert Organiser of experimental and electronic music and video-art; Director of SEM; Manager of sound studio of the Antwerp Music Conservatory and Professor of Electronic Music Composition; Producer, monthly radio programme dedicated to electro-acoustic music, 1992–; Co-founder and Vice President of BeFEM/FeBeMe, Belgian Federation of Electro-acoustic Music, 1994. *Compositions include:* Metrokunst, 1989; Watertoren-Installatie, 1989; Transparent Bodies, 1991; Commissioned works: Naderen, 1988, Blamis, 1990, Penetration, 1992, Irreversible, New Environment, 1992, Aural Silver, 1993, The Shift, 1994; Bruit Noir, 1995; Soleil Silencieux, 1996; Pigeon Piégé, 1997; Pièce de Résistance, 1998. *Recordings:* All music and video-art, including concerts of the SEM Ensemble. *Publications:* Editor, SEM magazine, 1975–79; Editor and part author, Documenta Belgicae II, 1985; Author of syllabus in use at Conservatory of Antwerp on Analogue Synthesis techniques, 1979; Various articles in newspapers and magazines. *Address:* Kapel Straat 44, 3140 Keerbergen, Belgium.

**DE LANCIE, John;** Oboist and Stage Director; b. 26 July 1921, Berkeley, CA, USA. *Education:* Curtis Institute, Philadelphia. *Career:* played oboe in Pittsburgh Symphony Orchestra, 1940–42; played with Philadelphia Orchestra from 1946, Principal Oboist 1954–74; teacher, Curtis Institute 1954–74, Dir 1977–85; commissioned and gave the premieres of Jean Francaix' Horloge de Flore in Philadelphia in 1961, and the Concerto by Benjamin Lees in 1963; Dir, New World School of Music 1987. *Recordings include:* Strauss Oboe Concerto 1987. *Current Management:* Harwood Management Group Inc., 509 W 110 Street, New York, NY 10025, USA. *Telephone:* (212) 864-0773. *Fax:* (212) 663-1129. *E-mail:* jim@harwood-management.com. *Website:* www .harwood-management.com.

**DE LARROCHA, Alicia;** pianist; b. 23 May 1923, Barcelona, Spain; m. Juan Torra; one s. one d. *Education:* studied with Frank Marshall in Barcelona. *Career:* performed in public from age 4; Concerto debut in 1934 with the Madrid Philharmonic; British debut in 1953 at Wigmore Hall; US debut in 1955 with the Los Angeles Philharmonic; Formed duo with cellist, Gaspar Cassado in 1956; Solo recitals and concerts with major orchestras in Europe, USA, Canada, Central and South America, South Africa, New Zealand, Australia and Japan; Director, Marshall Academy Barcelona from 1959; Recent British appearances with the City of Birmingham Symphony, Philharmonia and the London Symphony Orchestra; Played Falla's Nights in The Gardens of Spain at the 1986 Promenade Concerts also televised; Barbican Hall recital in 1989; Edinburgh Festival, 1995; Ravel's Concerto in G at the Barbican, 1997. *Recordings:* Works by Granados, Falla, Albeniz, Mozart and Romantic composers. *Honours:* Paderewski Memorial Medal, London, 1961; Decorated Spanish Orders of Civil Merit, 1962 and Isabella la Católica, 1972; Medalla d'oro of City of Barcelona, 1982; Gold Medal of Spanish National Assembly, 1982; Principe de Asturias Prize, 1994; Edison Award, 1968, 1978; Grammy Awards for recordings of Iberia by Albeniz, 1974 and 1989, Ravel Concertos 1975 and Granados Goyescas, 1991; Deutsche Schallplatten Prize, 1979; Grand Prix du Disque, 1991; Musician of the Year, USA, 1978. *Current Management:* Herbert H. Breslin Inc, 119 W 57th Street 1505, New York, NY 10019, USA.

**DE MAIN, John (Lee);** Conductor; b. 11 Jan. 1944, Youngstown, Ohio, USA. *Education:* BM 1966, MS 1968, Juilliard School of Music, New York; Studied Piano with Adele Marcus; Conducting with Jorge Mester. *Career:* Associate Conductor, St Paul (Minn) Chamber Orchestra, 1972–74; Music Director, Texas Opera Theater, 1974–76; Houston Grand Opera, 1979–94; Opera/Omaha, 1983–; Conducted the local premiere of Britten's A Midsummer Night's Dream, Houston, 1993; L'Elisir d'amore at Seattle, 1998. *Recordings:* For Composers' Recordings Inc; RCA. *Honours:* Julius Rudel Award, 1971; Grammy Award, 1977; Grand Prix de Disque, 1977. *Address:* c/o Houston Grand Opera, 510 Preston Avenue, Houston, TX 77002, USA.

**DE MEY, Guy;** Singer (Tenor); b. 4 Aug. 1955, Hamme, Belgium. *Education:* Studied at Brussels Conservatory and at Amsterdam with Erna Spoorenberg; Further study with Peter Pears and Eric Tappy. *Career:* Has appeared in Baroque Opera at such centres as Berlin, Hamburg, Strasbourg and Spoleto; Lully's Atys under William Christie in Paris, Florence and New York; Alidoro in Cesti's Orontea at Innsbruck 1986, returning for Aegus in Cavalli's Giasone, 1988; Rameau's Hippolyte at Regio Emilia and Eurymachus in Il Ritorno d'Ulisse at Mézières, 1989, conducted by Michel Corboz; London 1986 as Monteverdi's Orfeo; Brussels 1988, as the Painter in Lulu; Sang Don Polidoro in Mozart's La Finta Semplice at Innsbruck, 1991; Lully's Alceste at Opéra Comique, Paris, 1992; Further engagements at Utrecht Early Music Festival, Zürich, Venice and Bologna; Sang in the French version of Don Carlos at Brussels (1996) and Orpheus by Monteverdi for the English National Opera; Season 2000–01 as Carrado in A. Scarlatti's Griselda, at Innsbruck, M. Triquet in Eugene Onegin at Brussels and the Schoolmaster in The Cunning Little Vixen, for Netherlands Opera; Concert Repertoire includes the Evangelist in Bach's Passions. *Recordings:* Le Cinesi by Gluck; A Scarlatti's La Giuditta; Lully's Atys; Der Geduldige Sokrates by Telemann, Monteverdi's Orfeo and Poppea; Cavalli's Xerse and Giasone, Alessandro by Handel, Orontea and Rameau's Platée. *Address:* Théâtre Royale de la Monnaie, 4 Leopoldstrasse, 1000 Brussels, Belgium.

**DE MOOR, Chris;** Singer (Bass); b. 22 June 1946, Antwerp, Belgium. *Education:* Studied at the Brussels Conservatory. *Career:* Sang throughout Belgium and France, notably as Massenet's Don Quichotte, at Antwerp; Claudius in Hamlet by Thomas and Gounod's Frère Laurent at Antwerp, 1996; Zaccaria in Nabucco and Arkel in Pelléas. *Recordings:* Messiah; Mireille by Gounod. *Honours:* Vercelli and Barcelona, 1984. *Address:* Antwerp Opera, Ommeganchstrasse 59, 2018 Antwerp, Belgium.

**DE PALMA, Sandro;** Pianist; b. 14 Feb. 1957, Naples, Italy. *Education:* Classical studies in Latin, Greek; Studied Piano privately with Vincenzo Vitales, Naples. *Career:* Debut: Naples; Appeared ORF, Vienna, 1977; Carnegie Hall, New York, 1978; Other appearances include: Dvořák Hall, Prague; Interforum, Budapest; Gewandhaus, Leipzig; Dresden; East Berlin; Performances with major Italian Orchestras: RAI, Rome; San Carlo; Fenice Venice; Milan; Tours, France; Italy, Switzerland, USSR. *Recordings:* Liszt; 1st recording of Muzio Clementi's Gradus ad Parnassum, with Fonit Cetra. *Honours:* 1st Prize, Casella Competition, Naples, 1976; 1st Prize, Bruce Hungerford, New York, 1977. *Current Management:* Patrizia Garrasi, Via Manzoni 31, 20121 Milan, Italy. *Address:* Via del Colosseo 23, Rome, Italy.

**DE PEYER, Gervase Alan,** FRCM; British clarinettist and conductor; b. 11 April 1926, London; s. of Esme Everard Vivian de Peyer and Edith Mary Bartlett; m. 1st Sylvia Southcombe 1950 (divorced 1971); one s. two d.; m. 2nd Susan Rosalind Daniel 1971 (divorced 1979); m. 3rd Katia Perret Aubry 1980. *Education:* King Alfred's School, London, Bedales School and Royal Coll. of Music, London. *Career:* served HM Forces 1945, 1946; studied in Paris 1949; int. soloist 1949–; Founder mem. Melos Ensemble 1950–72; Prin. Clarinet, London Symphony Orchestra 1955–72; Founder and Conductor Melos Sinfonia of Washington 1992; Dir London Symphony Wind Ensemble; fmr Assoc. Conductor Haydn Orchestra of London; solo clarinettist, Chamber Music Soc. of Lincoln Center, NY 1969–; fmr Resident Conductor Victoria Int. Festival, BC, Canada; Co-founder and Artistic Dir Innisfree Music Festival, Pa, USA; mem. Faculty, Mannes Coll. of Music, NY; also conductor; recording artist with all major companies (most recorded solo clarinettist in the world); gives recitals and master classes throughout the world. *Honours:* Gold Medallist Worshipful Co. of Musicians 1948, Charles Gros Grand Prix du Disque 1961, 1962, Plaque of Honor for Acad. of Arts and Sciences of America for recording of Mozart concerto 1962. *Address:* Porto Vecchio 109, 1250 S Washington Street, Alexandria, VA 22314, USA; 42 Tower Bridge Wharf, St Katherine's Way, London, E1W 1UR, England. *Telephone:* (703) 739-0824 (USA); (20) 7265-1110 (UK). *Fax:* (703) 739-0572 (USA); (20) 7265-1110 (UK). *E-mail:* gdepeyer@aol.com (office). *Website:* www.gervasedepeyer.com (office).

**DE PONT DAVIES, Rebecca;** singer (mezzo-soprano); b. 3 July 1962, London, England. *Education:* Guildhall School of Music and Drama. *Career:* debut, Death in Venice, Glyndebourne Touring Opera, 1989; Gaea in Strauss's Daphne at Garsington Festival, 1995; La Zia Principessa/Zita in Puccini's Il Triticco at Broomhill, 1995; Contemporary works by Judith Weir, Jonathan Dove, Henze, in the United Kingdom and Europe; Concert Appearances at major British venues, Canada and Columbia; 3rd Lady in The Magic Flute, Opera Factory, 1996; Die Muschel in the British premiere of Strauss's Die Agyptische Helena at Garsington, 1997; Moksada in Snatched by the Gods (Param Vir) for Scottish Opera, 1998; Emilia in Verdi's Otello for English National Opera, 1998; Leda in Strauss's Die Liebe der Danaë for Garsington, 1999; Martha/Pantalis in Boito's Mephistopheles, Annina in Der Rosenkavalier and Mrs Sedley in Peter Grimes all for English National Opera, 1999; Geneviève in Pelléas et Mélisande and 3rd Secretary to Chairman Mao in Adams's Nixon in China for English National Opera, 2000; Schwertleite, Die Walküre BBC Proms, 2000; For English National Opera: Flosshilde, Das Rheingold, 2001; Mistress Quickly, Falstaff, 2001; Princess Marya Bolkonskaya, War and Peace, 2001; Ulrica, Un Ballo in Maschera, 2002; Theatre Dresser/School Boy/Groom, Lulu, 2002. *Recordings:* Antigone; Fleurs Jetées; Falstaff, 2001. *Honours:* Many educational prizes including award from Countess of Munster Musical Trust; AGSM; PDVT; Violet Openshaw Memorial Prize for Contraltos; Dorothy Openshaw Prize for Melodie. *Current Management:* Robert Gilder & Co., Enterprise House, 59–65 Upper Ground, London, SE1 9PQ, England. *Telephone:* (20) 7928-9008. *Fax:* (20) 7928-9755. *E-mail:* rgilder@robert-gilder.com.

**DE PONTES-LEÇA, Carlos;** Portuguese writer on music and music manager; *Artistic Advisor, Music Department, Calouste Gulbenkian Foundation;* b. 26 Nov. 1938, Coimbra. *Education:* Coimbra Univ., Univ. of Navarra, Spain, Music Conservatories of Lisbon and Coimbra. *Career:* Asst Dir Music Dept, Calouste Gulbenkian Foundation 1978–2004, Artistic Advisor 2004–; Assoc. Ed. (for Music and Dance) of the cultural magazine Coloquio-Artes, Lisbon 1971–96; Artistic Dir Leiria Music Festival 1993–2001; writer of music programmes on Portuguese TV and radio, essays on history of music and music aesthetics, and programme notes for Gulbenkian Foundation, San Carlos Theatre (Lisbon Nat. Opera) and recordings; commentator of opera performances on radio and TV; Founder-mem. Portuguese Music Council. *Publications:* contrib. to The New Grove Dictionary of Music and Musicians, Verbo Encyclopedia. *Address:* Calouste Gulbenkian Foundation, 1067-001 Lisbon, Portugal.

**DE RIDDER, Anton;** Dutch singer (tenor); b. 13 Feb. 1929, Amsterdam. *Education:* Amsterdam Conservatory with H. Mulder and J. Keyzer. *Career:* after Dutch stage debut in 1952 sang in Karlsruhe from 1956, Munich Theater am Gärtnerplatz, 1962–66, with Cologne Opera in the premiere of Zimmermann's Die Soldaten in 1965 and at the Edinburgh Festival in 1972; Guest appearances in London, Germany and Amsterdam; Bregenz Festival in 1974 as Don José, Glyndebourne Festival in 1979 as Florestan in the Peter Hall production of Fidelio under Haitink, and Salzburg Festival in 1985 in Capriccio. *Recordings:* Busoni's Doktor Faust; Capriccio; La Traviata; Lucia di Lammermoor.

**DE SALAS, Sergio;** Singer (Bass-Baritone); b. 1947, Spain. *Education:* Studied in Madrid, Barcelona and Milan. *Career:* Sang at Opera Houses in Spain from 1971; Appeared as Rigoletto in Valencia and sang in Paris, Marseilles, Bologna and Seville; Liège 1987–88 as the four villians in Les Contes d'Hoffmann; Teatro Real Madrid, 1989, as Gerard in Andrea Chénier; Liège 1990, as Canio; Other roles include Wagner's Dutchman, Athanael in Thais, Mephistopheles in La Damnation de Faust and parts in operas by Verdi. *Honours:* Prizewinner at Beniamino Gigli Competition Macerata and the Voci Verdiane at Parma, 1974.

**DE SARAM, Rohan;** British cellist; b. 9 March 1939, Sheffield, Yorkshire, England; m.; two c. *Education:* studied in Ceylon, in Florence with Gaspar Cassado, in Puerto Rico with Casals, further study with John Barbirolli. *Career:* from age 11 gave recitals and concerts in Europe; US debut with New York Philharmonic, Carnegie Hall 1960; further concerts in Canada, USSR, Australia and Asia; as a soloist, in addition to standard repertoire has worked personally with Kodály, Walton, Shostakovich; premieres of works by Pousseur and others; has taught at Trinity Coll. of Music; mem., Arditti Quartet, with repertoire including works by Boulez, Carter, Ferneyhough, Henze, Ligeti and many other living composers, and premiers of works by Bose, Britten, Bussotti, Cage, Davies, Glass, Gubaidulina, Hindemith, Kagel, Nancarrow, Rihm and Schnittke; as soloist has given the British premieres of Kottos for solo cello by Xenakis and Ligeti's solo cello sonata; has given the world premiere of Pousseur's Racine 19, Xenakis' Epicycles for cello and ensemble and Roscobeck for cello and double bass, Dillon's Eos for solo cello, and Berio's Sequenza XIV for cello; founder, De Saram Clarinet Trio and a duo with his brother, Druvi; interested in the music of his native Sri Lanka and plays the Kandyan drum. *Honours:* Suggia Award 1957, Ernst Von Siemens Prize 1999. *E-mail:* rosiedesaram@hotmail.com.

**DE SIMONE, Bruno;** Italian singer (baritone); b. 1957, Naples. *Education:* studied with Sesto Bruscantini. *Career:* debut in Spoleto, 1980, as Valentin in Faust and Albert in Werther; La Scala Milan debut, 1990, in Pergolesi's Lo frate 'nnammurato; Teatro San Carlo, Naples, from 1991, in Pergolesi's Flaminio, Don Giovanni and Paisiello's L'Idolo cinese; Has also sung at Florence in Paisiello's Barbiere di Siviglia and Pergolesi's Livietta e Tracollo; Macerata, 1992, as Malatesta, Naples, 1994, in Haydn's Mondo della Luna; Other roles include Rossini's Figaro, Taddeo, Dandini, Magnifico, Rimbaud and Germano, Mozart's Figaro, Alfonso, Guglielmo, Count and Leporello, Donizetti's Dulcamara, Belcore and Sulpice; Sang Geronimo in Il Matrimonio Segreto at Rome, 1996; Season 2000–01 as Rossini's Bartolo at Zürich, Taddeo at Padua and in Cimarosa's Il marito disperato, at Naples. *Current Management:* Stage Door, Via Marconi 71, 40122 Bologna, Italy. *Telephone:* 051 19 98 47 50. *Fax:* 051 19 98 47 79. *E-mail:* info@stagedoor.it. *Website:* www .stagedoor.it.

**DE SMET, Raoul,** MPhil; Belgian composer and fmr academic; b. 27 Oct. 1936, Antwerp; m. Marisa Seys 1962; one s. three d. *Education:* Catholic Univ. of Louvain, Univ. of Salamanca, Spain, Music Acad., Deurne, studied composition with A. Verbesselt and Ton de Leeuw, electronic music with L. Goethals, Ipem Gent. *Career:* debut, Darmstadt Ferienkurse Neue Musik; Prof. of Spanish Linguistics and Translation, Kath Vlaamse Hogeschool, Antwerp 1969–97; founder, Orphische Avonden playing concerts of new chamber music 1974; publisher, EM-Reeks, new music of Flemish Composers 1981; Foundation of Orpheus-Prijs Contest for interpretation of new chamber music 1987; mem. SABAM, Unie Belgische Componisten, Stichting Orpheus, CeBeDeM, Music Council of Flanders. *Compositions:* Chamber Opera: Ulrike 1979, 1988, Vincent, 1990; Concerto for Alto Sax, Strings, Accordion and Percussion, 1992; Concerto for Violin and Symphonic Orchestra, 1993; 2 Symphonies, 1960, 1995; 2 String Quartets; Clarinet and String Quartet; Octopus for 8 Bass Clarinets; Track-Sack-Fantasy for 10 accordions; Logbook 1, cello suite; Gnomons 2 for 4 Trombones and Stereotape; Soledad Sonora for

Alto Sax; Concerto for accordion and string orchestra, 2000. *Recordings:* Publications: Chamber music. Numerous. *Honours:* Fuga Trophy 1995. *Address:* Ruytenburgstraat 58, 2600 Berchem, Belgium. *Telephone:* (32) 300-466 (office). *E-mail:* orpheusprys@belgacom.net (office).

**DE SOUSA DIAS, Antonio;** Portuguese composer; b. 13 Nov. 1959, Lisbon. *Education:* Lisbon Conservatory with Constança Capdeville, University of Paris VIII with Horacio Vaggione, studied electronics and musicology. *Career:* Partner in performance groups, ColecViva, directed by Constança Capdeville, as direction assistant, sound synthesis and percussion since 1985; and Opus Sic; Since 1992, collaboration with Grupo Música Nova, directed by Cândido Lima; Professor in composition and electro-acoustics at the Escola Superior de Música, Lisbon; Deputy director of Escola Superior de Música de Lisboa, 1995–2001. *Compositions:* Estudos para Decoração de Interiores for synthe-sizers controlled by computer, 1987; Para dois pianos, nos 1 & 2, 1986, 1992; Estilhaços, incidental music, 1989; Mise en page, tape, 1990; O Jardim das Chuvas de Todo o Sempre for flute, clarinet, guitar, harp, percussion, piano, 2 violins, viola and cello, 1991; Rumbinação, Definitivamente! for 2 flutes, oboe, 2 clarinets, soprano, viola, cello and piano, 1994; 5 Circumstancias for clarinet and piano, 1995; Komm, tanz mit mir ! for five instruments, 1997; Gamanço tape, 1997; Natureza Morta com Ruídos de Sala, Efeitos Especiais e Claquete, for tape, 1997; há dois ou, music theatre, 1998; ...há dois ou..., musical theatre, 1998; Le blanc souci de notre toile for oboe and cello, 1998; uma sombra também, for clarinet and electronics, 1999; Uma Nuvem Também for clarinet and Max/Roland S-760, 1999; Estranho movimento, tape, 2000; Dói-me o luar for flute, clarinet, harp, vibraphone, piano, 2 violins, viola, cello, 2001; Têtrês for tape, 2001; Quand trois poules vont au champ for tape, 2002; Trois Chansons Inachevées for Soprano, Tenor sax and tape, 2003; Ressonâncias-Memórias for flute, clarinet, vibraphone, piano, violin, viola, cello and tape, 2003; Music for film: Santo António do Todo o Mundo, 1996; Chá Forte com Limão, 1993; O Altar dos Holocaustos, 1992; A Maldição de Marialva, 1989; Transparências em Prata, 1988; Fernando Lanhas, Os Sete Rostos, 1988; Os Emissáros de Khálom, 1987; Os Abismos da Meia-Noite, 1984; Short Movies: Nature Morte/ Stilleben, 2004; Processo Crime 141/53, 2000; Detectim, 1991; Theatre: Rumor, 1996; Estilhaços, 1989. *Publications:* Translatins MusicV files to Csound format with the help of OpenMusic (www.ircam.fr/equipes/ repmus/OMBook); Transcription de fichiers MusicV vers Csound au travers de OpenMusic in Actes des 10es Journées d'Informatique Musicale, Montbéliard; Autómatos da Areia, 1978–1984. *Address:* Al. Linhas de Torres, 155 - 4Dto 1750-142 Lisbon, Portugal.

**DE SOUZA, Ralph;** British violinist; b. 1959, England. *Career:* founder member and second violinist of the Endellion String Quartet, 1979; Many concerts in Paris, Amsterdam, Frankfurt, Munich, Salzburg and Rome; Appeared at the South Bank Haydn Festival in 1990, the Wigmore Hall Beethoven Series in 1991 and the Quartet Plus Series on South Bank in 1994; Quartet-in-Residence at Cambridge University from 1992 and Residency at MIT, USA, 1995. *Recordings include:* Works by Haydn, Bartók, Dvořák, Walton and Smetana. *Current Management:* Hazard Chase Ltd, Norman House, Cambridge Place, Cambridge, CB2 1NS, England. *Telephone:* (1223) 312400. *Fax:* (1223) 460827. *Website:* www.hazardchase.co.uk.

**DE VAUGHN, Paulette;** Singer (Soprano); b. 8 Aug. 1951, California, USA. *Education:* Studied with Martial Singher at Santa Barbara, at Juilliard School and in Vienna. *Career:* Debut: As Elisabeth de Valois at Paris Opéra; Appearances at National Theatre Prague from 1980, as Tosca, the Trovatore Leonora, Mimi, Amelia, Ballo in Maschera, Lady Macbeth, Turandot, Violetta and Abigaille; Sang Tosca at Stockholm 1988 and in season 1989–90 appeared as Savonlinna, as Tosca at Graz, as Mozart's Electra at Mannheim, Manon Lescaut, Staatsoper Berlin, Elena in I Vespri Siciliani and Komische Oper Berlin, Dresden and Sofia; Saarbrucken as Aida, Salome, Senta, Elsa and Leonore in Fidelio; Sang Aida at Royal Opera Copenhagen, 1991, at the Montpellier Festival 1992 and Alexandria, Egypt, 1995; Concerts and Lieder recitals in Austria, Germany and Sweden. *Address:* c/o Det Kongelige Teater, Box 2185, 1017, Copenhagen, Denmark.

**DE VOL, Luana;** Singer (Soprano); b. 30 Nov. 1942, St Bruno, San Francisco, California, USA. *Education:* San Diego University with Vera Rozsa in London and with Jess Thomas. *Career:* Debut: San Francisco 1983, as Ariadne auf Naxos; European debut Stuttgart 1983, as Leonore in Fidelio; Sang the Forza Leonora at Seattle 1983 and appeared at Aachen and Amsterdam; Member of Mannheim Opera from 1986; Appearances in Berlin, Staatsoper and Deutsche Oper from 1986 as Euryanthe, Agathe, Rezia in Oberon, Leonore and Senta; Staatsoper, Hamburg 1989, as Irene in Rienzi; Zürich and Vienna 1989 as Ellen Orford in Peter Grimes and Eva in Schreker's Irrelohe; Further engagements in Bologna, Dortmund, Gelsenkirchen and Frankfurt and at Bregenz and Orange Festivals; Sang Amelia in Ballo in Maschera at Stuttgart and Leonore in a concert performances at Festival Hall 1990; Gutrune in Götterdämmerung concert in Rome and Elsa in Lohengrin at Taormina, both conducted by Sinopoli 1991; Sang Marina in Dvořák's Dimitrji at Munich, Leonore at Zürich and Andromache in Reimann's Troades at Frankfurt, 1992; Sang Strauss's Empress at the Paris Châtelet. 1994; Season 1995-96 as Maria in Friedenstag, Amelia (Ballo) and Wagner's Elsa and Isolde at Dresden; Brunswick 1996 and Ghent 1998 as Isolde; Season 2001–02 as the Dyer's Wife in Die Frau ohne Schatten, at Dresden, and Isolde at Antwerp; Other roles include Donna Anna, Isolde, Elisabeth de Valois and Elisabeth in Tannhäuser, Brünnhilde and the Marschallin; Concert reperoire includes the Britten War Requiem and Shostakovich's 14th Symphony. *Recordings include:* Eva in

Schreker's Irrelohe (Sony). *Address:* c/o Opéra et Concert, 1 rue Volney, F–75002 Paris, France.

**DE VRIES, Han;** Dutch oboist; b. 31 Aug. 1941. *Education:* studied in Amsterdam. *Career:* soloist with the Concertgebouw Orchestra and Netherlands Chamber Orchestra; founder mem., Netherlands Wind Ensemble 1960; Danzi Wind Quintet from 1973; concerto soloist and chamber music collaborations throughout Europe, America and the Far East; premiered Bruno Maderna's Third Concerto, and works by Morton Feldman and Louis Andriessen; Lecturer at Amsterdam Conservatory from 1964. *Recordings include:* albums of music by Bach, Mozart and Telemann. *Address:* c/o Sweelinck Conservatorium, Van Baerlesstraat 27, 1071 AN Amsterdam, Netherlands. *Telephone:* 20540 7911. *Fax:* 20540 7496.

**DE VRIES, Klass;** Dutch composer; b. 15 July 1944, Terneuzen. *Education:* Rotterdam Conservatory with Otto Ketting, Stuttgart Hochschule für Musik. *Career:* Lecturer at Rotterdam Conservatory, 1979–; Guest Composer at Tanglewood, 1995. *Compositions:* Refrains, for two pianos and orchestra, 1970; Difficulties, for ensemble, 1977; Movements, for 15 instruments, 1979; Areas, for mixed chorus, wind ensemble and orchestra, 1980; Discantus, for orchestra, 1982; Eréndira, opera, 1984; Phrases, for soprano, mixed chorus, wind ensemble and orchestra, 1986; Piano sonata, 1987; Diafonia, la creación for two female voices and ensemble, 1988; Songs and Dances I–IV, for violin and piano, 1989; Eclipse, for ensemble, 1991; De Profundis. for wind orchestra, 1991; String Quartet, 1994; A King, Riding, Scenic oratorio after The Waves by Virginia Woolf, 1996. *Honours:* Mathijs Vermeulen Prize, 1983. *Address:* c/o BUMA, PO Box 725, AS Amstelveen, Netherlands. *Telephone:* 0031 20540 7911. *Fax:* 0031 20540 7496.

**DE WAAL, Rian;** concert pianist; b. 1958, Netherlands. *Education:* Sweelinck Conservatory, Amsterdam; masterclasses with Rudolf Serkin and Leon Fleisher. *Career:* Regular concert appearances with the Concertgebouw Orchestra, Rotterdam and Stuttgart Philharmonics, Polish and Radio Chamber Orchestra and the State Orchestra of Lithuania; Further concerts and recitals in Boston, Washington, DC, Atlanta and Montreal and on tour to Poland; Performs works by Godowsky, Balakirev and Tausig, as well as contemporary Dutch composers, in addition to the standard repertoire. *Honours:* Prizewinner at Vianna da Motta Competition, Lisbon, 1979, and the Queen Elisabeth Competition in Brussels, 1983. *Current Management:* Robert Gilder & Co., Enterprise House, 59–65 Upper Ground, London, SE1 9PQ, England. *Telephone:* (20) 7928-9008. *Fax:* (20) 7928-9755. *E-mail:* rgilder@robert-gilder.com.

**de WAART, Edo;** Dutch conductor; *Artistic Director, Hong Kong Philharmonic Orchestra*; b. 1 June 1941, Amsterdam; s. of M. de Waart and J. Rose; one s. one d. *Education:* Amsterdam Music Lyceum with Haakon Stotijn, Hilversum with Franco Ferrara. *Career:* co-prin. oboe Amsterdam Philharmonic 1961, Concertgebouw Orchestra 1963; Asst Conductor, New York Philharmonic 1965–66, Concertgebouw Orchestra, Amsterdam 1966; Musical Dir Netherlands Wind Ensemble 1966; Conductor, Rotterdam Philharmonic 1967, Musical Dir and Prin. Conductor 1973–79; Prin. Guest Conductor, San Francisco Symphony Orchestra 1975–77, Music Dir 1977–85; Music Dir Minn. Orchestra 1986–95; Artistic Dir Dutch radio organization, Nederlandse Omroep Stichting; Chief Conductor, Netherlands Radio Philharmonic Orchestra 1989–; Prin. Guest Conductor, Santa Fe Opera 1991–92; Artistic Dir and Chief Conductor, Sydney Symphony Orchestra 1993–2003; Artistic Dir Hong Kong Philharmonic Orchestra 2004–; guest conductor with leading orchestras and at leading venues in the USA and Europe, and at festivals including Spoleto, Bayreuth and Holland. *Honours:* first prize Dimitri Mitropoulos Competition, New York 1964; Hon. AO 2005. *Current Management:* Harrison/Parrott Ltd, 12 Penzance Place, London, W11 4PA, England. *Telephone:* (20) 7229-9166. *Fax:* (20) 7221-5042. *Website:* www .harrisonparrott.com. *Address:* c/o Hong Kong Philharmonic Orchestra, Level 8 Administration Building, Hong Kong Cultural Centre, Tsim Sha Tsui, Kowloon, Hong Kong (office). *Telephone:* 2721 2030 (office). *Fax:* 2311 6229 (office). . *Website:* www.hkpo.com.

**DEAK, Csaba;** Swedish composer and teacher; b. 16 April 1932, Budapest, Hungary. *Education:* Bela Bartók Conservatory, Budapest, Budapest Acad. of Music with Ferenc Farkas, studied with Hilding Rosenberg, Sweden, Ingesund School of Music, Arvika, Stockholm Musikhögskolan. *Career:* teacher, Swedish State School of Dance, Stockholm 1969–, Univ. of Göteborg 1971–74. *Compositions:* Jubilemus Salvatori, chamber cantata, 1958; 2 string quartets, 1959, 1967; Duo Suite for flute and clarinet, 1960; The Fathers, chamber opera, 1968; 121 for winds, percussion, double bass, 1969; Etude on Spring, 1970; Trio for flute, cello, piano, 1971; Andante och Rondo for wind quintet, 1973; Lucie's Ascent into Heaven, astrophonic minimelodrama, 1973; Verbunk for brass sextet, 1976; Bye-bye, Earth, A Play About Death, 1976–77; Hungarian Dances for Wind Quintet, 1977; Octet for wind quintet and string trio, 1977; Eden for symphonic band, 1978; The Piper's Wedding for wind quintet and symphonic band, 1979; Herykon for brass quintet, 1981; Vivax for orchestra, 1982; 5 Short Pieces for symphonic band, 1983; Farina Pagus for symphonic band, 1983; Massallians for trumpet, trombone, brass ensemble, percussion, 1985; Saxophone Quartet, 1986; Quintet for alto saxophone and string quartet, 1988; Concerto Maeutro for trumpet, euphonium, marimba, symphonic band, 1989; Quartet for tubas, 1990; Ad Nordiam Hungarica for chamber ensemble, 1991; Concerto for clarinet and wind orchestra, 1992; Anémones de Felix for symphonic band, 1993; Magie Noire for clarinet and

string quartet, 1993; Novem for saxophone quartet and brass quintet, 1994; Memento Mare for mixed choir and wind orchestra, 1995; Symphony for wind orchestra, 1995; Gloria for mixed choir, 1996; Octet for saxophone quartet and string quartet, 1998; Mayinka for symphony orchestra, 1999; Brassonance for brass band, 2000; Piano pieces; Choruses; Songs; Symphony No 2 for wind orchestra, 2001; Recollection for wind ensemble, 2003, Concerto for flute and string orchestra 2004. *Honours:* Atterberg Music Prize 1992, Gustavus Adolphus Fine Art Award 1989. *Address:* Döbelnsgatan 56, 113 52 Stockholm, Sweden. *Telephone:* 46-8-16-02-17 (home). *Fax:* 46-8-16-02-17 (home). *E-mail:* csaba.deak@chello.se.

**DEAN, Brett;** Composer and Violist; b. 23 Oct. 1961, Brisbane, Queensland, Australia; m. Heather Betts, 2 d. *Education:* Queensland Conservatorium of Music; Hochschule der Künste, Berlin. *Career:* Debut: As Violist: Hindemith Concerto with Melbourne Symphony Orchestra (ABC Concerto Competition), 1981; As Composer: Ariel's Music with Queensland Symphony Orchestra, 1995; As Violist: Member of Berlin Philharmonic Orchestra, 1985–; Soloist with Berlin Philharmonic Orchestra under Abbado, 1995; Chamber music at major European festivals including Bath, Aldeburgh and Salzburg; As Composer: One of a Kind, music for Jiri Kylian Ballet, 1998; Carlo, with Berlin Philharmonic under Simon Rattle, 1999; His works performed throughout Europe, Japan, USA and Australia. *Compositions:* Voices of Angels, written for Imogen Cooper, 1996; 12 Angry Men, for the 12 cellos of Berlin Philharmonic Orchestra, 1996; Carlo, for the Australian Chamber Orchestra, 1997; Beggars and Angels, for Melbourne Symphony Orchestra, 1999. *Recordings:* Hindemith: Viola d'Amore Concerto, with Frankfurt Radio Symphony Orchestra and Albert; Frankel: Viola Concerto, with Albert; Brahms and Bruckner: String Quintets, with Brandis Quartet; Dean: Music for 'One of a Kind', with Pieter Wispelwey, cello. *Honours:* 1st Prize at ABC Concerto Competition, 1981; Queensland Conservatorium Medal for Excellence, 1982; Honoured as Selected Work at Unesco International Rostrum of Composers, Paris, 1999. *Current Management:* Boosey & Hawkes, Berlin.

**DEAN, Robert;** conductor and vocal coach; b. 4 Sept. 1954, Surrey, England. *Education:* Durham University, Royal College of Music, Royal Northern College of Music, National Opera Studio. *Career:* debut, as Baritone, Musica Nel Chiostro, Alidora, in Cesti's Orontea 1979, as Conductor, Batignano Festival, Leonora 1987; Appearances with Covent Garden, ENO, Glyndebourne Festival and Touring, Scottish Opera, Opera North, Welsh National Opera, 1979–86; Scottish Opera Music Staff, 1988–, Head of Music, 1990–; Conducted Over 100 Performances, 1993–; Freelance: Canadian Debut, Edmonton Opera, 1993; US debut, Kentucky Opera 1995, conducted Die Zauberflöte there 1998. *Recordings:* Coronation Anthems; Video, Rossini Barbiere di Siviglia from Glyndebourne. *Current Management:* Robert Gilder & Co., Enterprise House, 59–65 Upper Ground, London, SE1 9PQ, England. *Telephone:* (20) 7928-9008. *Fax:* (20) 7928-9755. *E-mail:* rgilder@robert-gilder .com. *Address:* 51 Lyndhurst Drive, Leyton, London, E10 6SB, England.

**DEAN, Roger (Thornton);** Composer and Double Bass Player; b. 6 Sept. 1948, Manchester, England. *Education:* BA, Cambridge University, 1970, MA, PhD, 1973; DSc, Brunel University, 1984. *Career:* Professor, Brunel University, 1984–88; University of Sydney, 1988–. *Compositions include:* Destructures, for trumpet and large ensemble, 1979; Breaking Worlds, for violin, clarinet and double bass, 1980; Heteronomy 1–4 for ensemble, 1982; BA and BA for brass quintet, 1985; Timestrain, for clarinet and piano, 1989; Reel Choice for ensemble, 1989; Time Dance Peace, for dancers and 8 instruments, 1991; It Gets Complicated, for speaking pianist, 1992; Poet Without Language, for voices and electronics, 1992; Nuaghic Echoes, for voice and electronics, 1993; Elektra Pulses for string quartet and tape, 1993; Three Bagatelles for piano, 1994; Sonopetal for orchestra, 1995. *Honours:* Development Fellowships from the Arts Council of Great Britain. *Address:* c/o APRA, 1A Eden Street, Crows Nest, NSW 2065, Australia.

**DEAN, Stafford Roderick;** British singer (bass); b. 20 June 1937, Surrey; s. of Eric E. Dean and Vera S. Bathurst; m. 1st Carolyn J. Lambourne 1963; four s.; m. 2nd Anne E. Howells 1981; one s. one d. *Education:* Epsom Coll., Royal Coll. of Music and privately with Howell Glynne and Otakar Kraus. *Career:* Opera for All 1962–64; Glyndebourne Chorus 1963–64, Prin. début as Lictor in L'Incoronazione di Poppea 1963; under contract to Sadler's Wells Opera/ English Nat. Opera 1964–70; Royal Opera House, Covent Garden 1969–, début as Masetto in Don Giovanni; int. début as Leporello in Don Giovanni, Stuttgart 1971; guest appearances with Metropolitan Opera, New York, Chicago Lyric, San Francisco, Berlin, Munich, Hamburg, Cologne, Frankfurt, Vienna, Paris, Turin operas etc.; specializes in Mozart bass repertoire; bass soloist in world première of Penderecki Requiem, Stuttgart 1984; concert appearances in choral works by Beethoven, Shostakovich, Verdi. *Address:* c/o IMG Artists, Lovell House, 616 Chiswick High Road, London, W4 5RX, England. *Telephone:* (20) 8233-5800. *Fax:* (20) 8233-5801.

**DEAN, Timothy;** Conductor; b. 1956, England. *Education:* Studied at Reading University and at the Royal College of Music. *Career:* Has worked with Opera North, the Buxton Festival Opera and the Royal Opera House, Covent Garden; Kent Opera, 1983–90, conducting Così fan tutte, Agrippina, The Magic Flute, La Traviata, Carmen, Le Comte Ory and Don Giovanni on the company's visit to the Singapore Festival; Conducted Martin's Le Vin Herbé for the London Music Theatre Group and the British première of Legrenzi's Giustino for the Chichester Festival; Vivaldi's Juditha Triumphans at the Camden Festival; Acis and Galatea for the English Bach Festival in

Italy; Music Director of British Youth Opera, conducting Don Giovanni and The Marriage of Figaro in London and on tour; Music Director of the London Bach Society from 1988, appearing with them at Chichester and City of London festivals and on the South Bank; Season 1990–91, Assistant Music Director of New D'Oyly Carte Opera Company (conducting in the United Kingdom and USA); English National Opera debut, 1991, with Bluebeard's Castle and Oedipus Rex; Scottish Opera debut, 1991, with Barber of Seville; Music Director of The Opera Company, Tunbridge Wells, 1991–94; Also with British Youth Opera, conducting Così fan tutte (1998), Eugene Onegin, La Bohème, Carmen and La Gazza Ladra; In 1994 conducted Kent Opera in The Prodigal Son at major British festivals and for the BBC; Since Sept 1994 Head of Opera at the Royal Scottish Academy of Music and Drama, Glasgow; (L'Assedio di Calais by Donizetti, 1998); Conducted British Youth Opera in Albert Herring, 1996; appointed artistic director British Youth Opera, 2001. *Address:* c/o RSAMD, School of Music, 100 Renfrew Street, Glasgow G2 3 DB, Scotland.

**DEAN, Winton Basil,** MA, FBA; British musicologist and author; b. 18 March 1916, Birkenhead; s. of Basil Dean and Esther (née Van Gruisen) Dean; m. Hon. Thalia Mary Shaw 1939 (died 2000); one s. (two d. deceased) one adopted d. *Education:* Harrow, King's Coll., Cambridge. *Career:* mem. Music Panel, Arts Council of GB 1957–60; Ernest Bloch Prof. of Music, Univ. of Calif., Berkeley, USA 1965–66, Regent's Lecturer 1977; mem. Council, Royal Musical Asscn 1965–98 (Vice-Pres. 1970–98, Hon. mem. 1998–); mem. Vorstand, GF Händel-Gesellschaft, Halle 1980– (Vice-Pres. 1991–99, Hon. mem. 1999), Kuratorium, Göttinger Händel-Gesellschaft 1982–97, Hon. mem. 1997–; Hon. mem. RAM; Corresp. mem. American Musicological Soc. *Publications:* Bizet 1948, Carmen 1949, Handel's Dramatic Oratorios and Masques 1959, Shakespeare and Opera 1964, Georges Bizet, his Life and Work 1965, Handel and the Opera Seria 1969, The New Grove Handel 1982, Handel's Operas 1704–1726 (with J. M. Knapp) 1987, Essays on Opera 1990, (co-ed.) Handel's Opera Giulio Cesare in Egitto 1999; maj. contribs to New Oxford History of Music, vol. VIII 1982 and Grove's Dictionary of Music and Musicians, 5th and 6th edns 1954, 1980. *Honours:* Hon. MusDoc (Cambridge) 1996; City of Halle Handel Prize 1995. *Address:* Hambledon Hurst, Godalming, Surrey GU8 4HF, England (home). *Telephone:* (1428) 682644 (home). *E-mail:* dean584@aol.com (home).

**DEATHRIDGE, John;** Musicologist; b. 21 Oct. 1944, Birmingham, England. *Education:* Studied at Oxford University with Egon Wellesz and Frederic Sternfeld. *Career:* Lived in Germany during 1970s working as Conductor, Organist and Broadcaster; Fellow of King's College, Cambridge, 1983–96; Visiting Professor, Princeton University, USA, 1990–91; University of Chicago, 1992; King Edward Professor of Music, King's College London, 1996; mem, Royal Musical Association; American Musicological Society. *Publications:* Study of Wagner's Sketches for Rienzi, 1977; New Grove Wagner, with Carl Dahlhaus, 1984; Verzeichnis der musikalischen Werke Richard Wagners und ihrer Quellen, with Martin Geck and Egon Voss, 1986; Editor, The Wagner Handbook; Essays on Wagner's Life and Work, 1992; Editor, Family Letters of Richard Wagner, 1991; Critical edition of Wagner's Lohengrin, 3 vols, 1996–2000. *Contributions:* Cambridge Opera Journal; New German Critique; Times Literary Supplement; Programme notes for Covent Garden, Lohengrin and Der Freischütz 1997–98. *Address:* King's College London, School of Humanities, Department of Music, Strand, London WC2R 2LS, England.

**DECKER, Franz-Paul;** German conductor; b. 22 June 1928, Cologne; m. Christa Terka; two d. *Education:* Cologne Hochschule für Musik with P. Jarnach and E. Papst, Univ. of Cologne with E. Bucken and K. Fellerer. *Career:* Music Dir, Krefeld 1946–50; First Conductor, State Opera Wiesbaden 1953–56; Municipal Music Dir, Wiesbaden 1953–56; Generalmusikdirektor, Bochum 1956–64; Chief Conductor, Rotterdam Philharmonic Orchestra 1962–68; Music Dir, Montreal Symphony Orchestra 1967–75; Prin. Guest Conductor and Music Adviser, Calgary (Alberta) Philharmonic Orchestra 1975–77; Artistic Adviser, Winnipeg Symphony Orchestra 1981–82; Prin Guest Conductor, New Zealand Symphony Orchestra, Wellington 1980–89; Music Dir, Barcelona Symphony 1986–92; Chief Conductor, New Zealand Symphony 1990–99; Prin. Guest Conductor, Nat. Arts Centre Orchestra, Ottawa 1991–99; conducted the Ring-Cycle by Wagner at the Teatro Colón, Buenos Aires 1995–98; guest conductor world-wide since 1960, including opera performances in Ottawa, Montréal, Houston Opera, Dallas Opera, Lyric Opera Chicago and Tulsa Opera; regular guest conductor at the Teatro Colón, Buenos Aires since 1961, presented complete Mahler works and two Wagner Ring Cycles 1991–98. *Honours:* Dr hc; Bundesverdienstkreuz First Class (Germany), Herscheppend Schep ik Roquette Pinto Medal (Brazil), Medal (Netherlands), Queen Elizabeth II Jubilee Medal (Canada). *Address:* Kronenburgerstrasse 2, 50935 Cologne, Germany; 486 B Mount Pleasant Avenue, Westmount, QC, Canada. *Fax:* (221) 439197 (home).

**DECKER, Richard;** Singer (Tenor); b. 1958, USA. *Education:* Studied at the Manhattan School of Music (master classes with Judith Raskin and Nan Merriman); Further study at the Zürich Opera studio. *Career:* Sang with Zürich Opera from 1985 and made guest appearances in Saarbrucken, at the Aix and Macerata Festivals (Ferrando in Così fan tutte) and at the Vienna Staatsoper (in Zimmermann's Soldaten); Other roles include Alwa in Lulu (at Aachen) and has made frequent concert appearances, in Germany and Switzerland; Season 1995–96 at Heidelberg as Thomas' Wilhelm Meister and Wagner's Erik at Eutin; Berg's Alwa at Mannheim, 1998; Season 2000–01 as

Alwa at Dusseldorf and Melot in Tristan at Amsterdam. *Address:* c/o Opernhaus Zürich, Falkenstrasse 1, 8008 Zürich, Switzerland.

**DECKERT, Hans Erik,** DipMus; cellist and conductor; b. 11 Jan. 1927, Hamburg, Germany. *Education:* Royal Danish Conservatory of Music, Copenhagen, studied with Pablo Casals, Maurice Gendron, Igor Markevitch and Sergiu Celibidache. *Career:* solo debut (cello), Royal Conservatory of Music, Copenhagen 1952; cellist, Royal Chapel, Denmark; Docent in Cello, Conducting and Chamber Music, Ingesunds Acad. of Music, Sweden; Docent in Cello and Chamber Music, Esbjerg Acad. of Music, Denmark; Docent in Cello and Conducting, Jutland Acad. of Music, Århus, Denmark; founder, Cello Academy (a 12-part cello ensemble of young European musicians); lectures and gives masterclasses throughout Europe; frequent radio broadcasts as cellist and conductor in Germany and Denmark; mem. ESTA (Danish section) (hon. pres. and founder 1981), Danish Soloists' Union. *Compositions:* Canzona Per Dodici Violoncelli and numerous compositions for choir. *Address:* Norsmindevej 170, 8340 Malling, Denmark. *Telephone:* 86931585. *Fax:* 86931555. *E-mail:* hed@os.dk.

**DECOUST, Michel;** Composer; b. 19 Nov. 1936, Paris, France; m. Irene Jarsky, 1969, 1 d. *Education:* Studied Paris Conservatory under Louis Fourestier, Olivier Messiaen, Darius Milhaud; Studies with Stockhausen and Pousseur, Cologne, 1964, 1965, conducting studies with Boulez, Basle, 1965. *Career:* Professor of Composition, Dartington College summer school, England, 1967–69; Set up regional French orchestra, Pays de la Loire, 1967–70; In charge of musical activities, Maisons de la Culture, Rennes and Nevers, 1970–72; Founder, Director, Pantin Conservatory, 1972–76; Head, Education Department IRCAM, 1976–79; Chief Inspector for Musical Research, Ministry of Culture and Communications, 1979–; His music performed at various festivals, Europe, Israel, New York, also broadcast on radio, Italy, Germany, Spain, England, Greece, Switzerland, Poland, USA; President, ISCM France. *Compositions:* Orchestral, small ensemble, wind band and vocal works; instrumental solos and duos, electro-acoustic music, etc; Si et Si Seulement, orchestra, 1972; L'application des Lectrices aux Champs, soprano and orchestra, 1977; Eole, flute quartet, 1985; Sept Chansons Erotiques, settings of poems for soprano and piano, 1986; Bleus, text Blaise Cendrars, soprano and piano, 1986; De la Gravitation Suspendue des Memoires, orchestra, 1986; Je qui d'Autre, 3 voices and ensemble, 1987; Sinfonietta, 1983, for 10 instruments; Sonnet, 1985 for 15 instruments; One plus One Equals Four, Piano Percussion, 1988; Spectre for Wind Band, 1978; Interphone, Magnetic Tape; Les Galeries de Pierre, Alto Solo, 1984; Le Cygne, flute Solo, 1982; Lierre, 12 Cordes, 1986; Cafe-theatre, Chant-piano, 1985; Violin Concerto, 1990; Ligne for clarinet and string quartet, 1992; Cent Phrases pour Eventail for six voices and ensemble, 1996. *Recordings:* Releve d'Esquisse, Le Cygne, sinfonietta, Harmonia Mundi France, HMC 5152-HM57. *Publications:* Cahiers Perspectives, 1987. *Address:* 35 Rue de Clichy, 75009 Paris, France.

**DECSENYI, Janos;** Composer; b. 24 March 1927, Budapest, Hungary. *Education:* Studied composition with Rezsö Sugar, Budapest Conservatory, 1948–52; Endre Szervanszky, Budapest Academy of Music, 1952–56. *Career:* Hungarian Radio, Budapest, 1952–92, latterly as Head, Department of Serious Music and Director, Electronic Music Studio; Script Editor, Department of Serious Music, 1992–. *Compositions:* Stage includes: An Absurd Story, ballet, 1962; Orchestral: Divertimento for Harpsichord and Chamber Orchestra, 1959; Csontvary Pictures, 1967; Melodiae Hominis for Chamber Orchestra, 1969; Thoughts by Day, by Night, 1971; Commentaries on Marcus Aurelius for 16 Solo Strings, 1973; Double for Chamber Orchestra, 1974; Variations for Piano and Orchestra, 1976; Concerto Boemo, 1976; Concerto Grosso for Chamber Orchestra, 1978; Who Understands the Speech of Crickets?, for Chamber Orchestra and Tape, 1983; Cello Concerto, 1984; The Third One for 15 Solo Strings, 1985; I Symphony, 1986; II Symphony, 1993; Keepsake Album, audiovisual oratorio for soprano, bass, chamber choir, chamber ensemble, electronic and projected images, 1998; Vocal: Love for Soprano and Orchestra, 1957; Metamorfosi for Soprano and Piano, 1964; Shakespeare Monologues for Bass and Piano, 1968; The Plays of Thought, cantata for Soprano and Chamber Orchestra, 1972; Roads, etudes for Soprano and Piano, 1979; Twelfth Symphony of S.W. for Soprano and Percussion, 1980; 2 Symphonies, 1988, 1993; Keepsake Album, audio-visual oratorio, 1997; Chamber: String Trio, 1955; Sonatina Pastorale for Flute and Piano, 1962; String Quartet No 1 1978; String Quartet No 2 2003; Old Hungarian Texts, for Soprano, Bass and Chamber Ensemble, 1992; Frauengesänge, on German Poems, 1998; The Tiger, the Donkey and the Lemmings, 1998; Choral Music: Incidental music for theatre, films and radio; Electronic: Stones, 1987; Prospero's Island, 1989; Birds of the Cathedral, 1991; Book of Verses, five electro-acoustic sound poems. Pedagogical pieces;Farewell to a Far-Away Century — oratorio 2001; Des Dichters R M Rilke Begegnung mit dem Tod — Song Cycle 2001; From the Distance to the Nowadays — cantata to lines from the poems of E Ady 2003; Four Preludes to Saint-Exupéry, with choir 2003. *Recordings:* Several compositions recorded. *Honours:* Merited Artist, Hungary; Bartók-Pásztory Prize, 1999. *Address:* Wesselenyi u.65, 1077 Budapest, Hungary.

**DĚD, Jan;** Composer; b. 22 June 1936, Plzeň, Czechoslovakia. *Education:* Plzeň Conservatory. *Career:* mem., Music Centre of West Bohemia, Plzeň, Czech Music Society, Prague. *Compositions:* Four songs on the words of folk poetry, chorus, op 1, 1962; Wistful Variations, small ballet for 5 dancers, 5 musicians and reciter, op 38; Short Czech Mass for combined chorus and symphonic orchestra, op 42; Sonatine for Solo Viola, op 43; Great Czech-Latin Mass to Our Lady for combined chorus, soloists, symphonic orchestra and organ, op 44, 1992; Concerto of a serenade in E flat for clarinet in B and piano, op 51, 1996; Christmas Songs for combined chorus and chamber orchestra, op 60, 2002. *Address:* Zelenohorská 2, 32600 Plzeň, Czech Republic. *E-mail:* j.ded@cbox.cz.

**DEDEN, Otto;** Composer, Conductor, Organist and Choirmaster; b. 19 Nov. 1925, Amsterdam, Netherlands; m. S.A.M van Dijk, 4 c. *Education:* Studied Composition with Henk Badings. *Career:* Appearances in Church Services on radio and television; Choral Concerts with various male, female and mixed choirs. *Compositions:* 29 Masses; 50 Motets; Te Deum; Hymns; Ballads; Oratorios; Arrangements of Folk Songs (commissions), Dirge, Soprano with Organ, 1993; 5 two ballads, 1992; Mysteria; Kain; 4 Cantatas for mixed choir and orchestra and solo; Magnificat for mixed choir, organ, flute and alto solo; Several Cantatas for choir and orchestra preludes and fugas for great organ; Requiem for a Killed Soldier. *Recordings:* Ballade v.d. Bezemsteel (male voices), Maastricht, 1958; Raamconcerto, 1973; Otto Deden Musica Collecta (collection of recent works). *Honours:* Royal Order of Knighthood of Oranje Nassau, 1982; Order of Knighthood of Gregorius Magnus, Vatican; Medal of Honour of the City of Dordrecht, Netherlands. *Address:* Polluxhof 16, 3318 BJ Dordrecht, Netherlands.

**DEERING, Richard,** FTCL, GTCL, LRAM, ARCM, PGCA; British concert pianist; b. 15 July 1947, London; four c. *Education:* Trinity Coll. of Music. *Career:* debut Wigmore Hall, London 1973, piano recitals and broadcasts in over 90 countries 1975–; founder mem. of piano 40 (8 hands at 2 pianos); premières of several works, with many composers writing and dedicating works to Richard Deering; examiner world-wide for Trinity Coll. London 1979–; piano music reviewer Music Teacher magazine; mem. Incorporated Soc. of Musicians, Adjudicators' Council of British and Int. Federation of Festivals (vice-chair. 2000–02). *Recordings:* Beatles Concerto with Tokyo Symphony Orchestra, English Piano Music, Mediterranean Inspired (Music of Charles Camilleri), Piano 40. *Publications:* ed. of Music Sales 'Composer' series and 'Century of Piano Music' series; contrib. to Classical Music magazine. *Honours:* Royal Philharmonic Soc. Award for distinguished services to British Music 1981, Chair.'s Award for services to Trinity Coll., London 2006. *Address:* 55 Dalmally Road, Croydon, CR0 6LW, England (home). *Telephone:* (20) 8656-6222 (home). *E-mail:* richard@malacca.demon.co.uk (home). *Website:* www .impulse-music.co.uk/deering.htm (office).

**DEGRADA, Francesco,** DipMus, BA; Italian musicologist, academic, writer and music editor; *Professor of Music History, University of Milan;* b. 23 May 1940, Milan. *Education:* Milan Conservatory, Univ. of Milan. *Career:* teacher, Bolzano Conservatory, Brescia Conservatory; Lecturer 1964–76, Prof. of Music History 1976–, Dir of the Arts Dept 1983–, Univ. of Milan; teacher, Milan Conservatory 1966–73; founder-Dir and harpsichordist, Complesso Barocco di Milano 1967–76; Consultant to the Publisher, G. Ricordi 1971–; mem. editorial bds of critical edns of Vivaldi, Pergolesi and Verdi; mem. Accademia Nazionale di Santa Cecilia, Roma, Academia Europaea, London. *Publications:* Al Gran Sole Carico d'Amore, Per Un Nuovo Teatro Musicale 1974, Sylvano Bussotti e il Suo Teatro 1976, Antonio Vivaldi da Venezia all'Europa 1977, Il Palazzo Incantato, Studi Sulla Tradizione del Melodramma dal Barocco al Romanticismo (two vols) 1979, Vivaldi Veneziano Europeo 1980, Illusione e disincanto. Mozart e altri percorsi settecenteschi 2000; editor: Studi Pergolesiani/Pergolesi Studies (four vols) 1986, 1988, 1999, 2000, Andrea Gabrieli e il Suo Tempo 1988; contrib. many articles to scholarly journals. *Address:* c/o Università degli Studi di Milano, Via Festa del Perdono 7, 20122 Milan (office); Via Gaudenzio Ferrari 3, 20123 Milan, Italy.

**DEKANY, Bela;** Hungarian violinist; b. 22 April 1928, Budapest; m. Dorothy Browning 1961; one s. one d. *Education:* Franz Liszt Acad., Budapest with Prof. Weiner, Acad. for Music, Vienna, Austria with Prof. E. Morawec. *Career:* debut, Budapest 1947; has given recitals and broadcast performances; soloist with orchestras in Hungary, Austria, Switzerland, Australia and the UK; formed Dekany String Quartet, Netherlands 1960–68; leader, BBC Symphony Orchestra, London, England 1969–92. *Recordings:* Haydn String Quartets with Dekany String Quartet. *Address:* 68 Woodside Avenue, London, N6, England.

**DEKLEVA, Igor,** PhD; Slovenian pianist; *Professor of Piano and Piano Duet, Academy of Music, Ljubljana;* b. 30 Dec. 1933, Ljubljana; m. Alenka Dekleva; two s. *Education:* Acad. of Music, Ljubljana, Musical Acad., Munich, studied in Siena, Salzburg. *Career:* concerts, recitals, performances with orchestras in Slovenia and abroad, with repertoire including baroque, romantic and contemporary works; frequent appearances as piano duo with Alenka Dekleva, including first appearance at Opatija Tribune 1967; several concert tours with violinist Michael Grube; directed masterclasses in piano in several countries; author, leader and performer, two television series about piano masterpieces throughout history, and Slovene piano works; Prof. of Piano and Piano Duet, Acad. of Music, Ljubljana 1998–; mem., Asscn of Musical Artists (vice-pres.), Kiwanis Int., European Piano Teachers' Asscn of Slovenia (pres.). *Compositions:* many works for piano, chamber orchestra and choirs. *Recordings:* some 30 albums. *Publications:* Slovene National Piano School (eight vols). *Honours:* numerous hon. memberships and fellowships, including Fellowship for Distinguished Service to Music, Madras Philharmonic and Choral Soc. 1984; Dr hc (World Univ. Arizona) 1987; Betetto Prize 1980, Grand Ambassador of Int. Achievement 1990, Award of Excellence, Lisbon 2001, Capital City of Ljubljana Award 2004. *Address:* Hruševo 77, 1356 Dobrova, Slovenia. *Telephone:* (1) 3649075 (home). *Fax:* (1) 2427320 (office); (1) 3649075 (home).

**DEL BIANCO, Tito;** singer (dramatic tenor); b. 3 July 1932, Trieste, Italy; one s. one d. *Education:* studied with Augusta Rapetti Bassi in Trieste, with Renata Cotogni in Rome. *Career:* debut, New York, USA in Stabat Mater by Rossini, director Thomas Schippers, 1965; in Italy as Otello by Verdi, 8th Festival of Two Worlds, Spoleto, 1965; Title role of Otello, Teatro Regio Parma, 1966–71; Bayerische Staatsoper Munchen, 1973; May Festival Wiesbaden, 1970; Festival Szeged, Hungary, 1971; Festival Varna Bulgaria, 1972; Maggio Musicale Florence, 1980; Sang Calaf in Turandot at Naples, 1965, Bologna, 1969, Parma Regio, 1970; Pollione in Norma, Genoa, 1967; Faone in Pacini's Saffo, Naples, 1967; Radames in Aida at Naples, 1968; Ismaele in Nabucco, Trieste, 1969; Canio in Pagliacci, Parma Regio, 1969; Festival Torre del Lago Puccini, 1971; Director of Studies Centre A Rapetti Bassi, Trieste; Professor of Music Academy, Conservatorio in Trieste; Director of Studies Centre Augusta Rapetti Bassi. *Recordings include:* Rossini's Stabat Mater; Pacini's Saffo; Tito Del Bianco: Opera Arias, 2000. *Publications:* A Festival for Giuseppe Verdi in Prima Pagina, Parma, Italy, 1981; La Voce Cantata: Tecnica Vocale ed Espressione dell' Anima, 1981; Il Canto e la Psiche, 1990; L'Approccio al canto come Terapia, 1991; Il Festival Verdiano a Parma, 1999; La Forza del Destino e Altre Storie, 1999; Verdi e i Segni dei Tempi, 2000; contrib. to La Scuola di Canto di Augusta Rapetti Bassi, 1988; L'Espressione del Canto Nella Lezione di Reynaldo Hahn, 1993; La Parabola di Tristan und Isolde, 1993; Misticismo in Musica: Bruckner, Schoenberg e Brahms, 1994; Lo Strumento voce: Aspetti, Didattici e docimologici, in Capriccio di Strauss, 1996. *Honours:* Gold Medal, Giuseppe Verdi Prize, Parma, 1967; Commendatore of the Italian Republic, 1998; Medal, City of Trieste, 2003. *Address:* c/o Centro Studi A. Rapetti Bassi, CP 2159-TS11, 34123 Trieste, Italy. *E-mail:* csarbeit@libero.it.

**DEL CARLO, John;** Singer (Bass-baritone); b. 21 Sept. 1951, USA. *Career:* Sang in The Love for Three Oranges at San Diego (1978) and appeared with Western Spring Opera, 1980–81; European career from 1980, in Donizetti's Olivo e Pasquale at Barga; member of the Cologne Opera from 1987, and Rossini's Cambiale di Matrimonio at the 1987 Schwetzingen Festival; San Francisco Opera from 1982, as Alidoro in Cenerentola and Wagner's Kothner; Sang Donner and Gunther in Ring cycles for Seattle Opera, 1984–92; Other roles include the Wanderer in Siegfried (Cologne, 1990), Mustafà, Don Alfonso, Dulcamara and Simon Boccanegra; Sang Dulcamara at Santiago, 1996; Sang Baron di Kelbar in Verdi's Un Giorno di Regno at the Festival Hall, London for the Royal Opera, 1999; Sang Rossini's Bartolo at Chicago, 2001. *Recordings include:* La Gioconda (Decca), La Cenerentola (Philips) and La Cambiale di Matrimonio (Warner video). *Address:* c/o Seattle Opera Association, PO Box 9248, Seattle, WA 98109, USA.

**DEL MAR, Jonathan Rene,** MA, ARCM; British conductor and musicologist; b. 7 Jan. 1951, London, England; m. Annabel Teh Gallop 1992; two s. *Education:* Christ Church, Oxford, Royal Coll. of Music, Teatro La Fenice, Venice, Accademia S. Cecilia, Rome. *Career:* debut, London Symphony Orchestra, Barbican 1984; conductor, performed with many British orchestras also throughout Europe; mem Dvořák Soc. *Publications:* Indicatore Anagrafico di Venezia 1996, New Bärenreiter Urtext Edition of Beethoven Symphonies 1–9 1996–2000, Beethoven Cello Sonatas 2004; contrib. to Tempo, BBC Music Magazine, Beethoven Journal, Das Orchester, Beethoven Forum, Early Music. *Honours:* Imperial Tobacco Int. Conductors' Award 1978, prize Nikolai Malko Competition 1980, prize First Leeds Conductors' Competition 1984. *Address:* Oakwood, Crescent Lane, London, SW4, England. *Telephone:* (20) 7622-2000. *Fax:* (20) 7622-2000.

**DEL MONACO, Giancarlo;** Stage Director; b. 27 Dec. 1943, Treviso, Italy. *Education:* Studied music and languages at Lausanne. *Career:* Debut: Siracusa, 1964, Samson and Delilah; Assistant to Gunther Rennert, Wieland Wagner and Walter Felsenstein at Stuttgart, 1965–68; Personal assistant of the General Director Vienna Staatsoper, 1968–70; Principal Stage Director at Ulm, 1970–73; Intendant at Kassel, 1980–82; Director, Macerata Festival, 1986–88; Staged Les Huguenots at Montpellier, 1990, and at Barcelona, Roberto Devereux, the first of a projected trilogy of Donizetti's Tudor Operas; L'Elisir d'amore at Helsinki, 1991, followed by Metropolitan Opera debut with La Fanciulla del West; Intendant and Principal Producer at Bonn, 1992–97; Further guest engagements at Bayerische Staatsoper, Zürich Opera and Vienna Staatsoper; Staged Montemezzi's L'Amore dei tre re at Kassel, 1992 and Otello at Reggio Emilia; Staged at the Metropolitan Madama Butterfly and Simon Boccanegra, 1994–95; La Forza del Destino, 1995–96; Verdi's Stiffelio, 1997. *Honours:* Bundesverdienstkreuz, 1st Class, 1987; Cavaliere Ufficiale della Repubblica, 1987; Commendatore Dell' Ordine al Merito della Repubblica Italiana, 1993; Chevalier des arts et lettres, France, 1995; Cruzeiro del Sul, Brazil, 1995. *Current Management:* Zemsky/Green Division, Columbia Artists Management inc, 165 West 57th Street, New York, NY 10019, USA. *Address:* c/o Oper der Stadt Bonn, Am Boselagerhof 1, 53111 Bonn, Germany.

**DEL POZO, Rodrigo;** Singer (Tenor); b. 1969, Chile. *Education:* Studied lute, guitar and singing; Scholarship to study with Jacob Lindberg, 1992; Continuation of studies with Nigel Rogers and David Mason. *Career:* Sang with most leading groups specialising in Baroque repertoire, including St James' Baroque Players, BBC Proms, 1996; Concerto Palatino, Bruges; Sang with The King's Consort in Purcell and Blow Anthems and Odes, Bratislava

Cantans Festival; Purcell with Tafelmusik, Toronto; Sang with Orchestra of the Age of Enlightenment, English Bach Festival Orchestra; Ensemble Baroque de Limoges; Performed and recorded Mondonville Motets and Draghi, Mondonville Festival, Versailles; Performed Rameau's Anacréon with Les Musiciens du Louvre, Cité de la Musique; Sang Monteverdi Madrigals, BBC Proms, Royal Albert Hall, and on tour in USA; Performed with the Harp Consort, Wigmore Hall; Baroque opera performances have included Oslo Sommeropera and Boston Early Music Festival with Andrew Parrott; Pastore I, in Monteverdi's L'Orfeo, Beaune Festival and the Festtage Alter Musik, Stuttgart, with Tragicomedia and Stephen Stubbs; Arcetro, in Peri's Euridice, Drottningholm Theatre and the London Lufthansa Baroque Festival with Combattimento; Solo roles in Indian Queen with the King's Consort, Schwetzinger Festspiele; Concerts and recordings in France, Germany, Austria, Portugal, Netherlands, Spain and Belgium with the Gabrieli Consort; The King's Consort, BBC Prom; The Harp Consort, Teatro Lirico; Tragicomedia, Le Parlement de Musique; L'Ensemble Baroque de Limoges, Versailles and on tour in France; Performed, Purcell Odes, Les Arts Florissants, 1999; Tour with King Arthur, Gabrieli Consort and the King's Consort. *Recordings:* Many recordings for leading recording companies as well as for BBC Radio 3 and television and radio stations in America and Europe; Live recital for BBC Radio 3. *Address:* 11 Sunnymead, Hernes Road, Oxford OX2 7PX, England.

**DEL PUERTO, David;** Spanish composer; b. 30 April 1964, Madrid; m. Karin Anita Burk 1991; one s. *Education:* studied in Madrid with Alberto Potin (guitar), Jesus Maria Corral (harmony), Francisco Guerrero (composition), Luis de Pablo (composition). *Career:* major works in Almeida Festival, London 1985, Ensemble Intercontemporain Season, Paris 1989, Geneva Summer Festival 1989, Alicante Festival 1991, 1996, Ars Musica Festival, Brussels 1992, 1993, 1996, Gaudeamus Week, Amsterdam 1993, 1996, Takefu Festival, Japan 1993; premiere of Concerto for violin and orchestra in Madison, Wisconsin 1998; composer-in-residence, Young Spanish Nat. Orchestra 1999; works performed at Strasbourg Festival 1999; premiere of chamber opera Sol de Invierno, Teatro San Joao, Portugal 2002; premiere of String Quartet, Liceo de Cámara de Madrid 2002; premiere of Symphony No. 1 Boreas, Festival de Canarias 2005. *Compositions:* Corriente Cautiva for orchestra 1991, Concerto for oboe and chamber ensemble 1992, Etude for wind quintet 1993, Vision del Errante for 12 mixed voices 1994, Concerto for marimba and 15 instruments 1996, Concerto for violin and orchestra 1997, Intermezzo for string orchestra 1998, Fantasía Primera for orchestra 1998, Mito for 13 instruments 1999, Fantasía Segunda for orchestra 1999, Sol de Invierno scene for mezzo, baritone and six percussionists (after Ibsen), String Quartet 2002, Alio Modo for piano 2002, Advenit 2003, Sobre la noche for soprano and accordion 2003, Symphony No. 1, Boreas 2004, Symphony No. 2 for piano and orchestra 2005. *Recordings:* Concerto for Oboe, by Ernest Rombout, Xenakis Ensemble and Diego Masson (conductor); Invernal and En la luz, by Orquestra del Teatre Lliure, Conductor, J. Pons; Consort, by Quartet de Bec Frullato; Verso III, by José Vicente (percussion); Verso I, Isabelle Duval (flute); Chamber Music, featuring M. Bernat (marimba), E. Rombout (oboe), A. Sukarlan (piano), F. Panisello (conductor); Complete Piano Music/Accordion Duos/Una Suite para Leo, feturing A. Sukarlan (piano), M. Bernat (percussion), C. Gurriarán (soprano), A. L. Castaño (accordion), J. Libardo (saxophone). *Address:* Azurita, 9 El Giujo, 28260 Galapagar, Madrid, Spain. *E-mail:* daviddelpuerto_mp@yahoo.es.

**DEL TREDICI, David (Walter);** Composer and Teacher; b. 16 March 1937, Cloverdale, California, USA. *Education:* Studied Piano as a youth; Took courses in composition with Seymour Shifrin, Andrew Imbrie and Arnold Elston, University of California, Berkeley, BA, 1959, and with Earl Kim and Roger Sessions, Princeton University, MFA, 1963. *Career:* Debut as Piano Soloist with the San Francisco Symphony Orchestra at age 16; Pianist, Aspen (Colorado) Music Festival, 1958, Berkshire Music Center, Tanglewood, 1964, 1965; Composer-in-Residence, Marlboro (Vermont) Music Festival, 1966, 1967; Teacher, Harvard University, 1966–72; State University of New York at Buffalo, 1973, Boston University, 1973–84; City College and Graduate School of the City University of New York, 1984–; Composer-in-Residence, New York Philharmonic Orchestra, 1988–; Professor, the Juilliard School, 1993–96; Professor, Yale University, 1999. *Compositions:* String Trio, 1959; I Hear an Army for soprano and string quartet, after James Joyce, 1963–64; Night Conjure-Verse, after James Joyce, 1965; Syzygy for soprano, horn and chamber ensemble, after James Joyce, 1966; The Last Gospel for soprano, chorus, rock group and orchestra, 1967, revised 1984; Pop-Pourri for amplified soprano, mezzo-soprano ad libitum, chorus, rock group and orchestra, 1968, revised 1973; An Alice Symphony, after Lewis Carroll, 1969–75; Adventures Underground, after Lewis Carroll, 1971, revised 1977; Vintage Alice: Fantascence on A Mad Tea Party for amplified soprano, folk group, and orchestra, after Lewis Carroll, 1972; Final Alice for amplified soprano and orchestra, after Lewis Carroll, 1977–81; March to Tonality for orchestra, 1983–85; Haddock's Eyes for soprano and chamber ensemble, 1985–86; Ballad in Yellow, for piano. 1997; Dracula, for soprano and ensemble, 1998–99; Gay Life for voice and orchestra, 2000. *Recordings:* Various Compositions recorded. *Address:* c/o Fine Arts Management Inc, 75 Lafayette Avenue, Brooklyn, NY 11217, USA.

**DEL VIVO, Graziano;** Singer (Bass); b. 1 Nov. 1937, Florence, Italy. *Education:* Studied at Florence University and Conservatory. *Career:* Debut: Spoleto, 1961, as Ramphis in Aida; Teatro Regio Parma, as Onofrio in

Galuppi's I tre amanti ridicoli, 1964, and as Achillas in Handel's Giulio Cesare and Sparafucile in Rigoletto; Florence, 1965, in Billy Budd and Katerina Izmailova, returning in Robert le Diable by Meyerbeer, 1968, and Spontini's La Vestale, 1970; La Scala Milan as Pluto in Casella's Orfeo; Edinburgh Festival, 1969 and 1972; Sang in The Nose by Shostakovich at Rome and at Genoa and Naples in the Verdi Requiem; Pisa, 1973, in a centenary concert for Titta Ruffo.

**DELACÔTE, Jacques;** conductor; s. of Pierre Delacôte and Renée Wagner Delacôte; m. Maria Lucia Alvares-Machado 1975. *Education:* Music Conservatoire, Paris, Acad. of Music, with Prof. Hans Swarowsky, Vienna. *Career:* was Asst to Darius Milhaud and Leonard Bernstein; among the orchestras conducted: Orchestre de Paris, Orchestre Nat. de France, New York Philharmonic, Vienna Philharmonic, Vienna Symphony, Israel Philharmonic, Orchestre Nat. de Belgique, London Symphony, San Francisco, Cleveland, Scottish Chamber, Scottish Nat. Opera, RIAS Berlin, WDR Cologne, SF Stuttgart, SWF Baden-Baden, Bavarian Radio, Munich, English Chamber, BBC, London, London Philharmonic, Royal Philharmonic, London, Japan Philharmonic, Yomiuri Symphony, Dresdner Staatskapelle, Royal Opera House, Covent Garden (including Far East tour, Korea and Japan), English Nat. Opera, Opernhaus Zürich, Teatro Real, Madrid, Teatro Liceo, Barcelona, La Fenice, Venice, Vienna State Opera, Deutsche Oper, Berlin, Pittsburgh Opera, Welsh Nat. Opera, Opéra de Paris, Teatro Colón, Buenos Aires, Canadian Opera Co., Royal State Opera, Copenhagen, State Opera, Hamburg, State Opera, Munich, Chicago Lyric Opera, Semper Oper, Dresden; also recordings with EMI, Philips London and Tring London. *Festivals include:* Flandernfestival, Macerata Festival, Klangbogen Vienna, Dresden Musiktage. *Honours:* 1st Prize and Gold Medal Mitropoulos Competition, New York 1971. *Address:* Praça Eugênio Jardim 34/602, Copacabana, 22061-040 Rio de Janeiro RJ, Brazil.

**DELAMBOYE, Hubert;** Singer (Tenor); b. 1945, Valkenburg, Netherlands. *Career:* Sang in opera at Bielefeld and Wiesbaden, 1974–76; Cologne Opera from 1979; Seattle, Paris and Metropolitan, New York, 1986–88, as Mimi in The Ring; Wiesbaden from 1991 in Katya Kabanova and as Wagner's Loge, Siegmund, Siegfried and Tristan; Salzburg Festival, 1993 as Mozart's Lucio Silla; Frankfurt from 1994 as Cornelius's Nureddin, Loge and Samson; Brussels 1995 as Herod in Salome; Other roles include Verdi's Otello; Season 1997–98 as Paul in Die Tote Stadt at Wiesbaden, Florestan at the Théâtre des Champs-Elysées, Paris and Tichon in Katya Kabanova at Salzburg; Season 2000–01 as Tristan for Reisopera, Netherlands, Lancelot in Le Roi Arthus by Chausson at Edinburgh (concert), in Schoenberg's Die Jakobsleiter at the Vienna Staatsoper and as Tannhäuser at Wiesbaden; Concert and broadcast engagements. *Address:* c/o Hepsisches Staatstheater, Christian Zais Strasse 33-5, 6200 Wiesbaden, Germany.

**DELGADO, Alexandre;** Portuguese violist and composer; b. 8 June 1965, Lisbon. *Education:* Fundação Musical dos Amigos das Crianças, Lisbon, Conservatório de Música, Lisbon and Nice Conservatoire. *Career:* conductor, Fundação Musical dos Amigos das Crianças string orchestra 1981–86; mem., European Community Youth Orchestra 1988–99; musical asst, Rádio de Portugal 1989–91; mem., Gulbenkian Orchestra 1991–95; founder mem., Lacerda String Quartet; guest composer, Maastricht Festival 2001. *Compositions include:* Prelúdio 1982, Turbilhão 1987, Flute Concerto 1988, Antagonia 1990, String quartet 1991, Langará 1992, O doido e a morte (chamber opera) 1994, Tresvariacões 1999, Viola Concerto 2000. *Recordings include:* recital with Bruno Belthoise, Arditti String Quartet. *Publications:* Luis de Freitas Branco e o 1º modernismo português 1990, A Sinfonia em Portugal. *Honours:* Young Musicians Award, Lisbon 1987, João de Freitas Branco Award 1992. *Address:* Av. Luís Bivar 38, 5º esq., 1050-145 Lisbon, Portugal. *Telephone:* 213 571 711. *E-mail:* alexandre.delgado@mail.telepac.pt.

**DELLA CASA-DEBELJEVIC, Lisa** (see Casa-Debeljevic, Lisa Della)

**DELLER, Mark Damian;** British singer (countertenor); b. 27 Sept. 1938, St Leonards-on-Sea, England; m. Sheelagh Elizabeth Benson; three s. *Education:* chorister at Canterbury Cathedral, choral scholar at St John's Coll., Cambridge. *Career:* Lay Vicar, Salisbury Cathedral, 1960–68; founder and Dir, Guildhall Winter Concerts, 1962; Artistic Dir, first festival of the arts, Salisbury, 1967; Vicar-Choral, St Paul's Cathedral, 1969–73; Choral Conductor; began recording with father Alfred Deller, 1962; joined Deller Consort in early 1960s; has toured extensively in Europe, USA, Canada and South America, as member of Deller Consort and as a solo singer; Director, Deller Consort, 1979–; Director, Stour Music, 1976–, Canterbury Festival, 1988–2003. *Recordings:* as member of Deller Consort, the Vanguard, Argo and Nonesuch labels; Purcell's The Fairy Queen, King Arthur and The Indian Queen (Harmonia Mundi). *Honours:* Hon. DMus (Univ. of Kent) 1995. *Address:* 2 Rural Terrace, Wye, Ashford, Kent TN5 5AP England.

**DELLO JOIO, Justin,** BM, MM, DMA; American composer; *Faculty Composer-in-Residence, New York University;* b. 18 Oct. 1960, New York, NY; s. of Norman Dello Joio and Grayce Dello Joio; m. Marianne Bachmann; one d. *Education:* Juilliard School of Music, New York. *Career:* Prof. of Composition, New York Univ., currently Faculty Composer-in-Residence; works performed by Detroit Symphony Orchestra, Juilliard Orchestra with Sixten Ehrling, mems of the Mendelssohn String Quartet, and Primavera String Quartet; Piano Sonata premiered in Nat. Gallery of Arts, Washington, DC (also broadcast); collaborated with American novelist, John Gardner, on opera The Holy Sinner. *Compositions:* String Quartet No. 1, Primavera String Quartet,

Sonata for Piano 1986, Musica Humana symphonic poem for orchestra, Two Concert Etudes, Music for Piano Trio; works for orchestra, chamber orchestra, string quartet, vocal music and solo piano. *Recordings:* Music of Justin Dello Joio. *Honours:* Nat. Inst. and American Acad. of the Arts Charles Ives Scholarship, New York State Council on the Arts grant 1983, NEA grant 1985, New York Foundation for the Arts grant 1986, J. Guggenheim Fellowship. *Address:* ASCAP, ASCAP House, 1 Lincoln Plaza, New York, NY 10023; 400 E 89th Street, New York, NY 10128, USA (home). *Telephone:* (212) 427-8182 (home). *Fax:* (212) 427-8182 (home). *E-mail:* jnd1@nyu.edu (home).

**DELOGU, Gaetano;** Italian conductor; b. 14 April 1934, Messina. *Education:* Univ. of Catania, studied conducting with Franco Ferrara, Rome and Venice. *Career:* guest conductor, Italian Radio, Rome, Milan, Turin and Naples, London Symphony Orchestra, BBC Orchestra, Royal Opera Covent Garden, Orchestre National de France, Japan Philharmonic, Czech Philharmonic, New York Philharmonic Orchestra and National Symphony Orchestra, Washington, DC, USA 1968–69; conductor, Teatro Massimo, Palermo, Italy 1975–78; Music Dir and Conductor, Denver Symphony, USA 1978–87, Prague Symphony Orchestra 1995–2000, apptd Hon. Dir 2000–. *Recordings include:* Bruckner's Seventh Symphony, Schubert's Great C Major Symphony, Orff's Carmina Burana, Haydn's Symphonies Nos 83 and 101, Mahler's 1st Symphony, Hindemith's Symphonic Metamorphoses and Nobilissima Visione, Smetana's Ma Vlast 2001. *Honours:* first prize Young Conductors' Competition, Florence 1964, Dimitri Mitropoulos Competition, New York 1968. *Current Management:* Connaught Artists Management Ltd, 2 Molasses Row, Plantation Wharf, London, SW11 3UX, England. *Telephone:* (20) 7738 0017. *Fax:* (20) 7738 0909. *E-mail:* classicalmusic@connaughtartists.com. *Website:* www.connaughtartists.com.

**DELUNSCH, Mireille;** Singer (Soprano); b. 1962, Mulhouse, France. *Education:* Studied with Evelyn Brunner, Strasbourg Conservatoire. *Career:* Sang at Opera du Rhin and in Schoenberg's Moses and Aron, Théâtre du Châtelet, Paris; Pamina at Lyon and Mimi at Bordeaux; Rameau's Hippolyte et Aricie, Palais Garnier; Gluck's Armide, Nice, Amsterdam and Paris; Season 1998 with Gluck's Eurydice at Bordeaux and Venus in Rameau's Dardanus at Lyons; Season 1999–2000 as La Folie in Rameau's Platée, at Antwerp, and Poppea at Aix and Vienna (Theater an der Wien). *Recordings:* French Cantatas; Lully's Acis et Galatée; Gluck's Armide and Iphigénie en Aulide, under Marc Minkowski. *Address:* c/o Opéra de Lyon, 1 Place de la Comedie, 69001 Lyon, France.

**DELVAUX, Albert;** Director and Music Professor; b. 31 May 1913, Louvain, Belgium; m. Fernande Tassignon, 4 April 1945, 2 s., 1 d. *Education:* Royal Conservatory, Liège (Diploma of Virtuosity on Violoncello); Higher Diploma, Chamber Music; 1st Prize, Harmony, Counterpoint and Fugue and History of Music. *Career:* Head, Counterpoint, Royal Conservtory, Liège, 1945; Professor, Conservatory of Louvain and Tirlemont Academy until 1945; Honorary Director, St Nicolas Academy, 1945–78; Honorary Professor, Brussels Royal Conservatory until 1978. *Compositions include:* Symphony orchestra: Scherzo; Poème; Symphonique Suite; Variations; Miniatures; Sinfonia II; Sinfonia Burlesca I; Mouvement Symphonique; Sinfonie III; Concerto I and II for violin; Sinfonia IV; Capriccio for orchestra; Chamber orchestra: Esquisses; Concerto da Camera I and II; 5 Bagatelles; Introduttione e allegro; Sinfonia Concertante for violin and alto; Concerto for violin and violoncello; Concerto I and II for violoncello; Prelude for flute; Concerto for viola. *Recordings:* Sinfonia Burlesca; Esquisses; Trio No. 2; Sonata a quattro; Concerto for oboe, clarinet, bassoon and flute. *Honours:* 1st Prize Queen Elizabeth Symphonisch Music; 3rd Prize, Queen Elizabeth Chamber Music. *Address:* Kwadeplas 3, 9180 Belsele, Belgium.

**DEMARINIS, Paul;** Composer; b. 8 Oct. 1949, Cleveland, Ohio, USA. *Education:* Studied at Antioch College, Ohio, and with Robert Ashley at Mills College, Oakland. *Career:* Taught composition and computer at Mills College, 1973–78; Wesleyan University, 1979–81, San Francisco State University, 1987–89; Collaborations as a performer with Robert Ashley and David Tudor in New York and Paris and at New Music America Concerts, 1980–85; Computer audio-graphic systems installed at Museum of Contemporary Art, Chicago and the Wadsworth Atheneum; Audio installations at the Exploratorium San Francisco and the Children's Museum, Boston. *Compositions:* Computer-processed speech works Kokole, 1985, and I Want You, 1986; Installations Pygmy Gamelin, Paris, New York and Los Angeles, 1976–80; Music Room, Faultless Jamming, San Francisco and Boston, 1982–; Laser Disk, Eindhoven, Netherlands, 1989. *Address:* c/o San Francisco State University, Music Department, 1600 Holloway Avenue, San Francisco, CA 94132, USA.

**DEMBSKI, Stephen Michael,** BA, MA, MFA, PhD; American composer; *Professor of Composition, University of Wisconsin, Madison;* b. 13 Dec. 1949, Boston, MA. *Education:* Phillips Acad., Andover, Clifton Coll., Bristol, England, Ecole Normale de Musique, Paris, Antioch Coll., State Univ. of New York, Stony Brook, Princeton Univ. *Career:* Prof., Dir of Advanced Composition Programme, School of Music, Univ. of Wisconsin, Madison; music presented by UNESCO, Denmark 1978, 5th Int. Festival of Electronic-Acoustic Music, Bourges, France 1976, Int. Soc. for Contemporary Music, Bonn 1976, New York New Music Ensemble, American Composers' Orchestra, Huddersfield Festival, England, Alan Feinberg, Ursula Oppens, Fred Sherry, Robert Black, Christopher Kendall, Jonathan Faralli, Mauro Castellano, Daniel Druckman, Bert Turetsky, Gregory D'Agostino. *Compositions:*

recorded: Pterodactyl for piano 1974, Tender Buttons for piano 1977, Trio 1977, Digit for clarinet and computer synthesized tape 1978, Stacked Deck for large chamber ensemble 1979, Alba for chamber ensemble 1980, Alta for piano 1981, Caritas for SATB chorus 1981, Singles for voice and piano 1983, Spectra for orchestra 1985, Sonata for violin and piano, So Fine for SATB chorus 1994, Of Mere Being for soprano and large orchestra, Sonotropism for saxophone, piano, electric guitar 1996, Another Day for six percussionists 2001, Contemplations for organ 2001, Only Yesterday for solo percussionist 2001, Pied Beauty for soprano and contrabass 2002, For Five for piano, On Ondine for piano, Fool's Paradise: 48 Proverbs of Hell for soprano, recorder and flute 2003; recorded as conductor: 48 Motives, 96 Gestures, From the Diary of Dog Drexel, all by Scott Fields; published: Sunwood for guitar 1976, Sonata for violin and piano 1987–88, The Show 1986, Fantasy for solo flute 1988, On Ondine for piano 1991–2000, Three Scenes from Elsaveta (opera) 1992, Memory's Minefield 1994, At Baia 1994, Out of my System 1995, For Five 1996, Brass Attacks 1997, Le Monde Merengue 1998, Another Day 2001, Only Yesterday 2002, Contemplations 2002, Pied Beauty 2002, Respite from the Roast 2002. *Publications:* International Musical Lexicon 1980, Milton Babbitt – Words About Music (with Joseph N. Straus) 1987, Collected Essays of Milton Babbitt (with Peles, Strauss and Mead) 2003. *Honours:* three commission-fellowships from the NEA 1979, 1981, 1986, American Acad. and Inst. of Arts and Letters Goddard Lieberson Award 1982, Howard Foundation Fellowship 1986. *Address:* 96 Perry Street B-22, New York, NY 10014, USA. *Telephone:* (608) 263-1900 (office). *Website:* www.stephendemdski.com.

**DEMETEROVÁ, Gabriela;** Czech violinist; b. 17 May 1971, Prague. *Education:* Prague Conservatoire, Acad. of Fine Arts, Prague. *Career:* has performed with leading Czech orchestras in France, Germany, UK, USA; Stringed Autumn Prague 2001, Int. Music Festival Čdeský Krumlov Honour to Baroque 2001. *Recordings include:* selection from Biber's Biblical Sonatas 1996, Italian Baroque, W.A. Mozart – Sonatas for Piano and Violin, Violin Magic, and numerous recordings for Czech Radio. *Honours:* winner Jaroslav Kocián Competition, Yehudi Menuhin Competition 1993. *Address:* Bilkova 21, 110 00 Prague 1, Czech Republic. *E-mail:* demeterovag@volny.cz; ars@arskoncert.cz (office). *Website:* www.gabrielademeterova.com.

**DEMIDENKO, Nikolai;** Concert Pianist; b. 1 July 1955, Anisimova, Russia; m. (1), 1 s., (2) Julya Dougyallo, 15 Aug 1994. *Education:* Studied at Moscow Conservatoire with Dmitri Bashkirov. *Career:* Debut: British debut with Moscow Radio Symphony Orchestra, 1985; Has performed in Russia and abroad in concert and recital from 1976; Frequent tours of Japan and concerts with Bolshoi Symphony, Polish National Radio Orchestra, London Philharmonic, BBC Philharmonic and BBC Scottish Symphony, London Proms debut 1992 with Rachmaninov's 4th Concerto; Resident in the United Kingdom from 1990, teacher at Yehudi Menuhin School; Season, 1992–93 in concerts with the St Petersburg Philharmonic and the Philharmonia Orchestra; Recitals in Paris, Milan and the Concertgebouw, Amsterdam; Two-Piano recital with Dmitri Alexeev at Wigmore Hall, March 1993, to mark the 50th Anniversary of Rachmaninov's death; Six Piano Masterworks solo recitals at Wigmore Hall, January to June 1993 recreating concerts given by Alkan and Rubinstein in the 19th Century: The Classicists, The Age of Beethoven, The Early Romantics, The High Romantics, The Baroque Revival and Legacies and Prophecies, Liszt, Berg, Gubaidulina and Messiaen; Returned to London for German Romantic concerts, 1997. *Recordings:* Albums of Bach-Busoni, Chopin and Liszt; Medtner 2nd and 3rd Concertos with BBC Scottish Symphony Orchestra, Medtner and Chopin Concertos with Philharmonia; Live recordings at Wigmore Hall Masterworks series. *Honours:* Medallist, 1976 Concours International de Montreal and 1978 Tchaikovsky International Competition, Moscow. *Address:* c/o Georgina Ivor Associates, 28 Old Devonshire Road, London SW12 9RB, England.

**DEMITZ, Hans-Jürgen;** Singer (Baritone); b. 1946, Hanover, Germany. *Career:* Sang in opera throughout North Germany from 1976; Hanover, 1983, as Wagner's Dutchman and Marschner's Hans Heiling; Bayreuth, 1983, as Donner; Season 1985 with the premieres of Boehmer's Dr Faustus in Paris and Sutermeister's Le Roi Berenger in Geneva; Spoleto Festival, 1987, as Amfortas, Cerha's Der Rattenfänger at the Vienna Staatsoper; Other roles include as Wagner's Kurwenal at Trieste and Gunther at Lisbon. *Recordings include:* Zemlinsky's Florentinische Tragödie. *Address:* c/o Staatsoper, Opernring 2, 1010 Vienna, Austria.

**DEMPSEY, Gregory;** Singer (Tenor); b. 20 July 1931, Melbourne, Victoria, Australia. *Education:* Studied in Australia with Mavis Kruger and Annie and Heini Portnoj. *Career:* Debut: National Opera of Victoria, 1954, as Don Ottavio; Sang with Sadler's Wells/English National Opera from 1962, notably as Wagner's Mime and David, Don José, Peter Grimes, Tom Rakewell, and in the premiere of Bennett's The Mines of Sulphur (1965); Sang in the first local productions of Janáček's The Makropulos Case (1966) and The Excursions of Mr Brouček (1979); Other roles include the Drum Major in Wozzeck, Dionysius in The Bassarids by Henze (British stage premiere), Aeneas in Les Troyens and the Shepherd in Szymanowski's King Roger (New Opera Company); US debut, San Francisco, 1966, in The Makropulos Case; Aldeburgh Festival, 1967, in the premiere of Musgrave's The Decision; Covent Garden debut, 1972, as Laca in Jenůfa; Sang Bob Boles in Peter Grimes, Sydney, 1986; Prince Populescu in Countess Maritza at Melbourne, 1986. *Recordings include:* Billy Budd; The Ring of the Nibelung, conducted by Reginald Goodall.

**DEMPSTER, Stuart (Ross);** Trombonist, Professor and Composer; b. 7 July 1936, Berkeley, California, USA; m. Renko Ishida, 19 Dec 1964, 2 s. *Education:* BA, Performance, 1958, MA, Composition, 1967, San Francisco State College; Private Trombone lessons with AB Moore, Orlando Giosi and John Klock. *Career:* Principal Trombonist, Oakland Symphony Orchestra, California, 1962–66; Member, Performing Group, Mills College, 1963–66; Tours as Soloist, 1962–; Teacher, San Francisco Conservatory of Music, 1961–66; California State College, Hayward, 1963–66; Assistant Professor 1968–78, Associate Professor 1978–85, Professor 1985–98, Emeritus Professor, 1998–, University of Washington, Seattle; Masterclasses, International Trombone Workshop, 1974–. *Compositions:* Sonata for bass trombone and piano, 1961; Adagio and Canonic Variations for brass quintet, 1962; Chamber Music 13 for voice and trombones, 1964; The Road Not Taken for Voice, chorus and orchestra, 1967; Ten Grand Hosery, Mixed Media Ballet, 1971–72; Pipedream, Mixed Media Piece, 1972; Life Begins at 40, Concert Series and Musical Gallery Show, 1976; Standing Waves for trombone, 1976; Didjeridervish for didjeridu, 1976; Monty for trombone, 1979; Fog Calling for trombone and didjeridu, 1981; Harmonic Tremors for trombone and tape, 1982; Hornfinder for trombone and audience, 1982; Roulette for trombone and audience, 1983; Aix en Providence for trombones, 1983; JDBBBDJ for didjeridu and audience, 1983; Don't Worry, It Will Come for garden hoses and audience, 1983; Sound Massage Parlor for didjeridu, garden hoses, shell and audience, 1986; SWAMI (State of Washington as a Musical Instrument), an Acoustic Guide to the State of Washington for the State's Centennial, 1987–89; Milanda Embracing for unspecified mixed ensemble, 1993–94; Underground Overlays for conches, chanters and trombone, 1994–95; Caprice for unicycle riding trombonist, 1995; Time Piece for solo of mixed ensemble, 1998; Alternate Realities for solo flute; Various co-composed compositions with Pauline Oliveros, others in the Deep Listening Band, 1988–. *Recordings:* Numerous for major labels. *Publications:* The Modern Trombone: A Definition of Its Idioms, 1979. *Address:* c/o School of Music 353450, University of Washington, Seattle, WA 98195, USA.

**DEMUS, Jörg;** Austrian concert pianist; b. 2 Dec. 1928, St Pölten, Lower Austria; s. of Dr Otto and Erika (Budik) Demus. *Education:* Vienna State Acad. of Music and studies with various musicians. *Career:* début at age 14; mem. Gesellschaft der Musikfreunde, Vienna; débuts in London and Switzerland 1950, tour of Latin America 1951, Paris 1953, New York 1955, Japan 1961; has composed music for piano, songs, chamber music, opera; has performed in almost all important musical centres; has made over 450 LP records and CDs. *Publications:* Abenteuer der Interpretation (essays), co-author of a book on Beethoven's piano sonatas. *Honours:* Dr hc (Amherst Univ.) 1981; Premier Busoni at Int. Piano Competition, Bolzano 1956; Harriet Cohen Bach-Medal 1958; Hon. Prof. of Austria 1977; Beethoven Ring, Vienna Beethoven Soc. 1977; Mozart Medal, Mozartgemeinde, Vienna 1979; several Edison Awards and Grand Prix du Disque; Schumann Award, Zwickau, E Germany, 1986. *Address:* c/o Mr Roland Sölder, Lyra Artists Management, Döblinger Hauptstrasse 77A/10, 1190 Vienna, Austria (office). *Telephone:* (1) 3687472 (office); (1) 3681226 (home). *Fax:* (1) 3687473 (office).

**DENCH, Chris;** Composer; b. 10 June 1953, London, England; m. Diana Palmer, 1 d. *Career:* Commissioned by Elision resulting in Driftglass, 1990–91, which represented Australia at '92 International Rostrum of Composers in Paris; The French Ministry of Culture; The ABC; The BBC; The Arditti String Quartet; austraLYSIS; Synergy; and others. His works have been performed by Ensemble Accroche Note of Strasbourg, the Berlin Radio Symphony Orchestra, Ensemble Exposé, Ensemble Intercontemporain, London Sinfonietta, Music Projects, London, the Xenakis Ensemble and such soloists as Andrew Ball, Laura Chislett, James Clapperton, Rolf Hind, Stephanie McCallum, and many others; He has had works presented at such events as the Brighton Festival, Darmstadt Ferienkurse für Neue Musik, the Hong Kong ISCM World Music Days, Insel Musik Berlin, many Festivals in France and Italy, the Sydney Spring Festival and the Venice Biennale. *Compositions:* Four large-scale solo flute works for Laura Chislett, including Sulle Scale della Fenice; Tilt for solo piano; several large ensemble pieces, including Enoncé and Afterimages, quattro frammenti and planetary allegiances; chamber music; atsiluth, heterotic strings; Propriocepts for four voices and orchestra; 4 Symphonies, 1980, 1982, 1987, 1997; flesh and the mirror for Elision; beyond status geometry for Synergy, 1995; The heart's algorithms for piano, 1999. *Recordings:* Numerous recordings. *Honours:* Kranichsteiner Musikpreis, 1984. *Address:* c/o Australian Music Centre, PO Box N690, Grosvenor Place, Sydney 2000, Australia.

**DENE, Joszef;** Singer (Bass); b. 31 March 1938, Budapest, Hungary. *Education:* Studied in Budapest; Sang at the Hungarian State Opera, notably as Alberich in Das Rheingold. *Career:* Many performances at the Zürich Opera, in works by Monteverdi, Berg, Verdi, Janáček and Wagner; Berlin Komische Oper, 1975, as Mozart's Figaro; Further engagements at La Scala, Bayreuth, San Francisco and the Metropolitan (Wagner's Alberich, 1981); Paris Opéra, 1982 and 1985, as Gloucester in Reimann's Lear and as Trithemius in the premiere of Boehmer's Docteur Faustus; Opéra du Rhin Strasbourg and Barcelona, 1985–96, as Des Grieux in Manon; Season 1987 at Graz as the Hangman in the premiere of Cerha's Rattenfänger and as Taddeo in L'Italiana in Algeri at the Schwetzingen Festival; Graz Opera, 1988–89, as Alberich in Siegfried and Götterdämmerung; Sang Mesner in Tosca at Zürich, 2000; Other roles include Mozart's Alfonso and Papageno, Don Pasquale, Pizarro, Kurwenal, Klingsor, Leporello and Handel's Claudius (Agrippina).

*Recordings:* Don Giovanni, Boito's Nerone and Juditha Triumphans by Vivaldi; Il Ritorno d'Ulisse, Zürich, 1982.

**DENES, Istvan;** Conductor and Composer; b. 1950, Budapest, Hungary. *Education:* Piano, Conducting and Composition, Franz Liszt Academy, Budapest; Vienna Musikhochschule (Scholarship from Georg Solti). *Career:* Conductor, Budapest State Opera and Lecturer in Harmony, Franz Liszt Academy, 1980–84; Principal Conductor, Bremen Opera, 1987–95; Salieri's Axur, re d'Ormus at Verona and Salome at Montpellier; Further engagements at Prague, Essen, Stuttgart, Jena, Berlin, Darmstadt, Vienna Volksoper and Bregenz Festival; Conducted the first production this century of Zemlinsky's first opera, Sarema (Trier Opera, 1996). *Compositions include:* Logarithmische Rhythmen for percussion; Trio in Memoriam Bela Bartók for piano, cello and violin; Mohacs 1526, Hommage à Beethoven; Funerailles for orchestra. *Recordings include:* Sarema (Koch International). *Address:* c/o Theater der Stadt Trier, Am Augustinerhof, 5500 Trier, Germany.

**DENÈVE, Stéphane;** Conductor; b. 1972, France. *Education:* Graduated Paris Conservatoire, 1995. *Career:* Assistant to Georg Solti for Bluebeard's Castle with Orchestre de Paris, 1995, and Don Giovanni at the Paris Opéra, 1996; Conducted Die Zauberflöte at the Deutsche Oper am Rhein, 1997 (Permanent Conductor from 1999); Engagements with Cologne Opera for Dialogues des Carmélites, Così fan tutte, La Traviata and Die Zauberflöte, 1998–2000; Pelléas et Mélisande for Cincinnati Opera; Season 2000–01 with St Petersburg Philharmonic, Orchestre de Paris and Washington National Symphony Orchestra; Music Dir, Royal Scottish Nat. Orchestra 2004–. *Honours:* First Prize in Conducting, Paris Conservatoire, 1995. *Address:* c/o IMG Artists, Lovell House, 616 Chiswick High Road, London W4 5RX, England.

**DENIZ, Clare (Frances);** Concert Cellist and Teacher; b. 7 April 1945, England. *Education:* Private piano study from age 5; Private cello study with Madeleine Mackenzie from age 11; Won Junior Exhibition to Royal Academy of Music after only one years tuition; Teachers: Lilley Phillips and Derek Simpson, gaining LRAM; Further study with Christopher Bunting, Jacqueline du Pré and Antonia Butler; Masterclasses with Paul Tortelier then became a pupil. *Career:* Debut: Purcell Room, London, 1983; Former Principal Cellist with Royal Ballet Orchestra and sub-principal cellist with English National Opera; Many recitals specializing in British and French music as well as standard repertoire; Appeared at: Cambridge Festival, Cheltenham Lunchtime Concerts, Fairfield Hall Centenary Concert for Arnold Bax; Concertgebouw Amsterdam debut 1987, an unaccompanied Bach recital, returning in 1990; Recording for BBC Radio Oxford, 1987 and recorded a recital of French music in 1991; Invited to take part in Counterpoint II recital series by Incorporated Society of Musicians, 1990; 3 Concerts of first performances for the Wessex Composers Group, 1990, conceived by Incorporated Society of Musicians; Children's concerts and workshops; Played Haydn's C Major Concerto in 1990 and gave a Virtuoso Recital in 1992 for the Jacqueline du Pré Appeal Fund; Solo recitals given in Amsterdam, 1990 and 1992 and in Paris, 1993; Concert given for the EEC Brussels Commission, 1994. *Honours:* Elected Fellow of The Royal Society of Arts, 1990. *Address:* 31 Friday Street, Henley-on-Thames, Oxfordshire RG9 1AN, England.

**DENIZE, Nadine;** French singer (mezzo-soprano); b. 6 Nov. 1943, d. of Jean Denize and Christiane Denize; m. Bernard Bovier-Lapierre 1971; one s. *Education:* Conservatoire Nat Supérieur de Musique de Paris. *Career:* Singer Opéra and Opéra Comique, Paris 1965–71, Opéra du Rhin, Strasbourg 1974–77, Vienna Opera 1977–79; Guest Singer Opéra de Paris 1974–89, Opéra Bastille, Paris 1989–93 and major opera houses in Germany, Italy, Portugal, Hungary, Yugoslavia, Netherlands, USA, Argentina, etc; has performed at the major opera houses and with major orchestras and concert groups in France and world-wide 1974–; appearances at numerous festivals; has performed the works of Wagner, Berlioz, Verdi, Beethoven, Mozart, Schoenberg, Mahler, Mussorgsky, Janacek and Richard Strauss; has recorded works by Wagner, Berlioz, Verdi and Mahler; teacher, Ecole Normale de Musique de Paris Alfred Cortot. *Honours:* Officier des Arts et Lettres; Officier de l'Ordre Nat. du Mérite 1986. *Current Management:* c/o Jean-Marie Polivé, 16 avenue Franklin-Roosevelt, 75016 Paris, France. *Address:* 35 rue François Bonvin, 75015 Paris, France (home). *Telephone:* (1) 47-34-98-59 (home). *E-mail:* bernard.bovier-lapierre@wanadoo.fr (home).

**DENLEY, Catherine;** Singer (Mezzo-Soprano); b. 1954, Northamptonshire, England; m. Miles Golding, 3 s. *Education:* Studied at Trinity College of Music, London. *Career:* Sang 2 years with the BBC Singers; Solo performances with major orchestras and conductors throughout Europe and as far afield as the USA, Canada, China, Japan and the Ukraine; US appearances at the Tanglewood Festival with the Boston Symphony Orchestra; San Francisco concerts with John Eliot Gardiner; Performances of Messiah with the Hallé Orchestra, City of Birmingham Symphony, the English Concert in Belgium and The Sixteen in Finland and Poland; Mozart's Requiem in Salzburg and Innsbruck; Elgar's The Music Makers and the Bliss Pastoral at South Bank; Bach B Minor Mass at Aldeburgh and York; Beethoven's Missa Solemnis at the Windsor Festival; Staged performances of L'Incoronazione di Poppea at Spitalfields; Operatic roles include: Olga in Eugene Onegin at the Aldeburgh Festival; Nutrice in Monteverdi's Poppea; Handel Operas: Giustino and Radamisto; Mrs Noah in Noye's Fludde; Radio and television recordings in the United Kingdom and Europe; Television recordings include appearances in Channel 4's Maestro series and Mahler's 8th Symphony from Dublin; Sang

Third Lady in Die Zauberflöte, 1990; Promenade Concerts; Sisera in Handel's Deborah at the 1993 Proms; Mahler 2 in Kiev and Odessa; Tucapsky Stabat Mater in the Czech Republic; Haydn Stabat Mater in Madrid and Handel Judas Maccabaeus in Berlin and Halle; Season 1999 with Mozart's Requiem and Schumann's Scenes from Faust at the London Prom concerts. *Recordings:* Monteverdi's L'Orfeo and L'Incoronazia di Poppea; Handel's Semele, Hercules, Il Duello Amorosa and Messiah; Vivaldi's Gloria; Requiem by Bruckner; In the Beginning by Copland; Die Zauberflöte. *Honours:* G.T.C.L.; F.T.C.L. *Address:* CDI, Lyndhurst, Denton Road, Ben Rhydding, Ilkley, West Yorkshire, LS29 8QR, England.

**DENNER, Bettina;** Singer (Mezzo-soprano); b. 5 Jan. 1960, Weimar, Germany. *Education:* Studied at the Leipzig Musikhochschule, notably with Hans Christian Polster. *Career:* Sang at the Leipzig Opera from 1983, as Zerlina, Carlotta in Die schweigsame Frau, and Nicklausse in Les Contes d'Hoffmann; Guest at the Berlin Staatsoper from 1987, as Cherubino and on tour to Japan; Other roles have included Dorabella, Idamante, Massenet's Charlotte, Hermia in A Midsummer Night's Dream and Orlovsky; Sang the Hostess in Boris Godunov at Leipzig, 1993; Many concert engagements, notably at the Leipzig Thomasschule and the Gewandhaus. *Address:* c/o Deutsche Staatsoper Berlin, Unter den Linden 7, 1060 Germany.

**DENNING, Angela;** Australian singer (soprano); b. 1952, Sydney, NSW. *Education:* New South Wales Conservatory. *Career:* sang with the State Opera of South Australia from 1976 and with the Australian Opera at Sydney from 1979; English National Opera, 1982–83, Deutsche Oper Berlin, 1984, and the Staatsoper, 1988; Sang Clorinda in La Cenerentola at Salzburg, 1988–89, and Dalila in Handel's Samson at the 1988 Göttingen Festival; Other roles include Donna Anna and Meyerbeer's Marguerite de Valois (both in Berlin), Lucia di Lammermoor, Gilda, Nannetta, the Queen of Night and Fiordiligi. *Recordings include:* La Cenerentola (video).

**DENNIS, Elwyn;** Composer; b. 10 Aug. 1941, Los Angeles, USA. *Education:* BA, University of California, 1965. *Career:* Sculptor, Lecturer, Department of Architecture, University of Melbourne, 1974–75; Lecturer, Ballarat University, 1990–92; Manager of Clouds, a nature conservation area. *Compositions include:* Evidence of Origin, performance with sculpture, 1982; Particle Flow, 1983; Space of Concern, 1983; Clouds Are, 1984; Wimmera, 1986; A Mother's Day, 1987; Time Again, 1987; Invention for Guitar, 1988; Details of a Morning, 1988; Dry Country, 1992; Waiting Winter Out, tape with harpsichord, 1994; Commissions Association of Australia and The Listening Room, ABC-FM. *Honours:* Caulfield Arts Centre Purchase Prize, 1979. *Address:* c/o APRA, 1A Eden Street, Crows Nest, NSW 2065, Australia.

**DENNISON, Robert;** Concert Pianist; b. 10 June 1960, Philadelphia, USA. *Education:* Studied in Philadelphia Music Academy, at Temple University and the Peabody Conservatory; Further Study with Claude Frank and Horszowski. *Career:* Debut: Philadelphia, with the Shostakovich Second Concerto, 1971; Concerts and recitals in Washington, Boston, Cleveland, Los Angeles, St Louis and Chicago; Russian Tours with concerts in Kiev, St Petersburg, Vilnius, Moscow and Novosibirsk, 1991–93; Further engagements at Chicago, New Jersey, Colorado, San Francisco, Boston, Essen, Berlin, Hamburg Music Festival, Lucerne Festival and in Hungary, Romania and Czechoslovakia, 1992–93; Repertoire includes contemporary works by American composers as well as the standard classics. *Address:* c/o Sonata, 11 Northgate Street, Glasgow G20 7AA, Scotland.

**DENNISTON, Patrick;** Singer (Tenor); b. 1965, New York, USA. *Education:* Studied at Syracuse University and the Lyric Opera Center, Chicago. *Career:* Engagements with the San Francisco Opera, Houston Grand Opera, New York City Opera, Opera Pacific, Kentucky Opera, New Israeli Opera, Bonn Opera and at the Spoleto Festival; Further appearances throughout Canada; Roles have included Pinkerton, Don Carlos, Don José, Edgardo, Dmitri, Lensky and Alfredo; Glyndebourne Festival 1997, as Des Grieux in a new production of Manon Lescaut; Season 1997–98 with Pinkerton and Ismaele in Nabucco at Chicago, Erik in Der fliegende Holländer, and Radames at Houston; Cavaradossi at Madison. *Address:* c/o Lyric Opera Chicago, 20 North Wacker Drive, Chicago, IL 60606, USA.

**DEPLUS, Guy Gaston Simon;** clarinettist; b. 29 Aug. 1924, Vieux Condé, France; m. Yvette Vandekerkhove 1946, one s. *Education:* Conservatoire National Superieur du Musique de Paris. *Career:* Guard Republican Band and Orchestra, 1947; Concerts Colonne, 1950; Domaine Musical, with Pierre Boulez, 1953; Ars Nova, with Marius Constant, 1963; Paris Octet, 1965; Opéra Comique, 1968; Opera, 1973; Professor, Chamber Music, Paris Conservatory, 1974; Concerts in Berlin, Salzburg, Vienna, 1977; Professor, Clarinet, Paris Conservatory, 1978; Judge, International Competitions; Professor Ecole Normale de Musique de Paris, 1991; mem. International Clarinet Assocn (French chair.). *Recordings:* Mozart, Concerto, Trio, Quintet; Weber, 1st Clarinet Concerto, Concertino, Grand Duo; Rossini, Introduction, Theme and Variations; Beethoven Septet; Brahms 2 sonatas and trio; Messiaen Quartet. *Contributions:* The Clarinet. *Honours:* Quoted by Stravinsky in Memories and Commentaries, 1959; 4 Prix de l'Academie du Disque Francais; Lifetime Achievement Award, International Clarinet Association for Outstanding Performance, Teaching, Research and Service to the Clarinet, 1999. *Address:* 37 Square Saint Charles, 75012 Paris, France.

**DEPOLTOVA, Eva;** Singer (soprano); b. 5 Aug. 1945, Bratislava, Czechoslovakia. *Education:* Univ. of Music Arts, Prague, with Zdenka Zika and Elena Obraztsova. *Career:* debut, Prague National Theatre 1974; sang in concert with Czech Philharmonic Orchestra, Vienna Symphony Orchestra and other major orchestras, in Prague, Vienna, Salzburg, Linz, Copenhagen, Vienna, Lyon, Switzerland, Italy, Japan, Germany, Tehran, Istanbul, Taiwan; Dvořák Requiem and Stabat Mater, Janáček Glagolitic Mass, Beethoven, The Ninth Symphony, 1976; roles include Lady Macbeth, Marenka, The Bartered Bride, Violetta, La Traviata, Aida, Donna Anna and many others; sang Krasava in Libuše by Smetana at the National Theatre, Prague, 100th Anniversary re-opening 1983. *Recordings:* Fibich-Sarka, Foerster's Eva; Smetana, Dalibor, Libuše and The Kiss, Mozart, Don Giovanni, Martinů's The Miracles of Our Lady and Gilgamesh. *Honours:* Prix Caecilia, Union de la Presse 1985. *Address:* NA Prikope 12, 110 01 Prague, Czech Republic.

**DEPREIST, James Anderson;** Conductor; b. 21 Nov. 1936, Philadelphia, PA, USA; m. 1st Betty Louise Childress 1963; two d.; m. 2nd Ginette Grenier 1980. *Education:* BS 1958, MA 1961, Univ. of Pennsylvania; studied with Vincent Persichetti, Philadelphia Conservatory of Music, 1959–61. *Career:* conductor, Contemporary Music Guild, Philadelphia, 1959–62; specialist in music, US State Dept, 1962–63; Conductor, Bangkok, Thailand, 1963–64; Asst Conductor, New York Philharmonic Orchestra, 1965–66; Principal Guest Conductor, Symphony of the New World, 1968–70; European debut, Rotterdam Philharmonic Orchestra, 1969; Assoc. Conductor, 1971–75; Principal Guest Conductor, National Symphony Orchestra, Washington DC, 1975–76; Music Dir, L'Orchestre Symphonique de Québec, 1976–83, Oregon Symphony Orchestra, Portland, 1980–, Malmö Symphony Orchestra, 1991–94, Philharmonique De Monte-Carlo, 1994–98; Guest Conductor with major orchestras in North America and Europe; engaged for Andrea Chénier at Monte Carlo. *Publications:* Book of Poems, This Precipice Garden, 1987; The Distant Siren (poems), 1989. *Honours:* First prize, Dimitri Mitropoulos International Conducting Competition, New York, 1964. *Current Management:* TransArt (UK) Ltd, Cedar House, 10 Rutland Street, Filey, YO14 9JB, North Yorkshire, England. *Telephone:* (1723) 515819. *Fax:* (1723) 514678. *E-mail:* transartuk@transartuk.com. *Website:* www.transartuk.com.

**DERENZI, Victor;** American conductor; *Artistic Director, Sarasota Opera*. *Career:* Artistic Dir and principal conductor, Sarasota Opera 1981–; conductor with Lyric Opera of Chicago, St Louis, Toledo, New Orleans and New York City operas, and Opéra du Montréal, Un Ballo in Maschera in Canary Islands, and Spoleto Festival; responsible for Sarasota Opera Verdi Cycle, a multi-year project to present all of Verdi's music. *Address:* Sarasota Opera, 61 N Pineapple Avenue, Sarasota, FL 34236, USA (office). *Telephone:* (941) 366-6645 (office); (941) 955-5571 (home). *E-mail:* info@sarasotaopera.org (office). *Website:* www.sarasotaopera.org (office).

**DERNESCH, Helga;** Austrian singer (soprano, mezzo-soprano); b. 3 Feb. 1939, Vienna; m. Werner Kramm; two c. *Education:* Vienna Conservatory. *Career:* sang many operatic roles in Berne 1961–63, Wiesbaden 1963–66, Cologne 1966–69; freelance guest appearances at all maj. opera houses in Europe 1969–; regular appearances at Bayreuth Festival 1965–69, at Salzburg Easter Festival 1969–73; since 1979 has sung as mezzo-soprano; regular appearances at San Francisco Opera 1982–; début Metropolitan Opera, New York 1985; has sung in operas and concerts throughout Europe, N and S America, Japan; many recordings. *Address:* Salztorgasse 8/11, 1013 Vienna (office); Neutorgasse 2/22, 1013 Vienna, Austria.

**DEROUBAIX, Jeanne;** Singer (Mezzo-soprano); b. 16 Feb. 1927, Brussels, Belgium. *Education:* Studied in Brussels. *Career:* Sang in ensemble Pro Musica, under the direction of Safford Cape (1947–53); Toured widely in Europe with repertoire specialising in music of 13th–16th centuries; Lieder recitals and programmes of French chansons; Often heard in contemporary music; Sang in the first performances of Stravinsky's Threni (Venice 1958) and A Sermon, a Narrative and a Prayer (Basle 1962); Also heard in Schoenberg's Pierrot Lunaire and works by Boulez; Professor at the Musikhochschule Detmold from 1957. *Recordings:* Lieder by Brahms; Beethoven's Missa Solemnis; Monteverdi's Orfeo; Le Marteau sans Maître by Boulez.

**DES MARAIS, Paul (Emile);** Composer and Professor; b. 23 June 1920, Menominee, Michigan, USA. *Education:* Studied with Leo Sowerby, Chicago, 1937–41; Nadia Boulanger, Cambridge, 1941–42 and Paris, 1949; BA, 1949, MA, 1953, Harvard University. *Career:* Teacher, Harvard University, 1953–56; University of California, Los Angeles, 1956–. *Compositions:* Stage: Epiphanies, chamber opera, 1968; Incidental music to Dryden's A Secular Masque, 1976; Shakespeare's A Midsummer Night's Dream, 1976; Sophocles's Oedipus, 1978; G B Shaw's St Joan, 1980; Dryden's Marriage à la Mode, 1981; Shakespeare's As You Like It, 1983; G Etherege's The Man of Mode, 1984. Dance: Triplum for organ and percussion, 1981; Touch for 2 pianos, 1984. Chamber: 2 piano sonatas, 1947, 1952; Theme and Changes for harpsichord, 1953; Capriccio for 2 pianos and percussion, 1962; 2 Movements for 2 pianos and percussion, 1972 revised and enlarged as 3 Movements, 1975; The Baroque Isles for 2 keyboard percussionists, 1986; Orpheus, theatre piece for narrator and instruments, 1987; The French Park, for two guitars, 1988. Choral: Six-part Mass for double chorus, 1947; Motet for mixed voices, cellos and double basses, 1959; Psalm 121, 1959; Organum 1–6 for chorus, organ and percussion, 1972, revised and enlarged, 1980; Brief Mass for chorus, organ and percussion, 1973; Seasons of the Mind for chorus, piano 4-hands and celesta, 1980–81. Vocal: Reflections on Faure for voice and piano, 1972; Late Songs for voice and piano, 1978; Slowsong for voice and piano, 1987; The

French Park for two guitars, 1988. *Publications:* Harmony, 1962. *Contributions:* Articles in Perspectives of New Music. *Address:* c/o Music Department, University of California at Los Angeles, Los Angeles, CA 90024, USA.

**DESCHÊNES, Bruno,** BMus; Canadian composer, musician and ethnomusicologist; b. 12 Oct. 1955, Cap-Chat, Quebec, Canada; m. Shizuko Toguchi, 18 April 1981. *Education:* BMus, Composition, McGill University, Montréal, 1979; Master in Composition, University of Montréal, 1983; Research on Music Perception, Listening and Teaching. *Career:* involved in ethnomusicological studies 1995–, specialising in Japanese traditional music; also performs Japanese music on the shakuhachi (traditional bamboo flute); performing and conducting on radio and concerts, 1980–; compositions performed in France, USA, Venezuela, Brazil and Montréal, 1979–; Gives lectures, workshops and writes articles on music perception and listening in Canada, USA and Europe; World Music Reviewer, The All Music Guide (website) 2000–02; Journalist, Critic and Reviewer, The Scena Musicale (music magazine) 2003–. *Compositions:* Improvised Music: Expansion, Horizon, Pyramide, Chakras; Electronic Music: Murmures for tape and percussion; Different Chamber Groups: Dimension, Innerance, Prisme, Poemes Luminescence, Calme En Soi, Double Jeu; Choir: Ondes, Ondes et Particules; Les Vagues for narrator and tape, 1994; Le Monde est une Bulle d'air, tape, 1994; several works for Japanese and Chinese traditional instruments. *Contributions:* The Perceptions of Colour Through Music, Musicwork 26, 1984; Regularly publishes articles in the bulletin of the Centre Québécois de la Couleur; numerous articles on the psychology, sociology and philosophy of music. *Address:* 561 Rue Clark, Montréal, QC H2T 2V5, Canada (home). *Telephone:* (514) 277-4665 (home). *E-mail:* bruno@musis.ca (home). *Website:* pages.infinit.net/musis.

**DESDERI, Claudio;** Singer (Baritone) and Conductor; b. 9 April 1943, Alessandria, Italy. *Education:* Studied at the Florence Conservatory. *Career:* Sang as first in concert; Opera debut as Guadenzio in Il Signor Bruschino at the 1969 Edinburgh Festival, with the Maggio Musicale; Has sung widely in Italy and in Munich, Salzburg, Paris, Amsterdam, Chicago, Philadelphia, and Vienna; Best known in opera by Verdi, Berlioz, Monteverdi, Nono, Rossini, Bellini, Mozart, Donizetti and Massenet; Regular appearances in the United Kingdom from 1981; Glyndebourne Festival (as Figaro and Alfonso), Promenade and Festival Hall concerts; Covent Garden debut as Mozart's Figaro, 1987; Alfonso in Così fan tutte, 1989; Conducts Chamber Orchestras in Italy; Masterclasses at Musica di Fiesole; Conducted Così fan tutte and Le nozze di Figaro at Turin, 1989, Piacenza, 1990, Royal College of Music, London, 1990; Sang Don Magnifico in La Cenerentola at Covent Garden, 1990; Glyndebourne Festival as Falstaff, Maggio Musicale Florence as Leporello; Met debut 1995, as Rossini's Bartolo; Los Angeles 1995, as Don Pasquale; Sulpice in La Fille du Régiment at Rome, 1998. *Recordings include:* Così fan tutte and Le nozze di Figaro, conducted by Haitink. *Address:* c/o Poilvé, 16 Avenue de Franklin D. Roosevelt, F–75008, Paris, France.

**DESIMONE, Robert A.;** Stage Director, Arts Administrator and Conductor; b. 1940, USA; m. Angela Carol Bonica, 21 July 1974, 1 s., 1 d. *Education:* Performance Certificate, Music Academy of the West; BM, MA, University of Southern California; Diploma International Opera Centre, Zürich, Switzerland; DMA, University of Washington, USA. *Career:* Debut: As Stage Director, Rome, Italy; Director of Opera, University of Texas, Austin; Director of Opera, College Conservatory of Music, Cincinnati; Assistant Director, School of Music, University of Washington; Executive Director, Visual Arts Center, Anchorage, Alaska; Administrative Co-ordinator, Music Center Opera Association, Los Angeles; Director: City of the Angels Opera, Los Angeles; John F Kennedy Center for the Performing Arts, Washington DC; Lincoln Center for the Performing Arts, New York; Seattle Opera Association, Seattle, Washington; Stage Director: Teatro del' Opera, Rome; Teatro Goldini, Rome; Opernhaus, Zürich, Switzerland; Resident Stage Director, Seattle Opera Association, Seattle, Washington; Guest Director, theatres in Germany, Switzerland, Italy, USA; mem, National Opera Association; Metropolitan Opera Guild; College Music Society; Central Opera Association. *Address:* 3601 72nd Avenue SE, Mercer Island, WA 98040, USA.

**DESJARDINS, Michaël (Anthony);** Pianist; b. 2 Dec. 1959, Boston, Massachusetts, USA. *Education:* National Conservatory of Nice; National Superior Conservatory of Paris; Mozarteum, Salzburg; Cleveland Institute of Music. *Career:* Debut: Piano recital at Princess Grace Theatre, Monte Carlo, 1983; Has performed in major halls and festivals in France, Germany, Italy, Switzerland, Thailand, elsewhere; Appearances as Soloist with French, Russian and Polish orchestras, such as Philharmonic Orchestras of Nice, Cannes and Czestochowa, Chamber Orchestra of Haute-Normandie, The Moscow Soloists; Television appearances: J Martin's Le Monde est à vous, on France 2, A Duault's Portée de Nuit, on France 3, on TV 5 Bangkok, and numerous programmes on Télé Monte-Carlo; Major radio broadcasts on France Musique, France Inter, Radio Nostalgie, Radio Monte-Carlo; Founder and Director of various musical festivals. *Recordings:* Voyage Musical. *Honours:* Honours Medal, City of Cannes, 1971; Grand Prix, City of Nice, 1975; Honours Medals, City of St-Jean-Cap-Ferrat, 1996, 1999; Lys d'Or Honorary Medal, 1996; Honours Medal, J Rodrigo Anniversary, 1999; Decorated by Srinakharinwirot University, Bangkok, 1999. *Current Management:* B P Com. *Address:* 37 rue Hoche, 06 400 Cannes, France.

**DESSAY, Natalie;** French singer (soprano); b. 19 April 1965, Lyon. *Education:* Bordeaux Conservatoire and Ecole de l'Art Lyrique. *Career:* began career with concert of Mozart arias at La Scala (Milan); has since sung at many leading opera houses in France, Switzerland, Austria, USA and UK. *Operas include:* Don Procopio (Paris Opéra-Comique), Ariadne auf Naxos (Montpellier), Si j'étais Roi (Liège) 1990, Le Roi l'a dit (Nantes) 1990, Schauspieldirektor (Opéra de Lyon) 1991, Die Entführung (Opéra de Lyon), Die Fledermaus (Geneva), Les Contes d'Hoffmann (Opéra Bastille) 1992, (La Scala, Milan) 1994, Ariadne, Der Rosenkavalier (Vienna Staatsoper) 1993, Die Zauberflöte (Aix-en-Provence) 1994, (Opéra de Lyon) 1996, (Salzburg Festival) 1997, Arabella (Metropolitan Opera, NY) 1994, Lakmé (Nimes) 1996, Candide (Glyndebourne Festival) 1997, Alcina (Opera Garnier) 1999, Lulu (Vienna Staatsoper) 2000, Hamlet (Toulouse) 2000, Olympia (Opéra Bastille) 2000, Ophélie (Châtelet) 2000, Queen of Night (Vienna) 2000, Constanze (Geneva Opera) 2000, Aminta (Opéra Bastille) 2000. *Honours:* winner Int. Mozart Competition, Vienna Staatsoper 1990; Premier Prix de Concours Les Voix Nouvelles Competition. *Current Management:* Agence Artistique Thérèse Cédelle, Boulevard Malesherbes 78, 75008 Paris, France. *Telephone:* 1 49 53 00 02. *Fax:* 1 45 63 70 23.

**DESSI, Daniela;** Singer (Soprano); b. 14 May 1957, Genoa, Italy. *Education:* Studied in Parma and Siena. *Career:* Sang at first in concert and made stage debut at Savona, in Pergolesi's Serva Padrona; Mozart roles have included the Countess and Fiordiligi (at La Scala and Genoa), Donna Elvira (at Florence) and Vitellia in Desdemona (to the Otello of Placido Domingo), Amelia Bocanegra (at Vienna, Venice, and Hamburg), and Elizabeth de Valois (notably with Pavarotti at La Scala, 1992); Sang Alice Ford at Boston and Amsterdam; Made debuts as the Trovatore Leonora and Violetta at Rome and Tokyo, 1993; Nedda in Pagliacci at Philadelphia and the New York Met, Mathilde (Guillaume Tell) at Pesaro and Mascagni's Iris in Rome; Zürich Opera as Aida (season 1996–97), Mimi, Donna Elvira, Desdemona and Ginerva in Giordano's La Cena della Beffe; Sang in Salieri's Danaides at Verona, 1996, Madama Butterfly in Florence and Tosca in Tokyo, 1997; Season 1998 as Dolly in Wolf Ferrari's Sly at Zürich and Tosca at the Verona Arena; Season 2000–01 as Butterfly at Verona, Lucia di Lammermoor at Geneva, Adriana Lecouvreur for La Scala, Maddalena in Andrea Chénier at Nice and Tosca for Chicago Lyric Opera. *Recordings include:* Video of Don Carlos, from La Scala. *Address:* c/o Opernhaus Zürich, Falkenstrasse 1, 8008 Zürich, Switzerland.

**DESYATNIKOV, Leonid Arkadievich;** Russian composer; b. 1955, Kharkov, Ukraine. *Education:* Leningrad State Conservatory. *Career:* mem. Composers' Union 1979–. *Works include:* opera: Poor Lisa; ballet: Love Song in Minor; tango-operetta: Astor Piazzola's Maria de Buenos Aires (Grammy Award); symphony: Sacred Winter; film scores: Sunset 1990, Lost in Siberia 1991, Capital Punishment 1992, Touch 1992, Moscow Nights 1994, Katia Izmailova 1994, Hammer and Sickle 1994, Giselle's Mania 1995, The Prisoner of the Mountains 1996, The One Who is More Tender 1996, Moscow 2000, His Wife's Diary 2000. *Honours:* Golden Sheep Prize 2000. *Address:* Nepokorennykh prosp. 16, korp. 1, apt 177, 195220 St Petersburg, Russia (home). *Telephone:* (812) 545-20-98 (home).

**DEUSSEN, Nancy (Bloomer);** Composer; b. 1 Feb. 1931, New York, NY, USA; m. (1) Charles J Webster, 1952. m. (2) John H Bloomer, 1962. m. (3) Gary R Deussen, 1982, 1 s., 2 d. *Education:* Juilliard School of Music, 1949–51; Manhattan School of Music, 1951–53; BM, Composition, University of Southern California, School of Music, 1957–59; BM Music Education; Graduate Studies in Composition, UCLA, University of Southern California, Long Beach State University, San Jose State University. *Career:* Original ballet music The Little Hill performed New York City, 1952; Reflections on the Hudson for orchestra, 1955; Missa Breve premiere, Redlands, California, 1957; Suite for clarinet and piano, 1959; Woodwind Quintet premiere, 1985; Concert of original chamber music and orchestra premiere of Three Rustic Sketches, 1989; mem, American Music Center; Mu Phi Epsilon; NACUSA; American Composers Forum, BMI. *Compositions:* Little Fugue and Harvest Suite, for recorders, 1956; Missa de Angelis, 1957; Suite for clarinet and piano, 1959; The Serpent, Cantata, 1965; Woodwind Quintet, 1983; Three Rustic Sketches, for orchestra, 1987; Prelude and Cascades for piano, 1987; Fanfare and Andante for winds, 1988; The Long Voyage, for soprano and recorders, 1988; Trio for violin, clarinet and piano, 1988; Two Pieces for violin and piano, 1990; Trio for violin, cello and piano, 1993; Peninsula suite for string orchestra, 1994; Concerto for clarinet and small orchestra, commissioned by Richard Nunemaker, clarinettist, premiered 1995 by Consortium of 5 orchestras; Musings: Circa 1940 for solo piano, 1995; Canticles for brass, 1997; Parisian Caper, 1997; Ascent to Victory, for orchestra, 1997; The Pegasus Suite for flute and piano, 1998; Tribute to the ancients for brass quintet, 1998; A Silver, Shining Strand, suite for orchestra, 2001; Celebration Octet, 2002; Et in Terra Pax (SATB/pf), 2002; Tico (Orchestra), 2004. *Recordings:* San Andreas Suite; One of Nature's Majesties; Two Pieces for violin and piano; The Pegasus Suite; Reflections on the Hudson. *Honours:* First Prize, Britten-on-the-Bay, 1996; Mu Phi Epsilon Composition Competition, 1999; Marmor Chamber Music Composition Competition, 2002. *Address:* 3065 Greer Road, Palo Alto, CA 94303, USA. *Website:* nancybloomerdeussen .com.

**DEUTEKOM, Cristina;** singer (soprano); b. 28 Aug. 1938, Amsterdam; one d. *Career:* first maj. appearance at Munich State Opera 1966, then at Vienna Festwochen; sang at Metropolitan Opera, New York 1967; has sung in all the maj. opera houses in Europe, especially Italy and USA; specializes in bel canto operas by Rossini, Bellini and Donizetti and the great Verdi operas; recordings for EMI, Decca and Philips. *Honours:* Grand Prix du Disque 1969, 1972.

**DEUTSCH, Helmut;** Pianist; b. 1945, Vienna, Austria. *Education:* Studied piano, composition and musicology in Vienna. *Career:* Chamber musician and accompanist to leading singers; Former partners include Irmgard Seefried, Rita Streich, Ileana Cotrubas, Hans Hotter and Hermann Prey; Recent recital partners include Olaf Bär, Anne Sofie von Otter, Ruth Ziesak, Peter Schreier, Bernd Weikl, Barbara Bonney, Dietrich Henschel, Juliane Banse, Angelika Kirchschlager and Bo Skovhus; Many major festival appearances; Teacher at the Vienna Music Academy, 1967–79; Munich Hochschule für Musik, 1979–; Masterclasses in Europe and Japan. *Honours:* Vienna Composition prize, 1967. *Address:* c/o IMG Artists, Lovell House, 616 Chiswick High Road, London W4 5RX, England. *E-mail:* hedeutsch@yahoo.com.

**DEVIA, Mariella;** Singer (Soprano); b. 1948, Imperia, Italy. *Education:* Studied at the Accademia di Santa Cecilia, Rome. *Career:* Debut: Spoleto 1972, as Despina in Così fan tutte; Rome Opera 1973, as Lucia di Lammermoor; Guest appearances in Italy and at Munich, Hamburg and Berlin; Has sung Donizetti's Adina in Dallas and Verdi's Oscar in Chicago; Metropolitan Opera from 1979, as Gilda, Constanze in Die Entführung, Nannetta in Falstaff; Concert performance of Lakmé in New York; Sang title role in Donizetti's Elisabetta al Castello di Kenilworth at Bergamo, 1989; Elvira in I Puritani at Rome and Madrid, 1990; Maggio Musicale Florence, 1990 as Donizetti's Parisina; Rossini roles include Adele in Le Comte Ory, Amenaide in Tancredi and Semiramide; Pesaro Festival 1995, Zelmira; Sang Lucia di Lammermoor at Florence, 1996; at Teatro alla Scala: Capuleti e Montecchi, Lodoïska (Cherubini), Lucia di Lammermoor, Die Entführung, La fille du régiment, Turco in Italia 1990–97; Covent Garden: Die Zauberflöte, 1988; Rigoletto, 1990; Season 1999–2000 at Covent Garden as Desdemona in Rossini's Otello; Season 2000–01 as Donizetti's Adelia at Carnegie Hall, Bellini's Amina and Elvira at Florence, Lucrezia Borgia in Bologna. *Recordings include:* Rossini Adelaide di Borgogna, Donizetti Elisabetta al Castello di Kenilworth, Bellini La Sonnambula and I Puritani (Fonit Cetra); L'Elisir d'amore; Lucia di Lammermoor, with Zubin Mehta. *Address:* c/o R Lombardo Inc, One Harkness Plaza, 61 West 62nd Street, Suite 6F, New York, NY 10023, USA.

**DEVICH, Janos;** Cellist and Professor; b. 3 April 1938, Szeged, Hungary; m. Sara Veslelszky, 12 Aug 1974, 3 s. *Education:* Liszt Ferenc Academy for Music, Budapest. *Career:* Concerts regularly in almost all the countries in Europe, USA (five times), Australia, Japan (seven times), China, South Korea; Festivals in Besançon, Bath, Estoril, Prague, Warsaw, Babilin, Como, Chamonix, Amiens, Devon; President, Magyar Zeneművészeti Társaság; Vice President, Magyar Muzsikus Forum. *Recordings:* Kodály, Mozart, Dohnányi, Contemporary composers string quartet; String Quartets (Debussy, Ravel, D'Indy); Piano Quintets (Brahms, Schumann, Schubert); Complete Quartets (Schubert, Haydn). *Honours:* Franz Liszt Prize, 1970; Merited Artist of Hungary, 1990; Bartók-Pasztory Prize, 1996. *Address:* Budapest, Pusztaszeri-ut 30, Hungary 1025.

**DEVINU, Giusy;** Singer (Soprano); b. 1960, Cagliari, Italy. *Education:* Studied at the Cagliari Conservatory. *Career:* Debut: Sang in 1982; Has sung Violetta at La Scala under Riccardo Muti and at other Italian centres; Further engagements in Rigoletto at Bologna, 1990, Rossini's L'Occasione fa il ladro at Pesaro, 1989, and in Don Pasquale and as the Countess in Le nozze di Figaro at the Teatro La Fenice Venice, 1990-91; Sang in the Seven Stars concert at the Baths of Caracalla, 1991; Trieste 1991 as Lucieta un Wolf-Ferrari's Il Campiolo, Rome 1992 as Marie in La Fille du Régiment; Macerata Festival 1992 as Traviata; Sang Bellini's Giulietta at Genoa, 1996; Season 1998 with Lehar's Eva at Naples and Liu in Turandot at Turin; Sang Elcia in Rossini's Mosè in Egitto at Monte Carlo, 2000. *Address:* c/o Teatro La Fenice, Campo S Fantin 1965, 30124 Venice, Italy.

**DEVLIN, Michael (Coles);** Singer (Bass-Baritone); b. 27 Nov. 1942, Chicago, Illinois, USA. *Education:* BMus, Louisiana State University, 1965; Vocal training with Treigle, Ferro, and Malas, New York. *Career:* Debut: Operatic debut as Spalanzani, Les Contes d'Hoffmann, New Orleans, 1963; First appearance with New York City Opera as the Hermit in US premiere of Ginastera's Don Rodrigo, 1966; On roster until 1978; British debut as Mozart's Almaviva, Glyndebourne Festival, 1974; Royal Opera Covent Garden, London, 1975, 1977, 1979; European debut, Holland Festival, 1977; Frankfurt Opera and Bavarian State Opera, Munich, 1977; Metropolitan Opera debut in New York as Escamillo, 1978; San Francisco Opera, 1979; Hamburg State Opera and Paris Opéra, 1980; Miami Opera and Monte Carlo Opera, 1981; Dallas Opera, 1983; Chicago Lyric Opera, 1984; Los Angeles Opera, 1986; Other roles have been Don Giovanni, Eugene Onegin, Golaud, Don Alfonso, Ford, Wotan and the villains in Les Contes d' Hoffmann; At Santa Fe has sung Altair in Strauss's Die Aegyptische Helena and the Commandant in Friedenstag; Sang Pizarro in Fidelio at Los Angeles, 1990; Jochanaan in Salome at Covent Garden, 1992; Sang Escamillo at Los Angeles, 1992 followed by Boris Godunov, 1994; Amsterdam 1995, in Schoenberg's Moses und Aron; The Doctor in Wozzeck at the Metropolitan, 1997; Season 1998 as Dikoy in Katya Kabanova at St Louis; Sang in Miss Havisham's Fire by Argento at Saint Louis, 2001; Numerous appearances as soloist with major orchestras. *Current Management:* New Century Artist Management. *Address:* c/o Opera Theatre of Saint Louis, PO Box 191910, 539 Garden Avenue, Saint Louis, MO 63119, USA.

**DEVOS, Louis;** Singer (Tenor); b. 15 June 1926, Brussels, Belgium. *Education:* Vocal studies in Graz, Austria. *Career:* Founded Ensemble Musica Polyphonica 1950, for the performance of early music; Sang in the first performance of Stravinsky's Cantata, Brussels 1952, and in the premiere of the radio opera Orestes by Henk Badings, 1954; Concerts with the Munich Philharmonic from 1956, under the direction of Pierre Boulez and Hermann Scherchen; Sang in the premieres of Martin's Mystère de la Nativité (Geneva 1959) and Pilatus (Rome 1964); Cologne 1972, in Penderecki's Utrejna; Vienna Staatsoper 1974, as Aron in Schoenberg's Moses und Aron; Guest appearances in London, Milan, Amsterdam and Brussels. *Recordings:* Vocal music by Lully; Der Tod Jesu by Graun; Zelenka's Magnificat; Les Indes Galantes by Rameau; Lutoslawski's Paroles tissées; Moses und Aron; Rousseau's Le Devin du Village. *Address:* c/o Staatsoper, Opernring 2, 1010 Vienna, Austria.

**DEVOYON, Pascal;** Pianist; b. 6 April 1953, Paris, France; m. 29 Feb 1992, 2 s. *Education:* French Baccalaureate Mathematics section; Ecole Normale de Musique Conservatoire de Paris. *Career:* Has played with major orchestras from 1975 including the Philharmonia, Leningrad Philharmonic, NHK Tokyo; Broadcasts over radio and television with Orchestre de la Suisse Romande, Orchestre National d'Espayne, Rotterdam, Stuttgart Philharmonic and RAI of Milan; Debussy Sonatas and Fauré's D Minor Trio for the London Prom concerts at the Victoria and Albert Museum; Professor at the Paris Conservatoire, 1991; Berlin Hochschule für Musik, 1995. *Recordings:* Ravel, Liszt, Tchaikovsky, Bach, Franck, Fauré, Schumann, Grieg, Saint-Saëns. *Honours:* Second Prize, Viotti, 1973; Busoni, 1973; Third Prize, Leeds, 1975; Second Prize, Tchaikovsky, 1978. *Current Management:* Charles Finch, 11a Queens Road, Wimbledon, London SW19 8NG, England. *Address:* 50 Avenue de la Paix 93270 Sevran, France.

**DEW, John;** stage director; b. 1 June 1944, Santiago de Cuba, Cuba. *Education:* Studied in Germany with Walter Felsenstein and Wieland Wagner. *Career:* Debut: The Rake's Progress, at Ulm, 1971; Directed Mozart and Wagner cycles at Krefeld in the 1970s; Head of Production at Bielefeld from 1981, with Maschinist Hopkins by Brand, Schreker's Irrelohe and Der Singende Teufel, Hindemith's Neues vom Tage, Der Sprung über den Schatten and Zwingburg by Krenek; Bakchantinnen by Wellesz, Fennimore and Gerda, Nixon in China and Boito's Nerone; Season 1987–88 at the Deutsche Oper Berlin with Les Huguenots and the premiere of Los Alamos by Neikrug; Les Huguenots seen at Covent Garden, 1991; Other productions include La Juive at Bielefeld and Nuremberg, Clemenza di Tito at Zürich, Death in Venice at Nuremberg, 1992, Aida at Hamburg, 1993; Puritani, Vienna, 1994; Andrea Chénier, Berlin; Leipzig production of Le nozze di Figaro seen at the Israel Festival, 1992; Appointed Artistic Director of the Theatres of the City of Dortmund, 1995; Directed the premiere of Schnittke's Historia von D Johann Fausten, Hamburg, 1995; Floyd's Susannah at the Deutsche Oper, Berlin, 1997; Season 1998 with Die Königin von Saba at Dortmund and Lehar's Paganini in Vienna. *Address:* c/o Theater Erfurt, Postfach 800554, 99031 Erfurt, Germany.

**DEWIS, Michael;** Singer (Baritone); b. 1970, England. *Education:* Guildhall School and National Opera Studio. *Career:* Appearances as Marcello for the Mananan Festival, Escamillo at Dartington and Renato (Un Ballo in Maschera) for Opera Holland Park; Season 1997–98 in Don Carlos and The Golden Cockerel for the Royal Opera; Other roles include Papageno, Jack Rance (La Fanciulla del West) and Don Alfonso; Concerts include Messiah at the Albert Hall, Beethoven's Ninth, Mendelssohn's Elijah, Verdi's Requiem and The Dream of Gerontius. *Honours:* Guildhall Schubert Prize. *Address:* c/o Harlequin Agency Ltd, 203 Fidlas Road, Cardiff CF4 5NA, Wales.

**DEXTER-MILLS, Christopher John,** BA, MMus, PGCE; British teacher, musicologist and organist; *Director of Music, The Netherhall School;* b. 11 Dec. 1956, Boston, England; m. Suzanne; one s. *Education:* Dartington Coll. of Arts, Durham Univ. School of Education, Goldsmiths Coll., London, Univ. of East Anglia. *Career:* assistant teacher of music, Ernulf Community School 1980–85; organist, St Mary's Parish Church, St Neots 1981–83; Head of Music, Soham Village Coll. 1986–94; conductor, Ely Choral Soc. 1992–2000; Dir of Music, The Netherhall School, Cambridge 1995–; GCE Examiner, Edexcel Foundation 1996–; mem. Royal Musical Asscn. *Address:* Music Department, The Netherhall School, Queen Edith's Way, Cambridge, CB1 8NN, England (office). *Telephone:* (1223) 242931 (office). *Fax:* (1223) 410473 (office). *E-mail:* c.dexter-mills@netherhall.cambs.sch.uk (office).

**DEYOUNG, Michelle;** American singer (mezzo-soprano); b. 1969, Colorado. *Education:* apprentice with the Santa Fe Opera and the Israel Arts Vocal Inst. *Career:* Met Opera Young Artists' Program, appearing in Carmelites, Aida and Die Zauberflöte 1993–94; concert appearances with the San Francisco Symphony in Beethoven's Ninth, Mahler's Third and Das klagende Lied, with the Boston Symphony in Mahler 2, the Houston Symphony in Schoenberg's Gurrelieder and the New York Philharmonic (David Del Tredici premiere); other repertory includes the Verdi Requiem; Ravel's Sheherazade and Wagner's Wesendonck Lieder, in London, Amsterdam and Paris; Jocasta in Oedipus Rex, in Paris 1996; sang Fricka at Seattle and Chicago 1997–98; sang Brangaene at Seattle and Fricka for the Royal Opera at the Albert Hall 1998; Mahler 3 at Los Angeles 2003. *Honours:* winner Marilyn Horne Foundation Wings of Song, Marian Anderson Award. *Current Management:* Askonas Holt Ltd, Lonsdale Chambers, 27 Chancery Lane, London, WC2A 1PF, England. *Telephone:* (20) 7400-1700. *Fax:* (20) 7400-1799. *E-mail:* info@askonasholt.co .uk. *Website:* www.askonasholt.co.uk.

**DI BELLA, Benito;** Singer (Baritone); b. 1942, Palermo, Sicily, Italy. *Education:* Studied at the Palermo Conservatory and in Pesaro. *Career:* Sang at Spoleto and elsewhere in Italy before La Scala Milan debut, 1971, as Marcello in La Bohème; Sang further in Naples, Genoa, Venice and Palermo; Amonasro at the 1989 Verona Arena, Jack Rance at the 1985 Macerata festival; Further appearances throughout North and South America as Verdi's Luna, Germont, Pietro (Simon Boccanegra) and Rigoletto, Gerard in Andrea Chenier, the Herald in Lohengrin and Escamillo; Taormina Festival, 1990. *Address:* c/o Arena di Verona, Pizza Bra 28, 3 Verona, Italy.

**DI BONAVENTURA, Anthony;** Pianist; b. 12 Nov. 1930, Follensbee, West Virginia, USA. *Education:* Studied at the Curtis Institute with Vengerova. *Career:* Debut: With the NY Philharmonic in 1943, playing Beethoven's C minor Concerto; Beethoven cycle under Otto Klemperer with the London Philharmonic, 1959; Has performed widely in the US with major orchestras in the standard repertory and in works by contemporary composers; Vincent Persichetti, Luciano Berio (Points on a Curve to Find), Alberto Ginastera and Milko Kelemen have written works for him; Teacher at the School of Music, Boston University, from 1973. *Recordings:* Works by Scarlatti, Chopin, Debussy and Prokofiev, Eighth Sonata.

**DI CESARE, Ezio;** Singer (Tenor); b. 1939, Rome, Italy. *Education:* Studied in Rome. *Career:* Sang with a vocal sextet and made tours of Italy; Stage debut, 1975, in Bellini's Beatrice di Tenda; Many appearances in Italy and elsewhere in Europe as Alfredo, Rodolfo, and Tom Rakewell in The Rake's Progress; La Scala Milan, 1980, 1984, in Vivaldi's Tito Manlio and Idomeneo; Arvino, in Verdi's I Lombardi; Appearances in Netherlands and at the Verona Arena; Sang at Rome, 1986, in Spontini's Agnese di Hohenstaufen; Teatro Liceo, Barcelona, 1987, in the Spanish premiere of Mozart's Lucio Silla; Pesaro Festival, 1988, as Iago in Rossini's Otello; Sang Carlo in Pergolesi's Lo Frate Innamorato at La Scala 1989; Gabriele Adorno at Cremona; Rome Opera, 1990, in Franco Mannino's Il Principe Felice; Season 1992 as Iarba in Jommelli's Didone Abbandonata at the Teatro Rossini, Lugo; Season 1994 as Ismaele in Nabucco at Verona; La Scala 1995, as Raffaela in Verdi's Stiffelio; Jesi 1998, as Sostrate in Pergolesi's II Prigionero Superbo; Sang the High Priest in Idomeneo at Florence, 1996; Season 2000-01 as Offenbach's Orphée at Turin and the Prince in Lulu at Palermo. *Recordings:* Verdi's Stiffelio; La Finta Giardiniera; Alfano's Cyrano de Bergerac. *Address:* c/o Arena di Verona, Piazza Bra 28, 37121, Verona, Italy.

**DI DOMENICA, Robert Anthony,** BS; flautist, teacher and composer; b. 4 March 1927, New York, NY, USA. *Education:* New York University. *Career:* New York City Opera Orchestra; Freelance Flautist, New York Philharmonic Orchestra; Various engagements as solo artist; Faculty Member, 1969–, Associate Dean, 1973–76, Dean, 1976–78, New England Conservatory of Music, Boston. *Compositions include:* Operas: The Balcony, 1972, The Scarlet Letter, 1986; Beatrice Cenci, 1993; The Cenci, 1995; Francesco Cenci, 1996; Orchestral: Symphony, 1961, Concerto for violin and chamber orchestra, 1962, Concerto for wind quintet, strings and timpani, 1964, Music for flute and string orchestra, 1967, Variations on a Theme by Gunther Schuller for 13 instruments, 1983, Dream Journeys, 1984; Variations Soliloquies, 1988; Gone are the Rivers and Eagles, 1992; Chamber: Sonata for flute and piano, 1957, Sextet for woodwind quintet and piano, 1957, Quartet for flute, violin, viola and cello, 1960, Quintet for clarinet and string quartet, 1965, Sonata for violin and piano, 1966, Saeculum aureum for flute, piano and tape, 1967, Sonata for saxophone and piano, 1968; Piano Pieces, Vocal: Wind Quintet for soprano and woodwind quintet, 1963, Songs from Twelfth Night for tenor, flute, viola da gamba and harpsichord, 1976, Hebrew Melodies for soprano, violin and piano, 1983. *Recordings:* Leona Di Domenica in live first performance of the Solo Piano Music of Robert Di Domenica; Three Orchestral Works by Robert Di Domenica conducted by Gunther Schuller and the Radio Philharmonic of Hannover. *Publications:* Dream Journeys for Orchestra, 1984. *Honours:* Guggenheim Fellowship, 1972; Opera The Balcony premiered by the Opera Company of Boston, 1990 and Moscow's Bolshoi Theater, 1991.

**DI FRANCO, Loretta;** Singer (Soprano); b. 28 Oct. 1942, New York, NY, USA. *Education:* Studied with Maud Webber and Walter Taussig in New York. *Career:* Sang in the chorus of the Metropolitan Opera until 1965; Solo appearances in New York in The Queen of Spades, Don Giovanni (Zerlina), Un Ballo in Maschera (Oscar), Gianni Schicchi (Lauretta), Le nozze di Figaro (Marcellina) and Lucia di Lammermoor (title role); Returned to Met 1990, as Marthe in Faust. *Address:* c/o Metropolitan Opera, Lincoln Center, New York, NY 10023, USA.

**DI GIUSEPPE, Enrico;** Singer (Tenor); b. 14 Oct. 1932, Philadelphia, PA, USA. *Education:* Studied with Richard Bonelli at Curtis Institute of Music, Philadelphia, with Hans Heinz at Juilliard School of Music, NY. *Career:* Debut: Operatic debut as Massenet's Des Grieux, New Orleans, 1959; Toured with Metropolitan Opera National Company; NY City Opera debut as Michele in The Saint of Bleecker Street, 1965; On roster, 1967–81; Metropolitan Opera debut in NY as Turiddu, 1970; Sang at the Met until 1985 as Pinkerton, Rossini's Almaviva and Lindoro, Mozart's Ferrando, Alfredo, the Duke of Mantua and Rodolfo; Guest appearances with opera companies in Baltimore, Boston, Cincinnati, Dallas, Houston, Ottawa, Philadelphia, Pittsburgh, San Francisco, Toronto and other cities; Various engagements as concert artist. *Recordings:* Several recordings. *Address:* c/o Metropolitan Opera, Lincoln Center, New York, NY 10023, USA.

**DI LOTTI, Silvana;** Composer; b. 29 Nov. 1942, Aglie Canavese, Turin, Italy. *Education:* Studied in Turin and Salzburg, with courses at Siena notably with Berio and Boulez. *Career:* Teacher at the Turin Conservatory; Performances of her music in Italy and elsewhere. *Compositions include:* Aragorn for clavicembalo and 5 strings; Contrasti for 2 clarinets, 1981; Capriccio for violin and piano, 1981; Duo In Eco for violin and guitar, 1982; Conversari for orchestra, 1982; Serenata for chamber orchestra, 1982; Groups for piano. 1983; In Nomine Domini for orchestra, 1983; Intonazione for saxophone and piano, 1983; Rapsodia for 2 chitarre, 1984; Surfaces for organ, 1985; Aura for piano, 1985; Piano Trio, 1986; C'est Pour Toi Seule for coro misto, 1987; Mattutino for harp, 1990; A Solo for clarinet and ensemble, 1991; Arabesque for cello, 1991; E Nessun Tempo Ha Memoria Di Echi Svelati for bass clarinet and harp, 1992; Musica per Giocare for piano, 1994; Terre Rare for orchestra, 1995. *Recordings:* Haide for violin, cello and piano. *Address:* c/o Viale Ovidio 5, 10090 Gassino, Fr Bardassano, (TO) Italy.

**DI PIANDUNI, Oslavio;** Singer (Tenor); b. 1939, Montevideo, Uruguay. *Education:* Studied in Montevideo. *Career:* Appeared at Montevideo 1961–65 as Rinuccio in Gianni Schicchi and Lionel in Martha; Klagenfurt 1968–70 and Alfredo, Riccardo, Hoffmann, Don José, Pinkerton and Calaf at Bielefeld, 1970–75; Further engagements at the Theater am Gärtnerplatz, Munich, 1975–76, Vienna Volksoper, 1976–78 and Kiel 1979–82; Bremen 1982–84, Zürich 1988 as Edmund in Reimann's Lear; Hanover 1989, as Andrea Chénier; Other roles include Luigi in Il Tabarro, Hermann in The Queen of Spades and Otello, Oslo, 1999; Has also sung in operettas by Lehar, Johann Strauss and Offenbach; Many concert appearances and Lieder recitals. *Address:* c/o Niedersachische Staatstheater, Opernplatz 1, 3000 Hannover, Germany.

**DI PIETRO, Rocco;** Composer; b. 15 Sept. 1949, Buffalo, New York, USA; m. Juli Douglass, 28 May 1973, 1 s. *Education:* BPS, State University of New York, 1985; Studied with Hans Hagen, Lukas Foss and Bruno Maderna. *Career:* Lecturer on Modern Music; Performances of his compositions have been played in major cities of Europe and USA by such Musicians and Ensembles as Christiane Edinger, Christobal Halffter, Lukas Foss, Bruno Maderna, Bavarian Radio Orchestra, Brooklyn Philharmonic, St Paul Chamber Orchestra. *Compositions:* Overture to Combats for History, for percussion orchestra, 1980–81; Melodia Arcana for percussion and tarot cards, 1980–83; Aria Grande for violin and orchestra, 1980; Tratto Bizzaro, opera, 1984; Beauty and the Beast, incidental music for theatre, 1986; Annales after Tasso for madrigal voices and percussion, 1987. *Publications:* Melodia Nera for Timpani, AM Percussion Publications, 1985. *Current Management:* Sheldon Soffer, New York. *Address:* c/o American Percussion Publications, PO Box 436, Lancaster, NY 14086, USA.

**DI VIRGILIO, Nicholas;** Singer (Tenor); b. 1937, New York, USA. *Education:* Studied at the Eastman School and in New York. *Career:* Debut: Sang Pinkerton with Chautauqua Opera, 1961; Sang at Baltimore from 1956, San Francisco, 1966–67, Cincinnati, New Orleans, 1969–70, San Diego, Pittsburgh and the New York City Opera, 1964–71; Metropolitan Opera from 1970, as Pinkerton and as Edgardo in Lucia di Lammermoor; European engagements at Brussels, Amsterdam and Lyon, 1968–70; London, 1978, in the Verdi Requiem; Other roles have included Mozart's Idomeneo, Don Ottavio and Ferrando, Verdi's Alfredo, Fenton and Riccardo, Faust, Rodolfo, Hoffmann, Don José, Laca in Jenůfa and Cavaradossi. Voice Teacher at the University of Illinois.

**DIADKOVA, Larissa;** Singer (Mezzo-soprano); b. 1954, Zelenodolsk, Russia. *Education:* Studied at the St Petersburg Conservatory. *Career:* Sang with the Kirov Opera, St Petersburg, and elsewhere in Russia as Ratmir in Ruslan and Lyudmilla, Konchakovna in Prince Igor, Tchaikovsky's Olga and Pauline and the Duenna in Prokofiev's Betrothal in a Monastery; Guest appearances at the Bregenz and Edinburgh Festivals; Florence, 1995 as Verdi's Ulrica, Bolshoi and Metropolitan, 1996 as Marfa in Khovanshchina and Madelon in Andrea Chénier; Lyon and Savonlinna Festival, 1996 as the Countess in The Queen of Spades and Liubov in Mazeppa; Season 1998 as Ulrica at Monte Carlo, in Tchaikovsky's Mazeppa at the New York Met and Marfa with the Kirov Opera at La Scala; Season 2000–01 as Ulrica at the Vienna Staatsoper, Mistress Quickly at Salzburg, Azucena at Verona and Amneris for San Francisco Opera; Jezibaba in Rusalka at Covent Garden (concert) 2003. *Recordings:* Rimsky's Sadko; Mazeppa by Tchaikovsky. *Address:* Kirov Opera, 1 Theatre Square, St Petersburg, Russia.

**DIANDA, Hilda;** Composer; b. 13 April 1925, Cordoba, Argentina. *Education:* Studied with Malipiero and Scherchen; Further study at Milan Electronic Music Studios and in Darmstadt. *Career:* Teacher at Cordoba until 1971; Performances of her music in Europe and North America; Educator and Lecturer. *Compositions include:* Requiem, 1984; Cantico, after St Francis of Assisi, 1985; Trio for clarinet, cello and piano, 1985; Encantanientos for tape, 1985; Viola Concerto, 1988; Paisaje for 4 percussion, 1992; Mitos for percussion and strings, 1993; Pitiales for marimba, 1994. *Honours:* Cultural Merit Medal, Italy. *Address:* c/o SADAIC, Lavalle 1547, Apartado Postal Number 11, Sucursal 44-B, 1048 Buenos Aires, Argentina.

**DIAZ, Justino;** singer (bass-baritone); b. 29 Jan. 1939, San Juan, Puerto Rico. *Education:* University of Puerto Rico, New England Conservatory and studied with Ralph Errolle and Frederick Jagel. *Career:* debut in Puerto Rico, 1957, in Menotti's The Telephone; Metropolitan Opera from 1963, as Monterone and Sparafucile in Rigoletto, Figaro, Rossini's Maometto II and

Colline; Festival Casals, Puerto Rico, 1964–65; Spoleto Festival, 1965; Salzburg Festival, 1966, as Escamillo; Created Antony in Barber's Antony and Cleopatra, New York Met, 1966; La Scala, Milan, 1969, in Rossini's L'Assedio do Corinto; New York City Opera, 1973, in Ginastera's Beatrix Cenci; Covent Garden, 1976, as Escamillo; Guest appearance in Hamburg, Vienna, Mexico City, Chicago and San Francisco; San Francisco and Milan, 1982, as Scarpia and Asdrubalo in La Pietra del Paragone; Sang Attila at Cincinnati, 1984, Iago at Covent Garden, 1990; Michele in Il Tabarro at Miami, 1989, Iago and Scarpia at Los Angeles; Sang Escamillo at Rio de Janeiro, 1990; Debut as Amonasro at Cincinnati, 1990; Sang Iago in Zeffirelli's film version of Otello, 1987; Greater Miami Opera, 1992 as Franchetti's Cristoforo Colombo; Sang Puccini's Jack Rance at Covent Garden, 1994, Scarpia in 1995 (and for Opera Pacific, 1998); Sang Iago for Washington Opera, 2000. *Recordings:* Medea and La Wally; Thais by Massenet; L'Assedio di Corinto and Otello; Semele; Videos of Zeffirelli's Otello, and Meyerbeer's L'Africaine, from San Francisco Opera.

**DIBAK, Igor,** MA, PhD; Slovak composer; *Reader Expert, Academy of Arts, Banská Bystrica;* b. 5 July 1947, Spisska Nova Ves; m. Katarina Ormisova 1970. *Education:* piano study, Conservatorie Zilina 1962–66; with Prof. Jan Cikker, Dept of Composition, Univ. of Arts, Bratislava 1966–71; Magister. *Career:* ed., Music Dept, Czech TV, Bratislava 1969–79; Ed.-in-Chief, Music Dept, Czech Radio, Bratislava 1979–87, Music Dept Czech TV 1987–90; Dir Music School 1990–96; Ed., Music Dept, Slovak TV 1996–98; Reader Expert, Acad. of Arts, Banská Bystrica 1998–; mem. Slovak Music Union, Bratislava, Slovak Protective Union of Authors, Bratislava. *Compositions:* Opera Candlestick, New Year's Eve Part, Ballet Portrait, symphonic works including Accordion Concerto 1996; chamber compositions and compositions for children. *Recordings:* Moments musicaux 1, Fantasy for Viola and Orchestra, Divertimento for Strings, Opera Candlestick, New Year's Eve Part, Ballet Portrait, Czech television; Symphonic and Chamber works, Czech Radio Bratislava. *Publications:* Methodics of Piano Improvisation 1981. *Contributions:* Hudobny zivot (Music Live). *Honours:* Jan Levoslav Bella Award 1979, Union of Slovak Music Composers Award 1987. *Current Management:* Music Fond, Medená 29, 811 02 Bratislava, Slovakia. *Address:* Bajzova 10, 821 08 Bratislava, Slovakia. *Telephone:* (2) 555-72-894 (home).

**DIBBLE, Jeremy Colin,** BA, PhD; British; *Professor of Music, University College Cork;* b. 17 Sept. 1958, Epping, Essex, England; m. Alison Jane Manning 1984. *Education:* Trinity College, Cambridge, Univ. of Southampton. *Career:* Lecturer in Music, Univ. College, Cork, Ireland, 1987–93, Lecturer in Music, 1993–98, Reader in Music, 1998–2003, Prof. of Music, 2003–; mem. Society of Fellows, Knott/Christopherson Fellowship, from October 2004; Univ. of Durham; Administrator and Secretary to Turnbull Memorial Trust; mem. Oxford and Cambridge Club. *Recordings:* Consultant, Editor and Sleeve-note Writer for many recordings of works by Parry, Stanford and others. *Publications:* C. Hubert H. Parry: His Life and Music 1992, Nineteenth-Century British Music Studies (with Zon) 2002, Charles Villiers Stanford: Man and Musician 2002, Parry Sonatas for violin and piano, Musica Britannica Trust, Vol. LXXX 2003; contrib. Essays on Vaughan Williams in Perspective; Irish Musical Studies II: Studies in Church Music; King Arthur and Music; Music and British Culture 1785–1914; Constructions of Nationalism; Nineteenth Century British Music Studies Vols I and II; Articles in Journal of the British Institute of Organ Studies; Brio; Journal of the Ralph Vaughan Williams Society; New Grove 2, New Dictionary of National Biography; Thoemmes Dictionary of Nineteenth Century British Philosophers; Musik in Geschichte und Gegenwart; Dictionary of Irish Biography; New Oxford Companion to Music; Grolier's Encyclopaedia of the Victorian Era; Musical Editor to Dictionary of Hymnology; Reviews in Music and Letters, Notes and journal of Victorian Studies. *Address:* 69 Beechfield Rise, Coxhoe, Durham DH6 4SD, England. *E-mail:* jeremy.dibble@durham.ac.uk.

**DICHTER, Misha,** BS; American concert pianist; b. 27 Sept. 1945, Shanghai, China; s. of Leon Dichter and Lucy Dichter; m. Cipa Dichter 1968; two s. *Education:* Juilliard School of Music under Rosina Lhevinne. *Career:* winner, Silver Medal, Tchaikovsky Int. Competition, Moscow 1966; since then has performed with leading orchestras and at festivals and given recitals worldwide; also performs with wife as piano duo. *Publications:* articles in New York Times, Ovation and Keyboard magazines. *Honours:* Grand Prix du Disque Liszt 1999. *Address:* c/o Connie Shuman, CAMI, Mushalla Division, 165 West 57th Street, New York, NY 10019, USA (office).

**DICK, James Cordell,** BMus; concert pianist; b. 29 June 1940, Hutchinson, Kansas, USA. *Education:* University of Texas at Austin, Royal Academy of Music, London; studied with Dalies Frantz, Clifford Curzon. *Career:* debut, Carnegie Hall, New York City, USA; performs professionally throughout the USA and abroad in orchestral, chamber and solo repertoire; performed with conductors Kondrashin, Barbirolli, Ormandy, Maazel, Levine, Comissiona, Lombard, Schwarz, Fleisher, de Priest, Fiedler, Foster, Robert Spano and Christopher Hogwood among others; has performed on radio in England, Germany, France, Netherlands, Switzerland, Mexico and US Commissions new music for piano and orchestra; founder and Artistic Director of International Festival-Institute at Round Top, Texas. *Compositions:* Etudes for piano and orchestra, by Ben Lees, gave world premiere, 1975; Shiva's Drum, by Dan Welcher, gave world premiere in 1994; Krishna, from Malcolm Hawkins (England), world premiere in 1996; Rising Light by Chinary Ung. *Recordings:* Beethoven's Concerto No. 4; Tchaikovsky Concerto No. 1; Chopin Concerto No. 1; Prokofiev Concerto No. 3; Saint-Saëns Concerto No. 2; Rachmaninov Rhapsody. *Honours:* Prize, Tchaikovsky Competition, Russia, 1965; Prize, Leventritt Competition, New York City, 1965; Prize, Busoni Competition, Italy, 1965; Chevalier des Arts et des Lettres, 1996; Texas State Musician, 2003. *Current Management:* Alain Declert & Associates, PO Box 89, Round Top, TX 78954, USA. *Address:* Festival Hill, Round Top TX 78954-0089, USA.

**DICKERSON, Roger Donald,** BA, MM; American composer, musician (piano and double bass) and academic; b. 24 Aug. 1934, New Orleans, LA. *Education:* Dillard Univ., New Orleans, Ind. Univ. at Bloomington, Akademie für Musik und Darstellende Kunst, Vienna, Austria. *Career:* grew up playing jazz and blues in New Orleans; toured with Joe Turner and Guitar Slim 1951–54; mil. service in US Army, based in Ark. and Heidelberg, Germany 1957–59; played double bass with Fort Smith Symphony Orchestra 1957; composer, arranger for US Army in Europe Headquarters Co. Band, Heidelberg 1957–59; performed extensively in French Quarter of New Orleans 1962–; composed for New Orleans Symphony and others 1962–; Program Assoc. and Consultant in Humanities, Inst. for Services to Educ., Washington, DC 1979; private teacher of composition and piano 1962–; Adjunct Prof., Xavier Univ. of La, New Orleans 1979–82; Adjunct Prof., Southern Univ., New Orleans 1979–85; Assoc. Prof. and Co-ordinator of Music, Div. of Fine Arts 1985–; Lecturer in Music, Dillard Univ., New Orleans 1986–; co-f., Creative Arts Alliance of New Orleans (CAANO) 1975; Mayor's Task Force on Arts Policy for the City of New Orleans 1978; Mayor's Advisory Bd Arts and Cultural Affairs for the City of New Orleans 1979; La State Div. of the Arts Grant Cttee 1981; panellist La State Arts Council 1981–, Nat. Endowment for the Arts 1984–; mem. ASCAP. *Compositions include:* Prekussion for percussion 1954, Variations for woodwind trio 1955, Fair Dillard for chorus 1955, Sonatina for piano 1956, Chorale Prelude (Das neugeborne Kindelein) for organ 1956, String Quartet 1956, Music I Heard (vocal) 1956, Music for string trio 1957, Concert Overture for orchestra 1957, Essay for band 1958, Fugue 'n Blues for jazz ensemble 1959, Movement for trumpet and piano 1960, The Negro Speaks of Rivers (vocal) 1961, Quintet for wind instruments 1961, Ten Concert Pieces for beginning string players 1973, A Musical Service for Louis (A Requiem for Louis Armstrong) 1973, Orpheus an' His Slide Trombone for orchestra 1974–75, New Orleans Concerto 1976, Psalm 49 for chorus 1979, African-American Celebration for chorus 1984. *Honours:* Dr hc (Inst. for Minority Nationalities, People's Repub. of China) 1990; Dave Frank Award 1955, American Music Center Award 1972, 1975, New Orleans Bicentennial Comm. Certificate 1977, Citation of Achievement and Key to the City of New Orleans 1977, New Orleans Recreation Dept Louis Armstrong Cultural Devt Fund Memorial Award 1977, Masons Enterprises of New Orleans Outstanding Musicianship Award 1977, City Council of New Orleans Special Commendation 1978, Univ. New Orleans Marcus-Christian Award 1979. *Address:* c/o ASCAP, ASCAP Building, One Lincoln Plaza, New York, NY 10023, USA (office).

**DICKIE, Brian James;** British opera director; *General Director, Chicago Opera Theater;* b. 23 July 1941, s. of the late Robert Kelso and of Harriet Elizabeth (née Riddell) Dickie; m. 1st Victoria Teresa Sheldon (née Price) 1968; two s. one d.; m. 2nd Nancy Gustafson 1989. *Education:* Trinity Coll., Dublin. *Career:* Admin. Asst Glyndebourne Opera 1962–66; Admin. Glyndebourne Touring Opera 1967–81; Opera Man. Glyndebourne Festival Opera 1970–81, Gen. Admin. 1981–89; Artistic Dir Wexford Festival 1967–73; Artistic Adviser Théâtre Musical de Paris 1981–87; Gen. Dir Canadian Opera Co. 1989–93; Artistic Counsellor Opéra de Nice 1994–97; Gen. Dir EU Opera 1997–99, Chicago Opera Theater 1999–; Chair. London Choral Soc. 1978–85, Theatres Nat. Cttee Opera Cttee 1976–85; Vice-Chair. Theatres Nat. Cttee 1980–85; Vice-Pres. Theatrical Man. Asscn 1983–85; mem. Bd Opera America 1991–93. *Address:* Chicago Opera Theater, 70 East Lake Street, Suite 540, Chicago, IL 60601 (office); 405 Edgemere Way North, Naples, FL 33999 (home); 2000 N Lincoln Park West, Apt 412, Chicago, IL 60614, USA. *Telephone:* (312) 7048420 (office); (773) 3276471. *Fax:* (312) 7048421 (office).

**DICKIE, John;** Singer (Tenor); b. 5 Sept. 1953, London, England. *Education:* Studied at the University of Music, Vienna and the Vienna Academy. *Career:* Engaged in Wuppertal, 1979–82, Mannheim, 1982–85; Hamburg Staatsoper from 1985–87; Bregenz Festival, 1981–86, in L'Incontro Improvviso, Lucia di Lammermoor, Der Vogelhändler and Die Zauberflöte; Member of the Wiener Staats and Volksoper since 1987; Guest appearances at Covent Garden, Deutsche Oper Berlin, Staatsoper Berlin, Geneva, Düsseldorf among others; Other roles include Mozart's Belmonte, Don Ottavio, Ferrando, Tito and Belfiore, Lionel in Martha, Nemorino in L'Elisir d'amore, Berlioz's Benedict, Lensky in Eugene Onegin and Wagner's Steuermann and Froh; Sang Don Fabrizio in the world premiere of Schnittke's Gesualdo, Vienna, 1995; Title role in Leopold I's Il figliol prodigo, Vienna, 1997; Season 2000–01 at the Vienna Staatsoper in Die Jakobsleiter by Schoenberg, as Monostatos and as Red Whiskers in Billy Budd; Also heard as concert singer. *Recordings:* Mozart Tenor Arias; Così fan tutte (complete);. Fledermaus, Eisenstein (complete); Apollo und Hyazinth, Mozart (complete); Television production of Gluck's Orpheus et Euridice (Paris version); Album of own songs, Timeslip, 1987. *Address:* c/o Vienna Staatsoper, Opernring 2, A1010 Vienna, Austria.

**DICKINSON, Meriel,** GRSM, ARMCM; British singer (mezzo-soprano); b. 8 April 1940, Lytham St Anne's, England; m. Robert J.H. Gardner 1991. *Education:* Vienna Academy, Austria. *Career:* debut, London 1964; frequent radio broadcasts, two BBC television documentary films; recital programmes with her brother, composer Peter Dickinson throughout Europe; mem, Park

Lane Group, Incorporated Society of Musicians. *Recordings:* Contemporary British Composers (Crosse, Berkeley, Dickinson); Erik Satie Songs and Piano Music; Brecht-Weill series with London Sinfonietta; Singing teacher and Adjudicator. *Honours:* Countess of Munster Musical Trust Scholarship 1964–66. *Address:* The Old Bakery, Grendon Underwood, Aylesbury HP18 0SW, England.

**DICKINSON, Peter,** MA, DMus, LRAM, ARCM, ARCO, FRCO; British composer, pianist and writer; b. 15 Nov. 1934, Lytham, Lancashire, England; m. Bridget Jane Tomkinson; two s. *Education:* Queens' Coll., Cambridge and Juilliard School of Music, New York, USA. *Career:* various teaching posts in New York, London and Birmingham; First Prof. of Music, Keele Univ. 1974–84, Prof. Emeritus 1984–; Prof., Goldsmiths' Coll., London 1991–97, Emeritus Prof. 1997–; Head of Music, Inst. of United States Studies, Univ. of London 1997–2004; performances, broadcasts and recordings as pianist, mostly with sister, mezzo-soprano Meriel Dickinson. *Compositions include:* Transformations for orchestra 1970, Organ Concerto 1971, Piano Concerto 1984, Merseyside Echoes for orchestra 1985, Violin Concerto 1986, chamber music, choral works, songs, keyboard music, church music. *Recordings include:* Piano Concerto, Outcry, Organ Concerto, Song Cycles (Auden, Dylan Thomas, Cummings, Heath-Stubbs, Lord Berners, Philip Larkin), Rags, Blues and Parodies (Burns, Corso, Lord Byron, Stevie Smith, Satie), American Trio, organ and piano works. *Publications:* 20 British Composers (ed.) 1975, The Complete Songs and The Complete Piano Music of Lord Berners (ed., two vols) 1982, Collected Works for Solo Piano of Lennox Berkeley (ed., aka The Music of Lennox Berkeley) 1989, Marigold: The Music of Billy Mayerl 1999, Copland Connotations: Studies and Interviews 2002, Cage Talk: Historic Interviews With and About John Cage 2005; contrib. to various books and journals, incl. book chapters and dictionaries. *Honours:* Hon. DMus (Keele Univ.) 1999. *Address:* c/o Novello & Company, 8–9 Frith Street, London, W1V 5TZ, England.

**DICKMAN, Stephen Allen,** BA, MFA; Composer; b. 2 March 1943, Chicago, Illinois, USA. *Education:* Studied composition with Jacob Druckman at Bard College, and theory and composition with Arthur Berger and Harold Shapero at Brandeis University; Further study with Ernst Krenek at Berkshire Music Center, Tanglewood, and with Golfredo Petrassi in Rome. *Career:* Has travelled widely in order to study the music of Asia and the Middle East. *Compositions include:* Musical Journeys, Song Cycle for three violins and three sopranos, Trees and Other Inclinations for piano 1983, Orchestra by the Sea 1983, The Wheels of Ezekiel for chamber orchestra 1985, Maximus Song Cycle 1986, Tibetan Dreams (opera, with librettist Gary Glickman; Artist as Producer of New American Works Award, Nat. Endowment for the Arts)) 1987, Rabbi Nathan's Prayer, soprano and violin, 1995; The Violin Maker, musical in progress; Theatre Pieces King Arthur, 1996, and Cyrano, 1997; Duets, for 2 singers a capella, 1992–98; Four for Tom, piano and baritone, 1997; The Music of Eric Zann, baritone solo, on a story by H P Lovecraft, 1998, Gilgamesh (chamber opera) 2002, setting of The Yellow Wallpaper by Charlotte Perkins Gillman for soprano, piano and cello 2003. *Recordings:* The Music of Eric Zann; Who Says Works; Four For Tom; Indian Wells; If There Were No Birds and Rabbi Nathan's Prayer, Trees and Other Inclinations and The Wheels of Ezekiel; The Song of the Reed, My Love Makes Me Lonely, Love, the Hierophant. *Honours:* Fulbright Fellowship, Rome 1971–72, CAP Award, 1987, 1990; Meet the Composer, 1995; SOS Grant, East End Arts Council and New York Foundation for the Arts, 1995, 1998, 1999; Meet the Composer Fund Award, 1990, 1995, 1996; Timeline Suffolk Decentralization Grant, 1998; American Composers Forum Commission, 1998. *Address:* 73 Squaw Road, East Hampton, NY 11937, USA.

**DICKSON, Grant;** Singer (Bass); b. 1940, New Zealand. *Career:* Debut: New Zealand Opera, 1962; Appearances with Australian Opera as Mozart's Sarastro and Bartolo; Don Basilio, Don Pasquale and Baron Ochs; Rocco, Mephistopheles and Trulove for New Zealand Opera; European engagements from 1991, including the Commendatore in Dresden, Pluto in Telemann's Orpheus at Berlin and Boris Godunov for Welsh National Opera; Season 1998–99 with Schigolch in Lulu for De Vlaamse Opera and King Mark in Tristan for WNO; Season 1999–2000 in The Greek Passion and La Bohème at Covent Garden; Concerts include the Verdi Requiem at the Albert Hall. *Address:* c/o Harlequin Agency Ltd, 203 Fidles Road, Cardiff CF4 5NA, Wales.

**DICKSON, Joan;** Cellist and Teacher; b. 21 Dec. 1921, Edinburgh, Scotland. *Education:* LRAM; ARCM; Studied in Paris and Rome. *Career:* Solo Cellist with major British Orchestras; Appearances at the London Promenade Concerts, Cheltenham Festival, Edinburgh Festival; Tours abroad; Regular Broadcaster; Television appearances; Professor of Cello, Royal College of Music, London; Teacher of Cello, Royal Scottish Academy of Music, Glasgow; Short Talks, BBC radio. *Recordings:* Iain Hamilton Cello Sonata; Cesar Franck Sonata. *Contributions:* Incorporated Society of Musicians Magazine. *Honours:* Fellow, Royal College of Music; Fellow, Royal Scottish Academy Music and Drama; Cobbett Gold Medal for services to Chamber Music.

**DICTEROW, Glenn;** American violinist; *Concertmaster, New York Philharmonic Orchestra*; b. Los Angeles, CA; m. Karen Dreyfus. *Education:* Juilliard School. *Career:* solo debut aged 11 with Los Angeles Philharmonic; Assoc. Concertmaster, then Concertmaster, Los Angeles Philharmonic 1971–79; Concertmaster and solo violin, New York Philharmonic 1980–; Lecturer, Manhattan School of Music 1982–, Juilliard School 1985–; co-f., Lyric Piano Quartet 1986; guest performances as soloist with symphony orchestras,

including Los Angeles, Baltimore, Birmingham, Chautauqua, Grant Park, Indianapolis, Kansas City, Mexico City, Miami, Montréal, Omaha, Tampa, Monterey, and with Leipzig Gewandhaus Orchestra, Hong Kong Philharmonic; has played with conductors including Bernstein, Maazel, Kostelanetz, Mehta, Slatkin, Davis. *Recordings include:* Copland: Violin Sonata, Largo and Piano Trio, Richard Strauss: Also Sprach Zarathustra, Op. 30/Four Last Songs 1990, Rimsky-Korsakov: Scheherazade 1993, Korngold: Chamber Works 1995, Ives: Chamber Works 1996, Goetz: Chamber Music 1999, New York Legends 1999, Holdridge Conducts Holdridge 2001, Shostakovich: Violin Concerto No. 1, Bernstein: Sonata for Violin and Piano. *Honours:* bronze medal Int. Tchaikovsky Competition 1970. *Address:* New York Philharmonic, Avery Fisher Hall, 10 Lincoln Center Plaza, New York, NY 10023-6990, USA (office). *Website:* www.newyorkphilharmonic.org (office).

**DIDONATO, Joyce;** American singer (mezzo-soprano); b. 1970, Prairie Village, KS. *Education:* Acad. of Vocal Arts, Philadelphia and the Houston Opera Studio. *Career:* sang Ino in Handel's Semele at Spoleto, Italy 1996; Houston Grand Opera 1996–97 as Siebel in Faust, Fyodor in Boris Gudonov and Grace Kelly in the premiere of Jackie O; season 1998–99 as Nicklausse in Les Contes d'Hoffmann and Cherubino at Houston; premiere of Tod Machover's Resurrection, after Tolstoy; Rosina for Kentucky Opera; Cherubino at Santa Fe and Dorabella at Houston 2001; Rossini's Isabella and Angelina for New Israeli Opera; Rosina at the Paris Opéra 2002; Covent Garden debut at the Fox in The Cunning Little Vixen 2003; Idamante in Idomeneo at Netherlands Opera 2004; title role in La Cenerentola in Kansas City 2004, and at La Scala 2005; Dejanira in Hercules and Rosina in Il Barbiere di Siviglia, both at Paris Bastille 2004; Elisabetta in Maria Stuarda at Geneva 2005; season 2005–06 as Cherubino in Le Nozze di Figaro at The Met, Rosina in Il Barbiere di Siviglia at the Royal Opera House, Covent Garden, and Sesto in La Clemenza di Tito at Geneva; also performed as Dejanira in Handel's Hercules in Paris and in Heggie's Dead Man Walking at New York City Opera. *Recording:* The Deepest Desire (Bernstein, Copland, Heggie) 2005. *Honours:* district winner Met Opera auditions 1996, Richard Tucker Award 2002. *Current Management:* IMG Artists, Lovell House, 616 Chiswick High Road, London, W4 5RX, England. *Telephone:* (20) 8233-5800. *Fax:* (20) 8233-5801. *E-mail:* artistseurope@imgworld.com. *Website:* www .imgartists.com; www.joycedidonato.com.

**DIDONE, Rosanna;** Singer (Soprano); b. 13 Feb. 1952, Galliera, Veneta, Italy. *Education:* Studied at the Benedetto Marcello Conservatory Venice. *Career:* Debut: Padua 1978, as Serpina in La Serva Padrona; Appearances at Venice in Idomeneo, as Rosette in Manon and Bianca in La Rondine; Clarice in Il Mondo Della Luna at Turin and Frasquita in Carmen at Padau, 1982; At Trieste (from 1982) has sung Gnese in Il Campiello, Amor (Orpheus ed Euridice), Barbarina, and a Naiad in Ariadne auf Naxos; Rome Opera 1982 and 1988 in Don Carlos and as Mme Silberklang in Der Schauspieldirektor by Mozart; Other roles include Musetta, Marie-Louise in Kodály's Háry János, Biancofiore in Francesca da Rimini, Gilda, Susanna, Carolina (Il matrimonio segreto), Norina (Don Pasquale), Oscar, Nannetta, Laura and Despina; Guest appearances in Netherlands and Bulgaria. *Recordings:* Egloge in Mascagni's Nerone, and Francesca da Rimni (Bongiovanni).

**DIEMER, Emma Lou,** BM, MM, PhD; American composer, pianist, organist and academic; b. 24 Nov. 1927, Kansas City, MO. *Education:* Yale School of Music, Eastman School of Music. *Career:* composer-in-residence, Santa Barbara Symphony, 1990–92; Professor of Composition, University of California, Santa Barbara, 1971–91; organist, First Presbyterian Church, Santa Barbara, 1984–2000. *Compositions include:* Concerto for marimba, 1990; Concerto for piano, 1991; Sextet, 1992; Four Biblical Settings for organ, 1992; Kyrie, 1993; Fantasy for piano, 1993; Gloria, 1996; Psalms for organ and flute, Psalms for organ and trumpet, Psalms for organ and percussion, 1998; Mass, 2000; Piano Trio, 2000; Homage to Tchaikovsky, 2001. *Recordings include:* Declarations for organ; Toccata and Fugue for organ; Toccata for piano; Summer of 82 for cello and piano; Quartet for piano, violin, viola and cello; Sextet for woodwind quintet and piano; Youth Overture; Encore for piano, 1991; Sextet, 1993; Concerto in One Movement for piano, 1995; String Quartet No. 1, 1995; Santa Barbara Overture, 1997; Concerto in One Movement for piano, 1998; Fantasy for piano, 1998; Suite of Homages, for orchestra 1999; Four Chinese Love Poems, 1999; Piano Concerto, 2000; Suite of Homages, 2001, Santa Barbara Overture, 2001, Concerto for Organ 2004. *Publications:* Over 100 including: Toccata for marimba, 1956; Sonata for violin and piano, 1968; Sextet for woodwind quintet and piano, 1968; Anniversary Choruses for chorus and orchestra, 1970; Concerto for flute, 1973; Symphony No. 2, 1976; Toccata for piano, 1979; Suite of Homages for orchestra, 1985; String Quartet No. 1, 1987; Choral–A Feast for Christmas, 1992; Marimba Concerto, 1994; Organ Works, 1957–2004; Kyrie and Gloria, 1997; Psalms for flute and organ, 1999; Psalms for percussion and organ, 1999; Mass, 2000; Piano Sonata No. 3, 2001, Concerto for Organ 2004, Santa Barbara Overture 2004, Homage to Tchaikovsky 2004. *Honours:* Kennedy Center Friedheim Award, for Concerto in One Movement for piano, 1995; American Guild of Organists Composer of the Year, 1995; Honorary Doctorate of Letters, Central Missouri State University, 1999. *Address:* 2249 Vista del Campo, Santa Barbara, CA 93101, USA. *E-mail:* eldiemer@cox.net.

**DIENER, Melanie;** Singer (Soprano); b. 1967, Germany. *Education:* Studied with Sylvia Geszty in Stuttgart and with Rudolf Piernay in Mannheim; Further study at Indiana University. *Career:* Concerts include the Brahms Requiem in Paris and Zürich, Mendelssohn's St Paul under Philippe

Herreweghe and Mahler's 2nd Symphony at Linz; Recitals in Stuttgart and Bonn; Opera debut as Mozart's Ilia at Garsington, England, 1996; Season 1996–97 with Elijah at the Berlin Philharmonie, Fiordiligi at Covent Garden and in Paris, First Lady in Die Zauberflöte at the Salzburg Festival; Asberta in Holzbauer's Gunther von Schwarzburg under Ton Koopman at the Amsterdam Concertgebouw; The Strauss Four Last Songs at Turin and the Verdi Requiem at St Gallen; Season 1997–98 with Korngold's Kathrin for the BBC, Agathe in Der Freischütz for the Royal Opera in concert and Donna Elvira at Aix; Elsa in Lohengrin at Bayreuth, 1999; Covent Garden as Donna Elvira, 2002, returned to London 2003, as Elsa. *Honours:* Prizewinner, International Mozart Competition, Salzburg, 1995; Winner, Kirsten Flagstad Prize, Oslo, 1995. *Current Management:* Balmer & Dixon Management AG, Kreuzstrasse 82, 8032 Zürich, Switzerland. *Telephone:* (43) 244-8644. *Fax:* (43) 244-8649. *Website:* www.badix.ch.

**DIESSELHORST, Jan;** Cellist; b. 1956, Marburg, Germany. *Education:* Studied in Frankfurt and with Wolfgang Boettcher in Berlin. *Career:* Joined the Berlin Philharmonic Orchestra, 1979; Co-founded the Philharmonic Quartet Berlin, giving concerts throughout Europe, the USA and Japan; British debut, 1987, playing Haydn, Szymanowski and Beethoven at Wigmore Hall; Bath Festival, 1987, playing Mozart, Schumann and Beethoven (Op. 127); Other repertoire includes quartets by Bartók, Mendelssohn, Nicolai, Ravel and Schubert; Quintets by Brahms, Weber, Reger and Schumann. *Address:* c/o Berlin Philharmonic Orchestra, Philharmonie, Matthäuskirchstrasse 1, 1000 Berlin 30, Germany.

**DIETRICH, Karl;** Composer and Teacher; b. 9 July 1927, Wachstedt/Eichsfeld, Germany; m. Gerda Lins, 29 April 1952, 2 d. *Education:* Matriculation and Study, University Jena and High School of Music, Franz Liszt, Weimar. *Career:* Professor for Composition, High School of Music, Franz Liszt, Weimar; mem, Ordentliches Mitglied Deutscher Komponisten-Interessenverband. *Compositions:* Seven Symphonies, 1969–92; Operas: Die Wette des Serapion, 1984; Pervonte, 1989; Orchestral: 3 Divertimenti for Orchestra, 1972–76; Piano Concerto 1964; Concerto for orchestra, 1969; Dramatic Scenes for 3 flutes (1 Soloist), and large orchestra, 1974; Violoncello Concerto 1982; Concertino giocoso for string orchestra, 1962; Konzert-Suite for string orchestra, 1967; Memorial for string orchestra in connection with the choral of J. S. Bach, Vergiá mein Nicht, 1994; Konzertantes Präludium für Orchestra, 1996; Chamber Music: Prokofiev-Variationen für Klavier 4-händig, 1970; Anregungen für Klavier, 1974; Etude capricieuse für Cello-Solo, 1993; Ton-triage für Flöte-Solo, 1986; 3 Liederzyklen für Singstimme und Klavier; 3 Bläserquintette; 6 Dialoge für 2 Oboen; Divertimento für Flöte und Streichtrio. Organ: Groáe Fantasie für Orgel, 1981; Vision für Flöte und Orgel, 1984; Rupert-Mayer-Reflexionen für Orgel. Church Music: Psalm 49, Die Vergänglichkeit des Menschen, für Bariton und Orgel, 1994; Deutsche Messe für Männerchor a cappella, 1995; Schöndorfer Messe, lateinischer Text, für mittlere Singstimme und Orgel, 1996, und Kirchenmusikalische Kompositionen diverser Art für Chöre und Soli. *Recordings:* Symphony No. 4, contra bellum, SSO Thüringen, Conductor Lothar Seyfarth; Dramatic Szenes, Rundfunk-Sinfonieorchestra Leipzig, Conductor Herbert Kegel; Symphony No. 7, Philharmonie Erfurt, Conductor Wolfgang Rögner. *Publications:* Opéra Comique Pervonte nach Ch M Wieland; Violoncello Concerto; Symphony No. 4; Vision for flute and organ; Konzertsuite for string orchestra; Concertino giocoso for string orchestra; Three Cheerful Stories, cappella choir; Prokofiev-Variationen für Klavier 4-händig. *Honours:* Kunstpreis des FDGB, 1971; Kunst Preis der DDR, 1975; Kunstpreis der Stadt Weimar, 1983. *Address:* Auf dem Dürbache 10, 99438 Legefeld/Stadt Weimar, Germany.

**DIETSCH, James William,** BME, MMus; American singer (baritone) and artist manager; b. 21 March 1950, Kansas City, MO; m. Susan Kay Schell 1980; one s. *Education:* Univ. of Missouri, Kansas City, Juilliard School of Music American Opera Center, Vienna Acad. of Music, Austria. *Career:* debut, Fargo-Moorhead Civic Opera 1975; New York Town Hall 1981; Carnegie Hall 1982; leading artist with numerous opera cos and concert appearances in USA and abroad, including San Francisco Opera, New York City Opera, English Opera North, Karlsruhe Badisches Staatstheater, Saarbrucken Saarländiches Staatstheater, Michigan Opera, Milwaukee Opera, Deutsche Oper am Rhein, Minnesota Opera, Hawaii Opera, Staatstheater Essen, Santa Fe Opera, Spoleto Festival USA, New York Philharmonic, Mexico City Philharmonic; Man., establishing Dietsch Division of Pinnacle Arts. *Recordings:* Il Corsaro by Verdi, Historical Recording Incorporate, 1981. *Address:* Pinnacle Arts: Dietsch Division, Thierschstrasse 11, 80538 Munich, Germany. *Telephone:* (89) 340-8630. *Fax:* (89) 3408-6310. *E-mail:* jdietsch@pinnaclearts.com. *Website:* www.pinnaclearts.com.

**DIJKSTRA, Hebe;** Singer (Mezzo-Soprano); b. 4 Sept. 1941, Tvijzelerheide, Netherlands; m. Jan Alofs. *Education:* Studied at the Hague Conservatory. *Career:* Debut: Sang Gluck's Orpheus at Enschede, 1975; Sang Mistress Quickly at Enschede, and appeared in Rimsky's Sadko at Bonn, 1976; Engaged at Detmold, 1976–79, Saarbrucken 1979–80, Freiburg, 1981–83; Krefeld, 1982–85, Wuppertal, 1987–89; Amsterdam, 1989, in Der Kreidekreis by Zemlinsky; Member of the Staatstheater am Gärtnerplatz, Munich from 1989; Sang Rossweise in Die Walküre at Bayreuth, 1988–91; Ulrica at Amsterdam 1992; Mary in Der fliegende Holländer at the 1992 Bayreuth Festival; Other roles include Carmen, Fricka, Waltraute, the Nurse in Boris Godunov, and La Comandante in I Cavalieri di Ekebù by Zandonai; Sang Margret in Wozzeck at Amsterdam, 1994; Witch in the premiere of Robert Heppener's Een Ziel van Hout, 1998; Sang Hecuba in Troades by Reimann at

Berlin and Berne, 2000. *Address:* c/o Staatstheater am Gärtnerplatz, Gärtnerplatz 3, 8000 Munich, Germany.

**DILBÈR, MA;** Finnish (b. Chinese) singer (lyric coloratura soprano); b. 1960, Finland. *Education:* Music Academy, Beijing. *Career:* debut as Gilda in Rigoletto with Finnish National Opera; Performed with major Chinese ensembles while at school and at the music academy; Numerous engagements throughout Europe and the rest of the world; Repertoire includes Adina, Amina, Angelica, Haydn's Orlando Paladino, Blondchen, Cucia, Marie, Königin der Nacht, Despina, Elvira, Gilda, Lakmé, Nannetta, Olympia, Rosina, Sophie in Werther and Der Rosenkavalier, Zerbinetta and Zerlina; Performances with major orchestras including the Symphony Orchestra of Beethovenhalle, Bonn, Orchestra Sinfonica di Milano della RAI, Singapore Symphony Orchestra, Taiwan Nat. Symphony Orchestra, Israel Sinfonietta, Radio Orchestras of Denmark, China, Finland, Frankfurt; Mitteldeutschen Rundfunk, Århus, Malmö, Helsinki; Performed in the major opera venues world-wide; Subject of documentaries with Swedish, Finnish and Chinese television. *Recordings:* Five albums in China; Coloratura arias; Folk Songs; Lieder with piano; Nannetta in Falstaff; Lisa in La Sonnambula; The Art of Coloratura with Malmö Opera Orchestra. *Honours:* Hon. Prof. Xinjiang Arts Coll. 2000–; Second Prize, International Mirjam Helin Singing Competition, Helsinki, 1984; Birgit Nilsson Prize, twice, Golden Record and Best Performer Awards, China 2003. *Address:* Bågängsvägen 53, 21620 Malmö, Sweden. *E-mail:* dilber@telia.com (home).

**DILKES, Neville,** FRCO; British conductor; b. 28 Aug. 1930, Derby, England; m. 1st D. Pamela Walton (died 1979); four d.; m. 2nd Christine M. Allen 1986. *Education:* private tuition and masterclasses, Netherlands Radio Union International Conductors' course; Fellow Trinity College, London. *Career:* founder conductor of Kettering Symphony Orchestra; Founder conductor of Opera Da Camera; Founder conductor English Sinfonia; Associate conductor Philomusica of London; International radio and television; mem, Royal Society of Musicians of Great Britain. *Recordings:* English and French music, Bax, Butterworth, Moeran, Honegger, Ibert and Jolivet. *Honours:* Watney, Sargent Award for Conductors, 1963. *Address:* La Graineterie, 23 rue des Huttes, 85370 Nalliers, France (home). *Telephone:* 2-51-30-96-34 (home). *Fax:* 2-51-30-96-34 (home). *E-mail:* ncm-dilkes@wanadoo.fr (home).

**DILLON, James;** Scottish composer; b. 29 Oct. 1950, Glasgow. *Education:* Glasgow School of Art, Polytechnic of Central London, Polytechnic of North London. *Career:* works performed and featured at festivals throughout the world, including Antidogma (Turin), Bath, Darmstadt, Gulbenkian (Lisbon), Huddersfield, ISCM (Toronto), La Rochelle, Musica Nel Nostro Tempo (Milan), Music of Eight Decades (London), Paris d'Automne, Warsaw, Zig-Zag (Paris), Châtelet (Paris), Donaueschingen (Germany), Musica Nova (Glasgow), Musica (Strasburg), Ars Musica (Brussels), Ultima (Oslo), Venice Biennale, Sydney Spring, ISCM World Music Days (Toronto, Stockholm, Seoul and Manchester); Guest Lecturer, Univs of Keele, London, New York, Nottingham, Oxford, Central England and Gothenburg; guest composer Darmstadt Ferienkurse 1982, 1984, 1986; jury mem., Gaudeamus Composers' Competition 1985, ISCM Int. 1988 and Besancon Int. Competition 1990. *Compositions:* Spleen 1980, Once Upon a Time 1980, Come Live With Me 1981, Parjanya-Vata 1981, East 11th Street 1982, String Quartet 1983, Sgothan 1984, La Coupure 1986, Helle Nacht 1987, Del Cuarto Elemento 1988, L'Ecran parfum 1988, Shrouded Mirrors 1988, La Femme Invisible 1989, L'Oeuvre au noir 1990, Blitzschlag 1991, String Quartet No. 2 1991, ignis noster 1991–92, Siorram 1992, Vernal Showers 1992, L'Evolution du Vol 1993, Viriditas 1993, Traumwerk Book I 1995, Redemption 1995, Oceanos 1996, Todesengel 1996, The Book of Elements Vol. I 1997, String Quartet No. 3 1998, Hyades 1998, Eos 1998–99, residue… 1999, Vapor 1999, La coupure 2000, Via Sacra 2000, Violin Concerto 2000, Book of Elements Vol. III 2000, La navette 2000–01, Book of Elements Vol. II 2001, Two Studies 2001, Two Studies 2001, Traumwerk Book 2 2001, Traumwerk Book 3 2001–02, Book of Elements Vol. IV 2002, Book of Elements Vol. V 2002, Piano Quintet 2002, New Work 2002–03, The Rape of Philomela 2002–04, The Soadie Waste (British Composer Award for choral work) 2004. *Recordings:* helle Nacht; ignis noster; Come Live with me; A Roaring Flame; Sgothan; Ti re-Ti Ke-Dha; Evening Rain; Crossing Over; Spleen; Del Cuarto Elemento; East 11th Street, NY 10003; La femme invisible; Windows and Canopies; Dillug Kefitsah. *Publications:* Problemas Discursivos en La Muska Contemporanea 1989, Speculative Instruments: Timbre, Métaphore pour La Composition 1991. *Honours:* Kraninsteiner Musikpreis (Germany) 1982, London Times Classical Music Personality of the Year 1989, Royal Philharmonic Soc. Award 1997. *Address:* c/o Peters Edition Ltd, 10–12 Baches Street, London, N1 6DN, England.

**DIMITROVA, Anastasia;** Singer (Soprano); b. 16 Nov. 1940, Pernik, Bulgaria. *Education:* Studied at State Conservatory, Sofia and in Zagreb. *Career:* Debut: Sang in Nabucco at Skopje, 1965; Many Appearances at Opera Houses in Bulgaria and Yugoslavia, notably, Belgrade, Sofia, Zagreb and Rijeka; Roles have included Verdi's Elisabetta and Leonora (Trovatore), Mimi, Yaroslavna (Prince Igor), Tatiana in Eugene Onegin, Marenka (Bartered Bride), Rusalka, Micaela, Euridice and Marguerite. *Honours:* Winner, Francisco Vinas (Barcelona 1969) and Bussetto Competitions. *Address:* c/o Sofia State Opera, Boulevard Dondoukov 58, 1000 Sofia, Bulgaria.

**DINDO, Enrico;** Cellist; b. 16 March 1965, Turin, Italy. *Education:* Conservatorio G Verdi, Turin; Mozarteum Salzburg, with Antonio Sangro.

*Career:* Debut: 1st Cellist with La Scala Orchestra, 1988; Soloist in Beethoven Triple Concerto at La Scala, 1996; Worked with conductors Roberto Abbado, Aldo Cecato, Gunter Neuhold, Peter Maag, Gianandrea Noseda, Riccardo Chailly, Riccardo Muti, Mstislav Rostropovich; Played with Orchestre Nationale de France, St Petersburg Philharmonic Orchestra, Orchestra Sinfonica Nazionale RAI, Chicago Symphony and Kirov Chamber Orchestra. *Recordings:* Brahms, Cello Sonatas; Haydn, Cello Concerti. *Honours:* 1st Prize, Rostropovich Cello Competition, Paris, 1987. *Current Management:* AMP, Milan. *Address:* V Mercadante 8, 20124 Milan, Italy.

**DINESCU, Violeta,** MA; German (b. Romanian) composer, musician and academic; *Professor of Composition, University of Oldenburg;* b. 13 July 1953, Bucharest; d. of Alfons Dinescu and Elena Dinescu; m. Nicolae Manolache 1993. *Education:* Ciprian Porumbescu Conservatory of Music. *Career:* Instructor of Theory, Piano, Harmony, Counterpoint and Aesthetics, George Enescu Music School 1987–90, Conservatory for Church Music, Heidelberg, Germany 1989–91, Conservatory for Music, Frankfurt, Germany 1989–92, Acad. of Church Music, Bayreuth 1990–94; currently Prof. of Composition Univ. of Oldenburg, Germany; Special Corresp. Music Section Romania Literară, Muzică 1975–82; European Corresp. Living Music, Calif., USA 1987–; Guest Lecturer univs in Germany, SA and USA; performances and radio recordings in Romania, Germany, France, UK, USA, Italy, Belgium, Switzerland, Austria, El Salvador, SA, Colombia, Finland, Czech Republic, Sweden, Portugal, Mexico, Luxembourg, Canada etc.; mem. Union of Composers of Romania 1982–, Int. Arbeitskreis Frau und Musik, Germany 1982–, Minnesota Composers' Forum, USA 1984–, Exec. Bd Int. League of Women Composers, USA 1985–. *Compositions include:* chamber music: Echoes I, Parra Quitarra, Din Cimpoiu, Dies Diem Docet, Scherzo da Fantasia III, Sleep Song, Kata, Ichthys, Figuren III, Stringquartet din Terra Lonhdana, Contraste, Alternances, Festspielfanfare, Fragment V, Letitae, Flutesplay II, In Search of Mozart!, Terra Lonhdana; orchestral music: Transformations, Anna Perenna, Memories, Joc, Fresco, Kybalion; voice and instrumental music: Amont, Quatrain, Psalm 125, Concertino, Fragment I, Euraculos, Arpagic, In my Garden, Spring Song, Latin Sentences, Flower Song, Zori de flori, Bewitch Me into a Silver Bird!, The Play; Pfinstoratorium, Friedensoratorium, Wie Tau auf den Bergen Zions; operas: Hunger and Thirst, Der 35 Mai, Eréndira, Schachnovelle; ballet: Der Kreisel, Effi Briest, Aus Deinem Herzen Kannst Du die Liebe nicht Ausreissen. *Recordings include:* Internationales Festival Heidelberg 1987 1988, Fanny Mendelssohn-Quartet 1988, Internationales Festival Neue Musik 1991, over 50 CDs . *Honours:* Composers' Asscn Prize, Romania 1975, 1976, 1980, 1983, First Prize, Int. Eisteddfod Festival, Roodepoort, SA 1991, Gregynog Composers Award, Wales, UK 1993, American-Romanian Acad. of Arts and Sciences Award, Calif., USA 1994, Int. New Music Consortium Award, New York, USA 1996, 1999, Delta Omicron Triennal Composition Competition 1996, Women in Music Award, Ohio, USA 1997 and other awards and prizes. *Address:* University of Oldenburg, Fakultät 3/Musik, 26111 Oldenburg (office); Presuhnstr. 39, 26133 Oldenburg, Germany (home). *Telephone:* (441) 7982027 (office); (441) 42979 (home). *Fax:* (441) 7984016 (office); (441) 94904555 (home). *E-mail:* violeta.dinescu@uni-oldenburg.de (office). *Website:* www.dinescu.net.

**DINITZEN, Kim Bak;** Cellist; b. 24 Oct. 1963, Haderslev, Denmark; m. Ursula Smith, 8 May 1993. *Education:* Studied at Royal Danish Conservatoire of Music with Erling Blondal Bengtsson; Private studies in London with Ralph Kirshbaum. *Career:* Debut: Copenhagen, 1986; Weill Recital Hall at Carnegie Hall, New York, 1988; Wigmore Hall, London, 1991; Soloist with all Danish symphony orchestras; Recitals and chamber music concerts throughout Europe; Member of Chamber Orchestra of Europe, 1990–; Teacher at Royal Northern College of Music, Manchester, England, 1996–. *Recordings:* Benjamin Britten: Complete Works for Cello; G Fauré: Complete Works for Cello and Piano, with Elisabeth Westenholz, piano; Prokofiev and Schnittke Sonatas, with Paul Coker, piano; Niels W Gade: String Quintet, Sextet and Octet with the Johannes Ensemble. *Honours:* Victor Borge Prize, Denmark, 1987; 1st Prize for Cello, Washington International Competition, 1988; East and West Artists' Prize for New York debut, 1988; 3rd Prize, Gaspar Cassapo International Cello Competition, Florence, 1990. *Current Management:* Tivoli Artists' Management. *Address:* Flat 1, 3 Randolph Place, Edinburgh EH3 7TQ, Scotland.

**D'INTINO, Luciana;** singer (mezzo-soprano); b. 1959, San vito al Tagliamento, Pordenone, Italy. *Education:* Benedeto Marcello Conservatory, Venice. *Career:* debut singing Azucena in Il Trovatore, 1983; appearances as Rossini's Rosina in Marcerata and Naples, 1984, 1986; Aida at Cagliari and Trieste; La Scala Milan from 1987 in Nabucco, Guillaume Tell; Jommelli's Fetonte, Adriana Lecouvreur and as Luggrezia in Pergolesi's Lo Frate 'nnamorato; sang Frederica in Luisa Miller at Rome, 1990 and on Metropolitan Opera debut, 1991; Turin 1990 as Eboli in Don Carlos and Savona 1991 as Arsace in Rossini's Auerliano in Palmira; sang Preziosilla in Forza del Destino at Naples, Sara in Roberto Devereux at Bologna, 1992; Preziosilla at the 1992 Maggio Musicale, Florence; Amneris in Aida at Covent Garden, 1994, and at Buenos Aires, 1996; sang Eboli at Bologna, 1998; season 2000–01 as Rossini's Isabella at Turin and Eboli for Zürich Opera; Verdi Requiem at Florence, Palermo, Rome and Saõ Paulo, 2001. *Recordings include:* Lo Frate 'nnamorato, conducted by Riccardo Muti. *Honours:* winner Spoleto Singing Competition 1993. *Current Management:* Atelier Musicale, Via Caselle 76, San Lazzaro di Savena 40068, Italy. *Telephone:* (051) 19 98 44 44. *Fax:* (051) 19

98 44 20. *E-mail:* info@ateliermusicale.com. *Website:* www.ateliermusicale .com.

**DIVALL, Richard Sydney Benedict,** OBE, FRAS, FRNS; Australian conductor; b. 9 Sept. 1945, Sydney, NSW. *Education:* Univ. of Melbourne, Conservatorium of Music, Sydney. *Career:* debut, Handel's Xerxes, Sydney; Producer of Music, ABC 1960–70; Musical Dir, Queensland Opera 1971–; guest conductor, ABC 1972–; Music Dir, Victoria State Opera 1972–95, Prin. Conductor 1995–97; Assoc. Prof. of Music, Univ. of Melbourne 1992–; Prin. Resident Conductor, Opera Australia 1997–2002; edited 18th-century symphonies, series of eight vols. of colonial Australian repertoire music and 15 operas; Chair. of Marshall-Hall Trust. *Recordings include:* repertoire of over 140 operas, Early Australian Music Vol. 1. *Publications:* Music of Carl Linger, 1998; Complete Music of Henry Handel Richardson, 1999; New Publications of 3 volumes of Music of Frederick Septimus Kelly; Volume of music of Dom Rosendo Salvado, Alfred Hill, GW Marshall-Hall, Alberto Zelman, Australia's First Piano Music; 2 Symphonies and 2 String Quartets of Charles Edward Horsley, 1 Symphony and String Quartet of Fritz Hart; 6 volumes of early Maltese music; Pergolesi "Stabat Mater" (Wignacourt ms). *Honours:* D Artes e Cul (Hon. SP), 1987; KM, 1989; Commendatore al Merito, 1989; D Lett (Hon Monash), 1992; Australian Centenary Medal, 2003; Senior Fellowship Inst. for Studies in Australian Music Melbourne Univ.; Fra' n The Order of Malta (Cav n di Giustizia); Doc Univ. (Hon Aust Cath U.); Sr Fellow, State Library of Victoria 2003–04; Sir Bernard Heinze Award 2005. *Current Management:* Jenifer Eddy, 11/596 St Kilda Road, Melbourne, 3004, Australia. *Address:* 301 Arcadia, 228 The Avenue, Parkville, Vic. 3025, Australia. *Telephone:* 3 9381 0789 (home). *Fax:* 3 9381 0790 (home). *E-mail:* maestro@spin.net.au.

**DIVES, Tamsin;** Singer (Mezzo-Soprano); b. 1968, England. *Education:* Studied at the Guildhall School. *Career:* Opera appearances with Glyndebourne Festival, English National Opera, Opera North, Chelsea Opera and Edinburgh and Harrogate Festivals; Roles include Fidalma in Il Matrimonio Segreto and Mrs Grose in The Turn Of The Screw; Concerts with the Hallé Orchestra, Northern Sinfonia and The Nash Ensemble; Sang in the British Premiere of Korngold's Die tote Stadt, Queen Elizabeth Hall, 1996. *Recordings include:* Davies' The Martyrdom of St Magnus; Macmillan's Visitatio Sepulchri.

**DIVOKY, Zdenek;** Horn Player; b. 1954, Brno, Czechoslovakia. *Education:* Studied at the Janáček Academy in Brno with Frantisek Socl. *Career:* Wind Section of the State Philharmonic Orchestra in Brno; Czech Philharmonic, 1979; Solo peformer in concert and member of such chamber ensembles as the Prague Brass Trio, the Horn Quartet of the Czech Philharmonic, the Collegium Musicum Pragense and the Stamic Quartet; Solo engagements in Germany, Australia, England, Spain and Canada; Repertoire includes concertos by M and J Haydn, Telemann, Mozart, Punto, Rosetti, Schumann, Weber and Strauss; Recitalist in Beethoven, Mozart, Reicha, Brahms, Britten, Hindemith and Burghauser; Tours with the Czech Philharmonic and with various chamber ensembles to Europe, the USA and Japan. *Honours:* Prizewinner at Prague Spring International Festival and competitions in Munich and Markneukirchen.

**DIXON, James;** Conductor; b. 26 April 1928, Estherville, Iowa, USA. *Education:* Studied at the University of Iowa and with Dimitri Mitropoulos, 1949–60. *Career:* Conducted the US 7th Army Band in Germany; Led the University of Iowa Symphony, 1954–59; New England Conservatory Symphony in Boston, 1969–61; Conductor of the Tri-City Symphony in Davenport, Iowa, and Rock Island, Illinois; Associate Conductor of the Minneapolis Symphony, 1961–62; Guest Conductor with the National Orchestra of Greece in Athens, the Norddeutscher Rundfunk, Hamburg, the Westdeutscher Rundfunk, Cologne, the Tanglewood Orchestra, the Chicago Civic Symphony and the Chicago Symphony (1972); Conducted a student group at the International Society for Contemporary Music Festival in Boston, 1976; Has led the premieres of Charles Wuorinen's Piano Concerto and works by T J Anderson and William Matthews. *Honours:* Gustav Mahler Medal, 1963.

**DJIOEVA, Irina;** Singer (Soprano); b. 1971, Magadan, Russia. *Education:* St Petersburg Conservatoire. *Career:* Appearances with the Kirov Opera from 1996, as Verdi's Violetta, Leonora (La Forza del Destino) and Elisabeth de Valois, Glinka's Lyudmilla, and Marfa in Rimsky's The Tsar's Bride; Mozart's Queen of Night, Susanna and Donna Anna, Woglinde in Das Rheingold, Stravinsky's Nightingale and Lucia di Lammermoor; Further roles at the Mariinsky Theatre, St Petersburg, include Amina (La Sonnambula), Volkhova in Rimsky's Sadko, and Mimi; Sang in the Verdi season with the Kirov Opera at Covent Garden, 2001; Further tours to Italy and the New York Met; Sang Flowermaiden in Parsifal at Salzburg, 1998. *Honours:* Prizewinner, 1995 Mario del Monaco Competition and Rimsky-Korsakov International, 1996. *Address:* c/o Kirov Opera, Mariinsky Theatre, 1 Theatre Square, St Petersburg, Russia.

**DJUPSJÖBACKA, Gustav Mikael;** Finnish pianist; *Principal, Sibelius Academy, Helsinki;* b. 21 Dec. 1950, Borgå; m. Lena von Bonsdorff 1977; one s. one d. *Education:* Sibelius Acad., Musical Acad., Prague, Hochschule für Musik, Vienna. *Career:* debut, Helsinki 1978; keyboard player, Radio Symphony Orchestra of Finland 1977–87; Lecturer in Lied Music, Sibelius Acad. 1987–; mainly lied recitals in Europe, N and S America with Ritva Auvinen, Monica Groop, Tom Krause, Jorma Hynninen, others; mem. Yrjö Kilpinen Soc., Madetoja Foundation, Académie Francis Poulenc, Nordic Music

Cttee; mem. of Rimski Korsakov Singing Contest Jury, St Petersburg 2002. *Recordings:* Winterreise and Sibelius Songs with Tom Krause, Sibelius Songs with Ritva Auvinen, Complete Madetoja Songs with Gabriel Suovanen and Helena Juntunen. *Publications:* Yrjö Kilpinen's Morgenstern Songs 1992, Aarre Merikanto Songs 2000, Kilpinen Songs 2002, Guide on Finnish Art Songs 2001. *Honours:* Sylvi Kekkonen Scholarship 1975, 1976. *Address:* Sibelius Academy, Töölönkatu 28, 00260 Helsinki (office); Töölöntorinkatu 3 A 2, 00260 Helsinki, Finland (home). *Telephone:* (9) 4054620 (office). *Fax:* (9) 4054600 (office). *E-mail:* gdjupsjo@siba.fi (office).

**DMITRIEV, Alexander Sergeevich;** Russian conductor; b. 19 Jan. 1935, Leningrad; m.; one s. *Education:* Leningrad Choir School, Leningrad State Conservatory, Vienna Akad. für Musik und darstellende Kunst. *Career:* Conductor Karelian Radio and TV Symphony Orchestra 1961, Prin. Conductor 1962–71; Prin. Conductor Maly Opera and Ballet Theatre, Leningrad (now St Petersburg) 1971–77, and Music Dir Symphony Orchestra of St Petersburg Philharmonia 1977–; Prin. Conductor Stavanger Symphony Orchestra (Norway) 1990–98. *Recordings include:* Handel's Messiah, Haydn's Creation, Schubert's Symphony Nos. 1–9, Tchaikovsky's Symphonies 4, 5, 6, Rachmaninov's Symphony No. 2, Debussy's 3 Nocturnes, Ravel's Valses nobles et sentimentales, Ma Mère l'Oye, Saeverud's Peer Gynt, Symphony dolorosa, Balakirev's Piano Concerto, Medtner's Piano Concerto No. 1, Rachmaninov's Piano Concerto No. 3, Britten's Violin concerto. *Honours:* Merited Worker of Arts of Karelian ASSR 1967, People's Artist of Russia 1976, USSR People's Artist; Prize 2nd USSR Competition for Conductors 1966. *Address:* Symphony Orchestra, St Petersburg Philharmonic Society, Mikhailovskaya str. 2, St Petersburg 091011, Russia (office). *Telephone:* (812) 114-64-17 (home). *Fax:* (812) 117-21-26 (office). *E-mail:* dmitriev@mail.spbnit.ru; alexanderdmitriev@hotmail.com.

**DOBBER, Andrzej;** Singer (Baritone); b. 26 May 1961, Wiecbok, Poland. *Education:* Studied in Warsaw (making his debut as Gremin while a student) and in Nuremberg. *Career:* Sang at Nuremberg Opera, 1987-91, debut as Tonio in Pagliacci; Frankfurt Opera from 1991, as Nardo in La finta giardiniera, Luna, the Herald in Lohengrin, Gremin and Marcello; Guest at the Vienna Staatsoper as Escamillo (1992) and frequent concert appearances; Cologne from 1995, as Eugene Onegin and Mozart's Count; Sang Fyodor in The Invisible City of Kitezh at the Komische Oper, Berlin, 1996; Season 2000-01 in Berlin as Danilo in Die Lustige Witwe at the Deutsche Oper, and as Orestes in Elektra at the Komische Oper. *Address:* c/o Alfernik, Apollolaan 181, NL–1077 AT Amsterdam, Netherlands.

**DOBBS, Mattiwilda,** BA, MA; American singer (coloratura soprano); b. 11 July 1925, Atlanta, GA; d. of John Wesley Dobbs and Irene Thompson Dobbs; m. 1st Luis Rodríguez García 1953 (died 1954); m. 2nd Bengt Janzon 1957 (died 1997). *Education:* Spelman Coll., Atlanta and Columbia Univ. *Career:* studied with Lotte Leonard 1946–50; Marian Anderson scholarship, soloist at Mexico Univ. Festival 1947; studied at Mannes Music School and Berkshire Music Center 1948, with Pierre Bernac, Paris 1950–52; debut La Scala, Milan in L'Italiana in Algeri 1953; sang at Glyndebourne 1953, 1954, 1956, 1961, Royal Opera House, Covent Garden, London 1953, 1954, 1955, 1956, 1959, San Francisco Opera 1955, Metropolitan Opera, New York 1956–64, Stockholm Royal Opera 1957–71, Hamburg State Opera 1961–63, Norwegian and Finnish Opera 1957–64; concert appearances in USA, Australia, New Zealand, Israel, USSR, Netherlands, France, Sweden, Mexico; Visiting Prof., Univ. of Texas at Austin 1973–74; Prof., Univ. of Illinois 1975–76, Univ. of Georgia 1976–77, Howard Univ., Washington, DC 1977–91. *Honours:* 1st Voice Prize, Geneva Int. Competition 1951; Order of the North Star (Sweden). *Address:* 1101 South Arlington Ridge Road, Apt. 301, Arlington, VA 22202, USA. *Telephone:* (703) 892-5234.

**DOBRÉE, Georgina,** FRAM; British clarinettist, basset hornist, teacher and editor; b. 8 Jan. 1930, London, England. *Education:* Royal Academy of Music, studied with Gaston Hamelin in Paris. *Career:* member of Chamber Music Ensembles; Recitals, broadcasts, lecture recitals and masterclasses in Europe and USA; Many premieres and recipient of numerous dedications; Professor, Royal Academy of Music, 1967–86; Director, Chantry Records, 1975–84, mainly of 19th and 20th Century works and own performances; mem. RMA; International Clarinet Association; CASS; RAM Club; Royal Society of Musicians; PAMRA. *Publications:* Chantry Publications formed 1988, editions of mainly 19th century music for clarinet and/or basset horn, assigned June 2000 to Emerson Edition Ltd; Editions of other works with clarinet for MR, OUP, Schott, Chester and Nova. *Honours:* French Government Scholarship, 1949; First Prize, Darmstadt, 1953. *Address:* 58 Ninesprings Way, Hitchin, Hertfordshire SG4 9NR, England.

**DOBRONRAVOVA, Svetlana;** Singer (Soprano); b. 1957, Taganrog, Russia. *Education:* Studied at the Rostov on Don Conservatoire. *Career:* Debut: Lvov State Opera in 1982 as Tosca; Sang with the Lvov Opera until 1989 notably as Santuzza, Yaroslavna and Gioconda; National Opera Kiev from 1989 as Abigaille, Elisabeth de Valois, Aida, Desdemona, Leonora in Forza del Destino, Elsa, Tatiana and Maria in Mazeppa; Guest engagements in Canada and throughout Europe, including concerts of the Mozart and Verdi Requiems; British debut in 1996 with the Perm Opera as Abigaille. *Address:* Sonata Ltd, 11 North Park Street, Glasgow G20 7AA, Scotland.

**DOBSON, John;** Singer (Tenor); b. 1930, Derby, England. *Education:* Guildhall School of Music, with Norman Walker; Study in Italy with Giovanni Inghilleri. *Career:* Debut: Bergamo 1957, as Pinkerton; New Opera Company

1958, in Sir John in Love and A Tale of Two Cities; Glyndebourne Festival 1959, in Der Rosenkavalier; Engagements with English National Opera, Welsh National Opera and Scottish Opera; Deutsche Oper am Rhein, Düsseldorf, Orange Festival and Maggio Musicale, Florence; Covent Garden, 1959–95, in 100 roles and 2000 performances: roles include Wagner's David, Mime, Loge and Melot, Beethoven's Jacquino and Mussorgsky's Shuisky; Sang Paris in the premiere of Tippett's King Priam, Coventry, 1962; Sang Luke in the 1977 premiere of Tippett's The Ice Break; With the Royal Opera at La Scala Milan, 1976 and the Far East, 1979, 1986 and 1992; Sang Mime in the first Japanese performances of Wagner's Ring with the Deutsche Oper, 1987; Sang in the British Premiere of Berio's Un Re in Ascolto, 1989; Borsa in Rigoletto, Inn Keeper in a new production of The Cunning Little Vixen, 1990, the Emperor in Turandot; Director of Young Singers Ensemble at Covent Garden; Sang Mime in Siegfried, 1991, Jakob Glock in a new production of Prokofiev's Fiery Angel, 1992; Sang Altoun in Turandot at Covent Garden, 1994; Freelance Singer from 1995; Abbate in Andrea Chénier with the Royal Opera at the Festival Hall, 1998; Retired from singing in 1998 after a performance of the Rector (Peter Grimes) with the Royal Opera House at the Savonlinna Festival. *Recordings include:* Videos of Peter Grimes, Otello, Samson et Dalila and La Fanciulla del West. *Honours:* O.B.E., 1985. *Address:* c/o Royal Opera House (Education), Covent Garden, London WC2E 9 DD, England.

**DODD, Geraint;** Singer (Tenor); b. 1958, Rhosllanerchrugog, Wales. *Education:* Royal Northern College of Music, with Joseph Ward. *Career:* Appearances with Welsh National Opera as the Duke of Mantua, Pinkerton and Macduff; Florestan, Werther and Rodolfo for English Touring Opera; Don José in concert for WNO, 1988, and Radames for Mid Wales Opera; Other roles include Pollione in Norma (Neath Opera), Calaf, Cavaradossi in Tosca and Captain Vere in Billy Budd; Concerts include Messiah, the Verdi Requiem and The Dream of Gerontius. *Address:* Harlequin Agency Ltd, 203 Fidlas Road, Cardiff CF14 5NA, Wales.

**DODERER, Gerhard,** PhD; musicologist and organist; b. 25 March 1944, Kitzingen, Germany; m. C. Rosado Fernandes 1970. *Education:* Univ. of Würzburg, Staatskonservatorium of Würzburg. *Career:* organ recitals since 1970 in Europe and elsewhere; Prof. of Musicology, Universidade Nova de Lisboa, Portugal 1981–; mem. American, Spanish, Portuguese and German Musicological Socs. *Recordings:* albums of historical Portuguese organs. *Publications:* Portuguese Clavichords of the 18th Century 1971, Organa Hispanica (nine vols) 1971–84, Orgelmusik und Orgelbau in Portugal 1976, Domenico Scarlatti: Libro di Tocate 1991, The Organs at Braga Cathedral 1992, J. de la Té y Sagau: Cantatas Humanas a Solo (1723) 1999, L. Giustini di Pistoia: Sonate di Cimbalo di piano e forte 2002, Portugese String Keyboard Instruments of the 18th Century: Clavichords, Harpsichords, Piano and Spinets (with J. H. van der Meer) 2004. *Address:* Rua do Borja 133-B, 3A, Lisbon 1350-046, Portugal. *E-mail:* gdoderer@mail.telepac.pt.

**DODGE, Charles;** Composer; b. 5 June 1942, Ames, Iowa, USA; m. Katharine Schlefer, 1 July 1978, 1 s., 1 d. *Education:* BA, University of Iowa; MA, DMA, Columbia University; Studied composition with Richard Hervig, Darius Milhaud, Philip Bezanson, Gunther Schuller, Otto Luening, computer music with Godfrey Winheim. *Career:* Major performances: Tanglewood, 1965, 1973, 1986; Warsaw Autumn Festival, Poland, 1978, 1985, 1986; New Music, New York Festival, USA, 1979; Stockholm Festival of Electronic Music, Sweden, 1980, 1982; Venice Biennale, Italy, 1981; Calarts Festival, USA, 1983; Olympic Arts Festival, Los Angeles, 1984; New York Philharmonic, 1984; Los Angeles Philharmonic, 1984. *Compositions:* Folia; Changes; Earth's Magnetic Field; Speech Songs; Extensions; The Story of Our Lives; In Celebration; Cascando; Any Resemblance Is Purely Coincidental; The Waves; The One and the Other for chamber orchestra, 1993; That Which I Should Have Done!... for organ and tape, 1996; Just Harmonies–for Christian Wolff, 1996. *Recordings:* Earth's Magnetic Field, Nonesuch; Charles Dodge-Synthetic Speech Music. *Publications:* Computer Music; Synthesis, Composition and Performing (with Thomas A Jerse), 1985. *Contributions:* Musical Fractals, Byte Magazine, 1986. *Address:* Conservatory of Music, Brooklyn College, City University of New York, NY 11210, USA.

**DOESE, Helena;** Singer (soprano); b. 7 Aug. 1946, Göteborg, Sweden. *Education:* Studied in Göteborg, with Luigi Ricci in Rome, with Erik Werba and Gerald Moore in Vienna and with Vera Rozsa in London. *Career:* Debut: Göteborg 1971, as Aida; Bern Opera 1972–75, as Jenůfa, Micaela and Donna Anna; Royal Opera Stockholm from 1973 as Liu in Turandot, Mimi, Katya Kabanova and Eva in the Friedrich production of Die Meistersinger; Glyndebourne debut 1974, as Mozart's Countess: Fiordiligi 1975; Covent Garden from 1974 as Mimi, Gutrune in Götterdämmerung, Agathe in Der Freischütz and Amelia in Simon Boccanegra; Tatiana in Eugene Onegin for Scottish Opera; Guest appearances in Marseilles (Elisabeth de Valois), Sydney, (Aida), Paris Opéra, (Fiordiligi), Hamburg, (Agathe), San Francisco, (Countess) and Zürich (Sieglinde); Member of Frankfurt Opera: has sung title roles in Ariadne auf Naxos, Jenůfa and Iphigénie en Tauride, Countess in Capriccio, the Marschallin, and Chrysothemis in Elektra; Deutsche Oper Berlin, 1987, as Agathe followed by the Marschallin at Copenhagen; Sydney, 1988, as Eva in Die Meistersinger; Sang Rosalinde at Oslo, 1988, Tosca 1989; Season 1991/92 as Fidelio at Toronto, Elsa at Frankfurt and Ariadne at Stuttgart; Season 1994–95 sang Chrysothemis at Frankfurt, and Sieglinde; Strauss's Ariadne auf Naxos at the Teatro Colón, Buenos Aires, 1995 and

Elisabeth in Tannhäuser by Wagner at Sau Paulo in 1996. *Recordings include:* Videos of Glyndebourne Così fan tutte and Covent Garden Bohème.

**DOGHAN, Philip;** Singer (tenor); b. 1949, London, England. *Education:* BA, Durham University. *Career:* Sang as a boy in premiere of Tippett's King Priam, 1962; Sang in chorus at Glyndebourne and with the English Opera Group and English Music Theatre; English National Opera in Orfeo, the premiere of The Plumber's Gift and The Return of Ulysses; Has sung with Opera Factory in the premiere of Birtwistle's Yan Tan Tethera, 1986, La Calisto, The Knot Garden and Reimann's The Ghost Sonata; Appearances in Il Matrimomio Segreto and Les Pêcheurs de Perles in Rennes; Tom Rakewell at Cologne Opera, Alessandro in Il Re Pastore at the Théâtre des Champs Elysées; Mignon, La Straniera, La Cena delle Beffe, Elisa e Claudio and Gazzaniga's Don Giovanni at the Wexford Festival; Don Juan in The Stone Guest for the Berlin Kammeroper; Così fan tutte in Tours and Idomeneo in Metz; Concert engagements include Stravinsky's Threni for Italian Radio and appearances with Janowski, Hager, Rattle, Malgoire and Hogwood in Netherlands, Germany, Italy, Belgium and France; Sang several roles in the ENO revival of Busoni's Doctor Faust, 1990; Regular broadcasts for the BBC, Radio France and RAI; Orpheo in Lord's Masque by Castiglioni at La Fenice; Paris Opéra debut as Le Duc in Offenbach's Les Brigands, 1993; Royal Opera House, Basilo in Figaro, 1994; Cologne Opera 1995, as Tom Rakewell; Sang Britten's Aschenbach at Lubeck and in Die Wände by A.Hölszky at Frankfurt, 2000. *Honours:* Winner, Premier Grand Prix at Toulouse, 1980. *Current Management:* Athole Still International Management, Forresters Hall, 25–27 Westow Street, London, SE19 3RY, England. *Telephone:* (20) 8771-5271. *Fax:* (20) 8768-6600. *Website:* www.atholestill.com.

**DOHMEN, Albert;** Singer (Bass-Baritone); b. 1955, Krefeld, Germany. *Education:* Studied in Cologne and with Gladys Kuchta, 1977–84. *Career:* Sang at the Deutsche Oper am Rhein, Düsseldorf, 1983–85; Wiesbaden from 1986, Hamburg, 1986–87, Vienna Volksoper, 1987–90; Guest appearances at Stockholm (Assur in Semiramide, 1988), Catania (Kaspar in Der Freischütz) and Cairo, in Haydn's La Vera Costanza; Sang in the premiere of Bose's Die Leiden des Jungen Werthers at Ludwigsburg, 1986 and in the German premiere of La Princesse de Cleve by Jean Francaix; Sang Don Giovanni in festivals at Prague and Macerata, 1991; Returned to Macerata 1992, as Don Parmenione in Rossini's L'Occasione fa il Ladro. Other roles include Mozart's Count and Alfonso, Don Magnifico, the Grand Inquisitor and Verdi's Procida and Paolo, Scarpia and Gianni Schicchi; Wagner's King Henry, Biterolf, Wotan, Donner, Gunther and Amfortas; Sang Simone in Zemlinsky's Eine Florentinische Tragödie at Florence, 1996; Season 1998, as Weber's Kaspar at Rome and Jeremiah in Weill's Propheten at the London Proms; Season 2000–01 as the Wanderer at Trieste, Wotan in Die Walküre at Geneva, Scarpia for Covent Garden and the Rheingold Wotan at the Vienna Staatsoper; Concert repertoire includes the Verdi Requiem and Zemlinsky's Sieben Sinfonische Gesänge. *Recordings:* Spirit Messenger in Die Frau ohne Schatten, conducted by Solti. *Address:* c/o Volksoper, Wahringerstrasse 78, 1090 Vienna, Austria.

**DOHNÁNYI, Christoph von** (see von Dohnányi, Christoph)

**DOIG, Christopher;** Singer (Tenor); b. 4 April 1948, New Zealand. *Education:* Studied in New Zealand and with Anton Dermota at the Vienna Music Academy. *Career:* Sang at the Vienna Staatsoper from 1976 as David, Jacquino, Steuermann, Dr Caius and Remendado in Carmen; Linz Opera from 1980 as Don Ottavio, Tamino, Lionel in Martha, Fenton, Nemorino and the Duke of Mantua; Guest engagements in Vienna and at La Scala and the Salzburg Festival; Debut with Australian Opera, 1988, as Nerone in L'Incoronazione di Poppea; Sang David in Meistersinger at Sydney, conducted by Charles Mackerras; Hamburg Opera 1991, as Elemer in Arabella; Director of the New Zealand International Festival of Arts; Also sang in Jenůfa at Sydney, 1992; Maurizio in Adriana Lecouvreur, Sydney, 1992; Don José in Carmen and Erik in Fliegende Holländer, Cologne, 1992; Wozzeck, Stuttgart; Salome, Melbourne and Don José in Barcelona; Walther von Stolzing at Sydney, 1994; Sydney 1995, as Boris in Katya Kabanova. *Current Management:* Haydn Rawstron Ltd, London. *Address:* c/o Opera Australia, PO Box 291, Strawberry Hills, NSW 2012, Australia.

**DOLEZAL, Karel;** Czech viola player; *Professor, Prague Conservatory*; b. 16 Jan. 1948, Prague; m. 1974; two s. *Education:* High School of Music with Profs Cerny and Maly. *Career:* debut in Knights Hall of The Waldstein Palace, Prague 1973; solo performances at Prague Spring Festival 1976, Bratislava Music Festival 1977; music festival performances at Brno, Karlovy Vary, T. Teplice, Poland, GDR, Romania; solo concert, BBC, TV Prague and 12 concerts for Radio Prague; made biographical film with the Dolezal String Quartet (Czech Film Corpn), programmes for TV Prague, Radio NY 1981; performances at Wigmore Hall, London, Birmingham, Dublin, Prague Spring Festival, Paris Festival, Bretagne, Tonhalle Zürich, Berlin, Halle; concert tours of Austria, Spain, Scandinavia, Hungary, Tunisia etc.; radio and television programmes for Hamburg, Bremen, Frankfurt, Wiesbaden, Saarbrucken; concert tour of USA 1980; with quartet, concert tours of Japan 1993, Spain 1997, Kangasniemi Festival, Finland 1997; Prof., Prague Conservatory 1993–; concert tour in BRD 1998–99; masterclasses in Seoul, Daegu, Republic of Korea 2000. *Recordings:* 2 String Quartets by Dvořák, 1983; 2 String Quartets by Leoš Janáček, 1984; 5 albums of works by Mozart, Dvořák, Janáček, Martinů, Shostakovich, and others; Solo: Viola and piano works by: Bloch, Rubinstein, Hindemith, Matousek, 1995, Mendelssohn, Reger, Weber,

1997; Quartet: Quartets by Janáček, 1992; 2 Quartets by Dvořák, 1994; Quartets by Smetana, Fibich, 1996. *Address:* Milesovska Street 6, 130 00 Prague 3 (office); 2A Stodolou 056, 252 31 Všenory-Prague-West, Czech Republic (home). *Telephone:* 257710858 (home); 603821585 (mobile). *E-mail:* dolezalkin@volny.cz (office); dolezalkin@centrum.cz (home). *Website:* www .iumira.cz/dolezal.

**DOLLARHIDE, Thomas;** Composer and Musicologist; b. 30 Aug. 1948, Santa Rosa, California, USA. *Education:* MA and PhD, University of Michigan; Study with Leslie Bassett and William Bolcom. *Career:* Faculty of La Trobe University, 1981–89. *Compositions include:* Shadows, wind quintet, 1973; Theme and Variations, for 2 cellos, flute, clarinet and 2 speaking voices, 1976; Other Dreams, Other Dreamers, for orchestra, 1976; Shoestrings for flute and clarinet, 1977; Pluriels for orchestra, 1979; Punk for piano, 1980; By Thunder Mill Pond by trombone, 1981; Ragings of a One Pot Screamer, for piano, 1982; A Back Street for violin, 1983; Two Pieces, for piano, 1984; Madness in Paradise, for violin, viola, double bass, clarinet, guitar, mandolin and percussion, 1986; Aria for cello and piano, 1990; The Dark Horse for orchestra, 1992. *Honours:* Broadcast Music Award to Young Composers, USA, 1975–76. *Address:* c/o APRA, 1A Eden Street, Crows Nest, NSW 2065, Australia.

**DOLMETSCH, Jeanne-Marie;** Recorder Player and Treble Viol Player; b. 15 Aug. 1942, Hindhead, Surrey, England. *Education:* violin and piano, Royal Acad. of Music, 1961–64; LRAM. *Career:* Debut: Queen Elizabeth Hall, London, 1973; toured USA, Colombia, Germany, France, Ireland and Sweden with the Dolmetsch Ensemble; recorder soloist and Asst Dir, Haslemere Festival; appearances at Bath Festival, English Bach Festival; numerous radio broadcasts and television programmes. *Recordings:* collections of early music with the Dolmetsch Ensemble. *Address:* Jesses, Grayswood Road, Haslemere, Surrey, England.

**DOLMETSCH, Marguerite Mabel,** LRAM; British recorder player and viola da gamba player; b. 15 Aug. 1942, Hindhead, Surrey, England; m. Brian E. Blood. *Career:* travelled widely with the Dolmetsch Ensemble and the Dolmetsch Concertante, touring America, France, Germany, Sweden, South Africa, Colombia; Has performed at the Three Choirs Festival, Bath Festival and Haslemere Festival; Has also appeared at Queen Elizabeth Hall, Purcell Room and Wigmore Hall; Radio broadcasts and television programmes in the United Kingdom, Germany, South Africa and South America. *Recitals:* Various recitals with the Dolmetsch Ensemble; Director of the Dolmetsch Summer School and Dolmetsch Musical Instruments; Assistant Director, Haslemere Festival; mem. National Federation of Decorative and Fine Arts Societies. *Recordings:* Choice Consorts for Recorders; A Christmas Tapestry, in Words and Music; A Chest of Viols. *Address:* Heartsease, Grayswood Road, Haslemere, Surrey GU27 2BS, England.

**DOLTON, Geoffrey;** Singer (Baritone); b. 30 Dec. 1958, Shrewsbury, England. *Education:* Studied at the Royal Academy of Music with Joy Mammen; At NOS and in Milan with Peter Moores Foundation. *Career:* Debut: With Opera North, as Guglielmo in Così fan tutte, 1983; Further roles with Opera North as Mozart's Count, Lescaut in Massenet's Manon Lescaut and Henrik in the British premiere of Nielsen's Maskarade; With Opera Factory has sung Guglielmo (also televised) and Orestes in Gluck's Iphigenia operas; Manoel Theatre Malta, Figaro in Il Barbiere di Siviglia; Season 1992 as Hector in Tippett's King Priam at Antwerp, Monteverdi's Otho for Opera Factory, in Krenek's What Price Confidence? at the Almeida Festival and as Alan in Birtwistle's Yan Tan Tethera; Other roles include Papageno for Welsh National Opera and Opera Northern Ireland; Schaunard in La Bohème for Scottish Opera; Hector in King Priam for Opera North, Malatesta in Don Pasquale for New Israeli Opera and the title role in Grétry's Le Huron at the Buxton Festival, 1990; Sang Guglielmo in Così fan tutte for ENO, 1990; Recitals with the pianist Nicholas Bosworth; Season 1994, ENO Eisenstein in Die Fledermaus; Opera Northern Ireland, Figaro in the Barber of Seville; Castleward Opera Dandini in La Cenerentola; Sang in La Traviata for GTO at Glyndebourne, 1996; Season 2000, Caseyflood in John Lunn's Zoë for Glyndebourne and Channel 4; First Mate in Billy Budd in Venice; Dr Malatesta in Don Pasquale for Opera Zuid. *Recordings:* Donizetti's Emilia di Liverpool, with the Philharmonia Orchestra (Opera Rara). *Honours:* Peter Pears Prize for Recital Singing at the RAM; Honorary ARAM, 1992. *Address:* Allied Artists Agency, 42 Montpelier Square, London SW7 1JZ, England.

**DOMANINSKA, Libuse;** Singer (Soprano); b. 4 July 1924, Brno, Czechoslovakia. *Education:* Studied at the Prague Conservatory with Hana Pirkova and Bohuslav Sobesky. *Career:* Debut: Brno 1946, as Vendulka in The Kiss by Smetana; Sang at Brno in operas by Smetana and Janáček (Jenůfa, Katya Kabanova and the Vixen); Prague National Opera, 1955–85; Visited Edinburgh with the company in 1964, as Milada in Dalibor; Komische Oper Brelin 1956, Vienna Staatsoper, 1958–68; Holland Festival 1959, as Katya Kababova; Roles in Russian operas and in Mozart, Puccini and Verdi; Marenka in The Bartered Bride, Smetana's Libuše, Jenůfa, Aida, Elisabeth de Valois, Euridice and Foerster's Eva; Many concert appearances, notably in Janáček's Glagolitic Mass at La Scala; Retired 1985. *Recordings:* Glagolitic Mass, The Cunning Little Vixen, The Devil's Wall by Smetana (Supraphon). *Honours:* Artist of Merit, 1966; National Artist, 1974. *Address:* c/o National Theatre, PO Box 865, 11230 Prague 1, Czech Republic.

**DOMANSKY, Hanus;** Composer; b. 1 March 1944, Novy, Hrozenkov, Czechoslovakia. *Education:* Studied piano with Jaroslav Shanel; Composition with Jan Duchan, Brno Conservatory; Composition with Dezider Kardos, graduated 1970, Bratislava Academy of Musical Arts. *Career:* Associated with Czech Radio; Bratislava. *Compositions:* Concerto piccolo for Orchestra, 1970; Symphony, 1980; Piano Concerto, 1984; Music for Trumpet, Flute and Bass Clarinet, 1966; Musica giocosa for Violin and Piano, 1971; Dianoia for Violin, 1976; Piano pieces; Organ music; About Winter, cantata for Narrator, Children's Choir and Orchestra, 1968; Fiat lux, oratorio for Narrator, Soprano, Chorus and Orchestra, 1970; Versifying for Chorus and Percussion, 1972; Recruiting Songs for Men's Chorus, 1978; Solo Songs. *Honours:* Slovak Composers Award, 1983. *Address:* c/o Czech Radio, Bratislava, Slovakia.

**DOMINGO, Plácido,** FRCM; Spanish opera singer; *General Director, Washington Opera;* b. 21 Jan. 1941, Madrid; s. of the late Plácido and Pepita (Embil) Domingo; m. Marta Ornelas; three s. *Education:* Nat. Conservatory of Music, Mexico City. *Career:* operatic début at Monterrey, Mexico 1961; with Israel Nat. Opera for over two years; début at Metropolitan Opera, New York 1968; British début in Verdi's Requiem at Festival Hall 1969; Covent Garden début in Tosca 1971, returned to sing in Aida, Carmen 1973, La Bohème 1974, Un Ballo in Maschera 1975, La Fanciulla del West; has taken leading roles in about 120 operas; with New York City Opera 1965–; Artistic Dir Washington Opera 1994–2003, Gen. Dir 2003–; Artistic Dir LA Opera 2000–; Artistic Adviser and Prin. Guest Conductor Los Angeles Opera; Fellow, Royal N Coll. of Music; recent engagements include Tosca (conducting), Romeo and Juliet at Metropolitan Opera, New York, NY, Aida, Il Trovatore in Hamburg, Don Carlos in Salzburg, I vespri siciliani and La forza del destino in Paris, Turandot in Barcelona, Otello in Paris, London, Hamburg and Milan, Carmen in Edin., Turandot at the Metropolitan; New York stage début in My Fair Lady 1988 (213 performances by 2000); Luigi in Il Tabarro at the Met 1989; Otello at Covent Garden 1990, Lohengrin at Vienna Staatsoper, Don José at Rio de Janeiro, Otello at the Met and Barcelona; Don Carlos at Los Angeles, Dick Johnson at Chicago, Riccardo in Un Ballo in Maschera at the 1990 Salzburg Festival; debut as Parsifal at the Met 1991 and 2001, Otello at Covent Garden 1992, Siegmund in Die Walküre at the Vienna Staatsoper 1992; 1997 season included Don José and Siegmund at the Met and Gabriele Adorno in Simon Boccanegra at Covent Garden; 1999 season Herman in the Queen of Spades at the Met, and at Covent Garden 2002; concert performance of Verdi's Battaglia di Legnano with the Royal Opera 2000; Canio in Pagliacci at Covent Garden 2003; Nero in premiere of Monteverdi's Poppea in Los Angeles 2003; Rasputin in premiere of Deborah Drattell's Nicholas and Alexandra, Los Angeles 2003; opened 2002/03 Los Angeles Opera Season in Puccini's Fanciulla des West. *Films include:* Madame Butterfly with Von Karajan, La Traviata 1982, Carmen 1984, Otello 1986. *Recordings:* has made well over 100 recordings, including Aida, Un Ballo in Maschera, Tosca, Tannhäuser 1989, Die Frau ohne Schatten 1993, Gounod's Roméo et Juliette 1996, Merlin by Albeniz 2000; has made more than 50 videos. *Publications:* My First Forty Years (autobiog.) 1983, My Operatic Roles 2000. *Honours:* Dr hc (Royal Coll. of Music) 1982, (Univ. Complutense de Madrid) 1989; Hon. DMus (Univ. of Oxford) 2003; Commdr Légion d'honneur, Hon. KBE 2002, Medal of Freedom, Star of the Order of Merit (Hungary) 2005; nine Grammy Awards, European Culture Foundation Culture Prize 2003, Classic FM Gramophone Listeners' Choice Award 2005, Opera News Award 2005. *Current Management:* Vincent and Farrell Associates, Suite 740, 481 8th Avenue, New York, NY 10001, USA.

**DOMINGUEZ, Guillermo;** Singer (Tenor); b. 1961, Caracas, Venezuela. *Education:* Studied with José Castro in Caracas, then at Rome and Turin. *Career:* Debut: Treviso, 1984, as Rodolfo; Sang Rodolfo at Paris, Amiens and Munich; Zürich Opera as Don Ottavio and Ferrando and in Guillaume Tell; Appearances at Monte Carlo as Edgardo in Lucia di Lammermoor and at Innsbruck as Cavaradossi and the Duke of Mantua, 1988; National Theatre Mannheim as Alfredo and Puccini's Edgar with the Dresden Staatskapelle; Engagements in Spain as the Duke of Mantua; Many concert appearances. *Address:* c/o National Theater, Am Goetheplatz, 6B00 Mannheim, Germany.

**DOMINGUEZ, Oralia;** Singer (Contralto); b. 15 Oct. 1927, San Luis, Potosi, Mexico. *Education:* Studied at the Mexican National Conservatory. *Career:* Sang in Debussy's La Demoiselle Elue while a student; Stage debut Mexico City 1950, appeared as Amneris in 1951; Sang in Europe from 1953, London debut at the Wigmore Hall; La Scala Milan 1953 in Adriana Lecouvreur; Covent Garden 1955, as Sosostris in the premiere of The Midsummer Marriage by Tippett; Glyndebourne Festival 1955–64, as Mistress Quickly, Isabella, and Arnalta in the Leppard-Monteverdi L'Incoronazione di Poppea; Venice 1960, in Alcina, with Joan Sutherland; Sang at the Deutsche Oper am Rhein, Düsseldorf, from 1960; Guest appearances in Buenos Aires, Vienna, Frankfurt, Paris, Rome, Naples, Florence, Chicago, Dallas and New Orleans; Stuttgart Opera 1972–76; Mexico City concert, 1973. *Recordings:* Erda in The Ring, Mozart's Coronation Mass, Verdi Requiem (Deutsche Grammophon); Il Tabarro, La Gioconda (Decca). *Address:* c/o Deutsche Oper am Rhein, Heinrich-Heine Allee 16, 4000 Düsseldorf, Germany.

**DOMINGUEZ, Ruben;** Singer (Tenor); b. 4 Sept. 1940, Caracas, Venezuela. *Education:* Studied in Milan. *Career:* Debut: As Cavaradossi, Mexico City, 1967; Sang throughout the USA and in Venezuela as Donizetti's Edgardo, The Duke of Mantua, Alfredo, Riccardo in Un Ballo in Maschera, Rodolfo and Andrea Chénier; Cincinnati, 1985–86 as Radames and Manrico; Milwaukee, 1988 as Calaf; Opera North, 1986 as Ramirez in La Fanciulla del West; Teatro Colón Buenos Aires, 1992 as Cavaradossi; Other roles include: Pollione in

Norma, Opéra Nancy. *Address:* c/o Opera de Caracas, Museo del Teclado, Parque Central, Edif, Tacaqua, Mezzanina, Caracas 1010, Venezuela.

**DONADINI, Giovanna;** singer (soprano); b. 1964, Italy. *Education:* studied in Venice and Ancona. *Career:* debut: Monteverdi's Selve Morale e Spirituale, at La Fenice Venice; Mozart's Countess and Fiordiligi at Treviso, 1990–91; Season 1994 with Pamela Nubile by Farinelli at Treviso, and Camilla in Leo's Amor vuol Sofferanza at Martina Franca; Donna Elvira in Switzerland, and Galuppi's Le Nozze at Vicenza, 1996; Rossalane in Cimarosa's I Turchi Amanti at Citta di Castello, Fiordiligi in Tokyo and Mozart's Susanna at the Teatro Verdi, Sassari; Concerts include Pergolesi's Stabat Mater, Bach's Magnificat, Haydn's Stabat Mater, Beethoven's Ninth and the Four Last Songs at Treviso and Toulouse. *Honours:* 1994 Concorso Internazionale, Bilbao. *Current Management:* Atelier Musicale, Via Caselle 76, San Lazzaro di Savena 40068, Italy. *Telephone:* 051 19 98 44 44. *Fax:* 051 19 98 44 20. *E-mail:* info@ ateliermusicale.com. *Website:* www.ateliermusicale.com.

**DONAT, Zdislava;** Singer (Soprano Coloratura); b. 4 July 1939, Poznań, Poland. *Education:* Studied with Zofia Bregy in Warsaw and Gino Bechi in Siena, Italy. *Career:* Debut: Poznan 1964, as Gilda from 1971 in Teatr Wielki, Warsaw; Theater am Gärtnerplatz, Munich, as Queen of Night; Bayerische Staatsoper Munich, Hamburg, Vienna Staatsoper; London Covent Garden; La Scala, Milan; Met-Opera, New York; Teatro Colón Buenos Aires; Deutsche Oper, Berlin; San Francisco Opera; Opera in Moscow, Naples, Zürich, Frankfurt and many others; Festivals in Salzburg, 1979–87; Bregenz, Orange, Munich, Tokyo, Athens, Wroclaw and others; Roles include: Lucia di Lammermoor, La Sonnambula, Giulia in Capuleti, Norina, Constanze, Blonde, Zerlina, Olympia, Gilda, Violetta, Manon (Massenet), Martha, (Flotow), Queen in Golden Cockerel, La Princesse and Le Feu in L'Enfant et les Sortilèges by Ravel, Hanna (Moniuszko), Marzelline (Beethoven), Adele (Johann Strauss) and others; Warsaw 1991, as Giulia in I Capuleti e i Montecchi; Television productions, recitals and appearances with symphony orchestras. *Recordings include:* Die Zauberflöte, RCA, conductor J Levine; Operatic Arias, Polski Nagrania, conductor J Dobrzanski; Requiem by R Maciejewski, conductor, T Strugala. *Honours:* Grand Prix in Toulouse; Kammersängerin, Munich, 1977. *Address:* Teatr Wielki, Moliere 3, 00 076 Warsaw, Poland.

**DONATH, Helen;** American singer (soprano); b. 10 July 1940, Corpus Christi, Tex.; d. of Jimmy Erwin and Helen Hamauei; m. Klaus Donath 1965; one s. *Education:* Roy Miller High School, Del Mar Coll., Texas. *Career:* studied with Paola Novikova, later with husband Klaus Donath (by whom all song-recitals are accompanied); début at Cologne Opera House 1962, at Hanover Opera House 1963–68, Bayerische Staatsoper, Munich 1968–72; guest appearances in London (Covent Garden), Vienna, Milan, San Francisco, Lisbon, New York, etc.; has given concerts in all maj. European and American cities; over 100 recordings 1962–. *Major roles include:* Pamina in Die Zauberflöte, Zerlina in Don Giovanni, Eva in Die Meistersinger, Sophie in Der Rosenkavalier, Susanna in Le Nozze di Figaro, Anne Trulove in The Rake's Progress, Ilia in Idomeneo, Micaela in Carmen. *Honours:* Pope Paul Medal, Salzburg 50 Year Anniversary Medal, Bratislava Festival Award, Deutscher Schallplattenpreis and Grosses Lob for her first song recital recording, Lower Saxony Prize for Culture 1990. *Address:* c/o Shaw Concerts, 1900 Broadway, New York, NY 10023, USA (office); Bergstrasse 5, D-3002 Wedemark 1, Germany.

**DONATI, Walter;** Singer (Tenor); b. 4 Sept. 1938, Potsdam, Germany. *Career:* Sang in Italy from 1983, notably at Treviso as Erik in Der fliegende Holländer, at La Scala in Tannhäuser, I Lombardi and Macbeth; Sang Don Carlos at Dublin (1985), Radames at Avignon (1986), and Dick Johnson at Buenos Aires; Further appearances at Venice as Foresto in Attila, at Florence as Dimitri in Boris Godunov, Paris Opéra as Raimbaut in Robert le Diable (1985), returning as Pollione (1988); Manrico at Covent Garden (1990); Baritone from 1995 (Nabucco at Lonigo near Verona); Amonasro at Earl's Court, London, 1998; Sang Gleb in Giordano's Siberia at Wexford, 1999, and Nabucco at St Margreth 2000. *Address:* c/o Théâtre National de l'Opéra, 8 Rue Scribe, 75009 Paris, France.

**DONCEANU, Felicia;** Composer; b. 28 Jan. 1931, Bacau, Romania. *Education:* Bucharest Conservatory. *Career:* former Ed. of Editura Musicala, Bucharest. *Compositions include:* Spinet Sonata 1983, Moldavian Echoes, suite for Strings 1985, Three Symphonic Sketches 1982, The Clever Bell, chorus 1986, Inscription On A Mast, for Harp 1989, The Music Lesson, song 1992. *Honours:* Composition Prize, Romanian Composers' Union. *Address:* GEMA, Postfach 301240, 10722 Berlin, Germany.

**DONNELLY, Malcolm (Douglas);** Opera Singer (Baritone); b. 8 Feb. 1943, Sydney, Australia; m. Dolores Ryles. *Education:* Sydney Conservatory and Opera School; London Opera Centre. *Career:* Debut: Australian Opera, 1966; Australian Opera, Scottish Opera, English National Opera, Opera North, Netherlands Opera, Victoria State Opera, State Opera South Australia, Welsh National Opera, Royal Opera House, Covent Garden, English National Opera Tour, Moscow, Leningrad, 1991, Adelaide Festival 1991; Appearances at Edinburgh Festival, 1975, 1976; Wexford Festival, 1977, 1978; Glyndebourne, 1979, 1981, 1985; Hong Kong Festival, 1987; Brighton International Festival, 1988; Roles include, Macbeth, Simon Boccanegra, Rigoletto, Pizarro (Fidelio); Sang Kurwenal in Tristan und Isolde for Australian Opera, 1990, Macbeth with ENO on tour to Russia, Scarpia with Scottish Opera and Shishkov in From the House of the Dead for Welsh National Opera, 1990; Season 1992 in

Ovations concert by ENO at the Barbican Hall, Don Carlos in Ernani for Welsh National Opera and Ford in Falstaff for the English National Opera; Boccanegra and Iago in Australia; Sharpless, Royal Opera House, Covent Garden; Kurwenal for Australian Opera, Macbeth and Telramund (Lohengrin) ENO, 1993; Di Luna (Il Trovatore) Victoria State Opera, Kurwenal (Tristan und Isolde) Scottish Opera; Verdi Requiem, Guildford Cathedral, 1994; Scarpia, Lyric Opera of Queensland; Nabucco, Australian Opera; Falstaff, State Opera South Australia, 1995; Sang Iago at Sydney, 1996; Janáček's Forester, 1997; Butterfly, Royal Albert Hall, Australian Opera, Alberich in Wagner's Ring Cycle, State Opera of South Australia, 1998. *Recordings:* Videos of Lucia di Lammermoor and Un Ballo in Maschera, Australian Opera. *Honours:* Sydney Sun Aria Competition, 1969; Australian Opera Auditions Scholarship, 1970. *Current Management:* Jenifer Eddy, Melbourne. *Address:* PO Box 464, Ryde 2112, New South Wales, Australia.

**DONNELLY, Patrick;** Singer (Bass-Baritone); b. 15 March 1955, Sydney, Australia. *Education:* Studied at the Conservatorium of Music, Sydney and at the Guildhall School of Music, London. *Career:* Concert debut at Sydney Opera House in Belshazzar's Feast by Walton; Also appeared at Tiresias (Oedipus Rex) and in the Monteverdi Vespers; Sang with Glyndebourne Chorus on the 1983 Tour, solo debut as Theseus in A Midsummer Night's Dream, 1985; Festival and Tour appearances in Idomeneo (Neptune), Don Giovanni (Masetto), La Traviata, Le nozze di Figaro (Bartolo) and L'Incoronzione di Poppea; Other roles include Mozart's Figaro for Opera 80, First Minister in Cendrillon at the Wexford Festival and Bartók's Bluebeard at the Barbican; Sang Polyphemus in Acis and Galatea on tour in France, Hayden in the premiere of 63 Dream Palace by Jurgen Bose in Berlin, 1990, and the Herald in Lohengrin for Australian Opera, October 1990; Licone and Caronte in Haydn's Orlando Paladino at Garsington, Oxford; Mozart's Figaro at Grange Park, 1998; Concerts at most major London centres, including Stravinsky's Renard at the Queen Elizabeth Hall. *Recordings:* Renard with the Matrix Ensemble; Pergolesi's La Serva Padrona (Meridan).

**DONOHOE, Peter Howard,** BMus, ARCM, FRNCM; British pianist; b. 18 June 1953, Manchester; s. of Harold Donohoe and Marjorie Donohoe (née Travis); m. Elaine Margaret Burns 1980; one d. *Education:* Chetham's School of Music, Royal Manchester Coll. of Music, Univ. of Leeds; teachers include Derek Wyndham and Yvonne Loriod, Paris. *Career:* professional solo pianist 1974–; appears several times each season with major symphony orchestras in London and rest of UK and performs regularly at the Promenade Concerts 1979–; performances with the LA Philharmonic, Chicago, Boston, Pittsburgh, Cincinnati, Dallas, Detroit and Cleveland orchestras and in Europe with Berlin Philharmonic and Symphony, Leipzig Gewandhaus, Dresden Philharmonic, Vienna Symphony, Czech Philharmonic, Swedish Radio and Radio France Philharmonic orchestras and Maggio Musicale Fiorentino; has also performed at Edin. Festival, Schleswig-Holstein Music Festival, La Roque d'Anthéron, France, and Festival of the Ruhr; recordings include Messiaen's Turangalila Symphony (EMI) 1986, Dominic Muldowney Piano Concerto 1986 and Tchaikovsky's Piano Concerto No. 2 1986 (Gramophone magazine's Concerto of the Year) 1988, Brahms Piano Concerto No. 1, Liszt, Berg and Bartok Sonatas, Beethoven, Diabelli Variations and Sonata Opus 101, Rachmaninov Preludes, Four British Concertos with Northern Sinfonia; Founder, Artistic Dir British Piano Concerto Foundation; Vice-Pres. Birmingham Conservatoire of Music. *Honours:* Hon. DMus (Birmingham) 1992, (Univ. of Cen. England); Hon. DLitt (Warwick) 1996; jt winner Moscow Int. Tchaikovsky Competition 1982, Grand Prix Int. du Disque (Liszt), Gramophone Concerto Award (Tchaikovsky). *Address:* c/o Askonas Holt Ltd, Lonsdale Chambers, 27 Chancery Lane, London, WC2A 1PF, England (office).

**DONOSE, Ruxandra;** Singer (Mezzo-Soprano); b. 2 Sept. 1964, Bucharest, Romania. *Education:* Academy of Music, Ciprian Porumbescu, Bucharest. *Career:* Debut: Bellini's Romeo and Varvara in Katya Kabanova at Basle, 1991; Rossini's Rosina at Vienna, Hamburg, Toulon and São Paulo; Carmen at Vienna, Leipzig and Prague; Mozart's Cherubino at Dresden, Dorabella in Vienna and Sesto at Covent Garden; Offenbach's Nicklausse and Monteverdi's Poppea at San Francisco; Appearances as Varvara in Vienna, Feodor (Boris Godunov) at the Salzburg Festival, Annio in La Clemenza di Tito at Glyndebourne (1998) and Covent Garden (2000); Season 1999 with Strauss's Composer at Minneapolis and L'Enfant et les Sortilèges at Carnegie Hall; Sang Mozart's Sesto at Glyndebourne, 1999, Annio at Covent Garden and Mèlisande at Cincinnati, 2000; Engaged as Charlotte in Werther at Covent Garden, 2004. *Recordings:* Das Lied von der Erde and Bach's B minor Mass. *Honours:* Best Young Singer of Romania, 1989; ARD Competition, Munich, 1990; Marian Anderson Vocal Arts Competition, Special Prize, 1991. *Current Management:* Columbia Artists, New York. *Address:* Hebragasse 4/10, 1090 Vienna, Austria.

**DOOLEY, Jeffrey Michael,** BA; American singer (countertenor) and choral conductor; b. 7 Oct. 1945, Milwaukee, WI. *Education:* Milton Coll., Milton, Wisconsin Conservatory, apprenticeship with Mark Deller, Deller Consort, Canterbury, England. *Career:* debut, Carnegie Hall, 1977; regular appearances in Early Music scene, New York: Basically Bach (Lincoln Center), Clarion Concerts, Amor Artis Ensemble, Waverly Consort, Boston Early Music Festival Orchestra, Milwaukee Symphony Orchestra, Connecticut Symphony; Recital-lecture presentations, The Art of the Counter-Tenor, duo with Richard Kolb, lutenist, founder of The Gotham Consort; Founder, Director, The Stuyvesant Singers, Toronto, Canada; Ongoing appearances with the following Baroque Orchestras: Tafelmusik, Toronto, Ars Musica,

Michigan, Levin Baroque Ensemble, Amor Artis Ensemble, Concert Royal, ARTEC Ensemble, New York; European appearances, Madeira Bach Festival, 1981; Stour Music, England, 1985; Amor Artis tour, Switzerland and Italy, 1991; Specialist in the Handel Oratorio, frequently giving masterclasses in interpretation of the arias, and performing; mem, Early Music, America; International Society of Early Music Singers. *Recordings:* Henry Purcell: Airs and Duets, Nonesuch; J. S. Bach: Mass in B Minor, Nonesuch; Johannes Ockeghem: Masses, Nonesuch; G Dufay: Masses, Nonesuch; J. S. Bach: St John Passion, Newport Classic; G F Handel: Acis and Galatea, Newport; H Schütz: St Matthew Passion, Newport. *Publications:* contrib. to The Counter-Tenor Voice Defined, 1977; The Counter-Tenor's Roles in Music, 1982. *Address:* 229 E 11th Street, New York, NY 10003, USA.

**DOOLEY, William;** Singer (Baritone); b. 9 Sept. 1932, Modesto, California, USA. *Education:* Studied at the Eastman School of Music and in Munich with Viktoria Prestel and Hedwig Fichtmuller. *Career:* Debut: Heidelberg 1957, as Posa in Don Carlos; Sang at Bielefeld 1959–62; Member of the Deutsche Oper Berlin from 1962, notably in the premieres of Montezuma by Sessions (1964), Gespenstersonate by Reimann (1984) and Rihm's Oedipus, 1987; Salzburg Festival 1964, as Lucio Silla and 1966 in the premiere of The Bassarids by Henze; Metropolitan Opera from 1964, as Amonasro, Eugene Onegin, the villains in Les Contes d'Hoffmann, Telramund, Orestes (Elektra) and Mandryka; Hamburg Staatsoper 1967, as Iago and 1979 in the premiere of Jakob Lenz by Wolfgang Rihm; Guest appearances at the Royal Opera Stockholm from 1967; Other roles include: Berg's Wozzeck and Dr Schön, Pizarro, Kothner, Macbeth, Escamillo, Nick Shadow, Captain Mary (Die Soldaten) and Goryanchikov in From the House of the Dead; Sang Eagle in the premiere of Los Alamos by Marc Neikrug at Berlin, 1989; Santa Fe 1991, as Tiresias in Oedipus by Wolfgang Rihm. *Recordings include:* Telramund in Lohengrin (RCA); Jakob Lenz (Harmonia Mundi). *Address:* c/o Deutsch Oper Berlin, Richard Wagnerstrasse 10, 100 Berlin, Germany.

**DOONER, Daniel;** stage director; b. 1955, Ottawa, Canada. *Education:* Universities of London and Toronto. *Career:* Associate director with many British opera companies; Revivals of Rigoletto, Così fan tutte and La Traviata (2001) for the Royal Opera; Janáček's The Makropulos Case at the Brooklyn Academy for Glyndebourne Festival; Lucia di Lammermoor for Welsh National Opera at Malaga and The Magic Flute for English Touring Opera; Rigoletto, Cav and Pag, Donizetti's Betly, Il Barbiere di Siviglia and Puccini double bill for Opera Europa at Holland Park, London. *Address:* c/o Royal Opera House, Bow Street, Covent Garden, London, WC2E 9DD, England.

**DOORNBUSCH, Paul;** Composer and Sonologist; b. 30 Dec. 1959, Melbourne, Australia. *Education:* BMus, University of Melbourne, 1984; Postgraduate degree, Computer Science, University of Melbourne, 1990; Postgraduate studies in Sonology, Electronic Music, and Composition, Royal Conservatory of Holland, 1993, 1994. *Career:* Staff member, Royal Conservatory of Holland, 1995; Sound installation, Alive, International Computer Music Conference, 1996; Compositional residency for Strepidus Somnus, STEIM, Amsterdam; Member, EU Committee to implement centre for aural art, Macedonia, 1998; Senior Sonologist, I-Cubed Virtual Reality Centre, RMIT University, 2000; Research Fellow, Department of Computer Science, University of Melbourne, 2000; mem, International Computer Music Association. *Compositions:* Continuity 2, for recorder, quartet and electronics; Continuity 1, for electronics; Strepidus Somnus, for voices and electronics; Oxidization, for percussion and electronics; Corrosion, for percussion and electronics; Lorenz, for piano; ACT 5, for bassoon and percussion; G4, for electronics; MFPG, for electronics; Structured Luck, for bassoon and electronics; Asfixiation, for flute and electronics; On The Fence, medium ensemble and electronics; Iceberg, for electronics; Preludes, for 4 voices; M1 and M2, for soloist and electronics. *Recordings:* Corrosion, The Works of Paul Doornbusch. *Publications:* The Frog Peak Collaboration Project, 1998; Corrosion, 2001; Book: The Music of CSIRAC, 2001; Computer software. *Contributions:* Numerous newspaper articles; Several for The Age. *Address:* 5 Newton Street, Glenroy, VIC 3046, Australia.

**DORAN, Seán;** Irish/Australian theatre director; b. 1958, Derry, Northern Ireland. *Education:* Univ. of East Anglia and Goldsmiths Coll., London. *Career:* dir music-theatre co., Bloomsbury, London 1988; Chief Exec. UK Year of Literature and Writing, NI 1995; Artistic Dir Belfast Festival, NI 1997–99; Dir Perth Int. Arts Festival, Australia 1999–2003; Artistic Dir and Chief Exec. ENO, London 2003–05.

**DORDI, Patrizia;** Singer (Soprano); b. 1956, Italy. *Education:* Studied at the Accademia di Santa Cecilia, Rome. *Career:* Debut: Rome, 1979, in Schumann's Manfred; Opera debut in Handel's Ariodante at La Scala, 1980; Guest at La Fenice, Venice, as Lisa in La Sonnambula and Mathilde in Guillaume Tell; Naples as Elmira in Jommelli's La schiava liberata and at Catania as Amor in Orfeo ed Euridice; Other repertory includes Micaela, Sabina in Cimarosa's Gli Orazi ed i Curiazi, Pamina (Ravenna Festival), Mimi and Musetta; Zürich Opera 1992, as Mathilde in Guillame Tell.

**DORFMÜLLER, Joachim,** DrPhilHabil; German academic; b. 13 Dec. 1938, Wuppertal; m. Ursula Petschelt 1976; one s. two d. *Education:* Univs of Cologne and Marburg, studied piano and organ with father, Musikhochschule, Cologne. *Career:* teacher of music, mathematics and Latin, Gymnasium 1969–78, Univ. of Duisburg 1978–84, Univ. of Münster 1984–, Music Acad., Cologne 1984–98; founder, Artistic Dir, Wuppertaler Orgeltage 1973–2002; over 2,800 concerts on organ and piano in 21 countries including the USA and

Japan; mem. Humboldt-Akademie der Wissenschaften 1990, Norwegian Agder Acad. of Sciences and Letters 2004; Pres., Deutsche Edvard Grieg-Gesellschaft 1993; Research Group of the Norwegian Acad. of Science and Letters 1997. *Recordings include:* Virtuoso organ music of the Romantic period; Famous Organ works by Saint-Saëns; Piano works by Grieg; Meditations: Bach, Bernstein and Messiaen; Bach to Rachmaninov; Bach to Ligeti. *Publications include:* Norweg Klaviermusik 1900–1950, 1968; Zeit-genöss Orgelmusik 1960–84, 1985; 300 Jahre Orgelbau im Wuppertal, 1988; Geschichte des Sinfonieorchesters Wuppertal, 1991; Wuppertaler Musik-geschichte, 1995; Geistl. Musik von Grieg, 2000; Geschichte der Orgelmusik, 2006; contrib. more than 500 articles for Herder-Musiklexikon, Rheinische Musikerbiographien; Musik in Geschichte und Gegenwart; national and international journals. *Honours:* Director of Church Music 1990, Cultural Prize of the Rhineland 1993, Bundesverdienstkreuz 2004. *Address:* Ring-elstraße 22, 42289 Wuppertal, Germany.

**DORFMÜLLER, Kurt,** DPhil; German musicologist and librarian; b. 28 April 1922, Munich; m. Liselotte Laubmann; two s. *Education:* Univ. of Munich. *Career:* Bavarian State Library 1954–84, including Head of Music Collection 1963, Head of Acquisitions Division 1969–, Vice-Dir 1972; hon. mem. Int. Asscn of Music Libraries, Int. Inventory of Musical Sources. *Publications:* Studien zur Lautenmusik in der ersten Hälfte des 16 Jahrhunderts, 1967; Beiträge zur Beethoven-Bibliographie, 1977; Bestandsaufbau an wissenschaf-tlichen Bibliotheken, 1989; Musik in Bibliotheken, 1997; New ed. (with Norbert Gertsch) of Das Werk Beethovens... von Georg Kinsky and Hans Halm 2006; contrib. musicology and library science articles to journals, Festschriften and library exhibition catalogues. *Honours:* Ars Jocundissima Festschrift für Kurt Dorfmüller 1984. *Address:* Gabriel-von-Seidl-Strasse 39, 82031 Grünwald, Germany (home).

**DORING, Ute;** Singer (Mezzo-soprano); b. 4 June 1963, Berlin. *Education:* Studied in Berlin with Luisa Bosabalian. *Career:* Sang in opera at Kassel, 1990; Ulm, 1991–95; Roles have included Mozart's Cherubino and Idamante, Rossini's Rosina and Angelina and Octavian in Der Rosenkavalier; Schuber-tiade concerts at Feldkirch from 1995; Season 1995–96 as Flower Maiden in Parsifal at Bayreuth and roles in Eugene Onegin, Die Zauberflote, Otello and Figaro, Cologne; Frequent concert engagements; Nicklausse in Les Contes d'Hoffmann at Cologne; 1994–1997 Schubertiade Concerts Feldkirch, 1999 Wiener Klangbogen: Lieder-Recital and Sycorax in Faust by Spohr; Marie in Wozzeck: 1997 at Wuppertal, 2000 at Osnabrück and at Bonn, 1998 at Milan Scala as 2. Dame in Zauberflöte and in 2000 as Margret in Wozzeck, 2002 Debut in U.S.A, San Francisco Opera as Varvara in Kat'a Kabanova; 1999 and 2000 as Hansel in Frankfurt, 2001 als Leonore in Fidelio at Osnabrück; Season 2003 as Orlofsky at Cologne, Wozzeck - Marie at Wiesbaden and Gutrune (Götterdämmerung) at Cologne. *Current Management:* Balmer & Dixon Management AG, Kreuzstrasse 82, 8032 Zürich, Switzerland. *Telephone:* (43) 244-8644. *Fax:* (43) 244-8649. *Website:* www.badix.ch.

**DORN, Dieter;** German theatre director; *Manager, Bayerisches Staatsschauspiel;* b. 31 Oct. 1935, Leipzig. *Education:* Theaterhochschule, Leipzig and Max-Reinhardt-Schule, Berlin. *Career:* actor, producer and dir in Hanover 1958–68; Dir in Essen and Oberhausen 1968–70; Dir at Deutsches Schauspielhaus, Hamburg 1971, Burgtheater, Vienna 1972, 1976; Dir at Staatliche Schauspielbühnen, Berlin 1972–75, Salzburg Festival 1974, 1982, 1986; Chief Dir Münchner Kammerspiele (producing works by Lessing, Goethe, Büchner, Shakespeare etc.) 1976–83, Man. (Intendant) 1983–2001; Man. (Intendant) Bayerisches Staatsschauspiel 2001–; has also directed opera productions in Vienna, Munich, Kassel, New York and at Salzburg, Bayreuth and Ludwigsburg festivals; mem. Akademie der Künste, Berlin, Bayerische Akademie der Schönen Künste. *Address:* Bayerisches Staatsschauspiel, Max-Joseph-Platz 1, 80539 Munich, Germany (office). *Telephone:* (21) 852000 (office). *Fax:* (21) 852005 (office). *E-mail:* annette.fiebelkorn@st-schauspiel .bayern.de (office). *Website:* www.bayerischesstaatsschauspiel.de (office).

**DORNBUSCH, Hans;** Swedish singer (tenor); b. 1946, Gothenburg. *Educa-tion:* Stockholm Acad., School of the Royal Opera. *Career:* debut, Stockholm 1969 as Calaf; mem., Royal Swedish Opera, Stockholm from 1970, notably as Manrico, Otello, Pinkerton, Turiddu, Andres in Wozzeck and the Steuermann in Fliegende Holländer; sang Pope Alexander VII in the premiere of Christina, by Hans Gefors 1986; character roles in Albert Herring and Hansel und Gretel; guest appearances in England and Germany; frequent concert engagements. *Address:* c/o Kungliga Operan AB, PO Box 16094, 103 22 Stockholm, Sweden.

**DOROW, Dorothy;** Singer (Soprano); b. 1930, London, England. *Education:* Studied at Trinity College, London. *Career:* Sang in London from 1958, notably in BBC Invitation Concerts (Webern conducted by John Carewe, and the British premiere of Herzgewächse by Schoenberg, 1960); Has sung in the premieres of works by Birtwistle, Nono, Maderna, Dallapiccola, Bussotti, Ligeti, Boulez, Goehr and Bennett (The Ledge, Sadler's Wells, 1961); Sang Hilde Mack in the British premiere of Henze's Elegy for Young Lovers, Glyndebourne 1961; Lived in Sweden 1963–77, Netherlands from 1977: Professor of Voice at the Conservatoire of Amsterdam and The Hague; Masterclasses in Europe and Scandinavia; Concerts and opera in Italy, at La Scala, Venice, Rome, Florence and Bologna (Le Grand Macabre by Ligeti); Repertoire from Monteverdi to the 20th Century; Covent Garden debut 1983, as Stravinsky's Nightingale.

**DOSS, Mark;** Singer (Bass); b. 1960, Chicago, USA. *Career:* Sang Merlin in Purcell's King Arthur at St Louis, 1989; Season 1990 as Sarastro at the Glyndebourne Festival and Mozart's Publio at Chicago; New Orleans, 1991, as Rossini's Basilio, and Britten's Collatinus at San Diego; Season 1992 as Sparafucile in Rigoletto with Canadian Opera, Toronto, and in the premiere of Alice by Anthony Davis, at Philadelphia; Escamillo in Carmen at Brussels; Nourabad in Les Pêcheurs de perles and Water Spirit in Rusalka at San Diego, 1993–95; Other roles include Hercules in Gluck's Alceste at Chicago; Season 1998 as Frère Laurent in Roméo et Juliette at San Diego, Escamillo at San Francisco and High Priest in Samson et Dalila for Cincinnati Opera; Sang Escamillo at Chicago and Ravenna, Rossini's Mustafà at Turin, 2000. *Honours:* Winner, George London Competition, Washington, 1987. *Address:* San Diego Opera, PO Box 988, San Diego, CA 92112, USA.

**DOUFEXIS, Stella;** singer (mezzo-soprano); b. 1968, Frankfurt am Main, Germany. *Education:* Hochschule der Künste, Berlin, studied with Anna Reynolds, masterclasses with Dietrich Fischer-Dieskau and Aribert Reimann. *Career:* debut in Dido and Aeneas, Berlin, 1992; concert engagements in Schubert's Lazarus, under Fischer-Dieskau, Pergolesi's Stabat Mater (Kon-zerthaus, Berlin), Ravel's Shéhérazade, under Ashkenazy, and Janáček's Glagolitic Mass; Season 1995–96 at the Heidelberg Opera, as Cherubino, Hansel, Nicklause, Gluck's Orfeo and in the German premiere of Birtwistle's Second Mrs Kong; British debut at the Wigmore Hall in the International Songmakers series; Season 1996–97 in Provenzale's La Stellidaura Vendicata and Second dame in Die Zauberflöte at La Monnaie, Brussels; Rosina at Heidelberg; Schubert Lieder in Berlin and Lucerne, the Masses with the Deutsches Symphony Orchestra; Season 1998–99 with Der Rosenkavalier for Scottish Opera, Falstaff under Claudio Abbado in Ferrara, Berlin and the Salzburg Easter and Sumer Festival, 2001; with Berlioz's Les Troyens and Janacek's Da schlaue Füchslein, Munich Staatsoper, 2002; debut Liceu Barcelona in Felipe Pedrell's Els Pirineus, 2003. *Recordings include:* Webern, Dessau, Blacher and Fortner Lieder; Glagolitic Mass; Schumann series with Graham Johnson; Orchestra Songs of Joseph Marx with Steven Sloane. *Current Management:* Künstlersekretariat amGasteig, Rosenheimer str. 52, 81669 Munich, Germany.

**DOUGLAS, Barry,** OBE; Irish pianist and conductor; b. 23 April 1960, Belfast, Northern Ireland; s. of Barry Douglas and Sarah Jane Douglas (née Henry); m. Deirdre O'Hara; two s. one d. *Education:* Royal Coll. of Music, London with John Barstow. *Career:* pvt. study with Maria Curcio; London debut, Wigmore Hall 1981; toured Europe 1986–; regularly performs in USA; other concerts in Japan, USSR, Australia, Iceland, Czechoslovakia; recital debut in Carnegie Hall, New York 1988; Artistic Dir Camerata Ireland; winner of Tchaikovsky Piano Competition, Moscow 1986; tours USA, S America, Russia, Europe, Australia; has given numerous premieres of contemporary music by Buckley, Wilson, McCabe, Penderecki and O'Leary. *Recordings include:* Tchaikovsky Concertos Nos 1, 2 and 3, Sonata in G, Brahms Concerto No. 1, Piano Quintet in F Minor, Liszt concertos and Sonata in B Minor, Beethoven, Mussorgsky, Prokofiev, Rachmaninov Concerto No. 2, Berg, Reger, Strauss, Debussy, Britten, Corigliano, Penderecki Piano Concerto (with composer conducting). *Television:* Rhapsody in Belfast (BBC documentary) 1978, After the Gold (ITV) 1987, Playing for Peace Sky Artsworld) 2001. *Honours:* Hon. FRCM; Hon. DMus (Belfast); Diploma Royal Coll. of Music, Emmy Award for Concerto, (Channel 4 TV programme) 1993, Diapason d'Or for Reger/Strauss recording 1998. *Current Management:* IMG Artists, Lovell House, 616 Chiswick High Road, London, W4 5RX, England. *Telephone:* (20) 8233-5800 (office). *Fax:* (20) 8233-5801 (office). *Website:* www .camerata-ireland.com (office); www.barrydouglas.com (home).

**DOUGLAS, James,** LRAM, ARCM; British composer, organist and accompa-nist; b. 4 July 1932, Dumbarton, Scotland; m. Helen Torrance Fairweather 1968; two s. one d. *Education:* Heriot Watt College, Edinburgh, Conservatoire, Paris, Hochschule, Munich, Mozarteum, Salzburg. *Career:* debut at Wiener-saal, Salzburg, 1951; Dir, Eschenbach Editions, Caritas Records, Caritas Voices and Caritas Ensemble; Professor, Académie des Sciences Humaines Universelles, Paris, 1992–; mem. MPA, PRS, MCPS, PPL, BPI, British Academy of Composers and Songwriters. *Compositions:* 15 symphonies, 15 string quartets, 20 orchestral works, 200 songs, organ works, piano and organ works, flute works, chamber and instrumental works; The Christ Church Sequence (75 chamber works), four operas: Mask, The King, Molière, Cuthbert; choral works. *Recordings:* A Vision 2000, Cloud of Unknowing 2001, Visions of Glory 2001, Cry of the Deer 2001, eight CDs in the Caritas Live series 2002–04. *Publications:* The Music of Hermann Reutter 1966. *Address:* c/o Eschenbach Editions, 28 Dalrymple Crescent, Edinburgh, EH9 2NX, Scotland. *E-mail:* eschenbach@caritas-music.co.uk. *Website:* www .caritas-music.co.uk.

**DOUGLAS, Nigel;** Singer (Tenor), Director, Writer, Broadcaster and Lecturer; b. 9 May 1929, Lenham, Kent, England; m. Alexandra Roper, 21 July 1973, 1 s., 2 d. *Education:* Magdalen College, Oxford University; Musikakademie, Vienna, Austria. *Career:* Debut: Rodolfo in La Bohème, Vienna Kammeroper, 1959; Leading roles in opera houses and festivals, Aldeburgh, Antwerp, Barcelona, Basel, Berne, Brussels, Buenos Aires, Covent Garden, Düsseldorf, Duisburg, Edinburgh, English National Opera, Garsing-ton, Glyndebourne, Hamburg; Sadler's Wells, Scottish Opera, Venice, Lisbon, Vienna Volksoper, Welsh National Opera, Wexford, Zürich, Tokyo, Catania, Paris-Bastille, Seoul, New York and others; Repertoire of 80 roles including Peter Grimes, Captain Vere (Billy Budd), Aschenbach (Death in Venice),

Eisenstein (Fledermaus), Danilo (Merry Widow), Loge (Rheingold), Herod (Salome), Captain (Wozzeck), Hauk-Sendorf (Makropulos Case); Has written and presented over 300 programmes on opera and operetta for BBC Radio 2, 3, 4 and World Service; Regular television appearances in the United Kingdom and Europe; Directed numerous productions for Sadler's Wells, Australian Opera, Royal Flemish Opera. *Recordings:* Owen Wingrave; Salome; Zigeunerbaron; Various recitals. *Publications:* English versions of Die Csardasfürstin (Kalman), 1982, Gräfin Mariza (Kalman), 1983, Merry Widow (Lehar), 1983; Legendary Voices, 1992; More Legendary voices, 1994; The Joy of Opera, 1997; Lectures on various aspects of opera and operetta in London, Edinburgh, Zürich, Vienna, New York, Cleveland, Los Angeles, Sydney, Canberra, Brisbane. *Contributions:* Numerous articles to Times Literary Supplement; Opera Magazine; BBC Music Magazine. *Honours:* Nominated for Royal Philharmonic Society Book Prize 1993, Worshipful Company of Musicians' Sir Charles Santley Memorial Prize 2003. *Current Management:* Music International, UK. *Address:* Eythorne House, Eythorne, Dover, Kent CT 15 4 BE, England.

**DOUŠA, Eduard,** PhD, MGA; Czech composer and teacher; *Vice-Director, Prague Conservatory*; b. 31 Aug. 1951, Prague; m. 1976; two s. *Education:* gymnasium, Charles Univ., Prague, Acad. of Musical Arts, Prague. *Career:* teacher of theory of music, Conservatoire, Prague; teacher of theory of music, Philosophical Faculty, Prague 1986–, Conservatoire Prague 1995–; mem. Soc. of Czech Composers, Collegium (soc. for contemporary music) (chair. 2003–). *Compositions include:* Sonata for Organ; Variations on a Baroque Theme for Strings; Miniatures for Piano (for children); Sonatine for clarinet and piano (for children); Rhapsody for Clarinet and Piano; Three short suites for guitar (for children); Concerto for four saxophones and orchestra, 1993; Romantic Fantasy for two pianos, 1995; Fantasia for trumpet and organ, 1995; Uno per quattro per flauto, oboe, chittern ed violoncello, 1996; Imaginations for violin and guitar, 1997; Motorico for violin solo, 1997; Summer Sonatine for soprano saxophone and piano, 1999; Sonata drammatica for piano, 2001; Sonata brevis accordion 2001; Concerto for violin, accordion, guitar and strings, 2000; Concert music for violoncello, 2000; Concerto for violin and chamber orchestra, 2003; Concert music for violoncello and brass instruments, 2003. *Recordings:* Rhapsody for clarinet and piano, 1989; Variations on a Baroque Theme for strings, 1988; Miniatures for flute, violin, violoncello and harpsichord, 1990; Concerto for four saxophones, 1995; Many compositions were recorded for Czechoslovak Radio: Concertino for trumpet and orchestra, Sonata for piano, String-quartet, Romantic Phantasy for violin and piano, Rhapsody for clarinet and piano, Dialogue for oboe and piano and many compositions for children, musical fairy tales, songs, choirs; theoretical work on the history of Czech music for children. *Publications:* articles and radio lectures on history of Czech music. *Address:* Tenisová 9, 102-00 Prague 10, Czech Republic. *Telephone:* 241767226 (home). *E-mail:* dousa@prgcons.cz (office); eda.dousa@seznam.cz (home).

**DOWLING, Richard William;** American concert pianist; b. 6 Sept. 1962, Houston, TX. *Education:* BM, Summa Cum Laude, University of Houston, 1985; MM, Yale University, 1987; DMA, Piano Performance, University of Texas, Austin, 1990; Principal Teacher, Abbey Simon; Additional Studies with Jeanne-Marie Darre at Le Conservatoire de Musique, Nice and at Ecole Normale de Musique, Paris, France; Yale Norfolk Summer School and Music Festival, Connecticut, USA. *Career:* Debut: With Fort Worth Symphony, Texas, 1981; Solo Recitals throughout USA; PBS television solo recital programme debut aired nationally, 1986; Recital tour, France, 1991; Concerto appearances with Oklahoma Symphony, Houston Civic Symphony, Shreveport (Louisiana) Symphony, Midland-Odessa (Texas) Symphony, Brazos Valley (Texas) Symphony, Yale Trumbull Symphony, Arkansas Symphony; Concerto appearances with Jupiter Symphony, Tully Hall, Lincoln Center, New York City, 1992; 1st Holder of Walles Chair in the Performing Arts, Lamar University, 1989–90; Artist Faculty (Piano), The Harid Conservatory of Music, Boca Raton, Florida, USA; Recitals: Austria, Australia, South Africa, 1992; 2nd Tour of France, 1992; Gina Bachaeur Festival, Salt Lake City, Utah, 1993; Paris Recital Debut: Salle Cortot, 1994; Recitals in Singapore, Kuala Lumpur, Hong Kong, 1997. 1998; Solo recital, Weill Recital Hall, Carnegie Hall, New York, 1998; 5th tour of France, 1998; 6th tour of France, 1999; 1998–99 performed all piano solos and works with orchestra by George Gershwin for centennial celebration with West Virginia Symphony; mem, Artist Roster; The Piatigorsky Foundation, 1994–. *Recordings:* Richard Dowling Plays Chopin, 1997; A Frog He Went A Courting: Pairs of Pieces with cellist Evan Drachman, 1999; Sweet and Low-Down, Richard Dowling Plays George Gershwin, 2001; Richard Dowling Plays Chopin, Vol. II, 2003; World's Greatest Rags, 2004. *Publications:* New critical edition of Maurice Ravel's Trio for Piano, Violin and Cello, 1990; Critical edns of complete solo piano works of Ravel, nocturnes of Fauré, and sonatas of Hummel; Transcriptions of Gershwin solo piano works. *Honours:* Chevalier of the Company of Musketeers of Armagnac, Gascony, France in recognition of dedication to French musical arts, 1996; Grand Prix, French Piano Inst., 1993. *Current Management:* Joseph H. Conlin Concert Management, 853 Seventh Avenue, New York, NY 10019, USA; Parker Artists, Thomas F. Parker, 382 Central Park West, Suite 9G, New York, NY 10025, USA. *Website:* www.parkerartists.com. *Address:* 261 West 71st Street, No. 3, New York, NY 10023, USA. *E-mail:* PianistNYC@aol.com (home). *Website:* www.Richard-Dowling.com (home).

**DOWNES, Andrew,** BA, MA; composer and lecturer; b. 20 Aug. 1950, Handsworth, Birmingham, England; m. Cynthia Cooper 1975; two d. *Education:* St John's College, Cambridge, Royal College of Music, studied singing with Gordon Clinton, composition with Herbert Howells, Sir Lennox Berkeley. *Career:* debut, Wigmore Hall, 1969; Established Faculty of Composition, 1975, Head of School, 1990, Professor, School of Composition and Creative Studies, 1992–, Birmingham Conservatoire; Chaired Symposium on Music Criticism, Indian Music Congress, University of Burdwan, 1994; Performances of own works include: Vienna, 1983, 1998, 2001, 2002; Israel Philharmonic Guest House, Tel-Aviv, 1989; Berlin Kaiser Willhelm Gedächtniskirche, 1990; New York, 1996, 2003; Calcutta School of Music, 1994; Paris, 1995, 1996, 1997, 1998, 2001; University of New Mexico, 1995, 1997; Barletta, Italy, 1996; Bombay and Delhi, 1996; Eugene Oregon, 1996; Chicago, 1997; Caracas, Venezuela, 1997; Phoenix, Arizona, 1998; Rudolphinum, Prague, 1998, 2001, 2002; Genoa, 2002; Washington, 2002; Colorado, N Carolina, Michigan, 2003; Dublin, 2003; BBC Radio 2, 3 and 4; French Radio; France Musique; Austrian Radio; Czech Radio; Dutch Radio; Italian television. *Compositions include:* Sonata for 8 Horns Opus 54, University of New Mexico commission, 1994, subsequently performed by the Horns of the Czech Philharmonic Orchestra, 1997, 1998, 2001; Sonata for 8 Flutes, premiered at the USA National Flute Association Convention in New York, 1996; Songs From Spoon River, performed in New York, at Tanglewood Festival and on Radio 3; Towards A New Age, performed by the Royal Philharmonic Orchestra in Symphony Hall, Birmingham, 1997; New Dawn, oratorio based on American Indian texts, performed in Birmingham, 2000, and King's Chapel, Cambridge, 2001; Runnymede Service, St George's Chapel, Windsor and Chapel of Royal Holloway, University of London, 2000; Sonata for 8 Pianists, Birmingham, 2000 and Genoa, 2002; Sonata for Horn and Piano and Suite for 6 Horns for the Vienna Horn Society; Concerto for 4 Horns and Symphony Orchestra for the Czech Philharmonic Orchestra, 2002; 5 Dramatic Pieces for 8 Wagner Tubas for The Horns of the Czech Philharmonic Orchestra, 2003; Songs of Autumn, commissioned by Symphony Hall, Birmingham, for 1200 children with players from the CBSO. *Recordings include:* Sonata for 8 Horns by Horns of Czech Philharmonic Orchestra; Concerto for 2 Guitars and Strings, with Simon Dinnigan, Fred T. Baker and Strings from the City of Birmingham Symphony Orchestra; The Marshes of Glynn, commissioned for Royal Opening of the Adrian Boult Hall, Birmingham; Centenary Firedances, commissioned for the Centenary of the City of Birmingham; Sacred Choral Music, performed by the Chapel Choir of Royal Holloway, University of London; Flute Choir music by USA Flute Choirs; Music for Horns and Piano by the Vienna Horn Society; Sonata for Oboe and Piano; Sonata for Violin and Piano; Sacred Mass for Solo Violin; 3 Song Cycles; O Vos Omnes, motet, Cantamus commission; Sonata for 2 Pianos; Fanfare for a Ceremony, commission for Open University; Shepherd's Carol; The Souls of the Righteous, anthem. *Publications:* 86 works including 5 symphonies, 5 choral works, 2 double concertos, 3 string quartets, 6 works for brass ensemble, 5 song cycles, 7 anthems, 5 works for flute choir, 3 works for horn ensemble, sonatina and 2 sonatas for piano, and 7 sonatas for solo instrument with piano. *Address:* c/o Lynwood Music, 2 Church Street, West Hagley, West Midlands DY9 0NA, England. *E-mail:* downlyn@globalnet.co.uk. *Website:* www.users.globalnet.co.uk/~downlyn.

**DOWNES, Craig;** Singer (Tenor); b. 1960, South Africa. *Education:* Studied at University of Cape Town Opera, 1988–89. *Career:* Studio Soloist, CAPAB Opera, Cape Town; Junior soloist, CAPAB Opera, 1991; Productions of opera, operetta and musicals; Sang in venues throughout South Africa and Mauritius, 1994; Appeared regularly in oratorio, concerts and cabaret; Involved in the development of opera in rural areas of South Africa; Performances included Ismaele, Eisenstein and Alfredo in La Traviata; Welsh National Opera, 1995; Performed as High Priest of Neptune, Pinkerton in Madama Butterfly and Borsa in Rigoletto; Sang Lensky for performances of Eugene Onegin, Holland Park Festival; Erik, The Flying Dutchman, English National Opera; Lensy, ENO; Skuratov, From The House of the Dead; Sang leading tenor role, Carlo in Masnadieri, Amici di Verdi; Pinkerton, Madama Butterfly, Royal Albert Hall; Taken part in several opera gala concerts; Alfredo, La Traviata, Castleward Opera; Concert performances of Candide, London Symphony Orchestra, Barbican Hall; Beethoven's Missa Solemnis, Chelmsford; The First Knight, Parsifal, English National Opera, 1999; Alfredo, Castleward Opera, Ireland, 1999; Performed Dvořák Requiem, Rochester Cathedral, 1999; Don José for Co-opera, Ireland, 1999. *Address:* 6 The Hop Gardens, Thornwell, Chepstow, Gwent NP6 5RX.

**DOWNES, Sir Edward Thomas,** Kt, CBE, FRCM; British conductor; b. 17 June 1924. *Career:* studied with Herman Scherchen; professional conducting debut in UK with Carl Rosa Co.; conductor at Royal Opera House, Covent Garden 1952–69; Musical Dir Australian Opera 1972–76; Prin. Conductor, BBC Northern Symphony Orchestra, subsequently BBC Philharmonic Orchestra 1980–91; Chief Conductor, Netherlands Radio Orchestra until 1983; Assoc. Music Dir and Prin. Conductor, Royal Opera House, Covent Garden 1991–; regular appearances abroad as guest conductor. *Honours:* Hon. DMus (Birmingham) 1994; Evening Standard Opera Award for production of Verdi's Attila at Covent Garden 1991. *Address:* Royal Opera House, Covent Garden, London, WC2E 7QA, England. *Telephone:* (20) 7240-1200.

**DOWNEY, John Wilham,** BM, MM, DèsL; composer and academic; b. 5 Oct. 1927, Chicago, Illinois, USA. *Education:* De Paul University, Chicago Musical College, Paris Conservatoire, Sorbonne, Univ. of Paris. *Career:* teacher, De

Paul University, Chicago City College; Roosevelt University; Professor of Composition and Composer-in-Residence, University of Wisconsin, 1964–; founder, Wisconsin Contemporary Music Forum. *Compositions:* Ageistics, ballet, 1967; Incidental music to Shakespeare's Twelfth Night, 1971; Orchestral: La Joie de la paix, 1956; Chant to Michelangelo, 1958; Concerto for harp and chamber orchestra, 1964; Jingalodeon, 1968; Symphonic Modules, 1972; The Edge of Space for bassoon and orchestra, 1978, Discourse for oboe, harpsichord and strings, 1984; Double Bass Concerto, 1987; Declamations, 1985; Symphony (in two movements), 1992; Chamber: String Trio, 1953; For Those Who Suffered, for chamber orchestra, 1995; Violin Sonata, 1954; Wind Octet, 1954; 2 string quartets, 1964, 1976; Cello Sonata, 1966; Crescendo for 13 percussionists, 1977; Agort for woodwind quintet, 1967; Almost 12 for wind quintet, string quintet and percussion, 1970; Ambivalences I for any chamber combination, 1972; High Clouds and Soft Rain for 24 flutes, 1977; Duo for oboe and harpsichord, 1981; Portrait No. 1 for piano solo, 1980 Portrait No. 2 for clarinet and bassoon, 1983 and Portrait No. 3 for flute and piano, 1984; Piano Trio, 1984; Prayer for violin, viola and cello, 1984; Recombinance for double bass and piano, 1985; Solo Pieces: Tabu for Tabu, 1967; Lydian Suite for cello, 1975; Silhouette for double bass, 1980; Call for Freedom for symphonic winds, 1990; Ode to Freedom, orchestral, 1991; Rough Road for flute and guitar, 1995; Angel Talk for eight cellos, 1995; Piano pieces: Adagio Lyrico for two pianos, 1953; Eastlake Terrace for solo piano, 1959; Edges, piano solo, 1960; Pyramids, piano solo, 1961; Portrait No. 1, piano solo, 1980; Yad Vashem–An Impression, solo piano, 1991; Memories, piano solo, 1991; Vocal music, including Tangents, jazz oratorio, 1981; Choral works: What If? for choir, brass octet and solo timpani, 1973; Suite of Psalms for a cappella choir, 1989; Ghosts, for twelve violins, 1996; Setting of Psalm 90 for choir, organ, brass octet, timpani and soprano soloist, 1997; Mountains and Valleys, solo piano, 1999; Irish Sonata, violin and piano, 1999. *Recordings:* The Edge of Space; Cello Sonata on CRI; String Quartet No. 2; John Downey Plays John Downey; A Dolphin Octet for Winds, What If?; Adagio Lyrico and Agort; John Downey played by the London Symphony Orchestra: Declamations, Discourse, Jingalodeon, Concerto for Double Bass and Orchestra. *Publications:* Eastlake Terrace, 1959; Pyramids, 1960; Cello Sonata, Agort, Jingalodeon, Billaudot in Paris; Prayer, Silhouette, Portrait No. 3, 1984; Theodore Presser; La musique populaire dans l'oeuvre de Bela Bartók, 1966; Lydian Suite, 1976; Discourse, 1984; Soliloquy, 1997. *Address:* 4413 N Prospect Avenue, Shorewood, WI 53211, USA.

**DOYLE, Grant;** Singer (Baritone); b. 1971, Australia. *Education:* Elder Conservatorium, Adelaide; Royal College of Music, London; Vilar Young Artist Programme, Covent Garden, 2001. *Career:* Appearances with State Opera of South Australia and Opera Australia as Luiz in The Gondoliers and as Yarmadori in Madama Butterfly; Mozart's Count and Britten's Owen Wingrave at RCM; Season 2001–2002 as Purcell's Aeneas with the Irish Chamber Orchestra, and concerts with Orlando PO, Florida; Enrico in Donizetti's Il Campanello for Les Azuriales Opera, France, and Forester in The Cunning Little Vixen with Deutsches SO, Berlin, under Kent Nagano, for BBC TV. *Honours:* Royal Overseas League Trophy and National Mozart Competition for Singers, 2000, prize-winner. *Address:* c/o Vilar Young Artists, Royal Opera House, Covent Garden, London, WC2, England. *Telephone:* (20) 7240 1200. *Fax:* (20) 7212-9502.

**DRABOWICZ, Wojciech;** Singer (Baritone); b. 1963, Poznán, Poland. *Education:* Studied at the Poznán Academy, 1984–89. *Career:* Won prizes at the 1990 Tchaikovsky Competition, Moscow, and the Belvedere, Vienna; Member of the Poznán Opera from 1989 (debut as Eugene Onegin) and sang Morales at the 1991 Bregenz Festival; Other roles include Mozart's Guglielmo and Pagageno, Malatesta in Don Pasquale and other lyric repertory; Recitalist in songs by Schumann, Chopin and Schubert; La nozze di Figaro, directed by Jerome Savary at Warsaw Opera House, 1993; Eugene Onegin at Glyndebourne Opera Festival including a BBC Prom, 1994; Così fan tutte at Monnaie, Brussels, 1994; Pelléas et Mélisande, Kiel State Opera, 1995; The Queen of Spades at Glyndebourne Opera Festival, 1995; Further engagements include King Roger by Szymanowski at Théâtre des Champs Elysées, 1996, Eugene Onegin at Glyndebourne Opera Festival in 1996 and Figaro in Le nozze di Figaro 1997; Season 1998 as Vershinin in the premiere of Three Sisters by Peter Eötvös at Lyon, and Eugene Onegin at Barcelona; Sang King Roger at Warsaw, 2000. *Address:* c/o Poznán Grand Theatre, Fredry 9, 60-967 Poznán, Poland.

**DRAGONI, Maria;** Singer (Soprano); b. 1958, Procida, Naples, Italy. *Education:* Studied in Naples. *Career:* Debut: Sang Imogene in Il Pirata at Naples, 1984 (Teatro di Jesi); Appeared in the title role of Pergolesi's Il Flamino at the Teatro San Carlo Naples, 1984; Season 1988–89, as Fenena in Nabucco at La Scala, Turandot at Nancy and Ravenna and Aida at Marcerata; Mathilde in Guillaume Tell and Bellini's Norma at the Théâtre des Champs Elysées and Mulhouse, 1989; Season, 1990–91, as Elisabeth de Valois at Turin and Donna Anna at the Teatro dell Opera at Rome; Sang Mimi at Naples and Elisabeth de Valois at the Verona Arena, 1992; Other roles include Paolina in Poluito by Donizetti, Donna Anna, and La Gioconda; Sang Aida at Florence, 1996; Season 1995–96 as Norma at Zürich and Elvira in Verdi's Ernani at Strasbourg; Season 1999–2000 at Jesy as Ines de Castro in the opera by Persiani, as Elvira in Ernani at Genoa and as Norma at Savona.

**DRAHEIM, Joachim,** PhD; German musicologist and pianist; *Teacher of Latin and Music, Lessing Gymnasium, Karlsruhe;* b. 26 July 1950, Berlin-Schmargendorf. *Education:* University of Heidelberg, studied piano with Ursula Draheim, violoncello with Annlies Schmidt-de Neveu. *Career:* concerts as solo, chamber music and lieder pianist in Germany, Austria and Switzerland; Freelance, many recordings of lieder and piano pieces, Süddeutscher Rundfunk Karlsruhe and Heidelberg, (Südwestrundfunk, Studio Karlsruhe) 1973–; Freelance, several German and foreign music publishers including Breitkopf und Härtel, Wiesbaden, and Wiener Urtext Edition, and recording companies, 1974–; Numerous editions including Brahms und seine Freunde-works for piano, works by Mozart, Beethoven, Loewe, Fanny Hensel, Liszt, Mendelssohn, Robert and Clara Schumann, Chopin, Carl Reinecke, Woldemar Bargiel, Brahms, Busoni, others; First editions: Mendelssohn: Albumblatt in A major, Sonata in D major and Sonata movement in G minor for two pianos; Brahms: Die Müllerin; Schumann: Der Korsar, Piano accompaniment to Bach's Suite in C major for solo cello, Violin setting of Schumann Cello Concerto in A minor op 129, Variations on a nocturne by Chopin for piano, others; Teaching at Lessing Gymnasium, Karlsruhe, 1978–; Works for the Neue Schumann-Gesamtausgabe, the Neue Weber-Gesamtausgabe, the Neue Mendelssohn-Gesamtausgabe and the new MGG. *Honours:* Robert Schumann Preis der Stadt Zwickau 2003. *Address:* Sophienstrasse 165, 76185 Karlsruhe, Germany (office). *Telephone:* (7211) 859435 (home). *Fax:* (7211) 854507 (home).

**DRAHOS, Béla;** Flautist and Conductor; b. 1955, Kaposvar, Hungary. *Education:* Studied with Henrik Prohle at the Györ Conservatory and with Lorant Kovacs at the Ferenc Liszt Academy, Budapest, graduated, 1978; From 1991 studied conducting with Professor Carl Osterreicher in Vienna. *Career:* Solo Flautist with the Budapest Symphony Orchestra from 1976, including many foreign tours; Solo Flautist with the Hungarian State Orchestra, 1990; Solo Career in Austria, Bulgaria, Belgium, Czechoslovakia, England, Finland, France, Soviet Union, Switzerland and Germany; Concerts with the New Zealand Symphony Orchestra, 1988; West Berlin Philharmonie, 1989; Leader and Founder Member, Hungarian Radio Wind Quintet; Music Director, Kaposvar Symphony Orchestra, 1990; Assistant Conductor, Hungarian State Symphony Orchestra, 1993; Guest Conductor of leading orchestras in Hungary; Conducts operas and concerts in Austria and Germany. *Recordings:* Mozart Concerto K314; Paganini 24 Caprices; Bach 4th Brandenburg Concerto and Concerto for Two Flutes in F; Vivaldi Concertos (Hungaroton); 16 Haydn Symphonies for Naxos; Beethoven's Symphonies 1–9 and Overtures, Naxos. *Address:* c/o Hungarian Symphony Orchestra, 10–12 Pava utca, H–1094 Budapest, Hungary.

**DRAKE, George (Warren James),** PhD; lecturer in music and musicologist; *Associate Professor, School of Music, University of Auckland;* b. 4 Aug. 1939, Auckland, New Zealand; m. Carla Maria Driessen, one s., one d. *Education:* Univ. of Auckland;, Univ. of Ill., USA. *Career:* Assoc. Prof. 1976–, Univ. of Auckland; Dean, Faculty of Music, 1985–88; Head of the School of Music, 1988–91; Founding Pres., New Zealand Musicological Soc., 1982–85; Musicological Soc. of Australia; Int. Musicological Soc. *Publications:* Liber Amicorum John Steele: A Musicological Tribute, editor, 1997; Petrucci, Motetti B (Monuments of Renaissance Music XI, Chicago) 2002. *Address:* c/o School of Music, University of Auckland, Auckland, New Zealand. *E-mail:* w.drake@auckland.ac.nz. *Website:* www.music.auckland.ac.nz.

**DRAKE, Julius;** Pianist; b. 1959, England; m., two d. *Career:* many appearances world-wide collaborating with leading performers; Recitals with singers Thomas Allen, Victoria de los Angeles, Olaf Bär, Barbara Bonney, Felicity Lott, Lorraine Hunt, Edith Mathis, Ian Bostridge, Hughes Cuenod, Gerald Finley, Wolfgang Holzmair, Simon Keenlyside, Angelika Kirchschlager, Thomas Quasthoff and Joan Rodgers; Festival engagements at Kuhmo (Finland), Saintes (France) and Perth, with Michael Collins (clarinet), Natalie Clein (cello), Nicholas Daniel, Steven Isserlis, Ernst Kovacic, Christian Poltera, Christian Altenburger (violin) and Robert Cohen (violin) and Belcea, Maggini and Szymanowski Quartets; Performances of Hans Werner Henze's Songs from the Arabian, with Ian Bostridge, 2000–01; Artistic Director, Perth International Music Festival, Australia, 2001–2003; Season 2001–2002 with piano trio concerts in Spain, accompanied by Robert Cohen and Massimo Quarta, tours of USA and Japan with Ian Bostridge, Wigmore Hall with Gerald Finley and Amsterdam Concertgebouw with Thomas Quasthoff; London Proms Chamber Music, 2002; Recent appearances include concerts at Edinburgh, Salzburg, Schubertiade Festivals and in Amsterdam, London, Paris, Vienna, NY, Tokyo and Washington. *Recordings include:* French chansons, with Hugues Cuenod; English Songbook, Schubert and Schumann Lieder, Britten Canticles and Henze's Songs from the Arabian, with Ian Bostridge (EMI); Sibelius Songs with Katarina Karneus; Mahler, Haydn and Schumann with Alice Coote; Britten Canticles with Ian Bostridge, David Daniels, Christopher Maltman. *Current Management:* IMG Artists, Lovell House, 616 Chiswick High Road, London, W4 5RX, England. *Telephone:* (20) 8233-5800. *Fax:* (20) 8233-5801. *E-mail:* artistseurope@imgworld.com. *Website:* www.imgartists.com.

**DRAKULICH, Stephen;** Singer (Tenor); b. 1958, Iowa, USA. *Education:* Studied at Southern Illinois University; Apprentice at the Lyric Opera of Chicago; Study with Norman Gulbranson at Northwestern University. *Career:* Sang in The Turn of the Screw, The Rake's Progress and Lucia di Lammermoor at Chicago; Wuppertal Opera as Mozart's Ferrando and Tamino, Rodolfo in Bohème and Britten's Albert Herring, Janáček's Fox, Ramiro (Cenerentola), Lensky, Steuermann in Fliegende Holländer and Jacquino, at Bremen Opera, 1982–89; Sergei in Lady Macbeth of the Mtensk

District, Peter Grimes, Captain Vere (Billy Budd) and Jimmy in Mahagonny, Freiburg Opera, 1989–92; Guest appearances as Arkenholz in Reimann's Gespenstersonate at Stuttgart and Hamburg; Sergei on tour to Japan with Cologne Opera; Tom Rakewell in Switzerland and Peter Grimes at the Glyndebourne Festival, 1992; Adam in the premiere of Der Garten by Josef Tal, 1988; Season 1996–97 in D'Albert's Tiefland and Wolf-Ferrari's Sly, in Germany; Essex in Roberto Devereux for Blackheath Opera, 1998. *Honours:* Award winner at the Metropolitan Opera National Council Auditions. *Address:* c/o Freiburg Opera, Bertoldstrasse 46, 79098 Freiburg in Breisgau, Germany.

**DRAN, Thierry;** Singer (Tenor); b. 17 Aug. 1953, Bordeaux, France. *Education:* Studied at the Bordeaux Conservatory and in Paris with Michel Sénéchal. *Career:* Appearances at the Paris Opéra-Comique, the Berlioz Festival at Lyon (as Benedict), Rouen (Nadir, and in Les Indes Galantes); Marseille (in Capuleti e i Montecchi) and Lyon, as Fenton in Falstaff; Grand Théâtre Geneva, in Offenbach's Les Brigands and Barbe Bleue; Sang in the Ravel double bill at Glyndebourne, 1987–88; Paris Opéra as Don Ottavio and as Mercure in Orphée aux Enfers; Guest appearances at Bordeaux, as Jean in Le Jongleur de Notre Dame and Liège (Ernesto, the Duke of Mantua and Rossini's Count Almaviva); Frequent concert engagements. *Recordings:* Messager's Fortunio and Duc de Mantoue in Les Brigands. *Address:* c/o Opéra Royal de Wallonie, 1 rue des Dominicains, B–4000 Liège, Belgium.

**DRASKOVIC, Milimir;** composer, conductor, multimedia artist, producer and publisher; b. 5 June 1952, Sarajevo; m. Biljana Vasilievic. *Education:* Belgrade Music Acad., Belgrade Opera with Borislav Pascan. *Career:* Composer of music for numerous ensembles, for film and television, video, performance installation and for graphics and multimedia packages; Performances of work includes Gaudeamus, Utrecht, 1978; Festival international des musiques experimentales, Bourges, 1982; Radio biennale, Paris, 1982; Esquiss' Art, Almada, Portugal, 1982; BITEF, Belgrade 1982; Die Glockenspielen, Essen, 1983; New Art in Serbia, Beograd-Zagreb-Pristina 1983; Video C.D. Ljubljana 1983; European Minimal Music Project, Belgrade, 1983; Planum '84, Budapest, 1984; Different New Music, Belgrade, 1984–86; Yugoslav Documentary and Short Film, Belgrade, 1986–2000; Festival of Alternative Film, Split, 1987; Aut Art Alternativa, Grisignana 1989; Computer Art, Belgrade, 1991; Byzanz und Danach, Berlin, 1992–95; Eight Weeks, Belgrade 1995; Eine Kleine Geschichtsmusik, Goethe Institut, Belgrade, 1996; Oktoih, Belgrade 1997; From the New World, Belgrade 1999; Triosonata, Belgrade, 2000; Serbian Music, Kol hamuzika Jerusalim 2001; Draskovic-Oktoih, Outaut, Toronto 2002; Images of Notations, Ljubljana 2003; Open October Salon, Toronto 2003–04; music at numerous film festivals throughout Europe, and for radio and television. *Compositions include:* D'orchestra 1–5; Musica linea 1–10; HPSCHD 1–6; Eine Kleine Geschichtmusik; Octoechos; Eight Weeks; From the New World; Opera, Orgelwerke, Unfinished Symphony. *Recordings:* Opus 4, 1981; Ensemble for Different New Music, 1981; Film Music, 1989; Serbian Music for Harpsichord, 1 and 2, 1996; Oktoih/Milimir Draskovic's Eight Weeks, 1997; From the New World, 1999; Triosonata, 2000; From the New Old World 2001. *Publications:* Dirigent, 1981; Portrait of a Young Musician, 1983; Examples of Ideosemas, 1983; Music Design, 2000; Opus 4 2001. *Contributions:* Beorama. *Address:* Brace Srnic 23, 11050 Belgrade, Serbia and Montenegro. *E-mail:* milimir .draskovic@EUnet.yu.

**DRATH, Janina (Nina) Irena Drath-Nowicka;** pianist; b. 14 Oct. 1954, Katowice, Poland; m. Jerzy Bogdan Nowicki 1981; one s. *Education:* Acad. of Music, Warsaw. *Career:* debut with Silesian Philharmonic Orchestra 1968, with WOSPRIT (Great Symphony Orchestra of Radio and Television) 1968; first recital, Katowice 1963; first recital abroad, Ostrava, Czechoslovakia 1965; regular concerts (solo and with orchestra) from age 14; concert tours and performances in Poland, Spain, Italy, Germany, Belgium, France, USA, Mexico, Czechoslovakia; many radio and television performances; guest artist, Annual Chopin Workshops, Texas A&M Univ., USA 1981–94; artist-in-residence, Central State Univ., OK 1985–87; debut at Carnegie Hall, NY New York 1998; founder and Pres., Fryderyk Chopin Soc. of Texas 1990, Int. Chopin Piano Competition, Corpus Christi 1993, Sonata and Sonatina Int. Youth Piano Competition, Corpus Christi 1994; Artistic Dir and founder, Virtuoso Piano Performance Studies; jury mem., int piano competitions. *Recordings:* with Vandor Music Group: works of Haydn, Chopin, Petroff and Mozart; three albums of piano music by P. Petroff. *Address:* 4610 Abner Drive, Corpus Christi, TX 78411, USA.

**DRESHER, Paul (Joseph);** Composer; b. 8 Jan. 1951, Los Angeles, California, USA; m. 8 Mar 1986. *Education:* BA, Music, University of California, Berkeley, 1977; MA, Composition, University of California, San Diego, 1979; Private studies: North Indian Classical Music with Nikhil Banerjee, 1974–77; Ghanaian Drumming with C K and Kobla Ladzekpo, 1975–79; Javanese and Balinese Gamelan. *Career:* Composer, Performer throughout USA, Canada, Europe; Works performed at New York Philharmonic, San Francisco Symphony, Minnesota Opera, Brooklyn Academy of Music, Cal Arts Festival, New Music America, 1981, 1983, 1985, London International Festival of Theatre, Munich State Opera, Festival d'Automne, Paris; Commissions include Nonsuch Commission Award from American Music Center, and radio composition for Olympic Arts Festival; Founder, Artistic Director, Paul Dresher Ensemble (electro-acoustic chamber ensemble), 1993–, premiere on six-city tour of Japan, and performing at Lincoln Center; mem, BMI; American Music Center, Board of Directors; Opera

America; Chamber Music America. *Compositions:* This Same Temple, 1977; Channels Passing, 1981; Night Songs, 1981; Liquid and Stellar Music, 1981; The Way of How, opera, 1981; Dark Blue Circumstance, electronic, 1982–84; Reaction, 1984; See Hear, opera, 1984; Other Fire, electronic, 1984; Slow Fire, opera, 1985–86; Water Dreams, electronic, 1986; Power Failure, opera, 1989; Double Ikat, trio, 1989; Cornucopia, chamber orchestra, 1990; Pioneer, opera, 1991; The Gates, 1993; Din of Iniquity, 6 instruments, 1994; Stretch, 6 instruments, 1995; Blue Diamonds for solo piano, 1995; Violin Concerto, 1996–97; Elapsed Time, violin and piano duo, 1998. *Recordings:* Liquid and Stellar Music, This Same Temple; Slow Fire, complete opera, 1992; Opposites Attract, 1992; Double Ikat, Channels Passing, Dark Blue Circumstance, Night Songs, 1993; Casa Vecchia, 1995. *Contributions:* Sounding Eleven. *Honours:* Commissioned by Saint Paul Chamber Orchestra and Meet the Composer; Commission from the Library of Congress, 1997–98. *Current Management:* Bernstein Artists Inc, Brooklyn, New York. *Address:* 51 Avenida Drive, Berkeley, CA 94708, USA.

**DREW, David,** BA; British writer on music, publisher, producer, editor and dramaturg; b. 19 Sept. 1930, London, England; m. Judith Sutherland 1960. *Education:* Univ. of Cambridge. *Career:* freelance writer, with part-time consultancy and editorial duties, Decca Record Co. 1955–59; Prod., BBC Music Dept 1960; music critic, New Statesman 1960–67; music consultant to the Calouste Gulbenkian Foundation, UK Branch, and Artistic Dir of the Foundation's recording series, Music Today, EMI/Argo 1961–75; European representative and adviser, The Kurt Weill Foundation for Music 1971–76; Ed., later Advisory Ed., Tempo 1971–92, Editorial Advisory Bd mem. 2003–;; mem. BBC Music Advisory Cttee and Arts Council Music Panel 1971–80; adviser to the Holland Festival 1971, Berlin Festival 1974–75; Dir Contemporary Music, Boosey & Hawkes Music Publishers 1975–92; mem. Programme Cttee of Mürztal Music Workshop, Austria 1983–91; mem. Exec. Cttee of Les amis du compositeur Igor Markevitch, Lausanne and London 1988–95; Trustee, Britten-Pears Foundation, Dir of Britten Estate Ltd 1989–99; Artistic Dir, Largo Records, Cologne 1993–98; Editorial Bd mem., The Kurt Weill Edition 1992–; Artistic Adviser, South Bank Centre Weill Centenary Series 1999–2000; dramaturg, Broomhill Opera 1999–2000; editions of many stage and concert works by Kurt Weill, notably Cry the Beloved Country, Carnegie Hall 1988; Roberto Gerhard's opera, The Duenna, Madrid, Barcelona, Opera North 1992. *Publications:* Über Kurt Weill 1975, Weill, Ausgewählte Schriften 1975, Essays on the Philosophy of Music 1985, The Kurt Weill Handbook 1987, Der Weg der Verheissung and the Prophecies of Jeremiah 1998; contrib. numerous articles on 20th century composers, such as Stravinsky, Messiaen, Gerhard, Spinner, Gorecki. *Address:* 12 Favart Road, London, SW6 4AZ, England.

**DREW, James;** Composer, Playwright, Pianist and Director; b. 9 Feb. 1929, St Paul, Minnesota, USA; m. Gloria Kelly, 26 Mar 1960, 1 s., 1 d. *Education:* Certificate, New York School of Music, 1956; MA, Tulane University, 1964; Private study with Wallingford Riegger, 1956–69 and Edgard Varèse, 1956. *Career:* Composer for concert hall, theatre and film; Composer, Northwestern University, 1964–66; Yale University, 1966–73; Tanglewood, Lennox, MA, summer 1973, LSU, 1973–75; Director, Ghost Puppet Theatre, 1970–; Visiting Composer, California State University, 1976–77, University of California at Los Angeles, 1977–78; Director of American Music Theatre, 1978–, Mysterious Travelling Cabaret, 1980–, No Sleep Theatre, 1984–, and Greywolf International, 1993–; Director, Blast Operatheater, 1996–. *Compositions include:* Symphonies; Concerto for small percussion orchestra; Mysterium, opera; Faustus–an Epilogue for 2 pianos, solo viola and chamber ensemble; The Orangethorpe Aria; Five O'Clock Ladies, stage work; Last Dance, video work; Whisper, video; Cantobosolo for contrabass solo; Cantobosolo for percussion and orchestra; Live From the Black Eagle, video work; Cello Concerto; In This Place of Half Lights, Gloria... Sotto Voce, a monodrama; In Memoriam of Gloria Kelly Drew, 1990; Piano Concerto, Formingreforming, 1991; Easter Concerto for violin grand and orchestra, 1992; Celestial Cabaret for piano and chamber orchestra, 1993; Inaudible Answers for orchestra, 1994; Book of Lights, 1994; Elephants Coming for string quartet, 1994; Walden Songs for chamber orchestra, 1995; Sacred Dances of the Tunnel Saints, 1995; Hypothetical Structures, 1996; Survivors in Pale Light, 1996; Viola Concerto (Cellar-Lise's Alléluias); Giggles, ballet, 1996–98; With Closed Eyes Danced the Raven, 1998; The Ringing Hour for voices, percussion, orchestra, 1998; Contrabass Concerto, chamber version, 1999. *Recordings:* Sonata Appassionata for Cello and Piano (Cello America vol. 2), 1994; Cantolobo Solo (monodrama); Contolobosolo (monodrama). *Honours:* Guggenheim Fellow, 1973–74. *Current Management:* Cooke Associates, Nicolaistraat 17, 2517 SX Den Haag, Netherlands. *Address:* Greywolf Arts Institute, 10830 So 1000 East, Sandy, Utah 84094, USA.

**DREYFUS, George,** AM; composer; b. 22 July 1928, Wuppertal, Germany; two s. one d. *Education:* Vienna Acad. of Music. *Career:* Composer-in-Residence, Tienjin, China 1983, Shanghai 1987, Nanjing 1991. *Compositions include:* Garni Sands, The Gilt-Edged Kid (operas); Symphonies Nos. 1 & 2; Symphonie Concertante 1977; Jingles ... & More Jingles; Reflections in a Glasshouse; The Illusionist; The Grand Aurora Australis Now Show; Galgenlieder; Songs Comic & Curious; Music in the Air; From within Looking out; The Seasons; Ned Kelly Ballads; Quintet after the Notebook of J.-G. Noverre; Sextet for Didjeridoo & Wind Instruments; Old Melbourne; several pieces for young people; The Sentimental Bloke (musical) 1985, Lifestyle 1988, Song of Brother Sun 1988 (choral pieces), Rathenau (opera) 1993, Die Marx

Sisters (opera) 1994; more than 100 scores for film and TV including The Adventures of Sebastian the Fox 1963, Rush 1974, Great Expectations 1986. *Television:* The Gilt-Edged Kid (Australian Broadcasting Corpn —ABC) 1975, Didjeridu in Deutschland (SBS) 1988, Bicycles and Bassoons (SBS) 1989, Life is Too Serious (ABC) 2000. *Publications:* The Last Frivolous Book (autobiog.) 1984, Being George – And Liking It! 1998; numerous commercial CDs on the Move label. *Honours:* Grosses Bundesverdienstkreuz (Germany); Henry Lawson Award 1972, Prix de Rome 1976, 2004, Mishkenot Sha'ananim, Jerusalem 1980, Don Banks Fellowship 1992. *Address:* 3 Grace Street, Camberwell, Vic. 3124, Australia. *Telephone:* (3) 9809-2671 (home). *Fax:* (3) 9809-2671 (home). *E-mail:* gdreyfus@pigpond.net.au (office).

**DREYFUS, Huguette Pauline;** French harpsichordist; b. 30 Nov. 1928, Mulhouse. *Education:* Ecole Normale de Musique, Paris, Conservatoire National Supérieur de Musique, Paris, Chigiana Acad., Siena. *Career:* soloist, ORTF and various other radio and television networks world-wide; harpsichord teacher, Conservatoire Nat. Supérieur de Musique de Lyon, Académie Musicale de Villecroze and Conservatoire Nat. de Région de Rueil-Malmaison. *Recordings:* J. S. Bach: 6 English Suites, 6 French Suites; Rameau: Pièces de Clavecin; Couperin: Pièces de Clavecin; Scarlatti: Chronological Anthology of 70 Sonatas; Seixas: 14 Sonatas; Bartók: Pieces from Mikrokosmos; Chamber music by J. S. Bach, Leclair, Rameau, Haydn, Vivaldi, Corelli, C P E Bach, W A Mozart; J. S. Bach: Italian Concerto, Chromatic Fantasy and Fugue, Inventions and Sinfonias, 6 Partitas, French Overture, 4 Duetti, Praeludium, Fuga and Allegro in E flat major, Goldberg variations; Wilhelm-Friedemann Bach: 9 Fantasien; J. S. Bach Harpsichord Transcriptions of 16 Concerti by various composers; J. S. Bach: The Well-Tempered Clavier, vol. I; Henri Dutilleux: Les Citations, Diptyque for oboe, harpsichord, double bass, percussion; JS Bach: The Well-Tempered Clavier, Vol. II. *Honours:* Grosse Ehrenzeichen für Verdienste um die Republik Österreich 1992, Chevalier, Légion d'Honneur 1995, Officier, Ordre des Arts et des Lettres 1999, Commdr, Ordre National du Mérite 2004; first medal in harpsichord Int. Competition, Geneva 1958, Prix du Président de la République, Académie Charles Cros 1985, numerous Grand Prix for recordings. *Address:* 91 Quai d'Orsay, 75007 Paris, France.

**DRISCOLL, F. Paul;** American opera director and writer; *Editor-in-Chief, Opera Now;* b. Scarsdale, NY. *Education:* Regis High School, Manhattan and Coll. of the Holy Cross, New England. *Career:* fmr actor, Foothills Theater, Worcester; freelance dir and designer for theatre; worked at dept store, Lord & Taylor in various roles 1978–85; Product Development Man., Metropolitan Opera Guild retail programme 1985–90; freelance writer and dir from 1990, contributing reviews, stories and essays to publs, including Chamber Music, Musical America, Opera News, Stagebill; Picture Ed., Opera News, then Asst Man. Ed. from 1998, later Man. Ed., now Ed.-in-Chief; Dir of some 20 musicals and operettas, Coll. Light Opera Co., Falmouth, MA until 1998; Artistic Dir, Scarsdale Summer Music Theater for two years; Dir, Working, by the Washington Chamber Symphony, Kennedy Center; Dir, Mariage Blanc, with the Riverside Shakespeare Co. in New York; Dramatic Dir, Blue Hill Troupe production of The Sorcerer 1998. *Television:* host, Tonight Is... Opera New York. *Publications:* 25 years at Highfield: A History of the College Light Opera Company 1992, Fantastic Opera (with artist, John Martinez) 1997. *Address:* Opera News, 70 Lincoln Center Plaza, New York, NY 10023, USA. *E-mail:* info@operanews.com. *Website:* www.metoperafamily.org/operanews.

**DRISCOLL, Loren;** Singer (Tenor); b. 14 April 1928, Midwest, Wyoming, USA. *Education:* Studied at Syracuse and Boston University. *Career:* Debut: As Caius in Falstaff, Boston, 1954; New York City Opera debut, 1957, as Timur in Turandot; Sang Tom Rakewell in The Rake's Progress at Santa Fe, 1957; Deutsche Oper Berlin from 1962, notably as Fenton, Pinkerton, Flamand (Capriccio), Don Ottavio and The Painter in Lulu; Sang in the premieres of Henze's Der junge Lord (1965) and Ulisse by Dallapiccola (1968); Glyndebourne Festival, 1962, Ferrando; Salzburg Festival, 1966, as Dionysos in the premiere of The Bassarids by Henze, repeating the role at La Scala and Santa Fe, 1968; Metropolitan Opera from 1966, as David, and Alfred in Die Fledermaus; Schwetzingen Festival, 1971, as the Architect in the premiere of Reimann's Melusine, repeated at Edinburgh; Brussels, 1973, in the premiere of Love's Labour's Lost by Nabokov; Santa Fe, 1977, in the US premiere of Boulevard Solitude by Henze; Rome, 1982, with the company of the Deutsche Oper, in Undine by Lortzing; Further appearances in Hamburg, Cologne and Edinburgh. *Recordings:* Der junge Lord and Lulu; Oedipus Rex, Renard and The Nightingale, conducted by Stravinsky. *Address:* c/o Deutsche Oper Berlin, Richard Wagnerstrasse 10, 1000 Berlin, Germany.

**DRIVALA, Jenny;** Singer (Soprano); b. 4 July 1965, Greece. *Education:* Studied at the Athens and Bremen Conservatories. *Career:* Appearances at the Vienna Staatsoper, La Scala Milan and in Naples, Rome, Melbourne, Paris Châtelet, Florence and Pretoria; Repertoire includes Donizetti's Lucia, Maria Stuarda and Lucrezia Borgia, Violetta, Thais and Mélisande; Sang title role in Gluck's Armide for ORF television, Strauss's Daphne and Salome for Greek Radio and Glauce in Médée by Cherubini; Season 1994–95 as Massenet's Thais at St Gallen and Glauce in Athens; Strauss concert with Charles Mackerras; Sang Anna Bolena at Athens, 2000.

**DRIVER, Danny,** MA (Cantab.), PGDipRCM, ARCM; British pianist; b. 1977, London. *Education:* Cambridge Univ., Royal College of Music. *Career:* solo recitals in London at Wigmore Hall, Queen Elizabeth Hall, Purcell Room, Fairfield Hall; recital and concerto appearances in UK, USA, Canada, Israel,

Norway and Germany; Teacher, junior dept of Royal Acad. of Music; Assistant to Head of Keyboard, Royal College of Music. *Honours:* BBC Radio 2 Young Musician of the Year, 2001; Royal Overseas League Coutts Bank Award for Keyboard, 2001; Royal College of Music Amerada Hess Junior Fellowship, 2001; Eric Falk Trust Award, 2002, First Prize, Robert William and Florence Amy Brant Int. Piano Competition 2004, Soroptimist Prize and Special Prize for Best Performance of the Commisioned Work, Scottish Int. Piano Competition 2004. *Address:* 146a Audley Road, London, NW4 3EG, England. *Telephone:* (20) 8202-9289 (office); (20) 82029289 (home). *Website:* www.dannydriver.co.uk.

**DROBKOVA, Drahomira;** Czech singer (mezzo-soprano); b. 1935. *Career:* sang at Ostrava Opera, 1966–83; Roles have included Verdi's Ebol, Amneris and Azucena; Wagner's Ortrud and Adriano; Octavian and Marina, Boris Godunov; Dorabella; Prague Nat. Theatre, from 1983 in operas by Puccini, Smetana, Janáček, Strauss, Verdi and Dvořák; Savonlinna Festival, 1991, as the Witch in Rusalka; Concerts at Prague and elsewhere in music by Zelenka, Janáček and Mozart. *Recordings:* Janáček's Glagolitic Mass; Dvořák's Rusalka, Supraphon; Dvořák's American Flag; Marfa in Dimitrij, Mass D Dur, Spiritual Songs – Ave Maria; B. Martinu, The Prophecy of Isaiah, Hymn to St. James, Supraphon; The Drahomira Drobkova Album. *Honours:* Thalia 1993, Verdi's Ebol. *Address:* Antošovicka 178, Ostrava 2-Koblov, 71100, Czech Republic.

**DRUCKER, Eugene;** American violinist; b. 17 May 1952, Coral Gables, FL. *Career:* founder and co-leader, Emerson String Quartet 1976–; public debut at Alice Tully Hall, New York 1979, playing works by Mozart, Smetana and Bartók; quartet-in-residence, Smithsonian Inst., Washington 1980, and the Hartt School of Music 1981–2002, the Aspen Music Festival 1983, State Univ. of New York at Stony Brook 2002–; faculty mem., SUNY Stony Brook 2002–; European debut at the Spoleto Festival 1981; noted for performances of the quartets of Bartók, including all six works in a single evening; has given the premieres of works by Mario Davidovsky, Gunther Schuller, Richard Wernick, John Harbison, Wolfgang Rihm and Maurice Wright; with Emerson Quartet 100 concerts annually in major musical capitals of Europe, USA and Canada; tours of Japan and Australia; resident quartet, Chamber Music Soc. of Lincoln Center 1982–89. *Recordings:* with the Emerson Quartet: Bartók complete Quartets, Mozart six Quartets dedicated to Haydn, Schubert Cello Quintet with Rostropovich, Ives and Barber Quartets, Prokofiev Quartets and Sonata for two violins, Complete Beethoven Cycle 1997, Ned Rorem's Quartet No. 4 and Edgar Meyer's Quintet for String Quartet and Double Bass 1998, Mozart and Brahms Clarinet Quintets with David Shifrin 1999, the complete Shostakovich Quartets 2000, Bach's Art of the Fugue 2003; as soloist: Bach Sonatas and Partitas for violin and complete Duos and Sonatas by Bartók. *Honours:* Naumburg Award for Chamber Music 1978, Gramophone Magazine Award for Best Chamber Music Record and Record of the Year (for Bartók Quartets) 1989, Grammy Award for Best Chamber Music and Classical Record of the Year (for Bartók Quartets) 1990, Grammy Award for Best Chamber Music Album (for Beethoven Quartets) 1998, Gramophone Magazine Award for Best Chamber Music Record (for Shostakovich Quartets) 2000, Grammy Awards for Best Chamber Music and Classical Record of the Year (for Shostakovich Quartets) 2001. *Current Management:* c/o Matthew Zelle, IMG Artists, 152 W 57th Street, Fifth Floor, New York, NY 10019, USA. *E-mail:* kirshdem@aol.com. *Website:* www.emersonquartet.com.

**DRUIETT, Michael;** Singer (bass); b. 23 Jan. 1967, London. *Education:* European Opera Centre, Belgium, Scuola Superiore, Italy and the National Opera Studio, London. *Career:* Appearances with English National Opera in The Love for Three Oranges, Wozzeck, Gianni Schicchi, Salome, Cunning Little Vixen, Rigoletto, Ariodante, Don Carlos, Masked Ball, Orfeo and Lohengrin; Wozzeck in Paris under Barenboim; Principal Bass with the Royal Opera, Covent Garden, from 1993–97; Season 2000–01 as Donner in Das Rheingold and Ferrando in Il Trovatore for Scottish Opera; Further performances Paris Bastille, Toulouse, Bordeaux, Lyon, Dublin, Brussels, Tel-Aviv, Welsh National Opera; Performs regularly with major symphony orchestras. *Recordings:* Floyd's Susannah, with the Opéra de Lyon; Puccini Experience with the Orchestra of the Royal Opera/Downes. *Current Management:* Hazard Chase, Norman House, Cambridge Place, Cambridge CB2 1NS, England. *Telephone:* (1223) 312400. *Fax:* (1223) 460827. *Website:* www.hazardchase.co.uk.

**DRUMM, Imelda;** Singer (mezzo-soprano); b. 1969, Ireland. *Education:* Dublin City University; Leinster School of Music with Dr Veronica Dunne; National Opera Studio, London, 1996–97. *Career:* Roles with Glyndebourne Opera include Cherubino, 1994, Isolier in Le Comte Ory, 1997, Dorabella in Così fan tutte, 1995, Tisbe in La Cenerentola for Opera Ireland and Theodata in Handel's Flavio for OTC Dublin; Season 1998 as Cenerentola for English Touring Opera and Abaces in a revival of Artaserses by Terradellas at Barcelona. *Honours:* Richard Lewis/Jean Shanks Award and Esso Touring Award, Glyndebourne Opera.

**DRUMMOND, Sir John Richard Gray,** Kt, CBE, MA, FRSA, FRCM; British arts administrator; b. 25 Nov. 1934, s. of the late Capt. A. R. G. Drummond and of Esther Pickering. *Education:* Canford School, Trinity Coll. Cambridge. *Career:* joined BBC 1958, Asst Head, Music and Arts, Controller of Music 1985–91, Controller BBC Radio 3 1987–91, Dir BBC Promenade Concerts 1985–95; Dir Edin. Int. Festival 1978–83, European Arts Festival 1992; Vice-Chair. British Arts Festivals Asscn 1981–83 (Vice-Pres. 1994–); Pres.

Kensington Soc. 1985–2001; Chair. Nat. Dance Co-ordinating Cttee 1986–95; Gov. Royal Ballet 1986–2000; mem. Theatres Trust 1989–99, Chair. 1998–2001. *Programmes produced include:* Tortelier Master Classes 1964, Leeds Piano Competition 1966, Diaghilev 1967, Kathleen Ferrier 1968, Music Now 1969, Spirit of the Age 1975, The Lively Arts 1976–78. *Publications:* A Fine and Private Place (with Joan Bakewell) 1977, The Turn of the Dance (with N. Thompson) 1984, Speaking of Diaghilev 1997, Tainted by Experience (autobiog.) 2000. *Honours:* Chevalier, Légion d'honneur. *Address:* 5 Walker's Lane, Lewes, East Sussex, BN7 2JR, England (home). *Telephone:* (1273) 474995 (home).

**DU, Ming-xin;** Chinese composer and music editor; b. 19 Aug. 1928, Qianjiang Co., Hubei Prov.; m. 1966; one s. one d. *Education:* Yu Cai Music School and Tchaikovsky State Conservatoire, USSR. *Career:* debut solo piano concert, Shanghai 1948; Prof. of Composition, Cen. Conservatory of Music 1978–; participated in the Asian Composers' Conference and Music Festival, Hong Kong 1981; travelled to USA for performance of Violin Concerto No. 1, John F. Kennedy Center 1986, and gave lectures in music insts; Exec. Dir Chinese Musicians' Asscn; mem. 11th CPPCC 1997–. *Compositions include:* Violin Concerto No. 1, Violin Concerto No. 2, Piano Concerto No. 1, Piano Concerto No. 2, Great Wall Symphony, Luoshen Symphony, Youth Symphony, The South Sea of My Mother Land (symphonic picture), The Goddess of the River Luo (symphonic fantasia), Flapping! the Flags of Army, The Mermaid (ballet suite), The Red Detachment of Women (ballet suite), Wonderful China (film soundtrack) 1982, piano trio, string quartet. *Address:* Central Conservatory of Music, 43 Baojia Street, Beijing 100031, People's Republic of China.

**DU BOIS, Mark;** Singer (Tenor); b. 9 Nov. 1953, Toronto, Canada. *Education:* Studied in Toronto. *Career:* Debut: Canadian Opera Company, Toronto; Don Curzio in Le nozze di Figaro, 1976; Opera roles in Canada and elsewhere have included Tamino, Ramiro in Cenerentola, Fenton, Laerte in Hamlet and Rossini's Almaviva; La Scala, Milan, 1982 in Stravinsky's Mavra; Belfast Opera, 1983 as Tonio in La Fille du régiment; San Diego Opera, from 1987 notably as Ernesto in Don Pasquale; Concerts in London and elsewhere. *Address:* San Diego Opera, PO Box 988, San Diego, CA 92112, USA.

**DU BOIS, Rob;** Dutch composer; b. 28 May 1934, Amsterdam. *Education:* studied piano and jurisprudence. *Compositions:* Orchestral: Piano Concerto, 1960, revised, 1968; Cercle for Piano, 9 Winds and Percussion, 1963; Simultaneous, 1965; Breuker Concerto for 2 Clarinets, 4 saxophones and 21 strings, 1968; A Flower Given to My Daughter, 1970; Le Concerto pour Hrisanide for piano and orchestra, 1971; Allegro for strings, 1973; 3 Pezzi, 1973; Suite No. 1, 1973; Violin Concerto, 1975; Skarabee, 1977; Zodiak, 1977; Concerto for 2 violins and orchestra, 1979; Sinfonia da camera for wind orchestra, 1980; Luna, for alto flute and orchestra, 1988; Elegia for oboe d'amore and strings, 1995; Chamber: 7 Pastorales, 1960–64; Trio for flute, oboe and clarinet, 1961; Rondeaux pour deux for piano and percussion, 1962, 2nd series for piano 4-hands and percussion, 1964; Chants et contrepoints, for wind quintet, 1962; Espaces à remplir for 11 musicians, 1963; Oboe Quartet, 1964; String Trio, 1967; Symposium for oboe, violin, viola and cello, 1969; Trio Agitate for horn, trombone and tuba, 1969; Reflexions sur le jour ou Perotin le Grand ressuscitera for wind quintet, 1969; Fusion pour deux for bass clarinet and piano, 1971; Tracery for bass clarinet and 4 percussionists, 1979; Sonata for violin and piano, 1980; Elegia for oboe d'amore, violin, viola and cello, 1980; String Quartet No. 3, 1981; Sonata for Solo Viola, 1981; Ars aequi for 2 double basses and piano, 1984; Autumn Leaves for guitar and harpsichord, 1984; Hyperion for clarinet, horn, viola and piano, 1984; Forever Amber for 2 guitars, 1985; Das Liebesverbot for 4 Wagner tubas; On a Lion's Interlude for alto flute, 1986; Symphorine for flute and string trio, 1987; 4 String Quartets, 1960–90; Gàberbocchus for 4 pianos, 1994; Fleeting for clarinet and ensemble, 1997; Songs for violin, cello and piano, 1998; Die Gretchenfrage for flute and piano, 2004. *Address:* Spruitenbosstraat 21, 2012 LJ Haarlem, Netherlands.

**DU PLESSIS, Christian;** British singer (baritone); b. 2 July 1944, Vryheid, South Africa. *Education:* Potchefstroom and Bloemfontein Univs, studied with Teasdale Griffiths and Esme Webb in South Africa, Otakar Kraus in London. *Career:* debut with the PACT Opera in Johannesburg as Yamadori in Madama Butterfly 1967; British debut in Andrea Chénier at Theatre Royal, Drury Lane 1970; Valentin in Faust at Barcelona 1971; Prin. Baritone, ENO 1973–81, notably as Cecil in Maria Stuarda and Verdi's Germont and Posa; USA debut in Les Pêcheurs de Perles, Texas 1984; Covent Garden debut in Rigoletto 1984; recipient, Ernest Oppenheimer Bursary 1968, 1969, 1970; major roles with cos in UK, USA, France, Netherlands, Hong Kong, Ireland; retd 1988. *Current Management:* Performing Arts, 1 Hinde Street, London, W1M 5RH, England.

**DUBÉ, Jean;** Pianist; b. Dec. 1981, Canada. *Career:* Debut: Italian Women's Society Gala, Edmonton, Alberta, Canada, 5 years of age; Mozart Concerto No. 5 with Radio France Philharmonic Orchestra, Mozart Bicentenary Gala, Paris, 9 years of age; World-wide recitalist, chamber musician and soloist with orchestra in Japan, Canada, Latvia, France, Ireland, Germany, Belgium, Switzerland, Netherlands, Hungary, Czechoslovakia, Italy and Romania, 1988; Canadian television, 1988; French television and radio; Japanese television, Fuji; Concert Châtelet, 1991; Toured with orchestra, south of France, 1992; Salle Gaveau, France Musique; Toured Germany with orchestra, NDR radio, 1993; Japanese television, NHK, 1995; Toured Canada, Japan, 1996; Invalides, Bagatelle (Paris), Chimay (Belgium), 1997; Toured

Western Europe; Czech television, 1998; French and German television, 1999; Hungarian Institute, Musée d'Orsay, Paris and Tokyo, 2000; Festivals: Messiaen Festival, Dublin, Riga, BBC Radio 3, Orléans, Nice, Utrecht and Dietzenbach, 2001; Bayreuth, St Petersburg; performed Sain-Saëns Concerto No. 2, Concertgebouw, Amsterdam, 2003. *Recordings:* Samuel Barber, Sonata for piano; Conservatory of Paris-Meyer Foundation records: XXth century piano music: Ginastera, Bartók, Mochizuki, Messiaen, Komulainen, Prokofiev; Videotape: 8 productions for French and European cable television (Grieg Piano Concerto and Saint-Saëns Concerto for piano No. 4) with Orchestra Le Sinfonia de Lyon, conducted by Jean-Claude Guerinot, recorded live in Cathedral of St John, Lyon, France; also recordings of Liszt, Franck, Sibelius, Ciurlionis and others. *Honours:* First Prize, 'Young Prodigies Mozart', Paris National Competition, 1991; Youngest graduate ever, Nice Conservatory, 1992; First Prize, National Superior Conservatory of Paris, 1996; First Prize, Francis Poulenc, 1997; First Prize, Jeunesses Musicales, Bucharest, 1998; Yvonne Lefèbure Scholarship Orléans XXth Century, 2000; Second Grand Prize, Olivier Messiaen, Paris, 2000; Second Prize, Takasaki, 2000; Best Show of the Year, for Turangalila concert, 2001; First Prize, Franz Liszt Piano Competition, 2002. *Current Management:* Marie Méli, 30 rue du Moulin Joly, 75011 Paris, France.

**DUBINBAUM, Gail;** Singer (Mezzo-Soprano); b. 1958, New York, USA. *Education:* Studied with Herta Glaz and with the Metropolitan Young Artists Program. *Career:* Sang at the Metropolitan from 1982, debut in L'Enfant et les Sortilèges; Appearances in New York and elsewhere in the USA as Rossini's Rosina and Isabella and as Mozart's Dorabella; Engagements at the Vienna Staatsoper 1986–88; Suzuki in Butterfly for Opera Pacific at Costa Mesa and again at Detroit, 1991; sang in the Jeremiah Symphony with Leonard Bernstein conducting Boston Symphony, Los Angeles Philharmonic and the Pittsburgh Symphony (40th Anniversary of premiere), sang Suzuki and Bach Magnificat with Zubin Mehta and Israel Philharmonic; sang Nefertiti in Akhnaten by Philip Glass at Chicago, 2000; sang Nefertiti with the Boston Lyric Opera, Suzuki with Arizona Opera and Maddalena with Montreal Opera. *Address:* 2430 W Barbie, Phoenix, AZ 85085, USA. *E-mail:* DuMass315@aol.com.

**DUBOSC, Catherine;** Singer (Soprano); b. 12 March 1959, Lille, France. *Education:* Studied at Strasbourg Conservatory, Ecole National in Paris from 1980 with Denise Dupleix and Hans Hotter; Further study with Eric Tappy at Lyon. *Career:* Sang at Lyon Opéra, 1985–87, as Mozart's Despina, Pamina and Susanna, Nannetta, Blanche in Dialogues des Carmélites and Marzelline (Fidelio); Sang Gretel at Geneva, 1987 and Isipile in Cavalli's Giasone at Utrecht, 1988, and the Théâtre des Champs Elysées, Paris, 1990; Appearances at Montpellier (Pamina, 1991), Avignon, Nancy, Edinburgh and Strasbourg; Sang Mélisande at Lausanne, 1992 and at Frankfurt, 1994; Sang Blanche in the Danish premiere of Poulenc's Carmelites, Copenhagen, 1997. *Recordings include:* Giasone, The Love for Three Oranges, Campra's Tancrède, Scylla et Glaucus by Leclair and Darande in Gluck's La Rencontre Imprevue (Erato).

**DUBROVAY, Laszlo;** Composer and Teacher; b. 23 March 1943, Budapest, Hungary. *Education:* Bartók Conservatory, Budapest; Graduated, Academy of Music, Budapest, 1966; Principal Teachers: Istvan Szelenyi, Ferenc Szabo, Imre Vincze; Completed training in Germany with Karlheinz Stockhausen, Composition and Electronic Music from Hans-Ulrich Humpert, 1972–74. *Career:* Teacher of Music Theory, Budapest Academy of Music, 1976–; Residence in Berlin, 1985; Professor of Theory, Franz Liszt Academy of Music, Budapest, 1998–; mem, Hungarian Arts Academy. *Compositions include:* Stage works: The Ransom, opera in one act, 1991; The Sculptor, dance-play in one act, 1993; Faust the Damned, dance-play, 1998; Orchestral: 2 concertos for piano, 1982, 1998; Concertos for: strings, 1979, flute, 1981, trumpet, 1981, violin, 1991, cimbalom, 1994; Triple concerto for trumpet, trombone and tuba, 1989; 4 suite of Faust the Damned, 1989; Hungarian Symphony, 1997; Cantata Aquilarum, 1999; Timbre Symphony, 2000; Concert for Hungarian folk instruments, 2000; Symphonic band music: Deserts, 1987; March, 1990; The Ransom, 1992; Buzzing Polka, 1993; The Death of Faust, 1996; Ballet Suite, 1996; Festive Music, 2000; Chamber music: 3 string quartets, 1970, 1976, 1983; 2 wind quintets, 1968, 1972; 3 brass quintets, 1971, 1980, 1998; Brass Septet, 1980; 13 solos for different instruments, 1975–2000; Paraphrasis for piano, 1999; choruses, tape, live electronic and computer music pieces. *Address:* c/o ARTISJUS, Meszaros u. 15–17, H–01539 Budapest 114, PoB 593, Hungary.

**DUDAMEL, Gustavo;** Venezuelan conductor, composer and violinist; b. 1981, Barquisimento. *Career:* Musical Dir Simón Bolívar Nat. Youth Orchestra, Venezuela 1999–; currently Music Dir Youth Orchestra of the Andean Countries; attended Int. Conductors' Acad. of the Allianz Cultural Foundation, London 2004–05; has conducted Bamberger Symphoniker, Israel Philharmonic Orchestra, NDR Radio Orchestra Hannover; 2005–06 season includes Royal Stockholm Philharmonic, City of Birmingham SO, Orchestre Philharmonique de Radio France, Royal Liverpool Philharmonic, Frankfurt Radio SO, Sächsische Staatskapelle Dresden, Gothenburg SO at BBC Proms, Los Angeles Philharmonic at Hollywood Bowl (US debut), Philharmonia Orchestra at the QEH. *Honours:* winner Bamberger Symphoniker Gustav Mahler Conducting Competition 2004. *Current Management:* Askonas Holt Ltd, Lonsdale Chambers, 27 Chancery Lane, London, WC2A 1PF, England. *Telephone:* (20) 7400-1700 (office). *Fax:* (20) 7400-1799 (office). *E-mail:* info@ askonasholt.co.uk (office). *Website:* www.askonasholt.co.uk (office).

**DUDDELL, Joe,** FRAM; British composer; b. 1972, England. *Education:* Salford Univ., Royal Acad. of Music with Steve Martland. *Career:* commissions include London Sinfonietta, BT Scottish Ensemble, ViVA! and the BBC, including three works for the Proms; works performed at Bath, Chester, Huddersfield, Spitalfields, Lichfield, Lucerne and Brisbane Festivals, South Bank and Barbican Centres in London, New York and Moscow, and at tours in Scotland and Taiwan; Lecturer in Composition, Exeter Univ. *Compositions include:* Circle Square, saxophone quartet 1997; Parallel Lines, tuned percussion and piano, 1999; The Realside, soprano, tenor, chorus and optional brass, 1999; Computation, counter-tenor and ensemble, 1999; Vaporize, piano 4 hands, 2000; Snowblind, percussion and strings, 2001; Ode to English, unaccompanied voices, 2002; Ruby, percussion and orchestra, 2002–03; Shadowplay, cello and chamber orchestra, 2003; Temporal Keys, solo organ, 2003, New Dawn Fades for string orchestra 2004, Mnemonic for flute, harp and strings 2004, Freaky Dancer for vibraphone and guitar quartet 2003, Arbor Low for string quartet 2004. *Current Management:* Schott Co Ltd, 48 Great Marlborough Street, London, W1F 7BB, England. *Telephone:* (20) 7494-1487. *Fax:* (20) 7287-1529. *Website:* www.schott-music.com.

**DUDZIAK, Francis;** Singer (Baritone); b. 1959, France. *Education:* Studied at the Paris Conservatoire. *Career:* Sang at the Opéra du Rhin, Strasbourg, 1982–85; Lyon Opéra, 1985–88; Guest appearances throughout France in Monteverdi's Orfeo and Ulisse as Mozart's Masetto and Guglielmo, Ramiro in L'Heure Espagnole and in operetta; Saint-Cere Festival, 1985 in Dalayrac's L'Amant statue and Maison à vendre; Strasbourg, 1991 as Papageno; Many concerts in Paris and elsewhere. *Address:* 8 Rue Charles Nodier, 75018 Paris, France.

**DUESING, Dale;** Singer (baritone); b. 26 Sept. 1947, Milwaukee, USA. *Education:* Began studies in Milwaukee as a pianist; Vocal studies at Lawrence University in Wisconsin. *Career:* San Francisco Opera as Britten's Billy Budd and Donizetti's Belcore; Seattle Opera as Wagner's Wolfram and Tchaikovsky's Eugene Onegin; Glyndebourne debut 1976, as Olivier in Capriccio; later sang Guglielmo in Così fan tutte, conducted by Bernard Haitink; Ottone in L'Incoronazione di Poppea, Lysander in A Midsummer Night's Dream, 1989, and Figaro, 1989; Metropolitan Opera debut 1979, as Harlekin in Ariadne auf Naxos; Concert engagements with the New York Philharmonic, Berlin Philharmonic, Boston Symphony, Concertgebouw Orchestra, BBC Symphony and Santa Cecilia of Rome; Conductors include Giulini, Levine, Leppard, Ozawa, Sawallisch, Dohnányi and Previn; Opera engagements include Ariadne at La Scala, Billy Budd and Peter Grimes at the Metropolitan, Die Meistersinger in Brussels and Così fan tutte at Santa Fe; Sang Figaro at Seattle, 1989; Goryanchikov in From the House of the Dead, at Brussels, 1990; Guglielmo at Barcelona and Olivier at the 1990 Glyndebourne Festival; Solo recitalist in the USA and Europe; World Premiere: Wade in Jonathan Wade by Carlisle Floyd, Houston Opera; Così fan tutte at Liceo, Barcelona; Marriage of Figaro, Glyndebourne Opera under Rattle; Metropolitan Opera, New York, Pelléas and Papageno; Season 1991/92 as Mozart's Count at Brussels, 'I' in the premiere of Schnittke's Life with an Idiot at Amsterdam and Nardo in La Finta Giardiniera at the Salzburg Festival; Prodocismo in Il Turco in Italia at Théâtre du Champs-Elysées, Paris, 1996; Brussels 1997, in Orphée aux Enfers; Season 1998 as Bill in Mahagonny at Salzburg and Toby Belch in the premiere of Trojahn's Was ihr Wollt at Munich; Sang Leontes in the premiere of Wintermärchen by Boesmans, Brussels 1999; Narrator in the premiere of Sophie's Choice at Covent Garden, 2002. *Recordings include:* Don Giovanni and Zemlinsky's Lyric Symphony; Così fan tutte; Arias and Barcaroles, Leonard Bernstein. *Current Management:* Askonas Holt Ltd, Lonsdale Chambers, 27 Chancery Lane, London, WC2A 1PF, England. *Telephone:* (20) 7400-1700. *Fax:* (20) 7400-1799. *E-mail:* info@askonasholt.co.uk. *Website:* www.askonasholt.co.uk.

**DUFFIELD, Alan,** FTCL, LRAM, ARCM, ABSM; singer (tenor); b. 1952, Ripon, England. *Education:* Birmingham School of Music, Nat. Opera Studio, London. *Career:* concerts include Bach's St John Passion and B minor Mass (Lufthansa Festival, London), Handel's Joshua, High Priest in Idomeneo, under Simon Rattle, and Britten's Serenade for tenor, horn and strings (CBSO); Mozart's Requiem and Haydn's Nelson Mass with the London Mozart Players, BBC recital of John Joubert songs; appearances at Glyndebourne in Orfeo (ENO), and as Don Basilio and Don Curzio (Le nozze di Figaro); roles in La Bohème, Madama Butterfly, Der Rosenkavalier, Death in Venice, Samson, Mathis der Maler (Hindemith) for the Royal Opera. *Honours:* Dr hc (Birmingham Conservatoire). *Address:* c/o Royal Opera House, Covent Garden, London, WC2, England.

**DUGDALE, Sandra;** Singer (Soprano); b. 4 Jan. 1946, Pudsey, Yorkshire, England. *Education:* Studied in Leeds and at the Guildhall School, London. *Career:* Debut: With Glyndebourne Touring Opera as Despina in Così fan tutte; Has sung with English National Opera in operas by Mozart, Janáček and Strauss; Welsh National Opera in The Greek Passion by Martinů; Four principal roles with the Handel Opera Society; Handel roles with the English Bach Festival; Covent Garden debut 1983 as Fire and The Nightingale in the Ravel/Stravinsky double bill; returned 1985, as Adele in Die Fledermaus; Festival appearances include Hong Kong, Camden, Batignano, Wexford and Vienna; Frequent broadcasts with the BBC, including the Much Loved Music Show and Lo Speziale by Haydn (ITV); Sang Adele for Opera Northern Ireland at the Grand Opera House, Belfast, 1990; Sullivan's Angelina for D'Oyly Carte at Bournemouth, 1990; Concert engagements with most major British orchestras, under the batons of Charles Mackerras, Roderick Brydon, Charles

Groves, David Atherton, Philip Ledger, Mark Elder, John Eliot Gardiner and Vernon Handley; Regular visits to the USA. *Recordings include:* Videos of operettas by Gilbert and Sullivan; Series, 100 Years of Italian Opera, with the Philharmonia Orchestra. *Address:* c/o Music International, 13 Ardilaun Road, London, N5 2QR, England.

**DUHAMEL, Antoine;** Composer; b. 30 July 1925, Valmondois, France. *Education:* Studied with Messiaen and Liebowitz in Paris. *Career:* Club d'Essai, 1950–52; Discophiles Français, 1954–57 (Yves Nat, Lily Kraus, studios A Charlin); Film music from 1961 for such directors as J D Pollet, J L Godard, Fr Truffaut, B Tavernier, and now F Trueba and P Leconte. Wrote the orchestral music with Pierre Jansen for D W Griffith's Intolérance, 1985; Founder, Ecole de Musique de Villeurbanne, 1980; mem, SACEM; Honorary President, Syndicat national des Auteurs et Compositeurs; Vice-President, Fondation Beaumarchais. *Compositions:* Operas and other works for stage: L'Ivrogne, (Baudelaire), 1953, staged Tours, 1984 as Le scieur de long; Lundi, Monsieur, vous serez riche (Forlani), Paris 1969; L'Opéra des Oiseaux (Aristophane), Lyon, 1971; Ubu a L'Opera (Jarry), Avignon, 1974; Gambara (Balzac), Lyon, 1978; Les Travaux d'Hercule, Vaise 1981, Adelaide, 1983 and Brisbane, 1998; Le Transsiberien (Cendrars), Paris, 1983; Requiem de Jean Cocteau, Milly la Forêt, 1983; Quatrevingt-treize (Hugo), Fourvières, 1989; Carmenmania, ballet, Nice, 1994. *Recordings:* Many albums of film music. *Publications:* Gambara, a book of the collection Avant-Scène Opéra. *Honours:* Prix Georges Enesco, 1977; Grand Prix Sacem, 1998. *Address:* 243 rue Georges Duhamel, 95760 Valmondois, France.

**DUIJCK, Johan;** Belgian choir conductor, composer and pianist; b. 1954. *Career:* Prin. Conductor, Flemish Radio Choir 1997–; Assoc. Conductor, Spanish Radio Television Choir, Madrid 1998–; founder-conductor, European Youth Choir 1994–; Prof., Koninklijk Conservatorium, Ghent, Muziekkapel Koningin Elisabeth, Waterloo; teacher, Dartington Int. Music Schools; directs conducting courses, Euskalerriko Abesbatzen Elkartea, Spain 2000–; Chorus Dir, Acad. of St Martin in the Fields 2002–; pianist, Hans Memling Trio. *Compositions:* Alma de la música, Cantate Domino canticum novum. *Honours:* Prize of the European Youth Festival, Neerpelt, prizes for vocal composition from East and West Flanders, European Piano Teachers' Asscn composition prize, Haec Olim prize. *Address:* Gouden-Boomstraat 51, 8000 Bruges, Belgium. *Telephone:* (325) 031-00-28.

**DUMAY, Augustin;** Concert Violinist; b. 17 Jan. 1949, Paris, France. *Education:* Studied at the Paris Conservatoire from 1959 with Roland Charmy. *Career:* Debut: Théâtre des Champs Elysées, Paris, 1963; Studied further with Arthur Grumiaux, 1962–67, then played regularly in public; Partnerships with Jean-Philippe Collard and Michel Beroff; Concert with Karajan and the Berlin Philharmonic 1979 followed by Bartók's 2nd Concerto conducted by Colin Davis; Further engagements with L'Orchestre National de France, Suisse Romande Orchestra, London Symphony and English Chamber, and at the Montreux, Bath, Berlin, Lucerne, Monaco, Aix, Leipzig and Montpellier festivals; Other conductors include Ozawa, Dutoit, Sanderling, Sawallisch, Fruhbeck de Burgos and Skrowaczewski; Chamber music collaborations with Maria Joao Pires, Michel Dalberto, Lynn Harrell, Jean-Bernard Pommier, Yo-Yo Ma and Richard Stoltzmann; Gave the premiere of Berio's Sequenza 9, for solo violin, and the premieres of the concertos by Marius Constant and Isang Yun; Director of the National Chamber Orchestra of Toulouse from 1988; Played a 1721 Stradivarius, formerly belonging to Fritz Kreisler, then a 1744 Guarneri instrument. *Recordings:* Lalo's Symphonie Espagnole, conducted by Michel Plasson, and Chausson's Concerto for piano, violin and string quartet, with Collard and the Muir Quartet; Mozart, Complete Violin Concertos; Tchaikovsky and Mendelsohn, Violin Concertos, London Symphony Orchestra; Mozart, Piano and Violin Sonatas; Brahms, Complete Violin and Piano Sonatas with Maria Joâo Pires. *Current Management:* TransArt (UK) Ltd, Cedar House, 10 Rutland Street, Filey, YO14 9JB, North Yorkshire, England. *Telephone:* (1723) 515819. *Fax:* (1723) 514678. *E-mail:* transartuk@transartuk.com. *Website:* www.transartuk.com. *Address:* Granjinha Do Meio, Excalos De Baixo, 6005 Alcains, Portugal.

**DUMITRESCU, Iancu (Ioan);** Composer, Music Critic, Conductor and Pianist; b. 15 July 1944, Sibiu, Romania; m. (1) Cristina Dumitrescu, 10 May 1979, (2) Ana-Maria Avram, Sept 1988. *Education:* High School of Music, Bucharest; Piano with Cici Manta; Composition with Alfred Mendelssohn, Stefan Niculescu, Aurel Stroe, and with Sergiu Celibidache, Trier, Germany. *Career:* Founder, Leader and Conductor, chamber music ensemble Hyperion; Pianist specialising in avant garde music; Compositions performed on television and radio, Romania, Austria, Netherlands, France, Italy, 1970–; Commands: Radio France, Paris; Commande d'Etat, Minister of Culture, France; Kronos Quartet, San Francisco and G Enescu Philharmonic Orchestra; World premieres: Amsterdam, Berlin, Bremen, Bucharest, Cluj, Paris (Radio France), London (Royal Festival Hall), Royan, Warsaw, Vienna, Lisbon (Gulbenkian Foundation), Milan (Piccola Scala), Rome, Boston, New York, San Francisco; Head, Radio France, Paris. *Compositions include:* Alternances, I, II, string quartet, 1968; Multiples, 3 groups of percussion, 1972; Apogeum for orchestra, 1973; Reliefs for two orchestras and piano, 1975; Orion I and II, for three groups of percussion, 1978; Perspectives au Movemur, string quartet 1979; Zenith, percussion, 1980; Nimbus, 3 trombones, percussion, tape, 1980; Cogito-Trompe L'oeil for ensemble, 1981; Grande Ourse for ensemble, 1982; Aulodie Mioritica, double bass, orchestra, 1984; Haryphonies (alpha, beta, gamma), double bass, percussion, harryphono, piano préparé, 1985; Holzwege, viola solo, 1986; Reliefs for orchestra;

Harryphonies (epsilon), large orchestra, 1986; Monades (gamma and epsilon), for 6 monocords and harryphone, 1988; Gnosis, for double bass and string ensemble, 1988–97; L'Orbite D'Uranus; Astrée Lointaine, bass saxophone, orchestra, 1991; L'Empire des Signes, 1992; Au De La De Movemur; Clusterum, percussion, 1993; Galaxy, 3 harryphones, 3 percussions, microprocessor, 1993; 5 Impulsions, large orchestra, 1993; A Priori, chamber ensemble, 1994; Mythos, chamber ensemble, 1994; Kronos/Holzwege, string quartet; Impuls, bass flute, percussion, 1994; Mnemosyne, chamber ensemble, 1994; Pulsar Perdu for Kronos Quartet, string quartet, 1995; Fluxus, for tapes and large orchestra, 1996; Sirius Kronos Quartet, for string quartet and tape, 1996; Meteorites, electronic music, 1997; Ouranos, for distorted spectral sounds, string orchestra and electronic tape, 1997; La Chute dans le Temps, for six groups of instruments, new distorted spectral sounds and tape, 1997; New Meteors, Oiseaux célestes and Colossus, 2000. *Recordings:* Opera Omnia. *Address:* 16 Dr Draghiescu nr 16, sector 5, 76224 Bucharest, Romania.

**DUNCAN, Martin;** Stage Director; b. 1960, London. *Education:* LAMDA, London. *Career:* Stagings of Die Zauberflöte and Ariadne auf Naxos for Scottish Opera; Serse and La Clemenza di Tito in Munich; The Barber of Seville for English Touring Opera; L'Heure Espagnole, Gianni Schicchi, The Thieving Magpie and Iolanta for Opera North; Artistic Director of Nottingham Playhouse, 1994–99; British premiere production of Birtwistle's The Last Supper for Glyndebourne, 2000–01; Season 2001–2002 with The Rake's Progress and Die Entführung for the Bayerische Staatsoper, Munich. *Address:* c/o Glyndebourne Festival Opera, Glyndebourne, Lewes, Sussex BN8 5UU, England.

**DUNDAS-GRANT, Deirdre,** FRAM; British bassoon player; b. 28 May 1927, Ewell, Surrey, England; d. of James H. Dundas-Grant and Katherine Galloway; one d. one s. *Education:* Royal Acad. of Music. *Career:* debut, Bournemouth Municipal Orchestra as Second, then Principal Bassoon; Principal Bassoon with BBC Concert Orchestra, 1961–69; Principal, London Bach Orchestra; Monteverdi Orchestra; Steinitz Bach Players; Menuhin Festival Orchestra; solo recitals and chamber music with BBC and music clubs; sessions and engagements with all major orchestras; founder member, National Youth Orchestra and Portia Wind Ensemble; retd from public performing, engaged in examining, adjudication and consultation; mem. RAM Guild, British Double Reed Soc. (chair. 1999–2002), Royal Soc. of Musicians. *Recordings:* Bach Art of Fugue; Christmas Music from Venice with John Eliot Gardiner; Philip Jones Brass and Ensemble; Bach's B minor Mass with Academy of St Martin in the Fields; Many orchestral recordings. *Publications:* Arrangements of Bach Trios for Woodwind; Liszt Quintet; contrib. numerous articles to British Double Reed Notes. *Honours:* Mem. Court of Assts, Royal Soc. of Music 2004; Bach, Beethoven Scholarship, Royal Academy of Music, 1947–49. *Address:* 24 Dora Road, London SW19 7HH, England.

**DUNK, Roderick;** Conductor; b. 1959, Birmingham, England. *Education:* Studied at the Birmingham Conservatory. *Career:* Played double bass in the BBC Symphony Orchestra and BBC Concert Orchestra, 1978–90; From 1990 regular guest conductor with the BBC Concert, Royal Philharmonic, London Symphony and Halle Orchestras; Since 1996 conducted London Symphony Orchestra, Royal Philharmonic, Philharmonia, London Philharmonic, Vienna Symphony and Prague Symphony orchestras in several series of Compact Discs; Arranger and Music Director for BBC television, conductor of the London production of Carmen Jones and music director for Travelling Opera; Directed numerous performances with London City Ballet and Birmingham Royal Ballet; In 1986 formed the London Palm Court Orchestra, giving performances of Edwardian and Victorian music. *Address:* c/o Travelling Opera, 114 St Mary's Road, Market Harborough, Leicestershire, LE16 7DT, England.

**DUNKI, Jean-Jacques;** Swiss pianist and composer; *Professor, Musikhochschule Basel*; b. 28 Feb. 1948, Aarau; m. Christine Baader 1994; one d. *Education:* studied in Aarau, Basel, Berlin, Paris, London, Baltimore, New York. *Career:* debut as pianist 1963, as composer 1978; performing in most European Countries, USA, 1979–, Japan, 1993–; Latin America, 1997; 1999– international career as fortepianist. *Compositions:* Lutezia, 1978; Tú... no tienes imaginación, 1979; Prokrustes, 1982; Tetrapteron O–IV, 1991; Pessoa, 1993; Nulla dies, 1994; Figures, 1997; Kammerstück I–VIII, 1985–99. *Recordings:* Piano Music of Berg, Webern, Schönberg and Zemlinsky; Chamber Music of Grieg, Reger, Schumann; Own music. *Publications:* Schönberg's Zeichen 2005; several articles on Schönberg, Schumann, Reger and Webern. *Honours:* 1st Prize, Arnold Schoenberg Piano Competition, 1981. *Address:* Bruderholzallee 12, 4059 Basel, Switzerland.

**DUNN, Mignon;** Singer (Mezzo-soprano); b. 17 June 1931, Memphis, Tennessee, USA; m. Kurt Klippstatter, 24 July 1972. *Education:* Southwestern University; University of Lausanne; Vocal studies with Karin Branzell and Beverly Johnson, New York. *Career:* Debut: Operatic debut as Carmen, New Orleans, 1955; New York City Opera debut, 1956, on roster until 1957, then 1972 and 1975; Metropolitan Opera debut, New York, as Nurse in Boris Godunov, 1958; regular appearances in over 50 major roles including Ortrud, Marie Mère (Carmélites), Amneris, Azucena, Marina, Fricka, Herodias and Anna (Les Troyens); Guest appearances with opera companies in Chicago, San Francisco, Boston, Miami, Berlin, Hamburg, Vienna, Florence and other cities; Sang the Kostelnicka in Jenůfa at the 1988 Spoleto Festival; Season 1988–89 as the Witch in Rusalka at Philadelphia and Amneris in Chicago; Created Madame Irma in the premiere of The Balcony by

Di Domenica, Boston, 1990; Clytemnestra in Nuria Espert's production of Elektra at Barcelona, 1990; Mistress Quickly in Falstaff for New York City Opera, 1996; Soloist with orchestras in USA and Europe; Faculty, University of Illinois, 1990. *Recordings:* For several labels. *Honours:* Honorary D.Mus, Southwestern University, 1974.

**DUNN, Susan Lorette,** BA; American singer (soprano); b. 23 July 1954, Malvern, AR. *Education:* Hendrix Coll. and Indiana Univ. *Career:* debut as Aida at Peoria (Ill.) Opera Co. 1982; subsequent appearances at La Scala, Milan, Italy, Carnegie Hall, Lyric Opera, Chicago, Ill., Vienna Staatsoper, Australian Opera, Washington Opera, San Diego Opera, Calif., Teatro Communale Bologna, Metropolitan Opera, New York, Sydney Opera House, Australia; has performed with leading orchestras, including New York Philharmonic, Chicago Symphony, Boston Symphony, Orchestre de Paris, Concertgebouw Orchestra, Netherlands; Lecturer of Voice, Shepherd School of Music. *Opera roles include:* Aida, Sieglinde in Die Walküre, Elena in I Vespri Siciliani, Elisabeth de Valois in Don Carlo, Leonora in La Forza del Destino, Leonora in Il Trovatore, Amelia in Un Ballo in Maschera, Amelia Boccanegra. *Honours:* Nat. Metropolitan Opera Council Award 1981, Winner Philadelphia Opera Co./Pavarotti Int. Vocal Competition 1981, Winner WGN-III Opera Competition 1983, Dallas Morning News-Dallas Opera G. B. Dealey Prize 1983, Richard Tucker Award 1983. *Current Management:* Herbert H. Brelin, Inc., 119 W 57th Street, New York, NY 10019, USA.

**DÜNNEBACH, Ulrich;** Singer (Bass-baritone); b. 21 April 1946, Limbach, Germany. *Career:* Debut: Hagen Opera, 1969; Sang in opera at Aachen, 1975–80, Detmold, 1980–85, Nuremberg from 1985; Guest appearances at Munich as the Hermit in Der Freischütz, 1995, and at Liège and Rome, 1996, as Rocco in Fidelio; Sang Wagner's Daland at Bologna and Liège, 2000–01; Other roles have included Mozart's Figaro, Leporello, Alfonso and Sarastro; Oroveso in Norma, the Doctor in Wozzeck, King Philip in Don Carlos, Banquo and Zaccaria (Nabucco); Concerts include Penderecki's Polish Requiem, conducted by the composer. *Address:* Nuremberg Opera, Richard-Wagner Platz 2-10, 90443 Nuremberg, Germany.

**DUNSBY, Jonathan (Mark);** Musician and Professor of Music, University of Reading; b. 16 March 1953, Wakefield, Yorkshire, England; m. (1) Anne Davis, 7 Sept 1974, 1 d., (2) Esther Cavett, 25 May 1983, 1 d. *Education:* ARCM, 1968; BA, Honours, New College, Oxford, 1973; PhD, Leeds University, 1976; Harkness Fellow, 1976. *Career:* Debut: Piano, Wigmore Hall, 1972; Bronze Medal, Geneva International Competition, 1970; Jury Prize, Munich International Competition, 1970; Winner, Commonwealth Competition, 1974; Regular appearances with Violinist, Vanya Milanova; Professor of Music, University of Reading. *Publications:* Structural Ambiguity in Brahms, 1981; Founding Editor of Journal of Music Analysis, 1981; Music Analysis in Theory and Practice (with Arnold Whittall), 1987; Schoenberg, Pierrot Lunaire, 1992; Performing Music, 1995. *Contributions:* Music and Letters; The Musical Quarterly; Journal of Music Theory; Perspectives of New Music; Journal of the Arnold Schoenberg Institute. *Address:* University of Reading, Department of Music, 35 Upper Redlands Road, Reading, Berkshire RG1 5JE, England.

**DUPHIL, Monique;** Pianist; b. 24 April 1936, France; m. Jay Humeston, 2 d. *Education:* Studied privately with Marguérite Long and at Paris Conservatoire National Supérieur de Musique with, Jean Doyen, Rose Lejour, Joseph Calvet and Pierre Pasquier. *Career:* Debut at 15: At Paris Théâtre des Champs Elysées with L'Orchestre des Concerts du Conservatoire (now Orchestre de Paris); Solo recitals in over 50 countries; Performances with orchestras in Europe, South America, Asia (Taiwan, Hong Kong, Japan, China, Korea), Australia, USA under conductors including Eugene Ormandy, George Hurst, Charles Dutoit, Maag, Sanderling, Verbitsky, Benzi, Akiyama, de Priest; Has performed with Pierre. Fournier, H. Szeryng, R. Ricci, J. P. Rampal, Michel Debost, K. Leister, the St Petersburg and American String Quartets and the Geistag and Mozarteum String Trios; Member of the Amici and Villa Lobos Trios; Prof. of Piano, Oberlin Music Conservatory, OH, USA. *Recordings:* JS Bach's French Suites; Piano Music by A Liadov; H Villa Lobos' Piano Trios Nos 1, 2 and 3 and Piano and Cello Sonata No. 2. *Current Management:* New Fine Arts (solo); Mariedi Anders (Amici Trio), San Francisco. *Address:* Oberlin College, Music Conservatory, Oberlin, OH 44074, USA. *E-mail:* mduphil@oberlin.edu.

**DUPONT, Stephen;** Singer (Bass); b. 29 July 1958, Houston, Texas, USA. *Education:* Studied at Memphis State University and the American Opera Center, New York. *Career:* Sang in La Bohème at New York and appeared in operas by Menotti at Spoleto and Palermo, 1984; Guest appearances at Venice in the Verdi Requiem and Don Carlos, in Paris and San Francisco; Mozart's Commendatore at La Scala, 1989, Colline and Ramphis at the Metropolitan, 1986–87; Sang Gremin at Strasbourg, 1990, Sparafucile at Bonn and Banquo for Miami Opera (1992). *Address:* c/o Metropolitan Opera, Lincoln Center, New York, NY 10023, USA.

**DUPRÉ, Heather,** LRAM; pianist; b. 30 March 1949, Channel Islands. *Education:* Royal Academy of Music. *Career:* debut, Wigmore Hall 1976; solo pianist, recitals in the UK, including several appearances at Edinburgh Festival Fringe, Wigmore Hall and Purcell Room; broadcast on Radio London, 1974; Jr Prof., Royal Academy of Music 1973–76; examiner, Associated Board of Royal Schools of Music 1979–2000; mem., solo performers section, Incorporated Society of Musicians. *Address:* 19c Abercorn Place, St Johns Wood, London NW8 9DX, England.

**DUPUY, Martine;** Singer (Mezzo-Soprano); b. 10 Dec. 1952, Marseilles, France. *Career:* Debut: Aix-en-Province 1975, as Eurydice in Campra's Le Carnaval de Venise; Has sung in the coloratura mezzo repertoire in Europe and North and South America; Marseilles Opera 1985, as Bellini's Romeo and as Isabella in L'Italiana in Algeri; Paris Opera 1985, as Neocles in Le Siège de Corinthe; Other Rossini roles include Malcolm (La Donna del Lago) at Nice 1985 and Bonn 1990, Cenerentola (Lausanne) and Arsace in Semiramide at Valle d'Itria and Nice, 1985; Metropolitan Opera debut 1988, as Sextus in Giulio Cesare; Sang in the opening concert at the Bastille Opera, Paris, 13 July 1989; Season 1990-91 as Mère Marie in Les Dialogues des Carmélites for Lyon Opera, Jane Seymour (Anna Bolena) at Marseilles and Madrid and Armando in a concert performance of Meyerbeer's Il Crociato in Egitto at Montpellier; Other roles include Monteverdi's Nero and Penelope; Mozart's Cecilio (Lucio Silla) and Sextus (La Clemenza di Tito); Adalgisa in Norma and Donizetti's Maffeo Orsini (Lucrezia Boria) and Ada (Il Diluvio Universale); Has also sung in Buenos Aires, Salzburg and Lausanne; Brussels 1996, as Eboli in the French version of Don Carlos; The Prince in Cendrillon at Turin; Cenerentola at Tel-Aviv, 1998; Sang the Mother in Charpentier's Louise at Toulouse 2000. *Honours:* Winner, International Singing Competition, Peschiera del Garda, 1975; Grand Prix 1985 from Opera International, France. *Address:* c/o Opéra de Lyon, 9 Quai Jean Moulin, F-69001, Lyon, France.

**DURMULLER, Jorg;** Singer (Tenor); b. 28 Aug. 1959, Berne, Switzerland. *Education:* Studied at Winterthur and Hamburg and with Christa Ludwig and Hermann Prey. *Career:* Appeared with the company of the Hamburg Staatsoper at the 1986 Schwetzingen Festival, in the premiere of Die Lieden des Jungen Werthers by Hans-Jurgen von Bose; Member of the Bielefeld opera from 1987, notably as Mozart's Ferrando and Tamino, Verdi's and Nicolai's Fenton, and Chateauneuf in Zar und Zimmermann; Sang Ramiro in Cenerentola, 1989; Tour of Russia and Spain, 1989, guest appearances in concert and opera in Brussels, Paris, Pesaro, Geneva and Mannheim; Innsbruck Early Music Festival, 1991, as Fracasso in Mozart's La Finta Semplice, conducted by René Jacobs; Komische Oper Berlin, 1996 as Mozart's Ferrando; Sang Wagner's Steuermann at Strasbourg, 2001. *Recordings:* Bruckner's Missa Solemnis in F. *Address:* St ädtisches Buhnen, Brunnenstrasse 3, 4800 Bielefeld 1, Germany.

**DÜRR, Alfred,** PhD; German musicologist and editor; b. 3 March 1918, Charlottenburg. *Education:* Univ. of Göttingen. *Career:* mem. 1951–83, Asst Dir 1962–81, Johann-Sebastian-Bach-Inst., Göttingen; Ed., Bach-Jahrbuch 1953–74; ed. of works for Bach Neue Ausgabe sämtlicher Werke; mem. Akademie der Wissenschaften, Göttingen 1976–; corresponding mem. American Musicological Soc. 1988–. *Publications:* Studien über die frühen Kantaten Johann Sebastian Bachs 1951, Zur Chronolgie der Leipzigir Vokalwerke J. Bachs (revised reprint from Bach-Jahrbuch 1957) 1976, Johann Sebastian Bach, Weihnachts Oratorium 1967, Die Kantaten von Johann Sebastian Bach 1971, Johann Sebastian Bach: Seine Handschrift-Abbild seines Schaffens 1984, Im Mittelpunkt Bach: Ausgewählte Aufsätze und Vorträge 1988, Die Johannes-Passion von Johann Sebastian Bach: Entstehung, Überlieferung, Werkeinführung 1988, Bachs Werk vom Einfall bis zur Drucklegung 1989, Johann Sebastian Bach – Das Wohltemperierte Klavier 1998; contrib. articles in scholarly journals. *Honours:* Dr hc (Baldwin-Wallace Coll., Berea, OH) 1982, (Oxford) 1995; Festschrift published in honour of 65th birthday 1983. *Address:* Charlottenburger Strasse 19, 37085 Göttingen, Germany.

**DÜRR, Karl Friedrich;** Singer (Bass-baritone); b. 1949, Stuttgart, Germany. *Education:* Studied German Literature and Political Science, receiving his PhD in 1978. *Career:* Debut: Sang Antonio in Le nozze di Figaro at Ludwigsburg; Studied further with Gunther Reich and sang with the Stuttgart Staatsoper from 1980, notably as Rihm's Jakob Lenz, Mozart's Figaro, Leporello, Don Alfonso, Klingsor (Parisifal) and Biterolf (Tannhäuser), Alfio (Cavalleria), Monterone, Zuniga in Carmen, Krishna in Satyagrapha by Philip Glass, Faninial (Rosenkavalier); Animal trainer and Athlete in Lulu by Berg; Kothner in Die Meistersinger; Appearances at the Ludwisburg and Schwetzingen Festivals and with the ensemble of the Stuttgart Staatsoper on tour to Russia (Zimmermann's Die Soldaten); Further engagements as Kaspar in Der Freischütz, Kurwenal, and Wozzeck; Concerts in Kassel, Trieste, Berlin and New York; 1989; Vienna Festival 1990, as Krenek's Diktator and as the Boxer in Schwergewicht; Sang Don Alfonso at Stuttgart, 1991; Also in Paris, Bastille Opera (Die Soldaten) and Semper-Oper, Dresden (Leporello) and other German opera houses such as Düsseldorf and Bonn; Sang in Debussy's Chute de la Maison Usher at Stuttgart, 1996; Sacristan in Tosca and Bartolo in Il Barbiere di Siviglia at Stuttgart, 1998; Appointed Kammersänger at Stuttgart Staatstheater, 1998; Season 2000–01 as Offenbach's Crespel at Stuttgart, and in Donizetti's Le Convenienze and I Pazzi per progetto. *Recordings:* Eisenhardt in Die Soldaten. *Address:* c/o Staatstheater Stuttgart, Oberer Schlossgarten 6, 7000 Stuttgart, Germany.

**DÜRR, Walther;** Musicologist; b. 27 April 1932, Berlin, Germany; m. Vittoria Bortolotti 1960; two d. *Education:* PhD, Tübingen Univ., 1956. *Career:* Lecturer, Bologna Univ., Italy, 1957; Asst, Tübingen Univ., Germany, 1962; Gen. Ed., Neue Schubert-Ausgabe, 1965; Hon. Prof., Tübingen Univ.; broadcasts for radio stations Deutsche Welle, Cologne, Südwestfunk, Baden-Baden; mem. Society for Musical Research, International Musicological Society. *Publications:* Rhythmus und Metrum im italienischen Madrigal insbesondere bei Luca Marenzio, 1956; Serie IV (Lieder) of Neue Schubert Ausgabe, 1966; Franz Schuberts Werke in Abschriften; Liederalben und Sammlungen, 1975; Der Kleine Deutsch (with Werner Aderhold and Arnold Feil), 1983; Das Deutsche Sololied im 19 Jahrhundert, 1984; Franz Schubert (with Arnold Feil), 1991; Zeichen Setzung Aufsätze zur Musikalischen Poetik, 1992; Musik und Sprache, 1994; Schubert Handbook, editor with Andreas Krause, 1997; Schubert und das Biedermeier, Festschrift Walther Dürr, 2002, ed. Michael Kube, Werner Aderhold, Walburga Litschaner. *Contributions:* Die Musikforschung; Archiv für Musikwissenschaft; Österreichische Musikzeitschrift; 19th Century Music; MGG; New Grove Dictionary of Music and Musicians; numerous hon. anniversary works and reviews. *Address:* Hausserstrasse 140, 72076 Tübingen, Germany.

**DUSSAUT, Thérèse;** Pianist; b. 20 Sept. 1939, Versailles, France; m. Claude Lemaréchal. *Education:* Conservatoire National Supérieur, Paris; Musikhochschule, Stuttgart. *Career:* Debut: 1951, Salle Gaveau, Paris, with orchestra conducted by Georges Tzipine; Regular concert appearances, both solo and orchestral; Has undertaken several world tours including one for the Ravel centenary, 1975; Professor at Toulouse Conservatory; mem, Juries of International Competitions: Tchaikovsky, Moscow; Munich; Szymanowski, Poland; Horowitz, Ukraine; Kraïnev, Ukraine; Member of Summer Music Academy, Kiev; Arts-Sciences-Lettres, Paris; Triptyque, Paris. *Compositions:* Rameau Pièces in Concert by Billaudot; Rameau Fêtes d'Hébé by Billaudot. *Recordings:* Rameau Complete Works; Works by Ravel, Tchaikovsky and Shostakovich. *Contributions:* French Pianism–an Historical Perspective, Charles Timbrell. *Honours:* First Prize, International Piano Competition, Munich. *Current Management:* Liegner, New York, USA. *Address:* 14 rue Saint Victor, 75005 Paris, France.

**DUSSEK, Michael;** Concert Pianist; b. 1958, England. *Career:* Chamber musician throughout Europe, Japan and Australia, and Canada, notably with such soloists as Cho-Liang Lin, Anne Akiko Meyers, Kurt Nikkanen and Ofra Harnoy; Recent recitals in the Amsterdam Concertgebouw, Tokyo, Madrid, Milan and Vienna; Engagements throughout the United Kingdom with the cellist Alexander Baillie, oboist Douglas Boyd and violinist Lorraine McAslan; Concerto soloist with the London Mozart Players at the Festival Hall and work for BBC Radio 3 as chamber musician and accompanist; Purcell Room recital 1993 with Markus Stocker, featuring music by Schumann, Brahms, Liszt and Martinů. *Recordings:* Brahms Piano Trios and Horn Trio with the Dussek Trio, contemporary Finnish music with the Edymion Ensemble, cello sonatas with Ofra Harnoy and cello sonatas by Reger; Professor, Royal Academy of Music.

**DUSSELJEE, Kor-Jan;** Singer (Tenor); b. 1965, Netherlands. *Education:* Graduated Dutch Academy of Arts, 1988; Masterclasses with Schwarzkopf and Hartmut Holl. *Career:* Concerts throughout the Netherlands, from 1988; Besançon and Savonlinna Festivals, Switzerland and Germany; Opera engagements in Germany as Wilhelm Meister, Tamino, Don Ottavio, Lancelot in Purcell's King Arthur and Leopold in La Juive; Architect in Reimann's Melusine at Dresden and Munich; Season 1998–99 as First Jew in Salome and Francesco in Benvenuto Cellini, both with Rotterdam Philharmonic under Gergiev; Further appearances with the Scottish CO, Dresden Staatskapelle and Bamberg Symphony Orchestra. *Address:* c/o Netherlands Opera, Waterlooplein 22, 1011 Amsterdam, Netherlands.

**DUTILLEUX, Henri;** French composer; b. 22 Jan. 1916, Angers; s. of Paul and Thérèse (née Koszul) Dutilleux; m. Geneviève Joy 1946. *Education:* Conservatoire Nat. de Musique, Paris. *Career:* Dir Service Créations Musicales Radiodiffusion Française 1945–63; Prof. of Composition Ecole Normale de Musique, Paris 1961–, Pres. 1969–74; Assoc. Prof. Conservatoire Nat. Supérieur de Musique, Paris 1970–71; fmr mem. UNESCO Music Council; assoc. mem. Royal Acad. of Music, Belgium. *Compositions:* Sonata for Piano 1948, First Symphony 1951, Le Loup (Ballet) 1953, Second Symphony (Le Double) 1959, Métaboles (for orchestra) 1964, Cello Concerto: Tout un monde lointain 1970, Figures de Résonances (for two pianos) 1971, Preludes for Piano 1974, Ainsi la Nuit (for string quartet) 1976, Timbres, Espace, Mouvement (for orchestra) 1978, 3 Strophes sur le nom de Sacher (for cello) 1981, L'Arbre des Songes (violin concerto) 1985, Le Jeu des contraires (for piano) 1988, Mystère de l'instant (for 24 strings and cimbalom) 1989, Les Citations (for oboe, harpsichord, double-bass and percussion) 1991, The Shadows of Time (for orchestra) 1997, Sur le même accord for violin and orchestra 2002, Correspondences for song and orchestra 2003. *Publications:* Mystère et Mémoire des sons 1997. *Honours:* hon. mem. American Acad. and Inst. of Arts and Letters, Accad. di Santa Cecilia, Rome, RAM, London; Grand Prix de Rome 1938, Grand Prix du Disque 1957, 1958, 1966, 1968, 1976, 1978, 1984, Grand Prix Nat. de la Musique 1967, Prix de la Ville de Paris 1974, Koussevitzky Int. Recording Award 1976, World Record Award (Montreux) 1983; Prix Int. Maurice Ravel 1987, Grand Prix, Music Council UNESCO 1987, Praemium Imperiale Japan 1994, Ernst von Siemens Music Prize for outstanding contribution to int. music life 2005; Grand-Croix de la Légion d'honneur 2004, Commdr Ordre Nat. du Mérite, des Arts et des Lettres, du Mérite Culturel de Monaco. *Address:* 12 rue St-Louis-en-l'Isle, 75004 Paris, France. *Telephone:* 1-43-26-39-14.

**DUTOIT, Charles E.;** Swiss conductor and music director; b. 7 Oct. 1936, Lausanne; s. of Edmond Dutoit and Berthe Dutoit (née Laederman); one s. one d. *Education:* Conservatoire of Lausanne and Geneva, Accademia Musicale Chigiana, Siena, Italy, Conservatorio Benedetto Marcello, Venice, Italy and Berks. Music Center, Tanglewood, USA. *Career:* Assoc. Conductor Berne

Symphony Orchestra 1964, Principal and Artistic Dir 1966–78; Associate Conductor Tonhalle Orchestra Zurich 1966; Conductor and Artistic Dir Zurich Radio Orchestra 1964; Artistic Dir Nat. Symphony Orchestra of Mexico and Göteborg Symphony Orchestra 1977–2002; Artistic Dir Montreal Symphony Orchestra 1977–2002; Prin. Guest Conductor Minn. Orchestra 1983–84, 1985–86; Artistic Dir and Prin. Conductor Philadelphia Orchestra summer season, Mann Music Center 1991–2001, Saratoga Springs 1991–; Music Dir Orchestre Nat. de France 1990–2001; Prin. Guest Conductor NHK Symphony Orchestra, Tokyo 1996–, Music Dir 1998–; over 125 recordings since 1980, winning over 40 int. awards; operatic début Covent Garden (conducting Faust) 1983; Principal Conductor 1996 and Music Dir, NHK Symphony Orchestra, Tokyo 1998–2003; Guest Conductor of all major orchestras in USA, Europe, South America, Far East Asia, Australia and Israel. *Recordings:* 120 discs with various orchestras including Falla's Three Cornered Hat and El amor Brujo, The Planets, Tchaikovsky's 1st Piano Concerto, Saint-Saëns 3rd Symphony, Bizet's L'Arlesienne and Carmen Suites, Gubaidulina Offertorium with Boston Symphony, Symphonies by Honegger, Roussel's Symphonies with French Nat. Orchestra, Saint-Saëns Piano Concertos, Suppé Overtures, Berlioz' Les Troyens. *Honours:* Honorary Citizen of the city of Philadelphia; Commdr Ordre des Arts et Lettres, Hon. OC; Hon. DMus (Montreal) 1984, (Laval) 1985; Grand Prix de l'Académie du disque français, High Fidelity Int. Record Critics' Award, Montreux Record Award, Japan Record Acad. Award, Artist of the Year (Canada Music Council) 1982, Grand Prix du Président de la République (France). *Address:* POBox 5088 St Laurent, Montréal, QC H4L 4Z7 Canada.

**DUTT, Hank;** Violist; b. 4 Nov. 1952, Muscatine, Iowa, USA. *Career:* Joined the Kronos String Quartet, 1977; Many performances of contemporary music, including the premieres of works of John Cage (30 Pieces for string quartet), Pauline Oliveros (The Wheel of Time) and Terry Riley (G-Song, Sunrise of the Planetary Dream Collector and Cadenzas on the Night Plain); Formerly Quartet-in-Residence at Mills College, Oakland; From 1982 resident quartet at the University of Southern California; Appearances at the Monterrey Jazz Festival, Carnegie Recital Hall, San Quentin Prison and London's South Bank; New York debut 1984; Noted for 'cross-over' performances of jazz and popular music in arrangement. *Address:* c/o UCLA Music Department, University Park, Los Angeles, CA 90089, USA.

**DUTTON, Brenton (Price);** Composer and Tubist; b. 20 March 1950, Saskatoon, Canada; 2 s., 1 d. *Education:* BM, MM, Oberlin Conservatory of Music. *Career:* Tubist with Cleveland Orchestra, 1968–74; L'Orchestra Symphonique de Quebec, 1971–74, San Diego Symphony, 1980–; Solo Recital appearances throughout Canada, USA, Europe; Professor of Music, San Diego State University, 1980–, California Institute of the Arts, 1981–84; Brass Coach for the Jeunesses Musicales World Orchestra, in Europe, North and South America, 1986–1992; Tubist and Artistic Director of Westwind Brass, 1993–. *Compositions:* Over 100 including Symphony No. 2, 1972; Symphony No. 3, 1974; Song of the Moon, solo flute; On Looking Back, Brass Quintet; December Set, Woodwind Quintet; Dialogues of the sybarites, 3 trumpets and organ; Circles; Chinese Reflections; A Rolling Silence; Songs of Love, all song cycles for baritone and chamber ensemble; Additional Works: Ecq theow Variants, brass quintet; On A Darkling Plain, brass quintet; Song of the Sun, solo viola; Hotel Europejski Suite, violin, piano; Gilgamesh, opera in 3 acts, 1977–78. *Recordings:* Symphony No. 5 Dark Spirals, 1985; Character Dances and proud Music of the Storm, 1986; Carnival of Venice, brass quintet, 1983; Olympic Entrance, Tuba Suite, 1984; The Siren of Urak for viola and brass quintet, 1998; Tuba Concerto I and II, 1998; many radio and television broadcasts; Kraków, Summer; Quebec, Spring, both for string orchestra. *Publications:* Over 70 including, Sonata in Fact for Trumpet, Piano; Resonances for Tuba Quartet; Madrigals, Book I, 1998; Tuba Concerto II, 1998; And the Halls Resound, 1998. *Address:* School of Music and Dance, San Diego State University, San Diego, CA 92182, USA.

**DUTTON, Lawrence;** American violist; *Professor of Chamber Music, State University of New York at Stony Brook;* b. 9 May 1954, New York; m. Elizabeth Lim-Dutton; two s. *Career:* mem., Emerson String Quartet 1976–; premiere concert at Alice Tully Hall, New York 1977, with works by Mozart, Smetana and Bartók; European debut at Spoleto, Italy 1981; quartet-in-residence Smithsonian Inst., Washington 1980–, at the Hartt School 1981–, and at Spoleto and Aspen Festivals 1981–; first resident quartet at Chamber Music Soc. of Lincoln Center 1982–83; tour of Japan and Australia 1987; many performances of works by Bartók, including all six quartets in a single evening, and contemporary works; premieres include Mario Davidovsky's 4th Quartet and works by Maurice Wright and George Tsontakis; Bartók's 4th quartet and Brahms' C minor, London 2001; currently Prof. of Chamber Music, State Univ. of New York at Stony Brook, and Manhattan School of Music; plays Pietro Giovanni Mantegazza viola, dated Milan 1796. *Recordings:* Walter Piston's Concerto for string quartet, winds and percussion; works by Andrew Imbrie, Henry Howell, Roy Harris and Gunther Schuller; Bartók's Six Quartets. *Honours:* Dr hc (Middlebury Coll., Vermont) 1995. *Current Management:* c/o Matthew Zelle, IMG Artists, 152 W 57th Street, Fifth Floor, New York, NY 10019, USA. *E-mail:* kirshdem@aol.com. *Website:* www .emersonquartet.com.

**DUVAL, Denise;** Singer (Soprano); b. 23 Oct. 1921, Paris, France. *Education:* Studied at the Bordeaux Conservatory. *Career:* Debut: Bordeaux 1943, as Lola in Cavalleria Rusticana; Sang at the Folies Bergères, Paris, 1944; Paris Opéra from 1947, notably as Salomé in Hérodiade by Massenet, and as Blanche in

the French premiere of Dialogues des Carmelites, 1947; Sang at the Opéra-Comique Paris in the 1947 premiere of Poulenc's Les Mamelles de Tiresias: returned 1959 for the premiere of La Voix Humaine (repeated at La Scala 1960); Paris 1949, in the premiere of Le oui des jeunes Filles, by Hahn-Busser; Other roles were Thais, the Princess in Marouf by Rabaud, Concepcion, and Portia in La Marchande de Venise by Hahn; Edinburgh Festival with the Glyndebourne company in 1960, as Elle in La Voix Humaine; Glyndebourne Festival 1962–63, as Mélisande; Guest appearances in Milan, Vienna, Brussels, Amsterdam and Buenos Aires; Retired 1965 and became Professor at the Ecole Française de Musique in Paris. *Recordings:* L'Heure Espagnole, Les mamelles de Tirésias (Columbia); Dialogues des Carmélites (HMV).

**DUVILLIER-WABLE, Laurent,** LLL; French composer; b. 7 Oct. 1947, Nîmes; m. Françoise Gripois 1975; one s. one d. *Education:* studied piano with Suzanne Joly, composition with Michel Puig, René Leibowitz and Arnold Schoenberg. *Career:* began composing, self-taught, 1960; Professor of Music, Ecole de l'Abbaye au Bois, Paris, 1966–68; Joined the Board, 1969, Director-General, 1981–97, Société des Gens de Lettres; Director-General, Société Civile des Auteurs Multimédia, 1981–; SACEM, Paris. *Compositions include:* Possibilités I for 2 pianos, 1971; Possibilités II for 2 tenor instruments, Possibilités III for violoncello and piano, Possibilités IV, Le chant de l'Unsui, for soprano and piano, 4 hands, Possibilités V, violoncello solo, Possibilités VI for piano, 4 hands, recorded by ORTF, broadcast on France-Culture, 1973; Approche I for flute and violin, Approche II for soprano and flute, Variable I for 2 pianos, 1973; Variable I, piano solo version, 1974; Rite, music for mime and dance, 1975; Parcours, film music, 1977; Sonata for flute and percussion, 1992; Concertino pour neuf, A mon ami musicien Jean Villatte, commission, recorded by Radio France, 1993; Sonata II, De la forêt des stèles, 1996. *Publications:* Sonata II, De la forêt des stèles. *Address:* 150 rue de Tolbiac, 75013 Paris, France.

**DUYKERS, John;** Singer (Tenor); b. 1941, Canada. *Career:* Seattle Opera from 1966 (Masetto in Don Giovanni, 1968); Vancouver Opera from 1968, Edmonton from 1969; Sang Mao Tse-tung in premiere productions of Nixon in China by John Adams at Houston, San Francisco and Edinburgh, 1987; St Louis, 1989, and Philadelphia, 1992, in the premieres of Under the Double Moon and Tania, by A Davis; Chicago and Long Beach Opera, 1994, in The Gambler by Prokofiev; Sellem in The Rake's Progress at the Théâtre du Châtelet, Paris, 1996; Season 2000–01 in the premiere of In the Penal Colony by Philip Glass, at Seattle, as Strauss's Herod at Philadelphia, and Weill's Fatty at Genoa; Other roles include Strauss's Herod and Aegisthus. *Address:* c/o Long Beach Opera, 6372 Pacific Coast Highway, Long Beach, CA 90803, USA.

**DVORACEK, Jiri;** Composer, Professor and Music Administrator; b. 8 June 1928, Vamberk, Czechoslovakia. *Education:* Studied organ, Prague Conservatory, 1943–47; Studied composition with Ridky and Dobias, Prague Academy of Music, 1949–53. *Career:* Teacher 1953–67, Senior Lecturer 1967–78, Professor of Composition and Head, Composition Department 1979–90, Prague Academy of Music; President, Union of Czech Composers and Concert Artists, 1987–89. *Compositions:* Opera: Aphrodite's Island, 1967; Orchestral: 2 Symphonies, 1953, 1986; Symphonic Suite, 1958; Concertante Suite, 1962; Ex Post for piano and orchestra, 1963; Quattro Episodi, 1971; I am Living and Singing, cantata for soloists, choir, reciter, children's choir and orchestra, 1978; Giubilo, 1983; Concert for violin and orchestra, 1989; Chamber: Sonata Capricciosa for violin and piano, 1956; Invention for trombone and piano or small orchestra, 1961; Meditations for clarinet and percussion, 1964; Music for harp, 1970; Due per duo for horn and piano, 1970; Dialogues for flute and piano, 1973; Brass Quintet, 1973; Music for viola and piano, 1976; Sonata for trumpet and piano, 1977; Organ Sonata, 1979; Accordion Sonata, 1979; Theme and Variations for trombone and piano, 1980; Prague Transformations for wind quintet, 1981; Clarinet and Piano Play, 1982; Violin and Organ Play, 1984; Partita for oboe and bassoon, 1986; Partita Piccola, for violin, guitar and harmonica, 1987; Three Movements for string quartet, 1990; Trio for clarinet, violin and piano, 1994; Choral music; Songs. *Recordings:* Various compositions recorded. *Address:* Antala Staska 1015/43, 140 00 Prague 4, Czech Republic.

**DVORÁKOVA, Ludmila;** Singer (Soprano); b. 11 July 1923, Kolin, Czechoslovakia; m. Rudolf Vasata, deceased 1982. *Education:* Studied with Jarmila Vavrdova at The Prague Conservatory. *Career:* Debut: Ostrava 1949, as Katya Kabanova; Sang in Ostrava as Rusalka, Elisabeth de Valois, Countess Almaviva and Aida; Sang in Bratislava and at the Smetana Theatre, Prague, from 1952; Member, Prague National Opera, 1954–57 as Milada in Dalibor, Elisabeth, Leonore, Senta, and in Czech operas; Sang Leonore at the Vienna Staatsoper, 1956; Sang at Berlin Staatsoper, 1960–84 as Brünnhilde, Venus, Elisabeth de Valois, Kundry, Isolde, Ortrud, Tosca and the Marschallin; Karlsruhe 1964 as Isolde; Bayreuth Festival, 1965–71 as Gutrune, Brünnhilde, Venus, Ortrud and Kundry; Covent Garden, 1966–71 as Brünnhilde, Isolde and Leonore; Metropolitan Opera, 1965–68; Paris Opéra, 1966; Elektra, Graz 1973; Opera München, La Scala, Opera Roma, San Francisco, Buenos Aires, Deutsche Oper am Rhein Düsseldorf, 1973–74; Vienna Staatsoper, 1964–85; Salome, Herodias, Berlin, 1979–; Jenůfa, Kostelnicka, 1980; Visited Japan, 1983, 1984, with the State Operas of Berlin and Hamburg; Jenůfa, Vienna, 1984; Other roles included: Katerina Izmailova, (Vienna, 1965), Ariadne and The Dyer's Wife in Die Frau ohne Schatten. *Recordings:* Gutrune in Götterdämmerung, from Bayreuth; Wagner Recital. *Address:* 16200 Prague 6, Na Orechovce 14, Czech Republic.

**DVORSKY, Miroslav;** Singer (Tenor); b. 1960, Partizánske, Czechoslovakia. *Education:* Studied in Bratislava and Milan. *Career:* Debut: Bratislava, 1983, as Nemorino; Sang in the 1987 premiere of Cikker's The Insect May and guested at Edinburgh, 1990, as Gounod's Faust; Theater am Gärtnerplatz, Munich, from 1994, notably as Des Grieux in Manon; Rome, 1994, as the Prince in Rusalka and Rodolfo in La Bohème; Toronto, 1996, as the Duke of Mantua; Many appearances in operettas by Lehar and Johann Strauss; Season 2000–01 as Smetana's Jeník at Toronto, Ismaele in Nabucco at the Vienna Staatsoper, Oronte in I Lombardi at Marseille and a production of the Verdi Requiem at the Deutsche Oper, Berlin; Rodolfo in Florence and the Dvořák Requiem with the Orchestre de Paris; Sang Števa in Jenůfa at Hamburg, 2000, Laca for Washington Opera; President, Alzheimer Foundation, Slovakia. *Recordings include:* Das Land des Lächelns; Miroslav Dvorsky–Arias. *Current Management:* Austroconcert International. *Address:* c/o Austroconcert International, Gluckgasse 1, 1010 Vienna, Austria.

**DVORSKÝ, Peter;** Slovak singer (tenor); b. 25 Sept. 1951, Partizánske, Topol'čany Dist; s. of Vendelín Dvorský and Anna Dvorská; m. Marta Varšová 1975; two d. *Education:* State Conservatoire, Bratislava. *Career:* studied with R. Carossi and M. di Luggo, Milan 1975–76; opera soloist, Slovak Nat. Theatre, Bratislava 1972–96, 1999; sang at Metropolitan Opera, New York 1977, Covent Garden, London 1978, Bolshoi Theatre, Moscow 1978, La Scala, Milan 1979; performs regularly at Bratislava, Vienna State Opera, Covent Garden, La Scala, New York Metropolitan Opera, Munich, Berlin, Prague, Geneva, Paris, Buenos Aires, Tokyo and in many other cities throughout the world; numerous radio and TV performances; many recordings; Chair. Council of Slovak Music Union 1991–; Pres. Harmony Foundation 1991–; performed charity concerts after floods in Czech Repub. 2002. *Honours:* awards include Tchaikovsky Competition, Geneva (5th Prize 1974, 1st Prize 1975), Leoš Janáček Memorial Medal 1978, Giuseppe Verdi Medal 1979, Artist of Merit 1981, Nat. Artist 1984, Kammersänger, Vienna 1986, Francisco Cilea Prize 1991, Wilhelm Furtwängler Prize 1992. *Address:* J. Hronca 1A, 841 02 Bratislava, Slovakia. *Fax:* (2) 64287626.

**DWORCHAK, Harry;** Singer (Bass-baritone); b. 1947, Hershey, Pennsylvania, USA. *Education:* AVA, Philadelphia, 1970. *Career:* Sang first at the Barcelona Opera (from 1970), then throughout North America, with a 1982 debut at the New York City Opera; Théâtre du Châtelet, Paris, 1982, as Banquo; Welsh National Opera, 1985, as Oroveso; Sang Ferrando in Trovatore at the Metropolitan in 1988, at the Munich Staatsoper, 1992; Der fliegende Holländer, Frankfurt, 1991, Washington DC, 1995; Scarpia, Covent Garden, 1996; Bayerische Staatsoper, 1997; Sang Jochanaan (Salome), Austin, Texas, 1999; Season 2000–01 engaged as Wotan in Rheingold; Season 2001–02, Metropolitan Opera as Count Waldner in Arabella and Geisterbote in Die Frau ohne Schatten; Der Landgraf in Tannhäuser for Tulsa Opera, 2001;

Other roles include the Commendatore, Monteverdi's Seneca, Bellini's Capulet, Mephistopheles (Faust), Don Quichotte, Daland, Wagner's Dutchman, and Dosifey in Khovanshchina; Further engagements as Wotan, Rheingold, Augsburg; Wotan, Walküre, Augsburg; Der Wanderer; Pizarro in Fidelio, Buenos Aires, entire Ring Cycle. *Recordings:* Das Schloss, Bayerische Staatsoper, Munich; Don Alfonso in Così fan tutte, European Television Broadcast. *Honours:* Richard Tucker Award, 1987; Carnegie Hall Concert, 1987. *Current Management:* John J. Miller, New York. *Address:* 15 West 72nd Street, New York, NY 10023, USA.

**DYACHKOV, Yegor;** Cellist; b. 1974, Moscow, Russia. *Education:* Studies with Alexander Fedorchenko, Moscow Conservatory, Radu Aldulescu, Rome, André Navarra, Vienna, Yuli Turovsky, Montreal, Boris Pergamenschikow, Cologne. *Career:* Numerous Recitals in the Former Soviet Union, Italy, Latin America, Taiwan, USA, Canada; Guest Soloist with Montreal Symphony Orchestra, Metropolitan Orchestra of Montreal, Orchestre Symphonique de Quebec, National Arts Centre Orchestra in Ottawa, I Musici de Montreal; Concert Performances in Quebec, Ontario, New Brunswick; Performances at the Lanaudiere International Music Festival, Domaine Forget International Music Festival, Chamber Music Festival in Ste-Pétronille, Orford International Music Festival, Scotia Festival of Music, Mozarteum in Caracas; Vancouver Chamber Music Festival; Evian Festival, 1999. *Recordings:* Glazunov's Concerto Ballata; Strauss and Pfitzner Sonatas. *Current Management:* Latitude 45 Arts Promotion Inc. *Address:* c/o Latitude 45, Arts Promotion Inc, 109 St Joseph Blvd West, Montreal, Quebec H2T 2P7, Canada.

**DYAKOVSKI, Lubomir;** Singer (Tenor); b. 1 March 1950, Dupnitza, Bulgaria; m. Rossitza Ivanova Dyakovska, 1 s., 1 d. *Education:* Graduated from Vocal Faculty, Bulgarian Musical Academy, 1973. *Career:* Debut: Ernesto in Don Pasquale by Donizetti, 1970; Permanently engaged in Russe and Pleven; Numerous performances throughout Europe; Over 40 tenor solo performances in Masses, Oratorios and Requiems including Lensky in Eugene Onegin, Nadir in the Pearl Fishers by Bizet and Almaviva in Il Barbiere di Siviglia by Rossini; Sang with all major symphony orchestras and choruses in Bulgaria; Performances with major Bulgarian and European television and radio companies; Sang in studio recording of The Suffering of Jesus for Radio Zagreb; Participated in opening of Summer Music Festival in Dubrovnik, 1991; Soloist for Bolshoi Don Kosaken Ensemble, performing throughout Switzerland, Austria and Germany; mem, Rotary International; Union of Musicians in Bulgaria. *Recordings:* Russian songs and arias; Songs of Petrarca by Liszt, St Matthew Passion, Night of Walpurgis and Bach's Magnificat; The Golden Cockerel, Rimsky-Korsakov; Eugene Onegin; Prince Igor by Borodin; Evangelist in Christmas Oratorio by J. S. Bach; Handel's Messiah. *Honours:* Numerous Government and state awards. *Address:* c-x Storgozia, bl 72, entr A, ap 15, 5800 Pleven, Bulgaria.

# E

**EAGLE, David (Malcolm);** Composer, Flautist and Teacher; b. 21 Dec. 1955, Montreal, QC, Canada; m. Hope Lee, 23 Aug 1980. *Education:* BMus, 1979, MMus, 1982, McGill University; Studied Flute with Cindy Shuter, Composition with Bengt Hambraeus and Donald Steven; Composition with Klaus Huber and Brian Ferneyhough, Hochschule für Musik, Freiburg, 1981–83; PhD, University of California at Berkeley, 1992. *Career:* Freelance Composer; Works played, Canada, Holland Festival, 1985, Germany, Switzerland; Broadcasts on CBC Radio Canada, BBC, Hessischer Rundfunk, Swiss Radio, KRO (Netherlands); Invited Guest Composer, Boswil Kunstlerhaus, Switzerland, 1985; Commissions from Montreal Chamber Orchestra, Array-Music, Toronto Consort, many individuals; Co-ordinator, Electro-acoustic Music Studio, Assistant Professor, Composition, Theory, University of Calgary, 1990–. *Compositions:* Zhu Fong, string quartet, 1978; Strata-Vari for 14 strings, 1980; Within for solo cello, 1982; Strahlen for organ, 1983; Aura for septet, 1984; Renew'd at ev'ry glance for variable instruments, 1985; Toccare for harpsichord, 1986; Luminous Voices for early music ensemble and tape, 1987–88; Crossing Currents for orchestra, 1991; Hsuan for guzheng and tape, 1992; Nohocki for flute and cello, 1993; Music for AXIO, Open This Door, for AXIO (midi-controller), 1993; Sounding after Time for violin, cello, piano, computer, synthesizer, 1993. *Address:* 27 Stradwick Rise SW, Calgary, Alberta T3H 1G6, Canada.

**EAGLEN, Jane;** British singer (soprano); b. 4 April 1960, Lincoln, England. *Education:* Royal Northern Coll. of Music, studied with Joseph Ward. *Career:* debut, ENO in Patience 1984; engagements with ENO as Leonora in Il Trovatore and Elizabeth I in Mary Stuart; Western Australia Opera, Perth, as Tosca; Lyric Opera of Queensland, Brisbane, as Madama Butterfly; Scottish Opera, as Donna Anna; London Promenade Concert debut 1989, as Sieglinde in Act III of Die Walküre; sang Brünnhilde 1991; Tosca for ENO 1990; Donna Anna and Amelia (Ballo), Bologne 1991; sang Mathilde in Guillaume Tell at Covent Garden, Geneva 1992; Scottish Opera as Norma in a new production of Bellini's opera; Tosca, Buenos Aires 1993, then Donna Anna in Don Giovanni, Vienna State Opera, and title role in Norma, Seattle Opera; Brünnhilde in Die Walküre, Opera Pacific, California, and Vienna State Opera 1994; Norma with Riccardo Muti, Ravenna Festival 1994; title role in Ariadne, with ENO 1994; Brünnhilde in Die Walküre, La Scala, Milan 1994, and with Lyric Opera of Chicago 1995; Amelia in Un Ballo in Maschera, Opéra de Paris Bastille 1995; La Gioconda, Chicago, and Tristan and Isolde at Seattle 1998; concert appearances at the Wigmore Hall, Festival Hall and the Barbican Centre; Verdi Requiem and Mahler 8th Symphony; recitals for the Wagner Socs of London, New York and Buenos Aires; sang Isolde and Turandot at the New York Met 2000, 2003, and in Puerto Rico 2004; Turandot at Covent Garden 2001; complete Ring Cycle for Seattle Opera 2001, Met and Lyric Opera of Chicago 2001–05; London Proms 2002; sang La Vestale for ENO 2003, Ortrud in Lohengrin, and Ariadne, in Seattle 2004. *Recordings:* Die Flammen; Medea in Corinto; Norma, with Muti; Tosca; Turandot; Mozart and Strauss; Bellini and Wagner; Song Cycles by Strauss, Berg and Wagner; Der fliegende Holländer, conducted by Barenboim 2002, Tannhauser (Gramophone Award for Best Complete Opera) 2002. *Honours:* Peter Moores Foundation Scholarship, Countess of Munster Award, Carl Rosa Trust Award. *Current Management:* AOR Management Inc., 6910 Roosevelt Way NE, PMB 221, Seattle, WA 98115, USA. *Telephone:* (206) 729-6160 (office). *Fax:* (206) 985-8499 (office). *E-mail:* jennyrose@aormanagementuk.com (office). *Website:* www .aormanagementuk.com (office).

**EARLE, Roderick;** British singer (baritone); b. 29 Jan. 1952, Winchester, England; s. of Dennis and Fenella Earle; 1 s., 1 d. *Education:* Chorister, Winchester Cathedral; St John's College, Cambridge; Royal College of Music, London; Further study with Otakar Kraus. *Career:* With English National Opera, 1978–80; debut Royal Opera Covent Garden as Antonio in Le Nozze di Figaro, 1980; joined Royal Opera, sung over 60 roles including Schaunard, Abimelech, Orestes, Monterone, the Bonze, Brander, Harasta (Cunning Little Vixen), Kothner, the Philosopher (Cherubin), King Fisher, (Midsummer Marriage), Alberich, Siegfried and Götterdämmerung; Has appeared with all major British companies, toured to Japan, South Korea, Greece and Finland with the Royal Opera and appeared at festivals at Edinburgh, Buxton, Israel, Athens, Flanders; Has sung Kothner, Rangoni and Abimelech at Teatro Regio, Turin, and Altair in British premiere of Strauss's Die Ägyptische Helena and Ford at Garsington; other appearances include A Midsummer Night's Dream and Turandot (Rome Opera), Der Fliegende Hollander (Opera de Massy), Amonasro, Alfio and Tonio (Royal Albert Hall), Germont and Scarpia (Holland Park Opera), Ford and the Count Figaro (New Zealand Opera), Rigoletto (Opera Zuid) and Monterone (ENO); Sang Melchior Amahl and the Night Visitors at Sadler's Wells. *Recordings include:* Ferneyhough's Transit; Rossini's Stabat Mater with Richard Hickox; Les Troyens with Sir Colin Davis. *Films:* appeared in videos of La Fanciulla del West, Manon Lescaut, Andrea Chenier, Der Rosenkavalier (Solti), Carmen (Mehta), Salome (Downes), Otello and Traviata (Solti); soundtrack of film Meeting Venus. *Honours:* Musician of the Year Award, Greater London Arts Asscn;; various Grammy Awards. *Current Management:* Musichall, Vicarage Way, Ringmer, BN8 5LA, England. *Address:* St Raphael, 155 Maldon Road, Colchester . CO3 3BJ (home). *Telephone:* (1206) 574476 (home). *E-mail:* earle@ukonline.co.uk (home).

**EAST, Leslie Charles,** BMus, MMus, FGSM; British music publisher; *Director of Publishing, ABRSM (Publishing) Ltd;* b. 8 July 1949, Doncaster; m. Lilija Zobens; two d. *Education:* Kingsbury County Grammar School, London, King's Coll. London. *Career:* visiting lecturer and concert organizer, City Univ. London 1973–75; Dir of Music, Guildhall School of Music and Drama, London 1975–87; Publishing Dir, Novello and Co Ltd 1987–98; Man. Ed. 1998–99 and then Dir of Publishing, Associated Board of the Royal Schools of Music (Publishing) Ltd 1999–; Chair., Soc. for the Promotion of New Music 1978–83; Arts Council Music Panel mem. 1988–92; Chair., New Macnaghten Concerts 1989–99, Early Music Centre and Network 1994–2001, City Music Soc. 1998–; mem. Worshipful Company of Musicians, Royal Soc. of Musicians, Royal Philharmonic Soc., Asscn of British Choral Directors, Royal Overseas League, Royal Musical Asscn, The Peter Warlock Soc. *Publications:* contrib. various articles and reviews to The New Grove, The Musical Times, Music and Musiciams. *Honours:* Freeman of the Musicians' Company 1986, Freeman of the City of London 1978. *Address:* ABRSM (Publishing) Ltd, 24 Portland Place, London, W1B 1LU, England (office). *Telephone:* (20) 7467-8234 (office). *Fax:* (20) 7467-8833 (office). *E-mail:* leslieeast@abrsm.ac.uk (office). *Website:* www.abrsmpublishing.co.uk (office).

**EASTBURN, Susanna de Martelly,** BA, MPhil; Festival Director; b. 6 Jan. 1969, Truro, England. *Education:* Penair School, Cornwall, Millfield School, Somerset, King's Coll. Cambridge. *Career:* International Promotions Man., Chester Music/Novello & Co. Ltd 1994–2001; Artistic Dir, Huddersfield Contemporary Music Festival 2001–; non-exec. positions include Yorkshire Regional Arts Council 2002–; mem. British Arts Festivals Asscns (exec. bd mem.), Réseau Varèse (exec. bd mem.), Soc. for Promotion of New Music (vice-chair.), Int. Soc. for Contemporary Music (chair., British Section). *Address:* Huddersfield Contemporary Music Festival, Department of Music, Huddersfield University, Huddersfield, HD1 4TY, England (office). *Telephone:* (1484) 425082 (office). *Fax:* (1484) 472957 (office). *E-mail:* info@hcmf.co.uk (office). *Website:* www.hcmf.co.uk (office).

**EATHORNE, Wendy;** Singer (Soprano) and Teacher; b. 25 Sept. 1939, Four Lanes, Cornwall, England; 1 d. *Education:* Studied at the Royal Academy of Music, 1959–65; ARAM; LRAM; ARCM; JP; Hon FCSM; FTCL; FRSA. *Career:* West End production, Robert and Elizabeth, 1965–67; Numerous concert appearances including Promenade Concerts, London; Engagements with the London Bach Choir, London Symphony Orchestra, Hallé Orchestra and other leading British orchestras; Repertoire includes works by Handel (Susanna and Belshazzar), Liszt (Missa Solemnis) and Haydn (The Creation); Appearances with Welsh National Opera, English National Opera and Royal Opera, Covent Garden; Glyndebourne, 1969–71, as Sophie in Werther, First Boy in Die Zauberflöte and Atalanta in The Rising of the Moon; Italian debut in Ariadne auf Naxos; Repertoire also includes Julia in La Vestale by Spontini and Marguerite in Faust; Festival Adjudicator; Many recitals with the pianist Geoffrey Pratley, programmes include groups of songs by Purcell to modern pieces; Head of Vocal Studies, Opera and Music Theatre at Trinity College of Music, 1989–94; Senior Lecturer, Trinity College of Music. *Recordings:* Masses by Bach; A Village Romeo and Juliet; Monteverdi Madrigals Libro IV; A Scarlatti Clori e Zeffiro and St Cecilia Mass, Schubert Mass in A flat; Vaughan Williams The Pilgrim's Progress and Sir John in Love; Bridge, The Christmas Rose. *Address:* 23 King Edward's Road, Ruislip, Middlesex HA4 7AQ, England.

**EATON, John C.;** Composer; b. 30 March 1935, Bryn Mawr, USA; m. Nelda Nelson, 31 May 1973, 1 s., 1 d. *Education:* AB, MFA, Princeton University. *Career:* Columbia Artists in USA, Hamburg Opera, Maggio Musicale, Venice Festival, Los Angeles Philharmonic, Tanglewood, many more. *Compositions:* Operas performed: The Tempest, 1985; The Cry of Clytaemnestra, 1980; Danton and Robespierre; The Lion and Androcles; Myshkin; Herakles; Don Quixote, 1996; Travelling with Gulliver, 1997; King Lear, 2000; 2 Symphonies; Duo, mixed chorus; Mass, 1997; Blind Man's Cry; Concert Music for Solo Clarinet; Piano Variations; Microtonal Fantasy; Piano Trio; Concert Piece. *Recordings:* Danton and Robespierre; The Music of John Eaton; Microtonal Fantasy; Electro Vibrations. *Publications:* New Music Since 1950, 1974. His work was reviewed in, Time; New Yorker; London Financial Times; New York Times; High Fidelity; Opera News. *Honours:* Prix de Rome, 1959–61; Guggenheim, 1962, 1965; Fromm Commission, 1966; Koussevitzky Commission, 1970; Citation, NIAL, 1972; Composer in Residence, AAR, 1975; PBC Commission, 1970; Peabody Award, 1973; National Music Theater Award, 1988; MacArthur Fellow, 1990. *Address:* c/o ASCAP, ASCAP House, 1 Lincoln Plaza, New York, USA.

**EBBECKE, Michael;** Singer (Baritone); b. 8 Dec. 1955, Wiesbaden, Germany. *Education:* Studied at the Richard Strauss Conservatory Munich and with Josef Metternich in Cologne. *Career:* Debut: Stuttgart 1982, as Mozart's Figaro; Member of the Stuttgart Staatsoper from 1982, notably as Belcore, Giulio Cesare, Eugene Onegin, Silvio, and Don Fernando in Fidelio; Guest appearances at the Berlin Komische Oper (Guglielmo, 1984) and Deutsche Oper (Orestes in Iphigénie en Tauride, 1988); Appearances at Karlsruhe, Paris, Lyon (Wolfram in Tannhäuser) and La Scala Milan (Scherasmin in Oberon, 1989); Sang Stolzius in Die Soldaten at Stuttgart, 1987, Papageno and Escamillo in Season, 1990–91, Guglielmo, 1991–92;

Season 1995–96 as Pantaleone in The Love for Three Oranges at Stuttgart; Melisso in Handel's Alcina, 1998; Sang Verdi in the premiere of Adriana Hölszky's Giuseppe Sylvia, Stuttgart 2000; Concert engagements include Bach's St John Passion at Amsterdam, 1987. *Recordings:* Die Soldaten. *Address:* c/o Stuttgart Staatsoper, Oberer Schlossgarten 6, 700 Stuttgart, Germany.

**EBEN, Petr;** Czech composer; b. 22 Jan. 1929, Žamberk; s. of Vilém Eben and Marie Ebenová-Kahlerová; m. Šárka Ebenová (née Hurníková) 1953; three s. *Education:* Acad. of Music Arts, Prague. *Career:* Music Dir, TV, Prague 1954; debut as pianist, Prague 1954; Lecturer, Inst. for Musicology, Charles Univ., Prague 1955–, Assoc. Prof. –1990; Prof. of Composition, Acad. of Music, Prague 1990–96; Lecturer, Royal Northern Coll. of Music (RNCM), Manchester, UK 1978, Sr Lecturer in Theory of Music 1988; active as performing artist, especially as improviser on piano and organ; concerts in Royal Festival Hall and Westminster Cathedral, London, Notre Dame, Paris and Festivals in Melbourne, Edinburgh, Vienna, Berlin and USA; Pres. Prague Spring music festival 1990–96; mem. Union of Composers, Prague; Pres. Czech Soc. for Spiritual Music, Endowment of Prague Nat. Theatre. *Compositions include:* church opera: Jeremiáš; (ballet) Curses and Blessings; oratorios: Apologia Socratus, Sacred Symbols, Oratorium Anno Domini 2000; symphonic works: Vox clamantis, Prague Nocturne, Night Hours, Improperia; concertos: Organ Concerto No. 2 1982, for piano and orchestra; music for organ: Sunday Music, Laudes 1964, Mutationes, Faust 1980, A Festive Voluntary: Variations on Good King Wenceslas 1986, Job 1987, Three Jubilations for organ, 2 trumpets, 2 trombones 1987, Two Invocations for trombone and organ 1988, Four Biblical Dances 1993, Labyrinth of the World and Heart's Paradise 1997, Chagall Windows (for trumpet and organ); cantatas: Pragensia, Bitter Earth; also song cycles, piano trio, string quartet, quintets, many choral works including Desire of Ancient Things for a cappella mixed choir 1985. *Recording:* The Music of Petr Eben with Dagmar Pecková 1999, Anno Domini – An Oratorio for choir, soloists, speaker, chant schola and orchestra 2002. *Publications:* Score-Reading and Playing (co-author); contributions to journals. *Honours:* Hon. FRNCM 1992; Chevalier Ordre des Arts et Lettres; Order of Cyril and Methodius; Dr hc (Charles Univ.) 1994; Czech Music Fund Prize 1991, 1992, Stamitz-Preis, Künstlergilde 1993, Medal of Merit 2002. *Address:* Academy of Music Arts, Malostranské nám. 12, 110 00 Prague 1, Czech Republic (office). *Telephone:* (257) 534205 (office). *Fax:* (257) 530405 (office).

**EBERHARDT, Cornelius;** Conductor; b. 3 Jan. 1932, Oberaudorf, Germany; m. Ursula Schade 1957; one d. *Education:* Univs of Munich and Hamburg, 1950–53; State Acad. of Music, Munich, 1953–56; Accademia Chigiana, Siena, Italy, 1958. *Career:* Chorus Master of Municipal Opera, Ulm, Germany, 1956–60; Assoc. Conductor, Munich State Theatre, 1960–69; Music Dir, Regensburg Symphony and Opera, 1969–77; founder of Regensburg Music School; co-founder of Bavarian Festival of Modern Composers, 1973; Music Dir of Corpus Christi Symphony, TX, USA, 1975–2000; Prof. of Opera and Conductor, State Acad. of Music, Munich, Germany, 1977–97; Music Dir of American Institute of Musical Studies, Dallas, TX, 1978–; Visiting Prof., 1979–80, Prof. and Music Dir, 1984–87, Univ. of Texas, Austin; Visiting Prof., Corpus Christi State Univ., 1981–82; Guest Conductor in Europe and North and South America; Music Dir, Mozart Festival International, 1991; Pres., State Acad. of Music, 1991–95; Principal Guest Conductor, Munich Symphony, 1996–2002. *Publications:* Das Regensburger Orchester, 1972; Der Dirigent in Handbuch der Musikberufe, 1987; Volksmusik und Kunstmusik in Südosteuropa, 1988. *Honours:* Bavarian State Award for Young Artists, 1969; Order of Merit, Germany, 1996. *Address:* Darmstaedterstrasse 11-7, 80992 Munich, Germany.

**EBERLEY, Helen-Kay,** MMus; American opera singer, record company executive and publisher; b. 3 Aug. 1947, Sterling, IL; d. of William Elliott and P. Eberley. *Education:* Northwestern Univ. *Career:* debut in Der Rosenkavalier with Lyric Opera, Chicago, IL 1973; has performed jazz with Duke Ellington and Dave Brubeck; numerous solo concerts including Continental Bank Concerts 1981–89; Chair., Pres., Artistic Co-ordinator Eberley-Skowronski Inc., Evanston, IL 1973–92; Founder EB-SKO Productions 1976; Exec. Dir, performance consultant E-S Management 1985; Founder HKE Enterprises 1993–; singing coach; Guest Lecturer at colls and univs; numerous appearances on TV and radio; F. K. Weyerhauser Scholar, Metropolitan Opera 1967; volunteer Art Inst. of Chicago 1995–. *Operas include:* Così fan Tutte, Le Nozze di Figaro, Dido and Aeneas, Tosca, La Traviata, Don Giovanni, Brigadoon; Producer, Annotator: Gentleman Gypsy 1978; Exec. Producer: Separate But Equal 1976, All Brahms 1977, Opera Lady 1978, Eberley Sings Strauss 1980, Helen-Kay Eberley: American Girl 1983, Helen-Kay Eberley: Opera Lady II 1984. *Publications:* Angel's Song 1993, The Magdaleva Poems 1994, Chapel Heart 1995, Desert Dancing 1998, Canyon Ridge 2000, River Voice 2002. *Honours:* Milton J. Cross Award, Metropolitan Opera Guild 1968; numerous poetry awards including Best of the Best Award for The Rose Garden, Poets and Patrons, Inc., Chicago, First Prize, Chicagoland Poetry Contest for The Pond. *Address:* HKE Enterprises, 1726 Sherman Ave, Evanston, IL 60201, USA (office). *Telephone:* (847) 869-8231 (office).

**EBRAHIM, Omar;** Singer (Baritone); b. 6 Sept. 1956, London, England. *Education:* Studied at the Guildhall School of Music, London. *Career:* Appearances with the Opera Factory in Punch and Judy, The Beggar's Opera, The Knot Garden, and La Calisto; Sang in the premieres of Birtwistle's Yan Tan Tethera, South Bank, 1986 and Nigel Osborne's The Electrification of the Soviet Union, Glyndebourne, 1986; Glyndebourne Touring Opera in Il

Barbiere di Siviglia and La Bohème; Has sung Hector in King Priam for Kent Opera; With Scottish Opera has appeared in Mahagonny, Die Fledermaus and Iolanthe; Covent Garden, 1989, in the British premiere of Un Re in Ascolto by Berio; Sang Don Giovanni with Opera Factory at the Queen Elizabeth Hall, 1990, Parkhearst in the premiere of Bose's 63: Dream Palace at the 1990 Munich Biennale; The Fool in the premiere of Birtwistle's Gawain, Covent Garden, May 1991; Sang the Voice of Goya in the premiere of Osborne's Terrible Mouth, Almeida Festival, 1992; Created Vermeer in Birtwistle's The Second Mrs Kong, Glyndebourne, 1994; Sang Horace Tabor in the British premiere of Moore's The Ballad of Baby Doe, Bloomsbury Theatre, 1996; Momo in Cesti's Il Pomo d'Oro at Batignano, 1998. Television appearances include Yan Tan Tethera, by Birtwistle, The Kiss by Michael Nyman and the title role in a BBC version of Marschner's Vampyr, 1992; Concert repertoire includes Morton Feldman/Beckett Words and Music, Aventures, Nouvelles Aventures (Ligeti), Enoch Arden (Strauss) and Ode to Napoleon Bonaparte (Schoenberg). *Address:* c/o Allied Artists, 42 Montpelier Square, London SW7 1JZ, England.

**ECHOLS, Paul Clinton,** BA, MA; American opera director, musicologist and editor; b. 13 Feb. 1944, Santa Monica, CA. *Education:* Duke Univ., Durham, NC, New York Univ. *Career:* Deputy Chair. Dept of Music, Brooklyn Coll., New York 1971–75, Asst Prof. of Music 1971–75; Editorial Co-ordinator, The Charles Ives Soc. 1976–82; Int. Dir Concert Music Division, Peer Southern Music Publishers, New York 1982–85; Dir Historical Performance Programme 1980–84; Dir Opera Program 1988–, The Mannes Coll. of Music, New York; Vice-Pres. and Dir of Publishing, G. Schirmer/Associated Music Publishers Inc., New York 1986–87; Ed., Historical Performance: The Journal of Early Music America 1987–; mem. Charles Ives Soc. Inc. (bd of dirs), Early Music America Inc., American Musicological Soc., Sonneck Soc. and others. *Publications:* contrib. numerous articles to scholarly journals and other publications, including New Grove Dictionary of Music in America, numerous edns of music, including Renaissance and Baroque Choral Music and The Orchestral Works of Charles E. Ives. *Address:* c/o The Mannes College of Music, 150 West 85th Street, New York, NY 10024, USA.

**ECKHARDT, Mária;** Hungarian musicologist and choral conductor; *Director, Liszt Frenec Memorial Museum and Research Centre;* b. 26 Sept. 1943, Budapest. *Education:* Liszt Ferenc Acad. of Music. *Career:* Librarian and Research Worker, Music Dept, Nat. Széchényi Library, Budapest, 1966–73; Research Worker, Inst. of Musicology, Hungarian Acad. of Sciences, Budapest, 1973–87; Dir, Liszt Ferenc Memorial Museum and Research Centre at Liszt Acad. of Music, Budapest, 1986–. *Publications:* Franz Liszt und sein Kreis in Briefen und Dokumenten aus den Beständen des Burgenländischen Landesmuseums, with Cornelia Knotik, 1983; Liszt Ferenc Memorial Museum Catalogue, 1986; Franz Liszt's Estate at the Budapest Academy of Music, 1, Books, 1986; Franz Liszt's Music Manuscripts in the National Széchényi Library, 1986; Liszt Ferenc válogatott levelei 1824–1861, (selected letters 1824–1861), Budapest, 1989; Franz Liszt's Estate at the Budapest Academy of Music, II, Music, 1993; Franz Liszt's Weimarer Bibliothek (with Evelyn Liepsch) 1999. *Contributions:* Books on Liszt, Schubert, Chopin and Schumann, 1996–2002; Studies on Liszt and 19th-Century musical life and composers in: Studia Musicologica, Magyar Zene, The New Hungarian Quarterly, Journal of The American Liszt Society, Muzsika and others; exhibition catalogues, forewords to Liszt editions by Henle (Munich). *Honours:* Award of Excellence, American Liszt Soc., 1985; Erkel Prize, 1987, Szaboksi Prize 2004, MAOE Musical Grand Prize 2004. *Address:* Vörösmarty atca 35, 1064 Budapest (office); Ruszti ut 11, 1022 Budapest, Hungary (home). *Telephone:* (1) 342 7320 (office). *Fax:* (1) 413 1526 (office). *E-mail:* eckhardt@lib.liszt.hu (office). *Website:* www.lisztmuseum.hu (office).

**ECKHART, Janis (Gail),** BA; American singer (mezzo-soprano); b. 21 July 1953, CA. *Education:* Univ. of California, Los Angeles and Academia Real de Música, Madrid, Spain. *Career:* debut at New York City Opera 1981; numerous roles at New York City Opera, including Nabucco 1981, Rigoletto 1981, 1984, 1988, 1989, Carmen 1986, 1988; in Rigoletto at Opéra de Monte Carlo 1983, and Aida, Opera Delaware 1984; sang in Il Trovatore 1987, and in Un Ballo in Maschera 1986, both at Nat. Grand Opera; Carmen, Seattle Opera 1982; Samson et Dalila, Nat. Philharmonic of the Philippines 1980; Les Contes D'Hoffmann at the Opera Metropolitana, Caracas 1981; Nabucco, Rigoletto, Teatro de Opera, Puerto Rico 1988; Rigoletto, Opera Carolina 1990; Carmen, Metro Lyric Opera 1992; Carmen, Cairo Opera, Egypt 1992; Mahler's Kindertotenlieder and Songs of a Wayfarer, Nashville Symphony, Verdi's Requiem, New York Chorale Soc. and Plymouth Church of the Pilgrims; concert tour, Instituto Technológico de México 1992; Kismet, Taipei Symphony 1993; Ambassadors of Opera, Far East concert tour 1993; Middle East concert tour 1993; Cavalleria Rusticana, Hong Kong 1994; Carmen, Madrid, Lisbon 1995; Aida, Cairo Opera 1996; Beethoven's 9th Symphony, Avery Fisher Hall 1997; Amneris in Aida, Dicapo Opera Theatre tour 2001; Carmen in Florida 2001, 2003. *Current Management:* c/o J. Dietsch, Pinnacle ArtsMGMI, 889 Ninth Avenue, Second Floor, New York, NY 10019, USA. *Telephone:* (212) 397-7911. *Fax:* (212) 397-7920. *Website:* www.pinnaclearts.com. *Address:* 15 West 72nd Street, New York, NY 10023, USA.

**EDDINS, William;** American conductor and pianist; *Music Director, Edmonton Symphony Orchestra;* b. 1964, Buffalo, NY; m.; two s. *Education:* Eastman School of Music with David Effron, Univ. of Southern Calif. with Daniel Lewis. *Career:* fmr Assoc. Conductor Minnesota Orchestra; fmr Asst to

Daniel Barenboim at Berlin State Opera; Asst Conductor Chicago Symphony Orchestra 1992, subsequently Assoc. and later the first Resident Conductor of the orchestra; Prin. Guest Conductor RTE Nat. Symphony Orchestra, Ireland 2002–; Music Dir Edmonton Symphony Orchestra 2005–; founding mem. New World Symphony, Miami; has conducted US symphony orchestras, including San Francisco, Cincinnati, Atlanta, Detroit, Dallas, Los Angeles, Houston, San Antonio, Kansas City, Austin, Hartford, Memphis, Colorado, St Louis, also Los Angeles, Jacksonville and Tulsa Philharmonics; int. appearances as guest conductor of Adelaide SO, Barcelona SO, Bergen Philharmonic, Royal Scottish Nat. Orchestra, RAI Orchestra Sinfonica, Berlin Staatskapelle, Lisbon Metropolitan; regularly conducts from the piano, and has performed as pianist on Chicago Symphony Orchestra's 'Symphony Center Presents' recital series; founder and Artistic Dir Prospect Park Players, Hamline Univ., St Paul. *Recordings:* piano: Bad Boys Vol. 1 2003. *Honours:* Seaver/NEA Conducting Award 2000. *Current Management:* Omicron Artist Management Inc., POB 11912, Milwaukee, WI 53211, USA. *Address:* c/o Edmonton Symphony Orchestra, 9720 102 Avenue, Edmonton, AB T5J 4B2, Canada (office). *Telephone:* (780) 428-1108 (office). *Website:* www.edmontonsymphony.com.

**EDDY, Jenifer;** Singer (Coloratura Soprano); b. 1933, Melbourne, Australia; m. David Beamish, one s. *Education:* Studied in Melbourne with Henri Portnoj and in London with Bertha Nicklauss Kempner and Roy Henderson. *Career:* Frequent Guest Soloist with Australian Broadcasting Corporation in Concerts, Studio Broadcasts and on Television and Major Choral Groups, 1953–58; Professional stage debut, 1954, as Mascha in The Chocolate Soldier, Princess Theatre, Melbourne; Opera debut, 1956, as Nedda in Pagliacci; Elizabethan Opera Company, 1956–57 as Mozart's Susanna, Despina, Papagena and as Polly Peachum, Beggar's Opera; Covent Garden, 1959–69, roles including Xenia (Boris Godunov), Amor (Gluck's Orpheus), Fiakermilli (Arabella), Olympia (Tales of Hoffmann), Sophie (Der Rosenkavalier), Tytania (A Midsummer Night's Dream); Guest appearances with Sadler's Wells Opera, English National Opera, Welsh National Opera, Scottish Opera, English Opera Group, Bordeaux Opera, Maggio Musicale, Edinburgh, Leeds, Bath and Schwetzingen Festivals; Roles include, Despina, Rosina, Norina, Blondchen, Madame Herz (The Impressario), Musetta, Zerbinetta, Adele (Die Fledermaus); Appearances for BBC on radio, television and in concert; Managing Director, Jenifer Eddy Artists' Management, Melbourne, 1975–; Director, Lies Askonas Ltd, London, 1982–97; Consultant Askonas Holt Ltd, 1998–. *Recordings include:* Die Entführung, Gypsy Baron, Hansel and Gretel. *Honours:* Medal, Order of Australia, 1997. *Address:* Jenifer Eddy Artists' Management, Suite 11, The Clivedon, 596 St Kilda Road, Melbourne 3004, Victoria, Australia. *Telephone:* (3) 9529-5410 (office). *Fax:* (3) 9529-5410 (office). *E-mail:* info@jeam.com.au (office).

**EDDY, Timothy;** Violoncellist; b. 1930, USA. *Education:* Studied with Bernard Greenhouse. *Career:* Duo recitals with pianist Gilbert Kalish and soloist with orchestras at Denver, Dallas, and the Maggio Musicale, Florence; Concerts with the Bach Aria Group and festival engagements at Santa Fe, Marlboro, Florida and at SUNY Stony Brook; Cellist with the Orion String Quartet, including appearances throughout the USA and at the Wigmore Hall, London; Further European appearances at the Lockenhaus and Turku (Finland) Festivals; Collaborations with Rudolf Serkin, Pablo Casals, and members of the Végh, Budapest and Guarneri Quartets; Professor of Cello at SUNY, Stony Brook. *Recordings:* Albums with Columbia, Angel Vox, Vanguard, Nonesuch, New World and Delos. *Current Management:* Orion String Quartet, c/o Ingpen & Williams Ltd, 7 St George's Court, 131 Putney Bridge Road, London, SW15 2PA, England.

**EDELMANN, Peter;** singer (baritone); b. 1962, Vienna, Austria. *Education:* Vienna Musikhochschule. *Career:* Sang Mozart's Figaro on tour in Europe; Member of the Koblenz Opera from 1985, notably in the title role at the premiere of Odysseus by Klaus Arp, 1989; Guest appearances in Mannheim, Dortmund, Wuppertal and Krefeld, as Mozart's Don Giovanni and Guglielmo, Marcello, the Forester in Cunning Little Vixen, Rossini's Figaro, Posa and Lord Tristan in Martha; Lieder recitals and concerts in Vienna, Budapest, Salzburg and Wexford; Member of the Deutsche Oper Berlin from 1990 (Papageno 1991); Sang in the premiere of Desdemona und ihre Schwestern by Siegfried Matthus, Schwetzingen 1991; Theseus in Enescu's Oedipe, Berlin, 1996; Albert in Werther, Berlin (concert), 1998; Sang Morales in Carmen, Gounod's Valentin and Melot in Tristan at the Deutsche Oper, 2000. *Honours:* Winner, 1989 Belvedere Competitions, Vienna. *Current Management:* Robert Gilder & Co., Enterprise House, 59–65 Upper Ground, London, SE1 9PQ, England. *Telephone:* (20) 7928-9008. *Fax:* (20) 7928-9755. *E-mail:* rgilder@robert-gilder.com.

**EDELMANN, Sergei;** Pianist; b. 22 July 1960, Lvov, Russia. *Education:* Studied with father, Head Piano Department, Lvov Conservatory; Studied with Rudolf Firkusny, Juilliard School, New York, 1979 with Claude Frank, Aspen (Colorado) Music School. *Career:* Debut: First public appearance as soloist, Beethoven Piano Concerto No. 1 with Lvov Philharmonic Orchestra, 1970; More than 50 concerts throughout Russia; Toured widely in Europe and North America as soloist with leading orchestras and as a Recitalist. *Recordings:* For RCA. *Honours:* Gina Bachauer Memorial Scholarship Award, 1979. *Address:* c/o Arien Arts & Music B.V.B.A., de Boeystraat 6, B–2018 Antwerp, Belgium.

**EDER, Claudia;** Singer (Mezzo-soprano); b. 7 Feb. 1948, Augsburg, Germany. *Education:* Studied at Munich and Frankfurt, with Marianne Scheck. *Career:* Debut: Bielefeld, 1973, as Offenbach's Nicklausse; Sang at Wiesbaden and Gärtnerplatz Theater, Munich from 1975; Vienna Volksoper from 1982, notably in Christoph Rilke by Matthus; Salzburg Festival, 1993, as Octavian, Düsseldorf, 1995, as Carmen; Other roles include Dorabella, Cenerentola, Meg Page and Hansel; Concert engagements throughout Austria and Germany. *Address:* c/o Deutsche Oper am Rhein, Heinrich-Heine Alle 16a, 40213 Düsseldorf, Germany.

**EDER, György;** Cellist; b. 2 Feb. 1949, Budapest, Hungary. *Education:* Franz Liszt Academy, Budapest, 1969–73; Yale University, 1978; The Banff Centre, 1983; University of Wisconsin, 1984. *Career:* Founding Member, Eder String Quartet, 1973–96; Kodály String Quartet, 1998–; Concert tours world-wide; Principal Cellist, Budapest Symphony Orchestra, and later Budapest Festival Orchestra, several years. *Recordings:* Over 40 albums. *Honours:* Prizewinner, Evian Competition, 1976; Prizewinner, Munich Competition, 1977. *Address:* Galoca utca 15, 1028 Budapest, Hungary.

**EDER, Helmut;** Composer and Teacher; b. 26 Dec. 1916, Linz, Austria. *Education:* Linz Conservatory; Training in composition from Hindemith in Salzburg, 1947, Orff in Munich, 1953–54, J N David in Stuttgart, 1954. *Career:* Teacher, Linz Conservatory, 1950–, co-founding its electronic music studio, 1959; Teacher, Salzburg Mozarteum, 1967, now Emeritus Professor Composer; mem. Programme Organiser, International Stiftung Mozarteum; Rotary Club, Salzburg-Nord. *Compositions:* Operas: Oedipus, 1958; Der Kardinal, 1962; Die weisse Frau, 1968; Konjugationen 3, 1969; Der Aufstand, 1975; Georges Dandin oder Der betrogne Ehemann, 1978–79; Mozart in New York, 3-act opera, Salzburg Festival, 1991; Ballets: Moderner Traum, 1957; Anamorphose, 1963; Die Irrfahrten des Odysseus, 1964–65; Orchestral: Symphony No. 1, 1950, No. 2, 1962, No. 3, 1969, No. 4, Choral Symphony, 1973–75, No. 5, Organ Symphony, 1979–80; Musica semplice, flute, harpsichord, strings, 1953; Music for 2 trumpets and strings, 1955; Concerto for piano, 15 wind instruments, double basses, percussion, 1956; Pezzo Sereno, 1958; Concerto semiserio, 2 pianos and orchestra, 1960; Oboe Concerto, 1962; 2 Violin Concertos, 1963, 1964; Danza a solatio, 1963; Concerto a dodici per archi, 1963; Nil admirari, 1966; Syntagma, 1967; Concerto for bassoon and chamber orchestra, 1968; L'Homme armé, concerto for organ and orchestra, 1968–69; Metamorphosen, flute, oboe, string quartet, orchestra, 1970; Melodia-ritmica, strings, 1973; Pastorale, strings, 1974; Divertimento, soprano, orchestral group, 1976; Jubilato, chamber orchestra, 1976; Serenade, 6 horns, 46 strings, 1977; Double Concerto, cello, double bass, orchestra, 1977–78; Cello Concerto, 1981; Concerto No. 3, violin and orchestra, 1981–82; Concerto A B, chamber orchestra, 1982; Notturno, flute, oboe, strings, 1983, revised, 1984; Haffner Concerto, flute and orchestra, 1984; Concertino, classical orchestra, 1984; Pièce de concert, strings, 1984; Duetto-Concerto, 2 flutes and orchestra, op 95; Symphony No. 6, 1994; Oboe Concerto, 1996; Chamber: String Quartet, 1948; Szene for 6 horns, 1977; Suite with Intermezzo for 11 winds, 1979; Quintet, clarinet, 2 violins, viola, cello, 1982; Quartet, flute, string trio, 1983; String Quartet No. 4, op 94, 1991; Trio for clarinet, viola and piano, 1994; Piano pieces; Organ music; Choral works. *Recordings:* Numerous. *Honours:* Several prizes; Various commissions. *Address:* c/o AKM, Baummanstrasse 10, 1031 Vienna, Postfach 259, Austria.

**EDGAR-WILSON, Richard;** Singer (Tenor); b. 1963, Ipswich, Suffolk, England. *Education:* Studied at Christ's College, Cambridge (choral exhibition); The Royal College of Music with Edward Brooks. *Career:* Opera includes: Albert Herring, Tamino (Magic Flute), Quint (Turn of the Screw), Beauty (The Triumph of Beauty and Deceit, Gerald Barry, C4 television); Concert repertoire includes Messiah, Bach's B minor Mass, the Monteverdi Vespers, Mozart's Coronation and C minor Masses and Carissimi's Jephtha; Works by Kodály, Stainer, Vaughan Williams, Berio and Britten; Solo appearances all over England and North America, France, Norway and Germany; Operatic roles include Handel's Acis and The Mad Woman in Britten's Curlew River; Work with conductors, Trevor Pinnock, Richard Hickox, Charles Mackerras, Robert King. *Recordings:* Purcell's Dioclesian, Pinnock; Stradella, San Giovanni Battista, Minkowski (winner Gramophone Award 1993); Schubert, Die schöne Müllerin. *Current Management:* Ron Gonsalves Management.

**EDLUND, Mikael;** Swedish composer; b. 19 Jan. 1950, Tranås; two d. *Education:* Univ. of Uppsala, State Coll. of Music, Stockholm with I. Lidholm and A. Mellnäs. *Career:* Producer at Fylkingen, Stockholm 1979; teacher in composition, State Coll. of Music, Gothenburg 1985–87; Pres., Swedish Section of ISCM 1996–98; mem. Soc. of Swedish Composers, Swedish Performing Right Soc., Int. Soc. for Contemporary Music (Swedish Section), Fylkingen. *Compositions:* The Lost Jugglery for mezzo-soprano, cello, piano and 2 percussionists, 1974–77; Trio Sun for clarinet, bassoon and piano, 1980; Leaves for 8 female voices, acoustic piano, electric piano, harp and 7 percussionists, 1977–81; Brains and Dancin' for string quartet, 1981; Fantasia on a City for piano, 1981–86; Jord for 5 percussionists, 1982; Små Fötter, a miniature for guitar, 1982; Music for double wind quintet, 1984; Orchids in the Embers for piano, 1984; Ajar for orchestra, 1988–91; Blue Garden for piano trio, 1992–94; Dissolved Window for 21 strings, 1986–96; Fanfara, trumpet solo, 1995; Un punto nel cortile for flute, 1997; Solo for violin, 1998–99; Così ballano; Cinghiali for flute, violin, violoncello and piano, 2000; Mannen och flugan from male choir, 2002. *Recordings:* Brains and Dancin'; Trio Sun; Orchids in the Embers; Små Fötter; Leaves; Fantasia on a city. *Honours:*

Christ Johnson 1985. *Address:* Backvägen 2, 19135 Sollentuna, Sweden. *E-mail:* edlund@minpost.nu.

**EDWARDS, George Harrison;** Composer; b. 11 May 1943, Boston, Massachusetts, USA; m. Rachel Hadas, 22 July 1978. *Education:* BA, Oberlin College, 1965; MFA, Princeton University, 1967. *Career:* Theory Faculty, New England Conservatory of Music, 1968–76; Assistant Professor of Music, 1976–86, Associate Professor of Music, 1986–93, Professor, 1993, Columbia University. *Compositions:* String Quartet, 1967; Kreuz und Quer, 1971; Monopoly, 1972; Giro, 1974; Exchange-Misere, 1974; Draconian Measures, 1976; Gyromancy, 1977; Veined Variety, 1978; Northern Spy, 1980; String Quartet 2, 1982; Moneta's Mourn, 1983; Suave Mari Magno, 1984; A Mirth but Open'd, 1986; Heraclitian Fire for string quartet and string orchestra, 1987; Piano Concerto, 1990; Plus ça change. . . for ensemble, 1992; The Isle is Full of Noises for 6 instruments, 1995; Trio for clarinet, viola and piano, 1996. *Address:* 838 West End Avenue, Apt 3A, New York, NY 10025, USA.

**EDWARDS, Joan;** Singer (Mezzo-soprano); b. 1944, London, England. *Education:* Studied at the London Opera Centre. *Career:* Debut: Schwertleite in Die Walküre at Covent Garden; Sang with the English Opera Group in Britain and abroad, often with Benjamin Britten conducting; Opera North from 1978 as Marcellina in Le nozze di Figaro, Third Lady (Magic Flute), Mother in Hansel and Gretel, Juno and Minerva in Orpheus in the Underworld, Berta in Il Barbiere di Siviglia and Mary in The Flying Dutchman; Many concert performances; Appeared on BBC television in La Traviata.

**EDWARDS, Owain Tudor,** BMus, MMus, PhD; musicologist; b. 10 Nov. 1940, Ruabon, Wales; m. Grete Strand 1965; one s. two d. *Education:* Univ. of Wales, Bangor. *Career:* Asst Lecturer 1965, Lecturer 1967, Music Dept, Univ. Coll. of Wales, Aberystwyth; Lecturer in Music, Open Univ. 1970; Lecturer in Music, Liverpool Univ. 1973; Reader and Head of Music History 1974, Prof. 1985–, Norges Musikkhogskole, Oslo, Norway; organist, Kroer Church, 1980–; mem. Norwegian Acad. of Science and Letters. *Compositions:* Adventsgudstjeneste 1986, 155 orgelsatser til gudstjeneste bruk 1992, Processional Music for brass 1995. *Publications:* Joseph Parry 1841–1903 1970, Beethoven 1972, People, Instruments and the Continuo 1974, Suite, Sonata and Concerto 1974, Matins, Lauds and Vespers for St David's Day 1990, The Penpont Antiphonal 1997, English Eighteenth-Century Concertos – an Inventory and Thematic Catalogue 2005; contrib. to New Grove Dictionary of Music and Musicians, The Music Review, The Musical Quarterly, Proceedings of the Royal Musical Association, Revue Bénédictine, Cantus Planus, Studia Musicologica Norvegica, Svensk tidskrift för musikforskning, Modern Asian Studies and Flerstemmige Innspill. *Address:* Norges Musikkhøgskole, Gydasv 6, Postboks 5190, Majorstua, 0302 Oslo 3, Norway. *Telephone:* 23-36-70-63 (office). *E-mail:* owain.edwards@nmh.no (office).

**EDWARDS, Ross;** Australian Composer; b. 23 Dec. 1943, Sydney, NSW; m. Helen Hopkins 1974; one s. one d. *Education:* New South Wales State Conservatory of Music, Univ. of Sydney; MMus, Univ. of Adelaide, 1970. *Career:* International Society of Contemporary Music Festivals, Stockholm, 1966, Basel, 1970; mem., numerous professional organisations. *Compositions:* Sonata for 9 instruments, Quem Quaeritis (children's nativity play) 1967, Etude for orchestra 1969, Monos I (cello solo), Monos II (piano solo) 1970, Mountain Village in a Clearing Mist for orchestra, Antifon for voices, brass ensemble, organ and percussion, 5 Little Piano Pieces, The Tower of Remoteness, Concerto for piano and orchestra, Christina's world (chamber opera), Shadow D-Zone 1977, The Hermit of Green Light 1979, Ab Estasis Foribus 1980, Maninya I 1981, II for string quartet, III 1985, IV 1985–86, V 1986, Kumari (solo piano), Laikan I and II, Ten Little Duets 1982, Marimba Dances 1982, Etymalong 1984, Reflections 1985, Flower Songs 1986, Maninyas for violin and orchestra 1988, Varrageh for solo percussion and orchestra 1989, Aria and Transcendental Dance for horn and string orchestra 1990, Sensing (dance piece) 1993, Guitar Concerto 1994, Veni Creator Spiritus (double string quartet) 1994, Enyato III for orchestra 1995, Binyang for clarinet and percussion 1996. *Contributions:* Music Now, Australian Contemporary Music Quarterly.

**EDWARDS, Sian;** British conductor; b. 27 Aug. 1959. *Education:* Royal Northern Coll. of Music, Manchester. *Career:* studied with Sir Charles Groves, Norman Del Mar and Neeme Järvi and with Prof. I.A. Musin, Leningrad Conservatoire 1983–85; won first Leeds Conductors' Competition 1984; has worked with many leading orchestras in UK including London Philharmonic (LPO), Royal Liverpool Philharmonic, Royal Scottish Orchestra, City of Birmingham Symphony, Hallé, BBC Philharmonic, English Chamber orchestras and London Sinfonietta; also with LA Philharmonic Orchestra, The Cleveland Orchestra, The Ensemble Modern, Rotterdam Philharmonic Orchestra and other orchestras; operatic debut, Mahagonny, Scottish Opera 1986; other operatic productions include La Traviata and L'Heure Espagnole (Glyndebourne) 1987–88, Katya Kabanova, New Year (Glyndebourne Touring Opera) 1988–90, The Knot Garden, Rigoletto, Il Trovatore (Royal Opera House, Covent Garden) 1988–91, world premiere Greek (Mark Anthony Turnage), Munich Biennale 1988, Edin. Festival 1988, The Gambler (ENO) 1990, Khovanshchina (ENO) 1994, Mahagonny 1995, La Clemenza di Tito 1998, Eugene Onegin 2000, Peter Grimes (ENO) 2001, Don Giovanni, Danish Royal Opera 2001, The Death of Klinghoffer, La Damnation de Faust, Finnish Nat. Opera 2001; Music Dir ENO 1993–95. *Recordings include:* Tchaikovsky orchestral music (Royal Liverpool Philharmonic Orchestra) and Peter and the

Wolf, Young Person's Guide to the Orchestra, Tchaikovsky's Fifth symphony (LPO). *Address:* c/o Ingpen and Williams Ltd, 26 Wadham Road, London, SW15 2LR (office); 70 Twisden Road, London, NW5 1DN, England. *Telephone:* (20) 8874-3222 (office).

**EDWARDS, Terry;** British choral director and conductor; b. 1939, London. *Education:* Trinity Coll. of Music. *Career:* formed and directed such groups as London Sinfonietta Voices, Electric Phoenix and London Voices; concerts and recordings with radio choirs, choral societies and choruses world-wide; Season 1988 with the BBC Singers and Choral Society at the Festival Hall, Bach's B minor Mass at Glasgow; concerts with the London Sinfonietta in the Prom Concerts and festival appearances in Berlin, Geneva and Turin; Chorus Master for Georg Solti in three Verdi concerts in Chicago; directed the chorus at the Michael Vyner Memorial at Covent Garden, 1990; Chorus Dir, Royal Opera, Covent Garden 1992–2004; concerts with the Danish Radio Choir, 1991 and works by Erik Bergmann in Finland; directed Sinfonietta Voices in Stockhausen's Stimmung at the Queen Elizabeth Hall, 1997; concerts in 2004 with Netherlands Radio Choir, NDR Choir, Budapest Radio Choir, Nat. Chamber Choir of Ireland. *Film soundtracks:* Harry Potter, Lord of the Rings, Star Wars. *Recordings include:* Messiaen Cinq Rechants, Rachmaninov and Tchaikovsky Vespers, A Boy was Born by Britten; Verdi Choruses and Otello; La Bohème; Ligeti-A-Capella Music; Holliger; Die Jahreszeiten; Don Carlos; Curlew River, and 200 others.

**EDWARDS, Warwick (Anthony);** University Lecturer and Performer on Early Instruments; b. 22 April 1944, Dewsbury, England; m. Jacqueline Freeman, 2 d. *Education:* King's College, University of Cambridge; MA; BMus; PhD. *Career:* Lecturer, 1971–, Senior Lecturer, 1986–, Glasgow University; Director, Scottish Early Music Consort, 1976–; Director, Glasgow International Early Music Festival, 1990–. *Recordings:* Mary's Music: Songs and Dances from the time of Mary Queen of Scots, Scottish Early Music Consort, W Edwards Director, 1984. *Publications:* Editor: Music for Mixed Consort (Musica Britannica 40), 1977; W Byrd: Latin Motets (from manuscript scores) (The Byrd Edition 8), 1984. *Contributions:* Grove's Dictionary, 6th edition; Music and Letters; Proceedings of the Royal Music Association; Early Music; The Consort; British Book News. *Address:* 22 Falkland Street, Glasgow G12 9 PR, Scotland.

**EDWORTHY, Joanne Elizabeth,** GMus, RNCM; British singer (mezzo-soprano) and singing teacher; b. 24 July 1970, Epsom, Surrey; m. Robert Allen; one s. one d. *Education:* Royal Northern Coll. of Music. *Career:* debut as Hansel, WNO 1995; Siebel in Faust, WNO 1996; Glyndebourne co. mem. 1996–2000; opera roles include Hansel and Meg Page at QEH, Xerxes, Ramiro and Amadigi at New Coll., Oxford 1998–2003, Cheubino in Mozart's Figaro at Edinburgh Festival 2002; recitals and oratorio include St Martin in the Fields, St John's, Smith Square, Royal Festival Hall, Sheldonian Theatre, Christchurch Cathedral; radio and television role of Siebel in Gounod's Faust for WNO 1996; vocal tutor at St Paul's Girls' School, Hammersmith, London. *Honours:* Wingate Foundation Scholarship, Countess of Munster Award, Thurston Memorial Award (RNCM), Oncken Song Prize (RNCM). *Address:* 83 Arundel Road, Sands, High Wycombe, Buckinghamshire, HP12 4ND, England (home). *Telephone:* (1494) 521969 (home). *E-mail:* jo@jedworthy.co.uk (office). *Website:* www.jedworthy.co.uk.

**EENSALU, Marika;** Singer (Mezzo-soprano); b. 20 Sept. 1947, Tallinn, Estonia. *Education:* Studied at Tallinn and with Irina Arkhipova in Moscow. *Career:* Sang at the Estonia Theatre, Tallinn, from 1980, as Rosina, Carmen, Dorabella, Bradamante in Alcina, Marfa and Ulrica; Savonlinna Festival, 1987, with guest appearances in Moscow and throughout Germany, Denmark and Hungary; Concert engagements in works by Estonian composers. *Address:* c/o Estonian State Opera, Estonian Boulevard, 20001 Tallinn, Estonia.

**EEROLA, Aulikki;** Singer (Soprano); b. 1947, Tuusula, Finland. *Education:* Studied at the Sibelius Academy, Helsinki, and with Hilde Zadek and Erik Werba in Vienna. *Career:* Debut: Sang in concert at Helsinki, 1975; Savonlinna Festival, 1977, as Pamina in Die Zauberflöte, and has appeared widely in Germany, Austria, England, France and North America as concert soloist. *Address:* c/o Finnish National Opera, Bulevardi 23-27, 00180 Helsinki 18, Finland.

**EEROLA, Lasse Olavi;** Composer and Music Teacher; b. 24 Sept. 1945, Kuusankoski, Finland; m. Päivi Irmeli, 27 August 1983, 2 s. *Education:* Sibelius Academy, Helsinki, Finland, 1970–77. *Career:* Clarinet and Saxophone Player, 1967–74; Teacher of Theory and Clarinet, 1969–; Composer, 1975–; mem, Society of Finnish Composers; The Finnish Clarinet Society. *Compositions:* Variations for wind orchestra, 1975, recorded 1980 and 1992; Variations for orchestra, 1977; Metamorphoses for orchestra, 1979; Suite for Orchestra, 1980–81; Music for clarinet and piano, 1980–82; Miniature for orchestra, 1982; Chamber Music, 1983–84; Aino, 1984–85; Ceremonial Fanfare for Kouvola, 1984, recorded 1988; Fantasy for orchestra, 1985; Two Pieces for orchestra, 1985–86; Syksyisia Kuvia, 1985; Fantasia for clarinet and wind orchestra, 1986; Brass Quintet, 1987. *Recordings include:* Quintet for Brass, 1992; Scenes from Northern Carelia, 1990; Suite for wind orchestra, recorded 1995; Music for tuba and orchestra, 1991; Rose Red Music for brass and percussion instruments, 1994; Three Pieces for wind quintet, 1994; Amordus Play for tuba and piano, 1994–95; Three Pieces for tuba and piano, 1993–94. *Honours:* Province of North Karelia Art Prize, 1986 and 1995. *Address:* Suutarinkatu 12, 80100 Joensuu, Finland.

**EFRATY, Anat;** Singer (soprano); b. 28 June 1966, Tel-Aviv. *Education:* Studied at the Rubin Academy, Tel-Aviv, and with Walter Berry in Vienna. *Career:* Debut: Mahler's 2nd Symphony, with the Israel Symphony, 1993; New Israeli Opera from 1993, as The Bird in Farber's The Journey to Polyphonia, Britten's Helena, Ninetta in The Love for Three Oranges and other roles; US debut, San Diego, 1995, in Vivaldi's Gloria; German debut, Stuttgart, 1995, as Flaminia in Haydn's Mondo della luna; Théâtre du Châtelet, Paris, 1995, as Tebaldo in Don Carlo; Other roles include Frasquita, Sophie in Werther, Nannetta and Despina; Season 2000–01 as Lulu and Sophie at the Vienna Staatsoper, Lulu at Palermo. *Current Management:* Athole Still International Management, Forresters Hall, 25–27 Westow Street, London, SE19 3RY, England. *Telephone:* (20) 8771-5271. *Fax:* (20) 8768-6600. *Website:* www .atholestill.com.

**EFREMOV, Alexander;** Pianist; b. 8 July 1962, Tomsk, Siberia, Russia. *Education:* Far Eastern Institute of Arts, Vladivostok; Pianist, solo-ensembleist, accompanist, Tchaikovsky Conservatory, Moscow; Piano, Aesthetics, Masters degree, Postgraduate studies with Professor Dimitri Bashkirov. *Career:* Debut: Far Eastern Philharmonic, solo concert, 1985; Far East television, Russia, 1980–85; Radio ORF, 1997–; American Broadway music concerts, Tonhalle, Zürich, 1993; Concert in tribute to Geza Anda, Geza Anda House, Zürich, 1993; Solo Concert at Grossmünster, 1993; Concert with Bruckner Orchester, Linz, 1995; Chamber concert at Gasteig, Munich, 1996; Concert with Yevgeny Nesterenko at Vienna Konzerthaus, 1996; Concert with the Vienna Symphonic Orchestra at the Bregenz Festival, 1996; Concert in Theatre de St Quentin en Yvelines, Paris, 1997; Répétiteur and solo pianist, Porgy and Bess with the Vienna Symphony Orchestra, Bregenz, 1998. *Publications:* Schumann and the Aesthetics of German Romanticism, Lenin State Library, Moscow, 1990. *Address:* c/o Vienna Symphony Orchestra, Lehargasse 11, A–1060 Vienna, Austria.

**EGERTON, Francis;** Singer (tenor); b. 14 July 1930, Limerick, Republic of Ireland. *Career:* Early appearances with Scottish Opera, the Glyndebourne Festival and at Sadler's Wells; Covent Garden from 1972 as Iopas in Les Troyens, Beppe, Flute, the Captain in Wozzeck and roles in Carmen, Les Contes d'Hoffmann and La Fanciulla del West; Has sung Mime in Siegfried for Scottish Opera and in San Francisco; Other roles include, Pedrillo, Strauss's Scaramuccio at Nice, Italian Tenor at Glasgow and Monsieur Taupe in Capriccio at Glyndebourne, Bardolfo in Falstaff at San Francisco, in concert at Chicago and at Los Angeles, conducted by Giulini; Sang Il Conte in Cimarosa's Il Fanatico Burlato at Drottningholm, the Captain in Wozzeck at Edinburgh and Los Angeles; Season 1990–91 with Mr Upfold in Albert Herring at San Diego, the four tenor roles in Hoffmann in Paris, Goro in Madama Butterfly and Eumaus in Il Ritorno d'Ulisse in Los Angeles; Appearances in Prokofiev's The Fiery Angel at the Proms and Covent Garden, 1991–92, as the Doctor; Season 1995–96 as M le Comte in La Belle Vivette, after Offenbach, for English National Opera; M. Taupe in Capricco at Glyndebourne, 1998; Other recent roles in Falstaff at the Oper der Stadt in Cologne, Billy Budd at the Bastille, Goro in Los Angeles and Missail for Washington Opera; Sang the Emperor in Turandot at Covent Garden, 2002. *Current Management:* Athole Still International Management, Forresters Hall, 25–27 Westow Street, London, SE19 3RY, England. *Telephone:* (20) 8771-5271. *Fax:* (20) 8768-6600. *Website:* www.atholestill.com.

**EGRI, Monika;** Pianist; b. 17 Oct. 1966, Budapest, Hungary; m. Attila Pertis, 28 June 1991. *Education:* Bartók Conservatory, Budapest; Music Academy, Vienna. *Career:* Performances, Hungarian Days, London, 1989, Musikverein, Vienna, 1991, Budapest Spring Festival, Carinthian Summer Festival, Austria; Television and radio recordings, Hungary, Austria, Italy; Founded Egri and Pertis Piano Duo, 1980s. *Recordings:* For Hungarian Radio and ORF, Austria; Journey Around the World, 1995; Liszt: Opera Fantasies and Transcriptions for 2 pianos, 1997–98. *Contributions:* Die Presse; Kronen Zeitung; Piano Journal. *Honours:* Magistra Artium, 1994; Grand Prix Internationale du Disque Liszt, 1998; Prizewinner, many international competitions. *Current Management:* Annart Artists Management, Barkacs utca 7, 1221 Budapest, Hungary; J A Ellison, International Artists Management, 135 Stevenage Road, Fulham, London SW6 6PB, England; Künstlermanagement Till Dönch, Weimarer Str 48, 1180 Vienna, Austria. *Address:* Kaltwasserstrasse 1, 3413 Unterkirchbach, Austria.

**EHDE, John Martin;** Swedish cellist and conductor; b. 25 April 1962, Stockholm. *Education:* Royal Acad. of Music, Århus, Denmark, Hochschule für Musik, Vienna. *Career:* debut recital, Royal Acad., Copenhagen 1987; first appeared on Swedish Radio aged 11; recitals and concertos with orchestras throughout Europe and Canada; radio and television broadcasts in Scandinavia, Iceland, Italy, Viet Nam, Hong Kong, Canada; solo cellist, Helsingborg Symphony Orchestra, Sweden 1989–99; speciality, performing the music of Frederick Delius; Cello Concerto, sonata; Young People's Concerts with most Swedish and Danish symphony orchestras (speaker, cellist, conductor); freelance soloist and chamber musician, with tours in Canada, Hong Kong, Viet Nam, Singapore 2000–; mem. Leopold Stokowski Soc., London, Frederick Delius Soc., England. *Recordings:* numerous with The Lin Ensemble and with the pianist Carl-Axel Dominique (Sonatas by Alkan, Debussy and Delius) 1997, Cello Concerto by Olof Lindgren 1997. *Honours:* first prize in many Swedish youth competitions, Malmö Lions Club cultural grant 1974, one-year grant for studies in Vienna, Swedish Inst. for Science and Art 1987, awarded scholarship from Foundation of Swedish Conductor, Sten Frykberg 1990.

*Address:* Mansasvej 22, 2500 Valby, Denmark. *E-mail:* john@ehde.dk (office). *Website:* www.ehde.dk.

**EHNES, James;** Canadian violinist; *Francis Chaplin Guest Professor of Violin, Brandon University;* b. 1976, Brandon, MB. *Education:* Meadowmount School of Music, The Juilliard School, studied with Francis Chaplin and Sally Thomas. *Career:* made his solo orchestral debut with Montréal Symphony Orchestra aged thirteen; has performed with numerous orchestras worldwide, including LSO, London Philharmonia, BBC Philharmonic, BBC SO, Royal Scottish Nat. Opera, Scottish Chamber Orchestra, Royal Liverpool Philharmonic, Deutsche Kammerphilharmonie, Berlin SO, Orchestre de Lyon, Residente Orkest of The Hague, Czech Philharmonic, Budapest Festival Orchestra, Finnish Radio Orchestra, NHK Symphony Orchestra, Tokyo, Malaysian Philharmonic, New York Philharmonic, Chicago Symphony, Nat. Arts Center Orchestra, and the major orchestras of Boston, Philadelphia, Los Angeles, San Francisco, Pittsburgh, Cincinnati, Detroit, Minnesota, St Paul, Houston, Dallas, Seattle, Fort Worth, Indianapolis, Vancouver, Calgary, Winnipeg, Toronto, Newfoundland and Montréal; has appeared at festivals, including Ravinia Festival, Marlboro Festival, Seattle Chamber Music Festival, Bravo! Vail Valley Music Festival, Tokyo Summer Music Festival, Bermuda Festival, Montreux Festival, Festival de la Chaise-Dieu, Festival Côte St André, Moritzburg Festival, Festival of the White Nights; frequent performances in a trio with Jan Vogler (cello) and Louis Lortie (piano); has also performed with Leif Ove Andsnes, Yo-Yo Ma; currently Francis Chaplin Guest Prof. of Violin, Brandon Univ. *Recordings:* Paganini, 24 Caprices 1995, Prokofiev, The Two Violin Sonatas and Five Melodies 2000, Ravel/Debussy/Saint-Saens (with Wendy Chen) 2000, Bach, The Six Sonatas and Partitas for solo violin (Juno Award 2001, Cannes Classical Award for Young Artist of the Year 2002) 2000, Max Bruch, Violin Concertos Nos 1 and 3 (Juno Award 2002, Canadian Independent Music Award 2002) 2001, French Showpieces 2001, Bruch, Concerto No. 2 and Scottish Fantasy (Juno Award 2003) 2002, Fritz Kreisler 2002, Piano Quintets 2003, Romantic Pieces (works of Janáček, Smetana, Dvořák) 2004, Wieniawski, Sarasate 2004, Dallapiccola 2004, Donhányi 2004, Hummel 2004. *Honours:* Canadian Music Competition grand prize in strings 1987, first prize in strings 1988, Ivan Galamian Memorial Award, Canada Council for the Arts Virginia Parker Prize 1997. *Current Management:* Walter Homburger, 278 Heath Street E, Toronto, ON M4T 1T4, Canada. *Telephone:* (416) 481-5021 (office). *Fax:* (416) 481-1143 (office). *E-mail:* wfh@sympatico.ca (office). *Website:* www.jamesehnes.com.

**EIRIKSDOTTIR, Karolina;** Composer; b. 10 Jan. 1951, Reykjavík, Iceland; m. Thorsteinn Hannesson, 1 Aug 1974, 1 d. *Education:* Graduated, Reykjavík College, 1971, Reykjavík College of Music, 1974; MMus Music History and Musicology, 1976, MMus Composition 1978, University of Michigan, USA. *Career:* Major performances of works: Iceland Symphony Orchestra (4 works), at Nordic Music Days in Helsinki 1980, Oslo 1982, Copenhagen 1984; At Scandinavia Today, Washington DC 1982; Opera, Nagon har jag sett in Vadstena in Sweden, 1988, Reykjavík, 1989; Sinfonietta performed by the BBC Scottish Symphony Orchestra during Breaking the Ice Festival in Glasgow, 1992; Six Movements for String Quartet performed by the Arditti String Quartet, London, 1992; Three Paragraphs for Orchestra performed by the Malmö Symphony Orchestra at Stockholm New Music Festival, Stockholm, 1993; Performances at Nordic Music Festival, Göteborg, 1991; Dark Music Days Festival in Reykjavík, 1993 and Kuhmo Festival in Finland, 1993; Commission, Icelandic State television, work for symphony orchestra, 1985; Several performances, Iceland and abroad; Opera, I Have Seen Someone (1988) given British premiere by Lontano, 1996; mem, Society of Icelandic composers. *Compositions include:* Notes, Sonans, Sinfonietta, for orchestra; 5 pieces for chamber orchestra; 6 movements for string quartet; Rondo and Rhapsody for piano; In Vultu Solis, violin; Trio, violin, cello, piano; 6 poems from the Japanese, and Some Days, voice and instruments; All pieces in manuscript at Iceland Music Information Centre, Reykjavík; Orchestral pieces, Notes, Sonans, Sinfonietta, Klifur, Three Paragraphs, Opera: Nagon har jag sett, chamber orchestra: Five pieces and Rhapsody in C; Land possessed by poems for baritone and piano, solo pieces for clarinet, harpsichord and guitar and chamber music; Concerto for clarinet and orchestra, 1994; Living by the sea: a Collection of Songs, 1997; Man Alive, chamber opera, 1999; Solos for cello and violin. *Recordings:* Sinfonietta, Iceland Symphony Orchestra, conductor Paul Zukofsky; Other works recorded by Iceland State Broadcasting Service; Karolina Eiriksdottir–Portrait; Icelandic Chamber Music. *Address:* Blatun 6, 225 Bessastadahreppur, Iceland.

**EISMA, Will Leendert;** Composer and Violinist; b. 13 May 1929, Sungailiat, Indonesia; m. Wilhelmina A Reeser, 30 Nov 1960, 1 s., 1 d. *Education:* Conservatory of Rotterdam; Composition, Accademia di Santa Cecilia, Rome; Institute for Sonology, Utrecht. *Career:* Violinist: Rotterdam Philharmonic, 1953–59, Chamber Orchestra, Società Corelli, 1960–61, Chamber Orchestra, Radio Hilversum, 1961–89; Member of electro instrumental group ICE; Director, Studio for Electronic Music, Five Roses. *Compositions:* 4 Concerti for orchestra, 1 for 2 violins and orchestra, 1961; Taurus-A, 1963, Volumina for orchestra, 1964; Concerti for oboe, horn, 1973; Chamber and electronic music, 1970; Concerto for string trio and orchestra, 1974; Concerto for percussion, 1979; Concerto for English horn, 1981; Concerto for 5 violas, 1982; Du dehors–Du dedans, 1983; Silver Plated Bronze, 1986; Te Deum, 1988; Passo del Diavolo, 1988; Mawar jiwa for gamelan, 1992; Uguisu for gamelan, 1997. *Address:* Oude Amersfoortseweg 206, Hilversum 1212 AL, Netherlands.

**EJSING, Mette;** Singer (Mezzo-soprano); b. 9 Nov. 1954, Silkeborg, Denmark. *Education:* Studied in Copenhagen with Ulrik Cold and Ingrid Bjoner. *Career:* Sang with the Stuttgart Staatsoper, 1991–95; St Gallen, 1992, as the Countess in The Queen of Spades; Erda in Wagner's Ring at Karlsruhe, Århus, Vienna Staatsoper (1995) and La Scala, Milan (1996); Staatsoper Berlin, 1995, in Der Rosenkavalier, Die Zauberflöte and Der fliegende Holländer; Bayreuth Festival in Parsifal and Die Walküre; Sang Erda in Siegfried at Helsinki, 1998; Season 1999–2000 as Erda in Siegfried at Sydney and Trieste, Erda and First Norn at Bayreuth; Concerts in San Francisco, Berlin and elsewhere. *Address:* c/o Finnish National Opera, PO Box 176, Helsingkatu 58, 00251 Helsinki, Finland.

**EK, Harald;** Tenor; b. 1936, Jonkoping, Sweden. *Education:* Studied in Gothenburg with G Kjellertz and R Jacobson. *Career:* Debut: Gothenburg in 1966 in Die Lustige Witwe; Sang at Drottningholm in 1967 as Almaviva in Paisiello's Il Barbiere di Siviglia, Stadtstheater Berne, 1969–72, and Bayreuth Festival in 1971 in Der fliegende Holländer and Das Rheingold; Member of the Staatsoper Hamburg, 1972–75, and Zürich Opera from 1975; Sang Don José at Gothenburg in 1988; Other roles include Don Ottavio, Tamino, Hoffmann, Comte Ory, Cavaradossi, Tom Rakewell and Alfred in Die Fledermaus. *Recordings include:* Der fliegende Holländer. *Address:* School of Theatre and Opera, University of Göteborg, Box 5439, 40229 Göteborg, Sweden.

**EKLÖF, Marianne;** Singer (Mezzo-soprano); b. 15 March 1956, Sweden. *Education:* Studied in Stockholm, at Juilliard (New York) and in London with Vera Rozsa. *Career:* Sang in opera at Malmö from 1985, as Carmen and in the premiere of Werle's Midsummer Night's Dream; Stockholm Folkoperan from 1990, in Samson et Dalila and Les Contes d'Hoffmann; Jutland Opera, Århus, 1995, as Waltraute in Götterdämmerung; Sang Mme de la Motte in the British premiere of Marie Antoinette by Daniel Börtz, at Brighton; Many concert engagements. *Recordings include:* Grieg's Peer Gynt and Sigurd Josalfar. *Address:* c/o Folkoperan, Hornsgatan 72, 11721 Stockholm, Sweden.

**EKLUND, Anna;** Soprano; b. 1964, Sweden. *Education:* Studied at the Stockholm College of Music and the State Opera School. *Career:* Debut: Stockholm Royal Opera as Papagena; Sang in staged version of Carmina Burana at Stockholm in 1991; Roles have included Isamene in Haeffner's Elektra at Drottningholm, Novis Elisabeth in Forsell's Riket ar Ditt, the Queen of Night and Serpetta in La Finta Giardiniera; Season 1991–92 in the St Matthew Passion under Philippe Herreweghe in Sweden, Barcelona and Madrid, Betty in Salieri's Falstaff at Drottningholm; Season 1992–93 as Zémire in Grétry's Zémire et Azor at Drottningholm, and the leading female role in the premiere of Amorina by Lars Runsten at the Royal Opera Stockholm. *Address:* Nordic Artists Management, Sveavagen 76, 11359 Stockholm, Sweden.

**EKLUND, Hans;** Composer and Professor; b. 1 July 1927, Sandviken, Sweden. *Education:* Studied with Lars-Erik Larsson, Stockholm Musikhogskolan, 1949–52; Ernst Pepping, Berlin, 1954; Rome, 1957. *Career:* Professor of Harmony and Counterpoint, Stockholm Musikhogskolan, 1964–. *Compositions include:* Opera: Mother Svea, 1972; Orchestral: Symphonic Dances, 1954, Musica da Camera, No. 1, 1955, No. 2, 1956, No. 3, 1957, No. 4, 1959, No. 5, 1970, No. 6, 1970; Symphonies: No. 1, Sinfonia Seria, 1958, No. 2, Sinfonia Breve, 1964, No. 3, Sinfonia Rustica, 1967–68, No. 4, Hjalmar Branting in memoriam, 1973–74, No. 5, Quadri, 1978, No. 6, Sinfonia Senza Speranza, 1983, No. 7, La Serenata, 1984, No. 8, Sinfonia Grave, 1985, No. 9, Sinfonia Introvertita, 1992, No. 10 'Sine Nomine', 1994, No. 11, Sinfonia piccola, 1995, No. 12, Freschi, 1996; Other: Toccata, 1966, Concerto for trombone, winds and percussion, 1972, Requiem Per Soli Coro Ed Orchestra, 1977–78, Horn Concerto, 1979, Concerto for tuba and brass orchestra, 1980, Divertimento, 1986; Chamber: 2 Sonatas for solo violin, 1956, 1982, 3 Preludes for piano, 1990, 2 Pastoral Songs for choir, 1993; Various solo pieces, piano music and organ works and choruses. *Honours:* Member, Royal Swedish Academy of Music, 1975–; Awarded degree, Litteris et Artibus from the King of Sweden, 1985; Christ Johnson Fund Music Prize, 1989. *Address:* Bjornskogsgrand 63, 162 46 Vallingby, Sweden.

**EL-DABH, Halim Abdul Messieh,** MM, MFA; American composer and teacher; b. 4 March 1921, Cairo, Egypt. *Education:* Sulcz Conservatory, Cairo, University of Cairo, Berkshire Music Center, Tanglewood with Aaron Copland and Irving Fine, New England Conservatory of Music, Boston, Brandeis University. *Career:* teacher, Haile Selassie University, Addis Ababa 1962–65, Howard University 1966–69; teacher 1969–, Co-Dir 1979–, Center for the Study of World Musics, Kent State University. *Compositions include:* 3 Symphonies, 1950–56; String Quartet, 1951; Fantasia-Tahmeel for darabukka or timpani and strings, 1954; Bacchanalia for orchestra, 1958; Juxtaposition No. 1 for percussion ensemble, 1959; Black Epic, opera-pageant, 1968; Opera Files, 1971; Drink Of Eternity, opera-pageant, 1981; Concerto for darabukka, clarinet and strings, 1981; Tonography III for 5 winds, 1984; Piano pieces and choruses. *Publications:* The Derabucca: Hand Techniques in The Art of Drumming, 1965. *Honours:* Fulbright Scholarship; two Guggenheim Fellowships. *Address:* c/o Center for the Study of World Musics, Kent University, Kent, OH 44242, USA.

**ELCHLEPP, Isolde;** Singer (Mezzo-soprano); b. 1952, Strasbourg, France. *Education:* Opera School of the Bavarian State Opera. *Career:* Sang first at Bremen, notably as The Woman in Schoenberg's Erwartung, 1985; Wiesbaden from 1986 as Wagner's Venus, Fricka and Waltraute, and Azucena in Il Trovatore; Hanover Opera as Carmen, Ortrud, Santuzza, Octavian, the Composer, Amneris and Kundry; Deutsche Oper Berlin, 1990, as Ortrud; Guest appearances in Düsseldorf, Mannheim, Brunswick, Karlsruhe, Basle (Herodias in Salome) and Brussels; Concert repertory includes Schoenberg's Pierrot Lunaire, which she has sung in Paris and Nuremberg; Guest in Tokyo in Erwartung; Also sang Elektra with the Oslo Philharmonic; Troades, Frankfurt Opera; Fricka in Das Rheingold and Die Walküre at Hanover, 1992 as well as Hostess in the premiere of Reimann's Das Schloss, Deutsche Oper Berlin; Debut at Bayreuth Festival as Ortrud in 1993; Sang the Woman in Erwartung in a Pierre Audi production for Netherlands Opera; Season 1996 at Hanover as Lady Macbeth and Orff's Antigonae; Marie in Wozzeck at Turin, 1998; Sang Brünnhilde at Hannover, 1999, and Elektra at the Komische Oper Berlin, 2001. *Current Management:* Haydn Rawstron Ltd, London. *Address:* c/o Staatstheater Hannover, Opernhaus, Opernplatz 1, D–30159 Hannover, Germany.

**ELDER, Mark Philip,** CBE, MA; British conductor; *Music Director, Hallé Orchestra;* b. 2 June 1947, Hexham, England; s. of John Elder and Helen Elder; m. Amanda Jane Stein 1980; one d. *Education:* Bryanston School and Corpus Christi Coll., Cambridge. *Career:* music staff Wexford Festival 1969–70; Chorus Master and Asst Conductor Glyndebourne 1970–71; music staff Royal Opera House, Covent Garden 1970–72; Staff Conductor Australian Opera 1972–74; Staff Conductor ENO 1974–77, Assoc. Conductor 1977–79, Music Dir 1979–93; Prin. Guest Conductor London Mozart Players 1980–83, BBC Symphony Orchestra 1982–85, City of Birmingham Symphony Orchestra 1992–95; Music Dir Rochester Philharmonic Orchestra, NY 1989–94, Hallé Orchestra 2000–. *Honours:* Dr hc (Royal Acad. of Music) 1984, Hon. Fellow Royal Northern Coll. of Music; Olivier Award for Outstanding Contribution to Opera 1990. *Address:* Hallé Concerts Society, The Bridgewater Hall, Manchester, M1 5HA (office); c/o Ingpen & Williams Ltd, 7 St George's Court, 131 Putney Bridge Road, London, SW15 2PA, England (office). *Website:* www.halle.co.uk.

**ELIAS, Brian David;** British composer; b. 30 Aug. 1948, Bombay, India. *Education:* Royal Coll. of Music, studied with Elisabeth Lutyens. *Career:* freelance ed., arranger and copyist; clerk and statistican assistant, 1972–78; composer, full-time with some teaching commitments; mem. British Acad. of Composers and Songwriters. *Compositions include:* La Chevelure for soprano and chamber orchestra; Somnia for tenor and orchestra; L'Eylah for orchestra, commissioned by BBC for Promenade Concerts, 1984; Tzigane for solo violin; Peroration for solo soprano; Geranos for chamber ensemble, commissioned by The Fires of London, 1985; 5 songs to Poems by Irina Ratushinskaya for mezzo-soprano and orchestra commissioned by BBC for Winter Season, 1989–; The Judas Tree, ballet score commissioned by The Royal Ballet choreographed by Kenneth MacMillan, 1992; Fanfare, Royal Ballet, choreographed by Matthew Hart, 1993; Laments for mezzo-soprano, 6 female voices and orchestra (commissioned by BBC for the Cheltenham Festival, 1998); The House That Jack Built for orchestra commissioned by the BBC for Winter Season 2001–02; Three Songs (Christina Rosetti); A Talisman for bass-baritone and chamber orchestra (commissioned by Cheltenham Int. Festival of Music. *Recordings:* Peroration – 5 Songs to Poems by Irina Ratushinskaya; The Judas Tree; Laments, Moto Perpetuo. *Honours:* Jt Second Prize for Proverbs of Hell, Radcliffe Music Award 1977. *Address:* c/o Chester Music, 8–9 Frith Street, London, W1D 3JB, England (office). *Telephone:* (20) 7434-0066 (office). *E-mail:* promotion@musicsales.co.uk (office). *Website:* www .chesternovello.com (office).

**ELIAS, Jorge;** Singer (Tenor); b. 1973, Spain. *Education:* Queen Sofia School of Music, Madrid with Alfredo Kraus. *Career:* Appearances throughout Spain from 1995, including Oviedo Opera, Il Barbiere di Siviglia, Bilbao and Madrid; Edgardo in Lucia di Lammermoor at Bergamo, 1997; Verdi's I Masnadieri at Piacenza, Don Carlos at the Santander Festival; Rodolfo in La Bohème at Lucca; Season 1999–2000 with Bruckner's Te Deum at the Teatro Comunale in Florence under Zubin Mehta; Other concerts include Donizetti's Requiem at Bergamo. *Honours:* Placido Domingo Trophy; 1st Prize, Ciudad de Logzaño Opera Contest; 2nd Prize, Francisco Slouso International Opera Contest. *Address:* c/o IMG Artists, Lovell House, 616 Chiswick High Road, London W4 5RX, England.

**ELIAS, Rosalind;** Singer and Opera Director; b. Lowell, MA, USA. *Education:* New England Conservatory, Boston, Accademia di Santa Cecilia, Rome; further study with Daniel Ferro in New York. *Career:* sang with New England Opera 1948–52; Metropolitan Opera from 1954 as Cherubino, Dorabella, Rosina and Hansel, and in the premieres of Barber's Vanessa, and Antony and Cleopatra; Scottish Opera in 1970 as Rossini's La Cenerentola; Vienna Staatsoper in 1972 as Carmen; Glyndebourne Festival in 1975 as Baba the Turk in The Rake's Progress; other appearances in Hamburg, Monte Carlo, Barcelona, Lisbon and Aix-en-Provence; other roles included Verdi's Amneris and Azucena, Massenet's Charlotte and Giulietta in Les Contes d'Hoffmann; sang Herodias in Salome at Houston in 1987; produced Carmen at Cincinnati in 1988 and Il Barbiere di Siviglia for Opera Pacific, Costa Mesa, in 1989; sang Mistress Quickly in Falstaff at Boston, 1996; Italian debut as Old Lady in Bernstein's Candide, Turin, 1997; sang the Baroness in Vanessa at Monte Carlo, 2001. *Recordings:* La Gioconda, La Forza del Destino, Il Trovatore, Falstaff, Madama Butterfly, Rigoletto, Der fliegende Holländer. *Address:* c/o Opera Pacific, 3187 Red Hill Avenue, Costa Mesa, CA 92626, USA.

**ELIASSON, Andreas;** Composer; b. 3 April 1947, Borlange, Sweden. *Education:* Studied with Ingvar Lilholm and Gyorgy Ligeti. *Compositions:* Hymn, for mens' voices; Winds and Percussion, 1970; Melos for String Quartet, 1970; Picnic for Wind Quintet, 1972; Glasdans for orchestra, 1973; En avoss, church opera, 1974; Disegno for string quartet, 1975; Canti in Iontananza for chamber orchestra, 1977; Impronta for orchestra, 1978; Turnings for orchestra, 1978; Ombra for clarinet and string quartet, 1980; Backanterna, incidental music, 1982; Symphony, 1988; Fantasia for orchestra, 1988; Sinfonia concertante, 1989; Farfalle e ferro for horn and strings, 1992; Stammor for string quartet, 1992; Clarinet Concerto, 1992; Violin Concerto, 1992; Kimmo for trumpet and 6 percussion, 1996; Bass Clarinet Concerto, 1996; Oratorio, 2000. *Honours:* Royal Swedish Academy Prize, 1983. *Address:* c/o STIM, Sankhamnsgaten 79, 102 54 Stockholm, Sweden.

**ELIASSON, Sven Olaf;** Singer (Tenor); b. 4 April 1933, Boliden, Sweden. *Education:* Royal Music Academy, Stockholm. *Career:* Sang at Oslo from 1961, Stockholm from 1965; Guest appearances at the Hamburg Staatsoper, 1968–74; Further engagements at Zürich, Düsseldorf and Frankfurt; Glyndebourne in 1967 as Don Ottavio; Drottningholm Opera in 1967 as Belmonte in Die Entführung; Zürich Opera in 1968 and 1975 as Pfitzner's Palestrina and in the premiere of Klebe's Ein Wahrer Held; Stockholm Opera in 1970 in the premiere of Rosenberg's Hus Med Dubbel Ingang; Sang Schoenberg's Aron with the Hamburg Staatsoper in Israel in 1974; Other roles included Don José, Riccardo in Un Ballo in Maschera, Peter Grimes and Tom Rakewell in The Rake's Progress; Director of Oslo Opera from 1983; Sang Siegmund at Århus, 1987. *Recordings include:* Il Ritorno d'Ulisse in Patria by Monteverdi; Video of Swedish Opera production of Die Meistersinger. *Address:* c/o Jutland Opera, Thomas Jensens Alle, DK-8000 Århus, Denmark.

**ELKINS, Margreta Ann Enid,** AM, MusD; Australian singer (mezzo-soprano) and teacher; b. 16 Oct. 1930, Brisbane; d. of George Geater and Elizabeth Smith Henderson; m. Henry James 1950; one d. *Education:* Morningside State School, Commercial High School and Sacred Heart Convent (Qld). *Career:* on tour with Nat. Opera of Australia, Australia and New Zealand 1954–55; resident mezzo-soprano Royal Opera House, Covent Garden, London 1957–67; voice coach Queensland Conservatorium 1982–; Head of Vocal Studies Hong Kong Acad. for Performing Arts 1990–94; numerous performances with Lyric Opera (Qld), Victoria State Opera, English Nat. Opera, etc. *Current Management:* Jennifer Eddy Artists Management, The Cliveden, Suite 11, 596 St Kilda Road, Melbourne, Vic. 3004, Australia.

**ELLIOTT, Alasdair;** Scottish singer (tenor); b. 1954, Hamilton. *Education:* Royal Scottish Acad., Glasgow, Guildhall School of Music, Pears-Britten School of Advanced Musical Studies, Nat. Opera Studio. *Career:* sang with Kent Opera; Curzio (Nozze di Figaro), Flich (Beggar's Opera); English Touring Opera: Ramiro (La Cenerentola), Belmonte (Entführung), also for Glyndebourne Touring Opera; Opera Northern Ireland: Leicester (Maria Stuarda), Pedrillio (Entführung); Scottish Opera: Squeak (Billy Budd), Basilio (Nozze di Figaro), Iopas (Les Troyens), Rector (Peter Grimes), Benda (The Jacobin); ENO: Jew (Salome), Priest (Christmas Eve), Andrés (Wozzeck), Servant (The Bacchae, John Buller, world premiere); Brighella (Ariadne auf Naxos), Vova (Life with an Idiot); Royal Opera House: Fisherman (Guillaume Tell), Gelsomina (Il Viaggio a Reims), Vogelgesang (Die Meistersinger von Nürnberg), Priest (Die Zauberflöte), Junger Diener (Elektra); Pong (Turandot), Don Curzio (Nozze di Figaro); CBTO: Calasis (Les Boréades, Rameau); Covent Garden Festival Opera: Tamino (Die Zauberflöte); Edinburgh International Festival: Gerry (Tourist Variations, James Macmillan, world premiere); Netherlands Opera: Host (Benvenuto Cellini); Drottningholm Court Theatre: Armida (Haydn); Opéra Comique: Azeste (Ascanio in Alba); concerts in Spain, Switzerland, Netherlands, Canada, Trevor Pinnock and the English Concert, London Mozart Players, Jane Glover (including the first performance of The Vessel, Stephen Oliver); recent roles include Roderigo in Otello and Gastone in Traviata, for the Royal Opera, Pong in Turandot at the Teatro Real in Madrid, David in Die Meistersinger at The Staatstheater, Stuttgart, Palestrina at the Metropolitan Opera, New York and Eurimachus in Il Ritorno d'Ulisse at Lisbon, Mime in The Ring for Scottish Opera, Vasek in The Bartered Bride at Glyndebourne, Valzacchi in Der Rosenkavalier for Frankfurt Opera, Nick in Fanciulla del West in the Netherlands, Andres in Wozzeck for ROH; Monostatos in The Magic Flute for ENO, Brighelle in Ariadne for ROH, Bardolph in Falstaff for ENO; recitals: Queen's Hall, Edinburgh, Jubilee Hall, Aldeburgh, Purcell Room, Wigmore Hall, Royal Opera House, London. *Recordings include:* various Baroque repertoire with Janiculum. *Current Management:* AOR Management Inc., 6910 Roosevelt Way NE, PMB 221, Seattle, WA 98115, USA. *Telephone:* (206) 729-6160 (office). *Fax:* (206) 985-8499 (office). *E-mail:* jennyrose@aormanagementuk.com. *Website:* www.aormanagementuk.com.

**ELLIOTT, Anthony;** Conductor and Concert Cellist; b. 3 Sept. 1948, Rome, New York, USA; m. Paula Sokol, 9 June 1975, 4 d. *Education:* Rome Free Academy, Rome, New York, USA; Performers Certificate, 1969, School of Music, Indiana University; Bachelor of Music with Distinction, 1970, Indiana University. *Career:* Debut: St Lawrence Centre of Performing Arts, Toronto, Ontario, Canada; Soloist with Detroit Symphony, New York Philharmonic, CBC Toronto Orchestra, Minnesota Orchestra, Vancouver Symphony, Colorado Philharmonic; Recitals broadcast on NET, NPR and CBC, including premiere performances of 20th century compositions; Former Musical Director, University Symphony Orchestra, Western Michigan University; Former Assistant Music Director, Marrowstone Music Festival; Former

Professor of Cello, University of Houston; Former Music Director of the Houston Youth Symphony and Ballet; Visiting Professor, Eastman School of Music, Indiana University; Presently Professor of Cello, University of Michigan. *Chamber music:* Appeared with present and former concertmaster of Berlin Philharmonic, Concertgebouw Orchestra, Philadelphia Orchestra, Chicago Symphony, Minnesota Orchestra, Toronto Symphony, Montreal Symphony, and with members of Juilliard, Emerson, and Concord String Quartets. Also appeared with members of Chamber Music Society of Lincoln Center, and with Quarter Canada. *Recordings:* Solo cellist: Ravel, Mother Goose (complete ballet) (2); Ravel, La Valse and Alborada del Gracioso; Rimsky-Korsakov, Russian Easter Overture; Holst, The Planets; Koch International Classics Series, Music by Slav Composers; Lamentations Suite by Coleridge Taylor; Sonata for cello and piano Op No. 3 by Paul Hindemith; Cello music by Rachmaninov, 2002; recordings available at cdbaby.com, Slavic Music for Cello, French Music for Cello. Music for Cello and Piano by African—American Composers and an all Rachmaninoff CD. *Honours:* Gold Medalist, Feuermann Memorial International Cello Solo Competition. *Address:* School of Music, University of Michigan, Ann Arbor, MI 48109-2085, USA. *E-mail:* aelliot@umich.edu.

**ELLIOTT, Marie;** Singer (Soprano); b. 1970, Devon, England. *Education:* Guildhall School, with Johanna Peters; Royal Academy of Music; Further study with Janet Baker, Sarah Walker and Brigitte Fassbaender. *Career:* Solo oratorio appearances in Mozart's Requiem at Gloucester Cathedral. The Apostles by Elgar at Wells, Mendelssohn's Elijah, Pergolesi's Stabat Mater at St Martin-in-the-Fields, and Bach's Christmas Oratorio; Opera debut as Teodata in Flavio, for the London Handel Festival, 2001; Other roles include Dorabella, Rosina, Britten's Lucretia, and Isolier in Le Comte Ory; solo recital at St James's Piccadilly and Verdi Requiem at Bedford, 2001. *Honours:* Lucille Graham Award and Isabel Jay Prize, RAM, London. *Address:* c/o Royal College of Music, Prince Consort Road, London SW7, England.

**ELLIOTT, Paul,** BA, MA; American (b. British) singer (tenor) and teacher; b. 19 March 1950, Macclesfield, Cheshire, England; m. Wendy Gillespie 1982; two s. *Education:* chorister at St Paul's Cathedral, London, The King's School, Canterbury, choral scholar Magdalen Coll., Oxford, studied with David Johnston and Peter Pears. *Career:* vicar choral, St Paul's Cathedral 1972–75; mem. John Alldis Choir 1972–76, Cantores in Ecclesia 1972–76, Schütz Choir of London 1972–78, Monteverdi Choir 1973–78; founder mem. Hilliard Ensemble 1974–78; London Early Music Group 1976–79; vocal consort mem. of various consorts; tours of Europe and USA as solo concert artist; operatic engagements include Handel's Acis in St Gallen 1984, Mozart's Belmonte, Indiana Univ. 1988, and Mozart's Arbace in Chicago 1988; artist-in-residence, Washington Univ., St Louis 1984–85; Visiting Lecturer, Indiana Univ. School of Music, Bloomington 1985–87; Assoc. Prof. of Music 1987–92, Prof. of Music 1992–, Early Music Inst., Indiana Univ. School of Music; mem. Theatre of Voices 1991–; various workshops and seminars; Pres., McClosky Inst. of Voice, Boston, USA 2003 (Certified McClosky Voice Technician 2000); mem. Nat. Early Music Asscn, Early Music America, Nat. Asscn of Teachers of Singing, America, American Asscn of Univ. Profs. *Recordings:* as member of various vocal ensembles; as soloist with works by Bach, Handel, Purcell. *Address:* School of Music, 1201 E Third Street, Bloomington, IN 47405-2200, USA. *Telephone:* (812) 855-8254 (office). *E-mail:* elliottp@indiana.edu. *Website:* mypage.iu.edu/~elliottp.

**ELLIS, Brent;** Singer (Baritone); b. 20 June 1944, Kansas City, MO, USA. *Education:* Studied with Daniel Ferro in New York and with Luigi Ricci in Rome. *Career:* Debut: Washington DC in 1967 in the premiere of Ginastera's Bomarzo; Santa Fe Opera from 1972 notably as Mozart's Figaro, in the 1982 premiere of Rochberg's The Confidence Man and as Kunrad in Strauss's Feuersnot; New York City Opera debut in 1974 as Ottone in L'Incoronazione di Poppea; Glyndebourne from 1977 as Ford in Falstaff, Marcello, Don Giovanni and Germont in the Peter Hall production of La Traviata; Metropolitan Opera from 1979 as Silvio in Pagliacci, Rossini's Figaro and Donizetti's Belcore; Opera North, Leeds as Scarpia and Macbeth; Welsh National Opera as Zurga in Les Pêcheurs de Perles; Cologne Opera from 1984 in La Gazza Ladra, Wozzeck, Rigoletto and Eine Florentinische Tragödie by Zemlinsky; Appearances in the premieres of Pasatieri's Washington Square for Michigan Opera and The Seagull for Seattle Opera; Sang Germont at Glyndebourne, 1987, Santa Fe, 1989, also Kunrad in Feuersnot, 1988; San Francisco in 1989 as Iago, followed by Rigoletto at Covent Garden; Season 1992 as Amonasro at Seattle; Sang Dandini in Cenerentola at Toronto, 1996; Sang Macbeth for New Israeli Opera, 2000; Concert appearances in Mahler's 8th Symphony with the Chicago Symphony and with orchestras in San Francisco, Minnesota, Baltimore, Houston and Denver; Great Woods Festival with Michael Tilson Thomas. *Address:* c/o New York City Opera, Lincoln Center, New York, NY 10023, USA.

**ELLIS, David;** singer (baritone); b. 1970, England. *Education:* Royal Northern College of Music. *Career:* debut as Silvio in Pagliacci with Iceland Opera; Appearances as Don Giovanni with English Touring Opera, and Marcello and Donizetti's Talbot for Scottish Opera; Member of Covent Garden Opera from 1994 in Carmen, Die Meistersinger, Un Ballo in Maschera, Peter Grimes, Fanciulla del West, Salome and Billy Budd; Other roles include Belcore, Guglielmo and Posa in Don Carlos.

**ELLIS, David,** FRNCM, ARMCM; composer; *Associate Director, Orquestra Sinfónica Portuguesa;* b. 10 March 1933, Liverpool, England. *Education:*

Royal Manchester Coll. of Music. *Career:* Music Producer, BBC 1964–77, Head of Music 1977–86; Artistic Dir, Northern Chamber Orchestra 1986–94; Assoc. Dir, Orquestra Sinfónica Portuguesa 1994–. *Compositions:* Sinfonietta 1953, String Trio 1954, Dewpoint for soprano, clarinet and strings 1955, Piano Sonata, Diversions on a theme of Purcell for strings 1956, Violin Concerto 1958, Piano Concerto 1961, Opera Crito 1963, Magnificat and Nunc Dimittis for choir and organ 1964, Elegy for orchestra 1966, Fanfares and Cadenzas for orchestra 1968, Carols for an Island Christmas 1971, Symphony No. 1 1973, Solus for strings 1973, L for orchestra 1977, Sonata for solo double bass 1977, String Quartet No. 1 1980, Berceuse for clarinet and piano 1981, Aubade for horn and piano 1981, Suite Française for strings 1987, Contraprovisations 1994, Symphony No. 2 1995, String Quartet No. 2 1996, Four Songs 1998, A Little Cantata 1998, Three Note Variables for Piano 1998, Symphony No. 3 1998–99, Shadows in Blue 1999, Epiphany Nocturne 1999, Island Seascape 1999, Old Willows 2000, Attleborough Tuckets 2000, Rondo in Blue Minor for brass band 2001, Contra Partita per Bassi 2001, String Quartet No. 3 2002, Concerto for bassoon and strings 2002, Vetrate di Ricercata for organ 2002. *Recordings:* An Image of Truth 1999, Fast Forward 1999, Old City: New Image 2002. *Honours:* Royal Philharmonic Prize 1956, Royal Coll. of Music Patrons' Award 1956, Theodore Holland Award 1957, Royal Manchester Institution Silver Medal 1957, Ricordi Prize 1957. *Address:* Vassaras, 14 Patch Lane, Bramhall, Cheshire, England. *E-mail:* delliscomposer@aol.com. *Website:* www .davidellis-composer.co.uk.

**ELLIS, Gregory (Charles);** Violinist; b. 3 Nov. 1960, Preston, Lancashire, England; m. Leslie Gail Toney, 22 Dec 1985, 1 s., 2 d. *Education:* Royal Academy of Music, London; DipRAM, 1983; ARAM, 1989; With Shmuel Ashkenasi at Northern Illinois University, USA; Also student of Carmel Kaine and Frederick Grinke. *Career:* Debut: Wigmore Hall, London; Violinist and Leader, Vanbrugh String Quartet, resident to Radio Telefis Eireann since 1986; Frequent tours, the United Kingdom, Europe, Far East North and South America; Broadcasts on Radio 3, BBC World Service, Radio Telefis Eireann television and radio, Sky Channel (Arts), US and Canadian Radio, French television, Brazilian and Mexican television. *Recordings:* Several labels. *Honours:* Vanbrugh String Quartet 1st British string quartet to win the London/Portsmouth International String Quartet Competition, 1988. *Current Management:* Christa Phelps. *Address:* Vanbrugh House, Castle Treasure, Douglas, Co Cork, Ireland.

**ELLIS, James (Antony);** Composer and Conductor; b. 5 March 1954, Ashton-under-Lyne, England; m. Fiona Anne Johnson, 25 Feb 1978, 4 d. *Education:* Music Scholar, King's College, Cambridge, 1972–75; MA (Cantab); MMus, King's College, London, 1982. *Career:* Violinist Member of the Royal Philharmonic Orchestra, 1977–80, and Philharmonia, 1980–81; Assistant Tutor, King's College, London, 1982–84; Lecturer in Music, University of Keele, 1984–86; Composer-in-Residence, National Centre of Orchestral Studies, Goldsmiths' College, London, 1986–87; Lecturer in Music, City University, 1989–; Conductor for Thames Chamber Players, Oxford Haydn Players and appearances with National Centre of Orchestral Studies, European Community Youth Orchestra, Capricorn. *Compositions include:* Chamber: String Quartet No. 1, Summer Song; Works for Piano: Sonata No. 1, Autumn Tale; Serenata; Variations for Orchestra, 1979; Festive Fanfare; Prelude, Dream Sequence and the Song Of The Washerwoman, from the opera Yerma; Appearances; The Name Of The Rose; Summer Cycle including Summer Night; Summer's Apotheose; String Quartet No. 2, L'Eveil Au Désir; Canti Cantici, Libro 1. *Contributions:* Editorial Assistant, Music Analysis; Various reviews. *Address:* 2 Stanley Avenue, Chesham, Buckinghamshire HP5 2JF, England.

**ELLIS, Osian Gwynn,** CBE, FRAM; British harpist; b. 8 Feb. 1928, Ffynnongroew, Flintshire, Wales; s. of Rev. T. G. Ellis; m. Rene Ellis Jones 1951; two s. *Education:* Denbigh Grammar School, Royal Acad. of Music. *Career:* Prin. Harpist London Symphony Orchestra 1960–94; mem. Melos Ensemble; Prof. of Harp Royal Acad. of Music 1959–89; recitals and concerts worldwide; radio and TV broadcasts; works written for him include harp concertos by Hoddinott 1957, Mathias 1970, Jersild 1972, Robin Holloway 1985, Rhian Samuel 2000, solos and chamber music by Gian Carlo Menotti 1977, William Schuman 1978 and music by Britten: Suite for Harp 1969, Canticle V 1974, Birthday Hansel 1975, Folk Songs for voice and harp 1976. *Publication:* Story of the Harp in Wales 1991. *Honours:* Hon. DMus (Wales) 1970; Grand Prix du Disque, French Radio Critics' Award and other awards. *Address:* Arfryn, Ala Road, Pwllheli, Gwynedd, LL53 5BN, Wales. *Telephone:* (1758) 612501.

**ELMING, Poul;** Singer (tenor); b. 21 July 1949, Aalborg, Denmark. *Education:* Studied at the Conservatories in Aalborg and Århus, and with Paul Lohmann in Wiesbaden. *Career:* Debut: Sang in recital from 1978; Performed baritone roles with Jutland Opera, Århus, from 1979; Royal Opera Copenhagen from 1984 in many roles including Mozart's Count, Eugene Onegin, Malatesta and Verdi's Germont and Posa; Further private studies at Royal Danish Music Conservatory and the Juilliard, New York; Made his tenor debut as Parsifal at the Royal Opera, Copenhagen in 1989; Has sung Erik in Der fliegende Holländer and Spalanzani in Les Contes d'Hoffmann; Bayreuth Festival, Covent Garden, Deutsche Oper Berlin and the Vienna Staatsoper; Hannover and Mannheim from 1990 as Siegmund in Die Walküre and Parsifal; Many recitals and concerts including appearances with the Danish Radio Symphony Orchestra in Copenhagen; Sang Siegmund at Covent Garden, 1994; Parsifal at the 1996 Bayreuth Festival; Lohengrin at

Copenhagen, 1998; Season 2000–1 as Siegmund at the New York Met, Parsifal at Bayreuth and Covent Garden, and as Luke in the premiere of The Handmaid's Tale by Poul Ruders, at Copenhagen. *Recordings include:* Video of Parsifal from the Berlin Staatsoper, 1995. *Current Management:* Ingpen & Williams Ltd, 7 St George's Court, 131 Putney Bridge Road, London, SW15 2PA, England.

**ELMS, Lauris Margaret,** OBE, AM; Australian singer (contralto); b. 20 Oct. 1931, Melbourne; d. of Harry Britton and Jean Elms; m. Graeme Ernest de Graaff 1958; one d. *Career:* London debut as Ulrica in Ballo in Maschera, Royal Opera House, Covent Garden 1957; performances with Victoria Philharmonic, Sutherland-Williamson Opera Co., Elizabethan Opera Co., Australian Opera Co., Musica Viva, Chamber Music Fed., London Philharmonic, Royal Philharmonic, Israel Philharmonic; Hon. D MUS (Sydney) 1988; Queen's Jubilee Medal 1977. *Operas include:* Peter Grimes (also recording), Orfeo, Julius Caesar, Lucretia Borgia, Il Trovatore, Trojans, Bluebeard's Castle, Carmen; numerous recordings for Decca. *Address:* 10A Strathmore Parade, Chatswood, NSW 2067, Australia. *Telephone:* (2) 411 6727.

**ELMS, Roderick (James Charles);** Pianist and Organist; b. 18 Oct. 1951, Ilford, England. *Education:* Licentiate, Guildhall School of Music, 1965; Licentiate, Royal Academy of Music, 1970; Fellow, Royal College of Organists, 1974. *Career:* Debut: Wigmore Hall and Purcell Room, 1976; Regular Recitalist on organ and piano; Participant in recordings and public concerts given by all major symphony orchestras, some broadcast on radio or television; Member of GNAFF Ensemble, which made successful television debut, Dec 1982. *Compositions:* Many arrangements and original compositions performed and broadcast by BBC; Original Music to Love is a Gift; 4 Season Nocturnes for horn and orchestra, 1999. *Recordings:* Numerous works recorded with orchestras and choirs including many solo recordings with London Symphony, London Philharmonic and Royal Philharmonic Orchestras; Organ Music of Percy Whitlock, album; Solo piano album; Christmas arrangements recorded on Christmas Gift; Magnificat; In Dulci Jubilo; Original Music to Love is a Gift recorded on Just For Today; Frank Martin Ballade for piano and orchestra, London Philharmonic Orchestra/Bamert, 1995. *Honours:* ARAM. *Address:* 23 Bethell Avenue, Cranbrook, Ilford, Essex IG1 4UX, England.

**ELOY, Jean-Claude;** Composer; b. 15 June 1938, Mount Saint Aignan, Seine Maritime, France. *Education:* Studied with Milhaud, Martenot and Boulez, 1950–61. *Career:* Cologne Electronic Music Studio with Stockhausen, 1972–73; Producer for Radio France, 1971–87. *Compositions:* Symphony no 1, 1962; Equivalences for 18 instruments, 1963; Poly-chronies I and II for wind and percussion, 1964; Faisceaux-Diffractions, for 28 instruments, 1970; Kamakela for 3 ensembles and 3 choruses, 1971; Vers l'etendue for orchestra, 1974; Fluctuante Imnnuable for orchestra, 1977; Reverberation for 4 tapes and percussion, 1980; Anahata for soloists and ensemble, 1986; Sapho Hiketis for women's voices and electronics, 1989; Gaia for soprano and electronics, 1992. *Address:* c/o SACEM, 225 Avenue Charles de Gaulle, 92521 Neuilly sur Seine Cédex, France.

**ELSNER, Christian;** Singer (Tenor); b. 1965, Freiburg im Breisgau, Germany. *Education:* Studied in Frankfurt am Main. *Career:* Lensky in Eugene Onegin at Oper Heidelberg, Tichon in Katya Kabanova, Pedrillo in Entführung, Macduff in Macbeth at Staatstheater Darmstadt and Idomeneo at Norwegian State opera in Oslo; Concerts include Lieder recitals at the Schubertiade Feldkirch and throughout Europe; Mahler's Lied von der Erde in Munich and at the Wiener Festwochen, Bruckner's Te Deum at the Salzburg Festival, Beethoven's Ninth in London and Schumann's Faustszenen in Tokyo with conductors such as Giulini, Jordan, Herreweghe, Nelson, Blomstedt and Honeck. *Recordings include:* Schumann's Dichterliebe; Mahler's Lieder eines fahrenden Gesellen; Schubert Songs, and Mahler's Lied von der Erde. *Honours:* Winner, International Walter Gruner Lieder Competition, London, 1993; Second Prize, International ARD competition, Munich, 1994. *Address:* Kunstler Sekretariat am Gasteig, Rosenheimerstrasse 52, 81669 Munich, Germany.

**ELSTE, (Rudolf Otto) Martin,** DPhil; German musicologist, discologist and music critic; *Curator, Staatliches Institut für Musikforschung*; b. 11 Sept. 1952, Bremen. *Education:* Univ. of Cologne, Rheinische Musikschule, Cologne, King's Coll., London, England, Technische Universität, Berlin. *Career:* Curator, Staatliches Institut für Musikforschung Preussischer Kulturbesitz 1982–; Review Ed., IASA Phonographic Bulletin 1982–93; panel mem., German Record Critics Award 1983–, Pres. 2000–; Chair., IASA Discography Cttee 1992–96; Vice-Pres., IASA 1996–99; consulting musicologist, Bach-Tage Berlin 1986–87; Advisory Bd mem., CIMCIM 1995–2001; Editorial Advisory Bd mem., Music in Performance 1997; Vice-Pres., Verein f. Musik Archiv-Forschung 1998–2001; Consultant Ed., Die Musik in Geschichte und Gegenwart; bd mem. RIdIM Commission Mixte 2004–. *Publications:* Internationale Heinrich Schütz Diskographie 1928–72 1972, Verzeichnis deutschsprachiger Musiksoziologie 1975, Bachs Kunst der Fuge auf Schallplatten 1981, Musikinstrumenten Museum Berlin (contrib.) 1986, Handwerk im Dienste der Musik (contrib.) 1987, 100 Jahre Berliner Musikinstrumenten Museum (contrib.) 1988, Kleines Tonträger-Lexikon 1989, Kielklaviere (contrib.) 1991, Musikalische Interpretation 1992, Modern Harpsichord Music: A Discography 1995, Baines, Lexikon der Musikinstrumente (ed. and trans.) 1996, Bach-Handbuch (contrib.) 1999, Meilensteine der Bach-Interpretation 2000, Ausgezeichnet! (ed.) 2004; contrib. to books and journals, including New Grove, Fono Forum, Fanfare, Die Musikforschung, Basler Jahrbuch für Historische Musikpraxis, Jahrbuch des Staatlichen Instituts für Musikforschung, Jahrbuch Preussischer Kulturbesitz, Klassik heute, Musik in Geschichte und Gegenwart, Frankfurter Allgemeine Zeitung, Die Zeit, Neue Zeitschrift für Musik, Hindemith-Jahrbuch. *Honours:* ARSC Award for Excellence in Historical Recorded Sound Research 2001. *Address:* SIMPK, Tiergartenstrasse 1, 10785 Berlin, Germany (office). *Telephone:* (30) 25481132 (office). *Fax:* (30) 25481172 (office). *E-mail:* elste@sim.spk-berlin.de (office). *Website:* www.martin-elste.de.

**ELWES, John;** Singer (Tenor); b. 1946, England. *Education:* Studied with George Malcolm at Westminster Cathedral; Further study at the Royal College of Music. *Career:* Chorister at Westminster Cathedral; Soloist in Britten's Missa Brevis and Abraham and Isaac; Frequent broadcaster for the BBC; Repertoire includes Baroque, Lieder and Contemporary Music on the concert platform and operas by Gluck, Handel, Mozart and Monteverdi on stage; Sang Orfeo in Monteverdi's opera with Phillippe Herreweghe and La Chapelle Royale at the Montpellier opera house and with Flanders Opera, Antwerp, 1989–90. *Recordings include:* Orfeo in The Death of Orpheus by Stefano Landi, with Tragicomedia directed by Stephen Stubbs.

**EMMERLICH, Gunther;** singer (bass); b. 18 Sept. 1944, Thuringia, Germany. *Education:* Studied in Weimar and Dresden and with Pavel Lisitsian. *Career:* debut, sang the Peasant in Die Kluge by Orff at the Dresden Staatsoper in 1978; Appeared as Kuno in Der Freischütz at the reopening of the Semper Oper, Dresden, and has sung with the Dresden Ensemble at the Vienna Volksoper and in Amsterdam as Don Alfonso in 1988; Other roles include Osmin in Die Entführung, Geronimo in Matrimonio Segreto, Rocco, Dulcamara and the Hermit in Der Freischütz; Many concert appearances. *Recordings:* Der Freischütz; Eugene Onegin.

**ENCINAS, Ignacio;** Tenor; b. 1958, Spain. *Education:* Studied with Enzo Costantini and in Madrid; Masterclasses with Gianni Poggi and Gino Bechi. *Career:* Sang in Trovatore and La Favorita at the Santander Festival; Rigoletto at the Zarzuela Theatre in Madrid and appeared further in Oviedo, Valladolid and Malaga; At Dijon has sung in Pollione in Norma, Alfredo in Traviata, Rigoletto, and Riccardo in Un Ballo in Maschera; Season 1989–90 as Maurizio in Adriana Lecouvreur at Liège, returning as Turiddu and Rodolfo in La Bohème; Sang in Verdi's Attila at the Teatro Romano of Benevento and as Macduff in a concert performance of Macbeth at the 1990 Gstaad Festival and at Naples, 1998; Performances of Nabucco in Nimes, and as Arturo at Marseille, 1990–91; Sang Rodolfo in Luisa Miller for the Royal Opera at Edinburgh, 1988; Season 2000–01 as Turiddu at Buenos Aires, Calaf at Liège and Cavaradossi at the Deutsche Oper, Berlin. *Honours:* Winner of numerous international competitions. *Address:* c/o Mondial Musique, 17 rue Brey, F–75017 Paris, France.

**ENDERLE, Matthias;** Violinist; b. 16 June 1956, Switzerland. *Education:* Studied at the Winterhur Conservatory, in Indiana, and at the University International Menuhin Academy in Gstaad. *Career:* Co-Founder and Leader of the Carmina Quartet, 1984; Appearances from 1987 in Europe, Israel, Japan and USA; Regular concerts at the Wigmore Hall from 1987; Concerts at the South Bank Centre, London, Amsterdam Concertgebouw, the Kleine Philharmonie in Berlin, and Konzertverein Vienna; Four engagements in Paris, 1990–91, and seven in London; Tours of Australasia, the USA and Japan; Concerts at the Hohenems, Graz, Hong Kong, Schleswig-Holstein, Montreux, Bath, Lucerne, and Prague Spring Festivals; Collaborations with Dietrich Fischer-Dieskau, Olaf Bär and Mitsuko Uchida. *Recordings:* Various. *Honours:* Joint Winner, with members of Carmina Quartet, Paolo Borciani String Quartet Competition in Reggio Emilia, Italy, 1987; Gramophone Prize for Best Chamber Music Recording, 1992. *Address:* c/o Intermusica Artists' Management, 16 Duncan Terrace, London N1 8BZ, England.

**ENDO, Akira;** Conductor; b. 16 Nov. 1938, Shido, Japan. *Education:* Studied violin with Vera Barstow, Eudice Shapiro, and Jascha Heifetz; BM, MM, 1962, University of Southern California, Los Angeles. *Career:* Violinist, Trojan String Quartet, 1960–62; 2nd Violinist, Pacific String Quartet, 1962–69; Conductor, Long Beach Symphony Orchestra, California, 1966–69, and West Side Symphony Orchestra, Los Angeles, 1968–69; Music Director, American Ballet Theatre, NY, 1969–79; Resident Conductor of Houston Symphony Orchestra, 1974–76; Music Director, Austin Symphony Orchestra, TX, 1975–82 and Louisville Orchestra, 1980–83.

**ENGEL, Karl;** Concert Pianist; b. 1 June 1923, Basle, Switzerland; m. Barbara Wackernagel, 26 Oct 1976, 1 s., 1 d. *Education:* Humanistisches Gymnasium Basle; Basle Conservatory with Paul Baumgartner; Ecole Normale Paris with Alfred Cortot. *Career:* International career as concert pianist since 1948; Cycles of all Mozart piano concertos in Paris, Berlin, Munich, Salzburg, Vienna and Zürich; Cycles of all Beethoven piano sonatas in West Germany and Tel-Aviv; Series of all Mozart piano sonatas in Salzburg; Concert tours in Europe, USA and Japan; Guest of all major music festivals in Europe; Chamber music with Pablo Casals (Prades), Menuhin, Tortelier and Fournier; Lieder recitals with Dietrich Fischer-Dieskau, Hermann Prey and Peter Schreier; Professor of Piano at Hochschule für Musik Hanover, 1959–86; Masterclass at Berne Conservatory; mem, Schweizerischer Tonkunstlerverein. *Recordings:* Complete piano works of Schumann; Complete Mozart piano concertos with the Mozarteum Orchestra conducted by Leopold Hager; Complete solo piano music by Mozart; Chamber music and Lieder. *Honours:*

Prize, Queen Elisabeth Competition in Belgium, 1952. *Address:* Chemin du Closalet Nr. 2, 1822 Chernex (VD), Switzerland.

**ENGELMANN, Hans Ulrich;** Composer and Professor; b. 8 Sept. 1921, Darmstadt, Germany. *Education:* Studied composition with Fortner, Heidelberg, 1945–49; With Leibowitz and Krenek, Darmstadt, 1948–50; Musicology with Gennrich and Osthoff, Philosophy with Adorno, University of Frankfurt am Main; PhD, 1952. *Career:* Music Adviser, Hessischen Landestheater, Darmstadt, 1954–61; Lecturer, 1969–73, Professor, 1973–, in composition, Hochschule für Musik, Frankfurt am Main; Music Adviser, Theater Bonn, 1972–73; President, Work-Commission, GEMA; President, German Composers' League. *Compositions include:* Stage Works: Doktor Fausts Hollenfahrt, 1949–50; Verlorener Schatten, 1960; Der Fall Van Damm, 1966–67; Magog, 1956–57; Serpentina, 1962; Ophelia, 1969; Revue, 1972–73; Orchestral Works: Music for strings, brass and percussion, 1948; Impromptu, 1949; Partita, 1953; Strukturen, 1954; 5 Orchestra Pieces, 1956; Polyfonica, 1957; Nocturnos, 1958; Ezra Pound Music, 1959 Trias for piano, orchestra and tape, 1962; Shadows, 1964; Sonata for jazz orchestra, 1967; Sinfonies, 1968; Capricciosi, 1968; Sinfonia da camera, 1981; Chamber: Cello Sonata, 1948; String Quartet, 1952; Integrate for saxophone and piano, 1954; Choir and Orchestra: Incanto, 1959; Missa Popularis, 1980–83; Stele for chorus soloists, symphony orchestra, 1987; Choral music including cantatas; New Works: Dialogue Piano Percussion, 1991; Clarinota, 1991, Tastenstück, 1991; Essay, 1992; Modus, 1992; Ciacona for chamber orchestra, 1993; Per Luigi, 1996. *Recordings include:* 99 Bars for Cembalo; Commedia Humana; Monographie "H.U.E. und sein Werk", 1985; Portrait Hans Ulrich Engelmann, 1999. *Publications:* Bela Bartók's Mikrokosmos, doctoral thesis; Autobiography: Vergangenheitsgegenwart, 2001. *Contributions:* Melos; Neue Zeitschrift für Musik; Musik und Bildung. *Honours:* Scholarship, Harvard University, 1949; Goethe Medaille, 1986; Kreuz der BRD, 1992; Hessischer Verdienstorden, 1997. *Address:* Park Rosenhohe, Engelweg 15, 64287 Darmstadt, Germany. *Telephone:* (6151) 77979. *Fax:* (6151) 77979.

**ENGERER, Brigitte Marie;** French pianist; b. 27 Oct. 1952, Tunis; d. of Edgard and Marie-Rose Engerer; m. Yann Queffelec 1982; one d. one s. *Education:* Coll. Notre-Dame de Sion (Tunis) and Conservatoire Nat. Supérieur de Musique (Paris). *Career:* studied under Lucette Descaves 1958–69, and Stanislav Neuhaus at Conservatory of Moscow (USSR, now Russian Fed) 1970–80; has given concerts in Europe and USA, with Berlin Philharmonic (with Herbert von Karajan) 1980–81 and Zubin Mehta, London Symphony Orchestra, New York Philharmonic Orchestra, and other major orchestras world-wide, including Canada, Czech Repub., Switzerland, Austria, Germany, Italy, Hungary, Netherlands, etc; gave recital at Théâtre des Champs-Elysées 1993; Prof. Paris Conservatoire 1994–. *Recordings include:* Les saisons (Tchaikovsky) 1982, Mélodie hongroise, Schubert's Klavierstücke D946 and Impromptus Opus 90 1983, Schumann's Carnaval and Carnaval de Vienne (Grand Prix, Acad. du Disque Français) 1983, Chopin's Sonata No 3 and posthumous works, Piano romantique 1985, Tableaux d'une exposition and Une nuit sur le Mont-Chauve (Mussorgsky) 1988. *Video:* Richard Strauss' Burlesque 1988. *Honours:* Prix Int. Marguerite Long, Prix Int. Tchaikovsky, Prix Int. de la Reine Elisabeth de Belgique, Prix du Royaume de la Musique, numerous other awards; Chevalier des Arts et des Lettres. *Address:* Concerts de Valmaléte, 7 rue Hoche, 92300 Levallois-Perret, France.

**ENGERT, Ruth;** Singer (Mezzo-Soprano); b. 9 Oct. 1946, Frankfurt-am-Main, Germany. *Education:* Studied at the Frankfurt Musikhochschule and with Josef Metternich in Cologne. *Career:* Sang at Koblenz, Freiburg and Hannover, 1969–79; Member of the Deutsche Oper Berlin from 1979, notably as Mozart's Cherubino and Dorabella, Verdi's Eboli and Meg Page, Wagner's Fricka, Brangaene and Waltraute, Octavian, Nicklausse in Les Contes d'Hoffmann and Charlotte in Die Soldaten; Guest appearances at Turin in Clytemnestra in 1987, at Venice as the Composer in Ariadne auf Naxos and at Genoa, Madrid and Lisbon; Bayreuth Festival in 1989 as Venus in Tannhäuser; Sang Kundry at the Spoleto Festival in Italy and in Charleston, USA, 1986–90, and Octavian in Rosenkavalier at Catania in 1992; Sang Kundry for Flanders Opera, 1996; Clytemnestra in Elektra at Catania, 1998; Sang Herodias in Salome at Gelsenkirchen 1999. *Recordings:* Strauss's Feuersnot; Parsifal at Bayreuth, 1985; Die Walküre at Bayreuth, 1987; Eugene Onegin; Funeral Cantata by Cherubini. *Address:* c/o Musiktheater im Revier, Kennedyplatz, Pf 101854, 4650 Gelsenkirchen, Germany.

**ENGLICHOVA, Katerina;** Harpist; b. 13 June 1969, Prague, Czechoslovakia. *Education:* Conservatoire, Prague; Curtis Institute of Music, Philadelphia. *Career:* Debut: New York, Weill Recital Hall at Carnegie Hall, 1998 Paris, 2000; Modern Art Museum, Los Angeles, 1996; Paris, France, 1994, 1996, 1998, Hong Kong, 1998, 2001, Boston 1999, England 1999; The VII World Harp Congress, Prague, 1999; Festivals: Pacific Music Festival, Japan; Music by the Red Sea, Israel; Tanglewood Music Festival, USA; Rencontres Musicales d'Evian, France; Prague Autumn, Czech Republic; Repertoire includes Ravel, Introduction and Allegro; Ginastera Concerto etc; mem, World Harp Society. *Recordings:* Britten, Voice and Harp; Hindemith, Sonata; Harmonia Mundi, A Roussel, with Czech Nonet; Panton, M Ravel, C Debussy, Solo and Chamber Recital; Koch, Discover, C Saint-Saëns, L Spohr, P Hindemith, with Josef Suk, Violin; Petr Eben, Music for Harp; Rossetti Sonatas, 2000; Granados-Danzas Espagnolas, Supraphon, 2002. *Honours:* Prize, E Herbert Hobin Harp Competition, USA, 1993; 1st Prize Concerto Soloists Competition, 1994; 1st Prize, Pro Musicis International Award, New York, 1995; European Broadcast Competition, 1997; International Music

Competition, Vienna, 1999; Tim Competition, Italy, 2002. *Website:* www .englichova.cz.

**ENGLISH, Gerald;** Singer (Lyric Tenor), Educator and Administrator; b. 6 Nov. 1925, England; m. (1) Jennifer Ryan, 1954, 2 s., 2 d., (2) Linda Jacoby, 1974, 1 s. *Education:* Royal College of Music. *Career:* After war service began career as lyric tenor, subsequently travelling USA, and Europe; Appeared at Sadler's Wells, Covent Garden and Glyndebourne; Often heard in operas by Mozart and Monteverdi, and concert music by Bach, Stravinsky, Fauré and Dallapiccola; Professor, Royal College of Music, 1960–77; Director, Opera Studio, Victorian College for the Arts, Melbourne, Australia, 1977–89; Sang the title role in Andrew Ford's Sigmund Freud, Adelaide 2000. *Recordings:* Schumann Song Cycles with Roger Smalley Piano; Whispers music by Andrew Ford and vocal music of Peggy Glanville Hicks. *Honours:* D.Mus honoris causa, Sydney University, 1989; Australian Creative Artist Fellowship, 1994. *Address:* PO Box 4177, Geelong, Victoria 3220, Australia.

**ENGLISH, Jon Arthur,** BM; composer, trombonist, percussionist and double bass player; b. 22 March 1942, Kankakee, Illinois, USA; m. Candace Natwig. *Education:* University of Illinois with Kenneth Gaburo. *Career:* member of the Harry Partch Ensemble, 1961–62, the Illinois Contemporary Chamber Players, 1963–66 and the Savannah Symphony Orchestra, 1967; Associate Artist of the University of Iowa Center for New Music and New Performing Arts until 1974; has worked from Cologne since 1976; Performances in Europe as soloist, with Candace Natwig, singer, and in new music groups. *Compositions include:* 404 1-2 East Green Street for Tape, 1965; Sequent Cycles for 6 players, 1968;... Whose Circumference Is A Nowhere, 1970; Used Furniture Sale for Tape, 1971; Summerstalks for Performer and Tape, 1973; Shagbolt for Trombone, 1978; Electrotrombonics, 1979; Foursome, 1979; Dog Dreams, 1982; Harmonies For Charlie Mingus, 1983.

**ENS, Phillip;** Singer (Bass); b. 1962, Canada. *Career:* Debut: Manitoba Opera, 1985 as the Marchese in La Forza del Destino; Many appearances throughout Canada as Sarastro, Masetto and Figaro, for Pacific Opera Verdi's Sparafucile and Banquo and Gounod's Frère Laurence; Canadian Opera Company debut, 1989 as Don Fernando in Fidelio; US debut in 1992 as Sparafucile with Philadelphia Opera; Stuttgart Opera, 1993 as Sparafucile, Sarastro, Banquo in Macbeth, Mozart's Commendatore and Pimen in Boris Godunov; Carontes in Monteverdi's Orfeo at Munich and Claggart in Welsh National Opera's Billy Budd; Season 1999–2000 as Padre Guardiano in La Forza del Destino at the Deutsche Oper Berlin, Hunding at the Metropolitan Opera; Sarastro in Hamburg and Gremin in Eugene Onegin at Brussels; Season 2002–03 as Fafner and Hunding in The Ring at Stuttgart; Ramfis in Brussels; Wurm in the Metropolitan Opera's new prodution of Luisa Miller; Hunding with the Lyric Opera of Chicago; Concerts include the Missa Solemnis in Brussels and Paris, and the Mozart Requiem at Salzburg and the BBC Proms. *Address:* c/o IMG Artists, Lovell House, 616 Chiswick High Road, London W4 5RX, England.

**ENSTRÖM, Rolf;** Composer; b. 2 Nov. 1951, Södertälje, Sweden; m. Karin Enströ m-Salomonsson, 3 May 1980, 2 s., 1 d. *Education:* Engineer, studied Musicology and Philosophy at the universities in Stockholm and Gothenburg; Studied Music in Örebro, Musicology in Gothenburg; Composition self-taught. *Career:* Debut: With multimedia piece Myr at the International Society for Contemporary Music Festival, Athens, 1979; As multimedia artist has collaborated with artists in adjacent fields, including photographer Thomas Hellsing; His music performed world-wide; Directions played at International Society for Contemporary Music, Athens, 1979; Teaching at EMS, Stockholm; Summer courses at Nordens Biskops Arnö, near Stockholm; Participant, DAAD cultural exchange programme, 1991, then Composer-in-Residence, Berlin. *Compositions:* Tape music, music for instruments and electronics and multimedia works, including: Slutförbannelser, text by Elsa Grave, 1981; Fractal, multimedia piece (with Thomas Hellsing); Tjidtjag och Tjidtjaggaise, based on Lapp joik, 1987; Skizzen aus Berlin, 1991; Asylum, multimedia piece (with Thomas Hellsing); Vigil, saxophone quartet, 1994; In Ice, Mirror, 1995; Spin, 1995; Charm, 1996; Io, intermedia, 1996; Open Wide, piano, percussion, tape, 1997; Strange, 1997; Rama, mixed choir and tape, 1998; Kairos, 1999; Up, 1999. *Recordings:* Directions, Final Curses, Tjidtjag och Tjidtjaggaise; Fractal; Dagbrott, Sequence In Blue, Tonal Nagual, Tsentsaks; In Ice, Mirror. *Address:* c/o STIM, Box 27327, 10254 Stockholm, Sweden.

**ENTREMONT, Philippe;** French pianist and conductor; b. 7 June 1934, Reims; s. of Jean and Renée (Monchamps) Entremont; m. Andrée Ragot 1955; one s. one d. *Education:* Inst. Notre-Dame à Reims, Conservatoire Nat. Supérieur de Musique de Paris. *Career:* has performed with all major orchestras of world 1953–; Pres. of Acad. Int. de Musique Maurice Ravel, Saint-Jean-de-Luz 1973–80; Musical Dir and Permanent Conductor, Vienna Chamber Orchestra 1976–; Dir New Orleans Symphony Orchestra 1980–86; Prin. Conductor Denver Symphony Orchestra 1986–88, Paris Orchestre Colonne 1987–90, Netherlands Chamber Orchestra 1993–, Israel Chamber Orchestra 1995–; Dir American Conservatory Fontainebleau 1994; Prin. Guest Conductor Shanghai Broadcasting Symphony Orchestra 2001–. *Honours:* Officier Ordre nat. du Mérite, Officier, Légion d'honneur, Commdr des Arts et Lettres; Österreichisches Ehrenkreuz für Wissenschaft und Kunst; Harriet Cohen Piano Medal 1951, Grand Prix Int. Concours Marguerite Long-Jacques Thibaud 1953, 4 Grand Prix du Disque Awards, Edison Award 1968; Grammy Award 1972. *Address:* c/o Bureau de concerts Dominique Lierner, 17 rue du 4 septembre, 75002 Paris (office); 10 rue de Castiglione, 75001 Paris, France. *Telephone:* 42-86-06-08. *Fax:* 42-86-86-61 (home).

**EÖSZE, László;** Former Art Director; b. 17 Nov. 1923, Budapest, Hungary; m. (1) 2 c., (2) 24 September 1983. *Education:* PhD, Aesthetics and Literature. *Career:* Music Teacher and Pianist; Concerts in Hungary and Europe, 1946–51; mem, Co-President, F Liszt Society; Executive Secretary, 1975–95, International Kodály Society; Hungarian Musicological Society, 1996–. *Publications:* 16 books including, Zoltán Kodály élete és munkássága (Life and Work of ZK), 1956; Zoltán Kodály élete képekben (K's Life in Pictures), 1957; Az opera utja (History of Opera), 1960; Giuseppe Verdi, 1961, 2nd edition, 1966; Enlarged, 1975; Zoltán Kodály, His Life and Work, English, 1962, in German, 1965; Zoltán Kodály, 1967; Kodály, His Life in Pictures and Documents, 1971, English and German; Richard Wagner, 1969; Richard Wagner, Eine Chronik seines Lebens und Schaffens, 1969; Zoltán Kodály, életének krónikája, 1977; 119 római Liszt dokumentum, 1980; Selected Studies on Z Kodály, 2000; Essays and articles in various languages. *Contributions:* The New Grove Dictionary of Music and Musicians; Brockhaus Riemann Musiklexikon; Numerous professional publications. *Honours:* Erkel Prize, 1977; Gramma Award, 1978; Medium Cross of the Order of the Hungarian Republic, 1998; Medal for Merit of the Pres. of the Repub., 2003; Grand Prize of the Nat. Soc. of Creative Artists, 2003. *Address:* Attila ut 133, 1012 Budapest, Hungary.

**EÖTVÖS, Peter;** German (b. Hungarian) composer, conductor and professor of music; *Chief Conductor, Netherlands Radio Chamber Orchestra*; b. 2 Jan. 1944, Székelyudvarhely, Hungary; s. of László Eötvös and Ilona Szücs; m. 1st Piroska Molnár 1968; one s.; m. 2nd Pi-Hsien Chen 1976; one d.; m. 3rd Maria Mezei 1995. *Education:* Budapest Acad. and Musikhochschule, Cologne. *Career:* played in Stockhausen's Ensemble, Cologne 1966–76; composer and producer at WDR Electronic Music Studio, Cologne 1971–79; Conductor and Musical Dir Ensemble Intercontemporain, Paris 1979–91; Prin. Guest Conductor BBC Symphony Orchestra, London 1985–88; First Guest Conductor, Budapest Festival Orchestra 1992–95; Chief Conductor Netherlands Radio Chamber Orchestra 1994–; Prof., Musikhochschule Karlsruhe, Germany 1992–, Cologne 1998–2002; f. Int. Eötvös Inst. for Young Conductors; mem. Akad. der Kunst, Berlin, Szechenyi Acad. of Art, Budapest, Sächsische Acad. der Künste, Dresden. *Compositions include:* (for orchestra): Chinese Opera, Shadows, Psychokosmos, Atlantis, Ima, Jet Stream, Zeropoints, Two Monologues, Replica; (for ensemble): Intervalles-Intérieures, Windsequenzen, Steine, Triangel; (for string quartet): Korrespondenz; (for vocal ensemble): Three comedy madrigals; (for percussion): Psalm 151; (for musical theatre/opera): Radames, Harakiri, Three Sisters, As I Crossed a Bridge of Dreams, Le Balcon, Angels in America. *Honours:* Commdr, Ordre des Arts et Lettres 2003; Bartok Award, Budapest 1997, Stephan Kaske Prize, Munich 2000, Kossuth Prize, Hungary 2002, Midem Classical Award 'Living Composer', Cannes 2004, European Composing Prize 2004. *Current Management:* c/o Harrison-Parrott, 12 Penzance Place, London, W11 4PA, England. *Address:* Cseppkő u. 53, 1025 Budapest, Hungary. *Telephone:* (1) 3259273. *Fax:* (1) 3355961. *E-mail:* eotvospeter@hotmail.com (home). *Website:* www.eotvospeter .com (home).

**EPSTEIN, David M.;** Composer, Conductor, Theorist and Professor; b. 3 Oct. 1930, New York, NY, USA; m. Anne Merrick, 21 June 1953, 2 d. *Education:* AB, Antioch College, 1952; MMus, New England Conservatory of Music, 1953; MFA, Brandeis University, 1954; PhD, Princeton University, 1968. *Career:* Guest conductor of well known orchestras, Germany, Austria, Czechoslovakia, Poland, Israel, France, Belgium, Mexico, USA and others; Member, Herbert von Karajan Musikgespräche, Salzburg, 1983–88; Board of Directors, The Conductors Guild; Alumni Board and Board of Trustees, Antioch College. *Compositions include:* String Trio; Sonority–Variations for Orchestra; Fantasy Variations for Solo Viola or Violin; The Seasons; String Quartet, 1971; The Concord Psalter, 1978; Music for theatre, film and television. *Recordings include:* Bloch, Concerto Grosso No. 2, Czech Radio Orchestra; Tillis, Festival Journey, The New Orchestra of Boston; Kurt Weill–Suite from Der Silbersee, MIT Symphony Orchestra; Copland–Dance Symphony, Piston–Incredible Flautist, MIT Symphony. *Publications:* Beyond Orpheus, Studies in Musical Structure, 1979; Shaping Time: Music, The Brain and Performance, 1995; Various articles and music arrangements. *Address:* Department of Music, Massachusetts Institute of Technology, Cambridge, MA 02139, USA.

**EPSTEIN, Matthew A.,** BA; American opera administrator; b. 23 Dec. 1947, New York, NY. *Education:* Univ. of Pennsylvania. *Career:* Vice-Pres. Columbia Artists Man. 1973–99; Artistic Dir Brooklyn Acad. of Music 1987–90; consultant for the opera cos of Chicago and Santa Fe; Artistic Dir Welsh Nat. Opera 1991–94; Artistic Dir Lyric Opera of Chicago 1999–2005; Artistic Dir Kennedy Center Gala honoring George London (televised by PBS, recorded by RCA) 1981; Dir Rossini 200th Birthday Celebration Gala, Lincoln Center (televised and recorded by EMI) 1990; Artistic Consultant 'Celebration of the American Musical', Lincoln Center (televised) 1997.

**EQUILUZ, Kurt;** Singer (Tenor); b. 13 June 1929, Vienna, Austria. *Education:* Studied in Vienna with Adolf Vogel. *Career:* Sang as chorister in Vienna from 1945; Solo career at the Vienna Staatsoper from 1957, notably as Mozart's Pedrillo, Beethoven's Jacquino and in operas by Strauss; Sang at the Salzburg Festival in the premieres of Liebermann's Penelope, 1954, Martin's Le Mystère de la Nativité, 1960 and Wagner-Régeny's Das Bergwerk zu Falun, 1961; Performed the Narrator in Schnittke's Historia von D. Johann

Fausten, Vienna, 2001; Many concert appearances as Lieder singer and in religious music; Professor, Graz Musikhochschule, 1971–; Professor of Lieder and Oratorio, Academy for Music in Vienna, 1982–. *Recordings:* Monteverdi's Orfeo and Il Ritorno d'Ulisse; Cantatas by Bach and the St John and St Matthew Passions (Telefunken); Cavalieri's La Rappresentazione di Anima e di Corpo (Deutsche Grammophon). *Address:* Schwenkgasse 8/4, 1120 Vienna, Austria.

**ERB, Donald James,** BS, MM, DMus; American composer and music educator; *Distinguished Professor Emeritus, Cleveland Institute of Music;* b. 17 Jan. 1927, Youngstown, OH; s. of Tod and Janet Erb; m. Lucille Hyman 1950; one s. three d. *Education:* Kent State Univ., Cleveland Inst. of Music, Indiana Univ. School of Music, studied with Harold Miles, Kenneth Gaburo, Marcel Dick, Bernhard Heiden in USA, with Nadia Boulanger in Paris. *Career:* teacher 1953–61, composer-in-residence 1966–81, Prof. of Composition 1987–, Cleveland Inst. of Music; composer-in-residence, Dallas Symphony Orchestra 1968–69; staff composer, Bennington Composers Conference, VT 1969–74; Visiting Prof. 1975–76, Prof. of Music 1984–87, Indiana Univ. School of Music; Meadows Prof. of Composition, Southern Methodist Univ. 1981–84; composer-in-residence, St Louis Symphony Orchestra 1988–90; Nat. Endowment for the Arts Composer-Librettist Panel 1973–77, Chair. 1977–79; American Music Center bd mem. 1979–82, pres. 1982–86; Guggenheim Fellowship 1956; Ford Foundation Residency (Bakersfield Schools) 1962–63; Nat. Council on the Arts Fellowship 1967–68; Rockefeller Bellagio Study and Conference Center Fellowships 1980, 1989; American Acad. in Rome Residency 1992. *Compositions include:* Orchestral: Chamber Concerto for piano and strings, 1958, Symphony Of Overtures, 1964, Stargazing for band and tape, 1966, Christmasmusic, 1967, The Seventh Trumpet 1969, Autumnmusic for orchestra and electronic sounds, 1973, Music For A Festive Occasion for orchestra and electronic Sounds, 1975, Trombone Concerto, 1976, Cenotaph (For EV) for symphonic band, 1979, Sonneries, 1981, Contrabassoon Concerto, 1984, The Dreamtime, 1985, Concerto for brass and orchestra, 1986; Ritual Observances for orchestra, 1991; Violin Concerto, 1992; Evensong for orchestra, 1993; Suddenly It's Evening for electronics and cello, 1997; Dance You Monster for trumpet, 1993; Three Pieces for Double Bass, 1999; Chamber music, choral works and piano pieces. *Honours:* Dr hc (Cleveland Inst. of Music) 1984; Naumburg Recording Award 1974, Ohio Arts Council Awards 1979, 1980, 1996, Nat. Endowment for the Arts Awards 1980, 1981, 1984, 1987, 1990, 1995, American Acad. and Inst. of Arts and Letters Award 1985, Aaron Copland Award 1993, 1996, Ohioana Career Award 1998, American Music Center Letter of Distinction 2001. *Address:* 4073 Bluestone Road, Cleveland Heights, OH 44121, USA (home). *Telephone:* (216) 381-3912 (home). *E-mail:* donalderb@aol.com (home).

**ERBE, Teresa;** Singer (Soprano); b. 1958, Oberschesien, Germany. *Education:* Studied in Katowice. *Career:* Sang at Gdansk from 1981; Bremerhaven Opera, 1986–87, and Bremen, 1987–92, as Salome, Arabella and Elisabeth de Valois; Essen from 1992, as Bartók's Judith, the Marschallin and Giulietta in Les contes d'Hoffmann (1996); Season 1999–2000 as Salome at Freiburg, and Natasha in Three Sisters by Peter Eötvös; Further appearances in Rusalka, and operetta; Guest engagements in Prague, Stockholm, Copenhagen and St Petersburg. *Address:* Essen Opera, Rolandstrasse 10, 4300 Essen 1, Germany.

**ERBEN, Valentin;** Cellist; b. 14 March 1945, Austria. *Education:* Studied in Vienna, Munich and Paris. *Career:* Co-Founder and Cellist of the Alban Berg Quartet from 1971; Many concert engagements world-wide, including complete cycles of the Beethoven Quartets in 15 European cities, 1987–88 and 1988–89 seasons; Bartók/Mozart cycle in London, Vienna, Paris, Frankfurt, Munich, Geneva and Turin, 1990–91; Annual concert series at the Vienna Konzerthaus and festival engagements world-wide; Associate Artist at the South Bank Centre in London; US appearances in Washington DC, San Francisco and at Carnegie Hall in New York; Professor, Musikhochschule, Vienna and Cologne. *Recordings include:* Complete Quartets of Beethoven, Brahms, Berg, Webern and Bartók; Late Quartets of Mozart, Schubert, Haydn and Dvořák; Quartets by Ravel, Debussy and Schumann; Live recordings from Carnegie Hall playing Mozart and Schumann, Konzerthaus in Vienna, and Opéra-Comique in Paris, playing Brahms. *Honours:* Grand Prix du Disque; Deutsche Schallplatenpreis; Edison Prize; Japan Grand Prix; Gramophone Magazine Award. *Address:* Intermusica Artists' Management, 16 Duncan Terrace, London N1 8BZ, England.

**ERBSE, Nebrio;** Composer; b. 27 Feb. 1924, Rudolstadt, Germany. *Education:* Studied at the Musikhochschule of Weimar and Berlin, with Boris Blacher. *Career:* Debut: Conducted in Berlin in 1961; Freelance Composer; Has conducted and directed opera; Moved to Salzburg in 1957, with his opera, Julietta, being performed there in 1959. *Compositions:* Stage: Juliena, opera, 1957, Ruth, ballet, 1958, Der Herr In Grau, comic opera, 1966; Orchestral: Symphony in 4 Movements, 1964, Das Hohelied Salomons, 1969, for string and wind players, 1971, Symphony No. 2, 1970, Triple Concerto, 1972; Chamber music and music for chorus. *Honours:* Beethoven Prize, Bonn, 1961; Appreciation Award for Music, Austrian Ministry for Education and Art, 1973. *Address:* c/o GEMA, Postfach 80 07 67, 81607 Munich, Germany.

**ERDÉLYI, Csaba;** Viola Player and Conductor; b. 15 May 1946, Budapest, Hungary; m. Ju-Ping Chi, 8 Oct 1989, 3 s. *Education:* Artist and Teacher Diplomas, Franz Liszt Academy of Music, 1970; Influential teachers: Pál Lukács, Yehudi Menuhin, Bruno Giuranna. *Career:* Franz Liszt Chamber Orchestra, 1968–72; Eszterházy Baryton Trio, 1973–78; Principal Viola,

Philharmonia Orchestra, London, 1974–78; Professor of Viola, Guildhall School of Music, London, 1980–87; Chilingirian String Quartet, 1981–87; Professor of Viola: Indiana University, Bloomington, 1987–91, Rice University, Houston, TX; Soloist in RFH, Promenade Concerts; Frequent Partner with Yehudi Menuhin; Masterclasses world-wide including: RAM London, Aldeburgh, Alaska, Beijing, Mexico, Budapest, USA; Annual summer classes in Gubbio Festival, Italy; Jury Member of BBC Young Musician of The Year and Lionel Tertis Viola Competition, Isle of Man; First US performance of Brahms/Berio Sonata for Viola and Orchestra; Opening recital at International World Viola Congress in Redlands, CA, 1989, and Vienna, 1992; mem, Institute for the Development of Intercultural Relations through the Arts, Geneva. *Recordings:* Hoddinott, Viola Concerto; Strauss Songs with Jessye Norman. *Publications:* Bartók: Viola Concerto; Bach: Suite Pour La Luth for Viola; Hummel: Fantasia; Mozart: Sinfonia Concertante KV 364 for String Sextet; Arrangement of Brahms' Sonata Op 78; Viola part to Schubert's Arpeggione Sonata. *Contributions:* Music and The Fear of Violence in Classical Music. *Honours:* 1st Prize, Carl Flesch Competition, 1972. *Address:* 2420 Boston Road, Bloomington, IN 47401, USA.

**ERDING-SWIRIDOFF, Susanne;** Composer; b. 16 Nov. 1955, Schwabisch Hall, Germany; m. Paul Swiridoff, 11 Mar 1988. *Education:* Stuttgart University, 1975–77; Oxford and Cambridge, England in summers, 1976–80; Yale University, USA, 1976; Universite de Montreal, Canada, 1978; Studied music, piano and composition with Milko Kelemen, Stuttgart Academy of Music, 1974–79 and composition with Dieter Acker, Munich, 1980; Seminars on composition at Buenos Aires, 1981; International Summer School of Music with Peter Maxwell Davies, Dartington, England, 1985; Composition with Agosto Benjamin Rattenbach, Buenos Aires, 1985. *Career:* Many television appearances, 1983–88. *Compositions include:* Orchestra: Yellan, 1981, Event, 1985, Il Visconte Dimezzato, 1994; Concertos: Konzert, 1983, Tierra Querida, 1986; Operas: Joy, chamber opera, 1983, Die Wundersame Geschichte Des Peter Schlemihl, marionette opera, 1991; Ballet: Yellan, 1981; Piano: Klaviersuite, 1982, Maske Und Kristall IV, 1992; Chamber Music: Grotesques Arabesques, 1980, Rotor, 1982, Homage To The City Of Dresden, 1985, Variations Serieuses, Fayence, 1986, Labirinto Del Sole, 1987, Gioielli Rubati, 1987, Blumen Und Blut, 1988, Zeitstimmen, 1993; Vocal: Okteondo, 1979, Initialen, 1986, Maske Und Kristall X, 1993, XII, 1994. *Address:* Am Postgutle 14, Post Box 620, 74506 Schwabisch Hall, Germany.

**ERICKSON, Kaaren;** Singer (Soprano); b. 9 Feb. 1953, Seattle, USA. *Education:* Studied at Western Washington University, Bellingham, WA, 1970–74 and the Music Academy of the West with Martial Singher and Maurice Abravanel. *Career:* Sang Gilda in 1982 and won 1st prize 1982 Munich Competition; Sang at the Deutsche Oper Berlin and the Munich Staatsoper; Piccola Scala 1983, in Les Pélerins de la Mecque; US engagements at Seattle, San Francisco, Houston, Cincinnati and the City Opera New York; Metropolitan Opera from 1985 as Susanna in new production of Le nozze di Figaro; Appears in the Met videos of Wagner's Ring, Parsifal and Elektra; Blanche in Dialogues of the Carmelites, as Zerlina in Don Giovanni and a Flowermaiden in a new production of Parsifal (1991); Other roles have included Mozart's Pamina and Fiordiligi, Micaela, Contessa, Ellen Orford and Marschallin in Der Freischütz; Sang in the premiere of The Voyage by Philip Glass, Metropolitan, 1992; Many Lieder recitals and concert appearances; mem, National Association of Teachers of Singing. *Recordings:* Le Cinesi by Gluck; The White Election by Gordon Getty; Messiah (Handel) with the Atlanta Symphony, Robert Shaw; Dvořák Stabat Mater with NJ Symphony, Zdenek Macal. *Current Management:* Thea Dispeker Artist Management. *Address:* c/o Thea Dispeker Artists Management, 59 E 54th St, NY 10022, USA.

**ERICSDOTTER, Siw;** Singer (Soprano); b. 9 Feb. 1919, Norrkoping, Sweden. *Education:* Studied in Stockholm with Nanny Larsen-Todsen. *Career:* Member of the Royal Opera Stockholm, 1951–54; Sang with the Hamburg Staatsoper, 1954–59; Appeared in Berlin from 1959 notably as Wagner's Elsa, Eva and Sieglinde; Guest appearances in Vienna, Paris and in Italy; Stuttgart Opera, 1962–70; Other roles include Leonore, Amneris, Tosca and the title role in Judith by N Berg. *Recordings include:* Herodias in Salome and Der Evangelimann by Kienzl.

**ERICSON, Barbro;** Singer (Mezzo-Soprano); b. 2 April 1930, Halmstad, Sweden. *Education:* Studied in Stockholm with Arne Sunnegard. *Career:* Debut: Stockholm in 1956 as Eboli in Don Carlos; Guest appearances in London, Berlin, Hamburg, Edinburgh, Helsinki, France, Netherlands and Italy; Sang at Paris Opéra in 1964 as Venus in Tannhäuser, Bayreuth Festival from 1964 as Kundry and Venus, and Salzburg Easter Festival in 1967 in Die Walküre under Karajan; Metropolitan Opera debut in 1968 as Fricka, returning to New York in 1976 as Herodias in Salome; Sang in the premiere of Ligeti's Le Grande Macabre, 1978. *Recordings include:* Die Walküre; Requiem and other works by Ligeti.

**ERKOREKA, Gabriel,** DipRAM, MA, ARAM; composer; *Composition Teacher, Musikene Conservatoire;* b. 27 Feb. 1969, Bilbao, Spain. *Education:* Conservatorio Superior de Música, Bilbao, Royal Acad. of Music, London. *Career:* performances include Festival Internacional de Alicante, Auditorio Nacional de Música (Madrid), Wigmore Hall, ICA and South Bank Centre, London, ISCM World Music Days 1998 in Manchester, Musikverein in Vienna, Chicago, New York, Amsterdam, Paris, Rome, Sydney, Tokyo; teacher of composition, Musikene Conservatoire, Basque Country. *Compositions:* over

40 pieces, including Kantak for piccolo and chamber ensemble, Bizitiza for mezzo soprano and ensemble, Izaro for piano quintet, Afrika for solo marimba and orchestra, Océano for symphony orchestra. *Recordings:* Kantak, Krater, Nubes, Cuatro Diferencias for accordion. *Honours:* SGAE prize 1996, INAEM prize 2001, Spanish Acad. Rome Prize 2001. *Current Management:* Repertoire Promotion Department, Oxford University Press, 70 Baker Street, London, W1U 7DN, England. *Telephone:* (20) 7616-5900 (office). *Fax:* (20) 7616-5901 (office). *E-mail:* repertoire.promotion@oup.com (office). *Website:* www.oup.co.uk/music/repprom (office).

**EROD, Ivan;** Composer, Professor and Pianist; b. 2 Jan. 1936, Budapest, Hungary; m. Marie-Luce Guy, 11 April 1969, 3 s., 2 d. *Education:* Academy of Music, Budapest, 1951–56; Academy of Music, Vienna, 1957–61. *Career:* Debut: Budapest; Coach for Vienna State Opera, 1962–64; Concert Pianist on 5 continents; Appearances include: Salzburg Festival, and Vienna Philharmonic with Karl Bohm; Full Professor for Composition and Music Theory at Hochschule für Musik und Darstellende Kunst, Graz, Austria, 1971–89, and Hochschule für Musik, Vienna, 1989–. *Compositions:* 2 Operas; Orchestral works, Concertos, Chamber Music, Cantatas, Lieder, Chorus works. *Recordings:* As pianist, 10 records with Rudolf Schock, tenor; Pierrot Lunaire (Die Reihe, Vienna), recordings in 10 countries; As composer, with various labels; Numerous radio recordings for BBC. *Contributions:* Articles in Osterreichische Musikzeitschrift. *Honours:* Several Austrian State Prizes; Bart ók Pasztory Prize, 1993. *Current Management:* Verlag Doblinger, Vienna, Austria. *Address:* Gumpendorfer Strasse 9-13, 1060 Vienna, Austria.

**ERÖS, Peter;** conductor; b. 22 Sept. 1932, Budapest, Hungary; m. 1st Georgia Weiser 1956; two s.; m. 2nd Jasmin Fay Roberts 1985 (divorced). *Education:* Franz Liszt Music Academy, Budapest; studies with Zoltan Kodály, Leo Weiner, Laszlo Somogyi. *Career:* Assistant to: George Szell (Cleveland Orchestra), Otto Klemperer (Holland Festival), Ferenc Fricsay, Assistant to Bayreuther Festival, 1957–60; Associate Conductor, Amsterdam Concertgebouw Orchestra, 1960–65; Music Director, Malmö Symphony Orchestra, Sweden, 1966–68; Principal Guest Conductor, Melbourne Symphony Orchestra, 1968–70; Music Director, San Diego Symphony Orchestra, Music Director, La Jolla Chamber Music Society, 1972–80; Principal Conductor, Western Australia Symphony Orchestra, Perth, 1975–79; Music Director, Peabody Symphony and Opera, Baltimore, USA, 1982–85; Music Director, Aalborg Symphony Orchestra, Denmark, 1983–89; Music Director, University of Washington Symphony Orchestra and Opera Department, 1989–; Numerous guest engagements with leading orchestras throughout the United Kingdom, Europe and the USA. *Recordings:* Siegfried Wagner, Orchestral Works; Gabriel von Wayditch, Jesus before Herod; Many recordings for Australian Broadcasting Commission and Swedish Radio. *Publications:* contrib. to various professional journals and newspapers. *Address:* c/o University of Washington, Department of Music, Seattle, WA 98195, USA.

**ESCHENBACH, Christoph;** German conductor and concert pianist; *Music Director, Philadelphia Orchestra, Orchestre de Paris*; b. 20 Feb. 1940, Breslau (now Wrocław, Poland). *Education:* Musikhochschulen, Cologne and Hamburg. *Career:* Musical Dir of Philharmonic Orchestra, Ludwigshafen 1979–83; Chief Conductor Tonhalle Orchestra, Zürich 1982–86; Co-Artistic Dir Pacific Music Festival 1992–98; Artistic Dir Schleswig-Holstein Music Festival 1999–2002; Musical Dir Houston Symphony Orchestra 1988–99 (Conductor Laureate 1999–), Ravinia Festival 1994–2003; Prin. Conductor NDR Symphony Orchestra 1998–2004; Musical Dir Orchestre de Paris 2000–, Philadelphia Orchestra 2003–; has appeared as conductor Boston Symphony, Chicago Symphony, Houston Symphony, LA Philharmonic, New York Philharmonic, Philadelphia Orchestra, San Francisco Symphony (US conducting debut 1975), Berlin Philharmonic, Danish Nat. Radio Orchestra, Hamburg NDR Symphony Orchestra, Kirov Orchestra, all five London orchestras, Orchestre de Paris, Vienna Philharmonic; as pianist with Atlanta Symphony, Radio Orchestras of Munich and Stuttgart, Israel Philharmonic and Israel Chamber Orchestras, NHK Orchestra Tokyo; operatic engagements include Bayreuth, Houston Grand Opera, NY Metropolitan Opera, Hessian State Theatre, Darmstadt (operatic conducting debut 1978); festivals include Bayreuth, Ravinia Festival and Schleswig-Holstein Musical Festival. *Honours:* Officer's Cross with Ribbon, German Order of Merit 1990, Commdr's Cross 1993, Officer's Cross with Star of the German Order of Merit 2002, Chevalier de la Légion d'honneur 2002; 1st Prize, Steinway Piano Competition 1952, Munich Int. Competition 1962, Clara Haskil Competition 1965, Leonard Bernstein Award 1993. *Current Management:* M. L. Falcone, Public Relations, 155 W 68th Street, New York, NY 10023, USA. *Telephone:* (212) 580-4302. *Fax:* (212) 787-9638 (office).

**ESCHKENAZY, Vesko;** Violinist; b. 3 Dec. 1970, Sofia, Bulgaria. *Education:* Studied with Yfrah Neaman in London, Pierre Amoyal in Lausanne and at the Bulgarian Conservatory, leaving with an Honours degree. *Career:* Leader, Pioneer Youth Philharmonic Orchestra in Sofia, 1979, touring France, Italy, Germany and Brazil; Solo performances with the English Chamber Orchestra, Royal Philharmonic Orchestra, Sofia Philharmonic, Bulgarian Festival Symphony, Monte Carlo Symphony, City of London Sinfonia, Philharmonia and London Philharmonic (Beethoven Concerto, 1992); Festival engagements in Sofia, Varna, Cannes, Montpellier and Nantes, with tours to the former Soviet Union, throughout Europe, India, Brazil and China; Repertoire includes concertos by Bach, Brahms, Mozart, Prokofiev, Sibelius and Shostakovich; Sonatas by Tartini, Bach, Mozart, Beethoven, Franck and

Schumann. *Recordings include:* Bruch and Mendelssohn Concertos, conducted by Emil Tchakarov; Brahms Violin Concerto with Sofia Philharmonic Orchestra and Emil Tabakov conducting. *Honours:* Winner of various competitions in Europe and China. *Address:* World Wide Artists Ltd, 6 Petersfield Crescent, Coulsdon, Surrey CR5 2JQ, England.

**ESCHRIG, Ralph;** Singer (Tenor); b. 2 April 1959, Dresden, Germany. *Education:* Studied at the Musikhochschule Dresden. *Career:* Sang at the Dresden Staatsoper 1984–87, notably in the local premiere of The Nose by Shostakovich; Lyric Tenor at the Berlin Staatsoper from 1987, notably as Mozart's Ottavio, Belmonte, Tamino and Ferrando, Fenton by Nicolai and in the Singspiels Erwin und Elmire by Reichardt and Zar und Zimmerman by Lortzing; Concert appearances as the Evangelist in Bach's Passions, Lieder by Schubert and Schumann and The Diary of One who Disappeared by Janáček; Engagements with the Dresden Kreuz Choir and Chorus of St Thomas's Leipzig and broadcasting stations in Germany and Finland. *Recordings include:* Mendelssohn Motets and Bastien und Bastienne by Mozart. *Honours:* Prizewinner, 1984 International Bach Competition; 1987 Mozart Competition at Salzburg. *Address:* c/o Berlin Staatsoper, Unter den Linden 7, 1086 Berlin, Germany.

**ESCOBAR, Roberto B.;** University Professor and Musician; b. 11 May 1926, Santiago, Chile; m. Marta Cruchaga, 19 Mar 1950, 2 s. *Education:* MA, Philosophy, Catholic University, Valparaiso; Conservatorio Nacional and Escuela Moderna de Musica, Santiago; Manhattan School of Music, New York. *Career:* Composer; Conductor, Chilean Modern Music Ensemble, 1973–78; Musicologist; President, Chilean Composers' Association, 1974–78; President, Sociedad Chilena de Filosofia, 1985–88. *Compositions:* Over 60 works performed publicly, including: Laberinto, 1971, first performed in USA, 1976; Symphonia de Fluminis, 1987, first performed in USA, 1992; Tower of the Winds, first performed in USA, 1989; Sinfonia Andres Bello, 1992, first performed in Chile, 1993; Prometheus, first performed in Chile, 1996; Cantos Cecilianos, first performed in Chile, 2000. *Recordings:* Preludios Franceses; Homenaje a Amengual; Talagante; Cuarteto Estructural, Cuarteto Funcional, Macul, La Granja, Elegia, Quinteto La Paloma. *Publications:* Catalogue of Chilean Music, 1969; Chilean Musicians and Their Music, 1971; Study in Black and White, 1973; Chilean Composers, 1997. *Contributions:* Various journals. *Honours:* Goethe Prize for Composition, 1982; Honorary Professor, University of Missouri, 1989; Claudio Arrau Prize, Chile, 1993, Distinguished Professor (Life Appointment) Universidad de Chile 1997. *Address:* PO Box 16360, Santiago 9, Chile.

**ESCOT, Pozzi;** American composer, teacher and writer on music; *Professor of Graduate Theoretical Studies & Composition, New England Conservatory*; b. 1 Oct. 1933, New York, NY. *Education:* BS, 1956, MS course, 1957, Juilliard School of Music, New York; Studied with Philipp Jarnach at Hamburg Hochschule für Musik, 1957–61. *Career:* teacher New England Conservatory of Music, Boston 1964–67, Prof. of Graduate Theoretical Studies & Composition 1980–; Ed. Sonus Journal 1980–, now Ed.-in-Chief; Visiting Lecturer, Harvard, Princeton, Chicago, Columbia, Stanford, Berkeley, Illinois, Northwestern Universities, also London, Edinburgh, Nice, Eichstatt, Augsburg, Helsinki, Hamburg, Leuven, Sorbonne, Dublin Inst. of Tech., Darmstadt, Milan, Paris, Beijing, Shanghai, Hanyang, Yonsie, Kunitachi, Hiroshima; Pres. Int. Soc. of Hildegard von Bingen Studies 1993–; Woodrow Wilson Visiting Fellow 1999–. *Compositions:* 5 Symphonies, 1952–57; 5 String Quartets; A Trilogy for chamber ensembles; Concerto for piano; Diverse chamber and solo works; 3 Poems of Rilke for narrator and string quartet, 1959; 3 Movements for violin and piano, 1959–60; Lamentus, Trilogy No. 1 for soprano and 8 players, 1962; Visione, Trilogy No. 3 for soprano, speaker and 5 players, 1964; Sands… for orchestra, 1965; Neyrac Lux for 2 guitars and electric guitar, 1978; Eure Pax for violin, 1980; Concerto for piano and chamber orchestra, 1982; Trio In Memoriam Solrac for violin, cello and piano, 1984; Jubilation for string quartet, 1991; Mirabilis III for low voice, 3 flutes and 3 violins, 1995; Visione 97 for chorus, 1997; Piano pieces and pieces for instrument and tape, Fifth Symphony 2000, Sixth Symphony 2001. *Publications:* Sonic Design: The Nature of Sound and Music, with Robert Cogan, 1976, 1981; Sonic Design: Practice and Problems, 1981, The Poetic Simple Mathematics in Music, Oh How Wondrous: Hildegard von Bingen Ten Essays. *Contributions:* Mystics Quarterly; Interface; New York Theory Society Music and Practice; Edinburgh University Musical Praxis; Perspectives of New Music; Stanford University Humanities Review; University of Leuven, Belgium. *Honours:* Radcliffe Inst., Rockefeller, Bellagio, Ford, Marshall Plan, Outstanding Educator of America, Woodrow Wilson Nat. Foundation Visiting Fellow. *Address:* 24 Avon Hill, Cambridge, MA 02140, USA. *Telephone:* (617) 585-1374 (office); (617) 868-0215 (home). *Fax:* (617) 868-0215 (home). *E-mail:* pescot@newenglandconservatory.edu (office). *Website:* www.newenglandconservatory.edu (office); www.sonicdesign.org (office).

**ESCRIBANO, María;** Composer and Pianist; b. 24 Jan. 1954, Madrid, Spain. *Education:* Studied, Real Conservatorio Superior de Musica de Madrid, 1963–73; Study with Rodolfo Halffter, Curso Internacional de Musica Manuel de Falla de Granada, 1971; Studied techniques of contemporary composition with Cristobal Halffter, Tomas Marco and Carmelo A Bernaola, Real Conservatorio Superior de Musica de Madrid; Also complete courses in the analysis of contemporary music and attended the Darmstadt International Courses, 1974–76. *Career:* Premiere of first work for instrumental ensemble, 1975; Resided in France as member of the Roy Hart Theatre, worked as composer, actress and pianist, 1978–80; Toured France, Belgium and Spain, 1980; Co-founder Theatrical Group, Agada, 1983; Composition and Music Teaching, 1989–; mem, Society of Authors. *Compositions include:* Muñecas de mimbre, 1974; Sin Seso, 1978; Concierto para Imma, 1976; L'histoire d'un s., 1978; Cuentos y canciones de la media lunita, 1987; Madrid de noche 1992; El sonido viajero, 1992; Memoria del viento, 1992; Desde la otra orilla, 1993; Sortilegio, 1993; Solar, 1994. *Publications:* Dictionary of Iberoamerica Music–dos mujeres en la musica/Historia de la musica española. *Honours:* Several scholarships. *Address:* c/o SGAE, Fernando VI 4, Apartado 484, 28080 Madrid 4, Spain.

**ESHAM, Faith;** singer (soprano); b. 6 Aug. 1948, Vanceburg, Kentucky, USA. *Education:* Studied at Juilliard School with Jennie Tourel and Beverly Johnson. *Career:* Debut: New York City Opera in 1977 as Cherubino; European debut as Nedda in Nancy; Sang Cherubino at Glyndebourne in 1981 and at La Scala in 1982; Vienna Staatsoper in 1984 as Micaela in Carmen; Geneva Opera in 1984 as Mélisande; New York City Opera as Pamina in Die Zauberflöte, Leila in Les Pêcheurs de Perles, Marguerite in Faust and Massenet's Cendrillon; Washington DC as Zerlina in Don Giovanni; Pittsburgh Opera as Gilda; Las Palmas as Antonia in Les Contes d'Hoffmann; Metropolitan Opera debut in 1986 as Marzelline in Fidelio; Season 1990–91 as Musetta at Cologne, Pamina for Washington Opera and Susanna at Fort Lauderdale; Micaela for Cincinnati Opera, Butterfly at St Louis and Cherubino at the Dallas Opera, 1992; Sang Butterfly for Welsh National Opera, 1995; Concert appearances at the Mostly Mozart Festival, New York, Requiem and Schubert's A flat Mass, and Fauré's Requiem with the Pittsburgh Symphony under Charles Dutoit. *Recordings include:* La nozze di Figaro conducted by Haitink; Video of Carmen, with Domingo. *Honours:* Young Artists Award from the National Opera Institute, 1978–79; Concours International de Chant de Paris Prize, 1981.

**ESHPAI, Andrey (Yakoulevitch);** Composer and Pianist; b. 15 May 1925, Kozmodemiansk, Russia; m. Alexandra Stempnevski, 2 s. *Education:* Studied with Miashoveky, Sofronitsky and Khachaturian at the Moscow Conservatory. *Career:* Regular television and radio appearances; Secretary, Union of Russian Composers; First Secretary, Union of Composers of RSFSR. *Compositions include:* 4 Symphonies, 1959–82; 2 Violin Sonatas, 1966, 1970; Concerto for orchestra, 1967; Festival Overture, 1970; The Circle, ballet, 1981; Oboe Concerto, 1982; Symphony No. 5, 1985–86, No. 6, (Liturgy) 1988–89, No. 7, 1991; Concerto for soprano saxophone and orchestra, 1986; Viola Concerto, 1988; Cello Concerto, 1989; Cello-Sonate, 1990; Violin Concerto No. 3, 1990; Hungarian Tunes for viola and orchestra. 1953; Symphonic Dances, 1949; 2 Piano Concertos; Violin Concerto No. 4, 1991; String Quartet (Concordia Discordans), 1992–95; Flute Concerto, 1994; Concerto for trumpet and trombone with symphony orchestra; Horn Concerto, 1995; Four Poems for orchestra, 1998; I Loved You for low voice and piano, 1999; Chamber Music includes: Rondeau-Etude for 4 saxophones; Music for over 60 films. *Address:* Apartment No. 121, Studentcheskaya st 44/28, 121 165 Moscow, Russia.

**ESPERIAN, Kallen;** Singer (Soprano); b. 8 June 1961, Waukegan, Illinois, USA. *Education:* Studied at the University of Illinois. *Career:* Sang in various opera houses and concert halls in the USA then won the 1985 Pavarotti Competition and toured with the tenor to China, singing Mimi in La Bohème; Further appearances as Mimi at the Berlin and Vienna Staatsopers in 1986, the Lyric Opera of Chicago and the Metropolitan, NY, 1989; Returned to the Metropolitan as Elena in I Vespri Siciliani; Has sung Verdi's Luisa Miller in Vienna, 1986, Verona and Geneva, 1993; Sang Desdemona at the Opéra Bastille in Paris and Reggio Emilia, 1992; Mozart's Countess at St Louis, the Trovatore Leonora at Chicago and Nedda for Connecticut Grand Opera; San Francisco in 1991 as Donna Elvira in Don Giovanni; Sang Desdemona at Covent Garden, 1997, and Amelia in the original version of Simon Boccanegra; Season 1999–2000 as Alice Ford in Falstaff at Chicago and Elisabeth de Valois at Munich. *Address:* c/o Grand Théâtre de Geneve, 11 Boulevard du Théâtre, 1211 Geneva 11, Switzerland.

**ESPERT ROMERO, Nuria;** Spanish actress and director; b. 11 June 1935, Hospitalet (Barcelona); m. Armando Moreno 1955; two d. *Career:* professional actress since 1947; first maj. success in Medée aged 19; created her own co. 1959; has appeared in works by Calderón, Shakespeare, O'Neill, Lope De Vega, Genet, Lorca, Espriu, Valle Inclán, Sartre etc.; Dir The House of Bernarda Alba (Lorca) with Glenda Jackson and Joan Plowright, London 1986 (Evening Standard Drama Award); has also directed operas Madame Butterfly, Elektra, Rigoletto, La Traviata and Carmen at Covent Garden and in Scotland, Brussels, Israel and Japan; Artistic Dir Turandot, Liceo Theater, Barcelona 1999. *Theatre includes:* The Seagull 1997, Master Class 1998, Who's Afraid of Virginia Woolf 1999, 2000, Medée 2002. *Publications:* numerous int. theatre publications. *Honours:* more than 100 Spanish honours and awards; 17 int. awards. *Address:* Pavia 2, 28013 Madrid, Spain. *Telephone:* (91) 7154958. *Fax:* (91) 3511177.

**ESPINOSA, Pedro;** Pianist; b. 13 Oct. 1934, Galdar, Gran Canaria, Canary Islands. *Education:* Teachers: His mother (Juana Lorenzo) Alfred Cortot, Marguérite Long, Edward Steuermann, Witold Malcuzynski, David Tudor. *Career:* Debut: Teatro Perez-Galdos, Las Palmas de Gran Canaria, 16 Nov 1949; Has played at Venice and Paris Biennials and Enescu Festival, Bucharest; Other festivals include Darmstadt, Granada, Santander and San Sebastian; Has appeared with the Orquesta Sinfónica de Bilbao, Orquesta de RTVE and Orquesta Sinfónica de Madrid; Spanish premiere of Messiaen's Les

Oiseaux Exotiques, with the Orquesta Nacional, 1963; Other notable performances include Bartók's Sonata for 2 pianos and percussion (1955), complete works for piano of Schoenberg, Berg and Webern (1956), 2nd and 3rd Sonatas by Boulez (1961, 1967), Stockhausen's Klavierstück VI (1972) and first complete performance of Mompou's Música callada (1980); Lecture-concerts with Theodor Adorno; Professor at the Royal Conservatories of Madrid, Pamplona and Guadalajara; Classes at Lyon, Freiburg and Geneva Conservatories and various Spanish institutions; Piano works dedicated to him by many distinguished composers; mem, Royal Academy of Fine Arts of the Canary Islands; Hijo Predilecto of City of Galdar. *Recordings:* For many European broadcasting companies; Records in Germany and Spain, notably the complete Klavierstücke of Stockhausen. *Honours:* Kranichstein Prize, Kranichsteiner Musikinstitut, Darmstadt; 1st Prize, Real Conservatorio de Madrid; Fine Arts Award for interpretation of 20th century piano music, Fundación Arnhem, 1965; 1 of 3 Most Distinguished Interpreters of Ravel's Concerto for left hand, Ravel Academy, 1975; Annual Piano Competition in Galdar named after him, 1988. *Address:* c/o Rafaela Bonilla 19, 28028 Madrid, Spain.

**ESPOSITO, Valeria;** Singer (soprano); b. 10 April 1961, Naples, Italy. *Education:* Salerno Conservatoire. *Career:* Debut: Teatro del Giglio in Lucca as Zerlina in Don Giovanni in 1986; Appeared in concert productions at La Scala of Riccardo III by Flavio Testi and Berg's Lulu; Amsterdam in 1987 as Nausicca in Ulisse by Dallapiccola; Lucca in 1987 in Domenico Puccini's Il Ciarlatano; Teatro Lirico Milan as Sophie in Werther; US debut at Houston in 1988 in Werther; Teatro San Carlo Naples in 1988 as Amor in Orfeo e Euridice; La Scala in 1989 in Pergolesi's Lo Frate Innamorato; Radio France in 1989 in the title role of Linda di Chamounix by Donizetti; Welsh National Opera in 1989 as Amina in La Sonnambula; Sang Ippodamia in Paer's Achille at Lugo di Romagna in 1988; Sang Amina at the 1992 Macerata Festival and at Rome 1996; Season 1995–96 as Adina at Rome, Rossini's Fiorilla at Catania and Constanze at the Vienna Staatsoper; Offenbach's Olympia at Catania, 1998; Lucia di Lammermoor at Toulouse, 1998; Sang Gilda at St Gallen and the Queen of Night at Barcelona, 2000; Featured Artist, Opera Now Magazine, 1992. *Honours:* Winner, Aslico Competition, Milan, 1987; Winner, Cardiff Singer of the World Competition, 1987. *Current Management:* Athole Still International Management, Forresters Hall, 25–27 Westow Street, London, SE19 3RY, England. *Telephone:* (20) 8771-5271. *Fax:* (20) 8768-6600. *Website:* www.atholestill.com.

**ESSER, Hermin;** Singer (Tenor); b. 1 April 1928, Rheydt, Germany. *Education:* Studied at the Schumann Conservatory Düsseldorf with Franziak Martiensen-Lohmann. *Career:* Debut: Krefeld 1954; Sang at Gelsenkirchen, the Komische Oper Berlin and Wiesbaden; member of the Deutsche Oper am Rhein, Düsseldorf, 1964–; Bayreuth Festival from 1966, as Froh, Erik, Tristan, Tannhäuser, Siegmund and Loge; Sang Tristan at Monte Carlo in 1973 and Parsifal at Rome in 1974; Sadler's Wells Opera 1973, with Scottish Opera as Tristan; Guest appearances in Paris, Moscow, Warsaw, Brussels, Zürich, Chicago, Geneva and Zürich; Sang Herod in Salome at the Staatsoper Berlin, 1988. *Recordings:* Das Rheingold; Der fliegende Holländer. *Address:* c/o Deutsche Staatsoper, Unter den Linden 7, 1086 Berlin, Germany.

**ESSWOOD, Paul Lawrence Vincent,** ARCM; British singer (countertenor) and conductor; b. 6 June 1942, Nottingham; s. of Alfred W. Esswood and Freda Garatt; m. 1st Mary L. Cantrill 1966 (divorced 1990); two s.; m. 2nd Aimée Désirée Blattmann 1990; one s. one d. *Education:* West Bridgford Grammar School and Royal Coll. of Music. *Career:* Lay Vicar, Westminster Abbey 1964–71; Prof. Royal Coll. of Music 1973–85, Royal Acad. of Music 1985–; Co-founder, Pro Cantione Antiqua – A Cappella 1967; opera debut, L'Erismena, Univ. of Calif., Berkeley 1968; debut at La Scala, Milan with Zürich Opera in L'Incoronazione di Poppea and Il Ritorno d'Ulisse 1978; Scottish opera debut in Dido and Aeneas 1978; world premiere, Penderecki's Paradise Lost, Chicago Lyric Opera 1979, Philip Glass's Akhnaton, Stuttgart 1984; Herbert Will's Schlafes Bruder, with Zurich Opera 1996; world première, Schnittke's Faust Cantata, Vienna, 1986; Handel's Riccardo Primo, Covent Garden, 1991; has appeared at many maj. int. festivals; specialist in performance of baroque music and has made many recordings of works by Bach, Handel, Purcell, Monteverdi, Cavalli, Britten (Abraham and Isaac), folksongs etc.; Prof. at 'Maîtrise de Notre Dame', Paris, conducting debut at Chichester Festival with Purcell's The Fairy Queen 2000, Kraków, Poland 2001. *Honours:* Hon. RAM 1990; Handel Prize (Germany) 1992. *Address:* Jasmine Cottage, 42 Ferring Lane, Ferring, West Sussex, BN12 6QT, England. *Telephone:* (1903) 504480. *Fax:* (1903) 504480. *Website:* www.themusickecompany.com.

**ESTEP, Craig;** Singer (Tenor); b. 1962, USA. *Career:* Sang Rinuccio in Gianni Schicchi at Charlotte Opera, 1987; San Francisco Opera as Ferrando in Così fan tutte, Alfredo, Nemorino, and Noburo in the 1991 US premiere of Henze's Das verratene Meer; Washington Opera, 1992–95, as Nemorino, and Tonio in La fille du Régiment; Calgary Opera, 1994, as Edgardo; Cologne, 1995, as Anfinomo in Monteverdi's Ulisse; Other roles include Pong in Turandot, Cassio in Otello and Ernesto in Don Pasquale. *Address:* c/o Washington Opera, John F. Kennedy Center, Washington DC, 20566, USA.

**ESTES, Simon;** Singer (Bass-Baritone); b. 2 March 1938, Centreville, IA, USA. *Education:* Studied with Charles Kellis at the University of Iowa and at the Juilliard School, NY. *Career:* Sang at various German opera houses from 1965 with debut at the Deutsche Oper Berlin as Ramfis in Aida; Member of Zürich Opera, 1976; Metropolitan Opera from 1976 in roles including Oroveso in Norma, La Scala in 1977 as Arkel in Pelléas et Mélisande, Hamburg Staatsoper in 1978 as King Philip in Don Carlos, Bayreuth Festival from 1978 as the Dutchman and Amfortas, Geneva Opera in 1984 as Jochanaan in Salome, and Covent Garden debut in 1986 as Wagner's Dutchman; Sang Wotan in new productions of Der Ring des Nibelungen at Berlin, 1984–85 and the Metropolitan, 1986–88; Appearances at San Francisco, Glyndebourne Festival, Paris Opéra, Munich and Vienna; Other roles include the Villains in Les Contes d'Hoffmann, Escamillo, King Mark, Mephistopheles, the Pharoah in Rossini's Moses and Boris Godunov; Concert engagements include the US premiere of the 14th Symphony by Shostakovich with the Philadelphia Orchestra; Other concerts with the New York Philharmonic, Chicago Symphony, Boston Symphony and the Berlin Philharmonic; London Promenade concerts debut in 1989 in Act III, Die Walküre; Sang title role in musical King, in London in 1990; Season 1992 included Macbeth for Greater Miami Opera and Wotan at Bonn; Sang Zaccaria in Nabucco at the 1994 Orange Festival, Porgy at Cape Town, 1996. *Recordings include:* Simon Boccanegra; Oberto by Verdi; Mahler's 8th Symphony; Fauré's Requiem.

**ETHUIN, Paul;** Conductor; b. 24 Sept. 1924, Bruay-sur-Escaut, France. *Education:* Studied at the Paris Conservatoire, 1943–46. *Career:* Professor of flute at the Rheims Conservatoire, 1944–51; Second Conductor at the Rheims Opéra, 1948, Principal from 1955; Capital Théâtre, Toulouse, 1955–61; Opéra d'Avignon, 1962–66; Director of music at the Théâtre des Arts, Rouen, 1966; Paris Opéra and Opéra-Comique, 1968–71; Led the premiere of Bondeville's Antony and Cleopatra, 1974, and returned to Rouen, 1984–89.

**EUBA, Akin,** PhD; Nigerian composer, musician (piano) and lecturer; b. 28 April 1935, Lagos. *Education:* CMS Grammar School, Lagos, Trinity Coll. of Music, London, England, Univ. of Calif., Los Angeles, and Univ. of Ghana, Legon. *Career:* Sr Programme Asst, Nigerian Broadcasting Corpn 1957–60, Head of Music and Music Research 1960–65; performer, numerous recitals in Europe, USA, Africa; organizer, numerous concerts of African music at home and abroad; lecturer in Africa and abroad 1966–; teacher, Univ. of Lagos 1966–68, Univ. of Ife 1968–77; Dir Center for Cultural Studies, Univ. of Lagos 1978–81; Dir Elekoto Music Centre, Lagos 1981–86; Research Scholar, Univ. of Bayreuth, Germany 1986–91; Dir Centre for Intercultural Music Arts, London 1988–; Hon. Visiting Prof., Dept of Music, City Univ., London 1993–96; Andrew Mellon Prof., Univ. of Pittsburgh, PA, USA 1997–; Overseas Fellow, Churchill Coll., Cambridge 2000–01; composer-in-residence, Ensemble Noir, Toronto, Canada 2003; World Music Scholar-in-Residence, Azusa Pacific Univ. 2004. *Compositions include:* Introduction and allegro 1956, String Quartet 1957, Two Yoruba Folk Songs 1959, The Wanderer for cello 1960, Igi nla so 1963, Five Pieces for English Horn and Piano 1963, Dance to the Rising Sun for chamber orchestra 1963, Three Songs for voice, piano and Iyalu drum 1963, Four Pieces 1964, Four Pictures from Oyo Calabashes for piano 1964, Impressions from an Akwete Cloth for piano 1964, Saturday Night at the Caban Bamboo for piano 1964, Tortoise and the Speaking Cloth (dramatic music) 1964, Abiku I (incidental music, for Iya–Abiku) 1965, Four Pieces for African Orchestra 1966, Legend 1966, Olurounbi: A Symphonic Study on a Yoruba Legend 1967, Wind Quartet 1967, Abiku II 1968, The Fall of the Scales 1970, Dirges 1970, Chaka (opera) 1970, The Laughing Tree 1970, Scenes from Traditional Life for piano 1970, Music for violin, horn, piano and percussion 1970, Ice Cubes for string orchestra 1970, Six Yoruba Folk Songs 1975, Two Tortoise Folk Tales in Yoruba 1975, FESTAC 77 1977, Black Bethlehem (opera) 1979, West African Universities Games Anthem 1981, Two Songs for orchestra with chorus 1983, Bethlehem (opera) 1984, Time Passes By 1985, Seven Modern African Poems 1987, Two Modern African Poems 1987, Wakar Duru: Studies in African Pianism Nos 1–3 1987, Themes from Chaka No. 1 1996, Orunmila's Voices 2002, Study in African Jazz No. 3 2002, Themes from Chaka 2 2003, Below Rusumo Falls 2003. *Honours:* first prize in piano performance Nigerian Festival of the Arts 1950–52, Fed. Govt of Nigeria Scholarship 1952–57, Rockefeller Foundation scholarship for study at Univ. of Calif., Los Angeles 1962. *Address:* 204 Music Building, Department of Music, University of Pittsburgh, Pittsburgh, PA 15260, USA (office). *E-mail:* aeuba@pitt.edu (office). *Website:* www.pitt.edu/~musicdpt (office).

**EULER, Christian;** Violist; b. 12 May 1956, Kassel, Germany; m., 1 s. *Education:* Bachelor and Master of Music degrees, Juilliard School of Music. *Career:* Philadelphia Orchestra, under Riccardo Muti, 1984–91; Member of Philadelphia Chamber Ensemble; Professor for Viola and Chamber Music at Universität für Musik und darstellende Kunst, Graz, Austria, 1991–; Solo and chamber music appearances in Europe. *Address:* Clemensstr 8, 80803 Munich, Germany.

**EVAN, Allan;** Singer (Baritone); b. 1941, Macon, Georgia, USA. *Education:* Studied at Juilliard and in Munich, Salzburg and Vienna. *Career:* Sang at Trier and elsewhere in Germany from 1968, as Crown in Porgy and Bess; Bremen Opera, 1973–76, Zürich, 1976–79, Basle, 1977–87, Mannheim from 1987; Other roles have included Escamillo and Pizarro (at Graz), Don Giovanni, Amonasro (Wiesbaden, 1996), Wotan, Amfortas and Scarpia in Tosca (Mannheim, 1994); Strauss's Barak and D Schnyder's The Tempest, Berne, 1996; Sang Dr Schön in Lulu at Mannheim, 1998. *Address:* c/o Nationaltheater Mannheim, Mozartstrasse 9, 68161 Mannheim, Germany.

**EVANGELATOS, Daphne;** Singer (Mezzo-Soprano); b. 1952, Athens, Greece. *Education:* Studied in Athens, Munich and Vienna. *Career:* Sang first at the Bayerische Staatsoper, Munich then in Vienna, Cologne, Frankfurt, Hamburg and Vienna; Théâtre de la Monnaie Brussels in 1982

in La Clemenza di Tito; Hamburg Staatsoper in 1984 in Cavall's L'Ormindo; Salzburg Festival in 1985 in Henze's version of Monteverdi's Il Ritorno d'Ulisse, as Melanto; Cologne in 1986 as the Prince in Massenet's Cendrillon; Other roles include Octavian in Der Rosenkavalier, Mozart's Cherubino, Sextus and Annius, Preziosilla in La Forza del Destino, the Composer in Ariadne auf Naxos and Wagner's Waltraute; Sang Tisbe in La Cenerentola at the 1988 Salzburg Festival; Wolf-Ferrari's Le Donne Curiose at the 1990 Munich Festival; Has also appeared in Campra's Tancrède, at Aix, Ramiro in La Finta Giardiniera, Orpheus, Mozart's Annius and Sextus, Fricka, Waltraute, and Varvara in Katya Kabanova. *Address:* c/o Music International, 13 Ardilaun Road, London N5 2QR, England.

**EVANGELIDES, Petros;** Singer (Tenor); b. 1949, Limasol, Cyprus. *Education:* Studied in Athens and Vienna. *Career:* Sang at Klagenfurt, 1973–74 and as Ernesto on tour in Switzerland, Germany and Netherlands, 1974; Stadttheater Berne, 1976–82, National Theatre Mannheim, 1982–84, Glyndebourne Festival in 1983 as Pedrillo in Die Entführung, Deutsche Oper Berlin as Monostatos and Pedrillo; Further appearances in Stuttgart, Amsterdam and Berlin, returned to Glyndebourne, 1984–91, in L'Incoronazione di Poppea, Falstaff, Die Entführung and Carmen; Vienna Staatsoper from 1984 notably in 1986 tour to Japan in Manon Lescaut and Tristan und Isolde; La Scala debut in 1986 as Monostatos; Sang Johannes in the premiere of Der Rattenfänger by Friedrich Cerha, Graz in 1987; Guest engagements at Hamburg as Brighella in Ariadne, Bonn, Zürich as Singer in Rosenkavalier, Strasbourg and Vichy. *Recordings include:* Video of L'Incoronazione di Poppea. *Address:* c/o Staatsoper, Opernring 2, 1010 Vienna, Austria.

**EVANS, Dame Anne;** Singer (soprano); b. 20 Aug. 1941, London, England. *Education:* Royal College of Music, London; Conservatoire de Musique, Geneva. *Career:* Principal Soprano, English National Opera, 1968–78; Debut as Mimi in La Bohème, then Mozart's Fiordiligi, Verdi's Violetta, Strauss's Marschallin, Wagner's Elsa and Sieglinde and Smetana's Mlada; With Welsh National Opera sang Strauss's Chrysothemis, Empress and Dyer's Wife, Beethoven's Leonore, Mozart's Donna Anna; Has sung extensively in Germany, Italy, France and America including Brünnhilde in Berlin, Nice, Paris, Turin, Zürich, Vienna, Buenos Aires and at the 1989–92 Bayreuth Festivals; Isolde in Brussels, 1994, Berlin, 1996, Dresden, 1997 and Paris 1998; Sieglinde in San Francisco; Elsa in Buenos Aires; Leonore in Stuttgart; Made Metropolitan debut with Elisabeth in Tannhäuser in 1992 and returned for Leonore in Fidelio in 1993; Recitals at Edinburgh Festival 1993 and Wigmore Hall, 1995; Sang Brünnhilde in Siegfried, 1995, and Götterdämmerung, 1996 at Covent Garden; Ariadne in Ariadne auf Naxos (original version), Edinburgh Festival, 1997; Madame Lidoine in Les dialogues des Carmélites, Glimmerglass Opera Festival, 2002. *Recordings:* Helmwige and Third Norn in ENO Ring under Goodall; Brünnhilde's Immolation scene; Brünnhilde in Der Ring des Nibelungen from Bayreuth; Mrs Grose in The Turn of the Screw. *Honours:* D.B.E., 2000. *Current Management:* Ingpen & Williams Ltd, 7 St George's Court, 131 Putney Bridge Road, London, SW15 2PA, England.

**EVANS, Damon;** Tenor; b. 1960, Baltimore, MD, USA. *Education:* Studied at the Interlochen Arts Academy on a Reader's Digest Foundation Scholarship. *Career:* Sang Amon in Akhnaten by Philip Glass at the New York City Opera in 1985; Virginia Opera Association in 1985 as Benji in the premiere of Musgrave's Harriet: The Woman Called Moses; Glyndebourne Festival in 1986 as Sportin' Life in Porgy and Bess; Has also sung Sportin' Life at Charleston, Boston, London with Philharmonic Orchestra and Moscow with the Finnish National Opera in 1988; Concert engagements include Beethoven's Ninth and Pulcinella, conducted by Simon Rattle; Bernstein's West Side Story at the Usher Hall in Edinburgh and a Bernstein Celebration at Alice Tully Hall in New York; Sang in the British premiere of Blitzstein's Airborne Symphony with the London Symphony, A Child of Our Time at the City of London Festival and Weill's 3 Concert Suites at the Almeida Festival; Carnegie Hall debut in 1989 in the premiere of a suite from Weill's Lost In The Stars; Has also sung Janáček's Diary of One Who Disappeared with Matrix at the Queen Elizabeth Hall; Sang Don José in Carmen Jones in London, 1991; Sang in Porgy and Bess at Covent Garden in 1992 and in the Weill/Grosz concert at the 1993 London Proms; Sang Sporting Life at Costa Mesa, CA, 1996. *Address:* c/o Opera Pacific, 9 Executive Circle, Suite 190, Irvine, CA 92714, USA.

**EVANS, Edgar;** Opera Singer (Tenor); b. 9 June 1912, Cardiganshire, Wales; m. Nan Walters, 1 s. *Education:* Private study with Dawson Freer, London, and Luigi Ricci, Rome Opera. *Career:* Debut: London, 1947 at Covent Garden in Massenet's Des Grieux; Professor of Singing, Royal College of Music; Founder Member and Principal Tenor, Royal Opera House, from 1946, as Don José, Alfredo, Mussorgsky's Dimitri, Calaf, Captain Vere, Tchaikovsky's Herman and Janáček's Laca; Numerous radio and television programmes; Sang Andres in the British stage premiere of Wozzeck (1952), Števa in the first British Jenůfa (1956) and Helenus in the first Covent Garden Troyens by Berlioz (1957); Narraboth in the Brook/Dali production of Salome and Zinovy in the British premiere of Katerina Izmailova by Shostakovich (1963), Herman in The Queen of Spades; Invited to Covent Garden 2002 as guest at Tchaikovsky's opera, in his 90th year; mem, Incorporated Society of Musicians. *Recordings:* Tristan und Isolde; Albert Herring. *Honours:* Honorary RCM, 1977. *Address:* The White House, 110 Preston Hill, Harrow, Middlesex HA3 9 SJ, England.

**EVANS, (D.) John O.,** BMus, MA, PhD; British broadcaster and musicologist; *Head of Music Programming, BBC Radio 3*; b. 17 Nov. 1953, Morriston, Wales. *Education:* Univ. Coll., Cardiff, Univ. of Wales. *Career:* First Research Scholar, Britten-Pears Library and Archive, Red House, Aldeburgh 1980–85; Music Producer, BBC Radio 3 1985–89, Chief Producer (series) 1992–93, Head of Music Dept 1993–97, Head of Classical Music 1997–2000, Head of Music Programming 2000–; Postgraduate Music Tutor, Univ. Coll., Cardiff 1986–87; Artistic Dir, Volte Face Opera Project 1986–89; Exec. Trustee, Peter Pears Award 1989–92; Artistic Dir, Covent Garden Chamber Orchestra 1990–93; guest lecturer, Nat. Film Theatre, ENO, Fairfield Halls, Croydon, Britten-Pears School, Aldeburgh Festival, Royal Coll. of Music, Goldsmiths' Coll. London, Hull Univ., Camden Festival, Bath Festival, Int. Brown Symposium on Benjamin Britten at Southwestern Univ., Georgetown, TX, USA; Chair., Royal Philharmonic Soc. Awards Opera Jury; juror Int. Conductors' Competition, Lisbon 1995, Kondrashin Conducting Competition 1998, BBC Singer of the World Competition, Cardiff 2003–, Tosti Int. Singing Competition; Dir, Britten Estate; Trustee, Britten Pears Foundation; Chair., Concentric Circles Theatre Bd. *Publications:* Benjamin Britten: Pictures from a Life 1943–1976 (with Donald Mitchell) 1978, Benjamin Britten: his Life and Operas (ed.) 1982; contrib. to A Britten Companion 1984, A Britten Source Book 1987, ENO, Royal Opera and Cambridge Opera Guides on Britten's Peter Grimes, Gloriana, The Turn of the Screw, Death in Venice; articles in magazines, including Opera Quarterly. *Honours:* Prix Italia 1989, Charles Heidsieck Award 1989, Royal Philharmonic Soc. Award 1994, Sony Radio Award 1997, Vienna TV Award 2004. *Address:* Room 4126, Broadcasting House, Portland Place, London, W1A 1AA, England. *Telephone:* (20) 7765-0481 (office). *Fax:* (20) 7765-0546 (office). *Website:* www.bbc.co.uk/radio3 (office).

**EVANS, Joseph;** Singer (Tenor); b. 13 Aug. 1945, Brookhaven, Missouri, USA. *Career:* Sang with the New York City Opera, 1976–, in Les Pêcheurs de Perles, Maria Stuarda, Don Giovanni, The Love of Three Oranges, Attila and La Traviata; Appearances with the Opera Company of Boston in Don Pasquale, Rigoletto, Benvenuto Cellini, War and Peace, I Capuleti e i Montecchi, Ruslan and Lyudmilla, Die Soldaten by Zimmermann, Montezuma by Sessions and Orphée aux Enfers; Has also sung with Houston Grand Opera and with opera companies in San Diego, Palm Beach, Cincinnati, Cleveland, Hawaii, Fort Worth and Colorado; Sang in The Love of Three Oranges in Geneva, The Prodigal Son in Venice, Persephone by Stravinsky at Nancy, and Guidon in Rimsky's Tsar Saltan at La Scala; Season 1988–89 with The Devil and Kate and Marschner's Der Templar und die Jüdin at Wexford; Sang Alwa in Lulu for the Opéra de Nantes, and Max in Der Freischütz for Welsh National Opera; Concert engagements with Bernstein and the New York Philharmonic, Lukas Foss and the Brooklyn Philharmonic and with Julius Rudel and Michael Tilson Thomas; Has also sung with the Pittsburgh, Atlanta and Indianapolis Symphony Orchestras and appeared in concerts with the Orchestre de l'Ile de France; Sang Lucas Wardlaw in Floyd's Passion of Jonathan Wade, Santa Fe, 1996; Sang Captain Vere in Billy Budd at Seattle, 2001. *Address:* Music International, 13 Ardilaun Road, London N5 2QR, England.

**EVANS, Peter;** Singer (Tenor); b. 1962, England. *Education:* Studied at the Royal Northern College of Music and the Royal Scottish Academy. *Career:* South Bank debut as Purcell's Aeneas with the English Chamber Orchestra, 1988; Further concerts with the Bournemouth Sinfonietta, London Bach Orchestra and Royal Liverpool Philharmonic; Repertory has included Elijah, Messiah (at Gdańsk, Poland), Mozart's Requiem (Aix Festival), Purcell's King Arthur with the English Concert and Hindemith's Das Nusch-Nuschi with the BBC Symphony Orchestra, 1995; Sang Monteverdi's Orfeo at the Aldeburgh festival, 1993; First Shepherd with ENO, 1996; Covent Garden Festival as Mozart's Schauspieldirektor and Lurcanio in Handel's Ariodante, 1996–97; Concert venues include the Queen Elizabeth Hall, St John's Smith Square and the Wigmore Hall. *Honours:* NFMS Concert Artists Award, 1987.

**EVANS, Peter Angus;** Musicologist; b. 7 Nov. 1929, West Hartlepool, England. *Education:* Studied with Arthur Hutchings and A E Dickinson at Durham University, 1947–51, BA in 1950; FRCO, 1952; BMus, Durham, 1953; MA, 1953; DMus, 1958. *Career:* Music Master, Bishop Wordsworth's School, Salisbury, 1951–52; Lecturer, Durham University, 1953–61; Professor of Music, Southampton University, 1961–90. *Publications include:* Articles on Britten and Jonathan Harvey in Tempo and The Musical Times; Chapter: The Vocal Works in Michael Tippett: A Symposium, 1965; The Music of Benjamin Britten, 1979; Articles on Britten and Rawsthorne in The New Grove Dictionary of Music and Musicians, 1980; Instrumental Music, chapter in Blackwell History of Music in Britain, 20th century volume, 1995. *Honours:* Honorary Member, Guildhall School of Music, 1998. *Address:* Pye's Nest Cottage, Parkway, Ledbury, Herefordshire HR8 2JD, England.

**EVANS, Peter Geoffrey,** BMus, ARCM; British pianist, teacher and conductor; b. 13 Jan. 1950, Redhill, Surrey, England. *Education:* University of Edinburgh, Hochschule für Musik, Vienna, Austria. *Career:* performances as solo pianist and in various duos and ensembles throughout the United Kingdom, including Aldeburgh and Edinburgh Festivals, London's South Bank and Wigmore Halls, St John's Smith Square, also in Austria, Germany, France, Poland, Ireland, USA, former USSR and Japan, 1974–; Appearances on Scottish, Tyne-Tees and BBC television, including BBC 2 Beethoven cello/piano sonata series; Recordings for French and Swedish Radio and Radio 3; Soloist with all major orchestras in Scotland; Principal Conductor, Edinbur-

gh's Meadows Chamber Orchestra, 1972–; Conducting debut in Spain at Festival of Torroella de Montgri, Catalonia, 1986; Close association with International Musicians Seminar, Cornwall, 1982–93; Masterclasses, Oberlin College, Ohio, USA, 1980, Deal Summer Music Festival, 1985–88; Membership of London-based Premiere Ensemble, 1990–; Artistic Co-Director of Hebrides Ensemble, 1991–2003. *Recordings:* Brahms and Martinů sonatas for cello and piano, with Steven Isserlis, cello; Cello and piano recital, with Alexander Baillie, cello, 1988; Solo piano in Britten's Young Apollo, with Scottish Chamber Orchestra, Serebrier, 1990; Recital of French music for cello and piano; Works by Webern, Lutoslawski and Rachmaninov for cello and piano, with William Conway; Over 70 for BBC, including large number for Radio 3. *Address:* 49 Spottiswoode Road, Edinburgh, EH9 1DA, Scotland. *Telephone:* (131) 4476414. *Fax:* (131) 4476414. *E-mail:* peterevans49@hotmail.com.

**EVANS, Rebecca (Ann);** Singer (Soprano); b. 19 Aug. 1963, Neath, Wales. *Education:* Guildhall School of Music and Drama, London. *Career:* Debut: As Gretel in Hansel and Gretel, Welsh National Opera in 1990; Has appeared in television series, Encore and Rebecca Evans; Roles include Ilia in Idomeneo, Oscar in Un Ballo in Maschera, Inez in La Favorita, the title role in Massenet's Cendrillon, and the Countess in Rossini's Count Ory; Season 1994 as Strauss's Sophie and Berlioz's Hero for Welsh National Opera, Marzelline in Leonore at the Edinburgh Festival; Janáček's Vixen with Scottish Opera, 1997; Season 1998 as Susanna for the Royal Opera, Massenet's Cendrillon at Ghent and Nannetta at the London Proms; Season 2000–01 as Anne Trulove at San Francisco and Sophie at Munich (also Susanna, and Zdenka in Arabella); Sang Zerlina at Covent Garden, 2002, Nannetta in 2003. *Recordings:* Mabel in The Pirates of Penzance; Belinda in Dido and Aeneas; Barbarina in Le nozze di Figaro; Nannetta in Falstaff conducted by John Eliot Gardiner; Italian Song Recital; Delius, Requiem; Finzi, Dies Natalis. *Honours:* Prizewinner, BP Peter Pears, 1990; Young Welsh Singer of the Year, 1991; Honorary Doctorate, University of Glamorgan. *Current Management:* Harlequin Agency Ltd. *Address:* 203 Fidlas Road, Llanishen, Cardiff CF14 5NA, Wales.

**EVANS, Tecwyn;** New Zealand chorus master and conductor; b. 1970, Auckland. *Education:* University of Otago, University of Kansas with Brian Priestman. *Career:* debut, Dunedin Sinfonia, 1997; Led Die Fledermaus for Kansas University Opera; Chorus Master at Glyndebourne Festival, from 1999; Glyndebourne Festival from 2000, with youth opera Zoë, and La Bohème for the Tour; Engagements with Netherlands Radio Choir, and choral workshops in New Zealand, USA and England; Assistant Conductor at Glyndebourne 2001 for Otello (Festival) and Le nozze di Figaro (Tour); Fidelio at the Paris Châtelet, 2000. *Honours:* Fulbright Fellowship.

**EVANS, Wynne;** Singer (Tenor); b. 1972, Carmarthen, Wales; m. Tanwen, 1999, 1 d. *Education:* Studied at the Guildhall School and the National Opera Studio, London. *Career:* Opera performances for Welsh National Opera include Liberto in Poppea, 1997, Tamino in the Magic Flute, 1998, Le Chevalier in Dialogues of the Carmelites, 1999, Alfredo in La Traviata, 2000–01, Rodolfo in La Bohème, 2001, Jaquino in Leonore, 2001, 1st Jew in Salome, 2001, Schoolmaster in The Cunning Little Vixen, 2001 and Alfred in Die Fledermaus, 2002; Roles for Opera North include Fenton in Falstaff, 1999, Prunier in La Rondine, 2000, and Paulino in The Secret Marriage, 2003; Roles for Scottish Opera include Tamino in the Magic Flute, 1998 and the Italian Tenor in Der Rosenkavlier, 1999; Other roles include Peacock in Broken Strings for the Almeida Opera and BBC Radio 3, 1996, Fracasso in La Finta Semplice for the Classical Opera Company, 1999, and Arvino in Lombardi for Chelsea Opera, 2001; Concert work includes Tippett's A Child of Our Time in Besançon; Charpentier's Orphée; Messiah in Handel Hall, Halle, Royal Albert Hall, London and St David's Hall, Cardiff; Verdi Requiem in the Royal Albert Hall, London; Wigmore Hall recital; BBC Proms Debut 2001; Operas for television: Salome & The Little Sweep and Rodolfo in the BBC drama The Beggar Bride. *Address:* c/o Doreen O'Neill, Harlequin Agency Ltd, 203 Fidlas Road, Cardiff CF4 5NA, Wales. *Telephone:* 02920 750821. *E-mail:* wynne@wynneevans.co.uk.

**EVERETT, Paul (Joseph);** Lecturer in Music; b. 6 May 1955, London, England; m. Margaret Mary Bernadette McLoughlin, 21 July 1979, 1 s. *Education:* BMus (Hons), Sheffield University, 1976; PhD, Liverpool University, 1984. *Career:* Lecturer in Music, Liverpool University, 1980–81; Lecturer in Music, University College, Cork, 1981–; mem, RMA. *Publications:* Editor of various modern editions of music by D Purcell, J C Schickhardt, J B Loeillet and several works by Vivaldi for the Istituto Italiano Antonio Vivaldi; Scholarly articles on Italian sources, especially those of Vivaldi's music; The Manchester Concerto Partbooks, 2 vols, 1989. *Contributions:* Music and Letters; Musical Times. *Address:* Music Department, University College, Cork, Ireland.

**EVROVA, Katia (Ekaterina);** Pianist; b. 5 Oct. 1947, Sofia, Bulgaria. *Education:* Diploma of Excellence in Piano and Musical Pedagogy, Bulgarian Superior Conservatoire of Music, Sofia, 1971; Diploma of Excellence in Chamber Music, Debussy Conservatoire, Paris, 1982. *Career:* first appearance with aunt Yova Kallova, teacher of piano, Sofia, 1952; concerts as member of violin and piano duo and trio with piano, 1976–81; concerts as violin and piano duo with Vladimir Lazov, 1983–89, performances including cycle of Schubert sonatas, 1987, cycle of 19 sonatas for piano and violin by Mozart, 1989; concert tours, Europe and Asia; piano teacher, Chaumont, France, 1989; founded the Mezzo-Forte Ensemble (piano, flute, classical guitar) with Franck Douvin and

Gérard Montaudoin, 1989; Piano and Chamber Music Teacher at School of Music, Pays de Langres, 1990; concerts with the Mezzo-Forte Ensemble at Chaumont and 4th European Congress of Jewish Studies, Troyes, 1990; debut, cycle of Mozart works for piano and violin as duo with Svetoslav Marinov, 1990; tours of Brazil and Mexico, 1991, France, 1992, 1993, Brazil, 1993; concerts in France in duo with Svetoslav Marinov, 1994, 1995–; concerts, 1996, and the integral of Beethoven's sonatas for piano and violin, duo with S. Marinov, 1997; concert tour as soloist with Orchestral Ensemble of the Sofia Philharmonia in 1998 at Sofia; concert tours in France as Duo Amadeus 91 (with S. Marinov) at Arc-en-Barrois, 1999, 2002, Chaumont and Joinville, 2000; Concert tour with Vocalys Ensemble in the Rossini's Petite messe solennelle, France, 2003; mem., Former Dramaturgist, Sofia Weeks of Music, Bulgarian International Festival, RBA of ABI. *Address:* 28 rue du Château Paillot, 52000 Chaumont, France.

**EVSTATIEVA, Stefka;** Singer (Soprano); b. 7 May 1947, Rousse, Bulgaria. *Education:* Sofia Conservatoire with Elena Kiselova. *Career:* Member of Rousse Opera, 1971–79; Roles have included Verdi's Amelia, Elisabeth de Valois, Aida and Desdemona, Margarita in Mefistofele, Yaroslavna in Prince Igor, Puccini's Mimi and Suor Angelica; Member of Bulgarian National Opera in Sofia from 1978; Guest appearances in Vienna, Frankfurt, Munich, Hamburg, New York, Berlin, Milan, Verona, Madrid and Paris; Roles include, Leonora in Il Trovatore, Elvira in Ernani, Madeleine de Coigny in Andrea Chénier, Donna Elvira in Don Giovanni and Lisa in Queen of Spades; Royal Opera debut in Manchester as Desdemona in Otello; London 1983 as Elisabeth de Valois; Metropolitan debut in 1983 as Elisabeth de Valois; San Francisco in 1984 and 1986 as Aida; Toronto, 1989–90 as Tosca, Mimi, Leonora in La Forzo del Destino and Desdemona; Appeared at Nimes in 1986 as Medora in the French premiere of Verdi's Il Corsaro; Sang at the Savonlinna Festival in 1990 as Aida; Season 1991–92 as Amelia in Ballo in Maschera at Antwerp, Tosca at Buenos Aires and the Forza Leonora at Florence; Sang Giordano's Maddalena at Buenos Aires, 1996; Elisabeth de Valois at Trieste, 1997; Many engagements as concert singer. *Recordings:* Rimsky-Korsakov's Boyartinya Vera Sheloga and The Maid of Pskov; 2 Recitals of Italian arias. *Address:* c/o San Francisco Opera, War Memorial Opera House, San Francisco, CA 94102, USA.

**EWENS, Craig R. R.;** English pianist and piano teacher; b. 26 March 1966, Wokingham, England. *Education:* Royal Coll. of Music Jr Dept, 1979–84; Guildhall School of Music and Drama, 1984–90. *Career:* debut, St John's Smith Square, London, 1988; many recitals for nat. music socs and in London; solo recitals at St John's Smith Square, Barbican Centre, St Martin in the Fields, St James's Piccadilly, St Bride's Fleet Street, Purcell Room; mem., Incorporated Soc. of Musicians, European Piano Teachers' Asscn; Fellow, Guild of Musicians and Singers. *Recordings:* Prokofiev 2nd Piano Concerto; Beethoven Sonatas op 57, 81a, 109, 110; Mozart Sonata K.457; Chopin Ballades; Schubert Wanderer Fantasy; Schumann Fantasy op 17; Prokofiev Sonatas Nos 2, 3 and 6; Berg Sonata op 1; Liszt Variations on Weinen, Klagen, Sorgen, Zagen; Ravel Scarbo. *Honours:* AGSM, Concert Recital Diploma (Premier Prix) GSMD 1988, Teresa Carreno Memorial Piano Prize 1984. *Address:* Flat 16, Howitt Close, Howitt Road, London NW3 4LX, England. *Telephone:* (20) 7483-4405. *E-mail:* craigewens@onetel.com.

**EWING, Alan;** Singer (Bass); b. 1959, Northern Ireland. *Education:* Read Music at University of East Anglia; Choral Scholar, Norwich Cathedral Choir; Guildhall School of Music with Rudolf Piernay, 1980–84. *Career:* Roles at the Guildhall School of Music include Sarastro, Colline, Bottom, Collatinus in The Rape of Lucretia, and Falstaff in The Merry Wives of Windsor; Has sung widely with Renaissance and Baroque groups, notably with the Consort of Musicke at major festivals in the USA, Australia, Japan, Israel and Europe; Has sung in oratorios throughout Europe and with the 1989 Young Songmakers' Almanac Concert; Appearances in The Rape of Lucretia at the Aldeburgh Festival and as the Voice of Neptune in Idomeneo with Rattle at the Queen Elizabeth Hall; Sang Trulove in The Rake's Progress conducted by John Lubbock and in Kopernicus by Claude Vivier in a Pierre Audi production at the Almeida Festival; Sang Osmin in Die Entführung at the 1991 Buxton Festival; Sang Rocco in Fidelio for Opera Northern Ireland, 1996; Season 1998 as the Priest in The Cunning Little Vixen at Spoleto and Vengeance in Rameau's Zoroastre on tour with Les Arts Florissants; Season 2000–01 in the premiere of Rêves d'un Marco Polo, at Amsterdam, as Handel's Polyphemus at the Salzburg Easter Festival, and as Britten's Collatinus at Florence.

*Recordings:* Various albums with the Consort of Musicke. *Address:* Allied Artists Agency, 42 Montpelier Square, London SW7 1JZ, England.

**EWING, Maria Louise;** American singer (soprano); b. 27 March 1950, Detroit; d. of Norman I. Ewing and Hermina M. Veraar; m. Sir Peter Hall 1982 (divorced 1989); one d. *Education:* Cleveland Inst. of Music. *Career:* début at Metropolitan Opera, New York singing Cherubino in The Marriage of Figaro 1976, closely followed by débuts with major US orchestras including New York Philharmonic and at La Scala Milan; performs regularly at Glyndebourne including the Barber of Seville, L'Incoronazione di Poppea and Carmen; repertoire also includes Pelléas et Mélisande, The Dialogues of the Carmelites, Così fan Tutte, La Perichole, La Cenerentola, The Marriage of Figaro (Susanna); performed Salome, Covent Garden 1988, Carmen, Earl's Court, London 1989, Tosca, Los Angeles 1989, Salome, Washington 1990, Madame Butterfly, Los Angeles, Tosca, Seville, Salome, Covent Garden 1992, Tosca, Los Angeles, Chicago, Salome, San Francisco, The Trojans, Metropolitan New York 1993, Madame Butterfly, Tosca, Vienna, The Trojans, Metropolitan, New York 1993/94; also appears as concert and recital singer; début Promenade Concerts, London 1987, Lady Macbeth of Mtsensk with Metropolitan Opera 1994. *Address:* c/o David Godfrey, Mitchell-Godfrey Management, 48 Gray's Inn Road, London, WC1X 8LT, England (office); c/o Herbert Breslin, 119 West 57th Street, Room 1505, New York, NY 10019, USA. *Telephone:* (20) 7831-3027 (London) (office). *Fax:* (20) 7831-5277 (London) (office). *E-mail:* davidgodfrey@mariaewing.com (office).

**EWINGTON, John,** OBE, MA, ACertCM, DipChMus, FGCM, FGMS; British music director; *General Secretary, Guild of Church Musicians;* b. 14 May 1936, Goodmayes, Essex; m. Hélène Mary Leach; two s. *Education:* South East Essex County Technical School, Lambeth and Goldsmiths' Coll., London. *Career:* nat. service in RN 1954–56; Admin Asst, Inst. of London Underwriters 1953–67; Underwriting Asst, PCW Agencies Lloyd's 1967–86; sr broker, HSBC Gibbs 1986–97; Dir of Music and organist, Blechingley Parish Church 1966–97; Dir of Music, City Singers, London 1968; Dir of Music, St Mary Woolnoth 1970–93; Gen. Sec., Guild of Church Musicians 1979–; organist and Dir of Music, St Katherine Cree, London 1998–; Conjoint Sr Lecturer, Conservatorium School of Music and Drama, Univ. of Newcastle, NSW 2004–; Gov. De Stafford School, Surrey 1979–84; Gov., Oxted School 1984–2005, Vice Chair. 1995–2005; mem. Friday Club, City Livery Club, Lloyds of London Three Rooms Club. *Compositions:* Hillbrow (hymn tune). *Publications:* Landmarks in Christian Worship and Church Music (with Canon Arthur Dobb); contrib. to magazines, journals, Church Times. *Honours:* Freeman City of London 1980, Hon. FFCM 1993, Hon. FCSM 1990, Hon. mem. RSCM 2002, Liveryman Worshipful Co. of Musicians 2001, Hon. Fellow Univ. of Newcastle, NSW 2004; OLJ Order of St Lazarus of Jerusalem 2002. *Address:* Hillbrow, Godstone Road, Blechingley, RH1 4PJ, England (home). *Telephone:* (1883) 743168 (home). *Fax:* (1883) 743168 (home). *E-mail:* JohnMusicsure@orbix.co.uk (office). *Website:* www.churchmusicians.org (office).

**EYSER, Eberhard;** Swedish composer and violist; b. 1 Aug. 1932, Marienwerder, Prussia, Germany. *Education:* Akademie für Musik und Theater, Hanover, Mozarteum, Salzburg, Accademia Chigiana, Siena, Italy. *Career:* violist, Royal Swedish Opera Orchestra. *Compositions:* about 360 works, including chamber and orchestral music, vocal and electronic music, computer music; Operas and chamber operas include Molonn, 1970, The Death of a Bird, 1971, A Man's Dream, 1972, Last Voyage, 1973, King of Hearts, 1973, Abu Said, 1976, Summer's Day, 1979, The Deep Water, 1980, Bermuda Triangle, 1981, Via Gravis, 1981, The Ravens, 1982, Roses and Ruins, 1982, The Last Day on Earth, 1982, The Red Book Mystery, 1984, Twilight in Granada, 1984, It Was Raining Yesterday, 1985, The Picture of Dorian Gray, 1986; The Aspern Papers, 1989; 5 saxophone quartets, orchestral works, Itabol, Metastrophy, Macbeth Overture; Charley McDeath, chamber opera, 1992. *Recordings:* King of Hearts, Last Voyage, The Deep Water, Overture, Circus Overture, Duo 3 G The Bard. *Address:* Karlbergsv 71B, 11335 Stockholm, Sweden. *Telephone:* 46 8308425. *E-mail:* eyser.eb@swipnet.se. *Website:* www.sami.se/art/eyser/home.htm.

**EZZAT, Mohammed Amin;** Iraqi; *Conductor, Baghdad Symphony Orchestra. Compositions include:* Three Fragments. *Address:* Iraqi National Symphony Orchestra, Baghdad Convention Center, Green Zone, Baghdad, Iraq.

# F

**FABBRI, Franca;** Singer (Soprano); b. 28 May 1935, Milan, Italy. *Education:* Studied in Milan with Adelina Fiori, Adelaide Saraceni and Giuseppe Pais. *Career:* Debut: Spoleto in 1963 as Violetta; Has sung widely in Italy and in Berlin, Hamburg, Cologne, Budapest, Warsaw, San Francisco and Aix-en-Provence; Sang in the premieres of L'Idiota and Riva delle Sirti by Chailly, Orfeo Vedevo by Savino and Al Gran Sole Carico d'Amore by Nono, 1975; Repertoire included Lucia di Lammermoor, Musetta, Nedda, Fiordiligi, Gilda, Marguerite de Valois in Les Huguenots, the Queen of Night and Pamira in L'Assedio di Corinto by Rossini; Roles in operas by Britten, Shostakovich, Maderna and Malipiero. *Address:* c/o Conservatorio Giuseppe Verdi, Via del Conservatorio 12, I–20122 Milan, Italy.

**FABBRICINI, Tiziana;** Singer (Soprano); b. 1961, Asti, Piemont, Italy. *Education:* Studied in Milan and other centres in Italy. *Career:* Won various singing competitions, 1982–85, and sang minor roles in provincial Italian opera houses; Made La Scala debut in 1990 as Violetta; Season 1991 in La Traviata at Naples and Elvire in a revival of La Muette di Portici by Auber at Ravenna; Sang Lucia di Lammermoor at La Scala in 1992 and at Houston, 1994, Fiorilla in Il Turco in Italia at the Théâtre des Champs-Elysées, 1996; Sang Tosca at Savona, 1997; Season 1999–2000 at Genoa as Arianna in Nasso, in the opera by Porpora and as Tosca at the Balbeck Festival. *Address:* c/o Théâtre des Champs Elysée, (Artist Contracts), 15 Avenue Montaigne, F–75008 Paris, France.

**FABER, Lothar;** Oboist; b. 7 Feb. 1922, Cologne, Germany. *Education:* Studied at the Cologne Musikhochschule and at the Paris Conservatoire. *Career:* Played with the WDR Orchestra, Cologne, from 1946, and has made many appearances at festivals throughout Europe: Berlin, Venice, Warsaw, Netherlands and Darmstadt; Has premiered works by Maderna, K Mayer, Baird, Fortner, Schuller and Zimmermann; Has given summer courses at Darmstadt and Siena, 1972–77. *Address:* c/o WDR Sinfonie-Orchester, D 50600 Koln, Germany.

**FABIAN, Marta;** Dulcimer Player; b. 1946, Budapest, Hungary. *Education:* Started playing the dulcimer at age 8; Studied at Béla Bartók Conservatory, 1960–64 and Ferenc Liszt Academy of Music, Budapest, 1967. *Career:* Soloist with Budapest Chamber Ensemble; Has made numerous guest performances in Austria, Belgium, Bulgaria, Czechoslovakia, Finland, France, Germany, the United Kingdom, the Netherlands, Italy, Latin America, Mexico, Poland, Russia, Spain, Sweden, Switzerland, Turkey, USA and Yugoslavia and appeared at the Bratislava, Darmstadt, Netherlands, Lucerne, IGNM (SIMC) of Athens and Graz Festivals, Warsaw Autumn Festival of Modern Music, the Witten Festival and the Zagreb Biennial Festival of Modern Music. *Recordings include:* Cimbalom Recital. *Honours:* Grand Prize, French National Record Academy, 1977; Liszt Prize.

**FAERBER, Jorg;** Conductor and Composer; b. 18 June 1929, Stuttgart, Germany. *Education:* Studied at the Hochschule für Musik, Stuttgart. *Career:* Theatre conductor and composer in Stuttgart and Heilbronn, 1952–60; Founded Württemberg Chamber Orchestra, 1960; Tours to Austria, the United Kingdom, France, Italy, USA and South Africa; Many performances in the Baroque repertory; Appearances with the European Community Chamber Orchestra, various BBC Orchestras, the Bournemouth Sinfonietta, the Thames Chamber Orchestra, and the Northern Sinfonia; Festival engagements at Swansea and with the English Bach Festival. *Recordings:* Bach Brandenburg Concertos; Boyce Symphonies; Vivaldi Four Seasons and other concertos; Bassoon Concertos by Weber, Graun, J C Bach, K Stamitz, Boismortier and Mozart; Concertos for cello, clarinet, viola and flute by Stamitz; Trumpet concertos by Torelli, Albinoni, Biber, Stölzel and Manfredini; Mozart piano concertos K413 and K450, violin concertos K218 and K219, flute concertos, Sinfonia Concertante K297b and overtures. *Address:* Postfach 3730, 7100 Heilbronn/Neckar, Germany.

**FAGÉUS, Kjell;** Clarinettist; b. 25 July 1949, Lönneberga, Sweden; m. Lena Fagéus, 23 Aug 1993, 2 s. *Education:* University study in Mathematics, 1 year; Student, 1970–74, Solo Diploma and Pedagogical Examination, 1974, Royal Music Academy, Stockholm; Studied with Stanley Drucker, Juilliard School of Music, New York, 1975–76. *Career:* Debut: Waldemars udde, Stockholm, 1974; Principal Clarinet, Royal Opera, Stockholm, 1976–90; Chamber music and solo performances throughout the world; Coach in Mental Training, Royal Academy, Stockholm, and for professional musicians at SAMI; mem, SYMF; SAMI, Sweden. *Recordings:* 3 albums with Stockholm Wind Quintet; Mozart Clarinet Concerto and Swedish Concertos with Royal Opera Orchestra; Mozart and Brahms Clarinet Quintets. *Publications:* Lek på fullt allvar, 1998. *Contributions:* Visions of Excellence, for International Society for Mental Training and Excellence. *Honours:* Swedish Government Scholarship, 10 years. *Address:* Skvattramstigen 19, 14264 Trångsund, Sweden.

**FAGGIONI, Piero;** Opera Producer; b. 12 Aug. 1936, Carrara, Italy. *Education:* Worked under Jean Vilar and Luchino Visconti in Italy. *Career:* Debut: La Bohème at Venice in 1964; Produced Alceste at La Scala in 1972, La Fanciulla del West in Turin in 1974 and at Covent Garden, Norma at Vienna in 1977, Carmen at Edinburgh in 1977, Macbeth at Salzburg in 1984, Francesca da Rimini at Metropolitan Opera in 1984 and production of Boris Godunov at Barcelona; Staging of Massenet's Don Quichotte seen at Paris

Opéra in 1986, and Florence and Monte Carlo in 1992; Produced Il Trovatore at Covent Garden in 1989; Principal Guest Producer at Covent Garden until 1990; Don Quichotte at the Rome Opera, 1997. *Address:* c/o Teatro dell Opera, Piazza B Gigli 00184 Rome, Italy.

**FAHBERG, Antonia;** Singer (Soprano); b. 19 May 1928, Vienna, Austria. *Education:* Studied at the Vienna Music Academy. *Career:* Sang at Innsbruck from 1950, and Munich from 1952; Opera engagements in Hamburg, Vienna, Brussels and Amsterdam; Radio and television engagements; Noted interpreter of works by Rossini (Stabat Mater), Beethoven (Christ at the Mount of Olives), Bruckner (Te Deum) and Bach. *Recordings include:* St Matthew Passion and Cantatas by Bach; Alexander Balus by Handel; Il Ritorno d'Ulisse and L'Incoronazione di Poppea; Diana in Gluck's Iphigénie en Tauride. *Address:* c/o Bayerische Staatsoper, Postfach 745, 8000 Munich 1, Germany.

**FÄHNDRICH, Walter;** Swiss musician and composer; b. 1 April 1944, Menzingen; one d. *Education:* studied in Lucerne. *Career:* international activities as Viola Player, Composer and Improviser; Solo Concerts; Music Installations, Music For Spaces; Improvisation; Professorship for Improvisation, Basel; Since 1990 organisation of the International Congresses for Improvisation, Lucerne; mem, Schweizerischer Tonkünstler-Verein. *Compositions:* Works for viola solo; Music For Spaces; Musical landscape projects; Chamber music; Electro-acoustic music; Music for radio plays, theatres, ballets. *Recordings:* Viola, ECM; Spaces, UNIT; Music For Spaces, Reihe Cantz; Various radio and television recordings. *Publications:* Improvisation, 1992; Improvisation II, 1994; Improvisation III, 1998; Zur geschichte und gegenwart der Elektronischen Musik, 1999; Improvisation IV, 2001; Improvisation V, 2003; Various publications on Music and Space. *Current Management:* Katherin Fähndrich, Piodina 20, 6614 Brissago, Switzerland.

**FAIRBAIRN, Clive (Stuart);** Conductor; b. 21 April 1946, London, England; m. Nicola Swann, 18 Aug 1979, 1 d. *Education:* Royal Academy of Music, London. *Career:* Debut: St Johns, Smith Square, London, 1977; Principal Conductor, New Mozart Orchestra, 1977–; Principal Conductor, Lindstrom Philharmonic Orchestra, 1984–; Guest appearances include London Symphony Orchestra, London Philharmonic, Philharmonia, and Wren Orchestra; Has broadcast with New Mozart Orchestra, London Symphony Orchestra, and Wren Orchestra; Conducted in Germany, Switzerland, Turkey and Portugal; mem, Incorporated Society of Musicians.

**FALCON, Ruth;** singer (soprano); b. 2 Nov. 1946, Residence, LA, USA. *Education:* studies in New Orleans, and Italy with Tito Gobbi and Luigi Ricci. *Career:* debut, New York City Opera in 1974 as Micaela in Carmen; Title role in Mayr's Medea in Corinto, Bern, 1975; Bayerische Staatsoper Munich, 1976–80 as Leonora in Trovatore and La Forza del Destino, and Mozart's Countess and Elettra; Guest artist in New York, Canada, Germany and France as Puccini's Manon Lescaut and Weber's Agathe; Paris Opéra debut in 1981 as Mozart's Donna Anna; Covent Garden and Vienna Staatsoper in 1983 as the Trovatore Leonora; Sang Anna Bolena at Nice in 1985; Nancy Opéra in 1986 as Norma; Aix-en-Provence Festival as Ariadne; Covent Garden in 1987 and Metropolitan in 1989 as the Empress in Die Frau ohne Schatten; Buenos Aires 1993 as Turandot; Sang the Trovatore Leonora at New Orleans, 1997; Concert repertory includes Mahler's 8th Symphony, Beethoven's Missa Solemnis, Verdi's Requiem and works by Handel, Mozart, Brahms, Dvořák and Strauss. *Recordings include:* Die Walküre; Götterdämmerung. *Current Management:* Robert Gilder & Co., Enterprise House, 59–65 Upper Ground, London, SE1 9PQ, England. *Telephone:* (20) 7928-9008. *Fax:* (20) 7928-9755. *E-mail:* rgilder@robert-gilder.com.

**FALEWICZ, Magdalena;** Singer (Soprano); b. 11 Feb. 1946, Lublin, Poland. *Education:* Studied at the Warsaw Conservatory with Olga Olgina and Maria Kuninska-Opacka. *Career:* Member of the Warsaw Chamber Opera, 1971–72; Solo debut as Oscar in Un Ballo in Maschera at the Komische Oper Berlin in 1973; Sang Madama Butterfly with Welsh National Opera in 1978 and for ENO at the London Coliseum in 1986; Member of the Staatsoper Berlin from 1984 with guest appearances in Frankfurt and Leipzig, and in the USA, Bulgaria, Finland and Netherlands; Dresden Staatsoper in 1985 as the Countess in the premiere of Siegfried Matthus' Weise von Liebe und Tod des Comten Christoph Rilke; Mozart's Countess at Dresden, 1988. *Recordings include:* Schubert's Alfonso und Estrella; Amor in Gluck's Orfeo ed Euridice; Die Kluge by Orff. *Address:* c/o Deutsche Staatsoper, Unter den Linden, 1086 Berlin, Germany.

**FALIK, Yuri Aleksandrovich;** Russian composer and conductor; b. 30 July 1936, Odessa; s. of Aleksander Yefimovich Falik and Yevgeniya Mikhailovna Bochko; m. Valentina Alexandrovna Papkova; one s. one d. *Education:* Odessa Specialized School, Leningrad State Conservatory as cellist (teachers A. Shtrimer and M. Rostropovich), as composer (B. Arapov). *Career:* teacher Leningrad (now St Petersburg) Conservatory 1965–88, Prof. of Composition and Instrumentation 1988–; toured as conductor with orchestras in Russia and USA. *Compositions:* for musical theatre: Orestea (choreographic tragedy) 1968, Scapin Antics (opera) 1981; for symphony orchestra: Symphony No. 1 1963, No. 2 (Kaddish) 1993, Light Symphony 1971, Concertos 1967, 1977, Mass over Igor Stravinsky 1975, Symphonietta for strings 1984, Canto in memoria for orchestra 2004; for instruments with orchestra: Concertino for oboe 1961, Violin Concerto 1971, Chamber Concerto for three flutes 1983, Concertino for bassoon 1987, Concerto della Passione for cello 1988, Lyrical Concertino for cello and orchestra 2002; vocal-symphony works: Five Poems by Anna Akhmatova for soprano and chamber orchestra 1978, Ringaday for mezzo-soprano and orchestra 1986, Polly and Dinosaurs (musical fairy-tale over Geraldine Freund) 1989, Mass 1996; works for choir a cappella, including Liturgy Chants 1992; chamber ensembles, including, "Buffoons", a Concerto for Winds and Percussion 1966, 8 Quartets 1955–2001, Brass quintet 2003; romances, instrumental pieces; 4 Concertos for chorus a capella 1979–98, Elegies: Concerto for soprano solo and chorus a capella 2001. *Honours:* First Prize Int. Cellists Competition Helsinki 1962, Merited Worker of Arts of Russia 1981, People's Artist of Russia 2002. *Address:* Finlyandsky prospekt 1, Apt 54, 194044 St Petersburg, Russia. *Telephone:* (812) 542-63-06 (home). *Fax:* (812) 311-58-11 (home). *E-mail:* afalik2000@mail.ru (home).

**FALKMAN, Carl Johan;** Singer (Baritone); b. 24 July 1947, Stockholm, Sweden. *Education:* Studied in Stockholm, and with Gino Bechi in Florence. *Career:* Debut: Stockholm, 1973, in the premiere of Werle's Tintomara; Drottningholm Festival from 1973, as Guglielmo, Pacuvio in Kraus's Proserpina; Guest engagements in Scandinavia and elsewhere as Dandini in La Cenerentola, Mozart's Figaro and Masetto, Eugene Onegin and Marcello; Don Giovanni at the Prague bicentenary performances, Prague, 1987; Grétry's Zémire et Azor at Drottningholm, 1993; Sang Wozzeck and Papageno at the Royal Opera Stockholm, 2000. *Address:* c/o Drottningholms Slottstheater, PO Box 270505, 10251 Stockholm, Sweden.

**FALLETTA, JoAnn;** Conductor; b. 27 Feb. 1954, New York, NY, USA. *Education:* Studied at Juilliard, Queens College and Mannes College. *Career:* Soloist with orchestras on classical guitar, lute, mandolin; Has conducted leading orchestras at Denver, Indianapolis, Phoenix, St Paul, Richmond, Toledo, Tucson and Columbus; European engagements in Italy, France, Switzerland and Denmark; Music Director of the Long Beach Symphony Orchestra, 1989; Music Director of the Virginia Symphony Orchestra, 1991, with guest appearances with the Symphony Orchestras of San Francisco, Savannah, Delaware, Hamilton and Antwerp; German debut with the Mannheim National Theatre Orchestra, in works by Barber, Gershwin and Brahms; Music Director of the Buffalo Philharmonic, 1998–. *Honours:* Winner of Stokowski, 1985, Toscanini, 1985, and Bruno Walter Awards, 1982–87. *Current Management:* ICM Artists. *Address:* 40 West 57th Street, New York, NY 10019, USA.

**FALLOWS, David Nicholas,** BA, MMus, PhD, FBA; British musicologist; *Professor of Music, University of Manchester*; b. 20 Dec. 1945, Buxton, England; m. Paulène Oliver 1976 (separated); one s. one d. *Education:* Jesus Coll., Cambridge, King's Coll., London, Univ. of California at Berkeley. *Career:* Asst, Studio der Frühen Musik, Munich 1967–70; Lecturer in Music, Univ. of Wisconsin at Madison 1973–74; Lecturer in Music, Univ. of Manchester 1976–82, Sr Lecturer 1982–92, Reader in Music 1992–97, Prof. of Music 1997–; Reviews Ed., Early Music 1976–95, 1999–2000; Visiting Assoc. Prof., Univ. of N Carolina at Chapel Hill 1982–83; founder and Gen. Ed., Royal Musical Assn Monographs 1982–98; Visiting Prof. of Musicology, École Normale Supérieure, Paris 1993; corresponding mem. American Musicological Soc. 1999–; mem. Int. Musicological Soc. (vice-pres. 1997–2002, pres. 2002–(07)), Royal Musical Assn (vice-pres. 2000–). *Publications:* Dufay 1982, Chansonnier de Jean de Montchenu (co-author) 1991, Companion to Medieval and Renaissance Music (ed. with T. Knighton) 1992, The Songs of Guillaume Dufay 1995, Oxford Bodleian Library MS Canon Misc. 213: Late Medieval and Early Renaissance Music in Facsimile, Vol. 1 (ed.) 1995, Songs and Musicians in the Fifteenth Century 1996, The Songbook of Fridolin Sicher 1996, A Catalogue of Polyphonic Songs 1415–1480 1999; contrib. to reference works, scholarly books and professional journals, including Gramophone, The Guardian, Early Music, New Grove Dictionary of Music and Musicians 1980, 2001. *Honours:* Ingolf Dahl Prize in Musicology 1971, Dent Medal 1982; Chevalier, Ordre des Arts et des Lettres 1994. *Address:* 10 Chatham Road, Manchester, M16 0DR, England. *E-mail:* david.fallows@man.ac.uk.

**FALVAY, Attila;** Violinist; b. 7 Sept. 1958, Budapest, Hungary; m. Maria Farnadi, 28 June 1983, two d. *Education:* Liszt Ferenc Academy of Music, Budapest with Professor Semyon Snitkowsky and Vienna Music Academy with Professor Josef Sivo. *Career:* 1st Violinist of Kodály Quartet, 1980–; Leader of Budapest Symphony Orchestra, 1989–. *Recordings include:* Complete Haydn Quartets; Complete Beethoven Quartets; Complete Schubert Quartets; Ravel; Debussy; d'Indy Quartets 1,2; Schumann; Brahms Piano Quintet; Schubert Forellen QUintet; Hofstetter Quartets 1–6; Mozart; Brahms Clarinet Quintet; Kodály Quartets 1,2; Mendelssohn Octet; Motzart Horn Quintet; Oboe Quartet; Musical Joke. *Honours:* Szigeti Competition, Budapest 2nd Prize 1978, Hubay Prize, 1980, Merited Artist of Hungary 1990; Bartók-Pásztory Prize 1996. *Address:* 1121 Budapest, Kázmér utca 40, 1121, Budapest, Hungary. *E-mail:* falvay@axelero.hu. *Website:* www.kodalyquartet .org.

**FALVO, Robert;** Percussionist; b. 27 Aug. 1963, New York City, USA. *Education:* BM, Music Education, Performer's Certificate, State University of New York, Fredonia, 1985; MM, Percussion Performance, 1987; DMA, Percussion Performance, Manhattan School of Music; Studied with Fred Hinger, Christopher Lamb, James Presiss, Claire Heldrich, Lynn Harbold, and Theodore Frazeur among others. *Career:* Performances with The New

Music Consort, New York City, 1987–, NOA, Carnegie Hall, New York City, 1988–, English Chamber Orchestra with US tour in 1988, Pierre Boulez and the Scotia Festival Orchestra, Nova Scotia, Canada, 1991, Frick Hawkins Dance Company Orchestra with tour to Tokyo, Shanghai, Hong Kong and throughout USA, 1991–, and Tokyo Symphony with world tour in 1991; Has also appeared with Erie Chamber Orchestra, Hudson Valley Symphony Orchestra, and New Music Orchestral Project; Xylophone Soloist with Fredonia Symphony Orchestra; Many contemporary music recitals in New York area including Carnegie Hall, Merkin Hall, Miller Hall, Hubbard Hall and Town Hall; Has conducted the Manhattan School of Music Contemporary and Percussion Ensembles; Frequent lectures on contemporary composition techniques for percussion instruments; Assistant Professor of Music, teaching percussion at School of Music, Appalachian State University in North Carolina. *Recordings:* Various. *Address:* PO Box 368 DTS, Boone, NC 28607, USA.

**FANDREY, Birgit;** Singer (Soprano); b. 1963, Vorpommern, Germany. *Education:* Studied at the Carl Maria von Weber Musikhochschule in Dresden. *Career:* Associated with the Opera Studio of the Dresden Staatsoper, then appeared with the main company from 1987 notably as Mozart's Susanna, Papagena, Pamina and Zerlina, Euridice, Mimi, Gretel, Sophie Scholl in Udo Zimmermann's Die Weisse Rose and in parts in operas by Siegfried Matthus; Sang Handel's Galatea at the Halle Festival in 1987, Amor in Orfeo ed Euridice at the Leipzig Gewandhaus, Mozart's Constanze at Amsterdam and Pamina at St Gallen; Constanze at Munich, 1993; Lieder recitals in works by Schubert, Schumann, Brahms and Strauss; Concert repertoire includes Beethoven's Mass in C at Amsterdam Concertgebouw, Bach's St John Passion, Messiah and Mozart's Exsultate Jubilate. *Address:* c/o Dresden Staatsoper, 8012 Dresden, Germany.

**FANNING, David John,** BMus, PhD, GNCM; Academic and concert pianist; *Professor of Music, Manchester University*; b. 5 March 1955, Reading, Berkshire, England; m. 1st 26 July 1975 (divorced 1994), 1 s., 2nd 1994 (divorced 2004). *Education:* Manchester Univ., Royal Northern Coll. of Music 1973–77. *Career:* fmr Reader Manchester Univ., now Prof. of Music 2004–; mem. Royal Musical Assn. *Publications:* The Breath of the Symphonist: Shostakovich's Tenth 1988, Carl Nielsen Symphony No. 5 1997, Shostakovich: String Quartet No. 8 2004. *Contributions:* Gramophone, Music and Letters, The Daily Telegraph, The Musical Times. *Address:* c/o School of Music and Drama, Coupland Street, Manchester M13 9PL, England. *Telephone:* (161) 275-4989. *Fax:* (161) 275-4994. *E-mail:* david.fanning@manchester.ac.uk. *Website:* www.arts.manchester.ac.uk/subjectareas/music/academicstaff/ davidfanning.

**FANSHAWE, David Arthur;** British composer, explorer, sound recordist and ethnomusicologist, writer, photographer and record producer; b. 19 April 1942, Paignton, Devon, England; m. 1st Judith Grant 1971; one s. one d.; m. 2nd Jane Bishop 1986; one d. *Education:* St George's Choir School, Stowe, Royal College of Music. *Career:* debut as composer and cantor soloist, Queen Elizabeth Hall, London 1970; composer for BBC, ITV, British Film Inst., documentaries, feature films and private commissions; multi-media presenter on indigenous and traditional music and own compositions 'One World One Music', active promoter and participant in concerts of own works world-wide; researcher and founder of The Fanshawe Collections 1965–94, with 3,000 tapes of traditional music from Arabia, Africa South-East Asia and the Pacific; publishing, copying and cataloguing The Pacific Collections, establishing The World Music Foundation, completing major work, Pacific Odyssey for world premiere at Sydney Opera House; BBC autobiographical documentaries include African Sanctus, Musical Mariner and Tropical Beat. *Compositions include:* African Sanctus, Dover Castle, Requiem For The Children Of Aberfan, The Clowns' Concerto, Arabian Fantasy, The Awakening;. *Television music includes:* When the Boat Comes In (BBC), Tarka the Otter, Flambard (ITV). *Recordings include:* African Sanctus, Dona Nobis Pacem, Salaams; ethnic compilations include Music of the River Nile, Spirit of Polynesia, Micronesia and Melanesia, Music of the South Pacific, Music of Kenya Tanzania, Music of Thailand and Laos, Heiva I Tahiti, Pacific Chants; contribs to many other albums. *Address:* PO Box 574, Marlborough, Wiltshire SN8 2SP, England. *E-mail:* music@fanshawe.com.

**FARBACH, Kent;** Composer; b. 2 Aug. 1961, Southport, Queensland, Australia. *Education:* BMus, 1989, MMus, 1995, Queensland Conservatory. *Career:* Senior Teacher, Forte Music School; Queensland Conservatory, 1992–. *Compositions include:* Mini Overture with Fanfares, for brass Septet and organ, 1989; Beneath the Forest Canopy, for ensemble, 1989; Life Stratum for orchestra, 1990; Tears for string orchestra, 1991; 1845: An Irish Elegy, for orchestra, 1992; From Quiet Places, for violin, cello, flute, clarinet, wind chimes, percussion and piano, 1993; Into the Landscape, for orchestra, 1994; Commissions from the Melbourne and Sydney Symphony Orchestras (1992), Queensland Symphony Orchestra (1994) and Sydney Philharmonia Choir (1995). *Honours:* Adelaide Chamber Orchestra Prize, 1992. *Address:* c/o APRA, 1A Eden Street, Crows Nest, NSW 2065, Australia.

**FARBERMAN, Harold;** Conductor and Composer; b. 2 Nov. 1929, New York City, USA; m. Corinne Curry, 22 June 1958, 1 s., 1 d. *Education:* Scholarship student, diploma, Juilliard School of Music, NY, 1951; BS, 1956, MS, 1957, New England Conservatory of Music, Boston. *Career:* Percussionist, Boston Symphony Orchestra, 1951–63; Conductor, New Arts Orchestra, Boston, 1955–63, Colorado Springs Philharmonic Orchestra, 1967–68, Oakland

Symphony Orchestra, CA, 1971–79; Principal Guest Conductor, Bournemouth Sinfonietta, 1986–; Founder, First President, Conductors' Guild, 1975; Founder, Conductors' Institute, University of West Virginia, 1980, relocated to University of South Carolina in 1987. *Compositions include:* Opera: Medea, 1960–61; Mixed-Media, If Music Be, 1965; Ballets, film scores; Orchestral: Concerto for bassoon and strings, 1965; Timpani Concerto, 1958; Concerto for alto saxophone and strings, 1965; Violin Concerto, 1976; War Cry on a Prayer Feather, 1976; Shapings for English horn, strings and percussion, 1984; Concerto for cello and orchestra, 1998–99; Chamber: Variations for percussion and piano, 1954, Music Inn Suite for 6 percussion, 1958, Quintessence for woodwind quintet, 1962, Images for 5 brass, 1964, Alea for 6 percussion, 1976; Concerto for flute and chamber orchestra, 1996; Little Boy and the Tree Branch, 1998. Vocal works. *Recordings include:* Symphonies by Mozart, Schumann and Beethoven; Bartók's Divertimento and Sonata for two pianos and percussion; Schoenberg/Handel Concerto; Bassoon Concertos by Weber and Hummel; Mahler, 1, 2, 4, 5, 6, 10; 22 Michael Haydn Symphonies; Glière No. 3, Bournemouth Symphonietta. *Publications include:* The Art of Conducting Technique: A New Perspective, 1997. *Honours:* Winner Belgium's St Helena award for best recording of the year. *Address:* 176 E 71st Street 7C, New York, NY 10021, USA.

**FARINA, Franco;** Singer (Tenor); b. 1957, Connecticut, USA. *Career:* Sang widely in opera in USA from 1986; Tamino at Cincinnati, Pinkerton at Pittsburgh (1989); Houston, Chicago and New Orleans; European engagements at the Paris Opéra (Pollione in Norma at the Bastille, 1996), Glyndebourne (Stravinsky's Tom Rakewell, 1989) and Frankfurt (Duke of Mantua, 1990); Metropolitan Opera from 1990 as Rodolfo, Alfredo and Pinkerton (1995); Toulouse, 1993, as Lensky in Eugene Onegin, Deutsche Oper Berlin, 1995, as Riccardo; Season 1998 as Manrico at Geneva, Cavaradossi in Cincinnati and Carlo in Verdi's Masnadieri for the Royal Opera at Baden-Baden, Edinburgh and Savonlinna; Cavaradossi at the NY Met, 2002; Season 2002–03 as Carlo in I Masnadieri at Covent Garden, Manrico at the Met, Radames at Barcelona and Gabriele Adorno for the Vienna Staatsoper. Concerts include the Verdi Requiem and Beethoven's Missa Solemnis. *Address:* Metropolitan Opera, Lincoln Center, New York, NY 10023, USA.

**FARKAS, Andras;** Conductor; b. 14 April 1945, Budapest; m. Francoise Viquerat, 23 June 1973, 1 s., 1 d. *Education:* Béla Bartók Academy, Budapest; Franz Liszt Academy, Budapest; Orchestra conducting with Hans Swarowsky, and horn at Akademie für Musik und Darstellende Kunst, Vienna. *Career:* Debut: Budapest, 1973; Settled in Switzerland in 1974 and performed in concerts throughout Europe; Invited Conductor, Orchestra of Hungarian Radio, Budapest Philharmonic, Orchestre de la Suisse Romande, Orchestre de Chamber de Lausanne, Orchestra of Slovakian Radio, Bratislava, Orchestra of Pilzn Radio, and Orchestre de Seville; Artistic Director and Founder, Nouvel Orchestre de Montreux, 1987; mem, Swiss Musicians Association; Centre Europeen de la Culture, Geneva. *Recordings:* Several for Hungarian and Swiss television and radio. *Contributions:* Swiss Musical Review, 1975–77. *Honours:* Vermeil Medal, Arts, Sciences et Lettres, Paris, 1990. *Address:* Chemin des Bouvreuils 12. 1009 Pully, Switzerland.

**FARKAS, Andrew,** BA, MLS; American librarian and educator; *Library Director Emeritus, University of North Florida;* b. 7 April 1936, Budapest, Hungary; m. (divorced). *Education:* Eötvös Lóránd Univ. of Law, Budapest, Occidental Coll., Los Angeles, Univ. of California, Berkeley. *Career:* Gift and Exchange Librarian, Chief Bibliographer and Asst Head, Acquisitions Dept, Univ. of California, Davis 1962–67; Music Ed. Daily Democrat, Woodland, Calif. 1965–67; Asst Man. Walter J. Johnson, Inc., New York 1967–70; Dir of Libraries and Prof. of Library Science, Univ. of N Florida, Jacksonville 1970–2003, Distinguished Prof. 1991, Library Dir Emer. 2003–; Contributing Ed., The Opera Quarterly 1993–; mem. American Library Asscn. *Publications:* Advisory Ed.: 42-vol. series, Opera Biographies 1977, Series Ed. 1989–; Titta Ruffo – An Anthology 1984, Opera and Concert Singers – An Annotated International Bibliography 1985, Lawrence Tibbett, Singing Actor (ed.) 1989, Enrico Caruso – My Father and My Family (co-author with Enrico Caruso, Jr) 1990, Jussi (co-author with Anna-Lisa Björling) 1996, Librarians' Calendar and Pocket Reference (annual) 1984–; adviser and contrib. to International Dictionary of Opera 1993. *Address:* Library Director Emeritus, University of North Florida, 4567 St John's Bluff Road South, Jacksonville, FL 32224, USA. *Telephone:* (904) 620-2554 (office). *Fax:* (904) 620-2719 (office). *E-mail:* afarkas@unf.edu (office).

**FARKAS, Katalin;** Singer (Soprano); b. 5 Jan. 1954, Budapest, Hungary. *Education:* Studied in Budapest. *Career:* Has sung at the Hungarian State Opera from 1982 as Rosina, Sophie (Werther), Sophie (Der Rosenkavalier), Mozart's Blondchen, Belinda, Nannetta (Falstaff), Oscar, Norina and Flotow's Martha; Glyndebourne Festival debut in 1985 as Zdenka in Arabella; Season 1986–87 in Liszt's Don Sanche at Naples and Amaryllis in Il Pastor Fido at the Göttingen Festival; Other roles include Beethoven's Marzelline, Donizetti's Gianetta (L'Elisir d'amore) and Serafina (Il Campanello), Zerbinetta; Göttingen 1990 in Handel's Floridante. *Recordings include:* World premiere recordings with Hungaroton; Handel: Terpsicore-Erato (conductor Nicholas McGegan, with Derek Lee Ragin); Handel: Atalanta, title role (conductor Nicholas McGegan); Telemann: Der geduldige Socrates-Erato (conductor Nicholas McGegan, with Paul Esswood, Guy de Mey); Don Sanche (Liszt, under Tamás Pál); Other important recorded roles are Serpina (Pergolesi: La serva padrona); Amarilli (Handel: Il pastor fido, also with Esswood and

McGegan). *Address:* Hungarian State Opera House, Andrassy ut 22, 1061 Budapest, Hungary.

**FARLEY, Carole,** MusB; American singer (soprano); b. 29 Nov. 1946, Le Mars, IA; d. of Melvin Farley and Irene Farley (née Reid); m. José Serebrier 1969; one d. *Education:* Indiana Univ. and Hochschule für Musik, Munich (Fulbright Scholar). *Career:* operatic début in USA in title role of La Belle Hélène, New York City Opera 1969; début at Metropolitan Opera as Lulu 1977; now appears regularly in leading opera houses of the world and in concert performances with major orchestras in USA and Europe; Metropolitan Opera première of Shostakovich's Lady Macbeth of Mitzensk (Katerina Ismailova); Wozzeck (Marie), Toulouse Opera. *Recordings include:* Le Pré aux Clercs, Behold the Sun, French songs by Chausson, Duparc, Satie and Fauré, Prokofiev songs, Poulenc's The Human Voice, Menotti's The Telephone, Britten's Les Illuminations, Prokofiev's The Ugly Duckling, Kurt Weill songs, Milhaud songs (with John Constable), Tchaikovsky opera arias, Delius songs with orchestra, Les Soldats Morts 1995 (Grand Prix du Disque), Grieg songs with orchestra, Ned Rorem Songs with Ned Rorem, Piano, Der Wampyr by Marschner. *Roles include:* Monteverdi's Poppea, Massenet's Manon, Mozart's Idomeneo, Verdi's La Traviata, Offenbach's Tales of Hoffmann and Strauss's Salome, Shostakovich's Lady Macbeth of Mtsensk, Wagner's Parsifal; (videos) Poulenc's La Voix Humaine, Menotti's The Telephone, Strauss's Four Last Songs and Songs with orchestra; mem. American Guild of Musical Artists; several awards and prizes including Grand Prix du Disque 1995 for Les Soldats Morts (by A. Lemeland) and Diapason d'Or (France) 1997. *Honours:* numerous prizes and awards. *Current Management:* Robert Lombardo Associates, Suite 6F, 61 W 62nd Street, New York, NY 10023, USA. *Telephone:* (212) 586-4453. *Fax:* (212) 581-5771. *Website:* www.rlombardo.com. *Address:* 20 Queen's Gate Gardens, London, SW7 5LZ, England; 270 Riverside Drive, New York, NY 10025, USA (home). *E-mail:* caspi123@aol.com (home).

**FARMAN, Raphaëlle;** Singer (soprano); b. 1965, France. *Education:* Paris Conservatoire, 1985–1990; Opera School of the Opéra Bastille, 1990–92. *Career:* Debut: Mozart's Susanna, 1989; Gilda in Rigoletto and Bellini's Elvira for Radio France; Appearances in The Queen of Spades and Carmen (as Frasquita) at the Opéra Bastille; Arminta in La Finta Giardiniera at Nantes, Gluck's Euridice at Lille, Mozart's Countess in Rennes, Poulenc's Blanche in St Etienne, and Micaela for Opera La Havana, Cuba (2001); British debut as Massenet's Esclarmonde, for Chelsea Opera Group, London; Engagements as Offenbach's Antonia, and the Countess, at Tours, Anna in La Dame Blanche, Poulenc's Thérèse and Donna Anna for the Opéra Comique, Paris; Season 2001–2002 as Venus in Cherubini's Anacreon in Venice, Donna Anna at Toulon, and Mozart's Sandrina at the Opéra Comique; Concerts with Armin Jordan, Charles Dutoit, Michel Plasson and Myung Whun Chung. *Current Management:* Athole Still International Management, Forresters Hall, 25–27 Westow Street, London, SE19 3RY, England. *Telephone:* (20) 8771-5271. *Fax:* (20) 8768-6600. *Website:* www.atholestill.com.

**FARNCOMBE, Charles Frederick;** Conductor; b. 29 July 1919, London, England; m. Sally Mae Felps, 23 May 1963, 1 d. *Education:* BSc in Engineering, London University, 1940; Royal School of Church Music, 1947–48; Royal Academy of Music, 1948–51; LRAM, 1952. *Career:* Musical Director, Handel Opera Society, 1955–85; Conducted first modern British performances of Rinaldo, Alcina and Deidamia, Rodelinda, Radamisto, Riccardo Primo, Scipione, Ottone, Atalanta, Ariodante, Ezio, Giustino and Rodrigo; Artistic Director Llantilio Crossenny Festival, 1962–; Chief Conductor, Royal Court Theatre, Drottningholm, Sweden, 1970–79; Guest Conductor, London Chamber Opera, 1974–; Chief Guest Conductor of Badisches Staatstheater, Karlsruhe, 1979–95; Musical Director, London Chamber Opera, 1983–95; Musical Director, Malcolm Sargent Festival Choir, 1986–; Guest Conductor Komische Oper in Berlin, 1995–98; Artistic Director Madley Festival, 1996–; Fellow, Royal Swedish Academy, 1972. *Recordings:* Rameau's Castor and Pollux; Great Handel Choruses; Drottningholm Music; Handel's Rodrigo; Handel Highlights, 1993. *Honours:* Royal Gold Medal of Drottningholm, 1971; C.B.E., 1977; Order of the Royal Northern Star, Sweden, 1982; Gold Medal from the Handel Academy in Karlsruhe, 1992. *Current Management:* Werner Kühnly, Wörthstrasse 31, 70563 Stuttgart, Germany. *Address:* 32 Trinity Court, 170A Gloucester Terrace, London W2 6HS, England. *Telephone:* (711) 7802764 (office). *Fax:* (711) 7804403 (home). *E-mail:* kuehnly@aol.com (office).

**FARNES, Richard;** British conductor; *Music Director, Opera North;* b. 1964, England. *Education:* King's Coll., Cambridge, Nat. Opera Studio, Royal Acad. of Music, Guildhall School. *Career:* music staff, Glyndebourne and with Scottish Opera and Opera Factory; English Touring Opera with Falstaff, La Bohème and The Barber of Seville; Gloriana, Figaro, Giovanna D'Arco, La Traviata, The Nightingale's to Blame (Simon Holt) and The Secret Marriage for Opera North; Bastien und Bastienne and La Serva Padrona for European Chamber Opera; Macbeth for City of Birmingham Touring Opera; season 1997–98 with The Makropulos Case at Glyndebourne, Die Entführung, Figaro and La Bohème for Glyndebourne Touring Opera; The Magic Flute, Param Vir double bill and world premiere of David Horne's Friend of the People for Scottish Opera 1999; also Nabucco for New Israeli Opera, Tel-Aviv, Albert Herring at Guildhall School 1998 and The Rake's Progress in Dublin 1999; founded Equinox 1992, for the performance of modern chamber ensemble pieces; Music Dir, Opera North 2004–. *Honours:* RAM Henry Wood and Philharmonia Chorus conducting scholarships. *Address:* Opera North, Grand

Theatre, 46 New Briggate, Leeds, LS1 6NU, England. *Website:* www .operanorth.co.uk.

**FARNON, David Graham,** MA, DipMus; composer, conductor and producer; b. 12 Oct. 1956, London, England; m. Susie Best 1989; two s. *Education:* Univ. of Cambridge, Royal Academy of Music, Royal College of Music, Trinity College of Music, London. *Career:* performances at The Barbican, Royal Festival Hall, London Palladium, the Queen Elizabeth Hall with orchestras including, London Symphony Orchestra and London Philharmonic Orchestra; numerous television and radio appearances. *Compositions:* approximately 400 for KPM, Chappell, Carlin, Destiny and Kanda Music Libraries; 2 Pieces for Orchestra, 1980; Overture: London By Day, 1981; Musical, Songs for Loving Swingers, 1991; Beyond The Furthest Star, for the Royal Choral Society, 1993; Pastourelle for violin and orchestra, 1993; 10 Pieces for wind band, 1989–94; 30 Pieces for woodwind ensemble, 1988–94; Various shows, television and radio commissions. *Recordings:* Conducting with the Royal Philharmonic Orchestra, including Holst, Elgar, Strauss, Albinoni and various operatic arias; First performance of Robert Farnon's Piano Concerto, Cascades to the Sea, with the Bratislava Radio Symphony Orchestra. *Address:* Les Villets Farm, Les Villets, Forest, Guernsey GY8 0HP. *Telephone:* (1481) 265712. *E-mail:* david@farnon.co.uk.

**FARQUHAR, David (Andross);** New Zealand composer; b. 5 April 1928, Cambridge, NZ; m. Raydia d'Elsa 1954; one s. one d. *Education:* BMus, Univ. of NZ; MA, Cambridge Univ.; Guildhall School of Music. *Career:* Lecturer, 1953–; Prof. of Music, Victoria Univ. of Wellington, NZ 1976–93; Founding Pres. and mem. Composers Asscn of NZ; mem. Bd NZ Music Centre. *Compositions:* And One Makes Ten; Anniversary Duets, (2 sets); Concertino for piano and strings; Evocation; Suite for guitar; Five Scenes for guitar; On Your Own; Partita; Ring Round the Moon, dance suite; Three Pieces for double bass; Three Scots Ballads; Concerto for Wind Quintet; Three Pieces for Violin and Piano; Three Improvisations; Six Songs of Women; Three Songs of Cilla McQueen; Eight Blake Songs; Three Echoes, String Quartets Nos 1, 2, and 4; Waiata Maori; Ode for piano; Five Canons for two clarinets; Symphony No. 1; Symphony No. 2; Symphony No. 3; Scherzo for orchestra; Folksong Trio (recorders); In Despite of Death, Symphony No. 3 – Remembered Songs 2003, Black, White and Coloured 2003. *Recordings:* Concerto for wind quintet; Symphonies nos 1–3; Three Improvisations; Three Pieces for violin and piano; Concertino for piano and strings; Evocation; Partita; Ring Round the Moon; Three Scots Ballads; In Despite of Death; Scherzo for orchestra; Magpies and Other Birds, Echoes and Reflections; String Quartet No. 1; Suite for guitar; Auras, 1987; Anniversary Suite No. 2, 1998; Homage to Stravinsky, 1998; Serenade for Strings; Six Songs of Women; Eight Blake Songs, Writing in the Sand, Three Medieval Carols, Three Songs of Cilla McQueen, Five Songs of e e cummings, Three Symphonies 2004. *Honours:* Companion New Zealand Order of Merit, 2004. *Address:* 15 Nottingham Street, Wellington, New Zealand.

**FARR, Gareth,** BMus; New Zealand composer and percussionist; b. 29 Feb. 1968, Wellington. *Education:* Victoria Univ., Weelington, Auckland Univ., Eastman School of Music. *Career:* composer-in-residence, Chamber Music New Zealand. *Compositions include:* Pembukaan 1990, works for Javanese gamelan, including Kebyar moncar and Reongan, Lilith's Dream of Ecstasy 1995, From the Depths Sound the Great Sea Gongs 1996, Hikoi 1998, Concerto for four percussionists 2005. *Recordings include:* album: Ruaumoko, Beowulf, Orakau, Rangitoto and Te Papa played by New Zealand Symphony Orchestra. *E-mail:* gareth@drumdrag.com. *Website:* www.garethfarr.com.

**FARRELL, Eibhlis;** Composer; b. 27 July 1953, Rostrevor, County Down, Ireland. *Education:* Studied at Queen's University, Belfast and at Bristol University. *Career:* Deputy Principal at the College of Music, Dublin Institute of Technology, 1983. *Compositions include:* Concerto Grosso, 1988; Sinfon for orchestra, 1990; Exultet, oratorio, 1991; Exaudi Voces and A Garland For The President for solo voices and chorus, 1991; Soundshock for concert band, 1993; Solo vocal music including, The Silken Bed for mezzo, violin, cello and harpsichord, 1993; Caritas Abundar for 2 sopranos and chorus, 1995; Island of Women for orchestra, 1996; Chamber and instrumental pieces including, Earthshine for harp, 1992. *Address:* c/o IMRO, Pembroke Row, Dublin 2, Ireland.

**FARREN-PRICE, Ronald (William);** Pianist and University Academic; b. 2 July 1930, Brisbane, Australia; m. Margaret Lillian Cameron, 15 Jan 1982, 3 s., 2 d. *Education:* Diploma in Music, University of Melbourne, 1951; Studies with Claudio Arrau on a personal scholarship donated by him, 1952–55, London and New York. *Career:* Debut: Melbourne Symphony Orchestra, Concerto, 1947; Wigmore Hall, London, 1955; Has played in over 50 countries including 12 concert tours of the former USSR and many performances at London's Wigmore Hall, Queen Elizabeth Hall, Purcell Room and St John's Smith Square; Performances at Carnegie Recital Hall, New York, National Gallery, Washington, and Tchaikovsky Hall, Moscow; Reader in Music, 1975, Dean, Faculty of Music, 1986–90, Head of Keyboard, 1991–97, Associate Professor, 1989–, Senior Associate of the Faculty, 1998–, Fellow of Queen's College, 1991–, Council Member of Queen's College, 1986–, Music Patron, Trinity College Music Foundation, University of Melbourne; Patron St Paul's Cathedral Old Christians Association; Director, Australian National Academy of Music, 1999; Federal Examiner for the Australian Music Examinations Board, 1984–85, 1994–97; Has performed concertos with many leading conductors including Antal Dorati, Ferdinand Leitner, Eugene Goossens,

Charles Groves, Willem van Otterloo, John Hopkins and Harry Blech; Has broadcast recitals in many countries and also appeared in television recitals; mem, Melbourne Club, University House, University of Melbourne. *Current Management:* Impresaria Pty Ltd. *Address:* Faculty of Music, University of Melbourne, Parkville, Victoria 3052, Australia.

**FARRER, John;** Conductor; b. 1950, USA. *Career:* Many performances with leading orchestras in the USA, notably with the San Francisco Symphony Orchestra and as guest conductor elsewhere; Music Director of the Roswell Symphony Orchestra in New Mexico; Faculty Member of the Conducting Workshops of the American Symphony Orchestra League; London debut in 1986 with the London Philharmonic; Senior Guest Conductor with the English Sinfonia and further concerts with the Royal Philharmonic Orchestra and the Bournemouth Symphony Orchestra. *Recordings include:* Tchaikovsky album with the London Philharmonic, Dvořák with the RPO and Copland and Gershwin with the Bournemouth Symphony Orchestra. *Address:* c/o Bournemouth Symphony Orchestra, 2 Seldown Lane, Poole, Dorset, BH15 1UF, England.

**FARULLI, Piero;** Italian professor of viola; *Teacher, Scuola di Musica di Fiesole;* b. 13 Jan. 1920, Florence; s. of Lioniero Farulli and Maria (née Innocenti) Farulli; m. Antonia Parisi 1945. *Education:* Conservatorio Statale Luigi Cherubini, Florence (under Gioacchino Maglioni). *Career:* Prof. of Viola 1957–77; for thirty years a mem. of Quartetto Italiano; has also collaborated with Amadeus and Berg Quartets; appeared with Trio di Trieste 1978; has lectured at Accad. Chigiana di Siena and at Salzburg Mozarteum; mem. of judging panel at several int. competitions and is active in many aspects of musical life and education in Italy, notably at the Scuola di Musica di Fiesole, which he founded in 1974; Medaglia della Cultura e dell'Arte. *Honours:* Grand 'Ufficiale della Repubblica 1994. *Address:* Scuola di Musica di Fiesole, Via delle Fontanelle, 24, 50016 S. Domenico di Fiesole, Florence, Italy (office); Via G. d'Annunzio 153, Florence, Italy. *Telephone:* (055) 597851 (office); (055) 608007 (office). *Fax:* (055) 599686 (office). *Website:* www.scuolamusica.fiesole .fi.it (office).

**FASHAE, Alycia;** Singer (soprano); b. 1970, England. *Education:* Royal Northern College of Music, with Ryland Davies and Honor Shepherd; L'Opéra National de Paris. *Career:* Appearances in Paris as Mozart's Servilia, Pamina and Fiordiligi; Adina in L'Elisir d'Amore, Lucia di Lammermoor, Gounod's Juliette, Micaela, Bizet's Leila, Massenet's Sophie and Cendrillon, Violetta, Gilda and Nannetta; Engagements on tour of Britain as Violetta, with European Chamber Opera and Pamina with Diva Opera; Leila in The Pearl Fishers for English National Opera; Season 2001–2002 as Donna Anna and Offenbach's Antonia with Diva Opera, Frasquita in Carmen for ENO and Gilda for European Chamber Opera; Tour of USA as Hanna Glawari in the Merry Widow. *Current Management:* Athole Still International Management, Forresters Hall, 25–27 Westow Street, London, SE19 3RY, England. *Telephone:* (20) 8771-5271. *Fax:* (20) 8768-6600. *Website:* www.atholestill.com.

**FASSBAENDER, Brigitte,** FRNCM; German singer (mezzo-soprano); b. 3 July 1939, Berlin; d. of the late Willi Domgraf-Fassbaender and Sabine Peters. *Education:* Nuremberg Conservatoire and studied with father. *Career:* début Bavarian State Opera, Munich 1961; has appeared at La Scala Milan, Vienna State Opera, Covent Garden London, Metropolitan Opera, New York, San Francisco and Salzburg; Teacher of Solo Vocal Music Musikhochschule, Munich; soloist, Dir of Opera, Braunschweig 1995–97; Intendantin Tiroler Landestheater, Innsbruck 1999. *Recordings:* over 100 recordings since 1964. *Honours:* Bundesverdienstkreuz am Bande, Bayerischer Verdiensторden. *Address:* c/o Sekretariat, Haiming, 83119 Obing, Germany (office).

**FAST, George Allen,** BMusA; Canadian singer (countertenor), voice professor and writer on music; b. 27 March 1954, Leamington, ON. *Education:* Univ. of Western Ontario. *Career:* debut with Waverly Consort, Kennedy Center, Washington DC, USA 1979; soloist with Tafelmusik Baroque Orchestra, The Bach Ensemble, Nat. Arts Centre Orchestra (Ottawa), CBC Vancouver Orchestra, Smithsonian Chamber Players, New York Oratorio Soc., Oregon Symphony, Opera Atelier (Toronto), Casals Festival, Madeira Bach Festival, Wratislavia Cantans, Pacific Opera Victoria, Les Violons du Roy, Studio de Musique Ancienne de Montréal, L'Orchestre de la Nouvelle France, Edmonton Symphony, Louisville Bach Soc. and others; Asst Prof. of Early Music Voice, Dir of Cappella Antica, McGill Univ. *Recordings:* The Christmas Story (with The Waverly Consort) 1983, Renaissance Favorites (with The Waverly Consort) 1985, Bach Cantatas 8, 78 and 99 (with Bach Ensemble, Joshua Rifkin) 1989, Complete Alto Cantatas of Buxtehude 1989. *Current Management:* Colwell Arts Management, 1580 Line 37, New Hamburg, ON N3A 4B7, Canada. *Address:* 263 Bourchemin Ouest, St Hugues, QC J0H 1N0, Canada.

**FATH, Karl;** German singer (bass); b. 1941. *Career:* Sang at Giessen, 1963–67, Koblenz, 1968–72, Brunswick, 1972–74 and Saarbrucken, 1974–77; Engaged at Gelsenkirchen from 1977 and has made guest appearances at Stuttgart, Karlsruhe, Frankfurt, 1984–86 and Cologne, 1987–88; Tour of Brazil in 1982 singing in Jakob Lenz by Wolfgang Rihm; Appeared as Don Magnifico in La Cenerentola at Bielefeld, 1989, Lunardo in I Quattro Rusteghi by Wolf-Ferrari at Hannover in 1991; Sang Truffaldino in Ariadne auf Naxos at Hannover, 2000; Many lieder recitals and concert appearances. *Recordings:* Petite Messe Solennelle by Rossini. *Address:* c/o Niedersachsiche Staatstheater, Opernplatz 1, 3000 Hannover, Germany.

**FAULKNER, Julia;** Singer (Soprano); b. 1962, St Louis, Missouri, USA. *Education:* Studied with Margaret Harshaw at Bloomington. *Career:* Sang Arminda in Mozart's Finta Giardiniera at Lyon, returning for Alice Ford in Falstaff; Mozart and Strauss roles at the Munich Staatsoper (Marschallin, 1995); Vienna, 1993–95, as Arabella and the Countess in Capriccio; Miami Opera, 1991, as Fiordiligi; Sang Marianne in Der Rosenkavalier at the Met, 2000; Other roles include Ariadne and Wagner's Gutrune (Vienna Staatsoper); Further engagements at Hamburg, Amsterdam, Geneva and Stockholm. *Recordings include:* Die Zauberflöte and Pergolesi's Stabat Mater. *Address:* c/o Bayerische Staatsoper, Max-Joseph-Platz, 80539 Munich, Germany.

**FAUST, Isabelle;** German violinist; b. March 1972, Esslingen. *Education:* Colleges of Music in Saabrücken, Detmold and Berlin. *Career:* Played with major orchestras: Hamburg Philharmonic, Yehudi Menuhin conducting, Württemberg Chamber Orchestra, Württemberg Philharmonic, Stuttgart Radio Symphony, Stuttgart Philharmonic, State Philharmonic of Rheinland-Pfalz, Bremen Philharmonic, Orchestra of Padua, West German Radio Symphony of Cologne, Stockholm Sinfonietta; US debut with Utah Symphony in 1995, Paganini Concerto No. 1; Has toured: Germany, Israel, Spain, Italy, Japan; Chamber Music with: B Giuranna, B Pergamenschikow, N Brainin, J Goritzki, N Gutman, J Silverstein, L Hokanson, Ph Hirschorn; Played at festivals of: Schleswig-Holstein, Bad Kissingen, Colmar, Lyon, Berlin, Sarasota. *Recordings:* Radio: Bartók's Solo Sonata for Violin; Mozart's Violin Concerto in A Major; Prokofiev's Concerto No. 1; Dvořák's Violin Concerto in A Minor; Mendelssohn's Violin Concerto in E Minor; Bruch's Violin Concerto in G Minor; Several recitals. *Honours:* 1st Prize, International Leopold Mozart Competition for Violinists, Augsburg, 1987; Premio Quadrivio Award in Rovigo, Italy for Outstanding Musical Achievement, 1990; 1st Prize in Paganini Competition in Genoa, Italy, 1993; Prize for Highly Talented Young Artists in Nordhein-Westfalen, 1994. *Current Management:* Hazard Chase, 25 City Road, Cambridge CB1 1DP, England. *Telephone:* (1223) 312400. *Fax:* (1223) 460827. *Website:* www.hazardchase.co.uk. *Address:* Lontelstrasse 19, 70839 Gerlingen, Germany.

**FAUST, Michael;** Flautist; b. 16 Jan. 1959, Cologne, Germany; m. Debora Bendocchi Alves, 30 Dec 1985, 1 s., 1 d. *Education:* Hochschule für Musik, Hamburg. *Career:* Principal Flautist with the Santa Cecilia Orchestra in Rome, the Hamburg Philharmonic (conductor C v. Dohnányi), Stuttgart Opera (conductor D R Davis), Munich Philharmonic (conductor S Celibidache), and Cologne Radio Symphonie (conductors Gary Bertini, Hans Vonk and Semyon Bychkov); Major Solo Concerts in New York, St Louis, Boston, Tokyo, Moscow and Paris; Ibert-concerto with the Moscow Symphony, conductor V Fedossejew, 1985; Gunther Schuller's Flute-concerto with the St Louis Symphony Orchestra, 1998; Premiere of Mauricio Kagel's flute concerto Das Konzert, 2003; Founding member of Ensemble Contrasts Köln; Professor for flute, Robert-Schumann-Hochschule Düsseldorf. *Recordings:* H W Henze El Cimarron; J. S. Bach to Mozart; 20th Century Flute Concertos, Ibert, Bernstein, Nielsen, Elliott Carter, French Flute Music. *Honours:* Prizes and Awards at Competitions in Bonn, Rome, Prague, New York. *Current Management:* Rolf Sudbrack, Hamburg. *Address:* Worringer Strasse 21, 50668 Köln, Germany. *Website:* www.mfaust.de.

**FEATHERSTONE, Gary Maxwell;** Composer and Performer; b. 2 Sept. 1949, Sydney, Australia. *Education:* piano and music education, Sydney Conservatorium. *Career:* debut, Radio 2CH, Sydney, aged 15; performances in England, France, Poland, Germany and Australia; recordings for ABC Radio and 2MBS, FM Radio, Sydney. *Compositions:* Piano Concerto No. 1, Piano Concerto No. 2, Rhapsody on Original Theme for Piano and Orchestra, Serenade for Strings 1999, Symphonic Fantasia – Peter Ibbetson (full orchestra) 2000. *Recordings:* Serenade for Strings (Nevsky Quartet, St Petersburg, Russia), Symphonic Fantasia (Peter Ibbetson, Slovak Radio Orchestra), Australian Piano Music (three compositions), Barcarolle (for ABC-FM, Australian Composers Concert) 1995. *Publications:* Piano Pieces for Children 1989, Idyll, for flute and piano 1990, Prelude in E Flat major, for piano 1990, Improvisation, for piano 1993, Pieces for Musical Children 1993, I Need Love, for voice and piano 1995, Four Nocturnes 1995, The Waltzes, for piano 1995, Barcarolle, for piano 1995, Berceuse, for piano 1996, Scherzo, for piano 1996, Two Dance Songs, piano 1997, 24 Preludes, piano 1999, Romance for Violin and Piano 2001, Dance in the Moonlight, for oboe and piano 2002.

**FEDDERLY, Greg;** Singer (tenor); b. 1961, California, USA. *Education:* Studied at the University of Southern California. *Career:* Appearances with the Los Angeles Opera have included Britten's Albert Herring, Mozart's Monostatos, Pinkerton, Hylas in Les Troyens and Arturo in Lucia di Lammermoor, 1988–; European debut as Tom Rakewell at the Aldeburgh Festival, 1992; Engagements at the Théâtre du Châtelet, Paris, in Die Frau ohne Schatten and Moses und Aron; Philidor's Tom Jones at the Drottningholm Festival, 1995; Gluck's Orpheus, 1996; Further roles include Mozart's Ferrando, Alfredo in La Traviata, Washington, 1996, Rossini's Almaviva, Seattle, 1997 and David in Die Meistersinger at Los Angeles, season 1997–98; Sang in the premiere of Florencia of the Amazons, at the Houston Opera, 1996; Tamino at Los Angeles, 1998; Season 1999–2000 included Telemaco in Ulisse at Glimmerglass; Concerts of The Creation in Barcelona; Alfredo in La Traviata at Los Angeles Opera and Pinkerton in Madama Butterfly in Santa Barbara. *Recordings include:* The Rake's Progress, for Swedish Television. *Honours:* First recipient of the Marilyn Horne Scholarship at UCLA. *Current Management:* Askonas Holt Ltd, Lonsdale Chambers, 27 Chancery Lane, London, WC2A 1PF, England. *Telephone:* (20) 7400-1700. *Fax:* (20) 7400-1799. *E-mail:* info@askonasholt.co.uk. *Website:* www.askonasholt.co.uk.

**FEDER, Donn-Alexandre;** Concert Pianist and Teacher; b. 23 June 1935, Philadelphia, PA, USA; m. Janet Landis, 26 Aug 1960, 1 d. *Education:* BS, 1958, MS, 1959, DMA, 1973, Juilliard School of Music; Studies with Rosina Lhevinne, Kabos and Gorodnitzki; Study at Eastman and with Jorge Bolet. *Career:* Debut: New York Town Hall in 1963; Extensive concerting throughout Europe, Mexico, Canada and USA, and for NBC and ABC television and BBC, England; Appearances with major European and American orchestras; Faculty, Philadelphia College of Performing Arts, 1971–81; Piano Faculty, Manhattan School of Music, 1978–; Member of 2-piano team, Feder and Gilgore; Co-director of Musicisti Americani Festival and Institute, Rome and Sulmona, Italy; Artist-Teacher, Taiwan International Festival, China, 1988 and 1989. *Recordings:* With the Netherlands Radio Philharmonic under Allers and Van Otterloo. *Recordings include:* Szymanowski Piano Music, Excursions for Two Pianos, Music of Barber, Copland and Gershwin (with Elisha Gilgore), Bartók Sonata for 2 Pianos and Percussion, Stravinsky's Concerto for 2 Solo Pianos, with Elisha Gilgore. *Address:* c/o Manhattan School of Music, Piano Faculty, 120 Claremont Avenue, New York, NY 10027, USA.

**FEDIN, Alexander;** Singer (Tenor); b. 11 Sept. 1954, Russia. *Career:* Sang at first in concert, then appeared at the Bolshoi, Moscow, from 1986, notably as Werther, Rossini's Almaviva and the Holy Fool in Boris Godunov; Guested with the Bolshoi at Glasgow, 1990, as the King in Tchaikovsky's Maid of Orleans, and at Rome, 1989, in a concert performance of Rachmaninov's Aleko; Berlin Staatsoper, 1991, as the Duke of Mantua; Further appearances at the Vienna Staatsoper, in Dortmund and at the Teatre Liceu, Barcelona; Cologne Opera 1995–96 as Tamino, Steuermann and Cassio; Season 2000–01 as Faust at Essen, Wagner's Erik at Freiburg and the Prince in The Love for Three Oranges at Cologne. *Address:* c/o Bolshoi Opera, 103009 Moscow, Russia.

**FEDOSEYEV, Vladimir Ivanovich;** Russian conductor; b. 5 Aug. 1932, Leningrad; s. of Ivan Fedoseyev and Elena Fedoseyeva; m. Olga Dobrokhotova; two c. *Education:* conductors' class of Moscow Musical Pedagogical Inst., Moscow Conservatoire. *Career:* mem. CPSU 1963–91; Artistic Dir and Chief Conductor Moscow Radio Symphony Orchestra of USSR Radio Network (now Tchaikovsky Acad. Symphony Orchestra) 1974–; concurrently Music Dir Vienna Symphony Orchestra 1997–; first Perm. Guest Conductor Tokyo Philharmonic Orchestra 1996–; Perm. Guest Conductor Zürich Opera 1997–; works with Bolshoi and Mariinsky Theatres, opera productions and concerts abroad, including Italy, France, Austria, Germany, Japan, Switzerland, Spain, UK, USA. *Honours:* People's Artist of USSR 1980, RSFSR State Prize 1989, Crystal Award of Asahi Broadcasting Corpn, Osaka 1989, Golden Orpheus, for recording of opera May Night. *Address:* Moscow House of Recording and Broadcasting, Malaya Nikitskaya 24, 121069 Moscow, Russia. *Telephone:* (095) 222-00-24 (office); (095) 229-57-68(Moscow) (home); (1) 406-54-96 (Vienna) (home). *Fax:* (095) 202-49-85.

**FEENEY, Angela;** Singer (Soprano); b. 19 Oct. 1954, Belfast, Northern Ireland. *Education:* Studied at Belfast, Dublin and Munich. *Career:* Debut: Irish National Opera, 1977, as Cherubino; English National Opera from 1978, as Micaela, Marenka in The Bartered Bride, Nedda, and Donna Elvira (1986); Munich Staatsoper, 1983–86, as Papageno, Gretel, and Ingrid in Egk's Peer Gynt; Deutsche Oper Berlin, 1985, as Butterfly, Dublin Grand Opera, 1986, as Gluck's Euridice; Wexford Festival, 1986, as Giulietta in Verdi's Un giorno di Regno; Other roles include Mimi and the Trovatore Leonore. *Address:* c/o Opera Theatre Company, 18 St Andrew Street, Dublin 2, Ireland.

**FEGRAN, Espen;** Singer (Baritone); b. 1960, Oslo, Norway. *Education:* Studied at the Oslo Academy with Nicolai Gedda. *Career:* Sang at the Norwegian National Opera in Oslo as Papageno (1987), Marcello, Guglielmo, Mozart's Count and similar repertory; Wiesbaden Opera from 1988, as Eugene Onegin, Belcore, Beckmesser, and in Henze's Verratene Meer; Bonn, 1992, in Jakob Lenz by Rihm; Leipzig 1996, in Greek by Turnage. *Address:* c/o Hessisches Staatstheater, Christian Zeds-Strasse 3–5, W-6200 Wiesbaden, Germany.

**FEIGIN, Joel;** American composer; *Associate Professor of Composition, University of California, Santa Barbara;* b. 23 May 1951, New York, NY; m. Severine Neff, 7 June 1986. *Education:* BA, Columbia University; DMA, The Juilliard School; Studied with Nadia Boulanger, Fontainebleau; Mellon Fellowship, Cornell University; Aaron Copland-American Society of Composers, Authors and Publishers Fellowship, Tanglewood Music Center. *Career:* Professor of Music, University of California at Santa Barbara; Senior Fulbright Scholar at Moscow Conservatory, Russia, 1998–99. *Compositions:* Mysteries of Eleusis, opera; Twelfth Night, opera; Elegy, in Memoriam Otto Luening for orchestra; Echoes from the Holocaust for chamber ensemble; Mosaic in Two Panels for strings; Transience for oboe and percussion; Nexus for flute and piano; Four Poems of Linda Pastan for soprano and ensemble; Five Ecstatic Poems of Kabir for soprano and ensemble; Veränderungen for violin and piano; Variations on a Theme by Arnold Schoenberg for piano; Festive Overture for orchestra 1996; Six Sonnets to Orpheus (Rilke) for mezzo and piano, 1996; Music for 'Mountains and Rivers', 1996; Tapestry, for French horn, violin and piano, 1996; Meditations on Dogen for Piano 1998. *Recordings:* Transience (2-CD set) includes 10 chamber and vocal works. *Publications:* Transience for oboe and percussion, 1997. *Contributions:* Stil oder Gedanke? Die Schoenberg-Nachfolge in Europa und Amerika; Roger

Sessions Newsletter, Vol. I; Perspectives of New Music, Vol. 12. *Address:* c/o Rosalie Calabrese Management, Box 20580 Park West Station, New York, NY 10025-1521, USA. *Telephone:* (212) 663-6620. *Fax:* (212) 663-5941. *E-mail:* rcmgt@yahoo.com. *Website:* www.joelfeigin.com.

**FEIGIN, Sarah;** Israeli Composer; b. 1 July 1928, Riga, Latvia. *Education:* Studied at the Riga Music Academy. *Career:* Emigrated to Israel in 1972 and was director of the Music Conservatory at Holon from 1973. *Compositions include:* The Golden Tree, ballet, 1956; The House Of The Cat, children's opera, 1959, revised 1988; Violin Sonata, 1968; The Storm, ballet, 1969; Music for piano and organ, for educational use. *Current Management:* c/o ACUM Ltd, 9 Tuval Street, Ramat-Gan 52117, Israel.

**FEJER, András;** Cellist; b. 1950, Hungary. *Education:* Studied with András Mihaly at the Franz Liszt Academy, with the Amadeus Quartet and Zoltán Szekeley. *Career:* Founder Member of the Takacs Quartet in 1975; Many concert appearances in all major European centres and the USA; Tours include New Zealand, Japan, England, Sweden, Belgium and Ireland; Bartók Cycle for festival at South Bank in 1990, and at the Théâtre des Champs-Elysées in 1991; Great Performers Series at Lincoln Center and Mostly Mozart Festival at Alice Tully Hall, NY; Visits to Japan in 1989 and 1992; Mozart Festivals at South Bank, Wigmore Hall and Barbican Centre in 1991; Beethoven cycles at the Zürich Tonhalle, in Dublin, at the Wigmore Hall and in Paris, 1991–92; Plays Amati cello made for the French Royal Family and loaned by the Corcoran Gallery, Washington DC. *Recordings:* Schumann Quartets, Opus 41, Mozart String Quintets with Denes Koromzay, 6 Bartók Quartets, Schubert's Trout Quintet with Zoltán Kocsis, Haydn, Opus 76, Brahms, Opus 51, Nos 1 and 2, Chausson Concerto with Joshua Bell and Jean-Yves Thibaudet; Works by Schubert, Mozart, Dvořák and Bartók. *Honours:* Winner, International Quartet Competition, Evian, 1977, and Portsmouth International Quartet Competition, 1979. *Address:* Artists Management International, 12–13 Richmond Buildings, Dean Street, London W1V 5 AF, England.

**FELCIANO, Richard (James);** Composer and Teacher; b. 7 Dec. 1930, Santa Rosa, California, USA. *Education:* Pupil of Milhaud, Mills College, Oakland, California, MA, 1955; Continued studies with Milhaud and Ple-Caussade, Paris Conservatory, 2 diplomas, 1955; Private studies with Dallapiccola, Florence, 1958–59, with Bezanson, University of Iowa, PhD, 1959. *Career:* Composer-in-Residence, National Center for Experiments in Television, San Francisco, 1967–71, City of Boston, 1971–73; Chairman of Music Department, Lone Mountain College, San Francisco, 1959–67; Professor, University of CA, Berkeley, 1967–; Founder, Center for New Music and Audio Technologies, University of CA, Berkeley, 1987. *Compositions include:* Chamber Opera: Sir Gawain and The Green Knight, 1964; Orchestral: Mutations, 1966, Galactic Rounds, 1972; Orchestra, 1980; Concerto for organ and orchestra, 1986; Symphony for strings, 1993; Overture Concertante for clarinet and orchestra, 1995; Chamber: Evolutions for clarinet and piano, 1962, Glossolalia for baritone, organ, percussion and tape, 1967, Chod for violin, cello, double bass, piano, percussion and live electronics, 1972, Alleluia to The Heart of Stone for reverberated recorder, 1984, Shadows for flute, clarinet, violin, cello, piano and percussion, 1987, Palladio for violin, piano and percussion, 1989, Responsory for solo male voice and live electronics, 1991, Camp Songs for chamber orchestra (15 instruments), 1992, Cante Jondo for bassoon, clarinet and piano, 1993, String Quartet, 1995; Piano pieces and various choral works. *Recordings:* Conducted own works; In Celebration of Golden Rain, for Indonesian gamelan and organ, 1977; Concerto for organ and orchestra, 1986. *Publications:* Analysis and commentary on sketches for Edgard Varèse's Poème électronique in Space Calculated in Seconds (Treib), 1997. *Honours:* Fulbright Fellowship, 1958; Guggenheim Fellowship, 1969; American Academy of Arts and Letters Award, 1974; Various grants and commissions; Library of Congress Koussevitzky Commission, 1999. *Address:* c/o Music Department, University of California, Berkeley, CA 94720, USA.

**FELD, Jindrich;** Czech composer and music teacher; b. 19 Feb. 1925, Prague, Czechoslovakia; m. Helena Feldova, 22 July 1955, 1 d. *Education:* Prague Conservatoire, 1945–48; Academy of Music, Prague. 1948–52; PhD, Charles University, Prague, 1952. *Career:* Composer; Music Teacher; Viz Composer-in-Residence, University of Adelaide, Australia, 1968–69; Professor, Conservatoire of Prague, 1972–86; Head, Department of Music, Czechoslovak Radio Prague, 1990–92; Guest lectures in Germany, Denmark, Norway, France, UK, and several univs in the USA and Japan. *Compositions include:* Orchestral: Three Frescoes for symphony orchestra, 1963; Symphony No. 1, for symphony orchestra, 1967; Dramatic Fantasy, The Days of August, for symphony orchestra, 1968–69; Symphony No. 2, for symphony orchestra, 1983; Cosmae Chronica Boemorum, oratorio-cantata for Soloists, mixed chorus and symphony orchestra, 1988; Symphony No. 3, Fin de Siècle, for symphony orchestra, 1994–98; Sinfonietta for symphony orchestra, 2001; Solo concertos: Flute concerto, 1954; Violoncello Concerto, 1958; Piano Concerto, 1973; Violin Concerto, 1977; Saxophone Concerto, 1980; Concertino for flute, piano and orchestra, 1991; American Concertino for soprano saxophone and chamber orchestra, 2002; Chamber solos: Sonatas for flute and piano, 1957; Piano, 1972; Cello and Piano, 1972; Violin and piano, 1985; Saxophone and piano, 1990; Concert Music for viola and piano, 1983; Partita concertante, for violoncello solo, 1991; Chamber Ensembles: 6 string quartets, 1949–93; Chamber Suite for nonet, 1960; Wind Quintet No. 2, 1968; Brass Quintet, 1970; String Quintet, 1972; Saxophone Quartet, 1981; Concerto da camera, for

two string quartets, 1987; Flautarchia, Music for Flute and String Quartet, 2000; Vocal music: Three Inventions for mixed chorus, 1966; Gloria cantus, mixed chorus on Latin text, 1984; Laus Cantus for soprano and string quartet, 1985; Stage work: A Postman's Tale, children's opera, 1956. *Publications:* Numerous compositions published and recorded. *Contributions:* Hudebni Rozhledy (Musical Review), Prague. *Honours:* Czechoslovak State Prize 1968; numerous prizes in competitions in Czech Repub. and abroad. *Address:* Peckova 17, 186 00 Prague 8, Karlin, Czech Republic (home). *Telephone:* 22481-7089 (home). *Fax:* 22481-5826 (home). *Website:* www.musica.cz/feld (office).

**FELDBUSCH, Eric;** Belgian composer and cellist; *Honorary Director,* Conservatoire Royal de Musique de Bruxelles; b. 2 March 1922, Grivegnee. *Education:* Liège Conservatory. *Career:* Active as concert cellist and teacher; Prof. de Violoncello, Mons Conservatory 1953–63, Dir 1963–73; Dir, Brussels Conservatory, 1974–87; mem., Académie Royale des Sciences des Lettres et des Beaux Arts de Belgique, 1982–; Hon. Dir Conservatoire Royal de Musique de Bruxelles. *Compositions include:* Opera: Orestes, 1969, Ballet El Diablo Cojuelo, 1972; Orchestral: Contrastes, 1956, Les Moineaux De Baltimore, suite, 1958, Mosäique for cello solo, 1961, Three Lorca Poems for voice and orchestra, 1964, Violin Concerto, 1967, Fantaisie–Divertissement, 1967, Cantique Des Cantiques for soprano and orchestra, 1970, Piccola Musica for strings, 1971, Triade for chamber orchestra, 1977, Concertante for 2 pianos and orchestra, 1986, Cello Concerto, 1988; Chamber: Violin Sonata, 1957, 4 String Quartets, 1955–71, Duo for flute and piano, 1959, Trio for flute, cello and violin, 1961, Septet for soprano and ensemble, 1969, Cheminement for violin and strings ensemble, 1984; Remembrance pour deux violons et piano, 1995; Mirages for orchestra, 2001; Quartet No. 5, 2002; Piano music and incidental music for plays. *Honours:* Resistance Medal 1940–45, Prix Int. Pablo Casals 1945, Winner, Prague Int. Cello Competition 1950. *Address:* Rue Vergot 29/4, 1030 Brussels, Belgium. *Telephone:* (2) 7311-39-65.

**FELDERER, Ingeborg;** Singer (Soprano); b. 28 Nov. 1933, Innsbruck, Austria. *Education:* Studied in Vienna and Milan. *Career:* Engaged at the Basle Stadttheater, 1955–59, notably in the premiere of Titus Feuerfuchs by Sutermeister and the local premiere of The Fiery Angel by Prokofiev, 1957, Wuppertal, 1959–62, Karlsruhe, 1962–65, and Basle, 1962–67; Sang minor roles at the Bayreuth Festival, 1961–63, and made guest appearances in Copenhagen, Frankfurt, Barcelona, Brussels, Zürich and Paris; Metropolitan Opera, NY, 1967–70 as Santuzza and the Trovatore Leonora; Vienna Staatsoper as Senta, Chrysothemis in Elektra and Woglinde; Barcelona in 1969 as Elisabetta in Maria Stuarda; Other roles include Hecuba in King Priam with the German premiere at Karlsruhe in 1963, Tosca, Katya Kabanova and the Duchess of Parma in Doktor Faust by Busoni; Frequent concert appearances. *Address:* c/o Bayerische Staatsoper, Postfach 100148, 8000 Munich 1, Germany.

**FELDHOF, Gerd;** Singer (Baritone); b. 29 Oct. 1931, Radvormwald, Cologne, Germany. *Education:* Studied in Detmold. *Career:* Debut: Essen in 1959 as Mozart's Figaro; Guest engagements at Buenos Aires in 1960; Sang at St ädtische Oper Berlin and Frankfurt Opera from 1961 and Metropolitan Opera from 1961 with debut as Kaspar in Der Freischütz; Further appearances in Helsinki, Hamburg, Copenhagen, Amsterdam, Montreal, Mexico City, Japan and Korea; Bayreuth Festival 1968–78, notably as Amfortas; Also sings Barak in Die Frau ohne Schatten (Karlsruhe, 1992); Deutsche Oper Berlin, 1996, as Wagner's Kurwenal. *Recordings include:* Lulu; Kothner in Die Meistersinger; Beethoven's 9th Symphony; Jonny Spielt Auf by Krenek; Hindemith's Mathis der Maler. *Address:* Festspielhaus, 85008 Bayreuth, Germany.

**FELDHOFF, Heinz;** Singer (Bass); b. 1939, Radvormwald, Cologne, Germany. *Career:* Sang at Essen, 1964–66, Bremen, 1966–70, Mannheim, 1970–87; Bayreuth Festival, 1967–78, as Hans Ortel, Reinmar and Fafner; Other roles have included Leporello, Baculus in Lortzing's Wildschütz, Ochs, and Riedinger in Mathis der Maler; Guest at Lisbon (1981) Antwerp (1983) and Dublin (1984); Sang Schigolch in Lulu at Heidelberg, 2000. *Address:* c/o Nationaltheater Mannheim, Am Goetheplatz, D-6800 Mannheim, Germany.

**FELDMAN, Barbara (Monk);** Canadian Composer and Theorist; b. 18 Jan. 1953, Quebec, Canada; m. Morton Feldman, 6 June 1987. *Education:* McGill University, Montreal, studied with Bengt Hambraeus; PhD, Composition, State Univ. of NY, Buffalo, 1987, studied with Morton Feldman. *Career:* Compositions performed by the Arditti Quartet, Clarinettist Roger Heaton, pianists Yvar Mikhashoff, Ursula Oppens, Frederic Rzewski, Aki Takahashi, percussionists Steven Schick, Robyn Schulkkowsky and Jan Williams, and cellist Frances-Marie Uitti; her music has been premiered at Darmstadt and festivals including Inventionen in Berlin, Nieuwe Muziek in Middelburg, Other Minds in San Francisco, Toronto New Music and in the Rotonda in Tokyo; Faculty, Internationale Ferienkurse für Neue Musik, Darmstadt, 1988, 1990; guest lectured at Hochschule der Künste in Berlin; Founder, Artistic Dir, Time Shards Music Series, Georgia O'Keefe Museum, Santa Fe, 2001–. *Compositions:* Trio for violin, cello and piano, 1983; Variations for six string instruments, 1986; Variations for string quartet and chorus, 1987; Duo for piano and percussion, 1988; The I and Thou for solo piano, 1988; Two Pianos, 1989; The Immutable Silence for instrumental ensemble, 1990; Pure Difference for instrumental ensemble, 1991; Infinite Other for choir and instruments, 1992. *Compositions include:* Orchestral: Design for String Orchestra, 1980 The Northern Shore for Piano, Percussion and Orchestra or Chamber Orchestra, 1997; Chamber music: Movement for Solo Viola, 1979;

Trio for violin, cello and piano, 1984; Pure Difference, clarinet, bassoon, violin, piano, synthesizer, percussion, 1990; Shadow, string quartet, 1991; Verses for Five, flute, bass clarinet, French horn, piano (and celesta), percussion, 1996; Proche et lointaine...la femme, bass clarinet, accordion, 2001; Choral: Variations for String Quartet and Chorus (text by Ludwig Wittgenstein), mixed chorus, string quartet, 1987; Infinite Other (text by Homer), 2 sopranos, mixed chorus, flute, clarinet, string quartet, piano, film adlibitum (by Stan Brakhage), 1992; Piano: The I and Thou, 1988; Two Pianos, 1989; Clear Edge, 1993; In the Small Time of a Desert Flower, 2000. *Publications:* Article, All Things Being Unmeasured, in New Observations, 1989. *Honours:* Edgard Varese Fellowship, SUNY Buffalo, 1984–87. *Address:* c/o SOCAN, 41 Valleybrook Drive, Don Mills, Ontario M3B 2S6, Canada.

**FELDMAN, Jill;** Singer (Soprano); b. 21 April 1952, Los Angeles, CA, USA. *Education:* Studied at San Francisco, Basle and Paris; Studied Musicology at the University of California at Santa Barbara. *Career:* Has sung in Europe and the USA in many performances of early music; US opera debut in 1979 as Music in Monteverdi's Orfeo; European opera debut in 1980 as Clerio in Cavalli's Erismena at Spoleto; Concerts with William Christie include Charpentier's Médée at the Salle Pleyel, Paris in 1984; Edinburgh Festival 1985, as Arthebuse in Charpentier's Actéon and Priestess in Rameau's Anacréon; Sang Vita in the first modern revival of Marco Marazzolli's La Vita Humana, at the Tramway, Glasgow, with the Scottish Early Music Consort, 1990. *Recordings:* Rameau's Anacreon; Cesti's Orontea; Cavalli's Xerse; Charpentier's Médée, Acteon and Les Arts Florissants; Incidental music for Molière's Le Malade Imaginaire, Purcell's Orpheus Britannicus and Harmonia Sacra; Solo Recital, Udite Amanti; Italian trecento, Ensemble Mala Punica; Van Eyck: French and English Lute Songs. *Address:* Località Campodalti, 52020 Pergine Valdarno, (AR) Italy.

**FELENCHAK, Vladimir;** Singer (Tenor); b. 1972, Yalta, Russia. *Education:* Graduated Glinka Academic Choir School 1990, St Petersburg Conservatoire 1998. *Career:* Young Singers Academy at the Mariinsky Theatre, St Petersburg, from 1998; Appearances with the Kirov Opera as Mozart's Basilio, the Duke of Mantua, Alfredo, the Indian Merchant in Sadko and Rimsky-Korsakov's Kaschchei and Berendai (The Snow Maiden); Sang Tamino and Monostatos in Die Zauberflöte in Midia, Lithuania, 1998; Other roles include the Simpleton in Boris; Sang with the Kirov Opera in summer season at Covent Garden, 2000. *Address:* c/o Kirov Opera, Mariinsky Theatre, Mariinsky Square, St Petersburg, Russia.

**FELIX, Václav;** Composer, Musicologist and Educator; b. 29 March 1928, Prague, Czechoslovakia; m. Danuse Felixová, 1 s., 2 d. *Education:* Graduate, Musical Faculty, Academy of Musical Arts, Prague, 1953; PhD and Candidate of Science, Charles University, Prague. *Career:* Editor, Hudební Rozhledy, Prague, 1959–61; Assistant, Musical Faculty, 1951–54, Special Assistant, 1960–73, Docent in Music Theory, 1973–84, Professor, Composition and Music Theory, 1985–92, Dean of Musical Faculty, 1985–90; mem, Association of Musical Artists and Scientists, 1990. *Compositions include:* Sonata Capricciosa for flute and piano, 1981; Concerto for trumpet and orchestra, 1984; Symphony No. 1 for female voice and orchestra, 1974; The Advertisement, chamber mini-opera, 1977; Sonata Lirica for oboe and piano, 1978; Double Concerto for violoncello, piano and string orchestra, 1978; Quartetto Amoroso for string quartet, 1979; Symphony No. 2 for small orchestra, 1981; Mariana, Opera in 4 acts, 1982; Sonata Poetica for piano solo, 1988; Sonata Concertante for viola and piano, 1989; Sonata Melodiosa for English horn and piano, 1993; Concerto for violoncello and orchestra, 1990; Symphony No. 3 for mixed choir and large orchestra, 1986; Symphony No. 4 for large orchestra, 1987; Symphony No. 5 for chamber orchestra, 1987; Symphony No. 6 for large wind orchestra, 1990; Sententiae Nasonis for mixed choir, 1995; Numerous other published compositions. *Publications:* Janáček's Sonata Style, 1980; The Fundamental Problems of Musical Forms, 1983. *Contributions:* Hudební Rozhledy; Zivá hudba. *Address:* K Betáni 1099, 148 00 Prague 4-Kunratice, Czech Republic.

**FELLER, Carlos;** Singer (Bass); b. 30 July 1922, Buenos Aires, Argentina. *Education:* Opera Studio of Teatro Colón. *Career:* Debut: Sang the Doctor in Pelléas et Mélisande, Buenos Aires, 1946; Sang widely in South America and toured Europe with Argentinian Chamber Orchestra, 1958; Resident in West Germany from 1958, notably at Cologne Opera where he has sung Don Pasquale, Dulcamara, Dr Bartolo, Leporello and Don Alfonso; Glyndebourne Festival, 1959–60, as Don Alfonso, Figaro, the Speaker in Die Zauberflöte and Dr Bombasto in the British premiere of Busoni's Arlecchino; Appearances at the Salzburg, Edinburgh and Holland Festivals and in most major opera houses in Europe and the Americas; Metropolitan Opera debut, 1988 as Don Alfonso, followed by Dr Bartolo, 1990; Buenos Aires and Santiago, 1990–91; Other roles in Il Matrimonio Segreto, Venice and Washington; Wozzeck at Seattle; Zar und Zimmermann, Der Rosenkavalier, La Cambiale di Matrimonio and Il Signor Bruschino at Cologne; Season 1992 as Don Alfonso in performances of Così fan tutte in Paris and Lisbon conducted by John Eliot Gardiner; Season 1992–93, Nozze di Figaro on tour with John Eliot Gardiner to Lisbon, Paris, London; La Bohème, Opéra Nationale, Paris, 1995; Season 1995–96, sang Alcindoro/Benoit in La Bohème, Opéra Nationale in Paris, also for season, 1996–97; Season 1997–98 included Le nozze di Figaro, La Traviata and Lulu, Opéra National, Paris, and from 1998–99 performances of Nozze di Figaro at the Brussels Opera and further performances of La Bohème in Paris; Sang Schigolch in Lulu, Opéra Bastille, 1998; Season 2000–01 included La Nozze di Figaro at the Brussels Opera, Merry Widow at the Teatro Colón in

Buenos Aires and La Bohème in Florence; Season 2001–02: Engaged to sing Tales of Hoffmann in Geneva. *Recordings:* Don Alfonso and Mozart's Bartolo with the Drottningholm Ensemble, conducted by Arnold Oestmann; Videos of Il Barbiere di Siviglia, Il Matrimonio Segreto, La Gazza Ladra and Agrippina. *Current Management:* Haydn Rawstron Ltd, London. *Address:* c/o Haydn Rawstron UK Ltd, 36 Station Road, London SE20 7BQ, England.

**FELLINGER, Imogen,** PhD; German musicologist; b. Munich; d. of Wolfgang and Lola Margarete Fellinger. *Education:* Gymnasium (Munich), Univs of Munich and Tübingen. *Career:* Research Collaborator Int. Inventory of Musical Sources (RISM) for W Germany and W Berlin 1957–62; Chair. Research Dept for Music Bibliography (19th Century), Inst. of Musicology, Univ. of Cologne 1963–70; Chair. 19th Century Music Archive, State Inst. for Music Research, Prussian Culture Collection, Berlin 1970–93, Sr Lecturer 1983–93; Chair. Working Group on Music Periodicals, Int. Asscn of Music Libraries, Archives and Documentation Centres (IAML) 1979–, Rep. to Répertoire Int. de la Presse Musicale 1992–; Founder-mem. Johannes Brahms Gesamtausgabe 1983–; mem. Kuratorium Österreichische Johannes Brahms Gesellschaft 1991–. *Publications:* Über die Dynamik in der Musik von J. Brahms 1961, Verzeichnis der Musikzeitschriften des 19. Jahrhunderts 1968, Klavierstücke, Opus 118 und 119 von J. Brahms (ed) 1974, Periodica Musicalia 1789–1830 1986, R. Fellinger, Klänge um Brahms 1997; numerous contribs to music periodicals, dictionaries, congress reports and collections. *Address:* St Anna-Platz 10, 80538 Munich, Germany. *Telephone:* (89) 225287.

**FELLNER, Till;** Austrian concert pianist; b. 1972, Vienna. *Education:* Vienna Conservatory with Helene Sedo-Stadler, studied with Alfred Brendel and Oleg Maisenberg. *Career:* performances with a number of leading orchestras, including Acad. of St Martin in the Fields, BBC Symphony Orchestra, Camerata Academica Salzburg, Chicago Symphony Orchestra, City of Birmingham Symphony Orchestra, Los Angeles Philharmonic, Orchestre de Paris, Vienna Philharmonic, Vienna Symphony, London Philharmonia; has worked under many noted conductors, including Claudio Abbado, Andrew Davis, Nikolaus Harnoncourt, Heinz Holliger, Leonard Slatkin, Neville Marriner and Kent Nagano; chamber work with Thomas Zehetmair, Alban Berg Quartet, Heinrich Schiff and the Virtuose Bläser Wien; solo recitals and concerts in many cities, including Amsterdam, Berlin, London, Moscow, Munich, New York, Paris, Salzburg and Vienna; appearances at Schubertiade Feldkirch, Wiener Festwochen, Mostly Mozart in New York, Tanglewood Festival, Edinburgh Festival, Festival d'Antheron, Festival Montreaux-Vevay, Klavier-Festival Ruhr, Salzburg Festival and others; season 1997–98, solo cycle of three concerts with works by Schubert, Berg, Schoenberg and Webern, with performances in London, Paris, Vienna and Vevey; tour of Japan with the Alban Berg Quartet, the USA with the Mozarteum Orchestra Salzburg, and Australia, performing with the Symphony Orchestras of Melbourne, Queensland, Sydney and Tasmania 1998–99; season 1999–2000, three-concert cycle playing Book 1 of The Well-Tempered Klavier by J. S. Bach and the five last piano sonatas of Beethoven in Brussels, London Wigmore Hall, Lyon, Rome, Paris, Vienna and many other cities; season 2003–04 played J. S. Bach's The Well-Tempered Clavier Book 2 and works by Brahms, Liszt, Kurtág, Ligeti, Franck and Messiaen, performing in Vienna, London, Vevay, Amsterdam, Barcelona, Milan and Vancouver. *Recordings include:* Schubert: Four Impromptus for Piano, Schoenberg: Suite für Klavier op 25, Beethoven: Piano Sonata in F minor, opus 57, Mozart: Piano Concerto K482, Rondo in A minor, K511, Beethoven: Piano Sonata in C minor op 10, Schumann: Kreisleriana op 16, Reubke: Sonata in B minor, Schubert: Sonata in A minor op 143, Mozart: Piano Concertos No. 25, K503 and No. 19, K459, J. S. Bach: The Well-Tempered Clavier Book 1. *Honours:* first prize Clara Haskil Int. Competition 1993, Mozartinterpretationspreis of the Mozartgemeinde Wien 1998. *Address:* c/o Künstlermanagement Till Dönch, Rögergasse 24–26/G2, 1050 Vienna, Austria. *Website:* www.doench.at.

**FELTSMAN, Vladimir;** Pianist and Teacher; b. 8 Jan. 1952, Moscow, Russia. *Education:* Piano lessons from age 6 with mother; Studied at Central Music School Moscow and with Yakov Flier at Moscow Conservatory. *Career:* Debut: Soloist with Moscow Philharmonic in 1963; Toured Russia and Eastern Europe from 1971; Played in Japan in 1977 and France in 1978; Emigrated to USA in 1987; Performed at The White House in 1987; New York recital debut at Carnegie Hall in 1987; Professor, State University of New York, New Paltz, 1987–. *Recordings:* Various. *Honours:* 1st Prize, Prague Concertino Competition, 1967; Joint 1st Prize, Marguérite Long-Jacques Thibaud Competition, Paris, 1971. *Address:* c/o Music Department, State University of New York, New Paltz, NY 12561, USA.

**FENNELLY, Brian;** Composer, Theorist, Pianist and Professor of Music; b. 14 Aug. 1937, Kingston, New York, USA; m. 1st, one s.; m. 2nd Jacqueline Burhans Baczynsky. *Education:* Bachelor of Mechanical Engineering, 1958, BA, 1963, Union College; MMus, Yale School of Music, 1965, PhD, Yale University Graduate School, 1968. *Career:* USAF, 1958–61; teacher, Union College and Yale University Faculty 1962–68; Professor 1968–97, Professor Emeritus 1997–, New York University; Editor, Contemporary Music Newsletter 1969–77; Composers' Forum 1968; Performances, USA, Europe, Canada, South America and International Society for Contemporary Music International Festival 1973, 1980, 1981, 1984; commissions from Koussevitsky Foundation 1983, 1999, Fromm Music Foundation 1999; Rockefeller Foundation Bellagio Center residency 1999; Camargo Foundation residency 2002; Copland House residency 2004. *Compositions:* numerous including: SUNYATA, 1970; String Quartet in 2 Movements, 1971–74; Tesserae I–IX,

1971–80; In Wildness is the Preservation of the World, 1976; Quintuplo, 1977–78; Tropes and Echoes, 1981; Canzona and Dance, 1982–83; Thoreau Fantasy No. 2, 1985; Corollaries I–IV, 1986–2000; Brass Quintet, 1987; Keats on Love, 1988–89; Lunar Halos, 1990; A Sprig of Andromeda, 1991–92; On Civil Disobedience. 1993; Locking Horns, Brass Quintet No. 2, 1993–94; Skyscapes I–III, 1996–2002; Chrysalis, 1997; Sonata Serena, 1997–98; Velvet and Spice, Brass Quintet No. 3, 1999; Three's Company, 2000; Arias and Interludes (String Quartet No. 2), 2001, Quincunx 2003, Sasquatch 2003–04; others recorded. *Recordings:* Wind Quintet; Evanescences; String Quartet in 2 movements; In Wildness Is The Preservation Of The World; Sonata Seria; Scintilla Prisca; Prelude and Elegy; Empirical Rag; Tesserae VII; For Solo Flute; Concerto for saxophone and string orchestra; Tesserae VIII; Tesserae II; Fantasy Variations; Two Poems of Shelley; On Civil Disobedience; A Sprig of Andromeda; Paraphrasis; Chrysalis, Thoreau Fantasy No.2, Concert Piece for Trumpet and Orchestra, Lunar Halos, Reflections/Metamorphoses. *Contributions:* Dictionary of Contemporary Music, 1974; New Grove Dictionary of Music and Musicians; Perspectives of New Music; Journal of Music Theory. *Honours:* Nat. Endowment for the Arts Composer Fellowships 1977, 1979, 1985, Guggenheim Foundation Fellowship 1980, First Prize Louisville Orchestra Competition 1986, American Acad. of Arts and Letters Lifetime Achievement Award 1997. *Address:* 2 Schryver Court, Kingston, NY 12401, USA. *E-mail:* Brian.Fennelly.MUS.65@aya.yale.edu (office); FennellyBL@aol.com (home). *Website:* sai-national.org/phil/composers/bfennell.html.

**FENOUILLAT, Christian;** Set Designer; b. 1940, Grenoble, France. *Career:* Stage designs include Fidelio and Gluck's Orpheus for Welsh National Opera; Bellini's I Capuleti at Lisbon, Gluck's Armide and Mozart's Clemenza di Tito at the Théâtre des Champs Elysées and Jenůfa at Spoleto; Wozzeck, Hamlet by Thomas, Der Rosenkavalier and Wagner's Ring, for Geneva Opera; Pelléas et Mélisande at Brussels and Ariane et Barbe-Bleue by Dukas for Opéra de Lyon; Designs for La Cenerentola at Covent Garden, Hamlet at Barcelona and Lucia di Lammermoor for Chicago Lyric Opera (2001–2002 season). *Address:* c/o Opéra de Lyon, 1 place de la Comédie, F–69001 Lyon, France.

**FERGUS-THOMPSON, Gordon;** British pianist; b. 9 March 1952, Leeds; s. of the late George Thompson and Constance Webb. *Education:* Temple Moor Grammar School, Leeds and Royal Northern Coll. of Music. *Career:* debut, Wigmore Hall 1976; has appeared as soloist with orchestras, including Orchestra of the Hague, Gothenburg Symphony Orchestra, Royal Liverpool Philharmonic, The Philharmonia, City of Birmingham Symphony, Hallé, BBC Symphony; extensive tours in Europe, N America, Australia, Far East and S Africa; Prof. of Piano, Royal Coll. of Music 1996–; Gulbenkian Foundation Fellowship 1978. *Recordings include:* The Rachmaninoff Sonatas 1987, Balakirev and Scriabin Sonatas 1987, Complete Works of Debussy (five vols), Complete Works of Scriabin (five vols) 1990–2001, Rachmaninoff's Etudes-Tableaux 1990, Bach Transcriptions 1990, Complete Works of Ravel (two vols) 1992, Headington: Piano Concerto 1997. *Honours:* MRA Prize for Best Instrumental Recording of the Year 1991, 1992. *Address:* 12 Audley Road, Hendon, London, NW4 3EY, England (home). *Telephone:* (20) 8202-5861 (home).

**FERMANI, Simone;** Conductor; b. 1954, Italy. *Education:* Studied at the Perugia Conservatory, Santa Cecilia Conservatory Rome and with Franco Ferrara; Assistant to Leonard Bernstein and the Vienna Philharmonic Orchestra, 1986; Mozart repertory in Bologna, Padua, Venice and Milan; Artistic Director, 1991–, Orchestra Sinfonica Del Sacro Cuore, Milan; Further concerts in Rome, Würzburg, Bangkok, Montreal, Canada, and Il Barbiere di Siviglia at Marseille; Other opera repertory includes works by Mozart, Wagner, Bizet, Rossini, Puccini and Verdi. *Honours:* Perrenoud Prize, 1995 Conductor's Competition, Vienna. *Current Management:* Athole Still International Management, Forresters Hall, 25–27 Westow Street, London, SE19 3RY, England. *Telephone:* (20) 8771-5271. *Fax:* (20) 8768-6600. *Website:* www.atholestill.com.

**FERNANDEZ, Nohema;** Pianist; b. 23 May 1944, Havana, Cuba; 1 d. *Education:* Diploma, Conservatorio Internacional, Havana, 1960; BMus, DePaul University, USA, 1965; MMus, Northwestern University, 1966; DMA, Stanford University, 1983; Piano studies with Jorge Bolet, Adolph Baller, and duo-pianists Vronsky and Babin. *Career:* Debut: Havana in 1960; New York debut at Carnegie Recital Hall in 1983; Appearances at Festival de Musica Latino-Americana, Mexico City, Cabrillo Festival, and Sunriver Festival and recitals in Glasgow, Edinburgh, Vienna, Amsterdam, New York, Miami and San Francisco; Radio broadcasts in Mexico City, New York and San Francisco and television appearances in Chicago and San Jose; Soloist with orchestras in US, Seoul; Recitals in Cuba, USA, Canada, Europe, South America; Member, Jaffe-Fernández Duo (cello and piano); Radio broadcasts in Mexico, USA, Korea; Television appearances. *Recordings:* Various including Latin-American music for the Saarländisches Rundfunk. *Contributions:* Articles in Piano Quarterly and Latin American Music Review. *Honours:* NEA Solo Recitalist Award, 1990–91; Distinction of Honour, La Rosa Blanca, Los Angeles, 1996. *Current Management:* Joanne Rile Artists Management. *Address:* c/o Joanne Rile Artists Management, 801 Old York Road, Noble Plaza, Suite 212, Jenkontown, PA 19046-1611, USA.

**FERNANDEZ, Wilhelmenia;** Singer (Soprano); b. 5 Jan. 1949, Philadelphia, Pennsylvania, USA. *Education:* Studied at Philadelphia, 1969–73, and at the Juilliard School. *Career:* Debut: Houston Opera, 1977, as Gershwin's Bess; Sang in Porgy and Bess on tour in the USA and Europe; Pa ris Opéra, 1979, as

Musetta in La Bohème; Appearances at the New York City Opera, in Boston and Michigan, and at Toulouse as Aida; Opéra du Rhin, Strasbourg, and Liège, 1987–88, as Marguerite; Theater des Westens, Berlin, 1988, as Bess; Bonn Opera, 1989, as Aida; Sang the title role in Carmen Jones, London, 1991; Winner of the Evening Standard Award for Best Actress in a Musical; National Indoor Arena, Birmingham, 1992; 1994–96, Aida at Deutsche Oper Berlin; Other roles include Mozart's Countess and Donna Anna, Purcell's Dido and the title role in Luisa Miller; Concert engagements include Beethoven's Ninth; Recital at Kensington Palace in the presence of HRH Princess of Wales; Regular recitalist throughout Europe and USA; Appeared in the film Diva. *Address:* c/o Marks Management Ltd, 14 New Burlington Street, London W1X 1FF, England.

**FERNANDEZ-GUERRA, Jorge;** Composer; b. 17 July 1952, Madrid, Spain. *Education:* Studied at the Madrid Conservatory. *Career:* From 1970 has worked as musician, composer and actor in the Independent Theatre Movement; Opera, Sin Demonio No Hay Fortuna, based on the Faust legend and performed at Madrid's Sala Olimpia in 1987. *Compositions include:* Sin Demonio No Hay Fortuna, opera; Incidental music to plays by Aeschylus, Wilde, Beckett, Brecht and others; Chamber and orchestral music. *Address:* c/o SGAE, Fernando VI 4, Apartado 484, 28080 Madrid 4, Spain.

**FERNEYHOUGH, Brian John Peter,** ARAM; British composer and academic; *William H. Bonsall Professor of Music, Stanford University;* b. 16 Jan. 1943, Coventry; s. of Frederick George Ferneyhough and Emily May Ferneyhough (née Hopwood); m. 1st Barbara J. Pearson 1967; m. 2nd Elke Schaaf 1980; m. 3rd Carolyn Steinberg 1984; m. 4th Stephanie Jan Hurtik 1990. *Education:* Birmingham School of Music, RAM, Sweelinck Conservatory, Amsterdam, Music Acad., Basle. *Career:* composition teacher, Musikhochschule, Freiburg, Germany 1973–78, Prof. of Composition 1978–86; Prin. Composition Teacher, Royal Conservatory of The Hague 1986; Prof. of Music, Univ. of California, San Diego 1987–99; Leader of Master Class in Composition, Civica Scuola di Musica, Milan 1985–87; Visiting Artist, Berlin 1976–77; Guest Prof., Musikhögskolan, Stockholm 1980, 1981, 1982, 1985; Visiting Prof., Univ. of Chicago 1986; Lecturer in Composition, Darmstadt Int. Courses 1976–96; Guest Prof. of Poetics, Mozarteum, Salzburg, Austria 1995; mem. Akad. der Künste, Berlin 1996; Fellow, Birmingham Conservatoire 1996; William H. Bonsall Prof. of Music, Stanford Univ. 2000–. *Works include:* Sonatas for String Quartet 1967, Firecycle Beta 1969–71, Transit 1972–74, Time and Motion Study III 1974, La Terre Est Un Homme 1976–79, Second String Quartet 1979–80, Lemma-Icon-Epigram 1981, Carceri d'Invenzione 1981–86, 3rd String Quartet 1987, Kurze Schatten II 1988, La Chute d'Icare 1988, Fourth String Quartet 1989–90, Allgebrah 1991, Bone Alphabet 1991, Terrain 1992, Maisons Noires 1993, On Stellar Magnitudes 1994, String Trio 1995, Incipit 1995–96, Kranichtänze II 1996, Allgebrah 1996, Flurries 1997, Unsichtbare Farben 1999, The Doctrine of Similarity 2000, Opus Contra Naturam 2000, Stele for Failed Time 2001, Shadowtime (opera) 2005. *Publications:* Complete Writings on Music 1994, Collected Writings 1996; various articles published separately. *Honours:* Chevalier, Ordre des Arts et des Lettres 1984; Koussevitsky Prize 1979, Grand Prix du Disque 1978, 1984 and other awards and prizes. *Address:* Office 225, Department of Music, Braun Music Center, Stanford University, 541 Lasuen Mall, Stanford, CA 94305-3076 (office); 848 Allardice Way, Stanford, CA 94305, USA. *Telephone:* (650) 725-3102 (office); (650) 565-8842. *Fax:* (650).725-2686 (office); (650) 565-8842. *E-mail:* brian.ferneyhough@stanford.edu (office). *Website:* www.stanford.edu/group/Music (office).

**FERRAND, Emma;** Cellist; b. 1 Oct. 1948, London, England; m. Richard Deakin, 6 Sept 1969, 3 c. *Education:* International Cello Centre, London, 1965–66; Royal Academy of Music, London; Pupil of Pierre Fournier, Geneva. *Career:* debut: Wigmore Hall 1974; solo concerts; BBC recordings; BBC television with Elgar Concerto 1975; chamber music concerts; member, Deakin Piano Trio and Deakin Chamber Players; Senior Lecturer, Royal Northern College of Music, Manchester 1983–; Artist in Residence, Stowe Summer School and Lake District Summer Music 1999–2004; Visiting Professor, Eastman School of Music, NY, USA, 1994; Jury Member, South Africa International String Competition; appearances on BBC 2, Radio 3; tour and masterclasses in USA 2001; concerts throughout Canada and UK 2003. *Recordings:* C Hubert Parry's complete piano trios, piano quartet; Parry's Chamber Works with Piano; Bach Suites for Solo Cello Vol. I. *Honours:* Associate of RAM. *Address:* Ings Cottage, Berrier, Nr Penrith, Cumbria CA11 0XD, England. *Website:* www.emmaferrand.co.uk.

**FERRANDIS, Bruno;** Conductor; b. 1960, France (Algiers). *Education:* Guildhall School, London, and Juilliard School, New York; Further study with Leonard Bernstein and Franco Ferrara. *Career:* Associate Conductor, Juilliard Opera Center, –1993; Resident Conductor, Canadian Opera Company, Toronto, 1993–; repertoire: Lulu, Pelléas, Jenůfa, Katya Kabanova, Erwartung, Fidelio, and works by Verdi, Puccini and Strauss; Dir, New York ensemble Music Mobile, –1996, Contemporary Opera Training in Banff, –2001; Symphonic repertoire with BBC Northern, Polish Radio, Monte Carlo and Jerusalem Symphony, Hong Kong and Seoul Philharmonics, Madrid RTVE, French orchestras particularly Radio France Philharmonique; Specialist in Gurlitt's Wozzeck and Die Soldaten. *Honours:* Grand Prix de la Critique, 1997. *Address:* c/o Musicaglotz, 11 rue le Verrier, 75006 Paris, France.

**FERRARI, Elena;** Singer (Soprano); b. 1970, England. *Education:* National Opera Studio, London. *Career:* Appearances with Opera North as Musetta (1996) and Bice in Korngold's Violanta (also at the 1997 London Proms); Mozart's Countess for English Touring Opera 1997 and Fiordiligi for Opera North, 1997–98; Other roles include Adina (L'Elisir d'amore) Violetta, Donna Elvira, Marguerite, Mélisande, Cherubini's Medea and Polly Peachum in The Threepenny Opera; Jenny in Weill's Mahagonny Songspiel at the London Proms, 1997; Season 1998, as Cinna in Mozart's Lucio Silla for Garsington Opera; Other concerts include the Verdi Requiem, Elijah, Italian Songs and French Melodies. *Honours:* Gerald McDonald Award, National Opera Studio. *Address:* c/o Opera North, Grand Theatre, New Briggate, Leeds, Yorks, LS1 6NU, England.

**FERRARINI, Alida;** Singer (Soprano); b. 9 July 1946, Villafranca, Verona, Italy. *Education:* Studied at the Verona Conservatory and in Venice. *Career:* Debut: Trevisto in 1974 as Mimi; Appearances at the Verona Arena from 1975 as Mércédes and Micaela in Carmen, Oscar and Gilda; Further performances in Rigoletto at Parma in 1987, Paris Opéra in 1988 and Bilbao in 1990; Sang Micaela and Adina at La Scala, Milan; Other roles have included Xenia in Boris Godunov and Liu in Turandot at Verona, Norina, Euridice, Ines in La Favorita at Bregenz, Nannetta and Lauretta in Gianni Schicci; Season 1984 sang Gilda at Covent Garden, and made American debut as Adina at San Francisco; Appeared as Marie in La Fille du Régiment at the Paris Opéra and the Teatro São Carlos in Lisbon, 1988–89; Sang Pergolesi's Serpetta at Reggio Emilia, Micaela at Genoa and Liu at the Festival of Caracalla, 1992; Verona Arena 1996, as Micaela; Verdi's Oscar, 1998. *Address:* c/o Arena di Verona, Piazza Bra 28, 37121 Verona, Italy.

**FERRÉ, Susan (Ingrid);** Concert Organist and Harpsichordist; b. 5 Sept. 1945, Boston, Massachusetts, USA; d. of Gustave A. Ferré and Dorothy Fredericks Ferré; m. Kenneth Charles Lang 18 June 1980; one s. *Education:* BA, Philosophy and Music Literature, BMus, Texas Christian University, 1968; Diplome d'Orgue et Improvisation, Schola Cantorum, Paris, France, 1969; MMus, Eastman School of Music, New York, USA, 1971; DMA, North Texas State University, 1979; Studies with Jean Langlais, Marcel Dupré in France and David Craighead, USA. *Career:* Formerly Adjunct Faculty Member, North Texas State University, Denton and Southern Methodist University, Dallas; Musical Director, Texas Baroque Ensemble, 1980–2001; Director of Early Music at Round Top Festival, 1986–2000; Organ and Harpsichord performances in North and South America, Europe and Scandinavia; Featured Artist, Lahti Organ Festival, Finland and at the World Council of Churches, Switzerland; Recitals at the Cathedral of Notre-Dame, Paris, France; Numerous radio broadcasts, USA; Visiting Assistant Professor of Music and University Organist, Pacific Lutheran University, Tacoma, Washington, 2001–2002; Board Pres., Westfield Center for Keyboard Studies, 1999–2004; Board mem., Jehan Alain Soc., 2002–04; Past Dean, Dallas Chapter, American Guild of Organists, 1991–93. *Compositions:* Numerous compositions published and recorded by Avant Quart Company, France. *Recordings:* Works of Langlais on the Cavaillé organ at Ste Clotilde, Paris; Messe Solennelle by Louis Vierne (VQR Digital Recordings); Preludes & Postludes for the year beginning 9-11-2001; Recordings for national radio and television, France, Hungary, Sweden, Finland, USA; Works by Karg-Elert, Langlais, Alain, Duruflé, Fanny Mendelssohn, Liszt, Ethel Smyth, Tournemire, Messiaen and Bolcom. *Honours:* Fulbright Scholar, 1968–69; Distinguished Alumna Award, Univ. of N Texas School of Music, 2001. *Current Management:* Independent Concert Artists, Garland, Texas, USA. *E-mail:* iconcertartists.com. *Address:* HC 72, Box 199, Kingston, OK 73439, USA. *E-mail:* susanferre@earthlink.net (home). *Website:* home.earthlink.net/~susanferre/ (home).

**FERRERO, Lorenzo;** composer; b. 17 Nov. 1951, Turin, Italy. *Education:* studied with Massimo Bruni and Enore Zaffiri at Bourges (electronic resources), Turin Univ. *Career:* collaboration with the Musik Dia Licht Galarie in Munich from 1974, producing multimedia works; Artistic Consultant at the Puccini Festival at Torre del Lago, 1980–84; Artistic Director of the Arena di Verona 1991–94; Works to attempt a reconciliation between opera and pop/rock music. *Compositions:* Piano Concerto, 1991; Paesaggio con figura for orchestra, 1994; Tempi di quartetto, 1996–98; Three Baroque Buildings, concertino for trumpet, bassoon and strings, 1997; Theatre pieces, Rimbaud, Avignon, 1978; Marilyn, Rome, 1980; La Figlia del Mago, Montepulciano, 1981; Charlotte Corday, Rome, 1989; Le Bleu-blanc-rouge Et Le Noir, Paris, Centre George Pompidou, 1989; Nascita di Orfeo, Verona Filharmonico, 1996. *Address:* Via Lanfranchi 17, 10131 Turin, Italy.

**FERREYRA, Beatriz Mercedes;** Argentine composer; b. 21 June 1937, Cordoba. *Education:* studied with C. Bronstein in Buenos Aires, with Nadia Boulanger, Edgardo Canton, with György Ligeti and Earle Brown in Darmstadt, Groupe de Recherches Musicales (GRM), Paris and Radiotelevisione Italiana (RAI) with Pierre Schaeffer. *Career:* debut with Groupe de Recherches Musicales (GRM), Paris 1964; Asst Prof., GRM 1965–70, Groupe de Musique Experimentale de Bourges (GMEB) 1973; B. Baschet Musical Instrument Development 1971; Music Therapy 1973–76, 1989; Dartmouth Coll. Computer System 1975; jury mem. at fourth Int. Music Competition, GMEB 1976, second Int. Radiophonic Competition Phonurgia Nova, Arles 1987, Royal Conservatory of Music, Mons, and at the 'Metamorphoses' 2000–01. *Compositions:* Demeures Aquatiques 1967, Médisances (Diplome du meilleur disque pour 'Loisir des Jeunes', Paris 1971) 1968, L'Orvietan 1970, Etude aux sons flegmatiques 1971, Le Récit 1971,

Antartide (film score) (Prix du Centre Nat. du Cinéma Français 1972) 1971, Siesta Blanca (third prize Electronic Music Competition, Fylkingen 1975) 1972, Mutations (film score) 1972, A la lueur de la lampe (ballet) 1973, Canto del Loco 1974, Homo Sapiens (for television) (Prix Rissolli 'Della Prima Opera', Italy 1978) 1974, Tierra Quebrada 1976, Echoes 1978, La Baie St James (for television) 1980, Jeux des Rondes 1980–84, Musiques en Feu (for television) 1981, Cercles des Rondes 1982, La Calesita 1982, Boucles, rosettes et serpentines 1982, Bruissements 1983, Arabesque autour d'une corde raide 1984, Passacaille déboitée pour un lutin 1984, Petit Poucet Magazine (Concours Int. de Création Radiophonique Phenourgia Nova Prix France Culture de l'Innovation, Arles 1986) 1985, The UFO Forest (hon. mention Concours Int. du GMEB, Bourges 1987) 1986, L'Autre... ou le chant des marécages 1987, Souffle d'un petit Dieu distrait (Laureat du concours UPIC dans le cadre des Journées d'Informatique Musicale, Paris 1999) 1988, 1997, Brise sur une fourmillère 1988, Tata, tocame la toccata 1990, Remolinos 1990, Mirage Contemplatif? 1991, Ríos de Sueño: No. 1 Río de los pájaros (Concours int. de musique et d'art sonore électroacoustique Prix Magisterium, Bourges 2000) 1998, No. 2 Río de los pájaros escondidos 1999–2000, No. 3 Río de los pájaros azules 1993, 1998, Jazz't for Miles 2001, La Ba-balle du chien-chien à la mé-mère 2001, Cantos de antes (Radio Bulgarie second prize 2004) 2002, Les Chemins du vent des glaces 2002, Murmureln 2003, Le Solfegiste solfeté 2003. *Publications:* Souffle d'un petit Dieu distrait 1997, Chrysopée electronique 1998, Le solfège sonore de Pierre Schaeffer et la composition musicale (article in LYRE magazine, December 1999), Le 'groupe solfège' du G.R.M. et le Traité des Objets Musicaux (article in Du sonore au musical of Sylvie Dallet and Anne Veitl) 2001, Musikhören: Theorie un Praxis Elektroakustischer Musik, and Klänge und Klangstrukturen - Finden, Erfinde, Verarbeiten (two chapters in Welt Musik) 2004; contrib. to articles, reports and album notes. *Address:* 600 Chemin des Logis, 76270 Nesle Hodeng, France (home). *Telephone:* (2) 32-97-10-16 (home).

**FIALA, George;** Composer, Pianist and Conductor; b. 31 March 1922, Kiev, Ukraine, Russia. *Education:* Tchaikovsky State Conservatory, 1939–41; Studied composition with Hansmaria Dombrowski and conducting with Wilhelm Furtwängler, Akademische Hochschule für Musik, Berlin, 1942–45, and with Leon Jongen at Conservatoire Royal de Musique. *Career:* Active member of well-known Seminare des Arts Brussels, participated in many musical events as composer, pianist and conductor; Settled in Montreal, Canada, in 1949 and active as composer, pianist, organist and teacher; Producer for Radio Canada International. *Compositions include:* Soloist with orchestra: Capriccio, 1962, Divertimento Concertante, 1965, Musique Concertante, 1968, Sinfonietta Concertata, 1971; Voices with orchestra: Canadian Credo, 1966; Orchestral: Autumn Music, 1949, Symphony No. 4, 1973, Overtura Buffa, 1981, The Kurelek Suite, 1982; Flute Concerto, 1991; Sinfonico II, 1992; Chamber music: Cantilena and Rondo, 1963, Duo Sonata for Violin and Harp, 1971, Concertino Canadese, 1972, Partita Concertata, 1982, Quintet, 1982; Musique à 7, 1992; Voice: Four Russian Poems, 1968, My Journey, 1982; Requiem, 1995; Piano solos and duos. *Recordings:* Chamber Music for Five Wind Instruments; Montreal; Concertino; Suite Concertante; Three Movements; Sonata Breve; Sonata l for Two Pianos; Duo Sonata; The Kurelek Suite; Quartet No. 2 for Saxophones; Sinfonietta Concertata. *Address:* PO Box 66, Station B, Montreal, Quebec, H3B 3J5, Canada.

**FIALKOWSKA, Janina;** Pianist; b. 1951, Canada. *Education:* Baccalaureate and Maîtrise, University of Montreal; Studies in Paris with Yvonne Lefébure; At the Juilliard School with Sasha Gorodnitzki and privately with Arthur Rubinstein. Has performed with all major North American orchestras and most major European orchestras. Recitals World-wide. Premiered Liszt's Concerto No. 3 opus posthumus with Chicago Symphony, 1990. Premiered the Andrzej Panufnik Concerto; Renowned for Chopin and Liszt interpetations and promotes 20th century Polish and Canadian music; Founder of Piano 6, a group of internationally renowned Canadian Pianists who are committed to a programme that affordably brings important recitals to areas throughout Canada where classical music performances are a rarity. *Recordings:* Musicaviva: Moszkowski Concerto; Szymanowski solo piano works; Chopin 24 Etudes; Paderewski, Piano and orchestra works. *Honours:* Top Prizewinner, A Rubenstein Piano Competition, 1974; Opus Award, 1998; Awarded with the Officer of the Order of Canada, 2002. *Current Management:* Ingpen & Williams Ltd, 7 St George's Court, 131 Putney Bridge Road, London, SW15 2PA, England.

**FIDDES, Ross Ashley;** Composer and Conductor; b. 20 Nov. 1944, Newcastle, New South Wales, Australia. *Education:* AMusA, 1971; Dip Law, 1968. *Career:* Solicitor, 1968–95; Musical Director, Novocastrian Arts Orchestra, 1991–95; Principal Conductor, Opera Hunter, 1992–95; Conductor and Musical Director, The Sound Construction Company, 1988–94. *Compositions include:* Four Ceremonies, for piano, 1982; Never Again, for male chorus, 1984; White Birds Flying, for female chorus, 1984; Children, for chorus, 1984; The Proposal, 1 act chamber opera, 1985; Combination Permutations, for piano duet, 1985; Suite for Brass Quintet, 1985; Trumpet Sonata, 1985; Ceremony, for symphonic wind band, 1987; Image and Refraction, for clarinet, bassoon, horn and string quintet, 1987; Bird Song, song cycle for soprano and clarinet, 1991; Abelard and Heloise, 2-act musical, 1997–. *Honours:* Festival of Emerging Composers, USA, 1995; City of Newcastle Drama Award (CONDA), for outstanding achievement in Newcastle Theatre, for Abelard and Heloise, 1997. *Address:* PO Box 375, New Lambton, NSW 2305, Australia.

**FIELD, Helen;** British singer (soprano); b. 14 May 1951, Wrexham, Clwyd, Wales. *Education:* Royal Northern Coll. of Music, Manchester and Royal Coll. of Music, London. *Career:* studied FRG; won triennial Young Welsh Singers' Competition 1976; roles with Welsh Nat. Opera include Musetta, Poppea, Kristina, Gilda, Marzelline, Mimi, Tatyana, Jenůfa, the Vixen, Marenka and Desdemona; has also appeared with Opera North and Scottish Opera; début at Royal Opera House, Covent Garden as Emma in Khovanschina 1982; début with ENO, as Gilda 1982, at Metropolitan Opera, New York, as Gilda; has also appeared with Netherlands, Cologne and Brussels opera cos; concert performances with several leading orchestras and regular radio and TV appearances; recordings include Rigoletto, A Village Romeo and Juliet and Osud. *Address:* c/o Athole Still International Management Ltd., Foresters Hall, 25–27 Weston Street, London, SE19 3RV (office); c/o Askonas Holt Ltd, 27 Chancery Lane, London, WC2A 1PF, England.

**FIELDSEND, David;** Singer (tenor); b. 1947, Yorkshire, England. *Education:* Guildhall School of Music and Drama. *Career:* Debut: Vanja in Katya Kabanova at the 1972 Wexford Festival; Appearances with Scottish Opera as Jacquino in Fidelio, Arturo (Lucia di Lammermoor) and Rossini's Almaviva; Further engagements with the D'Oyly Carte Opera, Opera North, Travelling Opera, Chelsea Opera Group and Dorset Opera; Covent Garden debut, 1983, in Der Rosenkavalier, Bardolph (Falstaff) in Paris and Borsa (Rigoletto) at Jerusalem; Concerts and oratorios with orchestras and choral societies throughout the United Kingdom and Europe; Season 1996 included gala concert with the Royal Philharmonic and Gilbert and Sullivan evening at the Albert Hall. *Recordings include:* Five operetta albums with the D'Oyly Carte Opera. *Honours:* Gold Medal at the GSMD, London. *Current Management:* Musicmakers International Artists Representation, Tailor House, 63–65 High Street, Whitwell, Hertfordshire SG4 8AH, England. *Telephone:* (1438) 871708. *Fax:* (1438) 871777. *E-mail:* musicmakers@compuserve.com. *Website:* www.operauk.com.

**FIERENS, Guillermo;** classical guitarist; b. 1940, Argentina. *Education:* studied with Andres Segovia. *Career:* debut in Spain 1963; US debut in 1965 with concert tour of Mexico in 1967; Regular engagements in the United Kingdom with the London Symphony Orchestra, Hallé Orchestra, English Chamber, Royal and London Philharmonics, Philharmonia and Orchestra of the Welsh National Opera; Played at Queen's Hall in Edinburgh in 1983 and festival appearances at Norwich, St Andrews, Harrogate, Lichfield, Newbury and Belfast; Further concerts in Netherlands, Switzerland, Spain, Hong Kong, Czechoslovakia, USA, Italy and Canada. *Recordings:* Music by Castelnuovo-Tedesco, Albeniz, Turina, Sor and Villa-Lobos. *Honours:* Caracas International Guitar Competition 1967; Citta d'Alessandria Competition in Italy; Gold Medal, Villa-Lobos Competition, Rio de Janeiro, 1971.

**FIFIELD, Christopher George,** MusB, ARCO, ARMCM; British conductor and writer on music; *Music Director, Lambeth Orchestra;* b. 4 Sept. 1945, Croydon, Surrey, England; m. Judith Weyman 1972 (divorced); three c. *Education:* Manchester Univ., Royal Manchester Coll. of Music, Guildhall School, Cologne Musikhochschule. *Career:* fmrly Asst Dir of Music Capetown Opera, music staff Glyndebourne for 12 years, Music Dir London Contemporary Dance Theatre, Dir Northampton Symphony Orchestra, Central Festival Opera, Reigate and Redhill Choral Soc. and Jubilate Choir; frequent conductor at Trinity Coll. of Music; Dir of Music, Univ. Coll. London 1980–90; fmrly chorus master Chelsea Opera Group; currently Music Dir and Conductor, Lambeth Orchestra. *Publications:* Max Bruch: his Life and Works 1988, Wagner in Performance 1992, True Artist and True Friend: A Biography of Hans Richter 1993, Letters and Diaries of Kathleen Ferrier 2003, Ibbs and Tillett: the Rise and Fall of a Musical Empire 2005; contrib. to reference books and journals, including Viking Opera Guide, International Opera Guide, New Grove Dictionary of Opera 1992, Grove 7, Dictionary of National Biography, Oxford Companion to Music. *Address:* 162 Venner Road, London, SE26 5JQ, England. *E-mail:* christopherfifield@ntlworld.com. *Website:* www.lambeth-orchestra.org.uk.

**FIGUERAS, Montserrat;** Singer (Soprano); b. 7 March 1940, Barcelona, Spain. *Education:* Studied in Barcelona and Basle. *Career:* Performances with Ars Musicae and research into early singing techniques; Has worked with the Schola Cantorum Basiliensis and sung with members of the ensemble Hesperion XX and the Capella Reial; Sang in Martin y Soler's Una Cosa Rara at the 1997 Vienna Festival (Grosser Saal).

**FIGUEROA, Rafael;** Cellist; b. 27 March 1961, San Juan, Puerto Rico; m. Irma I. Justicia 1987. *Education:* BM and Performer's Certificate, Indiana Univ. School of Music; violoncello studies with Janos Starker and Gary Hoffman. *Career:* recital debut at Terrace Theater, Kennedy Center for The Arts, Washington DC; recitals in major concert halls including Library of Congress, Kennedy Center, National Gallery of Art, Jordan Hall, Shriver Hall, Merkin Hall, Caslas Hall in Tokyo, Carnegie Recital Hall; numerous radio broadcasts on national public radio. *Recordings:* F. Mendelssohn's Concerto for Violin and Piano with Orpheus Chamber Orchestra, 1989; Schoenberg's Verklärte Nacht, 1990; Strauss's Le Bourgeois Gentilhomme and Divertimento Op 86, 1992; Weber's Clarinet Concertos and Rossini's Variations, 1992. *Contributions:* The Strad Magazine, Strings Magazine.

**FILATOVA, Ludmila Pavlovna;** Russian singer (mezzo-soprano); b. 6 Oct. 1935, Orenburg; d. of Pavel Filatov and Valentina Semoylova; m. Rudakov Igor 1971. *Education:* Faculty of Mathematics, Leningrad Univ. *Career:* mem. CPSU 1969–91; began singing in choir; mem. of Kirov Opera choir 1958–60; soloist with Kirov (now Mariinsky) Opera 1962–; teacher of singing, Leningrad Conservatoire 1973–; gives chamber concerts: Shostakovich, Tchaikovsky, Rachmaninov, Glinka etc. *Major roles include:* Lyubasha in A Bride for the Tsar, Marfa in Khovanshchina, Carmen, Marta-Ekaterina in Petrov's Peter I, Countess in The Queen of Spades. *Honours:* Glinka Prize 1960, People's Artist of USSR 1983. *Address:* Mariinsky Theatre, Teatralnaya pl. 1, St Petersburg, Russia.

**FILIANOTI, Giuseppe;** Singer (Tenor); b. 1973, Italy. *Education:* With Alfredo Kraus in Milan and at the academy of La Scala. *Career:* Debut: Sang in Donizetti's Dom Sébastien at Bologna; Appearances at La Scala in Gluck's Armide and Paisiello's Nina and as Donizetti's Edgardo at Turin; Alfredo at Florence, Tokyo and Covent Garden (2001); Engagements in Rossini's Le Siège de Corinthe and Tancredi at Pesaro, Un giorno di regno by Verdi at Bologna and La Favorita at Las Palmas, 2001; Season 2001–2002 as Tamino and Rinuccio in Gianni Schicchi at Rome, and Fenton in Falstaff at Bologna. *Honours:* Winner, Francisco Viñas and Placido Domingo Operalia Competitions. *Address:* c/o Teatro Comunale di Bologna, Largo Respighi 1, 40126 Bologna, Italy.

**FILIP, Ana Felicia;** singer; b. 1959, Romania. *Education:* Bucharest Academy. *Career:* debut as Antonia in Les Contes d'Hoffmann, with Romanian Opera; Sang at first at Brasov, then at the National Opera in Bucharest (debut, 1986, as Antonia in Les Contes d'Hoffmann); Guest appearances in Basle (as Violetta, 1991), Frankfurt and elsewhere including Covent Garden, 1994; Nancy 1998, as Violetta; Season 2000–01 as the Trovatore Leonora at Dortmund and Contessa de Folleville in Il Viaggio a Reims, at Liège and Bologna; Many concert engagements.

**FILIPOVA, Elena;** Singer (Soprano); b. 2 Dec. 1957, Pasardjk, Bulgaria. *Education:* Sofia Music High School; Piano and oboe at Sofia Music Conservatory. *Career:* Debut: Marenka in Bartered Bride, Bad Staatstheater Karlsruhe, 1981; Badisches Staatstheater, 1981–86; Sang at Salzburg Festival in 1983; Guest performances at Hamburg, Frankfurt, Barcelona, Luxemburg, Hannover as Violetta in 1988, Bern, Vienna, and Nuremberg; Has also sung Donna Anna, Amelia Boccanegra and Tatiana, and sang Aida at Hanover in 1990; Concerts in Germany, Austria, France, Italy, and Switzerland, and television appearances on ORF Salzburg Festival in 1983, ZDF, Berlin in 1983, SWF, Baden Baden in 1985 with Mozart and Handel Arias; Sang Manon Lescaut at Sydney, 1998; Sang Puccini's Minnie at Toronto, 2001. *Honours:* 1st Prize, Karajan Foundation, Salzburg Festival, 1982. *Address:* Staatstheater, Opernplatz 1, 3000 Hannover, Germany.

**FILIPOVIC, Igor;** Singer (Tenor); b. 18 April 1951, Ljubljana, Slovenia. *Education:* Studied in Ljubljana and in Italy. *Career:* Debut: Sang Ernesto in Don Pasquale, 1976; Member of the Vienna Kammeroper, 1976–77, Lucerne Opera, 1977–78; Guest appearances in Europe, the USA and Canada as Rossini's Amenofi in Mosè in Egitto and Arnoldo in William Tell, Arturo in I Puritani, Edgardo in Lucia di Lammermoor, Enrico in Maria di Rohan, Tonio in La Fille du Régiment, the Duke of Mantua in Rigoletto, Alfredo in La Traviata, Riccardo in Un Ballo in Maschera, Rodolfo in Luisa Miller, Cavaradossi in Tosca, and Don José at Bregenz Festival in 1992; Also sang at Prague, Venice, Milan, Rome, Turin, Palermo, Vienna Staatsoper and Volksoper, Stuttgart, Mannheim, Frankfurt, Brussels, Chicago and New York at the City Opera; Verdi's Riccardo at Ljubljana, 1998; Broadcasting engagements throughout Europe. *Address:* c/o Opernhaus Dortmund, Kuhstrasse 12, 44137 Dortmund, Germany.

**FINCH, Catrin;** Welsh harpist; b. 1980, Llanon, Ceredigion; m. Hywel Wigley 2003. *Education:* Purcell School, RAM. *Career:* performed at BBC proms aged 11, while mem. of Nat. Youth Orchestra; Royal Harpist 2000–04; has performed in concerts with Bryn Terfel and Sinfonia Cymru in Dublin and Birmingham, English Chamber Orchestra, London Acad. Symphony Orchestra, RPO, Acad. of St Martin-in-the-Fields, London Mozart Players, Nat. Polish Radio Symphony Orchestra, BBC Nat. Orchestra of Wales, Manchester Camerata Orchestra, European Union Chamber Orchestra, Peoria Symphony, Canton Symphony, Cedar Rapids Symphony Orchestra, North Carolina Symphony Orchestra, Yakima Symphony Orchestra, Boston Pops, Charlotte Symphony; has given recitals at Wigmore Hall, Carnegie Hall, Young Concert Artists Series, New York and Boston; formed the Catrin Finch Band 2005–, debut performance Koh Samui Festival, Thailand 2005. *Recordings:* Harp Recital 2000, Carnaval de Venise 2001, Crossing the Stone 2003, The Harpist 2004. *Honours:* Royal Overseas League Music Competition Marisa Robles Harp Prize, London 1999, first prize Lily Laskine Int. Harp Competition, France 1999, winner Young Concert Artists Int. Auditions 2000, Princeton Univ. Concerts Prize 2000, Echo Klassik Award for Best Crossover Artist in Germany 2004. *Current Management:* Young Concert Artists Inc., 250 W 57th Street, Suite 1222, New York, NY 10107, USA. *Telephone:* (212) 307-6655. *Fax:* (212) 581-8894. *E-mail:* yca@yca.org. *Website:* www.yca.org. *E-mail:* catrin@harpingon.com. *Website:* www.catrinfinch.com.

**FINCKEL, David;** American cellist; b. 6 Dec. 1951, Kutztown, PA. *Career:* mem., Emerson String Quartet 1977–; premiere concert at Alice Tully Hall in New York 1977, with works by Mozart, Smetana and Bartók; European debut at Spoleto, Italy 1981; quartet-in-residence, Smithsonian Inst., WA 1980, at the Hartt School 1981, and the Spoleto and Aspen Festivals 1981; first resident quartet, Chamber Music Soc. of Lincoln Center 1982–83; many performances of works by Bartók, including all six quartets in a single evening, and contemporary works; premieres include Mario Davidovsky's 4th

Quartet and works by Maurice Wright and George Tsontakis, Beethoven series at South Bank, London 1996; Haydn, Beethoven, Razumovsky Quartets 2001. *Recordings include:* Walter Piston's Concerto for string quartet, winds and percussion, works by Andrew Imbrie, Henry Cowell, Roy Harris and Gunther Schuller, Bartók's Six Quartets. *Current Management:* c/o Matthew Zelle, IMG Artists, 152 W 57th Street, Fifth Floor, New York, NY 10019, USA. *E-mail:* kirshdem@aol.com. *Website:* www.emersonquartet.com.

**FINDLAY, Jane;** Singer (mezzo-soprano); b. 1960, England. *Education:* Royal Northern Coll. of Music and with Peter Harrison and Paul Hamburger. *Career:* sang with the Glyndebourne Festival Chorus, then as Hermia and Dorabella with the Touring Opera, and Third Boy in Die Zauberflöte at the Festival; sang Dorabella with the Northern Ireland Opera Trust in Belfast and with Opera 80 in tour; appearances at the Wexford Festival and with Opéra Nancy; sang in Margot-la-Rouge at the Camden Festival in 1984 and in Monteverdi's L'Orfeo at Florence under Roger Norrington; tour of Germany with the Monteverdi Choir in 1985, including Irene in Handel's Tamerlano at the Göttingdon Festival and concert performances in Cologne; Season 1987–88 in Opera 80's Cenerentola and appearances in The Gondoliers and La Belle Hélène for New Sadler's Wells Opera; WNO debut in 1989 in La Traviata and Covent Garden debut in 1990 as Magdalena in Die Meistersinger; concert repertoire includes The Dream of Gerontius, Shéhérazade by Ravel, Bach's Christmas Oratorio and Messiah. *Honours:* South East Arts Award; Miriam Licette Award, 1985.

**FINE, Wendy;** Singer (soprano); b. 19 Dec. 1943, Durban, South Africa. *Education:* Studied with John van Zyl in Durban and with Christian Mueller, Erik Werba and Maria Hittorf at the Vienna Music Academy. *Career:* Debut: Stadttheater Berne as Madama Butterfly; Appearances at opera houses in London, Hamburg, Munich, Stuttgart, Berlin, Lisbon, Vienna and Geneva; Sang at Bayreuth Festival in 1971; Roles include Nedda, Micaela, Marguerite, Mimi, Sophie in Der Rosenkavalier, Desdemona, Fiordiligi, Donna Elvira, Pamina, Luise in Der Junge Lord (British premiere in 1965), Ophelia in Szokolay's Hamlet, and Maria in The Miracles of Our Lady by Martinů; Sang at Covent Garden, 1971–77 as Musetta, Gutrune, Donna Elvira, Fiordiligi and Jenůfa, and at La Scala Milan in 1977 as Berg's Marie.

**FINGERHUT, Margaret;** Pianist; b. 30 March 1955, London, England. *Education:* Royal College of Music, London; Peabody Conservatory, Baltimore. *Career:* Performed in the United Kingdom, America, Europe, Scandinavia, Africa, India, Turkey and Israel; Played with London Symphony, Royal Philharmonic, London Philharmonic and Philharmonia Orchestras; Broadcasts for BBC radio and WFMT, Chicago; Appeared on film and television; Professor of Piano, Royal Northern College of Music, 1998–. *Recordings:* Chandos Records; Several with the London Philharmonic and London Symphony Orchestras, including world premiere recording of Arnold Bax's Winter Legends; Has also recorded music by Grieg, Dukas, Falla, Howells, Suk, Stanford and Moeran; Collections of Russian and French Composers. *Honours:* Hopkinson Gold Medal, 1977; Boise Foundation Scholarship, 1977; Greater London Arts Association, Young Musician of the Year, 1981. *Current Management:* Helen Houghton. *Address:* 9 Cromwell Road, Burgess Hill, Sussex RH15 8QH, England.

**FINK, Bernarda;** Argentine singer (mezzo-soprano); b. 29 Aug. 1955, Buenos Aires; m.; two c. *Education:* Instituto Superio de Arte del Teatro Colón, Buenos Aires and studied with Michel Corboz in Europe. *Career:* sang Rossini's Cenerentola at Buenos Aires 1986; concerts of Baroque music with Michel Corboz as conductor in Paris, Geneva, Berlin, Lisbon and Tokyo; sang Penelope in Monteverdi's Ulisse at Innsbruck 1993, Montpellier and Barcelona (also the Messenger in Orfeo); Amsterdam as Proserpina in Orfeo 1995; Cenerentola at the Berlin Staatsoper 1994; season 2000 as Dorabella at Aix-en-Provence and European tour as Gluck's Orpheus, with René Jacobs; recitals at Carnegie and Wigmore Halls, Paris, Vienna and Sydney Opera Houses. *Recordings include:* Rossini's Zelmira and Handel's Amadigi, Handel's Giulio Cesare and Flavio, Monteverdi's Orfeo and Ulisse, Messiah. *Current Management:* Impulse Art Management, PO Box 15401, MK Amsterdam, Netherlands. *Telephone:* (20) 626 69 44. *Fax:* (20) 622 71 18.

**FINK, Manfred;** Singer (Tenor); b. 15 April 1954, Frankfurt am Main, Germany. *Education:* Studied in Frankfurt. *Career:* Chorus of the Cologne Opera, 1979–81 then soloist with the Mainz Opera from 1981 with debut as Tamino; Deutsche Oper am Rhein, Düsseldorf, from 1982 as Mozart's Ferrando, Belmonte and Don Ottavio; Guest appearances from 1984 at Buenos Aires, Venice, Rome, Nice, Florence as David in Die Meistersinger in 1985, Frankfurt and Vienna; Other roles have included Edgardo in Lucia di Lammermoor, Des Grieux in Manon Lescaut, Rinuccio and Nemorino; Sang the Steuermann in Der fliegende Holländer for Cologne Opera in 1991, and Pedrillo in Die Entführung at the Schwetzingen Festival in 1991; Sang Verdi's Macduff at the Komische Oper, Berlin, 1997. *Recordings:* Handel Dettingen Te Deum. *Address:* c/o Komische Oper, Behrenstrasse 55–57, D–10117 Berlin, Germany.

**FINK, Michael (Jon);** Composer and Teacher; b. 7 Dec. 1954, Los Angeles, USA. *Education:* Studied at the California Institute of the Arts with William Kraft, Harold Budd, Barney Childs and Mel Powell (MFA 1980). *Career:* Performances with the Negative Band and Stillife; Composer-in-Residence, North Michigan University, 1985; Teacher at California Institute of the Arts from 1982. *Compositions include:* Two pieces for piano, 1983; Work for chamber orchestra, 1986; Living to be Hunted by the Moon, for clarinet, bass

clarinet, electronics, 1987; A Temperament for Angels, electronics and keyboards, 1989; Sound Shroud Garden, with Jim Fox, 1989; Epitaph, bass clarinet, 1990. *Recordings include:* Album vocalise. *Publications include:* Business Music in Contemporary Life, 1989. *Address:* c/o ASCAP, ASCAP Building, 1 Lincoln Plaza, NY 10023, USA.

**FINK, Myron S.;** composer; b. 19 April 1932, Chicago, USA. *Education:* Juilliard School with Bernard Wagenaar and Castelnuovo-Tedesco, Burrill Phillips at the University of Illinois, Cornell University with Robert Palmer and in Vienna. *Career:* former teacher at Alma College, Hunter College New York, the Curtis Institute and the City University of New York; Opera, The Conquistador, premiered at San Diego, 1997. *Compositions:* Operas: The Boor, after Chekhov, 1955, Susanna And The Elders, 1955, Jeremiah, 1962, Judith And Holofernes, 1978, Chinchilla, 1986, The Island Of Tomorrow, 1986; The Conquistadors, 1997. *Honours:* Woodrow Wilson Memorial Fellowship 1954.

**FINK, Richard-Paul;** Opera Singer (Dramatic Baritone); b. 23 March 1955, USA. *Education:* Kent State University; Oberlin College. *Career:* Worked and performed with the Houston Symphony, Pops, Houston Ballet; Other productions include Falstaff, Boris Godunov, Eugene Onegin at Houston Opera, Scarpia at Bremer Stadt Theater in Germany, 1988, Jokanaan in Salome, Enrico in Lucia di Lammermoor and Tchelio in The Love for Three Oranges at Bremen Opera, 1988–89, Kaspar in Der Freischütz, 1988–89, Escamillo in Carmen and as Rigoletto for Welsh National Opera, 1990–91, the Water Gnome in Rusalka and Klingsor in Parsifal at Houston Grand Opera, 1991–92; 1992–93 season opened as Sid in Albert Herring with the Atlanta Opera, Kurwenal in Tristan, Count di Luna in Il Trovatore, Pizarro in Fidelio and Sebastiano at the Washington Opera Kennedy Center's staging of D'Albert's Tiefland; Sang Wagner's Dutchman at Sydney, 1996; The Forester in The Cunning Little Vixen at Toronto, 1998; Alberich in Wagner's Ring Cycle (Met, Dallas, Seattle), 1999, 2000, 2001; Title role in Flying Dutchman in Sydney, Toronto and Mexico City; Leading roles with Metropolitan Opera, New York, Opéra Bastille, Paris, Seattle, Dallas, Los Angeles and others; Engaged for Rigoletto for Opéra du Montreal, 2003. *Current Management:* Columbia Artists Management, Inc. (Zemsky-Green Division), 165 West 57th Street, New York, NY 10019. *Address:* 1310 Bridle Spur Lane, Houston, TX 77055, USA.

**FINK, Walter;** Singer (Bass); b. 1949, Vienna, Austria. *Education:* Studied at the Vienna Conservatory. *Career:* Sang at the Vienna Staatsoper from 1977 (Baron Ochs, 1982); Bregenz Festival, 1989–95, as Daland, and Rocco in Fidelio; Brussels, 1992, in Rossini's La Donna del Lago; Vienna, 1991–95, as Mozart's Osmin and Pogner in Die Meistersinger; Other roles include Kaspar in Der Freischütz, Wagner's Landgrave and Hunding, Sarastro, Ramphis (Aida), Orestes and La Roche in Capriccio; Season 1997–98 as the Father in Leopold I's Il Figliol Prodigo at the Vienna Redoutensaal and Colonna in Rienzi at the Staatsoper; Season 2000–01 as General Polkan in The Golden Cockerel at Bregenz and as Sarastro at Antwerp. *Recordings include:* Fafner in Das Rheingold. *Address:* c/o Vienna Staatsoper, Opernring 2, 1010 Vienna, Austria.

**FINKE, Martin;** Singer (Tenor); b. 1948, Rhede bei Bocholt, Germany. *Education:* Studied with Hilde Wesselman at the Folkwang Hochschule Essen. *Career:* Sang first at opera houses in Augsburg, Cologne Stuttgart; and at Bayreuth Festival, 1975; Sang at Barcelona in 1983 as Jacquino in Fidelio and Bregenz Festival in 1984; Sang David in Die Meistersinger at the Théâtre de la Monnaie in Brussels, 1985 and at Salzburg Festival in 1986 in the premiere of Penderecki's Die schwarze Maske; Other roles include Mozart's Pedrillo and Monostatos and Mime in Der Ring des Nibelungen, Nice Opéra, 1988; Cologne Opera 2000, as Hauk in The Makropulos Case and Mime in Das Rheingold; Concert singer in the Passions of Bach, Messiah and the Missa Solemnis. *Recordings:* Pagliacci, Intermezzo and Ariadne auf Naxos; Die Verschworenen by Schubert; Operettas by Lehar. *Address:* c/o Oper der Stadt Köln, Offenbachplatz, 5000 Cologne, Germany.

**FINKO, David;** Composer and Conductor; b. 15 May 1936, Leningrad, Russia. *Education:* Studied at the Leningrad School of Performing Arts, 1950–58 and Leningrad Conservatory, 1960–65. *Career:* Emigrated to the USA in 1979; Visiting Lecturer, University of Pennsylvania, 1979–81; Lecturer and Composer-in-Residence, University of Texas, El Paso, 1981. *Compositions:* Polinka, after Chekhov, 1965; In A Torture Chamber Of The Gestapo, 1970; The Enchanted Tailor, 1983; Orchestral: 6 Tone Poems, 1965–78, Symphony No. 1, 1969, Piano Concerto, 1971, Viola Concerto, 1971, Symphony No. 2, 1972, Double Concerto for Violin, Viola and Orchestra, 1973, Double Concerto for Viola, Double Bass and Orchestra, 1975, Harp Concerto, 1976, Concerto for 3 Violins and Orchestra, 1981, Pilgrimage To Jerusalem, 1983; Hear, O Israel for soloists, chorus and orchestra, 1987; Violin Concerto, 1988; Chamber: Piano Sonata, 1964, Mass Without Words for Violin and Organ, 1968, Lamentations of Jeremiah for Violin, 1969, Fromm Septet, 1983. *Honours:* Grants and fellowships, ASCAP, The Fromm Foundation and the Memorial Foundation of Jewish Culture. *Address:* Music Department, University of Texas, El Paso, TX, USA.

**FINLEY, Gerald Hunter,** MA, ARCM; Canadian singer (baritone); b. 30 Jan. 1960, Montreal; s. of Eric Gault Finley and Catherine Rae Hunter; m. Louise Winter 1990; two s. *Education:* Glebe Collegiate Inst., Ottawa, Univ. of Ottawa, Royal Coll. of Music, London, UK, Nat. Opera Studio, London, King's Coll. Cambridge. *Career:* chorister St Matthew's Church, Ottawa 1969–78; mem. Ottawa Choral Soc., Cantata Singers, Ont. Youth Choir 1977–78,

Glyndebourne Festival Chorus, UK 1986–89; debut as opera soloist, Papageno in The Magic Flute, London 1989; roles at Glyndebourne: Sid (Albert Herring) 1989, Papageno, Guglielmo, Count Dominik (Arabella), Kuligin (Katya Kabanova) 1990–93, Figaro (Marriage of Figaro) at opening of new opera house 1994; Owen Wingrave, Olivier (Capriccio), Nick Shadow; Agamemnon (Iphigénie en Avlide), debut Canadian Opera Co., Sid (Albert Herring) 1991; has sung Figaro at Covent Garden London and many other opera houses worldwide 1992–; other roles at Covent Garden include Pilgrim (Pilgrim's Progress), Achilla (Giulio Cesare), Creonte (L'Anima del Filosofo), Forester (Cunning Little Vixen), Don Giovanni; roles at Opéra de Paris include Valentin, Sharpless, Papageno, Figaro, Don Giovanni 2001; debut Metropolitan Opera, New York, Papageno (Magic Flute) 1998; role of Mr. Fox in Fantastic Mr. Fox, LA Opera 1998; debut ENO, Harry Heegan (The Silver Tassie) 2000; concert soloist and lieder singer; Visiting Prof. Royal Coll. of Music (RCM) 2000. Film: Owen Wingrave 2001. Recordings: Papageno, Guglielmo, Sid, Masetto, Haydn's Creation, Brahms' Requiem, Silver Tassie, Pilgrim's Progress, Dido and Aeneas; Songs of Travel 1998, Schubert Complete Songs 1817–1821, Complete Songs of Henri Duparc 2002. Radio: numerous recordings with BBC and CBC. Honours: John Christie Award, Glyndebourne 1989; Juno Award for Best Vocal Peformance (Canada) 1998; Singer Award Royal Philharmonic Soc. 2001. Address: c/o IMG Artists Europe, 616 Chiswick High Road, London, W4 5RX, England; c/o IMG Artists, 825 Seventh Avenue, New York, NY 10019, USA. Telephone: (20) 8233-5800 (London); (212) 489-8300 (USA). Fax: (20) 8233-5801 (London); (212) 246-1596 (New York).

**FINNIE, Linda Agnes;** British singer (mezzo-soprano); b. 9 May 1952, Paisley; d. of William Finnie and Agnes Finnie. Education: John Neilson Institution, Paisley, Carrick Acad., Maybole, Royal Scottish Acad. of Music and Drama. Career: concert performances in many European countries, Australasia, the Far East and USA and regular radio broadcasts; has sung with all the maj. British orchestras and with Chicago, Boston, Pittsburgh and San Francisco Symphony orchestras, Hong Kong Philharmonic, Orchestre de Paris, Orchestre Philharmonique de Radio France, RAI Orchestra (Turin) and Danish Radio Orchestra, under many leading conductors, including Claudio Abbado, Lorin Maazel, Daniel Barenboim, André Previn, Michael Tilson-Thomas, Jeffrey Tate, Sir John Pritchard, Sir Colin Davis, Simon Rattle, Andrew Davis, Esa Pekka Salonen, Neemi Jarvi and Richard Hickox; opera roles with ENO include Amneris, Eboli, Brangäne and Ulrica, with Royal Opera House, Waltraute, Mme. Larina, Second Norn; has also sung at Geneva, Nice, Bayreuth and Frankfurt; Hertogenbosch Concours, John Noble Bursary, Countess of Munster Scholarship. Recordings include: Alexander Nevsky, Elijah, Beethoven's 9th Symphony, Songs of the British Isles, Armide, La Rondine and l'Enfant et les Sortilèges. Honours: Kathleen Ferrier Memorial Award; Kathleen Ferrier Prize. Address: 16 Golf Course, Girvan, Ayrshire, KA26 9HW, Scotland, UK.

**FINNILA, Birgit;** Singer (Contralto); b. 20 Jan. 1931, Falkenberg, Sweden; m. Allan Finnila, 2 s., 3 d. Education: Studied in Goteborg with Ingalli Linden and at Royal Academy of Music with Roy Henderson. Career: Concerts in Sweden from 1963; London debut in 1966 followed by concerts in Berlin, Hamburg, Hanover, Stuttgart and Düsseldorf; Tours of USA, Australia, Russia and Israel from 1968; Opera debut at Goteborg in 1967 as Gluck's Orpheus; Guest appearances at La Scala Milan and the Munich Staatsoper; Salzburg Easter Festival, 1973–74 as Erda in The Ring, under Karajan; Sang Brangaene in Tristan und Isolde at the Paris Opéra in 1976. Recordings: Cimarosa's Requiem; Mozart's Betulia Liberata; Bach's Magnificat; Bruckner's Te Deum; Dvořák's Requiem; Strauss's Aegyptischa Helena; Bach's B minor Mass; Vivaldi's Tito Manlio. Honours: Grand Prix du Disque for Juditha Triumphans by Vivaldi. Address: c/o Svensk Konsertdirektion AB, Box 5076, 40222 Goteborg, Sweden.

**FINNISSY, Michael Peter;** Composer; b. 17 March 1946, London, England. Education: Royal Coll. of Music, London. Career: Dir of Music, London School of Contemporary Dance, 1969–74; Lecturer, Chelsea Coll., Chelsea School of Art, Dartington Summer School; guest artist, The Victorian Coll. of The Arts, Melbourne, 1982–83; composition teacher, Winchester Coll., 1987–, Sussex Univ., 1989–2000; Chair in Composition, Univ. of Southampton, 1999–; Sr Fellow, KBC-Chair in New Music, Catholic Univ. of Leuven, 2000–02; Royal Acad. of Music, 1991–2001; Chair., British Section ISCM, 1989–90; Pres., ISCM, 1991–96; Exec. Councillor, ISCM, 1990–96; hon. mem., International Society for Contemporary Music. Compositions: World, 1968–74; Folk-Song Set, 1969–70; Tsuru Kame, 1971–73; Mysteries, 1972–79; Cipriano, 1974; seven piano concertos, 1975–81; Offshore, 1975–76; Mr Punch, 1976–77; English Country-Tunes, 1977; Alongside, 1979; Sea and Sky, 1979–80; Kelir, 1981; Dilok, 1982; Whitman, 1981–2005; Vaudeville, 1983; Ngano, 1983–84; String Quartet, 1984; Cabaret Vert, 1985; The Undivine Comedy, Stage Work, 1988; Red Earth, 1987–88; Gershwin Arrangements and More Gershwin, 1975–90; Obrecht Motetten, 1988–; Unknown Ground, 1989–90; Thérèse Raquin, stage work, 1992–93; Folklore, 1993–95; Shameful Vice, Stage Work, 1994; Liturgy of Saint Paul, 1995; The History of Photography in Sound, 1995–2001; Onbevooroordeeld Leven, 2000–01; four organ symphonies 2002–; Verdi Transcriptions (for Book 4, British Composer Award Instrumental category British Acad. of Composers and Songwriters 2005) 1972–2005, Molly-House (Making Music Award British Composer Awards 2005). Current Management: Oxford University Press Repertoire Promotion Department, 70

Baker Street, London, W1U 7DN, England. Telephone: (20) 7616 5900. Fax: (20) 7616 5901. Website: www.michaelfinnissy.info.

**FINSCHER, Ludwig,** PhD; German musicologist, lexicographer and academic (retd); b. 14 March 1930, Kassel. Education: Univ. of Göttingen, Univ. of Saarbrücken. Career: Asst Lecturer, Univ. of Kiel 1960–65, Univ. of Saarbrücken 1965–68; Ed., Die Musikforschung 1961–68, Co-Ed. 1968–74; Prof. of Musicology, Univ. of Frankfurt am Main 1968–81, Univ. of Heidelberg 1981–95; mem. Akademie der Wissenschaften, Heidelberg, Akademie der Wissenschaften und der Literatur, Mainz, Academia Europaea; corresponding mem. American Musicological Soc. Publications: Collected Works of Gaffurius (ed., two vols) 1955, 1960, Collected Works of Compère (ed., five vols) 1958–72, Loyset Compère (c.1450–1518): Life and Works 1964, Geschichte der Evangelischen Kirchenmusik (co-ed., second edn) 1965, Studien zur Geschichte des Streichquartetts: I, Die Entstehung des klassischen Streichquartetts: Von den Vorformen zur Grundlegung durch Joseph Haydn 1974, Collected Works of Hindemith (ed. with K. von Fischer) 1976–, Renaissance-Studien: Helmuth Osthoff zum 80. Geburtstag (ed.) 1979, Quellenstudien zu Musik der Renaissance (ed., two vols) 1981, 1983, Ludwig van Beethoven (ed.) 1983, Claudio Monteverdi: Festschrift Reinhold Hammerstein zum 70. Geburtstag (ed.) 1986, Die Musik des 15. und 16. Jahrhunderts: Neues Handbuch der Musikwissenschaft (ed., vol. 3/1–2) 1989–90, Die Mannheimer Hofkapelle im Zeitalter Carl Theodors (ed.) 1992, Die Musik in Geschichte und Gegenwart (ed., second edn, 26 vols) 1994–, Bach's Posthumous Role in Music History 1998, Joseph Haydn 2000; contrib. editorially to the complete works of Mozart and Gluck, contrib. to scholarly books and journals. Honours: Dr hc (Univ. of Athens) 2002, (Univ. of Zürich) 2003;hon. mem. Int. Musicological Soc., Gesellschaft für Musikforschung, hon. foreign mem. Royal Musical Asscn, London 1978–; Akademie der Wissenschaften Prize, Göttingen 1968; Ordre pour le mérite 1994, Grand Order of Merit, Germany 1997. Address: Am Walde 1, 38302 Wolfenbüttel, Germany (home). Telephone: 5331-32713 (home). Fax: (5) 33133276 (home).

**FINSTERER, Mary;** Composer; b. 25 Aug. 1962, Canberra, Australia. Education: Studied with Brenton Broadstock and Riccardo Formosa in Melbourne and Louis Andriessen in Amsterdam; BMus, MMus, Melbourne University, undertaking a PhD in composition. Career: Lecturer at various universities including Montreal, Dusquene in Pittsburgh, Wollongong, Melbourne and Victorian College of Arts, Australia; Her work has been performed at major festivals and concerts Throughout the world including New York, Paris, Amsterdam, Pittsburgh, Los Angeles, Montreal, Zürich, Essen, Berlin, Frankfurt, Manchester, London, Sydney and Melbourne; Many commissions and performances from leading ensembles in Australia, Europe, Canada and the USA including the Queensland, Melbourne and Sydney Symphony Orchestras, Australian Chamber Orchestra, Le Nouvel Ensemble Modern, Ensemble Modern, Arditti String Quartet and Ensemble Intercontemporain. Compositions include: Scat, for chromatic harmonica and orchestra, 1992; Catch, for soprano saxophone, bass clarinet and piano, 1992; Omaggio alla Pieta, for 6 voices, double bass (optional) and percussion, 1993; Tract for solo cello, 1993; Constans, violin concerto, 1995; Nyx, concerto grosso, 1996; Magnet, for solo tuba and tape, 1997; Ether, for solo flute, 1998; The Door in the Wall for solo piano with multimedia, 1999; Pascal's Sphere, for chamber orchestra and multimedia, 1999. Honours: Le Nem Forum, 1991; Paris Rostrum, 1992; Has represented Australia in 4 ISCM World Music Day Festivals: Switzerland, 1991; Germany, 1995, England, 1997 and Romania, 1998.

**FIORILLO, Elisabetta;** Singer (Mezzo-soprano); b. 1960, Naples, Italy. Career: Appeared as Ulrica at Naples, Musetta in Leoncavallo's Bohème at Venice and Azucena at Zürich, Macerata, Turin, Verona, and Parma, 1984–; Guest appearances in Berlin, Hamburg, Verona and Philadelphia as Amneris in Aida, 1993–96; Preziosilla in La Forza del Destino at Barcelona, Azucena at Munich, Eboli in Turin and Fenena in Nabucco at Naples; Sang Eboli at Trieste, 1997; Concert repertory includes the Verdi Requiem and song recitals; Further engagements at the Vienna Staatsoper and the Caracalla Festival, Rome. Honours: Winner, Mattia Battistini Competition, 1983; Prizewinner, Voci Verdiane Competition Busseto and the Vincenzo Bellini Competition, 1984. Address: c/o Opernhaus Zürich, Falkenstrasse 1, 8008 Zürich, Switzerland.

**FIRSOVA, Elena Olegovna;** Russian composer; b. 21 March 1950, Leningrad (now St Petersburg); d. of Oleg Borisovich Firsov and Victoria Evgenievna Firsova; m. Dmitri Smirnov 1972; one s. one d. Education: Moscow Conservatory with Alexander Pirumov and Yury Kholopov, also studied with Edison Denisov. Career: mem. Composers' Union, Russia 1976–; British debut with Petrarch's Sonnets 1980; moved to UK 1991; freelance composer 1991–; Prof., composer-in-residence, Keele Univ. 1993–; Tutor in Composition, Royal Northern Coll. of Music, Manchester 1999–2001; featured composer, Park Lane Group Jan. 2004. Compositions include: String Quartet No. 1 1972, String Quartet No. 2 1974, Violin Concerto No. 1 1976, Chamber Concerto for flute and strings 1978, String Quartet No. 3 Misterioso 1980, Chamber Concerto for cello and orchestra 1982, Violin Concerto No. 2 1983, Earthly Life cantata for soprano and ensemble 1984, Fantasie for violin solo 1985, Chamber Concerto for piano and orchestra 1985, Music for 12 1986, Piano Sonata 1986, Forest Walks for soprano and ensemble 1987, Chamber Concerto for horn and ensemble 1987, Augury for orchestra and chorus 1988, Autumn Music 1988, Monologue for bassoon 1989, Nostalgia for orchestra 1989, String Quartet No. 4 Amoroso 1989, Stygian Song for soprano and ensemble 1989, Odyssey for seven performers 1990, Verdehr-Terzett for violin, clarinet and piano 1990, The Nightingale and the Rose (chamber opera after Wilde) 1991, Seven Haiku for voice and lyre 1991, Far Away saxophone quartet, Sea Shell for voice and ensemble 1991, Whirlpool for voice, flute and percussion 1991, Silentium for voice and string quartet 1991, String Quartet No. 5 Lagrimoso 1992, Secret Way for orchestra and voice 1992, Distance for voice and ensemble 1992, Meditation in the Japanese Garden for flute, viola and piano 1992, You and I for cello and piano 1992, Starry Flute 1992, Vigilia for violin and piano 1992, Otzvuki for flute and guitar 1992, Cassandra for orchestra 1992, Phantom for four viols 1993, The Night Demons for cello and piano 1993, Crucifixion for cello and bayan 1993, Hymn to Spring for piano 1993, Monologue for solo saxophone 1993, The Enchanted Island 1993, Album Leaf for cello and piano 1993, Piano Trio No. 2 Mad Vision 1993, Insomnia for four singers 1993, Before the Thunderstorm for soprano and ensemble 1994, String Quartet No. 6 1994, String Quartet No. 7 Compassione 1995, String Quartet No. 8 The Stone Guest 1995, String Quartet No. 9 The Door is Closed 1996, Chamber Concerto for cello and orchestra 1996, Temple of Mnemosyne chamber concerto for piano and orchestra 1996, The River of Time for mixed chorus and chamber orchestra 1997, The Secrets of Wisdom for soprano, flute, recorder and percussion 1997, The Sound of Time Passing for orchestra 1997, The Captivity for wind orchestra, Leaving for strings, Equinox for choir, The Scent of Absence for bass, harp and flute 1998, String Quartet No. 10 La Malinconia 1998, Frozen Time for piano quartet, Winter Elegy for counter-tenor and string trio, The Singing Forest for four recorders and strings, Das Erste ist vergangen for soprano, bass, mixed choir and chamber orchestra, Vernal Equinox for violin and piano 1999, Perpetual Return for ensemble 2001, The Rest is Silence for cello (from poem by Mandelstam), Epitaph for string trio, Romantische Fragmente for ensemble, Prrok (Prophet) for baritone, chorus and accordion, Euphonisms for euphonium and piano 2003, Requiem on Anna Akhmatova Poem 2003. *Current Management:* Boosey & Hawkes PLC, First Floor, Aldwych House, 71–91 Aldwych, London, WC2B 4HN, England. *Telephone:* (20) 7299-1919. *Fax:* (20) 7299-1991. *Website:* www .boosey.com/firsova.

**FIRTICH, Georgy (Ivanovich);** Composer; b. 20 Oct. 1938, Russia; Divorced, 2 s. *Education:* Leningrad Music College; Leningrad Conservatoire. *Career:* Debut: Leningrad in 1953 as composer and musician; Composer of symphonies, film scores, and music for radio and theatre; Chairman of St Petersburg Association of Modern Music; Professor, Music Faculty, St Petersburg State Pedagogical University; mem, Composers' Union of St Petersburg; Association of Modern Music, St Petersburg. *Compositions include:* 7 Sonatas for Piano and for Viola and Piano, 1960–90; Bug, 1961 and Return, 1964, ballets; About Motherland, symphony, 1963; Baths, opera, 1971; Concerto-Symphony, 1986; Vocal Cycle for Baritone, 1988; Vocal Cycle for Soprano and Piano, 1990; Choral works include: Leningrad, cantata in 6 movements, for Soprano, Baritone, Chorus and Symphony Orchestra, 1976; 10 Sonatas for Piano and for flute and piano, 1996–99; Concerto Fanasia for 2 pianos, 1997; Quintet-fantasia Music Therapy, 1999; Young Ignoramus, musical play, 1999; The Reminiscences of Mikhailovskoye, symphonic poem, 1999. *Recordings include:* Adventures of Captain Vrungel, 1986; Edwards; Sonata No. 4 for piano, 1985; Concerto-symphony for piano and symphony orchestra, 1986; Doctor Aibolit, 1999. *Honours:* Laureate of Leningrad Competitions; Honoured Worker of Arts, Russia, 1993. *Address:* Novoalexandrovskaya St 11-29, St Petersburg 193012, Russia.

**FISCH, Asher;** Israeli conductor; *Music Director, New Israeli Opera;* b. 1965, Jerusalem. *Career:* engagements with Don Giovanni at Munich, Tristan and La Forza del Destino at Copenhagen and Katya Kabanova at Houston; British and US debuts 1995–1996, with Der fliegende Holländer at Los Angeles and Gala with the Royal Opera; Music Dir, Vienna Volksoper –2000, with Die Meistersinger and Zemlinsky's Der König Kandaules; Vienna Staatsoper performances include Parsifal, Tosca, and Eugene Onegin; Metropolitan Opera debut 2000, with The Merry Widow; season 2001–02 with Parsifal for Seattle Opera, Les Contes d'Hoffmann in Berlin and The Ring in Adelaide (Helpmann Award for Best Musical Dir 2005) 2004–05; Music Dir, New Israeli Opera, Tel-Aviv 2001–, with Otello, Aida and Norma; concerts with the Munich, Israel and Radio France Philharmonics, Detroit Symphony, Philharmonica Hungarica and NHK SO, Japan. *Current Management:* Askonas Holt Ltd, Lonsdale Chambers, 27 Chancery Lane, London, WC2A 1PF, England. *Telephone:* (20) 7400-1700. *Fax:* (20) 7400-1799. *E-mail:* info@ askonasholt.co.uk. *Website:* www.askonasholt.co.uk. *Address:* New Israeli Opera, The Opera House, Tel-Aviv Performing Arts Centre, 28 Leonardo da Vinci Street, PO Box 33321, Tel-Aviv 61332, Israel. *Website:* www.israel-opera .co.il.

**FISCHER, Adam;** Austrian conductor; b. 9 Sept. 1949, Budapest, Hungary; m. Doris Fischer 1979; one s. one d. *Education:* Budapest School of Music. *Career:* conducting and composition studies in Budapest and Vienna with Swarowsky; held posts at Graz Opera, Karlsruhe; Gen. Music Dir Freiburg; work with Bavarian State Opera; regular conductor with Vienna State Opera 1973–, recently with Zurich Opera; major debuts Paris Opera 1984, La Scala 1986, Royal Opera House 1989, ENO 1991, San Francisco Opera 1991, Chicago Lyric Opera 1991, Metropolitan Opera, New York 1994; has conducted many world-class orchestras, particularly Helsinki Philharmonic, Boston and Chicago Symphony and LA Philharmonic and Vienna Chamber Orchestra; concert tours to Japan and USA; Music Dir Kassel Opera 1987–92, Founder and Artistic Dir first Gustav Mahler Festival, Kassel 1989; f. Austro-

Hungarian Haydn Orchestra (AHHO) and Festival, Eisenstadt, Austria 1987, later Music Dir AHHO; Music Dir Mannheim Opera 2000–; Conductor Bayreuth Festival (Ring Cycle) 2001–; Chief Conductor Danish Radio Sinfonietta. *Film:* BBC TV film of Bartok's Bluebird's Castle with London Philharmonic Orchestra (Italia Prize 1989 and Charles Heidsieck Prize). *Music:* numerous recordings including complete Haydn symphonies, and Lucio Silla and Des Knabaen Wunderhorn with Danish Radio Sinfonietta. *Honours:* won Jt First Prize, Milan Cantelli Competition 1973. *Address:* c/o Askonas Holt Ltd, Lonsdale Chambers, 27 Chancery Lane, London, WC2A 1PF, England. *Telephone:* (20) 7400-1700. *Fax:* (20) 7400-1799.

**FISCHER, György;** Conductor, Pianist and Harpsichordist; b. 12 Aug. 1935, Budapest, Hungary. *Education:* Franz Liszt Academy, Budapest; Salzburg Mozarteum. *Career:* Assistant to Karajan at the Vienna State Opera where he conducted Die Zauberflöte and Die Entführung; Principal Conductor at the Cologne Opera, notably in a Mozart cycle produced by Jean Pierre Ponnelle; Bavarian State Opera with Don Giovanni, Idomeneo and Die Zauberflöte in South America, and Cimarosa's Le Astuzie Femmnili at Wexford; British debut with the Welsh National Opera in 1973 returning for Così fan tutte and Le nozze di Figaro; London debut in 1979 with the British premiere of Mozart's Mitridate at the Camden Festival; English Chamber Orchestra from 1980; Debut with Australian Opera, 1987–88, conducting Così fan tutte in 1990; Don Giovanni for Vancouver Opera in 1988; Season 1992 with Le nozze di Figaro at Sydney; Accompanist to leading singers including his former wife, Lucia Popp. *Recordings include:* Mozart Arias for soprano voice with Kiri Te Kanawa, Teresa Berganza and Cecilia Bartoli.

**FISCHER, Hanne;** Singer (mezzo-soprano); b. 1968, Denmark. *Education:* Royal Danish Acad. of Music, Copenhagen, studied with Ingrid Bjoner and Vagn Thordal. *Career:* debut, Royal Opera, Copenhagen 1993, as Cherubino in Le Nozze di Figaro; engaged as member of the ensemble at the Opera in Kiel, Germany 1993–97, where she sang Siebel (Faust), Second Lady (The Magic Flute), Dorabella (Così fan tutte), Cherubino (Le Nozze di Figaro), Hänsel (Hänsel and Gretel), Angelina (Rossini's La Cenerentola) and Idamante (Idomeneo); guested at the Royal Opera, Copenhagen, singing Rosina (The Barber of Seville) 1993, 1994, Dorabella (Così fan tutte) 1995, and Zerlina (Andreas Homoki's staging of Don Giovanni) 1996; debut at the Glyndebourne Festival as Annio (Nicholas Hytner's staging of La Clemenza di Tito) 1995, she was reinvited there to sing Isolier (Le Comte Ory) 1997, 1998; further engagements at the Flemish Opera, Antwerp, as Annio 1997, Idamante (Idomeneo) 1998; member of the ensemble at the Royal Opera, Copenhagen 1997–, where she has sung Suzuki (Madama Butterfly), Idamante (Idomeneo), Der Komponist (Ariadne auf Naxos), Dorabella (Così fan tutte), Cherubino (Le Nozze di Figaro), Offred's Double (The Handmaid's Tale), Pauline (Queen of Spades), Amando (Le Grand Macabre) and Marchesa Melibea (Il Viaggio a Reims); numerous concerts all over Europe, several of which broadcast on radio and TV, including the title role in Offenbach's Perichole and the final gala concert at Euromusicale, Munich; soloist in the first performance of Vølvens Spaadom by Andy Pape, with Copenhagen Philharmonic Orchestra 2000; soloist in the Philharmonie Berlin with the RSO Berlin in the performance of Franz Léhar's opera Tatjana 2001; season 2000–01 at the Flemish Opera, Antwerp and Gent, singing The Fox in Robert Carsen's staging of The Cunning Little Vixen by Janáček, also guested at the Staatsoper Hamburg and the Opera in Bonn; season 2002–03, debut at the Théâtre des Champs-Elysées, Paris as The Fox (The Cunning Little Vixen), at the Flemish Opera singing Dorabella (Guy Joosten's staging of Così fan tutte), with both the Copenhagen Philharmonic and the Danish National Radio Symphony Orchestra as soloist in Mahler's Rückert-Lieder, and with the Royal Opera, Copenhagen singing Waltraute (Kasper Holten's new production of Die Walküre); season 2003–04 debut as Sextus (David McVikar's new La Clemenza di Tito), and performances in Il Viaggio a Reims, Das Rheingold, and The Handmaid's Tale at the Royal Opera, Copenhagen. *Recordings:* Tatjana (with the RSO, Berlin) 2001, The Handmaid's Tale 2000, Archipel des solitudes (with the Danish National Radio Symphony Orchestra and Leif Segerstam) 2000, Des Sänger's Fluch (with the Danish National Radio Symphony Orchestra and Michael Schönwandt) 1999, Vom Pagen und der Königstochter (with the Danish National Radio Symphony Orchestra and Michael Schönwandt) 2000. *Honours:* Noilly Prat Music Prize. *Address:* Opern- und Konzertagentur Kursidem & Tschaidse, Am Tal 28, 80331 München, Germany. *Telephone:* (89) 29 16 16 61. *Fax:* (89) 29 16 16 67. *E-mail:* kursidem@opern-agentur.com.

**FISCHER, Iván;** Hungarian/Dutch conductor; *Music Director, Budapest Festival Orchestra;* b. 20 Jan. 1951, Budapest; s. of Sándor Fischer and Éva Boschán; two d. *Education:* B. Bartók Music Conservatory, Budapest and Wiener Hochschule für Musik under Hans Swarowsky, Mozarteum, Salzburg under Nikolaus Harnoncourt. *Career:* Jt Music Dir Northern Sinfonia of England, Newcastle 1979–82; Music Dir Kent Opera 1984–; Prin. Guest Conductor Cincinnati Symphony Orchestra 1989–96; Music Dir Lyon Opera House 1999–; co-founder and Music Dir Budapest Festival Orchestra 1983–; debut in London with Royal Philharmonic Orchestra 1976; concert tours with London Symphony Orchestra to Spain 1981, USA 1982, world tour 1983; concerts with Berlin Philharmonic Orchestra, Concertgebouw Orchestra etc.; main performances in USA: Los Angeles Philharmonic, Cleveland, Philadelphia, San Francisco Symphony and Chicago Symphony Orchestras; operas: Idomeneo, Don Giovanni, Julius Caesar, La Bohème, La Clemenza di Tito, Marriage of Figaro, Magic Flute, in London, Paris, Vienna. *Honours:* Premio

Firenze 1974, Rupert Foundation Award, BBC, London 1976, Gramophone Award for Best Orchestral Recording of the Year (for The Miraculous Mandarin), Philips 1998. *Address:* Budapesti Fesztiválzenekar Alapítvány (BFO Foundation), Alkotás utca 39/c., 1123 Budapest, Hungary. *Website:* www.bfz.hu.

**FISCHER, Jan F.;** Composer; b. 15 Sept. 1921, Louny, Czechoslovakia; m. 1969, 1 d. *Education:* Studied at the Prague Conservatory, 1940–45; Master School for Composers, with Jaroslav Rídky, Prague University, 1945–48. *Career:* Committee member of the Pritomnost Association for Contemporary Music, 1945–49, and of the Union of Czechoslovak Composers, 1949–70; mem, Guild of Czech Composers, Presidium, 1959–671 VP FIAF, 1964–66; Society Present Time, 1991–97, chairman, 1997–98. *Compositions include:* Operas: The Bridegrooms, Brno, 1957; Romeo, Juliet and Darkness, 1962; Oh, Mr Fogg (after Around the World in 80 Days), 1971; The Miracle Theatre, Radio Prague, 1973; Dekameron, 1977; Copernicus, 1983; The Bridge for Klara, television 1988; The Rites, 2001; Ballets: Marionetteer, 1980; Battallion, 1997; Orchestral: Symphony, 1959; Clarinet concerto, 1963; Harp concerto, 1973; Commemoration, 1973; Night Music for strings, 1973; Concerto for orchestra, 1980; Partita for string orchestra, 1983; Piano Quintet, 1949; Conversations with Harp for string trio, harp and flute, 1979; Brass Quintet, 1983; Sextet for harp and wind quintet, 1993; Concertos for two harps and string orchestra, 1997; Arietti for soprano and harp, 1996; Armonioso for violin and piano, 1998; Concerto for flute, harp and string orchestra, 1999; Chamber operas: Excitement, 1996; Guard, 1996, Concerto for trumpet and orchestra 2003, Dialogues for harp and piano 2005. *Recordings:* Prague Preludes for 5 harps; Suite for Flute and Harp; Etudes for harp solo; Monologues for harp solo; 130 works for theatre, music for film and television; Songs. *Honours:* State Award, Laterna Magica, Brussels, 1959; Prize, City of Prague, 1966; Prize, Guild of Composers, 1986. *Address:* 147 00 Prague 4, Jasna 18, Czech Republic (home).

**FISCHER, Julia;** German violinist; b. 1983, Munich. *Education:* Leopold Mozart Conservatory, Augsburg with Lydia Dubrowskaya, Munich Acad. of Music with Ana Chumachenco. *Career:* has performed with orchestras in USA, Japan, Brazil and throughout Europe, including New York Philharmonic, Boston Symphony Orchestra, Acad. of St Martin-in-the-Fields, RPO, Berlin Radio Symphony Orchestra, Bavarian Radio Symphony Orchestra, Gewandhaus Orchestra, Dresden Philharmonic, Real Orquesta Sinfónica de Sevilla; chamber music pnrs include Christoph Eschenbach, Jean-Yves Thibaudet, Daniel Müller-Schott, Tabea Zimmermann, Gustav Rivinius, Lars Vogt, Oliver Schnyder, Milana Chernyavska. *Recordings:* Brahms, Piano Quartets 2003, Russian Violin Concertos (Gramophone magazine Editor's Choice 2005) 2004, Bach, Sonatas and Partitas for Solo Violin 2005. *Honours:* first prize and special prize Int. Yehudi Menuhin Competition 1995, Eurovision Competition for Young Instrumentalists 1996, Foundation of European Industry Prix d'Espoir 1997. *Current Management:* Mastroianni Associates Inc., 161 W 61st Street, Suite 17E, New York, NY 10023, USA. *Telephone:* (212) 586-6210 (office). *Fax:* (212) 586-5963 (office). *E-mail:* info@ jfmartists.com (office). *Website:* www.jfmartistsonline.com (office). *E-mail:* julia@juliafischer.com. *Website:* www.juliafischer.com.

**FISCHER, Klaus Peter;** Musicologist; b. 16 Jan. 1937, Breslau, Silesia, Germany. *Education:* Diploma in School Music, Franz-Liszt Hochschule, Weimar, 1958; PhD, Cologne University, 1970. *Career:* German Historical Institute, Rome, Italy, 1970–72; German Research Association, 1972–76; Scientific Collaborator, Institute for Hymnological and Ethnological Studies, Cologne-Maria Laach, Germany, 1977–78; Lecturer, 1982–87, Associate Professor, 1988–, University of Pavia, Italy; mem, Gesellschaft für Musikforschung; International Musicological Society; Società Italiana di Musicologia; Associazione fra Docenti Universitari Italiani di Musica. *Publications:* Die Psalmkompositionen in Rom um 1600 (ca 1570–1630), 1979. *Contributions:* Analecta Musicologica; Archiv für Musikwissenschaft; Studi Musicali; Die Musikforschung; New Grove's Dictionary of Music and Musicians, 6th edition; Kirchenmusikalisches Jahrbuch; Die Musik in Geschichte und Gegenwart (MGG), 2nd edition; Congress Reports; Articles in: The New Grove Dictionary of Music and Musicians, second edition, 2001. *Address:* Via Villa Glori 5, 26100 Cremona, Italy.

**FISCHER, Miroslav;** Stage Director and Opera Regisseur; b. 6 Dec. 1932, Slovakia; m. (1) Olga Hanakova, 17 Oct 1977, (2) Jitka Saparova, 19 Oct 1977, 1 s., 1 d. *Education:* School of Musical Arts, Bratislava, 1955. *Career:* Debut: Traviata, at Slovak National Theatre, Bratislava, 1955; More than 130 operas and operettas performed in Bratislava, Banska, Bystrica, Kosice, Brno, Plzeň, Ankara, Bilbao, Brussels, most notably: The Consul, 1956; Fliegende Holländer, 1957; Pelléas et Mélisande, 1958, Fidelio, 1960; Midsummer Night's Dream, 1963; La Forza del Destino, 1964; The Greek Passion, 1969; Salome, 1976; Lohengrin, 1976; Falstaff, 1978, Elektra, 1980; Don Carlos, 1981; Katarina Izmailova, 1984; Un Ballo in Maschera, 1985; Wozzeck, 1985; Donizetti's Caterina Cornaro at Bratislava, 1997. *Address:* Dankovskeho 14, 811 03 Bratislava, Slovakia.

**FISCHER, Norman;** Cellist; b. 25 May 1949, Plymouth, MI, USA. *Education:* Studied at the Interlochen Arts Academy and with Richard Kapuscinski at the Oberlin College Conservatory. *Career:* Member of the Concord String Quartet from 1971; Nationwide performances in a wide repertory, including many works by American composers; George Rochberg has written his Piano Quintet, String Quintet and String Quartets Nos 3–7 for the ensemble; Other composers who have been premiered include Lukas Foss

(Third Quartet), Ben Johnston (Crossing) and Jacob Druckman (Third Quartet); Quartet in Residence at Dartmouth College, New Hampshire, from 1974. Scholar in Residence at Dartmouth College. *Honours:* Naumburg Award, 1971. *Address:* c/o Music Department, Dartmouth College, Hanover, NH 03755, USA.

**FISCHER, Thierry;** Swiss conductor; *Principal Conductor, BBC National Orchestra of Wales;* b. 1957. *Education:* studied flute with Aurèle Nicolet. *Career:* fmr flautist with Zürich Opera; fmr Prin. Flute, Chamber Orchestra of Europe, where he also began conducting; devoted career solely to conducting from 1992; fmr Prin. Conductor Netherlands Ballet Orchestra; Prin. Conductor Ulster Orchestra 2001–06, BBC Nat. Orchestra of Wales 2006–; has appeared as guest conductor with orchestras including the Philharmonia, CBSO, Halle, BBC Symphony, Bournemouth Symphony, Scottish Chamber, Northern Sinfonia, Philharmonique de Radio France, Hanover Radio, Düsseldorf Symphoniker, Berlin Symphony, Sinfonica di Milano, Stavenger Symphony, Copenhagen Philharmonic, Monte-Carlo, RSI Lugano Chamber, Zürich Chamber, Australian Chamber; made N American debut with Nat. Arts Centre Orchestra, Ottawa and Colorado Symphony 2003–04; tours with Ulster Orchestra include Prague and New York, also BBC Proms 2005. *Recordings:* Frank Martin, Polyptyque 1992, Mozart, Serenades 1997, Netherlands Wind Ensemble plays Janáček 1999, Stravinsky, Mavra and Chamber Works 1999, Prokofiev, Violin Concerto No. 2 2003, Jean Françaix, Symphony in G Major, Françaix, Orchestral Works 2004, Françaix, Le Roi Nu and Les Demoiselles de la Nuit 2005. *Current Management:* c/o Susie McLeod, Intermusica Artists' Management Ltd, 16 Duncan Terrace, London, N1 8BZ, England. *Telephone:* (20) 7278-5455 (office). *Fax:* (20) 7278-8434 (office). *E-mail:* mail@intermusica.co.uk (office). *Website:* www.intermusica.co.uk (office).

**FISCHER-DIESKAU, Dietrich;** German singer (baritone) and conductor; b. 28 May 1925, Berlin; s. of Dr Albert Fischer-Dieskau and Dora Klingelhöffer; m. 1st Irmgard Poppen 1949 (died 1963); three s.; m. 2nd Ruth Leuwerik 1965 (divorced 1967); m. 3rd Kristina Pugell 1968; m. 4th Julia Varady 1978. *Education:* high school in Berlin, singing studies with Profs Georg Walter and Hermann Weissenborn. *Career:* mil. service 1943–45; POW in Italy until 1947; First Lyric and Character Baritone, Berlin State Opera 1948–; mem. Vienna State Opera Co. 1957–; Prof. of Singing Musikhochschule Berlin 1981–; numerous concert tours in Europe, USA and Asia; has appeared at a number of festivals: Bayreuth, Salzburg, Lucerne, Montreux, Edin., Vienna, Holland, Munich, Berlin, Coventry, etc.; best-known roles in Falstaff, Don Giovanni, The Marriage of Figaro, etc.; first performances of contemporary composers Britten, Henze, Tippett, etc.; mem. Akad. der Künste, Bayerische Akad. der Schönen Künste, Munich, Int. Mahler-Gesellschaft (Vienna) and German Section, Int. Music Council, High School for Music and Theatre, Munich 1999. *Publications:* Texte deutscher Lieder 1968, Auf den Spuren der Schubert-Lieder 1971, Wagner und Nietzsche, der Mystagoge und sein Abtrünniger 1974, Franz Schubert, ein Portrait 1976, Robert Schumann—Wort und Musik 1981, Töne sprechen, Worte klingen-Zur Geschichte und Interpretation des Gesanges 1985, Nachklang 1987, Wenn Musik der Liebe Nahrung ist: Künstlerschicksale im 19 Jahrhundert 1990, Johann Friedrich Reichardt: Kapellmeister dreier Preussenkönige 1992, Claude Debussy und seine Welt 1994, Schubert und seine lieder 1998. *Honours:* Hon. mem. Wiener Konzerthausgesellschaft 1963, RAM (London), Royal Acad. (Stockholm), Deutschen Oper, Berlin 1978, Royal Philharmonic Soc.; Bundesverdienstkreuz 1st Class 1958, Grosses Verdienstkreuz des Verdienstordens der Bundesrepublik Deutschland 1974, Chevalier Légion d'honneur 1990; Hon. DUniv (Oxford) 1978, Hon. DMus (Paris-Sorbonne) 1980, (Yale) 1980; Int. Recording Prizes almost every year since 1955, Berlin Kunstpreis 1950, Mantua Golden Orpheus Prize 1955, Edison Prize 1960, 1962, 1964, 1965, 1967, 1970, President's Prize Charles Gros Acad., Paris 1980, Förderungspreis der Ernst-von-Siemens-Stiftung 1980, Mozart Medal 1962, Golden Orpheus 1967, Grammy Award (several times), Prix Mondial Montreux (several times), Ernst-Reuter-Plak 1993, Polar Music Prize 2004, Lotte Lehmann Foundation World of Song Award 2005. *Address:* c/o Deutsche Verlanganstalt, Stüttgart, Germany (office).

**FISCHER-MÜNSTER, Gerhard;** German composer, conductor, musician (piano, clarinet) and lecturer; b. 17 Nov. 1952, Münster-Sarmsheim; m. Bettina Fischer-Münster 1979; one s. one d. *Education:* Peter Cornelius Konservatorium, Mainz; Staatliche Musikhochschule und Johannes Gutenberg Universität, Mainz; Staatsexamen (lecturer, soloist), 1974; seminar for conducting, Bingen. *Career:* first compositions in 1965; concerts as soloist (piano, clarinet); concerts as conductor of a number of orchestras and ensembles; radio and television performances and recordings in Germany, Italy, Austria, Switzerland, France, Belgium, USA, and Japan; guest conductor with the European Symphony Orchestra, Luxembourg, 1993; performances at international festivals; jury member of music competitions; guest lecturer at Universität Mainz and various institutes; founder of wind chamber ensemble, 1981; founder of Symphonic Wind Orchestra of Mainz Conservatory, 1991; lecturer at Peter Cornelius Konservatorium, Mainz (clarinet, improvisation, composition, symphonic wind orchestra, wind chamber ensemble) 1975–. *Compositions include:* symphonies: Psychodrom; Im Anfang war das Wort; Daliphonie; Haiku-Lieder; Psalm 99; Schizophonie; Geldschein-Sonate; Piano Concertino; Symphonic Pictures; Sonatas, lieder, and orchestral works. *Recordings include:* Haiku-Lieder; Philosophie eines Filous; Musique de table; Süd-Freak-Idyll; Adoration and more. *Publications:*

Harmonie aus dem Einklang; Lehrplan Klarinette; Kreativ Üben; Lexikon Komponisten der Gegenwart; Lexikon des Blasmusikwesens; Wer ist Wer Deutschland. *Honours:* numerous prizes from Germany, Switzerland, UK, USA. *Address:* Auf den Zeilen 11, 55424 Münster-Sarmsheim, Germany. *Telephone:* (6721) 46727 (home). *E-mail:* fischer-muenster@gmx.de (home). *Website:* www.fischer-muenster.de.

**FISHER, Gillian;** Singer (Soprano); b. 1955, England; m. Brian Kay. *Education:* Studied with John Carol Case at the Royal College of Music and with Jessica Cash. *Career:* Appearances in the world's leading concert halls, including Albert, Festival and Barbican Halls, London; Amsterdam Concertgebouw, Lincoln Center, New York and Suntory Hall, Tokyo; Handel Festivals in London and in Maryland, USA; Frequent broadcasts with repertoire ranging from Baroque music to the vocal symphonies of Milhaud; Featured in Central Television series Man and His Music; Sang in Theodora and other works by Handel for tercentenary year, 1985; Sang in Messiah with Ton Koopman and the Amsterdam Baroque Orchestra, Japan, 1987; Appearances in Italy, Japan and Australia with vocal group The Sixteen; Gluck's Euridice at Covent Garden, 1989. *Recordings include:* Purcell's King Arthur and Dioclesian with John Eliot Gardiner and the Monteverdi Choir; The Triumph of Time and Truth by Handel with Denys Darlow and the London Handel Orchestra; Great Baroque Arias and Pergolesi's Stabat Mater with the King's Consort and Michael Chance; Purcell's Fairy Queen and Bach cantatas with The Sixteen and Harry Christophers and Handel duets with the King's Consort and James Bowman. *Current Management:* Magenta Music. *Address:* c/o Brian Kay, Radio 3, BBC Broadcasting House, Portland Place, London W1A 1AA, England.

**FISHER, Jonathan;** Singer (Baritone); b. 1963, England. *Education:* Guildhall School, London, with Bernard Dickerson, and Cologne Musikhochschule. *Career:* Appearances for the Royal Opera, Covent Garden, in The Pilgrim's Progress and La Battaglia di Legnano (concert), Chérubin by Massenet, Der Rosenkavalier, Simon Boccanegra and The Midsummer Marriage; Henry Higgins in My Fair Lady for the Covent Garden Festival; Associated with Royal Opera House education projects. *Recordings:* The Pilgrim's Progress, Peter Grimes, Christmas from Covent Garden. *Publications:* By George, musical about the Gershwins. *Honours:* Painter prize, Guildhall School. *Address:* c/o Royal Opera House (contracts), Covent Garden, London, WC2, England. *Telephone:* (20) 7240 1200. *Fax:* (20) 7212-9502.

**FISHER, Norma;** Concert Pianist; b. 11 May 1940, London, England; m. Barrington Saipe, 3 Sept 1967, 2 s. *Education:* Guildhall School of Music with Sidney Harrison, 1951–57 and privately with Ilona Kabos, 1957–68 and Jacques Fevrier, Paris, 1962. *Career:* Debut: Wigmore Hall, 1956; Proms, Royal Albert Hall, 1963; Performances throughout the United Kingdom, Europe, USA, Canada and Israel in recitals, concertos and chamber music; Regular performer for BBC, London; Represented the United Kingdom twice at International Jeunesses Musicales Congress; Jury Member of many major international piano competitions; Invited to give Masterclasses world-wide; Founded London Masterclasses in 1988. *Honours:* 2nd Prize, Busoni International Piano Competition, Italy, 1961; Piano Prize (Joint holder with Vladimir Ashkenazy), Harriet Cohen International Awards, 1963. *Current Management:* J. Audrey Ellison, International Artists Management, London, England. *Address:* 5 Lyndhurst Gardens, Finchley, London N3 1TA, England.

**FISHER, Stephen (Carey);** Musicologist; b. 18 May 1948, Norfolk, Virginia, USA. *Education:* BA, University of Virginia, 1969; PhD, University of Pennsylvania, 1985. *Career:* Assistant Professor, Widener University, 1985–87; Lecturer, University of Pennsylvania, 1989–; mem, American Musicological Society; International Musicological Society; Music Library Association. *Publications:* The Symphony 1720–1840, series B, vol. IX, 1983; Joseph Haydn Werke, series 1, vols 9, Sinfonien um 1777–79, 2002,. *Contributions:* Haydn-Studien; Mitteilungen der Internationalen Stiftung Mozarteum; Current Musicology; Haydn Studies, 1975; The Haydn Yearbook; The Eighteenth Century: A Current Bibliography; Eighteenth Century Studies; Journal of Musicology; New Grove Dictionary of Opera; Notes; Journal of the American Musicological Society; New Grove Dictionary of Music. *Honours:* Fulbright-Hays Grant, 1976–77. *Address:* Department of Music, University of Pennsylvania, 201 South 34th Street, Philadelphia, PA 19104-6313, USA. *E-mail:* docsfisher@aol.com (home); fisher@pobox.upenn .edu (office).

**FISICHELLA, Salvatore;** Singer (Tenor); b. 1948, Italy. *Education:* Studied in Catania and Rome. *Career:* Debut: Spoleto Festival, as Werther; Sang in Rigoletto and I Puritani at the Rome Opera and appeared widely in Europe and America as Arturo, Arnoldo (Guillaume Tell) and Gualtiero (Il Pirata); New York Met debut as Arturo, opposite Joan Sutherland; Engagements at the Zürich Opera under Nello Santi in I Puritani, Il Pirata and Guillaume Tell; Further leading roles in such operas as Traviata, Butterfly, La Favorita, Roberto Devereux, Faust, Mefistofele and Attila; Season 1996–97 as the Duke of Mantua at Zürich, Pinkerton and Alfredo at Palermo, Edgardo (Luci di Lammermoor) at La Scala and Fernando (La Favorita) at Catania; Further roles in Rossini's Mosè in Egitto and Otello, I Capuleti e i Montecchi, and The Two Widows; Season 2000–01 as the Duke of Mantua at St Gallen and Gualtiero in Bellini's Pirata at Catania. *Honours:* Premio Bellini d'Oro in Catania; Premio Internazionale Giacomo Lauri Volpi, at Rome. *Address:* c/o Opernhaus Zürich, Falkenstrasse 1, 8008 Zürich, Switzerland.

**FISK, Eliot Hamilton,** MA; American classical guitarist and professor of music; *Professor, Salzburg Mozarteum;* ; *New England Conservatory, Boston;* b. 10 Aug. 1954, Philadelphia, Pa. *Education:* Yale Univ., Aspen Music School with Oscar Ghiglia, studied with Andres Segovia, Ralph Kirkpatrick, Albert Fuller. *Career:* solo recital debut, Alice Tully Hall, New York 1976; toured throughout the world as soloist with orchestras, as recitalist and chamber music performer; teacher, Aspen Music School 1973–82, Yale University 1977–82, Mannes Coll. of Music 1978–82; Prof., Cologne Hochschule für Musik 1982–89, Mozarteum, Salzburg 1989–, New England Conservatory, Boston 1996–; prepared transcriptions of works by J. S. Bach, Scarlatti, Mozart, Paganini, Mendelssohn, E. Halffter, I. Albeniz, E. Granados, for guitar; new works for guitar composed for him by Robert Beaser, Luciano Berio, Cristóbal Halffter, Nicholas Maw, Xavier Montsalvatge, George Rochberg, Kurt Schwertsik. *Recordings:* first recordings of Paganini Caprices Op. 1, Rochberg: Caprice Variations, Balada: Concierto Magico, Segovia: Canciones Populares, Berio: Sequenza XI, Beaser: Mountain Songs, Rochberg: Muse of Fire, Castelnuovo-Tedesco: Suite Op. 133. *Publications:* transcriptions of Bach, Mozart, Frescobaldi, Scarlatti, Paganini; edns of Beaser, Berio, Rochberg, Halffter, Montsalvatge, Maw and others. *Honours:* Winner, Int. Classical Guitar Competition, Gargnano, Italy 1980. *Current Management:* c/o Vantage Artists, 131 Varick Street, Suite 937, New York, NY 10013, USA. *E-mail:* probles@vantageartists.com. *Website:* www.vantageartists.com; www .eliotfisk.com.

**FISSORE, Enrico;** singer (bass-baritone); b. 23 Jan. 1939, Piemonte, Italy. *Education:* Milan and Turin Conservatories. *Career:* debut, Teatro Nuovo Milan 1964, as Don Giovanni; Many appearances in Europe and North America in Italian operas of the 17th and 18th centuries; Glyndebourne debut 1967, as Schaunard in La Bohème; USA debut at San Francisco, as Rossini's Bartolo; La Scala Milan 1979, in Vivaldi's Tito Manlio; Further engagements as Verdi's Melitone and Dulcamara in L'Elisir d'amore at the Metropolitan, Don Magnifico (La Cenerentola) with Florida Opera and Leporello at Portland (season 1997–98); Other appearances at the Chicago Lyric Opera, Vienna Staatsoper, Opéra Bastille, Salzburg Festival and Munich; Glyndebourne 1997, as Bartolo in Le nozze di Figaro, followed by Puccini's Trittico in Brussels. *Current Management:* Robert Gilder & Co., Enterprise House, 59–65 Upper Ground, London, SE1 9PQ, England. *Telephone:* (20) 7928-9008. *Fax:* (20) 7928-9755. *E-mail:* rgilder@robert-gilder.com.

**FITKIN, Graham;** British composer; b. 19 April 1963, Crows-an-Wra, Cornwall. *Education:* Univ. of Nottingham, Koninglijk Conservatorium, The Hague. *Career:* co-founder piano ensemble, The Nanquidno Group 1985; Programme Dir, Soc. for the Promotion of New Music 1993; PRS Composer in Education 1995, 1996, 1998; composer-in-residence, Royal Liverpool Philharmonic Orchestra 1994–96; founder sextet, Graham Fitkin Group 1996; composer-in-residence, The Harbourside Centre, Bristol 1997–98; featured composer for Park Lane Group and at Presteigne Festival 1999, at Mixing Music Festival 2000, at Int. Guitar Festival 2001; composer-in-residence, The Lemon Tree, Aberdeen 2000, 2001; various collaborative projects with different organizations, including The Geography Project, Scotland 1999–. *Compositions include:* Drum (music theatre) 1989, Loud 1989, Log 1990, Line 1991, Nasar 1992, Ghosts (opera) 1993, Huoah 1994, Length 1994, Metal 1995, Henry 1995, Granite 1995, Bebeto 1995, North 1998, Bob 1998, Timber 2000, Ending 2000, Ascendant 2001, Circuit concerto for two pianos 2002. *Honours:* Int. Grand Prix Music for Dance Video Award 1994. *Address:* c/o G. Ricordi & Company, Bedford House, 69–79 Fulham Street, London, SW6 3JW, England (office). *E-mail:* info@fitkin.com. *Website:* www.fitkin.com.

**FITZGERALD, Daire;** Concert Cellist; b. 1966, Dublin, Ireland. *Education:* Studied with Rostropovich, at the Menuhin School with William Pleeth and the Menuhin Academy with Radu Aldulescu. *Career:* Concerts throughout Western Europe, China, India, Israel and Czechoslovakia, while a student at the Society of Lincoln Center, New York, and concerts with such orchestras as the Royal Philharmonic, Warsaw Sinfonia, Central Philharmonic of Peking, Hallé and Berlin Radio Symphony; Soloist with the Camerata Lysy Gstaad on tour to Japan and Canada; Berlin debut with the Saint-Saëns A minor concerto; New Year's Concert for Finnish television, tour of USA playing chamber music with Menuhin and participation on Julian Lloyd Webber's Cellothon at South Bank, London.

**FITZPATRICK, Martin;** music administrator; *Head of Music, English National Opera.* *Education:* Balliol Coll. *Career:* Head of Music, Royal Danish Opera 1994–2001; Chorus Master Opera North 2001–05; Head of Music ENO 2003–; conducting posts at ENO include The Magic Flute 2004, In the Beginning, Carmen (asst). *Address:* English National Opera, London Coliseum, St Martin's Lane, Trafalgar Square, London, WC2, England (office). *Telephone:* (20) 7836-0111 (office). *Fax:* (20) 7845-9296 (office). *Website:* www.eno.org.

**FLAGELLO, Ezio;** Singer (Bass); b. 28 Jan. 1931, New York, NY, USA. *Education:* Studied with Friedrich Schorr and John Brownlee at the Manhattan School of Music; Further study with Luigi Ricci in Rome. *Career:* Debut: Concert performance of Boris Godunov at Carnegie Hall, 1952; Sang Dulcamara in Rome, 1956; After winning Metropolitan Auditions of the Air (1957) appeared in New York until 1987, as Leporello, Fiesco in Simon Boccanegra, Pogner, Philip II and Rossini's Basilio; Sang Enobarbus in the inaugural production of the Metropolitan Opera at Lincoln Center, Antony and Cleopatra by Barber (1966); Guest appearances in San Francisco, Dallas,

Houston, Milan, Vienna, Berlin, Prague and Florence; Screen debut, Francis Ford Coppola's Godfather II; Sang Sarastro for Pennsylvania Opera Theater, 1991. *Recordings include:* Così fan tutte; Lucrezia Borgia; Lucia di Lammermoor; Un Ballo in Maschera; Ernani; Luisa Miller; Rigoletto; La Forza del Destino; Alcina; I Puritani; Don Giovanni. *Address:* 2005 Samontee Road, Jacksonville, FL 32211, USA.

**FLANAGAN, Leslie John;** Singer (Baritone); b. 1969, Rockhampton, Australia. *Education:* Studied in Australia and at the Scottish Academy of Music. *Career:* Appearances at the Mananan Festival as Schaunard in La Bohème and as Malatesta in Don Pasquale for Clonter Opera; Junior Principal with English National Opera, 1999–2000 season; Other roles include Papageno, Demetrius (A Midsummer Night's Dream), Don Giovanni and Escamillo; Concerts include the Fauré and Brahms Requiems, Mendelssohn's St Paul, Elgar's Apostles and Puccini's Messa di Gloria. *Honours:* Marianne Mathy Award, 1996. *Address:* Harlequin Agency, 203 Fidlas Road, Cardiff CF4 5NA, Wales.

**FLECK, William;** Singer (Bass); b. 28 Aug. 1937, Tyrone, Pennsylvania, USA. *Education:* Studied at the Eastman School and at the Manhattan School of Music. *Career:* Sang widely in the USA, at first as guest in Boston, Minneapolis and Hawaii; Metropolitan Opera from 1980, in Die Zauberflöte, Tannhäuser, Traviata, Bohème and Tosca; Sang Rocco at Mexico City, 1983; Sang in the US premiere of Ruslan and Lyudmilla at Boston and elsewhere as Leporello, Alfonso, Don Magnifico, and Morosus in Die schweigsame Frau; Baron Ochs in Der Rosenkavalier, directed by Jonathan Miller, New York City Opera debut, 1996. *Current Management:* Sardos Artists Management Corp, 180 West End Avenue, New York, NY 10023. *Address:* 24 Riverside Drive, Ridgefield, CT 06877, USA.

**FLEET, Marlene (Rose);** Concert Pianist; b. 13 Feb. 1942, Grimsby, South Humberside, England; m. Harry Terence Harvey Taylor, 5 June 1972. *Education:* LRAM, ARCM, Grimsby Technical College; Royal Academy of Music, 1960–65. *Career:* Debut: Wigmore Hall, 1964; Numerous concerts in the United Kingdom, Europe and America; Appearances at Wigmore Hall, Purcell Room, Queen Elizabeth Hall, Royal Festival Hall, London; Plays regularly for BBC and has performed on BBC television; Played with most of the leading British orchestras and with many distinguished conductors. *Recordings:* Numerous recordings for BBC Radio 3. *Honours:* Winner of most of solo pianist prizes, Royal Academy of Music, 1960–65; Countess of Munster Scholarship; Martin Musical Scholarships. *Address:* 22 Fairefield Crescent, Glenfield, Leicester LE3 8EH, England.

**FLEISCHER, Tsippi;** Composer; b. 20 May 1946, Haifa, Israel. *Education:* Studied at the Tel-Aviv and New York Universities and the Rubin Academy of Music; PhD, Musicology, Bar Ilan University, Ramat Gan, Israel, 1995. *Career:* Teacher at the Tel-Aviv and Bar-Ilan Universities; Professor, Music Department Levinsky Institute, Tel-Aviv. Member, Levinsky Institute Pedagogical Committee. *Compositions include:* A Girl Named Limonad, music theatre, 1977; Girl-Butterfly-Girl, song cycle, for soprano and ensemble, 1977; Lamentation for soprano, women's chorus, 2 harps and percussion, 1985; In The Mountains Of Armenia for children's chorus, 1988; Cantata, Like Two Branches, 1989; Oratorio 1492-1992, 1992; Four Old Winds, 4 multimedias in ancient Semitic languages), 1993–96; Medea, chamber opera, 1995; Salt Crystals, 1st Symphony, 1995; The Train Symphony, 2nd Symphony, 1998; Regarding Beauty, 3rd Symphony, 1998; A Moving Shadow, 4th Symphony (incl. folk wind and percussion), 2000; An Israeli-Jewish Collage, 5th Symphony 2002–2003; Ethnic Silhouettes, 1988–98; Lead Life (song cycle), 2001Opera: Medea, 1995; Cain and Abel, 2001; Victoria, 2003–2004;. *Recordings include:* Tsippi Fleischer Vocal Music, 1992; Tsippi Fleischer Art Music Settings of Arab Poetry, 1993; Around the World with Tsippi Fleischer, 1997; Israel at 50 a Celebration of the Music of Tsippi Fleischer, 1999. *Honours:* ACUM prize for Music, 1994; Prime minister's Award for Composers, 50th Anniversary of the State of Israel, 1998; ACUM Prize for life time achievement in composition for the concert hall, 2002. *Address:* PO Box 8094, Haifa 31080, Israel.

**FLEISHER, Leon;** Pianist and Conductor; b. 23 July 1928, San Francisco, California, USA. *Education:* Studied piano with Artur Schnabel, 1938–48; Conducting with Pierre Monteux. *Career:* First public recital, 1934; Played Liszt's A Major Concerto with the San Francisco Symphony, 1942; Brahms D Minor Concerto in San Francisco and New York, 1943, 1944; International career from 1952; Gave concerts with George Szell and the Cleveland Orchestra; Joined faculty of the Peabody Conservatory of Music, Baltimore, 1959; Premiered Leon Kirchner's Concerto, Seattle, 1963; Lost use of right hand, 1965, and later played Piano Left Hand repertoire; Co-Director of the Theatre Chamber Players, Washington DC, 1968; Associate Conductor of the Baltimore Symphony Orchestra, 1973–78; Guest engagements as conductor with leading orchestras in the USA; Resumed bimanual solo pianist career, 1982; Artistic Director of the Tanglewood Music Center, 1986–97. *Address:* ICM Artists Ltd, 10 Barley Mow Passage, London, W4 4PH, England.

**FLEMING, Renée,** MMus; American singer (soprano); b. 14 Feb. 1959, Indiana, PA; d. of Edwin Davis Fleming and Patricia (Seymour) Alexander; m. Richard Lee Ross 1989 (divorced 2000); two d. *Education:* Potsdam State Univ., Eastman School of Music of Univ. of Rochester, Juilliard School American Opera Center. *Career:* debuts Houston Grand Opera (Marriage of Figaro) 1988, Spoleto Festival, Charleston and Italy 1987–90, New York City Opera (La Bohème) 1989, San Francisco Opera, Metropolitan Opera, Paris

Opera at Bastille, Teatro Colon, Buenos Aires (all Marriage of Figaro) 1991, Glyndebourne (Così fan tutte) 1992, La Scala Milan (Don Giovanni) 1993, Vienna State Opera (Marriage of Figaro) 1993, Lyric Opera of Chicago (Susannah) 1993, San Diego Opera (Eugene Onegin) 1994, Paris Opera 1996, Massenet's Thaïs at Nice and Gounod's Marguerite at the Met 1997, Floyd's Susannah at the Met 1999, Louise at Barbican Hall, London and the Marschallin at Covent Garden 2000; premiered Previn's A Streetcar Named Desire 1998; recital tour with Jean-Yves Thibaudet 2001–02; London Proms 2002, Dvořák's Rusalka in concert at Covent Garden 2003, Bellini's Il Pirata at the Met 2003; Fulbright Scholar to Germany 1984–85. *Recordings include:* Sacred Songs 2005, R. Strauss's Daphne (with Cologne Radio Chorus and Symphony Orchestra) 2005. *Publication:* The Inner Voice: the Making of a Singer (autobiog.) 2005. *Honours:* George London Prize 1988, Richard Tucker Award 1990, Solti Prize, Acad. du Disque Lyrique 1996, Vocalist of the Year, (Musical America) 1997, Prize Acad. du Disque Lyrique 1998, Grammy Awards 1999, 2002, creation of the dessert 'La Diva Renée' by Master Chef Daniel Boulud 1999, Classical BRIT Awards for Top-selling Female Artist 2003, for Outstanding Contribution to Music 2004. *Current Management:* M. L. Falcone Public Relations, 155 West 68th Street, Apt. 1114, New York, NY 10023-5817, USA. *Telephone:* (212) 580-4302. *Fax:* (212) 787-9638.

**FLETZBERGER, Matthias;** Pianist; b. 24 Aug. 1965, Vienna, Austria. *Education:* Hochschule für Musik, Vienna. *Career:* Musikverein Wien; Mozarteum Salzburg Festival; Festivals, Puerto Rico, Lockenhaus, Athens, Naples; Soloist, Israel Philharmonic, Orchestre de Bordeaux, R Schumann Philharmonie, Hochschulorchester Vienna, Orquesta Sinfonica de Chile; Recitals in Europe, America, Australia; Musical Assistant to Elisabeth Schwarzkopf and Renata Tebaldi; Musical Director and Principal Conductor of the Superstiltheater in Vienna. *Recordings:* Production of video clips for ORF; Radio and television recordings; Conductor of the television production of The Magic Flute at the Vienna Festival, 1991. *Honours:* Recipient, various prizes and awards. *Address:* Alban Bergweg 11, A 1130 Vienna, Austria.

**FLIMM, Jürgen;** German theatre director; *Artistic Director, Festival Ruhrtriennale;* b. 17 July 1941, Giessen; s. of Werner Flimm and Ellen Flimm; m. Susanne Ottersbach 1990. *Career:* early work at the Munich Kammerspiele; Dir Nationaltheater, Mannheim 1972–73; Prin. Dir Thalia Theater, Hamburg 1973–74; directed plays in Munich, Hamburg, Bochum, Frankfurt 1974–79 and in Zürich, Amsterdam, Salzburg, Vienna, Milan; Dir Cologne Theatre 1979–85, Thalia Theatre, Hamburg 1985–2000; Pres. German Bühnenvereins 1999–; Acting Dir Salzburg Festspiele 2001–06, Artistic Dir 2006–; Artistic Dir Festival Ruhrtriennale 2005–; Salome at the Met, New York 2004, Monteverdi's Poppea Zürich Opera 2005. *Films:* Wer zu spät kommt – die letzten Tage des Politbüros 1990, Käthchens Traum 2004. *Publications:* Theatergänger 2004. *Honours:* Dr hc (Hildesheim) 2002; Bundesverdienstkreuz 1992, Konrad-Wolf-Preis, Berlin 1995. *Address:* c/o Salzburger Festspiele, Mönchsberg 1, 5020 Salzburg, Austria (office).

**FLOR, Claus Peter;** German conductor; b. 16 March 1953, Leipzig; adopted s. of Richard Flor and Sigrid Langer; m. Sabine Winni 1985; one s. *Education:* Music School, Weimar and High School of Music, Weimar/Leipzig. *Career:* studied under Rolf Reuter, Rafael Kubelik and Kurt Sanderling; learnt violin and clarinet before commencing conducting studies; Chief Conductor, Suhl Philharmonic 1981–84; Chief Conductor, Music Dir Berliner Sinfonie Orchester 1984–92; Prin. Conductor, Artistic Adviser, Zürich Tonhalle Orchestra 1991–; Prin. Guest Conductor, Philharmonia Orchestra, London 1991–; US debut with Los Angeles Philharmonic 1985; debut with Berlin Philharmonic 1988; Prin. Guest Conductor Dallas Symphony Orchestra; regular appearances with Vienna Symphony, Orchestre de Paris, Royal Concertgebouw, Rotterdam Philharmonic and major German orchestras; frequent guest engagements with leading orchestras in UK, USA, Canada etc.; conductor of opera at many German opera houses including Berlin Staatsoper and Deutsche Oper, Berlin. *Recordings include:* Mendelssohn, Cherubini, Dvořák, Mozart, Shostakovich. *Address:* c/o Intermusica Artists' Management Ltd, 16 Duncan Terrace, London, N1 8BZ, England. *Telephone:* (20) 7278-5455. *Fax:* (20) 7278-8434.

**FLÓREZ, Juan Diego;** Peruvian singer (tenor); b. 1973, Lima. *Education:* studied in Lima and at the Curtis Inst., Philadelphia. *Career:* debut in Matilde di Shabram at the Rossini Opera Festival, Pesaro 1996; signed exclusive contract with Decca Music Group 2001; appearances include La Scala, Milan (in Armide, Falstaff, Cappello di Paglia di Firenze, Barbiere di Siviglia, Nina Pazza per Amore, La Sonnambula), Comunale, Firenze (in Le Comte Ory, Falstaff), Covent Garden, London (in Elisabetta by Donizetti, Otello by Rossini, La Cenerentola), Konzerthaus, Vienna (in La Semiramide), Carlo Felice, Genoa (in La Cenerentola, Le Comte Ory), Rossini Opera Festival, Pesaro (in Matilde di Shabram, Il Signor Bruschino, Petite Messe Solennelle, La Cenerentola, Viaggio a Reims), Regio, Turin (in La Sonnambula, Maria Stuarda), La Maestranza, Seville (in Donizetti's Alahor in Granata), Filarmonico, Verona (in Italiana in Algeri), Vienna Staatsoper (in Barbiere di Siviglia, Italiana in Algeri, Gianni Schicchi), Opera di Roma (in Barbiere di Siviglia), Las Palmas (in Italiana in Algeri), Vienna Musikverein (in Stabat Mater), Bayerische Staatsoper (in Italiana in Algeri), Gran Teatro del Liceo, Barcelona (in Stabat Mater), Opera National, Paris (in Italiana in Algeri), Bilbao (in Barbiere di Siviglia); engaged at La Scala, Opéra Bastille, Covent Garden, Paris Châtelet, New York Met, Salzburg Festival and San Francisco Opera until 2005. *Honours:* Abbiati Prize 2000, Rossini d'Oro (Pesaro) 2000, Opera Actual magazine Award for best tenor 2005. *Current Management:*

Ernesto Palacio, Via Donizetti 11, Lurano, Italy. *Telephone:* (35) 800623. *Fax:* (35) 4877812. *E-mail:* ernestopalacio@tiscali.it. *Website:* www.ernesto palacio .com; www.JuanDiegoFlorez.com.

**FLOROS, Constantin;** German/Greek musicologist; b. 4 Jan. 1930, Salonika, Greece. *Education:* Studied composition and conducting, Vienna Music Acad. and musicology at Vienna Univ. *Career:* Prof. of Musicology, Univ. of Hamburg, 1972–95; Pres. Gustav Mahler Vereinigung, Hamburg 1988; mem. European Acad. of Sciences and Arts 2002. *Compositions:* compositions for chamber music, choir, organ. *Publications:* 22 books including 3 vols on medieval notations; 3-vol. treatise on Gustav Mahler; 2 vols on Johannes Brahms; 2 vols on Alban Berg; Der Mensch, die Liebe und die Musik, 2000. *Honours:* Dr hc (Univ. of Athens) 1999. *Address:* Schlangenkoppel 18, Hamburg, Germany. *Telephone:* (40) 7133308 (also fax) (office).

**FLOWERS, Kate;** Singer (soprano); b. 1950, Cheshire, England. *Education:* Studied at the Northern School of Music and the Royal Northern College of Music; Further study in Paris. *Career:* Glyndebourne Festival from 1976, as Despina, Isotta in Die schweigsame Frau, Norina in La Fedeltà Premiata and the title role in The Cunning Little Vixen; Appearances with Opera North as Gretel, Despina, Susanna, Zerlina, Aennchen in Der Freischütz and Thérèse in Les mamelles de Tirésias; Polly Peachum in The Beggar's Opera for Scottish Opera; Micaela, Marenka and Jenůfa for the Welsh National Opera; Concert engagements in Europe, and on London's South Bank with the Philharmonia, the English Chamber Orchestra, Royal Philharmonic, Hallé Orchestra, London Philharmonic and the Academy of St Martin in the Fields; Sang Jenny in The Threepenny Opera for Opera North, 1990; Sang Mrs Ford in Falstaff with City of Birmingham Touring Opera, 1995; Sang Marianne in Der Rosenkavalier at Covent Garden, 2000. *Honours:* John Christie Award and Royal Society of Arts Scholarship, 1977. *Current Management:* Music-makers International Artists Representation, Tailor House, 63–65 High Street, Whitwell, Hertfordshire SG4 8AH, England. *Telephone:* (1438) 871708. *Fax:* (1438) 871777. *E-mail:* musicmakers@compuserve.com. *Website:* www .operauk.com. *Address:* c/o The Grand Theatre, 46 New Briggate, Leeds LS1 6NH, England.

**FLOYD, Carlisle,** BA, MA; American composer; b. 11 June 1926, Latta, SC. *Education:* Converse Coll., Spartenberg, Syracuse Univ. with Ernest Bacon, studied piano with Rudolf Firkusny and Sidney Foster. *Career:* teacher, Florida State Univ. 1947–76; M. D. Anderson Prof. of Music, Univ. of Houston 1976–. *Compositions:* operas: Slow Dusk 1949, Susannah 1951, Wuthering Heights 1958, The Passion of Jonathan Wade 1962, The Sojourner and Mollie Sinclair 1963, Markheim 1966, Of Mice and Men 1969, Bilby's Doll 1976, Willie Stark 1981, Cold Sassy Tree 2000; other: Pilgrimage (song cycle) 1956, Piano Sonata 1957, The Mystery (song cycle) 1960, Flower and Hawk monodrama for soprano and orchestra 1972, Citizen of Paradise (song cycle) 1983, A Time to Dance for baritone, chorus and orchestra 1994. *Honours:* Nat. Medal of Honour 2005. *Current Management:* Boosey & Hawkes, Aldwych House, 71–91 Aldwych, London, WC2B 4HN, England.

**FLURY, Urs Joseph;** Swiss composer, violinist and conductor; b. 25 Aug. 1941, Bern. *Education:* Bern and Basel Univs, Conservatory Biel and Basel. *Career:* stage appearances, TV and radio broadcasts in Switzerland and other European countries. *Compositions:* chamber music: Variations on a Christmas Carol, Fantasia and Sonata for violin solo, Two Suites for violin and piano, Variations and Duo for violin and viola, Wind Quintet, Quartet for oboe, violin, viola and cello, Lieder; orchestral works: Vineta (Symphonic Poem), Three Suites, The Little Mermaid, Concerto di carnevale for rag band and orchestra, Three Fantasies on Carols for organ and strings; instrumental concertos: Concertino Veneziano for violin and strings, Concerto for violin in D, Cello Concerto; vocal music: Christmas Cantata, Christmas Oratorio, three masses, salve regina. *Recordings:* as violinist and conductor: Cello Concerto, Concertino Veneziano, Concerto for violin in D, Sonata for Violin Solo, Suite Nostalgique, Christmas Oratorio, The Little Mermaid, Vineta, Lieder, Quartet for oboe, violin, viola and cello, Duo for violin and viola. *Publications:* Pahlen Kurt: Oratorien der Welt 1985, Pahlen Kurt, Neue Musikgeschichte der Welt 1990, Hartnack Joachim: Grosse Geiger unserer Zeit 1983, Schweizer Chorkomponisten 1999, Musik in Geschichte und Gegenwart 2002; contrib. to several professional journals and magazines. *Honours:* Music Prize, Canton Solothurn 1993. *Address:* Zelglistrasse 5, 4562 Biberist, Switzerland. *Website:* www.urs-joseph-flury.ch.

**FOCCROULLE, Bernard;** Belgian organist, composer and theatre director; *Director-General, Théâtre Royal de la Monnaie, Brussels*; b. 1953, Liège. *Education:* Conservatoire de Liège, studied organ under Hubert Schoonbroodt, Xavier Darasse, Bernard Lagacé, Gustav Leonhardt. *Career:* fmr teacher of musical analysis; has toured worldwide as a soloist; mem. Ricercar Consort early music ensemble from 1982; Dir-Gen. Théâtre Royal de la Monnaie, Brussels 1992–(2007); f. Culture and Democracy arts org. 1993. *Recordings:* J. S. Bach's complete works for organ (with Ricercar Consort), Mozart, Keyboard Works 1992, Bruhns/Reinken, Sämtliche Orgelwerke 2002, Organ Recital at Grenzing Organ Brussels Cathedral 2003, Tunder, Organ Works 2004. *Honours:* Fondation Alfred Töpfer Prix Montaigne 2001. *Address:* Théâtre Royal de la Monnaie, Place de la Monnaie, Brussels 1000, Belgium (office). *E-mail:* info@lamonnaie.be (office). *Website:* www.@ lamonnaie.be (office).

**FOCILE, Nuccia;** Singer (Soprano); b. 25 Nov. 1961, Militello, Sicily, Italy. *Education:* Turin Conservatory. *Career:* Season 1986–87, as Oscar in Ballo in Maschera at Turin and Philadelphia, Thalia in Rameau's Platée at Spoleto, Elvira (L'Italiana in Algeri) at Schwetzingen and Mistress Ford in Salieri's Falstaff at Peralade; Further engagements at Buenos Aires as Musetta, Valencienne in The Merry Widow at Venice and Nannetta at Covent Garden, 1988; Rio de Janeiro in 1989 as Rossini's Rosina, and Oscar at Naples, and Ascanio in Pergolesi's Lo frate 'nnamorato at La Scala; Returned to Milan in 1990 as Servilia in La Clemenza di Tito and appeared at Bergamo as Eleanora in Donizetti's L'Assedio di Calais; Pesaro Festival, 1990, as Giulia in La Scala di Seta, Teatro Valle Rome as Countess in Paisiello's Don Chisciotte; Returned to Philadelphia, 1991, as Norina, sang Mozart's Susanna at Houston and appeared at the Opéra Bastille, Paris, as Ilia in Idomeneo; Barcelona and Dallas, 1992, as Adina in L'Elisir d'amore, Oscar at the Opéra Bastille, Paris, Tatiana at the Théâtre du Châtelet and Carolina (Matrimonio Segreto) at the 1992 Ravenna Festival; Sang Gounod's Juliette at the Paris Opéra-Comique, 1994; La Traviata for WNO, 1995; Season 1996–97 with Mozart's Ilia at Florence, Liù and Susanna for the Royal Opera, Mimi in Paris and Tel-Aviv, and Amelia Boccanegra for WNO; Season 2000–01 as Amelia Grimaldi at Wellington, Susanna for WNO and Mimi at the Met. *Recordings include:* Lo frate 'nnamorato (Pergolesi) and L'Assedio di Calais (Donizetti); Le nozze di Figaro, Così fan tutte and Don Giovanni with Charles Mackerras. *Honours:* Turin International Competition, 1983; Pavarotti Competition, Philadelphia, 1986. *Current Management:* Askonas Holt Ltd, Lonsdale Chambers, 27 Chancery Lane, London, WC2A 1PF, England. *Telephone:* (20) 7400-1700. *Fax:* (20) 7400-1799. *E-mail:* info@askonasholt.co.uk. *Website:* www .askonasholt.co.uk.

**FODOR, Eugene Nicholas, Jr;** Violinist; b. 5 March 1950, Turkey Creek, Colorado, USA. *Education:* Studied with Harold Wippler, Denver; Ivan Galamian, Juilliard School of Music, New York, 1966–68; Josef Gingold, Harry Farbiman and William Primrose, Indiana University School of Music, diploma 1970; Jascha Heifetz, University of Southern California at Los Angeles, 1970–71. *Career:* Debut: Soloist at age 10 with Denver Symphony Orchestra; Soloist with major orchestras, 1974–; Recitalist, Performed at the White House, Washington DC 1974, 1986. *Honours:* 1st Prize, Merriweather Post Competition, 1967; Paganini Competition, Genoa, 1972; Co-2nd Prize, Tchaikovsky Competition, Moscow, 1974. *Current Management:* Hillyer International Inc, 888 Seventh Avenue Suite 300, New York, NY 10106, USA.

**FOLAND, Nicolle;** Singer (Mezzo-soprano); b. 1968, Des Moines, USA. *Education:* University of Northern Iowa. *Career:* Appearances with the Western Opera Theater on tour and in San Francisco as Adele and Rosalinda (1993), Donna Anna, and Tina in Argento's The Aspern Papers (Opera Center); San Francisco Opera, 1995–, as Kate Pinkerton, Clorinda (La Cenerentola), Gerhilde, Musetta, multiple roles in the premiere of Harvey Milk, and High Priestess in Aida; Guest with Indianapolis Opera as Adina in L'Elisir d'amore; Season 1996–97 as Micaela with Cincinnati Opera, Musetta with Los Angeles Music Center Opera and Seattle Opera; Micaela at San Francisco, 1998; Concerts include Placido Domingo special at San Francisco. *Address:* c/o San Francisco Opera, War Memorial Opera House, Van Ness Avenue, San Francisco, CA 94102, USA.

**FÖLDES, Imre;** Musicologist and Professor of History; b. 8 March 1934, Budapest, Hungary; m. Dr Zsuzsa Vadász, 1 d. *Education:* Graduate in composition, Ferenc Liszt Academy of Music, Budapest. *Career:* Musicologist, Professor of Music History and Theory, Ferenc Liszt Academy of Music, Department of Teachers Training Institute; Educational Lecturer on Music for the general public and radio; mem, Hungarian Musicians Association; Society for Propagating Sciences and Arts; Hungarian Ferenc Liszt Society; Hungarian Kodály Society; Lajos Bárdos Society. *Publications:* Harmincasok, Beszélgetések magyar zeneszerzőkkel (Generation of The Thirties–Talks with Hungarian Composers), 1969; Life and Works of J. S. Bach, 1976; The Melody Dies Irae, 1977. *Contributions:* Az ének-zene tanítása; Muzsika; Parlando. *Honours:* Art Prize for Socialist Culture, 1974; Art Prize, National Council of Trade Unions, 1975; Szabolcsi Prize, 1977; Ferenc Erkel Prize, 1986. *Address:* Kresz Géza utca 26, 1132 Budapest, Hungary.

**FOLDI, Andrew (Harry);** Opera Director and Singer (Bass); b. 20 July 1926, Budapest, Hungary; m. Marta Justus, 19 May 1977, 1 s., 1 d. *Education:* MA, Musicology, 1948, PhD, Philosophy, 1945, University of Chicago. *Career:* Debut: La Bohème, 1950; Director of Music, Department of Adult Education, University of Chicago, 1949–61; Chairman of the Opera Department, DePaul University, 1951–57; Adviser, Netherlands Opera, 1977–80; Chairman and Artistic Director, Opera Department, Cleveland Institute of Music, 1981–91; Director, Chicago Lyric Opera Center for American Artists, 1991–95; Stage direction includes: The Barber of Seville (Atlanta Opera), 1989; The Merry Wives of Windsor, (Chicago Opera Theatre), 1990; La Tragédie de Carmen (Lyric Opera Center, Chicago), 1992; Television performances of Il Barbiere di Siviglia, 1967, The Merry Widow, 1977, Elixir of Love, 1978, and Lulu, 1980; Other performances include: Alberich in the Ring and Schigolch in Lulu at the Metropolitan Opera, Bartolo in Il Barbiere de Siviglia, Vienna Staatsoper and San Francisco, Cardillac at La Scala; mem, American Musicological Society. *Recordings include:* Fiddler on the Roof, 1974; A Modern Psalm, 1975. *Publications:* Articles in Opera News, Alban Berg Society. *Address:* Chicago Opera Theater, 20 East Jackson Boulevard, Suite 1400, Chicago, IL 60604, USA.

**FOLWELL, Nicholas,** ARAM; singer (baritone); b. 1953, England. *Education:* Studied with Raimund Herincx; Royal Academy of Music and London Opera

Centre. *Career:* Sang with Welsh National Opera from 1978 as Mozart's Figaro and Leporello, Pizarro, Melitone, Escamillo, The Poacher in The Cunning Little Vixen, Alberich in The Ring of the Nibelung (also at Covent Garden with Welsh National Opera, 1986) and Wagner's Melot and Klingsor; As guest with other British companies has sung the Villians in The Tales of Hoffmann, Tonio, Beckmesser, Schaunard, Creon and The Messenger in Oedipus Rex, Alberich and Papageno (English National Opera 1990); Sang in Weill's Seven Deadly Sins with the London Sinfonietta, 1988; Debuts in France, Italy, Austria and West Germany, 1987–90; Created Koroviev in York Höller's Master and Margarita in Paris, 1989; Covent Garden and Glyndebourne, 1990, as The Poacher (conducted by Simon Rattle) and Beethoven's Pizarro; Sang in The Weill Event at the 1990 Almeida Festival; Promenade Concerts, 1991, in Prokofiev's The Fiery Angel; Alberich in Rheingold (Opéra de Nantes), 1992; Mozart's Figaro for Glyndebourne Touring Opera at Sadler's Wells; Cecil, Maria Stuarda, Buxton Festival, 1993; Alberich in Siegfried at the Opéra de Nantes, 1993; Sang Sancho Panza in Don Quichotte for ENO, 1996; Van Tricasse in the premiere of Dr Ox's Experiment by Gavin Byars, ENO, 1998; Alberich in The Ring at the Longborough Festival, 2000–02. *Recordings:* Tristan and Isolde and Parsifal, conducted by Reginald Goodall; Poacher (Cunning Little Vixen); Pish-Tush (The Mikado). *Current Management:* Robert Gilder & Co., Enterprise House, 59–65 Upper Ground, London, SE1 9PQ, England. *Telephone:* (20) 7928-9008. *Fax:* (20) 7928-9755. *E-mail:* rgilder@robert-gilder.com.

**FONDA, Jean (Pierre);** Concert Pianist; b. 12 Dec. 1937, Boulogne-sur-Seine, Paris, France. *Education:* Virtuosity Prize, Piano Instrumentation, Geneva Conservatory, Switzerland. *Career:* Debut: Germany, 1958; Concert tours in Europe, South America, USA, Japan, Middle East, Turkey, elsewhere; Television in Paris, Munich; Major European Summer Festivals including Lucerne, Montreux, Edinburgh and Monte Carlo. Compositions; Cadenzas for various piano concertos. *Honours:* Recipient, Harriet Cohen Medal, London, 1968; Chevalier des Arts et des Lettres, awarded by French Minister of Culture, 1980. *Current Management:* Ingpen & Williams Ltd, 7 St George's Court, 131 Putney Bridge Road, London, SW15 2PA, England. *Address:* 20 Parc Château Benquet, Geneva, Switzerland.

**FONDRAY, Alain;** Singer (Baritone); b. 1932, Bangolet, France. *Education:* Studied in Paris. *Career:* Debut: Tonio in Pagliacci, Cherbourg, 1968; Sang in many provincial French opera houses in 1970s; Appearances at the Paris Opéra, 1985 and 1991, in Jerusalem by Verdi and as the High Priest in Samson et Delila; Royal Opera House, Covent Garden, in La Fanciulla del West, La Scala Milan as Amonasro, Metropolitan Opera in Cavalleria Rusticana; Sang Scarpia at San Francisco, returning in 1990 as Renato in Un Ballo in Maschera; Vienna Staatsoper and Barcelona, 1991, as the High Priest and Scarpia; Festival engagements include Orange, 1992, as Count Luna, and Bregenz, 1993, as Nabucco; Sang Massenet's Sancho Panza at Toulouse, 1992, and Count Luna at Orange; La Scala, 1993, as Scarpia; Sang in Massenet's Thais at Nice, 1997; Season 2000–01 as Iago at Brussels, Comte de Toulouse in Verdi's Jérusalem at Genoa, and in the premiere of Cecilia by Charles Chayne at Monte Carlo; Amonasro at Maastricht and Massenet's Hérode at St Etienne. *Recordings include:* Sancho Panza in Don Quichotte, conducted by Michel Plasson. *Address:* c/o Opéra de La Bastille, 120 Rue de Lyon, F-75012 Paris, France.

**FONSECA, Regina;** Singer (Mezzo-soprano); b. 1932, Portugal. *Career:* Sang at Düsseldorf, 1958–59, Bremen, Saarbrucken, Mainz, Kiel and Kassel, 1959–69; Engaged at the Mannheim National Theatre, 1969–81, Gelsenkirchen, 1981–82, Dortmund, 1983–84; Guest appearances at Cologne and Nuremberg, Naples, Hamburg (Brangaene in Tristan und Isolde, 1967), Monte Carlo and the Deutsche Oper Berlin, 1975; Sang Kundry at the 1976 Bayreuth Festival and the Composer in Ariadne auf Naxos at the Vienna Staatsoper; Deutsche Oper am Rhein, Düsseldorf, 1983; Other roles have included Wagner's Venus, Ortrud, Waltraute and Fricka, Strauss's Clytemnestra and Nurse, Countess Geschwitz in Lulu, Verdi's Eboli, Lady Macbeth and Azucena, Zenobia in Handel's Radamisto and the Countess in Zimmermann's Die Soldaten.

**FONTANA, Bill;** Composer, Sound Sculptor and Radio Producer; b. 25 April 1947, Cleveland, Ohio, USA. *Education:* Studied at John Carroll University and at the New School for Social Research; BA, 1970; Private study with Louis Lane and Philip Corner. *Career:* Composer-in-Residence and music director for the Toronto Free Theater, 1972–73; Compiled archive of natural sounds for the Australian Broadcasting Commission, 1975–78; Natural sound archive for the Oakland Museum in California, 1979; Assembled material for series of 365 programmes broadcast in San Francisco, 1983, as Soundscapes; Composer, sound sculptor and radio producer on various broadcasting stations. *Compositions include:* Phantom Clarinets, 1975; Handbell Sculptures, 1977; Wave Spiral, 1977; Music for a Resonant Space, 1977; Music for Carillon; Standing Wave Sculpture, 1978; Piano Sculpture, 1978; Ocarina Sculpture; Sound Sculpture for Brass Band; Space between Sounds, 1980; Flight Paths out to Sea; Grid Projections; Landscape Sculpture with Foghorns, 1981; Oscillating Steel Grids along the Brooklyn Bridge, 1983; Sound Recycling Sculpture, 1983; Soundscapes, 1983; Metropolis Köln, 1985; Vertical Water, 1991; Earth Tones, 1992; Spiralling Sound Axis, 1993; Sound Island, 1994; Wave Trains, 1996; Acoustical Visions of Venice, 1999; Wave Memories, 1999; Music Information Network Lyon, 2001. *Address:* c/o ASCAP, ASCAP Building, 1 Lincoln Plaza, Lincoln Center, New York, NY 10023, USA.

**FONTANA, Carlo;** Italian opera house director and journalist; b. 15 March 1947, Milan; s. of Ciro Fontana; m. Roberta Cavallini. *Education:* Univ. Statale di Milano. *Career:* journalist 1968–77; responsible for youth activities, Piccolo Teatro di Milano 1968–71; Asst to Gen. Man. Teatro all Scala, Milan 1977–79, mem. Admin. Council 1980–84; Deputy Admin. Fonit Cetra 1979–84; Pres. Associazione Lirica Concertistica Italiana (AS.LI.CO.) 1980–83; Dir Music Section, Venice Biennale 1983–86; Dir Ente Autonomo Teatro Comunale di Bologna 1984–90; Pres. Associazione Nazionale Enti Lirici e Sinfonici 1986–; mem. Commissione Centrale Musica, Consiglio Nazionale dello Spettacolo; Sovrintendente, Teatro alla Scala, Milan 1990–2005; Prof., Univ. of Pavia. *Honours:* Grand 'Ufficialle della Repubblica Italiana; Ambrogino d'Oro, Milan 1999.

**FONTANA, Gabriele;** Austrian singer (soprano); b. 1958, Innsbruck. *Education:* Vienna Musikhochschule with Ilse Rapf. *Career:* sang Echo in Ariadne and Lauretta in Gianni Schicchi at the Opera Studio of the Vienna Staatsoper; sang Pamina at Frankfurt; Hamburg Staatsoper from 1982, as Susanna, Servilia in La Clemenza di Tito and Sophie in Der Rosenkavalier; sang in the premiere of Udo Zimmermann's Die Weisse Rose, revised version; guest appearances in Bremen and Hanover; Glyndebourne 1984, as the Countess in Le nozze di Figaro; Bregenz Festival 1985, as Pamina; Vienna Staatsoper and Glyndebourne Festival 1987, as Fiordiligi; sang in Die weisse Rose at Innsbruck 1989; Lieder recitals in London, Berlin, Brussels and Vienna; season 1996–97 with First Lady in Die Zauberflöte at Amsterdam; Bruckner's Mass in F Minor, with Radio Symphony Orchestra of Leipzig, and with Düsseldorf Sinfoniker 1997; season 2000–01 at Hannover as Martinů's Katerina, Poppea, and Ursula in Mathis der Maler; Countess in Capriccio at Amsterdam. *Recordings include:* Schubert Lieder and Bach Cantatas, Idomeneo, Arabella, Gluck's Paride ed Elena, Die grossmütige Tomyris by Reinhard Keiser, Rheintochter in Das Rheingold with Dohnányi and the Cleveland Symphony Orchestra. *Current Management:* Haydn Rawstron Ltd, 36 Station Road, London, SE20 7BQ, England. *Website:* www.haydnrawstron.com.

**FONTANA, Sergio;** Singer (Bass); b. 14 Feb. 1950, Berne, Switzerland. *Education:* Studied in Milan and with Mario del Monaco. *Career:* Stage career from 1972, with appearances in Geneva, Bologna, Florence, Milan, Metz and Berne; Roles have included Verdi's Zaccaria and Sparafucile, Wurm in Luisa Miller, Rodolfo in La Sonnambula, Sarastro, Timur in Turandot, Zuniga in Carmen and Biterolf in Tannhäuser. *Recordings include:* Macbeth; Madama Butterfly.

**FONTYN, Jacqueline;** Belgian composer; b. 27 Dec. 1930, Antwerp; m. Camille Schmit (deceased); two c. *Education:* studied piano with Ignace Bolotine, theory and composition with Marcel Quinet; studied in Paris with Max Deutsch and in Vienna with Hans Swarowski. *Career:* Prof. of Composition, Conservatoire Royal de Bruxelles 1971–90; has given lectures and seminars around the world; commission from the Serge Koussevitzky Music Foundation, Library of Congress Washington; mem. Royal Acad. of Belgium. *Compositions include:* symphony orchestra: Evoluon 1972, Quatre Sites 1977, In the Green Shade 1991, On a Landscape by Turner 1992, L'Anneau de Jade 1996, Goeie Hoop 1998, Au Fil des Siecles 2000; chamber or string orchestra: Galaxie 1965, Pour 11 Archets 1971, Evoluon 1972, Per Archi for string orchestra 1973; solo and orchestra: Mouvements Concertants for two pianos and strings 1957, Violin Concerto 1974, Quatre Sites 1976, Halo for harp and 16 instruments 1978, Colinda for cello and orchestra 1991, Vent d'Est for classical accordion and strings, Es ist ein Ozean concerto for flute, harpsichord and string orchestra 1999; symphonic band: Frises 1975, Creneaux 1983, Aratoro 1992, Blake's Mirror 1993; vocal music: Psalmus Tertius for baritone, choir and orchestra, Ephemeres for mezzo-soprano and orchestra 1979, Alba for soprano, clarinet, cello, harp or percussion, piano 1981, Pro and Antiverb(e)s for soprano and cello 1984, Cheminement for soprano and and eight players 1986, Rosa, Rosae for soprano, contralto, clarinet, violin, harp and piano 1986, In the Green Shade 1988, Rose des Sables for mezzo-soprano, speaker, female choir and orchestra 1990, On a Landscape by Turner 1992, Sieben Galgenlieder for soprano or mezzo-soprano, oboe or clarinet, cello and piano 1994, L'anneau de Jade 1996, Ich Kannte Meine Seele Nicht for six mixed voices or six female voices 1997, Goeie Hoop 1998, Au Fil des Siecles 2000, Naïra for mezzo and piano 2000; solos and duos: Capriccio 1954, Ballade 1963, Le Gong 1980, Aura 1982, Spirales for two pianos 1971, Six Climats for cello and piano 1972, Controverse for bass clarinet and percussion 1983, La Deviniere for violin and piano 1987–88, Polissonnerie for percussion and piano 1991, La Quinta Stagione for violin solo 1991, Analecta for two violins 1981; instrumental and chamber music: Piano Trio 1957, Horizons for string quartet 1977, Zones for flute, clarinet, cello, percussion and piano 1979, Meglio Tardi for flute, bass clarinet and piano 1994, La Fenêtre Ouverte for traverso, gamba and harpsichord 1996, Aube for flutes, guitar and piano 1998, En luminures for organ 2000, Koba for violin and piano 2000, Ein (Kleiner) Winternachtstraum 2002, Battements D'ailes 2001, Rivages Solitaires 1989, Virus Alert (opera) 2002. *Recordings:* Concerto pour violon et orchestre, Michaël Bezerchny, Orchestre National de Belgique, Georges Octors, DGG; Spirales, Ballade, AUa, Capriccio, Le Gong, Mosaici, Bulles, Robert Groslot and Daniel Blumenthal, CD Duchesne; Ephemeres, Per Archi, Halo, Psalmus Tertius, Koch Schwann/ Aulos; Créneaux, Blake's Mirror, Aratoro, Frises, Grand Orchestre d'Harmonie 'Musique Royale des Guides', Norbert Nozy, WWM; Alba, Intermezzo, Mime 5, Fougeres, Filigrane sul Cuor Della Terra, Compagnon de la Nuit, Ottavo

Records; Pro and Antverb(e)s, Sieben Galgenlieder, Le Gong, Six Climats, Mosaïques, Musica a Quattro, Mime 2, Cyprès. *Honours:* Fondation de France Prix Arthur Honegger 1988; awarded title of Baroness by the King of Belgium in recognition of her artistic merits. *Address:* rue Léon Dekaise 6, 1342 Limelette, Belgium. *E-mail:* performourmusic@wanadoo.com.

**FORBES, Elizabeth;** Critic, Writer on Music and Translator; b. 3 Aug. 1924, Camberley, Surrey, England. *Education:* Autodidactic. *Career:* Freelance Music Critic, Financial Times, 1970–80. *Publications:* Opera from A to Z, 1977; Observer's Book of Opera, 1982; Mario and Grisi, 1985; Old Scores, detective story; Translations for Nottingham University of Spontini's La Vestale, Auber's La Muette de Portici, Meyerbeer's Robert le Diable and Berwald's Queen of Golconda; Translations for Radio 3: Schubert's Claudine von Villa Bella, Brand's Maschinist Hopkins and Wagner-Régeny's Die Bürger von Calais. *Contributions:* Opera Now/The Independent; Encyclopedia of Opera, 1976; New Grove Dictionary of Music and Musicians, 1980, 2001; The Performing Arts, 1980; New Grove Dictionary of American Music, 1986; Whitaker's Almanack, 1991–2004; New Grove Dictionary of Opera, 4 vols, 1992; Viking Opera Guide, 1993; New Dictionary of National Biography, and The Collins Classical Music Encyclopedia, 2001. *Address:* Flat 3, 1 Bryanston Square, London W1H 2 DH, England.

**FORBES, Elliot;** American professor of music (retd); b. 30 Aug. 1917, Massachusetts, USA; m. Kathleen Brooks Allen, 7 June 1941, 3 d. *Education:* BA, 1941, MA, 1947 Harvard; Mozarteum, Salzburg, 1937; Westminster Choir College, 1946. *Career:* Debut: Conductor, Harvard Glee Club and Radcliffe Choral Society, 1958; Teacher at Cate School, California, 1941–43, Belmont Hill School, Massachusetts, 1943–45; Assistant Professor, 1947–54, Associate Professor, 1954–58, Princeton University; Professor of Music at Harvard University, 1958–84; mem, AAAS; American Musicological Society; College Music Association. *Publications:* Editor: Thayer's Life of Beethoven, 1964, Beethoven's Fifth, 1971, A History of Music at Harvard to 1972, 1988, A Report of Music at Harvard, 1972–90, 1993. *Contributions:* Articles in American Choral Review and Music Quarterly. *Honours:* Phi Beta Kappa; Signet Society Medal, 1985; Harvard Medal, 1991; Hon D.Mus, New England Conservatory, 1996, Harvard Univ., 2003. *Address:* 975 Memorial Drive, Apt 210, Cambridge, MA 02138, USA. *Telephone:* (617) 864-6787.

**FORBES, Rupert Oliver;** Singer (Tenor), Conductor and Stage Director; b. 27 Jan. 1944, London, England; m. Elisabeth Burnett, 10 July 1976, 2 s. *Education:* St John's College, Cambridge University; With Pierre Bernac, Paris, and Luigi Ricci, Rome; Opera Studio, Zürich; Arturo Merlini, Milan. *Career:* Sang at the Zürich Opera 1970–75; Engaged at the Stadttheater Basel from 1975, singing Mozart's Monostatos and Pedrillo, Jacquino in Fidelio, Tybalt in Roméo et Juliette, Lindoro, (Haydn's La Fedelta Premiata), the comic roles in Les contes d'Hoffmann, Wagner's Steuermann, Hauptmann in Wozzeck (Berg) and Lord Barrat in Der Junge Lord; Guest appearances in Mannheim, Wiesbaden, Kassel, Bremen and Freiburg; Since 1990, freelance singer with Covent Garden, Scottish Opera, Glyndebourne, Rome, Wexford; Stage Director, Of Mice and Men (Carlisle Floyd) Opéra de Nantes; Many engagements in concert and oratorio, notably in works by Bach. *Recordings:* As tenor: Visitatio Sepulchri by James MacMillan; Salome by Strauss; Conductor: Fauré Requiem, Opera Choruses, My Fair Lady, Fiddler on the Roof, Oliver, Carmen. *Address:* 10 Mount Vernon Road, Edinburgh EH16 6BW, Scotland. *Telephone:* 0131 6643030.

**FORBES, Sebastian;** Composer and University Professor; b. 22 May 1941, Amersham, Buckinghamshire, England; m. (1) Hilary Spaight Taylor, 2 d., (2) Tessa Brady, 24 Sept 1983, 1 s., 1 d. *Education:* Royal Academy of Music, 1958–60; Kings College, Cambridge University, 1960–64; MA, Cantab; BMus, Cantab; D.Mus, Cantab; LRAM; ARCO; ARCM. *Career:* Treble Soloist, 1953–56; BBC Producer, 1964–67; Organist, Trinity College, Cambridge, 1968; Lecturer, Bangor University, 1968–72; Conductor, Aeolian Singers, 1965–69; Seiriol Singers, 1969–72; Horniman Singers, 1981–90; Lecturer, University of Surrey, 1972–; Professor of Music, 1981–; Compositions and commissions: Essay for clarinet and orchestra, Proms, 1970; Symphony, Edinburgh Festival, 1972; Sinfonia I–III, 1979, 1989, 1990; 8 ensemble sonatas, 1976–2001; Much organ and piano music including Sonata-Rondo for piano, 1996; Much chamber music including 5 string quartets, 1969, 1979, 1982, 1996, 2000; Numerous works of church music; mem, Performing Right Society. *Recordings:* String Quartet No. 1, 1971; Capriccio for organ, 1980; Bristol Mass, 1992; Hymn to St Etheldreda, 1996. *Publications:* String Quartet No. 1, 1970; Organ sonata, 1970; Violin Fantasy No. 2, 1980; Seasonal Roundelay, 1985; Numerous choral pieces, Cathedral Music. *Honours:* McEwen Memorial Prize, 1962; Clements Memorial Prize, 1963; Radcliffe Music Award, 1969; SPNM Carl Flesch Prize, 1980; ARAM, 1990; FRSA, 1997. *Address:* Octave House, Boughton Hall Avenue, Send, Woking, Surrey GU23 7 DF, England. *Website:* www.sebastianforbes.com.

**FORBES-LANE, Andrew;** Singer (Tenor); b. 1960, Walton-on-Thames. *Education:* Manchester University; Royal Northern College of Music, with Nicholas Powell. *Career:* Appearances with Opera North, City of Birmingham Touring Opera, and Crystal Clear Opera; English National Opera 1993, in the premiere of Jonathan Harvey's Inquest of Love; Roles have included Don José, Alfredo, Tamino, Pinkerton, Lensky, Jenik in The Bartered Bride, Ferrando, Rodolfo, and Tichon in Katya Kabanova; Glyndebourne Festival and Tour debut 1999, as Ringmaster in The Bartered Bride; Don Curzio in Le nozze di Figaro, 2000; Concerts with the RTE, Dublin, Hanover Band, London Proms,

Salisbury Festival and in Antwerp. *Address:* c/o Glyndebourne Festival Opera, Glyndebourne, Lewes, Sussex BN8 5UU, England.

**FORD, Andrew;** Composer, Conductor, Writer and Broadcaster; b. 18 March 1957, Liverpool, England. *Education:* Graduated with honours, Composition, University of Lancaster, 1978; Composition study with Edward Cowie and John Buller; Doctor of Creative Arts, University of Wollongong, 1994. *Career:* Fellow in Music, University of Bradford, 1978–82; Founder, Music Director, Performer, Big Bird Music Theatre, 1982; Lecturer, Faculty of Creative Arts, University of Wollongong, New South Wales, Australia, 1983–95; Many world and Australian premieres with the Faculty's contemporary music ensemble SCAW, 1984–90, including Stockhausen's Stimmung, 1986; Conductor, Australia Ensemble, Seymour Group, Magpie Musicians, Australian Chamber Orchestra; Composer in residence, Bennelong Programme, Sydney Opera House, 1985; Own works played in Australia, Europe, America, South East Asia; Commissions; Writer and broadcaster on music; Featured composer, many festivals, including Aspekte, Salzburg, 1984, Ferrara 1985, Istanbul, Buffalo, Up-Beat to The Tate, Liverpool, Aspen, 1988; Composer in residence, Australian Chamber Orchestra, 1993–94, also Conductor. *Compositions:* Music theatre: Songs for the Lady Pan, 1981–83; From Hand to Mouth, 1984–85; Poe, opera, 1981–83; Whispers, 1990; Casanova Confined, 1995; Children's opera: The Piper's Promise, 1986–87; The World Knot, 1987–88; Orchestral: Concerto for Orchestra, 1980; Prologue, Chorale and Melodrama, 1981; Epilogue to an Opera, 1982; The Big Parade, 1985–86; Imaginings, piano and orchestra, 1991; The Widening Gyre, chamber orchestra, 1993; The Great Memory, cello and orchestra, 1994; The Furry Dance, 1999; Chamber ensemble: Sonata for 4 Instruments, 1978; Chamber Concerto No. 1, 1979, No.2 Cries in Summer, 1983; Bright Ringing Morning, 1981, Pit, 1981; Boatsong, 1982; Rant, 1984, Pea Soup, 1984; Four Winds, saxophone quartet, 1984; Foolish Fires, 1985; String Quartet, 1985; Deep Blue, 1986; On Canaan's Happier Shore, 1987; The Art of Puffing, 1989; Parabola, 1989; Ringing the Changes, 1990; Pastoral, 1991; Clarion, 1991; Dance Maze for large ensemble, 1996; Tattoo for 12 timpani and 4 pianos, 1998; The Unquiet Grave for viola and ensemble, 1998; Solo instruments: Les débris d'un rêve, piccolo and reverb, 1992; Portraits, piano, 1981; Like Icarus Ascending, violin, 1984; A Kumquat for John Keats, piano, 1987; Swansong, viola; Several vocal works; The Laughter of Mermaids, vocal ensemble; Insomnia, chorus and ensemble; Vocal: Harbour, tenor and strings. *Address:* c/o The Music Show, ABC Radio National, GPO Box 9994, Sydney, NSW 2001, Australia.

**FORD, Anthony Dudley,** BMus; British musician; b. 19 Sept. 1935, Birmingham; m. Diane Clare Anwyl; one s. one d. *Education:* Birmingham Univ. *Career:* Sr Lecturer in Music, Univ. of Hull 1964–99; conductor, Hull Bach Choir 1969–; freelance harpsichordist and pianist; mem. Royal Musical Assocn, Assocn of Univ. Teachers. *Compositions:* various songs and choral pieces. *Publications:* editions: Giovanni Bononcini: When Saul was King, Aeterna Fac, Arias from the Vienna Operas; Purcell: Fantazias and In Nomines; contrib. to The Musical Times, Proceedings of the Royal Musical Association, Current Musicology, Die Musik in Geschichte und Gegenwart, Dictionary of National Biography. *Honours:* Barber Post-graduate Scholarship in Music 1957. *Address:* 199 Victoria Avenue, Hull, HU5 3EF, England (home). *Telephone:* (1482) 343199 (home).

**FORD, Bruce;** American singer (tenor); m. H. Ypma 1982; one s. *Education:* Texas Tech. Univ., Houston Opera Studio. *Career:* sings in major opera houses in N America and Europe, specializing in Mozart and bel canto composers; Rossini's Otello (Covent Garden), Ermione (Glyndebourne), Zelmira, Ricciardo e Zoraide (Pesaro) revived for him; concert appearances include La Scala, Edin. Festival, Covent Garden, San Francisco Opera, Düsseldorf Symphonic, Chicago Lyric Opera and Amsterdam Concertgebouw; extensive recording career including many rare 19th century operas. *Honours:* Seal of Tex. Tech. Univ. 1997. *Address:* c/o Athole Still International Management Ltd, 25–27 Westow Street, London, SE19 3RY, England (office). *Telephone:* (20) 8771-5271 (office). *Fax:* (20) 8771-8172 (office). *E-mail:* lucy@atholestillopera.co.uk (office); TenorBruceFord@compuserve.com (home). *Website:* www.bruce-ford.com (office).

**FORD, Trevor,** ARAM, ARSCM, FRSA; British music administrator, editor and flautist; b. 28 Nov. 1951, London, England; m. Marianne Barton 1979; two s. *Education:* Royal Acad. of Music. *Career:* orchestral flautist 1976–; Personnel Man. English Sinfonia 1979–2003; Orchestral Man. Philomusica of London 1981–2002, Midland Philharmonic 1982–96, Ambache Chamber Orchestra 1984–89; Gen. Man. English Festival Orchestra 1984–; Bd Dirs Asscn of British Orchestras 1985–88, mem. of Council 2004–; Dir of Music, St John's Church, Palmers Green 1992–2003; Chair. Organists' Working Party 1993–95; Treasurer Inc. Soc. of Musicians 1996–2003; mem. of Council and Exec. Under-Treasurer Royal Coll. of Organists 1995–2004; Prof. Guildhall School of Music and Drama 1996–; Prof. Birmingham Conservatoire 1999–2004; mem. of Council Royal School of Church Music 2001–; mem. Musicians' Union, Inc. Soc. of Musicians, Asscn of British Choral Dirs, Church Music Soc. *Publications:* The Musician's Handbook (ed.) 1986, The Art of Auditioning 1988, Church Music Quarterly 1989–2000. *Honours:* Hon. RCO. *Address:* 151 Mount View Road, London N4 4JT, England.

**FORRESTER, Maureen,** CC, DMus; Canadian singer (contralto) and administrator; b. 25 July 1930, Montréal, PQ; d. of Thomas and Mary Domican Forrester; m. Eugene Kash 1957 (separated); four d. one s. *Education:* Dawson School, Montreal, privately and Univ. of Western Ontario.

*Career:* Trustee Nat. Arts Centre Corpn 1973; Gov. Thomson Hall 1982; Chair. Canada Council 1984–1989; Fellow Strong Coll., York Univ. *Honours:* numerous hon. degrees; Nat. Award in Music (Banff School of Fine Arts) 1967, Harriet Cohen Int. Music Award 1968, Molson Prize 1971, Yale school of Music Samuel Simons Sanford Award 1983, Toronto Arts Award 1989, Royal Bank Award 1995. *Address:* Canada Council, POB 1047, 99 Metcalfe Street, Ottawa, Ontario, K1P 5V8, Canada.

**FORSBERG, Bengt;** Pianist; b. 1950, Sweden. *Education:* Gothenburg Music Academy; London, with Peter Feuchtwanger; Copenhagen with Herman D. Koppel. *Career:* Chamber musician, and accompanist to leading soloists; Chamber Music Society of Lincoln Center, New York, concerts 1999–2000 with Anne Sofie von Otter, featuring music by Korngold; Further engagements at the Wigmore Hall, London, Lisbon, Paris Châtelet, Graz and Gothenburg; Season 1999–2000 with Stravinsky's Piano Concerto and Medtner's 2nd Concerto, with the Royal Philharmonic, in Stockholm; Other repertoire includes Mozart and Martinů Concertos, Bach's Well-Tempered Klavier, and works by Grieg, Sibelius, Fauré and Franck. *Recordings include:* Songs by Stenhammar and Sibelius, with Anne Sofie von Otter; Schumann's Frauenliebe und Leben, Lieder by Berg, Korngold, Strauss and Schubert; Songs by Grieg and Weill; Albums with Mats Lidström, cello. *Address:* c/o IMG Artists, Lovell House, 616 Chiswick High Road, London, W4 5RX.

**FORSBERG, Roland;** Director of Music and Organist; b. 18 Sept. 1939, Stockholm, Sweden; m. (1) Margaretha Widlund, 1967–91, (2) Lisbeth Carlborg, 1992, 2 s., 1 d. *Education:* Professor of Music, Royal Academy of Music, Stockholm, 1961; Higher Organist Exam, 1963; Higher Cantor Exam, 1964; Diploma, Organist, 1968. *Career:* Director of Music: Norrmalm Church, Stockholm, 1964–89; Organists, Immanuel Church, Stockholm, 1989–; Musical Expert, Swedish State Psalm Committee, 1976–86; mem, Kammarmusikföreningen Samtida Musik; Föreningen Svenska Tonsättare, Stockholm. *Compositions include:* Liten Svit for organ, 1959; Passacaglia for organ, 1960; Verbum Christi, vocal, 1963; 12 Sacred Songs, 1964; Musica solenne for organ, 1965; Orgeljojk for 2 organs, 1975; Sicut Cervus Organ Symphony, 1977; Sonata lapponica for violin and piano, 1980; Sonatina da cappella for violin and organ, 1983; 3 piano sonatas; Concertos for flute and oboe; Sacred concertos for solo voices and organ; Songs; Hymns; Motets; Cantatas; Oratorios; Masses and other choral works; 8 organ suites; Psalm sonata for mixed chorus (English words), 1984; Credo Triptych for organ, 1988; Memoria for violin and piano or organ, 1988; Symphonic Pictures for Archipelago for organ and brass orchestra, 1995; Missa in Millennium Immanuel, 1998–99. *Recordings include:* Kärlekens musik; Tre orglar i Västervik; En gång blir allting stilla; Sjögrens Legender; Autography, Swedish Composers play their own works; Orgelmusik i Sjövik; Skärgårdsorgel, Archipelago the Mid-Eighteenth Century Organ of Utö. *Publications:* Editions: Sjung svenska kanon, 1977; Fader wår (Gustaf Duben), 1980; Seven Sacred Songs (Anders Bond), 1981; Organ Fantasy (Otto Olsson), 1983; Two Organ Pieces (Anders Bond), 1985; 88 Preludes (Anders Bond); Organ Preludes I–III; Concerto grosso g-moll transcription for organ (Archangelo Corelli); Sinfonia IB26 transcription for organ solo (Johan Helmich Roman); Sinfonia in G Major, 1994. *Honours:* Numerous including Composers Scholarships, STIM, Stockholm, 1974, 1981, 1985; Föreningen Svenska Tonsättare, 1996. *Address:* Dalarö Prästgård, 13054 Dalarö, Sweden.

**FORST, Judith Doris,** OC, BMus; Canadian singer (mezzo-soprano); b. 7 Nov. 1943, New Westminster, BC; d. of Gordon Stanley and Euna Jessie Lumb; m. Graham N. Forst 1964; one s. one d. *Education:* Univ. of British Columbia. *Career:* Has appeared in USA with New York Metropolitan Opera, New York City Opera, Seattle Opera, San Francisco Opera, New Orleans Opera, Fort Worth Opera, Santa Fe Opera, Washington, DC Opera, Miami Opera, Baltimore Opera and San Diego Opera Soc., in Canada with Canadian Opera Co. (Toronto), Vancouver Opera, Calgary Opera, Montréal Symphony Orchestra, Vancouver Symphony Orchestra and Hamilton Symphony Orchestra, and in Europe with Munich State Opera (Germany), Symphony Orchestra of Barcelona (Spain) and Orchestre de Radio France (Paris); Guest Lecturer Univ. of British Columbia, Univ. of Montréal; mem. Asscn of Canadian TV and Radio, American Guild of Musical Artists. *Honours:* Hon. LLD (Univ. of British Columbia) 1992; Hon. DMus (Univ. of Victoria) 1995; won Metropolitan Opera auditions 1968, CBC Cross-Canada Talent Contest 1968, Canadian Woman of the Year 1978, Greater Miami Opera Asscn Performer of the Year 1980, Univ. of British Columbia Distinguished Alumnus of the Year 1986, Freeman City of Port Moody 1992. *Address:* 428 Princeton Ave, Port Moody, BC V3H 3L3, Canada.

**FORSTER, Andreas;** Singer (Baritone); b. 17 Sept. 1949, Naumburg, Germany. *Education:* Studied in Berlin and in Essen with Gladys Kuchta. *Career:* Debut: Detmold, 1974, as Schaunard in La Bohème; Sang at Kaiserslautern, 1975–76, Saarbrucken, 1976–78, Nuremberg, 1978–88; Staatstheater Hanover from 1988; Guest appearances at the Staatsoper Berlin, Düsseldorf, Cologne, Dortmund, Stuttgart, Munich, Wiesbaden and Orlando, Florida, USA; Roles have included Verdi's Nabucco, Rigoletto, Macbeth and Simon Boccanegra, Germont, Renato, Iago and Amonasro, Rodrigo, Luna, Donizetti's Enrico, Belcore and Dulcamara, Gerard, Escamillo, Eugene Onegin, Wolfram, Amfortas, Marcello, Olivier in Capriccio and Mozart's Don Giovanni and Count; Concert engagements in works by Bach, Handel, Beethoven, Brahms, Mahler and Penderecki; Lieder recitals and broadcast concerts in Germany, France and Italy; Sang Grigoris in The Greek

Passion and Telramund in Lohengrin at Hannover, 2000. *Address:* Niedersachische Staatstheater, Opernplatz 1, 30159 Hannover, Germany.

**FORSYTH, Malcolm (Denis);** Composer and Conductor; b. 8 Dec. 1936, Pietermaritzburg, South Africa; m. (1) Lesley Eales, 1965, divorced 1984, one d. *Education:* BMus, 1963, MMus, 1966, D.Mus, 1972, University of Cape Town; Conductors class, Canford Summer School of Music, 1980–84. *Career:* Conductor: Chamber Choir and Orchestra, University of Cape Town, 1962–64; St Cecilia Orchestra, 1977–86; Edmonton Wind Sinfonia, 1978–79; West Wind Chamber Ensemble, 1980–83; Chamber Choir, University of Witwatersrand, 1983; Guest Conductor: Cape Town, CAPAB and Edmonton Symphony Orchestras, Alberta Ballet Orchestra, National Orchestra, SABC, Johannesburg; As Trombonist: Assistant Principal Cape Town Symphony Orchestra, 1961–67; Co-Principal, CAPAB Symphony Orchestra, 1971–72; Principal, Edmonton Symphony Orchestra, 1973–80; Junior Lecturer, College of Music, University of Cape Town, 1967; Assistant Professor, 1968–71, Associate Professor, 1971–77, Professor of Music, 1977–, Division Chairman, Concert Activity Chairman, 1984–86, Artistic Director, Music Department, 1987–89, McCalla Professor, 1990–91, University of Alberta, Edmonton, Canada; Visiting Professor, Cape Town and Witwatersrand Universities; Composer-in-Residence: Banff Centre, 1975–78; Festival of the Sound, 1991; University of Alberta, 1997; Juror; Commissions include Canada Council, CBC and University of Cape Town; Fellow of the Camargo Foundation, Cassis, France, 1993; Composer-in-Residence, University of Alberta, 1996–; Saskatchewan New Music Festival, 1997. *Compositions:* Works for orchestra, band, ensembles, piano, vocal solos and choir including Valley of a Thousand Hills for orchestra, 1989; These Cloud Capp'd Towers for trombone and orchestra, 1990; Electra Rising for cello and chamber orchestra, 1995. *Recordings:* Electra Rising, 1997; Soaring with Agamemnon. 1998. *Honours:* Composer of the Year, Canada, 1989; JUNO Winner for Best Classical Composition, 1987, 1995, 1998; Queen's Jubilee Medal 2003; Order of Canada 2003. *Current Management:* BMG Ariola, Counterpoint Musical Services. *Address:* 9259 Strathearn Drive, Edmonton, Alberta T6C 4E1, Canada.

**FORTE, Allen,** BA, MA; American musician and writer; *Battell Professor Emeritus of the Theory of Music, Yale University New Haven;* b. 23 Dec. 1926, Portland, OR. *Education:* Columbia Univ. *Career:* Faculty, Teachers Coll., Columbia Univ. 1953–59, Manhattan School of Music 1957, Mannes Coll. of Music 1957–59; Instructor, Yale Univ. 1959–61, Asst Prof. 1961–64, Assoc. Prof. 1964–68, Prof. 1968–91, Battell Prof. of the Theory of Music from 1991, now Prof. Emer.; Ed., Journal of Music Theory 1960–67; Gen. Ed., Composers of the Twentieth Century 1980–; Fellow American Acad. of Arts and Sciences 1995; mem. American Musicological Soc., Soc. for Music Theory (pres. 1977–82). *Publications:* Contemporary Tone-Structure 1955, Schenker's Conception of Musical Structure 1959, Bartók's 'Serial' Composition 1960, The Compositional Matrix 1961, Tonal Harmony in Concept and Practice 1962, A Theory of Set-complexes for Music 1964, A Program for the Analytical Reading of Scores 1966, Computer-implemented Analysis of Musical Structure 1966, Music and Computing: The Present Situation 1967, The Structure of Atonal Music 1970, The Harmonic Organization of The Rite of Spring 1978, Introduction to Schenkerian Analysis (with S. Gilbert) 1982, The American Popular Ballad of the Golden Era 1924–1950 1995, The Atonal Music of Anton Webern 1998, Olivier Messiaen as Serialist 2002, Listening to Classic American Popular Songs 2001, Songs of Yesterday for Today (pianist-arranger) 2005; contrib. to learned books and journals. *Honours:* Hon. PhD (Eastman School of Music) 1988; Sr Marshal Yale Univ. Commencement Ceremony 2004; Guggenheim Fellowship 1981, Festschrift published in his honour: Music Theory in Concept and Practice 1997. *Address:* c/o Department of Music, PO Box 208310, Yale University, New Haven, CT 06520 (office); 10 Mulberry Hill, Hamden, CT 06517, USA (home). *Telephone:* (203) 288-8888 (home). *E-mail:* allen.forte@yale.edu (office). *Website:* www.allenforte.com.

**FORTE, Cinzia;** Singer (Soprano); b. 1968, Italy. *Career:* Appearances at La Scala Milan as Lisette in La Sonnambula, as Pamina at La Coruña, Gilda (Rigoletto) in Venice and Lucia di Lammermoor; Teti in Rossini's Le nozze di Teti e di Peleo at Pesaro, Traviata in Modena and Lisette in Puccini's La Rondine at Covent Garden (2002); Baroque repertory includes Vivaldi's Farnace (at Madrid), Messiah, Te Deum by Charpentier and Pergolesi's Stabat Mater; Season 2002–03 as Corina in Rossini's Il viaggio a Reims in Oviedo, Lucia in Tokyo and Adina in L'elisir d'amore at Venice; Other roles include Susanna and Musetta. *Address:* c/o Ouverture, Via Braccianese Claudia 44, 1–00062, Bracciano, Rome, Italy.

**FORTIN, Lyne;** Canadian singer (soprano); *Soprano and Voice Teacher, Montreal Opera Apprentice Program;* b. 28 April 1962, Quebec, Canada. *Education:* Studied in Quebec and with Marlena Malas. *Career:* Sang with Canada Piccola Opera 1985–; frequent concert appearances; Soprano and Voice Teacher, Montreal Opera Apprentice Program. *Opera appearances include:* Susanna (Marriage of Figaro) and Gilda (Rigoletto), Quebec Opera, 1987, 1989; Montreal Opera 1990–, including Olympia (Les Contes d'Hoffman), Gounod's Juliette and Leila in The Pearl Fishers 1996; Norina (Don Pasquale), Philadelphia 1991; Micaela (Carmen), Portland Opera 1994; Adina (Elisir d'Amore), Seattle and Countess (Marriage of Figaro), Montreal, 1988; Donna Anna (Don Giovanni) with Scottish Opera, 2001; Countess (Marriage of Figaro), Electra (Idomeneo), Vlaamse Opera, Antwerp. *Recordings include:* Les Grands Duos d'Amour de l'Opéra Française (with Richard Margison) 1987; Noel 1993; Lyne Fortin Live 1995; Mozart 1999. *Honours:* Special Prize, CBC National Competition for Young Performers 1986; Winner, Pavarotti

International Vocal Competition 1988; First Prize and Grand Prize, CIBC National Competition Festival of Music, Concourse de musique de Quebec; Medal of 125th Anniversary of Canada, for Contributions to Community 1992. *Address:* c/o L'Opéra de Montréal, 260 de Maisonneuve Boulevard West, Montréal, Quebec H2X 1Y9, Canada. *Telephone:* (450) 670-9274. *E-mail:* kaskou@sprint.ca (office).

**FORTIN, Viktor;** Austrian composer and academic; b. 14 May 1936, Fohnsdorf, Steiermark; m.; one s. *Education:* Steiermarkisches Landes Konservatorium; University of Vienna; Academie für Musik und Kunst, Graz. *Career:* mem. President of Steirischer Tonkunstlerbund; Osterreichischer Komponistenbund. *Compositions include:* Appalachian sonata for flute and piano 1970, Happy Suite for strings, piano and percussion 1978, Maja's Orchestra for strings and piano, Ohhh Pinocchio!, Opera House, Graz 1994–95, Tartu, Estonia 1999, Kraków, Poland 2005, Concerto for speaker and orchestra, with texts from Mozart letter, Graz 1994, Lublin 1997, Quito, Ecuador 1998, Archibalds Adventures for 2 speakers and orchestra 1997, 1998, Cairo and Graz 1999 5 Love Songs with texts from Erich Fried, Marginals to the Spring 1986, Der Kleine Klabautermann, Blacksmith Variations, Concerto for soprano recorder and strings, Hafer Quartet. *Recordings include:* Ohhh Pinocchio! 1994, Viktor Fortin and Friends 1996, Archibald's Adventure 2000, Missa duri montis 2003, Concertino for bassoon & strings 2004, Concert amusant (flute & strings) 2004. *Publications:* Doblinger, Vienna, Concert for soprano recorder and string orchestra, 1992, Brass Light, Not Easy, Moeck Germany, Lambsborner Nuesse for recorder-orchestra, 1997. *Contributions:* Musik aus Osterreich, 1998. *Honours:* Goldenes Ehrenzeichen des Landes Steiermark 1995. *Address:* 8054 Graz, Halmweg 13, Austria (home). *Telephone:* (316) 296207 (home). *E-mail:* fortin@aon.at (home). *Website:* www.fortin.at (home).

**FORTUNATO, D'Anna;** Singer (Mezzo-soprano); b. 21 Feb. 1945, Pittsburgh, Pennsylvania, USA. *Education:* Studied with Frederick Hagel and Gladys Miller at the New England Conservatory, 1965–72; Further study with Phyllis Curtin at the Berkshire Music Center. *Career:* Concert appearances in Pittsburgh, Detroit, Louisville, Atlanta and Minnesota; Recitals with the Chamber Music Society of Lincoln Center and with the Boston Musica Viva ensemble; Taught at Longy School of Music, Cambridge, 1974–82; Member of the Liederkreis Ensemble; European debut, Paris, 1980, as Purcell's Dido with the Boston Camerata; Sang in the premiere of John Harbison's opera Full Moon in March, New York, 1979; New York recital debut, 1981; New York City Opera debut, 1983, as Ruggiero in Handel's Alcina. *Honours:* Co-winner, Naumburg Chamber Music Prize, 1980. *Address:* c/o New York City Opera, Lincoln Center, New York, NY 10023, USA.

**FORTUNE, George;** American singer (baritone) and voice teacher; b. 13 Dec. 1935, Boston, Massachusetts. *Education:* Brown University, Providence, Boston University; vocal studies with Todd Duncan. *Career:* debut: Ulm 1960, as Fluth in Die Lustigen Weiber von Windsor; guest appearances in Bordeaux, Brussels, Strasbourg, Hamburg and Munich; Glyndebourne 1964, as the Count in Le nozze di Figaro; Santa Fe 1967, in the US premiere of Henze's Boulevard Solitude; Member of the Deutsche Oper Berlin from 1967; roles include Mozart's Figaro and Guglielmo, Rigoletto, Giulio Cesare, Iago, Amonasro, Posa, Scarpia, Gerard and Wolfram; further appearances in Dusseldorf, Frankfurt, Milan and Zürich; debut at the Metropolitan Opera New York in 1985 with Tonio, further parts include Jack Rance and Alfio; sang Scarpia at the Teatro San Carlos, Lisbon 1988, the High Priest in Samson et Dalila at the Deutsche Oper Berlin 1989; Barnaba in La Gioconda 1998; season 2000–01 as Scarpia at the Prague State Opera, Gounod's Capulet at Strasbourg, Count Luna for the Deutsche Oper; many concert engagements. *Recordings include:* Thérèse by Massenet, Olympie by Spontini, Christus by Liszt, Armida by Dvorak. *Address:* c/o Konzert-Direktion Hans Alder, Auguste-Viktoria-Strasse 64, D-14199 Berlin; Keithstrasse 12, D- 12307 Berlin, Germany (home). *E-mail:* fortune@p-soft.de (home).

**FORTUNE, Nigel (Cameron);** Musicologist; b. 5 Dec. 1924, Birmingham, England. *Education:* Studied Music and Italian at Birmingham University (BA, 1950) and researched Italian monody at Cambridge under Thurston Dart (PhD, 1954). *Career:* Music Librarian at London University, 1956–59; Lecturer in Music at Birmingham University, 1959–69, Reader in Music from 1969; Secretary of the Royal Musical Association, 1957–71, Vice-President, 1991; Member of editorial committee, Musica Britannica, 1975–77; Senior member, editorial committee, New Grove Dictionary of Music and Musicians, 1970–80; Editorial work for the New Oxford History of Music. *Publications include:* Continuo Instruments in Italian Monodies, 1953; Italian Secular Song from 1600 to 1635, 1954; Italian 17th Century Singing, 1954; Purcell's Autographs (with F B Zimmerman), 1959; A New Purcell Source, 1964; Philip Rosseter and his Songs, 1965; Editor, with Denis Arnold, The Monteverdi Companion, 1968, and The Beethoven Companion, 1971; Opera and Church Music, 1630–1750 (editor with Anthony Lewis), 1975; Editions of John Dowland and sacred music by Purcell (with Thurston Dart and Anthony Lewis).

**FOSS, Lukas;** American composer, conductor, pianist and academic; *Professor of Composition, Boston University*; b. 15 Aug. 1922, Berlin, Germany; s. of Martin Foss and Hilda Schindler; m. Cornelia B. Brendel 1950; one s. one d. *Education:* Lycée Pasteur, Paris, Curtis Inst. of Music, Yale Univ. Music School. *Career:* Prof. of Conducting and Composition, Univ. of Calif. at Los Angeles 1951–62; Founder Dir Center for Creative and

Performing Arts, Buffalo Univ. 1963–; Musical Dir, Conductor Buffalo Philharmonic Orchestra 1962–70; Musical Dir, Conductor Brooklyn Philharmonic Orchestra 1971–90 (Conductor Laureate 1990–), Jerusalem Symphony Orchestra 1972–76, Milwaukee Symphony Orchestra 1981–87; Dir, Conductor Ojai Festival, Calif. 1955, 1956, 1957, Festival of the Arts Today, Buffalo 1960–67, Franco-US Festival (New York Philharmonic Orchestra) 1964, Stravinsky Festival (New York Philharmonic Orchestra) 1965; Visiting Prof. Harvard Univ. 1969–70, Manhattan School of Music 1972–73, Carnegie Mellon Univ. 1987–90; Prof. of Composition, Boston Univ. 1991–; Visiting Prof. of Composition, Tanglewood 1989, 1990, Yale Univ. 1991; mem. Nat. Acad. of Arts and Letters. *Compositions include:* Time Cycle, Echoi, Baroque Variations, Paradigm, Geod, three operas, Orpheus, Map, Percussion Concerto, String Quartets, American Cantata, Night Music for John Lennon, Thirteen Ways of Looking at a Blackbird, Solo Observed, Flute concerto, Clarinet concerto, Guitar concerto, Symphony No. 3 (Symphony of Sorrows), Griffelkin (opera). *Recordings:* all above compositions and others. *Honours:* 19 hon. degrees; New York Music Critics' Circle Awards; Prix de Rome; Guggenheim Fellowship; Ditson Award 1973, Gold Medal, American Acad. of Arts and Letters 2001. *Address:* 1140 Fifth Avenue, New York, NY 10128, USA. *Telephone:* (212) 722-8003.

**FOSTER, Anthony;** Composer; b. 11 April 1926, Gravesend, Kent, England; m. Barbara Foster, 26 July 1952, deceased 1991, 1 d. *Education:* LRAM, ARCO; Piano with Anne Collins, Arthur Tracy Robson, Organ with John Cook, John Webster, Composition with Gordon Jacob, Richard Arnell. *Career:* Composed many works, secular and sacred for solo and choral voices, solo instruments and orchestra; Composed incidental music for BBC productions; mem, The British Academy of Composers and Songwriters; The Performing Right Society. *Recordings:* Jonah and the Whale, Harrow School of Young Musicians, Royal Albert Hall, London, 1983; A Child is Born, 1987, Christ the Lord is Risen Again, 1997, Child of Heaven, 1999, Chichester Cathedral Choir, directed by Alan Thurlow; Jubilate Deo for Organ, Alan Thurlow, Organist, Chichester Cathedral, 1988; Magnificat, Blessed Virgin Mary Service, Carlisle Cathedral Choir, directed by Jeremy Suter 2000. *Publications:* 55 published works (including all the above-mentioned titles). *Honours:* Honorary Vice-President, Brighton Schools Music and Drama Association, 1977. *Address:* 1 Cawley Road, Chichester, West Sussex PO 19 1UZ, England.

**FOSTER, Catherine;** Singer (Soprano); b. 1975, Nottingham, England. *Education:* Studied at Royal Northern College of Music and the National Opera Studio. *Career:* Appearances as Britten's Governess in Nottingham, Donna Anna at Dartington and Musetta for the Mananan Festival; Welsh and English National Operas with the Queen of Night; Concerts include Mozart's Requiem and C Minor Mass, Schubert's Mass in G, Elijah, the Brahms Requiem and Haydn's Theresienmesse, 1999–2000 season. *Honours:* Dame Eva Turner Award, 1997; Mario Lanza Opera Prize. *Address:* Harlequin Agency, 203 Fidlas Road, Cardiff CF4 5NA, Wales.

**FOSTER, Donald H.;** American professor emeritus; b. 30 April 1934, Detroit, Michigan, USA. *Education:* BS, Wayne State University, 1956; MMus, 1960, PhD, 1967, University of Michigan. *Career:* Music Faculty, Olivet College, Michigan, 1960–67; Professor of Musicology, College-Conservatory of Music, University of Cincinnati, Ohio, 1967–99; mem, American Musicological Society; American Association of University Professors. *Publications:* L'histoire de la femme adultère by Louis-Nicolas Clérambault, 1974; Louis-Nicolas Clérambault 1676–1749: Two Cantatas for Soprano and Chamber Ensemble, 1979; Symphonies concertantes of Jean-Baptiste Davaux; Overtures of Franz Beck; Jean-Philippe Rameau: A Guide to Research, 1989; Sourcebook for Research in Music (co-author) 1993, revised edn 2005. *Contributions:* Symphony Orchestras of the USA: Selected Profiles, 1986; Opera Quarterly; Recherches sur la musique française classique; The Diapason; Acta Musicologica; Current Musicology; L'orgue–cahiers et mémoires. *Honours:* Fulbright Grant, 1962. *E-mail:* dfoster@fuse.net. *Address:* 393 Amazon Avenue, Cincinnati, OH 45220, USA.

**FOSTER, Jillian;** Singer (Soprano); b. 1970, England. *Education:* Studied at the Royal Academy of Music. *Career:* Has sung with Kent Opera, Wexford Festival, Dublin Grand Opera and the Richard Strauss Society; Roles have included Tosca, Mimi, Donna Elvira, Violetta, Agathe and Arabella; Sang Garsenda in Francesca da Rimini with the Chelsea Opera Group and Messiah and Beethoven's Ninth with the Tokyo Philharmonic. *Honours:* Winners' Concert at the 1992 Pavarotti Competition. *Address:* Helen Sykes Artists Management, 100 Felsham Road, Putney, London SW15 1DQ, England.

**FOSTER, Lawrence Thomas;** American conductor; *Music Director, Gulbenkian Orchestra*; b. 23 Oct. 1941, Los Angeles; m. Angela Foster 1972; one d. *Career:* studied with Fritz Zweig and Karl Böhm and at Bayreuth Festival and Tanglewood Master Classes; Music Dir Young Musicians Foundation, Los Angeles 1960–64; Conductor San Francisco Ballet 1960–64; Asst Conductor LA Philharmonic Orchestra 1965–68; Chief Guest Conductor Royal Philharmonic Orchestra, London 1969–74; Music Dir Houston Symphony Orchestra 1971–78; Music Dir Orchestre Philharmonique, Monte Carlo 1978–96; Music Dir Duisburg Orchestra, FRG 1982–86; Music Dir Chamber Orchestra of Lausanne 1985; conductor Jerusalem Symphony Orchestra 1990; music Dir Aspen Music Festival and School 1990–96; Music Dir Orquestra Ciutat de Barcelona 1995–2002, Prin. Guest Conductor 2002–; Artistic Dir Georg Enescu Festival 1998–2001; Music Dir Gulbenkian Symphony Orchestra, Lisbon 2002–. *Honours:* Koussevitsky Memorial Conducting Prize, Tanglewood 1966; Pres.'s decoration for services to Romanian music 2003. *Address:* c/o ICM Artists Ltd, 8942 Wilshire Boulevard, Beverly Hills, CA 90211-1934, USA; c/o Harrison Parrott Ltd, 12 Penzance Place, London, W11 4PA, England.

**FOTEK, Jan;** Composer; b. 28 Nov. 1928, Czerwinsk nad Wisla, Poland. *Education:* Studied with Stanislav Wiechowicz in Kraków and Szeligowski in Warsaw. *Compositions:* Operas: The Sea of Recovered Unity, Polish Radio, 1967; Galileo, 1969; The Spoons and the Moon, 1973–76; The Woodland Princess, opera-ballet, Warsaw, 1978; Man and Angels, misterium sacrum, 1982; Vir sapiens dominabitur astris, after Dante, Copernicus, St Francis and Michelangelo, Polish Radio, 1983; Opus Concertante for organ, piano and percussion, 1959; Gregorian Hymn for chorus and orchestra; A Cycle of Verses for children's chorus and orchestra, 1963; Epitasis for orchestra, 1967; The Last War for narrator, chorus and orchestra, 1971; Partita for 12 bassoons and 3 double bassoons, 1973; Musica Chromatica for strings, 1982; Sonata for tuba and piano, 1984; Czarnolas Suite for strings, 1986; Ecloga for counter-tenor and ensemble, 1987. *Address:* c/o Society of Authors ZAiKS, 2 Hipoteczna Street, 00 092 Warsaw, Poland. *Telephone:* (4822) 828 17 05. *Fax:* (4822) 828 13 47. *E-mail:* sekretariat@zaiks.org.pl. *Website:* www.zaiks.org.pl.

**FOU, Ts'ong;** Pianist; b. 10 March 1934, Shanghai, China. *Education:* Studied in China with Mario Paci and at the Warsaw Conservatory with Zbigniew Drzewiecki. *Career:* Debut: With the Shanghai Municipal Orchestra, playing Beethoven's Emperor Concerto, 1951; Gave 500 concerts in Eastern Europe while studying in Poland; Moved to London, 1958; Solo appearances in Europe, Scandinavia, the Far East, Australia and New Zealand, North and South America. *Recordings include:* Concertos by Beethoven, Haydn, Chopin, Mozart; Solo recitals of Chopin, Debussy, Bach, Handel, Mozart, Beethoven, Schubert, Scarlatti, Schumann; Chopin: Mazurkas (complete); Chopin: Nocturnes and Solo Piano works. *Honours:* 3rd Prize, Bucharest Piano Competition, 1953; 3rd Prize, International Chopin Competition, Warsaw, 1955. *Address:* 62 Aberdeen Park, London N5 2BL, England.

**FOUCHECOURT, Jean-Paul;** Singer (Tenor); b. 10 Aug. 1958, Blanzy, France. *Education:* Trained as conductor and saxophone player; Vocal studies under the influence of Cathy Berberian. *Career:* Many appearances with such early music groups as Les Arts Florissants, and Les Musiciens du Louvre; Rameau's Les Indes Galantes, Les Fêtes d'Hébé and Zoroastre, Lully's Atys and Charpentiers's David et Jonatas under the direction of William Christie, Concerts in France and on tour throughout Europe, America and Japan; Rameau's Hippolyte et Aricie and Lully's Phaëton under Marc Minkowski; Further engagements in Purcell's Fairy Queen at the Aix Festival, Monteverdi's Orfeo under René Jacobs at Salzburg, L'Incoronazione di Poppea with Christophe Rousset for Netherlands Opera and Monteverdi's Ulisse with Michel Corboz at Geneva; Other repertory includes the Berlioz Roméo et Juliette (with John Eliot Gardiner), Offenbach's Orphée aux Enfers, Mozart's Nozze di Figaro and Poulenc's Les Mamelles de Tiresias with Seiji Ozawa, (on tour to Japan, 1996); Season 1997–98 in the title role of Rameau's Platée with the Royal Opera and at Edinburgh; L'Enfant et les Sortilèges at Florence, 1998; Debut at the Met in New York with Tales of Hoffmann; Season 1999–2000 included Golden Cockerel at Covent Garden, Madama Butterfly with Boston Symphony Orchestra, Poppea at Aix en Provence Festival and Platée at the Bastille; Engaged as Arnalta in Poppea for Netherlands Opera, 2001; Ravel's L'Heure Espagnole at the London Proms, 2002. *Recordings include:* Lully's Atys and Phaëton; Mondonville's Titon et L'Aurore and Les Fêtes de Paphos; Rameau's Les Indes Galantes, Pygmalion and Hippolyte et Aricie; Socrate by Satie; Les Mamelles de Tiresias. *Current Management:* Askonas Holt Ltd, Lonsdale Chambers, 27 Chancery Lane, London, WC2A 1PF, England. *Telephone:* (20) 7400-1700. *Fax:* (20) 7400-1799. *E-mail:* info@askonasholt.co.uk. *Website:* www.askonasholt.co.uk.

**FOUNTAIN, Ian;** British pianist; b. 15 Oct. 1969, Welwyn Garden City, England. *Education:* chorister at New Coll., Oxford, Winchester Coll., Royal Northern Coll. of Music with Sulamita Aronovsky. *Career:* has performed widely in the UK, in major London recital halls and in Europe and the USA from 1986, with recitals at festivals including Sintra, Stresa, Montpellier, Davos, Kuhmo, Berlin, Schleswig-Holstein, Prague Spring and Ravello; worked with leading orchestras, including the London Symphony Orchestra, Czech Philharmonic, Israel Philharmonic, City of Birmingham Symphony Orchestra, Philharmonic Orchestra, Bournemouth Symphony Orchestra, English Chamber Orchestra, Royal Liverpool Philharmonic Orchestra, Britten Sinfonia, Deutches Symphonie-Orchester, Singapore Symphony Orchestra, Polish Nat. Radio Symphony, Slovak Philharmonic and Jerusalem Symphony; Prof. of Piano, Royal Acad. of Music, London. *Recordings:* Beethoven: Diabelli Variations, Non-Beethoven Diabelli Variations. *Honours:* winner Viotti-Valessia Int. Piano Competition (Italy) 1986, jt winner Arthur Rubinstein Int. Piano Competition 1989. *Current Management:* Connaught Artists Management Ltd, 2 Molasses Row, Plantation Wharf, London, SW11 3UX, England. *Telephone:* (20) 7738-0017. *Fax:* (20) 7738-0909. *E-mail:* classicalmusic@connaughtartists.com. *Website:* www.connaughtartists.com.

**FOUNTAIN, Primous, III;** composer; b. 1 Aug. 1949, St Petersburg, Florida, USA. *Education:* DePaul University in Chicago. *Career:* freelance composer from 1968, including association with the Arthur Mitchell Dance Theatre of Harlem. *Compositions include:* Manifestations for orchestra, 1969; Grudges for orchestra, 1972; Ritual Dance of the Amaks for orchestra, 1973; Duet for

flute and bassoon, 1974; Cello Concerto, 1976; Ricia for violin, cello and piano, 1980; Harp Concerto, 1981; Symphony No. 1, Epitome of the Oppressed, 1984. *Honours:* BMI Composition Award, 1968; Guggenheim Fellowships, 1974, 1977; Award, American Academy and Institute of Arts and Letters.

**FOURNET, Jean;** Conductor; b. 14 April 1913, Rouen, France. *Education:* Studied with Philippe Gaubert at the Paris Conservatoire. *Career:* Debut: Rouen, 1936; Conducted in Rouen and Marseilles until 1944; Music Director of the Opéra-Comique, Paris, 1944–57; Conducting courses at Ecole Normale, Paris, 1944–62; Conducted Pelléas et Mélisande in Tokyo, 1958; Conductor of the Netherlands Radio Orchestra, 1961–68; Chicago Lyric Opera, 1965; Principal Conductor of the Rotterdam Philharmonic from 1968–73; Guest conductor in Europe, South America, USA and Israel; Metropolitan Opera debut, 1987, Samson et Dalila; Conducted Les Dialogues des Carmélites at Seattle, 1990. *Recordings include:* Berlioz Grande Messe des Morts, 1943; Louise by Charpentier; Pelléas et Mélisande and Les Pêcheurs de Perles; Mignon; d'Indy Symphonie; Saint-Saëns Piano Concertos; Fauré Requiem; Franck Symphonic Poems; Debussy La Damoiselle élue (Janine Micheau), Nocturnes, Ibéria and Prélude. *Address:* c/o Seattle Opera Association, PO Box 9248, Seattle, WA 98109, USA.

**FOURNIER, Brigitte;** Singer (Soprano); b. 14 June 1961, Nendaz, Switzerland. *Education:* Studied in Berne, Essen and Lausanne. *Career:* Sang in concert in works by Bach, Handel, Mozart, Schubert, Rameau and Honegger; Concert and lieder venues at the Aix and Montpellier Festivals, and throughout Switzerland; Sang Musetta in La Bohème at Biel/Solothurn, Naiad in Ariadne auf Naxos at Lausanne and Zerbinetta at Klagenfurt (1991); Toulouse, 1995, as Constance in Dialogues des Carmélites, Geneva, 1996, as Mozart's Blondchen; Season 2000–01 as Lucia in The Rape of Lucretia at Lausanne and the Woodbird in Siegfried at Geneva. *Recordings include:* Zelenka Requiem.

**FOURNILLIER, Patrick;** Conductor; b. 26 Dec. 1954, Neuilly-sur-Seine, France. *Education:* Studied with Louis Fourestier and Pierre Dervaux in Paris; Strasbourg Conservatoire with Jean-Sebastian Bereau, Salzburg Mozarteum with Leopold Hager, and with Franco Ferrara at the Accademiana Chigiana, Siena. *Career:* Assistant Conductor to Jean-Claude Casadesus at L'Orchestre National de Lille, 1983–85, Artistic Director, until 1986; Music Director, Nouvel Orchestre de St Etienne, 1988–, and Director, Sinfonietta d'Amiens, 1989–92; Music Director, Massenet Festival, St Etienne, 1988–; Important revivals of such neglected Massenet operas as Amadis, Thérèse, Cléopâtre, Esclarmonde and Grisélidis; Le Roi de Lahore by Massenet, 1997; Premieres have included Quatre-Vingt-Treize by Antoine Duhamel, 1989. *Honours:* Hans Haring Prize, Salzburg, 1982; Second Prize, Besancon International Conductors Competition, 1984; Prizewinner, Vaclav Talich Competition Prague, 1985; Second Prize, Grzerorz Fitelberg Competition at Katowice, 1987.

**FOWKE, Philip Francis,** FRAM; British concert pianist; b. 28 June 1950, Gerrards Cross, Bucks.; s. of Francis H. V. Fowke and Florence L. (née Clutton) Fowke. *Education:* Downside Abbey School. *Career:* began piano studies with Marjorie Withers 1957; awarded RAM Scholarship to study with Gordon Green 1967; Wigmore Hall debut 1974; UK concerto debut with Royal Liverpool Philharmonic 1975; Royal Festival Hall debut 1977; BBC Promenade Concert debut 1979; US debut 1982; debuts in Denmark, Bulgaria, France, Switzerland, Hong Kong, Belgium and Italy 1983; Austrian debut at Salzburg Mozart week 1984; German debut 1985; New Zealand debut 1987; now appears regularly with all the leading orchestras in UK and gives regular recitals and concerto performances for BBC Radio; Prof. RAM 1984–91, Welsh Coll. of Music and Drama 1994; Head of Keyboard Dept, Trinity Coll. of Music, London 1995–98, Sr Fellow 1998; recordings of Bliss, Chopin, Delius, Finzi, Rachmaninoff and Tchaikovsky piano concertos; Recitalist and Piano Tutor, Dartington Int. Summer School 1996, 1997, 2000; Concerto appearances with the Hallé Orchestra and in USA 1997; 50th Birthday Recital, Wigmore Hall, London 2000; soloist, BBC Proms 2001; mem. London Piano Quartet; Vice-Chair. European Piano Teachers' Asscn (UK) presenter and contrib. to music programmes on BBC Radio and to nat. press. *Recordings include:* Hoddinott Piano Concerto, CD album of film scores 1998. *Publications:* reviews and obituaries in nat. press. *Honours:* Countess of Munster Musical Trust Award 1972, Nat. Fed. of Music Socs. Award 1973, BBC Piano Competition 1974, Winston Churchill Fellowship 1976 and numerous other awards and prizes. *Current Management:* Patrick Garvey Management, Cedar House, 10 Rutland Street, Filey, North Yorkshire YO14 9JB, England. *Website:* www.patrickgarvey.com.

**FOWLER, Bruce;** Singer (Tenor); b. 1965, West-Monroe, Louisiana, USA. *Career:* Chicago Opera from 1990, notably as Nemorino in L'Elisir d'amore; Lindoro in Il Turco in Italia at Cleveland and Tonio in La Fille du régiment at Toronto (1994); Pesaro Festival, 1993, as Carlo in Rossini's Armida, and as Ferrando in Così fan tutte at Catania; Bonn Opera, 1995–96, in La Rondine and as Rossini's Almaviva; Sang Ferrando for Palm Beach Opera, 1998; Season 2000–01 as Rossini's Lindoro at the Deutsche Oper Berlin, Idreno in Semiramide at St Paul and Ramiro in Cenerentola at Cincinnati; Alfredo for Finnish National Opera. *Recordings include:* Armida.

**FOWLER, Jennifer;** Composer; b. 14 April 1939, Bunbury, Western Australia, Australia. *Education:* BA Hons, 1961, Dip Ed, 1962, BMus, 1967, University of Western Australia; Further study, Studio for Electronic Music, Utrecht, 1968–69. *Career:* Resident, London, 1969–; Music Teacher, schools,

1962–72; Freelance Composer; mem, Women in Music; International Alliance for Women in Music; Sonic Arts Network; British Academy of Composers and Songwriters. *Compositions include:* Hours of the Day, 4 mezzos, 2 oboes, 2 clarinets, 1968; Chimes, Fractured, ensemble, 1971; Veni Sancte Spiritus, chamber choir, 1971; Chant with Garlands, orchestra, 1974; Voice of the Shades, soprano, ensemble, 1977; Piece for EL, solo piano, 1981; The Arrows of St Sebastian, II, bass clarinet, cello, tape, 1981; Line Spun with stars, piano trio, 1983; When David Heard..., choir, piano, 1983; Echoes from an Antique Land, ensemble, 1983; Threaded Stars, solo harp, 1983; Blow Flute, solo flute, 1983; Letter from Haworth, mezzo, clarinet, cello, piano, 1984; Answer Echoes, 4 flutes, 1986; Lament, baroque oboe, bass viol, 1987; Restless Dust, cello, piano, 1988; And Ever Shall Be, mezzo, ensemble, 1989; Reeds, Reflections..., oboe, string trio, 1990; Plainsong for Strings, string orchestra, 1992; Lament for Mr Henry Purcell, ensemble, 1995; Singing the Lost Places, soprano and orchestra, 1996; Lament for Dunblane, chamber choir, 1996; Eat and Be Eaten, 6 singers and harp, 2000; Magnificat 2, soprano, flute, cello and harp, 2000; Freewheeling, solo harp, 2001; Echoes..., flute, cello, violin, cello and piano, 2001; Magnificat & Nunc Dimittis, 2002; Hymn for St Brigid, for SATB, 2002; Apsaras Flying, 3 recorders, cello and harpsichord, 2003; Towards Release, violin, marimba and guitar, 2003, Streaming Up, flute, oboe, clarinet, cello and piano 2004. *Recordings:* Chimes Fractured on Australian Festival of Music Vol. 10; Blow Flute on The Flute Ascendant; Threaded Stars on Awakening; Echoes from an Antique Land on Mizu to Kori; Veni Sancte Spiritus on Sydney Dreaming. *Contributions:* New Music Articles, Vol. 4, 1985; Contemporary Music Review, Vol. II, 1995. *Honours:* Prize for Hours of the Day, Berlin Academy of the Arts 1970; Radcliffe Award 1971; 1st Prize, Chamber Music, International Contest for Women Composers, Mannheim 1974; Miriam Gideon Prize 2003. *Address:* 21 Deodar Road, London SW15 2NP, England. *E-mail:* 100611.2060@compuserve.com. *Website:* www.impulse-music.co.uk/fowler.htm.

**FOWLER, John;** Singer (Tenor); b. 1956, USA. *Career:* Sang in the USA as Edgardo in Lucia di Lammermoor, and in Norma; European engagements from 1983, including Rodolfo at Cologne and Hoffmann at Liège, 1985; Vienna Staatsoper, 1984–85, as Des Grieux, Leicester in Maria Stuarda and Arturo in I Puritani; Hamburg Staatsoper, 1984–85, in Rosenkavalier, Traviata and La Bohème; Welsh National Opera, 1986–87, as Edgardo and as Tonio in La Fille du Régiment; Further appearances in New Orleans, Houston (as Faust), Miami (Hoffmann, 1989), with Edmonton Opera (Duke of Mantua) and Liège (Gounod's Romeo, 1988); Concert showings in works by Respighi, Verdi (Requiem) and Mendelssohn (Elijah); Sang Percy in Anna Bolena at Barcelona and Donizetti's Edgardo at Dublin, 1991; Sang Hoffmann at Cincinnati, 1992; Gounod's Faust at Saint Louis, 1998. *Honours:* Winner, Metropolitan Opera Auditions, 1981. *Address:* c/o Herbert Barrett Management, 1776 Broadway, Suite 1610, New York, NY 10019, USA.

**FOWLES, Glenys;** Singer (Soprano); b. 4 Nov. 1946, Perth, Western Australia. *Education:* Studied with Margarita Mayer in Sydney, Kurt Adler in New York and Jani Strasser in London. *Career:* Debut: Sang Oscar (Ballo in Maschera), Australian Opera in Sydney, 1969; Sang in the USA, 1974–81, notably at the New York City Opera as Poppea, Susanna, Mélisande, 1976, Mimi and Micaela; European engagements have included Ilia in Idomeneo at Glyndebourne (1974), Sophie and Titania for Scottish Opera (Midsummer Night's Dream); Other roles include Gounod's Juliette, Mozart's Zerlina and Pamina, Marzelline, Marguerite (Faust), Nannetta, Anne Trulove, Mimi and Lauretta; Sang Liu in Turandot for Australian Opera, 1991; Marschallin, 1992. *Address:* Australian Opera, Sydney Opera House, Sydney, New South Wales, Australia.

**FOX, Donal Leonellis;** American composer and jazz and classical musician (piano); b. 17 July 1952, Boston, MA. *Education:* New England Conservatory of Music, Berklee Coll. of Music, Berkshire Music Center, Tanglewood; theory and counterpoint with Avram David, composition and harmony with T. J. Anderson, composition and orchestration with Gunther Schuller. *Career:* debut, premiere of Refutation and Hypothesis II for chamber orchestra, Festival of Contemporary Music at Tanglewood 1983; piano and improviser, world premiere of Oliver Lake's Movements Turns and Switches for violin and piano, Library of Congress, Washington 1993; piano and improviser, world premiere, The Demon, Int. Ottawa Jazz Festival, Nat. Gallery of Canada 1995; piano and improviser, world premiere of Anthony Kelley's Africamerica for piano and orchestra 1999; publisher and writer, BMI 1993–; Pres., Leonellis Music 1994–, Harry Fox Agency Inc 1996–; mem. Massachusetts Cultural Council (educational collaborative 1984–). *Television:* Donal Fox and David Murray in Session 1993, The Fox/Troupe Project (PBS) 1993, Say Brother (WGBH) 1993. *Compositions:* Refutation and Hypothesis I: a Treatise for piano solo 1981, Dialectics for two grand pianos 1988, Variants on a Theme by Monk for alto saxophone and piano 1990, Jazz Sets and Tone Rows for alto saxophone and piano 1990, Vamping with T. T. for bass clarinet and piano 1993, T-Cell Countdown for voice, piano and double bass 1993, River Town Packin House Blues, The Old People Speak of Death, Following the North Star Boogaloo for piano and poet 1993, Gone City: Ballet in Three Movements for clarinet, piano and double bass 1994. *Recordings include:* Boston Duets 1992, Videmus 1992, Ugly Beauty 1995, Donal Fox: Mellow Mood 1996, Donal Fox: Gone City 1997. *Honours:* Meet the Composer/Rockefeller Foundation/NEA grant 1991, Guggenheim Fellowship in Music Composition 1997, Bogliasco Fellowship in Music Composition 1998, Djerassi Foundation Fellowship in

Music Composition 1999. *Current Management:* Leonellis Music, 14 Highland Park Avenue, Roxbury, MA 02119, USA.

**FOX, Erika;** Composer; b. 3 Oct. 1936, Vienna, Austria; m. 1961, 1 s., 1 d. *Education:* ARCM, Royal College of Music, London; Also private study with Jeremy Dale Roberts and Harrison Birtwistle. *Career:* Numerous commissions from leading contemporary music groups; Works performed at London's South Bank, Canada, Greece, Turkey, Czechoslovakia, festivals and broadcasts; Rehearsed orchestra at Menuhin School; Teaching includes Centre for Young Musicians, Pimlico; Junior Department, Guildhall School of Music and Drama; Composition workshops in various schools and privately; Sometime ballet pianist for Arts Educational Schools. *Compositions include:* Lamentations for Four, 1973; The Slaughterer, chamber opera, 1975; Paths Where the Mourners Tread, 1980; Litany for Strings, 1981; Movement for String Sextet, 1982; Shir, 1983; Kaleidoscope, 1983; Quasi Una Cadenza, 1983; Nick's Lament, 1984; Osen Shomaat, 1985; Silver Homage, 1986; Rivka's Fiddle, 1986; On Visiting Stravinsky's Grave at San Michele, 1988; Hungarian Rhapsody, 1989; The Bet, puppet music drama, 1990; The Dancer Hotoke, chamber opera, Garden Venture commission, 1992 (Olivier Award Nomination); The Moon of Moses, 1992; Davidsbündler Lieder for flute and piano, 1999; David Singt vor Saul for piano and ensemble, 2000; Piano concerto commissioned by Julian Jacobson, 1993; Tuned Spheres, 1995. *Current Management:* Elinor Kelly, Westbrook Farm Cottage, Boxford, Nr Newbury, Berkshire RG16 8DL, England. *Address:* 78 Peterborough Road, London SW6 3EB, England.

**FOX, Fred(erick Alfred);** Composer; b. 17 Jan. 1931, Detroit, Michigan, USA. *Education:* Studied at Wayne State University, The University of Michigan, Indiana University, Bloomington with Bernhard Heiden. *Career:* Teacher at Franklin College, Indiana and Sam Houston University, Huntsville; Worked in Minneapolis; Assistant, Contemporary Music Project, Washington DC; Teacher, California State University, Hayward, 1964–74 and at Indiana University, 1974–97, Chairman of Composition Department, 1980–97; mem, ASCAP; American Music Center; Composers' Forum. *Compositions include:* A Stone, A Leaf, an Unfound Door for soprano and ensemble, 1966; BEC for chamber ensemble, 1968; The Descent for chorus and percussion, 1969; Violin Concerto, 1971; Matrix for cello, strings and percussion, 1972; Ternion for oboe and orchestra, 1973; Variables No. 5 for orchestra, 1974; Variables Nos 1–4 and 6 for instruments, 1976; Time Excursions for soprano, speaker and instruments, 1976; Beyond Winterlock for orchestra, 1977; Ambient Shadows for 8 instruments, 1978; Night Ceremonies for orchestra, 1979; Sonaspheres Nos 1–5 for chamber ensemble, 1980–83; Nilrem's Odyssey for baritone, speaker and chorus, 1980; Tracings for orchestra, 1981; Bren for 13 brass, 1982; Januaries for orchestra, 1984; Shaking the Pumpkin for saxophone, piano and percussion, 1989; Auras for chamber ensemble, 1989; Nightscenes for strings and percussion, 1989; Devil's Tramping Ground for chamber ensemble, 1991; Echo Blues for orchestra, 1992; Dreamcatcher for 13 players, 1994; Impressions for orchestra, 1995; When the Thunder Speaks for saxophone and piano 1998. *Recordings:* Music of Frederick Fox; Music of Frederick Fox, Volume 2; Shaking The Pumpkin. *Address:* 711 South Clifton Street, Bloomington, IN 47401, USA.

**FOX, Leland Stanford;** Music Professor and Administrator; b. 25 Jan. 1931, Worcester, MA, USA; m. Wanda R. Nelson 1 March 1955; one s. one d. *Education:* BM, 1956, MM, 1957, Baylor Univ.; PhD, Florida State Univ., 1962. *Career:* Hearst Publications, New York, 1948–51; Graduate Asst, 1956–57, Instructor of Music, 1957–60, Baylor Univ.; Graduate Asst, Florida State Univ., 1960–62; Principal Tenor, Asolo Festival, 1962; opera and oratorio performances; Instructor in Music, Pensacola Junior Coll., 1962–63; Assoc. Prof. of Music, Univ. of Oklahoma, 1963–66; Assoc. Prof. to Prof., Dir of Opera Theater, 1966; Editor, The Opera Journal, 1968–88; Assoc. Dean of Graduate School, Univ. of Mississippi, 1986–. *Publications include:* Index of Italian Opera 1900–1970; Opéra Comique: A Vehicle for Classic Style, 1964; From Out of the Ashes: Santa Fe Opera's New Theater, 1968; La Belle Arsène 1773 by Pierre Alexandre Monsigny, 1969; The State of Opera: A Dialogue Between Boris Goldovsky and Carlisle Floyd, 1971; ed. of numerous books. *Contributions:* New Grove Dictionary of Music and Musicians; Opera Quarterly.

**FOX, Malcolm;** Composer; b. 13 Oct. 1946, Windsor, England; m. Pauline Elizabeth Scholz, 5 April 1980, 1 s. *Education:* Royal College of Music, University of Lndon; ARCM 1966; BMus (Hons), 1967; MMusRCM, 1968. *Career:* Music Director, Cockpit Theatre, London, 1972–74; Lecturer in Music, 1974–79, Senior Lecturer, 1980–, University of Adelaide, South Australia; mem, Australasian Performing Right Association; Australia Music Centre; Fellowship of Australian Composers; Association of Professional Composers (UK). *Compositions:* Sid the Serpent, opera, 1976; Six Miniatures, violin and piano, 1977; Violin Concerto, 1980; The Iron Man, opera, 1987; Pathways of Ancient Dreaming, string orchestra, 1990; Ten Thousand Years Goodbye, soprano, piano and clarinet, 1992. *Publications:* Music Education in South Education (1836–1986), chapter in From Colonel Light into the Footlights–The Performing Arts in South Australia from 1936 to the present, 1988. *Contributions:* Siegfried's Death, 1989; The Swan Knight in Wagner's Lohengrin, 1989; Wotan's Spear, 1993. *Address:* 13 Whinham Street, Fitzroy, Adelaide, South Australia 5082, Australia.

**FOX, Sarah;** British singer (soprano); b. 1973, Giggleswick, Yorkshire. *Education:* Studied with Margaret H Clark at London Univ. and with Margaret Kingsley at Royal Coll. of Music (graduated Opera School, 1999). *Career:* Debut: Wigmore Hall recital with Roger Vignoles, 1998; St John's Smith Square recital with Malcolm Martineau, March 1999; Recitals for BBC Radio 3; Concerts and Festival engagements throughout the UK and abroad including BBC Proms, Edinburgh Festival, and tours of Israel and Japan;. *Recordings include:* Boccherini's Stabat Mater with the King's Consort, Vivladi Sacred Music with Kings Coll., Cambridge. *Operatic appearances include:* Woglinde (Wagner's Ring Cycle), Covent Garden; Susanna (Le Nozze de Figaro), Glyndebourne; Zerlina (Don Giovanni), Glyndebourne and Cincinnati Opera. *Honours:* Numerous prizes including Thomas Allen Opera Scholarship, 1997; Royal Coll. of Music Queen Elizabeth Rose Bowl, 1998; Kathleen Ferrier Award 1997; John Christie Award, Glyndebourne 2000. *Current Management:* Askonas Holt Ltd, Lonsdale Chambers, 27 Chancery Lane, London, WC2A 1PF, England. *Telephone:* (20) 7400-1700. *Fax:* (20) 7400-1799. *E-mail:* info@askonasholt.co.uk. *Website:* www.askonasholt.co.uk.

**FOX, Tom;** Singer (Baritone); b. 1950, USA. *Education:* Studied at the College Conservatory of Music in Cincinnati Opera Company. *Career:* Appeared with Texas Opera Theater, 1974, then with Houston Grand Opera; Resident member of Cincinnati Opera, 1976–80; Frankfurt Opera from 1981 as Orestes (Elektra), Amonasro, Don Pizarro, Escamillo, Klingsor, Ford, Figaro and Nick Shadow in The Rake's Progress; Wiesbaden, 1981, as Don Giovanni; Hamburg Staatsoper, 1983, as Arcalems in Amadis de Gaule by J C Bach; Has sung with Canadian Opera as Orestes, Jochanaan and Escamillo; Welsh National Opera, 1985, as Escamillo; Other roles include Iago (Teatro Colón, 1986), Claudius in Hamlet by Thomas (Pittsburgh), Alberich in The Ring for Nice Opera, at the Théâtre des Champs Elysées and in San Francisco; Gessler in Guillaume Tell in Nice; Dutchman, Amonasro, the villains in Hoffmann and Scarpia (Pittsburgh); Giovanni (Francesca di Rimini) in Turin; Barnaba in La Gioconda with Rome Opera; Invited to San Francisco for the US premiere of Henze's Das Verratene Meer; Season 1992/93 with debut in Washington as Iago, the role of Vesco di Blois in Massenet's Esclarmonde in Palermo, Telramund in Montpellier; Debut at the Metropolitan Opera, New York as Alberich, Jochanaan in San Francisco; 1993/94, Prus (Makropulos Case) in San Francisco and Bologna, his debut at the Lyric Opera of Chicago as Scarpia, his debut as Wotan at the Santiago Opera in Chile, Klingsor in a new production of Parsifal at the Munich Staatsoper and Kurwenal in a new production of Tristan at La Monnaie in Brussels; Sang Pizarro in Fidelio at the 1996 Salzburg Festival; Sang Scarpia at Cincinnati, 1998; Season 2000–01 as Kurwenal and Klingsor for San Francisco Opera and Prus in The Makropulos Case at the New York Met. *Address:* Kaye Artists Management Ltd, Barratt House, 7 Chertsey Road, Woking GU21 5 AB, England.

**FRACCARO, Walter;** Singer (Tenor); b. 1968, Italy. *Career:* Many appearances at leading opera houses from 1993; Season 1994–95 as Ismaele in Nabucco at Barcelona, Cavaradossi at Valencia and Lisbon, and Raffaele in Stiffelio at Madrid; Further engagements as Alfredo at Lisbon, Radames at Pittsburgh, Riccardo in Ballo in Maschera at Tenerife and Marseilles; Alfredo and the Verdi Requiem at the International Festival of Peralada in Spain; Season 1996–97 as Faust in Mefistofele at Pittsburgh, Radames at San Francisco, Pinkerton at the Metropolitan Opera and Verdi's Macduff in Hamburg; Don José at San Francisco, 1998. *Honours:* Winner, 1993 Concorso di Vorallo Valesia (Jury Prize from Carlo Bergonzi); Placido Domingo Prize at the 1993 Concorso Internazionale di Canto Francisco Vinas, Barcelona. *Address:* c/o Metropolitan Opera, Lincoln Center, New York, NY 10023, USA.

**FRACKENPOHL, Arthur Roland;** American composer and professor; b. 23 April 1924, Irvington, New Jersey. *Education:* studied with Bernard Rogers, Eastman School of Music, BA 1947, MA 1949; Darius Milhaud, Berkshire Music Center, Tanglewood, summer 1948; Nadia Boulanger, Fontainebleau 1950; D.Mus, McGill University, Montreal 1957. *Career:* Teacher 1949–61, Professor 1961–85, Crane School of Music, State University of New York at Potsdam; mem. ASCAP. *Compositions:* chamber opera: Domestic Relations (To Beat or Not to Beat) 1964; orchestral: A Jubilant Overture 1957, Largo and Allegro for Horn and Strings 1962, Short Overture 1965, Concertino for Tuba and Strings 1967, Suite for Trumpet and Strings 1970, Concerto for Brass Quintet and Strings 1986; band music: Brass Quartet 1950, 5 Brass Quintets 1963, 1972, 1986, 1994, 1997, Trombone Quartet 1967, Brass Trio 1967, String Quartet 1971, Breviates for Brass Ensemble 1973, Suite for Brass Trio and Percussion 1973, Trio for Oboe, Horn and Bassoon 1982, Tuba Sonata 1983; Concerto for bassoon and band 1998; choral works: Te Deum 1962, Gloria 1968, Mass 1990; piano pieces; song cycles; solo songs. *Recordings:* The Art of Brass, with Potsdam Brass Quintet, The Art Collection: Caroline Brass. *Publications:* Harmonization at the Piano 1962, 6th edition 1991. *Address:* c/o 13 Hillcrest Drive, Potsdam, NY 13676, USA (home).

**FRANCESCH, Homero;** Concert Pianist; b. 6 Dec. 1947, Montevideo, Uruguay. *Education:* studied in South America and with Ludwig Hoffmann at the Munich Acad. *Career:* many appearances as concert soloist throughout Europe, notably with the Ravel concertos and in the premiere of Henze's Tristan, London 1974; frequent radio and television appearances. *Current Management:* Concerto Winderstein GmbH, Postfach 44 04 46, 80753 München, Germany. *Telephone:* (89) 38 38 46. *Fax:* (89) 33 79 38. *E-mail:* artists@winderstein.de. *Website:* www.concerto.de.

**FRANCESCHETTO, Romano;** Singer (Bass-baritone); b. 1957, Italy. *Education:* Studied at the Parma Conservatory. *Career:* Has sung widely in Italy from 1981, notably at La Scala in Milan, Rome, Verona, Venice, Turin, Palermo, Bologna, Trieste and Catania; Further engagements in Hamburg, Dresden, St Petersburg, Bordeaux, Tel-Aviv, Rio de Janeiro, Seoul and elsewhere; Has performed all the major buffo roles such as Don Bartolo, Dulcamara, Don Magnifico; Leporello; Geronimo; Don Pasquale; Gianni Schicchi; Also leading roles in many baroque and classical operas. *Recordings include:* Morlacchi's Barbiere di Siviglia (Bongiovanni); Paisiello's Don Chisciotte; Rossini's Adina; Salieri's Falstaff. *Current Management:* Alberto Mirri, Rome. *Address:* Via Fornio 6/C, 43036 Fidenza, Italy.

**FRANCI, Carlos;** Composer, Conductor; b. 18 July 1927, Buenos Aires, Argentina. *Education:* Studied at the Rome Conservatory and with Fernando Previtali at The Academy of St Cecilia. *Career:* Conducted symphonic music at first, then Hänsel und Gretel at Spoleto in 1959; Appearances at many opera houses in Italy and abroad, including the Vienna Staatsoper; led the Company of Rome Opera in Rossini's Otello at the NY Metropolitan, 1968, returning as guest, 1969–72; Other repertoire includes: Spontini's Fernand Cortez and Verdi's Nabucco, Berne, 1990; Conducted the Seven Stars concert at the Baths of Caracalla, 1991; Verdi's I Masnadieri at Piacenza, 1998. *Compositions include:* L'Imperatore, Opera, produced at Bergamo, 1958. *Address:* c/o Teatro dell Opera di Roma, Piazza B Gigli 8, 00184 Rome, Italy.

**FRANCI, Francesca;** singer (mezzo-soprano); b. 1962, Rome, Italy. *Education:* studied with Rodolfo Celletti and Tito Gobbi. *Career:* debut singing Mahler's Lieder eines fahrenden Gesellen at Verona, 1984; appeared as Maddalena in Rigoletto at Genoa and Naples, Rosina at Bari and Suzuki in Bologna, 1988; Festival della Valle d'Itria 1988 in Donizetti's Maria di Rohan, as Armando; Edvige in Guillaume Tell at La Scala, Milan, returning as Fatima in Oberon; sang Ernestina in Rossini's L'Occasione fa il Ladro at Pesaro; further engagements at Rome and Naples (from 1987), Florence, Monteverdi's Otho, 1992, Paris and Wiesbaden; France 1992 as Stephano in Gounod's Roméo et Juliette; season 1996 as Contessa d'Arco in Rossini's Matilde di Shabran at Pesaro and Fenena in Nabucco at the Verona Arena; Season 1998 as La Cieca in La Gioconda at Genoa, Fenena at Rome and Beppe in L'Amico Fritz at Naples; sang Verdi's Preziosilla at Verona Arena and Adalgisa in Norma at Catania, 2000. *Recordings include:* Maria di Rohan. *Current Management:* All'Opera Artists Management, Viale Giuseppe Mazzini 41, 00195 Rome, Italy. *Telephone:* (06) 3215772. *Fax:* (06) 3215252. *E-mail:* info@allopera.net. *Website:* www.allopera.net.

**FRANCIS, Alun;** Conductor; b. 1943, Kidderminster, England. *Education:* Royal Manchester College of Music, 1960–63. *Career:* Played the horn in Hallé and Bournemouth Symphony Orchestras; From 1966 has conducted more than 60 orchestras in over 20 countries; Guest conductor at the Vienna Festival, Hong Kong Arts Festival with the BBC Scottish Symphony, Arhus Festival in Denmark with the Philharmonia Hungarica, Promenade Concerts, London, with the Royal Philharmonic, and Festival Hall, 1983, in Henryk Szeryng Golden Jubilee concert; Chief Conductor and Artistic Director of the Ulster Orchestra, 1966–67, and the Northern Ireland Opera Trust, 1974–84; Director, Northwest Chamber Orchestra in Seattle, 1980–85; Director and Artistic Adviser, Overijssells Philharmonic in Netherlands, 1985–87; Chief Conductor of the NordwestDeutsche Philharmonie and Principal Conductor of Berlin Symphony (from 1989); Repertoire includes Bel Canto opera (1978 revival of Donizetti Gabriella di Vergy, premiere of revised version, at Belfast) and 20th century music ranging from Berio to Stockhausen; Has composed music for the concert hall, films and theatre. *Recordings:* Donizetti's Ugo, Conte di Parigi, with the Philharmonia Orchestra; Offenbach's Christopher Columbus, with the London Mozart Players (Opera Rara); Other albums with the London Symphony, Royal Philharmonic, English Chamber and Northwest Chamber Orchestras. *Address:* c/o London Artists, 10 Guild Street, Stratford-upon-Avon, CV 37 6RE, England.

**FRANCIS, Jeffrey;** Singer (Tenor); b. 1958, Poplar Bluff, Missouri, USA. *Education:* Sang in Seattle. *Career:* Sang at the Berlin Staatsoper from 1990, as Lentolo in Graun's Cleopatra e Cesare, Tamino, Paolino in Il Matrimonio Segreto, Jupiter in Semele (1996) and in Gassmann's L'Opera Seria; Rossini Festival at Pesaro, 1993–95, as Gernando in Armida and Rodolphe in Guillaume Tell; Season 1993–94 as Evander in Alceste at Vienna, Argirio in Rossini's Tancredi in Berlin and Rossini's Almaviva at Santa Fe; Season 1998 with Rossini's Ramiro in Tel-Aviv and Chapelou in Le Postillon de Lonjumeau at the Berlin Staatsoper; Season 2000 in Roméo et Juliette by Berlioz at Salzburg and as Almaviva at the Vienna Staatsoper. *Recordings include:* Armida.

**FRANCIS, Sarah Janet,** ARCM, FRCM, RSA; British oboist; *Professor of Oboe, Royal College of Music;* b. 1939, London, England; m. Michael D. C. Johnson; two d. *Education:* Royal Coll. of Music, London, French government scholarship, Paris, Boise Foundation Scholarship to study with Pierre Pierlot, Paris. *Career:* debut, BBC 1959; principal oboe, BBC Nat. Orchestra of Wales; BBC recitalist; soloist, chamber music and orchestral player; Prof. of Oboe, Royal Coll. of Music, London 1974–; Dir, London Harpsichord Ensemble; dedicatee of many concert and chamber music works; masterclasses in Amsterdam, Cologne, Geneva, Moscow, Copenhagen and Stockholm Conservatoires; mem. British Music Soc., Royal Soc. of Musicians, Inc. Soc. of Musicians; fmr Chair. British Double Reed Soc. *Compositions:* Seven Dedications: Gordon Jacob, Seven Bagatelles 1971, Gordon Crosse, Ariadne for solo oboe and 12 players

1972, Phyllis Tate, The Rainbow and the Cuckoo for oboe quartet 1975, Crosse, Little Epiphany Variations for oboe and cello 1977, Anthony Payne, Concerto 1980, William Mathias, Oboe Concerto 1989, Stephen Dodgson, Oboe Quartet 1994. *Recordings:* Britten Metamorphoses, Quartet, Crosse Ariadne; Boccherini Quintets; Crusell, Reicha Quintets; Howells, Rubbra Sonatas; Rutland Boughton Oboe Concerto, RPO; Mozart and Krommer Concertos, LMP; Britten complete oboe music; Bax, Holst Quintets; Moeran, Jacob Quartets, Chandos; Complete Albinoni, Handel and Telemann Concertos LHE; Vanhal Quartets; Telemann Complete Oboe Sonatas. *Publications:* Going Solo 1995, Oboe Music to Enjoy 1996; contrib. to Joy Boughton: A Portrait, Double Reed News. *Honours:* Royal Coll. of Music Somerville Prize for Wind Instruments 1959. *Address:* 10 Avenue Road, London N6 5DW, England. *Telephone:* (20) 8340-5461 (home). *Fax:* (20) 8347-5907 (home). *Website:* sarahfrancisoboe.co.uk (home).

**FRANCK, Mikko;** Finnish conductor; *General Music Director, Finnish National Opera;* b. 1979, Helsinki. *Education:* Sibelius Acad. and studied in New York, Israel and Sweden. *Career:* children's chorus mem., Finnish Nat. Opera; appeared as the young Sibelius at the Helsinki Swedish Theatre 1992; conductor with several Finnish orchestras, including the Vaasa, Lappeenranta, Pori and the Chamber Orchestra of the Sibelius Acad., Helsinki; season 1997–98 with the Turku Philharmonic, Tapiola Sinfonietta, Tampere Philharmonic and Netherlands Radio Philharmonic; Japanese tour with the Sibelius Acad. Symphony Orchestra; conductor, The Magic Flute at the Finnish Nat. Opera; US debut at the Aspen Festival; season 1999–2000 included return visits to the Stockholm Philharmonic, Finnish Radio Symphony, Swedish Radio Symphony, Bergen Philharmonic and a tour of Japan with the Bamberg Symphony in 2000; Music Dir and Chief Conductor of the Orchestre Nat. de Belgique 2002–; season 2002–03 debuts with Chicago, San Francisco Symphony and Berlin Philharmonic orchestras and tour of Japan with the Orchestre Nat. de Belgique; concerts with the Scottish Chamber, BBC Nat. Orchestra of Wales, Hessischer Rundfunk, Stuttgart Opera and Tokyo Symphony Orchestras; premiere of Rautavaara's Rasputin, Helsinki 2003; 2003–04 season included concerts with Hamburg Staatsoper Orchestra, La Scala Orchestra, Milan, Staatsoper Berlin, Munich Philharmonic, Isreal Philharmonic; Gen. Music Dir, Finnish Nat. Opera 2006–. *Recordings:* Sibelius En Saga and Lemminkainen Legends (with the Swedish Radio Symphony), Tchaikovsky's Sixth Symphony. *Current Management:* Harrison/Parrott Ltd, 12 Penzance Place, London, W11 4PA, England. *Telephone:* (20) 7229 9166. *Fax:* (20) 7221 5042. *Website:* www.harrisonparrott.com.

**FRANDSEN, John;** Composer and Organist; b. 13 March 1956, Aalborg, Denmark; m. Kirsten Grove, 5 Jan 1985, 1 d. *Education:* Aalborghus Statsgymnasium; MA in Music at Århus University; Composition and Organ at Royal Academy of Music, Århus. *Career:* Teacher at Århus University, 1979–83 and The Royal Academy of Music, Århus, 1980–; Organist at Ellevang Church, 1982–84 and Holy Ghost Church, Århus, 1984–; Conductor of Cantilena Choir, 1983–; mem, Chairman of Young Nordic Music, Danish Section, 1983–87; Chairman of Århus Unge Tonekunstnere, 1983–; Danisher Composers' Society. *Compositions:* String Song for String Quartet, 1980; Wo Immer Wir Soielen for Mixed Choir, 1982; Songs of Innocence for Soprano and Guitar, 1984; Amalie Lever, opera, 1984; Avers/Revers for Wind Quintet, 1985; Deux Poèmes Sur Le Temps for Mixed Choir, 1985; Amalie Suite for Chamber Orchestra, 1985; Stabat Mater for Tenor and Organ, 1986; Petite Suite for Guitar, 1986; De/Cadences for Wind Quintet, 1987. *Recordings:* Songs of Innocence with soprano Ellen Lunde and guitarist Erling Moldrup. *Contributions:* Organistbladet; Dansk Mussiktidsskrift. *Address:* Odinsvej 7, 8230 Aabyhoj, Denmark.

**FRANK, Claude;** Pianist; b. 24 Dec. 1925, Nurnberg, Germany; m. Lilian Kallir 1959, one d. (Pamela Frank). *Education:* studied in France and USA with Artur Schnabel, K. U. Schnabel. *Career:* debut, New York Philharmonic 1959; appearances with most major orchestras, including New York Philharmonic, Boston Symphony, Chicago Symphony, Cleveland Orchestra, Philadelphia Orchestra, Berlin Philharmonic, Concertgebouw, London Symphony, Royal Philharmonic; performed with conductors, including Bernstein, Giulini, Leinsdorf, Mehta, Szell; tours of Australia, Africa, Israel, Taiwan; appearances at most major music festivals; New York memorial concert for Artur Schnabel 1981. *Recordings:* 32 Beethoven Piano Sonatas, Mozart Concertos, Beethoven Trios, numerous other works. *Publications:* contrib. to Piano Quarterly, Keynote Magazine. *Honours:* Beethoven Society Award 1979. *Current Management:* Columbia Artists Management LLC, 165 West 57th Street, New York, NY 10019-2276, USA. *Telephone:* (212) 841-9500. *Fax:* (212) 841-9744. *E-mail:* info@cami.com. *Website:* www.cami.com.

**FRANK, Pamela;** Violinist; b. 20 June 1967, New York, USA; d. of Claude Frank and Lillian Kallir. *Education:* studied with Szymon Goldberg and Jaime Laredo; Graduated Curtis Institute, Philadelphia, 1989. *Career:* debut, Carnegie Hall, New York, with the New York String Orchestra, conducted by Alexander Schneider 1985; many appearances with leading orchestras worldwide, including Boston Symphony, Cleveland Orchestra, Tonhalle Orchestra (Zürich) and Orchestre de Paris; Soloist with the Academy of St Martin-in-the-Fields, London, and leader of Academy Chamber Ensemble; engagements with chamber musicians, including Peter Serkin and Yo-Yo Ma and frequent recital tours with her father; contemporary repertoire includes music by Takemitsu, Ellen Taafe Zwilich and Aaron Jay. *Recordings include:* albums with the Academy of St Martin-in-the-Fields. *Current Management:* IMG

Artists, Lovell House, 616 Chiswick High Road, London, W4 5RX, England. *Telephone:* (20) 8233-5800. *Fax:* (20) 8233-5801. *E-mail:* artistseurope@imgworld.com. *Website:* www.imgartists.com.

**FRANK, Susanne;** Violinist; b. 2 Nov. 1962, Switzerland. *Education:* Studied at the Winterthur Conservatory in Paris and the International Menuhin Academy. *Career:* 2nd violin of the Carmina Quartet since 1987; Appearances from 1987 in Europe, Israel, Japan and the USA; Regular concerts at the Wigmore Hall from Oct 1987; Concerts at the South Bank Centre, London, Amsterdam Concertgebouw, the Kleine Philharmonie in Berlin, Konzertverein Vienna; Four engagements in Paris, 1990–91, seven in London; Tours to Australasia, USA, Japan, and concerts at the Hohenems, Graz, Hong Kong, Montreux, Schleswig-Holstein, Bath, Lucerne and Prague Spring Festivals; Collaborations with Dietrich Fischer-Dieskau, Olaf Bär and Mitsuko Uchida. *Recordings:* Albums for several labels (from 1991). *Honours:* Joint winner (with members of Carmina Quartet), Paolo Borciani String Quartet Competition in Reggio Emilia, Italy, 1987; Gramophone prize for best recording of chamber music, 1992. *Address:* c/o Intermusica Artists' Management, 16 Duncan Terrace, London N1 8BZ, England.

**FRANKE-BLOM, Lars-Åke (Harry);** Composer; b. 4 April 1941, Norrköping, Sweden; m. Gunilla Marie-Louise Dalin 1965, 1 s., 2 d. *Education:* Master's degree, Romance Languages, University of Uppsala, 1965; Logopede, Karolinska Institute, Stockholm, 1967; Composition with Nils Eriksson and Daniel Börtz. *Career:* Debut: With orchestral work Motions, 1975; Active in Norrköping, collaborating with the local symphony orchestra on several occasions; The troll battle commissioned and performed by the Folkopera, Stockholm, 1979; The well of the virgins, ballet, commissioned by Swedish Television, 1982; The web of yearning commissioned by Norrköping Symphony Orchestra, 1984, presented on Swedish Television, 1988; HP, opera commissioned by the Royal Theatre, Stockholm, 1990, first performance, 2001; mem, Association of Swedish Composers, 1978. *Compositions:* Motions for orchestra, 1973; Music for mobile for orchestra, 1975–77; Concertos for violoncello, 1977, viola, 1980, contrabasso, 1983; The troll battle, opera for children, 1979; 3 symphonies, 1982, 1993, 1994; Web of yearning, symphonic poem, 1984; Impossible reality, chamber music, 1986; HP, opera in 2 acts, 1990–95; Music for art, chamber music, 1991; The 3rd Symphony Fire on the Earth, commissioned and performed by the Swedish Radio Symphony Orchestra in 1998; Music for the film, Bathers, presented on Swedish television, 1999, A Mansion Tale opera 2004. *Recordings:* Endymion; Music for mobile; Web of yearning, music and television film; Music for art; Several radio recordings. *Honours:* Prizewinner, International New Music Composers' Competition, 1989–90. *Address:* Mastgatan 15, 60385 Norrköping, Sweden.

**FRANKL, Peter;** British concert pianist; b. 2 Oct. 1935, Budapest, Hungary; s. of Tibor and Laura Frankl; m. Annie Feiner 1958; one s. one d. *Education:* High School, Franz Liszt Acad. of Music, Budapest. *Career:* began career in late 1950s, London debut 1962, New York debut with Cleveland Orchestra under George Szell 1967; has performed with world's major orchestras, including Berlin Philharmonic, Amsterdam Concertgebouw, Israel Philharmonic, Leipzig Gewandhaus and all the London and major American orchestras, under conductors, including Abbado, Boulez, Colin Davis, Antal Dorati, Haitink, Herbig, Leinsdorf, Maazel, Masur, Muti, Rozhdestvensky, Salonen, Sanderling and Georg Solti; Visiting Prof. of Piano Yale Univ., USA 1987. *Recordings include:* complete works for piano by Schumann and Debussy, a solo Bartók and Chopin album, a Hungarian Anthology, Mozart concertos with mems of the English Chamber Orchestra, Brahms piano concertos nos 1 and 2, the complete four-hand works by Mozart with Tamás Vásáry, the three Brahms violin sonatas with Kyung Wha Chung, Brahms, Schumann, Dvořák and Martinů recordings, quintets with the Lindsay Quartet. *Honours:* won first prize in several int. competitions; Officer's Cross Order of Merit (Hungary) 1972. *Address:* 5 Gresham Gardens, London, NW11 8NX, England. *Telephone:* (20) 8455-5228. *Fax:* (20) 8455-2176. *Website:* www.peterfrankl.co.uk (home).

**FRANKLIN, James (Jim),** PhD; Australian lecturer in music technology, composer and musician (shakuhachi performer); b. 14 Feb. 1959, Sydney, NSW. *Education:* Univ. of Sydney; Shihan (master performer), Int. Shakuhachi Research Centre, Japan, 1996; studies with Peter Sculthorpe 1978–81, Milko Kelemen 1982–85, Ton de Leeuw 1985–86, Riley Lee 1988–98, Katsuya Yokoyama 1996. *Career:* Univ. of Sydney 1987–93; Lecturer in Music Tech., Univ. of Western Sydney 1994–2003; Founder-mem. OHM, Electronic Music Group; freelance composer, shakuhachi performer and music educator 2003–. *Compositions include:* Corno Inglese for choir 1979, Talisman for piano 1980, Three Glimpses of Aquilon for piano 1980, Across the Swan's Riding for piano and orchestra 1981, The Unliving Seed (chamber opera) 1983, Boundaries for the Child of Flame for string quartet 1984, Fragments of a Broken Land for orchestra 1984, Triptych for 8 voices and ensemble 1984, Dream Within a Dream for tape 1988, Raising Dust for synthesizer 1988, The Hours of the Sea-Bird for voices, keyboard, synthesizer, sampler and sequencer 1988, Fountain of Light for Shakuhachi and electronics (with Riley Lee) 1991, Middle Dance for voices and ensemble 1992, Naratic Visions (dance theatre) 1993, Heart for shakuhachi, voice and live electronics 1994, Three Treasures: Columns and Webs for koto quartet, percussion, shakuhachi and electronics 1996, Peace Bell for 3 shakuhachi and collaged pre-recorded bells 1996, Songs for the Not-Born #1 for shakuhachi and live electronics 1996, Water Spirits for koto, shakuhachi and electronics (with Satsuki Odamura) 1994–96, Thoughts of

Distant Clouds for koto and shakuhachi 1998, Butsuga for shakuhachi 1999, Moon Road to Dawn (with Antony Wheeler) 1999, Abundance (with Michael Atherton) 2001, Flötenspiel for shakuhachi 2002, Songs for the Not-Born #2 for shakuhachi, theremin and live electronics 2002, #3 2003, A Lattice of Winds for shakuhachi and koto 2003, Aurora for shakuhachi, koto, ruined piano, guitars, marimba and double bass (with Michael Atherton) 2003, Zen-Geschicthen for shakuhachi and narrator 2004. *Publications:* The Ongaku Masters – An Anthology of Japanese Classical Music (ed. five CDs and booklets) 2004. *Honours:* Best Original Soundtrack, Munich Int. Multi-Media Festival 1990. *Address:* Ottensooser Weg 1, 91207 Lauf, Germany. *E-mail:* dr_jim_franklin@t-online.de.

**FRANKLIN, Peter (Robert);** University Teacher; b. 19 Dec. 1947, London, England. *Education:* BA, DPhil, University of York, 1966–72. *Career:* Teacher of Music and German, Harlaxton College, Lincolnshire, 1974–79, and at William Jewell College, Liberty, Missouri, USA, 1979; Lecturer, Department of Music, University of Leeds, 1980–1995. *Publications:* Natalie Bauer-Lechner–Recollections of Gustav Mahler (editor, annotator), 1980; The Idea of Music, Schoenberg and Others, 1985. *Contributions:* Many journals including The Music Review, Music and Letters, Opera (1992), The Musical Quarterly and The Musical Times, on Mahler and Schreker; Programme Notes (e.g. Pfitzner's Palestrina at Covent Garden, 1997); Article on Mahler in New Grove Dictionary, 2001. *Address:* c/o St Catherine's College, Oxford, OX1 3UJ.

**FRANOVA, Tatiana;** Pianist; b. 3 Aug. 1945, Czechoslovakia; m. Eduard Ihring, 20 Aug 1966, 1 d. *Education:* Bratislava Conservatoire, 1959–64; Academy of Music and Dramatic Arts, Bratislava, 1964–69; Music Academy, Vienna, 1969–73; Postgraduate studies in Bratislava, 1980–83. *Career:* Concert tours in Austria, Brazil, Cuba, Egypt, France, Germany, Hungary, India, Italy, Luxembourg, Poland, Romania, Spain, Gran Canaria, Switzerland, Sweden, USSR; Professor, Academy of Arts, Cairo, Egypt, 1983–87; Professor of Piano, Academy of Music Arts, Bratislava, 1987–; mem, Slovak Music Union. *Recordings:* Brahms: Sonata in F sharp minor Op 2, 1975; Rachmaninov: Sonata in B minor Op 36, 1975; Etudes–Chopin, Liszt, Scriabin, Rachmaninov, 1978; Rachmaninov: Concerto No. 1 in F sharp minor, 1982; De Falla: Nights in the Gardens of Spain, 1982; Complete works of Glazunov, 1991. *Honours:* 1st Prize in Radio Competition, Young People's Studio, 1964; Silver Medal at International Festival, Bordeaux, 1974; F Kafenda Prize, 1980. *Current Management:* Slovkoncert. *Address:* Gorkeho 7, 81101 Bratislava, Slovakia.

**FRANTZ, Justus;** German pianist; b. 18 May 1944, Hohensalza. *Education:* under Prof. Eliza Hansen in Hamburg and Wilhelm Kempf in Positano. *Career:* prizewinner, Int. Music Competition, Munich 1967; since 1969 has appeared at all major European concert venues and toured USA, Far East and Japan; has made many tours and recordings in piano duo with Christoph Eschenbach and received Edison Int. Award for their recording of Schubert marches 1983; Co-Founder and Dir Schleswig-Holstein Music Festival; Prof. Hamburg Musikhochschule 1985–; Founder Schleswig-Holstein Music Festival 1986, Dir 1986–94; performed complete cycle of Mozart concertos in several European cities 1987–88. *Recordings include:* works by Scarlatti, Beethoven, Mozart and concertos for two, three and four pianos by J. S. Bach.

**FRANZÉN, Olov (Alfred);** Swedish composer, cellist and recitalist; b. 22 Jan. 1946, Umeå, Sweden; m. Ingeborg Axner, 12 Nov 1977. *Education:* Stockholm Music Acad., 1966–73; Music Teacher Examination, 1970; Cello with Gunnar Norrby, 1966–72; Composition with Ingvar Lidholm, 1969–73. *Career:* Debut: As composer, A Wind Quintet in Lund, 1963; As Cellist, Nyströ m, 1971; Cellist in Norrköping Symphony Orchestra, 1971–72; Harpans Kraft, Stockholm, 1971–77; Swedish television Film, Sundcreme with Harpans Kraft, 1976; Freelance in Härnösand and Founder, HND Ensemble, 1977–92; Cellist, Sundsvall Chamber Orchestra, 1983–90; Teacher of Composition, Kapellsberg Music School, Härnösand, 1983–92; In 1986 started Faimo Edition for publishing music scores and recordings; Freelance in Skokloster, 1992–; hundreds of solo recitals throughout Sweden, 1993–; Has played with Harpans Kraft and HND in Sweden, Finland, Austria on radio; Composition played in all Nordic countries and abroad; Cellist, Duo Franzén, 1978–; Skokloster Chamber Soloists, 1994–97; Trio Concordia, 1999–. *Compositions include:* Cytoplasma for song and piano, 1968; Fiesta for percussion ensemble, 1982; Har for soprano and harp, 1983; The Vacuum State for symphony orchestra, 1983; From The Junction Point for bassoon and live electronics, 1985; Suite for 3 flutes, 1986; Agnim for symphony orchestra, 1987; It's Getting Sunny for brass band, 1988; Gaps for violin and piano, 1990; Apmel for flute, clarinet, percussion, piano and string quartet, 1992; The Unseen Present for cello and reciter, 1993; Opus NN for mezzo soprano, guitar and cello, 1994; Clouds on Blue Sky for symphony orchestra, 1995; Organic music No. 2 for cello solo, 1995; String Quartet, 1996; Lamentode, for soprano, bass clarinet and piano, 1997; Autumn Duo for 2 violins, 1997; Four Realities for reciter and symphony orchestra, 1998; La terza via for cello solo, 2000; In Fondo for mezzosoprano, flute and cello, 2001; Organic Music No. 4 for string sextet, 2002; Strigi Aluconi Gratias for saxophone quartet, 2003; Suite Grande for cello solo 2004. *Recordings:* Beyond, with 6 Pieces for winds and piano, 1991; Gaps, 1997; Four Realities, 2000; La Terza Via, four pieces for solo cello, 2002. *Address:* Abbotvägen 18, 74695 Skokloster, Sweden. *Telephone:* (18) 386268 (office). *Fax:* (18) 386268 (office). *E-mail:* of@kreativamusikskolan.nu (office). *Website:* www.oloffranzen.org (office).

**FRASER, Malcolm (Henry);** Opera Director; b. 1 Aug. 1939, Kingston-upon-Thames, England; m. 25 April 1964, 4 s. *Career:* Assoc. Dir, Lincoln Repertory, 1966–68; Resident Dir, Welsh National Opera Company, 1968–76; Senior Lecturer, Royal Northern College of Music, 1976–87; Founder, Artistic Dir, Buxton Int. Festival, 1979–87; J Ralph Corbett Distinguished Prof. of Opera, Univ. of Cincinnati, 1986–2003; Guest Dir, London Opera Centre, New Sadler's Wells Opera, Portland Opera, Seattle Opera, Calgary Opera, Edmonton Opera, Virginia Opera, Arkansas Opera, until 1990; Permanent Guest Dir, Arkansas Opera, 1988–; Associate Artistic Dir, Buxton International Festival, 1988–; Florentine Opera of Milwaukee; Artistic Dir, Opera Theatre of Lucca, 1996–; Directed World Premiere of Hermann's Wuthering Heights for Portland Opera, as well as Falstaff with Sir Geraint Evans and Don Giovanni with James Morris for the same company. *Honours:* Churchill Fellow, 1969; Prize for Mise-en-Scène, Prague International Television Festival, 1975; Kodály Medal, Hungarian Government, 1982; 14 times winner, National Opera Association Prize for best college production in USA; Manchester Evening News Award and Sunday Times (London); Prof. Professor Emeritus of the University of Cincinnati. *Address:* Madeira House, Tideswell, Derbyshire SK17 8NU.

**FREDMAN, Myer,** LRAM; British conductor and author; b. 29 Jan. 1932, Plymouth, Devon, England; m. Jeanne Winfield, 26 Aug 1954, 2 s. *Education:* Dartington Hall; The Opera School, London. *Career:* debut: Cork; Glyndebourne Festival with operas by Mozart, Verdi, Maw and Von Einem; Glyndebourne Touring Opera 1968–74; State Opera of South Australia; Seymour Group; Guest Conductor throughout Europe, America and Australia; BBC television; Wexford, Perth and Adelaide Festivals also at Hong Kong Fest; Conductor in Poland, Belgium, Romania and Germany; Conducted Cavalli's L'Ormindo at Brussels in 1972, Bizet's Carmen in Hamburg 1973 and Il Barbiere di Siviglia in Sydney 1974; season 1992 with La Bohème for the Canadian Opera Company, Toronto and Le nozze di Figaro in Sydney; Head of Opera at the New South Wales Conservatorium 1981–92 including the premiere of Lawrence Hargrave by Nigel Butterfly in 1988; Associate Artist of The Australian Opera 1991–99; concert debut South America 1992 at Montevideo and Buenos Aires; conducted Australian premieres of Midsummer Marriage, Death in Venice and One Man Show; Dialogues des Carmélites 1997. *Recordings:* Bax Symphonies 1 and 2, London Philharmonic Orchestra, No. 3 with Sydney Symphony; H Brian Symphonies 16 and 22 with London Philharmonic Orchestra; Delius Paradise Garden with London Philharmonic Orchestra; Benjamin Overture to an Italian Comedy; Respighi Sinfonia Drammatica, Piano Concerto with Sydney Symphony; Puccini Le Villi with Adelaide Symphony; Britten and Delius recordings. *Publications:* The Conductor's Domain 1999, From Idomeneo to Die Zauberflöte 2002 The Drama of Opera 2003. *Honours:* Bronze Medal by Italian Government 1965. *Address:* 18A Nietta Road, Lindisfarne, Tasmania 7015 (home). *Telephone:* (3) 6243-1368. *E-mail:* mfredman@netspace.net.au. *Website:* www.netspace.net .au/~mfredman.

**FREDRIKSSON, Karl-Magnus;** Singer (Baritone); b. 6 Feb. 1968, Stockholm, Sweden. *Education:* Music High School; Opera High School, 1989–91; Masterclass with D Fischer-Diskau, 1991. *Career:* Debut: Stockholm Royal Opera, 1996; Recital at Wigmore Hall, 1994, 1995; Recitals at Helsinki Opera Stage, 1996; and in Stockholm Opera Stage, 1997; Die Lustige Weiber von Windsor, Stockholm Opera, 1997; Radio Opera in Swedish Radio, 1997; Several tours with Eric Ericson in Europe; Figaro in Il Barbiere di Siviglia, Royal Opera Stockholm, 1998; mem, The Swedish Theatre Order. *Recordings:* Kullervo (Sibelius) with Colin Davis; Die Lustige Witwe (Lehar) with John Eliot Gardiner; Nordic Romances (solo recording); Summer Night, 1999. *Honours:* Major soloist prize from the Swedish Royal Music Academy, 1993; Miriam Helin Competition in Helsinki. *Current Management:* Scandinavian Artists Management AB. *Address:* Vastmannag 76, 113 26 Stockholm, Sweden.

**FREEDMAN, Gertrud;** Singer (Soprano); b. 1933, Germany. *Education:* Studied at the Augsburg Conservatory. *Career:* Sang at Passau and Mainz, 1957–60, Munich Staatsoper, 1960–80; Guest appearances at Lisbon and Barcelona as Sophie and Blondchen, Komische Oper Berlin as Rosina in Paisiello's Barbiere di Siviglia; Other roles include Mozart's Papagena and Despina, Anna in Intermezzo, Zdenka, Oscar, Musetta, and Adele in Die Fledermaus. *Address:* c/o Bayerische Staatsoper, Max-Joseph-Platz, D-80539 Munich 1, Germany.

**FREEMAN, David;** Stage Director; b. 1 May 1952, Sydney, New South Wales, Australia; m. Marie Angel. *Career:* f. Opera Factory, Sydney 1973, in Zürich 1976, with 20 Swiss productions; productions for Opera Factory, London 1981–98 included The Knot Garden, Punch and Judy, The Beggar's Opera, Cavalli's La Calisto, Birtwistle's Yan Tan Tethera (world premiere 1986); Eight Songs for a Mad King by Peter Maxwell Davies, Ligeti's Adventures/Nouvelles Aventures and Reimann's The Ghost Sonata; Mozart's 3 Da Ponte operas presented at the Queen Elizabeth Hall as part of the bicentenary celebrations; has also produced Osborne's Hells Angels; f. Opera Factory Films 1991; directed Prokofiev's The Fiery Angel for Marinsky Theatre, St Petersburg, Covent Garden and Metropolitan, New York; operas by Birtwistle, Maxwell Davies, Ligeti and Mozart have been shown on BBC and Channel 4 television; for English Nat. Opera has produced Orfeo, Akhnaten by Glass (British premiere), The Mask of Orpheus (world premiere) and The Return of Ulysses; productions elsewhere have included La Bohème for Opera North, Manon Lescaut at the Opéra-Comique, Paris, and work in

Germany, Houston and New York; The Magic Flute, for Opera Factory, 1996; Butterfly and Tosca, Raymond Gubbay (1998–2001); Nabucco for Opera Australia 2005. *Honours:* Chevalier, l'Ordre des Arts et Lettres, 1985. *Current Management:* Allied Artists. *Address:* c/o English National Opera, St Martin's Lane, London WC2N 4ES, England.

**FREEMAN-ATTWOOD, Jonathan,** BMus, MPhil; British educator, musician (trumpet), producer and writer; *Vice-Principal, Royal Academy of Music;* b. 4 Nov. 1961, Woking, England; m. Henrietta Parham; one s. one d. *Education:* Univ. of Toronto, Christ Church, Oxford. *Career:* Dean of Undergraduate Studies, RAM 1991–95, Vice-Principal and Dir of Studies 1995–; Prof., Univ. of London 2001–. *Recordings:* 70 recordings as producer for independent labels (ASV, BIS, Channel Classics, Naxos, Avie, Simax, GNN, Chandos); recordings as trumpet soloist: Albinoni Sonatas and Concertos with Ian Simcock, Bach Connections with Colm Carey, Rheinberger with John Wallace and Colm Carey. *Publications:* contrib. to New Grove (2nd edn), Music and Letters, Musical Times, Early Music, Gramophone. *Honours:* Hon. RAM; Diapason d'or and Gramophone Awards as producer 1997, 2001, 2003. *Address:* Royal Academy of Music, Marylebone Road, London, NW1 5HT, England (office). *Telephone:* (20) 7873-7351 (office). *Fax:* (20) 7873-7451 (office). *E-mail:* K.McKiernan@ram.ac.uk (office).

**FREIBERG, Christine;** Singer (soprano); b. 1966, England; m., two c. *Education:* Royal College of Music, with Marion Studholme and in Paris with Bruce Brewer. *Career:* Clori in Cavalli's L'Egisto for St James's Opera; First Niece in Peter Grimes in Nantes and Cologne; Cherubino for Reisopera in Netherlands; Appearances with Opéra de Nantes in Ariadne auf Naxos; Kullervo by Sallinen; Götterdämmerung and Parsifal; Season 1998–99: Flower Maiden in Parsifal for Reiseopera, Netherlands; Italian Singer in Capriccio for Opera Nantes; Nele in Till Eulenspiegel for Nantes, 1999; Fyodor in Boris Godunov for Opera Ireland, 1999; Il re pastore: Aminta, for Musiek theater, Transparant, Belgium, 2002 and 2003 Tour; Many concert appearances. *Address:* Music International, 13 Ardilaun Road, London N5 2QR, England. *Telephone:* 01727 766432. *E-mail:* pc.raymond@virgin.net.

**FREIER, Jurgen;** Singer (Baritone); b. 3 Feb. 1943, Danzig, Germany. *Career:* Debut: Dresden Staatsoper, 1973, as Silvio in Pagliacci; Dresden until 1980, as Papageno, Rossini's Figaro and Belcore; Guest appearances throughout eastern Europe; Berlin Staatsoper from 1980, notably as Lysiart in Weber's Euryanthe, in the title role of Graf Mirabeau by Matthus (premiere, 1989) and Eugene Onegin; Düsseldorf, 1991, in Schreker's Die Gezeichneten; Hamburg, 1995, in the premiere of Schnittke's Historia von Dr Johann Fausten, Munich, 1996, in the premiere of Bose's Schlachthof 5; Komische Oper Berlin as Pizarro and Cologne Opera as Kurwenal, 1998; Season 1999–2000 as Wagner's Donner and Gunther at Hamburg, Kurwenal for Cologne Opera, and Alberich at Chemnitz. *Address:* Berlin Komische Oper, Behrenstrasse 55-57, 10177 Berlin, Germany.

**FREIRE, Nelson;** Brazilian pianist; b. 18 Oct. 1944, Boa Esperança. *Education:* studied with Nise Obino and Lúcia Branco in Brazil, with Bruno Seidlhofer in Vienna. *Career:* debut at Vienna Acad. of Music, performing Brahms' Sonata in F sharp minor 1959; duo partner Martha Argerich 1959–; has appeared with orchestras, including the Berlin Philharmonic, Munich Philharmonic, Royal Concertgebouw, Rotterdam Philharmonic, Vienna Symphony, London Symphony, Royal Philharmonic, Orchestre de Paris; signed exclusive recording contract with Decca 2001. *Recordings include:* Chopin 24 Preludes; Piano duos with Martha Argerich. *Honours:* prizewinner Int. Piano Competition of Rio de Janeiro 1957, First Prize Vianna da Motta competition, Lisbon 1972, Dinu Lipatti medal, London, Edison Prize for Chopin recording. *Address:* c/o Decca Classics, Universal Music (UK) Ltd, Elsinore House, 77 Fulham Palace Road, London, W6 8JA, England.

**FREITAG, Erik;** Composer and Violin Teacher; b. 1 Feb. 1940, Vienna, Austria. *Education:* Studied at the Vienna Hochschule für Musik and with Karl-Birger Blomdahl, Stockholm. *Career:* Violinist Swedish Radio, 1964–66; Philharmonic Orchestra, Stockholm, 1967–1970; Section Leader, Conservatory of Vienna; Composer-in-Residence at the University of North Western Michigan in association with the International Festival Earth/Arts Traverse, Michigan, 1996; mem, Austrian Society of Composers; ISCM Austrian Section; Ensemble Wiener Collage (adminstration). *Compositions:* Quintet for clarinet, horn, violin, cello and piano; Circuits magiques for string quartet; Limericks– 5 songs for medium voice and 6 instruments; Immagini for violin solo, flute, oboe, violin, viola, cello, double bass and piano. *Recordings:* Helle Nacht for strings, 1990; Sonata for cello and piano, 1990; Triaphonie I for horn, violin and piano, 1995; Soul-Sky for violin solo, 1995; El retablo de la catedral de Tarragona for chamber ensemble, 1992; Radio: Yoziguanatzi for Orchestra, 1994; Triaphonie II for saxophone, violin and piano; Passages in the Wind, Poems by John Gracen Brown for baritone and 7 instruments; Reflections in Air for string trio; 3 pieces for string quartet; Strindburg-ljus och skugga for chamber orchestra; Idun for violin and piano; Sonata Nachtstücke for violin and viola. *Honours:* Competition Prize Nordelbische Tage, Hamburg, 1975; Prize, Austrian Ministry of Education. 1975; Prize, City of Vienna, 1979; Theodor Körner Prize, 1981. *Address:* Schippergasse 20, 1210 Vienna, Austria.

**FRÉMAUX, Louis Joseph Félix;** French orchestral conductor; b. 13 Aug. 1921, Aire-sur-la-Lys; m. 1st Nicole Petitbon 11948; four s. one d.; 2nd Cecily Hake 1999. *Education:* Conservatoire Nat. Supérieur de Musique, Paris. *Career:* Musical Dir and Perm. Conductor of Orchestre Nat. de l'Opéra de

Monte-Carlo, Monaco 1955–66; Prin. Conductor, Rhône-Alpes Philharmonic Orchestra, Lyons 1968–71; Prin. Conductor and Musical Dir, City of Birmingham Symphony Orchestra 1969–78; Chief Conductor, Sydney Symphony Orchestra 1979–81, Prin. Guest Conductor 1982–85; guest appearances in Austria, Belgium, Holland, France, Italy, New Zealand, Norway, Switzerland, South America and Germany. *Honours:* Hon. DMus (Birmingham Univ.) 1978; Hon. mem. RAM 1978; 8 Grand Prix du Disque Awards; Koussevitsky Award; Chevalier Légion d'honneur; Croix de Guerre (twice). *Address:* 25 Edencroft, Wheeley's Road, Birmingham, B15 2LW, England (home).

**FRENI, Mirella;** Italian singer; b. (Mirella Fregni), 27 Feb. 1935, Modena; d. of Ennio Fregni and Gianna (née Arcelli) Fregni; m. 1st Leone Magiera 1955; one d.; m. 2nd Nicolai Ghiaurov (died 2004). *Career:* debut 1955 as Micaëla in Carmen, debut at La Scala, Milan 1962, Glyndebourne Festival 1961, Royal Opera House, Covent Garden 1961, Metropolitan Opera, NY 1965; has sung at Vienna State Opera, Rome Opera, Barcelona Gran Teatro del Liceo, Boston Opera, La Scala and at Salzburg Festival and leading opera houses throughout the world. *Recordings include:* Carmen, Falstaff, La Bohème, Madame Butterfly, Tosca, Verdi Requiem, Aïda, Don Giovanni. *Major roles include:* Nanetta in Falstaff, Mimi in La Bohème, Zerlina in Don Giovanni, Susanna, Adina in L'Elisir d'amore, Violetta in La Traviata, Desdemona in Otello. *Current Management:* Cæcilia Lyric Department, Rennweg 15, 8001 Zurich, Switzerland. *Telephone:* (1) 221 33 88. *Fax:* (1) 211 71 82. *E-mail:* caecilia@caecilia-lyric.ch. *Website:* www.caecilia.ch.

**FRENI, Rose;** Singer (Mezzo-soprano); b. 1941, USA. *Career:* Sang at Wuppertal, Düsseldorf and Karlsruhe, 1965–75; Schwetzingen, 1969, in the premiere of Klebe's Das Märchen; New York City Opera from 1977, debut as Santuzza; Boston Opera from 1982, in the US premiere of Zimmermann's Die Soldaten, and Adalgisa in Norma; Giessen Opera, 1993, as Ariadne; Other roles have included Maddalena in Rigoletto, Jocasta in Oedipus Rex and the Witch in Dido and Aeneas. *Address:* c/o New York City Opera, Lincoln Center, New York, NY 10023, USA.

**FRENKLOVA, Jana;** Pianist; b. 17 Sept. 1947, Prague, Czechoslovakia; 1 d. *Education:* Prague Conservatoire, 1962–67, Honours Graduate; Leningrad Conservatoire, 1967–68 (studies curtailed after Russian invasion of Czechoslovakia). *Career:* Debut: Prague, 1956; Pianist in Residence, Lancaster University, 1975–79; Pianist in Residence, University College of North Wales, 1979–; Recording Artist for BBC Radio 3, 1977–. *Honours:* Numerous first prizes in Czechoslovakia up to 1968; Finalist, Alfredo Casella Competition, Naples, 1970; Winner, Dudley Competition, 1971. *Current Management:* Encore Concerts. *Address:* Maen Hir Bach, Dwyran, Anglesey, Gwynedd LL61 6UU, North Wales.

**FRETWELL, Elizabeth,** OBE; Australian singer (soprano) and vocal coach; b. 13 Aug. 1920, Melbourne; m. Robert Simmons; one s. one d. *Education:* Privately. *Career:* joined Nat. Theatre, Melbourne 1950; joined Sadler's Wells, London 1956; mem. Elizabethan Opera Co., Australia 1963; toured W. Germany 1963, Canada, UK, USA 1964, Europe 1965; Guest Soprano Durban and Cape Town Opera Cos, S. Africa 1970; mem. Australian Opera 1970–87; appeared opening season Sydney Opera House 1973; professional adjudicator; mem. music bd Opera Foundation, Australia 1982–. *Operas include:* La Traviata, Fidelio, Ariadne auf Naxos, The Flying Dutchman, The Girl of the Golden West, Il Trovatore, Aida, Peter Grimes, Forza del Destino, Falstaff, Masked Ball, Il Tabarro. *Address:* 47 Kananook Ave, Bayview, NSW 2104, Australia.

**FREUD, Anthony,** LLB; British opera administrator and barrister; *General Director, Houston Grand Opera;* b. 30 Oct. 1957, London; s. of the late Joseph Freud and Katalin Freud (née Löwi). *Education:* King's Coll. School, Wimbledon and King's Coll., London. *Career:* trained as barrister before joining Sadler's Wells Theatre Co. 1980–84; Co. Sec., Welsh Nat. Opera 1984, Head of Planning 1989–92, Gen. Dir 1994–2005; Exec. Producer, Opera, Philips Classics 1992–94; Chair. of the Jury BBC Cardiff Singer of the World Competition 1995–; Chair. Opera Europe 2001–05; Trustee Nat. Endowment for Science, Technology and the Arts 2004–; Gen. Dir Houston Grand Opera 2006–. *Honours:* Hon. Fellow Cardiff Univ. 2002. *Address:* Houston Grand Opera, 510 Preston Street, Houston, TX 77002, USA. *Website:* www .houstongrandopera.org.

**FREUDENTHAL, Otto;** Composer, Pianist and Violist; b. 29 July 1934, Gothenburg, Sweden; 1 s. *Education:* TCL, England; Studied piano with Ilona Kabos. *Career:* Debut: (as pianist) Wigmore Hall, London; Recitals and Concerts in England, Germany, Switzerland, Netherlands, Scandinavia, Japan, China, USA; Broadcasts; Teacher, Royal College of Music, Manchester; Assistant to Dr Otto Klemperer to 1973; mem, Swedish Society of Composers, STIM. *Compositions:* Chamber music, viola concerto, concert piece for trombone and orchestra; In Highgate Cemetery for strings; Chamber opera; A BankoMat cantata; The Song About Our Town; A cantata to Linkopings 700 year jubilee; Symphony, 1989; String Quartet, 1991; Saxophone Quartet, 1992. *Recordings:* Coliseum records, BBC, Swedish Radio; Wir Wandelten, with Cheryl Jonsson, soprano. *Publications:* (essay) Music and Equity (with Irene Lotz); Chamber Music with Wollenweber Edition, Munich, Plucked String Music. *Honours:* Harriet Cohen Memorial Medal for interpretation of Beethoven; Swedish State Cultural Stipend, 1977, 1987. *Address:* Bäckfall, 590 41 Rimforsa, Sweden (office); 6 Hillsborough, Corris Uchaf, Powys, SY20

9RG, Wales (home). *Telephone:* (1654) 761405. *E-mail:* otto@cooptel.net (home).

**FREY, Alexander (James);** Organist, Pianist, Music Director and Conductor; b. 5 Oct. 1961, Chicago, Illinois, USA. *Education:* BMus (honours), organ, piano, conducting, 1984, MMus (honours), organ, conducting, 1986, University of Michigan, Ann Arbor; Teachers include Gavin Williamson (piano), Robert Glasgow (organ), Gustav Meier (conducting); Dietrich Fischer-Dieskau (opera and lieder accompanying), Berlin. *Career:* Appeared as Pianist and Organist with Berlin Philharmonic Orchestra, Hollywood Bowl Orchestra, Deutsches Sinfonie Orchester, Rundfunk-Sinfonie Orchester Berlin, Brandenburg Chamber Orchestra (also Guest Conductor, 1993–94), Ars Longa Chamber Orchestra of Germany (also Principal Guest Conductor, 1991–94), Ensemble Europa (also Conductor, 1995), members of Chicago Symphony Orchestra, (under Mauceri, Abbado and others); Annual world-wide recital tours; Music Director, Hamburg Kammerspiele Theater, 1992–93, Berliner Ensemble, 1992–95, collaborating with Peter Zadek; Music Director, Antony and Cleopatra at Edinburgh Festival, Vienna Festwochen, Holland Festival, Berlin, 1994, Das Wunder von Mailand, Venice Festival, 5th European Festival, Berlin, 1995, Ich bin das Volk, Heidelberg Festival, Berlin, 1995; Conducted Ensemble Europa, Israel, Berlin, to commemorate end of WW II, 1995; Chamber music with Ruggiero Ricci, Vermeer Quartet and Donald McInnes; Featured pianist or organist in 3 films; Television and radio, USA, Canada, Europe including Germany. Principal Conductor, Philharmonia Orchestra of Berlin, 1995–; Principal Conductor, Artist-in-Residence and Artistic Adviser, Festival Ruidoso, 1995–. *Current Management:* Artist Recitals, 3427 Fernwood Avenue, Los Angeles, CA 90030, USA.

**FREY-RABINE, Lia;** Dramatic Soprano; b. 12 Aug. 1950, Crosby, Minnesota, USA; m. Eugene Rabine, 27 June 1976, 1 s. *Education:* BMus, MMus, Indiana University, Bloomington; Private vocal studies with Eugene Rabine (Founder and Director of the Rabine Institute for Functional Voice Pedagogy, Bonstadt, Germany). *Career:* Debut: Municipal Theatre, Bern, Switzerland, 1973; Principal Singer, Bern, 1973–75, Flensburg, Germany, 1975–77, Nürnberg, 1977–79, Hagen, 1979–84, Frankfurt, 1984–; Guest appearances in numerous other German, Austrian and Swiss theatres and in Barcelona, Ghent, Rome, Naples, Vienna State Opera and other European cities; Sang the Siegfried Brünnhilde at Dortmund, 1991; and Elektra there, 1996. *Honours:* Metropolitan Opera Auditions National Finalist, 1971; Outstanding Musician of 1983, State of Nordrhein-Westfalen. *Current Management:* Kühnly Agency, Stuttgart, Germany. *Address:* Kleinstrasse 6, 61194 Niddatal-2, Germany.

**FREYER, Achim;** Stage Director and Theatre Designer; b. 30 March 1934, Berlin, Germany. *Education:* Studied at the Akademie der Kunste, East Berlin. *Career:* Debut: Designed sets and costumes for the Ruth Berghaus production of Il Barbiere di Siviglia at the Berlin Staatsoper, 1967; Emigrated to the West, 1973, and created designs for Cardillac and Pelléas et Mélisande at the Cologne Opera 1973–75; Directed and designed Iphigénie en Tauride at the Munich Staatsoper 1979 (seen at Amsterdam and Basle, 1990); Philip Glass's Satyagraha and the premiere of Akhnaten at the Stuttgart Staatsoper (1981, 1984); Orfeo ed Euridice at the Deutsche Oper Berlin, 1982, Die Zauberflöte at Hamburg (seen at the Vienna Festival 1991); Iphigénie en Tauride at the Deutsche Staatsoper, 1994; Die Zauberflöte for Salzburg, 1997 and Don Giovanni 1998, at Schwetzingen. *Address:* c/o Deutsche Staatsoper, Unter den Linden 7, 1086 Berlin, Germany.

**FRIED, Anneliese;** Singer (Mezzo-soprano); b. 1962, Germany. *Education:* Studied in Karlsruhe. *Career:* Sang at Aachen Opera, 1985–91; Munster, 1991–93, Cologne from 1993; Guest appearances at Düsseldorf (Mistress Quickly in Falstaff, 1995), Dresden (Fidalma in Il Matrimonio Segreto, 1996), Paris, Zürich and Geneva; Other roles have included Mary in Der fliegende Holländer, Ericlea in Monteverdi's Ulisse, Mrs Sedley in Peter Grimes, and Orlofsky in Die Fledermaus; Professor at the Cologne Musikhochschule from 1995. *Address:* c/o Staatliche Hochschule fur Music, Vocal Faculty, Dagobertstrasse 38, D–50668, Germany.

**FRIED, Joel (Ethan);** Conductor; b. 22 April 1954, California, USA; m. Mary Anne Massad, 9 Dec 1990, 1 step-d. *Education:* BMus, 1973; MMus, Piano Performance, DMA, University of Southern California, 1979. *Career:* Debut: Hidden Valley Opera, 1978; European debut, Heidelberg Castle Festival, 1981; Assistant Conductor, New York City Opera, 1980–82; Resident Conductor, Heidelberg Castle Festival, 1981–; Studienleiter, Saarland State Theatre, 1983–86; Chorus Master, Cleveland Opera, 1990–92; Chorus Master and Music Administrator, Pittsburgh Opera, 1992–; Conducting appearances with Zürich Opera, Fort Worth Opera and Cleveland Opera. *Honours:* 2nd Prize, American Conductors Competition, 1978; Special Prize for Contemporary Music, Hans Swarowsky International Conducting Competition, Vienna, 1984. *Address:* c/o Pittsburgh Opera, 711 Penn Avenue, Pittsburgh, PA 15222, USA.

**FRIED, Miriam;** Violinist; b. 9 Sept. 1946, Satu-Mare, Romania. *Education:* Rubin Academy of Music, Tel-Aviv; Graduate Studies, Europe and USA (Juilliard School, Ivan Galamian). *Career:* Debut: Carnegie Hall, New York, 1969; Royal Festival Hall, England; Appearances, orchestras world-wide including, Los Angeles Philharmonic; Philadelphia, Cleveland, Chicago, Boston Symphonies; New York Philharmonic; Berlin and Munich Philharmonics; Vienna Symphony; Zürich Tonhalle; Orchestre Nationale de France; Recent appearances include Stuttgart Radio Orchestra (conducted Neville Marriner); Danish Radio (Kurt Sanderling); Jerusalem Symphony at Berlin Festival; Orchestre Nationale, Belgium; Philharmonic Orchestras, Monte Carlo, Stuttgart, Nuremburg; Nouvel Orchestre Philharmonique, Paris; Opened Helsinki Festival (with Helsinki Philharmonic conducted by Gennadi Rozhdestvensky), 1988; Hollywood Bowl (Yuri Temirkanov), 1988; Cleveland Orchestra (Mariss Jansons), 1989; Santa Cecilia (Temirkanov), 1989; Orchestre de Paris (Kurt Sanderling), 1989; American engagements for 1994–95, Chicago Symphony Orchestra, Cleveland Orchestra, Boston Symphony Orchestra, Philadelphia Orchestra; Frequent engagements, Royal Philharmonic Orchestra; BBC television and Promenade Concerts; Edinburgh Festival; Scottish National Orchestra; Bournemouth Symphony; Numerous recitals. *Recordings:* Recital album, Deutsche Grammophon; Solo Violin Works, Bach; Sibelius Violin Concerto, Helsinki Philharmonic (Okko Kamu), 1988. *Honours:* Scholarship, overseas studies, American Israel Cultural Foundation; 1st Prizes, Paganini International Competition, Genoa Italy, 1968, Queen Elisabeth Competition, Belgium, 1971. *Current Management:* Agence de Concerts et Spectacles Caecilia. *Address:* c/o Mauroy Concerts, 19 rue des Primevères, L–2351, Luxembourg.

**FRIEDE, Stephanie;** Singer (Soprano); b. 1959, New York, USA. *Education:* Studied at the Juilliard School and the Oberlin Conservatory. *Career:* Debut: Houston Opera, 1985, as Siebel in Faust; Sang further at Houston as Zerlina, Micaela and Manon; European debut as Stuttgart 1987, as Adina; Amsterdam, 1987, as Massenet's Cendrillon; Season 1991 as Donna Anna at Munich and Elettra in Idomeneo at Glyndebourne; Liège, 1992, as Salome in Herodiade by Massenet; Further engagements at the Buxton Festival as Eleanore d'Este in Torquato Tasso by Donizetti, at Cologne as Violetta and elsewhere in Europe as Gounod's Juliette, Anne Trulove, and Mimi; Season 2000–01 as Giulietta at Antwerp, Salome and Sieglinde for Zürich Opera, and Amelia (Ballo in Maschera) at Hamburg. *Address:* c/o Oldani, Viale Legioni Romane 26, 1–20147 Milan, Italy.

**FRIEDEL, Martin (Kurt);** Composer; b. 3 Aug. 1945, Warwateil, Germany. *Education:* BSc (Hons), 1967, PhD, 1972, University of Melbourne. *Career:* Fellowships and Residences in Australia and Germany, 1976–95; Commissions from theatres in Australia, and the Adelaide Festival of the Arts, 1992. *Compositions include:* Sin, 7 act opera for 4 voices and orchestra, 1978; Two Songs, for soprano and ensemble, 1982; South of North, 1 act chamber opera, 1985; Conversations Before the Silence, cantata, 1989; Foxy, 1 act chamber opera, 1991; The Heaven Machine and Seduction of a General, 1 act operas for soprano and electronics, 1991; Four Choral Fragments for Walter Benjamin, 1992; Songs from the Astronauts, for soprano, baritone and ensemble, 1994; The Third Planet, oratorio, 1995; Three Night Pieces, string quartet, 1995. *Honours:* Best Score, Chicago International Film Festival, 1994. *Address:* c/o APRA, 1A Eden Street, Crows Nest, NSW 2065, Australia.

**FRIEDERICH, (Albert) Matthias;** oboist, recorder player and composer; b. 16 June 1954, Heidelberg, Germany; m. Margaret Joy Stone 1980; one s. *Education:* Cologne Music College with G. Hoeller, H. Hucke and A. Meidhof. *Career:* debut, recorder soloist, Vivaldi's Sopranini Recorder Concerto in C major, Heidelberg, 1966; Concerts with George Malcolm, Amadeus Quartet, Mozarteum Quartet, Munich String Trio, and Sinfonia Varsovia, Poland; Since 1988, member of Pifferari di Santo Spirito Trio, Heidelberg (with Margaret Friederich and Peter Schumann); Concerts, Berlin, Paris, Dallas and Tokyo; mem, International Double Reed Society. *Compositions:* Happy Birthday Variations, 1989; Highstreet Dixie, 1990; Enigma Blues for FGB, 1991; Jubilee Stomp, 1992; Amusement, 1994. *Recordings:* Music for Fun, 1991; Pifferari Safari, 1993. *Contributions:* Article, Jazz on the oboe and the cor anglais, to Rohrblatt. *Address:* Floringasse 2, 69117 Heidelberg, Germany.

**FRIEDLI, Irene;** Singer (Mezzo-soprano); b. 1965, Rauchlisberg, Switzerland. *Education:* Studied with Kurt Widmer at the Basle Music Academy and attended master classes with Dietrich Fischer-Dieskau and Brigitte Fassbaender. *Career:* Shepherd and Hope in Monteverdi's Orfeo and Dryad in Ariadne auf Naxos, Lucerne Opera, 1993–94; Zürich Opera as Gertrude in Roméo et Juliette, Suzuki, Third Lady in Die Zauberflöte, Mercédès (Carmen) and the title role in L'Enfant et les Sortilèges, 1994; Opera and concert engagements with such conductors as Helmuth Rilling, Horst Stein, Michel Corboz and Neeme Järvi; Has appeared widely as guest in Switzerland and abroad, notably in contemporary concert music. *Honours:* Prizewinner at the Hugo Wolf (Stuttgart), Schubert (Graz) and Othmar Schoeck (Lucerne) Competitions. *Address:* c/o Opernhaus Zürich, Falkenstrasse 1, 8008 Zürich, Switzerland.

**FRIEDMAN, Gérard;** Singer (Tenor); b. 3 April 1926, Paris, France. *Education:* Studied at the Paris Conservatoire with Roger Bourdin and Charles Panzera. *Career:* Sang Don Curzio in Don Giovanni at the 1955 Aix Festival, Théâtre des Champs Elysées, Paris, 1954, in the premiere (concert) of Prokofiev's Fiery Angel; Sang widely in France until 1988 as Spalanzani in Les Contes d'Hoffmann, a Brahmin in Padmâvatî by Roussel and Torquemada in L'Heure Espagnole by Ravel; Professor at the Metz Conservatory from 1970. *Recordings include:* Auber's Manon Lescaut, Samson et Dalila, Fauré's Pénélope and Chausson's Le Roi Arthus, Te Deum by Lully, Masses by M A Charpentier and songs by Fauré. *Address:* c/o Conservatoire National de Région Metz, 2 Rue Paradis, 57036 Metz, France.

**FRIEDMAN, Leonard (Matthew);** Violinist; b. 11 Dec. 1930, London, England; m. twice, 2 s., 3 d. *Education:* Guildhall School of Music and Drama. *Career:* Debut: Central Hall, 1938; Conway Hall, 1949; Joint Founder, Haydn Orchestra and Cremona Quartet; Member, Adolph Busch Chamber Orchestra, English Chamber Orchestra, Rostal, Hurwitz, Bath Festival; Founder Leader, Northern Symphony; Deputy Leader, Royal Philharmonic Orchestra and Leader, Bremen Philharmonic; Leader, Westphalia Symphony; Founder, Scottish Ensemble; Guest Leader, Scottish Chamber; London Festival; Member, Melos of London; Duo with Allan Schiller, and with son Richard Friedman; Director, Friedman Ensemble; mem, Honorary Member, Royal Overseas; Scottish Arts; New Club. *Recordings:* Director, Music at Hopetoun; Director, Music at Drumlanrig; Scandinavian Serenade; String Orchestra Music by Mozart; Baroque Cello Concertos; English Serenade; Schubert String Quintet; Bach Concertos; Tribute to Kreisler. *Honours:* Gold Medal, Guildhall School of Music, 1953; Royal Patronage of Duke of Edinburgh, 1975; Citizenship Prize of Edinburgh, 1980–81; Founder/Director, Camerata of St Andrew, 1988. *Address:* 17a Dublin Street, Edinburgh EH1 3PG, Scotland.

**FRIEDRICH, Reinhold;** German trumpeter; b. 14 July 1958, Weingarten, Baden; m. Annette Friedrich; two s. *Education:* studied with Edward Tarr, Pierre Thibaud in Paris. *Career:* debut with Berlin Philharmony; numerous television and live performances, including the EBU Opening Concerto with B. A. Zimmermann's Nobody Knows De Trouble I See, Biennale Berlin 1997; Trumpet Concerto by Benedict Mason; Hummel's First Recordings of the Concerto in E Major with the Historical Keyed Trumpet 1996; teacher, Hochschule fur Musik, Karlsruhe; mem. Int. Trumpet Guild. *Recordings:* B. A. Zimmermann's Nobody Knows De Trouble I See, Hummel and Puccini Recordings with the Historical Keyed Trumpet, Sequenza X by Berio, Gubaidulina's Trio. *Honours:* first prize German Music Competition 1981, winner ARD Competition, Munich 1986. *Current Management:* Künstlersekretariat Astrid Schoerke, Grazer Strasse 30, 30519 Hannover, Germany.

**FRIEND, Caroline;** Singer (Soprano); b. 1950, England. *Career:* Concert appearances in the United Kingdom, Switzerland, Belgium, France, Germany and the Netherlands; Repertoire includes Handel's Oratorios, Bach's Oratorios and Cantatas, Schubert's A flat Mass, Britten's War Requiem under Stephen Cleobury in King's College, Vaughan Williams' Sea Symphony, Howells' Hymnus Paradisi, Rossini's Stabat Mater, Dvořák's Stabat Mater; Mahler's 4th Symphony and Les Nuits d'Eté with the Netherlands Philharmonic under Franz-Paul Decker; Appearances with the Songmakers' Almanac in England and Ireland, performing Robin Holloway's Women in War; Sang Diane in Rameau's Hippolyte et Aricie for the English Bach Festival under Jean-Claude Malgoire in Athens and Versailles and at Covent Garden; Other roles include Mozart's Donna Anna, Susanna, Pamina, Countess and Fiordiligi (Pavilion Opera), Rosalinde (Die Fledermaus), Norina (Don Pasquale), Hannah in The Merry Widow, Tosca and Mimi, (Puccini), Berta in The Barber of Seville and performances of Balfe's The Siege of Rochelle; Engagements in all the major London concert halls and with many choral societies; Conductors include Adrian Boult, John Eliot Gardiner and Charles Mackerras. *Address:* 33 Wetherby Mansions, Earls Court Square, London SW5 9BH, England.

**FRIEND, Lionel;** British conductor; *Conductor-in-residence, Birmingham Conservatoire*; b. 13 March 1945, London; s. of Norman A. C. Friend and Moya L. Dicks; m. Jane Hyland 1969; one s. two d. *Education:* Royal Grammar School, High Wycombe, Royal Coll. of Music (RCM), London, London Opera Centre. *Career:* with Welsh Nat. Opera 1969–72, Glyndebourne Festival/Touring Opera 1969–72; 2nd Kapellmeister, Staatstheater, Kassel, FRG 1972–75; Conductor ENO 1976–89; Musical Dir New Sussex Opera 1989–96; Guest Conductor BBC Symphony, Philharmonia, Nash Ensemble, Scottish Chamber, Royal Ballet and in Australia, Brazil, Denmark, France, Hungary, Norway, Spain, Germany, Netherlands, Belgium, Sweden, USA. *Address:* 136 Rosendale Road, London, SE21 8LG, England (home). *Telephone:* (20) 8761-7845 (home). *E-mail:* lionelfriend@hotmail.com (home).

**FRIGERIO, Ezio;** Stage Designer; b. 16 July 1930, Como, Italy. *Education:* Studied architecture at Milan Polytechnic. *Career:* Costume Designer, Giorgio Strehler's Piccolo Teatro d'Arte from 1955; Collaborations with Strehler, Eduardo de Filippo and other directors in Italy and elsewhere; Designed Don Pasquale at the Edinburgh Festival, 1962, Tosca at Cologne, 1976, and Carmen at Hamburg, 1988; Collaborations with Nuria Espert for Madama Butterfly and Traviata at Scottish Opera (1987 and 1989), Rigoletto at Covent Garden, 1988, and Elektra at Barcelona, 1990; La Scala Milan, 1990, with Fidelio and The Queen of Spades; Designs for Il Turco in Italia and Anna Bolena at Madrid, season 1990–91; Andrea Chénier for Buenos Aires, 1996; Aida at Palermo, 1998; Frequent associations with costume designer Franca Squarciapino. *Address:* c/o Royal Opera House (Contracts), Covent Garden, London WC2E 9 DD, England.

**FRIMMER, Monika;** Singer (Soprano); b. 1955, Marburg, Germany. *Education:* Studied in Hanover. *Career:* Staatstheater, Hanover, 1981–93, notably in operas by Mozart and the Baroque repertoire; Herrenhausen Festival, 1981, as Morgana in Handel's Alcina; Hanover, 1989, as Matilde in a revival of Steffani's Enrico Leone; Deutsche Oper Berlin, 1991–92; Sang in Handel's Radamisto at Göttingen, 1993; Concert engagements throughout Europe, and in the USA and Israel. *Recordings include:* Messiah, Mozart Masses and Pergolesi Stabat Mater; Radamisto. *Address:* c/o Göttingen Handel Festival (contracts), Augustplatz 8, 7010 Leipzig, Germany.

**FRISCH, Walter M.;** Professor of Music; b. 26 Feb. 1951, New York, NY, USA; m. Anne-Marie Bouché 1981, 2 s. *Education:* BA, Yale University, 1973; MA, 1977, PhD, 1981, University of California, Berkeley. *Career:* Assistant Professor of Music, 1982–88, Associate Professor, 1988–94, Professor, 1994–, Columbia University; Research in music of 19th and 20th centuries, especially the Austrian tradition (Schubert, Brahms, Schoenberg); mem, American Musicological Society; American Brahms Society. *Publications:* Brahms' Alto Rhapsody (editor, facsimile edition), 1983; Brahms and the Principle of Developing Variation, 1984; Schubert: Critical and Analytical Studies (editor), 1986; The Early Works of Arnold Schoenberg, 1993. *Contributions:* Co-editor, 19th Century Music, 1984–92. *Honours:* Winner, American Society of Composers, Authors and Publishers-Deems Taylor Award for outstanding book on music, 1985, 1995. *Address:* Department of Music, Columbia University, New York, NY 10027, USA.

**FRISELL, Sonja;** Stage Director; b. 5 Aug. 1937, Richmond, Surrey, England. *Education:* Studied piano and acting at the Guildhall School. *Career:* Associated with Carl Ebert at the St ädtische Oper Berlin and at Glyndebourne; Staff Producer, La Scala, solo producer in North and South America and Europe; Directed La Favorite at the 1977 Bregenz Festival, Vivaldi's Tito Manlio at La Scala, 1979, and Handel's Agrippina at Venice, 1985; Marriage of Figaro, San Francisco, 1982; Directed Carmen at Buenos Aires, 1985, Aida at the Metropolitan, 1988; Lyric Opera of Chicago, 1989–90; Don Carlos: Khovanshchina at San Francisco, 1990; Don Giovanni, Capetown, 1991; Directed: Die Zauberflöte for Washington Opera at Kennedy Center, 1991 (revived 1998); Forza del Destino at San Francisco, 1992; Otello at Washington, 1992; Ballo at Chicago, 1992; Rigoletto at Gothenburg, 1993; Trovatore at Chicago, 1993; Lucia at Calgary, 1994; Eugene Onegin, Calgary, 1996; La Gioconda, La Scala, 1997; Elena da Feltre, by Mercadante, Wexford, 1997; Turandot, Seville, 1998 and Trieste, Cagliari, Santander and Cordoba, 1999; Eugene Onegin, Phoenix, 2000; Otello, Washington, 2000; Eugene Onegin with Arizone Opera, 2000; La traviata in Rio de Janeiro, 2001; Don Carlos, Washington, 2001; Carmen, Iceland, 2001; LaTraviata, Rio de Janeiro, 2001; Otello, Tokyo, 2002; Otello in Tokyo, 2002; Salome with Arizona Opera, 2003; Turnadot in Helsinki, 2004mem, AGMA. *Current Management:* CAMI New York, USA. *Address:* Quinta do Refugio, Pincho 8600-090 Bensafrim, Algarve, Portugal.

**FRITH, Benjamin;** Concert Pianist; b. 11 Oct. 1957, Sheffield, England; m. Donna Sansom, April 1989, 3 d. *Education:* Private study with Fanny Waterman since childhood; BA (Hons) 1st Class, Music, Leeds University, 1979. *Career:* Debut: Official London debut in recital at Wigmore Hall, 1981, sponsored by Countess of Munster Trust; Performing career of recitals, concertos and participation in chamber music ensembles in London and the Provinces including South Bank, Wigmore Hall, Usher Hall Edinburgh, Aldeburgh, Harrogate and many major festivals; Television and radio appearances; Concerts in Italy, Spain, Germany, Poland, Israel and America; mem, Incorporated Society of Musicians. *Recordings:* Diabelli and 32 variations by Beethoven; Chamber music; Schumann piano music, Davidsbündlertänze (opus 6), Fantasiestücke (opus 12); Martin Ellerby, piano and chamber works, and Collage, French and English, clarinet and piano music with Linda Merrick; Mendelssohn, complete solo piano works and complete works for piano and orchestra; Messiaen, Visions de l'Amen, with Peter Hill, Malcolm Arnold, complete piano works. *Honours:* Joint Top Prizewinner, Busoni International Pianoforte Competition, 1986–; Gold Medallist and joint 1st Prizewinner, Arthur Rubenstein International Piano Masters Competition, 1989. *Current Management:* Modena International Music, Italy; Rosalia Heifetz, Israel. *Address:* 6 Carisbrook Road, Carlton in Lindrick, Nottinghamshire S81 9 NJ, England.

**FRITTOLI, Barbara;** Singer (Soprano); b. 1967, Milan, Italy. *Education:* Studied at the Giuseppe Verdi Conservatory, Milan. *Career:* Sang first at the Teatro Comunale, Florence, and has appeared as Mozart's Countess under Abbado, Fiordiligi in Vienna and Ravenna, 1996; Donna Elvira at Naples; Desdemona with Antonio Pappano at Brussels and with Abbado at the Salzburg Easter Festival, 1996; New York Met and Covent Garden debuts as Mimi and Micaela; Medora in Verdi's Il Corsaro, Turin, 1996; Concerts include Strauss's Vier Letzte Lieder in Milan, Rome and London, Rossini's Stabat Mater, Ein Deutsches Requiem and the Verdi Requiem; Sang Fiordiligi in Così fan tutte at Covent Garden and Glyndebourne, 1998; Season 1999–2000 in new production of Falstaff at Covent Garden; Season 2002–03 as Donizetti's Maria Stuarda at Edinburgh (concert) and Vitellia in La Clemenza di Tito at Covent Garden, returning for Luisa Miller. *Recordings include:* Il Trittico, with Mirella Freni; Il Barbiere di Siviglia; Pergolesi's Stabat Mater, with Riccardo Muti. *Honours:* Winner of several international competitions. *Current Management:* Askonas Holt Ltd, Lonsdale Chambers, 27 Chancery Lane, London, WC2A 1PF, England. *Telephone:* (20) 7400-1700. *Fax:* (20) 7400-1799. *E-mail:* info@askonasholt.co.uk. *Website:* www.askonasholt.co.uk.

**FRITZSCH, Johannes;** German conductor; *Chief Conductor, Oper Graz*; b. 1960, Meissen. *Education:* studied with his father and Carl Maria von Weber Music Acad., Dresden. *Career:* second Kapellmeister, Rostock Opera 1982–87; conducted Il Barbiere di Siviglia and Il Matrimonio Segreto at the Semper Opera Dresden 1987; Kapellmeister, Staatsoper Dresden 1987–, with more than 350 opera and ballet performances; guest conductor, Royal Swedish Opera, Stockholm; regular orchestra concerts in fmr E Germany; West German debut 1990 with Beethoven's Fifth Piano Concerto and the New World Symphony with the Nat. Theatre Orchestra, Mannheim; Danish debut with the Orchestra of Danish Radio at Copenhagen 1991; also Don Giovanni, Royal Opera, Stockholm 1991; Rialto Theatre, Copenhagen 1991; Entführung, Nozze di Figaro and Don Giovanni, Royal Opera, Stockholm 1991; La Traviata, Hanover 1991; Hansel and Gretel at Sydney, with Australian

Opera 1992; Kapellmeister, Staatsoper Hannover 1992–93; Die Bassariden at Freiburg 1993; Der Freischütz at Cologne 1997; Music Dir and Chief Conductor, Städtische Bühnen and the Philharmonische Orchester, Freiburg 1992–99; guest appearances with orchestras, including Berliner Sinfonie Orchester, Copenhagen Radio Orchestra, Düsseldorfer Sinfoniker, Hamburger Sinfoniker, Nationaltheater-Orchester Mannheim, Norddeutsche Philharmonie Rostock, Orchestre Philharmonique Montpellier, Orchestre Philharmonique Strasbourg, Orchestre Philharmonique Toulouse, Oslo Radio Orchestra, Philharmonie Essen, Staatskapelle Dresden, Staatskapelle Schwerin, Staatsorchester Halle, State Orchestra of Victoria, Stockholm Radio Orchestra, Sydney Symphony Orchestra, Tasmanian Symphony Orchestra, West Australian Symphony Orchestra; and with opera cos, including Bastille Opera Paris, Deutsche Oper Berlin, Komische Oper Berlin, Opera Australia, Opera Cologne, Opera Malmö, Royal Opera Stockholm; Conductor of Der Rosenkavalier, Barber of Seville for Opera Australia in Sydney, La Bohème for Royal Opera Stockholm and The Rake's Progress and Entführung for Staatsoper Dresden 2004; Conductor of Don Giovanni in Sydney, Falstaff in Dresden and Der Rosenkavalier in Graz 2005; Chief Conductor Oper Graz 2006–. *Current Management:* Patrick Togher Artists Management, Suite 25, 450 Elizabeth Street, Surry Hills, NSW 2010, Australia. *Telephone:* (2) 93196255. *Fax:* (2) 93197611. *E-mail:* pjtogher@ozemail.com.au. *Website:* www.patricktogher.com. *Address:* c/o Oper Graz, Theater Graz, Kaiser Josef Platz 10, 8010 Graz, Austria. *Telephone:* (316) 8008. *Website:* www.theater-graz.com/opernhaus/.

**FROBENIUS, Wolf;** Musicologist; b. 1 June 1940, Speyer/Rhein, Germany. *Education:* Studies in Musicology, History of Art and History, Freiburg i/Br, Germany and Paris, France; PhD, Freiburg i/Br, 1968; Habilitation, Freiburg i/Br, 1988. *Career:* Staff Member, Handwörterbuch der musikalischen Terminologie, Akademie der Wissenschaften und der Literatur, Mainz, 1968–88; Teacher, University of Freiburg i/Br, 1971–88; Professor, University of Saarbrücken. *Publications:* Hohannes Boens Musica und seine Konsonanzenlehre, 1971. *Contributions:* Handwörterbuch der Musikwissenschaft; The New Grove; Die Musik in Geschichte und Gegenwart. *Address:* Akazienweg 56, 66121 Saarbücken, Schafbrücke, Germany.

**FRONTALI, Roberto;** Singer (Baritone); b. 1963, Italy. *Career:* Sang at the Rome Opera from 1986, in Spontini's Agnese di Hohenstaufen, Valentin in Faust and Massenet's Albert; Season 1992–93 as Belcore at Dallas and Ford in Falstaff at La Scala; Sang Rossini's Figaro at Florence and Naples, 1993; San Francisco, 1993, as Riccardo in I Puritani; Season 1995–96 with Marcello in La Bohème at the Metropolitan; Florence, 1996, as Enrico in Lucia di Lammermoor; Other roles include Nottingham in Roberto Devereux by Donizetti, Verdi's Miller and Puccini's Sharpless; Season 1998 with Alphonse in La Favorite at Rome and Rossini's Figaro at Genoa and for the Royal Opera, London; Season 2000–01 as Count Luna at the New York Met, Eugene Onegin at Florence, Germont for the Opéra Bastille, Falstaff at Frankfurt and Ernesto in Il Pirata by Bellini at Catania. *Recordings include:* Falstaff; L'Elisir d'amore. *Address:* c/o Teatro dell Opera di Roma, Piazza B. Gigli 8, 00184 Rome, Italy.

**FROUNBERG, Ivar;** Composer; b. 12 April 1950, Copenhagen, Denmark; m. Inge Sínderskov Madsen, 1 s. *Education:* Organist and Choirleader, 1976; MA, Composition, State University of New York, USA, 1981; Royal Danish Academy of Music, 1986. *Career:* Lecturer, Electro-acoustic Music, 1986–90, Assistant Professor, Musical Composition, 1991–, The Royal Danish Academy of Music; Board of the Danish Composers' Society, 1982–94; Board of KODA, 1988–94; Music Co-ordinator at the 1994 ICMC; Chairman ISCM Festival, 1996; Chairman, DIEM, 1998–; Councillor at the Danish Arts Council, 1999–; Prof., Norwegian State Acad. of Music, Oslo, 2000–. *Compositions:* Drei-Klang, 1982; Henri Michaux preludes, 1985; Embryo, 1985; Multiple Forms, 1986; A Dirge: Other echoes inhabit the Garden, 1988; What did the Sirens sing as Ulysses sailed by?, 1989; A Pattern of Timeless Motion, 1989; Time and the Bell, 1990; SHâTaLè, 1991; World Apart 1992–94;... to arrive where we started, 1993; Hydra, 1996; Droemmespor, 1997; The Anatomy of a Point, 1990–95/97; Hoodoos 1997; Quasi una sonata, 1998; Cancion, no cantado, 1998; Voyelles, 1999; SAXO, 2000; Prélude-Voyage-Jotunheim, 2002; Logogriphes, 2003. *Recordings:* A Pattern of Timeless Motion; What did the Sirens Sing as Ulysses sailed by?, A Dirge: Other Echoes Inhabit the Garden, Multiple Forms; Other Echoes Inhabit the Garden (solo version); Worlds Apart;... to arrive where we started. *Publications:* Theory and Praxis in the compositional methods of Iannis Xenakis–an exemplification; Komponisten Pierre Boulez, 1985; Ein Schwebender Stein... Positionen 37. *Contributions:* Dansk Musiktidskrift; Nutida Musik. *Honours:* The Ancker Grant, 1994; 3 Year Grant of the Danish State Arts Council, 1994–96; Prize in Honour of Carl Nielsen, 1995; The Poul Schierbeck Prize of Honour, 1998. *Address:* POB 5190, Gydasvei 6, Majorstua, 0302, Norway (office); Melchiorsvej 1, 3450 Alleríd, Denmark. *Telephone:* 23-36-71-08 (office). *E-mail:* if@nmh.no (office).

**FRUGONI, Orazio;** Pianist; b. 28 Jan. 1921, Davos, Switzerland. *Education:* Graduated Milan Conservatory, 1939; Attended master classes of Alfredo Casella at the Accademia Chigiana, Siena, and Dinu Lipatti at the Geneva Conservatory. *Career:* Played in concerts in Italy from 1939 and in the USA from 1947; Piano professor at the Eastman School, Rochester, until 1967; Director, 1967–72; Teacher of piano at the Luigi Cherubini Conservatory at Florence from 1972. *Recordings include:* Beethoven's E flat concerto of 1784 (premiere recording); Mendelssohn's Piano Concerto. *Honours:* Prix de Virtuosité, Geneva Conservatory, 1945. *Address:* Conservatorio di Musica L Cherubini, Piazzetta delle Belle Arti, Florence, Italy.

**FRÜHBECK DE BURGOS, Rafael;** Spanish conductor; b. 15 Sept. 1933, Burgos; s. of Wilhelm Frühbeck and Stephanie Frühbeck (née Ochs); m. María Carmen Martínez 1959; one s. one d. *Education:* music acads in Bilbao, Madrid and Munich, Univ. of Madrid. *Career:* Chief Conductor, Municipal Orchestra, Bilbao 1958–62; Music Dir and Chief Conductor, Spanish Nat. Orchestra, Madrid 1962–78, Hon. Conductor 1998; Music Dir of Düsseldorf and Chief Conductor Düsseldorf Symphoniker 1966–71; Music Dir Montreal Symphony Orchestra 1974–76; Prin. Guest Conductor Yomiuri Nippon Symphony Orchestra 1980–90, Hon. Conductor 1991; Prin. Guest Conductor Nat. Symphony Orchestra, Washington, DC 1980–90; Music Dir Vienna Symphony Orchestra 1991–96; Gen. Music Dir Deutsche Oper Berlin 1992–97; Gen. Musik Dir Rundfunk Symphony Orchestra, Berlin 1994–2000; Chief Conductor RAI Symphony Orchestra, Turin 2001; Prin. Guest Conductor, Dresdner Philharmonic Orchestra 2003–04; mem. Real Academia de Bellas Artes, Madrid 1975. *Orchestrations:* Suite Española (Albéniz) 1965, Tema y Variaciones (Turina) 1985. *Honours:* Gran Cruz al Mérito Civil Orden de Alfonso X 1966, Orden de Isabel la Católica 1966, Grand Cross of Civil Merit (Germany) 2001, Gold Medal Labour Merit (Spain) 2004; Dr hc (Univ. of Navarra) 1994, (Univ. of Burgos) 1998; Prize for Musical Interpretation, Larios Foundation CEOE (Confed. Española de Orgs Empresariales), Madrid 1992, Fundación Guerrero Prize for Spanish Music, Madrid 1996, Gold Medal City of Vienna 1995, Medal of Civil Merit (Austria) 1996, Gold Medal Int. Gustav Mahler Soc., Vienna 1996, Gold Medal State of Vienna 2000, hon. mem. Israel Philharmonic Orchestra 1999. *Address:* Avenida del Mediterráneo 21, Madrid, 28007, Spain (home). *Telephone:* (341) 5016933 (home).

**FRYKBERG, Susan;** Composer; b. 10 Oct. 1954, Hastings, New Zealand. *Education:* Studied at the University of Canterbury; University of Otago; Simon Fraser University. *Career:* Freelance Composer; Teacher in Vancouver, the University of Auckland and Simon Fraser University; mem, Canadian Music Centre; New Zealand Music Centre. *Compositions include:* Electro-acoustic music theatre pieces: Saxarba, 1985, Caroline Herschel Is Minding The Heavens, 1988, Woman And House, 1990, Mother Too, 1991; Birth/Rebirth/Bearing Me, 1991; Insect Life, 1993; Audio-Birth Project, 1996–97; Sue and Kathy Telecompose Across the Country, 1997. *Recordings:* Astonishing Sense of Being Taken Over by Something Far Greater Than Me; Harangue 1. *Publications:* Acoustic Dimensions of Communication, Study Guide; Simon Fraser University. *Address:* c/o New Zealand Music Centre, PO Box 10042, Level 13, Brandon Street, Wellington, New Zealand.

**FU, Haijing;** Singer (baritone); b. 1960, China. *Education:* Studied in London and New York. *Career:* Concert engagements include Mozart's Requiem with the Montreal Symphony Orchestra, Zemlinsky's Lyric Symphony, Beethoven's Ninth, Carmina Burana with the Pacific Symphony and the Cleveland Orchestra, Verdi's Requiem in Geneva; Mendelssohn's Erste Walpurgisnacht with the Boston Symphony and Mozart's C minor Mass with the Cincinnati Orchestra; Metropolitan Opera debut 1990, as Germont, followed by Sir Richard Forth in I Puritani; Renato with Atlanta Opera, Enrico and Verdi's Miller at Philadelphia and Filippo in Bellini's Bianca e Fernando at Catania, Italy, 1992; Appearances as Rigoletto with the San Diego and Edmonton Opera companies; Other roles include Marcello in La Bohème, and Posa in Don Carlos; Sang Germont at Philadelphia, 1992; Season 1998 as Germont at Miami and in Stiffelio at the New York Met. *Honours:* Second Prize, Benson and Hedges Gold Award International Competition, London, 1987; Winner, Metropolitan Opera National Council Competition, 1988. *Address:* c/o Metropolitan Opera House, Lincoln Center, New York, NY 10023, USA.

**FUCHS, Barbara;** Singer (Soprano); b. 1959, Zürich, Switzerland. *Education:* Studied at Frankfurt and Zürich, with masterclasses by Erik Werba, Sena Jurinac and Elisabeth Schwarzkopf. *Career:* Sang at the Ulm Opera, 1983–85, as Blondchen, Adele, Olympia, Rosina and Susanna; Gelsenkirchen, 1985–87, as Sophie, the Queen of Night and Annina in Eine Nacht in Venedig; Frankfurt from 1990, as Zerbinetta, Helena in Reimann's Troades and other coloratura roles; Guest appearances throughout Germany and frequent concert engagements.

**FUCHS, Olivia;** Opera Director; b. 15 Aug. 1963, London, England; m. Nigel Robson; one s. one d. *Education:* BA, German and Drama, Westfield Coll., Univ. of London; Postgraduate Diploma, Drama Studio, London. *Career:* debut, Johnny Johnson by Kurt Weill for Opera Factory Zürich, 1992; Britten's Turn of the Screw, for Bath Theatre Royal, 1993; Handel's Arminio for the London Handel Society, 1996; Mozart's Marriage of Figaro at the Queen Elizabeth Hall, 1996; La Bohème, 1997, and Il Trovatore, 1998, both for Opera South, Ireland; Mozart's Apollo and Hyacinth for the Classical Opera Company, 1998; Premiere of John Lunn's The Maids for ENO/Lyric Theatre, Hammersmith, 1998; Britten's The Turn of the Screw for the Brighton Festival, 2000; Verdi's La Traviata for English Touring Opera, 2001–02; Janáček's Osud and Sarka for Garsington Opera, 2002; Beethoven's Fidelio for Opera Holland Park, 2003; Wolf's Italian Songbook for Royal Opera House, 2003; Dvorak's Rusalka for Opera North, 2003; Tchaikovsky's Cherevichki for Garsington Opera 2004; Verdi's Luisa Miller for Opera Holland Park 2004; Peter Sellar's Theodora for Opera du Rhin 2004; Don Giovanni for Opera North 2005 fmr Assoc. Dir, Glyndebourne and Opera Factory; mem., Directors' Guild of Great Britain. *Current Management:* Music Hall, Vicarage

Way, Ringmer, BN8 5LA, England. *Telephone:* (1273) 814240 (office). *Fax:* (1273) 813637 (office). *E-mail:* info@musichall.co.uk (office).

**FUGE, Katharine;** Singer (Soprano); b. 1968, Jersey. *Education:* Studied in London. *Career:* Engagements with the English Bach Soloists, notably on the Bach Cantata Pilgrimage tour, 2000, throughout Europe and in New York; St Matthew Passion with De Nederlande Bachvereniging, 2001; Handel and Zelenka with Collegium Vocal Gent, Handel's Athalia with Frieder Bernius in Göttingen, Acis and Galatea in Denmark; Season 2000-01 in Britain at Symphony Hall, Birmingham, Wigmore Hall, and Liverpool and Southwark Cathedrals; Repertory includes Poulenc's Gloria, Stabat Mater by Stanford and Pergolesi, and Messiah; Sang First Mermaid in Weber's Oberon at the Barbican Hall, London 2002. *Recordings include:* Albums in DG Archiv collection, Bach Cantata Pilgrimage; Vivaldi Gloria and Handel Dixit Dominus (Philips Classics); Dvořák Mass in D. *Address:* c/o English Baroque Soloists, 57 Kingswood Road, London, SW19 3 ND, England.

**FUGELLE, Jacquelyn;** Singer (Soprano); b. 1949, London, England; m. George Johnston, 1975, 1 d. *Education:* Studied at Guildhall School of Music; Vienna Academy and in Rome. *Career:* Debut: Wigmore Hall, London, 1975; Extensive repertoire in oratorio, recital and opera; Appearances in England, Canada and Europe; Television and radio appearances in the Netherlands, Sweden and for the BBC; Debut at Royal Opera House, Covent Garden, 1991 as Arbate in Mozart's Mitridate; Other roles at Royal Opera House include Falcon, in Die Frau ohne Schatten; Debut with Scottish Opera, 1993; Major oratorio performances include Elijah with London Philharmonic Orchestra, conducted by Kurt Masur; Broadcasts include Messiah in Norway, Mendelssohn's 2nd Symphony in Paris and B Minor Mass in Iceland; mem, ISM; Equity. *Recordings:* Operatic Favourites with Joan Sutherland, Luciano Pavarotti; Music by Bottesini with Tomas Martin on double bass and Anthony Halstead on piano. *Honours:* Silver Medal, Worshipful Company of Musicians; Countess of Munster; Royal Society of Arts Scholarships; 2nd Prize, Kathleen Ferrier Competition. *Address:* 38 Wadham Road, Portsmouth, Hampshire, PO 2 9EE, England.

**FUJIKAWA, Mayumi;** Violinist; b. 27 July 1946, Asahigawa City, Japan. *Education:* Toho Conservatoire, Tokyo; Antwerp Conservatory, Belgium; further study with Leonid Kogan in Nice. *Career:* concerts with leading orchestras in South America, Australia, Israel, Asia, Japan and Europe; American orchestras in Philadelphia, Boston, Chicago, Pittsburgh and Cleveland; festival engagements at Aldeburgh with Previn, Edinburgh with the Concertgebouw Orchestra and Kondrashin; other conductors include Barenboim, Dutoit, Foster, Haitink, Levine, Ormandy, Sanderling and Rattle; television appearances playing the Mozart Concertos with the Scottish Chamber Orchestra; Promenade Concerts, London, 1991, in Mozart's Sinfonia Concertante. *Recordings:* Mozart Concertos with the Royal Philharmonic conducted by Walter Weller; Beethoven's Kreutzer and Franck's Sonata with Michael Roll; Tchaikovsky and Bruch Concertos with the Rotterdam Philharmonic; Sonatas by Prokofiev and Fauré. *Honours:* Second Prize, Tchaikovsky International Competition, Moscow, 1970; First Prize, Henri Vieuxtemps Competition, Verviers, Belgium, 1970. *Current Management:* Terry Harrison Artists Management, The Orchard, Market Street, Charlbury, Oxfordshire OX7 3PJ, England. *Telephone:* (1608) 810330. *Fax:* (1608) 811331. *E-mail:* artists@terryharrison.force9.co.uk.

**FUJIOKA, Sachio;** Conductor; b. 1962, Tokyo, Japan. *Education:* Studied in Japan with Kenichiro Kobayshi and Akeo Watanabe; Royal Northern College of Music, 1990–. *Career:* Assistant Conductor of the BBC Philharmonic, 1994; Season 1995–96 as Conductor of the Japan Philharmonic and Principal Conductor of the Manchester Camerata; Season 1996–97 with Royal Philharmonic Bournemouth, Norwegian Radio, Stavanger and Singapore Symphony Orchestras; Royal Liverpool and Guildford Philharmonics, the Ulster Orchestra and the Orchestra National du Capitole de Toulouse. *Recordings include:* Album with the BBC Philharmonic, 1996. *Honours:* Charles Grove Conducting Fellowship, 1993. *Address:* c/o IMG Artists, Lovell House, 616 Chiswick High Road, London W4 5RX, England.

**FUKAI, Hirofumi;** Violist; b. 10 Feb. 1942, Saitama, Japan. *Education:* Studied with Ivan Galamian at Juilliard, at the Toho School, Tokyo, and the Basle Conservatory. *Career:* Soloist with the Berne Symphony and the Hamburg Philharmonic, 1970–87; NDR Symphony from 1988; Concert performances throughout Europe, notably in the premieres of works by Zimmermann, Rihm and Henze (Compases para preguntas ensimismadas); Professor at the Hamburg Musikhochschule from 1974. *Address:* Hochschule für Musik, Harvesthuderweg 12, 2000 Hamburg 12, Germany.

**FUKASAWA, Ryoko;** Pianist; b. 22 June 1938, Togane City, Chiba Prefecture, Japan; m. Tomoyuki Fukasawa, 2 Oct 1967, deceased. *Education:* Hochschule für Musik und darstellende Kunst, Vienna, 1956–59. *Career:* Debut: Recital in Tokyo with Tokyo Symphonia Orchestra, 1953; Recital in Vienna, 1959; Regular concerts with Tonkünstler Orchester conducted by E Merzendorfer, Musikverein, 1960; NHK Symphony Orchestra conducted by S Ozawa in Tokyo, 1963; Wiener Kammer Orchester conducted by A Quadri, 1965; NHK Symphony Orchestra, conducted by L von Matacic, 1966; Concert tours of Switzerland, Hungary and Japan, 1965–68; Concert tours in Japan, South America and Asia; Television and radio appearances in Japan and Europe; Numerous premieres of contemporary music in Japan and Europe. *Recordings:* Encore Album, 1988; Piano Recital, 1989; Beethoven Violin Sonata, 1991; Schubert and Beethoven, 1992; Trout Quintet with Wiener

Kammer Ensemble, 1992; Moments Musicaux, 1997; Mozart Recital, 1999. *Publications:* Diary for the Piano, 1955; Diary from Vienna, 1957; Schubert and Vienna, pocketbook on music, 1980; The Piano and Me, 1991. *Honours:* 1st Prize at the Student Music Competition in Japan, 1950; 1st Prize, Japan Music Competition organised by NHK and Mainich, Newspaper, 1953; Top Prize, Geneva International Music Competition, 1961. *Address:* 2-18-1 Chome, Tamagawa Denenchofu, Setagaya-ku, Tokyo 158-0085, Japan.

**FUKUHARA, Kan;** Japanese flautist; b. Nagoya. *Education:* Tokyo Fine Arts Univ., studied with Sanzaemon Takara. *Career:* specializes in traditional Japanese music, often playing the nokan, a double-barrelled flute. *Recording:* Splendour of the Shamisen 1999. *Address:* c/o Playasound Records, Sunset France Productions, 96 rue du Château, Boulogne 92100, France (office).

**FULGONI, Sarah;** Mezzo-Soprano; b. 1970, London, England. *Education:* Studied at the Royal Northern College of Music. *Career:* Has sung with the Welsh National Opera from 1994 as Prince Charming in Cendrillon and Beatrice in Beatrice and Benedict; Season 1995 as Dorabella with English National Opera, Strauss's Composer at Broomhill Opera, Celia in Haydn's Fedeltà Premiata at Garsington and Hyppolita in A Midsummer Night's Dream at the Ravenna Festival; Further engagements at the Harrogate and Schleswig-Holstein Festivals, at La Scala in Elektra and in Berlin in Mahler's Third Symphony; Sang Carmen with Welsh National Opera, 1997 and Ino in Semele for Flanders Opera, 1998; Engaged in Carmen at Santa Fe; Other roles include Charlotte in Werther (at Tel-Aviv), Monteverdi's Penelope (Geneva) and Leonora in La Favorita (Nice); Sang Berlioz's Béatrice for WNO and Netherlands Opera, 2001; Covent Garden debut as Federica in Luisa Miller, 2003. *Honours:* Frederic Cox Award, Curtis Gold Medal, Runner-up in 1993 Kathleen Ferrier Awards. *Address:* c/o IMG Artists, Lovell House, 616 Chiswick High Road, London, W4 5RX, England.

**FULKERSON, James Orville,** MM; composer and trombonist; b. 2 July 1945, Manville, Illinois, USA. *Education:* Illinois Wesleyan University, University of Illinois. *Career:* Fellow at the Center for Creative Performing Arts, State University of New York at Buffalo, 1969–72; Residencies at the Deutscher Akademischer Austauschdienst in Berlin, 1973, and the Victorian College of the Arts, Melbourne, 1977–79; From 1981 resident at Dartington College, South Devon. *Compositions include:* Guitar Concerto, 1972; To See a Thing Clearly for orchestra, 1972; Co-ordinative systems Nos 1–10, 1972–76; Orchestral Piece, 1974; Music for Brass Instruments Nos 1–6, 1975–78; Raucasity and the Cisco Kid or, I Skate in the Sun, theatre piece, 1978; Concerto for amplified cello and chamber orchestra, 1978; Vicarious Thrills for amplified trombone and pornographic film, 1979; Symphony, 1980; Force Fields and Spaces for trombone, tape and dancers, 1981; Cheap Imitations IV for soloist, tape and films, 1982; Put Your Foot Down Charlie for 3 dancers, speaker and ensemble, 1982; Rats Tale for 6 dancers, trombone and ensemble, 1983; Faust for tape, 1992; Antigone, tape, 1993; Eden, electronics, 1992; Wood-Stone-Desert for trumpet, live electronics and tape, 1996; Mixed-media works, television and film music; Various instrumental pieces under the titles Space Music, Patterns, Metamorphosis and Chamber Musics.

**FULLER, Albert;** Harpsichordist and Conductor; b. 21 July 1926, Washington DC, USA. *Education:* Studied organ with Paul Callaway at the national Cathedral in Washington; Peabody Conservatory; Georgetown, Johns Hopkins and Yale Universities (Ralph Kirkpatrick and Paul Hindemith); Studied French Baroque Keyboard Music in Paris. *Career:* Performer on the harpsichord in New York from 1957, Europe from 1959; Repertoire includes French music and the sonatas of Scarlatti; Professor of Harpsichord at the Juilliard School from 1964; President and Artistic Director of the Aston Magna Foundation (for the study of Baroque music), 1972–83; Summer Academies at Great Barrington, Massachusetts; Conductor of Rameau's Dardanus and Les Sauvages (Les Indes Galantes); Handel's Acis and Galatea and Xerxes, 1978, 1985; Assoc. Prof. Yale Univ., 1977–80; Founder, 1985, Helicon Foundation. *Publications include:* Edition of the harpsichord music of Gaspard Le Roux. *Address:* c/o Juilliard School of Music, Lincoln Plaza, NY 10023, USA.

**FULLER, David Randall,** AB, AM, PhD; American musicologist, organist and harpsichordist; b. 1 May 1927, Newton, MA. *Education:* Harvard Univ.; studied organ with E. Power Biggs, William Self and André Marchal, harpsichord with Albert Fuller. *Career:* Instructor, Robert Coll., Istanbul 1950–53; Asst Prof., Dartmouth Coll. 1954–57; Prof. of Music, State Univ. of New York, Buffalo 1963–98; John Knowles Paine Travelling Fellowship, Harvard 1960–61; Nat. Endowment for the Humanities Sr Fellowship 1976–77; CIES-Fulbright Research Award (Western European Regional Research Programme) 1985; mem. American Musicological Soc., American Guild of Organists, Soc. for Seventeenth-Century Music. *Recordings:* music by Armand-Louis Couperin (with William Christie), organ music of Widor, Reubke, Liszt, Stehle and others. *Publications:* A Catalogue of French Harpsichord Music 1699–1780 (with Bruce Gustafson) 1990, edns of keyboard works by Armand-Louis Couperin and Handel; contrib. numerous articles on French baroque music and historical performance to The New Grove Dictionary of Music and Musicians 2001, The New Harvard Dictionary of Music 1986, Early Music and others. *Honours:* Westrup Prize of the Music and Letters Trust 1997. *Address:* c/o State University of New York, Buffalo, NY 14260, USA.

**FULLER, Louisa;** Violinist; b. 1964, England. *Education:* Studied at the Royal Academy of Music with Emanuel Hurwitz; Further study with David Takeno. *Career:* Extensive tours of Europe as Principal second Violin of the

Kreisler String Orchestra, winner in 1984 of Jeunesses Musicales Competition in Belgrade; Co-founder and Leader of the Duke String Quartet, 1985–, performing throughout the United Kingdom, with tours of Germany, Italy, Austria and Baltic States and South Bank series, 1991 with Mozart's early quartets, made the soundtrack for Ingmar Bergman documentary, The Magic Lantern, for Channel 4 television, 1988, BBC debut feature, features for French television, 1990–91 playing Mozart, Mendelssohn, Britten and Tippett works, Brahms Clarinet Quintet for Dutch radio with Janet Hilton, Live Music Now series with concerts for disadvantaged people, The Duke Quartet invites... at the Derngate Northampton, 1991 with Duncan Prescott and Rohan O'Hora, Resident Quartet of the Rydale Festival in 1991, Residency at Trinity College, Oxford, with tours to Scotland and Northern Ireland and a concert at Queen Elizabeth Hall in 1991, appeared on Top of the Pops and Radio 1, Number 1 album in 1993 with, Little Angels, featured on BBC Def ll and in German television documentary, String parts for Lloyd Cole, Blur, the Cranberries and Pretenders, 1994–95 and extensive work with choreographers, Bunty Mathias, Union Dance and Rosas, 1994–95. Recordings include: With Duke Quartet: Quartets by Tippett, Shostakovich and Britten, Dvořák (American) Barber Quartet and Kevin Volans Works, 1995. Honours: Poulet Award from RAM; Top 3 Newcomers Cannes Classical Music Award, for Duke's American disc, 1994. Current Management: Scott Mitchell. Address: 81B Sarsfeld Road, London SW12 8HT, England.

**FURLANETTO, Ferruccio;** Singer (Bass); b. 16 May 1949, Pordenone, Sicily, Italy. Education: Studied with Campogaliani and Casagrande. Career: Sang at Vicenza in 1974 as Sparafucile in Rigoletto; Trieste, 1974, as Colline in La Bohème, with José Carreras and Katia Ricciarelli; Appearances at La Scala, Banquo, Turin, Leporello, and San Francisco as Alvise in La Gioconda; Metropolitan Opera, 1980; Salzburg Festival from 1986, as Philip II and Leporello, 1990, conducted by Riccardo Muti; San Diego and Covent Garden, 1988, as Mephistopheles and Leporello; In 1989 sang Mozart's Figaro at Geneva and Fernando in La Gazza Ladra at the Pesaro Festival; Season 1991–92 included Le nozze di Figaro in Paris, London, Salzburg and New York; Sang in Semiramide and Don Giovanni at the Metropolitan; Concert performances of Mozart's Da Ponte operas with the Chicago Symphony; Other roles include Philippe II, Don Giovanni, Leporello with Karajan, Figaro (Salzburg), Figaro, Bastille, Procida in Vespri Siciliani, Scala; Festival appearances 1996 at Salzburg (Don Giovanni) and Florence (Orestes); Philip II in Don Carlos for the Royal Opera at Edinburgh, 1998; Season 2000–01 as Don Giovanni at Salzburg, Gremin in Eugene Onegin at Florence, Leporello for the New York Met and Attila at Trieste; mem, Ambassador of Honour of the United Nations. Recordings include: Don Alfonso in Così fan tutte, conducted by James Levine; Roles in Mozart's Da Ponte operas, conducted by Daniel Barenboim; Videos of Don Carlos, Metropolitan and Salzburg, Rigoletto, Metropolitan, Vespri Siciliani at La Scala, and Don Giovanni at the Metropolitan and Salzburg; Also many films. Address: Musicaglotz, 11 Rue de Verrier, 75006 Paris, France.

**FURLANETTO, Giovanni;** Italian singer (bass-baritone); b. 1958. Career: sang in Italian opera houses from 1982; Trieste, 1989, in Donizetti's Linda di Chamounix, Florence, 1989, as Mozart's Figaro; Philadelphia Opera as Wurm in Luisa Miller; Season 1990 as Leporello at Trieste and Ircano in Rossini's Ricciardo e Zoraide at Pesaro; Salzburg Festival, 1995, as Masetto; Season 1995–96 as Escamillo at Nice and Wurm in Santiago; Mozart's Figaro at San Francisco, 1997; Season 1998 as Nonancourt in Rota's Italian Straw Hat, at La Scala; Sang Mozart's Figaro at Hamburg and Leporello in Baltimore, 2000. Current Management: Atelier Musicale S.r.l., via Caselle 76, 40068 San Lazzaro di Savena (Bo), Italy. Telephone: (051) 199844 44. Fax: (051) 199844 20. E-mail: info@ateliermusicale.it. Website: www.ateliermusicale.it. E-mail: giovannifurlanetto@giovannifurlanetto.com. Website: www .giovannifurlanetto.com.

**FURMANSKY, Abbie;** Singer (Soprano); b. 1969, USA. Education: Juilliard School, New York; Santa Fe Opera School. Career: New York City Opera from 1993, as Micaela, Musetta, Janáček's Fox, and Lisette in La Rondine; Engagements with Canadian Opera, at Frankfurt, Washington (Esmerelda in The Bartered Bride) and New Jersey; Deutsche Oper Berlin from 1995, as Pamina, Zerlina, Sophie in Werther, Gretel, and Junge Mädchen in Schoenberg's Moses and Aron (season 1999–2000). Concerts include Elijah, Haydn's Lord Nelson Mass, Mahler's 4th Symphony, Beethoven's Missa Solemnis and Mozart's Requiem and Vespers; Schoenberg's 2nd Quartet and Rossini's Petite Messe. Recordings include: Ines in La Favorite by Donizetti. Honours: Prizewinner, 1999 Francesco Vinas Competition, Barcelona. Address: c/o Theateragentur Dr G. Hilbert, Maximilianstrasse 22, 80539 Munich, Germany.

**FURRER-MÜNCH, Franz;** Composer; b. 2 March 1924, Winterthur, Switzerland; m. Cécile Brosy. Education: First artistic training, Zürich and Basel; studied Flute, Piano, Harmony, Counterpoint and Composition, Basel Konservatorium; Scientific studies, ETH, Zürich; Musicology with K von Fischer and P Müller, Zürich Univ.; Study visits: Federal Repub. of Germany including Studio für elektronische Musik, Freiburg, and USA including State Univ. of New York at Stony Brook for research work with Prof. G W Stroke at the Electro-optical Sciences Center and Univ. of Bennington, Vermont. Compositions include: Intarsia, for cello solo, 1972; Silben for organ, 1977; Von Dort nach Dort for four percussion, piano, tape and film, 1981–82; L'Oiseau en papier–Vier Versuche, Ikarus zu begreifen for solo cello, string orchestra and piano, 1984–85; Souvenir mis en scène for two cellos, 1988–89; Trio for violin,

cello and piano, 1991–92; Skizzenbuch for chamber ensemble, 1992–93;... hier auf dieser Strasse, von der sie sagen, dass sie schön sei, for voice, flute, cello and four timpani, 1993; Erwarten im Flachland, Nebengesänge für Violine solo, 1994; Wort Jahr Stunde for alto flute in G, cello and piano, 1995–96; adagio, adagio cantabile for solo cello, for P. Sacher, 1997/98; Gesänge vom schwebenden Turm for flute, oboe, violin and cello, for the 60th birthday of Heinz Holliger, 1999; Von weit/schreiben ins Meer, for chamber- and percussion-ensemble and voice, 1999–2000; ans ungereimte verdingt, for tenor sax solo, 2000; eng/weit/lento I-XII, 2001 for bass flute, two grancassa and some percussion instruments; Symphonische Blätter for string orchestra, 2002; Auftrags werk der schweizer kulturstiftung pro Helvetia und Präsid. Dep. Stadt Zurich; Freundliche Landschaft, for solo viola 2003, Streichtrio 2003, Mouvement, for four kettledrums 2004, Senza misura, se piace for two flutes 2004, Legenden/Melismen 2004. Recordings include: Dialogue for oboe and clarinet, 1972; Timbral Variations, 1973; Images sans cadres, for voice and clarinet quartet, 1982, 1990; Souvenir mis en scène, for 2 cellos, Thomas and Patrick Demenga, 1988–89; Skizzenbuch for ensemble, 1993; Erwarten in Flachland for violin, 1994; Canti Velati for flute and cello, 1998; Portrait-CD Franz Furrer-Münch, 1999; Musikszene Schweiz/ Grammont Portrait. Publications: Zur Semiotik graphischer Notation 1978; Instrumentation in der Musik des 20. Jahrhunderts 1985; Harmonik in der Musik des 20. Jahrhunderts 1996. Honours: Kunstpreis Zollikon 2002. Address: Hohfurristrasse 4, 8172 Niderglatt, Switzerland.

**FÜRST, Janos Kalman;** British orchestral conductor; b. 8 Aug. 1935, Budapest, Hungary; s. of Lajos Fürst and Borbala Spitz; m. 1st Antoinette Reynolds 1962 (divorced 1977); two s.; m. 2nd Ingeborg Nordenfelt. Education: Franz Liszt Acad. of Music, Budapest and Brussels Conservatory. Career: Dir Irish Chamber Orchestra 1963–66; Resident Conductor Ulster Orchestra 1967–71; Chief Conductor Malmö Symphony Orchestra 1974–78; Music Dir Marseilles Opera 1981–; Music Dir Aalborg Symphony Orchestra 1980–83; Dir Marseilles Philharmonic Orchestra 1985–; fmr Chief Conductor Irish Radio and TV Symphony Orchestra 1987. Honours: Swedish Gramophone Prize 1980. Address: c/o EMI Classics, 30 Gloucester Place, London, W1A 1ES, England (office).

**FUSSELL, Charles C(lement);** Composer, Conductor and Teacher; b. 14 Feb. 1938, Winston-Salem, North Carolina, USA. Education: Piano with Clemens Sandresky, Winston-Salem; BM, Composition, 1960, with Thomas Canning, Wayne Barlow and Bernard Rogers; Piano with José Echaniz; Conducting with Herman Genhart, Eastman School of Music, Rochester, New York; Pupil of Boris Blacher, Berlin Hochschule für Musik, 1962; MM, Eastman School, 1964. Career: Teacher, Theory, Composition, University of Massachusetts, 1966, Founder-Director of its Group for New Music, 1974, later renamed Pro Musica Moderna; Teacher, Composition, North Carolina School of the Arts, Winston-Salem, 1976–77; Boston University, 1981; Conductor, Longy School Chamber Orchestra, Cambridge, Massachusetts, 1981–82; Artistic Director, New Music Harvet/Boston, Boston's first city-wide contemporary music festival, 1989. Compositions: Orchestral: Symphony No. 1, 1963, No. 2, 1964–67, No. 3, Landscapes, 1978–81; 3 Processionals, 1972–73; Northern Lights, chamber orchestra, 1977–79; 4 Fairy Tales, 1980–81; Dance Suite, 5 players, 1963; Ballades, cello and piano, 1968, revised, 1976; Greenwood Sketches: Music for String Quartet, 1976; Free-fall, 7 players, 1988; Julian, drama, 1969–71; Voyages, soprano, tenor, women's chorus, piano, winds, recorded speaker, 1970; Eurydice, soprano and chamber ensemble, 1973–75; Resume, song cycle, soprano and 3 instruments, 1975–76; Cymbeline, drama, soprano, tenor, narrator, chamber ensemble, 1984; The Gift, soprano and chorus, 1986; 5 Goethe Lieder, soprano or tenor and piano, 1987, for soprano or tenor and orchestra, 1991; A Song of Return, chorus and orchestra, 1989; Wilde, symphony No. 4, baritone and orchestra; Last Trombones, 5 percussionists, 2 pianos, 6 trombones, 1990; Symphony No. 5, for large orchestra, 1994–95; Night Song, for piano solo, 1995; Specimen Days, a cantata, for baritone solo, chorus and orchestra, 1993–94; Being Music (Whitman) for baritone solo and string quartet, 1993; Venture, four songs for baritone and piano, 2001; Right River for cello solo and string orchestra, 2001; Infinite Fraternity for baritone solo, chorus, flute and viola, 2002; High Bridge, a choral symphony, 2003–04. Recordings: Goethe Lieder; Specimen Days; Being Music; Symphony No. 5; The Astronaut's Tale, chamber opera. Honours: Ford, Fulbright, Copland Grants and commissions. Address: ASCAP, ASCAP House, 1 Lincoln Plaza, New York, NY 10023, USA.

**FUSSELL, Louis;** British music teacher and composer; b. 8 Oct. 1925, Manchester. Education: English and German studies; Trinity College of Music, London; Fellowship, 1954. Career: Debut: Bamberg, 14 July 1998; Teacher, stringed instruments, various schools; mem, Incorporated Society of Musicians, 1974–84. Compositions include: Bamberg Festive Overture, 1998; Overture for the Year 2000, 2000; Symphony No. 1, 2001; Symphony No. 2, 2001; Symphonies No 3 and No 4, 2002–03; overtures, concerto for trumpet and orchestra, chamber music; concerto for flute and orchestra; Symphony No 5, Romanian. Recordings include: Bamberg Festliche Ouverture, 1998; Symphonies 1, 2, 3, 4, 5 and 6 2000–04), 4 overtures, 3 string quartets, 2 concertos. Address: 35 Rutland Road, Bedford, MK40 1DG, England. Telephone: (1234) 307520 (home).

**FUTRAL, Elizabeth;** Singer (Soprano); b. 1968, Louisville, USA. Education: Studied at the Opera Center of Chicago Opera. Career: Debut: New York City Opera, 1992, as Gilda; Sang Bella in The Midsummer Marriage, and Lakmé at the City Opera; Season 1995–96 as Gounod's Juliette at Miami, Valencienne in The Merry Widow at the City Opera and Lucia di Lammermoor at Florence; Rossini's Matilde di Shabran at Pesaro, Musetta at Covent Garden and Catherine in Meyerbeer's Etoile du Nord, at Wexford, 1996; Other roles include Tytania in A Midsummer Night's Dream; Season 1999 with Gounod's Juliette at Chicago, Gilda at Pittsburgh and Brussels, Susanna at Munich and Strauss's Zerbinetta at Santa Fe; Season 2000–01 as Donizetti's Adina for Chicago Opera, Gilda at Santa Fe, Nannetta in Munich and Baby Doe in the Opera by Douglas Moore for the New York City Opera; Lucia di Lammermoor at New Orleans. *Address:* c/o IMG Artists, Lovell House, 616 Chiswick High Road, London W4 5RX, England.

# G

**GABOS, Gábor;** Pianist; b. 4 Jan. 1930, Budapest, Hungary; m. Ingeborg Sandor, 20 Oct 1951, 1 s., 1 d. *Education:* Performer's Diploma, Ferenc Liszt Academy of Music, Budapest. *Career:* Debut: Budapest, 1952; Festival Hall, London; Musikverein, Vienna; Châtelet, Paris; Palais des Beaux-Arts, Brussels; Further appearances in Italy, Russia, Japan, Germany, Sweden, Greece, Switzerland, Peru, South America and throughout Europe. *Recordings:* Various. *Honours:* Liszt Ferenc Award of Hungarian Government, 1959; Lauréat du Concours International Reine Elisabeth, Brussels, 1960; 1st Prize, International Liszt-Bartók Competition, 1961; Top Award for the Japan Record Academy, 1968; Merited Artist of the Hungarian People's Republic, 1976. *Current Management:* Interkoncert, Budapest, Hungary. *Address:* Nyul utca 10, 1026 Budapest, Hungary.

**GADD, Stephen;** Singer (Baritone); b. 18 Sept. 1964, Berkshire, England. *Education:* St John's College, Cambridge; Royal Northern College of Music. *Career:* Ping in Turandot at Covent Garden; Yeletsky in Queen of Spades for Scottish Opera; Count in Marriage of Figaro for Scottish Opera; Marcello (La Bohème), Peking Festival; Escamillo (Carmen) for BBC; Other appearances at Geneva Opera, Châtelet (Paris), Opéra Comique (Paris), New Israeli Opera and Opéra du Rhin; Concert repertoire includes: Britten, War Requiem; Walton, Belshazzar's Feast; Mendelssohn, Elijah. *Recordings include:* Mozart's Coronation Mass; Purcell's Dioclesian for DGG with Trevor Pinnock and the English Concert; La Bohème and Madama Butterfly (excerpts) with RPO; Hamish Maccun Works. *Honours:* Kathleen Ferrier Memorial Scholarship.

**GADDES, Richard;** Opera Administrator; b. 23 May 1942, Wallsend, England. *Education:* Studied at Trinity College of Music, London. *Career:* Co-founded Wigmore Hall Lunchtime Concerts, 1965; Emigrated to USA, 1969; Artistic Administrator of Santa Fe Opera, 1969–76, Gen. Dir, 2000–; Founded Opera Theater of St Louis, 1976, Gen. Dir, 1976–85; Production of Britten's Albert Herring for WNET and BBC television, 1978; Visited Edinburgh with the St Louis Company in 1983, with Fennimore and Gerda by Delius and The Postman Always Rings Twice by Stephen Paulus, the first American opera to be performed at the Edinburgh International Festival; American premiere of Saariaho's L'Amour de loin, 2002; world premiere of Sheng's Madame Mao, 2003; mem, Board of Directors, Pulitzer Foundation for the Arts; William Matheus Sullivan Foundation. *Honours:* Honorary Doctor of Musical Arts, St Louis Conservatory, 1983; Honorary DFA, University of Missouri, St Louis, 1984; Honorary DA, Webster University, 1986. *Address:* Santa Fe Opera, PO Box 2408, Santa Fe, NM 97504-2408, USA.

**GADENSTÄTTER, Clemens;** Austrian composer, conductor and flautist; b. 26 July 1966, Zell am See. *Education:* Universität für Musik und darstellende Kunst, Vienna with Erich Urbanner, Musikhochschule Stuttgart with Helmut Lachenmann. *Career:* founder (with Florian Müller), Ensemble Neue Musik, Vienna 1990; Lecturer, Darmstadt Ferienkurse für Neue Musik 1994; teacher, Universität für Musik und darstellende Kunst, Vienna 1995–, and in Graz 1998–; Ed. bi-annual journal, Ton 1995–2000. *Compositions include:* Trio 1990, Musik für Orchesterensembles 1990–94, Versprachlichung; dreaming of a land an arm's length away – die arie des vogelnestaushebers (with film installation by Joseph Santarromana) 1992–94 (version without film entitled Versprachlichung) variationen und alte themen 1996, Ballade L 1997, Polyskopie 2000–01, Wir müssen einzelne irgendwann bitten, alle jetzt aufzupassen (electroacoustic) 2001, Comic sense 2002–03. *Recordings:* Polyskopie, Streichtrio II, Variationen und alte themen, Comic sense, Versprachlichung, schniTt, Musik für Orchesterensembles. *Publications:* tag day. ein schreibspiel (with Lisa Spalt) 2000; contrib. to Stellwerk I 2002. *Honours:* winner Forum junge Komponisten competition, WDR 1992, Publicity-Preis of the SKE-Fond 1997, Vienna Förderungspreis 1997, first prize 2003. *Address:* 2. Bez, Gr. Sperl-G. 32-34, 1020 Vienna, Austria. *E-mail:* mailport@aon.at.

**GAEDE, Daniel;** violinist; b. 25 April 1966, Hamburg, Germany; m. Xuesu Liu 1992. *Education:* Studienstiftung des Deutschen Volkes and Abbado European Musicians Trust, studied with Thomas Brandis in Berlin, Max Rostal in Switzerland, Josef Gingold in the USA. *Career:* regular performances as soloist and chamber musician in Europe, Asia, N and S America; soloist with Philharmonia Orchestra, London, City of London Sinfonia, Vienna Philharmonic Orchestra; leader, Vienna Philharmonic Orchestra 1994–. *Honours:* 1st Prize, German National Competition, Jugend musiziert, 1983; Prizewinner, Carl Flesch Competition, London and Artist International Competition, New York; Eduard Söring Prize, 1987; Joseph Joachim Prize, 1989. *Address:* Mariahilferstrasse 49-1-14, 1060 Vienna, Austria.

**GAETA, Luis;** Singer (Baritone); b. 1953, Buenos Aires, Argentina. *Education:* Studied in Buenos Aires and with Tito Gobbi. *Career:* Many appearances at the Teatro Colón, Buenos Aires, notably as Verdi's Rigoletto, Posa (1996) and Germont, Marcello, Jack Rance (La Fanciulla del West), Valentin and Rossini's Figaro; Prus in The Makropulos Case, Mozart's Count and the Villains in Les Contes d'Hoffmann; Premieres of works by local composers and guest appearances throughout South America; Season 1998 as Malatesta in Don Pasquale; Many concert engagements; Season 2000 as Puccini's Sharpless at Buenos Aires and Donizetti's Enrico at Córdoba. *Address:* Teatro Colón, Buenos Aires, Argentina.

**GAGE, Irwin;** Pianist; b. 4 Sept. 1939, Cleveland, Ohio, USA. *Education:* Studied with Eugene Bossart at the University of Michigan; Yale University with Ward Davenny; Vienna Akademie with Erik Werba, Klaus Vokurka and Hilde Langer-Rühl. *Career:* Accompanist to leading singers, including Hermann Prey, Dietrich Fischer-Dieskau, Christa Ludwig, Gundula Janowitz, Jessye Norman, Elly Ameling, Lucia Popp, Brigitte Fassbaender, Tom Krause, Arleen Auger, Anna Reynolds, René Kollo, Peter Schreier and Edita Gruberova plus younger singers François Le Roux, Cheryl Studer, Thomas Hampson, Siegfried Lorenz and Francisco Araiza; Festival appearances at every major festival in the world; Professor at the Zürich Conservatory and master classes throughout the world; Anniversary concerts of Brahms, Ravel, Schubert and Mendelssohn, 1997. *Recordings:* Over 50 recordings, some of which have won prizes such as the Gramophone Award (3 times), Grand Prix du Disque, Deutsche Schallplatten Preis (5 times), Edison Prize, recording prizes from Spain, Belgium, Finland and Japan and the Ovation-MUMM Awards in USA. *Address:* Kunstler Sekretarat am Gasteig, Rosenheimer Strasse 52, 81669 Munich, Germany.

**GAGNE, Marc;** Professor and Composer; b. 16 Dec. 1939, Saint Joseph de Beauce, Quebec, Canada; m. Monique Poulin, 27 Dec 1969, 1 s., 2 d. *Education:* Doctor of Letters, University Laval, Quebec, 1970; 3 years at School of Music, University Laval with Jacques Hétu, José Evangélista and Roger Matton. *Career:* Symphonie de chants paysans created at Moncton Choralies Internationals, 1979; His Symphonie-itineraire was principal work by Quebec Symphony Orchestra at Festival marking 375th anniversary of the discovery of Canada; L'opéra Menaud was given on television in the form of a scenic Cantata, May 1992. *Compositions:* Les Chansons de la tourelle, in the folklore mode, 1975; Jeu a deux faces, Piano Sonata No. 1; Ceremonial d'orgue pour la fete du Tres Saint-Sacrement, 1976; Deux chorals pour la temps de la Passion for organ, 1976; Les Jeunes Filles a marier, suite for a capella choir on folklore themes, 1977; Short Mass, Du Peuple de Dieu, 1981; Messe, Des enfants de Dieu, 1993; Sonate du roi Renaud for alto saxophone and piano, 1983; Vari-anes et moulin-ations for solo marimba, 1983; Symphonie-itineraire, 1983–84; Menaud, opera in 3 acts and a prologue, 1984–86; Évangéline et Gabriel, opera in 2 acts, 1987–90; Le Père Noël, la sorcière et l'enfant, conte de Noël for chamber orchestra, choir and soloists, 1993; Les Verdi (opera in 3 acts), 1999; Trio with piano No. 1 (Le rossignol y chante), 1999; Trio with piano No. 2 (Au bois du rossignolet), 1999; Horn Sonata (The Winter), 1999. *Address:* 677 Avenue du Chateau, Sainte-Foy, QC G1X 3N8, Canada.

**GAGNON, Alain;** Composer; b. 1938, Trois-Pistoles, Québec, Canada. *Education:* Ecole de Musique, Laval University; Graduate degree in Composition studying under Jeanne Landry, Jocelyne Binet and Roger Matton; Studied with Henri Dutilleux, Ecole Normale de Musique, Paris; Studied with Olivier Alain, Ecole César-Franck, Paris; Studied composition and orchestration with André-François Maresconi, Geneva Conservatory; Initiated into electro-acoustic music at University of Utrecht. *Career:* His works have been performed in France, Switzerland, Germany, Latin America and Canada and several have been recorded or published; Sat on several juries including Competition for Young Composers, 1980, with Murray Schafer, Barbara Pentland and Toru Takemitsu; Teacher, Techniques of Composition, Ecole de Musique, Laval University, 1967–; Director of Composition Programme, Laval University, 1977–. *Compositions include:* Works for orchestra, chamber music, string quartets and piano; Trio pour flûte, violon et violoncello; Septuor; Les oies sauvages; Prélude pour orchestra, 1969; Ballet score, 1983. *Honours:* Received Prix d'Europe, 1961; Association de musique actuelle de Québec honoured him by performing 3 of his works including Incandescence, 1982.

**GAHL, Dankwart (Arnold);** Cellist and Professor; b. 18 Dec. 1939, Korbach, Germany; m. Irmgard Schuster (deceased 1996), 23 May 1964, 1 s., 1 d. *Education:* Private cello and viola da gamba instruction (with Johannes Koch/ Kassell); Summer class with Casals, 1959; Entry to the Akademie für Musik und darstellende Kunst, Vienna, Oct 1959; Student of Wilfried Boetticher; Theory with Erwin Ratz; Pedagogics Diploma, 1963; Final Concert Diploma with 1st class honours. *Career:* Foundation member of the Vienna Soloists, 1959, touring with this formation all over the world, participating in many famous festivals, for example playing with Casals at Prades Festival; Originating from this same ensemble is the Alban Berg Quartet and the Austrian String Quartet, of which he has been a member since 1972; Quartet in residence at Mozarteum, Salzburg, 1972–, holder of the cello class, 1972–; Foundation member of the piano trio Trio Amade, Salzburg, 1979; Ordinary Professor at the Hochschule, 1984–; Concerts in the USA and several tours to the Far East; Guest classes in South Korea on many occasions; Has given classes with the Quartet at Salzburg Summer Academy, Mozarteum for many years; Invited jurist of international chamber music competitions on many occasions; mem, Vienna Symphony Orchestra. *Honours:* Scholarship, Studienstiftung des Deutschen Volkes. *Address:* Carl Storch-Strasse 10, Salzburg, Austria.

**GÄHMLICH, Wilfried;** Singer (Tenor); b. 14 July 1939, Halle, Germany. *Education:* Studied at the Musikhochschule Freiburg and with Alfred Pfeifle in Stuttgart. *Career:* Debut: Giessen, 1968, as Pedrillo in Die Entführung; Sang at Wuppertal, 1973, in the premiere of Blacher's Yvonne, Prinzessen von Burgund; Appearances in Düsseldorf, Zürich, Vienna, Stuttgart, Wiesbaden and London; Salzburg, 1983, in Dantons Tod by Von Einem; Other roles include Florestan, the Drum Major in Wozzeck, Tamino, Andrea Chénier, Don José and Max in Der Freischütz; Bregenz Festival, 1987–88, in Les Contes d' Hoffmann; Sang Pedrillo in Die Entführung at the Theater an der Wien, Vienna, 1989; The Sailor in Krenek's Orpheus und Eurydike for the Austrian Radio; Salzburg Festival, 1992, as The Hunchback in Die Frau ohne Schatten; Valzacchi in Der Rosenkavalier at the Opéra Bastille; Sang in the premiere of K... by Philippe Manouri at the Opéra Bastille, 2001. *Recordings:* Dantons Tod; Die Entführung; Video of Elektra conducted by Abbado (as the Young Servant). *Address:* c/o Staatsoper, Ringstrasse, Vienna, Austria.

**GAJEWSKI, Jaromir (Zbigniew);** Conductor, Musician and Composer; b. 2 April 1961, Pryzyce, Poland. *Education:* MA, Academy of Music, Poznan. *Career:* Debut: Poznan, 1986; Teacher of Conducting, Composition and Harmony, 1988–; Founder of Academy Orchestra, 1991–; mem, Polish Composers' Society; Polish Society for Contemporary Music. *Compositions:* Altana–Songs for voice and piano, 1986; 2 String Quartets, 1986, 1988; Penetration for symphony orchestra, 1989; From Dawn to Dusk for orchestra, 1989; In Cage, opera, 1990; Overture, 1993; 3rd string quartet, 1995; Requiem Symphony, 1997; Fantasy, 1998; Why Has Thou Forsaken Me?, 1999. *Recordings:* Altana–Songs; 2 String Quartets. *Address:* ul Boguslawa 24/3, 79-200 Pyrzyce, Poland.

**GAL, Zahava;** singer (mezzo-soprano); b. 29 Aug. 1948, Haifa, Israel. *Education:* Rubin Acad., Jerusalem, Juilliard School with Jennie Tourel and Daniel Fero. *Career:* Feodor in Boris Godunov, La Scala, 1979; Salzburg Easter Festival production of Parsifal, 1980; Angelina in La Cenerentola, Netherlands Opera, Amsterdam, 1980; Feodor in Boris Godunov, Carmen, Paris Opéra, 1981; Sang Carmen in Peter Brook's Carmen, Hamburg, Zürich; Rosina in Barber of Seville, Washington DC (2 seasons), Glyndebourne Festival Opera, at Santiago de Chile, Scottish Opera in Lyon, Avignon, Nantes, Dario Fo's Amsterdam production, Frankfurt Opera (2 seasons); Isolier in Le Comte Ory, Pesaro, Italy; Cherubino in Marriage of Figaro at Monte Carlo, Vienna Staatsoper and Santa Fe Festival; Ariodante in Nancy, Paris, Lausanne, Dejanira in Hercules, title role in Teseo, Covent Garden, Siena, Athens Summer Festival, Handel Year, 1985; Nicklausse, Rosina, Carmen with New Israeli Opera, 1988–89; Rinaldo, Paris; Elmira in Floridante with Tafel Baroque Orchestra in Toronto, San Francisco; Zerlina in Don Giovanni, Nancy; Concert repertoire includes Schéhérazade, L'Enfant et les Sortilèges (Ravel), Songs of a Wayfarer, 3rd and 4th Symphonies (Mahler), Romeo and Juliet (Berlioz), Requiem, C-minor Mass (Mozart), Bruckner's Te Deum, Beethoven's 9th, Pergolesi's Stabat Mater; Has sung with Mehta and Israel Philharmonic, Barenboim and New York Philharmonic, Abbado with La Scala Orchestra and Chicago Symphony, Armin Jordan and Orchestre de la Suisse Romande, Mata with Pittsburgh and Dallas Symphonies; Television appearances in Switzerland, Italy, France, Israel. *Recordings include:* Mussorgsky's choral works with Abbado; Amaltea in Moses in Egypt; L'Incoronazione di Poppea; Duet selection; Donizetti cantata. *Honours:* Grand Prix, 1st Prize, Mélodie Française Concours International de Chant, Paris; Top Prize, Lieder, Munich International Competition; 1st Place, Kathleen Ferrier Young Artists Award. *Current Management:* Robert Lombardo Associates, Suite 6F, 61 W 62nd Street, New York, NY 10023, USA. *Telephone:* (212) 586-4453. *Fax:* (212) 581-5771. *Website:* www .rlombardo.com.

**GAL, Zoltan;** Violist; b. 1960, Hungary. *Education:* Studied at the Franz Liszt Academy, Budapest, and with Sandor Devich, György Kurtág and András Mihaly. *Career:* Member of the Keller String Quartet from 1986, debut concert at Budapest, Mar 1987; Played Beethoven's Grosse Fuge and Schubert's Death and the Maiden Quartet at Interforum 87; Series of concerts in Budapest with Zoltán Kocsis and Deszo Ranki (piano) and Kalman Berkes (clarinet); Further appearances in Nuremberg, at the Chamber Music Festival La Baule and tours of Bulgaria, Austria, Switzerland, Italy (Ateforum 88, Ferrara), Belgium and Ireland; Concerts for Hungarian Radio and Television. *Recordings:* Albums (from 1989). *Honours:* 2nd Prize, Evian International String Quartet Competition, May 1988. *Address:* c/o SullivSweet, 28 Albion Street, London, W2 2AX, England.

**GALANTE, Inessa;** Singer (Soprano); b. 1959, Riga, Latvia. *Education:* Studied at the Riga conservatory. *Career:* Sang at the Riva National Opera, 1982–91, notably as Gilda, Adina, L'Esilir d'Amore, Rosina, Micaela, Rimsky's Snow Maiden, Marguerite, Lucia di Lammermoor and Olympia in Les Contes d'Hoffmann; Guest appearances in St Petersburg as Lucia and Marguerite; Mannheim Opera from 1991 as Pamina, Nedda, Freia in Das Rheingold, Mimi, and Gluck's Euridice; Sang Micaela at Frankfurt, 1993 and Donna Elvira at Düsseldorf, 1996; Violetta at Nancy, 1998; Sang Mimi for Miami Opera, 1999; Concert repertory in Russia, Germany and North America includes Requiems by Brahms, Faure, Verdi and Mozart; Beethoven Ninth. *Address:* c/o Opera de Nancy, 1 Rue St Catherine, 54000 Nancy, France.

**GALÁS, Diamanda;** American singer and poet; b. San Diego, CA. *Education:* Univ. of Calif. *Career:* played in her father's band at mil. bases and bars from age of 13; first live performance, Festival d'Avignon, France 1979; performed lead in opera Un Jour Comme un Autre, Avignon 1980; performed at Theatre Gerard Philippe Saint-Denis; solo tour at European festivals including Donaueschingen, Inventionen, Biennale de Paris, Musica Oggi, Festivale de la Voce; performed at Int. AIDS Conf., San Francisco 1990, Olympic Festival, Barcelona, Spain 1990, Helsinki Festival, Festival delle Colline, Italy, Serious Fun Festival, Lincoln Center, USA 1993, Royal Festival Hall (RFH), London, UK 1996, Defixiones, London 1999, La Serpenta Canta, RFH, London 2001. *Recordings include:* The Litanies of Satan 1982, Panoptikon, The Masque of the Red Death (triptych) 1989, Plague Mass (trilogy), Wild Women with Steak Knives, Tragouthia apo to Aima Exon Fonos (Song from the Blood of those Murdered), Vena Cava 1992, The Divine Punishment, Saint of the Pit, There are No More Tickets to the Funeral, The Singer, Insekta 1993, The Sporting Life 1994, Schrei X Live/Schrei 27 1996. *Publications include:* The Shit of God 1996. *Address:* c/o Asphodel Records, 763 Brennan Street, San Francisco, CA 94103, USA. *E-mail:* garth@diamandagalas.com (office). *Website:* www .diamandagalas.com (office).

**GALE, Elizabeth;** Singer (Soprano); b. 8 Nov. 1948, Sheffield, Yorkshire, England. *Education:* Studied at the Guildhall School of Music, London, with Winifred Radford. *Career:* Debut: With the English Opera Group, in Purcell's King Arthur; Appeared in The Turn of the Screw with the EOG; Scottish Opera (Glasgow) as the Queen of Shemakha in The Golden Cockerel and Despina and Tytania; Welsh National Opera (Cardiff) as Blondchen in Die Entführung; Glyndebourne, 1973–86, as Barbarina, Papagena, Susanna, Nannetta, Zerlina, Marzelline in Fidelio, Drusilla in L'Incoronazione di Poppea, Titania (A Midsummer Night's Dream, 1984) and Miss Wordsworth (Albert Herring, 1985) also Amor in Orfeo; Marzelline at the Paris Opéra and the Vienna Staatsoper; Covent Garden as Zerlina and as Adele in Die Fledermaus, also as Woodbird (Siegfried) and Xenia (Godunov); Zürich Opera as Susanna, Ilia (Idomeneo), Ismene (Mitridate), Nannetta, Drusilla and Marzelline; Frankfurt, 1980, in Castor et Pollux by Rameau also as Aennchen (Freischütz) and Marzelline; Guest appearances in Amsterdam, Geneva and Cologne; Sang at San Diego, in La Voix Humaine by Poulenc, 1986, US debut; Appeared with Chelsea Opera Group at the Queen Elizabeth Hall, 1989, as Massenet's Thais; Glyndebourne Festival, 1990, as Miss Wordsworth, repeated at Los Angeles, 1992; Sang in Owen Wingrave at Glyndebourne, 1997; Season 1998 as Alice Ford at Garsington and Despina for Glyndebourne Touring Opera; Sang Susanna, Tytania and Oscar in Ballo at Hong Kong Festival; Despina in Los Angeles and Donna Elvira in Belfast; Sang Despina at Glyndebourne, 2000; Many concert engagements, in particular in works by Handel; Guest, Opera Houses, Vienna and Paris. *Recordings include:* Le nozze di Figaro and Don Giovanni; Amor in Orfeo ed Euridice; Israel in Egypt; Handel's Messiah, Saul, and Jephtha conducted by Harnoncourt; Dido and Aeneas; Semele in Die Liebe der Danaë, in a BBC recording of Strauss's opera; Recital of Bliss Songs with Nash Ensemble. *Honours:* John Christie Award, Glyndebourne, 1973. *Address:* c/o Musichall, Vicarage Way, Ringmer, East Sussex, BN8 5 LA, England.

**GALIMIR, Felix;** Violinist; b. 20 May 1910, Vienna, Austria; m. Suzanne Hirsch, 18 Feb 1945. *Education:* Pupil of Adolf Bak, Vienna Conservatory, Diploma, 1928; Carl Flesch, Berlin and Baden-Baden, 1929–30. *Career:* Founder, Galimir String Quartet, Vienna, 1929; US debut, Town Hall, New York, 1938; Founder, reconstituted Galimir String Quartet, New York, 1938; First Violinist, NBC Symphony Orchestra, New York, 1939–54; Concertmaster, Symphony of the Air, New York, 1954–56; Teacher-Performer, Marlboro (VT Festival and Music School, 1954–); Teacher, Juilliard School of Music, New York, 1962; Head, Chamber Music Department, Curtis Institute of Music, Philadelphia, 1972–; Teacher, Mannes College of Music, New York, 1977–. *Recordings:* Various. *Honours:* Grand Prix du Disque, 1937, 1938; Honorary D.Mus, New School of Music, Philadelphia, 1984 and Mannes College of Music, 1987. *Address:* 225 East 74th Street, New York, NY 10021, USA.

**GALINDO, Juan;** singer (baritone); b. 1947, San Sebastian, Spain. *Education:* San Sebastian Conservatory, La Scala Milan with Giuseppe di Stefano. *Career:* debut in Barcelona 1973, as Enrico in Lucia di Lammermoor, with Pavarotti; has sung widely in Italy as Carlos in Forza del Destino, Rigoletto, Macbeth and Iago; guest appearances in Liège, Berne, Zürich, Graz, Copenhagen and Munich, notably as Marcel in Puccini's Il Tabarro; season 1984–85 as Iago and Nabbucco at St Gallen, Rigoletto at Zürich.

**GALL, Hugues R.;** French opera house director; b. 18 March 1940, Honfleur; s. of Max Gall and Geneviève Carel. *Education:* Inst. des Sciences Politiques, Sorbonne. *Career:* fmr official, Ministries of Agric., Educ. and Culture; Sec.-Gen. Réunion des Théâtres Lyriques 1969–73; Deputy Dir-Gen. Paris Opéra 1973–80; Dir-Gen. Grand Theatre, Geneva 1980–94; Dir-Gen. Paris Opéra 1995–2004; elected mem. Acad. des Beaux-Arts, Inst. de France 2002. *Honours:* Prix Montaigne 1996, Prix Grand Siècle-Laurent Perrier 1999; Officier Légion d'honneur, Ordre nat. du Mérite, des Palmes académiques, Chevalier du Mérite agricole, Commdr des Arts et des Lettres.

**GALL, Jeffrey Charles,** BA, MPhil; American singer (countertenor); b. 19 Sept. 1950, Cleveland, OH; m. Karen Rosenberg 1978. *Education:* Princeton University, Yale University with Blake Stern, Arthur Burrows. *Career:* member, Waverly Consort, 1974–78; Debuts: Brooklyn Academy of Music in Cavalli's Erismena, Spoleto Festival, Italy, 1980, La Scala, 1981, Edinburgh Festival, 1982, San Francisco Opera, 1982, La Fenice, 1984, Teatro di San Carlo Naples, 1984, Canadian Opera, 1984, Handel Festival at Carnegie Hall,

1984, Chicago Lyric Opera, 1986, Sante Fe Opera, 1986, and Metropolitan Opera, 1988; Has sung in operas by Jommelli, Lully, Pergolesi, Cesti, Purcell, Scarlatti and Mozart; Television appearances include the title role in Handel's Giulio Cesare; Season 1992 included Britten's Oberon at Los Angeles and in Conti's Don Chisciotte at the Innsbruck Festival of Early Music; Performed Oberon in Britten's Midsummer Night's Dream with the Frankfurt Opera, Ottone in Monteverdi's Poppea for the Cologne Opera, David in Handel's Saul with the Boston Caecelia Society, 1993; Returned to Metropolitan Opera in Britten's Death in Venice in 1994; Sang Medieval Carmina Burana for Clemencic Consort, Oberon in for the New Israeli Opera and Ottone for the Dallas Opera, repeated at Amsterdam, 1996. *Recordings include:* Flavio conducted by René Jacobs. *Honours:* First Prize, Bodky Award for Performance of Early Music, 1977. *Current Management:* William Knight, 309 Wood Street, Burlington, NJ 08016, USA.

**GALLA, Jan;** Singer (Bass); b. 21 Dec. 1955, Nova Zahky, Czechoslovakia. *Education:* Studied at the Bratislava Conservatory. *Career:* Member of the National Theatre Bratislava, in the Italian and Slavonic opera repertory; Guest appearances in Rio de Janeiro (as Ramphis in Aida, 1986), the Paris Opéra and Opéra-Comique, and Opera North, Leeds; Sang Verdi's Attila with the Bratislava company at Edinburgh, 1990; Season 1992–93 as Donizetti's Raimondo in Dublin and the Commandant in From the House of the Dead at the Barbican Hall; Bratislava 1995, as Massenet's Don Quichotte. *Address:* c/o Slovak National Theatre Opera, Gorkého 4, 815 06 Bratislava, Slovakia.

**GALLARDO-DOMÂS, Cristina;** Chilean singer (soprano); b. 1968, Santiago. *Education:* studied in Santiago and at Juilliard, New York. *Career:* sang at Santiago Opera as Butterfly, Nedda, Mimi and Liu in Turandot; Spoleto Festival 1993 as Suor Angelica; Rome Opera 1994 as Traviata; Hamburg 1995; Detroit 1994 and La Scala 1994–95 as Antonia in Les Contes d'Hoffmann; season 1995–96 as Mimi at the Metropolitan, at the Opéra Bastille, Paris and Hamburg; season 2000–01 as Violetta and Mimi at the Met, Amelia Grimaldi for Munich Opera and Liu in Turandot at Covent Garden (debut); returned to London 2003, as Madama Butterfly; other roles include Marie in La fille du Régiment and Magda in La Rondine by Puccini; many concert engagements. *Honours:* Olivier Award 2004, Opera Actual magazine Premio de la Mejor Soprano 2005. *Current Management:* DM Artist Management, Mario Dradi Bundesgasse 26, 3011 Bern, Switzerland. *Telephone:* (31) 3121314. *Fax:* (31) 3121312. *E-mail:* gall@dmartist.com. *Address:* Canarias Lyric C/ Leon y Castillo 421 2-B, 35007 Las Palmas de Gran Canaria, Spain (office). *Telephone:* 928 224 113 (office). *Fax:* 928 225 568 (office). *E-mail:* canarias_lyric@yahoo.es (office). *Website:* www.gallardo-domas.com.

**GALLEGO, Maria;** Singer (Soprano); b. 1962, San Fernando, Spain. *Education:* Studied in Cadiz and at the Barcelona Conservatory. *Career:* Debut: Barcelona, 1985 as Sidonie in Gluck's Armide; Appearances at Barcelona as Celia in Mozart's Lucio Silla, Monica in Respighi's La Fiamma and in Strauss's Capriccio; Telemaco by Gluck, 1987; Guest appearances in Bologna and Ravenna as Rosaura in Le Maschere by Mascagni, 1988; Pisa and Madrid; Bonn Opera, 1991–92; Other roles include Betty in Salieri's Falstaff. *Address:* c/o Bonn Opera, Am Boeselagerhof 1, 53111 Bonn, Germany.

**GALLI, Dorothea;** Singer (Soprano); b. 11 Nov. 1951, Zürich, Switzerland; m. Rudolf Bamert. *Education:* Studied with Elsa Cavelli and Elisabeth Schwarzkopf and at the Salzburg Mozarteum. *Career:* Sang at the Zürich Opera, 1976–78, Kaiserlautern, 1978–79, Gelsenkirchen, 1979–82; Guest appearances at the Deutsche Oper am Rhein Düsseldorf, Karlsruhe, Mannheim, Dortmund, Heidelberg and Amsterdam; Roles have included Mozart's Donna Elvira, Fiordiligi and Ramiro (La Finta Giardiniera), Leonore, Marguerite, Mimi, Tatiana, the Marschallin, Arabella, Emilia Marty and Giorgietta in Gianni Schicchi; Many Lieder recitals and performances of oratorio. *Address:* c/o Opernhaus Zürich, Falkenstrasse 1, 8008 Zürich, Switzerland.

**GALLIANO, Richard;** French accordionist; b. 12 Dec. 1950, Le Cannet. *Education:* studied with Claude Noel. *Career:* renowned for creating a fusion of jazz, classical and traditional styles of accordion music; composer, arranger and conductor with Claude Nougaro Orchestra 1973–76; formed trio with Daniel Humair and J. F. Jenny-Clark 1994; has performed at Umbria Jazz Festival with Joe Zawinul, Charlie Haden, New York Tango Quartet, Montréal Jazz Festival 1997, 1998, 1999 and other int. festivals, including Antibes, Montreux, Vienna, San Francisco, North Sea, Melbourne, Tokyo, Peking, Shanghai; collaborations with artists including Juliette Greco, Charles Aznavour, Ron Carter, Chet Baker, Enrico Rava, Martial Solal, Miroslav Vitous, Trilok Gurtu, Jan Garbarek, Michel Petrucciani, Michel Portal, Toots Thielemans. *Recordings:* New Musette 1992, Spleen 1993, Viaggio 1993, Panamanhattan, Live, with Ron Carter (Classical and Jazz Award for Best Jazz Album 1996) 1994, Laurita 1995, New York Tango (Victoire de la Musique 1996) 1996, Blow Up (Victoire de la Musique 1997, Classical and Jazz Award for Best Jazz Album 1997) 1997, French Touch (Musica Jazz Award for Best Int. Jazz Album) 1998, Passatori 1999, Concerts Inédits 2000, Blues Sur Seine (with Jean-Charles Capon) 2001, Gallianissimo 2001, Face to Face (with Eddy Louiss) 2001, Piazolla Forever 2003, Concerts (with Michel Portal) 2004, Blue Hat (with Wasilewski Cronholm) 2005, Ruby My Dear 2005. *Current Management:* M.G.M. Produzioni Musicali, Via C. Battisti 21, Foligno 06034, Italy. *Telephone:* (742) 355588. *E-mail:* margui@bcsnet.it. *Website:* www.ejn.it/mgm; www.richardgalliano.com.

**GALLO, F. Alberto;** Professor of History of Music; b. 17 Oct. 1932, Verona, Italy. *Education:* LLD; PhD. *Publications include:* Antonii Romani Opera, 1965; Mensurabilis Musicae Tractatuli, 1966; Il Codice Musicale 2216 della Biblioteca Universitaria di Bologna, 1968–70; Franchini Gafurii Extractus Parvus Musicae, 1969; Petrus Picardus Ars Motettorium Compilata Breviter, 1971; Johannes Boen Ars Musicae, 1972; La Prima Rappresentazione al Teatro Olimpico, 1973; Italian Sacred Music, 1976; Storia della Musica: Il Medioevo, 1977; Il Codice Musicale Panciatichi 26 della Biblioteca Nazionale di Firenze, 1981; Geschichte der Musiktheorie, 1984; Music of the Middle Ages, 1985; Musica e Storia tra Medio Evo e Età Moderna, 1986; Italian Sacred and Ceremonial Music, 1987; Musica nel castello Bologna, 1992; Il Codice Squarcialupi, Firenze, 1992. *Address:* L Alberti 34, 40137 Bologna, Italy.

**GALLO, Lucio;** Singer (Bass-baritone); b. 1958, Taranto, Italy. *Education:* Studied in Turin. *Career:* Sang Marcello to Pavarotti's Rodolfo in Peking, China; Escamillo in Turin and Leporello at the Vienna Staatsoper, 1989; Returned to Vienna as Valentin in Faust, Marcello, and Paolo in Simon Boccanegra; Further appearances at the Hamburg Staatsoper as Mozart's Count (also at Covent Garden), Dandini in Cenerentola at Bologna and Don Alvaro in Il Viaggio a Reims at Pesaro; Metropolitan Opera New York debut, 1991, as Guglielmo; Mozart's Figaro, 1992, with the Covent Garden company on tour to Japan; Sang Dallapiccola's Prigioniero at Florence, 1996; Puccini's Lescaut at La Scala, 1998; Season 2000–01 at the Deutsche Oper Berlin as Eugene Onegin and Macbeth at the Staatsoper; Amonasro at Macerata, Mozart's Count at Munich and Ford in Falstaff for the Salzburg Easter Festival; Covent Garden 2001 and 2003, Dandini and Sharpless; Concert repertory includes Les Béatitudes by Franck, Winterreise, and Lieder by Wolf. *Recordings include:* Bartolo in Il Barbiere di Siviglia. *Address:* c/o Staatsoper, Opernring 2, 1010 Vienna, Austria.

**GALSTIAN, Juliette;** Singer (soprano); b. 1970, Armenia. *Education:* Graduated, Piano and Voice, Yerevan Conservatoire, 1995. *Career:* Appearances in Armenia as piano recitalist and concert soloist; From season 1996 engagements at leading opera houses, including Mimi in the centenary production of La Bohème at Turin; Zerlina in Don Giovanni at La Fenice, Susanna in Le nozze di Figaro and Xenia in Boris Godunov at Turin; Flowermaiden in Parsifal at the Opéra Bastille, Paris, Valencienne in The Merry Widow at with the Royal Opera, London. *Honours:* Laureate, Maria Callas Grand Prix, Athens; Winner, Viotti International Competition; Prizewinner, Jose Carreras Competition at Pamplona. *Current Management:* Athole Still International Management, Forresters Hall, 25–27 Westow Street, London, SE19 3RY, England. *Telephone:* (20) 8771-5271. *Fax:* (20) 8768-6600. *Website:* www.atholestill.com.

**GALTERIO, Lou,** BA; American opera director and administrator; b. 29 Nov. 1942, New York, NY. *Education:* Marquette University, Milwaukee. *Career:* worked as an actor and theatre director; Opera productions for the Opera Theater of St Louis include Così fan tutte, Le nozze di Figaro, Albert Herring, Ariadne auf Naxos and the US premiere of Prokofiev's Maddalena, 1982; Director of opera production at the Manhattan School from 1977; Santa Fe Opera, Il Barbiere di Siviglia and Hindemith's Neues vom Tage, 1981; Kennedy Center, Washington, Argento's Postcard from Morocco, 1979; New York City Opera, 1980, La Cenerentola; Chicago Opera Theater, 1984, Don Giovanni; Staged Don Giovanni at Santa Fe, 1992. *Address:* c/o Santa Fe Opera, PO Box 2408, Santa Fe, NM 87504, USA.

**GALUZIN, Vladimir;** Singer (Tenor); b. 1957, Novosibirsk, Siberia, Russia. *Education:* Studied at Novosibirsk Conservatoire. *Career:* Sang at the Novosibirsk Opera, 1988–90, Kirov Theatre St Petersburg, 1990–; Tours with the Kirov to Spain, Italy, France and the Edinburgh Festival; Appearances as Otello in St Petersburg and as Guest in Stuttgart, Dresden, Amsterdam, Brussels and Japan; Grishko in the Kupfer production of Rimsky's Invisible City of Kitezh (Bregenz, 1995), and Sergei in the Graham Vick production of Lady Macbeth of the Mtsensk District, at the Metropolitan, 1996; Season 1996–97 as Pinkerton at Cologne and Alexei in The Gambler by Prokofiev at La Scala; Many engagements at the Vienna Staatsoper (debut as Hermann in The Queen of Spades); Season 1997–98 with Otello at Brussels and for the New Israeli Opera, Lensky in Eugene Onegin at Buenos Aires; Other roles include Radames, Don Carlos, Calaf, Cavaradossi, Chevalier des Grieux, Andrei in Tchaikovsky's Mazeppa and Vladimir in Prince Igor; Season 1998 as Khovansky in Khovanshchina at La Scala and Calaf at Madrid; Returned to Madrid 2000, for Alvaro in La Forza del Destino; Season 2000–01 as Pinkerton, Shostakovich's Sergei and Alexei in The Gambler by Prokofiev at the New York Met; Cavaradossi at Orange, Radames at the Verona Arena and Hermann in The Queen of Spades at Covent Garden. *Recordings include:* Video of title role in Rimsky's Sadko (Philips). *Address:* Bureau de Concert Maurice Werner, 7 Rue Richerance, 75008 Paris, France.

**GALVANY, Marisa;** Singer (Soprano); b. 19 June 1936, Paterson, New Jersey, USA. *Education:* Studied with Armen Boyajian. *Career:* Debut: Seattle Opera, 1968, as Tosca; New York City Opera from 1972, as Elizabeth I in Maria Stuarda, Anna Bolena, Médée, Santuzza and Violetta; Mexico City and San Francisco, 1972–73, Aida; New Orleans, 1974, as Rachel in La Juive; Guest appearances in Philadelphia, Warsaw, Prague, Belgrade and Rouen; Metropolitan Opera from 1979, as Norma, Ortrud, and the Kostelnicka in Jenůfa; Other roles include Verdi's Hélène, Abigaille and Elvira, Turandot, Mozart's Countess, Massenet's Salomé and Tchaikovsky's Iolanta; Sang

Verdi's Ulrica in New York Central Park, 2000. *Recordings include:* Title role in Medea in Corinto by Giovanni Simone Mayr. *Address:* c/o Metropolitan Opera, Lincoln Center, New York, NY 10023, USA.

**GALVEZ-VALLEJO, Daniel;** Singer (Tenor); b. 1967, Spain. *Education:* Studied in Spain and Italy. *Career:* Many appearances in Italy as Alfredo and Rodolfo in La Bohème; Montpellier Festival, 1991–95, as Igor in Bizet's Ivan IV, and in Sacchini's Oedipe a Colone; Riccardo in Verdi's Oberto; Sang in Les Brigands by Offenbach at the Paris Opéra, Bastille, 1994; Season 1995 as Hoffmann at Lyon and Don José at Lille; Other roles include Pollione in Norma and Wagner's Steersman. *Recordings:* Samson et Dalila. *Address:* c/o Opera de Montpellier, 11 Boulevard Victor Hugo, 34000 Montpellier, France.

**GALWAY, Sir James,** Kt, KBE, FRCM, FRCO, FGSM; British flautist and conductor; b. 8 Dec. 1939, Belfast; s. of James Galway and Ethel Stewart Galway (née Clarke); m. 1st 1965; one s. m. 2nd 1972; one s. two d. (twins); m. 3rd Jeanne Cinnante 1984. *Education:* Mountcollyer Secondary School, Royal Coll. of Music, Guildhall School of Music, Conservatoire National Supérieur de Musique, Paris. *Career:* first post in Wind Band of Royal Shakespeare Theatre, Stratford-on-Avon; later worked with Sadler's Wells Orchestra, Royal Opera House Orchestra, BBC Symphony Orchestra; Prin. Flute, London Symphony Orchestra and Royal Philharmonic Orchestra; Prin. Solo Flute, Berlin Philharmonic Orchestra 1969–75; int. soloist 1975–; soloist/conductor 1984–; Prin. Guest Conductor, London Mozart Players 1997–; performances worldwide include appearances in The Wall, Berlin, and at the Nobel Peace Prize Ceremony, 1998; as conductor, toured Germany with Wurttembergisches Kammerorchester and Asia with Polish Chamber Orchestra, 2000–01; has premiered many contemporary flute works commissioned by and for him; numerous recordings; James Galway Rose named after him by David Austin. *Film music:* flute soloist, soundtrack of Lord of the Rings – Return of the King. *Publications:* James Galway: An Autobiography 1978, Flute (Menuhin Music Guide) 1982, James Galway's Music in Time 1983, Flute Studies – Boehm 12 Grand Studies 2003. *Honours:* Hon. MA (Open Univ.) 1979, Hon. DMus (Queen's Univ., Belfast) 1979, (New England Conservatory of Music) 1980, (St Andrew's Univ.) 1982; Officier, Ordre des Arts et des Lettres 1987; Grand Prix du Disque 1976, 1989, Nat. Acad. Recording, Arts & Sciences Pres. Merit Award 2004, Classical BRIT Award for Outstanding Contribution to Music 2005. *Address:* c/o Lisa Baglieri, Benzeholzstr. 11, 6045 Meggen, Switzerland. *E-mail:* lisabag@earthlink.net (office). *Website:* www.superflute.com (home).

**GAMBA, Piero;** Conductor; b. 16 Sept. 1936, Rome, Italy. *Education:* Studied piano and score reading with his father. *Career:* Conducted Beethoven's 1st Symphony at the Rome Opera House, aged 8; Tours of Europe and North and South America whilst a child; British debut 1948, conducting Beethoven and Dvořák in London; Moved to Madrid in 1952; Guest engagements in London, 1959–63 often with the London Symphony Orchestra; Musical Director of Winnipeg Symphony Orchestra, Canada, 1970–81; Principal Conductor, Adelaide Symphony Orchestra from 1982–88. *Recordings include:* Rossini's Overtures with the London Symphony Orchestra; Beethoven's Piano Concertos with Julius Katchen as soloist.

**GAMBA, Rumon;** Conductor; b. 1970, England. *Education:* Royal Academy of Music, with Colin Metters. *Career:* Associate conductor of the BBC PO, from 1998; Music Director of the Iceland SO, 2002–; Appearances with all the BBC Orchestras, City of Birmingham SO, Britten Sinfonia, Bournemouth SO and Royal Scottish National Orchestra; Season 2001–02 with Munich PO (Shostakovich 8th Symphony) Toronto SO, Bergen PO, London PO, Melbourne and Dusseldorf Symphonies and NDR Hannover; Season 2002–03 with US debut (Florida PO), New York PO youth series concerts and 2003 Sydney Festival (most leading Australian orchestras); Further engagements with Barcelona and Basle Symphonies, Orquesta de Valencia and Singapore SO; Blue Peter concerts with the BBC PO at the London Proms, 2002. *Recordings include:* Malcolm Arnold Symphonies and music by Vaughan Williams, Auric, Bliss, Alwyn and Richard Rodney Bennett (film music) (Chandos). *Current Management:* Harrison/Parrott Ltd, 12 Penzance Place, London, W11 4PA, England. *Telephone:* (20) 7229 9166. *Fax:* (20) 7221 5042. *Website:* www.harrisonparrott.com.

**GAMBERONI, Kathryn;** Soprano; b. 11 June 1955, Pennsylvania, USA. *Education:* Studied at the Curtis Institute. *Career:* Debut: St Louis in 1981 as Gerda in the US premiere of Fennimore and Gerda by Delius; Sang with the St Louis Company at the Edinburgh Festival in 1983 as Margot la Rouge by Delius; Seattle Opera from 1985 as Adina, Despina, Adele, Juliette, Zerbinetta and Marzelline, 1991; Santa Fe in 1985 in the US premiere of The English Cat by Henze, returning in 1989 in Judith Weir's A Night At The Chinese Opera and as Satirino in La Calisto; Guest appearances in Paris, Dallas, Cologne, Chicago and Melbourne; Other roles include Mozart's Blondchen, Susanna and Papagena, and Fanny in Rossini's La Cambiale di Matrimonio; Sang Rosina in Paisiello's Il Barbiere di Siviglia for Long Beach Opera in 1989 and the title role in The Cunning Little Vixen at the New York City Opera in 1991. *Address:* c/o New York City Opera, Lincoln Center, New York, NY 10023, USA.

**GAMBILL, Robert;** Tenor; b. 11 March 1955, Indianapolis, Indiana, USA. *Education:* Studied at the Hamburg Musikhochschule with Hans Kagel. *Career:* Debut: Milan 1981 as Michael in the premiere of Stockhausen's Donnerstag aus Licht; Sang at Frankfurt from 1981 notably in Die Gezeichneten by Schreker; Sang at Wiesbaden as Ernesto, Tamino, Don

Ottavio and Nicolai's Fenton; Glyndebourne in 1982–85 as Almaviva in Il Barbiere di Siviglia and Don Ramiro in La Cenerentola, La Scala Milan in 1982, Teatro La Fenice, Venice as Ferrando in Così fan tutte in 1983; Sang David in Die Meistersinger at the renovated Zürich Opera in 1984; Geneva and Aix-en-Provence in 1984 as Rossini's Lindoro and Almaviva; Season 1987–88 as Belmonte at Buenos Aires and the Steersman in Fliegende Holländer at La Scala, also at the Metropolitan in 1989; Schwetzingen Festival in 1987 as Rossini's Almaviva, Theater an der Wien Vienna in 1988 in Schubert's Fierrabras, sang Almaviva at Munich in 1990 and Wagner's David at Covent Garden; Other roles include Mozart's Ferrando, Renaud in Armide, Verdi's Fenton and Iopas in Les Troyens; Sang in Rossini double bill at Cologne and Schwetzingen in 1992; Sang Offenbach's Barbe-bleue at Stuttgart, 1996; Season 1997–98 with Max at Frankfurt and Florestan at Stuttgart; Sang Tannhäuser at Dresden, 2001; London Proms, 2002; Engaged as Tristan at Glyndebourne (2003). *Recordings include:* Rossini's Stabat Mater; Evander in Gluck's Alceste ed Euridice; Tenor Solo in Messiah. *Address:* c/o Staatstheater Stuttgart, Oberer Schlossgarten 6, 7000 Stuttgart 1, Germany.

**GAMMON, Philip (Greenway),** ARCM, FRAM; British pianist and conductor; *Principal Pianist, The Royal Ballet;* b. 17 May 1940, Chippenham, Wiltshire, England; m. Floretta Volovini, 1963, 2 s. *Education:* Royal Academy of Music, 1956–61; Pupil of Harold Craxton; Badische Musikhochschule, 1961–64; Pupil of Yvonne Loriod. *Career:* Joined Royal Ballet, Covent Garden, 1964; Ballet for All Principal Pianist, 1968–71; Teaching appointments at Watford School of Music and Trinity College; Returned to Royal Ballet, 1972; Solo Pianist for many ballets including Elite Syncopations, A Month in the Country and Return to the Strange Land; Conducting debut with Ballet for All at Richmond Theatre, 1970; At Covent Garden, 1978, Sleeping Beauty; Radio 3 broadcasts in recitals as soloist and accompanist; Debut Festival Hall and Barbican Hall in 1984 as Piano Soloist; Solo pianist for Rhapsody, Mr Worldly Wise, Ballet Imperial, Concerto, La Fin du Jour, Winter Dreams; The Concert, Margaurite and Armand; Guest conducting with the English National Ballet, Hong Kong Ballet, 1996 and National Ballet of Portugal, 1997 and 1998; Principal Pianist and Conductor of the Royal Ballet, 1999–; Presents a lecture-recital, Music and Reminiscence, A Pianist's Life with the Royal Ballet; Solo Pianist at Entente Cordiale Gala, Palais Garnier, Paris 2004, Gala des Etoiles, La Scala, Milan 2004. *Recordings:* Elite Syncopations, with musicians from the Covent Garden Orchestra; A Month in the Country, Chopin/Lanchbery; Winter Dreams; DVD of Margaurite and Armand (Liszt Sonata), 2004. *Publications:* First orchestral arrangement of La Chatte Metamorphosée en femme, premiered in 1985 at the Royal Opera House. *Honours:* Recital Diploma 1960, MacFarren Gold Medal 1961, Karlsruhe Culture Prize 1962, Badische Musikhochschule Diplom 1963. *Address:* 19 Downs Avenue, Pinner, Middx, HA5 5AQ, England. *Telephone:* (20) 8866-3260.

**GANASSI, Sonia;** Italian singer (mezzo-soprano); b. 1967, Reggio Emilia. *Career:* debut, Spoletto 1991 as Rossini's Cenerentola; Rome Opera from 1992, as Rossini's Isabella and Rosina; season 1995 as Rosina at Venice, Adalgisa in Norma at Bologna, Carmen at Monte Carlo and Emma in Zelmira at Pesaro; US debut Washington 1993 as Cenerentola; season 1996 as Isabella at Genoa; Giovanna in Anna Bolena at Bologna and as Mascagni's Zanetta at Florence; season 1997–98 as Rosina for the Royal Opera in London; Bellini's Romeo at Reggio Emilia and Maffeo Orsini in Lucrezia Borgia at La Scala; other roles include Elisabetta in Maria Stuarda, Dorabella, Nicklausse in Les Contes d'Hoffmann and Massenet's Charlotte; season 2001–02 as Cenerentola, and Romeo in I Capuleti e i Montecchi at Covent Garden; Adalgisa at Turin, Donizetti's Leonora at Bologna, Cenerentola in Madrid, Milan and San Francisco, Elisabetta in Barcelona; London Proms 2002. *Recordings:* Il Barbiere di Siviglia, Rossini's Sigismondo. *Address:* Theateragentur Dr Germinal Hilbert, Maximilianstrasse 22, 80539 Munich, Germany. *Telephone:* (89) 290 747-0. *Fax:* (89) 290 747-90. *Website:* www.hilbert.de.

**GANTER, Martin;** Singer (Baritone); b. 15 May 1965, Freiburg, Germany. *Education:* Studied in Berlin, Germany. *Career:* Debut: Mozart's Count at Coblenz, 1989; Sang in the premiere of Henze's Das verratene Meer, Berlin, 1990; Appearances at the Bavarian State Opera, Munich, from 1991, as Ned Keene in Peter Grimes, Schaunard (La Bohème), Papageno, Silvio and Malatesta; Guglielmo (Così fan tutte) in Basle, Barcelona and Dresden (1997); Don Giovanni at Hof and Rossini's Figaro at Baden-Baden (1985), Dandini in La Cenerentola at the Dresden Staatsoper, 1996. *Honours:* Winner, VDMK Competition, Berlin, 1988. *Address:* c/o Haydn Rawstron Ltd, 38 Station Road, London SE20 7BQ, England.

**GANZAROLLI, Wladimiro;** singer (bass); b. 9 Jan. 1932, Venice, Italy. *Education:* Bendetto Marcello Conservatory, Venice. *Career:* debut at Teatro Nuovo in Milan in 1958 as Mephistopheles in Faust; Sang at La Scala Milan from 1959, notably as Falstaff and as Bottom in the local premiere of Britten's A Midsummer Night's Dream, Spoleto in 1959 in a revival of Il Duca d'Alba by Donizetti, Monte Carlo in 1960, Vienna Staatsoper from 1964, Teatro Colón Buenos Aires in 1966 as Leporello in Don Giovanni and as a guest in the USA, notably in San Francisco, Chicago, Dallas and at the Metropolitan Opera in 1968; sang at Teatro Regio, Turin, 1955–82. *Recordings:* Le nozze di Figaro; Così fan tutte; Don Giovanni, conducted by Colin Davis; La Vera Costanza by Haydn under Antal Dorati; Un Giorno di Regno and Stiffelio by Verdi; Les Huguenots by Meyerbeer; Luisa Miller.

**GARAVANTA, Ottavio;** Tenor; b. 26 Jan. 1934, Genoa, Italy. *Education:* Studied with Rosetta Noli and Vladimiro Badiali. *Career:* Debut: Milan in 1954 as Don Ottavio; Sang major roles in Italy at La Scala and in Rome, Florence and Verona; Guest engagements in Vienna, Buenos Aires, Berlin, Marseilles, Brussels, Chicago, San Francisco, Lisbon and Belgrade; Glyndebourne Festival in 1967 as Rodolfo in La Bohème; Has often appeared in revivals of neglected Italian operas; Sang at Théâtre de la Monnaie, Brussels, in 1980 in Donizetti's Il Duca d'Alba, Genoa in 1985 as Cadmo in Donizetti's Il Diluvio Universale and sang Carlo in a concert performance of Verdi's Giovanna d'Arco with Margaret Price at Festival Hall in London, 1989; Sang at Teatro Regio Turin in 1990 as Radames; Livorno 1992, as Giorgio in I Rantzau by Mascagni. *Recordings:* Scenes from Rossini's Otello with Virginia Zeani; Mosè in Egitto by Rossini; Admeti in Dejanice by Catalani. *Honours:* Winner of the Verdi Competition at Bussetto and competitions at Genoa and Modena. *Address:* c/o Teatro di Torino, Piazza Castello 215, 10124 Turin, Italy.

**GARAZZI, Peyo;** Tenor; b. 31 March 1937, St Jean Pied de Port, Basses Pyrenees, France. *Education:* Studied in Bordeaux and Paris. *Career:* Sang first at the Théâtre de la Monnaie in Brussels; Sang at Royal Opera Ghent in 1962 as Nadir in Les Pêcheurs de Perles, Paris, 1977 in Gwendoline by Chabrier and guest appearances in Bordeaux, Munich and Berlin; Covent Garden Opera in 1983 as Don Carlos in a French language revival of Verdi's opera; Other roles include Florestan, Aron in Moses und Aron by Schoenberg and parts in operas by Delibes, Donizetti, Offenbach and Puccini. *Recordings include:* Don Quichotte by Massenet.

**GARCIA, Jose;** Singer (Bass); b. 1959, USA. *Career:* Season 1987 as Sarastro for Pennysylvania Opera and the Commendatore in a Peter Sellars production of Don Giovanni; Season 1988–89 as the Grand Inquisitor in Don Carlos at Bologna; Polidoro in Rossini's Zelmira at Venice; Gounod's Frère Laurent at Seattle; Season 1990 as Roger in the British premiere of Verdi's Jérusalem for Opera North; Sarastro for Glyndebourne Touring Opera. *Recordings:* Zelmira. *Address:* Opera North, Grand Theatre, 46 New Briggate, Leeds LS1 6NU, England.

**GARCIA, Navarro Luis;** Conductor; b. 30 April 1941, Chiva, Valencia, Spain. *Education:* Studied at Valencia and Madrid Conservatories and in Italy with Franco Ferrara and at Vienna Academy with Hans Swarowsky. *Career:* Founded the Spanish University Orchestra in 1963; Permanent Conductor of the Valencia Symphony, 1970–74; Musical Director of San Carlos Theatre at Lisbon, 1980–82; Principal Guest Conductor of the Radio Symphony Orchestra, Stuttgart, 1984–87, the Vienna State Opera, 1987–91, and the Tokyo Philharmonic Orchestra, 1992–; Generalmusikdirektor of the Stuttgart State Opera, 1987–91; Musical and Artistic Conductor of the Barcelona Symphony Orchestra, 1991–93; Permanent Guest Conductor at Deutsche Oper Berlin, 1992–; Appearances in most major international opera theatres including Covent Garden La Bohème in 1979 and Tosca in 1983, La Scala Milan, Madama Butterfly in 1987 and Vienna State Opera, Falstaff, La Bohème, Tosca, La Forza del Destino and Andrea Chénier; Has also conducted many leading orchestras including the Vienna Philharmonic, London Symphony and Philharmonia, Leningrad Philharmonic, Chicago Symphony, Pittsburgh Symphony, and Los Angeles Philharmonic; mem, Royal Academy of San Carlos, Spain. *Recordings:* Several. *Honours:* 1st Prize, Madrid Conservatory, 1963; Prizewinner, International Competition Besançon, 1967; Gold Medal, Paris City, 1983. *Address:* Conciertos Vitoria, Amaniel 5-50-2, 28015 Madrid, Spain.

**GARCÍA ASENSIO, Enrique;** Spanish conductor; *Conductor and Music Director, Municipal Symphonic Band of Madrid*; b. 22 Aug. 1937, Valencia, Spain. *Education:* Master's degree, Violin, Harmony, Counterpoint, Fugue, Chamber Music, Composition, Royal Conservatory of Music, Madrid; Orchestra Conducting, Munich Higher School of Music, with Professors Lessing, Eichhorn and Mennerich; Further study, Accademia Chigiana, with Sergiu Celibidache. *Career:* Has conducted all leading Spanish orchestras; Music Director, Conductor: Las Palmas Philharmonic, Canary Islands, 1962–64, Valencia Municipal Orchestra, 1964–65, Spanish Radio and Television Orchestra, Madrid, 1966–84; Assistant Conductor, National Symphony Orchestra, Washington DC, season 1967–68; Principal Guest Conductor, Valencia Orchestra; Conductor Madrid Municipal Symphonic Band, 1994–98, Conductor and Music Dir 2002–; Music Director and Conductor of the Radio and Television Symphony Orchestra, 1998–; Led orchestras in Canada, USA, Mexico, Dominican Republic, Brazil, Uruguay, Argentina, Portugal, France, Italy, England, Belgium, Russia, Japan, Northern Ireland, Israel, Netherlands, Greece, Denmark, Romania, Puerto Rico, Austria, Germany, Bulgaria, Switzerland, Iceland; Turkey, Luxemburg, South Africa, Slovakia and the Czech Republic; Symphonic and operatic repertory; Assistant to Celibidache at master classes, Bologna, Munich; Professor of Conducting, Royal Conservatory of Music, Madrid, 1970–; International master classes, Netherlands, Dominican Republic; Presenter, The World of Music educational television programme, 4 years. *Recordings:* numerous including: Zarzuela, Teresa Berganza and English Chamber Orchestra 1976, Ernesto Halffter, English Chamber Orchestra, 1991, Banda Sinfónica Municipal de Madrid, Orquesta Sinfónica RTVE. *Address:* Gavilan 8, 28230 Las Rozas, Madrid, Spain. *Telephone:* (915) 263231 (office); (916) 302572 (home). *Fax:* (916) 303810 (home). *E-mail:* gasensio@hotmail.com (office); maestro@garciaasensio.com (home). *Website:* www.garciaasensio.com (home).

**GARCISANZ, Isabel;** Singer (Soprano); b. 29 June 1934, Madrid, Spain. *Education:* Studied with Angeles Ottein in Spain and with Erik Werba in Vienna. *Career:* Debut: Vienna Volksoper in 1964 as Adèle in Le Comte Ory; Sang in Paris at the Opéra and the Opéra-Comique; Guest appearances in Bordeaux, Marseille, Nancy, Nice, Cologne, Barcelona and Miami; Glyndebourne, 1966–68, 1970 as Concepcion in L'Heure Espagnole, Nerillo in L'Ormindo and Zaida in Il Turco in Italia; Toulouse, 1972–73 in the premieres of operas by Casanova and Nikiprowetsky; Strasbourg in 1974 in the premiere of Delereue's Medis et Alissio; Engagements with French Radio, Paris, in the first performances of works by Mihalovici; Was the first singer of Hahn's Sybille; Sang in the premiere of Le Château des Carpathes, by Philippe Hersant, Montpellier, 1993; mem, Acanthes; Union des Femmes Artists Musiciennes. *Recordings:* L'Ormindo; Le Maître de Chapelle by Paer; Le Roi Malgré Lui by Chabrier; Cantigas; Sybille; Mass by Ohana; 3 Centuries of Spanish Melodies; Spanish Songs by Rodrigo, Falla, and Garcia. *Current Management:* Agence Thérèse Cedelle, 78 Boulevard Makesherres, 75008 Paris, France. *Address:* c/o Opéra du Rhin, 19 Place Broglie, 67008 Strasbourg Cédex, France.

**GARD, Robert;** Singer (Tenor); b. 7 March 1927, Cornwall, England. *Education:* Studied with Dino Borgoli, Walter Hyde at the Guildhall School of Music and Kaiser Breme in Bayreuth. *Career:* Debut: English Opera Group in Lennox Berkeley's Ruth, 1957; Sang for Welsh Opera then at Aldeburgh and in Australia as Britten's Peter Quint in the Turn of The Screw, Albert Herring, Male Chorus and Aschenbach; Sang Anatol in War and Peace at the opening of the Sydney Opera House in 1973, appearing on television in this production, and Charpentier's Louise and Manon; Sang Aschenbach in a film version of Britten's Death in Venice in 1981, commissioned by the Britten Foundation; Other roles included Aegisthus, Herod, Loge, Siegmund, Tamino, Steva in Jenůfa, Peter Grimes, Tom Rakewell, and Le Mesurier in the premiere of Meale's Voss, 1986; Sang Mr Upfold in Albert Herring at Sydney, 1996. *Honours:* O.B.E., 1981. *Address:* c/o Australian Opera, Sydney Opera House, Sydney, NSW, Australia.

**GARDINER, Sir John Eliot,** Kt, CBE, MA, FRSA; British conductor and musical director; b. 20 April 1943, Fontmell Magna, Dorset; s. of the late Rolf Gardiner and of Marabel Gardiner (née Hodgkin); m. 1st Cherryl Anne Ffoulkes 1971 (divorced 1981); m. 2nd Elizabeth Suzanne Wilcock 1981 (divorced 1997); three d.; m. 3rd Isabella de Sabata 2001. *Education:* Bryanston School, King's Coll., Cambridge, King's Coll., London, and in Paris and Fontainebleau with Nadia Boulanger. *Career:* Founder and Artistic Dir Monteverdi Choir, 1964, Monteverdi Orchestra 1968, English Baroque Soloists 1978, Orchestre Révolutionnaire et Romantique 1990; concert debut Wigmore Hall, London 1966; youngest conductor Henry Wood Promenade Concerts, Royal Albert Hall 1968; operatic debut Sadler's Wells Opera, London Coliseum 1969; Prin. Conductor CBC Vancouver Orchestra 1980–83; Musical Dir Lyon Opera 1982–88, Chef fondateur 1988–; Artistic Dir Göttingen Handel Festival 1981–90, Veneto Music Festival 1986; Prin. Conductor NDR Symphony Orchestra, Hamburg 1991–94; residency at the Châtelet, Paris Oct. 1999–; Bach Cantata Pilgrimage, with performances throughout Europe 2000; conducted Handel's Israel in Egypt at the London Proms 2002, The Cunning Little Vixen at Covent Garden 2003; regular guest conductor with major orchestras in Amsterdam, Paris, Brussels, Geneva, Frankfurt, Dresden, Leipzig, London, Vienna, Berlin; appearances at European music festivals, including Aix-en-Provence, Aldeburgh, Bath, Berlin, Edinburgh, Flanders, Netherlands, London, Salzburg, BBC Proms; over 200 recordings. *Publications:* Claude le Jeune Hélas, Mon Dieu (ed.) 1971, contrib. Gluck's Orfeo 1980. *Honours:* Hon. Fellow, King's Coll., London 1992, Royal Acad. of Music 1992; Commdr, Ordre des Arts et des Lettres 1997, City of Leipzig and Bach Archiv Bach Medal for lifetime achievement in the performance of music by J. S. Bach 2005; Dr hc (Univ. Lumière de Lyon) 1987; 15 Gramophone awards, including Record of the Year 1991, Artist of the Year 1994, Edison Awards 1982, 1986, 1987, 1988, 1989, 1996, 1997, Grand Prix du Disque 1978, 1979, 1980, 1992, Prix Caecilia 1982, 1983, 1985, Arturo Toscanini Music Critics' awards 1985, 1986, Deutscher Schallplattenpreis 1986, 1994, 1997, Classic FM Gramophone Award and Gramophone Magazine Record of the Year (for recording of Bach Cantatas) 2005, Leonie Sonning Music Prize 2005.

**GARDNER, Edward;** British conductor; *Music Director, Glyndebourne Touring Opera. Education:* King's Coll., Cambridge, RAM. *Career:* fmr Asst Conductor Hallé Orchestra; Music Dir Glyndebourne Touring Opera 2004–, with productions including La Bohème 2004, La Cenerentola 2005, The Turn of the Screw 2006, Fidelio 2006; has conducted Camerata Salzburg, London Philharmonic, Melbourne Symphony, Belgrade Philharmonic, Royal Scottish Nat. Orchestra, BBC SO, Philharmonia, Alabama Symphony, Orchestre de Bretagne; season 2005–06 appearances included BBC Scottish SO, BBC Nat. Orchestra of Wales, Vancouver Symphony, Orquestra Nacional do Porto, MDR Leipzig, Orchestre Philharmonique de Liege; opera highlights include Tchaikovsky's Eugene Onegin with Glyndebourne Touring Opera 2002, Meyerbeer's L'Africaine with Strasbourg Opera 2004, Mozart's Cosi fan Tutte with ENO 2005, Adams' The Death of Klinghoffer with Scottish Opera 2005, Weill's Seven Deadly Sins with Paris Opera 2005, Donizetti's L'Elisir d'Amore, Paris Opera 2006, Stravinsky's The Rake's Progress, Paris 2007–08. *Honours:* Royal Philharmonic Soc. Award for Best Young Artist 2005. *Current Management:* c/o Wray Armstrong, IMG Artists, Lovell House, 616 Chiswick High Road, London, W4 5RX, England. *Telephone:* (20) 7957-5800 (office). *Fax:*

(20) 7957-5801 (office). *E-mail:* artistseurope@imgartists.com (office). *Website:* www.imgartists.com (office). *Address:* Glyndebourne Productions Ltd, Glyndebourne, Lewes, East Sussex BN8 5UU, England (office). *Telephone:* (1273) 812321. *Fax:* (1273) 812783. *E-mail:* info@glyndebourne.com. *Website:* www.glyndebourne.com.

**GARDNER, Jake;** singer (baritone); b. 14 Nov. 1947, Oneonta, NY, USA; m. Cynthia Clarey 1978; one s. *Education:* State University of New York, Potsdam, Syracuse University. *Career:* spent first 10 years of career studying and performing with the tri-Cities Opera, Binghamton, New York; Sang Valentin in Faust at Houston, 1975; Carnegie Hall, 1976, in a concert performance of Le Cid by Massenet; Sang James Stewart in premiere of Thea Musgrave's Mary, Queen of Scots at 1977 Edinburgh Festival, and repeated the role at Norfolk, Virginia, 1978 and elsewhere; Appeared with Boston Opera in 1979 US premiere of Tippett's The Ice Break and has sung at opera houses in Washington, Detroit, San Diego, San Francisco, New Orleans and St Louis; Has sung Mozart's Guglielmo and Figaro with Netherlands Opera, Escamillo in Peter Brook's version of Carmen throughout Europe and at Lincoln Center; Wexford Festival debut 1987 as Valdeburgo in La Straniera; Has also sung the title role of Il Ritorno d'Ulisse conducted by Nicholas McGegan for Long Beach Opera and in the premiere of Musgrave's Incident at Owl Creek Bridge, for BBC Radio 3; Principal baritone at Cologne Opera from 1989, as Valentin, Nardo in La Finta Giardiniera, Mozart's Count, Puccini's Lescaut and Marcello, Belcore in L'Elisir d'amore; Concert performances of Figaro and the Glagolitic Mass, conducted by Simon Rattle; Glyndebourne Festival debut 1991, as Guglielmo; Other roles in Shostakovich The Nose for Cologne Opera and title role in Don Giovanni for Dresden Opera, 1994; Ned Keene in Peter Grimes, Châtelet, 1995; Schwetzingen Festival, 1995, in Salieri's Falstaff; Sang Kolenaty in The Makropulos Case at Aix, 2000. *Recordings include:* El Cid, Mary, Queen of Scots. *Current Management:* Askonas Holt Ltd, Lonsdale Chambers, 27 Chancery Lane, London, WC2A 1PF, England. *Telephone:* (20) 7400-1700. *Fax:* (20) 7400-1799. *E-mail:* info@askonasholt.co.uk. *Website:* www.askonasholt.co.uk.

**GARDNER, John Linton,** CBE, BMus; British composer; b. 2 March 1917, Manchester, England; m. Jane Margaret Mary Abercrombie 1955 (died 1998); one s. two d. *Education:* Exeter College, Oxford. *Career:* Music Staff, Royal Opera House, 1946–52; Tutor, Morley College, 1952–76 (Director of Music 1965–69); Professor, Royal Academy of Music, 1956–86; Deputy Chairman, PRS, 1983–88; Chairman, 1963, Composers' Guild; Honorary Member, Royal Philharmonic Society, 1998. *Compositions:* 5 operas, including The Moon and Sixpence, 1957; 3 symphonies; 3 string quartets; 3 piano sonatas, concertos for piano, trumpet, organ, oboe and flute; Brass Chamber Music; 12 major Cantatas for chorus and orchestra, including, The Ballad of the White Horse; Music for smaller groups; Concerto for flute and strings, 1994; Sextet for piano and wind, 1995; Much unaccompanied choral music. *Recordings:* A Latter-Day Athenian Speaks; Theme and Variations for brass; Quartet for saxes; Tomorrow Shall Be My Dancing Day; Ecossaises; Burns Sequence; Flute Concerto; Third Symphony; Oboe concerto; 2nd Oboe Sonata. *Publications:* contrib. to Schumann, A Symposium; Musical Companion; Journals including Listener, Musical Times, RAM Magazine, Tempo, Dublin Review. *Honours:* Gold Medal, Bax Society, 1958. *Address:* 20 Firswood Avenue, Epsom, Surrey KT19 0PR, England.

**GARDOW, Helrun;** Singer (Mezzo-soprano); b. 8 Jan. 1944, Eisenach, Germany. *Education:* Studied in Berlin and Milan and with Josef Metternich in Cologne. *Career:* Sang at the Bonn Opera, 1969–76, and Zürich Opera, 1976–87 in various roles including Orpheus and Dorabella; Appeared in the premieres of Kelterborn's Ein Engel Kommt nach Babyon, 1977 and Der Kirschgarten in 1984; Guest appearances at Copenhagen, Düsseldorf, Edinburgh, Berlin, Dresden, Munich, Milan and Vienna; Concert engagements at Frankfurt, Madrid, Amsterdam, Cologne and Naples; Active in Seoul, Korea from 1987 as singer and director of Art-Com, in computer visual art and music. *Recordings:* Minerva in Il Ritorno d'Ulisse; L'Incoronazione di Poppea; Dido and Aeneas; Bach Cantatas and Magnificat; Haydn's Theresa Mass; Mozart's Missa Brevis in D. *Address:* c/o Opernhaus Zürich, Falkenstrasse 1, 8008 Zürich, Switzerland.

**GARETTI, Helene;** Singer (Soprano); b. 13 March 1939, Roanne, Loire, France. *Education:* Studied at the Paris Conservatoire and with Regine Crespin. *Career:* Sang first at Nice then Paris Opéra from 1968 as Marguerite, Iphigénie en Tauride, Médée, Chrysothemis in 1987 and Desdemona in 1988; Sang Massenet's Grisélidis at Strasbourg in 1986; Appearances at the Paris Opéra-Comique as Mimi, Butterfly, Katya Kabanova and Donna Elvira in 1988; Sang Sieglinde at Rouen and elsewhere in France; Other roles have included Leonore, Ariadne and Marguerite in Damnation de Faust.

**GARIBOVA, Karine;** Violinist; b. 1965, Moscow, Russia. *Education:* Studied at the Central Music School, Moscow. *Career:* Co-Founder, Quartet Veronique, 1989; Many concerts in the former Soviet Union and Russia, notably in the Russian Chamber Music Series and the 150th birthday celebrations for Tchaikovsky, 1990; Masterclasses at the Aldeburgh Festival, 1991; Concert tour of the United Kingdom in season 1992–93; Repertoire includes works by Beethoven, Brahms, Tchaikovsky, Bartók, Shostakovich and Schnittke. *Recordings include:* Schnittke's 3rd Quartet. *Honours:* Winner, All-Union String Quartet Competition, St Petersburg, 1990–91; Third Place, International Shostakovich Competition at St Petersburg, 1991, both with the

Quartet Veronique. *Address:* c/o Sonata (Quartet Veronique), 11 Northpark Street, Glasgow G20 7AA, Scotland.

**GARILLI, Fabrizio;** Pianist and Composer; b. 29 July 1941, Monticelli d'Ongina, Placenza, Italy; m. Anna Paola Rossi, 8 Sept 1968, 1 s. *Education:* Diploma in Piano, Composition and Choral Music; Teaching qualification. *Career:* Debut: Piano Soloist with orchestra, Beethoven's 3rd Concerto, Teatro Municipale, Piacenza; Concerts as solo pianist with orchestra and chamber music; Conservatory Director. *Compositions:* Fantasie for Piano; Cantico delle Creature for Soloists, Choir and Organ; Contrappunti Su Temi Gregoriani for Organ and Orchestra; Metamorfosi for 2 Pianos and Percussion; Laude for Female Choir, Narrator and Orchestra. *Recordings:* Music of 17th Century Italians, Ciampi, Galuppi and Scarlatti, and JS Bach Well-Tempered Klavier, 2 records. *Publications:* Studi per Pianoforte; La Cartellina; Pezzi Per Cordo di Voci Bianche; Pezzi per Organo. *Honours:* 1st Prize, FM Neapolitano Composition Competition, Naples; 2nd Prize, Pedrollo, Milan; 1st Place, Assisi Prize; Various compositions commended in other composition competitions. *Address:* Via A da Sangallo 22, 29100 Piacenza, Italy.

**GARINO, Gerard;** Singer (Tenor); b. 1 June 1949, Lancon, Provence, France. *Education:* Studied at the Bordeaux Conservatoire and in Italy. *Career:* Debut: Bordeaux, 1977 as Rossini's Almaviva; Appearances at Bordeaux as Gerald in Lakmé and in La Dame Blanche and Gounod's Mireille; Further engagements as Mozart's Ferrando in Toulouse and Nadir in Les Pêcheurs de Perles at Aix; Paris Opéra and Liège 1981, in Il Matrimonio Segreto and Don Pasquale (Ernesto); Returned to Liège 1982 and 1987, as Idomeneo and in Grétry's Zemire; Portrait de Manon, Monte Carlo 1989; Season 1991, as Nadir at the Opéra-Comique, Paris, Pylades in Iphigénie en Tauride by Piccinni at Rome and Masaniello in La Muette de Portici at Marseille; Other roles include Tonio (La Fille du Régiment), Macduff, Ismaele (Nabucco) and Nicias (Thais); Traviata and Romeo and Juliette at Liège, Bohème at Toulouse, Thérèse (Massenet) at Monte Carlo, 1989; Manon (Massenet) at Bordeaux, Anna Bolena at Marseille, 1990; Werther at Festival Massenet and Festival de La Coruna, Spain, 1993; St Gallen 1994, as Nicias in Thais by Massenet. *Recordings:* L'Abandon d'Arianne by Milhaud; Don Sanche by Liszt; Messiaen's St François d'Assise; Il Pitor Parigino by Cimarosa; Video of Carmen (as Remendado); La Mort d'Orphée, Berlioz. *Honours:* Winner, 1973 Enrico Caruso Competition. *Address:* Teatro dell'Opera, Piazza B Gigli, 00184 Rome, Italy.

**GARNER, Françoise;** singer (soprano); b. 17 Oct. 1933, Nerac, Lot-et-Garonne, France. *Education:* Paris Conservatoire, Accademia di Santa Cecilia, Rome and in Vienna. *Career:* debut, Paris Opéra-Comique in 1963 in the premiere of Menotti's Le Dernier Sauvage; sang in Paris as Rosina, Leila, Lakmé and Olympia; Paris Opéra as Gilda and Lucia di Lammermoor, and Aix-en-Provence Festival in 1971 as the Queen of Night in Die Zauberflöte; sang Marguerite in Faust at La Scala Milan in 1977, and at Verona Arena as Butterfly and Gounod's Juliette, 1977–79; many performances in France and Italy in operas by Bellini; Metropolitan Opera 1986 as Elvira in I Puritani.

**GARO, Edouard;** Chorus Master and Composer; b. 6 July 1935, Nyon, Switzerland; m. Verena Rellstab, 2 April 1963, 1 s., 1 d. *Education:* Arts, History, Philology, University of Lausanne; Composition, Singing, Academy of Lausanne; Studies, Pierre Mollet and Maroussia Le Mar Hadour, Geneva and Sylvia Gähwiller, Zürich. *Career:* Founder, Conductor, Ensemble Choral de la Côte; Music Master, Gymnase Cantonal de Nyon; Professor, Séminaire Pédagogique de l'enseignement secondaire, Lausanne; mem, ASM; SUISA; SSA. *Compositions:* Prospectrum, piano and tape, 1971; Les Sept contre Thèbes, 8 female voices and percussion, 1978; Incantation a 3, clarinet solo and tape, 1980; Agamemnon, opera, 1982; Le Masque blanc sur fond rouge, opera-ballet, 1984; Un Instant seul, 1989; Petra cantat, 1994; Joutes, 1996; La Grande Eclipse, 1996; String Quartet No. 1, 1993–97, No. 2, 1995–97, No. 3, 1998; Violin Concerto, 1999; Joutes rhapsodiques, cello, clarinet, piano, 2001; Requiem, S.T.B. solo; boy's choir, choir, instr. ensemble, 2001. *Publications:* Invention for Music Teaching: SOLMIPLOT. *Honours:* Grand Prix UFAM, with Medal from Ville de Paris, 1972; Silver Medal, International Exhibition of Inventions and New Techniques, Geneva, 1974. *Address:* 16 rue de la Porcelaine, 1260 Nyon, Switzerland.

**GARRARD, Don;** Singer (Bass); b. 31 July 1929, Vancouver, Canada. *Education:* Studied at the Toronto and Vancouver Conservatories and Opera School, Toronto; Music Academy of the West at Santa Barbara with Lotte Lehmann; Final 2 years study in Milan. *Career:* Debut: Toronto in 1952 as the Speaker in Die Zauberflöte; Sang Don Giovanni for Canadian television; Sadler's Wells Opera London from 1961 as Attila, Sarastro, Rocco, Raleigh in Gloriana, Trulove in The Rake's Progress and in the British premiere of Pizzetti's L'Assassinio nella Cattedrale in 1962; Scottish Opera in 1963 in the British premiere of Dallapiccola's Volo di Notte; Aldeburgh Festival in 1964 in the world premiere of Curlew River by Britten; Glyndebourne Festival, 1965–76 as Rochefort in Anna Bolena, Gremin, Pastor in the local premiere of Von Einem's The Visit of The Old Lady, Trulove and Arkel in Pelléas et Mélisande; Hamburg Staatsoper debut in 1968 as Padre Guardiano in La Forza del Destino and Covent Garden debut in 1970 as Ferrando in Il Trovatore followed by Prince Gremin in E Onegin, 1971–72; English National Opera as Sarastro; Mephisto (Faust); Rocco (Fidelio); Beckett in Murder in the Cathedral; Attila; Guardiano (Forza); Daland in Flying Dutchman; The Wanderer in Siegfried; Guest appearances in Santa Fe, Johannesburg,

Toronto, Ottawa, Washington and Edinburgh; Sang the Grand Inquisitor in Don Carlos at Toronto in 1988, Daland in Der fliegende Holländer for Pacific Opera at Victoria BC, in 1989; Sang King Mark in Tristan und Isolde for Capab Opera at Cape Town in 1992; Season 1994–95, as Rocco and Sarastro; Crespel in Les Contes d'Hoffmann, 1998; many concert appearances. *Recordings include:* The Rake's Progress. *Honours:* 1st Prize Singing, Stars of Tomorrow and NOS Futures Etoiles, Canada, 1953, 1954; Vercelli Concours, 1961; Queen's Jubilee Medal, 1977. *Address:* The Villa, 18 Van Der Poll Avenue, Tokai 7945, Cape Town 8000, South Africa.

**GARRETT, David;** Concert Violinist; b. 1981, USA. *Career:* Appearances with the Chamber Orchestra of Europe under Abbado and the Munich Philharmonic under Mehta; British debut at the 1993 Brighton Festival with the Bournemouth Symphony, returned in 1994 with the London Philharmonic under Matthias Bamert and in 1995 with City of Birmingham Symphony Orchestra under Stefan Sanderling; US debut with Los Angeles Philharmonic under Zubin Mehta 1994, with Munich Philharmonic Orchestra under Zubin Mehta 1997, Berlin debut with Rundfunk Sinfonieorchester Berlin 1999; performed at Expo 2000, Hannover; recent engagements have included Royal Philharmonic Orchestra under Leonard Slatkin and Orchestre Philharmonique de Liège under Louis Langrée. *Recordings include:* exclusively for Deutsche Grammophon: Mozart Violin COncertos (Abbado), 24 Paganini Caprices, Tchaikovsky Violin Concert (Pletnev), Pure Classics. *Current Management:* Askonas Holt Ltd, Lonsdale Chambers, 27 Chancery Lane, London, WC2A 1PF, England. *Telephone:* (20) 7400-1700. *Fax:* (20) 7400-1799. *E-mail:* info@askonasholt.co.uk. *Website:* www.askonasholt.co.uk.

**GARRETT, Eric;** singer (bass-baritone); b. 1935, Yorkshire, England. *Education:* Royal College of Music, London and studied with Eva Turner and Tito Gobbi. *Career:* debut at Covent Garden in 1962 in La Bohème; many character roles at Covent Garden from 1962; Appearances with Scottish Opera and the Welsh National Opera, Brussels and Ghent, 1978–79 as Bartolo in Il Barbiere di Siviglia, Dulcamara in L'Elisir d'amore and in Adriana Lecouvreur; Antwerp, 1981 as Baron Ochs in Der Rosenkavalier; Sang Mustafà in L'Italiana in Algeri at Covent Garden in 1988, Ceprano in Rigoletto in 1989, Skula in a new production of Prince Igor in 1990, followed by Don Pasquale and Alcindoro; Other roles at Covent Garden include Gianni Schnicci, Don Fernando, Sacristan, Swallow, Varlaam and Frank; Has also sung Falstaff, Melitone, Scarpia, Ochs, Kecal, Schigolch in Lulu and Rocco; Guest appearances include San Francisco, Los Angeles, Marseilles, Montpellier and Munich; Flemish Deputy in Don Carlos at Covent Garden, 1996; Mozart's Antonio with the Royal Opera, 1998. *Recordings include:* La Fanciulla del West; Billy Budd.

**GARRETT, Lesley,** CBE, FRAM; British singer (soprano); b. 10 April 1955, d. of Derek Arthur Garrett and Margaret Wall; m. 1991; one s. one d. *Education:* Thorne Grammar School, Royal Acad. of Music, Nat. Opera Studio. *Career:* winner Kathleen Ferrier Memorial Competition 1979; performed with Welsh Nat. Opera, Opera North, at Wexford and Buxton Festivals and at Glyndebourne; joined ENO (Prin. Soprano) 1984. *Television:* appeared in BBC TV series Lesley Garrett... Tonight. *Major roles include:* Susanna in The Marriage of Figaro, Despina in Così Fan Tutte, Musetta in La Bohème, Jenny in The Rise and Fall of The City of Mahagonny, Atalanta in Xerxes, Zerlinda in Don Giovanni, Yum-Yum in The Mikado, Adèle in Die Fledermaus, Oscar in A Masked Ball, Dalinda in Ariodante, Rose in Street Scene, Bella in A Midsummer Marriage, Eurydice in Orpheus and Eurydice and title roles in The Cunning Little Vixen and La Belle Vivette; numerous concert hall performances in UK and abroad (including Last Night of the Proms); TV and radio appearances. *Publication:* Notes From a Small Soprano (autobiog.) 2001. *Honours:* Hon. DArts (Plymouth) 1995; Best Selling Classical Artist, Gramophone Award 1996. *Address:* The Music Partnership Ltd, Suite 6, Riverside House, 27–29 Vauxhall Grove, London, SW8 1SY, England (office). *Telephone:* (20) 7840 9590. *Fax:* (20) 7735 5252.

**GARRISON, Jon;** Tenor; b. 11 Dec. 1944, Higginsville, Missouri, USA. *Career:* Has sung widely in North America notably at opera houses in Houston, Montreal, Santa Fe and San Diego; Metropolitan Opera from 1974 in Death in Venice, Manon Lescaut, Così fan tutte as Ferrando and Die Zauberflöte as Tamino; New York City Opera from 1982 as Admète in Alceste, Don Ottavio, Rodolfo, Nadir, the Duke of Mantua, Tom Rakewell, Tamino and Nicholas in the premiere of Reise's Rasputin in 1988; Sang Prince Edmund in the premiere of Stewart Copeland's Holy Blood and Crescent Moon at Cleveland, 1989, and sang Shuratov in the US stage premiere of From The House of The Dead, in New York, 1990; Sang the title role in Oedipus Rex at the Festival Hall, London, 1997; Idomeneo at the 1996 Garsington Festival. *Address:* c/o New York City Opera, Lincoln Center, New York, NY 10023, USA.

**GARRISON, Kenneth;** Singer (Tenor); b. 6 Dec. 1948, West Monroe, Louisiana, USA. *Education:* Studied at the Salzburg Mozarteum and with Hans Hopf in Munich. *Career:* Debut: Regensburg, 1977, as Mozart's Basilio; Sang at Regensburg until 1980, Oldenburg, 1980–82, Karlsruhe, 1982–84 (Wagner's Mime and Steersman); Munich Staatsoper from 1984, as Luzio in Wagner's Das Liebesverbot, Dvořák's Dimitri, the Prince in Love for Three Oranges, Max and Narraboth; Guest engagements as Strauss's Emperor at Karlsruhe, Radames at Saarbrucken and Parsifal at Brunswick and Essen; Mainz, 1990, as Otello; Season 1993 at Brunswick as Strauss's Emperor, Strasbourg 1996 in From the House of Death; Many concert appearances,

notably in Beethoven's Ninth and Rossini's Stabat Mater; Season 2000–01 as Mime in Siegfried at Mannheim and Tannhäuser at Cape Town. *Address:* c/o Bayerische Staatsoper, Max-Joseph-Platz, Pf 100148, W-8000 Munich 1, Germany.

**GASCO, Daniel;** Singer (Tenor); b. 1961, Valencia, Spain. *Education:* Studied in Valencia and with Waldemar Kmentt in Vienna. *Career:* Appearances in Vienna as Nicolai's Fenton and Mozart's Ferrando and in Rossini's Il Viaggio a Reims; Bregenz Festival, 1989–93 as Rossini's Ramiro and Lindoro, Fenton, and in Rossini's Stabat Mater; Berne, 1993 as Daniel in Judith by Matthus; Season 1994 as Ferrando at Lubeck and Verdi's Fenton at Brunswick. *Address:* c/o Staatsoper, 1010 Vienna, Austria.

**GASDIA, Cecilia;** Soprano; b. 14 Aug. 1960, Verona, Italy. *Education:* Studied classics and piano in Verona. *Career:* Debut: Florence in 1982 as Giulietta in I Capuleti e i Montecchi by Bellini; La Scala in 1982 as Anna Bolena in the opera by Donizetti; Perugia and Naples in 1982 in Demophoon by Cherubini and as Amina in La Sonnambula; Paris Opéra debut in 1983 as Anais in Moise by Rossini; Pesaro in 1984 in a revival of Il Viaggio a Reims by Rossini; US debut in Philadelphia in 1985 as Gilda in a concert performance of Rigoletto; Chicago Lyric Opera and Metropolitan Opera in 1986 as Giulietta and as Gounod's Juliette; Other roles include Violetta, Liu in Turandot, Hélène in Verdi's Jérusalem and Mrs Ford in Salieri's Falstaff; Sang Rosa in Fioravanti's Le Cantatrici Villane, Naples, 1990; Season 1991–92 as Adina at Chicago, Mimi at Bonn, Nedda at Rome, Elena in La Donna del Lago at La Scala and Rosina at the Festival of Caracalla; Pesaro Festival 1994, as Semiramide; Zürich 1997, as Gounod's Marguerite; Season 1998 as Euridice at Florence, Giulietta in Un Giorno di Regno at Parma, Handel's Cleopatra at Glimmerglass, New York, and Suzel in L'Amico Fritz at Naples; Season 2000–01 as Jean in Le Jongleur de Notre Dame by Massenet in Rome, Elcia in Rossini's Mosè in Egitto at Verona and as Suzel in Mascagni's L'Amico Fritz. *Recordings include:* Catone in Utica; Motets by Vivaldi; Il Viaggio a Reims; Video of Turandot; Rossini's Armida and Ermione. *Address:* c/o Teatro San Carlo, Via San Carlo 98F, 80132 Naples, Italy.

**GASSIEV, Nikolai Tengizovich;** Russian singer (tenor); b. 2 Feb. 1952, Tskhinvali, Georgia. *Education:* Leningrad State Conservatory. *Career:* soloist Mariinsky Opera and Ballet Theatre 1990–; debut in Metropolitan Opera as Yurodivy (Boris Godunov) and Agrippina (Fairy Angel) 1992, Dresdner Staatsoper 1993, Brooklyn School of Music 1995, Edinburgh Festival 1995, Albert Hall 1995, La Scala 1996. *Honours:* Prize of Union of Theatre Workers Best Actor of the Year 1994. *Address:* Mariinsky Theatre, Teatralnaya pl. 1, St Petersburg, Russia (office). *Telephone:* (812) 315-57-24 (office).

**GASTEEN, Lisa;** Australian singer (soprano); b. 1957, Queensland. *Education:* Queensland Conservatorium with Margaret Nickson, studied in San Francisco, London Opera Studio. *Career:* debut, Lyric Opera of Queensland as the High Priestess in Aida and Diana in Orpheus in The Underworld 1985; appearances with Australian Opera as Miss Jessel in The Turn of the Screw, Frasquita, Madame Lidoine in Carmelites, both Leonoras, Elsa, Donna Elvira and Leonore in Fidelio; Victorian State Opera as Elisabeth in Tannhäuser, Elisabeth de Valois and Desdemona, Leonora Trovatore 1993; season 1991–92 as the Trovatore and Forza Leonoras for Scottish Opera, Amelia in Un Ballo in Maschera for WNO and Washington Opera, Donna Anna in Prague and Fidelio Leonore in Stuttgart; concert repertoire includes Rossini's Stabat Mater and Elijah for the Sydney Philharmonia, Beethoven's Ninth in Sydney, Melbourne and Tasmania, Tokyo Philharmonic; sang Verdi's Requiem for Hungarian radio 1993, Maddelena in Andrea Chénier for Deutsche Oper Berlin 1994, Aida for Australian Opera 1995; sang the Trovatore Leonora at Sydney 1996; sang the Empress in Die Frau Ohne Schatten for Melbourne Festival 1996; season 1999–2000 as Brünnhilde in Siegfried at Stuttgart, Verdi's Elisabeth de Valois and Strauss's Chrysothemis at Sydney; season 2001–2002 all three Brünnhilde at Meiningen and Isolde for Opera Australia in Melbourne; sang Brünnhilde at Covent Garden 2005. *Honours:* Covent Garden Scholarship 1984, Metropolitan Opera Educational Fund grant winner Australian Regional Finals Metropolitan Opera, NY Competition 1982, Advance Australia Award 1991, winner Cardiff Singer of the World Competition 1991, Helpmann Award (for role of Isolde with Opera Australia) 2002. *Current Management:* Jenifer Eddy Artists' Management, Suite 11, The Clivedon, 596 St Kilda Road, Melbourne 3004, Vic., Australia.

**GASZTECKI, Marek;** Singer (Bass); b. 1953, Poland. *Career:* Debut: Poznan, 1977, as Theseus in A Midsummer Night's Dream; Sang at Poznan until 1980, then with Darmstadt Opera as Don Magnifico in Cenerentola, the Water Spirit in Rusalka and many other roles; Many guest appearances elsewhere in Germany, notably at Bonn as Cecil in Donizetti's Maria Stuarda and in The Lighthouse by Maxwell Davies; Has also sung in contemporary works by Klebe and Cerha and has sung in concert in works by Bach, Handel and Haydn; Season 1994–95 in Prokofiev's Fiery Angel at Kassel and as Lothario in Mignon by Thomas at Heidelberg; Season 1999–2000 in Busoni's Faust at Salzburg and in Szymanowski's King Roger for Netherlands Opera. *Address:* c/o Oper der Stadt Bonn, Am Boeselagerhof 1, Pf 2440, W-5300 Bonn, Germany.

**GASZTOWT-ADAMS, Helen (Catriona);** Soprano; b. 29 Sept. 1956, Geelong, Victoria, Australia. *Education:* Victorian College of The Arts, Melbourne; National Opera Studio, London, 1989; Studied with Audrey Langford and Janice Chapman. *Career:* Debut: Pamina in Die Zauberflöte,

State Opera of South Australia, 1983; Sang in Don Giovanni, Manon, Countess Maritza, and Figaro for State Opera of South Australia, 1985–86; Debut with Australian Opera as Nanetta in 1986 then in Suor Angelica, Il Tabarro, Médée, Poppea, and Carmen; London debut, Anna Bolena at National Opera Studio Showcase, Queen Elizabeth Hall in 1989; BBC Cardiff Singer of the World finals in 1989; European concert debut, Grusse aus Wien, Robert Stolz Club, recorded for Belgian radio and television, 1990; Sang Gilda in Rigoletto, Australian Opera in 1990; English National Opera debut as Donna Elvira in 1991; Other appearances include Rossini's Petite Messe Solennelle, Netherlands and Belgian tour, Strauss's Vier Letzte Lieder, Koninklijk Ballet van Vlaanderen, Antwerp, Belgium, Mozart's Requiem, English String Orchestra, Bath Mozart Festival, and as Pamina in Die Zauberflöte, Victoria State Opera, Melbourne; Extensive radio and television recital and concert work including Handel's Messiah, Mendelssohn's Elijah, A Midsummer Night's Dream, Orff's Carmina Burana, and Vier Letzte Leider; Performed with Melbourne and Sydney Symphony Orchestras, Australian Chamber Orchestra, and opera and concert performances in the United Kingdom, Barbados, Australia, France and Spain. *Address:* c/o English National Opera, St Martin's Lane, London WC2N 4ES, England.

**GATES, Crawford;** Conductor and Composer; b. 29 Dec. 1921, San Francisco, California, USA; m. Georgia Lauper 1952; two s. two d. *Education:* BA, San Jose State Coll.; MA, Brigham Young Univ.; PhD, Music, Eastman School of Music, Univ. of Rochester; conducting studies with Eleazar de Carvalho and Hans Swarowsky. *Career:* debut, Stanford Univ., as composer, 1938; Utah Symphony, as conductor; Chair., Music Dept, and Conductor, Symphony Orchestra and Opera, Brigham Young Univ., 1960–66; Artist-in-Residence, Prof., Chair of Music Dept, Beloit Coll., Beloit, Wisconsin, 1966–89; Music Dir, Beloit Janesville Symphony, 1966–1999, Quincy Symphony, 1969–70, Rockford Symphony Orchestra, 1970–86. *Compositions include:* six stage works, seven symphonies, Tone Poems, Suites, Concertos, numerous choral arrangements, four major choral works, trumpet concertino and horn sonata; Pentameron for piano and orchestra (commissioned by Grant Johannesen); over 100 titles published including Suite for String Orchestra. *Recordings:* Symphony No. 2, Orchestral Setting of Beloved Mormon Hymns, included on Philadelphia Orchestra Album; The Lord's Prayer and A Jubilant Song; Music to the New Hill Cumorah Pageant, 1988; Promised Valley. *Address:* 2108 Scenic Drive, Salt Lake City, UT 84109, USA.

**GATI, Istvan;** Tenor; b. 29 Nov. 1948, Budapest, Hungary. *Education:* Studied at the Franz Liszt Academy, Budapest. *Career:* Member of the Hungarian State Opera from 1972 notably in the premieres of Csongor and Tunde by Attila Bozay in 1985 and Ecce Homo by Sandor Szokolay, 1987; Appearances at the Vienna Staatsoper from 1986; Sang Don Giovanni at Liège in 1988, Nick Shadow at the Deutsche Oper Berlin in 1989 and Antonio in Le nozze di Figaro at the 1991 Vienna Festival; Season 1999–2000 as Ruggiero in Halévy's La Juive and Marco in Gianni Schicchi; Guest appearances in Italy, France, Poland, Spain, Netherlands and Austria and concert engagements in works by Bach, Handel, Mozart, Beethoven and Liszt. *Recordings include:* Cantatas by Bach, Don Sanche and The Legend of St Elisabeth by Liszt; Salieri's Falstaff; Paisiello's Barbiere di Siviglia; Don Pasquale; Simon Boccanegra; Telemann's Der Geduldige Sokrates; Balthazar and Jonas by Carissimi; Ein Deutsches Requiem; Mahler's Lieder eines Fahrenden Gesellen; Oronte in Handel's Floridante. *Honours:* Competition Winner at Salzburg, Vienna, Trevisto and Moscow at Tchaikovsky International in 1974. *Address:* c/o Hungarian State Opera, Nepoztarsasag utja 22, 1061 Budapest, Hungary.

**GATTI, Daniele;** Italian conductor; *Music Director, Royal Philharmonic Orchestra*; b. 6 Nov. 1961, Milan; m. Silvia Chiesa 1990. *Education:* Giuseppe Verdi Conservatory, Milan. *Career:* conducted Verdi's Giovanna d'Arco 1982; appearances with the Maggio Musicale Fiorentino Orchestra, Milan Angelicum, Bologna Municipal Orchestra, regional orchestras of Italian radio; f. Stradivari Chamber Orchestra 1986; debut at La Scala, Milan with Rossini's L'occasione fa il Ladro 1987–88 season; US debut with American Symphony Orchestra, Carnegie Hall, New York 1990; Covent Garden debut with I Puritani 1992; Music Dir Santa Cecilia, Rome 1992–; Prin. Guest Conductor, Royal Opera House, Covent Garden 1994–96; debut at Metropolitan Opera, New York with Madama Butterfly 1994–95 season; debut with Royal Philharmonic Orchestra 1994, Music Dir 1995–(2009); debut with New York Philharmonic 1995; Music Dir Teatro Communale, Bologna 1997–; has led many orchestras in Europe and USA, including the Bavarian Radio Symphony, London Philharmonic, Cleveland Orchestra, Boston and Chicago Symphonies and the Accademia Santa Cecilia, Rome; has conducted at many of the world's leading opera houses; conducted the RPO at the London Proms 1999, 2002. *Recordings:* Tschaikovsky's Fourth and Fifth Symphonies, Pathétique Symphony No. 6 2005. *Current Management:* Columbia Artists Management Ltd, 28 Cheverton Road, London, N19 3AY, England. *Telephone:* (20) 7272-8020. *Fax:* (20) 7272-8991. *E-mail:* info@cami.co.uk. *Address:* Via Scaglia Est 134, 41100 Modena, Italy (office); c/o Royal Philharmonic Orchestra, 16 Clerkenwell Green, London, EC1R 0DP, England (office).

**GATTI, Giorgio;** Singer (Bass-Baritone); b. 1 April 1948, Poggio a Caino, Italy. *Education:* Studied in Florence and Rome. *Career:* Opera engagements throughout Italy in operas by Pergolesi, A Scarlatti, Salieri, Anfossi, Piccinni, Morlacchi and Sacchini, Florence, 1994 in La Bohème; Opera and concert appearances in France, Germany, Switzerland, Japan and North America; Member of group Recitar Cantando, 1980–90. *Recordings:* Il Barone di Rocca

antica by Anfossi; Fioravanti's La Servascaltra. *Address:* c/o Teatro Comunale, Via Solferino 15, 50123 Florence, Italy.

**GAUCI, Miriam;** Maltese singer (soprano); b. 3 April 1957, Vittoriosa, Gozo; d. of Carmel Cutajar and Rosette Tabone; m. Michael Laus 1987; one d. *Education:* Conservatoio G. Verdi and Centro di Perfezionamento Artisti Lirici, Milan, Italy. *Career:* debut at La Scala, Milan, Italy in La Sonnambula, L'Orfeo, Die Frau ohne Schatten; debut in USA in Madame Butterfly at Santa Fe 1987; appeared in La Bohème with Placido Domingo, Los Angeles, USA, Hamburg, Germany; appeared in La Traviata, Geneva, Switzerland, Dresden, Germany; also sang in Madrid, Lisbon and Berlin, Manon at Vienna Staatsoper 1996 and in Boito's Mefistofele; in Falstaff at the Hamburg Staatsoper 1997, Mimi at the New York Met 2001. *Video:* Carmen 1989. *Recordings include:* Madame Butterfly 1992, Manon Lescaut, Pagliacci (Naxos), La Bohème, Deutsches Requiem, Verdi's Requiem, Egmont, Operatic Arias. *Honours:* first prize in various int. competitions, including Treviso, Bologna, Milan, Italy 1979. *Address:* c/o Grand Théâtre de Genève, 11 Boulevard du Théâtre, 1211 Geneva, Switzerland; Villa No. 5, Salini Street, Marsascala, Malta. *Telephone:* 820033. *Fax:* 690477.

**GAVANELLI, Paolo;** Singer (Baritone); b. 1959, Monselice, near Padua, Italy. *Career:* Debut: Sang Leporello at the Teatro Donizetti, Bergamo in 1985; Season 1988–89 as Mephistopheles at Barcelona and Marcello in La Bohème in Madrid; Further engagements as Marcello at Venice, Bologna and the State Operas of Munich and Vienna in 1991; Sang Luna in Trovatore at the Metropolitan in 1990 returning in Puritani and as Germont in 1992; Sang Gerard in Andrea Chénier at San Francisco and Stuttgart, Renato in Un Ballo in Maschera at Chicago and Verdi's Falstaff at the Rome Opera; Festival appearances at Pesaro as Germano in La Scala di Seta, 1990 and the Arena Verona; Has also appeared at La Scala from 1991 and Genoa as Renato; Other roles include Rossini's Figaro and Verdi's Iago, Rigoletto and Amonasro; Festival appearances 1996 at Ravenna (as Alfio) and Rome (Gerard); Renato (Ballo in Maschera) at Verona, 1998; Season 2000–01 at the Munich State Opera as Riccardo in I Puritani, Germont, and Posa; Nabucco at Verona, Falstaff at Covent Garden and Simon Boccanegra for San Francisco Opera; Germont for the Royal Opera, 2002. *Recordings:* Marcello in La Bohème. *Address:* c/o Metropolitan Opera House, Lincoln Center, New York, NY 10023, USA.

**GAVAZZI, Ernesto;** singer (tenor); b. 7 May 1941, Seregno, Monza, Italy. *Education:* Milan Conservatoire with Bruno Carmassi, Scuola della Scala with Vladimiro Badiali. *Career:* debut in Treviso in 1971 as Nemorino in L'Elisir d'amore; many appearances in Italy and elsewhere in Europe as Elvino in La Sonnambula, Paolina in Il Matrimonio Segreto and Rossini's Almaviva, Don Ramiro, Giocondo in La Pietra del Paragone, Edward Milfort in Il Cambiale di Matrimonio, Rodolphe in Guillaume Tell and Don Eusebio in L'Occasione fa il Ladro; has sung at Pesaro and La Scala in several Rossini revivals including Zefirio in Il Viaggio a Reims, 1984–85; sang Goro in Madama Butterfly and Chekalinsky in The Queen of Spades at La Scala, 1990–97; Normanno in Lucia di Lammermoor at La Scala, 1997; season 2000–01 at La Scala in Tosca, Rigoletto, Il Trovatore and Falstaff. *Recordings include:* Il Viaggio a Reims; Captain in Simon Boaccanegra; Borsa in Rigoletto; Uldino in Attila; Guillaume Tell under Riccardo Muti.

**GAVIN, Julian;** Singer (Tenor); b. 1965, Melbourne, Victoria, Australia. *Education:* Studied in Melbourne (BMus) and at the National Opera Studio, London. *Career:* Has appeared widely in the United Kingdom and Ireland as Alfredo, Des Grieux, Nemorino, Rodolfo, Tamino, Don José and the Duke of Mantua; Further appearances in Franck's Hulda, Alvaro in La Forza del Destino, Ismaele in Nabucco, Arrigo in Verdi's Battaglia di Legnano, Pinkerton, and Laca in Jenůfa (Opera North, 1995); Pollione in Norma at Lucerne, 1996; Steersman in The Flying Dutchman, Alfredo in La Traviata for Australian Opera, 1996, 1997; Concert repertoire includes Messiah, Rossini's Stabat Mater, The Dream of Gerontius, the Verdi Requiem with David Willcocks, Mahler's 8th Symphony at the Festival Hall; Tippet, A Child of Our Time, Ulster Orchestra; Sang Beaumont in Maw's The Rising of the Moon for the BBC; Season 1996–97 as the Duke of Mantua, Alfredo and Pinkerton for ENO; Sang Hoffmann, 1998; Carlo VII in Verdi's Giovanna d'Arco for Opera North, Don Carlos in Leeds, at the Edinburgh Festival and for the Royal Opera, 1998 with Haitink, and for Opera Australia, 1999; Season 1999–2000, Roméo in Gounod's Roméo et Juliette and Don José in Carmen, Puccini's Des Grieux at Genoa, with the ENO Rodolfo in La Bohème and the title role in Ernani; Pinkerton for Opera North; Concert performances of Kodály's Psalmus Hungaricus with the BBC Symphony Orchestra and Berlioz Roméo et Juliette with the Sydney Symphony Orchestra; Manrico for ENO 2001; mem, International Society of Musicians. *Recordings:* Godvino in Verdi's Aroldo; Don José in Carmen; Roméo et Juliette; Les Contes d'Hoffmann. *Honours:* Lady Turner Prize, University of Melbourne, 1978; L Mus A, 1985. *Address:* c/o English National Opera, St Martin's Lane, London, WC2, England.

**GAVRILOV, Andrei Vladimirovich;** Russian pianist; b. 21 Sept. 1955, Moscow. *Education:* Moscow Conservatory. *Career:* winner of the Tchaikovsky Competition in Moscow 1974; performs regularly throughout Europe, America and Japan, including recitals at Salzburg, Roque d'Antheron, Schleswig-Holstein, Istanbul and Chichester Festivals; has performed in England with the Philharmonia, London Philharmonic, Royal Philharmonic, BBC Symphony and London Symphony Orchestras, in America with the Baltimore

Symphony, Detroit Symphony, New York Philharmonic and Philadelphia Orchestras; lives in Germany. *Honours:* disc awards include the French suites of J. S. Bach and the Etudes of Chopin; several int. prizes. *Address:* c/o Konzertdirektion Schlote, Danreitergasse 4, 5020 Salzburg, Austria.

**GAWRILOFF, Saschko;** Violinist; b. 20 Oct. 1929, Leipzig, Germany. *Education:* Early studies with his father; Leipzig Conservatory, 1942–44 with Gustav Havemann and Martin Kovacz in Berlin, 1945–47. *Career:* Leader of the Dresden Philharmonic, 1947–48, Berlin Philharmonic, 1948–49, Berlin Radio Symphony, 1949–53, Museum Orchestra of Frankfurt am Main, 1953–57, and Hamburg Radio Symphony, 1961–66; Teacher at the Nuremberg Conservatory, 1957–61; Professor at the North-West German Music Academy, 1966–69, at the Folkwanghochschule in Essen from 1969; Head of masterclasses for violin at the Cologne Musikhochscule; Appearances with leading orchestras include Germany and the United Kingdom and concerts in Vienna, Milan, Madrid, Rome, Paris, India and Japan; Conductors include Boulez in Berg Concerto, Solti, Dohnányi, Gielen and Inbal; Has given the premieres of works by Maderna, Dieter Kaufmann and Schnittke; Formed a trio with Alfons Kontarsky and Klaus Storck in 1971; Member of the Robert Schumann Trio with Johannes Goritzki and David Levine; Contemporary music with Siegfried Palm and Bruno Canino. *Honours:* Winner, International Competitions at Berlin and Munich in 1953; Genoa Paganini Competition and City of Nuremberg Prize, 1959. *Current Management:* Ingpen & Williams Ltd, 7 St George's Court, 131 Putney Bridge Road, London, SW15 2PA, England.

**GAYER, Catherine;** Soprano; b. 11 Feb. 1937, Los Angeles, California, USA. *Education:* Studied in Los Angeles. *Career:* Sang in the premiere of Nono's Intolleranza in 1960, at Venice in 1961, Covent Garden in 1962 as the Queen of Night, Deutsche Oper Berlin from 1963 notably as Hilde Mack in Henze's Elegie für Junge Liebende, Berg's Lulu and Marie in Zimmermann's Die Soldaten and Nausicca in the 1968 premiere of Dallapiccola's Ulisse, and Scottish Opera from 1968 as Susanna, Hilde Mack, the Queen of Shemakha in The Golden Cockerel and in the 1975 premiere of Orr's Hermiston; Sang at Schwetzangni Festival in 1971 in the premiere of Reimann's Melusine, at Edinburgh Festival in 1972 with the company of the Deutsche Oper Berlin in Die Soldaten; Sang the leading role in the premiere of Joseph Tal's Der Versuchung at Munich in 1976; Other roles include Ulisse at La Scala, Zerbinetta, Gilda and Mélisande, sang the Woman in Schoenberg's Erwartung at the Komische Oper Berlin in 1988, songs by Reimann and Szymanowski at the 1990 Aldeburgh Festival, Berlin Kammeroper in 1991 with Berio's Sequenza III, Tal's Die Hand, The Medium by Maxwell Davies and Weisgall's The Stronger; Sang at Stuttgart in 1992 as the Grand-Mother in Dinescu's Eréndira and in Rag Time, an arrangement of Joplin's Treemonisha at the 1992 Schwetzingen Festival and in 2 productions of Schoenberg's Pierrot Lunaire; Sang in Manon at the Deutsche Oper, 1998. *Recordings:* Woodbird in Siegfried; Elegie für Junge Liebende; Die Israeliten in Der Wüste by CPE Bach; Il Giardino d'Amore by Scarlatti. *Honours:* Winner, San Francisco Opera Auditions, 1960 and Berlin Kammersängerin in 1970. *Address:* c/o Deutsche Oper, Richard Wagnerstrasse 10, Berlin, Germany.

**GAYFORD, Christopher;** Conductor; b. 1963, Wilmslow, England. *Education:* Royal Coll. of Music with Christopher Adey, John Forster and Norman del Mar. *Career:* repetiteur at Graz Opera, 1987; Jr Fellow in Conducting at the Royal Northern Coll. of Music, 1988; conducted Don Carlos and A Midsummer Night's Dream at the Royal Northern Coll. of Music, 1990; debut with the London Mozart Players at the Barbican Hall, 1990, in L'Elisir d'amore for Royal Northern Coll. of Music and Don Giovanni for Opera North; Asst Conductor to Royal Liverpool Philharmonic Orchestra, 1992–93; conducted Così fan tutte for British Youth Opera at Sadler's Wells, 1992. *Honours:* Besançon International Competition for Young Conductors, 1989.

**GEBHARDT, Horst;** Singer (tenor); b. 17 June 1940, Silberhausen, Germany. *Education:* Studied in Weimar and Berlin. *Career:* Debut: Schwerin in 1972 as Chateauneuf in Lortzing's Zar und Zimmermann; Sang at Leipzig, the Staatsoper Dresden and Berlin; Member of the Leipzig Opera from 1985 including role as Erik in Fliegende Holländer in 1989, and has made guest appearances in France, Italy, Spain, England, Yugoslavia, Russia, Poland, Japan and Cuba; Other roles have included Max, Mozart's Belmonte, Ottavio, Titus, Tamino and Ferrando, Lensky, Fenton, Strauss's Narraboth and Flamand, Jacquino in Fidelio, David in Die Meistersinger, Alfredo and Sextus in Giulio Cesare; Kiel Opera 1991, in Vincent by Rautavaara. *Recordings:* Idomeneo; Parsifal; Palestrina; Alfonso und Estrella. *Honours:* Prizewinner, International Bach Competition, Leipzig and National Opera Competition, Germany, 1972. *Address:* St ädtische Theatre, 7010 Leipzig, Germany.

**GEDDA, Nicolai;** Swedish singer (tenor); b. 11 July 1925, Stockholm; s. of Michael Ustinov and Olga Ustinov (née Gedda); m. Anastasia Caraviotis 1965; one s. one d. *Education:* Musical Acad., Stockholm. *Career:* debut, Stockholm 1952; concert appearances Rome 1952, Paris 1953, 1955, Vienna 1953, Aix-en-Provence 1954, 1955; first operatic performances in Munich, Lucerne, Milan and Rome 1953, Paris, London and Vienna 1954; Salzburg Festival 1957–59, Edin. Festival 1958–59; with Metropolitan Opera, NY 1957–, Tokyo Opera 1975–; worldwide appearances in opera, concerts and recitals; numerous recordings. *Address:* Valhallavagen 110, 114 41 Stockholm, Sweden.

**GEDGE, Nicholas (Paul Johnson);** Singer (Bass-baritone); b. 12 March 1968, Brecon, Wales; m. Kate Robinson, 16 Sept 1995, 1 d. *Education:* St John's College, Cambridge, 1987–90; MA, Law, University of Cambridge;

Royal Academy of Music, 1990–94. *Career:* Debut: Theseus in Midsummer Night's Dream, Covent Garden Festival, 1994; Sang Leporello at Royal Academy of Music, Charon at Batignano, Dr Bartolo and Don Magnifico with English Touring Opera; Concerts with London Philharmonic Orchestra, Ulster Orchestra, CLS; Recitals, Buxton Festival and Wigmore Hall. *Honours:* Queen's Commendation for Excellence, Royal Academy of Music. *Address:* 28 Vestry Road, London SE5 8NX, England.

**GEERTENS, Gerda;** Composer; b. 11 Aug. 1955, Wildervank, Netherlands. *Education:* Studied with Klaas de Vries, 1981–85. *Career:* Performances of works at the Concertgebouw in Amsterdam, in Darmstadt, Israel, Ireland and the US. *Compositions include:* Mexitli for mixed choir and ensemble, 1982; Trope for cello, 1987; As En Seringen for ensemble with percussion, 1988; String Trio, 1990; Contrast for saxophone quartet, 1990; Heartland for symphony orchestra, 1994; Transitions for flute trio, 1998; New Era, electronic music, 2001. *Address:* c/o Vereniging Buma, PO Box 725, 1180 AS Amstelveen, Netherlands.

**GEFORS, Hans;** Composer; b. 8 Dec. 1952, Stockholm, Sweden. *Education:* Studied composition with Per-Gunnar Alldahl and Maurice Karkoff; Pupil of Ingvar Lidholm at Stockholm Academy of Music, 1972; Per Norgård at Jutland Conservatory of Music, Diploma in 1977. *Career:* Active as composer, music critic and editor; Professor of Composition at Malmö College of Music, 1988; Der Park premiere at the 1992 Wiesbaden Festival; Clara, premiere at the 100th anniversary of the Opéra Comique, Paris, 1998; mem, STIM; Royal Academy of Music. *Compositions:* Operas: The Poet And The Glazier, 1979, Christina, 1986, Der Park, 1991; Vargen Kommer, 1997; Clara, 1998; Music Theatre: Me Morire En Paris, 1979, The Creation No. 2, 1988; Orchestral: Slits, 1981, Christina Scenes, 1987, Twine, 1988, Die Erscheinung Im Park, 1990; Lydias Sånger for mezzo and orchestra, 1996; Njutningen for soprano, baritone, choir and orchestra, 2002; The Knight of the Boy's Gaze, 2003; Chamber: Aprahishtita, 1970–71, La Boîte Chinoise, 1976, L'Invitation Au Voyage for Voice, Guitar and Violin, 1981, Krigets Eko for Percussionist, 1982, Tjurens Död, 1982, Flickan Och Den Gamle, 1983, Galjonsfiguren, 1983, One Two, 1983; A Hunting for the Wind for organ, 1994; Vocal: Singer On Förtröstan for Voice and Guitar, 1970, Whales Weep Not! for 16 Part Choir, 1987, En Obol, sonnets, for Voice, Clarinet, Cornet, Cello and Piano, 1989; Total Okay, 1992. *Recordings:* Scenes from Christina; Vargen Kommer. *Honours:* Christ Johnson Fund Prize, 1994, 2002. *Address:* STIM, Sandhamnsgatan 79, PO Box 27327, 102 54 Stockholm, Sweden.

**GEIGER, Ruth;** pianist; b. 30 Jan. 1923, Vienna, Austria. *Education:* studied in Vienna with Hans Gal and Julius Isserlis, Juilliard School, New York with Josef Lhevinne. *Career:* debut at the Town Hall, New York, 1944; recitals and appearances with orchestras in USA; radio and television broadcasts in New York; annual concert tours of Europe from 1957; orchestras include Suisse Romande, New Philharmonia, English Chamber Orchestra; BBC Series, My Favourite Concertos; appearances on BBC solo recital series at St Johns Smith Square, London; numerous live broadcasts; live concerto broadcasts with Glasgow BBC Orchestra; Complete Schubert Sonatas for Basle Radio; Toured Sweden, Netherlands, Belgium, Switzerland, Austria, England; Masterclasses at University of Sussex, 1971; Chamber Music with the Allegri Quartet; Concert and teaching week's residency at Yale University, USA; Most recent appearances on Live BBC Concert series; Lunchtime Recital at St David's Hall, Cardiff, 1992; Live Broadcast of Lunchtime Recital at St John's Smith Square, London, 1992; 1995 includes recital on Sunday Morning Coffee Concerts, Wigmore Hall, London; Masterclass and Recital, Newton Park College, Bath; Recital in Tours, France; Solo recitals in Tours, France, 1995, 1997, also collaboration in Tours with French mezzo-soprano in Lieder by Schubert and Brahms. *Recordings include:* Schubert Sonatas for Critics Choice Records. *Honours:* Naumburg Award, New York, 1943; Finalist, Leventritt Competition, 1944 and Rachmaninov Competition, 1948. *Address:* 160 W 73 Street, New York, NY 10023, USA.

**GELB, Peter;** American business executive and film and television producer; *President, Sony Classical International Operations;* b. 1959, s. of Arthur Gelb. *Career:* fmr man., Vladimir Horowitz; Pres. Sony Classical USA 1993–95, Pres. Sony Classical Int. Operations 1995–; Man. Dir Metropolitan Opera, New York 2006–. *Honours:* Emmy Awards for Outstanding Classical Program in the Performing Arts 1987, 1990, 1991, Emmy Awards for Outstanding Individual Achievement in Int. Programming 1991, Int. Documentary Asscn Award 1991, Grammy Award 2002. *Address:* Sony Classical USA, 550 Madison Avenue, New York, NY 10022, USA (office). *Website:* www .sonyclassical.com (office).

**GELIOT, Michael,** BA; British opera director and theatre director; b. 27 Sept. 1933, London, England; m. Diana Geliot; two c. *Education:* Univ. of Cambridge. *Career:* Staged first British production of Liebermann's School For Wives, while at Cambridge in 1958; Sadler's Wells from 1960; Burt's Volpone for the New Opera Company in 1961 and Weill's Mahagonny in 1963; Resident Producer then Director of Productions with Welsh National Opera, 1965–78; Productions for Scottish Opera, Kassel, Zürich, Barcelona, Wexford, Amsterdam, Ottawa, Lausanne, Netherlands Opera with Wozzeck in 1973, and Munich Opera with Fidelio in 1974; Staged the premiere of Maxwell Davies's Taverner at Covent Garden in 1972; Translations of Mozart's Zauberflöte and Nozze di Figaro; Stagings at Kassel Opera include Le nozze di Figaro in 1980; Collaborations with the designer, Ralph Koltai. *Honours:* Critics' Prize, Barcelona 1974.

**GELLMAN, Steven D.;** Composer, Pianist and Professor of Music; b. 16 Sept. 1947, Toronto, Canada; m. Cheryl Gellman, 18 Oct 1970, 1 s., 1 d. *Education:* Juilliard School of Music, New York, USA; Conservatoire de Paris. *Career:* Soloist with CBC Symphony Orchestra in own Concerto for Piano and Orchestra, aged 16; Compositions performed in USA, Canada, France, Europe, South America and Japan; European tour with Toronto Symphony, 1983; Gellman's Awakening performed 10 times throughout Europe; Universe Symphony, Inaugurated the International Year of Canadian Music, 1986; From 1994 appointed Full Professor of Composition and Theory, Faculty of Music, University of Ottawa; mem, Associate of Canadian Music Centre; Canadian League of Composers. *Compositions include:* Orchestral: Odyssey, 1971, Symphony No. 2, 1972, Chori, 1976, The Bride's Reception, 1983; Jaya Overture, 1995; Chamber Music: Mythos ll for flute and string quartet, recorded, 1968, Wind Music for brass quintet, recorded, 1978, Dialogue for solo horn, 1978, Transformation, 1980, Chiaroscuro, 1988, Concertino for guitar and string quartet, 1988, Red Shoes, 1990, Musica Eterna for string quartet, 1991, Child-Play for chamber orchestra, 1992, Sonata for cello and piano, 1995; Piano: Melodic Suite, 1972, Poeme, recorded, 1976, Waves and Ripples, 1979, Keyboard Triptych for piano-synthesizer, 1986; Orchestra: Love's Garden for soprano and orchestra, 1987, Piano Concerto, 1988–89; Canticles of St Francis for choir and orchestra, 1989; Opera: Gianni, 1996–99. *Publications:* Album for Piano, 1994. *Honours:* Named Composer of The Year, 1987. *Address:* c/o Music Department, Stewart Street, University of Ottawa, Ottawa, Ontario, K1N 6N5, Canada.

**GELMETTI, Gianluigi;** Conductor; b. 11 Sept. 1945, Rome, Italy. *Education:* Studied at the Accademia di Santa Cecilia in Rome with Franco Ferrera, with Sergiu Celibidache and in Vienna with Hans Swarowsky. *Career:* Musical Director of Pomeriggi Musicale of Milan, and teacher at the Conservatory until 1980; Artistic Director of RAI Symphony Orchestra at Rome, 1980–84; Musical Director of Rome Opera, 1984–85; Chief Conductor of the South German Radio Symphonie Orchestra, 1989; Musical Director, Orchestre Philharmonique of Monte Carlo in 1990; Has conducted the first performances of Castiglioni's Sacro Concerto in 1982, Donatoni's In Cauda in 1983 and Henze's 7th Symphony in 1984; Conducted Tosca at La Fenice in Venice, 1989 and a double bill of Rossini's La Cambiale di Matrimonio and Il Signor Bruschino at the 1989 Schwetzingen Festival, Rossini's La Gazza Ladra with Katia Ricciarelli at Pesaro in 1989 and Salieri's Les Danaides at the 1990 Ravenna Festival; Season 1992 with Tancredi at Bologna, Rossini double bill at Schwetzingen and Il Matrimonio Segreto at the Ravenna Festival; Conducted Mascagni's Iris at Rome, 1996; Royal Opera premiere of Rossini's Otello, Covent Garden, 2000; Returned to Covent Garden for La Rondine and Turandot, 2002; Chief Conductor and Artistic Director, Sydney SO, 2004. *Recordings include:* Telerecording of Rossini double bill; La Gazza Ladra; Il Barbiere di Siviglia. *Address:* Symphonie Orchester des Suddeutsche Rundfunk, Neckarstrasse 230, Postfach 837, 7000 Stuttgart, Germany.

**GELT, Andrew (Lloyd);** Composer, Conductor and Performer; b. 2 Feb. 1951, Albuquerque, New Mexico, USA. *Education:* BM, cum laude with distinction, Music Theory, University of New Mexico, 1973; MM, Clarinet Performance, University of Southern California, 1975; DMA, Theory and Composition, University of Miami, 1978; Studied at University of Denver; Clarinet student of Mitchell Lurie; Studied with Stanley Drucker. *Career:* Professor of several Universities and Colleges including University of Miami, University of North Carolina, Richmond Technical College, Temple University, Princeton University; Specialises in the analysis of microprocessor devices as applied to music; Main expertise in theory and composition of music in the eclectic vein. *Compositions:* Symphony No. 1, Op 34, The Art of Eclecticism, premiered by Frederick Fennell, second performance by the Orchestra Society of Philadelphia; Lamento for strings, Op 22; Homage to Gesualdo, Op 33; Suite Eclectique, Op 35; Concerto-Quintet for five clarinets assorted, Op 19; Sonatina Veehemente, Op 26; Armageddon; Works housed at the American Music Center in New York. *Current Management:* The American Music Center, 30 West 26th Street, Suite 1001, New York, NY 10010-2011, USA. *Address:* PO Box 922, Hollywood, FL 33022, USA. *E-mail:* andrew@gelt.net. *Website:* www.gelt.net.

**GEMROT, Jiri;** Composer; b. 15 April 1957, Prague, Czechoslovakia; m. 16 Oct 1982. *Education:* Prague Conservatorium, 1972–76; Graduated in Composition, Academy of Musical Arts, Prague, 1981; Master Composers Course with Franco Donatoni, Accademia Chigiana, Siena, Italy, 1981. *Career:* Producer of Radio Prague, 1982–86, 1990–; Editor, Panton Publishing House, 1986–90. *Compositions:* Published: Sonata for piano No. 1, 1981; Tributes for orchestra, 1983; 5 Lyrical Songs To Poems by Ingeborg Bachmann for soprano and piano, 1984; Inventions for violin and viola, 1984, Sonata for piano No. 2, 1985; Maxims for 15 strings, 1986; Rhapsody for bassoon and piano, 1986; Preludium and Toccata for harpsichord, Rhapsody for oboe and piano, 1988; Sonatina for violin and piano, 1990; Inventions for cello and double bass, 1991; Concerto for flute and orchestra, 1992; Psalmus 146 for mixed chorus and orchestra, 1992;' Lauda, Sion, for baritone and wind orchestra, 1994; Schalmeiane for 6 oboes, 1996; IV Sonata for piano, 1996; The American Overture, 1996; Concertino for orchestra, 1997; Bachman lieder for soprano and orchestra, 1998; Concertino for harp and orchestra, 1998; V sonata for piano, 1999; Quintet for piano and strings, 2001; Sonata for cello and piano, 2001; Trio for violin, cello and piano, 2001; Concertino for flute, timpani, bagpipe and orchestra, 2002; Double-Concerto for cello, piano and orchestra, 2002; Sapporiana for flute and guitar, 2003, Piano Concerto, 2003.

*Recordings:* Tributes; Dances And Reflections; Cello Concerto; Sonata for harp; Bucolic for string quartet; Meditation for viola and Organ; Invocation for Violin and Organ; Sonatina for flute and piano; Maxims for 15 strings; Piano Sonatas. *Address:* Na Valech 32, Prague 6, Czech Republic.

**GENAUX, Vivica;** American singer (mezzo-soprano); b. Fairbanks, AK. *Career:* noted for her singing of baroque and bel canto opera; numerous worldwide performances of Rosina in Il Barbiere di Siviglia, Angelina in La Cenerentola and Isabella in L'Italiana in Algeri (all Rossini); other performances include Hasse's Marc Antonio e Cleopatra, in Brussels and Paris, Scarlatti's oratorio La Santissima Trinità, in Paris, Palermo and Lyon, Gluck's Orfeo ed Euridice, at Los Angeles Opera, Mendelssohn's A Midsummer Night's Dream with the Orchestre Nat. de France, in Paris and Hong Kong, Hassem in Donizetti's Alahor in Granata, in Seville, Selimo in Hasse's Solimano for the Deutsche Staatsoper, Berlin, Penelope in Monteverdi's Il ritorno d'Ulisse, at the Bayerische Staatsoper; season 2005–06 included Mozart's Vesperae Solennes de Confessore with Orchestre Nat. de France conducted by Richard Muti, Vivaldi's Bajazet with Europa Galante in Vienna, as well as Rossini roles with San Francisco Opera, Anchorage Opera, Opera Carolina, Michigan Opera Theatre, and at Menorca's Teatre Principal de Maó and Lisbon's Teatro Nacional de São Carlos. *Recordings:* Rossini, Rossiniana 1998, Rossini, An Evening of Arias and Song 1999, Donizetti, Alahor in Granata 1999, Handel, Arminio 2001, Arias for Farinelli 2002, Bel Canto Arias 2003, Handel, Rinaldo 2003, Scarlatti, La Santissima Trinità 2004, Vivaldi, Il Bajazet 2005. *Honours:* Dresden Music Festival Artist of the Year 1999, Florentine Opera Marie Z. Uihlein Artist Fund 2004. *Current Management:* c/o Dominique Riber, Opéra et Concert, 7 rue de Clichy, Paris 75009, France. *Telephone:* 1-42-96-18-18 (office). *Fax:* 1-42-96-18-00 (office). *E-mail:* d.riber@opera-concert.com (office). *Website:* www.opera-concert.com (office). *Address:* c/o Karen Kriendler Nelson, KKN Enterprises, 277 West End Avenue, Suite 11A, New York, NY 10023, USA (office). *Telephone:* (212) 496-5154. *Fax:* (212) 721-9566. *E-mail:* kknenterp@aol.com.

**GENCER, (Ayse) Leyla;** Turkish singer (soprano); b. 10 Oct. 1924, Istanbul. *Education:* Istanbul Conservatory; further study with Giannina Arangi Lombardi and Apollo Granforte. *Career:* debut: Ankara as Santuzza 1950; Teatro San Carlo Naples as Madama Butterfly 1954, and soon after in opera houses of Europe and USA; Palermo and Trieste as Violetta in La Traviata 1955; Trieste, as Agata in Il franco cacciatore 1956; San Francisco as Francesca da Rimini 1956; with La Scala, Milan 1956–1980: notably in the premieres of Poulenc's Dialogues des Carmélites 1956; soloist in Verdi's Requiem to Toscanini's Funeral, Milan Cathedral; performed as Leonora in La Forza del Destino, Cologne, Paolina in Poliuto 1960, Elisabetta in Don Carlos and Lisa in La Dama di Picche 1961, Aida 1963, Lady Macbeth 1964, Norma 1965, Amelia in Simon Boccanegra 1966, Ottavia in Incoronazione di Poppaea 1967, Elettra in Idomeneo 1968, Lucrezia Borgia, Elena in I vespri siciliani 1970, Gluck's Alceste 1972; performances elsewhere include Lucrezia in I due Foscari, La Fenice, Venice 1957, Lida in La battaglia di Legnano, Florence 1959, Donna Elvira in Don Giovanni, Rome 1960, Amelia in Simone Boccanegra, Salzburg Festival 1961, Elisabetta in Don Carlos and Donna Anna in Don Giovanni, Covent Garden, London 1962, The Countess in Figaro's Hochzeit and Donizetti's Anna Bolena, Glyndebourne Festival 1962–63, Amelia in Un ballo in maschera, Verona 1962, Aida 1963, Norma 1965, Leonora in Il trovatore 1968, Donizetti's Maria Stuarda, Edinburgh Festival 1969, Rossini's Elisabetta Regina d'Inghilterra 1972, Lady Macbeth in Verdi's Macbeth, Florence 1975, Medea in Mayr's Corinto, Tearo San Carlo, Naples 1977, Donna Elvira in Mozart's Don Giovanni 1978, title role in Donizetti's Lucrezia Borgia, Florence 1979, Lady Billows in Britten's Albert Herring, Reggio 1980, Corilla in Gnecco's La Prova d'un opera seria, Venice 1983; further appearances in Vienna, Munich, Moscow, Warsaw, Oslo, Buenos Aires and Rio de Janeiro; pioneer of Donizetti and Bellini renaissance; Artistic Dir, Teacher, Singing and Interpretation Acad., La Scala Theatre 1997–; Istanbul Int. Singing Competition Leyla Gencer named after her 1995. *Recordings include:* Mozart's Don Giovanni, Nozze di Figaro, Idomeneo; Donizetti's Anna Bolena, Maria Stuarda, Roberto Devereux, Lucrezia Borgia; Belisario, Lucia di Lammermoor; Caterina Cornaro, Les Martyrs, Messa di Requiem for Bellini; Bellini's I Puritani, Norma, Beatrice di Tenda; Pacini's Saffo; Spontini's La Vestale; Verdi's Il Trovatore, Erneni, Macbeth, La Forza del Destino, Aida, Attila, I due Foscari, La Battaglia di Legnano, Gerusalemme, Simon Boccanegra, Don Carlos, Un Ballo in Maschera, Rigoletto; Massenet's Werther; Zandonai's Francesca da Rimini; Ponchielli's La Gioconda; Rossini's Elisabetta Regina d'Inghilterra; Poulenc's Dialoghi delle Carmelitane; Pizzetti's Assassinio nella Cattedralle; Tschaikovsky's La Dama di Picche; songs: Chopin, Bellini, Donizetti, Schumann-Liszt. *Publications:* several articles in music journals. *Honours:* Commendatore della Repubblica italiana 1967; Dr hc (Istanbul) 1989; more than 50 int. awards, including Ambrogino d'Oro, Milan 1988, Renowned Artist of Repub. of Turkey 1989, Bronze Statue, Ankara 1995, Bellini Gold Medal 1995, Puccini Prize 2002, Le Muse Int. Prize, Florence (jtly). *Address:* c/o Viale Majno 17A, 20122 Milan, Italy. *Telephone:* (02) 799837 (home). *Fax:* (02) 799837 (home).

**GENS, Veronique;** French singer (soprano); b. 19 April 1962, Orleans. *Education:* Paris Conservatoire. *Career:* has sung with Les Arts Florissants from 1986; solo engagements include Mozart's Cherubino and Vitellia, under Jean-Claude Malgoire, the Countess with Opéra de Lyon 1994, and Donna Elvira at Tourcoing; sang Venus in King Arthur with Les Arts Florissants in Paris and at Covent Garden 1995; Mozart's Idamante in Lisbon 1995; has also worked with such conductors as William Christie, Marc Minkowski and René Jacobs; season 1996 with Les Talens Lyriques at the Versailles Baroque Days as Venus in Les Fêtes de Paphos by Mondonville, Beaune Festival with Les Musiciens du Louvre as Lully's Galatée; solo engagements include Fiordiligi with Vlaamse Opera, Belgium 1997 and Donna Elvira at Aix-en-Provence, Milan, La Monnaie and Tokyo with Claudio Abbado and Peter Brook 1998–99; as Vitellia (Clemenza di Tito) in Madrid 1999 and Fiordiligi there 2002; Wigmore Hall, London recital 2000; Alcina in Hamburg 2002; Donna Elvira in Don Giovanni, Glyndebourne 2002 and Liceu Barcelona 2003, Fiordiligi in Tokyo 2005, Vitellia (Clemenza) in Dresden 2005. *Recordings:* Dido and Aeneas; Les Arts Florissants, William Christie; Hippolyte et Aricie by Rameau; Les Musiciens du Louvre, Marc Minkowski; Campra Motets, Requiem and Te Deum; Charpentier David et Jonathas, Miserere and Missa Assumpta Est; Jommelli Armida Abbandonata and Lamentations; Lully Acis et Galatée, Alceste, Armide, Atys, Phaeton; Marais, Alcyone; Mondonville Les Fêtes de Paphos; Mozart's Così fan tutte and Don Giovanni; Purcell King Arthur and Fairy Queen; Rameau Castor et Pollux, Dardanus and Platée; Mozart Arias; Handel's Cantatas; Così fan Tutte with Jacobs; French Songs with Roger Vignoles; Berlioz: Les Nuits d'Eté, Les chants d'Auvergne under J.C. Casadesus orchestre de Lille 2004. *Honours:* Revelation Musicale de l'année 1995, Artiste Lyrique of the Year 1999. *Current Management:* Hilbert Agentur, Maximillianstrasse 22, 80539 Munich, Germany.

**GENTILE, Ada;** Composer; b. 26 July 1947, Avezzano, Italy; m. Franco Mastroviti, 2 July 1972. *Education:* Diploma in Piano, 1972 and Composition in 1974, S Cecilia Conservatoire, Rome; Advanced course with Goffredo Petrassi, Accademia di Santa Cecilia, 1975–76. *Career:* Participant in international composition competitions; Her works performed throughout Europe, Canada, USA, China, Japan and Australia; Invited to festivals of contemporary music including Huddersfield, Århus, Zagreb, Warsaw, Alicante, Bacau and Kassel; Commissions from RAI, French Ministry of Culture, Opera theatre in Rome and Accademia di Santa Cecilia; Artistic Director, G Petrassi Chamber Orchestra, 1986–88, and Nuovi Spazi Musicali Festival, Rome; Teacher at S Cecilia Conservatoire and presenter of contemporary music festivals for RAI-Radiotre. *Compositions:* About 60 published works and several recorded works. *Recordings:* 12 titles. *Address:* Via Divisione Torino 139, 00149 Rome, Italy. *E-mail:* ada.gentile@tin.it.

**GENTILE, Louis;** Singer (Tenor); b. 2 Sept. 1957, Connecticut, USA. *Education:* Studied in New York. *Career:* Guest appearances in opera and broadcasting houses in Europe and the USA; Sang at Darmstadt, 1983–86; Krefeld, 1986–88 as Alfredo, among other roles; Netherlands Opera at Amsterdam, 1988, in Fidelio, Berlin Staatsoper, 1986, in Judith by Siegfried Matthus; Appeared at the Deutsche Oper Berlin 1990, as Schwalb in Mathis der Maler; Pedro in Tiefland at the Theater am Gärtnerplatz, Munich, 1991; Sang Don José at Oslo, 1991; Other roles include Tamino, Rossini's Almaviva, Boris in Katya Kabanova, Cavalli's Ormindo, Rodolfo, and Erik in Der fliegende Holländer; Sang Bibalo's Macbeth for Norwegian Opera at Oslo, 1992; Season 1995 at Bielefeld in the premiere of Der Sturz des Antichrist by Ullmann and at Leipzig as Boris in Katya Kabanova; Wagner's Tristan at Ghent, 1998; Sang Max at Bonn and Tristan in Antwerp, 2001. *Honours:* Winner Young Talent Presents, Competition, 1981. *Address:* c/o Deutsche Oper Berlin, Richard Wagnerstrasse 10, 1000 Berlin, Germany.

**GEORG, Mechthild;** Singer (Mezzo-soprano); b. 1956, Germany. *Education:* Studied in Düsseldorf with Ingeborg Reichelt: and at the Cologne opera studio. *Career:* Sang at first in concert, then at the Essen Opera from 1989; Guest engagements throughout Germany as Monteverdi's Octavia and Penelope, Cherubino, the Composer in Ariadne auf Naxos, Flosshilde (Hamburg, 1992) and Henrietta in Graf Mirabeau by Matthus; Concerts in Belgium, Austria and Switzerland; Sang Atalanta in Handel's Serse at Copenhagen, 1996; Magdeburg Telemann Festival 1996, in Der Neumodische Liebhaber Damon. *Recordings:* Suor Angelica and Gianni Schicchi; Messiah and Schumann Requiem; Udolin in Schubert's Die Verschworenen. *Address:* c/o Theater Essen, Rolandstrasse 10, D-4300 Essen 1, Germany.

**GEORGE, Alan Norman,** MA; violist; b. 23 Dec. 1949, Newquay, Cornwall, England; m. Lesley Schatzberger; one s. two d. *Education:* King's College, Cambridge. *Career:* debut as member of Fitzwilliam Quartet, Purcell Room, London, 1973; Member, Fitzwilliam Quartet, 1968–, Quartet in Residence, University of York, 1971–74, 1977–86, University of Warwick, 1974–77, Fitzwilliam College, Cambridge, 1998–, Univ. of Wales, Bangor 1999–; Lecturer, University of York, 1986–88, Finchcocks Quartet, 1992–96; Participant, 1st performance of Quartets, No. 2 by Sebastian Forbes, Edward Cowie, David Blake, Cuaderna by Bernard Rands, No. 1 by Michael Blake, Rachel Stott, Matthew King, Nos 1 and 3 by Liz Johnson, No. 1 by Jeremy Thurlow, Stone by Peter Dyson, No. 4 by Duncan Bruce; Long Hidden by Jackson Hill; Clarinet Quintet by David Blake; Michael Blake Clarinet Quintet, 1st British performances, Shostakovich Quartets 13, 14, 15; Alfred Schnittke, Canon in Memory of I F Stravinsky; Fitzwilliam Quartet, affiliate artists at Bucknell University, Pennsylvania, USA, 1978–86, 1998–; Tutor in Viola, Royal Northern College of Music, 1998–; Principal Viola, English Baroque Soloists, Orchestre Révolutionnaire et Romantique; Member, New London Consort, Lumina contemporary music group; 1st performances,... et Quart by John Paynter, Clarinet Trio by William Sweeney; Concerts and recordings, London Classical Players, Age of Enlightenment, Academy of Ancient Music, English Baroque Soloists, New London Consort, King's Consort, Hanover Band, Yorkshire Baroque Soloists. *Recordings:* Shostako-

vich Quartets Nos 1–15; Franck Quartet in D; Borodin Quartets Nos 1 and 2; Delius Quartet; Sibelius Voces Intimae; Brahms Clarinet Quintet; Wolf Italian Serenade; Schubert String Quintet; Beethoven Quartets ops 127, 130, 132, 133, 135; Shostakovich Piano Quintet with V Ashkenazy; Mozart Clarinet Trio with A. Hacker and K. Evans; Schumann Piano Quintet and Piano Quartet with R. Burnett; Mozart Clarinet Quintet with L. Schatzberger; Chamber version of Beethoven's Piano Concerto No. 4, with R Levin; Haydn Seven Last Words from the Cross; Chamber versions of Mozart Piano Concertos K413, K415 and Piano Quartet K452a, with Richard Burnett; Haydn Quartets Op 1/6, 71/2, 77/2. *Publications:* Shostakovich Chamber Music; Performing Haydn's Quartets, 2001; Russian and Soviet Quartets in the 20th Century, 2001. *Address:* 10 Bootham Terrace, York, YO30 7DH, England.

**GEORGE, Donald;** singer (tenor); b. 13 Sept. 1955, San Francisco, USA. *Education:* Louisiana State University, studied in Berlin and with Josef Metternich in Munich. *Career:* sang lyric tenor roles at the Theater am Gärtnerplatz, Munich, Brussels and the Vienna Staatsoper, 1986, in the premiere of Das Schloss by André Laporte and as Belmonte; Deutsche Oper Berlin, 1988–89, as Bernstein's Candide and as Fenton in Die Lustigen Weiber von Windsor; Guest appearances at Madrid in the local premiere of Lulu, Würzburg (as Belmonte), Komische Oper Berlin (Tamino); Leopold in La Juive (Bielefeld 1989); Giessen (Mozart's Titus) and Bregenz (Steuermann in Der fliegende Holländer); Other roles include Faust, Ferrando, Leukippos (Daphne), Jason in Médée and Jenik in The Bartered Bride; Sang Antonio in Prokofiev's The Duenna at the 1989 Wexford Festival; Title role in Rossini's Aureliano in Palmira at Bad Wildbad, 1996; The Prince in The Love for Three Oranges, Komische Oper Berlin, 1998; Season 1999–2000 as Mozart's Ferrando at Naples and Bob Boles in Peter Grimes at La Scala; Concerts at the Barbican Hall, London; Other repertoire includes works by Bach, Handel, Orff and Vaughan Williams. *Recordings include:* Alzira by Verdi. *Current Management:* Stafford Law, Candleway, Broad Street, Sutton Valence, Kent ME17 3AT, England. *Website:* www.stafford-law.com.

**GEORGE, Michael;** Singer (Baritone); b. 10 Aug. 1950, Thetford, England. *Education:* Chorister at King's College Cambridge; Royal College of Music, London. *Career:* Debut: The Maltings, Snape, in Handel's Saul, 1972; Solo engagements and as member of leading early music ensembles in the United Kingdom and Europe; Sang in Handel's L'Allegro at the 1988 Promenade Concerts, Brahms Requiem with the London Symphony Orchestra and Kurt Sanderling, Haydn's Creation in Madrid, Beethoven's Missa Solemnis and Choral Symphony with the Hanover Band, Purcell's Dioclesian with John Eliot Gardiner, and performances of Messiah with The Sixteen in London, Italy, Spain, Poland and France; Engagements at the Three Choirs Festival, Royal Festival Hall, Oslo, Brussels and tour of Austria, Germany and Yugoslavia with the Orchestra of St John's; Twentieth century repertoire includes Threni by Stravinsky for the BBC, A Child of Our Time with the Bournemouth Symphony Orchestra, the premiere of John Metcalf's The Boundaries of Time for the BBC at the Swansea Festival and Christus in the St John Passion by Arvo Pärt during a tour of the United Kingdom with the Contemporary Music Network; Sang in 3 Promenade Concerts in 1990, and in Bach's Cantata Herz und Mund und Tat und Leben, Bonfire of the Vanities and Janáček's Glagolitic Mass; Sang Abinoam in Handel's Deborah at the 1993 Proms; Grimbald in Purcell's King Arthur at Rome, 1996; Sang in Oswald von Wolkenstein concert at the Purcell Room, London, 1997; Sang in staged version of Bach's St John Passion for ENO, 2000; Handel's Samson at the London Proms, 2002. *Recordings include:* Medieval Carmina Burana; Monteverdi's Vespers of 1610 and Orfeo; At The Boar's Head by Holst; Purcell's St Cecilia Ode; Handel's Ottone; Complete Purcell Odes with the King's Consort. *Current Management:* IMG Artists. *Address:* c/o IMG Artists Europe, Lovell House, 616 Chiswick High Road, London W4 5RX, England.

**GEORGIADIS, John (Alexander);** Violinist and Conductor; b. 1939, Rochford, Essex, England. *Education:* Royal Liberty; RAM, London. *Career:* Concertmaster, CBSO, 1962–65; Concertmaster, London Symphony Orchestra, 1965–79; Music Director, London Virtuosi, 1972–; Bristol Sinfonia, 1982–84; 1st violin Gabrieli Quartet, 1987–90; Music Director, Bangkok Symphony Orchestra, 1994–96; Website Builder, 1996–; mem, RAM Guild. *Recordings:* London Symphony Orchestra, Chandos and Pickwick; Gabrieli Quartet, Chandos; Various Naxos. *Honours:* FRAM, 1968; FGSM, 1969; Honorary Doctorate, Essex University, 1990; Dove Prize 1960; Gulbenkian Award 1961. *Address:* Shoreline House, Wellington Parade, Walmer, Deal, Kent CT14 8AB, England. *E-mail:* johngeorgiadis@musicgallery.co.uk (home). *Website:* www.johngeorgiadis.com.

**GEORGIAN, Karine;** Cellist; b. 5 Jan. 1944, Moscow, Russia; m. Anthony Philips, 15 Dec 1990, 1 s. *Education:* Gnessin School, Moscow, 1950–61; Private studies with Armen Georgian, father, 1949–61; Moscow Conservatory with Mstislav Rostropovich, 1961–68. *Career:* Regular appearances with leading Soviet, European and American orchestras and festivals; Debut tour in 1969 at Carnegie Hall with Chicago Symphony, returning in 1970 in a performance of Khatchaturian Cello Rhapsody; Recital at Prague in 1970; Played with Berlin Philharmonic Orchestra in 1970, Leningrad Philharmonic Orchestra in 1973, and Royal Philharmonic Orchestra in 1982; Professor of Cello at Staatliche Hochschule für Musik since 1984; Played at BBC Proms, Henry Wood Promenade Concerts in 1985 and 1990, and with Philadelphia Orchestra in 1990. *Recordings:* Brahms Trio in B with Dmitri Alexyev and Liane Isakadze; Denisov Concerto in C with Moscow Philharmonic and Dmitri

Kitayenko; Khatchaturian Cello Rhapsody with Bolshoi Radio Symphony and Aram Khatchaturian; Sonatas by Shostakovich and Locatelli, Aza Amintayeva; Couperin Music for 2 Cellos with Natalia Gutman; Brahms Trio in A minor with Thea King and Clifford Benson. *Honours:* 1st Prize, All Union Music Competition, 1966; 1st Prize and Gold Medal, Tchaikovsky International Competition, Moscow, 1966. *Address:* c/o Olivia Ma Artists' Management, 65 Campden Street, London W8 7EL, England.

**GERBER, Steven (Roy);** Composer and Pianist; b. 28 Sept. 1948, Washington, USA. *Education:* BA, Haverford College, 1969; MFA, Princeton University, 1971; Composition with Robert Parris, Milton Babbitt, JK Randall, Earl Kim; Piano with Robert Parris, Agi Jambor, Irwin Gelber. *Career:* Received 3 commissions; World premiere of his compositions Symphony No. 1 and Serenade for String Orchestra during tour of Russia in 1990, returning in 1991 to perform several more concerts of his orchestral and chamber works including a concert at Tchaikovsky Hall in Moscow, since then has returned numerous times; US premiere of Symphony No. 1 by Louisville; mem, Several professional organizations. *Compositions include:* Dirge and Awakening for Orchestra premiered by the Russian National Orchestra under Mikhail Pletnev; Violin Concerto written for the American violinist Kurt Nikkanen who premiered it in Moscow and Novosibirsk in 1994 and playing it again at Kennedy Center in Washington with National Chamber Orchestra, 1995. *Recordings:* Many of his compositions have been recorded including Une Saison en Enfer. *Honours:* Fellowship, Princeton University; Winner of competitions held by The New Music Consort with String Quartet No. 2 and Musicians' Accord with Concertino; Duo in 3 Movements for Violin and Piano won The American Composers' Alliance 50th anniversary recording award. *Address:* 639 West End Avenue 10D, New York, NY 10025, USA.

**GERELLO, Vassily;** Singer (Baritone); b. 1950, Chernivtsi, Ukraine. *Education:* Studied at the St Petersburg Conservatory. *Career:* Sang as professional while a student, and with the Kirov Opera as Verdi's Germont and Posa, Valentin (Faust), Napoleon in War and Peace, Balearalz in Mussorgsky's Salammbô and the Venetian Guest in Rimsky's Sadko; On tour to Edinburgh Festival, 1991; Season 1993–94 as Papageno and Mozart's Figaro in St Petersburg, Rossini's Figaro with Netherlands Opera; Season 1994–95 as Paolo in Simon Boccanegra at the Bastille Opéra and Covent Garden; Eugene Onegin for Toronto Opera and the Vienna Staatsoper, 1998; Yeletsky in The Queen of Spades at Buenos Aires and Posa at the São Paulo Opera; Season 1995–96 with Bohème, Giulio Cesare and Boccanegra at the Bastille Opéra; New York Met debut, as Alfio in Cavalleria Rusticana, 1997; Rachmaninov's Aleko at the 1999 London Proms. *Recordings include:* Dr Pustrpalk in Salatán by Pavel Haas; Tchaikovsky's Moscow Canatata. *Current Management:* Askonas Holt Ltd, Lonsdale Chambers, 27 Chancery Lane, London, WC2A 1PF, England. *Telephone:* (20) 7400-1700. *Fax:* (20) 7400-1799. *E-mail:* info@askonasholt.co.uk. *Website:* www.askonasholt.co.uk.

**GERGALOV, Alexander;** Singer (Baritone); b. 1960, Russia. *Career:* Performances at the Kirov Opera, St Petersburg from 1990 including Eugene Onegin; Robert in Tchaikovsky's Iolanta; Yeletsky in The Queen of Spades; Andrei in War and Peace; Germont; Yeletsky at Lyon Opéra, 1996; Other roles include: Figaro in Il Barbiere di Siviglia; Don Carlo in La Forza del Destino; Renato in Un Ballo in Maschera; Papageno; Rodrigo in Don Carlos; Many guest engagements in Europe with the Kirov Company; Numerous concert appearances. *Recordings:* The Queen of Spades; Rimsky's Sadko; War and Peace (Bolkonsky); Betrothal in the Monastery (Ferdinand); Kashchey the Immortal (Ivan Korolevich). *Address:* c/o Kirov Opera, Theatre Square 1, St Petersburg, Russia.

**GERGIEV, Valery Abesalovich;** Russian conductor; *Artistic Director, Mariinsky Theatre;* b. 2 May 1953, Moscow; m. Natalia Gergieva; one s. one d. *Education:* Leningrad Conservatory. *Career:* prize winner at All-Union Conductors' Competition, Moscow (while still a student) and at Karajan Competition, Berlin; Chief Conductor Armenian State Orchestra 1981–84; Asst Conductor (to Yuriy Temirkanov) Kirov Opera, Leningrad; Music Dir Kirov (now Mariinsky) Opera Theatre 1988–, also Artistic and Gen. Dir 1996–; Prin. Guest Conductor Rotterdam Philharmonic 1989–92, Prin. Conductor 1992–; Prin. Guest Conductor New York Metropolitan Opera 1998–(2008); Prin. Conductor London Symphony Orchestra (2007–); Artistic Dir St Petersburg Stars of the White Nights festival, Moscow Easter festival, Gergiev Festival Rotterdam, Mikkeli Int. Festival, Finland; tours extensively in Europe and the USA; has guest-conducted Berlin Philharmonic, Dresden Philharmonic, Bayerischer Rundfunk, Royal Concertgebouw, London Philharmonic, City of Birmingham Symphony, Royal Philharmonic, London Symphony, Orchestra of Santa Cecilia, Japan Philharmonic; orchestras of Boston, Chicago, Cleveland, New York, San Francisco and Toronto; operas at Covent Garden, Metropolitan and San Francisco. *Honours:* State Prize of Russia 1994, 1999, Musical Life Magazine Musician of the Year 1992, 1993, Classical Music Award 1994, Musical America Yearbook Conductor of the Year 1996, People's Artist of Russia 1996, Triumph Prize 1999, Order of Friendship, Russia 2000, Order of St Mesrop Mashtots, Armenia 2000, Russian Presidential Prize 2002, UNESCO Artist of the World 2003, Nat. Pride of Russia Award 2003, For Work and the Fatherland Award 2003, World Econ. Forum Crystal Prize 2004, People's Artist of Ukraine 2004, Royal Swedish Acad. of Music Polar Music Prize 2005. *Current Management:* Columbia Artists, 165 West 57th Street, New York, NY 10019, USA. *Telephone:* (212) 841-9506. *Fax:* (212) 841-9599. *Address:* Mariinsky Theatre, Teatralnaya pl. 1, St Petersburg, 190000, Russia. *Telephone:* (812) 326-41-41.

*Fax:* (812) 314-17-44. *E-mail:* post@mariinsky.ru. *Website:* www.mariinsky .ru/en.

**GERGIEVA, Larissa;** pianist; b. 1959, Beltsy, Moldova. *Education:* Vladikavkas with Zarama Lolaeva. *Career:* Repetituer at the Vladikavkas Opera, then at the Tchaikovsky Opera House Perm, 1987–; Russian recitals at Moscow and St Petersburg and partnerships with leading singers in Italy, Germany, USA and the United Kingdom (Edinburgh, Wigmore Hall and Queen Elizabeth Hall); Season 1994–95 included recitals at the Edinburgh Festival with Olga Borodina and Galina Gorchakova, and at the Wigmore Hall in the Wigmore/Kirov series; Coaching engagements have included The Fiery Angel and Ruslan and Ludmila with the San Francisco Opera, 1994–95; Accompanied Kirov artists in Shostakovich Songs for the BBC, 1995; Masterclasses for singers at Perm, and general director of Rimsky-Korsakov Competition for singers at St Petersburg. *Recordings include:* Tchaikovsky Songs, and the Mighty Handful, with Olga Borodina. *Honours:* First prize at the Kazan and Tallinn National Competitions. *Current Management:* Askonas Holt Ltd, Lonsdale Chambers, 27 Chancery Lane, London, WC2A 1PF, England. *Telephone:* (20) 7400-1700. *Fax:* (20) 7400-1799. *E-mail:* info@ askonasholt.co.uk. *Website:* www.askonasholt.co.uk.

**GERHAHER, Christian;** German singer (bass-baritone); b. 1969, Straubing. *Education:* received a medical degree, Munich Music Acad., masterclasses with Dietrich Fischer-Dieskau and Elisabeth Schwarzkopf;. *Career:* mem., Municipal Theatre Würzburg 1998–2000; operas include The Magic Flute at Strasbourg Opera, Ruhr Triennale, Gärtnerplatztheater Munich, Salzburg Festival, Così fan tutte at Baden-Baden Festival, Freischütz with Capella Coloniensis; concert appearances with the Berlin Philharmonic singing various Schubert cycles, Britten's War Requiem; debut with Royal Concertgebouw Orkest, Amsterdam, singing Dvorak's Biblical Songs 2004; performances at Wigmore Hall, London, including Schubert recital 2005; other concert performances with Gewandhausorchester, Leipzig, Vienna Philharmonic, Bayerische Rundfunk, Philharmonie Cologne, Los Angeles Philharmonic Orchestra, and at the Schubertiade in Vilabertran, Schwetzingen Festival. *Recordings:* Abert, Ekkehard 2000, Gerhaher sings Lieder 2002, Weber, Der Freischütz 2002, Schubert, Winterreise 2002, Mahler, Kindertotenlieder 2002, Schubert, Die Schöne Müllerin 2003, Schubert, Schwanengesang 2003, Haydn, The Creation 2004, Schubert, Song Cycles 2004, Schumann, Lieder 2004, Orff, Carmina Burana 2005. *Honours:* Prix Int. Pro Musicis, Paris/New York 1998. *Current Management:* KünstlerSekretariat am Gasteig, Rosenheimer Str. 52, Munich 81669, Germany. *Telephone:* (89) 444-8879-0 (office). *Fax:* (89) 448-9522 (office). *E-mail:* team@ks-gasteig.de (office). *Website:* www.gasteig.de (office).

**GERINGAS, David;** Concert Cellist and Conductor; b. 29 July 1946, Vilna, Russia; m. Tatiana Schatz. *Education:* Studied with Rostropovich at the Moscow Conservatoire, 1963–71. *Career:* Concert tours of Germany in 1970 and Hungary in 1973; Resident in Germany from 1976; Many recitals with pianist, Tatiana Schatz; Played in the orchestra of the North German Radio and has given solo performances of works by Honegger, Milhaud, Hindemith and Kabalevsky; Premiered the Sonata for Solo Cello by Gottfried von Einem in 1987; Piano trio performances with Gerhard Oppitz and Dmitri Sitkovetsky; Also plays the baryton and has formed the Trio Geringas with the violinist, Vladimir Mendelssohn and the cellist, Emil Klein; Concerts with the Berlin PO, Vienna SO, Montreal SO, Philadelphia Orchestra, Chicago Symphony, NHK SO (Tokyo), London PO, Philharmonia and Israel PO, with conductors such as Ashkenazy, Gerd Albrecht, Eschenbach, Kondrashin, Leitner, Rattle, Rostropovich, Sawallisch and Tilson Thomas; as conducor performances include with North German Radio Symphony, Orchestra da Camera di Padova and the Forum Philharmonic in Netherlands; currently guest conductor of the South-West German CO in Pforzheim and the Lithuanian CO; Active career in chamber music working with his wife pianist Tatjana Geringas and British pianist Ian Fountain; Commissioned works from composers including Sofia Gubaidulina, Peteris Vasks, Erkki Sven Tüür, and was a pioneer in introducing the music of many Russian avant-garde composers to the west, including Gubaidulina, Denisov and Schnittke; Professor of Cello at the Musikhochschule in Lübeck, 1980–2000 and at the Hochschule für Musik "Hanns Eisler", 2000–. *Recordings include:* Gubaidulina Offertorium with the Boston Symphony under Dutoit; Concertos by Boccherini and Pfitzner. *Honours:* Winner, Tchaikovsky International Competition, 1970; Preis der Deutschen Schallplattenkritik, 1994. *Current Management:* Connaught Artists Management Ltd, 2 Molasses Row, Plantation Wharf, London, SW11 3UX, England. *Telephone:* (20) 7738 0017. *Fax:* (20) 7738 0909. *E-mail:* classicalmusic@connaughtartists.com. *Website:* www .connaughtartists.com.

**GERMAIN, Alan;** French stage director, choreographer, author and set and wardrobe designer; b. 1948, France. *Education:* studied music, choreography and architecture in Paris. *Career:* f. dance and theatre company, 1972, for historically authentic performances throughout France; Productions include Mozart's Requiem at the Opéra Comique, 1995; Opéra Côté Costume at the Palais Garnier, 1995; Le Triomphe de la Vertu at the Musée National du Moyen Age, 1999; Cesti's Il Tito at the Opéra du Rhin, Strasbourg, with Les Arts Florissants; Lehar's The Merry Widow at the Opéra de Saint-Etienne, Opéra de Vichy, 1999/2003, Opéra de Massy, 2003; Productions for the English Bach Festival include Gluck's Iphigénie en Tauride at the Royal Opera and for Athens Festival; Rossini's Le Siège de Corinthe in Madrid and Oresteia by Xenakis at the Linbury Studio Theatre, Covent Garden, 2000;

Lully/Molière Bourgeois Gentilhomme at the Château de Chambord 1995, and at the Linbury, 2001, Château de Blois and Grand Théâtre de Reims, 2002; Gluck's Telemaco at the Covent Garden and the Athens Festival, 2003, Charpentier/Molière Le Malade imaginaire, Château de Blois and Grand Théâtre de Reims; Gounod/Molière le Médicin malgré lui, Opéra de Tours, Massy, Vichy, Tourcoing, Limoges. *Exhibitions:* Costumes de scène en liberté, Grand Théâtre de Reims 2001, Memoires de scène, Bibliotheque de l'Opéra de Paris 2003, Fantômes d'opéra, Reims 2004. *Publications:* Le Tour du Monde en 80 Langues, 1995; Les Origines de l'Homme, 1997; La Ville Invisible, 1999; Les Grenouilles de Saint-Pierre, 2001 L'Affaire Callas, 2002; Meurtre à la Française, 2004, Fantômes d'opéra 2004. *Honours:* Fondation de la Vocation Prize 1978. *Address:* 29 rue de Paradis, 75010 Paris, France. *Telephone:* 1-42-46-37-83. *Fax:* 1-42-46-67-85. *E-mail:* compagnie@alaingermain.com. *Website:* www.alaingermain.com.

**GESSENDORF, Mechthild;** German singer (soprano); m. Ernö Weil. *Career:* performances with Bayerische Staatsoper (Munich), Hamburgische Staatsoper, Deutsche Oper (Berlin), Wiener Staatsoper (Vienna), Royal Opera House (Covent Garden, London), Grand Opéra (Paris), La Scala (Milan), Metropolitan Opera (New York), Monte Carlo Opera etc.; numerous appearances at int. festivals including Salzburg (Austria), Aix-en-Provence (France) and Edinburgh (UK). *Operas include:* Der Rosenkavalier, Ariadne auf Naxos, Lohengrin, Die Walküre, Der fliegende Holländer, Jenufa, Die Frau ohne Schatten, Tannhäuser. *Address:* Nibelungen Str. 23, 75179 Pforzheim, Germany.

**GESSI, Romolo;** Conductor; b. 25 March 1960, Trieste, Italy; m. Alessandra Carani, 4 Mar 1995, 1 d. *Education:* Conducting studies at the State Conservatoire, St Petersburg, with Kukuskin; Wiener Meisterkurse, Vienna, with Kalmar; Accademia Musicale, Pescara, with Renzetti. *Career:* Debut: Symphonic, Teatro Rossetti, Trieste, 1991; Opera, Teatro Lirico di Spoleto, with Puccini's La Bohème, 1995; Music Director, Chamber Orchestra of Friuli Venezia-Giulia, 1991–, and Serenade Ensemble, 1994–2000; Professor of Conducting, State Conservatoire, Milan, 1995; Professor of Chamber Music, State Conservatoire, Trieste, 1997–; Professor, European Masterclass in Spoleto; Conductor, Orchestra del Teatro Lirico di Spoleto; Guest Conductor with Milano Classica, Filarmonia Veneta; Numerous concerts in Italy, Austria, Spain, Hungary, Russia, Sweden, Switzerland, Slovenia and Croatia. *Recordings:* Rimsky-Korsakov, Dvořák, Strauss and Music in the 20th Century, with Serenade Ensemble. *Honours:* Second Prize, Gusella Conducting Competition, Pescara, 1993; First Prize, Austrian-Hungarian International Conducting Competition, Vienna and Pécs, 1994; Best Classified, Opera Conducting Competition, Caserta, 1994. *Address:* Via Brunner 9, 34125 Trieste, Italy.

**GESZTY, Sylvia;** Singer (Soprano); b. 28 Feb. 1934, Budapest, Hungary. *Education:* Studied at the Budapest Conservatory and the Budapest Music Academy with Erszébet Hoor-Tempis. *Career:* Sang at the Berlin Staatsoper from 1961 with debut as Amor in Orfeo ed Euridice, Komische Oper Berlin, 1963–70, and Hamburg Staatsoper, 1966–72; Covent Garden and Salzburg Festival debuts in 1966 and 1967 as the Queen of Night; Sang at Stuttgart Opera from 1971, Glyndebourne Festival, 1971–72 as Zerbinetta and Constanze, Luzern Festival in Paisiello's Barbier, Los Angeles in 1973 with the company of the New York City Opera as Sophie in Der Rosenkavalier and Schwetzingen Festival in 1976 as Gismonda in Cimarosa's Il Marito Desperato; Sang Rosina in Haydn's La Vera Costanza at Vienna in 1984, also televised; Guest appearances in Buenos Aires, Vienna, Paris, Amsterdam, Moscow, Cairo, Helsinki, Stockholm, Lisbon, Venice, Rome; Many concert appearances. *Recordings include:* Ariadne auf Naxos; Die Israeliten in der Wüste by CPE Bach; Cantatas by JS Bach; La Rappresentazione di Anima e di Corpo by Cavalieri; Die Zauberflöte; Così fan tutte; Barbier von Bagdad by Cornelius; Mozart's Die Schuldigkeit des Ersten Gebotes; Handel's Imeneo; Mozart's Kolatur-Konzertarien; Songs by Debussy, Ravel, Kodály, Bartók; Dessau Lieder; Beethoven's Christus am Ölberg; Television productions: Hoffmann's Erzählunen; Barbier von Bagdad; Eine Nacht in Venedig. *Honours:* Since 1988, biennial International Coloratura Singing Competition held in her name. *Address:* c/o Secretary ICSC, PO Box 1163, 75390, Gechingen, Germany.

**GEYER, Gwynne;** Singer (Soprano); b. 1965, USA. *Career:* Season 1991 as Tatiana in Eugene Onegin at St Louis; Rosalinde in Die Fledermaus at Toronto and Nedda at the New York City Opera; Season 1993–94 as Rusalka at the Metropolitan Opera; Smetana's Marenka at Toronto and Mimi in Geneva; Sang in Kalman's Gräfin Mariza at Santa Fe, 1995; Musetta at the Opéra Bastille, Paris and the title role in Landowski's Galina at Lyon; Sang Jenůfa at Cincinnati, 1998; Many concert appearances. *Address:* c/o Cincinnati Opera, Music Hall, 1241 Elm Street, Cincinnati OH 45210 USA.

**GHAZARIAN, Sona;** Singer (Soprano); b. 2 Sept. 1945, Beirut, Lebanon. *Education:* Studied at the Armenian College in Beirut; Psychology at the American University in Beirut; Masterclasses in Music at the Accademia Chigiana, Siena, and at the Accademia Santa Cecilia in Rome. *Career:* Member of the Vienna Staatsoper from 1972 notably as Oscar in Un Ballo in Maschera and as Violetta in La Traviata, during the same period appeared in the title role in Lucia di Lammermoor at the Grand Théâtre of Geneva; Bregenz Festival in 1983 as Aennchen in Der Freischütz; Guest appearances in Hamburg, Paris, Brussels, Geneva and Salzburg; Sang at Verona Arena in 1985, Barcelona in 1988, and Metropolitan Opera in 1989 as Musetta in La

Bohème; Sang in JC Bach's Adriano in Siria for Austrian Radio, conducted by Charles Mackerras; Susanna in Paisiello's Nina at Zürich, 1998. *Recordings:* Il Re Pastore by Mozart; Marzelline in Fidelio; Un Ballo in Maschera; Mozart Gala in Tokyo; Beethoven's Missa Solemnis–Live Concert at the Vatican. *Honours:* Many International Prizes. *Current Management:* Dr Raab and Dr Böhm, Plankengasse 5, 1010 Vienna, Austria. *Address:* c/o Vienna State Opera House, Opernring 2 1010 Vienna, Austria.

**GHEORGHIU, Angela;** Romanian singer (soprano); b. 7 Sept. 1965, Adjud; m. 1st Andrei Gheorghiu 1988; m. 2nd Roberto Alagna (q.v.) 1996. *Education:* Bucharest Acad. *Career:* debut at Bucharest as Solveig in Grieg's Peer Gynt 1983; appearances at Covent Garden from 1992, Met debut 1993, and in Washington, Vienna, Monte Carlo, Berlin, Nat. Opera Cluj; repertoire includes Zerlina, Mimi, Nina (all in Cherubin), Suzel (L'Amico Fritz), Juliette (Roméo et Juliette), Magda (La Rondine), Nedda (Pagliacci), and roles in Don Giovanni, La Bohème, Turandot, Carmen, La Traviata, L'Elisir d'Amore, Falstaff. *Recordings include:* La Traviata (as Violetta) 1994, Tosca (solo) 2001, selection of arias. *Honours:* Belvedere Prize, Vienna, Schatzgraber-Preis, Hamburg State Opera, Gulbenkian Prize. *Current Management:* Il Trittico, Via Rocche 4, 37121 Verona, Italy. *Telephone:* (045) 8001500. *Fax:* (045) 8046801. *Website:* www.iltrittico.net.

**GHEORGHIU, Stefan;** Romanian violist; b. 13 Aug. 1951, Constanta; m. Cornelia Gheorghiu 1975; two s. *Education:* Music High School, Bucharest, Music Academy, Bucharest. *Career:* debut recital, 1973; first concert as soloist (Arad) 1975; soloist with George Enescu, Philharmonic Orchestra, 1976; mem. of George Enescu Philharmonic Orchestra 1974–, First Viola 1985–; solo career in Romania and Italy; founder member of Romantica String Trio; Professor at Darmstadt Summer Courses for Contemporary Music 1986–; Professor at the Music Academy, teaching viola 1993–; President, Romanian Federation on the Musicians Union; President, Union of Interpretative Creation of Romanian Musicians. *Recordings:* 1975–95 recordings as Soloist and Chamber Music at Romanian Radio and Television Broadcasting System; 1984, Mozart-Sinfonia Concertante for violin and viola. *Honours:* Medal, Markneukirchen (DDR), 1977; Special Prize for Interpretation of a French Piece, Evian, France, 1979; Prize, Darmstadt, Germany, 1984. *Address:* Str Frumoasa 52, et 4, ap 18, 78116 Bucharest, Romania.

**GHEZZO, Dinu;** Composer and Conductor; b. 2 July 1941, Tuzla, Romania; m. Marta Ghezzo, 3 Oct 1961, 1 d. *Education:* State Diploma in Education, 1964, in Composition, 1966, Romanian Conservatory, PhD, University of California, Los Angeles, 1973. *Career:* Program Director, Composition, Director, Professor of Composition, New York University; Director, George Enescu International Composition Competition; Co-Director, New Repertory Ensemble of New York. *Compositions include:* Aphorisms; Structures; Sketches, recorded; Breezes Of Yesteryear; Sound Shapes l and ll; From Here To There; Two Prayers for Soprano and Tape; A Book Of Songs; Ostrom; Doina; Five Village Scenes for chamber ensemble, 1995; Checkmate for John Cage, for ensemble and dancers, 1995; Wind Rituals, 1995; In Search of Euridice for saxophone, piano and tape, 1995; Five Corrado Songs for bass and tape, 1996; Italian Love Songs, 1997; Sound and Etchings for clarinet, 1997; Imaginary Voyages for clarinet, cello and percussion, 1997. *Recordings:* Several. *Publications:* Most works published. *Contributions:* Tomis; Living Musician. *Address:* New York University, Music Department, 35 West 4th Street, New York, NY 10003, USA.

**GHIGLIA, Lorenzo;** stage designer; b. 26 Nov. 1936, Florence, Italy. *Education:* studied in Florence. *Career:* worked at the Bergamo Festival in 1958 then designed the premiere of Pizzetti's Il Calzare d'Argento at La Scala in 1961 for director Margherita Wallmann; Has also collaborated with Franco Enriquez, Mario Missiroli and Filippo Crivelli; Designed La Bohème at Palermo in 1961, Attila at Florence in 1962 and Petrassi's Il Cordovano at Turin in 1966; US commissions include Pagliacci and Rigoletto for Houston Opera and Samson et Dalila at Dallas; Glyndebourne, 1965–66 with Anna Bolena and Dido and Aeneas; Further designs at Florence with Le Villi and Busoni's Arlecchino in 1972 and 1975, La Scala and Suor Angelica in 1973 and Catania with Médée in 1977.

**GHIGLIA, Oscar;** classical guitarist; b. 13 Aug. 1938, Livorno, Italy; m. Anne-Marie d'Hauteserre 1966; one d. *Education:* Santa Cecilia Conservatory, Rome. *Career:* concert tours in N America 1965–; performed with Juilliard, Tokyo, and Emerson String Quartets, Julius Baker, Victoria de los Angeles, and Jean Pierre Rampal; performances worldwide include Turkey, Israel, Japan, Australia and New Zealand; artist-in-residence, Hartt School of Music, Univ. of Hartford, USA, and Musik Akademie de Stadt, Basel; summer instructor at Aspen, Colorado Music Festival 1969, Academia Musicale Chigiano, Siena, Italy 1976, and Banff Centre for the Arts, Canada 1978–. *Recordings include:* Paganini Sonata, The Guitar in Spain, The Spanish Guitar of Oscar Ghiglia. *Address:* 197 South Quaker Lane, West Hartford, CT 06119, USA (office); Helfenberg Strasse 14, Basel 4059, Switzerland.

**GHINDIN, Alexander;** Concert Pianist; b. 1977, Moscow. *Education:* Tchaikovsky State Conservatory, Moscow. *Career:* Concert and recital engagements in Russia, USA and Europe, from 1994; Festival apearances in Stockholm, Luxembourg, Moscow and Brussels; Soloist with the Moscow Virtuosi, the London Philharmonic Orchestra under Ashkenazy, Philharmonic de Liège, St Petersburg Camerata and Philharmonia, London; Season 2001–2002 with the Monte Carlo Philharmonic, Munich Philharmonic and the London Philharmonica at Lincoln Center (Rachmaninov's 3rd Concerto);

Recitals under the auspices of UNESCO, for the Pope and English Royalty. *Recordings include:* Albums for Decca and Harmonia Mundi. *Honours:* Prizewinner, 1994 Tchaikovsky International and 1999 Queen Elisabeth Competition. *Address:* c/o Musicaglotz, 11 Rue le Verrier, 75006 Paris, France.

**GHIUSELEV, Nicola;** Bulgarian singer (bass); b. 17 Aug. 1936, Pavlikeni; s. of Nicolai Ghiuselev and Elisaveta Ghiuseleva; m. 1st Roumiana Ghiuseleva 1960; m. 2nd Annamaria Petrova-Ghiuseleva 1984; two s. one d. *Education:* Acad. of Fine Arts, Sofia and singing studies under Christo Brumbarov. *Career:* won vocal competitions in Sofia 1959, Prague 1960, Helsinki 1962; joined State Opera Co., Sofia; debut as Timur in Puccini's Turandot, State Opera, Sofia 1961; has since appeared at most of the major opera houses of the world; major roles include Philip II, Boris Godounov, Don Giovanni, Attila, Wotan and the Mefistofele roles of Gounod, Berlioz and Boito; noted for Russian roles such as Dositheus, Prince Igor, Ivan the Terrible and the bass repertoire of Verdi, Rossini, Bellini, Donizetti, Mozart, Berlioz, Cherubini, Ponchielli, etc. *Recordings include:* Turandot 1961, Les Huguenots 1969, Offenbach: Les contes d'Hoffmann, Mefistofele 1983, Orthodox Chants 1997. *Address:* Villa Elpida, 1616 Sofia, Bulgaria; Via della Pisana 370/B2, 00163 Rome, Italy. *Telephone:* (2) 562929 (Sofia); (06) 66162834 (Rome). *Fax:* (2) 562929 (Sofia); (06) 66162834 (Rome).

**GHONEIM, Mauna,** BMus; Egyptian composer, musician (piano) and teacher; *Associate Professor of Composition, Cairo Conservatoire;* b. 21 Aug. 1955, Cairo. *Education:* Cairo Conservatoire, Hochschule für Musik und darstellende Kunst Vienna, Austria. *Career:* composer from 1977; teacher and Research Asst Cairo Conservatoire 1978–81, Assoc. Prof. of Composition 1988–. *Compositions include:* Sonata for piano 1977, Aria for voice and piano 1977, Fantasy for piano and strings 1978, Sahara Safari 1978, Hadith El Hajar (Talking Stones) 1979, Hadith El Karya (The Village) 1979, El Adkar El Dameya (Blood Density) 1980, Small Pieces for percussion instruments 1984, Concerto for piano and orchestra 1984, Two Pieces for woodwinds and string orchestra 1984, String Quartet 1985, String Trio 1985, Lied for soprano and piano 1985, Suite for flute, oboe and string orchestra 1986, Piano Pieces for two voices 1986, Quartet for woodwinds 1986, Tanz für klavier and zwei schlagzeuger (Dance for piano and two percussionists) 1988, El Mashrabia for string orchestra 1988, Two Portraits for string orchestra 1988, Die Däume der Nacht for voice with instrumental ensemble 1988, Elegy for orchestra 1990, Sunlight Fishing 1990, Little Songs for Children 1991, Nacht Bäume Suite for flute solo 1991, Three Pieces for two pianos 1993, Suite for flute and harp 1993. *Honours:* winner Syndicate of the Arts Prize 1991, Acad. of Arts Award 1991, Ismaelia Festival Prize for Film Music 1990. *Address:* Cairo Conservatoire, Avenue of the Pyramids, Giza, Egypt (office).

**GIACOMINI, Giuseppe;** Tenor; b. 7 Sept. 1940, Veggiano, Padua, Italy. *Education:* Studied with Elena Fava Ceriati in Padua, Marcello del Monaco in Treviso and Vladimiro Badiali in Milan. *Career:* Debut: In 1966 as Pinkerton in Madama Butterfly; Sang in Berlin and Vienna from 1972, Hamburg from 1973, La Scala debut in 1974, Paris Opéra debut in 1975, and US debut at Cincinnati Opera from 1976 as Alvaro in La Forza del Destino, Verdi's Macduff, Don Carlos and Manrico, Puccini's Cavaradossi and Canio in Pagliacci; Further appearances in Barcelona, Boston, Budapest, London, Munich and Tokyo; Sang Verdi's Otello at San Diego in 1986; Season 1992 as Alvaro at Naples, Canio at Rome and Radames at the festival of Caracalla; Other roles include Puccini's Calaf, Luigi, Rodolfo and Des Grieux, Pollione in Norma, Turiddu in Cavalleria Rusticana, Giordano's Andrea Chénier, Verdi's Radames in Aida, and Ernani; Sang Radames at the Verona Arena, Manrico at the Vienna Staatsoper and Calaf at Covent Garden, 1996; Season 2000–01 as Canio in Pagliacci at the Vienna Staatsoper and Cavaradossi at Covent Garden. *Recordings include:* Norma; Fausta by Donizetti; Manon Lescaut; Cavalleria Rusticana; Il Tabarro and Tosca, both new editions, recorded in Philadelphia under Riccardo Mutio. *Honours:* Prizewinner in competitions at Naples, Vercelli and Milan. *Address:* c/o Patricia Greenan, 19b Belsize Lane, London NW3 4DU, England.

**GIAIOTTO, Bonaldo;** Singer (Bass); b. 25 Dec. 1932, Ziracco, Udine, Italy. *Education:* Studied in Udine and with Alfredo Starno in Milan. *Career:* Debut: Teatro Nuovo Milan in 1957; Sang widely in Italy then appeared as Rossini's Bartolo at Cincinnati in 1959; Metropolitan Opera debut in 1960 as Zaccaria in Nabucco and has sung in New York for 25 years in 300 performances, notably as Ramphis, Raimondo and Timur; Further engagements in Paris, London, Bordeaux, Rome, Geneva, Vienna, Hamburg and Madrid; Concert tour of South America in 1970; Season 1985 as Banquo in Zürich, Attila at the Verona Arena and in a revival of Donizetti's Il Diluvio Universale at Geneva, as Noah; La Scala Milan debut in 1986 as Rodolfo in La Sonnambula; Season 1988–89 as Ramphis in Aida at Chicago, Fiesco in Simon Boccanegra at Piacenza and Padre Guardiano in Miami and Verona; Sang Timur in Turandot at Turin in 1990; Season 1992 as Alvise in La Gioconda at Rome and Philip II and Ramphis at the Verona Arena; Sang in the French version of Don Carlos at Brussels, 1996. *Recordings:* Ferrando in Il Trovatore; Brogni in La Juive; Luisa Miller; Aida; La Traviata; Turandot; La Cieco in Massenet's Iris conducted by Patanè. *Address:* c/o Arena di Verona, Piazza Bra 28, 37121 Verona, Italy.

**GIBAULT, Claire;** French conductor; b. 31 Oct. 1945, Le Mans; d. of Louis and Suzanne Gibault. *Education:* Conservatoire du Mans and Conservatoire Nat. Supérieur de Paris. *Career:* at Opéra de Lyon 1971–74, Conductor 1990–; fmr Dir Office de Radiodiffusion-Télévision Française (ORTF) Orchestra,

Orchestre du Conservatoire de Paris, and Toulouse, Angers, Nantes and Mulhouse orchestras; Dir Opéra de Chambéry; conductor at concerts in France and abroad, and with orchestras including Orchestre de la Suisse Romande, Monte-Carlo, Nice-Provence-Côte-d'Azur, Turin, Rome, Lausanne, Brussels, Québec and San Francisco orchestras, at Royal Opera House, Covent Garden, London, Berlin Philharmonic Orchestra (first woman conductor) etc. *Works conducted include:* The Magic Flute 1974, 1994, L'enlèvement au sérail 1987, Pelléas et Mélisande 1993, La station thermale (world première) 1995; numerous contemporary works. *Recordings:* Les mariés de la Tour Eiffel 1990, Les Brigands d'Offenbach (first woman conductor) etc. *Honours:* Chevalier de l'Ordre Nat. du Mérite; Prix de la Fondation de la Vocation 1969 and numerous prizes from Conservatoire du Mans and Conservatoire Nat. Supérieur de Paris. *Address:* Opéra de Lyon, 1 place de la Comédie, 69001 Lyon, France.

**GIBB, James;** Pianist, Teacher and Professor Emeritus; b. 7 March 1918, Monkseaton, Northumberland. *Education:* Merchiston Castle School, Edinburgh, Scotland; Taught piano by Mabel Lander, a pupil of Leschetizky. *Career:* Debut: Promenade Concert 1949 in Royal Albert Hall; Concerto Soloist, Berlin Philharmonic Orchestra and North-West German Radio Orchestra under Hans Schmidt-Isserstedt; Extensive tours in Central America and the Caribbean; Concert with BRNO State Radio Symphony Orchestra, conducted by Carlo Maria Giulini, Prague Spring Festival. Schubert Piano Sonatas for Musicians; mem, Incorporated Society of Musicians. *Publications:* Article in Penguin's Keyboard Music edited by Denis Matthews (later issued by David and Charles). *Honours:* Professor Emeritus, Guildhall School of Music and Drama, 1995; Fellow, Guildhall School of Music and Drama, 1967. *Current Management:* Anthony Purkiss. *Address:* 35 Fonthill Road, Hove, E Sussex BN3 6HB, England.

**GIBBONS, Jack;** Pianist; b. 2 March 1962, England. *Career:* Debut: London Solo Debut, 1979; Numerous solo and concert appearances from the age of 10; Annual solo concert at the Queen Elizabeth Hall, London, since 1990; Performances at the Barbican, London; Symphony Hall, Birmingham; New York and Washington DC Debuts, 1994; Debut, Lincoln Center, New York, 1997; Many appearances on BBC radio, television and Classic FM radio, and with various orchestras. *Compositions:* Solo piano arrangements of Gershwin's Concert Works and Overtures, and transcriptions of Gershwin's original piano improvisations from recordings and piano-rolls. *Recordings:* For series of solo piano albums; The Authentic George Gershwin vols 1, 2, 3 and 4; Alkan's Complete Opus 39 Etudes, vols 1 and 2; Lambert's Rio Grande with the English Northern Philharmonia Orchestra, Opera North, conductor David Lloyd-Jones. *Honours:* First Prize, Newport International Pianoforte Competition, 1982; MRA Award for best solo instrumental recording for The Authentic George Gershwin, 1993. *Current Management:* Carolyn Sachs, Trillium Productions Inc, New York, USA. *Address:* c/o Carolyn Sachs, Trilium Productions Inc, 345 Riverside Drive, Suite 6A, New York, NY 10025, USA.

**GIBIN, João;** singer (tenor); b. 1929, Lima, Peru. *Education:* studied in Lima and at the Scuola della Scala, Milan, Italy. *Career:* sang first in Italy then guested with the Netherlands Opera in Amsterdam as Andrea Chénier and Calaf; Vienna Staatsoper from 1958; Covent Garden 1959, as Edgardo opposite Joan Sutherland's Lucia; leading roles at La Scala from 1960; New York City Opera and Maggio Musicale, Florence, 1961, as Radames and Don Carlos. *Recordings:* Fanciulla del West (with Birgit Nilsson), Lucia di Lammermoor (with Sutherland). *Honours:* winner MGM South American Caruso Competition 1954.

**GIBSON, Jon (Charles);** Flautist, Saxophonist and Composer; b. 11 March 1940, Los Angeles, California, USA. *Education:* Studied at Sacramento and San Francisco State Universities. *Career:* Co-founded the New Music Ensemble in 1961; Associated with minimalist group of composers including participation in the premiere of Terry Riley's In C, 1964, and membership from 1968 of the Philip Glass Ensemble; Visual arts involved in compositions, some of which written for dancers; Solo appearances as instrumentalist in the USA and Europe. *Compositions include:* Opera: Voyage Of The Beagle, 1985; Who Are You, Vocal and Tape Delay; Visitations: An Environment Soundscape And Radioland for Tape, 1966–72; Instrumental: Multiples, 1972, Song I–IV, 1972–79, Melody I–IV, 1973–75, Cycles for Organ, 1973, Recycle I and ll, 1977, Call, 1978, Return, and Variations both for Small Ensemble, 1979–80, Extensions, dance score, 1980, Relative Calm, dance score, for Small Ensemble and Tape, 1981, Interval for Video Tape, 1985; Southern Climes for ensemble, 1993; Chorales from Relative Calm for ensemble, 1993; Chrome, 1995; Lines, for ensemble, 1996; Unfinished Business I for small ensemble, 1997; A Rose It Isn't, solo instrument, 1997. *Recordings include:* Einstein On The Beach, with the Philip Glass Ensemble. *Honours:* Grantee, Creative Artist Public Service Program, 1974, 1981 and Rockefeller Foundation, 1982. *Address:* c/o ASCAP, ASCAP Building, 1 Lincoln Plaza, New York, NY 10023, USA.

**GIEBEL, Agnes;** Singer (Soprano); b. 10 Aug. 1921, Heerlen, Netherlands; m. Herbert Kanders, 1 s., 2 d. *Education:* Studied at the Folkwang-Schule Essen with Hilde Wesselmann. *Career:* Gave first public concert in 1933 with Lieder by Strauss and Reger; Adult career from 1947 giving many concerts and recitals in Europe and North America; Bach Cantatas series with Karl Ristenpart for Berlin Radio, 1950–51; Church concerts in Cologne until 1982, Duet concert there; 1989; Repertoire included 20th century works, Mozart arias and much Baroque music. *Recordings include:* Bach's Christmas Oratorio; St Matthew Passion; St John Passion; Beethoven's Missa Solemnis; Die Schöpfung; Bach Cantatas; Ein Deutsches Requiem; Song recitals, and album with Hermann Prey and Celibidache. *Address:* c/o Cologne Musi-khochschule, Dagoberstrasse 38, D–50668 Cologne, Germany.

**GIELEN, Michael Andreas;** Austrian conductor and composer; b. 20 July 1927, Dresden, Germany; m. Helga Augsten 1957; one s. one d. *Education:* Univ. of Buenos Aires. *Career:* studied composition under E. Leuchter and J. Polnauer; pianist in Buenos Aires; on music staff of Teatro Colón 1947–50; with Vienna State Opera 1951–60, Perm. Conductor 1954–60; First Conductor, Royal Swedish Opera, Stockholm 1960–65; conductor and composer in Cologne 1965–69; Musical Dir Nat. Orchestra of Belgium 1969–73; Chief Conductor Netherlands Opera 1973–75; Music Dir and Gen. Man. Frankfurt Opera House Sept. 1977–87; Music Dir Cincinnati Symphony 1980–86; Prin. Conductor SWF Radio Orchestra, Baden-Baden 1986–99; Prof. of Conducting, Mozarteum, Salzburg 1987–95, Emer. 1995–; Chief Guest Conductor, BBC Symphony Orchestra 1979–82; Perm. Guest Conductor, Berlin State Opera 1998–, Berlin Symphony Orchestra 1998–. *Honours:* Dr hc (Berlin Hochschule der Künste) 2000; State Prize, Hessen 1985, Adorno Prize, Frankfurt 1986, Vienna Music Prize 1997, Frankfurt Music Prize 1999. *Address:* AU 57, 5311 Loibichl, Austria. *Telephone:* (6232) 2082 (home).

**GIERHARDT, Heike;** Singer (Soprano); b. 8 Aug. 1964, Frankfurt, Germany. *Education:* Studied at the Frankfurt Musikhochschule. *Career:* Sang at the Mannheim Opera, 1987–92; Essen from 1992; Roles have included Nicolai's Frau Fluth, Mozart's Constanze, Donna Anna, Pamina and Fiordiligi; Marenka in The Bartered Bride, Freia in Das Rheingold and Saffi in Der Zigeunerbaron; Guest engagements at Dresden, Frankfurt, Dortmund and Weimar; Season 1998 as Mme Lidoine in Les Dialogues des Carmélites at Essen; Season 1999 as the Empress in Die Frau ohne Schatten at Essen and Barcelona; Numerous concert appearances. *Address:* Essen Opera, Roland-strasse 10, 4300 Essen 1, Germany.

**GIERLACH, Robert;** Polish singer (bass-baritone); b. 1965. *Education:* Chopin Conservatoire, Warsaw. *Career:* appearances in title role of Szyma-nowski's King Roger at Carnegie and Festival Halls and at Salzburg Festival; Rossini's Basilio and Alidoro for Rome Opera; Mozart's Count in Venice and Trieste, Faraone in Rossini's Mosè in Egitto at Verona, Don Giovanni at Amsterdam and Don Profondo in Il Viaggio a Reims at Bologna; Stravinsky's Oedipus Rex (as Creon) in Paris, and Pulcinella; Mozart's Figaro at Glyndebourne (debut, 2001), Florida, Geneva and Detroit. *Honours:* Winner, Viotti Contest at Vercelli and Alfredo Kraus Competition, Las Palmas. *Current Management:* Pinnacle Arts, Thierschstrasse 11, 80538 Munich, Germany. *Telephone:* 49-89-340-8630. *Fax:* 49-89-3408-6310. *Website:* www .pinnaclearts.com.

**GIERSTER, Hans;** Musical Director; b. 12 Jan. 1925, Germany. *Education:* Musikhochschule, Munich; Mozarteum, Salzburg. *Career:* Formerly Musical Director of Freiburg-im-Breisgau Municipal Theatres; General Musical Director, Nuremberg, 1965; Director, Musiktheater Nuremberg, 1971; Conductor at Munich Staatsoper; Guest Conductor at State Operas of Hamburg, Munich and Vienna; Guest appearances at festivals in Munich, 1964, Edinburgh with Bavarian State Opera in Così fan tutte in 1965, Glyndebourne with Magic Flute in 1966, Zürich in 1971 and Vienna in 1972; Concerts with Philharmonic Orchestras of Bamberg, Berlin, Munich, Vienna, London, and Mexico City. *Address:* Musiktheater Nürnberg, 8500 Nuremberg, Hallerweisse 4, Germany.

**GIERZOD, Kazimierz;** Polish pianist; *Professor, Frederic Chopin Academy of Music;* b. 6 Aug. 1936, Warsaw; m. Jolanta Zegadlo 1974. *Education:* Frederic Chopin Acad. of Music, Warsaw, with Prof. Margerita Trombini-Kazuro, Accad. Chigiana, Siena, Italy with Prof. Guido Agosti. *Career:* regular recitals and concerts in Europe, Canada, China, Cyprus, Japan, USA, S America, Australia and Kuwait from 1964; tutor, Frederic Chopin Acad. of Music, Warsaw 1969–73, Asst Prof. 1973–86, Prof. 1986–, Dean of Piano Dept 1975–87, elected Rector of Acad. 1987, 1990–93; lectures on musical interpretation, masterclasses in Poland, Japan, USA, Venezuela, Cyprus, China, Germany, Taiwan and Lithuania; radio and TV commentator during Int. Frederic Chopin Piano Competition, Warsaw 1985, 1990; radio and TV interviews and interviews for local and foreign press; Visiting Prof., Soai Univ., Osaka, Japan 1988–; Chief of Piano Chair 1999–; mem. Jury of Piano Competititon, Europe, Japan and Venezuela; Pres. Frederic Chopin Int. Foundation, Warsaw, Poland 1992–98; Vice-Pres. Frederic Chopin Soc., Warsaw 1997, Pres. 2002. *Recordings:* archival recordings for Polish radio of Polish music, recordings for American, Cypriot, Polish and Japanese radio and television, album released in Poland and Germany. *Publications:* numerous articles in music journals, including Ruch Muzyczyy. *Honours:* Officer's Cross, Order of Polonia Restituta 2002; First Prize, Gdansk Piano Competition 1964, Ministry of Culture Medals for Artistic and Pedagogic Achievements. *Address:* 2 Okolnik str., 00-368, Warsaw (office); ul Sygie-tynskiego 36, 05-805 Otrebusy, Poland (home). *Fax:* (22) 8278308 (office); (22) 7585562 (home).

**GIETZ, Gordon;** Singer (Tenor); b. 1968, Canada. *Education:* Studied in Calgary, Toronto and New York. *Career:* Artist en Residence with Opera de Montréal; Recent engagements: Sang Don Ottavio in Don Giovanni, Opéra National de Paris; Števa in Jenůfa, Grand Théâtre de Genève; Tamino in Die Zauberflöte, De Nederlandse Opera; Idamante in Idomeneo, Chevalier in Dialogues des Carmélites and Benedict in Beatrice and Benedict, all with Santa Fe Opera; Sam Polk in Susannah, Grand Théâtre de Genève; Tom Rakewell in The Rake's Progress, Edmonton Opera, Duke in Rigoletto, Hennessy Opera, Beijing and Hanoi; Fenton in Falstaff, New York City Opera; Alfredo in La Traviata, Opera Company of Philadelphia; Hoffmann in Les Contes d'Hoffmann and Tamino in Die Zauberflöte, l'Opéra de Montréal; Roméo in Roméo et Juliette, Western Australia Opera; Danceny in Dangerous Liaisons, Washington Opera; Recent concert engagements: Sang Števa in Jenůfa, Philadelphia Orchestra, Carnegie Hall; Das Lied von der Erde, Mainly Mozart Festival; Klaus-Narr, Gurre lieder, Ravinia Festival; Beethoven's Ninth Symphony, Houston Symphony and at BBC Proms, Royal Albert Hall; Jacquino in Fidelio, New York Philharmonic; Schubert's Mass in E Flat, Philadelphia Orchestra; Mahler's Eighth Symphony, Winnipeg Symphony; Frère Mass ée in Saint François d'Assise, VARA Radio Orchestra, Concertgebouw; Season 2000–01: Lysander in Britten's A Midsummer Night's Dream, Glyndebourne Festival Opera; Carmina Burana, Tanglewood Festival; Engaged to sing Jack in The Midsummer Marriage, Royal Opera House, Covent Garden; Valinace in Arshak II, San Francisco Opera; Števa in Jenůfa, Théâtre du Châtelet; Camille in Thérèse Raquin, Dallas Opera; Rinuccio in Gianni Schicchi, De Vlaamse Opera; Duke in Rigoletto, Edmonton Opera; Covent Garden debut as Stingo in the premiere of Sophie's Choice, 2002. *Recordings include:* L'Enfance du Christ and Berlioz's Lelio; Les Mamelles de Tirésias. *Address:* c/o IMG Artists, Lovell House, 616 Chiswick High Road, London W4 5RX, England.

**GIFFORD, Anthea;** British classical guitarist; b. 17 Feb. 1949, Bristol, England; m. John Trusler 1970; one s. one d. *Education:* Accademia Musicale Chigiana, Siena, Italy, Royal College of Music, London. *Career:* debut, Purcell Room, London; Many solo recitals and over 30 programmes on BBC Radio 3 with violinist, Jean-Jacques Kantorow; Recitals at the Purcell Room, Wigmore Hall, Fairfield Hall, Barbican Centre, Queen Elizabeth and Festival Halls; Television appearances on Channel 4, BBC 2, and TSW among others, frequent chamber music recitals with Delmé String Quartet and adjudicator for Overseas League; Performances in Italy, France, Spain and Germany; Director of Droffig Recordings; mem, Incorporated Society of Musicians; Overseas League. *Recordings:* Paganini and his Contemporaries by Kantorow-Gifford Duo, 1991; Solo Recital, 1991; Paganini Ensemble, 1991; Kantorow-Gifford Violin and Guitar Duos, 1993; Dodgson Duo Concerto with Northern Sinfonia, 1994. *Publications:* contrib. to Guitar International. *Honours:* Young Musician of the Year, Greater London Arts Association Award. *Address:* 24 Donovan Avenue, London, N10 2JX, England.

**GIFFORD, Helen;** Composer; b. 5 Sept. 1935, Melbourne, Australia. *Education:* BMus, Melbourne University Conservatorium of Music, 1958. *Career:* Composer in Residence, Melbourne Theatre Company, 1970–; Commissions from Melbourne Chorale, Astra Chamber Music Society, Australian Broadcasting Commission, Australian Percussion Ensemble. *Compositions include:* Chamber Music: Fantasy for Flute and Piano, 1958, Skiagram for Flute, Viola and Vibraphone, 1963, String Quartet, 1965, Canzone for Chamber Orchestra, recorded, 1968, Sonnet for Flute, Guitar and Harpsichord, 1969, Overture for Chamber Orchestra, 1970, Images For Christmas for Speaker, Electric Guitar, Small Organ with Percussion, Celesta and Effects for 5 Players, 1973; Point of Ignition for mezzo and orchestra, 1997; The Western Front, World War I, for choir and ensemble, 1999; Piano: Piano Sonata, 1960, Waltz, 1966, Cantillation, 1966; Orchestral: Phantasma for String Orchestra, recorded, 1963, Imperium, 1969; Vocal, Choral: As Dew In Aprille, Christmas carol for Boy or Female Soprano, Piano or Harp or Guitar, 1955, Vigil, a cappella, 1966, Bird Calls From An Old Land for 5 Soprano Soloists, a Cappella Female Choir, 1971; Brass: Company Of Brass for Ensemble, 1972; Theatre: Incidental music and songs, Jo Being, 1-act opera, 1974; Music for the Adonia, theatre, 1992. *Address:* c/o J Albert and Son, 139 King Street, Sydney, New South Wales 2000, Australia.

**GILAD, Jonathan;** Concert Pianist; b. 1981, Marseilles, France. *Education:* Marseilles Conservatory, and with Dimitri Bashkirov in Colmar and Madrid. *Career:* Concerts with the Israel Philharmonic under Zubin Mehta, Monte Carlo Philharmonic Orchestra, The Ulster Orchestra and Lausanne Chamber Orchestra; US debut, 1996 with the Chicago Symphony Orchestra, returned 1997 with the Chopin E minor Concerto; Berlin recital debut, 1988; Season 1998–99 included USA tour with the St Petersburg Philharmonic Orchestra; Boston Symphony Orchestra concerts, appearances with the Israel Philharmonic Orchestra and at the Maggio Musicale, Florence; Schumann Concerto with the Chicago Symphony Orchestra in Berlin under Daniel Barenboim; Wigmore Hall debut, 2000. *Recordings:* Numerous. *Honours:* Prizes at the Paris Mozart Competition, 1991; Salzburg Mozarteum Competition, 1992. *Address:* c/o Konzertdirektion Hörtnagel Berlin GmbH, Oranienburger Strasse 50, D–10117 Berlin, Germany.

**GILBERT, Alan;** American conductor; *Music Director, Santa Fe Opera;* b. 23 Feb. 1967, New York. *Education:* Harvard Univ., Curtis Inst. of Music, Juilliard School. *Career:* Chief Conductor and Artistic Adviser, Royal Stockholm Philharmonic Orchestra 2000–; Music Dir, Santa Fe Opera 2003–; Principal Guest Conductor, NDR Hamburg Symphony Orchestra 2003–; guest conducting engagements include performances with the Bayerischer Rundfunk, Orchestre de Paris, Tonhalle, New York Philharmonic, Los Angeles Philharmonic, NHK Symphony, Royal Concertgebouw Orchestra debut 2003, BBC Proms debut with the Mahler Chamber Orchestra 2003, and debut with Zurich Opera 2003. *Honours:* First Prize in the Int. Competition for Musical

Performance, Geneva 1994, Seaver/Nat. Endowment for the Arts Conductors Award 1997. *Current Management:* c/o IMG Artists, Lovell House, 616 Chiswick High Road, London, W4 5RX, England. *Telephone:* (20) 8233-5800. *Fax:* (20) 8233-5801. *E-mail:* cdennes@imgworld.com. *Address:* c/o The Santa Fe Opera, PO Box 2408, Santa Fe, NM 87504-2408, USA. *Website:* www .santafeopera.org.

**GILBERT, Anthony,** MA, DMus, FRNCM; British composer; b. 26 July 1934, London, England; two s. one d. *Education:* Univ. of Leeds, studied composition with Anthony Milner, Matyas Seiber, Alexander Goehr and Gunther Schuller, studied conducting with Lawrence Leonard at Morley Coll., London. *Career:* Lecturer in Composition, Goldsmiths' Coll. 1968–73; composer-in-residence, Univ. of Lancaster 1970–71; Lecturer in Composition, Morley Coll. 1972–75; Sr Lecturer in Composition, Sydney Conservatorium, Australia 1978–79; composer-in-residence, City of Bendigo, Victoria 1981; Head of School of Composition and Contemporary Music, Royal Northern Coll. of Music –1999; mem. Soc. for the Promotion of New Music, Performing Right Soc., Mechanical Copyright Protection Soc., British Acad. of Composers and Songwriters. *Compositions:* operas: The Scene-Machine 1971, The Chakravaka-Bird 1977; orchestral: Symphony, Sinfonia, Ghost and Dream Dancing, Crow Cry, Towards Asavari, On Beholding a Rainbow violin concerto 1997, Another Dream Carousel, Sheer, Palace of the Winds; for wind orchestra: Dream Carousels; chamber: four string quartets, Saxophone Quartet, Quartet of Beasts, Nine or Ten Osannas, Vasanta with Dancing; instrumental: Ziggurat, Reflexions, Rose Nord, Moonfaring, Dawnfaring, three piano sonatas, Spell Respell, The Incredible Flute Music, Treatment of Silence, Osanna for Lady O; vocal: Certain Lights Reflecting, Love Poems, Inscapes, Long White Moonlight, Beastly Jingles; music theatre: Upstream River Rewa 1991, Handles to the Invisible for chorus 1995, Vers de Lune 1999. *Recordings:* Moonfaring; Beastly Jingles; Nine or Ten Osannas; Towards Asavari; Dream Carousels; Igorochki; Quartet of Beasts; Six of the Bestiary; Farings; Another Dream Carousel. *Address:* 4 Oak Brow Cottages, Altrincham Road, Styal, Wilmslow, Cheshire SK9 4JE, England. *E-mail:* anthonygilbert@anthgilbert.demon.co .uk.

**GILBERT, Jane;** Singer (mezzo-soprano); b. 1969, New York, NY, USA; m. John Hancock. *Education:* Studied at the Juilliard Opera Center. *Career:* Season 1993–94 at Cenerentola at Kansas City, Varvara in Katya Kabanova for Canadian Opera, Britten's Lucretia at the Brooklyn Academy and Ragonde in Comte Ory at Spoleto Festival, USA; Season 1994–95 as Bartók's Judith at Melbourne (also at Edinburgh), Olga in Eugene Onegin at Toronto, (1996), Cuniza in Oberto for Opéra de Nice and Federica in Luisa Miller for Washington Opera; Concert repertoire includes the Berlioz Mort de Cléopâtre. *Current Management:* Athole Still International Management, Forresters Hall, 25–27 Westow Street, London, SE19 3RY, England. *Telephone:* (20) 8771-5271. *Fax:* (20) 8768-6600. *Website:* www.atholestill.com.

**GILBERT, Kenneth Albert,** OC, DMus, FRCM; Canadian harpsichordist and organist; b. 16 Dec. 1931, Montreal; s. of Albert George Gilbert and Reta Mabel (Welch). *Education:* Conservatoire de Musique, Montreal and Conservatoire de Paris. *Career:* Prof. Conservatoire de Musique, Montreal 1965–72; Assoc. Prof. Laval Univ. 1970–76; Guest Prof. Royal Antwerp Conservatory 1971–73; Dir Early Music Dept Conservatoire de Strasbourg 1981–85; Prof. Staatliche Hochschule für Musik, Stuttgart 1981–89, Hochschule Mozarteum, Salzburg 1984–2000, Paris Conservatoire 1988–96; Adjunct Prof., McGill Univ. 1998–; Instructor at other music acads, summer schools etc.; Pres., Editions de l'Oiseau-Lyre Monaco 2001–; Fellow, Canada Council 1968, 1974, Calouste Gulbenkian Foundation 1971; has recorded complete harpsichord works of Couperin, Scarlatti and Rameau, suites and partitas of J.S. Bach, Well-tempered Clavier of Bach and concertos for 2, 3, 4 harpsichords by Bach; Fellow Royal Coll. of Music. *Publications:* editions of complete harpsichord works of Couperin, Scarlatti and Rameau, Bach's Goldberg Variations, Frescobaldi Toccatas. *Honours:* Fellow, Royal Society of Canada; Hon. mem. RAM; Officier Ordre des Arts et des Lettres, Cross of Honour 1st Class (Austria). *Address:* 11 rue Ernest-Psichari, 75007 Paris, France (office). *Telephone:* 1-45-56-04-93 (office). *Fax:* 1-45-56-04-93 (office). *E-mail:* kengil@ online.fr.

**GILCHRIST, Diana;** Soprano; b. 1970, Canada. *Education:* Studied at Banff School of Fine Arts and in Los Angeles and London. *Career:* Founded Opera Lyra at Ottawa and sang at Koblenz Opera from 1989, notably as Susanna, Janáček's Vixen and Gilda; Sang Mozart's Blondchen with Mainz Opera, followed by Zerbinetta; Bielefeld in 1991 as Grétry's Zemire, Vienna Volksoper in 1992 as the Queen of Night, returning as Offenbach's Olympia; Concerts in Canada and Germany have included Orff's Carmina Burana. *Address:* Helen Sykes Artists Management, 100 Felsham Road, Putney, London SW15 1DQ, England.

**GILCHRIST, James;** Singer (tenor); b. 1970, England. *Education:* Chorister at New College, Oxford; Choral Scholar, King's College, Cambridge. *Career:* Concerts include: Haydn's Creation at the Queen Elizabeth Hall, London, Elijah at St David's Cathedral, Solomon in Buxton and Mozart's Requiem at the Barbican with the English Chamber Orchestra; Engagements with the King's Concert in Purcell Odes at the Wigmore Hall, and Bach's B minor Mass at the Queen Elizabeth Hall, 2000; Messiah in Oslo, Bach's Magnificat with The Sixteen in Spain and the Christmas Oratorio in Italy; Opera includes Mozart's Ferrando and Strauss's Scaramuccio, under Richard Hickox, and Gomatz in Mozart's Zaide in Istanbul; Season 2000–01 with the Britten War

Requiem in King's College Chapel, Monteverdi Vespers and Messiah with The Sixteen, Bach Passions with the Australian Chamber Orchestra and various Bach touring projects, notably with the Monteverdi Choir and Orchestra. *Current Management:* Hazard Chase, Norman House, Cambridge Place, Cambridge CB2 1NS, England. *Telephone:* (1223) 312400. *Fax:* (1223) 460827. *Website:* www.hazardchase.co.uk.

**GILES, Alice;** concert harpist; b. 9 May 1961, Adelaide, Australia. *Education:* studied with June Loney and Alice Chalifoux. *Career:* extensive concert performances in Australia, the USA, Israel and Germany; Festival engagements at Schleswig-Holstein, Bayreuth (International Youth Festival) and Düsseldorf New Music Festivals, Adelaide (Britten's Canticles with Barry Tuckwell and Gerald English), Sydney, Marlboro Music Festival (USA), and Bath Mozartfest; New York Merkin Hall debut, 1983, 92nd Street 'Y' Concert, 1988; Wigmore Hall debut, June 1989, and tour with Luciano Berio; Featured Soloist at festivals including Salzedo Centennial, Austin, Texas, World Harp Congress, Copenhagen, and World Harp Festival, Cardiff, Wales; Frankfurt Hochschule, 1990–98; School of Music at Canberra, Australia, 1999–; Concertos with Collegium Musicum Zürich, Badische Staatskapelle Karlsruhe, English Symphony Orchestra, all major symphony orchestras in Australia and tour of North and South America with Australian Youth Orchestra; Chamber concerts with violinist Thomas Zehetmair and pianist Arnan Wiesel; mem, Co-Founder, Director, EOLUS–International Salzedo Society. *Recordings include:* Recital, Fauré's Impromptu in D flat major, 2 Preludes of Debussy, Tournier's 2nd Sonatine, 5 Preludes of Salzedo; Recital of works for solo harp by Carlos Salzedo; Chamber music for flute and harp with Geoffrey Collins, flute. *Honours:* Churchill International Fellowship, 1980; Winner, International Harp Competition, Israel, 1982. *Current Management:* Robert Gilder & Co., Enterprise House, 59–65 Upper Ground, London, SE1 9PQ, England. *Telephone:* (20) 7928-9008. *Fax:* (20) 7928-9755. *E-mail:* rgilder@robert-gilder.com.

**GILFEDDER, John (Francis);** Composer; b. 27 Jan. 1925, Melbourne, Victoria, Australia. *Education:* BMus, 1958, BEd (Hons), 1962, University of Melbourne. *Career:* Faculty Member, Queensland Conservatorium, 1970–; Concert Presenter and Producer. *Compositions include:* The Trojan Doom for speaking voice, string quartet, flute, cor anglais and horn, 1972; Orbits About a Theme for piano, 1981; Colours of the Cosmos, for percussion ensemble, 1985; The Legend of Tibrogargan, for orchestra, 1986; Raga of the Morning for cello, 1989; Reedy Rivers, for woodwind, 1992; Transparencies in Violet, for viola and string orchestra, 1994; Conversazione Pastorale, for saxophone quartet, 1994; Te Deum in Montage, for choir, 1995; Commissions from the Queensland Philharmonic (1994) and others. *Address:* c/o APRA, 1A Eden Street, Crows Nest, NSW 2065, Australia.

**GILFRY, Rodney;** Singer (Baritone); b. 11 March 1959, California, USA. *Career:* Sang in opera at Los Angeles as Guglielmo, Mozart's Figaro, the Villains in Contes d'Hoffmann and Ford in Falstaff, 1990; European engagements as Figaro at Hamburg, Tel-Aviv and Zürich; Frankfurt Opera from 1989, as Gounod's Mercutio, Ernesto (Il Pirata) and Massenet's Herod; Geneva, 1988, as Lescaut in Manon, Santa Fe, 1991, in the US premiere of Oedipus by Rihm; Concert engagements include Bach's B minor Mass in Paris and at La Scala, Milan; Season 1992 as Guglielmo in Barcelona and at the Holland Festival, Don Giovanni at the Opéra de Lyon; Sang Sharpless in Butterfly at Los Angeles, 1996; Guglielmo at Covent Garden, 1997; Met debut as Demetrius in A Midsummer Nights Dream, 1997; Season 1998 as the Count in Capriccio at Glyndebourne and Stanley in the premiere of Previn's A Streetcar Named Desire at San Francisco; Season 2000–01 as Billy Budd and Dandini at Los Angeles, Valentin in Faust at Munich and Guglielmo for the New York Met; Nathan in the premiere of Sophie's Choice, Covent Garden, 2002. *Recordings:* Ein Deutsches Requiem; Così fan tutte. *Address:* c/o Opéra de Lyon, 9 Quai Jean Moulin, 69001 Lyon, France.

**GILHOOLY, John;** Irish music administrator; *Director, Wigmore Hall;* b. Castleconnell, Co. Limerick. *Education:* Univ. Coll. Dublin, Dublin City Coll. of Music and Leinster School of Music and Drama. *Career:* fmr history teacher Univ. Coll. Dublin; man. positions include with Harrogate Int. Centre, ExCel in Docklands, London, Univ. Coll. Dublin Admin and Services Dept; Exec. Dir Wigmore Hall, London 2000–05, acting Artistic Dir 2005, now has overall title of Dir 2005–; has appeared as a soloist on TV and radio in Ireland; fmrly presented radio programmes for Lyric FM, Ireland. *Address:* Wigmore Hall, 36 Wigmore Street, London, W1U 2BP, England (office). *Telephone:* (20) 7258-8200 (office). *Fax:* (20) 7258-8201 (office). *E-mail:* info@wigmore-hall.org.uk (office). *Website:* www.wigmore-hall.org.uk (office).

**GILL, Timothy;** Cellist; b. 1960, England. *Career:* Co-founded the Chagall Piano Trio at the Banff Centre for the Arts in Canada, resident artist; Debut concert at the Blackheath Concert Halls in London in 1991; Further appearances at the Barbican's Prokofiev Centenary Festival, the Warwick Festival and the South Place Sunday Concerts at the Conway Hall in London; Purcell Room London recitals in 1993 with the London premiere of piano trios by Tristan Keuris, Nicholas Maw and Ethel Smyth (composed in 1880); Premiere of Piano Trio No. 2 by David Matthews at the Norfolk and Norwich Festival in 1993; Engaged for the Malvern Festival in 1994. *Address:* Chagall Trio, South Bank Centre, Press Office (Pamela Chowham Management), London SE1, England.

**GILLES, Marie-Louise;** Singer (Mezzo-Soprano); b. 1937, Duren, Germany. *Education:* Studied at the Folkwang-Hochschule Essen with Hilde Wesselmann. *Career:* Wiesbaden Opera from 1962 as Octavian, Dorabella and the Composer in Ariadne auf Naxos; Staatsoper Munich, 1964–66, Bremen, 1966–68 and from 1968 at Hannover notably as Azucena, Brangaene, Eboli, Waltraute, Fricka, Ortrud, Berg's Marie and Countess Geschwitz, and Santuzza; Bayreuth Festival, 1968–69, appearances at the Dubrovnik and Salzburg Easter Festivals and concert engagements in Washington, New York, Vienna, Paris and Lisbon; Professor at the Hannover Musikhochschule from 1982. *Recordings:* Petite Messe Solennelle by Rossini; Bach Cantatas; Hans Heiling by Marschner. *Address:* Hochschule für Musik und Theater, Emmichplatz 1, 3 Hannover, Germany.

**GILLESPIE, Neil;** Singer (Tenor); b. 1968, Glasgow, Scotland. *Education:* Royal Scottish Academy, with Duncan Robertson; Britten-Pears School and European Centre for Opera and Vocal Studies, Belgium; further studies with Nicolai Gedda. *Career:* Appearances with Opéra de Lyon, New Israeli Opera and English National Opera; Royal Opera, Covent Garden in Mathis der Maler by Hindemith, Verdi's Il Corsaro, Luisa Miller, Paul Bunyan and The Pilgrim's Progress; Giuseppe in La Traviata, 2001; Other roles include Bacchus in The Olympians by Bliss, Rossini's Almaviva, Tamino, and Sailor in Dido and Aeneas. *Address:* c/o Royal Opera House (contracts), Covent Garden, London. WC2, England. *Telephone:* (20) 7240 1200. *Fax:* (20) 72129502.

**GILLESPIE, Rhondda (Marie),** BMus; British concert pianist; b. 3 Aug. 1941, Sydney, Australia; d. of David Gillespie and Marie Gillespie; m. Denby Richards 1972. *Education:* NSW Conservatorium with Alexander Sverjensky and in London with Louis Kentner and Denis Matthews. *Career:* debut on Australian radio aged eight 1949; first public recital 1953; winner NSW Concerto Competition, Sydney 1959; European debut in London with Tchaikovsky Piano Concerto 2 1960; since then has played with major orchestras throughout UK, Netherlands, Germany, Scandinavia, Far East and USA and made many festival appearances. *Address:* 2 Princes Road, St Leonards-on-Sea, East Sussex, TN37 6EL, England. *Telephone:* (1424) 715167. *Fax:* (1424) 712214. *E-mail:* musicalopinion2@aol.com.

**GILLESPIE, Wendy;** Viol Player; b. 1950, New York, USA. *Career:* Member of Fretwork with first London concert at the Wigmore Hall in 1986; Appearances in the Renaissance and Baroque repertoire in Sweden, France, Belgium, Netherlands, Germany, Austria, Switzerland and Italy; Radio broadcasts in Sweden, Netherlands, Germany and Austria and a televised concert on ZDF, Mainz; Tour of Russia in 1989 and Japan in 1991; Festival engagements in the United Kingdom; Repertory includes In Nomines and Fantasias by Tallis, Parsons and Byrd, dance music by Holborne and Dowland including Lachrimae, six-part consorts by Gibbons and William Lawes, songs and instrumental works by Purcell; Collaborations with vocal group, Red Byrd in verse anthems by Byrd and Tomkins, London Cries by Gibbons and Dering, Resurrection Story and Seven Last Words by Schütz; Gave George Benjamin's Upon Silence at the Queen Elizabeth Hall in 1990; Wigmore Hall concerts, 1990–91 with music by Lawes, Purcell, Locke, Dowland and Byrd. *Recordings:* Heart's Ease, late Tudor and early Stuart; Armada, courts of Philip II and Elizabeth II; Night's Black Bird by Dowland and Byrd; Cries And Fancies (fantasias, In Nomines and The Cries Of London by Gibbons); Go Nightly Cares, consort songs, dances and In Nomines. *Address:* c/o OWM, 14 Nightingale Lane, London N8 7QU, England.

**GILLETT, Christopher;** Singer (Tenor); b. 1958, London, England. *Education:* Studied at the Royal College of Music with Robert Tear and Edgar Evans; National Opera Studio, London. *Career:* Debut: Sadler's Wells as Edwin in The Gypsy Princess, 1981; sang with New Sadler's Wells Opera in Gilbert and Sullivan; Has appeared with Glyndebourne Touring Opera as Ferrando and Albert Herring; Hermes in King Priam for Kent Opera; Royal Opera House Covent Garden from 1984 as Flute in Midsummer Night's Dream, Roderigo in Otello, Dov in Knot Garden, Pang and Hermes and in Parsifal, Un Re in Ascolto and Idomeneo; Sang Nooni in The Making of the Representative for Planet 8 by Glass at the London Coliseum and in Amsterdam; Season 1990–91 with the Martyrdom of St Magnus by Maxwell Davies in London and Glasgow; Mozart's Ferrando at Garsington Manor and Arbace with the English Bach Festival at Covent Garden and in the Vichy Festival, France; Pysander in Netherlands Opera Ulisses; Sang Musil in the premiere of Broken Strings by Param Vir, Amsterdam, 1992; Tichon in Katya Kabanova for Glyndebourne Touring Opera and Britten's Flute at the 1992 Aix-en-Provence Festival; Concert engagements include Elgar's The Kingdom with the London Philharmonic, Tippett's Mask of Time with the Hallé; Bach's St John Passion in Hong Kong, Cambridge and Greenwich and Elijah with the Bach Choir; Season 1997 with Britten's Flute and Pirzel in Die Soldaten for English National Opera and M Triquet for Netherlands Opera; Season 1999 as Britten's Flute in Rome and in the premiere of Rêves d'un Marco Polo by Claude Vivier at Amsterdam; Oliver Knussen's Where the Wild Things Are and Higglety, Pigglety, Pop! at the London Proms, 2002. *Honours:* Winner, Grimsby Singing Competition, 1980; Countess of Munster Award, 1981. *Address:* c/o IMG Artists, Lovell House, 616 Chiswick High Road, London, W4 5RX, England.

**GILLIES, Malcolm George William,** BA, DipEd, MA, MMus, PhD, DMus; Australian professor of music and university administrator; *Deputy Vice-Chancellor (Education), Australian National University;* b. 23 Dec. 1954, Brisbane, Australia. *Education:* Australian Nat. Univ., Univ. of Queensland, Royal Coll. of Music, London, Univs of Cambridge and London, UK, Univ of Melbourne. *Career:* Tutor in Music, Univ. of Melbourne 1981–83; Lecturer in

Music, Victorian Coll. of Arts 1983–86; Lecturer in Music 1986–90, Sr Lecturer, Univ. of Melbourne 1991–92; Prof. of Music, Univ. of Queensland 1992–99; Exec. Dean, Humanities and Social Sciences and Pro-Vice-Chancellor, Univ. of Adelaide 1999–2001; Deputy Vice-Chancellor (Educ.) ANU 2002–; Fellow, Australian Acad. of the Humanities 1992, Pres. 1998–2001; Pres. Nat. Acads Forum, Australia 1998–2002, Australian Council for Humanities, Arts and Social Sciences 2004–. *Publications include:* Bartók in Britain 1989, Notation and Tonal Structure in Bartók's Later Works 1989, Bartók Remembered 1990, Bartók im Spiegel Seiner Zeit 1991, The Bartók Companion (ed.) 1993, Halsey Stevens's The Life and Music of Béla Bartók (3rd edn) 1993, The All-Round Man: Selected Letters of Percy Grainger (co-ed.) 1994, Northern Exposures 1997, Grainger on Music (co-ed.) 1999, Gen. Ed. (series) Oxford Studies in Musical Genesis, Structure and Interpretation, Portrait of Percy Grainger (co-author) 2002, El Mundo de Bartók 2004. *Honours:* Centenary Medal (Australia) 2003. *Address:* Chancery, Australian National University, ACT 2000 (office); 1501 Capital Tower, 2 Marcus Clarke Street, Canberra City, ACT 2601, Australia (home). *Telephone:* (2) 6125-3386 (office); (2) 6262-5498 (home). *Fax:* (2) 6125-9614 (office). *E-mail:* dvc.ed@anu.edu.au (office). *Website:* www.anu.edu.au (office).

**GILLINSON, Sir Clive Daniel,** CBE, ARAM, FRAM, FRNCM; British cellist; *Executive and Artistic Director, Carnegie Hall;* b. 1946, Bangalore, India; m. Penny; three c. *Education:* Frensham Heights School, Royal Acad. of Music. *Career:* played in Nat. Youth Orchestra of Great Britain 1963–65, Philharmonia Orchestra –1970, London Symphony Orchestra 1970–84; elected to Bd of Dirs London Symphony Orchestra 1976–79, 1983–, Finance Dir 1979, Man. Dir 1984–2005; Exec. and Artistic Dir Carnegie Hall, New York 2005–; owned an antique shop, Hampstead, London 1978–86; Chair. Asscn of British Orchestras 1992–95; Gov. and mem. of Exec. Cttee Nat. Youth Orchestra 1995–; founding pnr Masterprize 1997–; founding trustee Nat. Endowment for Science, Technology and the Arts 1998–; mem. Int. Music Council of the Children's Hearing Inst., New York 1998–. *Honours:* Dr hc (City Univ.) 1995; Royal Acad. of Music May Mukle Cello Prize, ABSA Garrett Award 1992, Hon. GSMD 1992, Freeman of the City of London 1993. *Address:* c/o Carnegie Hall, 881 Seventh Avenue, New York, NY 10019-3210, USA.

**GILMORE, Gail Varina,** MMus; American singer (mezzo-soprano); b. 21 Sept. 1951, Washington, DC. *Education:* In New Orleans (LA) and Univ. of Indiana at Bloomington. *Career:* Appearances at Oper am Rhein (Düsseldorf, Germany), Teatro la Fenice (Venice, Italy), Arena di Verona (Italy), Opernhaus Frankfurt (Germany), Houston Opera (TX), Metropolitan Opera (New York), Bolshoi Theatre (Moscow); performances with José Carreras; numerous concert appearances. *Operas include:* Les Troyens, Carmen, Orfeo ed Euridice, Cavalleria Rusticana, Ariadne auf Naxos, Der Rosenkavalier, Aida, Macbeth, Il Trovatore, Don Carlos, Tannhäuser, Parsifal, Lohengrin. *Address:* Apollolaan 123, NL 1077 Amsterdam, Netherlands.

**GILMOUR, Russell (Scott);** Composer; b. 21 May 1956, Penrith, New South Wales, Australia. *Education:* BA, University of New England, 1986; Australian Chamber Orchestra's Composer Workshop, 1987, 1993. *Career:* Faculty Member, All Saints College, Bathurst, 1987–90; Canterbury College, Queensland, 1990–; Commissions from Bathurst City and Chamber Orchestras, 1987, 1989. *Compositions include:* A Peaceable Kingdom, for chamber orchestra, 1987; Mud, for tuba, 1989; Songlines, for orchestra, 1989; Edge, for flute, 1990; Wood Dance, for marimba, 1991; Point II, for recorder, 1991; Blowpipes, for flute quartet, 1993; Cantate Domino, for choir, 1993; String Quartet: The Art of Reckoning, 1993; A Way Along, for choir and marimba, 1994. *Contributions:* Sounds Australian (Spring 1992). *Address:* c/o APRA, 1A Eden Street, Crows Nest, NSW 2065, Australia.

**GILVAN, Raimund;** Singer (Tenor); b. 1938, Manchester, England. *Education:* Studied at the Cologne Musikhochschule. *Career:* Sang at the Mainz Opera from 1961, Mannheim, 1963–74; Among his best roles have been Capito in Mathis der Maler, Lensky, Henze's Junge Lord, Adrasto in Traetta's Antigone, David in Die Meistersinger and Pfitzner's Palestrina; Many concert appearances. *Recordings:* Beethoven Missa solemnis, Bach B minor Mass, Lieder by Wolf.

**GIMENEZ, Eduardo;** Singer (tenor); b. 2 June 1940, Mataro, Barcelona. *Education:* Studied with Carmen Bracons de Clomer and Juan Sabater in Barcelona and Vladimiro Badiali in Rome. *Career:* Debut: Reggio Emilia in 1967 as Nemorino in L'Elisir d'amore; Has sung widely in Italy and at the Teatro Liceo, Barcelona; Holland Festival in 1970 in La Fedelta Premiata by Haydn; Guest appearances in Brussels, Nice, Monte Carlo, Venice, Budapest, Bordeaux, Tel-Aviv, Seattle and Washington; Sang at Pesaro and La Scala Milan, 1984–85 in a revival of Rossini's Il Viaggio a Reims; Well known in operas by Cimarosa, Bellini, Paisiello, Galuppi, Mozart, Verdi and Puccini; Has sung in Paisiello's Il Barbiere di Siviglia at Leningrad, and at Barcelona in 1988 in the premiere of Libre Vermell by Xavier Benguere, returning as Ferrando in Così fan tutte in 1990; Covent Garden debut 1990, as Ernesto; Season 1992 as Rossini's Don Ramiro at the Semper Oper Dresden and in Barcelona. *Recordings include:* Elvino in La Sonnambula; Don Pasquale; L'Atlantida by Falla; Rossini's Armida.

**GIMENEZ, Raul;** Tenor; b. 14 Sept. 1950, Argentina. *Education:* Studied in Buenos Aires. *Career:* Debut: Teatro Colón Buenos Aires in 1980 as Ernesto in Don Pasquale; Sang in concert and opera throughout South America before his European debut as Filandro in Cimarosa's Le Astuzie Femmineli at the 1984 Wexford Festival; Sang in Paris and Venice as Roderigo in Rossini's

Otello and appeared as Elvino in La Sonnambula in 1989 at the Théâtre des Champs-Elysées; Season 1987 sang at the Pesaro Festival in Rossini's L'Occasione fa Il Ladro, at Amsterdam as Ernesto and as Alessandro in Il Re Pastore at Rome; Aix-en-Provence in 1988 as Gernando and Carlo in Rossini's Armida; Toronto and Zürich in 1989 as Almaviva; US debut at Dallas as Ernesto, Lisbon in 1989 as Tonio in La Fille du Régiment and Covent Garden 1990–93 as Almaviva, Ernesto and Ramiro; Season 1990 with appearances as Argirio in Tancredi at Geneva, Così fan tutte at Buenos Aires and Salieri's Les Danaides at the Ravenna Festival as Lyncée; Debuts at Vienna State Opera in 1990 as Almaviva, La Scala in 1993 as Argirio in Tancredi, and at Florence in 1993 in La Cenerentola; Further guest appearances in Munich, Rome Geneva, Naples, Bologna, Verona, Turin, Frankfurt, Toulouse, Monte Carlo, Lausanne, Schwetzingen Festival and Brussels; Season 1996 sang Appio in Pacini's L'Ultimo giorno di Pompei, Martina Franca; Lindoro in L'Italiana in Algeri at the Vienna State Opera, 1996; Season 1998 debut at Paris Opéra Bastille as Tebaldo in Capuleti ed i Montecchi and Edgardo in Lucia di Lammermoor, as Il Turco in Italia at Monte Carlo and Almaviva at Geneva; Season 2000 as Don Ottavio at La Coruña and as Ramiro in La Cenerentola at the Met and in Madrid. Recordings include: Arias by Mozart, Rossini, Bellini and Donizetti; Les Danaides; L'Occasione fa il Ladro conducted by Michelangelo Veltri; Il Turco in Italia; Rossini's Messa di Gloria, 1992; Il Barbiere di Siviglia; Viaggio a Reims; La Cenerentola; L'italiana in Algeri; L' Inganno Felice; Rossini's Stabat Mater; La Sonnambula. Address: c/o Patricia Greenan, 19b Belsize Park, London NW3 4DU, England.

**GIMSE, Havard;** Pianist; b. 15 Sept. 1966, Kongsvinger, Norway. Education: Norway State Academy of Music; Bergen Music Conservatory; Mozarteum, Salzburg; Musikhochschule, Berlin. Career: Debut: Trondheim Symphony Orchestra, 1981; Soloist with Major Scandinavian orchestras, such as Oslo Philharmonic, Bergen Philharmonic, Helsinki Radio, since 1981; Concerts in Europe and North and South America; Played with conductors including Kitajenko, Talmi, Schonwandt, Iona Brown; Several chamber music appearances; Oslo Philharmonic Tour of the United Kingdom, 1995–96; Schleswig-Holstein Festival, 1997; Valdemossa Chopin Festival, 1997. Recordings: Liszt: Piano Sonata; Chopin: Piano Music; Grieg: Piano and chamber music; Tveitt: Piano Music. Honours: Princess Astrid's Music Prize, 1985; Robert Levin Festival Prize, 1986; Jugend Musiziert Frankfurt, 1987; Steinway Prize, Berlin, 1995; Grieg Prize, Norway, 1996. Current Management: Pro Arte International Management. Address: Fosswinchelsrt 9, N5007 Bergen, Norway.

**GINTY, Eugene;** Singer (Tenor); b. 10 Dec. 1965, London, England. Education: BA Hons Degree in Music, Durham University; Studies under Ian Barr. Career: Debut: Japan and France, 1994; Don Jose, 1997; Cavaradossi, for Midwales Opera, 1997; Don Ramiro for English Touring, 1997; Sandy, The Lighthouse, 1998; Tonio, La Fille du Régiment for English Touring Opera, 1998; 4 appearances on BBC Radio 2's Friday Night is Music Night; Numerous appearances on BBC Radio 3 including Rossini's Petite Messe Solennelle; 1 appearance on Radio 4, Seeds of Faith; Concert Repertoire: Evangelist (St John), Sheffield Cathedral (St Matthew), Durham Cathedral and St Anne's, Belfast; Britten's Abraham and Isaac, Eton College, 1994; Bach Cantata 191 at Queen Elizabeth Hall, 1995; Schubert's Mondschein at Wigmore Hall under Stephen Cleobury; Britten's Serenade for Tenor, Horn, and Strings, Cleveland Chamber Orchestra, 1996; Elgar's Dream of Gerontius, Guildford Civic Hall, 1998; mem, Equity; Pamra. Recordings: Psalms and Part Songs, BBC Singers/Jane Glover; Pärt and Tormis, BBC Singers/Bo Holton; Richard Strauss, BBC Singers/Stephen Cleobury. Current Management: O.C.A. Address: 270 Shrub End Road, Colchester, Essex CO3 4RL.

**GINZER, Frances;** Singer (Soprano); b. 19 Sept. 1955, Calgary, Alberta, Canada. Education: Studied at Calgary, North Texas State and Toronto Universities. Career: Debut: Canadian Opera Toronto, as Clothilde in Norma; Sang Antonia in Les Contes d'Hoffmann at Toronto, followed by the Verdi Requiem, Messiah, Beethoven's Ninth and Die Schöpfung; European opera debut Karlsruhe, 1983 as Antonia; Engaged at Düsseldorf from 1987 and has made guest appearances at Hamburg, Stuttgart, Cologne, Bonn, London (English National Opera), Munich State Opera, Frankfurt, Zürich, Warsaw, Maastricht, Vancouver, Calgary, Edmonton, Winnipeg and USA debut in Dallas, Texas; Welsh National Opera 1991, as Violetta; Duisburg 1991, as Frau Fluth in Die Lustige Weiber von Windsor; Washington Opera 1995, as Senta; Brünnhilde in Siegfried at Düsseldorf, 1996; Elsa in Lohengrin at Tokyo, 1997; Early roles included Micaela, Constanze, Donna Anna and Mozart Countess; Lucia, Cleopatra, Sophie in Der Rosenkavalier, Aminta (Die schweigsame Frau), Jenůfa, Leila (Les Pêcheurs des perles) and Mimi; Present Repertoire includes Turandot, Ariadne, Senta and Tosca; Sang Brünnhilde for San Francisco and Dallas Opera, 1999–2000; Turandot at Covent Garden, 2002. Recordings include: Handel's Rodrigo; Adriana Lecouvreur. Address: c/o Welsh National Opera, John Street, Cardiff CF1 4SP, Wales.

**GIORDANI, Marcello;** Singer (Tenor); b. 1963, Catania, Sicily. Career: Debut: Spoleto Festival 1986, as Duke of Mantua; La Scala debut 1988, as Rodolfo, and US debut at Portland, as Nadir; Season 1991 in Live from Lincoln Center (New York) concert and debut at the Verona Arena, as the Duke; Recent engagements as Nemorino, Rodolfo and Alfredo at the Metropolitan (season 1996–97), Pinkerton, Edgardo and Gounod's Roméo at Houston,

Alfredo at Covent Garden under Georg Solti, Tonio (La Fille du Régiment) and Hoffmann at Portland and Faust at the Opéra Bastille, Paris; Further engagements at San Francisco Seattle, Chicago, Vienna (in Rosenkavalier and I Puritani), Hamburg, Munich and Berlin; Season 1997–98 as Werther at the Metropolitan, in Lucrezia Borgia at La Scala, L'Elisir d'amore in Dallas and as Pinkerton at San Francisco; Season 2000–01 as Faust at Los Angeles, Gabriele Adorno for San Francisco Opera, Rodolfo at the Met, Cavaradossi for Chicago Opera and Raoul in Les Huguenots at Carnegie Hall. Address: c/o Metropolitan Opera, Lincoln Center, New York, NY 10023, USA.

**GIOVANINETTI, Christoph;** Violinist; b. 1960, France. Education: Studied at the Paris Conservatoire with Jean-Claude Pennetier and with members of the Amadeus and Alban Berg Quartets. Career: Member of the Ysaÿe String Quartet from 1984; Many concert performances in France, Europe, America and the Far East; Festival engagements at Salzburg, Tivoli in Copenhagen, Bergen, Lockenhaus, Barcelona and Stresa; Many appearances in Italy notably with the Haydn Quartets of Mozart; Tours of Japan and the USA in 1990 and 1992. Recordings: Mozart Quartet K421 and Quintet K516; Ravel, Debussy and Mendelssohn Quartets. Honours: Grand Prix Evian International String Quartet Competition, 1988; Special prizes for best performances of a Mozart quartet, the Debussy quartet and a contemporary work; 2nd Prize, Portsmouth International String Quartet Competition, 1988. Address: c/o Phelps, Ysaÿe Quartet, 6 Malvern Road, London, E8 3LT, England.

**GIRAUD, Suzanne;** Composer; b. 31 July 1958, Metz, France. Education: Studied at the Strasbourg and Paris Conservatoires; Further study with Tristan Murail, Brian Ferneyhough and Franco Donatoni. Compositions include: Tentaive-Univers for percussion, 1983; String Quartet, 1983; Terre Essor for Orchestra, 1984; Ergo Sum for 15 Instruments, 1985; L'Offrande a Venus for 8 instruments, 1985; Le Rouge Des Profondeurs for 6 Instruments, 1990; L'Oeil Et Le Jour for Percussion, 1990; String Trio, 1991; Envoûtements 1 for violin, 1996; Petraca for 6 voices. 1996; Envoûtements 4 for string quartet, 1997; Ton Coeur sur la Pente du Ciel for orchestra, 1998; To One in Paradise for mezzo-soprano and orchestra, 1999; Zéphyr for piano, 1999; Au Commencement était le Verbe, for 16 voices and 6 percussionists, 2002; Le Bel été for baritone and piano, 2002; Envoûtements V for guitar and string quartet, 2001; Duos pour Prades for clarinet and cello, 2002; Envoûtements VI for 6 percussionists, 2003; Le Vase de Parfums, opera, 2004; Concerto for cello and orchestra 2004, Envoûtements VII for soprano and 6 instruments 2005, Envoûtements VIII for 8 cellos (cello octet) 2005. Recordings: To One in Paradise; Envoûtements I, II, III and IV. Honours: First Prizes at the Paris Conservatory; Diploma from the Accademia Chigiana in Sienna for Composition; In residence at the Villa Medici, Rome; Chosen for performance by the ISCM (Budapest, Manchester). Address: 125 Avenue du General de Gaulle, 94500 Champigny-sur-Marne, France. Telephone: (6) 08-30-40-63 (office). E-mail: suzanne.giraud@free.fr (office). Website: www.resmusica.com/suzanne (office); www.suzannegiraud.com (office).

**GIROLAMI, Renato;** Baritone; b. 1959, Amelia, Torino, Italy. Education: Studied in Germany with Ernst Haefliger and Dietrich Fischer-Dieskau and in Italy with Sesto Bruscantini. Career: Sang Mozart's Figaro and Leporello at Passau, Germany, St Gallen, Switzerland and at Salzburg Landestheater, 1987–89; From 1989 with ensemble at Vienna Volksoper singing Figaro, Leporello and Guglielmo in Così fan tutte; From 1991 member of Vienna Staatsoper where he added Bartolo in Barber of Seville, also in Stuttgart, 1992–94, Belcore in L'Elisir d'amore, Sharpless in Madama Butterfly and Taddeo in L'Italiana in Algeri; Other roles include Somarone in Béatrice et Bénédict with Neville Marriner in London, 1990, Papageno at Barcelona in 1991, the Count in Le nozze di Figaro at Bari, 1991, Schaunard in La Bohème at Naples in 1992 and at Tokyo in 1993, and Enrico in Lucia di Lammermoor at Marseilles in 1994; Sang at Essen 1999–2000 as Don Alfonso and Don Pasquale. Address: Friedgasse 57-2, 1190 Vienna, Austria.

**GISCA, Nicolae,** DMus; Romanian conductor and university professor; Professor of Conducting and Orchestration, George Enescu Academy of Arts; b. 30 Sept. 1942, Tibirica, Romania; m. Elena Gisca 1965; one d. Education: Music Conservatory George Enescu, Iasi, Romania. Career: conducting debut with Conservatory Choir 1962; conductor of over 900 choral, chamber and symphony concerts with Conservatory Symphony and Chamber Orchestras, Conservatory Choir and Chamber Choir, Bacau and Botosani Philharmonic Orchestras; performances and tours of concerts in Romania, Austria, Germany, Belgium, Luxembourg, Switzerland, Wales, France, Italy and Spain with Chamber Choir, Cantores Amicitae; TV and radio appearances; Prof. of Conducting and Orchestration, George Enescu Acad. of Arts 1965–. Compositions: arrangements and choral processing of European, American, African and Asian Folksongs for Choir; 145 musical pieces. Recordings: The Tour of The World in 16 Melodies; Winter Songs From Everywhere; The Festival of Political Song; Christmas Carols from Romania and From the World; Romanian Choral Music; Cantores Amicitae Sings the World; Christmas Carols from Everywhere; Kripenspiel; P. Constantinescu: The Byzantine Oratorio for Christmas; Negro Spirituals; The Liturgies of the World. Publications: The Conductor's Art 1982, The Treaty of Instruments Theory Vol I 1987, Vol II 1998, The COnductor of the CHoir 1992, The Interpretation of Choral Music 2004, Unity and Variety in Christian Spirituality Reflected in Choral Liturgical Music 2004. Honours: six first prizes at Nat. Festival of Singing, Romania 1979, 1981, 1983, 1985, 1987, 1989, First Prize, Int. Competition "Youth and Music", Vienna 1980, Third Prize, Int. Music Eisteddfod, Llangollen, Wales 1991, Second Prize 1995,

Excellent Mention, Int. Competition, Montreux 1995, Special Prize, Int. Music Festival, Cantonigros, Spain 1995, two First Prizes, Int. Music Festival "World Music", Fivizzano, Italy 2002. *Address:* George Enescu Academy of Arts, Str. Horia 7–9, 700126, Iasi (office). *Telephone:* (232) 212548 (office). *Fax:* (232) 212551 (office). *E-mail:* enescu@arteiasi.ro (office). *Website:* www .arteiasi.ro (office); romania-on-line.net/whoswho (office).

**GITECK, Janice;** Composer and Pianist; b. 27 June 1946, New York, USA. *Education:* Studied at Mills College with Darius Milhaud and Morton Subotnick; Paris Conservatoire with Olivier Messiaen, 1969–70; Aspen School with Milhaud and Charles Jones; Has also studied electronic music, Javanese gamelan and West African percussion. *Career:* Teacher at Hayward State University, the University of California at Berkeley, 1974–76, and Cornish Institute, Seattle from 1979; Co-Director of the Port Costa Players, 1972–79. *Compositions include:* Piano Quintet, 1965; 2 String Quartets; How To Invoke A Garden, cantata, 1968; Traffic Acts for 4-track tape, 1969; Sun Of The Center, cantata, 1970; Magic Words, 1973; Messalina, 1973; Helixes for ensemble, 1974; A'gita, opera, 1976; Sandbars On The Takano River, 1976; Thunder Like A White Bear Dancing, 1977; Callin' Home Coyote, burlesque, 1978; Far North Beast Ghosts The Clearing, 1978; Peter And The Wolves for trombone with actor and tape, 1978; Breathing Songs From A Turning Sky, 1980; When The Crones Stop Counting for 60 flutes, 1980; Tree, chamber symphony, 1981; Hopi: Songs Of The Fourth World, 1983; Loo-Wit for viola and orchestra, 1983. *Honours:* Grants from The California Arts Council, 1978 and The National Endowment For The Arts, 1979 and 1983; Commissions from soloists and ensembles. *Address:* c/o ASCAP, ASCAP Building, 1 Lincoln Plaza, New York, NY 10023, USA.

**GITLIS, Ivry;** Concert Violinist; b. 22 Aug. 1922, Haifa, Israel; m. Paule Deglon. *Education:* Studied at the Ecole Normale de Musique, Paris, and with Flesch, Enescu and Thibaud. *Career:* First played in public at age 8 in Israel; Worked in British Troop entertainment during the War; Debuts with the London Philharmonic, BBC Symphony and other British orchestras during the 1940s; Paris debut in 1951, Israel debut in 1952 and US debut in 1955; Many recitals and concert appearances with leading orchestras; Often heard in works by 20th century composers. *Recordings include:* Concertos by Berg, Stravinsky, Bartók and Tchaikovsky. *Honours:* Winner, Thibaud Prize, 1951.

**GIURANNA, Bruno;** Italian viola player and conductor; b. 6 April 1933, Milan. *Education:* Coll. S. Giuseppe and Conservatorio di Musica Santa Cecilia, Rome and Conservatorio di Musica S. Pietro a Maiella, Naples. *Career:* Founder mem. I Musici 1951–61; Prof. Conservatorio G. Verdi, Milan 1961–65, Conservatorio S. Cecilia, Rome 1965–78, Prof. Acad. Chigiana, Siena 1966–83; Prof. Nordwest-deutsche Musikakademie, Detmold, Germany 1969–83; Prof. Hochschule der Künste, Berlin 1981–98; Prof. W. Stauffer Foundation 1985–; Prof. Royal Music Acad., London 1994–96; Prof. Acad. S. Cecilia, Rome 1995–97; mem. Int. Music Competition jury, Munich 1961–62, 1967, 1969, Geneva 1968, Budapest 1975; soloist at concerts in festivals including Edinburgh Festival, Holland Festival and with orchestras including Berlin Philharmonic, Amsterdam Concertgebouw and Teatro alla Scala, Milan; Artistic Dir of Orchestra da Camera di Padova 1983–92; Academician of Santa Cecilia 1974. *Honours:* DLit hc (Univ. of Limerick) 2003. *Address:* Via Bembo 96, 31011 Asolo, TV, Italy. *Telephone:* (423) 55734. *Fax:* (423) 520115. *E-mail:* info@giuranna.it (home). *Website:* www.giuranna.com (home).

**GIZBERT STUDNICKA, Bogumila;** Harpsichordist; b. 16 March 1949, Kraków, Poland; 1 s. *Education:* MMus with honours, Academy of Music, Kraków, 1973; Study with Jos Van Immersel, Conservatoire Royal, Antwerp, Belgium; Diploma with special honours, Conservatoire Royal, 1979; Master-classes with Zuzana Ruzickova, Kenneth Gilbert, and Ton Koopman. *Career:* Numerous concert appearances including with Polish Orchestra of Wojciech Rajski, Poland and other European countries; Active participant in many chamber music ensembles; Assistant Professor, Department of Harpsichord and Early Instruments and Department of Chamber Music, Academy of Music, Kraków; mem, Polish Society of Musicians. *Recordings:* Concertos of Antonio Vivaldi, JS Bach's transcriptions, Polskie Nagrania Musa; Recordings for Polish and Belgian radio and television and Dutch radio. *Honours:* Prize, Polish Piano Festival, Slupsk, 1974; Prize with Distinction, International Harpsichord Competition, Bruges, Belgium, 1977. *Address:* ul Meissnera 4m 66, 31462 Kraków, Poland.

**GJEVANG, Anne;** Norwegian singer (contralto); b. 24 Oct. 1948, Oslo. *Education:* Conservatorio Santa Cecilia (Rome) and Hochschule für Musik und Darstellende Kunst (Vienna). *Career:* Operatic debuts in Austria and Germany, Bayreuth Festival 1983, Metropolitan Opera, New York 1987, Victoria Music Festival, London 1991; mem. Zurich Opera House 1987–91; guest performer Berlin and London Philharmonics, Chicago Symphony Orchestra, USA, Orchestre de Paris; performed with famous conductors including Solti, Barenboim, von Karajan, Giulini, Abbado, Chailly, Albrecht, Perick, Haitink and Pappano; renowned for appearances as Erda in Wagner's Ring des Nibelungen; awarded Norsk Kritikerpris 1986. *Recordings include:* Anne Gjevang in Recital, Mahler's 3rd Symphony, Schumann's Das Paradies und die Peri, Handel: Messiah 1985, (Arias and Choruses) 1990, (Highlights) 1998. *Address:* Leinv 3, 1453 Bjørnemyr, Norway. *Telephone:* (9) 96-09-35. *Fax:* (9) 91-07-66.

**GLANERT, Detlev;** German composer; b. 6 Sept. 1960, Hamburg. *Education:* studied with Hans Werner Henze in Cologne. *Career:* co-organizer, Cantiere Internazionale d'Arte, Montepulciano 1989–92. *Compositions:*

Symphonie 1 1984, Mahler/Skizze for 11 instruments 1989, Der Spiegel des großen Kaisers (opera) (Rolf Liebermann Opera Prize) 1993, Klavierkonzert 1994, Symphonie 3 1996, Joseph Süß (opera) 1998–99, Scherz, Satire, Ironie und tiefere Bedeutung (opera) (Bavarian Theatre Prize 2001) 1999–2000, Burleske for orchestra 2000, Chamber Sonata No. 3 Geheimer Raum 2002, Die drei Rätsel 2002–03. *Recording:* Portrait. *Address:* c/o Boosey and Hawkes, Komponisten Abt., Lützowufer 26, 10787 Berlin, Germany (office). *Website:* www.boosey.com (office).

**GLANVILLE, Mark;** Singer (bass); b. 24 May 1959, London, England. *Education:* Studied at Oxford University and the Royal Northern College of Music. *Career:* Debut: Sang the 2nd Soldier in Les Troyens and the Doctor in Macbeth for Opera North, 1987; Has sung Nourabad (Les Pêcheurs de Perles), the King (Aida), the King of Clubs in The Love for Three Oranges, Hobson in Peter Grimes and Betto di Signa in Gianni Schicchi for Opera North; Scottish Opera debut, 1988, as the Commendatore in Don Giovanni; Radio Vara, Amsterdam, as Lord Rochefort in Anna Bolena; Omaha Opera as Ferrando in Il Trovatore; Sang Iago at Haddo House, 1996; Concert engagements include Bruckner's Te Deum for the Hallé Orchestra and Messiah with the Royal Liverpool Philharmonic; Opera: King (Oranges) in Lisbon, 1991; Father (Jewel Box) for Opera North, 1991; New Israeli Opera, 1992; Concerts of Beethoven 9 (Ulster Orchestra conducted by Tortelier and Netherlands Philharmonic, conducted by Menuhin); Mozart Requiem, Bournemouth Sinfonietta conducted by Menuhin, City of London Orchestra conducted by Judd, Stravinsky's Oedipus (RAI Milano conducted by Gatti). *Recordings include:* Donizetti's L'Assedio di Calais (Opera Rara); Schubert's Mass in G. *Honours:* Scholarships from the Peter Moores Foundation and the Countess of Munster and Ian Fleming Trusts; Ricordi Opera Prize and Elsie Sykes Fellowship, Royal Northern College of Music. *Current Management:* Athole Still International Management, Forresters Hall, 25–27 Westow Street, London, SE19 3RY, England. *Telephone:* (20) 8771-5271. *Fax:* (20) 8768-6600. *Website:* www.atholestill.com.

**GLANVILLE, Susannah;** Singer (Soprano); b. 1964, England. *Education:* Studied with Margaret Field at the Birmingham Conservatoire and with Margaret Kingsley at the Royal College of Music; Further study at the National Opera Studio. *Career:* Season 1994–95 with Glyndebourne Touring Opera singing Musetta in La Bohème; Mimi for English Touring Opera; Luisa Miller at Opera North; European debut in Nice as Mozart's Countess. Season 1996–97 Fiordiligi in Così fan tutte for Opera North and Mozart's Pamina for English National Opera; Season 1998–99 sang Verdi's Giovanna D'Arco for Opera North; American debut as Blanche Dubois in André Previn's Streetcar Named Desire with San Francisco Opera; Title role in Strauss's Arabella for Opera North and Vitellia in Mozart's La Clemenza di Tito for Glyndebourne Touring Opera; Concert Appearances include Britten's War Requiem with the Bournemouth Symphony Orchestra, Hindemith's Das Nusch-Nuschi and Mörder, Hoffnung der Frauen with the BBC Symphony Orchestra and Andrew Davies;Verdi's Requiem with the English Northern Philharmonia and Paul Daniel and Blanche Dubois in Streetcar Named Desire Suite with André Previn at the Tanglewood Festival; Sang Schumann's Genoveva for Garsington Opera, 2000; First Lady in Die Zauberflöte at Covent Garden 2003. *Current Management:* Askonas Holt Ltd, Lonsdale Chambers, 27 Chancery Lane, London, WC2A 1PF, England. *Telephone:* (20) 7400-1700. *Fax:* (20) 7400-1799. *E-mail:* info@askonasholt.co.uk. *Website:* www .askonasholt.co.uk.

**GLASER, Werner (Wolf);** Composer, Pianist and Conductor; b. 14 April 1910, Cologne, Germany; m. Renée Glaser, 4 c. *Education:* University; Pupil of: Abendroth; Dahmen; Jarnach; Hindemith. *Career:* Debut: Pianist, 1918; Conductor, Opera of Chemnitz, 1929–31; Teacher in Denmark; Teacher, Västerås, Sweden, 1945–; Composer; Critic; Soloist; Various programmes at the Swedish Broadcasting Service; Series of recitals; Conferences; Vice Director, Town Music School, Västerås. *Compositions:* 13 Symphonies; 5 Operas; 14 String Quartets; Col Legno, German Recital; Chamber Music; 2 Ballets; Cantatas; Work for solo instruments; Concertos; Stage Work Performances at: Stockholm; Gothenberg; Västerås. *Recordings:* Phono Suecia, Linnea rezza for Solo; Opus 3: for duo; Fermat, for duo; Coronet, for saxophone quartet; Caprice, for trio. *Publications:* Trumma och triangel, 1946; Den sköna leken, 1947; Poems 1–7, 1969–77; Poems, 1981; Poems, 1992. *Honours:* Medal of the Swedish Royal Academy of Music, 1993. *Address:* Djäknegatan 16, 722 15 Västerås, Sweden.

**GLASS, Beaumont;** Opera Coach, Stage Director, Recital Accompanist, Author and Lecturer and University Professor; b. 25 Oct. 1925, New York, NY, USA; m. Evangeline Noël Young, 7 June 1958; one d. *Education:* BS, US Naval Academy, Annapolis, 1949; Graduate studies, San Francisco State College and University of California at Berkeley, 1955; Private music study in Piano, Violin and Theory. *Career:* Debut: As Stage Director, Northwest Grand Opera, Seattle, 1956; Northwest Grand Opera, 1956–57; Assistant to Lotte Lehmann, Music Academy of the West, 1957–59, 1961; Coach, New York City Opera, 1959; Coach, Studienleiter, Zürich Opera, 1961–80; Accompanist, Grace Bumbry Recital Holland Festival, 1965; Accompanist, Grace Bumbry Brahms Lieder Recital, Salzburg Festival, 1965; Coach, Harpsichordist, Recital Accompanist, Festival of Aix-en-Provence, 1974, 1976–78; Director of Opera, University of Iowa, 1980–98; Stage Director, Utah Opera Company, autumn 1988; Stage Director, Cedar Rapids Symphony opera productions, 1987–2001; 3 week residency Mason Gross School of the Arts, Rutgers University, 1999; Masterclasses, Indiana University, 2000, Univ of SOuthern Maine, Southeastern Oklahoma State Univ, Univ of Maine in Orono; Coach, opera and lieder, AIMS, Graz, Austria, 2000–; Stage Director, Maine Opera Company, 2000–. *Accompaniments on CDs:* Grace Brumby – A Portrait, Luba Tcheresky – In This Life. *Publications:* Biography of Lotte Lehmann, 1988; Schubert's Complete Song Texts, Vol. I, 1996, Vol. II, 1997; Brahms' Complete Song Texts, 1999; Hugo Wolf's Complete Song Texts, 2000; Robert Schumann's Complete Song Texts, 2001, Richard Strauss' Complete Song Texts 2004, Selected Song Texts of Great German Lieder 2004. *Contributions:* Contributing and consulting editor, The Opera Quarterly, 1983–89. *Honours:* University of Iowa Presidential Lecturer, 1988. *Address:* The Steeples, 2 Mountain Street, Camden, ME 04843-1649, USA.

**GLASS, Paul Eugène,** BMus; Composer; b. 19 Nov. 1934, Los Angeles, CA, USA; m. Penelope Margaret Mackworth-Praed 1977. *Education:* piano, trombone, composition, theory from early age; Univ. of Southern California; composition with Boris Blacher, Ingolf Dahl, Hugo Friedhofer, Goffredo Petrassi (Accademia di Santa Cecilia), Roger Sessions (Princeton Univ.), Witold Lutoslawski (Warsaw). *Career:* first public performance of compositions 1956; composer of concert music, film and television music; Prof., Conservatorio di Musica della Svizzera Italiana and Franklin Coll., Switzerland. *Compositions:* (all works published) orchestral works include: Sinfonia No. 3 1986, No. 4 1992, Lamento dell'acqua 1990, Quan Shi-qu 1994, Corale per Margaret 1995, Omaggio per piano 1995, How to Begin, for orchestra 1995, Sinfonia No. 5 ad modum missae 1999; chamber works include: Quartet for flute, clarinet, viola, violoncello 1966, Wie ein Naturlaut for 10 instruments 1977, Saxophone Quartet 1980, String Quartet No. 1 1988; vocal works include: 3 Songs for baritone and piano 1954, 5 chansons pour une Princesse errante for baritone and piano 1968, baritone and orchestra 1992, Sahassavagga, for children's chorus (text from the Dhammapada) 1976, Un sogno, for children's chorus (text Alberto Nessi) 1981, Deh, spiriti miei, quando mi vedete for chorus (text Guido Cavalcanti) 1987, Pianto de la Madonna for soprano, baritone, chorus, orchestra (text Jacopone da Todi) 1988; film scores include: The Abductors 1957, Lady in a Cage 1962, Bunny Lake is Missing 1965, Catch My Soul 1972, Overlord 1974, The Late Nancy Irving 1983, Die Abzocker 2000, Kakapo, ballet pour enfants 2001, Soggetti migranti for three percussionists and orchestra 2002, Prisma for solo dancer and jazz ensemble 2002, Sinfonia No. 6: quinto giorno 2003. *Recordings:* Portrait Paul Glass; Sinfonia No. 3, Quartetto I, 5 pezzi per pianoforte, Lamento dell'acqua; Jan Fryderyk, 2 concerts, Cologne; Concerto per pianoforte estemporaneo e orchestra; I Cantori della Turrita, Guilys; Sahassavagga; many for Swiss radio. *Address:* Presso Conservatorio della Svizzera Italiana, via Soldino 9, 6900 Lugano-Besso, Switzerland.

**GLASS, Philip;** American composer; b. 31 Jan. 1937, Baltimore, MD; s. of Benjamin Glass and Ida Glass (née Gouline); m. 1st JoAnne Akalaitis (divorced); m. 2nd Luba Burtyk (divorced); one s. one d.; m. 3rd Candy Jernigan (died 1991); m. 4th Holly Critchlow 2001; two s. one d. *Education:* Peabody Conservatory, Baltimore, Univ. of Chicago and Juilliard School of Music. *Career:* Composer-in-Residence, Pittsburgh Public Schools 1962–64; studied with Nadia Boulanger, Paris 1964–66; f. Philip Glass Ensemble 1968–, concert tours USA and Europe; f. record co. Chatham Square Productions, New York 1972, Dunvagen Music Publrs, Orange Mountain Music record co. 2002; mem. ASCAP. *Film scores include:* North Star 1977, Koyaanisqatsi 1983, Mishima 1985, Powaqqatsi 1987, The Thin Blue Line 1988, Hamburger Hill 1989, Mindwalk 1990, A Brief History of Time 1991, Anima Mundi 1991, Candyman 1992, The Voyage 1992, Orphée 1993, Candyman II: Farewell to the Flesh 1994, Monsters of Grace 1998, Bent 1998, Kundun 1998, The Hours (BAFTA Anthony Asquith Award 2003, Classical BRIT Award for Contemporary Music 2004) 2002. *Compositions include:* String Quartets (1–4), Violin Concerto, Low Symphony, The Palace of the Arabian Nights, The Fall of the House of Usher, Einstein on the Beach 1976, Madrigal Opera: The Panther 1980, Satyagraha 1980, The Photographer 1982, The Civil Wars: A Tree Is Best Measured When It Is Down 1983, Akhnaten 1983, The Juniper Tree 1985, A Descent Into The Maelstrom 1986, In The Upper Room 1986, Violin Concerto 1987, The Light for Orchestra 1987, The Making of the Representative for Planet 8 1988, The Fall Of The House Of Usher 1988, 1,000 Airplanes on the Roof (with David Henry Hwang) 1988, Mattogrosso 1989, Hydrogen Jukebox (with Allen Ginsberg) 1989, The White Raven 1991, Orphée, chamber opera after Cocteau 1993, La belle et la bête, after Cocteau 1994, Witches of Venice (ballet) 1995, Les enfants terrible (dance opera) 1996, The Marriages Between Zones Three, Four and Five 1997, Symphony No. 5 1999, Symphony No. 6 (Plutonian Ode) 2000, In the Penal Colony (theatre) 2000, Tirol Concerto, piano and orchestra 2000, Concerto Fantasy for two timpanists and orchestra 2000, Voices for Organ, Didgeridoo and Narrator 2001, Concerto for Cello and Orchestra 2001, Danassimo 2001, The Man in the Bath 2001, Passage 2001, Diaspora 2001, Notes 2001, Galileo Galilei (opera) 2002, Waiting for the Barbarians (opera) 2005. *Publications:* Music by Philip Glass 1987, Opera on the Beach 1988. *Honours:* BMI Award 1960, Lado Prize 1961, Benjamin Award 1961, 1962, Ford Foundation Young Composer's Award 1964–66, Fulbright Award 1966–67, Musical America Magazine Musician of the Year 1985, New York Dance and Performance Award 1995. *Current Management:* Dunvagen Music, 632 Broadway, Suite 902, New York, NY 10012, USA. *Telephone:* (212) 979-2080 (office). *Fax:* (212) 473-2842 (office). *E-mail:* info@dunvagen.com (office). *Website:* www.philipglass.com.

**GLASSMAN, Allan;** Singer (Tenor and Baritone); b. 1950, Brooklyn, New York, USA. *Education:* Studied at Hartt College of Music and Juilliard School. *Career:* Sang as a baritone at Michigan Opera from 1975, then at Philadelphia, Washington and the City Opera, New York; Roles have included Dandini in La Cenerentola, Rossini's Figaro, Belcore, Enrico in Lucia di Lammermoor, Ford and Schaunard; Studied further in New York and sang tenor roles at the Metropolitan from 1985 with debut as Edmondo in Manon Lescaut; Further appearances in USA and at Frankfurt as Tybalt in Roméo et Juliette, Cassio, Bacchus, Alfredo, Hoffman, Faust and Eisenstein; Sang Tichon in Katya Kabanova at the Metropolitan in 1991, Marcello in Leoncavallo's La Bohème at St Louis, Dimitri in Boris Godunov at Pittsburgh in 1991, and Arrigo in I Vespri Sicilani at Nice in 1992; Season 1995–96 as Kardinal Albrecht in Mathis der Maler, and Cavaradossi at the New York City Opera, Bacchus in Ariadne auf Naxos for Miami Opera; Tichon at Dallas, 1998; Sang Boris in Katya Kabanova at Montreal, 2000. *Address:* 1704 Garnet Lane #3002, Ft Worth, TX 76112, USA.

**GLAUSER, Elisabeth;** Mezzo-Soprano; b. 1 June 1943, Interlaken, Switzerland. *Education:* Studied in Berne, Stockholm and Italy. *Career:* Sang in Pforzheim, 1971–73, Freiburg, 1973–75, Dortmund, 1975–82, and Staatsoper Stuttgart, 1982–88; Sang Rossweise at Bayreuth Festival, 1976–80, Adelaide in Arabella at Glyndebourne Festival in 1985; Guest appearances at Rome Opera as Herodias in Salome in 1988 and Komische Oper Berlin in Düsseldorf, Zürich, Bologna, Venice, Cologne, Lisbon, Hanover and Schwetzingen Festival; Other roles have been Marcellina, Maddalena, Kundry, Fricka, Waltraute, Octavian, Clytemnestra and the Countess Geschwitz in Lulu; Concert soloist in works by Bach, Handel, Mozart, Brahms, Beethoven and Liszt; Teacher, Berne Conservatory, 1988–. *Address:* c/o Hochschule für Musik und Theater, Papiermüthlestr 13, CH –3000 Bern, Switzerland.

**GLAZER, Gilda;** Pianist; b. 1949, New York, NY, USA; m. Robert Glazer. *Education:* BA, Music, Queens College, City University of New York; MA, Music, Columbia University; Piano student of Nadia Reisenberg. *Career:* Debut: Kaufman Concert Hall, New York; Resident Keyboardist, Chicago Symphony; Resident Keyboardist, St Louis Symphony; Guest Soloist, Chicago, St Louis, North Carolina Symphonies; Resident Soloist, New York String Symphony; Pianist, Glazer Duo, 1970–; Pianist, New York Piano Quartet; Guest Pianist with Mendelssohn Quartet; World premieres of works by Leo Ornstein, David Ott; Piano Faculties: Hartt College of Music; Chicago Musical College; Extensive solo tours; Appearances in Lincoln Center, Carnegie Hall and Ravinia Festival; Pianist, New Friends of Chamber Music, New York. *Recordings:* Piano solos and chamber music of Leo Ornstein, Joaquin Turina, Easley Blackwood and David Amram. *Publications:* Album of works for Piano and Viola, edited, 1980; Schubert Arpeggione Sonata, edited 1993. *Contributions:* American Piano Magazine. *Honours:* Judge, Heida Hermanns International Competition. *Current Management:* Robert M Gewald Management. *Address:* Prestige Concerts International, 14 Summit, Englewood, NJ 07632, USA.

**GLAZER, Robert;** Violist and Conductor; b. 1945, Anderson, Indiana, USA; m. Gilda Glazer. *Education:* BMus, MMus, Chicago Musical College; Studied Viola with William Primrose, Conducting with Franco Ferrara. *Career:* String Faculty, Columbia University; Member, Chicago Symphony; Co-Principal Viola, St Louis Symphony; Violist, Hartt String Quartet; Music Director, New York String Symphony; Violist of Glazer Duo, 1970–; Guest Soloist: St Louis Symphony, Louisville Orchestra, Hartford Symphony; Guest Violist with Lenox Quartet, Manhattan and Mendelssohn Quartets; Extensive solo tours; World premieres of works by David Epstein and Leo Ornstein; Conductor, American Chamber Orchestra, Brevard Music Festival. *Recordings:* Soloist, Morton Gould Viola Concerto with Louisville Orchestra; Violist, Lyric by George Walker; Works by Joaquin Turina and Easley Blackwood. *Publications:* Editor: Album for Viola and Piano, 1980; Schubert Arpeggione Sonata, 1993. *Contributions:* Conductors Guild Journal; Instrumentalist. *Honours:* Tanglewood Award; Judge, Washington International Competition; Judge, Primrose Memorial Competition; Robert Glazer Viola Award created at Chicago Musical College of Roosevelt University. *Current Management:* Robert M Gewald Management. *Address:* Prestige Concerts International, 14 Summit, Englewood, NJ 07632, USA.

**GLENN, Bonita;** Singer (soprano); b. 1960, Washington, USA. *Education:* Philadelphia Academy of Music. *Career:* sang with the Vereingen State Orchestra under Eugene Ormandy, the Oakland Symphony, Toronto Symphony and Rochester Orchestra; recitals at Carnegie Hall, Avery Fisher Hall, Tully Hall, and Kennedy Hall and in Canada and Costa Rica; sang in La Bohème with Philadelphia Grand Opera and in Turandot at the Salzburg Landestheater under Leopold Hager; sang Manon in Houston and Pamina with Santa Fe Opera; appeared as Musetta, Suppé's Galatea, and Corilla in Viva La Mamma at Berne and St Gallen in Switzerland; concert engagements in Europe, Canada and the USA, in Germany with the Nuremberg Symphony Orchestra, the Stuttgart Symphony in Four Last Songs under Neville Marriner, and the Bavarian Radio Symphony Orchestra; sang Clara in Porgy and Bess with the Royal Liverpool Philharmonic conducted by Libor Pešek and with the Scottish Chamber Orchestra under Carl Davis, 1989–90. *Honours:* Winner, Philadelphia Orchestra Vocal Competition.

**GLENNIE, Evelyn Elizabeth Ann,** OBE, GRSM, FRAM, FRCM, FRNCM; British timpanist, percussionist and composer; b. 19 July 1965, Aberdeen, Scotland; d. of Isobel Glennie and Herbert Arthur Glennie. *Education:* Ellon Acad.,

Aberdeenshire, Royal Acad. of Music, London. *Career:* solo debut at Wigmore Hall, London, 1986; concerto, chamber and solo percussion performances worldwide; gave Promenade concerts' first-ever percussion recital 1989; numerous TV appearances, including three documentaries on her life; composer of music for TV and radio; many works written for her by composers, including Bennett, Rouse, Heath, Macmillan, McLeod, Muldowney, Daugherty, Turnage and Musgrave; f. Evelyn Glennie Nat. Music Scholarship; Munster Trust Scholarship 1986. *Films:* wrote and played music for The Trench, Touch the Sound (Critics' Prize, Locarno Int. Film Festival). *Play:* Playing from the Heart. *Recordings include:* Rhythm Song, Dancin', Light in Darkness, Rebounds, Veni Veni Emmanuel, Wind in the Bamboo Grove, Drumming, Her Greatest Hits, The Music of Joseph Schwantner, Sonata for Two Pianos and Percussion (Bartók), Last Night of the Proms – 100th Season, Street Songs, Reflected in Brass, Shadow Behind the Iron Sun, African Sunrise, Manhattan Rave, UFO, Bela Fleck-Perpetual Motion, Oriental Landscapes, Fractured Lines. *Television includes:* music for Trial and Retribution 1–5 (Yorkshire TV), music for Mazda commercial Blind Ambition, Survival Special (Anglia) and others. *Publications:* Good Vibrations (autobiog.) 1990, Great Journeys of the World, Beat It!, Marimba Encores, 3 Chorales for Marimba. *Honours:* Hon. DMus (Aberdeen) 1991, (Bristol, Portsmouth) 1995, (Leicester, Surrey) 1997, (Queen's, Belfast) 1998, (Southampton) 2000; Hon. DLitt (Warwick) 1993, (Loughborough) 1995, (Salford) 1999; Hon. LLD (Dundee) 1996; Hon. DUniv (Essex, Durham) 1998; Hon. Fellow Welsh Coll. of Music and Drama; many prizes and awards, including Shell/LSO Music Gold Medal 1984, Queen's Commendation Prize at RAM 1985, Grammy Award 1988, Scotswoman of the Decade 1990, Charles Heidsieck Soloist of the Year, Royal Philharmonic Soc. 1991, Personality of the Year, Int. Classical Music Awards 1993, Young Deaf Achievers Special Award 1993, Best Studio Percussionist, Rhythm Magazine 1998, 2000, 2002, 2003, 2004, Best Live Percussionist, Rhythm Magazine 2000, Classic FM Outstanding Contribution to Classical Music 2002, Walpole Medal of Excellence 2002, Musical America 2003. *Current Management:* IMG Artists Europe, Lovell House, 616 Chiswick High Road, London, W4 5RX, England. *Telephone:* (20) 8233-5800. *Fax:* (20) 8233-5801. *E-mail:* info@imgartists.com. *Website:* www.imgartists.com. *Address:* PO Box 6, Sawtry, Huntingdon, Cambs., PE17 5YF, England (office). *Telephone:* (1480) 891772 (office). *Fax:* (1480) 891779 (office). *E-mail:* carla@evelyn.co.uk (office). *Website:* www.evelyn.co.uk (office).

**GLENNON, Jean;** Singer (Soprano); b. 1960, USA. *Career:* Professional career from 1983 when she was a winner of the Metropolitan Opera Auditions; Many appearances with opera companies in Miami, Virginia and New York; Season 1993 gave her British concert debut with the Academy of St Martin in the Fields and further concerts at Düsseldorf, Brescia and Montreux; Season 1994 with Musetta at Antwerp, Aida at Würzburg, and Mimi in Dortmund; Concerts of the Verdi Requiem at Bordeaux and Beethoven's Ninth in Strasbourg; Season 1995–96 as Tosca at St Gallen, Butterfly at Malmö and Donna Anna for New Zealand Opera. *Recordings include:* Floyd's Susannah, with Opéra de Lyon; Sang Turandot at Auckland, 1997. *Address:* Helen Sykes Artists Management, 100 Felsham Road, Putney, London SW15 1DQ, England.

**GLICK, Jacob;** American violist, viola d'amore player, mandolinist and educator; b. 29 Jan. 1926, Philadelphia, PA; m. Lilo Kantorowicz 1949; two d. *Education:* New School of Music, Philadelphia, Peabody Conservatory, Baltimore, MD, Yale Summer School of Music, Norfolk, CT, Kneisel Hall, Blue Hill, MN. *Career:* debut at Carnegie Recital Hall, New York City, 1962; Town Hall recital, New York City, 1964; Performance of Hindemith's Schwanendreher Concerto with Clarion Orchestra, Avery Fisher Hall, Lincoln Center, 1965; Soloist in Vivaldi's Concerto for Mandolines with New York Philharmonic under Bruno Maderna, 1972; Performance of Schoenberg's Serenade with Boulez at New York Philharmonic Rug Concert, 1974; Guest Faculty at Shanghai Conservatory, 1985–86. *Compositions:* Mandolinear, 1965; Octet–Four Hands, 1968; Row for Lou, 1992. *Recordings:* Variazioni Sopra Una Melodia, by Robert Moevs; Aldebaran, by Jean Eichelberger Ivey; Serenade, Op 24, by Arnold Schoenberg; Various with Contemporary Quartet and Beaux-Arts Quartet; contrib. to Contemporary Music Newsletter; Record Album Notes, CRI-SD 135; Concertante for Piano and Orchestra, 1944, Vivian Fine. *Address:* RR! Box 80-S, North Bennington, VT 05257, USA.

**GLICK, Srul (Irving);** Composer; b. 8 Sept. 1934, Toronto, Canada; m. 18 Sept 1957, 1 s., 2 d. *Education:* BMus, 1955, MMus, 1958, University of Toronto; Continued studies with Darius Milhaud, Louis Saguer and Max Deutch. *Career:* Teacher of Theory and Composition, Royal Conservatory of Music and York University; Composer-in-Residence at Beth Tikvah Synagogue, Toronto, 1969–. *Compositions include:* Chamber music, orchestral, works for solo instruments with orchestra, vocal, choir with instruments, and piano; Violin concerto, 1976; Divertimento for strings, 1987; String Quartet No. 1, 1984, and No. 2, 1994; Cello sonata, 1989; The Reawakening for orchestra, 1991; Piano Concerto, 1992; Piano Quintet, 1994; Piano Sonatina, 1996. *Recordings:* 4 Preludes for piano; Petite Suite for solo flute; Suite Hebraique No. 1; Songs from The Sabbath Festivals and High Holy Days; I Never Saw Another Butterfly; Gathering In, a symphonic concept for strings; Suite Hebraique No. 2; 2 Landscapes for tenor and piano; Music for Passover; Suite Hebraique No. 4; Prayer and Dance for cello and piano; String Quartet No. 1; Violin Concerto; Anthology including 17 works including Northern Sketches and Fantasy for Violin and Orchestra (Vision of Ezekiel).

**GLOBOKAR, Vinko;** Composer and Trombonist; b. 7 July 1934, Anderny, Meurthe et Moselle, France; m. Tatjana Kristan, 27 June 1963, 2 s. *Education:* Diploma, Ljubljana Conservatory, 1954; Trombone at Conservatoire National de Musique, Paris, 1954–59; Composition and Conducting with René Leibowitz, 1959–63; Composition with Berio, 1965; University Physics, 2 years. *Career:* Trombone Soloist; Conductor; Played with group for new music, Buffalo University, 1966; Teacher of Trombone, Staatliche Hochschule für Musik, Cologne, 1968–76, and Composition, New Music Courses, Cologne; Founder, New Phonic Art Quartet, 1969; Director of Department for Instrumental and Vocal Research, IRCAM, Paris, 1973–79; Professor, Scuola di Musica, Fiesole-Florenna, 1983–; Solo performer of works written for him by Stockhausen, Berio, Kagel and others; British premiere with Heinz Holliger of Gemeaux by Toru Takemitsu, Edinburgh, 1989; Played his Kolo at Dartington Summer School, 1992. *Compositions include:* Accord for soprano and ensemble, 1966; Concerto Grosso for 5 instruments, chorus and orchestra, 1970; Laboratorium for ensemble, 1973; Les Emigres, 1982–86; Labour, 1992; Blinde Zeit for ensemble, 1993; Dialog Über Feuer, 1994; Dialog Über Erde, 1994; Dialog Über Wasser, 1994; Dialog Über Luft, 1994; Masse, Macht und Individuum, 1995. *Recordings include:* Les Emigrées; Vinko Globokar; Globokar by Aulos. *Publications:* Vzdih-Izdih; Einatmen-Ausatmen Komposition und Improvisation by Vinko Globokar. *Contributions:* About 30 articles in musical magazines. *Honours:* 1st Prize: Trombone, Paris, 1959, Gaudeamus, Composition, 1968 and Radio Yugoslavia, 1973. *Address:* 2 rue Pierre et Marie Curie, 75005 Paris, France.

**GLONTI, Felix (Phillip);** Composer and Professor; b. 8 Nov. 1927, Batumi, Georgia; m. Eteri Ahvlediani, 1 s. *Education:* Conservatory of St Petersburg. Debut; World premiere of Dawn, a ballet in 2 acts, libretto and staging by V Chabukiani, in Tbilisi, 29 Oct 1967. *Career:* World premiere in Brussels Symphony No. 1 Romantic (Horizons du Monde), 1966; Symphony No. 6 Vita Nova, world premiere, Tbilisi, 1979; Symphonic Meditations on a theme by Francesco Petrarca, world premiere in Prague, 1980; Symphony No. 7, Fiat Lux, world premiere, Tbilisi, 1981; Symphony Concertante, Wanderjahre for pianoforte and full symphonic orchestra, world premiere Tbilisi, 1983; Symphony No. 10, Pax Humana, world premiere Tbilisi, 1987. *Compositions:* Symphonies: No. 6, Vita Nova, 1979, No. 7, Fiat Lux, 1981, No. 8, Symphonic Groups, 1982, No. 10, Pax Humana, 1984, No. 1, Romantic, 1986, No. 11, The Open World, 1987, No. 12, Symfoniya-Liturgiya for soprano, baritone, chorus and orchestra, 1989; Sinfonia Concertante for cello and orchestra, 1990; Concertante for violin and orchestra, 1993; Concertante for piano and orchestra, 1997; Opera, Kleopatra, after Shakespeare, 1976, revised 1994; Three Sonnets for vocal soloists and piano, 1997. *Recordings:* Romantic Symphony No. 1; Vita Nova, Symphony No. 6; Symphonic Meditations on a theme by Francesco Petrarca; Marienbadische Elegie (Symphonic Concerts); Wanderjahre (Symphony concertante); Symphony Concertante for pianoforte and full symphony orchestra, 1998; Ode to Life Happiness and Love, words by Plato and Shakespeare, for soloists, chorus and organ. *Publications:* The Anthropology of Post-Serial Musical Thinking for Characterization of Conceptual Paradigm, 2000. *Contributions:* Georgian Literature, 1981; Soviet Music, 1983. *Address:* Alexander Kazbegi str No. 20/9, Tbilisi 380077, Georgia.

**GLOSSOP, Peter;** British opera singer (baritone) (retd); b. 6 July 1928, Sheffield, England; s. of Cyril Glossop and Violet Elizabeth Wright; m. 1st Joyce Blackham 1955 (divorced 1976); m. 2nd Michelle Yvonne Amos 1977 (divorced 1987); two d. *Education:* High Storrs Grammar School, Sheffield. *Career:* joined Sadler's Wells Opera 1952, notably singing Rigoletto, di Luna, Silvio, Scarpia and Eugene Onegin; with Covent Garden Opera Co 1962–66, notably in Verdi roles of Amonasro, Iago, di Luna, Posa, Renato, Rigoletto, Simon Boccanegra, and in the title role of Billy Budd; sang Verdi roles each season at La Scala, Milan 1965–72, notably Rigoletto; freelance singer 1966–86; Iago at Salzburg with Herbert von Karajan 1970; sang at Metropolitan Opera 1971–86, notably as Scarpia, Don Carlo in La forza del destino, Wozzeck and Falstaff; Flying Dutchman at Opera North 1979; Mandryka at ENO 1980. *Films:* Tonio in I Pagliacci, conducted by Herbert von Karajan, Iago in Otello, conducted by Karajan. *Television includes:* Billy Budd (BBC) 1966, Rigoletto (BBC) 1972, Otello (BBC) 1973. *Recordings:* Billy Budd, conducted by the composer, Chorebus in Les Troyens, conducted by Sir Colin Davis, Macbeth. *Publications:* autobiography 2004. *Honours:* First Prize Bulgarian First Competition for Young Opera Singers 1961; Hon. DMus (Sheffield) 1970; 'Amici di Verdi' Gold Medal 1965, Verdi Gold Medal of Parma 1967, Silver Cross of St George 1996. *Address:* End Cottage, 7 Gate Close, Hawkchurch, Axminster, Devon, England.

**GLOVER, Jane Alison,** CBE, MA, DPhil, FRCM; British conductor; *Music Director, Music of the Baroque, Chicago;* b. 13 May 1949, d. of the late Robert Finlay Glover and Jean Muir. *Education:* Monmouth School for Girls and St Hugh's Coll., Oxford. *Career:* Jr Research Fellow St Hugh's Coll. 1973–75, Lecturer in Music 1976–84; Sr Research Fellow 1982–84; Lecturer St Anne's Coll., Oxford 1976–80, Pembroke Coll. 1979–84; mem. Oxford Univ. Faculty of Music 1979–; professional conducting debut at Wexford Festival 1975; operas and concerts for BBC, Glyndebourne 1982–, Royal Opera House 1988–, Covent Garden, English Nat. Opera 1989–, London Symphony Orchestra, London Philharmonic Orchestra, Royal Philharmonic Orchestra, Philharmonia, Royal Scottish Orchestra, English Chamber Orchestra, Royal Danish Opera, Glimmerglass Opera, New York 1994– and Australian Opera 1996– and many orchestras in Europe and USA; Prin. Conductor London Choral Soc.

1983–2000; Artistic Dir London Mozart Players 1984–91; Prin. Conductor Huddersfield Choral Soc. 1989–96; Music Dir Music of the Baroque, Chicago 2002–; mem. BBC Cen. Music Advisory Cttee 1981–85, Music Advisory Cttee Arts Council 1986–88; Gov. RAM 1985–90, BBC 1990–95. *Television:* documentaries and series and presentation, especially Orchestra 1983, Mozart 1985. *Radio:* talks and series including Opera House 1995, Musical Dynasties 2000. *Publications:* Cavalli 1978, Mozart's Women: His Family, His Friends, His Music 2005; contribs to The New Monteverdi Companion 1986, Monteverdi 'Orfeo' Handbook 1986; articles in numerous journals. *Honours:* Hon. DMus (Exeter) 1986, (CNAA) 1991, (London) 1992, (City Univ.) 1995, (Glasgow) 1996; Hon. DLitt (Loughborough) 1988, (Bradford) 1992; Dr hc (Open Univ.) 1988, (Brunel) 1997. *Address:* c/o Askonas Holt Ltd., Lonsdale Chambers, 27 Chancery Lane, London, WC2A 1PF, England. *Telephone:* (20) 7400-1700. *Website:* www.baroque.org.

**GLUBOKY, Pyotr;** Singer (Bass); b. 1947, Gordiyenki, near Volgograd, Russia. *Education:* Studied at the Moscow Conservatoire and the Bolshoi Theatre. *Career:* Appearances at the Moscow Bolshoi from 1975, as Rossini's Bartolo and Basilio, Leporello and Alfonso, Pimen, King Philip, Mendoza in Prokofiev's Betrothal in a Monastery and parts in his War and Peace; Guested with the Bolshoi at the 1991 Edinburgh Festival as Panas in Rimsky-Korsakov's Christmas Eve; Concert appearances in Greece, England, Canada, USA, Australia, France, Italy and Japan. *Address:* c/o Bolshoi Theatre, 10309 Moscow, Russia.

**GLUSHCHENKO, Fedor Ivanovich;** Russian conductor; b. 29 March 1944, Rostov Region; m. 1st; one s. one d.; m. 2nd Galina Baryshnikova; one d. *Education:* Moscow and Leningrad State Conservatories, Vienna Acad. of Music; studied under Herbert von Karajan. *Career:* Chief Conductor, Karelian Radio and TV Symphony Orchestra, Petrozavodsk 1971–73; Chief Conductor and Artistic Dir, Ukrainian State Symphony Orchestra, Kiev 1973–87; British debut in 1989 with BBC Scottish Symphony, also appeared with Royal Liverpool Philharmonic and Scottish Chamber Orchestra; Conductor, Istanbul Opera 1990–91; Chief Conductor and Artistic Dir, J. S. Bach Chamber Orchestra, Yekaterinburg 1996–; Guest Conductor, Moscow Philharmonic Orchestra, Russian State Symphony Orchestra, Moscow Symphony, Ministry of Culture Orchestra and orchestras in Riga, Vilnius, Sverdlovsky, Tbilisi and Tashkent; tours in UK, Sweden, Italy, Denmark, People's Repub. of China, Germany, France and Spain. *Address:* 1st Pryadilnaya str. 11, apt. 5, 105037 Moscow, Russia. *Telephone:* (095) 165-49-46 (home).

**GLYNN, Gerald,** BA, MA; composer; b. 3 Sept. 1943, Brisbane, Qld, Australia. *Education:* University of Queensland, University of Sydney, electronic studios of French Radio, studied with Peter Maxwell Davies, Olivier Messiaen, Larry Sitsky, composition seminars with Iannis Xenakis and Henri Pousseur. *Career:* NSW Conservatory, 1981; Commissions from Seymour Group (1982) and Symeron (1992). *Compositions include:* Masses, for organ, 1972; Chanson de Ronsard, for soprano, countertenor and percussion, 1974; Changes, for cello, 1975; Syntheses, for string quartet, 1977; Interplay for cello and piano, 1980; William Blake Triptych for chorus, 1981; Chamber Concerto, 1982; Love's Coming, song cycle for medium voice and piano, 1986; Toccata-Sonata, for piano, 1989; Filigrees 1, 2 and 3, for piano, 1981–91; The Rose of Amherst, song cycle for medium voice and piano, 1991; Strata for violin and piano, 1994; Filigrees 4 for piano, 1997. *Address:* 13 Rue Chaligny, 75012 Paris, France.

**GNAM, Adrian;** Conductor, Music Director and Oboist; b. 4 Sept. 1940, New York, NY, USA; m. Catharine Dee Morningstar, 16 Aug 1983, 1 s., 1 d. *Education:* BMus, 1961, MMus, 1962, College Conservatory of Music, Cincinnati; BS, D.Mus, ABD, University of Cincinnati, 1962. *Career:* Debut: Carnegie Recital Hall and Town Hall, New York, 1962; Principal Oboe: American Symphony Orchestra under Stokowski, Cleveland Orchestra under Szell; Heritage Chamber Quartet, Carnegie Wind Quintet, Chamber Arts Ensemble; Faculty: University of Cincinnati College-Conservatory of Music, 1967–76, Ohio University, 1969–76; Distinguished Artist in Residence, Mercer University 2001; Guest Conductor throughout the USA; Orchestras in Romania, Yugoslavia, Venezuela, Mexico City, Japan, Italy, Brazil, Spain; Congress of Strings, Temple and Georgetown Universities, Peabody Conservatory, Universities of Michigan, Georgia and Houston, Colorado Philharmonic; Assistant Music Director, 1976–82, Music Director, 1982–84, National Endowment for the Arts; Principal Guest Conductor, Philadelphia Concerto Soloists Chamber Orchestra, 1977–88; Music Director: Midland Symphony, Michigan, 1982–86, Macon Symphony, Georgia, 1983–, Eugene Symphony, Oregon, 1985–89, Tuscaloosa Symphony, Alabama, 1993–96; Music Director, Macow Sinfonia 2000; President, Conductors' Guild; AFM; American Symphony Orchestra League. *Recordings:* For several labels. *Address:* 85440 Appletree Court, Eugene, OR 97405, USA.

**GOBLE, Theresa;** Singer (Mezzo-soprano); b. 1970, England. *Education:* Studied at the Guildhall School, National Opera Studio, Britten-Pears School and European Opera Centre, with Vera Rozsa and Nicolai Gedda. *Career:* Concert repertoire includes the Verdi Requiem, Rossini Stabat Mater and Petite Messe, Messiah, Dvořák Stabat Mater and Tippett's Child of Our Time; Created the Aunt in Param Vir's Snatched by the Gods, for ENO Contemporary Opera Studio; Sang Flosshilde in Das Rheingold for Scottish Opera, and appeared as Baba the Turk in The Rake's Progress at the Queen Elizabeth Hall (1997); Ulrica (Ballo in Maschera) for Opera Holland Park; Other roles include Dorabella, Verdi's Amneris, Eboli and Mistress Quickly, Charlotte (Werther), Carmen, Adalgisa, Leonora (La Favorita) and Laura in

La Gioconda. *Address:* c/o Karen Durant Management, 298 Nelson Road, Whitton, Middlesex, TW2 7BW, England.

**GOCKLEY, (Richard) David,** BA, MBA; American opera director; *General Director, San Francisco Opera*; b. 13 July 1943, Philadelphia, PA; s. of Warren Gockley and Elizabeth Gockley; m. Adair Lewis; two s. one d. *Education:* Brown Univ., Columbia Univ., New England Conservatory, Boston. *Career:* Dir of Music, Newark Acad. 1965–67; Dir of Drama, Buckley School, New York 1967–69; Box Office Man., Santa Fe Opera 1969–70; Asst Man.-Dir Lincoln Center, New York 1970; Business Man., Houston Grand Opera 1970–71, Assoc. Dir 1971–72, Gen. Dir 1972–2006; co-founder Houston Opera Studio 1977; Gen. Dir San Francisco Opera 2006–; mem. Bd of Dirs Texas Inst. of Arts in Educ.; mem. Opera America (pres. 1985–); fmr Chair. Houston Theater Dist. *Operas produced include:* Pasatieri's The Seagull 1974, Porgy and Bess (Grammy Award 1977) 1976, Floyd's Bilby's Doll 1976, Willie Stark 1981, Harvey Milk (by Stewart Wallace and Michael Korie), Glass's Akhnaten 1984, John Adams' Nixon in China (Emmy Award 1988) 1987, Tippett's New Year 1989, The Passion of Jonathan Wade 1991, Meredith Monk's Atlas 1991, Robert Moran's Desert of Roses 1992, Florencia en el Amazonas, Treemonisha, A Quiet Place, Resurrection, Carmen. *Honours:* Hon. DHL (Univ. of Houston) 1992, Hon. DFA (Brown Univ.) 1993; League of New York Theaters and Producers Tony Award 1977, Columbia Business School Dean's Award 1982, Nat. Inst. of Music Theater Award 1985, Brown Univ. William Rogers Award 1995. *Address:* San Francisco Opera, 301 Van Ness Avenue, San Francisco, CA 94102, USA. *Website:* www.sfopera.com.

**GODAR, Vladimir;** Composer; b. 16 March 1956, Bratislava, Czechoslovakia. *Education:* Bratislava Conservatory; Academy of Music and Drama, 1980. *Career:* Editor, OPUS Publishing House. *Compositions include:* Trio for oboe, violin and piano, 1973; Fugue for string orchestra, 1975; Three Songs, 1977; Overture for symphony orchestra, 1978; Symphony, 1980; Wind Quintet, 1980; Trio for violin, clarinet and piano, 1980; Ricercar, 1980; Melodarium, 20 dances, 1980; Melodarium, 72 duets, 1981; Lyrical Cantata, 1981; Partita, 1983; Talisman, 1983; Grave Passacaglia for piano, 1983; Four Serious Songs, 1984; Orbis Sensualium Pictus, oratorio, 1984; Concerto Grosso Per Archi e Cembalo, 1985; Sonata In Memoriam Viktor Shklovski, 1985; Symphony No. 2, 1992; Via Lucis for orchestra, 1994; Déploration sur la mort de Witold Lutoslawski, piano quintet, 1994; Tombeau de Bartók for orchestra, 1995. *Honours:* Jan Levoslav Bella Prize, Slovak Music Fund. *Address:* SOZA, Kollarova nam 20, 813 27 Bratislava, Slovakia.

**GODFREY, Daniel Strong,** BA, PhD; Composer and Music Professor; b. 20 Nov. 1949, Bryn Mawr, PA, USA; m. Diana Carol Bottum 1976; one s. *Education:* Yale Univ.; Yale School of Music, 1975; Univ. of Iowa, 1982. *Career:* Dir, Yale Russian Chorus, including tours of USA and USSR, 1969–72; Visiting Asst Prof., Music Composition and Theory, Univ. of Pittsburgh, PA, 1981–93, Asst Prof., 1983–88, Assoc. Prof., 1988–93, Prof., 1993–, Dir, 1997–99; Composer in Residence, Syracuse Univ. School of Music, Syracuse, NY, 2002–. *Compositions:* String Quartet, 1974; Progression, 1975; Trio, 1976; Five Character Pieces for viola and piano, 1976; Celebration for solo piano, 1977; Music for marimba and vibraphone, 1981; Scrimshaw for flute and violin, 1985; Concentus for small orchestra, 1985; Intermedio for string quartet, 1985; Dickinson Triptych for soprano and piano, 1986; Three Marian Eulogies for high voice, viola and piano, 1987; Mestengo for orchestra, 1988; Numina for 6 instruments, 1991; Clarion Sky for orchestra, 1992; String Quartet No. 2, 1993; Two Scenes in Chiaroscuro for 10 performers, 1994; Serenata Ariosa for clarinet, viola and piano, 1995; Festoons for piano solo; From a Dream of Russia, for clarinet, violin and piano, 1996; Jig, for wind ensemble/concert band, 1996; Sinfonietta for string orchestra, 1996; Lightscape for orchestra, 1997; Symphony in Minor, 1999; String quartet No. 3, 2000, revised, 2001; Shindig for solo horn and wind ensemble, 2000, revised 2001; Breath and Shadow for bassoon and string quintet, 2001; Romanza for string quartet, 2001; Concerto for piano and chamber winds, 2003; Pomp and Revelry for wind quintet, 2004. *Recordings:* String Quartet No. 3; String Quartet No. 2; Romanza; Lightscape for orchestra; Jig; Festoons; Scrimshaw; Trio; Five Character Pieces; Celebration; String Quartet No. 1; Progression; Music for Marimba and Vibraphone; Intermedio. *Publications:* Music Since 1945, Elliott Schwartz (co-author). *Contributions:* Elliott Carter's String Quartet No.3: A Unique Vision of Musical Time, in Sonus, Vol. 8, No. 1. *Honours:* New York Foundation for the Arts Award, 1991; Winner, Spirit of Today's West Competition, 1991; Indiana State University Festival Award, 1992; American Acad. of Arts and Letters, 1998; Barlow Endowment for Music Composition, 1999; Big Ten Band Directors Association, 1999; Koussevitzky Music Foundation Award, 2000; J. S. Guggenheim Foundation Award, 2001–02. *Current Management:* American International Artists. *E-mail:* cynthia@artists.com. *Address:* 222 Kensington Place, Syracuse, NY 13210, USA. *E-mail:* dsgodfre@syr.edu.

**GODFREY, Victor;** Singer (Bass-baritone); b. 10 Sept. 1934, Deloraine, Canada. *Education:* Studied with Gladys Whitehead in Winnipeg and Joan Cross in London; Further study with Hans Hotter in Munich and with Giovanni Inghilleri. *Career:* Debut: Covent Garden in 1960 as the Doctor in Macbeth; Appeared with the Covent Garden Company at Coventry in 1962 in the premiere of King Priam by Tippett, and Aldeburgh Festival in 1966 in the premiere of The Burning Fiery Furnace by Britten; Guest appearances at Drottningholm and at opera houses in Glasgow with Scottish Opera, Edinburgh, Florence, Naples, Berlin, Düsseldorf, Montreal, Nice and Amsterdam; Other roles included Scarpia, Amonasro, Zaccaria in Nabucco,

Wotan, Wolfram, Orestes and Jochanaan; Also sang in operas by Busoni, Dallapiccola and Hindemith; Many concert engagements.

**GODSON, Daphne;** Violinist; b. 16 March 1932, Edinburgh, Scotland. *Education:* LRAM; ARAM; Royal Academy of Music, London; Brussels Conservatoire. *Career:* Principal Soloist for Scottish Baroque Ensemble, 1969–87; Principal for Scottish Chamber Orchestra, 1974–76; Member of Bernicia Ensemble, Scottish Early Music Consort; Leader, Edinburgh Bach Players; Soloist with BBC Scottish, Scottish National Orchestra and the Bournemouth Symphony Orchestra; Teacher, RSAMD, City of Edinburgh Music School; mem, Incorporated Society of Musicians; Soroptimist International. *Recordings:* Various. *Honours:* Premiere Prize, Brussels Conservatoire, 1956; ARAM, 1988. *Address:* 48-11 Learmonth Avenue, Edinburgh, EH4 1HT, Scotland.

**GODZISZEWSKI, Jerzy,** MA; pianist; b. 24 April 1935, Wilno, Poland. *Education:* Superior Music School, Warsaw; summer masterclasses in piano with Benedetti Michelangeli, Arezzo, Italy. *Career:* regular appearances as soloist and with orchestras in Poland and abroad; performed complete piano works of Maurice Ravel 1975, of Karol Szymanowski 1982; chamber music appearances; teacher of piano, Superior Music School, Wroclaw 1967–77; teacher of piano 1978–, Prof. 1988–, Acad. of Music, Bydgoszcz; appearances in int. music festivals, including Warsaw Autumn, Chopin festivals; mem. Polish Artists' and Musicians' Asscn. *Recordings:* piano works of Chopin, Szymanowski, Debussy, Ravel, Prokofiev and others for Polish radio and television, and for Muza and Wifon record companies; Complete Piano Works of K. Szymanowski. *Honours:* Distinction, Sixth Chopin Int. Piano Competition, Warsaw 1960, Szymanowski Memorial Foundation Award 1998, Fryderyk Prize for Best Solo Record for Complete Piano Works of K. Szymanowski 1998. *Current Management:* Maria Blaszczak Artists' Management, ul. Ogrody 13/246, 85-870 Bydgoszcz, Poland. *Telephone:* (52) 3713211. *Fax:* (52) 3713211. *Address:* ul. W. Lokietka 54, 85-200 Bydgoszcz, Poland. *E-mail:* iamb@lazi.pl.

**GOEBBELS, Heiner;** German composer; b. 17 April 1952, Neustadt. *Education:* studied in Frankfurt. *Career:* co-founded Duo Heiner Goebbels Alfred Harth 1976–88; Music Director, Frankfurt Schauspiel 1978–88; Founded performance group, Cassiber 1982. *Compositions include:* Tränen des Vaterlands, ballet, 1987; Red Run, ballet, 1988–91; Befreiung for narrator and ensemble, 1989; Newtons Casino, music theatre, 1990; Black on White, music theatre, 1995; Surrogate Cities for orchestra, 8 movements, 1995; Industry and Idleness, for chamber orchestra 1996; Roman Dogs, radio play, 1996; Nichts Weiter, for orchestra, 1996. *Honours:* Prix Italia (for Roman Dogs) 1996. *Current Management:* c/o Klaus Schäffer, Ulrichstr. 18, 60433 Frankfurt, Germany. *Website:* www.heinergoebbels.com.

**GOEBEL, Reinhard;** German violinist; b. 31 July 1952, Siegen, Westphalia. *Education:* studied in Cologne and Amsterdam; teachers include Maier, Gawriloff and Leonhardt. *Career:* Founder of Musica Antiqua Köln in 1973 for the performance of early music, touring in Europe, North and South America, the Far East and Australia; London debut at the Queen Elizabeth Hall, 1978; Played in a concert at the 1989 York Festival in England with music by Legrenzi, Schmelzer and Biber; Season 1996 with Gluck's Orphée et Eurydice at Drottningholm and Handel's Serse at Copenhagen; tour of N America and S America for 30th anniversary of ensemble 2003. *Recordings include:* Bach's Art of Fugue and Musical Offering; Biber's Mensa Sonora and Solo Violin Sonata in A; Orchestral Suites by Telemann (ECHO Award for Sinfonia Spituosa 2002); soundtrack of Gérard Corbiau's film, Le Roi danse, with music by Lully (ECHO Award 2001); Bachiana (music by the Bach family); Charpentier's Musique Sacrée, Biber's Harmonia Artificiosa. *Publications:* Johann David Heinichen: Sacred Vocal Music 2003, Johann David Heinichen: Lamentations Jeremiae. *Address:* Brüsseler Str. 94, 50672 Köln, Germany (office). *Telephone:* (221) 9232030 (office). *Fax:* (221) 9232031 (office). *E-mail:* management@musica-antiqua-koeln.de (office). *Website:* www.musica-antiqua-koeln.de (office).

**GOEBELS, Franzpeter;** Pianist, Harpsichordist and Professor; b. 5 March 1920, Mülheim-Rhur, Germany; m. Gertraud Kockler, 1 s., 1 d. *Education:* Univs of Cologne and Berlin. *Career:* Debut: 1940; Solo Pianist, Deutschlandsenderm, Berlin; Docent, Robert Schumann Konservatorium, Düsseldorf; Professor, Hochschule für Musik, Detmold; mem, VDMK. *Compositions:* (as Angfied Traudger) Dependances for Harpsichord and Strings, 1970; Byrd-Boogy, 1971; Bach: Goldberg Variations for Harpsichordist and Strings. *Recordings include:* 6 Sonatas by Bach and Bach Concertos for Harpsichord, Publications: Das Sammelsurium, 1968; Handbuch der Pianistik, 1973. *Contributions:* Melos; Musica; Musik und Bildung. *Honours:* Honourable Professor, University of Barcelona; IAM; Ruhr Preis für Kunst und Wissenschaft, 1969. *Address:* An Der Pyramideneiche, (Privatzufahrt: Clara Schumann Weg), Postfach 4023, 493 Detmold 14, Germany.

**GOEHR, Alexander,** MA; British composer; b. 10 Aug. 1932, Berlin; s. of Walter Goehr and Laelia Goehr; m. 1st Audrey Baker 1954; m. 2nd Anthea Felicity Staunton 1972; m. 3rd Amira Katz; one s. three d. *Education:* Berkhamstead School, Royal Manchester Coll. of Music, Paris Conservatoire (with Olivier Messiaen) and privately with Yvonne Loriod. *Career:* composer, teacher, conductor 1956–; held classes at Morley Coll., London; part-time post with BBC, being responsible for production of orchestral concerts 1960–; works performed and broadcast world-wide; awarded Churchill Fellowship 1968; Composer-in-Residence, New England Conservatory, Boston, Mass.

1968–69; Assoc. Prof. of Music, Yale Univ. 1969–70; Prof. West Riding Chair of Music Univ. of Leeds 1971–76; Prof. of Music, Univ. of Cambridge 1976–99, Prof. Emer. 1999–, Fellow of Trinity Hall, Cambridge 1976–; Reith Lecturer 1987. *Works include:* Songs of Babel 1951, Sonata 1952, Fantasias 1954, String Quartet 1956–57, Capriccio 1957, The Deluge 1957–58, La belle dame sans merci 1958, Variations 1959, Four Songs from the Japanese 1959, Sutter's Gold 1959–60, Suite 1961, Hecuba's Lament 1959–61, A Little Cantata of Proverbs 1962, Concerto for Violin and Orchestra 1961–62, Two Choruses 1962, Virtutes 1963, Little Symphony 1963, Little Music for Strings 1963, Five Poems and an Epigram of William Blake 1964, Three Pieces for Piano 1964, Pastorals 1965, Piano Trio 1966, Arden muss sterben (Arden Must Die, opera) 1966, Warngedichte 1967, String Quartet 1967, Romanza 1968, Naboth's Vineyard 1968, Konzertstück 1969, Nonomiya 1969, Paraphrase 1969, Symphony in One Movement 1970, Shadowplay 1970, Sonata about Jerusalem 1970, Concerto for Eleven Instruments 1970, Piano Concerto 1972, Chaconne for Wind 1974, Lyric Pieces 1974, Metamorphosis/Dance 1974, String Quartet No. 3 1976, Psalm IV 1976, Fugue on the Notes of the Fourth Psalm 1976, Romanza on the Notes of the Fourth Psalm 1977, Prelude and Fugue for Three Clarinets 1978, Chaconne for Organ 1979, Das Gesetz der Quadrille 1979, Babylon the Great is Fallen 1979, Sinfonia 1980, Cello Sonata 1984, Behold the Sun 1984, Two Imitations of Baudelaire 1985, Symphony with Chaconne 1986, Eve Dreams in Paradise 1987, Carol for St Steven 1989, . . . in real time 1989, Sing, Ariel 1989, String Quartet No. 4 1990, Still Lands 1990, Bach Variations 1990, The Death of Moses 1991, The Mouse Metamorphosed into a Maid 1991, Colossus or Panic 1992, I Said, I Will Take Heed 1993, Cambridge Hocket 1993, Arianna (opera) 1995, Schlussgesang 1997, Kantan (opera) 2000, Piano Quintet 2001, Second Musical Offering (GFH) 2001. *Honours:* Hon. Prof. Beijing Univ. 2001; Hon. mem. American Acad. and Inst. of Arts and Letters; Hon. ARCM 1976; Hon. FRNCM 1980; Hon. FRCM 1981; Hon. DMus (Southampton) 1973, (Manchester), (Nottingham) 1994, (Siena) 1999; Dr hc (Cambridge) 2000. *Address:* Trinity Hall, Cambridge, CB3 9DP; University Music School, 11 West Road, Cambridge CB3 9DP; c/o Schott and Co. Ltd, 48 Great Marlborough Street, London, W1V 2BN, England.

**GOEKE, Leo;** Tenor; b. 6 Nov. 1936, Kirksville, Missouri, USA. *Education:* Studied at Louisiana State University, State University of Iowa with David Lloyd and New York with Hans Heinz and Margaret Harshaw. *Career:* Debut: Metropolitan Opera in 1971 as Gaston in La Traviata; Sang Tamino, Edgardo, Alfredo, the Duke of Mantua, Ferrando and Don Ottavio in New York; Glyndebourne Festival, 1973–78 as Flamand in Capriccio, Idamante, Tom Rakewell, Don Ottavio and Tamino; Stuttgart in 1981 in the German premiere of Satyagraha by Philip Glass, repeated in 1990; Other roles include Ernesto in Don Pasquale, Almaviva, Rodolfo, Belmonte, Pinkerton and Massenet's Des Grieux; Guest engagements at the New York City Opera and in Seattle, Strasbourg, Baltimore and Amsterdam; Television appearances include Gandhi in the Stuttgart production of Satyagraha in 1983. *Address:* Staatstheater Stuttgart, Oberer Schlossgarten 6, 7000 Stuttgart 1, Germany.

**GOENNENWEIN, Wolfgang;** Conductor and Educator; b. 29 Jan. 1933, Schwabisch-Hall, Germany. *Education:* Studied music in Stuttgart, and philosophy at Heidelberg and Tubingen Universities. *Career:* Director of the South German Madrigal Choir at Stuttgart, 1959; Tours throughout Europe from 1964 and to South America in 1971; Director of the Cologne Bach Choir, 1969–73; Repertoire has included Palestrina, Bach, Schütz and Stravinsky; Chair of Choirmastership at Stuttgart Musikhochschule, 1968; Artistic Director at the Ludwisburg Castle Festivals from 1972 conducting Die Zauberflöte, Fidelio and Der Freischütz, 1972–89; Principal of the Hochschule für Musik und Darstellende Kunst at Stuttgart, 1973; Has also conducted the Bach Passions and Christmas Oratorio, Haydn Oratorios and Masses by Mozart and Bruckner; General Director, Staatstheater Stuttgart in opera, ballet and theatre, 1985, and at Ludwigsburg Festival in 1990 with Die Entführung; Conducted L'elisir d'amore at the 2002 Ludwigsburg Festival. *Recordings include:* Bach Cantatas, St Matthew Passion and Magnificat; Mozart's Requiem, with the Consortium Musicum; Handel's Dettinger Te Deum; Haydn's Creation and Seasons, with the Ludwigsburg Festival Orchestra; Mozart's Mass in C minor; Beethoven's Missa Solemnis, with the Collegium Aureum; Brahms' Ein Deutsches Requiem; Bruckner's E minor Mass. *Address:* Staatstheater Stuttgart, Oberer Schlossgarten 6, 7000 Stuttgart 1, Germany.

**GOERGEN, Viviane;** Luxembourg/Swiss pianist; b. 17 June 1948, Paris, France. *Education:* Studied French and German, Nancy University; Graduated, Conservatoire de la Ville de Luxembourg, 1965; Graduated, Conservatory of Nancy, France, 1967; Licence de Piano, Paris Conservatory and Ecole Nationale de Musique, Paris. *Career:* Debut: Luxembourg; First appeared, Paris, 1971; London, 1973; Zürich, 1974; Bonn, 1975; Brussels, 1976; Prague, 1978; Vienna, 1979; Frankfurt, 1982; Madrid, 1983; Berlin, 1991; Since 1978 has taken part in regular foreign tours; Numerous radio appearances; first performances of works, partly especially composed for her; Devotes attention to the music of Claude Debussy and to reviving pianoworks of forgotten composers; lectured in Berlin, Frankfurt, Cythira and Madeira 2000–05; mem, Founded the Center for the Mental Training of Musical Performers, 1994. *Recordings:* Schumann: Davidsbündlertänze, Drei Romanzen Op 28; Johannes Brahms: Sonata Op 5 and Sonata Op 38; César Franck: Sonata in A Major; Ludwig van Beethoven: Sonatas Op 5; Dimitri Shostakovich: Sonata Op 40.; Lyonel Feininger, The Piano Works, 1994; Kurt

Dietmar Richter, Feiniger Impulse, 1994; Claude Debussy, Images, 1997; Erwin Schulhoff, 3rd Sonata for piano, 1997; Ernst Toch, 10 recital and 10 concert studies (op 56 and 55), Burlesques (op 31), 1999. *Film:* film of the Center for the Mental Training of Musical Performers (RTL) 2002. *Honours:* Order of Merit, for artistic achievements, Luxembourg, 1993. *Address:* Nelkenstr. 1, 63322 Rödermark, Germany. *E-mail:* viviane.goergen@gmx.net (office).

**GOERNE, Matthias;** German singer (baritone); b. 31 March 1967, Karl-Marx-Stadt. *Education:* studied with Hans Beyer, Elisabeth Schwarzkopf, Dietrich Fischer-Dieskau. *Career:* Bach St Matthew Passion under Kurt Masur launched his reputation 1990, followed by opera debut with the title role in Henze's Der Prince von Homburg, Cologne 1992; Wigmore Hall recital 1994; performances with Dresden Staatsoper 1997; Salzburg debut 1997, Metropolitan Opera debut 1998, both as Papageno; Edinburgh Festival performance of Schubert's Winterreise with Alfred Brendel 1998; Wozzeck in Zürich 1999, at Covent Garden 2002; created role of Kasim in Henzes L'Upupa 2003, repeated in Teatro Real, Madrid 2004; tour of USA, including performances with Philadelphia Orchestra, Los Angeles Phiharmonic and the Nat. Symphony Orchestra, Washington, as well as Lieder evenings with Alfred Brendel in Los Angeles and with Christoph Eschenbach in Carnegie Hall 2004; sang Bluebeard in Bartók's Duke Bluebeard's Castle in concert performance with the Berliner Philharmoniker 2005; returned to Metropolitan Opera as Papageno 2005. *Recordings include:* Bach Cantatas, Schubert's Winterreise with Alfred Brendel, Dichterliebe, Schumann's Heine and Eichendordd Leiderkreise and Kerner songs, German operatic arias, Schubert songs, Mahler songs with the Concertgebouw Orchestra, Schumann Lieder. *Honours:* winner Hugo Wolf Competition 1990. *Current Management:* Michael Kocyan Artists Management, Wielandstr. 37, 10629 Berlin, Germany. *E-mail:* info@matthiasgoerne.de. *Website:* www.matthiasgoerne.de.

**GOERNER, Stephan;** Cellist; b. 23 Oct. 1957, Switzerland. *Education:* Studied at the Winterhur Conservatory, at Juilliard and the International Menuhin Academy in Gstaad. *Career:* Co-Founder and Cellist of the Carmina Quartet, 1984 with appearances from 1987 in Europe, Israel, Japan and USA; Regular concerts at the Wigmore Hall from 1987 and at the South Bank Centre in London, Amsterdam Concertgebouw, the Kleine Philharmonie in Berlin, and Konzertverein Wien in Vienna; Four engagements in Paris, 1990–91, seven in London and tours to Australasia, USA, and Japan with concerts at the Hohenems, Graz, Hong Kong, Montreux, Schleswig-Holstein, Bath, Lucerne, and Prague Spring Festivals; Collaborations with Dietrich Fischer-Dieskau, Olaf Bär and Mitsuko Uchida. *Recordings:* Various. *Honours:* Joint winner with members of Carmina Quartet, Paolo Borciani String Quartet Competition in Reggio Emilia, Italy, 1987. *Address:* c/o Intermusica Artists' Management, 16 Duncan Terrace, London N1 8BZ, England.

**GOERTZ, Harald,** DrPhil; Austrian conductor, musicologist, pianist, manager and university professor; *Vice-President, Österreichische Gesellschaft für Musik;* b. 31 Oct. 1924, Vienna; m. Carola Renner; one s. one d. *Education:* Univ. of Vienna, advanced piano studies with Wührer and conducting studies with Reichwein, Krips and Swarowsky, Acad. of Music, Vienna. *Career:* asst to Herbert von Karajan, Scala di Milano, Lucerne and others; Music Dir opera and concerts, Ulm, Germany 1955–63; Guest Conductor, Stuttgart, Vienna, Berlin and elsewhere; teacher, Acad. of Music, Stuttgart and Salzburg Mozarteum; Prof. and Leader of Conductor's Class, Opera Section, Hochschule für Musik, Vienna and seminars for interpretation; Chorus Dir Vienna Opera –1991; Pres. Austrian Soc. of Music 1963–97; writer and commentator, Austrian TV and Salzburger Festspiele. *Publications:* Österreichisches Musikhandbuch (ed.), Dictionary of Contemporary Austrian Composers (ed.) 1989, Mozart's Dichter Lorenzo da Ponte 1988, Gerhard Wimberge (monograph) 1990, Österreichische Komponisten der Gegenwart (ed.) 1994, Hanns Eisler Symposion (ed.) 2000, Verdi für Opernfreunde 2001, Musikhandbuch für Österreich 2003; contribs to Grove Dictionary of Music and Musicians. *Honours:* Officer of the British Empire (Civil Section); Bundesverdienst-Kreuz, Germany. *Address:* Österreichische Gesellschaft für Musik, Hanuschgasse 3, 1010 Vienna (office); Wiedner Hauptstrasse 40, 1040 Vienna, Austria (home). *Telephone:* (1) 5123143 (office); (1) 5876406 (home); (676) 6052706 (Mobile) (home). *Fax:* (1) 5124299 (office). *E-mail:* oegm@music.at (office). *Website:* www.music.at/oegm (office).

**GOETHALS, Lucien (Gustave Georges);** Composer; b. 26 June 1931, Ghent, Belgium; m. Maria De Wandelaer, 12 July 1958, 1 s. *Education:* Royal Conservatory of Ghent; Studied composition with Norbert Rosseau and modern technics with Godfried Michael Koenig. *Career:* Organist, 1958–62; Producer, IPEM, 1962; Professor, Analysis, Royal Conservatory, Ghent; Producer, BRT 3, 1964. *Compositions:* Cellotape for cello, piano and electronic music, 1969; Endomorfie for violin, piano and electronic music, 1969; Contrapuntos, electronic music, 1974; Llanto por Salvador Allende for trombone solo; Klankstrukturen organ solo; Triptiek, violin and harpsichord; Sinfonia en Grismayor, 2 orchestras and electronic music, 1966; Many electronic compositions, chamber music and compositions for orchestra; Concerto for Orchestra, 1972; Concerto for 2 clarinets and orchestra, 1983; Concierto de la luz aj las tinublas, for organ and orchestra, 1989; 2 string quartets, 1967, 1992. *Publications:* Lucien Goethals, Le Constructivisne Bifuntionel by Dr H Sabbe; Lucien Goethals, Composer, by H Sabbe. *Contributions:* Professional journals. *Honours:* Mathieu Prize, 1956; Provin-

cial Composition Prize, 1960; Koopal Prize, 1977; Culture Prize, City of Ghent, 1981. *Address:* Verschansingsstraat 32, Mariakerke, 9030 Ghent, Belgium.

**GOLAN, Itamar;** Pianist; b. 1970, Vilnius, Lithuania. *Education:* Studied in Israel with Lara Vodovoz and Emmanuel Krasovsky; Further study in Boston, 1985–88. *Career:* Recitals and chamber music performances in Israel and the USA 1977–; Collaborations with Mischa Maisky, Ivry Gitlis and the Aurora Piano Quartet; Appearances at the Ravinia, Edinburgh, Besançon, Ludwigsburg and Wyoming Festivals; Concert partners have included Maxim Vengerov, Shlomo Mintz and Tabea Zimmerman; Trio formation with Mintz and Mat Haimovitz (violin and cello); Solo engagements with the Israel Philharmonic under Zubin Mehta and the Jerusalem Symphony Orchestra with David Shallon; Faculty member of the Manhattan School of Music, 1991–; Paris Conservatoire, 1994–. *Current Management:* Askonas Holt Ltd, Lonsdale Chambers, 27 Chancery Lane, London, WC2A 1PF, England. *Telephone:* (20) 7400-1700. *Fax:* (20) 7400-1799. *E-mail:* info@askonasholt.co.uk. *Website:* www.askonasholt.co.uk.

**GOLANI, Rivka;** Canadian violist and painter; b. 22 March 1946, Israel; d. of Jacob and Lisa Gulnik; m. Jeremy Fox 1993; one s. *Education:* Univ. of Tel-Aviv. *Career:* studied with Oedon Partos; concerts as soloist worldwide; has inspired many new works including viola concerti by Holloway, Hummel, Fontajn, Colgrass, Holmboe, Yuasa and Turner, solo works by Holliger, Holmboe and others; has collaborated with composers as a visual artist in presenting multimedia performances; art exhbns in Israel, Britain, Germany and N America. *Recordings include:* three-album set of solo works by J. S. Bach. *Publication:* Birds of Another Feather (book of drawings). *Honours:* Grand Prix du Disque 1985. *Address:* c/o Margaret Barkman, 54 Long Point Drive, Richmond Hill, Ontario, L4E 3W8, Canada. *Telephone:* (416) 722-6977. *Fax:* (905) 773-6261. *E-mail:* mbarkman@compuserve.com. *Website:* members.rogers.com/aaionline.

**GOLDBERG, Reiner;** Singer (Tenor); b. 17 Oct. 1939, Crostau, Germany. *Education:* Carl Maria von Weber Hochschule für Musik, Dresden, with Arno Schellenberg. *Career:* Debut: As Luigi in Il Tabarro at Dresden in 1966; Dresden State Opera, 1973–77 and Deutsche Staatsoper East Berlin from 1977; Roles include Florestan, Turiddu, Cavaradossi, Hermann in The Queen of Spades, Aron in Schoenberg's Moses und Aron, and Sergei in Katerina Izmailova; Guest appearances in Leipzig, Leningrad, Vienna, Prague and Italy; Toured Japan with Dresden Company in 1980; Covent Garden debut in 1982 as Walther in Die Meistersinger; Paris 1982 in a concert performance of Strauss's Die Liebe der Danaë, Bayreuth Festival in 1988 in a new production of The Ring produced by Harry Kupfer, New York debut in 1983 in a concert performance of Strauss's Guntram, La Scala Milan in 1984 as Tannhäuser, and Teatro Liceo, Barcelona in 1985 as Siegfried; Sang Walther at Covent Garden in 1990, Erik in Der fliegende Holländer at Bayreuth in 1990 and Bayreuth Festival in 1992, Florestan and Tannhäuser at the Metropolitan in 1992; Aegisthus in Elektra at Florence, 1996; Tannhäuser at the Berlin Staatsoper, 1999; Season 2000–01 as Max in Der Freischütz at the Berlin Staatsoper and Walther von Stolzing in Madrid. *Recordings:* Drum Major in Wozzeck; Parsifal in the film version of Wagner's opera by Syberberg, with role mimed by a woman; Max in Der Freischütz; Guntram; Siegmund in Haitink's recording of Die Walküre. *Address:* c/o Allied Artists Ltd, 42 Montpelier Square, London SW7 1JZ, England.

**GOLDENTHAL, Elliot;** American composer; b. 2 May 1954, New York, NY. *Education:* Manhattan School of Music with John Corigliano. *Career:* freelance composer of theatre, film and choral music; collaborations with Yo-Yo Ma, Julie Taymor and Neil Jordan; mem. ASCAP. *Compositions include:* Brass Quartet 1983, The Transposed Heads (musical after Thomas Mann) 1987, Pastime Variations for chamber orchestra 1988, Shadow lay Scherzo for orchestra 1988, Juan Darien, A Carnival Mass 1988, Fire Water Paper: A Vietnam Oratorio 1995, Concerto for trumpet and piano 1996, Othello (for San Francisco Ballet) 2003, incidental music for A Midsummer Night's Dream, The Taming of the Shrew, The Tempest, Titus Andronicus. *Film scores:* Cocaine Cowboys 1979, Blank Generation 1980, Drugstore Cowboy 1989, Pet Cemetery 1989, Grand Isle 1991, Alien 3 1992, Demolition Man 1993, Interview with the Vampire 1994, Golden Gate 1994, Cobb 1994, Voices 1995, Batman Forever 1995, Heat 1995, Michael Collins 1996, A Time to Kill 1996, Batman & Robin 1997, The Butcher Boy 1998, Sphere 1998, In Dreams 1998, Titus 1999, Final Fantasy: The Spirits Within 2001, Frida (Golden Globe for Best Score 2003) 2002, The Good Thief 2002, S.W.A.T. 2003. *Television music:* Criminal Justice 1990, Fool's Fire 1992, Behind the Scenes (series) 1992, Roswell 1994. *Current Management:* Gorfaine/Schwartz Agency Inc., 13245 Riverside Drive, Suite 450, Sherman Oaks, CA 91423, USA.

**GOLDING, Robin Mavesyn,** MA (Oxon); British writer and editor; b. 4 June 1928, London, England; m. 1st Claire Simpson 1956 (divorced); one d.; m. 2nd Felicity Lott 1973 (divorced). *Education:* Christ Church, Oxford (Westminster Scholar). *Career:* freelance writer on musical subjects; experience of local journalism (The Kensington News); the record industry (Vox), music and general publishing (George Rainbird); Librarian, Boyd Neel Orchestra 1953–56; Admin. Asst 1961–65, Registrar 1966–87, Royal Acad. of Music; Ed., Royal Acad. of Music Magazine 1963–87; mem. Savage Club, Garrick Club, Chelsea Arts Club, Royal Musical Asscn, Royal Soc. of Musicians, Royal Philharmonic Soc., Critics' Circle. *Publications:* Ernest Closson's History of the Piano (revised from 1947 edn); compiled innumerable programme notes 1953–; contrib. to Gramophone, CRC, Classical Record Collector, Musical

Times, Music and Musicians, Records and Recording, The Strad, Arts Review. *Honours:* Hon. ARAM 1965, Hon. RCM 1971, Hon. RAM 1976. *Address:* 33 Prentice Street, Lavenham, Sudbury, Suffolk CO10 9RD, England. *Telephone:* (1787) 247817. *Fax:* (1787) 248485.

**GOLDMANN, Friedrich;** German composer and conductor; b. 27 April 1941, Siegmar-Schönau, Chemmitz. *Education:* studied in Darmstadt with Karlheinz Stockhausen, at Dresden Musikhochschule, Akademie der Künste, Berlin, and Humboldt Univ. *Career:* President of German section of ISCM 1990–97; Professor of Composition, Hochschule der Künste, Berlin 1991–. *Compositions include:* Essays for orchestra, I–III 1963, 1968, 1971; Oedipus Tyrann for chorus and orchestra, 1969; 4 Symphonies 1973, 1973, 1986, 1988; Concertos for Trombone (1977), Violin (1977), Oboe (1979), Piano (1979); 2 string quartets, 1975, 1997; Zusammenstellung, wind quintet 1976; Piano Trio, 1978; Piano Sonata 1987; Wind Quartet, 1991; Klangszenen I and II for orchestra, 1990, 1992; Fast erstarrte Unruhe for ensembles, I–III, 1991, 1992, 1995; Ketten for flute, 1997; Schubert Heine Lieder, arranged for baritone and orchestra, 1997; Trio for oboe, cello and piano, 1998. *Honours:* Sächsische Akademie der Künste, Dresden 1995. *Address:* c/o Hochschule der Künste, Postfach 12 05 44, 10595 Berlin, Germany.

**GOLDSMITH, Barry;** Concert Pianist; b. 4 June 1959, New York, USA. *Education:* Peabody Conservatory of Music; Johns Hopkins University, BM, DMA, Piano Scholarship; MM, Piano, Indiana University School of Music; Piano Scholarship, Manhattan School of Music. *Career:* Debut: Carnegie Recital Hall, New York City, 1982; Solo Recitals in USA, Canada and Europe; Cities include, New York, Philadelphia, Washington DC, Baltimore, San Francisco, Vancouver, London, Oslo, The Hague, Brussels, Milan; Performed in Major Concert Halls: Carnegie Recital Hall, New York City; Wigmore Hall, London; Diligentia Hall, The Hague; University Hall, Oslo; Solo Recitals at Interlochen Arts Academy; Guest Appearances at Universities on the East Coast and Midwest, USA; Soloist with Peabody Symphony, The Queensborough Symphony and Orchestras in New York; Live Performances on WNYC FM Radio in New York City; Taped Performances on National Public Radio, USA; Solo recitals in Edinburgh (Scotland) and with orchestras in New York's Town Hall (USA); Professor of Piano at Queensborough Community College in New York. *Compositions:* Works for Piano, Voice or Violin and Piano; The Heritage, Suites for Violin and Piano. *Recordings:* Recording Artist with CRS Records; Piano Concerti by Russian-Jewish composers with Royal Scottish Nat. Orchestra, David Amos conducting (Helicon). *Current Management:* International Artists Alliance. *Address:* 75-07 171 Street, Flushing, NY 11366, USA.

**GOLDSTEIN, Malcolm;** Composer and Violinist; b. 27 March 1936, Brooklyn, New York, USA. *Education:* Studied at Columbia University with Otto Luening. *Career:* Has taught at Columbia-Princeton Electronic Music Center, 1959–60, Columbia University, 1961–65, New England Conservatory, 1965–67, Goddard College, Vermont, 1972–74, and Bowden College, Brunswick, Maine, 1978–82; Co-Director of the concert series, Tone Roads, 1967–69, giving performances of works by Ives, Varése and Cage; Director of the New Music Ensemble and Collegium at Dartmouth College, 1975–78; Has toured Europe and North America as violinist. *Compositions include:* Emanations for violin and cello, 1962; Ludlow Blues for wind and tape, 1963; Overture To Fantastic Gardens, 1964; Majority for string trio, 1964; Sirens For Edgard Varése, 1965; Sheep Meadow for tape collage, 1967; Frog Pond At Dusk, 1972; Upon The Seashore Of Endless Worlds, 1974; Yosha's Morning Song Extended, 1974; Hues Of The Golden Ascending for flute and ensemble, 1979; On The First Day Of Spring There Were 40 Pianos, 1981; A Breaking Of Vessels, Becoming Song, flute concerto, 1981; The Seasons, Vermont, 1980–82; Of Bright Mushrooms Bursting In My Head for ensemble, 1984; Cascades Of The Brook (Bachwasserfall) for orchestra, 1984; Through the deserts of time, string quartet, 1990; Aparicion con vida, theatre piece, 1993; Regarding the Tower of Babel, for speaker and ensemble, 1997; Divisions of Ground for woodwind instruments, piano and percussion, 1998. *Publications include:* Edition of the 2nd Symphony by Ives; From Wheelock Mountain, scores and writings, 1977. *Address:* c/o ASCAP, ASCAP Building, 1 Lincoln Plaza, New York, NY 10023, USA.

**GOLDSTONE, Anthony (Keith);** Concert Pianist; b. 25 July 1944, Liverpool, England; m. Caroline Clemmow, 26 July 1989. *Education:* Royal Manchester College of Music. *Career:* Debut: Wigmore Hall, London, 1969; Appearances throughout England with all major symphony orchestras and in recital; Many festivals; Several London Promenade Concerts including the Last Night in 1976; Very frequent broadcaster; Tours, North and South America, Africa, Asia, Europe, Australasia; Flourishing piano duo with wife Caroline Clemmow and numerous chamber activities including founding Musicians of the Royal Exchange in 1978; mem, Incorporated Society of Musicians. *Recordings:* Solo piano: Schubert, Lyapunov, Arensky, Glière, Parry, Elgar, Holst, Lambert, Moussorgsky, Britten, Bridge, A Moyzes and others; Chamber: Beethoven, Sibelius, Mendelssohn, Holst, others; Piano Duo: Two-piano works by Holst (Planets), Brahms (Sonata), Gál, Britten, George Lloyd, Soler, others; Piano duets by Schubert (complete), Rimsky-Korsakov, Tchaikovsky, Stravinsky, Elgar, virtuoso variations, romantic sonatas, others; Concertos: Beethoven (from London Promenade Concerts), Alkan, Saint-Saëns Pitfield. *Honours:* International Piano Competitions, Munich, Vienna, 1967; BBC Piano Competition, 1968; Gulbenkian Fellowship, 1968–71; Fellow, Royal Manchester College of Music, 1973. *Address:* Walcot Old Hall, Alkborough, North Lincolnshire DN15 9JT, England.

**GOLDTHORPE, (John) Michael,** MA; British singer (tenor); b. 7 Feb. 1942, York; two s. two d. *Education:* Trinity College, Cambridge; Certificate of Education, King's College, London; Guildhall School of Music and Drama, London. *Career:* Debut: Purcell Room, London, January 1970; Paris debut, 1972; Opera Royal, Versailles, 1977; Royal Opera, Covent Garden and BBC television, 1980; Regular Broadcaster, BBC radio; US debut, Miami Festival, 1986; Appearances in Singapore, Iceland, most countries Western Europe; Concertgebouw, Amsterdam, 1986; Directed Medieval Concert in Rome, 1987; Noted Bach Evangelist and exponent of French Baroque; Lucerne Festival's performance of Frank Martin's Golgotha, 1990; Series of concerts for the Sorbonne, Paris, 1992; Examiner, Trinity College of Music and Royal College of Music, London; Lecturer, Teacher, Univ. of Roehampton, London; Founder and Artistic Dir, specialist Victorian music group and charity, The Bold Balladiers, 1995; mem, Hon Fellow, Cambridge Society of Musicians, 1993; Member of the Royal Society of Musicians of Great Britain, 1999. *Recordings include:* Rameau: Hippolyte et Aricie, La Princesse de Navarre and Pygmalion; Charpentier: Missa Assumpta est Maria; Mondonville Motets; Cavalli: Ercole Amante; Delius: Irmelin; Monteverdi: L'Incoronazione di Poppea, Madrigali; Blanchard: Cantatas; Stuart Ward: St Cuthbert of Lindisfarne and Other Songs. *Honours:* Choral Exhibition, Cambridge, 1961; Lieder Prize GSM, 1967; Greater London Arts Asscn Young Musicians Award, Inc. Soc. of Musicians Young Musicians Award, Park Lane Group's Young Musicians Award, early 1970s; Wingate Scholarship, 1994; SEDA accreditation as Teacher in Higher Education, 2000. *Address:* 23 King Edward's Road, Ruislip, Middx, HA4 7AQ, England. *Telephone:* (1895) 635737 (office); (7761) 247617 (home). *E-mail:* info@michaelgoldthorpe.com (office). *Website:* www.michaelgoldthorpe.com (office).

**GOLESORKHI, Anooshah;** Singer (Baritone); b. 1962, Tehran, Iran. *Education:* Studied in California. *Career:* Debut: Opera Pacific Costa Mesa, 1988 as Amonasro in Aida; Sang Escamillo at Bergen Opera, Norway; Iago on tour with the Company in Israel, 1993; Connecticut Opera 1991 as Garriso in Massenet's Navarriase; San Jose Opera as Rossini's Figaro and Marcello in La Bohème; St Gallen 1993 as Barnaba in La Gioconda and Canterbury Opera, New Zealand as Scarpia; Other roles include Verdi's Nabucco, Renato, Luna and Macbeth and Gerard in Andrea Chénier. *Address:* c/o Opera Bergen, Kommediebakan 9, 5016 Bergen, Norway.

**GOLIGHTLY, David Frederick,** BA, AMusM; British composer; b. 17 Nov. 1948, Co. Durham, England. *Education:* Huddersfield University; Guildhall School of Music and Drama; Leeds University; Nottingham University. *Career:* Composer. *Compositions include:* The Eye, a Chamber Opera premiered 1992; Symphony No. 1; Rites of Passage and The St Petersburg Mass premiered 1994 in the State Capella Hall, St Petersburg, Russia; Frontiers (Five arrangements of American folk songs for male voice choir); Songs of the Cliff Top for baritone and piano; Star Flight, Northumbrian Fantasy, Crimond arrangement, and A Weardale Portrait for brass band; Septet for brass; Little Suite for brass quintet; Three Pieces for tombone quartet (Vol. 1 and 2); Concert Fanfare for brass and percussion; Four Preludes for flute and guitar; Three Shadow Portraits for piano; Piano Sonata No. 1; Flute concerto; Trumpet concerto; Concerto for strings; Three Pan Love Songs for solo flute; Piano Trio Letters of Regret; Dances for Showgirls for piano trio; Music for the Theatre and Film. *Current Management:* Modrana Music Promotions Ltd, Mill Isle House, 4 The Batts, Frosterley, Wear Valley, Bishop Auckland, County Durham, DL13 2SB, England. *Telephone:* (1388) 527068. *E-mail:* info@modranamusicpromotions.com. *Website:* www .modranamusicpromotions.com (office).

**GOLIJOV, Osvaldo,** PhD; Argentine composer; *Composer-in-Residence, Chicago Symphony Orchestra;* b. 5 Dec. 1960, La Plata. *Education:* Jerusalem Rubin Acad., Univ. of Pennsylvania, Tanglewood Inst., studied with Gerardo Gandini in La Plata, Mark Kopytman in Jerusalem, George Crumb in Pennsylvania, Oliver Knussen at Tanglewood. *Career:* moved to USA 1986; numerous collaborations with the Kronos Quartet, including a series of arrangements of music from all over the world; collaborations with artists including Taraf de Haïdouks, Mexican rock band Café Tacvba, Klezmer master David Krakauer, tabla virtuoso Zakir Hussain, Argentine musician and prod. Gustavo Santaolalla, Mexican film dir Alejandro González Iñarritu; composer-in-residence posts include Merkin Hall, New York, Spoleto Festival, Los Angeles Philharmonic Music Alive series, Marlboro Music Festival, Ravinia Festival; teacher Coll. of the Holy Cross, Worcester, MA 1991–, currently Assoc. Prof.; Visiting Lecturer Boston Conservatory, Tanglewood Music Center; composer-in-residence Chicago Symphony Orchestra 2006–(08). *Compositions:* Yiddishbbuk for string quartet 1992, The Dreams and Prayers of Isaac the Blind for klezmer clarinet and string quartet 1994, K'vakarat for clarinet and string quartet 1994, Last Round for string orchestra 1996, Oceana (choral work) 1996, Din for bells and ensemble 1998, Doina for string quartet 1999, Mariel for cello and marimba 1999, St Mark Passion for soloists, chorus, percussion and orchestra 2000, Tenebrae for soprano, clarinet and string quartet 2002, Three Songs for soprano and orchestra 2002, Ainadamar (one-act opera) 2003, Ayre for soprano and ensemble 2004, Tekyah for klezmer ensemble 2004. *Film soundtracks:* The Man Who Cried 2000, Darkness 2002. *Current Management:* c/o Jonathan Brill, ICM Artists, 40 W 57th Street, New York, NY 10019, USA. *Telephone:* (212) 556-5620 (office). *Fax:* (212) 556-5677 (office). *E-mail:* jbrill@icmtalent .com (office). *Website:* www.icmtalent.com (office). *E-mail:* nfo@osvaldogolijov .com. *Website:* www.osvaldogolijov.com.

**GÖLLNER, Theodor,** PhD; German musicologist; *Director, Commission of Music History, Bavarian Academy of Sciences*; b. 25 Nov. 1929, Bielefeld; s. of Friedrich Göllner and Paula Brinkmann; m. Marie Louise Martinez 1959; one s. one d. *Education:* Univs of Heidelberg and Munich. *Career:* Lecturer, Univ. of Munich 1958–62, Asst Prof., Assoc. Prof. 1962–67; Prof., Univ. of Calif. Santa Barbara 1967–73; Prof., Chair. Inst. of Musicology, Univ. of Munich 1973–97; mem., Dir Comm. of Music History, Bavarian Acad. of Sciences 1982–; mem. European Acad. of Sciences and Arts 1991–. *Publications:* Formen früher Mehrstimmigkeit 1961, Die mehrstimmigen liturgischen Lesungen 1969, Die Sieben Worte am Kreuz 1986, Et incarnatus est in Bachs h-moll-Messe und Beethovens Missa solemnis 1996, Die Tactuslehre in den deutschen Orgelquellen des 15. Jahrhunderts 2003; (ed.) Münchner Veröffentlichungen zur Musikgeschichte 1977–, Münchner Editionen zur Musikgeschichte 1979–. *Address:* Institute of Musicology, University of Munich, Geschwister-Scholl-Platz 1, 80539 Munich (office); Bahnweg 9, 82229 Seefeld, Germany (home). *Telephone:* (1089) 21802364 (office). *E-mail:* TheodorGoellner@aol.com (home).

**GOLOVIN, Andrei;** Composer and Conductor; b. 11 Aug. 1950, Moscow, Russia. *Education:* Moscow Conservatoire, 1971–76; Postgraduate Course, 1977–79. *Career:* Teacher of Composition at Gnesins' State Musical College, 1975–, and Gnesins' Russian Academy of Music, 1989–; mem, Russian Composers' Union. *Compositions:* Published: Cadence and Ostinato for 5 timpani, bells, tam-tam and piano, 1979, Concerto Symphony for viola, cello and symphony orchestra, 1980, Sonata for oboe and cembalo, 1980, Sonata for piano, 1981, Duet for violin and piano, 1981, Duet for viola and cello, 1981, Sonata Breve for viola and piano, 1982, Japanese edition, 1992, 2 Pieces for piano, 1982, Sonata for cello solo, 1983, 2 Pieces for flute and piano: Portrait, and, Landscape, 1983, Prelude for vibraphone, 1984, Legend for piano, 1984, 3 Easy Pieces for piano, 1985, 1st Quartet for 2 violins, viola and cello, 1986, Music for string quartet, 1986, Sonatina for piano, 1986, Japanese edition, 1991, Fairy-Tale for horn and piano, 1987, Concert Symphony for viola, piano and orchestra, 1988, Symphony for full symphony orchestra, 1990, Elegy for cello solo, 1990, Poeme Nocturne for viola and piano, 1991, Plain Songs: Canata to Verses by N Rubtsov for mezzo-soprano, bass, piano and chamber orchestra, 1991, Remote Past for piano, 1991; Symphony No. 4, for cello and orchestra, 1992; On the Hills of Georgia, chorus, 1992; Spring Song for trombone and piano, 1993; First Love, opera after Turgenev, 1996. *Recordings:* Simple Songs: Cantata, Elegy for cello solo; Sonata Breve for viola and piano; Elegy for cello solo; Concert Symphony for viola, piano and orchestra; Quartet for 2 violins, viola and cello; 2 Pieces for flute and piano; Music for strings. *Address:* Shumkin St 3, k2, Ap 45, Moscow 107113, Russia.

**GOLTZ, Christel;** Singer (Soprano); b. 8 July 1912, Dortmund, Germany; m. Theodor Schenk. *Education:* Studied with Ornelli-Leeb in Munich and with Theodor Schenk. *Career:* Sang first at Plauen as Eva, Santuzza and Octavian; Sang at the Dresden Staatsoper from 1936 notably as Reiza in Oberon, in the premiere of Sutermeister's Romeo und Julia in 1941 and in the local premiere of Orff's Antigonae in 1950; Sang in Berlin from 1947, then in Munich and Vienna as Salome, Elektra, the Countess in Capriccio, Tosca and Leonore; Covent Garden, 1951–52 as Salome and as Marie in the local stage premiere of Wozzeck; Salzburg Festival from 1954 in the premiere of Liebermann's Penelope and as Elektra and Leonore, and as Salome at the Metropolitan Opera in 1954; Guest engagements in Paris, Brussels and Milan; Sang at the State Operas of Munich and Vienna until 1970. *Recordings:* Salome; Die Frau ohne Schatten. *Honours:* Ehrenmitglied of the Dresden Staatsoper, 1996. *Address:* c/o Vienna State Opera, Ring Strasse, Vienna, Austria.

**GOLUB, David;** Pianist and Conductor; b. 22 March 1950, Chicago, USA. *Education:* Studied with Alexander Uninsky in Dallas and with Beveridge Webster at the Juilliard School, New York; Graduated, 1974. *Career:* Debut: With Dallas Symphony Orchestra, 1964; Appeared with orchestras in Philadelphia, Cleveland, Dallas, St Louis, Pittsburgh, Cincinnati, Chicago, Minnesota, Washington and Atlanta; Solo appearances also with orchestras of Toronto, Ottawa, Edmonton, Montreal, Calgary and Vancouver; Has performed at all major North American music festivals; International appearances with such conductors as Maazel, Mata, Horst Stein, Zinman, Conlon, Chailly, Levine, Dutoit, Bychkov, DeWaart, Foster, Skrowaczewski and Albrecht; European engagements with orchestras in London, Rome, Paris, Milan, Geneva, Florence, Rotterdam, Amsterdam and Prague; Appeared in film From Mao to Mozart, which documented tour to China in 1979 with Isaac Stern and formed a piano trio with Colin Carr and Mark Kaplan. *Recordings:* Gershwin and Rachmaninov with London Symphony Orchestra and complete piano trios of Schubert, Mendelssohn and Brahms; Haydn's L'Isola Disabitata, as conductor; The Complete Trios of Dvořák, Rachmaninov with Golub-Kaplan-Carr Trio. *Current Management:* Herbert Barratt Management. *Address:* 1776 Broadway, New York, NY 10019, USA.

**GOMBRICH, Carl;** Singer (Bass); b. 1975, England. *Education:* Guildhall School, and National Opera Studio, London, with Neil Howlett; King's College, London and Morley Opera. *Career:* Early roles included Ribbing (Ballo in Maschera), Gounod's Mephistopheles, Sparafucile (Rigoletto) and Guglielmo; Appearances as the Commendatore in Don Giovanni for Pavilion Opera and on Japanese Tour; Don Pasquale for Opera Italiana and Blansac in La Scala di Seta at the 1999 Wexford Festival; The Monk in Don Carlos, Oroveso (Norma) and Mozart's Osmin, for British Youth Opera, Linbury Studio Theatre, Covent Garden. *Address:* c/o National Opera Studio, Morley College, 61 Westminster Bridge Road, London, SE1 7XT, England.

**GOMEZ, Jill,** FRAM; British opera and concert singer (soprano); b. 21 Sept. 1942, New Amsterdam, British Guiana. *Education:* Royal Acad. of Music, Guildhall School of Music. *Career:* operatic début as Adina in L'Elisir d'Amore with Glyndebourne Touring Opera 1968 and has since sung leading roles with Glyndebourne Festival Opera incl. Mélisande, Calisto and Ann Truelove in The Rake's Progress; has appeared with The Royal Opera, English Nat. Opera and Scottish Opera in roles including Pamina, Ilia, Fiordiligi, the Countess in Figaro, Elizabeth in Elegy for Young Lovers, Tytania, Lauretta in Gianni Schicchi and the Governess in The Turn of the Screw; cr. the role of Flora in Tippett's The Knot Garden, at Covent Garden 1970 and of the Countess in Thea Musgrave's Voice of Ariadne, Aldeburgh 1974; sang title role in Massenet's Thaïs, Wexford 1974 and Jenifer in The Midsummer Marriage with Welsh Nat. Opera 1976; cr. title role in William Alwyn's Miss Julie for radio 1977; performed Tatiana in Eugene Onegin with Kent Opera 1977; Donna Elvira in Don Giovanni, Ludwigsburg Festival 1978; cr. title role in BBC world premiere of Prokofiev's Maddalena 1979; Fiordiligi in Così fan tutte, Bordeaux 1979; sang in première of the Eighth Book of Madrigals in Zürich Monteverdi Festival 1979; Violetta in Kent Opera's production of La Traviata, Edin. Festival 1979; Cinna in Lucio Silla, Zurich 1981; The Governess in The Turn of the Screw, Geneva 1981; Cleopatra in Giulio Cesare, Frankfurt 1981; Teresa in Benvenuto Cellini, Berlioz Festival, Lyon 1982, Leila in Les Pêcheurs de Perles, Scottish Opera 1982–83; Governess in The Turn of the Screw, English Nat. Opera 1984; Helena in Glyndebourne's production of Britten's A Midsummer Night's Dream; Donna Anna in Don Giovanni, Frankfurt Opera 1985 and with Kent Opera 1988; Rosario in Goyescas by Granados 1988, Helena in Midsummer Night's Dream, London Opera 1990; cr. role of Duchess of Argyll in Thomas Adès's Powder Her Face, Cheltenham Int. Music Festival and London 1995; regular engagements including recitals in France, Austria, Belgium, Netherlands, Germany, Scandinavia, Switzerland, Italy, Spain and the USA; Festival appearances include Aix-en-Provence, Spoleto, Bergen, Versailles, Flanders, Netherlands, Prague, Edin. and BBC Promenade concerts; masterclasses Pears-Britten School, Aldeburgh, Trinity Coll. of Music, London, Dartington Summer Festival, Meridian TV. *Recordings include:* Vespro della Beata Vergine 1610 (Monteverdi), Acis and Galatea (Handel), A Child of Our Time (Tippett), three recital discs of French, Spanish and Mozart songs, Quatre Chansons Françaises (Britten), Trois Poèmes de Mallarmé (Ravel), Chants d'Auvergne (Canteloube), Les Illuminations (Britten), Bachianas Brasileiras No. 5 (Villa Lobos), Cabaret Classics with John Constable, Knoxville-Summer of 1915 (Barber), South of the Border (Down Mexico Way...) arranged by Christopher Palmer for Jill Gomez, Britten's Blues (songs by Britten and Cole Porter); première recordings of Cantiga – The Song of Inês de Castro commissioned by her from David Matthews, Seven Early Songs (Mahler), A Spanish Songbook (with John Constable), The Knot Garden (Tippett), Miss Julie (William Alwyn), Powder Her Face (Thomas Adès). *Address:* 16 Milton Park, London, N6 5QA, England. *Telephone:* (20) 8348-4193 (home); (1954) 267353 (home). *Fax:* (20) 8348-4193 (home). *E-mail:* jillgomez@btopenworld.com (home).

**GOMEZ-MARTINEZ, Miguel-Angel;** Conductor and Composer; b. 17 Sept. 1949, Granada, Spain. *Education:* Studied at the Granada and Madrid Conservatories, in USA and Vienna with Hans Swarowsky. *Career:* Conducted opera in Lucerne, Berlin, Frankfurt, Munich and Hamburg, at Covent Garden in London, Paris, Geneva, Berne, Houston, Chicago, Florence, Rome, Venice and Palermo; Resident Conductor for Berlin Deutsche Oper, 1973–77, and Vienna Staatsoper, 1977–82; Festivals in Berlin, Vienna, Munich, Macerata in Italy, Granada, Santander, San Sebastián, Savonlinna in Finland and Helsinki; Repertoire of over 50 operas including works by Mozart, Puccini, Rossini, Verdi and Wagner; Conductor for Radiotelevision Española Orchestra, 1984–87; Artistic Director and Chief Conductor, Teatro Lirico Nacional Madrid, 1985–91; General Musikdirektor, Nationaltheater Mannheim and Chief Conductor of the Nationaltheater Orchestra, 1990–93; Chief Conductor of Hamburg Symphony, 1992–, and General Music Director of the Finnish National Opera, Helsinki, 1993–; Concerts with most major orchestras in Europe, Far East and America; Chief Conductor, Orchestra of Valencia. *Compositions include:* Suite Burlesca; Sinfonia del Descubrimiento, first performed in 1992, at Mozart Saal, Rosengarten, Mannheim; Five Canciones sobre poemas de Alonso Gamo, for soprano and orchestra, first performed Grosse Musikhalle, Hamburg, 1996. *Current Management:* Balmer & Dixon Management AG, Kreuzstrasse 82, 8032 Zürich, Switzerland. *Telephone:* (43) 244-8644. *Fax:* (43) 244-8649. *Website:* www.badix.ch.

**GONDA, Anna;** Singer (Mezzo-soprano); b. Jan. 1950, Miskole, Hungary. *Education:* Studied at Franz Liszt Academy in Budapest and in Berlin. *Career:* Debut: Sang Gluck's Orpheus in Berlin, 1976; Sang at Rostock, 1976–78, Vienna Staatsoper from 1981 notably on tour to Japan in 1986 and at Salzburg Festival in 1984 in the premiere of Un Re in Ascolto by Berio; Appeared in Zigeunerbaron at Zürich Opera conducted by Nikolaus Harnoncourt in 1990; Lieder recitals and concerts in Austria, France and Switzerland; Other roles include Verdi's Azucena, Ulrica, Mistress Quickly, Amneris, Maddalena and Preziosilla, Wagner's Erda and Brangaene, Marina in Boris Godunov, Clytemnestra and Penelope in Il Ritorno d'Ulisse; Vienna Staatsoper 1995–96 as Erda, Ulrica and Zulma in L'Italiana in Algeri. *Recordings include:* Zulma in L'Italiana in Algeri; Margret in Wozzeck. *Address:* c/o Opernhaus Zürich, Falkenstrasse 1, 8008 Zürich, Switzerland.

**GONDEK, Juliana (Kathleen);** Singer (Soprano); b. Pasadena, California, USA; 1 d. *Education:* Violin study; BM, 1975, MM, 1977, University of

Southern California School of Music; Britten-Pears School of Advanced Musical Studies, Aldeburgh, England. *Career:* Debut: San Diego Opera; Sang Contessa in Le nozze di Figaro with Netherlands Opera in 1986, Heroines in The Tales of Hoffmann in 1986, Alcina in 1987 at Opera Theatre of St Louis, title role in Bianca e Falliero at Greater Miami Opera in 1987, Fiordiligi in Così fan tutte at Hawaii Opera in 1989, Vitelia in La Clemenza di Tito for Scottish Opera in 1991, title role in Beatrice di Tenda in 1991, Elvira at Seattle Opera in 1991 and Gismonda in Othone, 1992; Zenobia in Radamisto, 1993; Title role in Esther, 1994; Ginevra in Ariodante at the Handel Festival, Göttingen, 1995; Aspasia in Mozart's Mitridate, 1993; Leyla in Bright Sheng's The Song of Majnun with San Francisco Symphony, 1992; Triple role of Diane Feinstein/Harvey's Mama/The Hooker in world premiere of Harvey Milk with Houston Grand Opera, New York City Opera and San Francisco Opera, 1995–96; Ela in world premiere of Dreamkeepers by David Carlson with Utah Opera, 1996; Title role in the world premiere of Hopper's Wife by Stewart Wallace and Michael Korie, 1997; Ginevra in Ariodante with Dallas Opera, 1998; Sang Mozart's Countess at Cologne, 2000; Appeared in concert in Canada, USA and in Europe; Appeared as soloist at Edinburgh, Caramoor, Marlboro, Mostly Mozart, Newport, Lincoln Center, Göttingen and Avignon Festivals and as recitalist in USA and Europe; Sang as soloist with New York Philharmonic, Minnesota Orchestra, symphonies of St Louis, San Francisco, Montreal, Toronto, Detroit, Dallas, Seattle, Indianapolis and Baltimore; Philharmonia Baroque and Freiburger Barock Orchestras; Professor of Voice and Opera Studies, University of California at Los Angeles, 1997–. *Recordings:* As Gismonda in Handel's Ottone, 1992; Video, Live From The Met, as 1st Lady in Die Zauberflöte with Metropolitan Opera, 1992; As Zenobia in Handel's Radamisto, 1993; Fortuna in Handel's Giustino, 1994; Ginevra in Handel's Ariodante, 1995; Premiere recording of Harvey Milk with San Francisco Symphony Orchestra and Chorus under Donald Runnicles. *Current Management:* Colbert Artists Management Inc. *Address:* c/o Colbert Artists Management Inc, 111 West 57th Street, New York, NY 10019, USA.

**GONG, Dong-Jian;** Opera Singer (bass); b. 1 Dec. 1957, Nanchang, China. *Education:* Shanghai Conservatory of Music, China, 1980–84; Artist Diploma, Indiana University, USA, 1988–90; Opera music Theatre International, USA, 1991. *Career:* Debut: Colline in La Bohème, Vienna Staatsoper, 1991; Colline, Opera de Nice, France, Sparafucile in Rigoletto, Bilbao, Spain, Ramfis in Aida with Palm Beach Opera, Giorgio in I Puritani with Opera Malaga, Spain and as Timur with the Teatro Municipal in Santiago, 1992–93; Asdrubila, an opera premiered at 1993 Barcelona Summer Festival; Zaccaria in Nabucco with the Opera de Bellas Artes in Mexico City, Ferrando in Il Trovatore with Minnesota Opera, Raimondo in Lucia di Lammermoor with the New Jersey State Opera, Il Frate in Don Carlos in Bilbao, 1993–94; Sparafucile in Rigoletto, Timur in Turandot and Colline in a new production of La Bohème, he also appeared with the Virginia Opera as Basilio in Il Barbiere di Siviglia, performed the Boatsman in Bruch's Odysseus with the American Symphony Orchestra at Avery Fisher Hall, soloist in the Verdi Requiem with the Kennedy Opera, 1995–96; Returned to Vancouver Opera as Zaccaria in Nabucco, concert appearances included a performance of Beethoven's Missa Solemnis with the Richmond Symphony, 1994–95; Performances of Philip II in Don Carlos with the Kentucky Opera, the Grand Inquisitor in Don Carlos with Opéra de Lyon and Opéra de Nice, Ramfis with Oper der Stadt Köln and performances in Munich, Amsterdam and Hong Kong in the role of Kublai Khan in Marco Polo, 1996–97; Oper der Stadt Köln for performances of Ramfis in Aida, 1997–98; Ramfis at the Deutsche Oper Berlin, performances of Beethoven's Symphony No. 9 with the Columbus Symphony Orchestra, Biterolf in Tannhäuser in Seville, Oroveso in Norma with Opera Memphis, soloist in the Verdi Requiem with the Nashville Symphony, 1998–99. *Recordings:* Marco Polo by Tan Dun as Kublai Khan. *Current Management:* Pieter G. Alferink Artists Management Amsterdam BV, Apollolaan 181, 1077 AT Amsterdam, Netherlands.

**GONLEY, Stephanie,** FGSM; British violinist; *Leader, English Chamber Orchestra;* b. 1966. *Education:* Chetham School of Music, Guildhall School of Music, with Dorothy DeLay at Juilliard School and in Berlin. *Career:* Mozart Concertos with Manchester Camerata, Mendelssohn, Walton, Brahms and Bruch with Royal Philharmonic, Walton with the London Philharmonic Orchestra and Beethoven in the Netherlands with Adrian Leaper; Further engagements with English Chamber Orchestra (ECO) in 1990, Philharmonia and Halle, at Montpellier Festival and in Hong Kong, Belgium and Canada, played Vivaldi's Four Seasons with English Chamber Orchestra at Festival Hall in 1993; Prom Debut in 1995 with BBC Scottish Symphony Orchestra; Leader, English Chamber Orchestra 1991–; (Masterclasses at Banff, Canada, Aspen, USA and Prussia Cove, Cornwall, England); Co-Founded the Vellinger String Quartet in 1990; (Particpated in master classes with the Borodin Quartet, Pears-Britten School in 1991); Concerts at Ferrara Musica Festival in Italy and debut on South Bank with the London premiere of Roberts Simpson's 13th Quartet; BBC Radio 3 debut in 1991; Season 1994–95 with concerts in London, Germany, Spain, USA, Italy at Sweden, Paris, at Davos Festival, Switzerland; Played at Wigmore Hall several times (with Haydn Op 54 No. 2, Gubaidulina and Beethoven Op 59 No. 2), and at the Purcell Room with Haydn's Seven Last Words. *Recordings include:* Elgar's Quartet and Quintet with Piers Lane, Dvorak Romance with ECO and Charles Mackerass, Sibelius Concerto with Adrian Leaper and Orchestra of Gran Canaria, Schubert Quintet with Bernard Greenhouse. *Honours:* Winner of London International String Quartet Competition 1994. *Current Management:* Robert Gilder & Co., Enterprise House, 59–65 Upper Ground, London, SE1 9PQ,

England. *Telephone:* (20) 7928-9008. *Fax:* (20) 7928-9755. *E-mail:* rgilder@robert-gilder.com.

**GONNEVILLE, Michel;** Lecturer and Composer; b. 1950, Montreal, Canada. *Education:* Studied piano at an early age; Studied at Ecole de Musique Vincent-d'Indy, 1968–72; BMus, 1972; Doctorate in Composition, University of Montreal. *Career:* Composer, studying analysis and composition with Giles Tremblay at Conservatoire de Musique de Montreal, 1973, obtaining first prizes in Analysis and Composition in 1974 and 1975; Attended Stockhausen's seminars in Darmstadt in 1974 and his composition classes in Cologne for three semesters, also working in the Electronic Studio at Cologne Musikhochschule; Student and Personal Assistant to Henri Pousseur at Liège; His professors included Frederic Rzewski and Joh Fritsch; Returning to Canada in 1978 he lectured on analysis and composition at Montreal and Rimouski Conservatories and at the Universities of Montreal and Ottawa; Professor of Composition and Analysis, Conservatoire de Musique de Montreal. Composed works for Louis-Philippe Pelletier, Michael Laucke, Robert Leroux, Gropus 7, L'Ensemble d'Ondes de Montreal, the SMCQ and a recent work premiered by the Orchestre des Jeunes du Quebec; His works have been performed in Montreal, Quebec, Toronto, Metz, Cologne, Bonn, Liège and Paris and several have been recorded including Adonwe and broadcast by CBC and WDR in Cologne. *Compositions include:* Chute/Parachute for piano and band, 1989; Adonwe for piano and orchestra, 1994; Attirévers le haut par le menu for alto solo, 1995; Le Cheminement de la baleine, 1998. *Address:* 6812 20th Avenue, Montreal, Quebec, H1X 2J7, Canada.

**GONZAGA, Otoniel;** Singer (Tenor); b. 1944, Philippines. *Career:* Has appeared at opera houses in Europe and North America, 1967–; Engaged at Trier, 1973–77, Frankfurt am Main, 1977–88; Member of Cologne Opera, 1988–; Guest engagements at Stuttgart, Munich (Theater am Gärtnerplatz), Vienna (Volksoper), Barcelona, Berne and Genoa; Sang Otello at Aachen, Edgardo in Lucia di Lammermoor at Cincinnati, 1990; Other roles have included Ferrando, Faust, Almaviva and Luigi in Il Tabarro; Season 1993–94 as Calaf at Bergen and Manrico at Cincinnati; Many concert appearances. *Address:* c/o Stadttheater, Theaterstrasse 1–3, 5100 Aachen, Germany.

**GONZALES, Dalmacio;** singer (tenor); b. 12 May 1945, Olot, Spain. *Education:* studied in Barcelona and at the Salzburg Mozarteum with Arleen Auger and Paul Schilharsky; Further study with Anton Dermota in Vienna. *Career:* debut at the Teatro Liceo Barcelona in 1978 as Ugo in Parisina by Donizetti; New York City Opera and San Francisco in 1979 as Alfredo and in Rossini's Semiramide and Tancredi; Metropolitan Opera from 1980 as Ernesto in Don Pasquale and later as Almaviva, Fenton and Nemorino; Sang at La Scala Milan and Aix-en-Provence in 1981 in Ariodante and Tancredi, at Pesaro and La Scala, 1984–85 in a revival of Rossini's Il Viaggio a Reims and further appearances in Rome, Los Angeles, Chicago, Berlin, Zürich, Trieste and London; Sang Ford in Salieri's Falstaff at Parma in 1987 and at Munich Festival in 1990 as Catullus in Catulli Carmina by Orff; Sang Ugo at the 1990 Maggio Musicale, Florence; Other roles include Rossini's Argiro in Tancredi, Idreno in Semiramide, Lindoro, James V in La Donna del Iago and Rinaldo in Armida; Season 1992 as Nemorino at Barcelona and Demetrio in Rossini's Demetrio e Polibio at Martina Franca; Madrid 1995, as Stravinsky's Oedipus; Sang Calaf in Turandot at the reopening of the Teatre Liceo, Barcelona, 1999. *Recordings:* Verdi's Requiem, Falstaff and Il Viaggio a Reims; La Donna del Lago by Rossini.

**GONZALEZ, Carmen;** Singer (Mezzo-soprano); b. 16 April 1939, Vallodid, Spain. *Career:* Studied at the Madrid Conservatory and with Magda Piccarolo and Rodolfo Celetti in Milan. *Recordings:* Orlando Furioso by Vivaldi; Anacreon by Cherubini. *Address:* c/o Netherlands Opera, Waterlooplein 22, 1011 PG, Amsterdam, Netherlands.

**GONZALEZ, Manuel;** Singer (Baritone); b. 30 April 1944, Madrid, Spain. *Education:* Studied at the Madrid Conservatoire. *Career:* Debut: Théâtre de la Monnaie Brussels in the lyric baritone repertoire at opera houses in Brussels, Antwerp, Ghent and Liège; Guest engagements in Dortmund, Essen, Frankfurt, Hamburg, Stuttgart and Mannheim; Barcelona, Lisbon, Paris, Nice, Marseilles and Geneva, and at the Vienna Volksoper; Sang roles in operas by Donizetti, Bizet, Mozart, Puccini, Rossini, Massenet and Verdi; Wagner's Wolfram von Eschenbach and Tarquinius in Britten's The Rape of Lucretia; Wexford Festival 1973, in Donizetti's L'Ajo nell'imbarazzo (The Tutor in a Fix); Many concert appearances. *Address:* c/o Théâtre de la Monaie, 4 Leopoldstrasse, 1000 Brussels, Belgium.

**GOODALL, Howard (Lindsay);** Composer and Broadcaster; b. 26 May 1958, London, England. *Education:* Chorister, New College, Oxford; ARCO, 1975; Music Scholar, Christ Church, Oxford (MA Hons). *Career:* Composer TV themes and scores: Blackadder, Mr Bean, Vicar of Dibley, The Gathering Storm, The Borrowers, Red Dwarf; Composer and Performer in: Rowan Atkinson in Revue, the United Kingdom Tours 1977–87, World Tour 1982, West End, 1981, 1986, Broadway, 1986; TV programmes (writer and presenter); Howard Goodall's Big Bangs; Howward Goodall's Oragn Works; Howward Goodall's Chorla Works; Howward Goodall's Great Dates; BBC Choir of the Year; mem, BASCA; Liberal Club; PRS; MU; European Movement; Liberal Club. *Compositions:* Musicals: The Hired Man, with Melvyn Bragg, 1984; Girlfriends, 1987; Days of Hope, 1991; Silas Marner, 1991, The Kissing-Dance, 1999, The Dreaming, 2001; Choral: In Memoriam Anne Frank; Missa Aedis Christi; Psalm 23; Dover Beach, Jubilate Deo, I am not I, Marlborough Canticles, Salisbury Cantciles. *Honours:* Ivor Novello

Award, Best Musical, 1985; BAFTA Huw Weldon Award, 2001; Peabody Award for Journalism & Mass Communication; IMZ TV Best Arts Documentary Award; British Television Advertising Craft Award Best Original Music. *Current Management:* PBJ Management. *Address:* 7 Soho Square, London, W1D 3DQ, England. *Telephone:* (20) 7287-1112. *Website:* www.howardgoodall .co.uk.

**GOODALL, Valorie;** Singer (Soprano), Voice Teacher and Opera Director; b. 23 Sept. 1936, Waco, Texas, USA; m. William P Mooney, 21 Jan 1962, 2 s. *Education:* BM cum laude, Baylor University, 1958; MM, University of Colorado, 1959. *Career:* Debut: Graz Opera House, Austria; Leading Lyric Soprano, roles of Mimi, Micaela, Mélisande, Zdenka, Composer, Fiordiligi, Cherubino, Graz Opera; Performances at opera houses of Graz, Geneva, Bern, Theater an der Wien in Vienna, Prague; Star/producer, State museum tour of Venus and Adonis with early instruments, New Jersey, USA, 1981; Founder/ director of Opera at Rutgers; Performer in oratorio, song recital and musical theatre; Resident Stage Director: New England Lyric Operetta, Stamford, Conn. *Recordings:* Land des Lächelns by Lehar, opposite Giuseppe di Stefano, London Records. *Address:* Voice Department, Mason Gross School of the Arts, Rutgers University, New Brunswick, NJ 08903, USA.

**GOODE, Richard Stephen,** DipMus, BSc; American pianist; b. 1 June 1943, New York, NY; m. Marcia Weinfeld 1987. *Education:* Mannes Coll. of Music, Curtis Inst., studied with Nadia Reisenberg and Rudolf Serkin. *Career:* debut, New York Young Concert Artists 1962; Carnegie Hall recital début 1990; founding mem., Chamber Music Soc. of the Lincoln Center; mem. Piano Faculty, Mannes Coll. of Music 1969–; concerts and recitals in USA, Europe, Japan, South America, Australia, Far East; has played with Baltimore, Boston, Chicago, Cleveland, New York, Philadelphia, Berlin Radio, Finnish Radio and Bamberg Symphony Orchestras, New York, Los Angeles, Baltimore, Orpheus, Philadelphia, ECO and Royal Philharmonic Orchestras. *Honours:* Young Concert Artists Award, First Prize Clara Haskil Competition 1973, Avery Fischer Prize 1980, Grammy Award (with clarinettist Richard Stoltzman). *Current Management:* Frank Salomon Associates, 201 W 54th Street, Apt 1c, New York, NY 10019, USA. *Address:* 12 East 87th Street, Apt 5A, New York, NY 10128, USA (office).

**GOODING, Julia;** Singer (Soprano); b. 1965, England. *Education:* Studied at the Guildhall School. *Career:* Opera appearances at the Innsbruck Festival and the Opéra-Comique, Paris; Dido and Aeneas in Mexico; Concerts with such conductors as Malgoire, Minkowski, Leonhardt, Bruggen and Mackerras in Europe, North America and the Far East. *Recordings include:* King Arthur; Handel's Belshazzar; Handel's Teseo; Purcell Odes; Monteverdi's Orfeo; Blow Venus and Adonis. *Address:* c/o Ron Gonsalves Management, 7 Old Town, Clapham, London, SW4 0JT, England.

**GOODLOE, Robert;** Singer (Baritone); b. 5 Oct. 1936, St Petersburg, Florida, USA. *Education:* Studied at Simpson College Indianola (Iowa) and with Harvey Brown and Armen Boyajian. *Career:* Debut: Des Moines, Iowa, 1963, as Mozart's Figaro; Has sung principally at the Metropolitan Opera, also in Hartford, Baltimore, Philadelphia and San Francisco; Roles include Puccini's Scarpia, Michele and Marcello; Enrico (Lucia di Lammermoor); Mercutio in Roméo et Juliette; Germont in La Traviata and Paolo in Simon Boccanegra. *Address:* c/o Metropolitan Opera, Lincoln Center, NY 10023, USA.

**GOODMAN, Alfred;** Composer and Musicologist; b. 1 March 1920, Berlin, Germany; m. Renate Roessig, 14 July 1966, 1 s. *Education:* BS, Columbia College, New York; MA, Composition, Musicology, Columbia University; PhD, Technische Universität, Berlin. *Career:* Editor, Westminster Records, New York City; Composer, Movietone, New York City; Music Editor, Bavarian Broadcasting Commission; Lecturer, Academy of Music, Munich Service, 1971–; Lecturer, Academy of Music, College of Music, Munich, 1976–. Gave lecture at Arnold Schoenberg Symposium, Duisburg, Germany, 1993. *Compositions:* Psalm XII; The Audition, opera in 1 act; Pro Memoria for orchestra; Individuation, symphonic work; Chamber works, songs, choral compositions, television and film scores, orchestral works; The Lady and the Maid, opera in 1 scene; Across the Board for brass ensemble (for Locke Brass Consort, London); Brassology for Eleven (for Brunn Brass Ensemble, Czechoslovakia); Works for organ and brass; Timpani; Works for organ and saxophone, organ and flute or trumpet; Universe of Freedom-Orchestrology, 1991; Orchestrette in 7 parts, 1992; Orchesterology, 1994; Reflections: Manhattan Survey, for orchestra, 1997. *Publications:* Musik im Blut; Lexikon: Musik von A–Z; Die Amerikanischen Schuler Franz Liszts; Dictionary of Musical Terms, 1982. *Address:* Bodenstedt Strasse 31, 81241 Munich, Germany.

**GOODMAN, Craig (Stephen);** Flautist, Conductor and Educator; b. 6 July 1957, Pittsburgh, Pennsylvania, USA. *Education:* BA, Yale University, 1978; MM, Yale School of Music, 1979; Private study with Marcel Moyse and theory with Narcis Bonet. *Career:* Debut: Konzerthus, Vienna, Austria, 1975; Solo Flutist, Opera Company, Philadelphia, 1978–79; Freelance, American Symphony, New York City Ballet, St Luke's Chamber Orchestra, Musica Aeterna, 1979–86; Solo engagements, Australia, Europe, USA; Musical Director, The Players of the New World, New York; Chamber Music performances with L'Ensemble, New York City, Bach Aria Group, New York City and Ensemble i, Vienna, Austria; Solo videos of Bach and Gossec, WYNC Television, New York; Featured artist on Sunday Morning with Charles Kuratt, CBS television. *Recordings:* Bach Aria Group, Bach

Brandenburg Concerto No. 4 with James Buswell, Samuel Baron and Festival Strings, Ensemble I recording, Bach Trio Sonata in G for 2 flutes and continuo; Musical Heritage Society recording, Morton Gould's Concerto for wind quartet, piano and violin.

**GOODMAN, Erica;** Canadian harpist; b. 19 Jan. 1948, Toronto. *Education:* Royal Conservatory of Music, Toronto; National Music Camp, Interlochen, Michigan; Univ. of Southern California, Los Angeles; Curtis Institute of Music, Philadelphia. *Career:* debut, Alice Tully Hall-Lincoln Center, New York, 1972; child prodigy, accompanied opera singer Teresa Stratas on national television at the age of 13, 1961; played for Pres. Kennedy at the White House, 1962; youngest musician ever to join the Toronto Musicians' Asscn, 1962; mem. of Toronto and CBC Symphony Orchestras, 1962–66; conducted by Igor Stravinsky, 1964; soloist, Philadelphia Orchestra, 1968; toured Japan with flautist Robert Aitkin at invitation of Toru Takemitsu to perform his work, 1995; performed at the Royal Palace in Stockholm with horn player Sören Hermansson, 1996; one of the most active studio harpists on the continent and played on numerous scores of films, television and radio productions. *Recordings include:* Erica Goodman In Concert; Erica Goodman And Friends; The Virtuoso Harp; Flute and Harp; Erica Goodman Plays Canadian Harp Music; Horn And Harp Odyssey; Trio Lyra. *Address:* 9 York Ridge Road, Toronto, Ont., M2P 1R8, Canada. *E-mail:* erigo78@hotmail.com. *Website:* ericagoodman.tripod.com.

**GOODMAN, Roy,** FRCO, ARCM; British conductor, director and violinist; *Principal Conductor, Holland Symfonia;* b. 26 Jan. 1951, Guildford, Surrey; s. of Peter Goodman and Mary Sheena Goodman; m. 1st Gillian Dey 1970 (divorced) 1992; two s. one d.; m. 2nd Sally Jackson 1992 (divorced 1999). *Education:* chorister King's Coll., Cambridge, Royal Coll. of Music, Berkshire Coll. of Educ. *Career:* Head of Music, Alfred Sutton Boys' School, Reading 1971–74, Bulmershe Comprehensive School, Reading 1974–76; founder and Dir Brandenburg Consort 1975–2001; Sr String Tutor for Berkshire 1976–78; co-founder and Co-Dir The Parley of Instruments 1979–86; Dir of Music, Univ. of Kent, Canterbury 1986–87; Principal Conductor The Hanover Band 1986–94; Dir of Early Music, RAM 1987–89; Musical Dir European Union Baroque Orchestra 1988–2003; Principal Conductor Umeå Symphony Orchestra and Swedish Northern Opera 1994–99, Manitoba Chamber Orchestra, Winnipeg 1999–2005, Holland Symfonia, Amsterdam 2004–; Principal Guest Conductor English Chamber Orchestra 2004–; seven tours of USA 1988–94 including Lincoln Center and Carnegie Hall; Guest Conductor with Finnish and Swedish Radio, Lahti, Tampere, Ulster, Norrköping, Reykjavík and Stavanger Symphony Orchestras, Royal Liverpool and Rotterdam Philharmonic Orchestras, English Northern Philharmonia, Orchestre de Bretagne, New Queen's Hall Orchestra, Scottish, English, Swedish, Netherlands Radio, Netherlands, Geneva, Lausanne and Manitoba Chamber Orchestras, City of London Sinfonia, Västerås Sinfonietta, German Handel Soloists, Freiburg Baroque Orchestra, Netherlands Wind Ensemble and the Amsterdam Bach Soloists; conducted complete Beethoven Symphonies in Hannover, Handel's Tamerlano in Paris and Aldeburgh and with Opera North in Leeds, Scipione, Tamerlano, Ezio and Amadigi in Karlsruhe, Mozart's Bastien and Bastienne in Portugal, Don Giovanni in Belfast, La Clemenza di Tito for Flanders Opera, Gluck's Orfeo for ENO at the London Coliseum and Trädgården by Jonas Forssell at the Drottningholm Court Theatre in Sweden; revival of Arne's Artaxerxes, London 1995; conducted New Queen's Hall Orchestra at Barbican Hall, 1997, La Clemenza di Tito at Antwerp 1997. *Recordings:* as conductor, violinist and keyboard player, has directed some 100 recordings of repertoire ranging from Monteverdi to Holst, including major orchestral works by Purcell, Corelli, Bach and Handel, and the symphonies of Haydn, Beethoven, Schubert, Weber, Berwald and Schumann. *Honours:* Hon. DMus (Hull) 2002. *Address:* 217 Birchanger Lane, Birchanger, Bishops Stortford, Herts., CM23 5QJ, England. *Telephone:* (1279) 647467. *Fax:* (1279) 647466. *E-mail:* roy@roygoodman.com. *Website:* www.roygoodman.com.

**GOODWIN, (Trevor) Noël,** BA; British critic and writer on music and dance; b. 25 Dec. 1927, Fowey, Cornwall, England; m. Anne Mason Myers 1963; one step-s. *Career:* Assistant Music Critic: News Chronicle, 1952–54, Manchester Guardian, 1954–55; Music and Dance Critic, Daily Express, 1956–78; Associate Editor, Dance and Dancers, 1958–; Executive Editor, Music and Musicians, 1963–71; London Dance Critic, International Herald Tribune, Paris, 1978–83;Music Reviews, The Times, 1978–98; London Correspondent, Opera News, New York, 1980–91; Overseas News Editor, 1985–91, Editorial Board, 1991–99, Opera; Planned and presented numerous radio programmes of music and records for BBC Home and World Services since 1954; Frequent contributor to music and arts programmes on Radios 3 and 4. *Publications:* London Symphony, portrait of an orchestra, 1954; A Ballet for Scotland, 1979; A Knight at the Opera (with Geraint Evans), 1984; Royal Opera and Royal Ballet Yearbooks (editor), 1978, 1979, 1980; New Grove Dictionary of Music and Musicians (area editor, writer), 1980; A Portrait of the Royal Ballet (editor), 1988. *Contributions:* Numerous journals and magazines; Encyclopaedica Britannica, 15th edition, 1974; New Grove Dictionary of Music, 1980, 2000; Encyclopaedia of Opera, 1976; New Oxford Companion to Music, 1983; Pipers Enzyklopädie des Musiktheaters, 1986–91; New Grove Dictionary of Opera, 1992; Viking Opera Guide, 1993; International Dictionary of Ballet, 1993; Metropolitan Opera Guide to Recorded Opera, 1993; International Encyclopedia of Dance, 1998; Larousse Dictionnaire de la Danse, 2000; Oxford

Dictionary of National Biography 2004. *Address:* 76 Skeena Hill, London, SW18 5PN, England. *Telephone:* (20) 8788-8794.

**GOODWIN, Paul;** Conductor and Oboist; b. 2 Sept. 1956, England. *Education:* City of London School, Temple Church Choir, Nottingham University; Guildhall School of Music; Vienna Hochschule für Musik. *Career:* Associate Director of the Academy of Ancient Music; Director, Dartington Festival Baroque Orchestra and the Royal College of Music Baroque Orchestra; Principal Guest Conductor of the English Chamber Orchestra, 1998–2003; Guest engagements with Ulster Orchestra, Hallé, BBC Symphony Orchestra, Scottish Chamber Orchestra, RTE Dublin, CBSO, English Chamber Orchestra, Swedish Chamber Orchestra, Comiische Oper Berlin, Lyon opera Orchestra, Nurenburg Philharmonic, SWR Rundfunk Orchester, Hessiche Rundfunk Orchester, Orchestra National de Lille, European Baroque Orchestra, and in the USA with the Portland Baroque Orchestra and St Pauls Chamber Orchestra; Conducted staged production of the Bach St Matthew Passion in collaboration with Jonathan Miller; Opera productions include Karlsruhe Opera, Opernhaus Halle and Opera North and at the Megaron, Athens; Conducted Handel's Poro at Halle and Il Re Pastore at Leeds, 1998; London Proms 1999, with Haydn's 64th Symphony and excerpts from Handels Triumph of Time and Truth; Featured at the London Proms 1999, 2002 and 2004 with the Academy of Ancient Music. *Recordings:* Solo recordings on the oboe: (Bach, Telemann, Albinoni, Vivaldi, Haydn, Mozart); As a Conductor with the AAM (Mozart, Handel, Schütz and Tavener), Elgar's Nurdery Suite, Ikon of Gros (Taverner), Lotorio (Handel), CD of Christmas Music with SWR Kaiserslautern Orchestra. *Current Management:* Askonas Holt Ltd, Lonsdale Chambers, 27 Chancery Lane, London, WC2A 1PF, England. *Telephone:* (20) 7400-1700. *Fax:* (20) 7400-1799. *E-mail:* info@askonasholt.co.uk. *Website:* www.askonasholt.co.uk.

**GORBENKO, Pavel;** Violinist; b. 1956, Moscow, Russia. *Education:* Studied at Gnessin Music Institute with Dr Kiselyev. *Career:* Co-founder, Amistad Quartet, 1973, now Tchaikovsky Quartet; Many concerts in Russia with repertoire including works by Haydn, Mozart, Beethoven, Schubert, Brahms, Tchaikovsky, Borodin, Prokofeiv, Shostakovich, Bartók, Barber, Bucci, Golovin and Tikhomirov; Recent concert tours to: Mexico; Italy; Germany. *Recordings include:* Recitals for a US-Russian company. *Honours:* Winner with Amistad Quartet: Bela Bartók Festival, 1976; Bucchi Competition, Rome, 1990. *Address:* c/o Sonata (Tchaikovsky Quartet), 11 Northpark Street, Glasgow G20 7AA, Scotland.

**GORCHAKOVA, Galina Vladimirovna;** Russian singer (soprano); b. 1962, Novokuznetsk; m. Nikolai Petrovich Mikhalsky (divorced); one s. *Education:* Novosibirsk State Conservatory. *Career:* soloist Sverdlovsk (now Yekaterinburg) Theatre of Opera and Ballet 1987–91, Kirov (now Mariinsky) Theatre 1990–96; leading roles in opera productions Madam Butterfly, Prince Igor, The Invisible City of Kitezh, Queen of Spades, Aida, Don Carlos, Tosca, Cavalleria Rusticana; regularly performs in European and American opera theatre including Covent Garden (debut Renata, The Fiery Angel by Prokofiev 1991), La Scala, Metropolitan Opera, Opera Bastille, also in Tokyo. *Honours:* Merited Artist of Russia. *Address:* c/o Askonas Holt, Lonsdale Chambers, 27 Chancery Lane, London, WC2A 1PF, England. *Telephone:* (20) 7400-1700.

**GORDEI, Irina;** Singer (Soprano); b. 1968, Russia. *Education:* Graduated Byelorusia State Academy 1991. *Career:* Ekaterinburg Opera and Ballet Theatre from 1993, as Tosca, Aida, Amelia (Un ballo in Maschera), Lisa (The Queen of Spades) and Verdi's Elisabeth and Lady Macbeth; Teatro Comunale, Floreance, 1994 as Amelia (repeated at Vienna Staatsoper 1995); Appearances with Kirov Opera, St Petersburg, from 1999, including Verdi season at Covent Garden, 2001; Concert repertoire includes Verdi Requiem and works by Shostakovich (Festival Medal, 1997). *Honours:* Prizewinner, International F. Vignas Competition, Barcelona, 1993. *Address:* c/o Kirov Opera, Mariinsky Theatre, 1 Theatre Square, St Petersburg, Russia.

**GORDIEJUK, Marian (Stanislaw Wlodzimierz);** Composer, Music Theory Lecturer, Music Journalist and Musicologist; b. 9 Feb. 1954, Bydgoszcz, Poland; m. 2 July 1977, 1 s., 2 d. *Education:* State College of Music, Łódź, Pedagogic studies with Assistant Professor Antoni Kedra, 1976; Studies in Music Theory under Professor Franciszek Wesolowski, 1977; Studies in conducting vocal-instrumental groups with Professor Zygmunt Gzella, 1978; Studies in Composition, with Professor Jerzy Bauer, 1979. *Compositions include:* Suite, Birds, for two transverse flutes (Łódź) 1976, published: Edition Agencja Autorska Warszawa, 1986, Contemporary Polish Music, Series of Chamber Music Compositions; Games for flute and harp (Gdansk) 1987, recorded: Polskie Radio, Gdansk, 1987; Children's Quart Miniature for Oboe or Flute and Piano (Łódź) 1987, recorded: Telewizja Polska, Łódź, 1987; String Quartet (with amplifier) Gdansk, 1991. *Address:* ul Tczewska 12, 85-382 Bydgoszcz, Poland.

**GORDON, Alexandra;** Singer (Soprano); b. 1945, Dannevirke, New Zealand. *Education:* Studied at London Opera Centre and with Walter Midgley. *Career:* Debut: Sang First Boy in Die Zauberflöte and Despina in Così fan tutte for New Zealand Opera, aged 19; Sang with Opera for All at Glyndebourne and with Scottish Opera, notably as the Queen of Night and Flotow's Martha, and in The Nightingale by Stravinsky; Many concert appearances and radio broadcasts; Sang Delia in new production of Rossini's Il Viaggio a Reims, Covent Garden, 1992. *Honours:* Friends of Covent Garden Scholarship, at London Opera Centre. *Address:* c/o New Zealand National Opera, State Opera House, PO Box 6588, Tel Aro, Wellington, New Zealand.

**GORDON, David Jamieson;** American concert and opera singer (tenor); b. 7 Dec. 1947, Philadelphia; m. Barbara Bixby 1969. *Education:* College of Wooster, McGill University, Conservatoire de Quebec, Canada. *Career:* debut with Lyric Opera of Chicago, 1973; frequent appearances with North American and European orchestras and opera companies, including Metropolitan Opera, Lyric Opera of Chicago, San Francisco Opera, Hamburg Staatsoper, Boston Symphony, Philadelphia Orchestra, Cleveland Orchestra, Los Angeles Philharmonic; Specialist in music by J. S. Bach; Also appears regularly as master class teacher and lecturer; Bach Festivals of Bethlehem, Carmel, Oregon and Winter Park (USA) Stuttgart, Tokyo. *Recordings:* Bach Magnificat–R Shaw/Atlantic Symphony; Acis and Galatea, Seattle Symphony; Pulcinella, St Paul Chamber Orchestra; other recordings on Telarc, London Decca, Delos, RCA Red Seal and Nonesuch/Electra. *Current Management:* Thea Dispeker Inc, 59 East 54 Street, New York, NY 10022, USA. *Address:* 84 South Clinton Street, Doylestown, PA 18901, USA.

**GÓRECKI, Henryk Mikołaj;** Polish composer; b. 6 Dec. 1933, Czernica, nr Rybnik; s. of Otylia Górecka and Roman Górecki; m. Jadwiga Górecka 1959; one s. one d. *Career:* studied composition at State Higher School of Music, Katowice, under Boleslaw Szabelski; Docent, Faculty of Composition, State Higher School of Music, Katowice, Rector 1975–79, Extraordinary Prof. 1977–79. *Compositions include:* Four Preludes for piano 1955, Sonata No. 1 for piano, Op. 6 1956–90, 3 Diagrams for flute solo, Op. 15 1959, Diagram No. 4 for flute solo, Op.18 1961, Genesis cycle 1962–63, Scontri for large symphony orchestra 1960, Cantata for organ, Op. 26 1968, Old Polish Music 1969, Canticuum graduum for orchestra, Op. 27 1969, Symphony No. 1 "1959" for string orchestra and percussion, Op. 14 1959, Ad Matrem 1971, Symphony No. 2, Copernican 1972, Symphony No. 3 (Threnodies for soprano and orchestra) 1976 (more than 700,000 records sold), Beatus Vir 1979, Concerto for harpsichord (piano) and string orchestra, Op. 40 1980, Lerchenmusik (trio) 1984, Three Cradle Songs for unaccompanied mixed choir, Op. 49 1984, Totus Tuus for unaccompanied mixed choir, Op. 60 1987, Concerto-Cantata for flute and orchestra, Op. 65 1992, Quasi una Fantasia String Quartet No. 2, Op. 64 1992, Little Requiem for a Polka for piano and 13 instruments, Op. 66 1993, Valentine Piece for flute and little bell 1996, Three Fragments to Words of Stanisław Wyspianski for voice and piano 1996, Little Fantasy for violin and piano, Op. 73 1997, Salve Sidus Polonorum, Cantata of St Adalbert, Opus 72, for large mixed choir, two pianos, organ and percussion ensemble 1997–2000, String Quartet No. 3 1999, Niech nam żyją i śpiewają for vocal ensemble 2000. *Honours:* Dr hc (Acad. of Catholic Theology, Warsaw) 1993, (Warsaw Univ.) 1994, (American Catholic Univ., Washington, DC) 1995, (Ann Arbor Univ., Mich.) 1996, (Concordia Univ., Montreal) 1998; First Prize, Young Composers' Competition, Warsaw, for Monologhi 1960, Paris Youth Biennale, for 1st Symphony 1961, Prize, UNESCO Int. Tribune for Composers for Refrain 1967, for Ad Matrem 1973, First Prize, Composers' Competition, Szczecin, for Kantata 1968, Prize of Minister of Culture and Arts 1965, 1969, 1973, Prize of Union of Polish Composers 1970, of Cttee for Polish Radio and TV 1974, of Minister of Culture and Arts 1965, 1969, 1973, State Prize 1st class for Ad Matrem and Nicolaus Copernicus Symphony 1976, Award of the Ministry of Foreign Affairs 1992. *Address:* ul. H. A. Górnika 4 m.1, 40-133 Katowice, Poland. *Telephone:* (32) 258-17-58.

**GORITZKI, Ingo;** German oboist and academic; *Professor of Oboe, Staatliche Musikhochschule, Stuttgart;* b. Berlin. *Education:* Detmold Music Acad., studied flute with Gustav Schech, piano with E. Picht-Axenfeld, oboe with Helmut Winschermann. *Career:* fmr prin. oboist, Basel Symphony Orchestra, Frankfurt Radio Symphony Orchestra; apptd Prof., Staatliche Hochschule für Musik und Theater, Hannover 1976; currently Prof., Staatliche Musikhochschule, Stuttgart; co-founder, Musikalische Akademie Stuttgart; Artistic Dir Sommersprossen Festival, Rottweil; has appeared at numerous int. festivals, including Oregon Bach Festival, USA, Kasarsu Festival, Japan, Isang Yun Festival, Korea, Crusell Festival, Finland; gives masterclasses at Int. Bach Acad., Stuttgart and worldwide. *Recordings include:* Bach, Orchestral Suites Nos 1–3 1990, Hindemith, Sonatas, Vol. 5 1996, Oboe Concertos from Bohemia 1999, Mozart, Oboe Concertos 1999, R. Strauss, Wind Concertos 1999, Bach, Restored Oboe Concerti 2000, Bach, Oboe Works 2000, Bach, Sonatas, The Art of Fugue 2002. *Address:* Staatliche Musikhochschule, Raum 6.26, Landhausstr. 20, Stuttgart 70190, Germany (office). *E-mail:* ingogoritzki@netscape.net (office).

**GORMLEY, Clare;** Soprano; b. 1969, Australia. *Career:* Frequent concert and recital appearances throughout Australia and in Europe; Repertory includes Lieder by Mozart and Schumann, Bach's St Matthew Passion and Goyescas by Granados; Contestant at the 1995 Cardiff Singer of the World Competition; Season 1995–96 as Alexandra in the premiere of The Eighth Wonder, at Sydney and Gretel at Brisbane (also at the Met); Debut with Royal Opera, London, as Despina (1998, also at the New York Met). *Honours:* Winner, Metropolitan Opera Auditions. *Address:* c/o Jennifer Eddy Artists' Management, Suite 11, The Clivedon, 596 St Kilda Road, Melbourne, Victoria 3004, Australia.

**GÖRNE, Matthias;** German singer (baritone); b. 1966, Chemnitz. *Education:* in Leipzig from 1985, then with Dietrich Fischer-Dieskau and Elisabeth Schwarzkopf. *Career:* performed with the children's choir at Chemnitz Opera; sang in Bach's St Matthew Passion under Kurt Masur, Leipzig 1990; appearances with Hanns Martin Schneidt and Munich Bach Choir and with NDR Symphony Orchestra Hamburg; further engagements under Horst Stein, with Bamberg Symphony Orchestra and in Hindemith's Requiem under Wolfgang Sawallisch; concerts at Leipzig Gewandhaus under Helmuth Rilling and in Amsterdam and Paris; Lieder recitals with pianist Eric Schneider; sang title role in Henze's Prinz von Homburg, Cologne 1992, Marcello in La Bohème at Komische Oper, Berlin 1993, Wolfram in Tannhäuser, Cologne 1996, Die Schöne Müllerin, Bath 1997; engaged for Die Zauberflöte, Salzburg Festival 1997. *Recordings include:* Winterreise 1997, Entarte Musik. *Current Management:* IMG Artists, Lovell House, 616 Chiswick High Road, London W4 5RX, England.

**GOROKHOVSKAYA, Yevgena;** Singer (Mezzo-soprano); b. 1944, Baku, Russia. *Education:* Studied at Leningrad Conservatory. *Career:* Debut: Maly Theatre, Leningrad, as Lehl in The Snow Maiden by Rimsky-Korsakov, 1969; Member, Maryinsky Opera Leningrad (now St Petersburg), 1976–; Roles have included Lubasha in The Tsar's Bride by Rimsky, Eboli (Don Carlos) and Azucena; Guest appearances, Germany, Romania, Spain, France, Greece, USA, Switzerland, Czechoslovakia; On Tour to the United Kingdom, 1991, sang Mme Larina in Eugene Onegin at Birmingham and Marfa in Khovanshchina at Edinburgh Festival; Salzburg Easter Festival 1994 as the Nurse in Boris Godunov. *Recordings:* Several albums. *Address:* c/o Maryinsky Opera and Ballet Theatre, St Petersburg, Russia.

**GORR, Rita;** Singer (Mezzo-soprano); b. 18 Feb. 1926, Zelzaete, Belgium. *Education:* Studied in Ghent and at the Brussels Conservatory. *Career:* Debut: Antwerp 1949, as Fricka in Die Walküre; Strasbourg Opera 1949–52, as Orpheus, Amneris and Carmen; Paris Opéra-Comique and Opéra debuts 1952, as Charlotte (Werther) and as Magdalene in Die Meistersinger; Bayreuth Festival 1958, as Ortrud and Fricka; La Scala Milan 1960, as Kundry; Covent Garden 1959–71, debut as Amneris; Edinburgh Festival 1961 in Iphigénie en Tauride, with the Covent Garden company; Metropolitan Opera from 1962, as Amneris, Eboli, Santuzza, Azucena and Dalila; London Coliseum 1969, in a concert performance of Roussel's Padmavati (British premiere); Other roles have included Margared (Le Roi d'Ys), Massenet's Hérodiade, the title role in Médée by Cherubini and Didon in Les Troyens by Berlioz; Sang the Mother in Louise by Charpentier at Brussels, 1990; First Prioress in Dialogues des Carmélites at Lyon, 1990 followed by Herodias in Salome; Toronto 1997, in The Carmelites; Sang the Nurse in Eugene Onegin at Barcelona, 1998; Countess in Queen of Spades at Munich, 2001. *Recordings:* Pelléas et Mélisande; Dialogues des Carmélites, Iphigénie en Tauride; Aida, Lohengrin; Louise by Charpentier. *Honours:* Winner, Competition at Verviers, 1946; Winner, Lausanne International Singing Competition, 1952. 21. *Address:* c/o Opéra de Lyon, 9 Quai Jen Moulin, 69001 Lyon, France.

**GORRARA, Riccardo (Richard),** DipMus; classical guitarist, lutenist and conductor; b. 29 May 1964, Metz, France. *Education:* studied in Italy and England, Guildhall School of Music, Royal Academy of Music, Paris Music College. *Career:* debut in Genoa Cathedral, Italy; appeared in most European halls and festivals, Milan, Rome, Turin, London, Paris, Madrid; Paris Festival, Edinburgh Festival; mem, Royal Philharmonic Society; National Early Music Association; Lute Society; Dutch Lute Society; Brussels Philharmonique Society. *Compositions:* Varied; Music for guitar and lute from 15th Century to present, including Dowland, Frescobaldi, Ferrabosco, Couperin, Weiss, Bach, Sor, etc. *Recordings:* Various major recordings for guitar and lute, particularly works from 15th Century to 20th Century rarely played; 7 Gramophone recordings, also for radio broadcasting; Various national radio stations in Italy, Denmark, Switzerland. *Publications:* contrib. various reviews of Guitar and lute method, technique, interpretation for Italian guitar and music magazines.

**GORTON, Susan;** Singer (Mezzo-soprano); b. 1946, Cheshire, England. *Education:* Studied at the Royal Manchester College of Music. *Career:* Debut: Feklusha in Katya Kabanova for the Glyndebourne Tour, 1992; Further appearances with GTO, as Filippyevna in Eugene Onegin and Marcellina in Le nozze di Figaro; Glyndebourne Festival 1995–97, as the Chambermaid in The Makropulos Case; Further engagements as Mistress Quickly and Mrs Sedley in Peter Grimes, for English National Opera; Florence Pike in Albert Herring for English Touring Opera, Martha in Faust and Mamma Lucia in Cavalleria Rusticana for Welsh National Opera; Premieres include Julian Grant's A Family Affair for the Almeida Festival and The House of Crossed Desires by John Woolrich for Music Theatre Wales, 1996; Season 1997–98 as the Hostess in Boris Godunov and Grandmother in Jenůfa for WNO, and Mrs Sedley for the Lyric Opera, Chicago. Season 1998–99 Mrs Sedley in Peter Grimes and Mamma Lucia in Cavalleria Rusticana for Welsh National Opera and Chambermaid in The Makropulos Case for Gran Teatre del Liceu; Grandmother Burja in Jenůfa and Auntie in Peter Grimes for Glyndebourne Festival Opera, 2000; Countess in The Queen of Spades, Welsh National Opera, 2000; Mary in Der fliegende Holländer, Lyric Opera of Chicago, 2001; Mrs Herring, Glyndebourne Festival Opera, and Florence Pike, GTO, in Albert Herring, 2002. *Address:* c/o Harlequin Agency Ltd, 203 Fidlas Road, Cardiff CF4 5NA, Wales.

**GORTSEVSKAYA, Maria;** Singer (Mezzo-soprano); b. 1965, Russia. *Career:* Many appearances in solo recitals in France, Belgium, Germany and Spain; Mariinsky Theatre, St Petersburg, from 1990, as Siebel in Faust, Fyodor in Boris Godunov, Rossini's Rosina, Bizet's Mercédès and roles in The Fiery Angel and War and Peace; Sang Adjutant to Marshal Murat in War and Peace with the Kirov Opera at Covent Garden, 2000; Appearances as guest with the

Kirov in Japan and the USA (Metropolitan Opera). *Address:* c/o Kirov Opera, Mariinsky Square, St Petersburg, Russia.

**GORZYNSKA, Barbara,** MA; Polish violinist; b. 4 Dec. 1953, Cmielow; d. of Zygmunt and Janina (née Nowak) Gorzynski; m. Ryszard Rasinski 1982; one s. *Education:* Acad. of Music, Łódź. *Career:* debut with Great Symphony Orchestra of Polish Radio 1969; performances as soloist with London Philharmonic Orchestra, Royal Philharmonic Orchestra (UK), Staatskapelle Dresden (Germany), Warsaw Philharmonic Orchestra, English Chamber Orchestra, Halle Orchestra (Germany) 1981–; London debut Royal Festival Hall 1981; Prof. of Violin Acad. of Music, Łódź; Visiting Prof. Hochschule für Musik und Darstellende Kunst, Graz, Austria; recordings with Le Chant du Monde, WIFON, Polskie Nagrania. *Recordings include:* Chopin's Trio in G Minor 1986, Wieniawski's Pieces for Violin and Piano 1988, Mozart's Violin Concerto in D 1991. *Honours:* First Prize and Henryk Szeryng Special Prize Zagreb Int. Violin Competition 1977, First Prize Carl Flesch Int. Violin Competition 1980. *Address:* Sienkiewicza 101–109 m. 48, 90-301 Łódź, Poland.

**GOSMAN, Lazar;** Violinist and Conductor; b. 27 May 1926, Kiev, USSR; m. Eugenia Gosman, 16 April 1950, 1 s. *Education:* Central Music School, Moscow, 1934–44; Diploma, Honours, Tchaikovsky Conservatory of Music, Moscow, 1945–49. *Career:* Violinist, Leningrad Philharmonic Orchestra; Music Director, Leningrad Chamber Orchestra, 1962–77; Associate Concertmaster, St Louis Symphony, USA, 1977–82; Music Director, Tchaikovsky Chamber Orchestra, formerly Soviet Emigré Orchestra; Professor, Violin, State University of New York, Stonybrook. *Recordings:* Over 40 with Leningrad Chamber Orchestra; Two records with Tchaikovsky Chamber Orchestra. *Current Management:* Herbert Barrett Management, New York. *Address:* 3 East Gate Street, Setauket, NY 11733, USA.

**GOSSETT, Philip,** BA, MFA, PhD; American musicologist, academic and writer; *Robert W. Reneker Distinguished Service Professor, University of Chicago*; b. 27 Sept. 1941, New York, NY; m. Suzanne S. Gossett 1963; two s. *Education:* Amherst Coll., Columbia Univ., Princeton Univ. *Career:* Asst Prof., Univ. of Chicago 1968–73, Assoc. Prof. 1973–77, Prof. 1977–84, Chair Dept of Music 1978–84, 1989, Robert W. Reneker Distinguished Service Prof. 1984–, Dean Division of Humanities 1989–99; Visiting Assoc. Prof., Columbia Univ. 1975; Direttore dell'edizione, Edizione critica delle Opere di Gioachino Rossini 1978–; Meadows Visiting Prof., Southern Methodist Univ. 1980; General Ed., Works of Giuseppe Verdi 1981–; Assoc. Prof., Universitá degli Studi, Parma 1983, and Rome 1994; Visiting Prof., Univ. of Paris 1988; Five-Coll. Visiting Prof. 1989; Gauss Seminars, Princeton Univ. 1991; 'Consulenza musicologica', Verdi Festival, Parma 2000–; Hambro Visiting Prof. of Opera Studies, Univ. of Oxford 2001; Visiting Scholar, Phi Beta Kappa 2002–03; Fellow American Acad. of Arts and Sciences 1989; Woodrow Wilson Fellowship 1963–64; Fulbright Scholar, Paris 1965–66; Martha Baird Rockefeller Fellowship 1967–68; Guggenheim Fellowship 1971–72; Nat. Endowment for the Humanities Sr Fellowship 1982–83; mem. American Inst. of Verdi Studies, American Musicological Soc. (pres. 1994–96), Int. Musicological Soc., Società Italiana di Musicologia, Soc. for Textual Scholarship (pres. 1993–95). *Publications:* The Operas of Rossini: Problems of Textual Criticism in Nineteenth-Century Opera (two vols) 1970, Treatise on Harmony, by Jean-Philippe Rameau (trans. and ed.) 1971, The Tragic Finale of Tancredi 1977, Early Romantic Opera (ed. with Charles Rosen) 1978–83, Le Sinfonie di Rossini 1981, Rossini Tancredi (critical edn) 1983, Italian Opera 1810–1840 (ed., 25 vols) 1984–92, 'Anna Bolena' and the Maturity of Gaetano Donizetti 1985, Il barbiere di Siviglia 1992, Rossini Ermione (with P. Brauner) 1995, Don Pasquale 1999, Semivanide (with A. Zedda) 2001; contrib. to reference works, scholarly books and professional journals. *Honours:* Hon. DHL (Amherst Coll.) 1993; hon. mem. Accademia Filarmonica di Bologna 1992, Accademico Onorario Accademia di Santa Cecilia Rome 2003; American Musicological Soc. Alfred Einstein Award 1969, Medaglio d'Oro prima classe, Italy 1985, American Acad. of Composers, Authors and Publishers Deems Taylor Award 1986; Grand Ufficiale dell'Ordine al Merito 1997, Cavaliere di Gran Croce 1998, Order of Rio Branca, Brazil 1998, Socio Straniero, Ateneo Veneto 2001. *Address:* c/o Department of Music, University of Chicago, 1010 E 59th Street, Chicago, IL 60637, USA. *E-mail:* phgs@midway.uchicago.edu.

**GOTHONI, Ralf;** Finnish pianist, conductor and composer; b. 2 May 1946, Rauma; m. Elina Vähälä; two s. *Education:* Sibelius Academy, Helsinki; Folkwang-Hochschule, Essen. *Career:* Soloist with leading orchestras worldwide, guest at major festivals; Debut: Jyvaskyla Festival; Principal Guest Conductor, Turku Philharmonic, 1994–2000; Principal Conductor, English Chamber Orchestra, 2000–; Music Dir Northwest Chamber Orchestra, Seattle, 2001–; Prof. for chamber music, Musikhochschule Hamburg, 1986–96; Hanns Eisler-Hochschule Berlin, 1996–2000; Sibelius-Acad. Helsinki, 1992–; Guest Prof., Royal College of Music, London, 2000–. *Compositions:* 3 chamber operas, chamber music and songs. *Recordings:* more than 100 recordings including music by Britten; Piano concerto, Rautavaara; 2 piano concertos, Villa Lobos; Chorus XI Schubert; Chamber music and piano sonatas, Brahms; Piano quartets; music by Sallinen and Schnittke, etc. *Publications:* Book, The Moment of Creativity, 1997, Does the Moon Rotate, 2001, Piano book, 2003. *Honours:* Gilmore Award, 1994; Pro Finlandia medal, 1992; Schubert medal, 1977.

**GOTSINDER, Mikhail;** Violinist; b. 1950, Moscow, Russia. *Education:* Studied at Moscow Conservatoire with David Oistrakh. *Career:* Co-founder, Amistad Quartet, 1973, now Tchaikovsky Quartet; Many concerts in Russia with repertoire including works by Haydn, Mozart, Beethoven, Schubert, Brahms, Tchaikovsky, Borodin, Prokofiev, Shostakovich, Bartók, Barber, Bucci, Golovin and Tikhomirov; Recent concert tours to: Mexico; Italy; Germany. *Recordings include:* Recitals for a US-Russian company; All Tchaikovsky's quartet works. *Honours:* Winner with Amistad Quartet: Bela Bartók Festival, 1976; Bucchi Competition, Rome, 1990. *Address:* c/o Sonata (Tchaikovsky Quartet), 11 Northpark Street, Glasgow G20 7AA, Scotland.

**GOTTLIEB, Gordon;** Percussionist, Conductor and Composer; b. 23 Oct. 1948, Brooklyn, NY, USA. *Education:* total musicianship with James Wimer, 1961–71; High School of Performing Arts, 1966; timpani and percussion with Saul Goodman, 1966–71; BMus, 1970, MMus, 1971, Juilliard School of Music. *Career:* extensive performing with New York Philharmonic, including solo appearances in 1974 and 1986; commissioning and performing new works for piano and percussion with brother Jay, active in contemporary music and has played with Contemporary Chamber Ensemble, Speculum Musicae, the Juilliard Ensemble, the Group for Contemporary Music and others; as conductor performed the New York premiere of Vesalii Icones by Peter Maxwell Davies and made his Carnegie Hall debut conducting William Walton's Facade with Anna Russell narrating, 1981; conducted Histoire du Soldât of Stravinsky with L'Ensemble and Shaker Loops of John Adams at the Santa Fe Chamber Musical Festival, 1986; performed with Stevie Wonder, Ray Charles, Patti LaBelle, Tony Bennett, Paula Abdul, Michael Bolton, Bette Midler, Sarah Vaughan, Quincy Jones, Al Jarreau, Paul Winter; mem. Percussive Arts Society, NARAS, Recording Musicians' Asscn. *Compositions:* Graines gemellaires, improvisation 1; Traversées, improvisation 2, Saudades do Brasil; The River Speaker; Improvisations with Jay Gottlieb; Ritual Dancer; Fanfare, with Paul Winter; various jingles. *Recordings:* History, Michael Jackson; Kingdom of the Sun, film with Sting; Bulletproof Heart, with Grace Jones; A Secret Life, with Marianne Faithfull; Romulus Hunt, My Romance, with Carly Simon; Sostice Live!, Prayer for the Wild Things, with Paul Winter; Pete, Pete Seeger; many films and jingles; Bartók, Sonata for 2 Pianos; Histoire du Soldât, I Stravinsky; Two Against Nature, Steely Dan (four Grammy awards, including Album of the Year 2001); Everything Must Go, Steely Dan, 2003. *Publications:* The Percussion of Carnival, for Modern Percussionist magazine, 1984; World Influences: Africa and South India, 1985; three articles on studio playing, 1985. *Honours:* Martha Baird Rockefeller Grant, 1980; four Grammy Awards, including for Paul Winters, Prayer for the Wild Things, 1994, Pete Seeger, Pete; NARAS Most Valuable Player Award, New York Studios, 1989; Meet the Composer Grant, 1989. *E-mail:* gorgot@earthlink.net.

**GOTTLIEB, Jack S.,** BA, MFA, DMA; American composer; b. 12 Oct. 1930, New Rochelle, NY. *Education:* Queens Coll., NY, Brandeis Univ., Univ. of Illinois, Berkshire Music Center with Aaron Copland, Boris Blacher; studied composition with Karol Rathaus, Irving Fine, Robert Palmer and Bun-ill Phillips. *Career:* encouraged to become a composer by Max Helfman; Asst to Leonard Bernstein, New York Philharmonic 1958–66; taught at Loyola Univ., New Orleans 1966; Music Dir, Temple Israel, St Louis 1970–73; in residence nine times at MacDowell Colony, Peterborough, NH, once at Yaddo, Saratoga Springs, NY 1960s–70s; Composer-in-Residence, Hebrew Union Coll. 1973, Prof. at its New York School of Sacred Music 1975; Publs Dir, Amberson Enterprises 1977; consultant, Bernstein Estate and Ed. Prelude, Fugue & Riffs, the Bernstein Newsletter; fmr Pres. American Soc. for Jewish Music; f. Theophilous Music, Inc. 1978; fmr Pres. American Soc. for Jewish Music; reviewer and author of articles on musical topics; annotator for concert programs and recordings; his lectures, From Shtetl to Stage Door, and Sing Along –The Jewish Influence on Tin Pan Alley, form the basis for Funny, It Doesn't Sound Jewish, a lecture-entertainment presented more than 50 times at Library of Congress, Smithsonian Institution, Village Gate, New York, various univs and Jewish centres, and various venues in Israel and Canada; mem. ASCAP. *Compositions include:* orchestral works: Articles of Faith for orchestra and memorable voices 1965, Psalmistry 1979, Scenes from the Song of Songs (cantata) 1997; chamber works: String Quartet (prize winner in a BMI, Inc. competition) 1954, Twilight Crane for woodwind quintet and narrator 1961, revised 2000, Letting Go, Vocalise for Soprano Saxophone or Flute and Piano 1997, Fantasy on High Holy Day Themes for Solo Violoncello 1998, Sessionals for Brass Quintet 1998; piano and organ: Piano Sonata 1960, The Silent Flickers, 13 Diversions for one piano four-hands 1968, revised 1996, Two Interludes: Travel to the Garden and The Family Together 1996, A Rag, A Bone and A Hank of Hair (3 pieces) 2000, Gershwin Medley: 3 by 2 for piano four-hands 2000; choral: Quodlibet: Kids' Calls for chorus and piano (First Prize, Nat. Fed. of Music Clubs Contest) 1957, In Memory Of... (cantata) (First Prize, Brown Univ. Contest) 1960, Love Songs for Sabbath, Friday Evening Service 1965, Shout for Joy, Psalm settings 1967, New Year's Service for Young People 1970, Verses from Psalm 118 1973, Sharing the Prophets, A Musical Happening 1975, setting of the entire Biblical The Song of Songs 1976, Set Me As A Seal, with violin or flute and piano 1976, revised 1991, Two Affirmations, with keyboard or brass sextet 1976, Psalmistry, for Choir, Soloists and Jazz Ensemble 1979 (revised), Presidential Suite (seven pieces for a capella chorus) 1989, May the Words (a Cappella), Two Nigunim for Two-Part Singing, Your Hand, O God, Has Guided 1999, Grant Us Peace (anthem) 2000, In the Palace of Time 2004; song cycles: Yes is a pleasant country (song cycle on poems of E. E. Cummings) 1998, Songs of Godlove (two-vol. set of 51 solos and duets including some of the following listed titles: Hoofprints, 3 songs (Tennessee Williams 1954), Two Blues for voice and clarinet (Williams 1954), Heavenly Grass (Williams, revised 2000), Downtown

Blues for Uptown Halls, 3 songs for female voice, clarinet and piano (words by the composer 1967, revised 1999), Three Night Songs: May We Lie Down (Gates of Prayer 1973), Acquainted With the Night (Robert Frost 1975) and It Is Evening (Gates of Prayer 1977), I Think Continually (Stephen Spender 1978) and Light and Splendour for voice, flute and clarinet (Leonard Cohen 1981) 2004, two cabaret song cycles, words by the composer: Solitaire and Scrapbook 1988–91, incidental music for Twelfth Night (Gallery Players 1995), and the cycles: Songs of Loneliness (7 poems of Constantine Cavafy 1962), Haiku Souvenirs (5 poems by Leonard Bernstein 1967), and yes is a pleasant country (13 poems of E. E. Cummings 1999); other stage works: one-act operas: Tea Party (libretto by Erik Johns) (Winner, Ohio Univ. opera competition, Nat. Fed. of Music Clubs Award 1955), The Movie Opera (words by the composer) 1982, revised 1994, Death of a Ghost (based on The Canterville Ghost 1988), musical theatre works also include The English Lesson, a scene from Shakespeare's Henry V 1993, Monkey Biz'nis, A Musical Diversion in one act for three male singers 1991–93, and After the Flood, A Musical Journey in Two Acts for a cast of six (SATTBB) 1990–91, revised 2001. *Recordings:* Evening, Morn & Noon – The Sacred Music of Jack Gottlieb 1991, Presidential Suite with the Gregg Smith Singers 1994, and with the Carolina Chamber Choir, Conductor Timothy Koch, Love Songs for Sabbath and six other choral works with four different choirs and Tovah Feldshuh as Reader, Monkey Biz'nis. *Publications:* Leonard Bernstein, Young People's Concerts (ed.) 1992, Funny, It Doesn't Sound Jewish: How Yiddish Songs and Synagogue Melodies Influenced Tin Pan Alley, Broadway and Hollywood 2004; numerous writings on Bernstein and other musical topics. *Honours:* Hon. mem. American Conf. of Cantors 2003; Center for Jewish Creativity and Culture Ahad Ha'am Award 1993; awards from Brown and Ohio Univs . *Address:* c/o ASCAP, ASCAP Building, 1 Lincoln Plaza, New York, NY 10023, USA. *E-mail:* Theophi@ix.Netcom.com. *Website:* www.jackgottlieb.com.

**GOTTLIEB, Jay (Mitchell);** American pianist and composer; b. 23 Oct. 1954, New York. *Education:* BA, Hunter College, 1970; MA, Harvard University, 1972; Chatham Square Music School, New York; Conservatoire Americain de Fontainebleau, France with Nadia Boulanger; Festivals of Tanglewood and Darmstadt with Messiaen, Loriod, Ligeti, Kontarsky. *Career:* Recitals in New York: Alice Tully Hall, Merkin Hall, Carnegie Recital Hall, Third Street Settlement, Cooper Union, Radios WQXR, WNYC, New York University, Theatre des Champs-Elysées, Centre Pompidou, Paris, Alte Oper, Frankfurt; Soloist with Boston Symphony, Orchestra Della Radiotelevisione in Italy, Nouvel Orchestre Philharmonique, Paris, L'Orchestre Philharmoni-que d'Europe, Paris, L'Orchestre du Rhin, Geneva and radio and television in New York, Boston, Washington, Paris, Switzerland, Frankfurt, Cologne, Rome; Festivals of Berlin, Rome, Milan, Venice, Paris, Almeida, Aldeburgh, Autumn in Warsaw, Musica in Strasburg, Avignon, Toulouse, Frankfurt, Amsterdam; International Piano Festival of La Roque d'Anthéron, France, Int. Keyboard Inst. and Festival, New York; Guest Prof., Paris Conservatory, France, Music School of Indiana Univ., Bloomington. *Compositions:* Syn-chronisms for two percussionists and tape; Sonata for violin and piano; Improvisations for piano and percussion; Essay for orchestra; Soundtrack for film, La Discrète. *Recordings:* Trois Contes de L'Honorable Fleur of Maurice Ohana; Lys de Madrigaux; Piano and Percussion-Jay and Gordon Gottlieb; Appello of Barbara Kolb; Harawi of Messiaen; Figure of Michèle Reverdy; La Discrète, soundtrack; Arcane of Allain Gaussin; Concord Sonata of Ives; Piano Works of John Adams; Piano Sonata of Solbiati; Piano Works of John Cage; Recital, 2003, for Signature series Radio-France; Jazz Connotation of Bruno Mantovani, Piano Music of Nicolas Obouhov. *Publication:* 10 Ans avec le Piano du XXe siècle 1998. *Honours:* C. D. Jackson Prize, Berkshire Music Center Tanglewood 1975, First Prize, Int. Improvisation Competition, Lyons, France 1976, Martha Baird Rockefeller Foundation Grant 1980, Nat. Endowment for the Arts Grant 1980, Laureate, Yehudi Menuhin Foundation 1982, Grand Prix du Disque 1995, 2002, 2004, Recording of the Month, Le Monde de la Musique 1998, 1999, 2000, Diapason d'or 2001. *Address:* 29–31 Rue des Boulets, 75011 Paris, France. *Telephone:* 1-43-48-59-71. *Fax:* 1-43-48-58-30. *E-mail:* jaygottlieb@freesurf.fr (office). *Website:* www.jaygottlieb.freesurf.fr (office).

**GOTTLIEB, Peter;** Singer (Baritone); b. 18 Sept. 1930, Brno, Czechoslova-kia. *Education:* Studied in Rio de Janeiro and in Florence with Raoul Frazzi. *Career:* Sang at first in Italy, Belgium and North America; Paris Opéra in 1962 premiere of L'Opéra d'Aran by Becaud and as Don Giovanni, Figaro, Papageno, Scarpia and Wozzeck, 1985; Glyndebourne Festival 1966–79 as Albert in Werther, Barber in Die schweigsame Frau, Mercurio in the first modern performance of Cavalli's Calisto, (1970) and Zastrow in the premiere of The Rising of the Moon by Nicholas Maw; Théâtre de la Monnaie Brussels 1983, in the premiere of La Passion de Gilles by Boesmans; Opéra du Rhin Strasbourg in 1984 premiere of H H Ulysses by Jean Prodromidès; Other roles include Iago, Don Carlos in La Forza del Destino and the Count in Capriccio; Professor, Paris Conservatoire from 1982. *Recordings include:* La Calisto (Decca); Opéra D'Aran (Pathe); La Passion de Gilles (Ricercare); H H Ulysses (Harmonia Mundi); La Cocarde de Mimi Pinson (Decca); La Traviata (Sofca). *Address:* 361 rue Lecourbe, 75015 Paris, France.

**GÖTZ, Cornelia;** Singer (soprano); b. 2 March 1965, Waiblingen, Germany. *Education:* Studied in Karlsruhe, Vienna and Munich. *Career:* First major role as Mozart's Zaide, at the Munich Staatsoper; Appearances as the Queen of Night in Die Zauberflöte throughout Germany and at the Wiener Festwochen; Nuremberg Opera 1992–94, as Mozart's Serpetta and Zerlina, Suppe's

Galathée, and Rosina; Further roles include Mozart's Papagena, Blondchen and Constanze; Adele in Die Fledermaus and Olympia; First Flower Maiden in Parsifal at Covent Garden; Sang in Zimmermann's Die Weisse Rose at the Vienna Odeon, 1998; Concerts include Bach Passions, Messiah, Haydn Creation and Seasons, Mozart's C Minor Mass, and Carmina Burana; Schoenberg's Herzgewäcsche and Second String Quartet with Bavarian Radio; Season 1999–2000 as Constanze at Kassel and Frasquita in Carmen for the Deutsche Oper Berlin. *Current Management:* Athole Still International Management, Forresters Hall, 25–27 Westow Street, London, SE19 3RY, England. *Telephone:* (20) 8771-5271. *Fax:* (20) 8768-6600. *Website:* www .atholestill.com.

**GÖTZ, Werner;** Singer (Tenor); b. 7 Dec. 1934, Berlin, Germany. *Education:* Studied with Friedrich Wilcke and W Kelch in Berlin. *Career:* Debut: Oldenburg 1967, as Alvaro in La Forza del Destino; Sang in Düsseldorf, Karlsruhe, Munich, Stuttgart and Hamburg; Roles included Wagner's Erik, Lohengrin and Parsifal, Mozart's Tamino, Lionel in Martha by Flotow and parts in operas by Puccini, Janáček and Verdi; Further engagements in London, Zürich, Łódź, Barcelona, Amsterdam and Frankfurt; Munich Opera 1978, in the premiere of Lear by Reimann; Karlsruhe Opera until 1984. *Recordings include:* Lear (Deutsche Grammophon); Melot in Tristan und Isolde; Eine Florentinische Tragödie by Zemlinsky (Fonit-Cetra). *Address:* c/o Bayerische Staatsoper, Postfach 745, 8000 Munich 1, Germany.

**GÖTZEN, Guido;** Singer (Bass); b. 1959, Düsseldorf, Germany. *Education:* Studied in Cologne with Joseph Metternich. *Career:* Sang first at the Cologne Opera Studio and at Berne, as Angelotti in Tosca, the Major Domo in Capriccio, Hobson in Peter Grimes, and Sarastro, 1988–89; Bayerische Staatsoper Munich, as the King in Aida, Colline, Masetto and roles in Palestrina, Meistersinger, Mathis der Maler, Parsifal, Orff's Trionfi, Dvořák's Dimitri and The Love for Three Oranges, 1989–94; Zürich Opera as Sparafucile in Rigoletto (under Nello Santi), Mozart's Commendatore and Sarastro, and the Bonze in Madama Butterfly, from 1994; Zürich Opera 2000 as Lamoral in Arabella and Schigolch in Lulu. *Recordings include:* Die Meistersinger, conducted by Sawallisch. *Honours:* Prizewinner at the Belvedere Competition, 1987. *Address:* c/o Opernhaus Zürich, Falkenstrasse 1, 8008 Zürich, Switzerland.

**GOULD, Clio;** British violinist; b. 1968, England. *Education:* studied with Emanuel Hurwitz, Pauline Scott and Igor Ozim. *Career:* concerto debut at Royal Festival Hall, aged 17; recitalist and soloist at Bath, Cheltenham, Harrogate, Spitalfields (London) and Huddersfield festivals; Artistic Dir of the BT Scottish Ensemble –2004; currently principal violinist of the London Sinfonietta; concerto soloist with the Ulster Orchestra; Nat. Symphony Orchestra of Ireland and Royal Philharmonic (Barbican Hall, London); Proms debut 1999, with Inside Story by Piers Hellawell; Festival d'Automne, Paris, and chamber recitals in Japan; season 2000–01 with European tour of the Weill Concerto (London Sinfonietta) and concertos with the London Philharmonic Orchestra, Ulster Orchestra and Royal Scottish Nat. Orchestra; plays "Rutson" Stradivarius of 1694. *Recordings include:* Tears of the Angels, by John Tavener. *Honours:* Hon. RAM 1999. *Address:* c/o London Sinfonietta, Third Floor, Dominion House, 101 Southwark Street, London SE1 0JF, England. *Telephone:* (20) 7928-0828. *Fax:* (20) 7928-8557. *E-mail:* info@ londonsinfonietta.org.uk. *Website:* www.londonsinfonietta.org.uk.

**GOWLAND, David;** British music coach; b. 1953. *Education:* Royal Coll. of Music and Nat. Opera Studio, London. *Career:* mem., Glyndebourne music staff 1987, as repetiteur and asst conductor in a wide repertory; Paris Opéra with La Clemenza di Tito and La Bohème, pianist in Porgy and Bess; Head of Music Staff at the Geneva Opera 1989–96, and appointments with Royal Danish Opera, Netherlands Opera, Covent Garden and Dublin Grand Opera; Festivals of Aix, Orange and Wexford; Weill's Threepenny Opera at RADA, London; concerts include Edinburgh and Aldeburgh Festivals, London Proms and BBC orchestras; season 1997–98 with The Ring in Australia, and Tristan, Idomeneo and Lohengrin in Copenhagen; Lucia di Lammermoor, Turandot and Porgy and Bess at Orange; La Traviata for the Opéra Bastille, Paris; Chief Coach of the Vilar Young Artists' Programme, Royal Opera House; visiting tutor, Nat. Opera Studio. *Honours:* Jani Strassi Award, Glyndebourne 1988. *Address:* c/o National Opera Studio, The Clore Building, 2 Chapel Yard, Wandsworth High Street, London, SW18 4HZ, England.

**GRAEBNER, Eric Hans;** Composer, Pianist, Lecturer and Conductor; b. 8 Jan. 1943, Berrington, England; one s. *Education:* MA, Cambridge University; PhD, York University; ARCO. *Career:* Lecturer in Music, University of Southampton, 1968–98; Visiting Fellow, Princeton, New Jersey, USA, 1973, 1981–82, 1983; Assistant Professor, William Paterson College, New Jersey, 1981–82; Director, Resurge Studio, 1998–; mem, EMAS (Sonic Arts Network), PRS; NMB (New Music Brighton). *Compositions:* Thalia, 1975; Between Words, 1976; String Quartet No. 1, 1979; String Quartet, No. 2, 1984; 4 Songs and an Aria, 1980; Aspects of 3 Tetrachords, 1973 Quintet, 1981; La mer retrouvée, 1985–86; 3rd Quartet, 1985; Dollbreaker, 1987; Trapeze Act, 1988; Berenice, 1990–91; Introduction and Passacaglia, 1993; Venus in Landscape, 1995; Resurge, 1997; Conversation with Clarinet, 1999; Morphologies, 2001; Wind Quintet, 2002; Naughty Plautus, 2002. *Recordings include:* Divertimento of the Statues, 1993; Resurge, 1997; Venus in Landscape; 1998; Fulminar, 1998. *Publications:* New Berlioz Edition, 1971–72. *Contributions:* Soundings; Perspectives of New Music; In Theory Only; Music Analysis. *Honours:* Fulbright-Hayes Fellowship, 1973; Dio Award, 1977; Fellow,

Salzburg Seminar of American Studies, 1976. *Address:* Resurge Studio, 30 Dyke Road Drive, Brighton, East Sussex, BN1 6AJ, England.

**GRAEME, Peter;** Oboist; b. 17 April 1921, Petersfield, England; m. Inge Anderl 1952; one s., three d. *Education:* Royal College of Music. *Career:* London Philharmonic Orchestra, from 1938; Military service 1942–46, then freelance oboist; First Oboe in various orchestras including Kalmar Orchestra; Haydn Orchestra; Boyd Neel Orchestra; Philomusica; Goldsborough Orchestra; English Chamber Orchestra; Melos Ensemble of London; Oboe Professor, Royal College of Music, 1949–91; Royal Northern College of Music, 1974–90; mem, Musicians Union. *Recordings:* Various with Kalmar Orchestra, Melos Ensemble of London, English Chamber Orchestra. *Honours:* Hon. ARCM 1959, FRCM 1979, FRNCM 1989. *Address:* 32 Bimport, Shaftesbury, Dorset, SP7 8AZ, England.

**GRAF, Hans;** Austrian conductor and administrator; b. 15 Feb. 1949, Linz. *Education:* Bruckner Conservatory, Linz, Academy of Music, Graz. *Career:* Music Dir Iraqi Nat. Symphony Orchestra 1975, Mozarteum Orchestra, Salzburg 1984–94, Calgary Philharmonic Orchestra 1995–, Nat. Orchestre de Bordeaux-Aquitaine 1998–, Opéra de Bordeaux 1998–, Houston Symphony Orchestra 2001–; guest conductor with several orchestras including Vienna Symphony, Vienna Philharmonic, Orchestre Nat. de France, Leningrad Philharmonic, Pittsburgh Symphony, Boston Symphony. *Honours:* First Prize, Karl Böhm Conductors Competition, Salzburg 1979. *Address:* Brunnhausgasse 21, 5020 Salzburg, Austria.

**GRAF, Judith;** Singer (Soprano); b. 1967, Switzerland. *Education:* Studied in Zürich, at Juilliard, New York and London. *Career:* Sang at Biel Opera from 1989 in Gianni Schicchi and as Donna Elvira, Monteverdi's Poppea, Anne Trulove, Pamina, Fiordiligi, Mozart's Vitellia, the Composer in Ariadne and Tchaikovsky's Tatiana; Pforzheim, 1991 as Marguerite in Faust; Landstheater Slazburg, 1993 in the premiere of Glaube, Liebe, Hoffnung by G Schedle; Biel 1995 as Sonja in Der Zarewitsch; Concert appearances throughout Switzerland. *Address:* Biel Opera, Burggasse 19, 2502 Biel, Switzerland.

**GRAF, Maria;** Singer (Mezzo-soprano); b. 1929, Germany. *Education:* Studied at the Vienna Academy with Anny Konetzni. *Career:* Sang in the chorus of the Vienna Staatsoper, 1950–55, solo debut at Innsbruck, 1955; Sang at Munster and Frankfurt, then Karlsruhe Opera, 1969–69; Guested at Bayreuth, 1955 (as Flosshilde and Rossweise) and Italy in operas by Wagner (Die Walküre at La Scala, 1963); Sang Helen in the German premiere of Tippett's King Priam, 1963; Other roles included Mozart's Marcellina, Herodias in Salome, Marie (Wozzeck) and Mistress Quickly (Falstaff); Teatro La Fenice, Venice, 1968, in the Ring.

**GRAF, Peter-Lukas;** Flautist and Conductor; b. 5 Jan. 1929, Zürich, Switzerland. *Education:* Studied at the Paris Conservatoire with Marcel Moyse (flute) and Eugene Bigot (conducting). *Career:* First flautist with the Winterthur Orchestra, 1951–57; Conductor at the Lucerne State Theatre 1961–66; Played in the Lucerne Festival Orchestra 1957–, and toured as soloist with the Edwin Fischer and Gunther Ramin; Performances with the English Chamber Orchestra, the Academy of St Martin in the Fields and the Lucerne Festival Strings; As Soloist and Conductor, tours of Europe, South America, Australia, Japan and Israel; Teacher at the Basle Conservatory 1973–. *Recordings include:* Spohr Concertante for violin, harp and orchestra; Bach A minor Triple Concerto and Saint-Saëns A minor Concerto (English Chamber Orchestra); Mozart Flute Concertos and Concerto K299 (Lausanne Chamber Orchestra); Swiss music with Orchestra della Radio Svizzera, and the Zürich Tonhalle. *Honours:* First prizes in flute and conducting, Paris Conservatoire, 1950, 1951; Winner, International ARD Competition, 1953; Bablock Prize, Harriet Cohen International Music Award, London, 1958.

**GRAFFMAN, Gary;** American pianist; b. 14 Oct. 1928, s. of Vladimir and Nadia (Margdin) Graffman; m. Naomi Helfman 1952. *Education:* Curtis Inst. of Music, Philadelphia under Mme. Isabelle Vengerova. *Career:* professional début with Philadelphia Orchestra 1947; concert tours all over the world; appears annually in America with major orchestras; Dir Curtis Inst. 1986–, Pres. 1995–; year offstage to correct finger injury 1980–81; gramophone recordings for Columbia Masterworks and RCA Victor including concertos of Tchaikovsky, Rachmaninoff, Brahms, Beethoven, Chopin and Prokofiev. *Publication:* I Really Should be Practising (autobiog.) 1981. *Honours:* Leventritt Award 1949; several hon. degrees. *Address:* Office of the Director, Curtis Institute of Music, 1726 Locust Street, Philadelphia, PA 19103-6187, USA (office). *Telephone:* (215) 893-5252 (office). *Fax:* (215) 893-0897 (office).

**GRAHAM, Alasdair;** Pianist and Professor; b. 19 April 1934, Glasgow, Scotland. *Education:* BMus, Edinburgh University; Performers Diploma, Vienna Hochschule für Musik; Royal Academy of Music with Peter Katin. *Career:* Debut: Bishopsgate Hall, 1958; Soloist with Scottish National Orchestra, London Philharmonic Orchestra, BBC Symphony Orchestra (Proms, 1963), Royal Liverpool Philharmonic, Hallé Orchestra, Sydney Symphony Orchestra, Melbourne Symphony Orchestra (Australian tour), 1967; Recitals, BBC television, the United Kingdom, Turkey, India; As Accompanist with Elisabeth Söderströ m, Josef Suk, John Shirley-Quirk; Professor, Royal College of Music, London; mem, Royal Society of Musicians of Great Britain. *Recordings:* Schubert: Sonata in B flat, 8 Ecossaises. *Honours:* Harriet Cohen Commonwealth Medal, 1963; Honorary RCM, 1973. *Address:* 184 Can Hall Road, London E11 3 NH, England.

**GRAHAM, Colin;** Stage Director, Librettist and Artistic Director; b. 22 Sept. 1931, Hove, Sussex, England. *Education:* New Covenant School of Ministry, St Louis, 1985–87, ordained Minister in 1988; Diploma, Royal Academy of Dramatic Art; Private study. *Career:* Debut: Playhouse Theatre, Nottingham, England; Artistic Director, Aldeburgh Festival, 1969–82, English Music Theatre, 1976–, Opera Theater of St Louis, 1982–; Director of Productions, English National Opera, Sadler's Wells Opera, 1976–82; Over 400 productions in opera, television and theatre, including 54 world premieres; staged the premiere of Corigliano's The Ghosts of Versailles at the Metropolitan, 1991, production of Britten's Death in Venice at Covent Garden, 1992, and Metropolitan Opera, 1993 and world premiere of Susa's The Dangerous Liaisons at San Francisco, 1994; The Barber of Seville at St Louis, 1996; staged premiere of Previn's A Streetcar Named Desire, San Francisco, 1998; staged plays, opera, television for Oled Vic Co, Royal Shakespeare Co, Bristol Old Vic, Nottingham Plyhouse, Oxford Playhouse, BBC TV, ITV, Belgian TV, Royal Opera Covent Garden, Glyndebourne Opera, Sadlers Wells Opera, English National Opera, Belgian National Opera La Monnaie; mem, Equity; Canadian Equity; American Guild of Musical Artists; Arts and Educational Council, 1993; Award of Personal Achievement in the Arts. *Publications:* Opera Libretti: The Golden Vanity by Britten, 1970, Penny for a Song by Bennett, 1970, King Arthur by Purcell, 1972, The Postman Always Rings Twice, by Paulus, 1983, Joruri by Miki, 1985, The Woodlanders by Paulus, 1985; The Tale of Genji by Miki, 1999; Silk by Previn, 1999; Anna Karenina by Carlson; Madame Mao by Sheng (libretto and world premiere productgion for Santa Fe Opera). *Contributions:* Opera Magazine; Musical Times; Opera News, 1992. *Honours:* Winston Churchill Fellowship, 1975; Prize for Opera Production for Orpheus, Germany, 1977; Honorary Doctor of Arts, Webster University, 1985 and University of Missouri, 1992; O.B.E., 2002. *Address:* PO Box 191910, St Louis, MO 63119, USA.

**GRAHAM, Peter John;** Arranger and Composer; b. 5 Dec. 1958, Bellshill, Scotland; m. Janey Buchan, 1 s., 1 d. *Education:* BMus, Edinburgh University, 1980; PGCE, Moray House College, 1981; MMus, Goldsmiths' College, 1994; PhD, University of Salford, 1999. *Career:* Arranger, Composer, New York, London, 1986–91; Lecturer, University of Salford, 1991–97; Senior Lecturer, 1997–2001; Reader in Composition, 2001–. *Compositions:* Numerous publications for brass and wind including: Dimensions, 1983; Montage, 1994; Harrison's Dream, 2000; Arrangements for BBC television and radio, commercial television and various recordings including Reflected in Brass, Evelyn Glennie meets the Black Dyke Band. *Honours:* Reflected in Brass nominated Best Classical Crossover Album, Grammy Awards, 1999; ABA/ Ostwald Composition Prize, 2002. *Address:* c/o Gramercy Music, PO Box 41, Cheadle Hulme, Cheshire SK8 5HF, England.

**GRAHAM, Susan;** American singer (mezzo-soprano); b. 23 July 1960, Roswell, NM. *Education:* Manhattan School of Music, Texas Technical Univ. *Career:* sang Massenet's Chérubin while a student; engagements with St Louis Opera as Erika in Vanessa, Charlotte and at Seattle as Stephano in Roméo et Juliette; season 1989–90 included Chicago Lyric Opera debut as Annius in La Clemenza di Tito, Sonia in Argento's Aspern Papers at Washington, Dorabella and the Composer at Santa Fe; Carnegie Hall debut in Des Knaben Wunderhorn and Bernstein concert in New York; season 1990–91 as Octavian with San Francisco Symphony, Minerva in Monteverdi's Ulisse with San Francisco Opera, Berlioz's Beatrice at Lyon, Cherubino at Santa Fe; Mozart's C minor Mass under Edo de Waart and with Philadelphia Orchestra under Neville Marriner; season 1991–92 at Metropolitan as Second Lady, Cherubino, and Tebaldo in Don Carlos; L'Opera de Nice as Cherubino and Les Nuits d'Été in Lyon; Beethoven's 9th in Spain conducted by Marriner; Salzburg Mozart Week 1993, as Cecilio in Lucio Silla, Easter and Summer Festivals as Meg Page in Falstaff; season 1993–94 as Massenet's Chérubin and Dorabella at Covent Garden, Ascanio in Les Troyens at the Met, Annius in Tito at San Francisco and 1994 Salzburg Festival; Octavian for WNO, and Vienna State Opera and Marguerite in La Damnation de Faust for L'Opéra de Lyon; season 1995 as Dorabella and as Arianna in the premiere of the opera by Goehr at Covent Garden; season 1997 with Chérubin at Covent Garden and in Lucio Silla at Salzburg; sang Octavian at Covent Garden 2000; created Sister Helen Prejean in Jack Heggie's Dead Man Walking, San Francisco 2000; season 2001 as Mignon at Toulouse and Dorabella at the New York Met. *Recordings include:* Falstaff conducted by Solti, La Damnation de Faust conducted by Kent Nagano, Béatrice et Bénédict conducted by John Nelson, Stravinsky's Pulcinella, Charles Ives Songs (Grammy Award for Best Classical Vocal Performance 2005) 2005) Poèmes de l'amour 2005. *Honours:* Opera News Award 2005. *Current Management:* IMG Artists, Lovell House, 616 Chiswick High Road, London, W4 5RX, England. *Telephone:* (20) 8233-5800. *Fax:* (20) 8233-5801. *E-mail:* info@imgartists.com. *Website:* www .imgartists.com; www.susangraham.com.

**GRAHAM-HALL, John;** Singer (Tenor); b. 23 Nov. 1955, Middlesex, England. *Education:* Studied at King's College, Cambridge and Royal College of Music. *Career:* Debut: Opera North, as Ferrando in Così fan tutte, 1983; Has sung Albert Herring at Covent Garden and Glyndebourne, Pedrillo for Kent Opera, Cassio for Welsh National Opera and Don Ottavio for Opera Northern Ireland; Glyndebourne Touring Opera as Britten's Aschenbach, Lysander, Basilio and Ferrando; English National Opera debut as Cyril in Princess Ida, 1992, returning as Basilio, Tanzmeister in Ariadne and Schoolmaster in Cunning Little Vixen; Engagements at Lyon as Lensky and Frère Mass ée in Messiaen's St François d'Assise, Vancouver as Ferrando, Brussels and Lisbon as Cassio and Antwerp as Achilles in King Priam; Glyndebourne Festival as Kudrjas in Katya Kabanova and Flute in Midsummer Night's Dream; Scottish Opera as Eisenstein, and Schoolmaster in Cunning Little Vixen; Aix-en-Provence as Lysander and Bordeaux as Tanzmeister in Ariadne; Amsterdam as Basilio and Curzio; Conductors have included Haitink, Janowski, Tate, Rattle and Abbado; Concert career with all major British orchestras including Pulcinella with BBC Symphony, 1993; Further recent appearances include Moses and Aron in Amsterdam, La Belle Hélène with English National Opera, and Shapkin in House of the Dead in Nice; Season 1996 with Narciso in Il Turco in Italia at Garsington and in Moses and Aron at Salzburg; Basilio in Figaro for the Royal Opera, London; Recent engagements include Alwa, Herod for ENO, Tanzmeister for ROH, Mime for ENO; Further plans include Perela at Paris Bastille; Season 2000–01 in the premiere of The Silver Tassie, by Turnage, for ENO, and as Monostatos and Mime; Britten's Bob Boles at Amsterdam; Dancing Master in Ariadne at Covent Garden, 2002. *Recordings include:* Carmina Burana; L'Incoronazione di Poppea; A Midsummer Night's Dream; As Bob Boles in Peter Grimes. *Address:* c/o Musichall, Ivydene, Vicarage Way, Ringmer, East Sussex, BN8 5 LA, England.

**GRAHN, Ulf (Ake Wilhelm);** Composer; b. 17 Jan. 1942, Solna, Sweden; m. Barbro Dahlman, 15 Aug 1969, 1 s. *Education:* Degree in Violin Pedagogy, SMI, Stockholm, 1968; MM, Catholic University, Washington DC, USA, 1973; Business Administration, Development Studies, Uppsala University, Sweden, 1986. *Career:* Music Instructor, Stockholm and Lidingo Schools, 1964–72; Teaching Assistant, Instructor, Catholic University, Washington, 1972–76; Founder, Music Director, Contemporary Music Forum, 1973–85; Lecturer, Northern VA Community College, 1975–79; Lecturer, Associate Professor, George Washington University, 1983–87; Founder, Artistic Director, The Aurora Players, 1983–; Artistic and Managing Director, Lake Siljan Festival Sweden, 1988–90; Composer-in-Residence, Charles Ives Center, USA, 1988; Publisher and Owner, Edition NGLANI, 1985–; mem, STIM Sweden; Society of Swedish Composers. *Compositions:* Major orchestral works including Symphonies Nos 1 and 2; Concertos for piano, guitar and double bass; Chamber and Choral Music; Solo works for Guitar, Piano, Violin; Three Dances with Interludes, premiered in Stockholm, 1990; Blå Dunster, 1990, an instrumental opera premiered in Örebro, Sweden, 1991; As Time Passes By for orchestra, 1993; Aron's Interlude for 6 instruments, 1994; Summer '61 for ensemble, 1995; Morning Rush for orchestra, 1995; Cikadas for 4 instruments, 1996. *Recordings:* Cinq Preludes; Snapshots; Sonata for Piano with Flute and Percussion; In The Shade, Caprice; Sonata for Piano. *Contributions:* Many articles, and reviews in Europe; Tonfallet; Musik Revy and Ord och Ton. *Honours:* Stockholm International Organ Days, 1973; League International Society for Contemporary Music Piano Competition, 1976; First Prize in Music for, Toccata for Carillon, Dalarna Composition Contest, 1990. *Address:* PO Box 5684, Takoma Park, MD 20913-5684, USA.

**GRANDISON, Mark;** Composer; b. 9 Dec. 1965, Adelaide, South Australia. *Education:* BMus (Hons) 1987, MMus 1990, University of Adelaide; Study with Richard Meale, 1983–87. *Career:* Teacher and Acting Co-ordinator, Marryatville Special Interest Music Centre, Adelaide, 1992–93; Kambala School, Sydney, 1994–. *Compositions include:* Four Poems of Wilfrid Owen for contralto and ensemble, 1985; Contrasts for orchestra, 1987; Night Interiors for orchestra, 1988; Los Caprichos for chamber orchestra, 1989; Five Blake Songs for soprano and piano, 1990; Toccata for chamber ensemble, 1992; Three Dances for string orchestra, 1993; Surface Tension for string quartet, 1996; Kinetica for youth orchestra, 1997; Tarantella for Orchestra, 1998; Commissions from the Adelaide Chamber Orchestra, Vrizen and Australian Broadcasting Association. *Honours:* South Australia Young Composer's Award, 1993. *Address:* c/o APRA, 1A Eden Street, Crows Nest, NSW 2065, Australia.

**GRANGE, Philip (Roy);** British composer; *Professor of Composition, University of Manchester;* b. 17 Nov. 1956, London; m. Elizabeth Caroline Hemming 1986; two c. *Education:* York University, 1976–82; BA, 1979; Doctorate in Composition, 1984; Dartington Summer School of Music, Composition class with Peter Maxwell Davies, 1975–81. *Career:* Promenade Concert debut, 1983; Fellow in the Creative Arts, Trinity College, Cambridge, 1985–87; Northern Arts Fellow in Composition, Durham University, 1988–89; Appointed Lecturer in Composition, 1989–95, Reader in Composition, 1995–99, Professor of Composition, 1999–2000, Exeter University; Professor of Composition, Univ. of Manchester 2001–; Performances of music at most major festivals in the United Kingdom, and in Europe, USA and the Far East; British Council sponsored tour of Taiwan as both composer and lecturer 1997, 2000; featured composer, TWCAT Conf., Taiwan 2003, Music Factory Festival, Bergen, Norway 2003. *Compositions:* Cimmerian Nocturne, 1979; Sextet, 1980; The Kingdom of Bones, 1983; La Ville Entière, 1984; Variations, 1986; Out in the Dark, 1986; In Memorian HK, 1986; The Dark Labyrinth, 1987; Concerto for Orchestra, Labyrinthine Images, 1988; In A Dark Time, 1989; Changing Landscapes, 1990; Focus and Fade, 1992; Lowry Dreamscape, 1992; Piano Polyptich, 1993; Bacchus Bagatelles, 1993; Des fins sont des commencements, 1994; Piano Trio: Homage to Chagall, 1995; A Puzzle of Shadows for soprano, violin and piano, 1997; Sky-Maze with Song Shards, 1999; Lament of the Bow, 2000, Clarinet concerto 2000, Daedalus's Lament 2001, String Quartet 2003, Duet Movement 2003, Eclipsing 2004. *Recordings:* La Ville Entière for clarinet and piano, Dark Labyrinths (recording of six pieces), Diptych, The Knell of Parting Day. *Current Management:* c/o Maecenas Music, 5 Bushey Close, Old Barn Lane, Kenley, Surrey CR8 5AU,

England. *Address:* Music Department, University of Manchester, Denmark Road, Manchester, M15 6HY, England (office).

**GRANT, Clifford (Scantlebury);** Australian singer (bass); b. 11 Sept. 1930, Randwick, NSW; m. 1st Jeanette Earle; one s. two d.; m. 2nd Ruth Anders 1992. *Education:* Studied at Sydney Conservatorium with Isolde Hill; Melbourne with Annie Portnoj; London with Otakar Kraus. *Career:* Debut: New South Wales Opera Company, as Raimondo in Lucia di Lammermoor, 1952; Sang with Sadler's Wells/English National Opera from 1966, debut as Silva in Ernani; Leading roles in Oedipus Rex, The Mastersingers, Peter Grimes, The Magic Flute, Madama Butterfly, The Barber of Seville, The Ring of the Nibelung, Don Giovanni, The Coronation of Poppea, and Don Carlos; Sang in San Francisco, 1966–78; Glyndebourne Festival as Nettuno in Il Ritorno d'Ulisse, 1972; Further engagements with Covent Garden Opera, Welsh National Opera and in Europe; Sang in Sydney from 1976, as Nilakantha (Lakmé), 1986; Season 1990 as Marcel in Les Huguenots with Australian Opera; Returned to the United Kingdom, 1992 and sang Alvise in new production of La Gioconda, Opera North, 1993; Many concert appearances. *Recordings:* Don Giovanni; Rigoletto; Esclarmonde; L'Oracolo; Fafner in The Rhinegold and Hunding in The Valkryie, conducted by Reginald Goodall; Bartolo in Le nozze di Figaro; Il Corsaro; The Apostles by Elgar; Tosca; Les Huguenots. *Address:* c/o Opera Australia, Sydney Opera House, Sydney, NSW, Australia.

**GRÄSBECK, Manfred;** Violinist; b. 16 July 1955, Åbo, Finland; m. Maija Lehtonen, 14 May 1989, 1 s., 1 d. *Education:* Åbo Konservatorium, Åbo, Finland, 1962–79; Académie Internationale de Musique, Maurice Ravel, 1972–76; Académie Internationale d'été, Nice, France, 1974–77; Tjajkovskij-konservatoriet Kiev, Ukraina, 1978–81; Sibelius Academy, 1981–91; MMus, 1997, Postgraduate Studies, Sibelius-Akademin, Helsingfors, Finland. *Career:* Debut: Ludwig van Beethoven sonatas Nos 5, 7 and 9, Salle Gaveau, Paris, 1978; As soloist with orchestras: Århus, 1972; Copenhagen, 1972; Bordeaux, 1972; Toulouse, 1973, 1974; Västerås, 1977; Stockholm, 1983; Hamburger Symphoniker, 1983; Reykjavík, 1986; Volgograd, 1990; Beethoven Violin Concerto (with cadenzas by M. Gräsbeck), Vilnius and Kaunas, 1992; mem, Liszt Gesellschaft Ky, Helsinki; Attended Professor Jorma Panula Conducting Competition, Vaasa, Finland, November, 2003. *Compositions:* 7 symphonies; 6 violin concertos HRF op 23 and Integrity op 34; film music; and others. *Recordings:* Ellis B Kohs: Conductor, Passacaglia K 11 for organ and strings; Piano and organ, Kreisler with Love, vol. 1 and 2, with Maija Lehtonen; Paganini caprices op 1; K Aho violin concerto; L Bashmakov violin concerto No. 2, Manfred Gräsbeck Plays Sibelius 2005. *Address:* Nalleback-avägen 1B, 00700 Helsinki, Finland.

**GRAUBART, Michael;** Composer, Conductor and Lecturer; b. 26 Nov. 1930, Vienna, Austria; m. (1) Ellen Barbour, 1962, 1 s., 2 d., (2) Valerie Coumont, 1996. *Education:* BSc, Physics, Univ. of Manchester, England, 1952; Studied Composition privately with Matyas Seiber, 1953–57; Flute with Geoffrey Gilbert, 1953–56. *Career:* Conductor, Ars Nova Chamber Orchestra, 1960; Conductor, Hampstead Chamber Orchestra, 1962–66; Music Director, Focus Opera Group, 1967–71; Director of Music, Morley College, 1966–91; Adjunct Professor of Music, Syracuse University London Centre, 1989–91; Senior Lecturer, School of Academic Studies, Royal Northern College of Music, Manchester, 1991–96. *Compositions include:* Sonata for cello and piano; Sinfonia a 10 for 10 winds; Quintet for flute, clarinet, viola, cello and vibraphone; Canzonetta for triple chamber orchestra; Declensions for 10 instruments; To a Dead Lover for soprano and 7 instruments; Untergang for baritone, chorus and 11 instruments; Quasi una Sonata for piano; Three Bagatelles for cello and piano; Sure I am only of uncertain things for a cappella chorus; Two songs for mezzo-soprano and piano; Concertino da Camera for viola and four woodwinds; Diptych (The Seed and the Harvest, Broken Mirror) for 4 winds; Scena and Capriccio for piano; Variants and Cadenzas for orchestra; Nightfall for chorus and piano; Elegy for orchestra; Speculum Noctuinum for 9 winds, cello and bass; Scena II and Finale for euphonium, 2 flutes, viola and cello, 1992 and 1995; Ricordanze for recorders and piano, 1995, 1997; String Quartet, 2000; Sonata for cello and piano; The Meridian Angel for counter tenors, 2 tenors and baritone; Scena III for solo cello; Editions: Music by Pergolesi, Dufay and Josquin. *Publications:* 4 articles on Leopold Spinner, including one for the revision of New Grove's Dictionary of Music; Numerous articles and reviews on Bach, Beethoven, Schubert, Mendelsohn, Schoenberg, Berg and Webern for Tempo and Musical Times. *Address:* 18 Laitwood Road, Balham, London SW12 9QL, England. *E-mail:* michael.graubart@btinternet.com.

**GRAUNKE, Kurt;** Violinist, Conductor and Composer; b. 30 Sept. 1915, Stettin, Germany. *Education:* Pupil in violin of Gustav Havemann; Berlin Hochschule für Musik; Received training in composition from Adolf Lessle and Hermann Grabner, in violin from Hanns Weiss and Hans Dunschede, and in conducting from Feliz Husadel; Completed violin studies with Wolfgang Schneiderhan. *Career:* Played violin in the Vienna Radio Orchestra; Founder-Conductor, Graunke Symphony Orchestra, Munich, 1945–. *Compositions:* 8 symphonies: 1969, 1972, 1975, 1981, 1982, 1983, 1985; Violin Concerto, 1959; Other orchestral works. *Recordings:* Numerous albums, film and television soundtracks. *Address:* c/o Symphonie Orchester Graunke, Schornstrasse 13, 8000 Munich 30, Germany.

**GRAVES, Denyce;** American singer (mezzo-soprano); b. 1963, Washington DC. *Education:* Oberlin Coll. Conservatory and New England Conservatory.

*Career:* early roles included Maddalena at Washington and Giuletta in Les Contes d'Hoffmann at the Spoleto Festival; further engagements as Dalila in Philadelphia and Montréal, Honegger's Antigone, the High Priestess in La Vestale at La Scala, Adalgisa in Zürich and Donizetti's Leonora (La Favorita) at Catania; appearances as Carmen at San Francisco, Vienna, the Bergen Festival, Covent Garden, Berlin, Zürich, Houston, Los Angeles, Buenos Aires and Munich; season 1995–96 as Carmen in Zürich and at the Met, Dalila in Washington, Carmen at San Francisco 1998; season 2000 as Carmen at Chicago, Amneris in Cincinnati, Dalila at the Met and Dulcinée in Don Quichotte for Washington Opera; The Nation's Favourite Prom at the London Proms 2002; concert repertory includes Messiah, the Verdi Requiem, Rossini's Stabat Mater, Ravel's Shéhérazade and Mahler's Kindertotenlieder. *Recordings include:* Gertrude in Hamlet by Ambroise Thomas, Emilia in Otello. *Honours:* Met Opera nat. finalist, Grand Prix du Concours Int. du Chant de Paris, Marian Anderson Award. *Address:* 616 Chiswick High Road, London, W4 5RX, England. *Telephone:* (20) 8233-5917. *Fax:* (20) 8742-8758. *E-mail:* jvanderveen@imgworld.com. *Website:* www.imgartists.com; www.denycegraves.com.

**GRAVS, Leonard;** Singer (Bass-baritone); b. 28 Jan. 1944, Maastricht, Netherlands. *Career:* Debut: Sang Sparafucile in Rigoletto at Maastricht, 1966; Sang with Netherlands Opera, Opéra de Wallonie at Liège, 1973–82; Hannover Opera, 1982–86; Saarbrucken, 1986–88; Geneva, 1988–94; Guest appearances at Marseille, Cologne, (Pallante in Agrippina), 1985 and Montreal; Other roles have included Puccini's Colline and Angelotti, Nourabad in Les Pêcheurs de perles and the Minister in Fidelio, Liège, 1996; Zuniga in Carmen, Verdi's Zaccaria, Grand Inquisitor and Ramphis; Escamillo and Kaspar; Season 1997–98 as Gessler in Guillaume Tell at Liège. *Address:* Opéra de Wallonie, 1 Rue des Dominicains, 4000 Liège, Belgium.

**GRAY, George;** Singer (Tenor); b. 26 May 1947, USA. *Career:* Sang Cavaradossi at Colorado Springs, 1984, Cairo and Radames with North Carolina Opera, 1986, 1988; New Jersey Festival, 1987, as Bacchus, Seattle, 1987, as Otello, Tristan at Columbus, Ohio; Season 1988 in Schoenberg's Gurrelieder at Frankfurt, and Pollione in Norma; Tristan at Nancy, 1990, with Aeneas at the opening of the Bastille Opéra, Paris; Sang Parsifal at Chicago, 1990, Siegfried at Zürich, 1988; Further appearances as Bacchus at Kassel, in Schreker's Schatzgräber at the Holland Festival and Meyerbeer's Vasco da Gama at the Berlin Staatsoper, 1992; Lohengrin at Leipzig; Season 1999–2000 at the San Francisco and Dallas Operas as Siegfried. *Address:* c/o Berlin Staatsoper, Unter den Linden 7, 1060 Berlin, Germany.

**GRAY, James;** Singer (countertenor), Keyboard player and Conductor; b. 1 Jan. 1956, London, England. *Education:* Royal Acad. of Music, London; private study with Maria Curcio, London; Acad. of Fine Arts, Prague; Centro Studio Musicali Rinascimento, Florence. *Career:* debut, Prague, 1976, Czech Philharmonic Society; Guest Dir of Prague Madrigalists, 1980–81 (Berlin television debut 1981); Repétiteur Nationaltheater, Mannheim, 1981–82; La Chaise-Dieu Festival, 1984 (French television); Domenico Scarlatti Tercentenary Celebrations, 1985 (Radio Madrid, Spanish television); many subsequent appearances as singer, conductor and accompanist throughout mid and Eastern Europe. *Recordings:* Domenico Scarlatti 5 Cantate Inedite 1985, Monteverdi: Lamento d'Arianna (awarded Grand Prix Acad. du Disque Français) 1985, O Primevera 2002, Guillaume de Machaut: La Messa de Nostre Dame 1989, Benedetto Marcello; Cantate a 1, 2, 3 voci 1990. *Address:* Via Romana 34, 50125 Florence, Italy. *E-mail:* horti_annalenae@tin.it.

**GRAY, Linda Esther;** British singer (soprano); b. 29 May 1948, d. of James and Esther Gray; m. Peter McCrorie 1971; one d. *Education:* Greenock Acad. and Royal Scottish Acad. of Music and Drama. *Career:* London Opera Centre 1969–71, Glyndebourne Festival Opera 1972–75, Scottish Opera 1974–79, ENO 1979, Welsh Opera 1980; debut American performance 1981; appeared Royal Opera House, London 1982, 1983. *Operas include:* Tristan und Isolde, die Walküre, Tosca, Parsifal, Fidelio. *Recordings:* Tristan und Isolde 1981, Die Feen 1983. *Honours:* Cinzano Scholarship 1969, Goldsmith Scholarship 1970, James Caird Scholarship 1971, Christie Award 1972, Kathleen Ferrier Award 1972. *Address:* 35 Green Lane, New Malden, Surrey, KT3 5BX, England.

**GREAGER, Richard;** Singer (tenor); b. 5 Nov. 1946, Christchurch, New Zealand. *Education:* Studied in Australia. *Career:* Junior Principal at Covent Garden until 1975; Lyric Tenor at Scottish Opera from 1975, then sang widely in Germany, notably at Hanover, Dortmund, Wiesbaden, Karlsruhe and Bonn; Roles included Don Ottavio, Ferrando, Tamino, Rodolfo, the Duke of Mantua, Fenton and Ernesto; Australian Opera from 1980, as The Painter in Lulu, Edgardo (opposite Sutherland's Lucia), Peter Grimes, Lensky, Don José and Peter Quint (The Turn of the Screw); Guest appearances at the Grand Théâtre Geneva as Peter Quint, the Painter and the Negro in Lulu (Jeffrey Tate conducting) and Edgardo; Opéra de Lyon as Huon in Oberon; Season 1988–89 as Rodolfo at Melbourne and Covent Garden; Eisenstein in Die Fledermaus for Scottish Opera; Peter Quint in Schwetzingen and Cologne; Covent Garden 1991 as Arthur in the world premiere of Gawain by Harrison Birtwistle; Other roles include Tonio (La Fille du Régiment) and Werther; Season 1991–92 as Arbace in Idomeneo at Helsinki, Herod in Salome at Wellington and Mozart's Basilio with the Royal Opera in Japan; Sang Don José and Don Ottavio for Wellington City Opera, 1997; Torquemada in L'Heure Espagnole at Auckland, 1998; Captain in Wozzeck (Barrie Kosky's production), Sydney; Dr Caius in Falstaff for NBR New Zealand Opera, Roger in Love in the Age of Therapy for OzOpera, Melbourne and Sydney Festivals,

2001; Prince Shuisky in Boris Godunov for NBR New Zealand Opera; Herod in Salome for Opera Australia, 2003. *Recordings:* video: Gawain, Lucia di Lammermoor, La Traviata, Un Ballo in Maschera, Turn of the Screw, Dialogue of the Carmelites; also recorded Berlioz's Requiem and Schubert's 6 Masses. *Honours:* Winner, Sun Aria Competition, Australia. *Current Management:* Arts Management, Level 2, 420 Elizabeth Street, Surry Hills, NSW 2010, Australia.

**GREEN, Anna,** ARCM; Opera Singer; b. 27 Jan. 1933, Southampton, England; m. Howard Vanderburg 1965. *Education:* Royal Coll. of Music. *Career:* debut, Amelia in Verdi's Un Ballo in Maschera, Deutsche Oper am Rhein, Düsseldorf 1961; sang Aida, Tosca and Abigaille; later sang German roles, including Fidelio, Marschallin, Isolde, Brünnhilde and Elektra; appeared as Hecuba in King Priam at Royal Opera House, Covent Garden, London, Brünnhilde for ENO and WNO, Elektra for Vienna State Opera and in Karslruhe and Mannheim, Brünnhilde in Barcelona, Florence, Naples, Nice, Warsaw, Lisbon, Hamburg, Stuttgart and Cologne, Isolde in Berlin, Mannheim, Karlsruhe and Wiesbaden, Kostelnicka in Jenůfa in Stuttgart; also sang in Canada and USA, as Brünnhilde at founding of Pacific Northwest Wagner Festival and in subsequent four seasons; concert appearances include Stravinsky's Les Noces at Albert Hall, London, under Pierre Boulez, Schoenberg's Erwartung in Scotland, under Gari Bertini, Altenberg Lieder for RAI, Rome, Wagner concert with Los Angeles Philharmonic conducted by Zubin Mehta; mem. Genossenschaft Deutscher Bühnen. *Recordings:* Aus dem Essener Musikleben; Betulia Liberata KV 118 Mozart.

**GREEN, Barry,** BMus, MMus; American bassist, academic and writer; b. 10 April 1945, Newark, NJ; m. Mary Tarbell Green 1984; two s. one step-s. *Education:* Indiana University School of Music, University of Cincinnati. *Career:* Principal Bassist, Nashville Symphony, 1965–66; Principal Bassist, Cincinnati Symphony, 1967–; Faculty, University of Cincinnati, 1967–; Cassals Festival Orchestra, 1979–87; International Workshops, 1982–86; mem, International Society of Bassists, Founder Director, Life Member; ASTA; Founder-Executive Director, International Society of Bassists. *Recordings:* (Solos) Baroque Bass; Romantic Music for Double Bass; New Music for Double Bass; Bass Evolution; Sound of Bass, Vol. 1 (Chamber Music Recordings) Heritage Chamber Quartet; Music Now; What of My Music Opus One. *Publications:* Fundamentals of Double Bass Playing; Advanced Techniques of Double Bass Playing, 1976; Inner Game of Music, 1986; contrib. to Suzuki Journal; American Music Teacher; Instrumentalist; Bass World. *Address:* 3449 Lyleburn Place, Cincinnati, OH 45220, USA.

**GREEN, Barton;** American singer (tenor); b. 1967, New Orleans. *Education:* Washington and Yale Univs. *Career:* sang Tamino at Tacoma Opera, 1986; Pinkerton for Sarasota Opera, 1994; Season 1995 with Alfredo for Pittsburgh Opera; Faust at Conneticut; Rossini's Almaviva for Da Capo Opera and Tonio in La Fille du régiment for Augusta Opera; Eugene Opera, 1996 as Rodolfo, and Gennaro in Lucrezia Borgia at Manhattan Opera; Giessen Opera, 1996 as Edgardo in Lucia di Lammermoor; Alfred in Die Fledermaus for Florida Grand Opera, 1998. *Honours:* Richard Tucker Award 1994.

**GREEN, Paul Jay;** Clarinettist; b. 19 Dec. 1948, New York, USA; m. Lisa Dolinger Green, 19 December 1993. *Education:* BA, Yale College, 1970; MS, Performance, Juilliard School of Music, 1972; JD Brooklyn Law School, 1978; LLM, New York University School of Law, 1982; Studies with Leon Russianoff, Keith Wilson, Joseph Allard. *Career:* Debut: Young Concert Artists, Carnegie Recital Hall, 1966; Soloist: New York Philharmonic; Hartford Symphony Orchestra; New Haven Symphony Orchestra; Colorado Music Festival; Festival of Two Worlds in Spoleto, Italy; International Festival of Contemporary Music, Kraków, Poland; The Days of New Music Festival in Chisinau, Moldova; Chamber music performances with: Jacqueline Du Pré; Richard Goode; The Lark Quartet; The Borromeo Quartet; The Ying Quartet; The Alexander Quartet; The St Lawrence Quartet; The Miami String Quartet; The Eroica Trio; Founder and Artistic Director, Gold Coast Chamber Music Festival; Principal clarinettist of The New Haven Symphony Orchestra, 1989–90; Colorado Music Festival Orchestra; Symphony of the Americas; American Sinfonietta; Atlantic Classical Orchestra; Associate Professor of Music, Clarinet and Chamber Music, Conservatory of Music, Lynn University, Boca Roton, Florida, 1992–; Instructor of Music, Clarinet and Chamber Music, School of Music, Florida International University, Miami, Florida, 1996–. *Recordings:* Carnival of the Animals with Leonard Bernstein and the New York Philharmonic; Return to the Concert Stage, 1990; Quintet for Clarinet and Strings with the Miami String Quartet, 2001. *Current Management:* Marilyn Gilbert, Artists Management. *Address:* 717 Heron Drive, Delray Beach, FL 33444, USA.

**GREENAN, Andrew,** MA; singer (bass); b. 5 Feb. 1960, Birmingham, England; m. Susannah Davies 1989, two s. one d. *Education:* St Marys Coll., Liverpool, St Johns Coll., Cambridge, Royal Northern Coll. of Music with John Cameron. *Career:* debut, La Scala, Milan, 1983; Bayreuther Festspielchor, 1985–87; British Opera debut, Mozart's Bartolo Opera 80, 1989; Principal Bass, English National Opera, 1992–97; Roles include: King Henry, Sarastro, Rocco, Commendatore, Timur, Sparafucile, Swallow; Other engagements include: Bottom in Midsummer Night's Dream at Teatro Regio, Turin, 1995; Landgraf in Tannhäuser at Queen Elizabeth Hall; For Royal Opera Covent Garden: Swallow with Mackerras, Ataliba in Alzira with Elder, 1st Nazarene in Salome with Dohnányi, Pietro in Simon Boccanegra with Solti, Rocco for Welsh National Opera, Abimélech in Samson et Dalila for New

Israeli Opera (1998), Swallow for Hamburg State Opera and Welsh National Opera; Recent concert work includes Verdi Requiem with Belgian National Orchestra and appearances with the English Chamber and BBC Symphony Orchestras. *Recordings:* The Nightingale by Stravinsky, with the Philharmonia and Robert Craft; Video recordings of Peter Grimes with ENO and Salome with the Royal Opera; Appears as Raymond/Larimondo in the film Lucia based on Donizetti's opera. *Current Management:* Robert Gilder & Co., Enterprise House, 59–65 Upper Ground, London, SE1 9PQ, England. *Telephone:* (20) 7928-9008. *Fax:* (20) 7928-9755. *E-mail:* rgilder@robert-gilder.com. *Address:* 3 Wheatsheaf Gardens, Lewes, East Sussex BN7 2UQ, England.

**GREENAWALD, Sheri (Kay);** Soprano; b. 12 Nov. 1947, Iowa City, Iowa, USA. *Education:* Studied with Charles Matheson at the University of Northern Iowa and with Hans Heinz, Daniel Ferro and Maria DeVarady in New York; Further studies with Audrey Langford in London. *Career:* Debut: Manhattan Theater Club 1974, in Les mamelles de Tirésias by Poulenc; Sang in the premieres of Bilby's Doll by Carlisle Floyd and Washington Square by Thomas Pastieri (Houston and Detroit, 1976); European debut with Netherlands Opera as Susanna in Le nozze di Figaro, 1980; Regular concert appearances with the St Louis and San Francisco Symphony Orchestras and the Rotterdam Philharmonic; Sang in the premiere of Bernstein's A Quiet Place, Houston 1983; Other roles include Violetta, Ellen Orford (Peter Grimes), Mozart's Despina and Zerlina, Sophie in Werther and Norina in Don Pasquale; Season 1991/92 at Chicago as Pauline in the US Stage premiere of Prokofiev's The Gambler and Mozart's Donna Anna, Fiordiligi at Seattle; Sang the Marschallin with Welsh National Opera, 1994; Susa's Transformations at St Louis, 1997; Los Angeles Opera debut 1998 as Catán's Florencia. *Address:* c/o Houston Grand Opera Association, 510 Preston Avenue, Houston, TX 77002, USA.

**GREENBAUM, Stuart (Geoffrey Andrew);** Composer; b. 25 Dec. 1966, Melbourne, Australia. *Education:* Studied at the University of Melbourne; BMus, hons, MMus, PhD (pending), Teachers include Brenton Broadstock and Barry Conyngham. *Career:* Debut: Upon the Dark Water (text by Ross Baglin), premiered at Sydney Opera House, 1990, by the Song Company; Works performed by groups including: The Modern Wind Quintet, I Cantori di New York, The Song Company, Melbourne Symphony, The Oxford University Philharmonia, The Arcadian Singers, Ormond College Choir, The Pacific Ocean Symphony Orchestra; mem, AMC; FAC; CPCF. *Compositions:* Ice Man, solo piano, 1993; The Killing Floors, orchestra, 1995; Four Minutes in a Nuclear Bunker, orchestra, 1995; Nelson, soprano, baritone, string quartet, 1997; The Foundling, choir, string quartet, vibraphone, 1997. *Recordings:* CDs: Upon the Dark Water, song company; Greenbaum, Hindson, Peterson, anthology; Music for Theatre, playbox; Portrait and Blues Hymn; Polar Wandering, Fairfield Days. *Honours:* ANA Composition Award, 1991; Dorian Le Galliene Composition Award, 1993. *Address:* 4/111 Rushall Crescent, North Fitzroy, Vic 3068, Australia.

**GREENBERG, Sylvia;** singer (soprano); b. 1951, Romania. *Education:* Tel-Aviv Acad. of Music and studied with Marc Belfort in Zürich. *Career:* debut in a Tel-Aviv concert, conducted by Zubin Mehta; stage debut Zürich 1977, as the Queen of Night; later sang Zerbinetta, Olympia in Les Contes d'Hoffmann, and in operas by Monteverdi; Guest appearances in Hamburg, Berlin, Vienna, Munich and Cologne; Glyndebourne Festival 1978, Die Zauberflöte; US debut Chicago 1981, in Die Schöpfung, conducted by Solti; Bayreuth Festival 1983, as Waldvogel in Siegfried; Salzburg Festival 1984, premiere of Un Re in Ascolto by Berio; At La Scala in 1985 sang the Queen of Night; Aix-en-Provence as Ilia in Idomeneo, 1986; Sang in Doktor Faustus by Giacomo Manzoni at La Scala, 1989; Olga in Fedora at Bologna, 1996; Sang Donna Elvira for New Israeli Opera, 2000. *Recordings include:* Die Schöpfung; Te Deum by Bizet; Poulenc's Gloria; Carmina Burana. *Current Management:* Franz Hainzl Artists' Management, Postfach 17, 1043 Vienna, Austria. *Telephone:* (1) 586 4536. *Fax:* (1) 585 5551. *E-mail:* office@hainzl.net. *Website:* www.sylviagreenberg.com.

**GREENFIELD, Edward (Harry),** OBE, MA; British music critic; b. 30 July 1928. *Education:* Trinity Hall, Univ. of Cambridge. *Career:* joined Staff of Manchester Guardian 1953, Record Critic 1955, Music Critic 1964, succeeded Sir Neville Cardus as Chief Music Critic 1977–93; broadcaster on music and records for BBC Radio 1957–; mem. Critics Panel, Gramophone 1960–; Pres. Fed. of Recorded Music Socs 1997–. *Publications:* Puccini: Keeper of the Seal 1958, Monographs on Joan Sutherland 1972, André Previn 1973, Stereo Record Guide (with Robert Layton, Ivan March and initially Denis Stevens, nine vols) 1960–74, Penguin Stereo Record Guide 1975, Penguin Guide to Compact Discs 1986. *Honours:* Hon. GSM 1991; Goldener Verdienstzeichen, Salzburg 1980, Gramophone Special Award 1993. *Address:* 16 Folgate Street, London, E1 6BX, England. *Telephone:* (20) 7377-7555 (office).

**GREENHOUSE, Bernard;** American cellist and teacher; b. 3 Jan. 1916, Newark, NJ; m. Aurora Greenhouse; two d. *Education:* Juilliard Graduate School of Music, New York, studied with William Berce, Felix Salmond, Emanuel Feuermann, Diran Alexanian, Pablo Casals. *Career:* principal cellist, CBS Symphony Orchestra, New York 1938–42; mem., Dorian String Quartet 1939–42; solo cellist, US Navy Symphony Orchestra; mem., Navy String Quartet 1942–45; annual recitals, Town Hall, New York 1946–57; mem., Harpsichord Quartet 1947–51, Bach Aria Group 1948–76; founder-mem., Beaux Arts Trio 1955–87; guest artist, Juilliard, Guarneri and

Cleveland String Quartets; numerous appearances on major concert series and with festivals worldwide; Prof., Manhattan School of Music, New York 1950–82, Juilliard School of Music, New York 1951–61, Indiana Univ. School of Music, Bloomington summers 1956–65, State Univ. of New York, Stony Brook 1960–85, New England Conservatory of Music, Boston 1986–92, Rutgers, State Univ. of New Jersey 1987–92; masterclasses around the globe; mem. Cello Soc. (pres. 1955–59, 1987–92). *Honours:* Dr hc (State Univ. of New York, Stony Brook) 1988; hon. faculty mem. Central Conservatory, Beijing, China 2003, hon. mem. American String Teachers Asscn; Indiana Univ. Eva Jantzer Award 1980, Chamber Music America Nat. Service Award 1988, Distinguished Cellist Award, Manchester, UK 1996, Prix Mondial du Disque, Union de la Presse Musicale Belge, Gramophone Record of the Year, Stereo Review Record of the Year, three Grand Prix du Disques, American String Teachers' Asscn Teacher of the Year Award 1982, US Presidential Citation 1982, US Presidential Medallion 1985. *Address:* 12 E 86th Street, New York, NY 10028, USA.

**GREENLAW, Kevin;** Singer (Baritone); b. 1965, USA. *Education:* Interlocken Arts Academy; Eastman School of Music; Opera School of the Royal Scottish Academy. *Career:* Early appearances as Mozart's Guglielmo and Nardo, Schaunard in La Bohème, Britten's Tarquinius, and Papageno (at Aldeburgh); Concerts include Carmina Burana, Des Knaben Wunderhorn by Mahler, Messiah and the Fauré Requiem; Paris Opéra Bastille in Manon, Parsifal, Don Carlos and War and Peace; Ned Keene in Peter Grimes at Montpellier 2001; Elsewhere in France as Belcore, Ramiro in L'Heure Espangole and Odoardo in Handel's Ariodante at the Paris Palais Garnier, 2001; Juan in Massenet's Don Quichotte and Morales in Carmen at the Bastille; Has sung at Dortmund Opera as Don Giovanni and Marcello; Festival engagements at Edinburgh (Fringe), Isle of Mann, Aldeburgh and Orange. *Address:* Chemnitzer Straße 30, D–44139, Dortmund, Germany. *Telephone:* 49 231 545 0083. *Fax:* 49 231 545 0083.

**GREENWOOD, Andrew;** Conductor; b. 1954, Todmorden, Yorkshire, England. *Education:* Studied at Clare College, Cambridge and at the London Opera Centre. *Career:* Opera For All, 1976; Member of the music staff of Covent Garden 1977–84, studying with Edward Downes and conducting the Dutch Radio and Television Orchestra; Principal Guest Chorus Master of the Philharmonia Chorus from 1981: concerts with Previn, Davis, Giulini, Sinopoli and Solti; Conducted Rossini's Petite Messe Solennelle at the Istanbul Festival 1985; Chorus master at Welsh National Opera from 1984, and has conducted performances of operas by Mozart, Bizet, Puccini, Verdi, Berlioz (The Trojans), Beethoven, Strauss and Smetana; Many concerts on BBC Radio 2 and 3, notably with the BBC National Orchestra of Wales; Debut with the Rotterdam Philharmonic 1990, Cologne Opera 1990, The Bartered Bride and Die Fledermaus; English National Opera 1990–92, The Magic Flute and Madama Butterfly; Conducted Manon Lescaut for the Chelsea Opera Group, 1992, Don Giovanni for ENO; The Pearl Fishers for English Touring Opera, 1996. *Current Management:* Athole Still International Management, Forresters Hall, 25–27 Westow Street, London, SE19 3RY, England. *Telephone:* (20) 8771-5271. *Fax:* (20) 8768-6600. *Website:* www.atholestill.com.

**GREER, David (Clive),** BA, MA, MusD, FRSA; British professor of music; b. 8 May 1937, London; m. 1st Patricia Regan 1961 (died 1999); two s. one d.; m. 2nd Harriet Marling 2002. *Education:* Dulwich Coll., Univ. of Oxford, Univ. of Dublin. *Career:* Lecturer in Music, Univ. of Birmingham 1963–72; Hamilton Harty Prof. of Music, Queen's Univ., Belfast 1972–84; Prof. of Music, Univ. of Newcastle 1984–86; Prof. of Music, Univ. of Durham 1986–2001, Prof. Emer. 2001–; Mellon Visiting Fellow, Huntington Library, Calif. 1989, Mayers Visiting Fellow 1991; Folger Visiting Fellow, Folger Shakespeare Library, Washington DC 1994, 1998; Chair. Accreditation Panel, Hong Kong Baptist Univ. 1994; Ed. Journal (fmrly Proceedings) of the Royal Musical Association, Vols 103–115. *Publications:* Ed. with F. W. Sternfeld, English Madrigal Verse (3rd edn) 1967, English Lute Songs (facsimile series) 1967–71, Hamilton Harty, His Life and Music 1979, Songs from Manuscript Sources 1979, Collected English Lutenist Partsongs (Musica Britannica, Vols 53–54) 1987–89, A Numerous and Fashionable Audience: The Story of Elsie Swinton 1997, John Dowland: Ayres for Four Voices (Musica Britannica, Vol. 6) 2000, Musicology and Sister Disciplines 2000. *Contributions:* Music and Letters, Proceedings of the Royal Musical Association, Lute Society Journal, Musical Times, Shakespeare Quarterly, English Studies, Notes and Queries, Early Music, Music Review. *Address:* Department of Music, University of Durham, Palace Green, Durham, DH1 3R L, England (office). *E-mail:* d.c.greer@durham.ac.uk (office).

**GREEVY, Bernadette;** Irish singer (mezzo-soprano); b. 3 July 1940, Dublin; d. of Patrick J. Greevy and Josephine F. Miller; m. Peter A. Tattan 1965 (died 1983); one s. *Education:* Convent of the Holy Faith, Clontarf, Dublin. *Career:* London début, Wigmore Hall 1964; has since appeared on maj. concert platforms in Europe, USA, Canada and Far East; recordings of works by Brahms, Handel, Haydn, Bach, Berlioz, Britten, Elgar and Mahler; mem. Bd Nat. Concert Hall 1981–86, 1991–. *Honours:* Hon. DMus (Univ. Coll., Dublin), (Trinity Coll., Dublin); Harriet Cohen Int. Music Award; Order of Merit (Order of Malta); Dame of the Holy Sepulchre; Pro Ecclesia et Pontifice (Vatican). *Address:* c/o Trinity College, Dublin (office); Melrose, 672 Howth Road, Dublin 5, Ireland.

**GREGOR, Bohumil;** Conductor; b. 14 July 1926, Prague, Czechoslovakia. *Education:* Studied with Alois Klima at the Prague Conservatory. *Career:*

Worked at the Prague 5th May (Smetana) Theatre from 1947; Conducted at the Brno Opera 1949–51; Musical Director Ostrava Opera 1958–62; Performances of Janáček's Katya Kabanova and The Excursions of Mr Brouček and premieres of works by Pauer, Kaslik and Trojan; Conductor at the Prague National Theatre from 1962: led the company in the first British productions of Janáček's From the House of the Dead (Edinburgh 1964 and 1970); Royal Opera Stockholm 1966–69, Hamburg Staatsoper 1969–72: premiere of Kelemen's Belagerungzustand (after The Plague by Camus, 1970) and operas by Verdi, Smetana and Janáček; Performances of The Cunning Little Vixen in Vienna, Edinburgh, Brussels and Amsterdam; San Francisco Opera from 1969, Jenůfa, Otello and Salome; Conducted The Cunning Little Vixen at Zürich, 1989 and at the Bayreuth Youth Festival, 1990; New production of Dvořák's The Devil and Kate at Prague, 1990; Season 1993 with Katya Kabanova and a new production of The Bartered Bride; Principal Guest Conductor, National Theatre, Prague; Brandenburgers in Bohemia by Smetana, 1997; Premiere of Burian's Bubu from Montparnasse (composed 1927), 1999; Music Director, The Prague State Opera, 1999–. *Recordings:* Several sets of Czech opera: The Makropulos Case, The Cunning Little Vixen, Jenůfa and From the House of the Dead; Dvořák Symphonic Poems; Concert overtures; Slavonic rhapsodies. *Address:* Janackovo Nabrezi 7. 150 00 Prague 5, Czech Republic.

**GREGOR, Joszef;** Singer (Bass); b. 8 Aug. 1940, Rakosliget, Hungary. *Education:* Studied in Budapest with Endreh Poessler and sang in choir of Hungarian army. *Career:* Appearances at the Szeged Opera from 1964; Sang Sarastro at the Hungarian State Opera, Budapest, 1966; Played title role in Hungarian premiere of Attila, 1972 and appeared in operas by Goldmark, Rossini, Donizetti, Puccini and Bartók (title role in Duke Bluebeard's Castle); Visited the Wiesbaden Festival 1970 and sang elsewhere in Germany as guest; Houston Grand Opera 1986 as Varlaam in Boris Godunov, Monte Carlo Opera 1988, in Cimarosa's Il Pittore Parigino; New York Met debut 1994, as a Priest in Lady Macbeth of the Mtsensk District; Sang the King in Aida at Szaged, 1997; Sang Dulcamara at the Erkel Theatre, Budapest, 1995; Sang Rossini's Bartolo at Antwerp, 1999, and in Jenůfa at Geneva, 2001; Many radio and television performances from 1975; Frequent concert engagements. *Recordings:* Goldmark's Die Königin von Saba; Haydn's L'Infedeltà delusa and La Fedeltà Premiata; Paisiello's Barbiere di Siviglia; Guntram (Strauss), Nerone (Boito) and Mosè in Egitto (Rossini); Don Pasquale, Gianni Schicchi and La Fiamma by Respighi; Duke Bluebeard's Castle; Liszt's Missa solemnis and Legend of St Elisabeth; Beethoven's Missa solemnis and 9th Symphony; Salieri's Falstaff; La Serva Padrona; Il Pittore Parigino; Andrea Chénier and Fedora; Der Geduldige Sokrates by Telemann (Hungaroton). *Address:* Hungarian State Opera House, Nepoztarsasag utja 22, 1061 Budapest, Hungary.

**GREGSON, Edward;** Composer; b. 23 July 1945, Sunderland, England; m. Susan Carole Smith, 30 Sept 1967, 2 s. *Education:* Royal Academy of Music, 1963–67; LRAM, 1966; GRSM, 1967; BMus, University of London, 1977;. *Career:* Lecturer, 1976, Reader in Music, 1989, Professor of Music, 1994, Goldsmiths' College, University of London; Principal, Royal Northern College of Music, 1996–; Director: Associated Board of the Royal Schools of Music, Performing Right Society, Hallé Orchestra; Governor, Chetham's School of Music; As Composer commissioned by numerous orchestras, organisations, ensembles, the United Kingdom and abroad, 1970–, including English Chamber Orchestra, 1968, York Festival, 1976, Royal Shakespeare Company, 1988, 1990, Bournemouth Festival, 1991, Hallé Orchestra, 1999, also National Centre for Orchestral Studies, Wren Orchestra of London, BBC, Royal Liverpool Philharmonic, 1991; Extensive judging panel work includes BBC Young Musician of the Year and Royal Philharmonic Society, amongst others. *Compositions include:* Orchestral: Music for Chamber Orchestra, 1968; Horn Concerto, 1971; Tuba Concerto, 1976; Trombone Concerto, 1979; Metamorphoses, 1979; Contrasts, concerto for orchestra 1983, revised 2001; Trumpet Concerto, 1983; Celebration, 1991; Blazon, 1992; Clarinet Concerto, 1994; Concerto, piano and wind, 1995–97; And the Seven Trumpets, 1998; Violin Concerto, 2000; Choral, vocal: In the Beginning, 1966; 5 Songs of Innocence and Experience, 1980; Missa Brevis Pacem, 1988; Make a Joyful Noise, anthem, 1988; A Welcome Ode, 1997; The Dance, forever the Dance, 1999; Instrumental, chamber: Divertimento, 1967; 6 Little Piano Pieces, 1967; Piano Sonata in one movement, 1986; Alarum, 1993; Three Matisse Impressions, 1993; Romance for Recorder and string quartet, 1964, revised 2003; Brass Quintet, 1967; Equale Dances from brass quintet, 1983; Brass Band: Variations on Laudate Dominum 1976, Connotations, 1977; Dances and Arias, 1984; Of Men and Mountains, 1990; The Trumpets of the Angels, 2000, An Age of Kings 2004; Symphonic Wind Band: Festivo, 1985; The Sword and the Crown, 1991; The Kings Go Forth, 1997, Serenata Notturna for violin and piano 1999, for cello and piano 2004; Educational music. *Recordings:* most of these compositions have been commercially recorded. *Publications include:* The Contemporary Repertoire of Brass Bands in the 20th Century, 1979. *Honours:* FRAM, 1990; FRNCM, 1999; FRCM, 2000, Hon. FLCM, 1997; Hon. DMus (Sunderland) 1996; Fellow Dartington College of Arts, 1997; Hon. Doctor of Arts (Manchester Metropolitan) 2003. *Address:* c/o The Royal Northern College of Music, 124 Oxford Road, Manchester M13 9RD, England (office). *Telephone:* (161) 907-5273 (office). *E-mail:* edward.gregson@rncm.ac.uk (office).

**GRELA-MOZEJKO, Piotr;** Composer and Music Critic; b. 15 March 1961, Bytom, Poland; m. Kasia Zoledziowski 30 June 1990. *Education:* MA,

University of Silesia, Katowice; Studied Composition with Dr Edward Boguslawski, Katowice, Dr Boguslaw Schaeffer, Kraków, Dr Alfred Fisher, University of Alberta. *Career:* Debut: The Silesian Tribune of Composers, 1982; 1st performance of work, 1977; Works performed at major festivals such as Warsaw Autumn Festival, Poznan Music Spring Festival, Gdansk Meetings of Young Composers; Founder, Fascinating Music Festival, Katowice, 1983–86; Co-Founder, J. S. Bach Festival, Kraków-Katowice, 1985; Took part in many exhibitions of musical scores, Institut Polonais, Paris, Royal Academy of Music, London, Warsaw, Salzburg, Katowice; Numerous interviews, Polish television and radio, also CBC; Polish television documentary on activities and the Fascinating Music Festival, 1992; Completed MMus Degree in Composition at the University of Alberta, Edmonton, 1992. *Compositions:* Archival radio recordings, Poland, Canada, USA: Ravenna, harpsichord; minimum-optimum-maximum, chamber ensemble; en attendant Bergson, string quartet; The Dreams of Odysseus, tape (performed in Warsaw, Poland, as part of the first exhibition of Polish artists in exile, Jestesmy); Epitaph for Jerzy, for tape included in A BEAMS Compilation; Xylotet Concerto, saxophone, orchestra; Horror Vacui, strings; Ordines, saxophone, organ, cello; Melodramas I–VI, solo instruments; Festivals: Canada, Pacific Market, Fringe, The Edmonton Music Festival, Warsaw. *Address:* No. 8 8807 101st Street, Edmonton, Alberta T6E 3Z9, Canada.

**GRIBENSKI, Jean;** Musicologist; b. 5 Aug. 1944, Castelmoron-sur-Lot, Lot-et-Garonne, France; m. Isabelle Serrand, 10 Sept. 1980, 1 s., 3 d. *Education:* History, Musicology, Sorbonne, Paris, 1963–68; Studied Piano, Musical Theory and Harmony. *Career:* Teaching, History of Music, Sorbonne, Université Paris IV, 1970–2003, Université de Poitiers, 2003–; Editor-in-Chief, Revue de Musicologie, 1974–86; mem, Société française de musicologie, Board of Directors, 1974–, President, 1995–2001. *Publications:* Thèses de doctorat en langue française relative à la musique/French language dissertations in music, 1979; D'un opéra l'autre, 1996. *Address:* 23 avenue de Breteuil, 75007 Paris, France. *E-mail:* jean.gribenski@wanadoo.fr (home).

**GRICE, Garry (Bruce);** Opera Singer (Tenor); b. 25 Jan. 1942, Dayton, Ohio, USA; m. Patricia A Michael, 9 July 1983, 1 s., 2 d. *Education:* BA, History, University of Daytn, 1964; Musical studies with Hubert Kockritz, Cincinnati and Adelaide Saraceni, Milan. *Career:* Debut: National Opera, USA, 1970–71; 8 seasons in German and Swiss opera houses including: Debut, Stadttheater, St Gallen, Switzerland, 1974, Debut, Bavarian State Opera, 1974; Debut as Don José in Carmen, Florentine Opera, Milwaukee, 1980; Bacchus in Ariadne auf Naxos, Des Moines Metro Opera, 1980; Debut, New York City Opera, 1981; Bermuda Festival, 1981; Debut, Chicago as Don José in Carmen, 1983; Debut, Calgary Opera Association, 1985; Debut, Cairo, 1990; Has sung with conductors Kleiber, Prêtre, Guadagno, Keene and Rescigno; Has appeared in over 50 roles including Otello, Florestan, Bacchus, Canio, Max and Radames; Has sung throughout USA, also Canada, Bermuda and Europe mainly Germany, Austria, Switzerland; Faculty Voice and Opera, University of Notre Dame, 1991; Artistic Director, Indian Opera North since 1990; Performance: New Orleans Debut, Verdi Requiem, 1992. *Recordings:* Title role in Otello, Television Public Broadcasting, 1984; Turiddu in Cavalleria Rusticana, Canadian Public Radio, 1985. *Publications:* Translations into English of Otello, Il Trovatore and Tales of Hoffmann. *Current Management:* Warden Associated INc, 127 W 72nd Street, Suite 2-R, New York, NY 10023, USA.

**GRIER, Francis;** Organist, Pianist and Composer; b. 1955, England. *Education:* Chorister at St George's Chapel, Windsor Castle; Eton College; Organ Scholar at King's College, Cambridge; Piano Studies with Joseph Cooper, Fanny Waterman and Bernard Roberts; Organ with Gillian Weir. *Career:* Assistant Organist to Simon Preston, at Christ Church Cathedral, Oxford; Organist and Director of Music, 1981; Organ recitals throughout the United Kingdom; First Organ recital at the BBC Promenade Concerts, 1985; Sudied in India from 1985; Then worked with mentally handicapped in London and Bangladore; Resident in England from 1989; Works as psychodynamic counsellor; mem, FRCO. *Compositions:* Advent Responsories for King's College Chapel, 1990; Mass with motets for Westminster Abbey; Sequences of Readings and Music for Ascension, for the 550th anniversary of Eton College, 1990; The Cry of Mary, for BBC2, 1992; St Francis, opera, for Eton College and National Youth Music Theatre, 1993; Mass in Time of Persecution, for soloists, chorus and orchestra, including poems of Ratushinskaya, 1994; My Heart Dances, settings of Tagore, for soloists, chorus and orchestra, commissioned by 3 Choirs Festival, 1995. *Recordings:* Bach; Mendelssohn; Couperin, Franck; Messiaen: Messe de la Pentecôte and L'Ascension, all on the Rieger organ at Christ Church Cathedral. *Address:* 65 Tynemouth Road, London N15 4AU, England.

**GRIEVES-SMITH, Jonathan Mark,** BA; British conductor and artistic director; b. 14 Dec. 1962, Kendal, England; m. Sally; two s. one d. *Education:* Kingswood School, Bath and Univ. of Sussex. *Career:* Artistic Dir and Prin. Conductor, Melbourne Chorale; Artistic Admin., The Queensland Orchestra; Music Dir, Brighton Festival Chorus; Chorus Master, Huddersfield Choral Soc., Halle Choir, Reading Festival Chorus; guest conductor, Royal Philharmonic Orchestra, Royal Liverpool Philharmonic, London Mozart Players, Bournemouth Symphony Orchestra, New Zealand Symphony Orchestra, Melbourne Symphony Orchestra, Orchestre Nat. de Lille, Bochum Symphoniker, Europa Cantat in Denmark and Austria, Dartington Int. Summer School; Conductor Emer., Melbourne Chorale. *Recordings:* as chorus master for Bax/Handley, Beethoven/Menuhin, Walton/Previn, Tippett/Previn, Mar-

tin/Bamert, Lloyd/Lloyd, Patterson/Simon. *Address:* 14 Lambert Road, Toorak, Vic. 3142, Australia (home).

**GRIFFEL, Kay;** American singer (soprano); b. 26 Dec. 1940, Eldora, IA; m. Eckhard Sellheim. *Education:* Northwestern Univ., IL, studied in Berlin and at Santa Barbara with Lotte Lehmann. *Career:* debut, Chicago 1960, as Mercédès in Carmen; sang at the Deutsche Oper Berlin and in Bremen, Mainz, Karlsruhe, Hamburg and Düsseldorf; Salzburg 1973 in the premiere of De Temporum fine Comoedia by Orff; Glyndebourne Festival 1976–77, as Alice Ford in Falstaff; tour of Japan with the Staatsoper Berlin 1977, as the Marschallin, Donna Elvira and Mozart's Countess; Lisbon 1978, Eva in Die Meistersinger; Metropolitan Opera from 1982, as Electra in Idomeneo, Rosalinde, Arabella, Tatiana and the Countess; further appearances in Brussels, Moscow, Cologne and at the Orange Festival; sang Eva in Die Meistersinger at Wellington, New Zealand 1990. *Recordings:* Janáček Diary of One who Disappeared, De Temporum fine Comoedia, Italian Arias. *Honours:* Hon. DFA (Simpson Coll., Indianola, IA) 1982. *Current Management:* Theateragentur Dr Germinal Hilbert, Maximilianstrasse 22, 80539 Munich, Germany.

**GRIFFEY, Anthony Dean;** American singer (tenor); b. 1968, North Carolina. *Education:* Metropolitan Young Artist Development Program. *Career:* debut, New York Met 1995, as First Knight in Parsifal; Appearances at the Met in Manon, Don Carlos, Aida, Billy Budd, Salome, Boris Godunov and The Queen of Spades; Further engagements as Peter Grimes and Sam Polk in Floyd's Susannah at the Met, Mitch in Previn's A Streetcar named Desire at San Francisco, and Mozart's Idomeneo for the Mainly Mozart Festival, New York; Season 2000–01 with Peter Grimes at Glyndebourne, Ferrando in Così fan tutte and Laca in Jenůfa at the Saito Kinen Festival, Japan, and The Dream of Gerontius with the New York Philharmonic; Other concerts include Britten's War Requiem, at Tanglewood. *Recordings include:* A Streetcar Named Desire. *Current Management:* Columbia Artists Management LLC, 165 W 57th Street, New York, NY 10019-2276, USA. *Telephone:* (212) 841-9500. *Fax:* (212) 841-9744. *E-mail:* info@cami.com. *Website:* www.anthonydeangriffey.com.

**GRIFFIN, Judson;** Violist and Violinist; b. 7 Sept. 1951, Lewes, Delaware, USA; m. Mara Paske, 7 May 1988. *Education:* DMA 1977, MM 1975, Juilliard School of Music; BM, Eastman School of Music, 1973. *Career:* Debut: Carnegie Recital Hall, New York City, January 1981; Violist, Rochester Philharmonic Orchestra, 1970–73; Freelance Violist, New York City, 1973–77; Assistant Professor, University of North Carolina at Greensboro, 1977–79; Principal Viola, Aspen Chamber Symphony, 1977–80; Freelance Violinist and Violist, New York City, 1979–; Current activities, Violist of Smithson String Quartet and Smithsonian Chamber Players (Smithsonian Institution, Washington DC); Atlantis Ensemble (Europe); Violinist of Four Nations and Sonata a quattro (New York); Regular appearances with almost all period-instrument organisations in USA. *Recordings:* Chamber music on labels, Nonesuch, Harmonia Mundi (France, USA), L'Oiseau-Lyre, Reference, Harmonia Mundi (Germany), Columbia, CRI, CP2, Pro Arte, Newport; Many radio recordings. *Address:* 170 Claremont Avenue No. 7, New York, NY 10027, USA.

**GRIFFITH, Lisa;** Singer (Soprano); b. 1959, USA. *Education:* Studied at Indiana University and the Cincinnati Conservatory. *Career:* Debut: Seattle Opera, 1984; Sang at Wiesbaden Opera, 1984–89, Hanover, 1989–91, notably as Zerbinetta; Deutsche Oper am Rhein, Düsseldorf, from 1991, as Susanna in The Marriage of Figaro and Sophie in Rosenkavalier (1993); Other roles include Gilda and Pamina; Guest at the Munich Staatsoper, the Komische Oper Berlin and Staatsoper Stuttgart; Frequent concert appearances; Sang in premiere production of Beuys by Franz Hummel, Vienna, Berlin and Düsseldorf, 1998; Sang Irina in Three Sisters by Peter Eötvös at Dusseldorf, 1999, and Gounod's Juliette at Lubeck, 2000. *Address:* c/o Deutsche Oper am Rhein, Heinrich-Heine-Allee 16a, 40213 Düsseldorf, Germany.

**GRIFFITH-SMITH, Bella;** American singer and conductor; b. 1920. *Education:* studied with Howard Thain, Franco Iglesias, Dr Paul Csonka. *Career:* debut at the Civic Opera of the Palm Beaches; appeared with Louis Quilico, Metropolitan artist, Robert Merrill, Giuseppe Campora; television: Concert Version-Spanish Translation, Channel 2, Miami; Madama Butterfly; radio: La Traviata; leading roles in Madama Butterfly; La Bohème, Tosca, Cavalleria Rusticana, Pagliacci, Suor Angelica, Il Tabarro, Faust, Carmen (Micaela), Così fan tutte (Fiordiligi), Tales of Hoffmann (Antonia), Don Pasquale-Norina, L'Oca del Cairo (Celidora), La Traviata, Oratorio-Elijah, L'Enfant Prodigue, Messiah, Vivaldi's Gloria, Stabat Mater, Rossini; concerts: Salome, Otello, Turandot, with Alain Lombard/Greater Miami Philharmonic; guest soloist; Pres., Coral Gables Civic Opera and Orchestra, Inc. *Address:* 700 Santander Avenue, Coral Gables, FL 33134, USA.

**GRIFFITHS, Graham (Charles Thomas);** Conductor, Pianist and Lecturer; b. 13 May 1954, Tiverton, England; m. Miriam Regina Zillo, 18 Jan 1985, 2 s. *Education:* Bryanston School 1967–72; BMus (hons) Edinburgh University, 1976; PGCE (Cantab) Cambridge University, 1977. *Career:* Founder-Member, Edinburgh Experimental Arts Society, 1972–76; Founder-member, Grand Toxic Opera Company, Edinburgh, 1974–76; Member, Cambridge Contemporary Music Ensemble, 1976–78; Marketing/Education Officer, Scottish National Orchestra, 1978–81; Co-Administrator, International Musica Nova Festival, Glasgow, 1978–81; Arts Journalist, Scottish Television, 1981–86; Principal Conductor, Glasgow Chamber Orchestra, 1985–86; Lecturer in Twentieth Century Music, São Paulo State University,

Brazil, 1987–89; Founder-Director, Jardim Musical Arts Centre, 1987–; Founder-Conductor, Ensemble Grupo Novo Horizonte, 1988–; Director of Education, Mozarteum Brasileiro, 1987–; Conductor, Choir of Cultura Inglesa, São Paulo, 1988–90; Choral Director, 1st National Festival of Brazilian Colonial Music (Juiz de Fora) 1990; Guest Conductor, Campos do Jordao Festival, 1990; Guest Conductor, Orquestra Sinfonica e Madrigal da Universidade Federal da Bahia, Salvador, 1990–; Director of Conducting Course, Festival Seminarios Internacionais Salvador, 1991; Lecture-Recital piano tours: 1990 Bridges Across Time, Brazil, Denmark, United Kingdom; 1991 New World Experience, Brazil, Denmark (25 concerts); Co-Founder-Director, Mostra de Musica Contemporanea, Ouro Preto, 1991; Regular broadcasts on Radio e Televisao Cultura, São Paulo, 1988–; Visiting Lecturer, Federal Universities of Rio de Janeiro, 1990, Bahia 1990/91, Uberlandia 1992; Guest Conductor, Camerata Antigua de Curitiba, 1993. *Compositions:* Sacred Choral Works include: Anglican Hymn Collection, 1988–; The Lords Prayer, 1990; Ta Voix, 1991; Cançao de Quatá for Trombone Quartet, 1993. *Current Management:* Jardim Musical, São Paulo. *Address:* Rua Angatuba 97, Pacaembu, 01247-000 São Paulo, SP, Brazil.

**GRIFFITHS, Hilary;** Conductor; b. 1950, Leamington Spa, England; m. Andrea Andonian, 28 June 1978, 2 s. *Education:* Studied at the Royal Academy of Music, London Opera Centre and in Siena and Milan. *Career:* Former principal staff conductor at the Cologne Opera, with appearances also in Dresden, Düsseldorf, Nuremberg and Basle; Former music director of Oberhausen Opera with further engagements in Oslo, Antwerp, Leeds (Opera North) and at the Edinburgh, Prague and Schwetzingen Festivals; Conductor at the State Opera Prague from 1992 (operas by Zemlinsky and Strauss), music director at Regensburg from 1993 and at the Eutin opera festival (Die Zauberflöte, Il Trovatore, Der Freischütz and Turandot); Season 1997 with Don Giovanni and Intermezzo at Regensburg, Die Zauberflöte and Aida in Cologne and Otello and Butterfly in Prague; Don Giovanni at the Perth Festival, Australia and Der Prinz von Homburg to open the Wiesbaden May Festival; Concerts with the Rotterdam Philharmonic, the BBC National Orchestra of Wales, and the West German Radio Orchestra. *Recordings:* CD, Jommelli, Mass in D and Te Deum. *Publications:* World Premieres: Das Gauklermärchen and Lulu; German Premieres, A Christmas Carol and Simon Bolivar both by Thea Musgrave. *Contributions:* TV and Video: Il matrimonio segreto, from the Schwetzingen Festival, Lulu from Cologne. *Address:* Graf-Adolf-Strasse 28, 51065 Cologne, Germany.

**GRIFFITHS, Howard Laurence,** MBE, ARCM; British conductor; b. 24 Feb. 1950, Hastings, England; m. Semra Griffiths 1971; one s. one d. *Education:* Royal Coll. of Music, London with Cecil Aronowitz, studied conducting with Leon Barzin, Paris, Erich Schmid, Zürich. *Career:* debut at QEH, English Chamber Orchestra 1989; Royal Festival Hall, Royal Philharmonic Orchestra 1991; Principal Viola, Ankara State Opera until 1979; mem., Lucerne String Quartet; Principal Guest Conductor, Oxford Orchestra da Camera 1994; Dir and Principal Conductor, Zürich Chamber Orchestra 1996–; has conducted many prominent orchestras, including Royal Philharmonic Orchestra, English Chamber Orchestra, Warsaw Philharmonic Orchestra, Basel Radio Symphony Orchestra, Istanbul State Symphony Orchestra, Northern Sinfonia of England, Stadtorchester Winterthur, Polish Chamber Orchestra, Tonhalle Orchestra Zürich, Nat. Orchestra of Spain, London Mozart Players, Slovak Radio-Symphony Orchestra, Tchaikovsky SO of the Moscow Radio, Orchestre Nationale de Paris, Orchestre Philharmonique de Montpellier, Tapiola Sinfonietta; repertory includes music by Henze (Requiem), Crumb, Kagel and Pärt; Artistic Dir, Allensbach Chamber Music Festival, Germany 1992–98; Artistic Director, Orpheum Foundation for the Promotion of Young Soloists 2000–. *Recordings include:* 18th Century Swiss Composers Stalder and Reindl, English Chamber Orchestra; Instrumental Works of Othmar Schoeck, English Chamber Orchestra; Mozart Horn Concertos, Kalinski and Polish Chamber Orchestra; works of Max Bruch, Royal Philharmonic Orchestra; three albums of music by Turkish composers Saygun, Erkin, Rey, with Northern Sinfonia of England; Baroque Oboe Concertos and Mozart Sinfonia Concertante; Caspar Fritz Violin Concerto, English Chamber Orchestra; Ferdinand Ries Complete Symphonies 1–8 with Zürich Chamber Orchestra. *Current Management:* Konzertgesellschaft, Hochstrasse 51, Postfach, 4002 Basel, Switzerland.

**GRIFFITHS, Paul Anthony,** BA, MSc; British music critic and writer; b. 24 Nov. 1947, Bridgend, Glamorgan, Wales. *Education:* Lincoln Coll., Oxford. *Career:* music critic for various journals 1971–; Area Ed. 20th Century Music, New Grove Dictionary of Music and Musicians 1973–76; music critic, The Times 1982–92, New Yorker 1992–96, New York Times 1997–; compiled Mozart pasticcio The Jewel Box for Opera North 1991, Purcell pasticcio Aeneas in Hell 1995. *Publications:* A Concise History of Modern Music 1978, Boulez 1978, A Guide to Electronic Music 1979, Cage 1981, Peter Maxwell Davies 1982, The String Quartet 1983, György Ligeti 1983, Bartók 1984, Olivier Messiaen 1985, New Sounds, New Personalities: British Composers of the 1980s 1985, An Encyclopedia of 20th Century Music 1986, Myself and Marco Polo (novel) 1987, The Life of Sir Tristram (novel) 1991, The Jewel Box (opera libretto) 1991, Stravinsky 1992, Modern Music and After 1995, libretti for Tan Dun's opera, Marco Polo 1996, libretti for Elliott Carter's opera, What Next? 1999, The Sea on Fire 2004. *Address:* University of Rochester Press, 668 Mount Hope Avenue, Rochester, NY 14620-273, USA.

**GRIFFITHS, Paul Wayne;** Conductor; b. 1958, England. *Education:* Studied at Royal Northern College of Music and London Opera Centre.

*Career:* Conducted The Judgement of Paris by John Woolrich in Royal Opera House Garden Venture Series, Orchestra of Royal Opera at Windsor Festival and Symphony Hall, Birmingham; Paris debut at Théâtre du Champs Elysées, with Orchestre du Conservatoire National; Further concerts with Royal Philharmonic, English Chamber Orchestra and Tokyo Philharmonic; Season 1992–93 with Il Trovatore for Scottish Opera, L'Elisir d'amore at Gothenburg, concert in Athens with Grace Bumbry and London with Josephine Bartsow and Montserrat Caballé; Covent Garden debut with Rigoletto (1994), returning for La Bohème and Turandot; Artistic Director and Accompanist of Luciano Pavarotti Masterclass; Recital Accompanist with Geraint Evans, José Carreras, Katia Ricciarelli, James King, Thomas Allen and Yevgeny Nesterenko; Staff Conductor, Royal Opera House, Covent Garden.

**GRIGOREV, Alexei;** Singer (tenor); b. 1968, Russia. *Education:* Sweelinck Conservatory; Netherlands International Opera Studio. *Career:* Appearances throughout Europe in Billy Budd, Antwerp; The Nose, Lyon; Mozart's Mitridate at Lyon; Meistersinger, Parsifal and Figaro, Netherlands; Season 1998–99 in Moses und Aron, Die Zauberflote and La finta giardiniera, Darmstadt; Marzio, Mozart's Mitridate, Lyon, 1998; Season 1999–2000 at Châtelet, Paris, Amsterdam and Antwerp; Sang Innkeeper, Benvenuto Cellini, Festival Hall Concert, 1999; Season 2000–01: Le grand macabre, Antwerp; Boris Godounov, Capriccio, DNO, Amsterdam; Don Pasquale, Luxembourg; Three Sisters by Eötvös; Bastien und Bastienne, Concertgebouw, Amsterdam; Season 2001–02: Le Coq d'or in Nantes; Three Sisters by Eötvös in Brussels, Lyon and Vienna; Pulcinella in Brussels and Amsterdam; Lucia di Lammermoor in Basel; Dido and Aeneas, Netherlands; Lustigen Weiber; Concert repertory includes Bach's St John and St Matthew Passions, Berlioz Messe solennelle and Mahler's Klagende Lied; Season 2001–02: Orff's Carmina Burana, Rossini's Stabat Mater, Debussy's L'invocation, Shostakovich's From Jewish Folk Poetry. *Current Management:* Athole Still International Management, Forresters Hall, 25–27 Westow Street, London, SE19 3RY, England. *Telephone:* (20) 8771-5271. *Fax:* (20) 8768-6600. *Website:* www .atholestill.com. *Address:* Sleewijkstraat 78, 1107 TW Amsterdam, Netherlands. *E-mail:* a.grigorev@freeler.nl.

**GRIGORIAN, Gegam;** Singer (Tenor); b. 29 Jan. 1951, Erevan, Armenia. *Education:* Studied at the Opera School of La Scala, Milan. *Career:* Debut: Lwów Opera, 1989, as Cavaradossi; Kirov Opera, St Petersburg, from 1990, notably as Vladimir in Prince Igor and Dimitri in Boris Godunov; Amsterdam from 1991, as Gennaro in Lucrezia Borgia, Andrea Chénier and Cilea's Maurizio; Pierre in War and Peace at the Opéra Bastille, Paris; Covent Garden debut, 1993, as Lensky; Season 1994–95, as Radames at Rome, Pollione in Norma at Genoa and Rimsky's Sadko in Paris; Sang Verdi's Riccardo at Santiago, Cavaradossi at Wiesbaden and Turiddu at Florence; Metropolitan Opera debut as Hermann in The Queen of Spades, 1995; Season 1998 as Riccardo at Monte Carlo, Vasily Golitsin in Khovanshchina at La Scala (Kirov Opera) and Alvaro in La Forza del Destino at St Petersburg (also televised); Sang Canio at Buenos Aires, 2000, Golitsin on tour with the Kirov to Covent Garden, and Pierre in War and Peace at La Scala. *Address:* Kirov Opera, 1 Theatre Square, St Petersburg, Russia.

**GRIGORIU, Theodor;** Composer; b. 25 July 1926, Galatzi, Romania; m. 28 Mar 1951. *Education:* Studied with Mihail Jora, Conservatory of Bucharest, Romania, and Aram Khachaturian, P I Tchaikovsky, Moscow, USSR; Faculty of Architecture, Bucharest. *Career:* Secretary-General, Union of Romanian Composers; Freelance Composer; His works performed world-wide. *Compositions:* Orchestral works include: Sinfonia Cantabile, Op 1, 1950, revised 1966; Variations Symphoniques sur une Chanson d'Anton Pann, (Six Tableaux d'Epoque), 1955; Concerto pour Double Orchestre de Chamber et Hautbois, 1957; Rêve Cosmique-poéme orchestral, 1959; Hommage à Enesco, 8(16) violons, 1960; Orchestral version of Sept Chansons (works Clement Marot), 1964; Tristia, in memoriam Ionel Perlea, Melodie Infinie, 1972; Suite Carpatine, string orchestra, 1980; Pastorale si Idylles de Transylvanie, 1984; Concerto pour violon et orchestre Byzance aprés Byzance, 1994; Chopin Orchestral, 25 Pieces pour un ballet imaginaire, 1995; Requiem for a Poetess, 1999; Aeterna verba im 2000 for mixed chorus and orchestra, 2000; Choral Music: Elegia Pontica, (vers d'Ovide), choir, baritone-bass, 1969; Canti per Europa (oratorio), mixed choir and orchestra, 1976; Les Vocalises de la Mer (choral symphony), mixed choir, organ and orchestra, 1984; Chamber music: Columna Modala (Cahiers I, II), investigations dans l'ethos roumain, piano, 1984; Quatuor à cordes A la recherche de l'echo, 1983; Film Music: Codine, 1963; La Foret des Pendus, 1965; Theatre music. *Recordings:* Various works, Electrocord. *Publications:* Muzica si Numbul Poeziei. *Address:* Str Pictor Rosenthal 2, Bucharest 71288, Romania.

**GRIGSBY, Beverly;** Composer; b. 11 Jan. 1928, Chicago, Illinois, USA. *Education:* Studied in California with Ernst Krenek and Ingolf Dahl and at Stanford University and the Royal College, London. *Career:* Teacher at California State University, Northridge, 1963–92. *Compositions include:* Stage works: Augustine The Saint, 1975, Moses, 1978, The Vision Of St Joan, 1987; Trio for violin, clarinet and piano, 1984; Wind Quintet, 1990; Keyboard Concerto, 1993; Concerto for orchestra, 1994; Computer music. *Address:* c/o ASCAP, ASCAP Building, 1 Lincoln Plaza, New York, NY 10023, USA.

**GRILLO, Joann;** Singer (Mezzo-Soprano); b. 14 May 1939, New York, USA; m. Richard Kness, 1 s. *Education:* BS, Hunter College, New York; Private study with Loretta Corelli, Franco Iglesias and Daniel Ferro. *Career:* Debut: New York City Opera 1962, as Gertrude in Louise; Metropolitan Opera, as

Carmen, Meg Page in Falstaff, Preziosilla in La Forza del Destino, Santuzza, Laura in La Gioconda, Neocle in The Siege of Corinth and Suzuki (226 performances); Sang Massenet's Charlotte at Barcelona in 1963; Amneris at Frankfurt (1967); Carmen at the Vienna Staatsoper and in Paris (1978, 1981); Guest appearances in Essen, Hamburg, Zürich, Dallas, Philadelphia, Lisbon and Marseille; Other roles include Marguerite in The Damnation of Faust, Saint-Saëns's Dalila, Olga in Eugene Onegin, Fricka in The Ring and Verdi's Eboli, Ulrica and Azucena; Sang Amneris at Rio de Janeiro, 1988; Concert appearances as Jocasta in Oedipus Rex. *Current Management:* Eric Semon Associates, 111 W 57th Street, New York, NY 10019, USA. *Address:* c/o Rio de Janeiro Opera, Teatro Municipal, Rio de Janeiro, Brazil.

**GRIMAUD, Hélène;** American (b. French) pianist; b. Aix en Provence, France. *Education:* studied in Marseille with Pierre Barbizet, Conservatoire Nat. Supérieur de Musique, Paris, studied with Jacques Rouvier, Gyorgy Sandor and Leon Fleischer. *Career:* Paris debut recital 1987; performances at MIDEM, Cannes, and at La Roque d'Anthéron Piano Festival 1987; has performed with orchestras worldwide, including Boston Symphony, Cleveland Orchestra, Los Angeles Philharmonic, New York Philharmonic, Philadelphia Orchestra, Montréal Symphony, London Symphony Orchestra, City of Birmingham Symphony Orchestra, London Philharmonic Orchestra, English Chamber Orchestra, Berlin Philharmonic, Bavarian Radio Symphony, Deutsches Symphonie-Orchester, Gewandhausorchester Leipzig, Tonhalle Zurich, Göteborg Symphony, Oslo Philharmonic, Tokyo NHK Symphony, St Petersburg Philharmonic, Concertgebouw Orchestra, Rotterdam Philharmonic, Orchestre Philharmonique de Radio France, Orchestre de Paris; recent performances include the première of a work for piano and orchestra by Arvo Pärt at the Tate Modern gallery, London, concerts in Amsterdam, London, Paris and Japan with the Czech Philharmonic and Ashkenazy, performances with the Philharmonia Orchestra under Christoph von Dohnányi, the Danish National Radio Symphony under Thomas Dausgaard, Detroit Symphony under Neeme Järvi and Netherlands Radio Philharmonic under Peter Eötvös; signed an exclusive contract with Deutsche Grammophon 2002; season 2003/04 appearances included performances with Orchester der Bayerische Staatsoper, San Francisco Symphony, Deutsches Symphonie Orchester Berlin, Tokyo Philharmonic, and tours with the Australian Youth Orchestra, the Chamber Orchestra of Europe and the Philharmonia Orchestra. *Recordings:* Rachmaninoff's Sonata No. 2 (Grand Prix du Disque 1986) 1985, Ravel Concerto in G and Rachmaninov Concerto No.2 with the Royal Philharmonic and Jesus Lopez-Cobos, Schumann Concerto and Strauss Burleske with David Zinman and the Deutsches Symphonie-Orchester Berlin, Brahms opus 116–119 1996, Gershwin Concerto in F and the Ravel Concerto in G with David Zinman and the Baltimore Symphony, Brahms Piano Concerto No.1 with Berlin Staatskapelle Orchester and Kurt Sanderling (Cannes Classical Recording of the Year 1999) 1997, Beethoven sonatas opus 109/110 and concerto No.4 with the New York Philharmonic under Kurt Masur 1999, Rachmaninov Etudes-Tableaux and concerto No.2 with the Philharmonia Orchestra and Vladimir Ashkenazy 2001, Credo 2002. *Honours:* Officier, Ordre des Arts et des Lettres 2002. *Current Management:* Jasper Parrott, HarrisonParrott Ltd, 12 Penzance Place, London, W11 4PA, England. *Telephone:* (20) 7229-9166. *Fax:* (20) 7221-5042. *E-mail:* jasper.parrott@harrisonparrott.co.uk. *Website:* www.harrisonparrott.com; www.helenegrimaud.com.

**GRIMM, Hans-Gunther;** Singer (Baritone) and Professor; b. 1925, Germany. *Education:* Studied in East Berlin. *Career:* Sang at Berlin Staatsoper, 1950–52, Bremen, 1952–54, Mannheim, 1954–60; Engaged at Cologne, 1960–64, Theater am Gartnerplatz, Munich, 1964–66, Dortmund, 1966–70; Sang in Cologne, 1961, in German premiere of Nono's Intolleranza 60; Guest appearances as concert and opera singer, Frankfurt, Japan, North America, France and Barcelona; Roles included Mozart's Count, Don Giovanni, Guglielmo and Papageno, Malatesta, Marcello, Wolfram, Escamillo, Don Fernando in Fidelio and Carlos in Forza del Destino; Professor at Maastrich Conservatory, Netherlands, 1973–82. *Recordings include:* Undine by Lortzing; Eine Nacht in Venedig; Rossini's Petite Messe solennelle; Beethoven's Ninth.

**GRIMSLEY, Greer;** Singer (baritone); b. 1962, New Orleans, Louisiana, USA. *Career:* Sang Jochanaan in Salome with Scottish Opera, 1988; Saratoga Opera, 1988, as Alfonso in Così fan tutte and Wexford Festival in Der Templer und die Jüdin by Marschner; Tour of Australia, Canada and Europe in Peter Brook's La Tragédie de Carmen, 1991, as Escamillo; Bregenz Festival, 1991, as Escamillo; Santa Fe in the US premiere of Henze's English Cat and appearances with the Lake George Festival as Pizarro and Don Giovanni; Italian debut, Bologna, 1995, as Escamillo; Metropolitan Opera, 1995–96, as Balstrode (Peter Grimes) and Jochanaan; Escamillo at Vancouver, 1996; Engaged as Donner and Gunther in The Ring, Seattle 2001. *Current Management:* Athole Still International Management, Forresters Hall, 25–27 Westow Street, London, SE19 3RY, England. *Telephone:* (20) 8771-5271. *Fax:* (20) 8768-6600. *Website:* www.atholestill.com.

**GRINDENKO, Tatyana Tikhonovna;** Russian violinist; b. 29 March 1946, Kharkov, Ukraine; m. 1st Gidon Kremer (q.v.); m. 2nd Vladimir Martynov. *Education:* Moscow State Conservatory. *Career:* Prize, World Int. Youth Competition in Bulgaria 1968, Wieniawski Competition in Poland 1972; repertoire includes baroque, avant-garde, jazz, rock, experimental music; co-f. (with A. Lyubimov) and Artistic Dir. Moscow Acad. of Ancient Music. *Address:*

Moscow State Philharmonia, Tverskaya str. 31, 103050 Moscow, Russia. *Telephone:* (095) 253 7425 (home).

**GRINGOLTS, Ilya;** Violinist; b. 1982, Russia. *Education:* Studied at the St Petersburg Special Music School with Tatiana Liberova and Jeanna Metallidi and at the Juilliard School New York with Itzhak Perlman and the late Dorothy Delay, from 1999. *Career:* Appearances with the St Petersburg Philharmonic Orchestra; Moscow Symphony and BBC Scottish Symphony Orchestras; Further engagements 1999–2000 with the National Symphony Orchestra, Washington, Melbourne Symphony Orchestra, Minnesota Orchestra, Royal Liverpool Philharmonic Orchestra and Tapiola Sinfonietta Finland; Recitals for the BBC 's Verbier Festival, The Louvre, Palais des Beaux Arts and Oleg Kagan Festival; Engaged for concerto tour of Italy with Moscow Soloists and Yuri Bashmet, 2000; Shostakovich's Concerto No.1 at the London Proms, 2002; Recent engagements include performances with the Chicago Symphony Orchestra under Daniel Barenboim, UBS Verbier Orchestra/ Kurt Masur and Mstislav Rostropovich, Israel Philharmonic with Zubin Mehta, the St Petersburg Philharmonic Orchestra and Yuri Temirkanov, Deutsche Symphonie Orchester Berlin, at the Proms with the BBC Philharmonic and Vassily Sinaisky, Rotterdam Philharmonic with Vladimir Jorowski, London Philharmonic, Atlanta Symphony, City of Birmingham Symphony, BBC Symphony, Warsaw Philharmonic, Swedish Chamber Orchestra, Minnesota Orchestra and New Zealand Symphony Orchestra. *Recordings:* Paganini Concerto no.1; Works by Ysaÿe, Ernst and Schnittke; Tchaikovsky and Shostakovich No. 1 concertos and Solo Bach for Deutsche Grammophon. *Honours:* Winner, 1998 International Violin Competition; Premio Paganini, and given special honours for being the youngest ever competitor to be placed in the final and the best interpreter of Paganini's Caprices; Has been selected as one of the twelve young artists on the BBC's New Generation Artists Scheme. *Address:* c/o Tom Carrig, Assistant, IMG Artists, Lovell House, 616 Chiswick High Road, London W4 5RX, England. *E-mail:* tcarrig@imgworld.com.

**GRIST, Reri;** Coloratura Soprano; b. 29 Feb. 1932, New York, USA. *Education:* Music and Art High School, New York; Queens College. *Career:* Debut: Consuelo, West Side Story, 1957; Appeared at: Metropolitan Opera, New York, 1966–77; Vienna State Opera Austria, 1963–88; Munich State Opera, Germany, 1965–83; San Francisco Opera Association, 1963–76, 1983, 1990; Royal Opera House, Covent Garden, London, 1962–1974; La Scala, Milan, 1963, 1977–78; Opernhaus Zürich, Switzerland, 1960–66; Netherlands Opera, Amsterdam, 1990–91; Chicago Lyric Opera, 1964; Deutsche Oper, Berlin; Washington Opera Society; European Debut, Cologne, Germany, 1960; New York City Opera, 1959; Santa Fe Opera, New Mexico, 1959; Festival Appearances include: Salzburg, Austria, 1964–77; Munich Festival, 1967–83; Vienna Festival, 1963–80; Holland Festival, 1963; Glyndebourne Festival, 1962; Spoleto Festival, Italy, 1961; The most important new productions were with the stage directors Guenther Rennert, Giorgio Strehler, Pierre Audi, Lofti Mansouri, Otto Schenk, Carl Ebert, Joshua Logan and Jerome Robbins; Repertoire: Mozart: Susanna, Queen of Night, Despina, Zerlina, Blondchen, Madame Herz; R Strauss: Zerbinetta, Sophie, Aminta, Italian Singer; Verdi: Gilda, Oscar, Nannetta; Donizetti: Adina, Norina, Marie; Rossini: Rosina, Fanny, Elvira; J Strauss: Adele; Offenbach: Olympia; Delibes: Lakmé; Poulenc: Constance; D Moore: Baby Doe; Britten: Titania; Morton Feldman: The Woman (Neither); Stravinsky: Le Rossignol; Concert appearances with NY Philharmonic, Wiener Philharmoniker, Boston Symphony, Munich Philharmonic, Die Reihe, etc and others with conductors: Bernstein, Ozawa, Boulez, Sawallisch, Paumgartner, Cerha, etc; Song recitals in Austria, France, Germany and USA; Pedalogical activities: Professor of Voice, IN Univ, Bloomington, IN, 1981–83, Hochschule für Musik, Munich, Germany, 1984–95; Steans Institute, Ravinia, IL, Song interpretation 1992–; Tanglewood Festival, London Opera Centre, Hochschule der Kuenste: Basel, Switzerland. *Recordings:* Marriage of Figaro, Don Giovanni, Die Entführung, Così fan tutte, The Impressario, Il Re Pastore; Ariadne auf Naxos; Ballo in Maschera, Rigoletto; Scarlatti's Endimione e Cintia; Le Rossignol. *Honours:* Bayerische Kammersaengerin. *Address:* c/o Columbia Artists Management, 165 West 57th Street, New York, NY 10019, USA.

**GRITTON, Peter William,** MA, LRAM; Composer, Arranger, Accompanist, Singer and Teacher; b. 7 Dec. 1963, Redhill, Surrey; m. Harriet; one s. one d. *Education:* chorister at Salisbury Cathedral; Reigate Grammar School; principal horn of the National Youth Orchestra; academic exhibitioner and choral scholar at Clare Coll., Cambridge. *Career:* countertenor lay clerk at Christ Church Cathedral, Oxford 1985–87; has sung with The Sixteen, Hanover Band, I Fagiolini, Gabrieli Consort, The Light Blues, Tenebrae, Flash Harry, Cambridge Singers; accompanist to Ian Partridge, Henry Herford, Nicholas Clapton, Christopher Purves; Asst Dir of Music, St Paul's Boys School, London. *Compositions:* Run with Torches, Away in a Manger, Stille Nacht: Portraits of Peace, Love Songs, Mary Seacole. *Publications:* Follow that Star (Christmas Songs), With a little help from my friends (Beatles), Encores for Choirs (two vols), G & S for Choirs, Folksongs from around the world (India, Far East, Caribbean and Australia and the South Pacific); contrib. to The Faber Carol Book, Jazz Piano Time, Spooky Piano Time, Fingerprints, Here's a Howdy-do. *Address:* 89 Devonshire Road, London, SE23 3LX, England (home). *E-mail:* petergritton@tiscali.co.uk (office).

**GRITTON, Susan;** Singer (soprano); b. 31 Aug. 1965, Reigate, England. *Education:* Studied Botany at London and Oxford Universities, before a career in music. *Career:* Debut: Mozart Requiem, Wigmore Hall, 1994; Many engagements in such repertory as Mozart's C Minor Mass, Brahms Requiem, Handel's Theodora and Schubert's Der Hirt auf dem Felsen; Orchestras include the London Symphony Orchestra under Colin Davis, London Philharmonic Orchestra under Haitink, Hallé under Nagano, City of London Sinfonia under Hickox, Gothenburg Symphony under Järvi and the Orchestra of the Age of Enlightenment under Steuart Bedford; Opera roles include Mozart's Susanna and Zerlina at Glyndebourne, Marzelline for Rome Opera; Fulvia in Handel's Ezio at the Théâtre des Champs-Elysées; Tiny in Britten's Paul Bunyan for ROH, Atalanta in Xerxes and Xenia in Boris Godonov at English National Opera; Sister Constance in The Carmelites, 1999; Other ENO roles include Caroline in The Fairy Queen, Pamina, Monteverdi's Drusilla, Nannetta and Janáček's Vixen; Season 2001–02 with Euridice and Marenka for the Royal Opera, Handel's Cleopatra and Romilda (Xerxes) at Munich; Bach's St Matthew Passion at the London Proms, 2002. *Recordings include:* Messiah and Solomon; Haydn's Nelson's Mass and Vivaldi's Ottone in Villa; Miss Wordsworth in Albert Herring; Holst Songs; Handel; Vivaldi; Purcell; Handel's Theodora. *Honours:* Winner, Kathleen Ferrier Memorial Prize, 1994; Arts Foundation Fellowship, 1994. *Current Management:* Askonas Holt Ltd, Lonsdale Chambers, 27 Chancery Lane, London, WC2A 1PF, England. *Telephone:* (20) 7400-1700. *Fax:* (20) 7400-1799. *E-mail:* info@askonasholt.co.uk. *Website:* www.askonasholt.co.uk.

**GRIVNOV, Vsevolod;** Singer (Tenor); b. 1968, Russia. *Education:* Studied at the Russian Chorus Academy and the Russian Music Academy. *Career:* Soloist with the New Opera company of the Moscow Municipal Theatre, from 1990; Roles have included Bayan in Ruslan and Lyudmilla, Lensky (Eugene Onegin) and Leicester in Maria Stuarda; Concerts with the Toscanini Orchestra, Italy, under Rudolf Barshai, with Beethoven's Missa solemnis and Bach's B minor Mass, 1991–92, Ghent 1992, as Don José in Peter Brook's Tragédie de Carmen; Fenton in Falstaff at Copenhagen, 1997; Engaged in Rachmaninov's Aleko at the 1999 London Proms. *Recordings include:* Filmed version of Eugene Onegin, 1993. *Current Management:* Askonas Holt Ltd, Lonsdale Chambers, 27 Chancery Lane, London, WC2A 1PF, England. *Telephone:* (20) 7400-1700. *Fax:* (20) 7400-1799. *E-mail:* info@askonasholt.co.uk. *Website:* www.askonasholt.co.uk.

**GROBEN, Françoise;** cellist; b. 4 Dec. 1965, Luxembourg. *Education:* Köln Musikhochschule with Boris Perganenshikov, Amadeus (also William Pleeth, Daniel Shafran). *Career:* debut, Musikverein, Vienna, Festspielhaus, Salzburg; Major concert halls in Europe, Russia, Japan and Israel including Suntory Hall, Tokyo, St Petersburg Philharmonic Hall, Hamburg Musikhalle, Brussels Palais des Beaux Arts, Berlin Philharmonie; Soloist of St Petersburg Philharmonic Orchestra, Moscow Radio-TV Orchestra, Russian State Orchestra, NHK Orchestra, Tokyo; Jerusalem Philharmonic Orchestra, Conductor, Svetlanov, Kitajenko, Rostropovich; Bavarian Radio Sinfonia; Festivals: Berliner Festwochen, Schleswig-Holstein Festival, Radio France Montpellier, Kuhmo, St Petersburg Spring, Wallonie, MDR, Bratislava; Member of Zehetmair String Quartet. *Recordings:* many radio and television recordings, Busoni and Poulenc cello music; Zemlinsky Chamber Music. *Honours:* 2nd Prize (Silver Medal) International Tchaikovsky Competition, Moscow, 1990; Several special prizes. *Address:* Moltkestr 31, 50674 Cologne, Germany.

**GROOP, Monica;** Singer (Mezzo-soprano); b. 4 April 1958, Helsinki, Finland. *Education:* Studied at the Conservatory and Sibelius Academy in Helsinki; Masterclasses with Kim Borg, Hartmut Holl, Mitsuko Shirai and Erik Werba. *Career:* Has appeared with the Savonlinna Opera Festival from 1986 and the Finnish National Opera in Helsinki from 1987; Sang Dorabella in a production of Così fan tutte conducted by Salvatore Accardo at Naples, 1989; Concert performance of Così fan tutte in Rome, 1991; Concert engagements with leading Finnish and other Scandinvian orchestras under Erich Bergel, Jukka-Pekka Saraste, Leif Segerstam and Walter Weller; Tour of West Germany 1989 with the Drottningholm Baroque Orchestra in Bach's St John Passion (Bachwoche Ansbach Festival); Season 1989–90 with the Bach B minor Mass and St John Passion in Stockholm, Berlin and Edmonton, Canada; Mozart's Betulia Liberata with the Bachakademie in Stuttgart under Helmuth Rilling, 1991; Mahler/Schoenberg project with Philippe Herreweghe and the Ensemble Musique Oblique; Season 1991/92 with Cherubino at Aix-en-Provence, Wellgunde and the Walküre Waltraute at Covent Garden (debut), the Missa Solemnis at Aix, 1992; Tour of Così fan tutte with Sigiswald Kuijken to Spain, France and Portugal and appearances with the Drottningholm Theatre at the Barbican; Season 1993 with Cherubino at Toulouse, the Composer at the Paris Opéra Comique and Bach's St John Passion in Spain, Lucerne and Stockholm; Sang Mélisande for Netherlands Opera, 1996; Cherubino for the Royal Opera, 1998; Glyndebourne Festival 1999, as Sesto in La Clemenza di Tito; Sang in the premieres of works by Olli Kortekangas and Kalevi Aho at Savonlinna 2000; Dorabella at Tokyo, 2001; Wigmore Hall recital, 2002. *Recordings include:* Bach B minor Mass; Così fan tutte for television. *Current Management:* IMG Artists Europe (GM); Nordic Artists Management (Nordic Countries). *Address:* c/o IMG Artists Europe, Lovell House, 616 Chiswick High Road, London W4 5RX, England.

**GROSCHEL, Werner;** Singer (Bass); b. 18 Sept. 1940, Nuremberg, Germany. *Education:* Studied at the Richard Strauss Conservatory Munich with Marcel Cordes and Josef Metternich. *Career:* Debut: Flensburg 1967, as Fiesco in Simon Boccanegra; Member of the Zürich Opera from 1972, as Rocco, Mephistopheles, Falstaff (Nicolai) and Dikoy in Katya Kabanova; Mozart's Osmin, Don Giovanni and Sarastro; Verdi's King Philip, Silva (Ernani) and

Zaccaria (Nabucco); Wagner's Daland, Landgrave, King Henry and Pogner; Sang in the 1975 premiere of Klebe's Ein Wahrer Held and the premiere of Kelterborn's Ein Engel kommt nach Babylon, 1977; Guest appearances elsewhere in Switzerland and in Germany; Sang Don Inigo in Ravel's L'Heure Espagnole at the Zürich Opera, 1996; Sang the Theatre Director in Lulu at Zurcih, 2000; Many concert engagements, notably in music by Bach and Monteverdi. *Recordings include:* Plutone in Monteverdi's Orfeo, L'Incoronazione di Poppea and Il Ritorno d'Ulisse. *Address:* c/o Opernhaus Zürich, Falkenstrasse 1, 8008 Zürich, Switzerland.

**GROSGURIN, Daniel;** Cellist; b. 13 July 1949, Geneva, Switzerland; m. Ferhan Güraydin, 21 June 1990. *Education:* Classical Baccalaureate, Geneva, 1967; Conservatoire Geneva, 1st Prize, 1968; Master of Music, Indiana University, 1972. *Career:* Debut: London, 1976; Lucerne Festival, 1975; Festival Strings, Lucerne, 1975–78; Regular appearances with Orchestre de la Suisse Romande, 1978–; Chamber music with several well-known artists including Martha Argerich; Professor, State Music College, Heidelberg, Mannheim, Germany, 1978–90; Tours with Stuttgart Philharmonic, 1987; Professor, Geneva Conservatory of Music, 1990; Salzburg Festival, 1990; London Festival Hall with LSCO, 1991; Tibor Varga Festival, 1991; Eastern Music Festival, USA, 1992–98; Founder of Les Solistes de Genève, 1995. *Recordings:* G. Cassadó: Pièces favorites, Le Violoncelle et l'Opéra. *Current Management:* Becker, Herdecke, Germany. *Address:* Unterer Rheinweg 46, 4057 Basel, Switzerland.

**GROSS, Eric;** Composer and Lecturer; b. 16 Sept. 1926, Vienna, Austria; m. Pamela Davies. *Education:* MA, MLitt, D.Mus, University of Aberdeen, Scotland; FTCL, LMusTCL, Trinity College of Music, London. *Career:* Freelance Pianist, Arranger, Conductor, Composer, 1941–58; Lecturer, New South Wales, Australia, 1959–60; Lecturer, Senior Lecturer, Associate Professor, Department of Music, Sydney University, New South Wales, 1960–91, retired 1991; Visiting Professor of Music, University of Guyana, Georgetown, 1989; Now Freelance Composer. *Compositions:* Symphonies Nos 1 and 2; Violin Concerto; Piano Concerto; Oboe Concerto; 2 Mandolin Concertos; The Amorous Judge, opera; Pacem in Terris, cantata; The Shepherd of Bethlehem, cantata; 5 Burns Songs, 6 Henry Lawson Settings. *Recordings:* Symphony No. 1, 1975; Quintet for alto saxophone and string quartet; Klavierstücke I, II, III, 1990; Concerto No. I for mandolin and chamber orchestra; Concerto No. II for mandolin and chamber orchestra; 6 Henry Lawson Settings and 5 Burns Songs. *Publications:* Background and Problems for an Historical and Critical Edition of the String Quartets of F X Dusek, 1972; Music Manuscripts in the Library of St Bonifaz, Munich–a Preliminary Catalogue, 1975. *Contributions:* The Contemporary Australian Composer and Society, 1971. *Current Management:* Inquiries to Australian Music Centre, Sydney, New South Wales. *Address:* 54/84 St George's Crescent, Drummoyne, NSW 2047, Australia. *E-mail:* egross@pacific.net.au.

**GROSS, Ruth;** Singer (Soprano); b. 1959, Kleve, Germany. *Education:* Studied Viola at Essen, Voice with Edda Moser, Cologne. *Career:* Debut: Regensburg, as Leonore in Fidelio, 1987; Sang at Ulm, 1988–89, notably in Golem by d'Albert and in operetta; Bayreuth Festival, 1989–90, as Ortlinde in Die Walküre; Sang Leonore at Basle, 1989; Has appeared at Staatsoper Stuttgart, 1989–, as Iphigénie (in Aulide), Arabella and Elsa in production of Lohengrin conducted by Silvio Varviso; Season 1995–96 at Kaiserslantern as Wagner's Elisabeth and in the premiere of Gesualdo by Franz Hummel. *Address:* Staatsoper Stuttgart, Oberer Schlossgarten 6, 7000 Stuttgart, Germany.

**GROSSNER, Sonja Elizabeth,** MA; Violinist and Composer; b. 14 Dec. 1942, Maidenhead, England; one d. *Education:* Berkshire Junior Music School, Reading, Carl Maria von Weber Hochschule für Musik, Dresden, Germany, DeMontford Univ., Leicester, Birmingham Conservatoire. *Career:* violinist, State Theatre Orchestra, Freiberg Sachsen 1968–73; music teacher and violinist, Dresden 1974–84; teaching appointments, Leicestershire 1985–87; self-employed music teacher, Loughborough 1986–88; peripatetic violin and viola teacher, Derbyshire LEA 1988–91; instrumental teacher, Bedfordshire LEA 1991–92; violin and viola teacher, Nottingham LEA 1992–95; Northamptonshire Music Service 1996–97; private music teacher, PhD student 1997–; mem. Incorporated Soc. of Musicians, British Acad. of Composers and Songwriters, Central Composers' Alliance. *Compositions:* Sad Prelude and Carefree, for orchestra 1992, Summer Suite, for string orchestra 1993, Musical Moments, for five clarinets, Fantasy Fragments, for trumpet solo and electroacoustics 1996, Parody, for two pianos and percussion 1996, To each other strangers, for woodwind quintet, Elegy 2, for full orchestra, Dark Adagio, String Quartet No. 3 1999, Appassionato, for cello and piano, Destiny, for full orchestra. *Publications:* Sonata for viola and piano in one movement 1996, Four Kinds, for four clarinets 1997, I Am Nobody, four songs of poems by Emily Dickinson 1998. *Honours:* Birmingham Chamber Music Prize 1999, Almira String Quartet Prize 2002. *Address:* 85 Maple Road, London, W11 2JN, England. *Telephone:* (1509) 215960. *Fax:* (1509) 215960. *E-mail:* vontuba@onetel.net.uk.

**GROTH, Konradin;** trumpeter and academic; *Professor of Trumpet, Hochschule der Künste, Berlin.* *Career:* joined the Berlin Philharmonic Orchestra 1968, prin. trumpet 1974–98 (performed world premiere of Siegfried Matthaus' Concerto for trumpet 1984), trumpet teacher Orchestra Akademie 1974–; prin. trumpet German Opera 1971–74; Prof. of Trumpet, Hochschule der Künste, Berlin 1998–; lectures and masterclasses worldwide, including 6th Hamamatsu Int. Wind Instrument Acad. and Festival, Japan 2000, Int. Trumpet Guild Conf., New York 2000; has recorded with ensembles, including German Brass, Berlin Philharmonic Brass Ensemble, Berlin Philharmonic Brass Quintet. *Recordings:* Brass in Berlin 1990, Christmas Adagio 1996, Das Deutsche Blechbläserquintett 2004. *Publication:* Etudes on New Tonguing and Breathing Techniques 1990. *Address:* Hochschule der Künste, Universität der Künste, Ansprechpartner/-in, Postfach 12 05 44, Berlin 10595, Germany (office).

**GROVES, Glenys;** Singer; b. 28 July 1949, Hillingdon, Middlesex. *Education:* Studied with Mavis Bennett, 1959–80, then Eduardo Asquez. *Career:* Debut: D'Oyly Carte Opera Company, 1968; Royal Opera House, Covent Garden, 1988; Regularly works with Ambrosian Singers, 1967–; West End Shows, The Great Waltz, Drury Lane, 1970; The Card, Tom Brown's School Days; Chichester Festival, 1983; Justinus, 1984; The Lily Maid; Wexford Festival, 1984, 1985, 1987; Royal Opera, Covent Garden, as Chief Hen, Cunning Little Vixen, Lady in Waiting, Les Huguenots; Solo Voice, Prince Igor; Newspaper Seller, Death in Venice; Modestina, Il Viaggio a Reims; Milliner, Der Rosenkavalier; Page, Lohengrin; Olga, Merry Widow; Ida, Die Fledermaus; BBC radio, roles in Gilbert and Sullivan; Operettas; Songs From The Shows, Friday Night is Music Night; Regular guest soloist with Black Dyke Band; Extensive concert and oratorio repertoire; Performs throughout the United Kingdom and Europe with The Garden Party; mem, The Friends of Robert Stolz. *Recordings:* Royal Opera, Cunning Little Vixen, Prince Igor; Vox Ottone, Trumpet and Soprano in Duet. *Current Management:* AHF Rigby. *Address:* Chapmans Barn, The Lee, Buckinghamshire HP16 9NA, England.

**GROVES, Paul;** Singer (Tenor); b. 24 Nov. 1964, Lake Charles, Los Angeles, USA; m. Charlotte Hellekant. *Education:* Louisiana State University; Juilliard Opera Center. *Career:* Debut: Steuermann in Der fliegende Holländer, Metropolitan Opera, 1992; Appearances in New York as Mozart's Ferrando and Verdi's Fenton, and roles in Ariadne, Death in Venice, Les Troyens, Parsifal, Die Zauberflöte and The Ghosts of Versailles; European debut as Belfiore in La Finta Giardiniera, for Welsh National Opera; Mozart's Don Ottavio at Salzburg, Idamante at Geneva and Tamino at Munich; Season 1995–96 with Tamino at La Scala, Tom Rakewell for WNO and New York recital debut at Alice Tully Hall; Season 1996–97 with Tom Rakewell at the Paris Châtelet, Nemorino, Flamand in Capriccio and Rossini's Almaviva at the Vienna Staatsoper; Recitals throughout the USA; Further roles include Nadir for Vancouver Opera, Lensky at St Louis and Arturo in I Puritani for Boston Lyric Opera; Sang Des Grieux in Manon at Berlin, 1998; Berlioz Faust at Salzburg, 1999; Season 2000–01 as Bellini's Arturo at Munich, Gluck's Pylades at Salzburg and Ferrando at the Met; Haydn's the Creation at the London Proms, 2002; Engaged as Tamino at Covent Garden, 2003. *Recordings include:* Rigoletto; Alceste; Parsifal and Idomeneo (DGG); Der fliegende Holländer (Sony); Manon Lescaut (Decca). *Address:* c/o Vienna Staatsoper, Opernring 2, A–1010 Vienna, Austria.

**GRUBE, Michael;** Violin-Virtuoso and Violin Professor; b. 12 May 1954, Uberlingen. *Education:* Privately with his violinst father, Professor Max-Ludwig Grube; Further violinistic studies with Henryk Szeryng and Ivan Galamin; Conservatory Diploma, 1975; Studies of Musicology and Composition (Professor Gunther Becker). *Career:* Debut: West Berlin, 1964; Concert Soloist in 110 countries of all continents, performances before His Majesty King Tupou IV of Tonga and Queen of Tonga; Concerts and Festival Performances in Vienna, Copenhagen, Prague, Warsaw, Leningrad, Moscow, New York, Washington DC, Jerusalem, Caracas, Buenos Aires, Canberra, Singapore, Osaka, Bangkok, Bogota, São Paulo, Delhi, Panama City, Madrid, Istanbul; Pro Musica International UK. *Compositions:* Souvenir de Senegal for Solo Violin (Radio Dakar); Hommage a Colville Young an Olanchito (Landestonkunstler Festival 1986–87). *Recordings:* Garnet Records, Düsseldorf; Violin Concertos by Bruch, Mendelssohn, Mozart; Violin Music by Dvořák; Smetana, Suk, Handel, Paganini, Reger, Haas, also with Max Ludwig Grube (violin) and Helen Grube (Piano). *Current Management:* Konzertdirektion Olga Altmann. *Current Management:* Konzertdirektion Olga Altmann, Jaquingasse 37/55, 1030 Vienna, Austria.

**GRUBER, Andrea;** Singer (Soprano); b. 1965, New York, NY, USA. *Career:* Debut: Scottish Opera, 1990, as Leonore in Forza; Sang Third Norn in Götterdämmerung at the Metropolitan, 1990, followed by Elisabeth de Valois and Aida at the Met; Amelia (Ballo), Amelia (Simon Boccanegra); Opera debut as Leonora in Forza with Scottish Opera; Professional debut as Soprano Soloist in Verdi's Requiem with James Levine, Chicago Symphony, Ravinna Festival, 1989; Seattle Opera, 1992, as Aida, Cologne, 1993, as Amelia (Ballo in maschera); Further guest appearances in Toronto, at the Vienna Staatsoper and in Italy; Covent Garden debut 1996, Arabella; Sang Chrysothemis in Elektra at Seattle, 1996; Season 1998 as Amelia (Ballo in Maschera) at Monte Carlo; Elvira (Ernani) at Marseilles, 1999; Sang Odabella in Attila at Chicago, 2001. *Recordings:* Götterdämmerung. *Address:* c/o Metropolitan Opera, Lincoln Center, New York, NY 10023, USA.

**GRUBER, Heinz Karl;** Austrian composer; b. 3 Jan. 1943, Vienna. *Education:* Vienna Hochschule für Musik and with Gottfried von Einem. *Career:* Sang in Vienna Boys' Choir 1953–57; Double Bass player in ensemble Die Reihe from 1961; Principal Double Bass Tonkünstler Orchestra 1963–69; Co-Founder of MOB Art and Tone ART ensemble 1968–71; Has worked with Austrian Radio, Vienna, from 1969; conducted the premiere of his opera Gomorra at the Vienna Volksoper, 1993; Trumpet Concerto premiered at the

1999 London Proms. *Compositions:* 4 pieces for solo violin 1963; Manhattan Broadcasts 1962–64; 5 Kinderlieder for female voices 1965, revised 1980; The Expulsion from Paradise for speakers and 6 solo instruments 1966, revised 1979; 3 MOB Pieces for 7 instruments and percussion 1968, revised 1977; 6 Episodes from a Discontinued Chronicle for piano 1967; Frankenstein !! for baritone, chansonnier and orchestra 1976–77, ensemble version, 1979; Phantom-Bilder for small orchestra 1977; Violin Concerto 1977–78; Demilitarized Zones for brass band 1979; Charivari for orchestra 1981; Castles in the Air for piano 1981; Rough Music, concerto for percussion and orchestra 1982; Anagram for 6 cellos 1987; Nebelsteinmusik (2nd Violin Concerto) 1988; Cello Concerto 1989; Gomorra (opera), 1992; Gloria von Jaxtberg, music theatre, 1992–94; Trumpet Concerto, 1998; Television appearances include Nekrophilius the Pawnbroker in Bring Me the Head of Amadeus (for the Mozart Bicentenary, 1991), Dancing in the Dark for orchestra 2002, Der Herr Nordwind (opera) 2004, Zeitfluren for ensemble 2004. *Current Management:* c/o Boosey & Hawkes Ltd, First Floor, Aldwych House, 71–91 Aldwych, London, WC2B 4HN, England. *Website:* www.boosey.com/gruber.

**GRUBEROVA, Edita;** Singer (soprano); b. 23 Dec. 1946, Bratislava, Czechoslovakia. *Education:* Studied with Maria Medvecká in Prague and with Ruthilde Boesch in Vienna. *Career:* Debut: Bratislava 1968, as Rosina; Sang at the Vienna Staatsoper 1970, as the Queen of Night: sang Zerbinetta in Vienna 1976; Glyndebourne Festival 1973; Salzburg Festival from 1974, as the Queen of Night, conducted by Herbert von Karajan; Metropolitan Opera debut 1977, as the Queen of Night; Covent Garden 1984, as Giulietta in a new production of I Capuleti e i Montecchi by Bellini; Guest appearances at the Bregenz Festival and at La Scala, the Munich Staatsoper (Massenet's Manon) and the Hamburg Staatsoper; Other roles include Gilda, Lucia, Constanze and Violetta; Sang Lucia at La Scala, 1984, Chicago 1986 and Barcelona 1987; La Scala 1987, Donna Anna, Zürich Opera 1988, as Marie in La Fille du Régiment; Metropolitan Opera 1989, as Violetta; Sang Rossini's Rosina and Semiramide (concert) at Munich 1990; Barcelona 1990, as Ariadne; Vienna Staatsoper Oct 1990, as Elizabeth I in Donizetti's Roberto Devereux, Season 1992 as Lucia at Munich and Semiramide at Zürich; Linda di Chamounix, 1995; Anna Bolena at the 1997 Munich Festival; Season 1997–98 as Linda di Chamounix at Vienna and La Scala, Milan; Season 2000–01 as Anna Bolena at Zürich, Elvira in Puritani at the Vienna Staatsoper and Elizabeth I in Roberto Devereux in Hamburg (concert). *Recordings:* Video of Rigoletto, with Luciano Pavarotti; Lucia di Lammermoor; La Traviata; I Puritani; Roberto Devereux; Linda di Chamounix; La Fille du Régiment; Don Giovanni; Die Zauberflöte.

**GRUBERT, Naum;** Pianist; b. 1951, Riga, USSR. *Education:* Studied at the Riga Conservatory and with Professor Gutman in Moscow. *Career:* Performed first in Russia, Eastern Europe, Italy and Finland; Emigrated from USSR 1983 and has performed with the London Symphony, the Hague Philharmonic, Netherlands Philharmonic Orchestre de la Suisse Romande, Helsinki Philharmonic and orchestras in Germany and Spain; Conductors include Paavo Berglund, Sergiu Commisiona, Franz-Paul Decker, Valeri Gergiev, Hartmut Haenchen, Vernon Handley, Thomas Sanderling, Horst Stein and Christopher Seaman; Further engagements with the Rotterdam Philharmonic, the Tonkunstler Orchestra Vienna and the Scottish National Orchestra. *Honours:* 2nd Prize, International Piano Competition, Montreal, 1977; Prizewinner at the 1978 Tchaikovsky Competition, Moscow. *Current Management:* Ingpen & Williams Ltd, 7 St George's Court, 131 Putney Bridge Road, London, SW15 2PA, England.

**GRUDZIEŃ, Jacek;** Polish composer; b. 7 Feb. 1961, Warsaw. *Education:* Akademii Muzycznej, Warsaw with Włodzimierz Kotoński (composition) and Szabolsca Esztényi (piano improvisation), studied composition at Darmstadt, Patras, Kazimierz and Dartington, studied in London with Paul Paterson and Giles Swayn, electronic studio work with Barry Anderson. *Compositions include:* Tristaniana 1984, Turdus musicus 1984, Dla Elizy czyli Straszny sen pewnego pianisty (For Elise, or The Terrible Dream of a Certain Pianist) 1985, Sonosfera 1985, Androvanda, gui 1986, Interludium 1986, Dźwięki nocy (Night Sounds) 1987, Lumen, chorus 1987, Hologram II 1988, Somnus 1988; Drzewa (Trees) 1992, Missa brevis 1992, Movement II 1992, Tritonos 1993, Wiatr od morza (Wind from the Sea) 1993, Pavana 1994, Hyacinth Girl 1995, One Jubilee Rag 1995, Gagliarda 1996, Nonstrom 1996, Saxophone Concerto 1996, Światła Pochylenie 1997, Pangea 1997. *Recordings include:* Vivienne Spiteri, Wiatr od morza. *Honours:* Konkursu Młodych Kompozytorów Polskich 1988, Ogólnopolskiego Konkursu Kompozytorskiego 1995. *E-mail:* Jacek .Grudzien@ddg.art.pl. *Website:* all.art.pl/all.art.pl/on-line/Grudzien/Jacek .html.

**GRUENBERG, Erich,** OBE, FRCM, FGSM; British violinist and music teacher; b. 12 Oct. 1924, Vienna, Austria; s. of Herman and Kathrine Gruenberg; m. Korshed Madan 1956; two d. *Education:* in Vienna, Jerusalem and London. *Career:* Leader, Philomusica of London 1954–56, Stockholm Philharmonic Orchestra 1956–58, London Symphony Orchestra 1962–65, Royal Philharmonic Orchestra 1972–76; leader of London String Quartet and mem. Rubbra-Gruenberg-Pleeth Piano Trio in 1950s; now appears as soloist with leading orchestras in Britain and abroad; taught at Royal Coll. of Music 1960–65; fmr Prof., Guildhall School of Music and Drama 1981; Prof., RAM; winner, Carl Flesch Int. Violin Competition. *Address:* c/o Intermusica Artists' Management, 16 Duncan Terrace, London, N1 8BZ; 80 Northway, Hampstead Garden Suburb, London, NW11 6PA, England. *Telephone:* (20) 7278-5455; (20) 8455-4360. *Fax:* (20) 7278-8434.

**GRUENBERG, Joanna;** Concert Pianist; b. 1957, Stockholm, Sweden. *Education:* Studied with Fanny Waterman, Louis Kentner and Peter Frankl; Guildhall School of Music with James Gibb. *Career:* Appearances at the Aldeburgh and Harrogate Festivals, at the Fairfields Hall, Croydon and for the City Music Society, London; Festival Hall debut 1978, with the Royal Philharmonic Orchestra; Recital tours with her father, Erich Gruenberg; Concerts with the GLC series at Ranger House and visits to Ireland and Spain; Played with the Bournemouth Symphony and Sinfonietta 1983–85; Barbican Centre with Tchaikovsky's 1st Concerto and the Grieg Concerto with the Royal Liverpool Philharmonic, 1984–85; Further engagements with the Hallé Orchestra (Mendelssohn's 1st Concerto, 1988) and the Philharmonia at the Barbican. *Recordings include:* Album for Unicorn. *Honours:* RAOS, Silver Medal 1980. *Address:* Intermusica Artists' Management, 16 Duncan Terrace, London N1 8BZ, England.

**GRUESSER, Eva;** Violinist; b. 1965, Black Forest, Germany. *Education:* Studied at: Freiburg Hochschule; Rubin Academy in Jerusalem; Juilliard School, USA. *Career:* Leader of Lark Quartet, USA; Recent concert tours to: Australia; Taiwan; Hong Kong; China; Germany; Netherlands; US appearances at: Lincoln Center, NY; Kennedy Center, Washington DC; Boston; Los Angeles; Philadelphia, St Louis; San Francisco; Repertoire includes quartets by Haydn, Mozart, Beethoven, Schubert, Dvořák, Brahms, Borodin, Bartók, Debussy and Shostakovich. *Honours:* With Lark Quartet: Gold Medals at 1990 Naumberg and 1991 Shostakovich Competitions; Prizewinner: Premio Paulio Borciani, Reggio Emilia, 1990; Karl Klinger Competition, Munich, 1990; London International String Quartet, 1991; Melbourne Chamber Music, 1991. *Address:* c/o Sonata (Lark Quartet), 11 Northpark Street, Glasgow, G20 7AA, Scotland.

**GRUFFYDD JONES, Angharad;** Singer (Soprano); b. 1973, Wales. *Education:* Univ. of Cambridge; Royal College of Music, with Margaret Kingsley. *Career:* concert engagements with conductors Ivor Bolton, Richard Hickox, Roy Goodman and Roger Norrington; Mozart Exsultate Jubilate at Greenwich and York Minster, Messiah in Spain with Harry Christophers and the Monteverdi Vespers at Washington DC; song recitals in London (Purcell Room) and elsewhere; opera appearances in Orlando by Handel for the Cambridge Handel Opera Group, and Fidalma in Muzio Scevola for the London Handel Festival, 2001; sings with chamber choirs The King's Consort, The Sixteen and the Monteverdi Choir; soloist in John Eliot Gardiner's Bach Cantata Pilgrimage, 2000. *Honours:* Prizewinner, Young Welsh Singer of the Year Competition, 2000. *Address:* c/o Royal College of Music, Prince Consort Road, London SW7, England.

**GRUMBACH, Raimund;** Singer (Baritone); b. 20 Jan. 1934, Eibelstadt, Würzburg, Germany. *Education:* Studied in Würzburg. *Career:* Sang at the Stadttheater Würzburg 1956–59; Nuremberg Opera 1959–62; Bayerische Staatsoper Munich from 1962, as Mozart's Sharples and Marcello; Wolfram in Tannhäuser; Guest appearances in Edinburgh (1965, with the Munich company), Paris, Vienna, Madrid and Tokio; Many concert appearances; Teacher at the Munich Hochschule from 1972. *Recordings:* Il Barbiere di Siviglia; Der Mond by Orff; Leoncavallo's La Bohème; Feuersnot by Strauss; Sutermeister's Romeo und Julia; Der Freischütz; Tristan und Isolde; Intermezzo. *Address:* c/o Staatliche Hochschule für Musik, Arcisstrasse 12, Munich 12, Germany.

**GRUNDHEBER, Franz;** singer (baritone); b. 27 Sept. 1937, Trier, Germany. *Education:* studied in Trier and Hamburg, Indiana University, USA, Music Academy of the West, San Diego. *Career:* has sung at the Hamburg Staatsoper from 1966, opening the 1997/98 season with a new production of Macbeth, playing the leading role and opening the 2000/01 season with a new production of Tosca, playing the role of Scarpia; Tours of the USA and many appearances in European opera houses; Vienna Staatsoper 1983, as Mandryka in Arabella; Salzburg Festival 1985, as Olivier in Capriccio; Other roles include Mozart's Masetto and Guglielmo, Faninal in Der Rosenkavalier, and Escamillo; Salzburg and Savonnlina Festivals 1989, as Orestes and Amonasro; Sang Barak in Die Frau ohne Schatten at the Holland Festival, 1990; Season 1992 as Germont at Barcelona; Wozzeck at the Châtelet, Paris, and Macbeth at Cologne; Sang Wozzeck at Chicago, 1994; Rigoletto at Covent Garden, 1997; Season 2000–01 as Wozzeck at the Vienna Staatsoper, Simon Boccanegra in Munich, Amfortas for the San Francisco Opera and Scarpia in Hamburg; Dr Schön in Lulu at Vienna, 2002; Contracted by Vienna State Opera until 2006; Has sung Rigoletto at the Metropolitan Opera in 1999, 2001 and 2004. *Recordings include:* Video of Elektra (as Orestes) conducted by Abbado, Don Giovanni; Video of Wozzeck conducted by Barenboim, 1997; Doktor Faust by Busoni; Die drei Pintos by Weber/Mahler. *Honours:* 'Kammersänger' from Hamburg State Opera, Vienna State Opera. *Address:* c/o Royal Opera House (Contracts), Covent Garden, London WC2E 9DD, England.

**GRUNEWALD, Eugenie;** Singer (Mezzo-soprano); b. 1962, USA. *Career:* Appearances as Amneris in Aida at Michigan, Orlando, Austin, Miami and for the San Francisco Opera (1997); European debut as Giovanna Seymour in Anna Bolena at Barcelona; Dido in Les Troyens at Toulouse and Athens, Tchaikovsky's Joan of Arc and Lyubov (Mazeppa) with the Opera Orchestra of New York; Azucena and Wagner's Venus with Austin Lyric Opera, the mezzo roles in Puccini's Trittico with the Chicago Lyric Opera and Santuzza with Tulsa Opera; Fenena in Nabucco with Connecticut Opera, Preziosilla at Barcelona and the Nurse in Dukas' Ariane et Barbe-bleue at Hamburg (1997);

Concerts with the New World Symphony under Michael Tilson Thomas, the Boston Philharmonic, Little Orchestra Society and the Pacific Symphony at the Aspen Festival. *Address:* c/o Austin Lyric Opera, PO Box 984, Austin, TX 78767, USA.

**GRUSKIN, Shelley;** Flautist and Recorder Player; b. 20 July 1936, New York, USA. *Education:* Studied at Eastman School, Rochester, graduated 1956. *Career:* Member, New York Pro Musica, 1961–74, playing recorder and other early wind instruments; Associated with such singers as Charles Bressler, Bethany Beardslee, Jan De Gaetani, Russel Oberlin; Premiere of liturgical drama The Play of Herod at the Cloisters, New York 1963; Tour of Europe, 1963, USSR 1964; Final performances with group in Marco da Gagliano's La Dafne, 1974; Formed Philidor Trio 1965, with soprano Elizabeth Humes and harpsichordist Edward Smith; Performances with group until 1980; Teacher of music history and early music performance practice at various institutions; Artist-in-Residence, College of St Scholastica, Duluth, Minnesota 1978–1998, faculty Emeritus 1998–; President of the American Recorder Society, 1980–88. *Recordings include:* Albums with New York Pro Musica and Philidor Trio. *Address:* College of St Scholastica, Duluth, Minnesota 55811, USA.

**GRUZIN, Boris;** Conductor; b. 1940, Tashkent, Russia. *Education:* Moscow Conservatoire. *Career:* Principal Conductor of the Novosibirsk and Odessa Opera and Ballet Theatres; Mariinsky Theatre, St Petersburg, from 1993; Professor at the St Petersburg Conservatoire 1986–; Repertoire includes Tchaikovsky's Mazeppa, Eugene Onegin, Swan Lake and Sleeping Beauty, Prince Igor, The Maid of Pskov by Rimsky-Korsakov and Giselle; Season 1999–2000 with War and Peace at St Petersburg and the Kirov Ballet at Covent Garden; other ballet repertoire includes Romeo and Juliet and Le Corsaire; Symphonic Concerts in Moscow, Odessa, Kiev, Tomsk and abroad. *Honours:* Honoured Artist of the Russian Federation, 1992. *Address:* c/o Kirov Opera, Mariinsky Theatre, 1 Theatre Square, St Petersburg, Russia.

**GUACCERO, Giovanni;** Composer; b. 25 Sept. 1966, Rome, Italy. *Education:* Graduate, Conservatory of music of Rome, Santa Cecilia in composition, 1995, and in electronic music, 1997. *Career:* Debut: Rome, Folkstudio, 1991; Salmo Metropolitano, chorus and orchestra, Rome, Conservatorio, Santa Cecilia, 1995; Trane's Way, Rome, 1996; Theatre: Filottete, music for stage, Academie d'Arte Drammatica, Rome, 1991; Radio: Alquimia, 1998; mem, Nuova Consonanza. *Compositions:* Salmo Metropolitano, 1995; Infedelis Peregrinatio, 1996; Per Versi Diversi, 1997; Flute Dance, 1997; Il Canto dei Popoli, 1998. *Recordings:* Salmo Metropolitano, 1998; Flute Dance, 1999; Ascoltate e capire la luna, 1999. *Publications:* Dal Centro Del Corpo, 1999; Per Versi Diversi, 1999; Pincelada, 1999; Danza No. 2, 1999. *Contributions:* La Musica contemporanea è un genere musicale, NC News 2, 1999. *Honours:* Nuove Generazioni, project of Nuova Consonanza, 1997. *Current Management:* Alberto Giraldi. *Address:* Via Lidia 5, 00179 Rome, Italy.

**GUARNERA, Piero;** Singer (baritone); b. 1962, Rome, Italy. *Career:* Debut: Spoleto, 1987, as Belcore; Has sung at Spoleto as Malatesta, Enrico (Lucia di Lammermoor) and Ned in Treemonisha; Rome Opera debut, 1989, as Masetto, followed by Gluck's Oreste and Verdi's Ford; Other roles include Rossini's Figaro (at Naples), Mozart's Figaro (Florence), Fabrizio in Salieri's La locandiera at Lugo, Dandini in Malaga, Marcello on tour to Netherlands (1994), and Tarquinius in The Rape of Lucretia; La Scala Milan from 1990, in Idomeneo, Henze's Das verratene Meer and Arabella. *Current Management:* Athole Still International Management, Forresters Hall, 25–27 Westow Street, London, SE19 3RY, England. *Telephone:* (20) 8771-5271. *Fax:* (20) 8768-6600. *Website:* www.atholestill.com.

**GUARRERA, Frank;** Singer (Baritone); b. 3 Dec. 1923, Philadelphia, Pennsylvania, USA. *Education:* Studied with Richard Bonelli at the Curtis Institute, Philadelphia. *Career:* Debut: New York City Opera 1947, as Silvio in Pagliacci; Metropolitan Opera from 1948, as Escamillo, Amonasro, Don Alfonso, Eugene Onegin, Gianni Schicchi, Germont and Ford, 34 roles in 427 performances; La Scala Milan 1958, as Zurga in Les Pêcheurs de Perles; Other appearances in London, San Francisco, Paris, Chicago, and Los Angeles. *Recordings include:* Faust (Philips); Cavalleria Rusticana, Così fan tutte and Lucia di Lammermoor (CBS); Falstaff conducted by Toscanini (RCA). *Address:* 423 Second Avenue, Bellmawr, NJ 08031, USA.

**GUBAIDULINA, Sofia Asgatovna;** Russian (b. Tatar) composer; b. 24 Oct. 1931, Chistopol; d. of Asgat Gubaidulin and Fedossia Gubaidulina; m. Peter Meschaninov; one d. *Education:* Kazan and Moscow Conservatories, private studies with Nikolai Peiko, Vissarion Shebalin and Grigori Kogan. *Career:* first noticed abroad, Paris 1979; British debut playing Symphony in 12 Movements 1987; freelance composer in Moscow 1963–91, in Germany 1991–. *Compositions:* instrumental: Piano quintet 1957, Allegro rustico for flute and piano 1963, Five Etudes for harp, double bass and percussion 1965, Vivente non vivente for synthesizer 1970, Concordanza for chamber ensemble 1971, String Quartet No. 1 1971, Music for harpsichord and percussion 1971, Fairytale Poem 1971, Stufen (The Steps) 1971, Detto II for cello and ensemble 1972, Rumore e Silenzio for percussion and harpsichord 1974, Ten Preludes for solo cello 1974, Quattro for 2 trumpets and 2 trombones 1974, Concerto for bassoon and low strings 1975, Sonata for double bass and piano 1975, Light and Darkness for solo organ 1976, Dots, Lines and Zigzag for bass clarinet and piano 1976, Trio for 3 trumpets 1976, Concerto for orchestra and jazz band 1976, Duo-Sonata for 2 bassoons 1977, Quartet for 4 flutes 1977, Misterioso for 7 percussionists 1977, Te Salutant capriccio for large light orchestra 1978,

Introitus concerto for piano and chamber orchestra 1978, Detto I sonata for organ and percussion 1978, De profundis for solo bayan 1978, Sounds of the Forest for flute and piano 1978, In Croce for cello and organ 1979, Jubilatio for 4 percussionists 1979, Offertorium concerto for violin and orchestra 1980, Garten von Freuden und Traurigkeiten for flute, harp and viola (speaker ad lib) 1980, Rejoice sonata for violin and cello 1981, Descensio for ensemble 1981, Seven Words for cello, bayan and strings 1982, In the Beginning there was Rhythm for 7 percussionists 1984, Et exspecto sonata for solo bayan 1985, Quasi Hoquetus for viola, bassoon, cello and piano 1985, Stimmen... vetummen..., symphony in 12 movements 1986, String Quartet No. 2 1987, String Quartet No. 3 1987, Answer without Question collage for 3 orchestras 1988, String Trio 1988, Pro et Contra for large orchestra 1989, Silenzio 5 pieces for bayan, violin and cello 1991, Even and Uneven for 7 percussionists 1991, Tatar dance for 2 double basses and bayan 1992, Dancer on a Tightrope for violin and piano 1993, Meditation on the Bach-Choral Vor deinen Thron tret ich hiermit for harpsichord, 2 violins, viola, cello and double bass 1993, String quartet No. 4 1993, Early in the Morning, Right Before Waking for 7 kotos 1993, The Festivities at Their Height for cello and orchestra 1993, Now Always Snow for chamber ensemble and chamber choir on poems of Gennady Aigi 1993, 2nd cello concerto 1994, In anticipation... for saxophone quartet and 6 percussion 1994, Zeitgestanten symphony in 4 movements 1994, Music for flute, strings and percussion 1994, Viola concerto 1996, Quaternion for 4 cellos 1996, Galgenlieder à 3 15 pieces for mezzo, double bass and percussion 1996, Galgenlieder à 5 1996, Ritorno perpetuo for harpsichord 1997, Canticle of the Sun for cello, chamber chorus and 2 percussionists 1997, Two Paths for 2 violas and orchestra 1998, Im Schatten des Baumes for koto, bass-koto, cheng and orchestra 1998; vocal: Phacelia vocal cycle for soprano and orchestra 1956, Night in Memphis cantata for mezzo-soprano, male chorus and chamber orchestra 1968, Rubaiyat 1969, Roses 5 romances for soprano and piano 1972, Counting Rhymes 5 children's songs 1973, Hour of the Soul for mezzo-soprano and large orchestra 1976, Perception for soprano, baritone and 7 string instruments 1981, Hommage à Marina Tsvetava suite in 5 movements for chorus a cappella 1984, Hommage à T. S. Eliot for soprano and octet 1987, Two Songs on German Folk Poetry for soprano, flute, harpsichord and cello 1988, Witty Waltzing in the style of Johann Strauss for soprano and octet 1987, for piano and string quartet 1989, Jauchzt vor Gott for chorus and organ 1989, Alleluja for chorus, boys soprano, organ and large orchestra 1990, Aus dem Stundenbuch for cello, orchestra, male chorus and female speaker 1991, Johannes Passion 2000. *Honours:* Royal Swedish Acad. of Music Polar Prize 2002. *Address:* Ziegeleiweg 12, 25482 Appen, Germany; 2d Pugachevskaya 8, Korp. 5, Apt. 130, 107061 Moscow, Russia.

**GUBBAY, Raymond,** CBE, FRSA; British music promoter; b. 2 April 1946, London; s. of David Gubbay and the late Ida Gubbay; m. Johanna Quirke 1972 (divorced 1988); two d. *Education:* Univ. Coll. School, Hampstead. *Career:* concert promoter 1966–; f. and Man. Dir Raymond Gubbay Ltd 1966–; presents regular series of concerts at major London and regional concert halls including Royal Albert Hall, Royal Festival Hall, Barbican Centre, Symphony Hall Birmingham, Bridgewater Hall Manchester, Royal Concert Hall Glasgow and in Ireland, Belgium and Scandinavia; has presented productions of: (operas and operettas) The Ratepayer's Iolanthe 1984, Turandot 1991–92, La Bohème (centenary production) 1996, Carmen 1997, Madam Butterfly 1998, 2000, 2003, The Pirates of Penzance 1998–99, 2000, Tosca 1999, Aida 2001; (ballets) Swan Lake 1997, 1999, 2002, 2004, Romeo and Juliet 1998, The Sleeping Beauty 2000, Cavallaria Rusticana and Pagliacci 2002, D'Oyly Carte Opera Co. Seasons 2000, 2001, 2002, 2003, Savoy Opera 2004. *Honours:* Hon. FRAM 1988, Hon. FTCL 2000. *Address:* Dickens House, 15 Tooks Court, London EC4A 1QH, England. *E-mail:* info@raymondgubbay.co.uk (office). *Website:* www.raymondgubbay.co.uk (office).

**GUBRUD, Irene (Ann);** Singer (Soprano); b. 4 Jan. 1947, Canby, Minnesota, USA. *Education:* Studied at St Olaf College, Northfield, Minnesota, and at Juilliard, New York. *Career:* Concert engagements with leading US orchestras; Tour of Germany with the Baltimore Symphony; Premiere of Star-Child by George Crumb with the New York Philharmonic conducted by Pierre Boulez, 1977; European engagements with the Stuttgart and Bavarian Radio Orchestras; Opera debut 1981, as Mimi with the Minnesota Opera, St Paul; Recitals at Lincoln and Kennedy Centers 1981; Appearances at the Aspen, Blossom and Meadowbrook Festivals; Teacher at Washington University, St Louis, 1976–81. *Honours:* First Prize, Concert Artists Guild competition 1970; Ford Foundation performance competition 1971; Rockefeller and Minna Kaufmann Ruud competitions, 1972; Winner, Naumburg International Voice Competition, 1980.

**GUDBJORNSSON, Gunnar;** Singer (Tenor); b. 1965, Reykjavík, Iceland. *Education:* Studied at New Music School, Reykjavík, with Hannelore Kuhse in Berlin, and with Nicolai Gedda in London. *Career:* Debut: Icelandic Opera, as Don Ottavio, 1988; Sang Clotarco in Haydn's Armida at Buxton Festival, 1988; Appearances with Opera North and Welsh National Opera; Opera galas at St David's Hall, Cardiff, and with Royal Philharmonic; Sang the Lawyer in Punch and Judy at Aldeburgh Festival and engaged with Wiesbaden Opera as Almaviva, Ottavio and Tamino; Concert repertoire includes St Matthew Passion (Queen's Hall, Edinburgh), Britten's Serenade, Die schöne Müllerin; Recitals at Covent Garden and Wigmore Hall, 1993; Further appearances at the BBC Proms (Les Noces, 1996), the Opéra Bastille, Bregenz Festival, Aix-en-Provence, Geneva and Lisbon; Wagner's Steersman at Lille, 1998; Season 2000–01 as Don Ottavio at the Deutsche Oper Berlin, Belmonte, and Fenton in

Falstaff at the Berlin Staatsoper. *Recordings include:* Die schöne Müllerin; Albums in Mozart complete edition; Radio recordings for BBC, Radio France and Hessische with broadcasts in most of Europe. *Honours:* Gunnar Thoroddson Scholarship, 1987; Leoni Sonnering Prize, 1988. *Current Management:* Askonas Holt Ltd, Lonsdale Chambers, 27 Chancery Lane, London, WC2A 1PF, England. *Telephone:* (20) 7400-1700. *Fax:* (20) 7400-1799. *E-mail:* info@askonasholt.co.uk. *Website:* www.askonasholt.co.uk.

**GUDMUNDSEN-HOLMGREEN, Pelle;** Composer; b. 21 Nov. 1932, Copenhagen, Denmark; m. (1) Gunvor Kaarsberg, 21 Nov 1959, 1 s., 1 d., (2) Karin B. Lund, 29 Aug 1997. *Education:* Studied Theory and History of Music at The Royal Danish Conservatory of Music, 1953–58. *Career:* Teacher, Royal Danish Academy of Music in Århus, 1967–73; Works have been played at Scandinavian Music Days, international festivals, ISCM, on Danish Television and on Radio world-wide; Music for plays and films. *Compositions include:* Frère Jaques for orchestra, 1964; Recapitulations for small ensemble, 1965; Je ne me tairai jamais. Jamais, for voices and instruments, 1966; Piece by Piece for chamber orchestra, 1968; Tricolore IV for orchestra, 1969; Terrace in 5 Stages for woodwind quintet, 1970; Plateaux pour Deux for cello and percussion, 1970; Mirror II for orchestra, 1973; Songs Without for mezzo soprano and piano, 1976; Symphony, Antiphony for orchestra, 1977; Prelude to Your Silence, octet, 1978; Your Silence, septet and soprano, 1978; Mirror Pieces for clarinet trio, 1980; String Quartet V Step by Step, 1982; VI Parting, 1983; VII Parted, 1984; Triptycon, concerto for percussion, 1985; String Quartet VIII Ground, commissioned by the Kronos Quartet, 1986; Concord, Sinfonietta, 1987; Octopus for organ and 2 players, 1989; Trois Poèmes de Samuel Beckett for vocal group, 1989; Concerto Grosso for string quartet and symphonic ensemble, 1990; The Creation, the 6th day, for double choir and violin solo, 1991; For Piano, 1992; Turn for guitar, bass flute, harp and soprano, 1993; Traffic, Sinfonietta, 1994; Double, for violin and piano, 1994; Album, for saxophone quartet, 1994; For Cello and orchestra, 1996; Blow on Odysseus for vocal soloists, chorus, brass instruments and percussion, 1998; Stepping Still, for string sextet, 1999; Still, Leben, for organ, 2000; Countermove I II III, for organ, 2000; In Triplum, for organ, 2000; Sound/Sight, for choir, 2001; Two Madrigals for vocal ensemble 2001, For Violin and Orchestra, 2002; Three Stages for vocal ensemble, 2003, Moving, Still. Hans Christian Andersen 200 for baritone and string quartet 2004, Portrait for saxophone quartet and bass drum 2004. *Recordings:* Solo for electric guitar; Mirror Pieces; Symphony, Antiphony; Octopus; For cello and orchestra, Frère Jaques, Concerto Grosso; Music for voices and instruments, chamber music, organ music, all on his label dacapo; Triptycon on BIS. *Contributions:* Dansk Musiktidsskrift; Nutida Musik. *Honours:* Antiphony, Symphony was awarded the 1980 Music Prize of the Nordic Council. *Address:* Eggersvej 29, 2900 Hellerup, Denmark. *Telephone:* 39656393 (home); 86596848 (home).

**GUELFI, Giangiacomo;** Singer (Baritone); b. 21 Dec. 1924, Rome, Italy. *Education:* studied in Florence and with Titta Ruffo. *Career:* Debut: Spoleto 1950, as Rigoletto; Sang at the Teatro Fenice Venice and in Catania; La Scala Milan from 1952; Chicago Lyric Opera from 1954; Appearances in Rome, Paris, Cairo, Naples, Berlin and Dallas; Covent Garden 1975, as Scarpia, Chénier; Verona Arena 1960, 1970, 1972; Rio de Janeiro 1964, as Macbeth and Scarpia; Lisbon 1965, as Guillaume Tell; Metropolitan Opera 1970, as Scarpia, and Jack Rance in La Fanciulla del West; Appeared at the Maggio Musicale, Florence, in revivals of L'Africaine by Meyerbeer, 1971, and Agnese di Hohenstaufen by Spontini; Sang in Giordano's La Cene delle Beffe at La Scala 1977. *Recordings include:* Tosca and Aida (Cetra); Cavalleria Rusticana (Deutsche Grammophon); Verdi's I Due Foscari, I Lombardi, Nabucco and Attila. *Address:* c/o Teatro alla Scala, Via Filodrammatici 2, 20120 Milan, Italy.

**GUÉRINEL, Lucien;** Composer; b. 16 Aug. 1930, Grasse, France; m. Marie-Claire, 22 Dec 1958, 1 s. *Education:* Studied piano with Yvonne Studer in Marseille; Studied harmony with Marcel Prévot in Marseille and André Jouve in Paris; Composition with Louis Saguer in Paris. *Career:* Mem, Sciences, Letters and Arts Academy of Marseille. *Compositions:* 7 Fragments d'Archiloque, for 12 voices; 4 poèmes d'E Montale, for 12 voices; 4 chants pour un visage, for 12 voices and four instruments; Canti Corali, Ungaretti, choir and orchestra; Les Sept Portes, choir, 16 strings and 2 percussionists; Prendre corps, string quartet with soprano and mezzo-soprano; Séquence, for reeds trio. *Recordings:* Strophe 21, 2nd string quartet; Ce chant de brume, for cello; 7 Fragments d'Archiloque; 4 poèmes d'E Montale; 4 chants pour un visage; Chants-Espaces, for 2 pianos; 8 préludes, for piano; Appels, for vibraphone; Cadence, for harpsichord; 6 Bagatelles, for wind quintet; Soleil ployé, for violin. *Publications:* Poetry: La parole échouée, 1969; La sentence nue, 1973; Acte de présence, 1997; Music published by several publishers. *Contributions:* Music critic for La Provence. *Honours:* Second Prize, Competition for string quartets, Philip Morris, Paris, 1983; Finalist, International Competition, Piano en Creuse, 1990, 1994. *Address:* 56 rue Paradis, F 13006 Marseille, France.

**GUHL, Helmut;** Singer (Baritone); b. 1945, Hamburg, Germany. *Education:* Studied in Hamburg. *Career:* Debut: Eutin Festival, 1973, as the Count in Lortzing's Wildschütz; Sang with Oldenburg Opera, 1974–78, notably as Sharpless, Papageno, Germont and Wolfram; Eutin Festival as Guglielmo, Rossini's Figaro and Belcore; Hanover Opera from 1978, as Don Giovanni, Orpheus, Rossini's Mosè (1991), and Beckmesser; Guest appearances at the Deutsche Oper am Rhein, Düsseldorf, and in Hamburg, Mannheim and

Stuttgart. *Address:* c/o Staatstheater Hanover, Opernhaus, Opernplatz 1, W-3000 Hanover 1, Germany.

**GUIDARINI, Marco;** Conductor; b. 1952, Genoa, Italy. *Education:* Studied conducting with Franco Ferrara, and at the Academy of Pescara. *Career:* Led regional orchestras in Italy, then assisted John Eliot Gardiner at the Lyon Opéra, making debut 1986 with Falstaff; Wexford Festival and London 1988–89, with the local premieres of Mercadante's Elisa e Claudio and Mozart's Mitridate; Season 1990–91 with Tosca at English National Opera, Figaro for Welsh National Opera, La Bohème for Scottish Opera and Manon Lescaut in Dublin; Vancouver and Sydney debuts with Don Pasquale and Tosca; Season 1993–94 with La Traviata at Stockholm, I Lombardi at Bologna and Il Barbiere di Siviglia at the Berlin Staatsoper; Season 1997 with Don Giovanni at Copenhagen, Rigoletto in Geneva, Barbiere at Los Angeles (US debut) and Don Carlos in Marseilles; Other repertory includes Così fan tutte (Australian Opera), Die Zauberflöte, Un Ballo in Maschera and Nabucco (Nice Opéra); Bellini's Capuleti at Reggio Emilia, 1998. *Address:* Allied Artists, 42 Montpelier Square, London SW7 1JZ, England.

**GUILLAUME, Edith;** opera and concert singer (lyric mezzo); b. 14 June 1943, Bergerac, France; m. Niels Hvass; two c. *Education:* Royal Danish College of Music, Copenhagen, private studies in Copenhagen and Paris. *Career:* opera debut as Thérèse, Dreaming of Therese, Jutland Opera; Sang with opera in Copenhagen, Århus, Hamburg, Mannheim, Geneva, Montpelier, Nancy, Metz, Lille, Liège, Le Havre; resident member, Royal Danish Opera, Copenhagen; roles with these companies include Bartók, Judith (Bluebeard's Castle); Bibalo, Julie (Miss Julie); Bizet, Carmen (Carmen); Campra, Clorinde (Tancrède); Davies, Miss Donnithorne's Maggott; Gluck, Orfeo; Gounod, Siebel (Faust); Mascagni, Santuzza (Cavalleria Rusticana); Massenet, Charlotte (Werther); Monteverdi, Ottavia and Poppea (L'Incoronazione di Poppea), Penelope (Ritorno d'Ulisse); Mozart, Cherubino (Le nozze di Figaro), Dorabella (Così fan tutte), Idamante (Idomeneo); Offenbach, La perichole (La Perichole); Penderecki, Jeanne (The Devils of Loudun); Poulenc (Voix Humaine); Ravel, Concepcion (L'Heure Espagnole); Rossini, Zaida (Turco in Italia), Angelina (Cenerentola); Strauss, Octavian (Der Rosenkavalier); Verdi, Maddalena (Rigoletto), Meg (Falstaff); Jutland Opera 1996, as Mozart's Marcellina; Sang in Die schweigsame Frau at Århus, 2000. *Recordings:* various Danish songs. *Honours:* Critics Prize of Honour, 1970; Tagea Brandt Memorial Fund, 1977. *Address:* Ellebakken 2, 2900 Hellerup, Copenhagen, Denmark.

**GUILLOU, Jean;** Organist, Composer and Pianist; b. 18 April 1930, Angers, France. *Education:* Paris Conservatoire from 1945 with Dupré, Duruflé and Messiaen. *Career:* Professor, Instituto de Alta Cultura, Lisbon, 1953–57; recitalist in residence in West Berlin. 1958–62; Organist, St Eustache, Paris, 1963; Professor, International Masterclass, Zürich, 1970–. *Compositions:* Organ: Toccata, op 9, 1962; Sagas, op 20, 1968; Symphonie Initiatique, 1969; La Chapelle des Abimes, 1970; Scènes d'Enfants, op 28; Hyperion, op 45; Eloge, op 52; Alice au Pays de l'Orgue, 1995; Instants, op 57; Orchestra: Judith-Symphonie for mezzo and orchestra; Concerto Grosso, op 32; Concerto Héroïque; Concerto 2000, op 62; 5th Concerto (King Arthur); Missa Interrupa, op 51; Piano and organ: Colloques Nos 2, 4 and 5; Concertos for cello and organ, violin and organ; Peace, for 8 voices and organ, op 43; Aube, for 12 voices and organ, op 46; Andromeda, for soprano and organ, op 39; Fête, for clarinet and organ, op 55. *Recordings:* J. S. Bach, Complete Organ Works, Goldberg Variations, Musical Offering; Vivaldi, 5 Concertos; C. Franck, Complete Organ works; Mussorgsky, Pictures at an Exhibition; Stravinsky, Petrushka; Julius Reubke, piano and organ sonatas; Guillou Plays Guillou, 7 CDs, Philips. *Publications:* Author of the book about organ, history and design, L'Orgue, Souvenir et Avenir, Ed Buchet, Chastel. *Honours:* Gramophon Critics Prize, 1980; International Performer of the Year, USA, 1980; Prize of the Liszt Academy, Budapest, 1982; Diapason d'Or and Prix Choc of Le Monde, 1991. *Address:* 45 rue de l'Arbre Sec, 75001 Paris, France.

**GULEGHINA, Maria;** Belarusian/Armenian singer (soprano); b. 1959, Odessa; m. Mark Gulegin. *Education:* Odessa Conservatory (studied with Yevgeni Ivanov). *Career:* soloist Minsk Opera Theatre 1983–90; taught in Minsk Conservatory 1986–90; regular appearances at La Scala (since 1986), Wiener Staatsoper, Metropolitan Opera 1990, other major European theatres. *Music:* video-audio: Tosca, Manon Lescaut, Macbeth (all at La Scala, Milan); Andrea Chenier, Nabucco (both at Metropolitan Opera, New York); audio Tabarro, Oberto, Francesca di Rimini, Picovcia Dama. *Radio:* many live broadcasts from the Met, La Scala, Vienna etc. *Television:* Nabucco (Vienna Met), Andrea Chenier, Tosca, Manon Lescaut, Macbeth (all at La Scala), Verdi Arias, Italian Arias (both for NHK). *Opera roles include:* parts in Tosca, Manon Lescaut (Puccini), Due Foscari, Il Trovatore, Un Ballo in Maschera, Ernani, Aida, Otello, Nabucco (Verdi), Cavalleria Rusticana (Mascagni), Andrea Chenier, Fedora (Giordano), Yolanta, Eugene Onegin, Queen of Spades (Tchaikovsky); concert performances of Verdi's Requiem; solo recitals in Germany, Italy, Switzerland, Austria, France, Hungary, USA, Japan. *Honours:* First Prize All-Union Glinka Competition 1984, Zanatello Award, Verona 1997. *Address:* c/o Askonas Holt, Lonsdale Chambers, 27 Chancery Lane, London, WC2A 1PF, England. *Telephone:* (20) 7400-1700. *Fax:* (20) 7400-1799.

**GULKE, Peter;** Conductor; b. 29 April 1934, Weimar, Germany. *Education:* Studied at the Franz Liszt Hochschule Weimar, the Friedrich Schiller University Jena and the Karl Marx University, Leipzig (PhD 1958). *Career:*

Repetiteur at the Rudolstadt Theatre 1959; Music Director at Stendal 1964 and Potsdam 1966; Stralsund 1972–76; Kapellmeister at the Dresden Opera 1976; Musical Director at Weimar 1981; as Musicologist Technical University, Berlin 1984; Musical Director, Wuppertal Opera, 1986–96; Work as musicologist includes edition of Symphonic Fragments by Schubert, from sketches, broadcast at the Schubert Congress in Detroit, 1978; Lecturer at the Hochschule für Musik in Dresden; Conducted Poulenc's Dialogues des Carmélites at Wuppertal 1989, to commemorate the bicentenary of the French Revolution and numerous other operas including the Ring at Wuppertal, Graz, Kassel; Professor Staatliche Hochschule für Musik Freiburg, 1996–2000. *Recordings include:* Beethoven Piano Concerto of 1784 and Udo Zimmermann's Der Schuhu und der fliegende Prinzessin, works by Schreker, Ravel, Schoenberg, Berg, Webern, Baird; Symphonic Fragments by Schubert, Schumann. *Publications:* Bruckner, Brahms, Zwei Studien, 1989; Schubert und seine Zeit, 1991; Fluchtpunkt Musik, 1994; Triumph der neuen Tonkunst. Mozarts späte Sinfonien und ihr Umfeld, 1998. *Address:* Zum Rebberg 10, 79112 Freiburg.

**GULLI, Franco;** Concert Violinist; b. 1 Sept. 1926, Trieste, Italy; m. Enrica Cavallo. *Education:* Studied with father and at Trieste Conservatory, Accademia Chigiana, Siena. *Career:* Debut: 1932; World-wide appearances with leading orchestras, including Cleveland, Pittsburgh, Ottawa; Chamber music activity with wife and with Trio Italiano d'Archi; Former member, Pomeriggi Musical Orchestra of Milan and of I Virtuosi di Roma; Gave premieres of concertos by Malipiero and Viozzi and of Paganini's 5th Concerto (1959); Masterclasses, Accademia Chigiana, Siena, 1964–72; Professor of Music, Lucerne Conservatory, 1971–72; Professor of Music, Indiana University from 1972, Distinguished Professor of Music; mem. Accademia Nazionale Santa Cecilia, Rome. *Recordings include:* Duos with Bruno Giuranna; String Trios by Beethoven with the Italian Trio; Paganini's Concerto No. 5; Beethoven Sonatas, with Enrica Cavallo; Mendelssohn Sonata in F; Mozart Violin Concerti (complete). *Honours:* Premio dell'Accademia Chigiana, Siena. *Current Management:* Columbia Artists New York, 165 West 57th Street, NY 10019, USA.

**GULYÁS, Dénes;** Hungarian singer (tenor); b. 31 March 1954, s. of Dénes Gulyás and Mária Szitár; m. Judit Szekeres; two s. one d. *Education:* Liszt Ferenc Acad. of Music, Budapest. *Career:* joined State Opera, Budapest 1978; debut as Rinuccio in Gianni Schicchi; debut in USA, Carnegie Hall and Avery Fisher Hall, New York: concert performances; numerous tours in the USA. *Repertoire includes:* Faust, des Grieux (Manon), Werther, Hoffman, Titus (La Clemenza di Tito), Percy (Anne Boleyn), Ernesto (Don Pasquale), Duke of Mantua (Rigoletto), Fenton (Falstaff), Ferrando (Così fan tutte), Don Ottavio, Tamino, Alfredo (La Traviata), Edgardo (Lucia di Lammermoor), Nemorino, Rodolfo (La Bohème), Tom Rakewell (The Rake's Progress). *Recordings include:* Caldara, Albinoni, Sammartini, Vivaldi: Magnificat, Erkel: Hunyadi László 1994. *Honours:* 1st Prize, Parma 1979, won Luciano Pavarotti singing competition, Philadelphia 1981, Holder of Liszt Prize, titled Merited Artist. *Address:* Hungarian State Opera, Andrássy ut 22, 1062 Budapest, Hungary (office). *Telephone:* (1) 131-2550 (office).

**GULYAS, György;** Conductor; b. 11 April 1916, Korostarca, Hungary; m. Eva Manya, 6 Nov 1958, 3 d. *Education:* Composition and Conducting, Academy of Music, Budapest, 1942. *Career:* Teacher, Music Teachers' Training College, Debrecen, 1942–46; Founder-Director, Music High School, Bekestarhos, also conductor, Tarhosi Korus, 1946–54; Director, Music High School, Debrecen, 1954–66; Debrecen Academy of Music, Budapest, 1966–76; Founder, Chief Conductor, Kodály Choir, Debrecen, 1955–83; Békéstarhosi Zenei Napok, music director 1976–. *Publications:* Author, Bekestarhos Zenei tanulsagai, 1968; Az enekkari intonacio kerdesei, 1972; Articles in various professional journals; Büneim... Büneim?, biography, 1988. *Address:* 8 Blaháné, Debrecen 4024, Hungary.

**GUNDE, Peter;** Conductor; b. 1942, Budapest, Hungary. *Education:* Studied Oboe at the Budapest Conservatory; Composition, Coducting, Franz Liszt Academy, Budapest; Seminars in Weimar and Petersburg with Arvid Jansons, 1965–75. *Career:* Oboist, National Orchestra, Budapest, 1961–63; Kapellmeister in Miskolc, Hungary, 1972–73; Opera Kapellmeister, Hungarian State Opera, 1973–75; Founder, Director, Corelli Chamber Orchestra, Budapest, 1975–77; Conductor, Artistic Director, Chorus and Orchestra, Kapisztran and Palestrina Choir, Budapest, 1973–77; Director of the Chamber Orchestra and Lecturer at the International Youth Festival, Bayreuth, 1975–77; Assistant to Peter Maag, Christoph von Dohnànyi, Herbert von Karajan, Salzburg Festival, 1977–78; Lecturer, University of Bielefeld and University of Osnabrück; Guest Conductor, Stavanger, Oslo and Hungary, 1981–83; Concerts with the Sudwesteutschen Kammerorchester in Pforzheim and Reutlingen; Concerts in Hungary and USA, 1984; Guest Conductor in Tokyo and Israel; Broadcasts with the Westdeutschen Rundfunk Cologne, 1985–89; Concert Tour with the Hungarian Virtuosi Orchestra, 1990–93, 1993–. *Address:* Heeperstrasse 52a, 33607 Bielefeld 1, Germany.

**GUNN, Jacqueline;** Stage Designer; b. 1959, Scotland. *Career:* Opera designs have included The Rake's Progress for Opera Integra, La Voix Humaine at the Bloomsbury Festival, La Pietra del Paragone at Wuppertal, Tannhäuser for New Sussex Opera, Henze's Labirinto at the Munich Biennale, Otello, L'Elisir d'amore and Trovatore for Lucerne Opera and Così fan tutte for English National Opera in 1994. *Address:* Phoenix Artists Management, 6 Windmill Street, London, W1B 1HF, England.

**GUNN, Nathan;** American singer (baritone); b. 1970. *Education:* Univ. of Illinois. *Career:* debut, New York Met 1995, as Morales in Carmen; appearances at the Metropolitan include Guglielmo, Paris in Roméo et Juliette, Strauss's Harlequin and Schaunard in La Bohème; European debut as Prince Andrei in Prokofiev's War and Peace at the Opéra Bastille, Paris: Season 2000–01 as Guglielmo at Glyndebourne, Mozart's Count in Brussels and Harlequin for the Royal Opera, Covent Garden; concerts with the Chicago Symphony and Cleveland Orchestras and recitals at the Wigmore Hall. *Recordings include:* American Anthems. *Current Management:* ICM New York, 40 W 57th Street, New York, NY 10019, USA. *Telephone:* (212) 556-5600. *Website:* www.icmtalent.com; www.nathangunn.com.

**GUNS, Jan;** Belgian bass clarinettist; b. 22 Nov. 1951, Antwerp, Belgium; one s. two d. *Education:* Royal Flemish Conservatorium, Antwerp, summer courses in Nice, France. *Career:* debut with Royal Flemish Opera, Antwerp, 1971; Assistant Professor of Clarinet, Royal Conservatorium, Gent, 1979; Played with Opera of Flanders, 1980; BRT Philharmonic Orchestra, 1983; Associate Professor, 1984, Professor of Bass Clarinet, 1991–, Royal Flemish Conservatorium, Antwerp; Bass Clarinet Player and Percussionist with Gemini Ensemble, 1990–: Professor of bass clarinet-basset horn at the Belgian Flanders Exchange Center in Osaka, Japan. *Recordings:* Introduction and Concertante for Bass Clarinet and Clarinet Choir, opus 58 (Norman Heim), with Walter Boeykens Clarinet Choir, 1986; Harry's Wonderland for Bass Clarinet and 2 Tapes (André Laporte), 1987; Mladi sextet (Leoš Janáček), with Walter Boeykens Ensemble, 1992; Spotlights on the Bass Clarinet, Concerto for Bass Clarinet and Concert Band (Jan Hadermann), with Concert Band of the Belgian Guides, conducted by N Nozy, 1993; With Gemini Ensemble, 1993; Sonata (Frits Celis); Van Heinde en Verre (Wilfried Westerlinck); Due Concertante (Ivana Loudova); Giuco per Due (Dietrich Erdmann); Exercises (Jean Segers); Tango (Frédéric Devreese); with Moscow Chamber Soloists, Trio Classicum and Gemini Ensemble, 2000; Elegie (Dirk Brossé); Zebus (Johan Favoreel); Divertimento (Alain Craens); Pierrot (Wilfried Westerlinck); Fantasy Quintet (York Bowen); Divertimento (Akira Yuyama); Duo-Sonata (Charles Camilleri); Experience (Alain Craens). *Address:* Hagelandstraat 48, 2660 Hoboken (Antwerp), Belgium. *Telephone:* (3) 288-9184. *E-mail:* guns.jan@pandora.be.

**GUNSON, Ameral Blanche Tregurtha;** British singer (mezzo-soprano); b. 25 Oct. 1948, London; d. of Charles Cumbria and Auriol Cornwall; m. 1st Maurice Powell 1969 (divorced 1974); m. 2nd Philip Kay 1979; two s. *Education:* Convent of Jesus and Mary, London and Guildhall School of Music and Drama. *Career:* freelance singing career 1972–74, with BBC Singers 1976–80; solo singing career in Britain and abroad, Proms Seasons 1979, 1985, 1988, 1989, 1990; Assoc. Guildhall School of Music and Drama. *Honours:* Gramophone Award for recording of Peter Grimes 1997; Lubslith Asscn (Finland) Award for vocal teaching 1997. *Address:* 40 Brooklands Way, Redhill, Surrey, RH1 2BW, England. *Telephone:* (1737) 762726.

**GUNSON, Emily Jill;** Australian flautist and musicologist; b. 28 Jan. 1956, Melbourne. *Education:* BMus, 1980, PhD, 2000, Univ. of Western Australia; postgraduate study with William Bennett, 1981–82; performance diplomas, LMusA, 1978, LRAM, LGSM, ARCM, 1980. *Career:* concerto debut, 1973; Principal Flute, West Australian Arts Orchestra, 1982–83; performances with West Australian and Sydney Symphony Orchestras; Artistic Dir, Leader, Australian chamber ensembles, Wendling Quartet, Cambini Quintet, Emanuel Ensemble, Music Autentica, performing on both modern and historical flutes; Dir Avon Valley Spring Chamber Music Festival; guest artist, Mozart Gesellschaft Kurpfalz; musicological research in field of 18th century flute history, performance and repertoire; international authority on Wendling family of musicians and singers in 18th century Mannheim and Munich. *Publications:* Johann Baptist Wendling (1723–1797): Life, Works, Artistry and Influence, Including a Thematic Catalogue of all his Compositions, 1999. *Contributions:* The Court of Carl Theodor: A Paradise for Flautists, in Quellen und Studien zur Geschichte der Mannheimer Hofkapelle, vol. eight, 2002; seven articles in New Grove Dictionary (second edn); RISM errata; 18th and 19th Century Flute Music (ed.). *Honours:* Médaille d'Honneur de la Ville de Ribeauvillé (France) 2000. *Current Management:* Flutissimo, PO Clackline 6564, WA, Australia. *Telephone:* 0417 984887. *Address:* Emanuel Farm, Clackline WA 6564, Australia (home). *Telephone:* (8) 9574-1591 (home).

**GÜNTER, Horst;** Voice Teacher, Professor of Voice and Singer (Baritone); b. 23 May 1913, Leipzig, Germany; m. 4 May 1938, 2 s., 2 d. *Education:* Choirboy, St Thomas, Leipzig; Musicology and Philosophy, Universities of Leipzig and Bologna; Voice, Leipzig Conservatory; Most influential teachers: Karl Straube, Fritz Polster, Emmi Leisner. *Career:* Debut: Matthäus-Passion, St Thomas, Leipzig, 1939; Count in Marriage of Figaro, Schwerin State Opera, 1941; Leading Lyric Baritone, Hamburg State Opera, 1950–68; Knappertsbusch and Böhm, Munich State Opera, 1958–63; Edinburgh Festival, 1952, 1956; Holland Festival, 1961; Guest Singer: Vienna State Opera, Frankfurt, with Solti; Ansbach Bach Festival, 1951–58; Numerous radio recordings; For television, 12 operas; First performance of Moses and Aaron in Hamburg, 1954; Teaching: Nordwest-deutsche Musikakademie, Detmold, 1959–65; Professor, 1963; Staatliche Musikhochschule, Freiburg, 1965–68; University of Southern California, Los Angeles, 1978–80; University of California, Los Angeles, 1981; Visiting Professor: Many US universities including Southern Methodist University, Dallas, North Texas State University, Denton, Oberlin Conservatory of Music, University of Minnesota, University of Alaska; Musashino Academia Musicae, Tokyo, 1984, 1986, 1987, 1990, 1991, 1992;

Frequent Judge, international voice competitions such as Munich, Budapest, Leipzig, 's-Hertogenbosch, Los Angeles, Dallas, Osaka; Founder of EVTA, European Voice Teacher Association, 1991; Voice Teacher at Studio Opera, Zürich, Switzerland, 2001–. *Recordings include:* Lohengrin, Schüchter; Moses und Aron, Rosbaud; Zillich, Così fan tutte, Jochum, Don Giovanni, Klemperer, Zauberflöte, Rother, La Traviata, Wagner, Die Fledermaus, Schüchter; Weihnachts Oratorium; Karl Richter, Matthäus Passion; Kurt Redel, Zar und Zimmermann; La Bohème, Erede; CD: Dokumente einer Sängerkarriere: 18 Operatic Arias; Hansel und Gretel; Lortzing, Zar und Zimmerman; Telemann: Matthäus Passion; Wagner Lohengrin. *Address:* Unterer Heimbach 5, 79280 Au bei Freiburg, Germany.

**GUNTER, John;** British stage designer; b. 1938, England; m.; two d. *Education:* Central School of Art and Design (now Central St Martin's School of Art), London. *Career:* Diploma of Theatre Design with Distinction; Head of Theatre Department at the Central School, then Head of Design at the National Theatre, London; Opera designs for the Glyndebourne Festival include Albert Herring, Simon Boccanegra, Porgy and Bess (British company premiere, 1986), La Traviata and Falstaff; Le nozze di Figaro 1994, revived 1997, Peter Grimes and Otello (also for Chicago Lyric Opera); Further engagements with English National Opera, Welsh National Opera, Scottish Opera, Opera North and the Salzburg Festival; La Scala, Milan, and opera houses at Munich, Cologne, Hamburg, Buenos Aires, Sydney and Los Angeles; Original 1857 version of Simon Boccanegra for Covent Garden, 1997; Season 1996–97 with Samson et Dalila for Queensland Opera; Also, Ernani for National Reise Opera, Netherlands, and Der fliegende Holländer for Covent Garden; Revival of Albert Herring at Glyndebourne Festival, and tour with GTO, 2002 (from 1985 production at Glyndebourne); Anything Goes, musical, Drury Lane Theatre, London; Romeo and Juliette, opera for Los Angeles; Peter Grimes, opera for Salzburg (sets and costumes), 2003–05. *Honours:* SWET Award for Best Designer (Guys and Dolls, Nat. Theatre) 1982, Olivier Award for Best Designer (Wild Honey, Royal Nat. theatre) 1984, Primetime Emmy Award for Best Design (Porgy and Bess) 1994. *Current Management:* c/o Richard Haigh, Performing Arts, 6 Windmill Street, London, W1T 2JB, England.

**GUO, Wenjing;** Chinese composer; b. 1 Feb. 1956, Chongqing; one d. *Education:* Central Conservatory of Music, Beijing. *Career:* violinist Dance and Choral Ensemble of Chongqing 1970–77; Dean and Prof., Composition Dept, Central Conservatory of Music, Beijing 1983–; works performed at major festivals in Europe; works performed by orchestras world-wide, including BBC Scottish Symphony Orchestra, China National Symphony Orchestra, Cincinnati Percussion Group, Göteborg Symphony Orchestra, Hong Kong Chinese Orchestra, Hong Kong Philharmonic Orchestra, HuaXia Chinese Ensemble, Lincoln Center Chamber Music Soc., London Sinfonietta, New York Music Consort, Nieuw Ensemble, Taiwan Symphony Orchestra; Visiting Scholar, Asian Cultural Council, USA; guest lecturer, Swedish Royal Inst. of Music, Univ. of Cincinnati, Manhattan School of Music; mem. Asscn of Chinese Musicians. *Film appearance:* Broked Silence. *Composition for film and television includes:* Hong fen 1994, Yangguang Canlan de Rizi 1994. *Compositions:* Ba 1982, The River of Sichuan 1981, Concerto 1986, Shu Dao Nan 1987, Shou Kong Shan 1991, Yun Nan 1993, The Wolfcub's Village (opera) 1993 (orchestral suite) 1994, Drama op. 23 1995, Inscriptions on Bone op. 24 1996, Concertino pour violoncelle et ensemble op. 26 1997, Echoes of Heaven and Earth op. 31 1998, The Night Banquet (opera) 1998, Journeys 2004. *Address:* c/o Central Conservatory of Music, 43 Baojia Street, Western District, Beijing 100031, People's Republic of China. *Telephone:* (10) 6641 2585. *Fax:* (10) 6641 3138. *E-mail:* imecwy@public.bta.net.cn. *Website:* www .ccom.edu.cn.

**GURIAKOVA, Olga;** Singer (Soprano); b. 1971, Novokuznetsk, Russia. *Education:* Graduated Moscow Conservatoire 1995. *Career:* Appearances at the Stanislavsky Musical Theatre, Moscow, from 1994; Kirov Opera, St Petersburg, from 1996, as Mimi, Natasha in War and Peace, Tatiana, Maria in Tchaikovsky's Mazeppa, Donna Anna, Desdemona and Elvira in Ernani; Further engagements as Gorislava in Ruslan and Lyudmila and Militrissa in Rimsky-Korsakov's Tsar Saltan; Tours of Europe, Israel and the Far East with the Kirov; Tchaikovsky's Maria at the New York Met and Iolanta at Carnegie Hall, 1998; Season 1999–2000 with Maria and Donna Anna in St Petersburg and Natasha at the Opéra Bastille, Paris; Sang with the Kirov at Covent Garden, 2000. *Honours:* Winner 2nd Rimsky-Korsakov International Competition; Russian Golden Mask and Casta Diva Competition, 1996. *Address:* c/o Kirov Opera, Mariinsky Theatre, 1 Theatre Square, St Petersburg, Russia.

**GUSCHLBAUER, Theodor;** Conductor; b. 14 April 1939, Vienna, Austria. *Education:* Vienna Acad. of Music. *Career:* conducted the Vienna Baroque Ensemble 1961–69; Asst at the Vienna Volksoper 1964–66; Conductor of the Salzburg Landestheater 1966–68, Lyon Opéra 1969–75; General Musik-Direktor, Linz-Bruckner Symphony Orchestra and the Landestheater Linz 1975–83; Chief Conductor, Strasbourg Philharmonic 1983–97, Rhineland-Palatinate Philharmonic 1997–2001; guest appearances at many festivals, including those at Salzburg, Aix-en-Provence, Prague, Bregenz, Flanders, Oxford, Lucerne, Montreux, Ascona, Maggio Musicale Fiorentino; regular guest conductor with the Vienna and Hamburg Operas, Geneva, Paris (Bastille), Munich, Cologne, Lisbon and Zürich. *Recordings:* Symphonies by Mozart, Haydn, Schubert and Beethoven; Concertos by Strauss, Mozart, Haydn, Mendelssohn and Weber; Mozart's Divertimento K287, Cassation K99, Masses K194 and K220, Vesperae Solennes, Sinfonia Concertante

K297b, Bassoon Concerto, Flute Concertos (Rampal), and Piano Concertos K271, K453 and K467 (Maria Joao Pires); K415; K488; Strauss Burleske, Horn Concerto No. 2 and Oboe Concerto; Beethoven's 6th Symphony and Schubert's Ninth, with the New Philharmonia; Bruckner 7, D'Indy, Hindemith, Grieg, Rachmaninov, Waldteufel, Dvořák, Scriabin, Vieuxtemps. *Honours:* Chevalier, Légion d'honneur 1997; seven Grand Prix du Disque; Mozart Prize, Goethe Foundation, Basel 1988.

**GUSSMANN, Wolfgang;** stage designer and costume designer; b. 1953, Germany. *Career:* collaborations from 1985 with Willy Decker at Cologne, including designs for La Finta Giardiniera, Billy Budd, Der fliegende Holländer, Eugene Onegin and Il Trittico; Capriccio at Florence, Bibalo's Macbeth (premiere) and Così fan tutte at Oslo; Partnership with Johannes Schaaf on Boris Godunov at Munich and Die Entführung aus dem Serail at Hamburg; Season 1996–97 with Freischütz and Don Giovanni at Dresden, the premiere of Das Schloss by Reimann in Berlin, Die Frau ohne Schatten in Geneva and at the Paris Châtelet, Eugene Onegin at the Paris Opéra Bastille, Idomeneo in Munich and Tristan at Leipzig; Season 1997–98 with La Bohème at Cologne, Tosca at Stuttgart, Lulu at the Bastille, Katya Kabanova in Amsterdam, Lohengrin at Bayreuther Festspiele, Pelléas et Mélisande at Hamburg, Billy Budd and Lulu at the Vienna Staatsoper and The Ring in Brussels. Season 1998–99 with Der Rosenkavalier and The Ring in Dresden and Der fliegende Holländer at the Opéra National in Paris; Most recent projects include: Freischütz, Don Giovanni, Die Soldaten and Lear in Dresden; Billy Budd in Antwerp; Tosca in Stuttgart; Carmen in Amsterdam; Pelléas et Mélisande in Hamburg; Macbeth with Oper Leipzig; Merry Widow at the Hamburg Staatsoper. Further productions include: Boris Godunov in Amsterdam and Paris; Billy Budd and Lulu at the Vienna Staatsoper, Rheingold in Dresden, Arabella and Manon Lescaut in Munich, Jenůfa at the Komisches Oper, Berlin, and Katya Kabanova at the Hamburg Staatsoper. *Address:* c/o Haydn Rawstron Ltd, 36 Station Road, London SE20 7BQ, England.

**GUSTAFSON, Nancy;** Singer (Soprano); b. 27 June 1956, Evanston, Illinois, USA; m. Brian Dickie. *Education:* Studied in San Francisco on the Adler Fellowship Program. *Career:* San Francisco Opera debut as Freia in Das Rheingold: returned as Musetta in La Bohème and Antonia in Les Contes d'Hoffmann and Elettra in Idomeneo; Opera Colorado as Donna Elvira; Minnesota Opera as Leila in Les Pêcheurs de Perles; Canadian debut as Violetta for Edmonton Opera; Festival performances as Rosalinda in Sante Fe and Britten's Helena for Chataugua Opera; European debut as Rosalinde in Paris, season 1984–85; Glyndebourne debut as Donna Elvira, while tour to Hong Kong: Festival appearances as Katya Kabanova, in a new production of Janáček's opera, 1988, returned 1990; Chicago Lyric Opera debut as Marguerite in Faust; Covent Garden debut 1988, as Freia; Scottish Opera 1989, as Violetta; Metropolitan Opera debut 1989, as Musetta; Sang Freia in Rheingold at Munich, 1990; Seattle Opera 1989, as Elettra in Idomeneo, Antonia in Les Contes d'Hoffmann 1990; Sang Eva at La Scala and Amelia in a new production of Simon Boccanegra at Brussels 1990; Sang Lisa in The Queen of Spades at Glyndebourne 1992; Season 1991–92 as Violetta and Alice Ford at Toronto; Sang the Letter Scene from Eugene Onegin at the 1993 London Proms; Eva in a new production of Die Meistersinger at Covent Garden, 1993; Concert engagements in Mahler's 8th Symphony, with the San Francisco Symphony, and at the Carmel Bach Festival, California; Engaged as Floyd's Susannah, Houston, 1996; Returned to Covent Garden as Eva, 1997; Season 2000–01 as Laurie Moss in Copland's The Tender Land, at the Barbican, Ellen Orford in Los Angeles, and Mathilde in Guillaume Tell for the Vienna Staatsoper. *Address:* c/o Theateragentur Dr G. Hilbert, Maximillanstrasse 22, D–80539 München, Germany.

**GUSTAVSSON, Jan;** Trumpeter; b. 8 Dec. 1959, Vadstena, Sweden; m. Jessica Gustavsson, 13 July 1996, 1 s. *Education:* Studied at Gothenburg Music Conservatory; Trumpet Soloist. *Career:* Debut: Lisbon, Portugal, 1989; Principal Trumpet, Norrköping, 1982–92; Principal Trumpet, Royal Stockholm Philharmonic Orchestra, 1992–; Trumpet Soloist appearances in Sweden, Portugal, Austria and Switzerland. *Recordings:* Leopold Mozart, Giuseppe Tartini, Trumpet Concertos as Soloist with Winterthur Stadtorchester, conductor Franz Welser-Möst, 1989. *Honours:* 2nd Prize, Budapest International Trumpet Solo Competition, 1984. *Address:* Kungliga Filharmoniska Orkestern, Box 7083, 103 87 Stockholm, Sweden.

**GUTIERREZ, Horacio;** Pianist; b. 28 Aug. 1948, Havana, Cuba; m. Patricia Asher. *Education:* Juilliard School of Music, New York City, USA, 1967–70. *Career:* Debut: At age 11 with Havana Symphony Orchestra; Performed most major symphony orchestras as soloist in recitals throughout the world; Appearances on BBC television and also in France and USA; Tours in USA, Canada, Europe, South America, Israel, USSR, Japan. *Recordings:* Numerous including Rachmaninov Pian Concertos No. 2 and 3 with Lorin Maazel and Pittsburgh Symphony (nominated for a Grammy in 1992); Brahms Nos 1 and 2 and Tchaikovsky No. 1. *Honours:* Recipient, 2nd Prize, Tchaikovsky Competition, 1970; Avery Fisher Prize, 1982. *Current Management:* Cramer Marder Artists. *Address:* 3426 Springhill Road, Latayette, CA 94549 USA.

**GUTMAN, Natalia Grigorievna;** Russian cellist; b. 14 Nov. 1942; m. Oleg Kagan (deceased); three c. *Education:* Gnessin Music School, Moscow (under R. Shposhnikov), Moscow Conservatory (under Prof. Kozolupova and Mstislav Rostropovich). *Career:* tours include: visits to Europe, USA and Japan, appearing with the Berlin Philharmonic Orchestra, Vienna Philharmonic Orchestra, London Symphony orchestra, Orchestre Nat. de France and Orchestre de Paris; played chamber music in USSR and Europe with Eliso Virsaladze and Oleg Kagan 1982–; played sonatas, trios and quartets with Sviatoslav Richter; plays sonata and concerto written for her by Alfred Schnittke; solo tours include: the USA with USSR State Symphony Orchestra and Yevgeny Svetlanov, Italy with BBC Symphony and Yuri Temirkanov, USSR with Sir John Pritchard; performed with Royal Philharmonic Orchestra under Yuri Temirkanov, Royal Festival Hall, London, the Concertgebouw, the London Philharmonic, the Munich Philharmonic, the Berlin Philharmonic, the Orchestre Nat. de France, the LA Philharmonic under André Previn, the Chicago Symphony under Claudio Abbado 1988–89; teacher at Moscow Conservatory 1967–77; Prof. Stuttgart Conservatory 1997–; f. Oleg Kagan Memorial Festival, Krems, Moscow. *Honours:* prizes at the Vienna Student Festival Competition, the Tchaikovsky Competition, the Munich Chamber Music Competition and the Dvořák Competition, Prague. *Address:* Askonas Holt, Lonsdale Chambers, 27 Chancery Lane, London, WC2A 1PF, England. *Telephone:* (20) 7400-1700 (London); (095) 203-33-91 (Moscow).

**GUTTLER, Ludwig;** Trumpeter, Conductor and Professor; b. 13 June 1943, Sosa, Germany. *Education:* Degree in Architecture; Studied trumpet with Armin Mennel, Leipzig Hochschule für Musik, 1961–65. *Career:* Debut: Soloist with orchestra in 1958; Solo Trumpeter, Handel Festival Orchestra, Halle, 1965–, and Dresden Philharmonic, 1969–81; Founder, Director, Leipziger Bach-Collegium, 1976–, Blechbläserensemble Ludwig Guttler, 1978–; Virtuosi Saxoniae, 1985–; Solo tours throughout the world; Lecturer, 1972–80, Professor, 1980–, Head of Masterclasses in wind playing, 1982–, Dresden Hochschule für Musik; Guest Teacher at Weimar International Music Seminar, 1977–, also in Austria, Japan and the USA. *Recordings:* Over 21 albums. *Honours:* National Prize, German Democratic Republic, 1978; German Phonoakademie Recording Prize, 1983; Music Prize, City of Frankfurt, 1989. *Address:* c/o Gotthart Wilke, Edinger Konzer-und Kunstleragentur, Lindenstrasse 26, 8011 Zorneding, Germany.

**GUTTMAN, Albert;** Pianist; b. 12 Oct. 1937, Galati, Romania. *Education:* Conservatoire of Music, Bucharest; Graduate in Piano, Florica Musicescu; Studied Piano Accompaniment under Dagobert Buchholz; Graduate, Biennial Masterclasses, magna cum laude, Santa Cecilia Conservatoire, Rome with teacher Guido Agosti. *Career:* Professor of Piano, Chamber Music and Piano Accompaniment, Bucharest Conservatoire of Music, 1960–76; Official Assistant for Chamber Music, Santa Cecilia National Academy in Rome, 1972; Invited by Yehudi Menuhin to teach chamber music at International Menuhin Academy of Music, Gstaad, Switzerland, 1982–84; Taught summer courses in Italy and Switzerland between 1969 and 1983; Professor of Piano, Musikschule Saanenland, Gstaad and Professor of Piano Accompaniment, including permanent Masterclass for Graduate Pianists specializing in Piano Accompaniment, Musik Akademie der Stadt Basel, 1983–; World-wide tours and participant in numerous festivals; Recitals with Radu Aldulescu and Silvia Marcovici, and often performed with Yehudi Menuhin, Pierre Fournier, Ruggiero Ricci, Enrico Mainardi, Jean Pierre Rampal, Christian Ferras, Lola Bobesco, Pina Carmirelli, Ivry Gitlis, Raphael Sommer. *Recordings include:* Radio and Television recordings world-wide; Discopgraphy: Beethoven, Complete Edition Five Sonatas for Piano and Cello, Radu Aldulescu on cello; Schumann, Frauen Liebe und Leben; De Falla, Siete Canciones Populares Españolas, Elena Cernei, mezzo; Shostakovich Sonata Op 40 for Cello and Piano; Hindemith Sonata Op 11 No. 3 for Cello and Piano, Radu Aldulescu on Cello; Bach Sonata No. 4 for Violin and Piano BWV 1017; Beethoven Sonata Op 30 No. 3 for Piano and Violin, Lola Bobesco on Violin; Brahms Sonata No. 2 Op 100 in A major and No. 3 Op 108 in D minor for Piano and Violin, Angela Gavrila Dieterle on Violin; Beethoven Seven Variations in E flat WoO46 for Piano and Cello, Mirel Iancovici on Cello. *Honours:* The Hephzibah Menuhin International Prize for Pianists, 1981. *Address:* Chalet Bel Air, App 216, 3780 Gstaad, Switzerland.

**GUY, Barry John;** British musician (double bass, baroque bass) and composer; b. 22 April 1947, Lewisham, London. *Education:* AGSM. *Career:* Freelance Bassist; principal, City of London Sinfonia; Academy of Ancient Music, London Classical Players until 1995; Solo recitalist; Artistic Director, London Jazz Composers Orchestra; Barry Guy New Orchestra; Plays with improvisation groups Parker/Guy/Lytton, Guy/Gustafsson/Strid, Cecil Taylor, Bill Dixon Quartet, Marilyn Crispell, Homburger-Guy Duo, Demierre/Guy/Niggli; mem, Musicians Union, PRS, MCPS, BACS. *Compositions include:* Statements ll, 1972; String Quartet III, 1973; Anna, 1974; Play, 1976; EOS for double bass and orchestra, 1977; Details, 1978; Hold Hands and Sing, 1978; Waiata, 1980; Pfiff, 1981; Flagwalk, 1974; Voyages of the Moon, 1983; RondOH!, 1985; Circular for solo oboe, 1985; The Road to Ruin, 1986; Harmos, 1987; The Eye of Silence, 1988; UM 1788, 1989; Look Up!, 1990; Theoria, 1991; After the Rain, 1992; Bird Gong Game, 1992; Mobile Herbarium, 1992; Portraits, 1993; Witch Gong Game, 1993; Witch Gong Game ll, 1994; Un Coup Dés, 1994; Buzz, 1994; Celebration, 1995; Ceremony, 1995; Three Pieces for orchestra, 1995; Concerto for orchestra, Fallingwater, 1996; Double Trouble Two, 1996; Holyrood, 1998; Redshift, 1998; Bubblets, 1998; Remembered Earth, 1998; Octavia, 1999; Dakryon, 1999; Inscape (Tableaux), 2000; Nasca Lines, 2001; Switch, 2001; Inachis, 2002; Aglais, 2002; Anaklasis, 2002; Folio, 2002, Oort-Entropy 2004, Lysandra 2004. *Recordings include:* Over 100 albums including: Ode, 1972; Endgame, 1979; Incision, 1981; Tracks, 1983; Zürich Concerts, 1988; Double Trouble, 1990; Elsie jo Live, 1992; Theoria, 1992; After the Rain, 1993; Fizzles, 1993; Portraits, 1994; Vade Mecum, 1994;

Imaginary Values, 1994; Witch Gong Game ll, 1994; Cascades, 1995; Obliquities, 1995; Iskra 1903, 1995; Three Pieces for orchestra, 1997; Sensology, 1997; Frogging, 1997; Natives and Aliens, 1997; Bingo, 1998, Double Trouble Two, 1998; At the Vortex, 1998; Ceremony, 1999; In Darkness Let Me Dwell, 2000; Melancholy, 2000; Nailed, 2000; Dividuality, 2001; Inscape – Tableaux 2001, Odyssey, 2002, Symmetries, 2002, Celebration 2002, Ithaca 2004, Gubbröra 2004, Dakryon 2005. *Honours:* Radcliffe Award 1st Prize, 1973; Royal Philharmonic Prize for Chamber Scale Composition, 1991; Joint Prizewinner, Hilliard Composition prize, 1994; Abendzeitung (Munich) Sterne des Jahres, 1999. *Address:* POB 52, CH-8477 Oberstammheim, Switzerland (home). *Telephone:* (52) 7402972 (home). *Fax:* (52) 7402972 (home). *E-mail:* barry@maya-recordings.com (home). *Website:* www.maya -recordings.com (home).

**GUY, (Ruth) Maureen;** singer (mezzo-soprano); b. 10 July 1932, Penclawdd, Glamorgan, South Wales; m. John Mitchinson 1958. *Education:* Guildhall School of Music and Drama. *Career:* debut as Dryad in Ariadne auf Naxos, Sadler's Wells; Principal Mezzo-Soprano at Sadler's Wells, Royal Opera House Covent Garden and Frankfurt Opera; Recitals, oratorio and orchestral concerts world-wide; Tours of New Zealand, Australia and Europe; Performed in opera in New Zealand, Spain, Portugal, France and Budapest; Her roles included Delilah, Eboli, Amneris, Azucena, Fricka, Erda, Orpheus, Mrs Sedley and Adriano in Rienzi; Performed Oedipus Rex in Herodus Atticus in Athens, conducted by Stravinsky; Vocal Tutor at the Welsh College of Music and Drama. *Recordings:* Solti, Götterdämmerung; Leinsdorf, Die Walküre; Sadler's Wells, Rigoletto, as Maddalena. *Honours:* Glamorgan County Scholarship to Guildhall School. *Address:* The Verzons Granary, Munsley, Ledbury, Hertfordshire, England.

**GUYER, Joyce;** Singer (Soprano); b. 1961, USA. *Career:* Sang Mozart's Constanze at Washington, 1987; Chicago Opera, 1988, as Gluck's Euridice, Buxton Festival, 1989, as Livia in Cimarosa's L'Italiana in Londra; Metropolitan Opera, New York, from 1993, in Jenůfa, Ariadne auf Naxos, Parsifal and Idomeneo; Season 1991 at Montpellier and Nice, as Constanze and Donna Anna; Bayreuth Festival, 1995–96, in The Ring and Parsifal. *Recordings include:* Videos of Parsifal and Idomeneo. *Address:* c/o Metropolitan Opera, Lincoln Center, New York, NY 10023, USA.

**GWYNNE, David;** singer (bass); b. 1945, Pontnewydd, Cwmbran, Wales. *Education:* Guildhall School, London. *Career:* appearances with Welsh National Opera as Verdi's Zaccaria, and Grand Inquisitor, Wagner's Daland, Pimen in Boris Godunov, Mozart's Basileo and Rocco in Fidelio; Scottish Opera in The Trojans, Peter Grimes, Schnittke's Life with an Idiot, Katya Kabanova, Aida, Oedius Rex and Don Giovanni, as the Commendatore; Engagements with English National Opera in Henze's The Prince of Homburg and Gianni Schicchi; Opera North in Katya Kabanova, Attila, The Love for Three Oranges, Fidelio (Fernando) and Gloriana; Arkel in Pelléas et Mélisande, Ferrando in Il Trovatore and Hermit in Der Freischütz are other roles: Glyndebourne Festival 2000, as Antonio in Le nozze di Figaro.

**GYSELYNCK, Jean-Baptiste;** Professor; b. 22 March 1946, Ghent, Belgium; m. Bruyneel Arlette, 1 June 1946, 1 s., 1 d. *Education:* Royal Atheneum of Ghent; Royal Music Conservatory of Ghent, 1962–66; Conservatory of Brussels, 1966–78. *Career:* Teacher of Counterpoint, Royal Flemish Music Conservatory of Antwerp, 1970; Professor of Harmony, Counterpoint and Composition at Lemmens Institute of Louvain, 1970–79; Professor Written Harmony, 1970–, Professor of Harmony, Art Humanities Department, 1974–75, Royal Music Conservatory of Brussels. *Compositions include:* Recorded: Simfonia Da Camera, radio and television, 1975, Intermezzi for Wood Instruments, LP and radio, 1977, Trio for Strings, radio, 1979, Adagio En Allegro for Alto Saxophone, radio, 1979, Adagio En Allegro for Alto Saxophone, Diptyque for Violin and Piano, radio, 1980, Diptyque for Violin and Piano, radio, 1982; Published: Intermezzi, Illuminatio, Diptyque, Music for 6 poems written by Johan Daisne. *Honours:* International Music Competition Queen Elisabeth Laureat of Composition, 1980; Silver Prize of Her Majesty Queen Fabiola Composition Competition Sabam, 1980; 6 Poems of Johan Daisne given at the Albertine, Brussels, 1985. *Address:* Kortrijksesteenweg 934, 9000 Ghent, Belgium.

# H

**HAAN, Richard;** Singer (Baritone); b. 1959, Kosice, Slovakia. *Career:* Sang at Usti nad Labem and Olomouc, Slovak National Opera at Bratislava, 1990–93, Janáček Opera at Brno and National Theatre, Prague, as guest (Verdi's Amonasro and Renato, 1994–96); Edinburgh Festival, 1990, as Valentin in Faust, Salzburg, 1992, in Janáček's From the House of the Dead; US debut, 1996, at Virginia Opera, Norfolk, as Wagner's Dutchman; Sang Mathis in The Polish Jew by Karel Weis at the Prague State Opera, 2001; Other roles include Don Giovanni and Gershwin's Porgy; Numerous concert appearances. *Address:* c/o Virginia Opera, PO Box 2580, Norfolk, VA 23501, USA.

**HAAS, Kenneth;** Symphony Orchestra Executive; b. 8 July 1943, Washington DC, USA; m. (1) Barbara Dooneief, 14 Feb 1964, divorced 1990, 2 d., (2) Signe Johnson, 23 Mar 1990, 1 s. *Education:* BA, Columbia College, 1964. *Career:* Assistant to Managing Director, New York Philharmonic, 1966–70; Assistant General Manager, 1970–75, General Manager, 1976–87, Cleveland Orchestra; General Manager of Cincinnati Symphony Orchestra, 1975–76; Managing Director of Boston Symphony Orchestra, 1987–; Chairman of Orchestra Panel, National Endowment for The Arts, 1982–85; Co-Chairman of Music Overview Panel, National Endowment for The Arts, 1983–85; Chairman of Challenge Grant Panel, Ohio Arts Council, 1985–86; mem, American Symphony Orchestra League, Executive Committee, 1980–82, Board of Directors, 1993–94; Managers of Major Orchestras, US, Chairman, 1980–82. *Address:* Symphony Hall, 301 Massachusetts Avenue, Boston, MA 02115, USA.

**HABBESTAD, Kjell (Helge);** Teacher and Composer; b. 13 April 1955, Bomlo, Hordaland, Norway; m. Inger Elisabeth Brammer, 30 Dec 1976, 1 s., 2 d. *Education:* Studies of Church Music (organ), 1975–79; Studied Composition, Norwegian State Academy of Music, 1979–81. *Career:* Organist, Snaroya Church, Baerum 1977–81, Langhus Church, Ski 1986–87; Teacher of Harmony, Counterpoint, Composition, Bergen Conservatory of Music 1981–86, Ostlandets Conservatory of Music, Oslo, 1986–96; Norwegian State Academy of Music, 1996–. *Compositions:* 3 Cantica (Magnificat, Nunc Dimittis, Benedictus Dominus), 1978–83; Lament, soprano and orchestra, 1981; Mostraspelet, baritone solo, choir, orchestra and mediaeval instruments, 1983; Ave Maria, concerto for organ and string orchestra, 1984; Something New–Below Ground, concerto for tuba and brass band, 1985; Mostrasuite for baritone solo, unison choir and orchestra, 1986; Introduction and Passacaglia, over a theme by Fartein Valen, organ solo, 1987; Hammerklavier, piano solo, 1989; Orpheus, flute, piano and ballet dancer, 1993; One Night on Earth, oratorio, 1993; Hans Egedes Natt, opera, 1995; Ibsen Songs, song and piano, 1996; Liturgic dramas/church plays, choral works, chamber music, cantatas, organ chorals, motets. *Publications:* Cantate–Handbook of Norwegian Sacred Choral Works, 1989; Themes, Trends and Talents, 25 Years of Contemporary Norwegian Music, co-editor, 1992; Arrangements, Arenas and Actors in Contemporary Norwegian Music, editor and writer, 1992; Yearbook of Contemporary Norwegian Music, editor and writer, 1996 and 1997. *Address:* Wesselsvei 5, 1412 Sofiemyr, Norway.

**HABEREDER, Agnes;** Swiss/German singer (soprano); b. 1957, Kelheim, Germany. *Education:* Studied in Munich, Florence and Stuttgart. *Career:* Sang at Augsburg Mozart Festival, 1979 as Mozart's Donna Anna; Winner of Mozart Competition in Würzburg; Guest appearances at Florence and Paris as Wagner's Gutrune, 1981; Semper-Opera Dresden Musikfestspiele 1984–89, Marie in Berg's Wozzeck; Zürich Opera from 1984 as Strauss's Empress, Wagner's Senta, and Ursula in Hindemith's Mathis der Maler; Bayreuth Festival, 1983–86, in The Ring; Salzburg Festival, 1986, as Leonore in Fidelio; Other roles include Salome, Korngold's Marietta, and Cassandre in Les Troyens (Zürich, 1990); Other guest appearances at Vienna, Munich, Mannheim, RAI Turin; Concert performances all over the world; Teacher at Augsburg Music High School 1993–; Teacher at Munich Music High school, 1993–; mem, Bund Deutsche Gesangspädagogen; Muenchner Tonkuenstler EV; owner Gestnet Kirchberg, working with UNICEF. *Film:* Cassandre in Hector Berlioz by Tony Palmer. *Recordings:* Kantate, Von deutscher Seele, by Hans Pfitzner, Düsseldorfer Symphoniker, conductor Heinrich Hollreiser. *Publications:* Agnes Habereder: A Voice and its Presence (by Klaus Kirschner). *Address:* Stillnau 52, 86657 Bissingen, Germany. *Telephone:* (9084) 90466 (office); (1702) 061054 (home). *Fax:* (9084) 90455 (office). *E-mail:* L'AbelageMusic@hotmail.com (office). *Website:* www.gestnet.kirchberg.de (home).

**HABERMANN, Michael Robert,** AAS, BA, MA, DMA; American pianist, piano instructor and composer; b. 23 Feb. 1950, Paris, France. *Education:* Nassau Community College, Garden City, NY, Long Island University, Greenvale, NY, Peabody Conservatory, Baltimore, MD. *Career:* debut, Carnegie Recital Hall 1977; American Liszt Festival appearances in 1978, 1982, 1993; International Piano Festival, University of Maryland in 1979; Grand Piano Programme, National Public radio recital in 1981; McMaster University, Hamilton, Ontario, Canada, 1983; Rocky River Chamber Music Society, Ohio, 1984–2001; Lecturer, Elder Hostel Program, Peabody Conservatory, Baltimore, 1990–; International Concert Series, Hempstead, New York, 1999; Performing Arts Center, Purchase, New York, 2000. *Recordings:* Sorabji: A Legend in His Own Time; Sorabji: Le Jardin Parfumé; Sorabji: Piano Music,

vol. 3; Sorabji: The Legendary Works; Sorabji: Transcriptions and other works; Piano Music of Alexandre Rey Colaço Educo. *Publications:* Kaikhosru Shapurji Sorabji, The Piano Quarterly, 1983; The Exotic Piano Masterpieces of Sorabji, Soundpage and Score, Keyboard Magazine, 1986; A Style Analysis of The Nocturnes for Solo Piano by Kaikhosru Shapurji Sorabji with special emphasis on Le Jardin Parfumé, University Microfilms International; Author of Sorabji's Piano Music, in Sorabji: A Critical Celebration, 1993; Author, Essay for Remembering Horowitz: 125 Pianists recall a legend, 1993. *Address:* 4208 Harford Terrace, Baltimore, MD 21214, USA. *E-mail:* pf@ michaelhabermann.com.

**HACKER, Alan Ray;** British clarinettist, conductor and lecturer; b. 30 Sept. 1938, Dorking, Surrey; m. (1) Anna Maria Sroka, 1959, 2 d., (2) Karen Evans, 1977, divorced, 1 s., (3) Margaret Shelley 1995. *Education:* Royal Academy of Music; FRAM. *Career:* Joined London Philharmonic Orchestra, 1958; Professor, Royal Academy of Music, 1960–76; Co-Founder, Pierrot Players, 1965; Founded Matrix, 1971, Music Party for authentic performance of classical music, 1972, Classical Orchestra, 1977; Member, Fires of London, 1970–76; Guest Conductor, Orchestra La Fenice, Venice, 1981; Revived basset clarinet, restored original text to Mozart's concerto and quintet, 1967; Revived baroque clarinet, 1975; 1st modern authentic performances, 1977–, including: Mozart Symphonies 39, 40; Beethoven Symphonies 2, 3, 7, 9 and Egmont; Haydn Harmonie and Creation Masses, Symphony 104, Trumpet Concerto; Premieres, music by Birtwistle, Boulez, Feldman, Goehr, Maxwell Davies, Stockhausen, Blake, Mellers, Sciarrino; Conductor, 5 staged performances of Bach St John Passion, European Music Year, 1984; Directed Hallström's Den Bergtagna revival, Swedish National Opera (for Norrlands Operan), 1986–87, and 1st production of complete Keiser's Claudius, Vadstena Academy, Sweden, 1989; Premiered Judith Weir's The Vanishing Bridegroom, Scottish Opera, 1990; Così fan tutte, La Finta Giardiniera, Opera North, 1990–91; Stuttgart Opera, 1990–96, Don Giovanni and Monteverdi's Ulisse; Così fan tutte, La Cenerentola, Barcelona, 1992, Giulio Cesare, Halle Handel Festival; La Clemenza di Tito, Vienna, 1994; Opéra de Paris Bastille, Magic Flute; Stuttgart Opera, Purcell's King Arthur, 1996–97; Handel's Xerxes, Cologne, 1996–97; Handel's Alcina at Stuttgart and Edinburgh, 1998; Sir Robert Mayer Lecturer, Leeds University, 1972–73; Senior Lecturer, Music, York University, 1976–85; Orchestral work with major orchestras world-wide; Handel's Saul, Berlin, 1999. *Recordings:* Many including Brahms Clarinet Sonatas, 1989; Mozart and Weber Quintets. *Publications:* Mozart Concerto and Quintet scores, 1972; Reconstructed Mozart Concerto, 1st edition, 1973; Schumann's Soirestücke, 1985. *Honours:* O.B.E. 1988; Patron, Artlink 1993; Hon. doctorate (York) 2004. *Address:* Hindlea, Broughton, Malton, North Yorkshire YO17 6QJ, England. *Telephone:* (1653) 696163 (home). *E-mail:* clarinet@hackers-at-hindlea.freeserve .co.uk.

**HADARI, Omri,** FGSM; Israeli conductor; b. 10 Sept. 1941; m. Osnat Hadari 1965; one s. one d. *Education:* Tel-Aviv Music Coll., Guildhall School of Music and Drama, London. *Career:* debut, London 1974; conductor, London Lyric Orchestra; Principal Guest Conductor, Adelaide Symphony Orchestra; conducted Shostakovich's New Babylon in London 1982, New York and Helsinki and at the Flanders Festival; debut with Australian Opera 1988 in La Bohème; Music Dir and Principal Conductor, Cape Town Symphony Orchestra, S Africa 1989–; Guest Conductor for Royal Philharmonic Orchestra, London Symphony Orchestra, City of Birmingham Symphony Orchestra, Australian Opera, Sydney Symphony Orchestra, Melbourne Symphony Orchestra, South Australia Symphony Orchestra, Queensland Symphony Orchestra, Israel Chamber Orchestra, Jerusalem Symphony Orchestra, Beer-Sheva Sinfonietta, Het Brabant Symphony Orchestra, Dutch Nat. Ballet, Victorian State Opera, Ulster Orchestra, Nat. Symphony Orchestra of S Africa, Natal Philharmonic, Columbus Symphony Orchestra, Ohio, San Francisco Chamber Orchestra, Orchestra of Radio City New York, Lahti Symphony Orchestra, Avanti Orchestra, Tasmania Symphony Orchestra; mem. Incorporated Soc. of Musicians. *Honours:* Dr Leo Kestenberg Prize, Israel 1969, Guildhall School of Music Conducting Prize 1974, Capsalic Cup for Conducting 1974. *Address:* PO Box 128, Shdeima 76855, Israel. *Telephone:* (8) 869 3041. *E-mail:* hadario@013.net. *Website:* www.hadarimaestro.com.

**HADDOCK, Marcus;** Singer (Tenor); b. 19 June 1957, Fort Worth, Texas, USA. *Education:* Vocal Studies, Baylor University, Waco, Texas, with Carol Blaickner-Mayo; Texas Tech University with John Gillas; Boston University with Phyllis Curtin. *Career:* Roles include Count Almaviva in Il Barbiere di Siviglia, Ramiro in La Cenerentola, Lindoro in L'Italiana in Algeri, Tonio in La Fille du Régiment by Donizetti; International debut in Bordeaux as Ford in Salieri's Falstaff; Nemorino in L'Elisir d'amore; Festival appearances in Aachen, Karlsruhe and Bonn in La Bohème and Lucia di Lammermoor, La Traviata, Madama Butterfly, Werther and Les Contes d'Hoffmann; Debut with Opéra Paris de Bastille as Arbace in Idomeneo; 1992 debut with Teatro alla Scala as Matteo in Arabella with Wolfgang Sawallisch; 1994–95 season as Lenski in Eugene Onegin for Lausanne Opera, then Rodolfo in La Bohème in Geneva, Pinkerton in Madama Butterfly in Los Angeles and Don Carlo in Antwerp; Season 1995–96 included Ruggero in La Rondine, Roméo in Roméo et Juliette in Geneva and appearance in Gran Teatro la Fenice to sing Don

Carlo in Warsaw; Season 1996–97 included appearance with Deutsche Oper Berlin as Faust, Tebaldo in I Capuleti e i Montecchi at Opera de Bastille and Lenski in debut with Nederlandse Opera in Amsterdam; Verdi Requiem with Orchestre de Paris; Season 2000–01 as Puccini's Ruggiero in Los Angeles, Julien in Louise at Toulouse, Pinkerton at the Teatro Colón, Buenos Aires, and the Duke of Mantua for Dallas Opera; Sang Don José at Glyndebourne 2002. Concert repertoire includes Missa Solemnis and Janáček's Glagolitic Mass. *Recordings:* Orazi e Curiazi with London Philharmonic Orchestra; Il Guarany, with Oper der Stadt Bonn. *Address:* 1000 The Lane, Skaneateles, NY 13152, USA.

**HADJINIKOS, George,** DipMus; British conductor, pianist and lecturer; b. 3 May 1923, Volos, Greece; m. Matina Crithary (deceased); one s. *Education:* Athens University, Athens Conservatoire, Mozarteum at Salzburg, studied with Carl Orff, Munich, Ed Erdmann, Hamburg and G. Chavchavadze, Paris. *Career:* concert soloist, conductor, lecturer in Europe, USA, South Africa, India and Brazil; world premieres of works by Nikos Skalkottas; soloist with many international orchestras including: Berlin Philharmonic, BBC Orchestra with Antal Dorati, Hallé Orchestra with John Barbirolli, NDR with Herman Scherchen, Suisse Romande, Zürich and Copenhagen Radio; Conductor of many orchestras world-wide including: London Bach Festival Ensemble, RAI Milan Orchestra (Athens Festival opening concert), Rio de Janeiro, Copenhagen, Stockholm and Athens Radio Orchestras, Sinfonie Orchester Berlin and numerous international youth orchestras; Concert tour of US universities; Prepared and Conducted 1st Greek performance of Brahms' German Requiem, 1992, Stravinsky's Persephone 1996, Les Noces 1997; Nexus Opera Workshop; Lectured, Wuerzburg European Council Symposium; Developed fresh approach, Essence and Origins of Musical Interpretation presented at open seminars and articles; Musical Director of the Hortos International Seminars, where Greek musical youth meets musical youth from Europe, Russia, America and other countries, 1983–; Teacher, Royal Manchester and Royal Northern Colleges of Music, 1961–88. *Recordings:* Album with works by Bach, Bartók, Skalkottas, Konstantinidis and Poniridis; CD, Conducting Skalkottas Fairy Tale. *Publications:* Monographs on Skalkottas, 1981 and Mozart's Recitative, 1991; Co-editor, The Complete works by Nikos Skalkottas; Series of articles on Essence and Origins of Musical Interpretation (to be published in Greek, 2005); Centenary guide to the work and personality of Nikos Skalkottas (1904–2004). *Honours:* Ugo Foscolo Medal for services to European Music, Pavia Univ., Italy 1992.

**HADLEY, Jerry;** Singer (Tenor); b. 16 June 1952, Peoria, Illinois, USA; m. Cheryll Drake Hadley. *Education:* Studied at University of Illinois and with Thomas LoMonaco. *Career:* Debut: Sarasota, FL in 1978 as Lionel in Martha; New York City Opera debut in 1979 as Arturo in Lucia di Lammermoor, returning as Werther, Tom Rakewell, Rodolfo, Pinkerton and Nadir; Vienna Staatsoper debut in 1982 as Nemorino in L'Elisir d'amore; Glyndebourne debut in 1984 as Idamante in Trevor Nunn's production of Idomeneo; Covent Garden in 1984 as Fenton in Falstaff; Metropolitan Opera debut in 1987 as Des Grieux in Manon; Stage engagements in Chicago, Hamburg, Berlin, Munich and Geneva; Other roles include Gounod's Faust, the Duke of Mantua and the tenor leads in Anna Bolena and Maria Stuarda; Hamburg in 1987 as Tamino and sang Edgardo at the Deutsche Oper Berlin and Washington, 1988–89; Candide in a concert performance of Bernstein's work in London in 1989; Sang Hoffmann in London in 1992; Sang Tom Rakewell at the 1994 Salzburg Festival; Created the title role in Myron Fink's The Conquistador, San Diego, 1997; Concert engagements with the Pittsburgh Symphony, Boston Symphony, Chicago Symphony, Philadelphia Orchestra, Vienna Philharmonic and Los Angeles Philharmonic; Recitals with pianist, Cheryll Drake Hadley; Sang Weill's Jimmy Mahoney at Salzburg, 1998; Created the title role in The Great Gatsby by John Harbison at the New York Met, 1999; Engaged as Idomeneo at Baden-Baden, 2000; Sang Števa in Jenůfa at Covent Garden, 2002. *Recordings include:* Schubert Mass in E flat; La Bohème; Beethoven's Choral Symphony; Requiems of Mozart and Verdi with the Robert Shaw Chorale; Britten's Serenade, Nocturne and Les Illuminations; Il Re Pastore conducted by Neville Marriner. *Address:* c/o IMG Artists, Lovell House, 616 Chiswick High Road, London W4 5RX, England.

**HAEBLER, Ingrid;** Austrian pianist; b. 20 June 1929, Vienna. *Education:* Vienna Acad., Salzburg Mozarteum and Geneva Conservatory. *Career:* specializes in Haydn, Mozart, Schubert and Schumann; mem. Faculty, Salzburg Mozarteum 1969–; concerts with Concertgebouw Orchestra, London Symphony, Royal Philharmonic, Vienna and Berlin Philharmonics, Boston Symphony, Lamoureux Orchestra, Stockholm and Warsaw Philharmonics, London Mozart Players; has appeared in festivals worldwide. *Honours:* won 1st Prize, Int. Competition Munich 1954; Mozart Medal, Vienna 1971, Mozart Medal, Salzburg 1979, Gold Medal of Honour, Vienna 1986, Gold Medal 'Viotti d'oro', Vercelli, Italy 2000. *Address:* 5412 St Jakob am Thurn, Post Puch Bei Hallein, Land Salzburg, Austria.

**HAEFLIGER, Andreas;** Swiss pianist; b. Berlin, Germany. *Education:* Juilliard School, New York. *Career:* studied with Herbert Stessin, twice won Gina Bachauer Memorial Scholarship; has appeared with many of world's leading orchestras in N America, Europe and Japan; numerous recital appearances including Great Performers Series, Lincoln Center, New York, Wigmore Hall, London and in Germany, Austria, France and Italy; has performed twice at BBC Proms, London; tours USA with Takacs String Quartet; performs frequently with baritone Matthias Goerner. *Recordings include:* Mozart Piano Sonatas, Schumann's Davidsbündlertanze and Fanta-

siestücke, Schubert's Impromptus, music by Sofia Gubaidulina, Schubert's Goethe Lieder (with Matthias Goerne). *Honours:* Preis der Deutschen Schallplattenkritik (for recording of Schubert's Goethe Lieder). *Current Management:* Intermusica Artists Management Ltd, 16 Duncan Terrace, London, N1 8BZ, England. *Telephone:* (20) 7278-5455 (office). *Fax:* (20) 7278-8434 (office). *E-mail:* mail@intermusica.co.uk (office). *Website:* www .intermusica.co.uk.

**HAEFLIGER, Ernst;** Singer (tenor); b. 6 July 1919, Davos, Switzerland. *Education:* Studied in Zürich and with Fernando Carpi in Geneva; Further study with Julius Patzak in Vienna. *Career:* Debut: In 1942 as the Evangelist in Bach's St John Passion; Sang with Zürich Opera, 1943–52; Many concert appearances in Switzerland, Germany, Austria, France and Netherlands, notably in the St Matthew Passion and Lieder cycles by Schubert; Salzburg Festival in 1949 as Tiresias in the premiere of Antigonae by Orff, returning for Idomeneo and the Choral Symphony; Glyndebourne Festival, 1956–57 as Tamino in Die Zauberflöte and as Belmonte in Die Entführung; Guest appearances in Munich, Hamburg, Florence, Aix-en-Provence, Brussels and Berlin at the Deutsche Oper, 1952–74; Sang in the first performances of the oratorios Le Vin Herbé, Golgotha and in Terra Pax, by Frank Martin; Visited Moscow and Leningrad with the Munich Bach Choir in 1968; Professor at the Musikhochschule Munich from 1971; Sang the Shepherd in Tristan und Isolde at Munich, 1996; London Prom Concerts 2002, as the Speaker in Schoenberg's Gurrelieder. *Recordings:* St Matthew Passion; Missa Solemnis; Oedipus Rex; Pelléas et Mélisande; Die Entführung; Fidelio; Don Giovanni; Die Zauberflöte; Der fliegende Holländer; Brockes Passion by Handel; Die Israeliten in der Wüste by CPE Bach. *Publications:* Die Singstimme, 1984. *Current Management:* Ingpen & Williams Ltd, 7 St George's Court, 131 Putney Bridge Road, London, SW15 2PA, England.

**HAEFLIGER, Michael,** BMus, MBA; musician; b. 2 May 1961, West Berlin. *Education:* Juillard School of Music, St Gallen Univ., Harvard Business School. *Career:* Artistic and Exec. Dir, Davos Music Festival 1986–98, Lucerne Festival 1999–; mem. Int. Soc. of Performing Arts, Lions Club. *Honours:* World Economic Forum Global Leader for Tomorrow 2000, European Cultural Initiative Award 2003. *Address:* c/o Lucerne Festival, Hirschmattstr 13, 6002 Lucerne (office); Spissenstr 2, 6047 Kastanienbaum, Lucerne, Switzerland (home). *Telephone:* 412264400 (office). *Fax:* 412264460 (office). *Website:* www .lucernefestival.ch (office).

**HAENCHEN, Hartmut;** Conductor; b. 21 March 1943, Dresden, Germany. *Education:* Member of the Dresden Kreuzchor, 1953–60, under Rudolf Mauersberger and at the Dresden Musikhochschule, 1960–66. *Career:* Directed the Robert-Franz-Singakademie and the Halle Symphony, 1966–72; Music Director at the Zwickau Opera, 1972–73; Permanent Conductor of the Dresden Philharmonic, 1973–76, Philharmonic Chorus of Dresden, 1974–76 and 1985–1987 permanent guest conductor of the Staatsoper Dresden; Musical Director of the Schwerin Staatstheater and conductor of the Mecklenburg Staatskapelle, 1976–79; Professor of Conducting, Dresden Musikhochschule, 1980–86; Permanent Guest Conductor at Komische Oper Berlin and Berlin Staatsoper; Guest appearances in Europe, USA, Canada, Japan and China at leading opera houses in Europe, New York and at Kirishima Festival in Japan; From 1980 Artistic Director of the CPE Bach Chamber Orchestra, Berlin; From 1986 to 1999 Musical Director of the Netherlands Opera and 1986–2002 Chief Conductor of the Netherlands Philharmonic Orchestra and the Netherlands Chamber Orchestra; Conducted Bluebeard's Castle, La Damnation de Faust, Elektra, Salome, Rosenkavalier, Le nozze di Figaro, Entführung, Don Carlos, Tristan, Parsifal, Boris Godunov, Orphée et Eurydice; Conducted Gluck's Orfeo ed Euridice at Covent Garden in 1991 followed by Mozart's Mitridate; Die Frau ohne Schatten, Mitridate, La Damnation de Faust and Samson et Dalila at Amsterdam in 1992; Opened the 1994 season for Netherlands Opera with Lady Macbeth of the Mtsensk District; Elektra at Amsterdam, 1996, and Götterdämmerung 1998; After completion of his Ring for the Netherlands Opera in 1999, he changed from Musical Director to First Guest Conductor and conducted Alceste, Meistersinger, Capriccio, King Roger, Onegin, Lear, Lulu and Titus; Season 2002–03 with La Clemenza di Tito, Die Zauberflöte and Die Soldaten in Amsterdam and until 2005 the complete Ring cycle; From 2003, Intendant of the Dresdner Musik Festspiele. *Recordings:* Numerous including Gluck's Orfeo ed Euridice, earning the Preis der Deutschen Schallplatten and Gramophone Award Nomination. *Address:* Dresdner Musikfestspiele, Tiergartenstrasse 36, D 01219 Dresden, Germany.

**HAENDEL, Ida,** CBE; British (b. Polish) violinist; b. 15 Dec. 1928, Chelm, Poland. *Education:* Warsaw Conservatoire, pvt. tuition in Paris and London. *Career:* studied with Carl Flesch and Georges Enescu; London debut at Queen's Hall with Sir Henry Wood, Queen's Hall 1937; USA debut 1946; moved to Montreal, Canada 1952, Miami, Fla, USA 1979; performances throughout world with many noted conductors including tour with London Philharmonic Orchestra to first Hong Kong Festival of Arts and China and three tours of USSR; participated in centenary anniversary Festival of Bronislav Huberman, Tel-Aviv 1982; celebrated 50th anniversary of debut at Promenade Concerts, London 1987; numerous recordings of works by all the major composers. *Publication:* Woman with Violin (autobiog.) 1970. *Honours:* Hon. mem. RAM 1982–; Dr hc (Royal Coll. of Music) 2000; Sibelius Medal (Finland) 1982. *Address:* c/o Ernest Gilbert Associates, 109 Wheeler Avenue, Pleasantville, NY 10570, USA. *Telephone:* (914) 769-3691. *Fax:* (914) 769-5407. *E-mail:* ejgilbert@msn.com (office).

**HAENEN, Tom;** Singer (Bass); b. 1959, Amsterdam, Netherlands. *Education:* Studied at Amsterdam Conservatoire. *Career:* Debut: As Don Alfonso in Così fan tutte for Netherlands Opera; Appearances in the Netherlands and elsewhere as the General in Prokofiev's The Gambler, Arkel in Pelléas et Mélisande and Ferrando in Il Trovatore, Osmin in Die Entführung for Opera North and Leporello and Geronte in Manon Lescaut in Dublin; Further engagements as Sparafucile in Rigoletto, Don Cassandro in La Finta Semplice and Tom in Un Ballo in Maschera for Flanders Opera in 1992; Guest appearances at Spoleto, Israel and Las Palmas Festivals. *Honours:* Prizewinner at the International 's-Hertogenbosch and Rio de Janeiro Competitions.

**HAFIDH, Munther Jamil;** Iraqi musician (viola, cello); m. *Career:* viola player, Baghdad Symphony Orchestra 1959–. *Address:* Iraqi National Symphony Orchestra, Baghdad Convention Center, Green Zone, Baghdad, Iraq.

**HAGEGÅRD, Erland;** Baritone; b. 27 Feb. 1944, Brunskog, Sweden; m. Anne Terelius. *Education:* Studied in Sweden with Arne Sunnegaard, Erik Werba in Vienna and Gerald Moore in Vienna. *Career:* Debut: Vienna Volksoper in 1968 in Trois Opéras Minutes by Milhaud; Sang with Frankfurt Opera, 1971–74; Member of the Hamburg Staatsoper from 1974; Guest with the Vienna Staatsoper from 1976; Appearances at the Drottningholm Court Opera in Sweden; Danish television in Xerxes by Handel; Roles include Escamillo, Valentin, Don Giovanni, Eugene Onegin, Albert in Werther and Germont in La Traviata; Lieder singer in works by Schubert; Television appearances include Suppé's Boccaccio.

**HAGEGÅRD, Håkan;** Baritone; b. 25 Nov. 1945, Karlstad, Sweden; m. Barbara Bonney, dissolved, 2 c. *Education:* Music Academy of Stockholm; Student of Tito Gobbi, Rome, Gerald Moore, London, and Erik Werba, Vienna. *Career:* Debut: As Papageno in The Magic Flute, Royal Opera, Sweden, 1968; Metropolitan Opera debut in 1978 as Donizetti's Malatesta; Member of Royal Opera Stockholm; Appeared with major opera companies throughout Europe, in film of The Magic Flute in 1975 and at Glyndebourne from 1973 as the Count in Figaro and Capriccio and as Mozart's Guglielmo; Created role of Crispin in Tintomara, Royal Opera Stockholm in 1973; Covent Garden debut in 1987 as Wolfram in Tannhäuser, also at Chicago in 1988; Metropolitan Opera in 1988 as Guglielmo; Sang Eisenstein in Die Fledermaus at Chicago in 1989; Created Beaumarchais in The Ghosts of Versailles by Corigliano at the Metropolitan in 1991; Deutsche Oper Berlin in 1992 as Wolfram; Season 1996 at the Met as Prus in The Makropulos Case and in April Gala; The Officer in the US premiere of Lindberg's A Dream Play, Santa Fe, 1998; Sang Scarpia at Sydney, 2000; Recitalist. *Recordings include:* Die Zauberflöte under Armin Jordan; Don Giovanni, in title role, from Drottningholm. *Current Management:* Thea Dispeker. *Address:* c/o Thea Dispeker Artists' Management, 59 East 54th Street, New York, NY 10022, USA.

**HAGEN, Christina;** Singer (Mezzo-Soprano); b. 1956, Hamburg, Germany. *Education:* Studied singing with Naan Pold and Hilde Nadolowitsch; Concert Diploma, Exam as Private Music Instructor, Opera Diploma with Distinction, Hochschule für Musik und Darstellende Kunst, Hamburg; Masterclasses including with Sena Jurinac and at International Studio for Singing, Herbert von Karajan Stiftung, with Christa Ludwig. *Career:* Engaged at Staatstheater Oldenburg, 1983–84, then Deutsche Oper am Rhein, Düsseldorf-Duisburg, 1984–; Guest appearances in Germany at Berlin, Hamburg and Cologne, at Bolshoi Theatre in Moscow, Antwerp, Amsterdam and Staatsoper Berlin, National Theater Munich; Participant at Bayreuth Festival in 1989, 1990, 1991; Has sung Rosina in Barber of Seville, Micha in Samson by Handel, Judith in Bluebeard's Castle by Bartók and Jocasta in Oedipus Rex at Oldenburg, Olga in Eugene Onegin and Second Woman in Die Zauberflöte at Oldenburg and Düsseldorf, the Composer in Ariadne auf Naxos, Dorabella in Così fan tutte, Nicklausse in Tales of Hoffmann, Orlowsky in Die Fledermaus, Maddalena in Rigoletto, Fatima in Weber's Oberon, Sextus in Julius Caesar by Handel, Flosshilde, Erda and Fricka in Rheingold and in Walküre, Second Norn and Waltraute, Fenena in Nabucco, Britten's Lucretia, Olga in Das Schloss, Ottavia in Monteverdi's L'Incoronazione di Poppea, Eboli at Düsseldorf, Clytemnestra (Gluck) at Düsseldorf and Berlin, Fricka in Walküre at Munich, Santuzza in Cavalleria Rusticana at Eutiner Festival; Season 1995–96 at Düsseldorf as Wagner's Venus and Fricka; Many lieder recitals and concert appearances. *Honours:* Nominated Chamber Singer of Deutsche Oper am Rhein at Düsseldorf, 1992. *Address:* c/o Deutsche Oper am Rhein, Heinrich-Heine Allee 16, 40213 Düsseldorf, Germany.

**HAGEN, Daron Aric,** MMus; American composer and pianist; b. 4 Nov. 1961, Milwaukee. *Education:* Univ. of Wisconsin, Curtis Inst., Julliard School. *Career:* founding Dir, Perpetuum Mobile New Music Ensemble 1983–93; debut as concert pianist with Denver Chamber Orchestra 1986; composer-in-residence, Long Beach Symphony Orchestra 1994; composition teacher, Curtis Inst. 1996; Pres., Lotte Lehmann Foundation, New York 2004–; composer-in-residence, Princeton Univ. Atelier 2005. *Compositions include:* Prayer for Peace 1981, Echo's Songs 1983, Symphony No. 1 1985–88, Dear Youth 1991, Shining Brow (opera) 1990–92, Muldoon songs 1992, Vera of Las Vegas (cabaret opera) 1995, Symphony No. 3 1997, Chamber symphony 2003, The Antient Concert (opera) 2004. *Recordings include:* Vera of Las Vegas, Songs of Daron Hagen, Strings Attached (complete music for solo strings). *Honours:* Bearns Prize 1985, Barlow Int. Composition Prize for Chamber Music 1985, Friedheim Award 1994. *Address:* c/o Carl Fischer, Director of Concert Music, 65 Bleecker Street, New York, NY 10012, USA (office). *E-mail:* daron@daronhagen.com. *Website:* www.daronhagen.com.

**HAGEN, Reinhard;** Singer (Bass); b. 1966, Bremen, Germany. *Education:* Studied at Karlsruhe. *Career:* Sang at Kassel Opera, 1989–90, Dortmund, 1991–94, Deutsche Oper Berlin from 1993; Season 1991 as Sarastro at the Landestheater Salzburg and at Brussels; Salzburg Festival, 1993, as Plutone in Monteverdi's Orfeo; German premiere of Casken's The Golem, 1993; Season 1996 as Cadmus in Semele at Aix-en-Provence, Gounod's Frère Laurent at Geneva and Ferrando in Il Trovatore at Berlin; Sang Titurel in Parsifal at the Deutsche Oper, 1998; Season 2000–01 as Verdi's Banquo and Count Walter at the Deutsche Oper, King Henry in Lohengrin at San Diego, Sarastro in Barcelona, Rocco at Glyndebourne and bass solos in the St Matthew Passion for La Scala, Milan. *Recordings include:* Les Béatitudes, by Franck. *Address:* c/o Deutsche Oper Berlin, Richard Wagner Strasse 10, 1060 Berlin, Germany.

**HAGEN-GROLL, Walter;** Choral Conductor; b. 15 April 1927, Chemnitz, Germany. *Education:* Studied at the Stuttgart Musikhochschule, 1947–52. *Career:* Assistant Conductor at the Stuttgart Opera, 1952; Chorus Master at the Heidelberg Opera, 1957, and Deutsche Oper Berlin, 1961; Directed the chorus of the Berlin Philharmonic from 1961; Assisted Wilhelm Pitz at Bayreuth, 1960–62; Chorus Master at Salzburg Festival from 1965, Philharmonia Chorus, London, 1971–74; Chorus Master at the Vienna Staatsoper 1984, Vienna Singakademie 1987; Choral Director at the Salzburg Mozarteum from 1986.

**HÄGER, Claus;** Singer (Baritone); b. 1963, Wuppertal, Germany. *Education:* Studied in Cologne and Freiburg; Masterclasses with Dietrich Fischer-Dieskau. *Career:* Hamburg Staatsoper, 1991–92; Sang Papageno at the Berlin Staatsoper, 1994; Schwetzingen Festival, 1995; Other roles have included Mozart's Guglielmo, Silvio in Pagliacci, Puccini's Schaunard and Falke in La Bohème; Broadcast and concert engagements; Season 1998 as Marquis de Corcy in Le Postillon de Lonjumeau at the Berlin Staatsoper. *Honours:* Prizewinner, 1992 Oberdörfer Competition, Hamburg. *Address:* c/o Berlin Staatsoper, Unter den Linden 7, 1060 Berlin, Germany.

**HAGER, Leopold;** Conductor; b. 6 Oct. 1935, Salzburg, Austria; m. Gertrude Entleitner, 2 July 1960, 1 d. *Education:* Graduated in organ, piano, conducting, harpsichord, High School for Music (Mozarteum), Salzburg. *Career:* Assistant Conductor, Staedtische Buhnen, Mainz, Germany, 1957–62; Principal Conductor: Landestheater, Linz, Austria, 1962–64; Opernhaus, Cologne, Germany, 1964–65; General Music Director: Staedtische Buhnen, Freiburg, Germany, 1965–69; Principal Conductor, Mozarteum Orchestra, Salzburg, 1969–81; Has conducted many performances of early operas by Mozart; Led the first modern performance of Mitridate, Salzburg, 1971; Symphony Orchestra, Radio Luxembourg, 1981–96; Guest Conductor: Vienna Opera; Munich Opera; Metropolitan Opera; Covent Garden; Teatro Colón, Buenos Aires; Berlin and Vienna Philharmonics; Conducted Così fan tutte at the Metropolitan, 1991; Figaro, 1997. *Recordings:* Mozart Piano Concertos, with Karl Engel; Bastien und Bastienne, Lucio Silla, Il re Pastore, Ascanio in Alba, Mitridate Re di Ponto; CD of La Finta Semplice released 1990. *Honours:* Decorated, Ehrenkreuz 1 klasse für Kunst und Wissenschaft, Austria. *Address:* Morzgerstr 102, 5034 Salzburg, Austria.

**HÅGGANDER, Mari Anne;** Swedish singer (soprano); b. 23 Oct. 1951, Trokorna. *Education:* Opera School, Gothenburg. *Career:* debut as Micaela in Carmen, Ponelle production, Royal Opera, Stockholm; has sung Cherubino, Elisabetta in Don Carlo at Savonlinna in Finland, Pamina and the Countess in Figaro at Bonn and Buxton Festival, Eva in Meistersinger at Bayreuth 1981, Mimi at Stockholm and Hamburg, Eva at the Metropolitan 1985, and Elsa in Lohengrin at San Francisco; guest appearances include Berlin, Munich, Paris, Brussels, Vienna, New York, Seattle and Toronto; other roles include Butterfly, Amelia in Un Ballo in Maschera and Simon Boccanegra, Marschallin, Tatiana in Eugene Onegin, Lisa in The Queen of Spades, Sieglinde, Arabella, and Donna Anna. *Recordings:* Das Rheingold with Levine; Peer Gynt with Blomstedt; Several lieder and sacred music recordings. *Honours:* Court Singer to His Majesty the King of Sweden. *Current Management:* Artistsekretariat Ulf Tornqvist, Sankt Eriksgatan 100 2 tr, 113 31 Stockholm, Sweden.

**HAGLEY, Alison;** British singer (soprano); b. 9 May 1961, London, England. *Education:* Guildhall School of Music, National Opera Studio. *Career:* Sang in Handel's Rodelinda at the Aldeburgh Festival and Handel's Flavio with Musica nel Chiostro at the 1985 Batignano Festival in Italy; Camden Festival in 1986 in La Finta Giardiniera by Mozart; Sang Clorinda in Opera 80s 1987 production of La Cenerentola; Glyndebourne debut in 1988 as the Little Owl in L'Enfant et Les Sortilèges, returning in Jenůfa and as Susanna, Nannetta, Papagena and Zerlina; Glyndebourne Tour as Varvara in Katya Kabanova, Despina and Papagena; Covent Garden as a Flowermaiden in Parsifal and in Peter Grimes; English National Opera in 1991 as Lauretta in a new production of Gianni Schicchi and Gretel in Hansel and Gretel; Scottish Opera appearances as Musetta in La Bohème and Adele in Die Fledermaus; Sang Mélisande in 1992 with Boulez and Peter Stein, WNO; Sang Nannetta for ENO in 1992; Glyndebourne 1994, as Susanna; Covent Garden 1997, in Massenet's Chérubin; Bella in The Midsummer Marriage at Munich. 1996; Munich Opera Festival, 2000. *Honours:* FPC Opera Singer of the Year, National Opera Studio. *Current Management:* IMG Artists, Lovell House, 616 Chiswick High Road, London, W4 5RX, England. *Telephone:* (20) 8233-5800.

*Fax:* (20) 8233-5801. *E-mail:* info@imgartists.com. *Website:* www.imgartists .com.

**HAHN, Barbara;** German singer (mezzo-soprano); b. 1965, Stuttgart. *Education:* studied in Stuttgart and at Salzburg Mozarteum. *Career:* sang at Bielefeld from 1987 as Dorabella, Cherubino and Orlofsky; Nicklausse in Les contes d'Hoffmann at Bregenz Festival, 1987; Appeared as Dorabella and Nicklausse at Hanover, 1988; Sang Grimgerde in Die Walküre at Bologna; Angelina, in La Cenerentola at Passau; Freiburg Opera, 1989–91, as Octavian, Idamantes, Hansel and Sonja in Der Zarewitsch; Concert performance of Schreker's Der ferne Klang in Berlin, 1990; Frankfurt Opera, 1992–, debut as Dorabella. *Recordings:* Der ferne Klang, conducted by Gerd Albrecht. *Address:* Steinachstr. 2, 97082 Würzburg, Germany. *E-mail:* pphahnpp@gmx.de. *Website:* barbarahahn.de.

**HAHN, Hilary;** Violinist; b. 27 Nov. 1979, Lexington, Virginia, USA. *Education:* BMus, Curtis Institute of Music, Philadelphia. *Career:* Debut: Age 6 years, Baltimore, 1986; First Full Recital, Age 10 years, 1990; Major Orchestra Debut with Baltimore Symphony Orchestra, 1991; Utah and Florida Symphonies, 1992; Philadelphia Orchestra, 1993; New York Philharmonic Orchestra and Cleveland Orchestra, 1994; European concerto debut in Budapest, with Budapest Festival Orchestra, and European Recital debut at Festival de Sully et d'Orleans, France, 1994; German debut at 15 Playing Beethoven Violin Concerto with Bavarian Radio Symphony Orchestra and Lorin Maazel, Munich, 1995; Carnegie Hall debut at 16 with Philadelphia Orchestra and Christoph Eschenbach, 1996; Concerto Debuts in Berlin, Frankfurt, Hannover and Rotterdam, 1996; Recital debuts in Kennedy Center (DC), Alice Tully Hall, New York, Munich, Rotterdam and Paris, 1997; Concerto debuts in London, Glasgow, Birmingham, Zürich and Vienna with Bavarian Radio Symphony, and in Paris with French Radio Symphony Orchestra, 1998; As Chamber Musician Appears Regularly at Marlboro Music Festival, Skaneateles Festival and with the Chamber Music Society of Lincoln Center, New York. *Recordings include:* Solo Sonatas and Partitas of J. S. Bach; Concertos of Beethoven, Bernstein (Serenade), Samuel Barber, Edgar Meyer, Brahms and Stravinsky. *Honours:* Avery Fisher Career Grant, 1995. *Current Management:* IMG Artists. *Address:* c/o IMG Artists, 450 West 45th Street, New York, NY 10036, USA.

**HAIDER, Friedrich;** Pianist and Conductor; b. 1961, Austria. *Education:* Acad. of Music, Vienna; Mozarteum,Salzburg. *Career:* Theatrical debut: Klagenfurt, with Johann Stzrauss: Wiener Blut, 1984; Engagements from 1989 with Der fliegende Holländer at Barcelona, La Bohème in Stockholm, Figaro at Aix, Salome in Lisbon and Die Entführung at Bonn; Chief Conductor of the Opéra du Rhin, Strasbourg, 1991–95, with Il Trovatore, Rigoletto, La Traviata and Madama Butterfly; Debut, Vienna Staatsoper in Die Fledermaus, 2003–04; Chief Conductor, City of Oviedo Orchestra, Spain, 2004–(2007); Guest appearances at Nice, with Faust and Tristan und Isolde, Barcelona (Lohengrin, Beatrice di Tenda), Lisbon (Norma, I Puritani), Hamburg (Don Giovanni) and Cologne (I Capuleti e I Montecchi); Concerts in Tokyo, Amsterdam, Munich, Milan and Budapest; Recital accompanist to Renata Scotto, Charlotte Margiono, Vesselina Kasarova and Rainer Trost. *Recordings include:* Roberto Devereux; Die schöne Müllerin, with Rainer Trost (Nightingale); Strauss Orchestral Lieder; Die Fledermaus; Richard Strauss: Eine Alpensinfonie, Ein Heldenleben, Till Eulenspiegel and world premiere recording of the integral Orchestral Songs; Brahms Serenade, op. 11. *Address:* c/o Theateragentur Dr G. Hilbert, Maximilianstrasse 22, 80539 Munich, Germany.

**HAIGH, Andrew Wilfred;** Pianist and teacher; *Head of Piano, Kent Music Academy;* b. 26 April 1954, Lagos, Nigeria. *Education:* Student, 1969–74; Associate, Royal College of Music, London, 1975; Studied with Cyril Smith, Phyllis Sellick, Albert Ferber, 1974; Licenciate, Royal Academy of Music, 1975. *Career:* Debut: London Philharmonic Orchestra, Royal Festival Hall, 1965; Wigmore Hall, 1971; Soloist with all major British orchestras including: London Symphony; London Philharmonic; Philharmonia; Royal Philharmonic; BBC Philharmonic Orchestra; Soloist, Herbert von Karajan Festival, Berlin, 1970; Recitals in Europe; Head of Piano Kent Music Acad. (fmrly Kent Centre for Young Instrumentalists); Examiner, Trinity College of Music, and Adjudicator. *Honours:* Gold Medallist, 1969; Winner, BBC Mozart Competition, 1969; Winner, Royal Overseas Competition; National Piano Competition; Hopkinson Silver Medal, 1973; Dannreuther Concerto Prize, Royal College of Music. *Address:* 15 Dornden Drive, Langton Green, Tunbridge Wells, Kent TN 3 0AA, England (home). *Telephone:* (1892) 862187 (home).

**HAILSTORK, Adolphus Cunningham,** MMus, PhD; American composer; b. 17 April 1941, Rochester, NY. *Education:* Howard Univ., Washington DC, Manhattan School, Michigan State Univ., with Nadia Boulanger in France. *Career:* teacher, Michigan State Univ. 1969–91, Youngstown State Univ. 1971–76, Norfolk Virginia State Coll. 1977–. *Compositions include:* The Race For Space, theatre piece, 1963; Phaedra, tone poem, 1966; Horn Sonata, 1966; Statement, Variation And Fugue for Orchestra, 1966; Sextet for Strings, 1971; Violin Sonata, 1972; Bagatelles for Brass Quintet, 1973; Pulse for Percussion Ensemble, 1974; Bellevue and Celebration, both for Orchestra, 1974; Concerto for Violin, Horn and Orchestra, 1975; Spiritual for Brass Octet, 1975; American Landscape, Nos 1, 3 and 4 for Orchestra, 1977–84; American Landscape for Violin and Cello, 1978; Piano Sonata, 1981; Sport of Strings, 1981; Piano Concerto, 1992; Symphony No. 2, 1996; Trumpet Sonata, 1996; Let the Heavens be Glad, for chorus, 1996; Unaccompanied choral music, and

with brass and percussion accompaniment. *Honours:* Ernest Bloch Award, 1971; Commissions from the Edward Tarr Brass Ensemble and the Virginia Symphony. *Address:* 521 Berrypick Lane, Virginia Beach, VA 23462-1927, USA.

**HAÏM, Emmanuelle;** Conductor, Harpsichordist and Pianist; b. 1967, Paris, France. *Education:* harpsichord with Kenneth Gilbert and Christophe Rousset; coach and assistant to William Christie, Simon Rattle (Les Boréades by Rameau, Salzburg, 1999), Mark Minkowski and Christophe Rousset. *Career:* founded Paris-based early music group, Le Concert d Astrée, 2000; conducted Rodelinda for the Glyndebourne Tour, 2001; Season 2002–03 with Handel's Agrippina in Chicago and Poro at the Edinburgh Festival; guest conductor with Les Muses Galantes and the Orchestra of the Age of Enlightenment; appearances at the Beaune and Poitiers Festivals, recitals with Natalie Dessay, Sandrine Piau and Patricia Petibon; engaged for Theodora with GTO for 2003, and Rodelinda at the 2004 Festival; conducted Monteverdi's Orfeo at the London Barbican, 2003 and engaged for European and US tours, 2004–05; Handel's Tamerlano for Opéra Lille, 2004–05. *Recordings include:* Handel Arcadian Duets and Cantata Aci Galatea e Polifemo; Purcell's Dido and Aeneas, with Ian Bostridge and Susan Graham. *Current Management:* IMG Artists (UK) Ltd, 616 Chiswick High Road, London, W4 5RX, England.

**HAIMOVITZ, Matt;** cellist; b. 3 Dec. 1970, Tel-Aviv, Israel. *Education:* Juilliard School, New York, Collegiate School, New York, Princeton Univ. and Harvard Univ., studied with Gabor Rejto, Leonard Rose, Carl Schahter. *Career:* appeared with Israel Philharmonic Orchestra under Mehta at Mann Auditorium, Tel-Aviv, broadcast on Israel nat. TV 1985; London debut with English Chamber Orchestra under Barenboim at the Barbican 1985; appearances with many conductors and orchestras and regular recitals throughout USA and Europe since 1985; debut with Philharmonia Orchestra and Giuseppe Sinopoli at Royal Festival Hall in London 1987; debut with Chicago Symphony Orchestra under James Levine at Ravinia Festival 1988; first tour to Japan 1988, to Europe 1989, and to Australia with Sydney and Melbourne Symphony Orchestras 1991; live concert appearance, The Performing Arts Pay Tribute to Public Television (PBS) 1988; first American recital tour 1990; debut with Berlin Philharmonic under James Levine in Berlin 1990; Lucerne Festival debut with solo recital programme 1990; recital debuts with solo cello repertoire at Montreux Festival, Washington, DC, New York and Paris 1991; debut with Dallas Symphony 1992. *Recordings include:* Lalo and Saint-Saëns Concerti with Chicago Symphony under Levine 1989, Solo Cello in works by Reger, Britten, Crumb and Ligeti 1991, Bach Cello Suites. *Honours:* Avery Fisher Career Grant Award 1985. *Current Management:* TransArt UK Ltd, Cedar House, 10 Rutland Street, Filey, North Yorkshire Y014 9JB, England.

**HAITINK, Bernard John Herman,** CH, KBE; Dutch conductor; b. 4 March 1929, Amsterdam. *Career:* Conductor Netherlands Radio Philharmonic Orchestra 1955–61; appeared regularly as Guest Conductor for Concertgebouw Orchestra, Amsterdam 1956–61, Joint Conductor 1961–64, Chief Conductor and Musical Dir 1964–88, Hon. Conductor 1999–; Prin. Conductor London Philharmonic Orchestra 1967–79, Artistic Dir 1970–78, Pres. 1990–; Musical Dir Glyndebourne Festival Opera 1978–88, Royal Opera House, Covent Garden 1987–2002, European Union Youth Orchestra 1994; Prin. Guest Conductor Boston Symphony Orchestra 1995–; Chief Conductor and Music Dir, Sächsische Staatskapelle, Dresden 2002–04; tours with Concertgebouw in Europe, N and S America, Japan, with London Philharmonic in Europe, Japan, USA; Guest Conductor Los Angeles Philharmonic, Boston Symphony, Cleveland, Chicago Symphony, New York Philharmonic, Berlin Philharmonic, Vienna Philharmonic, Dresden Staatskapelle, Concertgebouw and other orchestras; Hon. mem. RAM, London 1973, Int. Gustav Mahler Soc.; records for Philips, Decca and EMI. *Honours:* Hon. DMus (Oxford) 1988, (Leeds) 1988; Medal of Honour, Bruckner Soc. of America 1970, Gold Medal of Int. Gustav Mahler Soc. 1971, Erasmus Prize 1991; Royal Order of Orange-Nassau, Chevalier des Arts et des Lettres, Officer, Order of the Crown (Belgium); Conductor Laureate, Concertgebouw 1999, CH 2002–. *Address:* c/o Lisa Perry, Askonas Holt Ltd., 27 Chancery Lane, London, WC2A 1PF, England. *Telephone:* (20) 7400-1700. *Fax:* (20) 7400-1799.

**HAJDU, Andre;** Composer; b. 5 March 1932, Budapest, Hungary. *Education:* Studied with Kodály and Kosa in Budapest, 1947–56 and with Milhaud and Messiaen in Paris. *Career:* Teacher at Tel-Aviv Academy of Music, 1967–70; Teacher, Bar Ilan University, 1970–. *Compositions:* Plasmas, 1957 for piano; Petit enfer for orchestra, 1959; Journey Around My Piano, 1963; 2 piano concertos, 1968, 1990; Ludus Paschalis for soloists, chorus and 9 instruments, 1970; Mishnayoth for voice, choir, orchestra and piano, 1972–73 Terouath Melech for clarinet and strings, 1974; The Unbearable Intensity of Youth for orchestra, 1976; Bashful Serenades, clarinet and orchestra, 1978; On Light and Depth for chamber orchestra, 1983; The Story of Jonas, opera for children, 1985–86; Dreams of Spain, cantata for orchestra and choir; Symphonie concertante for 6 soloists and strings, 1994; Ecclesiaste for narrator, solo cello and cello ensemble, 1994; Continuum, for piano and 15 instruments, 1995; Merry Feet, nursery songs, 1998. *Publications:* Milky Way, 4 vols piano pedagogic, 1975; The Art of Piano Playing, piano pedagogic, 1987. *Honours:* Israel prize for composition, 1997. *Address:* c/o ACUM Ltd, PO Box 14220, Acum House, Rothschild Blvd 118, Tel-Aviv 61140, Israel.

**HAJOSSYOVA, Magdalena;** Singer (Soprano); b. 25 July 1946, Bratislava, Czechoslovakia. *Education:* Studied at the Bratislava Music Academy. *Career:* Debut: Slovak National Theatre Bratislava, 1971, as Marenka in The Bartered Bride; Sang at the National Theatre Prague and elsewhere in Czechoslovakia; Berlin Staatsoper from 1975, as Mozart's Pamina, Fiordilgi, Contessa, Donna Anna, Handel's Alcina, Wagner's Eva, Elsa, Strauss's Arabella, Marschallin, Capriccio, Dvořák's Rusalka; Has also sung in the operas of Jan Cikker; Guest appearances as opera and concert singer in England, Belgium, Spain, Netherlands, Greece, Italy, France, USA, Japan, Russia, Austria, Iran and German Capitals. *Recordings include:* The Cunning Little Vixen, Don Giovanni and Mahler's 4th Symphony; Erindo by Sigismund Kusser; Beethoven's 9th Symphony; Mozart's Requiem; Dvořák's Requiem, Stabat Mater; Britten: Illuminations; Janáček: Missa Glagolitica; Dvořák: Dimitri; Mahler's 2nd Symphony; Schumann: Paradies und der Peri; Gounod: Margarethe in Faust; Wagner: Wesendonk-Lieder; Strauss: Brentano-Lieder, 4 Letzte Lieder; Bruckner: Te Deum, and F minor Mass; Schubert: G major Mass and Stabat Mater; H Wolf, Italienisches Liederbuch; Mahler G and Alma: Lieder; Brahms, Lieder. *Current Management:* Deutsche Staatsoper Berlin, Unter den Linden 7, Germany. *Address:* Kopenicker Str 104, Berlin 19179, Germany.

**HAKALA, Tommi;** Finnish singer (baritone); b. 9 Aug. 1970, Riihimäki. *Education:* Sibelius Acad. and Staatliche Hochschule für Musik, Karlsruhe. *Career:* fmr mem., Finnish Nat. Opera; worked at Nuremberg Opera 1998–2001, 2001–04; has appeared as guest at Savonlinna Opera Festival, Bayerische Staatsoper, Aalto Theater Essen, Semperoper Dresden, Opera du Rhin; other concert appearances in Belgium, Estonia, Italy, USA, Israel, Wales; opera roles include Schaunard and Marcello in La Bohème, Papageno in The Magic Flute, Guglielmo in Così fan tutte, Graf in Der Wildschutz, Dandini in La Cenerentola, The Count and Figaro in Le Nozze di Figaro, Besenbinder in Hänsel and Gretel, Wolfram in Tannhäuser, Silvio in Pagliacci, Germont in La Traviata, Man from Minsk in The Flight; Matti Salminen grant; Richard Wagner Foundation scholarship. *Recording:* Great Baritone Arias 2005. *Honours:* first prize Merikanto Singing Competition 2001, winner BBC Cardiff Singer of the World 2003. *Current Management:* c/o Simon Goldstone, IMG Artists, Lovell House, 616 Chiswick High Road, London, W4 5RX, England. *Telephone:* (20) 7957-5800 (office). *Fax:* (20) 7957-5801 (office). *E-mail:* sgoldstone@imgartists.com (office). *Website:* www.imgartists.com (office).

**HAKOLA, Riikka;** Singer (Soprano); b. 1962, Finland. *Education:* Studied at the Sibelius Academy, Helsinki, in Italy and Berlin, New York and London. *Career:* Sang in the 1989 premiere of The Knife by Paavo Heininen, at the Savonlinna Festival; National Opera, Helsinki, 1990, as Lucia di Lammermoor; Guested in London in Haydn's opera Orfeo; Sang Marzelline in Fidelio at Savonlinna, 1992, and other roles have included Rosina, Gilda, Susanna, the Queen of Night and Violetta; Debut at the Bolshoi in Moscow, 1995; Frequent concert engagements in Finland and abroad; Turku 1996, as Zetulbe in Crusell's The Little Slave Girl. Has sung several world premieres by Finnish contemporary composers at Savonlinna Opera Festivals including the title role in Frieda by Tikka and Hilda in Alexis Kivi by Rautavaara; Sang Jenny in Weill's Mahagonny and First Nymph in Linkola's Angelika in recordings for Finnish television. *Address:* c/o Finnish National Opera, Bulevardi 23–27, 00180 Helsinki 18, Finland.

**HALA, Tomás;** Conductor and Composer; b. 6 Sept. 1963, Prague, Czechoslovakia. *Education:* Prague Conservatory, Piano, Composition, 1978–84; Prague Academy of Music, Piano, Conducting, 1984–90. *Career:* Conductor of Opera House, Ceskè Budejovice, 1990–91; Conductor, Prague National Theatre Opera, from 1991, Mozart: Don Giovanni (Assistant to Charles Mackerras), Die Zauberflöte, Le nozze di Figaro; Verdi: La Forza del Destino; mem., Czech Musical Fund. *Compositions:* Chamber Opera: Vejstupny Syn (Disobedient s.); Composition with Baritone Solo–Rough Sea; Variations for Cello; Piano Concerto. *Recordings:* Chamber Opera, Vejstupny Syn, Czech radio and television, 1985. *Publications:* Score of Opera Vejstupny syn, 1986. *Address:* Zavadilova 13, 160 00 Prague 6, Czech Republic.

**HALBREICH, Harry (Leopold);** Musicologist; b. 9 Feb. 1931, Berlin, Germany; m. Helène Chait, 11 April 1961, separated, 1 s., 2 d. *Education:* Geneva Conservatory, 1949–52; Studies with Arthur Honegger at Ecole Normale de Musique, Paris, 1952–54, and at Paris Conservatoire, 1955–58. *Career:* Teacher of Musical Analysis at Royal Conservatory, Mons, Belgium, 1970–; General Musical Adviser to the Brussels Philharmonic Society with about 180 concerts annually; Numerous lectures and seminars in Italy including Turin, Cagliari and Venice, in Spain at Madrid and Granada, in Japan at the Akiyoshidai Festival of Contemporary Music, and elswhere; Artistic Board (programme adviser), at the Venice Biennale for Contemporary Music; International jury member for International Record Critics Award, High Fidelity, New York, Academie Charles-Cros, Paris, Prix Cecilia, Brussels, and for several composition competitions at Parma, Turin and Cagliari; Regular Producer of radio programmes for RTB, Brussels and RSR in Geneva. *Publications include:* Edgard Varèse, in French, 1970; Olivier Messiaen, in French, 1980, revised edition, 1996; Claude Debussy, in French, 1980; Arthur Honegger, Un Musicien dans la Cité des Hommes, 1992; L'Oeuvre d'Arthur Honegger, 1993; Arthur Honegger, in the series, Les Grands Suisses, 1995; Founding Member and Co-Editor of the music magazine, Crescendo, Brussels; Large participation to the Fayard Music Guides, Paris: Piano Music, 1987, Chamber Music, 1989 and Choral Music,

1993, also several titles in the series, L'Avant-Scène Opéra, including Moses und Aron. *Contributions:* Harmonie, Paris, 1965–84; Le Monde de la Musique, Paris, 1982–89; Encyclopaedia Universalis; Crescendo. *Address:* Avenue Brugmann 513, 1180 Brussels, Belgium.

**HALE, Robert;** Singer (bass-baritone); b. 22 Aug. 1943, Kerrville, TX, USA; m. Inga Nielsen. *Education:* New England Conservatory of Music with Gladys Miller, Boston Univ. with Ludwig Bergman; Oklahoma Univ.; with Boris Goldovsky in New York. *Career:* debut with New York City Opera 1967; Metropolitan debut in the title role in Der Fliegende Holländer 1990, returning there as Wotan in Die Walküre 1993, 1996, Pizzaro in Fidelio 1993, Orest in Elektra 1994; performances as Wotan in Richard Wagner's Der Ring des Nibelungen include Vienna, La Scala, Paris, Berlin, Munich, Hamburg, Cologne, Tokyo, Sydney, San Francisco, Washington, DC and New York; other roles include Pizzaro in Fidelio, Salzburg Festival 1990, Barak in Die Frau ohne Schatten at the Easter and Summer Festival (televised) 1992, the title role in Béla Bartók's Bluebeard's Castle at the Summer Festival 1995, Handel's Saul at the Ludwigsburg Festival 2000–01; sings regularly with Vienna State Opera, Royal Opera Covent Garden, La Scala Milan, Paris, Munich State Opera, Deutsche Oper Berlin, Hamburg State Opera; guest appearances include performances with the orchestras of Boston, Philadelphia, Cleveland, Chicago, San Francisco, New York, Houston, Dallas, Los Angeles, Washington, DC, Toronto and Montréal, the Berliner Philharmonie, Musikverein Vienna, the Royal Albert Hall and the Barbican Centre in London, Concertgebouw Amsterdam; festival engagements include Ravinia, Tanglewood, Cincinnati and Wolftrap in the USA, and Salzburg, Munich, Bregenz, Bergen, Lausanne, Orange, Bordeaux, Ravenna and Athens in Europe. *Recordings include:* Der Fliegende Holländer, Das Rheingold, Die Walküre, The Messiah, Siegfried, Verdi Requiem, Das Paradies und die Peri, Song of Love (with Inga Nielsen) 1997, Salome 1999. *Video recordings include:* Die Frau ohne Schatten, Der Fliegende Holländer, Der Ring des Nibelungen. *Honours:* Singer of the Year, Nat. Asscn of Teachers of Singing. *Current Management:* Dr Germinal Hilbert Theateragentur, Maximillianstrasse 22, 80539 Munich, Germany.

**HALEVI, Hadar;** Singer (Mezzo-soprano); b. 1966, Israel. *Career:* Appearances in Israel and throughout Europe in concerts and opera; Repertory includes Carmen, Bizet, Werther, Massenet, Il Barbiere, Rossini, Mozart operas, Ravel; Contestant at the 1995 Cardiff Singer of the World Competition. *Address:* 10 rue St Bernard, Toulouse, 31000 France.

**HALFFTER, Cristobal;** composer and conductor; b. 24 March 1930, Madrid, Spain; m. Maria Manuela Caro; two s. one d. *Education:* Madrid Conservatory with Del Campo, private studies with Alexander Tansman. *Career:* Studied harmony and composition with Conrado del Campo and at the Real Conservatorio de Musica in Madrid, graduated in 1951; 1961–1966 teacher of composition and musical forms at the Real Conservatorio de Musica in Madrid and director of this institute 1964–66; scholarships for the USA (Ford Foundation) and Berlin (DAAD); 1970–1978 Lecturer at the University of Navarra; Lecturer at the Internationale Ferienkurse für Neue Musik at Darmstadt; 1976–1978 president of the Spanish section of the ISCM; 1979: Artistic Director, Studio for electronic music at the Heinrich Strobel-Stiftung in Freiburg, 1980; Member, European Academy of Science, Arts and Humanities, Paris; 1981: was awarded the Gold Medal for Fine Arts by King Juan Carlos of Spain, 1983; Member, Royal Academy of the Fine Arts San Fernando, Madrid; Since 1989 Principal Guest Conductor of the National Orchestra, Madrid, since 1970 conductor of the chief orchestras in Europe and America; lives in Madrid; mem, Real Academia De Bellas Artes, Spain; Akademie Der Künste, Berlin; Kungl Musikaliska Akademien, Sweden, Stockholm. *Compositions:* Stage: Ballet Saeta 1955; Orchestral: Piano Concerto 1955; 5 Microformas 1960; Rhapsodia espanola de Albeniz for piano and orchestra 1960; Sinfonia for 3 instrumental groups 1963; Secuencias 1964; Lineas y Puntos for 20 winds and tape 1967; Anillos 1968; Fibonaciana for flute and strings 1970; Plaint for the Victims of Violence 1971; Requiem por la libertad imaginada 1971; Pinturas negras 1972; Processional 1974; Tiempo para espacios for harpsichord and strings 1974; Cello Concerto 1975; Elegias a la muerte de tres poetas espanoles, 1975; Officium defunctorum 1979; Violin Concerto; Tiento 1980; Handel Fantasia 1981; Sinfonia Ricercata 1982; Versus 1983; Parafrasis 1984; 2nd Cello Concerto 1985; Double Concerto for violin, viola and orchestra 1984; Tiento del Primer tono y Batalla Imperial 1986; Concerto for Cello and Orchestra, No. 2 (first performed by Rostropovich), 1986; Dortmund Variations 1987; Piano Concerto 1988; Preludio and Nemesis 1989; Concerto for saxophone quartet and orchestra 1989; Violin Concerto No. 2, 1991; Daliniana for chamber orchestra, 1994; Odradek, Homage à F. Kafka, for orchestra, 1996; Vocal: Regina Coeli 1951; Misa Ducal 1956; In exspectatione resurrectionis Domini 1962; Brecht-Lieder 1967; Symposium 1968; Yes Speak Out 1968; Noche pasiva del sentido 1971; Gaudium et Spes for 32 voices and tapes 1972; Oracion a Platero 1975; Officium Defunctorum 1978; Noche Pasiva del Sentido 1979; Leyendo a Jorge Guillen 1982; Dona Nobis Pacem 1984; Tres Poemes de la Lirica Espanola 1984–86; Dos Motetes para Caro a Cappella, 1988; Muerte, Mudanza y Locura, for tape and voices, 1989 (text by Cervantes); La del alba seria, after Cervantes, for solo voices, chorus and orchestra, 1997; Opera, Don Quijote, premiered at Madrid, Teatro Real, 2000; Chamber: 2 String Quartets 1955, 1970; Solo Violin Sonata 1959; Codex for guitar 1963; Antiphonismoi for 7 players 1967; Noche activa del espiritu 1973; Mizar for 2 flutes and electronic ensemble 1980; String Sextet, 1994; Piano Music. *Recordings:* For Soprano,

Baritone and Orchestra: 2nd Cello Concerto Rostropovich and Orchestra National De France, Erato. *Address:* Bola 2, Madrid 28013, Spain.

**HALFVARSON, Eric;** Singer (Bass); b. 1953, Texas, USA. *Education:* Studied at Houston Opera Studio. *Career:* Sang at Houston from 1977, notably as Sarastro, 1980; Carnegie Hall, New York, in Hamlet by Ambroise Thomas, 1981; San Francisco, 1982–, notably as Hagen in The Ring, 1990; Spoleto 1983, in European premiere of Barber's Antony and Cleopatra; Further appearances at Chicago, Toronto, Miami, St Louis (US premiere of Il Viaggio as Reims, 1986) and Dallas (premiere of The Aspern Papers by Dominick Argento, 1988); Sang Raimondo in Lucia di Lammermoor at Washington, 1989, Wagner's King Henry at Dallas and the Landgrave in Tannhäuser at Montpellier, 1991; Engagements at Santa Fe as Baron Ochs, 1989, 1992, and Morosus in Die schweigsame Frau, 1991; Other roles include Ramphis (Dallas 1991), Banquo, Rocco, Sparafucile (New York Met, 1995), the Commendatore in Don Giovanni, Puccini's Colline, Alvise in La Gioconda and Gremin in Eugene Onegin; Sang the King in Schreker's Der Schatzgräber at the 1992 Holland Festival; Pogner in Die Meistersinger at the 1996 Bayreuth Festival; Hagen at Buenos Aires, 1998; Season 2000–01 as Fafner and Hunding at the Met, Sarastro and the Grand Inquisitor at the Vienna Staatsoper; Claggart at Covent Garden and King Henry in Lohengrin at Bayreuth; Sang Sparafucile in Rigoletto at Covent Garden, Doctor in Wozzeck, 2002. *Recordings include:* Enobarbus in Antony and Cleopatra. *Address:* c/o Santa Fe Opera, PO Box 2408, Santa Fe, NM 87504, USA.

**HALGRIMSON, Amanda;** Singer (Soprano); b. 28 Nov. 1956, Fargo, North Dakota, USA. *Education:* Studied at Northern Illinois University. *Career:* Appearances at opera houses in 32 American States, notably as Fiordiligi, Norina, Clarice in Il Mondo della Luna and Rosalinde; Sang with Texas Opera on tour, 1987–88, as Lucia di Lammermoor; European debut 1988, as the Queen of Night with Netherlands Opera; Further engagements in Vienna (Volksoper and Staatsoper), St Gallen and Düsseldorf; Concert performances include Mozart's Schauspieldirektor and Salieri's Prima la musica, poi le parole with Houston Symphony; Sang the Queen of Night in a new production of Die Zauberflöte at the Deutsche Oper Berlin, 1991; Member of the ensemble of the Deutsche Oper Berlin, 1992–93; Sang Beethoven's Missa Solemnis with the Boston Symphony Orchestra under Roger Norrington, 1993; Sang Beethoven's 9th Symphony at the reopening of the Liederhalle in Stuttgart under G Gelmetti, 1993; Schumann's Faust/Gretchen with the Minnesota Orchestra as well as Beethoven's Missa Solemnis with the Boston Symphony Orchestra at the Tanglewood Festival; Sang Donna Anna with the Birmingham Symphony Orchestra under Simon Rattle, 1993; Concerts of Mozart's Requiem in London, Berlin and Paris with the Chamber Orchestra of Europe, 1993; Queen of Night at the Grand Théâtre de Genève, 1994; Sang the Trovatore Leonora and Donna Anna at the Deutsche Oper Berlin, 1996; Other roles include Strauss's Empress (Berlin, 1998) and Aithra in Die Aegyptische Helena; Season 2000 as Trovatore Leonora at Bonn and the Empress in Die Frau ohne Schatten at Essen; mem, Deutsche Oper, Berlin, 1992–2001. *Honours:* Prizewinner at Voci Verdiana (Bussetto) Competition, 1985 and the Metropolitan Auditions, 1987. *Address:* Sybelstr. 67, 10629 Berlin, Germany.

**HALIM, Mohammed;** Indonesian composer; b. 1963, Bukittinggi, Sumatra. *Education:* Acad. for Indonesian Performing Arts, Padangpanjang, and in Surakarta. *Career:* collaboration with dance ensemble, Gumarang Sakti 1990–; concert tours to Europe, America and Asia 1994; teacher of composition, Acad. for Indonesian Performing Arts (Sekolah Tinggi Seni Indonesia), Padangpanjang. *Compositions include:* Amai-Amai 1992, Awuak Tongtong 1993. *Address:* Sekolah Tinggi Seni Indonesia, Padangpanjang, West Sumatra, Indonesia (office). *E-mail:* mitramus@indo.net.id (office).

**HALL, Aled;** Singer (Tenor); b. 1970, Pencader, Wales. *Education:* Studied in Aberystwyth and London, National Opera Studio. *Career:* Sang as boy soprano then at Wexford Festival, 1995–96 in Pacini's Saffo and Meyerbeer's L'Etoile du Nord; Appearances in Falstaff and Le Pescatrici for Garsington Opera; Carmen and Poppea for Welsh National Opera and as Monostatos for Scottish Opera; Butterfly and Tosca for Raymond Gubay productions; Concerts include Janáček's Diary at Wexford; Messiah at the Festival Hall and Mozart's Requiem. *Honours:* Joseph Maas prize at the Royal Academy. *Address:* c/o Harlequin Agency Ltd, 203 Fidles Road, Cardiff CF4 5NA, Wales.

**HALL, Janice;** Singer (Soprano); b. 28 Sept. 1953, San Francisco, USA. *Education:* Studied in Boston with Grace Hunter. *Career:* Sang in Cavalli's Egisto for the Wolf Trap Opera Company, 1977; New York City Opera 1978–81, as Ann in Die Lustigen Weiber von Windsor and Mozart's Servillia; European debut with the Hamburg Opera, 1982; Further appearances in Tel-Aviv, Venice and Drottningholm; Salzburg Festival 1985, as Fortuna in the premiere of Henze's version of Il Ritorno d'Ulisse; Cologne 1985, as Poppea in Handel's Agrippina; Has returned to the USA to sing at Houston, Washington DC, Santa Fe (Cavalli's Calisto 1989); Sang La Cambiale di Matrimonio at the 1989 Schwetzingen Festival and Micaela at the 1995 Eutin Festival; Other roles include Verdi's Oscar, Gilda and Violetta, Rosina, Pamina and Lauretta.

**HALL, John;** Singer (Bass); b. 1956, Brecon, Wales; m. Julie Crocker, 1 s., 2 d. *Education:* Studied at the Birmingham School of Music and at the Royal College of Music with Frederick Sharp. *Career:* Sang Rossini's Basilio and Mozart's Bartolo for Opera 80; Appearances with the English Bach Festival at Covent Garden and the Athens Festival; Glyndebourne Festival from 1981; Glyndebourne Touring Opera as Masetto in Don Giovanni (Hong Kong 1986), Mozart's Figaro and Quince in A Midsummer Night's Dream; Théâtre du

Châtelet, Paris, 1985, in The Golden Cockerel; Opera North, 1986, in The Trojans and Madama Butterfly, and returned in Carmen, Tosca, Nielsen's Maskarade and Don Giovanni (as Leporello); Kent Opera, 1989, in The Return of Ulysses; Almeida Festival, 1989, in the premiere of Golem by John Casken; Glyndebourne Touring Opera, 1989–90, as Basilio and Rocco in Fidelio; Covent Garden, 1991, in Boris Godunov, as Mitiukha; English National Opera, 1992, in Return of Ulysses, as Time, Antinous; Throughout France in Midsummer Night's Dream, 1993–94; Premiere of Gruber's Gloria at Huddersfield Contemporary Music Festival, 1994; Midsummer Night's Dream at Torino and Ravenna, 1995; Sang Mozart's Antonio for GTO at Glyndebourne, 1996; Concert repertory includes Vaughan Williams's Serenade to Music (Last Night of the Proms, 1987), Messiah and Elijah. *Recordings:* Title role in Casken's Golem. *Address:* Ivydene, Vicarage Way, Ringmer. East Sussex BN8 5 LA, England.

**HALL, Peter (John);** Singer (Tenor); b. 7 April 1940, Surbiton, England. *Education:* BA 1964, MA 1968, King's College, Cambridge; Choral Scholarship, Private vocal study with Arthur Reckless, John Carol Case. *Career:* Lay-Vicar, Chichester Cathedral, 1965–66; Vicar-Choral, St Paul's Cathedral, London, 1972–2001; Member, various professional choral groups including John Alldis Choir, Schütz Choir of London, London Sinfonietta Voices; Sang Ugo and Il Prete in La Vera Storia (Berio), Florence 1986, un Prete and Reduce in Outis (Berio) at La Scala, Milan, 1996 and Dr Chebutykhin in Three Sisters (Eötvös) in Lyon, 1998 at the composers' personal request; mem, Incorporated Society of Musicians. *Recordings:* Carmina Burana (Orff), with Hallé Orchestra; Transit (Ferneyhough), with London Sinfonietta; At the Boar's Head (Holst), with Royal Liverpool Philharmonic Orchestra; Christmas Vespers (Monteverdi) with Denis Stevens; Prometeo (Nono) with the Ensemble Modern, Frankfurt and The Flood (Stravinsky) with the London Sinfonietta. *Honours:* Choral Scholarship, Cambridge. *Address:* 51 Treachers Close, Chesham, Bucks HP5 2HD, England.

**HALL, Sir Peter Reginald Frederick,** Kt, CBE, MA; British theatre director and film director; b. 22 Nov. 1930, Bury St Edmunds, Suffolk; s. of late Reginald Hall and Grace Hall; m. 1st Leslie Caron 1956 (divorced 1965); one s. one d.; m. 2nd Jacqueline Taylor 1965 (divorced 1981); one s. one d.; m. 3rd Maria Ewing (q.v.) 1982 (divorced 1989); one d.; m. 4th Nicola Frei 1990; one d. *Education:* Perse School and St Catharine's Coll., Cambridge. *Career:* produced and acted in over 20 plays at Cambridge; first professional production The Letter, Windsor 1953; produced in repertory at Windsor, Worthing and Oxford Playhouse; two Shakespearean productions for Arts Council; Artistic Dir Elizabethan Theatre Co. 1953; Asst Dir London Arts Theatre 1954, Dir 1955–57; formed own producing co., Int. Playwright's Theatre 1957; Man. Dir Royal Shakespeare Co., Stratford-upon-Avon and Aldwych Theatre, London 1960–68 (resgnd), Assoc. Dir –1973; mem. Arts Council 1969–73; Co-Dir, Nat. Theatre (now Royal Nat. Theatre) with Lord Olivier April-Nov. 1973, Dir 1973–88; f. Peter Hall Co. 1988; Artistic Dir Glyndebourne 1984–90; Artistic Dir The Old Vic 1997; Wortham Chair in Performing Arts, Houston Univ., Tex. 1999; Chancellor Kingston Univ. 2000–; Dir Kingston Theatre 2003–; Assoc. Prof. of Drama, Warwick Univ. 1964–67; mem. Bd Playhouse Theatre 1990–91; acted in The Pedestrian (film) 1973. *Productions:* Blood Wedding, The Immoralist, The Lesson, South, Mourning Becomes Electra, Waiting for Godot, Burnt Flowerbed, Waltz of the Toreadors, Camino Real, Gigi, Wrong Side of the Park, Love's Labours Lost, Cymbeline, Twelfth Night, A Midsummer Night's Dream, Coriolanus, Two Gentlemen of Verona, Troilus and Cressida, Ondine, Romeo and Juliet, The Wars of the Roses (London Theatre Critics' Award for Best Dir 1963), Becket, The Collection, Cat on a Hot Tin Roof, The Rope Dancers (on Broadway), The Moon and Sixpence (opera, Sadler's Wells), Henry VI (parts 1, 2 and 3), Richard III, Richard II, Henry IV (parts 1 and 2), Henry V, Eh?, The Homecoming (London Theatre Critics' Award for Best Dir 1965, Antoinette Perry Award for Best Dir 1966), Moses and Aaron (opera, Covent Garden), Hamlet (London Theatre Critics' Award for Best Dir 1965), The Government Inspector, The Magic Flute (opera), Staircase, Work is a Four Letter Word (film) 1968, Macbeth, Midsummer Night's Dream (film) 1969, Three into Two Won't Go (film) 1969, A Delicate Balance, Dutch Uncle, Landscape and Silence, Perfect Friday (film) 1971, The Battle of Shrivings, La Calisto (opera, Glyndebourne Festival) 1970, The Knot Garden (opera, Covent Garden) 1970, Eugene Onegin (opera, Covent Garden) 1971, Old Times 1971, Tristan and Isolde (opera, Covent Garden) 1971, All Over 1972, Il Ritorno d'Ulisse (opera, Glyndebourne Festival) 1972, Alte Zeiten (Burgtheater, Vienna) 1972, Via Galactica (musical, Broadway) 1972, The Homecoming (film) 1973, Marriage of Figaro (opera, Glyndebourne) 1973, The Tempest 1973, Landscape (film) 1974, Akenfield (film) 1974, Happy Days 1974, John Gabriel Borkman 1974, No Man's Land 1975, Judgement 1975, Hamlet 1975, Tamburlaine the Great 1976, Don Giovanni (opera, Glyndebourne Festival) 1977, Volpone (Nat. Theatre) 1977, Bedroom Farce (Nat. Theatre) 1977, The Country Wife (Nat. Theatre) 1977, The Cherry Orchard (Nat. Theatre) 1978, Macbeth (Nat. Theatre) 1978, Betrayal (Nat. Theatre) 1978, Così Fan Tutte (opera, Glyndebourne) 1978, Fidelio (opera, Glyndebourne) 1979, Amadeus (Nat. Theatre) 1979, Betrayal (New York) 1980, Othello (Nat. Theatre) 1980, Amadeus (New York) (Tony Award for Best Dir 1981) 1980, Family Voices (Nat. Theatre) 1981, The Oresteia (Nat. Theatre) 1981, A Midsummer Night's Dream (opera, Glyndebourne) 1981, The Importance of Being Earnest (Nat. Theatre) 1982, Other Places (Nat. Theatre) 1982, The Ring (operas, Bayreuth Festival) 1983, Jean Seberg (musical, Nat. Theatre) 1983, L'Incoronazione di Poppea (opera, Glyndebourne) 1984, Animal Farm (Nat. Theatre) 1984,

Coriolanus (Nat. Theatre) 1984, Yonadab (Nat. Theatre) 1985, Carmen (opera, Glyndebourne) 1985, (Metropolitan Opera) 1986, Albert Herring (opera, Glyndebourne) 1985, The Petition (New York and Nat. Theatre) 1986, Simon Boccanegra (opera, Glyndebourne) 1986, Salome (opera, Los Angeles) 1986, Coming in to Land (Nat. Theatre) 1986, Antony and Cleopatra (Nat. Theatre) 1987, Entertaining Strangers (Nat. Theatre) 1987, La Traviata (Glyndebourne) 1987, Falstaff (Glyndebourne) 1988, Salome (Covent Garden) 1988, Cymbeline (Nat. Theatre) 1988, The Winter's Tale (Nat. Theatre) 1988, The Tempest 1988, Orpheus Descending 1988, Salome (opera, Chicago) 1988, Albert Herring 1989, Merchant of Venice 1989, She's Been Away (TV) 1989, New Year (opera, Houston and Glyndebourne) 1989, The Wild Duck 1990, Born Again (musical) 1990, The Homecoming 1990, Orpheus Descending (film) 1990, Twelfth Night 1991, The Rose Tattoo 1991, Tartuffe 1991, The Camomile Lawn (TV) 1991, The Magic Flute 1992, Four Baboons Adoring the Sun (New York) 1992, Siena Red 1992, All's Well That Ends Well (RSC) 1992, The Gift of the Gorgon (RSC) 1992, The Magic Flute (LA) 1993, Separate Tables 1993, Lysistrata 1993, She Stoops to Conquer 1993, Piaf (musical) 1993, An Absolute Turkey (Le Dindon) 1994, On Approval 1994, Hamlet 1994, Jacob (TV) 1994, Never Talk to Strangers (film) 1995, Julius Caesar (RSC) 1995, The Master Builder 1995, The Final Passage (TV) 1996, Mind Millie for Me 1996, The Oedipus Plays (Nat. Theatre at Epidaurus and Nat. Theatre) 1996, A School for Wives 1995, A Streetcar Named Desire 1997, The Seagull 1997, Waste 1997, Waiting for Godot 1997, 1998, King Lear 1997, The Misanthrope 1998, Major Barbara 1998, Simon Boccanegra (Glyndebourne) 1998, Filumena 1998, Amadeus 1998, Kafka's Dick 1998, Measure for Measure (LA) 1999, A Midsummer Night's Dream (LA) 1999, Lenny (Queens Theatre) 1999, Amadeus (LA, NY) 1999, Cuckoos 2000, Tantalus (Denver, Colo) 2000, Japes 2000, Romeo and Juliet (LA) 2001, Japes 2001, Troilus and Cressida (NY) 2001, Tantalus 2001, A Midsummer Night's Dream (Glyndebourne) 2001, Otello (Glyndebourne) 2001, Japes (Theatre Royal) 2001, The Royal Family (Theatre Royal) 2001, Lady Windermere's Fan (Theatre Royal) 2002, The Bacchai (Olivier Theatre) 2002, Design for Living (Theatre Royal, Bath) 2003, Betrayal (Theatre Royal, Bath) 2003, The Fight for Barbara (Theatre Royal, Bath) 2003, As You Like It (Theatre Royal, Bath) 2003, Cuckoos (Theatre Royal, Bath) 2003, The Marriage of Figaro (Lyric Opera of Chicago) 2003, Happy Days (Arts Theatre, London) 2003, Man and Superman (Theatre Royal, Bath) 2004, Galileo's Daughter (Theatre Royal, Bath) 2004. *Publications:* The Wars of the Roses 1970, Shakespeare's three Henry VI plays and Richard III (adapted with John Barton), John Gabriel Borkman (English version with Inga-Stina Ewbank) 1975, Peter Hall's Diaries: The Story of a Dramatic Battle 1983, Animal Farm: a stage adaptation 1986, The Wild Duck 1990, Making an Exhibition of Myself (autobiog.) 1993, An Absolute Turkey (new trans. of Feydeau's Le Dindon, with Nicki Frei) 1994, The Master Builder (with Inga-Stina Ewbank) 1995, Mind Millie for Me (new trans. of Feydeau's Occupe-toi d'Amélie, with Nicki Frei), The Necessary Theatre 1999, Exposed by the Mask 2000, Shakespeare's Advice to the Players 2003. *Honours:* Hon. Fellow St Catharine's Coll. Cambridge 1964; Chevalier, Ordre des Arts et des Lettres 1965; Dr hc (York) 1966, (Reading) 1973, (Liverpool) 1974, (Leicester) 1977, (Essex) 1993, (Cambridge) 2003; Hon. DSocSc (Birmingham) 1989; Hamburg Univ. Shakespeare Prize 1967, Evening Standard Special Award 1979, Evening Standard Award for Outstanding Achievement in Opera 1981, Evening Standard Best Dir Award for The Oresteia 1981, Evening Standard Best Dir Award for Antony and Cleopatra 1987, South Bank Show Lifetime Achievement Award 1998, Olivier Special Award for Lifetime Achievement 1999, New York Shakespeare Soc. Medal 2003. *Address:* 48 Lamont Road, London, SW10 0HX, England. *E-mail:* phpetard@aol.com (office).

**HALL, Anthony (Tony) William,** CBE, MA, FRSA; British business executive; *Executive Director, Royal Opera House, London;* b. 3 March 1951, Birkenhead; s. of Donald William Hall and Mary Joyce Hall; m. Cynthia Lesley Davis 1977; one s. one d. *Education:* King Edward's School, Birmingham, Birkenhead School, Merseyside, Keble Coll., Oxford. *Career:* joined BBC 1973, News Ed. 1987–90, Dir News and Current Affairs 1990–93, Man. Dir News and Current Affairs 1993–96, Chief Exec. BBC News 1996–2001; Exec. Dir Royal Opera House 2001–; mem. Council Brunel Univ. 1999–; Fellow, Vice-Chair. Royal TV Soc. (Chair. 1998–2000); Dir (non-exec.) Customs and Excise 2002–; Hon. Visiting Fellow City Univ. 1999–2000; Patron Newsworld 1999–2000; Chair. Theatre Royal Stratford East. *Publications:* King Coal: A History of the Miners 1981, Nuclear Politics 1984, articles in various periodicals. *Address:* Royal Opera House, Covent Garden, London, WC2E 9DD, England (office). *Telephone:* (20) 7240-1200 (office). *Fax:* (20) 7212-9502 (office). *Website:* www .royaloperahouse.org (office).

**HALL, Vicki;** Singer (Soprano); b. 13 Nov. 1943, Jefferson, Texas, USA. *Education:* Studied in New York and with Josef Metternich in Cologne. *Career:* Sang at New York City Opera, 1970–; Made guest appearances in Vienna (Volksoper), Munich (Theater am Gärtnerplatz), Cologne, Wuppertal and Bregenz; Roles have included Mozart's Susanna and Blondchen, Carolina in Matrimonio Segreto, Frau Fluth in Die Lustige Weiber von Windsor, Olympia, Strauss's Sophie, Adele in Fledermaus, Gretel, and Janáček's Vixen; Many concert appearances.

**HALLGRIMSSON, Haflidi;** Icelandic composer and cellist; b. 18 Sept. 1941, Akureyri, Iceland; m. 1975; three s. *Education:* The Music School, Reykjavík, Iceland; Academia Sancta Cecilia, Rome; Royal Acad. of Music, London; private studies in composition with Alan Bush and Peter Maxwell Davies.

*Career:* mem., Haydn String Trio, 1967–70; English Chamber Orchestra, 1971–76; Principal Cellist, Scottish Chamber Orchestra, 1977–83; Mondrian Trio, 1984–88; many recitals, appeared as soloist with Symphony Orchestras and performed on BBC Radio 3; mem., Society of Promotion for New Music, Society of Scottish Composers, Performing Right Society. *Compositions:* Poemi; Verse I; Five Pieces for Piano; Seven Folksongs from Iceland; Scenes from Poland; Words in Winter, 1987; Ríma, 1994; Herma, 1995; Still-Life, 1995; Crucifixion, 1997; Mini-Stories, 1997; Ombra, 1999, Passia, 2000. *Recordings:* Strond; Poemi; Vers I; Daydreams in Numbers; Tristia; Jacob's Ladder; String Quartet No. 1; String Quartet No. 2; solitaire; Offerto; Seven Epigrams; Intarsia, The World of Incidences (D. Kharms), Cello Concerto No.2, Passia (choral work), Homage to Mondrian (piano solo). *Honours:* Suggia Prize for Cello playing, 1967; Viotti Prize, Italy, 1975; Nordic Council Prize, 1986. *Address:* 5 Merchiston Bank Gardens, Edinburgh, EH10 5EB, Scotland. *Telephone:* (131) 447-5752 (home). *E-mail:* h.hallgrimsson@ btinternet.com (home).

**HALLIN, Margareta;** Swedish singer (soprano) and composer; b. 22 Feb. 1931, Karlskoga. *Education:* Royal Stockholm Conservatory with Ragnar Hulten. *Career:* sang at the Royal Opera, Stockholm 1954–84, in the premieres of Blomdahl's Aniara 1959 and Drommen om Therese 1964 and Tintomora 1973, by Werle; also as Constanze, Blondchen, Lucia di Lammermoor, Gilda and Leonora in Il Trovatore; sang Anne Trulove in the Swedish premiere of The Rake's Progress 1961; Glyndebourne Festival 1957, 1960, as the Queen of Night; Covent Garden 1960 with the Stockholm Co. in Alcina by Handel; Drottningholm Court Opera from 1962, notably in the Abbé Vogler's Gustaf Adolf och Ebba Brahe 1973; appearances in Florence, Edinburgh, Hamburg, Zürich, Rome and Munich; later in career sang Elsa, Elisabeth de Valois, Mathilde in Guillaume Tell, the heroines in Les Contes d'Hoffmann, Violetta, Donna Anna, Senta, Butterfly and the Marschallin; sang Cherubini's Médée 1984; Drottningholm 1991, as Clytemnestra in Electra by Haeffner. *Compositions include:* Miss Julie, opera after Strindberg. *Honours:* Swedish Court Singer 1966, Order Litteris et artibus 1976. *Address:* c/o Kungl. Musikaliska Akademien, Blasieholmstorg 8, 111 48 Stockholm, Sweden.

**HALLSTEIN, Ingeborg;** German singer (coloratura soprano); b. 23 May 1939, Munich; one d. *Career:* Mem. Bayerische Staatsoper 1961–; numerous guest appearances in Germany and abroad, including Teatro Colón (Buenos Aires), Wiener Staatsoper (Vienna), Royal Opera House (Covent Garden, London), Royal Opera House (Stockholm), Concertgebouw (Amsterdam); has performed at many festivals in Austria, Germany, the Netherlands and Ireland; has performed operas, operettas and oratorios for radio and TV broadcasts; Prof. Hochschule für Musik, Würzburg 1979; title Bayerische Kammersängerin conferred; Bundesverdienstkreuz 1976. *Operas include:* Die Schweigsame Frau, Die Zauberflöte, Der Rosenkavalier, Ariadne auf Naxos, Idomeneo. *Film:* Wälsungenblut. *Address:* Tengstr 35, 80796 Munich 40, Germany.

**HALMEN, Petre;** stage designer, costume designer and stage director; b. 14 Nov. 1943, Talmaciu, Romania. *Education:* studied in Berlin. *Career:* worked at Kiel and Düsseldorf, then collaborated with director Jean-Pierre Ponnelle at Zürich from 1975 in cycles of operas by Monteverdi and Mozart; Munich 1978–, with premieres of Reimann's Lear and Troades, 1986, Das Liebesverbot by Wagner and Berg's Lulu, 1985; Designs for Aida at Berlin; Chicago and Covent Garden 1982–84; Parsifal at San Francisco 1988 and 2 Ring Cycles; Designed and Directed Lohengrin at Düsseldorf 1987, Paer's Achille at Bologna 1988, La Straniera at Spoleto Festival, Charleston, 1989, and Nabucco for Munich Festival, 1990; Designs for Parsifal seen at Mainz 1991, Mozart's Lucio Silla at Vienna Staatsoper; Directed The Golden Cockerel at Duisburg, 1991, La Clemenza di Tito at Toulouse, 1992; Directed and designed Turandot at Deutsche Oper am Rhein, Düsseldorf, 1993; Directed and designed: Aida at Staatsoper Berlin, 1995, Turandot at Opéra de Nice, France, 1995, Don Giovanni at Staatsoper Hamburg, 1996, Rosenkavalier at Staatstheater Darmstadt, 1997, Orfeo by Gluck at Opernhaus Halle, 1997, Ariadne auf Naxos at Toulouse, France, 1988, Idomeneo at Salzburg Festspielhaus, 1998 and Ezio by Handel at Festspiele Halle, 1998. *Address:* Tengstrasse 26, 80798 Munich, Germany.

**HALMRAST, Tor;** Composer; b. 26 April 1951, Sarpsborg, Norway. *Education:* MSc, Engineering (Acoustics), 1976; BMus, University of Trondheim, 1978; Private studies in Composition, State Scholarship, Sweelinck Conservatory, Amsterdam, 1988. *Career:* Composer-in-Residence, Music Conservatory, Tromsoe, 1988–90; Festival Composer, Northern Norwegian Festival, 1990; In charge of acoustic design of several buildings for music, concerts and theatre, and studios; mem, Vice-Chairman, Society of Norwegian Composers. *Compositions:* Works for symphony orchestra, chamber works, solo works, music for television, films and records and sound installation, including the prize-winning music for the Norwegian Pavillion at the World's Fair, Expo92 in Seville, Spain, and for ice/music sculpture for the Olympics in Lillehammer, 1994; Alfa and Romeo, radiopera for Norwegian Radio, 1997. *Recordings:* Hemera 2901; Music for EXPO92 and other electro-acoustic works: Aquaduct, Icille, Oppbrudd, Varang, Motgift; Alfa and Romeo (Radiopera). *Publications:* Several papers on room acoustics. *Address:* Spaangberg v 28a, 0853 Oslo, Norway.

**HALSEY, Simon Patrick,** MA; Conductor; b. 8 March 1958, Kingston, Surrey, England; m. Lucy Lunt 1986. *Education:* King's Coll., Cambridge,

Royal Coll. of Music. *Career:* Conductor, Scottish Opera-Go-Round 1980, 1981; Dir of Music, Univ. of Warwick 1980–88; Chorus Dir, City of Birmingham Symphony Orchestra 1982–; Assoc. Dir, Philharmonia Chorus 1986–97; Music Dir, Birmingham Opera Company 1987–2000; Wagner's Ring 1990–91; Britten's Church Parables in London and elsewhere 1997; Dir, Acad. of Ancient Music Chorus 1988–92; Dir, Salisbury Festival 1989–93; Chorus Dir, Flanders Opera, Antwerp 1991–95; Consultant Ed., Faber Music Ltd 1996–; Artistic Dir, BBC National Chorus of Wales 1995–2000; Guest Conductor, Chicago Symphony Chorus 1993–94; Principal Guest Conductor, Netherlands Radio Choir 1995–2002, Chief Conductor 2002–; Principal Guest Conductor, Sydney Philharmonic Choirs 1997–; Chief Conductor, European Voices 2000–; Principal Conductor, Berlin Radio Choir 2001–. *Recordings include:* Rossini's Petite Messe Solennelle, Bruckner's Mass in E Minor 1990. *Publications:* Ed., Choral Music, Faber Music. *Honours:* Gramophone Record of the Year 1989, Deutsche Schallplatten Prize 1993; Hon. doctorate, Univ. of Central England 2000. *Current Management:* Hazard Chase Ltd, Norman House, Cambridge Place, Cambridge, CB2 1NS, England. *Telephone:* (1223) 312400. *Fax:* (1223) 460827. *Website:* www.hazardchase.co.uk.

**HALSTEAD, Anthony George,** FRMCM, FGSM; British conductor, horn player, harpsichordist and composer; b. 18 June 1945, Manchester, England; m. 1st Lucy Mabey 1969; two s.; m. 2nd Ellen O'Dell 1985; one d. *Education:* Chetham's School, Royal Manchester Coll. of Music, studied with Dr Horace Fitzpatrick, Myron Bloom, George Malcolm, Sir Charles Mackerras and Michael Rose. *Career:* mem., Bournemouth Symphony Orchestra 1966, BBC Scottish Symphony Orchestra 1966–70, London Symphony Orchestra 1970–73, English Chamber Orchestra 1972–86; Prof., Guildhall School of Music 1971–; fmr Artistic Dir, Hanover Band; mem. Musicians' Union, British Horn Soc., Int. Horn Soc., ISM. *Compositions:* Divertimento Serioso 1973, Prologue and Passus 1976, Serenade for oboe and strings 1978, Concertino Elegiaco 1983, Suite for solo horn or trumpet. *Recordings:* Weber-Horn Concertino 1986, Mozart Horn Concertos 1987, L'Oiseau-Lyre 1993, Haydn Horn Concertos 1989, Britten-Serenade 1989, 12 harpsichord and 14 fortepiano concertos by J. C. Bach, 16 albums of J. S. Bach's complete orchestral works. *Current Management:* Patrick Garvey Management, Cedar House, 10 Rutland Street, Filey, North Yorkshire YO14 9JB, England. *Website:* www.patrickgarvey.com.

**HALTON, Richard;** Singer (Baritone); b. 1963, Devon, England. *Education:* Studied at the University of Kent and the Guildhall School of Music with Johanna Peters. *Career:* Has sung with most leading British opera companies including: Capriccio and Romeo and Juliette with the Royal Opera, Novice's Friend (Billy Budd) and Harry Easter (Street Scene) with English National Opera, Schaunard with Glyndebourne Touring Opera, Ravenal in Showboat at the London Palladium and on 2 national tours with Opera North/RSC, Glyndebourne Festival Opera, 1989, Opera 80, as Danilo in The Merry Widow; Other operatic appearances include: Capriccio at Covent Garden, 1991, in Billy Budd (ENO) and La Bohème (GTO); Holofernes in the world premiere of Ian McQueen's Line of Terror at the Almeida Festival, Harlequin (Ariadne auf Naxos) and Perrucchetto (La Fedeltà Premiata) for Garsington Opera; Repertoire also includes Mozart's Count in Figaro, Tarquinius in The Rape of Lucretia; Street Scene, by Kurt Weill, ENO, 1992; Italian Girl in Algiers by Rossini, Buxton Festival, 1992; Dancairo, Carmen, Dorset Opera, 1992; Janko in Petrified by Juraj Beneš for Mecklenburg Opera, 1992–93; Papageno, The Magic Flute, Scottish Opera, 1993; Sang Sid in Albert Herring at Garsington, 1996; Concert engagements include: A Child of Our Time, St John Passion and Messiah with the City of London Sinfonia conducted by Richard Hickox and Carmina Burana in Perugia and the Royal Albert Hall; Recital works includes Schumann's Dichterliebe with Stephen Barlow at St John's Smith Square; Further engagements include Jason in Gavin Bryars' Medea (Glasgow and BBC Radio 3), Valentin in Faust and Dandini in La Cenerentola. *Honours:* Walter Hyde Memorial Prize; Schubert Prize; Lawrence Classical Singing Bursary. *Address:* c/o Garsington Opera, Garsington, Oxfordshire OX44 9 DH, England.

**HALTON, Rosalind;** Harpsichordist and Musicologist; b. 4 Oct. 1951, Dunedin, New Zealand; m. David Halton 1979. *Education:* New Zealand Junior Scholarship, BA, Otago Univ. 1969–72; Commonwealth Scholarship to Oxford Univ. 1973–80, DPhil, St Hilda's Coll.; harpsichord study with Colin Tilney. *Career:* research and editing of Classical Symphonies (Beck-Holzbauer) and Cantatas of Alessandro Scarlatti; concerts of 17th and 18th century chamber music using period instruments; solo performances on harpsichord and pianos of 18th and early 19th centuries; Lecturer, Performance 1986–90, Senior Lecturer 1990–99, Univ. of New England, Armidale, Australia; Senior Lecturer in Performance and Musicology, Univ. of Newcastle, NSW 1999–; founder mem. of Chacona, baroque chamber ensemble; mem. Musicology Society of Australia. *Recordings:* The French Harpsichord: Music by F. and L. Couperin 1996, Olimpia and other cantatas by Alessandro Scarlatti 2001. *Publications:* Olimpia, A Scarlatti Cantata 1996, Toccata 1998, Clori mia, Clori bella 1998. *Contributions:* various reviews, Music and Letters. *Honours:* Soundscapes Award 1997. *Address:* c/o The Conservatorium, University of Newcastle, Auckland St, NSW 2300, Australia; 26 Rhondda Road, Teralba, NSW 2294, Australia. *E-mail:* R.Halton@newcastle.edu.au.

**HAMARI, Julia;** Hungarian singer (mezzo-soprano); b. 21 Nov. 1942, Budapest; d. of Sándor Hamari and Erzsébet Dokupil; m. Lajos Pető. *Education:* Franz Liszt Music Acad. of Budapest, Hochschule für Musik.

*Career:* debut as soloist Bach's St Matthew Passion in Vienna under Karl Richter 1966; specializes in Rossini, Mozart, Bellini; lieder recitalist and oratorio performer; has appeared world-wide with conductors including Herbert von Karajan, Sergiu Celibidache, Rafael Kubelik, Georg Solti, Karl Böhm and Pierre Boulez; debut in USA as soloist with Chicago Symphony Orchestra 1967; opera debut at Salzburg Festival as Mercedes in Bizet's Carmen 1967; has appeared with Deutsche Oper am Rhein in various baroque and classical operas 1968–; has appeared at major opera houses including La Scala, Covent Garden and Vienna State Opera; opera roles include Celia in La fedeltř premiata (J. Haydn), Orpheus (Gluck), Dorabella and Despina (Così fan tutte), Angelina in La Cenerentola (Rossini), Rosina in Il Barbiere di Siviglia (Rossini), Sesto in La clemenza di Tito (Mozart), Cherubino in Nozze di Figaro (Mozart), Sinaide in Mosč in Egitto (Rossini), Romeo in I Capuleti ed I Montecchi (Bellini); Prof., Staatliche Hochschule für Musik, Stuttgart 1989–. *Participation in festivals:* performed in festivals of Edinburgh, Glyndebourne, Florence (Maggio Musicale). *Recordings include:* Matthäus-Passion by J.S. Bach), Oberon by Weber, Il matrimonio segreto by Cimarosa, Giulio Cesare by Händel, Roméo et Juliette by Berlioz, Mozart's Requiem, Mass in C major by Beethoven, Ernani by Verdi, Tito Manlio by Mozart, Bach Cantatas, Cavalleria rusticana, I Puritani by Bellini, Beethoven's 9th Symphony, Bach's Mass in B Minor, Orpheus by Gluck, Stabat Mater by Pergolesi, Don Sanche by F. Liszt, Mosč in Egitto by Rossini, Prima la musica by A. Salieri, Hänsel und Gretel, Eugen Onegin, Meistersinger, Czipra in Zigeunerbaron, Eugen Onegin from the Munich Opera (video) 1972. *Honours:* prizewinner, Erkel International Singing Competition, Budapest 1964, Kodály Prize 1987. *Address:* Max Brodweg 14, Stuttgart 40, Germany.

**HAMBLETON, Tristan;** Singer (Bass); b. 1988, London. *Career:* St Paul's Cathedral Choir, from 1996; Appearances as the youth in Mendelssohn's Elijah under Andrew Davis in Rome and with Richard Hickox; Engagements at English National Opera Studio and in Britten's War Requiem and Mahler's Third Symphony at the Royal Festival Hall; Handel's L'Allegro, il Penseroso ed il Moderato with Les Arts Florissants; Sang Amor in Gluck's Orfeo ed Euridice at Covent Garden, 2001. *Recording:* soloist on The Armed Man, by Carl Jenkins (CD). *Address:* c/o Music Dept, The King's School, Canterbury, CT1 2ES, England. *Telephone:* (1227) 595556 (office). *Fax:* (1227) 595559 (office). *E-mail:* music@kings-school.co.uk (office).

**HAMBLIN, Pamela;** Singer (Soprano); b. 14 June 1954, Cookeville, Tennessee, USA. *Education:* Studied at North Texas State University and Salzburg Mozarteum. *Career:* Debut: Karlsruhe, as Euridice in Orphée aux Enfers by Offenbach, 1980; Has sung at Karlsruhe in such roles as Handel's Florinda (Rodrigo), Almirena (Rinaldo) and Romilda (Serse); Micaela, Mozart's Susanna, Pamina, Constanze and Sandrina, Verdi's Gilda and Oscar, Constance in Cherubini's Les Deux Journées, Strauss's Sophie and Aminta (Die schweigsame Frau) and Titania in A Midsummer Night's Dream; Guest appearances at Dresden, Stuttgart, Zürich, Essen, Heidelberg, Strasbourg, Madrid, Barcelona and Athens. *Recordings include:* Rodrigo. *Address:* Schillerstr. 15, 76275 Ettlingen, Germany.

**HAMBRAEUS, Bengt;** Composer, Organist and Musicologist; b. 29 Jan. 1928, Stockholm, Sweden. *Education:* Studied organ with Alf Linder, 1944–48; Uppsala University, PhD, 1956; Summer Courses at Darmstadt 1951–55, with Krenek, Messiaen and Fortner; Worked for Swedish Broadcasting Corporation from 1957, Director of Chamber Music 1965–68, Production Director 1968–72; Composed at Electronic Studios of Cologne, Munich, Montreal and Milan; Professor at McGill University, Montreal from 1972, Professor Emeritus, 1995–. *Compositions:* Chamber Operas Experiment X, 1971; Se Människan, 1972; Sagan, 1979; L'oui-dire, 1986; Concerto for organ and harpsichord, 1951; Antiphones en rondes for soprano and 24 instruments, 1953; Crystal Sequence for soprano choir and ensemble, 1954; Rota for 3 orchestras and tape, 1956–62; Transfiguration for orchestra, 1962–63; Constellations I–V, 1958–83; Segnali for 7 instruments, 1960; Mikrogram for ensemble, 1961; Interferences for organ, 1962; Klassiskt spel, electronic ballet, 1965; Fresque Sonore for soprano and ensemble, 1967; Rencontres for orchestra, 1971; Pianissimo in due tempi for 20 string instruments, 1972; Ricercare for organ, 1974; Advent for organ 10 brass instruments and percussion, 1975; Ricordanza for orchestra, 1976; Continuo for organ and orchestra, 1975; Livre d'orgue, 1980–81; Symphonia Sacra for 5 soloists, choir, wind instruments and percussion, 1986; Apocalypsis cum figuris for bass solo, choir and organ, 1987; Five Psalms for choir, 1987; Litanies for orchestra, 1988–89; Nocturnals for chamber orchestra, 1989; Piano Concerto, 1992; St Michael's Liturgy, 1992; Missa pro Organo, 1992; Organum Sancti Jacobi, 1993; Meteoros, 1993; Songs of the Mountain, The Moon and Television, 1993; Eco dalla montagna lontana, 1993; Triptyque pour orgue avec MIDI, 1994; Due Rapsodie, 1994; Concentio, 1995; Quatre tableaux, 1995; Horn Concerto, 1995–96; Archipel for 15 soloists, 1997; FM 643765 for organ, 1997. *Publications:* Codex Carminum Gallicorum, 1961; Om Notskifter (On Notation) 1970; Numerous articles and essays published since 1948. *Address:* RR1, Apple Hill, Ontario K0C 1B0, Canada.

**HAMEENNIEMI, Eero (Olavi);** Composer; b. 29 April 1951, Valkeakoski, Finland; m. Leena Peltola, 7 Oct 1977, (divorced Oct 1989), 1 d. *Education:* Diploma, Sibelius Academy, 1977; State Higher School of Music, Kraków, 1979; Eastman School of Music, Rochester, New York, USA, 1980–81. *Career:* Commissions for the Finnish Radio Symphony Orchestra, Swedish RSO, Helsinki Festival, Finnish National Ballet; Works performed by (the above) and Scottish National Orchestra, Malmö Symphony Orchestra, Gothenburg

Symphony Orchestra; Senior Lecturer, Sibelius Academy, 1982–. *Compositions:* Symphony, 1982–83, 1984; Dialogue for Piano and Orchestra, 1987; Sonata for Clarinet and Piano; Loviisa, a ballet in two acts, premiere 19 Mar 1987, Finnish National Ballet; Second Symphony, 1988; 2 String Quartets, 1989, 1994; Leonardo, ballet in 2 acts; The Bird and the Wind for strings, soprano and two Indian classical dancers (choreography by Shobana Jeyasingh), 1994; The Dances of the Wind for strings, 1994; Valkalam for 2 viols and harpsichord, 1996; Chamber Concerto, 1997. *Recordings:* Duo l, for flute and cello; Pianosonata, 1979; Sonata for clarinet and piano, 1987. *Publications:* ABO–johdatus uuden musiikin teoriaan, Sibelius Academy Publications, 1982 (An Introduction to the Theory of Contemporary Music); Tekopalmun alla (Under an Artificial Palm Tree), essays on the interaction of cultures. *Honours:* Nattuvanar for male voice choir won the UNESCO Rostrum of Composers in 1994. *Address:* Lapilantie 8B7, 04200 Kerava, Finland.

**HAMELIN, Marc-André,** OC; Canadian concert pianist; b. 1961, Verdun; m. Judy Karin Applebaum. *Education:* Vincent d'Indy School of Music and Temple Univ., Philadelphia. *Career:* recitals in Montréal, Toronto, New York and Philadelphia; concerto appearances in Toronto, Québec, Ottawa, Albany, Detroit, Indianapolis, Minneapolis, New York (Manhattan Philharmonic and Riverside Symphony) and Philadelphia; toured with the Montréal Symphony to Spain, Portugal and Germany 1987; duo partnership with cellist, Sophie Rolland from 1988; Beethoven cycles in New York, Washington, Montréal and London (Wigmore Hall 1991); soloist, Turangalîla Symphony with the Philadelphia Orchestra and Andrew Davis 1996–97; played with the Tokyo Philharmonic conducted by Okko Kamu, gave a recital in Seoul 2004; Hong Kong Arts Festival debut, with the Hong Kong Philharmonic 2004. *Recordings include:* Works by Leopold Godowsky, William Bolcom Twelve New Etudes, Stefan Wolpe Battle Piece and Ives Concord Sonata, Sorabji Sonata No. 1, Rzewski The People Will Never Be Defeated, Albéniz's Iberia 2005. *Honours:* first prize Carnegie Hall Int. American Music Competition 1985, Virginia P. Moore Prize, Canada 1989. *Current Management:* Georgina Ivor Associates, 28 Old Devonshire Road, London, SW12 9RB, England. *Telephone:* (20) 8673-7179. *Fax:* (20) 8675-8058. *E-mail:* info@giamanagement.com. *Website:* www .giamanagement.com.

**HAMILTON, David;** Singer (Tenor); b. 1960, USA. *Career:* Appearances with opera companies at Philadelphia, San Diego, Tulsa, Sarasota, Hawaii, New York (City Opera), Milwaukee and St Louis; Metropolitan Opera debut, season 1986–87; Season 1991–92, as Tamino for Opéra de Nice, Lensky with Manitoba Opera, and Pinkerton with Chattanooga Opera; Season 1992–93, as Tamino with Vancouver Opera, Peter Quint in Turn of the Screw for Edmonton Opera and Lensky with Scottish Opera; Concert repertoire includes Messiah, Rinaldo by Brahms, Mozart's Requiem, Dvořák's Stabat Mater, the Berlioz Roméo et Juliette and Schumann's Scenes from Faust; Soloist with Israel Philharmonic, Baltimore Symphony, Mostly Mozart Festival Orchestra and Indianapolis Symphony under Raymond Leppard; As recitalist gave premiere of Hugo Weisgall's cycle Lyric Interval; Sang Belmonte in Die Entführung with the Metropolitan Opera. *Honours:* Winner, Paris International Voice Competition, 1984. *Address:* c/o Metropolitan Opera House, Lincoln Centre, New York, NY 10023, USA.

**HAMILTON, David (Peter);** Music Critic and Writer on Music; b. 18 Jan. 1935, New York, USA. *Education:* Princeton University; AB 1956, MFA in Music History, 1960. *Career:* Music and Record Librarian, Princeton University, 1961–65; Assistant Music Editor 1965–68, Music Editor 1968–74, W W Norton & Company, New York; Music Critic, The Nation, 1968–; Music Correspondent, Financial Times, London, 1969–74; Associate Editor, Musical Newsletter, 1971–77. *Publications:* The Listener's Guide to Great Instrumentalists, 1981; The Music Game: An Autobiography, 1986; Editor, Metropolitan Opera Encyclopedia: A Guide to the World of Opera, 1987. *Contributions:* Many articles and reviews in periodicals. *Address:* c/o The Nation, 72 Fifth Avenue, New York, NY 10011, USA.

**HAMILTON, Ronald;** Singer (Tenor); b. 1947, Hamilton, Ohio, USA. *Career:* Sang in opera at Ulm, 1975–77, Düsseldorf, 1977–85; Guest appearances throughout Germany, and in Stockholm, Geneva and Paris; Metropolitan Opera, 1988, as Alwa in Lulu, and Salzburg Festival, 1990, as Krenek's Orpheus; Paris Opéra Bastille, 1992, in Messiaen's St François d'Assise; Brussels, 1993, in From the House of the Dead, and the premiere of Reigen by Boesmans; Trieste and Montpellier, 1996, as Tristan; Other roles include Florestan, Wagner's Lohengrin and Walther, Strauss's Emperor and Bacchus, and Enée in Les Troyens; Sang Tannhäuser at Palermo, 1998; Season 2000–01 as Tristan at Hamburg and Wagner's Erik in Trieste. *Address:* Teatro Massimo, Via R Wagner 2, 90139 Palermo, Sicily, Italy.

**HAMMES, Lieselotte;** Singer (Soprano) and Professor; b. 1932, Siegburg, Germany. *Education:* Studied in Cologne. *Career:* Debut: Cologne, as Amor in Orfeo ed Euridice, 1957; Guest appearances at Stuttgart, Hamburg, Berlin (Deutsche Oper), Naples, Rome, Lisbon and Paris (1971); Glyndebourne Festival 1965, as Sophie in Der Rosenkavalier; Sang at Cologne until 1975 as Mozart's Pamina, Susanna and Papagena, Marzelline, Mimi, Manon Lescaut, Nedda, Marenka in The Bartered Bride and Anne Trulove in The Rake's Progress; Teacher at Bonn then Siegburg from 1973; Professor at Cologne Musikhochschule, 1985–. *Address:* Staatliche Hochschule für Musik, Dagobertstrasse 38, 5000 Cologne 1, Germany.

**HAMMOND-STROUD, Derek,** OBE; British singer (baritone); b. 10 Jan. 1926, London, England; s. of Herbert William Stroud and Ethel Louise Elliott. *Education:* Trinity Coll. of Music, London with Elena Gerhardt, Gerhard Hüsch. *Career:* debut in London 1955, in the British Premiere of Haydn's Orfeo et Euridice; Guest Artist with numerous opera companies; Principal Baritone, English National Opera, 1961–71, as Rossini's Bartolo, Verdi's Melitone and Rigoletto, Wagner's Alberich and Beckmesser; Royal Opera, Covent Garden, 1971–89; Glyndebourne, 1973–86; Broadcasts on BBC and European radio; Opera and Recital appearances: Netherlands; Denmark; Iceland; Germany; Austria; Spain; USA; opera appearances: Metropolitan Opera, New York, 1977–89; Teatro Colón, Buenos Aires, 1981; National Theatre, Munich, 1983; Other roles included: Publio, in La Clemenza di Tito; Don Magnifico; Roles in the British premieres of La Pietra del Paragone, Der Besuch der Alten Dame, and Faninal in Der Rosenkavalier; mem, Incorporated Society of Musicians; retd teacher. *Recordings:* many recordings for various companies including the ENO Ring of the Nibelung and Der Rosenkavalier. *Honours:* Hon. mem., RAM; Honorary Fellow, Trinity Coll. of Music, London; Sir Charles Santley Memorial Award by Worshipful Company of Musicians. *Address:* 18 Sutton Road, Muswell Hill, London N10 1HE, England. *Telephone:* (20) 8883-2120 (home).

**HAMON, Deryck;** Singer (Bass); b. 1965, Guernsey. *Education:* Royal Northern College of Music. *Career:* Concert performances throughout the United Kingdom of Messiah, Elijah, Samson, Haydn's Nelson Mass, Five Elizabethan Songs by Vaughan Williams and the Mozart and Fauré Requiems; Member of the D'Oyly Carte Opera, notably as The Mikado; Rossini's Basilio and Escamillo for Travelling Opera, Dikoy in Katya Kabanova at the Opera Theatre, Dublin, and Banquo in Macbeth for City of Birmingham Touring Opera; Other roles include Mozart's Sarastro, Commendatore and Alfonso, Rossini's Bartolo, Puccini's Angelotti (Tosca) and Colline (La Bohème). *Address:* Karen Durant Management, 298 Nelson Road, Whitton, Twickenham TW2 7BW, England.

**HAMPE, Christiane;** Singer (Soprano); b. 1948, Heidelberg, Germany. *Education:* Studied in Heidelberg and in Munich with Annelies Kupper. *Career:* Sang at the Hagen Opera, 1971–73, Basle, 1974–76, Wuppertal, 1976–78, and Karlsruhe, 1979–80; Bregenz Festival, 1974, as Clarice in Haydn's Il mondo della luna, Vienna Staatsoper as Susanna and further guest appearances in Karlsruhe, throughout Europe and in the USA; Professor at the Karlsruhe Musikhochschule from 1988. *Recordings include:* Lortzing's Undine (Capriccio). *Address:* c/o Musikhochschule, Wolfortsuieies Strasse 7, 76131 Karlsruhe, Germany.

**HAMPE, Michael,** DPhil; German theatre, opera and television director and actor; b. 3 June 1935, Heidelberg; s. of Hermann and Annemarie Hampe; m. Sibylle Hauck 1971; one d. *Education:* Falckenberg Schule, Munich, Univs. of Vienna and Munich and Syracuse Univ., USA. *Career:* Deputy Dir Schauspielhaus, Zürich 1965–70; Dir Nat. Theatre, Mannheim 1972–75; Cologne Opera 1975–95; Dresden Music Festival; directs opera at La Scala, Milan, Covent Garden, London, Paris Opera, Salzburg and Edin. Festivals, Munich, Stockholm, Cologne, Geneva, San Francisco, Sydney, Los Angeles, Buenos Aires, Tokyo; directs drama at Bavarian State Theatre, Munich Schauspielhaus, Zürich, etc.; directs and acts in film and TV; Prof. State Music Acad., Cologne and Cologne Univ.; mem. Bd European Acad. of Music, Vienna; theatre-bldg consultant; teaches at Vienna Univ., UCLA and Univ. of Southern California, USA, Kunitachi Coll. of Music, Tokyo. *Publications:* Oper in Köln 1975–95, Cologne Alles Theater; articles in newspapers and periodicals. *Honours:* Bundesverdienstkreuz, Commendatore Ordine al Merito (Italy), Goldenes Ehrenabzeichen des Landes Salzburg; Olivier West End Award 1983. *Address:* Odinweg 52, 51429 Bergisch Gladbach, Germany.

**HAMPSON, (Walter) Thomas,** BA; American singer (baritone); b. 28 June 1955, Elkhart, Ind.; s. of Walter Hampson and Ruthye Hampson; one d. *Education:* Eastern Washington Univ., Fort Wright Coll., Music Acad. of West. *Career:* with Düsseldorf Ensemble 1981–84; title role in Der Prinz von Homburg, Darmstadt 1982; debut in Cologne, Munich, Santa Fé 1982–84; Metropolitan Opera, NY, Vienna Staatsoper, Covent Garden 1986, La Scala, Milan, Deutsche Oper, Berlin 1989, Carnegie Hall, San Francisco Opera 1990; has performed with Wiener Philharmoniker, NY Philharmonic, London Philharmonic and Chicago Symphony orchestras; f. The Hampsong Foundation 2003. *Roles include:* Guglielmo in Così fan tutte, the Count in Le Nozze di Figaro, Billy Budd (title role), Hamlet (title role) 1976, Il Barbiere di Siviglia (title role), Posa in Don Carlos, Riccardo in I Puritani 1997. *Recordings include:* Schubert's Winterreise 1997, Das Lied von der Erde 1997, Belshazzar's Feast 1998, Operetta Album with London Philharmonic 1999, No Tenors Allowed: Opera Duets (with Samuel Ramey) 1999, Verdi Arias with Orchestra of the Age of Enlightenment 2001, Wagner's Tannhäuser 2002, Cole Porter's Kiss Me Kate 2002,. *Honours:* Dr hc (Whitworth Coll., Washington, San Francisco Conservatory) Hon. RAM 1996; Edison Prize, Netherlands 1990, 1992, Grand Prix du Disque 1990, 1996, Cannes Classical Award 1994, Echo Klassik 1995, EMI Artist of the Year 1997, Deutsche Schallplattenkritik Award 1999, Cecilia Award 2000, Diapason D'Or Award 2000; Citation of Merit, Vienna Kammersänger 1999. *Address:* c/o IMG Artists Europe, Media House, 616 Chiswick High Road, London W4 5RX, England (office). *Website:* www.hampsong.com (office).

**HAMPTON, Christopher James,** CBE, MA, FRSL; British playwright; b. 26 Jan. 1946, Fayal, the Azores, Portugal; s. of Bernard Patrick and Dorothy

Patience (née Herrington) Hampton; m. Laura Margaret de Holesch 1971; two d. *Education:* Lancing Coll., New Coll., Oxford. *Career:* wrote first play When Did You Last See My Mother? 1964; Resident Dramatist, Royal Court Theatre 1968–70; freelance writer 1970–. *Plays:* When Did You Last See My Mother? 1967, Total Eclipse 1969, The Philanthropist 1970, Savages 1973, Treats 1976, Able's Will (TV) 1978, Tales from Hollywood 1983, Les Liaisons Dangereuses 1985, White Chameleon 1991, Alice's Adventures Underground 1994, The Talking Cure 2002. *Translations include:* Marya (Babel) 1967, Uncle Vanya, Hedda Gabler 1970, A Doll's House 1971 (film 1974), Don Juan 1972, Tales from the Vienna Woods 1977 (film 1979), Don Juan Comes Back from the War 1978, The Wild Duck 1980, Ghosts 1983, Tartuffe 1984, Faith, Hope and Charity 1989, Art 1996, An Enemy of the People 1997, The Unexpected Man 1998, Conversations After a Burial 2000, Life × Three 2001, Three Sisters 2003. *Directed:* (films) Carrington 1995, The Secret Agent 1996, Imagining Argentina 2003. *Opera libretto:* Waiting for the Barbarians (music by Philip Glass) 2005. *Publications:* When Did You Last See My Mother? 1967, Total Eclipse 1969 (film 1995), The Philanthropist 1970, Savages 1973, Treats 1976, Able's Will (TV) 1978, The History Man (TV adaptation of novel by Malcolm Bradbury) 1981, The Portage to San Cristobal of A.H. (play adaptation of novel by George Steiner) 1983, Tales from Hollywood 1983, The Honorary Consul (film adaptation of a novel by Graham Greene) 1983, Les Liaisons Dangereuses (adaptation of a novel by Laclos) 1985, Hotel du Lac (TV adaptation of a novel by Anita Brookner) 1986, The Good Father (film adaptation of a novel by Peter Prince) 1986, Wolf at the Door (film) 1986, Dangerous Liaisons (film) 1988, The Ginger Tree (adaptation of novel by Oswald Wynd, TV) 1989, White Chameleon 1991, Sunset Boulevard (book and lyrics with Don Black) 1993, Alice's Adventures Underground (with Martha Clarke) 1994, Carrington (film) 1995, Mary Reilly (film) 1996, The Secret Agent (film) 1996, Nostromo (screenplay) 1997, The Quiet American (film) 2002, Collected Screenplays 2002, The Talking Cure 2002. *Honours:* Officier, Ordre des Arts et des Lettres 1998; Evening Standard Award for Best Comedy 1970, 1983, for Best Play 1986, Plays and Players London Critics' Award for Best Play 1970, 1973, 1985; Los Angeles Drama Critics' Circle Award 1974, Laurence Olivier Award for Best Play 1986, New York Drama Critics' Circle Award for Best Foreign Play 1987, Prix Italia 1988, Writers' Guild of America Screenplay Award 1989, Academy Award for Best Adapted Screenplay 1989, BAFTA Award for Best Screenplay 1990, Special Jury Award, Cannes Film Festival 1995, Tony Awards for Best Original Score (lyrics) and Best Book of a Musical 1995, Scott Moncrieff Prize 1997. *Address:* 2 Kensington Park Gardens, London, W11, England. *Telephone:* (20) 7229-2188. *Fax:* (20) 7229-7644 (office).

**HAMVASI, Sylvia;** Singer (Soprano); b. 1972, Budapest, Hungary. *Education:* Franz Liszt Academy and Leo Weiner Conservatory, Budapest. *Career:* Roles with Budapest Youth Opera have included Mozart's Blonde and Mme Herz, Serpina in La Serva Padrona and Olympia; Concert tour with the Youth Opera Studio to Kuwait; Repertory includes Bach's St John Passion, Christmas Oratorio and Masses, Mozart, Liszt and Kodály Masses, Carmina Burana and Handel's Messiah, Dixit Dominus and Solomon. *Recordings include:* Album with the Hungarian Radio Youth Orchestra, conducted by Tamas Vasary. *Honours:* European Mozart Foundation Award, at the 1996 Hommage á Lucia Popp Competition, Bratislava. *Current Management:* Ingpen & Williams Ltd, 7 St George's Court, 131 Putney Bridge Road, London, SW15 2PA, England.

**HAN, Derek;** Concert Pianist; b. 1951, USA. *Education:* Juilliard School, New York. *Career:* Many appearances in USA and Europe from 1976 notably with the Moscow Philharmonic, Berlin Symphony, Sinfonia Varsovia (conducted by Yehudi Menuhin), Frankfurt State Orchestra, Moscow State Symphony Orchestra and London Philharmonic; Season 2000–01 on tour with the Warsaw Philharmonic in the Far East, Netherlands tour with the Budapest Symphony and concerts in Berlin and New York; Tour of the United Kingdom with the Bolshoi Symphony and South America with Residentie Orchestra, the Hague; Further concerts with the Philharmonie der Nationen. *Recordings include:* Complete Concertos of Haydn, Mozart, Beethoven and Mendlessohn; Tchaikovsky and Shostakovich Concertos; Complete Mozart Violin and Piano sonatas, with Joseph Silverstein. *Honours:* Winner, 1977 Athens International Piano Competition. *Address:* c/o IMG Artists, Lovell House, 616 Chiswick High Road, London W4 5RX, England.

**HANAK, Bohus;** Singer (Bass-Baritone); b. 8 Jan. 1925, Banovce, Czechoslovakia. *Education:* Studied in Bratislava. *Career:* Sang at Bratislava from 1950 and made guest appearances with the company at Prague, Sofia and Wiesbaden; Engaged at Linz, 1958–60 and at Stadttheater Basle, 1968–88; Further performances at the Komische Opera Berlin, Bolshoi Moscow, Leningrad, State Operas of Dresden and Munich, Naples, Geneva, Innsbruck, Berne and Paris at Théâtre des Champs Elysées; Roles have included Mozart's Figaro and Don Giovanni, Pizarro, Rigoletto, Renato, Amonasro, Count Luna, Macbeth, Simon Boccanegra, Wolfram, Telramund, the Dutchman, Alberich, Prince Igor, Eugene Onegin, Scarpia, Cardillac, Nabucco and Mandryka. *Address:* c/o Theater Basel, Theaterstrasse 7, 4010 Basel, Switzerland.

**HANANI, Yehuda;** Cellist; b. 19 Dec. 1943, Jerusalem, Israel; m. Hannah Glatstein, 21 Mar 1971, 1 s. *Education:* Rubin Academy of Music, Israel; Juilliard School, USA. *Career:* Guest Performer with Chicago Symphony, Philadelphia Orchestra, Baltimore Symphony, St Paul Chamber Orchestra, Berlin Radio Symphony, Israel Philharmonic, BBC National Orchestra of Wales, etc; Aspen Music Festival; Chautauqua; Marlboro; Artistic Director,

Chamber Music Series, Miami Center for the Fine Arts; Cello Faculty, The Peabody Conservatory and Cincinnati College-Conservatory. *Recordings:* Miaskovsky Cello Sonatas; Alkan Cello Sonata; Vivaldi Cello Sonatas; Aleksander Obradovic Cello Concerto; Leo Ornstein Sonata; Samuel Barber Sonata; Lukas Foss Capriccio. *Honours:* Nomination for Grand Prix du Disque; Recipient of 3 Martha Baird Rockefeller Grants for Music; America Israel Cultural Foundation Award.

**HANCOCK, Gareth,** ARAM; British pianist and conductor; b. 1960, England. *Education:* Clare Coll., Cambridge, Royal Acad., London. *Career:* engagements as repetiteur at English National Opera, playing harpsichord in The Barber of Seville; conducted Rigoletto for English Touring Opera 1996, and Misper for Glyndebourne Education 1997; repetiteur and assistant at Glyndebourne from 1995, including Chief Coach for Jonathan Dove's Flight 1999; teacher at the Royal Academy; Lieder recital accompanist in Britain, France, Germany and USA. *Recordings include:* The Barber of Seville, ENO. *Address:* c/o Royal Academy of Music, Marylebone Road, London, NW1 5HT, England.

**HANCOCK, John;** American singer (baritone); b. 1968, New York, NY; m. Jane Gilbert. *Education:* Juilliard Opera Center, New York. *Career:* sang Oreste in Iphigénie en Tauride at Strasbourg, 1993, Rossini's Dandini in Kansas City and Raimbaud for the Spoleto Festival, USA; La Haine in Lully's Armide in Paris and Antwerp, Marcello in La Bohème at Glyndebourne and with the Canadian Opera Company, 1995, Rossini's Barber for the New Israeli Opera and Valentin in Philadelphia; Other roles include Silvio in Pagliacci, Malatesta and Tarquinius; Sang Lord Henry Wootton in the premiere of Lowell Liebermann's The Picture of Dorian Gray, Monaco, 1996; Belcore for Florida Grand Opera, 1998; Concert repertoire includes Mahler's Kindertotenlieder at Alice Tully Hall and Des Knaben Wunderhorn. *Current Management:* Columbia Artists Management LLC, 1790 Broadway, New York, NY 10019-1412, USA. *Telephone:* (212) 841-9500. *Fax:* 212 841-9744. *E-mail:* info@cami.com. *Website:* www.cami.com.

**HANCOCK, Paul;** Composer; b. 6 May 1952, Plymouth, Devon, England; m. Joan Baigent, 11 Oct 1986, sep, 3 step-s., 1 step-d. *Education:* MA, BMus, Trinity Hall, Cambirdge, 1971–76. *Career:* Composing and Private Music Teaching in Plymouth 1976–79, York 1979–83, Oxford 1983–85, Cambridge 1985–87; First London Recital at BMIC, Jan 1986; mem, Composers Guild of Great Britain. *Compositions:* Main Compositions: 24 Preludes, piano solo, 1979–81; String Quartet, 1982; Who? Songs for children, 1981; With The Mermaids, wind quartet, 1983; The Gift Of A Lamb, children's opera, 1985; Maen Tans-Boskednan, piano solo, 1984; Silent Love, song cycle, 1985; Zennor, clarinet and viola, 1986; Little Gidding Variations, orchestra, 1985–86; Viola Concerto, 1986; The Mermaid of Zennor, opera, 1986–88;... O Very Most The Hidden Love..., song cycle, 1986; The Voice of the Hidden Waterfall, ensemble, 1987; Nocturne for Ragnhild, soprano and piano duet, 1988; Dancing On A Point Of Light, ensemble, 1988; Round 12 O'Clock Rock, baritone and piano; Sea Change, percussion ensemble, 1989; Vespers of St Mary Magdalene, soprano and organ, 1990, piano sonatas 1, 2 and 3, 1990–91; Ogo Pour, percussion solo, 1991; Matrice, piano duet, 1991; The Ring of Fire, piano solo, 1992; Journey Out of Essex, baritone and ensemble, 1993. *Recordings:* Two cassettes of piano music. *Address:* Brunnion Farmhouse, Lelant Downs, Hayle, Cornwall TR27 6 NT, England.

**HANCORN, John;** singer (baritone); b. 1954, Inverness, Scotland. *Education:* Trinity Coll. of Music, National Opera Studio; further studies with Hans Hotter in Munich and London. *Career:* debut, Edinburgh 1981, as Masetto in Don Giovanni; Aldeburgh from 1981 in Albert Herring, The Rape of Lucretia and Eugene Onegin; Glyndebourne Touring Opera from 1983 in The Love of Three Oranges, Kent Opera as Masetto in Don Giovanni and Fidelio; Debut at Covent Garden as Hermann in Les Contes d'Hoffmann; Tour of Italy 1986 with Monteverdi's L'Orfeo conducted by Roger Norrington; Concert performance of Charpentier's Médée with the Orchestra of the Age of Enlightenment, 1987; Season 1989–90 with Welsh National Opera as Kilian in Der Freischütz, Hector in King Priam with Musica nel Chiostro in Batignano, Italy, Handel's Israel in Egypt with the Royal Choral Society, 1990; Concert repertory also includes the Brahms Requiem; Appearances with the Royal Philharmonic Orchestra, Scottish Chamber Orchestra, Bournemouth Sinfonietta and at the festivals of Camden, Greenwich, Brighton, Aldeburgh, Flanders and Frankfurt; Sang in Weber's Oberon at the Edinburgh and Tanglewood Festivals and at the Alte Oper, Frankfurt, conducted by Ozawa; Season 1992–94 worked with Welsh National Opera and English National Opera in many major roles; Sang Jove in Semele by John Eccles, for Mayfield Chamber Opera, 1996; The Devil in Ordo Virtutum by Hildegard of Bingen for Vox Animae at the 1996 York Early Music Festival. *Recordings:* with Consort of Musicke and Anthony Rooley, 1994. *Current Management:* Robert Gilder & Co., Enterprise House, 59–65 Upper Ground, London, SE1 9PQ, England. *Telephone:* (20) 7928-9008. *Fax:* (20) 7928-9755. *E-mail:* rgilder@robert-gilder .com.

**HAND, Richard,** ARAM; British musician (guitar); b. 27 Nov. 1960, Marsden, Yorkshire, England. *Education:* Royal Acad. of Music. *Career:* mem., English Guitar Quartet (tour of Israel); mem. flute and guitar duo, The Lightfingered Gentry (tours of Germany, Holland, Egypt, Dubai, Brunei, Malaysia); mem. guitar duo, Hand/Dupré (tours of Norway, Poland, India, Bangladesh, Sri Lanka, Philippines, Malaysia, Indonesia, Singapore, Hong Kong, USA, Turkey, Azerbaijan); mem., Pro Arte Trio (tour of Sweden); mem., Tetra

Guitar Quartet (tour of Saudi Arabia, India); concerts in Wigmore Hall, St John's Smith Square, Purcell Room, Barbican and BBC Proms at Royal Albert Hall; numerous television and radio broadcasts world-wide; has performed premieres of new works by Peter Dickinson, Tim Souster, Jonathon Lloyd, David Bedford, Roger Steptoe, Michael Ball, Brian May, Judith Bingham, Wilfred Josephs; mem. ISM, Musicians' Union. *Recordings:* Carey Blyton: Complete Guitar Music, Lyric Pieces (Hand-Dupré Duo), Scenes from Childhood (with Pro Arte Guitar Trio), Summer Waves (with English Guitar Quartet), Carmen (with Tetra Quartet); world premières of works by Edward Cowie, Malcolm Williamson, Peter Dickinson, David Bedford, Tim Souster. *Honours:* RAM Open Scholarship 1979, RAM Julian Bream Prize 1981, RAM String Players' Prize 1981, RAM John Munday Prize 1981. *Address:* 61 Balcome Street, Marylebone, London, NW1 6HD, England (home). *Telephone:* (20) 7724-3806 (office). *E-mail:* info@richardhand.net (home). *Website:* www .richardhand.net (office).

**HANDLEY, Vernon George,** CBE, BA, FRCM; British conductor; b. 11 Nov. 1930, Enfield; s. of Vernon Douglas and Claudia Lillian Handley; m. 1st Barbara Black 1954 (divorced); one d. one s. (deceased); m. 2nd Victoria Parry-Jones (divorced); one s. one d.; m. 3rd Catherine Newby 1987; one s. *Education:* Enfield School, Balliol Coll., Oxford, Guildhall School of Music. *Career:* Conductor, Oxford Univ. Musical Club and Union 1953–54, Oxford Univ. Dramatic Soc. 1953–54, Tonbridge Philharmonic Soc. 1958–61, Hatfield School of Music and Drama 1959–61, Proteus Choir 1962–81; Musical Dir and Conductor, Guildford Corpn and Conductor, Guildford Philharmonic Orchestra and Choir 1962–83; Assoc. Conductor, London Philharmonic Orchestra 1983–86 (Guest Conductor 1961–83); Prof. for Orchestra and Conducting, Royal Coll. of Music 1966–72, for Choral Class 1969–72; Prin. Conductor, Ulster Orchestra 1985–89, Malmö Symphony Orchestra 1985–89; Prin. Guest Conductor Royal Liverpool Philharmonic Orchestra 1989–95 (Conductor Laureate 1995–), Melbourne Symphony Orchestra 1992–95; Chief Conductor W Australian Symphony Orchestra 1993–; Assoc. Conductor Royal Philharmonic Orchestra 1994– (Guest Conductor 1961–94); Bournemouth Symphony Orchestra, BBC Welsh Orchestra, BBC Northern Symphony (now BBC Philharmonic) Orchestra, Ulster Orchestra, BBC Scottish Symphony Orchestra, New Philharmonia (now Philharmonia) Orchestra; conducted London Symphony Orchestra in int. series, London 1971; Fellow Goldsmiths' Coll., London 1987; tours of Germany 1966, 1980, S Africa 1974, Holland 1980, Sweden 1980, 1981, Germany, Sweden, Holland and France 1982–83, Australia 1986, Japan 1988, Australia 1989, 1991, 1992. *Recordings include:* Elgar Violin Concerto (Kennedy), Wand of Youth and 2nd Symphony (London Philharmonic), Vaughan Williams 5th Symphony and Flos Campi (Liverpool Philharmonic), Bridge the Sea and Britten Sea Interludes (Ulster Orchestra), Bax Enchanted Summer, Walsingham and Fatherland (Royal Philharmonic), Delius Florida Suite, North Country Sketches, Violin Concerto, Suite and Legende (Ralph Holmes), Dvořák Overtures and Scherzo Capriccioso, Finzi Cello Concerto (Rafael Wallfisch), Moeran Symphony, Simpson 2nd, 4th, 6th, 7th, 9th and 10th Symphonies, all Vaughan Williams Symphonies, Elgar Dream of Gerontius, Bantock: Part I of Omar Khayyám 2006, Bax 2006. *Honours:* Hon. RCM 1970; Hon. mem. Royal Philharmonic Soc. 1989; Hon. DUniv (Surrey) 1980; Hon. DMus (Liverpool) 1992; Hon. DLitt (Bradford) 1998; Arnold Bax Memorial Medal for Conducting 1962; Conductor of the Year, British Composer's Guild 1974; Hi-Fi News Audio Award 1982; Gramophone Record of the Year 1986, 1989; British Phonographic Industry Award 1988. *Address:* Cwm Cottage, Bettws, Abergavenny, Monmouthshire, NP7 7LG, Wales; Hen Gerrig, Pen-y-Fan, nr Monmouth (Gwent), Wales. *Telephone:* (1873) 890135.

**HANDT, Herbert;** Tenor, Conductor and Musicologist; b. 26 May 1926, Philadelphia, Pennsylvania, USA. *Education:* Juilliard School New York; Vienna Academy. *Career:* Debut: Vienna Staatsoper, 1949; Sang in the premieres of Venere Prigioniera by Malipiero (Florence 1957) and Maria Golovin by Menotti (Brussels 1958); Appeared in the Italian and French premieres of works by Henze, Berg, Busoni and Britten; Debut as Conductor, Rome, 1960; Founded own opera group and gave revivals of works by Boccherini, Rossini and Geminiani; Also heard in Haydn's Orfeo ed Euridice (L'Anima del Filosofo); Settled in Lucca, Italy and founded the Associazione Musicale Lucchese and the Lucca Chamber Orchestra. *Recordings:* Maria Golovin (RCA); Don Giovanni, Haydn's Orfeo, Idomeneo (Nixa); Giuseppe, Figlio di Giacobbe by Luigi Rossi; Rossini's Otello; Temistocle by JC Bach; Sesto in Giulio Cesare by Handel (Vox). *Publications include:* Performing editions of early Italian vocal music.

**HANKEY, Tom;** Violinist; b. 1975, England. *Education:* Royal College of Music, London. *Career:* Co-founded Tavec String Quartet at RCM, 1999; Coached by Simon Rowland-Jones and the Chillingirian Quartet; Performances at St Martin-in-the-Fields, Serpentine Gallery (BBC Proms) and National Gallery, London; Music Society concerts throughout Britain; Festival Engagements at Lower Wye Valley Chamber Music Festival, 2000–2001; Workshops and concerts in educational establishments; Concert at National Gallery, September 2001, with Octet by Schubert and Strauss's Till Eulenspiegel; Member and leader of the Piros Ensemble, 2000. *Honours:* Winner, Helen Just String Quartet Prize; Rio Tinto Ensemble Prize and NET4 music Prize. *Address:* c/o Royal College of Music, Prince Consort Road, London, SW7 2 BS, England.

**HANLEY, Regina;** Singer (Soprano); b. 1970, Dublin. *Education:* Dublin College of Music; Royal Northern College of Music. *Career:* Appearances with

Glyndebourne Festival Opera as Micaela, Jenůfa, Katya Kabanova, Nedda and Tatiana; Season 1998–99, as Janáček's Emilia Marty for Scottish Opera, Go Round and Donna Anna for the Perth Festival; Concerts include Beethoven's Mass in C, Messiah, Verdi Requiem, Vivaldi's Gloria, Mozart Mass in C Minor, Strauss's Four Last Songs and Rossini's Stabat Mater. *Address:* Music International, 13 Ardilaun Road, London N5 2QR, England.

**HANLON, Kevin (Francis);** Composer; b. 1 Jan. 1953, South Bend, Indiana, USA. *Education:* Studied at Indiana University, the Eastman School of Music and the University of Texas, DMA 1983; Further study with Mario Davidovsky at the Berkshire Music Center. *Career:* Taught at the University of Kentucky, 1982–83; Composition and electronic music faculty at the University of Arizona, Tucson; Director of the Arizona Contemporary Music Ensemble; Appearances as Singer and Conductor. *Compositions include:* Through to the End of the Tunnel for low voice and tape delay 1976, revised 1980; Second Childhood for soprano and ensemble, 1976; Cumulus numbus for orchestra, 1977; Variations for alto saxophone and tape delay, 1977; Toccata for piano, 1980; String Trio, 1981; An die ferne Geliebte for low voice and piano, 1980; Lullaby for my Sorrows for chamber orchestra, 1982; Ostinato Suite for harpsichord, 1982; Centered for chamber ensemble and tape, 1983; A E Housman Song Cycle for low voice and chamber ensemble, 1982; Choral Introits for chorus and ensemble, 1982; Trumpet Sonata, 1983; Sratae for orchestra, 1983; Relentless Time for small orchestra, 1984; Kaleidoscopic Image for orchestra, 1986; On an Expanding Universe, 1986; Chronological Variations for strings, 1987; The Lark of Avignon for wind ensemble and piano, 1993; Clairon for orchestra, 1997. *Honours:* Joseph H Bearns Prize, 1978; Koussevitzky Prize, 1981. *Address:* c/o ASCAP, ASCAP Building, 1 Lincoln Plaza, NY 10023, USA.

**HANLY, Brian (Vaughan);** Concert Violinist and Music Professor; b. 3 Sept. 1940, Perth, Australia; m. Jeri Ryan Hanly, 25 Aug 1968, 2 s. *Education:* Performers Diploma 1960, Teachers Diploma 1961, Australian Music Examinations Board. *Career:* Violinist, Arts Trio, in residence at University of Wyoming and University of Houston, Texas, USA; Numerous tours with Western Arts Trio, Europe, USA, Mexico, also concerts throughout South America and Australia; Soloist with orchestras throughout Australia, Mexico, USA, with particular success with Beethoven and Prokofiev Concertos. *Recordings:* 1st recording of Claude Debussy's recently discovered piano trio; 7 albums with Western Arts Trio. *Honours:* Winner, Australian Broadcasting Commission Concerto Competition. *Address:* Music Department, University of Wyoming, Laramie, WY 82071, USA.

**HANNAH, Ron;** Composer and Teacher; b. 14 Dec. 1945, Moose Jaw, Saskatchewan, Canada. *Education:* BSc, Chemistry, 1969, BMus, Theory, Composition, 1973, MMus, Composition, 1975, EdDip, 1980, University of Alberta, Edmonton; Student of Violet Archer, Manus Sasonkin, Malcolm Forsyth. *Career:* Member, Da Camera Singers, 1973–; Instructor, Department of Extension, University of Alberta, 1975–76; Instructor, Harmony, Ear Training, Red Deer College, 1977–78; Music Instructor, Edmonton Public Schools, 1980–; Founder, Owner, Composer Publications, Edmonton, 1989; Commissions include 1 from Edmonton Symphony Orchestra and 2 from Canadian Broadcasting Corporation; Founding Editor, The Alberta New Music Review, magazine of Edmonton Composers' Concert Society; mem, Co-founder and Co-ordinator, Edmonton New Music Festival. *Compositions include:* From Song of Solomon, SATB, piano, 1972; An Immorality, SATB, piano, 1972; The Dinner Party, song cycle, soprano, clarinet, piano, 1973; String Quartet No. 1, 1973; Sonata for violoncello and piano, 1973; Three African Songs, tenor, piano, 1974; The Shrine of Kotje, chorus and orchestra, 1975; Variations on a Theme of Violet Archer, piano, 1975; Concert Piece, flute, piano, 1975; Visions of Nothingness, piano sonata in 2 movements, 1975; Sonata for French horn and piano, 1976; Prelude and Meditation on Coventry Cathedral, trumpet, organ, 1978; Five Preludes, organ, 1978; Songs of Myself, song cycle, soprano, violin, piano, French horn, 1979; The Lonely Princess, flute, guitar, 1981; Suite for Elan, piano, 1982; Piano Trio No. 1, 1982; Four Canons for three Voices, mixed chorus, piano, 1983; Mademoiselle Fifi, chamber opera, 1983; Three Songs on Poems of Robert Graves, voice, electronic tape, 1984; Fantasia on Ein Feste Burg, organ, 1984; Hypatia, a play with songs, 1984; Three Romantic Madrigals, 1985; Concerto for piano and tape, 1986; Morning's Minion: 4 songs after G M Hopkins, soprano, piano, 1987; Alleluia, SATB, 1989; Credo, mezzo-soprano, viola, piano, 1990; Divertimento for strings, 1991; Pastoral Suite for solo guitar, 1992–93; Suite of Orchestral Dances, 1992; Toccatissimo! for 2 pianos and 2 percussionists, 1993–94. *Recordings:* 5 Preludes for organ; Concert pieces for flute and piano; Meditation for cello and piano. *Address:* 11627 46th Avenue, Edmonton, Alberta T6H 0A6, Canada.

**HANNAN, Eilene;** Singer (Soprano); b. 4 Nov. 1946, Melbourne, Australia. *Education:* Studied in Australia and London. *Career:* Debut: Australian Opera 1971, as Barbarina in Le nozze di Figaro; Sang Natasha in Prokofiev's War and Peace at the opening of the Sydney Opera House, 1973; Other Australian roles have been Janáček's Vixen, Santuzza, Mozart's Zerlina and Cherubino and Leila in Les pêcheurs de Perles, Glyndebourne and Wexford 1977, as the Vixen and as Salomé in Herodiade by Massenet; English National Opera from 1978, as Janáček's Mila (Osud) and Katya Kabanova, the Duchess of Parma in Busoni's Doctor Faust, Mozart's Pamina and Susanna, Mélisande, Poppea (Monteverdi) and Natasha; Covent Garden debut 1978, in the British premiere of The King Goes Forth to France, by Sallinen; Sang in Britten's The Turn of the Screw at Brisbane in 1988; Season 1992, as Jenůfa at Sydney,

Pat Nixon for the State Opera of South Australia and at Düsseldorf; Sang Katya Kabanova at Sydney, 1995; Emma in the premiere of Summer of the Seventeenth Doll, at Sydney, 1999. *Current Management:* Ingpen & Williams Ltd, 7 St George's Court, 131 Putney Bridge Road, London, SW15 2PA, England.

**HANNAN, Michael (Francis);** Composer, Writer, Educator and Keyboard Performer; b. 19 Nov. 1949, Newcastle, New South Wales, Australia. *Education:* BA 1972, PhD 1979, University of Sydney; Graduate Diploma of Musical Composition, University of Sydney, 1982. *Career:* Teacher, University of New South Wales 1975–76, University of Sydney 1977–83; Lecturer in Composition, Queensland Conservatorium of Music, 1985–86; Head of Music, Northern Rivers College of Advanced Education, 1986–; Research, Post-doctoral Scholar, University of California, Los Angeles, 1983–84; Research Affiliate, University of Sydney, 1985–. *Compositions:* Voices in the Sky for piano, 1980; Rajas for solo cello, 1982; Zen Variations for piano, 1982; Island Song for recorders, percussion and organ, 1983; In the Utter Darkness, for solo flute, 1983; Callisto for piano, 1986. *Recordings:* The Piano Music of Peter Sculthorpe, Move Records, 1982. *Publications:* Peter Sculthorpe: His Music and Ideas, 1929–79, 1982. *Contributions:* Various publications. *Address:* c/o School of the Arts, Northern Rivers College of Advanced Education, Lismore, NSW 2480, Australia.

**HANNAY, Roger Durham;** American composer, conductor and teacher; *Professor Emeritus, University of North Carolina;* b. 22 Sept. 1930, Plattsburg, New York; m. Janet Roberts, 1 d. *Education:* BMus, Syracuse University, 1948–52; MMus, Boston University, 1952–53; PhD, Eastman School of Music, 1954–56; Berkshire Music School, 1959; Princeton Seminar for Advanced Studies, 1960; Bennington Composers Conferences 1962–65. *Career:* Debut: Music in Our Time, New York City, 1964; Teacher on the faculties of SUNY, Hamilton College, University of Wyoming, Concordia College; Teacher, University of North Carolina, where founded and directed Electronic Studio and the New Music Ensemble, 1967–82; Conducted the North Carolina Symphony Orchestra in his Symphony No. 4, American Classic, 1983, Greensboro Symphony Orchestra premiere of his orchestral suite, The Age of Innocence, 1985, Peter Fuchs Conductor; Winston-Salem Symphony Orchestra premiere of Symphony No. 6, 1994; Univ. of N Carolina Symphony Orchestra premiere of Symphony No.7 2000; Residencies, Charles Ives Center for American Music, MacDowell Colony, Yaddo. *Compositions include:* 10 symphonies, 1953–2004, 5 chamber operas, 4 string quartets; Sphinx, trumpet and tape; Pied Piper, clarinet and tape; Clarinet Voltaire, saxophone, percussion and speaker; The Journey of Edith Wharton, opera in 2 acts for 5 voices and chamber orchestra, 1982; Rhapsody, flute and piano; Souvenir and Souvenir ll, 1984 and 1986; Ye Musick for the Globe Theatre, 1985; The Nightingale and the Rose, chamber opera after Wilde, 1986; Prologue to Chaucer's Canterbury Tales, commissioned. *Recordings:* Symphony for Band; Architecture in Sound, 1997, 10 symphonies 1953–2004, Rhapsody for flute and piano 1952, Symphony for Band 1963, Modes of Discourse 1994, Journey of Edith Wharton (opera) 1982. *Publications:* Transcribed and edited, Sonate for viola and piano by Mrs H H Beach, 1984; My Book of Life, collection of autobiographical essays, 1997. *Honours:* grants: Nat. Endowment for the Arts 1975, The Kenan Foundation 1975, NC Arts Council 1992, Pogue Foundation 1992; Honigman comp. publ. awards 1982, 2002. *Address:* University of North Carolina, Chapel Hill, NC 27599 (office). *Website:* www.lib.unc.edu/mss/inv/htm (office).

**HANNIKAINEN, Ann-Elise;** Composer and Pianist; b. 14 Jan. 1946, Hangö, Finland. *Education:* Academia Moderna de Música, Peru; Sibelius Acad., Finland; studies with composer, Ernesto Halffter, Spain. *Career:* debut, as composer, orchestral piece, Anerfálicas, Valencia, Spain, 1973; Tournée as pianist, Andalucia, 1975; performance, world premiere, Piano Concerto, Helsinki, 1976; Anerfálicas, Teatro Real, Madrid, Spain, 1977; Finnish and Spanish radio broadcasts; piano recitals; Festival Kuhmoinen, Andalucia, Madrid and others; mem., Société des Auteurs, Compositeurs et Editeurs de Musique (Paris), Society of Finnish Composers. *Compositions include:* Anerfálicas, orchestral, 1973; Pensamientos for piano, 1974; Toccata Fantasia for piano, 1975; Concerto for piano and orchestra, in memoriam Manuel de Falla's 100th Anniversary, 1976; Cosmos for orchestra, 1977; Trio, Sextetto, 1979; Chachara for flute and piano, 1980; Solemne for solo piano, 1982; Zafra for violin and piano, 1986. *Publications:* Pensamientos, 1974; Toccato Fantasia; Chachara; some works included in Centre de Documentation de la Musique Contemporaire, Paris, France. *Honours:* First Prize, Second Contest for Young Composers, JJMM Barcelona, 1980. *Address:* Kokonniementie 14B 3, 17800 Kuhmoinen, Finland.

**HANNULA, Kaisa;** Singer (Soprano); b. 1959, Finland. *Education:* Studied at the Sibelius Academy, Helsinki, and in London and Vienna. *Career:* Sang at first in concert and appeared at the 1989 Savonlinna Festival, in the premiere of The Knife by Paavo Heininen; Savonlinna, 1991, as Marenka in The Bartered Bride and Helsinki, 1992, in Pohjalaisia by Madetoja; Other roles include Marguerite and Violetta; Sang Schoenberg's Erwartung at Savonlinna, 1995; Princess in the premiere of Erik Bergman's The Singing Tree, Helsinki, 1995; Season 2000–01 as Papageno at Savonlinna and Wagner's Gunther in Bonn. *Address:* c/o Finnish National Opera, Bulevardi 23–27, SF 00180 Helsinki 18, Finland.

**HANNULA, Tenno;** Singer (Baritone); b. 1950, Vehmaa, Finland. *Education:* Studied in Finland with P Salomaa, in Rome with Luigi Ricci and at

Musikhochschule Vienna. *Career:* Sang Escamillo and Posa in Don Carlos at Kaiserslautern, 1976; Nationaltheater Mannheim from 1977, as Wolfram, Enrico, Counts Luna and Almaviva, Eugene Onegin, Marcello, Rossini's Figaro and Lortzing's Tsar; Sang Almaviva at Ludwigsburg 1980–81, Savonlinna Festival 1981–89, as Papageno and in the 1984 premiere of Sallinen's The King Goes Forth to France; Stuttgart Staatsoper 1982–, notably in the 1984 premiere of Akhnaten by Philip Glass; Guest appearances at Hamburg, Hanover, Karlsruhe, Aachen, Vienna, Munich, Leningrad and Munich; Finnish National Opera, Helsinki, as Rigoletto, Deutsche Oper Berlin as Thoas in Iphigénie en Aulide; Sang Blancsac in La Scala di Seta at Stuttgart Staatsoper, 1991; Forester in The Cunning Little Vixen at Karlsruhe, 1996, and Dunois in The Maid of Orleans, 1998. *Recordings include:* Akhnaten. *Address:* c/o Stuttgart Staatsoper, Oberer Schlossgarten 6, 7000 Stuttgart, Germany.

**HANSELL, Kathleen Amy Kuzmick,** BA, MMus, PhD; American musicologist and music editor; b. 21 Sept. 1941, Bridgeport, CT; one s. one d. *Education:* Wellesley Coll., MA, Univ. of Illinois at Urbana, Univ. of California at Berkeley, studied piano organ and harpsichord with private teachers. *Career:* instructor in music history, by correspondence, Univ. of Illinois 1967–68; organist, Lutheran Church of the Good Shepherd, Sacramento, CA 1969–71, Gloria Dei Lutheran Church, Iowa City 1973–74; instructor in musicology, harpsichord and organ, Grinnell Coll., Iowa 1975–76; instructor in music history, Cornell Coll., Mt Vernon, Iowa 1979; archivist, Swedish Music History Archive, Stockholm 1982–88; in-house Ed. for critical edns, G. Ricordi and Co, Milan, Italy 1988–92; Music Ed., Univ. of Chicago Press, Chicago, IL 1992–; Man. Ed., The Works of Giuseppe Verdi 1992–; mem. American and Italian Musicology Socs, Soc. of Dance History Scholars. *Publications:* Editor, Mozart: Lucio Silla for Neue Mozart Ausgabe, 1986; Franz Berwald Complete Works, Vol. 14, Duos (Bärenreiter), 1987, Hindemith, Organ Concerto, 1962 for Hindemith-Ausgabe in preparation; Il balletto e l'opera italiana, in Storia dell'opera italiana (Turin), 1988; Editor, Rossini: Zelmira, for Tutte le opere di Gioachino Rossini; Editor, Verdi: Stiffelio for The Works of Giuseppe Verdi; Compositional Techniques in Stiffelio: Reading the Autograph sources in Verdi's Middle Period: Source Studies, Analysis and Performance Practice, 1997; Galetano Gioia, il ballo teatrale e l'opera del primo Ottocento in Creature di Prometeo: Il ballo teatrale dal divertimento al dramma, 1996; Gluck's Orpheus och Euridice in Stockholm: Performance practices on the way from Orpheo to Orphée in Gustavian Opera: An Interdisciplinary Reader in Swedish Opera Dance and Theatre, 1771–1809, 1991; contrib. to numerous professional magazines and publications including Grove's Dictionary, 6th edition; The New Grove Dictionary of Opera. *Address:* 4940 S East End Avenue, Chicago, IL 60615, USA.

**HANSFORD, Andrew,** BMus, MA, ARCM, ARCO, LRSM, LGSM, LTCL, FLCM, FRSA; British pianist, organist and harpsichordist; b. 25 May 1973, Taplow, Berkshire, England. *Education:* Univ. of Surrey, Guildford, Univ. of Bristol and Univ. of Wales, Cardiff. *Career:* professional keyboard accompanist, choral accompanist, continuo player, chamber and orchestral pianist (including celesta), piano duet player, also flautist; resident organist, Sacred Hearts Roman Catholic Church, Charlton Kings, Cheltenham 1989–95; private piano tutor 1990–97; piano tutor, King's Coll., Guildford 1991–94; pianist, Royal Ballet School, London 1996–97; piano accompanist and music lecturer, Morley Coll., London 1998; piano tutor, Cheltenham Coll. 1998–2004, Cirencester Coll. 1998–; music examiner for grade and diploma examinations, including some examiner training 1998–; GCE Advanced/AS-Level examiner, Univ. of London Examinations Bd practical and written music papers 1999–2001, Oxford and Cambridge Examinations Bd music papers 2001–; fmr asscn as piano accompanist, harpsichordist and celesta player for rehearsals and/or public performances with Cirencester Choral Soc., Charlton Kings Choral Soc., Cheltenham Bach Choir, Cheltenham Choral Soc., Bath Philharmonia 1998–; mentor in piano, Associated Bd of the Royal Schools of Music, London (mem. of mentor panel 2000–); music adjudicator for competitive music festivals, including Cheltenham Coll. Dept of Music 2000, 2002; resident organist, St Peter's Roman Catholic Church, Cirencester 2001–; music lecturer, Univ. of Bath, Swindon 2001–; resident piano accompanist (and tenor), 'Jubilate' Chamber Choir, Cheltenham 2002–04; performances include Cirencester Parish Church (St John the Baptist), Cheltenham Town Hall, Cheltenham Pittville Pump Room, Cheltenham Coll. Chapel, Thirlestaine Long Gallery (Cheltenham Coll.), New Assembly Hall (Cheltenham Coll. Jr School), Bath Assembly Rooms, St Giles's Cathedral, Edinburgh, Eisteddfod of Wales 1995; mem. Royal Coll. of Organists, RSA. *Honours:* Int. Hedy King Robinson Grade 8 Theory of Music Prize from the Associated Bd of the Royal Schools of Music 1999, Hon. FMusICMA diploma 2000. *Address:* 62 Roberts Close, Stratton, Cirencester, Gloucestershire GL7 2RP, England. *E-mail:* andhmusic@yahoo.co.uk.

**HANSLIP, Chloë;** Concert Violinist; b. 1987, Guildford, England. *Education:* studied with Natasha Boyarskaya, 1991–; masterclasses in Vienna with Zakhar Bron, 1993–; further studies in Cologne and Madrid. *Career:* played child violinist in 1996 film, Onegin (Devil's Trill Sonata); recitals in Europe, Scandinavia and the USA; TV appearances at Europe, Russia and Israel; Bruch First Concerto at the Barbican, London, 2002; Sarasate's Carmen Fantasy at the 2002 London Proms; Wigmore Hall concert and concertos with the London Mozart Players. *Recordings include:* Paganini and Bloch (with John Williams) 2002. *Honours:* First Prize, Junior International Competition; Novosibirsk, 1997; Scholarship with Sibelius Foundation, 2001. *Current*

*Management:* Hazard Chase, Norman House, Cambridge Place, Cambridge CB2 1NS, England. *Telephone:* (1223) 312400. *Fax:* (1223) 460827. *Website:* www.hazardchase.co.uk.

**HANSMANN, Christine;** Singer (Mezzo-soprano); b. 1964, Thuringia, Germany. *Education:* Studied in Leipzig. *Career:* Sang at Weimar Opera from 1989; Guest appearances at Leipzig, Kassel and elsewhere in Germany, as Mozart's Dorabella and Cherubino, Fricka, Ottavia in Poppea, the Composer in Ariadne auf Naxos and Hansel; Leipzig Opera from 1993 in Le Grand Macabre by Ligeti, Satyricon by Maderna and Schoenberg's Moses und Aron; Other roles include Wagner's Kundry and Brangaene; Concerts with the Leipzig Gewandhaus Orchestra, including US debut at New York in the Wesendonck Lieder. *Address:* c/o Leipzig Opera, Augustusplatz 12, 7010 Leipzig, Germany.

**HANSON, Robert (Frederic);** Composer, Musicologist and Teacher; b. 24 Oct. 1948, Birmingham, England; m. (1) Anthea Judith Carter, 11 July 1970, 1 d., (2) Rosalind Thurston, 1 Nov 1980, 2 s. *Education:* ARCO, 1967, BA, 1970, PhD, 1976, Southampton University. *Career:* Founder, Conductor, Southampton University Chamber Orchestra, 1970–72; Analytical research into the music of Webern, 1970–73; Freelance Teacher and Composer, 1973–74; Lecturer in Music, Dartington College of Arts, 1974–91; Degree Course Leader, 1983–91; Acting Head of Music, 1990–91; Director of Studies, Morley College, 1991–; mem, Society for the Promotion of New Music; Performing Right Society. *Compositions:* Metaphysical Verses for soprano and orchestra, 1980; Changes for string orchestra, 1982; Chamber Concerto, 1986; Song Cycles: Auguries of Innocence, 1988; Clarinet Concerto, 1991; Thanksgiving Music, 1994; String Quartet, 1997; Exequiae Muniae, 1999. *Contributions:* Tempo; Lutoslawski's Mi-Parti; Music Analysis; Webern's Chromatic Organisation. *Address:* Morley College, 61 Westminster Bridge Road, London, England.

**HARA, Kazuko;** Composer; b. 10 Feb. 1935, Tokyo, Japan. *Education:* Studied in Japan, with Dutilleux in Paris and with Tcherepinn, 1962; Singing at Venice Conservatory, 1963, Gregorian Chant in Tokyo. *Career:* Her operas have been successfully performed in Tokyo. *Compositions include:* Operas, The Casebook of Sherlock Holmes, the Confession, 1981; On the Merry Night, 1984; A Selection for Chieko, 1985; Sute-Hime: The Woman who Bit off a Man's Tongue, 1986; A Love Suicide at Sonezaki, 1987; Beyond Brain Death, 1988; Yosakoi-bushi: Junshin and Omma, 1990; Princess Iwanaga, 1990; Pedtro Kibe: recanted not, 1992; Nasuno-Yoichi, 1992; Tonnerre's miraculous tree, 1993; The Life of the Virgin Mary, oratorio, 1993; Lord Sansho, opera, 1995; Princess Nukata, opera, 1996; Crime and Punishment, opera after Dostoyevsky, 1998.

**HARADA, Sadao;** Japanese cellist; b. 4 Jan. 1944, Tokyo. *Education:* Juilliard School. *Career:* cellist of the Tokyo Quartet, 1969–1999; regular concerts in the USA and abroad; First cycle of the complete quartets of Beethoven at the Yale at Norfolk Chamber Music Festival, 1986; Repeated cycles at the 92nd Street Y (NY), Ravinia and Israel Festivals and Yale and Princeton Universities; Season 1990–91 at Alice Tully Hall, the Metropolitan Museum of Art, New York and in Boston, Washington DC, Los Angeles, Cleveland, Detroit, Chicago, Miami, Seattle, San Francisco, Toronto; Tour of South America, two tours of Europe including Paris, Amsterdam, Bonn, Milan, Munich, Dublin, London, Berlin; Quartet-in-Residence at Yale University, the University of Cincinnati College-Conservatory of Music. *Recordings:* Schubert's Major Quartets; Mozart Flute Quartets with James Galway and Clarinet Quintet with Richard Stoltzman; Quartets by Bartók, Brahms, Debussy, Haydn, Mozart and Ravel; Beethoven Middle Period Quartets (RCA). *Honours:* Grand Prix du Disque du Montreux; Best Chamber Music Recording of the Year from Stereo Review and the Gramophone; Four Grammy Nominations. *Current Management:* Kajimoto Concert Management, 8-6-25 Ginza, Chuo-ku, Tokyo, 104-0061, Japan.

**HARBISON, John (Harris);** Composer and Conductor; b. 20 Dec. 1938, Orange, New Jersey, USA. *Education:* Pupil of Walter Piston, Harvard College, BA 1960, Boris Blacher, Berlin Hochschule für Musik 1961, and Roger Sessions and Earl Kim, Princeton University, MFA 1983; Studied conducting with Eleazer de Carvalho, Berkshire Music Center, Tanglewood, Massachusetts and with Dean Dixon, Salzburg. *Career:* Teacher, Massachusetts Institute of Technology, 1969–82; Conductor, Cantata Singers and Ensemble, 1969–73, 1980–82; Composer-in-Residence, Reed College, 1968–69; Pittsburgh Symphony Orchestra 1982–84; Berkshire Music Center, 1984; New Music Adviser 1985–86, Composer-in-Residence 1986–88, Los Angeles Philharmonic Orchestra. *Compositions:* Operas: The Winter's Tale, 1974; Full Moon in March, 1977; The Great Gatsby, 1999. Ballets: Ulysses' Bow, 1984; Ulysses Raft, 1983; Orchestral: Sinfonia for violin and double orchestra, 1963; Confinement for chamber ensemble, 1965; Elegiac Songs for mezzo-soprano and chamber orchestra, 1973; Descant-Nocturne, 1976; Diotima, 1976; Piano Concerto, 1978; Snow Country for oboe and strings, 1979; Violin Concerto, 1980; Symphony No. 1, 1981; Deep Potomac Bells for 250 tubas, 1983; Remembering Gatsby, 1986; Viola Concerto, 1989; Symphony No. 2, 1987; Oboe Concerto, 1991; Symphony No. 3, 1991; 14 Fabled Folksongs for violin and marimba, 1992; Suite for cello, 1993; Flute Concerto, 1993; Cello Concerto, 1993; The Most Often Used Chords, for orchestra, 1993; Emerson, for double chorus, 1995; Four Psalms for vocal soloists, chorus and orchestra, 1999; Chamber: Serenade for 6 instruments, 1968; Piano Trio, 1969; Bermuda Triangle for amplified cello, tenor saxophone and electric organ, 1970; Die

Kurze for 5 instruments, 1970; Woodwind Quintet, 1979; Organum for Paul Fromm for chamber group, 1981; Piano Quintet, 1981; Exequien for Carlo Simmons for 7 instruments, 1982; Overture, Michael Kohlhass for brass ensemble, 1982; Variations for clarinet, violin and piano, 1982; String Quartet No. 1, 1985, No. 2, 1987, No. 3, 1993; Choral Pieces; Songs. *Recordings:* Several compositions recorded. *Honours:* Guggenheim Fellowship, 1978; Pulitzer Prize in Music, 1986; Many commissions including opera The Great Gatsby, for performance at the Metropolitan on January 1 2000. *Address:* 4037 Highway 19, De Forest, WI 53532, USA.

**HARBOTTLE, Guy;** Singer (Baritone); b. 1960, England. *Education:* Royal College of Music, London. *Career:* Appearances with Kent Opera, Wexford Festival, European Chamber Orchestra and Travelling Opera as Bizet's Escamillo and Zurga, Germont, Amonasro, Gianni Schicchi, Marcello and Belcore; Further engagements with British Youth Opera, Pavilion Opera, at Gothenburg and the Edinburgh Festival; Sang Fritz in the British premiere of Korngold's Die tote Stadt (concert) at the Queen Elizabeth Hall, 1996; Orestes in the British premiere of Oresteia by Xenakis for the English Bach Festival, Linbury Studio, Covent Garden, 2000; Britten roles include Balstrode, Sid (Albert Herring) and Tarquinius in The Rape of Lucretia. *Address:* c/o English Bach Festival, 15 South Eaton Place, London SW1W 9ER, England.

**HARDENBERGER, Håkan;** Swedish trumpeter; b. 27 Oct. 1961, Malmö. *Education:* studied with Bo Nilsson in Malmö, Royal Coll. of Music, Malmö, Paris Conservatoire with Pierre Thibaud. *Career:* prizewinner at competitions in Paris, Munich, Toulon and Geneva; extensive tours of Europe and N and S America; British debut playing the Howarth Trumpet Concerto, Crystal Palace 1984; tour of Germany with the Dresdner Baroque Soloists 1984; Bournemouth Sinfonietta with Andrew Parrott playing Hummel and Bach 1985; Harrogate and Warwick Festivals 1985, and S American tour with the Munich Bach Collegium; London Promenade Concert debut 1986, with the premiere of Array by Gordon Crosse conducted by James Loughran; premiere of Harrison Birtwistle's Endless Parade with the Collegium Musicum Zürich conducted by Paul Sacher 1987; premiere of John McCabe's Rainforest II at the Harrogate Festival 1987; concerts with the Scottish Nat. Orchestra and Neeme Jarvi, and the Northern Sinfonia with George Malcolm; other conductors with whom he has worked include Peter Eötvös, Charles Mackerras, John Pritchard, Seiji Ozawa and Rostropovich; Edinburgh Festival debut 1989, playing the Haydn Concerto with Esa-Pekka Salonen conducting the Swedish Radio Symphony; premiered Henze's Concerto in Japan 1992; season 1993–94 with S American tour, appearances at Salzburg and the London Proms, tour of Europe with the London Sinfonietta; played Michael Haydn's Concerto at St John's, London 1997; premiere of Gruber's Concerto at the London Proms 1999. *Recordings:* Concertos by Haydn, Hummel, Hertel, Stamitz and Telemann (with the Acad. of St Martin in the Fields under Neville Marriner), Birtwistle Endless Parade Concertos by Davies and Watkins, Mysteries of the Macabre, Baroque Trumpet Recital, At the Beach. *Honours:* RPO Charles Heidseele Music Award for best instrumentalist 1988, 1989. *Current Management:* KDS UK Ltd, 4 Addison Bridge Place, London, W14 8XP, England. *Telephone:* (20) 7602-3648. *Fax:* (20) 7602-3780. *Website:* www.kdschmid.de; www.hakanhardenberger.com.

**HARDING, Daniel;** British conductor; *Music Director, Mahler Chamber Orchestra;* b. 31 Aug. 1975, Oxford, England; m. Beatrice; one d. *Education:* Univ. of Cambridge. *Career:* season 1993–94 conducted The Miraculous Mandarin Suite with the City of Birmingham Symphony, followed by Schnittke's Viola Concerto with Yuri Bashmet; other CBSO repertory includes Das Lied von der Erde, The Rite of Spring and Stockhausen's Gruppen; season 1994–95 with the Rotterdam Philharmonic, London Symphony, Scottish Chamber Orchestra and BBC Philharmonic Orchestra; tour of the UK 1995 with the Birmingham Contemporary Music Group in The Soldier's Tale; further engagements with the Netherlands Wind Ensemble and the Jeunesse Musicales World Orchestra; London Proms debut 1996 (as youngest ever conductor), Prin. Conductor, Trondheim Symphony Orchestra 1997, Prin. Guest, Norköpping Symphony Orchestra; conducted Don Giovanni at Aix and Jenůfa for WNO 1998; guest conductor, Santa Cecilia Orchestra of Rome, Royal Stockholm Philharmonic, Frankfurt Radio Symphony Orchestra and the Residentie Orchestra of the Hague 1997–98; season 1998–99 conducted the London Philharmonic and Leipzig Gewandhaus Orchestras; Music Dir Deutsche Kammerphilharmonie, Bremen 2000–03; further engagements include returns to the City of Birmingham and London Symphony Orchestras, Berlin Philharmonic and the Frankfurt and Swedish Radio Orchestras; debut at the Royal Opera House with Turn of the Screw 2001; season 2001–02 with San Francisco Symphony Orchestra, Philadelphia Orchestra, Los Angeles Philharmonic Orchestra, London Symphony Orchestra, Gewandhaus Orchestra, Dresden Staatskapelle and Concertgebouw Orchestra; Wozzeck at Aix 2003; co-f. and Music Dir, Mahler Chamber Orchestra 2003–; prin. guest conductor LSO 2004, 2006–07; opened 2005–06 season with Mozart's Idomeneo at La Scala, Milan; Music Dir Swedish Radio Symphony Orchestra 2007–. *Recordings:* works by Lutoslawski with soprano Solveig Kringelborn and the Norwegian Chamber Orchestra, works by Britten with Ian Bostridge and the Britten Sinfonia 1998, The Turn of the Screw (Gramophone Opera Award 2003) 2002. *Honours:* Royal Philharmonic Soc. Best Debut award 1994, Choc de L'Année 1998, Le Monde de la Musique 1998; Chevalier, Ordre des Arts et des Lettres 2002. *Current Management:* Askonas Holt Ltd, Lonsdale Chambers, 27 Chancery Lane, London, WC2A 1PF, England. *Telephone:* (20) 7400-1700. *Fax:* (20) 7400-1799. *E-mail:* info@askonasholt.co.uk. *Website:*

www.askonasholt.co.uk. *Address:* Mahler Chamber Orchestra, Heinrich-roller-strasse 16–17, 10405 Berlin, Germany. *Website:* www.mahler -chamber.de.

**HARDY, Janet;** Singer (Dramatic Soprano); b. 1940, Atlanta, Georgia, USA. *Education:* Studied at the Mississippi Southern and Louisiana Colleges; BM in Music Education, Louisiana College; Further study with Dorothy Hulse, Dominique Modesti, Gladys Kuchta and Hilde Zadek. *Career:* Has sung in Gelsenkirchen, Kassel and Augsburg as Elektra, Ortrud, Leonore in Fidelio, the Kostelnicka in Jenůfa, Kundry, Isolde, Senta and Turandot; Guest appearances in Frankfurt, Salzburg, Copenhagen, the Berlin Staatsoper, Trieste, Leipzig, Berne, Mannheim, Toulon and Düsseldorf; Season 1988–89 with the title role in new productions of Mona Lisa by Schillings in Augsburg and Elektra in Innsbruck; Sang Elektra at the Vienna Staatsoper, June 1991; Brünnhilde in Die Walküre at Liège, the Dyer's Wife in Die Frau ohne Schatten at Augsburg, Nov 1991; Sang Elektra with Welsh National Opera, 1992; Sang with the Augsburg Opera until end of season 2000–01. *Address:* Music International, 13 Ardilaun Road, London N5 2QR, England.

**HARDY, Rosemary;** Singer (Soprano); b. 1949, England. *Education:* Studied at the Royal College of Music and at the Franz Liszt Academy, Budapest. *Career:* Performances with Roger Norrington, Michel Corboz and John Eliot Gardiner in The Baroque repertoire; Solo cantatas with the Drottningholm Baroque Ensemble, Sweden, at the Berlin Staatsoper and the Wigmore Hall; Sang in Jonathan Miller's production of Orfeo by Monteverdi; Modern repertoire includes Webern's music for voice at the Venice Biennale 1983 and the Cheltenham Festival; Webern recital at the Vienna Konzerthaus 1983; Schoenberg's 2nd Quartet (Arditti) for the Maggio Musicale, in Geneva and in London (BBC); Premieres of Jonathan Harvey's Passion and Resurrection and Song Offerings; Tours of France with Ensemble Inter-contemporain, performing Boulez, Ravel, Varèse and Kurtag (Scenes from a Novel): has also given Kurtag's Sayings of R V Troussova; Appearances at the Glyndebourne Festival in Knussen's Where the Wild Things Are and Higgelty Piggelty Pop; Concert showings with the Hallé, City of Birmingham, San Diego, Danish Radio, BBC Symphony and London Symphony Orchestras; Has sung in Henze's The English Cat for the BBC and in Frankfurt and Italy; Concert with the Schoenberg Ensemble and the Nieuw Ensemble at the Holland Festival; Pierrot Lunaire in Milan, 1991; Tour with Capricorn on the Contemporary Music Network; Has also sung in Schubert Masses with the London Philharmonic, Mozart and Handel concert for the Cambridge Festival and concerts at the Aldeburgh Festival; Knussen's Where the Wild Things Are and Higglety Pigglety Pop at the London Proms, 2002. *Recordings:* Cavalli's Ercole Amante (Erato); Monteverdi's Combattimento, Il Ballo delle Ingrate and Scherzi Musicale. *Honours:* Artijus Prize, Hungary, 1983. *Address:* Phoenix Artists Management, 6 Windmill Street, London W1P 1HF, England.

**HARE, Ian Christopher,** MA, MusB, FRCO, ADCM, ARCM; musician; *Director of Music, Crosthwaite Church, Keswick;* b. 26 Dec. 1949, Kingston upon Hull, England; m. (divorced 2002); two d. *Education:* Hymers Coll., Hull, King's Coll., Cambridge, Royal Coll. of Music. *Career:* Lecturer in Music, subsequently Organist, Lancaster Univ.; Organist and Master of Choristers Cartmel Priory 1981–89; sub-organist Carlisle Cathedral 1989–95; founded and Musical Dir Lancaster Singers 1975–89; currently Dir of Music Crosthwaite Church; directs the Keswick and Wigton Choral Socs; Chorus Master Cumbria Rural Singers; Associated Bd examiner; adjudicator for organ competitions; performed in Britain and abroad, including France, Germany, USA as organ recitalist and accompanist; played at many of the major London venues, including the Proms; mem. Incorporated Soc. of Musicians, Royal Coll. of Organists, Incorporated Asscn of Organists. *Compositions:* Thou, O God Art Praised in Sion, anthem 1973, Beethoven's Hymn to Joy, organ arrangement 1974, A Child is Born, anthem 1987, Three Dances for Organ, Except the Lord build the house, anthem for SATB and Organ. *Recordings:* Handel's Messiah, Bach Cantata 147 and motets, Britten's Missa Brevis, St Nicholas, Once in Royal David's City, Hymns for all Seasons, King's Coll. Choir Cambridge 1968–72; In Pastures Green (The Organ of Crosthwaite Church Keswick). *Current Management:* J. Audrey Ellison, International Artists' Management, 135 Stevenage Road, Fulham, London, SW6 6PB, England. *Telephone:* (20) 7381-9751 (office). *Fax:* (20) 7381-2406 (office). *E-mail:* Audrey-Ellison@Intel.freeserve.co.uk (office). *Address:* The Porch, Skiddaw Lodge, Crosthwaite Road, Keswick, Cumbria, CA12 5QA, England (home). *Telephone:* (1768) 773342. *Fax:* (1768) 773342. *E-mail:* ian .hare@btopenworld.com.

**HAREWOOD,** 7th Earl of, cr. 1812; **George Henry Hubert Lascelles,** KBE; British musical administrator; b. 7 Feb. 1923, London; s. of the late 6th Earl of Harewood and HRH Princess Mary, The Princess Royal (d. of HM King George V); m. 1st Maria Donata Stein 1949 (divorced 1967); three s.; m. 2nd Patricia Tuckwell 1967; one s. *Education:* Eton Coll. and King's Coll., Cambridge. *Career:* Capt. Grenadier Guards 1942–46; POW 1944–45; ADC to Earl of Athlone, Gov.-Gen. of Canada 1945–46; Counsellor of State during absence of the Sovereign 1947, 1954, 1956; mem. Bd Dirs Royal Opera House, Covent Garden 1951–53, 1969–72, Admin. Exec. 1953–60; Dir-Gen. Leeds Musical Festival 1958–74; Artistic Dir Edinburgh Int. Festival 1961–65; Chair. British Council Music Advisory Cttee 1956–66, Arts Council Music Panel 1966–72; Artistic Adviser New Philharmonia Orchestra, London 1966–76; Pres. English Football Asscn 1964–71, Leeds United Football Club; Chancellor, York Univ. 1963–67; mem. Gen. Advisory Council of BBC 1969–77, Gov. of BBC 1985–87; Man. Dir ENO 1972–85, Chair. 1986–95, Pres. 1995–; Man. Dir

Opera North 1978–81, Vice-Chair. 1981–; Pres. British Bd of Film Classification 1985–97; Artistic Dir Adelaide Festival for 1988; Artistic Adviser, Buxton Festival 1993–98; Ed. Opera 1950–53, Kobbé's Complete Opera Book 1954, 1976, 1987, 1997. *Publications:* The Tongs and the Bones (autobiog.) 1981, Kobbé's Illustrated Opera Book 1989, Pocket Kobbé 1994. *Honours:* Austrian Great Silver Medal of Honour 1959, Lebanese Order of the Cedar 1970; Janáček Medal 1978. *Address:* Harewood House, Leeds, Yorkshire, LS17 9LG, England (home).

**HARGAN, Alison;** Singer (Soprano); b. 1943, Yorkshire, England. *Education:* Studied piano and singing at the Royal Northern College of Music. *Career:* Debut: With Welsh National Opera, as Pamina in Die Zauberflöte; Concert performances of music by Strauss and Mahler, Four Last Songs and Resurrection Symphony, and Verdi (Requiem); Appearances include Tippett's A Child of our Time with Neville Marriner, the Fauré Requiem with the Royal Philharmonic Orchestra and Bach's B Minor Mass in Lisbon; Britten's War Requiem with the Boston Symphony Orchestra and Mahler's 8th Symphony at La Fenice, Venice, conducted by Eliahu Inbal; Has also worked with Andrew Davis, Eugen Jochum, Erich Leinsdorf, Leppard, Ozawa, Pritchard, Colin Davis, Lorin Maazel, Simon Rattle, Richard Hickox and Rozhdestvensky; Orchestras include the Vienna Philharmonic, Munich Philharmonic and Los Angeles Philharmonic, as well as leading orchestras in the United Kingdom. *Address:* c/o City of Birmingham SO, CBSO Centre, Berkeley Street, Birmingham, B1 2LF, England.

**HARGITAI, Geza;** Violinist; b. 1940, Hungary. *Education:* Studied at the Franz Liszt Academy, Budapest. *Career:* Second Violinist of the Bartók Quartet from 1985; Performances in nearly every European country and tours of Australia, Canada, Japan, New Zealand and the USA; Festival appearances at Adelaide, Ascona, Aix, Venice, Dubrovnik, Edinburgh, Helsinki, Lucerne, Menton, Prague, Vienna, Spoleto and Schwetzingen; Tour of the United Kingdom 1986 including concerts at Cheltenham, Dartington, Philharmonic Hall Liverpool, RNCM Manchester and the Wigmore Hall; Tours of the United Kingdom 1988 and 1990, featuring visits to the Sheldonian Theatre, Oxford, Wigmore Hall, Harewood House and Birmingham; Repertoire includes standard classics and Hungarian works by Bartók, Durko, Bozay, Kadosa, Soproni, Farkas, Szabo and Lang. *Recordings include:* Complete quartets of Mozart, Beethoven and Brahms; Major works of Haydn and Schubert (Hungarton); Complete quartets of Bartók (Erato). *Current Management:* Ingpen & Williams Ltd, 7 St George's Court, 131 Putney Bridge Road, London, SW15 2PA, England.

**HARGREAVES, Glenville,** BMus, GRSM, ARMCM; Singer (Baritone); b. 26 July 1950, Bradford, England. *Education:* Studied at St John's College, York, Royal Northern Coll. of Music, London Opera Centre, Liverpool Univ. *Career:* debut: title role in Il Barbiere di Siviglia 1981; Covent Garden debut in Les Contes d'Hoffmann 1982; with English National Opera from 1982, notably in Magic Flute, War and Peace, Salome; modern repertory includes The Old Man, in Purgatory by Gordon Crosse; Walworth in Wat Tyler by Alan Bush; Ullmann's Emperor of Atlantis; Mittenhofer in Henze's Elegy for Young Lovers (Queen Elizabeth Hall, London and Opéra de Lausanne); Sir Charles Keighley in John Metcalf's Tornrak (creation, 1990); appeared with Opera North as The Dark Fiddler in A Village Romeo and Juliet, Kothner in Meistersinger and roles in Tosca, The Bartered Bride and Germont (La Traviata) 2004; Welsh National Opera debut as Marcello in La Bohème, also the Guardian in Elektra, Don Pasquale 1992 and Ankarstroem 1993; debut as Falstaff with City of Birmingham Touring Opera; Don Alfonso and Music-master in Ariadne 2003 for English Touring Opera; other roles include Nick Shadow, Sharpless (Cork Opera and Paris), Tonio, Scarpia and Michele (Holland Park); concert repertory includes Elijah, Judas Maccabaeus, The Kingdom, Messiah, Sea Drift by Delius, Gerontius, Lieder eines fahrenden Gesellen by Mahler, Bach Passions, Carmina Burana; has sung with Hallé Orchestra, Nat. Orchestra of Spain, Royal Philharmonic Orchestra, RLPO, Nat. Orchestra of Argentina; frequent broadcasts; appearances at Garsington Opera: Musiklehrer in Ariadne 1993, Count Capriccio 1994, Schumann's Genovena 2000; Rigoletto for Pimlico Opera, English Touring Opera 1996, Roubaix 1997, Belfast 2004; for Grange Park Opera: Andre in Messager's Fortunio 2001, Mountararat in Iolanthe 2003; Opera Holland Park seasons: Michele in Il Tabarro 1997, Baldassare in L'Arlesiana 1998, Don Alfonso 2000, Tonio in I Pagliacci 2003; recently The Rake's Progress for Opera de Lausanne and Opera de Bordeaux 2003; for the Netherlands: Kolenaty in Macropulos Case 2001, all seven Traveller roles in Death in Venice 2002. *Recordings:* Old Man, in Purgatory. *Honours:* Hon. RAM. *Address:* c/o Musichall Ltd, Vicarage Way, Ringmer, East Sussex, BN8 5 LA, England.

**HARJANNE, Jouko;** Finnish trumpeter; *Artistic Director, Lieksa Brass Week;* b. 21 June 1962, Rauma. *Education:* Tampere Conservatory with Raimo Sarmas, studied with Henri Adelbrecht and Timofey Dokshitser. *Career:* concerto debut with Finnish Radio Symphony Orchestra 1978; co-principal trumpeter, Tampere Philharmonic Orchestra 1978–84; principal trumpet, Finnish Radio Symphony Orchestra 1984–; chamber musician with many ensembles, including Finnish Brass Ensemble, Brasstime Quartet and Protoventus Ensemble; Prof., Sibelius Acad., Helsinki 1989–; Artistic Dir, Lieksa Brass Week 1996–; has given first performances of concertos by Segerstam 1984, Gruner 1987, 1992, Linkola 1988, 1993, Wessman 1991, Bashmakov 1992, European première of Schedrin's Concerto 1995. *Recordings include:* concertos by Haydn, Hummel, Shostakovich, Jolivet, Goedicke, Harut'unyan, Vasilenko, Tamberg and Zimmermann, and works by Finnish composers. *Honours:* second prize Prague Spring Int. Competition 1987, Lieksa Brass Week Brass Player of the Year Award 1989, first place Int. Trumpet Guild Ellsworth Smith Trumpet Competition 1990. *Address:* c/o Lieksa Brass Week, Koski-Jaakonkatu 4, 81700 Lieksa, Finland (office). *Telephone:* 13 689 4147. *Fax:* 13 689 4915 (office). *E-mail:* brass.week@lieksa.fi (office). *Website:* www.joukoharjanne.com.

**HARLE, John (Crofton);** Saxophonist, Composer, Arranger and Conductor; b. 20 Sept. 1956, England; m. 1985, Julia Jane Eisner, 2 s. *Education:* Royal College of Music, Foundation School; ARCM, Hons 1978; Private study in Paris, 1981–82; FGSM 1990. *Career:* Leader of Myrha Saxophone Quartet, 1977–82; Formed duo with Pianist John Lenehan, 1979; Saxophone soloist, 1980–, with major international orchestras including, London Symphony Orchestra, English Chamber Orchestra; Basel Chamber Orchestra; San Diego Symphony Orchestra; Principal Saxophone, London Sinfonietta, 1987–; Professor of Saxophone, GSMD, 1988–; Formed Berliner Band, 1983, John Harle Band, 1988; Premiered Birtwistle's Panic at the Last Night of the London Proms, 1995; Opera Angel Magick premiered at the 1998 London Proms; World premiere of The Little Death Machine at the London Prom, 2002. *Compositions:* Several Ensembles, 1983–, including London Brass and London Symphony Orchestra; Opera, Angel Magick, London Proms, 1998; Frequent composer and soloist on television and feature films; Regular broadcaster on BBC radio; Featured in One Man and his Sax, BBC2, 1988. *Recordings:* Has made many recordings; Major works written for him by Dominic Muldowney, Ned Rorem, Richard Rodney Bennett, Luciano Berio, Michael Nyman, Gavin Bryars, Mike Westbrook and Stanley Myers. *Publications:* John Harle's Saxophone Album, 1986. *Honours:* Dannreuther Concerto Prize, Royal College of Music, 1980; GLAA Young Musician, 1979, 1980. *Website:* www.johnharle.com.

**HARNONCOURT, Nikolaus;** Austrian cellist and conductor; b. 6 Dec. 1929, Berlin, Germany; s. of Eberhard and Ladislaja Harnoncourt (née Meran); m. Alice Hoffelner 1953; three s. one d. *Education:* Matura Gymnasium, Graz, Acad. of Music, Vienna. *Career:* cellist mem. of Vienna Symphony Orchestra 1952–69; solo concerts on viola da gamba; int. debuts 1966; Prof., Mozarteum and Inst. of Musicology, Univ. of Salzburg 1972–; founder-mem., Concentus Musicus, Ensemble for Ancient Music 1954; Conductor, Zürich Opera and Amsterdam Concertgebouw Orkest; conducted Schubert's Alfonso, Vienna Festival 1997, La Perichole, Zürich 1998; Die Fledermaus, Vienna 2001; conducted Le nozze di Figaro at Salzburg 2005; has given numerous concerts in Europe, Australia and the USA. *Recordings include:* many works with Concentus Musicus, notably Handel's Messiah, Bach's Brandenburg Concertos and Cantatas, operas by Monteverdi and Rameau (Castor et Pollux), Bach's B Minor Mass, Don Giovanni 1990, Die Schöpfung with Vienna Symphony Orchestra, Idomeneo with Zürich Opera, Telemann Tafelmusik. *Publications:* Musik als Klangrede, Wege zu einem neuen Musikverständnis 1982, Der musikalische Dialog 1983. *Honours:* Hon. DMus (Edin.) 1987; shared Erasmus Prize 1980, H. G. Nägeli Medal, Zürich 1983, Kyoto Prize (arts and philosophy category, for life's work) 2005. *Address:* c/o Styriarte, Steirische Kulturveranstaltungen GmbH, Sackstraße 17, 8010 Graz (office); 38 Piaristengasse, 1080 Vienna, Austria. *Website:* www.harnoncourt.info.

**HARNOY, Ofra,** CM; Israeli/Canadian cellist; b. 31 Jan. 1965, Hadera, Israel; d. of Jacob Harnoy and Carmela Harnoy; m. Robert S. Cash. *Career:* studied with her father in Israel, William Pleeth in London, Vladimir Orloff in Toronto and in master classes with Mstislav Rostropovich, Pierre Fournier and Jacqueline du Pré; professional début, aged 10, with Boyd Neel Orchestra, Toronto; solo appearances with many maj. orchestras in the USA, Canada, Japan, Europe, Israel and Venezuela; TV appearances in Canada, the UK and other European countries, Japan and Australia; played world premiere performance Offenbach cello concerto, N American premiere Bliss cello concerto, world premiere recording of several Vivaldi cello concertos; many solo recordings. *Honours:* prizes and awards include: JUNO Award for Best Classical Soloist (Canada) 1987/88, 1988/89, 1991, 1992, 1993; First Prize Montreal symphony competition 1978, Canadian Music Competition 1979, Concert Artists Guild, New York 1982; Young Musician of the Year, Musical America magazine, USA 1983; Grand Prix du Disque; Critics' Choice, Best Records of the Year, The Gramophone, UK 1986, 1988, 1990. *Address:* PO Box 23046, 437 Spadina Road, Toronto, Ont., M5P 2W0, Canada; Suite 1000, 121 Richmond Street West, Toronto, Ont., M5H 2KA (office). *Telephone:* (416) 863-1060. *Fax:* (416) 861-0191.

**HARPER, Edward James,** BA, BMus, ARCM, LRAM; British composer; b. 17 March 1941, Taunton, Somerset; m. 1st Penelope Teece 1969 (divorced 1984); m. 2nd Dorothy C. Shanks 1984; one s. one d. *Education:* King Edward VI Grammar School, Guildford, Royal Coll. of Music and Christ Church, Oxford. *Career:* Lecturer in Music, Univ. of Edin. 1964, Sr Lecturer 1972–90, Reader 1990–; Dir New Music Group of Scotland 1973–91. *Compositions include:* Bartok Games 1972, Fanny Robin (chamber opera) 1975, Ricercari 1975, 7 Poems by E. E. Cummings 1977, Symphony 1979, Clarinet Concerto 1981, Hedda Gabler (opera) 1985, Qui creavit coelum (mass) 1986, The Mellstock Quire (opera) 1987, Homage to Thomas Hardy (orchestra, song cycle) 1990, The Lamb (soprano, chorus and orchestra) 1990, Overture for chamber orchestra 1992, And Winds, Austere and Pure (three songs for choir and piano duet) 1993, Chanson Minimale (for chamber orchestra) 1994, chamber opera based on William Golding's The Spire 1996, Psalm 150 (for unaccompanied choir) 1996, Scena (for solo cello) 1996, Trio (for clarinet, cello and piano) 1997, Souvenir for Two Pianos and Percussion 1998, Etude for Orchestra 1999,

Lochinvar Opera for Schools 2000. *Address:* 7 Morningside Park, Edinburgh, EH10 5HD, Scotland.

**HARPER, Heather,** CBE, FRCM; British singer (soprano); b. 8 May 1930, Belfast; d. of Hugh and Mary Eliza Harper; m. 2nd Eduardo J. Benarroch 1973. *Education:* Trinity Coll. of Music, London. *Career:* created soprano role in Britten's War Requiem, Coventry Cathedral 1962; toured USA with BBC Symphony Orchestra 1965, USSR 1967, soloist opening concerts at the Maltings, Snape 1967, Queen Elizabeth Hall 1967; annual concert and opera tours USA 1967–91 (retd); prin. soloist BBC Symphony Orchestra on 1982 tour of Hong Kong and Australia; prin. soloist Royal Opera House US visit 1984; also concerts in Asia, Middle East, Australia, European Music Festivals, S. America; prin. roles at Covent Garden, Bayreuth Festival, La Scala (Milan), Teatro Colón (Buenos Aires), Edinburgh Festival, Glyndebourne, Sadler's Wells, Metropolitan Opera House (New York), San Francisco, Frankfurt, Deutsche Oper (Berlin), Japan (with Royal Opera House Covent Garden Co.), Netherlands Opera House, New York City Opera; renowned performances of Arabella, Ariadne, Chrysothemis, Kaiserin, Marschallin (Richard Strauss); TV roles include Ellen Orford (Peter Grimes), Mrs. Coyle (Owen Wingrave), Ilia (Idomeneo), Donna Elvira (Don Giovanni), La Traviata, La Bohème; 25 consecutive years as prin. soloist at the Promenade concerts; Dir Singing Studies at the Britten-Pears School for Advanced Musical Studies, Aldeburgh, Suffolk 1986–; Prof. of Singing and Consultant Royal Coll. of Music, London 1985–93; First Visiting Lecturer in Residence, Royal Scottish Acad. of Music 1987–; retd from operatic stage 1986 (operatic farewell, Teatro Colón, Buenos Aires 1986), from concert stage 1991; mem. BBC Music Panel 1989, Royal Soc. of Arts 1989–. *Recordings include:* Les Illuminations (Britten), Symphony No. 8 (Mahler), Don Giovanni (Mozart), Requiem (Verdi) and Missa Solemnis (Beethoven), Seven Early Songs (Berg), Marriage of Figaro, Peter Grimes, Four Last Songs (Strauss), 14 Songs with Orchestra. *Honours:* Hon. Fellow Trinity Coll. of Music; Hon. mem. RAM; Hon. DMus (Queen's Univ.); Edison Award 1971, Grammy Award 1979, 1984, 1991. *Address:* c/o Royal Scottish Academy of Music and Drama, 100 Renfrew Street, Glasgow, G2 3DB, Scotland.

**HARPER, John Martin,** MA, PhD; *Director-General, Royal School of Church Music;* b. 11 July 1947; m. Sally Harper. *Education:* King's Coll. School, Cambridge, Clifton Coll., Bristol, Selwyn Coll., Cambridge, Birmingham Univ. *Career:* music tutor West Bromwich Arts Centre 1970–71; Dir Edington Festival 1971–78; Dir of Music St Chad's Cathedral, Birmingham 1972–78; Lecturer in Music Birmingham Univ. 1974–75, 1976–81; Asst Dir of Music King Edward's School, Birmingham 1975–76; Fellow, organist, Informator Choristarum and tutor in music, Magdalen Coll.; Univ. Lecturer, Oxford 1981–90, Univ. Coll. of North Wales, Univ. of Wales, Bangor; Prof. of Music 1991–98; RSCM Resident Prof. in Christian Music and Liturgy 1998–; Leverhulme Fellow 1997–98; Dir of Centre for Advanced Welsh Music Studies 1994–; Ed. Welsh Music History 1996–; mem. Plainsong and Medieval Music Soc. (chair. 1998–), Guild of Church Musicians, Cathedral Organists Assocn (sec. 1998–), Cathedral Music Working Party, Early English Organ Project (trustee 1999–), Panel of Monastic Musicians (adviser 1976–), General Synod Liturgical Commission (consultant 2001–). *Compositions:* Choral Compositions 1974–ed Orlando Gibbons; Consort Music 82; The Forms and Orders of Western Liturgy 1991; ed Hymns for Prayer and Praise 1996; ed RSCM Music for Common Worship Series 2000. *Recordings:* The English Anthem (five vols), Magdalen Coll. Choir (Benemerenti Papal Award 1978). *Publications:* New Grove Dictionary of Music and Musicians 1980, Frescobaldi Studies 1987, Die Musik in Geschichte und Gegenwart 1994, Blackwell History of Music in Britain Vol. 2 1995, articles and reviews in music journals and papers. *Honours:* Hon. Fellow Guild of Church Musicians 1996. *Address:* Royal School of Church Music, Cleveland Lodge, Westhumble, Dorking, Surrey RH5 6BW, England (office). *Telephone:* (1306) 872800 (office). *Fax:* (1306) 887260 (office). *E-mail:* enquiries@rscm.com (office). *Website:* www.rscm.com (office).

**HARPER, Thomas;** Singer (Tenor); b. 1950, Oklahoma, USA. *Education:* Studied in Los Angeles, Kansas City, Paris and Italy. *Career:* Sang in opera at Coburg, 1982–85, Kaiserslautern, 1985–87, in buffo and character roles; Stadttheater Hagen, 1987–, as the Duke of Mantua, Radames, Almaviva, Don Ottavio, Alwa in Lulu and Daniel in Belshazar by David Kirchner; Sang Fritz in Der Ferne Klang by Schreker, 1989; Seattle Opera, 1991 and 1995, as Mime in Der Ring des Nibelungen; Dortmund Opera, 1991–92, as Mime and in premiere of Sekunden und Jahre des Caspar Hauser, by Reinhard Febel; Sang Mime in Siegfried at Turin, 1998; Season 2000–01 as Mime for Dallas and Geneva Operas. *Recordings include:* Der Ferne Klang (Marco Polo). *Address:* c/o Seattle Opera Association, PO Box 9248, Seattle, WA 98109, USA.

**HARRELL, Lynn;** American cellist; b. 30 Jan. 1944, New York; s. of Mack Harrell and Marjorie Fulton; m. Linda Blandford 1976; one s. one d. *Education:* Juilliard School of Music, New York and Curtis Inst. of Music, Philadelphia. *Career:* principal 'cellist, Cleveland Orchestra (under George Szell) 1963–71; now appears as soloist with the world's major orchestras; Piatigorsky Prof. of Cello, Univ. of Southern California 1987–93; Prof. of Int. Cello Studies, RAM, London 1988–93, 1993–95; Artistic Dir LA Philharmonic Inst. 1988; soloist, Memorial Concert for Holocaust Victims, Vatican 1994; Music Adviser, San Diego Symphony Orchestra 1988–89. *Music:* recordings include works by J. S. Bach, Beethoven, Bloch, Boccherini, Brahms, Bruch, Debussy, Dutilleux, Dvořák, Elgar, Fauré, Haydn, Herbert, Hindemith, Lalo, Mendelssohn, Prokofiev, Rachmaninov, Rosza, Saint-Saëns, Schoenberg, Schubert, Schumann, Shostakovich, Strauss, Tchaikovsky, Villa-Lobos,

Vivaldi, Walton. *Current Management:* ICM Artists, 4–6 Soho Square, London, W1D 3PZ, England. *Telephone:* (20) 7432-0800. *Fax:* (20) 7432-0808. *E-mail:* infoUK@icmtalent.com.

**HARRHY, Eiddwen;** Singer (Soprano); b. 14 April 1949, Trowbridge, Wiltshire, England; m. Gregory Strange, 22 Jan 1988, 1 d. *Education:* Studied at the Royal Manchester College of Music and in London and Paris. *Career:* Debut: Royal Opera House, Ring Cycle, 1974; English National Opera 1975, Marriage of Figaro, Magic Flute, Carmen, Le Comte Ory; Appeared with all the major British orchestras and opera companies; Sang in Europe (Paris, Amsterdam, Berlin, Barcelona and many other venues), USA, Hong Kong, Sydney and Wellington; Vocal Tutor at Welsh College of Music and Drama, 1996–2001; Professor at Royal College of Music, London, 2001–; mem, Musicians Benevolent Fund. *Recordings:* Handel's Alcina and Amadigi, Beethoven's 9th Symphony, Fairy Queen for major record companies. *Honours:* Miriam Licette, 1972; Imperial League of Opera, RMCM, 1972. *Current Management:* Phoenix Artists Management, 6 Windmill Street, London W1P 1HF, England.

**HARRIES, Kathryn;** Singer (Soprano); b. 15 Feb. 1951, Hampton Court, Middlesex, England. *Education:* Studied at the Royal Academy of Music with Constance Shacklock. *Career:* Presented BBC television series Music Time; Festival Hall, London, debut 1977: concert repertoire ranges from Monteverdi to the 20th Century; Operatic debut with the Welsh National Opera 1982, as Leonore: returned as Sieglinde and Gutrune (also at Covent Garden, 1986), Adalgisa, and the Composer in Ariadne auf Naxos; English National Opera as Eva, Female Chorus in The Rape of Lucretia, Irene (Rienzi) and Donna Anna in The Stone Guest by Dargomyzhsky; Appearances with Scottish Opera as Leonore, the title role in the premiere of Hedda Gabler by Edward Harper, and Senta; Metropolitan Opera 1986, as Kundry in Parsifal: returned 1989, as Gutrune in a new production of Götterdämmerung; Sang Dido in the first complete performance of Les Troyens in France, Lyon 1987, Senta for Paris Opéra, Sieglinde in Nice and Paris and Leonore in Buenos Aires; Covent Garden debut 1989, in the British premiere of Un Re in Ascolto by Berio; returned 1991 as Gutrune in a new production of Götterdämmerung; Dido in Les Troyens for Scottish Opera, 1990, also at Covent Garden; season 1990–91 with Katya Kabanova at ENO, Bartók's Judith for Scottish Opera, Dukas' Ariane, Netherlands Opera, Massenet's Cléopâtre in St Etienne and Giulietta in Les Contes d'Hoffmann at the Châtelet in Paris; Season 1992 with the Berlioz Dido in Brussels and Carmen at Orange; Sang Brangaene for Scottish Opera, 1994 and 1998; Kundry in Parsifal at the Opéra Bastille, Paris, 1997; Engaged for the Kostelnicka in Jenůfa at Chicago 2000; Season 2000–01 in the premieres of Rêves d'un Marco Polo by Claude Vivier, at Amsterdam, and David Sawyer's From Morning to Midnight, for ENO. *Current Management:* Ingpen & Williams Ltd, 7 St George's Court, 131 Putney Bridge Road, London, SW15 2PA, England.

**HARRIS, Donald,** BMus, MMus; American composer and musicologist; b. 7 April 1931, St Paul, MN; m. Marilyn Hackett 1983; two s. (from previous marriage). *Education:* University of Michigan; studied with Paul Wilkinson, St Paul, Minnesota, Ross Lee Finney, University of Michigan, Nadia Boulanger, Max Deutsch and André Jolivet in Paris, France. *Career:* Administrator, New England Conservatory, 1968–77; Dean, Hartt School of Music, University of Hartford, 1980–88; Dean, College of Fine Arts, The Ohio State University, 1988–97, Prof. of Composition and Theory School of Music; Incidental Music, Poet with the Blue Guitar, Connecticut Public Radio, 1979; Incidental Music, Fires, Connecticut Public Radio, 1983. *Compositions include:* Piano Sonata; Violin Fantasy; Symphony in Two Movements; On Variations; For the Night to Wear; Balladen; Little Mermaid, opera; Two String Quartets; Ludus I; Ludus II; Of Hartford in a Purple Light (Wallace Stevens); Les Mains (Marguerite Yourcenar), Second String Quartet, Lyric Fanfare for Orchestra, Five Tempi (Ludus III). *Publications:* Co-Editor, Correspondence between Alban Berg and Arnold Schoenberg, New York. *Contributions:* Journal of the Arnold Schoenberg Institute; Perspective of New Music; Newsletter, International Alban Berg Society; Music Journal; Alban Berg Studien, Universal Edition. *Address:* 5257 Courtney Place, Columbus, OH 43235-3474, USA.

**HARRIS, Ellen,** BA, PhD; American musicologist; b. 4 Dec. 1945, Paterson, NJ. *Education:* Brown Univ., Univ. of Chicago, with Edward Lowinsky and Howard M. Brown. *Career:* Columbia Univ. 1977–80; Univ. of Chicago from 1980, Prof. 1988; Massachusetts Inst. of Technology 1989–; active as singer in the Baroque repertory; musical consultant, Santa Fe Opera 2001; Renee Fleming 2003; Fellow, American Acad. of Arts and Sciences 1998; mem., Inst. for Advanced Study 2004. *Publications:* Handel and the Pastoral Tradition 1980, Henry Purcell's Dido and Aeneas 1987, Handel as Orpheus: Voice and Desire in the Chamber Cantatas 2001; editions: Purcell, Dido and Aeneas 1987, The Librettos of Handel's Operas (ed.) 1989, G. F. Handel, Alto Cantatas 2001; articles: The Italian in Handel 1980, Handel's London Cantatas 1984, Shakespeare in Music 1985, Handel's Ghost: The Composer's Posthumous Reputation in the Eighteenth Century 1992, Harmonic Patterns in Handel's Operas 1994, Integrity and Improvisation in the Music of Handel 1990, Why Study the Arts – Along with Science and Math 1992, King Arthur's Journey into the Eighteenth Century 1995, Twentieth Century Farinelli 1997, Metastasio and Sonata Form 1999, Jaames Hunter, Handel's Friend 2000. *Honours:* ACLS Fellowship 1980–81, NEH Fellowship 1988–89, Bunting Inst. Fellowship 1995–96, American Musicological Soc. Otto Kinkeldey Award

2002. *Address:* c/o Music Department, Massachusetts Institute of Technology, Boston MS, USA. *E-mail:* eharris@mit.edu (office).

**HARRIS, Hilda;** Singer (Mezzo-soprano); b. 1930, Warrenton, North Carolina, USA. *Education:* Studied at North Carolina State University and in New York. *Career:* Sang in musicals on Broadway; Made opera debut at St Gallen, Switzerland, 1971, as Carmen; Returned to New York, 1973, as Nicklausse in Les Contes d'Hoffmann at City Opera and in Virgil Thomson's Four Saints in Three Acts (as St Theresa) at the Metropolitan; Further roles at the Met have included the Child in L'Enfant et les Sortilèges, Cherubino, Hansel, Stephano in Roméo et Juliette and parts in Lulu; Sang Nicklausse at Seattle, 1990, Cherubino at the 1990 Spoleto Festival; Frequent concert appearances. *Address:* c/o Metropolitan Opera, Lincoln Center, New York, NY 10023, USA.

**HARRIS, John;** Singer (Dramatic Tenor); b. 5 Dec. 1944, England. *Education:* Studied at the Birmingham Conservatoire. *Career:* Appearances with the Royal Opera House, Covent Garden, Welsh National Opera, English National Opera, Scottish Opera and Opera North, Glyndebourne, The Old Vic; Performances in New York, Tokyo, Tel Aviv, Milan, Paris, Munich, Dortmund, Dublin; Concert work includes Messiah and Verdi's Requiem at the Royal Albert Hall; Roles have included: Mime, Wagner's Ring Cycle; Don José, Carmen; Peter Grimes; Lensky, Eugene Onegin; Skuratov, From the House of the Dead; Tichon in Katya Kabanova; Bardolfo, Falstaff; Goro, Madama Butterfly; Laca in Jenůfa; Vitek, Makropoulos Case; Don José, Carmen; Monostatos, The Magic Flute; Florestan, Fidelio; Melot, Tristan und Isolde; The Ringmaster, The Bartered Bride; Mime in Siegfried at Covent Garden for WNO; Red Whiskers in Billy Budd; Television performances for BBC, Channel 4, HTV, RTE; BBC Radio 3. *Recordings include:* Opera recordings for EMI, Decca and Suprafon (Czech Republic). *Address:* 41 Queen's Road, Penarth, Vale of Glamorgan CF64 1 DL, Wales. *Telephone:* (0)29 20 700823.

**HARRIS, Matthew;** Composer; b. 18 Feb. 1956, North Tarrytown, New York, USA; m. 4 Dec 1988. *Education:* New England Conservatory, with Donald Martino, 1974–75; Fontainebleau School, with Nadia Boulanger, France, 1976; BM, 1978, MM, 1979, DMA, 1982, Juilliard School of Music; Harvard Graduate School, 1985–86. *Career:* Major performances: New York New Music Ensemble, 1983; Houston Symphony, 1986; Minnesota Orchestra, 1987; League/ISCM, New York, 1987; Florida Symphony Orchestra, 1988; Alea III, Boston, 1988; Assistant Professor, Fordham University, 1982–84; Instructor, Kingsborough College, City University of New York, 1985; Music Editor, Carl Fischer Inc, 1987–; mem, Broadcast Music Inc; Composers Forum; American Music Center; Board Member, League-International Society for Contemporary Music. *Compositions:* Music After Rimbaud; Songs of the Night, soprano, orchestra; Ancient Greek Melodies, orchestra; As You Choose, monodrama; Starry Night, piano trio; Invitation of the Waltz, string quartet; string Quartet No. 7. *Recordings:* Music After Rimbaud, Opus One Commissions: Casa Verde Trio, 1984; Haydn-Mozart Orchestra, 1985; Scott Stevens: Leigh Howard Stevens, marimbist, 1986; Minnesota Composers Forum: Omega String Quartet, 1988; The Schubert Club; Anthony Ross, cellist, 1988. *Address:* American Composers Edition, 170 W 74th Street, New York, NY 10023, USA.

**HARRIS, Paul,** ARAM, GRSM, ARCM, LRAM; British composer, teacher, performer and examiner and adjudicator; b. London. *Education:* Haberdashers' Aske's School, Royal Acad. of Music, Univ. of London. *Career:* mem. Incorporated Soc. of Musicians (ISM), Royal Soc. of Musicians. *Compositions:* five Buckingham Concertos, Arrows of Desire (ballet), The Meal (children's opera), the Improve your Sight Reading, Improve your Scales, Improve your Practice series. *Publications:* The Music Teachers' Companion 2000, Clarinet Basics, Malcolm Arnold – Rogue Genius 2004; contrib. to Libretto (ABRSM), ICA Magazine, The Strad, BBC Music Magazine, ISM Journal, Clarinet and Saxophone Soc. Magazine, Beckus (Malcolm Arnold Soc.). *Honours:* Hon. TCL . *Address:* 15 Mallard Drive, Buckingham, MK18 1GJ, England (home). *Telephone:* (1280) 813144 (home). *E-mail:* paulharris@dial.pipex.com (home).

**HARRIS, Ross;** Composer; b. 1 Aug. 1945, Amberley, New Zealand. *Education:* University of Canterbury, and with Douglas Lilburn at Victoria University, Wellington. *Career:* Associate Professor at Victoria University from 1989; Freelance composer, notably with electronic resources. *Compositions include:* Trio, for flute, viola and harp, 1973; To a Child, for tape, 1973; Shadow Music, 1977; Skymning, 1978; Echo, 1979; The Hills of Time, for orchestra, 1980; Incantation, soprano and tape, 1981; Life in Peace, for choir and synthesizer, 1983; Waituki, opera, 1984; Evocation, for flute, cello and synthesizer, 1985; Flüchtig, flute and tape, 1986; Kaiku, 1987; Dreams, Yellow Lions, for baritone and chamber ensemble, 1987; Mosaic (Water), 1990; Tanz der Schwäne, chamber opera, 1989; Wind Quintet, 1989; Harmonicity, 1991; Horn Call on Makara Cliff, horn and tape, 1991; 2 string quartets, 1991, 1998; 2 Chamber Concertos, 1994, 1996; Piano Trio, 1995; Sinfonietta for strings, 1996; Inharmonicity, piano and tape, 1998. *Address:* c/o Music Faculty, Victoria University, Wellington, New Zealand.

**HARRISON, Jonty;** Composer and Lecturer; b. 27 April 1952, Scunthorpe, England; m. Alison Warne 1985. *Education:* BA, DPhil, University of York, 1970–76; British Youth Symphony Orchestra, National Youth Orchestra of Great Britain; Studied composition with Bernard Rands. *Career:* National Theatre, London; Visiting Composer, University of East Anglia Recording and Electronic Music Studio, 1978; Visiting Lecturer, City University, London, 1978–80; Reader in Composition and Electro-acoustic Music, Director of

Electro-acoustic Music Studio, The University of Birmingham, 1980–; Hungarian Radio, 1982; IRCAM, 1985; Groupe de Recherches Musicales, Paris, 1986, 1993; Groupe de Musique Expérimentale de Bourges, 1987, 1995. *Compositions:* Q, 1976; Lunga, 1977; Pair/Impair, 1978; SQ, 1979; Rosaces 3, 1980; EQ, 1980; Monodies, 1981; Rosaces 4, 1982; Klang, 1982; Sons transmutants/sans transmutant, 1983; Hammer and Tongs, 1984; Paroles hérétiques, 1986; Tremulous Couplings, 1986; Farben, 1987; Aria, 1988; Concerto Caldo, 1991; . . . et ainsi de suite. . ., 1992; Ottone, 1992; Hot Air, 1995; Unsound Objects, 1995; Sorties, 1995; Hot Air, 1996; Surface Tension, 1996; Splintering, 1997; Abstracts, 1998. *Recordings:* Sons transmutants/sans transmutant (Fine Arts Brass Ensemble); Ottone (Fine Arts Brass Ensemble); Klang; EQ (Daniel Kientzy); . . .et ainsi de suite. . . EQ (Stephen Cottrell); Pair/Impair; Aria; Unsound Objects; Streams, 1999. *Publications:* Q; Sons transmutants/sans transmutant; Hammer and Tongs; Concerto Caldo; Rosaces 4; Paroles hérétiques; Paroles plus hérétiques; Tremulous Couplings; EQ; Ottone, all 1996. *Contributions:* Electro-Acoustic Music; Music and Letters; The Musical Times; Lien (Musiques et Recherches-Belgium); Upbeat to the Tate 88–Liverpool (Programme Book); The Journal of Electro-acoustic Music; Organised Sound. *Address:* 9 Prospect Road, Moseley, Birmingham B13 9TB, England.

**HARRISON, Sally;** singer (soprano); b. 1968, England. *Education:* Univ. of Oxford and Royal Northern College of Music; further study with Ava June. *Career:* sang Morgana in Alcina, Manon and Gilda in Rigoletto with Royal Northern College of Music, 1987–88; engagements with ENO: Micaëla in Carmen, Romilda in Xerxes, Despina in Così fan Tutte, Pamina in The Magic Flute, Yum-Yum in The Mikado; Maggie in Hey! Persephone with Almeida Opera; Poppaea in Agrippina at Buxton Festival; Galatea in Acis and Galatea at English Bach Festival; Yum-Yum in The Mikado at La Fenice, Venice; Musetta in La Bohème for Opera Soc. of Hong Kong; Countess Almaviva in The Marriage of Figaro with OTC, Dublin; Despina in Così fan Tutte, Musetta in La Bohème, Polly Peachum in The Threepenny Opera with Scottish Opera; Lucia in Lucia di Lammermoor with Stowe Opera; performances of music of Hans Werner Henze in Germany and UK with English Chamber Orchestra and others; further concert appearances include Baravian Radio Symphony Orchestra, Bournemouth Sinfonietta, Symphony Hall, Birmingham, Greenwich and Harrogate Festivals, Hallé Proms; Carlotta in The Phantom of the Opera Her Majesty's Theatre, London 2004–05. *Recordings include:* Mercedes in Carmen, Sultana Rose-in-Bloom in The Rose of Persia. *Honours:* Peter Moores Foundation Scholarship. *Current Management:* James Black Management, 3/26 Denmark Street, London, WC2H 8NN, England. *Telephone:* (20) 7209-0397. *E-mail:* james@jamesblackmanagement.com. *Website:* www.jamesblackmanagement.com.

**HART-DAVIS, Michael;** Singer (tenor); b. 1968, Worcester, England. *Career:* Glyndebourne Festival from 1995, as Atallo in Rossini's Ermione, Messenger in Theodora, Lamplighter in Manon Lescaut, and Thomas in The Last Supper by Birtwistle, 2001; Glyndebourne Tour as Mozart's Don Curzio, Janek in The Makropulos Case and Rossini's Comte Ory; Further appearances as Don Curzio for Netherlands Opera, Agenor in Il Re Pastore for Opera North and Rossini's Almaviva for English National Opera and Mid-Wales Opera; Chelsea Opera Group as Innkeeper in Benvenuto Cellini and Pallas in Cherevichki by Tchaikovsky; Concerts include Messiah at the Albert Hall under David Willcocks, and engagements at Verbier, Geneva, Lyon and Annecy; Season 2001–2002 as Ramiro in La Cenerentola for Opera Zürich. *Current Management:* Musicmakers International Artists Representation, Tailor House, 63–65 High Street, Whitwell, Hertfordshire SG4 8AH, England. *Telephone:* (1438) 871708. *Fax:* (1438) 871777. *E-mail:* musicmakers@compuserve.com. *Website:* www.operauk.com. *Address:* c/o Glyndebourne Festival Opera, Lewes, Sussex BN8 5UU, England. *Telephone:* 01273 812321. *Fax:* 01273 812783.

**HARTELIUS, Malin;** Singer (Soprano); b. 1961, Vaxjo, Sweden. *Education:* Studied at the Vienna Conservatory with Margaret Bence. *Career:* Debut: Vienna (Raimund-Theater) as Christel in Der Vogelhändler, 1986; Sang at Baden and St Gallen, then Ludwigsburg Festival, 1990, as Blondchen; Vienna Staatsoper from 1990, notably as Esmerelda in The Bartered Bride; Member of the Zürich Opera, 1991–92, as Papagena, Sophie and Adele; Salzburg Festival, 1992, as Barbarina in Le nozze di Figaro; Many appearances in operetta and on the concert platform; Salzburg Festival 1993 as Nausikaa in Dallapiccola's Ulisse; Zürich from 1994 as Pamina, Rossini's Elvira and Cimarosa's Elisette; Salzburg 1998 as Mozart's Blondchen; Season 2000 as Schubert's Estrella at Zürich, Dirce in Cherubini's Médée at Salzburg and Marzelline in Munich. *Address:* c/o Zürich Opera, Falkenstrasse 1, 8008 Zürich, Switzerland.

**HARTEROS, Anja;** Singer (Soprano); b. 1972, Germany. *Education:* Studied at Cologne and Perugia. *Career:* Debut: 1996; Appearances in Germany and throughout Europe as Mozart's Countess and Fiordiligi; Mimi in La Bohème; Season 1999–2000: Cardiff Singer of the World Winner's Concert at the Barbican Hall, London and Fiordiligi in Così fan tutte for Bonn Opera; Engaged as Fiordiligi for the 2001 Edinburgh Festival; Sang Agathe and Mimi, Munich and Vienna State Operas, 1999; Season 2000–01 as Fiordiligi at Frankfurt and Lyon, Mozart's Countess at Munich and Mimi for the Deutsche Oper Berlin. *Honours:* Winner, Cardiff Singer of the World Competition, 1999. *Address:* c/o Bonn Opera, Am Boeselagerhof 1, 53111 Bonn, Germany.

**HARTH, Sidney;** Violinist, Conductor and Professor; b. 5 Oct. 1929, Cleveland, Ohion, USA; m. Teresa Testa Harth. *Education:* Cleveland Institute of Music, MB, 1947; Pupil of Joseph Fuchs and Georges Enesco. *Career:* Debut, Carnegie Hall, New York, 1949; Concertmaster and Assistant Conductor, Louisville Orchestra, 1953–58; Faculty Member, University of Louisville; Concertmaster, Chicago Symphony Orchestra, 1959–62; Faculty Member, De Paul University; Concertmaster, Casals Festival Orchestra, San Juan, 1959–65, 1972; Professor of Music and Chairman of the Music Department, Carnegie-Mellon University, Pittsburgh, 1963–73; Concertmaster and Associate Conductor, Los Angeles Philharmonic Orchestra, 1973–79; Music Director, Puerto Rico Symphony Orchestra, 1977–79; Interim Conductor, New York Philharmonic Orchestra, 1980; Orchestral Director, Mannes College of Music, New York, 1981–; Professor of Violin at SUNY, Stony Brook. *Address:* c/o Mannes College of Music, 150 West 85th Street, New York, NY 10024, USA.

**HARTKE, Stephen Paul,** BA, MA, PhD; American composer; b. 6 July 1952, New Jersey; m. Lisa Stidham 1981; one s. *Education:* Yale Univ., Univ. of Pennsylvania, Univ. of California, Santa Barbara, studied composition with James Drew, George Rochberg and Edward Applebaum. *Career:* Fulbright Prof. of Composition, Univ. of São Paulo, Brazil 1984–85; Prof. of Composition, Univ. of Southern California 1987–; composer-in-residence, Los Angeles Chamber Orchestra 1988–92; mem. American Music Center. *Compositions:* Alvorada, Iglesia Abandonada, The King of the Sun, Maltese Cat Blues, Oh Them Rats is Mean in My Kitchen, Pacific Rim, Sonata Variations, Songs for an Uncertain Age, Caoine, Night Rubrics, Post-Modern Homages, Symphony No. 2, Four Madrigals on Old Portuguese Texts, Wir Küssen Ihnen Tausendmal die Hände, Violin Concerto, Wulfstan at the Millennium 1995, Concerto for violin and orchestra, The Ascent of the Equestrian in a Balloon 1995, Sons of Noah 1996, The Horse with the Lavender Eye 1997, Piano Sonata 1998, The Rose of the Winds 1998, Boule de Suif 2006. *Publications:* contrib. to Caderno de Musica 1985, Minnesota Composers Forum Newsletter 1988. *Honours:* Rome Prize 1992, American Acad. of Arts and Letters Award 1993, Chamber Music Soc. of Lincoln Center Stoeger Award 1997, Guggenheim Fellowship 1997–98. *Address:* c/o School of Music, University of Southern California, Los Angeles, CA 90089, USA.

**HARTLIEP, Nikki;** Singer (Soprano); b. 22 Sept. 1955, Naha, Okinawa, Japan. *Education:* Studied at San Francisco Conservatory. *Career:* Debut: Western Opera, San Francisco, 1982; Appearances at Chicago Opera, 1987–88, as Ellen Orford in Peter Grimes (Tatiana in Eugene Onegin, 1990); Madama Butterfly at San Francisco Opera and elsewhere, from 1989 (Dublin, 1990); Other roles include Micaela, Antonia in Les contes d'Hoffmann, Alice Ford (Long Beach Opera, 1994) and Mimi; Numerous concert engagements. *Address:* c/o Long Beach Opera, 6372 Pacific Coast Highway, Long Beach, CA 90803, USA.

**HARTMAN, Vernon,** DipA; American singer (baritone) and opera producer; b. 12 July 1952, Dallas, TX. *Education:* Southwest Texas State Univ., North Texas State Univ. *Career:* debut, Philadelphia as Masetto 1977; sang with New York City Opera from 1977 and made guest appearances at Cincinnati, San Antonio and Seattle; Spoleto Festival 1977–78, as Guglielmo; Cincinnati 1990, as Enrico in Lucia di Lammermoor; Metropolitan Opera from 1983, as Rossini's Figaro, Count Almaviva, Schaunard and Guglielmo; other roles have included Rigoletto, Malatesta, Silvio, Marcello, Frank in Die Tote Stadt and Falke in Fledermaus; sang Almaviva and Marcello at Milwaukee 1991; created title role in Boston Lyric Opera's Elmer Gantry; sang the role of Fred Moore in the world premiere of Anton Coppola's epic Sacco and Vanzetti for Opera Tampa; frmly Gen./Artistic Dir, Opera Birmingham, Artistic Adviser, Boheme Opera, NJ; guest dir for numerous companies and organizations throughout the USA; currently Prod. of Opera for Opera Tampa, Evansville Philharmonic Orchestra, Indiana, and Bardavon 1869 Opera House, Poughkeepsie; currently Exec. Prod., Nickel City Opera, Buffalo; founder and Pres., Impresario Productions LLC, opera, musical theatre and concert production co. *Address:* Impresario Productions LLC, 2582 Church Lane, Kintnersville, PA 18930, USA. *Telephone:* (267) 980-3961. *Fax:* (610) 847-7014. *Website:* www.impresarioproductions.com.

**HARTMANN, Rudolf A.;** Singer (baritone); b. 19 Jan. 1937, Bad Windsheim, Germany. *Education:* Munich Musikhochschule. *Career:* Sang at first as a bass, at Augsburg, then at Nuremberg in the baritone repertory; Member of the Zürich Opera from 1972, as Fluth in Die Lustige Weiber von Windsor, Faninal, Sharpless, Schaunard, Frank in Die Fledermaus (season 1996–97) and in the Swiss premiere of Jakob Lenz by Wolfgang Rihm; Guest engagements as Beckmesser at the Vienna and Hamburg State Operas and the Dresden Semperoper; Concert and recital engagements at Bayreuth, Florence, Salzburg, Munich and Vienna; Teacher of Voice at Zürich Conservatory and Musikhochschule. *Recordings:* Radio and CD recordings as Papageno, in the Solti Meistersinger, and the Eighth Book of Madrigals by Monteverdi, under Nikolaus Harnoncourt. *Address:* c/o Opernhaus Zürich, Falkenstrasse 1, 8008, Switzerland.

**HARTMANN, Will;** Singer (Tenor); b. 1968, Siegen, Germany. *Education:* Graduated Musikhochschule, Cologne, 1993. *Career:* Opera Studio, Cologne, 1991–93; Roles at Cologne Opera, 1993–96, included Papageno, Guglielmo, Schaunard, Morales (Carmen) and Harlequin in Ariadne auf Naxos; Hannover State Opera from 1996 as Dandini in Cenerentola, Monteverdi's Orfeo, Marcello and Rossini's Figaro; Further appearances at Munich, Bonn, Leipzig,

Rome and Orange; Royal Opera debut 1998 as Da-ud in Die Aegyptische Helena (Concert); Title role in Birtwistle's Gawain, 2000; Concerts with Sinopoli, Janowski, and Christian Thielemann; Season 2002 engaged as Stewa in Jenůfa and Tom Rakewell in The Rake's Progress in Hannover; Macduff in Macbeth at Covent Garden; Season 2003 engaged as Tamino in Die Zauberflöte at Covent Garden and Pelléas in Pelléas et Mélisande in Hannover. *Honours:* Winner, Alexander Girandi Competition, Coburg, and International Wagner Singing Competition, Strasbourg. *Address:* c/o Theateragentur Dr G. Hilbert, Maximilianstrasse 22, Munich, Germany.

**HARVEY, Jonathan Dean,** MA, PhD, DMus, FRCM, FRSCM; British composer and professor of music; *Composer in Association, BBC Scottish Symphony Orchestra*; b. 3 May 1939, Sutton Coldfield; s. of Gerald Harvey and Noelle Harvey; m. Rosaleen Marie Barry 1960; one s. one d. *Education:* St Michael's Coll., Tenbury, Repton, St John's Coll., Cambridge, Glasgow Univ., Princeton Univ. *Career:* lecturer, Southampton Univ. 1964–77; Reader, Sussex Univ. 1977–80, Prof. of Music 1980–94; Prof. of Music, Stanford Univ. 1995–2000; Visiting Prof. Imperial Coll. 1999–2002; Composer in Asscn BBC Scottish Symphony Orchestra 2004–; mem. Arts Council of England's Music Advisory Panel 1995–97, British Council's Music Advisory Panel 1993–95, Academia Europaea 1989, Acad. Cttee of RCM 1990–94. *Compositions include:* Four Quartets 1977, 1989, 1995, 2003, Mortuos plango, vivos voco (for tape) 1980, Passion and Resurrection 1981, Bhakti 1982, Gong Ring 1984, Song Offerings 1985, Madonna of Winter and Spring 1986, Lightness and Weight 1986, Tendril 1987, Time Pieces 1987, From Silence 1988, Valley of Aosta 1989, Ritual Melodies 1990, Cello Concerto 1990, Inquest of Love (opera) 1991, Serenade in Homage to Mozart 1991, Scena 1992, One Evening 1993, The Riot 1993, Missa Brevis 1995, Percussion Concerto 1996, Ashes Dance Back 1997, Wheel of Emptiness 1997, Death of Light/Light of Death 1998, Calling Across Time 1998, Tranquil Abiding 1998, White as Jasmine 1999, Mothers Shall Not Cry 2000, Bird Concerto with Pianosong 2001, The Summer Cloud's Awakening 2001, Songs of Li Po 2002, Jubilus 2003, String Trio 2004; about 20 works for choir. *Publications:* The Music of Stockhausen 1975, Music and Inspiration 1999, In Quest of Spirit 1999. *Honours:* Hon. RAM; Hon. Fellow, St John's Coll. Cambridge; Hon. Research Fellow, Royal Coll. of Music 2001–; Hon. DMus (Southampton, Bristol, Sussex); The Britten Award 1993. *Address:* c/o Faber Music, 3 Queen Square, London, WC1N 3AU, England. *Telephone:* (020) 7833-7911. *Fax:* (020) 7833-7939.

**HARVEY, Keith;** Cellist; b. 1950, England. *Education:* Studied with Douglas Cameron at Royal Academy of Music and with Gregor Piatigorsky in Los Angeles. *Career:* Formerly youngest ever principal cellist of London Philharmonic Orchestra, then principal of English Chamber Orchestra; Plays cello by Montagnana of 1733, formerly belonging to Bernard Romberg; Founder member of Gabrieli Ensemble, with chamber music performances in the United Kingdom and abroad; Co-founded the Gabrieli Quartet, 1967, and toured with them to Europe, North America, Far East and Australia; Festival engagements in the United Kingdom, including Aldeburgh, City of London and Cheltenham; Concerts every season in London, participation in Barbican Centre's Mostly Mozart Festival; Resident Artist at University of Essex, 1971–; Has co-premiered by William Alwyn, Britten, Alan Bush, Daniel Jones and Gordon Crosse, 2nd Quartets of Nicholas Maw and Panufnik (1983, 1980) and 3rd Quartet of John McCabe (1979); British premiere of the Piano Quintet by Sibelius, 1990. *Recordings include:* 50 CDs including early pieces by Britten, Dohnányi's Piano Quintet with Wolfgang Manz, Walton's Quartets and the Sibelius Quartet and Quintet, with Anthony Goldstone. *Honours:* Emmy Award for solo playing in films.

**HARVEY, Peter;** Singer (Baritone); b. 1958, England. *Education:* Choral Scholar at Magdalen College Oxford, Guildhall School of Music. *Career:* Concert appearances with the St James Baroque Players in Telemann's St Matthew Passion at Aldeburgh and London; Visit to Lisbon with The Sixteen; Concerts of Monteverdi and Purcell in Poland and the Flanders Festival with London Baroque; Sang with Joshua Rifkin and the Bach Ensemble at St James Piccadilly, 1990; Engagements with La Chapelle Royale and Collegium Vocale in Belgium, France and Spain; Bach Cantatas for French television and tour of Messiah with Le Concert Spirituel; Other repertoire includes the War Requiem, Elijah and the Five Mystical Songs of Vaughan Williams; St John in The Cry of the Ikon by John Tavener (also televised); Bach's St John Passion (Westminster Abbey) and Christmas Oratorio; Schubert's E flat Mass; Visited Brazil 1989 with The Sixteen for Messiah; Belgium 1991 in Teixeira's Te Deum, conducted by Harry Christophers; Sang with Les Talens Lyriques at Versailles Baroque Days in Mondonville's Les Fêtes de Paphos, 1996. *Recordings:* Dido and Aeneas (with CPE Bach with La Chapelle Royale (Virgin Classics); Gilles Requiem with Le Concert Spirituel. *Honours:* Walther Gruner International Lieder Competition, 2nd Prizewinner; Nonie Morton Award (leading to Wigmore Hall debut). *E-mail:* enquire@peterharvey .info.

**HARVEY, Richard (Allen);** Composer and Performer; b. 25 Sept. 1953, London, England. *Education:* Associate, Royal College of Music, 1971. *Career:* Debut: Conductor, London Symphony Orchestra, Barbican Centre, 1985; Recorder/Woodwind Player; Conductor and Composer; Founder, London Vivaldi Orchestra; Guest Conductor, Royal Philharmonic and London Symphony Orchestras; Toured with guitarist John Williams, 1984–; Conductor and Performer with English Chamber Orchestra, Barbican Centre, London, 1987. *Compositions:* Concerto Antico for guitar and orchestra; Reflections on A Changing Landscape, viola concerto; Plague and the

Moonflower, eco-oratorio; A Time of Miracles, children's opera; Compositions for films and television include Game, Set and Match, G.B.H, Jake's Progress and Defence of the Realm. *Recordings:* Italian Recorder Concertos; The Genteel Companion; Brass at La Sauve-Majeure; Four Concertos for Violins and Recorder; GBH soundtrack; Jake's Progress soundtrack. *Current Management:* Ian Amos, Tyringham House, Spring House, Brightlingsea, Essex, CO7 0PJ, England.

**HARWOOD, Richard;** English cellist; b. 8 Aug. 1979, Portsmouth. *Education:* Royal Northern Coll. of Music, Manchester with Prof. Ralph Kirshbaum; cello with Joan Dickson, Steven Doane, David Waterman, Heinrich Schiff; piano with Diana Bell and Joyce Rathbone. *Career:* debut, Kabalevsky op49 in G minor at Adrian Boult Hall, Birmingham 1990; Purcell Room debut with Julius Drake 1999; performed concerti in Royal Albert Hall, Queen Elizabeth Hall, St John's Smith Square and St George's Brandon Hill; collaborated with conductors, including David Parry, En Shao, and Yehudi Menuhin; soloist with numerous orchestras, including Bournemouth Symphony Orchestra and Philharmonia; toured New Zealand with Elgar Concerto 1993; recital performances include Schoenbrunn Palace Theatre, Vienna 1997, Wigmore Hall Recital debut 1998, Purcell Room debut 1999. *Recordings:* Elgar Concerto (BBC Radio 3) 1993, Tchaikovsky's Variations on a Rococo Theme (BBC Radio 3). *Honours:* Audi Junior Musician (youngest ever winner) 1992, Pierre Fournier Award for cellists 2004, numerous scholarships winner Pierre Fournier Award 2004, Bachpreisträger XIV Internationaler Johann-Sebastian-Bach-Wettbewerb, Leipzig 2004. *Current Management:* c/o Libby Sutton, Hazard Chase, 25 City Road, Cambridge, CB1 1DP, England. *Telephone:* (1223) 312400 (office). *Fax:* (1223) 460827 (office). *E-mail:* libby .sutton@hazardchase.co.uk (office). *Website:* www.hazardchase.co.uk (office); www.richardharwood.com

**HASELBÖCK, Martin;** Organist and Conductor; b. 23 Nov. 1954, Vienna, Austria. *Education:* Studied at the Musikhochschule, Vienna, and with Jean Langlais and Daniel Roth in Paris. *Career:* Debut: Konzerthaus, Vienna, 1973; Organist at Augustinekurche, Vienna, 1976; Vienna Hofkapelle, 1977; Solo appearances with leading orchestras in Berlin, Vienna and elsewhere in Europe; Premieres of organ concertos by Ernst Krenek Cristobàl Halffter and William Albright; Professor of Organ at the Lubeck Musikhochschule, 1986–2003; Vienna Music Univ., 2003–; Founded the Wiener Akademie 1985, giving many performances of Baroque and early Classical music; Guest Conductor with the Vienna Symphony, Philadelphia, Los Angeles, Pittsburgh Orchestra and many other orchestras; Opera engagements in Prague (Mozart Festival) and Zürich. *Recordings include:* Works by Haydn, Mozart, Bach, Biber and Telemann, with the Wiener Akademie; Complete organ works of Bach, Schoenberg and Liszt. *Honours:* Winner, Vienna-Melk International Organ Competition, 1992; Deutscher Schallplattenpreis, Ehrenkreuz für Wissenschaft und Kunst, Vienna, 1997; Hon. doctorate, Luther College, Iowa, USA, 2003. *Address:* c/o Universität für Musik, 1030 Vienna, Germany. *E-mail:* haselboeck@chello.at.

**HASHIMOTO, Eiji;** Harpsichordist; b. 7 Aug. 1931, Tokyo, Japan; m. Ruth Anne Laves, 8 June 1963, 1 s., 2 d. *Education:* BM in Organ, 1954, Graduate Diploma in Organ, 1955, Tokyo University of Fine Arts; MA in Composition, University of Chicago, 1959; MM, Harpsichord, Yale University School of Music, 1962. *Career:* Harpsichord Instructor at Toho Gakuen School of Music, Tokyo, 1966; Assistant Prof. of Harpsichord and Artist-in-Residence, 1968–72, Assoc. Prof. of Harpsichord and Artist in Residence, 1972–77, Prof. of Harpsichord and Artist in Residence, 1977–2001, Prof. Emeritus of Harpsichord, 2001–, Univ. of Cincinnati College Conservatory of Music; Concerts: recitals and or solo appearances in Australia, Austria, Belgium, Brazil, Canada, Chile, China, England, Finland, France, Germany, Netherlands, Iran, Italy, Japan, Luxembourg, Mexico, New Zealand, Philippines, Spain, Switzerland, USA and Venezuela. *Recordings:* 18 recordings (including 8 CDs) of solo, solo with orchestra, conducting and ensemble performances. *Publications:* Editions: D Scarlatti, 100 Sonatas, in 3 vols, 1975 and 1988; C P E Bach, Sonatas in 3 vols, 1984, 1988; J B Loeillet, Pièces pour Clavecin, 1985; D Scarlatti, 90 Sonatas in 3 vols, 1999–. *Honours:* Prize of Excellence, Japanese Ministry of Cultural Affairs, 1978, 1982; Rockefeller Foundation Bellagio Residency Grant, 1998; Distinguished Research Professorship, Univ. of Cincinnati, 1998. *Address:* 4579 English Creek Drive, Cincinnati, OH 45245, USA. *E-mail:* eiji.hashimoto@uc.edu. *Website:* www.eijihashimoto .com.

**HASKIN, Howard;** singer (tenor); b. 1958, Kansas City, USA. *Education:* studied at Bloomington, Illinois and Zürich. *Career:* sang Monostatos in Die Zauberflöte at Orange, 1981; Wexford Festival, 1982, in Griselidis by Massenet, and Opera North, 1983, as Ramphis in Aida; Kent Opera from 1984, as Paris in King Priam, Don José and Peter Grimes; Buxton Festival, 1984, as Jason in Cherubini's Médée; Amsterdam, 1989, as Dimitri in Boris Godunov and 1992 in the premiere of Schnittke's Life with an Idiot; Glyndebourne, 1990–91, as Monostatos, and Covent Garden, 1992, as Robbin in Porgy and Bess. *Current Management:* Stafford Law, Candleway, Broad Street, Sutton Valence, Kent ME17 3AT, England. *Website:* www.stafford-law .com.

**HASSAN, Ustad Mehdi;** Pakistani singer; b. 1927, Luna, Rajasthan, India; s. of Azeem Khan. *Education:* studied with his father, Azeem Khan and uncle, Ismail Khan. *Career:* singer in a range of styles, including Ghazal, Dhrupad, Khayal, Thumri and Dadra; classical singer on Radio Karachi 1952–55;

playback singer for films early 1960s–late 1980s; tours worldwide. *Recordings:* numerous albums of classical, popular and film music. *Honours:* Pride of Performance medal (Govt of Pakistan) 1985, Pakistan Broadcasting Corpn lifetime achievement award. *Address:* c/o Sony Music Entertainment India Pvt Ltd, Span Centre, South Avenue, Santacruz (w), Mumbai 400054, India. *Website:* www.sonymusic.co.in.

**HASSON, Maurice;** French/Venezuelan violinist; b. 6 July 1934, Berck-Plage; m. Jane Hoogesteijn, 1969; one s. three d. *Education:* Conservatoire Nat. Supérieur de Musique, Paris, further studies with Henryk Szeryng. *Career:* Prof., RAM, London 1986; concert artist in major concert halls throughout world, also in TV and radio performances. *Recordings include:* Concerto No. 1 (Paganini), Concerto No. 2 (Prokofiev), Debussy Sonatas, Fauré Sonatas, Concerto No. 1, Scottish Fantasy (Bruch), Concerto for 2 and 4 violins (Vivaldi), Double Concerto (Bach), Concerto (Brahms), Brilliant Showpieces for the Violin, Tzigane (Ravel), Rondo Capriccioso (Saint Saëns), Poème (Chausson), Gypsy Airs (Sarasate), Violin Concerto (Castellanos-Yumar), Sonata (Franck), virtuoso pieces. *Honours:* Hon. mem. RAM; Orden Andrés Bello; Orden Tulio Febres Cordero (Venezuela); First Prize Violin, Prix d'honneur and First Prize Chamber Music, Conservatoire Nat. Supérieure de Musique, Paris 1950, Int. Prize Long Thibaut 1951, Int. Prize Youth Festival, Warsaw 1955, Grand Prix Musique de Chambre 1957, Médaille de Vermeil de la Ville de Paris. *Address:* 18 West Heath Court, North End Road, London, NW11 7RE, England (home). *Telephone:* (20) 8458-3647 (home). *Fax:* (20) 8455-8317 (home). *E-mail:* jdehasson@btinternet.com (home).

**HASTINGS, Baird;** Musician, Writer and Educator; b. 14 May 1919, New York City, USA; m. Louise (Lily) Laurent, 22 Dec 1945, deceased 7 Mar 1997. *Education:* AB, Harvard College, 1939; Diploma, Paris Conservatory, 1946; Diploma, Tanglewood, 1957; Diploma, Mozarteum, Salzburg, 1961; MA, Queens College, 1966; PhD, Sussex College, 1976. *Career:* Conductor, Mozart Chamber Players, 1957–60; Conductor, Mozart Festival Orchestra, 1960–; Music Adviser, Eglevsky Ballet, 1961–78; Lecturer in Music, Conductor of Band and Orchestra, Trinity College, 1965–70; Administrator, Juilliard School of Music, New York City, 1972–85; Music Adviser, School of American Ballet, New York City, 1973–85; Music Director, Westport Point, Massachusetts, Summer Episcopal Church, 1974–92; Guest Conductor, American Symphony; Consultant, Royal Academy of Music, London; Panelist, Hofstra Mozart Conference, New York; mem, The Bohemians; Musicians Union; American Musicological Society. *Compositions:* Arranger of Music by Mozart, Wagner, Thomson and others including re-orchestration Act IV, La Vie Parisienne, Offenbach, 1984. *Recordings:* Music for Strings; Mozart Concerto No. 27 for piano and orchestra, with Beveridge Webster; Michael Haydn Symphony; Other Mozart works. *Publications include:* Berard, 1950; Sonata Form in Classic Orchestra, 1966; Treasury of Librettos, 1969; Don Quixote by Minkus, 1975; Choreographers and Composers, 1983; Mozart Research Guide, 1989. *Contributions:* American Record Guide; Carnegie Hall programmes; Alice Tully Hall programmes; Prose of Distinction to Ballet Review; Juilliard Journal; Guide to Thamos by Mozart, Conductor's Journal. *Honours:* Fulbright Fellowship, 1949–50, Tanglewood, 1957. *Address:* 33 Greenwich Avenue, New York, NY 10014, USA.

**HATRIK, Juraj;** Composer; b. 1 May 1941, Orkucany, Presov, Czechoslovakia; m. 17 April 1965, 2 s. *Education:* Academy of Music and Dramatic Arts, Bratislava. *Career:* Debut: Sinfonietta, 1963; Musical Education, Aesthetics and Psychology of Music, Academy of Music; Professor of Composition, Academy of Music and Dramatic Arts, Bratislava, 1997–; mem, Slovak Roma Club. *Compositions include:* Double Portrait for Orchestra, 1971; Da Capo al Fine for Orchestra, 1976; Diary of Tanja Savitchova for brass quintet and Soprano, 1976, television version 1983; Happy Prince, opera after Oscar Wilde, 1978; Sans Souci, 1st symphony, 1979; Vox Memoriae, cycle for 4 instruments, 1983; Canzona for organ, alto and viola, [after John Roberts], after R Tagore, 1984; Submerged Music for soprano and strings, 1985; Moment Music avec J. S. Bach for soprano and chamber group, 1985; Victor, 2nd symphony, 1988; Compositions for children, choirs and 4 monologues for accordion; Adam's Children, chamber opera after Slovak national proverbs and bywords, 1991; Diptych for violin, cello and piano, 1989; The Lost Children for string quartet with basso solo after Gregory Orr, 1993; The Brave Tin Soldier, musical by Hans Andersen, 1994; An die Musik, sonata-depèche for Schubert for clarinet, violin, cello and piano, 1995–96; Requiem for Iris, for actress and chamber ensemble, 1998; Skatingring 1951, 1998; Liebe, Sinn und Not, sonata for contrabasso and piano (in memoriam R M Rilke), 1999; Litany of While (after Arthur Lundkvist, symphonic poem for large orchestra), 2001; Ecce quod Natura, phantasy for piano and orchestra, 2002; Eeee quod Natura..., concerto for piano and orchestra, 2002. *Publications:* Jewel of Music: Pedagogical texts about music, 1997. *Contributions:* Slovak Music; Musical Life. *Honours:* Premio di città Castelfidardo (Composition for Accordion Solo), 1993. *Current Management:* Academy of Music and Dramatic Arts, Bratislava, music analysis and composition. *Address:* Dubnická 2, 85102 Bratislava, Slovakia. *E-mail:* hatrik@vsmw.sk.

**HATTORI, Joji;** Concert Violinist and Conductor; b. 1969, Japan. *Education:* Studied in Vienna with Rainer Küchl; Further lessons with Lord Menuhin and Vladimir Spivakov. *Career:* Concert engagements throughout Europe; British debut with the Royal Philharmonic Orchestra; Concerts with Yehudi Menuhin at the Festival Hall and with Vienna Chamber Orchestra at the Vienna Konzerthaus; Appearances with the English Chamber Orchestra, the BBC National Orchestra of Wales and the Scottish Chamber Orchestra,

London Mozart Players, Israel and Zürich Chamber Orchestras, Orchestre de la Suisse Romande, Munich Radio Symphony and most major Japanese orchestras including New Japan Philharmonic under Seiji Ozawa; Wigmore Hall, London, debut 1996, with pianist Bruno Canino; Plays a Guarneri del Gesu violin (Hämmerle 1733); Music Director of Tokyo Ensemble; Visiting Professor at Royal Academy of Music, London; Associate Conductor of Vienna Chamber Orchestra; Artistic Director of the Genius of the Violin Festival and the Menuhin International Violin Competition. *Recordings:* Bach Violin Concertos with the Scottish Chamber Orchestra, 1997; Kreisler with Joseph Seiger, 1998; Mozart Violin Concertos with London Mozart Players, 2001. *Honours:* Hon. RAM; Winner of a Carnegie Hall conducting debut and Lincoln Maazel Fellowship at the Maazel-Vilar Conducting Competition, 2002; Winner, Young Musician of the Year in Japan, 1992; Menuhin International Violin Competition, Folkestone, 1989. *Address:* 72 Leopold Road, London SW19 7JQ, England. *E-mail:* hatoff@attglobal.net. *Website:* www.jojihattori.com.

**HATZIANO, Markella;** Singer (Mezzo-soprano); b. 1960, Athens, Greece. *Education:* Studied with Gogo Georgilopoulu at the Athens National Conservatory and Tito Gobbi in Rome. *Career:* Sang Eboli in Don Carlos with the National Opera of Greece and made her US debut, as Azucena at Boston, in 1987; Returned to Boston as Suzuki, Amneris, Neris in Cherubini's Médée and in Verdi's Requiem; French repertory includes Carmen (Mexico 1992, under Enrique Batiz), Massenet's Charlotte (Malaga, 1993) and Marguerite in La Damnation de Faust (Trieste, 1993); Sang Dido in Les Troyens with the London Symphony Orchestra at the Barbican Hall, under Colin Davis, 1993; Further appearances as Judith in Bluebeard's Castle at the Salzburg Festival, Dido at La Scala, 1996, Amneris at Florence, under Zubin Mehta; Sang Dalila and Amneris at Covent Garden, 1996; Concert repertory includes Mahler's Das Lied von der Erde, Kindertotenlieder and 2nd and 3rd Symphonies; Season 1996–97 concerts with the New York Philharmonic, Chicago Symphony Orchestra, Los Angeles Philharmonic and the Orchestre de la Suisse Romande; Debut with the London Symphony in Schoenberg's Erwartung, 1997; Season 2000–01 with Giovanna Seymour in Anna Bolena at Athens and the Verdi Requiem for the Granada Festival. *Recordings include:* Verdi Requiem, with the London Symphony Orchestra under Richard Hickox. *Honours:* Winner, Tito Gobbi International Competition, 1983; American-Israel Competition, 1987. *Address:* c/o Steven Larson, PO Box 575, Creighton, Nebraska 68729, USA.

**HAUBOLD, Ingrid;** Singer (Soprano); b. 1943, Berlin, Germany; m. Heikki Toivannen. *Education:* Studied in Detmold and at the Munich Musikhochschule with Annelies Kupper. *Career:* Sang at the Munich Theater am Gärtnerplatz, 1965–66; Detmold Landestheater 1970–72, Bielefeld 1972, Lubeck from 1979; Guest engagements at Hanover (from 1981) and Karlsruhe (1981–84); Sang Isolde at Madrid 1986, Turin and Berlin 1988, Lucerne Festival 1989, Kassel 1992; Has also appeared at the Teatro Massimo Palermo, Teatro Comunale Bologna, the Vienna Staatsoper, Schwetzingen Festival (Ariadne, 1989) and the Metropolitan Opera, 1990–91; Other roles include Senta (Savonlinna Festival 1990), Pamina, Wagner's Elsa, Elisabeth, Brünnhilde (Wiesbaden, 1996), Gutrune, Eva, Freia, Sieglinde, Irene (Rienzi) and Ada (Die Feen); Leonore, Strauss's Chrysothemis and Marschallin, Janáček's Jenůfa and Katya Kabanova; Many concert appearances. *Address:* c/o Deutsche Oper Berlin, Richard Wagnerstrasse 10, Berlin, Germany.

**HAUDEBOURG, Brigitte;** French harpsichordist, pianofortist and teacher; b. 5 Dec. 1942, Paris; m. Paul Cousseran; one s. one d. *Education:* studied piano with Marguérite Long and Jean Doyen, masterclass with R. Veyron-Lacroix. *Career:* debut in Paris; Many television and radio appearances in France, USA, Canada, Europe, Russia, Tunisia, Hong Kong, Bangkok, Tahiti; Artistic Director of a French baroque festival in Tarentaise. *Recordings:* 70 Albums and CDs, including Daquin, Dandrieu, 2 albums of suites; Devienne, for flute and harpsichord; Chevalier de St Georges, for violin and harpsichord; Jean Pierre Baur, for harp and harpsichord; W F Bach, 2 albums, No. 1, 3, 4, 5; CDs include, Louis Couperin, for harpsichord; Josse Boutmy for harpsichord, world premiere; Padre Antonio Soler; J Schobert for pianoforte; J A Benda for pianoforte; E N Mehul for pianoforte; J G Eckardt for pianoforte; L Kozeluh for pianoforte; Boutmy for harpsichord. *Publications include:* 2nd book of Josse Boutmy, (harpsichord). *Address:* 10 Avenue F. Roosevelt, 92150 Suresnes, France.

**HAUG, Halvor;** Composer; b. 20 Feb. 1952, Trondheim, Norway. *Education:* Degree, School Music Teacher, Conservatory of Music, Veitvet, Oslo, 1970–73; Sibelius Academy, Helsinki, 1973–74; Studies with Kolbjörn Ofstad, Oslo, 1974–75, London, 1978. *Career:* Performances in Norway and abroad with major musicians and orchestras; numerous radio and television performances in Norway and overseas; mem, Society of Norwegian Composers. *Compositions include:* Orchestra: 3 Symphonies, 1981–82, 1984, 1991–93; Symphonic Picture, 1976; Silence for Strings, 1977; Poema Patetica and Poema Sonora, 1980; Song of the Pines, 1987; Insignia, 1993; Glem aldri henne, song cycle for mezzo-soprano and orchestra, 1997; Il Preludio dell'Ignoto, 2000; Chamber: Brass Quintet, 1981; 2 String Quartets, 1985, 1996; Piano Trio, 1995. *Recordings include:* Symphony No. 1; Silence for Strings; Sinfonietta with the London Symphony Orchestra and Dreier; Symphonic Picture and Poema Patetica, with the London Philharmonic Orchestra and Dreier; Symphony No. 2, with Norwegian Youth Symphony Orchestra and Andersen; Symphony No. 3; Insignia; Song of the Pines; Silence for Strings, with Norrköping Symphony Orchestra, English Chamber Orchestra and Ruud. *Current Management:*

Warner Chappell Music Norway A/S. *Address:* c/o PO Box 4523 Torshov, 0404 Oslo, Norway.

**HAUNSTEIN, Rolf;** Singer (Baritone); b. 18 Jan. 1943, Dresden, Germany. *Education:* Studied with Johannes Kemter in Dresden and Kurt Rehm in Berlin. *Career:* Sang in Bautzen, Freiberg and Cottbus, before engagement at the Dresden Staatsoper, 1971; Roles have included Germont, Posa, Ford, Scarpia, Beckmesser, Rigoletto, Pizarro, Klingsor, Telramund, Onegin and Wagner's Dutchman; Guest engagements at Leipzig, the Komische Oper Berlin, Kiel, Wiesbaden and Strasbourg; Member of the Zürich Opera from 1991; Season 1996–97, Telramund, the Minister in Fidelio and Dikoj in Katya Kabanova; Sang Kdenatý in The Makropulos Case, Toulouse, 1998; Sang the Animal Trainer and Athlete in Lulu at Zürich, 2000; Conductors have included Harnoncourt, Dohnànyi, Masur and Suitner and opera producers such as Ruth Berghaus, Robert Wilson, Joachim Herz and Harry Kupfer, 1976. *Address:* c/o Opernhaus Zürich, Falkenstrasse 1, 8008 Zürich, Switzerland.

**HAUPTMANN, Cornelius;** Singer (Bass); b. 1951, Stuttgart, Germany. *Education:* Graduated Stuttgart Musikhochschule 1982; Berne Conservatoire with Jakob St ämpfli; Further study with Dietrich Fischer-Dieskau in Berlin and masterclasses in Salzburg with Eric Tappy and Elisabeth Schwarzkopf. *Career:* Sang at Stuttgart from 1981, notably as Masetto; Heidelberg Opera 1985–87, as King Philip in Don Carlos and Osmin; Stadttheater Karlsruhe from 1987, as Sparafucile (Rigoletto), Plutone (Orfeo), Sarastro and Mozart's Figaro; Festival appearances at Lucerne, Salzburg, Singapore, Sapporo, Schwetzingen (1983 premiere of Henze's The English Cat) and Ludwigsburg (recital 1991); Further engagements in Munich, Paris, Berlin, Leipzig, Orleans, London, Lyon and Amsterdam (Publio and Sarastro in concert performances of La Clemenza di Tito and Die Zauberflöte, 1990); Sang Sarastro at Ludwigsburg, 1992; Conductors include John Eliot Gardiner, Hogwood, Janowski, Tilson Thomas, Masur, Barenboim, Maazel, Lothar Zagrosek, Roger Norrington, Neville Marriner, Pierre Boulez, Philippe Herreweghe; Concert performances include the St Matthew Passion (Gardiner) and Mozart's Requiem (Bernstein) in 1988; Frequent Lieder recitals, and other concerts under Nikolaus Harnoncourt, Trevor Pinnock, Helmut Rilling and Gary Bertini; Sang Rocco in a concert performance of Fidelio at Lyon, 1996; Gave masterclasses in Wales, Japan and England (Britten-Pears School of Advanced Music Studies, Aldeburgh). *Recordings:* Bach St John and St Matthew Passion, Mozart C minor Mass, Idomeneo, La Clemenza di Tito, and Die Entführung, with Gardiner and Mozart Requiem and C minor Mass (Bernstein) for Deutsche Grammophon; Beethoven: Missa Solemnis (Herreweghe); Schoenberg's Jakobsleiter (Inbal); Haydn Stabat Mater, with Pinnock (DG) and Die Zauberflöte with Norrington; Enescu Oedipe with Foster (EMI); Akhnaten by Philip Glass (CBS); Lieder by Loewe, Mozart, Schubert, Mendelssohn, Monteverdi; Schütz with Frieder Bernius. *Current Management:* IMG Artists, 54 avenue Marceau, 75008 Paris, France. *Address:* Waldburgstr 121, 70563 Stuttgart, Germany.

**HAUSCHILD, Wolf-Dieter;** Conductor; b. 6 Sept. 1937, Greiz, Germany. *Education:* Studied at Franz Liszt Musikhochschule, Weimar, with Ottmar Gerster and Hermann Abendroth; Further study with Hermann Scherchen and Sergiu Celibidache. *Career:* Conductor of the Deutsche National Theater Weiners and from 1963 Chief Conductor of the Kleist Theatre at Frankfurt Oder (also of Frankfurt Philharmonic); Chorus Master for RDA Radio, 1971–74; joint conductor of Berlin Radio Symphony Orchestra, 1974–78; Chief Conductor of the Symphony Orchestra of Radio Leipzig, 1978–85; Professor of Conducting at the Musikhochschule of Berlin and Leipzig from 1981; Guest Conductor of Berlin Symphony Orchestra; Chief Conductor of Stuttgart Philharmonic Orchestra, 1985–91; Professor of Conducting at Karlsruhe Musikhochschule, 1988; Artistic Director and Chief Conductor at Essen Opera, 1991–98 (1806 Version of Fidelio, 1998); Guest appearances at Berlin Staatsoper and Komische Opera and the Semper-Oper Dresden; Conducted a new production of Tristan und Isolde at Essen, 1992. *Address:* c/o Theater und Philharmonie, Rolandstrasse 10, 45128 Essen, Germany.

**HAUSER, Alexis;** Music Director; b. 1947, Vienna, Austria. *Education:* Student at the Conservatory and the Academy of Music and Performing Arts in Vienna; Graduated summa cum laude in the masterclass of Professor Hans Swarowsky; Also studied with Franco Ferrara in Italy and Herbert von Karajan, Salzburg, Mozarteum. *Career:* Debut: With Vienna Symphony, 1973; Several concerts and broadcasts with Vienna Symphony; Invitations to conduct many other European orchestras including the Berlin RIAS Symphony, Belgrade Philharmonic and the Vienna Chamber Orchestra; Invited by Seiji Ozawa to spend summer of 1974 in Tanglewood; USA Debut with New York City Opera, 1975; Conducted Atlanta Symphony with Itzhak Perlman as soloist, 1975; Subsequently conducted with Symphonies of San Francisco, Minnesota, Seattle, Kansas City (with Maureen Forrester as soloist) and the Rochester Philharmonic; Music Director, Orchestra London Canada, 1981–; Led orchestra on its first European tour to the Festival Internationale dell Aquila in Italy; Directed Conductors' Seminar at the Royal Conservatory of Music in Toronto; Conducted the Toronto, Winnipeg and Kansas City Symphonies; Appeared at Chicago's Grant Park Festival. *Honours:* Winner of several conducting awards in Austria including 1st International Hans Swarowsky Conducting Competition in Vienna; Awarded Koussevitzky Conducting Prize at Tanglewood, 1974; In 1984 Orchestra London Canada received the Award of Merit presented by the Canadian Performing Right Organization.

**HAUTZIG, Walter;** Concert Pianist; b. 28 Sept. 1921, Vienna, Austria; m. Esther Rudomin, 10 Sept 1950, 1 s., 1 d. *Education:* State Academy of Vienna; Jerusalem Conservatory; Curtis Institute, Philadelphia; Principal Teacher, Mieczyslaw Munz; Private Study with Artur Schnabel. *Career:* Debut: Town Hall, New York, 31 Oct 1943; Recitals and Orchestral Appearances in over 50 Countries; Soloist with Berlin Philharmonic, Orchestra National Belgique, Oslo, Stockholm, Copenhagen, Helsinki, Zürich, New York, Baltimore, St Louis, Buffalo, Vancouver, Honolulu, Tokyo, Sydney, Melbourne, Auckland, Wellington, Mexico, Bogota, Jerusalem and Tel-Aviv; Played for BBC, Australian, New Zealand, Japanese, USA and Canadian Radio; Professor of Piano, Peabody Conservatory of the Johns Hopkins University, Baltimore, USA, 1960–87. *Recordings:* Numerous for labels, including Americus, Connoisseur Society, RCA, Vox Records. *Publications:* Playing Around–A Pianist Remembers, 1996. *Contributions:* Musical America; American Record Guide.

**HAVERINEN, Margareta;** Singer (soprano); b. 1951, Finland. *Education:* Studied with Pierre Bernac in Paris, Anita Välkki in Helsinki, Gladys Kuchta in Düsseldorf and Vera Rozsa in London. *Career:* After winning the 1978 Geneva International Competition sang in opera at Helsinki and Oslo as Gilda, Violetta, Tosca and Donna Anna; Welsh National Opera, 1988, and Dublin, 1992, as Tosca; London, 1992, in the British premiere of Sibelius's opera The Maiden in the Tower; Savonlinna Festival, 1994, as Judith in Bluebeard's Castle; Many concerts and Lieder recitals in Europe and the USA (Carnegie Hall, New York, and the Westminster Artsong Festival in Princeton). *Address:* c/o Dublin Grand Opera Society, John Player Theatre, 276–288 Circular Road, Dublin 8, Republic of Ireland.

**HAVLAK, Lubomir;** Violinist; b. 27 Feb. 1958, Prague, Czechoslovakia; m. Jarmila Havlakova, 26 Aug 1983, 1 s., 1 d. *Education:* Conservatoire in Prague; Academy of Music in Prague; Masterclasses: Nathan Milstein in Zürich; Masterclasses with leading ensembles: Tel-Aviv, Amadeus, Guarneri, Juilliard and Alban Berg Quartets. *Career:* Debut: Prague Spring Festival, 1980; Member, (Martinů) Quartet; Leader of Havlak and Martinů Quartet: Prague Spring Festival; UNESCO Hall in Paris, Kuhmo Festival (Finland), Wigmore Hall, London, Bath Festival, Brighton Festival; Festivals in Dartington, in Evian (France), Arjeplog (Sweden), Bratislava (Slovakia), Orlando Festival (Netherlands), Frankfurter Sonoptikum; Film: Meeting with Segerstam; Concerts in Europe, USA and Japan; Television, radio. *Recordings:* Leader of Martinů Quartet; Martinů Quartets (Naxos); Debussy, Martinů (Panton); Early Czech Composers–Krommer, Richter; Dvořák, Smetana-String Quartets; Antonin Wranitsky–Concertante Quartets; Janáček, String Quartets; Honegger. *Honours:* With Havlak Quartet: Prague Spring Competition, 2nd Prize, 1979; Evian: Contemporary Music, 1st Prize, 1978; Portsmouth, 2nd Prize, 1982; München, 2nd Prize, 1982; Florence, 2nd Prize, 1984. *Address:* Pod Vlastnim Krovem 27, 182 00 Prague 8, Czech Republic. *Telephone:* +42 (286) 884294; +42 (606) 888373. *E-mail:* lubomir.havlak@volny.cz. *Website:* www.musikerportrait.com/martinu-quartet.

**HAVLIK, Jiri;** Horn Player; b. 20 July 1956, Tabor, Czecholovakia; m. Helena Havlikova, 18 Mar 1978, 2 d. *Education:* French Horn, Composition, Conservatoire, Prague, 1971–77; Composition, 1977–78, Horn, 1978–81, Academy of the Musical Arts. *Career:* Member, Czech Philharmonic, 1979–, Horn Trio Prague, 1985–; Chamber and Solo Performances in Czech Republic, Switzerland, Netherlands, Japan, Canada; Founder, Horn Music Agency, Prague, 1991. *Compositions:* Concerto for Horn and Orchestra, 1976; The Cycle of the Piano Compositions, 1978; Three Fugues for Three Horns and Piano, 1997. *Recordings:* Czech Philharmonic Horn Section, 1989; Old Czech Concertos for 2 and 3 Horns, 1992. *Honours:* 2nd Prize, Concertino Prague International Competition, 1970; Special Prize, Czech Ministry of Culture, 1978; 3rd Prize, Prague Spring International Competition, 1978. *Current Management:* Pragoart Prague. *Address:* Na Spravedlnosti 1152, 27101 Nove Straseci, Czech Republic.

**HAWES, Patrick,** BMus; British composer; b. 1958, Lincolnshire. *Education:* Durham Univ. *Career:* fmr conductor Durham Univ. Chamber Choir and Symphony Orchestra; fmr music and English teacher, Pangbourne Coll.; fmr composer-in-residence Charterhouse; own choir, Conventus. *Compositions include:* A King's Ransom (children's opera, with Andrew Hawes), The Land (folk song-based choral work, with Andrew Hawes), The Wedding at Cana, The Far Seeing Land, The Call (song cycle) 1999, The Incredible Mrs Ritchie (film score) 2002, Chorus a cappella, Quanta Qualia, Lazarus Requiem 2005. *Recording:* Blue in Blue (album) 2002. *Current Management:* Novello Publishing Ltd, 8–9 Frith Street, London, W1D 3JB, England. *E-mail:* info@patrickhawes.com. *Website:* www.patrickhawes.com.

**HAWKES, Tom;** Stage Director; b. 21 June 1938, England. *Education:* Trained at the Royal Academy of Music. *Career:* Resident Staff Producer at Sadler's Wells 1965–69; For English National Opera has produced Un Ballo in Maschera, Madama Butterfly, La Vie Parisienne, La Gazza Ladra and Die Fledermaus; English Bach Festivals (seen at Covent Garden and in France, Greece, Italy and Spain) include Rameau's Castor et Pollux and Platée, Handel's Teseo and Gluck's Alceste and Orphée et Eurydice; Dido and Aeneas in London and at the Athens Festival; Artistic Director for Phoenix Opera and Director of Productions for the Handel Opera Society; La Finta Giardiniera for the English Music Theatre; Wat Tyler by Alan Bush, Hansel and Gretel and operettas at the Sadler's Wells Theatre; Season 1990–91 with The Maid of Orleans for Northern Opera, La Bohème in Hong Kong, Mitrate in Monte

Carlo and Handel's Riccardo Primo at the Royal Opera House and in Limasol for the English Bach Festival; Has also conducted in Dublin, Nottingham, Oxford, Belgium and Guelph and St Louis, USA; Season 1993/94 with Rigoletto and Die Fledermaus at Singapore, L'Orfeo, for EBF at Royal Opera House, Covent Garden, and in Spain; Director of Productions for the Singapore Lyric Theatre and for Crystal Clear Productions. *Address:* c/o Music International, 13 Ardilaun Road, London N5 2QR, England.

**HAWKINS, Brian,** FRCM; British viola player and teacher; *Head of Strings Faculty, Royal College of Music (retired);* b. 13 Oct. 1936, York, England; m. Mavis Spreadborough, 30 Dec 1960, 1 s., 1 d. *Education:* St Peter's School, York, National Youth Orchestra, 1951–54, Royal College of Music, 1954–60. *Career:* Chamber Music, Edinburgh Quartet; Martin Quartet; Vesuvius Ensemble; Nash Ensemble; London Oboe Quartet; Gagliano String Trio; Member, English Chamber Orchestra, Academy of St Martin-in-the-Fields, London Sinfonietta, London Virtuosi; Professor, Viola and Chamber Music, Royal College of Music, 1967–; String Faculty Adviser, Royal College of Music, 1989; Head of String Faculty, Royal College of Music, 1992–2000; Cttee mem. European String Teachers' Asscn; mem. Royal Society of Musicians, Incorporated Society of Musicians. *Recordings:* With the Nash Ensemble, London Virtuosi, London Oboe Quartet and Gagliano Trio, London Sinfonietta, English Chamber Orchestra, Acad. of St Martin's-in-the Fields, Nat. Philharmonic Orchestra. *Honours:* Silver Medal, Worshipful Company of Musicians, 1960; Fellowship of The Royal College of Music, 1991. *Address:* The Old Vicarage, 129 Arthur Road, London, SW19 7DR, England (home). *Telephone:* (20) 8946-4511 (home). *Fax:* (20) 8946-9183 (home). *E-mail:* violahawk@aol.com (home). *Website:* www.brianhawkinsviola.com (home).

**HAWKINS, John;** Composer and Pianist; b. 26 July 1944, Montreal, Canada. *Education:* Studied under Istvan Anhalt and received Master's degree in Composition, McGill University. *Career:* Joined Faculty of Music, University of Toronto, teaches theory and composition, 1970–; Remained active as pianist and performed frequently in the concerts of Societe de Musique Contemporaine du Quebec as well as Toronto's New Music Concerts, of which he is a member of Board of Directors; Conductor, Pierre Boulez' conducting seminar, Switzerland 1969. *Compositions:* Composed over 70 new works which include pieces for harpsichord and organ; Music for an Imaginary Musical, for chamber ensemble, 1994; Night Song for baritone, marimba and string quartet, 1995; If There Are Any Heavens for soprano and chamber ensemble, 1996. *Honours:* Won several major awards including first John Adaskin Memorial Fund Award, 1968 and BMI Student Composers' Award, 1969. *Address:* c/o SOCAN, 41 Valleybrook Drive, Don Mills, Ontario M3B 2S6, Canada.

**HAWKINS, Osie;** Singer (Baritone); b. 16 Aug. 1913, Phoenix City, Alabama, USA. *Education:* Studied in Atlanta and with Friedrich Schorr in New York; Sang at the Metropolitan Opera from 1942, as Wagner's Telramund, Kurwenal, Bitterolf, Wotan, Amfortas, Donner and Gunther; Zuniga in Carmen and Monterone in Rigoletto; Also sang with Central City Opera, Colorado and the Cincinnati Summer Opera; Many concert appearances; Executive Stage Manager at the Metropolitan 1963–78; 926 performances with the Metropolitan Opera, played 54 roles in 39 different operas in German, Italian, French and English. *Honours:* Awarded Metropolitan Opera National Council Verdi Memorial Award of Achievement, 1978; Inducted into Philadelphia Academy of Vocal Arts Hall of Fame, 1987. *Address:* c/o Metropolitan Opera, Lincoln Center, New York, NY 10023, USA.

**HAWKSLEY, Deborah;** Singer (mezzo-soprano); b. Singapore. *Education:* Royal Northern Coll.; Guildhall School of Music. *Career:* appearances in Death in Venice, with GTO; as Third Lady, Mozart; Prince Orlofsky, Composer, Ariadne auf Naxos for ENO; Dorabella for Opera Theatre, Dublin; Cenerentola for European Chamber Opera; Baba the Turk, in The Rake's Progress, Aldeburgh Festival; Carmen for First Act Opera, 1998–99; Season 1999, as Prince Orlofsky on tour to the USA, Armelinde in Massenet's Cendrillon for Central Festival Opera and Rossini's Petite Messe for Northern Sinfonia; gala concerts for City of London Sinfonia in the UK and Germany. *Current Management:* Music International, 13 Ardilaun Road, London, N5 2QR, England.

**HAWLATA, Franz;** Singer (Bass); b. 26 Dec. 1963, Eichstatt, Germany. *Education:* Munich Musikhochschule, with Ernst Haefliger, Hans Hotter and Erik Werba. *Career:* Debut: Gärtnerplatztheater, Munich, 1986; Engagements at the Komische Oper Berlin and in Munich, with guest appearances as Altoum in Busoni's Turandot in Dortmund; Baron Ochs in Der Rosenkavalier at Würzburg, for Welsh National Opera, New York Metropolitan (1995) and the Paris Opéra Bastille (1998); Peneios in Strauss's Daphne at Hamburg, Wozzeck at Bad Urach, Rocco in Beethoven's Leonore, on tour with John Eliot Gardiner, Leporello at Covent Garden and Osmin in Die Entführung at Salzburg (1996); Vienna State Opera 1994–95 as Nicolai's Falstaff, Kaspar, Don Pasquale, Sarastro and Baron Ochs; The Monk in Don Carlos at the Opéra Bastille, 1998, and Kecal in The Bartered Bride for the Royal Opera; Ochs at Covent Garden, 2000; Season 2001 as the Dutchman in Chicago and Wotan in Meiningen. *Recordings include:* Mephisto in Spohr's Faust, from the Bad Urach Festival. *Honours:* Prizewinner, 1987 Belvedere International Singing Competition, Vienna. *Address:* c/o IMG Artists, Lovell House, 616 Chiswick High Road, London W4 5RX, England.

**HAYASHI, Yasuko;** Singer (Soprano); b. 19 July 1948, Kanagawa, Japan; m. Giannicola Piglucci. *Education:* Studied in Tokyo with Shibata and Rucci;

Studied with Lia Gurani and Campogalliani in Milan. *Career:* Debut: La Scala 1972, as Madama Butterfly; Appearances in Florence, Rome, London, Venice, Turin, Barcelona, Chicago and Aix-en-Provence; Other roles include Donna Anna, Fiordiligi, Carolina in Il Matrimonio Segreto, Luisa Miller, Anne Trulove and Liu, in Turandot; Turin 1976, in Bianca e Fernando by Bellini; Sang Donna Anna at reopening of Stuttgart Staatsoper, 1984; Genoa 1985, in a revival of Il Diluvio Universale by Donizetti; Season 1987–88 as Butterfly at Verona and Leonora in La Forza del Destino in Tokyo; Appearances on television and in concert. *Recordings:* I Lituani by Ponchielli; Rachel in La Juive; Requiem by Bottesini, Fonit-Cetra; Video of Madama Butterfly from La Scala. *Address:* c/o Staatsoper Berlin, Unter den linden 7, 1060 Berlin, Germany.

**HAYES, Jamie;** Stage Director; b. 1959, England. *Career:* Productions of The Gondoliers, The Magic Flute and Midsummer Night's Dream at Freemason's Hall; Aida, Opera Northern Ireland; Il Barbiere di Siviglia and La Cenerentola for Garsington Opera, Thieving Magpie, Figaro, Così fan tutte and Albert Herring for British Youth Opera at Sadler's Wells and Edinburgh; Former Director of productions for Clonter Opera For All, with La Traviata, La Bohème and Carmen; Buxton Festival with L'Italiana in Algeri, Le Huron and L'Italiana in Londra; Wexford Festival with Zaza and Le Rencontre Imprévue; Other productions include Alcina for Royal Northern College of Music and The Pearl Fishers for Victorian State Theatre, Robinson Crusoe, British Youth Opera, The Bear, RSAMD; Appointed Director of Productions, British Youth Opera, in 1996; La Bohème, for BYO, 1998. *Address:* Park House, 33 Brackley Road, Towcester, Northamptonshire NN12 6 DH, England.

**HAYES, Malcolm Lionel Fitzroy;** British music journalist, writer and composer; b. 22 Aug. 1951, Overton, Marlborough, Wiltshire. *Education:* St Andrews University; BMus Honours, Edinburgh University, 1974. *Career:* Music Critic, The Times, 1985–86; Music Critic, The Sunday Telegraph, 1986–89; Music Critic, The Daily Telegraph, 1989–95; Frequent broadcasts (talks) for BBC Radio 3, 1985–, and Radio 4, 1986–; Music performed at Bath Festival, 1985, ICA, London, 1985, BBC, London, 1986, Viitasaari Festival, Finland, 1987; Edinburgh Contemporary Arts Trust, 2002. *Compositions:* Into the Night for unaccompanied chorus 1984, Stabat Mater for soloists and orchestra 2001, Odysseus Remembers for soloists and orchestra 2004. *Publications:* New Music 88 (co-editor), 1988; Anton von Webern, 1995; 20th-Century Music, 6 vols 2001, Selected Letters of William Walton, 2002. *Contributions:* Numerous articles for Tempo, 1982–92; The Listener, 1985–89; Musical Times, 1985–86; International Opera Guide, 1987; New Music 87, 1987; Opera Now, 1991–1996; BBC Music Magazine, 1995–; Classic FM Magazine, 1995–. *Honours:* Tovey Prize for Composition, Edinburgh University, 1974. *Address:* Sunday Telegraph, 1 Canada Square, Canary Wharf, London E14 5DT, England. *Telephone:* (20) 7538-7391 (office). *E-mail:* starts@ telegraph.co.uk (office).

**HAYES, Quentin;** Singer (Baritone); b. 27 Nov. 1958, Southend, England. *Education:* Studied at Dartington College, the Guildhall School with Arthur Reckless and Rudolph Pernay, and at the National Opera Studio. *Career:* Created Eddy in Mark-Anthony Turnage's Greek, Munich, 1988, repeated it at Edinburgh and the London Coliseum; Rossini's Figaro with Glyndebourne Touring Opera, Verdi's Ford for CBTO, Morales in Carmen for Welsh National Opera, and Angelotti for Scottish Opera; Ford, Papageno and Marcel Proust in Schnittke's Life with an Idiot for English National Opera, 1995; Nachtigal in Die Meistersinger for Royal Opera House Covent Garden; Concerts include Les Troyens at the Amsterdam Concertgebouw, Elijah in Wells Cathedral, L'Enfance du Christ in Spain and music by Purcell with Collegium Vocale; Season 1997 with The Dream of Gerontius at Bath, Handel's Semele at the Berlin Staatsoper, Britten's Church Parables for CBTO and Henze's Elegy for Young Lovers with the London Sinfonietta; Frère Léon in Messiaen's St François d'Assise for Concertgebouw, Amsterdam; Season 2003 at Covent Garden as Yamadori in Butterfly and the Herald in Lohengrin. *Recordings include:* Pepusch Death of Dido for the BBC; Greek; Britten, Rejoice in the Lamb; Where the Wild Things Are, Knussen; Donald in Billy Budd with Hickox and the London Symphony Orchestra. *Honours:* Winner VARA Dutch Radio Prize at the Belvedere Singing Competition, Vienna, 1992; Winner Vara Dutch Radio Prize and Belvedere Singing Competition, 1993. *Address:* c/o Royal Opera House (contracts), Covent Garden, London, WC2, England.

**HAYMON, Cynthia;** Singer (Soprano); b. 6 Sept. 1958, Jacksonville, Florida, USA; m. Barrington Coleman. *Education:* Graduate, Northwestern University. *Career:* Debut: Santa Fe Opera, as Diana in Orpheus in the Underworld, 1985; Sang Xanthe in US premiere of Die Liebe der Danaë, Santa Fe, 1985; Has sung Micaela for Seattle Opera and Liu in Boston; Created Harriet, A Woman Called Moses, Virginia, 1985; European debut, 1986, as Gershwin's Bess at Glyndebourne; With Covent Garden has sung Liu on tour to Far East and Mimi in London; State Operas, Hamburg, Munich, as Liu, Theatre de la Monnaie, Brussels, as Gluck's Amor; Israel Philharmonic as Micaela, conducted by Zubin Mehta; Season 1988–89 with Eurydice at Glyndebourne, Mimi for Baltimore Opera, Marguerite with Opera Grand Rapids; Season 1989–90 included Susanna for Seattle Opera, Canadian Opera debut as Micaela; Coretta King opposite Simon Estes, West End; 1990–91 highlights: Lauretta in Gianni Schicchi at Seattle, Liu in Miami, and Mozart's Pamina at Bastille Opéra, Paris; 1991–92 highlights: San Francisco Opera debut as Micaela in Carmen, premiere of Rorem's Swords and Plowshares with Boston Symphony, Pamina at Opéra Bastille, Liu at Royal Opera House, Covent

Garden, Gershwin in concert at Teatro La Fenice, Venice, recital at Northwestern University, Carmina Burana with Detroit Symphony Orchestra, Mendelssohn's Symphony No. 2 for RAI, Rome, Gershwin and Tippett concert with London Symphony Orchestra, Gala concert, Glyndebourne Festival, 1992–93 highlights: Bess in Porgy and Bess, Royal Opera House, Pamina at Opéra Bastille, Micaela in Birmingham and Dortmund, Marguerite at Deutsche Oper Berlin, Mimi at Santa Fe Opera; Sang Musetta at Amsterdam, 1996; Liu in Turandot at Dallas, 1997; Sang Gluck's Euridice at Leipzig, 2000; Concert engagements in Brahms Requiem conducted by Kurt Masur, Rossini's Stabat Mater (London debut) with London Symphony Orchestra conducted by Michael Tilson Thomas; Other conductors: Seiji Ozawa, Bernard Haitink, Isaiah Jackson. *Recordings include:* Tippett's A Child of Our Time, London Symphony Orchestra, Richard Hickox, conductor; Bess in Porgy and Bess, Glyndebourne Festival Opera, Simon Rattle, conductor. *Honours:* Grammy Award, 1990. *Address:* c/o Columbia Artists Management Inc, 165 West 57th Street, New York, NY 10019, USA.

**HAYS, Sorrel Doris,** MMus; American composer, keyboard player and multimedia artist; b. 6 Aug. 1941, Memphis, TN. *Education:* Hochschule für Musik, Munich, Germany, University of Wisconsin, studied with Hilda Somer, Paul Badura-Skoda, Harold Cadek, Hedwig Bilgram. *Career:* in 80s added film and video to media art; Commissions from West German Broadcasting Cologne; Film, music video production shown at Museum of Modern Art, New York and Stedelijk Museum, Amsterdam; premiered Henry Cowell's Concerto for Piano and Orchestra 1978; commissions from Westdeutscher Rundfunk, Cologne, 1988; Echo, Whatchasay Wie Bitte, 1989; The Hub, Megopolis Atlanta and Sound Shadows, commissioned as opening work for Whitney Museum Acoustica Festival, April 1990; Bits, NY City premiere, 1993, Merkin Hall; Performances of Opera, The Glass Woman, NYC, Interart Theater, 1993; Premiere, The Clearing Way, Chattanooga Symphony, 1992; commission/premiere A Birthday Book for baritone, oboe, tuba, Cowell Centennial Festival, Merkin Hall 1997; Queen Bee-ing, The Bee Opera, comic opera commissioned by Cary Trust, premiered by Medicine Show Theater, New York City, 2003; mem, ASCAP. *Compositions:* Southern Voices for Orchestra and Soprano, 1982, 21 minutes; Celebration of No, tape, Soprano, Violin, Piano, Cello, 1983; Sunday Nights, Piano, 1979; HUSH, Soprano, 2 Percussion, 1986; The Clearing Way, for full orchestra, contralto, SATB chorus; 3 act opera, 11 soloists and chorus, The Glass Woman, 1993; Dream in Her Mind, opera, Commission/premiere West Deutsche Rundfunk, 1995; Mapping Venus, 2 act opera, 1998; The Bee Opera, 2003. *Recordings:* Dreaming the World, Voicings (Smithsonian Folkways), Sorrel Hays Plays Henry Cowell. *Publications:* Tunings for string quartet; Southern Voices for Orchestra. *Honours:* Opera America, production award for opera, The Glass Woman, 1989 and National Endowment for the Arts, 1992; New York Foundation on the Arts, Fellowship on Music Composition, 1998, and Media 1985. *Address:* 697 West End Avenue, PHB, New York, NY 10025, USA. *E-mail:* hays2ries@mindspring.com (office).

**HAYWARD, Marie (Pauline);** Opera Singer (Soprano) and Teacher; b. 1940, England; m. Michael Segal, deceased, 1 s. *Education:* Royal Academy of Music; London Opera Centre; Tito Gobbi, Italy; MA; ARAM; LRAM; RAMDipl. *Career:* Debut: Royal Opera House; Numerous world-wide appearances, including Royal Albert Hall, Festival Hall, Musikverein, Vienna, London Coliseum, Kiel Opera House, Germany; Also Ring Cycle at Lubeck, Mannheim and Kiel; Also Isolde; Engaged by Klaus Tennstedt as Dramatic Soprano, Kiel, for roles including Desdemona, Mozart's First Lady, Donna Anna (Don Giovanni); Verdi and Wagner roles; Major roles include: Abigail, Northern Ireland Opera, Brünnhilde for English National Opera, Elvira and Fiordiligi at Glyndebourne; Miss Jessel in Turn of the Screw at Geneva and Sadler's Wells, English Opera; Oratorio performances in England and Europe; BBC broadcasts, Melodies for You, Friday Night is Music Night; Workshops and Masterclasses at Milan and Heidelberg Universities; mem, ISM. *Recordings:* Serenade to Music; Pilgrim's Progress; Adrian Boult, Ave Maria. *Honours:* ARAM, 1993; 2nd Prize, 's-Hertogenbosch International Competition; Medal of Distinction, Geneva.

**HAYWARD, Robert;** Singer (Bass-baritone); b. Nov. 1956, Surrey, England. *Education:* Studied at the Guildhall School of Music and the National Opera Studio. *Career:* Sang Falstaff and Mozart's Figaro while at college; Glyndebourne Touring Opera, 1986, as Don Giovanni; Has sung Figaro, Don Giovanni, Marcello, Count and Sharpless for Welsh National Opera; Theseus and Haushofmeister (Capriccio) for Glyndebourne Festival; English National Opera appearances as Tomsky in The Queen of Spades, Escamillo (1995) and Jochanaan (1996); US debut as Figaro for Houston Grand Opera, 1988; German debut, 1990, as Don Giovanni for the Bayerische Staatsoper on tour to Teatro Liceo Barcelona; For Opera North Guglielmo, Figaro, Count, Escamillo, Don Giovanni, Malatesta, Marcello, Robert in Iolanta, Debussy's Golaud; For Royal Opera House, Spirit Messenger (Frau); For Glyndebourne Tour Count and Onegin; Sang Germont for GTO at Glyndebourne, 1996; Sang Iago in Otello for ENO, 1998; Concert engagements include Messiah with the Royal Liverpool Philharmonic, Hallé and London Philharmonic Orchestras; The Mask of Time, Elijah, Beethoven's Ninth and the Brahms Requiem with the Hallé; Das klagende Lied and Gurrelieder with the English Northern Philharmonia; The Dream of Gerontius with the Scottish National Orchestra; Haydn's Creation with the Bournemouth Sinfonietta and the Philharmonia conducted by Claus Peter Flor; Mozart Requiem with Georg Solti; New Israeli Opera as: Malastesta, Guglielmo; Season 2000–01 as Escamillo for WNO, Golo in Pelléas for ENO and Jochanaan in Salome at Glasgow. *Recordings:*

Beethoven's 9th Symphony; Das klagende Lied. *Current Management:* Ingpen & Williams Ltd, 7 St George's Court, 131 Putney Bridge Road, London, SW15 2PA, England.

**HAYWOOD, Lorna;** Singer (Soprano); b. 29 Jan. 1939, Birmingham, England; m. Paul Crook. *Education:* Royal College of Music, with Mary Parsons and Gordon Cinton; Juilliard School with Sergius Kagen and Beverly Johnson. *Career:* Debut: Juilliard 1964, as Katya Kabanova; Covent Garden debut 1966, in Die Zauberflöte: sang Jenůfa in 1972; English National Opera from 1970, notably Janáček's The Makropulos Case and Katya Kabanova; Appearances with Welsh National Opera and at the Glyndebourne Festival; Guest engagements in Prague, Brussels, New York, Chicago, Dallas, Washington and Seattle: roles include Marenka in The Bartered Bride, Mimi, Micaela in Carmen, Sieglinde, Elizabeth Zimmer in Elegy for Young Lovers, Mozart's Countess, Madama Butterfly, Ariadne, the Marschallin and Lady Billows in Albert Herring (Los Angeles, 1992); Masterclass for Ohio Light Opera, 1996. *Address:* c/o English National Opera, St Martin's Lane, London, WC2, England.

**HAZELL, Andrea;** Singer (Mezzo-soprano); b. 1965, Southampton, England. *Education:* Studied at Royal Academy of Music. *Career:* Many appearances throughout the United Kingdom in oratorio; Sang Second Witch in Dido and Aeneas for Amersham Festival, Offenbach's Perichole in Reading and Dorabella at the 1990 Cheltenham Festival; Sang in Carmen at Earl's Court, 1989, and on tour to Japan; Royal Opera, Covent Garden, 1990–, in Les Huguenots and Die Frau ohne Schatten and as Tefka in Jenůfa, 1993; Other roles include Marcellina in Le nozze di Figaro. *Address:* c/o Royal Opera House (Contracts), Covent Garden, London WC2E 9 DD, England.

**HAZELL, Richard;** Singer; b. 1940, Staffordshire, England. *Education:* Royal College of Music. *Career:* Debut: Film, Phantom of the Opera, 1961; Theatre and television work until 1973; Appearances with Royal Opera, Covent Garden, in Manon, Carmen, The Merry Widow, Andrea Chénier, La Rondine, Der Rosenkavalier, La Bohème and Paul Bunyan; Servant in La Traviata, 2001; Orge in the British premiere of Henze's Policino; International tours with the D'Oyly Carte Opera Company; Former chairman of the Amici di Verdi and founder member of the Royal Opera House Education advisory council. *Address:* c/o Royal Opera House (contracts), Covent Garden, London, WC2, England. *Telephone:* (20) 7240 1200. *Fax:* (20) 72129502.

**HAZLEWOOD, Charles;** British conductor, music director and broadcaster; *Founder and Artistic Director, Dimpho Di Kopane Opera Company*; m.; three c. *Education:* Christ's Hospital, Univ. of Oxford. *Career:* Music Dir Broomhill Opera 1993–96; jt Artistic Dir Wilton's Music Hall, London 1999–2003; co-founder and jt Artistic Dir Dimpho Di Kopane Opera Co., Cape Town, South Africa 2000–, conducting Carmen and West Side Story, conceived music for Yiimimngaoliso (The Mysteries), Ibali Loo Tsotsi (The Beggar's Opera), The Snow Queen; collaborations with Steve Reich, Peter Maxwell Davies, Badly Drawn Boy; Music Dir and Conductor, Excellent Device and Harmonieband chamber orchestras; conducted Orchestra of St Luke's, Carnegie Hall 2003; Prin. Guest Conductor, BBC Concert Orchestra 2005–. *Television:* presenter Vivaldi Unmasked, The Genius of Mozart, The Genius of Beethoven, The Culture Show (all BBC). *Radio:* presenter Charles Hazlewood Discovering Music (BBC). *Film:* Music Dir on U-Carmen e-Khayelitsha. *Honours:* winner European Broadcasting Union conducting competition 1995, Sony Music Broadcaster of the Year Bronze Award 2005. *Current Management:* c/o Ian Stones, HarrisonParrott, 12 Penzance Place, London, W11 4PA, England. *Telephone:* (20) 7229-9166 (office). *Fax:* (20) 7221-5042 (office). *E-mail:* Ian .Stones@harrisonparrott.co.uk (office). *Website:* www.harrisonparrott.com (office). *E-mail:* enquiries@charleshazlewood.com. *Website:* www .charleshazlewood.com.

**HAZUCHOVA, Nina;** Singer (Mezzo-soprano); b. 24 May 1926, Czechoslovakia. *Education:* Conservatory, Bratislava. *Career:* Appeared with Slovak National Theatre; Roles included: Carmen, Amneris in Aida; Azucena in ll Trovatore; Eboli in Don Carlos; Maddalena in Rigoletto; Suzuki in Madama Butterfly; Rosina, in The Barber of Seville; Marina in Boris Godunov; Cherubino in The Marriage of Figaro; Nancy in Martha; Isabella in The Italian Girl in Algiers; Catherine in The Taming of the Shrew; Appeared as a Concert Singer performing with the best Czech orchestras; Has toured many countries including USSR, Germany, Austria, Belgium, Italy, Yugoslavia, Arabia, China, Mongolia; Vocal-Teacher, Academy of Music Arts (Vysoka skola muzickych umeni) Bratislava; mem, Slovak Music Foundation, Bratislava. *Recordings:* Has made numerous records. *Honours:* Meritorious Artist, 1968. *Address:* c/o Bratislava Academy of Music Arts, Vocal Faculty, Jiráskova 3, 81301 Bratislava, Slovakia.

**HEADLEY, Erin;** lirone player and viola da gamba player; b. 1948, Texas, USA. *Career:* Member of Tragicomedia, three musicians performing in the Renaissance and Baroque repertory; Concerts in the United Kingdom and at leading European early music festivals; Gave Stefano Landi's La Morte d'Orfeo at the 1987 Flanders Festival; Francesca Caccini's La liberazione di Ruggiero dall'isola d'Alcina at the 1989 Swedish Baroque Festival, Malmö. *Recordings include:* Proensa (troubadour songs), My Mind to me a Kingdom is (Elizabethan ballads, with David Cordier); A Musicall Dreame (duets from Robert Jones's 1609 collection); Biber's Mystery Sonatas; Concert programmes include The Lyre of Timotheus (incidental music by Handel, Bach, Vivaldi and Abel); Orpheus I Am (music based on the Orpheus myth by Landi, Monteverdi, Lawes and Johnson); Il Basso Virtuoso (songs by Landi,

Monteverdi, Strozzi, Huygens and Purcell, with Harry van der Kamp); Three Singing Ladies of Rome; Monteverdi Madrigals from Book VIII and L'Orfeo; Early Opera: Peri's Euridice, Landi's La Morte d'Orfeo and Rossi's Orfeo. *Address:* c/o 14 Nightingale Lane, London N8 7QU, England.

**HEALEY, Derek;** Composer; b. 2 May 1936, England. *Education:* Studied organ with Harol Darke and composition with Herbert Howells at Durham University; Further study at the Royal College of Music and with Petrassi and Celibidache in Italy. *Career:* Tutor: University of Victoria, BC, Australia, 1969–71, College of Arts, University of Guelph, 1972–78; Professor of Composition and Theory, University of Oregon, 1979, returning to the United Kingdom in 1988. *Compositions include:* Opera Seabird Island, 1977, and children's opera, Mr Punch, 1969; Ballets Il Carcerato 1965 and The Three Thieves, 1967; Orchestral: The Willow Pattern Plate, 1957; Concerto for organ, strings and timpani, 1960; Butterflies for mezzo and chamber orchestra, 1970; Arctic Images, 1971; Tribulation, 1977; Music for a Small Planet, 1984; Mountain Music, 1985; Gabriola (A West Coast Canadian Set), 1988; Salal (An Idyll), 1990; Triptych, 1996; Chamber: String Quartet, 1961; Cello sonata, 1961; Mobile for flute and ensemble, 1963; Laudes for flute and ensemble, 1966; Maschere for violin and piano, 1967; Wood II for soprano and string quartet, 1982; English Dances for percussion sextet, 1987; Piano music including Lieber Robert, 1974; Organ music and songs; 3 organ sonatas, 1961, 1992, 1996. *Address:* 29 Stafford Road, Ruislip Gardens, Middlesex HA4 6PB, England.

**HEARTZ, Daniel Leonard;** Educator; b. 5 Oct. 1928, Exeter, New Hampshire, USA. *Education:* AB, University of NH, 1950; MA, 1951; PhD, 1957, Harvard University. *Career:* Assistant Professor, Music, University of Chicago, 1957–60; Assistant Professor, 1960–64, Associate Professor, 1964–66, Professor, 1966–, Chairman, 1968–72, Music, University of CA, Berkeley; mem, American Musicological Society, Vice President, 1974–76; IMS; RMA; Societe Française de Musicologie; Gesellschaft für Musikforschung. *Publications:* Pierre Attaingnant, Royal Printer of Music, 1969; Edition of Mozart's Idomeneo, Neue Mozart Ausgabe, 1972; Mozart's Operas, 1990; Haydn, Mozart and The Viennese School 1740–1780, 1995; Music in European Capitals: The Galant Style 1720–1780, 2003, From Garrick to Gluck: Essays on Opera in the Age of Enlightenment. *Contributions:* Professional Journals including The Beggar's Opera and opéra-comique en vaudevilles, 1999. *Honours:* Dent Medal, RMA 1970, Kinkeldey Prize, American Musicological Society 1970, 2004, Guggenheim Fellowship 1967–68, 1978–79, Fellow of American Academy of Arts and Sciences 1988. *Address:* 1098 Keith Avenue, Berkeley, CA 94708, USA.

**HEASTON, Nicole;** Singer (Soprano); b. 1965, Ohio, USA. *Education:* University of Akron, Ohio; Cincinnati Conservatory. *Career:* Debut: Houston Grand Opera as Gounod's Juliette; As Pamina, Washington Opera; Anne Trulove, The Rake's Progress, on her European debut at Montpellier, 1997; Concerts with Marc Minkowski at Halle, Brussels and Barcelona, 1995; Created Jacqueline Onassis in Michael Daugherty's Jackie O at Houston; Concert repertory includes works by Handel and Bach. *Recordings:* Une Bergère in Gluck's Armide. *Honours:* William Matheus Sullivan Foundation award, 1998. *Address:* c/o Music International, 13 Ardilaun Road, London N5 2QR, England.

**HEATER, Claude;** Singer (Tenor); b. 1930, Oakland, California, USA. *Education:* Studied in Los Angeles; Further study in Europe with Mario del Monaco and Max Lorenz. *Career:* Sang at first as baritone, on radio and tv and in Broadway Musicals; Bayerische Staatsoper 1964, in König Hirsch by Henze; Sang Wagner roles in Amsterdam, Brussels, Hamburg, Berlin and Milan; Bayreuth Festival 1966, as Siegmund and Melot; Other roles included Turiddu, Otello, Florestan and Samson; Guest appearances in South America; Sang Tristan at Spoleto, 1968 and appeared at Dresden, 1968, Barcelona, Bordeaux and Geneva, 1968–69; Budapest and Venice, 1970. *Recordings:* As Melot in Tristan und Isolde, conducted by Karl Böhm (Deutsche Grammophon).

**HEBERT, Bliss;** American stage director; b. 30 Nov. 1930, Faust, NY. *Education:* Syracuse Univ. with Robert Goldsand, Simone Barrere, Lelia Gousseau. *Career:* debut as Stage Dir, Santa Fe 1957; Gen. Man., Washington Opera Soc. 1960–63; Stage Dir, New York City Opera 1963–75, Metropolitan Opera, New York 1973–75 (debut with Les Contest d'Hoffmann); guest Dir, Juilliard School 1975–76; Dir of opera cos of San Francisco 1963, Washington 1959, Houston 1964, Fort Worth 1966, Caramoor Festival, Katonah, NY 1966, Seattle Opera 1967, Cincinnati 1968, La Gune Festival 1968–, Portland, Oregon 1969, Vancouver 1969, San Diego 1970, New Orleans 1970, Toronto 1972, Baltimore 1972, Tulsa 1975, Miami, FL 1975, Charlotte, NC 1975, Dallas 1977, Shreveport, Los Angeles 1977, Chicago 1983, Montréal 1984, Boston 1984, Cleveland 1988, Opera Northern Ireland 1988, Virginia Opera 1991, Opera Mexico City 1993, Austin Opera 1993, Florentine Opera, Milwaukee 1994; Don Giovanni 1996; Roméo et Juliette at San Diego 1998. *Address:* Pinnacle Arts Management Ltd, 889 Ninth Avenue, Second Floor, New York, NY 10019, USA. *Telephone:* (212) 397-7915. *Fax:* (212) 397-7920.

**HEBERT, Pamela;** Singer (Soprano); b. 31 Aug. 1946, Los Angeles, California, USA. *Education:* Studied at the Juilliard School with Maria Callas, Tito Capobianco, Margaret Hoswell and Boris Goldovsky. *Career:* Debut: New York City Opera 1972, as Donn Anna; Appearances in New York as Mimi, title role in L'Incoronazione di Poppea, Vespina in Haydn's L'Infedeltà delusa and the Composer in Ariadne auf Naxos; Frequent concert engagements. *Address:* c/o New York City Opera, Lincoln Center, New York, NY 10023, USA.

**HECHT, Joshua;** Singer (Baritone); b. 1928, New York City, USA. *Education:* Studied with Lili Wexberg and Eva Hecht in New York and with Walter Tassoni in Rome. *Career:* Debut: Baltimore 1953, as Des Grieux in Manon; Sang in Boston, Chicago, Miami, Pittsburgh, San Francisco, Seattle and New Orleans; Metropolitan Opera from 1964; Further appearances at the New York City Opera and in Graz, Johannesburg, Barcelona, Bucharest, Dublin and Vancouver; Roles include the Wanderer in Siegfried, Amfortas, Rigoletto, Iago, Scarpia and the title role in Einstein by Dessau (Gelsenkirchen 1980); Sang Prospero in Martin's Der Sturm (The Tempest), Bremen, 1992; Australian Opera at Sydney (1994) as Schigolch in Lulu.

**HECKMANN, Harald;** German musicologist; b. 6 Dec. 1924, Dortmund, Germany; m. Elisabeth Dohrn, 25 August 1953, 1 s. *Education:* Gymnasium, Dortmund, 1934–43; Musicology, Freiburg/Breisgau, 1944–52; Assistant to Wilibald Gurlitt, Freiburg/Breisgau, 1952–54. *Career:* Teacher of Church Music History, College of Music, Freiburg/Breisgau, 1950–54; Director, German History of Music Archives, Kassel, 1955–71; Director, German Broadcasting Archives, Frankfurt am Main, 1971–91; mem, Honorary President, International Association of Music Libraries; Hon. President, International Inventory of Musical Sources; Board Member, Robert-Schumann Society; Co-President, International Repertoire of Music Iconography; History of Music Commission, FRG; Hon. mem. Int. Schubert Soc., Rotary. *Publications:* Deutsches Musikgeschichtlichs Archiv, Katalog der Filmsammlung, 1955–72; W A Mozart, Thamos, Koenig in Aegypten, Choere und Zwischenaktmusiken, 1956; W A Mozart, Musik zu Pantomimen und Balletten, 1963; Ch W Gluck, La Rencontre imprévue, Editor and Critic, 1964; Elektronische Datenverarbeitung in der Musikwissenschaft, 1967; Das Tenorlied, 3 vols, co-editor, 1979–86; Musikalische Ikonographie, co-editor, 1994; various essays on musicology including La sventurata musica, 1996, Nachschlagewerke zur Musik 1998. *Honours:* Stadtmedaille der Stadt Kassel 1979, Goldene Mozart Medaille der Int. Stiftung Mozarteum, Salzburg 1993, Bundesverdienstkreuz 1st Class 2000. *Address:* Im Vogelshaag 3, D65779 Ruppertshain/Ts, Germany.

**HEDGES, Anthony John;** Reader in Composition and Composer; b. 5 March 1931, Bicester, England; m. Delia Joy Marsden, 1957, 2 s., 2 d. *Education:* Keble College, Oxford, MA, BMus, LRAM. *Career:* Teacher, Lecturer, Royal Scottish Academy of Music, 1957–63; Lecturer in Music, University of Hull, 1963, Senior Lecturer 1968; Reader in Composition, 1978–95; Founder-conductor, The Humberside Sinfonia, 1978–81; Chairman, Composers' Guild of Great Britain, 1972, Joint Chairman 1973; Executive Committee of Composers' Guild 1969–73, 1977–81, 1982–87; Council Member, Composers' Guild. *Compositions include:* Orchestral: Comedy Overture, 1962; Sinfonia Semplice, 1963; Expressions, 1964; Concertante Music, 1965; Variations on a theme of Rameau, 1969; An Ayrshire Serenade, 1969; Celebrations, 1973; Symphony, 1972–73; Sinfonia Concertante, 1980; Scenes from the Humber, 1981; Showpiece, 1985; Symphony No. 2, 1997; Divertimento for String Orchestra, 1997; Choral: Gloria, unaccompanied, 1965; Epithalamium for chorus and orchestra, to text by Spenser, 1969; Bridge for the Living, for chorus and orchestra, to text by Philip Larkin, 1976; I Sing The Birth, for chorus and chamber orchestra, 1985; I'll Make Me a World, chorus and orchestra, 1990; Symphony No. 2, 1997; Chamber: Five preludes for piano, 1959; Sonatinas for flute, viola, bassoon, trumpet and trombone, 1982; Flute Trios, 1985, 1989; Piano Quartet, 1992; Many anthems, partsongs, albums of music for children; Music for television, film and stage. *Recordings:* Scenes from the Humber; Kingston Sketches; Bridge for the Living; Four Breton Sketches; Four Miniature Dances; Overture: Heigham Sound; Cantilena; Divertimento for string orchestra; An Ayrshire Serenade; Fiddlers Green; A Cleveland Overture; Piano Sonata; various solo and chamber works. *Publications:* Basic Tonal Harmony, 1987, Comprehensive Archive in Hull Central Music Library. *Contributions:* regular contributor to The Guardian, The Scotsman, The Glasgow Herald, The Musical Times, 1957–63; The Yorkshire Post, 1963–73. *Honours:* Honorary D.Mus, University of Hull, 1997. *Address:* 76 Walkergate, Beverly, East Yorkshire HU17 9ER, England. *E-mail:* ahedges@westfieldmusic.karoo.co.uk. *Website:* westfieldmusic.karoo.net.

**HEDWALL, Lennart;** Composer, Conductor and Musicologist; b. 16 Sept. 1932, Gothenburg, Sweden; m. Ingegerd Henrietta Bergman, 13 April 1957, 4 s. *Education:* Royal College of Music, Stockholm, 1951–59; Composing and Conducting at Darmstadt, Vienna, Hilversum and Paris. *Career:* Debut: As composer, 1950; As professional conductor, Messiah, 1954; Conductor: Riksteatern, 1958–60; Great Theatre Gothenburg, 1962–65, Drottningholm-teatern, 1966–70, Royal Theatre, 1967–68, Orebro Orchestra Society, 1968–74; Teacher, Dramatic School in Gothenburg, 1963–67, State Opera School, 1968–70, 1974–80, 1985–97; Director of Swedish National Music Museum, 1981–83; Member of the Royal Swedish Academy of Music and the Accademia Filarmonica of Bologna. *Compositions:* 2 Operas: Herr Sleeman Kommer and America, America; The Dress of Birgitta, church opera; Symphony 1 (retrospettiva), 2 (elegiaca), 3 (semplice); Sagan, symphonic phantasy; Legend and Pezzo pastorale for orchestra; Jul igen, a Christmas Rhapsody; Several works for String Orchestra; Concertos for Flute, Oboe, Violoncello; Chamber Music: 3 String Quartets and 2 String Trios and others; Organ and Piano works; Several Song Cycles; Choir pieces and cantatas; Stage and television works; Many editions of old Swedish music. *Recordings:*

As conductor with Orebro Chamber Orchestra, Värmland Sinfonietta, Musica Vitae and Östersunds Serenade Ensemble; As accompanist, several song recitals; Also others as Organist and Pianist. *Publications:* Hugo Alfvén, monography, 1973; Operettas and Musicals, 1976; The Swedish Symphony, 1983; Wilhelm Peterson-Berger, a biography in pictures, 1983; The Concert Life in Åbo 1872–76, 1989; Hugo Alfvén, a biography in pictures, 1990; The Musical Life in the Manors of Vermland 1770–1830, 1992; Form Structures in Roman's Sinfonias, 1995; A Survey of The Music in Vermland, 1995; Swedish Music History, 1996; The Composer Erik Gustav Geijer, 2001; Oscar Byström, a biography, 2003. *Contributions:* Dagen Nyheter, 1957–78; Musikrevy and others. *Address:* Mårdvägen 37, 16756 Bromma, Sweden. *Telephone:* 8269450 (home).

**HEELEY, Desmond;** Stage Designer; b. 1 June 1931, West Bromwich, England. *Education:* Trained at the Shakespeare Memorial Theatre, Stratford, 1947–52. *Career:* Debut: La Traviata for Sadler's Wells, 1960; Productions for Glyndebourne (I Puritani, 1960) and English National Opera (Maria Stuarda, 1973); Work for the Metropolitan Opera includes Norma 1970, Pelléas et Mélisande 1972, Don Pasquale 1978 and Manon Lescaut 1980; Chicago designs for La Traviata seen at Detroit and Seattle, 1996. *Address:* c/o Lyric Opera of Chicago, 20 North Wacker Drive, Chicago, IL 60606, USA.

**HEGAARD, Lars;** Composer; b. 13 March 1950, Svendborg, Denmark; m. Susanne Taub, 10 Oct 1984, 4 s. *Education:* Diploma in Guitar, 1973; BA, Music, 1975; Examination of Teaching, 1977; Diploma in Composition, 1980. *Career:* Has played at all major festivals in Denmark and Scandinavia including on Radio; Has several commissions through The Danish Arts Foundation and 3 year Stipendium, 1983. *Compositions include:* Orchestra: Symphony Nos 1 and 2, Letter To My Son; Chamber Orchestra: Decet, Intersections; The Rolling Force, cello concerto; The Seasons According to I Ching; Triptych with Objects; Chamber Works: Five Fragments for String Quartet; The Four Winds, clarinet, cello, piano; Music For Chameleons, wind quintet; Configurations, alto flute, guitar; Six Studies for Two Guitars, Songlines, guitar trio; 13 short pieces for flute, viola, harp; Dreamtracks, flute, clarinet, horn, percussion, guitar, cello; Four Square Dances for Saxophone Quartet; Partials' Play, flute, guitar, cello; Inside for bass clarinet, percussion and electronics; Beings for flute, clarinet, vibraphone, piano, guitar, violin, cello; Rituals for solo guitar, flute, clarinet, percussion, piano, violin, cello; Solo works: Variations, guitar; The Conditions of a Solitary Bird, guitar; Canto, cello; The Great Beam…, piano; Worldes Bliss, organ; Labyrinthus, electric guitar; Chains, organ; Vocal: Hymns, baryton, sinfonietta; Haiku, soprano, violin, piano; Far Calls, Coming Far, mezzo soprano, electric guitar, percussion, Text: James Joyce; The Dimension of Stillness, soprano, flute, guitar, cello, Text: Ezra Pound; Orchestra: Symphony No. 3; Chamber Orchestra: Twine for 9 instruments; Chamber works: Four visions for string quartet; Invocations for organ and 2 saxophones; Short Cuts for oboe, clarinet, saxophone and bassoon; Singing Sculpture for recorder, violin, cello and guitar; Ambient Voices for violin, clarinet, cello and piano; Octagora Room for guitar and string quartet; Vocal: Night Flower; Four Poems by Sylvia Plath for mezzo-soprano, percussion, piano, viola, double-bass; Nogle Lykkelige Sekunder: 4 Poems by Poul Borum for organ and basso. *Recordings include:* The Great Beam of the Milky Way, piano; 5 Fragments for string quartet; Decet for wind and string quintet; Partials Play for flute, guitar, cello; Four Square Dances for saxophone quartet; Triptych with objects; 13 Short Pieces; Twine; The Four Winds; Ambient Voices. *Contributions:* Interviews in Dansk Musiktidskrift. *Current Management:* Publishers: The Society for Publication of Danish Music, Gråbrodrestraede 18,1, 1156 Copenhagen, Denmark. *Address:* c/o Danish Composers' Society, Gråbrodre Torv 16, 1154 Copenhagen K, Denmark.

**HEGARTY, Mary;** Singer (soprano); b. 1960, Cork, Republic of Ireland. *Education:* Cork School of Music, at Aldeburgh and the National Opera Studio in London; further study with Josephine Veasey. *Career:* Has sung for Radio Telefis Eireann in Britten's Quatres chansons Françaises and the Brahms Requiem; Bach's Christmas Oratorio with Harry Christophers; Recitals in Ireland, the USA and at the Aix-en-Provence Festival (Une Heure avec Mary Hegarty); Covent Garden debut as a Flowermaiden in Parsifal, followed by Pousette in Manon; English National Opera as Nannetta and Naiad (Ariadne); Appearances with Opera Factory in La Calisto; With Opera North as Leonora in the British premiere of Nielsen's Maskarade (1989) in Ariane et Barbe-Bleue, the Mozart pasticcio The Jewel Box (1991) and as Frasquita; Buxton Festival 1991, in Mozart's Il Sogno di Scipione; Requiem for RTE; Princess Laula in Chabrier's Etoile, (Opera North); Papagena in Magic Flute (ENO); Eurydice in Orpheus in The Underworld, (D'Oyly Carte); Adele in Die Fledermaus, (Dublin Grand Opera Society); Eurydice in Orpheus In the Underworld; Cherubino in The Marriage of Figaro, Elisa in Mozart's Il Re Pastore, The Italian Soprano in Strauss's Capriccio and Gloria in world premiere of Gloria-A Pigtale, Nerina in La Fedelta Premiata, Tanterabogus in The Fairy Queen; 1996–97 with the English National Opera included Norina in Don Pasquale, Blonde in Die Entführung aus dem Serail and Elvira in L'Italiana in Algeri; Fiorilla in Il Turco In Italia for Garsington in 1996; Susanna in The Marriage of Figaro at Grange Park, 1998; Season 2000 as Jessie in the premiere of Turnage's The Silver Tassie, for ENO, Puccini's Lisette and Donizetti's Adina for Opera North. *Recordings:* Debut solo album, A Voice is Calling; Title role in Gilbert and Sullivan's Patience; Eurydice in Offenbach's Orpheus in the Underworld; Mendelssohn Lobgesang with Naxos.

*Honours:* Winner, Golden Voice of Ireland, 1984; Bursary for study at Aldeburgh; Irish Life, Sunday Independent Classical Music Award, 1988; Allied Irish Bank, RTE National Entertainments Award for Classical Section, 1987.

**HEGEDUS, Olga;** Cellist; b. 18 Oct. 1920, London, England. *Education:* London Violoncello School; Private Study, Pierre Fournier. *Career:* Debut: Recital, Wigmore Hall, London; Solo recitals; Many BBC and television appearances with trios, chamber ensembles and others; Member, Davey String Quartet; mem, Incorporated Society of Musicians; Musicians Union. *Recordings:* Art of Fugue, Bach, and Musical Offering, with Tilford Festival Ensemble; The Curlew, Warlock, with Haffner Ensemble; Vivaldi Motets with Teresa Berganza and English Chamber Orchestra; Dvořák Serenade, with English Chamber Orchestra Wind Ensemble; Schubert Quintet in C, with Gabrieli Quartet. *Contributions:* A Pictorial Review, English Chamber Orchestra, 1983. *Address:* 8 Kensington Place, London W8 7PT, England.

**HEGGEN, Almar;** Singer (bass); b. 25 May 1933, Valldal, Norway. *Education:* studied at Oslo Conservatory, with Paul Lohmann in Wiesbaden and with Clemens Kaiser-Breme in Essen. *Career:* debut, Oslo, 1957, as Masetto in Don Giovanni; sang in Wuppertal, Berlin, Frieburg, Wiesbaden, Nuremburg, Munich; guest performances in Sweden, Yugoslavia and others; Nuremburg 1969, in premiere of The Dream of Liu-Tung by Isang Yun; roles include: Rocco (also filmed), King Philip, Padre Guardiano, Sarastro, Don Alfonso, Tiresias (in Oedipus Rex), Daland, Pogner, Fafner, Hagen, Baron Ochs, Ptolomeo, in Giulio Cesare; Wagner: Landgraf, King Henry, Marke, Hunding; Verdi: Zacharias, Ramphis; Mozart: Osmin; Rossini, Don Basilio; Smetana, Kezal; many oratorios including: Creation and Seasons of Haydn, Verdi's Requiem, Mozart's Requiem; teacher of singing; mem., Norsk Operasangerforbund, Norsk Musikerforening; Norsk Tonekunstnersamfunn, Kunsterforeningen. *Address:* Hareveien 40A, 1413 Tårnasen, Norway.

**HEICHELE, Hildegard;** Singer (soprano); b. Sept. 1947, Obernburg am Main, Germany; m. Ulrich Schwalb. *Education:* Studied at the Munich Musichochschule. *Career:* Debut: Klagenfurt, as Jennie in Aufstieg und fall der Stadt Mahagonny; Munich Staatsoper from 1971, notably as Mozart's Zerlina, Despina, Susanna and Ilia; Appearances in Vienna, Cologne (as Gretel), Karlsruhe (as Adina), Berlin, Zürich and Barcelona; Covent Garden 1977, 1983, as Adele in Die Fledermaus; Frankfurt 1981, in the Symphony of a Thousand, by Mahler; Monte Carlo 1982, Brussels 1984, as Susanna; Bayreuth Festival 1984, as the Woodbird in Siegfried; Sang at Kassel and Hanover 1988, as Elsa and Elisabeth; Concert engagements in Vienna, Graz and Venice (1985). *Recordings include:* Mahler's 8th Symphony; Egisto by Cavalli; Bach Magnificat; Handel Dettinger Te Deum; Video of Die Fledermaus (Covent Garden 1983).

**HEIDEMANN, Stefan;** Singer (Baritone); b. 1961, Germany. *Education:* Studied in Hanover and with Joseph Greindl. *Career:* Sang at Nuremberg Opera, 1988–91, Düsseldorf from 1991; Komische Oper Berlin, 1993, as Guglielmo, Ford in Falstaff, 1996; Season 1995–96 at Düsseldorf as Wagner's Wolfram, Falke in Die Fledermaus, and in the premiere of Gervaise Macquart by Klebe; Other roles include Lortzing's Tsar Peter, Mozart's Count, Nicolai's Herr Fluth, and Marcello in La Bohème; Guest engagements in concert and opera throughout Germany; Sang in the premiere production of Beuys by Franz Hummel, Düsseldorf and Vienna, 1998. *Address:* Deutsche Oper am Rhein, Heinrich-Heine Alle 16a, 40213 Düsseldorf, Germany.

**HEIDSIECK, Eric;** Pianist; b. 21 Aug. 1936, Reims, France. *Education:* Studied at the Ecole Normale de Musique, Paris and with Marcel Ciampi at the Paris Conservatoire; Private study with Alfred Cortot and Wilhelm Kempff. *Career:* Many appearances in London, France and elsewhere from 1955; Mozart's last twelve concertos in Paris, 1964, and the Beethoven Sonatas (1969, 1979); Frequent chamber music engagements, notably with Paul Tortelier; Repertory also includes the Suites of Handel; Professor at the Lyon Conservatoire, 1980–98. *Recordings include:* Le Tombeau de Couperin, by Ravel; Concertos by Mozart and Beethoven's Sonatas. *Publications include:* Cadenzas to Mozart's Piano Concertos. *Honours:* Premier Prix, Paris Conservatoire, 1954. *Address:* c/o Conservatoire National Supérieur de Lyon, 3 Rue de Angile, 69005 Lyon, France.

**HEIFETZ, Daniel (Alan);** Violinist and Teacher; b. 20 Nov. 1948, Kansas City, Missouri, USA. *Education:* Pupil of Theodore Norman; Studied with Sascha Jacobson, Israel Baker, and Heimann Weinstine, Los Angeles Conservatory, 1962–65, and with Efrem Zimbalist, Ivan Galamian, and Jascha Brodsky, Curtis Institute of Music, 1966–71. *Career:* Debut as soloist in the Tchaikovsky Violin Concerto with the National Symphony Orchestra of Washington DC, on tour in New York; Thereafter regular tours of North America and the world; Appointed to the faculty of the Peabody Conservatory of Music, Baltimore, 1980. *Recordings:* For Leonarda. *Honours:* 1st prize, Merriweather-Post Competition, Washington DC, 1969; 4th prize, Tchaikovsky Competition, Moscow, 1978. *Address:* c/o Shaw Concerts Inc, ASCAP Building, 1900 Broadway, New York, NY 10023, USA.

**HEIFETZ, Robin (Julian);** Composer; b. 1 Aug. 1951, Los Angeles, California, USA. *Education:* Studied at UCLA with Paul Chihara and Roy Travis; University of Illinois with Salvatore Martirano and Ben Johnston, DMA 1978. *Career:* Composer-in-Residence at Shiftelsen Electronic Studio, Stockholm, 1978–79; Worked at various music departments in Canada and the USA; Director of the Centre for Experimental Music at the Hebrew

University of Jerusalem, 1980. *Compositions include:* 2 Pieces for Piano 1972; Leviathan for piano 1975; Chirp for euphonium and piano 1976; Susurrus for computer and tape 1978; Child of the Water for piano 1978; For Anders Lundberg Mardrom 29 30 10 for tape 1979; A Clear and Present Danger for tape 1980; Spectre for tape 1980; Wanderer for synthesizer 1980; The Unforgiving Minute for 9 instruments 1981; In the Last, Frightened Moment for tape 1980; The Vengeance for Synthesizer 1980; The Arc of Crisis for tape 1982; A Bird in Hand is Safer than one Overheard for 2 or more performers 1983; At Daggers Drawn for tape 1983. *Honours:* Awards at the Concours International de Musique Electro-Acoustique, Bourges, France, 1979, 1981; International Computer Music Competition at Boston, 1983. *Address:* c/o ASCAP, ASCAP Building, 1 Lincoln Plaza, New York, NY 10023, USA.

**HEILGENDORFF, Simone;** Violist and Musicologist; b. 4 April 1961, Opladen, Germany. *Education:* Graduated. Final Artistic Examination (Viola Performance), Staatliche Hochschule fuer Musik im Rheinland, Cologne, Germany, 1987; Magister Artium (Musicology), Albert-Ludwigs-University in Freiburg, Germany, 1989; Master of Music (Viola Performance), University of Michigan, USA, 1991; PhD (Musicology), Humboldt Universität zu Berlin, 1999. *Career:* Violist and founding member of the Kairos Quartet; Former member of symphonic orchestras: Junge Deutsche Philharmonie, Serenata Basel (chamber orchestra); Work in Progress; Performances: Contemporary Music: Ensemble Modern (ISCM-Ens); Aventure Freiburg, Contemporary Ensemble (Aspen Music Festival 1991); Early Music: Ensemble für Alte Musik, Dresden; Concerto Köln; Faculty, Universität der Künste, Berlin; Member of the Kairos Quartet specializing in contemporary music in Berlin. *Recordings:* Numerous CD productions. *Publications:* Various musicological publications; Experimentelle Juszenierung Von Sprache und Musik, Vergleichende Analysen zu Dieter Schnebel und John Cage, Freiburg, Germany 2002. *Address:* Jagowstr 16, 10555 Berlin, Germany.

**HEILMANN, Uwe;** Singer (tenor); b. 7 Sept. 1960, Darmstadt, German; m. Tomoko Nakamura. *Education:* Studied in Detmold with Helmut Kretschmar. *Career:* Sang at Detmold from 1981 as Tamino, Don Ottavio and the Italian Singer in Rosenkavalier; Stuttgart Staatsoper from 1985, notably as Tamino, Belmonte, Don Ottavio, Cassio in Otello and Max in Der Freischütz; Munich Staatsoper as Don Ottavio, Vienna as Tamino; Sang Pylades in Iphigénie en Tauride at the Deutsche Oper Berlin; Appearances at the Salzburg and Ludwigsburg Festivals, 1988–89, including Max; Concert engagements and Lieder recitals, notably in works by Schubert and Wolf; Sang Cassio in Metropolitan Opera Gala, 1991; Season 1993–94 as Belmonte at La Scala and Steuermann at the Met. *Recordings include:* Tamino in Die Zauberflöte, conducted by Solti; Belmonte in Die Entführung conducted by Hogwood; Die schöne Mullerin, with James Levine; Haydn's Orfeo ed Euridice, with Cecilia Bartoli (L'Oiseau Lyre, 1997). *Current Management:* Askonas Holt Ltd, Lonsdale Chambers, 27 Chancery Lane, London, WC2A 1PF, England. *Telephone:* (20) 7400-1700. *Fax:* (20) 7400-1799. *E-mail:* info@askonasholt.co .uk. *Website:* www.askonasholt.co.uk.

**HEIMANN, Robert;** Singer (Baritone); b. 1958, Boston, USA. *Education:* Studied at Stanford University and in New York. *Career:* Sang in musicals on Broadway from 1981; Concert appearances at Carnegie Hall, including Linda di Chamounix, 1993; European debut, Belfast Opera, 1991, as Mozart's Figaro; Leipzig Opera from 1991, as Rossini's Figaro, Guglielmo, Papageno, Count Luna in Il Trovatore, and Leporello; Guest engagements in Brussels, 1992, Israel and Brunswick (as Silvio in Pagliacci). *Address:* c/o Leipzig Opera, Augustusplatz 12, 7010 Leipzig, Germany.

**HEININEN, Paavo;** Composer; b. 18 Jan. 1938, Järvenpää, Finland. *Education:* Studied Theory and Composition, Sibelius Academy, Helsinki, Finland, College of Music, Cologne, Germany and at Juilliard School of Music, New York, USA, 1956–62; Training as Pianist, Conductor and Musicologist. *Career:* Teacher of Theory and Composition, Turku Institute of Music, Turku, Finland, and at Sibelius Academy, Helsinki, 1966–. *Compositions include:* Orchestral Works: Symphony No. 1, 1958, revised 1960, Piano Sonata, Symphony No. 3, 1969, revised 1977, Dia, 1979; Works for Solo Instrument and Orchestra: Concerto for Piano and Orchestra No. 3, 1981; Cello Concerto, 1985; Violin Concerto, 1993; Lightings, 1998; Muraski in Casa Ando, 1998; Chamber Music: Jeu l and ll, 1980; Works for Solo Instrument: Gymel for Bassoon and Tape, 1978; What an Evening, What a Lightning for ensemble, 1999; Bluekeys for piano, 1999; Vocal and Choral Works: The Silken Drum, opera, 1980–83, Floral View with Maidens Singing, folk melody, 1980–83, Dicta, computer music, 1980–83; Another Heaven, Blooming Earth for male chorus, 1999. *Recordings include:* Adagio with Royal Philharmonic Orchestra under Walter Süsskind; Da Camera Magna; Sonatine, 1957; Sonatina Della Primavera; The Autumns, Finnish Radio Chamber Choir under Harald Andersén; Maiandros, tape composition; Discantus II; Touching; Concerto III with Paavo Heininen on Piano, the Sibelius Symphony Orchestra under Ulf Söderblom. *Address:* TEOSTO, Lauttassarentie 1, 00200 Helsinki 20, Finland.

**HEINIÖ, Mikko;** Composer and Professor of Musicology; b. 18 May 1948, Tampere, Finland; m. Riitta Pylvänäinen, 2 April 1977, one s., one d. *Education:* MA, 1972, PhD, 1984, University of Helsinki; Hochschule der Kunste, West Berlin, 1975–77; Diploma in Composition, Sibelius Academy, 1977. *Career:* Composer, 1972–; Teacher, University of Helsinki, 1977–85; Professor, Musicology, University of Turku, 1985–; President, Finnish Composers' Society, 1992–; Board Member, Copyright Organisation TEOSTO,

1984–. *Compositions include:* orchestral: 6 piano concertos; Concerto for French horn and orchestra; Concerto for Orchestra; Possible Worlds, Symphony No. 1; Dall'ombra all'ombra; Trias; Symphony No. 2 (Songs of Night and Love); On the Rocks for orchestra, 1998; Minne, for sting orchestra, 1996; Envelope for Haydn's Trumpet Concerto, 2002; chamber music: Duo for Violin and Piano; Brass Mass; Piano Trio; In G, violoncello and piano; Wintertime, harp and marimba/vibraphone; Piano Quintet; Relay for cello and violin, 1998, Treno della notte, clarinet, violin, cello and piano, 2000, Sextet for baritone, flute, clarinet, violin, cello and piano 2000; vocal: Landet som icke är, children's choir and piano; Vuelo de alambre, soprano and orchestra; The Shadow of the Future, soprano and brass instruments; La, piano and 4 voices; Wind Pictures, choir and orchestra; Hermes, piano, soprano, string orchestra and dance theatre, 1994, Three Morning Songs for baritone and piano 2000; works for the stage: The Knight and the Dragon, church opera, 2000; Khora, Piano, 5 percussionists and dance theatre, 2001, The Hour of the Snake opera in two acts 2003–05. *Recordings include:* Notturno di fiordo for flute and harp; Champignons à l'hermeneutique; Genom kvällen; Vuelo de alambre; Possible Worlds; Wind Pictures; Duo for Violin and Piano; Piano Quintet; Hermes; Piano Trio; In G; Wintertime; The Knight and the Dragon; Sextet. *Publications:* Contemporary Finnish Composers and their background, 1981; Contemporary Finnish Music, 1982; The Idea of Innovation and Tradition, 1984; The Reception of New Classicism in Finnish Music, 1985; The Twelve Tone Age in Finnish Music, 1986; Postmodern Features in New Finnish Music, 1988; Contextualisation in the research of art music, 1992; Finnish Composers (co-author), 1994; Finnish Music History 4: Music of Our Time, 1995; From Tones to Words, 1997; The Reception of New Finnish Operas 1975–1985, 1999. *Honours:* mem. Royal Swedish Acad. of Music 2004. *Address:* Mustainveljestenkuja 2a, 20700 Turku Finland. *E-mail:* mikko .heinio@composers.fi (home). *Website:* www.fimic.fi/contemporary/composers/ heinio+mikko (home).

**HEINRICH, Siegfried;** Conductor and Künstlerischer Direktor für Oper und Festspielkonzerte Bad Hersfeld; b. 10 Jan. 1935, Dresden, Germany. *Education:* Studied in Dresden and Frankfurt am Main, 1954–61. *Career:* Debut: Sänger im Dresdner Kreuzchor, 1948; Conductor, Frankfurt Chamber Orchestra, 1957; Since 1961, Artistic Director, Hersfeld Festival Operas and Concerts; Lecturer, Music Academy of Kassel; Künstlerischer Leiter des J. S. Bach-Institutes und Bachchores Frankfurt (M), 2000; Conductor, Radio Symphony Orchestras, Prague, Frankfurt am Main, Hanover, Luxemburg, ORTF, France, Budapest, Warsaw, Katowice, Kraków, Venice, Stuttgart; Concert Tours throughout Europe; New Interpretations of Bach's The Art of the Fugue, Beethoven's opera Fidelio with parts of Leonore I, Handel's Messiah, Monteverdi's Marian Vespers, Orfeo, Poppea, Il ritorno d'Ulisse. *Recordings:* Bach, Beethoven, Bizet, Brahms, Britten, Bruckner, Carissimi, Dvořák, Honegger, Liszt, Mahler, Mozart, Monteverdi, Ockeghem, Spohr, Telemann, Weber. *Publications:* Prospectuses and press reviews from Jubilate Schallplatten; Bärenreiter, Koch International. *Honours:* Bundesverdienstmedaille, 1976; Goethe-Medaille, 1983; Bundesverdienstkreuz, 1988. *Current Management:* Rainer Zagovec, Rathausstr 42, 65428 Rüsselsheim. *Address:* Arbeitkreis Für Musik e V, Nachtigallenstr 7, 36251 Bad Hersfeld, Germany.

**HEINSEN, Geerd;** German journalist; *Editor, Orpheus. Career:* Ed., Orpheus Oper International magazine. *Address:* Orpheus, Ritterstraße 11, 10969 Berlin, Germany. *Telephone:* (30) 6 14 68 40. *Fax:* (30) 6 14 68 65. *E-mail:* info@orpheusoper.de. *Website:* www.orpheusoper.de.

**HEISSER, Jean-François;** pianist; b. 7 Dec. 1950, St Etienne, France. *Education:* Paris Conservatoire with Vlado Perlemuter. *Career:* many appearances in Europe and North America from 1975; Recital engagements from 1976 (Lincoln Center, New York) with violinist Regis Pasquier; Soloist with the Nouvel Orchestre Philharmonique de Radio-France, 1976–85; Professor at the Paris Conservatoire from 1986 and Director of the Maurice Ravel Summer Academy 1993–; Repertory includes Beethoven, Schubert, Dukas, Berio and Schoenberg. *Recordings include:* Albeniz, Granados, Turina, Falla, and Martinů's Double Concerto, with Georges Pludermarker. *Honours:* Premier Prix, Paris Conservatoire, 1973; Winner, International Competition at Jaén, Spain, 1974. *Address:* c/o Paris Conservatoire, 14 rue de Madrid, 75008 Paris, France.

**HEJA, Domonkos;** Conductor; b. 20 Dec. 1974, Budapest. *Education:* Piano, violin, trumpet, percussion at Bartók Conservatory, 1997; Conducting degree, Ferenc Liszt Music Academy, 1998. *Career:* Debut: Budapest, 1993; Founder and Music Director, Danubia Youth Symphony Orchestra, 1993–; Conductor, Hungarian National Philharmonics; Budapest Philharmonic; Budapest Symphony; Franz Liszt Chamber Orchestra; Kosice Philharmonic. *Recordings:* M Haydn St Theresienmesse Hungaroton. *Honours:* First prize, National Percussion Competition, 1990; First prize, 9th International Conductors Competition, Budapest, 1998; Caripodis Prize, Mitropoulos Competition, Athens. *Current Management:* Budapest Artists Management. *Address:* 1118 Budapest, Somloi ut 39, Hungary.

**HELD, Alan;** Singer (bass-baritone); b. 1959, Washburn, Illinois, USA. *Education:* Studied at Millikin and Wichita State Universities. *Career:* Appearances with the Met Opera New York, in Billy Budd, Boris Godunov, Rigoletto, Tannhäuser and Tosca, from 1989; European debut at the Spoleto Festival, as the Villains in Les Contes d'Hoffman, 1989; Frankfurt Opera, as Šiškov in From the House of the Dead, the Rheingold Wotan and Leporello, from 1993; Royal Opera Covent Garden, as Gunther in Götterdämmerung,

Borromeo in Palestrina and Orestes in Elektra, from 1996; Season 1997–98 with San Francisco Opera as Orestes and in Wagner's Ring, Gunther at Munich, London and Birmingham and Kurwenal for Chicago Lyric Opera; Further appearances with Washington Opera (ten roles), Seattle Opera and the Théâtre de la Monnaie, Brussels; Season 2001 Bass soloist, Beethoven's 9th with Simon Rattle and the Vienna Philharmonic; Chicago Symphony, Houston Symphony, Pittsburgh Symphony, Metropolitan Opera Orchestra; Leporello in Don Giovanni at Covent Garden, 2002; Sang Wotan at the 2002 Bayreuth Festival. *Honours:* Richard Tucker Music Foundation Career Grants; Winner Birgit Nilsson Competition. *Current Management:* Askonas Holt Ltd, Lonsdale Chambers, 27 Chancery Lane, London, WC2A 1PF, England. *Telephone:* (20) 7400-1700. *Fax:* (20) 7400-1799. *E-mail:* info@askonasholt.co.uk. *Website:* www.askonasholt.co.uk.

**HELESFAY, Andrea;** Violinist; b. 18 Nov. 1948, Budapest, Hungary. *Education:* Béla Bartók Conservatoire, 1968–73; Franz Liszt University of Music; Study with Vilmoš Tatrai, Andras Mihály. *Career:* Debut: Aged 11, Budapest; Member, Hungarian Chamber Orchestra, Budapest Chamber Ensemble, often as Soloist; Zürich Chamber Orchestra, Tonhalle Orchestra, Zürich, 1973–; Many appearances as soloist in Germany, Switzerland; frequent appearances on radio and television; Founder, Trio Turicum; mem, Various professional organisations. *Honours:* Award Winner, International Mozart Violin Competition, Salzburg. *Address:* Hadlaubstrasse 148, CH 8006 Zürich, Switzerland.

**HELEY, John;** Cellist; b. 1948, London. *Education:* Studied at the Guildhall School of Music with William Pleeth. *Career:* Sub-Principal Cellist of the Royal Philharmonic Orchestra, 1970–80; Freelance career from 1981 with chamber recitals London Sinfonietta and other ensembles; Associate Principal Cellist of the Academy of St Martin-in-the-Fields from 1986 including solo appearances; Principal cello of Orchestra of St John's, Smith Square,1977–. *Address:* c/o Academy of St Martin in the Fields, Raine House, Raine Street, London, E1W 3RJ, England.

**HELFRICH, Paul M.;** Composer; b. 5 May 1955, Philadelphia, USA. *Education:* BMus, Pennsylvania State University, 1978; MMus, Composition, Temple University, 1980; DMA, Composition, Temple University, 1986, studied with Clifford Taylor and Maurice Wright. *Career:* Owner, Nu Trax Recording Studio, Upper Darby, PA, 1981–; Senior Project Manager, 1987–91, Assistant Director, Exhibit Development, 1991–, Franklin Institute Science Museum, PA. *Compositions include:* Sine Nomine for brass chorale, 1974; Metamorphosis 1 for string orchestra, 1976; Theme and Five Variations for string orchestra and percussion, 1977; Five Short pieces for piano, 1977; Sonata Allegro in G for symphonic wind ensemble, 1978; Winds from a longer Distance, for tape and seven dancers, 1989; Song for healing, tape and solo dancer, 1990; The Robot Game Show, for tape, 1990; Movie soundtracks: Spirits in the Valley II, 1991, The Alchemist's Cookbook, 1991. *Address:* 130 Cunningham Avenue, Upper Darby, PA 19082, USA.

**HELIN, Jacquelyn;** Concert Pianist; b. 24 Sept. 1951, Chicago, Illinois, USA. *Education:* BM, University of Oregon, 1973; Graduate Studies, Yale University School of Music, 1973–74; MA, Stanford University, 1976; DMA, University of Texas, 1982. *Career:* Performances at Wigmore Hall, London, The Chagall Museum, Nice, American Embassy, Paris, Merkin Hall and Town Hall, New York, Dumbarton, Oaks, The Corcoran Gallery, Hirshhorn Museum, Washington DC and The Brooklyn College Conservatory of Music; The Dame Myra Hess Series; The Beethoven Discovery Series, The Aspen Music Festival; Featured Artist, PBS television programme honouring Virgil Thomson's 90th birthday; Premiered Joan Tower's Piano Concerto with Hudson Valley Philharmonic, 1986; Numerous radio appearances; WFMT Chicago, WNCN New York, WGMS Washington and throughout USA on National Public Radio. *Recordings:* For Musical Heritage, Virgil Thomson Ballet and Film Scores for Piano.

**HELLAWELL, Piers;** Composer and University Lecturer; b. 14 July 1956, Chinley, Derbyshire, England. *Education:* New College, Oxford, 1975–78; BA (Hons 1st Class), 1978; MA, 1984. *Career:* Composer-in-Residence, 1981–85, Lecturer in Music, 1986–, Queens University of Belfast; Northern Ireland Co-ordinator, European Music Year, 1985; Regular broadcasts, BBC, Radio 3. *Compositions:* Xenophon, commissioned, performed Belfast, elsewhere, Radio 3, by Ulster Orchestra, 1985; How Should I Your True Love Know, 1st performed by The Fires of London, Queen Elizabeth Hall, Peter Maxwell Davies conducting, 1986; Sound Carvings From Rano Raraku, commission (ACNI), 1st performed Northern Ireland tour and BBC, Martin Feinstein Quartet, 1988; Das Leonora Notenbuch, commissioned North West Arts, 1st performed Buxton Festival by William Howard, 1989, 1st broadcast BBC Radio 3, 1990; The Erratic Aviator's Dance, commissioned, performed at the Dance Place, Washington DC and elsewhere by Alvin Mayes Dance and Collaborations Ensemble, 1989; Memorial Cairns, commission, premiere, Ulster Orchestra, 1992, BBC Radio 3, 1993; River and Shadow, commission, premiere, Hilliard Ensemble, Antwerp, 1993, CBC Radio Canada, 1994; Victory Boogie-Woogie, commission, premiere, Riga Piano Duo, Riga, 1993; High Citadels, commission, premiere, Jorg Vögel, Meerbusch Kunst Expo (Germany), 1994; Truth or Consequences, BBC broadcast, 1994; Camera Obscura, commission, premiere, Philip Mead, Rainbow Over Bath, 1994; Sound Carvings from the Ice Wall, BBC commission, premiered by Psappha, Manchester, 1995, BBC, 1995; Takla Makan, commission, premiere, Evelyn Glennie at Cheltenham Festival, 1995, BBC, 1995; Do Not Disturb, youth

chorus, 1996; Let's Dance, for percussion, 1996; Sound Carvings from the Water's Edge, for 11 strings, 1996; The Building of Goves for piano quartet, 1998. *Current Management:* Maecenas Music, London. *Address:* Department of Music, Queens University of Belfast, Belfast BT7 1NN, Northern Ireland.

**HELLEKANT, Charlotte;** Singer (Mezzo-soprano); b. 15 Jan. 1962, Hogalid, Sweden. *Education:* Eastman School of Music, with Jean DeGaetani, at the Curtis Institute. *Career:* Opera engagements include Cherubino for Portland and Washington Operas, Dorabella for the Canadian Opera Company, Charlotte and the Composer in Ariadne for Glimmerglass Opera and Musetta in Leoncavallo's Bohème at St Louis; Season 1995–96 as Bartók's Judith with the Orchestre de Paris, Charlotte at Washington, the Page in Salome for the Metropolitan Opera (debut role) and Ino in Semele at Aix-en-Provence; Contemporary roles include Lotte in Bose's Werther at Santa Fe, Erika in Barber's Vanessa, Cherubino in Corigliano's Ghosts of Versailles, at Chicago, the leading role in Bergman's The Singing Tree, for Finnish National Opera and Nastassja in Krasa's Verlobung in Traum; Concerts include Marguerite in La Damnation de Faust (Stockholm Philharmonic Orchestra), Mahler's 2nd Symphony (San Francisco Symphony Orchestra), Les Nuits d'Eté (Cleveland) Mahler's Rückert Lieder and Das Lied von der Erde (Netherlands Radio Philharmonic Orchestra); Berlioz L'Enfance du Christ with John Nelson and Mozart's Requiem under Neeme Järvi; Berio's Epiphanies with the composer conducting, Des Knaben Wunderhorn with the Swedish Radio Symphony Orchestra and Le Martyre de Saint Sebastien; Season 1997 as Cherubino at the Opéra Bastille, Salzburg debut as Amando in Ligeti's Le Grand Macabre, and Charlotte for New Israeli Opera; Season 1999–2000 as the Berlioz Marguerite at Salzburg, Nicklausse in Hoffmann at Antwerp and Varvara in Katya Kabanova at Amsterdam. *Recordings include:* Krasa's Verlobung in Traum; Mahler's 2nd Symphony; Ligeti's Le Grand Macabre. *Address:* c/o IMG Artists, Lovell House, 616 Chiswick High Road, London W4 5RX, England.

**HELLELAND, Arild;** Singer (Tenor); b. 29 Nov. 1949, Norway. *Education:* Studied in Oslo, Bergen and Gothenburg. *Career:* Concert appearances throughout Scandinavia; Norwegian State Opera at Oslo from 1989, as Janek in The Makropulos Case, Eisenstein in Die Fledermaus, and Mime in Wagner's Ring (also at Helsinki, 1996); Deutsche Oper Berlin, 1994–95, as Shuisky in Boris Godunov, Monostatos in Die Zauberflöte; Royal Opera, Stockholm, in A Dreamplay by Lidholm; Sellem in The Rake's Progress on Swedish television; Edinburgh, and other Festival engagements; Sang Mime in Siegfried at Helsinki, 1998. *Address:* c/o Finnish National Opera, PO Box 176, Helsingkatu 58, 00251 Helsinki, Finland.

**HELLER, Richard (Rainer);** Composer; b. 19 April 1954, Vienna, Austria; m. Shihomi Inoue, 26 Aug 1980. *Education:* Diploma in Composition, 1979; Final Examination in Composition for Audio-Visual Media, 1978, Final Examination for Cultural Management, 1979, Hochschule für Musik und Darstellende Kunst, Vienna. *Career:* Numerous performances of own works in Argentina, Austria, Belgium, Bulgaria, Czechoslovakia, Denmark, Egypt, France, Germany, Greece, Hungary, Italy, Japan, Kazakhstan, Netherlands, Romania, Russia, Switzerland, Spain, Saudi Arabia, South Africa, Turkey, Uruguay, Yugoslavia; Teaching Composition and Music Theory, Music Academy, Augsburg, Germany, 1979–. *Compositions include:* Concerto for violin; Concerto for 2 pianos and orchestra; Sinfonietta for wind orchestra; Concerto for bass clarinet; Concerto for marimba; Concertino for orchestra; Concerto per fiati; Toccata for wind orchestra; Novelette, piano trio; 3 moments musicaux, guitar quartet; string quartet; Cellophonie, 8 violoncellos; Statement, string trio; Elegy on texts out of Duineser Elegien by R M Rilke; Ballade, piano 4 hands; Various pieces for chamber ensembles; Songs; Solo pieces for piano, organ, bass clarinet; Numerous commissions. *Recordings:* Augsburger Gitarrenquartett; Organ-piano; MC, live documentations; Numerous radio recordings. *Address:* Reichenberger Strasse 24, 86161 Augsburg, Germany.

**HELLERMANN, William,** MA, DMA; composer; b. 15 July 1939, Wisconsin, USA; m. 1985; one s. one d. *Education:* Columbia University School of Arts; private study with Stefan Wolpe. *Career:* mem. BMI; ACA. *Compositions:* Time and Again, for orchestra, 1967; Anyway..., for orchestra, 1976; But the Moon..., for guitar and orchestra, 1975; Tremble, for solo guitar; Squeek for desk chair, 1978; Post/Pone for guitar and 5 instruments, 1990; Hoist by Your Own Ritard, 1993. *Recordings:* Ariel, for electronic tape, 1967; At Sea; Ek-Stasis I; Passages 13–The Fire. *Publications:* Articles published; Beyond Categories, 1981; Experimental Music, 1985; Scores: Row Music, Tip of the Iceberg, Time and Again for symphony orchestra; Long Island Sound; Distances/Embraces; Circle Music 2 and 3; Passages 13–The Fire; To the Last Drop; Ek-Stasis I. *Honours:* Prix de Rome, American Academy, 1972; NEA Fellowship, 1976–79; Composer in Residence, Center for Culture and Performing Arts, State University of New York at Buffalo. *Address:* PO Box 31, Philmont, NY 12565, USA.

**HELLMANN, Claudia;** Singer (Mezzo-soprano); b. 1931, Berlin, Germany. *Education:* Studied in Berlin. *Career:* Debut: Oper, Munster, 1958–60; Stuttgart Staatsoper, 1960–66, Nuremberg, 1966–75; Appearances at Bayreuth Festival, 1958–61, as Wellgunde and a Flower Maiden; La Scala Milan, 1963, as Flosshilde; Sang in concert at the Salzburg Festival, 1961–85; Hamburg Staatsoper from 1960, Théâtre de la Monnaie Brussels, 1963–67; Other roles have included Marcellina, Magdalena in Die Meistersinger, Mistress Quickly, Fidalma in Matrimonio Segreto and Frau von Hufnagel in

Henze's Der Junge Lord; Many concert and oratorio appearances. *Recordings:* Ismene in Orff's Antigonae, Bruckner's F minor Mass; Die Walküre; Bach's Easter Oratorio; Bach Church Cantatas. *Address:* c/o Stuttgart Staatsoper, Oberer Schlossgaten 6, 7000 Stuttgart, Germany.

**HELLWIG, Klaus;** Pianist and Educator; b. 3 Aug. 1941, Essen, Germany; m. Mi-Joo Lee. *Education:* Folkwang Hochschule Essen with Detlek Kraus, in Paris with Pierre Sancan; summer courses with Guido Agosti and Wilhelm Kempff. *Career:* concerts throughout Europe, USA, Canada, Asutralia, Brazil, Far and Middle East, all German radio stations, BBC London, NHK Tokyo; Prof., Univ. of the Arts, Berlin. *Recordings:* FX Mozart Concerti in C and E Flat, Cologne Radio Orchestra, conductor Roland Bader (Schwann); Haydn Concerto in D, Mozart Concerto KV 537; Bach Inventions; recordings of 20 other works; Carl Reinecke: The Four Piano Concerti. *Honours:* Prize at the Concours Internationale M. Long–J. Thibaud, Paris, 1965; First Prize, Concorso Internazionale G. B. Viotti, Vercelli, Italy, 1966. *Address:* Mommsenstr 58, 10629 Berlin, Germany. *E-mail:* hellwig.lee@t-online.de.

**HELM, E(rnest) Eugene;** Musicologist and Professor; b. 23 Jan. 1928, New Orleans, Louisiana, USA. *Education:* Southeastern Louisiana College, BME, 1950; Louisiana State University, MME, 1955; North Texas State University, PhD, 1958. *Career:* Faculty Member, Louisiana College 1953–55, Wayne (Neb) State College 1958–59, University of Iowa 1960–68; Associate Professor 1968–69, Professor 1969–, of Music, Chairman, Musicology Division 1971–87, University of Maryland; Co-ordinating Editor, Carl Philipp Emanuel Bach Edition, 1982–89. *Publications:* Music at the Court of Frederick the Great, 1960; With A Luper, Words and Music, 1971, 2nd edition 1982; A Thematic Catalogue of the Works of Carl Philipp Emanuel Bach, 1987; The Cannon and the Curricula, 1994. *Contributions:* Articles in numerous periodicals and other publications. *Address:* c/o Department of Music, University of Maryland, College Park, MD 20742, USA.

**HELM, Hans;** Singer (Baritone); b. 12 April 1934, Passau, Germany. *Education:* Studied with Else Zeidler and Franz Reuter-Wolf in Munich, Emmi Muller in Krefeld. *Career:* Debut: Graz 1957, in Boris Godunov; Sang in Vienna, Cologne, Frankfurt, Munich, Düsseldorf and Hanover; Salzburg Festival 1973, in the premiere of De Temporum fine Comoedia by Orff; Glyndebourne Festival 1976, as the Count in Le nozze di Figaro (also at Covent Garden, 1976 and 1991); Vienna Staatsoper, 1987 and 1990, as Agamemnon in Iphigénie en Aulide, and in Die Soldaten; Munich 1989, as Faninal in Der Rosenkavalier; Sang The Forester in The Cunning Little Vixen at the Vienna Volksoper, 1992; Season 1995–96 as Donner in Das Rheingold at Vienna and Strauss's Faninal in Munich; Many concert appearances. *Recordings:* Otello (EMI); De Temporum fine Comoedia and Die Frau ohne Schatten (Deutsche Grammophon). *Address:* c/o Staatsoper, Opernring 2, 1010 Vienna, Austria.

**HELM, Karl;** Singer (Bass); b. 3 Oct. 1938, Passau, Germany. *Education:* Studied with Else Zeidler in Dresden and with Franz Reuter-Wolf in Munich. *Career:* Debut: Berne 1968, as Don Alfonso in Così fan tutte; Member of the Bayerische Staatsoper, Munich; Guest appearances in Geneva, Paris, Düsseldorf, Hamburg and Stuttgart; Other roles include Arkel in Pelléas et Mélisande, Rocco, King Philip, Zaccaria, Varlaam, Fasolt, Falstaff in Die Lustigen Weiber von Windsor, Dulcamara, and Melitone in La Forza del Destino; Berlin Staatsoper 1987, in La Cenerentola; Munich 1990, as First Nazarene in Salome; Sang Swallow in Peter Grimes at Munich, 1991; Many concert appearances. *Recordings include:* Die Feen by Wagner. *Address:* Bayerische Staatsoper, Postfach 745, 8000 Munich 1, Germany.

**HELMS, Dietrich,** MA, DPhil; Musicologist; b. 23 July 1963, Westfalan, Germany. *Education:* Westfälische Wilhelms, Universität Münster, Germany, St Peter's Coll., Oxford. *Career:* editorial work for the Hallesche Händel-Ausgabe 1996–7; lecturer at the Institut für Musik und Didaktik at Dortmund Univ. 1997–; lectureships at the Univs of Münster, Hamburg and Bremen; mem. Gesellschaft für Musikforschung, Royal Musical Asscn, Arbeitskreis Studium Populäres Musik, Arbeitskreis musikpädagogische Forschung. *Publications:* Heinrich VIII und die Musik: Überlieferung, musikalische Bildung des Adels und Kompositionstechniken eines Königs 1998, Beiträge zur Popularmusikforschung (ed.), Samples: Notizen, Projekte und Kurzbeiträge zur Popularmusikforschung (ed.); contrib. to Die Musikforschung, Beiträge zur Popularmusikforschung, Hamburger Jahrbuch für Musikwissenschaft. *Address:* Institut für Musik und ihre Didaktik, Universität Dortmund, 44221 Dortmund, Germany (office). *Telephone:* (231) 755-2975 (office). *Fax:* (231) 755-6236 (office). *E-mail:* Dietrich.Helms@Uni-Dortmund.de (office).

**HELMS, Joachim;** Singer (Tenor); b. 24 June 1943, Rostock, Germany. *Education:* Studied at the Franz Liszt Musikhochschule Weimar and in Dresden. *Career:* Debut: Erfurt, 1974, as Ernesto in Don Pasquale; Sang at Erfurt, 1974–83, as Mozart's Ferrando and Tamino, the Duke of Mantua, Nemorino, Don Carlos, Max in Der Freischütz and Sergei in Katerina Izmailova; Dresden Staatsoper from 1984, as Rodolfo, Alfredo and Don Ottavio; Guest appearances in the former Soviet Union, Poland, Bulgaria, Austria and Switzerland; Sang Ernesto at Leipzig, 1989; Many concert appearances and broadcasting engagements. *Address:* c/o Staatsoper, 8012 Dresden, Germany.

**HELPS, Robert;** Composer, Pianist and Professor; b. 23 Sept. 1928, New Jersey, USA. *Education:* Juilliard Preparatory Department and Institute of Musical Arts, 1936–43; Private study with Abby Whiteside, piano; and Roger Sessions, composition, 1943–60. *Career:* Debut: Recital, New York, 1990; Active piano and chamber music performances including many premieres with leading contemporary music groups in New York, Boston, Chicago, San Francisco, Los Angeles; Tours with Bethany Beardslee, Soprano, Rudolf Kolisch, Isidore Cohen, Jorja Freezanis, Violin. *Compositions:* Symphony, Two Piano Concertos, various chamber music and songs; Many solo piano pieces, voice and orchestra. *Recordings include:* Nocturne, 3 Hommages; Hommage a Faure; 3 Hommages, Nocturne for string quartet. *Publications include:* Nocturne, 1975; Valse Mirage, 1978; Eventually the Carousel Begins, 1991; The Running Sun, 1976; Symphony No. 1; Piano Concerto No. 1. *Address:* 4202 E Fowler Avenue, USF 30838, Tampa, FL 33620-9951, USA.

**HELTAY, Laszlo (Istvan);** British (b. Hungarian) Conductor; b. 5 Jan. 1930, Budapest, Hungary. *Education:* MA, Franz Liszt Academy of Music, Budapest, with Kodály and Bardos; BLitt, Merton Coll., Oxford. *Career:* Director of Music, Merton Coll., Oxford, 1960–64; Founded the Kodaly Choir, and Schola Cantorum of Oxford (subsequently Collegium Musicum Oxoniense), 1960 and gave premiere of Kodaly's The Music Makers, 1964; Associate Conductor, New Zealand Broadcasting Corporation Symphony Orchestra 1964–65; Musical Dir, New Zealand Opera Company, 1964–66; Conductor, Phoenix Opera Company, London, 1967–69, 1973; Conductor, Collegium Musicum of London, 1970–89; Dir of Music, Gardner Centre, Sussex Univ. 1968–78; Founder and Music Dir Brighton Festival Chorus 1967–94, Conductor Emeritus 1994–; Music Dir, Chorus of the Academy of St Martin in the Fields, 1975–99; Dir of Royal Choral Society, 1985–94; Dir, Coro de RadioTelevision Española, Madrid 1997–2000; concerts with Norddeutscher Rundfunk Chor; the Philharmonia, the Royal Philharmonic, London Philharmonic and Dallas Symphony Orchestras; masterclasses for young choral conductors in Europe and USA. *Recordings:* Choral works of Kodály, Respighi, Rossini and Haydn (Stabat Mater and Salve Regina) on Argo and Decca Labels; Paco Peña, Misa Flamenca for Virgin; recordings for CBS and Nimbus; Chorus Director for film 'Amadeus'. *Honours:* International Kodály Medal, 1982; Hon. DMus Univ. of Sussex, 1995; Hon. Fellow of Merton Coll., Oxford, 1997. *Address:* Can Lleuger, Apto 43 08318 Canyamars Spain.

**HEMM, Manfred;** Singer (Baritone); b. 1961, Mödling, Austria; m. Amanda Roocroft, 1995. *Education:* Studied at the Vienna Conservatory with Waldemar Kmentt. *Career:* Debut: Klagenfurt 1984, as Mozart's Figaro; Sang at Augsburg 1984–86, Graz, 1986–88, notably as Papageno, Leporello and Polyphemus in Acis and Galatea; Vienna Staatsoper from 1988 (title role in the premiere of Von Einem's Tuliphant, 1990); Guest appearances as Bayreuth, Basel, Berne, Zürich, Salzburg (Figaro, 1989–91) and Orange; Sang Figaro at the Deutsche Oper Berlin, 1990, Aix-en-Provence Festival, 1991; Metropolitan Opera debut 1991, as Papageno; Salzburg Festival, 1992, as the One Eyed Brother in Die Frau ohne Schatten; Philadelphia 1995, as Giorgio in I Puritani; Sang Kuno in Der Freischütz in concert with the Royal Opera, 1998; Sang Amfortas for Scottish Opera and Mozart's Figaro in Munich 2000; Frequent Lieder recitals and concert appearances. *Recordings include:* Video of Die Zauberflote, from the Met. *Address:* c/o Metropolitan Opera, Lincoln Center, New York, NY 10023, USA.

**HEMSLEY, Thomas,** CBE, FGSM; British opera and concert singer, producer and educator; b. 12 April 1927, Coalville, Leicestershire, England; m. Gwenllian James 1960; three s. *Education:* Brasenose College, Oxford, private music studies. *Career:* opera debut, Mermaid Theatre, London, 1951; St Paul's Cathedral, London, 1950–51; Stadttheater, Aachen, 1953–56; Deutsche Oper am Rhein, 1957–63; Opernhaus Zürich, Switzerland, 1963–67; Performed at Glyndebourne, 1953–83, as Hercule (Alceste), Masetto (Don Giovanni), Sprecher (Zauberflöte), Minister (Fidelio), Dr Reischmann (Elegy for Young Lovers), Musiklehrer (Ariadne), Aeneas (Dido), Arbace (Idomeneo); Edinburgh and Bayreuth Festivals, (1968–70, as Beckmesser), Covent Garden, Scottish Opera, Welsh Opera, English National Opera, English Opera Group, Kent Opera (Falstaff, 1980); Created Demetrius in A Midsummer Night's Dream (Aldeburgh 1960), Mangus in The Knot Garden at Covent Garden, 1970, and Caesar in Iain Hamilton's Catiline Conspiracy, 1974; Produced The Return of Ulysses for Kent Opera, 1989; Soloist with many major orchestras; Frequent broadcast on radio and television; Repertoire includes more than 150 Operatic Roles; Masterclasses, BBC television, Danish television, Music colleges in the United Kingdom, Denmark, Sweden, Norway; Visiting Professor, Royal College of Music, London and Royal Northern College of Music; Guest Professor, Royal Danish Academy of Music; Director of Opera, Dartington International Music Summer School; mem, Equity; ISM; Garrick Club; Member, Royal Philharmonic Society; Fellow Royal Society of Arts. *Recordings:* Operas: Dido and Aeneas; The Fairy Queen; Saul; Xerxes; Alcina; Alceste; Midsummer Night's Dream; Savitri; The Knot Garden; Meistersinger; The Olympians; The Wandering Scholar. Cantatas: Bach; Handel; Schütz; Songs: Schubert; Schumann; Wolf; Berkeley; Fauré, Duparc, Roussel; Choral: Delius Requiem. *Publications include:* Singing and Imagination 1998. *Honours:* Honorary RAM, 1974; Hon FTCL, 1988. *Address:* 10 Denewood Road, London N6 4AJ, England.

**HENCK, Herbert;** Pianist and Writer on Music; b. 28 July 1948, Treysa, Hesse, Germany. *Education:* Studied in Mannheim and Stuttgart, and at the Hochschule für Musik, Cologne, with Aloys Kontarsky. *Career:* Many appearances in Germany and elsewhere in 20th Century repertory, notably with music by Cage, Stockhausen, Boulez and Schoenberg; leader of courses at Darmstadt, Cologne and other avant-garde centres. *Recordings include:*

Boulez Sonatas; Music of Changes, Cheap Imitation and Music for Piano, 1–84, by John Cage; Stockhausen's Klavierstücke I–IX; Les Heures persanes, by Koechlin; Music by Schoenberg and Charles Ives. *Publications include:* Neuland, Ansätze zur Musik der Gegenwart, 1980–85; Experimentelle Pianistik, 1994. *Address:* c/o Hochschule für Musik, Dagoherstrasse 38, 50688 Cologne, Germany.

**HENDERSON, Gavin Douglas,** CBE; British; *Principal, Trinity College of Music;* b. 3 Feb. 1948, Brighton, England; m. Mary Jane Walsh 1992; two s. *Education:* Brighton Coll. of Art, Kingston Art Coll., Slade School of Fine Art, Univ. Coll. London. *Career:* debut as soloist, Wigmore Hall 1972; performer, BBC radio and television, festivals including City of London, Brighton; Artistic Dir, Brighton, York, Portsmouth, Crawley, Bracknell (jazz, folk and early music), Bournemouth festivals; Chief Exec., the New Philharmonia and Philharmonia Orchestra 1975–79; Chair., Music Panel, Arts Council of England; Vice-Pres., British Arts Festivals Assen; Vice-Pres., European Festivals Assen, Pres. 2004–; Principal and Chief Exec., Trinity Coll. of Music, London; Artistic Dir, Dartington Int. Summer School 1985–; Chair., Nat. Foundation for Youth Music 1998–; mem. RSA, ISM, Musicians' Union, Worshipful Co. of Musicians, RSM. *Publications:* Picasso and the Theatre 1982, Festivals UK Arts Council 1986, National Arts and Media Strategy (Festivals Section) 1991; contrib. to Musical Times, Classical Music, Tempo, The Listener. *Honours:* Hon. MA (Sussex); Hon. Fellow, Sussex Univ., Univ. of Brighton. *Address:* Trinity College of Music, King Charles Court, Old Royal Naval College, Greenwich, London, SE10 9JF, England. *Website:* www.tcm.ac .uk.

**HENDERSON, Katherine;** Singer (Mezzo-soprano); b. 1970, Cape Town, South Africa. *Education:* University of Cape Town; National Opera Studio, 1998. *Career:* Debut: Beethoven's Choral Fantasia, Cape Town Symphony Orchestra, 1994; Sang title role in Peter Brook's La Tragédie de Carmen, Cape Town; Concert for Nelson Mandela, 1996; Appearances at Cape Town as Lola in Cavalleria Rusticana and as Maddalena in Rigoletto; Carmen for Castleward Opera, Belfast; Bess in Porgy and Bess Suite, Peterborough; Mercédès in Carmen for Opera North and Mozart's Requiem at Basingstoke; Season 1999 at Mercedes, at Leeds; The Kingdom by Elgar, Isle of Wight; Further concerts. *Honours:* Winner, Wendy Fine Opera Prize Competition, 1994. *Address:* Music International, 13 Ardilaun Road, London N5 2QR, England.

**HENDERSON, Moya;** Composer; b. 2 Aug. 1941, Quirindi, New South Wales, Australia. *Education:* Studied at the University of Queensland and with Maurice Kagel in Cologne. *Compositions include:* Sacred Site for Organ and Tape, 1983; The Dreaming for Strings, 1985; Celebration 40,000, piano concerto, 1987; Currawong: A Symphony Of Bird Sounds, 1988; Waking Up The Flies, piano trio, 1990; Wild card for Soprano, Cello and Piano, 1991; Anzac Fanfare for soprano and orchestra, 1995; Lindy, opera, 1997; In Paradisum for chorus, 1997; I Walked into my Mother, music drama for radio, 1998; Music theatre pieces, chamber and vocal music. *Address:* c/o 1A Eden Street, PO Box 567, Crows Nest, NSW 2065, Australia.

**HENDL, Walter;** Conductor, Pianist and Composer; b. 12 Jan. 1917, West New York, New Jersey, USA; m. Barbara Helsley, 1 d. by previous marriage. *Education:* Studied piano with Clarence Adler; Piano scholarship student of David Saperton and conducting scholarship student of Fritz Reiner, Curtis Institute of Music, Philadelphia; Conducting student of Serge Koussevitzky, Berkshire Music Center, Tanglewood, Massachusetts, summers 1941–42. *Career:* Assistant Conductor, New York Philharmonic Orchestra, 1945–49; Music Director, Dallas Symphony Orchestra, 1953–72; Associate Conductor, Chicago Symphony Orchestra, 1958–64; Music Director, Ravinia Festival, 1959–63; Director, Eastman School of Music, Rochester, New York, 1964–72; Music Director, Erie (Pennsylvania) Philharmonic Orchestra, 1976–. *Recordings:* Several. *Address:* c/o Erie Philharmonic Orchestra, 409 G Daniel Baldwin Building, Erie, PA 16501, USA.

**HENDRICKS, Barbara Ann,** BSc, BMus; Swedish singer (soprano); b. 20 Nov. 1948, Stephens, Ark.; d. of M. L. and Della Hendricks; m. Ulf Englund 1978; one s. one d. *Education:* Univ. of Neb. and Juilliard School of Music, New York, studying with Jennie Tourel. *Career:* operatic debut, San Francisco Opera (L'Incoronazione di Poppea) 1976; has appeared with opera companies of Boston, Santa Fe, Glyndebourne, Hamburg, La Scala (Milan), Berlin, Paris, LA, Florence and Royal Opera, Covent Garden (London), Vienna; recitals in most maj. centres in Europe and America; has toured extensively in USSR and Japan; concert performances with all leading European and US orchestras; has appeared at many maj. music festivals including Edin., Osaka, Montreux, Salzburg, Dresden, Prague, Aix-en-Provence, Orange and Vienna; nearly 90 recordings; nominated Goodwill Amb. for Refugees at UNHCR 1987; Founder of the Barbara Hendricks Foundation for Peace and Reconciliation in 1998. *Film appearance:* La Bohème 1988, The Rake's Progress 1994. *Honours:* Hon. mem. Inst. of Humanitarian Law, San Remo, Italy 1990; Commdr des Arts et des Lettres; Hon. DMus (Nebraska Wesleyan Univ.) 1988; Dr hc (Univ. of Louvain, Belgium) 1990, 1993, (Juilliard School, New York) 2000; Prince of Asturias Foundation Award 2000, Lions Club International Award for the Defense of Human Rights 2001, Premio Internacional Xifra Heras (Univ. of Gerona, Spain) 2004, La Medaille D'Or de la ville de Paris 2004. *Address:* B H Office, c/o Fondberg Produktion, Dalagatan 48, 11324, Stockholm, Sweden (office). *E-mail:* bh.office@bluewin.ch (office). *Website:* www.barbarahendricks .com (office).

**HENDRICKS, Marijke;** Singer (Mezzo-soprano); b. 18 April 1956, Schinveld, Netherlands. *Education:* Studied in Maastricht and Cologne. *Career:* Sang at the Cologne Opera 1981–85, notably as Nancy in Martha, Cherubino, Hansel, Meg Page and Olga in Eugene Onegin; Sang the Marchesa in Musgrave's The Voice of Ariadne at the 1982 Edinburgh Festival; Guest appearances at Geneva 1985, as Cherubino, Salzburg, 1986 as Second Lady in Die Zauberflöte and Innsbruck, 1986 in the title role of Cesti's Orontea; Bordeaux and Lyon 1987, as Ramiro in La Finta Giardiniera; Amsterdam 1987, in a concert performance of Tancredi, as Isaura; Visits to the Orange Festival and to Israel with the company of Cologne Opera, 1984; Antwerp 1988, as Dulcinée in Massenet's Don Quichotte; Maastricht 1989 in La Belle Hélène; Television appearances in Austria and Switzerland. *Address:* Oper der Stadt Köln, Offenbachplatz, 5000 Cologne, Germany.

**HENDRICKS, Scott;** Singer (Baritone); b. 1970, San Antonio, Texas. *Education:* University of Arkansas. *Career:* Season 1997–98 as Mozart's Count, and in Billy Budd and Carmen, at Houston; Season 1998–99 as Dmitry in the premiere of Todd Machover's Resurrection and as Sharpless in Butterfly; other roles include Ford in Falstaff, Gianni Schicchi, Papageno and Don Giovanni; Season 1999–2000 as Dandini in La Cenerentola at Santa Barbara, Rossini's Figaro at Kansas City and Messiah in New York; Complete Songs of Franz Schubert Recital Series, with John Wustmann; Season 2000–01 as Eugene Onegin for Utah Opera, Wagner's Donner, Posa in Don Carlos and Malatesta in Don Pasquale, for Cologne Opera; Ford at Santa Fe, Marcello in San Diego and Don Giovanni for Arizona Opera, 2001. *Address:* c/o IMG Artists, Lovell House, 616 Chiswick High Rd, London W4 5RX, England.

**HENDRIKX, Louis;** Singer (Bass); b. 13 March 1927, Antwerp, Belgium. *Education:* Studied at the Antwerp Conservatory and with Willem Ravelli. *Career:* Debut: Antwerp 1963, as Samuel in Un Ballo in Maschera; Sang in Antwerp and Kassel; Further appearances in Hannover, Cologne; Dortmund; Munich; Hamburg, Nuremberg, Lyon, Bordeaux, Toulouse, Venice, Palermo, Milan, Monte Carlo, Stockholm, Glasgow and London (Gurnemanz at Covent Garden); Promenade Concerts 1972; Théâtre de la Monnaie and Rome Opera 1973, as Boris Godunov and as King Mark in Tristan und Isolde; Also Salzburg, Fafner in Rheingold and Pogner in Meistersinger for the Easter Festivals. *Recordings include:* Gessler in Guillaume Tell (EMI); Rheingold with Herbert von Karajan. *Address:* c/o Théâtre de la Monnaie, 4 Léopold-strasse, 1000 Brussels, Belgium.

**HENKEL, Kathy,** BA, BM, MA; American composer, writer and lecturer; b. 20 Nov. 1942, Los Angeles, CA; d. of Norman Nicholas Henkel and Lila Rhea Lee; m. Michael E. Manes (divorced). *Education:* Univ. of California at Los Angeles, California State Univ. at Northridge. *Career:* music reviewer, Los Angeles Times 1979; scriptwriter and producer for radio station, KUSC-FM 1984–89; programme annotator, education co-ordinator, Chamber Music/LA Festival 1987–95; programme annotator, Los Angeles Chamber Orchestra 1988–98; liner notes writer, Pro Piano Records 1993–2003; owner, Sign of the Silver Birch Music 2003–; works premiered and performed at Gubbio Music Festival, Italy, Montevarchi Festival, Italy, Alaska Women Festival, Fairbanks, Dana Festival, Ohio, Toronto Guitar Society, live broadcasts on KFAC, Los Angeles, London, England, Greenwich Village, New York; commission from State of Alaska 1993; mem. Chamber Music America, Phi Beta Women's Professional Arts Fraternity, Nat. Acad. of Recording Arts and Sciences. *Compositions:* Pioneer Song Cycle 1968, Trumpet Sonata 1979, Lost Calendar Pages 1984, Moorland Sketches 1985, Piano Sonata 1986, Bass Clarinet Sonata 1987, River Sky for solo guitar 1988, Book of Hours for solo harp 1990, Sonata for flute and organ 1992, Alaskan Fantasy and Fanfare 1993, Sea Songs 1997, Suite Spice for clarinet, bassoon and piano 2001, Gotta Minute Suite 2003, Tango for bassoon and piano 2005, Bestiary for bassoon quartet 2006. *Publications:* contrib. to Performing Arts Magazine. *Address:* 2367 Creston Drive, Los Angeles, CA 90068-2201, USA (office).

**HENN, Brigitte;** Singer (Soprano); b. 21 Oct. 1939, Freudenthal, Czechslovakia; m. Raymond Henn. *Education:* Studied in Frankfurt, in Wiesbaden with Helena Braun and in Basle. *Career:* Sang at the Basle Opera, 1968–75, Deutsche Oper Berlin, 1976–80; Guest appearances at Basle from 1982, and in Düsseldorf, Frankfurt, Zürich and Hanover; Roles have included Mozart's Countess, Donna Anna and Fiordiligi, Agathe, Euridice, Marenka in The Bartered Bride, Wagner's Senta, Elsa and Sieglinde, Elisabeth de Valois, Alice Ford and Amelia in Un Ballo in Maschera; Operetta engagements in works by Lehar and Zeller; Many concert appearances.

**HENRY, Antoni Garfield;** Singer (Tenor); b. 1970, England. *Education:* Studies with Ludmilla Andrew and Nicholas Powell. *Career:* Debut: Luigi in Il Tabarro for Broomhill Opera; Appearances as Don José for Opera North, 1999; Rodolfo for European Chamber Opera and at Holland Park, 1998–99; The Duke of Mantua for English Touring Opera; Canio in Pagliacci for Central Festival Opera; Alfred in Die Fledermaus and Pinkerton for European Chamber Opera; Carmen Jones, Old Vic and West Side Story for Pimlico Opera. *Address:* c/o Music International, 13 Ardilaun Road, London N5 2QR, England.

**HENRY, Claire;** Singer (Mezzo-soprano); b. 1970, England. *Education:* Studied at Trinity College, London and with Ryland Davies. *Career:* Appearances as Mozart's Sesto, Bloomsbury Theatre; Cherubino for Clonter Opera; Périchole for Dorset Opera; Kate Pinkerton, English National Opera; In Die Meistersinger, Covent Garden; Concerts include Elgar's The Kingdom; Messiah and works by Haydn, Mendelssohn, Bach, Mozart and Vivaldi;

Season 1999: With Herr Mozart and Doctor Strauss for the Covent Garden Festival. *Honours:* First Prize, English Song Competition, TCM. *Address:* Music International, 13 Ardilaun Road, London N5 2QR, England.

**HENRY, Didier;** France singer (baritone); b. 24 May 1953, Paris. *Education:* Paris Conservatoire and the studio of the Grand Opéra. *Career:* sang at St Etienne 1988, in a revival of Massenet's Amadis; Aix-en-Provence 1989, in The Love for Three Oranges and in Belfast as Valentin the same year; season 1990 as Marc-Antoine in Massenet's Cléopâtre at St Etienne, followed by Blondel in Grétry's Richard Coeur de Lion; has sung in Moscow in Pelléas et Mélisande, in Marseille as Pietro in La Muette de Portici by Auber and at the Paris Théâtre du Châtelet in L'Enfant et les Sortilèges; other roles include Gluck's Orestes (La Scala 1991), Puccini's Lescaut, Pelléas and Hamlet; Marquis de la Force in Poulenc's Carmelites at the 1999 London Proms; sang Gluck's Oreste at Marseille 2000. *Recordings include:* Pelléas et Mélisande, The Love for Three Oranges and Massenet's Amadis and Cléopâtre, Mélodies de Ravel, Massenet, Poulenc and Saint-Saëns. *Address:* c/o Chorégies d'Orange, BP 205, 84107 Orange Cédex, France.

**HENSCHEL, Dietrich;** German singer (baritone); b. 1967, Berlin. *Education:* studied with Hanno Blanschke in Munich and with Dietrich Fischer-Dieskau in Berlin. *Career:* debut at the Munich Biennale in Michèle Reverdy's Le Précepteur 1990; concert appearances in festivals at Stuttgart, Urach and Feldkirch (Schubertiade); Kiel Opera 1993–96, as Mozart's Papageno and Count, Rossini's Figaro, Valentin in Faust, Pelléas, Henze's Prince of Homburg, and Monteverdi's Orfeo; engagements with leading orchestras in Germany, Netherlands and Austria; numerous guest appearances at opera houses from 1996, including in Bonn, Stuttgart, Lyons, Deutsche Oper, Berlin (debut in the title role of Hans Werner Henze's Der Prinz von Homburg 1997); other opera roles include the title role of Nixon in China, Tuzenbach in the premiere of Trois Soeurs by Peter Eötvös, Olivier in Capriccio, the Barber in Die schweigsame Frau, and Faust in Busoni's Doktor Faust; concert repertory includes Messiah, Gounod's St Cecilia Mass, Carmina Burana, numerous song recitals of Lieder repertory. *Recordings:* Carmina Burana, Mozart's Messiah, songs by Othmar Schoeck, Humperdinck's Königskinder, Brahms's German Requiem, Haydn's Four Seasons, Mahler orchestral songs (with Kent Nagano and the Hallé Orchestra), Bach's St Matthew Passion (with Nikolaus Harnoncourt and Concentus Musicus Wien), Korngold Lieder, Schubert's Die Winterreise (with Irwin Gage) 2000, Mahler's Des Knaben Wunderhorn (with Philippe Herreweghe and the Orchestre des Champs-Elysées) 2005. *Address:* c/o Christian Lange, Langemusic, Ludwig-Behr-Str. 7, 82327 Tutzing, Germany. *Website:* www.dietrichhenschel.de.

**HENSCHEL, Jane Elizabeth,** BA; American singer (mezzo-soprano); b. 2 March 1952, Appleton, Wis.; d. of Lester Haentzschel and Betty Haentzschel (née Lau). *Education:* Univ. of Southern California. *Career:* debut with the Netherlands Opera as the Nurse in Die Frau ohne Schatten 1992; ensemble mem. Aachen Oper 1977–80; joined Wuppertal Opera, Germany 1980, later with Dortmund and Düsseldorf Operas; appearances at the Glyndebourne, Salzburg and Saito Kinen Festivals and at La Scala, Milan, Deutsche Oper, Berlin, Amsterdam Opera, Paris Opera, Bayerische Staatsoper, Munich, Staatsoper, Berlin, Royal Opera House, Covent Garden, London and the San Francisco Opera; has performed with numerous conductors including Seiji Ozawa, Sir Colin Davis, Daniel Barenboim, Bernard Haitink, Riccardo Muti, Christian Thielemann, Sir Andrew Davis, Lorin Maazel; Baroque repertoire includes Vivaldi's oratorio Juditha Triumphans (Radio France). *Operatic roles include:* Die Amme (the nurse) in Die Frau ohne Schatten (Netherlands Opera, Royal Opera House, London 1992, Los Angeles, Bavarian State Opera, Munich, Vienna, Paris, Deutsche Oper Berlin, Metropolitan Opera), Fricka in Das Rheingold and Die Walküre (Royal Opera House, London 1996), Ulrica in Un Ballo in Maschera (Royal Opera House, London), Klytemnestra in Elektra (Bavarian State Opera, Munich, Royal Opera House, London), Herodias in Salome (Bavarian State Opera, Munich, La Scala, Milan, San Francisco Opera), Brangäne in Tristan und Isolde (Orange Festival, Los Angeles Music Center Opera, Paris Opera), Queen of Sheba in Königin von Saba (Concertgebouw, Amsterdam), Genevieve in Pelléas et Mélisande (Japan), Cassandre in Les Troyens (La Scala, Milan), Waltraute in Götterdämmerung (Royal Opera House, London), Mrs Grose in The Turn of the Screw (Royal Opera House, London), Judy in Birtwistle's Punch and Judy (Netherlands Opera 1993), Kostelnicka in Jenufa (Japan), Mistress Quickly in Falstaff (Vienna, Munich, with the London Symphony Orchestra), The Witch in Rusalka, Ottavia in L'Incoronazione di Poppea (Aachen Oper), Erda in Ring (Royal Opera House, London) 2004. Auntie in Peter Grimes (Salzburg) 2004, Mistress Quickly (LA Opera) 2004; Amneris, Eboli, Ortrud, Carmen, Azucena, Venus. *Recordings include:* Mahler's 8th Symphony with CBSO and Simon Rattle, The Rake's Progress with Ozawa, Krasa's Die Verlobung im Traum, Die Drei Groschen Oper, Britten's The Turn of the Screw with Daniel Harding, Albeniz' Merlin with Placido Domingo. *Honours:* Grammy Award 2001, Gramophone Award 2003. *Current Management:* c/o Askonas Holt, Lonsdale Chambers, 27 Chancery Lane, London, WC2A 1PF, England. *Telephone:* (20) 7400-1700 (office). *Fax:* (20) 7400-1799 (office). *E-mail:* peter .bloor@askonasholt.co.uk (office). *Website:* www.askonasholt.co.uk (office).

**HENZE, Hans Werner;** German composer and conductor; b. 1 July 1926, Gütersloh; s. of Franz Henze and Margarete Geldmacher. *Education:* Staatsmusikschule, Braunschweig, Kirchenmusikalisches Institut, Heidelberg. *Career:* musical collaborator Deutsches Theater in Konstanz 1948; Artistic Dir and Conductor Ballet of the Hessian State Theatre in Wiesbaden

1950; living in Italy as an ind. artist since 1953; Prof. of Composition, Mozarteum, Salzburg 1962–67; Prof. of Composition, Hochschule für Musik, Cologne 1980–91; Artistic Dir Accad. Filarmonica Romana 1982–91; Prof. of Composition RAM, London 1987–91; founder and Artistic Dir Munich Biennale for Contemporary Music Theatre 1988–; composer-in-residence Berlin Philharmonic Orchestra 1990; 'Voices' series of concerts to celebrate 75th birthday, London 2001; mem. Akad. der Künste, Berlin 1960–68, Bayerische Akad. der Schönen Künste, Munich, Akad. der Künste, Hamburg. *Compositions include:* opera and music theatre: Das Wundertheater 1948, Boulevard Solitude 1951, Ein Landarzt 1951, Das Ende einer Welt 1953, König Hirsch (revised as Il Re Cervo) 1953, Der Prinz von Homburg 1958, Elegy for Young Lovers 1959, Der Junge Lord 1964, Die Bassariden 1964, Das Ende einer Welt 1964, Ein Landarzt 1964, Der langwierige Weg in die Wohnung des Natascha Ungeheuer 1971, La Cubana 1973, We Come to the River 1974, Don Chischiotte della Mancia 1976, Pollicino (for children) 1979, The English Cat 1980, Il ritorno d'Ulisse in Patria 1981, Das verratene Meer 1986, Il re Teodoro in Venezia 1991, Venus and Adonis 1993, L'Upapa–oder der Triumph der Sohnesliebe 2003; ballet: Jack Pudding 1949, Ballet-Variationen 1949, Das Vokaltuch der Kammersängerin Rosa Silber 1950, Die Schlafende Prinzessin 1951, Labyrinth 1951, Der Idiot 1952, Maratona 1956, Undine 1956, Des Kaisers Nachtigall 1959, Tancredi 1964, Orpheus 1978, Le disperazioni del Signor Pulcinella 1992, Le fils de l'air 1995, Labyrinth 1996, Tanzstunden, Ballet Triptych 1997; oratorio: Novae de Infinito Laudes 1962, The Raft of the Medusa 1968; cantata: Being Beauteous 1963, Ariosi 1963, Cantata della Fiaba Estrema 1963, Moralities 1967; vocal music: Whispers from Heavenly Death 1948, Der Vorwurf 1948, Apollo and Hyacinth 1949, 5 Neapolitan Songs 1956, Nachtstücke and Arien 1957, Kammermusik 1958, Novae de Infinito Laudes 1962, Ariosi 1963, Being Beateous 1963, Lieder von einer Insel 1964, Musen Siziliens 1966, Versuch über Schweine 1968, Das Floss der Medusa 1968, El Cimarrón 1969, Voices 1973, Jephte 1976, El Rey de Harlem 1979, Canzoni for Orpheus 1980, Paraphrasen über Dostoiewsky 1990, Richard Wagnersche Klavierlieder 1998, Six Songs from the Arabic 1998; orchestral: Sinfonie 1947, three concertos for violin 1947, 1971, 1997, two concertos for piano 1950, 1967, Symphonic Variation 1950, Ode to the West Wind 1953, Quattro Poemi 1955, Concerto per il Marigny 1956, Jeux des Tritons 1957, Quattro Fantaise 1958, Sonata for Strings 1958, 3 Dithyrambs 1958, Antifone 1960, Los Caprichos 1963, Double Bass Concerto 1966, Telemanniana 1967, Compases para preguntas ensimisadas 1970, Heliogabalus Imperator 1971, Tristan 1973, Ragtimes and Habaneras 1975, In Memoriam: Amicizia 1976, Aria de la Folía española 1977, Il Vitalino raddoppiato 1977, Barcarola 1979, Apollo Trionfante 1979, Le Miracle de la Rose 1981, Canzona 1982, I Sentimenti di Carl P. E. Bach 1982, Sonata for 6 1984, Guitar Concerto 1986, Sieben liebeslieder 1986, Allegro brillante 1989, Requiem 1990, Quintetto 1990, Fünf Nachtstücke 1990, Trumpet Concerto 1992, Sieben Boleros 1998, Trio in drei Sätzen 1998, Fraternité 1999, Tempest 2000, Scorribanda Sinfonica 2001, L'heure bleue 2001, Scornbanda 2001, 10th Symphony 2002. *Publications:* Das Ende einer Welt 1953, Undine, Tagebuch eines Balletts 1959, Essays 1964, El Cimarrón: ein Werkstattbericht 1971, Musik und Politik 1976, Die Englische Katze—Ein Arbeitsbuch 1978–82 1983, Reiselieder mit böhmischen Quinten 1996, Komponieren in der Schule 1998, Bohemian Fifths: An Autobiography (trans. by Stewart Spencer) 1998, Briefe Einer Freundschaft (with Ingeborg Bachmann) 2004. *Honours:* Hon. FRNCM 1998; Hon. DMus (Edin.) 1971; Robert Schumann Prize 1951, North-Rhine-Westphalia Art Prize 1957, Prix d'Italia 1954, Sibelius Gold Medal, Harriet Cohen Awards, London 1956, Music Critics Prize, Buenos Aires 1958, Kunstpreis, Berlin, Niedersächsischer Kunstpreis 1962, Ludwig-Spohr-Preis 1976, Heidelberg-Bach-Preis 1983, Siemens-Preis 1990, Apollo d'Oro, Bilbao 1990, Preis des Internationales Theaterinstituts 1991, Grosses Bundesverdienst-kreuz 1991, Kultureller Ehrenpreis, Munich 1996, Hans-von-Bülow Medal of the Berlin Philharmonic Orchestra 1997, Bayerischer Maximiliansorden für Wissenschaft und Kunst 1998, Praemium imperiale, Tokyo 2000, Best Living Composer, Cannes Classical Award 2001, German Dance Prize 2001. *Address:* c/o Künstler Sekretariat Christa Pfeffer, Schongauer Str. 22, 81377 Munich, Germany (office); c/o Chester Music, 8–9 Frith Street, London, W1D 3JB, England. *Telephone:* (20) 7432-4238 (London) (office); (89) 718041 (Munich). *Fax:* (20) 7287-6329 (London) (office). *E-mail:* com@schott-musik.de (office); wiebke.busch@musicsales.co.uk. *Website:* www.hanswernerhenze.de (home).

**HEPPNER, Ben,** OC, BMus, LLD; Canadian singer (tenor); b. 14 Jan. 1956, Murrayville, BC. *Education:* Univ. of British Columbia. *Career:* many oratorio and concert performances in Canada; Opera Bacchus in Ariadne auf Naxos; Canadian Opera Co. as Zinovy in Lady Macbeth of Mtsensk; American debut in Tannhäuser at the Chicago Lyric Opera 1988; has sung the Prince in Rusalka with the Philadelphia Opera Co., Seattle Opera 1990, and at the Vienna State Opera 1991; European debut at the Royal Opera Stockholm 1989, as Lohengrin; sang Walther von Stolzing on his La Scala and Covent Garden debuts 1990, and in Seattle; San Francisco Opera debut 1989, as Lohengrin; season 1991–92 with Janáček's Laca at Brussels, the Emperor in Die Frau ohne Schatten at Amsterdam and the premiere of William Bolcom's McTeague in Chicago; season 1992 with Dvořák's Dimitrij at Munich, Mozart's Titus at Salzburg; sang Lohengrin at Seattle 1994; Walther at the Met, New York 1995; debut as Tristan at Seattle 1998 and under Abbado at Salzburg 1999; sang Aeneas in Les Troyens with the London Symphony Orchestra at the Barbican Hall 2000; Schoenberg's Gurrelieder at the London Proms 2002; Otello at the Vienna Staatsoper 2003. *Recordings:* Fidelio (conducted by Colin Davis) 1996, two of Die Meistersinger (conducted by Wolfgang Sawallisch and by Solti) 1997, Rusalka (conducted by Charles Mackerras) 1998, Les Troyens (conducted by Sir Colin Davis) 2001. *Honours:* Birgit Nilsson Prize 1988, ECHO Deutscher Schallplattenpreis for Singer of the Year 1993, Juno Award for Best Classical Album, Vocal or Choral Performance 1996, Seattle Opera Artist of the Year 1996, Grammy Awards for Best Opera Recording 1998, Best Opera Recording and Best Classical Album 2002, Royal Philharmonic Soc. Award for best singer 2005. *Current Management:* Columbia Artists Management, 165 W 57th Street, New York, NY 10019, USA. *Address:* Administrative Office, 35 Kearney Drive, Toronto, ON M9W 5J5, Canada (office). *Telephone:* (416) 743-2761 (office). *E-mail:* eldonmcbride@sympatico.ca (office). *Website:* www.benheppner.com.

**HERBERT, Trevor,** *PhD, CertEd, ARCM, LGSM;* Musician and Musicologist; b. 18 Oct. 1945, Cwmparc, Wales; pnr Helen Grace Barlow. *Education:* Tonypandy Grammar School, St Luke's Coll., Exeter, Royal Coll. of Music, Open Univ. *Career:* trombone player (modern and period instruments), BBC Symphony Orchestra, Royal Philharmonic Orchestra, WNO, Musica Reservata, Taverner Players, Wallace Collection 1969–76; Music Department, Open Univ. 1976–, Prof. of Music 1998–; freelance performer, writer, composer and broadcaster; mem. Royal Musical Asscn, American Musicological Soc., Historic Brass Soc., Galpin Soc. *Compositions:* several TV scores, including Wales! Wales? (BBC 1993) and Under Milk Wood (Syriol/BBC 1992). *Recordings:* with major orchestras, Taverner Players, Musica Reservata. *Publications:* Cambridge Companion to Brass (ed with J. Wallace), The British Brass Band: A Musical and Social History, An introduction to the Cultural Study of Music (ed with M. Clayton and R. Middleton); contrib. to New Grove Dictionary of Music and Musicians, New Dictionary of National Biography, The Encyclopaedia of Popular Music of the World. *Honours:* Foundation scholar, Royal Coll. of Music 1967, Martin Scholarship 1968, Christopher Monk Award (Historic Brass Soc.) 2002.

**HERBIG, Gunther;** German conductor; b. 30 Nov. 1931, Aussig, Czechoslovakia; s. of Emil Herbig and Gisela (née Hieke) Herbig; m. Juttta Czapski 1958; one s. one d. *Education:* Franz Liszt Conservatory for Music, Weimar. *Career:* conductor, Nat. Theatre, Weimar 1957–62; Music Dir Hans Otto Theatre, Potsdam 1962–66; Conductor Berlin Symphony Orchestra, Berlin, GDR 1966–72; Gen. Music Dir 1977–83; Gen. Music Dir Dresden Philharmonic, Dresden, GDR 1972–77; Music Dir Detroit Symphony Orchestra, Detroit, Mich, USA 1984–90, Toronto Symphony Orchestra 1988–94, Toronto, Ont., Canada 1990–91; Prin. Guest Conductor Dallas Symphony Orchestra, Dallas Tex. 1979–81, BBC Philharmonic Orchestra, Manchester, UK 1981–84. *Honours:* Theodor Fontane Prize 1964, Cultural Award (GDR) 1970.

**HERCHERT, Jörg;** Composer; b. 20 Sept. 1943, Dresden, Germany. *Education:* Studied at the Dresden and East Berlin Conservatories, 1962–69, and with Paul Dessau at the Berlin Academy, 1970–74. *Career:* Freelance composer from 1975; Professor of Composition at the Dresden Conservatory 1992–. *Compositions:* Ode an eine Nachigall, for soprano and oboe, 1972; Komposition, for soprano, baritone and 12 instruments, 1975; Seligpreisungen I–VIII for organ 1974–85; Flute Concerto, 1976; Sextet, 1978; Das geistliche Jahr, cantata cycle, 1978–96 (9 works for soloists, chorus and ensemble with percussion); Horn Concerto, 1980; Octet, 1984; 2 String Quartets, 1981, 1986; Nonet, 1990; Nachtwache, opera, 1993; Abraum, opera, 1997; Namen Gottes I–XXI, for organ, 1990–97. *Address:* c/o Hochschule für Musik (Carl Maria von Weber), Blochmannstrasse 2–4, 01001 Dresden, Germany.

**HERFORD, (Richard) Henry,** *MA, ARNCM, GRNCM;* singer (baritone); b. 24 Feb. 1947, Edinburgh, Scotland; m. Lindsay John 1982; two s. one d. *Education:* King's College, Cambridge, Royal Northern College of Music. *Career:* Glyndebourne Chorus, 1977–78; Forester in Janáček's Cunning Little Vixen; Roles with Royal Opera House, Covent Garden, Scottish Opera, Handel Opera, Chelsea Opera Group, Batignano, Nancy, English Bach Festival; Frequent concerts with leading orchestras in the United Kingdom, Europe and North and South America; Appearances with many ensembles and on radio and television (Maxwell Davies: The Lighthouse, BBC 2); Numerous recitals; Visiting Professor at Royal Northern College of Music, Royal College of Music, Birmingham Conservatoire. *Recordings:* Recital of American Songs; High Priest in Rameau's Castor and Pollux; Handel's Messiah, excerpts with Scottish Chamber Orchestra and George Malcolm; Dickinson, A Dylan Thomas Song Cycle; Handel's Dixit Dominus and Israel in Egypt with King's College Cambridge Choir; Joubert, The Instant Moment with English String Orchestra; Vaughan Williams's Five Tudor Portraits, Five Mystical Songs; Britten's A Midsummer Night's Dream; Charles Ives: Songs, 2 vols; Songs with Instruments with Ensemble Modern; Maxwell Davies, Resurrection; Bridge, The Christmas Rose; Michael Berkeley, Père du doux repos; George Lloyd, Iernin; Stravinsky, Pulcinella; Edward Gregson, Missa Brevis Pacem; Bliss, Complete Songs; John Manduell: Songs of the Renaissance. *Honours:* Curtis Gold Medal (RNCM); Benson & Hedges Gold Award (Suape); First prize, American Music Competition (New York); British Retailers Record of the Year. *Address:* Pencots, Northmoor, Oxford OX29 5AX, England.

**HERINCX, Raimund (Raymond Frederick);** British singer (bass-baritone) and voice teacher and therapist; b. 23 Aug. 1927, London; s. of Florent Herincx and Marie Cheal; m. Margaret J. Waugh (known as Astra Blair) 1954; one s. two d. *Education:* Thames Valley Grammar School and Univ. of London. *Career:* Educ. Officer, Household Cavalry 1946–48; studied singing in

Antwerp, Brussels, Barcelona and London with Giovanni Valli, Samuel Worthington and Harold Williams 1949–53; mem. Royal Opera House chorus; joined Welsh Nat. Opera 1956; Prin. Baritone, Sadler's Wells Opera 1957–67; début Royal Opera House, Covent Garden 1968; joined Metropolitan Opera House, New York 1976, subsequently appearing in most major US opera houses mainly in works of Wagner and Richard Strauss; Prof. of Voice RAM 1970–77; Sr Voice Teacher, North East of Scotland Music School 1979–; voice therapist 1979–; voice teacher Trinity Coll. of Music, London 1993–; lecturer, Univ. Coll., Cardiff 1984–87; Music Critic for Music and Musicians. *Honours:* Hon. RAM 1971; Opera Medal, Int. Music Awards 1968. *Address:* c/o English National Opera, St. Martin's Lane, London, WC2N 4ES, England (office).

**HERING, Karl-Josef;** Singer (Tenor); b. 14 Feb. 1929, Westonnen, Germany. *Education:* Studied with Fred Husler, Max Lorenz and Franz Volker. *Career:* Debut: Hanover 1958, as Max in Der Freischütz; Engagements at the Deutsche Oper Berlin and in Cologne, Karlsruhe, Stuttgart, Vienna and Hamburg; Royal Opera House Covent Garden, as Siegfried in Der Ring des Nibelungen, 1966; Further appearances in Trieste, Toronto, Barcelona, Marseille and Buenos Aires; Other roles include Florestan, Canio, Aegisthus, Hermann in The Queen of Spades and Erik in Der fliegende Holländer; Many concert performances. *Address:* c/o Deutsche Oper Berlin, Richard Wagnerstrasse 10, 1000 Berlin, Germany.

**HERMAN, Silvia;** Singer (Soprano); b. 1954, Vienna, Austria. *Education:* Studied in Vienna with Anton Dermota: worked at the Opera Studio of the Vienna Staatsoper, 1976–79. *Career:* Appearances in Vienna 1979–82, Hamburg 1983–85; Guest engagements in Stuttgart, Geneva, Barcelona, Madrid and Cologne, 1989–90; Salzburg Festival, 1978–81; Bayreuth Festival 1978 as a Flowermaiden, 1985–88 as Wellgunde and Waltraute in Die Walküre; Bruckner Festival in Linz, 1982–88, and elsewhere, in Lieder recitals and concert showings. *Recordings:* Das Rheingold and Die Walküre, conducted by Haitink; Schumann's Das Paradies und der Peri. *Address:* Oper der Stadt Koln, Offenbachplatz, 5000 Cologne, Germany.

**HERMAN, Vasile;** Romanian composer and teacher; b. 10 June 1929, Satu Mare, Romania; s. of Vasile Herman and Elena Pop; m. Titina Herman, 2 c. *Education:* Diploma of Composition, 1957, Doctor of Musicology, 1974, High School; Diploma of Teacher of Music, 1954. *Career:* Television and radio appearances; mem. Composers' Union of Romania. *Compositions:* Double Concerto; Poliphony; Concert of Strings; Chamber works: Melopee, Variante, Epsodi, 5 Symphonies, Concerto for Strings and Percussion; Paos, 1993; Sysma, 1993; Refractus for violin and percussion, 1993; Fonolophion for oboe, harp, string and percussion, 1993; Gelou Quidam Blacus, 1996; Paos, 1996; Hora Lunga for clarinet piano and percussion, 1997; Variazioni for oboe, piano and percussion, 1998; Monocantata for tenor solo, clarinet solo and percussion, 1998; Akes Samenos for flute solo, Hestia for percussion 1999, Sonata for cello 2002. *Recordings:* Cantilations; Rimes Nostalgique; Variante. *Publications:* Form and Style in Contemporary Romanian Music 1977, The Musical Forms 1982; contrib. to Muzica, Steaua, Tribuna, Utunk (Romania). *Honours:* Order of Cultural Merit; Prize, Composers' Union, Romania; Prize, Romanian Academy, two Medals of Cultural Merit. *Address:* Str Octavian Goga No. 33 Apt 4, 3400 Cluj-Napoca, Romania.

**HERMAN, Witold Walenty,** *MA, DPhilMus;* Polish cellist; *Professor, State Academy of Music, Kraków;* b. 14 Feb. 1932, Toruń; m. Catherine Bromboszcz 1970; one s. one d. *Education:* Szymanowski Conservatory, Torun, Academy of Music, Kraków, Ecole Normale de Musique, Paris, France, World University, Tucson, AZ, USA. *Career:* debut with State Philharmonic, Kraków, May 1954; cello concerts with orchestras, cello recitals, masterclasses in Poland and other European countries; Professor, Music Academy, Kraków, Dir Cello and Double Bass Dept; Visiting Professor of the Franz Liszt Musik Akademie in Weimar, 1972; mem. Jury of the International Pablo Casals Cello Competition in Budapest 1968, int. cello competition Markneukirchen, Germany. *Recordings:* For radio and television in Poland and the rest of Europe including Radio Luxembourg; As a solo cellist with major symphony orchestras. *Publications:* Notes for Cello, edited in Poland, Polish Music Edition. *Honours:* Chevalier Cross of the Order of Polonia Restituta; Special Prize of the Polish Minister of Culture, Golden Cross of Merit, Poland, Excellence in Teaching Award Palm Beach Univ., Florida (USA) 2001, Honoured Guest Tchaikovsky Competition, Moscow (Russia), J. S. Bach Competition, Leipzig (Germany). *Address:* Academy of Music, ul sw. Tomasza 43, 31027 Kraków, Poland; ul Friedleina 49 m 5, 30-009 Kraków, Poland. *Telephone:* (12) 422-32-50 (office); (12) 634-53-73 (home). *Fax:* (12) 422-66-94 (office).

**HERMANN, Roland;** Singer (Baritone); b. 17 Sept. 1936, Bochum, Germany. *Education:* Vocal studies with Paul Lohmann, Margarethe von Winterfeldt and Falmino Contini. *Career:* Debut: Trier 1967 as Count Almaviva; Member of the Zürich Opera from 1968; Guest appearances in Munich, Paris, Berlin and Cologne; Buenos Aires 1974, as Jochanaan in Salome and Wolfram in Tannhäuser; US debut 1983, with the New York Philharmonic; La Scala Milan debut 1986, with Claudio Abbado; Roles include Don Giovanni, Amfortas, Germont, Gunther in Götterdämmerung and the title roles in Karl V by Krenek and Doktor Faust by Busoni; Apollo (L'Orfeo), Cinna (Lucio Silla), Morald (Die Feen), Forester (The Cunning Little Vixen); Mauregato (Alfonso und Estrella); Beckmesser, Achille (Penthesilea); Vendramin (Massimila Doni), Orff's Prometheus; Took part in the European stage premiere of Die Jakobsleiter by Schoenberg (Hamburg 1983) and the world premiere of Kelterborn's Der Kirschgarten (Zürich 1984); Sang in the premiere of Krenek's Oratorio Symeon der Stylites at the 1988 Salzburg Festival, conducted by Lothar Zagrosek; BBC London 1989, in the title role of Der Prinz von Homburg by Henze; sang the Forester in The Cunning Little Vixen at Zürich 1989, The Master in the premiere of York Höllier's Der Meister und Margarita (Paris 1989) and Gunther at a concert performance of Götterdämmerung at the Holland Festival; Sang Busoni's Doktor Faust at Leipzig, 1991; Season 1992 as Nekrotzar in Le Grand Macabre at Zürich, followed by the Count in Capriccio; Sang Paolo in Simon Boccanegra at Zürich, 1996; Gurlitt's Wozzeck at Florence, 1998; Many Lieder recitals and concert appearances. *Recordings include:* Penthesilea by Schoeck (BASF); Prometheus and Trionfi by Orff, Die Meistersinger, CPE Bach's Magnificat (Deutsche Grammophon); Moses und Aron by Schoenberg (CBS); Zemlinsky's Der Kreidekreis; Mathis der Maler by Hindemith; Peer Gynt by Werner Egk; Der Vampyr by Marschner; Schumann's Genoveva. *Current Management:* Ingpen & Williams Ltd, 7 St George's Court, 131 Putney Bridge Road, London, SW15 2PA, England.

**HERMANOVA, Vera;** Organist; b. 9 Sept. 1951, Brno, Czechoslovakia; m. Zdenek Spatka, 8 July 1977. *Education:* Conservatoire in Brno, 1967–73; Master's degree, Janáček Academy of Performing Arts in Brno, 1973–77; Postgraduate study at the Janáček Acdemy, 1978–81; Conservatoire National de Saint-Maur, Paris (with Professor Gaston Litaize), 1980–81; Postgraduate study of musical science, Doctor's degree, Masaryk University in Brno Faculty of Philosophy, 1991–97. *Career:* Special attention to French and Czech organ music of all periods; Master course with prominent European organists (Gaston Litaize, Piet Kee, Lionel Rogg); Radio and television recordings in Czech Republic, Denmark, Germany, Austria, Slovenia; Organ recitals in a number of European culture centres including Prague, Paris, Vienna, Linz, Berlin, Munich, Hamburg, Dresden, Copenhagen, Oslo, Ljubljana, Haarlem, Utrecht, and in festivals at home and abroad (the United Kingdom, Germany, Denmark, Netherlands, Austria); mem, Association Jehan Alain, Romainmôtier, Switzerland. *Recordings:* French Organ Works (Messiaen, Dupré, Alain); Les Grandes Orgues de Notre Dame de Chartres (French Organ Music); Musica Nova Bohemica (Eben, Kohoutek); Musik der Gegenwart (Bodorová); Czech Organ Music of the 18th Century; Czech Organ Music of the 20th Century; F. X. Brixi (1732–1771) Organ Concertos (with authentic period instruments), 1999. *Honours:* Finalist, International Organ Competition, Bologna, 1975; Premier Prix à l'Unanamité, Saint-Maur, 1981; Czech Music Fund Prize for CD recordings, Prague, 1992. *Address:* Udolní 13, 602 00 Brno, Czech Republic.

**HERNANDEZ, Cesar;** Singer (Tenor); b. 13 Oct. 1960, Puerto Rico. *Career:* Debut: New Jersey, 1989, as Rodolfo in La Bohème; Spoleto Festival, 1991, in Menotti's Goya; Appearances in opera houses at Trieste, Catania and Genoa; Season 1995 as Pinkerton at Hamburg, Alfredo at Vienna and Cavaradossi at Helsinki; Further engagements as the Duke of Mantua at Tel-Aviv and for Miami Opera, Edgardo in Lucia di Lammermoor and San Diego as Cavaradossi (1996); Sang Paco in La Vida Breve at Brussels, 1998; Season 2000 as Pinkerton at the Deutsche Oper Berlin, Cavaradossi in Brussels, Faust at the Salzburg Landestheater and Falla's Paco in Venice; Concerts include the Verdi Requiem. *Address:* c/o Théâtre Royale de la Monnaie, 4 Leopoldstrasse, 1000 Brussels, Belgium.

**HERNANDEZ-IZNAGA, Jorge;** Violist; b. 1950, Havana, Cuba; m. Lozano Carola, 1972, 1 s., 1 d. *Education:* National School of Art, Havana, 1964–72; Conservatory Tchaikovsky, Moscow, 1976–79, 1981–83. *Career:* Debut: Havana, 1972; Professor, Viola, Conservatory Roldan, Havana, 1972–76; Superior Institute of Arts, Havana, 1983–92; Principal Viola, National Symphonic Orchestra of Cuba; Founder, The Havana String Quartet; Television and radio appearances in Cuba, 1972–92, Moscow, 1977, 1979, Hungary, 1979, Argentina, 1987, 1988, Uruguay, 1988, Korea, 1988, Bulgaria, 1990, Mexico, 1990, Spain, 1992–97; Co-Principal, Orchestra of Cordova, Spain; mem, Writers and Artists Union of Cuba; Individual Member, Chamber Music of America. *Recordings:* Havana String Quartet, L Brouwer's Quartets and M Ravel-H Villa Lobos No. 1. *Honours:* Prize, Interpretive Mastery, Chamber Music Festival of Havana, 1987. *Current Management:* KH Productions SL. *Address:* Basilica No. 18, Madrid 28020, Spain.

**HERNANDEZ-LARGUIA, Cristian;** Choir Conductor; b. 6 Oct. 1921, Buenos Aires, Argentina; m. Eugenia Barbarich 1953. *Education:* Studied with T. Fuchs, E. Leuchter, R. Shaw, N. Greenberg and G. Graetzer. *Career:* Debut: Madrigal Group, Asoc Ros de Cultura Inglesa 1941; Conductor, Coro Estable de Rosario, since 1946; Founder and Conductor, Pro Musica de Rosario, 1962; Appearances in concert tours to North, Central and South America and Europe, 1967–92, Hunter College, NY, Coolidge Auditorium, Washington DC and St Martin in the Fields, London; Professor of Choir Conducting, Musical Morphology and Acoustics, University of Litoral, University Rosario. *Recordings:* 35 titles. *Publications:* Performances: Mass in B Minor, Bach's first version with Argentine cast, 1985; St John Passion, Bach, 1977; First Argentine performance of complete and original version Messiah, 1973, Brocke's Passion, 1980, Handel. *Honours:* Numerous personal and joint awards (with Pro Musica and CER) as well as National Culture Glory, 1984, Illustrious citizen, 1985, Concorso Internazionale Guido D'Arezzo, Italy, 1967–81. *Address:* San Luis 860, 4J 2000 Rosario, Argentina.

**HERNON, Paul;** Director and Designer; b. 1947, Northumberland, England. *Career:* Co-founded the London Music Theatre Group, 1982, and directed the British stage premieres of Martin's Le Vin Herbé and Vivaldi's Juditha Triumphans at the Camden Festival, London; British premieres of Salieri's Prima la Musica and Ward's The Crucible; Directed a tercentenary production of Handel's Acis and Galatea for the English Bach Festival in Reggio Emilia, Seville and Madrid; In Northern Ireland has directed Don Giovanni, Così fan tutte, Le nozze di Figaro, Die Zauberflöte and Der Schauspieldirektor and works by Haydn, Donizetti, Puccini and Purcell; Has designed productions of Hansel and Gretel at Sadler's Wells, La Favorita in Dublin, Offenbach operas in Belfast and Crispino e la Comare at the Camden Festival; Designed the Yuri Lyubomov productions of Jenúfa (first in Zürich, 1986) and Das Rheingold at Covent Garden, 1986, 1988; Eugene Onegin for Bonn, 1987, and Tannhäuser for Stuttgart, 1988. *Address:* Music International, 13 Ardilaun Road, London N5 2QR, England.

**HERR, Karlheinz;** Singer (Bass); b. 27 Dec. 1933, Zellhausen, Germany. *Education:* Studied with Paul Lohmann in Frankfurt. *Career:* Sang first in opera at Mainz 1959, then appeared at Darmstadt, 1960–63, Mannheim from 1963 until 1988; Among his best roles have been Klingsor, Osmin, Mozart's Bartolo, Leporello, Rocco, Daland, and Varlaam in Boris Godunov; Guest appearances at the Paris Opéra, 1974, Bayreuth Festival, 1974, and in The Ring at Warsaw, 1988–90; Concert engagements in Haydn's Seasons and Creation, Messiah, Rossini's Stabat Mater and the Verdi and Fauré Requiems. *Address:* c/o Nationaltheater Mannheim, Am Goetheplatz, W-6800 Mannheim, Germany.

**HERREWEGHE, Phillippe;** Conductor and Choral Director; b. 2 May 1947, Ghent, Belgium. *Education:* studied piano at Ghent Conservatory; Studied medicine and psychiatry, graduated 1975. *Career:* Founder, Collegium Vocale of Ghent, 1975; Founder, La Chapelle Royale, 1977; Orchestre des Champs Elysées, 1991; Ensemble Vocal Européen; Performances include: St Matthew's Passion, Bach, with La Chapelle Royale; C Minor Mass and Requiem, Mozart; Elias, Paulus, A Midsummer Night's Dream, Mendelssohn; Missa Solemnis, Beethoven; German Requiem, Brahms; Les Nuits d'Eté, L'Enfance du Christ, Berlioz; guest conductor with many orchestras including Concertgebouw Orchestra, Rotterdam Philharmonic Berlin Philharmonic, Leipzig and Vienna Philharmonic; Artistic Director, Saintes Festival, 1982–; Cultural Ambassador for Flanders, 1993–; Musical Director, Royal Flanders Philharmonic Orchestra, 1998. *Recordings:* Over 60 with the above ensembles including music by Rameau, Lalande and Lully, Mahler's Des Knaben Wunderhorn (with Orchestre des Champs-Elysées) 2005. *Honours:* Officier des Arts et Lettres, Doctor Honoris Causa, Leuven University, 1997–. *Address:* c/o Stephane Maciejewski, 10 rue Coquillere, 75001 Paris, France.

**HERRICK, Christopher;** British organist. *Career:* fmr organist Westminster Abbey, London; freelance concert organist 1984–; numerous int. performances, including complete organ works of J. S. Bach at Lincoln Center Festival, USA 1998, BBC Proms, London, St Olav's Festival, Norway, Stockholm Int. Festival, Sweden, Eskilstuna Kloster, Sweden, Toledo Int. Organ Festival, Spain, concerts and tours in New Zealand, Australia, Canada, Denmark, Switzerland. *Recordings:* Organ Fireworks Vols 1–10 1984–2004, Bach, The Six Trio Sonatas 1990, Bach, The Orgelbüchlein 1994, Daquin, Douze Noëls 1995, Bach, The Italian Connection 1995, Bach, Organ Miniatures 1997, Organ Dreams I 1998, Bach, Organ Cornucopia 1999, Bach, The Clavierübung Chorales 1999, Organ Dreams II 2000, Bach, Attributions 2000, Organ Dreams III 2002, Bach's Complete Organ Works (16 CDs) 2002, Sweelinck, Keyboard Music 2003, Organ Dreams IV 2005. *E-mail:* enquiries@herrick.musician.org.uk (office). *Website:* www.herrick .musician.org.uk.

**HERRMANN, Anita;** Singer (Mezzo-soprano); b. 1947, Karlsruhe, Germany. *Education:* Studied in Strasbourg and with Joseph Metternich in Cologne. *Career:* Sang with the Bonn Opera, 1971–79, Karlsruhe, 1980–86, with further engagements at the Staatsoper Stuttgart, the Berlin Deutsche Oper and the Vienna Volksoper; Bregenz Festival, 1987–90, in Contes d'Hoffmann and Fliegender Holländer; Roles have included Mozart's Marcellina, Ino in Semele, Mistress Quickly in Falstaff, Lubasha in Sadko, Carolina in Elegy for Young Lovers and Mirza in Judith by Matthus (Berne, 1992); Sang Strauss's Annina at Deutsche Oper, Berlin, 1993. *Address:* c/o Stadttheater Bern, Nägelistrasse 1, 3011 Bern, Switzerland.

**HERRMANN, Karl Ernst;** stage director and stage designer; b. 1936, Neukirch, Upper Lusatia, Germany. *Education:* Hochschule für Bildende Kunst, Berlin. *Career:* designed for theatre at Ulm from 1961 and associated with Peter Stein at Bremen and Berlin, 1969–78; Designed Das Rheingold and Die Walküre at the Paris Opéra, 1976; Théâtre de la Monnaie, Brussels, from 1978, with a cycle of seven operas by Mozart, La Traviata and Orfeo ed Euridice; Eugene Onegin at Hamburg, 1979; Die Zauberflöte at the Salzburg Landestheater, to inaugurate the Mozart Bicentenary, 1991; Die Entführung at the Vienna Staatsoper, 1991; Brussels productions of La Clemenza di Tito and La finta Giardiniera seen at Salzburg Festival, 1992; Designed sets for the Peter Stein production of Pelléas et Mélisande at Welsh National Opera, 1992. *Address:* Théâtre Royale de la Monnaie, 4 Leopoldstrasse, 1000 Brussels, Belgium.

**HERSANT, Philippe;** Composer; b. 21 June 1948, Rome. *Education:* Studied at the Paris Conservatoire, with André Jolivet, in Madrid (1970–72) and at the Villa Médici, Rome, 1978–80. *Career:* Producer, Radio France, 1973–; Composer-in-Residence with the Orchestre National de Lyon, 1998–2000. *Compositions include:* Les Visites Espacées, chamber opera, 1982; Stances, for orchestra, 1992; Aztlan, for orchestra, 1983; String Quartet no. 1, 1985; Missa

Brevis, 1986; Nachtgesang, for clarinet, violin, cello and piano, 1988; String Quartet No.2, 1988; 2 Cello Concertos, 1989, 1997; Sextet, 1994; Le Chateau des Carpathes, opera, 1991; Landschaft mit Afgonauten, cantata, 1994; L'Infinito, for 12 voices, 1994; 5 Pièces, for orchestra, 1997; Piano Trio, 1998; Paysage avec ruines, for mezzo and orchestra, 1999. *Honours:* Prix Arthur Honegger, 1994; Prix Maurice Ravel, 1995; Grand Prix de la Musique Symphonique, 1998. *Address:* c/o Orchestre National de Lyon, 82 Rue de Bonnel, 69431 Lyon Cédex, France.

**HERSETH, Adolph;** trumpeter; b. 25 July 1921, Lake Park, MN. *Education:* Luther Coll., IA, New England Conservatory. *Career:* began career as mil. bandsman during World War II; prin. trumpet Chicago Symphony Orchestra 1948–2001. *Recordings include:* Ives, Holidays Symphony 1990, Mussorgsky, Pictures at an Exhibition 1992, Prokofiev (with Alexander Nevsky and Claudio Abbado) 1996, Asbury Brass Quintet (with Adolph Herseth) 1998, Scriabin, Symphonies 2, 3 and 4 1999, Prokofiev, Greatest Hits 2005. *Honours:* Dr hc (DePaul Univ.), (Luther Coll.), (New England Conservatory of Music), (Rosary Coll.), (Valparaiso Univ.); Living Art of Music Symphonic Musician Award 1994, Musical America Instrumentalist of the Year 1996.

**HERZ, Joachim;** German, professor and producer; b. 15 June 1924, Dresden; m. 1st Charlotte Kitze 1954 (died 1994), one s.; m. 2nd Dr Kristel Pappel 2000. *Education:* Kreuzschule Dresden, Colls of Music, Leipzig and Dresden, Humboldt Univ., Berlin. *Career:* producing debut Die Bremer Stadtmusikanten Coll. of Music, Dresden 1950; Producer, Dresden Touring Opera 1951–53, Berlin Komische Oper 1956, Cologne 1957; Dir, Leipzig Opera 1976; Man. Dir, Berlin Komische Oper 1981; Dir of Productions Dresden Nat. Opera 1981–; Music Coach, Dresden 1946–49; teaching asst, Dresden Drama Studio 1949–51, teacher 1951–53; teacher, Berlin 1953–56, Cologne 1957; Lecturer, Berlin Univ. 1956; Prof., Leipzig Univ. 1976–96; Visiting Lecturer, Univs of Munich, Salzburg, Eichstätt, Paris VIII, London, California, Göttingen, Lisbon, Heidelberg. Cincinnati, British Columbia, New York City, Banff Centre, Stockholm, Tokyo, Osaka, Tartu, Vienna, Bamberg, Nice, Fribourg; Visiting Lecturer Colls of Music in Tallinn, Leipzig, Dresden, Tokyo; Visiting Lecturer Wagner Societies New York, Nagoya, and London; guest producer Buenos Aires, London, Moscow, Stockholm, Cardiff, Belgrade, Bern, Munich, Glasgow, Essen, Hamburg, Frankfurt, Vienna, Helsinki, Tartu; consulting producer Taipei; produced Tell, Clemenza di Tito at Buenos Aires, Flying Dutchman, Marriage of Figaro at Bolshoi Theatre, Katja Kabanowa, Lohengrin, Zauberflöte in Vienna, Figaro at La Habana, Madame Butterfly (using original version) for Welsh Nat. Opera, Zurich, Vancouver, Salome for ENO, Peter Grimes for Scottish Opera, Belshazar in Hamburg, Der Rosenkavalier, Don Giovanni in Salzburg; Lulu, Mahogonny, Flying Dutchman, Schwejk, Forza del Destino, Albert Herring, Turandot, Young Lord, Bum-Bum for Komische Oper, Ring des Nibelungen, Hugenotten, Grand Macabre, Meistersinger, War and Peace, Frau ohne Schatten, Boris, Zauberzeige, Jungfrau von Orleans, Don Carlos, Katerina Ismailowa in Leipzig, Nose, 3 Oranges, Wozzeck, Osud, Salome, Ariadne, Der goldene Topf in Dresden; producer at opening of Semperopera Dresden 1985, new opera house Leipzig 1960; tours with Salzburg Così fan tutte Japan, with Leipzig Xerxes through 13 countries; mem. Acad. of Arts, Berlin and Saxony. *Film:* The Flying Dutchman. *Television:* Xerxes, Copenhagen; BBC4 Butterfly (original version), Nose, Salome, Mahagonny, BumBum, Zauberflöte, Rosenkavalier. *Recordings:* Freischütz (with Carlos Kleiber), Zauberflöte (with Colin Davis). *Publications:* Musiktheater (with others) 1970, Joachim Herz über Musiktheater 1974, Herz' Ring des Nibelungen at Opera Leipzig 1975, 1980, Figaro lässt sich scheiden 1985, Herz' Don Giovanni in Salzburg 1990; libretti trans.; contrib. to congresses, programmes, magazines, books. *Honours:* Hon. bd mem. Music Theatre Cttee (iTi), Hon. mem. Bolshoi Theatre, Opera Leipzig; Grand prix du disque, Freischütz 1974; Orpheus Magazin, West Berlin Best production of the year for Salome, London 1976; 4 times City of Leipzig Kunstpreis1961–86,. *Address:* Seestr. 8, 01067 Dresden, Germany. *Telephone:* (351) 495-4197. *Fax:* (341) 878-0088. *E-mail:* pappelk@aol.com.

**HESS, Andrea,** ARAM; British cellist; *Artistic Director, Glenilla Arts Foundation;* b. 7 May 1954, London, England; m. John Leonard 1985. *Education:* Royal Acad. of Music, Nordwestdeutschemusikakademie, Detmold, Germany. *Career:* debut at Wigmore Hall, London 1979; numerous performances as a soloist throughout UK, Europe, Canada and the Far East; performed as a mem. of several chamber ensembles, notably the Kreisler Trio of Germany and the Raphael Ensemble; appeared on stage as solo cellist in Nat. Theatre production of The Elephant Man 1980–81; solo cellist for RSC 1982–87; appearances in drama productions for BBC and major independent TV cos; several broadcasts for BBC Radio 3; composer and onstage solo cellist in the Nat. Theatre and West End for Arthur Miller's Broken Glass 1994–95; currently mem. of Swartzentruber piano trio. *Recordings:* Volker David Kirchner Trio, Wergo; Chopin cello works and Chamber Music with the Kreisler Trio, Pantheon; Hyperion recordings of both Brahms sextets, Dvořák, Quintet and Sextet, Korngold Sextet and Schoenberg's Verklärte Nacht, Martinů and Schulhoff Sextets, Arensky Quartet, and Tchaikovsky's Souvenir de Florence Sextet, Strauss Sextet from Capriccio, Bruckner Quintet, Schubert String Trio and Double Cello Quintet and both Brahms Quintets and the Mendelssohn Quintets; Frank Bridge Quintet and Sextet with the Raphael Ensemble. *Address:* 10 Belsize Park, London, NW3 4ES, England.

**HESSE, Ruth;** Singer (Mezzo-soprano); b. 18 Sept. 1936, Wuppertal, Germany. *Education:* Studied with Peter Offermans in Wuppertal and with Hildegard Scharf in Hamburg. *Career:* Sang in Lübeck from 1958; Hamburg Staatsoper from 1960; Operas by Wagner, Verdi and Strauss at the Deutsche Oper Berlin from 1962; Bayreuth Festival as Mary, Magdalene and Ortrud; Berlin, 1965, in the premiere of Der junge Lord by Henze; Vienna Staatsoper, 1966, Ortrud, Brangaene and Eboli; Paris Opéra, 1966, 1972, as Kundry and as The Nurse in Die Frau ohne Schatten; Salzburg Festival, 1974–75, as The Nurse; Sang Clytemnestra in Elektra at the Deutsche Oper Berlin, 1988; Concert and oratorio appearances. *Recordings:* Die Meistersinger; Die Frau ohne Schatten; Der junge Lord; Fricka in Der Ring des Nibelungen; Violanta by Korngold. *Address:* c/o Deutsche Oper Berlin, Richard Wagnerstrasse 10, 1000 Berlin, Germany.

**HESSE, Ursula;** Singer (Mezzo-soprano); b. 1970, Cologne, Germany. *Education:* Studied at the Berlin Musikhochschule with Ingrid Figur and Gundula Hintz-Lukas; Masterclasses with Hilde Rössl-Majdan and Brigitte Fassbaender; Lieder study with Aribert Reimann. *Career:* Komische Oper Berlin, in the song cycle Love, Life and Death by Siegfried Matthus, 1995; Toured Brussels, London, Dresden and Copenhagen in Mozart concert arias for the ballet Un Moto di Gioa, 1995; Concerts at the Berlin Festival with the Berlin Singakademie and with the New Bach Collegium in Brussels and Amsterdam; Season 1996–97 as Carmen at Lübeck and in Die Zauberflöte at Brussels; Alcina, Handel, Amsterdam. *Recordings include:* Webern Lieder, with Aribert Reimann. *Honours:* Prizewinner, Paula-Saloman-Lindberg Lieder Competition, 1993; Deutscher Musikweitbewer, 1995. *Address:* c/o Netherlands Opera, Waterlooplein 22 1011 PG, Amsterdam, Netherlands.

**HETHERINGTON, Hugh;** Singer (Tenor); b. 1958, England. *Education:* Studied at the Guildhall School of Music, at St John's College, Cambridge, and with Frederick Cox in Manchester; Further studies with Audrey Langford. *Career:* With Glyndebourne Festival and Touring Companies has sung Dr Caius (Falstaff), Truffaldino (Love of Three Oranges), Where the Wild Things Are and Idomeneo; Appearances with Scottish Opera as Dema in Cavalli's L'Egisto, Pang in Turandot, The Devil in The Soldier's Tale, Basilio in Le nozze di Figaro and roles in Iolanthe, Lulu, La Vie Parisienne and Eugene Onegin; With English National Opera as Piet in Ligeti's Le Grand Macabre and in The Return of Ulysses and L'Orfeo (1992); Covent Garden from 1985 in King Priam and Samson et Dalila; Further engagements with University Opera, New Sussex Opera, Opera Factory, Zürich and London Sinfoniettas, the Singers' Company, Channel 4 television and the Endymion Ensemble double bill of Monteverdi and Michael Nyman (1987); New York debut, 1989, in HMS Pinafore with New Sadler's Wells Opera at the City Center Theater; Concerts with the City of Birmingham Symphony and the Matrix Ensemble.

**HETHERWICK, Gilbert;** American label manager; *President, Sony BMG Masterworks Classical Division. Career:* fmr Gen. Man. Angel Records/EMI Classics USA; fmr man. at Sony Classical and Telarc Records; Vice-Pres. and Gen. Man. BMG Classics 2003–05; Pres. Sony BMG Masterworks Classical Division 2005–, responsible for labels, including RCA Red Seal, Sony Classical, Odyssey, Deutsche Harmonia Mundi, Arte Nova. *Address:* Sony BMG Music Entertainment, 550 Madison Avenue, New York, NY 10022, USA (office). *Website:* www.sonybmgmasterworks.com.

**HEUCKE, Stefan;** Composer; b. 24 May 1959, Gaildorf, Germany. *Education:* Studied Piano with Professor Renate Werner, Stuttgart, 1978–82; Piano with Professor A von Arnim, Composition with Professor G Schafer, Musikhochschule, Dortmund, 1982–86. *Career:* Debut: Premiere of Vier Orchesterstücke, op 5, performed by Saarland State Orchestra, Saarbrucken, 1985; Dozent (University Lecturer) in Theory of Music, Musikhochschule, Dortmund, 1989–; Production and editing live for WDR, SDR and Saarlandischer Rundfunk broadcasting stations; Numerous performances in Germany, Russia, Netherlands, France and Chile; mem, GEMA; Interessenverband deutscher Komponisten. *Compositions:* Self-published: Vier Orchesterstücke, op 5, 1983; Variations on a theme of Webern for orchestra, op 10, 1988; Piano trio, op 11, 1989; Symphony No. 1, op 12, 1990; Symphony No. 2, op 19, 1993; The Selfish Giant for narrator and orchestra, op 20, 1994; Sonata for bass clarinet and piano op 23, 1995; Quartet for violin, viola, violoncello, double bass and piano op 25, 1995; The Happy Prince, 21 Easy Piano Pieces op 28. *Recordings:* CD, Abendgebete, op 14, with Berthold Schmid, tenor, and Sinfonietta Tubingen. *Honours:* Prize, Forum of Young German Composers Competition, 1985; Grant, City of Dortmund, 1990. *Address:* Markt 10a, 59174 Kamen, Germany.

**HEWITT, Angela,** BMus; Canadian pianist; b. 26 July 1958, Ottawa. *Education:* Royal Conservatory of Music, Toronto, Univ. of Ottawa. *Career:* debut recital aged 9, Toronto; appeared around the world as soloist with orchestra (Canada, USA, UK, Japan, Australia) and in recitals (in China, Mexico and throughout Europe); New York debut, Alice Tully Hall 1984; Wigmore Hall debut 1985; Proms debut 1990. *Recordings:* First Bach recording in 1986; Cycle of Bach on CD: Inventions, 1994, French Suites, 1995, Partitas, 1997; Granados' Spanish Dances; Bach, Well-Tempered Klavier Book I, 1998, Book II, 1999, Bach Keyboard Concertos 2005. *Honours:* Int. Bach Piano Competition 1985, prizewinner Washington DC (Bach, 1975; Leipzig, 1976; Zwickau, 1977; Cleveland, 1979; Milan, 1980; First Prize in Viotti Competition, Italy, 1978; First Prize in Toronto International Bach Piano Competition, 1985; Honorary Doctorate, University of Ottawa, 1995; Key to the City of Ottawa, 1997; Royal Philharmonic Soc. BBC Radio 3 Listeners' Award 2003. *Address:* 3436 Springhill Road, Lafayette, CA 94549, USA.

**HEYER, John (Hajdu);** Musicologist and Conductor; b. (John H. Hajdu), 4 Jan. 1945, Altoona, PA, USA; m. Sandra Lee Heyer 1973; two s. *Education:* BMus, Composition, DePauw Univ., 1966; MA, PhD, Musicology, Univ. of Colorado, 1971–73; studied with Nadia Boulanger, 1967–70. *Career:* teacher, Univ. of Colorado 1971–73; teacher, 1973–87, Chair., Music Department, 1980, Univ. of California, Santa Cruz; Lecturer, Programme Annotator, Carmel Bach Festival, 1979–; Dean, Coll. of Fine Arts, Indiana Univ. of Pennsylvania, Indiana, PA, 1987–; mem. of International Committee preparing the New Collected Works of Jean-Baptiste Lully for publication; Pres., Rocky Ridge Music Center Foundation, 1989–; Dean, Coll. of Arts and Communication, Univ. of Wisconsin, Whitewater, 1997–. *Recordings:* Conducted J. Gilles, Messe des Morts, Musical Heritage Society, 1981. *Publications:* Critical Edition: Jean Gilles, Messe des Morts, 1983; Lully and the Music of the French Baroque, 1989; Critical edition: J.-B. Lully, Notus in Judaea, 1996; Lully Studies, 2000. *Contributions:* Notes; The New Grove. *Address:* College of Arts and Communication, University of Wisconsin Whitewater, Whitewater, WI 53190, USA.

**HEYNIS, Aafje;** Singer (Contralto); b. 2 May 1924, Krommenie, Netherlands. *Education:* Studied with Aaltje Noordewier-Reddingius, Laurens Bogtman and Bodi Rapp; Further study with Roy Henderson in England. *Career:* Sang at first in oratorio and other sacred music; Amsterdam, 1956, in Der Wildschütz by Lortzing; Concertgebouw Amsterdam from 1958, in the Alto Rhapsody, Mahler, Bach (St Matthew Passion, B Minor Mass), Monteverdi, Schubert, Handel, Beethoven and Frank Martin; Retired 1984. *Recordings:* Orfeo ed Euridice by Gluck; Madrigals by Monteverdi; Music by Bach. *Honours:* Harriet Cohen Medal, 1961. *Address:* c/o Concertgebouworkest, Jacob Obredhstrasse 51, 1017 Amsterdam, Netherlands.

**HICKEY, Angela;** singer (mezzo-soprano); b. 1949, England. *Education:* Guildhall School of Music. *Career:* appearances with Royal Opera House, English National Opera, Scottish Opera, Opera North, Glyndebourne, City of Birmingham Touring Opera, Opera Northern Ireland, Monte Carlo Opera, Teatro Carlo Felice, Genoa; Roles include: Verdi's Preziosilla, Mistress Quickly and Azucena; Kabanicha in Katya Kabanova; Jocasta in Oedipus Rex; Carmen; Hélène in War and Peace with ENO; Annina in Der Rosenkavalier with Monte Carlo Opera; Mrs Sedley in Peter Grimes; Madame Larina in Eugene Onegin; Marcellina in Figaro with Opera Northern Ireland, 1991, Glyndebourne, 1992, Opera North, 1996; Mother Goose at Glyndebourne, 1994; Sang Mrs Sedley at Genoa, 1998; Mrs Trapes in Beggar's Opera in Caen and Rouen, 1999; Concerts include: Stabat Mater, Rossini; Requiem, Verdi; The Dream of Gerontius and Sea Pictures, Elgar; Ninth Symphony and Missa Solemnis, Beethoven; 2nd Symphony, Mahler; Nuits d'Eté; Appearances throughout Spain, France, Germany, Italy, Brazil, Czech Republic and Denmark. *Recordings include:* Hippolyte et Aricie, Rameau; Street Scene, Weill; Arianna, Alexander Goehr; Sea Pictures, Elgar.

**HICKOX, Richard Sidney,** CBE, MA, FRCO, LRAM; British conductor; *Music Director, Opera Australia;* b. 5 March 1948, Stokenchurch, Bucks.; s. of Rev. S. E. Hickox and Jean Millar; m. 1st Frances Ina Sheldon-Williams 1976; one s.; m. 2nd Pamela H. Stephen 1995; one s. *Education:* Royal Grammar School, High Wycombe, Royal Acad. of Music, London and Queens' Coll. Cambridge (Organ Scholar). *Career:* Dir of Music, High Wycombe Parish Church 1970–71, St Margaret's, Westminister 1972–82, Barbican Summer Festival 1984–85; Artistic Dir Woburn Festival 1967–89, Christ Church Spitalfields Festival 1978–94, St Endellion Festival 1974–, Truro Festival 1981–, Chester Summer Festival 1989–, City of London Festival 1994–; Artistic Dir Northern Sinfonia 1982–90, Prin. Guest Conductor 1990–; Music Dir, City of London Sinfonia and Richard Hickox Singers (now City of London Sinfonia Singers) 1971–, Bradford Festival Choral Soc. 1978–, London Symphony Chorus 1976–; Assoc. Conductor, London Symphony Orchestra 1985–; co-f. Opera Stage 1985; Prin. Conductor BBC Nat. Orchestra of Wales 2001–06, Conductor Emer. 2006–; Music Dir, Opera Australia 2005–; has conducted opera at Covent Garden, ENO, Opera North and Scottish Opera. *Recordings include:* Bach Masses, Albinoni Adagio, music by Finzi, Delius and Duruflé, Burgon Requiem, Haydn Nelson Mass (all for Decca, Argo Label), Gluck Armide, Handel Alcina, music by Vaughan Williams, Gilbert and Sullivan, Elgar Miniatures, Delius Miniatures and Berkeley Or Shall We Die? (all for EMI), Prokofiev The Love for Three Oranges (Chandos) 2005. *Honours:* Gramophone Award for Best Choral Recording 1992, Royal Philharmonic Soc. Music Award 1995, Gramophone Opera Award 1995, Deutsche Schallplattenpreis, Diapason d'Or. *Current Management:* Intermusica Artists' Management, 16 Duncan Terrace, London, N1 5BZ, England. *Telephone:* (20) 7278-5455 (office). *Fax:* (20) 7278-8434 (office). *Address:* Opera Australia, The Opera Centre – Sydney, 480 Elizabeth Street, Surry Hills, NSW 2010, Australia (office); 35 Ellington Street, London, N7 8PN, England (home). *Website:* www.opera-australia.org .au.

**HIDALGO, Manuel;** Composer; b. 4 Feb. 1956, Antequera, Andalusia, Spain. *Education:* Studied at the Zürich Conservatory, 1976–78, with Hans Ulrich Lehmann, and in Hanover and Stuttgart with Helmut Lachenmann, 1979–84. *Career:* Freelance composer from 1982, with performances at Donaueschingen, Stuttgart, Saarbrücken and elsewhere. *Compositions include:* Hacia, string quartet, 1980; Harto, for orchestra, 1982; Al componer, for viola, cello, double bass and orchestra, 1986; Alegrias piano concerto, 1987; Gloria, for six voices and orchestra, 1989; Trio esperando, 1989; Fisica, for orchestra, 1991; Vomitorio, Stage, 1991; Desastres de la guerra, after Goya, for narrator and 19 instruments, 1996; Des Kaisers neues Kleid, after Andersen, 1996; String

Quartet No. 2, 1996; Musik nach Gedichten, for soprano, alto and orchestra, 1996; Dali, opera, 1999. *Address:* c/o Saarländisches Staatstheater, Schillerplatz, 66111 Saarbrücken, Germany.

**HIDAS, Frigyes;** Composer; b. 25 May 1928, Budapest, Hungary; m. Erzsebet Zombori, 5 July 1966, 1 d. *Education:* Degree in Composing, Academy of Music, Budapest, 1946–51. *Career:* Music Director, Budapest National Theatre, 1951–66; Music Director, Budapest Operetta Theatre, 1974–79; Freelance Composer. *Compositions include:* Cedar, ballet in 2 acts, 1975; Three Movements for orchestra, 1987; The Undanced, ballet, 1989; Chamber music: Three Sketches, 1982; Divertimento, 1982; Hungarian Folksongs, 1985; Pian-Org, 1985; Musique pour six, 1985; Alteba Trio, 1986; Brass chamber music: Trio, 1980; Six Etudes, 1980; Play, 1981; Three Little Scherzos, 1982; Movement, 1982; Septet, 1982; Training Patterns, 1982; 5 x 5, 1983; Trumpet Fantasy, 1983; Little Suite, 1983; Academic Quintet, 1983; Musik für Bläser, 1983; Four-in-Hand, 1985; Sextets Nos 1 and 5 for bass trombone and wind quintet; Tuba Quartet, 1990; Saxophone Quartet, 1990; Works for concert band: Ballet Music, 1980; Merry Music, 1980; Concertino, 1981; Suite, 1981; Fantasy and Fugue, 1984; Folksong Suites Nos 1 and 2, 1985; Circus Suite, 1985; Festive Music, 1985; 17 concertos including: Ballad, 1982; Rhapsody, 1982; Flute Concerto No. 2, 1983; Trumpet Concerto No. 2, 1983; Baroque Concerto, 1984; Széchenyi Concerto, 1984; Quintetto concertante, 1985; Requiem for symphonic band, 4 soloists and mixed choir, 1996; Save the Sea, symphonia for symphonic band, 1997; Concerto for symphonic band, 1998; Saxophonia in E flat for alto saxophone, symphonic band and symphonic orchestra, 1998; Sax-Fantasy for symphonic band, 1998; Concerto for saxophone quartet and symphonic band, 1998; Birthday Concerto for trombone, symphonic band and symphonic orchestra, 1998; History of Vriezenveen, concerto for symphonic band, 1998; Swiss Rhapsody for symphonic band, 1998; Oboe Concerto No. 2, for oboe and wind ensemble, 1999; Missouri Overture for symphonic band, 1999; Oratorios; Music for films, television and theatre. *Recordings:* Wind Concerto No. 2; Flute Concerto No. 2; Toccata, Movement No. 3 of Organ Sonata; Violin Concertino; Oboe Concerto; Rhapsody for Brass Trombone; Training Patterns, excerpts; Four-in-Hand. *Honours:* Erkel Prize, 1958, 1982; Merited Artist of the Hungarian Republic, 1987; Bartók Pásztory Prize, 1993. *Address:* Attila ut 133, 1012 Budapest, Hungary.

**HIDJOV, Plamen;** Singer (Bass); b. 20 March 1953, Sofia, Bulgaria. *Education:* Studied in Sofia, and in Rome with Boris Christoff. *Career:* National Opera, Sofia, 1981–88, Kaiserslautern from 1994; Prokofiev's Napoleon in War and Peace, Theatre Champs-Elysées, Paris, Teatro Massimo, Palermo, 1986; Wexford Festival and Queen Elizabeth Hall, London, 1988, in Mercadante's Elisa e Claudio; Scottish Opera, 1989, and Madrid, 1991, as Leporello; Other roles include Rossini's Bartolo, Basilio, Don Magnifico, Donizetti's Dulcamara, Don Pasquale, Raimondo, Verdi's Philip II, Procida, Attila and Mussorgsky's Boris Godunov, Pimen, Dosifey and Varlaam; Wagner's Daland, King Marke and Wotan, Baron Kelbar in Verdi's Un Giorno di Regno, Kaiserslautern, 1996; Glinka's Ivan Susanin at Kaiserslautern, 1997; Concerts include Bach's B minor Mass, Messiah, and Mozart's Coronation Mass; Beethoven's 9th Symphony at Paris and Medellin, Colombia, 1987; Liszt Festival Tour, Oratorio Christus, 1990; Verdi's Requiem in Granada, 1993. *Address:* c/o Pfalztheater Kaiserslautern, 6750 Kaiserslautern, Germany.

**HIELSCHER, Ulrich;** Singer (Bass); b. 29 April 1943, Schwarzengrund, Germany. *Education:* Studied in Düsseldorf and with Paul Lohmann in Wiesbaden. *Career:* Sang at Essen from 1967, member of the Cologne Opera from 1974; Guest appearances at Hamburg, Hanover, Wuppertal, Frankfurt, Düsseldorf, Stuttgart and the Vienna Staatsoper, Ghent Opera, 1984–85, and further appearances as concert singer in Netherlands, Belgium, France, Switzerland and Colombia; Further guest appearances, Stadtstheater Schwerin, Staatsoper Berlin, Staatsoper Dresden, Theatre in Kiel and Freiburg; Opera roles have included Mozart's Osmin, Figaro, Leporello, Alfonso, Sarastro and Speaker, Verdi's Falstaff and Padre Guardiano, Kecal in The Bartered Bride, Mephistopheles in Faust, Plunket in Martha; Wagner's Daland, Hagen and Gurnemanz, Baron Ochs, the Doktor in Wozzeck, Don Pasquale, Rodrigo in Lulu, Rocco in Fidelio, Pogner in Die Meistersinger and Massenet's Don Quichotte; Season 1994–95 at Schwerin as Don Quichotte and Pogner; Season 2000–01 at Cologne in Werther, Billy Budd, Falstaff, Carmen and The Love for Three Orange; Concert showings in works by Bach, Handel, Haydn, Mozart, Beethoven and Bruckner; Lied repertoire includes Schubert, Schumann, Beethoven, Richard Strauss, Wolf, Brahms, P Cornelius, Dvořák, F Martin, C Loewe, Paul Gräner, Hans Pfitzner, Moussorgsky, Mendelssohn and Robert Franz. *Recordings include:* Messa di Gloria by Puccini. *Address:* Oper der Stadt Köln, Offenbachplatz, 50667 Cologne, Germany.

**HIERHOLZER, Babette;** Pianist; b. 27 March 1957, Freiburg, Breisgau; m. D. Michael Simpler, 31 Aug 1990. *Education:* Studied with Elisabeth Dounias-Sindermann, Berlin, 1964–73; With Herbert Stessin, pre-college of Juilliard School of Music, New York, 1973–74; With Lili Kraus, Texas Christian University, Fort Worth, 1973–74; With Wolfgang Saschowa, Berlin, 1974–76; With Maria Tipo, Florence, Italy, 1975; With Paul Badura-Skoda, Folkwang-Hochschule Essen (Künstlerische Reifeprüfung Diploma, 1981), and Vienna, 1976; With Bruno Leonardo Gelber, Buenos Aires, Argentina, 1979. *Career:* Debut: With orchestra at age 11 at Philharmonic Hall, Berlin; Regular appearances with orchestra and solo recitals in Berlin, Hamburg, Bonn, Frankfurt, Munich, Salzburg, Lausanne, Torino, Bordeaux, Caracas, Santiago, New York, Chicago, St Louis, Pittsburgh, Washington DC; Numerous engagements with the Berlin Philharmonic Orchestra with conductors: Colin Davis, Klaus Tennstedt, Leopold Hager, Semyon Bychkov, Lothar Zagrosek, Gerd Albrecht, Sixten Ehrling, Paavo Berglund; USA debut with Pittsburgh Symphony Orchestra, 1984; Recital-debut at Carnegie Hall, New York, 1991; Canadian debut with Saskatoon Symphony Orchestra, 1994; Several Performances of the Clara Schumann Piano Concerto (on the occasion of the 100th anniversary of Clara Schumann's death) in Berlin, Winnipeg, Ottawa, Festivals at Merida and Maracaibo, Venezuela; Solo recitals with an original recital programme of Clara Schumann at Schumann Houses at Bonn and Zwickau. *Recordings:* CDs: Music by Couperin, Debussy, Schumann, Mozart, Schubert, Scarlatti Piano Sonatas Vols. 1, 2 and 3; Played Soundtrack and Double for Clara Wieck (played by Natassja Kinski) in the Schumann Movie: Spring Symphony (by Peter Schamoni); CD Kinderszenen (Scenes of Childhood), 1999. *Current Management:* Konzert-Direktion Hans Adler, Berlin, Germany; Del Rosenfield Associates Inc. USA. *Address:* 46 Aspinwall Road, Red Hook, New York 12571, USA.

**HIESTERMANN, Horst;** Singer (Tenor); b. 14 Aug. 1934, Ballenstadt, Harz, Germany. *Career:* Stadttheater Brandenburg from 1957, debut as Pedrillo in Die Entführung; Sang in Leipzig, Weimar, Berlin and Dresden; Deutsche Oper am Rhein Dusseldorf, 1976–84; Salzburg Festival from 1978 as Monostatos, as the Dancing Master in Ariadne auf Naxos, and as Robespierre in Dantons Tod, 1983; Dallas Opera, 1982, as Loge in Das Rheingold; Tokyo, 1983, as Mime in Siegfried; Other appearances in Geneva, Rouen, Amsterdam, Houston and New York (Metropolitan Opera); Barcelona, 1984, as Aegisthus in Elektra; Member of the Zürich Opera from 1984; Deutsche Oper Berlin, 1984, in the premiere of Reimann's Gespenstersonate; Vienna Staatsoper, 1987, as Herod in Salome; Sang Mime in a new production of The Ring at the Metropolitan, 1988–90; Shuisky in Boris Godunov at Barcelona, 1990; Herod in Berlin; Sang Aegisthus at Athens, 1992; Other roles include the Captain in Wozzeck (Catania, 1998) and David in Die Meistersinger. *Recordings:* Wozzeck; The Duenna by Prokofiev; Puntila by Dessau; Carmina Burana; Trionfi by Orff; Die Zauberflöte; Karl V by Krenek; Die Meistersinger conducted by Karajan. *Publications:* E: Mime bist du so witzig?, 2000. *Address:* c/o Deutsche Oper Berlin, Richard Wagnerstrasse 10, D-1000 Berlin, Germany.

**HIETIKKO, Jaakko;** Singer (Bass); b. 16 May 1950, Kurikka, Finland. *Education:* Studied at the Helsinki Sibelius Academy. *Career:* Sang in the chorus of the Finnish National Opera from 1975 and was appointed as a soloist in 1980; Has appeared in most of the classical bass roles; Has specialised in such modern repertory as The Red Line by Sallinen (premiere, 1978), Vincent by Rautavaara (premiere, 1990); Sang in the premiere of The Book of Jonah by Olli Kortekanges, Helsinki, 1995 and The Last Temptations by Kokkonen; Many appearances at the Savonlinna Festival and as a concert singer. *Address:* c/o Finnish National Opera, PO Box 176, 00251 Helsinki Finland.

**HIGBEE, Dale Strohe,** AB, PhD; American music director and musician (flute, recorder); *Music Director, Carolina Baroque;* b. 14 June 1925, Proctor, VT; one d. *Education:* Harvard Univ., Univ. of Texas at Austin; studied flute with Georges Laurent, Arthur Lora, Marcel Moyse, recorder with Carl Dolmetsch. *Career:* freelance flautist 1942–77, recorder player 1956–; clinical psychologist, South Carolina State Hospital, Columbia 1954–55, VA Medical Center, Salisbury, NC 1955–87; book and record review editor, The American Recorder 1967–89; Music Dir and recorder soloist, Carolina Baroque 1988–; mem. American Bach Soc., American Handel Soc., American Musical Instrument Soc. (bd of dirs 1972–74, 1985–88), American Musicological Society, American Recorder Soc. (bd of dirs 1963–65), Dolmetsch Foundation (gov. 1963–), Early Music America, Galpin Soc., Mozart Soc. of America, Music Library Asscn, Royal Musical Asscn, Soc. for Eighteenth-Century Music. *Recordings with Carolina Baroque:* The Great Mr Handel, Three Baroque Titans and a Minor Master, Handel and his Contemporaries, Music of the French Court and Chapel, Solo, Double and Triple Concertos of Bach and Telemann, Bach and Handel: Baroque Prometheans, Songs and Sonatas of Handel, Bach and his Peers, Cantatas and Concertos of Bach, Bach and Handel: Baroque Masters, Viva Voce! Two Mini Operas by Handel, Bach: Music to Challenge the Intellect and Touch the Heart, Arias, Duets and Ballet Music from Handel Operas, Sacred and Secular Cantatas of J. S. Bach, Bach Arias, Duets and Chamber Music. *Publications include:* A Survey of Musical Instrument Collections in the United States and Canada (with William Lichtenwanger, Cynthia Adams Hoover and Phillip T. Young) 1974; numerous articles and book, record and music reviews in American Recorder, Consort, Continuo: The Magazine of Old Music, Early Music, Galpin Society Journal, Journal of the American Musical Instrument Society, MLA Notes, Music & Letters, Music Journal, National Flute Association Newsletter, Newsletter of the American Musical Instrument Society, Southeastern Historical Society Newletter, Woodwind World. *Honours:* Combat Infantry Badge, Purple Heart. Pfc., 314th Infantry Regiment, 79th Division, 1943–45. *Address:* c/o Carolina Baroque, 412 South Ellis Street, Salisbury, NC 28144-4820, USA (office). *Telephone:* (704) 633-9311 (office). *E-mail:* info@carolinabaroque.org (office). *Website:* www.carolinabaroque.org (office).

**HIGDON, Jennifer,** BM, PhD; American composer; b. 31 Dec. 1962, Brooklyn, NY. *Education:* Bowling Green State Univ., Univ. of Pennsylvania. *Career:* composer-in-residence, American Composers' Forum Continental Harmony Project 2000, Nat. Youth Orchestra Festival 2002, Bravo! Vail Valley Music Festival 2002, 2003, Tanglewood Festival of Contemporary Music 2002, Bard

Conductor's Inst. 2003, Cabrillo Festival of Contemporary Music 2004, Composers' Conference at Bennington Coll. 2004, Philadelphia Singers; featured composer, Tanglewood Festival of Contemporary Music 2003; mem. composition faculty, Curtis Inst. of Music. *Compositions include:* Shine 1995, Blue Cathedral 1999, Wind Shear 2000, City Scape 2002, Concerto for Orchestra 2002, Machine 2002, Piano Trio (Ithaca Coll. Heckscher Prize 2003), Dooryard Bloom 2004, Logo 2004. *Recordings include:* Blue Cathedral (with Atlanta Symphony Orchestra), City Scape and Concerto for Orchestra (with Atlanta Symphony Orchestra). *Honours:* winner ASCAP Foundation Commission Project 1995, Pennsylvania Council on the Arts Fellowship 1996, 2000, American Acad. of Arts and Letters Charles Ives Fellowship 1997, Guggenheim Fellowship 1997, Pennsylvania Council on the Arts Artist's Fellowship 2000. *Address:* c/o Cheryl Lawson (Artist Representative), Lawdon Press, 1008 Spruce Street, Suite 3F, Philadelphia, PA 19107, USA (office). *Telephone:* (215) 592-1847 (office). *Fax:* (215) 592-1095 (office). *E-mail:* lawdonpress@aol.com (office). *Website:* jenniferhigdon.com.

**HIGGINBOTTOM, Edward,** BMus, MA, PhD, FRCO; British university lecturer; *Director of Music, New College, Oxford;* b. 16 Nov. 1946, Kendal, Cumbria, England; m. Caroline M. F. Barrowcliff 1971; three s. four d. *Education:* Corpus Christi College, Cambridge. *Career:* Research Fellow, Corpus Christi College, Cambridge 1973–76; Dir of Music and Fellow of New College, Oxford 1976–. *Recordings:* over 80 recordings. *Publications:* various edns of music, contribs to Grove 6 and 7, Musical Times, Organists Review, Music and Letters. *Honours:* Hon. Fellowship, Royal School of Church Music 2002, Guild of Church Musicians 2003; Royal College of Organists Harding and Read Prizes; Commdr, Ordre des Arts et des Lettres. *Address:* New College, Oxford, England.

**HILEY, David;** University Professor; b. 5 Sept. 1947, Littleborough, England; m. Ann Fahrni, 28 Feb 1975, 2 d. *Education:* BA (Oxon), 1973; PhD, London, 1981. *Career:* Assistant Music Master, Eton College, 1968–73; Lecturer, Royal Holloway College, London, 1976–86; Professor, Regensburg University, Germany, 1986–; mem. Plainsong and Mediaeval Music Soc., Gesellschaft für Musikforschung, American Musicological Soc., Academia Europaea. *Publications:* New Oxford History of Music II (co-editor), 1990; Western Plainchant: A Handbook, 1993; Die Offizien des Mittelalters (co-editor), 1999; Das Repertoire der normanno-sizilischen Tropare I: Die Sequenzen, 2001. *Address:* Sonnenstrasse 10, 93152 Nittendorf, Germany. *E-mail:* david.hiley@psk.uni-regensberg.de.

**HILL, David Neil,** MA; British master of music and organist; b. 13 May 1957, Carlisle; s. of Brian and Jean Hill; m. 1st Hilary Llystn Jones 1979; one s. one d.; m. 2nd Alice Mary Wills 1994; one d., one s. *Education:* Chetham's School of Music, Manchester; St John's Coll., Cambridge. *Career:* Conductor, Alexandra Choir, London, 1979–80, Musical Dir, 1980–87; Sub-Organist, Durham Cathedral, 1980–82; Organist, Master of Music, Westminster Cathedral, 1982–88; Organist, Dir of Music, Winchester Cathedral, 1988–2002; Artistic Dir, Philharmonia Chorus, 1990–98; Musical Dir, Waynflete Singers, 1988–2002; Musical Dir, The Bach Choir, 1998–; Dir of Music, St John's College, Cambridge, 2003–; frequently directs choral workshops and summer schools, in UK, USA and Australia; regularly conducts the BBC Singers; Chief Conductor, Southern Sinfonia. *Recordings:* three albums of Choral Works by Stanford (with Westminster Cathedral Choir) 1997–98. *Publications:* Giving Voice (co-author) 1995; contrib. several articles on choir training. *Honours:* Hon. DMus (Southampton); Gramophone Award, 1985; Grammy Award, 1997. *Address:* St John's College, Cambridge, CB2 1TP, England. *Telephone:* (1223) 338683 (office). *E-mail:* dnh21@cam.ac.uk (office).

**HILL, George R.;** Musicologist and Music Bibliographer; b. 12 July 1943, Denver, Colorado, USA. *Education:* AB, Music, with Department Honours, Stanford University, 1965; AM, Library Science, University of Chicago, 1966; PhD, Historical Musicology, New York University, 1975. *Career:* Librarian, Music Division, New York Public Library, 1966–70; Assistant Music Librarian, New York University, 1971–72; Fine Arts Librarian, University of California, Irvine, 1972–73; Associate Professor of Music, Baruch College, City University of New York, 1973–. *Publications:* A Thematic Locator for Mozart's Works as Listed in Kochel's Chronologisch-Thematisches Verzeichnis - 6th Edition (principal author), 1970; A Preliminary Checklist of Research on the Classic Symphony and Concerto to the Time of Beethoven (excluding Haydn and Mozart), 1970; A Thematic Catalogue of the Instrumental Music of Florian Leopold Gassmann, 1976; Florian Leopold Gassmann, Seven Symphonies, 1981; Joseph Haydn Werke, Floetenuhrstuecke, 1984; A Handbook of Basic Tonal Practice, 1985, Indes to Printed Music: Collections and Series (database ed.) 2004–. *Contributions:* Articles and Reviews to various professional journals, including The New Grove Dictionary of Music and Musicians. *Address:* 84 Highgate Terrace, Bergenfield, NJ 07621-3922, USA.

**HILL, Jackson;** Composer and University Professor of Music; b. 23 May 1941, Birmingham, Alabama, USA; m. Martha Gibbs 1966, 1 s. *Education:* AB, 1963, MA, 1966, PhD, Musicology, 1970, University of North Carolina; Composition with Iain Hamilton, 1964–66, and Roger Hannay, 1967–68. *Career:* Assistant/Associate Professor of Music, 1968–80, Head of Department of Music, 1980–90, Associate Dean of Faculty, 1990–95, Presidential Professor 1996–, Bucknell University, Lewisburg, Pennsylvania; Conductor, Bucknell Symphony Orchestra, 1969–79; Member, Research Unit, Manchester College, Oxford, England, 1975; Choral Conductor Assistant, Exeter College, Oxford; Hays/Fulbright Fellow, Japan, 1977; Visiting Fellow, Clare

Hall, Cambridge, England, 1982–83. *Compositions:* More than 100 works including: Serenade, 1970; Three Mysteries, 1973; Paganini Set, 1973; Missa Brevis, 1974; English Mass, 1975; By the Waters of Babylon, sonata, 1976; Whispers of the Dead, 1976; Streams of Love, 1979; Enigma Elegy, 1987; Symphony No. 1, 1990; Symphony No. 2, 1993; Symphony No. 3, 1997, Long Hidden Deep 2001, Philomel 2002, In Winter's Keeping 2002, Remembered Love 2004, When Spring is Born 2004, Sky of Birds 2005. *Recordings:* Sonata: By the Waters of Babylon; Ecce vidimus eum; Rhapsody, 1995; Tholos, 1998; Tango, 1998, Tango II 2002, Voices of Autumn 2003. *Publications:* The Music of Kees van Baaren, 1970; The Harold E Cook Collection of Musical Instruments; numerous articles on music and mysticism, Japanese music and Buddhist liturgical music. *Contributions:* Ethnomusicology; Studia Mystica; Notes. *Honours:* Harriman Award 2004. *Address:* Bucknell University, Lewisburg, PA 17837, USA.

**HILL, Jenny;** British opera and concert singer (soprano); b. 20 June 1944, London, England; m. (divorced); two d. *Education:* Nat. School of Opera, London Opera Centre. *Career:* debut, Sandman, Hansel and Gretel, Sadler's Wells Opera Company (now known as ENO); English Opera Group with Benjamin Britten performing in London, Russia and Canada; created role of Pretty Polly in Punch and Judy premiere, Aldeburgh and Edinburgh Festivals, 1968, and Mrs Green in Birtwistle's Down by the Greenwood Side, premiere at the London and Brighton Festivals, 1969; repertory operas performed include Traviata, Lucia, La Sonnambula, Rigoletto, Marriage of Figaro, Magic Flute, A Midsummer Night's Dream; concert appearances include A Mother Goose Primer, with the Pierrot Players, and Petrassi's Magnificat, with Giulini, both British premieres at the Royal Festival Hall, 1972; City of London Opening Concert, Bach's B minor Mass with Giulini at St Paul's Cathedral; opening concert, English Bach Festival, Blenheim Palace; performances on radio and television as well as numerous song recitals of classical and avant-garde music; teaching singing from home as well as performing; mem., Equity, Incorporated Society of Musicians, Asscn of Singing Teachers. *Recordings include:* The Rape of Lucretia, as Lucia; Schumann's Faust; Bach's St John Passion, Bach's B Minor Mass – Giulini; other recordings now available in Italy of concerts and performances with Giulini (EMI) and Britten (Universal). *Honours:* Leverhulme Scholarship 1960–63, Gulbenkian Fellowship for Most Outstanding Young Performer 1969–72. *Address:* 5 Oaklands Grove, London, W12 0JD, England. *Telephone:* (20) 8743-3646. *E-mail:* jennyhill@3rdrock.co.uk.

**HILL, Martyn;** Singer (Tenor); b. 14 Sept. 1944, Rochester, Kent, England; m. Marleen De Maesschalck, 1974, 3 s., 1 d. *Education:* Royal College of Music; ARCM; Vocal Studies with Audrey Langford. *Career:* Established a reputation as one of the most distinguished international tenors of his generation; He is known throughout the world as a concert and oratorio soloist and recitalist; Repertoire includes Elgar's Dream of Gerontius, Berlioz's Damnation of Faust, Brucker's Te Deum, Verdi's Requiem and Mahler's Das Lied von der Erde; Performs regularly the works of Benjamin Britten; Glyndebourne 1985 and 1988, as Idomeneo and Belmonte; Recently sang War Requiem with the Sydney Symphony and Edo de Waart, Spring Symphony with the Hallé Orchestra and Kent Nagano, and Serenade with the Czech Philharmonic and Christopher Seaman; Evangelist in Bach's St John Passion, Festival Hall, 1997; Sang Eumete in Monteverdi's Ulisse at Florence, 1999. *Recordings include:* Britten's Serenade with the RPO and Vladimir Ashkenazy; Herbert Howells's Missa Sabrinensis with the London Symphony Orchestra and Rozhdestvensky for Chandos and Bach's St Matthew Passion with the choir of King's College, Cambridge for Columns Classics. *Address:* Owen/White Management, 14 Nightingale Lane, London N8 7QU, England.

**HILL, Peter;** Pianist and University Lecturer; b. 14 June 1948, Lyndhurst, England; m. Charlotte Huggins, 21 April 1981, 2 d. *Education:* MA, Oxford University; Royal College of Music. *Career:* Debut: Wigmore Hall, London, 1974; Regular broadcasts, BBC; International festival appearances include: Harrogate, Bath, English Bach, Dublin, Stuttgart; Founder Member, Ensemble Dreamtiger; Professor, University of Sheffield. *Recordings:* Complete Piano Music of Havergal Brian; Dreamtiger; East-West Encounters; Nigel Osborne: Remembering Esenin; Piano Works by Nigel Osborne, Douglas Young, Howard Skempton; Messiaen: The Complete Piano Music; Beethoven: Diabelli Variations; The Complete Piano Works of Schoenberg, Berg and Webern; Stravinsky: Music for Four Hands; Stravinsky: Solo Piano Music. *Publications:* The Messiaen Companion (editor); Stravinsky: The Rite of Spring. *Contributions:* Tempo. *Honours:* Chappell Gold Medal, Royal College of Music, 1971; 1st Prize, Darmstadt Ferienkurs, 1974. *Address:* c/o Department of Music, University of Sheffield, Sheffield S10 2 TN, England.

**HILL, Robert (Stephen);** Harpsichordist, Fortepianist and Musicologist; b. 6 Nov. 1953, Philippines. *Education:* Solo Diploma, Amsterdam Conservatory, 1974; Licentiate, Trinity College of Music, London, 1974; MA, 1982, PhD, 1987, Harvard University, USA. *Career:* Tours with Musica Antiqua Köln; Radio and television broadcasts for West German, British, Dutch, Belgian and French networks, and National Public Radio and CBC, USA. *Recordings:* J. S. Bach. Sonatas for Violin and Harpsichord with Reinhard Goebel; J. S. Bach, Art of Fugue, early version; Solo Harpsichord. *Contributions:* Early Music; Bach Jahrbuch. *Honours:* Erwin Bodky Award, 1982; Solo Recitalist Award, National Endowment for the Arts, 1983; Noah Greenberg Award, American Musicological Society, 1988. *Current Management:* Andreas Braun, Cologne, Germany. *Address:* Staatliche Hochschule für Musik Freiburg, Freiburg, Germany.

**HILL SMITH, Marilyn,** AGSM; British singer (soprano); b. 9 Feb. 1952, Carshalton, Surrey; d. of George Smith and Irene Smith. *Education:* Nonsuch High School, Ewell and Guildhall School of Music and Drama. *Career:* cabaret, pantomime, concerts 1971–74; toured Australia and NZ with Gilbert & Sullivan for All 1974, USA and Canada 1976; Prin. Soprano, ENO Opera 1978–84; Covent Garden début in Peter Grimes 1981; has appeared at several major European music festivals including Versailles, Granada, Aldeburgh, London Promenade Concerts etc., also with New Sadler's Wells Opera, Canadian Opera Co., Welsh Nat. Opera, Scottish Nat. Opera, New D'Oyly Carte Opera, Lyric Opera of Singapore, etc. and on television and radio and has made several recordings particularly of operetta; Patron Cen. Festival Opera, Epsom Light Opera; singing teacher and adjudicator for music festivals. *Honours:* Hon. Life mem. Johann Strauss Soc. of GB; Young Musician of the Year 1975 and other prizes. *Current Management:* c/o Music International, 13 Ardilaun Road, Highbury, London, N5 2QR, England. *Telephone:* (20) 7359-5183.

**HILLEBRAND, Nikolaus;** Singer (Bass); b. 1948, Oberschlesien, Germany. *Education:* Studied with Rolf Dieter Knoll in Cologne and Hanno Blaschke in Munich. *Career:* Debut: Lubeck, 1972; Israel, 1972, as Mosè in the opera by Rossini; Salzburg Easter Festival, 1974, in Die Meistersinger; Vienna Staatsoper, 1974; Bayreuth Festival, 1974–75, in Parsifal and Die Meistersinger; Further engagements in Munich (Lohengrin), Karlsruhe, London, Paris, Rome and Brussels; Taormina Festival 1991, as Telramund; Many concert appearances, notably in music by Bach; Conductors include Abbado, Böhm, Kleiber, Karajan and Muti. *Recordings include:* Stefano Colonna in Rienzi; St John Passion by Bach; Egisto by Cavalli; Romeo und Julia by Sutermeister; Reger's Requiem. *Current Management:* Ingpen & Williams Ltd, 7 St George's Court, 131 Putney Bridge Road, London, SW15 2PA, England.

**HILLEBRANDT, Oskar;** Singer (Baritone); b. 15 March 1943, Schopfheim, Baden, Germany. *Education:* Studied at Cologne Musikhochschule with Josef Metternich. *Career:* Sang at the Stuttgart Staatsoper from 1969; Appearances at Saarbrucken, Kiel and Brunswick from 1971; Member of the Dortmund Opera from 1985; Guest appearances at Hamburg, Munich, Düsseldorf, Mannheim and Zürich; La Scala Milan as Telramund and the Teatro Zarzuela Madrid as Achillas in Giulio Cesare by Handel; Seattle Opera as Alberich in the Ring; Further engagements in Antwerp, Copenhagen and at the Santander Festival, Marseilles and Turin, 1986, as Kaspar and Donner; British debut, 1989, as Mandryka at the Glyndebourne Festival; Other roles include Pizarro, Scarpia, Count Luna, Amonasro, Simon Boccanegra and Jochanaan in Salome, Wagner's Dutchman, Amfortas and Klingsor; Sang Alberich at Santiago, 1996; Season 1995–96 as Wotan at Dortmund, Pizarro at Rome and Alberich in Oslo; Sang Alberich and Gunther in Götterdämmerung at Buenos Aires, 1998; Sang Alberich in Siegfried, and Falstaff at the Komische Oper Berlin, 2000; Concert showings in Paris, London, New York, Barcelona and Rome. *Address:* Opernhaus, Kuhstrasse 12, 4600 Dortmund, Germany.

**HILLEBRECHT, Hildegard;** Singer (Soprano); b. 26 Nov. 1927, Hanover, Germany. *Education:* Studied with Margarethe von Winterfeld, Franziska Martianssen Lohmann and Paul Lohmann. *Career:* Debut: Freiburg, 1951, as Leonora in Il Trovatore; Sang at Zürich, 1952–54, notably in the premiere of the revised version of Hindemith's Cardillac (1952); Düsseldorf, 1954–59, Cologne, 1956–61; Sang Maria in Strauss's Friedenstag at Munich, 1961; Many appearances at the State Operas of Vienna, Hamburg and Munich; Salzburg Festival, 1946, 1964, as Ilia, Chrysothemis and Ariadne; Deutsche Oper Berlin, 1968, in the premiere of Ulisse by Dallapiccola; Covent Garden, 1967, as the Empress in Die Frau ohne Schatten; Metropolitan Opera, 1968–69; Sang with the Zürich Opera from 1972; Appearances in Rio de Janeiro, Paris, Rome, San Francisco, Edinburgh, Copenhagen, Barcelona, Dresden, Brussels and Prague; Repertoire includes works by Wagner, Puccini (Tosca), Verdi and Strauss, Elena in I Vespri Siciliani, Elisabeth de Valois, Desdemona, Sieglinde, Jenůfa and Ursula in Mathis der Maler. *Recordings:* Excerpts from Don Giovanni and Tannhäuser; Cavalleria Rusticana; Der Rosenkavalier; Ariadne auf Naxos; Don Giovanni; Duchess of Parma in Doktor Faust by Busoni; Die Zauberflöte.

**HILLER, Wilfried;** Composer; b. 15 March 1941, Weissenhorn, Swabia, Germany. *Education:* Studied with Günther Bialas at the Munich Musikhochschule (1963–68), with Boulez and Stockhausen at Darmstadt (1963) and with Carl Orff, from 1968. *Career:* Founded concert series Musik Unserer Zeit, 1968; Editor at Bavarian Radio, from 1971; Composition Department of the Richard Strauss Conservatory, Munich, from 1993. *Compositions include:* Katalog I–V for percussion 1967–74, An diesem heutigen Tage, theatre 1973, Schumamit, from the Song of Songs, for soloists, choruses and orchestra 1977–93, Niobe, theatre 1977, Der Josa mit der Zauberfiedel, for speaker, violin and chamber orchestra 1985, reconstruction of Karl Amadeue Hartmann's Chaplin-Ford-Trott (from Waxworks), opera 1930/87, Das Traumfresserchen, singspiel 1990, Chagall-Zyklug, for clarinet and chamber orchestra 1993, Der Rattenfänger, opera 1993, Peter Pan, theatre 1997, Der Schimmelreiter, stage 1997, Der Geigenseppel, melodrama for marionettes 1999, Eduard auf dem Seil, opera 1999, Aias, after Sophocles and Ovid, for mezzo, baritone, speaker and orchestra 2000, Pinnochio, opera 2001, Wolkenstein, opera 2003, Augustinus, oratorio for 2 sopranos, boy soprano, 6 male voices, choir and ensemble 2004. *Honours:* Richard Strauss Prize,

Munich, 1968; Schwabinger Arts Prize, 1978. *Current Management:* c/o Schott & Co Ltd, 48 Great Marlborough Street, London, W1F 7BB, England.

**HILLIER, Paul Douglas,** OBE, AGSM; British singer, conductor and writer; b. 9 Feb. 1949, Dorchester, England; m. Lena-Liis Kiesel 1977; two d. *Education:* Guildhall School of Music. *Career:* debut at the Purcell Room, London 1974; Vicar-Choral, St Paul's Cathedral 1973–74; Dir, Hilliard Ensemble 1974–90; Early Music Masterclasses, York, London, Vancouver, Canada; Visiting Lecturer, Univ. of California, Santa Cruz 1980–81; television debut, Music in Time 1983; Copland Fellow, Amherst Coll., MA 1984; Dir, Theatre of Voices 1989–; Prof. of Music, Univ. of California, Davis 1990–96; Dir, Early Music Inst., Indiana Univ. School of Music 1996–. *Publications:* 300 Years of English Partsongs 1983, Romantic English Partsongs 1986, The Catch Book 1987, Arvo Pärt 1997. *Honours:* Edison Klassik 1986. *Address:* c/o Harmonia Mundi, 45 Vyner Street, London, E2 9DQ, England.

**HILLMAN, David;** Singer (Tenor); b. 1936, England. *Education:* Studied at the National School of Opera. *Career:* Sang at Sadler's Wells, London, from 1962 as Tamino, Ferrando, Hoffmann, Rodolfo and Essex in Gloriana; Sang also in the premieres of Benjamin's Tartuffe, 1964, Bennett's The Mines of Sulphur, 1965, Williamson's The Violins of St Jacques, 1966, and Musgrave's Mary Queen of Scots (Edinburgh, 1977); English premiere of Nielsen's Saul and David, 1977, as David, and in Szymanowski's King Roger with the New Opera Company, 1975; Guest appearances as Macduff at Covent Garden, at Stuttgart, Bonn, with Netherlands Opera (as Tom Rakewell, 1972), Santa Fe (Oliver's Duchess of Malfi, 1978) and at Glyndebourne (Elemer in Arabella, 1985); Also appeared in operettas by Gilbert and Sullivan.

**HILTON, Janet;** British clarinettist; b. 1 Jan. 1945, Liverpool; d. of H. Hilton and E. Hilton; m. David Richardson 1968; two s. (one deceased) one d. *Education:* Belvedere School, Liverpool, Royal Northern Coll. of Music, Vienna Konservatorium. *Career:* BBC concerto début 1963; appearances as clarinet soloist with major British orchestras including Royal Liverpool Philharmonic, Scottish Nat., Scottish Chamber, City of Birmingham Symphony Orchestra (CBSO), Bournemouth Symphony, Bournemouth Sinfonietta, City of London Sinfonia, BBC Scottish and Welsh Symphony, BBC Philharmonic; guest at Edinburgh, Aldeburgh, Bath, Cheltenham, City of London Festivals, Henry Wood Promenade concerts; appearances throughout Europe and N America; Prin. Clarinet Scottish Chamber Orchestra 1974–80, Kent Opera 1984–88; teacher Royal Scottish Acad. of Music and Drama 1974–80, Royal Northern Coll. of Music 1983–87; Head of Woodwind, Birmingham Conservatoire 1992–; Head of Woodwind, RCM, London 1998–; Prof., Univ. of Cen. England 1993; Dir Camerata Wind Soloists; several recordings for Chandos, including all Weber's music for clarinet with the CBSO, Lindsay Quartet and Keith Swallow, the Neilsen and Copland Concertos with the Scottish Nat. Orchestra, Stanford Clarinet Concerto with Ulster Orchestra, Mozart Clarinet Quintet with the Lindsay Quartet 1998; recordings of McCabe, Harper, Maconchy and Hoddinott concertos with BBC Scottish Symphony Orchestra on Clarinet Classics 2001; dedicatee of works by Iain Hamilton, John McCabe, Edward Harper, Elizabeth Maconchy, Alun Hoddinott, Malcolm Arnold. *Address:* 5B Belsize Park Gardens, London, NW3 4ND, England. *Telephone:* (20) 7586-7374. *E-mail:* jhilton@rcm.ac.uk (office).

**HIMMELBEBER, Liat;** Singer (Mezzo-soprano); b. 27 April 1956, Stuttgart, Germany. *Education:* Studied in Berlin, and in Hamburg with Judith Beckmann; Masterclasses with Aribert Reimann and Dietrich Fischer-Dieskau. *Career:* Sang at the Eutin Festival, 1982–83; Oldenburg, 1984–85, and from 1985 as member of the Theater am Gärtnerplatz, Munich; Among her best roles have been Rosina, Mozart's Dorabella and Cherubino, and Hansel; Guest with the Hamburg Staatsoper and appearances with the Augsburg Opera from 1992; Concerts include premieres of works by Reimann, Von Bose and Manfred Trojahn; Sang also in the Munich 1987 premiere of Miss Julie by A Bibalo. *Address:* c/o St ätdische Buhnen Augsburg, Kasernstrasse 4–6, Pf 111949, 86159 Augsburg, Germany.

**HIND, Rolf;** Pianist, Composer; b. 1964, England. *Education:* Studied at Royal College of Music with John Constable and Kendall Taylor; Los Angeles with Johanna Harris-Heggie. *Career:* Has premiered works by Ligeti, Kurtag, Berio, Ruders, McMillan, Holt, Unsuk Chin and many others; played in festivals and major venues throughout Europe and Australasia under conductors including Sir Simon Rattle, Oliver Knussen, Vladimir Ashkenazy and Franz Welser-Most. *Compositions:* composed works for piano and for ensemble, BBC Radio and WDR; chamber collaborations with cellist Frances-Marie Uitti and David Alberman. *Recordings include:* solo works by of Messiaen and John Adams. *Address:* c/o Clarion/Seven Muses, 47 Whitehall Park, London N19 3TW, England.

**HIND O'MALLEY, Pamela,** ARCM; fmr composer, cellist and pianist; b. 27 Feb. 1923, London, England; m. Raymond O'Malley (died 1996); two s. one d. *Education:* studied cello with Ivor James, Piet Lentz and Pablo Casals, piano with Dorothea Aspinall and Imogen Holst, composition with Herbert Howells. *Career:* debut at Wigmore Hall, 1963; Cello Soloist and Ensemble Player; As One Pair of Hands, gave recitals for solo cello and solo piano in programmes that always include one contemporary work; Solo recitals playing Cello and Piano from 1967; Wigmore Hall 1969 and 1970; fmr Teacher of Cello and Piano, Cambridge; Part time Cello Teacher, Kings College School; Part time Ensemble Coach, Cambridge University Music Society. *Compositions:* Keyboard Music, Songs, Duo for Violin and Cello, Trio for Flute, Viola and Cello;

Suite for String Orchestra. *Publications:* Cycle of Four Rounds for Four Violins; Arrangements of two Fauré songs for either Viola or Cello with Piano; contrib. to Royal College of Music Magazine; Casals as Teacher (Royal College of Music Magazine, 1950); Casals and Intonation (ESTA News and Views, 1981, and re-printed in the STRAD, 1983). *Address:* c/o 94 Fernside Road, London, SW12 8LJ, England.

**HINDS, Esther;** Singer (Soprano); b. 3 Jan. 1943, Barbados, West Indies. *Education:* Studied with Clyde Burrows in New York, and at Hartt College, Hartford, with Helen Hubbard. *Career:* Debut: New York City Opera, 1970, as First Lady in Die Zauberflöte; Has sung in New York as Donna Elvira, Madama Butterfly and Gershwin's Bess (on Broadway); Engagements at opera houses in Houston, Cincinnati and San Diego; Other roles include Liu (Turandot) and Micaela; Spoleto Festival, 1983, as Cleopatra in Antony and Cleopatra by Samuel Barber; Many concert performances. *Address:* c/o New York City Opera, Lincoln Center, New York, NY 10023, USA.

**HINDS, Geoffrey (William John);** Composer and Piano Teacher; b. 2 April 1950, Auckland, New Zealand. *Education:* BA, Auckland, 1974; MPhil (Mus) Auckland, 1976; BDiv, Melbourne College of Divinity, 1980; LRSM (Piano Teachers), 1983. *Compositions:* Held in New Zealand Music Archive Canterbury University - Sonata for viola and pianoforte, 1975; Suite for string quintet, 1975; String Quartet, 1976; Cantata Upon This Rock, 1982; Held in Music Library, Radio New Zealand, Wellington Motet for the Lord has Purposed, 1980–81; Overture into a Broad Place, 1981; String Quartet, 1981; Symphonic Moments of Our Time, 1982; And His Name Shall Be Called, 1981; Through The Grapevine, 1982; Anthems written for St Barnabas Choir; Song Cycle, Water Water Everywhere, 1985; Song Cycle, Pieces of Peace, 1986; Colyton Overture, 1986–87, written for Manawatu Youth Orchestra; String Quartet 1983–84; Song cycle, Innocence and Experience, 1987; Blowing in the Wind for wind quintet, 1987; Song Cycle, Nine Mystical Songs, 1988–89; Godzone Re-evaluated for Youth Orchestra, 1989; Great Outdoors Suite for piano, 1989; String Quartet, 1989; Symphony, St Barnabas Ballads (Tenor and piano); Creation Cantata; The Good Life (Musical), 1990; Piano Sonata; Two Edged Sword (Song Cycle for soprano and piano); Sonata for trombone, organ, 1991–; Flights of Fancy, for clarinet and string quartet; Gardens (SATB); Suite for viola; Our Good Keen Men (Song cycle for tenor and piano), 1992; A Tree For All Seasons (soprano, cello and piano); City of. . . (Song cycle for tenor, piano), 1993; String Quartet No. 2, 1995; The Mind, canticle (soprano, piano), 1995; Reflections, 1995; From the Rising of the Sun, 1996; Solitude: A Pilgrim's Progress; Creation in Reverse, 1997; Spiritual, suite for guitar, 1997; From Dawn to Dusk, wind quintet; 1997; Piano Suite, 1997; At Akito for SATB, 3 trombones and timpani, 1997; Tension for alto, tenor and pianoforte, 1997; The Cave for SATB, 1998; Rhapsody in White for clarinet, trombone, pianoforte, 1998; On Watching the Sailboats for tenor and pianoforte, words by J G Brown, 1998; String Quartet No. 6 (. . . of Ages), 1998; Bully Boys for tenor solo, men's chorus, 3 trombones and percussion, 1999. *Address:* 72 Valley Road, Mount Eden, Auckland 1003, New Zealand.

**HINTERMEIER, Margareta;** Austrian singer (mezzo-soprano); b. 11 April 1954, St Polten; one s. *Education:* studied in Vienna with Hilde Konetzi. *Career:* Peter Musikus at Theater an der Wien 1972; engaged at Wiener Staatsoper from 1976; debut as Hirte in Tosca 1976; roles include the Composer in Ariadne auf Naxos, Clairon in Capriccio, Lola, Annio, Dorabella, Orlofsky, Federica in Luisa Miller, Wagner's Magdalena, Cherubino, Silla, Lucrezia Borgia, Fricka in Das Rheingold and Die Walküre, Octavian, Jocaste, Emilia, Herodias, Venus in Tannhäuser, Adriano in Rienzi; guest appearances include the opening of Dresden Opera, Salzburg Festival, Schubert Festival Hohenems, Carinthia Summer, Istanbul Festival, Altafulla (Barcelona, Spain), Flanders Festivals. *Recordings include:* Maidservant in video of Elektra, conducted by Abbado; Die Walküre; Beethoven's Ninth. *Honours:* Preis der Freunde der Wiener Staatsoper, Kammersängerin 1991. *Address:* c/o Staatsoper, Opernring 2, 1010 Vienna, Austria (office).

**HIRAI, Motoki,** BPhil, MA; Japanese pianist and composer; b. Tokyo. *Education:* Keio Univ., Tokyo, RAM, City Univ. and Guildhall School of Music and Drama, London. *Career:* Japanese govt artistic emissary on tours of Sri Lanka 1994, Portugal 1996, Malaysia 1997; resident in UK from 1996; numerous concerts and broadcasts throughout the UK; concert tour of Europe and Japan 2005; solo recital, St John's, Smith Square, London 2005. *Compositions include:* Valse Pathétique 1993, Hommage à Chopin 1999. *Honours:* Sir Jack and Lady Lyons Performance Award. *E-mail:* info@motokihirai.com. *Website:* www.motokihirai.com.

**HIROKAMI, Jun'ichi;** Japanese conductor; b. 5 May 1958, Tokyo. *Education:* Studies, Tokyo Music University. *Career:* Debut: Israel Philharmonic Orchestra, 1988, London Debut, London Symphony Orchestra, 1989; Assistant Conductor, Nagoya Philharmonic Orchestra, 1983; International career from 1984; Conducted the NHK Symphony Orchestra, 1985, Orchestre National de France, 1986; Royal Philharmonic Orchestra, 1990; Further engagements with the Stockholm Philharmonic, Norrkoeping Symphony Orchestras (Principal Conductor from 1991), Malmö and Gothenburg Symphony Orchestras and radio orchestras in Netherlands and Italy; Operatic debut (July 1989), Un Ballo in Maschera followed by Rigoletto and La Forza del Destino, all with the Australian Opera; International concert activities spread to other countries: Spanish National Orchestra, Berlin Radio Symphony, Royal Concertgebouw Amsterdam, Montreal Symphony and with many European Orchestras; Conducted all major Japanese orchestras and appointed Principal Guest Conductor of the Japanese Philharmonic Orchestra, 1995. *Recordings:* Debut with the London Symphony Orchestra (BMG) and subsequent recordings with BIS Records of Sweden and Fun House Records, Japan, mainly made with his own Norrkoping Symphony Orchestra. *Honours:* Winner, 1st International Kondrashin Conducting Competition, Amsterdam, 1984. *Current Management:* Hazard Chase, 25 City Road, Cambridge CB1 1DP, England. *Telephone:* (1223) 312400. *Fax:* (1223) 460827. *Website:* www.hazardchase.co.uk.

**HIRSCH, Michael;** Musician and Composer; b. 1958, Munich, Germany. *Career:* Composer, 1976–; Member of several groups for contemporary music; Collaboration with Dieter Schnebel, Josef Anton Hledl, Helmut Lachenmann; Performances and broadcasts for European radio and television; Actor, Stage Director, several European theatres and festivals; Translates works from music to speech, theatre to music; Work performed at several international festivals including Donaueschingen Festival, Klangaktionen, Musica Viva, in Munich; Witten Festival for new chamber music, Grenzenlos; Berlin in Moscow, 1996; XIII Cigle de música del segle XX, Barcelona; Dresden Festival for Contemporary Music; Music Biennale, Berlin. *Compositions include:* Il Viaggio, music theatre, 1982–83; Memoiren 1. Buch, string quartet, 1983–85; Memoiren 3. Buch, concert for 6 instruments, 1986–91; Beschreibung eines Kampfes, music theatre, 1986–92; Hirngespinste, nocturnal scene for 2 players and accordion, 1996; Odradek, novel for chamber ensemble, 1994–97; Passagen/Szenen, for flute, clarinet, piano and string trio, 1997; Le carnet d'esquisse, for chamber ensemble, 1997–98; Das stille Zimmer, opera, 1998–99. *Address:* Gleditschstr 38, 10781 Berlin, Germany.

**HIRSCH, Peter;** Conductor; b. 1956, Cologne, Germany. *Education:* Studied at the Hochschule, Cologne. *Career:* Assistant to Michael Gielen at the Frankfurt Opera, 1979; First Conductor at Frankfurt Opera, 1983–87; Debut at La Scala with Prometeo by Luigi Nono; World premiere of Stephen Climax by Hans Zender, 1986; Guest conductor at many German theatres as well as Welsh National Opera, English National Opera, Netherlands Opera; Chief Conductor of Jeune Philharmonie de Belgique, 1993–95; Regular Guest amongst others at Staatsoper unter den Linden, Berlin, Deutsches Symphonie-Orchester Berlin, Berliner Sinfonie-Orchester, Residentie Orkest Den Haag, Orchestre National de Belgique, Bournemouth Symphony, Radio Orchestras of WDR Cologne and MDR Leipzig, ensemble recherche, at Bologna Festival, Berliner Festwochen and Munich Biennale. Many world premieres of works by Nono, Lachenmann, Zender, Knaifel and others. *Recordings:* CD recordings of Mahler 5th Symphony, Nono, Brahms, Schoenberg. *Address:* Weinbergstr. 26, 14548 Caputh, Germany.

**HIRSCH, Rebecca;** British violinist. *Education:* Royal Coll. of Music, London with Jaroslav Vanecek. *Career:* debut with the London Sinfonietta at the Barbican, playing Strauss' Bougeois Gentilhomme; has appeared as soloist with numerous orchestras in the UK and elsewhere in Europe, including Ålborg Symphony Orchestra, Bournemouth Symphony Orchestra, BBC Concert Orchestra, BBC Philharmonic, BBC Scottish Orchestras, Danish National Radio Symphony Orchestra, London Sinfonietta, Philharmonia, Ulster Orchestra. *Honours:* English Speaking Union scholarship 1984. *Address:* c/o London Sinfonietta, Third Floor, Dominion House, 101 Southwark Street, London, SE1 0JF, England.

**HIRST, Grayson;** Singer (Tenor); b. 27 Dec. 1939, Ojai, California, USA. *Education:* Studied at the Music Academy of the West with Martial Singher and at the Juilliard School with Jennie Tourel. *Career:* Debut: Sang Cavalli's Ormindo with the Opera Society of Washington, 1969; Sang Tonio in La fille du régiment at Carnegie Hall, 1970; New York City Opera debut, 1970, in Britten's The Turn of the Screw; Kennedy Center, Washington, in the premiere of Ginastera's Beatrix Cenci; Other premieres include works by Robert Aitken, Ned Rorem, Robert Starer, Virgil Thomson (Lord Byron) and Jack Beeson; Sang Tonio in Pagliacci at Carnegie Hall, New York, 1990; Further appearances in France, Brazil, England and Switzerland; Other roles include Don José, Pelléas, Faust and Mozart's Tamino, Ferrando and Belmonte. *Recordings include:* Schubert's Die schöne Müllerin.

**HIRST, Linda;** Singer (Mezzo-soprano); b. 1950, Yorkshire, England. *Education:* Flute and singing at the Guildhall School of Music, London. *Career:* Joined Swingle Singers and often appeared with Cathy Berberian; Concerts with the London Sinfonietta with Berio, Ligeti and Henze conducting their works; Premiere performances of Muldowney's Duration of Exile, Osborne's Alba, Simon Holt's Canciones and Judith Weir's The Consolations of Scholarship; Performances of Schoenberg's Pierrot Lunaire in Paris and Florence and for Channel 4 television; Glyndebourne Festival debut, 1985, Knussen's Where the Wild Things Are; 1986 world premiere of Osborne's The Electrification of the Soviet Union; Appearances at Bath and Almeida Festivals; Frankfurt Opera, Henze's Elegy for Young Lovers; Arts Council Network Tour with the London Sinfonietta; Also performs earlier music such as Incoronazione di Poppea in Spitalfields for Opera London; Sang in the premiere of Vic Hoyland's La Madre (written for her), London, 1990. *Recordings:* Songs Cathy Sang; Ottavia in L'Incoronazione di Poppea. *Fax:* (20) 7680-0665.

**HIRSTI, Marianne;** Singer (Soprano); b. 1958, Oslo, Norway. *Education:* Studied in Oslo and Lubeck. *Career:* Sang at Kiel, 1980–81; Staatsoper Hamburg, 1981–85; Cologne, 1985–87; Staatsoper Stuttgart from 1987; San Meroe in Reinhard Keiser's Die grossmütige Tomyris at Ludwigshafen, followed by Constanza in Bononcini's Griselda and Blondchen in Die

Entführung; Cologne Opera as Maire in Zar und Zimmermann; Ludwigsburg Festival as Susanna in Le nozze di Figaro; Théâtre de la Monnaie, Brussels, as Berta in Il Barbiere di Siviglia, 1992; Other roles have included Despina, Marzelline, Gretel, Sophie in Werther and Tytania in A Midsummer Night's Dream; Many Lieder recitals and concert appearances, including Wigmore Hall, London, 1988. *Recordings include:* Beethoven Missa Solemnis; Die Grossmütige Tomyris; Der Zwerg by Zemlinsky; Blondchen in Die Entführung, conducted by Hogwood. *Address:* c/o Staatsoper Stuttgart, Oberer Schlossgarten 6, 7000 Stuttgart, Germany.

**HIRTE, Klaus;** Singer (Baritone); b. 28 Dec. 1937, Berlin, Germany. *Education:* Studied at the Stuttgart Musikhochschule with Hans Hager. *Career:* Sang at the Stuttgart Staatsoper from 1964; Bayreuth Festival, 1973–75, as Beckmesser in Die Meistersinger; Salzburg Festival as Antonio in Le nozze di Figaro; Ludwigsburg Festival, 1972, as Papageno; Further appearances in Nuremberg, Munich, Düsseldorf, Mannheim, Venice, Chicago and San Antonio; Other roles include Don Pasquale and Dulcamara by Donizetti; Wagner's Kurwenal and Klingsor and parts in operas by Strauss, Gluck, Mascagni and Weber; Sang Oberon in the premiere of Der Park by Hans Gefors, Wiesbaden, 1992; Stuttgart Staatsoper 1993, in Don Quichotte by Hans Zender; Sang the Impresario in Donizetti's Convenienze Teatrali at Stuttgart, 2001. *Recordings include:* Tannhäuser; Die Meistersinger; Le Cadi Dupé by Gluck; Der Schauspieldirektor; Cavalleria Rusticana; Intermezzo; Die schweigsame Frau. *Address:* c/o Staatstheater Stuttgart, Oberer Schlossgarten 6, 7000 Stuttgart 1, Germany.

**HIRVONEN, Anssi;** Singer (Tenor); b. 1948, Finland. *Education:* Qualified as Cantor-organist, 1976, Singing Teacher and leaving certificate from the General Department, 1978, Singing Diploma, 1986, Sibelius Academy, Helsinki; Studied at the Conservatoire of Tampere, Helsinki; Private studies with Jolanda di Maria Petris; Further studies in Berlin and Vienna. *Career:* Appearances as Oratorio and Concert Soloist in Finland, Sweden, Germany, Hungary, USA, Estonia, Russia, Latvia and the Faroe Islands; Opera Debut at Tampere Opera, 1975; Solo engagements at the Heidelberg Opera, 1979–80, the Savonlinna Opera Festival 1978–, the Finnish National Opera 1980–, and provincial operas in Finland; Sang in the world premieres of Ilkka Kuusisto's The War of the Light, 1982, Rautavaara's Thomas, 1986 and his Vincent, 1990, Atso Almila's 30 Silver Coins 1988; Guest Soloist at the operas of Stockholm and Tallinn; Numerous television and radio appearances and recordings; Professor and Lecturer of Singing, Sibelius Academy; Guest Soloist, Finnish National Opera; Sang Don Ottavio in Don Giovanni for St Michael Opera, 1999. *Recordings include:* Contemporary Finnish Choir Music; Sacred Songs of C Franck, T Kuusisto, Y Karanko, E Linnala, A Maasalo and L Madetoja; Christmas Songs of O Kotilainen, A Maasalo, S Palmgren and S Ranta; Musica Humana, Sacred Songs of P Kostiainen and J Sibelius; Rautavaara's Vincent, 1986 and Thomas, 1990; Jean Sibelius: The Tempest op 19, 1992. *Honours:* Director Musices, 1998. *Address:* Satamasaarentie 7, 00980, Finland.

**HIRZEL, Franziska;** Swiss singer (soprano); b. 28 Nov. 1952, Zürich. *Education:* studied in Basel, Fribourg, Frankfurt am Main and Zürich. *Career:* sang at Darmstadt Opera from 1980, notably in the 1983 premiere of Klebe's Die Fastnachtsbeichte and as Mozart's Blondchen, Donna Elvira, Fiordiligi and Pamina, Micaela, Martha, Euridice, Gilda, Musetta and Gretel; concert repertoire has included sacred works by Bach, Beethoven, Mozart, Haydn and Schoenberg; many Lieder recitals and broadcasting engagements; guest appearances at concert halls and opera houses throughout Germany; sang Marie in Gurlitt's Wozzeck at Turin 2000. *Address:* c/o Noord Nederlands Orkest, Palmslag 20, 9724 CS Groningen, Netherlands.

**HITCHCOCK, Hugh Wiley,** BA, MMus, PhD; American musicologist, writer and editor; b. 28 Sept. 1923, Detroit, MI. *Education:* Dartmouth Coll., Univ. of Michigan. *Career:* faculty mem., Univ. of Michigan 1947–61; Prof. of Music, Hunter Coll., CUNY 1961–71; Ed., Prentice-Hall History of Music Series 1965–, Earlier American Music 1972–98, Recent Researches in American Music 1976–94; mem. of exec. cttee and area ed. for the Americas, The New Grove Dictionary of Music and Musicians 1980; co-ed., The New Grove Dictionary of American Music 1986; Prof. of Music, Brooklyn Coll., CUNY 1971–80, Distinguished Prof. of Music 1980–93; Founder-Dir, Inst. for Studies in American Music, Brooklyn Coll. 1971–93; J. Paul Getty Center for Art History and the Humanities scholar 1985–86; mem. American Musicological Soc. (pres. 1991–92, hon. mem. 1994–), Charles Ives Soc. (pres. 1973–93), Music Library Asscn (pres. 1966–68). *Publications:* Music in the United States: A Historical Introduction 1969, Charles Ives Centennial Festival-Conference 1974, Ives 1977, An Ives Celebration: Papers and Panels of the Charles Ives Centennial Festival-Conference (ed. with Vivian Perlis) 1977, The Phonograph and Our Musical Life 1980, The Music of Ainsworth's Psalter 1612 (with L. Inserra) 1981, The Works of Marc-Antoine Charpentier: Catalogue Raisonné 1982, Ives: A Survey of the Music 1983, Marc-Antoine Charpentier 1990, critical edn of Charles Ives, 129 Songs 2004; contrib. to scholarly books and professional journals. *Honours:* Hon. mem. American Musicological Soc. 1994; Chevalier, Ordre des Arts et des Lettres 1995; Fulbright Sr Research Fellowships 1954–55, 1968–69, Guggenheim Fellowship 1968–69, Nat. Endowment for the Humanities grant 1982–83; Soc. for American Music lifetime achievement award 2003. *Address:* 1192 Park Avenue, No. 10-E, New York, NY 10128, USA.

**HJORTSO, Merete;** Singer (Soprano); b. 1944, Denmark. *Education:* Studied in Copenhagen and Vienna. *Career:* Debut: Royal Opera Copenhagen, 1971 in Kagel's Halleluja; Sang frequently with the Jutland Opera at Århus, notably in the 1983 premiere of Det guddommelige Tivoli by Norgaard; Major roles have included Marguerite in Faust, Susanna and Cherubino in Le nozze di Figaro, Zdenka, Micaela, Massenet's Thaïs and Leonora in Nielsen's Maskarade; Guest engagements in Strasbourg, Brussels and elsewhere; Frequent concert appearances. *Recordings:* Nielsen's Maskarade. *Address:* c/o Den Jyske Opera, Thomas Jensens Alle, DK 8000 Århus, Denmark.

**HO, Allan (Benedict);** Musicologist; b. 30 March 1955, Honolulu, Hawaii, USA. *Education:* BA, Music History, 1978, MA, Musicology, 1980, University of Hawaii; PhD, Musicology, University of Kentucky, 1985. *Career:* Discovered a copy of the lost full score of Wilhelm Stenhammar's First Piano Concerto, the manuscript of which was believed destroyed during WWII, and which was the most widely performed Swedish composition at the turn of the century; mem, American Musicological Society; Pi Kappa Lambda. *Publications:* A Biographical Dictionary of Russian/Soviet Composers, 1989; Music for Piano and Orchestra: The Recorded Repertory; Critical editions of the 2-piano score and full score of Wilhelm Stenhammar's First Piano Concerto; Shostakovich Reconsidered, 1998. *Contributions:* Journal of the American Liszt Society; Notes; The New Grove Dictionary of American Music; New Grove Dictionary of Opera; New Grove Dictionary of Women Composers; New Grove Dictionary, new version. *Address:* Box 1771, Music Department, Southern Illinois University, Edwardsville, IL 62026, USA.

**HOARE, Peter;** Singer (Tenor); b. 1965, Bradford, England. *Education:* Huddersfield School of Music. *Career:* Appearances with Welsh National Opera from 1992, as Jacquino, Mozart's Tito, Arbace and Basilio, and the Shepherd in Tristan und Isolde; Nemorino for Mid Wales Opera and Sellem in The Rake's Progress at Lausanne; Bardolfo in Falstaff at Covent Garden, 1999; Concerts include the Mozart and Berlioz Requiems, Messiah with George Malcolm, Bach's Christmas Oratorio, Britten's Serenade and the Verdi Requiem; Season 1999 with Vitek in The Makropulos Case at Aix-en-Provence. *Address:* c/o Harlequin Agency Ltd, 203 Fidlas Road, Cardiff CF4 5NA, Wales.

**HOBKIRK, Christopher;** Singer (Tenor); b. 1965, Henley-on-Thames, England. *Education:* Studied at the Royal Scottish Academy and at Royal College of Music with Neil Mackie. *Career:* Concert engagements in Finland and Norway with Britten's St Nicolas and Bach's St John Passion; Bach's Magnificat with the Las Palmas Philharmonic, the B minor Mass at Edinburgh and Telemann's Luke Passion at St John's Smith Square; Created Eochd in Edward McGuire's opera The Loving of Etain, 1990, at Glasgow; Season 1991 with Britten's Serenade at Palma, Bach's St Matthew Passion at Darmstadt and Bergen, Mozart's Requiem with the Manchester Camerata and the B minor Mass conducted by William Boughton; Sang Misael in The Burning Fiery Furnace for St James's Opera, 1991.

**HOBSON, Ian,** BA, MA, DMus; pianist and conductor; b. 1953, Wolverhampton, England; m.; four s. one d. *Education:* Magdalene College, Cambridge, Yale University. *Career:* Finalist in 1978 Baltimore Symphony Conducting Competition; Silver Medals at Artur Rubinstein and Vienna-Beethoven Competitions; 1st Prize, Leeds International Piano Competition, 1981; Soloist with Royal Philharmonic Orchestra, Philharmonia and Scottish National Orchestra; USA with Orchestras of Chicago, Philadelphia, Pittsburgh, St Louis, Baltimore, Indianapolis and Houston; Complete cycles of Beethoven's Sonatas; Founded Sinfonia da Camera, 1984; The Age of Anxiety for Bernstein's 70th birthday, 1988; As conductor led Mozart's Concertos from the keyboard with English National Orchestra on its Far Eastern tour; Illinois Opera Theatre in Così fan tutte and Die Fledermaus; 1988–89 season engagements with San Diego Chamber Orchestra and in Israel; Professor, University of Illinois, 1983–. *Recordings:* Chopin/Godowsky Etudes and the complete piano sonatas of Hummel; Strauss's Burlesque and the Paregon on the Symphonia Domestica, with the Philharmonia; Concertos by Françaix, Saint-Saëns and Milhaud, with the Sinfonia da Camera; 24 Chopin Etudes, Rachmaninov Transcriptions and Mozart's Concertos Nos 23 and 24. *Fax:* (20) 8287-9428.

**HOCH, Beverly;** American singer (soprano); b. 1956, Kansas City, Kansas. *Education:* studied in New York. *Career:* Concert performances from 1980, notably at Carnegie Hall, New York, and the Kennedy Center, Washington; European concerts in Madrid, Gothenburg and Brussels; Opera appearances at Spoleto, the Wexford Festival (Philine in Mignon), and Santa Fe; Her best known role is Mozart's Queen of Night, which she sang in the 1991 Glyndebourne Festival. *Recordings include:* Die Zauberflöte.

**HOCH, Francesco;** Composer and Professor of Music; b. 14 Feb. 1943, Lugano, Switzerland; m. 1 May 1971, 2 s. *Education:* G Verdi Conservatory, Milan; Composition, Padua, Darmstadt. *Career:* Professor of Music, Lugano; Assistant, Composition Course, Chigiana Academy, Siena Italy, 1974; Invited, International Laboratory, Venice Biennial, 1975; Founder Oggimusica Association of Contemporary Music, 1977; Regular radio broadcasts of compositions, Europe, Israel, Canada, USA, Australia, Japan, Russia, Latin America; Television recordings. *Compositions:* 63 published works including: Dune, 3 instruments, 2 percussion, 2 voices, 1972; L'Oggetto Disincantato, 13 instruments, 1974; Trittico, clarinet, viola; Leonardo e/und Gantenbein, opera-ballet, 1980–82; Ostinato variabile, I, bass clarinet, 1981, II, bass clarinet, piano, III, 2 guitars, IV, piano, violin, 1982; Sans, oboe, orchestra, 1985; Un Mattino, 2 flutes, 1986; Der Tod ohne des Mädchen, string quartet, 1990; Memorie da Requiem, choir, orchestra, 1989–91; Postludio degli Spettatori, choir, 1991; Péché d'outre-tombe, for clarinet and string quartet, 1993; La Passerelle des Fous, opera, for 3 sopranos, 5 actors and 8 instruments, 1994–95; Canti e danze dai nuovi gironi for 13 instruments, 1995; Der hoffnungsvolle Jean und der Moloch for narrator and chorus, 1995; Suite Palomar for 5 instruments, 1995–97; L'isola dell'amore for 3 voices and mandolin orchestra, 1997–98; The Magic Ring opera, for 6 voices, 3 e-guitars, 3 percussions, electronic tape and video scenes, 1995–2000; Su Gentile Invito for violin and cello, 2000; Es ist Zeit for flute, 2000; Doppio Concerto for cello, piano and orchestra, 2001–02; Duo dal doppio for cello and piano, 2002; Ave lucanum for choir, 2003. *Recordings include:* Chamber and orchestral works, CD; Il Mattino Dopo, CD, 2000; Memorie da Requiem, CD Doron, 2002; Fantasia da L'isola dell'amore, Cd Altrisuoni, 2003; The Magic Ring, opera, CD, MGB, CH, 2004; Video Recordings include: Trasparenza per nuovi elementi, Video TSI, CH, 1977; Leonardo e/und Gantenbein, opera, video TSI, CH, 1985; F.Hoch- Ritratto and Suite Palomar PARS MEDIA, Munich, 2001. *Publications:* Enc Musica UTET (Torino); Enc Grove; Francesco Hoch, Swiss Composer, by Pro Helvetia, 1994; Donazione opere, Zentralbibliothek, Zurich, 2001; F.Hoch: Influssi sulla mia musica in Entre Denge et Denzy, P Sacher Stiftung, Basel; Carlo Piccardi: La sfida musicale di F.Hoch in CdT, CH, 15/04/ 2002' Paolo Petazzi: Magie de la Bourse in Dissonanz, CH, 2003; Paolo Repetto: Utopie und Erinnerung in Dissonanz, CH, 2003; Carlo Piccardi: Il futuro nel passato (F.Hoch) in bloc notes 48, 2003. *Address:* Campo dei Fiori 9, 6942 Savosa, Switzerland.

**HOCHMANN, Klaus;** German composer; b. 29 Dec. 1932, Angerbürg, Ostpreußen, Poland. *Education:* Composition and Conducting at Stuttgart and Salzburg. *Career:* Piano Teacher, Music School of Herrenberg; mem., Society for Promotion of Radio Symphony Orchestra Stuttgart, Leoš Janáček Society Bern. *Compositions include:* Der Findling, opera, 1970; Midsummer Night, 5 choirs ac, 1963; Requiem für einen Unbekannten, 3 songs for bass and organ, 1965; Concertino I for percussion, 1969; Concertino III for percussion solo and tutti, 1974; Bilder des Todes for recorder and percussion, 1991; one to four for string quartet, 1991; Mary, poem with music, text by Dorothea Spears, 1992. *Recordings:* Requiem für einen Unbekannten, 1968; Tenebrae factae sunt for mixed choir ac, 4 speaker, percussion, 1992; In Memoriam, song cycle for baritone and piano, 1980; Und suche Gott, for mixed choir ac and speaker, 1991; Mein Bruder Tod for mixed choir a cappella, after Agnes Miegel, 1985; Intrada for organ, 1993; Selbst die Steine umarmen wir; Strophen for 5 solo voices a cappella, after Nelly Sachs, 1994. *Honours:* Composition Prizes, Kassel, 1965, Bern, 1975, Bonn, 1984; Promotion Prizes, 1971, 1977. *Address:* Beethovenstrasse 62, 71083 Herrenberg, Germany.

**HOCKNEY, David,** CH, RA; British artist and stage designer; b. 9 July 1937, Bradford; s. of the late Kenneth Hockney and Laura Hockney. *Education:* Bradford Coll. of Art and Royal Coll. of Art. *Career:* taught at Maidstone Coll. of Art 1962, Univ. of Iowa 1964, Univ. of Colorado 1965, UCLA 1966 (Hon. Chair. of Drawing 1980), Univ. of California, Berkeley 1967; has travelled extensively in Europe and USA; Assoc. mem. Royal Acad. 1985. *Film:* A Bigger Splash (autobiographical documentary) 1974. *Exhibitions:* first one-man Exhbn, Kasmin Gallery, London 1963; subsequent one-man exhbns at Museum of Modern Art, New York 1964, 1968, Laundan-Alan Gallery, New York 1964, 1967, Kasmin Gallery 1965, 1966, 1968, 1969, 1970, 1972, Stedeljik Museum, Amsterdam 1966, Palais des Beaux-Arts, Brussels 1966, Studio Marconi and Galleria dell'Ariete, Milan 1966, Galerie Mikro, Berlin 1968, Whitworth Art Gallery, Manchester 1969, André Emmerich Gallery, New York 1972–96, Gallery Springer, Berlin 1970, Kestner-Ges., Hanover 1970, Whitechapel Gallery (retrospective exhbn), London 1970, Kunsthalle, Bielefeld 1971, Musée des Arts Décoratifs, Louvre, Paris 1974, Galerie Claude Bernard, Paris 1975, Nicholas Wilder, Los Angeles 1976, Galerie Neundorf, Hamburg 1977, Warehouse Gallery 1979, Knoedler Gallery 1979, 1981, 1982, 1983, 1984, 1986, Tate Gallery (retrospective Exhbn) 1980, 1986, 1988, 1992, Hayward Gallery (photographs) 1983, 1985, Museo Tamayo, Mexico City 1984, LA County Museum of Art (retrospective) 1988, 1996, The Metropolitan Museum of Art (retrospective) NY 1988, Knoedler Gallery, London 1988, LA Louver Gallery, Calif. 1986, 1989–, Venice 1982, 1983, 1985, 1986, 1988, Nishimura Gallery, Tokyo, Japan 1986, 1989, 1990, 1994, Royal Acad. of Arts, London 1995, Hamburger Kunsthalle 1995, Manchester City Art Galleries (retrospective exhbn) 1996, Nat. Museum of American Art, Washington, DC 1997, 1998, Museum Ludwig, Cologne 1997, Museum of Fine Arts, Boston 1998, Centre Georges Pompidou, Paris 1999, Musée Picasso, Paris 1999, Annely Juda Fine Art 2003, Nat. Portrait Gallery 2003; group exhbns include ICA, Second and Third Paris Biennales of Young Artists, Musée d'Art Moderne 1961, 1963, Third Inst. Biennale of Prints, Nat. Museum of Art, Tokyo 1962, London Group Jubilee Exhbn 1914–1964, Tate Gallery 1964, Painting and Sculpture of a Decade, Gulbenkian Foundation, Op and Pop, Stockholm and London 1965, Fifth Int. Exhbn of Graphic Art, Ljubljana 1965, First Int. Print Biennale, Cracow 1966, São Paulo Biennale 1967, Venice Biennale 1968, Pop Art Redefined, Hayward Gallery, London 1969, 150 Years of Photography, Nat. Gallery, Wash., DC 1989–90; touring show of prints and drawings Munich, Madrid, Lisbon, Tehran 1977, Saltaire, Yorks, New York, LA 1994, Royal Acad. (drawings) 1995–96. *Stage design:* set: Ubu Roi, Royal Court Theatre, London 1966, Rake's Progress, Glyndebourne 1975, Die Zauberflöte, Glyndebourne 1978, La Scala 1979, Nightingale, Covent Garden 1983, Varii Capricci, Metropolitan Opera House, New York 1983, Tristan and Isolde, LA Music Centre Opera, LA 1987, Turandot, Lyric Opera 1992–, San

Francisco 1993, Die Frau Ohne Schatten, Covent Garden, London 1992, LA Music Centre Opera 1993; costume and set: Les Mamelles de Teresias, Metropolitan Opera House, New York 1980, L'Enfant et les sortilèges, Metropolitan Opera House, New York 1980, Parade, Metropolitan Opera House, New York 1980, Oedipus Rex, Metropolitan Opera House, New York 1981, Le Sacre du Printemps, Metropolitan Opera House, New York 1981, Le Rossignol, Metropolitan Opera House, New York 1981. *Publications:* Hockney by Hockney 1976, David Hockney, Travel with Pen, Pencil and Ink 1978 (autobiog.), Paper Pools 1980, Photographs 1982, China Diary (with Stephen Spender), 1982, Hockney Paints the Stage 1983, David Hockney: Cameraworks 1984, Hockney on Photography: Conversations with Paul Joyce 1988, David Hockney: A Retrospective 1988, Hockney's Alphabet (ed. by Stephen Spender) 1991, That's the Way I See It 1993 (autobiog.), Off the Wall: Hockney Posters 1994, David Hockney's Dog Days 1998, Hockney on Art: Photography, Painting and Perspective 1999, Hockney on 'Art': Conversation with Paul Joyce 2000, Secret Knowledge: Rediscovering the Lost Techniques of the Old Masters 2001, Hockney's Pictures 2004; illustrated Six Fairy Tales of the Brothers Grimm 1969, The Blue Guitar 1977, Hockney's Alphabet 1991. *Honours:* Hon. PhD (Aberdeen) 1988, (Royal Coll. of Art) 1992; Hon. DLitt (Oxford) 1995; Guinness Award 1961, Graphic Prize, Paris Biennale 1963, First Prize 8th Int. Exhbn of Drawings and Engravings, Lugano 1964, prize at 6th Int. Exhbn of Graphic Art, Ljubljana 1965, Cracow 1st Int. Print Biennale 1966, First Prize 6th John Moores Exhbn 1967, Hamburg Foundation Shakespeare Prize 1983, Praemium Imperiale, Japan Art Asscn 1989, Fifth Annual Gov.'s Award for Visual Arts in Calif. 1994. *Address:* c/o 7508 Santa Monica Boulevard, Los Angeles, CA 90046-6407, USA.

**HODDINOTT, Alun,** CBE, DMus, FRNCM; Welsh composer; *Artistic Director, Cardiff Festival of Twentieth Century Music*; b. 11 Aug. 1929, Bargoed, S Wales; s. of Thomas Ivor Hoddinott and Gertrude Jones; m. Beti Rhiannon Huws 1953; one s. *Education:* Gowerton Grammar School and Univ. Coll., Cardiff. *Career:* Lecturer, Cardiff Coll. of Music and Drama 1951–59; Lecturer Univ. Coll., Cardiff 1959–65, Reader 1965–67, Prof. of Music 1967–87; Artistic Dir Cardiff Festival of Twentieth Century Music 1966–89, Pres. 1989–; Fellow, Univ. Coll., Cardiff 1981, Welsh Coll. of Music and Drama 1990. *Works include:* seven symphonies 1955–77; four sinfoniettas, eleven concertos 1951–69, six piano sonatas 1959–72, four violin sonatas 1969–76, sonatas for harp, cello, clarinet, horn, sonata for Cello and Piano 1977, Welsh Dances, Investiture Dances, Black Bart, Dives and Lazarus 1965, Variants 1966, Fioriture 1968, The Tree of Life 1971, Ritornelli 1974, The Beach at Falesa (opera) 1974, The Magician (opera), Ancestor Worship, Five Landscapes (song cycles), A Contemplation upon Flowers (songs for soprano and orchestra), What the Old Man Does is Always Right (opera), Passaggio for orchestra 1977, Dulcia Iuventutis 1977, Sonata for Organ, Voyagers (for baritone solo, male voices and orchestra) Sonatina for guitar, Sonatina for two pianos, The Rajah's Diamond (opera), Scena for string quartet, Ritornelli for brass quintet, Hymnus Ante Somnum, Nocturnes and Cadenza for solo 'cello, The Heaventree of Stars (for violin and orchestra) 1980, The Trumpet Major (opera in three acts) 1981, Nocturnes and Cadenzas for solo flute, Ritornelli for four double basses, Te Deum (for mixed voices and organ), Lanterne des Morts (for orchestra), Six Welsh Folk Songs (soprano and piano), Doubles (for oboe, harpsichord and strings), Five Studies (for orchestra), Four Scenes from the Trumpet Major (for orchestra), Quodlibet for orchestra 1982, Quodlibet for brass quintet 1983, Masks (oboe, bassoon and piano) 1983, Ingravescentem aetatem (chorus and piano duet) 1983, Lady and Unicorn: Cantata for mixed voices and piano, Piano Trio No. 2, Bagatelles for oboe and harp, String Quartet No. 2, Piano Sonata No. 7, Scenes and Interludes: Concertante for trumpet, harpsichord and strings, Symphony No. 6, Hommage à Chopin (orchestra), Bells of Paradise: Cantata for baritone, mixed chorus and orchestra 1984, Welsh Dances, Third Suite (orchestra), Divertimenti for flute, bassoon, double bass and percussion, Scena for string orchestra, Sonata for two pianos, The Silver Hound: Cycle for tenor and piano, Passacaglia and Fugue for organ, Fanfare with Variants for brass band, Green Broom: Ballad for male voices and piano, Sonata for four clarinets, Sing a New Song (anthem for mixed voices and organ) 1985, Flower Songs (women's voices and piano), Concerto for violin, cello and orchestra, Sonata No. 8 for piano, Divisions: Concertante for horn, harpsichord and strings, Concerto for orchestra, Concerto for clarinet and orchestra 1986, Aspiciens A Longe (anthem for mixed voices and organ) 1987, Welsh Dances (for brass band) 1987, Cantata: Legend of St Julian 1987, String Quartet No. 3 1988, Dr. Faustus: Scena (for mixed voices and brass) 1988, lines from Marlowe's Dr. Faustus 1988, Noctis Equi (cello and orchestra), Songs of Exile, Piano Sonata No. 9, Star Children, Piano Sonata No. 10, Symphony for organ and orchestra 1989, Emynau Pantycelyn (cantata) 1990, Three Advent Carols 1990, Novelette for flute, oboe and piano 1991, Sonata for flute and piano 1991, Sonata No. 5 for violin and piano 1992, Vespers Canticle 1992, Symphony for brass and percussion 1992, Chorales, Variants and Fanfares for organ and brass quintet 1992, Gloria 1992, A Vision of Eternity 1992, Three Motets for chorus and organ 1993, Wind Quintet 1993, Sonata No. 11 for piano 1993, Mass for St David 1994, Sonata No. 12 for piano 1994, Six Bagatelles for string quartet 1994, Three Hymns for mixed chorus and organ 1994, Shakespeare Songs for unaccompanied chorus 1994, The Silver Swimmer for soprano and ensemble 1994, Five Poems of Gustavo Adolfo Bécquer for baritone and piano 1994, One Must Always Have Love (song for high voice and piano) 1994, Mistral (concerto for violin and orchestra) 1995, Shining Pyramid (concerto for trumpet and orchestra) 1995, Sonata for oboe and harp 1995, Tymhorau (four

poems for Gwyn Thomas for baritone and piano) 1995, The Poetry of Earth (songs for mixed choir and piano duet) 1995, Camargue Mass 1996, Sonata No. 3 (cello and piano) 1996, Magnificat and Nunc Dimittis 1996, String Quartet No. 4 1996, Piano Trio No. 3 1996, Sonata No. 2 (clarinet and piano) 1996, Sonata No. 6 (violin and piano) 1997, Tempi: Sonata for Harp 1997, The Poetry of Earth (songs for baritone and harp) 1997, Island of Dragons (variants for cello) 1998, Dragon Fire (concertante for timpani, percussion and orchestra), Grongor Hill (scena for baritone, string quartet and piano), Lizard (variants for recorder), Tower (opera in three acts) 1998–99, Celebration Dances (orchestra), To the Poet (Pushkin songs for baritone and piano), Symphony No. 10 1999–2000, La Serenissima (songs for baritone and piano), Quintet for oboe, piano and string trio, Concerto for percussion and brass; Piano Sonata No. 13 2000; String Quartet No. 5 2001; Dream Wanderer for violin, horn and piano 2001, Bagatelles for 11 instruments 2001, Concerto for euphonium and orchestra 2001, Three Welsh Folk Songs (cello and piano) 2002, Lizard (concerto for orchestra) 2002, Sonata (euphonium and piano) 2003, Concerto for trombone and orchestra 2003–04, Promontory of Dreams (song cycle) 2004, Badger in the Bag (overture) 2004, Bagatelles for 4 trombones 2004, Concerto Grosso for brass 2004, Sonata for piano duet 2004, 7 Folk Songs arranged for baritone and harp. *Honours:* Hon. mem. RAM; Hon. DMus (Sheffield) 1993; Walford Davies Prize 1954, Bax Medal 1957, Hopkins Medal of the St David's Soc. of New York 1981, Glyndŵr Medal 1997. *Address:* 64 Gowerton Road, Three Crosses, Swansea, SA4 3PX, Wales. *Telephone:* (1792) 873702 (home). *E-mail:* hoddinott@croesau.fsnet.co.uk (home).

**HODGES, Nicolas;** Composer and Pianist; b. 4 June 1970, London, England. *Education:* Studied composition at Dartington and Winchester with Morto Feldman and Michael Finnissy; Piano with Robert Bottone and privately with Susan Bradshaw; Music at Cambridge University. *Career:* As pianist, premieres including music by Finnissy, Weir, Skempton, Toovey, Powell, Holloway, Bill Hopkins, some as part of the Bach project, broadcast on Radio 3. *Compositions:* Piano Studies, solo piano, 1988–92; Small Shadows, 1990; Twothreefourfive, violin and piano, 1991–92; Do I detect a silver thread between you and this young lady, solo viola, 1993; Concertino, 1993; Scripture for soprano, oboe d'amore and 2 percussion, 1994. *Recordings:* Bach Project released on CD. *Contributions:* Various articles and reviews to Tempo, Musical Times, including The Music of Bill Hopkins, 1993, The Music of Luigi Nono 1950–58 - Analytical investigations. *Address:* Flat 3, 68 Norwood Road, Herne Hill, London SE24 9BB, England.

**HODGSON, Julia;** Viol Player; b. 1960, England. *Career:* Member of Fretwork, first London concert at the Wigmore Hall, London, July 1986; Appearances in the Renaissance and Baroque repertoire in Sweden, France, Belgium, Netherlands, Germany, Austria, Switzerland and Italy; Radio broadcasts in Sweden, Netherlands, Germany and Austria; Televised concert on ZDF, Mainz; Tour of Soviet Union, Sept 1989, and Japan, June 1991; Festival engagements in the United Kingdom; Repertory includes In Nomines and Fantasias by Tallis, Parsons and Byrd; Dance music by Holborne and Dowland (including Lachrimae); Six-part consorts by Gibbons and William Lawes; Songs and instrumental works by Purcell; Collaborations with vocal group Red Byrd in verse anthems by Byrd and Tomkins, London Cries by Gibbons and Dering, Resurrection Story and Seven Last Words by Schütz; Gave George Benjamin's Upon Silence at the Queen Elizabeth Hall, Oct 1990; Wigmore Hall concerts, 1990–91, with music by Lawes, Purcell, Locke, Dowland and Byrd. *Recordings:* Heart's Ease (late Tudor and early Stuart); Armada (Courts of Philip II and Elizabeth I); Night's Black Bird (Dowland and Byrd); Cries and Fancies (Fantasias, In Nomines and The Cries of London by Gibbons); Go Nightly Care (consort songs, dances and In Nomines by Byrd and Dowland). *Address:* c/o Fretwork, 16 Teddington Park Road, Teddington, Middlesex, TW11 8 ND, England.

**HODKINSON, Juliana;** Composer; b. 17 March 1971, Exeter, England. *Education:* King's College, Cambridge, 1990–93; MA Double Honours, Music and Philosophy, University of Cambridge, 1993; Diploma in German; Private studies under Hans Abrahamsen and Per Nørgård; MA, Japanese Studies, Sheffield University, 1997. *Career:* Debut: 1st professional performance of composition Recalling Voices of the Child, Capricorn ensemble, ICA, London, 3 Mar 1994; Works performed at ICA, London, Den Anden Opera, Copenhagen, Nordic Music Days, 1998, Stockholm, Musikhalle, Hamburg, Paul Gerhardt Kirche and Neuköllner Saalbau, Berlin, Tokyo University of Fine Arts, La Machine à Eau, Mons, Belgium; Works performed by Capricorn (London), Athelas Sinfonietta (Copenhagen), Sonanza (Stockholm), Orchestre Royal de Chambre de Mons (Belgium), Contemporary Alpha (Tokyo), Matthias Arter (Zürich), Prisma (Berlin), Ensemble 2000 (Denmark), Danish Radio Concert Orchestra; mem, Dansk Komponist Forening; Koda-NCB, Denmark. *Compositions:* In Slow Movement, 1994; Water Like a Stone, 1996; Machine à Eau, 1998; Music for Gilles Requiem, 1999. *Contributions:* Dansk Musik Tidsskrift, 1994, 1997; Japanese Society Proceedings, 1996. *Honours:* Danish Arts Council Grants, 1994, 1998, 1999; Daiwa Foundation, Scholarship, 1995–97; Pépinières Européens Jeunes Artistes residency, 1997–98; Kongegaarden Centre for Music and Visual Arts, residency, 1999. *Address:* Kongegaarden, Algade 25, 4220 Korsír, Denmark.

**HOEL, Lena;** Singer (Soprano); b. 1957, Sweden. *Education:* Studied at the Stockholm Music High School. *Career:* Sang at the Stockholm Royal Opera, from 1984 as Gilda, Sophi in Der Rosenkavalier and in the premieres of Backanterna by Daniel Börtz, 1991; Festival of Drottningholm from 1989; In Soliman II by JM Kraus and Isme in Elektra by JC Haeffner; Mozart: Pamina/

Magic Flute, Fiordiligi/Così fan tutte; Puccini: Mimi/La Bohème; Bizet: Carmen; Janáček: The Cunning Little Vixen; Lidholm: A Dreamplay/Indra's d.; Sandström: Staden/Cecilia; Other roles in Aniara by Blomdahl; Sang Dorinda in Handel's Orlando at Stockholm, 2000; Recitals and chamber music as well as oratorios. *Recordings:* Sandström/The High Mass; Blomdahl/Aniara; Börtz/The Bacchantes. *Honours:* The Jenny Lind Scholarship, until 1983. *Current Management:* The Royal Opera, Stockholm. *Address:* Kungliga Operan, PO Box 16094, 10322 Stockholm, Sweden.

**HOELSCHER, Ulf;** Violinist; b. 17 Jan. 1942, Kitzingen, Germany. *Education:* Privately with father and Bruno Masurat; Studied with Max Rostal in Cologne; Studied 3 years in USA with Josef Gingold, Indiana University, and with Ivan Galamian, Curtis Institute, Philadelphia, USA. *Career:* Member, International Geiger Elite; Violin Concertos of Kirchner with Berlin Philharmonic, 1984; Franz Hummel's Violin Concerto, Baden-Baden, 1987; Performed Double Concerto by Aribert Reimann, with Wolfgang Reimann, Hannover, 1989; Performances and recordings from a wide repertoire featuring Frankel, Tchaikovsky, Schumann, Mendelssohn, Richard Strauss, Brahms and Beethoven, and the chamber music of Bartók, César Franck, and Szymanowski. *Recordings:* Hummel's Violin Concerto, with USSR State Symphony Orchestra. *Current Management:* Astrid Schoerke. *Address:* c/o Monckebergalee 41, 30453 Hannover, Germany.

**HOENE, Barbara;** Singer (Soprano); b. 4 Feb. 1944, Cottbus, Germany. *Education:* Studied at the Leipzig Musikhochschule and with Johannes Kempter. *Career:* Debut: Dessau, 1966 as Laura in Der Bettelstudent; Sang at Halle/Saale, 1968–73; With the Dresden Opera roles have included Mozart's Fiordiligi and Pamina, Sophie in Der Rosenkavalier, Carolina in Il Matrimonio segreto, Orff's Die Kluge and Verdi's Nannetta; Many further roles in operas by Handel; Guest appearances in Berlin, St Petersburg, Italy, France and Japan; Season 1994–95 as Marcellina in Le nozze di Figaro; Sang in the premiere of Reimann's Melusine; Sang in the premiere of Celan by Peter Ruzicka at Dresden, 2001; Lieder recitals and oratorios by Bach and Handel. *Address:* c/o Staatsoper Dresden, Theaterplatz 2, 01067 Dresden, Germany.

**HOEPRICH, Thomas (Eric);** Clarinettist; b. 5 Sept. 1955, Baltimore, Maryland, USA. *Education:* AB cum laude, Harvard University, 1976; Solo Diploma, Royal Conservatory of Music, Netherlands, 1982. *Career:* Principal Clarinet, Orchestra of the 18th Century, 1983–; Founding Member of Amadeus Winds, Stadler Trio (basset horns), Nachtmusik and Trio d'Amsterdam; Regular appearances with London Classical Players, Tafelmusik and The Orchestra of the Handel and Haydn Society; Professor, Royal Conservatory of Music, Netherlands. *Recordings:* Mozart Clarinet Concerto and Quintet with Orchestra of the 18th Century, Philips; Other recordings as soloist: Taverner Players, EMI; Musica Antiqua Cologne, DGG-Archiv; Other recordings for Decca, Harmonia Mundi, Accent, Erato and SONY Classical. *Contributions:* Early Music; Tibia; Galpin Society Journal; NOTES. *Honours:* Mozart Clarinet Concerto and Quintet recording named one of the best 15 CDs of 1988, Le Monde de la Musique. *Address:* Bredeweg 39-2, 1098 BN Amsterdam, Netherlands.

**HOFFMAN, Gary;** Concert Cellist; b. 1956, Vancouver, Canada. *Education:* Indiana University School of Music. *Career:* faculty member at Bloomington, Indiana, 1980s; soloist with major orchestras in Chicago, London, San Francisco, Montreal, Cleveland, Philadelphia; English Moscow and Los Angeles Chamber Orchestras, Orchestre National de France, Suisse Romande and Rotterdam Philharmonic; conductors include Previn, Dutoit, Andrew Davis, Kent Nagano and James Levine; festival engagements at Ravinia, Aspen, Marlboro, Bath, Helsinki, New York (Mostly Mozart) and Verbier; chamber music as guest with the Emerson, Tokyo, Brentano and Ysaye String Quartets; Artist Member of the Lincoln Center Chamber Music Society, New York. *Recordings:* albums for BMG, Sony, EMI and Chant du Monde labels. *Honours:* Winner, Rostropovich International Competition, Paris, 1986. *Address:* c/o Musicaglotz, 11, rue le Verrier, 75006 Paris, France.

**HOFFMAN, Grace;** American singer (mezzo-soprano); b. 14 Nov. 1925, Cleveland, Ohio; d. of Dave Hoffman and Hermina Hoffman. *Education:* Western Reserve Univ. and Manhattan School of Music, New York. *Career:* completed musical studies in Italy (Fulbright Scholarship); appeared at Maggio Musicale, Florence; guest performance as Azucena (Il Trovatore) Zürich Opera and subsequently mem. of this company for two years; debut at La Scala, Milan as Fricka (Die Walküre); with Stuttgart Opera 1955–; given titles Württembergische Kammersängerin 1960, Austrian Kammersängerin 1980; has appeared at Edinburgh and Bayreuth festivals; numerous guest appearances in leading roles at Teatro Colón, Buenos Aires, San Francisco Opera, Chicago Lyric Opera, Covent Garden, Metropolitan Opera, the Vienna Opera, in Berlin, Brussels, etc.; numerous oratorio and concert appearances in the maj. European music centres; Prof. of Voice, Hochschule für Musik, Stuttgart 1978. *Honours:* Vercelli Prize, Medal of State of Baden-Württemberg 1978. *Address:* c/o Staatstheater Stüttgart, Oberer Schlossgarten 6, 7000 Stuttgart 1 (office); Bergstrasse 19, 72666 Neckartailfingen, Germany (home).

**HOFFMAN, Irwin;** Symphony Conductor and Violinist; b. 26 Nov. 1924, New York City, USA; m. Esther Glazer Hoffman, 3 s, 1 d. *Education:* Juilliard School of Music. *Career:* Conductor of Vancouver Symphony, BC, Canada, 1952–64; Associate Conductor and Acting Music Director, Chicago Symphony, IL, USA, 1964–70; Music Director of The Florida Orchestra, 1968–87; Chief permanent conductor of Belgian Radio and Television Symphony, 1972, 1976;

Guest Conductor for various leading orchestras in Europe, North America, Israel and South America. *Recordings:* Several. *Address:* c/o Everett Wright, 3876 Oak Grove Drive, Sarasota, Florida, USA.

**HOFFMAN, Joel (Harvey);** Composer, Pianist and Teacher; b. 27 Sept. 1953, Vancouver, British Columbia, Canada; m. 30 Dec 1988. *Education:* BM, University of Wales, Cardiff, Wales, 1974; MM, 1976, DMA, 1978, Juilliard School, New York, USA. *Career:* Graduate Teaching Assistant, Juilliard School, New York, 1976–78; Professor of Composition, College-Conservatory of Music, University of Cincinnati, Ohio, 1978–; Commissions: Cincinnati Symphony Orchestra, 1993; Shanghai String Quartet, 1993; National Chamber Orchestra, 1993; Golub-Kaplan-Carr Trio, 1991; Artistic Director, Music Ninety-eight, Music Ninety-nine and Music 2000 Festivals. *Compositions:* Variations for violin, cello and harp, 1975; Music from Chartres for 10 brass instruments, 1978; September Music for double bass and harp, 1980; Chamber Symphony, 1980 Sonata for harp. 1982; 5 Pieces for two pianos, 1883; Double Concerto, 1984; Violin Concerto, 1986; Fantasia Fiorentina, for violin and piano, 1988; Hands Down, for piano, 1986; Crossing Points for string orchestra, 1990; Partenze, for solo violin, 1990; Each for Himself, for piano solo, 1991; Cubist Blues for violin, cello and piano, 1991; Music in Blue and Green, for orchestra, 1992; Metasmo for percussion trio, 1992; Self-Portrait with Mozart, violin, piano and orchestra, 1994; Music for Chamber Orchestra, 1994; ChiaSsO for orchestra, 1995; L'Immensitá dell'Attimo, song cycle for mezzo and piano, 1995; The Music Within the Words, 1996; Portogruaro Sextet, 1996; Millennium Dances, for orchestra, 1997; Self-Portrait with Gebirtig for cello and orchestra, 1998; Kraków Variations for viola sola, 1999; Reyzele: A portrait for chamber ensemble, 1999. *Recordings:* Duo for viola and piano, 1991; Partenze, 1992; Music for Two Oboes, 1995; Tum-Balalaykę, 1996; Fantasy Pieces, 1999. *Honours:* National Endowment for the Arts Commissions, 1985, 1991; BMI Award, 1972; Bearns Prize, Columbia University, 1978; American Academy Institute of Arts and Letters, 1987. *Address:* College-Conservatory of Music, University of Cincinnati, Cincinnati, OH 45221, USA.

**HOFFMAN, Stanley;** Violinist and Violist; b. 8 Dec. 1929, Baltimore, Maryland, USA. *Education:* Private study with Arthur Grumaux, Belgium; BSc, Juilliard School of Music; Study with Mischa Mischakoff, Raphael Bronstein and Oscar Shumsky. *Career:* Debut: Carnegie Recital hall, New York City; Regular Member, New York Philharmonic Orchestra under Leonard Bernstein, 1961–64, Jerusalem Radio Symphony Orchestra, Israel, 1981–83; Bohemians, New York; Local 802 Association Federation of Musicians. *Recordings:* Vocal Chamber Music, Vol. I with Susan Reid-Parsons as soprano, 1971, Vol. II with Elinor Amlen and Rose Macdonald, sopranos, 1973; Taping session for Radio Kol Israel, 1984, 1986; Solo violin sonatas, Béla Bartók, Honegger, Hindemith, Ralph Shapey, Paul Ben-Haim, Bach C Major, Roger Sessions. *Address:* Poste-Restante, Tel-Aviv, Israel.

**HOFFMANN, Anke;** Singer (Soprano); b. 19 Sept. 1969, Siegen, Germany. *Education:* Musikhochschule Cologne from 1989. *Career:* Deutsche Oper am Rhein, Düsseldorf, from 1990 as Gounod's Juliette, Papagena in Die Zauberflöte, Nicolai's Anne, Frasquita in Carmen and Olympia in Les contes d'Hoffmann; Wiesbaden, 1992, in the premiere of Der Park by Hans Gefors; Further guest engagements in Mainz, as Zerbinetta and in Henze's Der junge Lord at Saarbrucken, as Zerlina, and at Bremerhaven, as Gilda; Other roles include Mozart's Blondchen and Queen of Night, Nannetta, Adele, and Philene in Mignon; Bonn Opera from 1993; Sang Aennchen in Der Freischütz at Eutin, 2000; Concerts include Bach's Passions, Handel's Messiah and Joshua, Mozart's Requiem and Mendelssohn's Elijah. *Honours:* Medal Winner in competitions at Berlin and Salzburg (1990, 1993). *Address:* c/o Oper der Stadt Bonn, Am Boeselagerhof 1, Pf 2440, 53111 Bonn, Germany.

**HOFFMANN, Horst;** Singer (Tenor); b. 13 June 1935, Oppeln, Germany. *Education:* Studied with Thilde Amelung in Hildesheim and Otto Kohler in Hanover. *Career:* Debut: Hanover, 1961, in Zar und Zimmermann; Has sung at the Stuttgart and Munich State Operas and the Deutsche Oper am Rhein, Düsseldorf; Komische Oper Berlin and the Opéra du Rhin, Strasbourg; Bayreuth Festival, 1967–68; Further appearances in Cologne, Lisbon, Zürich, Vienna (Volksoper) and Sydney, 1984 (Lohengrin and Siegmund, 1987 and 1989); Teatro Regio, Turin, 1987, as Don Ottavio; Otello, Sydney and Melbourne, 1988, and in Sydney, 1992; From the House of the Dead, Cologne, Germany, 1992; Sang Florestan at Sydney, 1992; Tristan and Isolde, Sydney and Melbourne, 1993, and Essen, Germany, 1993; Die Meistersinger, Sydney, 1993; Roles include Tamino, Belmonte, Nemorino, Edgardo, Pinkerton, Alfredo in La Traviata and Alfred in Die Fledermaus; Sang Otello at Sydney, Lohengrin at Dresden, Walküre at Düsseldorf and Tristan at Trieste, 1996; Season 1997–98 Tannhäuser at Sydney and Melbourne, Bacchus in Ariadne and Samson at Sydney, and Erik in The Flying Dutchman in Melbourne; Season 1999–2000 Florestan in Fidelio in Capetown, Andres in Wozzeck and Aegisthus in Elektra in Sydney and Tristan in Sydney and Melbourne; Season 2003: Gurrelieder in Perth; Messiah in Tampa, 2004. *Recordings include:* Bruckner Te Deum and CD Great Opera Heroes, 1996. *Current Management:* Jenifer Eddy Artists' Management, Melbourne. *Address:* 2504 Gulf Blvd #506, Indian Rocks Beach Fl 33785 USA.

**HOFFMANN, Richard;** Composer and Musicologist; b. 20 April 1925, Vienna, Austria. *Education:* Studied at the University of New Zealand and the University of California at Los Angeles; Composition studies with Arnold Schoenberg. *Career:* Secretary and assistant to Schoenberg, 1948–51; Teacher of University of California at Los Angeles, 1951–52, Oberlin College from 1954; Visiting Professor at the University of California, Berkeley, 1965–66; Co-editor of the complete works of Schoenberg, 1961, edited the score of Von Heute auf Morgen. *Compositions include:* Prelude and Double Fugue for strings, 1944; Piano Sonata, 1946; Violin Concerto, 1948; 4 String Quartets, 1947, 1950, 1974, 1977; 3 Songs, 1948; Duo for violin and cello, 1949; 3 Songs, 1950; Piano Quartet, 1950; Fantasy and Fugue for organ, 1951; Piano Sonatina, 1952; Piano Concerto, 1954; Cello Concerto, 1956–59; String Trio, 1963; Memento Mori for male voices and orchestra, 1966–69; Music for strings, 1971; Decadanse for 10 players, 1972; Changes for 2 chimes, 4 performers, 1974; Souffler for orchestra, 1976; In memorium patris for computer-generated tape, 1976; Intavolatura for strings and percussion, 1980. *Honours:* Guggenheim Fellowships, 1970, 1977. *Address:* c/o ASCAP, ASCAP Building, 1 Lincoln Plaza, New York, NY 10023, USA.

**HOFFMANN-ERBRECHT, Lothar;** Professor; b. 2 March 1925, Strehlen Schlesien, Germany; m. Margarete Fischer, 2 d. *Education:* Graduate, Academy of Music, Weimar, 1949; PhD, University of Jena, 1951; Habilitation, Department of Musicology, University of Frankfurt, 1961. *Career:* Professor of Musicology, University and Academy of Music of Frankfurt am Main, University of Technology of Darmstadt; mem, Society for Music Research; International Musicological Society. *Publications include:* Deutsche und italienische Klaviermusik zur Bachzeit, 1954; Thomas Stoltzer, Leben und Schaffen, 1964; Thomas Stoltzer, Ausgewaehlte Werke II–III; Heinrich Finck, Ausgewaehlte Werke, I–II; Beethoven Klaviersonaten (with Claudio Arrau); Henricus Finck-musicus excellentissimus, 1445–1527, 1982; Musikgeschichte Schlesiens, 1986; Jüdische Musiker aus Breslau, 1996; Schlesisches Musiklexikon, 2001. *Contributions:* Various professional journals. *Honours:* Bundesverdienstkreuz, 1997. *Address:* 9 Amselweg, 63225 Langen, Germany.

**HOFMAN, Srdjan;** Composer; b. 4 Oct. 1944, Glina, Serbia. *Education:* Studied at the Belgrade Academy, 1963–72. *Career:* Assistant 1974, and Professor, 1986–, at the Belgrade Academy of Music; Electronic Music Festivals at Bourges and Helsinki; Further performances at ISCM Festivals in Essen and Stockholm. *Compositions include:* Symphony in Two Movements, 1969; Concerto Dinamico, 1971; Konzertanntne epizode, for violin and orchestra, 1972; The Legal Code of Succession; for clarinet and 2 string sextets, 1974; Cantus de Morte, for speaker, mezzo and orchestra, 1978; Who Am I? fairy tale, for actors, mezzo, female chorus ensemble and tape, 1986; Rebus I and II for electronics, 1988–89; Replika for violin and piano, 1990; Koncertantna muzika for piano, 13 strings and electronics 1993; Duel, for piano and live electronics, 1996. *Honours:* First prize, Belgrade International Composers' Forum, 1994, 1995. *Address:* c/o Union of Bulgarian Composers, Iv Vazov 2, 1000 Sofia, Bulgaria.

**HOFMANN, Manfred;** Singer (Bass); b. 10 Oct. 1940, Kahl am Main, Germany. *Education:* Studied at the Frankfurt Musikhochschule. *Career:* Sang at Saarbrucken, 1970–71, Lucerne, 1972–74, Mainz Opera, 1974–77, St Gallen, 1977–80, and Berne, 1980–84; Member of the Graz Opera from 1985, notably in the 1987 premiere of Der Rattenfänger by Friedrich Cerha; Major roles have included Mozart's Bartolo, Alfonso and Sarastro, Rocco in Fidelio, Donizetti's Raimondo and Dulcamara, Rossini's Bartolo, Alidoro in La Cenerentola and Geronimo in Il Turco in Italia; Waldner in Arabella, the Grand Inquisitor in Don Carlo and Wagner's Landgrave; Many buffo and character roles. *Address:* c/o Graz Opera, Kaiser Josef Platz 10, 8010 Graz, Austria.

**HOFMANN, Peter;** German singer (tenor); b. 12 Aug. 1944, Marienbad. *Education:* Hochschule für Musik, Karlsruhe. *Career:* operatic début as Tamino, Lübeck 1972; mem. Stuttgart Opera 1973–; sang Siegmund, centenary production of The Ring, Bayreuth 1976, Covent Garden London 1976; US début as Siegmund, San Francisco Opera 1977; début Metropolitan New York (Lohengrin) 1980; pop artist 1984–; seven week tour across Germany performing Phantom of the Opera 1999. *Address:* c/o Fritz Höfman, Schloss Schönreuth 8581, Germany.

**HOFMANN, Rosmarie;** Singer (Soprano); b. 1 July 1937, Lucerne, Switzerland. *Career:* Concerts, throughout Europe, overseas; Appeared, many regular international festivals; Many recent world premieres, including works composed for her; Extensive repertoire includes: J. S. Bach: Johannes, Matthäus and Markus Passions, Mass in B minor, Mass No. 2 A major, Weihnachts-Oratorium, Magnificat plus Einlagesätze, 6 solo soprano and some 60 other cantatas; Beethoven: 9th Symphony, Christus am Oelberge, Missa solemnis, Mass C major, lieder; Brahms: Ein Deutsches Requiem, lieder, duets, quartets; Bruckner: Requiem D minor, Te Deum, Grosse Messe No. 3 F minor, Grosse Messe D minor; Carissimi: Historia de Jephther; Charpentier: Te Deum, Messe de Minuit; Durufle: Requiem; Dvořák: Te Deum, Stabat Mater, Mass in D, Zigeunerlieder; Fauré: Requiem; Handel: Israel in Egypt, Dettinger and Utrechter Te Deums, Brockes and St John Passions, Messias, Joshua, Saul, Jephtha, Judas Maccabaeus, Das Alexanderfest, Belshazzar, Psalms 96, 109, 112, 51, German arias, duets, cantatas Cäcilien Ode, Ode for Queen Anne, Salve Regina; J Haydn: L'incontro improvviso (1st soprano), L'anima del Filosofo (Genio, Euridice), Die Schöpfung, Die Jahreszeiten, Die sieben Wörte des Erlösers am Kreuz, Stabat Mater, 6 Grosse Messen, many other Masses; Honegger: Le Roi David, Jeanne d'Arc au bûcher, La Vierge, La danse des morts; Frank Martin: In Terra Pax, Golgotha; Mendelssohn: Paulus, Elias, 2nd Symphony Lobgesang,

Hochzeit des Camacho (main role), lieder, duets; Monteverdi: Vespreae della Maria Vergine, Magnificat, Psalm 111, solo motet, duets; Mozart: Solo motet Exsultate jubilate, oratorio La Betulia liberata, Die Schuldigkeit des ersten Gebots, cantatas, funeral music, Requiem, Regina Coeli KV 108, KV 127, many small works, C minor Mass, Davidde penitente, many masses, lieder; Pergolesi: Stabat Mater, Salve Regina, Psalm 112; Poulenc: Gloria, Stabat Mater; Schubert: Magnificat, Salve Regina, Masses Der Hirt auf dem Felsen, Auf dem Strom; Saint-Saëns: Christmas Oratorio, Requiem Mass, oratorio Le Déluge; Schütz: Die Weihnachts-Historie, Die Auferstehungs-Historie, sacred concertos and duets; Telemann: Matthaus-Passion 1746, Lukas-Passion 1744, Magnificat, Grosse Kantate, many solo cantatas; Vivaldi: Gloria, Magnificat, Psalm Laudate pueri, cantatas, solo motets. *Recordings:* Phyllis und Thirsis, C P E Bach; Canzonette amorose, Rossi; Stabat Mater, Dvořák; Sacred music, J and M Haydn; Bach cantatas; Mozart motets, Scholar Cantorum Basiliensis Orchestra, conductor Peter Sigrist; Quiteria (main role), Die Hochzeit des Camacho, 1993; Many more. *Address:* Mozartstrasse 46, 6006 Lucerne, Switzerland.

**HOFMEYR, Hendrik (Pienaar);** Composer; b. 20 Nov. 1957, Cape Town, South Africa. *Education:* Univ. of Cape Town, 1976–1981; Studied at the Conservatoires of Florence and Bologna, 1982–91. *Career:* Freelance Composer in South Africa and elsewhere, from 1986; Lecturer, Univ. of Stellenbosch, 1992–; Senior Lecturer, Univ. of Cape Town, 1998–2000; Assoc. Prof., Univ. of Cape Town, 2001–. *Compositions include:* The Fall of the House of Usher, opera, 1987 (premiered at Pretoria, 1988); Vala, ballet after William Blake, 1998; Missa Sancti Ignatii de Loyala, for soprano, chorus and orchestra 1989; The Land of Heart's Desire, opera after W.B. Yeats, 1990; Alice, ballet 1991; Cadenza for cello, 1994; Lumukanola, opera 1995; Raptus for violin and orchestra, 1996; Alleenstryd, for medium voice and piano, 1997; String Quartet, 1998; Flute Concerto, 1999; Piano Concerto, 1999; Of Darkness and the Heart for soprano and orchestra, 2000; Concerto for violin and flute, 2001; Die Laaste Aand, opera, 2002; Sinfonia africana, 2003; Die Stil Avontuur for soprano and piano, 2003. *Honours:* Winner, Queen of Belgium Composition Competition, 1997; winner of the Dimitri Mitropoulos Competition, Greece. *Address:* SA College of Music, UCT Private Bag, Rondebosch, 7700 South Africa. *E-mail:* mushhh@protem.uct.ac.za.

**HOGLUND, Paul;** Swedish singer (bass-baritone); b. 1927, Alno. *Education:* studied in Stockholm and Essen. *Career:* debut as Rossini's Bartolo, Royal Opera, Stockholm 1948; sang as Leporello, Stora Theater 1955–60; Sparafucile in Rigoletto and the villains in Les Contes d'Hoffmann; sang Mozart's Masetto and Figaro, Don Pasquale, Leporello, the Sacristan in Tosca, Schigolch in the local premiere of Berg's Lulu at the Royal Opera Stockholm 1960–83; premiere of Berwald's Queen of Golconda 1968; many buffo and character roles in other operas.

**HÖGMAN, Christina;** Singer (Soprano); b. 18 Feb. 1956, Danderyd, Sweden; m. Nils-Erik Sparf, 17 May 1991, 2 s. *Education:* Musicology, History of Art, University of Uppsala, Sweden, 1974–78; Royal Music Academy, Stockholm, 1978–83; State Opera School, Stockholm, 1984–86; Masterclasses: Elisabeth Schwarzkopf, Nicolai Gedda, Geoffrey Parsons, Vera Rozsa. *Career:* Debut: Drottningholm Court Theatre, 1985; Hamburg State Opera, Germany, 1986–88; Guest Contracts, 1988–97; Basel Opera, Innsbruck Opera, Opéra du Rhin, Strasbourg, Monte Carlo Opera, Montpellier Opera, Royal Opera in Stockholm; Major Roles: Donna Elvira, Countess Almaviva, Cherubino, Annio, Erste Dame (Mozart; Soloist with Academy of Ancient Music, Mozart Tour, Japan, 1991); Folkoperan Stockholm 1992, 1996 as Elisabeth de Valois and Donna Elvira; Sang title role in premiere of Marie Antoinette by Daniel Börtz, Stockholm, 1998. *Recordings:* Donna Elvira in Don Giovanni; Vitige in Flavio (Handel); Telemacho in Il Ritorno d'Ulisse in Patria and Valelto in L'Incoronazione di Poppea (Monteverdi); English Lute Songs with Jakob Lindberg; Lieder by Clara Schumann; Les Illuminations by Britten; 2nd String Quartet by Schoenberg; Matthew Passion and John Passion (Bach); Neun Deutsche Arien (Handel). *Current Management:* Kristina Hennel-Lee, Scherzo Stockholm Management. *Address:* c/o Scherzo Stockholm Management, Högbergsgatan 66A, 11854 Stockholm, Sweden.

**HOGWOOD, Christopher Jarvis Haley,** CBE, MA, FRSA; British musician, conductor, musicologist and keyboard player, writer, editor and broadcaster; b. 10 Sept. 1941, Nottingham; s. of Haley Evelyn and Marion Constance Hogwood (née Higgott). *Education:* Univ. of Cambridge, Charles Univ., Prague, Czechoslovakia. *Career:* keyboard continuo, The Acad. of St Martin-in-the-Fields 1965–76, keyboard soloist 1970–76, Consultant Musicologist 1971–76; Founder-mem. Early Music Consort of London 1965–76; Writer and Presenter, The Young Idea (BBC Radio) 1972–82; Founder and Dir Acad. of Ancient Music 1973–; mem. Faculty of Music, Cambridge Univ. 1975–; Artistic Dir. King's Lynn Festival, England 1976–80; Series Ed., Music for London Entertainment 1983–97; Dir Handel and Haydn Soc., Boston, USA 1986–2001, Conductor Laureate 2001–; Hon. Prof. of Music, Keele Univ. 1986–90; Editorial Cttee, CPE Bach Edn (Md) 1986–98; Dir of Music, St Paul Chamber Orchestra, Minn., USA 1987–92, Prin. Guest Conductor 1992–98; Visiting Artist, Harvard Univ. 1988–89, Tutor, Mather House 1991–93; Artistic Adviser, Australian Chamber Orchestra 1989–93; Int. Prof. of Early Music Performance, RAM, London 1992–; Visiting Prof. Dept of Music, King's Coll., London 1992–96; Ed. Bd Early Music (Oxford Univ. Press) 1993–97; Artistic Dir Summer Mozart Festival, Nat. Symphony Orchestra, USA 1993–2001; Assoc. Dir Beethoven Acad., Antwerp 1998–2002; Chair. Advisory Bd CPE Bach Complete Works 1999–; Prin. Guest Conductor, Kammerorchester Basel, Switzerland 2000–; Kayden Visiting Artist, Learning from Performers Programme, Harvard Univ. 2001; Prin. Guest Conductor, Orquesta Ciudad de Granada 2001–04, Ed. Bd, Early Music Performers, Peacock Press 2002; Bd of Eds., Bohuslav Martinu Foundation 2003–; Advisory Panel, Eighteenth-Century Music, Cambridge Univ. Press 2003; Orchestra Sinfonica di Milano Giuseppi Verdi 2003–; Pres., Early Music Wales 1996–, Nat. Early Music Asscn (NEMA) 2000, The Handel Inst. 2000–. *Publications:* Music at Court 1977, The Trio Sonata 1979, Haydn's Visits to England 1980, Music in Eighteenth Century England (co-author) 1983, Handel 1984, Holmes' Life of Mozart (ed.) 1991, The Keyboard in Baroque Europe (ed.) 2003; many edns of musical scores; contribs to The New Grove Dictionary of Music and Musicians 1980 and 2001; numerous recordings. *Honours:* Hon. Fellow Jesus Coll., Cambridge 1989, Pembroke Coll., Cambridge 1992; Hon. Prof. of Music, Univ. of Cambridge 2002–; Hon. mem. Royal Acad. of Music 1995; Freeman Worshipful Co. of Musicians 1989; Hon. DMus (Keele) 1991; Winner, Yorkshire Post Music Book Award 1984, Walter Willson Cobbett Medal (Worshipful Co. of Musicians) 1986, UCLA Award for Artistic Excellence 1996, Scotland on Sunday Music Prize, Edin. Int. Festival 1996, Distinguished Musician Award (Inc. Soc. of Musicians) 1997, Martinu Medal (Bohuslav Martinu Foundation) Prague 1999; Handel & Haydn Soc. Fellowship named 'The Christopher Hogwood Historically Informed Performance Fellowship' 2001, Regione Liguria per il suo contributo all'arte e alla filogia della musica 2003. *Address:* 10 Brookside, Cambridge, CB2 1JE, England. *Telephone:* (1223) 363975. *Fax:* (1223) 327377. *E-mail:* office@hogwood.org (office). *Website:* www.hogwood.org (office).

**HÖH, Volker;** German musician (guitar) and guitar teacher; b. 24 April 1959, Altenkirchen, Pfalz; m. Jutta Maria Höh 1980; two d. *Education:* Univ. Rheinland-Pfalz, Koblenz, Staatliche Hochschule für Musik, Westfalen-Lippe, Münster. *Career:* recitalist and soloist with orchestras; radio and TV engagements; performed in most major cities and festivals; guitar teacher, Univ. of Koblenz, Landesmusikgymnasium Rheinland-Pfalz; masterclasses and workshops; mem. EGTA, BDZ. *Recordings:* solo: Cantos de Cuba, Danzas Fantásticas, Triops-Botschaft, Matthias Drude: Kammermusik, Operngala, Zypern-Variationen; duets: Calliope-Calls (with Christina Ascher), Annette Schlünz: Kammermusik, 7. und 8. Dresdner Tage der zeitgenössischen Musik; played on The Straits of Magellan (Turfan Ensemble), Fünf Stücke op. 10 (RSO Frankfurt), Zwei Suiten für Jazzorchester (RSO Frankfurt), Von Heute Auf Morgen (RSO Frankfurt), Die Jakobsleiter (RSO Frankfurt), Cristoforo Colombo (RSO Frankfurt). *Publications:* editor of pedagogic and chamber music guitar literature, contrib. articles on guitar to music periodicals. *Honours:* stipends and scholarships from Kultusministerium Rheinland-Pfalz, Darmstädter Ferienkurse, Richard Wagner Verband, Deutscher Musikrat, Keutscher Orchesterwettbewerb (with cantomano guitar ensemble) 2004. *Address:* Am Nörrenpfad 30 A, 56337 Eitelborn, Germany (office). *Telephone:* (2620) 2744 (office). *Fax:* (2620) 2459 (office). *E-mail:* volkerhoeh@git_art.de (office). *Website:* www.volker-hoeh.de.

**HOHEISEL, Tobias;** Stage Designer; b. 1956, Frankfurt, Germany. *Education:* Studied in Berlin. *Career:* Collaborations with director Nikolaus Lehnoff include Janáček Trilogy (Katya, Jenůfa and Makropulos Case) at Glyndebourne and Pfitzner's Palestrina at Covent Garden (season 1996–97, also seen at the Metropolitan, New York); Debut as set and costume designer with Salome at Rio de Janeiro; Britten's Death in Venice for the Glyndebourne Tour, La Bohème, and the Tales of Hoffmann for English National Opera (1997–98); Further engagements at Berlin (Deutsche and Staats-Oper), Vienna, La Scala Milan, San Francisco, Chicago, Amsterdam, Antwerp, Zürich and Cologne; Lohengrin at Théâtre de la Monnaie Brussels, for Anja Silja's debut as producer; Season 1997 with Der Freischütz in Berlin, Ariadne at Brussels, Macbeth in Hamburg and Don Carlos at the Opéra Bastille, Paris; Designs for Henze's Boulevard Solitude at Covent Garden, 2001. *Address:* c/o English National Opera, St Martin's Lane, London WC2N 4ES, England.

**HÖHN, Carola;** Singer (Soprano); b. 3 March 1961, Erfurt, Germany. *Education:* Studied at the Franz Liszt Musikhochschule, Weimar. *Career:* Sang at Eisenach, 1984–87, Altenburg, 1987–88; Berlin Staatsoper from 1988, notably as Marie Antionette in the 1989 premiere of Graf Mirabeau by Siegfried Matthus; Other roles have included Antonia, Mozart's Fiordiligi and Pamina, Gretel, Marie in Zar and Zimmermann and Sophie in Der Rosenkavalier; Agathe, Eva, the Countess in Capriccio and Albertine in Die Brautwahl by Busoni; Concert repertoire includes Carmina Burana by Orff; Guest engagements elsewhere in Germany and broadcasting commitments; Pamina in Die Zauberflöte at Bordeaux, 1992; Season 2000–01 in Berlin as Eva and Donna Elvira. *Address:* Deutsche Staatsoper Berlin, Unter den Linden 7, 1086 Berlin, Germany.

**HOIBY, Lee;** Composer and Pianist; b. 17 Feb. 1926, Madison, Wisconsin, USA. *Education:* BA, University of Wisconsin, 1947; MA, Mills College, 1952; Diploma, Curtis Institute, 1952; Private study with Egon Petri and Gunnar Johansen. *Career:* Debut: As Pianist at Alice Tully Hall, New York City, 1978; Commissions from Ford Foundation, Curtis Institute, St Paul Opera, Des Moines Metro Opera, USIA, Dorian Wind Quintet, G Schirmer, Library of Congress; mem, Yale Univ. American Society of Composers, Authors and Publishers. *Compositions:* Operas: The Scarf, 1954, A Month in the Country, 1964, Summer and Smoke, 1971, Something New for the Zoo, 1980, The Tempest, 1986, This is the Rill Speaking, 1993; Romeo and Juliet, 2003; What is this Light?, melodrama, 1995; Sonata for Violin and Piano; Serenade for Violin and Orchestra; The Italian Lesson, musical monologue; Galilo Galilei,

oratorio; For You O Democracy; A Hymn of the Nativity, Cantatas; The Tides of Sleep, symphonic song; Various solo piano works, songs and choral pieces; St Mary Magdalene, 1995. *Recordings:* After Eden, ballet; Piano Concerto; Choral Music of Lee Hoiby. *Honours:* Fulbright Fellow, 1952; Arts and Letters Award, 1957; Guggenheim Fellow, 1958; Honorary Member, American Guild of Organists; Honorary DFA, Simpson College, 1983. *Address:* 9807 CH28, Long Eddy, NY 12760, USA (home). *Telephone:* (845) 887-4321 (home). *Fax:* (845) 887-6067 (home). *E-mail:* aquarius@catskill.net (home). *Website:* leehoiby.com (home).

**HOJSGAARD, Erik;** Danish composer; b. 3 Oct. 1954, Århus. *Education:* Royal Academy of Music, Århus with Per Norgård, Cantiere Internazionale d'Arte, Royal Academy of Music, Copenhagen. *Career:* Manager, Århus Young Composers' Society, 1974–76; Member of Organising Committee, Young Nordic Music Festival, 1974–81; Music Committee, Århus Regional Council, 1977–78; Music Copyist, 1977–82; Professor (ear training), Royal Academy of Music, Copenhagen, 1982–; Member of Governing Body, Society for the Publication of Danish Music, 1982–92; His works performed at various music festivals in the Nordic countries, also at International Society for Contemporary Music festivals (1980, 1983). *Compositions:* Orchestral: Untitled symphony, 1974; Cello Concerto, 1975; Refleksion, 1977; Scherzo e notturno, 1982; Piano Concerto, 1984–85; Four Sketches, 1990; Nocturne, 1994; Fragment, 1995; Symphony No. 1, 2000; Symphony No. 2, 2003; Chamber music: Dialogues, 1972; Solprismer, 1974; The Sunflower, 1978; Intrada, 1981; Fantasy Pieces, 1982–84; Watercolours, 1983; Intermezzi, 1983; Carillon, 1986; Two Mobiles, 1990; Paysage blême, 1991; Paysage triste, 1994; Equali, 1996; Four Small Pieces, 1996; Paysage, 1997, Images oubliées I-III 2004; Solo instruments: Cendrée, 1976; Sonata in C major, 1980; C'est la mer mêlée au soleil, 1981; Corellage, 1992; Epreuve, 1993; Violin Sonata, 1997; Etude, 1999; Three small pieces, 2000; Solo voice with instruments: Landet som icke är, 1974; Tuan's Songs, 1976; Variations: 6 Songs of Autumn, 1976; Vise, ballad, 1977; Täglich kommt die gelbe Sonne, 1977; Joyous, 1979; Fragments, 1979; The Lost Forest, 1980; Summer Songs, 1981; The Rose, 1981; Two Songs, 1985; Le città continue, 1986; Two songs for mixed choir, 1985–86; Don Juan kommt aus dem Krieg, opera, 1991. *Honours:* Carl Nielsen Prize 1993. *Address:* Esbern Snaresvej 16, 4180 Soro, Denmark. *E-mail:* erik@hojs.dk. *Website:* www.hojs.dk.

**HOLDEN, Amanda Juliet,** MA (Oxon.), LRAM, ARCM, LGSM; British musician, translator, writer and librettist; b. 1948, London; d. of Sir Brian Warren and Dame Josephine Barnes; m. (divorced); three s. *Education:* Univ. of Oxford, Guildhall School, American University, Washington, DC. *Career:* freelance accompanist and Teacher at Guildhall School, 1973–86; Freelance Translator and Writer; Opera translations include Haydn's Armida, Handel's Ariodante and Alcina, Rameau's Les Boréades; Verdi's Rigoletto, Un Ballo in Maschera, Aida and Falstaff; Wagner's Lohengrin, Mozart's La finta giardiniera, Il re pastore, Idomeneo, Die Entführung, Le nozze di Figaro, Don Giovanni and La clemenza di Tito; Rossini's La Cenerentola, The Barber of Seville; Puccini's La Bohème, Tosca, Madama Butterfly and Il Trittico; Donizetti's L'Elisir d'amore and Mary Stuart; Gounod's Faust; Bizet's The Pearl Fishers and Carmen; Massenet's Werther; Rachmaninov's Francesca da Rimini; General Editor, The Viking Opera Guide, 1993, The Penguin Opera Guide, 1995, The New Penguin Opera Guide, 2001, The Penguin Concise Guide to Opera 2005; Librettos for The Silver Tassie by Mark Anthony Turnage, English National Opera, 2000, Family Matters, Tête-à-Tête 2005; piano tuner for Nigel Osborne 2005. *Recordings:* Translations of: The Barber of Seville; Don Giovanni; A Masked Ball; Falstaff (for Chandos Opera in English Series). *Publication:* contrib. to The Mozart Compendium 1990. *Honours:* Olivier Award for Outstanding Achievement in Opera 2001. *Address:* 107 Sotheby Road, London N5, England.

**HOLDORF, Udo;** Singer (Tenor); b. 10 July 1946, Bonn, Germany. *Education:* Studied in Cologne with Josef Metternich, and in Düsseldorf. *Career:* Debut: Würzburg, 1971, as Otello; Deutsche Oper am Rhein, Düsseldorf, from 1973 as Edgardo in Lucia di Lammermoor, Puccini's Calaf and Luigi (Il Tabarro), Strauss's Herod and Matteo, the Captain in Wozzeck and Janáček's Boris, Albert Gregor and Mr Brouček; Guest appearances in Frankfurt, Stockholm, Paris and Lisbon; Sang in the 1985 Duisburg premiere of Goehr's Behold the Sun and at Bayreuth, 1981–88, in Die Meistersinger; US engagements in New York, Atlanta and Los Angeles; Season 1995–96 in Athens as Berg's Captain and at Amsterdam in The Nose by Shostakovich; Sang Jack in Weill's Mahagonny at Salzburg, 1998; Season 2000–01 as Vitek in The Makropulos Case at Dusseldorf and Aegithus in Elektra at Essen; Many concert engagements. *Recordings include:* Der Silbersee by Weill. *Address:* c/o Netherlands Opera, Waterlooplein 22, 1011 PG Amsterdam, Netherlands.

**HOLECEK, Heinz;** Singer (Baritone); b. 13 April 1938, Vienna, Austria. *Education:* Studied in Vienna with Elisabeth Höngen. *Career:* Debut: Vienna Volksoper, 1960 as Papageno; Sang at the Vienna Staatsoper from 1962, debut there as Papageno; Other roles have included Mozart's Leporello and Guglielmo, Rossini's Figaro; Gianni Schicchi; Frosch in Die Fledermaus at Turin, 1993; Salzburg Festival, 1981 in the premiere of Baal by Cerha; Concert appearances in music by Haydn, Mozart and Beethoven; Cabaret engagements in Moscow and Montreal and throughout Europe; Television appearances in Austria. *Recordings:* Der Rosenkavalier; Salome; Die Fledermaus; Land des Lächelns. *Address:* c/o Staatsoper, Opernring 2, 1070 Vienna, Austria.

**HOLECEK, Sebastian;** Singer (Baritone); b. 1965, Vienna, Austria. *Education:* Studied in Vienna. *Career:* Vienna Volksoper, 1987–90, notably in Die Weise von Liebe und Tod by Matthus; Theater am Gärtnerplatz, Munich, 1990–92; Monte Carlo, 1991, as Papageno; The Speaker in Die Zauberflöte at Ludwigsburg, 1993; Further appearances in Paris, Santiago and Turin; Vienna Volks and Staatsoper, from 1992; Other roles include Mozart's Masetto and Figaro; Schaunard in La Bohème; Sang Papageno at St Margareth, 1999. *Recordings:* Irrelohe by Schreker. *Address:* c/o Staatsoper, Opernring 2, 1010 Vienna, Austria.

**HOLEK, Vlastimil;** Violinist; b. 1950, Czechoslovakia. *Education:* Studied at the Prague Conservatory. *Career:* Founder member of the Prazak String Quartet, 1972; Tour of Finland, 1973, followed by appearances at competitions in Prague and Evian; Concerts in Salzburg, Munich, Paris, Rome, Berlin, Cologne and Amsterdam; Tour of the United Kingdom, 1985, including Wigmore Hall debut; Tours of Japan, the USA, Australia and New Zealand; Tour of the United Kingdom, 1988, and concert at the Huddersfield Contemporary Music Festival, 1989; Recitals for the BBC, Radio France, Dutch Radio, the WDR in Cologne and Radio Prague; Appearances with the Smetana and LaSalle Quartets in Mendelssohn's Octet. *Honours:* 1st Prize, Chamber Music Competition of the Prague Conservatory, 1974; Grand Prix, International String Quartet Competition, Evian Music Festival, 1978; 1st Prize, National Competition of String Quartets in Czechoslovakia, 1978; Winner, String Quartet Competition of the Prague Spring Festival, 1978. *Current Management:* Ingpen & Williams Ltd, 7 St George's Court, 131 Putney Bridge Road, London, SW15 2PA, England.

**HOLENDER, Ioan;** Romanian opera house director; *Director, Vienna State Opera;* b. 18 July 1935, Timisoara; m.; two s. one d. *Education:* Timisoara Polytechnic Inst., Vienna Conservatory. *Career:* expelled from Romanian higher educ. system on political grounds 1956; worked as tennis trainer and stage dir's asst 1956–59; moved to Vienna and began singing studies 1960; opera singer, Vienna and Klagenfurt 1962–66; joined Starka Theater Agency 1966, later took control of agency and renamed it Holender Opera Agency; Gen. Sec. Vienna State Opera and Vienna Volksoper 1988–92, Dir Vienna Volksoper 1992–96, Dir Vienna State Opera 1992–; guest lecturer Vienna Univ. *Publications:* Ioan Holender: Der Lebensweg des Wiener Staatsoperndirektors (autobiog.) 2001. *Honours:* hon. mem. Romanian Acad., Hon. Citizen of Timisoara; Vienna Municipality Golden Medal of Merit, Golden Medal for Services to Vienna Community, Grand Golden Hon. Medal of Austrian Repub., Austrian Hon. Cross for Science and Art, First Class, Officier, Ordre des Artes et des Lettres; Dr hc (Gheorge Dima Music Acad.); Vienna Philharmonic Franz Schalk Gold Medal. *Address:* Wiener Staatsoper, Opernring 2, Vienna 1010, Austria (office). *Telephone:* (1) 51444-2250 (office). *Website:* www.staatsoper.at (office).

**HOLICKOVA, Elena;** Singer (Soprano); b. 1950, Czechoslovakia. *Education:* Conservatory of Music, Bratislava; Academy of Music and Drama, Bratislava. *Career:* Slovak National Theatre; Musetta in La Bohème, Lisa in The Queen of Spades, Rusalka in Rusalka, Jenůfa, Julietta, Adriana in Adriana Lecouvreur, Marina in Dimitriy; Verdi's Gilda; Feodor in Mussorgsky's Boris Godunov; Small Shepherd in Suchon's The Whirlpool; Nuri in The Lowlands; Queen in Dance over the Crying; Swallow in The Happy Prince; A Servant in Elektra; Marenka in The Bartered Bride; Orphan in The Siege of Bystrica; Amelia Grimaldi in Simon Boccanegra, 1984–85. *Recordings:* Songs by Mikulus Schneider-Trnavsky; Cycles by Alexander Moyzes; Glimpse into the Unknown; Mutations by Ilja Zeljenka, 1980; Ode to Joy, 1983; Submerged Music. *Honours:* Slovak Music Fund Prize, 1984. *Address:* c/o Slovak National Theatre, Gorkého 2, 815 06 Bratislava, Slovakia.

**HÖLL, Hartmut;** German pianist; b. 24 Nov. 1952, Heilbronn. *Education:* Studied in Milan, Stuttgart and Munich. *Career:* many lieder recitals from 1972 in Europe, Japan and the Americas with Mitsuko Shirai and other leading singers; accompanist for Dietrich Fischer-Dieskau 1982–90; chamber music engagements with violist Tabea Zimmermann 1985–; toured with Renée Fleming in Europe, Asia, USA 2001–; worked with Thomas Hampson, Jochen Kowalski, Christoph Prégardien, Hermann Prey, David Wilson Johnson, Urszula Kryger, Jadwiga Rappé, Peter Schreier, Roman Trekel; fmr Prof. Frankfurt, Cologne, currently Prof. Karlsruhe; masterclasses in Finland, Weimar Int. Music Seminar, Schleswig-Holstein Festival, Salzburg Mozarteum, in Jerusalem and USA; Visiting Prof. Helsinki 1998–99, Salzburg Mozarteum 1994–2003, Zurich 2004–Dir Int. Hugo Wolf Acad. fo rChant, Poetry and Lieder Art, Stuttgart; mem. jury Robert Schumann Contest, Zwickau, Naumburg Competition, New York and Int. ARD Music Contest, Munich. *Recordings include:* over 50 albums since 1985 including lieder albums with Mitsuko Shirai and Beethoven songs with Fischer-Dieskau; Sonatas and others by Brahms and Shostakovich with Tabea Zimmermann. *Honours:* Hon. mem. Robert Schumann Soc., St Petersburg Philharmonic Soc.; Joint winner, Hugo Wolf Competition, Vienna, Robert Schumann Competition, Zwickau 1974, 1990, prizes at Athens and 's-Hertogenbosch, Netherlands 1976, Louvre Carte Blanche, Paris (with Mitsuko Shirai) 1993, ABC Int. Music Award (with Mitsuko Shirai) 1997. *Address:* c/o Karlsruhe Staatlich, Hochschule fur Musik, Postfach 6040, 76040 Karlsruhe, Germany. *E-mail:* kivisaari@aol.com (office).

**HOLL, Robert;** Singer (Bass-baritone); b. 10 March 1947, Rotterdam, Netherlands. *Education:* Studied with Jan Veth and David Hollestelle. *Career:* Sang with the Bayerische Staatsoper Munich from 1973; Has concentrated on concert career from 1975; Appearances at the Vienna, Holland and Salzburg Festivals, the Schubertiade at Hohenems; Salzburg Mozartwochen, 1981–83, as the Priest in Thamos, König in Ägypten, as the Voice of Neptune in Idomeneo and Cassandro in La Finta Giardiniera; Many engagements as a singer of Lieder, in music by Schubert, Brahms and Wolf; Concert appearances with Bernstein, Giulini, Harnoncourt, Jochum, Karajan, Sawallisch, Stein and De Waart; Promenade Concerts, London, 1987, in the Choral Symphony; Judge, Walter Gruener International Lieder Competition, London, 1989; Sang in Schubert's Fierrabras at the Theater an der Wien, Vienna, 1988; Season 1992 at Zürich, as Assur in Semiramide and La Roche in Capriccio; Sang Hans Sachs at the Bayreuth Festival 1996–2002; Vienna Festival, 1997, Schubert's Des Teufels Lustschloss; Season 2000–01 as Hans Sachs at Bayreuth, Mozart's Commendatore and Wagner's Daland at the Berlin Staatsoper; Future engagements include the part of Gurnemanz (Parsifal) at the Weiner Staatsoper and Bayreuth Festival, 2004. *Recordings include:* Mozart's Requiem; Mozart and Salieri by Rimsky-Korsakov; Lieder by Pfitzner; Requiems by Bellini and Donizetti; Mozart's Zaide and La Finta Semplice; St Matthew Passion by Bach; Die Schöpfung; Utrecht Te Deum by Handel; Mozart's Mass in C Minor; Bach Mass in B Minor; Wagner's Die Meistersinger von Nuremberg (Sachs); Wagner's Der Fliegende Holländer (Daland). *Honours:* Winner, Munich International Competition, 1972. *Current Management:* Ingpen & Williams Ltd, 7 St George's Court, 131 Putney Bridge Road, London, SW15 2PA, England.

**HOLLAND, Ashley;** Singer (Baritone); b. 1969, England. *Career:* Many concert and opera engagements throughout the United Kingdom; Opera repertory includes Handel's Giulio Cesare and Walton's The Bear; Also sings Mahler's Rückert Lieder; Contestant at the 1995 Cardiff Singer of the World Competition; Season 1998 in Mozart's Grabmusik for the Classical Opera Company and Cecil in Mary Stuart for ENO. *Address:* c/o IMG Artists, Lovell House, 616 Chiswick High Road, London, W4 5RX, England.

**HOLLAND, Mark;** singer (baritone); b. 19 Sept. 1960, Salford, England. *Education:* Royal Northern College of Music with John Cameron, and with Roberto Benaglio in Italy. *Career:* joined Welsh National Opera in 1984 and has appeared as Rossini's Figaro, Mozart's Count, Eugene Onegin, Schaunard in La Bohème, Don Carlo in Ernani and Enrico in Lucia di Lammermoor; Sonora in La Fanciulla del West, 1991; Festival engagements include Piccinni's La Buona Figliola at Buxton; Season 1989–90 as Falke in Fledermaus for Opera Northern Ireland and Masetto for Dublin Grand Opera; Season 1990–91 as Ford in Falstaff at the Théâtre des Champs Elysées, tour to Japan with La Bohème and Carmina Burana with the Royal Philharmonic; Sang Puccini's Marcello and Mozart's Allazim (Zaide) with the City of Birmingham Touring Opera, 1991–92; Bregenz Festival, 1992, as Morales in Carmen; Minister in Fidelio at Bregenz, 1995; Sang Andrei in Three Sisters by Peter Eötvös at Hamburg, 2000. *Current Management:* Robert Gilder & Co., Enterprise House, 59–65 Upper Ground, London, SE1 9PQ, England. *Telephone:* (20) 7928-9008. *Fax:* (20) 7928-9755. *E-mail:* rgilder@robert-gilder.com.

**HOLLANDER, Julia;** Stage Director; b. 1965, Bristol, England. *Education:* St Catherine's College, Cambridge, and also in Paris. *Career:* Opera productions have included Orfeo ed Euridice for The Cambridge Arts Theatre, Les Mamelles de Tiresias at The Edinburgh Festival, Giovanna d'Arco at the Bloomsbury Theatre in London, Samson and Delilah for Northern Opera in Newcastle, The Rake's Progress for Aldeburgh, Acis and Galatea for Gregynog and Manchester Festivals, Turn of The Screw at the Britten Theatre in London, La Bohème for Mid Wales Opera, La Wally at the Bloomsbury Theatre and Love of Three Oranges in London; Staff Producer at ENO, 1988–91, working on numerous productions and reviving Xerxes, Lear and Macbeth in London and abroad; Solo production debut for ENO with Fennimore and Gerda, 1990, returning for the premiere of John Buller's Bakxai, 1992 and Eugene Onegin in 1994; Directed Margareta Hallin's Miss Julie for Operate at Hammersmith, 1996. *Current Management:* Ingpen & Williams Ltd, 7 St George's Court, 131 Putney Bridge Road, London, SW15 2PA, England.

**HOLLANDER, Lorin D.;** Pianist; b. 19 July 1944, New York, NY, USA. *Education:* Studied with Eduard Steuermann at the Juilliard School and with Leon Fleisher and Max Rudolf. *Career:* Debut: Carnegie Hall, 1955; Has performed with leading orchestras in the USA including the New York Philharmonic, Philadelphia Orchestra, Washington National and Chicago Symphony Orchestra; European engagements with the Warsaw Philharmonic, Orchestre de la Suisse Romande, London Philharmonic and Concertgebouw; Has performed in prisons, hospitals and other institutions; Series of programmes on television; Adviser to the Office of the Gifted and Talented for the US Government; Lecturer on psychological aspects of musical performance.

**HÖLLE, Matthias;** Singer (Bass); b. 8 July 1951, Rottweil am Nekkar, Germany. *Education:* Studied in Stuttgart with Georg Jelden and in Cologne with Josef Metternich. *Career:* Sang first in concerts and oratorios; Sang in opera at Cologne from 1976; Ludwigsburg Festival, 1978, as the Commendatore in Don Giovanni; Has appeared at the Bayreuth Festival from 1981 as the Nightwatchman, Titurel, Fasolt and Hunding (1988 in Der Ring des Nibelungen, conducted by Daniel Barenboim); King Marke in Tristan und Isolde at Bologna (1983), Florence (1989) and Cologne (1990); Sang in the premiere of Stockhausen's Donnerstag (1981) and created Lucifer in Stockhausen's Samstag aus Licht at the Palazzo dello Sport with the company of La Scala Milan, 1984; Guest appearances in Hanover, Geneva, Tel-Aviv and New York (Fidelio at the Metropolitan, 1986); Season 1989 as Don Fernando in Fidelio at Brussels, Daland in Stuttgart and the Commendatore at Parma; Sang Hunding at Bonn and the Bayreuth Festival, 1992; Fafner in The Ring at Covent Garden, 1996; Hermit in Der Freischütz at Rome, 1998; Season 2000–01 as Pogner and Gurnemanz at Bayreuth, Speaker in Die Zauberflöte at Barcelona and Fasolt at Toulouse; Television appearances in Die Schöpfung and Beethoven's Christus am Olberge. *Recordings include:* Don Giovanni; Haydn's Seven Last Words on the Cross; Handel's Saul; Lieder by Schumann; Fourth Shepherd in Daphne, conducted by Haitink; Samstag aus Licht by Stockhausen; Gurnemanz in Parsifal, conducted by Barenboim. *Address:* Vischerweg 11, 7290 Freudenstadt, Germany.

**HÖLLER, York Georg;** Composer; b. 11 Jan. 1944, Leverkusen, Germany. *Education:* Studied at the Cologne Musikhochschule, 1963–70, with B A Zimmermann and Herbert Eimert; Ferienkurse Darmstadt, 1965, with Boulez; Worked at the Electronic Music Studios, Cologne, with Stockhausen. *Career:* Freelance composer from 1965; First orchestral work, Topic, performed at Darmstadt, 1970; Invited by Boulez to work at the studios of IRCAM, 1978; Piano Concerto given French premiere by Daniel Barenboim, Paris, 1988; Der Meister und Margarita last new production at the Paris Opéra, Salle Garnier, before the opening of the Opéra de la Bastille; Professor for analysis and music theory at the College Musikhochschule, 1975–89; Director of the Electronic Studio at WDR Cologne, 1990–. *Compositions:* 5 Pieces, piano, 1964; Diaphonie, 2 pianos, 1965; Topic, orchestra, 1967; Sonate Informelle, 1968; Cello Sonata, 1969; Epitaph, violin, piano, 1969; Piano Concerto, 1970, No. 2, 1983–84; Chroma, orchestra, 1972–74; Horizont, electronics, 1972; Tangent, electronics, 1973; Klanggitter, electronics, 1976; Antiphon for string quartet, 1977; Arcus, orchestra, 1978; Moments Musicaux, flute, piano, 1979; Umbra, orchestra, 1979–80; Mythos, orchestra, 1979–80; Résonance, orchestra, tape, 1981–82; Schwarze Halbinselu, orchestra, tape, 1982; Traumspiel, soprano, orchestra, tape, 1983; Magische Klanggestalt, orchestra, 1984; Improvisation sur le nom de Pierre Boulez, 1985; Der Meister und Margarita, opera, 1985–89; Piano Sonata No. 2, Hommage à Franz Liszt, 1987; Fanal, trumpet, orchestra, 1990; Pensée, piano, orchestra, electronics, 1991; Aùna, large orchestra, 1992; Caligùla, opera after A Camus, 1992; String quartet No. 2, 1997; Aufbruch for orchestra, 1999, ervige Tag for chorus, orchestra and electronics 2001, Ex Tempore for 9 players 2001, Trias for saxophone, percussion and piano 2001, Klangzeichen for piano and wind quartet 2003. *Recordings:* Schwarze Halbinselu; Résonance; Arcùs. *Publications:* Composition of the Gestalt on the making of an organism, 1984; B A Zimmermann Moine et Dionysos, 1985; Auf der süche nach den Klang von Morgan, 1990. *Honours:* Chevalier, Ordre des Arts et des Lettres, Paris; Rolf-Liebermann Preis für Opera Komponisten. *Current Management:* c/o Boosey & Hawkes Ltd, 1st floor, Aldwych House, 71–91 Aldwych, London, WC2B 4HN, England. *Website:* www.boosey.com/holler.

**HOLLEY, William;** Singer (tenor); b. 4 Dec. 1930, Bristol, Florida, USA. *Education:* Studied in Florida. *Career:* Debut: As Gounod's Faust, Salzburg Landestheater, 1961; Sang as Gelsenkirchen Opera, 1962–65; Deutsche Oper Berlin, 1971–79; Bavarian State Opera, 1971–76; Stuttgart, 1973–82; Deutsche Oper am Rhein, Düsseldorf, 1966–84; Guest appearances in San Francisco, Don Ottavio, 1968; Vienna, Copenhagen, Barcelona and Houston; Salzburg Festival, 1969–71 in Cavalieri's La Rappresentazione di Anima e di Corpo; Other roles have included Mozart's Tamino, Ferrando and Belmonte, Verdi's Duke of Mantua and Alfredo, Hoffman, Froh in Das Rheingold, Puccini's Cavaradossi and Calaf, Andrea Chénier, Don José, Lensky and Laca in Jenůfa; Des Grieux in Manon Lescaut, Don Carlos and Verdi's Riccardo. *Address:* c/o Deutsche Oper am Rhein, Heinrich Heine Alle 16a, 40213 Düsseldorf, Germany.

**HOLLIDAY, Melanie;** Singer (Soprano); b. 12 Aug. 1951, Houston, Texas, USA. *Education:* Studied at Indiana University School and at the Graz Academy of Music. *Career:* Sang at Hamburg and Klagenfurt from 1973; Basle Opera as Zerbinetta in Ariadne auf Naxos; Vienna Volksoper from 1976, as Olympia in Les Contes d'Hoffmann, Frau Fluth, Constanze, Philine in Mignon, Adele (Die Fledermaus), Valencienne (Die Lustige Witwe) and in Die Schöne Galatea by Suppé; Tours of Japan with the Volksoper, 1979, 1982, 1985; Guest appearances in Germany, Italy, Netherlands, Spain and Switzerland; Vienna Staatsoper; Houston Opera, 1983; Operetta tour of West Germany with René Kollo, 1984; Theater am Gärtnerplatz, Munich, 1986, as Musetta in La Bohème; Turin and Berlin 1994, 1996, Adele and Valencienne. *Recordings include:* Die Fledermaus; Film of L'Elisir d'amore. *Address:* c/o Volksoper, Währingerstrasse 78, 1090 Vienna, Austria.

**HOLLIER, Donald Russell;** Composer and Conductor; b. 7 May 1934, Sydney, Australia. *Education:* Studied at the NSW State Conservatorium, the RAM in London and the University of London (D Mus, 1974). *Career:* Head of Academic Studies at the Canberra School of Music, 1967–84; Musical Director of the Canberra Choral Society and Canberra Opera; Australian premieres of works by Vaughan Williams, Walton, Britten and Poulenc. *Compositions include:* Operas, The Heiress (1975, staged Melbourne 1988); The Beggar's Bloody Opera, 1991; For the Term of his Natural Life, 1993; Myra Breckinridge; The Revelation of St John the Divine, oratorio, 1974; 7 Psalms and Lamentations of David, 1979; 7 New Psalms, 1986; 9 Concertos, 1966–89; All Between the Earth and Sphere, for orchestra, 1991; Variations on a theme of Debussy for trumpet and piano, 1998; Many songs and piano pieces.

*Honours:* Churchill Fellowship, 1973. *Address:* c/o Australian Music Centre Ltd, 1st Floor, Argyle Stores, 18 Argyle Street, The Rocks, Sydney, Australia.

**HOLLIGER, Heinz;** Swiss oboist and composer; b. 21 May 1939, Langenthal; m. Ursula Holliger. *Education:* in Berne, Paris and Basel under Emile Cassagnaud (oboe) and Pierre Boulez (composition). *Career:* Prof. of Oboe, Freiberg Music Acad. 1965–; has appeared at all the major European music festivals and in Japan, USA, Australia, Israel, etc.; conducted Chamber Orchestra of Europe, London 1992, London Sinfonietta 1997; Composer-in-Residence, Lucerne Festival 1998; recorded over 80 works, mainly for Philips and Deutsche Grammophon. *Compositions include:* Der magische Tänzer, Trio, Siebengesang, Wind Quintet, Dona nobis pacem, Pneuma, Psalm, Cardiophonie, Kreis, String Quartet, Atembogen, Die Jahreszeiten, Come and Go, Not I. *Honours:* recipient of several int. prizes. *Address:* c/o Ingpen & Williams, 26 Wadham Road, London, SW15 2LR, England (office); Konzertgesellschaft, Hochstrasse 51/Postfach, 4002 Basel, Switzerland.

**HOLLIGER, Ursula;** Harpist; b. 8 June 1937, Basle, Switzerland; m. Heinz Holliger. *Education:* Studied in Basle and at the Brussels Conservatoire. *Career:* World-wide appearances with leading orchestras, including the Philharmonics of Berlin, Vienna and Los Angeles, the Orchestre de Paris, English Chamber Orchestra, Orchestra of South German Radio and the Schweizerisches Festspielorchester Luzern; Conductors have included Pierre Boulez, Michael Gielen, Simon Rattle, André Previn and Neville Marriner; Composers who have written for her and her husband include Edison Denisov, Henze (Doppio Concerto, 1966), André Jolivet, Ernst Krenek, György Ligeti (Double Concerto, 1972), Witold Lutoslawski (Double Concerto, 1977); Several works written for her by her husband; Professor at the Basle Music Academy. *Recordings include:* Spohr Concertos for Harp and Concertos for Violin and Harp. *Current Management:* Ingpen & Williams Ltd, 7 St George's Court, 131 Putney Bridge Road, London, SW15 2PA, England.

**HOLLOP, Markus;** Singer (Bass); b. 1968, Berlin, Germany. *Education:* Studied at the Munich Musikhochschule. *Career:* Major roles with the opera studio of the Bayerische Staatsoper from 1991; Sarastro in Die Zauberflöte and Rossini's Basilio in Gorlitz; Ulm Opera as the King in The Love for Three Oranges, Offenbach's Crespel at Wiesbaden and engagements with the Bayerische Staatsoper, from 1993; Further appearances in Schumann's Genovena (Zürich), Hamlet and Wozzeck (Geneva) and Salome (Paris Châtelet, under Semyon Bychkov, 1997); Concerts include Weill's Ozeanflug in Munich and Solo Voice in Schoenberg's Moses und Aron with the Philharmonia Orchestra under Christoph von Dohnányi at the Festival Hall, London, 1996. *Honours:* Winner, Carl Maria von Weber Competition, Munich, 1993. *Address:* c/o Bayerische Staatsoper, Max-Joseph Platz, Pf 100148, 8000 Munich 1, Germany.

**HOLLOWAY, David;** Singer (Concert Baritone) and Teacher; b. 12 Nov. 1942, Grandview, Missouri, USA; m. Deborah Seabury, 25 May 1975, 4 s., 1 d. *Education:* Bachelor's Degree, Master's Degree in Voice, University of Kansas, 1967; Studied with Luigi Ricci in Rome, 1972–81; Voice training with Richard Torigi in New York; French repertoire with Janine Reiss and Jacqueline Richard; German repertoire with Frank Eggermann. *Career:* Debut: With Kansas City Lyric Opera, 1968; Sang with Deutsche Oper am Rhein, 1981–91, Metropolitan Opera, 1974–87, New York City Opera, 1972–80, Glyndebourne Opera Festival, 1985, 1987, Chicago Lyric Opera, Dallas Opera, Houston Opera, National Opera Center, Ottawa, Canada, Santa Fe Opera, Central City Opera Festival, San Francisco, Cincinnati Opera; Voice/Opera Faculty, North Park University and Music Institute of Chicago. *Recordings:* Escamillo in Carmen with Glyndebourne Festival Opera; The Face on the Barroom Floor by Mollicone; Songs by Frederick Rzewsky; Songs by Karl and Vally Weigl. *Honours:* Winner, San Francisco Opera audition, 1968; Martha Baird Rockefeller Docent, 1970; HiFidelity/Musical America Award, Tanglewood Festival, 1971; National Opera Institute Grantee, 1973–74. *Address:* 936 Sunset Road, Winnetka, IL 60093, USA.

**HOLLOWAY, John;** Violinist; b. 19 July 1948, Neath, Wales. *Education:* Studied with Yfrah Neaman at the Guildhall School, London; Further study with William Pleeth, Sándor Végh and Sigiswald Kuijken. *Career:* Leader of Kent Opera Orchestra, 1972–79, Taverner Players (1977–91) and London Classical Players, 1978–92; Founded L'Ecole d'Orphée 1975, with many performances of Baroque music in London and elsewhere; Professor of the GSM, London, and guest professor at the Schola Cantorum, Basle, and Indiana University. *Recordings include:* Chamber Music by Handel, with L'Ecole d'Orphée; Biber's Mystery Sonatas, Buxtehude Chamber Music, with Jaap ter Linden and Lars Ulrik Mortensen. *Honours:* Gramophone Award, 1991. *Address:* Guildhall School of Music and Drama, Silk Street, Barbican, London EC 2Y 8DT, England.

**HOLLOWAY, Robin Greville,** PhD, DMus; British composer, writer and academic; *Professor of Musical Composition;* b. 19 Oct. 1943, Leamington Spa; s. of Robert Charles Holloway and Pamela Mary Holloway (née Jacob). *Education:* St Paul's Cathedral Choir School, King's Coll. School, Wimbledon, King's Coll., Cambridge and New Coll., Oxford. *Career:* Lecturer in Music, Univ. of Cambridge 1975–, Reader in Musical Composition 1999–, Prof. 2001–; Fellow of Gonville and Caius Coll., Cambridge 1969–. *Compositions include:* Garden Music opus 1 1962, First Concerto for Orchestra 1969, Scenes from Schumann opus 13 1970, Evening with Angels opus 17 1972, Domination of Black opus 23 1973, Clarissa (opera) opus 30 1976, Second Concerto for Orchestra opus 40 1979, Brand (dramatic ballad) opus 48 1981, Women in War opus 51 1982, Seascape and Harvest opus 55 1983, Viola Concerto opus 56 1984, Peer Gynt 1985, Hymn to the Senses for chorus 1990, Serenade for strings 1990, Double Concerto opus 68, The Spacious Firmament for chorus and orchestra opus 69, Violin Concerto opus 70 1990, Boys and Girls Come Out To Play (opera) 1991, Winter Music for sextet 1993, Frost at Midnight opus 78, Third Concerto for Orchestra opus 80 1994, Clarinet Concerto opus 82 1996, Peer Gynt opus 84 1984–97, Scenes from Antwerp opus 85 1997, Gilded Goldberg for two pianos 1999, Symphony 1999, Missa Caiensis 2001, Cello Sonata 2001, Spring Music opus 96 2002, String Quartet no. 1 2003, String Quartet no. 2 2004. *Recordings:* Sea Surface Full of Clouds chamber cantata, Romanza for violin and small orchestra opus 31, 2nd Concerto for Orchestra opus 40, Horn Concerto Opus 43, Violin Concerto opus 70, Third Concerto for orchestra, Fantasy Pieces opus 16, Serenade in DC opus 41, Gilded Goldberg opus 86, Missa Caiensis, Organ Fantasy, Woefully Arrayed. *Publications:* Wagner and Debussy 1978, On Music: Essays and Diversions 1963–2003 2004; numerous articles and reviews. *Address:* Gonville and Caius College, Cambridge, CB2 1TA, England. *Telephone:* (1223) 335424. *E-mail:* rgh1000@cam.ac.uk (home). *Website:* www.rhessays.co.uk (home).

**HOLLOWAY, Stephen;** Singer (bass); b. 1951, England. *Education:* studied at the Guildhall School and with Vera Rozsa; Christ's Coll., Cambridge. *Career:* appearances with Scottish Opera as Don Fernando in Fidelio, Private Willis in Iolanthe, Doctor Grenvil in La Traviata and Thanatos/The Oracle in Alceste; Sparafucile and Mozart's Bartolo for European Chamber Opera; The Speaker in The Magic Flute under Jane Glover at the Covent Garden Festival; Chub in Tchaikovsky's Cherevichki and The Chamberlain in Stravinsky's Nightingale for Chelsea Opera Group. *Current Management:* Musikmakers. *Address:* Little Easthall, St Paul's Walden, Hertfordshire SG4 8DH, England.

**HOLLREISER, Heinrich;** Conductor; b. 24 June 1913, Munich, Germany. *Education:* Akademie der Tonkunst Munich. *Career:* Conducted at opera houses in Wiesbaden, Mannheim, Darmstadt and Duisburg; Munich Opera from 1942, notably with operas by Strauss, then Musical Director in Düsseldorf; Hamburg Opera, 1947, with the local premiere of Peter Grimes by Britten; Vienna Staatsoper from 1952; Principal Conductor at the Deutsche Oper Berlin, 1981–64; Blacher's Zweihunderttausend Thaler, 1969; Modern repertory includes operas by Bartók, Hindemith and Berg; Bayreuth Festival, 1973–75, Tannhäuser and Die Meistersinger; Wagner's Ring at the Vienna Staatsoper, 1976; Guest Conductor with the Cleveland Orchestra, 1978. *Recordings include:* Mozart Piano Concertos; Tchaikovsky and Mendelssohn Violin Concertos; Bartók Cantata Profana and Concerto for Orchestra; Symphonies by Schubert, Brahms, Dvořák, Tchaikovsky, Bruckner, Stravinsky, Apollo, Pulcinella and Jeu de Cartes. *Address:* c/o PO Box 100262, Bayreuther Festspiele, 8580 Bayreuth 1, Germany.

**HOLLWEG, Werner;** Singer (Tenor); b. 13 Sept. 1936, Solingen, Germany; m. Constance Daucha, 2 c. *Education:* Studied in Detmold, Munich and Legano. *Career:* Debut: Vienna Kammeroper, 1962; Bonn, 1963–67; Gelsenkirchen, 1967–68; Maggio Musicale, Florence, 1969, as Belmonte in Die Entführung; Guest appearances in Hamburg, Munich, Berlin, Rome, Paris, New York and Los Angeles; Salzburg Festival as Mozart's Tamino, Ottavio, Ferrando and Belmonte; Osaka, Japan, 1970, in Beethoven's 9th Symphony; Covent Garden debut, 1976, as Mozart's Titus; Paris Opéra, 1986, as Jason in Cherubini's Médée; Promenade Concerts, London, 1989, in Psalmus Hungaricus by Kodály; Created Matthew Levi in Höller's Der Meister und Margarita, Paris, 1989; Sang the High Priest in Idomeneo at Salzburg, 1990; Acted in Henze's Il Re Cervo at Wuppertal, 1996; Wuppertal 1993, as Vova in Schnittke's Life with an Idiot; Berne 1996, as Prospero in the premiere of The Tempest by Daniel Schnyder. *Recordings:* Haydn, Die Jahreszeiten; Mozart, Le nozze di Figaro; Mahler, Das klagende Lied; Mozart, La Finta Giardiniera and Zaide; Lehar, Die lustige Witwe; Mozart, Mitridate and Idomeneo; Monteverdi, Il Combattimento; Ballads by Schubert, Schumann and Loewe. *Current Management:* Ingpen & Williams Ltd, 7 St George's Court, 131 Putney Bridge Road, London, SW15 2PA, England.

**HOLM, Mogens (Winkel);** Composer; b. Oct. 1936, Copenhagen, Denmark. *Education:* Studied Oboe and Composition, Royal Danish Academy of Music, Copenhagen. *Career:* Oboe player in various Copenhagen orchestras including the Danish Radio Light Orchestra, 1964–65; Choreographer to his own ballet scores, 1975–. *Compositions include:* Opera: Aslak, 1961; Sonata for Four Opera Singers, 1967–68; Ballet: Tropisms, 1963; Chronicle, 1968; Galgarien, 1970; Report, 1972; Tarantel, 1975; Eurydice Hesitates, 1977; Whitethroat under an Artificial Firmament, 1979–80; To Bluebeard, 1982; Orchestra: Kammerkoncertante, 1959; Concerto piccolo, 1961; Cumulus, 1965; Ricercare, 1966; The Glass Forest, 1974; Aiolos, symphony in 1 movement, 1972–77; Cries, 1983–84; Chamber Music: Abracadabra, 1960; Tropismer, 1960; Sonata, 1965; Transitions, 1972; Seven Letters to Silence, 1976; Adieu, 1982; Note-book, 1983; Vocal: October Morning, 1964; Transitions, 1971; Nightmare, 1973; For Children, 1984. *Recordings:* Has made numerous recordings. *Address:* KODA, Rosenvaengets Hovedvej 14, 2100 Copenhagen, Denmark.

**HOLM, Peder;** Composer and Educator; b. 30 Sept. 1926, Copenhagen, Denmark. *Education:* Graduate in Violin and Theory, Royal Danish Conservatorium, 1947; Teacher's Examination in Piano and Violin. *Career:* Director, Western Jutland Conservatorium; Director, West Jutland Symphony Orchestra; mem, Programme Committee, Danish Radio, 1963–67; Music Committee, State Cultural Foundation, 1965–68. *Compositions include:* Pezzo

Concertante for orchestra, 1964; VYL for orchestra, 1967; Khebeb for 2 pianos and orchestra, 1968; 2 pieces for wind quintet, 1968; Music for brass band, 1969; Ole Wivel, children's song for children's choir, 1970; Concertino for clarinet and chamber orchestra, 1970; Legend, Erik Knudsen, for children's choir, 1971; Ene Mene, Inscription, Mobile, September Evening, Regards to Borge, 5 choral songs for mixed choir; Pikkutikka for children's choir and orchestra, 1973; Arrangements: Works by Schumann, Grieg, Couperin and Mozart; Pieces for the Musica Ensemble Series; Works for solo voice, orchestra, symphonic works, concertos and chamber music; The Wandering Prince and the Poor Maiden, drama, 1984; Ode for the Year, 1988; Voices of Funen for mixed chorus and ensemble, 1995. *Publications include:* The String Method; Wind Method; Violin 1 and 2 (editor); All part of Wilhelm Hansen's MUSICA-Methods series. *Address:* c/o KODA, Maltegardsvej 24, 2820 Gentofte, Denmark.

**HOLM, Renate;** Singer (Soprano); b. 10 Aug. 1931, Berlin, Germany. *Education:* Studied with Marie Ivogun in Vienna. *Career:* Sang in films and entertainment programmes from 1953; Vienna Volksoper from 1957, debut as Gretchen in Der Wildschütz by Lortzing; Appearances at the Vienna Staatsoper, Bolshoi Theatre, Moscow, Covent Garden, London, and the Teatro Colón, Buenos Aires in the soubrette repertory, including Despina, Norina, Sophie, Zerlina and Marzelline; Salzburg Festival from 1961, as Blondchen in Die Entführung, Papagena and Musetta, 1975. *Recordings:* Die Fledermaus, Der Vogelhändler, Das Land des Lächelns; Die Zauberflöte; Die Entführung. *Address:* c/o Staatsoper, 1010 Vienna, Austria.

**HOLMAN, Peter;** Harpsichordist and Chamber Organist; b. 19 Oct. 1946, London, England. *Education:* King's College, London with Thurston Dart; D Mus (London), 1995. *Career:* As student, directed the pioneering early music group Ars Nova; Founded, The Parley of Instruments, with Roy Goodman, 1979, The Parley now recognised as one of the leading exponents of Renaissance and Baroque string consort music; Musical Director and co-founder, 1985, Opera Restor'd which specialises in authentic productions of eighteenth century English operas and masques; Past Professor, Royal Academy of Music in London for 10 years and has taught at many conservatories, universities and summer schools in England and abroad; Artistic Director of the annual Suffolk Village Festival; Joint Artistic Director, with Paul O'Dette, of the 1995 Boston Early Music Festival; Presently, Reader in Historical Musicology at the University of Leeds; Regular Broadcaster on BBC Radio 3; He spends much of his time in writing and research; Special interests in the early history of the violin family, in European instrumental ensemble music of the Renaissance and Baroque and in English seventeenth and eighteenth century music; Edition of Arne's Artaxerxes performed London, 1995; Directed Opera Restor'd in Lampe's The Dragon of Wantley, 1996, and double bill of Scarlatti's La Dirindina and Haydn's La Canterina, 1998. *Publications:* Many editions of early music; Four and Twenty Fiddlers; The Violin at the English Court 1540–1690, 1993; Ed, London: Commonwealth and Restoration in The Early Baroque Era, C A Price in the Man and Music (Music and Society in the USA) series (London), 1993; Paper on Monteverdi's string writing in the Nov 1993 issue of Early Music; Henry Purcell, A General Survey of Purcell's Music, 1st edition, 1994; Dowland, Lachrimae, 1999. *Contributions:* Various articles and reviews to a range of newspapers and journals. *Honours:* Hon ARAM, 1979. *Address:* 119 Maldon Road, Colchester, Essex CO3 3AX, England.

**HOLMES, Eugene;** Singer (Baritone); b. 7 March 1932, Brownsville, Tennessee, USA; m. Katja L Holmes. *Education:* BS, Music Education, Indiana University, Bloomington; Special award, Performer's Certificate; Studied with W D Walton in St Louis, Frank St Leger at the Indiana University in Bloomington, and with Dorothy Ziegler in Miami. *Career:* Debut: Goldovsky Opera, New York, 1963, in The Crucible by Ward; Kammersänger, Deutsche Oper am Rhein, Düsseldorf; Sang in San Diego, San Francisco, Seattle and New York (City Opera), 1971, in the premiere of The Most Important Man by Menotti); Washington, 1970, in the US premiere of Koanga by Delius; Düsseldorf, 1983, as Don Carlos in La Forza del Destino, Nabucco, and Enrico in Lucia di Lammermoor; Munich, 1983, in a concert performance of Porgy and Bess; Other roles include Amonasro, Macbeth, Iago, Rigoletto, Boccanegra, Jochanaan and parts in operas by Mozart, Wagner and Puccini; Verdi's La Traviata, Germont, Puccini's La Bohème, Marcello, Madama Butterfly, Sharpless, Manon Lescaut, Verdi's Il Trovatore, Count di Luna; Performed with the Deutsche Oper am Rhein in the USSR, Magic Flute; Concert tours in Japan and Israel; Sang the Minister in Fidelio at Dusseldorf, 1999. *Recordings include:* Porgy and Bess; Koanga. *Address:* c/o Deutsche Oper am Rhein, Heinrich Heine Allee 16, 4000 Düsseldorf, Germany.

**HOLOMAN, D(allas) Kern;** Musicologist, Conductor and Music Educator; b. 8 Sept. 1947, Raleigh, North Carolina, USA; m. Elizabeth R Holoman, 1 s., 1 d. *Education:* Studied bassoon and conducting, North Caroline School of the Arts; Accademia Musicale Chigiana, Siena, Italy, 1967, 1968; BA, Duke University, 1969; MFA, 1971, PhD, 1974, Princeton University. *Career:* Founding Director, Early Music Ensemble, 1973–77, 1979, Conductor, Symphony Orchestra, 1978–, Chairman, Music Department, 1980–88, University of California at Davis; Founding Co-Editor, 19th Century Music Journal, 1977; General Editor, Recent Researches in the Music of the Nineteenth and Early Twentieth Centuries, 1989; Guest Lecturer, various professional organisations; mem, American Musicological Society; Music Library Association; Association National Hector Berlioz. *Publications:* The

Creative Process in the Autograph Musical Documents of Hector Berlioz, c. 1818–1840, 1980; Musicology in the 1980s (edited with C Palisca), 1982; Dr Holoman's Handy Guide to Concert-Going, 1983; Catalogue of the Works of Hector Berlioz, 1987; Writing About Music: A Style-Sheet from the Editors of the 19th Century Music, 1988; Berlioz, 1989; Berlioz's Roméo et Juliette, New Berlioz Edition (editor). *Contributions:* Numerous articles and reviews to journals and other publications. *Address:* c/o Department of Music, University of California at Davis, Davis, CA 95616, USA.

**HOLSZKY, Adriana;** Composer; b. 30 June 1953, Bucharest, Romania. *Education:* Studied at the Bucharest Conservatory with Milko Kelemen, in Germany and with Franco Donatoni in Italy. *Career:* Teacher at the Stuttgart Hochschule, 1980–89. *Compositions include:* Space for 4 Orchestras, 1980; Erewhon for 14 Instruments, 1984; Bremer Freiheit, opera, 1987; Lichtflug for Violin, Flute and Orchestra, 1990; Gemalde Eines Erschlagenen for 74 Voices, 1993; The Rise of the Titanic, music theatre, 1998; Other vocal and chamber music. *Honours:* Prizewinner in competitions in Rome, Paris, Mannheim and Heidelberg.

**HOLT, Olivier;** Conductor; b. 1960, Paris, France. *Education:* Vienna Hochschule für Musik. *Career:* Assistant at Opéra de Nancy and Opéra de Paris; Conducted performances at the Paris Châtelet, Opéra-Comique and at Marseille Opéra; Music Director of the Orchestre Symphonique d'Europe, 1987–91, with tours to Vienna, Salzburg and Madrid; Guest with the Orchestre National de Lille, Marseille Philharmonique and Colonne Concerts; Season 1999/2000 with the Orchestre de Picardie (Haydn/Bach/Webern) and at Lille (Franck/Liszt/Saint-Saëns); Conductor at the Conservatoire de Rouen, 1997–; Season 2001 with concerts in Miami and throughout France. *Recordings include:* Albums with Nathalie Dessay, Françoise Pollet and Isabelle Vernet; Stabat Mater by Gouvy. *Address:* c/o Musicaglotz, 11 rue le Verrier, 75006, France.

**HOLT, Simon,** FRNCM; British composer; b. 21 Feb. 1958, Bolton, Lancs. *Education:* Bolton Coll. of Art, Royal Northern Coll. of Music. *Career:* featured composer at Bath Festival 1985; commissions from London Sinfonietta include Kites, Ballad of the Black Sorrow, from Nash Ensemble Shadow Realm, Era Madrugada, Canciones, Sparrow Night, All Fall Down, and Proms for 1987 and 1992; also featured at Music in London Now Festival in Japan 1986; featured at Huddersfield Festival 1998. *Compositions include:* Lunas Zauberschein for mezzo and bass flute 1979, Palace at 4am, Mirrormaze, Maiastra, Burlesca Oscura, Tauromaquia, Syrensong, Capriccio Spettrale, String Quartet: Danger of the Disappearance of Things 1989, Lilith, Walking With the River's Roar, Icarus Lamentations, A Knot of Time, Minotaur Games, A Book of Colours, Daedalus Remembers (for Cheltenham Festival) 1995, The Nightingale's to Blame (for Opera North) 1998, eco-pavan for ensemble 1998, Sunrise's Yellow Noise for soprano and orchestra 1999, Boots of Lead (texts by Emily Dickinson) for alto voice and orchestra 2002, Who Put Bella in the Wych Elm? (British Composer Award for Stage Work) 2004. *Recordings:* Era Madrugada, Canciones, Shadow Realm, Sparrow Night with Nash Ensemble, eco-pavan, Feet of Clay, Lilith, Boots of Lead, Kites. *Honours:* Ivor Novello Award for Classical Music 2003. *Address:* c/o Chester Music Ltd, 14–15 Berners Street, London, W1T 3LJ, England.

**HOLTEN, Bo;** Composer and Choral Director; b. 22 Oct. 1948, Rudkobing, Denmark. *Career:* conducts vocal group, Ars Nova, performances of rare works; music critic and ed., Dansk Musiktidsskrift; pioneer, many unusual concerts combining classical music/jazz; led the BBC Singers at the 1999 London Proms in Brumel's Mass Et ecce terra motus. *Compositions include:* works for symphony orchestras with/without chorus, works for large/small chamber ensembles; vocal and instrumental music; choral works with/without instruments; The Bond (opera) 1978–79; tape, film scores; symphonic works include: Mahler-Impromptu 1972–73, Caccia 1979, Symphony 1982, Tertia Die 1985, Imperia for soprano, bass, double chorus and orchestra 1997.

**HOLTENAU, Rudolf;** Singer (Baritone); b. 1937, Salzburg, Austria. *Education:* Studied in Linz and in Vienna with Alfred Jerger. *Career:* Sang in concert, 1959–61; Opera engagements at Klagenfurt, 1961–62, Regensburg, 1962–65, Bielefeld, 1965–67, Essen, 1967–75; Further appearances at Cologne, 1972–73, Vienna Staatsoper, 1973–75, Graz, 1977–79; Guest throughout the 1970s at Stockholm, Lyon, Brussels, Barcelona, Monte Carlo, Lisbon, Marseille and Bologna; Performances of Der Ring des Nibelungen at Seattle, 1978–79; Sang such roles as Wagner's Dutchman, Sachs, Wotan, Gunther, Kurwenal and Amfortas, Strauss's Mandryka and Verdi's Amonasro at Hamburg, Berlin (Deutsche Oper), Buenos Aires, Venice, San Francisco and Rio de Janeiro; Sang at Cape Town, 1982, 1985. *Recordings:* Ballads by Carle Loewe.

**HOLTHAM, Ian;** Concert Pianist and Educationalist; b. 1 Feb. 1955, Melbourne, Victoria, Australia. *Education:* BA, PhD, DipEd, Melbourne University; BMus, Durham University; Studied with Peter Feuchtwanger, Geza Anda and Geoffrey Parsons. *Career:* Debut: Purcell Room and Wigmore Hall, both 1977; Appearances in the United Kingdom, Switzerland, France, Austria, Italy, Thailand, Hong Kong and Australia; Concerto soloist and recitalist; Numerous radio and television appearances including frequently for Australian Broadcasting Corporation; Head of Keyboard and Practical Studies at the Faculty of Music, University of Melbourne. *Recordings:* Chopin: 24 Etudes, Op 10 and Op 25; Godowsky: Selection of transcriptions of Chopin Etudes; Imo pectore-music by Beethoven, Schubert, Schumann and Rachmaninov; Acts of Homage–Music by Brahms and Schubert. *Publications:* The Essentials of Piano Technique, 1992; Various articles in the Oxford Companion to Australian Music. *Current Management:* Alan Watkinson Management. *Address:* Heavitree, PO Box 412, Canterbury, Victoria 3126, Australia.

**HOLTMANN, Heidrun;** Pianist; b. 18 Oct. 1961, Munster, Westphalia, Germany. *Education:* Study with Eleonore Jäger, Münster, 1966–70; Professor Renate Kretschmar-Fischer, Musikhochschule Detmold/Westphalia, 1970–83; Nikata Magaloff, Geneva, Switzerland, 1978; Vladimir Ashkenazy, Lucerne, Switzerland, 1981. *Career:* Concerts in England, France, Germany, Israel, Italy, Japan, Yugoslavia, North Africa, Austria, Poland, Hungary, Switzerland, USA; Concerts at Festivals in Bordeaux, France; Brescia and Bergamo, Italy; Salzburg; Lockenhaus, Austria; Lucerne, Switzerland; Berlin, West Germany; Concerts with Detroit Symphony Orchestra (Ivan Fischer), Royal Philharmonic Orchestra, London (Antal Dorati), Mozarteum Orchestra/Salzburg, Tonhalle Orchestra/Zürich (Gerd Albrecht, Ferdinand Leitner, David Zinman), ARD/NDR-ZDF, West Germany; DRS-TV, Zürich, Switzerland; RTV Skopje, Yugoslavia; Television recordings at ARD and ZDF, West Germany; Radio Recordings several times with all Radio stations in West Germany. *Recordings:* Gidon Kremer Chamber Music Festival, 1983; Anneliese Rothenberger Presents, 1984; Bach, Goldberg Variations, 1986; Schumann, Carnaval and Kreisleriana, 1987. *Current Management:* Konzertagentur Fahrenholtz, Oberweg 51, 6000 Frankfurt/Main 1. *Address:* Büsingstrasse 1, 1000 Berlin 41, Germany.

**HOLTON, Ruth;** Singer (Soprano); b. 1961, England. *Education:* Choral exhibitioner at Clare College, Cambridge; Further study with Elizabeth Lane, Nancy Long and Julie Kennard. *Career:* Appearances from 1985 in Baroque music at Bruges, Turku (Finland), Berlin, Amsterdam, Rome, Vienna, Paris; Recitals in Cambridge, Oxford, London, Glasgow and at the Three Choirs Festival in Gloucester; Fauré's Requiem at the Théâtre du Châtelet, Paris, and Ilia in Idomeneo, 1991; Radio broadcasts, BBC Recital, Radio 3, 1992, 1994, 1995, 1996, 1997; WDR Recital, 1992; World-wide broadcast of Bach's St John Passion with choir of St Thomas', Leipzig, 1997; Concert work with Fretwork, Orchestra of the Age of Enlightenment, Ton Koopman, John Eliot Gardiner, Gustav Leonhardt, Taverner Consort. *Recordings:* Bach's St John Passion and Cantatas, Jephtha by Handel and Carissimi, Dido and Aeneas, Handel's Messiah, Mozart's Salzburg Masses, works by Schütz and Buxtehude; Angel in Schütz's Christmas Story with the King's Consort; Grand Pianola Music by John Adams, also music by Steve Reich. *Address:* 27 Casewick Road, London SE27 0TB, England.

**HOLZAPFEL, Marcela;** Singer (Soprano); b. 1960, Chile. *Education:* Studied in Chile. *Career:* Sang at Santiago Opera, 1985–88, as Clorinda in La Cenerentola, Mozart's Constanze, Strauss's Zerbinetta and Verdi's Nannetta; Rio de Janeiro, 1988, as Zerbinetta; Stuttgart Staatsoper from 1990, as Sophie in Werther, Antonoe in Henze's Bassarids, Puccini's Musetta and Oscar in Un Ballo in Maschera; Berlin Staatsoper, 1991, as Constanze in Die Entführung; Santiago from 1992, notably as Gilda and as Micaela in Carmen; Many concert engagements. *Address:* c/o Opera del Teatro Municipal, San Antonio 149, Santiago Central, Chile.

**HOLZMAIR, Wolfgang;** Austrian singer (baritone); b. 24 April 1952, Vöcklabruck. *Education:* Vienna Acad. of Music and Dramatic Arts with Hilde Rössel-Majdan and Erik Werba. *Career:* appearances in opera and concert halls throughout Germany, Austria and Switzerland; premiered Berio's orchestration of Mahler Lieder 1992; has sung with leading European and American orchestras, including the Israel Philharmonic, Berlin Philharmonic, Vienna Symphony, Leipzig Gewandhaus, Cleveland and Concertgebouw Orchestras, and the Orchestra of the Age of Enlightenment; Covent Garden debut, as Papageno 1993; other opera roles include Rossini's Figaro and Valentin, Gluck's Orpheus and Eugene Onegin, Udo Zimmermann's Die Weisse Rose, Ireo in Cesti's Semiramide, Serezha in Nigel Osborne's The Electrification of the Soviet Union, Peri's Orfeo, Creonte in Haydn's Orfeo and Enrico in Haydn's Isola disabitata in Lyon, Pelléas, the Count in Capriccio in Cagliari, Speaker of the Temple in Die Zauberflöte, the title role in Daniel Schnyder's Casanova; season 2003–04 included appearances in London, Lisbon, New York, Ottawa, Graz, Vienna and at the Risör and Bregenz festivals, and sang Lieder eines fahrenden Gesellen with the Minnesota Orchestra, Schubert songs with the Orchestra of St Luke's, Carnegie Hall, and Mahler's Das Lied von der Erde at the Vienna Festival; season 2004–05 included recitals in New York, Washington, Dublin, London, Vienna and at the Bath, Menuhin and Carinthian Summer Festivals; teacher of lied and oratorio, Mozarteum, Salzburg 1998–. *Recordings:* Lieder by Clara and Robert Schumann, Eichendorff songs, recordings of Schubert, Pelléas et Mélisande (with Haitink and the Orchestre National de France), Brahms' Ein deutsches Requiem (with Herbert Blomstedt) (Grammy Award). *Address:* Owen White Management, 59 Lansdowne Place, Hove, East Sussex BN3 1FL, England. *Telephone:* (1273) 727127. *Fax:* (1273) 328128. *E-mail:* info@owenwhitemanagement.com. *Website:* www.owenwhitemanagement.com.

**HOMOKI, Andreas;** German opera director; *Chief Director and Intendant, Komische Oper, Berlin;* b. 16 Feb. 1960, Marl. *Education:* Bremen Hochschule, Acad. of Fine Arts, Berlin. *Career:* Asst at Deutsche Oper Berlin, Theater des Westens and Komische Oper, Berlin; Asst to Harry Kupfer at Salzburg Festival, Stuttgart State Opera and Cologne Opera 1986–87; Asst to Michael Hampe, Willy Decker and Harry Kupfer, at Cologne Opera 1987; Asst to Michael Hampe at Salzburg Festival; opera productions have included

Mozart's Bastien und Bastienne in Oslo, Le nozze di Figaro for Kammeroper Herdecke 1988, Fidelio and Jakob Lenz by Wolfgang Rihm for the Cologne Music Acad. 1989–90; Dir, Michael Hampe Australian Opera production of Die Meistersinger 1990, for New Zealand Int. Festival of the Arts; Il Trovatore for Wellington City Opera 1991; Instructor of Drama Opera Dept, Cologne Music Acad. 1988–93; freelance director 1993–; Chief Dir, Komische Oper, Berlin 2002–, Intendant 2003–; opera productions have included L'Enfant et les Sortilèges for Cologne Music Acad. 1992, Die Frau ohne Schatten, Grand Théâtre de Genève 1992 and Le Châtelet, Paris (French Theatre Critics' Award for Best Opera) 1993, Cav and Pag in State Theatre, Mainz 1993, Madama Butterfly, Essen 1993, Das Schloss by Reimann, Hannover 1994, Frau ohne Schatten, Paris 1994, Wildschütz, Cologne 1994, Rigoletto, Hamburg 1994, Tristan und Isolde, Wiesbaden 1994, Idomeneo at the Nationaltheater, Munich 1996, Falstaff 1996, L'Amour pour les trois oranges 1998, The Merry Widow 2000, Arabella, Nationaltheater Munich 2001, The Bartered Bride 2002, Eine Florentinische Tragödie/Der Zwerg by Zemlinsky 2002, Manon Lescaut, Nationaltheater Munich 2002, The Gypsy Princess, Komische Oper Berlin 2003. *Honours:* French Theatre Critics Award for Best Opera 1994. *Current Management:* Haydn Rawstron (UK) Ltd, 36 Station Road, London, SE20 7BQ, England. *Address:* c/o Komische Oper Berlin, Behrenstr. 55–57, 10117 Berlin, Germany. *E-mail:* a.homoki@komische-oper -berlin.de.

**HONECK, Manfred;** Austrian conductor; b. 1963, Vienna. *Career:* Asst Conductor to Claudio Abbado, Gustav Mahler Youth Orchestra from 1987; Prin. Conductor, Jeunesse Orchestra, Vienna and regular concerts with the NDR Orchestra Hanover and the Radio Symphony Orchestras of Berlin, Leipzig, Munich, Frankfurt, Cologne, Saarbrucken and Stuttgart; Kapellmeister at the Zürich Opera from 1991; opera productions include Die Fledermaus, Figaro and Il Barbiere di Siviglia at the Vienna Volksoper 1989–90; Giordano's Fedora and Andrea Chénier, Massenet's Hérodiade at Zürich; Così fan tutte at Hamburg 1993; premiere of Herbert Willi's opera Schlafes Bruder 1996; ballet includes Pulcinella at the Vienna Staatsoper 1990; debut with the Vienna Philharmonic Orchestra and Houston Symphony 1994; season 1995 with the Chicago Symphony Orchestra and the BBC Symphony at the Festival Hall, London; season 1996–97 with the Dresden Staatskapelle, Oslo Philharmonic, Danish Radio Symphony and Royal Danish Orchestras; Music Dir, Norwegian Opera from 1997; further concerts with the BBC Symphony Orchestra 1997–98, conducted them in Strauss family concert at the London Proms 1999; Music Dir and Principal Conductor Swedish Radio Symphony Orchestra 2000–06; Music Dir Stuttgart State Opera (2007–). *Honours:* European Prize for Conducting 1993. *Address:* Swedish Radio Symphony Orchestra, Berwaldhallen, 105 10 Stockholm, Sweden. *Website:* www.sr.se.

**HONG, Hei-kyung;** South Korean singer (soprano); b. 1958, Seoul. *Education:* Juilliard School, New York. *Career:* debut, Houston, 1983, as Gilda in Rigoletto; Sang Musetta at Chicago, 1983, and at the Metropolitan Opera from 1985 (debut as Servilia in La Clemenza di Tito), followed by Mimi, Despina, Susanna, Lauretta (Gianni Schicchi), Ilia and Pamina; Toronto, 1992, as Gounod's Juliette; Other roles include Leila (Les Pêcheurs de Perles), Manon, Butterfly, Bellini's Giulietta and Woglinde in Das Rheingold; Sang Zerlina at Dallas, 1996. *Recordings include:* Rheingold and Götterdämmerung. *Address:* c/o Metropolitan Opera, Lincoln Center, New York, NY 10023, USA.

**HÖNIGSBERG, David;** Composer, Conductor and Pianist; b. 28 Oct. 1959, Johannesburg, South Africa; 1 d. *Education:* BMus, RAND, Hochschule für Musik und Darstellende Kunst, Vienna, Austria, 1987; (Roman Haubenstock-Ramati), 1988–89. *Career:* Debut: Market Theatre, Johannesburg, 1980; Assistant Conductor, Imilonji Kantu Choir Soweto, 1989 Frankfurt Choir Festival; Concerto for Evi and orchestra, Johannesburg; Tomas and the Rainbow Dragon, Zürich; Piano concerto, St Cecilia Players, Zürich; mem, Schweizersche Tonkunstler Verein; SUISA; SMPV; SME. *Compositions:* 8 canzoni for cello and piano; Stefan Thut, cello; D Honigsberg, piano; Tomas and the Rainbow Dragon (Tudor). *Publications:* Music critic The Star Tonight, 1988–93. *Honours:* Samro Overseas Scholarship, 1988; First Prize, Total Composition, 1987. *Address:* Marktgasse 3, 8180 Bulach, Switzerland.

**HONNA, Tetsuji;** Conductor; b. 19 Jan. 1957, Koriyama, Japan. *Education:* Tokyo University of Fine Arts and Music; Studied Conducting under Michiyoshi Inoue; Studied at the Concertgebouw, Amsterdam. *Career:* Debut: Tokyo, Japan Philharmonic Orchestra, 1986; Hungarian State Symphony Orchestra, Corinthian Summer, 1994; Netherlands Philharmonic Orchestra, Holland Music Session, 1997; Salzburg, Mozarteum Orchestra, 1998; Philharmonia Orchestra, 1997; Many recordings for NHK FM with Tokyo Philharmonic Orchestra; Permanent Conductor of the Orchestra Osaka Symphoniker, 1994–; Guest Permanent Conductor of the Nagoya Philharmonic Orchestra, 1998–; Conductor of the Shirakawa Symphonia, 2000–. *Recordings:* Akutagawa Works with Japan Philharmonic Orchestra; Dvořák and Schumann with New Japan Philharmonic Orchestra. *Address:* c/o Dr Raab und Dr Bohm GmBH, Plankengasse 7, 1010 Vienna, Austria.

**HOOKS, Bridgett;** Singer (Soprano); b. 1967, New York, USA. *Education:* Studied at the Manhattan School of Music and the Curtis Institute, Philadelphia. *Career:* Sang at the Ghent Opera from 1990 as Mozart's Countess, and Madame Cortese in Rossini's Viaggio a Reims; Philadelphia Opera, 1990–92, in Argento's Postcard from Morocco, Copland's The Tender

Land and Don Giovanni, as Donna Anna; Concerts include Alice Tully Hall, New York (1994), Aspen Festival (Verdi Requiem), Spoleto Festival (1995), and Mahler's 8th Symphony (Cologne, 1995); Further repertory includes Spirituals (at the Vatican), Beethoven's Ninth and Shostakovich's 14th Symphonies, and Poulenc's Stabat Mater; Many lieder recitals. *Address:* c/o Opera Company of Philadelphia, 510 Walnut Street, Suite 1600, Philadelphia, PA 19106, USA.

**HOOPER, Adrian John;** Australian conductor and mandolinist; b. 6 May 1953, Sydney, NSW; m. Barbara Michele Jackson 1975; two s. one d. *Education:* New South Wales Conservatorium of Music. *Career:* founder and conductor of Australia's foremost mandolin orchestra, The Sydney Mandolins; regular player with the Australian Opera and Ballet Orchestra which accompanies the Australian Opera, and performed in such works as Otello and The Merry Widow; Worked with Sydney Symphony Orchestra in such works as Agon by Stravinsky; Regularly takes part in radio and concert performances as a Mandolin Soloist and Conductor for the Australian Broadcasting Commission; Soloist, Australian Chamber Orchestra; Mandolin Teacher, New South Wales State Conservatorium of Music, 1983; Teacher in Performance, Sydney University, 1996–. *Recordings:* over 80 recordings of music by Australian composers. *Publications:* Published and edited a number of Ancient Mandolin works; Editing all Mandolin Concertos. *Address:* 24 Kitchener Street, Oatley, NSW 2223, Australia. *E-mail:* mail@ sydneymandolins.com.

**HOOVER, Katherine,** MM; American composer and flautist; b. 2 Dec. 1937, Elkins, W Va. *Education:* Eastmann School and the Manhattan School of Music. *Career:* Lecturer, Manhattan School and Juilliard School; organizer, Women's Interart Center music festivals, New York 1978–81. *Compositions include:* Homage to Bartók, for wind quintet 1975, Trio, for clarinet, violin and piano 1978, Piano Book 1977–82, From the Testament of François Villon, for baritone, bassoon and string quartet 1982, Lyric Trio, for flute, cello and piano 1983, Clarinet Concerto 1987, Wind Quintet 1987, Eleni: a Greek Tragedy, for orchestra 1987, Double Concerto for 2 violins and strings 1989, Da pacem, piano quintet 1989, Night Skies, for orchestra 1992, Dances and Variations for flute and harp 1996, Bounce, for orchestra 1997, Kyrie, for 12 flutes 1998, The Heart Speaks, 7 songs for soprano and piano 1998, String quartet 1998, Trio for 3 flutes 1999, Suite for flute, guitar and bassoon 2000. *Publications:* Requiem 1865/2001 for soprano, alto, tenor and bass soloists, brass, percussion and organ 2003, El Andalus, for cello and piano 2004, Three Sketches, for piccolo and piano 2004, To Greet the Sun, for flute 2005. *Honours:* Acad. of Arts and Letters Award in Composition 1994. *Address:* c/o Papagena Press, PO Box 20484, Park West Station, New York, NY 10025 (office); 160 West 95th Street, #5B, New York, NY 10025, USA (home). *Telephone:* (212) 749-3012 (office); (212) 666-4745 (home). *Fax:* (212) 316-2235 (office). *E-mail:* khoover@papagenapress.com (office). *Website:* www .papagenapress.com (office).

**HOPE, Daniel;** British violinist; *member, Beaux Arts Trio;* b. 1974, South Africa. *Education:* Menuhin School of Music and Royal Coll. of Music with Felix Andrievsky. *Career:* played duos with double-bassist Garry Karr 1983, Bartók duos with Yehudi Menuhin for German television 1984; int. debut with the Jyväskylä Symphony Orchestra of Finland, playing the Mendelssohn Concerto; Brighton Festival in Bach's Fifth Brandenburg Concerto, recitals at the Purcell Room, London, the Bach Violin Concertos with the Milton Keynes Chamber Orchestra and concert with the Hallé Orchestra under Menuhin; Vivaldi's Four Seasons with the Aachen City Orchestra, Prokofiev's First Concerto in Finland and London, and the Beethoven Concerto on tour in Europe; appearances at the Schleswig-Holstein Festival, Germany; mem., Beaux Arts Trio 2002–. *Recordings include:* Bach concertos. *Honours:* winner Hugh Bean Violin Competition 1986, Peter Morrison Concerto Competition 1989, Classical BRIT Award for Young British Classical Performer 2004. *Current Management:* Encore Arts Management, USA. *Telephone:* (812) 320-4389. *E-mail:* info@encoreartsmanagement.com. *Website:* www .encoreartsmanagement.com; www.danielhope.com; www.beauxartstrio.org.

**HOPFERWEISER, Josef;** Singer (Tenor); b. 25 May 1938, Graz, Austria. *Education:* Musikhochschule Graz. *Career:* Frequent appearances at the Vienna Volksoper, notably in Notre Dame by Schmidt; State Operas of Hamburg, Munich and Stuttgart; Further engagements in Nancy, Frankfurt, Graz, Milan, Rome and San Francisco; Sang in the premiere of Troades by Aribert Reimann, Munich, 1986; Sang Froh in Das Rheingold at Munich, 1987, Alwa in Lulu at Madrid, 1988; Vienna Staatsoper, 1990, as Walther in Die Meistersinger; Herod in Salome, 1994; Many concert appearances. *Recordings include:* Alwa in Berg's Lulu, conducted by Christoph von Dohnányi.

**HOPKINS, Antony,** CBE, FRCM; British composer, writer and broadcaster; b. 21 March 1921, London; s. of the late Hugh Reynolds and Marjorie Reynolds; m. Alison Purves 1947 (died 1991). *Education:* Berkhamsted School and Royal Coll. of Music with Cyril Smith. *Career:* fmr Lecturer, Royal Coll. of Music 15 years; Dir Intimate Opera Co. 1952–64; composed incidental music for theatre (Old Vic, Stratford-upon-Avon), radio and cinema; presenter of radio series, Talking About Music (BBC) 1954–92. *Compositions include:* operas: Lady Rohesia, Three's Company, Hands Across the Sky, Dr Musikus, Ten o'clock Call, The Man from Tuscany; ballet music: Etude, Café des Sports; others: Psalm 42, Magnificat and Nunc Dimittis for girls' choir), A Time for Growing, Early One Morning, Partita for solo violin, John and the Magic Music Man for narrator and orchestra (Grand Prix Besançon Film Festival) 1976, songs, recorder pieces, three piano sonatas; incidental music, including Oedipus, The Love of Four Colonels, Cast a Dark Shadow, Pickwick Papers, Billy Budd, Decameron Nights. *Publications:* Talking about Symphonies 1961, Talking about Concertos 1964, Music All Around Me 1967, Music Face to Face 1971, Talking about Sonatas 1971, Downbeat Guide 1977, Understanding Music 1979, The Nine Symphonies of Beethoven 1980, Songs for Swinging Golfers 1981, Sounds of Music 1982, Beating Time (autobiog.) 1982, Pathway to Music 1983, The Concertgoer's Companion Vol. I 1984, Vol. II 1986, The Seven Concertos of Beethoven 1996; contrib. to numerous books. *Honours:* Hon. FRAM; Hon. Fellow, Robinson Coll. Cambridge 1980; Hon. DUniv (Stirling) 1980; Italia Prizes for composition 1952, 1957, City of Tokyo Medal for services to music 1973, Royal Coll. of Music Chappell Gold Medal 1943, Royal Coll. of Music Cobbett Prize. *Address:* Woodyard Cottage, Ashridge, Berkhamsted, Herts., HP4 1PS, England (home). *Telephone:* (1442) 842257 (home).

**HOPKINS, John (Raymond);** Conductor and Director; b. 19 July 1927, Preston, England; m. (1) Ann Rosemary Blamey, deceased, 5 d., (2) Geraldene Catherine Scott, 1 July 1987. *Education:* Cello student, Associate Fellow, Royal Manchester College of Music. *Career:* Assistant Conductor, BBC Glasgow, 1949–52; Conductor, BBC Northern Orchestra, 1952–57; National Orchestra, New Zealand; Musical Director, New Zealand Opera Company, 1957–63; Director of Music, ABC, 1963–73; Dean, School of Music, Victoria College of Arts, Melbourne, Australia, 1973–86; Principal Conductor, Auckland Philharmonic Orchestra, 1983–; Director of New South Wales State Conservatorium of Music, 1986–93; Artistic Adviser, Sydney Symphony Orchestra, 1986–88; Education Consultant, Sydney Symphony Orchestra. *Recordings:* Various with Melbourne, New Zealand and Moscow Symphony Orchestras. *Honours:* O.B.E., 1970; Queen's Silver Jubilee Medal, 1977; Title of Professor, Sydney University, 1991. *Address:* 1290 Mountain Lagoon Road, Bilpin, NSW 2758, Australia.

**HOPKINS, Sarah;** Composer and Performer; b. 1958, Lower Hutt, New Zealand. *Education:* New South Wales Conservatorium of Music High School; Victorian College of the Arts Music School. *Career:* Toured extensively throughout Australia, the United Kingdom, Europe and the USA; Musician in Residence, GIAE, Gippsland, Victoria, Australia, 1978; Musician in Residence, CIT, Caulfield, Victoria, 1979; Composer in Residence, Arts Victoria Music '81, 1981; Musician in Residence, 1981, Guest Artist in Residence, 1983, Brown's Mart Community Art Project; Let's Make Music, Northern Territory, 1982; New Music ACTION Residency, Victorian College of the Arts, Melbourne, 1982; Composer-Performer in Residence, Darwin Theatre Group, 1984; Artist in Schools, 1985, 1986; Composer-Performer, Sky Song Project, Brown's Mart, Darwin, and major tour, 1987 and 1988; Performer in Residence, The Exploration San Francisco, 1988; Composer in Residence, Northern Territory Arts Council, Darwin, 1989. *Compositions:* Ensemble works: Cello Timbre, 1976; Seasons II, 1978; Cellovoice, 1982; Whirlies, 1983; Sunrise/Sunset, 1983; Interweave, 1984; Deep Whirly Duo, 1984; Aura Swirl, 1986; Eclipse, 1986; Bougainvillea Bells, 1986; Cello Chi, 1986; Flight of the Wild Goose, 1987; Ring, 1987; Songs of the Wind, 1989; Circle Bell Mantra, 1989; Spiral Bells, 1989; Soul Song, 1989; Transformation, 1989; Heart Songs, 1989. *Recordings:* Soundworks 1: Collaborative Works; Soundworks 2: Solo and Duo Works; Soundworks 3: Whirliworks Performance; Interweave; Soundworks Performance.

**HOPKINS, Tim;** Stage Director and Performer; b. 1963, London, England. *Education:* Graduated from Queen's College, Cambridge in 1986. *Career:* Productions at Musica nel Chiostro, Battignano, 1989–91; Peter Grimes for Dublin Grand Opera, 1990; The Gondoliers for New Doyle Carte in 1991; Falstaff for English Touring Opera in 1992, Mario and the Magician for Almeida Opera, 1992; Così fan tutte for Welsh National Opera, 1992; Zampa at the 1993 Wexford Festival; Staged the premiere of Judith Weir's Blond Eckbert for English National Opera in 1994 and Berio's Vera Storia at the Festival Hall; Yeomen of the Guard for Welsh National Opera in 1995 (also seen at Covent Garden and in the USA), Così fan tutte, also for Welsh National Opera and Rimsky's Golden Cockerel for Rome Opera; Iphigénie en Aulide for Opera North, 1996; Season 1997–98 with Il Trovatore at Graz Oper, Maria Stuarda at Basel Opera and at the Royal Opera with a new production of The Golden Cockerel; Season 1999–2000, Radamisto for Opera North, A-ronne for Almeida Opera and Eugen Onegin for Basel Opera; Season 2001–02, Forest Murmurs for Opera North, Kantan/Damask Drum by Goehr for Almeida Opera; Only the Names Have Been Changed for the Munich Festival; Mare Nostrum for Theatre Basel; The Rake's Progress, in Hanover. *Honours:* NESTA Fellowship, 2002. *Address:* c/o T.J.H., 26A Cole Street, London SE1 4YH, England. *E-mail:* thopkins@divcon.co.uk.

**HORACEK, Jaroslav;** Singer (Bass) and Teacher; b. 29 April 1924, Dehylov, Czechoslovakia. *Education:* Studied with Rudol Va šek, Karel Kugler and Peter Burja in Ostrava, Apollo Granforte in Prague. *Career:* Debut: Opava, 1945, as Kecal in The Bartered Bride; Sang in Ostrava, 1951–53, then at the National Theatre, Prague; Sang in the standard bass repertory, and in operas by Smetana, Janáček and Dvořák; Took part in the 1959 premiere of Mirandolina by Martinů; Guest appearances in Warsaw, Sofia, Amsterdam, Boston, Edinburgh (1964, with the Prague Company), Naples, Barcelona and Boston; Sang Debussy's Arkel at Prague, 1986; Don Giovanni at the bicentenary performance of the opera, 1987; Many concert appearances; Producer of Czech operas at La Scala Milan; Teacher at the Prague

Conservatory. *Address:* c/o National Theatre, PO Box 865, 112 30 Prague 1, Czech Republic.

**HORAK, Josef;** Bass Clarinettist and Music Educator; b. 24 March 1931, Znojmo, Czechoslovakia. *Education:* State High School of Musical and Dramatic Arts. *Career:* Clarinettist, Czech Radio Symphony Orchestra and State Philharmonic, Brno; Concert Soloist; Professor, State Music High School, Prague; Chamber Music Lecturer, Biberach, West Germany; Member, chamber music ensemble Due Boemi di Praga, with Emma Kovarnova, Prague, 1963–; Concerts in Europe, USA, Asia and Africa; Television programmes in Czechoslovakia, Germany and Romania; Radio programmes, many European countries and USA; Discovered the bass clarinet as a solo instrument, giving the first bass clarinet recital in the world (1955); Chamber soloist of the Czech Philharmonic Orchestra; mem, Union of Czech Interpreters; Honorary member, Jeunesses Musicales de Suisse. *Recordings:* Due Boemi di Praga; At the New Ways; Bass Clarinet, the New Solo Instrument; The Paganini of the Bass Clarinet; The Singing Bass Clarinet; CD: Horák-New Age of Bass Clarinet, Horák and his Bass Clarinet-New Sound, The Singing Bass Clarinet; Also about 85 single recordings on various records. *Honours:* Gold Medal, 1958; Prize, L Janáček Competition, 1959; Hi-Fi Festival, Paris, 1965; Pick of the Year, London, 1974; Clarinet Super Record, Tokyo, 1986. *Address:* Bubenska 39, 170 21 Prague 7, Czech Republic.

**HORIGOME, Yuzuko;** Violinist; b. 1960, Tokyo, Japan. *Education:* Studied at Toho Gakuen School of Music, Tokyo, with Toshiya Eto; Graduated, 1980. *Career:* Won Queen Elisabeth of the Belgians International Competition, 1980; London debut, 1983, concerts with London Symphony Orchestra under Claudio Abbado and André Previn; US debut, 1982, at Tanglewood, with Boston Symphony; Later appearances in Pittsburgh, Chicago, Los Angeles and Montreal; 1988/89 season included concerts in Europe and Japan with the Salzburg Camerata, Royal Liverpool Philharmonic and Scottish National Orchestras, and at the Prague Spring Festival; USA tour with the Chamber Music Players of Marlboro, 1995; Featured in film Testimony, on the life of Shostakovich. *Recordings:* Bach Concerti with the English Chamber Orchestra with A Litton; Bach's Solo Violin Sonatas; Sibelius and Mendelssohn Concertos with the Concertgebouw Orchestra and Ivan Fischer, music by Bruch (Tring, 1996); Mozart Concerti, Camerata Academic Salzburg with Sándor Végh; Takemitsu by Denon, 1999; Beethoven, Kakadu Variations with Rudolph Serkin and Peter Willey. *Current Management:* Cadenza Conzert, Salzburg; Kajimoto Management, Tokyo, Japan. *Address:* 26A Avenue Emile Van Becelaere, Box 90, 1170 Brussels, Belgium.

**HORN, Volker;** Tenor; b. 1945, Klagenfurt, Germany. *Education:* Studied at the Vienna Musikhochschule. *Career:* Sang as boy soprano in the Bayreuth production of Tannhäuser directed by Wieland Wagner, 1954–55; Has sung at the Deutsche Oper Berlin from 1976; Guest appearances in Lyon, Karlsruhe, Munich and Strasbourg as Max in Der Freischütz and Loge in Das Rheingold, and at Bayreuth and Salzburg Easter Festivals in 1980; Deutsche Oper Berlin in 1987 as Galba in Die Toten Augen by d'Albert; Sang Hans Kraft in Der Kobold by Siegfried Wagner, Rudolstadt, 1992; Other roles include Tamino, Florestan, Lohengrin and Tristan; Sang in premiere of Gesualdo by F Hummel at Kaiserslautern, 1996; Season 2000–01 as Malcolm in Macbeth and Hervey in Anna Bolena at the Deutsche Oper; Concert and oratorio appearances in Germany, Austria and Switzerland. *Recordings:* Die Zauberflöte; Nabucco. *Address:* c/o Deutsche Oper Berlin, Richard Wagnerstrasse 10, 1000 Berlin, Germany.

**HORNE, David;** Concert Pianist and Composer; b. 12 Dec. 1970, Tillicoultry, Stirling, Scotland. *Education:* Studied at St Mary's Music School in Edinburgh, the Curtis Institute, Philadelphia and Harvard University. *Career:* Soloist with BBC Philharmonic and Symphony, Welsh and Scottish Orchestras, CBSO, the Scottish National and London Sinfonietta; Festival engagements at Edinburgh, Aldeburgh, Almeida and London; BBC Promenade Concert debut in 1990 with Prokofiev's Third Concerto; Other repertory includes Ravel G major, Gershwin Concerto, Brahms Concerto in D minor, Beethoven 1st Concerto and Choral Fantasia, Iain Hamilton 2nd Concerto (world premiere), Mozart K271, Frank Symphonic Variations, and Tchaikovsky 1st Concerto. *Compositions:* String Quartet, 1988; Splintered Unisons for clarinet, violin, cello and piano, 1988; Towards Dharma for 6 instruments, 1989; Light Emerging for symphony orchestra, 1989; Out of the Air, 1990; Contraries and Progressions for ensemble, 1991; Northscape for chamber orchestra, 1992; Piano Concerto, 1992; Pensive, for mezzo, voices and chamber orchestra, 1998; Spike, for ensemble, 1998; Broken Instruments, 1999; Zip, for cello and piano, 1999; The Year's Midnight for tenor, chorus and orchestra 2000, Blunt Instruments for large ensemble 2000, Ignition for solo percussion and orchestra 2002, Concerto for Orchestra 2003, Disembodied Instruments for large ensemble 2003, Double Violin Concerto for 2 violins and strings 2003, Flight from the Labyrinth for string quartet 2004, Gossamer for saxophone quartet 2004; Vocal music: Jason Field (ENO Opera Studio), Travellers, cantata The Lie; Opera, Friend of the People (Scottish Opera, 1999). *Honours:* 1st Prize, National Mozart Competition, 1987; 1st Place for Piano, BBC Young Musician of The Year, 1988; Winner, Huddersfield Contemporary Music Festival Composers Competition, 1988. *Current Management:* c/o Boosey and Hawkes, 1st floor, Aldwych House, 71–91 Aldwych, London, WC2B 4HN, England. *Website:* www.boosey.com/horne.

**HORNE, Marilyn;** American singer (mezzo-soprano); b. 16 Jan. 1934, Bradford, PA; d. of Bentz and Berneice Horne; m. 1st Henry Lewis (divorced);

one d. *Education:* Univ. of Southern California with William Vennard. *Career:* debut as Hata in The Bartered Bride, Guild Opera Co. 1954; performed with several German opera cos in Europe 1956; has since appeared at Covent Garden, London, San Francisco Opera, Chicago Lyric Opera, La Scala, Milan, Metropolitan Opera, New York; repertoire includes Eboli (Don Carlo), Marie (Wozzeck), Adalgisa (Norma), Jane Seymour (Anna Bolena), Amneris (Aida), Carmen, Rosina (Barbiere di Siviglia), Fides (Le Prophète), Mignon, Isabella (L'Italiana in Algeri), Romeo (I Capuletti ed i Montecchi), Tancredi (Tancredi), Orlando (Orlando Furioso), Malcolm (La Donna del Lago), Calbo (Maometto II); retd from singing 1999, with galas in New York and San Francisco 1998; f. Marilyn Horne Foundation to coach and encourage young singers. *Publication:* My Life (autobiog., with Jane Scovell), The Song Continues (autobiog., with Jane Scovell) 2005. *Honours:* numerous hon. doctorates, including Hon. DMus (Univ. of Pittsburgh) 2005; Nat. Medal of Arts 1992, Kennedy Center Honor 1995, Musical American Musician of the Year 1995, Classic FM Gramophone Award for Lifetime Achievement 2005. *Current Management:* Colombia Artists Management Inc., Wilford Division, 165 W 57th Street, New York, NY 10019, USA.

**HORNIK, Gottfried;** Baritone; b. 5 Aug. 1940, Vienna, Austria. *Education:* Studied in Vienna. *Career:* Sang at Klagenfurt as Papageno and as Silvio in Pagliacci; Graz Opera as Mozart's Figaro, Don Giovanni and Alberich; Deutsche Oper Berlin and San Francisco as Beckmesser in Die Meistersinger; Salzburg Easter Festival as Kurwenal in Tristan und Isolde, under Karajan; Sang Alberich and other Wagner roles at the Vienna Staatsoper; Sang at Leipzig Opera as the Villains in Les Contes d'Hoffmann, Cologne Opera in 1983 as Klingsor in Parsifal, Covent Garden in 1987 as Faninal in Der Rosenkavalier, Deutsche Oper Berlin in 1988 as Alberich in The Ring and sang Wozzeck at the Metropolitan in 1990; Sang Orestes in Elektra at Athens in 1992; Vienna Staatsoper 1995, in the premiere of Schnittke's Gesualdo; Emperor in Turandot, 2001. *Recordings:* Die Zauberflöte, Tosca, and Die Meistersinger conducted by Karajan; Der Wildschütz by Lortzing.

**HOROVITZ, Joseph,** MA, BMus, FRCM; British composer and conductor; *Professor of Composition, Royal College of Music;* b. 26 May 1926, Vienna. *Education:* New Coll., Oxford Univ. and Royal Coll. of Music (RCM), London and studied with Nadia Boulanger, Paris. *Career:* resident in UK 1938–; Music Dir Bristol Old Vic 1949–51; Conductor Festival Gardens Orchestra and open-air ballet, London 1951; Co-Conductor Ballets Russes, English season 1952; Assoc. Dir Intimate Opera Co. 1952–63; Asst Conductor Glyndebourne Opera 1956; Prof. of Composition, RCM 1961–; mem. Council, Composers' Guild 1970–, Council, Performing Right Soc. 1969–96; Pres. Int. Council of Composers and Lyricists of Int. Fed. of Socs of Authors and Composers 1981–89. *Compositions:* 16 ballets including Alice in Wonderland, Les Femmes d'Alger, Miss Carter Wore Pink, Concerto for Dancers; one-act operas: The Dumb Wife, Gentlemen's Island; concertos for violin, trumpet, jazz harpsichord, oboe, clarinet, bassoon, percussion, tuba; other orchestral works include Horizon Overture, Jubilee Serenade, Sinfonietta for Light Orchestra, Fantasia on a Theme of Couperin, Toy Symphony; brass band music includes a euphonium concerto, Sinfonietta, Ballet for Band, Concertino Classico, Theme and Co-operation, The Dong with a Luminous Nose; music for wind band includes a divertimento Bacchus on Blue Ridge, Windharp, Fête Galante, Commedia dell'Arte, Dance Suite and Ad Astra in commemoration of the Battle of Britain; choral music includes Samson, Captain Noah and his Floating Zoo (Ivor Novello Award for Best British Music for Children 1976), Summer Sunday, Endymion, Sing Unto the Lord a New Song, 3 choral songs from As You Like It; vocal music includes Lady Macbeth (mezzo-soprano and piano) and works for the King's Singers (e.g. Romance); chamber music includes 5 string quartets, oboe sonatina, oboe quartet and clarinet sonatina; contribs to Hoffnung Concerts: Metamorphoses on a Bed-Time Theme and Horrortorio for chorus, orchestra and soloists; numerous scores for theatre productions, films and TV series (Ivor Novello Award for Best TV Theme of 1978 for the series Lillie); productions of Son et Lumière include St Paul's Cathedral, Canterbury Cathedral, Brighton Pavilion, English Harbour Antigua, Bodiam Castle. *Honours:* Commonwealth Medal Composition 1959, Leverhulme Music Research Award 1961, Gold Order of Merit of Vienna 1996, Nino Rota Prize (Italy) 2002. *Address:* Royal College of Music, Prince Consort Road, London, SW7 2BS, England.

**HORSLEY, Colin;** Pianist and Professor; b. 23 April 1920, Wanganui, New Zealand. *Education:* Royal College of Music. *Career:* Debut: At Invitation of Sir John Barbirolli at Hallé Concerts, Manchester, 1943; Soloist with all leading orchestras of Great Britain, the Royal Philharmonic Society, 1953, 1959, Promenade Concerts; Toured Belgium, Netherlands, Spain, France, Scandinavia, Malta, Sri Lanka, Malaysia, Australia and New Zealand; Festival appearances include Aix-en-Provence, International Contemporary Music Festival, Palermo, British Music Festivals in Belgium, Netherlands and Finland; Broadcasts frequently. *Recordings:* EMI Meridian; Symposium Records; CDs of John Ireland Piano Concerto and Mozart Quintet for Piano and Wind. *Honours:* O.B.E., 1963; FRCM, 1973; Hon RAM. *Address:* Belmont, Dreemskerry, Maughold, Isle of Man.

**HORTON, Peter Bernard,** MA, DPhil, DipLib; British music librarian and musicologist; *Reference Librarian, Royal College of Music;* b. 19 June 1953, Ashford, England; m. Elaine Wood; two s. one d. *Education:* Sir Roger Manwood's Grammar School, Sandwich, Magdalen Coll., Oxford, Univ. Coll., London. *Career:* Asst Reference Librarian, Royal Coll. of Music 1984–95; Reference Librarian and Research Co-ordinator, Royal Coll. of Music 1995–;

mem. Royal Musical Asscn, Hymn Soc., Church Music Soc. *Publications:* edns: Samuel Sebastian Wesley: Anthems 1 Musica Britannica 57 1990, Anthems 2 Musica Britannica 63 1992; books: Samuel Sebastian Wesley: A Life 2004. *Honours:* Hon. RCM . *Address:* Royal College of Music, Prince Consort Road, London, SW7 2BS (office); 13 Spencer Gardens, London, SE9 6LX, England (home). *Telephone:* (20) 7591-4324 (office); (20) 8850-3791 (home). *Fax:* (20) 7589-7740 (office). *E-mail:* phorton@rcm.ac.uk (office); PBHSpencerGdns@aol.com (home).

**HORVAT, Milan;** Conductor; b. 28 July 1919, Pakrac, Yugoslavia. *Education:* Studied at the Zagreb Music Academy, 1939–46. *Career:* Began as pianist and choral conductor; Conductor of the Zagreb Philharmonic, 1946–53 and 1958–59; Chief Conductor of the Radio Telefis Eireann Symphony, 1953–58; Principal Conductor of the Zagreb Opera, 1958–65 with many premieres of Yugoslav music; Guest Conductor with many major orchestras in Europe and the USA; Musical Director of the Dubrovnik Festival, 1965; Principal Conductor of the Austrian Radio Symphony, 1969–75; Professor of Conducting at the Graz Academy, 1975; Conductor of the Zagreb Symphony Orchestra, 1975–. *Recordings:* Haydn Harpsichord Concertos, with Robert Veryon-Lacroix; Mozart Violin and Piano Concertos, with Jean Fournier and Jörg Demus; Hindemith Mathis der Maler Symphony; Shostakovich Symphonies Nos 1 and 9, and 1st Piano Concerto with the Zagreb Philharmonic; Beethoven Violin Concerto, with Igor Ozim. *Address:* c/o Zagreb Philharmonic Orchestra, Trjanska 66, 4100 Zagreb, Croatia.

**HORVATH, László;** Clarinettist; b. 14 July 1945, Koszeg, Hungary; Divorced, 1 s., 1 d. *Education:* Music Gymnasium, Gyor, 1960–64; Studied with Professor György Balassa, 1964–69, MMus with distinction, 1969, Liszt Ference Academy of Music, Budapest; Bursary student, Conservatoire de Musique, Paris, 1969–70; Studied with Professor Ulysse Delecluse. *Career:* Debut: Competition in Budapest in 1965; Clarinettist, 1965–68, Soloist and Leading Clarinettist, 1968–, Hungarian State Symphony Orchestra, Budapest; Professor at Conservatory of Music Debrecen, 1974–79, and at Béla Bartók Conservatory of Music, Budapest, 1980–; Toured as soloist, Buffet-Crampon Company, Japan, 1981, 1986; Many solo recitals world-wide and appearances as clarinet duo with Klara Kormendi, and chamber music with Philharmonic Wind Quintet in Europe, USA, Canada, Australia and Japan, 1983–; Recitals at Claude Champagne Hall, Montreal, 1991 and 1993; Radio broadcasts in Budapest, Paris, London and Tokyo and television appearances in Hungary; Masterclasses at Montreal, 1991, 1993 and Jury Member for International Competition for Musical Performers, Geneva, 1990. *Recordings:* Works by Leo Weiner, 1970, Attila Bozay, 1976, 1979, Carl and Johann Stamitz, 1979, Johann Molter, 1979, 1991, Mozart, 1981; 20th Century Clarinet Music, 1991; Clarinetto all'Ungherese, 1992. *Current Management:* Interkoncert, Vorosmarty ter 1m, 1368 Budapest, Hungary. *Address:* 6 Jászai Mari Tér V-44, 1137 Budapest, Hungary.

**HORWOOD, Michael Stephen;** American/Canadian composer; b. 24 May 1947, Buffalo, New York, USA; m. Celia M. Roberts 1974, 2 s. *Education:* BA, Music, 1969, MA, Composition, 1971, State University of New York, Buffalo. *Career:* Debut: Performance of his works at Baird Hall, SUNY, Buffalo in 1966; Professor of Music and Humanities at Humber College of Applied Arts and Technology, Ontario, Canada, 1972–2003; Assoc. Composer Canadian Music Centre 1979; Featured Composer, Saskatoon Symphony, Saskatchewan, Canada, 1991–92; Featured Composer, Composers and Orchestras – What's the Score? conference, Kitchener, Ontario, 1995; Retrospective concerts of his works: Toronto, Ontario, 1982, 1990; Adjudicator: SOCAN Young Composers Competition, 1987, Alliance for Canadian New Music Projects Awards, 1989, Ontario Arts Council Music Commissioning Program, 1993; Contemporary Canadian Music Workshop for Emerging Composers Competition, 1997; mem. Canadian League of Composer 1979; Performing Arts affiliation: SOCAN (Canada), BMI (USA). *Compositions include:* Durations for 1–4 Keyboards, 1965; Piece Percussionique No. 1 for 6 percussionists and piano, 1965, revised 1979; Women Of Trachis, incidental music for chamber orchestra, 1966; Piece Percussionique No. 3 for 3 percussionists, 1966; Piece Percussionique No. 4 for 4 percussionists, 1967, revised 1981; Concerto for double bass and string orchestra, 1967, revised, 2002; Double Quintet for 2 wind quintets, 1968; Asteroids for brass quartet, 1969; 8 Microduets, 1969–83; Piece Percussionique No. 5 for 2 percussionists and Tape, 1970; Sextet for chamber ensemble, 1971; Little Bow Piece for percussion octet, 1972; 5, 3, 4 for jazz orchestra and percussion ensemble, 1973; Facets for augmented chamber group, 1974; Talos IV for solo accordion, 1975; Interphase for chamber sextet, 1975; Andromeda for wind ensemble, 1976, revised 1980; Bipolarity for accordion and string trio, 1979; Birds for piccolo, piano and optional visual program, 1979; Io for double bass and violin, 1979; Splinters for chamber sextet, 1981; Residue for tuba and vibraphone, 1981; Three Cadenzas for guitar and harpsichord, 1981; Exit To Your Left for wind quintet, 1982; String Quartet No. 1, 1982; Sonata for cello and piano, 1983; Brass-Fast for brass quintet, 1984; Symphony No. 1, 1984; Three Landscapes for solo piano, 1984; Suite for accordion and percussion, 1985; Amusement Park Suite, for orchestra, 1986; Nervous Disorder, chamber trio, 1988; Broken Chords for solo piano, 1990; National Park Suite for orchestra, 1991; Psalm 121 for SSA choir, 1991; Symphony No. 2, Visions of a Wounded Earth, for chorus and orchestra, 1995; Do You Live For Weekends? for chamber orchestra, 1996; Symphony No. 3, Andromeda, for tenor saxophone and orchestra, 1996; Intravariations for piano and orchestra, 1997; Quartzite Dialogues for narrator and wind quintet, 1999; T + I = Ewigkeit, for solo piano,

2000; Three Interludes for orchestra, 2000. *Recordings:* Overture for piano player and 2 assistants; Piece Percussionique No. 5, 1982; Birds, 1982; Dynamite, 1983; Six Pieces for piano; Broken Chords, 1998; Tantrum IV, 2000; Fugue for Sam, 2000; Motility, 2000; Brass Fast, 2001; Asteroids, 2001; Birds, 2001; Horizontal Tango, 2002. *Publications:* Birds, 1982; Music as History, The Representation of the Individual in Western Music (co-author), 1996; That Pioneering Spirit (co-ed.), 1998. *Honours:* Three times recipient Composer Residency Program, SOCAN Foundation, 1997, 1998, 1999. *Address:* POB 69, Cowley, Alberta, T0K 0P0, Canada (home). *E-mail:* Michael@HorwoodComposer.com (home). *Website:* www.HorwoodComposer.com (home).

**HORYSA, Inghild;** Singer (Mezzo-soprano); b. 2 Jan. 1944, Bielitz, Germany. *Education:* Studied with Helena Braun in Munich. *Career:* Debut: Munich Staatsoper in 1966 in Hansel and Gretel; Munich in 1969 in the premiere of The Play of Love and Death by Cikker; Sang at Nuremberg, the Vienna Volksoper, Düsseldorf, Frankfurt, Mannheim, Hamburg and Stuttgart; Other roles include Dorabella, Amneris, Eboli, Venus, Brangaene, Marina in Boris Godunov, Orsini in Lucrezia Borgia, Fricka in Walküre, Clytemnestra in Elektra, Baba the Turk in The Rake's Progress and Octavian; Frequent concert appearances. *Address:* c/o Nuremberg Opera House, Nuremberg, Germany.

**HOSE, Anthony (Paul);** Musician and Conductor; b. 24 May 1944, London, England; m. Moira Griffiths, 8 July 1977, 2 d. *Education:* Junior Exhibitioner, 1955–62, Student, 1962–66, Royal College of Music, London; ARCM. *Career:* Glyndebourne Festival, 1966–68; Bremen Opera, Federal Republic of Germany, 1968–69; Welsh National Opera, 1969–83; Music Director, Buxton Festival, 1979–87; Artistic Director, Welsh Chamber Orchestra, 1986–; Artistic Director, Beaumaris Festival, 1986–; Realisation of Cavalli's Giasone; Artistic Director, Buxton Festival, 1988–91; Professor, Royal College of Music, 1991–; Professor, Royal Academy of Music, 1992–98; Artistic Director, Rhyl Easter Festival, 1994–95; Artistic Director, Llandudno October Festival, 1994–2000; Artistic Director, Mount Dora Spring Festival, Florida, 1998–; Orchestra Conductor, Stetson University, Florida, 2000–. *Publications:* English translation: Grétry: Le Huron; Elektra (Strauss); Ariodante (Handel); Don Quixote (Conti). *Current Management:* Michael Brewer, 8 Edward Court, 317 Hagley Road, Birmingham B16 9LQ, England. *Address:* 6 Lôn-y-Celyn, Cardiff CF14 7BW, Wales. *Telephone:* (1386) 8228963. *Fax:* (1386) 8228948. *E-mail:* ahose@stetson.edu.

**HOSEK, Jiri;** Czech violoncellist; b. 20 Aug. 1955, Prague; m. Marie Kaplanova 1977; two d. *Education:* Prague Conservatory, Academy of Music, Prague, Conservatory National, Paris, and courses at Nice and Szombately. *Career:* debut in Tchaikovsky's Rococco Variations, 1974; Tours to Russia, Germany, France, Italy and Poland; Many television and radio appearances including Anton Kraft Concertos. *Recordings:* Elgar Concerto, 1985; Anton Kraft Concertos; Radio recordings of Vivaldi Concerto, D Popper Konzertstücke, Dvořák's Rondo, Tchaikovsky's Rococco Variations, Prokofiev Symphony Concerto and Elgar Concerto. *Address:* Sudomerska 29, 13000 Prague 3, Czech Republic.

**HOSIER, John;** College Principal; b. 18 Nov. 1928, England. *Education:* MA, St John's College, Cambridge, 1954. *Career:* Lecturer in Ankara, Turkey, 1951–53; Music Producer, BBC Radio for Schools, 1953–59 then seconded to ABC, Sydney to advise on educational music programmes, 1959–60; Music Producer and subsequently Senior and Executive Producer for BBC television, pioneering the first regular music broadcasts to schools, 1960–73; ILEA Staff Inspector for Music, Director of Centre for Young Musicians, 1973–76; Principal at Guildhall School of Music and Drama, 1978–88; Director, Hong Kong Academy for Performing Arts, 1989–93; mem, Founder Member, Vice Chairman, United Kingdom Council for Music Education and Training, 1975–81; Gulbenkian Enquiry into Training Musicians, 1978; Trustee, Hirnichsen Foundation, 1981–88; Music Panel, British Council, 1984–88; GLAA, 1984–86; Vice Chairman, Kent Opera, 1985–88; Council of Management, Royal Philharmonic Society, 1982–89; Governing Body, Chetham's School; Governing Body, NYO FRSA, 1976; Hong Kong Council for the Performing Arts; General Committee, Hong Kong Philharmonic Orchestra. *Compositions:* Music for Cambridge revivals of Parnassus, 1949 and Humourous Lovers, 1951; Something's Burning, Mermaid, 1974; Many radio and television productions. *Publications:* The Orchestra, 1961, revised edition, 1977; Various books, songs and arrangements for children. *Contributions:* Professional journals. *Honours:* FGSM, 1978; Honorary RAM, 1980; FRCM, 1989; C.B.E., 1984; FRNCM, 1985; Honorary D.Mus, The City University, 1986; Honorary FTCL, 1986. *Address:* c/o Chetham's School of Music, Long Millgate, Manchester, M3 1 SB, England.

**HOSKINS, Donald,** BMus, MA, PhD; British pianist and conductor; *Artistic Director and Conductor, Aminta Chamber Orchestra (of London)*; b. 9 June 1932, Abertillery, Wales; m. Dinah Patricia Stanton 1972. *Education:* Abertillery Grammar School, Univ. of Wales, Cardiff. *Career:* Nat. Service 1954–56; directed choral groups, gave lectures and piano recitals, performed on television; teacher, Tudor Grange Grammar School, Solihull 1956–60; presented piano recitals; adjudicated at school festivals; founded local arts orchestra; performed as soloist with the Birmingham Philharmonic Orchestra 1956–60; guest conductor, Birmingham Philharmonic Orchestra on a visit to Wales 1962; Dir of Music, Hayes Grammar School, Middlesex 1960–64; founded and conducted local chamber orchestras and ensembles; solo recital,

Paris; Lecturer, Eastbourne Coll. of Education, East Sussex 1964–67; soloist Hillingdon Festival 1964; Sr Lecturer, Dept of Education, Barking Regional Coll. of Technology 1967; song recital accompanist, Purcell Room, South Bank 1972; Head of NE London Polytechnic Music Centre 1978; established annual two-day Univ. of East London concert band festival 1980; guest conductor London Mozart Players 1983; piano recital, Athens 1984; founder Artistic Dir Conductor Aminta Chamber Orchestra (of London) 1985; soloist with combined Desford Dowty, Fodens and Coventry brass bands 1989; soloist at inaugural concert, Zweibrucken, Germany 1994; presented concert band performances, Witten, Germany 1995, Univ. of Kaiserslautern 1997, Royal Star and Garter Home, Richmond 1998–2002; Visiting Prof., Univ. of Provo, Salt Lake City 1994, Music Conservatorium, Univ. of Cincinnati, USA 1994; guest conductor, Royal Philharmonic Concert Orchestra 1995, 1996, BBC Concert Orchestra 1997, 1998, London Philharmonic Choir 1999; conducted concerts at the QEH, London 2000, 2002; guest conductor Cantus Firmus Chamber Orchestra, Moscow 2004; Pres., Redbridge Music Soc.; consultant and Dir of Concerts, Univ. of E London 1996; presented the 26th annual concert band performance at Univ. of E London, the 21st annual concert of the Aminta Chamber Orchestra in Church of St Martin-in-the-Fields, London 2005; children's concerts and open-air symphony concerts; guest conductor, 'Cantus Firmus' Chamber Orchestra, Bulgarian Cultural Centre, Moscow 2004. *Honours:* Hon. DMus (Univ. of E London) 2003. *Address:* 'Aminta', 12 Hurst Park, Midhurst, West Sussex GU29 0BP, England (home). *E-mail:* donald@donaldhoskins.wanadoo.co.uk (home).

**HOSOKAWA, Toshio;** Composer and Pianist; b. 23 Oct. 1955, Hiroshima, Japan. *Education:* Berlin with Isang Yun and in Frieburg with Klaus Huber and Brian Ferneyhough. *Career:* Composer in residence at festivals in Geneva, London, Darmstadt, Seattle and Warsaw. *Compositions:* Manifestation for violin and piano, 1981; In Tal der Zeit for string quartet and piano, 1986; Ferne Landschaft I for orchestra, 1987; Flute concerto, 1988; Ave Maria, 1991; Hiroshima Requiem for voices and orchestra, 1988–92; Fragmente for wind quintet, 1989; Landscape for string quartet, 1992; Landscape II for harp and string quartet, 1993; Landscape III for orchestra, 1993; Super flumina Babylonis for soloists and orchestra, 1995; String Trio, 1996; Cello Concerto, 1997; Seascapes-Night for chorus and ensemble, 1997; Voyage I–III for ensemble, 1997; Cloudscapes-Moon Night for sho and accordion, 1998; Memory of the Sea, Hiroshima Symphony, 1998; Seascapes-Oita for orchestra, 1998; Piano Concerto 'Ans Meer', 1999; Silent Flowers for string quartet, 1999; Voiceless Voice in Hiroshima for chorus and orchestra, 2000. *Honours:* Berlin Philharmonic Centenary Prize, 1982. *Address:* c/o Documentation Centre for Modern Japanese music, 8-14 Azabudai I-chome, Minato-ku, Tokyo 106, Japan.

**HOSSFELD, Christiane;** Singer (Soprano); b. 2 March 1961, Schwerin, Germany. *Education:* Studied at the Hanns-Eisler Musikhochschule, Berlin, 1977–83. *Career:* Sang at Halberstadt from 1983, Dresden Staatsoper from 1986, notably as Zerbinetta, Gilda, Nannetta (Falstaff), Gretel, and Olympia in Les contes d'Hoffmann; Premiere of Meyer's Der goldene Topf, 1989, and Zemlinsky's Der Zwerg, 1993; Guest engagements at the Berlin Staatsoper and elsewhere; Bayreuth Festival, 1989–95, in Parsifal and Tannhäuser; Sang Zerlina and Papagena at Dresden, 2000; Many radio and television engagements. *Recordings include:* Die Lockende Flamme by Künneke. *Address:* Staatsoper Dresden, Theaterplatz 2, 01067 Dresden, Germany.

**HOTEEV, Andrei;** Russian pianist; b. 2 Dec. 1946, St Petersburg. *Education:* St Petersburg Conservatoire, Moscow Conservatoire with Lev Naumov. *Career:* debut, Moscow 1983, Rotterdam 1990; recitals include Shostakovich in Concertgebouw, Amsterdam 1990, Prokofiev in Musikhalle, Hamburg 1991, Hommage a Schnittke, Hamburg 1992, manuscript version of Mussorgsky's Pictures at an exhibition, first British performance in Purcell Room, London 1993, the original versions of Tchaikovsky's four piano concertos, Moscow 1996, numerous television broadcasts. *Recordings:* Tchaikovsky Piano Concerto No. 3; All the Works of Tchaikovsky for Piano and Orchestra; Mussorgsky Pictures at an Exhibition–manuscript version; Boris Godunov Suite. *Publications:* contrib. to Fono Forum 1998, Klassik Heute 1998, Frankfurter Allgemein 1999, Fanfare 1999.

**HOU, Runyu;** Chinese orchestral conductor; *Principal Conductor, Shanghai Symphony Orchestra*; b. 6 Jan. 1945, Kunming; s. of Hou Zhu and Zhu Bangying; m. Su Jia 1971; one s. one d. *Education:* Music Middle School of Shanghai Conservatory, Shanghai Conservatory (conducting). *Career:* studied at Musikhochschule, Cologne, FRG and Mozarteum, Salzburg, Austria 1981–85; started playing piano aged 7; debut, Kunming 1954; Prin. Conductor Shanghai Symphony Orchestra 1990–; debut Carnegie Hall, New York 1990. *Honours:* Hon. mem. Richard Wagner Verband, Cologne. *Address:* 105 Hunan Road, Shanghai (office); RD. 1601 No. 12 Lane 125, Cao Xi Road, Shanghai, People's Republic of China; Gerhardus-von-Wassenburgstr. 8, 41468 Neuss, Germany (home). *Telephone:* (21) 64690942; (2131) 5234747 (home). *E-mail:* rhou@gmx.net (home).

**HOUGH, Stephen Andrew Gill,** MMus, FRNCM; British pianist; b. 22 Nov. 1961, Heswall, Cheshire. *Education:* Chetham's School of Music, Royal Northern Coll. of Music (RNCM) and Juilliard School, New York. *Career:* regular guest performer with London Symphony, New York Philharmonic, Cleveland, Philadelphia, Philharmonia, Royal Philharmonic and London Philharmonic Orchestras; Visiting Prof. RAM; Int. Chair of Piano, RNCM; regular appearances with other orchestras in USA, Europe, Australia, Far

East and at int. music festivals; MacArthur Foundation Fellowship 2001. *Recordings include:* complete Beethoven violin sonatas (with Robert Mann), Hummel piano concertos, recitals of Liszt and Schumann, Brahms concerto Nos 1 and 2, The Piano Album Vols I, II, Britten Music for One and Two Pianos, Scharwenka and Sauer concertos, Grieg, Liszt, Rubinstein cello sonatas (with Steven Isserlis), Brahms violin sonatas (with Robert Mann), York Bowen piano music, Franck piano music, Mompou piano music, Liebermann piano concertos, Mendelssohn piano and orchestral works, Schubert sonatas and New York Variations, Brahms Clarinet Trio, The New Piano Album, Liszt Sonata, Mozart Piano and Wind Quintet, Brahms F minor Sonata, Saint-Saëns Complete Music for Piano and Orchestra, English Piano Album, Hummel Piano Sonatas, Chopin Ballades and Scherzos, Rachmaninov and Franck Cello Sonatas (with Steven Isserlis), Rachmaninov piano concertos (with Dallas Symphony and A. Litton) (Classical BRIT Critics' Award 2005, Classic FM Gramophone Editor's Choice Award 2005) 2004, Brahms, Dvořák and Suk 2005. *Compositions:* Transcriptions, Suite R-B and Other Enigmas, Piano Album. *Honours:* Hon. mem. RAM; Dayas Gold Medal, RNCM, Terence Judd Award 1982, Naumburg Int. Piano Competition 1983, Gramophone Record of the Year 1996, 2002. *Current Management:* Harrison Parrott Ltd, 12 Penzance Place, London, W11 4PA, England. *Telephone:* (20) 7229-9166. *Fax:* (20) 7221-5042. *E-mail:* info-harrisonparrott.co.uk. *Website:* www.harrisonparrott.co.uk; www.stephenhough.com.

**HOVLAND, Egil;** Composer and Organist; b. 18 Oct. 1924, Mysen, Norway. *Education:* Studied at Oslo Conservatory, 1946–49, with Holmboe in Copenhagen, Copland at Tanglewood and Dallapiccola in Florence. *Career:* Music critic and organist in Fredrikstad. *Compositions:* Church opera the Well, 1982; Ballets Dona Nobis Pacem, 1982; Den Heliga Dansen, 1982; Veni Creator Spiritus, 1984; Danses de la Mort, 1983; 3 Symphonies, 1953, 1955, 1970; Concertino for 3 trumpets and strings, 1955; Music for 10 instruments, 1957; Suite for flute and strings, 1959; Missa Vigilate, 1967; Mass to the Risen Christ, 1968; All Saints' Mass, 1970; The Most Beautiful Rose, after Hans Christian Andersen, 1972; Trombone Concerto, 1972; Missa Verbi, 1973; Violin Concerto, 1974; Piano Concerto, 1977; Tombeau de Bach for Orchestra, 1978; Pilgrim's Mass, 1982; Concerto for piccolo and strings, 1986; Chamber music including Piano Trio, 1965, 2 Wind Quintets, 1965, 1980, and String Quartet, 1981; Opera Captive and Free, 1993; Oboe Concerto, 1996; Viola Concerto, 1997. *Recordings include:* Works for Choir; Concertos: Trombone, Violin and Piccolo; Chamber works; (all for Norwegian Aurora). *Honours:* Knight of the Royal Order of St Olav, 1983. *Address:* c/o Labråten 14 C, 1614 Fredrikstad, Norway.

**HOWARD, Ann;** British singer (mezzo-soprano); b. 22 July 1936, Norwood, London; d. of William A. Swadling and Gladys W. Swadling; m. Keith Giles 1954; one d. *Education:* with Topliss Green and Rodolfa Lhombino, London and Dominic Modesti, Paris. *Career:* repertoire includes Carmen, Dalila (Samson et Dalila), Dulcinée (Don Quichotte), Hélène (La Belle Hélène), Eboli (Don Carlo), Azucena (Il Trovatore), Amneris (Aida), Isabella (L' Italiana in Algeri), Proserpina (Orfeo), Ortrud (Lohengrin), Brangaene (Tristan und Isolde), Fricka (Das Rheingold and Die Walküre), Baba the Turk (The Rake's Progress), Katisha (The Mikado), Czipra (Gipsy Baron), Lilli Vanessi (Kiss Me Kate), Clytemnestra (Electra), La Grande Duchesse de Gerolstein, Stepmother (Into The Woods), Prince Orlofsky (Die Fledermaus), Old Lady (Candide), Auntie (Peter Grimes), Hostess (Boris Godunov), Jezi Baba (Rusalka), Marcellina (Marriage of Figaro), Emma Jones (Street Scene), performed in world premières of Mines of Sulphur (Bennett) 1970, Rebecca (Josephs) 1982, The Tempest (Eaton, USA) 1985, The Plumber's Gift (Blake) 1989, The Doctor of Myddfai (Maxwell Davies) 1996 and in UK première of Le Grand Macabre 1981; series of Gilbert and Sullivan operas Performing Arts Centre, NY State Univ. 1993–98; has appeared in UK, France, Canada, USA, Mexico, Chile, Portugal, Germany, Austria and Italy and on BBC radio and TV; teaches privately. *Honours:* The Worshipful Co. of Musicians Sir Charles Santley Memorial Award 2002.

**HOWARD, Brian (Robert);** Composer and Conductor; b. 3 Jan. 1951, Sydney, New South Wales, Australia. *Education:* BMus (Hons), University of Sydney, 1972; D.Mus, University of Melbourne, 1985; Composition studies with Peter Sculthorpe, Bernard Rands, Richard Meale and Maxwell Davies; Conducting with Neville Marriner and Michael Gielen, 1974–76. *Career:* Resident, Royal Danish Ballet 1980–81, State Opera of South Australia, 1989; Musical Director, Western Australia Ballet, 1983–85; Dean, WA Conservatory, 1992–95; Commissions from Festivals of Sydney and Perth, and from Opera Factory Zürich (1991), among others. *Compositions include:* A Fringe of Leaves, for chorus and orchestra, 1982; Metamorphosis, opera for 6 voices and chamber ensemble, 1983; The Rainbow Serpent, for ensemble, 1984; Fly Away Peter, for wind quintet, 1984; Sun and Steel, for string orchestra, 1986; The Celestial Mirror, for orchestra, 1987; Whitsunday, opera for 10 voices and chamber ensemble, 1988; Wildbird Dreaming for orchestra, 1988; The Enchanted Rainforest, musical, 1989; Masquerade, ballet, 1994; Wide Sargasso Sea, opera, 1996. *Recordings include:* Sun and Steel, Chandos. *Address:* c/o APRA, 1A Eden Street, Crows Nest, NSW 2065, Australia.

**HOWARD, Jason;** singer (baritone); b. 1960, Merthyr Tydfil, Wales. *Education:* Trinity College of Music, Royal College of Music with Norman Bailey. *Career:* gained early experience as Alfio, Blow's Adonis, Zurga, Don Giovanni and Sharpless; With Scottish Opera has sung Guglielmo, Don Giovanni, Germont and Figaro; Further engagements as Ned Keene for English National Opera, Billy Budd and Ezio in Attila for Opera North, and

Ramiro in L'Heure Espagnole for Scottish Opera; Concert appearances in Carmina Burana, L'Enfance du Christ, Messiah, Fauré's Requiem, The Kingdom, Elijah and Haydn's Lord Nelson Mass; Other engagements include Rossini's Figaro and Eugene Onegin for Seattle Opera, 1992–93; Television showings in Scotland and Wales; Sang Marcello at Covent Garden, 1996; Germont at Cincinnati, 1998; Sang Puccini's Sharpless for Scottish Opera, 2000. *Recordings include:* Student Prince; Song of Norway; A Little Night Music. *Honours:* Ricordi Prize, Rowland Jones Award and Singing Faculty Award, TCM. *Current Management:* IMG Artists, Lovell House, 616 Chiswick High Road, London, W4 5RX, England. *Telephone:* (20) 8233-5800. *Fax:* (20) 8233-5801. *E-mail:* artistseurope@imgworld.com. *Website:* www.imgartists .com.

**HOWARD, Jeffrey John;** Vocal Coach, Organist, Pianist, Conductor and Arranger; b. 19 March 1969, Cardiff, Wales; Rachael Jones 1992; two s. *Education:* piano studies, Welsh College of Music and Drama, 1983; BMus, Cardiff University, 1987; Advanced Organ studies, Royal Academy of Music, London, 1990. *Career:* accompanist to many male voice and mixed choirs; solo organist and pianist in recital and concert; appeared as accompanist on several recordings and television and radio work; foreign tours; Voice Coach at Welsh College of Music and Drama; has worked extensively with the Swansea Bach Choir, BBC Welsh Chorus, South Glamorgan Youth Choir and early music performances including the Orchestra of the Age of Enlightenment; performer on the Live Music Now scheme; Guest Artist-in-Residence at First United Methodist Church, Lubbock, Texas, USA, 1996–97; Visiting Professor of Organ, Texas Tech University, 1996–97; Repetiteur at WNO, 1999–; arranger for BBC's Songs of Praise; Repetiteur work on opera and music theatre; Royal Albert Hall solo debut in Shostakovich's 2nd Piano concerto, 2002. *Recordings:* several Christian recordings with Cambrensis (South Wales Baptist Choir) including Hymns, 1995; recording as Organist with Cor Meibion de Cymru, 1995; Bryn Terfel, organist with male voice choir and orchestra of the WNO; arranger for solo vocal albums with Royal Philharmonic Orchestra, 2000 and Budapest Symphony Orchestra, 2002. *Publications:* Kevin Mayhew–Welsh Folk Song Arrangements for flute and harp. *Honours:* Glynne Jones Prize for Organ, 1990; Michael Head Accompaniment Prize, 1991; Prizewinner, San Antonio Organ Competition, 1997. *Address:* 9 Clos Alyn, Pontprennau, Cardiff, CF23 8LB, Wales.

**HOWARD, John (Stuart);** Composer, Lecturer, Writer and Conductor; b. 22 Dec. 1950, Glasgow, Scotland; m. Ellen Jane Howard, 15 April 1974, 1 s., 1 d. *Education:* Ilford County High School; Junior Exhibitioner, Royal College of Music, 1965–69; BA, 1st Class Honours, University of Durham, 1969–72; PhD in Composition awarded, 1979. *Career:* School teaching, various posts; Senior Lecturer and Principal Lecturer, Kingston Polytechnic/University, 1979–92; Associate Professor and Head of Music, Nanyang Technological University, Singapore, 1993–; Honorary Senior Research Fellow, Kingston University, 1993–95; mem, PRS; ISME. *Compositions:* Dunstable Cantus for Piano, 1974; The Two Regions for Brass Band, 1976; Bubbles for Ever? for Flute, Clarinet, Violin and Cello, 1981; Games/End Game for Chinese Orchestra, 1983; Sonata for Brass Quintet, 1983; Fantasia and Dance, for Chinese Orchestra, 1985. *Publications:* Learning to Compose, Cambridge, 1990; Performing and Responding, Cambridge, 1995. *Contributions:* Various; Schools Council Magazine; Pears Encyclopedia; Music File, four articles, 1991–93; IJME, Reviewer; Proceedings of British-Swedish Ethnomusicology Conference, 1991. *Address:* Division of Music, National Institute of Education, Nanyang Technological University, 469 Bukit Timah Road, Singapore 259756.

**HOWARD, Leslie (John);** Pianist and Composer; b. 29 April 1948, Melbourne, Australia. *Education:* AMusA, 1962; LMus, 1966; BA, 1969; MA, Monash University, 1973 Piano Studies with June McLean, Donald Britton and Michael Brimer (Australia), Guido Agosti (Italy) and Noretta Conci (London). *Career:* Debut: Melbourne 1967; Staff, Monash University, 1970–73; Guildhall School of Music and Drama, London, 1987–92; Concertos with various orchestras in Australia, England, Europe, America, South America, Asia; Regular broadcasts as Pianist, Chamber Musician and Musicologist for BBC, ABC, RAI, and various American networks; Telecasts in the Americas, Australia and Southeast Asia; Council, Royal Philharmonic Society; Trustee, Geoffrey Parsons and Erich Vietheer Memorial Trusts; President, Liszt Society; Grainger Society; Prokofiev Foundation. *Compositions:* Fruits of the Earth, ballet; Hreidar the Fool, opera; Prague Spring, opera; Sonatas for violin, clarinet, percussion, double bass horn, cello and piano; Piano Solo; Canzona for brass ensemble; Missa Sancti Petri, 1993; Songs; Motets; Trios, String Quartets. *Recordings:* Complete keyboard works of Grainger; Works by Franck, Rachmaninov, Glazunov, Rubinstein, Granados, Mozart, Beethoven, Tchaikovsky, Stravinsky;96 CDs of the works and transcriptions of Liszt. *Publications:* Edition of complete works of Liszt for cello and piano, 1992, and Piano Trio, 1993 and Violin and Piano 2003; A Liszt Catalogue, with Michael Short, 1993; Volumes of piano and Choral Music and Songs, 1999–. *Contributions:* Liszt Society Journal, on Liszt; Music and Musicians, on Grainger; Musical Opinion, on Liszt; Viking Opera Guide, on Liszt and Rachmaninov; Dubal's Hovowitz Symposium. *Honours:* Diploma d'Onore, Siena, 1972, Naples, 1976; Ferenc Liszt Medal of Honour, 1986; Liszt Grand Prix du Disque, Liszt Academy Budapest, 5 times; Ferenc Liszt Medal of Honour, Hungarian Republic, 1989; Member of the Order of Australia, 1999. *Current Management:* Michael Brownlee Walker, BW Associates. *Address:* 128 Norbury Crescent, Norbury, London SW16 4JZ, England.

**HOWARD, Patricia,** MA, PhD; British writer; b. 18 Oct. 1937, Birmingham; m. David Louis Howard 1960; two d. *Education:* Lady Margaret Hall, Oxford and Univ. of Surrey. *Career:* Lecturer and Tutor of Music, Open Univ. 1976–; many broadcasts both on network and for Open Univ.; mem. Royal Musical Asscn. *Publications:* Gluck and the Birth of Modern Opera 1963, The Operas of Benjamin Britten: An Introduction 1969, Haydn in London 1980, Mozart's Marriage of Figaro 1980, C W Gluck: Orfeo 1981, Haydn's String Quartets 1984, Beethoven's Eroica Symphony 1984, Benjamin Britten: The Turn of The Screw 1985, Christoph Willibald Gluck: A Guide to Research 1987, Music in Vienna, 1790–1800 1988, Beethoven's Fidelio 1988, Music and the Enlightenment 1992, Gluck: An eighteenth century portrait 1995, Gluck's Orpheus Operas 1997, From Composition to Performance: The String Family 1998, The Solo Voice: Evidence for a Historical Investigation 1998, In Defence of Modern Music and its Celebrated Performers, translation and critical edition of Vincenzo Manfredini, Difesa della musica moderna (1788) 2002, An introduction to gender studies: Mozart's operas and sonatas 2002, Beethoven's Eighth Symphony; reception studies 2002, The Turn of the Screw: analysis and interpretation 2002. *Contributions:* Musical Times, Music and Letters, The Consort, The Listener, The Gramophone, Opera, ENO and Friends, Acta musicologica, Eighteenth-Century Fiction, Il Saggiatore musicale, Notes, Cambridge Opera Journal, The Opera Journal, Programme books for Covent Garden Opera, Glyndebourne Opera and The Barbican Centre. *Honours:* Susette Taylor Travelling Fellowship 1971, Leverhulme Research Award 1976, British Acad. Research Award 1988. *Address:* Stepping Stones, Gomshall, Surrey, GU5 9NZ, England (home).

**HOWARD, Yvonne;** Singer (mezzo-soprano); b. 1950, Staffordshire, England. *Education:* Studied at the Royal Northern College of Music. *Career:* Operatic appearances as Mozart's Marcellina with Glyndebourne Touring Opera, Cenerentola for English Touring Opera and Suzuki for Birmingham Music Theatre; Sang Fricka and Waltraute in The Ring of the Nibelungen, City of Birmingham Touring Opera; Season 1990–91 sang Mercedes at Covent Garden, and Meg Page in Falstaff for ENO; Sang Amastris in Xerxes, Meg Page and Maddalena in Rigoletto for ENO in 1992; Glyndebourne 1994, as Mrs Sedley in Peter Grimes; Royal Opera 1998, as Marcellina; Sang Meg Page for Opera North and in Rinaldo at Garsington, 2000; Concert engagements include Mozart's Requiem under Menuhin at Gstaad, Messiah with the Tokyo Philharmonic, Vivaldi's Gloria with the English Chamber Orchestra, Messiah with the Hallé Orchestra and Liverpool Philharmonic, De Falla's Three Cornered Hat at Festival Hall and with Ulster Orchestra; Song recitals include Wigmore Hall debut in 1989. *Honours:* Curtis Gold Medal, RNCM.

**HOWARTH, Elgar,** ARAM, DMus, FRCM, FRNCM; British trumpeter, conductor and composer; b. 4 Nov. 1935, Cannock, Staffs.; s. of Oliver Howarth and Emma Wall; m. Mary Bridget Neary 1958; one s. two d. *Education:* Eccles Grammar School and Manchester Univ. –Royal Northern Coll. of Music (jt course). *Career:* orchestral player 1958–70; Chair. Royal Philharmonic Orchestra 1968–70; Prin. Guest Conductor Opera North 1985–88; freelance orchestral conductor 1970–; Musical Adviser Grimethorpe Colliery Brass Band 1972–; compositions: Trumpet Concerto 1968, Trombone Concerto 1962, Music for Spielberg 1984, Songs for BL for brass band; Fellow Welsh Coll. of Music and Drama. *Honours:* Hon. FRNCM 1999; Hon. Fellow Royal Coll. of Musim 2001, Univ. Coll. Salford; Hon. DUniv (Cen. England, York); Hon. DMus (Keele) 1996, (York) 2000; Hon. DLitt (Salford) 2003; Eddison Award 1977, Olivier Award for Outstanding Achievement in Opera 1997. *Address:* 27 Cromwell Avenue, London, N6 5HN, England.

**HOWARTH, Judith;** British singer (soprano); b. 11 Sept. 1962, Ipswich; m. 1986. *Education:* Royal Scottish Acad. of Music and Drama and studies with Patricia Macmahon. *Career:* recipient of special bursary to join Royal Opera House, Covent Garden as prin. soprano in 1985–86 season; maj. roles with Royal Opera include Musetta, Ännchen (Der Freischütz), Gilda, Adela, Marguerite de Valois (Les Huguenots), Liu, Norina, Marzelline and Morgana (Alcina) 1989–96; now freelance; numerous concert and recital engagements in UK, USA, Far East, Australia and NZ; debut at Salzburg Festival in Mozart's Der Schauspieldirektor 1991; has also appeared with Florida Grand Opera, Drottningholm Festival, Opera North and Glyndebourne Touring Opera; debut with Deutsche Staatsoper, Berlin in Cavalli's La Didone 1996. *Address:* c/o Askonas Holt, Lonsdale Chambers, 27 Chancery Lane, London, WC2A 1PF, England. *Telephone:* (20) 7379-7700. *Fax:* (20) 7242-1831.

**HOWELL, Gwynne Richard,** CBE, BSc, DipTP, MRTPI; British singer (bass); b. 13 June 1938, Gorseinon, Wales; m. Mary Edwina Morris 1968; two s. *Education:* Univ. of Wales, Univ. of Manchester, Manchester Royal Coll. of Music with Gwilym Jones, studied with Otakar Kraus. *Career:* principal bass at Sadler's Wells, singing roles including Monterone and the Commendatore; sang at Glyndebourne and Covent Garden in debut as First Nazarene in Salome, 1969–70; Metropolitan House debut in 1985 as Lodovico in Otello and Pogner in Die Meistersinger; sang Gurnemanz in a new production of Parsifal at London Coliseum in 1986; sang the Parson and the Badger in a new production of The Cunning Little Vixen in 1990 and sang the Fliedermonolog at the Reginald Goodall Memorial Concert in London, 1991; sang at London Coliseum in 1992 as King Philip in a new production of Don Carlos, Daland at Covent Garden and Mozart's Bartolo on tour with the company to Japan; sang Dikoy in Katya Kabanova at Covent Garden 1997, Seneca in Poppea for WNO, Arkel in Pelléas et Mélisande at Glyndebourne and the London Proms 1999; sang in Martinů's Greek Passion, Covent Garden 2000, premiere of Turnage's The Silver Tassie for ENO and the Commendatore at Glyndebourne 2000;

sings in Europe and USA and records for BBC and major recording cos. *Repertory includes:* Verdi and Mozart Requiems and Missa Solemnis; other roles include the King in Aida, Mephisto in Damnation of Faust, High Priest in Nabucco, Hobson in Peter Grimes and Sparafucile in Rigoletto. *Address:* 197 Fox Lane, London, N13 4BB, England (home).

**HOWELLS, Anne Elizabeth,** FRNCM; British singer (mezzo-soprano); b. 12 Jan. 1941, Southport, Lancs.; d. of Trevor Howells and Mona Howells; m. 1st Ryland Davies (q.v.) 1966 (divorced 1981); m. 2nd Stafford Dean 1981 (divorced 1998); one s. one d. *Education:* Sale County Grammar School, Royal Northern Coll. of Music. *Career:* three seasons in Chorus with Glyndebourne Festival Opera 1964–66, took leading role at short notice in L'Ormindo (Cavalli) 1967; subsequent roles include Dorabella in Così fan tutte, Cathleen in world premiere Rising of the Moon (Nicholas Maw), Composer in Ariadne, Diana in Calisto; with Royal Opera House, Covent Garden 1969–71, appearing as Lena in world premiere of Victory (Richard Rodney Bennett), Rosina in The Barber of Seville, Cherubino in The Marriage of Figaro; Guest Artist with Royal Opera House 1973–; has also appeared with Welsh Nat. Opera, Scottish Opera, ENO, Chicago Opera, Geneva Opera, Metropolitan Opera, New York, Lyons Opera, Marseilles Opera, Nantes Opera, Netherlands Opera and in Naples, San Francisco, Hamburg, Berlin, La Scala, Milan, in Belgium and at the Salzburg Festival 1976 and 1980 (Tales of Hoffmann and film version of Clemenza di Tito); Prof. RAM 1997–. *Address:* c/o IMG Artists, Media House, 3 Burlington Lane, London, W4 2TH, England. *Telephone:* (20) 8233-5800. *Fax:* (20) 8233-5801.

**HOWIE, Alan Crawford,** MMus, PhD; British academic; b. 6 Nov. 1942, Stornoway, Scotland; m.; three c. *Education:* Coatbridge High School, Scotland, Royal Scottish Acad. of Music and Drama (jr student), Univ. of Edinburgh, Acad. of Music, Vienna, Austria, Univ. of Manchester. *Career:* Lecturer in Music, Univ. of Manchester, especially on the 19th century and research in the music of Schubert and Bruckner; Assoc. Ed. Bruckner Journal 1997–; Ed. the Schubertian 2002–; mem. Royal Musical Asscn, Inc. Soc. of Musicians, Internationales Franz Schubert Institut, Internationale Bruckner Gesellschaft. *Publications:* Perspectives on Anton Bruckner (co-ed. with Paul Hawkshaw and Timothy Jackson) 2001, Anton Bruckner: A Documentary Biography (two vols) 2002; contrib. to Music and Letters, Music Quarterly; papers at int. 19th-century music confs early 1980s–. *Address:* 27 Dalmore Road, Sheffield, South Yorks., S7 2EP (home); Martin Harris Centre for Music and Drama, University of Manchester, Coupland Street, Manchester, M13 9PL, England (office). *Telephone:* (161) 2754991 (office); (114) 2551655 (home). *Fax:* (161) 2754994 (office). *E-mail:* acrhowie@blueyonder.co.uk (home); crawford.howie@man.ac.uk (office).

**HOWLETT, Neil (Baillie);** Singer (Baritone); b. 24 July 1934, Mitcham, Surrey, England; m. Elizabeth Robson, 2 d. *Education:* MA (Cantab); St Paul's Cathedral Choir School; King's College, Cambridge; Hochschule für Musik, Stuttgart. *Career:* Debut: In the world premiere of Britten's Curlew River at Aldeburgh in 1964; Major roles with Sadler's Wells, English Opera Group, Royal Opera House, Covent Garden, Hamburg, Bremen, Nantes, Bordeaux, Toulouse, Nice, and Marseille; Principal Baritone for English National Opera, London; Has sung most major baritone roles; Sang title roles in the premieres of Blake's Toussaint and Crosse's The Story of Vasco; Appearances at most major festivals; Sang Hector in King Priam with the Royal Opera at Athens in 1985 and Amfortas in Buenos Aires in 1986; Sang Scarpia in Tosca with English National Opera, 1987–90; Holland Festival in 1990 as Ruprecht in Prokofiev's The Fiery Angel; Faninal in Der Rosenkavalier at Catania, 1992; Wotan in Das Rheingold and Die Walküre at Leicester, 1998–99; Other roles include Golaud in Pelléas, King Fisher in The Midsummer Marriage and Wagner's Dutchman; Recitalist, teacher and regular broadcaster; Professor at Guildhall School of Music. *Honours:* Kathleen Ferrier Memorial Prize. *Current Management:* Ingpen & Williams Ltd, 7 St George's Court, 131 Putney Bridge Road, London, SW15 2PA, England. *Address:* c/o English National Opera, London Coliseum, St Martin's Lane, London, WC2N 4ES, England.

**HOYLAND, Vic,** DPhil; British composer; b. 11 Dec. 1945, Wombwell, Yorkshire, England. *Education:* University of Hull, York University with Robert Sherlaw Johnson and Bernard Rands. *Career:* Hayward Fellow in Music, University of Birmingham, 1980–83; Visiting Lecturer at York University, 1984 and Lecturer 1985–93, Senior Lecturer, 1993–98, Reader in Composition, 1998–, the Barber Institute for Fine Arts, University of Birmingham; Founder Member and Co-Director of the Northern Music Theatre; Compositions have been featured at the Aldeburgh, Bath, Holland and California Contemporary Music Festivals; Survey of works at the 1985 Musica Concert Series in London; Commissions from the Northern Music Theatre, the Essex Youth Orchestra, New MacNaghten Concerts, Musica, the Barber Institute, BBC Promenade series, BCMG, Southbank Summerscope, Huddersfield Festival, Almeida Festival, York and Cheltenham Festivals. *Compositions include:* Em for 24 voices, 1970; Jeux-Theme for mezzo and ensemble, 1972; Esem for double-bass and ensemble, 1975; Xingu, music theatre, 1979; Reel for double-reed instruments, 1980; Michelagniolo for male voices and large ensemble, 1980; Quartet Movement, 1982; Head And Two Tails, 3 pieces for voice(s) and ensemble, 1984; String Quartet, 1985; Seneca/Medea for voices and ensemble, 1985; In Transit for orchestra, 1987; Work-Out for trombone, 1987; Work-Out for marimba, 1988; Trio, 1990; The Other Side Of The Air for Rolf Hind, piano solo, 1991; In Memoriam P.P.P., 1992; Piano Quintet, 1992; Concerto for pianoforte ensemble, 1993; String Quartet

No. 3, Bagatelles, 1994; Vixen, large scale work for full orchestra, 1997; QIBTI, full orchestra, 2002; Phoenix, full orchestra, 2003. *Address:* c/o University of York Music Press Ltd, Department of Music, University of York, Heslington, York YO1 5DD, England.

**HOYLE, Ted;** Cellist; b. 17 Aug. 1942, Huntsville, Alabama, USA. *Education:* BMus, Eastman School of Music; MMus, Yale University; DMA, Manhattan School of Music, 1981; Studied with André Navarra, Ecole Normale de Musique, Paris, France. *Career:* Cellist, Kohon Quartet; Professor of Music, Kean University, New Jersey; Cellist, Performing Arts Trio, New Jersey; Co-Director, Hear America First, Manhattan concert series, 1978–81; mem, Violoncello Society; American String Teachers' Association. *Compositions:* Edited works by Bach, Schumann, Scriabin for Belwin Mills. *Recordings:* A number with the Kohon Quartet including: String quartets by Walter Piston, Peter Mennin, Charles Ives, William Schuman, Aaron Copland, Julia Smith, Roger Sessions and Penderecki; Quartet of Joseph Fennimore; Quintet of Robert Baksa; Trio Sonatas of J. S. Bach, G F Handel, G Telemann. *Address:* 340 West 28th Street 15D, New York, NY 10001, USA. *E-mail:* tedhoy@aol.com (home).

**HRUBA-FREIBERGER, Venceslava;** Singer (soprano); b. 28 Sept. 1945, Dublocive, Czechoslovakia. *Education:* studied in Prague. *Career:* debut, Prague National Theatre, 1969, in Wranitsky's Oberon; sang at Pilzen Opera, 1970–72, Leipzig Opera, 1972–88; roles have included Verdi's Gilda, Mozart's Constanze and Queen of Night, Lucia di Lammermoor, Janáček's Vixen, Violetta, and Glinka's Lyudmila; Guest appearances at the Aix Festival, 1982, Nice and Prague; Staatsoper Berlin from 1987; Concerts in Austria, Spain, England, Poland and Japan. *Recordings include:* Bach's The Choice of Hercules; C. P. Bach's Magnificat, Handel's L'Allegro ed il Pensieroso and Mozart's Apollo et Hyacinthus. *Address:* c/o Staatsoper Berlin, Unter den Linden 7, 1060 Berlin, Germany.

**HSU, John T.;** Professor of Music and Performer on Cello, Viola da gamba, and Baryton; b. 21 April 1931, Swatow, China; m. Martha Russell, 31 July 1968. *Education:* BMus 1953, MMus 1955, New England Conservatory of Music. *Career:* Teacher, 1955–; Fellow, Cornell Society for the Humanities, 1971–72; Instructor, 1955–58; Professorial Staff, 1958–76; Chairman, Department of Music, 1966–71; Artist-Faculty, Aston Magna Foundation, 1973–90; Old Dominion Professor of Music and Humanities, Cornell University, Ithaca, New York, 1976–; Barytonist, Haydn Baryton Trio, 1982–; Artist-in-Residence, University of California, Davis, 1983; Regents Lecturer in Music, University of California, Santa Cruz, 1985; Viola da gamba Recitalist, including radio broadcast, in North America and Europe; Director, Aston Magna Performance Practice Institute, 1986–90; Artistic Director, Aston Magna Foundation for Music and the Humanities, 1987–90; Music Director and Conductor, Apollo Ensemble, 1991–; John Hsu in a course in French Baroqua Viol Playing, presented by The Viola da gamba Society of America. *Recordings include:* Pièces de Viole, by Louis de Caix d'Hervelois and Antoine Forqueray, Belgium, 1966; 3 Gamba Sonatas, by J. S. Bach, Germany, 1971; First complete recording of the 5 suites for viola da gamba by Antoine Forqueray, 1972; Pièces de viole by Maria Marais, 1973–76; Pièces de viole, by Charles Dollé and Jacques Morel, 1978; 2 vols of Baryton Trios by Joseph Haydn, London, 1988–89; Apollo Ensemble and John Hsu, Conductor; 3 vols of Symphonies by Joseph Haydn, USA, 1993–99; Baryton Trios by Haydn, 1996; Apollo Ensemble and John Hsu, conductor, Symphonies by Joseph Haydn. *Publications:* Editor, The Instrumental Works, by Marin Marais (1656–1728), Vol. I, 1980, Vol. II, 1987, Vol. III, 1995, Vol. IV, 1998, Vol. V, 2000, Vol. VI, 2001, Vol. VII, 2002; A Handbook of French Baroque Viol Technique, 1981. *Contributions:* Early Music, 1978. *Honours:* Doctor of Music, New England Conservatory of Music, 1971; Doctor of Arts, Ramapo College of New Jersey, 1986; Chevalier de l'Ordre des Arts et des Lettres, France, 2000. *Address:* 402 Hanshaw Road, Ithaca, NY 14850, USA.

**HSU, Ya-Ming,** DipMus, MA, DMus; Taiwanese composer; b. 5 Feb. 1963; m. Wen-Chi Lin 1994; one s. one d. *Education:* National Taipei Teachers' College, Tunghi University, Boston University, USA. *Career:* debut aged 17, received First Prize in Taiwan Composition Competition, Taiwan Educational Ministry; Lecturer, Chinese Culture University; Head of Chinese Music Talent Development Association; mem, ASCAP; Asian Composer League; National Association of Composers, USA. *Compositions:* Two Romantic Suites, Arts Trio commission, 1994; The Joyful News from Heaven, 1995; Bright be the Place of Thy Soul, 1997; Wind-Color, China Found Music Ensemble commission, 1998; A Tone Poem for Baritone, Chorus and String Quartet, Chinese Choral Society of Rochester commission, 1998; Four Choral Music, 1998; Snowing in June, 1999; Taiwan Mass, Taipei Philharmonic Chorus commission, 2000; Elegy, Arts Trio Taipei commission, 2000; Elegy for cello and piano, 2003; Twelve preludes for piano, 2003. *Recordings:* Snowing in June, Taipei Philharmonic Chamber Choir, 1999. *Publications:* Four Choral Music, 1998. *Honours:* Several Prizes, Taiwan Educational Ministry, Provincial Music Association, Chung Hwa Rotary Educational Association, National Taipei Teachers' College, Taipei International Community Cultural Association; Best Composition, The Golden Melody Award, 2000. *Address:* 2F, Nr 10 51st Alleyway, 102 Lane, Shei-fu Road, Tamshui, Taipei County, Taiwan. *Telephone:* (2) 26263274. *Fax:* (2) 26215713. *E-mail:* taiwanmass@yahoo.com.

**HUA, Lin;** Composer and Professor; b. 8 Aug. 1942, Shanghai, China. *Education:* Shanghai Conservatory of Music, piano and composition with

Sang Tong, Wang Jianzhong and Chen Mingzhi. *Career:* composer for Shanghai Wind Band 1967–76, Shanghai Opera and Ballet House 1976–79; Assoc. Prof., Counterpoint, Fugue, Shanghai Conservatory of Music 1979–; consultant, Shanghai Philharmonic Asscn 1982–. *Compositions include:* Bright Mountain Flowers In Full Bloom, ballet, 1976; Fantasy for piano and accordion, 1978; Love of The Great Wall for piano and accordion, 1978; Farewell Refrains At Yang Gate Pass for piano quartet, 1978; Beauty of Peking Opera for string quartet, 1979; Album of Woodcuts for piano quintet, 1979; Amid Flowers Beside a River Under the Spring Moon for 4 harps, 1979; Flower and Song, concertino for soprano and orchestra, 1980; Suite Tragedy for chamber symphony, 1988; 24 Preludes and fugues on reading Sikong Tu's Shipin (Personalities of Poetry in Tang Dynasty), 1990; Album of World Folk Songs for piano, 1991; stage, film and television music. *Publications:* Guide the Teaching of Polyphony by Using Creative Psychology 1980, Stravinsky Techniques in Polyphonic Writing 1987, The Sense of Ugliness and its Application in Western Music 1988, Abstraction of Art and Abstractionism 1989, Course of Polyphone 1994, The Pilgrimage to Music 1995, Talk on Music 1998, 101 World Folk Songs 1998. *Address:* 20 Fenyang Road, Shanghai, People's Republic of China.

**HUANG, An-Lun,** MM, FTCL; Chinese composer; b. 15 March 1949, Guangzhou City, Guangdong Prov.; s. of Huang Fei-Li and Zhao Fang-Xing; m. Ouyang Rui-Li 1974; one s. *Education:* Central Conservatory of Music, Beijing, Univ. of Toronto, Canada, Trinity Coll. of Music, London and Yale Univ., USA. *Career:* started piano aged five; studied with Shaw Yuan-Xin and Chen Zi; works have been widely performed in China, Hong Kong, Philippines, northern Africa, Australia, Europe, USA and Canada; Resident Composer, Cen. Opera House of China 1976–; Pres. Canadian Chinese Music Soc., Ont. 1987–; Deputy Dir State Bureau of Materials and Equipment 1987–88; Vice-Minister of Materials 1990; Fellowship in Composition, Trinity Coll. of Music, London 1983. *Compositions:* operas: Flower Guardian Op. 26 1979, Yeu Fei Op. 37 1986 and 6 others; symphonic, chamber, vocal, choral and film music, including: Symphonic Concert Op. 25, Symphonic Overture, The Consecration of the Spring in 1976 Op. 25a 1977, Piano Concerto in G Op. 25b 1982, Symphony in C Op. 25c 1984, The Sword (symphonic poem) Op. 33 1982, Easter Cantata (text by Semuel Tang) Op. 38 1986; Psalm 22-A Cantata in Baroque Style Op. 43c 1988, Piano Concerto in G; ballets: The Little Match Girl Op. 24 1978, A Dream of Dun Huang Op. 29 1980, The Special Orchestra Album 1997. *Honours:* Yale Alumni Asscn Prize, Yale Univ. 1986. *Address:* 15 Carlton Road, Markham, Ont., L3R 17E, Canada (office); The Central Opera House of China, Zuojia Zhuang, Out of Dongzhimen Gate, Beijing, People's Republic of China. *Telephone:* (416) 423-6396.

**HUANG, Zhun;** Composer; b. 25 June 1926, Huang Yan County, Zhe Jang Province, China. *Education:* Studied with composer Xian Xinghai and others. *Career:* Singer, mezzo-soprano, 1941–42; Composer, Peking Film Studio, 1949–51; Composer and music director at Shanghai Film Studio, 1951–87; mem, Standing Committee of Chinese Musicians Association; Vice-Chairman of China Film Music Society; Committee of Shanghai Artists Association; Standing Committee of Chinese Music Copyright Society. *Compositions:* Over 40 film scores which include Old Man and Nymph, 1956; Red Women Soldiers, 1960; Sisters on Stage, 1964; Horsekeeper, 1982; Numerous television music and songs. *Publications:* Selected songs of Huang Zhun; Life and Melodies; Music and My Life. *Honours:* The theme song for Red Women Soldiers, chosen as one of the 20th century masterpieces of Chinese Music, 1989; Winner, 50th anniversary of Chinese television and films music prize, 1999. *Address:* Apmt 9C, 34 Fu Xing Xi Lu, Shanghai 200031, People's Republic of China.

**HUANGLONG, Pan;** Composer; b. 9 Sept. 1945, Puli, Taiwan. *Education:* National Taiwan University, 1967–71; Studies with Ulrich Lehmann in Zürich, 1974–76, and Helmut Lachenmann in Hanover, 1976–78; Berlin Hochschule der Kunste with Isang Yun, 1978–80. *Career:* Professor at National Institute of Arts in Taipei, 1981–; Founded Modern Music Centre, 1984; Co-founded Taiwan branch of ISCM, 1989. *Compositions:* Night-Mooring near a Maple Bridge, for orchestra, 1974; Bird's Eye View for marimba and vibraphone, 1977; Metempsychose for 5 solo strings and orchestra, 1977; String Quartet, 1977; Paradise for orchestra 1978; Enlightenment for ensemble, 1979; Clarinet Quartet, 1980; 2nd String Quartet, 1981; Series: Expelling Yearnings, 1975–76; Elements of Change, 1979–86; Kaleidoscope, 1986–95; Formosa Landscape, 1987–95; Labyrinth Promenade, 1988–98; Ying-Yong, 1992–95; Cello Concerto, 1997; Concerto for cello and 3 instruments, 1997; Totem and Taboo for 6 percussion, 1997; East and West, for ensemble, 1998; Solo I for harpsichord, 1998. *Address:* c/o CHA, 2nd Floor, No. 7 Ching Dao East Road, Taipei, Taiwan.

**HUBER, Klaus;** Composer; b. 30 Nov. 1924, Berne, Switzerland. *Education:* Studied at the Zürich Conservatory 1947–49 with Stefi Geyer and Willy Burkhard; Further study with Boris Blacher in Berlin. *Career:* Taught violin at the Zürich Conservatory from 1950; Lucerne Conservatory 1960–63; Basle Music Academy from 1961. *Compositions:* Orchestral: Invention und Choral, 1956; Litania instrumentalis, 1957; Terzen-Studie, 1958; Alveare vernat, 1967; James Joyce Chamber Music, 1967; Tenebrae, 1967; Tempora for violin and orchestra, 1970; Turna, 1974; Zwischenspiel, 1986; Lamentationes, 1994; Choral: Quem terra, 1955; Das Te Deum Laudamus Deutsch, 1956; Antiphonische Kantate, 1956; Soliloquia, 1959–64; Cuius legibus rotantur poli, 1960; Musik zu eines Johannes-der-Taufer Gottesdienst, 1965; Kleine Deutsche Messe, 1969;... inwendig voller figur... after the Apocalypse and Durer, 1971; Hiob xix, 1971; Vocal: Abendkantate, 1952; Kleine Tauf Kantate für Christof, 1952; 6 Kleine Vokalisen, 1955; Der Abend ist mein Buch, 1955; Oratorio Mechtildis, 1957; Des Engls Anredung an der Seele, 1957; Auf die ruhige Nacht-Zeit, 1958; Askese, 1966; Psalm of Christ, 1967; Grabschrift, 1967; Der Mensch, 1968; Traumgesicht, 1968;... ausgespant..., 1972; Jot oder Wann kommt der Herr zuruck, opera, 1973; Im Pardies, opera pieces, 1975; A Prayer on a Prayer for women's voices and ensemble, 1996; Umkehr–im Licht Sein for mezzo, chorus and ensemble, 1997; Instrumental: Ciacona for organ, 1954; Concerto per la camerata, 1955; In Memoriam Willy Burkhard for organ, 1955; Partita, 1955; Noctes intelligibis lucis for oboe and harpsichord, 1961; Moteti-Cantiones for string quartet, 1963; 6 Miniaturen, 1963; In te Domine spervai for organ, 1964; Sabeth, 1967; Ascensus for flute, cello and piano, 1969; 3 kleine Meditationen for string trio and harp, 1969; Ein Hauch von Unzeit I–III, 1972; Chamber Concerto for piano and ensemble, 1994; Ecce homines for string quintet, 1998; L'ombre de notre âge for ensemble, 1999. *Honours:* First Prize at the 1959 ISCM Competition, Rome (for Die Engels Anredung an die Seele); Arnold Bax Society Medal, 1962; Beethoven Prize of Bonn, 1970 (for Tenebrae). *Address:* c/o SUISA, Bellariastrasse 82, CH –8038 Zürich, Switzerland.

**HUBER, Nicolaus A.;** German composer; b. 15 Dec. 1939, Passau. *Education:* studied in Munich with Gunter Bialas, at Darmstadt with Stockhausen and in Venice with Luigi Nono. *Career:* Professor at the Folkwanghochschule, Essen from 1974. *Compositions include:* Spärenmusik, for orchestra, 1981; 6 Bagatellen, for 10 instruments and tape, 1981; Nocturnes, for orchestra, 1984; La force du vestige, for ensemble, 1985; Vier Stücke, for orchestra and tape, 1986; Doubles, mit einem beweglickhen ton, for string quartet, 1987; Clash Music, for cymbals, 1988; Tote Metren, for baritone and ensemble, 1989; Off enes Fragment, for soprano and ensemble, 1991; First Play Mozart, for flute, 1993; En face d'en face, for orchestra and tape, 1994; Disappearances, for piano, 1995; Sein als Einspruch, for 8 solo voices, 1997;... in die Stille, for cello, 1998; Covered with Music, for soprano and ensemble, 1998; Ach, des Erhabene... beträubte Fragmente, for double chorus, 1999; Mixed Media works, including Eröffnung und Zertrümmerung, for ensemble and tape, 1992.

**HUBERMAN, Lina;** Violinist; b. 1955, Moscow, Russia. *Education:* Studied at Moscow Conservatoire with Yanketevich. *Career:* Member of the Prokofiev Quartet, founded at the Moscow Festival of World Youth and the International Quartet Competition at Budapest; Many concerts in the former Soviet Union and on tour to Czechoslovakia, Germany, Australia, the USA, Canada, Spain, Japan and Italy; Repertoire includes works by Haydn, Mozart, Beethoven, Schubert, Debussy, Ravel, Tchaikovsky, Bartók and Shostakovich. *Current Management:* Sonata, Glasgow, Scotland. *Address:* c/o Prokofiev Quartet, 11 Northgate Street, Glasgow G20 7AA, Scotland.

**HUDECEK, Vaclav;** Violinist; b. 7 June 1952, Rozmital, Czechoslovakia; m. Eva Trejtnarova, 8 Feb 1977. *Education:* Academy of Music Prague and private lessons for 4 years with David Oistrakh in Moscow. *Career:* Debut: With Royal Philharmonic Orchestra in London, 1967; Concert tours in Europe, Japan and USA since London debut, and tours in Europe, USA, Japan and Australia; Soloist with Czech Philharmonic Orchestra, 1983; mem, Central Committee, Union of Czech Composers and Concert Artists; Association of Czech Musicians. *Recordings:* Most of the world violin repertoire. *Honours:* Artist of Merit of Czechoslovakia, 1980; Record of the Year in 1992 for Vivaldi's Four Seasons and Best Selling Record of Czechoslovakia. *Current Management:* Dr Raab-Dr Böhm Künstleragentur, Plankengasse 7, 1010 Vienna, Austria. *Address:* Londynskà 83, 120 00 Prague 2, Czech Republic.

**HUDSON, Benjamin;** Violinist; b. 14 June 1950, Decatur, Illinois, USA. *Education:* Studied in New York. *Career:* Co-founded the Schoenberg String Quartet in 1977 becoming Columbia String Quartet in 1978; Has performed many modern works including the premieres of Charles Wuorinen's Archangel in 1978 with trombonist, David Taylor, and 2nd String Quartet in 1980, Berg's Lyric Suite in its version with soprano, Bethany Beardslee, New York, 1979, and Roussakis' Ephemeris in 1979; Further premieres include quartets by Morton Feldman in 1980, Wayne Peterson in 1984 and Larry Bell in 1985. *Recordings include:* String Quartet No. 3 by Lukas Foss and Ned Rorem's Mourning Song with baritone, William Parker. *Honours:* National Endowment of The Arts Grants, 1979–81.

**HUDSON, John;** Singer (Tenor); b. 1967, Barnsley, Yorkshire, England. *Education:* Studied at the Guildhall School with Laura Sarti; Further study with Josephine Veasey. *Career:* Debut: English National Opera, as Verdi's Macduff, 1993; Seasom 1993–94 with ENO as Rodolfo, Nadir in The Pearl Fishers and Don Ottavio; Alfredo in La Traviata for Welsh National Opera and for Auckland Opera, New Zealand; Concerts include Beethoven's Ninth at the Barbican and in Paris, Messiah in Ottawa with Trevor Pinnock and Mozart's Requiem with the English Chamber Orchestra; 50th Anniversary Concert with ENO and television appearance with Lesley Garrett in Viva la Diva, on BBC 2; Season 1996–97 as Alfredo and Nadir with ENO; Season 1998 as Des Grieux in Manon and Robert Dudley in Mary Stuart, for ENO. *Current Management:* Ingpen & Williams Ltd, 7 St George's Court, 131 Putney Bridge Road, London, SW15 2PA, England.

**HUDSON, Paul;** Singer (Bass); b. 24 June 1946, Barnsley, England. *Education:* Studied at the Royal College of Music and the London Opera Centre. *Career:* Debut: Sadler's Wells Opera, 1969, in the premiere of Williamson's Lucky Peter's Journey; Many appearances with English

National Opera and the Welsh National Opera, in works by Puccini, Britten and Wagner; Opera North, 1979, in Der fliegende Holländer and Peter Grimes; Guest appearances elsewhere in Baroque and contemporary music; Frequent concert engagements; Season 1998 as Rocco in Fidelio for English Touring Opera and Cacique in Il Guarany by Gomes for Chelsea Opera. *Recordings include:* Music by Stravinsky and La fanciulla del West; Laertes in Hamlet by Thomas; Scenes from Gilbert and Sullivan. *Address:* c/o Alexander Management, 38 Lytton Grove, Putney, London SW15 2HB, England.

**HUDSON, Richard,** FRSA; stage designer; b. 1954, Rhodesia (now Zimbabwe). *Education:* Wimbledon School of Art. *Career:* designs for ENO include The Force of Destiny, The Marriage of Figaro; premieres of Judith Weir's A Night at the Chinese Opera (Kent Opera) and The Vanishing Bridegroom (Scottish Opera); Glyndebourne debut 1992, The Queen of Spades, followed by Eugene Onegin, the British stage premiere of Rossini's Ermione, and Manon Lescaut 1997; Die Meistersinger von Nurnberg at Covent Garden 1993; further engagements with I Puritani at La Fenice, Venice, The Rake's Progress for the Lyric Opera Chicago, Lucia di Lammermoor at Zürich and Munich, Rossini's L'Inganno felice at the Pesaro Festival; Samson et Dalila at the Metropolitan Opera, New York; The Rake's Progress at the Saito Kinen Festival, Japan; Ernani and Guillaume Tell at the Vienna Staatsoper season 1997–98; other designs for Manon (Opera North), Mary Stuart (Scottish Opera) Les Contes d'Hoffmann (Staatsoper, Vienna); Così fan tutte, (Glyndebourne) 1998; season 2001–02 with Carlisle Floyd's Of Mice and Men at Bregenz, Houston and Washington; The Cunning Little Vixen for Opera North; Les Vêpres Siciliennes and Khovanschina in Paris; Tamerlano and Idomeneo in Florence; Benvenuto Cellini in Zürich; Peter Grimes in Amsterdam; Twilight of the Gods for ENO 2005; British Scenography Commissioner to the Organisation Internationale des Scenographes, Techniciens et Architects de Théâtre (OISTAT). *Honours:* Royal Designer for Industry, Laurence Olivier Award 1988, Tony Award 1998, Prague Quadreniale Gold Medal for set design 2003. *Address:* Judy Daish Associates, 2 St Charles Place, London, W10 6EG, England.

**HUEBER, Kurt (Anton);** Composer and University Lecturer; b. 9 July 1928, Salzburg, Austria. *Education:* Diploma, Piano and Conducting, Musik Hochschule Mozarteum, Salzburg, 1948. *Career:* Section Leader, Konservatorium der Stadt Wien; Works performed in concerts and on radio; Teacher, Musical Acoustics, Hochschule für Musik, Vienna, 1980–93. *Compositions:* Scenic Music for Stage, Linz, 1958–60; Schwarz auf Weiss, 1st opera composed for Austrian television, 1968; Symchromie I, 1970; Symchromie II, 1972; Formant spectrale for string orchestra, 1974; Sonata for viola solo; Sonata for trumpet and piano; Opera, The Canterville Ghost (O Wilde), 1990–91; Dankos Herz, string quartet, 1992–93; Völuspa, 3 mythological scenes for violin and string orchestra; Maskenspiel de Genien (F v Herzmanovsky-Orlando), opera op 50, 1995–98. *Recordings:* Glockenspektren for pipe-bells and piano; Iris for piano and percussion; Horn und Tuba, Requiem for 4 Wagner-Tubas and Contrabass Tuba, 1977; Osiris Hymnus; Schein und Sein; 22 songs for Baritone and Piano; CD: Musik for Violoncello and Piano, 1994; CD: Trondheim Bläserquintett Hören über Grenzen, Wind Quintet op 10, 1995; CD: Neue Orgelmusik aus Skandanavien und Mitteleuropa, 1 Fantasie für Orgel op 1, 1996; CD: Vienna Classic and Modern, Völuspa Violinkonzert op 39, 1997; CD: Neue Musik Österreich 2 Ekmelische Musik (Balance) string quartet Dankos Herz op 37, 1998. *Publications:* Pseudoharmonische Partialtonreihen, ihre ekmelischen Intervallstrukturen, ein neuer Klangraum der Musiktheorie, Mikrotöne I; Mathematisch-physikalische Grundlagen einer ekmelischen Intervallehre, Mikrotone II, 1988; Ekmelische Harmonik, Mikrotone III, 1990; Nachbildung des Glockenklanges mit Hilfe von Röhrenglocken und Klavierklängen, Acustica vol. 26, 1972; Instrumentenbau Musik International, 1975; Various other professional publications. *Address:* 3712 Grübern 34, Nö, Austria.

**HUFFSTODT, Karen;** singer (soprano); b. 31 Dec. 1954, Peru, Illinois, USA. *Education:* Illinois Wesleyan and Northwestern Universities. *Career:* sang with the New York City Opera from 1982 as Lehar's Merry Widow, Micaela, Violetta and Donna Anna; Santa Fe Opera in 1984 as the Soldier's Wife in the US premiere of Henze's We Come to The River, returning in 1989 as L'Ensoleillad in Massenet's Chérubin; Other engagements with Chicago Opera as Magda in La Rondine and Fiordiligi, Illinois Opera in title role in Mary, Queen of Scots by Thea Musgrave, Washington Opera in the premiere of Menotti's Goya in 1986, Cologne Opera as Constanze, Agrippina, Donna Anna and Mozart's Countess, and Metropolitan Opera as Violetta and Rosalinda in season 1989–90; Other roles include Musetta at Los Angeles and Hamburg, Thais at Paris Opéra, Nancy and Toulouse, Amalia in I Masnadieri by Verdi for Australian opera, Salome at Lyon, Agathe and Arabella at Catania, and Odabella in Attila for Opera North in 1990 and Covent Garden in 1991; Season 1992 as Tosca at Antwerp, Turandot at Lyon, and Chrysothemis at the Opéra Bastille Paris; Opened season at La Scala in 1993 as Spontini's Vestale; Sang Strauss's Ariadne at the Opéra Comique, Salome at the Bastille Opéra and Alice Ford at Antwerp in 1994; Season 1996–97 as Sieglinde at Covent Garden and Salome at San Francisco; Season 1998 as Elisabeth at Palermo, Isolde at Monte Carlo and Katerina Izmailova at Florence; Season 1999–2000 as Katerina Izmailova at Dresden, the Walküre Brünnhilde for Geneva Opera and Kundry in Washington. *Recordings include:* Salomé in a French language version of Strauss's opera. *Current Management:* Theateragentur Heidi Steinhaus, Auerfeldstr. 26, 81541

Munich, Germany. *E-mail:* Steinhaus@heidi-steinhaus.de. *Website:* www .heidi-steinhaus.de.

**HUFSCHMIDT, Wolfgang;** German composer; b. 15 March 1934, Mülheim. *Education:* studied church music and composition at Essen. *Career:* church organist at Essen 1954–68; Lecturer in Composition 1971–88, Folkwang Hochschule; Rektor 1988–96. *Compositions include:* Mass, for soprano and chorus, 1961; Easter Story, 1964; Meissner Te Deum, 1968; Verwandlungen, for string quartet, 1969; Stephanus, mixed media, 1972; Solo, for violin, 1972; Agende for 4 choruses and ensemble, 1973; Trio, I–IV, 1970–95; We Shall Overcome for speaker, low voice, chorus and 9 instruments, 1984; Lieder ohne Worte, 24 Klavierstücke, with tape, 1986; Double Woodwind quintet 1989; an E for low voice and piano, 1995. *Honours:* Ruhr Prize, Mülheim 1973.

**HUGGETT, Monica;** Violinist; b. 16 May 1953, London, England. *Education:* Studied at the Royal Academy of Music with Manoug Parikian; Early performance practice with Sigiswald Kuijken, Gustav Leonhardt and Ton Koopman. *Career:* Co-founded the Amsterdam Baroque Orchestra with Koopman, 1980, and was its leader until 1987; Many performances on authentic gut-string violins with such ensembles as the Hanover Band, Academy of Ancient Music, Raglan Baroque Players and Hausmusik; World-wide tours as soloist, director and chamber musician in a repertoire extending from the late Renaissance to the Romantic with performances and recordings of Mozart, Beethoven, Schubert, Mendelssohn and the concertos of Vivaldi and Bach; Played the Beethoven Concerto with the Orchestra of the Age of Enlightenment under Ivan Fischer at the Queen Elizabeth Hall, April 1991; The Mendelssohn Concerto under Charles Mackerras, 1992; Professor of Baroque and Classical Violin at the Hochschule für Kunste in Bremen and Artistic Director of the Portland Baroque Orchestra, USA; Founded The Greate Consort, 1995. *Recordings include:* Symphonies by Beethoven with the Hanover Band (as director); Vivaldi La Stravaganza and Schubert Octet with the Academy of Ancient Music; Vivaldi La Cetra and Schubert Trout Quintet with the Raglan Baroque Players and Hausmusik; Rameau Pièces de Clavécin en Concerts and Corelli Violin Sonatas Op 5 with Trio Sonnerie and Vivaldi Four Seasons, Mozart Violin Concertos; Bach Violin Concertos with the Amsterdam Baroque Orchestra; Beethoven Concerto and Mendelssohn Concerto with the Orchestra of the Age of Enlightenment. *Address:* c/o Francesca McManus, 71 Priory Road, Kew Gardens, Surrey TW9 3 DH, England.

**HUGH, Tim;** Concert Cellist; b. 1965, England. *Education:* Studied at Yale and with William Pleeth and Jacqueline Du Pré. *Career:* Former solo cellist with the BBC Symphony Orchestra and joint principal with the London Symphony Orchestra; Many concerts with the Liverpool Philharmonic Orchestra, the Royal and BBC Philharmonics, Bournemouth Symphony Orchestra and Sinfonietta, and London Mozart Players; Appearances at the Leipzig Gewandhaus, La Scala Milan and Amsterdam Concertgebouw; Solo cello suites by Bach and Britten at 1994 Glasgow Mayfest, tour of the United Kingdom with the Polish State Philharmonic and engagements at Aldeburgh and the London Proms; Chamber music by Fauré and others with Domus and the Solomon Trio. *Recordings include:* Britten's Suites; Sonatas by Beethoven and Grieg with Yonty Solomon; CP Bach and Boccherini Concertos. *Honours:* Prizewinner at 1990 Tchaikovsky International Competition, Moscow. *Telephone:* (20) 7602-1416. *Fax:* (20) 7371-2726. *E-mail:* lisapeacock@aol.com.

**HUGHES, Martin (Glyn);** Pianist; b. 23 March 1950, Hemel Hempstead, England; 1 s., 1 d. *Education:* Salisbury Cathedral Choir School, 1960–63; Music Scholar, Bryanston School, 1963–66; Paris Conservatoire, France, 1966–67; Private study with Yvonne Lefebure, 1967–70; Moscow Conservatory, Russia, 1970–71. *Career:* Debut: Wigmore Hall, London, England, 1972; Proms, 1972; French radio and television, 1972; Cheltenham Festival, 1973; Making a Name, BBC television, 1974; Tour of USSR, 1974; RPO and London Symphony Orchestra debuts, 1975; Chichester and Llandaff Festivals, 1975; Recital and Concerto debut, Queen Elizabeth Hall, 1977; Tours and radio recitals, Portugal and Germany, 1977; Beethoven Sonata Cycle, 1979; regular Radio 3 broadcasts, solo appearances including: Royal Festival Hall, European tours, 1980–; Founder, 1984, Artistic Director of Music, Fens Festival and summer school, 1984, 1986; Fengate Music trust; Director, Annual Summer School, Val de Saire, France, 1988, 1989; Bath Festival, 1983, 1985, 1986; Member, Kreutzer Piano trio, 1985; Tours of USA, Israel, 1987–88; Study with Wilhelm Kempff, 1980; Professor, Hochschule für der Kunste, Berlin, Germany, 1991–; Tour of Japan, 1993; Guest teacher, Academy of Music, Bucharest, 1993, 1994, 1995. *Publications:* Russian School of Piano Playing, translation and editing, 1976. *Contributions:* Chapter in Performing Beethoven, 1994. *Honours:* Bronze Medal, Marguerite Long Competition, 1969; British Council Scholar, 1970–71; Arts Council of Great Britain Award, 1975; Honorary MMus, University of Surrey, 1991. *Address:* Leibnizstrasse 58, 10629 Berlin, Germany.

**HUGHES, Owain Arwel,** OBE; British conductor; *Principal Associate Conductor, Royal Philharmonic Orchestra; Music Director, National Youth Orchestra of Wales and Camerata Wales;* b. 21 March 1942, Cardiff, Wales; m. Jean Bowen Lewis 1966; one s. one d. *Education:* Univ. Coll., Cardiff, Royal Coll. of Music with Adrian Boult and Harvey Philips, 1964–66, and with Kempe in London and Haitink in Amsterdam. *Career:* guest conductor with all UK orchestras and choirs esp. Hallé Orchestra; Assoc. Conductor BBC Nat. Orchestra of Wales 1980–86, Philharmonic Orchestra 1984–90; Music Dir Huddersfield Choral Soc. 1980–86; Principal Conductor Aalborg Symphony Orchestra 1994–99; Guest Conductor throughout Scandinavia esp. Danish Radio Symphony Orchestra, Helsinki Philharmonic Orchestra, Aarhus Symphony Orchestra; Founder and Artistic Dir Welsh Proms 1986–; Principal Assoc. Conductor Royal Philharmonic Orchestra 2004–; Music Dir Nat. Youth Orchestra of Wales 2003–, Camerata Wales 2005–; TV Presenter Conductor Music for the Masses and Much Loved Music Show (BBC) television; 50th anniversary VE Day, 60th anniversary Holocaust Memorial Palace of Westminster; on radio Royal Albert Hall concert series (Classic FM). *Television:* performances of Mahler 8, Verdi Requiem, Handel Messiah, Mendelssohn Elijah, Walton Belshazzar's Feat, Rossini Stabat Mater, Cherubini Requiem, Sibelius Kullervo Symphony. *Recordings include:* Music of Delius and Vaughan-Williams London Symphony (Philharmonia Orchestra), fourteen Symphonies, orchestral works and concertos by Holmboe (Aalborg Symphony Orchestra), Rachmaninov Symphonies (Royal Scottish Nat. Orchestra), Rachmaninov Piano Concertos (Malmö Symphony Orchestra), Holst Planets, Choral Classics, Opera Classics, Verdi Requiem and Messiah (Royal Philharmonic Orchestra), Carols Album and Hymns Album (Huddersfield Choral, both gold discs), Vaughan-Williams Hymns Album and Vaughan-Williams Carols Album (Cardiff Festival Choir), Sibelius Symphony No. 1 and Sullivan Irish Symphony (BBC Concert Orchestra), Ludwig Nielsen Oratorio Moses and Hermann D.Kottel Oratorio Tower of Babel (Danish Radio Symphony Orchestra and Chorus), Tchaikovsky Piano Concertos, Borressen Symphonies and Norby Orchestral Works (Aalborg Symphony Orchestra). *Honours:* Hon. DMus (Univ. of Wales, Council for National Academic Awards, London); Fellowships (Univ. Coll., Cardiff, Univ. of Wales Trinity Coll., Royal Welsh Coll. of Music and Drama. *Current Management:* Hazard Chase, 25 City Road, Cambridge CB1 1DP, England. *Telephone:* (1223) 312400. *Fax:* (1223) 460827. *E-mail:* info@hazardchase.co.uk. *Website:* www.hazardchase.co.uk.

**HULA, Pavel;** Violinist; *Artistic Director, Praga Camerata;* b. 23 Jan. 1952, Prague, Czechoslovakia; m. Helena Sirlova, 29 June 1976, one d. *Education:* Violin, 1970–74, and Chamber Music, 1980–82, Academy of Music Arts, Prague. *Career:* Debut: Prague Festival, Spring 1976; First Violin, Kocian Quartet, 1975–, with performances at over 3,000 concerts in 30 countries; Appearances on radio and television; Wigmore Hall debut, 1992; Artistic Director of Praga Camerata (String Orchestra) 2001–. *Recordings:* Virtuoso Violin Duets; Mozart's String Quartets; Dvořák's String Quartets; Haydn: Quartets; Hindemith's String Quartets. *Honours:* 1st Prize, Kocian Violin Competition, 1963, 1964; 2nd Prize, Concertino Praga, Radio Competition, 1969; Prize, Society of Chamber Music of Czech Philharmonic, 1981; Grand Prix du Disque de l'Académie Charles Cross, Paris, 1997. *Address:* Secská 1875/11, 100 00 Prague 10, Czech Republic.

**HULL, Eric;** conductor; b. 1967. *Education:* Vienna Hochschle für Musik. *Career:* Assistant at La Scala, Toronto Symphony, Florence and Salzburg Festivals; Opera and concerts with the Berlin Radio, Teatro San Carlo, Naples (Fioravanti's Le Cantatrici Villane), Teatro La Fenice, Genoa and Treviso; La Scala Milan from 1988, with the premiere of Donatoni's Il Vello Dissotto, La Clemenza di Tito, Iphigénie en Tauride and Pergolesi's Lo Frate 'nnamorato; Edition of Salieri's L'Europa Riconosciuta for La Scala; Belcanto Gala in Moscow, and engagements with the Milan Symphony and Monte Carlo Philharmonique; Modern premiere of Piccinni's L'Americano at Martina Franca, 1996. *Recordings include:* L'Americano Incivilito. *Current Management:* Opera-Connection Alste & Mödersheim, Leibnizstrasse 94, 10625 Berlin, Germay. *Telephone:* 30 31 99 66 88. *Fax:* 30 31 80 97 39. *E-mail:* info@opera-connection.com. *Website:* www.opera-connection.com.

**HULMANOVA, Stefania;** Singer (Soprano); b. 20 Jan. 1920, Dolné Dubové, Czechoslovakia; m. Cyril Hulman, 23 Feb 1943, 2 s. *Education:* State Conservatory, Bratislava. *Career:* Debut: Sang Rusalka in Dvořák's Rusalka, State Theatre, Kosice, 1948; Soloist, Opera of the State Theatre, Kosice, 1948–51; Soloist, Opera of the Slovak National Theatre, Bratislava, 1952–79; Core repertoire: Julia in Jakobin by A Dvořák, Marenka in The Bartered Bride, Vendulka in The Kiss by Smetana, Halka in Halka by Moniuszko, Santuzza in Cavalleria Rusticana by Mascagni, Countess in The Marriage of Figaro, Aida, Nella in Gianni Schicchi; Soloist, Opera of the Slovak National Theatre, Bratislava, 1952; Numerous other roles performed include Leonora in Trovatore, Elisabeth de Valois in Don Carlos, Desdemona in Otello, all by Verdi; Tosca; Guest Performances include The Whirlpool by Suchon at Dresden; Tosca, Moscow; Svätopluk, Perugia, Italy; Concert, Peking, China; Concert, Hanoi, Viet Nam; The Whirlpool, Budapest, Hungary; mem, Honorary Member, Opera of the Slovak National Theatre. *Address:* Ostravska 7, 811 04 Bratislava, Slovakia.

**HUMBLET, Ans;** Singer (Soprano); b. 17 Sept. 1957, Maastricht, Netherlands. *Education:* Studied with Elisabeth Ksoll and at Amsterdam. *Career:* Appearances with Netherlands Opera from 1983 and Wuppertal Opera, 1986–90 in such roles as the Queen of Night, Blondchen, Marie in Zar und Zimmermann, Woglinde, Despina and Musetta; Sang Kunigunde in the German premiere of Bernstein's Candide at Wuppertal in 1990; Enschede Holland in 1990 as Ninetta in Mozart's La Finta Giardiniera; Guest appearances at Düsseldorf and Aachen as the Queen of Night, and at Mönchengladbach as Frasquita in Carmen; Concert engagements in Beethoven's 9th, Mendelssohn's St Paul, Bruckner's Te Deum, Carmina Burana and Masses by Haydn and Mozart; Broadcasts in Netherlands, Germany and Belgium; Engaged at Maastricht from 1990. *Address:* De Nederlandse Opera, Waterlooplein 22, 1011 PG Amsterdam, Netherlands.

**HUMPERT, Hans Ulrich;** Composer; b. 9 Oct. 1940, Paderborn, Germany. *Education:* Studied at the Cologne Musikhochschule, with Petzold and Eimert; Darmstadt Courses, 1964, 1965, with Pierre Boulez and György Ligeti. *Career:* Co-founder, with Wolfgang Rihm and York Höller, of Gruppe 8, 1969; Performances of electronic music as percussionist and synthesizer, Professor of electronic composition at Cologne, 1972–; Commission for the KunstklangRaum, Gelsenkirchen, 1997. *Compositions include:* Clarinet Concerto, 1969, rev. 1980; Waves and Forms, 1971; Synesis, 1971; Das Ohr auf der Strasse, 1972; Electronic Maniac, 1973; Assonanzen, 1977; Approcia Petraca, 1985; Die Ehe der Andromache, 1991; Construction in MicroPoly-Gons 1994; Candide, radio play, 1995; KunstklangRaum 1997; Die Bandbrücke spricht, 1997; Strophen, flugelhn, 1998. *Address:* Elektronische Musik Studio, Musikhochschule Köln, Dagobnerstrasse 38, 50608 Cologne, Germany.

**HUNKA, Pavlo;** singer (bass); b. 7 April 1959, England. *Education:* Royal Northern College of Music with Joseph Ward. *Career:* has performed in concerts throughout the United Kingdom as soloist and conductor; Royal Albert Hall in London, 1988 in a concert celebrating 1000 years of Christianity in the Ukraine; Opera debut as Melisso in a 1989 production of Handel's Alcina at the RNCM; Has also sung Theseus in A Midsummer Night's Dream and Philip II in Don Carlos with the RNCM; Professional opera debut as Basilio in Il Barbiere di Siviglia with Welsh National Opera, 1990; Recent engagements as Rangoni in Boris Godunov for Basle Opera and Dulcamara in L'Elisir d'amore; Other roles include Colline in La Bohème and Prince Gremin in Eugene Onegin; Now on contract to Basel Stadttheater, Switzerland; Salzburg 1994–95, in Boris Godunov and Elektra, Bregenz Festival, 1995 as Pizarro; Bonn 1995–96, as Leporello and Tomsky in The Queen of Spades; Basle Opera 1996, as Rigoletto; Season 2000–01 as Verdi's Renato at Bregenz, Telramund in Munich, Wozzeck for Dallas Opera and Creon in Oedipus Rex at Naples; Weber's Euryanthe at the London Proms, 2002. *Honours:* Diploma with Distinction in Performance, RNCM, 1990; Ricordi Opera Prize; Peter Moores Foundation and Wolfson Foundation Scholarships. *Current Management:* Artists Management Zurich, Rütistrasse 52, 8044 Zürich-Gockhausen, Switzerland. *Telephone:* (1) 821 89 57. *Fax:* (1) 821 01 27. *Website:* www .artistsman.com.

**HUNT, Alexandra,** BA, BS; American opera and concert singer (soprano), librettist and libretto translator; b. 1940. *Education:* Vassar College, Juilliard School of Music, Sorbonne University, Paris, France. *Career:* debut as Marie in La Scala's first production of Wozzeck in German, 1971, conducted by Claudio Abbado; Sang title role of Lulu at Metropolitan Opera and Katya Kabanova sung in Czech, Janáček Festival, Brno; Jenůfa at Lincoln Center, NY; Soprano Soloist in Penderecki Passion According to St Luke, Philadelphia Orchestra; Amelia in Ballo in Maschera, Providence, RI and Bucharest; Title role of Tosca in Bulgaria, Romania and Czechoslovakia; Sang Marie in Wozzeck at Hamburg Staatsoper; Lady Macbeth in Macbeth at Florentine Opera and Kentucky Opera; Soprano Soloist in Mahler's Fourth Symphony, Bogota Filarmonica; In Beethoven's Ninth Symphony, Omaha and Des Moines Symphonies; many other roles. *Recordings:* Songs of John Alden Carpenter, Charles T. Griffes and Edward MacDowell. *Publications:* New English Translation of Mozart's Don Giovanni and Così fan tutte. *Address:* 170 West 74th Street, Apt 1106, New York, NY 10023, USA.

**HUNT, Fionnuala;** Concert Violinist; b. 1960, Belfast, Northern Ireland. *Education:* Studied at Ulster College of Music, Royal College of Music and The Vienna Hochschule für Musik with Wolfgang Schneiderhan. *Career:* Leader and Soloist with the Vienna Chamber; Former member of the Bavarian State Opera Orchestra in Munich; Co-Leader of the RTE Symphony Orchestra in Dublin; Guest Leader of the Ulster Orchestra; Duo recitals with pianist sister, Una Hunt, performing throughout: Ireland; Austria; Germany; Czechoslovakia; Italy; The United Kingdom; Member of the Dublin Piano Trio; Solo appearances with: The National Symphony Orchestra of Ireland; The RTE Concert Orchestra; The Ulster Orchestra; Played Lutoslawski's Partita at the Maltings Concert Hall, Snape; Artistic Director and Leader of the Irish Chamber Orchestra. *Address:* c/o Owen and White Management, 14 Nightingale Lane, London, N8 7QU, England.

**HUNT, Gordon;** British oboist and conductor; *Professor of Oboe, Guildhall School of Music and Drama;* b. 1950, London, England. *Education:* Royal Coll. of Music with Terence MacDonagh. *Career:* fmr principal, BBC Nat. Orchestra of Wales and London Philharmonic Orchestra; principal oboist, Philharmonia Orchestra; guest oboist, Berlin Philharmonic Orchestra; solo and chamber music appearances throughout Europe, USA, the Far East and in New Zealand; Music Dir, Swedish Chamber Winds 1991–97; Consultant Prof., Royal Acad. of Music; principal oboist, London Chamber Orchestra; Artistic Dir, Danish Chamber Players 2001–04; works regularly with the Danish Radio Sinfonietta; Prof. of Oboe in Dept of Wind, Brass and Percussion, Guildhall School of Music and Drama; mem. of jury, triennial Int. Oboe Competition, Tokyo; numerous radio and TV broadcasts; conducts and directs many orchestras and ensembles; gives masterclasses on four continents. *Recordings include:* Britten, Bax, Bliss 1997, Soliloquy 1998, Elevazione 2002. *Honours:* Hon. ARAM. *Address:* c/o Guildhall School of Music and Drama, Silk Street, Barbican, London, EC2Y 8DT, England. *Website:* www.oboist.co.uk.

**HUNT, Lorraine;** Singer (Mezzo-soprano); b. 1 March 1954, San Francisco, USA. *Education:* Studied in San Francisco and began career as a violist. *Career:* Concert appearances include Krasa's Chamber Symphony with the Boston Symphony Orchestra, tour of Australia with the Australian CO, Dido and Aeneas with the Philharmonia Baroque, San Francisco, and L'Enfance du Christ under Roger Norrington, at the Paris Théatre des Champs Elysées; Further concerts with the San Francisco, Houston, Boston and St Louis Symphonies; Mark Morris Dance Group, as singer, at the Adelaide, Edinburgh and Brooklyn Academy Festivals; Early opera appearances as Sextus in Giulio Cesare, Mozart's Donna Elvira, Octavia in Poppea and Handel's Serse, all directed by Peter Sellars; Season 1995–96 with Haydn's Scena di Berenice at Tanglewood, Charpentier's Médée with Les Arts Florissants in Europe and New York; Handel's Ariodante at the Göttingen Festival and Xerxes at the Los Angeles Music Center; Season 1996 with Irene in Handel's Theodora at Glyndebourne, the Berlioz Nuits d'Ete under Nicholas McGeegan, recitals with Dawn Upshaw in New York and tour of Europe with the Australian CO; Season 1996–97 with Sesto in Handel's Giulio Cesare and the title role in Carmen at the Paris Opéra Bastille, Massenet's Charlotte with the Opéra de Lyon; Further opera enagements in Vienna, Brussels, Lausanne, Aix, Amsterdam, Tokyo and Boston; Sang Handel's Serse with New York City Opera, 1997; Monteverdi's Ottavia at San Francisco, 1998; Sang Myrtle in the premiere of Harbison's The Great Gatsby, NY Met 1999; Premiere of El Niño by John Adams at the Paris Châtelet, 2000. *Recordings include:* Britten's Phaedra and Charpentier's Médée (Erato); Handel's Susanna, Theodora, Clori, Tirsi e Fileno, and Messiah, Purcell's Fairy Queen, Monteverdi's Ulisse (Harmonia Mundi); Videos of Peter Sellars productions of Don Giovanni (as Donna Elvira), Giulio Cesare (Sesto) and Theodora (Glyndebourne 1996). *Address:* c/o IMG Artists, 420 West 45th Street, New York, NY 10036-3503, USA.

**HUNT, Michael;** Stage Director; b. 1957, London, England. *Education:* Studied at Liverpool University. *Career:* Debut: Gounod's Mireille for Liverpool Grand Opera; Artistic Director of the Cheltenham Arts Centre from 1980, staging a number of plays and Così fan tutte; Directed the British premiere of Berwald's Queen of Golconda at Nottingham and The Rake's Progress at Cambridge; Staff Director at English National Opera, directing Aida and Orpheus in the Underworld, also Madama Butterfly for the Education Unit; Oedipus Rex for Opera North; Rossini's Tancredi at Las Palmas; Der Freischütz in an outdoor touring production; Oedipus Rex and Iolanthe for Scottish Opera; La Traviata for Dublin; Figaro for British Youth Opera; World Premieres of Giles Swayne's Le nozze di Cherubino and Harmonies of Hell; Artistic Director, Bloomsbury Festival; Director of Performing Arts, Riverside Studios in London; Teacher at The Royal Academy, Birmingham School of Music and various Drama Schools; In 1996 directed Puccini's La Bohème at the Royal Albert Hall. *Address:* Performing Arts, 6 Windmill Street, London W1P 1HF, England.

**HUNZIKER, Bernhard;** Swiss singer (tenor); *Teacher, Musikhochschule, Zürich;* b. 27 Aug. 1957, Thun. *Education:* Studied with Paul Lohmann in Wiesbaden, in Zürich with Irwin Gage, Munich with Ernst Haefliger and with Heather Harper and Peter Pears at Aldeburgh and London. *Career:* Zürich Opera Studio, 1987–88, Augsburg Opera, Athens Megaron, Lucerne, St Gall, including solo appearances; has worked with conductors including Jesus Lopes-Cobos, Marc Soustrot, K A Rickenbacher, Helmut Rilling, Yehudi Menuhin; concert engagements in Switzerland, Austria, Italy, Germany and France, and several performances at the Israel Festival, Lucerne Festival, Opera Festival, Bad Hersfeld, Germany and Aldeburgh Festival; repertory includes works from Monteverdi, Bach, Mozart, Schubert to Britten, masses and oratorios; Evangelist and Arias in Bach's St Matthew Passion, conducted by M. Corboz 2004, F.Martin: In Terra Pax with Liverpool Philharmonic 2004; Teacher Musikhochschule, Zürich; President, European Voice Teachers Association, Swiss Section, 2001–. *Recordings include:* Musikalische Exequien by Schütz; CD, Swiss Lieder by Schoeck, Huber and others, 2001; Lieder Quartets by Swiss composers, Zürich Vocal Quartet; St John Passion, J. S. Bach. *Honours:* Promotion Prize, Migros Company, Zürich, 1983; Kiefer-Hablitzel-Prize, 1985; Prize, Swiss Musicians Association, 1987. *Address:* c/o Kirchgasse 15, 8001 Zürich, Switzerland. *Telephone:* (44) 2525802. *E-mail:* hunziker.bretscher@bluewin.ch; bernhard.hunziker@doz.hmt.edu. *Website:* operissimo.com.

**HURD, Michael John,** BA, MA; British composer and writer; b. 19 Dec. 1928, Gloucester, England. *Education:* Pembroke Coll., Oxford. *Career:* Prof. of Theory, Royal Marines School of Music 1953–59; freelance composer and author 1959–. *Compositions include:* opera: Widow of Ephesus 1971, The Aspern Papers 1993, The Night of the Wedding 1998; choral: Missa Brevis 1966, Music's Praise 1968, This Day to Man 1974, Shepherd's Calendar 1975, The Phoenix and the Turtle 1975, Genesis 1987, Night Songs of Edward Thomas 1990, Five Spiritual Songs 1996, Five Songs of Praise 1999; orchestral: Sinfonia concertante 1968, Dance Diversions 1972, Concerto da Camera 1987, Overture to Unwritten Comedy 1987; chamber music: Flute Sonatina 1964, Violin Sonata 1987. *Publications:* Immortal Hour: The Life and Times of Rutland Boughton (revised edn as Rutland Boughton and the Glastonbury Festivals) 1962, The Composer 1968, An Outline History of European Music 1968, Elgar 1969, Vaughan Williams 1970, Mendelssohn 1970, The Ordeal of Ivor Gurney 1978, The Oxford Junior Companion to Music 1979, Vincent Novello and Company 1981, The Orchestra 1981, Letters of Gerald Finzi and Howard Ferguson 2001; contrib. New Grove Dictionary of Music and Musicians, New Oxford Companion to Music, Athlone History of British Music, Musik in Geschichte und Gegenwart. *Address:* 4 Church Street, West Liss, Hampshire GU33 6JX, England.

**HUREL, Philippe;** Composer; b. 24 July 1955, Domfront, France. *Education:* Studied with Betsy Jolas at the Paris Conservatoire, Computer Science with Tristan Murail, 1984; Research at IRCAM, electronic music studios (Paris), 1985–90. *Compositions include:* Eolia, for flute, 1982; Trames, for strings, 1982; Memento pour Marc, for orchestra, 1983; Diamants imaginaire, diamant lunaire, for ensemble and electronics, 1986; Pour l'image, for 14 instruments, 1987; Fragment de lune, 1987; Mémoire vive, for orchestra, 1989; Remanences, for 14 instruments, 1992; La celebration des invisibles, shadow theatre, 1992; Leçon des choses, 1993; Pour Luigi, for ensemble, 1994, Kits, for 6 percussion instruments and double bass, 1996;...... a mèsure, for flute and ensemble, 1997. *Honours:* Siemens Prize, Munich, 1995. *Address:* Centre de Musique Contemporaine, Cité de la Musique, 16 Place de la Fontaine, 75019 Paris, France.

**HURFORD, Peter John,** OBE, MusB, MA, FRCO; British organist; b. 22 Nov. 1930, Minehead, Somerset; s. of Hubert John Hurford and Gladys Winifred James; m. Patricia Mary Matthews 1955; two s. one d. *Education:* Blundell's School, Royal Coll. of Music (Open Foundation Scholar), Jesus Coll., Cambridge (organ scholar) and private studies with André Marchal, Paris. *Career:* commissioned, Royal Signals 1954–56; debut, Royal Festival Hall, London 1956; Organist and Choirmaster Holy Trinity Church, Leamington Spa 1956–57; Dir of Music, Bablake School, Coventry 1956–57; Master of the Music, Cathedral and Abbey Church of St Albans 1958–78; freelance concert and recording organist 1978–; Visiting Prof., Coll. Conservatory of Music, Cincinnati, USA 1967–68, Univ. of Western Ont., Canada 1976–77; Acting Organist, St John's Coll. Cambridge 1979–80; Visiting Artist-in-Residence, Sydney Opera House 1980–82; Prof., RAM 1982–88; John Betts Fellow, Univ. of Oxford 1992–93; Decca recording artist 1977–; concerts in USA, Canada, Australia, NZ, Japan, Far East, E and W Europe 1958–98; f. St Albans Int. Organ Festival 1963, Artistic Dir 1963–78, Hon. Pres. 1978–; Pres. Inc. Asscn of Organists 1995–97; mem. Council Royal Coll. of Organists 1964–2003, Pres. 1980–82; Fellow, Royal School of Church Music 1977. *Compositions include:* (organ music) Suite – Laudate Dominum, Chorale Preludes, (choral music) The Communion Service, Series III, The Holy Eucharist, Rite 2 (for American Episcopal Church), music for the Daily Office, miscellaneous anthems, songs, carols, etc. *Recordings include:* complete organ works of J. S. Bach, Handel, F. Couperin, P. Hindemith, music of Franck, Mendelssohn; numerous recitals for BBC, including 34 commentated programmes of J. S. Bach's complete organ works 1980–82, Bach organ music cycle (Herald Angel Critics Award), 50th Edin. Int. Festival 1997. *Publications:* Making Music on the Organ 1988, numerous forewords, contribs to journals. *Honours:* Hon. FRCM 1987; Hon. Fellow in Organ Studies, Univ. of Bristol 1997–98; Hon. mem. RAM 1982; Hon. DMus (Baldwin-Wallace Coll., Ohio, USA) 1981, (Bristol) 1992; Gramophone Award 1979. *Address:* Broom House, St Bernard's Road, St Albans, Herts. AL3 5RA, England.

**HURLEY, Laurel;** Soprano; b. 14 Feb. 1927, Allentown, PA, USA. *Education:* Studied with her mother. *Career:* Debut: Sang in the Student Prince at New York in 1943; New York City Opera debut as Zerlina in 1952; Sang at the Metropolitan Opera from 1955 as Oscar, Musetta, Mimi, Adele, Susanna, Olympia, Papagena, Zerlina and Perichole; Also sang in I Capuleti e i Montecchi by Bellini; Many concert appearances in North America. *Address:* c/o Metropolitan Opera, Lincoln Center, New York, NY 10023, USA.

**HURNÍK, Ilja;** Czech pianist and composer; b. 25 Nov. 1922, Ostrava-Poruba; m. Jana Hurníková 1966; one s. *Education:* Conservatoire, Prague. *Career:* composition; Acad. of Music and Dramatic Arts, Prague 1948–52; self-employed artist 1942–; one-man concerts since 1942, Poland, Switzerland, FRG, Cuba, USA. *Compositions:* orchestral works: Things. Divertimento for small orchestra 1977, Overture a la Klicpera 1985, Symphony in C 2001; concertos: Flute Concerto 1952, Concerto for Oboe and Strings 1959, Concerto for wind instruments, piano and timpani 1956, Concerto for piano and chamber orchestra 1972, New Clavecin, version for piano and strings 1975, Concertino for piano and strings (also for 2 violins and strings) 1981, Concerto for viola and strings 1994; chamber compositions: Motifs from Childhood 1934, revised 1944, Partita in A for flute and piano 1950, Sonata for viola and piano 1951, Four Seasons of the Year for 12 instruments 1952, Sonata da Camera for flute, oboe, cello and harpsichord or piano 1953, Moments musicaux for 11 wind instruments 1955, Eserzii for flute, oboe, clarinet and bassoon 1956, Little Faun, for flute and piano 1956, Stories of a Band, for narrator and chamber ensemble to the composer's own text 1968, Chamber music for strings 1962, Musicians – Suite for narrator and 18 soloists to poems by Frantisek Branislav 1963, Concertino for violin and piano 1971, Simfonia Facile, for strings and piano 1975, Wind Quintet No. 2 1985, Sonatina for double bass and piano 1986; piano compositions: The First Melodies 1931, Preludes for piano 1943, Sonatina for piano 1950, Piano Pieces in an easy style, Piano Duets for Homework 1963, Ditties for Keys. Easy pieces for the piano 1969, Waltzes, for piano duet 1971, Piano Duets – Exercises and studies 1972, New Clavecin, version for piano solo 1975, Studies for four hands 1975, Vorsil Alley – A cycle of easy party pieces 1976, Jazz-piccolo – A cycle of easy party pieces 1977, Fantasy for two pianos 1979, Variations on a theme by Pergolesi, as a piano duet 1984, Innocenza 1992; vocal works: Flowers – A song cycle for soprano and piano to lyrics by Frantiçek Vrba 1940, Ditties for the flute, for a higher voice, flute (violin) and piano to folk poetry lyrics 1953, cantata Maryka 1955, Choruses about Mothers for mixed choir 1955, Sun-Warmed Balk – A cycle of children's (girls) choruses with piano accompaniment 1955, Children's Tercets 1956, Noah – Oratorio for tenor solo, mixed

choir and orchestra to Biblical texts 1959, Three Daughters – Small cantata for children's (girl's) chorus to folk-poetry lyrics 1960, Solomon, for bass and string quartet or organ to the text of the Song of Songs 1961, Minute-Long Ditties, for soprano, flute and piano 1961, Children's Terzettos, for 3 children's voices, flute, harp and double bass to lyrics by Frantisek Branislav 1962, Sulamit, songs for alto and orchestra 1963, Aesop – Cantata suite for mixed choir and orchestra according to Aesop's Fables 1964, June Night – A cycle of duets for children's (girls) choir to piano accompaniment to folk poetry lyrics 1965, Pastorella for children's chorus and chamber ensemble 1965, Scenes for children's chorus to texts by Vaclav Fischer 1971, Echo – Chamber Cantata for soloists, girl's choir, chamber and string orchestra, oboe and piano to the composer's own text 1982, Conversation Between Mother And Child – Children's choruses to folk and the composer's own texts 1984, Seasonal Madrigals 1984, The Carp, The Flea And So On – Ditties for children's choruses with piano accompaniment to the composer's own texts 1985, Water, Little Water – Children's choruses to lyrics by Vaclav Fischer 1986, Oratorio for children's chorus and orchestra 1990, Missa Vinea Crucis for children's choir and orchestra/organ 1991; ballets: Ondráš 1949, Faux pas de quatre 1987; operas: The Lady and Robbers 1966, Diogenes 1973, Fishermen In Their Own Nets 1981, Oldřich a Boženka 1985, Wisemen and Fools 1986; recorded complete works of Debussy. *Publications:* The Journey with a Butterfly, Marshland, Childhood in Silesia (memoirs), Laurel Leaves 1987; children's books, including Kterak psáti a řečniti (How to Write and Speak) 1997, Final Report 2000. *Honours:* Dr hc (Univ. of Ostrava) 1992; Czech Musical Fund Prize 1967, Supraphon Prize 1971, Grand Prix, Piano Duo Asscn of Japan 1990, Int. Antonín Dvořák Prize 2001. *Address:* Český rozhlas, Vinohradská 12, 120 99 Prague 2; Národní třída 35, 110 00 Prague 1, Czech Republic. *Telephone:* (2) 2421-4226.

**HURSHELL, Edmund;** Singer (Bass-baritone); b. 1921, USA. *Education:* Studied in the USA and Germany. *Career:* Engaged at the Stadtische Oper Berlin, 1952–53, Kiel 1953–55, Vienna Staatsoper 1955–60, as Amonasro, Scarpia, Alfio, Pizarro Hans Sachs, Orestes and Mandryka; Théâtre de la Monnaie Brussels, 1961, as the villains in Les Contes d'Hoffmann, Bologna and Amsterdam 1963, as Wolfram and Wotan; Sang Handel's Giulio Cesare at Barcelona 1964, the Dutchman and the Wanderer at Buenos Aires and Lille, 1965; Further engagements at Nuremberg, Rome, Tel-Aviv, Athens and Philadelphia; Metropolitan Opera 1967, as Kurwenal in Tristan; Appearances at Graz 1967–69; Other roles included Kaspar, the Grand Inquisitor and Falstaff. *Address:* c/o Vereinigte Buhnen, Kaiser Josef Platz 10, 8010 Graz, Austria.

**HURST, George;** Conductor; b. 20 May 1926, Edinburgh, Scotland. *Education:* Various preparatory and public schools in England and Canada; Royal Conservatory, Toronto. *Career:* Assistant Conductor, Opera, Royal Conservatory of Music, Toronto, 1946; Lecturer, Harmony and Counterpoint, Composition etc, Peabody Conservatory of Music, Baltimore, USA, 1947; Conductor, York Pennsylvania Symphony Orchestra, 1950–55, concurrently of Peabody Conservatory Orchestra, 1952–55; Assistant Conductor, London Philharmonic Orchestra 1955–57 with tour of Russia, 1956; Associate Conductor, BBC Northern Symphony Orchestra, 1957; Principal Conductor, BBC Northern Symphony Orchestra (previously BBC Northern Orchestra), 1958–68; Artistic Adviser, Western Orchestral Society, 1968–73; Staff Conductor, Western Orchestral Society (Bournemouth Symphony Orchestra and Bournemouth Sinfonietta), 1973–; Principal Guest Conductor, BBC Scottish Symphony Orchestra, 1986–89; Principal Conductor, National Symphony Orchestra of Ireland, 1990–93; Frequent Guest Conductor, Europe, Israel, Canada, 1956–. *Address:* 21 Oslo Court, London NW8, England.

**HURST, John;** Singer (Tenor); b. 1958, Norfolk, West Virginia, USA. *Education:* Studied in the USA, in Vienna and at the Salzburg Mozarteum. *Career:* Sang at the Vienna Volksoper from 1987, notably as Mozart's Idomeneo, Max in Der Freischütz, Erik in Der fliegende Holländer and Lenski in Eugene Onegin (1990); Alwa in Berg's Lulu; Guest appearances at the Schwetzingen Festival, Hamburg Staatsoper, Cologne (as Eisenstein in Die Fledermaus), Strasbourg and Tokyo. *Honours:* Winner, 1982 Belvedere Competition, Vienna. *Address:* c/o Vienna Volksoper, Währingerstrasse 78, 1090 Vienna, Austria.

**HURWITZ, Emanuel,** CBE, FRAM, FRSAMD, FRSA; British violinist; b. 7 May 1919, London; s. of the late Isaac Hurwitz and Sarah Gabrilovitch; m. Kathleen Crome 1948; one s. one d. *Education:* Royal Acad. of Music, London. *Career:* Leader, Hurwitz String Quartet 1946–53, Melos Ensemble 1956–74; Leader Goldsborough Orchestra 1947–57, English Chamber Orchestra 1957–69, New Philharmonia Orchestra 1968–70, Aeolian String Quartet 1970–81; Prof., RAM 1968–87; Visiting Lecturer, Royal Scottish Acad. of Music and Drama 1987–, Univ. of Michigan 1995; recorded complete Haydn Quartets with Aeolian Quartet 1972–76; now active internationally in chamber music master classes; f. Emanuel Hurwitz Chamber Music Trust 1993; Pres. Inc. Soc. of Musicians 1995–96. *Honours:* Gold Medal, Worshipful Company of Musicians 1965. *Address:* 25 Dollis Avenue, London, N3 1DA, England (home). *Telephone:* (20) 8346-3936 (home). *Fax:* (20) 8343-1595 (home).

**HUS, Walter;** Composer and Pianist; b. 2 July 1959, Mol, Belgium. *Education:* Diploma supérieur, Brussels Royal Conservatory, 1984. *Career:* Recitals as classical pianist since early childhood, Italy, Germany, Poland;

Performances as improviser/interpreter of own compositions, 1982–; Concerts throughout Europe with group Maximalist, own compositions, 1984–; Member, Belgisch Pianokwartet, Simpletones, etc; Various radio and television appearances; Video film with Marie André and Walter Verdin; Composer, several works for ballet, full-sized opera. *Compositions include:* 8 etudes on improvisation, piano solo; Music for fashion show, Yamamoto, Brussels; Muurwerk, music for choreography, Roxane Huilmand; Die Nacht, opera, 2 acts, libretto by Wolfgang Klob (unfinished); Compositie, video film by Marie André and W Hus; Hus/Verdin, video tape by Walter Verdin; Liefde, composition for 4 pianists at 2 pianos; La Theorie, idem, both written for Belgisch Pianokwartet; Nox aeterna for piano, 1994; Kopnaad, incidental music, 1995. *Recordings:* 8 etudes on improvisation, 1984; Maximalist, 1985; Muurwerk, 1986; Die Nacht, radio recording, 1987. *Honours:* 1st Prize, Piano 1981, Paris Conservatory. *Current Management:* Lucifer Productions.

**HUSA, Karel;** American composer and conductor; b. 7 Aug. 1921, Prague, Czech Repub.; s. of the late Karel Husa and Bozena Husova; m. Simone Husa (née Perault); four d. *Education:* Prague Conservatory of Music, Prague Acad. of Music, Paris Conservatory of Music, Ecole normale de musique de Paris. *Career:* composer, conductor in Paris, guest conductor with European orchestras, Kappa Alpha Prof. of Music, Cornell Univ. 1954, Asst Prof. 1954, Assoc. Prof. 1957, Prof. 1961; conductor of the univ. orchestras, teacher of composition (retd 1992), guest conductor with American orchestras and lecturer; Prof. Ithaca Coll., School of Music 1967–86; mem. Belgian Royal Acad. of Arts and Sciences 1974–, American Acad. of Arts and Letters 1994–. *Dance:* Monodrama (ballet) for Butler Ballet, Indiana 1976, The Steadfast Tin Soldier for Boulder Philharmonic, Colorado 1974, The Trojan Women for Louisville Ballet, Kentucky 1980. *Film:* Young Generation 1946, Gen, Prague 2001, Karel Husa Comes Home 2002. *Music:* Music for Prague 1968, Apotheosis of this Earth 1972, four string quartets; concertos for piano, brass quintet, organ, viola, violin, cello, saxophone, percussion, trumpet, orchestra; symphonies (Mosaiques, Fantasies); chamber music includes quintets for wind, brass, works for piano, sonatas for violin, music for band. *Publications:* Music for Prague; Apotheosis of this Earth; Concerto for Orchestra; The Trojan Women; An American Te Deum; Concerto for Sax and Winds; Concerto for Wind Ensemble; Les couleurs fauves, Cayuga Lake; Four Quartets; Twelve Moravian Songs; Sonata a Tre; Symphony No. 1; Evocation de Slovaquie; Serenade. *Honours:* hon. degrees include Coe Coll. 1976, Cleveland Inst. of Music 1985, Ithaca Coll. 1986, Baldwin-Wallace Coll. 1991, St Vincent Coll. 1995, Hartwick Coll. 1997, New England Conservatory 1998, Masaryk Univ., Brno 2000, Acad. of Musical Arts, Prague 2000; awards include Pulitzer Prize 1969, Sudler Prize 1984, Friedheim Award 1985, Grawemeyer Award 1993, Guggenheim Award 1964, 1965, Sousa Order of Merit 1985, Czech Repub. Medal of Merit (First Class) 1995, Medal of Honor of the City of Prague 1998. *Address:* 4535 S. Atlantic Avenue, Apt. 2106, Daytona Beach, FL 32127 (office); 1 Belwood Lane, Ithaca, NY 14850, USA (home). *Telephone:* (386) 322-0635 (Winter) (office); (607) 257-7018 (Summer) (office). *Fax:* (607) 257-0616 (home).

**HUSS, Hugo Jan;** Symphony Orchestra Conductor; b. 26 Jan. 1934, Timisoara, Romania; m. Mirella Regis, 1 Aug 1970, 1 d. *Education:* Diplomat in Arts, speciality Symphony Orchestra Conducting, Bucharest Conservatory of Music, 1958; Master of Business Administration, Roosevelt University of Chicago, 1977. *Career:* Debut: Concert, Romanian Athenaeum, Bucharest; Television appearance, performance of Tosca with Placido Domingo; Radio broadcasts with La Crosse Symphony, Wisconsin; Radio Louisville with Louisville Symphony, Kentucky; Radio Birmingham with Alabama Symphony; Guest Conductor, Cape Town Symphony, South Africa; Tbilisi, Russia; Kraków, Poland; Brno, Czechoslovakia; Sarajevo, Yugoslavia; Veracruz, Mexico; Grand Rapids, Michigan and Huntsville, Alabama, USA; Music Director and Conductor of Arad Symphony, Romania; Principal Guest Conductor of Gunthe Symphony, Munich, Germany; Titular Director and Principal Conductor of Guadalajara Symphony, Mexico; Music Director of the La Crosse Symphony, Wisconsin, USA, Conductor Emer. 1998; Guest Conducting engagements around the world; Opened the Constantin Silvestri International Festival with a concert in Târgu-Mures, Romania, 1997. *Honours:* Order of Cultural Merit (Romania) 1968. *Address:* N1972 Hickory Lane, La Crosse, WI 54601, USA. *E-mail:* hugo@hugohuss.com. *Website:* www.hugohuss.com.

**HUSSON, Suzanne;** Pianist; b. 4 April 1943, Buenos Aires, Argentina. *Education:* Began musical studies at age 5 with Mrs E Westerkamp; Later attended Conservatoire M de Falla, Buenos Aires; Conservatory of Geneva (Prof Hilbrandt); Staatliche Hochschule für Musik, Köln (Prof B Seidhofer); Special Courses given by Arturo Benedetti Michelangeli (Italy and Switzerland). *Career:* Debut: 1st Public Recital at age 8, Buenos Aires; Various international performances in recitals and as soloist with conductors such as Marc Andreae, W Sawallisch, C Dutoit, and Orchestra Philarmonique de Lyon, Stuttgart Philharmonic, Orchestra de la Radio Suisse Italienne and Orchestra of Swiss Romande; Television and radio appearances in Germany and Switzerland; Radio appearances in Argentina, Poland and France. *Recordings:* Stravinsky, Les Noces, directed by Charles Dutoit, Erato Label, 1973; R Vuataz, Concert for Piano and Orchestra, Opus 112, Orchestra of Swiss Romande, directed by Wolfgang Sawallisch, CBS Label, 1981; Scarlatti-Ginastera-Debussy-Ravel, Fono Label, 1987; Latin American Classics, Guatemala, Manuel Martinez-Sobral piano music, Vols 3 and 5, 1999, 2003.

*Current Management:* Wismer-Casetti, Rue Merle-d'Aubigné 26, 1207 Geneva, Switzerland. *Address:* 24 rue de la Dôle, 1203 Geneva, Switzerland (office). *Telephone:* (22) 345-3470 (office). *E-mail:* shusson@bluemail.ch (office). *Website:* www.musicedition.ch/interpret (office).

**HUSZAR, Lajos;** composer; *Professor of Music Theory, University of Szeged;* b. 26 Sept. 1948, Szeged, Hungary. *Education:* Secondary Music School, Szeged, with Istvan Vantus, 1963–67; Academy of Music, Budapest, with Endre Szervanszky and Zsolt Durko, 1967–73; Academy of St Cecilia, Rome, Italy, with Goffredo Petrassi, 1975. *Career:* Prof. of Music Theory Univ. of Szeged 1990–; mem. Association of Hungarian Composers; Hungarian Society of Music. *Compositions include:* Musica concertante for 13 players 1975, 69th Psalm for tenor and piano 1976, 5 Pieces for piano 1977, Scherzo and Adagio for chamber orchestra 1979, Sonata for harpsichord 1979–85, Brass Quintet 1980, 3 Songs to poems by Else Lasker-Schüler for soprano and viola 1981–89, Serenata Concertante for flute and string orchestra, Songs of Solitude for soprano and percussion 1983, Notturno for piano 1984, Concerto Rustico for chamber orchestra 1985, Chamber Concerto for cello and 17 strings 1987, Libera me for organ 1993, The Silence, opera in 2 acts 1994–98, Trittico estivo for oboe and piano 1998, Icons to the memory of János Pilinszky for soprano and chamber orchestra 2000–01, Passio for soloists, choir, organ and percussion 2003–04. *Recordings:* Dies Sanctificatus, Chamber Concerto, 69th Psalm, Brass Quintet, Songs of Solitude. *Honours:* Erkel Prize 1994, Bartók-Pásztory Prize 2003. *Address:* Postás u. 12, 6729 Szeged, Hungary. *E-mail:* huszarla@hotmail.com.

**HUTCHESON, Jere Trent;** American composer and academic; *Professor of Music, Michigan State University;* b. 16 Sept. 1938, Marietta, Georgia; m. (1) Virginia Bagby, 1 d., (2) Mary Ellen Gayley Cleland, 21 June 1982, 1 s., 1 d. *Education:* BMus, Stetson University; MMus, Louisiana State University; PhD, Michigan State University; Berkshire Music Center. *Career:* Prof. Michigan State Univ. 1965–. *Compositions include:* Passacaglia for band; 3 Things for Dr Seuss; Shadows of Floating Life; Wonder Music I, II, III, IV, V; Sensations; Transitions; Construction Set; Colossus; 3 Pictures of Satan; Electrons; Fantaisie-Impromptu; Nocturnes of the Inferno; Passing, Passing, Passing; Patterns; Cosmic Suite; Earth Gods Symphony; Chromophonic Images for symphonic band; Will-O-The-Wisps for solo violin; The Song Book for tenor and flute; Duo Sonata for clarinet and percussion; Concerto for piano and wind orchestra; Metaphors for orchestra; Interplay for alto saxophone and mallet percussion; Ritual and Dance for female chorus; Five French Portraits for wind orchestra; Duo Concertante in memoria di Margot Evans for violin and piano; Concerto for violin and small orchestra; Long Live the Composer, chamber opera; Dance of Time Symphony, 1995; Caricatures for wind symphony, 1997; Portfolio for cello and chamber ensemble, 1997; More Caricatures for wind symphony, 1999; Glosses, Annotations and an Exegesis for cello and piano (also violin and piano), 1999; Mrs Dalloway's Party for mezzo-soprano and piano, 1999; Caricatures III for wind symphony, 2000; Three Notions for saxophone quartet, 2000; Three Visions for full orchestra, 2001; Quirky Etudes for piano; Sonata for Piano; Concerto for solo percussion and wind symphony; Divertimento for flute solo, winds and percussion; Three Pieces for Tuba and Piano, Gradus ad Parnassum – Caricatures IV for wind symphony; Petals Over Time for mezzo-soprano and piano; Variations and Excursions for string trio; Concerto for saxophone and wind symphony, Histwhist for mixed chorus and arranged for children's chorus SA, Lament for mixed chorus and arranged for women's chorus SSA, Taj Mahal for small orchestra, Desert Flower for wind symphony, Mist of Tears for mixed chorus and piano, Reflections-Caricatures V for wind symphony. *Recordings:* Deja View contains Caricatures for wind symphony 1997; DuoDenum (saxophone and percussion), Caricatures by Rutgers Univ. Wind Ensemble contains Caricature Suite 2004. *Publications:* Musical Form and Analysis, text, 1995. *Address:* 6064 Abbott Road, East Lansing, MI 48823, USA. *Telephone:* (517) 355-7664 (office); (517) 337-0295 (home). *E-mail:* hutcheso@msu.edu (office). *Website:* www.music.msu.edu/faculty/faculty.php?id=15 (office).

**HUTCHINSON, Nigel;** Concert Pianist; b. 1963, England. *Education:* University of Glasgow, Guildhall School with Craig Sheppard and Juilliard with Earl Wild. *Career:* Debut: Wigmore Hall, 1988; Concerts in France, Germany, Italy, Czechoslovakia and elsewhere in Europe; Concerto debut with the London Mozart Players under Jane Glover; Festival engagements at Harrogate and Glasgow, and recitals at the Salle Pleyel Paris, Barbican Centre and Festival Hall, London and Symphony Hall Birmingham; Broadcasts for BBC and Italian Radio; Purcell Room recital 1993, with Schubert (D664), Liszt and Debussy. *Recordings:* Rachmaninov music for six hands, with John Ogdon and Brenda Lucas, and Carnival of the Animals with the London Symphony Orchestra under Barry Wordsworth.

**HUTCHINSON, Stuart;** Conductor and Concert Accompanist; b. 3 March 1956, London, England. *Education:* Royal Academy of Music, London; Cambridge University; BMus (Honours), 1977; LRAM, 1979; ARAM, 1997; Studied with Bernstein and Pritchard. *Career:* Opera, Ballet and Music-Theatre Conductor: Productions for English National Opera, Scottish Opera, Theater des Westens Berlin, New Sadler's Wells Opera Company, Sadler's Wells Theatre/ROH, London International Opera Festival, Royal Academy of Music; Conductor, Scottish Ballet, 1991; Chorus Master, Dublin Grand Opera and Wexford Festival Opera; Music Staff, English National Opera, Opera North; Director of Music, Organist, University of London Chaplaincy, 1976–89; Music Director, Northcott Theatre, Exeter, 1982–84; Music Director, Artistic Director, Morley Opera, London, 1986–90; Music Director, Jonathan

Miller's Company/Old Vic Theatre, 1988–89; World premiere, Alice in Wonderland (Carl Davis), Lyric Theatre, Hammersmith, 1986; British premiere, Postcard From Morocco, (Dominick Argento) LIOF, 1988; World premiere, Tables Meet, (Stephen Oliver), Royal Festival Hall, 1990; Also productions for the Royal Shakespeare Company, (London), On Your Toes, with Makarova, West End, 1984; mem, Performing Right Society; Musicians Union. *Compositions:* Incidental theatre music including King Lear (Miller/Old Vic); Frequent arranger and orchestrator. *Recordings:* National Philharmonic Orchestra with James Galway; Philharmonia Orchestra with Michie Nakamaru; Several recordings for BBC Radio 3 and 4; Many for BBC Radio Drama; BBC and Independent Television. *Publications:* Prepared/Edited the 1995 (Opera North) Version of William Walton's Troilus and Cressida. *Contributions:* Opera magazine (Troilus and Cressida: Forty Years On), 1995. *Current Management:* Music International, 13 Ardilaun Road, London N5 2QR, England. *Address:* Suite 390, 37 Store Street, Bloomsbury, London WC1E 7QF, England.

**HUTTENLOCHER, Philippe;** Singer (Baritone); b. 29 Nov. 1942, Neuchatel, Switzerland. *Education:* Studied with Julette Bise in Fribourg. *Career:* Sang with the Ensemble Vocal de Lausanne and with the Choeurs de la Foundation Gulbenkian, Lisbon; Festival appearances in Montreux, Lausanne, Strasbourg and Ansbach in the Baroque repertory; Tour of Japan 1974; Zürich Opera 1975, as the title role in Monteverdi's Orfeo, produced by Jean-Pierre Ponnelle; London Bach Festival, 1978; Guest appearances in Vienna, Berlin, Hamburg, Milan and Edinburgh; Genoa 1987, in Dido and Aeneas and Les Malheurs d'Orphée by Milhaud. *Recordings include:* Bach Cantatas and operas by Monteverdi including Il Ritorno d'Ulisse and L'Orfeo (video); St Matthew Passion; Le Devin du Village by Rousseau; Die Jahreszeiten by Haydn, Bach B Minor Mass; Les Indes Galantes by Rameau, Così fan tutte, Il Maestro di Capella, Pénélope, St John Pasion, Handel Dettingen Te Deum and works by Carissimi, MA Charpentier and Gabrieli.

**HUYBRECHTS, Francois;** Conductor; b. 15 June 1946, Antwerp, Belgium. *Education:* Studied Cello and Clarinet at the Antwerp Conservatory; Conducting studies with Daniel Sternefeld, Bruno Maderna and Hans Swarowsky. *Career:* Debut: As Cellist, 1960; Conducting, 1963 The Fairy Queen by Purcell, Royal Flemish Opera; Conducted the Netherlands Chamber Opera, 1966–67; Concerts at the Salzburg Mozarteum 1967; Assisted Bernstein at the New York Philharmonic and conducted the Los Angeles Philharmonic and the Berlin Philharmonic; Musical Director of the Wichita Symphony 1972–79, San Antonio Symphony 1979–80. *Recordings include:* Janáček's Taras Bulba and Lachian Dances (London Philharmonic); Nielsen's 3rd Symphony (London Symphony Orchestra/Decca). *Honours:* Winner, Dimitri Mitropoulos Competition, New York, 1968; Prizewinner, Herbert von Karajan Foundation Competition, 1969. *Address:* c/o Polygram Classics, PO Box 1420, 1 Sussex Place, Hammersmith, London W6 9XS, England.

**HVOROSTOVSKY, Dmitri;** Russian singer (baritone); b. 16 Oct. 1962, Krasnoyarsk, Siberia. *Education:* Krasnoyarsk High School of Arts with Jekatherina Yofel. *Career:* soloist with Krasnoyarsk Opera 1986–; debut Wigmore Hall, London 1989, Alice Tully Hall, New York, Washington Kennedy Center 1990, BBC Promenade Concerts 1993; appeared in Aix-en-Provence and Salzburg Festivals 1992; has performed recitals in Europe, USA and Russia. *Roles include:* The Queen of Spades (Opéra de Nice) 1989, (Metropolitan Opera, New York) 1999, Eugene Onegin (La Fenice) 1991, (Châtelet, Paris) 1992, (Covent Garden) 1993, Il Barbiere di Siviglia (San Francisco Opera) 1991, I Puritani (Covent Garden) 1992, La Traviata (Chicago Lyric Opera) 1993, (Metropolitan Opera, New York) 2003, (Cagliari) 2004, (San Francisco Opera) 2004, (La Fenice) 2004, I Masnadieri (Covent Garden) 1998, 2002, Rigoletto (Novaya Opera, Moscow) 2000, (Covent Garden) 2005, Don Giovanni (Metropolitan Opera, New York) 2002, (Hamburg) 2003, Don Carlos (Zurich Oper) 2003, (Vienna) 2005, Pikovaya Dama (Metropolitan Opera, New York) 2004, (Teatro Real, Madrid) 2004, (La Scala, Milan) 2005, War and Peace (Salzburg Festival) 2004, Il Trovatore (Bastille Opera, Paris) 2004, Faust (Metropolitan Opera, New York) 2005. *Recordings include:* Tchaikovsky and Verdi Arias, Cavalleria Rusticana, Eugene Onegin, Don Carlos. *Honours:* First Prize USSR Nat. Glinka Competition 1987, Toulouse Singing Competition 1988, BBC Cardiff Singer of the World Competition 1989. *Current Management:* Askonas Holt Ltd, Lonsdale Chambers, 27 Chancery Lane, London, WC2A 1PF, England. *Telephone:* (20) 7400-1700. *Fax:* (20) 7400-1799. *E-mail:* info@askonasholt.co.uk. *Website:* www.askonasholt.co.uk.

**HWANG, Der-Shin;** Singer (Mezzo-soprano) and Teacher; b. 8 Feb. 1958, Taiwan. *Education:* BA in piano/voice, Taiwan University; Master of Fine Arts in Singing, University of California, Los Angeles; Associate of RCM honours in performing singing, Royal College of Music, London. *Career:* Debut: Suzuki, Holland Park; Serenade to Music with Hanley/RPO in Festival Hall and with Charles Groves/Philharmonia in the Barbican, 1989; Anitra in Peer Gynt with Neeme Järvi/Gothenburg Symphony Orchestra, Barbican, 1992–93; Haydn and Handel solo contatas with Tallis Chamber Orchestra, 1993; Mozart arias in Sandwich Festival, 1993; Christmass Magnificat with English Baroque Orchestra in Queen Elizabeth Hall, 1993; Judas Maccabaeus in Handel's Canon Park Church with London Mozart Players, 1994; Many other oratorio concerts with the choral societies in the United Kingdom including works such as Elgar's The Music Makers, Rossini's Stabat Mater, Petite Messe Solennelle, Mozart's C Minor Mass. Opera: Suzuki with many companies including Singapore Lyric Theatre, Crystal Clear and in Festival Mozart at Roubaix,

France; Other operatic roles including Prince Orlofsky, Siebel, Despina, Cherubino, Baba the Turk, Olga; Worked with companies such as Clonter Opera for All, City of Birmingham Touring Opera, Opera Factory and English National Opera; Solo Recitals. *Current Management:* Dal Segno Management. *Address:* Flat 2, 19 Woodstock Road, London NW11 8ES, England.

**HWANG, Sin-nyung;** South Korean singer (soprano); b. 21 Dec. 1972. *Career:* opera roles include Barbarina in Le Nozze di Figaro, Grand Théâtre, Geneva, Deuxième Dame in Dido and Aeneas, Opéra de Marseille 2005, Don Pasquale, Brescia, Italy 2005; performed a Haydn mass, Besançon, France 2005. *Honours:* second prize Valsesia Viotti Int. Competition 1998, Julian Gayarre Int. Singing Competition Orfeon Pamplones Prize, Pamplona 2002, first prize Arles Singing Competition 2003, winner Montréal Int. Singing Competition 2005. *Address:* Place de l'Octroi 10, Carouge 1227, Switzerland (office). *E-mail:* hwngsnyng@yahoo.it (office).

**HYDE-SMITH, Christopher;** Flautist and Teacher; b. 11 March 1935, Cairo, Egypt; 1 s., 1 d. *Education:* Royal College of Music, London. *Career:* Debut: Royal Festival Hall, 1962; Member, Camden Wind Quintet, London Mozart Players; Many flute and piano and/or harpsichord concerts with Jane Dodd; Appearances in Netherlands, Switzerland, Italy, France, Germany, Spain, Portugal, Scandinavia, Russia, North and South America; Professor, Royal College of Music; Dedicatee of works by Alwyn, Dodgson, Horovitz, Mathias and Rawsthorne; Judge at Leeds, Mozart and Tunbridge Wells Competitions; mem, Haydn Mozart Society; Chairman, British Flute Society. *Recordings:* Numerous recordings. *Current Management:* Lotte Nicholls, 16 Upper Wimpole Street, London WC1, England. *Address:* 94 Dorien Road, London SW20 8EJ, England.

**HYKES, David (Bond);** Composer; b. 2 March 1953, Taos, New Mexico, USA. *Education:* Studied Classical Azerbaijani and Armenian Music with Zevulon Avshalomov, 1975–77; North Indian Raga Singing with S Dhar from 1982. *Career:* Founded the Harmonic Choir, 1975; Resident at the Cathedral of St John the Divine, New York from 1979; Tours of the USA and Europe from 1980. *Compositions:* Harmonic Tissues for electronics, 1971; Shadow Frequencies for piano and electronics, 1975; Looking for Gold/Life in the Sun for children's voices and ensemble, 1975; Well-struck Strings for dulcimer, 1975–83; Special Delivery/Rainbow Voice for low voice, 1975–84; Test Studies for Harmonica Orchestra for ensemble, 1975–85; Hearing Solar Winds for voices, 1977–83; Outside of Being There for voices, 1981; Turkestan for synthesizer, 1979; Current Circulation for voices, 1984; Subject to Change for low voice and drones, 1983; Desert Hymns, 1984. *Honours:* Grants from the National Endowment for the Arts, 1978, 1983, The Rockefeller Foundation 1980–83, and UNESCO, 1983. *Address:* c/o ASCAP, ASCAP Building, 1 Lincoln Plaza, NY 10023, USA.

**HYNES, Rachel;** Singer (Soprano); b. 1965, South Wales. *Education:* Leeds University and Royal Scottish Academy of Music. *Career:* Appearances from 1997 with Scottish Opera in Rigoletto, The Queen of Spades, Aida and Macbeth (also at Vienna Festival); Company Principal from 2000, with Freia in Das Rheingold, Helmwige in Die Walküre and Third Norn in Götterdämmerung (2000-03); Further engagements as Inès in Il Trovatore, Giannetta (L'Elisir d'amore) and Mozart's Fiordiligi; Essential Scottish Opera tours, 2001–2002; Sang Anna Kennedy in Donizetti's Maria Stuarda (concert) at the 2002 Edinburgh Festival; Season 2002–2003 with Gluck's Euridice and Third Lady in The Magic Flute. *Honours:* Hobart Trust Award. *Address:* c/o Scottish Opera, 39 Elmbank Crescent, Glasgow, G2 4PT, Scotland.

**HYNNINEN, Jorma;** Finnish singer (baritone); b. 3 April 1941, Leppävirta; m. Reetta Salo 1961; one s. two d. *Education:* Sibelius Acad., Helsinki. *Career:* debut as Silvio in Pagliacci, Finnish Nat. Opera 1969; as Tonio in Pagliacci, Staatsoper Vienna 1977; La Scala, Milan 1977; Paris Opéra 1978; Bavarian State Opera, Munich 1979; Metropolitan Opera, New York 1984 as Posa; San Francisco Opera 1988; Lyric Opera of Chicago 1989; Deutsche Oper Berlin 1991 as Hindemith's Mathis der Maler; lieder recitals, New York, London, Europe and Beijing; soloist with Vienna Symphony, Boston Symphony and Israel Philharmonic; sang Amfortas in Parsifal at Antwerp 1996; Savonlinna Festival 1998, as Wagner's Wolfram; premieres include The Red Line and The King Goes Forth to France by Sallinen 1978, 1984, Thomas, and Vincent by Rautavaara 1985, 1990, and Sallinen's Kullervo 1992; season 2000 at Helsinki at Simon Boccanegra, Papageno, and Gloucester in the premiere of Lear by Aulis Sallinen; Tsar Nicholas in the premiere of Rautavaara's Rasputin, Helsinki 2003; Prof. of Arts, Finland 1990–. *Recordings:* Le nozze di Figaro with Riccardo Muti, Orestes in Elektra with Seiji Ozawa, Brahms' Requiem and Mahler's Eighth with Klaus Tennstedt, Winterreise, Die schöne Müllerin, Dichterliebe, Songs of Sibelius, Die schöne Magelone, Lieder eines Fahrenden Gesellen, Evergreen Love Songs. *Current Management:* Allied Artists, 42 Montpelier Square, London, SW7 1JZ, England. *Telephone:* (20) 7589-6243. *Fax:* (20) 7581-5269. *E-mail:* info@alliedartists.co.uk. *Website:* www.alliedartists.co.uk. *Address:* Ruskokuja 3B, 01620 Vantaa, Finland. *Telephone:* (40) 5212100 (home). *Fax:* (9) 893886 (home).

**HYPOLITE, Andée-Louise;** Singer (Mezzo-soprano); b. 1975, London, England. *Education:* Royal Scottish Academy, with Patricia McMahon, and National Opera Studio, London. *Career:* Early roles include Clarice in Rossini's La Pietra del Paragone, Mrs Herring, and Bizet's Mercedes; Other roles include Dorabella, and Mrs Grose, in The Turn of the Screw; Concerts include Ravel's Chansons madècasses, Elgar's Sea Pictures, Vier ernste Gesänge by Brahms and Berio's Folk Songs; Sang Mahler's Rückert Lieder for

Scottish Ballet. *Address:* c/o National Opera Studio, Morley College, 61 Westminster Bridge Road, London, SE1 7XT, England.

**HYTNER, Nicholas Robert,** MA; British theatre director; *Artistic Director, Royal National Theatre*; b. 7 May 1956, Manchester; s. of Benet A. Hytner and Joyce Myers. *Education:* Manchester Grammar School and Trinity Hall, Cambridge. *Career:* staff producer, ENO 1978–80; Assoc. Dir Royal Exchange Theatre, Manchester 1985–89; Assoc. Dir Royal Nat. Theatre 1989–97, Artistic Dir 2003–. *Theatre and opera productions include:* Wagner's Rienzi (ENO) 1983, Tippett's King Priam (Kent Opera) 1984, Handel's Xerxes (ENO) (Olivier Award 1985), The Scarlet Pimpernel (Chichester Festival) 1985, As You Like It, Edward II, The Country Wife, Schiller's Don Carlos, (Royal Exchange) 1986, Handel's Giulio Cesare (Paris Opera), Measure for Measure (RSC) 1987, Tippett's The Knot Garden (Royal Opera), The Magic Flute (ENO), The Tempest (RSC) 1988, The Marriage of Figaro (Geneva Opera), Joshua Sobol's Ghetto (Nat.Theatre), Miss Saigon (Theatre Royal, Drury Lane) 1989, King Lear (RSC) 1990, The Wind in the Willows (Nat.Theatre) 1990, Volpone (Almeida) 1990, The Madness of George III (Nat.Theatre) 1991, The Recruiting Officer (Nat.Theatre) 1992, Carousel (Nat.Theatre) (Tony Award for BestDirof a Musical 1994) 1992, The Importance of Being Earnest, Aldwych 1993, Don Giovanni (Bavarian State Opera) 1994, The Cunning Little Vixen (Paris) 1995, The Cripple of Inishmaan 1997, The Crucible 1997, The Lady in the Van 1999, Cressida 2000, Orpheus Descending 2000, The Winter's Tale (Nat.Theatre) 2001, Mother Clap's Molly House (Nat.Theatre) 2001, Sweet Smell of Success (Broadway) 2002, The History Boys (Nat.Theatre) (Olivier Award for Best Director) 2004, Così fan Tutte (Glyndebourne) 2006. *Films:* The Madness of King George 1994, The Crucible 1996, The Object of My Affection 1998. *Honours:* Evening Standard Opera Award 1985, Evening Standard Best Dir Award 1989. *Address:* c/o Royal National Theatre, South Bank, London, SE1 9PX, England.

# I

**IANNACCONE, Anthony;** Composer, Conductor and Teacher; b. 14 Oct. 1943, New York, USA; m. Judith Trostle, 1 s., 1 d. *Education:* BMus, MMus, Manhattan School of Music; PhD, Eastman School of Music. *Career:* Conducted Orchestras, Choruses, Wind Ensembles and Chamber Groups throughout the USA including: Lincoln Center, New York; Many University appearances as Guest Conductor and Composer; Teacher, Manhattan School of Music, 1967–68; Composition Professor, 1971, Director of Collegium Musicum, 1973; Record Debut as Conductor of Cornell Wind Ensemble, 1983. *Compositions include:* 3 Symphonies, 1965, 1966, 1992; Approximately 40 published works, 14 commercially recorded for orchestra, chorus, wind ensemble and chamber ensembles; Octet, 1985; Chautauqua Psalms, 1987; Concertante for clarinet and orchestra, 1994; Crossings for orchestra, 1996; Piano Quintet, 1995; 2 string quartets, 1965, 1997; West End Express for orchestra, 1997. *Recordings include:* Partita, for piano, 1967; Rituals for violin and piano, 1973; Aria Concertante for cello and piano, 1976; Walt Whitman Song, for chorus, soloists and winds, 1981; No. 2 Terpsichore, 1981; Images of Song and Dance, No. 1 Orpheus, 1982; Divertimento, for orchestra, 1983; Two Piano Inventions, 1985; Night Rivers, Symphony No. 3, 1992; Sea Drift, 1993; String Quartet No. 3, 1999; Waiting for Sunrise, 2002. *Address:* PO Box 981272, Ypsilanti, MI 48198, USA.

**ICHIHARA, Taro;** Singer (Tenor); b. 2 Jan. 1950, Yamagata, Japan. *Education:* Studied at the Juilliard School, New York, and in Italy. *Career:* Debut: Tokyo, 1980, as Gounod's Faust; Sang at the Teatro San Carlos, Lisbon, from 1982, notably as Calaf; Paris Opéra from 1983, as Verdi's Macduff, Don Carlos, Riccardo and Duke of Mantua; Salzburg Festival, 1984–85, as Malcolm in Macbeth; Further engagements at Nice, Turin, Naples, Buenos Aires (Verdi Requiem), Orange Festival (Ismaele in Nabucco) and Tokyo; Metropolitan Opera, New York, 1986–89, as the Italian Singer in Der Rosenkavalier and the Duke of Mantua; La Scala, 1989, as Gabriele Adorno; Cologne Opera, 1992; Other roles include Alfredo, Enzo in La Gioconda and Edgardo. *Address:* c/o Kajimoto Management Ltd, Kahoku Building, 8-6-25 Ginza, Chuo-Ku, Tokyo 104–0061, Japan.

**ICONOMOU, Panajotis;** Singer (Bass); b. 1971, Munich, Germany. *Education:* Guildhall School of Music from 1995; National Opera Studio in London. *Career:* Concert choir of the Tolzer Knabenchor, 1982–86, with the tours of Europe and solos under leading conductors; Bass with the Tolzer concert choir, 1988–92, with Mozart's Vespers at Versailles; Bach's Christmas Oratorio at the First Israel Bach Festival, under Peter Schreier; Further concerts at Munich, Hamburg, Milan and Vienna; Season 1997–98 with Bach and Telemann cantatas at the York Early Music Festival; Beethoven's Missa Solemnis at the Barbican; Christmas Oratorio in Munich; Mozart Sarastro at Holland Park and Osmin at Saar; Season 1999–2000 with Sparafucile for Welsh National Opera and Masetto for Scottish Opera. *Address:* c/o Welsh National Opera, John Street, Cardiff, CF1 ASP, Wales.

**IDANE, Yasuhiko;** Singer (Tenor); b. 1962, Japan. *Career:* Frequent appearances in the Far East and Europe, in operas by Puccini (Il Tabarro), Leoncavallo (La Bohème) and Mascagni (Cavalleria Rusticana); Also songs by Japanese composers, including Kobayashi; Contestant at the 1995 Cardiff Singer of the World Competition. *Address:* 6-23-3 Akatsuka, Itabashi-ku, Tokyo, Japan.

**IGOSHINA, Valentina;** Concert Pianist; b. 1972, Bryansk, Russia. *Education:* Moscow Conservatory Central Music School, 1990. *Career:* recitals and concerts throughout Russia and Western Europe 1993–, with repertory including Bach, Chopin, Brahms and Schumann; performed Rachmaninov Preludes in Tony Palmer's film biography, The Harvest, and appeared as Delfina Potocka in The Mystery of Chopin; Season 2000–01 with Hallé Orchestra and BBC Scottish Symphony Orchestra; London debut, 2002, at South Bank Harrods International Piano Series concert; Season 2002–03 with Hallé Orchestra concerts, debut with London Philharmonic and tours of Channel Islands and Yugoslavia. *Honours:* winner, Arthur Rubinstein International Piano Competition, 1993; Rachmaninov International Competition, Moscow, 1997. *Current Management:* Ingpen & Williams Ltd, 7 St George's Court, 131 Putney Bridge Road, London, SW15 2PA, England.

**IHLE, Andrea;** Singer (Soprano); b. 17 April 1953, Dresden, Germany. *Education:* Studied at Musikhochschule Dresden. *Career:* Debut: Dresden Staatsoper, 1976, as Giannetta in L'Elisir d'amore; Appearances in Dresden have included Aennchen and Marianne, in the productions of Freischütz and Rosenkavalier which opened the rebuilt Semperoper, 1985; Other roles in Dresden and elsewhere in Germany, have included Mozart's Papagena and Despina, Euridice, Gretel, Sophie (Der Rosenkavalier), Carolina (Il Matrimonio Segreto) and Marie in La Fille du Régiment; Concert and oratorio engagements; Season 1999–2000 at Dresden in Lady Macbeth of the Mtsensk District and Der Rosenkavalier. *Recordings:* Freischütz and Rosenkavalier; Bach's Christmas Oratorio; Missa Brevis by Carl Friedrich Fasch. *Address:* Semper Oper Dresden, 8012 Dresden, Germany.

**IHLOFF, Jutta-Renate;** Singer (Soprano); b. 1 Nov. 1944, Winteberg, Germany. *Education:* Studied with Marja Stein in Hamburg and with Giorgio Favaretto in Rome and Siena. *Career:* Debut: Staatsoper Hamburg 1973, as Zerlina in Don Giovanni; Has sung in Munich, Berlin, Vienna and Salzburg;

Frequent guest appearances elsewhere in Europe; Other roles include Mozart's Despina, Susanna, Blondchen and Pamina; Marzelline in Fidelio; Monteverdi's Poppea; Sophie and Zdenka; Mimi, Marie in Die Soldaten by Zimmermann, Adele in Die Fledermaus and Nannetta in Falstaff. *Recordings:* Serpetta in La Finta Giardiniera by Mozart.

**IKAIA-PURDY, Keith;** Singer (Tenor); b. 1956, Hawaii, USA. *Education:* Studied with Tito Gobbi, and with Carlo Bergonzi in Busetto. *Career:* Sang in opera throughout the USA from 1983, notably as Turiddu, the Duke of Mantua, Riccardo (Ballo in maschera), Cavaradossi, and Don José; Florestan in the original version of Fidelio at Berkeley, 1987; European debut at Bussetto, 1988, as Corado in Il Corsaro; Guested at Wiesbaden, 1989, as Alfredo, returning as Tebalo in Bellini's Capuleti; Vienna Staatsoper, 1993, Alfredo; Season 2000–01 as Arnold in Guillaume Tell, Ismaele, Macduff, Don Carlos and Hoffmann at the Vienna Staatsoper; Gaston in Jérusalem at Dresden (concert); Concert repertory includes Schubert's Die schöne Müllerin. *Address:* c/o Staatsoper, Opernring 2, 1010 Vienna, Austria.

**IKEDA, Kikuei;** Violinist; b. 31 Aug. 1947, Yokosuka, Japan; Studied at the Juilliard School with Dorothy DeLay and members of the Juilliard Quartet. *Career:* Second violin, Tokyo Quartet from 1974; Regular concerts in the USA and abroad; First cycle of the complete quartets of Beethoven at the Yale at Norfolk Chamber Music Festival, 1986; Repeated cycles at the 92nd Street Y New York, Ravinia and Israel Festivals, Yale, Princeton Universities; Season 1990–91 at Alice Tully Hall, the Metropolitan Museum of Art, New York, Boston, Washington DC, Los Angeles, Cleveland, Detroit, Chicago, Miami, Seattle, San Francisco, Toronto; Tour of South America, two tours of Europe including Paris, Amsterdam, Bonn, Milan, Munich, Dublin, London, Berlin; Quartet-in-residence at Yale University and at the University of Cincinnati College-Conservatory of Music. *Recordings:* Schubert's Major Quartets; Mozart Flute Quartets with James Galway and Clarinet Quintet with Richard Stoltzman; Quartets by Bartók, Brahms, Debussy, Haydn, Mozart and Ravel; Beethoven Middle Period Quartets. *Honours:* Grand Prix du Disque du Montreux; Best Chamber Music Recording of the Year from Stereo Review and the Gramophone; Four Grammy nominations. Address: Intermusica Artists' Management, 16 Duncan Terrace, London N1 8BZ, England.

**IKONOMOU, Katharine;** Singer (Soprano); b. 1957, Tashikent, Usbekistan, Russia. *Education:* Studied in Tashkent and at the Cologne Musikhochschule with Joseph Metternich. *Career:* Debut: Würzburg, 1984, as Salome; After further study in Italy sang Salome at Zürich, 1986, and Jenůfa at the 1988 Spoleto Festival (Chrysothemis, 1990); Sang Beethoven's Leonore at Trieste, 1990, and Fevronia in Rimsky's Invisible City of Kitezh (Florence, 1990); Rome, 1991, as Ariadne, Amelia in Ballo in Maschera at Genoa and Wagner's Senta at Catania, 1992. *Recordings include:* Songs by Russian composers. *Address:* c/o Theater Massimo Bellini, Via Perrotta 12, 95131 Catania, Italy.

**ILLES, Eva;** Singer (Soprano); b. 1939, Hungary. *Education:* Studied in Hungary. *Career:* Sang at the Regensburg Opera, 1967–69, Freiburg, 1969–71, Zürich, 1971–75, and Hanover, 1974–81; Guested at Covent Garden as Senta, 1972, at Barcelona and the Vienna Staatsoper; Other roles included Wagner's Elsa and Elisabeth, Ariadne, Amelia Grimaldi, Maddalena (Andrea Chénier), the Forza Leonora, and Turandot. *Address:* c/o Staatstheater Hanover, Opernhaus, Opernplatz 1, W-3000 Hanover 1, Germany.

**ILOSFALVY, Robert;** Hungarian singer (tenor); b. 18 June 1927, Hodmezovasarhely; m.; two c. *Education:* Budapest Acad. with Andor Lendvai. *Career:* soloist with the Artistic Ensemble of the People's Army from 1949; Budapest Opera from 1954, debut in the title role of Erkel's Hunyadi Laszlo; sang widely in Eastern Europe; San Francisco Opera 1964–68, New York Metropolitan Opera 1966; mem. Cologne Opera from 1966; Covent Garden 1968, as Des Grieux in Manon Lescaut; concerts with the Berlin Philharmonic and the Orchestra of the Accademia di Santa Cecilia; career centred on the Budapest Opera from 1981; Theatre de la Monnaie Brussels 1985, as Walther in Die Meistersinger; sang Walther von Stolzing at the 1986 Maggio Musicale, Florence; other roles include Rodolfo, Belmonte, Dick Johnson, Don José, Alfredo, Manrico, the Duke of Mantua, Lohengrin, Maurico, Don Alvaro, Conte Richard, Radamès, Hoffmann, Arnold, William Tell, Don Carlos, Florestan, Erbel's Bánk Bán, Kaiser (R. Strauss), Die Frau ohne Schatten, leading roles in Rigoletto, Un Ballo in Maschera, La Traviata, La Bohème, Hungaroton. *Recordings:* Madama Butterfly and Manon Lescaut, Hungaroton, Roberto Devereux (with Beverly Sills), Requiem by Dvořák (conducted by Kertesz), Rigoletto, Ballo del Mosca, Psalmus Hungaricus by Kodaly, Die Lustige Witwe by Lehár, Puccini's Il Tabarro and La Bohème, Puccini and Verdi. *Honours:* Lizst Prize 1961, Kossuth Prize 1965, Hungarian Repub. Honoured Artist 1987, eternal mem. Hungarian Opera House 1993, Hungarian Repub. Master Artist 2004. *Address:* c/o Hungarian State Opera House, Andrassy út 22, 1061 Budapest (office); Magyar Jakobinnsok Tere n/a, 1122 Budapest, Hungary (home). *Telephone:* (1) 3312-550 (office). *E-mail:* info@opera.hu (office).

**IMAI, Nobuko;** Japanese violist; b. 18 March 1943, Tokyo; m. Aart van Bochove 1981; one s. one d. *Education:* Toho School of Music, Tokyo, Juilliard School and Yale Univ., USA. *Career:* mem. Vermeer Quartet 1974–79; soloist with Berlin Philharmonic, London Symphony Orchestra, Royal Philharmonic, the BBC orchestras, Detroit Symphony, Chicago Symphony, Concertgebouw, Montreal Symphony, Boston Symphony, Vienna Symphony, Orchestre de Paris, Stockholm Philharmonic; festival performances include Marlborough, Salzburg, Lockenhaus, Casals, South Bank, Summer Music, Aldeburgh, BBC Proms, Int. Viola Congress (Houston), New York "Y", Festival d'Automne, Paris; conceived Int. Hindemith Viola Festival (London, New York, Tokyo) 1995; Prof. High School of Music, Detmold 1985–; Artistic Adviser, Casals Hall, Tokyo; over 20 recordings. *Honours:* First Prize Munich, Second Prize Geneva Int. Viola Competitions; Avon Arts Award 1993, Japanese Educ. Minister's Art Prize for Music 1993, Mobil Japan Art Prize 1995, Suntory Hall Prize 1996. *Address:* c/o Irene Witmer Personal Management in Classical Music, Leidsegracht 42, 1016 CM Amsterdam, Netherlands. *Telephone:* (20) 5244040. *Fax:* (20) 5244044.

**IMBRIE, Andrew W.;** American composer and academic; b. 6 April 1921, New York; m. Barbara Cushing 1953; two s. (one deceased). *Education:* studied piano with Leo Ornstein and Robert Casadesus, composition with Roger Sessions. *Career:* Prof., Univ. of California, Berkeley 1949–91, Jerry and Evelyn Hemmings Chambers Chair in Music 1989–91; visiting prof. at various univs and institutions; mem. American Acad. of Arts and Letters, American Acad. of Arts and Sciences; mem. bd of dirs, Koussevitzky Foundation. *Compositions include:* Orchestral: Violin Concerto, 1954; Three Symphonies, 1965, 1970; Cello Concerto, 1972; 3 Piano Concertos, 1973, 1974, 1992; Flute Concerto, 1977; Chamber: 5 String Quartets, 1942–87; 2 Piano Trios, 1946, 1989; Impromptu, for violin and pianoforte, 1960; To A Traveler for clarinet, violin and piano, 1971; Pilgrimage for flute, clarinet, violin, cello, piano and percussion, 1983; Dream Sequence for flute, oboe, clarinet, violin, viola, cello, piano and percussion, 1986; Spring Fever, for flute, oboe, clarinet, 2 violins, viola, violoncello, contrabass; pianoforte, percussion, 1996; Chicago Bells, for violin and piano, 1997; Piano Quartet, 1998; From Time to Time for flute, oboe, clarinet, bassoon, percussion, 2 violins, viola and 2 cellos, premiered at Chamber Music Society of Minnesota, 2001; Vocal: Operas; Christmas in Peebles Town (wincor), 1960; Angle of Repose, (Stegner-Hall), 1976, commissioned by San Francisco Opera; Requiem for Soprano, Chorus and Orchestra, 1984; 5 Roethke Songs for soprano and piano, 1990; Adam, cantata for Mixed Chorus, Soprano Solo, Chamber Orchestra, 1994; Songs of Then and Now for girls chorus, soprano, alto, flute, clarinet, violin, cello, piano and percussion, 1998. *Recordings:* Pilgrimage; Collage Ensemble, Gunther Schuller; Trio No. 2, Francesco Trio; Quartet No. 4, Emerson Quartet; Quartets No. 4 and No. 5, Pro Arte Quartet; Impromptu for violin and pianoforte; Parnassus Ensemble: Dream Sequence, Five Roethke Songs, Three Piece Suite, Campion Songs, To a Traveler, Symphony No. 3, London Symphony; Serenade; Piano Sonata; Requiem and 3rd Piano Concerto. *Publications:* Extra Measures and Metrical Ambiguity in Beethoven 1973. *Honours:* Guggenheim Fellowship 1953–54, 1959–60, Naumberg Award 1960, various grants and commissions. *Address:* 2625 Rose Street, Berkeley, CA 94708, USA.

**IMDAHL, Heinz;** Singer (Baritone); b. 9 Aug. 1924, Düsseldorf, Germany. *Education:* Studied with Berthold Putz in Krefeld and at the Cologne Musikhochschule. *Career:* Debut: Detmold 1948, as Morales in Carmen; Sang in Bremen, Berlin and Düsseldorf, the became a member of the Bayerische Staatsoper Munich; Guest appearances in Florence 1953, Rio de Janeiro, Turin 1972 and Oslo 1973; Repertoire included leading roles in operas by Wagner, Verdi, Strauss and Verdi. *Recordings:* Das Liebesverbot by Wagner.

**IMMELMAN, Niel,** FRCM; British pianist; b. 13 Aug. 1944, Bloemfontein, South Africa. *Education:* Royal College of Music with Cyril Smith, studied with Maria Curcio. *Career:* debut, Rachmaninov, London Philharmonic Orchestra, 1969; has given concerts at the Royal Festival Hall, London, and Amsterdam Concertgebouw with major orchestras and leading conductors; concert tours of all continents; teaching positions: Professor of Piano at Royal College of Music, 1980–; Masterclasses at Chopin Academy (Warsaw), Hong Kong Academy for Performing Arts, Moscow Conservatoire, Sibelius Academy (Helsinki), Toronto Royal Conservatory and the Universities of Berlin and Vienna; mem. Royal Society of Musicians of Great Britain, European Piano Teachers' Association. *Recordings include:* Complete Piano music of Suk; Works by Beethoven, Schubert, Schumann, Dale and Bloch; Featured in Classic CD Magazine's Pick of the Year. *Publications:* contrib. to International Piano Quarterly, Musicus, The Independent. *Honours:* Chappell Gold Medal 1969. *Address:* 41 Ashen Grove, London, SW19 8BL, England. *Telephone:* (20) 8947-7201. *Fax:* (20) 8946-8846. *E-mail:* immelman@lineone.net.

**INBAL, Eliahu;** British/Israeli conductor; *Chief Conductor, Berlin Symphony Orchestra;* b. 16 Feb. 1936, Jerusalem; s. of Jehuda Joseph Inbal and Leah Museri Inbal; m. Helga Fritzsche 1968; two s. one d. *Education:* Acad. of Music, Jerusalem, Conservatoire Nat. Supérieur, Paris, courses with Franco Ferrara, Hilversum and Sergiu Celebidache, Siena. *Career:* from 1963 guest conductor with numerous orchestras including Milan, Rome, Berlin, Munich, Hamburg, Stockholm, Copenhagen, Vienna, Budapest, Amsterdam, London, Paris, Tel Aviv, New York, Chicago, Toronto and Tokyo; Chief Conductor, Radio Symphony Orchestra, Frankfurt 1974–90, Hon. Conductor 1995–; Teatro La Fenice 1984–87; Hon. Conductor, Nat. Symphony Orchestra, RAI Torino 1996–; Chief Conductor Berlin Symphony Orchestra 2001–; has made numerous recordings, particularly of Mahler, Bruckner, Berlioz and Shostakovich. *Honours:* First Prize, Int. Conductors' Competition 'G. Cantelli' 1963; Officier des Arts des Lettres 1995; Goldenes Ehrenzeichen, Vienna 2001.

*Address:* Hessischer Rundfunk, Bertramstrasse 8, 6000 Frankfurt, Germany. *Telephone:* (611) 1552371.

**INCIHARA, Taro;** Singer (Tenor); b. 2 Jan. 1950, Yamagata, Japan. *Education:* Studied in Japan and at the Juilliard School, New York. *Career:* Debut: Tokyo, 1980, as Gounod's Faust; European debut, 1982, as Calaf at the Teatro San Carlo, Naples; Paris Opéra from 1983 as Macduff, Riccardo, Don Carlos and the Duke of Mantua; Guest appearances at Nice, Turin, Naples, Santiago and Buenos Aires, Verdi's Requiem, 1987; Macerata Festival, 1987, Orange, 1989, as Isamaele in Nabucco; Metropolitan Opera, 1987–89, as the Italian Singer and the Duke of Mantua; Further European engagements at Turin and Genoa; Sang Riccardo in Un Ballo in Maschera for Opera Pacific at Costa Mesa, California, 1991; Other roles include Gabriele Adorno, La Scala, 1989; Verdi's Rodolfo and Alfredo, Enzo in La Gioconda and Edgardo in Lucia di Lammermoor. *Address:* c/o Opera Pacific, 3187 Red Hill Avenue, Suite 230, Costa Mesa, CA 92626, USA.

**INCONTRERA, Roxana;** Singer (Soprano); b. 1966, Ploiesti, Romania. *Education:* Studied in Bucharest. *Career:* Sang at the Rudolstadt Opera, then at the Dresden Staatsoper (Queen of Night, Magic Flute, 1989); Guest appearances at Barcelona, in La Cenerentola, 1992, Salle Pleyel (Paris), Berlin, Essen, Düsseldorf, Hannover, Chemnitz, Leipzig, Halle; Other roles include Rossini's Rosina, Mozart's Sandrina (La finta giardiniera) and Constanze, Violetta, Zerbinetta, Fiakermilli (Arabella), Italian Singer (Capriccio), Olympia and Oscar; Sang Elvira in L'Italiana in Algeri at Dresden, 1998; Sang the Queen of Night and Verdi's Oscar at Dresden, 2000; Frequent concert engagements. *Address:* c/o Staatsoper Dresden, Theaterplatz 2, 01067 Dresden, Germany.

**INGLE, William;** Singer (Tenor); b. 17 Dec. 1934, Texhoma, Texas, USA. *Education:* Studied at the Academy of Vocal Arts in Philadelphia with Dorothy di Scala; With Sidney Dietsch in New York and Luigi Ricci in Rome. *Career:* Debut: Flensburg 1965, as Tamino; Sang at the Linz Opera, Düsseldorf, Kassel, Frankfurt, Graz, Leipzig, Montreal, Hanover, Wellington and Vienna; Other roles include Ernesto, Don Ottavio, Manrico, Lohengrin, Parsifal, Walther, Canio, Erik, Radames, Ferrando, Rodolfo, Almaviva, Flamand in Capriccio, the Duke of Mantua and Alfredo; Sang at Linz, 1976, in the premiere of Der Aufstand by Nikolaus Eder; Masaniello in La Muette de Portici by Auber, 1989; Television appearances as Herod, (Salome), in Canada and Tom Rakewell, (The Rake's Progress), in Austria.

**INGOLFSSON, Atli;** Composer; b. 21 Aug. 1962, Keflavik, Iceland; m. Thuridur Jonsdottir, 18 Aug 1990. *Education:* Diploma in Classical Guitar, 1983, BM, Theory and Composition, 1984, Reykjavík School of Music; BA, Philosophy, University of Iceland, 1986; Study with D Anzaghi, Milan Conservatory, 1985–88; Private study with G Grisey and Auditor at CNSMP, Paris, 1988–90. *Career:* Performances at Young Nordic music festivals, other Nordic music festivals and various occasions in Iceland, 1981–; His Due Bagatelle for Clarinet premiered in Milan, 1986 and widely performed; Various performances in Europe, 1990–, including Montreuil, May 1991, Varèse, July 1991; Amsterdam, Sept 1991, Milan, Nov and Dec 1991; Commissioned by IRCAM, Paris, to write for computer piano and ensemble, 1993. *Compositions:* Recorded on CD, Due Bagatelle for Clarinet; Et Toi Pale Soleil, for 4 voices and instruments; A Verso for piano, and O Versa for piano and 12 instruments, OPNA for bass clarinet and marimba; Le Pas Les Pentes for 8 instruments. *Address:* Borgarvegur 28, 260 Njardvik, Iceland.

**INGRAM, Jaime (Ricardo Jean);** Concert Pianist and Diplomat; b. 13 Feb. 1928, Panama City, Panama; m. Nelly Hirsch, 29 Jan 1950, 2 s., 1 d. *Education:* Piano Diploma, Juilliard Institute of Music, New York, USA, 1949, studied with Olga Samarof and Joseph Bloch; Piano Diploma, Conservatoire Nationale de Paris, France, 1950, studied with Yves Nat; Additional studies with Alberto Sciarretti, Panama, and Bruno Seidlhofer, Vienna. *Career:* Professor of Piano, National Conservatory of Music, Panama, 1952–56; Escuela Paulista de Musica, São Paulo, Brazil, 1958–60; Escuela Profesional, Panama, 1962–64, Conservatorio Jaime Ingram, 1964–69, University of Panama, 1972–74; Director of Culture, 1969–73; General Director of Culture, 1974–78, Panamanian Ambassador to Spain, 1979–82; Panamanian Ambassador to the Holy Sea, 1982–; Concert tours as soloist and piano duo with Nelly Hirsch; South and Central America, Cuba, Spain, Italy, Federal Republic of Germany; Bulgaria, Poland, Zürich and Geneva, Switzerland, London, England, Amsterdam, Netherlands, USSR, Israel. *Publications:* Hector Villa Lobos; Muzio Clementi, the Father of the Pianoforte, Antonio de Cabezon, Tientos y Diferencias; Orientacion Musical 1974, Historia, Compositores y Repertorio del Piano 1978.

**INOUE, Michiyoshi;** Conductor; b. 23 Dec. 1946, Tokyo, Japan. *Education:* Studies, Toho Gakuen Academy of Music with Professor Saitoh. *Career:* Associate Conductor of the Tokyo Metropolitan Symphony Orchestra, 1970; Conducted at La Scala, 1971; Conducted Orchestras in Paris, Vienna, Geneva, Berlin, Brussels, Hamburg, Munich, Stuttgart, Madrid, Naples, Turin, Florence, Lisbon, London, Helsinki, Leipzig, Copenhagen; Tours of Israel, Eastern Europe, Russia; Conducted the East Berlin Orchestra on tour to Japan; Concerts in Australia, New Zealand and with the Washington National Symphony in the USA; Conducted Opera in Vienna and at Cluj, Romania; Music Director, New Japan Philharmonic Orchestra, 1983–88; Music Director of the Kyoto Symphony Orchestra, 1990. *Recordings include:* Mahler's 6th, 5th and 4th Symphonies with the Royal Philharmonic; Albums with the Netherlands Chamber Orchestra (Nippon Columbia). *Honours:* First Prize,

Guido Cantelli Competition, Milan, 1971. *Current Management:* Kajimoto International, Tokyo, Japan. *Address:* 3–7–16–103, Uehara, Shibuyaku, Tokyo, 151–0064. *E-mail:* maestro@sc4.so-net.ne.jp.

**IOACHIMESCU, Calin;** Composer; b. 29 March 1949, Bucharest, Romania; m. Anca Vartolomei-Ioachimescu, 1 s., 1 d. *Education:* Graduate, Bucharest Music College, 1968; Graduate, 1st Place, Bucharest High School, Academy of Music, Composition with Stefan Niculescu, 1975; Computer music courses, IRCAM, Paris, 1985; International New Music Holiday Courses, Darmstadt, 1980, 1984. *Career:* Debut: In concert, Bucharest Radio Symphonic Orchestra, 1978; Symphonic, chamber and electronic works played throughout Romania and over the world; Compositions broadcast: Bucharest, France and Brussels; Sound Engineer, Romanian Broadcasting; Head, Computer Music Studio, Bucharest. *Compositions include:* Magic Spell for female voices, strings and percussion, 1974; String Quartet No. 1, 1974; Tempo 80, 1979; Oratio ll, 1981; Hierophonies, 1984; String Quartet No. 2, 1984; Spectral Music for saxophones and tape, 1985; Concerto for trombone, double bass and orchestra, 1986; Celliphonia for cello and tape, 1988; Palindrom/7, 1992; Concerto for saxophones and orchestra, commissioned by the Ministry of Culture, France, 1994; Les Eclats de l'Abîme for double bass, saxophone and tape, Radio France, 1995; Heptagrama for saxophones and tape, Ministry of Culture, France, 1998; Concerto for violin, cello and orchestra, 2002; Film music. *Recordings:* Various labels. *Publications:* Oratio ll, Paris; Bucharest: Tempo 80; String Quartet No. 2; Celliphonia. *Address:* Str Ardeleni 28, Sect 2, 72164-Bucharest, Romania. *Telephone:* 216104425. *E-mail:* ucmr@itcnet.ro.

**IONESCO-VOVU, Constantin,** PhD; Romanian pianist and academic; b. 27 May 1932, Floresti; m. Margareta Gabriel 1961 (died 1983). *Education:* Bucharest Superior Music Conservatory Hochschule, (Univ. of Music). *Career:* concerts as soloist with symphony orchestras, piano recitals and chamber music in Romania, France, Germany, Poland, Russia, Norway, Sweden, Denmark, Netherlands, Hungary, Czechoslovakia, Switzerland, Austria, Portugal, USA, Korea, Japan, Warsaw Autumn Festival, Evian Festival; Prof., (concert class, piano) Head of Piano Section, University of Music, Bucharest; Visiting Prof., Musikhochschule Tressingen, Germany, Nagoya Coll. of Music, Japan and Keimyung Univ., Taegu, Republic of Korea; masterclasses in Romania, Germany, Netherlands, Portugal, USA, Korea, Japan; mem. of int. juries for piano competitions in Romania, France, Germany, Italy, Portugal; Pres., European Piano Teachers' Assen, Romania. *Recordings:* radio recordings and albums in Romania, Germany, the Netherlands, Austria. *Publications:* Aurèle Stroë, concert music for piano, percussion and brass, 1968; C Silvestri, Piano Works, Vol. I 1973, Vol. II 1979; Romanian Piano Music, 1989; Dinu Lipatti Fantaisie, 1999; Essays about technique, aesthetics, and style of musical interpretation in musical periodicals. *Address:* Str Vasile Lascar 35, 020492 Bucharest, Romania. *Fax:* (21) 211-3095. *E-mail:* cionvovu@hotmail.com.

**IONITZA, Alexandru;** Singer (Tenor); b. 1953, Romania. *Education:* Studied Voice with Constantin Stroescu of the Bucharest Conservatory of Music. *Career:* Sang in opera at Bucharest and Munster, then the Deutsche Oper am Rhein, Düsseldorf, from 1984 (Rodolfo in La Bohème, 1993); Bregenz Festival, 1987–88, as Hoffmann; Cologne Opera, 1991, as Alfredo and Nemorino; Further engagements as Mozart's Belmonte at the Vienna Volksoper, at San Diego, the Theater am Gärtnerplatz, Munich, and Stuttgart; Many concert appearances. *Recordings include:* Elemer in Arabella; Oedipus Rex by Stravinsky; Beppo in Pagliacci; Alzira by Verdi; Narraboth in Salome. *Address:* c/o Deutsche Oper am Rhein, Heinrich-Heine Alle 16a, 40213 Düsseldorf, Germany.

**IRANYI, Gabriel;** Composer, Pianist and Lecturer; b. 6 June 1946, Cluj, Romania; m. Elena Nistor, 20 Aug 1969, 1 s. *Education:* Special School of Music, Cluj, 1955–65; George Dima High School of Music, Cluj, Composition and Musicology Department, Student of Prof D Sigismund Todutza. *Career:* Teaching Assistant, George Enesco High School of Music, Jassy, Romania, 1971–76; Lecturer, Cfar Saba Conservatoire, 1982–86; Since 1988 Professor of the Leo–Borchara–Musikschule in Berlin. *Compositions:* Segments, De Profundis; Bird of Wonder; Until the Day Breaks; Portraits of JS Bach; For solo piano; Laudae for 2 pianos; Song of Degrees for Chamber Ensemble; Alternances for percussion; Alef for soprano voice, clarinet, cello and piano; Realm for solo cello and electric amplification; Solstice for violin, cello and clarinet; Electric Amplication; Shir Hamaalot for organ; Tempora for string quartet, Meditation and Prayer, for violin and 15 strings; Laudae, for 2 pianos, or with chamber orchestra. *Address:* Gierkeplatz 10, Berlin 10585, Germany.

**IRELAND, Helen Dorcas,** BMus, MMus; British musician; b. 2 Nov. 1952; m. Gregory Rose; one s. *Education:* Purcell School London, Univ. of Birmingham, Royal Northern Coll. of Music, Peabody Conservatory, Baltimore, USA. *Career:* accompanist and ensemble player 1976–84; theatre musical dir in many English repertory theatres and the Royal Nat. Theatre; extensive work in Germany; education work in drama schools and summer schools; private coaching, on staff of Guildhall School of Music and Drama 1999–, Italia Conti Acad. 2004; mem. Musicians' Union, Incorporated Soc. of Musicians. *Address:* 57 Whitehorse Road, Stepney, London, E1 0ND, England (home). *Telephone:* (20) 7790-5883 (home). *Fax:* (20) 7265-9170 (home). *E-mail:* gregory-rose@tisl .co.uk (home).

**IRELAND, (William) Patrick,** ARCM; British viola player; b. 20 Nov. 1923, Helston, Cornwall, England; m. Peggy Gray; four c. *Education:* Wellington Coll., Worcester Coll., Oxford. *Career:* viola, Allegri String Quartet 1953–77,

1988; has taken part in the premieres of quartets by Martin Dalby 1972, Nicola LeFanu, Peter Sculthorpe, Elizabeth Maconchy, Robert Sherlaw-Johnson and Sebastian Forbes; two clarinet quintets by Jennifer Fowler and Nicola LeFanu 1971; four quartets by Barry Guy, Jonathan Harvey, Alison Bauld, Edward Cowie 1973; complete Beethoven Quartets at the 1974 Cheltenham Festival; taught and coached chamber music at the Menuhin School of Music in the 1960s; Asst Head of Strings, Royal Northern Coll. of Music 1977–80. *Recordings:* With Allegri String Quartet; Bach Brandenburg Concertos with Menuhin and Bath Festival Orchestra; two albums with Lindsay Quartet, as 2nd viola: Dvořák and Mozart Quintets. *Honours:* Hon. DMus (Southampton Univ.) 1975, Hon. MMus (Hull Univ.) 1995. *Address:* Hillgrove House, Dunkerton, Bath, Somerset BA2 8AS, England (home). *Telephone:* (1761) 470113 (home).

**IRMAN, Regina;** Swiss composer; *Lecturer, Thurgau University of Education;* b. 22 March 1957, Winterthur. *Education:* Winterthur Conservatory. *Career:* Lecturer, Thurgau Univ. of Education 2003–. *Compositions include:* Hügel bei Céret for two violas and double bass (also possible for other types of string ensemble) 1983, Ein vatter ländischer Liederbogen (based on texts by Adolf Wölfli) for mezzo and partly prepared grand piano 1985–86, Ein Trauermarsch (A Funeral March, based on texts by Adolf Wölfli) for spoken voice and percussion trio 1987, Requiem 'An den Tod' (To Death, based on a poem by Anna Achmatova) for 25 female and at least three male voices 1991–93, Wörter (Words) for saxophone ensemble and percussion 1994–95, '...wie eine Heuschrecke über die Meere...' (Like a Grasshopper over the Seas, based on text, pictures and an object by Meret Oppenheim) for large mixed choir and backing tape 1995–96, Drei Tänze (Three Dances, based on a text by Anna Achmatova) for soprano, female speaker/piano, clarinet and accordion 1996–97, Sculptures (for Bruce Nauman) for quarter-tone gamba quartet 1997, Surdina for altus solo 2000, Poem ohne Held (Poem without a Hero, opera based on a text by Anna Achmatova, libretto Peter Schweiger) 1997–2002, Landschaften (Landscapes) five pieces for percussion sextet 2003. *Recording:* Portrait 2001. *Address:* Wasserfurristrasse 48, 8406 Winterthur, Switzerland (home).

**IROSCH, Mirjana;** Singer (Soprano); b. 24 Oct. 1939, Zagreb, Yugoslavia. *Education:* Studied at the Zagreb Conservatory with Fritz Lunzer. *Career:* Debut: Linz 1962, as Mercedes in Carmen; Sang for many years at the Vienna Volksoper: Took part in the 1968 premiere of the revised version of Der Zerrissene by Von Einem; Tour of Japan 1982; Guest appearances in Graz, Frankfurt, Basle, Brussels and Munich; Other roles include Micaela, Marenka in The Bartered Bride, Fiordiligi, Donna Elvira, Judith in Duke Bluebeard's Castle, Concepcion in L'Heure Espagnole, Rosina and Rosalinde. *Recordings:* Die Lustige Witwe. *Address:* Volksoper, Wahringerstrasse 78, 1090 Vienna, Austria.

**IRVINE, Robert;** Cellist; b. 11 May 1963, Glasgow, Scotland. *Education:* Royal College of Music, London; Studied with Christopher Bunting, Amaryllis Fleming. *Career:* Member, Brindisi String Quartet, 1984–; Philharmonia Orchestra, 1986–; Appeared on Channel 4 television, and BBC television and radio; Principal Cello, London Soloists Chamber Orchestra, Britten-Pears Orchestra, 1985–86; mem, Musicians Union. *Recordings:* Britten 2nd Quartet; Berg Op 3 Quartet. *Honours:* Foundation Scholar, Royal College of Music; Ivor James Cello Prize; Stern Award for Diploma Recital; Dip.RCM; ARCM. *Address:* 8 Berwyn Road, London SE24 9 BD, England.

**IRWIN, Jane;** Singer (Mezzo-soprano); b. 1968, England. *Education:* Lancaster University and Royal Northern College of Music. *Career:* Early appearances in Mahler's 3rd Symphony, under Kent Nagano, and Des Knaben Wunderhorn; Tchaikovsky's Maid of Orleans at the RNCM, 1994; Recitals at the Paris Châtelet, Bienne, Poland, Japan and Geneva; Elgar's Sea Pictures in Scotland, Beethoven's Ninth and Missa Solemnis at the Edinburgh Festival, 1996–97; Rossini's Stabat Mater under Semyon Bychkov, Penderecki's Te Deum with the composer and The Dream of Gerontius conducted by David Willcocks; Covent Garden 1995–96, in Götterdämmerung and Die Walküre; Season 1997 in Die Zauberflöte and Ariadne auf Naxos at Aix, concert tour with the English Concert to Italy and Vienna and Hallé Orchestra concert. *Honours:* Decca Kathleen Ferrier Prize, 1991; Frederic Cox Award, 1992; Winner, 1993 Singers' Competition at the Geneva International Competition; Richard Tauber Prize, 1995. *Current Management:* Ingpen & Williams Ltd, 7 St George's Court, 131 Putney Bridge Road, London, SW15 2PA, England.

**ISAACS, Mark;** Australian composer and pianist; b. 22 June 1958, London, England. *Education:* BMus, New South Wales Conservatorium of Music, 1976; MMus, Eastman School of Music, 1986; study with Peter Sculthorpe, Josef Tal and Samuel Adler, among others. *Career:* mem., Mark Isaacs Jazz Trio; commissions from Musica Viva, Australia Ensemble, Sydney String Quartet and Seymour Group, among others; conductor and producer of various projects; toured Russia, 1994, 1995, 1996; established GraceMusic record label, 1997. *Compositions include:* Three Excursions for woodwind, 1971; Reverie for piano and orchestra, 1972; Reflections for piano and orchestra, 1973; Three to Go for big band, 1974; Interlude for flute and piano, 1975; Ballade for big band, 1976; D'Urbeville House for big band, 1976; Mad Jean: A Musical, 1977; Ode to Peace for big band, 1977; Footsteps for big band, 1977; Sad Girl for big band, 1977; Lamente for oboe and piano, 1978; Fantasy for violin and piano, 1979; Four Lyric Pieces for string trio, 1980; Liturgy for string orchestra, 1980; Ha Laitsun for two pianos, 1981; Quintet for Brass,

1981; Moving Pictures for piano and orchestra, 1982; Four Glimpses for orchestra, 1982; Diversion for six players, 1983; I Am for mixed chorus a cappella, 1984; Three Scherzi for winds and cello, 1984; String Quartet, 1984; So It Does for six players, 1985; Ballade for Orchestra, 1985; Three Songs for soprano and piano, 1985; Character References for violin and piano, 1985; Memoirs for percussion and piano, 1986; Preludes for piano, 1986; Visitation for solo piano, 1986; Four Comments for winds, 1986; Cantilena for bass clarinet and piano, 1987; Piece for flute and strings, 1987; Elegy for cello and piano, 1987; Variations for flute, clarinet and cello, 1988; Debekuth for violin and orchestra, 1988; Burlesque Miniatures for String Quartet, 1988; Drums of Thunder, 1988; Purple Prayer for jazz quartet and strings, 1989; Beach Dreaming (one-act opera for young people), 1990; Litany for piano and orchestra, 1991; Threnody for violin and cello, 1992; Lyric Caprice for cello and piano, 1993; Songs of the Universal for viola, cello, clarinet and piano, 1994; Scherzo for small orchestra, 1995; Voices The Passion of St Jeanne, 1996; The Burning Thread for mixed chorus a cappella, 1997; Scherzo for wind quintet, 1998; Three Excursions for concert band and strings, 1999; Chaconne/Salsa for cor anglais and orchestra, 2001; Three Days of Rain, 2001; Kensington Rags, 2002; Ave Maria for cello and piano, 2003; Canticle for trumpet and orchestra, 2003; various television and film themes. *Recordings:* Originals, 1981; Preludes, 1987; Encounters, 1990; For Sure, 1993; The Elements (four vols, Earth, Air, Water and Fire), 1996; Elders Suite (with Kenny Wheeler), 1997; On Reflection, 1998; Closer, 2000. *Honours:* 3rd Prize, 1st Tokyo International Competition for Chamber Music Composition, 1996; Fellowship Australia Council for the Arts, 1996–98; Commendation, Albert H Maggs Composition Prize, University of Melbourne, 1997; Membership: APRA. *E-mail:* gracemusic@bigpond.com. *Website:* www.listen.to/gracemusic.

**ISAKADZE, Liana;** Violinist and Conductor; b. 2 Aug. 1946, Tbilisi, Georgian Republic. *Education:* Tbilisi School for Most Educated Children, 1953–63; Tchaikovski Conservatory, Moscow, 1963–70. *Career:* Debut: International Festival Congregation, Moscow, 1956; Concerts all over the world; Russian television; Georgian television; Germany ZDF television film, Portrait Liana Ysakadze; Art Director and Conductor, Georgia State Chamber Orchestra, 1980–; mem, Leader of David Oistrakh School, Lenting bei Ingolstadt, Germany; Opened D Oistrakh Akademie Ingolstadt, 1993. *Compositions:* Many arranged for string orchestra; Sextets of Brahms, Tchaikovsky, Boccherini, Gershwin, Haydn, Bernstein, Dvořák, Mendelssohn and others. *Recordings:* Over 100 recordings and CDs including Firma Melodia, Firma Orfeusm Munich; Radio BR; MDR; Moscow radio. *Honours:* Folk Artist of USSR, 1988; Georgia State Prizes, 1982; Rustaveli prize, Taliashvili prize; First prizes at International violin competitions; Tchaikovsky, 1970; Paris, 1965; Sibelius, 1970. *Address:* Siegrune Str 1, 60639 Munich, Germany.

**ISAKOVIC, Smiljka;** Harpsichordist and Pianist; b. 23 March 1953, Belgrade, Yugoslavia. *Education:* Music secondary school, with honours, Belgrade 1965–69; American Community Schools, Athens, National Honour Society, 1969–71; Graduated, Belgrade Music Academy, 1974; Master's degree, Faculty of Music, Belgrade, 1979; Postgraduate piano studies, Tchaikovsky Conservatory, Moscow, USSR, 1978–79; Graduate, harpsichord, Royal Conservatory of Music, Madrid, Spain, 1984. *Career:* Debut: Belgrade, 1972; Performances throughout the former Yugoslavia, including festivals at Dubrovnik, Ljubljana, Ohrid, Belgrade, East and West Europe, the United Kingdom, USSR, USA, Cuba, Columbia; Masterclasses, harpsichord, international Centre des Jeunesses Musicales, Groznjan, Yugoslavia; Lectures, harpsichord; Music reviews, Evening News and Student newspapers, and Radio Belgrade; President, Association of Serbian Musicians. *Recordings:* Lady Plays–Keyboards, 1998; Radio and television appearances, Yugoslavia, Spain, Columbia. *Honours:* First Lady of the Harpsichord; Masaryk's Prize, artistic activities, Masaryk Academy of Arts, Prague, 1997; Title Queen of the Harpsichord, 1997. *Current Management:* Direccion artisitca Daniel, Los Madrazo, 16, 28014 Madrid, Spain. *Address:* Admirala Geprata 10, 11000 Belgrade, Serbia and Montenegro.

**ISBIN, Sharon,** BA, MMus; American guitarist; *Chair of Guitar Department, The Juilliard School;* b. Minneapolis. *Education:* Yale Univ., Yale School of Music, studied with Andrès Segovia, Oscar Ghiglia, Rosalyn Tureck. *Career:* has appeared as soloist with over 140 orchestras, including New York Philharmonic, Orchestre Nat. de France, LSO, BBC Scottish Symphony Orchestra, Milan Verdi Orchestra, Tonkünstler Orchestra, Tokyo, Jerusalem, Houston, National, Dallas, Baltimore, St Louis, Minnesota, Milwaukee Symphonies, St Paul, Los Angeles, Zürich, and Scottish Chamber Orchestras; has performed at festivals, including Mostly Mozart, Aspen, Ravinia, Interlochen, Santa Fe, Mexico City, Bermuda, Hong Kong, Montreux, Strasbourg, Paris, Athens, Istanbul, Prague Spring, Budapest; as chamber musician has collaborated with Nigel Kennedy, Denyce Graves, Benita Valente, Susanne Mentzer, Emerson String Quartet, Chamber Music Soc. of the Lincoln Center; performances include Ground Zero memorial concert, New York 11 Sept. 2002, the world premiere of John Duarte's Joan Baez Suite 2003, Concierto de Aranjuez with New York Philharmonic 2004, the world premiere of Steve Vai's Blossom Suite (with the composer), Paris 2005; Chair of Guitar Dept The Juilliard School 1989–; Dir guitar dept Aspen Music Festival; Dir Carnegie Hall Guitarstream Festival, New York 92nd St Y series, Nat. Public Radio Guitarjam. *Recordings:* Love Songs and Lullabies 1991, Road to the Sun 1992, Journey to the Amazon 1997, Dreams of a World (Grammy Award for Best Instrumental Soloist Performance without orchestra) 1999, Rodrigo and Latin Romances 2000, Rouse, Concert de Gaudi (Echo

Klassik Best Concert Recording 2002) 2001, Bach, Complete Lute Suites 2001, American Landscapes 2002, Baroque Favourites for Guitar 2003, Sharon Isbin 2004, Concierto de Aranjuez 2005. *Publication:* Classical Guitar Answer Book. *Current Management:* Jay K. Hoffman and Associates, 136 E 57th Street, Suite 801, New York, NY 10022, USA. *Telephone:* (212) 371-6690 (office). *Fax:* (212) 754-0192 (office). *E-mail:* hoffjayk@aol.com (office). *Address:* The Juilliard School, 60 Lincoln Center Plaza, New York, NY 10023-6588, USA. *Website:* www.juilliard.edu.

**ISEPP, Martin Johannes Sebastian,** ARCM; pianist, harpsichordist and conductor; b. 30 Sept. 1930, Vienna, Austria; m. Rose Henrietta Harris 1966; two s. *Education:* Lincoln Coll., Oxford, studied with Prof. Leonie Gombrich, Oxford. *Career:* English Opera Group 1950s; music staff, Glyndebourne Festival Opera 1957, Chief Coach 1973, Head of Music Staff 1978–93; Head of Opera Training, Juilliard School of Music, New York, USA 1973–77; Head of Music Studies, National Opera Studio, London 1978–95; Head of Acad. of Singing, Banff Centre School of Fine Arts, Banff, AB, Canada 1981–93; accompanist to leading singers including Ilse Wolf, Janet Baker, John Shirley-Quirk, Elisabeth Schwarzkopf, Elisabeth Söderström, Jessye Norman, Anne Howells, Sheila Armstrong and Hugues Cuenod; conductor, Le nozze di Figaro 1984, Don Giovanni 1986, Glyndebourne Touring Company, Entführung, Washington Opera 1986–87 season; Music Dir for The Actor in Opera courses, William Walton Foundation on Ischia 1992–96; Asst Conductor, Metropolitan Opera, New York 1996–; opera productions at Fondation, Royaumont, Centre de la Voix 1996–99, A New National Theatre, Tokyo, Peabody Conservatory, Baltimore, COC Ensemble, Toronto and l'Atelier de l'Opéra de Montréal. *Recordings:* as accompanist and continuo player. *Honours:* Carroll Donner Stuchell Medal for Accompanying, Harriet Cohen International Musical Foundation 1965, Hon. DFA, Wake Forest Univ. of North Carolina, USA 2002. *Address:* 37A Steeles Road, London, NW3 4RG, England. *E-mail:* miseppmusic@yahoo.co.uk.

**ISHII, Kan;** Composer; b. 30 March 1921, Tokyo, Japan. *Education:* Studied at the Mmasashino School of Music, 1939–43 and with Carl Orff in Munich, 1952–54. *Career:* Taught at the Toho Gakuen School of Music, 1954–56, the Aichi Prefectural Arts University at Nagoya, 1966–86, and 1939–43 and with Carl Orff in Munich, 1952–54. *Compositions:* The Mermaid and the Red Candle, 1 act opera, 1961; Princess Kaguya, 1 act opera, 1963; En no Gyoja, 3 act opera, 1965; Kesa and Morito, 3 act opera, 1968; Women are Wonderful, comic opera in 1 act, 1978; Kantomi, 3 act opera, 1981; Blue Lion, operetta, 1989.

**ISHIKAWA, Shizuka;** Violinist; b. 2 Oct. 1954, Tokyo, Japan; m. Jiri Schultz, 26 May 1978. *Education:* Diploma, Prague Music Academy, 1978; Studied with Professor Shin-ichi Suzuki and Saburo Sumi. *Career:* Performances at The Prague Spring Festival; Belgrade Music Festival; Warsaw Autumn Festival; Hungarian Music Week; Helsinki Music Festival; Czechoslovak Music Festival in Japan; Performances in Tokyo, Copenhagen, Prague, Vienna, Brussels, Bonn; Numerous Radio and Television broadcasts; Soloist with many major orchestras. *Recordings:* Concertos by Bartók, Bruch, Mozart, Myslivecek and Paganini. *Honours:* 2nd Prize, Wieniawski International Violin Competition, 1972; Silver Medal, Queen Elisabeth in Brussels, 1976; 3rd Prize, International Violin Competition of F Kreisler, 1979. *Current Management:* Konzerburo Andreas Braun, Koln 41, Lindenthal; Japan Arts Corp, Tokyo, Japan.

**ISOKOSKI, Soile;** Finnish singer (soprano); b. 14 Feb. 1957, Posio. *Education:* Sibelius Acad., Kuopio and studied with Dorothy Irving in Sweden. *Career:* fmr church organist, then gave concert debut as singer at Helsinki 1986; appearances at concert halls in Europe, Japan, USA; performances at La Scala, Milan, Paris Bastille, Covent Garden, London, state opera houses in Hamburg, Berlin, Munich, Vienna, also at the Salzburger Festspiele, Savonlinna Opera Festival; season 1993 with Salzburg Festival debut, as First Lady in Die Zauberflöte, and Mozart's Countess at Hamburg; Covent Garden debut 1997 as Fiordiligi in Così fan tutte; Strauss's Four Last Songs with the Bavarian State Orchestra under Zubin Mehta at the 1999 Prom concerts, London; season 2000–01 as Amelia Grimaldi at Helsinki, Wagner's Eva at Covent Garden, Liu in Turandot and Desdemona at the Vienna Staatsoper; New York Met debut as the Countess in Figaro 2002; Mahler's Symphony of a Thousand at the London Proms 2002. *Recordings:* Schumann, Frauenliebe und Leben, Liederkreis; Sibelius, Luonnotar, conducted by Neeme Järvi; Zemlinsky, Der Zwerg, conducted by James Conlon; Mozart, Donna Elvira in Don Giovanni conducted by Claudio Abbado; Beethoven, Fidelio conducted by Barenboim, Strauss: Four Last Songs (Gramophone Magazine Editor's Choice Award) 2002, Sibelius: Songs 2006. *Honours:* winner Lappeenranta Singing Competition 1987, second prize Cardiff Singer of the World Competition 1987, winner Elly Ameling and Tokyo Int. Competitions. *Current Management:* Allegro Artist Management, Lars Sonckin kaari 16, 02600 Espoo, Finland. *Telephone:* (9) 462-007. *Fax:* (9) 5259-4200. *E-mail:* allegro.artist@dlc.fi. *Website:* www.allegroartist.com.

**ISOMURA, Kazuhide;** Violinist; b. 27 Dec. 1945, Tokyohashi, Japan. *Education:* Studied at the Juilliard School with members of the Juilliard Quartet. *Career:* Violist of the Tokyo Quartet from 1969; Regular concerts in the USA and abroad; First cycle of the complete quartets of Beethoven at the Yale at Norfolk Chamber Music Festival, 1986; Repeated cycles at the 92nd Street Y, NY, Ravinia and Israel Festivals, Yale, Princeton Universities; Season 1990–91 at Alice Tully Hall, Metropolitan Museum of Art, NY, Boston,

Washington DC, Los Angeles, Cleveland, Detroit, Chicago, Miami, Seattle, San Francisco, Toronto; Tour of South America and two tours of Europe including Paris, Amsterdam, Bonn, Milan, Munich, Dublin, London, Berlin; Quartet-in-residence at Yale University; The University of Cincinnati College-Conservatory of Music. *Recordings:* Schubert's major Quartets; Mozart Flute Quartets with James Galway and Clarinet Quintet with Richard Stoltzman; Quartets by Bartók, Brahms, Debussy, Haydn, Mozart and Ravel; Beethoven Middle Period Quartets. *Honours:* Grand Prix du Disque du Montreux; Best Chamber Music Recording of the Year from Stero Review and the Gramophone; Four Grammy nominations. *Address:* Intermusica Artists' Management, 16 Duncan Terrace, London N1 8BZ, England.

**ISRAEL, Robert,** DipEd, DipMus; violist and teacher (retd) and composer; b. 12 June 1918, Berlin, Germany; m. Tamar Amrami 1951; one s. one d. *Education:* Rubin Acad., Jerusalem and Tel-Aviv, studied violin with Rudolph Bergmann, viola with Oedeon Partos, theory and harmony counterpoint composition with Yitshak Edel, Rosowsky and Mordecai Seter. *Career:* debut, Elegie for Viola with string orchestra by Mordecal Seter 1969; violist and tubist, Opera Orchestra, Tel-Aviv; violin teacher at various Kibbuzim 1946–48; Teacher of Violin, Viola and Theory, Conservatory Hadera 1952–; mem., Bass, Rinat Choir 1957–58; Principal Violist, Haifa Symphony Orchestra 1962–83; performed with many chamber music groups. *Compositions include:* Five verses from Song of Songs for two-voice choir 1955, six pieces for violin and piano 1988, Arrangement of Rosamunde, the Trout, Marche militaire (Schubert) for three violins or two violins and viola 1989, 14 songs, arrangement for popular orchestra 1990, Saraband, Bourrée, Polonais (J. S. Bach) Sonatine (Beethoven), arranged for two violas or viola and violoncello 1993, Diatonic three-octave scales with special fingering for violin 1997, and for viola 2000, Music for four violas, accompaniment parts for Mazas op. 36 Etudes, Four Basic Fingerings of One-Octave Scales for violin, the same for viola, Canons for four violins from J. S. Bach Choral verses, the same for viola and violoncello 1999, Sonatine (Telemann) adapted for two violas or viola and violoncello 1998, V for string quartet Marcia I, Marcia II Meditation, Dance 2004, arranged G. J. Gershwin, Soon for string quintet, S. Joplin, The Entertainer for string quintet 2005, Schubert Sonatine III (op. 137), Telemann Concerto for Viola, arranged for four violas 2005. *Honours:* Haifa Symphony Orchestra Award 1999. *Address:* Ytsiat-Europa st 11, Beth Eliezer PO Box 10772, Hadera 38484, Israel (home). *Telephone:* (4) 6201370.

**ISSERLIS, Steven John,** CBE; British cellist; b. 19 Dec. 1958, London; s. of George Isserlis and the late Cynthia Isserlis; m. Pauline Mara; one s. *Education:* City of London School, Int. Cello Centre, Scotland, Oberlin Coll., Ohio, USA. *Career:* London début Wigmore Hall 1977; London concerto début 1980; concerts and recitals throughout the world; Artistic Dir IMS Prussia Cove, Cornwall; Dir concert series Wigmore Hall, London, Salzburg Festival 1997, Berlin and Vienna 2000–01; featured soloist in Channel 4 TV series with Dudley Moore; visits to Minnesota, Philadelphia, St Petersburg, Israel Philharmonic Orchestras, recitals in Amsterdam, Warsaw Milan 2003–04; Artistic Dir Saint-Saëns Festival London 2004; TV documentary about Schumann and performance of Schumann's cello concerto, Channel 4 TV; numerous recordings. *Recordings:* Brahms Sonatas 2005. *Publications:* transcription Beethoven Variations in D arranged for violin or cello and piano or harpsichord, Edn of Saint-Saëns pieces for cello and piano, Steven Isserlis's Cello World, Unbeaten Tracks, Why Beethoven Threw the Stew 2001, Why Handel Waggled His Wig 2005. *Honours:* Hon. mem. RAM; Piatigorsky Award 1993, Royal Philharmonic Soc. Award 1993; Schumann Prize, Zwickau 2000. *Current Management:* Harrison Parrott Ltd, 12 Penzance Place, London, W11 4PA, England. *Telephone:* (20) 7229-9166. *Fax:* (20) 7221-5042. *E-mail:* info@harrisonparrott.co.uk (office). *Website:* www.harrisonparrott.com (office).

**ITAMI, Naomi;** Singer (Soprano); b. 1961, USA. *Education:* Guildhall School, London; Manhattan School, New York; Columbia University, New York. *Career:* Debut: As Zerlina in Don Giovanni under Charles Mackerras, Estates Theatre, Prague, 1991; Engagements at the Bach Festival, California; Tours of the USA and Far East with the Gregg Smith Singers; Covent Garden Young Artists' Recital series; Mozart's Blondchen with Scottish Opera; Lincoln Center Out-of-Doors Festival, New York; Divas' Tour of Europe; Despina at the Ludlow Festival, England; Susanna for Neath Opera, Wales and the European Centre of Vocal Arts, Belgium; Snape Maltings with the Borodin String Quartet; Buxton Festival; Maria, West Side Story, Dublin; Lady Thiang, The King and I, Broadway tour. *Recordings:* Four Lehar Operettas under Richard Bonynge. Honours; Maggie Teyte Prize, 1991; Prix de Maurice Ravel, France, 1991. *Address:* Music International, 13 Ardilaun Road, London N5 2QR, England.

**ITIN, Ilya;** Concert Pianist; b. 1970, Russia. *Education:* Studied with Natalia Litvinova at the Sverdlovsk Music School for Gifted Children; Tchaikovsky State Conservatoire, Moscow; New York with Yin Cheng Zong, from 1990. *Career:* Appearances with leading orchestras including the Cleveland under Dohnányi, and National Symphony under Skrowaczewski, from 1991; Recitals at Washington Kennedy Center and Lincoln Center, New York; Further concerts with European orchestras; Season 1997–98 debut at the London Proms with the BBC Philharmonic under Sinaisky, engagements associated with the Leeds Piano Competition, and European tour with the City of Birmingham Symphony under Simon Rattle. *Honours:* First Prize and Chopin Prize in the Ninth Robert Casadesus Competition, Cleveland; First Prize and Contemporary Music Prize in the Leeds International Piano

Competition, 1996. *Address:* c/o BBC Philharmonic Orchestra, New Broadcasting House, Oxford Road, Manchester, M60 1 SJ, England.

**IVALDI, Jean-Marc;** Singer (Baritone); b. 6 May 1953, Toulon, France. *Education:* Studied in Paris at the Conservatoire National and The School of the Grand Opera. *Career:* Debut: Paris Opéra in 1983 as Yamadori in Butterfly; Sang Rossini's Figaro at Liège, 1983, and appeared at Bordeaux, Toulouse, Nancy, Metz, Dijon, and Tours; As Bretigny in Manon and Ramiro in L'Heure Espagnole at Paris; Philadelphia in 1986 as Morales in Carmen, and Heidenheim 1989 as Escamillo; Other roles include Alfonso in La Favorite, Belcore, Albert in Werther, Ourrias in Mireille, Manuel in La Vida Breve, Germont, Paquiro in Goyescas, Frederic in Lakmé and Jarno in Mignon; Sang Valentin in Faust at St Etienne in 1990; Concert engagements include Carmina Burana at St Etienne and Joseph in L'Enfance du Christ at Nancy; Sang Escamillo at St Etienne, 1995. *Recordings:* La Favorite; Sonora in La Fanciulla del West, conducted by Leonard Slatkin. *Address:* Saison Lyrique de Saint Etienne, 8 Place de l'Hotel de Ville, 42000 St Etienne, France.

**IVAN, Monica;** Singer (Soprano); b. 1940, Stockholm, Sweden. *Education:* Studied in Stockholm, and in Siena with Luigi Ricci. *Career:* Debut: Stora Theater, Gothenburg, 1964, as the Queen of Night; Sang at the Hanover Opera, 1966–68; Zürich, 1968–69; Gothenburg from 1970; Sang the Queen of Night at the 1974 Savonlinna Festival; Guest appearances in Moscow and elsewhere in Russia from 1976, as Violetta, Gilda and Marguerite in Faust; Other roles have included Santuzza, Butterfly, the Trovatore Leonora and Amelia (Un Ballo in Maschera). *Address:* c/o Göteborgs Opera, C Nilssons Gatan, 41104 Göteborg, Sweden.

**IVANOV, Emil;** Singer (Tenor); b. 1960, Rome, Italy. *Education:* Studied in Sofia, Bulgaria. *Career:* Sang first at the National Opera, Sofia, then appeared as Don Carlos at Essen, 1987; St Gallen, 1988–89, as Ernani and Pollione in Norma; Macerata Festival as Manrico; Guest engagements as Cavaradossi and Radames at Frankfurt, Zamoro in Verdi's Alzira at Fidenza, as the Prince in Rusalka at Houston and Don José at the Bregenz Festival, 1991; Vienna Staatsoper, 1992, as Dvořák's Dimitri, Radames and in Carmen; Il Tabarro at Volksoper, 1993; Attila at Nice; Cavaradossi in Tosca at Metropolitan New York, 1993–94; 1994–95 Season: Carmen, La Traviata, Hérodiade, Madama Butterfly at Vienna-Staatsoper; Alfredo, Pinkerton, Don José, Carmen at Cologne, Il Tabarro at Birmingham and Don José at Pretoria; I Lombardi at St Gallen; Otello at Varna; Season 1999–2000 as Smetana's Dalibor at Cagliari, Alim in Le Roi de Lahore by Massenet at Bordeaux, Radames in Karlsruhe and Henri in Les Vêpres Siciliennes at St Gallen; Covent Garden debut 2002, as Carlo in I Masnadieri. *Address:* Karl Schweighofer 8/1/1, 1070 Vienna, Austria.

**IVASHKIN, Alexander Vasilevich,** BMus, MMus, PhD; cellist, conductor, writer and critic; *Professor of Music and Director of the Centre for Russian Music, University of London;* b. 17 Aug. 1948, Blagoveshchensk, Russia; m. Natalia Mikhailovna Pavlutskaya 1969. *Education:* Gnessin Special Music School, Russian Academy of Music, Moscow, Russian Art History Institute. *Career:* solo cellist, Bolshoi Theatre Orchestra, Moscow 1971–91; mem. Bd of Dirs, Bolshoi Opera Company 1987–91; solo recitals and appearances with orchestras, chamber music concerts, recording in over 30 countries in Europe, Russia, USA, Australia, Japan and New Zealand; Artistic Dir, Bolshoi Soloists 1978–91; Prof. of Cello, Univ. of Canterbury, New Zealand 1991–99; Artistic Dir, Adam Int. Cello Festival/Competition 1995–; Prof. of Music, Dir Centre for Russian Music, Univ. of London 1999–. *Recordings include:* Shostakovich, Cello Concertos Nos 1 and 2, 1998; Schnittke, Complete Cello Music, 1998–2002; Schumann, Gretchaninov, Cello Concertos, 1999–2000; Prokofiev, Complete Cello Music, 1996–2002; Tcherepnin, Complete Cello Music, 2000; Roslavets, Complete Cello Music, 2001; Rachmaninov, Complete Cello Music, 2003; Kancheli: Cello Concertos, 2002–04. *Publications:* Krzysztof Penderecki 1983, Charles Ives and 20th Century Music 1991, Conversation with A. Schnittke 1994, Alfred Schnittke 1996, Rostrospective (on M. Rostropovich) 1997, A. Schnittke Reader 2002. *Current Management:* Salpeter Artists Management, 28 Cheverton Road, London, N19 3AY, England; Ivy Artists, Postbus 592, 1200 AN Hilversum, Netherlands. *Address:* c/o Music Department, Goldsmiths College, University of London, London, SE14 6NW, England. *Telephone:* (20) 7919-7646. *Fax:* (20) 7919-7247. *E-mail:* a.ivashkin@gold.ac.uk.

**IWAKI, Hiroyuki;** Conductor; b. 6 Sept. 1932, Tokyo, Japan. *Education:* Studied percussion at the Tokyo Music Academy and conducting with Akeo Watanabe. *Career:* Assistant Conductor of the NHK, Japanese Broadcasting Symphony Orchestra, 1954; Conducted many premieres between 1957 and 1960; Conducted the Philharmonic Choir of Tokyo and was Musical Director of the Fujiwara Opera Company, 1965–67; Guest conductor of orchestras in Hamburg, Vienna and Berlin, 1966–69; Musical Director of the NHK Symphony from 1969, the Melbourne Symphony Orchestra from 1974; Director of the Orchestra-Ensemble Kanazawa, 1988; Conducted the first performances of works by Dallapiccola, (Concerto per la notte di natale de l'anno, 1956); Takemitsu: Marginilia, 1976, Dreamtime, 1982, A Way to Love, 1982 and Star-Isle, 1982; Isang Yun, (Symphony No. 4, 1986). *Recordings include:* Beethoven's 9th Symphony, with the NHK Orchestra; Bartók Concerto for Orchestra (Melbourne Symphony); Hungarian Rhapsodies by Liszt (Vienna State Opera Orchestra); Messiaen Couleurs de la cité céleste, Oiseaux Exotiques, Reveil des Oiseaux and Sept Hai-Kai (Decca); Dutch music with the Hague Philharmonic. *Address:* c/o Melbourne Symphony, PO Box 443, East Caulfield, Vic 3145, Australia.

**IWASAKI, Ko;** Japanese cellist; *Professor, Graduate School, Toho Conservatory, Tokyo;* b. 16 Aug. 1944, Tokyo; m. Yurie Ishio 1979; two s. *Education:* Toho Conservatory, Tokyo, Juilliard School of Music, USA, studied with Leonard Rose, Harvey Shapiro, Pablo Casals in Puerto Rico. *Career:* debut recital at Carnegie Recital Hall, New York 1966; recital at Wigmore Hall, London, England 1968; performed with London Symphony 1972; participant, Summer Festivals, including Marlboro, Portland (Oregon), Kuhmo (Finland), Lockenhaus (Austria); performances in USA, Europe, Russia and the Orient; Dir, Moonbeach Music Camp, Okinawa, Japan 1979–; Dir, Cello Masterclass, Southern Methodist Univ., USA; Prof., Toho Conservatory Graduate School, Tokyo. *Recordings:* Ko Iwasaki Plays Schubert Arpeggione Sonata; Beethoven Sonatas; Shostakovich Sonata; Japanese Contemporary Works for Cello; Ko Iwasaki and Staffan Scheja Play Sonatas by Rachmaninov and Grieg; Iwasaki, Requibros; 19 Short Pieces, Compact Disc; Beethoven: 2 Trios; Dvořák, Tchaikovsky with Polish National Radio Symphony; Haydn Cello Concerto No. 1 and No. 2, with Polish Chamber Orchestra. *Honours:* 3rd Prizes: Vienna International Cello Competition, 1967; Munich International Competition, 1967, Budapest International Cello Competition, 1968, Tchaikovsky International Competition; 2nd Prize, Cadao International Cello Competition. *Address:* 5732 Still Forest Drive, Dallas, TX 75252, USA.

**IZQUIERDO, Juan Pablo;** Musician and Conductor; b. 21 July 1935, Santiago, Chile; m. Trinidad Jimenez, 15 Dec 1973, 1 s., 1 d. *Education:* Graduate in Musical Composition, University of Chile, 1957; Conducting studies with Professor Hermann Scherchen, in Gravesano, Switzerland, 1958–61. *Career:* Debut: With National Symphony of Chile, Sept 1961;

Director of Music Department, Catholic University of Santiago; Principal Conductor, Gulbenkian Orchestra, Lisbon, Philharmonic Orchestra of Chile, National Symphony of Chile; Guest conducting, Berlin, Frankfurt, Hamburg, Vienna, Paris, Madrid, Jerusalem, Munich, elsewhere; Director of Orchestral Studies at Carnegie-Mellon University, Pittsburgh, USA; Music Director, National Symphony of Chile. *Recordings:* Bach: The Art of Fugue; Mozart: Requiem; Beethoven Symphonies; Brahms German Requiem; Mahler Symphonies: Britten: War Requiem; Stravinsky: Rite of Spring, and Firebird; Schoenberg: Transfigured Night; Messiaen: Turangalîla Symphony; Varèse: Amériques; Xenakis, Kagel, Scelsi, other contemporary composers. *Honours:* Critics Award, Santiago, 1963, 1999; 1st Prize, Dimitri Mitropoulos Competition, New York, 1966. *Current Management:* Conciertos Gama, Buenos Aires; MUSIESPANA, Madrid. *Address:* 1022 Murray Hill Avenue, Pittsburgh, PA 15217, USA.

**IZZO D'AMICO, Fiamma;** Singer (Soprano); b. 1964, Rome, Italy. *Education:* Studied at Santa Cecilia Conservatory, Rome, 1981–84. *Career:* Debut: Sang Mimi in La Bohème at the Teatro Regio, Turin, 1984; Sang Violetta at Treviso 1985, was discovered by Herbert von Karajan, Sang Elisabeth de Valois at the 1986 Salzburg Festival followed by Micaela in Carmen; US debut Philadelphia 1986 in La Bohème, with Luciano Pavarotti, celebrated his 15th anniversary with him at Modena, 1986; Bologna 1986 in La Traviata, conducted by Riccardo Chailly; Season 1987–88 with appearances in Bohème at Vienna, Metropolitan, New York; Manon in Genoa, Tosca and the Verdi Requiem at Salzburg; Further engagements at the Paris Opéra, London, Chicago, Monte Carlo, Monaco and Hamburg. *Address:* Metropolitan Opera, Lincoln Center, NY 10023, USA.

# J

**JABLONSKI, Krzysztof;** Pianist; b. 2 March 1965, Wrocław, Poland. *Education:* Karol Szymanowski Academy of Music in Katowice, 1986 with Professor Andrzej Jasinki. *Career:* Numerous concert engagements in Poland and abroad, including Austria, Belgium, Bulgaria, Canada, Czechoslovakia, Denmark, Germany, Finland, the United Kingdom, Netherlands, Israel, Italy, Japan, Norway, Soviet Union, Spain and USA. Many recordings for radio and television in Poland and abroad. *Recordings:* Chopin: 24 Preludes Op 28; Haydn: Sonata in C Minor No. 33, Beethoven: Sonata in C Minor Op 13, Pathetique; Mozart: Piano Concerto in F Major K 459, Orchester der Ludwigsburger Festspiele, W Goennenwein, Bayer Records; Chopin: 24 Preludes Op 28, Polonaise in A flat Major, Op 43, Heroique, Study in G flat Major Op 10-5 Black Keys, Study in C Minor Op 10-12, Revolutionary, Yamaha Piano Player; Chopin: Sonata in B Minor Op 58, Barcarolle in F sharp Major Op 60, Polonaises in A flat Major Op 53, Heroique in G Minor in B flat Major, in A flat Major, Nocturnes, in B flat Major Op 9-3 in F sharp Major Op 15,2; More recently: Mussorgsky: Piano solo, Pictures at an Exhibition; Schumann: Kinderszenen Op. 15; Debussy: Children's Corner, Kos Records, Kos CD 10 CD, 1993. *Address:* Ul Kwiska 43-9, 54-210 Wrocław, Poland.

**JABLONSKI, Peter;** Concert Pianist; b. 1971, Lyckeby, Sweden. *Education:* Studied at the Malmö Music College and the Royal College of Music, London. *Career:* Started as a percussionist; Performed Jazz with Thad Jones and Buddy Rich at Village Vanguard, New York, 1980; Has appeared with such orchestras as the Royal and Moscow Philharmonics, Philharmonia, Philadelphia, Cleveland and the Los Angeles and Japan Philharmonics in Berlin and Milan; Annual concert tours to Japan and Far East and America since 1992; Visits to Australia and New Zealand; Recent and future engagements include Deutsche Symphonie Orchestra, Philharmonia, Royal Stockholm Philharmonic, Swedish Radio, Hong Kong Philharmonic, Orchestre National de France and Czech Philharmonic under Ashkenazy; World premiere of Kilar's Piano Concerto, 1997. *Recordings include:* Concertos by Gershwin, Rachmaninov, Lutoslawski and Tchaikovsky; Chopin Waltzes and solo music by Liszt; Grieg recital, 1997. *Honours:* Edison Award, 1993; Årets Svensk I Varlden, 1996; Orpheus Award at Warsaw Autumn Festival, 1998. *Current Management:* Harrison/Parrott Ltd, 12 Penzance Place, London, W11 4PA, England. *Telephone:* (20) 7229 9166. *Fax:* (20) 7221 5042. *Website:* www .harrisonparrott.com.

**JACKIW, Stefan;** Concert Violinist; b. 1985, USA. *Education:* Studies with Zinaida Gilels, and with Michéle Auclair at the New England Conservatory. *Career:* Season 1997 with the Wieniawski Second Concerto at the Boston Pops, and with the Minnesota Orchestra and Pittsburgh Symphony; Further engagements with the Boston Symphony Orchestra's Youth Concert, conducted by Keith Lockhart; European debut with the Philharmonia, London, in Mendelssohn's Concerto, conducted by Benjamin Zander, April. 2000; Season 2000–01 with the Strasbourg Philharmonic conducted by Yoel Levi. *Address:* c/o IMG Artists, Lovell House, 616 Chiswick High Road, London W4 5RX, England.

**JACKMAN, Jeremy S.,** BMus; British conductor, composer and arranger; b. 22 April 1952, London, England; m. Angela; one s. one d. *Education:* Jr Exhibitioner Royal Coll. of Music, Hull Univ. *Career:* mem. of King's Singers 1980–90; Chorus Master, Belfast Philharmonic choir 1991–97, London Philharmonic Choir 1992–94; f. OSJ Voices in 1994 for the Orchestra of St John's Smith Square; Dir of Music, English Baroque Choir 2000–; mem. Assn of British Choral Dirs, Incorporated Soc. of Musicians. *Compositions:* 2 compositions, arrangements and edns for Harmonia; Veni Emanuel, Who Shall Hold the Heart of Man? for Maecenas, Music of the World for Novello. *Recordings:* many recordings for The King's Singers. *Publications:* contrib. to Meistersinger, Church Music Quarterly. *Address:* Palace Music, 64 Park Avenue North, London, N8 7RT, England (office). *Telephone:* (20) 8341-3408 (office). *Fax:* (20) 8341-3408 (office). *E-mail:* jeremy@jsjackman.e7even.com (office). *Website:* www.jeremyjackman.co.uk (office).

**JACKSON, Garfield;** Violist; b. 1955, England. *Career:* Founder-member and Violist of the Endellion Quartet, from 1979; Many concerts in Munich, Frankfurt, Amsterdam, Paris, Salzburg and Rome; South Bank Haydn Festival 1990 and Quartet Plus series 1994; Wigmore Hall Beethoven series 1991; Quartet in Residence at the University of Cambridge from 1992; Residency at MIT, USA, 1995. *Recordings include:* Works by Haydn, Barber, Bartók, Dvořák, Smetana and Walton (Virgin Classics). *Current Management:* Hazard Chase Ltd, Norman House, Cambridge Place, Cambridge, CB2 1NS, England. *Telephone:* (1223) 312400. *Fax:* (1223) 460827. *Website:* www .hazardchase.co.uk.

**JACKSON, Isaiah;** Conductor; b. 22 Jan. 1945, Virginia, USA; m. Helen Tuntland, 6 Aug 1977, 1 s., 2 d. *Education:* MS, Juilliard School of Music, 1969; DMA, 1973. *Career:* Assistant Director, American Symphony, 1970–71; Associate Conductor, Rochester Philharmonic, 1973–87; Music Director, Royal Ballet, Covent Garden, 1987–90; Music Director, Dayton Philharmonic, 1987–95; Principal Guest Conductor, Queensland Symphony, 1993–; Music Director, Youngstown Symphony, 1996–; Guest conducting, New York Philharmonic, Cleveland Orchestra, Boston Pops, San Francisco Symphony, Orchestre de la Suisse Romande, BBC Concert Orchestra, Berlin Symphony,

Royal Liverpool Philharmonic, Houston Symphony. *Recordings:* String orchestra compositions of Herrmann, Waxman, Rozsa, Berlin Symphony; Dance music of William Grant Still, Berlin Symphony; Gospel at the Symphony, Louisville Orchestra; Harp concerti of Ginastera and Mathias, English Chamber Orchestra. *Honours:* 1st Governor's Award for Arts, Virginia, 1979; Signet Society Medal for the Arts, Harvard University, 1991. *Address:* c/o United Arts, 3906 Sunbeam Drive, Los Angeles, CA 90065, USA.

**JACKSON, Laurence;** Concert Violinist; b. 1967, Lancashire, England. *Education:* Studied at Chetham's School of Music and at the Royal Academy with Maurice Hasson and Anne-Sophie Mutter. *Career:* Concerto repertoire includes works by Bruch, Mendelssohn, Vaughan Williams and Tchaikovsky; Aldeburgh Festival, 1988, in the Concerto Grosso by Schnittke; Soloist at the Casals Festival Hall, 1990, in The Four Seasons; Recitals at the Fairfields Halls, Queens Hall, Edinburgh, Brangwyn Hall and Turner Sims Hall; Member of Britten-Pears Ensemble tour of USA, 1991; As member of Borante Piano Trio has performed from 1982 at the Purcell Room and Wigmore Hall, in Dublin and Paris, and at the 1989 Festival Wiener Klassik (Beethoven's Triple Concerto); Season 1990 at the Bath and Perth Festivals, tour of Scandinavia, Russia and the Baltic States and master classes with Andras Schiff at Prussia Cove, Cornwall; Duo partnership with pianist Scott Mitchell; Solo concert tour of Chile, Colombia and Venezuela, 1991; Concerto and recital performances in Spain, 1992. *Recordings:* Solo recording with the ensemble Laureate, 1991. *Honours:* David Martin Concerto Prize, 1987, and Principal's Prize, 1988; The Royal English Heritage Award, 1983, 1985, 1986; 1st Prize at Vina del Mar, Chile, 1990; 3rd Prize, First Pablo Sarasate International Violin Competition, 1991. *Current Management:* Scott Mitchell Management, 26 Childebert Road, London SW17 8EX, England. *Address:* 23 Fulwell Park Avenue, Twickenham, Middlesex TW2 5HF, England.

**JACKSON, Sir Nicholas Fane St George (Bart),** Kt, LRAM, ARCM; organist, harpsichordist and composer; b. 4 Sept. 1934, London, England; m. Nadia Michard 1971; one s. *Education:* Radley College, Wadham College, Oxford, Royal Academy of Music with C. H. Trevor, George Malcolm, Gustav Leonhardt. *Career:* debut Wigmore Hall, 1964; Organist at St James's, London, 1971–74, St Lawrence Jewry next Guildhall, 1974–77; Organist and Master of the Choristers of St David's Cathedral, 1977–84; Organ recital at Royal Festival Hall, 1984; Director of Concertante of London, 1987–; Masterclasses at Segovia, Spain, 1989; Director of Festival Bach, Santes Creus, Spain; Tour of Croatia, 2002; Solo performances at South Bank, London and at Nôtre Dame Paris, Teatro Real Madrid and New York; World premiere of his opera The Reluctant Highwayman at Broomhill, 1995; mem. Master of the Worshipful Company of Drapers, 1994–95; Liveryman of the Worshipful Company of Musicans. *Compositions:* Mass for a Saint's Day; 4 Images for Organ; 20th Century Merbecke; Divertissement for Organ; Anthems and Choral Settings; Mass for Organ, 1984; Opera: The Reluctant Highwayman, 1992; Organ Sonata, 1995. *Recordings include:* The Organ of St David's Cathedral; Bach's Christmas Organ Music for Trumpet and Organ; 2 albums with Maurice Murphy; Complete Organ Works of Richard Arnell; Bach's 2 and 3 Part Inventions; François Couperin; Harpsichord Concertos; Mass for a Saint's Day; Own Organ Works and Works for Trumpet and Organ, played at Chartres Cathedral, 2000; Spanish Organ Music, Segovia Cathedral priory, 2001; Scarlatti CD. *Publication:* 'Recollections' of Sir T. G. Jackson RA (ed. and arranger). *Honours:* Honorary Fellowship, Hertford College, Oxford, 1995. *Address:* 42a Hereford Road, London, W2 5AJ, England.

**JACKSON, Richard;** singer (baritone); b. 1960, Cornwall, England. *Education:* studied with Pierre Bernac and Audrey Langford. *Career:* widely known as a concert singer, in song and oratorio; Founding mem., Songmakers' Almanac, with appearances in the USA, at the Saintes Festival, Three Choirs Festival and Wigmore and Queen Elizabeth Halls; solo recital with songs by Poulenc at Wigmore Hall, 1989; concerts with David Willcocks, Neville Marriner, Bertini, Rostropovich, Mackerras and Gardiner; has sung Bach and Handel in Spain and Portugal, Monteverdi's Vespers in Venice, The Starlight Express by Elgar; opera engagements at Glyndebourne and Aldeburgh Festivals and with Kent Opera, New Sadler's Wells Opera and with Handel Opera Soc.; sang Aeneas to the Dido of Janet Baker, Almeida Festival, London 1987–88, in British premiere of Jakob Lenz by Wolfgang Rihm and world premiere of The Undivine Comedy by Michael Finnissy. *Current Management:* Caroline Phillips Management, The Old Brushworks, Pickwick Road, Corsham, Wilts., SN13 9BX, England. *Telephone:* (1249) 716716. *Fax:* (1249) 716717. *E-mail:* cphillips@caroline-phillips.co.uk. *Website:* www.caroline -phillips.co.uk/jackson.

**JACOBS, Klaus J.;** Swiss business executive; *Chairman and CEO, Adecco SA.* *Education:* studies in Germany, Stanford Univ., USA. *Career:* Dir of Purchasing and Marketing, Jacobs AG 1962–73, Gen. Man. 1973–82; owner Jacobs Suchard (co. cr. following merger of Jacobs AG and Interfood 1982) – 1990; f. Barry Callebaut 1990; acquired Adia Personnel Services 1992; Jt Chair. Adecco SA (following merger of Adia and Ecco 1996) 1996–2002, Co-Chair. 2004–05, Chair. and CEO 2005–; founding Chair. The Jacobs Foundation 1988, now Hon. Chair.; founder and mem. Nat. Park of Hohe Tauern; mem. World Scout Foundation 1986–; Vice Chair. and Treasurer Carnegie Hall, acting Exec. Dir 2004–; mem. Bd Zürich Opera. *Address:*

Adecco SA, Sägereistrasse 10, 8152 Glattbrugg, Switzerland (office). *Telephone:* (1) 8788888 (office). *Fax:* (1) 8298888 (office). *Website:* www.adecco.com (office).

**JACOBS, René,** BPhil; Belgian conductor and singer (countertenor); *Artistic Director, Innsbrucker Festwochen der alten Musik*; b. 30 Oct. 1946, Ghent; m. Suzy Depporter. *Education:* Univ. of Ghent, studied singing with Louis Devos in Brussels, Lucie Frateur in The Hague. *Career:* recitals in Europe, Canada, USA, Mexico and the Philippines; performances with madrigal ensembles and with early music groups, including the Leonhardt Consort, Il Complesso Barocco, La Petite Bande and groups led by Alan Curtis and Nikolaus Harnoncourt; sings Baroque music and directs his own ensemble, Collegium Vocale; best known in operas by Monteverdi, Cesti, Handel, Gluck and Cavalli; sacred music by Charpentier and Couperin; teacher of performing practice in Baroque singing, Schola Cantorum, Basle; appointments at the Int. Summer School for Early Music, Innsbruck, and the Aston Magna Acad. for Baroque Music, USA; conducted Cavalli's Giasone in his own edition at the Innsbruck Festival 1988; Flavio 1989; L'Incoronazione de Poppea with the ensemble I Febi Armonici 1989; conducted Graun's Cleopatra e Cesare at the Baroque Festival, Versailles 1992; Conti's Don Chisciotte at the Innsbruck Festival of Early Music 1992; led Poppea at the Teatro Colón, Buenos Aires 1996; Monteverdi's Orfeo at the Barbican Theatre, London 1998; Artistic Dir Innsbrucker Festwochen der alten Musik. *Recordings:* Cesti's L'Orontea (from the 1982 Holland Festival), Arias by Monteverdi and Benedetto Ferrari, Motets by Charpentier, Bach's St Matthew Passion, Handel's Admeto and Partenope, Lully's Bourgeois Gentilhomme, Gluck's Orfeo ed Euridice and Echo et Narcisse, Giasone and La Calisto by Cavalli, Handel's Alessandro and Tamerlano, Charpentier's David et Jonathas, Handel's Giulio Cesare, Così fan tutte, Mozart's Le nozze di Figaro (MIDEM Classical Music Award for Recording of the Year 2005, Grammy Award for Best Opera 2005) 2004, Handel's Saul (with RIAS Chamber Choir) 2005, Haydn's Symphonies Nos 91 & 92 2005. *Honours:* MIDEM Classical Award for Artist of the Year 2005. *Address:* Innsbrucker Festwochen der alten Musik GmbH, Herzog-Friedrich-Straße 21, 1. Stock, 6020 Innsbruck, Austria. *Website:* www.altemusik.at.

**JACOBSON, Bernard (Isaac);** Writer on Music; b. 2 March 1936, London, England; m. (1) Bonnie Brodsky, 11 Aug 1968, dissolved 1982, 1 s., 1 d., (2) Dr Laura Dale Belcove, 3 Jan 1983. *Education:* City of London School, 1947–54; Corpus Christi College, Oxford as Open Scholar, 1956–60; Classical Honour Moderations, 1958; Lit Hum BA 1960; MA 1962. *Career:* Music Critic, Chicago Daily News, 1967–73; Director, Southern Arts Association, Winchester, England, 1973–76; Deputy Director of Publications, 1979–81, Director of Promotion, Boosey and Hawkes Music Publishers Ltd, London, 1982–84; Manager, Publications and Educational Programmes, 1984–88, Programme Annotater and Musicologist, 1988–91, Philadelphia Orchestra; Artistic Director, Residentie Orkest, Hague Philharmonic, 1992–94; Independent Associate, Joy Mebus Artists' Management, 1993–94; Artistic Adviser, North Netherlands Orchestra, 1994–. *Compositions:* Libretto, 16 poems, for Death of a Young Man, song cycle by Wilfred Josephs commissioned and performed by 1971 Harrogate Festival; Poems for Songs and other works by Richard Wernick. *Recordings:* Schoenberg Ode to Napoleon, 1968; Stravinsky, The Flood, 1995. *Publications include:* The Music of Johannes Brahms, USA and London, 1977; Conductors on Conducting, USA and London, 1979; A Polish Renaissance, in press; Many translations including Holofernes, Judith and Die Weise von Liebe und Tod des Cornets Christoph Rilke, all by Siegried Matthus, for Schott. *Contributions:* Dictionary of 20th Century Music, 1974; The New Grove, 1980. *Address:* Buys Ballotstraat 89, 2563 ZK Den Haag, Netherlands.

**JACOBSON, Julian;** Pianist; b. 1947, Scotland. *Education:* Studied piano with Lamar Crowson and Louis Kentner; Composition with Arthur Benjamin and Humphrey Searle; Graduate, Royal College of Music and Oxford University. *Career:* Debut: London, Purcell Room, 1974; Appearances in over 30 countries including concerto engagements with London Symphony, BBC Symphony, City of Birmingham Orchestra, English Chamber Orchestra, London Mozart Players, Bournemouth Sinfonietta; Chamber music recitals with: Nigel Kennedy, Lydia Mordkovitch, Zara Nelsova, Steven Isserlis, Colin Carr, Christian Lindberg, Ivry Gitlis, Brodsky and Arditti Quartets; Artistic Director, Paxos Festival, Greece; Teacher and Performer, Dartington International Summer School; Head of Keyboard Studies, Welsh College of Music and Drama, 1992–96; Solo recitals include five cycles of the complete Beethoven Sonatas; Concerts; Masterclasses in France, Germany, Malta, Hungary and China, 1994–95; Conductor, European Union Chamber Orchestra, 1999; Secretary, Beethoven Piano Society of Europe. *Compositions:* Songs; Piano Works; Chamber Music; 6 Film Scores. *Recordings include:* Albums on various labels; CD recordings of Complete piano sonatas of Weber. *Address:* 34 St Margaret's Road, London SE4 1YU, England.

**JACOBSSON, John-Eric;** Swedish singer (tenor); b. 6 Oct. 1931, Hogran. *Education:* studied in Stockholm with Toivo Ek, Arne Sunnegaard and Sonny Peterson. *Career:* debut, Royal Opera, Stockholm 1964, as Turiddu in Cavalleria Rusticana; sang at Stockholm in the premiere of Kalifens Son by Eiyser 1976, as Alwa in the local premiere of Berg's Lulu; other roles include Pedrillo in Die Entführung, Jacquino in Fidelio, Cavaradossi, Albert Herring, Eisenstein in Die Fledermaus and Ismaele in Nabucco, Števa in Jenůfa and title role in Xerxes and more than 100 different roles; guest appearances in Oslo, Copenhagen, Hamburg, Munich, Edinburgh, Moscow, Hong Kong and at the Drottningholm Festival; many concert appearances. *Address:* c/o

Stiftelsen Kungliga Teaterns Solister, PO Box 253, 103 24 Stockholm, Sweden. *E-mail:* info@operasolisterna.se.

**JAFFE, Monte;** Singer (Baritone); b. 5 June 1940, USA. *Education:* Studied at the Curtis Institute and with Giorgio Tozzi. *Career:* Appearances with Krefeld Opera as Wotan, Kaspar (Der Freischütz), Dr Schön (Lulu), Reimann's Lear, the Dutchman, and in Cerhaa's Baal and the premiere of Judith by Matthus. Further engagements at the Metropolitan in Death of Venice, Lear with English National Opera, the Hoffmann villains for Israel Opera and Bluebeard (Bartók) for Scottish Opera; Returned to English National Opera for the title role in the premiere of Timon of Athens by Stephen Oliver, 1991, and has also sung at Karlsruhe (Graf Mirabeau by Matthus), Berne (Nekrotaz in Le Grand Macabre), Tel-Aviv (Mephistopheles in Faust), Bonn (Gianni Schicchi), 1993, Turin (Walküre Wotan), Antwerp (Klingsor) and Bielefeld (Barak in Die Frau ohne Schatten); Other roles include Scarpia, Konchak (Prince Igor), Zaccaria (Nabucco) and Old Sam in Bernstein's A Quiet Place; Sang the Rheingold Wotan at Braunschweig and Osmin for New York City Opera, 1999; Nekrotzar in Ligeti's Le Grand Macabre for Flemish Opera, 2001. *Current Management:* Ingpen & Williams Ltd, 7 St George's Court, 131 Putney Bridge Road, London, SW15 2PA, England.

**JAFFE, Stephen;** Composer; b. 30 Dec. 1954, Washington DC, USA; m. Mindy Oshrain, 29 May 1988, 2 d. *Education:* AM, AB summa cum laude, University of Pennsylvania, with George Crumb, George Rochberg and Richard Wernick, 1973–78; Also at University of Massachusetts and Conservatoire de Musique, Geneva. *Career:* Director, Encounters with the Music of Our Time, Duke University, 1981–; Performances with San Francisco, New Jersey, New Hampshire Symphonies, Rome Radio Orchestra, New York New Music Ensemble, Spectrum concerts, Berlin, Aurora and Ciompi Quartets. *Compositions:* First Quartet, 1991; Double Sonata, two pianos, 1989; Four Songs with Ensemble, for mezzo soprano and ensemble, 1988; Four Images, 1983–87; The Rhythm of the Running Plough, 1988; Triptych, for piano and wind quintet, 1993; Pedal Point, baritone, low strings, harp and timpani, 1992; Pedal Point, baritone and consort of low instruments, 1994. *Recordings:* First Quartet; Centering for two violins; Three Figures and a Ground; The Rhythm of the Running Plough; Double Sonata; Four Songs with Ensemble; Fort Juniper Songs. *Publications:* First Quartet, 1991; Double Sonata, 1992; Three Figures and a Grand, 1993; Four Images for Orchestra, 1988. *Contributions:* Contemporary Music Review; Conversation between JS and SJ on the New Tonality, article, 1992. *Honours:* American Academy of Arts and Letters Prize, 1993; Brandeis University Creative Arts Citation, 1989. *Current Management:* Theodore Presser Co, Bryn Mawr, PA 19010, USA. *Address:* Box 90656, Durham, NC 27708, USA.

**JAFFEE, Kay;** Musician and Musicologist; b. 31 Dec. 1937, Michigan, USA; m. Michael Jaffee, 24 July 1961. *Education:* BA, University of Michigan, 1959; MA, New York University, 1965; PhD, New York University, 2001. *Career:* Debut: Carnegie Recital Hall, 1966; Founding Member and Associate Director, The Waverly Consort, 1964–; Performer on Renaissance wind and keyboard instruments, harps, psalteries and percussion; Annual tours of North America since 1967; Also tours to the United Kingdom and Latin America; Festival appearances include: Casals Festival, 1981 and 1983, Madeira Bach Festival, 1981, Hong Kong Festival, 1988 and Caramoor Festival; Television appearances in USA; mem, American Musicological Society; Society for 17th Century Music; Renaissance Society of America. *Recordings:* 13 with the Waverly Consort. *Publications:* Articles and reviews to the Journal of Musicology, The American Recorder and The Brass Quarterly. *Current Management:* Musicians Corporate Management Ltd, PO Box 589, Millbrook, NY 12545, USA. *Address:* PO Box 386, Patterson, NY 12563, USA.

**JÄGGI, Andreas;** Singer (Tenor); b. 30 March 1952, Basle, Switzerland. *Education:* Studied with Maria Stader in Zürich. *Career:* Singer and Designer with the Companie Alain Germain in Europe and the USA, from 1976; Sang at Kiel Opera from 1985, Paris from 1987 (Weill's Mahagonny at the Opéra Bastille, 1995); Guest appearances at Covent Garden, Cologne (from 1988), Paris Opéra-Comique (Handel's Theodora) and Strasbourg (Narraboth in Salome, 1994); Other roles include Mozart's Pedrillo, Wagner's David, Andreas in Wozzeck and Flute in A Midsummer Night's Dream; Further engagements at the Athens, Orange and Granada Festivals; Sang Sylvester in Turnage's The Silver Tassie at Dublin, 2001. *Address:* c/o Opéra de la Bastille, 120 Rue de Lyon, 75012 Paris, France.

**JAHN, Gertrude;** Singer (Mezzo-soprano); b. 13 Aug. 1940, Zagreb, Croatia. *Education:* Studied at the Vienna Music Academy with Elisabeth Rado and Lily Kolar; Further study with Erik Werba and Josef Witt. *Career:* Debut: Basle, 1963, as Gluck's Orpheus; Appearances at the State Operas of Vienna, Hamburg, Munich and Stuttgart; Glyndebourne, 1968, as Olga in Eugene Onegin; Salzburg Festivals from 1967, as Feodor in Boris Godunov, Mozart's Ascanio, Margret in Wozzeck and Countess Laura in the premiere of Penderecki's Die schwarze Maske, 1986; Munich and Madrid, 1988, as Adelaide in Arabella and the Countess Geschwitz in Lulu; Further engagements in Düsseldorf, Salzburg, Moscow, Trieste and Montreal; Other roles include Carmen, Giulietta in Les Contes d'Hoffmann, Octavian, Eboli, Preziosilla (La Forza del Destino), Fatima in Oberon and Magdalene in Die Meistersinger; Frequent concert appearances. *Recordings include:* Masses by Haydn and Schubert; Missa Choralis by Liszt; Wozzeck.

**JAHNS, Annette;** Singer (Mezzo-soprano); b. 1958, Dresden, Germany. *Education:* Studied at the Dresden Musikhochschule and with Judith Beckmann in Hamburg and Ute Niss in Berlin. *Career:* Sang with the Dresden Opera, 1982–99, as Mozart's Ramiro (Finta giardiniera), Dorabella and Cherubino, Nicklausse, Mistress Quickly, and Maddalena in Rigoletto; Carmen, Orpheus, Hansel and Olga; Has also performed in the Brecht/Weill Sieben Todsunden; Season 2000–01 as Sarah in Thomas Chatterton by Matthias Pintscher at the Vienna Volksoper and in the premiere of Celan by Peter Ruzicka. *Honours:* Berlin Reviewers' Award, 1987; Dresden Art Award, 1995. *Current Management:* Agentur Arias, Via Roma 15, 03912 Meran.Laubegaster Strasse 5, 01326 Dresden, Germany.

**JAHREN, Helen Mai Aase,** MFA; Swedish oboist; b. 2 May 1959, Malmö. *Education:* Malmö College of Music, Staatliche Hochschule für Musik, Freiburg, Konservatorium für Musik, Berne. *Career:* debut solo appearance with orchestra, age 17; Tours, France, Italy, Spain, Germany, Switzerland, Poland, Denmark, Norway, Finland, Iceland, Japan, 1980–; Belgian tour with Orchestre National de Belgique, 1982; Vienna debut, Grosses Konzerthaus, 1983; Toured Colombia, Ecuador, Peru, Argentina, Uruguay, Brazil, Venezuela, Costa Rica, Mexico, 1984; Debut with Stockholm Philharmonic Orchestra, 1987; Invited to Louisville Symphony Orchestra's 50th Anniversary, USA, 1987; Pan Music Festival, Seoul, 1988; Gala Opening Concert, with Hong Kong Philharmonic Orchestra, World Music Days, Hong Kong, 1988; Debut with Swedish Radio Orchestra, 1988; Many television and radio appearances world-wide; Artist Portrait by Swedish Television, 1991–93; Teaching: Malmö College of Music, 1984–87; Ingesund College of Music, 1991–93; Stockholm Royal College of Music, 1993–95; Masterclasses; Initiator and Artistic Director of Båstad Chamber Music Festival; Many pieces dedicated to her by composers such as Erik Bergman, Poul Ruders, Daniel Börtz; Jouni Kaipainen, Per-Henrik Nordgren, Sven-David Sandström and many others. *Recordings include:* Swedish music for oboe and organ with Hans-Ola Ericsson, 1986; Schnittke Double Concerto for oboe and harp, with Stockholm Chamber Orchestra, 1987; J H Roman, Oboe Concerto, 1988; L-E Larsson, Oboe Concertino, 1990; J Kaipainen, Oboe Concerto, 1995; Mozart, Oboe Concerto in C major, J C Bach: Oboe Concertos, Ferlendis: Oboe Concerto, 2000; Börtz: Oboe Concerto, Kithairon for Oboe Solo, Ekström: Oboe Concerto, The Accelerating Ice-cube, Gamstorp: Oboe Concerto, Pulse II for oboe solo, 2000. *Address:* Nybrogatan 81, 11441 Stockholm, Sweden.

**JAKSIC, Djura;** Conductor and Writer on Music; b. 30 April 1924, Karlovac, Yugoslavia; m. Slobondanka Ilic, 21 July 1962, 2 s. *Education:* School of Music, Belgrade, 1939–45; Music Science, Charles University, Prague and Prague Conservatoire, 1945–48; Diploma, Academic Musician-Conductor, Academy of Music, Zagreb, 1948–50. *Career:* Debut: Symphonic concert, Radio Belgrade Symphony, 1950; Conductor, Radio Symnphony, Radio Chamber and Radio Studio Orchestras, 1950–53; Associate Conductor, Belgrade Philharmonic Orchestra, 1953–66; Art Director, Principal Conductor, Chamber Orchestra Pro Musica, 1967–; Art Director, National Opera/Ballet, Belgrade, 1977–80; Concerts and tours in Yugoslavia, Austria, Belgium, Bulgaria, Czechoslovakia, Denmark, France, the United Kingdom, Hungary, Italy, Netherlands, Norway, Romania, Spain, Switzerland, Turkey and USSR; Autobiography broadcast on Belgrade Radio and Television, 1987, 1988. *Recordings:* Vivaldi, The Seasons, and J Slavenski, Suite of Dances, both with Chamber Orchestra Pro Musica; Pro Musica Plays Vivaldi, 1991; Over 300 radio recordings. *Publications:* On the Symphony Orchestra, 1954; State of Music in Serbia, 1969; Two Symphonies of Amando Ivancic; Revisions, editions and orchestrations of Yugoslav composers from the 15th to 19th century; Essays on Vivaldi, Telemann, Britten's War Requiem, Berg's Wozzeck, Finnish music, Bulgarian music; G B Shaw on Music: Selection of music criticisms, Serbocroat translation, selection and comment, 1989; Over 200 other articles. *Contributions:* Editor in chief, Pro Musica magazine, 1964–90; Yugoslav Music Encyclopaedia, 1958–. *Address:* Pozeska 92, 11031 Belgrade, Serbia and Montenegro.

**JAMES, Buddug Verona;** Singer (mezzo-soprano); b. 1963, Cardigan, Wales. *Education:* Guildhall School of Music and Drama; Nat. Opera Studio. *Career:* 50 operatic roles include Gluck's Orfeo in America and Canada; Dardano in Handel's Amadigi in New York and Europe; Cherubino in Mozart's Marriage of Figaro in Tokyo and Toronto; Has worked with Netherlands Opera, Cleveland Opera (USA), Glyndebourne; Almedia Opera; Opera Theatre Co.; Opera Northern Ireland; Opera North; Opera Atelier; Opera Circus; English Pocket Opera; Opera 80; Operavox Cartoons, Siobhan Davies Dance Co.; Music Theatre Wales and Mid Wales Opera; Premieres in operas by Gerald Barry, Jonathan Dove, Deirdre Gribbin, Wolfgang Rihm and John Woolrich; Concert repertoire includes Mozart's Ch'io mi scordi di te with BBC Welsh Symphony Orchestra and Jane Glover; Matthaus Passion with Paul Steinitz; Johannes Passion with Thomas Dausgaard; Theodora with Paul McCreesh; Bach Cantatas with John Georgiadis; Elijah with Owain Arwel Hughes. *Recordings include:* Thomas Chilcot Songs; Arias by Handel and Gluck; The James Sisters Sing Gospel. *Website:* www.buddug.co.uk.

**JAMES, Carolyn;** Singer (Soprano); b. 1963, USA. *Education:* Studied at Arizona State University and the Juilliard School. *Career:* Sang Mozart's Countess at Miami and the New York Metropolitan (1991–92); Vienna Volksoper, 1990, as Donna Anna, Fiordiligi at Cologne, 1993; Vienna Staatsoper, 1993–94, Metropolitan, 1995, as Ellen Orford in Peter Grimes; Verdi's Elisabeth de Valois at Seattle and Elettra in Idomeneo at the Paris Opéra Bastille, 1996; Other roles include Berlioz's Beatrice and Purcell's Dido;

Concerts include the Mozart and Verdi Requiems, Messiah, Elijah, and Mahler's 8th Symphony. *Address:* c/o Metropolitan Opera, Lincoln Center, New York, NY 10023, USA.

**JAMES, David;** Singer (countertenor); b. 1949, England. *Education:* Magdalen College, Oxford. *Career:* From 1978 has sung with the Hilliard Ensemble and other early music groups; Tours of Russia and Mexico, Schütz's Psalms of David and Cesti's Orontea in Innsbruck and at the Holland Festival; Handel's Orlando in Spain and Portugal with the Amsterdam Baroque Orchestra; Messiah in Finland and with The Sixteen (tours include visit to Utrecht 1990); Concerts with the Collegium Vocale Gent and La Chapelle Royale; Bach's St John Passion in London and Salzburg, the B minor Mass at Bruges and Cantatas in Finland (1991); Promenade Concerts 1990, in the cantata Herz und Mund und Tat und Leben; Contemporary Music Network tour with the Hilliard Ensemble in Pärt's St John Passion; Has sung at the Aldeburgh Festival, for Handel Opera in London, English National Opera and at Covent Garden; Frantz in the premiere of Dr Ox's Experiment, by Bryars, ENO, 1998; Gen. Dir, New Sussex Opera, mid-scale touring opera with emphasis on new or lesser known works. *Recordings:* Orlando; Messiah; Pärt St John Passion (ECM) Bach St John Passion. *Honours:* Winner, 's-Hertogenbosch Competition, Netherlands, 1978. *Current Management:* Hazard Chase Ltd, Norman House, Cambridge Place, Cambridge, CB2 1NS, England. *Telephone:* (1223) 312400. *Fax:* (1223) 460827. *Website:* www .hazardchase.co.uk; www.newsussexopera.com (office).

**JAMES, Eirian;** Singer (Mezzo-Soprano); b. 1952, Cardigan, Wales. *Education:* Royal College of Music with Ruth Packer. *Career:* Debut: Kent Opera, 1977, as Olga in Eugene Onegin, returned as Cherubino, Poppea, Rosina, and Meg Page in Falstaff; English National Opera in The Makropulos Case, War and Peace, Rigoletto and Rusalka; Buxton Festival in Handel's Ariodante; Lyon Opéra as Fatima (Oberon) and Rossini's Isolier; Genera Opera as Hansel; Houston Opera as Siebel in Faust and Sesto in Handel's Giulio Cesare; Aix-en-Provence as Dorabella (Così fan tutte); Covent Garden debut 1987 as Annina in Der Rosenkavalier, returned as Smeton in Anna Bolena, 1988 and Nancy in Albert Herring, 1989; Sang Dorabella at Aix-en-Provence, 1989, second Lady in Die Zauberflöte at the 1990 Prom Concerts; Ascanio in Benvenuto Cellini for Netherlands Opera, Cherubino at Houston; Concert Appearances at the BBC Promenades, Aldeburgh Festival, the Barbican and with the BBC National Orchestra of Wales; repertoire includes the Lieder eines fahrenden Gesellen (Lyon), Beethoven's Mass in C (London), Mozart's C Minor Mass (Edinburgh and Paris); Haydn's Harmoniemesse; Mendelssohn's Elijah; Gluck's La Corona (City of London Festival); Hermia, Midsummer Night's Dream, Aix-en-Provence, 1991; Orlofsky, Fledermaus, 1991, English National Opera; Rosina (Barber of Seville), 1992; Scottish Opera, Sextus (Julius Caesar), 1992; Sang Cyrus in Handel's Belshazzar at the 1996 Göttingen Festival; Sang Falsirena inMazzochi's La Catena d'Adone at Innsbruck and Britten's Hermia at Rome, 1999. *Recordings include:* Zerlina in Don Giovanni, conducted by John Eliot Gardiner, (Deutsche Grammophon); Sextus (Julius Caesar by Handel) conducted by Jean-Claude Malgoire. *Current Management:* IMG Artists Europe. *Address:* c/o Music International, 13 Ardilaun Road, London, N5 2QR, England.

**JAMES, Kevin G. G.;** Canadian modern and baroque violist, violinist, researcher and writer; b. 30 July 1961, Toronto. *Education:* summer sessions University of Toronto, Carleton University, University of Ottawa, Oberlin College, McGill University. *Career:* freelance orchestral and chamber player, recitalist; Staff writer, Encyclopedia of Music in Canada, 1989–92; Occasional Contributor on Canadian topics to The Strad, Early Music, Musick, Performing Arts in Canada, Continuo, Newsletter of the American Musical Instrument Society, Canadian Viola Society Newsletter. Premieres: Jan Jarvlepp, Encounter, 1991; Alyssa Ryvers, Two Songs for Viola and Voice, 1990, and Synergy for nine violas, 1994; Gilles Leclerc, Suite for Viola and Organ, 1997; Michael Spassov, Fantasy for Solo Viola, 1997; Brian Pantekoek, The Letter, for viola and percussion, 1998; Deirdre Piper, Fantasy for Solo Viola, 1999; Eldon Rathburn, Soliloquy for Solo Viola, 1999; Andrew Ager, Garden Shadows, for viola and chamber choir, 2000; Jan Jarvlepp, Street Scene, for viola and electric guitar, 2000; Peter Amsel, Poème pour Alto, for solo viola, 2000; Jan Jarvlepp, Suite for Viola and Strings, 2001; Peter Willsha, Intermezzo for Viola and Strings, 2002; mem, Association of Canadian Orchestras, 1985–; Canadian Viola Society, 1991–. *Recordings:* John Playford, The English Dancing Master, 1983; Jan Jarvlepp, Encounter, 1994, and Trio No. 2, 2000; The Mystical Music of Andalucia, with Barbara Solís, piano, 2003; Chamber and recital performances for Radio-Canada. *Address:* 505-455 Lisgar Street, Ottawa, ON K1R 5G9, Canada. *E-mail:* kggjames@canada.com.

**JAMES, Peter Haydn,** BMus, PhD, CertEd; Australian music editor; b. 17 Oct. 1940, Melbourne, Australia; m. A. Heather; one s. one d. *Education:* Univ. of Wales, Cardiff and Univ. of Bristol. *Career:* Lecturer then Dir of Studies, Birmingham School of Music (now Birmingham Conservatoire) 1970–83; Vice-Prin. RAM 1983–95; Series Ed., Cathedral Press Ltd 1997–; part-time Lecturer, Open Univ. 1973–81; Vicar Choral, Lichfield Cathedral 1969–74; Chorus Master, City of Birmingham Symphony Orchestra Chorus 1974–76; mem. Royal Musical Asscn. *Recordings:* Chorus Master for City of Birmingham Symphony Orchestra Chorus recordings 1975–77. *Publications:* more than 40 edns of early sacred music; contrib. to Music & Letters 1983, Annual Byrd Newsletter 1999, 2000, Johnson Society 1981, Thomas Tomkins: The last Elizabethan by Anthony Boden and others 2005. *Honours:* Fellow, Birmingham School of Music 1984; Hon. FRAM 1984; Hon. FRCM 1985. *Address:* Series Editor, Cathedral Press Ltd, Alltycham House Pontardawe, Swansea, SA8 4JT, Wales (office). *Telephone:* (1792) 865197 (office). *E-mail:* james@cathpress.fsnet.co.uk (office).

**JAMIESON, Peter;** British music executive; *Executive Chairman, British Phonographic Industry.* *Career:* fmr management trainee, EMI; Man. Dir EMI Greece four years; fmr sr exec. EMI and BMG; worked extensively in Europe, Australasia and Far East; helped established BMG Asia Pacific and MTV Asia; Exec. Chair. British Phonographic Industry (BPI) 2002–. *Address:* British Phonographic Industry, Riverside Building, County Hall, Westminster Bridge Road, London, SE1 7JA, England (office). *E-mail:* peter.jamieson@bpi.co.uk (office). *Website:* www.bpi.co.uk (office).

**JANACEK, Bedrich,** DipMus, BMus; organist; b. 18 May 1920, Prague, Czechoslovakia; m. Elisabet Wentz 1951; one s. *Education:* State Conservatory of Music, Prague, Royal High Music School, Stockholm, Sweden. *Career:* organist, various concerts in Europe and USA, including Royal Festival Hall, London, England, 1942–; soloist with orchestras; teacher of organ, State Conservatory of Music, Prague, 1946–48; Parish Musician, Cathedral Parish, Lund, Sweden, 1965–85. *Compositions:* organ compositions; choral works including two cantatas with orchestra; works for brass and organ. *Honours:* City of Lund Cultural Prize, 1980, 1988; Commander of Merit, Ordo Militaris et Hospitalaris Sancti Lasari Hierosolymitani, 1992; Litteris et Artibus, Sweden, 1993. *Address:* Kyrkogatan 17, 222 22 Lund, Sweden. *Telephone:* (46) 129602. *E-mail:* elisabet.wentzjanacek@telia.com.

**JANARCEKOVA, Viera;** Composer; b. 23 Sept. 1944, Svit, Czechoslovakia. *Education:* Studied at the Bratislava Conservatory and the Prague Academy. *Career:* Keyboard performer and composer in Germany from 1981. *Compositions include:* Radio drama Biomasse, 1984; 4 string quartets, 1983–89; Pausenfabrik for 2 clarinets and ensemble, 1987; Beschattungtheater for 4 cellos, 1990; Piano concerto, 1991; Vocal music including Donna Laura for mezzo and 15 instruments, 1989; Der Gehemnisvolle Nachen for mezzo cello, 1989. *Address:* c/o OSA. Cs armady 20, 160-56 Prague 6, Bubenec, Czech Republic.

**JANDER, Owen (Hughes);** Musicologist and Music Educator; b. 4 June 1930, Mount Kisco, New York, USA. *Education:* BA, University of Virginia, 1951; MA, 1952, PhD, 1962, Harvard University. *Career:* Faculty Member, 1960–1992, Chairman, 3 terms, Department of Music, Wellesley College; Founder Collegium Musicum, originated and oversaw project to build the Fisk Organ, Wellesley College; Editor, The Wellesley Edition and The Wellesley Edition Cantata Index Series, 1962–74; mem. American Musicological Society. *Publications:* Charles Brenton Fisk, Organ Builder (co-editor), 1986; Orpheus Revisited (Andante of Beethoven's 4th Piano Concerto), 1996. *Contributions:* Articles on 17th century Italian music and on Beethoven to various journals; 78 articles, The New Grove Dictionary of Music and Musicians, 1980. *Honours:* Guggenheim Fellowship, 1966–67; National Endowment for the Humanities Fellowship for Senior Scholars, 1985; Catherine Mills Davies Professorship in Music History, Wellesley College. *Address:* 72 Denton Road, Wellesley, MA 02181, USA.

**JANES, Fiona;** Singer (Mezzo-soprano); b. 1961, Sydney, NSW, Australia. *Education:* Studied at the New South Wales Conservatory and in Munich with Sena Jurinac. *Career:* Member of the Australian Opera 1988–91, notably as Mozart's Annio, Cherubino, Dorabella and Zerlina; Siebel in Faust for Victoria State Opera and Rosina for the Lyric Opera of Queensland; Buxton Festival 1992 as Nero in Handel's Agrippina and sang Rosina with English National Opera; Season 1993–94 at the Edinburgh Festival, as Sesto in La Clemenza di Tito for the Glyndebourne Tour, and Australian Opera as Cenerentola; Season 1995–96 at the Semperoper Dresden, Mozart's Idamantes with the Flanders Philharmonic Orchestra and Rossini's Isabella in Australia under Richard Bonynge; Sang Lucia di Lammermoor at Auckland, 1998; Concerts include Mozart's Requiem, Beethoven's Missa Solemnis (under Walter Weller), and Ninth Symphony under Charles Mackerras; Berlioz Faust with the Scottish National Orchestra. *Address:* c/o Arien Arts & Music B.V.B.A de Boeystraat 6, B–2018 Antwerp, Belgium.

**JANEVA-IVELIC, Veneta;** Singer (Soprano); b. 1950, Bulgaria. *Education:* Studied at Sofia Conservatory. *Career:* Sang at the Sofia Opera from 1973, National Opera Zagreb, from 1980; Guest appearances in Salzburg (with Zagreb company as Norma, 1985), Berlin Staatsoper, Paris Opéra (Abigaille in Nabucco), Luxembourg and Karlsruhe; Other roles have included Maddalena (Andrea Chénier), the Forza and Trovatore Leonoras, Violetta, Desdemona, Lady Macbeth, Butterfly and Elvira in I Puritani. *Honours:* Prizewinner, Rio International Competition, 1980. *Address:* Slovensko Narodno Gledaslisce, Zupancicava 1, 61000 Ljubljana, Serbia.

**JANICKE, Heike;** Violinist; b. 20 Dec. 1962, Dresden. *Education:* Diploma of Violin, Musikhochschule, Dresden, 1987; Soloist Degree, Musikhochschule Freiburg, 1990. *Career:* Violin Soloist with Philharmonic Dresden, Berliner Sinfonie Orchestra, Rundfunksinfonie Orchestra Berlin, Radio Sinfonieorchestra Stuttgart, Gewandhaus Orchestra, Leipzig, Odense Sinfonie Orchestra, Bucharest Philharmonic; Solo and Chamber Music Concerts throughout Europe, Middle East, Japan, Middle and South America; Television and radio productions; Member of Berlin Philharmonic Orchestra, 1991–93; Member, London Symphony Orchestra, 1993–; Concertmaster of Dresden Philharmonic Orchestra, 1995–. *Honours:* Scholarship, Mendelssohn, 1988; International Violin Competitions, Music Competition, Geneva, 1985; Fritz Kreisler, France, 1987; Georg Kulenkampff, Cologne, 1988; Carl Nielsen, Odense, 1988; Zino Francescatti, Marseille, 1989. *Address:* c/o London Symphony Orchestra, Silk Street, Barbican Centre, London, England.

**JANIS, Byron;** Pianist; b. 24 March 1924, McKeesport, Pennsylvania, USA; m. (1) June Dickson-Wright, 1 s., (2) Maria Veronica Cooper. *Education:* Studied with Josef and Rosina Lhevinne in New York and with Adele Marcus and Horowitz. *Career:* Debut: With Pittsburgh Symphony Orchestra, 1944, in Rachmaninov's 2nd Concerto; Carnegie Hall debut, 1948; European debut with Concertgebouw Orchestra, 1952; Toured Russian, 1960, 1962, appearing with Moscow Philharmonic Orchestra; Further engagements with Boston Symphony, Philadelphia Orchestra and Indianapolis Symphony; Liszt concerts in Boston and New York, 1962; Repertoire also includes Chopin, Prokofiev and Gottschalk; Career interrupted by illness in 1960s but resumed in 1972; White House concert, 1985; Discovered manuscripts of two Chopin waltzes in France, 1967. *Recordings include:* Concertos by Liszt and Rachmaninov. *Honours:* Harriet Cohen Award; First American to receive Grand Prix du Disque; Chevalier of the Order des Arts et Lettres, 1965; Ambassador for the Arts of the National Arthritis Foundation, 1985.

**JANK, Helena;** Concert Harpsichordist; b. 1955, Salvador, Bahia, Brazil; m. Eduardo Ostergren, 11 July 1992, 1 d. *Education:* Studied at Staatliche Hochschule für Musik, Germany. *Career:* Debut: Munich, 1967; Professor at Campinas State University, Brazil; Harpsichordist with Münchener Bach-Orchester; Performances as soloist and in chamber music ensembles in Germany, USA and Brazil; mem. International Bach Society. *Recordings:* Helena Jank Plays Bach, Scarlatti, Ligeti; The Finest Baroque Sonatas, Erich; Mozart Sonatas; J. S. Bach Goldberg Variations: A Guide for the Complete Person. *Publications:* Goldberg Variations. *Honours:* Academic Recognition for Excellence in Teaching. *Address:* Rua Alvaro Muller 150, Ap 32, 13023 180 Campinas, São Paulo, Brazil.

**JANKOVIC, Eleonora;** Singer (Mezzo-soprano); b. 18 Feb. 1941, Trieste, Italy. *Education:* Studied in Trieste and Milan. *Career:* Member of the Opera at Zagreb, then made Italian debut at Trieste, 1972, in Smareglia's Nozze Istriane; Appearances at La Scala from 1974, Bologna, 1975, Florence, 1976, Teatro Lirico Milan, 1975, in the premiere of Al gran sole carico d'Amore by Luigi Nono; Guest engagements at Turin, Venice, Naples and Catania; Verona Arena, 1975–78, 1983, 1987; Rio de Janeiro and Buenos Aires, 1982–83; Sang Enrichetta in I Puritani at Rome, 1990, and appeared in Luisa Miller at Trieste, 1990; Sang in Wolf-Ferrari's I Quattro Rusteghi, for Geneva Opera, 1992; Has also sung the Countess in The Queen of Spades, Ulrica, Amneris, Leonora in La Favorita, Carmen, Charlotte, Marina in Boris Godunov and Mother Goose in The Rake's Progress; Many concert appearances. *Address:* Teatro dell'Opera di Roma, Piazza B Gigli 8, 00184 Rome, Italy.

**JANOVICKY, Karel;** composer and broadcaster; b. 18 Feb. 1930, Plzeň, Czechoslovakia; m. Sylva Šimsová 1950; one s. one d. *Education:* Realné Gymnasium, Surrey Coll. of Music, England, studied with Jan Šedivka (chamber music) and Matyas Seiber (composition). *Career:* debut, Wigmore Hall, London 1956; many scores in MS. *Compositions include:* Passages of Flight song cycle, Sonata for bass clarinet and oiano, Three Cambridge Songs, Terzina for violin and piano 1988, three string quartets 1992, 1995, 1997, Saxophone Quartet 1996, Sonata for alto saxophone and piano 1999, Clarinet Quartet 2000, Harp Sonata 2000, In Praise of Rossini for flute and piano 2001, Concerto for Strings 2002, Symphony 2004. *Publications:* contrib. to new edn of Leoš Janáček: A Biography by Jaroslav Vogel 1981, Introducing Mr Brouček 1978. *Honours:* First Prize, Shakespeare Competition, Bournemouth Symphony Orchestra, 1957 for Variations on a Theme of Robert Johnson Op 17; Sonata for 2 Violins and Piano on SPNM Recommended List, London. *Address:* 18 Muswell Avenue, London, N10 2EG, England.

**JANOWITZ, Gundula;** Austrian singer (soprano); b. 2 Aug. 1937, Berlin, Germany; d. of Theodor and Else (née Neumann) Janowitz; m.; one d. *Education:* Acad. of Music and Performing Arts, Graz. *Career:* Début with Vienna State Opera 1960; has sung with Deutsche Oper, Berlin 1966, Metropolitan Opera, New York 1967, Salzburg Festival 1968–81, Teatro Colón, Buenos Aires 1970, Munich State Opera 1971, Grand Opera, Paris 73, Covent Garden Opera 1976, La Scala 1978; concerts in maj. cities throughout the world, appearances at Bayreuth, Aix-en-Provence, Glyndebourne, Spoleto, Salzburg, Munich Festivals; Opera Dir at Graz 1990–91; mem. Vienna State Opera, Deutsche Oper, Berlin; recordings with Deutsche Grammophon, EMI, Decca. *Address:* 3072 Kasten 75, Austria.

**JANOWSKI, Marek;** German conductor; *Artistic and Music Director, Orchestre de la Suisse-Romande;* b. 18 Feb. 1939, Warsaw, Poland. *Education:* Cologne Musikhochschule and studied in Siena, Italy. *Career:* fmrly Asst Conductor in Aachen, Cologne and Düsseldorf opera houses; Music Dir, Freiburg and Dortmund Operas 1973–79; Artistic Adviser and Conductor Royal Liverpool Philharmonic Orchestra 1983–86; Music Dir and Chief Conductor Orchestre Philharmonique de Radio France 1984–2000; Chief Conductor Gurzenich-Orchester, Cologne 1986–90; Artistic Dir Monte Carlo Philharmonic Orchestra 1999, Music Dir and Chief Conductor 2000–05; Principal Conductor and Artistic Dir Dresden Philharmonic Orchestra 2001–04; Chief Conductor and Artistic Dir Rundfunk Sinfonieorchester Berlin 2001–; Artistic and Music Dir Orchestre de la Suisse-Romande, Geneva 2005–; Endowed Guest Conductor Chair Pittsburgh Symphony Orchestra 2005–; regular guest conductor in Paris, West Berlin, Hamburg,

Cologne and Munich opera houses; has also conducted at Metropolitan Opera (New York), Chicago, San Francisco (American opera debut 1983), Dresden and Vienna State Operas, Teatro Colón (Buenos Aires), Orange Festival (France) and Théâtre du Châtelet (Paris); has conducted concerts with Berlin Philharmonic, Chicago Symphony, London Symphony Orchestra, Philharmonia, NHK (Tokyo), Dresden Staatskapelle, Boston Symphony Orchestra, Stockholm Philharmonic and BBC Symphony Orchestra. *Recordings include:* Wagner's Der Ring des Nibelungen (with the Dresden Staatskapelle), Weber's Euryanthe, Strauss's Die Schweigsame Frau, Penderecki's The Devils of Loudun, Korngold's Violanta, Hindemith's Die Harmonie der Welt, Bruckner Symphonies No. 4 and No. 6 (with Orchestre Philharmonique de Radio France), Roussel four symphonies (with Orchestre Philharmonique de Radio France) (Diapason D'Or 1996), Weber's Oberon 1997, Strauss's Four Last Songs (Gramophone magazine Editor's Choice Award 2002). *Current Management:* c/o Jessica Ford, Intermusica Artists' Management Ltd, 16 Duncan Terrace, London, N1 8BZ, England. *Telephone:* (20) 7278-5455. *Fax:* (20) 7278-8434. *E-mail:* mail@intermusica.co.uk. *Website:* www.intermusica.co.uk. *Address:* Orchestre de la Suisse Romande, Rue Bovy-Lysberg 2, 1204 Geneva, Switzerland (office). *Website:* www.osr.ch.

**JANSEN, Rudolf;** Dutch pianist; b. 19 Jan. 1940, Arnhem; s. of Simon C. Jansen; m. 1st Margreet Honig; two c.; m. 2nd Christa Pfeiler; two c. *Education:* Amsterdam Conservatory, studied piano with Nelly Wagenaar, organ with Simon C. Jansen and harpsichord with Gustav Leonhardt. *Career:* soloist; accompanist for numerous leading singers and other artists throughout the world, including Elly Ameling, Robert Holl, Han de Vries, Andreas Schmidt, Olaf Bär, Barbara Bonney, Tom Krause and Hans-Peter Blochwitz; conducts master classes for singers and accompanists in Europe, North America and the Orient; gave a masterclass at the Juilliard School, New York 1996; teacher, Amsterdam Conservatory, Nuremberg/Augsburg Hochschule für Musik. *Recordings:* more than 100 recordings as Lieder accompanist or chamber music player. *Honours:* Kt, Order of Orange-Nassau 1998; Prix d'Excellence for organ 1964, Toonkunst Jubileum Prize 1965, Prix d'Excellence for piano 1966, Zilveren Vriendenkrans, Friends of Amsterdam Concertgebouw 1966, Edison Prize (for recording made with Dorothy Dorow) 1987, Deutscher Schallplattenpreis (for recording made with Dietrich Fischer Dieskau/Netherlands Chamber Choir) 1992. *Address:* Schepenenlaan 2, 1181 BB Amstelveen, Netherlands (home). *Telephone:* (20) 641-6344 (home). *Fax:* (20) 647-0765 (home). *E-mail:* rudolfjansen.piano@planet.nl (home).

**JANSONS, Mariss;** Latvian conductor; *Chief Conductor, Royal Concertgebouw Orchestra;* b. 14 Jan. 1943, Riga; s. of Arvid Jansons and Erhaida Jansons; m. Irina Jansons 1967; one d. *Education:* studied with father, Leningrad Conservatory with N. Rabinovich, Vienna Conservatory with Hans Swarovsky, Salzburg with von Karajan. *Career:* Prin. Guest Conductor Leningrad (now St Petersburg) Philharmonic Orchestra; Chief Conductor Oslo Philharmonic 1979–2002; Guest Conductor Welsh Symphony Orchestra 1985–88; Salzburg debut with the Vienna Philharmonic 1994; Prin. Guest Conductor London Philharmonic Orchestra –1997; Music Dir Pittsburgh Symphony Orchestra 1995, Chief Conductor 1997–2002; Musical Dir Bavarian Radio Symphony Orchestra and Chorus 2002–; conducted the London Symphony Orchestra at the London Proms 2002; Prof. of Conducting, St Petersburg Conservatory 1995–; has appeared all over world, with Baltimore Symphony Orchestra, Berlin Philharmonic, Boston Symphony Orchestra, Chicago Symphony Orchestra, Cleveland Orchestra, London Philharmonia Orchestra, New York Philharmonic, Philadelphia Orchestra; Chief Conductor Royal Concertgebouw Orchestra 2004–. *Honours:* winner Herbert von Karajan Competition 1971, Anders Jahre Cultural Prize (Norway), RSFSR People's Artist 1986, Royal Philharmonic Soc. Conductor of the Year Award 2004; Commdr with Star Royal Norwegian Order of Merit. *Current Management:* c/o Stephen Wright, IMG Artists, Lovell House, 616 Chiswick High Road, London, W4 5RX, England. *Telephone:* (20) 8233-5800. *Fax:* (20) 8233-5801. *Website:* www.imgartists.com. *Address:* c/o Royal Concertgebouw Orchestra, Jacob Obrechtstraat 51, 1071 KJ Amsterdam, Netherlands.

**JANULAKO, Vassilio;** Singer (Baritone); b. 14 Sept. 1933, Athens, Greece. *Education:* Studied at the Athens Conservatory. *Career:* Debut: Athens, 1961, as the High Priest in Alceste; Engagements at opera houses in Stuttgart, Berlin, Düsseldorf, Hamburg, Munich, Vienna, Frankfurt, Nuremberg, Zürich, Toulouse and San Francisco; Roles include Pizarro, the Dutchman, Telramund, Amfortas, Don Giovanni, Mozart's Count, Gerard, Scarpia, Escamillo, Mandryka, Milhaud's Christopher Columbus and parts in operas by Verdi; Cologne, 1986, as Pandolfe in Cendrillon by Massenet; Spoleto and Philadelphia, 1988, in Jenůfa and Rusalka; Sang Paolo in Simon Boccanegra at Cologne, 1990. *Address:* c/o Oper der Stadt Köln, Offenbachplatz, 5000 Cologne, Germany.

**JAPE, Mijndert;** Dutch lutenist, classical guitarist, writer and music historian; b. 11 July 1932, Geleen, Limburg; m. Marie-Hélène Habets 1960 (died 1987). *Education:* Muzieklyceum Heerlen, Conservatory of Maastricht, Schola Cantorum, Paris, Royal Conservatory of the Hague; studied with Hans-Lutz Niessen, Ida Presti, Alexandre Lagoya, Toyohiki Satoh, Eugen Dombois, Thomas Binkley, Anthony Bailes. *Career:* soloist, accompanist on lute instruments, baroque operas, vocal groups, Belgium, Netherlands, France; Director, Delitiae Musicae, specialising in 1550–1650 music and poetry concerts, Netherlands, Belgium, France; Plays 1820 Moitessier guitar and 8 lute instruments; Guest Lecturer; Teacher of Lute and Guitar, 1955–92;

Musical director, 1986–92, Sittard Musical School, 1955–92; Teaching Lute and Guitar, Music Academy, Maasmechelen and Tongeren, Belgium. *Recordings:* 4 (solo, ensemble), Belgium, Netherlands. *Publications:* Fernando Sor–Opera Omnia for the Guitar; On Lute Tuition, 1987; Classical Guitar Music in Print, bibliography, 12 vols (with Marie-Hélène Habets), vols 5, 8 and 9, 1980–1989; Louys de Moy–le Petit Boucquet, 1990; Elementa Pro Arte, lute tutor, in progress; The 'Wilhelmus van Nassouwe', Dutch National Anthem, development and relationship to the lute music, 1994. *Address:* PO Box 81, 6190 Beek, Limburg, Netherlands.

**JAR, Valentin;** Singer (Tenor); b. 1950, Bucharest, Romania. *Education:* Bucharest and Hague Conservatories. *Career:* Sang at Gelsenkirchen Opera, 1981–82; Frankfurt, 1984–93; Roles have included Mozart's Monostatos and Pedrillo, Verdi's Macduff and Cassio, Apollo in Monteverdi's Orfeo, Mime in Siegfried and Janáček's Mr Brouček, Vitek and Luka for Opéra du Rhin Strasbourg; Iro in Monteverdi's Ulisse at Antwerp, Avignon and Lausanne; Strauss's Valzacchi at Toulouse; Weill's Fatty, Wexford; Season 1998–99 with Monostatos at Liège; Iro for Opera North and Lisbon. *Address:* Music International, 13 Ardilaun Road, London N5 2QR, England.

**JARMAN, Douglas,** BA, PhD; British lecturer and writer; b. 21 Nov. 1942, Dewsbury, Yorkshire, England; m. Angela Elizabeth Brown 1970; two d. *Education:* Hull Univ., Durham Univ., Liverpool Univ. *Career:* Lecturer in Music, Univ. of Leeds 1970–71; Lecturer 1974–86, Principal Lecturer 1986, Academic Studies, Royal Northern Coll. of Music, Manchester; Artistic Dir, Young Musicians' Chamber Music Festival; Chair., Psappha; mem. advisory bd, Music Analysis. *Recording:* Talk, Lulu, The Historical Background (recording of The Complete Lulu). *Publications:* The Music of Alban Berg 1979, Kurt Weill 1982, Wozzeck 1989, The Berg Companion 1989, Alban Berg, Lulu 1991, Expressionism Reassessed 1993, Alban Berg: Violin Concerto (critical edn) 1998, Hans Werner Henze at the RNCM (vols 1–3) 1999, The Twentieth Century String Quartet 2002, Alban Berg: Chamber Concerto (critical edn) 2004; contrib. to Perspectives of New Music, Musical Quarterly, Musical Times, Music Review, Journal of Royal Musical Association, Newsletter of International Alban Berg Society, Alban Berg Studien vol. 2. *Honours:* Hon. Fellow, Royal Northern Coll. of Music 1986; Hon. Prof. of Music, Univ. of Manchester 2002. *Address:* 1 Birch Villas, Birchcliffe Road, Hebden Bridge, HX7 8DA, England.

**JARRETT, Keith;** American pianist and composer; b. 8 May 1945, Allentown, PA. *Education:* Berklee School of Music. *Career:* gave first solo concert aged 7, followed by professional appearances; two-hour solo concert of own compositions 1962; led own trio in Boston; worked with Roland Kirk, Tony Scott and others in New York; joined Art Blakey 1965; toured Europe with Charles Lloyd 1966, with Miles Davis 1970–71; soloist and leader of own groups 1969–; Guggenheim Fellowship 1972. *Recordings include:* albums: Bach's Well-Tempered Klavier, Personal Mountains 1974, Luminessence 1974, Mysteries 1975, Changeless 1987, Nude Ants, The Cure 1990, Bye Bye Black 1991, At the Dear Head Inn 1992, Bridge of Light 1993, At the Blue Note 1994, La Scala 1995, Tokyo '96 1998, The Melody at Night With You 1999, Whisper Not 2000, Inside Out 2001, Always Let Me Go 2002, Selected Recordings 2002, Radiance 2005. *Honours:* Prix du Prés. de la République 1991, Royal Swedish Acad. of Music Polar Prize 2003; Officier, Ordre des Arts et des Lettres. *Current Management:* Vincent Ryan, 135 W 16th Street, New York, NY 10011, USA.

**JÄRVI, Neeme;** Estonian conductor; *Musical Director, New Jersey Symphony Orchestra;* b. 7 June 1937, Tallinn; s. of August Järvi and Elss Järvi; m. Liilia Järvi 1961; two s. one d. *Education:* Tallinn Music School, Leningrad Conservatorium and Leningrad Postgraduate Studium, studied with N. Rabinovich and Y. Mravinsky. *Career:* Conductor Estonian Radio Symphony Orchestra –1963; Chief Conductor Estonian State Opera House 1963–76, Estonian State Symphony Orchestra 1976–80; emigrated to USA 1980; Prin. Guest Conductor City of Birmingham Symphony Orchestra, UK 1981–83; Prin. Conductor Royal Scottish Nat. Orchestra 1984–88, Conductor Laureate for Life 1990–; Prin. Conductor Gothenburg Orchestra, Sweden 1982–; Music Dir Detroit Symphony Orchestra, USA 1990–2005, New Jersey Symphony Orchestra 2005–; Chief Conductor Residentie Orchestra, The Hague 2005–(09); First Prin. Guest Conductor Japan Philharmonic Orchestra; guest conductor of many int. symphony orchestras, including New York Philharmonic, Boston, Chicago, Royal Concertgebouw, Philharmonia, London Symphony, London Philharmonic; conducted Eugene Onegin 1979, 1984, Samson and Delilah 1982 and Khovanshchina 1985 at Metropolitan Opera House, New York; has held int. master classes in summer resort town of Pärnu, Estonia 2000–. *Recordings include:* more than 350 CDs including all Prokoviev, Sibelius, Grieg, Nielsen, Dvorak, Shostakovich, Franz Berwald and Stenhammar symphonies since 1983. *Honours:* Hon. mem. Royal Swedish Acad. of Music, Estonian Composers Union 1989; Hon. Citizen, City of Gothenburg 1987, State of Michigan 1992; Kt Commdr of North Star Order, Sweden 1990, Sash, Order of Nat. Coat of Arms 1996, Insignia, Coat of Arms, Tallinn 1997; Dr hc (Royal Swedish Acad. of Music) 1988, 1990, (Estonian Music Acad.) 1989, (Aberdeen|) 1990, (Gothenburg) 1985, 1991, (Tallinn Music Conservatory), Wayne State Univ., USA) 1994, (Michigan) 1999; First Prize, Young Conductors' Competition, Leningrad 1957, Estonian Soviet Socialist Repub. (ESSR) Honoured Artist 1965, First Prize, Accademia Nazionale di Santa Cecilia Conductors' Competition 1971, ESSR Peoples' Artist 1971, USSR State Prize 1978, Sibelius Soc. Medal 1986, Gramophone Magazine's Artist of the Year 1990, Gold Record, Chandos recording co. 1992,

Toblach's Mahler Prize (for recording of Mahler's Third Symphony) 1993, Grande Prix du Disque, Charles Gros Record Acad. of Paris (for CD of Stravinski's Symphony of Psalms) 1993. *Current Management:* Harrison Parrott Ltd, 12 Penzance Place, London, W11 4PA, England. *Telephone:* (20) 7229-9166. *Fax:* (20) 7221-5042. *Website:* www.neemejarvi.com; www .njsymphony.org.

**JÄRVI, Paavo;** Estonian conductor; *Artistic Director, Deutsche Kammerphilharmonie Bremen;* b. 1962, Tallinn. *Education:* studied in Tallinn, at the Juilliard School, in Los Angeles with Bernstein and at the Curtis Inst. with Max Rudolf. *Career:* has conducted most of the major orchestras, notably as Principal Guest Conductor of the Royal Stockholm Philharmonic and the City of Birmingham Symphony Orchestras; further engagements with the Philharmonia, Orchestra of the Age of Enlightenment, London, Munich, Czech, Israel, St Petersburg, BBC and Berlin Philharmonic Orchestras, Orchestre Nat. de France, Accademia Nazionale di Santa Cecilia, RAI Turin, Maggio Musicale Fiorentino, Orchestra Filarmonica della Scala, NHK, Boston, Vienna, London an Sydney Symphony Orchestras; Music Dir, Cincinnati Symphony Orchestra 2001–(09); Artistic Dir, Deutsche Kammerphilharmonie Bremen 2004–; Artistic Adviser, Estonian Nat. Orchestra; Music Dir, hr-Sinfonieorchester (Frankfurt Radio Symphony Orchestra) 2006–(10). *Recordings:* Sibelius album with the Royal Stockholm Philharmonic Orchestra, Sibelius Kullervo 1997, Britten and Shostakovich with the CBSO, Sibelius Cantatas, The Maiden in the Tower and two albums by Arvo Pärt with the Estonian Nat. Symphony Orchestra, albums of music by Berlioz, Sibelius, Tubin, Stravinsky and Prokofiev (Romeo and Juliet), with the Cincinnati Symphony Orchestra. *Current Management:* Harrison Parrott Ltd, 12 Penzance Place, London, W11 4PA, England. *Telephone:* (20) 7229-9166. *Fax:* (20) 7221-5042. *E-mail:* nicole.rochman@harrisonparrott.co.uk. *Website:* www.harrisonparrott.com.

**JARVLEPP, Jan Eric,** BMus, MMus, PhD; Canadian composer, teacher and cellist; b. 3 Jan. 1953, Ottawa, ON. *Education:* University of Ottawa, McGill University, Montréal, University of CA, San Diego, USA. *Career:* CBC Chamber Music Broadcasts; mem., Ottawa Symphony Orchestra 1981–, Nepean Symphony Orchestra 1981–91; electronic compositions performed on several different Canadian and US univ. campuses and radio stations; Music Dir, Espace Musique Concert Soc. 1993–99; mem. SOCAN, Canadian Music Centre. *Compositions:* Lento, 1975; Ice, 1976; Aurora Borealis, 1976; Buoyancy, 1977; Flotation, 1978; Transparency and Density, 1978; Trumpet Piece, 1979; Cello Concerto, 1980; Time Zones, 1981; Night Music, 1982; Harpsichord Piece, 1984; Evening Music for Carillon, 1984; Cadenza for Solo Cello, 1985; Guitar Piece, 1985; Morning Music for Carillon, 1986; Afternoon Music for Carillon, 1986; Sunrise, 1987; Sunset, 1987; Trio, 1987; Liquid Crystals, 1988; Camerata Music, 1989; Dream, 1990; Life in The Fast Lane, 1990; Encounter, 1991; Underwater, 1992; Music from Mars, 1993; Moonscape, 1993; Robot Dance, 1994; Pierrot Solaire, 1994; Garbage Concerto, 1995; Tarantella, 1996; Bassoon Quartet, 1996; Saxophone Quartet, 1996; Trio No. 2, 1997; Earth Song, 1998; Five-Way Crossover, 1998; Overture, 1999; Dilemma, 1999; Concerto 2000, 2000; Quintet 2000, 2000; Street Scene, 2000; Quintet 2001, 2001; Suite for Viola and Strings, 2001; Shinkausen, 2001; Quintet 2002, 2003; Comet, 2002; The Lord's Prayer, 2002; Quintet 2003, Quintet 2004, Procession and Auction 2004, Quintet 2005. *Recordings:* Chronogrammes; Soundtracks of The Imagination; Flights of Fancy; Garbage Concerto. *Publications:* Compositional Aspects of Berio's Tempi Concertati, Interface, vol. II, No. 4, 1982; Pitch and Texture Analysis of Ligeti's Lux Aeterna, ex tempore, Vol. 2-1, 1982; Alchemy in the Nineties, 1997. *Address:* PO Box 2684, Station D, Ottawa, ON K1P 5W7, Canada. *E-mail:* jarvlepp@magma.ca. *Website:* www.janjarvlepp.com.

**JASINKA-JEDROSZ, Elzbieta;** Polish musicologist; b. 11 Jan. 1949, Katowice; m. Janusz Jedrosz 1970; one s. *Education:* Warsaw Univ. *Career:* engaged in bibliographic documentation of Polish musical works and in other tasks at Archive of 20th Century Polish Composers, Polish Composers Archive, Warsaw Univ. Library Music Collection 1973–; mem. Polish Composers' Union, Karol Szymanowski Music Asscn, Zakopane, Polish Librarians' Asscn, Asscn of Polish Musicians. *Publications:* Music and Polish Musicians in French 1925–1950 1977, Karol Szymanowski 1882–1937 1983, The Manuscripts of Karol Szymanowski's Musical Works (catalogue) 1983, Karol Szymanowski in the Polish Collections (guide-book, co-author) 1989, Karol Szymanowski: Writer-Poet-Thinker 1997, The Manuscripts of the Young Poland's Composers (catalogue) 1997, Collection of the 20th Century Polish Composers' Archives 1999, Four Seasons: Selected Poetry 2004; contrib. to Muzyka 1981, Ruch Muzyczny 1980, 1981, 1983, 1988–89, 1998–99, 2002–05, Pagine 1989, Przeglad Biblioteczny 1989, 2002, Polski Rocznik Muzykologiczny 2004. *Honours:* hons for popularization of Karol Szymanowski's compositions 1998. *Address:* u. Janinówka 11m 122, 03562 Warsaw, Poland (home). *Telephone:* (22) 5525746 (office); (22) 6791952 (home). *Fax:* (22) 5525659 (office). *E-mail:* e.m.jasinska@uw.edu.pl (office). *Website:* www.buw.uw.edu.pl (office).

**JEDLICKA, Dalibor;** Singer (Bass-baritone); b. 23 May 1929, Svoyanov, Czechoslovakia. *Education:* Studied in Ostrava with Rudolf Vasek. *Career:* Debut: Opava, 1953, as Mumlala in The Two Widows by Smetana; Sang at the National Theatre, Prague, 1957–77, also guest appearances with the company in Brno, Amsterdam, Zürich and Edinburgh (1970 in the British premiere of The Excursions of Mr Brouček by Janáček); Engagements at Belgrade, Zagreb, Warsaw, Venice and Bologna; Repertoire included buffo roles and

German, French and Czech operas; Mozart's Figaro and Papageno, Don Pasquale and Kaspar in Der Freischütz; Opéra Comique, Paris, 1988, in From the House of the Dead. *Recordings include:* Janáček's Katya Kabanova, The Cunning Little Vixen and From the House of the Dead, conducted by Charles Mackerras; Pauer's Suzanna Vojirva and Don Giovanni; Another recording of Cunning Little Vixen.

**JEDLICKA, Rudolf;** Singer (Baritone); b. 22 Jan. 1920, Skalice, Czechoslovakia. *Education:* Studied with Tino Pattieri, Pavel Ludikar and Fernando Carpi in Vienna and Prague. *Career:* Debut: Dresden Staatsoper, 1944, as Marcel in La Bohème; Sang in Prague from 1945; Produced opera at Usti nad Labem, 1946–49; Guest with the Staatsoper Berlin from 1958; Appearances at the Vienna Staatsoper and in Russia, German and Polish opera houses as Mozart's Figaro and Don Giovanni, Posa in Don Carlos and Rossini's Figaro; Sang with the Prague National Opera at the Edinburgh Festival, 1964, 1970, in the British premieres of Janáček's From the House of the Dead and The Excursions of Mr Brouček; Professor at the Prague Conservatory, 1973–75; Director of the National Theatre, Prague, 1989; Sang Grigoris in Martinů's Greek Passion at Wiesbaden, 1990. *Recordings:* Jenůfa. *Address:* National Theatre, PO Box 865, 112 30 Prague 1, Czech Republic.

**JEFFERS, Gweneth-Ann;** Singer (Soprano); b. 1975, England. *Education:* University of Exeter; Goldsmiths College and Guildhall School, London; Royal Opera Vilar Young Artist Programme, from 2001. *Career:* Appearances with major London orchestras; Concert repertoire includes Schubert, Schumann, Ravel, Barber, Messiaen (Harawi at the Cheltenham Festival, 2000) and Cage; Verdi Requiem at Truro Cathedral, Brahms Requiem and Strauss's Vier Letzte Lieder in Canterbury Cathedral; Season 2000–2001 as Massenet's Navarraise at the Guildhall, Strauss's Ariadne with the Orchestre de Picardie and the original version of Berg's Lyric Suite with the Endellion Quartet at Aldeburgh. *Honours:* represented England at 2001 Cardiff Singer of the World Competition. *Current Management:* Askonas Holt Ltd, Lonsdale Chambers, 27 Chancery Lane, London, WC2A 1PF, England. *Telephone:* (20) 7400-1700. *Fax:* (20) 7400-1799. *E-mail:* info@askonasholt.co.uk. *Website:* www .askonasholt.co.uk.

**JEFFERS, Ronald Harrison;** Composer and Conductor; b. 25 March 1942, Springfield, Illinois, USA. *Education:* Studied composition with Ross Lee Finney at University of Michigan; University of California at San Diego, 1970–72, with Pauline Oliveros, Kenneth Gaburo and Robert Erickson; Choral conducting at Occidental College, Los Angeles, 1968–72. *Career:* Director of choral activities at Stony Brook, New York, and at Oregon State University; Tours of Europe, 1978 and 1982. *Compositions include:* Missa concrete for 3 choruses, 1969, revised, 1973; In Memoriam for chamber ensemble, 1973; Time Passes for mezzo, tape and ensemble, 1974–81; Transitory for chorus and tape, 1980; Arise My Love for 12 voices, chimes and gongs, 1981; Crabs for tape, 1981; This We Know, for chorus, 1987; Songs of the Sea, 1991; Salut au Monde! for chamber ensemble, 1993. *Address:* c/o ASCAP, ASCAP Building, 1 Lincoln Plaza, New York, NY 10023, USA.

**JEFFERSON, Alan (Rigby);** British writer; b. 20 March 1921, Ashtead, Surrey, England; m. 1st, one s.; m. 2nd two s. one d.; m. 3rd Antonia Dora Raeburn 1976; two s.; three s. one d. (from previous m.). *Education:* Rydal School, Colwyn Bay, Old Vic Theatre School. *Career:* administrator, London Symphony Orchestra 1968–69; Visiting Prof. of Vocal Interpretation, Guildhall School of Music and Drama, London 1968–74; Man., BBC Concert Orchestra, London 1969–73; Ed., The Monthly Guide to Recorded Music 1980–82; mem. Royal Soc. of Musicians, Soc. of Authors. *Publications:* The Operas of Richard Strauss in Great Britain 1910–1963 1964, The Lieder of Richard Strauss 1971, Delius (Master Musicians series) 1972, The Life of Richard Strauss 1973, Inside the Orchestra 1974, Strauss (Master Musicians series) 1975, Discography of Richard Strauss' Operas 1975, The Glory of Opera 1976, Strauss (Short Biographies series) 1978, Sir Thomas Beecham 1979, The Complete Gilbert and Sullivan Opera Guide 1984, Der Rosenkavalier 1986, Lotte Lehmann, A Centenary Biography 1988, Elisabeth Schwarzkopf (biog.) 1996, An Introduction to Classical Music (CD-ROM) 1996; contrib. to periodicals, including Blätter Internationale Richard Strauss Gesellschaft (Vienna), Classical Express.

**JEFFERY, Darren;** Singer (bass-baritone); b. 1976, England. *Education:* Royal Northern Coll. of Music; Vilar Young Artists Programme, Covent Garden 2001. *Career:* sang Falstaff and Der Sprecher (Die Zauberflote) with Royal Northern Coll. of Music; sang Antinöus in Monteverdi's Il ritorno d'Ulisse at the Creakes Festival and Solino in Gli Equivoci for the Batignano Festival, Italy; Glyndebourne Festival 2001, covering Don Fernando in Fidelio and Matthew in The Last Supper; sang Masetto in Don Giovanni at Covent Garden 2002; other roles with the Royal Opera, Covent Garden are Rambaldo, Mandarin (Turandot) 2002, Monterone (Rigoletto) 2002, Tutor (Elektra), Baron Douphol (La Traviata) 2002, Masetto (Don Giovanni) 2003, Bonzo (Madama Butterfly) 2003, Der Sprecher (Die Zauberflote) 2003, Gravedigger (Hamlet) 2003, Bartender (Sophie's Choice, world premiere) 2003; roles elsewhere include Cadmus in Handel's Semele, Donner in The Rheingold (ENO), Figaro in Le Nozze di Figaro (Savoy Opera Theatre). *Current Management:* Harlequin Agency Ltd, 203 Fidlas Road, Llanishen, Cardiff CF14 5NA, Wales. *Telephone:* (29) 2075-0821. *Fax:* (29) 2075-5971. *E-mail:* info@harlequin-agency.co.uk. *Website:* www.harlequin-agency.co.uk.

**JEFFERY, Peter;** Professor of Music; b. 19 Oct. 1953, New York, NY, USA; m. Margot Fassler, 1983, 2 s. *Education:* MFA, 1977, PhD, 1980, Princeton

University. *Career:* Hill Monastic Manuscript Library, 1980–82; Mellon Faculty Fellow, Harvard University, 1982–83; University of Delaware, 1984–92; Boston College, 1992–93; Princeton University, 1993–; mem, American Musicological Society; Medieval Academy of America; North American Academy of Liturgy; Societas Liturgica. *Publications:* A Bibliography for Medieval and Renaissance Musical Manuscript Research, 1980; Re-Envisioning Past Musical Cultures. *Contributions:* Journal of the American Musicological Society; Studia Liturgica; Archiv für Liturgiewissenschaft; Created Gregorian Chant website. *Honours:* Alfred Einstein Award, 1985; National Endowment for the Humanities Grant, 1986–88; John D MacArthur Fellowship, 1987–82. *Address:* Music Department, Princeton University, NJ 08544, USA.

**JEFFES, Peter;** Singer (Tenor); b. 1951, London, England. *Education:* Royal College of Music, London; Rome with Paolo Silveri. *Career:* Italian debut in Rome Opera in Spontini's Agnese di Hohenstaufen; Paris Opéra in Doktor Faust; With English Bach Festival at Covent Garden in Rameau's Castor et Pollux; Nero in L'Incoronazione di Poppea for Swiss television; European engagements as Lohengrin, Tamino and Lensky; Sang Mozart in Rimsky's Mozart and Salieri at Barcelona in 1987; Festival appearances at Aix-en-Provence, Orange, Monte Carlo, Athens and in the USA; Engagement with British companies in Roméo et Juliette, Les Contes d'Hoffmann, Die Zauberflöte, The Rake's Progress and A Midsummer Night's Dream; Opera North in the British premiere of Strauss's Daphne, 1987; Season 1988–89 in The Love for Three Oranges for Opera North; Since 1988, repertoire, roles in Cavalleria Rusticana, Pagliacci, Idomeneo, Faust, Werther, Salome, Fliegende Holländer, Macbeth, Attila and Eisenstein in Die Fledermaus; Now sings extensively in Europe and regularly in Israel; The Prince in the Love for Three Oranges, 1992; Sang Wagner's Rienzi for Chelsea Opera Group (concert) and the High Priest in Idomeneo at Lyon, 1999. *Address:* c/o Music International, 13 Ardilaun Road, Highbury, London N5 2QR, England.

**JEFFREYS, Celia;** Singer (Soprano); b. 20 Jan. 1948, Southampton, England. *Education:* Studied music at the Royal College of Music, ARCM. *Career:* Debut: Welsh National Opera, 1970, as Adele in Die Fledermaus; Sang at various regional opera houses in the United Kingdom; Appeared on BBC and Southern Television, United Kingdom; Sang at: Kassel and Darmstadt, Germany, Theater am Gärtnerplatz, Munich from 1976, Stadtheater Basel, 1978–81; From 1981–88 appeared as guest artist in: Bern, Berlin Koblenz, Salzburg, Theater an der Wien, Schlosspiele Heidelberg, Festspiele, Bregenz; From 1988–91 engagements in Linz, Austria; Appearing regularly in Salzburg and Linz, 1997–; Opera roles include Donna Elvira, in Don Giovanni; Mimi, La Bohème, the Marschallin in Rosenkavalier; Agathe in Der Freischütz; Nedda, in Pagliacci; Leonore, in Fidelio; Operetta roles include: Hanna Glawari, in The Merry Widow and Rosalinde in Die Fledermaus; Teacher, Bayerische Theaterakademie, Munich. *Recordings:* Student Prince; Brahms, German Requiem. *Current Management:* ASM, Obergütschrain 3, CH 6003 Lucerne, Switzerland. *Address:* Grasmeierstrasse 12 B, 80805 Munich, Germany.

**JEFFRIES, James Huw,** MA, ARCM, RSA; singer (countertenor); b. 1970, Canterbury, England. *Education:* Magdalen Coll., Oxford, Royal Coll. of Music, Britten-Pears School, studied with Valerie Masterson, Jennifer Smith, Geoffrey Mitchell, Nicholas Powell. *Career:* debut, Handel's Israel in Egypt, St John's, Smith Square, London; concerts in oratorio and concert repertoire throughout the UK; as well as in Canada, France, Germany, Ireland and The Netherlands; operatic performances in the UK, as well as in Denmark, Greece, Germany, The Netherlands and Norway. *Roles include:* Gluck's Orfeo, Rinaldo, Andronico in Tamerlano, Nero in L'Incoronazione di Poppea, Spirit in Dido and Aeneas, Caspar in world premiere of Alexander Knaifel's Alice in Wonderland, Oberon in A Midsummer Night's Dream, Nireno in Giulio Cesare. *Address:* 3/26 Denmark Street, London, WC2H 8NN, England (home). *Telephone:* (20) 7209-0397 (home). *E-mail:* jameshuwjeffries@blueyonder.co .uk (home). *Website:* www.jameshuwjeffries.com.

**JEHLICKOVA, Zora,** DiS; Czech singer (soprano); b. 10 April 1950, Brno. *Education:* Prague Conservatory. *Career:* sang at the Prague Nat. Theatre from 1974, notably as Natasha in War and Peace, Marenka in The Bartered Bride, Rusalka, Pamina, Donna Elvira, Tatiana in Eugene Onegin, and Mimi; title role in Dvořák's Armida 1987; Smetana Theatre, Prague 1992, as the Princess in Der Zwerg by Zemlinsky; guest appearances in Dresden, the Komische Oper, Berlin, La Scala, Milan, and the Nationaltheater Mannheim; many concert appearances. *Address:* c/o National Theatre Prague, PO Box 865, 11 230 Prague 1, Czech Republic. *E-mail:* jeelly@saznam.cz.

**JELEZNOV, Irina;** pianist; b. 4 Oct. 1958, Astrakhan, Russia; m. 1980; one s. *Education:* Tchaikovsky Conservatoire, Moscow. *Career:* debut in Tashkent Conservatoire Hall 1984; annual recitals and orchestra performances, Tashkent 1984–93; appearances in Moscow at The Maly Hall, Moscow Conservatoire 1986, 1987, Rachmaninov Hall and Shuvalova's Home 1991; piano duo festivals at Sverdlovsk 1989, Leningrad 1990, Nizny Novgorod 1991, Novosibirsk 1992; int. piano duo competitions in Belgrade, Yugoslavia 1989, Caltanissetta, Italy 1990, Hartford, CT 1990, Miami, FL 1991; television and radio appearances; Docent, Chair of Chamber Music, Tashkent Conservatoire; mem. Int. Piano Duo Asscn, Tokyo, Japan. *Address:* Prospekt Kosmonavtov d 12-106, 700015 Tashkent, Uzbekistan.

**JELEZNOV, Maxim;** Duo Pianist; b. 19 May 1958, Moscow, Russia; m. 29 Aug 1980, 1 s. *Education:* Piano Faculty, 1981, Postgraduate course as Piano Duo, 1987, Tchaikovsky Conservatoire, Moscow. *Career:* Debut: Tashkent Conservatoire Hall, 1984; Performances: Tashkent, yearly 1984–93; Maly Hall, Moscow Conservatoire, 1986, 1987; Sverdlovsk Piano Duo Festival, 1989; Belgrade, Yugoslavia, 1989; International Piano Duo Festival Leningrad, 1990; Hartford, USA, 1990; Caltanissetta, Italy, 1990; Rachmaninov Hall, Moscow, 1991; Shuvalova's Home, Moscow, 1991; Nizny Novgorod Piano Duo Festival, 1991; International Piano Duo Festival, Ekaterinburg, 1991–93; Piano Duo Festival, The Masters of Piano Duo, Novosibirsk, 1992; Television and radio appearances. *Address:* Prospekt Kosmonavtov d 12-106, 700015 Tashkent, Uzbekistan.

**JELINEK, Ladislav;** Czech concert pianist; b. 21 Feb. 1947, Brno, Czechoslovakia; m.; two s. *Education:* State Conservatory, Brno, Janáček Univ. of Musical Arts, Brno, majoring in solo piano under Prof. Frantisek Schäfer. *Career:* debut: Besedni Dum, Brno 1966; appearances as soloist with orchestra, solo pianist and chamber musician in Czechoslovakia and majority of Eastern European countries; radio and TV appearances in Eastern Europe 1968–81; numerous appearances (including radio and TV) in nearly all European countries, America, S Korea and Japan 1981–; Univ. Teacher, Frankfurter Hochschule für Musik und Darstellende Kunst 1984–; mem. Artistic Advisory Bd, Janáček Univ. of Musical Arts, Brno. *Recordings include:* Beethoven, Brahms, Chopin, Dvořák, Haydn, Janáček, Liszt, Liszt-Wagner, Mozart, Jan Novák, V. Novák, Prokofiev, Rachmaninov, Smetana and others. *Honours:* piano competitions: Acad. of Music, Czechoslovakia 1961, Hradec Kralove 1963. *Address:* Lerchenweg 2, 61350 Bad Homburg, Germany. *E-mail:* contact@classicalpiano.de. *Website:* www.classicalpiano.de.

**JENISOVA, Eva;** Singer (Soprano); b. 1963, Presov, Czecholovakia. *Education:* Studied at the Bratislava Conservatory. *Career:* Soloist with the National Theatre Bratislava from 1986; Further appearances (from 1988) with the Deutsche Oper Berlin, Bolshoi Moscow, Budapest State Opera, National Theatre Prague and the Israel and Edinburgh Festivals; Vienna Staatsoper from 1990, as Marguerite in Faust, Donna Elvira, Katya Kabanova and Rusalka; Elvira under Harnoncourt at Amsterdam, Pamina and Violetta at Trieste, and Janáček's Vixen at the Paris Châtelet; Covent Garden debut 1997, as Katya Kabanova; Season 1997–98 as the Duchess of Parma in Busoni's Faust at Lyon, the Vixen in Madrid and Paris, and Mozart's Vitellia at Nancy; Concerts include Mareiken in Martinů's Legends of Mary, with the Vienna Symphony Orchestra, the Missa Solemnis at Madrid, the German Requiem in Bologna, Carmina Burana in Munich, and Dvořák's Stabat Mater at Salzburg; Mahler's Second Symphony in Graz, and Rusalka at the Salle Pleyel, Paris; Teatro Regio Turin 1997, as Mélisande. *Address:* c/o 13 Ardilaun Road, London N5 2QR, England.

**JENKINS, Carol;** Violinist; b. 1965, Toronto, Canada. *Education:* Studied at University of Toronto with Rodney Friend and Victor Danchenki. *Career:* Associate Leader, Denver Symphony Orchestra and other orchestras; Second Violinist, Da Vinci Quartet from 1988, founded in 1980 under the sponsorship of the Fine Arts Quartet; Many concerts in USA and elsewhere in a repertoire including works by Mozart, Beethoven, Brahms, Dvořák, Shostakovich and Bartók. *Honours:* (With the Da Vinci Quartet), Awards and Grants from the NEA, the Western States Arts Foundation and the Colorado Council for the Humanities; Artist in Residence, University of Colorado. *Current Management:* Sonata, Glasgow, Scotland. *Address:* c/o Da Vinci Quartet, 11 Northpark Street, Glasgow G20 7AA, Scotland.

**JENKINS, Graeme James Ewers;** Conductor; b. 1958, England; m. Joanna, 2 d. *Education:* Studied at Dulwich College and Cambridge University; Royal College of Music with Norman Del Mar and David Willcocks; Adrian Boult Conducting Scholar. *Career:* Debut: Conducted Albert Herring and the Turn of the Screw at college; The Beggar's Opera, Die Entführung and Le nozze di Figaro for Kent Opera; Andrea Chénier, Brighton Festival; Cesti's La Dori (Spitalfields); Il Trovatore, Le nozze di Figaro and Così fan tutte with Scottish Opera; Così fan tutte with English National Opera (ENO debut), 1988; European debut, 1987, Hansel and Gretel and Ravel double bill with Geneva Opera; Simon Boccanegra, Netherlands Opera, 1989; As Music Director of Glyndebourne Touring Opera, 1986–91, has conducted A Midsummer Night's Dream, Albert Herring, Simon Boccanegra and Così fan tutte; La Traviata and Death in Venice (on BBC television), 1989; Glyndebourne Festival debut, 1987, with Carmen and Capriccio; Returned to Ravel double bill and Falstaff; Arabella, 1989; Oedipus Rex and Petrushka with Scottish Opera, 1989; Further engagements include Carmen and La Rondine with Canadian Opera in Toronto, La Bohème with Australian Opera, 1990; Concert appearances with the Hallé Orchestra, BBC Scottish, BBC Philharmonic, BBC Symphony, Royal Philharmonic, Kraków Radio Symphony and Scottish Chamber Orchestras; Fidelio (Glyndebourne Tour); Iphigénie en Tauride (Netherlands Opera); La Bohème (Australian Opera), 1990; Idomeneo (Glyndebourne Festival), 1991; Appearance at Hong Kong Festival, 1991; Conducted the world premiere of Stephen Oliver's Timon of Athens, London Coliseum, 1991; Residente Orkest The Hague, Netherlands Chamber Orchestra, 1991; Così fan tutte, US Opera debut, Dallas; Elektra, Dallas Opera, 1994; Death in Venice at the 1992 Glyndebourne Festival, Cologne Opera, 1996, Handel's Serse; Meistersinger, Australian Opera, 1993; Music Director, Dallas Opera, 1994; Chief Director, Cologne Opera, 1997–2002; Season 1997–98, numerous opera performances including Billy Budd, Katya Kabanova (with David Alden), Dallas; Macbeth (with Robert Carsen), Cologne; Appearances with Finnish Radio Symphony Orchestra; Debut with Utah and Dallas Symphony Orchestras; Work as orchestral conductor with major orchestras in the United

Kingdom and with broadcasts on radio; Conducted London Philharmonic Orchestra at Royal Festival Hall, 1998; Artistic Director, Arundel Festival, 1992–1998; Has strong reputation in Netherlands and has worked with many other leading European orchestras; Season 1998–99 with a new production of Parsifal in Cologne and the Ring Cycle in Dallas; Since 1999 Clemenza di Tito for Glyndebourne Festival; Makropolos Case and Love of three Oranges for Cologne Opera; Wozzeck, Simon Boccanegra and Acis and Galatea in Dallas; Cunning Little Vixen for Deutsche Oper Berlin, 2001; Ballo in Maschera, 2002; Paris concert debut 2001; Orchestra Philharmonique de Radio France; Houston Symphony Debut, 2001; Perth and Melbourne Symphony Debuts 2002. *Current Management:* Askonas Holt Ltd, Lonsdale Chambers, 27 Chancery Lane, London, WC2A 1PF, England. *Telephone:* (20) 7400-1700. *Fax:* (20) 7400-1799. *E-mail:* info@askonasholt.co.uk. *Website:* www .askonasholt.co.uk.

**JENKINS, Karl William Pamp,** OBE, FRAM, ARAM; Welsh composer, pianist and oboist; b. 17 Feb. 1944, Penclawdd. *Education:* Gowerton Grammar School, Univ. of Wales, Cardiff and RAM. *Career:* initially resident jazz oboist at Ronnie Scott's; co-founder, Nucleus, then played in Soft Machine; currently composer and conductor; Pres., Friends of the Nat. Youth Orchestra of Wales, Penclawdd Brass Band; patron, Nat. Youth Choir of Great Britain; Fellow, Royal Welsh Coll. of Music and Drama, Trinity Coll., Carmarthen, and Swansea Inst. *Compositions include:* Palladio 1992–95, Adiemus I: Songs of Sanctuary 1994, Adiemus II: Cantata Mundi 1996, Eloise 1997, Adiemus III: Dances of Time 1998, The Armed Man: A Mass for Peace 1999, Y Celtiaid (film score) (BAFTA Cymru Award for Best Original Music Soundtrack) 2000, Dying to Dance (TV score) 2001, Over the Stone 2002, Pwy Ysgrifennodd Y Testament Newydd? (film score) (BAFTA Cymru Award for Best Original Music Soundtrack) 2003, In These Stones Horizons Sing 2003, Quirk 2005, River Queen (film score) 2005. *Recordings include:* Adiemus (Songs of the Sanctuary), Palladio (with Smith Quartet and London Philharmonic Orchestra), Imagined Oceans, The Armed Man: A Mass for Peace (with Nat. Youth Choir of Great Britain and London Philharmonic Orchestra). *Honours:* first prize Montreal Jazz Festival (with Nucleus), two D&AD awards for best advertising music, Classic FM Red F Award for outstanding service to classical music. *Address:* Karl Jenkins Music Ltd, 46 Poland Street, London, W1F 7NA, England (office). *Telephone:* (20) 7434-2225. *Fax:* (20) 7494-4998. *E-mail:* info@karljenkins.com. *Website:* www.karljenkins.com.

**JENKINS, Katherine;** Welsh singer (soprano). *Education:* RAM. *Career:* fmr school teacher; fmr mem. Nat. Youth Choir of Wales; mem. Royal School of Church Music Cathedral Singers 1990–96; numerous public performances, including singing the Welsh nat. anthem at int. rugby matches, FA Cup Final at the Millennium Stadium, Cardiff 2005, VE Day celebration Trafalgar Square, London 2005. *Recordings:* Première 2004, Second Nature (Classical BRIT Award for Album of the Year 2005) 2004, Living For A Dream 2005. *Honours:* awarded Pelenna Valley Male Voice Choir scholarship, BBC Radio Two Welsh Choirgirl of the Year (twice), BET Welsh Choirgirl of the Year. *Current Management:* Bandana Management Ltd, 100 Goldborne Road, London, W10 5PS, England. *Telephone:* (20) 8969-0606 (office). *Fax:* (20) 8969-0505 (office). *Website:* www.banman.co.uk; www.katherinejenkins.co.uk.

**JENKINS, Neil,** MA; British opera and concert singer (tenor) and music editor; b. 9 April 1945, Sussex, England; m. Penelope Anne 1982; four s. one d. *Education:* King's Coll., Cambridge, Royal Coll. of Music, London. *Career:* debut in Purcell Room, London, Song Recital with Roger Vignoles 1967; Guest Soloist, Israel Chamber Orchestra 1968–69, London Bach Soc. 1971, 1973; mem. Deller Consort 1967–76; appearances at festivals in Israel, Paris, London and Spain; performances with Welsh Nat. Opera, Scottish Opera, Opera North, Glyndebourne, Edinburgh and Frankfurt, Kent Opera; new productions of Le nozze di Figaro and the Ravel double bill in Geneva; sang in Prokofiev's The Duenna, Wexford 1989, Bernstein's Candide, 1989; also heard in oratorio and concert, in orchestral version of Tippett's The Heart's Assurance at Canterbury 1990; debut at ENO in Monteverdi's Orfeo and Il Ritorno d'Ulisse 1992; sang the Marquis in Lulu at Glyndebourne Festival 199, Isaiah in Weill's Propheten, BBC Proms, London 1998, Vitek in The Makropolos Case at Acad. of Music, New York 2001; Guest Artist, Deutsche Oper Berlin and Opéra de Lyon 2004–05; Musical Dir Sussex Chorus 2002–; Cummins Harvey Visiting Fellow Commoner, Girton Coll. Cambridge 2002; mem. and Warden of PCS, Incorporated Soc. of Musicians, 1998–99. *Compositions include:* Christmas Carols for unaccompanied SATB singers in Christmas is Coming 1993. *Recordings include:* Bernstein's Candide and White House Cantata, King Priam, Mozart's Le nozze di Figaro, Henze's Kammermusik 1958, Britten's Serenade for tenor, horn and strings, with Oriol Ensemble, Britten's Peter Grimes conducted by Bernard Haitink; three tenor and guitar recital records. *Publications:* The Carol Singer's Handbook (ed.) 1993; Ed.: Bach St Matthew Passion, St John Passion 1998, Christmas Oratorio 1999, Sing Solo Sacred 1997; article in Haydn Soc. Journal. *Honours:* The Worshipful Co. of Musicians Sir Charles Santley Memorial Award 2004. *Address:* c/o Music International, 13 Ardilaun Road, London, N5 2QR, England; 10 Hartington Villas, Hove, Sussex, BN3 6HF, England (home). *Telephone:* (20) 7359-5183; (1273) 721577 (home). *E-mail:* music@musicint.co .uk (office); neil@neiljenkins.com (home). *Website:* www.neiljenkins.com.

**JENKINS, Speight;** American administrator; *General Director, Seattle Opera*; b. 31 Jan. 1937, Dallas, TX. *Education:* Univ. of Texas and Columbia Univ. Law School. *Career:* Ed., Opera News 1967–73; music critic New York Post 1973–81; host for the 'Live from the Met' broadcasts 1981–83; Gen. Dir,

Seattle Opera 1983–; has presided over such productions as The Ring Cycle 1986–87, 1991, 1995, War and Peace, Die Meistersinger, and Werther in the version for baritone 1989, the US premiere of Gluck's Orphée et Eurydice, Les Dialogues des Carmelites 1990, Glass Artist Dale Chihuly's scenic debut in Pelléas et Mélisande 1993, Norma 1994, Der Rosenkavalier 1997, Tristan und Isolde 1998. *Honours:* Dr hc (Seattle) 1992, (Univ. of Puget Sound) 1992. *Address:* Seattle Opera, PO Box 9248, Seattle, WA 98109-0248, USA. *E-mail:* mary.brazeau@seattleopera.org. *Website:* www.seattleopera.org.

**JENKINS, Terry;** Operatic Tenor; b. 9 Oct. 1941, Hertford, England; m. Pamela Ann Jenkins 1965, 1 s., 1 d. *Education:* BSc (Eng), University College London, 1964; Guildhall School of Music, 1964–66; London Opera Centre, 1967–68. *Career:* Debut: Opera for All, 1966–67, Nemorino (L'Elisir d'amore); Basilic Opera, 1968–71; Glyndebourne Touring Opera, 1969–71; Malcolm (Macbeth), M Triquet (Eugene Onegin), Schmidt (Werther), Scarramuccio (Ariadne auf Naxos); Glyndebourne Festival Opera, 1971, Major Domo (Queen of Spades), Officer (Ariadne auf Naxos); Glyndebourne Festival Opera, 1972, Scarramuccio; Sadler's Wells Opera, 1972–74; English National Opera, 1974–, roles include Basilio (Marriage of Figaro), Pedrillo (Entführung), Remendado (Carmen), Goro (Madama Butterfly), Gaston (La Traviata), Vanya (Katya Kabanova), Spoletta (Tosca), Schmidt (Werther), Fenney (Mines of Sulphur), Tchekalinsky (Queen of Spades), Loge (Rheingold), Borsa (Rigoletto), Duke (Patience); Orpheus (Orpheus in the Underworld); Various roles, Pacific Overtures, Hauk Sendorf (Makropulos Case), Schoolmaster (Cunning Little Vixen), Dr Caius (Falstaff); English National Opera tour, USA, 1984; New Opera Company, 1976, 1979, 1980; Royal Opera, Covent Garden, 1976, 1977, 1981; English Bach Festival, 1983, Versailles and Sadler's Wells; City of London Festival, 1978; Barbican Hall, 1984–88; Seattle Opera, 1983, Loge-Rheingold; Vienna Festival with English National Opera, 1985; Chelsea Opera Group, 1986; Boston Concert Opera, USA, 1986, Guillot-Manon; Aix-en-Provence Festival, 1991, 1992, Snout, A Midsummer Night's Dream, Britten; Sang Dr Caius at Garsington, 1998. *Recordings:* Justice Shallow in Sir John in Love, Vaughan Williams; Borsa in Rigoletto; Pacific Overtures, Street Scene; Several video recordings. *Contributions:* Musicians' Handbook. *Current Management:* Music International, Ardilaun Road, London N7, England. *Address:* 9 West End Avenue, Pinner, Middlesex, England.

**JENNINGS, Diane;** Singer (Soprano); b. 1959, California, USA. *Education:* Studied at the San Diego Opera School. *Career:* Sang small roles in opera at San Diego, then studied further in Munich, 1984–86; Sang at the Landestheater Salzburg 1986–87, as Marzelline in Fidelio, Susanna, Pamina and Marenka in The Bartered Bride; Aachen opera, 1988–91, as Mimi; Mainz, 1990, as Donna Anna, Concert engagements in Vienna, Graz, Munich and Verona. *Recordings include:* Suor Angelica and Brixi's Missa pastoralis. *Address:* c/o Stadtheater Aachen, Theaterplatz, W-5100 Aachen, Germany.

**JENSEN, Julian;** Singer (Tenor); b. 1968, Fowey, Cornwall. *Education:* Royal Academy of Music, London. *Career:* Principal with D'Oyly Carte Opera, 1992; Opera roles include: Mozart's Tamino, Basilo and Ferrando, Theatre Kernow, 1999; Verdi's Alfredo, Holland Park, 1999; Duke in Rigoletto; Wexford Festival, 1998, in Pavel Haas's Sarlatan and Zandonai's I Cavalieri di Ekebu; Laerte in Mignon, University College Opera; Bardolph in Falstaff, Palace Opera; Concerts include: Puccini's Messa di Gloria; Haydn's Creation; Pärt's St John Passion. *Address:* Music International, 13 Ardilaun Road, London N5 2QR, England.

**JENSON, Dylana (Ruth Lockington);** Violinist; b. 14 May 1961, Los Angeles, California, USA. *Education:* Began violin training with mother; Pupil of Manuel Compinsky, Jascha Heifetz and Josef Gingold; Masterclasses with Nathan Milstein in Zürich, 1973–76. *Career:* First public appearance as soloist in the Bach B Minor Concerto at age 7; Professional debut as soloist in the Mendelssohn Concerto with the New York Philharmonic Orchestra, 1973; European debut as soloist with the Zürich Tonhalle Orchestra, 1974; Thereafter regular tours world-wide as a soloist with leading orchestras, as a recitalist, and as a chamber music player. *Recordings:* Several. *Honours:* 2nd Prize in Tchaikovsky International Competition in Moscow, 1978. *Address:* c/o Konzertdirektion Jurgen Erlebach, Beim Schlump, 2000 Hamburg 13, Germany.

**JEPPSSON, Kerstin (Maria);** Composer; b. 29 Oct. 1948, Nyköping, Sweden. *Education:* BA, Musicology, Pedagogy, Social University of Stockholm, 1977; Studies, 1968–73, Music Teacher's Diploma, 1973, Stockholm Conservatory of Music; Composition with Maurice Karkoff, Stockholm, 1968–73, with Krzysztof Meyer and Krzysztof Penderecki, Kraków Conservatory of Music, Poland, 1974, 1977; Composition with Melvin Powell, 1978–79, MFA, 1979, California Institute of the Arts. *Compositions include:* Orchestral, chamber, solo instrumental, piano, vocal and choral works and songs, including: 3 Sentenzi for orchestra, 1970; Tre visor, choral, 1972; Blomstret i Saron, choral, 1972; Tre ryska poem for soprano and clarinet, 1973; 5 Japanese Images, choral, 1973; Hindemith in memoriam for clarinet and piano, 1974; Crisis for string orchestra and percussion, 1976–77; Vocazione, guitar solo, 1982; Prometheus for percussion, 1983; Tendenze for strings and piano, 1986; Kvinnosånger (female songs), published. *Recordings:* Various pieces. *Address:* Föreningen Svenska Tonsättare, Sandhamnsgatan 79, Box 27 327, 1002 54 Stockholm, Sweden.

**JEPSON, Kristine;** American singer (mezzo-soprano); b. 1965, USA. *Education:* Indiana Univ. *Career:* Season 1997–98 as Stephano in Roméo et Juliette at the Metropolitan, Hansel with the Canadian Opera Co. and

Schoolboy in Berg's Lulu at San Francisco; other roles include Bartók's Judith for Vancouver Opera, Strauss's Composer for Santa Fe Opera, Rosina with New York City Opera and Cherubino at the Met; Season 1999–2000 as Mozart's Annio in Dallas and Dorabella with Florida Grand Opera; Season 2000–01 as Octavian and Cherubino at the Met, Sister Helen in premiere of Jake Heggie's Dead Man Walking at San Francisco and Siebel in Faust at Paris Opéra; Octavian at the Monnaie, Brussels, Mozart's Sesto for Netherlands Opera and Nicklausse in Paris; concerts include Falla's El Amor Brujo at Alice Tully Hall and Bernstein's Jeremiah Symphony with the American Symphony Orchestra. *Current Management:* c/o Zemsky/Green Artists Management, 104 West 73rd Street, Suite #1, New York, NY 10023, USA. *Telephone:* (212) 579-6700. *Fax:* (212) 579-4723. *E-mail:* agreen@zemskygreen .com. *Website:* www.zemskygreen.com.

**JERSILD, Jörgen;** Composer; b. 1913, Copenhagen, Denmark. *Education:* Studied Composition and Music Theory with Poul Schierbeck and Piano with Alexander Stoffregen; Studied under Albert Roussel, Paris, France; Further studies in USA and Italy; MA, University of Copenhagen, 1940. *Career:* Danish Radio Music Department, 1939; Professor of Theory, Royal Academy of Music, Copenhagen, 1943–75. *Compositions:* Orchestral: Pastorale, 1916; Little Suite, 1950; The Birthday Concert, 1945; Harp Concerto, 1972; Ballet, Kings Theatre, 1954; Capricious Lucinda; Chamber Music; Music Making in the Forest, 1947; Fantasia e Canto Affetuoso, 1969; String Quartet, 1980; Für Gefühlvolle Spieler for Two Harps, 1982; Solo Instruments: Trois Pieces en Concert, for Piano, 1945; Pezzo Elegiaco, for Harp, 1968; Fantasia, for Harp, 1977; Fantasia, for Piano, 1987; 15 Piano Pieces for Julie, 1985; Jeu Polyrythmique for Piano, 1990; Lille Storstrom Suite for ensemble, 1995; Fantasia per Organo, 1985; Vocal Music: 3 Songs, 1944; 3 Danish Madrigals, 1958; 3 Danish Love Songs; 3 Romantiske Korsange, 1984; 3 Latin Madrigals, 1987; Il Cantico delle Creature, 1992; Music for Children: Quaretti Piccolo, 1950; Duo Concertante, 1956, 30 Polyrythmic Etudes, 1975. *Publications:* Laerebog i Rytmelaesning, 2nd edition, 1961; Laerbog i Melodilaesning, 2nd edition, 1963; Ear Training I–II, 1966; Elementary Rhythm Exercises; Advanced Rhythmic Studies, 1975; Romantic Harmony, 1970; Analytical Harmony I–II, 1989. *Honours:* several hon. appointments. *Address:* Söllerödvej 38, 2840 Holte, Denmark.

**JERUSALEM, Siegfried;** German singer (tenor); b. 17 April 1940, Oberhausen; m. 1980; one s. one d. *Career:* studied violin and piano at Folkwang Hochschule, Essen; played bassoon in German orchestras, including Stuttgart Radio Symphony Orchestra; studied voice and started singing career in Zigeunerbaron 1975; debut Metropolitan New York 1980, La Scala 1981, Vienna State Opera 1979; sang Loge and Siegfried, Wagner's Ring Cycle, Metropolitan New York 1990, Tristan, Bayreuth 1993, Wagner's Ring Cycle, Vienna 1994, Wagner's Rienzi, Vienna 1997, Tristana, Berlin Staatsoper 2000. *Honours:* Grammy for Wagner's Ring Cycle 1982, Grammy for Rheingold 1991, Bundesverdienstkreuz (1st Class) 1996. *Address:* Hochschule für Musik Nuremberg-Augsburg, Am Katharinenklaster 6, 90403 Nuremberg (office); c/o Dr G. Hilbert (Agent), Maximillianstrasse 22, 80538 Munich, Germany. *E-mail:* m.s.jerusalem@t-online.de (office).

**JEURISSEN, Herman G. A.;** Horn Player and Arranger; b. 27 Dec. 1952, Wijchen, Netherlands. *Education:* Soloist Diploma, Brabants Conservatorium, Tilburg, 1976. *Career:* co-first horn, Utrecht Symphony Orchestra, 1975–78; solo horn, The Hague Philharmonic Orchestra, 1978–; solo and concerto, radio and television appearances with orchestras in Netherlands, Austria, Germany, France and USA. *Recordings:* Mozart's Complete Horn Concertos; Complete Horn Music, by Leopold Mozart; Chamber Music, Franz and Richard Strauss; compositions for horn and organ; compositions for brass and carillon. *Publications:* Reconstruction and completion of Mozart's unfinished Horn Concertos K370b and K371, K 494A; compositions and arrangements for horns; Mozart and the Horn, 1978; Basic Principles of Horn Playing (three vols), 1997. *Contributions:* Mens en Melodie; Praeludium; Horn Call Brass Bulletin; Historic Brass Society Journal. *Honours:* Prix d'excellence, 1978; Silver Laurel of the Concertgebouw Friends, 1979. *Address:* Jacob Mosselstraat 58, 2595 RJ The Hague, Netherlands.

**JEWELL, Ian;** Violinist; b. 1950, England. *Education:* Studied at the Royal College of Music with Cecil Aronowitz and in Italy with Bruno Giuranna. *Career:* Solo performances of the Walton and Rubbra Concertos, Harold in Italy by Berlioz and the Mozart Concertante; Philharmonic at the Royal Academy of Music and Head of Strings, Purcell School; Co-founder, Gabrieli Quartet, 1967, and toured with them to Europe, North America, the Far East and Australia; Festival engagements in the United Kingdom, including the Aldeburgh, City of London and Cheltenham; Concerts every season in London in the Barbican's Mostly Mozart Festival; Resident Artist, University of Essex, from 1971; Co-premiered works by William Alwyn, Britten, Alan Bush, Daniel Jones and Gordon Crosse, 2 Quartets of Nicholas Maw and Panufnik, 1980, 1983, and the 3rd Quartet of John MacCabe, 1979; British premiere of the Piano Quintet by Sibelius, 1990. *Recordings include:* 50 CDs, including early pieces by Britten, Dohnányi's Piano Quintet with Wolfgang Manz, Walton's Quartets and the Sibelius Quartet and Quintet, with Anthony Goldstone.

**JIRIKOVSKY, Petr;** Pianist; b. 24 June 1971, Prague, Czechoslovakia. *Education:* Conservatory in Prague (Emil Leichner); Academy of Performing Arts in Prague (Ivan Klansky); Conservatoire De Paris (Solo Piano–Theodor Paraschivesco, Chamber Music–Itamar Golan); Hochschule für Musik in

Vienna (Chamber Music–Michael Schnitzler); Masterclasses and private lessons–Eugen Indjic. *Career:* Concerts all round the Czech Republic, Europe, Japan; Prague-Rudolfinum, Munich-Gasteig, Paris, London, Warsaw, Kyoto Concert Hall; Prague Spring Festival, Orlando Festival, Ohrid Summer Festival Member, Academia Trio; More than 40 recordings for Czech Radio. *Recordings:* B Smetana, CD, Czech Dances, 1994; B Smetana, CD, My Country (Piano Four Hands), 1995; B Smetana, Polkas (complete), 1997; A Dvořák, CD, Piano Trios (Academia Trio), 1997; Dvořák, Brahms, CD, Gypsy Songs (with Bernarda Fink–Mezzo Soprano), 1997; B Martinů, CD, Concerto Grosso for 2 Pianos and Chamber Orchestra (with Josef Hala, Prague Chamber Orchestra), 1997; B Smetana, CD, Works for 2 and 4 pianos (Live recording from Prague Spring Festival with other young Czech pianists, 1998; Beethoven, CD, Geister Trio, Shostakovich Trio No. 2, Academia Trio, 1999. *Honours:* 1st Prize, Beethoven Piano Competition, Czech Republic, 1986; 1st Prize, Chopin Competition, 1987; 3rd Prize, Smetana Piano Competition, 1988; 1st Prize, North London Festival, 1992; 1st Prize, Heerlen (Netherlands), with Academia Trio, 1995. *Address:* Grafická 44, 15000 Prague 5, Czech Republic.

**JO, Sumi;** Singer (soprano); b. 22 Nov. 1962, Seoul, Republic of Korea. *Education:* Studied in Seoul and at the Accademia di Santa Cecilia, Rome, 1983–86. *Career:* Debut: Teatro Verdi, Trieste, 1986, as Gilda; Sang at Lyon, Nice and Marseille, 1987–88; Appeared in Jomelli's Fetonte at La Scala, 1988; Discovered by Karajan and sang Barbarina at the 1988 Salzburg Festival; Oscar in Un Ballo in Maschera, 1989–90, conducted by Solti; Guest appearances at Munich from 1988, Vienna from 1989, and Paris; La Scala Milan in Ravel's L'Enfant et les Sortilèges, conducted by Lorin Maazel, and as Zerlina in Auber's Fra Diavolo, 1992; Metropolitan Opera as Gilda, 1988 and 1990; Royal Opera, Covent Garden, as Olympia in Tales of Hoffmann and as Elvira in I Puritani in 1991 and 1991; Chicago Lyric Opera as Queen of Night in 1990 and as Queen of Night with Danish Philharmonic conducted by Zubin Mehta in 1991; Season 1992 as Matilde in Rossini's Elisabetta at Naples, Olympia at Covent Garden (followed by Adina); Sang Zerbinetta at Lisbon, 1996; Season 1997–98 with L'Enfant et les Sortilèges at Boston, Zerbinetta at Lisbon and Turin, and in Mozart's Lucio Silla at Mozart Festival, New York. *Recordings:* Arias; Adèle in Le Comte Ory; Un Ballo in Maschera; Queen of Night in Die Zauberflöte, conducted by Armin Jordan and by Solti; Fiorilla in Rossini's Il Turco in Italia, conducted by Neville Marriner; Soprano soloist in Mahler Symphony No. 8, conducted by Sinopoli; Soprano soloist in Rossini's Messa di Gloria, conducted by Neville Marriner; Angèle d'Olivarès in Auber's Le Domino Noir, conducted by Richard Bonynge. *Current Management:* Columbia Artists Management, 165 West 57th Street, New York, NY 10019, USA.

**JOACHIM, Otto;** Composer, Violist, Violinist and Gambist; b. 13 Oct. 1919, Düsseldorf, Germany; Separated, 1 s. *Education:* Concordia School, Düsseldorf; Buths-Neitzel Conservatory, Düsseldorf; Rheinische Musikschule, Cologne. *Career:* CBC Soloist, Montreal String Quartet, L'Ensemble des Instruments Anciens de Montreal, Canada; 1st Violist, Montreal Symphony. *Compositions include:* Nonet, 1960; Psalm for Choir, 1960; Concertante No. 2 for string quartet and string orchestra, 1961; Fantasia for organ, 1961; 12 Twelve-tone Pieces for Children, 1961; Contrastes for orchestra, 1967; Kinderspiel for violin, cello, piano and speaker, 1969; 5,9 for 4-channel tape, 1971; Night Music for alto flute and guitar, 1978; 4 Intermezzi for flute and guitar, 1978; Requiem for violin or viola or cello, 1969; Paean for vioncello solo, 1989; Stacheldraht, melodrame, 1993; Metamorphoses for orchestra, 1995; String Quartet, 1997. *Address:* 7910 Wavell Road, Côte St-Luc, Montreal, Quebec Province H4W 1L7, Canada.

**JOBIN, André;** Singer (Tenor); b. 20 Jan. 1933, Quebec, Canada. *Education:* Studied as an actor in Paris and worked with Jean-Louis Barrault. *Career:* Sang at first as a baritone in Parisian musicals; Operatic roles as tenor from 1962, notably Pelléas at Marseilles, Nice, Paris, Madrid and San Francisco, 1965; Glyndebourne Festival, 1976, New York City Opera from 1970; Other roles have been Romeo, Don José, Massenet's Des Grieux, Rodrigo and John the Baptist, Julien (Louise) and Hoffmann; Many appearances at Quebec, Lyon, Brussels, Berlin and Madrid; Liège Opera, 1982–87, as Rodrigo in Le Cid, John the Baptist (Hérodiade) and Des Grieux; Cologne Opera, 1987, as Werther; Engaged in musical sand operettas in Chicago, London and Detroit; Sang in Bernstein's Candide at Turin 1997. *Recordings:* Several albums.

**JOCHUM, Veronica;** Pianist; b. 6 Dec. 1932, Berlin, Germany; m. Wilhelm Viggo von Moltke, 15 Nov 1961. *Education:* MA, 1955, Concert Diploma, 1957, Staatliche Musikhochschule, Munich, Germany; Private study with Edwin Fischer, Josef Benvenuti, 1958–59 and Rudolf Serkin, 1959–61. *Career:* Debut: Germany, 1954; Numerous appearances as soloist with orchestras in Europe North and South America, 1961–; Appeared with Boston Symphony, London Symphony Orchestra, London Philharmonic Orchestra, Berlin, Hamburg and Munich Philharmonics, Vienna Symphony and Concertgebouw Orchestra among others; Radio and television appearances; Recitals in over 50 countries in Europe, North and South America, Africa and Asia; Featured in a German film, Self-Attempt, on a novel by Christa Wolf. *Recordings:* Various labels. *Honours:* Cross of Order of Merit by German President (Bundesverdienstkreuz), 1994; Bunting Fellowship, Harvard-Radliff, 1996. *Address:* New England Conservatory of Music, 290 Huntington Avenue, Boston, MA 02115, USA.

**JOEL, Emmanuel;** Conductor; b. 1958, Paris, France. *Education:* Studied with at the Paris Conservatoire. *Career:* Early engagements with Opéra de Lyon and at the Aix-en-Provence Festival; Paris Opéra debut with Offenbach's Les Brigands, 1993; Semele and Les Pêcheurs de Perles in Melbourne and regular appearances with the Opéra de Nantes; Boildieu's La Dame Blanche at the Wexford Festival and Don Quichotte for English National Opera, 1996; La Belle Hélène for Scottish Opera, Carmen and Werther in Israel; Season 1996–97 with Chausson's Le Roi Arthus in Montpellier, Samson et Dalila in Sydney and Israel, Butterfly in Rouen, La Bohème for ENO and Eugene Onegin in Toulouse. *Address:* c/o Allied Artists, 42 Montpelier Square, London SW7 1JZ, England.

**JOËL, Nicolas;** Stage Director; b. 1945, Paris. *Career:* Opéra du Rhin, Strasbourg, from 1973, with Der Ring des Nibelungen, 1979; Stagings of Samson et Dalila at Chicago and San Francisco, Aida in Vienna, Lohengrin at Copenhagen and Eugene Onegin in Amsterdam; Rigoletto and La Traviata for Zürich Opera, Parsifal in San Francisco and Roméo et Juliette at Covent Garden, London; Artistic Director of Théâtre du Capitole, Toulouse from 1990: Falstaff, Elektra, Die Walküre and Il Trovatore; Further engagements for La Scala, Milan (Manon and La Rondine), New York Metropolitan (Andrea Chénier and Lucia di Lammermoor); Other stagings include Boris Godunov, Cav and Pag double bill and Salome (at Essen). *Address:* c/o Théâtre du Capitole, Place du Capitole, 31000 Toulouse, France.

**JOERES, Dirk;** Conductor and Pianist; b. 13 Aug. 1947, Bonn, Germany. *Education:* studied piano, conducting and composition, Berlin, Cologne, London and Paris. *Career:* Engagements with renowned orchestras; Repeat appearances at festivals in Berlin, London, Prague, Klavierfestival Ruhr and Schleswig-Holstein; Artistic Director, Westdeutsche Sinfonia, 1987; Recordings and television productions; World-wide orchestral tours; Guest conductor, London Royal Philharmonic. *Recordings:* Solo recording, Brahms and his Friends; Two Brahms Serenades, with Westdeutsche Sinfonia; Associate Conductor, Royal Philharmonic Orchestra. *Honours:* First prize, International piano competition, Vercello, 1972; Critic's Choice, two Brahms Serenades, Gramaphone Magazine, London; 100 Top CDs, BBC Music Magazine. *Address:* Humboldstr 17, 51379 Leverkusen, Germany.

**JOHANNSEN, Kay;** Organist and Church Musician; b. 1 Oct. 1961, Giengen, Germany; m. Andrea Ermer, 29 April 1987, one s., one d. *Education:* Studies at Freiburg in organ and conducting; Organ studies at NEC, Boston, with William Porter. *Career:* Concerts in major German cities and in foreign countries, broadcast concerts with almost all German stations, several concerts with orchestras such as the Nurnberg Symphonic, Radio Symphony Orchestra Prague, Radio Symphony Orchestra Hannover, Staatsphilharmonic Rheinland-Pfalz, Philharmonic Orchestra Gelsenkirchen, Berlin Philharmonic Orchestra and Stuttgart Philharmonic Orchestra; Guest Teacher, Freiburg Conservatory, 1992–93; Teacher, Karlsruhe Conservatory, 1994–2000; Organist of the Siftskirche Stuttgart, 1994–; Masterclasses in Frankfurt, Sofia, Kiev and Seoul. *Recordings:* CDs: Bach, Reger, Fortig, 1990; Christian Hommel, Bach, Mozart, Huber, ars musici; 1993; French organ music from the 19th century, 1993; Brahms, Complete Organ Works, 1996; Bach, Trio Sonatas, 1997; Bach Masterworks of Weimar, 1998; Bach III. Part of Clavierübung, 1999; Bach, the Young Bach–a Virtuoso, 1999; Bach, Neumeister–Chorales, 1999; Bach, Sonatas for violin and harpsichord, 2003. *Honours:* Various prizes in music competitions; German National Foundation Scholarship. *Address:* c/o Evang Bezirkskantorat, Altes Schloss, Schillerplatz 6, 70173 Stuttgart, Germany.

**JOHANNSSON, Kristjan;** Singer (Tenor); b. 1950, Akureyi Du, Iceland. *Education:* Studied at Nicolini Conservatory, Piacenza and with Campogalliani and Tagliavini. *Career:* Debut: National Theatre of Iceland, Reykjavík, as Rodolfo in 1961; Sang Pinkerton in a production of Madama Butterfly, by Ken Russell, at Spoleto, 1983; Engagements as guest artist at the Chicago Lyric Opera in Faust, Metropolitan New York, Vienna, Stuttgart and La Scala Milan; Roles have included Radames, Alvaro in La Forza del Destino, Cavaradossi and Dick Johnson; Sang Turiddu in Cavalleria Rusticana at Naples and Florence, season 1990–91; Calaf at the Verona Arena, 1991; Sang Manrico in the opening production at the New Teatro, Carol Felice, Genoa, 1991; Andrea Chénier at Florence, Calaf at Chicago, Cavaradossi at Rome and Manrico at Turin, 1992; Calaf at Torre del Lago, 1996; Dick Johnson at Zürich, 1998; Season 2000 as Otello at Budapest and Enzo in La Gioconda at the Deutsche Oper Berlin.

**JOHANOS, Donald;** Conductor; b. 10 Feb. 1928, Cedar Rapids, Iowa, USA; m. (1) Thelma Trimble, 27 Aug 1950, 2 s., 3 d., (2) Corinne Rutledge, 28 Sept 1985. *Career:* BMus, 1950, MMus, 1952; Eastman School of Music, Rochester, New York; Advanced conducting studies with Eugene Ormandy, George Szell, Thomas Beecham, Eduard van Beinum, Herbert von Karajan, Otto Klemperer, 1955–58.; Teacher, Pennsylvania State University, 1953–55; Music Director, Altoona (Pennsylvania) Symphony Orchestra, 1953–56; Johnstown (Pennsylvania) Symphony Orchestra, 1955–56; Associate Conductor, 1957–61, Resident Conductor, 1961–62, Music Director, 1962–70, Dallas Symphony Orchestra; Teacher, Southern Methodist University, 1958–62; Hockaday School, 1962–65; Associate Conductor and Director, Pittsburgh Symphony Orchestra, 1970–80; Music Director, Honolulu Symphony Orchestra, 1979–; Artistic Director, Hawaii Opera Theater, 1979–83; Guest conducting engagements with various orchestras at home and abroad.

*Recordings:* For various labels. *Address:* c/o Honolulu Symphony Orchestra, 1441 Kapiolani Boulevard, Suite 1515, Honolulu, HI 96814, USA.

**JOHANSSON, Eva;** Singer (Soprano); b. 25 Feb. 1958, Copenhagen, Denmark. *Education:* Studied at the Copenhagen Conservatory, 1977–81; Opera School of the Royal Opera, Copenhagen, 1981–84; New York, with Oren Brown. *Career:* Sang at the Royal Opera, Copenhagen, 1982–88, as the Countess in Figaro (debut), Tatiana, Pamina, Marie in Wozzeck and Chrysothemis (Elektra); Guest appearances in Oslo as Marie and Donna Anna (1985, 1987); Marie at the Paris Opéra, 1986; Sang in productions of Der Ring des Nibelungen at Berlin and Bayreuth, 1988, as Gutrune and as Freia and Gerhilde; Sang Freia in a concert performance of Das Rheingold at Paris, 1988, conducted by Daniel Baremboim; Vienna Staatsoper, 1989, as Fiordiligi; Tel-Aviv, 1990, as Donna Anna in Don Giovanni, conducted by Claudio Abbado; Since 1990: Elsa in Lohengrin at Bayreuth; Guest appearances in Barcelona, Munich, Dresden, Japan, Paris, Seville, Nice, Madrid, Stuttgart, Cologne and Hamburg; Debut as Donna Anna, at Covent Garden, 1992; Sang Elsa at the Accademia di Santa Cecilia, Rome, 1996; Chrysothemis in Elektra at Århus, 1998; Season 2000–01 at the Deutsche Oper Berlin as Sieglinde, Elsa, Tatiana, Eva, Liu, Senta, and Elisabeth in Tannhäuser. *Recordings:* Das Rheingold conducted by Bernard Haitink; Es War Einmal, by Zemlinsky. *Address:* Bühnenagentur Marianne Bottger, Dahlmannstrasse 9, 1000 Berlin 12, Germany.

**JOHNS, William;** Singer (Tenor); b. 2 Oct. 1936, Tulsa, Oklahoma, USA. *Education:* Studied in New York. *Career:* Debut: Lake George, 1967, as Rodolfo in La Bohème; Sang with the Bremen Opera as the Prince in The Love of Three Oranges and the Duke of Mantua; Welsh National Opera, 1970–72, as Radames and Calaf; Further appearances in Cologne, Düsseldorf, Dallas, Hamburg, Bregenz, Houston, Vienna, Aix-en-Provence, Rome and New York (Metropolitan Opera); Covent Garden debut, 1987, as Bacchus in Ariadne auf Naxos; Philadelphia Opera, 1988, as Florestan in Fidelio; Holland Festival, 1989, as Siegfried in a concert performance of Götterdämmerung; Other roles include Wagner's Lohengrin, Tannhäuser, Siegmund and Tristan, Huon (Oberon), the Emperor in Die Frau ohne Schatten, Jason in Medea in Corinto by Mayr, Hoffmann and Verdi's Otello; Sang Tristan at San Francisco, 1991. *Address:* c/o San Francisco Opera, War Memorial Opera House, San Francisco, CA 94102, USA.

**JOHNSON, Camellia;** Singer (Soprano); b. 1960, Delaware, USA. *Education:* Studied at Daytona Beach, Florida, and the Manhattan School of Music, New York. *Career:* Debut: Strawberry Woman, in Porgy and Bess at the Metropolitan, 1985; Sang in Porgy and Bess at Glyndebourne, 1986, and Helsinki, 1989, 1992; Season 1992–93, in Don Carlos at San Francisco and as Aida at Michigan; Beethoven's Ninth in Indianapolis and Montreal; Verdi's Requiem with the Saint Louis Symphony and the Long Island Philharmonic; Metropolitan Opera as Serena in Porgy and Bess, High Priestess in Aida and Madelon in Andrea Chénier; Mozart's Solemn Vespers and Requiem with the Cincinnati Symphony; Other repertoire includes the Four Last Songs of Strauss, Les Nuits d'Été, Schubert's Rosamunde, Rossini's Stabat Mater and Beethoven's Missa Solemnis. *Recordings:* Porgy and Bess. *Address:* c/o Metropolitan Opera, Lincoln Center, New York, NY 10023, USA.

**JOHNSON, David Cale;** Singer (Bass); b. 1950, Texas, USA. *Education:* New York; San Francisco, El Paso. *Career:* Opera engagements in Paris, Athens, Vienna, Geneva, Leipzig, São Paulo, Bogotá, Rio de Janeiro, Caracas, San Francisco also cover at the Metropolitan Opera; Concert soloist, New York Philharmonic, Honolulu, New Jersey, São Paulo Symphonies; Flensburg Opera, 1986–87; Hannover, 1987–91, notably König Heinrich in Lohengrin, Zaccaria in Nabucco, Colline in La Bohème and Don Pasquale; Mozart's Osmin and Sarastro at Lucerne in 1991, Bartered Bride (Kezal) in Basel and roles at the Vienna State and Volks Operas from 1991, including Fidelio (Rocco), Jerusalem (Roger), Prophète (Mathison), Zauberflöte (Sarastro), Aida (Il Re), Nabucco (Zaccaria). *Address:* c/o Vienna Staatsoper, Opernring 2, 1010 Vienna, Austria.

**JOHNSON, David (Carl);** Composer and Flautist; b. 30 Jan. 1940, Batavia, New York, USA. *Education:* Studied composition with Donald Keats and David Epstein at Antioch College; Leon Kirchner at Harvard University and Nadia Boulanger in Paris, 1964–65; Further study in Cologne. *Career:* Teacher at the Rheinische Musikschule Cologne, 1966–67; Worked with Stockhausen in the creation of Hymnen at the studios of West German Radio; Member of the Stockhausen ensemble at the Osaka World Fair, 1970; Cofounded Feedback Studio at Cologne, 1970; Director of the electronic music studio at the Basle Music Academy, 1975. *Compositions:* Five movements for flute, 1962; Bells for flute, guitar and cello, 1964; Thesis for string quartet, 1964; 3 Pieces for string quartet, 1964; 3 Pieces for string quartet, 1966; Tonantiton for tape, 1968; Process of Music for tape and instruments, 1970; Sound-environment pieces Music Makers, Gyromes mit und für Elise, Cybernet, Gehlhaar, Organica l'IV and Klangkoffer, 1969–74; Proganica for speaker and 2 electric organs, 1973; Audioliven for flute and electronics, 1976; In Memoriam Uschi for tape and 3 instruments, 1977; Jadermann incidental music to play by Hoffmansthal, 1980; Bach: Encounter of the Third Kind, stage piece, 1981; Calls in Search, for tape, 1981. *Address:* c/o ASCAP, ASCAP Building, 1 Lincoln Plaza, New York, NY 10023, USA.

**JOHNSON, David Charles,** MA, PhD; British composer, music historian, writer and music publisher; b. 27 Oct. 1942, Edinburgh, Scotland; one s. *Education:* Univs of Aberdeen and Cambridge. *Career:* organized recitals for

Edinburgh Festival 1975, 1985, 1986, 1988; cellist, McGibbon Ensemble 1980–96; Tutor in Musical History, Univ. of Edinburgh 1988–94; f. self-publishing co., David Johnson Music Edns 1990; mem. PRS, MCPS. *Compositions:* five operas, church music, Piobaireached for Solo Recorder, God, Man and The Animals (recorded by Alison Wells, soprano, and instrumental ensemble 2001, Metier, England), Piano Trio, Sonata for Cello and Piano, Trio for Recorders (published by Forsyth), Seven MacDiarmid Songs for Soprano, Trumpet, Piano, 12 Preludes and Fugues for Piano (recorded by Ian Hobson 1998, Zephyr, USA), three suites for solo cello; other songs, chamber and orchestral music. *Recordings:* The Art of Robert Burns (recorded by The Musicians of Edinburgh, Scotstown, USA) 2003, More Art of Robert Burns 2005. *Publications:* Music and Society in Lowland Scotland 1972, Ten Georgian Glees for Four Voices (ed.) 1981, Scottish Fiddle Music in the 18th Century 1984, The Scots Cello Book 1990, Stepping Northward 1990, Scots on the Fiddle 1991, Chamber Music of 18th Century Scotland 2000, Thistle and Minuet 2005, John Mahon Clarinet Concerto (ed.) 2006; contrib. to The New Grove Dictionary of Music and Musicians 1981, 2001, writes for Fiddler Magazine, Canada. *Address:* 8 Shandon Crescent, Edinburgh, EH11 1QE, Scotland. *Telephone:* (131) 337-4621 (office). *E-mail:* david@djmusiceditions.freeserve.co.uk (office).

**JOHNSON, Douglas;** Singer (Tenor); b. 1958, CA, USA. *Education:* Studied at the University of Los Angeles. *Career:* Appearances in Les Dialogues des Carmelites, La Fille du Régiment and La Clemenza di Tito while a student; Sang at Aachen, 1984–87, notably as Don Ottavio, Handel's Serse, Jacquino, Count Almaviva, Rinuccio in Gianni Schicchi, Belmonte and the Steuermann; Hanover, 1988–89, Frankfurt am Mainz, from 1989 notably as Tamino, 1991; Salzburg Festival, 1987, 1991 in Moses und Aron and as Arbace in Idomeneo; Guest appearances at Hamburg, Chateauneuf in Zar und Zimmermann, Deutsche Oper Berlin, Nicolai's Fenton, Vienna Staatsoper, Tamino, Cologne, Nemorino, 1987 and Ludwigshafen, Gualterio in Vivaldi's Griselda, 1989; Sang Rossini's Almaviva at Seattle, 1992. *Recordings include:* L'Oca del Cairo by Mozart.

**JOHNSON, Emma,** MBE; British clarinettist and conductor; b. 20 May 1966, Barnet, Hertfordshire, England. *Education:* Pembroke Coll., Cambridge, studied with John Brightwell, Sidney Fell. *Career:* debut, Barbican, London 1985; appearances with ECO, London Symphony Orchestra, Ulster Orchestra, Royal Liverpool Philharmonic Orchestra, Hallé Orchestra, City of London Sinfonia and Royal Philharmonic Orchestra; debut in Vienna at the Musikverein 1985; French debut with Polish Chamber Orchestra 1986; performances in Netherlands, Finland and Monte Carlo; TV and radio appearances in UK; Japanese debut, Tokyo 1990; New York debut 1992; Schumann Weekend concerts at Blackheath 1997; Visiting Prof., Royal Coll. of Music 1997–; conducting debut with London Mozart Players 2001; conducting debut with Royal Philharmonic Orchestra 2004. *Recordings:* Mozart Clarinet Concerto 1984, Crusell Clarinet Concerto No. 2 1985, Bottesini Duo for clarinet and double bass (with Tom Martin) 1986, Weber Clarinet Concerto No. 1 1987, Recital Disc La Clarinette Française (with Gordon Back) 1988, The Romantic Clarinet (concertos by Weber, Spohr and Crusell) 1992, Finzi and Stanford Concertos (with Royal Philharmonic Orchestra) 1992, Recital of Encores 1992, Michael Berkeley Concerto 1993, British Recital Disc 1994, Encores II 1994, Malcolm Arnold: Complete Clarinet Works 1995, Mozart and Weber Clarinet Quintets 2000, Voyage (classics and jazz) 2004, The Mozart Album 2005. *Honours:* Hon. Fellow Pembroke Coll., Cambridge 1999; BBC TV Young Musician of the Year 1984, bronze award European Young Musician of the Year Competition, Geneva 1984, Wavendon All Music Awards voted Young Professional All Music Musician 1986. *E-mail:* libbysutton@hazardchase.co.uk. *Current Management:* Hazard Chase Ltd, 25 City Road, Cambridge, CB1 1DP, England. *Telephone:* (1223) 312400. *Fax:* (1223) 460827. *E-mail:* info@hazardchase.co.uk. *Website:* www.hazardchase.co.uk. *Address:* Christa Phelps, 6 Malvern Road, London, E8 3LT, England. *Website:* www.emmajohnson.co.uk.

**JOHNSON, Graham Rhodes,** OBE, FRAM, FGSM; British pianist; b. 10 July 1950, Bulawayo, Rhodesia (now Zimbabwe); s. of the late John Edward Donald Johnson and of Violet May Johnson. *Education:* Hamilton High School, Bulawayo, Rhodesia, Royal Acad. of Music, London. *Career:* Artistic Adviser, accompanist Alte Oper Festival, Frankfurt 1981–82; Prof. of Accompaniment, Guildhall School of Music 1986–; Song Adviser, Wigmore Hall 1992–; Artistic Dir The Songmakers' Almanac; guest lecturer in several countries; writer, presenter BBC Radio 3 series on Poulenc, BBC TV series on Schubert 1978, Liszt 1986; concert début, Wigmore Hall 1972; has accompanied numerous singers including Dame Elisabeth Schwarzkopf, Jessye Norman, Victoria de los Angeles, Dame Janet Baker, Sir Peter Pears, Dame Felicity Lott, Ann Murray, Matthias Goerne, Christine Schäfer, Dorothea Roeschmann, François Le Roux; has appeared at festivals in Edin., Munich, Hohenems, Salzburg, Bath, Hong Kong, Bermuda; Chair. Jury Wigmore Hall Int. Singing Competition 1997, 1999, 2001; mem. Royal Swedish Acad. of Music 2000; numerous recordings. *Publications:* contrib. The Britten Companion 1984, Gerald Moore: The Unashamed Accompanist, The Spanish Song Companion 1992, The Songmakers' Almanac Reflections and Commentaries 1996, A French Song Companion 2000, articles and reviews. *Honours:* Chevalier, Ordre des Arts et des Lettres 2002; Gramophone Award 1989, 1996, 1997, Royal Philharmonic Prize for Instrumentalist 1998. *Address:* 83 Fordwych Road, London, NW2 3TL, England. *Telephone:* (20) 8452-5193. *Fax:* (20) 8452-5081 (home).

**JOHNSON, Marc;** Cellist; b. 1945, USA. *Education:* Studied at the Eastman School of Music and Indiana University. *Career:* Played with the Rochester Philharmonic while a student; Solo appearances in Rochester and with the Denver Philharmonic; Recital and chamber concerts in Washington DC, St Louis and Baltimore; Founder member of the Vermeer Quartet at the Marlboro Festival, 1970; Performances in all major US centres, Europe, Israel and Australia; Festival engagements at Tanglewood, Aspen, Spoleto, Edinburgh, Mostly Mozart (New York), Aldeburgh, South Bank, Santa Fe, Chamber Music West, and the Casals Festival; Resident quartet for Chamber Music Chicago; Annual master classes at the Royal Northern College of Music, Manchester; Member of the Resident Artists' Faculty of Northern Illinois University. *Recordings:* Quartets by Beethoven, Dvořák, Verdi and Schubert; Brahms Clarinet Quintet with Karl Leister. *Honours:* Denver Symphony and Washington International Competitions; Received title of Kämmersängen during the 1960s. *Address:* Allied Artists, 42 Montpelier Square, London SW7 1JZ, England.

**JOHNSON, Mary Jane;** American singer (soprano); b. 22 March 1950, Pampa, TX. *Education:* West Texas Univ. *Career:* debut, New York Lyric Opera as Agathe in Der Freischütz 1981; Philadelphia and Santa Fe 1982, as Musetta and Rosalinde; sang at the San Francisco Opera from 1983, as Freia in Das Rheingold, Jenifer in the US premiere of The Midsummer Marriage 1983, Marguerite, and the Empress in Die Frau ohne Schatten, Washington Opera from 1984, Boston and Cincinnati from 1986; European engagements with Opera North at Leeds, Torre del Lago (Puccini Festival), Bologna, Geneva and the Baths of Caraccala at Rome (Minnie in La Fanciulla del West); sang Salome at Santiago 1990, Desdemona at Pittsburgh and Minnie at the 1991 Santa Fe Festival; Helen of Troy in Mefistofele at Chicago 1991; La Scala and Opéra Bastille, Paris 1992, in the title role of Lady Macbeth of Mtsensk; Teatro Municipal Santiago as Senta in Der fliegende Holländer 1992; other roles include Mozart's Countess, Leonore, Alice in Falstaff, Tosca, Giulietta, the Duchess of Parma in Busoni's Faust, and Mrs Jessel in The Turn of the Screw; sang Janáček's Emilia Marty at Vancouver 1996, and Salome there in 1998; sang Elektra at Santa Fe 2000.

**JOHNSON, Nancy;** Singer (Soprano); b. 1954, California, USA. *Education:* Studied at California State University, Hayward. *Career:* Sang at the Landestheater Detmold, 1980–81, Wiesbaden, 1981–82, Mannheim, 1982–87; Engaged at the Stuttgart Staatsoper from 1987 and has made guest appearances at Düsseldorf, the Vienna Staatsoper, San Francisco (Eva in Die Meistersinger, 1988); Other roles have included Manon Lescaut, and the Empress in Die Frau ohne Schatten (Mannheim, 1984). *Address:* c/o Stuttgart Staatsoper, Oberer Schlossgarten 6, 7000 Stuttgart, Germany.

**JOHNSON, Robert;** Singer (Tenor); b. 10 Dec. 1940, Moline, Illinois, USA. *Education:* Studied at Northwestern University in Evanston and at New York. *Career:* Debut: New York City Opera, 1971, as Count Almaviva; Sang in New York, Chicago, Baltimore, Houston, New Orleans and Washington as Mozart's Ferrando, Belmonte and Tamino; Ernesto, Beppo in Donizetti's Rita, Alfredo, Fenton in Falstaff, Hoffmann, Rodolfo, Sali in A Village Romeo and Juliet, and Tom Rakewell; Frequent concert appearances. *Address:* c/o New York City Opera, Lincoln Center, New York, NY 10023, USA.

**JOHNSON, Russell;** American theatre designer and acoustician; *Chairman, Artec Consultants Inc.*; b. 1923, Briar Creek, PA. *Education:* Carnegie-Mellon Univ., Yale Univ. School of Architecture. *Career:* began career in research and consulting on the design, theatre planning, and acoustics of buildings for the performing arts 1946–; first professional projects under leadership of Prof. E. C. Cole 1946–50; Assoc. Bolt, Beranek and Newman (BBN), Cambridge, MA 1954–70, Founder and Prin. Consultant Theatre Planning and Consulting Div.; Founder Russell Johnson Assocs (renamed Artec Consultants) 1970, Chair. and Prin. Consultant, Artec Consultants Inc. 1970–; Fellow Acoustical Soc. of America, US Inst. for Theatre Tech. (USITT). *Designs include:* Culture and Congress Centre (Lucerne, Switzerland), Morton H. Meyerson Symphony Centre (Dallas), Sibelius Concert Hall (Lahti, Finland), Symphony Hall (Birmingham, UK), NJ Performing Arts Centre (Newark), Kravis Centre for the Performing Arts (W Palm Beach, FL), Derngate Centre (Northampton, UK), Kimmel Centre for the Performing Arts (Philadelphia), Pikes Peak Centre (Colorado Springs), Calgary Centre for the Performing Arts (Alberta), George Weston Recital Hall (Toronto, Ont.), Morsani Hall (Tampa Bay, FL), Performing Arts Centre (Tampa, FL), Royal Concert Hall (Nottingham, UK), Armenian Theatre, Centre-in-the-Square (Kitchener, Ont.), Crouse-Hinds Concert Theatre (Syracuse, NY), Hamilton Place (Ont.), Prudential Hall Opera House (Newark, NJ), Chan Shun Concert Hall (Vancouver BC), Toronto Centre for the Arts (Ont.), Concert Hall (Budapest, Hungary), Rose Hall for Jazz at Lincoln Centre (NY), Concert Hall and Opera House (Miami FL), Concert Hall and Opera House (Singapore), Concert Hall (Orange County, CA). *Honours:* USITT Award 1996, Wallace Clement Sabine Medal, Acoustical Soc. of America (ASA) 1997, Int. Citation of Merit, Int. Soc. of Performing Arts (ISPA) 1998. *Address:* Artec Consultants Inc., 114 West 26th Street, New York, NY 10001, USA (office). *Telephone:* (212) 242-0120 (office). *Fax:* (212) 645-8635 (office).

**JOHNSON, Tom,** BA, MMus; American composer; b. 18 Nov. 1939, Greeley, CO. *Education:* Yale Univ., studied with Morton Feldman. *Career:* music critic, Village Voice, New York 1971–82; freelance composer 1982–. *Compositions include:* Spaces, 1969; An Hour for Piano, 1971; The Four Note Opera, 1972; Septepede, 1973; Verses for alto flute, horn and harp, 1974; The Masque of Clouds, opera, 1975; Verses for viola, 1976; Trinity for SATB, 1978; Dragons in A, 1979; Movements for wind quintet, 1980; Harpiano, 1982; Predictables, 1984; Voicings for 4 pianos, 1984; Tango, 1984; Choral Catalogue, 1985; Pascal's Triangle, 1987; Riemannoper, 1988; Una Opera Italiana, 1991; Trigonometry, for 4 baritones and 4 percussion, 1995; Formulas, for string quartet, 1995. *Publications:* Imaginary Music, 1974; Private Pieces, 1976; Symmetries, 1981; Rational Melodies, 1982. *Address:* c/o Editions 75, 75 rue de la Roquette, 75011 Paris, France. *E-mail:* tom@johnson.org. *Website:* www .tom.johnson.org.

**JOHNSSON, Bengt Gustaf,** MA; Danish academic, pianist and organist; b. 17 July 1921, Copenhagen; m. Esther Paustian; one d. *Education:* University of Copenhagen, studied with Georg Vasarhely and Walter Gieseking, Royal Academy of Music, Copenhagen. *Career:* debut, Copenhagen, 1944; concert tours, broadcasts, Scandinavia, German Federal Republic, Switzerland, France, Netherlands; recitals in many European countries; US tour, 1964; organist, Danish Broadcasting, 1949–70; teacher, Royal Academy, Copenhagen, 1958–61; Professor, Royal Academy of Music, Århus, Jutland; numerous masterclasses; studied at Vatican Library, Rome, 1977, Benedictine Monastery, Montserrat, Spain, 1978, 1980–83; Spanish Cultural Department invitation to study in libraries in Barcelona and Montserrat, 1979, 1983. *Recordings include:* N. W. Gade Piano Music; Riisager, Complete Piano Works; Chamber Music of Beethoven, Brahms, Busoni; Roman Organ and Harpsichord Music from the 17th Century, 1982; Rued Langgaard: Piano Music, 1985; Catalan Organ Music, 1988. *Publications include:* History of the Danish School of Music until 1739, 1973; Roman Organ Music of the 17th Century; Roman Harpsichord Music from the 17th Century; Piano Music of Manuel Blasco de Nebra, 1984; 23 Piano Sonatas by Josep Galles, 1984; Editor: Heptachordum Danicum 1646 (translation, historical comments, source studies), 1977; Hans Mikkelsen Ravn: The Vatican Manuscript, 1981; Selected Sonatas of D Scarlatti including 1st edition of 4 new editions, 1985; Selected Piano Music of N W Gade, 1986; Catalan Organ Music of the 18th Century, 1986; Scarlatti Vol. II, 1988, vol. III, 1992; Niels W Gade: Klavierwerke, 1989; Piano Music by Franz Liszt, 1989; Selected Piano Works of Rued Langgaard, 1994. *Honours:* Cross of the Order of Knighthood, Medal of the Sibelius Acad., Helsinki 1976; Bronze Medal Winner, Piano Music of Manuel Blasco de Nebra, International Book Messe, Leipzig 1986. *Address:* Porsevænget 18, Kongens Lyngby, 2800 Copenhagen, Denmark (home). *Telephone:* 44-44-65-14.

**JOHNSSON, Catrin;** Singer (Mezzo-soprano); b. 1973, Sweden. *Education:* Royal University College of Music, Stockholm; Royal Academy of Music with Anne Howells. *Career:* Appearances for Diva Opera in Die Zauberflöte, La Traviata and The Tales of Hoffmann, as Nicklausse (2001); Idelberto in Handel's Lotario, Adalberto in Ottone, Purcell's Dido and Third Boy in Die Zauberflöte; Recitals at Aix-en-Provence and concerts in New Zealand, 1999; Bach's Magnificat in Vienna (2000) and St Matthew Passion for the London Handel Festival, 2001. *Honours:* Christine Nilsson Prize, Royal Academy of Music, Stockholm, 1997; Elena Gerhardt Lieder Prize, RAM, London. *Address:* c/o Royal College of Music, Prince Consort Road, London SW7, England.

**JOHNSTON, Benjamin (Ben) Burwell,** AB, MM, MA; American composer and teacher; b. 15 March 1926, Macon, GA. *Education:* College of William and Mary, Cincinnati Conservatory of Music, Mills College. *Career:* faculty mem., University of Illinois 1951–83. *Compositions:* Concerto for brass, 1951; St Joan, ballet, 1955; Passacaglia and Epilogue for orchestra, 1955–60; Septet for wind quintet, cello and bass, 1956–58; Gambit, ballet, 1959; Knocking Piece for 2 percussionists and piano, 1962; Gertrude, or Would She Be Pleased to Receive It?, opera, 1965; Quintet for groups, 1966; Carmilla, opera, 1970; Trio for clarinet, violin and cello, 1982; The Demon Lover's Doubles for trumpet and microtonal piano, 1985; Symphony, 1988; 10 string quartets, 1959–96; Piano pieces; Choruses; Songs; Sleep and Waking for percussion ensemble, 1994; Quietness, for speaking bass and string quartet, 1996. *Publications:* Maximum Clarity and Other Writings 2005. *Honours:* Guggenheim Fellowship 1959–60. *Address:* 120 Charlotte Street, Rocky Mount, NC 27804-3706, USA. *E-mail:* benbetjo@isp.com.

**JOHNSTONE, Harry (Diack),** BMus, MA, DPhil, FRCO, FTCL, ARCM, FSA; academic (retd); b. 29 April 1935, Vancouver, Canada; m. Jill Margaret Saunders 1960 (died 1989); one s. one d. *Education:* Royal Coll. of Music, London, Balliol Coll., Oxford. *Career:* Asst Organist, New Coll., Oxford 1960–61; Asst Lecturer in Music, Univ. of Reading 1963; Lecturer 1965, Sr Lecturer 1970, Tutorial Fellow in Music, Emeritus Fellow, St Anne's Coll., Oxford; Lecturer in Music, St John's 1980–2000; Visiting Prof. of Music, Memorial Univ., St John's, Newfoundland 1983; Reader in Music, Univ. of Oxford 1998–2000; Gen. Ed., Musica Britannica 2002–. *Publications:* Blackwell History of Music in Britain IV (ed. and co-author), The Eighteenth Century 1990, Maurice Greene: Cambridge Ode and Anthem (ed., Musica Britannica 58) 1991, Greene: Phoebe, a Pastoral Opera (Musica Britannica 82) 2004; numerous edns of 18th century music, mainly English; articles and reviews in The Journal of the Royal Musical Assocn, Notes, RMA Research Chronicle, The Musical Times, Music and Letters, Proceedings of the Royal Musical Association, Early Music, Early Music History, The New Grove, The New Oxford Dictionary of National Biography. *Address:* St Anne's College, University of Oxford, Oxford, OX2 6HS, England. *E-mail:* harry.johnstone@ music.ox.ac.uk (office).

**JOLAS, Betsy;** French composer; b. 5 Aug. 1926, Paris; d. of Eugène and Maria Jolas; m. Gabriel Illouz 1949; two s. one d. *Education:* Bennington Coll. (USA) and Conservatoire Nat Supérieur de Musique (Paris). *Career:* Pianist, organist and chorister Dessoff Choirs, USA; Prof. Conservatoire Nat Supérieur de Musique, Paris 1971–; has taught at Univs of Yale, Berkeley and Southern California, USA; Darius Milhaud Chair., Mills Coll., CA, USA; compositions have been performed by Boston Symphony Chamber Players, London Sinfonietta, Lincoln Center Chamber Music Soc., Ensemble Inter Comtemporain, Groupe Vocal de France, etc; mem. American Acad. of Arts and Letters 1983, American Acad. of Arts and Sciences 1995; Chevalier de l'Ordre Nat du Mérite; Commdr des Arts et des Lettres; other awards include Laureate Int. Orchestra Conducting Competition (Besançon) 1953, Copley Foundation Prize (Chicago, IL, USA) 1954, American Acad. of Arts Prize 1973, Fondation Koussevitsky Prize 1974, Grand Prix Nat de la Musique 1974, Grand Prix de la Ville de Paris 1981, Prix Arthur Honegger 2000. *Recordings of compositions:* D'un opéra de voyage, Episode quatrième, JDE, Points d'Aube, Quatuor II, Quatuor III, Sonate A 12, Stances, Episode huitième, Musique de jour, EA (petite suite variée). *Operas:* Le Pavillon au bord de la Riviere 1976, Le Cyclope 1986, Schliemann; numerous compositions for choirs, solo voices, orchestra, piano, etc. *Address:* c/o Conservatoire National Supérieur de Musique, 209 ave Jean Jaurès, 75019 Paris, France.

**JOLL, Philip;** Singer (Baritone); b. 14 March 1954, Merthyr Tydfil, Wales. *Education:* Studied at the Royal Northern College of Music with Nicholas Powell and Frederick Cox; Further study at the National Opera Studio in London. *Career:* Sang with English National Opera from 1979, as Donner and The Dutchman; Welsh National opera as Wotan (also with the company at Covent Garden, 1986), Kurwenal, Amfortas, Chorebus in The Trojans, The Forester (Cunning Little Vixen), Onegin, Orestes, Don Fernando in Fidelio, Jochanaan in Salome and Barak in Die Frau ohne Schatten; Covent Garden debut, 1982, in Salome, returning in Der Freischütz, Das Rheingold and Die Frau ohne Schatten; German debut, Frankfurt, 1983, as Amfortas, returning for The Dutchman; Guest appearances in Düsseldorf, 1985–86, Berlin and Wiesbaden (with the Welsh National Company in The Midsummer Marriage, 1986); Metropolitan Opera debut, 1988, as Donner in Das Rheingold; Australian debut as Jochanaan, for the Lyric Opera of Queensland, 1988; Bregenz Festival, 1989, in Der fliegende Holländer; Lyric Opera of Queensland, 1989–90, as Jochanaan in Salome and Marcello; Sang Orestes in Elektra and Rigoletto for Welsh National Opera, 1992–97; Season 2000 as Gurlitt's Wozzeck at Turin, Wotan for Seattle Opera and Britten's Balstrode at Amsterdam; Engaged as Wotan in The Ring, Seattle 2000–01. *Recordings include:* The Greek Passion by Martinů; Amfortas in Parsifal; Kurwenal in Tristan and Isolde, conducted by Reginald Goodall. *Address:* c/o IMG Artists, Lovell House, 616 Chiswick High Road, London W4 5RX, England.

**JOLLY, James;** British writer. *Education:* Univ. of Bristol, Univ. of Reading. *Career:* producer, Record Review (BBC Radio 3); Asst Ed. Gramophone –1989, Ed. 1990–2005, Ed.-in-Chief 2006–. *Publications as editor:* The Greatest Classical Recordings of All Time 1995, The Gramophone Opera 75: The 75 Best Opera Recordings of All Time 1997, The Gramophone Opera Good CD Guide 1998, The Gramophone Classical 2001 Good CD Guide (co-ed.) 2002. *Address:* Gramophone, Haymarket Magazines Ltd, PO Box 568, Haywards Heath, Sussex RH16 3XQ, England (office). *Website:* www.gramophone.co.uk.

**JOLY, Simon;** Conductor and Repetiteur; b. 14 Oct. 1952, Exmouth, Devon, England. *Education:* Organ Scholar, Corpus Christi Coll., Cambridge, 1971–74; BA, MA; ARCO. *Career:* music staff, Welsh National Opera, 1974–78; Assoc. Chorus Master, ENO, 1978–80; Asst, then Principal Conductor BBC Singers, 1980–95; conducted opera at ENO, BBC, Wexford Festival, Dublin, Berlin; conducted the Dutch, Irish, Finnish and French Radio Choirs; concerts with the BBC Singers include the Proms; many festivals including Warsaw, 2001; numerous programmes and concerts emphasising 20th Century music; Orchestral work includes concerts and BBC programmes with the BBC Symphony, Philharmonic and Concert Orchestras, National Orchestra of Wales, London Sinfonietta and Endymian Ensemble. *Recordings include:* Choral Works of Peter Maxwell Davies, Granville Bantock. *Address:* 49b Disraeli Road, Putney, London, SW15 2DR, England. *Telephone:* 020 8785 9617. *Fax:* 020 8785 2568. *E-mail:* simonjoly@ toadflax1.demon.co.uk.

**JONAS, Hilda Klestadt;** harpsichordist, pianist and teacher of harpsichord and piano; b. 21 Jan. 1913, Düsseldorf, Germany; m. Gerald Jonas 1938; two d. *Education:* Hochschule für Musik, Cologne, Gumpert Conservatory, studies with Michael Wittels in Cologne, Rudolf Serkin in Switzerland and Wanda Landowska in Paris, France. *Career:* concert soloist and recitalist world-wide, with recitals in France, Germany, Spain, Italy, Austria, Belgium, Australia, New Zealand, Hawaii, USA, at colls, univs, museums and art centres, including Harvard, Carnegie-Mellon, Cincinnati Taft Museum, Haifa Music Museum, Milano Centro Culturale San Fedele, Empire Saal of Schloss Esterházy, Eisenstadt, Brussel's Musée Instrumental, Castello Buonconsiglio, Trento, Palais Wittgenstein, Düsseldorf, Stanford Univ., California, Palace of the Legion of Honour San Francisco, San Francisco State Univ., Goethe Inst., California West Coast, from Olympia Evergreen State Coll. to Santa Barbara, Westmont, Ventura, Monterey Peninsula Colls, Sacramento Crocker Art Museum, Ojai Valley Art Center and other cultural centres in Marin County and San Francisco; soloist with major symphony orchestras, including Cleveland, Cincinnati; regular series and May festivals under Max Rudolf and Josef Krips, Honolulu, Oxford, Jerusalem, Strasbourg and elsewhere; owner of private piano studio, Honolulu 1938–42, and Cincinnati 1942–75; founder 1965, Dir 1965–75, Harpsichord Festival Put-in-Bay, OH; mem. Hadassah, Brandeis Univ. *Recordings include:* Listen Rebecca, The Harpsichord Sounds, for children of all ages; Johann Kuhnau: Six Biblical Sonatas, with text based on authentic edition; Hilda Plays Bach: Italian Concerto, Chromatic Fantasia and Fugue, Partita 1, Capriccio on the Departure of his Beloved Brother, and others; Johann Sebastian Bach: Goldberg Variations. *Publications:* contrib. to various music magazines. *Address:* 50 Chumasero Drive 1-L, San Francisco, CA 94132, USA. *Website:* www.hildajonas.com.

**JONAS, Sir Peter,** Kt, CBE, BA, LRAM, FRCM, FRNCM, FRSA; British arts administrator and opera company director; *Staatsintendant, Bavarian State Opera;* b. 14 Oct. 1946, London; s. of Walter Adolf and Hilda May Jonas; m. Lucy Hull 1989 (divorced 2001). *Education:* Worth School, Univ. of Sussex, Royal Northern Coll. of Music, Manchester, Royal Coll. of Music, London, Eastman School of Music, Univ. of Rochester, USA. *Career:* Asst to Music Dir, Chicago Symphony Orchestra 1974–76, Artistic Admin. 1976–85; Dir of Artistic Admin., The Orchestral Asscn, Chicago 1977–85; Gen. Dir English Nat. Opera 1985–93; Staatsintendant (Gen. and Artistic Dir) Bavarian State Opera, Munich 1993–2006; mem. Bd of Man. Nat. Opera Studio 1985–93; mem. Council Royal Coll. of Music 1988–95; mem. Council of Man., London Lighthouse 1990–92; mem. Kuratorium Richard Strauss Gesellschaft 1993–; mem. Advisory Bd Bayerische Vereinsbank 1994–2004; mem. Rundfunkrat, Bayerische Rundfunk 1999–, Athenaeum; Queen's Lecture, Berlin 2001; Visiting Lecturer, St Gallen Univ. 2003–, Univ. of Zurich 2004–. *Publications:* Powerhouse (with M. Elder and D. Pountney) 1993, Eliten und Demokratie 1999. *Honours:* Bayerische Verdienstorden (Germany) 2001; Hon. DMus (Sussex) 1993; Bavarian Constitutional Medal 2001, City of Munich Kulture-llen Ehrenpreis 2003. *Address:* c/o Bayerische Staatsoper, Nationaltheater, Max-Joseph-Platz 2, 80539 Munich; Fundsbergstrass 13, 80634 Munich, Germany (home). *Telephone:* (89) 2185-1001 (office); (89) 2185-1000 (home). *Fax:* (89) 2185-1003 (office). *E-mail:* peter.jonas@st-oper.bayern.de (office); sirpeterjonas@t-online.de (home).

**JONES, Bryn Terfel** (see TERFEL (JONES), Bryn)

**JONES, Della;** Singer (Mezzo-soprano); b. 13 April 1946, Neath, Wales. *Education:* Royal College of Music, London, and Centre Lyrique Music School, Geneva. *Career:* Sang first at Grand Théâtre, Geneva; Member of English National Opera, 1977–82, in La Gazza Ladra, Il Barbiere di Siviglia, La Cenerentola, Le Comte Ory, Figaro, Giulio Cesare, Orfeo, Carmen, L'Incoronazione di Poppea and La Forza del Destino; Appearances with Welsh National Opera in Les Troyens, Salome, Barbiere di Siviglia and Tristan und Isolde; Scottish Opera in L'Egisto, Hansel and Gretel and Don Giovanni; Opera North as Rosina and in La Cenerentola, Le Comte Ory, Die Meistersinger, Oedipus Rex and Salome; Other engagements with English Music Theatre (world premiere of Tom Jones by Stephen Oliver and The Threepenny Opera), Dublin Opera and Handel Opera Society; Baba the Turk in The Rake's Progress in Geneva and Venice; Ruggiero in Alcina for Los Angeles Opera; Sang Cecilio in Lucio Silla, also La Finta Giardiniera for Mostly Mozart Festival, New York; Other festivals in London (English Bach), Cheltenham, Aldeburgh, Chester, Salisbury, Athens, Orange, throughout France, Switzerland and Edinburgh; Sang Preziosilla in Forza del Destino for Scottish Opera, 1990; Ruggiero in Alcina at Geneva and Théâtre du Châtelet, Paris; Mrs Noye in Noyes Fludde at 1990 Promenade concerts, Hermia in Midsummer Night's Dream at Sadler's Wells, many other Prom appearances including Last Night, 1993; Marchesa Melibea at Covent Garden, 1992 (Il Viaggio a Reims); Sang Gluck's Armide at the Baroque Festival Versailles, 1992 and Clytemnestra in Iphigénie en Aulide for Opera North, 1996; Welsh National Opera, 1994, as Ariodante; Sang Rossini's Isabella for English National Opera, 1997; Aunt Hermance in the premiere of Dr Ox's Experiment, ENO, 1998; Sang Mozart's Marcellina at the Opéra Bastille, Paris, 2002; Concerts and recitals in USSR, USA, Europe and Japan. *Recordings include:* Haydn L'Incontro Improvviso and Il Ritorno di Tobia, conductor Dorati; Alcina, conductor Hickox; Marcellina in Figaro and Elvira in Don Giovanni, conductor Arnold Östmann; Donizetti L'Assedio di Calais; L'Incoronazione di Poppea; Rossini Stabat Mater and Arias, Bliss Pastoral, conductor Hickox; Recital of French Songs with Malcolm Martineau; The Bear by Walton; Dido in Dido and Aeneas; Video of ENO production of Giulio Cesare.

**JONES, Gareth;** Conductor; b. 1960, Port Talbot, Wales. *Education:* Studied at the Royal Northern College of Music with Gunther Herbig. *Career:* Assistant Conductor with Opera North; Associate with D'Oyly Carte Opera, from 1988; Welsh National Opera, 1990–98, with Nabucco, The Barber of Seville, Ernani, Faust, Fidelio and Un Ballo in Maschera; The Carmelites, 1999; Founder of the Cardiff Bay Chamber Orchestra, 1996, and concerts with the Scottish Chamber Orchestra at Edinburgh including Handel's L'Allegro and Purcell's Dido; Australian Chamber Orchestra at the Adelaide Festival; Season 1998–99 with the Royal Liverpool Philharmonic. *Address:* c/o Harlequin Agency Ltd, 203 Fidles Road, Cardiff CF4 5NA, Wales.

**JONES, Gordon;** Singer (Bass-baritone); b. 1960, Northampton, England. *Education:* Studied at York University; Choral Scholarship to York Minster. *Career:* Concert engagements include visits to the Lincoln Center in New York, the Royal Palace in The Hague, Hallé Orchestra, Martin's Le Vin Herbé at the Siena Festival and The Fairy Queen on tour in Italy; Performances of Berio's Sinfonia conducted by the composer, Simon Rattle and Esa-Pekka

Salonen; Bach's St John and St Matthew Passions with the Choir of King's College, Cambridge; Sang in Arvo Pärt's St John Passion at the 1986 Almeida Festival and on tour of the United Kingdom, 1988; Further engagements in Bristol and Aberdeen and at the Malvern and Aix-en-Provence Festivals; Bach's St John Passion with The Sixteen on tour in Spain. *Recordings:* Vièrne's Les Angelus; Lully's Idylle pour la Paix, BBC; Schütz Schwanengesang and Bach Motets with the Hilliard Ensemble; Pärt St John Passion.

**JONES, Gwyn Hughes;** Singer (Tenor); b. 1968, Llanbedrgoch, Wales. *Education:* Studied at the Guildhall and National Opera Studio, London. *Career:* Engagements with Welsh National Opera as Ismaele in Nabucco, 1995; The Duke of Mantua, Don Ottavio, Rodolfo in La Bohème; Rinuccio in Gianni Schicchi for English National Opera; Season 1999–2000 with Fenton in Falstaff at Brussels and Chicago, Ismaele for San Francisco Opera; concerts include Mozart's C Minor Mass with the London Symphony Orchestra; Verdi Requiem; Mendelssohn's Elijah; West Coast of USA tour with Orchestra of Royal Opera House, 1999; Sang Elektra at the Deutsche Oper Berlin, 1999. *Honours:* Winner, Neue Stimmen Competition, Gutersloh, 1995. *Address:* Harlequin Agency Ltd, 203 Fidlas Road, Cardiff CF14 5NA, Wales.

**JONES, Dame Gwyneth,** DBE, FRCM; British singer (soprano); b. 7 Nov. 1936, Pontnewynydd, Mon., Wales; d. of the late Edward George Jones and Violet Webster; one d. *Education:* Royal Coll. of Music, London, Accad. Chigiana, Siena, Zürich Int. Opera Centre. *Career:* with Zürich Opera House 1962–63; a Prin. Dramatic Soprano, Royal Opera House, Covent Garden 1963–; with Vienna State Opera House 1966–, Deutsche Oper Berlin 1966–, Bavarian State Opera 1967–; guest performances in numerous opera houses throughout the world including La Scala, Milan, Rome Opera, Berlin State Opera, Munich State Opera, Hamburg, Paris, Metropolitan Opera, New York, San Francisco, Los Angeles, Zürich, Geneva, Dallas, Chicago, Teatro Colón, Buenos Aires, Tokyo, Beijing, Hong Kong, Seoul, Bayreuth Festival, Salzburg Festival, Arena di Verona, Edin. Festival and Welsh Nat. Opera; known for many opera roles including Leonora, Il Trovatore, Desdemona, Otello, Aida, Aida, Leonore, Fidelio, Senta, The Flying Dutchman, Medea, Medea (Cherubini), Sieglinde, Die Walküre, Lady Macbeth, Macbeth, Elizabeth, Don Carlos, Madame Butterfly, Tosca, Donna Anna, Don Giovanni, Salome, Kundry, Parsifal and Isolde, Tristan und Isolde, Helena, Aegyptische Helena (R. Strauss), Färberin, Frau ohne Schatten, Elektra, Elektra (R. Strauss), Elizabeth/Venus, Tannhäuser, Marschallin, Der Rosenkavalier, Brünnhilde, Der Ring des Nibelungen, Ortrud, Lohengrin, Minnie, Fanciulla del West, Norma (Bellini), Erwartung (Schoenberg), La voix humaine (Poulenc), Kabanicha, Katia Kabanowa (Janacek), Kostelnicka Küstern, Jenůfa (Janacek); Pres. Richard Wagner Soc., London 1990; masterclasses in UK, Germany, France, Netherlands, Canada and Switzerland; debut as Stage Dir with new production of Der Fliegende Holländer by Richard Wagner at Deutsches Nat. Theater, Weimar; recordings for Decca, DGG, Philips, Chandos, EMI, CBS; Fellow, Royal Welsh Coll. of Music and Drama 1992. *Television films:* Fidelio, Aida, Flying Dutchman, Leonore, Beethoven 9th Symphony, Elisabeth and Venus in Tannhäuser, Poppea (Monteverdi), Rosenkavalier (R. Strauss), Die Walküre, Siegfried, Götterdämmerung, Die lustige Witwe, Don Carlos, Tristan und Isolde. *Honours:* Kammersängerin in Austria and Bavaria; Hon. mem. RAM 1980, Vienna State Opera 1989; Bundesverdienstkreuz (FRG) 1988, Commdr des Arts et Lettres (France) 1993, Österreichische Ehren Kreuz für Wissenschaft und Kunst, 1. Klasse 1998; Hon. DMus (Glamorgan) 1995, (Wales) 1998; Shakespeare Prize, Hamburg 1987, Golden Medal of Honour, Vienna 1991, Premio Pucci Award Torre del Lago 2003, Cymry for the World Honour, Wales Millennium Centre, Cardiff 2004. *Address:* PO Box 2000, 8700 Küsnacht, Switzerland.

**JONES, Ieuan;** Harpist; b. 1955, Wales. *Education:* Royal College of Music, with Marisa Robles. *Career:* Appearances, the United Kingdom, Dutch and Italian television; Soloist, London Rodrigo Festival, 1986; Soloist, Mozart Concerto for Flute and Harp, Bournemouth Sinfonietta, 1986; Invited performer, World Harp Congress, Vienna, 1987; Recitals, Spain, North America; Featured, premiere of Alan Hoddinott's Tarantella for Harp and Orchestra, St David's Day Concert, Cardiff, 1988; Mozart and Daniel Jones Concertos, Flute and Harp, Swansea, Aberystwyth, 1988; Replaced Marisa Robles, Mozart Flute and Harp Concerto, Debussy's Danses Sacrées et Profanes, Margam Festival, Swansea, 1988; USA Miami recital, North Wales tour; Promotional video, Welsh Development Board, 1990; Brussels, Mozart Concert Recordings release, 1990; Premiere, Rodrigo Concierto, Wales, 1991; Guest soloist of Enrique Batiz and the State Orchestra of Mexico, 1992; Soloist, Rodrigo Homage Concert, Seville EXPO celebrations, 1992; Welsh premiere of Sonata for Harp by William Mathias (dedicated to Ieuan Jones), at 1993 Machynlleth Festival. *Recordings:* The Uncommon Harp, selection of light classics and ballads, 1987; 2 Sides of Ieuan Jones 1988;. . . In The French Style, 1990; Mozart in Paris, 1990; All Through The Night, with Huw Rhys-Evans (tenor). *Honours:* All major prizes including Tagore Gold Medal and 1st-time award from HM the Queen Mother, Royal College of Music; All honours including overall Gold Medal, Royal Overseas League Music Competition; Joint winner, Israel International Harp Contest. *Current Management:* Neil Chaffey Concert Promotions, 8 Laxton Gardens, Baldock, Hertfordshire SG7 5DA, England.

**JONES, Isola;** Musician and Singer (Mezzo-soprano); b. 27 Dec. 1949, Chicago, Illinois, USA; m. Russell Thomas Cormier, 31 Mar 1984. *Education:* BA, Musical Education, Northwestern University, 1971. *Career:* Debut: Olga in Eugene Onegin, Metropolitan Opera, 15 Oct 1977; Live From the Met television series; Maddalena in Rigoletto, 1977, 1981; Lola in Cavalleria Rusticana, 1978; Girl in Mahagonny, 1979; Madrigal in Manon Lescaut, 1980; Recital with Placido Domingo, 1982; The Met Centennial Gala, 1983; Preziosilla in La Forza del Destino, 1984; Smaragdi in Francesca da Rimini; Spoleto Festival, 1989, as Giulietta in Les Contes d'Hoffmann. *Recordings:* Porgy and Bess, with Cleveland Orchestra conducted by Lorin Maazel; Flying Dutchman, with Chicago Symphony conducted by Georg Solti; Les Noces, with Chicago Symphony conducted by James Levine; Cavalleria Rusticana, with New Philharmonic Orchestra conducted by James Levine. *Honours:* Merit Award, Northwestern University, 1984. *Current Management:* Robert Lombardo Associates.

**JONES, Jonathan Hellyer,** MA, FRCO, ARCM ; British teacher and organist; b. 1 June 1951, Warwickshire, England. *Education:* Oakham School, Rutland, Royal Coll. of Music, St John's Coll., Cambridge. *Career:* taught at Perse School, Cambridge 1974–82, Anglia Polytechnic Univ. 1979–, Cambridge Univ. 1995–, Guildhall School of Music and Drama 1979, St John's Coll. School, Cambridge 1974–80; Fellow, Hughes Hall, Cambridge 2000–02; Fellow, Precentor and Organist, Magdalene Coll., Cambridge 2002–. *Recordings:* The Muse Delight'd 1981, The Organ in the Age of Reason 1983, Principia Musica 1988, Rare Baroque Flute Concertos 1991, Brandenburg Concertos 1998. *Honours:* Brian Runnett Prize (organ playing Cambridge Univ.) 1973, John Stewart of Rannoch Scholarship in Sacred Music (Cambridge Univ.) 1972. *Current Management:* Neil Chaffey Concert Promotions, 9 Munts Meadow, Weston, Herts SG4 7AE, England. *Telephone:* (1462) 790919 (office). *Fax:* (1462) 790920 (office). *Website:* www.cambridgebaroquecamerata .com.

**JONES, Karen;** Concert Flautist; b. 8 July 1965, Hampton, Middlesex, England. *Education:* Studied at the Guildhall School, in Vienna with Wolfgang Schulz and in New York. *Career:* Played the Ibert Concerto with the London Symphony Orchestra, 1985; Concerto performances with Neville Marriner at the Queen Elizabeth Hall, Andrew Litton at the Festival Hall and George Malcolm at the Snape Concert Hall; Further engagements with the Ulster Orchestra, the Philharmonia, the Wren Orchestra and London Musici; Solo recitals at the Purcell Room and Wigmore Hall; Member of the Pears-Britten Ensemble with performances in the United Kingdom and the USA; Guest Principal with the Australian Chamber Orchestra at the 1992 Promenade Concerts. *Recordings include:* Arnold's Concerto No. 1 and Panufnik's Hommage à Chopin; Malcolm Arnold Flute Concerto No. 2; The Flute Album–Karen Jones. *Honours:* Winner, Woodwind Section, BBC television Young Musician of the Year, 1982; Gold Medal of The Shell, London Symphony Orchestra Scholarship, 1985. *Current Management:* Owen/White Management. *Address:* c/o Owen/White Management, 14 Nightingale Lane, London N8 7QU, England.

**JONES, Leah-Marian;** Singer (Mezzo-soprano); b. 1964, Wales. *Education:* Studied at the Royal Northern College of Music and the National Opera Studio. *Career:* Appearances with the Royal Opera at Covent Garden as Mercédès (Carmen), Zulma (L'Italiana in Algeri), Flosshilde (Rheingold), Second Lady (Die Zauberflöte), Emilia (Otello), Rosette (Manon), Flora (La Traviata), Annina (Der Rosenkavalier), Dorotea (Stiffelio), Elena (Aroldo), Flosshilde (Götterdämmerung); Season 1995/96 with Welsh National Opera as Lola in Cavalleria Rusticana; Other roles include Maddalena, Carmen, Siebel, Isolier (Comte Ory) Adalgisa (Norma); Season 1996 with Royal Opera as Fenena (Nabucco) and Dorabella and Carmen for English National Opera; Sang Laura in Luisa Miller for the Royal Opera at Edinburgh, 1998; Season 2000–01 as Tisbe in La Cenerentola and Emilia in Otello, at Covent Garden; Flowermaiden in Parsifal at Covent Garden, 2002. *Recordings:* Solo CD: Intermezzo. *Address:* Harlequin Agency 203 Fidlas Road, Cardiff, CF4 5NA, Wales.

**JONES, Martin;** Concert Pianist; b. 4 Feb. 1940, England. *Education:* Studied in London. *Career:* Debut: Played at the Queen Elizabeth Hall, London, and Carnegie Hall, 1968; Regular appearances with major British orchestras at the Festival Hall, the Barbican and other venues; Tour of Canada with the BBC National Orchestra of Wales and recitals in Florida, Tennessee and California; Broadcasts in Britain, Ireland and the USA; Pianist-in-Residence at University College, Cardiff, 1971–88; Brahms recital at the Wigmore Hall, 1993; Repertoire includes many standard concertos and also those by Busoni, Benjamin, Barber, Mathias, McCabe, Lambert and Scharwenka; Played Grainger's Bridal Lullaby and Mock Morris on the soundtrack of the film Howard's End. *Recordings:* Extensively for Nimbus Records. *Address:* c/o Owen/White Management, 14 Nightingale Lane, London N8 7QU, England.

**JONES, Maureen;** Pianist; b. 1940, Australia. *Education:* Studied at the New South Wales Conservatorium, Sydney. *Career:* Formed Trio with Breton Langbein and Barry Tuckwell and gave the premiere of the Horn Trio by Don Banks at the 1962 Edinburgh Festival; Regular tours of Australia and Europe, including recent appearances in Dublin, Siena, Innsbruck, Paris, Sydney and Melbourne; Duo recitals with Barry Tuckwell; Concert debut playing Beethoven's 1st Concerto with the Sydney Symphony; Appearances at the Edinburgh Festival include concerts with the Berlin Philharmonic. *Address:* c/o Barry Tuckwell, Northern Sinfonia, Sinfonia Centre, 41 Jesmond Vale, Newcastle, NE1 1PG, England.

**JONES, Nerys;** Singer (Mezzo-Soprano); b. 1965, Wales. *Education:* Studied at the Royal Scottish Academy, RSAMD, and at the Guildhall School; Further study with David Pollard. *Career:* Debut: Karolka in Jenůfa for Scottish Opera; Appearances with Scottish Opera as Marzelline in Fidelio and Welsh National as Norina in Don Pasquale; English National Opera debut as Melissa in Ken Russell's production of Princess Ida, 1992; Further roles with ENO (Principal from 1994) include Cherubino, Despina, Zerlina, Proserpina (Orfeo), Mercédès (Carmen), Rosette (Manon), Flora (Traviata), Hansel, Flower Maiden (Parsifal), Sister Mathilde (Dialogues des Carmélites); Sang in the premiere of Blond Eckbert by Judith Weir, 1994; Cherubino at Grange Park Opera, and Kitchen Boy in Rusalka for ENO, 1998; Sang Rosina for Grange Park Opera, 1999; Sang Lisette in Haydn's Il mondo della luna, Garsington Opera, 2000; Dorabella in Così fan tutte, Grange Park Opera, 2001; Other roles include Flight (Jonathan Dove) for Reims Opera, 2001 and Antwerp, 2002; Many concert engagements. *Recordings:* CD Blond Eckbert. *Honours:* Peter Morrison Prize at the Royal Scottish Academy; John Noble Bursary. *Current Management:* Musichall. *Address:* Musichall, Vicarage Way, Ringmer, East Sussex, BN8 5 LA, England.

**JONES, Paul Carey;** Singer (Baritone); b. 1965, Cardiff, Wales. *Education:* Queen's College Oxford; Royal Academy of Music, with Mark Wildman and Julius Drake. *Career:* Appearances as Mozart's Figaro, Marcello and Schaunard in La Bohème, Enby in Purcell's The Indian Queen and Ariodates in Handel's Xerxes; Eleven baritone roles in Stephen Oliver's A Man of Feeling; Concerts recitals and broadcasts throughout the United Kingdom; Season 2001–2002 with Purcell's The Fairy Queen at the Linbury Theatre, Covent Garden, National Eisteddfod in Wales and St David's Hall, Cardiff. *Honours:* Hubert Kiver Prize, Royal Academy. *Address:* c/o English Bach Festival, Linbury Theatre, Royal Opera House, London WC2, England.

**JONES, Richard;** British producer; b. 7 June 1953, Lambeth, London, England. *Education:* Univs of Hull and London. *Career:* debut, A Water Bird Talk by Dominick Argento for Scottish Opera 1982; has directed for theatre and for opera companies; Musica nel Chiostro, Battingano (Mozart's Apollo et Hyacinthus 1984); Salieri's La Grotta di Trofonio and Paisiello's Il re Teodoro in Venezia, 1985; Opera Northern Ireland (Don Pasquale 1985); Wexford Festival (Mignon 1986); Cambridge Univ. Opera (The Magic Flute 1986); Opera 80 (The Rake's Progress 1986, Rigoletto 1987); Opera North (Manon 1987, Carmen and The Love for Three Oranges 1987); Scottish Opera-Go-Round (Macbeth and Die Entführung 1987); Scottish Opera (Das Rheingold 1989); Kent Opera (Le Comte Ory and A Night at the Chinese Opera 1988); The Love for Three Oranges and David Blake's The Plumber's Gift, world premiere for ENO 1989; Bregenz Festival, Austria (Mazeppa 1991); Netherlands Opera (The Flying Dutchman 1993); Bavarian State Opera (Julius Caesar 1994); Royal Opera House (Das Rheingold and Die Walküre 1994, Siegfried and Götterdämmerung 1995); Netherlands Opera (Mazeppa 1991); ENO (Die Fledermaus 1991); Scottish Opera (Die Walküre 1991); The Midsummer Marriage at Munich 1998; production of the Trojans for ENO 2003, Les Troyens for ENO 2003; Lady Macbeth of Mtsensk (Olivier Award for Best New Opera Production 2005) 2004. *Honours:* Laurence Olivier Award for Best Newcomer in Theatre 1988, Evening Standard Drama Award for Best Director 1990. *Address:* c/o English National Opera, London Coliseum, St Martin's Lane, Trafalgar Square, London, WC2, England.

**JONES, Roland Leo,** BMus; American violinist, violist and music teacher; b. 16 Dec. 1932, Ann Arbor, MI. *Education:* University of Michigan, Columbia University, National Orchestra Association Training Orchestra, Interlochen Music Camp, Meadowmount Music School and Tanglewood Music School. *Career:* soloist with Ann Arbor Civic Symphony, 1951, 1953; Violinist, Denver Symphony Orchestra, 1960–75; Jackson Hole, Wyoming Fine Arts Festival, 1964–65; Tours throughout USA and Canada; Founder, 1st Violinist, Highland Chamber Players, 1978–79; 1st Violinist, Highland String Quartet, 1979–2002; Tour with Denver Chamber Orchestra and San Francisco Opera, Western Opera Theater, 1987; Joined Musica Sacra Chamber Orchestra, Denver, Colorado, 2000; Toured Austria, Hungary and Italy, 2000. *Compositions:* New Cadenzas for all the Mozart Violin Concertos 1991, Two Cadenzas for the Telemann Concerto in G 2004. *Recordings:* with orchestra, Milena by Alberto Ginastera and Concertos No. 2 of Chopin. *Publications:* New Cadenzas for all the Mozart Violin Concertos 1992, 2003. *Address:* 3004 S Kearney, Denver, CO 80222, USA.

**JONES, Samuel;** Composer, Conductor and Educator; b. 2 June 1935, Inverness, Mississippi, USA; m. (1) 2 d., (2) Kristin Barbara Schutte, 22 Dec 1975. *Education:* BA, Millsaps College, 1957; MA, PhD, Eastman School of Music, University of Rochester, 1958–60. *Career:* Director of Instrumental Music, Alma College, Michigan, 1960–62; Music Director, Saginaw Symphony, 1962–65; Conductor, Rochester Philharmonic, 1965–73; Founding Dean, Shepherd School of Music, 1973–79; Professor of Conducting and Composition, Rice University, 1973–97; Composer in Residence, Seattle Symphony Orchestra, 1997–; Guest Conductor, Buffalo Philharmonic Symphonies of Detroit, Pittsburgh, Houston, Prague and Iceland. *Compositions:* In Retrospect; Symphony No. 1 (recorded); Elegy for String Orchestra (recorded); Overture for a City; Let Us Now Praise Famous Men (recorded); Spaces; Contours of Time; Fanfare and Celebration; A Christmas Memory; A Symphonic Requiem; Variations on a Theme of Howard Hanson; The Trumpet of the Swan; Listen Now, My Children (recorded); Two Movements for Harpsichord; Canticles of Time, Symphony No. 2; Symphony No. 3 (Palo Duro Canyon), 1992; The Seas of God, 1992; The Temptation of Jesus (oratorio), 1995; Janus, 1998; Roundings, 1999; Aurum Aurorae, 2001; Eudora's Fable (The Shoe Bird), 2002. *Recordings:* Symphony No. 3 recorded by Amarillo

Symphony; Let Us Now Praise Famous Men and Elegy recorded by Houston Symphony; Roundings recorded by Amarillo Symphony (with Cello Sonata); Piano Sonata recorded by John Perry; Two Movements for Hapischord recorded by Barbara Harbach. *Current Management:* Carl Fischer Inc. *Address:* 35247 34th Avenue S, Auburn, WA 98001, USA.

**JONES, Warren;** Vocal Coach and Accompanist; b. 11 Dec. 1951, Washington, District of Columbia, USA. *Education:* BM, New England Conservatory of Music, 1973; MM, San Francisco Conservatory of Music, 1977. *Career:* Accompanist to Luciano Pavarotti, Marilyn Horne, Frederica von Stade, Judith Blegen, Håkan Hagegård, Elisabeth Söderström, Martti Talvela, Carol Vaness, Lynn Harrell, Thomas Allen, Roberta Peters, Robert Alexander and Samuel Ramey; Appearances at Tanglewood, Ravinia, Caramoor and Salzburg Festivals; Assistant Conductor, Metropolitan Opera, San Francisco Opera; Classes at Harvard, San Francisco Conservatory of Music, Hartt School of Music, California State University; mem, Lifetime Member, Pi Kappa Lambda. *Address:* 711 West End Avenue, Apartment 6JN, New York, NY 10025, USA.

**JOOS, Martina;** Recorder Player; b. 15 Feb. 1972, Glarus, Switzerland. *Education:* Studied at the Hochschule für Musik und Theater in Zürich, Switzerland, with Kees Boeke and Matthias Weilenmann. *Career:* Member of 'Trio O'Henry' together with Claudia Gerauer and Barbara Nägele; Appearances (among others) at Bludenzer Tage für Zeitgemässe Musik, Austria, 1997; Festival of Ancient Music, Stary Sacz, Poland, 2000; Festival Musica Nova, Sofia, Bulgaria, 2001; Festival Bohemia-Saxony, Czech Republic, 2001; Cycle of premieres with works of Swiss composers, Zürich, 2000–01; Radio appearances (live recordings): St Peter's Church, Zürich, 1996; Great Hall of the HFMT, Zürich; Radio features: Austrian Radio ORF 1, 1998; Swiss Radio DRS 2, 2000; Bulgarian radio and television, Sofia, 2001; Premieres: Kees Boeke's The Unfolding, 1997; Martin Derungs's A Set of Pieces, 2000; Thomas Müller's Erste Etappe in Richtung farbiger Eindrücke, 2000; Giorgio Tedde's Medio Aevo, 2000; Andreas Nick's Trio pour flûtes à bec, 2000. *Address:* Hanfrose 19, CH 8055 Zürich, Switzerland.

**JORDAN, Armin (Georg);** Conductor; b. 9 April 1932, Lucerne, Switzerland; m. Kate Herkner, 1 s., 1 d. *Education:* University of Fribourg; Conservatoire de Lausanne (degrees in piano teaching and conducting). *Career:* Debut: Bienne Opera, 1957; Chief Conductor in Biene, 1961–63; First Conductor, Zürich Opera, 1963–71; Music Director, Basle Opera from 1971; Music Director, Orchestre de Chambre de Lausanne, 1973–85; Music Director, Orchestre de la Suisse Romande from 1985; Principal Guest Conductor, Ensemble Orchestral de Paris from 1986; Conducted Massenet's Manon at the Geneva Opera, 1989; Numerous appearances on television and radio in various countries; International career from 1963; Guest conductor at the Lyon, Vienna, Munich, Hamburg, Geneva, Brussels and Seattle Operas; Paris, Orchestre National de France and Nouvel Orchestre Philharmonique; Season 1991/92 with Die Fledermaus at Geneva and Don Giovanni at Aix-en-Provence; Led Parsifal at the Opéra Bastille, Paris, 1997; Tristan and Isolde at Seattle, 1998; Siegfried at Geneva, 2001; Engaged for the Ring at Seattle, 2001. *Recordings:* Actor and Conductor in Syberberg's film of Parsifal; Orchestral works by Dukas, Mozart, Dvořák, Ravel, Chausson, Schubert, Chopin and Franck; Mozart Violin Concertos, with Franco Gulli. *Honours:* Grand Prix, Académie Charles Cros, 1985; Cecilia Award, Belgium, 1985; Académie du Disque Lyrique, Paris, 1987; Prix de la Critique Internationale, 1987; Prix Académie du Disque Français, 1988. *Address:* Bunishoferstrasse 234, 8706 Feldmeilen (ZH), Switzerland.

**JORDAN, Irene;** Singer (Soprano); b. 25 April 1919, Birmingham, Alabama, USA. *Education:* Studied at Judson College, Alabama, and with Clyrie Mundy in New York. *Career:* Sang first as mezzo-soprano (Mallika in Lakmé at the Metropolitan, 1946), and after further study sang Donna Anna and Micaela at the Chicago Lyric Theatre, 1954; Appeared at the New York City Opera and the Metropolitan (the Queen of Night) in 1957; Elsewhere in America she sang Verdi's Aida and Lady Macbeth, Madama Butterfly, Weber's Euryanthe, Mozart's Vitellia (La Clemenza di Tito) and Leonore in Fidelio. *Recordings include:* Stravinsky's Pulcinella, conducted by the composer, and songs by Schoenberg.

**JORDAN, Philippe Dominique;** Swiss conductor; b. 18 Oct. 1974, Zürich. *Education:* studied piano, singing and violin, Konservatorium, Zürich with Boris Mersson, Karl Engel and Hans Ulrich Lehmann; *Career:* Asst to Jeffrey Tate, Théâtre du Châtelet in Paris and Festival of Aix-en-Provence; Theatre in Ulm; Opera Ireland, Dublin; Aalto-Theater Essen, Théâtre de la Monnie, Brussels; Kapellmeister and Asst to Daniel Barenboim, Staatsoper Unter den Linden in Berlin, opening with D. Milhaud's Christophe Colomb with Peter Greenaway, Teatro dell'Opera in Rome, Grand Théâtre Genève, Wiener Staatsoper, Théâtre du Châtelet Paris, Semperoper Dresden, Opéra National de Lyon, Festival d'Aix-en Provence, Salzburger Festspiele; Houston Grand Opera; Glyndebourne Festival; ROH; Metropolitan Opera NY; Metropolitan Opera; Royal Opera House Covent Garden; Opera Bastille; Berlin Philharmonic Orchestra; Philharmonic Orchestra; Orchestre Philharmonique de Radio France; Chamber Orchestra of Europe; Gen. Music Dir, Oper Graz 2001–04; Prin. Guest Conductor Staatsoper Unter den Linden 2005–. *Address:* c/o Staatsoper Unter den Linden, Unter den Linden 7, 10117 Berlin, Germany (office); Grieskai 2, 8020 Graz, Austria. *Website:* www.staatsoper -berlin.org.

**JORGENSEN, Jerilyn;** Violinist; b. 1960, New York, USA. *Education:* Studied at the Juilliard School with Joseph Fuchs. *Career:* Soloist with several orchestras in the Brahms and Tchaikovsky Concertos; Further study with members of the Juilliard Quartet and Co-founded the Da Vinci Quartet, 1980, under the sponsorship of the Fine Arts Quartet; Many concerts in the USA and elsewhere in the repertoire including works by Mozart, Beethoven, Brahms, Dvořák, Shostakovich and Bartók. *Honours:* With the Da Vinci Quartet: Awards and grants from the NEA, the Western States Arts Foundation and the Colorado Council for the Humanities; Artist in Residence at the University of Colorado. *Address:* 11 Northpark Street, Glasgow G20 7AA, Scotland.

**JOSEFOWICZ, Leila;** American violinist; b. 1978. *Career:* engagements with the Chicago Symphony Orchestra (Tchaikovsky Concerto, Philadelphia Orchestra under Sawallisch, Los Angeles Philharmonic and London Philharmonic with Franz Welser-Möst; Carnegie Hall debut with the Acad. of St Martin in the Fields under Neville Marriner 1994; returned to New York, with the Boston Symphony and Seiji Ozawa 1996; season 1996–97 with the Bamberg Symphony, the Rotterdam Philharmonic under Gergiev, the Danish Radio Symphony Orchestra, Monte Carlo Orchestra, Dallas Symphony Orchestra; tour of USA with Neville Marriner and Mendelssohn's Concerto at the London Proms 1997; season 1997–98 with Sydney Symphony Orchestra, Swedish RSO, tour of Germany with Neville Marriner and ASMF, Orchestre Nat. de France/Dutoit, Budapest Festival Orchestra, Finnish RSO; season 2003–04 soloist at Last Night of the Proms, London 2003; concerts with Hessischer Rundfunk, 2003, with the Oslo Philharmonic for Norwegian premiere of Knussen Violin Concerto 2004. *Recordings include:* Tchaikovsky and Sibelius Concertos with the Academy of St Martin in the Fields, Bartók's Solo Sonata and pieces by Paganini, Ysaÿe, Kriesler and Ernst, Bohemian Rhapsodies with Marriner/ASMF. *Current Management:* Harrison Parrott Ltd, 12 Penzance Place, London, W11 4PA, England.

**JOSELSON, Rachel;** Singer (Mezzo-soprano); b. 16 Sept. 1955, Englewood, New Jersey, USA. *Education:* Studied at Florida State and Indiana Universities, 1971–70; Further study with Mario del Monaco at Treviso. *Career:* Sang at Darmstadt Opera, 1982–84; Hamburg from 1984; Roles have included Mozart's Idamante, Cherubino and Dorabella, Gluck's Orpheus, and Siebel in Faust; Soprano roles include Mimi, Micaela, Eva in Die Meistersinger, Elisabeth de Valois and Gounod's Mireille; Debussy's Mélisande at Essen, 1990; Guest appearances at Berlin, Brussels, Barcelona and Atlanta; Frequent concert appearances. *Address:* Essen Opera, Rolandstrasse 10, 4300 Essen 1, Germany.

**JOSEPH, David (Robin);** Composer; b. 27 Jan. 1954, Melbourne, Victoria, Australia. *Education:* BMus (Hons), University of Melbourne, 1979. *Career:* Adelaide Chamber Orchestra, 1986–87; Tutor, University of Melbourne, 1993–95; Commissions from Kammermusiker Zürich, Adelaide CO, Queensland Ballet and others. *Compositions include:* Images for orchestra, 1983; The Dream, for orchestra, 1986; Clarinet Concerto, 1987; Horn Concerto, 1988; 2 String Trios, 1988, 1990; Symphony, 1989; The Haunting for orchestra, 1990; Chamber Concerto for strings, 1992; Dialogues for violin and strings, 1992; Pelléas and Mélisande, ballet, 1994; The Memory, for orchestra, 1994; From Endymion for 2 sopranos, alto, tenor, baritone, and bass, 1995. *Honours:* Alex Burnard Scholarship, 1980; AC International and AC Composers Fellowships, 1982, 1992. *Address:* c/o APRA, 1A Eden Street, Crows Nest, NSW 2065, Australia.

**JOSEPHSON, Kim Alan;** Singer (Baritone); b. 1954, Akron, Ohio, USA. *Career:* Debut: Sang in Strauss's Salome at Houston, 1977; Spoleto Festival, USA, 1991, in Menotti's Maria Golovin and Sarasota Festival, 1992, as Simon Boccanegra (both versions); Vancouver Opera as Rigoletto; Metropolitan Opera, New York, from 1991, as Sonora in La Fanciulla del West, Enrico in Lucia di Lammermoor, Germont in Traviata, Sharpless in Madama Butterfly, Silvio in Pagliacci, Count in Capriccio, the title role in Rigoletto and Marcello in La Bohème; Vienna Staatsoper debut, 1994, as Marcello in La Bohème followed by roles as Count di Luna in Il Trovatore, Germont in Traviata, Enrico in Lucia and Belcore in L'Elisir d'amore; Chicago debut as Marcello in La Bohème and in 1999 sang Eddie Carbone in the world premiere of A View from the Bridge by Bolcom; Many concert performances. *Honours:* Winner of many awards and competitions including Richard Tucker Foundation Grant; William Sullivan/George London Award; Puccini Foundation Award; Baltimore Opera Competition. *Address:* c/o Metropolitan Opera, Lincoln Center, New York, NY 10023, USA.

**JOSHUA, Rosemary;** Singer (Soprano); b. 16 Oct. 1964, Cardiff, Wales. *Education:* Studied in London at the Royal College of Music; Masterclasses with Thomas Allen, Graziella Sciutti and Claudio Desderi. *Career:* Debut at the Aix-en-Provence festival as Angelica in Orlando; Engagements with Opera Northern Ireland as Pamina, and at the 1992 Buxton Festival as Blondchen in Die Entführung; English National Opera as Adele in Die Fledermaus, Yum-Yum in The Mikado, Princess Ida, Norina, Sophie in Der Rosenkavalier and Susanna; Covent Garden Festival, 1993, as Pamina; Royal Opera debut, 1994, as Pousette in Manon; Angelica in Orlando at Aix-en-Provence Festival, Poppea in Agrippina and Susanna, Cologne Opera, 1994; Sang Sophie with ENO, 1997; Season 1999 as Handel's Semele for ENO and in Fauré's Requiem at the London Proms; Sang Poppea in Agrippina at Brussels, Sophie at the Deutsche Oper, Berlin; the title role of La Calisto at the Deutsche Staatsoper, Berlin, and in Brussels; Juliette in Romeo and Juliette and Ginevra in Ariodante in San Diego; The title role in The Cunning Little Vixen at the

Flanders Opera and at the Theatre des Champs Elysées in Le nozze di Figaro, the Glyndebourne Festival as Cleopatra in Giulio Cesare and to the Royal Opera House as Oscar in Un ballo in Maschera.Anne Trulove at Glyndebourne and Handel's Cleopatra for Florida Opera, 2000; Janáček's Vixen for Netherlands Opera, 2001 and at La Scala; Mahler's Symphony of a Thousand at the London Proms, 2002; Season 2002–03 in Die Fledermaus at the Met and in Handel's Saul and Der Rosenkavalier at Munich; Recent concert appearances include Bach's B Minor Mass with the London Philharmonic Orchestra under MArk Elder at the Royal Festival Hall, Beethoven's Symphony no. 9 with Sir Simon Rattle and the Orchestra of the Age of Enlightenment, Jephtha with René Jacobs and the Orchestra of the Age of Enlightenment in London, Brussels and New York, Mahler's Symphony no. 8 with Sir Simon Rattle and the National Youth Orchestra of Great Britain at the BBC Proms, Handel's Messiah with Daniel Harding and the Deutsche Kammerphilharmonie Bremen, Bach Cantatas with Nikolaus Harnoncourt and the Concentus Musicus Wien and Bach's B Minor Mass with Sir Roger Norrington and the Orchestra of the Age of Enlightenment. *Recordings:* 'Orlando' with Les Arts Florissants and William Christie for Erato; 'Venus and Adonis' and 'Dido and Aeneas' with René Jacobs for Harmonia Mundi; Sophie in Der Rosenkavalier for Chandos; the Sandman in 'Hansel und Gretel' for Teldec. *Honours:* Royal Philharmonic Award in debut category; Nominated for a Laurence Olivier Award in the category for Outstanding Achievement in Opera. *Address:* Askonas Holt Limited, Lonsdale Chambers, 27 Chancery Lane, London WC2A 1PF England. *Telephone:* 20 7400 1700. *Fax:* 20 7400 1799. *E-mail:* info@askonasholt.co.uk. *Website:* www.askonasholt.co.uk.

**JOSIPOVIC, Ivo;** Composer and Lawyer; b. 28 Aug. 1957, Zagreb, Croatia. *Education:* PhD, Law, University of Zagreb; Graduate, Music Academy, Zagreb. *Career:* Debut: 2 children's songs, 1978; Compositions performed in nearly all European countries, USA, Canada and Japan (EBU concert transmitted over 30 stations world-wide); Recordings for several radio and television stations; Performances at several European music festivals; Director of Music, Zagreb Biennale, 1981–; Docent, Music Academy, University of Zagreb, 1992–. *Compositions include:* Variations for piano; Play of the Golden Pearls for piano; Enypion for harp solo; Quartetto rusticano for string quartet; Per fiati for wind quintet; Passacaglia for string orchestra; Samba da camera for 13 strings; Dyptich for large orchestra; Epicurus' Garden for symphony orchestra; Man and Death for soloists, choir and orchestra; Pro musica for accordeon orchestra; The Most Beautiful Flower for voice and instrumental ensemble; Mrmesh for Mr Penderecki for folk orchestra; Thousands of Lotuses for choir and instrumental ensemble; Jubilus for piano solo; Elegaic Song for violin and piano; Dreams for voice and string orchestra. *Recordings:* Several compositions on CDs. *Address:* Palmoticeva 26, 10000 Zagreb, Croatia.

**JOUBERT, John Pierre Herman,** FRAM; Composer and University Lecturer; b. 20 March 1927, Cape Town, South Africa; m. Florence Mary Litherland 1951, one s. one d. *Education:* Diocesan Coll., Cape Town, Royal Acad. of Music, London. *Career:* Lecturer in Music, Univ. of Hull, England 1950–62; Lecturer (later Reader) in Music, Univ. of Birmingham 1962–86; mem. British Acad. of Composers and Songwriters, British Music Soc. *Compositions:* four String Quartets, 1950, 1977, 1987, 1988; Concertos, for violin, 1954, piano, 1957, bassoon, 1973; 2 Symphonies, 1955, 1969; two Sonatas for piano, 1957, 1972; Pro Pace Motets for unaccompanied choir, 1959; String Trio, 1960; Octet, 1961; Silas Marner, opera, 1961; Under Western Eyes, Opera, 1969; six Poems of Emily Brontë for soprano and piano, 1969; Déploration for orchestra, 1978; The Turning Wheel for soprano and piano, 1979; Herefordshire Canticles for choir and orchestra, 1979; Gong-Tormented Sea for choir and orchestra, 1981; Temps Perdu for orchestra, 1984; Rorate Coeli for unaccompanied choir, 1985; Piano Trio, 1987; Wings of Faith, orarorio, 2000. *Recordings:* Temps Perdu, Sinfonietta, The Instant Moment. *Honours:* Royal Philharmonic Soc. Prize, 1949; Hon. DMus, Univ. of Durham 1991. *Address:* 63 School Road, Moseley, Birmingham, B13 9TF, England.

**JUDD, James;** Conductor; b. 30 Oct. 1949, Hertford, England. *Education:* Trinity College of Music, London. *Career:* Assistant Conductor, Cleveland Orchestra, 1973–75; Associate Conductor, European Community Youth Orchestra, 1978–; Founder/Director, Chamber Orchestra of Europe; Music Director, Florida Philharmonic Orchestra; Artistic Director, European Communities Youth Orchestra, 1990; Artistic Director of Greater Miami Opera, 1993–; Guest Conductor with the Vienna and Prague Symphonies, Berlin Philharmonic, Orchestre National de France, Zürich Tonhalle and Suisse Romande Orchestra; Conducted La Cenerentola at Glyndebourne, 1985; Traviata, Il Trovatore, Il Barbiere di Siviglia, Rigoletto and Figaro for English National Opera; US Opera debut, 1988, with Don Giovanni in Miami; Season 1992/93 included tours with the Hallé and English Chamber Orchestras, London Symphony Orchestra, Royal Philharmonic and the Chamber Orchestra of Europe and Salzburg Festival; Conducted the Michael Nyman Band and the Philharmonia in the premiere of Nyman's Concerto for Saxophone and Orchestra, 1997. *Recordings:* With Chamber Orchestra of Europe; With English Chamber Orchestra; With Philharmonia Orchestra. *Current Management:* London Artists. *Address:* c/o Michael Emmerson, London Artists, 10 Guild Street, Stratford-upon-Avon, Warwickshire, CV 37 6RE, England.

**JUDD, Wilfred;** British opera director and opera translator; b. 1952, Hertford, Hertfordshire, England. *Education:* Oxford and London Opera Centre. *Career:* began as freelance director 1979; has been prod. with Royal

Opera 1984–, for which has staged Die Zauberflöte, Tosca, and La Fanciulla del West; notable production Finnissy's Thérèse Raquin for The Garden Venture; Artistic Dir, Royal Opera House Garden Venture 1988–93; wrote and dir, The Inner Ear, a concert drama premiered by Florida Philharmonic Orchestra 2002; Dir of Productions, Opera 80 1988–91. *Address:* 15 Cornwall Road, Twickenham, Middlesex TW1 3LS, England.

**JUDGE, Ian;** Stage Director; b. 21 July 1946, Southport, England. *Education:* Guildhall School of Music and Drama, London. *Career:* Joined the RSC in 1975, productions there include: The Wizard of Oz, The Comedy of Errors, Love's Labours Lost, The Relapse, Twelfth Night, A Christmas Carol, Troilus and Cressida and The Merry Wives of Windsor; Opera productions include: Faust, The Merry Widow, Cavalleria Rusticana, Pagliacci, Don Quixote La Belle Vivette and Mephistopheles for the ENO: Macbeth, Tosca, Acis and Galatea, Boris Godunov, Attila for Opera North; The Flying Dutchman (Royal Opera House); He has staged operas regularly in Europe, Australia and the USA: Macbeth (Cologne), Faust (Sydney), Les Contes d'Hoffmann (Houston), Tosca and Madama Butterfly (Los Angeles), Simon Boccanegra (Washington); Directed the original 1857 version of Verdi's Simon Boccanegra at Covent Garden, 1997; Staged Falstaff for the BBC Proms, 1998; Mephistopheles by Boito for ENO, 1999; Falstaff for Théâtre du Châtelet, Paris, 2001; La Bohème for Kirov Opera, St Petersburg, 2001; Ernani for National Reisoper, Netherlands, 2002. His credits include many plays and musicals, A Little Night Music (Piccadilly Theatre), Show Boat (London Palladium) and West Side Story in Australia. *Current Management:* Simpson Fox Association. *Address:* 52 Shaftesbury Avenue, London W1V 7DE, England.

**JUDSON, Colin;** Singer (Tenor); b. 1968, England. *Education:* Graduated Guildhall School of Music, 1992. *Career:* Engagements with touring opera companies, British Youth Opera, De Vlaamse Opera, Antwerp and at the Covent Garden Festival; Roles have included Remendado (Carmen), Isaac in La Gazza Ladra, Rossini's Almaviva, Purcell's Aeneas and Mozart's Monostatos, Tamino and Ferrando; Season 1996 with Werther for English Touring Opera, season 1997 as Coryphée in Le Comte Ory at Glyndebourne and in the Verdi Requiem at Hereford; Haydn's Nelson Mass for the Brighton Festival; Concerts include Schumann's Dichterliebe, Bach's Christmas Oratorio, The Dream of Gerontius, Puccini's Messa di Gloria and Stravinsky's Pulcinella. *Address:* C&M Craig Services Ltd, 3 Kersley Street, London SW11 4 PR, England.

**JUNE, Ava;** British singer (soprano); *Professor, Royal Northern College of Music;* b. 23 July 1934, London, England; m. David Charles Cooper (died 1982). *Education:* studied with Kate Opperman, Clive Carey and Joan Cross in London, and with Denice Dowling. *Career:* joined Sadler's Wells Chorus 1953; sang solo roles from 1957, Leila in The Pearl Fishers 1959; Covent Garden debut 1958, as the Heavenly Voice in Don Carlos; sang Mrs Schomberg in the 1970 premiere of Victory by Richard Rodney Bennett; appearances with WNO, Phoenix Opera, Scottish Opera and in Sofia, Vienna, Düsseldorf, Paris, Zagreb and Johannesburg; ENO 1973, as Sieglinde in The Ring, conducted by Reginald Goodall; US debut, San Francisco 1974, as Ellen Orford; sang Countess Vrouskaya in the premiere of Iain Hamilton's Anna Karenina, ENO 1981; other roles have included Countess Almaviva, Pamina, Agathe, Musetta, Butterfly, Violetta, Eva, the Marschallin, Elizabeth in Gloriana and in Maria Stuarda, Donna Anna, Marzelline, Micaela, Norina, Marguerite, Tosca, Aida and Santuzza; teacher of singing, later Prof., Royal Northern Coll. of Music 1985–; teacher of singing, Canterbury Christ Church Univ. Coll.; mem. of Bd, Carl Rosa Opera Co. *Recordings include:* Mrs Grosse in The Turn of the Screw, The Ring of the Nibelung, from the London Coliseum, La Traviata, The Bartered Bride. *Honours:* Queen's Prize RCM, London 1957, Gold Medal, Boris Cristoff Prize, Sofia (Bulgaria) 1963. *Address:* c/o English National Opera, St Martin's Lane, London, WC2N 4ES (office); 22 Mereway Road, Twickenham, Middx TW2 6RG, England (home).

**JUNG, Doris;** American singer (dramatic soprano) and teacher; b. 5 Jan. 1924, Centralia, IL; d. of John and May (née Middleton) Crittenden; m. Felix Popper 1951; one s. *Education:* Univ. of Illinois, Mannes Coll. of Music, Vienna Acad. of Performing Arts, Austria and under Julius Cohen, Emma Zador, Luise Helletsgruber and Winifred Cecil. *Career:* professional debut as Vitellia in Clemenza di Tito, Zurich Opera, Switzerland 1955; appearances with Hamburg State Opera and Munich State Opera, Germany, Vienna State Opera, Copenhagen Royal Opera, Stockholm Royal Opera, New York City Opera and Metropolitan Opera, New York, opera cos in Marseille and Strasbourg, France, Naples and Catania, Italy and with Syracuse Symphony 1981; teacher New York 1970–. *Address:* 40 West 84th Street, New York, NY 10024, USA. *Telephone:* (212) 873-3147 (home).

**JUNG, Manfred;** Singer (Tenor); b. 9 July 1940, Oberhausen, Germany. *Education:* Studied in Essen with Hilde Wesselmann. *Career:* Bayreuth Youth Festival, 1967, as Arindal in Die Feen by Wagner; Sang in the Bayreuth Festival Chorus, 1970–73; Sang in Dortmund and Kaiserslautern from 1971; Member of the Deutsche Oper am Rhein Düsseldorf from 1977; Bayreuth Festival from 1977, as Tristan, Parsifal and Siegfried (production of Der Ring des Nibelungen, 1983, by John Bury and Peter Hall); Sang in Wagner operas at the Salzburg Easter Festival, under Karajan (Tristan and Parsifal, 1980); Metropolitan Opera debut, 1981; Guest appearances in Zürich, Chicago, Toronto, Vienna; Hamburg, Munich, Barcelona, Cologne, Frankfurt, Lisbon, Rome and Montreal; Other roles include Walther, Florestan, Loge and

Siegmund; Sang Herod in Salome at Munich, 1990, Aegisthus in Elektra at the Spoleto Festival; Season 1991/92 as Herod at Barcelona and Valzacchi in Rosenkavalier at Catania; Season 1997–98 as Mime in The Ring, at Kassel. *Recordings include:* Siegfried in The Ring from Bayreuth. *Address:* c/o Hilbert Agentur, Maximilianstr 22, 8000 Munich 22, Germany.

**JUNGHÄNEL, Konrad;** German lutenist and musical director; *Professor, Hochschule für Musik, Cologne;* b. 1953; two s. two d. *Career:* appearances as soloist and member of early music ensembles throughout Europe, in the USA, Japan, South America and Africa; Collaborations with René Jacobs as soloist and continuo player in opera performances from the Baroque era and concerts with La Petite Bande, Musica Antiqua Köln, Les Arts Florissants and Tafelmusik; Founded Cantus Cölln 1987, with festival performances at Berne, Stuttgart, Utrecht, Innsbruck and Breslau; Conducted Francesco Cavalli's La Calisto in Cologne and Domenico Mazocchi's La Catena d'Adone in Innsbruck and Antwerp and a scenic production of Monteverdi's Madgrigals throughout Europe; Directed the production of Heinrich Schütz's Was liegt die Stadt so wüste at the Theater Basel, 2000 and at the Sächsische Staaatsoper Dresden, 2004–(06), Henry Purcell's Evening Hymn, Staatsoper Hannover, 2004 and Rameau's Les Paladins, Basel, 2004; conducted staged production of Bach cantatas at the Hamburg Opera, 2000; Directed Handel's Israel in Egypt at Basle, 2002; Handel's Semele and Monteverdi's L'Incoronazione di poppea, 2003; Repertory centres on Italian and German Renaissance and Baroque music. Recordings include Lute solos by Silvius Leopold Weiss; Schein's Diletti Pastorali; Rosenmuller's Vespro della beata Vergine; J. S. Bach: Lute Works; J. S. Bach: Motets; H Schütz: Psalmen Davids; Monteverdi: Vespro della beata Vergine. *Honours:* German Critics' Prize, for Weiss lute solos; Numerous Diapason d'Or Awards, 1991–98; Grand Prix du Disque, Académie Charles Cros, 1993; Editors Choice, Gramophone, 1999; Diapason d'Or and Lux du Monde de la Musique for CD Artus tragicus, 2000; Gramophone Award, Cecilia Award, Preis der deutschen Schallplattenkritik (CD, Monteverdi: Selva morale e spirituale), 2002, Preis der deutschen Schallplattenkritik, Echo Klassik (CD, Altbachisches Archiv) 2004. *Address:* Mittelstrasse 6a, 50321 Brühl, Germany (office). *Telephone:* (2232) 34433 (office); (2232) 370754 (home). *Fax:* (2232) 35113 (office). *E-mail:* cautus_coellu@t-online.de (office); k.junghaenel@web.de (home). *Website:* www.cautuscoellu.com.

**JUON, Julia;** Singer (mezzo-soprano); b. 28 Nov. 1943, St Gallen, Switzerland. *Education:* Zürich Conservatory. *Career:* sang in opera at St Gallen, 1975–80, Karlsruhe, 1980–83, and Kassel from 1984, notably as Ortrud and as Tina in the European premiere of The Aspern Papers by Dominick Argento; guest appearances as Fricks at Amsterdam and at the Hamburg Staatsoper as the Nurse in Die Frau ohne Schatten, 1989; other roles include Waltraute, Carmen, Agrippina, Donizetti's Leonora, Verdi's Ulrica, Eboli, Amneris and Azucena, Wagner's Kundry, Venus and Brangaene; modern repertoire includes Bartók's Judith, the Priestess in Schoeck's Penthesilea and Catherine in Jeanne d'Arc au Bûcher by Honegger; sang Kabanicha in Katya Kabanova at Basel in 1991 and Kundry at Essen in 1992; Countess Geschwitz in Lulu at Opéra Bastille, Paris, 1998; sang Waltraute and Azucena for Bonn Opera, 2000; Brangaene at Hamburg and Antwerp, 2000–01; concert engagements in Switzerland and Germany, at the Bregenz Festival and in Vienna. *Address:* Staatstheater, Friedrichplatz 15, 34117 Kassel, Germany.

**JURINAC, Srebrenka (Sena);** Austrian singer (soprano); b. 24 Oct. 1921, Travnik, Yugoslavia; d. of Dr Ljudevit Jurinac and Christine Cerv-Jurinac; m. Dr Josef Lederle. *Education:* Gymnasium and Music Acad., Zagreb, Yugoslavia. *Career:* studied under Maria Kostrenčić; first appearance as Mimi, Zagreb 1942; mem. Vienna State Opera Co. 1944–82; now works as a voice teacher; has sung at Salzburg, Glyndebourne Festivals, etc.; sang in Der Rosenkavalier 1966 and 1971, Tosca 1968, Iphigénie en Tauride 1973, Covent Garden; Austrian State Kammersängerin 1951; numerous tours and recordings; subject of biog. by Ursula Tamussino 2001. *Films:* Lisinski 1943, Der Rosenkavalier 1960. *Television:* Schwester Angelica (Puccini) (ORF) 1959, Otello (Verdi) (ORF) 1965, Wozzeck (Berg) (ZDF) 1970, Hänsel und Gretel (ORF) 1981. *Recordings:* Fidelio, Orfeo, Così fan tutte, Don Giovanni, Idomeneo, Le Nozze di Figaro, Ariadne auf Naxos, Der Rosenkavalier, Eugene Onegin, Lieder by Schumann and Richard Strauss. *Honours:* Ehrenkreuz für Wissenschaft und Kunst 1961, Grosses Ehrenzeichen für Verdienste um die Republik Österreich 1967, Ehrenring der Wiener Staatsoper 1968, Ehrenmitglied der Wiener Staatsoper 1971, Silver Rose of the Vienna Philharmonic Orchestra 2001. *Address:* c/o Wehrgasse 11A, 1050 Vienna, Austria. *Telephone:* (1) 5879295. *Fax:* (1) 5879295.

**JUROWSKI, Vladimir;** Russian conductor; *Music Director, Glyndebourne Festival Opera;* b. 1972, Moscow. *Education:* Music Acad., Berlin and Dresden, Germany. *Career:* chief conductor, Sibelius Orchestra, Berlin 1993–96; founder and conductor, United Berlin ensemble, performing modern music; int. debut conducting May Night by Rimsky-Korsakov, Wexford Festival 1995; fmr prin. guest conductor, Orchestra Sinfonica Verdi, Milan; prin. guest conductor Teatro Comunale, Bologna 2001; Music Dir Glyndebourne Festival Opera 2001–; Prin. Guest Conductor London Philharmonic Orchestra 2003–; Music Dir Russian Nat. Orchestra 2006–; has conducted in major venues worldwide, including Metropolitan Opera (New York), Opera Bastille (Paris), Komische Oper (Berlin), Teatro Comunale (Bologna), Teatro Real (Madrid), Royal Opera House (London), Welsh Nat. Opera (Cardiff), ENO (London), Edin. Festival. *Recordings include:* Werther by Massenet. *Current Management:* Stage Door, Via Marconi 71, 40122 Bologna, Italy. *Telephone:* (051) 19984750. *Fax:* (051) 19984779. *E-mail:* info@stagedoor.it. *Website:* www.stagedoor.it. *Address:* Russian National Orchestra, Orchestrion Garibaldi, 19 Moscow 117335, Russia. *Website:* www.rno.ru.

# K

**KAASCH, Donald;** Tenor; b. 19 Dec. 1968, Denver, Colorado, USA. *Education:* Studied at Colorado and Northwestern Universities. *Career:* Sang at the Chicago Lyric Opera, 1985–88; European engagements at Florence in 1989 in Idomeneo and at Geneva; Metropolitan Opera in 1989 in the character roles in Les Contes d'Hoffmann and returned for Jacquino in Fidelio and Mozart's Titus; Opéra Bastille in 1991 as Idamante in Idomeneo, Salzburg, 1992 as Argirio in Rossini's Tancredi; Other roles include Mozart's Tamino, Ferrando and Don Ottavio, Count Almaviva, the Prince in Lulu, Rinuccio and Argento's The Voyage of Edgar Allan Poe; Frequent concert performances including Leukippos in Strauss's Daphne at Antwerp, 1998; Sang the Priest in Stravinsky's Persephone at the Festival Hall, London, 1997; Royal Opera debut 1998, in The Golden Cockerel; Sang Gluck's Admète at Amsterdam 1999; Season 2000–01 as Britten's Male Chorus at Lausanne and Mozart's Mitridate in Sydney; Season 2002–03 in Thais at Chicago and in Der fliegende Holländer at Los Angeles. *Address:* c/o IMG Artists, Lovell House, 616 Chiswick High Road, London W4 5RX, England.

**KABAIVANSKA, Raina;** Bulgarian singer (soprano); b. 15 Dec. 1934, Burgas; d. of Joachin and Staika Kabaivanska; m. Franco Guandalini 1972; one d. *Education:* pvt. singing tuition and Conservatorium of Sofia. *Career:* debut in Puccini's Tabarro 1959; sang with Joan Sutherland and under direction of Maria Callas; has since performed with all major directors including Von Karajan in theatres world-wide; currently Prof. Chigiana Acad. of Music, Italy. *Films include:* Tosca, I Pagliacci, Falstaff, Il Trovatore, Madame Butterfly. *Records include:* Tosca, Madame Butterfly, Adriana Lecouvreur, Francesca da Rimini; numerous videos. *Honours:* Premio Puccini, Premio Viotti, Verdi d'Oro. *Address:* viale Fabrizio 81, Modena, Italy. *Telephone:* (59) 211170.

**KACZANOWSKI, Andrzej,** DipMus, MA; Polish double bassist; b. 22 April 1955, Białystok; m. 1974; two s. one d. *Education:* Chopin Acad. of Music, Warsaw. *Career:* debut, Domenico Dragonetti Concerto with Bilalystok Philharmonic Orchestra 1975; regular appearances as soloist or chamber player with numerous orchestras; Warsaw Chamber Orchestra under J. Kasprzyk 1978–84; Chamber Ensemble of the National Philharmonic under K. Teutsch, including concerts in Salle Pleyel (Paris), Santa Cecilia (Rome), Musikverein (Vienna), Tivoli (Copenhagen), Carnegie Hall (New York), among others; Polish Chamber Orchestra under Jerzy Maksymiuk 1984–85, numerous recordings and concerts; also collaboration with Warsaw Sinfonietta and Collegium Musicum; co-founder, Camerata Vistula Ensemble 1986; teacher, Josef Elsner First Music School in Warsaw 1991–96; co-producer, opening concert at Boguslawski Concer Hall, Warsaw 1997; Republic of Korea tour 1997; solo recitals, concerts and recordings 1998; first performance of Concerto by Emil Tabakov (with Sofia Philharmonic Orchestra) 1999; has played with musicians and conductors, including Claudio Abbado, Marek Drewnowski, Ruggiero Gerlin, Jacek Kspszyk, Konstanty Andrzej Kulka, Jerzy Maksymiuk, Janusz Olejniczak, Henryk Szeryng; performances at festivals, including Glasgow 1986, Berlin 1990, 1992, Warsaw Autumn 1985, 1986, 1988, 1989, Bialystok. *Recordings:* Polish Chamber Orchestra, Warsaw, Chamber Philharmonic Orchestra, Bach Keyboard Concerts, Ruggero Gerlin 1980, Lutoslawski, Prokofiev and Gorecki 1990, Schubert's Quintet op 114, Trout, Dvořák op 77 for Polish Radio SA, Fantasia Contrabasso 2004. *Address:* Pradzynskistr 20a 109, 05-200 Wotomin, Poland (office). *E-mail:* akaczan@ poczta.onet.pl (home).

**KAEGI, Dieter;** Stage Director; b. 1950, Zürich, Switzerland. *Education:* Musicology and German Literature at Zürich and Paris. *Career:* Assistant Director at English National Opera, 1980; Director of Productions at Aix-en-Provence Festival, 1989; Artistic Director, Opera Ireland; Der Rosenkavalier and Der Freischütz for Seattle Opera; Stagings of Tristan und Isolde at Monte Carlo, Idomeneo and Figaro at Copenhagen, Roméo et Juliette in Geneva and Anna Bolena by Donizetti at Metz; Bartók's Bluebeard's Castle at Strasbourg; Fidelio in Liège and Lady Macbeth of Mtsensk for Opera Ireland; Season 2001–2002 with Der Freischütz at Ulm, Don Carlos in Ireland and Die Entführung in Nancy. *Current Management:* Athole Still International Management, Forresters Hall, 25–27 Westow Street, London, SE19 3RY, England. *Telephone:* (20) 8771-5271. *Fax:* (20) 8768-6600. *Website:* www .atholestill.com.

**KAGEL, Mauricio;** Argentine composer; b. 21 Dec. 1931, Buenos Aires. *Education:* Univ. of Buenos Aires. *Career:* Artistic Dir Agrupación Nueva Música 1949; co-founder, Cinemathèque Argentine 1950; Dir and Conductor, Teatro Colón, Buenos Aires 1955; emigrated to Germany 1957; f. Kölner Ensemble für Neue Musik, Cologne 1959; Slee Prof. of Composition, State Univ. of New York 1964–65; Visiting Lecturer, Berlin Acad. of Film and TV 1967; Dir Scandinavian Courses for New Music, Gothenburg 1968–69; Dir Courses for New Music, Cologne 1969–75; Prof. of New Music and Theater, Cologne Conservatory 1974–97. *Compositions include:* Música para la Torre 1953, String Sextet 1953, Sur Scène 1959, Journal de théâtre 1960, Le Bruit 1960, Heterophonie 1959, Metapiece 1961, Antithese 1962, Die Frauen 1962, Diaphonie 1962, Phonophonie 1963, Mirum 1965, Match 1965, Tremens 1963, Camera Obscura 1965, Die Himmelsmechanik 1965, Musik für Renaissanceinstrumente 1965, String Quartet 1965, Variaktionen 1967, Kommentar Extempore 1967, Montage 1967, Phantasie 1967, Hallelujah 1968, Der Schall 1968, Acustica 1968, Unter Strom 1969, Ludwig Van 1969, Staatstheater (ballet) 1969, Tactil 1970, Klangwehr 1970, Zwei-Mann-Orchester 1971, Programm, Gasprache mit Kammermusik 1972, Exotica 1972, Variationen ohne Fuge 1973, 1898 1973, Kantrimusik 1975, Mare Nostrum 1975, Bestiarium 1975, Die Umkehrung Amerikas 1976, Variete 1977, An Tasten 1977, Die Erschöpfung der Welt (opera) 1979, Aus Deutschland 1981, Fragen 1982, Nach einer Lektüre von Orwell 1984, La trahison orale 1984, Two Ballads of Guillaume de Machaut 1984, Sankt Bach Passion 1985, Piano Trio 1985, Old/New 1986, A Letter 1986, Quodlibet 1988, Tantz-Schul (ballet) 1988, Osten 1989, Fragende Ode 1989, Nah und Fern 1993, Playback Play 1997, Entführung aus dem Konzertsaal 2000. *Television includes:* Sur Scène 1963, Match 1966, Duo 1968, Tactil 1971, Pas de Cinq 1978, Blue's Blue 1980, Dressur 1985, Repertoire 1989, Die Erschöpfung der Welt 2000. *Honours:* Koussevitzky Prize 1966, Karl Sczuka Prize for play Ein Aufnahmezustand 1969, Scotoni Prize for film Hallelujah, City of Zürich 1969. *Current Management:* c/o Universal Edition, Bösendorferstrasse 12, Postfach 3, 1015 Vienna, Austria.

**KAHANE, Jeffrey Alan,** BMus; American pianist and conductor; *Music Director, Colorado Symphony Orchestra*; b. 12 Sept. 1956, Los Angeles, CA; m. Martha Philips 1979; one s. *Education:* San Francisco Conservatory of Music. *Career:* debut as pianist, San Francisco, California 1973; soloist, New York and Los Angeles Philharmonics, Pittsburgh, San Francisco and Atlanta Symphonies; appearances with Cleveland Orchestra, New York, Los Angeles, Rotterdam and Israel Philharmonics, Boston, Chicago, Pittsburgh, San Francisco, Atlanta Symphonies; soloist in Bernstein's Age of Anxiety at the 1991 Promenade Concerts, London; Music Dir, Santa Rosa Symphony, Los Angeles Chamber Orchestra 1997–, Green Music Festival, Colorado Symphony Orchestra 2004–; mem. Piano Faculty, New England Conservatory of Music, Boston, Eastman School of Music, Rochester, NY. *Recordings:* Works of Gershwin and Bernstein with Yo-Yo Ma; Paul Schoenfield's Four Parables; Strauss' Burleske with the Cincinnati Symphony; Brandenburg Concerti (on harpsichord) with the Oregon Bach Festival Orchestra; Schubert's complete works for violin and piano with Joseph Swensen; Bach's Sinfonias and Partita No. 4 in D Major; Bernstein's Age of Anxiety. *Honours:* Grand Prize Arthur Rubinstein Int. Piano Competition, Tel-Aviv, Israel 1983, fourth prize Van Cliburn Int. Piano Competition 1981. *Current Management:* IMG Artists, 825 Seventh Avenue, Eighth Floor, New York, NY 10019, USA. *Telephone:* (212) 994-3540 (office). *Fax:* (212) 246-1596 (office). *E-mail:* bridget.wrathall@ imgworld.com.

**KAHLER, Lia;** Singer (Mezzo-soprano); b. 1952, USA. *Education:* Studied in Los Angeles, New York and Milan. *Career:* Sang at the Holland Festival, 1982, Detmold, 1983–85, notably as Eboli and Brangaene; Sang at Gelsenkirchen 1985–89, as Laura in La Gioconda, Monteverdi's Ottavia, the Witch and Mother in Hansel und Gretel, and in the premiere of Deinen Kopf, Holofernes by Blumenthaler, 1989; Other roles at Gelsenkirchen and elsewhere in Germany have included Ortrud, Maddalena, Marina in Boris Godunov, Dalila and Baba the Turk in The Rake's Progress; Many concert appearances. *Address:* Musiktheater im Revier, Kennedyplatz, 4650 Gelsenkirchen, Germany.

**KAHMANN, Sieglinde;** Singer (Soprano); b. 28 Nov. 1937, Dresden, Germany; m. Sigurdur Bjornsson. *Education:* Studied in Stuttgart. *Career:* Debut: Stuttgart Staatsoper 1959, as Aennchen in Der Freischütz; Engaged at the Theater am Gärtnerplatz, Munich, and sang at Hamburg, Vienna, Stuttgart, Leipzig, Karlsruhe and Kassel; Roles have included Mozart's Pamina, Donna Elvira, Countess and Cherubino, Lortzing's Gretchen and Mair, Martha and Musetta; Guest appearances at Lisbon, Strasbourg, Bucharest, Salzburg and Edinburgh, as Micaela, Lisa (Queen of Spades), Marenka (Bartered Bride) and Adele in Fledermaus. *Address:* c/o Stuttgart Staatsoper, Oberer Schlossgarten 6, 7000 Stuttgart, Germany.

**KAIN, Timothy,** DipMus; Australian classical guitarist; b. 25 Jan. 1951, Braidwood, NSW. *Education:* Canberra School of Music, Royal Northern College of Music, Manchester, and in Alicante, Spain. *Career:* debut, Purcell Room, 1982; Played all over the world for 20 years; Major tours of the United Kingdom and Australia with John Williams in 1992 and 1996, also Australia in 1996; Leader of Guitar Trek, a quartet playing a family of different sized guitars; Head of the Guitar Department at Canberra School of Music, Australian National University, 1982–; mem, Australian Music Centre. *Compositions:* has commissioned close to 30 new works for guitar, solo, chamber and concerto from Australian composers. *Recordings:* The Mantis and The Moon with John Wiliams; Guitar Trek, music for a guitar family; Guitar Trek II, the family continues; For Flute and Guitar; Music of the Americas with flautist Virginia Taylor. *Publications:* Three Preludes by Richard Vella is the first of a series, published 1998; Black Wattle Caprices, by Ross Edwards, 1999. *Honours:* First prize, Int GTR Competition, Spain, 1977; RNCM Bach Prize, 1979. *Address:* 84 Dryandra Street, O'Connor, ACT 2602, Australia.

**KAIPAINEN, Jouni Ilari;** Finnish composer; b. 24 Nov. 1956, Helsinki; m. Sari-Anne Liljendahl 1977; one s. *Education:* Sibelius Acad., Helsinki. *Career:* freelance composer 1981–. *Compositions:* The Miracle of Konstanz, television opera, 1985–87; Symphony, Opus 20, 1980–85; String Quartets, I 1973; II, 1974; III, 1984; IV, 1994; Ladders To Fire (A concerto for 2 pianos), 1979; Trios, I, 1983; II, 1986; III, 1987; Cinq poemes de René Char, Opus 12a, for soprano and orchestra, 1978–80. Chamber Music; Vocal Music; Incidental Music; Vernal Concerto for saxophone quartet and orchestra, 1996; Piano Concerto, 1997; Viola Concerto, 1997; Sestetto for ensemble, 1997; Remours for four flutes 1990–97; Clarinet Quintet 2000. *Publications:* contrib. numerous essays and articles in Finnish magazines, including Finnish Music Quarterly, Ammatti: säveltäjä 1981. *Honours:* UNESCO Int. Rostrum Chosen Work of the Year 1981, Union of Finnish Critics Spurs of Criticism (award for the most eminent debut of the year) 1982. *Address:* Finnish Music Information Centre, Lauttasaarent. 1, 00200 Helsinki (office); Kortelahdenkatu 22A 12, 33230 Tampere, Finland (home). *Website:* www.fimic.fi.

**KAISER, Barbara;** Conductor; b. 1 June 1947, Bremen, Germany. *Education:* Abitur; Studied in Schulmusik, Violin and Singing, Hochschule für Musik, Freiburg/Breisgau, 1967–73; Studies in Conducting, Hochschule der Künste, Berlin, 1979–85. *Career:* Debut: Guest Conductor, Philharmonisches Staatsorchester, Bremen, 1986; Founding Member, Musikfrauen Berlin, 1978; Manager, several projects with contemporary music of women composers; Manager of series of concerts with contemporary music at Hochschule der Künste Berlin, 1984–96; Neue Musik Berlin in cooperation, 1986; Lecturer at Hochschule der Künste Berlin, 1986–96; Guest Conductor, Philharmonisches Staatsorchester Bremen, Filharmonia Pomorska, Poland and Orchester der Stadt Heidelberg; mem. International Arbeitskreis Frau und Musik; Kulturinstitut Komponistinnen gestern-heute, Heidleberg. *Recordings:* Instrumental and Vocal, Musik von Komponistinnen, 1985; Komponistinnen in Berlin, 1987. *Contributions:* Some interviews on radio, magazines and journals. *Address:* Gneisenaustrasse 94, 10961 Berlin, Germany.

**KALABIS, Viktor,** PhDr; Czech composer; b. 27 Feb. 1923, Cerveny Kostelec; m. Zuzana Ruzickova 1952. *Education:* Prague Conservatory, Acad. of Arts and Music, Charles Univ., Prague. *Career:* Ed., Musical Producer, Czech Radio 1953–72; full-time composer 1972–; Pres. Int. Bohuslav Martinů Foundation 1990–2003; mem. Czech Musical Soc. *Compositions include:* orchestral works: five symphonies 1957, 1961, 1971, 1972, 1976, Concerto for large orchestra 1966, nine instrumental concertos, four compositions for chamber orchestra; chamber works: two nonets, Spring Whistles octet for wind 1979, two wind quintets, seven string quartets, sonatas for violin and harpsichord, violoncello and piano, clarinet and piano, trombone and piano, violin and piano 1967–82, seven string quartets 1949–93; solo works: three piano sonatas, three pieces for flute, Reminiscences for guitar 1979, Four Enigmas for Graham piano solo 1989, several choral works, five romantic love songs for higher voice and strings 1977, Two Worlds (Alice in Wonderland, ballet) 1980, Incantations for 13 wind instruments 1988, Carousel of Life songs for bass and piano 1989, Strange Pipers for ensemble 1990, Ludus per 4 for piano quartet 1996. *Recordings:* Diptych for strings, Chant du Monde. *Honours:* Musical Critics Portrait Prize 1967, State Prize 1969, Artist of Merit 1983, Parents' Choice Award, USA 1993. *Address:* Slezska 107, 130 00 Prague 3, Czech Republic. *Telephone:* (384) 363388 (office); (2) 6731-2104 (home).

**KALE, Stuart;** Singer (tenor); b. 27 Oct. 1944, Neath, Glamorgan, Wales. *Education:* Studied at the Guildhall School of Music and Drama and at the London Opera Centre. *Career:* Debut: With Welsh National Opera in 1971, as the Prince in the first production by a British company of Berg's Lulu; Sang with English National Opera notably as Don Ottavio and in Jonathan Miller's production of The Mikado; Sang Wagner's Siegfried at Bucharest in 1983 and appeared in the local premiere of Prokofiev's The Fiery Angel for South Australian Opera in 1988; Covent Garden debut 1988, in Manon, returning in 1989 as Bob Boles in Peter Grimes; has sung the Captain in Wozzeck at Strasbourg, 1987, Reggio Emilia, 1989 and Toronto 1990; In 1989 sang in L'incoronazione di Poppea at the Théâtre du Châtelet, Paris, the Drum Major in Wozzeck at Turin and Zinovy Ismailov in Lady Macbeth of the Mstensk District at Nancy, France; Sang Don Eusebio in Rossini's L'Occasione fa il ladro at the 1992 Schwetzingen festival; Sang Shuisky at Montpellier, 1996; Gafforio in Paisiello's Il Re Teodoro in Venezia at Padua, 1998; Season 1999–2000 as Diomedes in Penthesilea by Schoeck, at Lucerne, and the Captain in Wozzeck at La Scala. *Recordings:* Video of Idomeneo (title role) from Drottningholm. *Current Management:* Athole Still International Management, Forresters Hall, 25–27 Westow Street, London, SE19 3RY, England. *Telephone:* (20) 8771-5271. *Fax:* (20) 8768-6600. *Website:* www .atholestill.com.

**KALES, Elisabeth;** Singer (Soprano); b. 1952, Graz, Austria. *Education:* Studied at the Graz Conservatory. *Career:* Sang at the Graz Opera, 1975–79, Vienna Volksoper from 1979; Sang Papagena in Die Zauberflöte at Salzburg, 1980 and 1986; Bregenz Festival, 1984, as Christel in Zeller's Der Vogelhändler; Other roles have included Millöcker's Laura, and the Fox in The Cunning Little Vixen; Director of the Baden Opera from 1996; Further guest engagements at the Vienna Staatsoper. *Address:* c/o Stadtheater, Theaterplatz 7, 2500 Baden bei Wien, Austria.

**KALICHSTEIN, Joseph,** MSc; American/Israeli concert pianist; b. 15 Jan. 1946, Tel-Aviv; s. of Isaac Kalichstein and Mali Kalichstein; m. Rowain (née Schultz) Kalichstein; two c. *Education:* Juilliard School, New York. *Career:* New York debut 1967; European debut 1970; appearances with all the world's leading orchestras; recent engagements include Nat. Symphony Orchestra,

Washington, DC, Cincinnati Symphony, US tour with Jerusalem Symphony and Lawrence Foster, and return tours to Japan and Scandinavia; mem. Piano Faculty of Juilliard School 1985–. *Honours:* First Prize, Leventritt Int. Competition 1969, Edward Stevermann Memorial Prize 1969. *Current Management:* Harrison Parrott Ltd, 12 Penzance Place, London, W11 4PA, England.

**KALININA, Galina;** Singer (Soprano); b. 1951, Russia. *Education:* Studied in Moscow. *Career:* Member of the Bolshoi Opera, Moscow from 1977, notably as Donna Anna, Verdi's Trovatore Leonora, Elisabetta, Desdemona and Amelia (Ballo in Maschera); Tchaikovsky's Tatiana and Lisa and Madama Butterfly; Guest appearances in the West from 1982, notably as Tosca at Stuttgart 1988, and with Scottish Opera, Yaroslavna in Prince Igor at Wiesbaden and Zemfira in a concert performance of Rachmaninov's Aleko at Rome; Season 1987–88, as Tatiana at Buenos Aires, Butterfly in Oslo and Yaroslavna at Verona; Covent Garden 1991, as Tosca; Aida at Buenos Aires, 1996; Turandot at Toronto, 1997; Season 2000 as Lady Macbeth for Oslo Opera and Abigaille at St Margareth. *Recordings:* Fevronia in The Legend of the Invisible City of Kitezh by Rimsky Korsakov.

**KALISH, Gilbert;** Pianist and Teacher; b. 2 July 1935, New York, USA. *Education:* BA, Columbia Coll., 1956; Columbia University Graduate School of Arts and Sciences, 1956–58; Pupil of Isabelle Vengerova, Leonard Schure and Julius Herford. *Career:* New York Recital debut, 1962; European debut, London, 1962; Subsequent tours of the US, Europe and Australia; Pianist with the Contemporary Chamber Ensemble and the Boston Symphony Chamber Players; Regular accompanist to Jan DeGaetani until 1989; Artist-in-Residence, Rutgers, The State University of New Jersey, 1965–67; Swarthmore College, 1966–72; Head of Keyboard Activities, Chairman of Faculty, 1985–, Tanglewood Music Center, Tanglewood, Massachusetts; Faculty Member, Head of Performance Faculty, State University of New York at Stony Brook, 1970–. *Recordings:* as a soloist chamber player, and accompanist. *Honours:* Paul Fromm Award, University of Chicago for Distinguished Service to the music of our time, 1995. *Address:* c/o Music Department, State University of New York, Stony Brook, NY 11794, USA.

**KALJUSTE, Tonu;** Choral Director and Conductor; b. 1953, Tallinn, Estonia. *Education:* Studied at the Tallinn and Leningrad Conservatories. *Career:* Lecturer at the Tallinn Conservatory, 1978–81; Conducted works by Mozart, Britten and Weber with Estonian Opera; Founded the Estonian Philharmonic Chamber Choir, 1981; Artistic Director of choral festivals Tallinn '88 and Tallinn '91; Founded the Tallinn Chamber Choir, 1992; Founded the Tallinn Chamber Orchestra, 1993; Principal Conductor of the Swedish Radio Choir, from 1994; Guest conductor with choir and orchestras in Europe, Australia and North America; Has featured contemporary Estonian composers and concert series of Bach and other Baroque composers; Principal Conductor of the Netherlands Chamber Choir, 1998–; Concurrently Principal Conductor of the Estonian Philharmonic Chamber Choir and the Tallinn Chamber Orchestra. *Recordings:* Forgotten Peoples by Veljo Tormis, 1992; Te Deum by Arvo Pärte, 1993; Vespers Op 37 by Sergei Rachmaninov, 1995; Requiem by Alfred Schnittke and Miserere by Henryk Gorecki, 1995; Crystallisatio by Erkki-Sven Tüür, 1996; Casting a Spell by Veljo Tormis, 1996; Arvo Pärt's Litany, 1997, Beatus, 1997, Kanon Pokajanen, 1998; Psalms of Repentance by Alfred Schnittke, 1999. *Honours:* Nomination at 1995 Grammy Awards, for Best Choral Performance; The State Award of the Republic of Estonia, 1997; The Best Musician of Estonia, 1998; The ABC Music Award to Tonu Kaljuste and The Swedish Radio Choir for the year 1998. *Address:* Uus Str 22-5, Tallinn 10111, Estonia.

**KALLISCH, Cornelia;** Singer (Mezzo-soprano); b. 1955, Marbach am Neckar, Germany. *Education:* Studied in Stuttgart and Munich with Josef Metternich in Cologne. *Career:* Sang at first as Lieder recitalist, then sang in opera at Gelsenkirchen and elsewhere from 1984; Roles have included Orpheus, Octavian, the Composer in Ariadne auf Naxos, Monteverdi's Nero, Sesto in La Clemenza di Tito, (Ludwigsburg 1983–84), and Dorabella; Sang Cornelia in a concert performance of Tito at the Grosses Festspielhaus Salzburg, 1991; Arsace in Semiramide and Clairon in Capriccio at Zürich, 1992; Lieder recitals and concerts at Berlin, Vienna, Stuttgart and Frankfurt and in France and Italy; Performances of Wagner's Brangaene in concert with the Pittsburgh Symphony Orchestra and Kundry at Brussels, 1998; Bartók's Judith at Zürich, 1996; Season 1999–2000 as Paulina in the premiere of Wintermärchen by Boesmans at Brussels, and as solosit in the premiere of St Luke Passion by Rihm, at Stuttgart. *Recordings include:* Le Roi David by Honegger; Bach's Christmas Oratorio; Mozart's Requiem; Die Meistersinger by Wagner; F Schmidt, Das Buch mit sieben Siegeln; Klavierlieder by O Schoek; C Franck's Les Béatitudes. *Address:* Kunstler Sekretanat am Gasteig, Rosenheimer strasse 52, 81669 Munich, Germany.

**KALMAR, Magda;** Singer (Soprano); b. 4 March 1944, Budapest, Hungary. *Education:* Department of Singing, Béla Bartók Conservatory, Budapest. *Career:* Budapest State Opera, 1969–; Frequent performer in Hungary's concert halls and on Hungarian radio and television; Guest Performer at numerous operas including Austria, Belgium, Cuba, Czechoslovakia, Teatro la Fenice, Italy, Berlin, Leningrad, Stockholm and Paris; Roles include Mozart's Blondchen, Despina and Cherubino, Verdi's Oscar, Adele in Die Fledermaus, Don Pasquale and Norina by Donizetti, Adina in L'Elisir d'amore, Mozart's Pamina, Rossini's Rosina, Alban Berg's Lulu, Sophie in Der Rosenkavalier and Gilda in Rigoletto; Sang at Budapest 1987, in the premiere of Szokolay's Ecce Homo. *Recordings:* Has made numerous recordings including Haydn's Il Ritorno di Tobia, Rossini's Mosè in Egitto and Dittersdorf's oratorio Esther; Motets. *Honours:* Grand Prix du Disque, 1975, 1977; 1st Prize, International Rostrum for Young Performing Artists, Bratislava, 1972; Scholarship, Budapest State Opera, 1967. *Address:* c/o Hungarian State Opera House, Népöztarsasag utja 22, 1061 Budapest, Hungary.

**KALT, Frederic;** Singer (Tenor); b. 1963, Utah, USA. *Education:* Studied in Anchorage, Alaska. *Career:* Debut: New York City Opera, 1987, as Faust in Mefistofele; Puerto Rico, 1987, as Don José; Sang in Europe from 1991, notably Bacchus at Karlsruhe; Des Grieux in Manon Lescaut at La Scala and Otello at Cologne, 1996; Vienna Staatsoper from 1992, as Calaf, Cavaradossi and Verdi's Manrico; Other roles include Samson, Paolo in Francesca da Rimini (Bregenz, 1995), Pinkerton and Erik in Der fliegende Holländer (Los Angeles, 1995); Apollo in Daphne by Strauss at Santa Fe, 1996; Concerts include Verdi Requiem at Carnegie Hall. *Address:* c/o Santa Fe Opera, PO Box 2408, Santa Fe, NM 87504, USA.

**KALUDOV, Kaludy;** Singer (Tenor); b. 1953, Varna, Bulgaria. *Education:* Studied at Sofia Conservatory with Jablenska, graduating in 1976. *Career:* Member of the Sofia Opera from 1978; Guest engagements in Europe and North America, including Dimitri in Boris Godunov at Houston and Chicago, conducted by Abbado; Sang Faust in Mefistofele at Lisbon 1990, Alvaro in La Forza del Destino at Poznan, 1991; Riccardo (Ballo in Maschera) at Genoa 1991, Puccini's Des Grieux at Trieste and Radames at Tel-Aviv, 1992; Manrico in Trovatore at Salzburg 1992, Deutsche Oper Berlin 1992 and 1993, Wiener Staatsoper, 1994; Puccini's Des Grieux at La Scala, Milan, 1992 and at Palermo, 1993; Foresto in Attila at Wiener Staatsoper, 1984 and at La Scala 1991 (conducted by Riccardo Muti) and RAI Video; Singer in Rosenkavalier at Wiener Staatsoper, 1990 and at Deutsche Oper Berlin 1993, Staatsoper Berlin, 1992; Don Carlo at Bayerische Staatsoper, Munich 1993, National Opera, Sofia 1988, Madrid 1986; Requiem, G Verdi at London 1983 at Houston 1992, Tel-Aviv with Israel Philharmonic Orchestra conducted by Zubin Mehta; Radames in Aida at Staatsoper Berlin 1993, Finland 1994 and Philadelphia, 1996; Sang Alvaro at Savonlinna, 1998. *Recordings:* Golitsin in Khovanschchina and Vladimir in Prince Igor, with forces of the Sofia Opera conducted by Emil Tchakarov; Janáček's Glagolitic Mass with Charles Dutoit, Montreal, Decca, 1991; Rachmaninov's The Bells with Charles Dutoit, Philadelphia, Decca, 1992; Puccini's Des Grieux (Manon Lescaut) with BRT Philharmonic Orchestra, Brussels (conducted by Alexander Rahbari), Naxos, 1992. *Address:* Sreniawitow 7m 59, 03-188 Warsaw, Poland.

**KALUZA, Stefania;** Singer (Mezzo-soprano); b. 1950, Katowice, Poland. *Education:* Studies in Wroclaw and Vienna with Hans Hotter and Anton Dermota. *Career:* Debut: Opera, Wroclaw; Sang in Warsaw and Poznan; Also at the Landestheater Salzburg from 1984, and made guest appearances at the Vienna Staatsoper, Bregenz Festival and Brussels (in The Cunning Little Vixen); Versailles Festival, 1989, as Bersi in Andrea Chénier, Düsseldorf 1989, as Amneris; Appearances with the Zürich Opera from 1988, as Marcellina in Figaro, Martha in Mefistofele, Pamela in Fra Diavalo and Larina in Eugene Onegin, 1991; Sang Preziosilla at Zürich, 1992; Other roles include Dorabella, Frau Fluth, Ulrica and Rosina; Concert engagements in Poland, Hungary, Italy and Russia; Sang Amneris at San Diego, 1996; Season 1999–2000 at Zürich as Wagner's Venus, Enrichetta in I Puritani and Verdi's Maddalena. *Recordings include:* Frau Litumlei in Zemlinsky's Kleider Machen Leute. *Honours:* Winner, Belvedere International Competition, Vienna, 1983. *Address:* c/o Opernhaus Zürich, Falkenstrasse 1, 8008 Zürich, Switzerland.

**KAMBASKOVIC, Rastislav,** MA; professor of theory and music analysis; b. 20 June 1939, Prokuplje, Yugoslavia; m. (divorced); one s. one d. *Education:* Acad. of Music, Belgrade; diplomas in theory of music, composition. *Career:* debut, Serious Variation for Violins, Belgrade, 1965; Ed., Ed.-in-Chief, Chamber and Vocal, Symphonic Music, 1964–88; Chief Admin., Belgrade Radio-Television Symphony Orchestra, 1970–76; Prof. of Theory and Music Analysis, Theory Dept, Faculty of Music, Belgrade, 1988–, Head, Theory Dept, 1992–. *Compositions:* Solo Instrumental Music: Violin and Piano Sonata in G, 1964; Sonata for Two Violins, 1975; Six Piano Preludes, 1991; Chamber Music: Serious Variations for Flute and String Orchestra, 1966; Wood Wind Quintet, 1967; Piano Trio, 1975; Kumb Brass Wind Quintet, 1980; Pester Sketches for 14 Flutes, 1988; Four Harp Sonata, 1991; Jefimia Lamentoso for Cello and String Orchestra, 1993. *Publications:* Interaction—Diatonic and Chromatic in Prokofiev's Symphonies, 1992. *Honours:* Belgrade Music Festival Award, 1974; Serbian Asscn of Composers Awards, 1974, 1975, 1982, 1983; Belgrade Radio-Television Award, 1982. *Address:* 109 Nova 22, 11060 Belgrade, Serbia and Montenegro.

**KAMENIKOVA, Valentina (Jurijevna);** Pianist; b. 20 Dec. 1930, Odessa, Russia; m. Jaroslav Kamenik, 1954, 2 s. *Education:* Odessa Music High School; Prague Academy of Arts. *Career:* Prague Spring Festival; Salzburg Festival; Concerts in West Berlin, London, Madrid, Vienna, Palma de Mallorca; Chopin Festival in Polensa; Concert Tour, Europe; Professor, Prague Academy of Arts; mem, Jury Member, International Piano Competitions. *Recordings:* Tchaikovsky, Great Sonata and Dumka; Rachmaninov, Piano Concerto No. 1; Rhapsody on Paganini Theme; Chopin, Ballades; Mazurkas; Beethoven, Piano Sonatas No. 4 and No. 32; Tchaikovsky, Piano Concerto No. 1; Mozart, Sonatas No. 11 and 12; Haydn, 4 Piano Concertos;

Liszt, Sonata in B Minor; Mephisto Waltz; Brahms, Sonata No. 1; Rhapsodies; Liszt, Piano Concertos No. 1 and 2; Prokofiev, Sonatas No. 1 and 3. *Honours:* Prize Supraphon for Recording of Tchaikovsky Piano Concerto No. 1, 1973; Wiener Flotenuhr, Preis der Mozartgeminde, Wien. *Address:* Cechovo nam 9, 101 00 Prague, Czech Republic.

**KAMINKOVSKY, Rimma;** Violinist; b. 1940, Russia. *Education:* Studied in Odessa and Warsaw, at Tel-Aviv from 1969 and in the USA with Samuel Ashkenazi. *Career:* Teacher at the Rubin Academy of Music in Jerusalem, former co-leader of the Jerusalem Symphony Orchestra; Member of the Israel Philharmonic, with appearances as soloist; Co-Founder, Jerusalem String Trio, 1977, performing in Israel and Europe from 1981; Repertoire includes String Trios by Beethoven, Dohnányi, Mozart, Reger, Schubert and Taneyev, Piano Quartets by Beethoven, Brahms, Dvořák, Mozart and Schumann; Concerts with Radu Lupu and Daniel Adni.

**KAMINSKY, Laura;** American composer; *Dean, Conservatory of Music, Purchase College, State University of New York;* b. 28 Sept. 1956, New York, USA. *Education:* Oberlin Coll. and City Coll. of New York. *Career:* Co-founder Musicians Accord ensemble 1980; Assoc. Dir for the Humanities, 92nd Street, New York 1984–88; Artistic Dir New York Town Hall 1988–92; artistic consultant/educator, Nat. Acad. of Music, Winneba, Ghana 1992–93; Dir Music and Theatre Programs, The New School Univ., New York 1993–96; Dir European Mozart Acad., Poland 1996–97; Vice-Pres. for Programs, Meet the Composer, New York 1997–98; Chair. Music Dept, Cornish Coll. of the Arts, Seattle, Wash. 1999–2004; Dean, Conservatory of Music, Purchase Coll., State Univ. of NY 2004–. *Compositions include:* Proverbs of Hell for Soprano, Marimba and Piano 1989, Triftmusik for Piano 1991, Whitman Songs for Baritone and Piano 1992, Vukovar Trio for Violin, Cello and Piano 1999, River Music for Flute, Piano and Percussion 2000, Transformations for String Quartet 2000, The Full Range of Blue 2001, Libra for Chorus 2002, Danza Piccola for Solo Piano 2002, Transformations II for String Quartet 2002, Duo for Cello and Piano 2003, Runaway Anemone for Mandolin and Guitar 2003, Until a Name for Solo Flute 2003, The Seasons for Women's Chorus 2003, Piano Quartet 2003–04, Cadenza Variations for Woodwind Quintet 2004, Monotypes 2005, Music for Thelma for Violin and Piano 2005, L'arcipelago delle delizie for Solo Cello (in progress) 2005, Untitled for Flute and Piano (in progress) 2005, String Quartet No. 4 2005–06. *Address:* 735 Anderson Hill Road, Purchase, NY 10577, USA (office). *Telephone:* (914) 251-6705 (office). *Fax:* (914) 251-6739 (office). *E-mail:* Laura.Kaminsky@purchase.edu (office). *Website:* www.purchase.edu (office); www.LivingComposersProject.com.

**KAMMERLOHER, Katharina;** Singer (Mezzo-Soprano); b. 16 Nov. 1968, Munich. *Education:* Studied with Mechthild Böhme in Detmold; since 1998 with Vera Rozsa in London. *Career:* Member of the Staatsoper, Berlin from 1993, as Rosina, Costanza in Haydn's L'isola disabitata, Suzuki, as Meg Page under Claudio Abaddo, Mélisande under Michael Gielen, Octavian under Philippe Jordan. Under Daniel Barenboim she sang Magdalene, Wellgunde, Zerlina and Dorabelle in the Doris Dörrie-Production of Cosí fan tutte; Salzburg debut, Lulu, 1995; Schwetzingen Festival 1997, Anna in Cavalli's Didone, 1997; Concerts include Ravel's Shéhérazade, Kantscheli's Lamento (with Gidon Kremer, violin) and Beethoven's Ninth Symphony with Daniel Barenboim, Bach Cantatas under René Jacobs, Elijah with Wolfgang Sawallisch, Berlioz's Romeo with Luisi, Orchesterlieder by Schönberg in Munich and Vienna 2001 and Le Visage Nuptial by Boulez (Proms, London and Edinburgh 2001) both with Boulez; Tour of Japan with the Berlin State 2002; Second Lady in Magic Flute and Mozart Requiem at Salzburg, 2002; Anita in West Side Story with Kent Nagano, March 2003; Debut as Komponist in Ariadne auf Naxos with Fabia Luisi in Berlin, June 2003. *Recordings include:* Elektra (Teldec); Haydn's L'isola disabitata; Bach Cantatas (Harmonia Mundi); DVD of Cosí fan tutte (Barenboim/ Dörrie); DVD of Otello (Barenboim/ Flimm). *Address:* c/o Deutsche Staatsoper Berlin, Unter den Linden 9–11, 10117 Berlin, Germany.

**KAMMINGA, Martin;** Dutch organist; b. 23 Dec. 1933, Muiden; m. Renske van der Hauw 1957; two s. one d. *Education:* Amsterdam Conservatory with Piet Kee, Frans Moonen, Anton Kersjes. *Career:* organist, live and on radio, in major churches and cathedrals in Netherlands and France; Conductor, Royal Christian Choral Society, Amsterdam, 1967; Conductor, numerous major works for large orchestra, choir and soloists, Concertgebouw Amsterdam; Director, Hilversum Conservatory of Music, 1979–98; jury member, organ and choral conducting examinations, Conservatorium van Amsterdam, 1999–; mem. Royal Netherlands Society of Organists. *Honours:* Conductor of the Year, City of Amsterdam, 1981; Choir of the Year, City of Amsterdam, 1983; Ridder in de Orde van Oranje Nassau, on the 40th anniversary as a musician, Concertgebouw Amsterdam, 1999. *Address:* Prinses Beatrixlaan 12, 1381 AH Weesp, Netherlands.

**KAMNITZER, Peter;** Violist and College Professor; b. 27 Nov. 1922, Berlin, Germany. *Education:* Studied at the Juilliard and Manhattan Schools, New York. *Career:* Co-founded the La Salle String Quartet at the Juilliard School, 1949; Many concerts featuring modern composers and the quartets of Beethoven; European debut 1954; Composers who have written for the ensemble include, Hans Erich Apostel, Earle Brown, Henri Pousseur, Mauricio Kagel, György Ligeti, Penderecki and Witold Lutoslawski; Quartet-in-Residence, Colorado College 1949–53, the Quartet-in-Residence and Professor, Cincinnati College-Conservatory of Music; Quartet disbanded 1988. *Recordings include:* Works by Berg, Schoenberg, Webern and

Zemlinsky; Beethoven's Late Quartets. *Address:* c/o Cincinnati College-Conservatory of Music, Cincinnati, OH 45221, USA.

**KAMPE, Anja;** Soprano; b. 1968, Germany. *Career:* Many appearances in opera throughout Germany and elsewhere in Europe, notably in Rossini's Il Turco in Italia and as Fiordiligi in Così fan tutte; Also sings songs by Bizet and Wolf (Spanisches Liederbuch); Contestant in the 1995 Cardiff Singer of the World Competition. *Address:* c/o Via Alfieri No. 9, Cento (Fe) 44042, Italy.

**KAMU, Okko;** Finnish conductor and violinist; b. 7 March 1946, Helsinki; m. Susanne Kamu 1987; three s. three d. *Education:* Sibelius Acad. *Career:* leader, Suhonen Quartet 1964; began professional career with Helsinki Philharmonic Orchestra 1965; subsequently appointed leader, Finnish Nat. Opera Orchestra 1966–69, Third Conductor 1967; guest conductor, Swedish Royal Opera, Stockholm 1969; Chief Conductor, Finnish Radio Symphony Orchestra 1971–77; Music Dir Oslo Philharmonic 1975–79, Helsinki Philharmonic 1981–89; Prin. Conductor, Netherlands Radio Symphony 1983–86; Prin. Guest Conductor, City of Birmingham Symphony Orchestra 1985–88; Prin. Conductor, Sjaelland Symphony Orchestra, Copenhagen 1988–94; Music Dir Stockholm Sinfonietta 1989–93; Prin. Conductor Helsingborg Symphony Orchestra 1991–2000; First Guest Conductor, Singapore Symphony Orchestra 1995–2001; Music Dir Finnish Nat. Opera, Helsinki 1996–2000; Prin. Guest Conductor Lausanne Chamber Orchestra 1999–2002; conducted world premières of Sallinen's operas The Red Line and The King Goes Forth to France; numerous engagements with orchestras and opera houses worldwide; mem. Royal Swedish Acad. of Music 1996. *Honours:* First Prize, First Int. Karajan Conductor Competition, Berlin 1969. *Address:* Villa Arcadia, Calle Mozart 7, Rancho Domingo, 29639 Benalmedina Pueblo, Spain.

**KANAWA, Dame Kiri** (see Te Kanawa, Dame Kiri)

**KANCHELI, Giya (Georgy);** Georgian composer; b. 10 Aug. 1935, Tbilisi; s. of Alexander Kancheli and Agnessa Kancheli; m. Valentina Djikia; one s. one d. *Education:* Tbilisi State Conservatory with I. Tuskia. *Career:* Prof. Tbilisi Conservatory 1970–90; Music Dir Rustaveli Drama Theatre 1971–; First Sec. Georgian Composers' Union 1984–89; Composer in Residence, Berlin (German Academic Exchange Service) 1991–92; Composer in Residence, Royal Flemish Philharmonic Orchestra, Antwerp 1995–96. *Compositions include:* symphonies: First 1967, Second 1973, Third 1973, Fourth (in Memoriam Michelangelo) 1975, Fifth 1977, Sixth (In Memory of Parents) 1980, Seventh (Epilogue) 1986; other symphonic works: Mourned by the Wind for orchestra and viola 1989, Lament (in memory of Luigi Nono), for violin, soprano and orchestra 1995; opera: Music for the Living 1984; chamber works: Life Without Christmas 1989–90 (cycle of four works for chamber ensembles), Magnum Ignotum, for wind ensemble and tape 1994, Exil, for soprano, small ensemble and tape 1994; music to plays by Shakespeare, including King Lear, Richard III and other productions of Rustaveli Drama Theatre, incidental music. *Honours:* USSR State Prize 1976, USSR People's Artist 1988, State Prize of Georgia 1982, Nika Prize for film music 1987, Triumph Prize Moscow 1998. *Address:* Tovstonogov str. 6, 380064 Tbilisi, Georgia; Consience Straat 14, 2018 Antwerp, Belgium. *Telephone:* (3) 295-03-39 (Tbilisi); (3) 230-85-53 (Antwerp).

**KANG, Dong-suk;** American violinist; b. 28 April 1954, Seoul, Republic of Korea; m. Martine Schittenhelm; one s. one d. *Education:* Juilliard School, New York and Curtis Inst. Philadelphia (under Ivan Galamian). *Career:* prize winner, Queen Elisabeth of the Belgians, Montreal, San Francisco Symphony Foundation and Carl Flesch competitions; has appeared with maj. orchestras throughout USA, UK, Europe and Far East and at music festivals around the world including BBC Promenade concerts (debut 1987). *Recordings include:* complete repertoire for violin and orchestra by Sibelius, Nielsen Violin Concerto, Elgar Violin Concerto, Bruch Violin Concerto, Walton Violin Concerto. *Address:* 23 rue Daumesnil, 9430 Vincennes, France (office); c/o Clarion/Seven Muses, 47 Whitehall Park, London, N19 3TW, England. *Telephone:* (20) 7272-4413. *Fax:* (20) 7281-9687.

**KANG, Philip;** singer (bass); b. 10 April 1948, Seoul, Republic of Korea. *Education:* studied in Seoul and Berlin. *Career:* sang small roles at the Deutsche Oper Berlin from 1976; engagements at Wuppertal, Kiel and Nuremberg, Nationaltheater Mannheim from 1986; roles have included Sarastro, Rocco, Kaspar, Verdi's Sparafucile, Ramphis, Philip II, Ferrando and Padre Guardiano, Wagner's Daland, Pogner, Mark, King Henry and Gurnemanz; Sang in Italy from 1982, Rodolfo in Sonnambula at Toulouse 1983, Lisbon 1984, as Attila, Sarastro at the Théâtre des Champs Elysées, 1987; American engagements at New York and Philadelphia, European at Madrid, Rome, Frankfurt (as Rocco) and Cologne, as Rossini's Basilio; Théâtre de la Monnaie Brussels as Pimen in Boris Godunov and as Antonios in Stephen Climax by Hans Zender, 1990; Bayreuth Festival 1987–92, as Fafner, Hagen and Hunding; Season 1999–2000 as Verdi's King Philip at the Komische Oper, Berlin, and as Fafner and Hunding at Bayreuth. *Honours:* Mario del Monaco Competition winner 1979. *Address:* c/o Théâtre Royale de la Monnaie, 4 Leopoldstrasse, 1000 Brussels, Belgium.

**KANGA, Skaila;** Harpist; b. 8 Jan. 1946, Bombay, India; Divorced, 2 s., 2 d. *Education:* Royal Academy of Music, Junior Exhibitioner, 1959–64; Full-time Student, 1964–66; Studied Piano with Professor Vivian Langrish and Harp with Professor Tina Bonifacio. *Career:* BBC Concert Orchestra and Freelance with regional and major London orchestras; Solo career includes concertos

and broadcasts as well as numerous commercial recordings with such artists as Sutherland, Domingo, Pavarotti, Kiri te Kanawa and composers John Williams, Richard Rodney Bennett, Michel Legrand; Performed the Ravel Introduction and Allegro at the Proms, 4th time, 1994; Michael Tippett's 90th Birthday Celebrations, Barbican Hall, 1994; Fauré and the French Connection, festival in Manchester, 1995; Head of Harp, Royal Academy of Music; mem, PRS; BASCA; MCPS. *Compositions include:* Les saisons de la harpe, for solo harp; British Folk Songs Vol. I for flute and harp; Miniatures Bks I and II, harp duets for flute and harp; American Sketches for clarinet (or flute) and harp; Cadenzas for Mozart Concerto for flute and harp; all published by Alaw at www.alawmusic.ndo.co.uk. *Recordings include:* 3 Chamber works of Arnold Bax for Hyperion the Elegiac Trio, The Harp Quintet and the Nonet; French Chamber Music with Academy of St Martins; 2 Solo Albums with Tommy Reilly; Mozart Flute and Harp Concerto, City of London Sinfonia; Bax Chamber Music, Nash Ensemble. *Honours:* LRAM, 1966; ARAM, 1990; FRAM, 1994. *Address:* c/o Head of Harp, Royal Academy of Music, Marylebone Road, London NE1 5HT, England.

**KANI, Wasfi,** OBE, BMus; British violinist, conductor and opera director; *Chief Executive, Grange Park Opera;* b. 1956, London. *Education:* Univ. of Oxford. *Career:* played violin in Nat. Youth Orchestra; fmr programmer and designer financial computer systems, London; studied conducting with Sian Edwards 1980s; est. computer consultancy 1986–93; f. Pimlico Opera (touring co.) 1989, productions staged in banks, hosps, country houses, prisons (performance of Sweeney Todd was inspiration for BBC TV film Tomorrow La Scala 1991); Chief Exec. Garsington Opera 1992–97; cr. Grange Park rural opera festival, Hants. 1997, Chief Exec. 1997–, performances of Rinaldo, Eugene Onegin, I Capuletti e I Montecchi 2001, The Mikado, Iolanthe 2003. *Address:* General Administration, Grange Park Opera, The Coach House, 12 St. Thomas Street, Winchester, SO23 4HF, England (office). *Telephone:* (1962) 868600 (office). *Fax:* (1962) 868968 (office). *E-mail:* info@grangeparkopera.co.uk (office). *Website:* www.grangeparkopera.co.uk.

**KANKA, Michal;** Cellist; b. 23 May 1960, Prague, Czechoslovakia; m. 1982, 2 d. *Education:* Prague Conservatory and Academy of Performing Arts, University of Southern California. *Career:* Debut: Dvořák Concerto with Czech Philharmonic Orchestra, 1983; Regular appearances with Czech Orchestras, 1982–; Foreign tours to Europe, America, Japan and Australasia, 1982–; Member of the Prazak Quartet, 1986–; Berlin debut with RIAS, 1987; Regular concerts in Salzburg, Munich, London, Amsterdam, Milan, Tokyo and Sydney; Official soloist, Prague radio orchestra, 2003–. *Recordings:* Chopin, Sonata; Stravinsky's Italian Suite, 1984; Schubert's Sonata in C, 1989; Franck, Sonata, 1989; Mozart's Concertone with S Accardo, 1990; Martinů, 3 Sonatas, 1991; Beethoven, Mozart and Janáček works with Prazak Quartet, 1989–91; Vivaldi, 7 Cello Concertos, 1993; Complete works for cello and orchestra by B Martinů, 2 CDs, 1995; Boccherini, 7 Sonatas, 1998; Myslivecek, 6 Sonatas, world premiere recording, 1999; Rubinstein: Complete set for cello/piano; Haydn Cello Concertos. *Honours:* Laureate, Tchaikovsky Competition in Moscow, 1982; 1st Prize, Prague Spring Competition, 1983; Winner, Cello International Competition, ARD Munich, 1986; Soloist of the State Philharmony Brno, 1995; Diapason D'or, Chock de la Musique, Télérama, 1995. *Address:* Peckova 17, Karlin, 18600 Prague 8, Czech Republic.

**KANN, Hans;** Austrian pianist, composer and professor of piano; b. 14 Feb. 1927, Vienna; m. Kue Hee Ha 1953; one s. one d. *Education:* Vienna Music Academy, studied piano with Bloch, Göllner, Wührer, Schulhof, composition with Lechthaler, Polnauer. *Career:* debut in Brahmssaal, Vienna, 1946; Concerts in whole of Europe, Russia, Asia, China (3 concert tours), South America and USA, 1946–; Professor at Ueno University of Arts, 1955–58; big concerts in Japan, 1955–58, 1960, 1972, 1974, 1976, 1980–86; Professor at the Hochschule für Musik, 1977–95. *Compositions:* Sonatina for piano; Abschnitt; 10 Stücke ohne Bass-schlüssel; Fingerübungen; Concertino; Chamber Music; Music for Television; Experimental Music. *Publications include:* Sonatina; Abschnitt 37; Tägliche Fingerübungen für Pianisten; Models; 4 Stücke für Blockflöte und Klavier; Piano enso oboegaki, 1987; Pianists Memories; contrib. to Österreichische Musikzeitung; Gendai Ongaku (Tokyo). *Address:* Sonnenfelsgasse 11/14, Vienna 1010, Austria.

**KANTA, Ludovit;** Slovakian cellist; *Solo Cellist, Orchestra Ensemble, Kanazawa, Japan;* b. 9 July 1957, Bratislava; m. 1977; two s. one d. *Education:* Bratislava Conservatorium with G. Vecerny, Academy of Music, Prague with A. Vectomov. *Career:* debut in Strauss' Don Quixote, with Slovak Philharmonic, International Music Festival, Bratislava, Oct 1982; 1st Solo Cello, Slovak Philharmonic, Bratislava, 1983; Concert tours and international festivals as Soloist with Slovak Philharmonic, Bulgaria, 1984, USSR and Poland, 1985, Japan, 1987, Spain, 1988; Other foreign tours, Germany, 1980, 1983, 1986, Italy, 1981, Bulgaria, 1983, 1985, Yugoslavia, 1985, Romania, 1985, 1987, Sweden, 1985; Solo Cellist, Orchestra Ensemble, Kanazawa, Japan, 1990–; Associate Professor, Aichi Prefectural University of Arts, Nagoya, 1995–. *Recordings:* Dvořák-Cello Concerto, Haydn-Concerto in D Major, with Large Orchestra of Bratislava Radio, conducted by Kurt Hortnagel and Ondrej Lenárd; Igor Dibak-premiere recording of Cello Concerto, with Slovak Philharmonic, conductor Bystrik Rezucha; Haydn-Boccherini Concertos, Capella Istropolitana, conductor Peter Breiner; Cello Recital, 1997; Ludovit Kanta Cello Recital, with Heller on piano; Kodaly: Cello Solo Sonata op. 8; Dvořàk: Concerto h-mol op.104 with Orchestra Ensemble Kanazawa, conductor Jan Latham Koenig. *Honours:* 1st Prize, Beethoven Competition, OPAVA, 1977; 2nd Prize, Prague Spring International Competition, 1980; Concert Imagine; Concert Service Company. *Address:* Midorigaoka 1-2, 929-0322 Tsubata, Ishikawa, Japan (home). *Telephone:* (76) 288-7677 (home). *Fax:* (76) 288-7677 (home). *E-mail:* hanka@naa.att.ne.jp (home).

**KAPELLMANN, Franz-Josef;** Singer (baritone); b. 23 Sept. 1945, Cologne, Germany. *Education:* studied in Cologne. *Career:* sang at the Deutsche Oper Berlin, 1973–75, Dortmund from 1975, notably as Verdi's Luna, Posa, Germont, Iago and Amonasro, Scarpia, Gianni Schicchi, Wolfram, Beckmesser and Kurwenal; Alberich in a new production of Das Rheingold, 1990; Guest appearances at Düsseldorf, Wiesbaden, Karlsruhe, Klagenfurt, Lubeck and Paris (Alberich in Götterdämmerung); Other roles have included Riccardo in Puritani, Guglielmo, Papageno, Toby in The Red Line by Sallinen, Escamillo (at Regensburg), Mozart's Figaro (Gelsenkirchen) and Don Fernando in Fidelio (Granada Festival); Gala concert at the Alte Oper Frankfurt, 1989; Sang Alberich in Siegfried at Brussels, 1991, Beckmesser at Trieste, 1992; Pizarro in a concert of Fidelio, Edinburgh, 1996; Season 1998 at La Scala, Milan and Catania as Weber's Kaspar and Pizarro in Fidelio; Season 2000–01 as Alberich for Bonn Opera, Pizarro at La Scala and Kaspar in Der Freischütz at the Staatsoper Berlin. *Recordings:* Handel's L'Allegro, il Penseroso ed il Moderato. *Current Management:* Theateragentur Dr Germinal Hilbert, Maximilianstrasse 22, 80539 Munich, Germany. *Telephone:* (89) 290 747-0. *Fax:* (89) 290 747-90. *Website:* www.hilbert.de.

**KAPLAN, Abraham;** Conductor; b. 5 May 1931, Tel-Aviv, Israel. *Education:* Studied at the Israel Academy in Jerusalem and at the Juilliard School, 1954–57; Conducting studies with William Steinberg and Frederick Prausnitz, composition with Darius Milhaud. *Career:* Directed the Kol Israel Chorus, 1953–54 and 1958–59; Conductor of the Haifa Oratorio Society, 1958–59; Founded the Camerata Singers, USA, 1960; Director of Choral Music at Juilliard, 1961–77 and the Symphonic Choral Society of New York, 1968–77; Founded the Camerata Symphony Orchestra 1968 and appeared as Guest Conductor with leading orchestras in the US and Israel; Teacher at the Berkshire Music Center and at Union Theological Seminary New York, 1961–73; Director of Choral Studies at Chautauqua, New York, 1976; Professor of Music at University of Washington, Seattle, 1977; Many choral engagements and recordings with the New York Philharmonic. *Address:* University of Washington, Department of Music, Washington State, USA.

**KAPLAN, Lewis;** Concert Violinist; b. 10 Nov. 1933, Passaic, New Jersey, USA; m. Adria Goodkin, 6 Aug 1961, 1 s., 1 d. *Education:* Bachelor's degree, 1958, Master's degree, 1960, Juilliard School. *Career:* Debut: Town Hall, New York, 1961; Solo concerts, USA, Europe and Far East, 1953–; Violinist-Founder, Aeolian Chamber Players, 1961–; Violin and Chamber Music Faculties, the Juilliard School, 1964–; Artistic Director and Co-Founder, Bowdoin Summer Music Festival, 1964–; Violin Faculty, Summer Academy Mozarteum, Salzburg, Austria, 1987; Violin Faculty, Mannes College of Music, 1987–; Numerous conducting appearances in USA and Europe. *Recordings:* Numerous. *Publications:* Caprice Variations for Unaccompanied Violin by George Rochberg (editor), 1973. *Address:* 173 Riverside Drive, New York, NY 10024, USA.

**KAPLAN, Mark;** American violinist; b. 30 Dec. 1953, Boston, Mass, USA. *Education:* studied with Dorothy DeLay at Juilliard School, New York. *Career:* US engagements 1973–; performances with Cleveland, Philadelphia, Los Angeles, Pittsburgh and Baltimore Orchestras; Summer Festivals of Aspen, Blossom, Ambler, Grant Park and Santa Fe; European career 1980–; concerts with Berlin Philharmonic and Klaus Tennstedt; engagements in England and Israel with Rudolf Barshai, and thereafter with all major European Orchestras, gave European premiere of Marc Neikrug's Violin Concerto with Hallé Orchestra; BBC Promenade Concerts and Concerts with Royal Philharmonic in London and Italy; associations with conductors Marek Janowski, Michael Gielen and Charles Dutoit; piano recitals in Europe and America; recitals with Golub/Kaplan/Carr Trio playing each season in USA and Europe; trio toured Italy and UK 1994–95, appearing at St John's Smith Square. *Recordings:* Paganini and Wieniawski concertos repertoire, Mendelssohn, Brahms and Schubert Piano Trios, Sarasate Solo Violin Works. *Honours:* Fritz Kreisler Memorial Award, Award of Special Distinction, Leventritt Competition 1973. *Current Management:* c/o Jonathan Wentworth Associates Ltd, 10 Fisk Place, Suite 530, Mt Vernon, NY 10550, USA. *Telephone:* (914) 667-0707. *Fax:* (914) 667-0784. *E-mail:* office@jwentworth .com. *Website:* www.jwentworth.com.

**KARAI, József;** Hungary composer, pianist and conductor; b. 8 Nov. 1927, Budapest; m. Katalin Kertész. *Education:* Acad. of Music, Budapest. *Career:* debut 1950; mem. Asscn of Hungarian Composers, Hungarian Art Foundation, Hungarian Kodály Soc. *Compositions:* about 300 works for chorus based on 20th Century Hungarian Poets' poems and poems of Goethe, Shelley, C. Sandburg, Christina Rossetti, Petrarca, Edward Lear, Rilke, Trakl, J. R. Jimenez, Th Storm, Christian Morgenstern, G. Carducci; Works for wind instruments, strings, piano, organ and orchestra; 89 works published by Edition Musica and 80 by other publishers. *Publications:* Children and Female Choruses 1970, Mixed Choruses 1977, Twelve Spirituals 1978, Easy Children's Choruses 1978, Tenders of The Fire, 14 mixed choruses 1968–69, Selected Female Choruses, Zen-on, Tokyo 1992, Hungarian Christmas Songs (suite) 1993, Missa Brevis 1999. *Honours:* Erkel Prize 1972, SZOT Prize 1980. *Address:* Gyöztes u 19, 1151 Budapest, Hungary.

**KARAS, Joza;** Violinist and Musicologist; b. 3 May 1926, Warsaw, Poland (Czech Nationality); m. Anne Killackey, 14 Feb 1976, 5 s., 1 d. *Education:*

Academic Gymnasium, Prague, 1945; State Conservatory of Music, Prague, 1949; Hartt College of Music, University of Hartford, USA, 1957. *Career:* Violin Soloist, Recitalist, USA and Canada; Founder, Karas String Quartet; mem, Czechoslovak Society of Arts and Sciences in America. *Compositions:* Violin Method. *Recordings:* Hans Krása's Brundibár, 1993. *Publications:* Music in Terezín 1941–1945, 1985. *Contributions:* STTH; Jewish Digest; Journal of Synagogue Music; Review of the Society for the History of the Czechoslovak Jews; Theatrical Performances during the Holocaust. *Address:* 212 Duncaster Road, Bloomfield, CT 06002, USA.

**KARASEV, Grigory;** Singer (Bass); b. 1960, Russia. *Career:* Concert and opera performances throughout Russia: appearances at the Kirov Opera, St Petersburg, from 1987 as Ferrando in Il Trovatore, Mozart's Antonio (Figaro), Raimondo in Lucia di Lammermoor and Rossini's Don Basilio; Other roles include Don Pasquale, Orlik in Mazeppa, Nikitich in Boris Godunov and Storm Wind in Rimsky-Korsakov's Kashchei the Immortal; Guest appearances with New Israel Opera and La Fenice, Venice; Sang with the Kirov Opera in Summer Season at Covent Garden, 2000. *Address:* c/o Kirov Opera, Mariinsky Square, St Petersburg, Russia.

**KARASIK, Gita;** Concert Pianist; b. 14 Dec. 1952, San Francisco, California, USA; m. Lee Caplin, 25 June 1975. *Education:* Private study with Mme, Rosina Lhevinne, Juilliard; Karl Ulrich Schnabel; Lev Schorr; San Francisco Conservatory of Music. *Career:* Debut: San Francisco/SF Symphony, 1958; NYC/Carnegie Hall, 1969; First American Pianist to make official concert tour of People's Republic of China; Guest Soloist, National Television Debut, The Bell Telephone Hour, NBC, 1963; Guest Soloist, San Francisco Symphony, 1958, 1969, 1972, 1974; Los Angeles Philharmonic, 1971; St Louis Symphony, 1974–75; Boston Pops Orchestra with Arthur Fiedler, 1975; Indianapolis Symphony, 1972, 1976; Atlanta Symphony, 1972; Singapore Symphony, 1980–81; Hong Kong Philharmonic, 1980–82; Tours of Latin America, Far East, Europe, USA; Film Scores, Andy Warhol: Made in China, 1986; The Serpent and the Rainbow, 1988; To Die For, 1989; Son of Darkness, 1992. *Compositions:* Concerto for Gita Karasik No. 2 by Andrew Imbrie, as first prize Ford Foundation Artists Award, World Premiere with Indianapolis Symphony for Bicentennial, 1976. *Address:* 8332 Melrose Avenue, Hollywood, CA 90069, USA.

**KARAYANIS, Plato;** Opera Administrator; b. 26 Dec. 1928, Pittsburgh, USA. *Education:* Voice at Carnegie Mellon University, and at Curtis Institute; Administration and Stage Technology at the Hamburg Opera. *Career:* Six years as a leading baritone in major European houses; Director of Rehearsal Department, San Francisco Opera; Assistant Stage Director and Administrator for Metropolitan Opera National Company, 1965–67; Executive Vice President of Affiliate Artists Incorporated until 1977; General Director, the Dallas Opera, 1977–; President of Board of Directors, OPERA America, 1993–97; General Director, Dallas Opera 1977–2000, presiding over a complete Ring cycle and the world premiere of Argento's The Aspern Papers in 1988; US Premieres of operatic works by Vivaldi and Falla, and institutional stabilization of this major American opera company; Under his direction the company has committed to innovative productions of traditional repertoire, regular inclusion of major 20th century opera and new American works; Artistic Consultant, Palm Beach Opera, 2002–. *Honours:* Award for Excellence in the Creative Arts, Dallas Historical Society, 1993; TACA Award for Excellence in the Performing Arts, 1998; New rehearsal production centre for the Dallas Opera was named The Dorothy and Plato Karayanis Rehearsal Center. *Address:* 3327 Prescott Avenue, Dallas, TX 75219, USA. *Fax:* (214) 521-7084. *E-mail:* skarayan@swbell.net.

**KARCHIN, Louis;** Composer; b. 8 Sept. 1951, Pennsylvania, USA; m. Julie Sirota, 7 June 1987, 2 d. *Education:* BMus, Eastman School of Music, 1973; PhD, Harvard University, 1978. *Compositions:* Capriccio for Violin and Seven Instruments, 1979; Duo for Violin and Cello, 1981; Viola Variations, 1982; Songs of John Keats, 1984; Songs of Distance and Light, 1988; Sonata for Cello and Piano, 1989; String Quartet, 1990; Galactic Folds for Chamber Ensemble, 1992; String Quartet No. 2, 1994; Sonata da Camera for violin and piano, 1995; Rustic Dances, 1995; Rhapsody for orchestra, 1996; Cascades, 1997; American Visions: Two Songs on Poems of Yevgeny Yevtushenko, 1998; Romulus, an Opera in One Act, 1990; Quartet for Percussion, 2000; Deux Poemes de Mallarmé, 2001; Songs- Meditation, Interlude, Echoes, Memory, Carmen de Boheme, To the Sun, 2001–03; Voyages, for alto saxophone and piano, 2001; Orpheus a Masque for baritone, chamber ensemble and dancers, 2003. *Recordings:* Duo for Violin and Cello; Songs of John Keats; Capriccio for Violin and Seven Instruments; Galactic Folds, Songs of Distance and Light, American Visions, String Quartet #2, Rustic Dances, Sonata da Camera. *Honours:* Hinrichsen Award, American Academy of Arts and Letters, 1985; Koussevitzky-Tanglewood Award, 1971; Commission from Fromm Foundation at Harvard; Commission from Serge Koussevitzky Music Foundation, 1998; Hecksher Foundation Prize, 1999; Goddard Lieberson Award, American Academy of Arts and Letters, 2001; Barlow Endowment Commission, 2001;. *Current Management:* Howard Stokar Management, New York. *Address:* 24 Waverly Place, Rm 268, New York, NY 10003, USA.

**KARCZYKOWSKI, Ryszard;** Singer (Tenor); b. 6 April 1942, Tczew, Poland. *Education:* Studied in Gdansk with Halina Mickiewiczowna. *Career:* Sang in Gdansk and Stettin, then at the Landestheater Dessau (debut as Beppe in Pagliacci 1969); Other roles included Tamino, Ferrando, Fenton and Rodolfo; Sang in Leipzig from 1974, then in Berlin, Dresden (Tamino and Lensky),

Moscow, Zürich, Vienna, New York, Rome, Prague and Aix-en-Provence; Covent Garden debut 1977, as Alfred in Die Fledermaus, returned as the Duke of Mantua, Ferrando and Alwa in the first local production of Berg's Lulu, 1981; Sang in the 1981 stage premiere of Prokofiev's Maddalena (Graz) and the same year sang in Haydn's Orlando Paladino, at the Vienna Festival; Other roles include Ernesto, Nemorino, Rinuccio, Lionel (Martha), Jenik (Bartered Bride), Belmonte, Macduff and Elemer in Arabella; Further appearances in Boston (Duke of Mantua, 1981), Washington, Leningrad, Los Angeles, Zagreb and Lisbon; Sang in Rigoletto with the company of the Deutsche Oper Berlin at the Wiesbaden Festival, 1989; Star Guest at the Vienna Opernball, 1998. *Recordings include:* Szymanowski's 3rd Symphony, The Bells by Rachmaninov, Shostakovich 13th Symphony; Die Lustige Witwe and Die Fledermaus; Arias and Duets From Celebrated Operas, 1991; Laudate Dominum Omnes Gentes, 1992; A. Schoenberg–Von Heute auf Morgen, 1997; A. Berg–Lulu, 1998; F. Lehar–Gold and Silver, 1999. *Address:* Niederraeder Landstr. 6a, 60598 Frankfurt, Germany.

**KARIS, Aleck;** Pianist; b. 21 Jan. 1945, Washington DC, USA. *Education:* BM, Manhattan School 1976, with Charles Wuorinen; Juilliard School with Beveridge Webster; Private study with Artur Balsam and William Daghlian. *Career:* Latin American debut 1981 at São Paulo; New York debut 1984, playing Chopin, Schumann, Stravinsky and Elliott Carter; Has premiered works by Mario Davidovsky, Milton Babbitt and Morton Subotnick; Member of Speculum Musicae from 1983 and has performed with the Contemporary Chamber Ensemble, New York, St Luke's Chamber Ensemble and the Group Contemporary Music; Associate in Music Performances at Columbia University from 1983. *Honours:* Prizewinner, Rockefeller Foundation International Competition, 1978; fromm Foundation Grant, 1983. *Address:* Music Department, Columbia University, City University of New York, USA.

**KARKOFF, Maurice Ingvar;** Swedish composer; *Teacher of Theory and Composition, Stockholm Municipal Institute of Music;* b. 17 March 1927, Stockholm; two s. one d. *Education:* Music Theory with Karl-Birger Blomdahl, 1944–46; Studied Composition with Lars-Erik Larsson, Royal Conservatory of Music, Stockholm, 1948–53; Piano, 1945–46; Counterpoint, 1949–53; Conducting, 1950–52; Teacher's Degree, 1951; Additional composition studies with Erland von Koch, Hans Holewa, Wladimir Vogel, André Jolivet. *Career:* debut, Duo for Clarinet and Bassoon, Fylkingen 1951; Assistant Music Critic, Stockholmstidningen, 1962–66; Teacher, Stockholm Municipal Institute of Music, 1965–; mem. Royal Swedish Acad. of Music, Swedish Soc. of Composers. *Compositions include:* Lyric Suite for Chamber Orchestra; Nine Aphoristic Variants; 12 Symphonies and 5 Small Symphonies; 14 Solo Concertos; Dolorous Symphony for String Orchestra No. 9; Symphonic Reflections; Voices from the Past for Soprano and Strings; Quartet; 2 Tenor Horns and Trombone; Characters for Flute, Oboe, Clarinet, Bassoon, French Horn, Trombone, Euphonium, percussions; 4 Momenti for Violin and Piano; Aspects for Guitar; Spring in Hanger; Poem for Flute (or Alto Flute); Ballata, intermezzo e leggenda per Pianoforte; 15 Album leaves for piano; Glühende Rätsel, Fünf Lieder, Middle Voice and Piano; Early Summer, Songs for Middle Voice and Pianoforte: Scenes in the Desert, for low voice and pianoforte; When The Day Waned for High Voice and Pianoforte; 2 Fantasies for left hand; Kleine Music, English Horn; Chamber opera, The Frontier Kibbutz op 115. *Recordings include:* Six Chinese Impressions; 7 Pezzi per Grande Orchestra; Swedish Radio Symphony Orchestra; Vision Swedish Radio Orchestra, Serious Songs with Filharmonic Orchestra Kerstin Meyer; Symphony No. 4; Glühende Rätsel, soprano and piano; Dolorous Symphony (ninth) for strings; Symphony No. 11 (Sinfonia della Vita); 9 Chinese Songs, soprano, piano; Oriental Pictures for piano, (composer plays); Ernst und Spass for Saxophone Quartet; Sonatin for Alto Saxophone and Piano, new CD. *Honours:* City of Stockholm Prize of Honour 1976, Litteris et Artibus 1993, Alfven Prize 1999. *Address:* Tackjärnsvägen 18, 16868 Bromma, Sweden. *Telephone:* (8) 266876. *Fax:* (8) 266876.

**KARKOSCHKA, Erhard;** Composer and Composition Teacher; b. 6 March 1923, Mor Ostrava, Czechoslovakia; m. Rothraut Leiter, 27 July 1950, 3 s., 1 d. *Education:* DPhil. *Career:* Conductor, University Hohenheim, 1948–68; Professor, Musikhochschule Stuttgart, 1958–1996; Executive Board, Institut für Neue Musik und Musikerziehung, Darmstadt, 1964–72; President, IGNM, Section West Germany, 1974–80; Member of Academy of Free Art, Mannheim, 1980–; Lectures world-wide. *Compositions:* About 100 including music for orchestra, chamber music, chorus scenic works, opera, electronic music, organ music and multimedia projects; Chamber Opera, Orpheus oder Hadeshöhe, 1990; Paul Celan Variations I–V, 1996–98. *Recordings:* Ad Hoc 1; Bläsergedichte (Wind Poems) for woodwind quintet, 1988; Desideratio Dei for Organ, 1963; Quattrologe for string quartet, 1966; Antimony for wind quintet, 1968; Dialog for Bassoon and Electronics, 1982; Doch Fülle Zwei und Werde Vier, 1982; Entfalten for 4 soloists and big orchestra, 1983. *Publications:* Das Schriftbild Der Neuen Musik, 1965; Notation in New Music, 1972, Japanese translation 1977, Chinese translation, 1996; Analyse Neuer Musik, 1976; Hörerziehung Mit Neuer Musik, Ear Education With New Music, 1981. *Contributions:* Melos; Musik und Bildung; Musica; Musik und Kirche; Die Musikforschung. *Address:* Nellingerstrasse 45, 70619 Stuttgart, Germany. *Telephone:* 0771 445433. *Fax:* 0771 4403476. *E-mail:* karkoschkaerhard@aol .com.

**KARLINS, M(artin) William,** BM, MM, PhD; American composer and educator; *Harry N. and Ruth F. Wyatt Professor of Music Theory and Composition Emeritus, Northwestern University;* b. 25 Feb. 1932, New York,

NY; m. Mickey Cutler 1952; one s. one d. *Education:* Manhattan School of Music, Univ. of Iowa. *Career:* Asst Prof. of Music, Western Illinois Univ. 1965–67, Assoc. Prof. 1967–73; Dir Contemporary Music Ensemble, Northwestern Univ., Evanston, Illinois 1967–81, Prof. of Theory and Composition 1973–98, Harry N. and Ruth F. Wyatt Prof. of Music Theory and Composition 1998–2003, Emeritus 2003– music performed world-wide 1959–; composer-in-residence, 6éme Stage de Saxophone, Festival Lyrique et Musical de Duras, France 1991; composer-in-residence, World Saxophone Congresses in London, Bordeaux, Nuremberg and Washington, DC; guest composer and lecturer, Franz Liszt Acad. of Music, Budapest, and Franz Liszt Musical Coll., Györ, Hungary 1995; featured composer in a concert presented by American Cultural Center, Sofia, Bulgaria 1997; Lecturer, Wiener Hochschule für Musik 1999; composer and co-ordinator Stefan Wolpe Festival, Northwestern Univ. 2001; honoured composer and lecturer, Third Music Research Seminar, Escola de Música e Artes Cênicas da Universidade Federal de Goiás, Goiânia, Brasil 2003; mem. BMI, American Music Center. *Compositions:* for large ensemble: Concert Music No. 1 for orchestra 1959, Concert Music No. II for chorus and orchestra 1960, Concert Music No. III for woodwinds, brass, piano and percussion 1963, Concert Music No. IV for orchestra 1964, Lementations-in-Memoriam 1968, Passacaglia and Rounds for band 1970, Reflux concerto for amplified double bass and wind ensembler, piano and percussion 1971, Concert Music No. V for orchestra 1972, Symphony No. I for orchestra 1979, Catena I for little orchestra with clarinet obligato 1980, Concerto for alto saxophone and orchestra 1981, Catena II for soprano, saxophone and brass quintet 1982, Catena III concerto for horn and orchestra 1983, Nostalgie for saxophone ensemble 1991, Elegy for orchestra 1992, Academic Festival Fanfare 2001; chamber music: Concerto Grosso No. I for nine instruments 1959, String Quartet with soprano in the last movement 1960, Concerto Grosso No. II for seven solo instruments 1961, Birthday Music No. I 1962, String Trio 1962, Birthday Music No. II for flute and double bass 1963, Little Piece for four double basses 1962, Four Inventions and a Fugue for bassoon, piano and female voice 1962, Song for Soprano with alto flute and cello 1963, Variations on 'Obiter Dictum' for solo cello, piano and percussion 1965, Blues for saxophone quartet 1965, Music for oboe, bass clarinet and piano 1966, Quartet No. I for saxophones 1966, Three Songs for soprano, flute and piano 1967, Music for English horn and piano 1968, Music for alto saxophone and piano 1968, Music for tenor saxophone and piano 1969, Graphic Mobile 1969, Woodwind Quintet 1970, Celebration for flute, oboe and harpsichord 1970, Quintet for alto saxophone and string quartet 1973, Quartet No. II for saxophones 1975, 'and all our world is dew' Woodwind Quintet No. II 1977, Infinity for oboe d'amore, clarinet, viola and female voice 1978, Fantasia for tenor saxophone and percussion 1978, Fanfare with Fugato 1981, Returning the Scroll to the Arc for baritone and organ 1985, Impromptu for alto saxophone and organ 1985, Saxtuper for alto or soprano saxophone, tuba and percussion 1989, Introduction and Passacaglia for two saxophones and piano 1990, Night Light Quartet No. 3 for saxophone 1992, Under and Over for flute and contrabass 1994, Kindred Spirits for mandolin, guitar and harp 1997, Just a Line from Chameleon for two clarinets 2001, Under and Over for violin and contrabass 2003, Partners duo with solos for violin and piano 2004; solo pieces: Sonata No. I for piano 1959, Outgrowths – Variations for piano 1961, Sonata No. II for piano 1962, Obiter Dictum for organ 1962, Solo Piece with Passacaglia for clarinet 1964, Sonata No. III for piano 1965, Music for Cello Alone No. I 1966, Music for Cello Alone No. II 1969, Chameleon for harpsichord 1984, Seasons for solo saxophonist 1987, Suite of Preludes for piano 1988, Drei Kleine Cembalostücke for harpsichord 1994, Humble Harvest for piano 2000, Improvisations on 'Lines Where Beauty Lingers' for solo bass clarinet 2002, Improvisations on 'Lines Where Beauty Lingers' for solo saxophone 2003, Wally's Caprice for solo flute 2004; choral music: Children's Bedtime Songs for mixed chorus 1955, Three Love Songs for male chorus 1957, Three Poems for chorus 1966, Looking Out My Window for treble chorus and viola 1990. *Recordings of compositions:* Klecka Plays Broege and Karlins, Nostalgie: A Retrospective of Saxophone Music by M. William Karlins, Salvatore Spina Piano Music by Karlins, Lombardo and Stout, M. William Karlins, Works by M. William Karlins, Howard Sandroff, Charles Tomlinson Griffes, Carl Ruggles, Chicago Saxophone Quartet, Joseph Wytko Saxophones, Midwest Composers – Music for Winds, American Millennium Tribute to Adolphe Sax (vol. II), Lifting the Veil, Mixed Company, Heliosaxo, Shaking the Pumpkin, Conicality. *Address:* School of Music, Northwestern University, Evanston, IL 60208, USA (office). *E-mail:* m-karlins@ northwestern.edu (office).

**KARLSEN, Turid;** Singer (Soprano); b. 1961, Oslo, Norway. *Education:* Studied at the Maastricht Conservatory, Netherlands. *Career:* Prizewinner at the 1984 Francisco Vinas Competition, Barcelona and sang at the Weikersheim Festival in 1985 as Romilda in Xerxes and Gluck's Euridice; Karlsruhe Opera from 1986 in Wiener Blut and as Donna Elvira, which she has also sung in Stuttgart, Wiesbaden and Düsseldorf; Sang in the premiere of Graf Mirabeau by Matthus at Stuttgart in 1989; Guest at Dresden in 1989 as Isotta in Schweigsame Frau and Luxembourg in 1991 as Butterfly; Other roles include Mozart's Countess and Pamina, Mimi, Natasha in War and Peace and Violetta; Concert engagements include Bach's St Matthew Passion at Bogota. *Address:* c/o Badisches Staatstheater, Baumeisterstrasse 11, Pf 1449, W-7500 Karlsruhe, Germany.

**KARLSSON, Erik (Mikael);** Composer; b. 10 Dec. 1967, Nynäshamn, Sweden. *Education:* Studied composition and computer music with Tamas Ungvary, Anders Blomquist and others. *Career:* Composer at EMS, Stockholm, Swedish Broadcasting Corporation, Danish Institute for Electro-acoustic Music, Århus, also in Berlin and France; Appearances at festivals and concerts for electro-acoustic music in Europe and elsewhere and many international radio appearances. *Compositions:* Threads and Cords, 1990; Anchorings, Arrows, 1992; La Disparition de L'Azur, 1993; Interiors and Interplays, 1994; Épitaphe pour Iqbal Masih, 1995, all recorded. *Publications:* Author, Circle Almost Closing, and Fylkingen—60 Years of Experimental Art, 1994. *Contributions:* Various articles on contemporary music in Nutida Musik. *Address:* Junkergatan 16/ll, 126 53 Hägersten, Sweden.

**KARLSSON, Lars Olof;** Composer; b. 24 Jan. 1953, Jomala, Åland, Finland; m. Helena Hartikainen, 31 Dec 1994, 1 s., 1 d. *Education:* Studies at the Sibelius Academy, 1972–82; Cantor Organist, 1976; Higher Degree in Piano, 1979; Composition Studies at the Hochschule der Künste, West Berlin, 1982–83; Diploma in Composition, 1983. *Career:* Lecturer at the Sibelius Academy, 1983–; Co-founder of the Åland Culture Festival, 1983; mem, Society of Finnish Composers; Board Member, Scandinavian Guitar Festival, 1986–. *Compositions:* Five Aphorisms for Piano, 1973; Med Havet, song cycle for Baritone and Piano, 1976; Canto Drammatico, for Solo Violin, 1980; Concerto for Violin and Orchestra, 1993; Suite for Helena, for Wind Quintet, 1994; Toccata, Variations and Fugue on the Chorale Den Blomstertid Nu Kommer, for Organ, 1994; Ludus Latrunculorum, Oratorio, 1996; String Quartet, 1997; Two Love Scenes and a Daydream, for Voice, Soprano Saxophone and Big Band, 1997. *Recordings:* Arioso; Canto Drammatico; Composition for Organ; Passacaglia et Fuga B-A-C-H. *Contributions:* Critic for Hufvudstadsbladet, 1982–89; The Isle Is Full Of Noises, Nordic Sounds No. 3, 1996. *Honours:* 3-year grant from the Svenska Kulturfonden, 1986; 5-year State artists grant, 1995. *Address:* Landgränden 3 C 39, 02700 Helsingfors, Finland.

**KARMINSKI, Mark;** Composer; b. 30 Jan. 1930, Kharkiv, Ukraine; m. Irini Smichcovitch, 30 Aug 1955, 1 s. *Education:* Department of Philology and Literature, Kharkov State University; Composition, Kharkov State Conservatory. *Career:* 1st orchestral works and instrumental music performed in USSR cities; Opera Bukovinians premiered at Kharkov Opera House, 1957, Moscow, 1960; Other opera stagings: Ten days that shook the world, Donetsk, 1970, Prague National Theatre, 1972, Lvov, 1977, 1984; Irkutsk story, Kiev, Kharkov, Chelabinsk, Saratov, 1977–78; Only one day, Odessa, Lvov, 1987; Musical Robin Hood, Moscow, 1968, then 25 cities, USSR; Author, Philharmonic Concertos (radio, television). *Compositions include:* 4 operas; Rembrandt, ballet; Symphony; Oratorio; 5 Suites for string orchestra including Baroque faces and Play music in ancient style; 6 partitas for piano; Concertina for violin and piano, for flute and piano; Instrumental pieces; Vocal and choral works; Music for over 100 plays. *Recordings include:* The soldier forgot nothing, television film; Robin Hood; Songs from Robin Hood; O K Musketry, disco musical; Merri pencil, children's songs; M Karminsky's 9 songs; Symphony with Gorky Symphony Orchestra, conductor I Husman. *Publications:* Collected songs, 1970–85; Ten days that shook the world, 1973; Robin Hood songs, 1981; Irkutsk story, 1985; Choral music books, 15 choruses a cappella, 1988; Music for children, piano pieces, 1990; Kharkov Selected Works, 1995; 27 Pieces in Three-Part Rhythm, music for piano, 1996–. *Address:* Klotchkovskaja str 150a, ap 40, Kharkiv 310145, Ukraine.

**KARNEUS, Katarina;** Singer (Mezzo-Soprano); b. 1965, Stockholm, Sweden. *Education:* Trinity College of Music, London; National Opera Studio. *Career:* Varied concert repertoire including Beethoven's Ninth with Frans Brüggen and the Hallé Orchestra, Mozart's C Minor Mass in the Salzburg Festival with Roger Norrington, Les Nuits d'Eté and a Sylvester Concert with the Filharmonisch Orkest and Grant Llewellyn, Rossini-Mozart programme with Nicholas McGegan and the Hanover Band, Pergolesi Stabat Mater with the Netherlands Chamber Orchestra and Hartmut Haenchen and a concert at Buckingham Palace with Franz Welser-Möst; Prom debut with Rafael Frühbeck de Burgos and Edinburgh Festival debut with Charles Mackerras; Appearances at the Albert Hall with David Willcocks and at the Royal Festival Hall with the Bach Choir; Broadcast of Lieder eines fahrenden Gesellen with Grant Llewellyn and the Ulster Orchestra; Two concerts with Scottish Chamber Orchestra; South Bank debut in Purcell Room with a programme of Spanish and Scandinavian songs; Wigmore Hall recital as part of the Voices series; For Welsh National Opera: Angelina in La Cenerentola, Cherubino in Le nozze di Figaro and Rosina in Il Barbiere di Siviglia; Sesto in La Clemenza di Tito, Mercédès in Carmen for ENO and Opéra de Paris; Rosina and the title role in Carmen for Opéra Comique, Paris; The Page in Salome for Lyric Opera of Chicago; Tamiri in Il Re Pastore for Netherlands Opera; Further engagements include Sesto in La Clemenza di Tito for WNO; Debut with Glyndebourne Festival Opera as Dorabella; Cherubino at La Monnaie; Varvara in Katya Kabanova for Metropolitan Opera; Returned to the Bastille in 1999 to sing Dorabella, to the Opéra-Comique for Carmen and as Annio in La Clemenza di Tito at the Bayerische Staatsoper; Returned to WNO as Octavian in Der Rosenkavalier in 2000; Season 2000–01 as Gluck's Orpheus for WNO, as Dorabella at Munich and engaged as Olga in Eugene Onegin, New York Met; Also engaged to sing La Belle Hélène, Châtelet, Paris, 2001, Annio in La Clemenza di Tito at Covent Garden, 2002, and Adalgisa in Norma at Houston Grand Opera 2003. *Recordings:* R. Strauss, Mahler, Marx, Lieder. *Honours:* Christine Nilsson Award, 1994; Winner, Cardiff Singer of the World Competition, 1995. *Address:* Ingpen & Williams Ltd, 7 St George's Court, 131 Putney Bridge Road, London, SW15 2PA, England.

**KAROLYI, Sandor;** Professor; b. 24 Sept. 1931, Budapest, Hungary; m. 1st Suzanne Godefroid, 3 July 1954, 2 s., 1 d; 2nd Regina Bauer, 1 July 1998, one s. *Education:* Virtuosity Diploma, Franz Liszt Music Academy, Budapest, 1948; Virtuosity Diploma with distinction, Music Conservatory of Brussels, 1954; Teachers include Ede Zathureczky, Leo Weiner, Antal Molnar, André Gertler. *Career:* Debut: Franz Liszt Academy, 1941; Violin solo, Opera House in Frankfurt, 1956; Professor, Musikhochschule, Frankfurt am Main and at the Akademie Tonkunst Darmstadt; Concerts for the BBC and broadcasting companies in Europe; Television appearances in Germany, Japan, Philippines and Australia; mem, Deutsche Bachsolisten. *Recordings:* Paul Hindemith: 4 Violin Sonatas with Werner Hoppstock, piano, and Károlyi String Quartet recorded Quartets Nos 2 and 6 plus the Clarinet-Quartet of Paul Hindemith; Max Reger: Violin Sonatas A and C major with Suzanne Godefroid, piano; Prelude and Fugas for violin solo; Giuseppe Tartini Devil's Trill. *Publications:* Gustav Mahler Orchestra studies for the 10 symphonies, 1989. *Honours:* Diploma Contests in Geneva, 1947, Budapest, 1948, London, 1953; Contemporary Contest, Darmstadt, 1952; Vieuxtemps Prize, Belgium, 1959; Medaille Eugene Ysaye, Brussels, 1967. *Address:* Dehnhardtstrasse 30, 60433 Frankfurt am Main, Germany. *E-mail:* sandor.karolyi@t-online.de.

**KARPATI, Janos,** PhD, DSc; Hungarian musicologist; *Chief Librarian and Professor of Musicology, Ferenc Liszt Academy of Music;* b. 11 July 1932, Budapest. *Education:* Ferenc Liszt Acad., Budapest. *Career:* folk music research in Morocco 1957–58, in Japan 1988; recording production, Hungaroton 1959–61; Head Librarian and Lecturer, Ferenc Liszt Acad. of Music, Budapest 1961–, Prof. of Musicology 1983–. *Recordings:* Kagura: Japanese Shinto Ritual Music. *Publications:* A. Schoenberg 1963, Muzsikalo zenetortenet vol. II 1965, vol. IV 1973, Bartók String Quartets 1975, Music of the East 1981, Bartók's Chamber Music 1994, Music and Myth in the Japanese Ritual Tradition 1998, Bartók Analysis 2003, Képes Magyar Zenetörténet 2004. *Honours:* Erkel Prize 1971, Grand Prize Hungarian Artist 1995, Medal of the American Liszt Soc. 1996. *Address:* F. Liszt Academy, Liszt F. ter 8, 1061 Budapest (office); Felbo Zoldmali ut 61/65, 1025 Budapest, Hungary (home). *Telephone:* (1) 462-4671 (office); (1) 325-5747 (home). *Fax:* (1) 462-4672 (office). *E-mail:* karpati@lib.liszt.hu (office). *Website:* www.liszt.hu.

**KARR, Gary;** Double Bass Player; b. 20 Nov. 1941, Los Angeles, California, USA. *Education:* Studied with Herman Reinshagen, Warren Benfield and Stuart Sankey. *Career:* Debut: New York 1962 in concert with Leonard Bernstein, ad at New York Town Hall; European tour 1964, playing at Wigmore Hall London; Founded the International Institute for the String Bass, 1967; Teaching appointments at Juilliard School, Yale School of Music, Indiana University, New England Conservatory and Hartt School of Music, Hartford (1976); Formed duo with keyboard player Harmon Lewis in 1972, tours of Europe, the Far East, USA and Canada; Appearances as Soloist with the Chicago Symphony, New York Philharmonic, English Chamber Orchestra, London Symphony and Toronto Symphony; Composers who have written for him include Vittorio Giannini, Henze, Wilfred Josephs, Lalo Schifrin, John Downey and Gunther Schuller; Debut tour of Australia 1987–88; Television appearances include series Gary Karr and Friends on CBC in Canada and Bass is Beautiful for Channel 4, England; Further television engagements in France, Belgium, Japan, Norway, Switzerland and USA; Karr Doublebass Foundation Inc formed 1983 to provide valuable instruments for talented players. *Recordings:* Transcriptions of Paganini's Moses Fantasy and Dvořák Cello Concerto; Concerto by Lalo Schifrin. *Address:* Kaye Artists Management, 7 Chertsey Road, Woking, Surrey GU21 5 AB, England.

**KARR-BERTOLI, Julius;** German conductor; b. 11 June 1920, Munich; m. Charlotte Langesee; one d. *Education:* Acad. of Music, Munich. *Career:* first conducted aged 18 at the Bavarian State Theatre (Prinzregententheater) Grieg's Peer Gynt; conductor, Dortmund Opera 1942–45; freelance, Bavarian Radio, asst to Eugen Jochum 1945–60; Prof., Richard Strauss Conservatory, Munich 1972–85; concerts and music festivals in about 50 countries on four continents with some of the world's leading orchestras, including the Philharmonic Orchestras of Munich, Berlin, Beijing, Bucharest, Riga, Sofia, St Petersburg; numerous concert tours in Russia and the former USSR initiated by D. Shostakovich; anniversary of 60 years at the conductor's desk 1999, 80 years 2000 with festive concerts in Weimar and Munich; first concerts in Mexico City and Xalapa with first performance of works by Liszt and Dvořák 2001; principal concert for the Fesaam Music Festival with works by black composers, including William Grant Still and Powell Nash, and new concerts in Mexico, Belarus and Germany; 82nd birthday concerts in Ecuador 2002; Principal Guest Conductor Suk Chamber Orchestra, Prague. *Recordings:* Music of Pergolesi and Romanian Composers, Music of G. B. Pergolesi with the Suk Chamber Orchestra and Joseph Suk as violin soloist, Symphonies of L. van Beethoven and C. Franck, Symphonies Nos 3, 4 and 7 by Dvořák. *Current Management:* Artists International Management, PO Box 2146, Morristown, NJ 07961, USA. *Address:* Sommerstrasse 9, 81543 Munich, Germany (home). *Telephone:* (89) 6514789 (home). *Fax:* (89) 6514789 (home).

**KARSKI, Dominik,** MMus; Australian composer; b. 24 June 1972, Szczebrzeszyn, Poland. *Education:* West Australian Conservatorium of Music, Queensmald Conservatorium, Brisbane. *Career:* freelance composer; instrumental works from solo to orchestra commissioned and performed in Australia, N America, Asia and Europe; radio broadcasts in Australia and Europe; participant in World New Music Days 'Trans-it', Switzerland 2004. *Compositions:* Instrumental works from solo to orchestra include: Les Eruptions du Rêve, performed by Le Nouvel Ensemble Moderne, Forum

2000, Telstra Adelaide Festival; Glimmer, performed at Gaudeamus Music Week, 2002; Streams of Consciousness, performed by Ensemble Offspring, European tour, 2003; Inner Stream II, performed at Gaudeamus Music Week, 2003; Streams Within, Libra Ensemble commission performed Melbourne, 2003. *Recordings:* Floating on the River of Time, West Australian Symphony Orchestra 20th Century Ensemble; Les Eruptions du Rêve, Le Nouvel Ensemble Moderne. *Honours:* ABC Young Composers' Award, 1998; Ian Potter Music Commissions, Melbourne, 1999; Le Nouvel Ensemble Moderne, Forum 2000; First Prize, Panufnik Int. Young Composers Competition, Kraków, 2001; Hon. mention, Gaudeamus Music Week, Amsterdam, 2002; Albert H. Maggs Composition Award, 2003. *Address:* 2 Everett Lane, Currambine, WA 6028, Australia. *Telephone:* (8) 9304-2271 (office). *E-mail:* dominikk@echidna.id.au (office). *Website:* www.amcoz.com.au/comp/k/dkarski.htm (office).

**KARTTUNEN, Aussi (Ville);** Cellist; b. 30 Sept. 1960, Helsinki, Finland; m. Muriel Von Braun, 16 Aug 1985, 1 d. *Education:* Sibelius Academy, Helsinki; Teachers Vili Pullinen, Erkki Rautio, Private studies in London with William Pleeth; Jacqueline du Pré; In Netherlands with Tibor de Machula. *Career:* Soloist with all major Scandanavian Orchestras; Los Angeles Philharmonic, Philharmonia Orchestra, BBC Symphony, BBC Scottish, Orchestre de Paris, Dutch Radio Orchestra, London Sinfonietta, Ensemble Modern among others; Appearances in major festivals including: Edinburgh, Lockenhaus, Salzburg, Berlin, Vienna, Venice, Strasbourg, Montpellier, Helsinki; Artistic Director, Avanti! Chamber Orchestra, 1994–98; Artistic Director; Helsinki Biennale, 1995. Recordings include complete Beethoven works for cello; 20th Century Solo Cello; Concertos by Zimmermann, Hindemith, Lindberg and Saariaho with London Sinfonietta, the Los Angeles Philharmonia and Avanti!. *Honours:* First prize in Young Concert Artist Competition, Tunbridge Wells, England, 1981. First Prize and Gold Medal at the Festival Des Jeunes Solistes, in Bordeaux, 1982.

**KASAROVA, Vesselina;** Singer (Mezzo-Soprano); b. 1963, Stara Zagora, Bulgaria. *Education:* Studied at the Sofia Conservatory. *Career:* Appearances at the Sofia National Opera as Fenena, Rosina, Preziosilla and Dorabella; Member of the Zürich Opera, 1988–91 as Annio in Clemenza di Tito, Stephano in Roméo et Juliette, and Anna in Les Troyens; Salzburg Festival 1991–92 as Annio and Rossini's Tancredi; Further appearances as Rosina at the Vienna Staatsoper in 1991 and the Geneva Opera, and as Pippo in La Gazza Ladra at Barcelona in 1992; Season 1996 with Mozart's Zerlina at the Salzburg Festival and Idamante at Florence; Season 1998 as Cenerentola at Pesaro and Charlotte in a concert performance of Werther at the Deutsche Oper Berlin; Octavian at New York Met, 2000; Season 2000–01 as Mozart's Idamante at Salzburg and Sesto at Covent Garden (returned, 2002); Giovanna Seymour in Anna Bolena at Zürich and Rosina for Chicago Lyric Opera; Concert repertory includes Mozart's Requiem in Milan, and Agnese in Bellini's Beatrice di Tenda in Vienna. *Recordings include:* Romeo in Bellini's I Capuleti, 1998. *Address:* c/o Staatsoper, Opernring 2, 1010 Vienna, Austria.

**KASHKASHIAN, Kim;** violist and teacher; b. 31 Aug. 1952, Detroit, MI, USA. *Education:* Peabody Conservatory of Music, Baltimore with Walter Trampler and Karen Tuttle. *Career:* various engagements as a soloist with leading orchestras in N America and Europe; recitals, chamber music appearances notably with the Tokyo and Guarneri Quartets and the Beaux Arts Trio; faculty mem., New School of Music, Philadelphia 1981–86, Mannes Coll. of Music, New York 1983–86, Indiana Univ. School of Music, Bloomington 1985–87; Staatliche Hochschule für Musik, Freiburg 1989–; has prepared transcriptions and has commissioned various works for viola including music by Betsy Jolas, Schnittke and Sofia Gubaidulina. *Recordings:* as a soloist and chamber music artist, notably two unpublished sonatas by Hindemith. *Address:* Hartliebstr 2, 8000 Munchen 19, Germany.

**KASPSZYK, Jacek;** Polish conductor; *Artistic and General Director, Polish National Opera;* b. 1952. *Education:* Acad. of Music, Warsaw. *Career:* conducting debut at age 14; debut Warsaw Nat. Opera 1975; Prin. Guest Conductor Deutsche Oper am Rhein, Düsseldorf 1976–77; Prin. Conductor Polish Nat. Radio Symphony Orchestra 1978–80, Music Dir 1980–82; debut Berlin Philharmonic and New York 1978, London (with Philharmonia) 1982; conducted French Nat., Stockholm Philharmonic, Bavarian Radio Symphony, Rotterdam, Czech Philharmonic Orchestras; conducted Detroit Opera and San Diego Symphony Orchestra 1982; concerts at La Scala, Milan 1982; Australian tour with Chamber Orchestra of Europe 1983; conducted UK orchestras 1982–; debut Henry Wood Promenade Concerts 1984; Prin. Conductor and Artistic Adviser North Netherlands Orchestra 1991–95; Prin. Guest Conductor English Sinfonia 1992–; has toured with the Yomiuri Nippon Symphony and performed with Tokyo and Hong Kong Philarmonics, New Zealand, San Diego, Cincinnati, Winnipeg, Calgary Symphonies, and Detroit Opera; Prin. Guest Conductor Polish Philharmonic 1996–; Artistic and Musical Dir Polish National Opera Warsaw –1998; Artistic and Gen. Dir Polish National Opera Warsaw 2002–. *Music:* operas conducted include: Queen of Spades (Düsseldorf) 1977, Haunted Manor (Detroit) 1982, A Midsummer Night's Dream (Lyon) 1983, Eugene Onegin (Bordeaux) 1985, The Magic Flute (Opéra Comique, Paris and Stockholm) 1986, Seven Deadly Sins (Lyon) 1987, Die Fledermaus (Scottish Opera), Flying Dutchman (Opera North, UK) 1988, Barber of Seville (English Nat. Opera) 1992, Der Rosenkavalier (Warsaw) 1997, Don Giovanni (Warsaw) 1999, The Nutcracker (Zürich) 2000; many productions and recordings with Teatr Wielki, Warsaw, including performances in Luxembourg, Lvov, Beijing, Paphos, Japan (tour)

and Bolshoi Theatre in Moscow; recordings with London Symphony Orchestra, London Philharmonic Orchestra, Royal Philharmonic, Philharmonic Orchestras, Warsaw Symphony Orchestra; several other recordings. *Honours:* III Prize, Karajan Competition 1977. *Address:* Teatr Wielki, pl. Teatralny 1, 00-950, Warsaw, Poland (office). *Telephone:* (22) 6920500 (office). *Fax:* (22) 8260423 (office). *E-mail:* office@teatrwielki.pl (office); dyrnacz@teatrwielki.pl (office). *Website:* www.teatrwielki.pl (office).

**KASRASHVILI, Makvala;** Georgian singer (soprano); *Director, Bolshoi Theatre Opera;* b. 13 March 1948, Kutaisi; d. of Nina Nanikashvili and Filimon Kasrashvili; m. (divorced). *Education:* Tbilisi Conservatory. *Career:* joined Bolshoi Co., Moscow 1968, Dir Bolshoi Theatre Opera Dept 2002–; has performed internationally, including Covent Garden, London, Metropolitan Opera, New York, Verona, Vienna State Opera etc. *Roles include:* Lisa, Tatyana, Maria, Tosca, Lauretta, Donna Anna, Leonora, Aida, Turandot, Amelia. *Honours:* People's Artist of the USSR 1986; Grand Prix, Montreal Vocal Competition. *Address:* Bolshoi Theatre, Teatralnaya Pl. 1, Moscow, Russia. *Telephone:* (095) 200-58-00 (home).

**KASSEL, Wolfgang;** Singer (Tenor); b. 1930, Germany. *Career:* Sang at the Flensburg Opera, 1954–57; Engagements at Mainz, 1957–58, Wuppertal 1958–60, Krefeld 1960–66, Bielefeld 1967–74; Sang at Nuremberg, 1974–80 and made guest appearances at Munich 1973–76; Appeared as Tannhäuser at Covent Garden, 1973, Siegmund at Rouen, 1975; Other roles have included Lohengrin, Walther, Siegfried, Florestan, Max, Herod in Salome and Bacchus (Ariadne auf Naxos); Further engagements at Toulouse, Oslo, Würzburg and elsewhere in Europe. *Address:* c/o St ädtische Buhnen, Richard Wagnerplatz 2–10, 8500 Nuremberg, Germany.

**KASTON, Motti;** Singer (Baritone); b. 1965, Tel-Aviv, Israel. *Education:* Studied at the Tel-Aviv Conservatory and the Mannes College of Music, New York. *Career:* Sang Schaunard in La Bohème at Tel-Aviv, 1987; Germont and other roles at the Metropolitan, New York; Philadelphia, 1991, as Malatesta in Don Pasquale: Staatsoper Stuttgart from 1991, as Sharpless in Madama Butterfly, Dandini in La Cenerentola, Wolfram in Tannhäuser and Rossini's Figaro; Opéra-Comique, Paris, 1991, as Alphonse in La Favorite; Tel-Aviv, 1994, as Valentin in Faust and Stuttgart, 1996, as Roderick in La Chute de la Maison Usher, by Debussy; Season 1998 as Dandini in La Cenerentola at Tel-Aviv. *Address:* c/o New Israeli Opera, 28 Leonardo da Vinci St, PO Box 3321, Tel-Aviv 61332, Israel.

**KASTU, Matti;** Tenor; b. 3 Feb. 1943, Turku, Finland. *Education:* School of Royal Opera, Stockholm. *Career:* Principal Tenor at Stockholm Opera from 1973 with debut as Laca in Jenůfa at Edinburgh in 1974; Roles include Rodolfo in La Bohème, Bacchus in Ariadne auf Naxos, Walter in Die Meistersinger, Parsifal, and Florestan in Fidelio; Guest appearances in Vienna, San Francisco, Munich, Düsseldorf, Frankfurt and Berlin; Tour of USA in 1979 appearing in Detroit, Washington and New York; Welsh National Opera in 1981 as the Emperor in Die Frau ohne Schatten, Milan in 1983 in Mahler's Das klagende Lied; Created the Guide in Sallinen's The King Goes Forth to France, Savonlinna, 1984; Sang at Edinburgh Festival in 1990 as Tristan in a concert performance of Wagner's opera with the Jutland Opera; Sang Tristan at Århus in 1992. *Recordings include:* Menelaos in Aegyptische Helena. *Address:* c/o Den jske Opera, Thomas Jensens Allee, 8000 Århus, Denmark.

**KASZA, Katalin;** Singer (Soprano); b. 1942, Szeged, Hungary. *Education:* Graduate, Ferenc Liszt Academy, Budapest, 1967. *Career:* Debut: Abigail in Nabucco, Budapest State Opera, 1967; Judith in film of Duke Bluebeard's Castle and guest performer as Judith in the Edinburgh Festval, 1973 and at many other international venues; Brünnhilde in Wagner's Ring at Covent Garden Opera House, London, 1974–76, and at Geneva and several German cities, 1977–78; US debut in Duke Bluebeard's Castle, Los Angeles, CA, 1980; Sang Eudossia in Respighi's La Fiamma at Erkel Theatre, Budapest, 1989; Other roles include: Octavia in L'Incoronazione di Poppea, Leonore in Fidelio, Lady Macbeth, Title roles of Salome and Elektra, Senta in Der fliegende Holländer, Ortrud in Lohengrin, Fricka in Rheingold, Isolde in Tristan und Isolde and Kundry in Parsifal. *Recordings:* Radio and television film recording of Fidelio, 1969; As Judith in Duke Bluebeard's Castle, 1970, in television film and the same role for the complete Bartók edition; Kundry in Parsifal, 1983. *Honours:* The Best Dramatic Performer's Diploma, Sofia International Singing Concours, 1968; Liszt Prize 1, 1974; Béla Bartók–Ditta Pasztory Prize, 1992. *Address:* c/o Hungarian State Opera House, Andrássy ut 22, 1061 Budapest, Hungary.

**KATIMS, Milton;** Conductor and Violist; b. 24 June 1909, New York, NY, USA; m. Virginia Peterson, 7 Nov 1940, 1 s., 1 d. *Education:* BA, Columbia University; Private violin study from age 8; Conducting at National Orchestral Association with Leon Barzin, 1931–35. *Career:* Debut: NBC Symphony, 1947; Solo Violist and Assistant Conductor, WOR, Mutual Broadcasting Company, 1935–43; Faculty, Juilliard, 1946–54; NBC New York, First Desk Violist with Toscanini, Staff Conductor, 1943–54; Principal Guest Conductor with NBC Symphony, 1947–54 (52 broadcasts); Music Director, Seattle Symphony, 1954–76; Guest Conductor of orchestras on five continents; Solo viola appearances, chamber music with Budapest String Quartet, New York Piano Quartet, Pablo Casals and Isaac Stern; Artistic Director, University of Houston School of Music, 1976–84; mem, American Viola Society; American String Teachers Association. *Compositions:* Editions for Viola for International Music Company include 6 Solo Suites of Bach, 3 Gamba Sonatas of Bach, 2 Brahms Sonatas, Schubert Arpeggione Sonata and

25 other compositions. *Recordings:* Numerous as Conductor and Violist including: Bach Solo Viola Suites, Bach Gamba Sonatas, with Milton Katims and colleagues. *Publications:* Co-authored with his wife Virginia Peterson, cellist, The Pleasure Was Ours (Personal Encounters with the Greats, the NearGreats, and Ingrates), 2002; Contributions to: Various journals. *Honours:* Hon. doctorates (Seattle, Whitworth College, Cornish College of Arts, Columbia Univ. Medal of Excellence, 1954; Lifetime Achievement Award, Academy of Music Northwest, 1999; American Viola Soc. Career Achievement Award, 2002; Ditson and ASCAP awards for championing American composers. *Address:* Fairway Estates, 8001 Sand Point Way NE, Seattle, WA 98115, USA. *E-mail:* milvir@aol.com.

**KATIN, Peter Roy,** FRAM, ARCM; British pianist; b. 14 Nov. 1930, London; s. of the late Jerrold Katin and Gertrude Katin; m. Eva Zweig 1954; two s. *Education:* Henry Thornton School, Royal Acad. of Music, Westminster Abbey. *Career:* London debut, Wigmore Hall 1948; extensive concert tours in UK, Europe, Africa, Canada, USA and Far East; special interest in Chopin; recordings for Decca, EMI, Unicorn, Everest, Philips, CFP, Lyrita and Pickwick Int., Claudio, Olympia, Simax, Athene; Prof. Royal Acad. of Music 1956–60, Univ. of Western Ont. 1978–84, Royal Coll. of Music 1992–2001; Founder Katin Centre for Advanced Piano Studies 1991, Katin Trio 1997; Pres. Camerata of London 1994–. *Honours:* Hon. DMus (De Montfort) 1994; Eric Brough Memorial Prize 1944; Chopin Arts Award (New York) 1977. *Address:* TransArt (UK) Ltd, Cedar House, 10 Rutland Street, Filey, YO14 9JB, North Yorkshire, England; 4 Clarence Road, Croydon, Surrey, CR0 2EN, England (home). *Telephone:* (1723) 515819 (office). *Fax:* (1723) 514678 (office). *E-mail:* transartuk@transartuk.com (office); peter_katin@compuserve.com (home). *Website:* www.transartuk.com (office); ourworld.compuserve.com/homepages/peter_katin (home).

**KATS-CHERNIN, Elena;** composer and lecturer; b. 4 Nov. 1957, Tashkent, Uzbekistan. *Education:* State Conservatorium of Music, NSW, Hanover Musikhochschule with Helmut Lachenmann. *Career:* resident in Australia from 1975; composer of incidental music for dance theatre in Germany 1985–93; Lecturer, New South Wales Conservatory 1995; commissions from ZKM Karlsruhe 1993, Munchener Biennale 1994, Sydney Alpha Ensemble 1995, among others; Sehrayahn Resident, Ministry for the Arts Lower Saxony 1984–85; Iphis premiered by Music Theatre Sydney 1997. *Compositions include:* Piano Concerto, 1979; Bienie for orchestra, 1979; In Tension, for 6 instruments, 1982; Reductions, for 2 pianos, 1983; Duo I for violin and piano, 1984; Stairs, for orchestra, 1984; Transfer, for orchestra, 1990; Tast-en, for piano, 1991; Totschki: Dots, for oboe and clarinet, 1992; Clocks, for 20 musicians and tape, 1993; Retonica for orchestra, 1993; Clip for percussion, 1994; Concertino for violin and 11 players, 1994; Coco's Last Collection, dance theatre, for 2 pianos, 1994; Cadences, Deviations and Scarlatti for 14 instruments, 1995; Wild Rice for cello, 1996; The Schubert Blues for piano, 1996; Charleston Noir for double bass quartet, 1996; Purple Prelude for six instruments, 1996; Russian Rad for ensemble, 1996; Zoom and Zip for string orchestra, 1997; Iphis, opera after Ovid's Metamorphoses, 1997; Champagne in a Teapot for horn and 13 instruments, 1997; Matricide, the musical, 1998; Umcha for percussion ensemble, 1998; Sonata Lost and Found for piano, 1998; Stur in Dur for piano, 1999; Displaced Dances for piano and orchestra, 2000; Piano Concerto No. 2, 2001; Mr Barbeque, 12 cabaret songs, 2002; Garden Symphony for solo voices and orchestra, 2002; Wild Swans, ballet, 2002; Undertow, chamber dance-opera, 2004; Portrait CD, Clocks, 1997. *Honours:* Sounds Australian 1996. *Address:* c/o Boosey & Hawkes, First Floor, Aldwych House, 71–91 Aldwych, London, WC2B 4HN, England. *Website:* www.boosey .com/katschernin.

**KATZ, Arnold;** conductor; b. 18 Sept. 1924, Baku, Azerbaijan. *Education:* Central Music School, Moscow State Conservatoire; studied conducting at the Leningrad State Conservatoire. *Career:* conducting career in Russia from 1956; f. USSR Philharmonic of Novosibirsk and brought the orchestra on tour of England 1988; German tour 1989; guest appearances with the Stockholm Philharmonic, BBC Nat. Orchestra of Wales, Tivoli Orchestra (Copenhagen), Residentie Orchestra (Netherlands) and RT Luxembourg season 1990–91. *Recordings include:* music by Shostakovich and Siberian composers with the USSR Philharmonic of Novosibirsk; Russian music with the Leningrad Philharmonic. *Address:* c/o Residentie Orkest, PO Box 11543, 2502 AM, The Hague, Netherlands.

**KATZ, Martin;** Pianist and University Professor; b. 27 Nov. 1945, Los Angeles, California, USA. *Education:* Studied at the University of Southern California at Los Angeles, accompaniment with Gwendolyn Koldovsky. *Career:* Pianist for the US Army chorus in Washington, 1966–69; Accompanist to such leading singers as José Carreras, Kiri Te Kanawa, Teresa Berganza, Katia Ricciarelli and Nicolai Gedda; Concert tours of North and South America, Australia, Europe and Asia, notably with Marilyn Horne; Editions of Rossini operas performed by Houston Grand Opera and at the Rossini Festival, New York, 1982–83; Edition of Handel's Rinaldo performed at the Ottawa Festival 1982, Metropolitan Opera 1984; Associate Professor at Westminster Choir College, 1976; Professor at the University of Michigan, 1983. *Address:* Music Department, University of Michigan, Ann Arbor, MI 48109, USA.

**KATZ, Paul;** Cellist; b. 1941, USA. *Career:* Member of the Cleveland Quartet, 1969–94; Regular tours of the USA, Canada, Europe, Japan, Russia, South America, Australia, New Zealand and the Middle East; On Faculty of the Eastman School, Rochester and in residence at the Aspen Music Festival, co-founding the Center for Advanced Quartet Studies; Tour of the Soviet Union and five European countries, 1988; Season 1988–89 with appearances at the Metropolitan Museum and Alice Tully Hall, New York; Concerts in Paris, London, Bonn, Prague, Lisbon and Brussels; Festivals of Salzburg, Edinburgh and Lucerne; Many complete Beethoven cycles and annual appearances at Lincoln Center's Mostly Mozart Festival; In addition to standard repertory, has commissioned works by John Harbison, Sergei Slonimsky, Samuel Adler, George Perle, Christopher Rouse, Toru Takemitsu, Stephen Paulus, Libby Larsen, John Corigliano and Oswaldo Golyov. *Recordings:* Repertoire from Mozart to Ravel; Collaborations with Alfred Brendel (Schubert Trout Quintet), Pinchas Zukerman and Bernard Greenhouse (Brahms Sextets), Emanuel Ax, Yo-Yo Ma and Richard Stoltzman; Complete the Beethoven Quartets, 1982. *Publications:* Interpretation problems of the Beethoven Quartets, RCA, 1982. *Current Management:* ICM Artists, New York. *Address:* Eastman School of Music, 26 Gibbs Street, Rochester, NY 14604, USA.

**KATZ, Shelley;** Concert Pianist, Composer, Conductor and Accompanist; b. 1960, Montreal, Canada. *Education:* Studied at the Montreal Conservatoire and the Juilliard School in New York, BMus (Hon), 1982; MMus, 1983; PhD 1997. *Career:* Solo repetiteur at the Deutsche Oper am Rhein from 1987, Studienleiter in Koblenz from 1989, Kappelmeister and Assistant to the General Music Director at Mainz Opera; Accompanist to such singers as Nicolai Gedda, Gwyneth Jones and Jochen Kowalski; Musician-in-Residence, International Study Centre, Queen's University. *Compositions:* Drei Jüdische Lieder, 1988; Eyshes Chayil, 1998; Kaddish, 2000. *Recordings:* Songs by Canadian Composers with D. Gilchrist; Solo Piano Works by Canadian Composers; Of Fire and Dew, 21 Baritone Songs by John Jeffreys with J Veira; Lieder: Mozart Beethoven Schumann with J Kowalski. *Publications include:* A Description of Research into Electronically Generated Expressivity, with F Rumsey, 1994. *Address:* International Study centre, Queen's University, Herstmonceux Castle, Hailsham, East Sussex BN27 1 RP, England.

**KATZER, Georg;** Composer; b. 10 Jan. 1935, Habelschwerdt, Germany; m. Angelika Szostak, 13 May 1975, 3 s. *Education:* Hochschule für Musik, Berlin; AMU, Prague; Akademie der Kunste, Germany. *Career:* Freelance Composer, 1960; Professor of Composition, Academy of Fine Arts, Berlin. *Compositions:* Mainly published; Chamber music; More than 10 symphonic works; Solo concertos (with orchestra), for flute, oboe, piano, cello, harp and cello; Electro-acoustic works; Multi-media works; 2 ballets; 3 operas; Offene Landschaft for orchestra; Landschaft mit steigender Flut for orchestra. *Recordings:* Sound House, after F Bacon's The New Atlantis, for 3 orchestras, organ and tape; Kommen und Gehen, woodwind quintet and piano; Aide-Memoirem, tape composition; Harpsichord Concerto; Konzert für Orchester No. 1; Baukasten for orchestra; Empfindsame Musik; Streichermusik 1. *Address:* Weserstrasse 5, 15738 Zeuthen, Germany.

**KAUFMAN, Frederick;** Composer; b. 24 March 1936, Brooklyn, New York, USA. *Education:* Studied Composition with Vittorio Giannini at the Manhattan School, MMus, 1960; Juilliard School with Vincent Persichetti. *Career:* Played trumpet in the New York City Ballet Orchestra and for various New York bands; Composer-in-Residence at the University of Wisconsin, 1969; Director of Music for the city of Haifa, Israel, 1971–72; Music performed by major Israeli orchestras and dance companies; Chairman of the Music Department at Eastern Montane College, 1977–82; Professor of Composition at the Philadelphia College of the Performing Arts, 1982. *Compositions:* A Children's Opera, 1967; The Nothing Ballet, 1975; 3 Symphonies, 1966, 1971, 1978; Concerto for violin and strings, 1967; Interiors for violin and piano, 1970; Violin Sonata, 1970; And the World Goes On for percussion and ensemble, 1971; 3 Cantatas for chorus and organ, 1975; Triple Concerto, 1975; 5 Moods for oboe, 1975; Percussion Trio, 1977; Echoes for chorus, clarinet and percussion, 1978; 5 Fragrances for clarinet, harp and percussion, 1980; When the Twain Meet for orchestra, 1981; Metamorphosis for piano, 1981; Southeast Fantasy for wind ensemble, 1982; Mobile for string quartet, 1982; Stars and Distances, spoken sounds and chorus, 1981; Meditation for a Lonely Flute, 1983; Kiddish Concerto for cello and strings, 1984; A/V Slide Show for trombone, 1984; Masada for chorus, clarinet and percussion, 1985. *Publications include:* The African Roots of Jazz, 1979.

**KAUFMANN, Jonas;** German singer (tenor); b. 1969, Munich. *Education:* Munich Hochschule für Musik, masterclasses with Hans Hotter and James King. *Career:* sang with Saarbrucken Opera 1994–96; Salzburg Festival debut in Busoni's Dr Faust 1999; engagements from 1999, including Stuttgart, Chicago, Milan and Salzburg; season 2002 appearances included Flamand in Capriccio at Turin, Don Ottavio in Don Giovanni at Munich, Fierrabras at Zürich Oper; season 2003 appearances included Alfredo Germont in La Traviata at Chicago Opera, Rinaldo in Armida at Zürich Oper, Faust in La Damnation de Faust at Geneva, Belmonte in Die Entfuhrung aus dem Serail at Salzburg Festival, Tannhauser, Die Zauberflote and Die Entfuhrung aus dem Serail at Zürich Oper, and a recital at the Wigmore Hall, London; season 2004 included Max in Der Freischutz at Berlin, Fidelio at Zürich Oper, Cassio in Otello at Paris, Die Schopfung at Naples, and a recital in Brussels; other roles include Mozart's Ferrando, Belmonte, Tamino, Titus, Jacquino in Fidelio, Rossini's Almaviva, Alfredo in Otello. *Recordings include:* Carl Loewe's The Three Wishes. *Honours:* prizewinner Meistersinger Competition, Nuremberg 1993. *Current Management:* IMG Artists, Lovell House, 616 Chiswick High Road, London, W4 5RX, England. *Telephone:* (20) 8233-5800.

*Fax:* (20) 8233-5801. *E-mail:* sthomson@imgworld.com. *Website:* www .imgartists.com.

**KAUFMANN, Julie;** American singer (soprano); b. 25 May 1955, Iowa. *Education:* Iowa Univ., Zürich Opera Studio, Musikhochschule, Hamburg. *Career:* sang at Hagen, then at Frankfurt as Oscar in Un Ballo in Maschera, Blondchen, and Norina; Appearances in Hamburg, Bonn, Stuttgart, Berlin, Salzburg and Düsseldorf; Bayerische Staatsoper Munich, 1983, as Despina, Sophie and Zdenka; Aminta in Schweigsame Frau; Covent Garden debut, 1984, as Zerlina in Don Giovanni; Gave the premiere of Udo Zimmermann's Gib Licht meiner Augen, 1986; Sang at the Salzburg and Wiesbaden Festivals, 1987, as Blondchen and Despina; Aminta in Die schweigsame Frau at the Munich Opera, 1988 (tour of Japan, 1988 and at La Scala, Milan), Woglinde in the Ring, 1989 (also televised and available on video); Ludwigsburg Festival, 1989, as Susanna, and Carmina Burana at the 1990 Munich Festival; Sang Zdenka in Arabella at La Scala, 1992; Woglinde in Wagner's Ring at Paris Châtelet, 1994; World premiere of Manfred Trojahn's Frammenti di Michelangelo, 1995; Sang Pamina, 1996, Susanna, 1997 and Musetta, 1998 at the Opera Cologne; Sang Atalanta in Handel's Serse at the 1996 Munich Festival; Maria in the premiere of Trojahn's Was ihr Wollt (Twelfth Night), Munich 1998; Dalinda in Ariodante, Munich, 2000; Sang St Matthew Passion with Chicago Symphony, 1997; Brahms Requiem with NHK Orchestra, Tokyo, 1997; Mahler's 8th Symphony, San Francisco, 1998; Recital Tours and radio broadcasts Wolf's Italienisches Liederbuch in Italy, USA, and Germany; Hindemith's Marienleben in Germany; Professorship in Voice at the Universität der Künste, Berlin, 1999; Hindemith's Sancta Susanna, Cologne, 2001; Season 2000–01 at the Munich Staatsoper as Ginevra in Ariodante, and Despina; World premiere, Manfred Trojahn's 'Tritticino', Cologne, 2003; NATS, (USA); Paul Hindemith Gesellschaft, Berlin; Hans Pfitzner Gesellschaft. *Recordings:* Despina in Così fan tutte; Amor in Orfeo ed Euridice; Walther in La Wally; Woglinde in Das Rheingold, conducted by Haitink; Echo in Ariadne and Naxos, Schumann's Mignon Requiem and Mendelssohn's Lobgesang; Rezia in Pilgrims from Mecca; Nannetta in Falstaff, with Colin Davis; Solo Recital CD with Schoenberg, Debussy, Strauss, 1993, with Irwin Gage; Brahms Duette and Lieder with Marilyn Schmiege and Donald Sulzen; Beethoven Welsh, Scottish, Irish Songs with Neues Münchener Klavietrio; Hans Pfitzner Lieder with Donald Sulzen, 1999; Carl Loewe Lieder und Balladen with Cord Garben, 1999. *Honours:* Bayrischer Kammersängerin, 1991; Bayerischer Verdienstorden, 2000. *Address:* c/o Impresariat Sonia Simmenauer, Bornstrasse 12, 20146 Hamburg, Germany (office). *Telephone:* (40) 4231-3111 (office). *Fax:* (40) 4231-3113 (office). *Website:* www.impresariat-simmenauer.de.

**KAUPOVA, Helena;** Singer (Soprano); b. 1965, Czechoslovakia. *Education:* Studied at the Brno Conservatory; Bratislava Academy. *Career:* Slovak National Theatre, Bratislava, 1990, as Pamina and Micaela; National Theatre, Prague, 1992; As Mozart's Donna Anna; Donna Elvira; Pamina and Countess; Mimi, Jenůfa, Nedda and Tatiana; Guest appearances as Mimi at Toronto; Countess, Vancouver; Jenůfa in Santiago; Smetana's Marenka at Monte Carlo; Edinburgh Festival, 1993 as Janáček's Sarka and Krasava in Libuše, 1998. *Recordings:* Libuše and highlights from Don Giovanni and Die Zauberflöte. *Address:* Music International, 13 Ardilaun Road, London N5 2QR, England.

**KAVAFIAN, Ani;** violinist and teacher; b. 10 May 1948, Istanbul, Turkey; sister of Ida Kavafian. *Education:* studied with Ara Zerounian, Mischa Mischakoff in Detroit, Juilliard School of Music, New York with Ivan Galamian and Felix Galimir. *Career:* debut at Carnegie Recital Hall, New York 1969; European debut, Salle Gaveau, Paris 1973; soloist with many major orchestras; recitalist; duo recitals with sister, Ida Kavafian; artist mem. Chamber Music Soc., Lincoln Center, New York 1980–; teacher, Mannes Coll. of Music, New York 1982–, Manhattan School of Music, New York 1983, Queens Coll. CUNY 1983–. *Recordings:* as a recitalist and chamber music artist. *Honours:* Avery Fisher Prize 1976. *Current Management:* Herbert Barrett Management, 266 W 37th Street, 20th Floor, New York, NY 10018, USA. *Telephone:* (212) 245-3530. *Fax:* (212) 397-5860. *Website:* www .herbertbarrett.com.

**KAVAFIAN, Ida;** violinist; b. 29 Oct. 1952, Istanbul, Turkey; sister of Ani Kavafian. *Education:* studied with Ara Zerounian and Mischa Mischakoff, Detroit and with Oscar Shumsky and Ivan Galamian, Juilliard School, New York. *Career:* founding mem. chamber group, Tashi 1973; New York recital debut 1978; European debut, London 1982; appearances in duo recitals with sister, Ani Kavafian; mem., Beaux Arts Trio 1992–98; Artistic Dir, Music from Angel Fire festival; artist mem. Chamber Music Soc., Lincoln Center. *Recordings:* as a chamber music artist. *Honours:* winner Vienna da Motta Int. Violin Competition, Lisbon 1973, silver medal Int. Violin Competition of Indianapolis 1982, Avery Fisher career grant 1988. *Current Management:* Herbert Barrett Management, 266 W 37th Street, 20th Floor, New York, NY 10018, USA. *Telephone:* (212) 245-3530. *Fax:* (212) 397-5860. *Website:* www .herbertbarrett.com.

**KAVAKOS, Leonidas;** Violinist; b. 1967, Athens, Greece. *Education:* Studied at the Greek Conservatory with Stelios Kafantaris; Further studies with Joseph Gingold at the University of Indiana. *Career:* Debut: Athens Festival, 1984; Cannes Festival, 1985; US debut with the Santa Barbara Symphony, 1986; Athens Festival 1988, conducted by Rostropovich, leading to concerts with the National Symphony Orchestra in Washington DC; Concerts at the Helsinki Festival and with the Swedish Radio Symphony conducted by Esa-Pekka Salonen; European tour with the Helsinki Philharmonic conducted by Okku Kamu, 1989; Further appearances in Italy, Spain, France, Cyprus, Turkey, Hungary and Japan; Television and radio recordings in Greece, France, Germany, Spain and England; Dvořák's Concerto at the 1999 London Proms; London Proms, 2002. *Honours:* Winner, 1985 Sibelius Violin Competition, Indianapolis; 1986 International Competition; 1988 Winner, Naumburg Competition, New York; Winner 1988 Paganini Competition, Genoa. *Current Management:* Ingpen & Williams Ltd, 7 St George's Court, 131 Putney Bridge Road, London, SW15 2PA, England.

**KAVRAKOS, Dimitri;** Singer (Bass); b. 26 Feb. 1946, Athens, Greece. *Education:* Athens Conservatory of Music. *Career:* Debut: Athens Opera 1970, as Zaccaria in Nabucco; Athens Opera until 1978; US debut at Carnegie Hall, in Refice's Cecilia; Metropolitan Opera debut 1979, as the Grand Inquisitor in Don Carlos, returned to New York as Silva (Ernani), Walter (Luisa Miller), Ferrando (Il Trovatore), Capulet (Roméo et Juliette) and in I Vespri Siciliani; Chicago Lyric Opera in Aida, Lakmé, Les Contes d'Hoffmann and Fidelio; San Francisco Opera in La Gioconda; Guest engagements at La Scala, Paris Opéra, Aix-en-Provence, Spoleto, Lyon and Avignon; British debut Glyndebourne 1982, as the Commendatore in Don Giovanni; London debut at the Barbican Hall in Cherubini's Medée; Covent Garden debut 1984, as Pimen in Boris Godunov, returned in new productions of La Donna del Lago (Douglas 1985), Le nozze di Figaro (Bartolo) and Anna Bolena (Enrico VIII 1988); Rome Opera 1989, as Silva in Ernani, Bellini's Giorgio in Florence; Sang Fiesco in Simon Boccanegra at Cologne, 1990 and Prince Gremin in Eugene Onegin in Chicago; Maggio Musicale Florence, 1990 as Ernesto in Donizetti's Parisina; Season 1992–93 as Timur in Turandot at Chicago, Rossini's Mosè with the Israel Philharmonic, Banquo at Cologne and the Commendatore at Aix-en-Provence; Don Giovanni (Commendatore) and Le nozze di Figaro (Bartolo, Salzburg); I Puritani, Bregenz, 1985; Il Barbiere di Siviglia, Florence, 1994; Paris Opéra: Don Carlos and Puritani, 1987; Lucia, 1995; Lucrezia Borgia, Teatro San Carlo Naples, 1992; La Vestale, La Scala, 1993; Sang Banquo at Florence, 1995; La Scala 1997, in Lucia di Lammermoor; Season 1998–99 at Paris Opéra with Lucia di Lammermoor and I Capuleti e i Montecchi; Sang Arkel in Pelléas at Toronto, 2000. *Recordings include:* Don Giovanni; La Vestale, La Scala, 1993; Rigoletto, La Scala, 1994; Ravenna, Norma, 1994. *Address:* c/o Patricia Greenan, 19B Belsize Park, London NW3 4DU, England.

**KAWAHARA, Yoko;** Singer (Soprano); b. 3 Sept. 1939, Tokyo, Japan. *Education:* Studied with Toishiko Toda in Tokyo and with Ellen Bosenius at the Cologne Musikhochschule. *Career:* Debut: Niki Kai Opera Tokyo 1958, as Fiordligi; Sang in Bonn as Pamina, 1969; Bayreuth Festival 1972–77, as the Woodbird in Siegfried; Member of the Cologne Opera from 1975; Guest appearances in Frankfurt, Hamburg and Tokyo; Staatsoper Hamburg 1986, in La Clemenza di Tito; Other roles include Euridice, Sophie in Der Rosenkavalier, Desdemona, Freia and Liu; Many concert appearances. *Recordings include:* Reger's Requiem (Schwann). *Address:* c/o Oper der Stadt Köln, Offenbachplatz, 5000 Cologne, Germany.

**KAWALLA, Szymon (Piotr);** Conductor and Composer; b. 2 June 1949, Kraków, Poland; m. Hanna Kiepuszewska, 28 April 1973, 1 d. *Education:* Studies as Solo Concert Violinist 1972, as Conductor 1973, as Composer 1974, Chopin Academy of Music, Warsaw. *Career:* Debut: Philharmonic, Kraków, 1964; Conductor, Philharmonic Poherien, 1974–78; Conductor-Director, Torun Chamber Orchestra, 1978–80; Conductor-Director, Philharmonic and Opera Zielona Gora, 1980–86; Symphonic Orchestra and Chorus, RTV Kraków, 1985–; Concerts in Austria, Bulgaria, Canada, Cuba, England, Germany, Netherlands, France, Italy, Poland, Romania, Spain, Czechoslovakia, Russia, Vatican; Radio, television and films; Professor, Chopin Academy of Music, Warsaw. *Compositions:* Divertimento, Capriccio for violin solo, Oratorio, Pater Kolbe, Cantata, Wit Stwosz, Stabat Mater, Quartet for Strings. *Address:* Lazurowa 6/100, 01-315 Warsaw, Poland.

**KAWASAKI, Masaru,** DipMus; Japanese composer and conductor; *Professor Emeritus, Tokoha Gakuen University;* b. 19 April 1924, Tokyo; m. Taeko Koide 1953; two s. *Education:* Tokyo Acad. of Music. *Career:* first performance of Compos at Festliche Musiktage Uster, Switzerland 1971, 1974, 1977, 1981; Dir, Int. Youth Musicale, Shizuoka 1979, 1982 and 1985; Prof. Emer., Tokoha Gakuen Univ.; mem. Japanese Soc. Rights Authors and Composers, Nat. Band Asscn. *Compositions:* March Ray of Hope, 1963; March Forward for Peace, 1966; Essay on a Day for flute and piano, 1969; March Progress and Harmony, 1969; Warabe-Uta for symphony band, 1970; Prayer Music Number 1, Dirge, commissioned by Hiroshima City, 1975; Poem for symphony band, 1976; Prayer Music Number 2, Elegy, 1977; Romantic Episode, 1979; Romance for trumpet and symphony band, 1982; March Dedicated to Cupid, 1983; In the Depth of Night for flute and cello, 1993; La improvvisazione, for string trio 2004. *Publications:* Instrumentation and Arrangement for Wind Ensemble 1972, New Band Method 1979; contrib. to Band Journal, Tokyo. *Honours:* hon. mem. Int. Soc. of Contemporary Music, UNESCO Creative Artists Fellow 1966–67; Ministry of Education and President of NHK Composition Prize 1956. *Address:* 4-2-38 Hamatake, Chigasaki-shi 2530021, Japan (home). *Telephone:* (467) 866020 (home). *Fax:* (467) 866020 (home). *E-mail:* masaruk@jcom.home.ne.jp (home).

**KAY, Donald (Henry);** Composer; b. 25 Jan. 1933, Smithton, Tasmania. *Education:* BMus, University of Melbourne, 1955; Study with Malcolm Williamson, 1959–64. *Career:* Faculty member, Tasmanian Conservatorium,

1967–; Commissions from APRA, Lyrian String Quartet, Tasmanian Symphony Chamber Players, and others. *Compositions include:* Dance Movement for small orchestra, 1968; Four Australian Folk Songs, for women's or young voices, 1971; The Quest, for string quartet, 1971; There is an Island, for children's choir and orchestra, 1977; The Golden Crane, opera for children and adults, 1984; Dance Cameos, for mandolin, wind quintet, 1986; Hastings Triptych, for flute and piano, 1986; Northward the Strait, for chorus, soprano, baritone and wind band, 1988; Tasmania Symphony: The Legend of Moinee, for cello and orchestra, 1988; Dance Concertante for string orchestra, 1989; Haiku, for women's voices, piano and string quartet, 1990; Night Spaces, for flute, string trio and piano, 1990; Piano Concerto, 1992; Moonlight Ridge for string quintet or string orchestra, 1994; AEstivernal for mandolin, wind quintet or orchestra, 1994; River Views for trombone and string orchestra, 1995; The Edge of Remoteness for piano trio, 1996; Symphony–The South Land, 1997; Sonata for cello and piano, 1999; Sonata for piano, 1998; Different Worlds, for piano, 1999; Bird chants, for piano, 1999; Blue sky through still trees, for flute and piano, 1999; String Quartet No, 5, a trgaic life, 2002; The death of Ben Hall, for SATB chorus and concert band, 2002. *Recordings:* Tasmania Symphony–The Legend of Moinee. *Honours:* Sounds Australian Awards, 1989, 1990; Member of the General Division of the Order of Australia, 1991. *Address:* 4 Utiekah Drive, Taroona, Tasmania 7053, Australia.

**KAY, Serena;** British singer (mezzo-soprano); b. 1973, England. *Education:* Univ. of London, Royal Coll. of Music Opera School, currently studies with Philip Doghan. *Career:* opera roles include Hermia (Midsummer Night's Dream), English Touring Opera, Second Lady (Magic Flute), Opera North, Cenerentola, Mid Wales Opera, Rosina (Il Barbiere), Clonter Opera, Guido (Flavio), London Handel Soc., Dorabella (Così fan tutte), Mananan Opera, Sara (Tobias and the Angel), Young Vic/English Touring Opera, Nancy T'Ang (Nixon in China), ENO; concerts include Messiah (Handel), Huddersfield Choral Soc., Les Nuits d'ete (Berlioz), Oxford Sinfonia, Lieder eines fahrenden gesellen (Mahler), Barber of Seville highlights (with Gerald Finlay), Hansel (Hansel and Gretel highlights) BBC Concert Orchestra, Wesendonk Lieder (Wagner), OML-Portugal. *Honours:* Jr Fellowship, Royal Coll. of Music 2002–03. *Current Management:* c/o Ingpen and Williams Ltd, St George's Court, 131 Putney Bridge Road, London, SW15 2PA, England. *Telephone:* (20) 8874-3222. *Fax:* (20) 8877-3113. *E-mail:* info@ingpen.co.uk. *Website:* www .ingpen.co.uk.

**KAZARAS, Peter;** Singer (Tenor); b. 1956, New York, USA. *Career:* Debut: New York in 1981 in a concert performance of Khovanshchina; Houston in 1983 as Francois in the premiere of Bernstein's A Quiet Place; Santa Fe and Seattle in 1985 in Henze's English Cat and as Števa in Jenůfa; Returned to Seattle as Wagner's Froh and Erik, Hoffmann, Lensky and Pierre in War and Peace; New York City Opera debut in 1988 as Quint in The Turn of The Screw; Sang with Metropolitan Opera from 1990 as Narraboth in Salome, Shuisky in Boris Godunov and Almaviva in the premiere of Corigliano's The Ghosts of Versailles; Other modern repertory includes Udo Zimmermann's Die Weisse Rose, at Omaha in 1986, Pelegrin in the premiere of Tippett's New Year, at Houston in 1989, and Busoni's Die Brautwahl at Berlin Staatsoper in 1991; Sang Boris in the New Zealand premiere of Katya Kabanova, 1996; Captain Vere in Billy Budd at Dallas, 1997. *Address:* c/o Metropolitan Opera, Lincoln Center, New York, NY 10023, USA.

**KAZARNOVSKAYA, Lubov Yurievna;** Russian singer (soprano); b. 18 July 1956; m. Robert Roszik. *Education:* Moscow Gnessin School of Music and Moscow State Conservatory. *Career:* as student became soloist Moscow Stanislavsky and Nemirovich-Danchenko Musical Theatre 1981–86; soloist Leningrad Kirov (now Mariinsky) Opera Theatre 1986–89; debut outside USSR in Un Ballo in Maschera, Zürich Opera 1989, Desdemona in Otello, Covent Garden, London March 1990; moved to Vienna 1989; has performed in maj. opera houses of the world, in opera productions with Herbert von Karajan, Carlos Kleiber, Claudio Abbado, Riccardo Muti, Daniel Barenboim, James Conlon; also performs in concerts, including Requiem (Verdi), La Voix humaine by Poulenc and at festivals in Salzburg, Bregenz, Edin. and others. *Music:* operatic roles include leading parts in Eugene Onegin, Iolanthe, La Bohème, Pagliacci, Faust, Marriage of Figaro, Falstaff, Force of Destiny, Boris Godunov, La Traviata, Salome. *Honours:* prize winner All-Union competition of singers 1981, int. competition in Bratislava 1984. *Address:* Hohenberg-strasse 50, 1120 Vienna, Austria. *Telephone:* (1) 839106 (Vienna) (home); (095) 249-17-13 (Moscow) (home).

**KAZARNOVSKAYA, Lyuba;** Russian singer (soprano); b. 1960, Moscow. *Education:* Moscow Conservatory with Irina Arkhipova and Elena Shumilova. *Career:* debut, La Scala Milan 1989 in Verdi's Requiem under R. Muti; has sung at the Bolshoi, Moscow as Nedda, Mimi and Lida in La Battaglia di Legnano; tour of Italy with the Maily Theatre, Leningrad 1984; Kirov Theatre, Leningrad from 1986 as Leonora (La Forza del Destino and Trovatore), Marina, Violetta, Marguerite, Donna Anna and Tchaikovsky's Iolanta; Paris Opéra and Covent Garden 1987, as Tatiana with the Kirov Co.; Salzburg Festival 1989, in the Verdi Requiem, conducted by Karajan; Zürich Opera 1989–90, as Amelia Boccanegra and the Trovatore Leonora; Cologne Opera 1989–90, as Manon Lescaut and Amelia; Covent Garden 1990, as Desdemona; Metropolitan Opera as Tatjana in Eugene Onegin under Levine, Desdemona in Otello, Nedda in Pagliacci 1991–95; debut in Strauss' Salome 1995; new productions of Clemenza di Tito and Il Trovatore at San Francisco Opera and at Lyric Chicago, Tosca in Houston, Berlin and Vienna; recitals at the major music festivals; sang Pauline in Prokofiev's The Gambler at La Scala and in

Paris 1996–97; Aithra in Strauss' Aegyptische Helena under Thielemann with the Royal Opera at the Festival Hall 1998; first time ever singing two Manons in one evening; Massenet and Puccini premiere at the Bolshoi Theatre, Moscow and afterwards at opera festivals in Italy, Sweden, Germany and USA; personal television music show 'Glimpse of Love' 2000; concert and oratorio appearances, song recitals with works by Brahms, Wolf, de Falla, Dvořák and Rachmaninov; mem. Russian Opera Forum; Pres., Lyuba Kazarnovskaya Foundation. *Recordings include:* Shostakovich's 12th Symphony, Prokofiev's The Gambler, Tchaikovsky's The Complete Songs Op 103 (five vols), The Great Singers of Russia (video) 1901–99, Gypsy Love. *Honours:* The Voice of the Year, Russia 2001. *Address:* Arbat 35, Moscow 121002, Russia. *E-mail:* kazarnovskaya@888.ru.

**KEATING, Roderic Maurice,** MA, MMus, DMus, ARCO, ARCM; British singer (tenor); *Comprimario Tenor (Solo), Staatstheater Stuttgart;* b. 14 Dec. 1941, Maidenhead, Berks., England; m. Martha Kathryn Post 1968; one d. *Education:* Gonville and Caius Coll., Cambridge, Yale Univ. and Univ. of Texas, USA. *Career:* debut, Houston Grand Opera, Tales of Hoffmann 1970; Glyndebourne Touring and Festival Opera 1971–73; Theater an der Wien, Freddy, My Fair Lady 1971; perm. contracts in Lübeck 1972–74, Saarbrücken 1974–80, Wuppertal 1980–86, Bonn 1986–89, Stuttgart 1989–; more than 80 roles as lyric and character tenor; guest throughout Germany; guest appearances in Tbilisi, Georgia 1976, Interlaken Festspiel 1975, Wiesbaden 1977, Paris Opéra 1981, London Coliseum 1982, Warsaw 1983, Cologne 1985, Salzburg Festival 1986, Covent Garden 1988, Moscow 1989, Vienna and Schwetzingen Festivals 1990, Edinburgh Festival 2001; sang Tiresias in Henze's The Bassarids at Stuttgart 1989, Der Rosenkavalier, Théâtre Châtelet, Paris 1993 and Bologna 1995, Weill's Seven Deadly Sins, Tel-Aviv 1997; sang the Doctor in Three Sisters by Eötvös at Freiburg 2000; concerts and radio recordings for BBC, Bavarian Radio and SWF, WDR, SDR in Germany; oratorio and church concerts in Italy, France, Spain, Belgium, Netherlands, Germany. *Publications:* The Songs of Frank Bridge 1970; contrib. to Musical Times, Musical Opinion. *Address:* Staatstheater Stuttgart, 70183 Stuttgart, Germany (office); Lehenbühlstrasse 36, 71272 Renningen, Germany (home). *Telephone:* (7159) 18156 (home). *Fax:* (7159) 18156 (home). *E-mail:* RodericKeating@aol.com (home).

**KEATS, Donald (Howard);** Composer and Professor; b. 27 May 1929, New York, NY, USA; m. Eleanor Steinholz, 13 Dec 1953, 2 s., 2 d. *Education:* BMus primi honoris, Yale University School of Music, 1949; MA, Columbia University, 1952; Staatliche Hochschule für Musik, Hamburg, 1954–56; PhD, University of Minnesota. *Career:* Professor of Music, Antioch College, Ohio; Visiting Professor of Music, University of Washington, Seattle; Lawrence C Phipps Professor in the Humanities, University of Denver, 1982–85; Professor of Music, 1975–99, Professor Emeritus, 1999–, University of Denver, Colorado; Composer, Pianist, at concerts devoted solely to his music in USA, England and Israel. *Compositions include:* Symphonies No. 1 and No. 2 (An Elegiac Symphony); String Quartets No. 1, No. 2 and No. 3 (2001); Piano Sonata; The Hollow Men (T. S. Eliot), for chorus and instruments; Anyone Lived in a Pretty How Town (Cummings), for a cappella chorus; The Naming of Cats (T. S. Eliot), for chorus and piano; Tierras del Alma (Poemas de amor), song cycle for soprano, flute and guitar; Theme and Variations for Piano; Concerto for Piano and Orchestra; Diptych for cello and piano; Polarities for violin and piano; A Love Triptych (W B Yeats), song cycle; Musica Instrumentalis for 9 instruments; Elegy for full or chamber orchestra; Branchings for orchestra; Revisitations for violin, cello and piano. *Recordings:* String Quartet No. 2 (CD 1999); Piano Sonata, 1999. *Publications:* Many of above compositions published by Boosey and Harber. *Honours:* Fulbright Scholar, 1954–56; Guggenheim Fellowships, 1964–65, 1972–73; ASCAP Awards Annually since 1964. *Address:* 12854 West Buckhorn Road, Littleton, CO 80127, USA. *Telephone:* 303 948 3033. *E-mail:* dkeats@du.edu.

**KEBERLE, David (Scott);** Composer, Clarinettist and College Professor; b. 6 June 1952, Wausau, Wisconsin, USA. *Education:* BM, Composition, with distinction, Indiana University, 1975; BM, Education, with distinction, Indiana University, 1975; MMus, Composition, New England Conservatory of Music, Boston, 1977; Accademia di S Cecilia, Rome, 1980; Studied composition with Bernhard Heiden and Donald Martino, clarinet with Earl Bates, Joe Allard and W O Smith. *Career:* Instructor of Music, University of Wisconsin, Baraboo, 1977–81; Co-Founder of Electravox Ensemble, Rome, 1983; Instructor of Music, Loyola University, Chicago, Rome Centre, 1984–88; As Clarinet Soloist, performed in Brazil, Uruguay, Argentina, France, Italy, Israel, Austria and USA; Performed on National Italian Radio, 1987, 1988; Instructor of Music, St Mary's College, Rome Program, 1991–; mem, American Music Center, New York. *Compositions:* Incantation for clarinet and live electronics, 1986; Galoppando Attraverso il Vuoto for solo clarinet 1986; Concerto for Trumpet and Chamber Ensemble, 1980; Murmurs for solo flute, published by EDI-PAN Rome, 1989. *Recordings:* ElectraVox Ensemble Incantation for Clarinet and Live Electronics 1986, EDI-PAN Rome; Musicisti Contemporanei Clarinet and Piano EDI-PAN, 1989. *Honours:* Fulbirght Scholarship in Composition, 1979. *Address:* Via del Pellegrino 75, Int 18, 00186 Rome, Italy.

**KECHABIAN, Rafael;** Violinist, Concert Performer and Professor of Violin; b. 14 Feb. 1949, Yerevan, Armenia; m. Irene Kechabian, 25 Mar 1978, 2 s. *Education:* Special Musical School and Musical Secondary School, Sukhumi, 1957; State Yerevan Conservatory, Armenia, 1969; Postgraduate Course, State Yerevan Conservatory, Armenia, 1989–92; Diploma Violinist, Concert

Performer, Professor of Violin and Chamber Music. *Career:* Professor of Violin, Yerevan Music School, Armenia, 1970–83; Concertino, National Symphony Orchestra, Nicaragua, 1983–87; Professor of Violin, National Conservatory, Nicaragua, 1983–87; Soloist, State Chamber Ensemble of Armenia, 1987–93; Professor of Chamber Music, State Yerevan Conservatory, Armenia, 1987–93; Principal of the second violins, Symphony Orchestra of the Murcian Region, Spain, 1993–94; Professor of Violin, Musical Academy, Murcia, Spain, 1995; Violin Maker, Murcia, Spain, 1995. *Recordings:* Violinist, over 30 titles including: first recording of classical music in history of Nicaragua with National Symphony Orchestra, Miami, USA, 1984; Violinist, joint recordings with Orchestra Moscow Virtuosos of Spivakov, Moscow, 1983. *Honours:* Diploma, Ministry of Culture of the Republic of Nicaragua, 1987. *Address:* c/o Mariano Aroca, 7–4 1zq, 30011 Murcia, Spain.

**KEE, Piet;** Organist and Composer; b. 30 Aug. 1927, Zaandam, Netherlands; 2 c. *Education:* Studied with father, Cor Kee; Organ with Anthon van der Horst, Final Certificate cum laude and Prix d'excellence, 1948, Conservatoire of Amsterdam. *Career:* Debut: Zaandam, 1941; Organist of Schnitger organ, St Laurens Church, Alkmaar, 1952–87; Municipal Organist, St Bavo Church, Haarlem, 1956–89; Professor of Organ, Conservatoire of the Society Muzieklyceum, Sweelinck Conservatoire, Amsterdam, until 1987; Professor, International Summer Academy, Haarlem; Many concert tours world-wide; Television films of compositions Confrontation and Integration. *Compositions:* Two Songs (text Edgard Lemaire) for mezzo soprano and string quartet; Variations on a Carol, 1954; Triptych on Psalm 86, 1960; Two Organ Works, 1962; Four Manual Pieces, 1966; Music and Space for 2 Organs and 5 Brasswinds, 1969; Intrada for 2 Organs; Chamber Music; Valerius Gedenck-Clanck, 1976; Confrontation for 3 street organs and church organ, 1979; Integration for mixed choir, flageolet, mechanical birds, barrel organs and church organ, 1980; Frans Hals Suite for Carillon, 1990; Flight for flute solo, 1992; Bios for organ, 1994; Network for 2 organs, electronic keyboard, alto saxophone and descant recorder, 1996; Op-streek, for violin and piano, 1997; The World (text Henry Vaughan) for mixed choir and continuo instrument, 1999; Winds, for reed winds quintet, 2000; The Organ, homage to Pieter Saenredam, for organ, 2000; Heaven for mixed choir, 2001; Festival Spirit for five organs (commissioned by the International Organ Festival of St. Albans), 2001; Bios II for Organ, percussion and one violin, 2002; Heaven (text George Herbert) echo-fantasy for mixed choir and two solo sopranos; Festival Spirit for grand organ and 4 box organs; Bios II for organ, keyboard percussion, one violin and more percussion. *Recordings include:* Baroque music, romantic and modern music; New series of CDs including Bach organ works (4 vols); Franck organworks (San Sebastian); Piet Kee at Weingarten; Piet Kee at the Concertgebouw; Piet Kee plays Sweelinck and Buxtehude; Piet Kee plays Bruhns; Piet Kee plays Hindemith and Reger. *Publications:* The Secrets of Bach's Passacaglia, Musik und Kirche, 1982; Astronomy in Buxtehude's Passacaglia, The Diapason, Ars Organi, Het Orgel, 1984; Numbers and Symbolism in the Passacaglia and Ciacona, Het Orgel, 1986; Musik und Kirche, 1987; Loosemore Papers. *Honours:* Hon. FRCO. *Address:* Nieuwe Gracht 41, 2011 ND Haarlem, Netherlands.

**KEEFFE, Bernard,** BA; British conductor, broadcaster and academic; b. 1 April 1925, London; s. of Joseph Keeffe and Theresa Keeffe (née Quinn); m. Denise Walker 1954; one s. one d. *Education:* St Olave's Grammar School and Clare Coll., Cambridge. *Career:* served in Intelligence Corps 1943–47; mem. Glyndebourne Opera Co. 1951–52; BBC Music Staff 1954–60; Asst Music Dir, Royal Opera House 1960–62; Conductor BBC Scottish Orchestra 1962–64; Prof., Trinity Coll. of Music 1966–89; freelance conductor and broadcaster on radio and TV, concerts with leading orchestras 1966–; mem. int. juries, competitions in Sofia, Liège, Vienna and London; Warden solo performers section, Inc. Soc. of Musicians 1971; Chair. Anglo-Austrian Music Soc. *Radio:* Music in Japan (BBC World Service). *Television:* Elgar and the Orchestra (Best Music Programme of the Year) (BBC) 1979. *Publications:* Harrap's Dictionary of Music and Musicians (Ed.), ENO Guide to Tosca. *Honours:* Hon. Fellow Trinity Coll. of Music 1968. *Address:* 153 Honor Oak Road, London, SE23 3RN, England. *Telephone:* (20) 8699-3672.

**KEEGAN, Liane;** Singer (contralto); b. 1963, Australia. *Education:* Melba Conservatorium, Melbourne;National Opera Studio, London, Graz Summer School. *Career:* Appearances as Suzuki in Butterfly for Opera North (1996) Barbara in Korngold's Violanta at the 1997 London Proms and Waltraute in Act III of Die Walküre at the 1997 Edinburgh Festival; Other roles include Fricka, Dalila, Ulrica, Mistress Quickly, Dorabella and Rosina; Azucena for the State Opera of South Australia, 1999; Recitals throughout the United Kingdom and in France and Austria; Concerts include Mahler's Lieder eines fahrenden Gesellen, Das Lied von der Erde, Symphonies 2 and 3; Elijah, The Dream of Gerontius, Verdi Requiem, the Wesendonck lieder and Elgar's Sea Pictures; Schubert documentary on German television, 1995; Sang Erda, First Norn and Waltraute in Der Ring des Nibelungen for the State Opera of South Australia, 1998; Season 2002 Ulrica for Opera Australia (Un Ballo in Maschera), Gaea for Vara Radio Amsterdam Concertgebouw (Daphne); Season 2003, First Norn in The Ring, Offred's Mother in The Handmaid's Tale for ENO; Season 2004, Erda, 1st Norn and Waltraute in the Ring at Adelaide, Australia. *Current Management:* Arts Management. *E-mail:* enquiries@artsmanagement.com.au.

**KEEN, Catherine;** Singer (Mezzo-soprano); b. 1970, California, USA. *Education:* Adler Fellow, San Francisco Opera. *Career:* Appearances as Dalila at the Deutsche Oper Berlin and with Netherlands Opera as Federica in Luisa

Miller, Verdi's Emilia and Suzuki in Butterfly; Wagner's Flosshilde, 1999–2000; San Francisco Opera as Britten's Hermia, Magdelene, Venus in Tannhäuser, Fricka and Offenbach's Giulietta; Verdi's Amneris and Fenena at the 1998 Verona Arena and Brangaene in Tristan with the Cincinnati Symphony Orchestra; Season 1999–2000 with Waltraute and Fricka at Catania, Amneris in Houston and Kundry and Handel's Cornelia in Giulio Cesare at Washington; Concerts include Das Lied von der Erde in Paris, Mahler 8 at the Edinburgh Festival, Beethoven 9 and Schubert's Rosamunde. *Address:* c/o IMG Artists, Lovell House, 616 Chiswick High Road, London W4 5RX, England.

**KEENLYSIDE, Raymond;** Musician and Violinist; b. 9 May 1928, Southsea, Hampshire, England; m. Cynthia J Page, 2 s., 1 d. *Education:* Trinity College of Music, London. *Career:* Principal of Chamber Orchestras including: Boyd Neel; Philomusica; English Chamber Orchestra; Academy of St Martin-in-the-Fields; member of London Harpsichord Ensemble, 1959–62; David Martin String Quartet; Aeolian String Quartet, 1962–81; Professor of Violin, Royal College of Music; Senior Tutor, Royal College of Music Junior Department; Numerous radio appearances; Series on BBC television of late Beethoven String Quartets; Other television appearances. *Recordings:* Complete Haydn String Quartets, re-issued, 1997; Works by Schubert, Mozart, Elgar, Vaughan Williams, Ravel, Debussy, all with the Aeolian Quartet; Others with other groups. *Contributions:* Daily Telegraph Magazine. *Honours:* LTCL (TTD); Honorary MA, Newcastle University, 1970; Honorary FTCL, 1983; Honorary FRCM. *Address:* Bailiwick, Upper Woodford, Salisbury, Wiltshire SP4 6PF, England.

**KEENLYSIDE, Simon,** CBE; British singer (baritone); b. 3 Aug. 1959, London, England. *Education:* Royal Northern Coll. of Music. *Career:* gave concert performances, then engaged with Scottish Opera as Papageno and Billy Budd; season 1994–95 as Mozart's Count and Guglielmo at Covent Garden, Hamlet in the opera by Thomas at Geneva; sang Guglielmo at the reopened Palais Garnier, Paris 1996, and Thomas's Hamlet in Geneva; also sings lieder by Schubert; concerts include Britten's War Requiem at the Festival Hall (CBSO) 1997; Marcello and Figaro at the Vienna State Opera 1999; sang Monteverdi's Orfeo with Concerto Vocale under René Jacobs, Barbican Theatre 1998; sang Papageno at the New York Met 2001; season 2000–01 as Pelléas in Geneva, Marcello at the Met, Guglielmo at Salzburg and Billy Budd; Wagner's Wolfram in Munich and Belcore (L'Elisir d'amore) at La Scala. *Honours:* winner Richard Tauber Competition 1986. *Current Management:* Askonas Holt Ltd, Lonsdale Chambers, 27 Chancery Lane, London, WC2A 1PF, England. *Telephone:* (20) 7400-1700. *Fax:* (20) 7400-1799. *E-mail:* info@askonasholt.co.uk. *Website:* www.askonasholt.co.uk.

**KEHL, Sigrid;** singer (soprano, mezzo-soprano); b. 23 Nov. 1932, Berlin, Germany. *Education:* studied in Erfurt, Berlin Musikhochschule and with Dagmar Freiwald-Lange. *Career:* debut at Berlin Staatsoper 1956, in Prince Igor; Member of the Leipzig Opera from 1957, notably as Brünnhilde in Der Ring des Nibelungen, 1974; Engagements at the Berlin Staatsoper from 1971, Vienna Staatsoper from 1975; Further appearances at the Komische Oper Berlin and in Prague, Bucharest, Rome, Bologna, Geneva, Warsaw and Basle; Lausanne Festival 1983, as Isolde.

**KEINONEN, Heiki;** Singer (Baritone); b. 1951, Finland. *Education:* Studied in Helsinki. *Career:* Sang in concert from 1976, and at the Savonlinna Festival; Finnish National Opera at Helsinki from 1981, notably as Germont in La Traviata, 1993, and the premiere of Insect Life by Kalevi Aho, 1996; Vasa Opera, 1994, in the premiere of Miss Julie by Ilkka Kuusisto; Sang Pontto in the premiere of The Key, by Aho at Helsinki, 1995; Title role in Sweeney Todd, 1998. *Recordings include:* Kung Karls Jakt by Pacius. *Address:* c/o Finnish National Opera, PO Box 176, Helsingkatu 58, 00251 Helsinki, Finland.

**KEITH, Gillian;** Singer (Soprano); b. 1971, Canada. *Education:* McGill University, Montreal; Royal Academy, London, with Ian Partridge. *Career:* Concert repertoire includes Les Illuminations by Britten, Finzi's Dies Natalis, Strauss's Ophelia Lieder, Schubert's Mignon Lieder and Debussy's Quatre chansons de jeunesse; Soloist in Bach Cantatas on tour with John Eliot Gardiner, 2000, including Falsche Welt, dir trau ich nicht; Appearances in Brussels, New York, Edinburgh, London and Winchester; Season 2001 with Josabeth in Athalia for the London Handel Festival, Messiah and Israel in Egypt on tour to Austria, Germany and Turkey; Song recitals at Covent Garden, St George's Bristol and Tel-Aviv; Wigmore Hall debut June 2001; Handel's Israel in Egypt at the London Proms, 2002; Other repertory includes Purcell's Fairy Queen. *Recordings include:* Purcell's The Tempest; Hasse's Il Cantico de' tre fancuilli. *Honours:* Winner, Lieder, Early Music and French Song prizes, RAM. *Address:* Royal Academy of Music, Marylebone Road, London WC1, England.

**KEKULA, Josef;** violinist; b. 1952, Czechoslovakia. *Education:* studied with Václav Snítil and members of Smetana Quartet, Kostecky and Kohout. *Career:* co-founder and 2nd Violinist, Stamic Quartet of Prague, 1977; Performances at Prague Young Artists and Bratislava Music Festivals; Tours to: Spain, Austria, France, Switzerland, Germany, Eastern Europe; USA tour, 1980; Debut concerts in the United Kingdom at London and Birmingham, 1983; British tours, 1985, 1987, 1988 at Warwick Arts Festival, 20 concerts in 1989; Season 1991–92: Channel Islands, Netherlands, Finland, Austria, France, Edinburgh Festival, Debut tours of Canada, Japan and Indonesia; In 1994 visited Korea and Japan; In 1995 visited USA. *Recordings:* Shostakovich

No. 13; Schnittke No. 4 Panton; Mozart K589 and K370, Lyrinx; Dvořák; Martinů; Janáček complete quartets, Cadenza; Complete Dvořák String Quartets; Complete Martinů String Quartets; 1 CD, Clarinet Quintets by Mozart and Krommer. *Publications:* Complete Works of Smetana and Janáček String Quartet. *Honours:* with members of Stamic Quartet: Winner, International Festival of Young Soloists, Bordeaux, 1977, Winner, EBU International String Quartet Competition, 1986, Academie Charles Cros Grand Prix du Disque, 1989 for Dvořák Quartets, 1991 for Martinů Quartets; Diapason d'Or, 1994 for Dvořák Quintets. *Current Management:* Robert Gilder & Co., Enterprise House, 59–65 Upper Ground, London, SE1 9PQ, England. *Telephone:* (20) 7928-9008. *Fax:* (20) 7928-9755. *E-mail:* rgilder@robert-gilder.com.

**KELANI, Reem Yousef;** Palestinian singer and musicologist; b. 7 Aug. 1963, Manchester, England. *Education:* Kuwait Univ. *Career:* initially singer of jazz, subsequently Arab music; based in London 1989–, as performer and researcher of Palestinian music; research into traditional music from interviews in Palestine and in Lebanese refugee camps; featured vocalist, Gilad Atzmon and The Orient House Ensemble 2002–03; performed at Vossa Jazz Festival, Norway 2003. *Recordings:* Exile (BBC Jazz Award for Best CD) 2003. *Address:* The Miktab, PO Box 31652, London, W11 2YF, England (office). *Telephone:* (7092) 811747 (office). *E-mail:* reem@reemkelani.com. *Website:* www.reemkelani.com.

**KELEMEN, Barnabas;** Violinist; b. 12 June 1978, Budapest, Hungary. *Education:* Franz Liszt Academy, Budapest. *Career:* Appeared at Brabant Festival, Netherlands, and Cambridge Festival, England, 1992; Performances in Italy, 1995, Spain, 1996, on 3SAT television, Saarbrücken, Germany, 1997, and at Wigmore Hall, London, 1998. *Recordings:* F Liszt: Works for Violin and Piano, with Sergely Bogányi. *Honours:* 2nd Prize, Szigeti Competition, Budapest, 1997; 1st Prize, Mozart Competition, Salzburg, 1999. *Current Management:* Clemens Concerts Ltd, Attila út 61, 1013 Budapest, Hungary. *Address:* Széchenyi-emlek út 23, 1121 Budapest, Hungary.

**KELEMEN, Milko;** Composer; b. 30 March 1924, Slatina, Croatia. *Education:* Studies, Zagreb Academy of Music and with Messiaen and Aubin, Paris; Further study with Wolfgang Fortner, Freiburg, also Siemens Electronic Music Studio, Munich. *Career:* Taught Composition, Zagreb Conservatory, 1955–58, 1960–65; Founder, Zagreb Biennial Festival, President, 1961; Taught, Schumann Conservatory, Düsseldorf, 1972; Professor of Composition, Hochschule für Musik, Stuttgart, 1973; Professor of Composition, Hochschule Hans Eisler, Berlin, 1999. *Compositions include:* The Abandoned, ballet, 1964; O Primavera, tenor, strings, 1965; Words, cantata, 1966; Composé, 2 pianos, orchestra, 1967; Changeant, cello, orchestra, 1968; Motion, string quartet, 1969; The Siege, opera after Camus, 1970; Floreal, orchestra, 1970; Varia Melodia, string quartet, 1972; Gasho, 4 choir groups, 1974; Seven Agonies, mezzo, 1975; Mageia, orchestra, 1978; Apocalypse, ballet opera, 1979; Grand Jeu Classique, violin, orchestra, 1982; Love Song, strings, 1984; Dramatico, cello, orchestra, 1985; Fantasmus, viola, orchestra, 1986; Archetypon, orchestra, 1986; Landscapes, mezzo, string quartet, 1986; Memories, string trio, 1987; Sonnets, string quartet, 1987; Nonet, 1988; Requiem, speaker, ensemble, 1994; Salut au Monde, oratorio, soloists, 2 choruses, orchestra, projections, light actions, text Walt Whitman, 1995; Concerto for Oboe, English Horn, Oboe D'Amore and chamber orchestra; Good Bye My Fancy for violin and piano; Fantastic Animals for chorus, 1996; For Anton (Bruckner) for orchestra, 1996; Delicate Clusters for orchestra, 1999; Concerto 2000 for 5 singers and orchestra, 1999; Horn and Strings, 1999; Glissade, concerto for clarinet and orchestra, 2001; Tromberia, concerto for trumpet and orchestra, 2001; Aural, trio for violin, cello and piano, 2002; Orion, Venus, Andromeda, chorus for children; Inferno di Dante for bass solo; Intonazioni Poetiche for chamber orchestra; Pas de Deux, duo for violin and cello; Incanto for solo violin. *Recordings:* Various labels. *Publications:* Klanglabyrinthe, 1981, French, 1985, Croatian, 1994; Poruka Pateru Kolbu (Croatian), 1995, Message to Father Kolb (English), 1995; Klangwelten (German), 1995; Schreiben an Strawinsky (German). *Address:* Bergstrasse 62/II, 70186 Stuttgart, Germany.

**KELÉN, Peter;** Singer (Tenor); b. 27 July 1950, Budapest, Hungary. *Career:* Sang at the National Opera, Budapest, from 1974, notably as Werther, Edgardo in Lucia di Lammermoor, Alfredo, Don Carlos, the Duke of Mantua, Don Ottavio and Don José; Guest appearances at La Scala, Milan, as Fenton in Falstaff, 1983, Ernesto in Don Pasquale at the Vienna Staatsoper, Des Grieux in Rio de Janeiro and Riccardo at Milwaukee, 1990; Earl's Court, London, 1991, as Cavaradossi in Tosca; Budapest, 1995, in the premiere of Karl and Anna by Balassa. *Address:* Hungarian National Opera, Nepoztasarag utja 22, 1061 Budapest, Hungary.

**KELESSIDI, Elena;** Singer (Soprano); b. 1970, Kazakhstan. *Education:* Alma-Ata Conservatory. *Career:* Season 1991 at the Alma-Ata Opera as Bizet's Leila, Zerlina in Auber's Fra Diavalo, Wolf-Ferrari's Serafina and Amor in Orfeo ed Euridice; Mozart's Mme Herz and Constanze at the Athens State Opera, 1992; Donna Anna for Latvian Opera, under Gustav Kuhn; Royal Opera, Covent Garden from 1996, as Voice from Heaven in Don Carlos, Violetta and Handel's Cleopatra (1997); Season 1998–99 as Violetta for the Bavarian State Opera; Sang the Queen of Shemakha in The Golden Cockerel with the Royal Opera at Sadler's Wells (1991) and Giulietta in I Capuleti e i Montecchi at Covent Garden, 2001; Further engagements as Violetta in Monte Carlo and Hamburg, Tatiana (Eugene Onegin) at Montpellier and Gilda in Rio; Season 2001–2002 as Mimi at the Opéra Bastille and the New York Met, Susanna for Dallas Opera and Liu in Turandot for Netherlands Opera. *Address:* c/o Royal Opera (Contracts) Covent Garden, London WC2, England.

**KELLER, András;** violinist; b. 1960, Hungary. *Education:* Franz Liszt Acad., Budapest and with Sandor Devich, György Kurtág and András Mihaly. *Career:* member of the Keller String Quartet from 1986, debut concert at Budapest March 1987; Played Beethoven's Grosse Fuge and Schubert's Death and the Maiden Quartet at Interforum 87; Series of concerts in Budapest with Zoltan Kocsis and Deszö Ranki (Piano) and Kalman Berkes (Clarinet); Further appearances in Nuremberg, at the Chamber Music Festival La Baule and tours of Bulgaria, Austria, Switzerland, Italy (Ateforum 88 Ferrara), Belgium and Ireland; Concerts for Hungarian Radio and Television. *Recordings:* albums for Hungaroton (from 1989). *Honours:* 2nd Prize, Evian International String Quartet Competition, May 1988. *Address:* Vitorla U.3, 1031 Budapest, Hungary.

**KELLER, Heinrich;** flautist and composer; b. 14 Nov. 1940, Winterthur, Switzerland; m. 1968; three s. *Education:* Conservatory, Zürich. *Career:* debut, 1965; Philharmony, Bremen, 1965–66; Orchestra of St Gallen, 1967–72; Musikkollegium Winterthur, solo Flautist, 1972–; mem, Schweizerischer Tonkunstlerverein; Musikkollegium Winterthur, solo Flautist, 1972–1990; Musikhochschule Winterthur, Professor of Flute, 1972–2003. *Compositions:* Aleph, 1966; Blaserquintett, 1972; Puzzle, 1973; Streichquartett, 1973–74; Reduktion, 1974; Refrains, 1975; Ritual, 1979; Rencontre, flute and harpsichord, 1985; Verlorene Spur for piano, 1986; Rand for flute solo, 2002. *Recordings:* Flotenmusik aus Frankreich und Italien; Schubert, ihr Blumlein; Baroque and Rokoko, Flute music; 'Wie Risse im Schatten' by Mathias Steinauer; Sonata for Flute by Philipp Jarnach. *Honours:* Prize for composing String Quartet, Tonhalle, Zürich, 1974; Carl-Heinrich-Ernst Prize, 1998; Cultural Award of the City of Winterthur, 2000. *Address:* Grüzenstrasse 14, 8400 Winterthur, Switzerland.

**KELLER, Helen;** Singer (Soprano); b. 5 March 1945, Horgen, Zürich, Switzerland. *Education:* Studied in Zürich and with Agnes Giebel in Cologne. *Career:* Concert performances in Switzerland and elsewhere from 1971 with a repertoire including Rossini's Stabat Mater, L'Enfance du Christ, Schöpfung and Jahreszeiten, Elijah and St Paul, works by Bach and Handel and Honegger's Roi David; Appearances at Amsterdam, Antwerp, Paris, Milan, Annsbach, Karlsruhe and the USA in Britten, Brahms, Schubert, Monteverdi, Pergolesi, Vivaldi and Schumann; Stage engagements as Salome in San Giovanni Battista by Stradella at St Gallen and in Le Convenzione Teatrali by Donizetti at Zürich. *Recordings:* Messiah, Schubert's Mass in G and San Giovanni Battista. *Address:* c/o Peter Keller, Opernhaus Zürich, Falkenstrasse 1, 8008 Zürich, Switzerland.

**KELLER, Peter;** Singer (Tenor); b. 16 March 1945, Thurgau, Switzerland; m. Helen Keller. *Education:* Studied in Zürich, with Ernst Haefliger in Berlin and Agnes Giebel in Cologne. *Career:* Has sung at the Zürich Opera from 1973, notably in the Monteverdi series and as Pedrillo, Monostatos, Jacquino, Wagner's David and Steuermann, Valzacchi in Rosenkavalier and M Triquet in Eugene Onegin (1991); Guest engagements at Munich, Hamburg, Düsseldorf (Edgar in Reimann's Lear), Milan, Edinburgh, Berlin and Vienna; Concert singer in Europe and on tour with Helen Keller in the USA; Sang in Puccini's Trittico at Zürich, 1996; Season 2000–01 at Zürich in Lulu, Carmen, The Queen of Spades and Die Zauberflöte (Priest). *Recordings include:* Die Zauberflöte, Il Ritorno d'Ulisse and Monteverdi's Orfeo; Diary of One who Disappeared by Janáček; Handel's Israel in Egypt and Mendelssohn's Christus; Zemlinsky's Kleider Machen Leute. *Address:* c/o Peter Keller, Opernhaus Zürich, Falkenstrasse 1, 8008 Zürich, Switzerland.

**KELLER, Verena;** Singer (Mezzo-soprano); b. 8 Sept. 1942, Schwerin, Germany. *Education:* Studied in Vienna with Hans Hotter and in Berlin; Lieder with Erik Werba. *Career:* Engaged at Hanover 1963–66, Bonn 1979–88, Mainz 1983–86; Guest appearances at Cologne, Geneva, Naples, Herrenhausen and Göttingen; Roles have included Mozart's Ramiro, Carmen, Santuzza, Ortrud, Brangaene, Kundry, Venus, Fricka; Verdi's Amneris, Azucena and Ulrica, Strauss's Clytemnestra and Herodias, Janáček's Kabanicha and the Witch in Hansel and Gretel; Concert engagements in Baroque music throughout Germany and in Paris, Rome, Los Angles and Vancouver. *Recordings include:* Dvořák's Mass in D. *Address:* Staatstheater, Gutenbergplatz 7, 6500 Mainz, Germany.

**KELLERMAN, Julia Eleanor Margaret,** BA; British music book editor (retd); b. 10 March 1937, London, England; m.; one s. *Education:* Univ. of Bristol and Birkbeck Coll., London. *Career:* House Ed., Master Musicians Series, J. M. Dent & Sons Ltd 1972–94; freelance ed., Oxford Univ. Press 1994–99; Man. Music & Letters Trust 1996–2005; mem. Royal Musical Asscn. *Address:* 87 Hampstead Way, London, NW11 7LG, England (home). *Telephone:* (20) 8458-6113 (home). *E-mail:* jkellerman@compuserve.com (home).

**KELLOGG, Cal (Stewart);** Conductor and Composer; b. 26 July 1947, Long Beach, California, USA. *Education:* Conservatorio di Musica Santa Cecilia, Rome, Diplomas in Bassoon, Composition and Conducting. *Career:* Debut: Symphonic: Monte Carlo, 1975; Opera: Rome Opera, 1976; As Bassoonist, Toured with Renato Fasano's Piccola Teatro Musicale di Roma, 1967–72; Soloist with RAI Orchestra of Rome, 1972; Conductor of Symphonic Concerts with Baltimore Symphony, New World Symphony, Monte Carlo, Accademia

Nazionale di Santa Cecilia, Maggio Fiorentino, La Fenice, San Carlo, RAI Orchestras of Rome, Torino and Naples, Antwerp Philharmonic, Spoleto Festival Orchestra, Orchestra of Illinois, Seattle Symphony, Israel Sinfonietta of Beersheva; Director of Opera at Rome Opera, Teatro Communale di Firenze, San Francisco Opera, San Carlo, Teatro Regio di Parma, NYC Opera, Santa Fe, Washington Opera, St Louis, Houston Grand Opera, Canadian Opera Company, Opera Montreal, Seattle Opera, Edinburgh Opera Festival, Israel Festival, Spoleto Festival, Chautauqua Festival PBS television live from Lincoln Center, New York City Opera production of Menotti's The Saint of Bleecker Street; Radio broadcasts of Tosca, 1978, Houston Grand Opera, Ballo in Maschera, 1981, Canadian Opera Company, Il Trovatore, 1984 and Macbeth, 1986; Conducted Andrea Chénier at Philadelphia, 1997. *Compositions:* Sullivan Ballou's Letter to his Wife for Bass Baritone and Orchestra, a setting of a Civil War letter, 1990. *Recordings:* Thomas Pasatieri: Three Sisters, opera in 2 acts, 1986. *Address:* c/o Opera Company of Philadelphia, 510 Walnut Street, Suite 1600, Philadelphia, PA 19106, USA.

**KELLY, Bryan;** Composer, Pianist and Conductor; b. 3 Jan. 1934, Oxford, England. *Education:* Royal College of Music 1951–55, with Gordon Jacob and Herbert Howells; Paris with Boulanger. *Career:* Has taught at the Royal Scottish Academy of Music; Professor of Composition, Royal College of Music, 1962–84; Resident at Castiglione del Lago, Italy, 1984–. *Compositions:* Orchestral: The Tempest Suite, for strings, 1964; Cookham Concertino, 1969; Divertimento for brass band, 1969; Oboe Concerto, 1972; Edinburgh Dances for Brass Band, 1973; Guitar Concerto, 1978; Andalucia and Concertante Music or Brass, 1976, 1979; 2 Symphonies, 1983, 1986; Vocal: Tenebrae Nocturnes for tenor, chorus and orchestra, 1965; Magnificat and Nunc Dimittis for chorus and organ, 1965; The Shield of Achilles for tenor and orchestra, 1966; Sleep little Baby, carol, 1968; Stabat Mater, 1970; At the Round Earth's Imagin'd Corners for tenor, chorus and strings, 1972; Abingdon Carols, 1973; Let There Be Light for soprano, narrator, chorus and orchestra, 1973; Latin Magnificat, 1979; Te Deum and Jubilate for chorus and organ, 1979; Dover Beach for chorus, 1995; Piano Sonata, 1971; Prelude and fugue for organ, 1960; Pastorale and Paen for organ, 1973; Chamber music; Children's Pieces: Herod to your Worst, nativity opera, 1968; On Christmas Eve, suite of carols, 1968; The Spider Monkey Uncle King, opera pantomime, 1971. *Recordings:* The Choral Music of Bryan Kelly, Abbey Records. *Address:* c/o British Music Information Centre, 11 Stratford Place, London, W1, England.

**KELLY, Declan;** Singer (Tenor); b. 1965, Ireland. *Education:* Studied singing, Royal Irish Academy of Music; Singing, National Opera Studio, London. *Career:* Debut: Mozart's The Magic Flute, Opéra du Rhin, A Midsummer Night's Dream, 1998; Member, National Chamber Chior, Dublin; Member, St Patrick's Cathedral Choir, Dublin; Tamino, Mid Wales Opera; Wexford Festival Opera; Holland Park Opera; European Chamber Opera; Opera Theatre Company, Dublin; Ferrando, Young Dublin Opera; Camille, Clonter Opera; Borsa, Pimlico Opera and Holland Park Opera; Frederic, Carl Rosa Productions, and both La Chericia and the Villager, Wexford Arithmetic/Teapot/Frog in L'Enfant et les Sortilèges, National Concert Hall, Dublin; Spirit, and understudy of Pylade, English Bach Festival, Covent Garden and Athens; Regular soloist, National Symphony and RTE Concert Orchestra; Concerts, television and radio; Solo recitals in Ireland, the United Kingdom and USA; Charity concerts for Irish Youth Fund, New Jersey, 1991; Mozart Requiem, Ulster Orchestra, 1998–99, performances in Belfast, Wexford and at the NCH, Dublin; Festival Company Tenor, Buxton Festival, 1998; Tamino, Mid-Wales Opera on tour; Messiah, Fairfield Halls, London Mozart Players; Mozart Requiem with Vladimir Spivakov and Moscow Virtuosi, Madrid; Rossini Petite Messe Solennelle, Gower Chorale; Carmina Burana, Hastings; The Creation, Dublin; Scaramuccio, Opéra National du Rhin; Almaviva, The Barber of Seville, Mid-Wales Opera. *Recordings:* Te Deum with Myung-Whun Chung and L'Accademia di Santa Cecilia. *Current Management:* Helen Sykes Artists Management. *Address:* c/o Helen Sykes Artists Management, 100 Felsham Road, Putney, London SW15 1DQ, England.

**KELLY, Frances;** British harpist; b. 1955, England. *Career:* regular performances with the New London Consort in medieval and renaissance music; has toured in Europe and the Far East; Early Music Network tours in the UK 1986 and 1988; freelance engagements with the Consort of Musicke and the Gabrieli Consort and Players Recitals with soprano Evelyn Tubb; on modern harp was mem. of the Ondine Ensemble, giving performances in the UK and USA; partnership with the flautist Ingrid Culliford from 1977; BBC recital with tenor Ian Partridge; concerto soloist in the premieres of Edward Cowie's Concerto in Newcastle and London and for Tyne Tees Television; season 1988 included Debussy and Ravel with the Lindsay Quartet, chamber music by Bruch for the BBC and concerts in London, Denmark, Bruges and Utrecht as continuo player with the Consort of Musicke; South Bank Summer Music Festival with the New London Consort; played in Oswald von Wolkenstein concert 1997. *Recordings include:* Debussy's Trio Sonata with the Athena Ensemble, Britten's A Ceremony of Carols with the Choir of Christ Church Cathedral, Oxford, Mozart's Concerto K299 with the Academy of Ancient Music, Harp collection (solo, Amon Ra). *Address:* c/o Hyperion Records Ltd, PO Box 25, London, SE9 1AX, England.

**KELLY, Janis;** Singer (Soprano); b. 1955, Glasgow, Scotland. *Education:* Studied at Royal Scottish Academy of Music, the Royal College of Music and in Paris. *Career:* Represented Britain at the UNESCO Young Musicians' Rostrum at Bratislava, 1981; Operatic roles include Serpetta in La Finta Giardiniera (Glyndebourne, 1991); Flora in The Knot Garden and Mozart's

Despina, Zerlina and Susanna, 1991, for Opera Factory; English National Opera as Amor (L'Incoronazione di Poppea), Flora (The Turn of the Screw), Kitty (Anna Karenina by Iain Hamilton), Barbarina, Bekhetaten in Akhnaten, Woman/Fury in The Mask of Orpheus, Papagena, Yum-Yum, and Rose in Street Scene; Magnolia in Show Boat for Opera North; Concert appearances in the USA, Canada, Paris and Czechoslovakia; Season 1992 as Ottavia in The Coronation of Poppea, and Countess in Marriage of Figaro for Opera Factory, Governess in Turn of the Screw, Bath City Opera, Tatyana in Eugene Onegin for Kentish Opera; In 1995 sang the Countess in Figaro for ENO; Amaranta in La fedeltà Premiata (Garsington), and Fairy in Purcell's Fairy Queen, for ENO; Dorabella at Garsington and Romilda in Xerxes and the Countess in Figaro for ENO, 1997; Rosalinda in Die Fledermaus for Scottish Opera and Opera Ireland, 1998; Violetta in La Traviata with Opera North, 1998; Wigmore Hall Soiree Fauré, 1999; King Arthur in Concert in Portugal and St John Passion in Madrid; La Rondine with Opera North, 1999; Mrs Nixon in Nixon in China with ENO; The Cunning Little Vixen with Opera North, 2001; Directed Così fan tutte, Grange Park, 2001; Marschallin in Der Rosenkavalier with Opera North, 2002; Despina in Così fan tutte with ENO, 2002; Miss Jessel, Grange Park; Elettra in Mozart's Idomeneo with Opera North, 2003; Directed Iolanthe, Grange Park. *Recordings:* Magnolia, Show-boat; Rose, Street Scene; Mozart, Gluck, Puccini, Massenet Arias on Inspector Morse soundtrack albums. *Honours:* Anna Instone Award, Royal College of Music; Countess of Munster, Caird and Royal Society of Arts Scholarships. *Current Management:* Musichall, Vicarage Way, Ringmer, BN8 5 LA. *Address:* 159 Purves Road, London NW10 5TH, England.

**KELLY, Judith (Jude) Pamela,** OBE, BA; British theatre director; *Artistic Director, South Bank Centre, London;* b. 24 March 1954, Liverpool; d. of John Kelly and Ida Kelly; m. Michael Bird 1983; two s. (one deceased) one d. *Education:* Calder High School, Liverpool and Univ. of Birmingham. *Career:* freelance folk and jazz singer 1970–75; actress, Leicester Phoenix Theatre 1975–76; Founder Solent People's Theatre, Dir 1976–80; Artistic Dir Battersea Arts Centre (BAC) 1980–85; Dir of Plays Nat. Theatre of Brent 1982–85; freelance dir 1985–88; Festival Dir York Festival and Mystery Plays 1988; Artistic Dir West Yorkshire Playhouse 1988–2002, Chief Exec. 1993–2002; Founder and Artistic Dir Metal community arts lab., London, Liverpool, Bogota, Colombia 2002–; Visiting Prof. of Drama, Leeds and Kingston Univs; British Rep. on Culture for UNESCO 1997–; Chair. Common Purpose Charitable Trust 1997–, Qualifications and Curriculum Authority Advisory Group on the Arts 2001–03, Culture, Arts and Educ. Cttee, London 2012 Olympics 2004–; Artistic Dir South Bank Centre, London 2005–; Vice-Chair. Nat. Advisory Cttee on Creative and Cultural Educ. 1998; mem. Council RSA 1998–, Ind. TV Comm. 1999–. *Productions include:* West Yorkshire Playhouse: The Merchant of Venice 1994, Beautification of Area Boy 1996, The Seagull 1998, The Tempest 1998, Singin' in the Rain (Olivier Award for Outstanding Musical Production 2001) 1999, 2000, Half A Sixpence 2000; Sarcophagus (RSC) 1986, When We Were Married (Chichester Festival Theatre, transferred to Savoy Theatre) 1996, Othello (Shakespeare Theatre), Washington, DC 1997, The Elixir of Love (ENO) 1997, Johnson Over Jordan. *Honours:* Hon. Fellow Dartington Coll. of Arts; Hon. DLitt (Leeds Metropolitan) 1995, (Bradford) 1996, (Leeds) 2000, (York) 2001, (Open Univ.) 2001; Woman of the Year, Yorks. 1996, 2002, Yorkshire TV Personality of the Year 2002, Dream Time Fellowship, NESTA 2003. *Address:* South Bank Centre, Belvedere Road, London, SE1 8XX (office); Metal, 198A Broadhurst Gardens, London, NW6 3AY, England. *Telephone:* (20) 7921-0600 (office); (20) 7328-8551. *Fax:* (20) 7328-5552. *E-mail:* jude@metalculture.com. *Website:* www.southbankcentre.org.uk (office); www.metalculture.com.

**KELLY, Paul Austin;** Singer (Tenor); b. 1964, USA. *Career:* Debut: New York City Opera, as Tamino in Mozart's Die Zauberflöte; Roles in Rossini's Barbiere di Siviglia at Royal Opera, Rome Opera, Pesaro and New York Metropolitan Opera in 2000; In Zelmira at Pesaro, Opéra de Lyon and Paris; In Ermione at Glyndebourne; In Comte Ory at Canadian Opera and Glimmerglass; Cenerentola at Die Vlaamse Opera and Philadelphia; Turco in Italia at La Scala; Donizetti roles include Tonio at La Scala, Rome Opera, Opéra de Monte Carlo, Ernesto at Bologna and Austin Lyric Opera; Mozart roles include Tamino at La Scala, City Opera and Opera Pacific; Belmonte at Catania and Hawaii Opera; Don Ottavio at Dublin, Santiago and New York City Opera; Alessandro in Il Re Pastore at Opéra de Nice and Mostly Mozart Festival; Season 1999–2000 with Don Ottavio at New Israeli Opera; Ferrando at Glyndebourne; Bach B Minor Mass in Paris; Other repertoire includes roles in Bellini's La Sonnambula, Donizetti's Lucrezia Borgia, Offenbach's La Belle Hélène, and Rossini's Pietra del Paragone and Otello; Concerts include Rossini's Stabat Mater in Paris and Wexford, Mozart Requiem in Rome and Lisbon, Messiah, St Matthew Passion, Magnificat and Missa Solemnis. *Recordings include:* Three Rossini Tenors; Zoraide di Granata; La Romanzesco; Rossini Cantatas; Der Stein der Weise; The Holy Sonnets of John Donne by Britten. *Current Management:* Herbert Barrett Management. *Address:* c/o Herbert Barrett Management, 1776 Broadway, New York, NY 10019, USA.

**KELM, Linda;** Singer (soprano); b. 11 Dec. 1944, Utah, USA. *Education:* studied with Jennie Tourel at the Aspen School of Music and in New York. *Career:* debut, Seattle 1977, as Helmwige and Third Norn in the Ring; sang Turandot with Wilmington, 1979, followed by performances at Seattle, New York City Opera 1983, Chicago, San Francisco and Amsterdam; sang Salome at St Louis and Princess in Rusalka at Carnegie Hall; Perugia 1983, as Dirce in Cherubini's Demofoonte; Seattle Opera, 1985; as Brünnhilde; further guest appearances include Helmwige in the Ring.

**KELTERBORN, Rudolf,** DipMus; Swiss composer, conductor and academic; b. 3 Sept. 1931, Basel; m. Erika Kelterborn Salathe 1957; one s. one d. *Education:* Music Acad., Basel, studied composition with Blacher and Fortner, Salzburg and Detmold, conducting with Markevitch. *Career:* Teacher, Conductor, Basel, 1956–60; Professor of Composition: NW German Music Academy, Detmold, 1960–68, HS Zürich, 1968–75; Editor of Swiss Music Review, 1968–75; Head of Music Department, Swiss Radio, 1975–80; Professor of Composition, HS Karlsruhe, 1980–83; Director of Music Academy, Basel, 1983–94; Guest Prof. in USA 1970, 1980, Japan 1986, 1990, China 1993. *Compositions include:* Four Symphonies and five Operas Kaiser Jovian, 1967; Ein Engel Kommt nach Babylon, 1977; Der Kirschgarten, 1984; Ophelia, 1984; Julia, 1990; A ballet; Various works for Orchestra; Namenlos for ensemble and electronics, 1996; Herbstmusik, 7 pieces for orchestra, 2002; 4 Movements for Classical Orchestra, 1996; Concertos for various solo instruments; Chamber music including 6 string quartets, 1954–2001; Cantatas; piano and organ works. *Recordings:* Several under various labels. *Publications:* Komponist, Musikdenker, Vermittler (various authors), Zürich, Bern, 1993. *Honours:* Bernhard Sprengel Prize of the German Industry 1962; Arts Prize City of Basel 1984; Composition Prize, Swiss Musicians' Asscn. *Address:* Delsbergerallee 61, 4053 Basel, Switzerland (office). *Telephone:* (61) 261-8319.

**KEMENY, Alexander;** Violinist; b. 22 April 1943, Solna, Sweden; Divorced, 1 d. *Education:* Bratislava Conservatory, Czechoslovakia, 1960–66; Music Academy in Prague with Professor A Plocek, 1966–70. *Career:* Debut: 1970; Concertmaster, Innsbruck Symphonic Orchestra, 1973–75; Violinist, Prague Symphonic Orchestra, also Norrkoping Symphony Orchestra, Sweden; Freelance Concert Violinist, 1978–; Soloist with orchestra playing works by Myslivecek, Mozart, Beethoven, Brixi, Mendelssohn, Wieniawski, Eklund, and chamber music player of both classical and modern music, concerts in Czechoslovakia, Sweden, Denmark and Poland; Performed in Piano Trio and in Duo with guitarist Vladimir Vectomov; Radio performances, Czechoslovakia, Sweden and Austria; Performed at Bornholm Music Festival, Denmark, 1987. *Recordings:* Paganini, Giuliani, and Kowalski, Radio Prague and Bratislava; Smetana, Johansson and Telemann, Radio Sweden; Suk, Smetana, Foerster, and Suchoň, Radio Austria.

**KEMMER, Mariette;** Singer (Soprano); b. 1960, Luxembourg. *Education:* Studied at the Luxembourg Conservatoire and at the Rheinland National College of Music in Düsseldorf. *Career:* Sang at the Théâtre de la Monnaie, Brussels, as Mélisande, Sophie, Pamina, Micaela and Mozart's Countess; Guest appearances at the Vienna Staatsoper, Munich, Berlin, Hamburg, Frankfurt, Dresden, Stuttgart, Zürich, Geneva, Basle, Berne, Lausanne, Verona, Dublin, Karlsruhe, Mannheim, Nürnberg, Strasbourg, Marseille, Nancy, Montpellier, Nantes, Avignon, Metz and Liège; Has appeared at the festivals of Aix-en-Provence, Wexford and Bregenz; Other roles include Mozart's Ilia, Fiordiligi and Donna Elvira, Marguerite, Antonia, Tatiana and the Countess in Capriccio; Has appeared in concert, with major orchestras in Vienna, Paris Prague, Zürich, Brussels, Luxembourg, Monte-Carlo, Antwerp, Liège, Bregenz, Bonn, Nürnberg, Bamberg, Stuttgart, Heidelberg, Metz, Nancy, Nantes, Montpellier and the festival at Round Top, Texas. *Address:* Music International, 13 Ardilaun Road, London N5 2QR, England.

**KEMP, Nicola-Jane;** Singer (Coloratura Soprano); b. 1965, England. *Education:* Chetham's School of Music; Girton College, Cambridge; Royal College of Music; RSAMD, Glasgow; Further study with Margaret Hyde. *Career:* Appearances with British Youth Opera; Music Theatre Wales; London Opera Players; Central Festival Opera; Music Theatre Kernow; Aix-en-Province Festival; Covent Garden; Roles have included Verdi's Oscar; Mozart's Constanze and Queen of Night; Birtwistle's Pretty Polly in Punch and Judy; Season 1998, Covent Garden Festival; Jauchzet Gott (Bach) at the Purcell Room; Barbican with the London Soloists CO and at Crans Montana Festival; Season 1999 with Strauss's Zerbinetta, St John's Smith Square, and the Académie Européenne de Musique at Aix-en-Provence; A Mind of Winter (Benjamin) with Orchestre de Rouen, 2001; Lakmé (Belcanto Opera), 2001; Queen of Night and Papagena at Covent Garden, 2002; Jubilee Concert at Chatsworth House, 2002; UK Tour with Vienna Galan, 2002–03; Concerts throughout the United Kingdom. *Address:* Music International, 13 Ardilaun Road, London N5 2QR, England.

**KEMPF, Frederick;** Concert Pianist; b. 14 Oct. 1977, England. *Education:* Studied at the Royal Academy of Music, with Ronald Smith; Further study with Christopher Elton. *Career:* Debut: Mozart's Concerto K414, with the Royal Philharmonic, 1985; Concerto engagements with the Royal Liverpool Philharmonic Orchestra, London Mozart Players, European Community CO, Netherlands Radio Symphony Orchestra, BBC National Orchestra of Wales and the Hallé Orchestra; Conductors have included Libor Pešek, Ashkenazy, Taddaki Otaka and Feodor Gluschenko; Solo recitals at the Chichester, Canterbury, Bath, Guidlford and Exeter Fetsivals; Season 1996 with debut appearance at Berlin (Deutsches Symphonie Orchester), Munich and Prague recitals, and debut with the Philharmonia Orchestra; Season 1996–97 with tour of Japan, recitals in Washington and New York and concerts with American orchestras; Season 2001–02 with San Francisco Symphony Orchestra, Rotterdam Philharmonic Orchestra; Tours to Italy, France, Russia, Japan and Germany. *Recordings include:* Schumann and Rachmani-

nov recitals (BIS); Beethoven Sonatas Op. 109 and Op. 110 (BIS) and Chopin. *Honours:* Joint winner, National Mozart Competition, 1987; Winner, BBC Young Musician of the Year, 1992. *Address:* c/o Grant Rogers Musical Artists Management, 8 Wren Crescent, Bushey Heath, Hertfordshire, WD23 1AN, England.

**KEMPSTER, David;** Singer (Baritone); b. 1969, Wales; m. Charlotte Kinder, one s. *Education:* Royal Northern College of Music. *Career:* Engagements with English National Opera in Tosca, House of the Dead, 1997–98; Otello, La Traviata, Carmen, Salome and Dialogue of the Carmelites, 1998–99; Lescaut in Manon Lescaut; Schaunard in La Bohème, Toddy Foran in the world premiere of the Silver Tassie, Chouen Lai in the London premiere of Nixon in China, 1999–2000; Di luna in Il Trovatore, Poacher in A Cunning Little Vixen, 2000–01; Marcello in La Bohème, Pilate in St John Passion and Renato in Ballo in Maschera, 2001–02; Roles for Glyndebourne: Escamillo in Carmen, Germont in La Traviata; for Welsh National Opera: Belcore in L'Elisir d'Amore, Marcello in La Bohème; Other roles include Rigoletto, Barber's Figaro, Don Giovanni, and Mozart's Count Almaviva; Concert repertoire includes Handel's Messiah, Saul and Judas Maccabaeus, Elgar's The Dream of Gerontius, Fauré's Requiem, Mendelssohn's Elijah, Orff's Carmina Burana, Mozart's Requiem, Puccini's Messa di Gloria, Vaughan Williams' A Sea Symphony and Walton's Belshazar's Feast. *Address:* Harlequin Agency Ltd, 203 Fidlas Road, Cardiff CF4 5NA, Wales.

**KENDALL, Christopher (Wolff);** Conductor, Lutenist and Artistic Director; b. 9 Sept. 1949, Zanesville, Ohio, USA. *Education:* BA, Antioch College, 1972; MM, Conducting, University of Cincinnati Conservatory, 1974; Dalcroze School of Music, NY, 1969–70. *Career:* Director of 20th Century Consort in residence at the Smithsonian Institution, Washington, 1976–, Associate Conductor of the Seattle Symphony, 1987–; Founder and Lutenist of Folger Consort, Ensemble-in-Residence at Folger Shakespeare Library in Washington DC 1977–; Artistic Director of Millennium Inc, 1980–; Guest Conductor: Seattle Symphony, Chamber Music Society of Lincoln Center, Eastman Musica Nova, Da Capo Chamber Players, Washington Sinfonia. *Recordings:* 20th Century Consort Vols I and II, Smithsonian Collection; Into Eclipse (Stephen Albert) 20th Century Consort, Nonesuch; Shakespeare's Music, Folger Consort, Delos; A Distant Mirror, Carmina Burana, Folger Consort, Delos. *Honours:* Gold Award, Houston Film Festival for Millennium: 10 Centuries of Music 1986; Emmy Award for 20th Century Consort PBS Programme on Aaron Copland 1984.

**KENDALL, William;** Singer (Tenor); b. 1960, London, England. *Education:* King's School, Canterbury; Choral Scholar, Cambridge University; Further study with Robert Tear and Peter Pears. *Career:* Concert appearances under such conductors as Hogwood, Harnoncourt, Gardiner, Mackerras and Boulez; Works by Tippett and Tavener conducted by the composers; Sang in the world premiere of Penderecki's Polish Requiem; Tour of Germany, 1989 with the Monteverdi Choir and Orchestra in the Missa Solemnis and Beethoven's Mass in C; Further appearances in season 1990–91 as the Evangelist in the St John Passion, in The Dream of Gerontius and Britten's Serenade in Australia; Mozart Requiems in Oxford and Cambridge and Bach's B Minor Mass with The Sixteen at St John's Smith Square; London Promanade concert appearances and showings at the Holland Festival, Festival Berlin, 1987, and the 1989 Salzburg Festival. *Recordings:* Beethoven Missa Solemnis and Mass in C; Bach and Schütz with the Stuttgart Kammerchor; Sacred music by Haydn.

**KENGEN, Knud-Erik;** Organist, Pianist and Composer; b. 17 July 1947, Copenhagen, Denmark; m. Gerlinde Maria Pagel, 6 Dec 1969, 1 s., 1 d. *Education:* Studies in Musicology, University of Copenhagen, 1972–76; Final Diploma, Royal Danish Academy of Music, 1974; Studied under Professor Aksel Andersen; Consultations in Composition with Leif Kayser. *Career:* Assistant Organist, Dome of Copenhagen, 1974; Organist, Gladsaxe Church, Copenhagen, 1979–; Performances: Concert Organist at numerous concerts, mainly in Denmark but also in Germany, England and Sweden; also played as Soloist at first performance of Musica Autumnalis by Axel Borup Jorgensen in The Danish Broadcasting Corporation; as Pianist, Rehearser and Chorus Master; Accompanist at Lieder-Recitals. *Compositions:* Organ and Choir-Music in style somewhat indebted to modern French church-music since Langlais, Duruflé and early Messiaen; For Organ: Toccata, Opus 5; Choral Preludes, Opus 14 and 26, 7 Chorales for the Concert, Op 43, 1993; Rhapsody, Surrexit Dominus, Opus 22; Organ Fantasy, Victimae Paschali, Opus 24; Missa Fons Bonitatis, Opus 26; Proprium for Hallo-Mass, Opus 28; Choral Fantasy, Veni Creator Spiritus, Opus 40; For Choir: Psalm 12, Opus 21; Cantatas with Instruments, Opus 35; Stabat Mater, 1992; Psalm 23, 1999. *Publications:* Contributed to the lexical part of the History of Music in Denmark, 1978. *Address:* Tranegardsvej 69, 1 TV, DK 2900 Hellerup, Denmark.

**KENNEDY, (Nigel Paul),** ARCM; British violinist; b. 28 Dec. 1956, Brighton, England; s. of John Kennedy and Scylla Stoner; m. Agnieska; one s. *Education:* Yehudi Menuhin School, Juilliard School of Performing Arts, New York. *Career:* debut playing Mendelssohn's Violin Concerto at the Royal Festival Hall with the London Philharmonic Orchestra under Riccardo Muti 1977; subsequently chosen by the BBC as the subject of a five-year documentary on the devt of a soloist; other important debuts include with the Berlin Philharmonic 1980, New York 1987; has made appearances at all the leading UK festivals and in Europe at Stresa, Lucerne, Gstaad, Berlin and

Lockenhaus; tours to Australia, Austria, Canada, Denmark, Germany, Hong Kong, India, Ireland, Italy, Japan, Republic of Korea, New Zealand, Norway, Poland, Spain, Switzerland, Turkey and the USA; has given concerts in the field of jazz with Stephane Grappelli, including at the Edinburgh Festival and Carnegie Hall; runs his own jazz group; five-year sabbatical 1992–97; Artistic Dir, Polish Chamber Orchestra 2002–; Sr Vice-Pres. Aston Villa Football Club 1990–. *Television:* Coming Along Nicely (BBC documentary on his early career) 1973–78. *Recordings include:* Strad Jazz 1984, Elgar Sonata with Peter Pettinger 1985, Elgar's Violin Concerto with the London Philharmonic and Vernon Handley (Gramophone magazine Record of the Year, BPI Award for Best Classical Album of the Year) 1985, Vivaldi's Four Seasons, Bartók Solo Sonata and Mainly Black (arrangement of Ellington's Black Brown and Beige Suite), Sibelius Violin Concerto with the City of Birmingham Symphony Orchestra conducted by Sir Simon Rattle, Walton's Violin Concerto with the Royal Philharmonic Orchestra and André Previn, Bruch and Mendelssohn concertos with the English Chamber Orchestra conducted by Jeffrey Tate, Kafka (Kennedy's compositions), Tchaikovsky's Chausson Poème with the London Philharmonic Orchestra 1988, Brahms Violin Concerto with the London Philharmonic under Klaus Tennstedt 1991, Beethoven Violin Concerto with the NDR-Sinfonieorchester and Klaus Tennstedt 1992, chamber works by Debussy and Ravel, Berg's Violin Concerto, Vaughan Williams' The Lark Ascending with Sir Simon Rattle and the CBSO, works by Fritz Kreisler 1998, The Kennedy Experience, chamber works by Bach, Ravel and Kodaly (with Lynn Harrell) 1999, Classic Kennedy with the English Chamber Orchestra 1999, Bach's Concerto for Two Violins in D Minor, Concerto for Oboe and Violin in D Minor and the A Minor and E Major violin concertos the Berlin Philharmonic 2000. *Publication:* Always Playing 1991. *Honours:* Hon. DLitt (Bath) 1991; Golden Rose of Montreux 1990, Variety Club Showbusiness Personality of the Year 1991, BRIT Award for Outstanding Contribution to British Music 2000, Male Artist of the Year 2001. *Current Management:* Askonas Holt Ltd, Lonsdale Chambers, 27 Chancery Lane, London, WC2A 1PF, England. *Telephone:* (20) 7400-1700. *Fax:* (20) 7400-1799. *E-mail:* info@askonasholt.co.uk. *Website:* www.askonasholt.co.uk. *Address:* c/o John Stanley, Kennedy, 90–96 Brewery Road, London, N7 9NT, England.

**KENNEDY, Andrew;** Singer (Tenor); b. 1977, England. *Education:* Choral Scholar at King's College, Cambridge; Royal College of Music, with Neil Mackie. *Career:* Concerts include Cavalli's Messa Concertata with The Parley of Instruments, Messiah in Romsey Abbey, Haydn's Harmoniemesse in Canterbury Cathedral and Beethoven's 9th with the Hanover Band; Evangelist in Bach's St John and St Matthew Passions and Schubert's E flat Mass with the Brandenburg Consort; Modern repertory includes Britten's Nocturne and Serenade (King's College Chapel, St John's Smith Square) and Dies Natalis by Finzi. Principal conductor of The Allegri Singers; Stage appearances in Janàcek's Diary of One who Disappeared, Haydn's Die Feuerbrunst, The Rake's Progress and Holst's Savitri; Title role in Hugh the Drover by Vaughan Williams and tour of the United Kingdom as Mozart's Ferrando; Sang Ugone in Flavio for the London Handel Festival, 2001. *Address:* c/o Royal College of Music, Prince Consort Road, London SW7, England.

**KENNEDY, (George) Michael (Sinclair),** CBE, MA, CRNCM, FIJ; British journalist and music critic; b. 19 Feb. 1926, Chorlton-cum-Hardy, Manchester; s. of Hew G. Kennedy and Marian F. Kennedy; m. 1st Eslyn Durdle 1947 (died 1999); m. 2nd Joyce Bourne, 10 Oct. 1999. *Education:* Berkhamsted School. *Career:* staff music critic, The Daily Telegraph 1941–50, Northern Music Critic 1950–60, Northern Ed. 1960–86, Jt Chief Music Critic 1986–89; Chief Music Critic, The Sunday Telegraph 1989–2005; Gov. Royal Northern Coll. of Music. *Publications:* The Hallé Tradition: A Century of Music 1960, The Works of Ralph Vaughan Williams 1964, Portrait of Elgar 1968, Elgar: Orchestral Music 1969, Portrait of Manchester 1970, History of the Royal Manchester College of Music 1971, Barbirolli: Conductor Laureate 1971, Mahler 1974, The Autobiography of Charles Hallé, with Correspondence and Diaries (ed.) 1976, Richard Strauss 1976, Britten 1980, Concise Oxford Dictionary of Music (ed.) 1980, The Hallé 1858–1983 1983, Strauss: Tone Poems 1984, Oxford Dictionary of Music (ed.) 1985, Adrian Boult 1987, Portrait of Walton 1989, Music Enriches All: The First 21 Years of the Royal Northern College of Music, Manchester 1994, Richard Strauss: Man, Musician, Enigma (French critics prize for musical biog. 2003) 1999, The Life of Elgar 2004, Buxton: an English Festival 2004; contrib. to newspapers and magazines, including Gramophone, Listener, Musical Times, Music and Letters, The Sunday Telegraph, BBC Music Magazine. *Honours:* Hon. mem. Royal Manchester Coll. of Music 1971; Hon. MA (Manchester) 1975; Hon. MusD (Manchester) 2003. *Address:* The Bungalow, 62 Edilom Road, Manchester, M8 4HZ, England (home). *Telephone:* (161) 740-4528 (home). *E-mail:* majkennedy@bungalow62.fsnet.co.uk.

**KENNEDY, John,** OBE; British music industry executive; *Chairman and CEO, International Federation for the Phonographic Industry*; b. 1953, London. *Education:* Univ. of Leicester. *Career:* mem. Business Affairs dept, Phonogram 1978, Dir of Business Affairs 1979; then Dir of Business Affairs, CBS Records UK –1984; founding pnr entertainment law firm, J. P. Kennedy & Co. 1984–96; CEO PolyGram UK 1996–98 (merged with Universal Music 1998), Chair. and CEO Universal Music UK 1998–2001, Pres. and COO Universal Music Int. 2001–04; bd mem. Int. Federation for the Phonographic Industry (IFPI) 2002–04, and Chair. European Regional Bd 2002–04, Chair.

and CEO IFPI 2005–. *Address:* International Federation for the Phonographic Industry, 54 Regent Street, London, W1B 5RE, England (office). *Telephone:* (20) 7878-7900 (office). *Fax:* (20) 7878-7950 (office). *E-mail:* info@ifpi.org (office). *Website:* www.ifpi.org (office).

**KENNEDY, Nicki;** Singer (Soprano); b. 1968, England. *Education:* Bristol University; Royal Scottish Academy of Music and Drama; Royal College of Music. *Career:* Appearances with European Chamber Orchestra; Philharmonia; Les Musiciens du Louvre; Glasgow Philharmonia; London Festival Orchestra; London Handel Festival; Concertgebow Amsterdam, Snape Maltings; Glasgow Royal Concert Hall; Glasgow International Early Music Festival; Three Choirs Festival; Aix-en-Provence Festival; Appearances throughout Europe; Japan, Egypt, Dubai; 11 operatic roles; Broadcast with Camerata Hispanica; La Serenissima; Les Musiciens du Louvre; Founder, Cromata, specialising in 17th century Italian music. *Recordings:* Vivaldi Cantatas; Spanish Lute Songs; Les Musiciens du Louvre; The Musicians of the Globe; Modo Antiquo; Charivari Agreable. *Current Management:* Helen Sykes Artists Management, 100 Felsham Road, Putney, London SW15 1DQ, England.

**KENNEDY, Roderick;** Singer (Bass Baritone); b. 7 May 1951, Birmingham, England. *Education:* Studied at Guildhall School and with Otakar Kraus. *Career:* Debut: Covent Garden, 1975; Over 30 roles with the Royal Opera; Created Lt of Police in The Ice Break by Tippett, 1977; Appeared with Royal Opera on visits to La Scala, 1976, Korea and Japan in 1979 and 1986; Sang The Doctor in Wozzeck at Edinburgh and San Francisco, 1980–81, with further engagements at opera houses throughout Europe; Glyndebourne debut, 1981 as Don Fernando in Fidelio, followed by Alidoro, Rocco, Seneca in Poppea, and Britten's Theseus; Further festival appearances at Aldeburgh, Aix-en-Provence, Montpellier, Starasbourg and Florence; Regular performances with English National, Welsh National and Scottish Operas; Repertoire includes: The Coloratura Works of Handel and Rossini; Roles include: Don Alfonso, King Philip, Pogner, Bottom as well as many 20th century works; Regular Promenade and Concert appearances in the United Kingdom and abroad; Has worked with such conductors as Muti, Kleiber, Colin Davis, Ozawa, Harnoncourt, Solti, Haitink, Mehta, Prêtre and Mackerras; Sang Britten's Bottom for ENO, 1996; Director of the Winter Gardens, Charitable Trust, Bournemouth, England; General Director of Kent Opera, 1998–; Sang the Animal Trainer and Athlete in Lulu at Palermo, 2001. *Recordings include:* Messiah; La Traviata; Hérodiade; La Forza del Destino; Maria Padilla; Die Sieben Todessunden; Offenbach's Robinson Crusoe, The Immortal Hour and Le Comte Ory; Television films of Lucrezia Borgia, Giulio Cesare, Idomeneo, L'Egisto, Hérodiade, L'Incoronazia di Poppea, La Cenerentola and A Midsummer Night's Dream; The Complete Vocal and Piano Works of Lord Berners (One of Gramophone Magazine's Records of the Year, 1998); Berg's Lulu, 2001. *Current Management:* Music International. *Address:* The White House, Witchampton, Dorset BH21 5AU, England.

**KENNER, Kevin;** American/British concert pianist; b. 19 May 1963, California, USA. *Education:* Peabody Conservatory, Baltimore, Hochschule für Musik, Hannover, studied with Leon Fleisher. *Career:* has appeared in Europe, North and Central America, the Orient and former Soviet Union, since 1989 performing with St Paul Chamber Orchestra, Rochester Philharmonic and ensembles in San Diego, San Francisco, Kansas City and Baltimore; Recitals at the Salle Pleyel in Paris, the Châtelet, Queen Elizabeth Hall London (International Piano Series) and at the Kennedy Center, Washington, DC; Broadcasts in Japan, Australia, Poland, Germany and Costa Rica. *Honours:* winner: Gina Bachauer Competition, Utah, 1988; Van Cliburn Competition, Fort Worth, 1989; International Tchaikovsky Competition, Moscow, 1989; International Terence Judd Award, Manchester, 1990; International Chopin Piano Competition, 1990. *Current Management:* Künstlersekretariat Rolf Sudbrack, Gösselkoppel 54a, 22339 Hamburg, Germany. *Telephone:* (40) 5382165. *Fax:* (40) 5387720. *E-mail:* rolf .sudbrack@t-online.de. *Website:* www.sudbrackmusik.de. *E-mail:* kkenner@ csi.com (home). *Website:* www.kevinkenner.com.

**KENNY, Courtney Arthur Lloyd;** pianist, repetiteur and accompanist; b. 8 Nov. 1933, Dublin, Republic of Ireland; m. Caroline Anne Florence Arthur 1972; one s. *Education:* Wellington Coll., Berkshire, Royal Coll. of Music, London. *Career:* Musical Dir, Bristol Old Vic 1954–57; solo pianist, Royal Ballet 1957; mem., Glyndebourne Festival Opera music staff; founder, Western Opera, Ireland 1963; Wexford Festival Opera staff 1963–96, Head of music staff 1974; Senior Repetiteur 1982; New Sadler's Wells Opera Head of Music Staff 1983–89; Assoc. Music Dir, Ohio Light Opera 1983; mem. of various ensembles, including Bureau Piano Trio, Barbican Ensemble, Peter Lloyd Baroque Trio; Faculty, Blossom Festival School of Cleveland Orchestra and Kent State Univ. 1972–80; many concert appearances as soloist and accompanist in Europe, USA, Middle East; conducting debut, John Curry Theatre of Skating, then Ohio Light Opera, New Sadler's Wells Opera; cabaret-songs at the piano; appearances in USA, Canada, Middle East, England, Scotland and Ireland; mem. Incorporated Soc. of Musicians. *Recordings:* with Glyndebourne Festival Opera, recitals with Ian Wallace, two solo recitals (cabaret songs). *Publications:* contrib. to Opera. *Address:* Russets, Straight Mile, Etchingham, East Sussex TN19 7BA, England. *Telephone:* (1580) 819125. *Fax:* (1580) 819570. *E-mail:* ccfkenny@aol.com.

**KENNY, Jonathan (Peter);** Singer (Countertenor); b. 1960, England. *Education:* Studied at Exeter University and the Guildhall School. *Career:*

Appearances with English National Opera, Opera Theatre Company, Dublin, Opera Factory Zürich, Musica nel Chiostro and at Karlsruhe; Roles have included Bertarido in Rodelinda, Arsamenes in Xerxes, Guido in Flavio, Medoro in Orlando and Britten's Oberon; Other engagements as Andronico in Tamerlano for Glimmerglass Opera, (US debut 1995), Amadigi at Prague and Monteverdi's Ottone at the Brooklyn Academy; Royal Opera debut as Nireno in Giulio Cesare, 1997; Season 1998–99 as Handel's Amadigi at Lisbon, Hamor in Jephtha with the Netherlands Bach Society and Arsamenes in Handel's Serse with the Gabrieli Consort in France; Other roles include Gluck's Orfeo; Concerts throughout Europe including St Matthew Passion, in Jonathan Miller's dramatisation and Handel's Theodora in Berlin. *Recordings include:* Albums with John Eliot Gardiner (Philips) and Andrew Parrott (Sony). *Address:* c/o Musichall Ltd, Vicarage Way, Ringmer, East Sussex, BN8 5 LA, England.

**KENNY, Yvonne Denise,** AM, BSc; Australian singer (soprano); b. 25 Nov. 1950, Australia; d. of the late Arthur Raymond and of Doris Jean Kenny. *Education:* Sydney Univ. (Australia). *Career:* Debut Queen Elizabeth Hall, London 1975; prin. soprano Royal Opera House, London 1976; appearances with Berlin Staatsoper, Vienna State Opera, Australian Opera and at La Scala (Milan, Italy), La Fenice (Venice, Italy), Paris, Hamburg (Germany) and Zurich (Switzerland); performer Closing Ceremony Sydney Olympic Games 2000; numerous recordings. *Operas include:* Die Zauberflöte, Idomeneo, Fidelio, Le Nozze di Figaro, L'Elisir d'Amore, Turandot, Mitridate, Alcina, Semele, Giulio Cesare, Don Giovanni, The Fairy Queen, Capriccio, Der Rosenkavalier; Falstaff. *Current Management:* Jennifer Eddy Artists Management, Suite 11, The Clivedon, 596 St Kilda Road, Melbourne, Vic 3000, Australia.

**KENT, Christopher,** BMus, MMus, PhD, FRCO, FSA, ARMCM; British musicologist, organist and organ adviser; b. 12 Aug. 1949, London, England; m. 1st Angela Thomas 1973 (deceased); m. 2nd Susan Langston 2004. *Education:* Univ. of Manchester and King's Coll., London. *Career:* Asst Music Master, City of London School for Girls, 1975–80; Sr Lecturer in Music, Univ. of Reading 1980–2002, Hon. Fellow 2002–; mem. Editorial Bd Elgar Complete Edn 1979–; mem. Worshipful Co. of Musicians. *Recordings include:* Pachelbel's Hexachordum Apollinis, The Organ of Bowood Chapel 2005 and organ music by John Blow. *Publications:* Elgar Complete Edition: Symphony No. 1 (co-ed., five vols) 1981, The Dream of Gerontius 1982, The Apostles 1983, The Kingdom 1984, Music for Organ 1987, The Music of Edward Elgar: A Guide to Research 1993; contrib. to Musical Times, The Listener: Journal of British Institute of Organ Studies, The Organ Year Book, Music and Letters: Journal of the Royal College of Organists, Proceedings of the Royal Music Association, Cambridge Companion to the Organ 1998, Cambridge Companion to Elgar 2004, Early Keyboard Journal 2005. *Address:* The Laurels, Tytherton Lucas, Wilts., SN15 3RJ, England (home). *Telephone:* (1249) 740294 (home). *E-mail:* christopherkent@supanet.com (home).

**KENYON, Nicholas Roger,** CBE, BA; British broadcasting executive; *Controller, BBC Proms, Live Events and Television Classical Music*; b. 23 Feb. 1951, Altrincham, Cheshire, England; s. of Thomas Kenyon and Kathleen Holmes; m. Marie-Ghislaine Latham-Koenig 1976; three s. one d. *Education:* Balliol Coll., Oxford. *Career:* music critic, The New Yorker 1979–82, The Times 1982–85, The Observer 1985–92; Music Ed., The Listener 1982–87; Ed., Early Music 1983–92; programme adviser Mozart Now Festival, South Bank, London 1991; Controller, BBC Radio 3 1992–98, Dir BBC Proms 1996–, Controller, BBC Millennium Programmes 1998–2000, BBC Live Events and TV Classical Music 2000–; mem. bd ENO 2005–; Gov. Wellington School, Guildhall School of Music and Drama. *Publications:* The BBC Symphony Orchestra 1930–80 1981, Simon Rattle: The Making of a Conductor (revised edn as Simon Rattle: From Birmingham to Berlin 2001), Authenticity and Early Music (ed.) 1988, The Viking Opera Guide (co-ed.) 1993, The Penguin Opera Guide (co-ed.) 1995, Musical Lives (ed.) 2001, The BBC Proms Guide to Great Concertos (ed.) 2003, The BBC Proms Pocket Guide to Great Symphonies (ed.) 2003, The Faber Pocket Guide to Mozart 2006. *Honours:* Royal Philharmonic Soc. Awards for Fairest Isle (BBC Radio 3) 1996 and Sounding the Century 2000. *Address:* BBC, Broadcasting House, London, W1A 1AA, England (office). *Telephone:* (20) 7765-4928 (office). *Fax:* (20) 7765-0612 (office). *Website:* www.bbc.co.uk (office).

**KERMAN, Joseph Wilfred,** BA, PhD; American musicologist, writer, critic and editor; b. 3 April 1924, London, England; m. Vivian Shaviro 1945; two s. one d. *Education:* New York Univ., Princeton Univ. *Career:* Dir of Graduate Studies, Westminster Choir Coll., Princeton 1949–51; Asst Prof. 1951–56, Assoc. Prof. 1956–60, Prof. of Music 1960–71, 1974–94, Chair., Dept of Music 1960–63, 1991–93, Univ. of California at Berkeley; Heather Prof. of Music, Univ. of Oxford 1971–74; Fellow, Wadham Coll., Oxford 1972–74; founder/Co-Ed., 19th Century Music 1977–89; Ed. California Studies in 19th Century Music 1980–; Charles Eliot Norton Prof. of Poetry, Harvard Univ. 1997–98; Fellow, American Acad. of Arts and Sciences 1973, American Philosophical Soc. 2001. *Publications:* Opera as Drama 1956, The Elizabethan Madrigal: A Comparative Study 1962, Beethoven Quartets 1967, A History of Art and Music (with Horst W. Janson and Dora Jane Janson) 1968, Listen (with Vivian Kerman) 1972, Beethoven Studies (ed. with Alan Tyson) 1973, The Masses and Motets of William Byrd 1981, The New Grove Beethoven (with Alan Tyson) 1983, Contemplating Music: Challenges to Musicology 1985, Music at the Turn of the Century (ed.) 1990, Write All These Down: Essays on Music 1994, Concerto Conversations 1999, The Art of Fugue: Bach Fugues for

Keyboard 1715–1750 2005; contrib. to scholarly journals, including New York Review of Books. *Honours:* Guggenheim Fellowship 1960, Fulbright Fellowship 1966; National Inst. and American Acad. of Arts and Letters Award 1956, Hon. Fellow, Royal Acad. of Music, London 1972, hon. mem. American Musicological Soc. 1995. *Address:* Music Department, University of California, Berkeley, CA 94720 (office); 107 Southampton Avenue, Berkeley, CA 94707, USA (home).

**KERN, Patricia;** Singer (Mezzo-soprano); b. 14 July 1927, Swansea, Wales. *Education:* Guildhall School, London, with Parry Jones (1949–52). *Career:* Sang with Opera for All 1952–55; Sadler's Wells/English National Opera from 1959, debut in Rusalka; appearances as Rossini's Isolier, Rosina, Cinderella and Isabella; Mozart's Cherubino, Monteverdi's Messenger; Sang in the 1966 premiere of Malcolm Williamson's Violins of St Jacques; Covent Garden debut 1967, as Zerlina in Don Giovanni: returned as Cherubino and as Mrs Herring (1989); US debut 1969, Washington Opera; Scottish Opera in A Midsummer Night's Dream, L'Incoronazione di Poppea, Cenerentola and The Rape of Lucretia; Premiere of Iain Hamilton's Catiline Conspiracy, 1974; Foreign engagements include Cherubino at the New York City Center and Dallas Civic Opera; Rossini's Cenerentola in Stratford Ontario and Isolier in Washington; Isabella in Spoleto; Monteverdi's Ottone at Drottningholm; Concerts in Paris, Turin and Hong Kong; Chicago Lyric Opera, 1987, as Marcellina in Le nozze di Figaro, Repeated for Vancouver Opera, 1992. *Recordings:* Stravinsky, Cantata; Berlioz, Roméo et Juliette conducted by Colin Davis; Anna Bolena, Manon and Les Contes d'Hoffmann with Beverly Sills; Monteverdi Madrigals conducted by Raymond Leppard; Video of L'Incoronazione di Poppea, Glyndebourne, 1984. *Address:* c/o Music International, 13 Ardilaun Road, Highbury, London N5 2QR, England.

**KERR, Virginia;** singer (soprano); b. 1964, Ireland. *Education:* Royal Irish Academy and the Guildhall School, London. *Career:* appearances with Dublin Grand Opera as Leila, Liu (Turandot), Musetta, Micaela and Elvira in L'Italiana in Algeri (1996); Other roles include Fiordiligi for City of Birmingham Touring Opera, Anita in Krenek's Jonny Spielt Auf (at Leipzig), Mozart's Countess (Malta), and Grete in Schreker's Der ferne Klang (Opera North); Appearances with Scottish Opera as Jenůfa, Salome, Julia in Dvořák's Jacobin and the soprano lead in Judith Weir's The Vanishing Bridegroom; Ariadne for Castleward Opera, Tchaikovsky's Enchantress for New Sussex Opera and Donna Elvira at Leipzig (season 1996–97); Ortlinde in Die Walküre and Jenifer in The Midsummer Marriage at Covent Garden; Concerts include Stravinsky's Pulcinella, Schreker's Von Ewigen Leben (BBC Philharmonic Orchestra), Missa solemnis and Verdi Requiem (Mississippi Symphony Orchestra) and Carmina Burana at the Festival Hall; Beethoven's Ninth and Mahler's 2nd Symphony in Mexico. *Current Management:* Robert Gilder & Co., Enterprise House, 59–65 Upper Ground, London, SE1 9PQ, England. *Telephone:* (20) 7928-9008. *Fax:* (20) 7928-9755. *E-mail:* rgilder@robert-gilder .com.

**KERRY, Gordon,** BA; Australian composer, writer and critic; b. 21 Jan. 1961, Melbourne, Vic. *Education:* University of Melbourne, studied with Barry Conyngham. *Career:* freelance composer; music critic for the Sydney Morning Herald 1996–; commissions from Musica Viva, ABC, Adelaide Chamber Orchestra and others. *Compositions include:* Winter Through Glass, for piano, 1980; Canticles for Evening Prayer, for choir, 1983; Siderius Nuncius for Organ, 1985; Obsessions, for mezzo and piano, 1985; Phaselus, for ensemble, 1986; Ongaku, for mandolin, 1987; Paradi, for viola and piano, 1988; Cantata for chorus and chamber orchestra, 1989; Cipangu for choir and orchestra, 1990; Torquing Points, for string quartet, 1991; Viola Concerto, 1992; Medea, chamber opera in 3 scenes, 1992; Quadrivial Pursuits, for clarinet, piano, viola and cello, 1993; No Orphean Lute, piano trio, 1994; Harmonie for wind quintet, 1996; Concerto for cello, percussion and strings, 1996; Variations for orchestra, 1996; Breathtaking for soprano and ensemble, 1999; Such Sweet Thunder for orchestra, 1999. *Honours:* Sounds Australian Award 1990. *Address:* c/o APRA Ltd, 1A Eden Street, Crows Nest, NSW 2065, Australia.

**KERSJES, Anton (Frans Jan);** Conductor; b. 17 Aug. 1923, Arnhem, Netherlands; m. Margaretha van de Groenekan, 8 Aug 1946. *Career:* 1st Violinist, Arnhem Symphony Orchestra, 1941; Choir Conductor, 1945–46 and 1949; Co-founder, Kunstamaand Chamber Orchestra, 1953; Conductor, Netherlands Ballet Sonia Gaskell, 1953–61; 1st Conductor 1973–83, Principal Guest Conductor 1983–, Amsterdam Philharmonic Orchestra; Conductor, Netherlands Opera Company, 1955–60; Conductor, Amsterdam Ballet, 1960–62; Conductor of all Dutch symphony orchestras including Concertgebouw Orchestra, Orchestra Radio Hilversum; Guest Conductor, Netherlands Opera Company; Permanent Guest Conductor, Netherlands Philharmonic Orchestra, Amsterdam; Leader of conductors' class, Amsterdam Muzieklyceum, Sweelinck Conservatory, 1969–79; Leader conductors' and opera class, Deputy Director, Maastricht Conservatory; Tours in Europe, Scandinavia, the United Kingdom and USSR; Conductor of over 125 concerts, 5 operas on television. *Recordings:* For EMI and HMV. *Honours:* Decorated Officer, Order of Orange Nassau; Silver Medal, City of Amsterdam; Silver Medal, Concertgebouw. *Address:* 6 Honthorst Straat, 1071 Amsterdam, Netherlands.

**KERTESI, Ingrid;** Soprano; b. 1961, Budapest, Hungary. *Education:* Studied at the Franz Liszt Academy in Budapest and in Bayreuth. *Career:* Debut: Budapest in 1985 as Oscar in Un Ballo in Maschera; Sang Olympia at the Vienna Volksoper in 1987, Sophie in Budapest and Frasquita in Carmen at the 1991 Bregenz Festival; Other roles include Blondchen, Despina, Susanna and Mozart's Zerlina, Donizetti's Norina, Lucia and Adina, Amina in La Sonnambula, Gilda, Nannetta and Aennchen in Der Freischütz; Sang Adina at Budapest, 1996; Concert repertory includes works by Handel, Haydn, Mozart, Bach and Vivaldi. *Address:* c/o Bregenz Festival, Postfach 311, 6901 Bregenz, Austria.

**KERTESZ, Otto;** Cellist; b. 1960, Hungary. *Education:* Studied at the Franz Liszt Academy, Budapest and with Sandor Devich, György Kurtàg and András Mihaly. *Career:* Member of the Keller String Quartet from 1986, debut concert at Budapest March 1987; Played Beethoven's Grosse Fuge and Schubert's Death and the Maiden Quartet at Interforum 87; Series of concerts in Budapest with Zoltán Kocsis and Deszö Ranki (piano) and Kalman Berkes (clarinet); Further appearances in Nuremberg, at the Chamber Music Festival La Baule and tours of Bulgaria, Austria, Switzerland, Italy (Ateforum 88 Ferrara), Belgium and Ireland; Concerts for Hungarian Radio and Television. *Recordings:* Albums for Hungaroton (from 1989). *Honours:* 2nd Prize Evian International String Quartet Competitin, May 1988. *Address:* c/o SullivSweet, 28 Albion Street, London, W2 2AX, England.

**KESZEI, János;** Irish timpanist and percussionist; *Professor of Timpani, Royal College of Music;* b. 1 June 1936, Hungary; two s. one d. *Education:* Music High School, Budapest, Béla Bartók Conservatorium and Franz Liszt Academy of Music, Budapest. *Career:* debut as principal percussionist, RESO, Dublin 1957; principal timpanist, RESO, Dublin 1964, Ulster Orchestra 1966, City of Birmingham Symphony Orchestra 1969, P. Boulez, BBC Symphony Orchestra 1972–78; freelance 1978–, with ECO, RPO, LMP, CLS, English Symphonia, OAE, GTO; solo timpanist, Rotterdam Philharmonic 1984–87; toured and recorded ROH; contributed to more than 320 films, albums, lectures, masterclasses in the UK and abroad; involved in early and baroque, Hanover Band, King's Consort and OAE in Glyndebourne summer seasons, Salzburg, New York, Paris, Vienna, Berlin; Prof. of Timpani, Royal Coll. of Music, London 1973–; mem. Royal Soc. of Musicians of Great Britain. *Address:* 17 Grove Gardens, Tring, Herts HP23 5PX, England. *Telephone:* (1442) 828150. *Fax:* (1442) 828150.

**KETILSSON, Jon;** singer (tenor); b. 1970, Reykjavík, Iceland. *Education:* studied in Vienna. *Career:* debut in Offenbach's Barbe-bleue at Schönbrunn; sang Alfredo and Florestan at Prague State Opera, Max in Der Freischütz, Cavaradossi, Wagner's Erik and Candide at Dortmund; Strauss's Bacchus at Lausanne and Enée in Les Troyens at Lisbon; Cologne Opera as Tamino, Cavaradossi, Macduff, Don José, and Herr M. in Hindemith's Neues vom Tage; Other roles include Hoffmann, Pinkerton, Rodolfo and Sergei in Lady Macbeth of Mtsensk; Season 2001–2002 as Don José at Brussels and Geneva, Max in Lausanne and Enée at the Salzburg Festival; Concerts include Beethoven's Ninth, Carmina Burana, Messiah and Dvořák's Requiem. *Current Management:* Aria's di Novella Partacini & Alexandra Plaickner, Via Josef Weingartner 4, 39022 Lagundo, Italy. *Telephone:* (0473) 200 200. *Fax:* (0473) 222 424. *E-mail:* info@arias.it. *Website:* www.arias.it.

**KETTING, Otto;** Composer; b. 3 Sept. 1935, Amsterdam, Netherlands. *Education:* Studied at the Hague Conservatory, 1952–58. *Career:* Trumpeter in The Hague Philharmonic Orchestra 1965–60; Teacher of composition, Rotterdam Conservatory 1967–71 and at the Royal Conservatory in The Hague 1971–74; Artistic Adviser to the Utrecht Symphony Orchestra 1983; Opera Ithaka was premiered at the opening of the Muziektheater Amsterdam, 1989. *Compositions include:* Operas: Dummies 1974 and O, Thou Rhinoceros 1977; Ballets The Last Message 1962; Interieur 1963; Barriers 1963; The Golden Key 1964; Choreo-struction 1963; Theatre Pice 1973; Concerto for solo organ 1953; Sinfonietta 1954; Sonata for brass quartet 1955; Piano Sonatia 195; Passcagalia for orchestra 1957; Serenade for cello and piano 1957; Concertino 1958; Symphony 1959; Concertino for jazz quintet and orchestra 1960; Variations for wind, harp and percussion 1960; Series of works entitled Collage; Minimal Music for 29 toy instruments 1970; In Memoriam Igor Stravinsky for orchestra 1971; Time Machine for wind and percussion 1972; For Moonlight Nights for flute and 26 players 1973; Adagio for chamber orchestra 1977; Symphony for saxophones and orchestra 1978; Opera Ithaka 1986; Symphony No. 3, 1990; Medusa for saxophone and orchestra, 1992; Summer Moon for soprano and ensemble, 1992; Come, Over the Sea, for orchestra, 1994; Cheops for horn and orchestra, 1995. *Honours:* Guadeamus Prize 1958; Warsaw Autumn Festival Award 1963. *Address:* c/o BUMA/STERMA huis, Postbus 725, 1180 AS Amstelveen, Netherlands.

**KEYES, John;** Singer (Tenor); b. 1964, Illinois, USA. *Education:* Studied in Chicago. *Career:* Based with the Chicago Lyric Opera until 1991; Season 1991–92 with Siegmund in Die Walküre for Scottish Opera, Radames at Mexico City and Parsifal in Robert Wilson's production of Wagner's opera for Houston Grand Opera; Concert performances of Otello (as Roderigo) in Chicago an New York under Solti, 1991; Season 1992–93 as Siegmund at Hamburg and Nantes, Erik in Fliegende Holländer at Toulouse and Parsifal at Antwerp and Hamburg; Other roles include Walther von der Vogelweide and Eisenstein (Houston), Samson, Don Carlos, Don José and Dick Johnson; Sang Lohengrin in a new production of Wagner's opera for English National Opera, 1993; Season 1996–98 with Parsifal at Munich; Jean in Massenet's Hérodiade at San Francisco and Turiddu and Canio for Israel Opera; Florestan at Buenos Aires and Siegmund in Amsterdam; Sang Parsifal in Munich, Lohengrin in San Diego and Strauss's Emperor at the Deutsche Oper, Berlin. *Recordings include:* Otello. *Honours:* Winner, 1990, San Antonio Competition; Ruth Richards Grant in 1990 Richard Tucker Competition;

Concert repertoire includes Beethoven's Ninth. *Address:* c/o Tivoli Arists Management, 3 Vesterbrogade, DK –1630 Copenhagen, Denmark.

**KEYLIN, Misha;** Violinist; b. 5 March 1970, St Petersburg, Russia. *Education:* The Juilliard School. *Career:* Debut: Carnegie Hall in New York (aged 11), 1981; Performed both in recital and as soloist in major concert halls in over 30 countries. *Recordings:* The complete cycle of the Henri Vieuxtemps Violin Concertos. *Honours:* Winner of Hannover, Paganini, Sarasate and Sigall International Violin Competitions. *Current Management:* IMG Artists, Paris. *Address:* PO Box 230705, New York, NY 10023, USA.

**KEYTE, Christopher Charles;** British singer (bass-baritone); b. 11 Sept. 1935, Shorne, Kent, England; m. June Matthews. *Education:* choral scholar King's Coll., Cambridge. *Career:* oratorio, opera, concert and recital appearances; founder mem., Purcell Consort of Voices 1963–75; opera with The Fires of London; Prof. of Singing, Royal Acad. of Music 1982–87; Royal Opera House, Covent Garden 1989–. *Recordings:* Monteverdi Songs, Sacred Concertos; Purcell Anthems, Indian Queen; Haydn and Schubert Masses; Vaughan Williams Serenade to Music and Pilgrim's Progress; Songs by Quilter, Gurney and Glazunov; Mass of the Sea by Paul Patterson; The Lighthouse by Peter Maxwell Davies, Billy Budd by Benjamin Britten. *Honours:* Hon. RAM 1983. *Address:* 20 Brycedale Crescent, Southgate, London, N14 7EY, England.

**KHACHATRYAN, Sergei;** violinist; b. 1985, Yerevam, Armenia. *Education:* Taunus Music School, Eschborn, Germany, Wurzburg and Karlsruhe Music Acads, masterclasses in Keshet Eilon, Israel with Shlomo Mintz. *Career:* participation in music competitions in Rome, Krakow, Germany and Spain from 1995; appearances with symphony and chamber orchestras throughout Europe, including Bruch Concerto with English CO at Fairfields Hall, Croydon 2001; concerts throughout Finland, notably with the Sibelius Concerto, and in Israel, Ecuador, Brazil and Armenia; season 2001–02 with Music at Oxford recital, concerts with Bournemouth SO, Royal Philharmonic, Frankfurt Radio SO and Bochum Symphony. *Honours:* winner Louis Spohr Competition, Freiburg, Int. Team Sibelius Competition, Helsinki, first prize Queen Elisabeth Competition, Belgium 2005. *Current Management:* Askonas Holt Ltd, Lonsdale Chambers, 27 Chancery Lane, London, WC2A 1PF, England. *Telephone:* (20) 7400-1700. *Fax:* (20) 7400-1799. *E-mail:* info@askonasholt.co.uk. *Website:* www.askonasholt.co.uk.

**KHADEM-MISSAGH, Bijan;** violinist, conductor and composer; *President, GLOBArt;* b. 26 Oct. 1948, Tehran, Iran. *Education:* Univ. of Vienna, Austria, Acad. of Music, Vienna. *Career:* debut, as soloist with orchestra aged 13; concert tours, including radio and television appearances and festivals throughout Europe, Asia, Latin America and Australia; founder, Eurasia Quartet 1969–75; founder, The Dawnbreakers, Austrian Baha'i singing group 1970; founder, conductor and soloist, Tonkuenstler Chamber Orchestra, Vienna 1977–; Artistic Dir, Allegro Vivo, International Chamber Music Festival, Austria 1979–, Midsummer Music Festival, Sweden 1981–90; Badener Beethoventage 1980–86; Prof., J. M. Hauer Konservatory, Wiener Neustadt 1988; masterclasses for violin; Pres., GLOBArt, 1997–; Musical Dir, Music Forum Landegg, Switzerland 1991–2000. *Compositions:* instrumental and vocal works. *Recordings:* works by Beethoven, Schubert, Schoenberg, Weigl, Mendelssohn, Vitali, Paganini, Debussy, Szymanowski, Bach, Tchaikovsky, Haydn, Handel, Dvořák, Respighi, Bartók, Strauss, Kreisler; albums: Dawnbreakers 1976, The Child 1979, To A Friend 1982, Vision 1986, Call of the Beloved, Phoenix, Glad Tidings, Wie Sterne. *Publications:* Lieder – Book of Songs 1976, Das Musische als Lebensweise, Ein Credo 1998. *Honours:* Austrian Cross for Arts and Sciences 1998; Silbernes Ehrenzeichen Niederösterreich 1993, Kulturpreis der stadt Baden 1994. *Address:* Allegro Vivo. International Chamber Music Festival Austria, Wiener Strasse 16, 3580 Horn, Austria. *Telephone:* 2982-4319. *E-mail:* office@allegro-vivo.at. *Website:* www.allegro-vivo.at.

**KHALEMSKAIA, Marianna;** Singer (Soprano); b. 1960, St Petersburg, Russia. *Education:* Studied at St Petersburg State Conservatory and with soloists of the Mariinsky Theatre. *Career:* Concerts from 1992, including Mozart's Requiem and Kurt Weill songs; Opera debut in V Plesak's opera Tale of a Dead Princess, 1996; Paris Opéra-Comique as Elisetta in Il Matrimonio Segreto; Seasons 1996–98 as Annina in A Night in Venice, Rosina in Mozart's La Finta Semplice and Musetta in La Bohème. *Honours:* Prizewinner at Barcelona and Toulouse competitions. *Address:* Harlequin Agency Ltd, 203 Fidles Road, Cardiff CF14 5NA, Wales.

**KHAN, Ustad Bismillah;** Indian musician (shehnai); b. 21 March 1916, Bihar. *Career:* Hindustani shehnai player; performed All India Music Conf., Calcutta 1937; has performed in Europe, USA, Africa, USSR, Japan, Iran, Iraq, Afghanistan; features on more than 50 albums. *Recordings include:* on T Series: Bismillah Khan Vols 1–15, Shaan-E-Shenai, Shenai Samraat; on Navras: Live In London 1985 Vols 1 and 2, Live at the Queen Elizabeth Hall, Uphaar, Shenai, The Eternal Spirit 1993; on EMI India: An Exposition of Ragas, From Benaras- The Seat of Shenai, Fifty Golden Years, The Magnificence Of Shenai, Shaadi Ki Shenaiyan, Shenai Recital, The Enchanter, Majestic Ragas; on Music Today: Romantic Raga Vol. 2, Megh Malhar Vol. 4, Basant Bahar Vol. 1, Raga, Maestros Choice. *Honours:* Bharath Rathna (India's highest civilian honour), Padma Vibhushan, Tansen Award; Dr hc (Benares Hindu Univ.); Sangeet Natak Academi Award. *Address:* c/o Navras Records, 22 Sherwood Road, London, NW4 1AD, England. *Telephone:* (20)

8203-2553. *E-mail:* music@navrasrecords.com. *Website:* www.navrasrecords .com.

**KHANZADIAN, Vahan (Avedis);** Operatic Tenor; b. 23 Jan. 1939, Syracuse, New York, USA. *Education:* BEd, University of Buffalo, 1961; Curtis Institute of Music, 1963. *Career:* Debut: San Francisco Spring Opera as Ruggero in Puccini's La Rondine, 1968; Many roles in numerous productions including: Wozzeck, Fra Diavolo, Madama Butterfly, Lucia di Lammermoor; Appearances with major opera companies throughout USA and Canada including: NY City Center, Baltimore, Houston, Memphis, New Orleans, St Paul, Providence, Birmingham, Kentucky, Kansas City, Dayton, Toledo, Portland, Honolulu, Montreal, Edmonton, Vancouver; Guest soloist with major orchestras including: Boston, Chicago, Philadelphia, Baltimore, Boston Pops; Numerous recital tours; Masterclasses; Television and radio broadcasts; Tenor soloist in world premiere of Menotti's Lanscapes and Remembrances at Milwaukee, 1976; European debuts: Cavaradossi in Tosca at Aachen, 1992, Title role in Don Carlo at Basel, 1992, Metropolitan Opera debut as Riccardo in Ballo in Maschera, 1993, Lyric Opera, Chicago debut as Riccardo, 1993; Bavarian State Opera, Munich as Calaf in Turandot, 1995; Cincinnati Opera, USA as Radames in Aida, 1995. *Recordings:* Broadway cast recording of Follies, 1998. *Address:* Hunter Highlands, PO Box 741, Hunter, NY 12442, USA. *E-mail:* vahan@optonline.net.

**KHARITONOV, Dimitri;** Singer (baritone); b. 18 Oct. 1958, Kuibyshev, Russia. *Education:* Rimsky-Korsakov College of Music, Leningrad from 1976; Vocal studies, piano, with honours, Nezhdanova State Conservatory, Odessa, 1978–84. *Career:* Recital Singer, Odessa Philharmonic Society; Principal Baritone, Odessa State Opera, 1984; Sang 55 times at the Bolshoi Opera, Kremlin Hall, roles included: Prince Yeletsky, Queen of Spades, Duke Robert, Iolanta (Tchaikovsky), Duenna (Prokofiev); Also sang in Moussorgsky's Khovanshchina and Boris Godunov, Rimsky-Korsakov's Tzar Saltan, Germont (La Traviata) and Conte di Luna, Il Trovatore (Verdi), Figaro, Il Barbiere di Siviglia (Rossini), Silvio in Pagliacci; Sang in main opera houses and concert halls, Moscow, Leningrad, Kiev, Minsk; Appeared regularly on Russian television, settled in England, 1989; British debut as Jokanaan in Salome, Edinburgh Festival, 1989, returning for Tchaikovsky's Cantata Moskow; Season 1989–90 as Germont in Liège, Opera de Wallonie; In America sang at the Chicago Lyric Opera with Placido Domingo in La Fanciulla del West (Puccini) amongst others; In 1992 gave recital in Brussels at the Palais des Beaux Arts; In 1994 sang title role of Nabucco at Genoe; Also sang Oslo and Lillehammer in Rachmaninov lieder recitals; Sang in Buenos Aires at the Teatro Colón Sharpless in Madama Butterfly; In 1993 was Prince Yeletsky (The Queen of Spades) in the Glyndebourne Festival Opera and gave 3 recitals at the Risor Festival in Norway. *Recordings include:* Shostakovich's romances on Pushkin's poems with the City of Birmingham Symphony Orchestra; Tchaikovsky's Ode to Joy; Eugene Onegin; Khovanshchina; Prince Yeletsky in Queen of Spades, Glyndebourne production video. *Honours:* Winner All-Ukranian Lysenko Competition for Opera Singers, Kiel, 1983, Odessa, 1984; All-USSR M. I. Glinka Competition with special prize for best interpretation of Rimsky-Korsakov works, 1984; Grand Prix, Verviers International Opera Competition, Belgium, 1987; Gold Medal, Bastianini International Competition, Siena, 1988; Voci Verdiane Competition, Brusseto, 1988; Carlo Alberto Cappelli Competition, Arena di Verona, for International Competition Winners. *Current Management:* Allied Artists, 42 Montpelier Square, London SW7 4JZ, England.

**KHARITONOVA, Yelena;** Violinist; b. 1960, Moscow, Russia. *Education:* Studied at the Moscow Conservatoire with Andrei Shislov. *Career:* Co-Founder, Glazunov Quartet, 1985; Many concerts in the former Soviet Union and recent appearances in Greece, Poland, Belgium, Germany and Italy; Works by Beethoven and Schumann at the Beethoven Haus in Bonn; Further engagements in Canada and Netherlands; Teacher at the Moscow State Conservatoire and resident at the Tchaikovsky Conservatoire; Repertoire includes works by Borodin, Shostakovich and Tchaikovsky, in addition to the standard works. *Recordings include:* CDs of the six quartets of Glazunov. *Honours:* Prizewinner of the Borodin Quartet and Shostakovich Chamber Music Competitions with the Glazunov Quartet. *Address:* c/o Sonata (Glazunov Quartet), 11 Northgate Street, Glasgow G20 7AA, England.

**KHERSONSKAJA, Natalya (Mikhailovna);** Ukrainian musicologist, pianist and Organist; b. 1 Nov. 1961, Poltava; m. Sergei Zagny, 26 July 1986; one s. *Education:* piano and musicology at Poltava Music Coll. 1981, Preparatory Section of Philosophical Faculty of Moscow State M. Lomonosov Univ. 1982–83; studied organ with Prof. L. I. Roizman at Moscow State Conservatory 1984–89, musicologist 1990 and postgraduate 1993, Moscow State Conservatory. *Career:* Ed. chief edn of Ostankino, Television-Radio co. musical broadcasting, Moscow 1990–94; Chief Scientific Collaborator, Database Section (electronic musical encyclopaedia), Computer Centre, Moscow State Conservatory 1995–98; Instructor of Computer Courses by cathedra geofisique, Moscow State M. Lomonosov Univ. 1997. *Recordings include:* many broadcasts as author and interviewer including cycles, Music of 20th Century including Webern, Berg, Schoenberg, Scriabin, Mosolov and Boulez; Sviatoslav Richter plays Franz Schubert, Rondo; Masters of Antique Music including English virginalists and S. Scheidt and Schütz; 9 Hours of French Music from Perotin to Messiaen. *Publications include:* author of musicologic works including separate studies of the organ and klavier music of Samuel Scheidt (first in Russia) entitled, Word and Number as a Structural Idea of Organ Composition of S. Scheidt 1987, Tabulatura Nova of S. Scheidt (new concept) 1990, Word For Windows As Possible Cover for Database 1995, Notation and Forming Word and Number as a Structural Idea of Klavier Composition 1994, Unfinished Works by Franz Schubert and His Unfinished Sonatas Performed by Sviatoslav Richter 1997, Eclipses and the Tungussky Meter (and Meteors) 2000, Proportional Canon as a Basis of Movement of the Planets Around the Sun 2000. *Address:* Ul. Vagonoremontnaja 5 korpus 1, kv 23, 127411 Moscow, Russia.

**KHOLMINOV, Alexander;** Composer; b. 8 Sept. 1925, Moscow, Russia. *Education:* Studied with Golubev at the Moscow conservatory, graduated 1950. *Career:* Stage works have been widely performed in Moscow and Elsewhere in Russia. *Compositions:* Operas An Optimistic Tragedy Frunze, 1965; Anna Snegina, Gorky, 1967; The Overcoat, after Gogol, 1975; The Carriage, after Gogol, Moscow, 1975; Chapayev, Moscow Radio, 1977; The Twelfth Series, Moscow, 1977; The Wedding, after Chekhov, Moscow, 1984; Vanka, Monodrama after Chekhov, Moscow, 1984; The Brothers Karamazov, after Dostoyevsky, Moscow, 1985; Hot Snow, 1985; The Fruits of Enlightenment, after Tolstoy, 1990; 5 Symphonies, 1973, 1975, 1977, 1990, 1995; Viola Concerto, 1989; 3 string quartets, 1980, 1985, 1994; 24 Preludes for piano, 1994. *Honours:* USSR State Prize, 1978; People's Artist of the URSSR, 1984. *Address:* c/o RAO, Bolchaia Bronnai 6a, Moscow 103670, Russia.

**KHOMA, Natalia;** Cellist; b. 5 Dec. 1963, Lviv, Ukraine; m. Suren Bagratuni, 5 July 1986, 1 d. *Education:* BM, Lviv Music School; MM, DMA, Tchaikovsky Moscow Conservatory; Diploma, Boston University. *Career:* Debut: Soloist with Lviv Philharmonia Orchestra, 1975; Performances and Recitals at: Weill Recital Hall, Carnegie Hall, New York, Merkin Hall, New York, Jordan Hall, Boston, Rachmaninov Hall, Moscow, Moscow Conservatory Small Hall, Academy of Music Big Hall, Oslo, Norway, Palais des Beaux Arts, Brussels, Belgium, Schauspielhaus, Berlin, Germany, Grand Hall of Academy of Music, Budapest; Performed Throughout the Soviet Union, East Europe, Spain, Germany, Belgium, Italy, Norway, Canada, USA. *Recordings:* Numerous. *Honours:* 1st Prize, All Ukrainian Competition, 1981; Max Reger Special Prize, 1985; 2nd Prize, Markneukirchen International Competition, Germany, 1987; 1st Prize, Belgrade International Competition, 1990; 4th Prize, Tchaikovsky Competition, Moscow, 1990. *Address:* c/o Tchaikovsky Moscow Conservatory, Ul Gertzena 13, 103009 Moscow, Russia.

**KHRENNIKOV, Tikhon Nikolayevich;** Russian composer; b. 10 June 1913, Yelets, Lipetsk region; s. of Nikolay Khrennikov and Varvara Kharlamova; m. Klara Arnoldovna Vax (Khrennikova) 1936 (deceased); one d. *Education:* Moscow Conservatoire. *Career:* Dir of Music Central Theatre of Soviet Army 1941–54; Gen. Sec. Soviet Composers' Union 1948–57, First Sec., then Chair. 1957–91; Chair. Int. Asscn of Composers Unions 1991–92, Hon. Chair. 1995–; Pres. Tchaikovsky Int. Competition 1978–90, 1994–; Prof. Moscow Conservatory 1966–; mem. CPSU 1947–91; Deputy to USSR Supreme Soviet 1962–89; mem. Cttee USSR Parl. Group; mem. Cen. Auditing Comm., CPSU 1961–76; cand. mem. CPSU Cen. Cttee 1976–87; USSR People's Deputy 1989–91; Hon. mem. Santa Cecilia Acad., Tiberiana Acad. (Italy). *Principal compositions:* four piano concertos 1933, 1971, 1983, 1991, Five Pieces for Piano 1933, First Symphony 1935, Three Pieces for Piano 1935, Suite for Orchestra from Music for Much Ado About Nothing, In the Storm (opera) 1939, Second Symphony 1941, incidental music for play Long Ago 1942, Frol Skobeyev (opera) 1950, Mother (opera) 1956, Concerto for Cello and Orchestra 1959, A Hundred Devils and One Girl (operetta) 1961, two Concertos for Violin 1964, 1976, White Nights (operetta) 1967, Boy Giant (opera for children) 1969, Our Courtyard (ballet for children) 1970, Much Ado About Hearts (chamber opera) 1974, Third Symphony 1975, Love for Love (ballet) 1976, The Hussars' Ballad (Ballet) 1980, Dorothea (opera) 1982–83, The Golden Calf 1985 (opera), Napoleon Buonaparte (ballet) 1995, Captain's Daughter (ballet, after A. Pushkin) 1997; numerous popular songs and incidental music. *Honours:* State Prize 1942, 1946, 1951, 1967, 1979, People's Artist of the RSFSR 1955, of the USSR 1963; Hero of Socialist Labour 1973, Lenin Prize 1974, UNESCO Prize 1977, Glinka Prize 1983, Commdr des Arts et des Lettres (France). *Address:* Plotnikov per. 10/28, Apt. 19, 121200 Moscow, Russia. *Telephone:* (095) 244-71-72.

**KIBERG, Tina;** Singer (Soprano); b. 30 Dec. 1958, Copenhagen, Denmark. *Education:* Studied in Copenhagen. *Career:* Debut: Royal Opera Copenhagen, 1983, as Leonora in Nielsen's Maskarade; Sang Elsa in Lohengrin at Copenhagen, 1984, the Marschallin 1988, Mozart's Countess and Purcell's Dido, 1990, Hélène in Les Vepres Siciliennes, 1991; Guest appearances at Geneva and Frankfurt, 1988, as Agathe and the Countess, at Arhus as Mimi, Vienna Staatsoper 1990, as Elsa and Opéra Bastille Paris, 1991 as Lisa in The Queen of Spades; Lieder recitals in England, Germany and Italy from 1984; Sang Strauss's Ariadne at Copenhagen and Elisabeth in Tannhäuser at Bayreuth, 1992; Sang Wagner's Eva with the Royal Danish Opera, 1996; Other roles in opera have included Donna Elvira, Pamina, Desdemona, and Tatiana in Eugene Onegin; Sang Chrysothemis in Elektra at Catania, 1998; Concert repertoire includes Schmidt's Das buch mit Sieben Siegeln (Copenhagen), Beethoven's Mass in C (Lausanne), Haydn's Lord Nelson Mass (Vienna) and Elijah in Berlin; Tour of Moscow, Dresden, Berlin and London with Missa Solemnis conducted by Antal Dorati; Season 1999–2000 as Salome and Lisa in The Queen of Spades at Copenhagen, Sieglinde for Geneva Opera and Chrysothemis in Elektra for New Israeli Opera at Savonlinna. *Recordings include:* Lulu by Kuhlau. *Address:* c/o Det Kongelie Teater, Box 2185, DK 1017 Copenhagen, Denmark.

**KIEMER, Hans;** Singer (Bass-Baritone); b. 9 Feb. 1932, Munich, Germany. *Education:* Studied in Munich. *Career:* Engaged at Innsbruck, 1968–70, Augsburg, 1970–76, Wiesbaden, 1976–79; Appearances at Karlsruhe from 1979, notably at the Dutchman and Wagner's Kurwenal, Wotan and Amfortas, Verdi's Falstaff and Amonasro, in the 1986 premiere of Kunaud's Der Meister und Margarita and as Waldner in Arabella, 1989; Guest engagements at Amsterdam, Barcelona, Brussels, (the Wanderer in Siegfried, 1981), Bordeaux (as Jochanaan), Trieste (Pizarro), Vienna, Lisbon and Warsaw (Wanderer, 1989); Other roles include Strauss's Mandryka and Barak, Borromeo in Palestrina, Baron Ochs, Don Alfonso and Scarpia; Noted interpreter of the Ballades of Carl Loewe; Sang Mefistofele at Innsbruck, 1990. *Address:* Rebisches Staatstheater, Baumeisterstrasse 11, 7500 Karlsruhe, Germany.

**KIERNAN, Patrick;** Violinist; b. 1962, England. *Career:* Debut: Wigmore Hall, 1984 with Peter Pears; Co-Founder, Brindisi String Quartet, Aldeburgh, 1984; Concerts in a wide repertory throughout the United Kingdom and in France, Germany, Spain, Italy and Switzerland; Festival engagements at Aldeburgh (residency, 1990), Arundel, Bath, Brighton, Huddersfield, Norwich, Warwick and Prague Spring Festival; First London performance of Colin Matthews' 2nd Quartet, 1990, premiere of David Matthews' 6th Quartet, 1991; Quartet by Mark Anthony Turnage, 1992; World premiere of Colin Matthews' 3rd Quartet, Aldeburgh, 1994; Many BBC recitals and resident artist with the University of Ulster. *Recordings include:* Quartets by Britten, Bridge and Imogen Holst; Works by Pierné, Lekeu, Schoenberg, Berg and Webern. *Honours:* Prizewinner, Third Banff International String Quartet Competition in Canada, 1989, with Brindisi Quartet. *Address:* c/o Owen/White Management, 14 Nightingale Lane, London N8 7QU, England.

**KIKUCHI, Yoshinori;** Conductor; b. 16 Sept. 1938, Yawatahama, Japan. *Education:* Studied at Tokyo National University of Fine Arts and Music. *Career:* Chief Assistant at the Nikikai Opera, Tokyo, 1961–64; Studied further with Kasei Yamada in Japan, with Peter Maag at the Accademia Chigiana at Siena and with Franco Ferrara in Rome; Engagements at Palermo (Teatro Lirico and Teatro Massimo), 1973–77; Hessisches Staatstheater Wiesbaden, 1978–84; Guest Conductor in Japan, Italy, Germany, France, Spain and Belgium; La Scala, Milan, 1985–86; Verona Arena, 1987. *Address:* c/o Theateragentur Luisa Petrov, Glauburgstrasse 95, 60318 Frankfurt am Main, Germany.

**KILAR, Wojciech;** Polish composer; b. 17 July 1932, Lwów (now Lviv, Ukraine); m. Barbara Pomianowska. *Education:* State Higher School of Music, Katowice, (student of B. Woytowicz) Nadia Boulanger School. *Career:* mem. Cttee Int. Festival of Contemporary Music Warszawska Jesień 1975, Polish Composers Union 1953–; mem. Polish Acad. of Arts and Sciences 1998–. *Works include:* Sonatina for flute and piano 1951, Woodwind Quintet 1952, Mała uwertura 1955, I Symfonia 1955, II Symfonia 1956, Oda Bela Bartok in Memoriam 1957, Riff 62 1962, Générique 1963, Springfield Sonnet 1963, Diphthongs 1964, Solenne 1967, Training 68 for clarinet, trombone, and piano 1968, Upstairs Downstairs for soprano choir and orchestra 1971, Przygrywka i Kolęda 1972, Krzesany 1974, Bogurodzica 1975, Kościelec 1909 1976, Hoary Bog [Siwa Mgła] for baritone and orchestra 1979, Exodus 1981, Victoria for mixed choir and orchestra 1983, Angelus for soprano, for mixed choir and orchestra 1984, Orawa for string orchestra 1986, Choralvorspiel for string orchestra 1988, Requiem Father Kolbe for symphony orchestra 1994, Concerto for Piano and Orchestra 1996, Missa pro pace 2000; music for about 30 plays and 150 films including Illumination 1973, The Promised Land 1974, Dracula (ASCAP Award, Los Angeles 1992) 1991, Death and the Maiden 1994, Life at a Gallop 1995, The Portrait of a Lady 1996, The Ninth Gate 1999, Pamietam 2002, The Supplement 2002, The Pianist 2002, The Revenge 2002, Vendetta 2003. *Honours:* Dr hc (Opole Univ.) 1999; Lili Boulanger Memorial Fund Award, Boston 1960, Jurzykowski Foundation Award, New York 1983, State Award Grade I 1980, Award of Minister of Culture 1967, 1976, 1975, Prize of Polish Composers' Union 1975, ASCAP Award for his score from Coppola's Dracula in Los Angeles in 1992. *Address:* ul. Kościuszki 165, 40-524 Katowice, Poland. *Telephone:* (32) 2514965.

**KILDEA, Paul Francis,** BMus, MMus, DPhil; Australian conductor; b. 10 Feb. 1968, Canberra. *Education:* Univ. of Melbourne, Univ. of Oxford. *Career:* conductor on Young Artist Programme, Opera Australia 1996; conductor, The Cunning Little Vixen, Opera Australia 1997; Asst to Simone Young 1999–2002; conductor, Opera Australia, on The Barber of Seville 1998, La Bohème 2001, The Turn of the Screw 2002; Head of Music, Aldeburgh Productions 1999–2003; Artistic Dir, Wigmore Hall, London 2003–05. *Publications:* Selling Britten: Music and the Market Place 2002, Britten on Music 2003; contrib. to The Cambridge Companion to Britten 1999. *Current Management:* Intermusica, 16 Duncan Terrace, London, N1 8BZ, England. *Address:* Wigmore Hall, 36 Wigmore Street, London, W1U 2BP, England (office). *Telephone:* (20) 7258-8200 (office). *E-mail:* artisticdirector@wigmore-hall.org.uk (office). *Website:* www.wigmore-hall.org.uk (office).

**KILDUFF, Barbara (Jane);** Opera Singer (Soprano); b. 31 May 1959, Huntington, New York, USA. *Education:* BM, State University College, New York at Fredonia, 1981; MM, University of Connecticut, Storrs, 1983; MM, Yale University, 1984. *Career:* Debut: Washington Opera, Blonde; Performances include: Sang Blonde with Metropolitan Opera, conductor James Levine, 1990; With Baltimore Symphony, David Zinman, July 1990; With Zürich Opera, April–May 1990, Barenreiter–Carlos Kalmar; Sang Zerbinetta

in Munich 1987 and 1988; Conductors Bender, Sawallisch, Köhler in Vienna, 1987, 1991; Conductor Theodor Guschlbauer, Metropolitan Opera, 1987; James Levine, Hamburg, 1988; Julius Rudel, Basel, 1988; Vancouver, January 1989 (Martin André); In Vienna, April 1991 with Horst Stein; Olympia, Bregenz, Summer 1987 and 1988; Marc Soustrot, in Geneva, June 1990; Sang Adele at Metropolitan Opera, 1987, 1988, 1990, 1991; Julius Rudel; Cleopatra, Metropolitan, October 1988; Trevor Pinnock; Sophie in Der Rosenkavalier, Munich October 1989, 1990, 1991; Director: Brigitte Fassbaender, Heinrich Hollreiser; Metropolitan Opera, March 1991, Jiri Kout; Queen of Night, Oviedo, Spain, September 1991; Many concert appearances and television and radio performances; Season 1993 as the Countess in Capriccio at Vienna; Appears as Papagena in Met video of Die Zauberflöte; Sang Mozart's Blondchen at Bonn, 2000. *Address:* c/o CAMI, Crittenden Division, 165 West 57 Street, New York, NY 10019, USA.

**KILLEBREW, Gwendolyn;** Singer (Mezzo-Soprano); b. 26 Aug. 1939, Philadelphia, USA. *Education:* Templeton University; Juilliard School; Metropolitan Opera Studio. *Career:* Debut: Metropolitan Opera 1967, in Die Walküre; 1968–69 sang Carmen in Munich and at the New York City Opera; 1970 Copenhagen, Geneva and Prague in Handel's Tamerlano; 1972–73 Salzburg Festival, as Amneris and in the premiere of Orff's De Temporum fine Comedia; 1973 Washington Opera as Baba the Turk (The Rake's Progress) and San Francisco as Marina (Boris Godunov); Deutsche Oper am Rhein, Düsseldorf, from 1976, as Gluck's Orfeo, Verdi's Preziosilla and Azucena and Rossini's Isabella; Bayreuth debut 1978, as Waltraute in Götterdämmerung; Zürich 1981, as Mistress Quickly in Falstaff; Sang Frau Leimgruber in Klebe's Der Jüngste Tag, Duisburg, 1989; Season 1991–92 as the Nurse in Rimsky's Golden Cockerel and Strauss's Herodias at Duisburg; Also sings in concert. *Recordings:* Tamerlano; Orlando Paladino by Haydn; Edgar (Puccini), Schvanda the Bagpiper; De Temporum fine Comedia (Orff); Mahler's 3rd Symphony. *Honours:* Outstanding Musician, Temple University, 1971. *Current Management:* Ingpen & Williams Ltd, 7 St George's Court, 131 Putney Bridge Road, London, SW15 2PA, England.

**KILLMAYER, Wilhelm;** Composer; b. 21 Aug. 1927, Alunich, Germany. *Education:* Studied with Carl Orff, among others. *Career:* Ballet conductor at the Bavarian State Opera, 1961–64; Professor at the Munich Hochschule für Musik, 1973–91. *Compositions:* Operas La tragedie di Orfeo, 1961; Yolimba, 1963, 1970; Un lecon de francais, 1964; Der Weisse Hut, 1967; Ballets Encores, 1969; Paradies, 1974; 2 string quartets, 1969, 1975; 3 symphonies, 1968, 1969, 1973; Encore for orchestra, 1970; Kammermusik 1–3, 1970–73; The Broken Farewell for trumpet and chamber orchestra, 1977; Brahms-bildnis, piano trio, 1977; French songbook for soprano, baritone and ensemble, 1980; Im Freien, symphonic poem, 1980; Sostenuto for cello and strings, 1984; 4 songs in 4 European languages, 1993; Die Schönheit des Morgens for viola and piano, 1994; 8 Poesies for soprano and ensemble, 1995; La joie de vivre for small orchestra, 1996; Neue Heine-Lieder for tenor and piano, 1999; Pindar Odes for mixed chorus and organ, 1999. *Address:* c/o GEMA, Rosenheimer Str 11, 81667 Munchen, Germany.

**KIM, Ettore;** singer (baritone); b. 14 Nov. 1965, Republic of Korea. *Education:* studied in South Korea and Italy. *Career:* debut at Theatro Delle Erbe, Milan, in Salieri's Arlecchinata, 1990; sang in Henze's We Come to the River at La Scala and in the premiere of Ferroro's La Figlia del Mago at the Teatro San Carlo, 1992; Concert performances of Otello, as Iago, at Bordeaux, 1992; Engaged as Germont at Covent Garden, 1993; Chorebus in concerts of Les Troyens with the London Symphony Orchestra and on stage at La Scala, 1993–94; Belcore at Strasbourg, Antonio in Linda di Chamounix at Stockholm and Riccardo in Puritani for Bavarian Radio; Other roles include Scarpia, and Gerard in Andrea Chénier; Sang Camoëns in Donizetti's Don Sébastien at Aachen, 1998. *Recordings include:* Linda di Chamounix and I Puritani, both with Edita Gruberova. *Honours:* Gold Medal, International Giuseppe Verdi Competition at Bussetto, 1989.

**KIM, Hae-Jung;** Concert Pianist; b. 18 May 1965, New York, USA. *Education:* BM and MM, Juilliard School of Music; Peabody Conservatory; Moscow Conservatory. *Career:* Debut: Vienna Tonkunstler Orchestra, Vienna, 1985; Pittsburgh Symphony, St Louis; Royal Philharmonic, London Philharmonic, Moscow State Symphony, Barcelona Philharmonic, NHK Symphony, Lausanne Chamber, English Chamber, Monte Carlo Philharmonic. *Recordings:* Rachmaninov concertos no. 2 and 3; Prokofiev Concerto no. 1 and Tchaikovsky Concerto no.1, St Petersburg Symphony; Rachmaninov no. 4 and Rhapsody. *Honours:* 1st prize, Köln International Competition, 1998; D'Angelo Young Artist Competition; Medal award from Korean Government. *Current Management:* IMG Artists Management. *Address:* 3 Lincoln Center, NY 10023, USA.

**KIM, Michael (Injae);** Professor of Piano and Concert Pianist; b. 13 Feb. 1968, Quebec, Canada. *Education:* BMus, University of Calgary; MM, DMA, Juilliard School New York. *Career:* Debut: Calgary Philharmonic Orchestra, Canada, 15 years old; Performances with major orchestras of Canada and US, including Boston, Milwaukee, Cincinnati, Oklahoma City, Toronto, Vancouver, National Arts Centre, Calgary, Edmonton, Regina, Saskatoon, Winnipeg, London, toured Scotland with the Royal Scottish National Orchestra; Appearances in Glasgow, Edinburgh, Dundee, Aberdeen (1994); BBC Scottish Symphony, Glasgow (1992); Recitals throughout Canada and US, including appearances in virtually every series in Canada; Recital tour, Scotland, 1994; Recitals broadcast regularly by CBC, BBC, National Public Radio; As

Chamber Musician, appeared throughout Canada and US with sister violinist Helen Hwaya Kim (The Kim Duo), including appearances at Carnegie Hall, New York, 1992. *Recordings:* Chamber Works of Saint-Saëns; Ballades of Chopin and Grieg; Works of Stravinsky, Rachmaninov, Mussorgsky. *Honours:* Laureate of 1992 Scottish (Glasgow), 1993 Leeds, 1993 Ivo Pogorelich (Pasadena, California) International Piano Competitions; Grand Prizewinner, 1988 Canadian Music Competitions (Montreal, Quebec) and 1989 Canadian Broadcasting Corporation Competition for Young Performers, Toronto. *Address:* c/o Conservatory of Music, Lawrence University, 420 East College Avenue, Appleton, WI 54911, USA.

**KIM, Re Yang;** Singer (mezzo-soprano); b. 1953, Republic of Korea. *Education:* Studied in Seoul, Vienna and Augsburg. *Career:* Sang at the Berne Opera, 1977–78, Karlsruhe Staatstheater from 1978; Deutsche Oper am Rhein, Düsseldorf, 1982–87; Sang the Nurse in Die Frau ohne Schatten at Bonn, 1992, and Ulrica in Un Ballo in Maschera at Cologne, 1993; Other roles include Azucena in Il Trovatore, Eboli in Don Carlos, Carmen, Brangaene in Tristan und Isolde, Ortrud in Lohengrin and Herodias in Salome. *Address:* c/o Oper der Stadt Bonn, Am Boeselagerhof 1, Pf. 2440, 53111 Bonn, Germany.

**KIM, Sun-joo,** BMus; South Korean conductor and educator; b. 5 Oct. 1929, Sun Cheh Pyung an Buk-Do; m. Hye Sook Lee 1955; one c. *Education:* Kyung Hee Univ. *Career:* Principal Associate Conductor, Korean Broadcasting Symphony, Seoul, 1963–; Instructor, Yung-Hee University, Seoul, 1965; Principal Associate Conductor, Seoul Philharmonic, 1965–69; Principal Conductor, National Symphony Korea, 1969–70; Professor, Kyung Hee University; Conductor, Korean Symphony Orchestra, Seoul; mem, Board of Executives, 1975–82, Korean Musicians Union. *Address:* Kyung-Hee University, School of Music, Whoe Ki Dong, Seoul, Republic of Korea.

**KIM, Young-mi,** BA, MA; South Korean singer (soprano); b. 6 Nov. 1954, Seoul; m. Kim Sung-ha 1984. *Education:* Seoul Art School, Conservatory of Santa Cecilia, Rome, Academy of Santa Cecilia, Rome. *Career:* debut at Alice Tully Hall, New York Lincoln Center, 1980; Appearances with New York City Opera, Los Angeles Music Center Opera, Houston Grand Opera, Opera Company of Philadelphia, Opéra de Paris, Bastille Orchestra, National Symphony, Seattle Symphony, San Diego Symphony, Minnesota Orchestra, Colorado Symphony. *Recordings:* Sung-Eum Gramophone. *Honours:* Verona International Contest, 1977; Giacomo Contest, 1979; Maria Callas International Voice Competition, 1980; Luciano Pavarotti International Voice Competition, 1981. *Address:* c/o Seoul Arts Center, 700 Seocho-dong, Seocho-gu, Seoul 137-718, Republic of Korea (office).

**KIM, Young-uck;** South Korean violinist; b. 1 Sept. 1947, Seoul. *Education:* Curtis Institute, Philadelphia with Ivan Galamian. *Career:* debut, Philadelphia Orchestra conducted by Ormandy, 1963; tours of South America and Europe: appearances with the Berlin Philharmonic, Concertgebouw Orchestra, Vienna Philharmonic and London Symphony; Season 1987–88 in USA with the St Paul Chamber Orchestra, St Louis Symphony, Cleveland Orchestra, Pittsburgh Symphony and the New York Philharmonic; Concerts in Sweden, Italy and the United Kingdom; Season 1988–89, with the Hallé Orchestra and BBC National Orchestra of Wales; Tours to Eire, Sweden, Norway and Germany; USA recitals with Peter Serkin playing Beethoven sonatas; Piano Trio recitals with Emanuel Ax and Yo-Yo Ma: 1989 concerts in Switzerland, Germany and Italy; Concerto repertoire includes works by Bach, Berg, Mozart, Prokofiev, Sibelius, Stravinsky and Vivaldi; Concerts and Recitals American and Europe: New York Philharmonic, Los Angeles Philharmonic, London Symphony Orchestra, Hong Kong Philharmonic, Rotterdam Philharmonic; Tours, America and Far East; Season 1992 with World and European Premieres of newly commissioned concerto by Gunther Schuller (New York and Rotterdam). *Recordings include:* 5 Mozart Concertos with the London Philharmonic under Christoph Eschenbach; Ax/Kim/Ma Trio recording of Dvořák Trios (Sony Classical-Record of the Year Award, 1988); Mozart Piano Quartets with Previn, Heichiro and Gary Hoffman. *Current Management:* Gottschalk, Impresario A/S, Tollbugaten 3, 0152 Oslo, Norway.

**KIMBELL, David Rodney Bertram,** MA, DPhil, LRAM; British academic; *Professor Emeritus of Music, University of Edinburgh;* b. 26 June 1939, Gillingham, Kent; m.; one s. two d. *Education:* Worcester Coll., Oxford. *Career:* Lecturer, Univ. of Edinburgh 1965–78, Prof. of Music 1987–2001, Prof. Emer. 2001–; Prof. of Music, St Andrews Univ. 1979–1987. *Publications:* Verdi in the Age of Italian Romanticism 1981, Italian Opera 1991, Vincenzo Bellini: Norma 1998; contrib. to Hallische Händel-Ausgabe, New Oxford History of Music, Cambridge Companion to Verdi, Cambridge History of Italian Literature, Viking Opera Guide, The Classics of Music by D.F. Tovey (editorial contrib.). *Address:* 3 Bellevue Crescent, Edinburgh, EH3 6ND, Scotland (home). *E-mail:* d.kimbell@virgin.net (home).

**KIMBROUGH, Steven;** Singer (Baritone); b. 17 Dec. 1936, Athens, Alabama, USA. *Education:* Studied at Birmingham Southern College, Duke University, Princeton Theological seminary; Further study in Italy. *Career:* Debut: Mantua, 1968, as Marcel in La Bohème; Appearances in Mannheim, Frankfurt, London, San Francisco, New York and Philadelphia; Member of the Bonn Opera, 1971–; Sang in the premiere of Christophorus by Schreker, Freiburg, 1978; Essen 1989 as Mirabeau by Siegfried Matthus; Concert tours of the USA, Germany, Italy and Austria; Guest appearances at the opera houses of Vancouver, Cincinnati, Rio de Janeiro, Barcelona; Repertoire includes roles in operettas and musicals; German premiere Op 2 Zemlinsky, 1994; mem, American Guild of Musical Artists; Actors Equity. *Recordings*

include: Lieder by Korngold, Zemlinsky, Weill, Kienzl, Schreker, Schoenberg for EMI and Koch. *Address:* 128 Bridge Avenue, Bay Head, NJ 08742, USA.

**KIMM, Fiona;** Singer (mezzo-soprano); b. 24 May 1952, Ipswich, Suffolk, England. *Education:* Studied at the Royal College of Music, London. *Career:* Has sung at the Glyndebourne Festival in Die Zauberflöte, The Love for Three Oranges, Titus and L'Enfant et les Sortilèges; Appearances with Opera North as Hansel, Mercédès, Rosalind in The Mines of Sulphur, Hermia (A Midsummer Night's Dream) and Baba the Turk; Sang in the premiere of Edward Cowie's Kate Kelly's Road Show, Chester, 1983; With English National Opera has sung Orlofsky, Lola and Fyodor (Boris Godunov), and in Orpheus in the Underworld and Rusalka; Covent Garden debut in Boris Godunov; Berlioz Festival at Lyon in Dido and Aeneas; Sang in the premiere of Greek by Mark Anthony Turnage (Munich 1988) and again at the Edinburgh Festival; Scottish Opera in Lulu, Die Zauberflöte, Eugene Onegin and Das Rheingold; Bath Festival in El Rey de Harlem by Henze, with Ensemble Modern; Sang Smeraldina in The Love for Three Oranges, ENO 1989, Siebel in Faust, 1990; Opera North/RSC at Stratford as Julie in Showboat; Glyndebourne Festival 1990, as Third Lady in Die Zauberflöte; Michael Berkeley, Baa Baa Black Sheep, world premiere, 1993; Concert performances with the London Symphony, English Chamber Orchestra, City of Birmingham Symphony and London Sinfonietta; Conductors include Abbado, Haitink, Elder, Hickox, Andrew Davis, and Roger Norrington; Sang in Param Vir's Snatched by the Gods, for Almeida Opera, 1996; Mistress Quickly for Garsington Opera and Rosa Mamai in Cilea's L'Arlesiana for Opera Holland Park, 1998; Mrs Sedley in Peter Grimes for Frankfurt Opera; Markolfa in Simon Holt's The Nightingale's to Blame and in L'Enfant et les Sortilèges for Opera North and Larina in Onegin for Glyndebourne Touring Opera; Television appearances in The Gondoliers, L'Enfance du Christ and Man and Music series on Channel 4. *Current Management:* Connaught Artists Management Ltd, 2 Molasses Row, Plantation Wharf, London, SW11 3UX, England. *Telephone:* (20) 7738 0017. *Fax:* (20) 7738 0909. *E-mail:* classicalmusic@connaughtartists.com. *Website:* www.connaughtartists.com.

**KINCSES, Veronika;** Hungarian singer (soprano); d. of György Kincses and Etelka Angyal; m. József Vajda; one s. *Education:* Liszt Ferenc Music Acad. Budapest and Accademia Santa Cecilia, Rome. *Career:* soloist, State Opera, Budapest; song-recitals, also oratorio performances; guest performances in USA, Argentina, Venezuela, Hong Kong, Singapore etc. 1997–98; operatic roles include Madame Butterfly, Mimi (La Bohème), Manon Lescaut, Liu (Turandot), Le Villi (Puccini), Contessa (Le Nozze di Figaro), Fiordiligi (Così fan Tutte), Vitellia (La Clemenza di Tito), Elvira (Don Giovanni), Amelia (Simone Boccanegra), Leonora (La Forza del destino), Micaela (Carmen), Marguerita (Faust), Silvana (Fiamma–Respighi), Eva (Meistersinger von Nürnberg), Adriana (Adriana Lecouvreur), Tosca, Judit (Bluebeard's Castle). *Recordings:* Die Königin von Saba, Haydn's Der Apotheker and La Fedeltà Premiata, Songs by Bellini, Liszt's Hungarian Coronation Mass, Madame Butterfly, Orfeo ed Euridice, La Bohème (also DVD), Suor Angelica, Le Nozze di Figaro, etc. *Honours:* Winner, Dvořák Int. Singing Competition, Prague 1971, Liszt Prize, Kossuth Prize (Hungary), Prix de l' Acad. du Disque, Paris (four times). *Current Management:* International Management of the Hungarian State Opera, Andrássy ut 22, 1061 Budapest, Hungary; Robert Lombardo Associates, 61 West 62nd Street, New York, NY 10023, USA. *Telephone:* (1) 332-7372 (Hungary); (212) 586-4453 (New York).

**KING, Andrew (Graham),** BA, PGCE, ARCM; Singer (tenor) and Musical Director; b. 8 May 1953, Bury St Edmunds, England. *Education:* St John's Coll., Durham, Dunelm, King's Coll., Cambridge, vocal studies with Graham Watts, Ivor Davies, David Johnston, Eric Vietheer, Iris dell' Acqua. *Career:* Durham Cathedral Choir 1972–75, King's College Choir 1975–76; debut, Wigmore Hall, 1977; Proms, Baroque Cantatas, BBC Singers, 1978; Lay Clerk, Guildford Cathedral, 1976–77; BBC Singers, 1977–80; Sang with many emerging early music groups, including Tallis Scholars, Clerkes of Oxenford, The Sixteen, Medieval Ensemble of London, Landini Consort, Gothic Voices, Taverner Consort, King's Consort, New London Consort: Member of Consort of Musicke since 1978; Also performs with Ex Cathedra and Pro Cantione Antiqua; Performed contemporary works with the song group English Echoes and Singcircle; Noted as an Interpreter of Renaissance and Baroque Music and is in particular demand as Evangelist in the Bach Passions; Performances throughout Europe, also USA, Canada, Middle East, Japan and Australia; Festival appearances include Bruges, Edinburgh, Prague, Salzburg, Utrecht, York and many appearances at the Proms; Performances of early operas and masques in Austria, Belgium, UK, Germany, Netherlands, Italy, Norway, Spain and Sweden; Elected as a professional tenor of the Noblemen and Gentlemen's Catch Club, 2001; Has given a number of world premieres, most notably Leaving by Mark-Anthony Turnage with CBSO; Teacher, Birmingham Conservatoire; Masterclasses: England, Israel, Italy, Poland and Sweden; Musical Director, The Renaissance Ensemble, formed in 1997. *Recordings:* Over 80 including Monteverdi Vespers (New London Consort also Taverner Consort), Apollo and other roles in Monteverdi's Orfeo (NLC/Decca), many Monteverdi Madrigal recordings (Consort of Musicke/Decca/Harmonia Mundi/Musica Oscura/Virgin Classics), Handel's Esther (Academy of Ancient Music/Decca), Purcell's Ode on St Cecilia's Day (Taverner Consort/EMI), Purcell Late Songs (Mantle of Orpheus-Consort of Musicke/Musica Oscura), Bach's Christmas Oratorio (New London Consort/Decca); live recording of Mendelssohn's version of Bach's St Matthew Passion, with Choir and Orchestra of Swiss Italian Radio TV; Many other recordings of Medieval and Renaissance Music; Frequent radio broadcasts BBC Radio 3 and WDR; Video of Monteverdi Madrigals Banquet of the Senses with Consort of Musicke; Several television appearances including Proms and a series of Music in Venice with King's Consort (Channel 4). *Honours:* Choral Scholarship, Durham Cathedral, 1972–75. *Current Management:* Concert Directory International, Lyndhurst, Ben Rhydding, Ilkley, Yorkshire, LS29 8QR, England. *Address:* 49 Dalmeny Avenue, London SW16 4RS, England.

**KING, Mary;** Singer (Mezzo-soprano); b. 16 June 1952, Tonbridge Wells, England. *Education:* BA, English, Birmingham University; PGCE, St Anne's College, Oxford; Postgraduate Diploma, Guildhall School of Music. *Career:* Sang in opera at Glyndebourne, 1980, US debut, 1985, Covent Garden, 1990; Regular appearances with major British orchestras; Spanish tour with BBC Symphony Orchestra, 1991; Proms, 1991; New music a speciality with many first performances including: The Undivine Comedy by Finnissy in Paris and London, Valis, by Machover in Paris, Boston, and Tokyo; Teacher, Guildhall School of Music, London, 1990–; Artistic Director of Live Culture, a youth group of English National Opera, Baylis Programme; Formed Green Light Music Theatre, 1990; Has sung Marcellina and Baba the Turk at Glyndebourne, The Cockerel in The Cunning Little Vixen at Covent Garden; Sang Florence Pike in Albert Herring at Garsington, 1996 and Meg Page in Falstaff, 1998; Knussen's Where the Wild Things Are and Higglety, Pigglety, Pop! at the London Proms, 2002; mem, Equity; Association of Teachers of Singing. *Recordings:* Where the Wild Things Are, by Knussen; The Cunning Little Vixen; Britten's Praise We Great Men; Machover's Valis; Birtwistle's Meridian; Stilgoe's Brilliant the Dinosaur. *Current Management:* Mary Craig. *Address:* 34a Garthone Road, Honor Oak, London SE23 1EW, England.

**KING, Robert John Stephen,** MA; British conductor, harpsichordist and editor; b. 27 June 1960, Wombourne, England. *Education:* St John's Coll., Cambridge. *Career:* Dir, The King's Consort 1980–; guest conductor, Netherlands Chamber Orchestra, Orquesta Sinfonica Euskadi, Atlanta Symphony Orchestra, Minnesota Symphony, Nat. Symphony Orchestra of Washington, Houston Symphony Orchestra, English Chamber Orchestra, Madrid Symphony Orchestra, Granada Symphony Orchestra, Seville Symphony Orchestra, Royal Orchestra of Galicia, Norrköping Symphony Orchestra, Israel Camerata, Swiss Radio Choir, Netherlands Chamber Choir, Danish Radio Choir, Filharmonisch Orkest van Vlaanderen, RAI Nat. Symphony Orchestra, World Youth Symphony Orchestra; Artistic Dir, Purcell Tercentenary Festival, Wigmore Hall, London 1995; Artistic Dir, Nordic Baroque Festival 2002–; Artistic Dir, ION Festival Nürnberg 2003–. *Recordings:* 90 albums with The King's Consort. *Publications:* Henry Purcell 1994. *Address:* 34 St Mary's Grove, London, W4 3LN, England.

**KING, Terry B.;** Cellist, Conductor and Teacher; b. 20 Aug. 1947, Santa Monica, California, USA; m. Leslie Morgan 1976. *Education:* BM, Mt St Mary's College, Los Angeles, 1970; Postgraduate, Claremont Graduate School, 1974; University of Northern Iowa, 1989–91; Assistant Professor, University of Northern Iowa, 1990–. *Career:* Debut: Carnegie Recital Hall, New York, 1975; Assistant to Piatigorsky, University of Southern California, 1971–72; Instructor, San Francisco Conservatory, 1972; Lecturer, California University, Fullerton, 1972–75; Artist-in-Residence, Grinnell College, 1975–; Vienna Chamber Orchestra, 1978; St Paul Sunday Morning, 1984–87; Voice of America, America in Concert, Music from the Frick Museum, New York, Austrian Radio, NPR, PBS, several documentaries; Piatigorsky, McPhee, Harrison. *Compositions:* Arrangements, Trio music by Anderson, Enesco, de Falla, Fauré, Glinka; Voice and Instruments, Mozart, Bachelet, Godard; Cello Ensembles, Sibelius, Prokofiev, Shostakovich. *Recordings:* 17 recordings, Cello Music by Cowell, Barber, Cooper, Harris; Concertos by Harrison, Reale, Beethoven, Haydn; Trios with Mirecourt Trio, Beethoven to present day composers.

**KING, Dame Thea,** DBE, FRCM, ARCM, FGSM; British clarinettist; b. 26 Dec. 1925, Hitchin, Herts.; d. of Henry W. M. King and Dorothea L. King; m. Frederick J. Thurston 1953 (died 1953). *Education:* Bedford High School and Royal Coll. of Music. *Career:* Sadler's Wells Orchestra 1950–52; Portia Wind Ensemble 1955–68; London Mozart Players 1956–84; Prof. Royal Coll. of Music 1961–87, Guildhall School of Music 1988–; now mem. English Chamber Orchestra, Melos Ensemble of London, Robles Ensemble; frequent soloist, broadcaster and recitalist. *Recordings include:* works by Mozart, Brahms, Spohr, Mendelssohn, Bruch, Finzi, Stanford and 20th-century British music. *Publications:* Clarinet Solos (Chester Woodwind Series) 1977, Arrangement of J. S. Bach: Duets for Two Clarinets 1979, Schumann for the Clarinet 1991, Mendelssohn for the Clarinet 1993, The Romantic Clarinet: A Mendelssohn Collection 1994, Tchaikovsky 1995. *Address:* 16 Milverton Road, London, NW6 7AS, England. *Telephone:* (20) 8459-3453.

**KINGDOM, Elizabeth;** Singer (Soprano); b. 1932, USA. *Career:* Sang in opera at Bielefeld, 1958–63, notably in the 1962 German premiere of Scarlatti's Griselda, Nuremberg, 1962–68, (Hostess in the 1980 premiere of Zemlinsky's Der Traumgörge); Guest appearances at Cologne 1964, Oslo 1970, Graz 1982, and London 1988; Other roles have included Mozart's Donna Anna and Fiordiligi, Verdi's Elisabetta, Forza Leonora and Lady Elisabeth in Tannhäuser, Giulietta and Myrtocle in Die Toten Augen by d'Albert. *Recordings include:* Don Giovanni. *Address:* St ädtische Buhnen, Richard-Wagnerplatz 2–10, 8500 Nuremberg, Germany.

**KINGSLEY, Colin;** Lecturer and Pianist; b. 15 April 1925, London, England; m. 16 April 1955, 2 s., 2 d. *Education:* King's Scholar, Westminster School,

1938–43; BMus, Gonville and Caius College, Cambridge, 1946; D.Mus, Edinburgh, 1968; RCM, 1943–44, 1946–47; Leverhulme Scholar, ARCM, 1945. *Career:* Debut: 1947; Freelance Keyboard Playing, Broadcasting, 1948–; Solo Pianist, Royal Ballet, 1957–59; Several performances of contemporary music in the USA, Japan, Poland, France and the United Kingdom; Member of Macnaghten Committee, 1957–63; Associated Board Examiner, 1959–93; Pianist, University College of Wales, Aberystwyth, 1963–64; Principal Radio: Concertos, 1955–; University of Edinburgh Lecturer, 1964; Senior Lecturer, 1968, retired 1992; Series, Piano Music of P R Fricker, 1974 followed by premiere of his Anniversary for Piano, Cheltenham International Festival, 1978; Series, The English Musical Renaissance, Piano Music, 1977; mem, Incorporated Society of Musicians. *Recordings:* Lyrita, Sonatas for Piano by John White; Various BBC Recordings for broadcasting purposes. *Address:* 236 Milton Road East, Edinburgh EH15 2PF, Scotland.

**KINGSLEY, Margaret,** ARCM, FRCM, LRAM; British singer (soprano, mezzo-soprano); *Professor of Singing, Royal College of Music, London;* b. 20 Feb. 1939, Pool, Cornwall, England; m. W. A. Newcombe. *Education:* Royal Coll. of Music. *Career:* debut with Opera for All; Glyndebourne debut 1966, in Die Zauberflöte; appearances with Covent Garden Opera, ENO, Scottish Opera, Opera North, State Operas of Hamburg, Munich, Stuttgart and Vienna, Stockholm Royal Opera, Paris Opéra, Naples, Miami, Washington, Metropolitan Opera, New York; roles include Wagner's Gutrune, Beethoven's Leonore, Waltraute, Eboli, Elvira, Verdi's Amelia and Lady Macbeth, Mozart's Fiordiligi, Donna Anna and Electra, Cassandre in Les Troyens, Reiza in Oberon, Gluck's Euridice, Brünnhilde, title role in Ariadne auf Naxos, Azucena; ENO 1983–84, as Amneris, Marina (Boris Godunov), Akhrosimova (War and Peace) and Mrs Grose (The Turn of the Screw); concert appearances with leading British orchestras and on television; Prof. of Singing, Royal Coll. of Music; teacher at Centre de Formation Lyrique at the Opéra Bastille; giving masterclasses and teaching in Europe. *Address:* Montagu House, 8 White Court, Kings Ride, Alfriston, East Sussex BN26 5XP, England.

**KIRBY, James (Nicholas Joseph);** Pianist; b. 15 April 1965, Hull, England. *Education:* Royal Academy of Music; Moscow Tchaikovsky Conservatoire. *Career:* Debut: Wigmore Hall, London, 1991; As Recitalist, Chamber Musician and Concerto Soloist, performances throughout the United Kingdom including Wigmore Hall, South Bank Centre, Royal Albert Hall, London, and Europe; Performed with English Chamber Orchestra, Scottish Chamber Orchestra and Moscow Symphony Orchestra; Member, Barbican Piano Trio, performing on four continents. *Recordings:* Lalo: Complete piano trios, and Trios by Rachmaninov, Tchaikovsky and Schnittke with Barbican Piano Trio; Appassionato, pieces for violin and piano with Lydia Mordkovitch. *Honours:* Semi-finals, International Tchaikovsky Competition, 1990; 1st Prize, Città di Marsala International Competition, Sicily, 1992; Associate, Royal Academy of Music, 1997; Hon. Prof. of the Rachmaninov Institute, Tambov, Russia. *Address:* 3 Campbell Road, Bow, London E3 4 DS, England.

**KIRCHHOF, Lutz;** Lutenist; b. 15 May 1953, Frankfurt-on-Main, Germany. *Education:* Studied with Lother Fuchs; Musicology at Frankfurt University, with research on John Dowland and Sylvius Leopold Weiss. *Career:* Appearances throughout Germany and Europe from 1964; Studio der Frühen Musik, Frankfurt, 1973–80; Founded own Ensemble, 1976, for performances of early music; Repertoire from Renaissance to Contemporary music; Recitals with Max von Egmond (bass) and Derek Lee Ragin (Countertenor); Festival of Lute Music, Frankfurt, from 1988, as Founder and Director: later International Festival of Lute Music; Founded Research Society 1990, to assemble lute manuscript music from 16th–17th centuries. *Honours:* Winner, Jugend Musiziert Competition, 1972. *Address:* c/o Hochschule für Musik (Frankfurt am Main) Eschersheiner, Landstrasse 29–39, 60322 Frankfurt, Germany.

**KIRCHNER, Leon;** Composer, Pianist and Conductor; b. 24 Jan. 1919, Brooklyn, New York, USA. *Education:* Studies with Schoenberg at University of California, Berkeley (BA 1940) and in New York with Sessions; Further study at Berkeley (MA). *Career:* Lecturer at Berkeley from 1949; Lecturer, then Professor at the University of Southern California, 1950–54; Luther Brusie Marchant Professor at Mills College in Oakland, 1954–61; Appointed to Harvard Faculty, 1961, Walter Bigelow Rosen Professor of Music from 1966; Director of the Harvard Chamber Players, 1973; Director of the Harvard Chamber Orchestra and Friends, 1975; Pianist and Conductor of his own music and the Viennese Classics; Composer-in-Residence and Performer at the Santa Fe Chamber Music Festival, 1983; Tanglewood Music Center, 1985; Soloist and Conductor, Boston Symphony, New York Philharmonic, Philadelphia Orchestra, S F Symphony, St Paul Chamber Orchestra, Sudwest Funk Baden Baden, Tonhalle Zürich, London Sinfonietta, Buffalo Philharmonic; mem, National Institute of Arts and Letters; American Academy of Arts and Sciences. *Compositions:* Opera, Lily 1973–76; Orchestral, Sinfonia 1951; 2 Piano Concertos 1953, 1963; Toccata for strings, wind and percussion; Concerto for violin, cello, 10 wind instruments and percussion 1960; Music for Orchestra, 1969; Music for Flute and Orchestra; Music for Cello and Orchestra, 1992; Vocal, Words from Wordsworth for chorus, 1968; The Twilight Stood, song cycle after Emily Dickinson, 1983; Of Things Exactly As They Are, for soprano, baritone, chorus and orchestra, 1997; Instrumental, Duo for violin and piano, 1947; Piano Sonata, 1948; Little Suite for piano, 1949; 3 String Quartets, 1949, 1958, 1966; Sonata Concertante for violin and piano, 1952; Trio for violin, cello and piano, 1954; A Moment for Roger for piano; Five Pieces for piano, 1987; Interlude for piano, 1989; For Solo Violin II, 1987; For Solo Violin II, 1988; Triptych, Violin, Cello, 1988; Piano Trio, 1993;

Five Pieces for piano; Music for Twelve, 1985. *Honours:* George Ladd Paris Prize, University of California; Two Awards from New York Music Critics' Circle (First two string quartets); Naumburg Award for 1st Piano Concerto; Pulitzer Prize for 3rd String Quartet; Commissions from the Ford Foundation and the New York Philharmonic. *Address:* c/o ASCAP, ASCAP Building, 1 Lincoln Plaza, NY 10023, USA.

**KIRCHNER, Volker David;** Composer; b. 25 June 1942, Mainz, Germany. *Education:* studied with Gunther Kehr and Gunter Raphael, Peter Cornelius Conservatory, Mainz, 1956–59; Cologne Musikhochschule, 1959–63, with B. A. Zimmermann; Detmold 1964–65, with Tibor Varga. *Career:* violinist with the Kehr String Trio 1964–67, Frankfurt Radio Symphony Orchestra 1966–88; freelance composer 1989–. *Compositions include:* Music theatre: Riten für kleines klangtheater, 1971; Die Traung, 1975; Die funf Minuten des Isaak Babel, 1980; Belshazar, 1986; Das Kalte Herz 'Ein Deutsches Märchen', 1988; Erinys Threnos, 1990; Inferno d'amore 'Shakespearion I', 1995; Other works include Fragmente for orchestra, 1961–67; Chorale Variations for 15 solo strings, 1968, rev. 1990; Nachtmusik for ensemble, 1970; Nachtstück for viola and orchestra, 1980; Piano Trio, 1980; Bildnisse I–III for orchestra, 1981–1991; 2 Symphonies, 1980, 1992; String Quartet, 1982; Violin Concerto, 1982; Mysterion, for ensemble, 1985; Piano Sonata, 1986. Requiem, 1988; Saitenspiel for violin and viola, 1993; Missa Moguntina, 1993; Hortus Magicus for orchestra, 1994; Horn concerto, 1996; Ahasver, Scenic Oratorio, 2000. *Current Management:* Schott & Co Ltd, Promotion Department, 48 Great Marlborough Street, London, W1 F7BB, England.

**KIRCHSCHLAGER, Angelika;** Austrian singer (mezzo-soprano); b. 1965, Salzburg. *Education:* Musisches Gymnasium, Salzburg and Vienna Music Acad. *Career:* studied with Walter Berry in Vienna 1984; first performance in Die Zauberflöte, Vienna Kammeroper; concert performances in Austria, France, Germany, Italy, Czech Repub., Denmark, USA and Japan; recent recitals in London, Edinburgh, Amsterdam, Cologne, Frankfurt, Hohenems, Graz, Bilbao and in Scandinavia; composed Jonathan Miller production, Lausanne Opera 1998–99; sang with London Symphony Orchestra, New York Chamber Orchestra and Vienna Symphony Orchestra 1999–2000; feature appearances on Austrian Nat. Radio and TV (ORF); participated in film production about Hugo Wolf in role of Frieda Zerny 1992; signed exclusive contract with Sony label 1997. *Operatic title roles include:* Le nozze di Figaro, Schloss Schönbrunn, Vienna, Der Rosenkavalier, Geneva, Hänsel und Gretel, Graz, The Merry Widow, Vienna, Palestrina, Vienna, Don Giovanni, Ravenna and Milan, Les Contes d'Hoffman, Paris, Ariadne auf Naxos, London. *Recordings include:* album of lieder by Alma Mahler, Gustav Mahler and Erich Wolfgang Korngold (solo debut) 1997; featured on recording of Mendelssohn with Claudio Abbado and Berlin Philharmonic; When Night Falls (solo recital). *Honours:* winner of three prizes, Int. Belvedere Competition, Vienna 1991. *Address:* c/o Sony Music Entertainment (UK) Head Office/ European Regional Office, 10 Great Marlborough Street, London, W1F 7LP, England (office). *Telephone:* (20) 7911-8200 (office). *Website:* www.sonyclassical.com/artists/kirchschlager (office).

**KIRCHSTEIN, Leonore;** Singer (Soprano); b. 29 March 1933, Stettin, Germany. *Education:* Studied at the Robert Schumann Conservatory, Düsseldorf, with Franziska Martiensen-Lohman. *Career:* Sang first with the St ädtische Opera Berlin, from 1958; Kiel 1960–63, Augsburg 1963–65, Cologne 1965–68; Has sung with the Bayerische Staatsoper Munich from 1968; Salzburg Festival 1961 and 1970, Edinburgh Festival 1965 and 1971; Montreux Festival, 1965; Guest appearances in Hamburg, Stuttgart, Zürich and Vienna; Concert tours of USA, Argentina, England, Italy and Turkey. *Recordings include:* Die Zauberflöte and Cardillac; Bach Cantatas; Beethoven's Missa solemnis.

**KIRK, Vernon;** Singer (Tenor); b. 1966, England. *Education:* Royal Academy of Music and Actors Centre, London; Britten-Pears School, Aldeburgh. *Career:* Concerts include tour of Germany and Netherlands in Monteverdi's Christmas Vespers with the Academy of Ancient Music; Bach St Matthew Passion with the London Baroque Soloists, St John Passion in Norway; Messiah and The Creation under David Willcocks; Berlioz L'Enfance du Christ and Brahms Lieder at the London Proms; Schumann's Manfred at the Festival Hall, Die schöne Müllerin at St Martin in the Fields; Lutoslawski Paroles Tissées at the Barbican Hall; Opera roles include Mozart's Tamino, Ferrando and Don Ottavio, Donizetti's Ernesto and Nemorino; Lensky, and Gonslave in L'Heure Espagnole (season 1996–97). *Address:* C&M Craig Services Ltd, 3 Kersley Street, London SW11 4 PR, England.

**KIRKBRIDE, Simon;** British singer (baritone); b. 1970, Northamptonshire, England. *Education:* Peterborough Cathedral, Guildhall School and Royal College, London. *Career:* debut, Jankel in Arabella at Glyndebourne, 1996; Appearances as Publio in La Clemenza di Tito for Welsh National Opera, Masetto, and Morales in Carmen for Scottish Opera; Mozart's Figaro and Thaddeus in Birtwistle's The Last Supper (2001) at Glyndebourne; Concerts include the Requiems of Brahms, Mozart, Fauré and Duruflé, The Dream of Gerontius, Mozart's C Minor Mass, Bach's Passions and B Minor Mass, Belshazzar's Feast and Mendelssohn's Elijah; Soloist with the Britten Sinfonia, London and Calgary Philharmonics, London Handel Orchestra, Florilleguim, Montreal SO, London Baroque and London Mozart Players. *Address:* c/o Den Norske Opera, Storgaten 23, 0028 Oslo, Norway.

**KIRKBY, Emma,** OBE, MA; British singer (soprano); b. 26 Feb. 1949, Camberley, Surrey; d. of late Capt. Geoffrey Kirkby and of Beatrice Daphne

Kirkby; one s. with Anthony Rooley. *Education:* Sherborne School for Girls and Somerville Coll., Oxford and pvt singing lessons with Jessica Cash. *Career:* specialist singer of renaissance, baroque and classical repertoire; debut London concert 1974; full-time professional singer 1975–; since mid-1970s involved in revival of performances with period instruments and the attempt to recreate the sounds the composers would have heard; performances at the Proms from 1977; works as freelance with many groups and orchestras in the UK and Germany, including Consort of Musicke, Andrew Parrott's Taverner Players, Academy of Ancient Music, the Jaye Consort of Viols, London Baroque, Freiburger Barockorchester, Orchestra of the Age of Enlightenment; appearances at festivals, including Bruges, Utrecht, Luzern, Mosel, Rheingau, Passau, Schleswig-Holstein, Saintes, Beaune, Ottawa, Elora, Tanglewood, Mostly Mozart (New York) and many others. *Recordings include:* Complete songs of John Dowland 1976–77, Messiah (Handel) 1979, 1988, Madrigals by Monteverdi, Wert, Scarlatti and other Italians, Schütz, Grabbe, Wilbye, Ward and other English composers, Monteverdi Vespers, Mass in B Minor (Bach), Handel's Athalia, Joshua, Judas Maccabaeus, Sequences by Hildegarde of Bingen (Hyperion), Arie Antiche and Songs of Maurice Greene, Dido and Aeneas, Handel's German Arias, Italian Cantatas: Songs by Arne and Handel, Stabat Mater (Pergolesi), Haydn's Creation, Mozart Motets, Mozart Concert Arias, Vivaldi Opera Arias, Handel Opera Arias, Christmas Music with Westminster Abbey Choir, Christmas Music with London Baroque, Bach Cantatas with Freiburger Barockorchester, Handel, Sacred Contatas, Handel Gloria 2001. *Honours:* Hon. DLitt (Salford) 1985, Hon. DMus (Bath) 1994, (Sheffield) 2000; Hon. Fellow Guildhall School of Music, Royal Acad. of Music, Royal Coll. of Music; Handel Prize, Halle, Germany 1997, Classic FM Artist of the Year 1999. *Address:* c/o Consort of Musicke, 13 Pages Lane, London, N10 1PU, England. *E-mail:* consort@ musicke.net. *Website:* www.musicke.net.

**KIRKENDALE, Ursula,** DPhil; music historian; b. 6 Sept. 1932, Dortmund, Germany; m. Warren Kirkendale 1959; three d. *Education:* studied in Bonn. *Career:* Visiting Prof., Univ. of Southern California, Univ. of California, Duke Univ., Columbia Univ., USA. *Publications:* Antonio Caldara: Sein Leben und seine venezianisch-römischen Oratorien 1966; contrib. to Acta Musicologica, Journal American Musicological Society, Chigiana, Music and Letters, Studi musicali, Rivista Italiana di Musicologia, Dizionario Biografico degli Italiani. *Honours:* fellow, Deutscher Akademischer Austauschdienst; American Council of Learned Societies; Alfred Einstein Award; Deems Taylor Award; Elected Wirkendes Mitglied der Gesellschaft zur Herausgabe von Denkmälen der Tonkunst in Österreich; Festschrift: Musicologia Humana (with bibliography), 1994. *Address:* Via dei Riari 86, 00165 Rome, Italy.

**KIRKENDALE, Warren,** BA, DPhil; Canadian music historian; *Professor Emeritus, University of Regensburg*; b. 14 Aug. 1932, Toronto, Canada; m. Ursula Schöttler 1959; three d. *Education:* Univ. of Toronto, Univ. of Vienna, Austria. *Career:* Asst Prof., Univ. of Southern California 1963–67; Assoc. Prof., Duke Univ. 1967–75; Prof. 1975–82; Prof. Ordinarius, Univ. of Regensburg, Germany 1983–92, Prof. Emeritus 1992–; Visiting Prof., Harvard Univ. for Italian Renaissance Studies, Florence; mem. Italian and American Musicological Socs. *Publications:* Fuge und Fugato in der Kammermusik des Rokoko und der Klassik, 1967, English, 1979; L'Aria di Fiorenza, 1972; Madrigali a diversi Linguaggi, 1975; The Court Musicians in Florence during the Principate of the Medici, 1993; Emilio dei Cavalieri, 2001; contrib. to Journal of American Musicological Society, Acta Musicologica, Musical Quarterly, Mozart-Jahrbuch, Quadrivium, Dizionario Biografico degli Italiani, Volkswagen-Stiftung, Rivista italiana di musicologica, Studi musicali. *Honours:* Fellow, Deutscher Akademischer Austauschdienst; NEH; American Council of Learned Societies; Volkswagen-Stiftung; Elected Wirkendes Mitglied der Gesellschaft zur Herausgabe von Denkmälern der Tonkunst in Österreich; Doctor honoris causa, University of Pavia, 1986; Accademico Filarmonico honoris causa, Bologna, 1987; Medal, Collège de France, 1994; Medal, Univ. of Pavia; Festschrift: Musicologia Humana (with bibliography), 1994. *Address:* Via dei Riari 86, 00165 Rome, Italy.

**KIRSHBAUM, Ralph;** Cellist; b. 4 March 1946, Denton, Texas, USA. *Education:* Studied with his father Joseph Kirshbaum, with Lev Aronson in Dallas and with Aldo Parisot at Yale University. *Career:* Debut: With the Dallas Symphony, 1959; From 1970 has performed with most leading orchestras including those in: London, Berlin, Amsterdam and Paris; USA engagements with many American orchestras including the Boston Symphony, Chicago Symphony and the Los Angeles Philharmonic; Tours of Germany, Hungary, Switzerland, Israel, Scandinavia, New Zealand, Australia and Japan; Debut with the Orchestre de Paris in 1990; Festival appearances include: Edinburgh, London's South Bank and the Mostly Mozart Festival in NY; Promenade Concerts in London include premiere of Tippett's Triple Concerto in 1980; Premiered the Cello Concerto by Peter Maxwell Davies with Cleveland Orchestra under Christoph von Dohnányi in 1989; Has appeared with many renowned conductors including: Georg Solti, Yuri Temirkanov, Simon Rattle, André Previn and Colin Davis; Founder and Artistic Director of the RNCM Manchester International Cello Festival; Fellow and Tutor at The RNCM; Regular concerts with violinist György Pauk and pianist Peter Frankl; Frequent guest of the violinist and conductor Pinchas Zukerman, playing Brahms' Double Concerto in London, Edinburgh, Tokyo and Chicago; Played the Schumann Concerto at St John's, London, 1997; Elgar's Concerto with the BBC Philharmonic Orchestra at the 1999 London Proms. *Recordings include:* Barber Concerto; Elgar Concerto; Tippett

Triple Concerto; Bach Suites; Haydn Concertos. *Honours:* Winner, International Tchaikovsky Competition in Moscow, 1970. *Current Management:* Ingpen & Williams Ltd, 7 St George's Court, 131 Putney Bridge Road, London, SW15 2PA, England.

**KISER, Wieslaw (Maria);** Conductor, Critic and Composer; b. 20 July 1937, Poznań, Poland. *Education:* High School of Music, Poznan. *Career:* Debut: As composer, Poznan, 1965; As Conductor, Poznan, 1963; Over 750 concerts in Poland, Bulgaria, Finland, France, Germany, USSR and Czechoslovakia; Artistic Manager, The Boys Choir of Gniezno, Poland, 1989; Music Lecturer and Promotor of Music Life, 1990–; The Thrushes; Television and Radio broadcasts in Poland, Finland, France, USSR and Germany; Several concerts in Belgium as Conductor of The Starlings (Men's Choir). *Compositions:* From the Years 1989–1990; Scherzo for the violin and string orchestra; Aria to J. S. Bach's chorale for the violin and string orchestra; Trio for the viola, violoncello and contrabass; Impromptu for the viola, violoncello and contrabass; Six Children compositions for the piano Sonata for the piano; Over 70 choral compositions; Sonatina for string quartet, 1995; 12 Preludes for piano, 1996–98; 30 one choirs song, 1995–98. *Recordings:* Radio and television Poland, Finland, USSR, Germany and France. *Publications:* Organisation and Education of Children's Choirs, 1971; Aerials of Poznan, 1975; The Selected Problems of Music History, 1969; Watchword, The Music, in Encykloeadia Wielkopolska, The Great Poland Encyclopaedie; Watchword, The Music, in Dzieje Poznania, The Aets of Poznan, 1989–90; Mr Jerzy Kurczewski: The Man and the Artist, 1994; The Poznan Inhabitants on the records, 1994. *Current Management:* The Artistic Manager of the Men's Choir, The Starlings, Gniezno, Poland. *Address:* u Szelagowska 12, 61-626 Poznań, Poland.

**KISSIN, Evgeny Igorevich;** Russian pianist; b. 10 Oct. 1971, Moscow. *Education:* Moscow Gnessin Music School, studied piano with Anna Kantor. *Career:* debut playing Mozart's D-minor concerto aged 10; appeared with Moscow Philharmonic, playing Chopin concertos 1984; tour of Japan with the Moscow Virtuosi; debut in Western Europe with the Berlin Radio orchestra 1987; British debut at the Lichfield Festival with the BBC Philharmonic 1987; London Symphony Orchestra concert 1988; concerts with the Royal Philharmonic and Yuri Temirkanov 1990; promenade concert debut with the BBC Symphony, playing Tchaikovsky's First Concerto 1990; US debut with the New York Philharmonic 1990, subsequent US tour included Tanglewood, Carnegie Hall 1991; Grammy Award ceremony and performances with the Chicago Symphony and Philadelphia Orchestra 1991–92; performed with the Boston Symphony, London recital debut and concert with the Philharmonia, and Prokofiev Concertos with the Berlin Philharmonic 1992–93; played Chopin and Schumann at the Royal Festival Hall, London 1997; first pianist to perform a recital at the London Proms 1997; Chopin's First Concerto at the London Proms with the Bavarian State Orchestra 1999; first concerto soloist to play in the Proms Opening concert 2000; 10th anniversary tour of recitals in the USA, including Carnegie Hall 2000–01; appearances with the Warsaw Philharmonic, Philharmonia Orchestra, Bavarian Staatskapelle, Chicago Symphony, Boston Symphony, Metropolitan Opera, Bayerische Rundfunk, and the Leipzig Gewandhaus 1999–2001; Brahms' Concerto No. 2 in B flat major at the London Proms 2002. *Recordings include:* Rachmaninov 2nd Concerto and Etudes Tableaux with the London Symphony conducted by Gergiev, Rachmaninov Concerto No. 3, Chopin Vols I and II live recital from Carnegie Hall, Prokofiev Piano Concertos 1 and 3 with Berlin Philharmonic conducted by Claudio Abbado, Haydn and Schubert Sonatas 1995, Beethoven: Moonlight Sonata, Franck: Prelude, Choral et Fugue, Brahms: Paganini Variations 1998, Chopin: 4 Ballades, Berceuse op 57, Barcarolle op 60, Scherzo No. 4 op 54 1999, Chopin recital including 24 Preludes Op. 28, Sonata No, 2 and Polonaise in A-flat, Brahms 2003. *Honours:* Hon. DMus (Manhattan School of Music) 2001; Diapafon d'Or (France), Grand Prix Nobel Academie de Disque (France), Edison Klassiek Award (Netherlands) 1990, Chigiana Acad. Musician of the Year (Sienna) 1991, Musical America's Instrumentalist of the Year 1995, Triumph Award for outstanding contribution to Russia's culture 1997, Echo Award (Germany) 2002, Shostakovich Award (Moscow) 2003. *Current Management:* Askonas Holt Ltd, Lonsdale Chambers, 27 Chancery Lane, London, WC2A 1PF, England. *Telephone:* (20) 7400-1700. *Fax:* (20) 7400-1799. *E-mail:* info@askonasholt.co .uk. *Website:* www.askonasholt.co.uk.

**KIT, Mikhail;** Singer (bass); b. 1950, Russia. *Education:* Studied at the Odessa Conservatoire. *Career:* Sang first with the Perm Opera, then joined the Kirov Opera, 1966, singing Pimen, Boris, Prince Igor, Dosifei, Ivan Susanin, Gremin, Basilio, Leporello, Mephistopheles, Iago and Sarastro; Visited Edinburgh and the Metropolitan with the Kirov, 1991–92, Japan, 1993; Sang Dosifei in Khovanshchina with the Kirov Opera at Tel-Aviv, 1996; Engaged as Gremin at the Opéra Bastille, Paris, 1997; Season 1998 in Mazeppa with the Kirov Opera at the Metropolitan, as Mussorgsky's Dosifey at La Scala. *Recordings include:* The Fiery Angel and the title role in Prince Igor; Shostakovich songs with Larissa Gergieva for the BBC. *Current Management:* Askonas Holt Ltd, Lonsdale Chambers, 27 Chancery Lane, London, WC2A 1PF, England. *Telephone:* (20) 7400-1700. *Fax:* (20) 7400-1799. *E-mail:* info@askonasholt.co.uk. *Website:* www.askonasholt.co.uk.

**KITAYENKO, Dmitriy Georgievich;** Russian conductor; b. 18 Aug. 1940, Leningrad. *Education:* Leningrad Conservatory. *Career:* postgrad. study Moscow Conservatory (under Khazanov and Ginzburg); further study at Acad. of Music, Vienna 1966–67; conductor, Nemirovich-Danchenko Theatre

1969–, prin. conductor 1970–76; chief conductor, Moscow Philharmonic 1976–89; numerous appearances in Europe and USA; teacher at Moscow Conservatory 1969–, Prof. 1986–90; Music Dir, Frankfurt Radio Orchestra 1990–95; apptd Conductor, Bern Symphony Orchestra 1994; Perm. Conductor, Music Adviser, Bergen Philharmonic Orchestra 1991–. *Honours:* USSR People's Artist 1984; RSFSR State Prize 1988. *Address:* Chalet Kalimor, 1652 Botterens, Switzerland (home).

**KITCHEN, Linda;** British singer (Soprano); b. 1960, Morecambe, Lancs., England. *Education:* studied at Royal Northern Coll. of Music with Nicholas Powell, Nat. Opera Studio, later study with David Keren and Audrey Langford. *Career:* sang Blonde in Mozart's Die Entführung 1983 and Monteverdi's Amor at Glyndebourne Festival 1984; later sang Flora in The Knot Garden at Covent Garden and Barbarina in The Marriage of Figaro at London Coliseum; other roles include Mozart's Susanna, Papagena and Zerlina, and Adele; concert repertory includes Rossini's Stabat Mater, Mozart's Requiem, Poulenc's Gloria and Schoenberg's Pierrot Lunaire; sang Iris in Handel's Semele, at Covent Garden 1988; sang Oscar in Ballo in Maschera, Flora in The Knot Garden, Sophie in Werther, Jemmy in Guillaume Tell, Pamina, Magic Flute, Dublin, Cherubino, Zerlina, Serpetta in Finta Gardiniera and Magnolia in Showboat for Opera North; sang Eurydice in new production of Orpheus in the Underworld for Opera North 1992, followed by Susanna in The Marriage of Figaro, Despina and Martinů's Julietta for Opera North and Drusilla in Poppea for Welsh Nat. Opera 1997–98, Xenia in Boris Gounov at Brighton and Celia in Mozart's Lucio Silla for Garsington Opera 1998. *Recording:* Vaughan Williams: Serenade to Music 1990. *Honours:* Heinz Bursary. *Address:* c/o Hyperions Records Ltd, PO Box 25, London, SE9 1AX; c/o Musichall Ltd, Vicarage Way, Ringmer, East Sussex, BN8 5LA, England. *Telephone:* (20) 8318-1234 (London). *Fax:* (20) 8463-1230 (London). *E-mail:* info@hyperion-records.co.uk. *Website:* www.hyperion -records.co.uk.

**KITCHINER, John;** Singer (Tenor); b. 2 Dec. 1933, England. *Education:* Studied at the London Opera Centre with Joan Cross. *Career:* Debut: Glyndebourne 1965, as Count Almaviva; Appearances with English National Opera, Scottish Opera and Welsh National Opera; Roles include Guglielmo, Don Alfonso, Don Giovanni, Renato in Un Ballo in Maschera, Count di Luna, Figaro and Bartolo in Il Barbiere di Siviglia, Robert in Le Comte Ory, Marcello, Escamillo, and Count Eberbach in Der Wildschütz by Lortzing; Also sang in the British stage premieres of Prokofiev's War and Peace and The Bassarids by Henze, at the London Coliseum, 1972, 1974; Frequent concert engagements. *Address:* c/o English National Opera, London Coliseum, St Martin's Lane, London WC2N 4ES, England.

**KITSENKO, Dmitry;** Composer; b. 24 July 1950, Belay Tserkov, Kiev province, Moldovia. *Education:* Kishinyov Institute of Arts; Bucharest Music Academy. *Career:* Lecturer at Kishinyov Institute, 1977–82; Musicescu Academy, 1990–. *Compositions include:* concertos for Bayan (1977), Oboe (1977), Organ (1982), Trombone (1990, 1991) and Cello (1992); 4 Symphonies (1986, 1992, 1995, 1998); The Seasons for children's chorus and orchestra, 1980; Stabat Mater, for mezzo and chamber orchestra, 1989; Mariengebet, for women's chorus, 1989; Tinitatea Iupului for contralto and chamber orchestra, 1995; Ave Maria for soprano, clarinet and organ, 1993; Alleluja for soprano and trumpet, 1999; 2 string quartets, 1975, 1983; In Memoriam Oscar for 13 solo strings, 1988; Pastoral Games for ensemble, 1988; The Field for brass quintet, 1991; Transfiguration for ensemble, 1991; Exodus for ensemble, 1994; Kyrie, 1997; Concerto for 'Ars poetica' ensemble, 1999; Exodus 2 for ensemble, 1999; Strikhira for 4 cellos, 1999; keyboard and incidental music. *Address:* c/o Conservatorium de Muzic, Str. Stirbei Voda 33, 70732 Bucharest, Romania.

**KITTS, Christopher (Martin);** Conductor, Violinist and Educator; b. 7 April 1943, London, England; m. 16 Dec 1982. *Education:* Trinity College of Music, London, 1968; Conducting Studies with Dr Boyd Neel, Toronto, 1964–67, Dr Hans Lert, Virginia, 1966; Violin Studies with Bernard Robbins, New York Philharmonic, Clifford Evans, Toronto. *Career:* Conductor, Royal Conservatory Orchestra, Toronto, 1967, 1968, 1969; Conductor, Scarborough College Choir and Band, 1970; Concertmaster, North York Symphony Orchestra, 1971, 1972; Freelance Violinist, Toronto, 1972–85; Conducted Tours in England, France, West Germany, Netherlands, with Birchmount Park Collegiate, 1980, 1983, 1987, 1991; Adjudicator, Toronto International Music Festival, 1986, 1987; Music Director and Conductor, Scarborough Philharmonic Orchestra, 1985–93; Guest Conductor, Brampton Symphony, Mississauga Symphony, Scarborough Philharmonic, 1994–95. *Address:* 3663 Danforth Avenue, Scarborough, Ontario M1N 2GZ, Canada.

**KLAES, Armin;** Conductor; b. 17 Sept. 1958, Koblenz, Germany; m. Monika Hachmoller, 16 Mar 1982, 1 s. 1 d. *Education:* Conducting, Reinhard Peters at the Folkwang-Musikhochschulen Essen; Music pedagody and composition, Musikhochschule, Cologne; Musicology, University of Cologne; Chamber Music with Gunter Kehr. *Career:* Debut: Bedford Springs Festival for the Performing Arts, Pennsylvania, USA; Guest conductor with several orchestras since 1978; Founder and regular leader, Kolner Konzertgemeinschaft, 1978–85; Music Director, Mannesmann-Sinfonieorchester Duisburg, 1985–92; Founder and conductor of the Amadeus Kammerorchester, 1991; Since 1992, Artist leader of the Musikgemeinschaft Marl, symphonic orchestra and oratorio chorus. *Recordings:* Bach, Concert for organ with H Schauerte, Le Carnaval des Animaux. *Honours:* Folkwang–Forderpries, 1987. *Address:* Corneliusstrasse 167, 47918n Tonisvorst, Germany.

**KLANSKA, Vladimira;** Czech horn player; *Professor of Horn Class, Jan Neruda Gymnasium, Prague;* b. 9 Sept. 1947, Ceské Budejovice; m. Ivan Klansky 1973; two s. *Education:* Conservatory of Music, Prague, Academy of Music, Prague, masterclasses with Herrmann Baumann. *Career:* debut, Mozart II, Rudolfinum Hall, Prague, 1966; Co-Principal, Prague Symphony Orchestra, 1968–74; Concert Tours Throughout Europe in Duo Recitals with Pianist Ivan Klansky, Mozarteum Salzburg, 1972, Concertgebouw, Amsterdam, 1974; Member, Prague Wind Quintet, 1980; Member, Czech Nonet, 1982; Artistic Leader, PWQ and CN, 1991–, Concert Tours with Both Ensembles in Europe, USA and Japan, including Festivals in Salzburg, Edinburgh, Stresa, Sorrento; Radio Recordings in Prague, Stockholm, Brussels, Bremen, Genève, Montreux; President, Stich Punto Horn Society, 1989–; Prof. of Horn Class, Jan Neruda Gymnasium, Prague 1988–; masterclasses in the Czech Republic, France, USA, Brazil and Japan; practitioner in therapeutic One Brain System. *Recordings:* albums of both solo and chamber music. *Honours:* Prizewinner, International ARD Music Competition, Munich, 1973; Juror, International Horn Competitions. *Address:* Stronjnicka 9, 17000 Prague 7, Czech Republic. *Telephone:* (220) 807634; (606) 474570 (mobile). *E-mail:* vladimira.klanska@tiscali.cz.

**KLAPER, Michael;** German musicologist; b. 25 Dec. 1970, Bietigheim-Bissingen. *Career:* Asst, Univ. Erlangen-Nürnberg; mem. Royal Musical Assocn. *Publications:* Hildegard von Biyen: Lieder Facsimile Riesencodex (HS. 2) der Hessische Landesbibliotek Wiesbaden 1998, 'Die musikalische Überlieferung aus dem Kloster Reichenau im 11. Jahrhundert und die kompositorische Tätigkeit des Abtes Bern (1008–1048)' in Pass & Rausch, Beiträge zur Musik, Musiktheorie und Liturgie der Abtei Reichenau 2001, Die Musikgeschichte der Abtei Reichenau im 10. und 11. Jahrhundert: ein Versuch 2003. *Address:* Institut für Musikwissenschaft, Bismarckstr 1, 91054 Erlangen (office); Hartmannstr 105, 91052 Erlangen, Germany (home). *Telephone:* 9131 8522906 (office); 913132084 (home). *Fax:* 9131 8522403 (office).

**KLAS, Eri;** Estonian conductor; b. 7 June 1939, Tallinn; s. of Eduard Klas and Anna Klas; m.; one d. *Education:* Tallinn State Conservatory, studied at Leningrad State Conservatory with Nikolai Rabinovich. *Career:* percussionist, Estonian State Symphony Orchestra 1959–65; Asst Conductor to Boris Khaikin Bolshoi Theatre, Moscow 1969–72; Conductor Orchestra of Estonian Radio 1964–70; Conductor Nat. Opera Theatre Estonia 1965–, Music Dir 1975–95, Laureate Conductor 1996–; conducted more than 100 symphony orchestras in 40 different countries; Music Dir Royal Opera, Stockholm 1985–89; Prin. Guest Conductor Finnish Nat. Opera 1990–; Chief Conductor Århus Symphony Orchestra, Denmark 1991–96; Prof., Sibelius Acad. Helsinki 1994–; Music Dir Orchestra of Dutch Radio 1996–; Artistic Dir and Prin. Conductor Tampere Philharmonic Orchestra 1998–; Musical Adviser, Israel Sinfonietta 1999–; Chair. Bd Estonia Nat. Cultural Foundation 1991–; conducted at the Nobel Prize Ceremonial Concert in Stockholm 1989. *Repertoire includes:* more than 50 operas, operettas, musicals and ballets. *Honours:* Order of Nordstjernen (Sweden), Order of the Finnish Lion, Order of the White Star (Estonia); Dr hc (Estonian Acad. of Music) 1994. *Address:* Nurme str. 54, 11616 Tallinn, Estonia. *Telephone:* (2) 504-3444. *Website:* www .erkf.ee (office).

**KLATZOW, Peter;** Composer; b. 14 July 1945, Springs, South Africa. *Education:* Studied in Johannesburg, with Bernard Stevens at the RCM, London, and with Nadia Boulanger in Paris. *Career:* Rhodescan Broadcasting Corporation, producer; Cape Town University from 1973 (Associate Professor 1979); Founder of UCT Contemporary Music Society, 1974. *Compositions include:* Piano Sonata, 1969; In Memoriam, for soprano and strings, 1970; Interactions I for piano, percussion and ensemble, 1971; Symphony 'Phoenix', 1972; The Temptations of St Anthony for cello and orchestra, 1972; Time Structure I, for piano (1973), II for tape and orchestra, 1974; Still Life with Moonbeams for orchestra, 1975; Gardens of Memories and Discoveries for soprano and tape, 1975; 2 string quartets (1977, 1997); Concertos for Organ (1986), Marimba (1985) Clarinet (1989), and Piano with 8 instruments (1995); Hamlet, ballet, 1992; A Mass for Africa, 1994; Prayers and Dances from Africa, for chorus and brass quintet, 1996. *Publications include:* Composers in South Africa Today, editor, 1987. *Address:* c/o New Music SA, PO Box 7004, Grahamstown North 6148, South Africa.

**KLEBE, Giselher;** German composer; b. 28 June 1925, Mannheim; s. of Franz Klebe and Gertrud Michaelis Klebe; m. Lore Schiller 1946; two d. *Education:* Berlin Conservatoire and with Boris Blacher. *Career:* Composer in Berlin until 1957; Prof. of Composition and Theory of Music, Nordwest-deutsche Musik-Akademie, Detmold 1957–; mem. Acad. of Arts, Berlin and Hamburg, Bavarian Acad. of Fine Arts 1978; Pres. Berlin Acad. of Arts 1986–89. *Principal works:* Operas: Die Räuber (Schiller) 1957, Die tödlichen Wünsche (Balzac) 1959, Die Ermordung Cäsars (Shakespeare) 1959, Alkmene (Kleist) 1961, Figaro lässt sich scheiden (Ödön von Horvath) 1963, Jacobowsky und der Oberst (Werfel) 1965, Das Märchen von der Schönen Lilie (nach Goethe) 1969, Ein wahrer Held (Synge/Böll) 1975, Das Mädchen aus Domrémy (Schiller) 1976, Rendezvous (Sostshenkov) 1977, Der jüngste Tag (Ödön von Horvath) 1980, Die Fastnachtsbeichte (nach Zuckmayer) 1983, Gervaise Macquart (after Zola) 1995; Ballets: Signale 1955, Menagerie 1958, Das Testament (nach F. Villon) 1970; Orchestral Works: Zwitschermaschine 1950, Deux Nocturnes 1952, 7 symphonies 1952, 1953, 1967, 1971, 1977, 1995, 2003, Adagio und Fuge (with theme from Wagner's Walküre) 1962, Herzschläge (for Beatband and Symphony Orchestra), Konzert für Cembalo

mit elektrischen Klangveränderungen und kleines Orchester 1972, Orpheus (Dramatic scenes for orchestra) 1976, Salutations 1981, Boogie Agitato 1981, Concerto for Clarinet and Orchestra op. 92; Songs: Fünf Lieder 1962, Vier Vocalisen für Frauenchor 1963, La Tomba di Igor Stravinsky (for oboe and chamber orch.) 1979, Concerto for organ and orchestra 1980, Concerto for harp and orchestra 1988, Concerto for 'cello and orchestra 1989, Poema Drammatico 1999, Mignon, concerto for violin and orchestra 2000; Church music: Missa (Miserere Nobis) 1964, Stabat Mater 1964, Messe (Gebet einer armen Seele) 1966, Beuge dich, du Menschenseele (after S. Lagerlöf) for Baritone and Organ, Choral und Te deum for Solo Soprano, Choir and Orchestra 1978, Weihnachtsoratorium 1989; Chamber Music: 3 String Quartets 1949, 1963, 1981, 2 Solo Violin Sonatas 1952 and 1955, 2 Sonatas for Violin and Piano 1953 and 1974, 'Römische Elegien' 1953, Piano Trio Elegia Appassionata 1955, Introitus, Aria et Alleluja for Organ 1964, Quintet for Piano and Strings quasi una fantasia 1967, Fantasie und Lobpreisung (for organ) 1970, Variationen über ein Thema von Hector Berlioz (for organ and three drummers) 1970, Sonate für Kontrabass und Klavier 1974, 'Nenia' for solo violin 1975, Der Dunkle Gedanke for Clarinets and Piano 1980, Klavierstücke für Sonya (piano) 1980, Feuersturz für Klavier (op. 91) 1983, Otto canti con rime di Michelangelo 2000, Poema Drammatico, Concerto per due pianoforti ed orchestra (op. 130) 2000, Poema Lirico per violino e pianoforte con orchestra d'archi (op. 136) 2001, Dorneukrőning after Tizian (for mezzo-soprano and orchestra) 2003. *Honours:* Bundesverdienstkreuz (1st Class) 1975, Grosses Bundesverdienstkreuz 1999; Berliner Kunstpreis 1952, Preis Musik im XX Jahrhundert, Rome 1954, Mauricio Fürst Preis (Sweden) 1959, Rompreis Villa Massimo 1962, Premio Marzotto, Valdiagno 1964. *Address:* Bruchstrasse 16, 32756 Detmold, Germany (home). *Telephone:* (30) 3900070 (office); (5231) 23414 (home).

**KLEE, Bernhard;** Conductor; b. 19 April 1936, Schleiz, Germany. *Education:* Studied piano, composition and conducting at the Cologne Conservatoire; Assistant to Otto Ackermann and Wolfgang Sawallisch at the Cologne opera house. *Career:* Debut: Cologne 1960, Die Zauberflöte; Early appointments in Salzburg, Oberhausen and Hanover; Music Director in Lubeck 1966–73; British debut at the Hamburg Opera at the 1969 Edinburgh Festival, Der fliegende Holländer; Chief Conductor of the North German Radio in Hanover 1976–79; General Music Director in Düsseldorf from 1977; Chief Guest Conductor of the BBC Philharmonic Orchestra 1985–89; Conducted the orchestra at the 1989 Promenade Concerts, with Berg's Three Pieces from Wozzeck and Mahler's 6th Symphony; Has conducted all the major German and London orchestras, the English Chamber Orchestra, Stockholm and Rotterdam Philharmonics, Zürich Tonhalle, RAI Rome, Vienna Symphony, and NHK Tokyo; US debut 1974, with the New York Philharmonic: has since conducted in San Francisco, Chicago, Detroit and Washington; Regular guest conductor at opera houses in Hamburg, Munich, Berlin, Covent Garden and Geneva; Festival engagements at Edinburgh, Salzburg, Netherlands, Hong Kong and Dubrovnik; Promenade Concerts, London 1991, Mozart's Clarinet Concerto and Bruckner's 9th Symphony (BBC Philharmonic). *Recordings:* extensive catalogue with Polydor and EMI. *Current Management:* Ingpen & Williams Ltd, 7 St George's Court, 131 Putney Bridge Road, London, SW15 2PA, England.

**KLEIBERG, Ståle;** Composer and Associate Professor; b. 8 March 1958, Stavanger, Norway; m. Åsta Ovregaard, 25 June 1982, 1 d. *Education:* Degree in Musicology, University of Oslo; Diploma in Composing, State Academy of Music, Oslo. *Career:* Associate Professor, University of Trondheim; mem, Norwegian Society of Composers. *Compositions:* 32 Opuses since 1981, many of which have been commissioned by leading orchestras and ensembles; Compositions include large works for full orchestra and church music as well as chamber works for various ensembles and solo works; Main Works: String Quartet, 1985; Stilla for orchestra and soprano/tenor, 1986; Two Poems by Montale, 1986; The Bell Reef, Symphony No. 1, 1991; The Rose Window, 1992; Dopo for cello and strings, 1993; Chamber Symphony, Symphony No. 2, 1996; Sonanza e Cadenza, 1998; Concerto for double bass and orchestra, 1999. *Recordings:* Sonetto di Tasso, 1992; Chamber Music, 1997; Dopo, 1998; The Rose Window, 1999 Publications: Form in Impressionism, 1985; The Music of Hans Abrahamsen, 1986; CPE Bach and The Individual Expression, 1989; Sturm und Drang as Style and Period Designation in Music History, 1991; Grieg's Slåtter, Op. 72: Change of Musical Style or New Concept of Nationality, Journal of the Royal Musical Association, 1996; A National Music by French Means, 1999; Following Grieg, 1999. *Address:* Stokkanhaugen 201, 7048 Trondheim, Norway.

**KLEIN, Judith;** Composer; b. 14 April 1943, Chicago, USA. *Education:* BA at Berkeley, CA, 1967; Basle Conservatory; MA, New York University, 1987; Teachers included Charles Dodge and Ruth Anderson. *Career:* Director, computer music studios and Instructor, Computer Music Composition, New York University; Consultant for Electro-Acoustic Music at the New York Public Library for the Performing Arts; Guest Lecturer at Cincinnati College Conservatory, Studio for Electronic Music, Basle; Guest Composer at the Brooklyn College Center for Computer Music; Founder Electro-Acoustic Music Archives at New York Library for the Performing Arts; Guest and Artist-in-Residence at Dartmouth College and Studio for Electronic Music, Basle; Guest Composer at Computer Music Centre at Columbia University 2000–. *Compositions include:* Little Piece, 1979; Dead End, 1979; Dream/Song, 1980; Journeys, art installation collaboration, 1982; The Mines of Falum, Part 1, 1983; God Bites, 1983; The Tell-Tale Heart, film music, after

Edgar Allan Poe, 1983; From the Journals of Felix Bosonnet, 1987; 88" for Nick, 1992; Elements 1 and 2, sound installation, 1993; The Wolves of Bays Mountain, 1998; Music for radio plays and theatre productions include Family Play, 1981; Unheile Dreifaltigkeit, 1983; Sound installations in collaboration with visual artists include Journeys, 1982 and Elements 1.2, 1984. *Honours:* Honours at Bourges Electro-Acoustic Music Competition, 1988, for Journals; Finalist, 16th Electro-Acoustic Music Competition, Bourges, 1998. *Address:* c/o ASCAP, ASCAP Building, One Lincoln Place, New York, NY 10023, ; 130 West 17th Street, New York NY 10011 USA. *E-mail:* jakmail@earthlink.net.

**KLEIN, Kenneth;** Music Director and Conductor; b. 5 Sept. 1939, Los Angeles, California, USA. *Education:* Graduated Magna cum Laude, University of Southern California; Stanford University. *Career:* Debut: Europe, 1970; Paris, 1974; Moscow, 1974; Vienna, 1975; Conductor, Stuttgart Ballet in Stuttgart and then the Metropolitan Opera in all major cities of the USA; Toured USSR, Romania and Sweden, 1971, 1972; Invited by Pablo Casals to conduct 4 concerts in Puerto Rico, 1974; Conducted Suisse Romande Orchestra, Lamoureux Orchestra, Paris, France, Vienna Symphony, Montreux Festival; Debut with American Symphony Orchestra at Carnegie Hall, New York; Bruckner Orchestra, Austria, 1978; Debut at Rome Festival, 1979; Debut with Philharmonia Orchestra, Royal Albert Hall, London, England, 1979; Florida Philharmonic, Miami, Florida, USA, 1980–81; Edmonton Symphony; Louisville Orchestra; North Carolina Symphony; Kansas City Philharmonic; San Francisco Chamber Orchestra; Music Director, conducting over 60 concerts per season, Guadalajara, Mexico; Music Director, New York Virtuosi, South Dakota Symphony and the Waterville Valley Festival; Has made numerous guest appearances world-wide.

**KLEIN, Lothar;** Composer and Professor of Composition; b. 27 Jan. 1932, Hanover, Germany. *Education:* PhD, Degree in Musicology and Composition, University of Minnesota, 1961. *Career:* As an undergraduate wrote music for many theatre and film productions; Professor of Composition, University of Toronto; Chairman, Graduate Studies in Music; Guest Lectures for 150th anniversary of Hochschule für Musik, Berlin, American Society for Aesthetics and Fulbright Commission. *Compositions include:* Stage Works: Canadiana 1980; Last Love 1950–56; Orpheus 1976; The Prodigal Son 1966; Orchestral: Appassionata for Orchestra 1958; The Bluebird 1952; Charivari: Music for an Imaginary Comedy 1966; Epitaphs for Orchestra 1963; Fanfares for Orchestra 1978; Musique a Go-Go 1966; Orchestral Suite from The Masque of Orianna, 1971; Presto for Orchestra, 1958; Rondo Giocoso for Orchestra 1964; Symmetries for Orchestra 1958; Symphonic Etudes (Symphony No. 3) 1972; Symphony No. 1, 1955; No. 2, 1966; Band: Divertimento for Band, 1953; Eroica: Variations on A Promethean Theme 1970; Gloria for Band 1961; Small Orchestra: Janizary Music 1970; Sinfonia Concertante 1956; String Orchestra: Passacaglia of The Zodiac 1971; Soloists with Orchestra: Boccherini Collage for Cello and Orchestra 1978; Concerto for Winds, Timpani and Strings, 1956; Design for Percussion and Orchestra 1970; Ecologues for Horn and Strings, 1954; Invention, Blues and Chase, 1975; Musica Antiqua, 1975; Music for Violin and Orchestra, 1972; Paganini Collage for Violin and Orchestra, 1967; Scenes for Timpani and Strings, 1979; Slices of Time, 1973; Le Tresor des Dieux, 1969; Trio Concertante, 1961; Voices with Orchestra: Dorick Musick, 1973; Herbstlieder, 1962; The Masque of Orianna, 1973; Meditations on The Passyoun, 1961; The Philosopher in The Kitchen, 1974; Voices of Earth; Chorus: 8 Madrigals 1957; An Exaltation, 1960; Good Night, 1970; A Little Book of Hours, 1962; 3 Ancient Folksongs, 1959; 3 Chinese Laments, 1968; 3 Pastoral Songs, 1963; 3 Reflections, 1976; Travellers, 1981; 2 Christmas Madrigals, 1961; numerous works for Solo Voices; Solo Voice with Instrumental Ensemble; Instrumental Ensemble, Instrumental Solos; Piano Works; Concerti Sacro for viola and orchestra, 1980; Symphonic Partita, 1985; Centre-Stage for wind ensemble, 1991; Trocadero for winds and piano, 1994; Hachcava-Memorial Meditations for bass, voice, harps, 3 percussion, 1979; The Jabberwock in Ogden Nash's Dining Room, 1992; Birds, Bells and Bees: An Emily Dickinson Quilt for soprano, alto and pianist, 1986; String Quartet No. 2 on poems of Wallace Stevens, 1991; Danceries for large orchestra, 1995; Market Cries for mixed chorus, 1998; Symphonia Harmoniae Celestium Revelationem for soprano, viola, harps and percussion, 1998. *Address:* PROCAN, 41 Valleybrook Drive, Don Mill, Ontario M3B 2S6, Canada.

**KLEINDIENST, Stella;** singer (soprano); b. 1957, Germany; m. Johannes Schaaf. *Education:* Studied at the Cologne Opera Studio. *Career:* Sang at the Bremen Opera, 1981–88, Deutsche Oper Berlin, 1988–89 and the Vienna Staatsoper from 1990; Sang in Musgrave's Voice of Ariadne at the 1981 Edinburgh Festival and in Zemlinsky's Der Kreidekreis at Amsterdam in 1986; Covent Garden in 1987 and 1989 as Cherubino in a production of Figaro by her husband; Further guest appearances at Stuttgart as Ariadne and at Geneva and Antwerp; Other roles include Mila in Janáček's Osud, Anne Trulove, Belinda in Dido and Aeneas and Weber's Agathe; Sang Boulotte in Offenbach's Barbe-bleue at Stuttgart, 1996; Marzelline in Fidelio, 1998.

**KLEMENS, Adam;** Composer and Conductor; b. 14 Jan. 1967, Prague, Czechoslovakia. *Education:* Composition, 1989, Conducting, 1994, Conservatoire, Prague; Composition, Academy of Performing Arts, Prague, 1994. *Career:* Debut: Composer, Sinfonia Lacrimosa, Piano Concerto, 1989; Conductor, Prague Conservatoire Symphony Orchestra, 1994; Conductor, Amy, with Lynn Barber (US Percussionist); With George Crumb, Night of the Four Moons, 1994; Suk Chamber Orchestra, 1997; Bambini di Praga, 1997; Teacher, Musical Theory, Prague Conservatoire, 1996–; mem. Association of Musical Artists; Jeunesses Musicales of the Czech Republic. *Compositions:*

Clarinet Sonata, 1987; Sinfonia Lacrimosa, 1989; Perspectives for Oboe Solo, 1992; Music for Four Players, 1993; Piano concerto, 1994; Windy Music for Wind Orchestra, 1995; Fantasy for Wind Quintet and Harp, 1997; Composer of Film and Theatre Music. *Honours:* 1st Prize, Composers Competition, Generace, 1989, 1990; 3rd Prize, Composers Competition, Czech Ministry of Culture, 1990. *Address:* Chudenicka 1080/12, 02 10200 Prague 10, Czech Republic.

**KLIMOV, Valery (Alexandrovich);** Violinist; b. 16 Oct. 1931, Kiev, USSR. *Education:* Studied with Mordkovich in Odessa, then joined David Oistrakh at the Moscow Conservatory, graduated 1959. *Career:* Prizewinner at competitions in Paris and Prague 1956; Soloist with Moscow Philharmonic 1957; Gold Medal Tchaikovsky Competition Moscow 1958; British debut with BBC Symphony Orchestra at the Royal Festival Hall 1967; Regular visits to America, Canada, Australia, Italy, Germany, Switzerland, Sweden; Appearances with such conductors as Ormandy, Svetlanov, Rozdestvensky, Temirkanov and Arvid Yansons; Other than the standard repertoire, plays music by Prokofiev, Khachaturian, Hindemith and Schnittke; Head of violin studies at the Moscow Conservatory 1975–. *Recordings include:* CD of the Khachaturian Concerto (Olympia). *Honours:* National Artist of the RSFSR 1972.

**KLINKOVA, Zhivka;** Composer; b. 30 July 1924, Samokov, Bulgaria. *Education:* Studied at the Sofia Academy and with Wagner-Régeny and Blacher in Berlin, 1960–68. *Career:* Performances of her stage works in Germany and elsewhere. *Compositions include:* Ballets and musicals: Kaliakra, 1966, Vietnamese Poem, 1972, Isle Of Dreams, 1978, Cyril And Methodius, 1981, Vassil Levski, 1992; Symphony, 1974; Piano Concerto, 1992; Olympic Endeavour, opera-ballet, 1995; Sofia, opera, 1996; Chamber and keyboard music. *Address:* c/o Musicautor, 63 Tzar Assen Street, 1463 Sofia, Bulgaria.

**KLINT, Jorgen;** Singer (Bass-baritone); b. 6 April 1931, Elmelund, Denmark. *Education:* Studied at the Odense Conservatory, 1971–73. *Career:* Debut: Jutland Opera, 1975, as Luther in Les Contes d'Hoffmann; Sang at the Royal Opera Copenhagen, from 1975 including Boris in Lady Macbeth, 1991, Faninal in Der Rosenkavalier, 1994; Sang Alberich in The Ring at Arhus, 1983–87; Other Wagner roles include Daland, the Dutchman and Titurel; Sang in The Ring for Jutland Opera, 1994–96; Other roles include Gremin, Sarastro, Pizarro, Rocco and Banquo; Nielsen's Samuel in Saul and David. *Recordings:* Nielsen's Maskarade; Saul and David. *Address:* Den Jyske Opera, Thomas Jensens Alle, DK 8000 Århus, Denmark.

**KLOBUCAR, Berislav;** Conductor; b. 28 Aug. 1924, Zagreb, Yugoslavia. *Education:* Studied in Salzburg with Lovro von Matacic and Clemens Krauss. *Career:* Assistant at Zagreb Opera 1943–51; Conducted at the Vienna Staatsoper from 1953; General Director Graz Opera, 1960–71; Bayreuth Festival, 1968–69, Die Meistersinger and Lohengrin; Metropolitan Opera, 1968, Der fliegende Holländer, Die Walküre and Lohengrin; Music Director, Royal Opera Stockholm, 1972–81; Principal Conductor, Nice Opera, 1983–; Conducted L'amore dei tre re at Palermo, 1989; Many appearances as guest conductor with leading orchestras. *Address:* Orchestre Philharmonique de Nice, Opéra de Nice, rue Saint-François de Paule, 06300 Nice, France.

**KLOS, Wolfgang;** Austrian violist and viola professor; *Vice-President, Universität für Musik und Darstellende Kunst;* b. 15 July 1953, Vienna; m. Olga Sommer 1982. *Education:* Univ. of Vienna, Musikhochschule, Vienna, masterclasses with M. Rostal, U. Koch, B. Giuranna. *Career:* leader, Viola Sections, Tonhalle Orchestra, Zürich, Switzerland 1977–81, Vienna Symphony Orchestra 1981–89; teacher, viola, chamber music and orchestra, Vorarlberg State Conservatory of Music, Feldkirch, Austria 1977–89; Prof., viola and chamber music and masterclasses, Vienna Musikhochschule 1988–91, Head of String Dept 1991–2002; Vice-Pres., Universität für Musik und Darstellende Kunst (University of Music and Performing Arts), Vienna 2002–; masterclasses, various locations world-wide; soloist worldwide 1975–; mem. Vienna String Trio, numerous concerts, radio, television recordings world-wide. *Recordings include:* gradually recording entire string trio repertory; numerous recordings with various orchestras and chamber music groups. *Honours:* Das Große Ehrenzeichen für Verdienste um die Republik Österreich (Austria) 2003. *Address:* c/o Universität für Musik und Darstellende Kunst, Anton-von-Webern-Platz 1, 1030 Vienna; Hainbugerstrasse 35, 1030, Vienna, Austria (home). *Telephone:* (1) 711-55-60-30 (office); (1) 712-93-77 (home). *Fax:* (1) 711-55-60-39 (office); (1) 712-93-77 (home). *E-mail:* klos@mdw.ac.at (office). *Website:* www.mdw.ac.at.

**KLOSINSKA, Izabella;** Singer (Soprano); b. 1959, Poland. *Education:* Studied at the Warsaw Academy. *Career:* Appearances with Warsaw National Opera as Roxana in King Roger, Micaela, Pamina, Mozart's Countess, and Mimi; Season 1989 in Moniuszko's Haunted Castle at Vienna and Cassandra in Les Troyens at Amsterdam; Season 1993–94 as Roxana at Cincinnati and Buffalo, New York; Mozart Gala at Vienna; Carnegie Hall and Cologne concerts, 1995; Lieder recitals and further concerts at many venues; Sang in Penderecki's Polish Requiem at the Viva il Canto Festival, Cieszyn, 1997. *Address:* c/o National Theatre, Plac Teatrainy 1, 00-950 Warsaw, Poland.

**KLOUBOVA, Zdena;** Singer (Soprano); b. 1963, Czechoslovakia. *Education:* Studied at the Prague Academy and at Zwickau. *Career:* Sang at the Smetana Theatre, Prague, from 1992, National Theatre from 1993; Roles have included Mozart's Blondchen, Susanna, Servilia, Queen of Night and Despina, Verdi's Gilda; Strauss's Zerbinetta and Sophie and the title role in The Cunning Little

Vixen; Guest appearances in Denmark, Russia, Israel and Japan; Many concert appearances, in repertory from Baroque to contemporary. *Recordings include:* Carmina Burana; Schnittke's Requiem; Bach Mass in B minor; Kitchen Boy in Rusalka, conducted by Charles Mackerras, 1998. *Address:* Prague National Theatre, PO Box 865, 11230 Prague 1, Czech Republic.

**KLÜGL, Michael;** music administrator; *Intendant, Staatsoper Hannover.* *Career:* Intendant Landestheater Linz, Austria –2006; Intendant, Staatsoper Hannover 2006–. *Address:* Staatsoper Hannover, Opernplatz 1, Hannover 30159, Germany (office). *Telephone:* (511) 999-900 (office). *Website:* www.staatstheater-hannover.de (office).

**KLUSAK, Jan-Filip;** Composer; b. 18 April 1934, Prague, Czechoslovakia; m. Milena Kaizrova, 29 Mar 1979, 1 s. *Education:* Academy of Music, Dramatic Arts, Prague; Studied composition with Jaroslav Ridky and Pavel Borkovec, 1953–57. *Compositions include:* Published: Four Small Vocal Exercises, 1–11, for flute, 1965; Rondo for piano, 1967; Published and Recorded: Proverbs for Deep Voice and Wind Instruments, 1959; Pictures for 12 wind instruments, 1960; 1st Invention for chamber orchestra, 1961; 2nd String Quartet, 1961–62; Variation on a Theme by Gustav Mahler for orchestra, 1960–62; Sonata for violin and wind instruments, 1965–66; 6th Invention for Nonet, 1969; Invenzionetta per Flauto Solo, 1971; Monody in Memoriam Igor Stravinsky, 1972; 7th Invention for orchestra, 1973; 3rd String Quartet, 1975; Variations for two harps, 1982; Fantasia on Adam Michna of Otradovice for brass quintet and harp, 1983; Six Small Preludes for orchestra, Vor deinen Thron Tret ich Hiermit, 1984; What You Want, opera in 2 acts, 1984–85; The King with the Golden Mask, ballet, 1990; Hero and Leandros, ballet, 1988; Dämmerklarheit, Songs on Friedrich Rückert, 1988; 4th String Quartet, Mozart-Sickness, Fancy for chamber orchestra, 1991; Concerto for oboe and small orchestra, 1991; Tetragrammaton sive Nomina Eius for orchestra, 1992; Die Kunst des guten Zusammennspiels for wind, 1992; 5th string quartet, 1994; Ein Bericht für eine Akademie, opera in 1 act, 1993–97; It is a Paradise to Look At, symphonic poem, 1999; Bertram and Mescalinda, opera pasticcio in 1 act, 2002; GaDe, Fancy for violin, 2002; 6th String Quartet, 2003; Axiws temporum for orchestra, 2003. *Address:* Blanicka 26, 120-00 Prague 2, Czech Republic.

**KLUSON, Jospef;** Violist; b. 1953, Czechoslovakia. *Education:* Studied at the Prague Conservatory and Academy of Fine Arts. *Career:* Founder member of the Prazak-Quartet, 1972; Tours throughout Europe, America, Japan, Australia and New Zealand; Tours in the United Kingdom 1982, 1985, 1988, 1989, 1993 (Wigmore Hall, Queen Elizabeth Hall, Huddersfield Contemporary Music Festival); Recitals for BBC, Dutch Radio, Czech Radio, Radio France; Teaching: master classes at Orlando Festival, Mozart European Foundation, Antwerp, Bremen. *Honours:* First Prize in the Czech National String Quartet Competition, 1978; Grand Prix in Evian, 1978; Grand Prix at Prague Spring Competition, 1979. *Current Management:* Ingpen & Williams Ltd, 7 St George's Court, 131 Putney Bridge Road, London, SW15 2PA, England.

**KMENTT, Waldemar;** Singer (Tenor); b. 2 Feb. 1929, Vienna, Austria. *Education:* Studied at the Vienna Musikhochschule with Adolf Vogel, Elisabeth Rado and Hans Duhan. *Career:* Debut: Vienna 1950, in the Choral Symphony, conducted by Karl Böhm; Toured Europe with Viennese student group, appearing in Die Fledermaus and Le nozze di Figaro; Vienna Volksoper from 1951, debut as the Prince in The Love for Three Oranges: later roles in Vienna have included Belmonte, Don Ottavio, Ferrando, Idomeneo, Walther, Bacchus and the Emperor in Die Frau ohne Schatten; Sang Jacquino in Fidelio at the opening of the rebuilt Vienna Staatsoper, 1955; Salzburg Festival from 1955, in the premiere of Irische Legende by Egk and as Idamante (Idomeneo), Gabriel in Le Mystère de la Nativité by Martin, Ferrando and Tamino; Bayreuth Festival 1968–70, as Walther von Stolzing; Further engagements in Milan, Düsseldorf, Paris, Amsterdam, Munich and Stuttgart, and at the Drottningholm and Edinburgh Festivals; Sang Baron Zeta in Die lustige Witwe for Opéra National de Paris, 1997; Many concert appearances, notably in Das Lied von der Erde by Mahler. *Recordings:* Salome, Tiefland, Lulu, Bastien et Bastienne, Così fan tutte (Philips); Beethoven's Missa solemnis (Electrola); Die Fledermaus, Das Rheingold, Arabella, Tristan und Isolde (Decca); Video of Turandot from the Vienna Staatsoper, 1983. *Address:* c/o Staatsoper, Opernring 2, 1010 Vienna, Austria.

**KNAIFEL, Alexander Aronovich;** Russian composer; b. 28 Nov. 1943, Tashkent; s. of Aron Iosifovich Knaifel and Muza Veniaminovna Shapiro-Knaifel; m. Tatiana Ivanova Melentieva 1965; one d. *Education:* Moscow and Leningrad Conservatoires. *Career:* freelance composer; mem. Composers Union 1968–, Cinematographers Union 1987–. *Compositions:* Diada (Two Pieces) 1962, Classical Suite 1963, Ostinati 1964, Five Poems by Mikhail Lermontov 1964, Angel 1964, Musique militaire 1964, The Coming City of the Seeking After 1964, Passacaglia 1965, The Canterville Ghost 1965–66, Disarmament 1966, 150 000 000 1966, Lamento 1967, The Petrograd Sparrows 1967, Monodia 1968, Medea 1968, Argumentum de jure 1969, Joan 1970–78, A prima vista 1972, Status nascendi 1975, Ainana 1978, Rafferti 1980, Vera (Faith) 1980, Solaris 1980, Da (Yes) 1980, A Silly Horse 1981, A Chance Occurrence 1982, Pagan Fate 1982, Nika 1983–84, Counteraction 1984, God 1985, Agnus Dei 1985, Wings of a Serf 1986, Madness 1987, Through the Rainbow of Involuntary Tears 1987–88, Litania 1988, Shramy marsha (Scars of march) 1988, Voznosheniye (The Holy Oblation) 1991, Svete Tikhiy (O Gladsome Light) 1991, Postludia 1992, Once Again on the Hypothesis 1992, Scalae Iacobis 1992, Chapter Eight 1993, Maranatha

1993, Cantus 1993, Butterfly 1993, In Air Clear and Unseen 1994, Prayers to the Holy Spirit 1994–95, Alice in Wonderland 1994–2002, Psalm 51 (50) 1995, Amicta sole 1995, The Beatitudes 1996, Bliss 1997, Lux aeterna 1997, This Child 1997, Tabernacle 1998, With the White on the White 1998, Snowflake on a Spiderthread 1998, Daylight 1999, Small Blue Feathers 2001, Morning Prayers 2001, Entrance 2001, Fairytale of a Fisherman and a Little Fish 2002, Avowal of Love 2003, Nativiti 2003, Lukomoriye 2003, The Cherubimic Hymn 2004, Here! 2004, Old Photos 2004, The Little Beads for Charlie 2004, Fairytale of the Pope and of his Workman Balda 2004; incidental music for 40 films. *Publications:* Musique militaire 1974, Diada (Two Pieces) 1975, Classical Suite 1976, The Canterville Ghost 1977, Five Poems by Mikhail Lermontov 1978, Lamento 1979, The Petrograd Sparrows 1981, A Silly Horse 1985, Medea 1989, Vera (Faith) 1990, Passacaglia 1990, Da (Yes) 1991, O Comforter 1997, Bliss 1997. *Honours:* DAAD Honoured Grant-Aided Composer, Berlin 1993, Honoured Art Worker of Russia 1996. *Address:* Skobelevski pr. 5, Apt 130, 194214 St Petersburg, Russia (home). *Telephone:* (812) 553-82-68 (home). *Fax:* (812) 373-48-92 (office); (812) 553-53-97 (home). *E-mail:* knaifel@hotmail.com (office); knaifel@yahoo.de (home). *Website:* www.ceo.spb.ru/rus/music/knaifel.a.a (office).

**KNAPP, Peter;** Opera Singer (Baritone) and Director; b. 4 Aug. 1947, St Albans, England; m. Mary Anne Tennyson, 2 June 1984, 1 s. *Education:* St Albans School; St John's College, Cambridge. *Career:* Debut: Glyndebourne Touring Company; Kent Opera: Monteverdi's Orfeo (televised on BBC); Eugene Onegin; Don Giovanni; La Traviata; English National Opera: Don Giovanni; La Traviata; English National Opera: Don Giovanni; The Marriage of Figaro; Abroad: Sofia, Zürich, Frankfurt, Venice, Florence; Tour of Australia; Regular Broadcasts; 1978 began directing own opera company—La Périchole filmed for BBC television; 1988/89 2 week season at Sadler's Wells Theatre, London, 1989; sang Mozart's Figaro, 1989, Zelta in The Merry Widow for Scottish Opera, sang Wolfram in Tannhäuser for New Sussex Opera, 1990; Made version of Carmen for Travelling Opera, 1992. *Recordings:* Monteverdi Vespers; De Falla Master Peter's Puppet Show. *Publications:* Translations of Così fan tutte, The Marriage of Figaro, La Périochole, Orpheus in the Underworld, La Bohème, The Barber of Seville. *Honours:* First Benson and Hedges Gold Award, 1977. *Address:* Kaye Artists Management, Barratt House, 7 Chertsey Road, Woking GV21 5 AB, England.

**KNEZKOVA-HUSSEY, Ludmila;** Concert Pianist, Composer, Choral Conductor, Chamber Performer and Clinician; b. 22 April 1956, Mukacevo, Ukraine; m. Bernard Hussey, 17 Nov 1990, 1 d. *Education:* Doctorate in Music, Lvov Central Music School; Moscow Music School; Tchaikovsky Conservatory, Moscow; Academy of Music, Prague; Studies: France, 1986 and 1987; Germany, 1989 and 1990; Banff Centre School of Fine Arts, Canada, 1992. *Career:* Many recitals and concert engagements with leading orchestras in USA, Canada, Germany, Italy, Russia, Czech Republic, Slovakia, Austria, Hungary, Poland, Ukraine, Switzerland; Television and radio appearances in Canada, USA, Czech Republic, Russia, Latvia, Austria, Germany, Italy, Ukraine; In 1993 established the Ludmilla Knezkova-Hussey International Piano Competition which attracts many gifted and talented students from all over the world and is held every two years. *Recordings include:* Original compositions: Symphonic Fantasy for orchestra, 1985; Sonata for piano and flute, 1986; Compositions for a chorus, 1986; Symphonic Ballad for orchestra, 1988; Fantaisie for piano and orchestra, 1991; Moods of Mustique, 2000; If This Be Love, for piano, soprano and violin, 2000; St Andrews Anthology for piano, soprano and orchestra, 2001; CDs, Canada, 1994, 2000; Many recordings in Europe. *Address:* 155 Allison Crescent, Bathurst, NB E2A 3B4, Canada.

**KNIAZEV, Alexander A.;** Russian cellist; b. 21 April 1961, s. of Alexandre S. Schwarzmann and Ludmila P. Kniazeva; m. (deceased). *Education:* Moscow State Conservatory, Nyzhny-Novgorod State Conservatory. *Career:* Prof. Moscow State Conservatory 1995; masterclasses in France, Spain, Republic of Korea, Philippines; concerts 1978–, in Russia, UK, France, Germany, Italy, Spain, Belgium, Austria, USA, S Africa, S America, Republic of Korea, Japan and elsewhere; performed with partners V. Afanasyev, S. Milstein, E. Leonskaya, B. Engerer, Kun Woo Oark, V. Spivakov, V. Tretyakov, M. Brunello, Yu. Bashmet, Yu. Milkis. *Honours:* First Prize Nat. Competition, Vilnius, Lithuania 1977, Third Prize G. Cassado Int. Competition, Florence, Italy 1979, First Prize Int. Chamber Music Competition, Trapani, Italy 1987, Second Prize Tchaikovsky Int. Competition, Moscow, Russia 1990, First Prize Unisa Int. Competition, Pretoria, S Africa. *Address:* Skornyzhny per. 1, apt 58, Moscow 107078, Russia (home).

**KNIE, Roberta;** Singer (Soprano); b. 13 May 1938, Cordell, Oklahoma, USA. *Education:* Studied at Oklahoma University with Elisabeth Parham, Judy Bounds-Coleman and Eva Turner. *Career:* Debut: Hagen (Germany) 1964, as Elisabeth in Tannhäuser; Sang at Freiburg, 1966–69; Graz Opera, 1969, as Salome, Tosca and Leonore; Zürich and Nice, 1972–73, as Brünnhilde; Metropolitan Opera from 1975; Guest appearances in Kassel, Mannheim, Montreal, Buenos Aires, Brussels, Barcelona, Hamburg, Berlin, Munich and Stuttgart; Other roles include Isolde, Senta, Elsa, Sieglinde, Donna Anna, Elektra, the Marschallin, Lisa in The Queen of Spades, Electra in Idomeneo and both Leonoras of Verdi. *Recordings include:* Isolde in Tristan und Isolde.

**KNIGHT, Daniel,** BFA; British singer (bass, bass-baritone), voice teacher and artistic and musical director; b. (Nicolino Giacalone), 28 Nov. 1956, Montréal, Canada. *Education:* Marianopolis Coll., McGill Univ., Conservatoire de

Musique, Québec, Concordia Univ.; studied singing with Benjamin Luxon, Vera Rozsa, James Bowman, Rita Streich, Max van Egmond, Daniel Ferro and Emma Kirkby. *Career:* Dir, Dido and Aeneas, Waltham Abbey 1995; singing, St John's Smith Square, London 1997; BBC radio debut, Glenn Gould, Bach; private singing teacher, masterclasses in Canada, USA, Ireland, England 1974–; singing, modern world premiere singing title role of full staged complete performance of Purcell's Dioclesian, Dartington and Croatia with Paul Goodwin conducting 1995, 19th- and 20th-Century Austrian Lieder to mark Austria's Thousand Years 1996; Artistic Dir, founding mem., Handel Opera Company 1995; recital and voice masterclass, Houston, TX 1999; Musical Dir, Artistic Dir and Chair. of Handel Opera Company Ltd. *Recordings:* Music of the Second Generation 1995, Dioclesian by H. Purcell 1995, Baroque Opera Arias for Bass 1997. *Publications:* A Scarlatti Cantatas and Serenatas 1997, articles on singing in NODA London News. *Address:* Flat 3, Regina House, 65 Wimpole Street, London, W1G 8AN, England (home). *Telephone:* (20) 7487 2892. *E-mail:* danielknight@angelsong.co.uk. *Website:* www.danielknight.net.

**KNIGHT, Gillian,** LRAM, BA; Singer (mezzo-soprano); b. 1 Nov. 1939, Redditch, Worcestershire, England. *Education:* Royal Academy of Music, London, Open University. *Career:* D'Oyly Carte Opera, 1959–64, sang in contralto roles as Katisha (Mikado), Ruth (Pirates of Penzance), and Lady Jane (Patience); Sadler's Wells/English National Opera as Suzuki in Butterfly, Ragone (Comte Ory), Juno (Semele) and Carmen; Covent Garden from 1970, in the premiere of Maxwell Davies' Taverner, 1972, Der Ring des Nibelungen, Rigoletto, Eugene Onegin and Semele, 1988; Paris Opéra debut, 1978, in Die Zauberflöte; US debut, 1979, as Olga in Eugene Onegin at Tanglewood: Tours of USA singing Gilbert and Sullivan; Season 1986/87 Gertrude in Hamlet for Pittsburgh Opera; Nurse in Die Frau ohne Schatten for Welsh National Opera, 1989; Sang the Forester's Wife in The Cunning Little Vixen at Covent Garden; France: Rouen, Lile, Nantes, Avignon, Tours, Paris, Toulouse (Carmen, Don Quixote, Werther); Germany: Frankfurt, Ulrica in Ballo in Maschera; Spain: Carmen with Domingo in Valencia and Zaragoza; Switzerland: Rigoletto, Geneva; Sang Marguérite in La Dame Blanche at the 1990 Wexford Festival; Sang the title role in the British premiere of Gerhard's The Duenna, Opera North, 1992; Third Maid in Elektra at the First Night of the 1993 London Proms; Sang Annina in La Traviata at Covent Garden, 1996; Roméo et Juliette, 2000; Concert engagements with conductors such as Bertini, Boulez, Colin Davis, Charles Groves and Solti. *Recordings:* Six Gilbert and Sullivan roles; Messiah; Damnation of Faust and Mozart Masses with Colin Davis; Schoenberg's Moses und Aron with Boulez; Suor Angelica, Il Tabarro and Madama Butterfly with Maazel; La Forza del Destino with Levine. *Address:* c/o Royal Opera House (Contracts), Covent Garden, London WC2E 9DD, England.

**KNIGHT, Katherine;** Cellist; b. 1960, USA. *Education:* Johns Hopkins University; New England Conservatory. *Career:* Co-Founder, Da Vinci Quartet, 1980, under the sponsorship of the Fine Arts Quartet; Many concerts in the USA and elsewhere in a repertoire including works by Mozart, Beethoven, Brahms, Dvořák, Shostakovich and Bartók. *Honours:* With the Da Vinci Quartet: Grants from the NEA, Western States Arts Foundation and Colorado Council for the Humanities; Artist-in-Residence, University of Colorado. *Current Management:* Sonata, Glasgow, Scotland. *Address:* c/o Da Vinci Quartet, 11 Northpark Street, Glasgow G20 7AA, Scotland.

**KNIGHT, Mark Anthony;** British professor of violin and viola; b. 24 April 1941, Worcestershire, England; m. Patricia Noall 1965; one s. one d. *Education:* Guildhall School of Music and Drama, London, Tanglewood International Summer School, Massachusetts, USA. *Career:* debut in Brighton, 1962; freelance violinist, 1965–69, including London Philharmonic Orchestra; Leader, New Cantata Orchestra of London, 1966–69; Senior String Tutor, Wells Cathedral School, Wells, Somerset, 1975–88; Professor of Violin, Viola and Chamber Music, Guildhall School of Music and Drama, London, 1976–; several radio and television broadcasts. *Compositions:* Cadenzas: for Mozart's Violin Concertos No. 1 in B flat, K207, and No. 2 in D, K211; for Karl Stamitz's Viola Concerto in D; for Hoffmeister's Viola Concerto in D; for Haydn's Cello Concerto in C; for Mozart's Horn Concerto in E flat K495 for both valve and natural horn; Transcriptions for viola of Haydn's Cello Concerto in C with cadenzas; Geoffrey Burgon's Six Studies for solo cello. *Recordings:* A Boy Is Born, as Conductor of Wells Cathedral School Chamber Orchestra, 1977. *Publications:* Editor: Violin Sonatas Op 5 by Archangelo Corelli, 1991; 42 Violin Studies by Rodolphe Kreutzer, 1992. *Current Management:* Strings Attached Ltd, Great Skewes Cottage, St Wenn, Bodmin, Cornwall PL30 5PS, England.

**KNIPLOVA, Nadezda;** Singer (Soprano); b. 18 April 1932, Ostrava, Czechoslovakia. *Education:* Studied at the Prague Conservatory with Jarmila Vavrdova and at the Academy of Musical Arts with K Ungrova and Zdenek Otava. *Career:* Sang at Usti nad Labem 1956–59 and the Janáček Opera Brno (1959–64), notably as Renata in The Fiery Angel, Katerina in The Greek Passion and Katerina Izmailova; Principal of The Prague National Theatre from 1965: roles included the Kostelnicka in Jenůfa, Brünnhilde, Leonore, Milada (Dalibor), Libuše, Emilia Marty, Isolde, Tosca, Aida and Senta; Guest appearances in Salzburg (Brünnhilde, 1967), Barcelona (as Isolde), Turin (in Götterdämmerung) Berlin, Hamburg, New York and San Francisco (Die Walküre); Sang with the Berlin Staatsoper on tour in Japan; Janáček's Glagolitic Mass at the 1971 Salzburg Festival. *Recordings:* Jenůfa, Libuše, Dalibor, Orfeo ed Euridice; Katya Kabanova; Der Ring des Nibelungen.

*Honours:* Prizewinner at competitions in Geneva (1958), Vienna (1959) and Toulouse (1959); Czech Artist of Merit, 1970. *Address:* National Theatre, PO Box 865, 11230 Prague 1, Czech Republic.

**KNITTEL, Krzysztof;** Composer; b. 1 May 1947, Warsaw, Poland. *Education:* Warsaw Academy of Music, 1966–77, with Tadeusz Baird. *Career:* Experimental Studio of Polish Radio, 1973–; co-founder of various electro-acoustic and improvised music groups in Poland; Director of Warsaw Autumn Festival, 1995–98; President of Union of Polish Composers, 1999. *Compositions include:* String Quartet, 1976; Women's Voice, ballet, 1980; Low Sounds nos 1–5, 1979–91; Norcet 1 and 2, for tape, 1980; Black Water, White Water, Old Stream for instruments and tape, 1983; String quartet, with tape and percussion, 1985; 14 Variations on 14 Words by John Cage, 1986–92; Three songs Without Words, for soprano and tape, 1987; Nibiru, for strings and harpsichord, 1987; Histoire I–III, 1988–90; Borders of Nothing, computers, 1990; Instant reactions, for ensemble and computer, 1992; Satan in Goray, ballet, 1993; Legs, sound installation, 1993; Sonata da Camera 1–3, 1994–95; Radio Sculpture, 1994; Der Erwählte, ballet after Thoman Mann, 1995. *Honours:* Solidarity Prize, 1985. *Address:* c/o Polish Cultural Institute, 23 Portland Place, London WIN 4 HQ, England.

**KNIZIA, Martin;** Organist and Harpsichordist; b. 1960, England. *Education:* Organ with David Titterington and Martin Haselböck; Harpsichord and conducting at Lübeck and the Royal Academy, London. *Career:* Organ and harpsichord soloist, and continuo playing, with London Sinfonia, London Mozart Players and other orchestras; Founder of the Sweelink Ensemble, performing at St Martin-in-the-Fields, St James's Church, Brompton Oratory, and for the London Bach Festival; Assistant Director for the English Bach Festival, Lully/Molière Bourgeois Gentilhomme, Linbury Theatre Covent Garden, 2001; Teacher of figured bass and baroque organ improvisation, Royal Academy. *Publications include:* Editions of organ works by Orlando Gibbons (Universal). *Honours:* Foundation Fellowship, RAM. *Address:* c/o English Bach Festival, 15 South Eaton Place, London, SW1W 9ER, England.

**KNOBEL, Marita;** Singer (Mezzo-soprano); b. 1947, Johannesburg, South Africa. *Education:* Studied in Pretoria and at the London Opera Centre. *Career:* Sanga at the Cologne Opera 1973–85, notably as Auntie in Peter Grimes, Magdalene in Meistersinger and Mother Goose in The Rake's Progress; Guest appearances in Düsseldorf, Dresden, Basle, Barcelona and Edinburgh; Sang at the Munich Staatsoper 1990–91 and at the Vienna Staatsoper from 1992, in such roles as Suzuki, Fidalma (Matrimonio Segreto) and the Witch in Hansel and Gretel. *Address:* c/o Staatsoper, Opernring 2, 1010 Vienna, Austria.

**KNODT, Erich;** Singer (bass); b. 1945, Germany. *Education:* Studied in Koblenz. *Career:* Sang at the Stadttheater Koblenz, 1970–72; Wuppertal, 1972–76, Mannheim, 1976–87; Guest appearances at Düsseldorf, Hamburg, Stuttgrt, Brussels, 1989, Paris, Barcelona, Strasbourg and Madrid; Bregenz and Aix-en-Provence Festivals, 1985, 1989, as Sarastro; Wagner repertoire includes King Mark, Lisbon 1985, King Henry in Lohengrin, 1986, Hunding, Lisbon, 1989, Pogner and Hagen; also sang Mozart's Commendatore, Rocco, King Philip, Boris Godunov, Banquo and Ramphis (Bordeaux 1989); Sang Peneois in a concert performance of Daphne at Rome, 1991; Sarastro at Bordeaux, Pogner at Trieste and Roldano in Franchetti's Christoforo Colombo at the Montpellier Festival, 1992; Sang King Mark in Tristan und Isolde at Trieste, 1996. Many further concert engagements. *Address:* Nationaltheater, Am Goethplatz, 6800 Mannheim, Germany.

**KNOX, Garth Alexander,** ARCM; violist; b. 8 Oct. 1956, Dublin, Ireland. *Education:* Royal Coll. of Music, London, studied with Frederick Riddle, masterclasses with Paul Doktor and Peter Schidloff. *Career:* mem., English Chamber Orchestra 1979–81, and of London Sinfonietta; dedicatee and first performance of Henze's Viola Sonata, Witten 1981; first performance of James Dillon's Timelag Zero, Brighton 1981; guest principal viola, Opera La Fenice, Venice 1981–83; performances of Harold in Italy and Jonathon Lloyd's Viola Concerto with Danish Radio Symphony Orchestra, Copenhagen 1982; mem., Pierre Boulez's Ensemble Intercontemporain, Paris 1983–90; concertos by Luciano Berio and Marc-Andre Dalbavie conducted by Pierre Boulez in Bordeaux, Lisbon, Paris and New York; concerto by Karl-Amadeus Hartmann, Théâtre du Rond-Point, Paris 1987; tour of USSR with Jan Latham Koenig playing Shostakovich Viola Sonata 1987; first performance of Donatoni's La Souris sans Sourire with Quator Ensemble Intercontemporain, Paris 1989; mem., Arditti String Quartet 1990–98, premiering quartets by Ferneyhough (No. 4), Goehr (No. 4), Xenakis' Tetora and Feldman's Quintet; first performance of Ligeti's Loop for solo viola 1991; solo career 1998–. *Recordings:* Henze's Viola Sonata 1981, Schoenberg's Verklärte Nacht (supervised by Boulez), Embellie for solo viola (by Iannis Xenakis), Bruno Maderna. *Address:* 3 rue Saigne, 93100 Montreuil, France.

**KNUSSEN, (Stuart) Oliver,** CBE; British composer and conductor; b. 12 June 1952, Glasgow; s. of Stuart Knussen and Ethelyn Jane Alexander; m. Susan Freedman 1972; one d. *Education:* Watford Field School, Watford Boys Grammar School, Purcell School. *Career:* pvt. composition study with John Lambert 1963–68; conducted first performance of his First Symphony with London Symphony Orchestra 1968; Fellowships to Berkshire Music Center, Tanglewood, USA 1970, 1971, 1973; Caird Travelling Scholarship 1971; Head of Contemporary Music Activities, Tanglewood Music Center 1986–93; Co-Artistic Dir Aldeburgh Festival 1983–98; Music Dir London Sinfonietta 1998–2002, Conductor Laureate 2002–. *Compositions include:* operas: Where the Wild Things Are 1979–81, Higglety Pigglety Pop! 1984–85; symphonies: Symphony in one movement 1969, No. 2 (soprano and small orchestra) 1970–71, No. 3 1973–79; other works for chamber ensemble and for voice and ensemble, for orchestra and for piano. *Honours:* Hon. mem. American Acad. of Arts and Letters 1994, Royal Philharmonic Soc. 2002; Dr hc (Royal Scottish Acad. of Music and Drama) 2002; Countess of Munster Awards 1964, 1965, 1967; Peter Stuyvesant Foundation Award 1965; Watney-Sargent Award for Young Conductors 1969; Margaret Grant Composition Prize (for Symphony No. 2), Tanglewood 1971; Arts Council Bursaries 1979, 1981; winner, first Park Lane Group Composer Award 1982. *Address:* c/o Harrison/Parrott Ltd, 12 Penzance Place, London, W11 4PA (office); c/o Faber Music Ltd, 3 Queen Square, London, WC1N 3AR, England.

**KNUTSON, David;** Singer (Tenor); b. 19 March 1946, Wisconsin, USA. *Education:* Studied in Wisconsin. *Career:* Has sung in West Germany from 1971; Sang lyric roles at the Deutsche Oper Berlin from 1972; Guest appearances in Hamburg; Munich 1978, in the premiere of Lear by Reimann; Berlin 1975 and 1980, in the local premieres of La Calisto by Cavalli and Hippolyte et Aricie by Rameau; Spoleto Festival 1986, as the Witch in Hansel and Gretel; Sang Bishop Abdisu in Pfitzner's Palestrina, Berlin, 1996. *Recordings include:* Lear (Deutsche Grammophon). *Address:* c/o Deutsche Oper Berlin, Richard Wagner Strasse 10, 1000 Berlin, Germany.

**KOBAYASHI, Junko;** Concert Pianist; b. Sept. 1960, Kobe, Japan. *Education:* Osaka College of Music; Essen Musik Hochschule, Germany; Studied with Maria Curcio and Louis Kentner. *Career:* Debut: Royal Festival Hall, London, 1988; The Purcell Room Recitals, 1983–93; St John's, Smith Square concerts 1995–2001; Appearances in England, Germany, France, Denmark, Bulgaria, Poland, Thailand, Canada, USA, Venezuela, Zambia and Japan; Played with orchestras such as the London Philharmonic Orchestra, the Osaka Philharmonic Orchestra, the New Philharmonic Orchestra, The Academy of St Nicholas, Polish Baltic Symphony Orchestra; Broadcasts on BBC Radio 3, WKAR Televion, USA, ZDF Television, Germany; mem, Founder-Chairman, Takemitsu Society, 1997–. *Contributions:* Essays to Kansei Music newspaper; Monthly music column for Pelican Club Europe. *Address:* 26 Sandown Road, West Malling, Kent ME19 6NS, England.

**KOBAYASHI, Ken-Ichiro;** Conductor; b. 9 April 1940, Fukushima, Japan. *Education:* University of Fine Arts and Music at Tokyo, 1960–64, notably with Akeo Watanabe. *Career:* Debut: Tokyo Symphony Orchestra, 1972; Music Director of the Metropolitan Symphony Orchestra, Tokyo, then Symphony Orchestra of Kyoto (1985–90); Principal Guest with the Tokyo Symphony and Professor at the Tokyo College of Music; Many appearances with European orchestras, notably the Amsterdam Philharmonic and other Dutch ensembles; Succeeded Janos Ferencsik as Permanent Conductor of the Hungarian National Philharmonic Orchestra, 1987. *Honours:* Prizewinner, International Competition Min-On, Tokyo, 1970; Budapest International Competition, 1974. *Address:* c/o Hungarian Philharmonic Orchestra, Vorosmarty ter. 1 1051 Budapest, Hungary.

**KOBAYASHI, Marie;** Singer (Mezzo-soprano); b. 31 Aug. 1955, Kamakura, Japan. *Education:* Arts and Music National University, Tokyo; National Conservatory of Music, Paris. *Career:* Debut: With 2E2M, International Contemporary Music Festival, Strasbourg, 1983; Appearances: C R Alsina's Prima Sinfonia, Radio France concert with National Orchestra of France, 1985; Satie's La Mort de Socrate, Radio France concert with Nouvel Orchestre Philharmonique, 1989; Smeton in Donizetti's Anna Bolena, Nimes, 1989; Birtwistle's Meridian with Pierre Boulez, Châtelet Theatre, 1990; J Fontyn's Roses des Sable, Radio Brussels (RTBF), 1991; Has sung in many concerts of oratorios by Bach, Handel, Rossini, Mozart, others. *Recordings:* Les Madrigaux of G Arrgo, 1990; Motets of Vivaldi, 1990; Mozart's Requiem, 1991. *Address:* 49 rue Riquet, Apt 2, 75019 Paris, France.

**KOBEKIN, Vladimir;** Composer; b. 22 July 1947, Sverdlovsk, Russia. *Education:* Studied with Sergei Slonimsky at the Leningrad Conservatory, graduating in 1971. *Career:* Teacher, Urals Conservatory, 1971–80. *Compositions include:* Swan Song, chamber opera after Chekhov, Moscow, 1980; Dairy of a Madman, mono-opera, Moscow 1980; The Boots, chamber opera, 1981; Pugachyov, musical tragedy, Leningrad, 1983; The Prophet, a Pushkin Triptych, Sverdlovsk 1984; Play about Maximilian, Eleanor and Ivan, Moscow, 1989; The Jester and the King, chamber opera, 1991; The Happy Prince, chamber opera after Wilde, 1991; A Tale of Witchcraft, opera, 1992; N.F.B., after The Idiot by Dostoyevsky, 1995; The Young David, opera, 1997; Moses, monodrama, 1999; Instrumental, choral and chamber music including Cello Concerto, 1997; Fantasia for piano and orchestra, 1999; The Seventh of September: Demons, symphonic poem, 1999. *Honours:* USSR State Prize, 1987, Honoured Artist of the RSFSR. *Address:* c/o RAO, Bolchaia Bronnai 6-a, Moscow 103670, Russia.

**KOBEL, Benedikt;** Singer (Tenor); b. 1960, Vienna, Austria. *Education:* Studied at the Vienna Musikhochschule and the Studio of the Staatsoper. *Career:* Sang in concert performances of Gurlitt's Wozzeck and Reimann's Gespenstersonate, Vienna 1985; Appearances throughout Austria and the Theater am Gärtnerplatz, Munich, in operettas by Lehar, Zeller, Oscar Straus and Johann Strauss; Vienna Volksoper 1991–92, as Don Ottavio, Camille in Dantons Tod, Tamino, Belmonte, Ferrando, Almaviva and Rinuccio; Vienna Staatsoper 1992, as Cassio in Otello and Narraboth, Flamand (Capriccio), Steuermann (Flying Dutchman). *Address:* c/o Volksoper, Wahringerstrasse 78, 1090 Vienna, Austria.

**KOBILZA, Siegfried;** Austrian classical guitarist; b. 24 Aug. 1954, Villach, Carinthia; m. Vera Kobilza-Schweder 1983. *Education:* Musisch-Padagogisches Realgymnasium, Hermagor, Academy of Music, Vienna, studied with Karl Scheit. *Career:* first concert tour, Austrian cities including Vienna, 1979; Recitals in main Austrian venues including Wiener Musikverein, Wiener Konzerthaus, Grosses Festspeilhaus Salzburg, Mozarteum Salzburg, Brucknerhaus Linz; Soloist with orchestras including Vienna Symphony, Mozarteumorchester Salzburg, Vienna Chamber Orchestra; Television and radio recordings; Teaching master classes, various European countries and China; Debuts in London, Paris, New York, 1982; Concert tours, Germany, Switzerland, the United Kingdom, France, Netherlands, Iceland, Yugoslavia, Hungary, USA, USSR, Czechoslovakia, Turkey, Tunisia, China. *Address:* Servitengasse 7/16, 1090 Vienna, Austria.

**KOBLER, Linda;** Harpsichordist; b. 1952, New York City, USA; m. Albert Glinsky, 10 June 1979. *Education:* BM, Peabody Conservatory of Music; MM, Juilliard School, 1977. *Career:* Debut: Carnegie Recital Hall, 1984; Concerto Soloist with: Zürich Chamber Orchestra, New York Chamber Orchestra, Broadway Bach Ensemble, American Baroque Ensemble, Bach Gesellchaft, Seabrook Chamber Players, Cathedral Orchestra, New York Chamber Symphony, Toronto Symphony; Former Member, Ensemble Tafelmusik Quartet; performances in New York, Ohio, New Jersey, California, Washington DC, South Carolina, Louisiana, including Philips Collection, Cleveland Institute, University of California, Carnegie Recital Hall, Merkin Concert Hall, Spoleto Festival, Town Hall, New York City, Metropolitan Museum of Art, Indianapolis, Early Music Festival, Smithsonian Institute; Performances in Switzerland and Germany; Radio appearances in USA; World premiere of works by Zwillich and Persichetti; Faculty, Juilliard School, 1989–96; Harpsichord coach to film star Gwyneth Paltrow, 1994; Commentator, National Public Radio programme, Performance Today, 1997. *Recordings:* Musical Heritage Society; Works of Christophe Moyreau and Pancrace Royer; Classic Masters; Works of Frescobaldi, Strozzi. *Contributions:* Encyclopaedia of the Keyboard. *Address:* 4201 Sassafras Street, Erie, PA 16508, USA.

**KOC, Jozik;** Singer (Baritone); b. 1968, Oxford, England. *Education:* Studied at York University and the Guildhall School, London. *Career:* Concerts and recitals throughout the United Kingdom, 1991–92, leading to Wigmore Hall debut 1993; Opera debut as Fiorello in Il Barbiere di Siviglia, and Guide in Death in Venice, for Glyndebourne Touring Opera; Spirit in Monteverdi's Orfeo for English National Opera, Purcell's Aeneas for Opera Factory and Prince Lindoro in Haydn's Pescatrici (Garsington Festival Opera, 1997); Other roles include Mozart's Don Giovanni, Count and Guglielmo, Sancho in Massenet's Don Quichotte, and Schaunard (La Bohème); Concert repertoire includes Bach's B minor Mass, Messiah, Rossini's Petite Messe and the Fauré Requiem; Appearances with the London and Royal Philharmonics, and the English Chamber Orchestra. *Recordings include:* Baroque Anthems. *Address:* Music International, 13 Ardilaun Road, London N5 2QR, England.

**KOCH, Sophie;** Singer (Mezzo-soprano); b. 19 Feb. 1969, Versailles, France. *Education:* Paris Conservatoire, with Jane Berbié. *Career:* Appearances throughout France, notably in Marseille, Strasbourg, and Théâtre du Châtelet, Paris: Season 1998–99 as Rossini's Rosina and Mozart's Dorabella with the Royal Opera in London; Zerlina at the Schwetzingen Festival, in Monteverdi's Orfeo at the Vienna Festival, the Prince in Massenet's Cendrillon at Geneva, and Mercédès (Carmen) at the Opéra Bastille, Paris; Composer in Ariadne auf Naxos at Dresden and Zerlina in Munich, Season 1999–2000 with Cherubino and Octavian at the Vienna Staatsoper and the Composer at La Scala; other roles include Sextus in La Clemenza di Tito, Silla in Pfitzner's Palestrina and Cenerentola, all with the Royal Opera at Covent Garden, 2000–01; Mozart's Cherubino in Brussels and Paris, and on tour with the Bavarian State Opera to Japan; Engagements until 2005 include Siebel and the Composer at Covent Garden, and Octavian on tour with the Vienna State to Israel; Concerts include Beethoven's Missa Solemnis and Elgar's Sea Pictures. *Address:* c/o MusicaGlotz, 11, rue le Verrier, 75006 Paris, France.

**KOCMIEROSKI, Matthew;** American percussionist, conductor, historian and educator; b. 18 Aug. 1953, Roslyn, NY; m. Elaine S. Schmidt 1974. *Education:* Nassau Community College, Mannes College of Music. *Career:* Marimba concertos performed with: Atlantic Wind Symphony, New York, Broadway Chamber Symphony, Thalia Chamber Symphony, Seattle, Philharmonia Northwest, Midsummer Musical Retreat Festival Orchestra and The Bainbridge Orchestra; Numerous concerto and recital appearances in the Pacific North West including the Auburn Symphony; Chamber music performances include: New Music America, Seattle Chamber Music Festival, Bergen International Festival, Goodwill Arts Festival, Seattle Spring Festival of Contemporary Music, Moscow Autumn Festival, Moscow Alternativa Festival, Orcas Island Festival, Icicle Creek Festival, Icebreaker Festivals I and II, Methow Valley Festival; Aeolian Chamber Players, Seattle Chamber Players; Freelance performances with Martha Graham Dance Company, Seattle Symphony, Seattle Opera, Bolshoi Ballet, Joffrey Ballet, Northwest Chamber Orchestra; Instructor of Percussion and Music History, Classical New Music Programme, Cornish College of The Arts, Seattle; Member, New Performance Group, 1981–96; Artistic Director, New Performance Group, Seattle, beginning with the 1984–85 season; Principal Percussionist, Pacific Northwest Ballet Orchestra; Founding Member, Pacific Rims Percussion Quartet, 1995–; Pres. Int. Guild of Symphony, Opera and Ballet Musicians 2004–. *Recordings:* Paul Dresher's Night Songs, 1984; Atlas Eclipticalis, John

Cage conducting, 1986. *Address:* 12724 19th Avenue NE, Seattle, WA 98125, USA. *Telephone:* (206) 365-8925 (office).

**KOCSAR, Miklós;** Composer; b. 21 Dec. 1933, Debrecen, Hungary. *Education:* Studied with Farkas at the Budapest Academy of Music, 1954–59. *Career:* Teacher, Béla Bartók Conservatory, Budapest, 1972–; Deputy Head of Music, Hungarian Radio, 1983–. *Compositions:* Horn concerto, 1957; Capriccio for orchestra, 1961; Solitary song for soprano and chamber ensemble, 1969; Variations for orchestra, 1977; Capricorn concerto for flute and chamber orchestra, 1978; Metamophoses for orchestra, 1979; Sequenze for strings, 1980; Elegia for bassoon and chamber ensemble, 1985; Formazioni for orchestra, 1986; Visions of the Night, oratorio for mezzo-soprano solo, mixed choir and orchestra, 1987; Concerto for violoncello and orchestra, 1994; Choral music including I will invoke you, Demon, 1985; Missa in A for equal voices, 1991; Chamber: Wind Quintet, 1959; Brass Trio, 1959; Variziioni for woodwind quintet, 1968; Sestetto d'ottoni, 1972; 7 Variations for viola, 1983; Wind Quintet, No. 3, 1984; Quintetto d'ottoni, 1986; Rhapsody for Trombone, piano and percussion, 1989; Trio for strings, 1990; Music for 4 Trombones and Percussion, 1991; Songs and piano pieces; The Fire of St Anthony for orchestra, 1992; Salve Regina for voices and orchestra, 1995; Notturno for piano, 1996; Magnificat, 1996; Missa Seconde, 1997. *Honours:* Erkel Prize, 1973, 1980; Merited Artist of the Hungarian People's Republic, 1987; Merited Artist of the Hungarian People's Republic, 1987; Bartók-Pasztory Award, 1992. *Address:* Artisjus, PO Box 593, 1538 Budapest, Hungary.

**KOCSIS, Zoltán;** Hungarian pianist, conductor and composer; *General Music Director, Hungarian National Philharmonic Orchestra;* b. 30 May 1952, Budapest; s. of Ottó Kocsis and Mária Mátyás; m. 1st Adrienne Hauser 1986; one s. one d.; m. 2nd Erika Tóth 1997; one s. one d. *Education:* Budapest Music Acad. (under Pál Kadosa). *Career:* Asst Prof. Music Acad. Budapest 1976–79, Prof. 1979–; Producer of Archive Section of Hungaroton (record co.); co-founder, Artistic Co-Dir Budapest Festival Orchestra 1983–96; Gen. Music Dir Hungarian Nat. Philharmonic Orchestra 1997–. *Performances:* has appeared with Berlin Philharmonic Orchestra and performed in Germany, USSR, Austria and Czechoslovakia 1971; toured USA together with Dezsö Ranki and Budapest Symphony Orchestra (under George Lehel) 1971; recitals in Netherlands, Paris, London and Ireland 1972; concerts in Norway, with Svyatoslav Richter in France and Austria, with Claudio Abbado and London Symphony Orchestra and at BBC Promenade Concerts in London and Festival Estival, Paris 1977, Edin. Festival 1978. *Publications:* Miscellaneous Publs, Arrangements for Piano and 2 Pianos, etc. *Honours:* First Prize, Beethoven Piano Competition, Hungarian Radio and Television 1970, Liszt Prize 1973, Kossuth Prize 1978, Merited Artist's title 1984, Lifetime Achievement Award, MIDEM, Cannes 2004. *Address:* Hungarian National Philharmonic Orchestra, Komor Marcell u. 1, 1095 Budapest (office); Ringlò ùt. 75, 1121 Budapest, Hungary (home). *Telephone:* (1) 4116620; 4116623 (office). *Fax:* (1) 4116624 (office); (1) 424-5917 (home). *E-mail:* kocsis@ filharmonikusok.hu (office). *Website:* www.filharmonikusok.hu (office).

**KODALLI, Yelda;** Turkish singer (soprano); b. 20 Oct. 1968; m. *Education:* Hacettepe Univ., Ankara State Conservatory with Prof. Mustafa Yurdakul. *Career:* debut, ORF Austrian television 1991; Vienna State Opera 1992; Zauberflöte, Reykjavík 1991; performed in Vienna at Staatsoper and at Volksoper, Mannheim, Essen, Düsseldorf; Opéra Bastille, Paris; Munich Staatsoper; Strasbourg Festival; Schönbrunn Festival; La Scala; Hamburg and Wiener Staatsoper; Lyric Opera of Chicago; in Vienna in Hansel and Gretel, Arabella, Capriccio, Zauberflöte and Siegfried; new production of Zauberflöte, Teatro Regio, Turin 1994; Lucia di Lammermoor, Teatro Carlo Falice, Genoa; sang in Japan, Tel-Aviv and Haifa; opened La Zarzuela Theatre of Madrid in Stravinsky's Le Rossignol 1995; sang Gilda in Rigoletto in Japan, RAI orchestra of Turin; sang in concerts in Ankara and Istanbul, Zürich and Basel; on tour with the Orchestra della Toscana; performed Luciano Berio's Outis, La Scala; I Puritani, Tenerife; Christmas concert, ABAO, Bilbao; Zauberflöte, Vienna. *Recordings:* Constanze in Mozart's Die Entführung aus dem Serail with the Scottish Chamber Orchestra conducted by Charles Mackerras, Mozart in Turkey at the Topkapi Palace in Istanbul (film, dir by Elijah Moshinsky). *Publications:* Musica Viva, Lucia, Franca Cella 1994; contrib. to La Stampa 1994, Opera International Herald Tribune 1996, Readers Sun Times 1996, L'Opera TAA The Best Vocal of the Year 1996. *Current Management:* c/o Mario Dradi, via Isolalta Forette 11, 37068 Vigasio VR, Italy. *Telephone:* (045) 6649911. *Fax:* (045) 6649912.

**KODOMA, Momo;** Concert Pianist; b. 1972, Japan. *Career:* Concerts with Seiji Ozawa with the new Japanese Philharmonic, and with Boston Symphony Orchestra, 2000; Further concerts with Kent Nagano, Eliaha Inbal, Bernard Klee, Gerard Schwarz and Charles Dutoit, re-engaged for season 2000; Orchestras include Berlin Radio, Bayerische Rundfunk, Strasbourg Philharmonic and the Hallé; All major Japanese orchestras; Wigmore Hall recital debut, 1999, wth Chopin, Ravel and Messiaen; Festival engagements at Davos, 1999–2000, Berlin and Lucerne; Mostly Mozart and Marlboro, USA and Enescu Festivals; Further recitals at the Paris Châtelet and Tonhalle, Zürich; Repertory includes Messiaen's Vingt regards sur l'enfant Jésus. *Address:* c/o Kathryn Naish, IMG Artists, Lovell House, 616 Chiswick High Road, London W4 5RX, England.

**KOEHNE, Graeme (John);** Composer and University Lecturer; b. 1956, Adelaide, South Australia. *Education:* BMus, 1st class honours, MMus, University of Adelaide; Studied composition with Richard Meale, Tristam

Cary and Bernard Rands; Composition under Virgil Thomson and Louis Andriessen, School of Music, Yale University, USA. *Career:* Appointed Tutor in Piano and Composition, University of New England, Armidale, New South Wales, 1978; Collaborated with choreographer Graeme Murphy and Sydney Dance Orchestra; Commissions, Australian Bicentenary, West Australian Ballet Company, Queensland Ballet Company, Australian Chamber Orchestra, Seymour Group (Sydney), Australian Ballet; Lecturer in Composition, University of Adelaide. *Compositions:* Orchestral: The Iridian Plateau, 1977; First Blue Hours, 1979; Toccata, 1981; Fanfare, 1981; Rain Forest, 1981; riverrun…, 1982; Once Around the Sun, 1988; Unchained Melody, 1991; Powerhouse, 1993; Elevator Music, 1997; Ballet Suite from The Selfish Giant, 1985; Capriccio for Piano and Strings, 1987; Ensemble: Sextet, 1975; Cantilene, 1978; Crystal Islands, 1982; Divertimento Trois Pièces Bourgeoises, string quartet, 1983; Ricecare and Burletta, string trio, 1984; Miniature, 1985; String Quartet No. 2; Shaker Dances, 1995; Voice and ensemble: Cancion, text F Garcia Lorca, 1975; Fourth Sonnet, text S Mallarmé, Suite, 1984; Nearly Beloved, 1986; Nocturnes, 1987; Keyboard Music: Piano Sonata, 1976; Harmonies in Silver and Blue, piano, 1977; Twilight Rain, piano, 1979; Gothic Toccata, 1984 (aka Toccata Aurora). *Address:* c/o Boosey & Hawkes (Australia) Pty Ltd, Unit 12/6 (PO Box 188), Artarmon, NSW 2064, Australia.

**KOERPPEN, Alfred;** German composer; b. 16 Dec. 1926, Wiesbaden. *Education:* studied with Kurt Thomas in Frankfurt. *Career:* Professor, Staatliche Hochschule für Musik und Theater, Hanover 1964–91. *Compositions include:* Virgilius der Magier von Rome, opera, 1951; Der Turmbauzu Babel, oratorio, 1951; Das Feuer des Prometheus, oratorio, 1956; 17 Choralfantasien und Partiten, for organ, 1948–90; Wassermarken for soprano, tenor and string quartet, 1961; Joseph und seine Brüder, for female chorus and speakers, 1967; Arachne, ballet, 1968; Parabel vom Dornbusch, for mixed chorus and ensemble, 1969; Das Stadtwappen for solo voices, chorus and orchestra, 1973; Konzert im Dreieck, 1974; Donum Kinguarum, for 3 solo voices and chours, 1976; Ein Abenteuer auf dem Friedhof, chamber opera, 1980; Symphony, 1985; ECHO for solo voices and three chourses, 1985; Trio in zwei Sätzen for violin, cello and piano, 1986; Jona for chorus and organ, 1995; Abgesang for violin and orchestra 1995; Concerto for bass tuba and orchestra, 1998. *Honours:* Low Saxony Prize for culture 1983. *Website:* www.alfred -koerppen.de.

**KOETSIER, Jan;** Composer and Conductor; b. 14 Aug. 1911, Amsterdam, Netherlands; m. Margarete Trampe. *Education:* Academy of Music, Berlin. *Career:* Debut: As Composer and Conductor, Concertgebouw, Amsterdam, 1937; Second Conductor, Concertgebouw Orchestra, 1942–48; Conductor, Residentieorkest, The Hague, 1949–50; Conductor, Bavarian Radio Symphony Orchestra, Munich, 1950–66; Professor, Musikhochschule, Munich, 1966–76. *Compositions include:* 3 Symphonies; Orchestral Works; The Man Lot, cantata for Soli, Men's Choir and Orchestra; Concert Rondo for piano and strings, 1991; Opera, Frans Hal; Chamber Music; Various Solo Concertos with Orchestra; Piano Music; Lieder. *Recordings:* Petite Suite; Brass Quintet; Partita for English Horn and Organ; Concerto for Trumpet, Trombone and Orchestra; Brass Symphony; Die Abreise by D'Albert, reissued 1998. *Current Management:* Donemus, Paulus Potterstraat 14, Amsterdam, Netherlands. *Address:* Florianhaus, Unterkagn, 84431 Heldenstein, Germany.

**KOFRON, Petr;** Composer; b. 15 Aug. 1955, Prague, Czechoslovakia. *Education:* Janacek Academy Brno, 1974–79. *Career:* Founder and Director, Agon Orchestra, 1983–; Co-founder, Czech Society for New Music; Editor, Konzerva/Na Hudbu, music journal, 1989–. *Compositions include:* In Memoira I.O Dunayevsky, for speaker and brass quintet, 1975; Farewell Waltz, for orchestra, 1977; The Bow, for orchestra, 1979–81; String Quartet, 1982; For Soprano and Orchestra, after Georg Trakl, 1982; E.S.T. concerto for piano and ensemble, 1988; Liber LXXII, for 2 orchestras and tape, 1988; Alpha and Centaur, for violin and ensemble, 1989; Spira, for clarinet and ensemble, 1990; Enhexe, ensemble, 1991; The Golden Fern, opera, 1991; The Fire is Mine, for ensemble and electronics, 1993; Abram for 8 instruments, 1994; Tworl, string quartet, 1994; Big Dipper, for ensemble, 1996. *Publications include:* Graphic Scores and Concepts, 1996. *Address:* c/o Music Information Centre, Besedne 3, 11800 Prague 1, Czech Republic.

**KOGAN, Lev,** MA; composer and pianist; b. 6 March 1927, Baku, USSR; m. Ethel Kovensky 1969; two d. *Education:* Aram Khatchaturian diploma in piano composition. *Career:* Conservatory Teacher of Music Composition, Theory of Music, Moscow State Conservatory 1946–52; mem. League of Composers of the USSR and Israel. *Compositions:* 160 works; four ballets performed in the USSR; six musicals; 54 compositions for theatre; music for cinema and television; Jewish songs. *Recordings include:* Hassidic Music; 11 albums; six song collection albums 1958–99; ballet score 1960. *Honours:* Honoured Musician of the USSR; Recipient of the Prize of the Jewish Song Festival; Israel Acum Prize. *Address:* 55/9 Rubinstein Street, Jaffa D, Tel-Aviv, Jaffa 68212, Israel.

**KOGAN, Semjon;** Conductor; b. 24 April 1928, Bobruisk, Ukraine. *Education:* Studied violin and conducting at the St Petersburg Conservatoire. *Career:* Founded the State Symphony Orchestra at Omsk; Artistic Director, Rostov State Symphony Orchestra, 1976, participating in the 1990 Tchaikovsky International Competition, Moscow; Guest appearances with the USSR State Symphony, Moscow Philharmonic, Moscow Radio and St Petersburg Philharmonic Orchestras and invitations to conduct in Poland,

Czechoslovakia and Germany; Repertoire includes Stravinsky and Shostakovich in addition to the standard repertoire; Has given the premieres of works by Denisov, Shchedrin and Khrennikov; Professor, Rostov on Don Conservatoire; Founded Rostov Conservatoire Orchestra, 1993. *Recordings:* With the Rostov Symphony Orchestra. *Current Management:* Sonata, Glasgow, Scotland. *Address:* 11 Northpark Street. Glasgow G20 7AA, Scotland.

**KOHN, Karl-Christian;** Singer (Bass); b. 21 May 1928, Losheim, Saarbrucken, Germany. *Education:* Studied with Irene Eden at the Musikhochschule Saarbrucken. *Career:* Sang at the Deutsche Oper am Rhein, Düsseldorf, 1954–57; St ädtische Oper Berlin, 1956–58; Sang the title role in Le nozze di Figaro, at the reopening of the Cuvillies-Theater Munich, 1958; Member of the Bayerische Staatsoper Munich from 1958, notably in the 1963 premiere of Die Verlobung in San Domingo by Egk; Schwetzingen Festival, 1961, in the premiere of Elegie für junge Liebende by Henze; Guest appearances in Hamburg, Vienna, Berlin and elsewhere in Europe; Other roles included Mozart's Osmin, Sarastro and Commendatore. *Recordings:* Der Freischütz, Don Giovanni, Oedipus der Tyrann by Orff; Arabella, Doktor Faust, Don Giovanni, Wozzeck, Cardillac by Hindemith (Deutsche Grammophon); Bach's Christmas Oratorio. *Address:* c/o Bayerische Staatsoper, Postfach 745, 8000 Munich 1, Germany.

**KOHN, Karl George;** Pianist, Conductor and Composer; b. 1 Aug. 1926, Vienna, Austria. m. Margaret Case Sherman, 23 June 1950, 2 d. *Education:* Certificate, New York College of Music, 1944; BA, 1950, MA, 1955, Harvard University; Studied piano with Werschinger, conducting with Prüwer and composition with Piston, Ballantine, Fine and Thompson. *Career:* Instructor in Music, 1950–54, Assistant Professor, 1954–59, Associate Professor, 1959–65, Professor, 1965–85, William M Keck Distinguished Service Professor, 1985–95 now Professor Emeritus, Pomona College, Claremont, California; Teaching Fellow, Harvard University, 1954–55; Teacher, Berkshire Music Center, Tanglewood, summers 1954, 1955, 1957; Appearances as Pianist and Conductor. *Compositions include:* Orchestral: Sinfonia concertante for Piano and Orchestra, 1951; Castles and Kings, suite, 1958; Concerto mutabile for Piano and Orchestra, 1962; Episodes for Piano and Orchestra, 1966; Interlude ll for Piano and String Orchestra, 1969; Centone for Orchestra, 1973; The Prophet Bird l, 1976; Time Irretrievable, 1983; Lions on a Banner, Seven Sufi Texts for Soprano Solo, Chorus and Orchestra, 1988; Ode for String Orchestra, 1991; Concert Music for String Orchestra, 1993; End Piece for Chamber Ensemble, 1993; Ternaries for Flute and Piano, 1993; Middle Piece for Chamber Ensemble, 1994; Chamber Music: Encounters I–VI for various instrumental combinations; Choral Works, Songs, Piano pieces and Organ music; Reconnaissance for large chamber ensemble, 1995; Memory and Hope: Essay for Orchestra, 1996; Sax for 4, for saxophone quartet, 1996; More Reflections for clarinet and piano, 1997; Tripartita for vihuela and guitar, 1998; Number Play for two pianos, 1999; Trio, 2K for violin, cello and piano, 1999; Again, Again, for two pianos, 2000; Prelude for organ, 2000; Night Music for six guitars, 2000; Violaria for viola and piano, 2000; Night Music 2 for six guitars, 2000; After 09/11/01 for piano; November Piece for piano, 2001; Return – Symphonic Essay, transcribed for 2 pianos, 2001; Grand Fantasy for organ, 2002; Fourth Rhapsody for piano, 2003; Three Proverbs for chorus of mixed voices, a cappella, 2003; Sonata for cello and piano, 2003. *Publications:* End Piece, 1994; Ternaries, 1995; Set of Three, 1996; Reconnaissance, 1997. *Address:* 674 West 10th Street, Claremont, CA 91711, USA. *E-mail:* Kkohn@pomona.edu.

**KOHONEN, Jyrrki;** Singer (bass); b. 1965, Finland. *Education:* Sibelius Academy, Helsinki, with Tom Krause, Opera Studio of Zürich Opera. *Career:* Appearances with Finnish National Opera from 1994, as Mozart's Bartolo, Colline in La Bohème and Fafner in The Ring; Savonlinna Festival 1994, as Gremin and Banquo; Darmstadt Opera as Mozart's Osmin, Lord Plunkett in Martha, Raimondo, Sarastro and the Landgrave in Tannhäuser; Engagements at Cagliari in Wagner's Die Feen and at Bayreuth in Die Meistersinger; Season 2000–2001 in Beethoven's 9th and Mahler's 8th Symphonies under Riccardo Chailly, Rocco in Fidelio at Pisa and Truffaldino in Ariadne auf Naxos under Simon Rattle; Bayreuth 2001, in Lohengrin. *Current Management:* Athole Still International Management, Forresters Hall, 25–27 Westow Street, London, SE19 3RY, England. *Telephone:* (20) 8771-5271. *Fax:* (20) 8768-6600. *Website:* www.atholestill.com.

**KOHOUTEK, Ctirad,** PhDr, CSc; Czech composer, theorist and teacher (retd); b. 18 March 1929, Zábřeh na Moravě; s. of Hynek and Jarmila Kohoutek; m. Jarmila Chlebníčková 1953; one s. two d. *Education:* Brno Conservatory, Janáček Academy of Music Arts, Palacký University, Olomouc, Masaryk University, Brno. *Career:* debut, performance of symphonic poem Mnichov (Munich) 1953; Junior, Composition, 1953–59, Fellow, Composition, 1959–65, Senior Lecturer, Composition, Theory of Composition, 1965–80, Janáček Academy of Music Arts, Brno; Professor of Composition, Academy of Music Arts, Prague, 1980–90; Artistic Director, Czech Philharmonic, Prague, 1980–87; Full-time Composer, occasional Theorist and Pedagogue; mem., Asscn of Music Artists and Scientists, Prague; Club of Moravian Composers, Brno, 1992–. *Compositions include:* String Quartet, 1959; Concertino, violoncello, chamber orchestra, 1964; Rapsodia eroica, organ, 1965; Inventions, piano, 1965; Miniatures, 4 French horns, 1966; Memento, concerto for percussion and wind instruments, 1966; Teatro del mondo, large orchestra (Janáček Prize, Brno, 1975), 1969; Panteon, orchestra (Janáček Prize, Brno, 1975), 1970; Festive Prologue, large symphony orchestra, 1971; Celebration of Light, large orchestra, 1975; Symphonic Actualities, orchestra, 1976–78;

Tissues of Time, bass clarinet, piano, 1977; Minutes of Spring, wind quintet, 1980; Omaggio a vita, orchestra, 1989; About Cockerel and Little Hen, children's opera, 1989; Motifs of Summer, violin, violoncello, piano, 1990; Funs and Smiles, oboe, clarinet, bassoon, 1991; Winter Silences, brass, percussion, 1993; The Little Peach, mixed choir, piano, percussion, to text by Josef Kainar (1st Prize Jihlava, 1994), 1993; Autumn Songs, 2nd string quartet, 1995; The Water Metamorphoses, 4 flutes, 1996; L'unica speranza (The Only Hope), orchestra, 1997; Opposite Poles, 2 trumpets, 1998–99; The Magic of Wood, violin, piano, 1999–2000; Numerous pieces for choirs. *Publications include:* Modern Trends in Music Composition, 1965; Project Music Composition, 1969; Musical Styles from the Composer's Viewpoint, 1976; Music Composition, 1989. *Honours:* Second Prize in Composition, World Festival of Youth, Moscow 1957, Music Critics' Prize for Memento, Paris, 1967. *Address:* Helfertova 40, 613 00 Brno, Czech Republic (home). *Telephone:* (545) 573021 (home). *E-mail:* c.kohoutek@tiscali.cz (home). *Website:* www.musica.cz/comp/kohoutek.htm.

**KOITO, Kei;** Concert Organist, Composer and Professor; b. 4 Jan. 1950, Kyoto, Japan. *Education:* Studied organ, philosophy, musical aesthetics and psychology at Tokyo School of Fine Arts; Studied organ with Pierre Segond at the Geneva Conservatory, Analysis, orchestration and composition with Eric Gaudibert; Associated with electro-acoustic studios; Private study of organ with L F Tagliavani, Xavier Darasse and Reinhard Goebel. *Career:* Debut: Solo recitalist at Victoria Hall, Geneva, Maurice Ravel Auditorium, Lyons; Soloist with symphonic and chamber orchestras, regularly performing at festivals and on radio and television; Since 1978 has performed over 80 new works for organ, premiering a large number written especially for her; Professor of Organ at the Conservatoire in Lausanne; Adjudicator, guest lecturer and masterclasses in USA, Europe and Asia. *Compositions include:* Les Tours Du Silence for Narrator and Chamber Ensemble; Labryrinthe Dynamique for Brass Ensemble; Orestes-Stasimon for Choir; Esquisse Alpha for 2 Pianos; Wenn Aus Der Ferne for Organ; Splendid Rotation for 2 Amplified Harpsichords; In Step for String Quartet; Poème Pulvérisé for Voice and Percussion; Meta-Matic No. 22 for Tape. *Recordings:* 6 Trio Sonatas, 5 Concertos, Canonic Variations of JS Bach; Sonatas of CPE Bach and contemporary organ music. *Current Management:* Europe General: Camille Kiesgen, Bureau International de Concerts et de Conférences, Faubourg Saint-Honoré 252, 75008 Paris, France. *Address:* c/o Conservatoire de Musique de Lausanne, 6 rue du Midi, CH –1002 Lausanne, Switzerland.

**KOIZUMI, Kazuhiro;** Conductor and Music Director; b. 16 Oct. 1949, Japan; m. Masami. *Education:* University of The Arts, Tokyo; Hochschule für Musik, Berlin; Worked with Seiji Ozawa for 2 years. *Career:* Assistant Conductor, Japan Philharmonic, 1970–72; Music Director, New Japan Philharmonic, 1975–80, Winnipeg Symphony Orchestra, 1983–; Chief Conductor, Tokyo Metropolitan Orchestra, 1984–; Guest Conductor, Berlin Philharmonic, Chicago Symphony, National Orchestra of France, Royal Philharmonic, Vienna Philharmonic, Toronto Symphony, Tokyo Metropolitan, Kyoto Symphony, Nagoyo Symphony, Montreal Symphony, RAI in Naples and Munich Philharmonic; Adviser, Manitoba Conservatory of Music and Arts. *Recordings:* Lalo Concerto Russe/Concerto in F with Radio France, Decca label; Tchaikovsky, Kodály, Dvořák with WSO. *Honours:* First Prize, 2nd International Conductors Competition (MIN-ONO, 1970); First Prize, von Karajan Competition, 1972; Grand Prix du Disque. *Current Management:* Columbia Artists Management Inc. *Address:* c/o Columbia Artists Management Inc, New York, USA.

**KOK, Nicholas;** Conductor; b. 1962, England. *Education:* Organ Scholar at New College, Oxford; Royal College of Music as Repetiteur. *Career:* Music Staff of English National Opera from 1989–93; Music Adviser to Contemporary Opera Studio; Has conducted for English National Opera, The Return of Ulysses, The Marriage of Figaro, Così fan tutte and King Priam; The Fairy Queen, (Purcell) and Così fan tutte in 1995 and Orfeo in 1996; For English National Opera Bayliss Programmes he conducted Arion and the Dolphin, a new commission by Alec Roth; For Almeida Opera, Mario and The Magician by Stephen Oliver and A Family Affair, a new commission by Julian Grant; He has conducted Così fan tutte, The Coronation of Poppea, Reimann's The Ghost Sonata, Xenakis's The Bacchae and Nigel Osborne's Sarajevo for Opera Factory, London; For Opera Factory Zürich, Marschner's Der Vampyr in his own version for chamber orchestra and Cavalli's La Calisto; Further engagements with Opera Factory London include Dido and Aeneas and Britten's Curlew River; Other operatic engagements have included Don Giovanni for English Touring Opera, The Barber of Seville for Dublin Grand Opera, Gerald Barry's The Intelligence Park for the Almeida Festival/Opera Factory and Trois Operas Minutes by Milhaud and The Judgement of Paris by Eccles for Trinity College of Music; Has also worked with Scottish Opera; Philharmonia, Ulster Orchestra, London Sinfonietta; Scottish Chamber Orchestra; Royal Scottish National Orchestra; Bournemouth Sinfonietta; Endymion Ensemble; Almeida Ensemble; Cambridge University Chamber Orchestra; London Pro Arte Orchestra and the Philippines Philharmonic Orchestra; A number of Choral Societies; BBC engagements include The Soldier's Tale, The Carnival of the Animals, Reginald Smith Brindle's Journey Towards Infinity, Mondrial by Erollyn Wallen and several television and radio plays; The Marriage of Figaro for English National Opera, 1997. *Honours:* Countess of Munster Award and Lofthouse Memorial Prize. *Address:* Allied Artists, 42 Montpelier Square, London SW7 1JZ, England.

**KOKKOS, Yannis;** stage director and stage designer; b. 1944, Athens, Greece. *Education:* Nat. Theatre of Strasbourg. *Career:* has created designs for sets and costumes for productions of Macbeth, Lohengrin and Reimann's Lear at Paris Opéra Garnier, Pelléas et Mélisande at La Scala and the Vienna Staatsoper, Don Carlos at Bologna and Elektra at Geneva and San Francisco; Directed the Oresteia by Xenakis in Sicily; Directed and designed Boris Godunov in Bologna and Opéra Bastille, Paris, Ariane et Barbe Bleue in Geneva, La Damnation de Faust at the Théâtre du Châtelet, Paris, Nancy Opéra with Death in Venice, Festival d'Orange with Carmen, Tosca and Don Giovanni, Welsh National Opera and Scottish Opera with Tristan und Isolde, 1993, and Opera de Bordeaux with Salome; Pelléas et Mélisande and Tristan seen at Covent Garden, 1993; Norma, Opéra Bastille, Paris, 1996; Alceste, Scottish Opera, 1996; Tristes Tropiques by Aperghis, world premiere with Opéra Strasbourg, 1996; Elektra, Opéra de Lyon, 1997; Clemenza di Tito, Welsh National Opera, 1997; Hänsel and Gretel, Châtelet, Paris, 1997; Queen of Spades for Scottish Opera and Götterdämmerung at the Teatro Alla Scala, Milan, 1998; Outis, Luciano Berio, Châtelet, Paris, 1999; Pelléas et Mélisande in Bordeaux, 2000; Fliegende Holländer in Bologna, 2000; L'Orestie, Epidaure, 2001; Iphigénie en Avlide, La Scala, Milan, 2002; Phaedra, Dido and Aeneas, Opéra de Nancy, 2003; Les Troyens, Châtelet, Paris, 2003, Fenelon's Les Rois (world premiere), Opera Bordeaux 2004. *Publications:* Yannis Kokkos, Le Hèron et le Scénographe 1989. *Honours:* Commandeur, Ordre des Arts et des Lettres, France; Medaille d'or, Quadriennale of Prague, 1987; Laurence Olivier Award, 1997, Prix de la Critique, best opera production (for Les Troyens) 2003. *Address:* 7 rue Bourdaloue, 75009 Paris, France.

**KOLB, Barbara,** MM; American composer; b. 10 Feb. 1939, Hartford, CT. *Education:* Hartt Coll. of Music, Berkshire Music Center with Lukas Foss and Gunther Schuller. *Career:* played clarinet in the Hartford Symphony Orchestra 1960–66; composer-in-residence, Marlboro Music Festival 1973, American Acad. in Rome 1975; teacher of theory and composition, Brooklyn Coll. and Temple Univ.; Artistic Dir of Music New to New York, Third Street Music School Settlement 1979. *Compositions:* Rebuttal for two clarinets 1964, Chanson bas for voice, harp and percussion 1965, Three Place Settings for narrator and ensemble 1968, Trobar clus for 13 instruments 1970, Soundings for 11 instruments and tape 1972 (version for orchestra 1975 and 1977), Frailities for tenor, tape and orchestra 1971, Spring, River, Flowers, Moon, Night for two pianos and tape 1975, Appello for piano 1976, Musique pour un vernissage for ensemble 1977 (concert version 1979), Songs before an Adieu for flute, guitar and voice 1979, Chromatic Fantasy for narrator and ensemble 1979, Three Lullabies for guitar 1980, Related Characters for viola and piano 1980, Related Characters for viola and piano 1980, The Point that Divides the Wind for organ and four percussionists 1981, Cantico (film score) 1982, Millefoglie for ensemble and computer-generated sound 1985, Time... and Again for oboe, string quartet and tape 1985, Umbrian Colours for violin and guitar 1986, Yet That Things go Round for chamber orchestra 1986–88, Molto Allegra for guitar 1988, The Enchanted Loom for orchestra 1988–89, Extremes for flute and cello 1989, Voyants for piano and chamber orchestra 1991, Clouds for organ and piano, recorded tape 1992, All in Good Time for orchestra 1993, In Memory of David Huntley for string quartet 1994, New York Moonglow for ensemble 1995, Sidebars for bassoon and piano 1996, Criss Cross for percussion and orchestra 2000. *Honours:* Rome Prize 1969–71, Fulbright Scholarship 1966–67, MacDowell Colony and Guggenheim Fellowships, grants from the Ford Foundation and the NEA 1972–79. *Address:* Boosey & Hawkes Ltd, First Floor, 71–91 Aldwych, London, WC2B 4HN, England. *Website:* www.boosey.com/kolb.

**KOLLO, René;** German singer (tenor); b. 20 Nov. 1937, Berlin; s. of the late Willi and of Marie-Louise Kollodzieyski; m. 1st Dorthe Larsen 1967; one d.; m. 2nd Beatrice Bouquet 1982. *Career:* began career with Staatstheater, Brunswick 1965; First Tenor, Deutsche Oper am Rhein 1967–71; Dir Metropol Theater, Berlin 1996–97; guest appearances with numerous leading opera cos and at annual Bayreuth Wagner Festival. *Performances include:* The Flying Dutchman 1969, 1970, Lohengrin 1971, Die Meistersinger von Nürnberg 1973, 1974, Parsifal 1975, Siegfried 1976, 1977, Tristan (Zürich) 1980, (Bayreuth) 1981. *Publication:* Imre Fabian im Gespräch mit René Kollo 1982. *Honours:* Bundesverdienstkreuz, Goldene Kamera Award, Hörzu 2000. *Address:* c/o Pran Event GmbH, Ralf Sesselberg, An der Brücke 18, 26180 Rastede, Germany (office). *Telephone:* (4) 402-8687 (office).

**KOLLY, Karl-Andreas;** Pianist; b. 26 May 1965, Switzerland. *Education:* Music Academy, Zürich, 1988; Studied with Karl Engel and Mieczyslaw Horszowski. *Career:* Debut: Grieg Piano Concerto at Zürich, 1982; Concerto as soloist and chamber musician all over Europe, USA, Japan and Australia; Several radio and television programmes in Switzerland, Germany, Spain and Czech Republic, 1991; Professor, Hochschule für Musik, Zürich, 1991–. *Recordings:* CDs of Schumann piano works including Symphonic Etudes; Brahms, the Piano Trios, with Trio Novanta; The Piano Concertos of Skriabin, Glazunov, d'Albert, Wellesz, Schmidt; Liszt/Bach: The Complete Piano Transcription. *Honours:* First Prize, Jecklin Competition, 1975; University Competition of Zürich, 1988; Young Musicians Competition, Union of Swiss Banks, 1990; Tschumi prize for best soloist diploma of the year, 1991; Prix Maurice Sandoz, 1990. *Address:* Rosenrain 12, 8400 Winterthur, Switzerland. *Telephone:* 522133220. *Fax:* 522133220.

**KOLOMYJEC, Joanne;** Singer (soprano); b. 1955, Canada. *Career:* appearances in concert and opera throughout Canada, the USA and England

1983–; opera roles include the Countess and Susanna in Le Nozze di Figaro, Donna Elvira and Donna Anna in Don Giovanni, Fiordiligi in Cosi fan Tutti, Tatiana in Eugene Onegin, the title roles in Tosca and Jenůfa, Marguerite in Faust, Magda Sorel in The Consul, Violetta in La Traviata, Mimi in La Bohème, Agathe in Der Freischutz, Micaela in Carmen, Madame Lidoine and Blanche in Les Dialogues des Carmelites, Lia in L'Enfant Prodigue, Rosalinda in Die Fledermaus and Anna Glawari in The Merry Widow; concert engagements with Toronto Symphony and Calgary Philharmonic Orchestra; repertoire includes the Mozart and Verdi Requiems, Messiah, Rossini's Stabat Mater, Bruckner's Te Deum, Beethoven's Ninth and Shostakovich's 14th Symphony; sang David Del Tredici's Alice for the National Ballet of Canada at the London Coliseum, 1987, followed by Zemlinsky's Lyric Symphony. *Recordings include:* None But the Lonely Heart (with Janina Fialkowska), Song to the Moon (with Mario Bernardi and the Calgary Philharmonic Orchestra), A Night in Vienna, Raffi Armenian. *Current Management:* Dean Artists Management, 204 St George Street, Toronto, ON M5R 2N5, Canada.

**KOLTAI, Ralph,** CBE FRSA; British stage designer; b. 31 July 1924, Berlin, Germany; s. of Alfred Koltai and Charlotte Koltai (née Weinstein); m. Annena Stubbs 1954 (divorced 1976). *Education:* Cen. School of Art and Design, London. *Career:* Head of Theatre Design Dept, Cen. School of Art and Design 1965–72; Assoc. Artist RSC 1964–66, 1976–; Opera Dir The Flying Dutchman, Hong Kong Arts Festival 1987 and La Traviata 1990; over 200 productions of opera, drama and dance throughout Europe, the USA, Canada and Australia; Fellow Acad. of Performing Arts, Hong Kong, London Inst., Rose Bruford Coll. Art. *Exhibition:* retrospective exhbn London 1997, touring Asia, Europe 1998–99. *Designs include:* musical Metropolis 1989 (London), The Planets (Royal Ballet) 1990, The Makropulos Affair (Norwegian Opera) 1992, My Fair Lady (New York) 1993, La Traviata (Stockholm) 1993, Hair (London) 1993, Othello (Essen) 1994, (Tokyo) 1995, Madame Butterfly (Tokyo) 1995, Twelfth Night (Copenhagen) 1996, Carmen (Royal Albert Hall, London) 1997, Simon Boccanegra (Wales) 1997, Timon of Athens (Chicago) 1997, Nabucco (Festival Orange, France) 1998, Suddenly Last Summer (also Dir, Nottingham Playhouse) 1998, Dalibor (Edin. Festival) 1998, A Midsummer Night's Dream (Copenhagen 1998), Don Giovanni (St Petersburg) 1999, Genoveva (Edin. Festival) 2000, Katya Kabanova (La Fenice, Venice) 2003. *Publication:* Ralph Koltai: Designer for the Stage 1997. *Honours:* Royal Design for Industry, London Drama Critics' Award (for As You Like It) 1967, Gold Medal (Prague Quadriennale) 1975, Soc. of West End Theatres Designer of the Year (for Brand) 1978, Golden Triga (Prague) 1979, 1991, London Drama Critics' Award (for The Love Girl and The Innocent) 1981, Designer of the Year Award (for Cyrano de Bergerac) 1989, Silver Medal, Prague (for Othello) 1987, Distinguished Service to Theater, US Inst. of Theater Tech. 1993. *Address:* c/o London Management, 2–4 Noel Street, London W1; Suite 118, 78 Marylebone High Street, London, W1U 5AP, England. *Telephone:* (20) 7287-9000. *Fax:* (20) 7287-3436.

**KOMLÓS, Péter;** Hungarian violinist; *Professor of Violin, Liszt Ferenc Academy of Music, Budapest;* b. 25 Oct. 1935, Budapest; s. of László Komlós and Franciska Graf; m. 1st Edit Fehér 1960, two s.; m. 2nd Zsuzsa Arki 1984, one s. *Education:* Budapest Music Acad. *Career:* f. Komlós String Quartet 1957; First Violinist, Budapest Opera Orchestra 1960; Leader Bartók String Quartet 1963; Prof. of Violin, Liszt Ferenc Acad. of Music, Budapest 1981–. *Performances:* extensive concert tours to USSR, Scandinavia, Italy, Austria, German Democratic Repub. Czechoslovakia 1958–64, USA, Canada, NZ and Australia 1970, including Human Rights Day concert, UN HQ New York, Japan, Spain and Portugal 1971, Far East, USA and Europe 1973; performed at music festivals of Ascona, Edin., Adelaide, Spoleto, Menton, Schwetzingen, Lucerne, Aix-en-Provence. *Recordings:* recordings of Beethoven's string quartets for Hungaroton, Budapest and of Bartók's string quartets for Erato, Paris. *Honours:* 1st Prize, Int. String Quartet Competition, Liège 1964, Liszt Prize 1965, Gramophone Record Prize of Germany 1969, Kossuth Prize 1970, 1997, Eminent Artist Title 1980, UNESCO Music Council Plaque 1981; Order of Merit, Middle Cross of Repub. of Hungary 1995. *Address:* 2083 Solymár, Sport-u. 6, Hungary. *Telephone:* (6) 26-360-697. *Fax:* (6) 26-360-772. *E-mail:* stradivari@axelero.hu (office). *Website:* www.lfze.hu (office).

**KOMLOSI, Ildiko;** Singer (Mezzo-soprano); b. 1959, Békésszentandra's, Hungary. *Education:* Studied at Szeged Music Academy with Valeria Berdal and at Franz Liszt Academy, Budapest with András Miko; Guildhall School with Vera Rozsa and the Studio of La Scala with Giulietta Simionato. *Career:* Concert appearances have included the Verdi Requiem in Philadelphia, conducted by Lorin Maazel; Concerts with the BBC Symphony, the Royal Philharmonic with Antal Dorati and the Hungarian Radio and State Television Company; Engagements with the Hungarian State Opera Company, Budapest and the State Operas of Berlin, Vienna, La Scala and in America, San Francisco, Portland, Houston, Columbus, Ohio; Roles include Carmen, Sextus, Leonora in Favorita, Laura, Octavian, Giovanna Seymour (Anna Bolena) and Purcell's Dido; Sang Judit in a concert performance of Duke Bluebeard's Castle with the BBC Philharmonic conducted by András Ligeti, Feb 1991, and at the 1992 Prom Concerts London; Giovanna Seymour at Santiago; Sang Octavian at Palermo, 1998.

**KOMLOSSY, Erzsebet;** Singer (Contralto); b. 9 July 1933, Salgotarjan, Hungary. *Education:* Studied at the Bartók Conservatory in Budapest. *Career:* Member, Hungarian State Opera Budapest; Guest appearances in Moscow, London, Cologne, Edinburgh and elsewhere in Europe; Roles include Azucena (Covent Garden, 1970), Amneris, Ulrica, Preziosilla, Eboli, Carmen,

Dalila and parts in operas by Kodály, Szokolay and Erkel. *Recordings:* Aida, Madama Butterfly, Bank Ban by Erkel, The Spinning Room by Kodály and Blood Wedding by Szokolay (Hungaroton); Hungarian Coronation Mass by Liszt (Deutsche Grammophon); Háry János by Kodály (Decca). *Address:* c/o Hungarian State Opera House, Népöztársaśay utja 22, 1061 Budapest, Hungary.

**KOMOROUS, Rudolf;** composer and bassoonist; b. 8 Dec. 1931, Prague, Czechoslovakia. *Education:* Conservatory of Music; Academy of Musical Arts, Prague with Pavel Borkovec. *Career:* teacher, Central Conservatory of Peking, China, 1959–61; co-founder, Musica Viva Pragensis, Czechoslovakia; Emigrated to Canada 1969; Associate Professor of Composition and Theory, University of Victoria, 1971–. *Compositions:* Published by Universal Edition, Vienna and some of them have been issued on Supraphon Records; Mignon for string quartet, 1965; Gone for tape, 1969; Bare and Dainty for Orchestra, 1970; Lady Whiterose, Chamber opera, 1971; Anatomy of melancholy for tape, 1974; 4 Sinfonies, 1988, 1990, 1995, 1997; No, no, Miya, chamber opera, 1988; Hermione Dreaming for ensemble, 1992; The Seven Sides of Maxines' Silver Die for ensemble, 1998. *Honours:* First Prize, Concours International d'Exécution Musicale, Geneva, 1957.

**KONG, Joanne;** Pianist and Harpsichordist; b. 2 March 1957, Suffern, New York, USA; m. Paul Hanson 1981. *Education:* BMus, Piano and Harpsichord Performance, University of Southern California, 1979; MMus, Piano Performance, 1981, DMA, 1986, University of Oregon. *Career:* Critically acclaimed as Solo and Chamber Pianist and Harpsichordist; Special expertise in music of J. S. Bach, including performances of Goldberg Variations and complete Well-Tempered Klavier; Artist Faculty, University of Richmond, Virginia. *Honours:* Ruth Lorraine Close Fellowship Winner, Harpsichord, 1979, Piano, 1980, 1981; Laureate, Beethoven Foundation Fellowship Auditions, 1981; Fellowships to Bach Aria Festival and Institute, SUNY Stony Brook, 1982, 1984; 4th Place, J. S. Bach International Piano Competition, 1983. *Address:* 1211 Claremont Avenue, Richmond, Virginia 23227-4008, USA.

**KONGSTED, Ole Dan;** Danish musicologist, composer, church musician and jazz musician; *Senior Research Fellow, The Royal Library*; b. 22 Sept. 1943, Copenhagen; m. Ida Wieth-Knudsen 1967; one s. two d. *Education:* Univ. of Copenhagen. *Career:* holder of scholarship, Danish State 1976–80; freelance collaborator, Danish Radio 1976–; Conductor, Choir of the Jeunesses Musicales 1978–86; Asst Dir, Musikhistorisk Museum and Carl Claudius Samling, Copenhagen 1980–2000; Choirmaster, Church of the Sacred Heart, Copenhagen 1983–; Composer; founder and leader, Capella Hafniensis 1990–; holder of scholarship, Danish State/Royal Library 1994–2000; Sr Research Fellow, The Royal Library 2000–. *Compositions:* 35 opus numbers including: Opus 2, Puer natus est nobis for choir, soloists and organ; Opus 3a, Kyrie fons bonitatis for choir a cappella. *Recordings:* with Choir of the Jeunesses Musicales, with Ben Webster and Arnved Meyer Band, and Capella Hafniensis. *Publications:* E turri tibiis canere – Traek af taarnblaesningens historie, in Festskrift Johannes Simons (ed.) 1974, Census as Source Material for the History of Music 1976, Nils Schioerring: Musikkens Historie i Danmark (ed.) 1977–78, Music in Denmark at the Time of Christian IV 1988, Heinrich Schütz und die Musik in Dänemark zur Zeit Christians IV (co-ed.) 1989, Kronborg-Motetterne Tilegnet Frederik II og Dronning Sophie 1582, 1990, Kronborg-Brunnen und Kronborg-Motetten, Ein Notenfund des späten 16 Jahrhunderts aus Flensburg und seine Vorgeschichte 1991, Royal Danish Water Music 1582 1994, Gregorius Trehou in the Vatican Library 1998. *Honours:* Organist and Kantor Otto Koebkes Mindelegat, 1992. *Address:* The Royal Library, PO Box 2149, 1016 Copenhagen K, Denmark. *Telephone:* (33) 474701 (office). *E-mail:* ok@kb.dk (office).

**KÖNIG, Klaus;** Singer (Tenor); b. 26 May 1936, Beuthen, Germany. *Education:* Studied with Johannes Kemter in Dresden. *Career:* Sang in Cottbus in 1970; Dessau from 1973, as Max, Don Carlos, and Erik in Der fliegende Holländer; Sang at Leipzig 1978–82, Staatsoper Dresden from 1982; Guest appearances in Karlsruhe 1983–85 (Tristan and Tannhäuser), at La Scala and Covent Garden in 1984 (as Tannhäuser) and the Théâtre de la Monnaie Brussels 1985, as Tristan; Sang Max in Der Freischütz, at the opening of the restored Semper Opera House, Dresden (1985); Guest appearances in Paris, Parma, Strasbourg, Madrid, Venice and Barcelona; Other roles include Lensky, Florestan, Radames, Don José, Alvaro in La Forza del Destino, Lohengrin, Walther, Parsifal and Bacchus; Lisbon 1986, as Florestan; Sang Tannhäuser at Cologne and London 1987; Munich Opera 1988, as Menelaos in Die Aegyptische Helena by Strauss; Buenos Aires and Vienna Staatsoper 1988, as Florestan and Bacchus; Sang the Mayor in Friedenstag by Strauss, Dresden, 1998; Many engagements in concerts and oratorios. *Recordings:* Tannhäuser (EMI); Der Rosenkavalier (Denon); Choral Symphony (Philips). *Address:* c/o Allied Artists Agency, 42 Montpelier Square, London SW7 1JZ, England.

**KONSTANTINOV, Julian;** Singer (bass); b. 1966, Sofia, Bulgaria. *Education:* Sofia Academy, 1987–93. *Career:* Sang in The Rake's Progress and Il Barbiere di Siviglia while a student and represented Bulgaria at the 1992 Cardiff Singer of the World Competition; Appearances with the Sofia National Opera in Lucia di Lammermoor, Aida, Rigoletto, Luisa Miller and Turandot (as Timur); Season 1998 with the Royal Opera at Savonlinna and elsewhere as Massimiliano in Verdi's Masnadieri; Further engagements include Fiesco in Simon Boccanegra with the Berlin Philharmonic and Salzburg Festival conducted by Claudio Abbado, Padre Guardino in La Forza del Destino at the

Savonlinna Festival and Cardinal Brogni in La Juive at the New Israeli Opera, 1999–2000. *Current Management:* Askonas Holt Ltd, Lonsdale Chambers, 27 Chancery Lane, London, WC2A 1PF, England. *Telephone:* (20) 7400-1700. *Fax:* (20) 7400-1799. *E-mail:* info@askonasholt.co.uk. *Website:* www.askonasholt.co.uk.

**KONSULOV, Ivan;** Singer (Baritone); b. 29 May 1946, Varna, Bulgaria. *Education:* Studied with Jossifov in Sofia and with Aldo Protti in Italy. *Career:* Debut: Opera National Russe (Bulgaria) 1972; Sang in Berne from 1977, as Simon Boccanegra, Marcello (La Bohème), Scarpia, Don Giovanni, Mandryka, Tonio, Pizarro, Don Carlos (La Forza del Destino), Alfio and Iago; Bologna 1980, Zurga in Les pêcheurs de Perles; Philadelphia Opera 1982, Marcello: Bratislava 1984, as Eugene Onegin; Stuttgart and Berlin 1985, Don Giovanni; At the Monte Carlo opera in 1986 sang Gryaznoy in The Tsar's Bride by Rimsky-Korsakov; Engagements at Graz, Barcelona, Madrid and Karlsruhe; Sang Amfortas in Parsifal at Berne, 1989; Season 1992 as the Major-domo in Zemlinsky's Der Zwerg at Trieste. *Recordings include:* La Bohème-Marcello Opus-Bratislava Stereo with P Dvorsky and television film 1980; The Queen of Spades (Tomsky), Musik Mundial-Sofia with International Stars, 1988; Don Carlo-Posa, Balkanton, Sofia, 1988; Opera Recital Arias Balkanton, 1988. *Address:* c/o Stadttheater Bern, Nägeligasse 1, 3011 Bern, Switzerland.

**KONT, Paul;** Composer; b. 19 Aug. 1920, Vienna, Austria; 1 s. *Education:* Conductor's Diploma, 1947, Composer's Diploma, 1948, Vienna University of Music. *Career:* Professor of Composition, 1969–86, Emeritus, 1986–, Vienna Academy of Music. *Compositions:* Commissioned operas: Lysistrate (for Komische Oper Berlin), 1957; Peter und Susanne (for Austrian Television), 1959; For the Time Being (for Austrian Television), 1965; Celestina (for Stadt-Buhnen, Cologne), 1966; Plutos (for Austrian Government), 1976; Traumleben, musical, 1958; Ballets: Italia Passata; Die Traurigen Jäger; Amores; Il Ballo del Mondo; Monoballette, ballet film; Vom Manne und vom Weibe, oratorio; 4 Symphonies, 1979, 1981, 1981, 1983; Concertos; Chamber music; Lieder; Piano Sonatas; Roma, ballet, 1984; Lebenslauf, ballet, 1987; 3 Kleine Klavierkonzerte, 1989; Cronica Hungarica for orchestra, 1992; Sequenzen, 1994; Oesterreich for clarinet and piano trio, 1997. *Publications:* Antianiorganikum. *Address:* 47 Geusaugasse, Vienna 1030, Austria.

**KONTARSKY, Alfons;** Pianist; b. 9 Oct. 1932, Iserlohn, Germany. *Education:* Studied in Cologne with Else Schmidt-Gohr and Maurits Frank; Further study in Hamburg with Eduard Erdmann, 1955–57. *Career:* Many appearances with his brother in modern music programmes from 1955, including works by Earle Brown, Kagel, Stockhausen, Pousseur, Berio and Bussotti; Seminar at Darmstadt, 1962–69; Teacher at the Musikhochschule from 1969; Professor, Salzburg Mozarteum, 1983–; Formed Piano Trio with Saschko Gawriloff and Klaus Storck, 1971. *Recordings include:* Bartók's Sonata for two Pianos and Percussion. *Publications:* Pro Musica Nova: Studien zum Spielen neuer Musik für Klavier, 1973. *Honours:* First prize for Piano Duo at the 1955 Munich Radio International Festival. *Address:* Stacthiche Hochschule für Musik Rheinland, Degobertstrasse 38, 5000 Köln 1, Germany.

**KONTARSKY, Alois;** Pianist; b. 14 May 1931, Iserlohn, Germany. *Education:* Studied in Cologne with Else Schmitz-Gohr and Maurits Frank; Further study in Hamburg with Eduard Erdmann. *Career:* International performances with his brother from 1955 in modern repertoire: Michael Gielen, de Grandis, Henri Pousseur, Berio and Zimmermann; Gave premiere of Stockhausen's Klavierstücke I–XI, Darmstadt 1966; Concerts with the Stockhausen ensemble and duo with the cellist Siegfried Palm; Masterclass at the Cologne Musikhochschule from 1969; Premieres of music by Kagel, Stockhausen (Mantra), Berio and Bussotti. *Recordings include:* Bartók's Sonata for Two Pianos and Percussion; Klavierstücke I–XI by Stockhausen. *Honours:* First prize for Piano Duo at the Munich Radio International Festival, 1955. *Address:* Staatliche Hochschule für Musik Rheinland, Degobertstrasse 38, 5000 Köln 1, Germany.

**KONTARSKY, Bernhard;** Conductor; b. 1940, Germany. *Education:* Musikhochschule, Cologne. *Career:* Engagements at Bonn Opera and throughout Europe: Berg's Lulu for Flanders Opera and Wozzeck at the Deutsche Oper am Rhein; Adriana Hölszky's Die Wände and Henze's Boulevard Solitude for Frankfurt Opera; Henze's Der Prinz von Homburg at Antwerp and Schoenberg's Moses und Aron for the Deutsche Oper, Berlin; Productions for the Staatstheater Stuttgart include Zender's Don Quixote, Intolleranza by Nono, Bluebeard's Castle, and Zimmermann's Die Soldaten; Boulevard Solitude at Covent Garden, London, 2001; Professor at Academy of Frankfurt, 1981–. *Honours:* Mendelssohn Award, Cologne; International Disc Award of the German Press, 1992. *Address:* Staatstheater Stuttgart, Obererschlossgarten 6, 70173 Stuttgart, Germany.

**KOOPMAN, Antonius (Ton) Gerhardus Michael;** Dutch musician, professor of harpsichord and conductor; *Professor of Harpsichord, Royal Conservatory, The Hague*; b. 2 Oct. 1944, Zwolle; m. Christine H. H. Mathot 1975; three d. *Education:* Amsterdam Conservatory and Univ. of Amsterdam. *Career:* Prof. of Harpsichord, Royal Conservatory, The Hague; f. Amsterdam Baroque Orchestra 1979, Amsterdam Baroque Choir 1992; appears on concert platforms around the world and on radio and TV; has made over 200 recordings of harpsichord and organ works by Bach, Handel etc.; f. his own record label Antoine Marchand (Sub-label of Challenge Classics). *Publications:* Interpretation of Baroque Music 1985 and a small book about J. S. Bach 1985; The Harpischord in Dutch Paintings (co-), The World of the Bach Cantatas (co-ed with Christoph Wolff) 1996. *Honours:* Hon. mem. RAM,

London; Dr hc (Utrecht) 2000; winner of several prizes. *Address:* Meerweg 23, 1405 BC Bussum, Netherlands. *Telephone:* (35) 6913676. *Fax:* (35) 6939752. *E-mail:* ton.koopman@wxs.nl (office). *Website:* www.tonkoopman.nl (office).

**KOPCAK, Sergei;** Singer (Bass); b. 23 April 1948, Dacov, Carpathia. *Education:* Studied in Leipzig, Vienna and Milan. *Career:* Slovak National Opera at Bratislava, from 1974 in the Slav, French and German repertory; Metropolitan Opera, New York from 1983, as Ivan Khovansky, Wurm in Luisa Miller and Sparafucile in Rigoletto; The Commendatore, and Pimen in Boris Godunov; Salzburg Festival, 1986–87 in Moses und Aron; Edinburgh Festival, 1989 as Konchak in Prince Igor and Marseille, 1994, as Boito's Mephistopheles; Shostakovich's Boris at Florence, Maggio Musicale, 1998. *Recordings:* Janáček's Glagolitic Mass. *Address:* c/o Teatro Comunale, Via Solferino 15, 50123 Florence, Italy.

**KOPP, Miroslav;** Singer (tenor); b. 23 Feb. 1955, Plzeň, Czechoslovakia. *Education:* studied at the Prague Conservatory. *Career:* Prague National Theatre from 1981 as Alfredo, Ernesto, Don Pasquale, Pelléas, 1986 and the Prince in Rusalka, 1991; Vienna Staatsoper, 1986, in The Bartered Bride and Paris Opéra Comique in From the House of the Dead, 1988, (also at the Salzburg Festival); Geneva, 1992 as Boris in Katya Kabanova and Florence, 1993 as Števa in Jenůfa; Basle Opera as Don Carlos; Other roles include Wenzel in The Bartered Bride and Vitek in Smetana's Dalibor. *Recordings:* Dvořák's The Cunning Peasant; Smetana's Dalibor and Martinů's Ariane; Tikhon in Katya Kabanova, under Charles Mackerras. *Address:* Prague National Theatre, PO Box 865, 11230 Prague 1, Czech Republic.

**KOPPEL, Lone;** Danish singer (soprano); b. 20 May 1938, Copenhagen; m. Björn Asker 1983; one d. two s. *Education:* Royal Danish Acad. of Music. *Career:* debut, Copenhagen in 1962 as Musetta; sang at Kiel Opera 1964–65, and Royal Opera Copenhagen 1962–95; guest appearances at Sydney 1973–78, and Århus from 1972 as Leonore in Fidelio and the Trovatore Leonora; sang Salome at Bonn and Oslo 1973–74, and Lady Macbeth in Macbeth at Stockholm 1981; Copenhagen as Judith in Bluebeard's Castle and Shostakovich's Katerina Izmailova; other roles included Mikal in Saul and David, Wagner's Elisabeth, Kundry, Ortrud and Senta, Elektra, Jenůfa, Eboli, Donna Anna and Donna Elvira; sang Mme de Croissy in Poulenc's Carmélites at Copenhagen 1997; season 2002 as The Old Countess in The Queen of Spades and Herodias in Salome; directed Nabucco 2003. *Recording:* Lone Koppel: Live and Studio Recordings 1963–86 2004. *Address:* c/o Det Kongelige Teater, Box 2185, 1017 Copenhagen, Denmark.

**KOPTAGEL, Yuksel;** Pianist and Composer; b. 27 Oct. 1931, Istanbul, Turkey; m. Danyal Kerven, 30 Dec 1964. *Education:* Private studies with composer Djemal Rechid; Graduated, Real conservatorio de Music, Madrid, 1955; Diplome Superieur, Schola Cantorum, Ecole Superieure de Musique, Paris, 1958; Certificates on Composition and Spanish Music Interpretation, Santiago, 1959. *Career:* Debut: First public concert, Istanbul, aged 5; Concerts in Europe (Spain, France, Italy, Switzerland, Czechoslovakia, Germany) USA, India, Pakistan, Russia; Compositions published by Max Eschig, Paris and Bote and Bock, Berlin; International concert career with European Orchestras, 1953–; Member of Jury, Schola Cantorum, Paris; Participant, numerous music festivals. *Address:* Caddebostan Plajyolu 21/32, 81060 Istanbul, Turkey.

**KOPYTMAN, Mark;** Composer and Pianist; b. 6 Dec. 1929, Kamenetz-Podolski, USSR; m. Miriam Kopytman, 5 July 1955, 2 d. *Education:* MD, Tchernovitz, USSR, 1952; MMus, Lvow Academy of Music, USSR, 1955; PhD, Moscow Conservatory, USSR, 1958. *Career:* Senior Teacher, Theory and Composition, USSR State Academies of Music, 1955–72; Chairman of Theory and Composition Department, 1974–76, 1979–82, 1985–, Professor, 1976–, Rubin Academy of Music, Jerusalem, Israel; Deputy Head of Rubin Academy of Music and Dance, Jerusalem, Israel, 1985–; Guest Professor, Hebrew University Musicological Department, Jerusalem, 1979–; Guest Professor of Composition, University of Pennsylvania, USA, 1985 and 1989; Composer in Residence, Canberra School of Music, Australia, 1985; Music Director, the Doron Ensemble for the Performance of 20th Century music, 1990–93; Music Adviser, International Festival in St Petersburg, 1991–; Chairman, International Composers Contest in Moldova, 1992; Composer in Residence, Israel Camerata (Jerusalem), 1992–; Chairman, International Symposium, The Art of Composition, Jerusalem, 1998. *Compositions:* Case Mare (Opera), 1966; Songs of Kodr (oratorio), 1966; String Quartet III, 1969; Voices, 1974–75; October Sun, 1974; Monodrama (Ballet), 1975; Concerto for Orchestra, 1976; About an Old Tune, 1977; Rotations, 1979; Cantus II, 1980; Memory, 1981; Kaddish, 1982; Susskind von Trimberg (Opera), 1982–83; Cantus III, 1984; Life of the World to Come, 1985; Variable Structures, 1985–86; Letters of Creation, 1986; Dedication, 1986; Letters of Creation for voice and strings, 1987; Circles for voice, clarinet, cello and piano, 1987; Ornaments for harpsichord and orchestra, 1987; Scattered Rhymes for choir and orchestra, 1988; Eight Pages from the Book of Questions for voice solo, 1988; A Poem for the Numbers for the Dead for baritone and chamber ensemble, 1988; Love Remembered for choir and orchestra, 1989; To Go Away for mezzo-soprano and five instruments, 1989; Cantus V, 1990; Alliterations for piano, 1993; Tenero for cello solo, 1994; Strain, for string quartet, 1995; Beyond for chamber orchestra, 1997; Fermane for voice and three clarinets; String Quartet No. 4, 1997. *Recordings:* Six Moldavian Dances for Orchestra; String Quartet No. 2; About an Old Tune; October Sun; For Harp; Memory; Rotations; Cantus II; Lamentation; Cantus V; Strain, Beyond, Music for

strings. *Publications:* Choral Composition, 1971. *Address:* 4 Tchernichovsky Str, Jerusalem 92581, Israel.

**KORD, Kazimierz;** Polish conductor; *Music Director, Teatr Wielki, Warsaw*; b. 18 Nov. 1930, Pogórze nr. Cieszyn; m. *Education:* Leningrad Conservatory with Wladimir Nilsen, Acad. of Music, Kraków, State Higher School of Music in Kraków with Artur Malawski. *Career:* Artistic Man. Music Theatre, Kraków 1962–69; Man. and Music Man. Great Symphonic Orchestra of Polish Radio and TV in Katowice 1969–73; Artistic Dir and Principal Conductor Warsaw Philharmonic 1977–2001; Chief Conductor Südwestfunk Orchestra in Baden Baden 1980–86; six years' co-operation with Metropolitan Opera, New York; Music Dir Teatr Wielki, Warsaw 2005–; conducted in all important music centres of the world, toured in 57 countries. *Recordings:* complete Beethoven symphonies, Górecki's Symphony No. 3 and works by J.S. Bach, Chopin, Lutoslawski, Penderecki, Panufnik, Schumann, Richard Strauss, Szymanowski and Szymański. *Honours:* Critics' Award at Music Biennale Berlin 1971, Gold Orpheus Prize of Polish Musicians' Union 1972, Star of the Year, Munich 1975, Minister of Culture and Arts Prize (1st Class) 1977, 1998. *Address:* c/o Teatr Wielki, pl. Teatralny 1, Warsaw (office); ul. Nadarzyńska 37A, 05-805 Kanie-Otrebusy, Poland (home). *E-mail:* kama.kord@t-online.de (home). *Website:* www.teatrwielki.pl.

**KORDES, Heidrun;** Singer (Soprano); b. 1960, Germany. *Education:* Freiburg Musikhochschule. *Career:* Debut: Gelsenkirchen Opera; Engagement at the Hessichen Staatstheater, Wiesbaden, from 1986; Roles have included Mozart's Pamina and Susanna, Nedda in Pagliacci, Gilda in Rigoletto and parts in operas by Handel; Guest engagements at Leipzig, Dresden, Mannheim, Frankfurt and the Deutsche Oper am Rhein, Düsseldorf; Frequent concert appearances. *Recordings include:* Oreste and Xerxes by Handel; Albums of Lieder. *Address:* c/o Allied Artists, 42 Montpelier Square, London SW7 1JZ, England.

**KOREVAAR, David;** Pianist and Composer; b. 25 July 1962, Madison, Winsconsin, USA; m., 1 s., 1 d. *Education:* BMus, 1982, MMus, 1983, DMA, in progress, expected 2000, The Juilliard School. *Career:* Debut: Town Hall, New York, 1985; Recitals throughout USA, Japan; Chamber music appearances in USA, Japan, Australia, Europe; Founding member, Hexagon, piano and Wind Ensemble; Prometheus Piano Quartet; mem, Chamber Music America; College Music Society; American Liszt Society. *Compositions:* Piano concerto; 2 piano sonatas; Major works for piano trio; Violin and piano; string trio; Clarinet and piano. *Recordings:* Bach, Well-Tempered Klavier, Musicians showcase; Brahms, Later piano music; Liszt, Orchestral music transcribed for piano; Dohnànyi Etudes; Ruralia Hungarica. *Honours:* Top prize, William Kapell International competition, 1988; Peabody Mason music foundation award, 1985; French music award from Robert Casadesus international competition, 1989. *Current Management:* Jecklin Associates. *Address:* 3 Sasqua Pond Road, Norwalk, CT 06855, USA.

**KORF, Anthony;** Composer and Conductor; b. 14 Dec. 1951, New York City, USA. *Education:* BA, MA, Manhattan School of Music. *Career:* Artistic Director, Conductor, Parnassus, 1975–; Guest Conductor, Group for Contemporary Music; League ISCM; Co-Founder, Artistic Director, The Riverside Symphony; Commissioned by San Francisco Symphony, American Composers Orchester and others. *Compositions:* Symphony No. 2; Symphony in the Twilight; Oriole; A Farewell; Cantata; Double Take; Brass Quintet; Symphonia; Requiem, 3 Movements for Clarinet Solo. *Recordings:* A Farewell; Symphony No. 2; Conductor: Stefan Wolpe (Koch International); Andrew Imbrie (New World); Babbitt; Davidovsky; Korf; Lundborg; Olan. *Publications:* Stefan Wolpe Chamber Piece No. 2, Editor. *Honours:* Koussevitsky Commission, 1992; American Academy of Arts and Letters Lieberson Fellowship, 1988. *Address:* 258 Riverside Drive, New York, NY 10025, USA.

**KORHONEN, Erkki;** Finnish pianist; *General Director, Finnish National Opera*; b. 1956. *Career:* Gen. Dir Finnish Nat. Opera 2001–; jury mem. Polytech Choir 100th Anniversary Composition Contest 2003, Mirjam Helin Song Competition 2004, The Klaudia Taev Int. Competition for Young Singers 2005. *Recordings:* Tauno Marttinen, Vox Angelica 2002. *Address:* Finnish National Opera, Helsinginkatu 58, POB 176, Helsinki 00251, Finland (office). *E-mail:* erkki.korhonen@operafin.fi (office). *Website:* www.operafin.fi (office).

**KORHONEN, Ritva-Liisa;** Singer (Soprano); b. 1959, Finland. *Education:* Studied in Helsinki and Zürich. *Career:* Debut: Helsinki in 1984 as Gilda; After further study at the Sibelius Academy sang Musetta and Adina in Helsinki, Fiordiligi at Tampere, Traviata at Oulu and Adele in Die Fledermaus at Lahti; Further appearances at the Savonlinna Festival and in concert; Sang Pamina at Helsinki, 1998. *Address:* c/o Finnish National Opera, Bulevardi 23–27, 00180 Helsinki 18, Finland.

**KORN, Artur;** Singer (Bass); b. 4 Dec. 1937, Wuppertal, Germany; m. Sabine Hass. *Education:* Studied in Cologne, Munich and Vienna with Clemens Glettenberg and Schuch-Tovini. *Career:* Debut: Cologne Opera Studio 1963, in Un Ballo in Maschera; Sang in Graz 1965–68, Vienna Volksoper and Staatsoper from 1968; Glyndebourne Festival 1980–84, as Baron Ochs, Bartolo in Le nozze di Figaro and Waldner in Arabella; Metropolitan Opera from 1984, as Osmin, Bartolo and Ochs; Engagements in Chicago (debut 1984), San Francisco, Detroit, London and Toronto and in Germany, Italy, South Africa and Switzerland; Salzburg Festival 1987, in Schoenberg's Moses and Aron; Sarastro in Magic Flute, Buenos Aires; Ochs in Rosenkavalier, Santiago de Chile; Met Tour, Japan, 1988; State Opera Munich Tour, Japan,

1988; Vienna Festival State Opera Vienna with Harnoncourt (Osmin-Entführung), 1988; Sang 1991/92 as Hagen at Brussels and Mozart's Bartolo at the Salzburg Festival; Often heard in oratorios and Lieder. *Recordings include:* Alfonso und Estrella by Schubert; Le nozze di Figaro with Haitink; Vespro della Beata Vergine with Harnoncourt; Video. *Recordings:* Ariadne auf Naxos (Met/Levine); Arabella (Strauss) Glyndebourne/Haitink; Le nozze de Figaro; Die Entführung, Vienna State Opera/Harnoncourt. *Address:* c/o Staatsoper, Opernring 2, 1010 Vienna, Austria.

**KORONDI, Anna;** Singer (soprano); b. 1967, Budapest, Hungary. *Education:* studied in Budapest, Bartók Conservatory and Vienna. *Career:* concerts from 1991, notably at the Styriarte and Prague Spring Festivals; Komische Oper Berlin 1993–1997, as Mozart's Susanna and Zerlina, Lauretta in Gianni Schicchi; Sophie in Werther and Nannetta in Falstaff; concerts include Bach's Christmas Oratorio, Vienna 1994, Mendelssohn's St Paul, Carmina Burana, and appearances at the Leipzig Gewandhaus 1996; mem. of the Komische Oper Berlin 1993–97, Bonn Opera 1997–99; world premiere of opera Bernarda Albas Haus by Aribet Reiman, Bayerische Staatsoper 2000; Adele in Die Fledermaus, Salzburg Festival 2001; sang Lied at the Kissinger Sommer; has worked with orchestras across Europe, under Hans Neuenfels, Marc Minkowski, Howard Arman, Frans Brügen, Adam Fischer, Nikolaus Harnoncourt and Helmuth Rilling; Repertoire from baroque to modern, including Lieder; Season 2002–2003 included Mendelssohn's Athalia, Mozart's Requiem, Bach Cantatas and Brahms's Requiem; Season 2003–2004 included debut as Sophie in Der Rosenkavalier and Parsifal under Pierre Boulez. *Recordings* Mendelssohn's Athalia (Cappricio). *Honours:* Prizewinner, Schubert and Pavarotti International Competitions 1991, won ARD Competition, Munich 1993. *Current Management:* Boris Orlob Management, Jägerstrasse 70, 10117 Berlin, Germany. *Telephone:* 49 (30) 20450839. *Fax:* 49 (30) 20450849. *E-mail:* info@orlob.net. *Website:* www.orlob.net.

**KOROVINA, Tatiana;** Singer (Soprano); b. 1967, Kursk, Russia. *Education:* Studied at the Tchaikovsky Conservatory, Moscow. *Career:* Sang the Queen of Night in Die Zauberflöte at Staatsoper Vienna, 1990; Concert arias and Exultate Jubilate by Mozart, La Scala, Milan, Prague and Tokyo Suntory Hall, 1990–91; Komische Oper Berlin as Princess in The Legend of Tsar Saltan by Rimsky-Korsakov, 1994–2002; Blondchen in Die Entführung aus dem Serail, 1995; Adele in Fledermaus, 1996; Ninetta Prokofiev's Love for Three Oranges, 1998; Scolatella in Henze's König Hirsch, 1998; Zerbinetta in R Strauss's Ariadne auf Naxos, 1999; Sang at Rossini Festival in Wildbad with Cerere in Le Nozze di Teti e di Peleo, 1994; Aldimira in Sigismondo, 1995; Zenobia in Aureliano in Palmira, 1996; Argene in Un vero omaggio, 1997; Sang in Rossini's Stabat Mater at Philharmonic Berlin, 1996; Gabrielle and Eve in Die Schöpfung in Closter Chorin, 1998. *Recordings:* Abramo ed Isaaco by Myslivecek; Boccherini, Stabat Mater; Mozart's Concert Arias and Exultate jubilate; Rossini's Sigismondo; Aureliano in Palmira; Le nozze di Teti e di Peleo. *Address:* Komische Oper Berlin, Behrenstrasse 55–57, 10177 Berlin, Germany. *E-mail:* st_home@t-online.de. *Website:* st_home.bei.t-online.de/Korovina_Tatjana.htm.

**KORSAKOVA, Natasha;** Concert Violinist; b. 29 Jan. 1973, Moscow, Russia. *Education:* Studied at Central Music School, Moscow. *Career:* Debut: Concerts with Moscow Chamber Orchestra at the Conservatoire; Has given concerts in Bulgaria, Germany, Greece, Yugoslavia, China, Italy, Belgium and Japan, 1989–; Played at the Panatei Festival, Italy, 1991, and the Bruch Second Concerto with the Russian State Symphony Orchestra, October 1991; Repertoire also includes works by Vivaldi, Bach, Mendelssohn, Mozart, Tchaikovsky and Lalo; Chamber recitals in Japan, 1991 with her mother Iolanthe Miroshnikova as accompanist in works by Brahms, Saint-Saëns, Beethoven and Prokofiev; Based in Germany since 1993. *Honours:* awards at Wieniawski and Lipinski Competitions, Poland, 1988; Young Violinists International Competition, Kloster Schontal, Germany, 1989. *Current Management:* Sonata, Glasgow, Scotland. *Address:* 11 Northpark Street, Glasgow G20 7AA, Scotland.

**KORTE, Karl Richard;** American composer; b. 23 June 1928, Ossining, NY. *Education:* Juilliard School with Peter Mennin, Vincent Persichetti, Otto Luening, Goeffredo Petrassi and Aaron Copland. *Career:* teacher, Arizona State Univ. 1963–64, State Univ. of New York at Binghamton 1964–70; Prof. of Composition, Univ. of Texas at Austin 1971–96, Emeritus Prof. of Music 1996–; Visiting Prof., Williams Coll. 1996–99. *Compositions:* music in many categories, including chamber music, symphonic music, choral and piano; orchestral: Concertino on a Choral Theme, 1955; For a Young Audience, 1959; 2 Symphonies, 1961, 1968; Southwest, dance overture, 1963; Concerto for piano and winds, 1976; chamber: 2 string quartets, 1948, 1965; Quintet for oboe and strings, 1960; Matrix, 1968; Facets, 1969; Remembrances for flute and tape, 1971; Symmetrics, 1973; Piano Trio, 1977; Concertino for bass trombone, wind and percussion; The Whistling Wind for mezzo and tape, 1982; Double Concerto for flute, double bass and tape, 1983; Texarkana for band, 1991; Band music and works for chorus including Mass for Youth, 1963; Aspects of Love, 1968; Pale is this Good Prince, oratorio, 1973; Of Time and Seasons, 1975. *Honours:* two Guggenheim Fellowships, Fulbright Fellowships to Italy, 1953, to New Zealand, 1985; Gold Medal, Queen Elizabeth Int., 1969. *Address:* 545 Stage Road, Kuskirk, NY 12028, USA. *E-mail:* kkorte@aol.com. *Website:* www.kkorte.com.

**KORTEKANGAS, Jaakko;** Singer (baritone); b. 1961, Finland. *Education:* Sibelius Academy, Helsinki, and in Zürich. *Career:* sang at the Freiburg Opera

from 1989, notably as Posa in Don Carlos, Belcore, Rossini's Figaro, Billy Budd and Wolfram in Tannhäuser; Guest at Berne in 1992 in Shostakovich's Lady Macbeth and as concert singer in Europe and North America including New York in 1990; Guest at Zürich as Barber of Seville, 1993, also at the Finnish National Opera, and Savonlinna Opera Festival; The Captain in The Death of Klinghoffer by John Adams, 2001. *Recordings:* opera: Madetoja; Pohjalaisia, Finlandia; television opera: Rantavaara; Tietäjien lahja; solo: Me kiitämme sinua; Sibelius, Cantata for the Conferment Ceremony; Nuori Psyyke (Songs of Erkki Melartin). *Honours:* First Prize, 1989 Lappeenranta competition. *Address:* Leirikaari 2 C, 02600 Espoo, Finland.

**KORTEKANGAS, Olli;** Composer; b. 16 May 1955, Turku, Finland. *Education:* Studied Composition and Music Theory, Sibelius Academy, 1974–81, West Berlin, 1981–82. *Career:* Composer; Journalist; Choral Conductor, Pedagogue (Sibelius Academy, National Theatre Academy); mem, Founding Member, Korvat auki Society (society for promotion or new music), Board Member of Society of Finnish Composers, Finnish Composers' Copyright Bureau TEOSTO. *Compositions include:* Television opera Grand Hotel, 1984–85; Orchestral: Okologie1-Vorspiel, 1983; Okologie, 2; Konzert, 1986–87; Alba, 1988; Amores, 1989; Organ concerto, 1997; Ark, 1998; Instrumental Threnody, 1977; Sonata per organo, 1979, Emotion, 1988; Imaggio a M C Escher, 1990, Iscrizione, 1990, Choral MAA, 1984–85, Verbum, 1987, A, 1987–88, Movement Echoing, 1997, Electronic Memoria, 1988–89. *Recordings:* Has made several recordings of his work (on Finlandia and Ondine labels). *Honours:* Salzburg Opera Prize, 1989; Gianfranco Zaffrani Prize, 1989. *Address:* Ruohoahdenkatu 20, 00180 Helsinki, Finland.

**KOS, Bozidar,** BMus, MMus, PhD; Australian/Slovenian composer; b. 3 May 1934, Novo Mesto, Slovenia; m. Milana Karlovac 1963; one d. *Education:* Univ. of Adelaide, Univ. of Sydney. *Career:* teacher, cello, music theory, State Music School, Novo Mesto, 1953–54; Lecturer in Music, Torrens Coll. of Advanced Education, Adelaide, South Australia, 1975; Tutor in Composition, Electronic Music, 1976–77, Fellow in Composition, 1978–83, Univ. of Adelaide; Lecturer in Composition, 1984–91, Senior Lecturer in Composition, 1992–, Chair. Composition Division, 1994–2002, Sydney Conservatorium of Music, Univ. of Sydney, NSW; corresponding mem. Slovenian Acad. of Sciences and arts 2003–. *Compositions:* Orchestral: Axis 5-1-5, 1973; Mediations, 1974; Metamorphosis, 1978; Sinfonietta, 1983; Violin Concerto, 1986; Guitar Concerto, 1992; Crosswinds for jazz trumpet, alto saxophone and orchestra, 1993; Aurora Australis, 1997; Viola Concerto, 2000; Ensemble works: Integration, 1972; Chamber Piece, 1973; Little Fantasy, 1978; Quartet, 1980; String Quartet, 1982; Three Movements, 1982; Catena 1, 1985, Quasar, 1987; Catena 2, 1989; Ludus ex Nominum, 1989; Bravisssssimo, 1991, Catena 3 2003, Fatamorgana 2004; solo works: Reflections, piano solo, 1976; Piano Sonata, 1981; Kolo, piano solo, 1984; Evocations for solo cello, 1994; Evocations 2 for solo guitar, 1999; instrumental works with synthesiser, computer or tape: Modulations, 1974; Dialogue 1, tape, 1976; Spectrum, 1988. *Recordings:* Quasar for percussion quartet, on Synergy Percussion; Piano Sonata, on The Hands The Dream, Tall Poppies; Violin Concerto, on Forbidden Colours; Violin Concerto, Crosswinds; Guitar Concerto on Bozidar Kos Skladatelj-Composr; Evocations for solo cello, on Australian Cello, Tall Poppies; Catena 2, on Samsara/Australia Ensemble, Vox Australis and Anthology of Australian Music; Reflections on Musica Noster Amor: Musical Art of Slovenia. *Honours:* Adolf Spivakowsky Scholarship for Composition 1977, Third Prize, Premio Musicale Citta di Trieste Competition 1987, Albert H. Maggs Composition Award 1983, Best Australian Orchestral Work, Nat. Music Critics' Awards 1991, APRA/Australian Music Centre State Award for Long-Term Contribution to the Advancement of Australian Music 2004. *Address:* 62 Grand Boulevard, Blackwood Park, SA 2006, Australia (home). *Telephone:* (8) 8370-0419 (home). *Fax:* (8) 8278-3342 (home). *E-mail:* bozidar.kos@bigpond.com (home). *Website:* www.amcoz.com.au/k/bkos.htm (office).

**KOSMO, Ingebjørg;** singer (mezzo-soprano); b. 1967, Denmark. *Career:* frequent concert and opera engagements throughout Scandinavia and Europe; repertoire includes L'Enfant Prodigue by Debussy, the Composer in Ariadne auf Naxos, with songs by Schubert, Strauss and Stravinsky; contestant in the Cardiff Singer of the World Competition 1995. *Address:* c/o Den Norske Opera, Storgaten 23, 0028 Oslo, Norway.

**KOSTAS, Rudolf;** Singer (Baritone); b. 1950, Vienna, Austria. *Education:* Studied in Vienna, with Waldemar Kmentt. *Career:* Sang at the Vienna Kammeroper and Staatsoper from 1975; Salzburg Festival, 1981 in the premiere of Cerha's Baal; Stadttheater Freiburg, 1984–89; Season 1995–96 at Schwerin as Hans Sachs in Die Meistersinger and Westmoreland in Sly by Wolf-Ferrari; Other roles include Wagner's Amfortas and Wolfram; Mozart's Don Giovanni and Count; Berg's Wozzeck; Verdi's Luna; Rigoletto and Iago; Mozart's Figaro; Further appearances in Tel-Aviv, Munich and throughout Germany; Many concerts and Lieder recitals. *Address:* c/o Staatstheater Schwerin, Alter Garten, 19055 Schwerin, Germany.

**KOSTLINGER, Josef;** Singer (Tenor); b. 24 Oct. 1946, Braunau am Inn, Austria. *Education:* Studied at Salzburg and Stockholm. *Career:* Sang in the 1973 Stockholm premiere of Tintomora by Werle; Tamino in the Ingmar Bergman version of Die Zauberflöte; Salzburg Landestheater from 1974, in the premieres of König Ubu by F Hummel, 1994; Roles have included Mozart's Ferrando, Tamino and Belmonte; Ernesto in Don Pasquale; Many concert appearances. *Recordings:* Magic Flute. *Address:* c/o Landestheater, Schwarstrasse 22, 5020 Salzburg, Austria.

**KOSZEWSKI, Andrzej,** DipMus; Polish composer and musicologist; b. 26 July 1922, Poznań; m. Krystyna Jankowska 1959; one d. *Education:* Poznań Univ. with Adolf Chybinski, State Higher Schools in Poznań with Stefan B. Poradowski, studied with Tadeusz Szeligowski in Warsaw. *Career:* teacher of composition and theory of music as Professor of Academy of Music, Poznań; choral works are performed at numerous international festivals and competitions, mainly in Europe, America and Asia; mem. Polish Composer's Union, F. Chopin Soc. Polish Author's Soc. *Compositions include:* Concerto Grosso, 1947; Suita Kaszubska (Kashubian Suite), 1952; Trzy Kotysanki (Three Cradle Songs), 1952–69; Scena Tameezna 1953, Allegro Symfoniczne, 1953; Sinfonietta, 1956; Sonata Breve, 1954; 5 Dawnych Tancow (Five Old Dances) 1957, Muzyka Fa-Re-Mi-Do-Si, 1960; Tryptyk Wielkopolski (Great Poland Triptych), 1963; Zdronas Kralewno Wyborna 1963, La espero (The Hope), 1963; Nicolao Copernico dedicatum, 1966; Gry (Games), 1968; Makowe ziarenka (Poppy Seeds), 1969; Przystroje (Ornamentations), 1970; Ba-No-Sche-Ro, 1971–72; Da fischiare, 1973; Canzone e danza, 1974; Trzy koledy (Three Christmas Carols), 1975; Prologus, 1975; 3 Sonatinas, 1978; Ad musicam, 1979; Campana (The Bell), 1980; Angelus Domini, 1981; Three Euphonic Chorales, 1982; Suita Lubuska (Lubusz Suite), 1983; Zaklecia (Incantations), 1983; Strofy trubadura, 1985; Cantemus Omnes 1985, Tre pezzi, 1986; Trois chaconnes, 1986; Enigma 575, 1986; Krople teczy (Drops of a Rainbow) 1988; Wi-La-Wi, 1988–94; Serioso-Giocoso, 1989; Miserere, 1989; 3 Tance polskie (3 Polish Dances), 1989; Canti sacri, 1990; Tristis est anima mea, 1992; Ave Maria, 1992; Trittico di Messa, 1992; Carmina Sacrata, 1992–94; Et lux perpetua, 1992–96; Epitaphium, 1994; Iubilatio, 1994; O Swicie, O Zmooku (At Dawn, At Dark) 1996, Non sum dignus, 1996; From Dream and From Legend, 1997; Missa Gaude Mater, 1998, Pater Noster 1999, Unitis Viribus 2002, Magnificat 2004. *Publications:* author of many publications dealing with Chopinology and music education, including Melodics of Chopin's Walzes 1953, Materials for Piano Improvisation Training 1968. *Honours:* many awards and prizes. *Address:* ul Poznanska 37 m9, 60-850 Poznań, Poland (home).

**KOSZUT, Urszula;** Singer (Soprano); b. 13 Dec. 1940, Psycszyna, Poland; m. Gerhard Geist. *Education:* Studied with Maria Eichler-Cholewa in Katowice and with Bogdan Ruskiewicz in Warsaw. *Career:* Debut: Stuttgart in 1967 as Lucia di Lammermoor; Guest appearances in Germany, Warsaw, Geneva, Zürich, Lisbon, Chicago and Toronto; Roles include Regina in Mathis der Maler, Norma, Gounod's Juliette, Mozart's Donna Anna and Fiordiligi and parts in operas by Strauss, Verdi and Puccini; Concert engagements in works by Beethoven, Bach, Brahms, Handel, Haydn, Mozart and Mahler; Glyndebourne in 1970 as the Queen of Night; Member of the Vienna Staatsoper from 1971; Hamburg Staatsoper in the premieres of Ein Stern geht auf aus Jakob by Burkhard, Staatstheater by Kagel and Under Milkwood by Steffens; Further engagements at Cologne and Stuttgart. *Recordings:* Beethoven's 9th Symphony, conducted by Kempe; Roles in Don Giovanni, Mathis der Maler, Sutermeister's Romeo and Juliet and Paer's Leonora; Countess de la Roche in Zimmermann's Die Soldaten. *Address:* Lilienstrasse 26, 6670 St Ingbert, Germany.

**KOTCHERGA, Anatoly;** Singer (Bass); b. 1947, Ukraine, USSR. *Education:* Studied conducting at the Vinitza Conservatory, then singing at the Tchaikovsky Conservatory, Kiev; Further study with Marguerita Corosio and Giulio Cassaletta, 1975–76. *Career:* Leading soloist at the Kiev Opera from 1972, notably as Basilio, Mephistopheles, Pimen and Arkel; Guest appearances at La Scala Milan, and in Canada, Spain, France, Bulgaria, Czechoslovakia, Germany and Australia; Has sung Boris Godunov with the company of Warsaw Opera (also televised, 1986); Vienna Staatsoper 1988–91, as Shaklovity in Khovanshchina and in Don Carlos; Theater an der Wien, Vienna, as the Commendatore in Don Giovanni (1990); Season 1992 as Boris and The Sergeant in Lady Macbeth of the Mtsensk District at the Opéra Bastille, Paris and La Scala Milan; Concert appearances include Rimsky's Mozart and Salieri at the Vienna Konzerthaus and a recital of Russian songs in Lyons; Sang Boris Godunov at Montpellier, 1996; Pimen in Boris at Toulouse, 1998. *Recordings:* Khovanshchina by Mussorgsky, conducted by Abbado. *Honours:* Winner, Glinka Competition 1971 (Prize from the Ukrainian Ministry of Culture); Prizewinner at international competitions in Berlin 1973 and Moscow (Tchaikovsky Competition) 1974. *Address:* c/o Schaddeck Gasse 5/H, Anately, 1060 Vienna, Austria.

**KOTCHINIAN, Arutjun;** Singer (Bass); b. 1965, Armenia. *Education:* Tchaikovsky Conservatory, Moscow, with Yevgeny Nesterenko, and with Helmuth Rilling. *Career:* Principal of the Deutsche Oper Berlin from 1996, as Wurm in Luisa Miller, Zaccaria in Nabucco, Gounod's Mephistopheles and Henry VIII in Anna Bolena; Guest artist in Munich, Dresden, Barcelona and Bregenz as Don Giovanni, Leporello, Banquo, Sparafucile, Philip II and the Grand Inquisitor; Season 2001–2002 as Lodovico in Otello at Covent Garden, Verdi Requiem in Berlin, Zaccaria at Bilbao and Fiesco in Simon Boccanegra at San Diego. *Honours:* Winner, ARD Competition; Munich, 1996. *Address:* Deutsche Oper, Bismarckstrasse 35, 10627 Berlin, Germany.

**KOTIK, Petr;** Composer, Conductor and Flautist; b. 27 Jan. 1942, Prague, Czechoslovakia; m. 30 Sept 1966, 2 s. *Education:* Flute, State Conservatory, Prague, 1956–62; Flute, Music Academy, Prague, 1962–63, 1966–69; Composition, Flute, Music Academy, Vienna, 1963–66. *Career:* In 1964 performed with John Cage and Merce Cunningham Dance Company in Vienna, Prague and Warsaw; Founder of SEM Ensemble, group dedicated to performance of post-Cagean music including Kotik's compositions, 1970; Since 1972 SEM Ensemble performs yearly concerts, USA and Europe; In 1992 founded Orchestra of the SEM Ensemble, recording CD of works by Cage; Conducted the SEM Orchestra, to critical acclaim, in major concerts at Carnegie Hall, 1992, Schausspielhaus Berlin, Alice Tully Hall at Lincoln Center, Prague Spring Festival and Oji Hall, Tokyo; Performed and conducted at 400 Years of Music in Prague, 1994; Conducted Manhattan Book of the Dead, opera by David First, New York, 1995; Premiered works by Myers, Michell, Lewis and Smith in New York, 1995; Many performances in Europe and the USA with the SEM Ensemble. *Compositions include:* Music for Three, 1964; Kontrabandt, live electronic music, WDR Cologne commission, 1967; There is Singularly Nothing, text Gertrude Stein, 1971–73; John Mary, text Gertrude Stein, 1973; Many Many Women, text Gertrude Stein, 1975–78; Explorations in the Geometry of Thinking, text R Buckminster Fuller, 1978–80; Solos and Instrumental Harmonies, 1981–83; Wilsie Bridge, WDR Cologne commission, 1986–87; Letters to Olga, text Václav Havel, 1989–91; Quiescent Form for orchestra, 1994–95. *Recordings include:* 1st record: There is Singularly Nothing Nos 1 and 11, 1975; Entire Music by Marcel Duchamp, 1976; With John Cage, 1991; Petr Kotik: SEM Ensemble. *Address:* SEM Ensemble, 25 Columbia Place, Brooklyn, NY 11201, USA.

**KOTILAINEN, Juha;** Singer (Baritone); b. 1954, Finland. *Education:* Studied at the Kuopio Academy and the Sibelius Academy in Helsinki. *Career:* Sang at first in concert, then made opera debut at Helsinki in 1986 as Dandini in La Cenerentola; Has made many appearances as Mozart's Figaro and sang in the premieres of Rautavaara's Vincent at Helsinki in 1990 and Sallinen's Kullervo at Los Angeles in 1992; Engaged at the Aalto Theatre in Essen where roles have included Besenbinder in Humperdinck's Hansel and Gretel, Krushina in Smetana's The Bartered Bride and Pantalon in Prokofiev's The Love for Three Oranges; Recently he has appeared in title roles of Tchaikovsky's Eugene Onegin, Bartók's Duke Bluebeard's Castle and Guglielmo in Così fan tutte; Has also performed in Paul Dessau's opera Die Verurteilung des Lukullus and appeared as Paolo in Verdi's Simon Boccanegra; Title role of Mozart's Don Giovanni at the Aalto Theatre in 1995; Sang the Priest in Dallapiccola's Prigioniero, for Tampere Open, 1996; Season 2000–01 with Puccini's Sharpless and Marcello at Helskinki and Leontes in the premiere of Boesmans's Wintermärchen, at Brussels and the Paris Châtelet; Repertoire also includes solo songs and bass and baritone parts in great church music works; Has appeared in Bach's St Matthew Passion and the B minor Mass; Has given recitals in Finland, Scandinavia, Germany, Greece and Russia. *Recordings:* Numerous for various labels. *Address:* c/o Fazer Artists' Management Inc., Nervanderink, 5 E Y6, 00100 Helsinki, Finland.

**KOTKOVA, Hana;** Violinist; b. 3 May 1967, Olomouc, Czechoslovakia. *Education:* Conservatory Ostrava; Music Academy, Prague; International Menuhin Music Academy, Gstaad; Masterclasses with W Marschner, J Gingold, P Amoyal. *Career:* Debut: Opava with Opava Chamber Orchestra, 1977; Recitals and solos with orchestras in Czech Republic, Switzerland, Sweden, Italy and France, 1985–; Plays with Camerata Lysy, Yehudi Menuhin and A Lysy in Europe and USA, 1990–93; Chamber Music with N Magaloff, Jeremy Menuhin, P Coker; Recital in Prague, Rudolfinum (Dvořáks Hall) for Y Menuhin's 80, 1996; Duo with English Pianist S Mulligan, 1996–. *Recordings:* 1 CD with Enescu and Janáček, Sonatas; 1 CD with Martinů, 3 Sonatas. *Honours:* Laureat of Kocian's International Competition, 1977; 1st Prize, Beethoven International Competition, 1985; Winner, Prague Spring Competition, 1997; The Gideon Klein Foundation Prize, 1997; City of Prague Prize, 1997. *Current Management:* Prague Autumn, Prague. *Address:* Case di Sopra, 6935 Bosco Luganese, Switzerland.

**KOTONSKI, Wlodzimierz;** Composer; b. 23 Aug. 1925, Warsaw, Poland; m. Jadwiga Chlebowska, 1951, 1 s. *Education:* MMus, Warsaw State Highter School of Music. *Career:* With Experimental Music Studio of Westdeutscher Rundfunk, Cologne, Federal Republic of Germany, 1966–67; Professor of Composition, Head of Electronic Music Studio, Academy of Music, Warsaw, Poland, 1967–; Chief Music Director, Polish Radio and Television, 1974–76; Lecturer on Composition, USA, 1978; 1983–89, President of the ISCM Polish Section. *Compositions include:* Orchestral and chamber music, electronic and tape music and instrumental theatre; Guitar Concerto, 1994; Winter Journey for ensemble, 1995; Symphony, 1995; Speculum vitae, for orchestra and tape, 1996; Violin Concerto, 1996; Mijikayo, for Japanese instruments, 1996. *Publications:* Goralski and Zbojnicki, 1958; Percussion Instruments in the Modern Orchestra, 1967; Muzyka elektroniczna, 1989. *Address:* Academy of Music, Okolnik 2, Warsaw 00-368, Poland.

**KOTOSKI, Dawn;** Singer (Soprano); b. 1967, Maryland, USA. *Education:* Studied in New York. *Career:* Sang in the YCA concert series in Washington and New York, 1990–91; Further concerts at Carnegie Hall, Avery Fisher Hall, with the Atlanta, Baltimore and Chicago Symphony Orchestras and at the Metropolitan Opera; Sang Mozart's Susanna with the Canadian Opera Company at Calgary, in Handel's Partenope at Omaha and as Massenet's Sophie at St Louis; European engagements as Pamina, Oscar and Musetta at the Vienna Staatsoper, Susanna at Munich, Gilda in Strasbourg and Oscar at the Opéra Bastille, Paris; Gilda, Adele in Die Fledermaus, Sophie and Musetta, Zürich Opera season 1996–97; Engaged as Jemmy in a new production of Guillaume Tell in Vienna and as Zdenka in Arabella at Santa Fe; Concert repertory includes Die Schöpfung, by Haydn. *Recordings include:* Handel's Acis and Galtaea, and Giustino; Lisa in La Sonnambula, with Edita

Gruberova. *Address:* c/o Opernhaus Zürich, Falkenstrasse 1, 8008 Zürich, Switzerland.

**KOUBA, Maria;** Singer (Soprano); b. 1924, Altenmarkt, Austria. *Education:* Studied at the Graz Conservatory. *Career:* Debut: Graz, 1957, as Salome; Sang at Graz, 1957–61, Frankfurt from 1961: roles included Madama Butterfly, Salome, both Leonoras of Verdi, Alice Ford, Jenůfa, Senta, Eva, Tosca and Octavian; Guest appearances in Paris, 1962, London 1963 as Salome; Metropolitan Opera 1964–65; Brussels, Vancouver, Santa Fe, Naples, Vienna, Hamburg and Berlin; Other roles include Donna Anna, Liu, and Marenka in The Bartered Bride.

**KOUKL, George;** Pianist and Composer; b. 23 March 1953, Origlio, Switzerland. *Education:* Milan Conservatory; Diploma, Zürich Conservatory; Masterclasses. *Career:* Debut: 1972; Radio recordings for BBC London, NRK Oslo, Radio Vienna, SR6 Zürich, SSR Lausanne; Television appearances for Swiss television; Concerts in Europe, USA, Japan, South America; Festivals; Masterclasses; mem, Schweizerischer Tonkunstlerverein; Mensa Music, USA. *Compositions:* Pandora's Box; Te Deum; Quartet for wind instruments; Sonata for clarinet and piano; Ideograms, 1991, Radio Lugano. *Recordings:* Various. *Honours:* Alienor Award, Washington, 1986. *Current Management:* Music Play Management, 6947 Vaglio, Switzerland. *Address:* Casa La Campagnola, 6945 Origlio, Switzerland.

**KOUKOS, Periklis;** Composer and Opera Director; b. 3 Jan. 1960, Athens, Greece. *Education:* Studied Composition with Yannis Papaionnou and Dimitris Dragatakis in Athens, with Hans Werner Henze and Paul Patterson in London. *Career:* Composer; Professor of Piano, Advanced Theory and Composition at the National and the Athens Conservatories, 1990–; Artistic Director, Greek National Opera, 1997–99; Artistic Director and Supervisor of Millennium Advent, Acropolis, 1999–2000; President of the Hellenic Festival SA, 2000–. *Compositions include:* Merlin the Magician, children's opera, 1987–89; Conroy's Other Selves, opera in 1 act, Athens, 1990; The Manuscript of Manuel Salinas, opera in 3 acts; A Midsummer Night's Dream, opera-ballet, 1982. *Address:* c/o Hellenic Festival SA, Hadjichristou 23 and Mauriyanni S, 11742 Athens, Greece.

**KOUNADIS, Arghyris;** Composer; b. 14 Feb. 1924, Constantinople, Turkey. *Education:* Studied Piano at Athens Conservatory and with Yanni Papaionnou at the Hellenic Conservatory; Further studies with Wolfgang Fortner in Freiburg. *Career:* Director of Musica Viva concerts at Freiburg from 1963, Professor at Hochschule für Musik, 1972. *Compositions include:* Operas: The Return (performed Athens, 1991); Der Gumminsarg, Bonn, 1968; Die verhexten Notenstander, Freiburg, 1971; Tirésias, Heidelberg, 1975; Der Ausbruch, Bayreuth, 1975; Die Bassgeige, Freiburg, 1979; Lysistrate, Lubeck, 1983; Der Sandmann, Hamburg, 1987. *Address:* c/o Staatliche Hochschule für Musik, Freiburg im Breisgau, Schwarzwaldstrasse 141, 7800 Freiburg im Breisgau, Germany.

**KOUT, Jiri;** conductor; *Music Director, St Gallen Theater;* b. 26 Dec. 1937, Novedvory, Czechoslovakia. *Education:* Prague Conservatory, Nat. Acad. of Music, Prague. *Career:* first engagement as resident conductor, Pilsen Opera and Symphony Orchestra; Principal Conductor of the Nat. Opera in Prague, also appearing with the Prague Symphony Orchestra and the Nat. Radio Orchestra; Principal Conductor, Deutsche Oper am Rhein, Düsseldorf 1978–84; Musical Dir, Saarbruck 1985; conducted Der Rosenkavalier at Munich 1985, leading to engagements in Stuttgart, Berlin and Vienna; debut with the Berlin Philharmonic 1987; regular appearances in Saarbrucken, Venice, Naples, Florence, Cincinnati and Birmingham; conducted Katya Kabanova in Paris and Los Angeles 1988; Principal Resident Conductor, Deutsche Oper Berlin 1990, with Lady Macbeth, Tristan und Isolde and Mathis der Maler; Bluebeard's Castle at the Vienna Staatsoper; returned to Los Angeles with Boris Godunov and Parsifal; Metropolitan Opera debut 1991 (Der Rosenkavalier); season 1992 with Tannhäuser at the Deutsche Oper Berlin and The Makropulos Case at Los Angeles; Covent Garden debut 1993, with Jenůfa; Musical Dir, Leipzig Opera 1993; Wagner's Ring at the Deutsche Oper 1997; Elektra at San Francisco 1997–98; Der Rosenkavalier at the Met 2000; conducts leading orchestras, including Berliner Philharmonic, Gewandhausorchester Leipzig, München Philharmoniker, Gürzenichochester Köln, Orchestre Nat. de France, Orchestre de Paris, Orchestre Nat. du Capitole de Toulouse, Orchestre Nat. de Bordeaux Aquitaine, Los Angeles Philharmonic Orchestra, Birmingham Symphony Orchestra, NHK Symphonie Orchestra of Tokyo, Orchestra Sinfonica Nationale della RAI Torino, Orchestra Filarmonica della Scala Milano, Orchestra dell'Accademia di Santa Cecilia Roma, and Orquesta Nacional de España, Madrid; currently Music Dir, St Gallen Theater and Chief Conductor, St Gallen Symphony Orchestra. *Honours:* winner of conducting competitions at Besançon and Brussels 1965, 1969. *Current Management:* c/o Peter Wiggins, IMG Artists, 44 rue Blanche, 75009 Paris, France. *Telephone:* 1 44 31 00 10. *Fax:* 1 44 31 44 40. *E-mail:* pwiggins@imgartists.com. *Website:* www.imgartists.com. *Address:* Theater St Gallen, Museumstrasse 1/24, 9004 St Gallen, Switzerland. *Website:* www.theaterstgallen.ch.

**KOVACEVICH, Stephen;** American pianist; b. 17 Oct. 1940, San Francisco; s. of Nicholas Kovacevich and Loreta Kovacevich (née Zuban). *Education:* Berkeley High School, Calif. *Career:* studied under Lev Shorr and Dame Myra Hess; London début 1961; subsequently appeared at int. music festivals in Edin., Bath, Harrogate, Berlin, San Sebastián and Salzburg; a soloist at Henry Wood Promenade Concerts for fourteen seasons; tours frequently in Europe, America and Australasia; fmr Prin. Guest Conductor of Australian Chamber Orchestra; fmr Music Dir of Irish Chamber Orchestra; has conducted City of Birmingham Symphony, BBC Philharmonic, Bournemouth Symphony, Royal Liverpool Philharmonic orchestras, Chamber Orchestra of Europe, London Mozart Players, Nat. Youth Chamber Orchestra; numerous recordings. *Publication:* Schubert Anthology. *Honours:* winner of Kimber Award, Calif. 1959, Mozart Prize, London 1962, Edison Award (for recording of Bartok's 2nd Piano Concerto), Gramophone Award 1993 (for recording of Brahms' 1st Piano Concerto). *Current Management:* Van Walsum Management Ltd, 4 Addison Bridge Place, London, W14 8XP, England. *Telephone:* (20) 7371-4343. *Fax:* (20) 7371-4344. *Website:* www.vanwalsum.co.uk.

**KOVACIC, Ernst;** Austrian violinist and conductor; b. 12 April 1943, Kapfenberg; m. Anna Maria Schuster 1968; four s. *Education:* Acad. of Music, Univ. of Music, Vienna. *Career:* teacher Univ. of Music, Vienna 1975–; prizewinner, int. competitions, Geneva 1970, Barcelona 1971, Munich 1972; appears throughout Europe, UK and USA with leading orchestras and has appeared at many festivals including Salzburg, Berlin, Vienna, Bath, Edin., Aldeburgh and London Proms; first performances of works by composers including H. K. Gruber, K. Schwertsik, E. Krenek, F. Cerhe, I. Erod, R. Holloway, B. Furrer, G. F. Haas, N. Osbourne, K. H. Essl, H. Eder; repertoire includes maj. works of baroque, classical and romantic periods and contemporary works; Artistic Dir Vienna Chamber Orchestra 1996–98; Pres. Ernst Krenek Privatstiftung. *Address:* Kriehuberpasse 29/5, 1050 Vienna, Austria (home).

**KOVACK, Eszter;** Singer (Soprano); b. 18 May 1939, Tiszanana, Hungary. *Education:* Studied at the Franz Liszt Academy, Budapest. *Career:* Debut: Budapest National Opera, 1965, as Mercédès in Carmen; Sang in the dramatic repertory throughout Hungary, and as a guest in Prague, Warsaw, Moscow, Berlin and Washington; Metropolitan Opera, New York, 1982–84, notably as Brünnhilde in Die Walküre; Other roles include Leonore in Fidelio; Wagner's Elisabeth, Elsa, Eva and Sieglinde; Frequent concert appearances. *Address:* c/o National Opera, Nepoztarasag utja 22, 1061 Budapest, Hungary.

**KOVÁCS, Dénes;** Hungarian violinist; b. 18 April 1930, Vác; s. of József Kovács and Margit Juhász; m.; one s. one d. *Education:* Budapest Acad. of Music under Ede Zathureczky. *Career:* First Violinist, Budapest State Opera 1951–60; leading Violin Prof. at Budapest Music Acad. 1957–, Dir Budapest Music Acad. 1967; Rector Ferenc Liszt Acad. of Music 1971–80, Dean of String Dept 1980–; concert tours all over Europe, in USA, USSR, Iran, India, China and Japan; mem. jury in int. competitions: Tchaikovsky, Moscow, Long-Thibaud, Paris, Jean Sibelius, Helsinki, Joseph Joachim, Vienna, Wieniawski, Warsaw, and in Tokyo. *Recordings include:* Vivaldi – The Four Seasons 1962, Buxtehude – Trio Sonata in E major (Op. 2, No. 6) 1963, Gluck – Trio Sonata in G minor 1963, Vivaldi – Twelve Sonatas for Violin and Continuo (Op. 2) 1967–68, Corelli – Twelve Sonatas for Violin and Continuo (Op. 5) 1970, Caldara – Trio Sonata 1972, Gluck – Trio Sonata 1972, Gluck – Trio Sonata in E major 1980, Leffloth – Concerto for Violin and Harpsichord in D major 1980, Stölzel – Trio Sonata in F minor 1980, J. S. Bach – Trio Sonata for Flute, Violin and Continuo from The Musical Offering (BWV 1079), Beethoven – Sonatas for Violin and Piano, Beethoven – Violin Concerto Op. 61, Beethoven – Romances in F major Op. 50 and in G major Op. 40, Mendelssohn-Bartholdy – Violin Concerto in E minor Op. 64, Mozart – Four Sonatas for Violin and Piano, Nos 18, 21, 26 and 34. *Honours:* Golden Medal of Labour 1974; Kossuth Prize 1963, awarded Eminent Artist title 1970. *Address:* Music Academy, Liszt Ferenc tér 8, 1061 Budapest VI (office); Irányi utca 12, Budapest V, Hungary (home). *Telephone:* (1) 141-4788 (office).

**KOVACS, Janos;** Conductor; b. 1951, Budapest, Hungary. *Education:* Study under Professor Andràs Korodi, Ferenc Liszt Academy of Music, Budapest, 1971. *Career:* Coach, Conductor, Budapest State Opera; Musical Assistant, Bayreuth Festival, 1978, 1979; Frequent Conductor of top Hungarian Symphony Orchestras; Has conducted several guest performances given by the Budapest State Opera at the Dresden Festival and in the Berlin State Opera House; Two guest performances with Hungarian State Symphony Orchestra and festive concert series marking opening of Berlin's reconstructed Neues Konzerthaus, 1984; Conductor of several performances at Vienna Chamber Opera, 1984; Suisse Romande Orchestra, Geneva, Switzerland, 1985. *Honours:* Liszt Prize, 1985; Conducted Le nozze di Figaro at Budapest, 1998. *Address:* Hungarian State Opera, Nepotarsasag utja 22, 1061 Budapest, Hungary.

**KOVACZ, Peter;** Singer (Baritone); b. 1952, Budapest, Hungary. *Education:* Studied in Budapest, Dortmund and Munich. *Career:* Sang in opera at Munich and Pforzheim, followed by Gelsenkirchen and Dortmund; Appearances throughout Germany in operas by Mozart, Verdi and Wagner, notably as Gunther in Götterdämmerung, 1994, Dortmund. *Honours:* Treviso Singers Competition, 1978, winner for performances as Silvio in Pagliacci. *Address:* Dortmund Opera, Kuhstrasse 12, 4600 Dortmund, Germany.

**KOVATS, Kolos;** Singer (Bass); b. 1948, Hungary. *Education:* Ferenc Liszt Academy of Music, Budapest. *Career:* Budapest State Opera. Has made numerous appearances including operas The Magic Flute, Eugene Onegin, Boris Godunov, Don Carlos, La Forza del Destino, Ernani, Simon Boccanegra, Norma and title role in Rossini's Moses, in concert halls and opera houses around the world; Title role in Bartók's Duke Bluebeard's Castle; Sang Zaccaria in Nabucco at Brussels, 1987; Bluebeard at Turin, 1989; Sang Catalani's La Wally at the 1990 Bregenz Festival; Other roles include Verdi's

Philip, Banquo, Sparalucile, Fiesco, Padre Guardiano, Pagno (Lombardi), Fernando, Silva and Ramphis; Also Mozart's Sarastro and Commendatore, Mephistopheles, Creon, Oroveso, Pimen, Gremin and Henry VIII in Anna Bolena; Sang Bluebeard at the Théâtre du Châtelet, Paris, 1996; Has appeared in television and films; Oratorios. *Recordings include:* Has made numerous records: Medea, Ernani, Don Carlos, Lombardi, Macbeth, Liszt's St Elizabeth, Masses by Mozart and Schubert, Guillaume Tell; Video of Bluebeard's Castle, conducted by Solti. *Honours:* 1st Prize, Erkel International Voice Contest, 1973; 1st Prize, Rio de Janeiro International Vocal Competition, 1973; 2nd Prize, Moscow Tchaikovsky International Vocal Concurs, 1974; Recipient, Liszt Prize; Kossuth Prize, 1992. *Address:* c/o Hungarian State Opera House, Andrássy u 22, 1061 Budapest, Hungary.

**KOWALKE, Kim H.,** BA, MA, MPhil, PhD; American academic and musicologist; *Richard L. Turner Professor of Humanities, University of Rochester;* b. 25 June 1948, Monticello, Minnesota, USA; m. Elizabeth Keagy, 19 Aug 1978, 1 s. *Education:* Macalester Coll., Yale Univ. *Career:* Asst Prof. of Music 1977–82, Assoc. Prof. 1982–86, Occidental Coll., Los Angeles, CA; Prof. of Music and Musicology, Eastman School of Music, Univ. of Rochester, NY 1986–, Richard L. Turner Prof. of Humanities 2004–; Pres., Kurt Weill Foundation for Music Inc.; mem. editorial bd, Kurt Weill Edition 1992–. *Publications:* Kurt Weill in Europe 1979, A New Orpheus: Essays on Kurt Weill (ed.) 1986, Accounting for Success: Misunderstanding Die Dreigroschenoper 1990, A Stranger Here Myself: Kurt Weill Studien (ed.) 1993, Speak Low: The Letters of Kurt Weill and Lotte Lenya (ed. 1995. *Honours:* five times winner ASCAP-Deems Taylor Award for Excellence in Writing about Music, Theatre Library Asscn Friedley Award, two times winner of Sonneck Soc. for American Music Irving Lowens Prize for best article on American Music, Univ. of Rochester Goergen Award for Distinguished Achievment and Artistry in undergraduate education. *Address:* 888 Quaker Road, Scottsville, NY 14546-9757, USA. *Telephone:* (585) 275-8340 (office); (585) 889-3615 (home). *Fax:* (585) 273-5337 (office); (585) 889-3615 (home). *E-mail:* kkwk@mail.rochester.edu (office).

**KOWALSKI, David (Leon);** Composer; b. 29 March 1956, New Haven, Connecticut, USA; m. Michelle Disco, 2 Sept 1983, deceased 29 April 1994. *Education:* BA, University of Pennsylvania, 1978; MM, Composition, New England Conservatory of Music, 1981; PhD, Composition, Princeton University, 1985; Private studies with Donald Martino, Arthur Berger, Milton Babbitt. *Career:* Freelance Composer, 1978–. *Compositions include:* Quintus Obscurus, bass flute, viola, celeste and 2 percussion, 1977; Metamorphosis, jazz trio and orchestra, 1978; Dichotomies, solo viola, 1979, revised 1983; Come Sopra, oboe and cello, 1979; Les Voyageurs, horn and 3 celli, 1979, revised 1991; Quintetino, string quartet and piano, 1980; Concertino, flute/piccolo, clarinet, horn, violin, cello, bass, harp, piano and 2 percussion, 1980; Double Helix, orchestra, 1980, revised 1991; Alle Tode, soprano and piano, 1981; String Quartet No. 2, 1982; Chamber Concerto, 1982, revised 1984; Toccata, organ, 1982; Circonspection, soprano and clarinet, 1983; Four Frames, percussion quartet, 1983; Clarinet Quartet, clarinet, violin, cello and piano, 1983; Variations, wind quartet, 1983, revised 1991; Premonitions, piano solo, 1983; Skid Row, computer-generated tape, 1983; Masques, oboe, 1984; Echoes, soprano and computer-generated tape, 1984; Windhover, soprano and piano, 1985; Masques II, solo flute, 1986; Masques III, solo clarinet, 1987; Two Sonnets for soprano and piano, 1988; A Memory of Evening, mezzo and piano, 1989. *Recordings:* Double Helix performed by Silesian Philharmonic, with Joel Suben conducting, CD, 1995. *Address:* 32 Academy St, PO Box 501, Kingston, NJ 08528, USA.

**KOWALSKI, Jochen;** German singer (countertenor); b. 30 Jan. 1954, Wachow, Brandeburg. *Education:* Berlin Musikhochschule with Heinz Reeh, studied with Marianne Fischer-Kupfer. *Career:* sang at the Handel Festival Halle 1982, in the pasticcio Muzio Scevola; Has appeared with the Komische Oper Berlin from 1983, debut as Feodor in Boris Godunov; Guest appearances at the State Operas of Munich and Hamburg; Paris Opéra 1987 as Ptolomeo in Giulio Cesare; Vienna Staatsoper 1987 as Orlofsky in Die Fledermaus; Vienna Volksoper in Giustino by Handel; Has also sung in Düsseldorf, 1989, Amsterdam and Minneapolis; Sang Gluck's Orpheus with the Komische Oper at Covent Garden 1989, returned as Orlofsky 1990, in performances which also featured Joan Sutherland's retirement; Other roles include Daniel in Handel's Belshazzar, and Annio in La Clemenza di Tito; Sang Farnace in Mozart's Mitridate, Covent Garden 1991, Amsterdam 1992; Ottone in L'Incoronazione di Poppea at the 1993 Salzburg Festival; Sang Britten's Oberon at the Met, 1996–97 and at the Vienna Volksoper, 1998. *Recordings include:* Baroque Arias by Prussian composers; Handel and Mozart Arias; Gluck's Orfeo and Euridice; Symphoniae Sacrae by Schütz (Capriccio). *Address:* c/o Komische Oper, Behrenstrasse 55–57, 1080 Berlin, Germany.

**KOX, Hans;** Composer; b. 19 May 1930, Arnhem, Netherlands. *Education:* Studied at Utrecht Conservatory and with Henk Badings, 1951–55. *Career:* Director of Doetinchem Music School, 1957–71; Teacher at Utrecht Conservatory, 1971–. *Compositions include:* Over 200 symphonic, operatic and chamber music works including: Dorian Gray, opera, 1974, Lord Rochester, opera, 1978, 3 Symphonies, 1959, 1966 and 1985, Le Songe du Vergier for Cello and Orchestra, 1986, Magnificat I and II for Vocal Ensemble, 1989–90, Das Grune Gesicht, opera, 1981–91, Sonate for Violoncello and Piano, revised 1991, Face to Face, concerto for Altosaxophone and Strings, 1992, Cyclophony XIV, The Birds of Aengus for Violin and Harp, 1992, Oratorium Sjoah, 1993, Violin Concerto No. 3, 1993, Orkester Suite Aus der Oper Das Grune Gesicht,

1994, Ballet Suite for Orchestra, revised 1994, Das Credo Quia Absurdum for Soprano Solo, Bass Solo, Choir and Orchestra, 1995. *Recordings:* 3 CDs: L'Allegria, Oratorium Sjoah and Chamber music 'Through a Glass, Darkly'. *Honours:* Visser Neerlandia Prize for Symphony No. 1, 1959; Prix Italia for In Those Days, 1970; 1st Prize, Rostrum of Composers for L'Allegria, 1974. *Address:* c/o Hans Kox Foundation, Vier Heemskinderenstraat 42 hs, 1055 LL Amsterdam, Netherlands.

**KOZAR, John;** Concert Pianist and Conductor; b. 12 June 1946, Indiana, USA. *Education:* Academy of Music, Zagreb, Croatia; BMus, MMus, Indiana University, USA. *Career:* Debut: New York, 1978; British Concerto Debut, 1981; Teacher: University of Kansas, Indiana University, New England College, State University of New York, Ball State University; Recitals: New York City, London, Chicago, Munich, Vienna, Zagreb, Hong Kong, Johannesburg, Paris, Vancouver, Sydney; Concertos: Australia, London Philharmonic, Brooklyn Philharmonic; Television: Public Broadcasting Systems, Hong Kong Television, Scottish Television, SABC, CBC, Vancouver; Radio: Numerous radio performances, Nationally and Internationally; Conducting: Music Director, Kentish Opera Group, England; Music Director, Opera Program, State University of New York, Potsdam; Program Director, The Beethoven Foundation, Indiana; Freelance, Conductor, Opera, Ballet; Founded Piano Productions, 1989; Music Director and Conductor of Grand Piano Orchestra, including three tours of China. *Recordings:* Various albums. *Publications:* Annotated Bibliography of American Composer Emerson Whithorne, in progress. *Contributions:* Articles in professional journals. *Current Management:* Piano Productions Inc, 2063 Lombard Street, Philadelphia, PA 19146, USA.

**KOŽELUHOVA, Jitka;** Composer, Pianist and Singer; b. 19 Nov. 1966, Prague, Czechoslovakia; m. Marcus Gerhardts 1996; one s. *Education:* Conservatory of Prague; Music Faculty of the Acad. of Performing Arts in Prague. *Compositions:* Sonatine for pianoforte, 1986; Touzeni (Longing) cycle of songs for soprano and pianoforte, 1987; Obrazy (Images), string quartet, 1990–91; Six Songs On The Texts Of The Poems Of Emily Dickinson, cycle for soprano and pianoforte, 1991–92; Three Sentences About The Story Of Christmas, quartet for oboe, clarinet, bassoon and pianoforte, 1992–93; further compositions: Pierres (Stones) (cycle of women's choirs), 1992; Aus Der Tiefe (de Profundis) for mixed choir with soprano solo, 2 narrators and organ, 1994; Secret Dolour, Fantasy on themes from Schubert's Rondo Op 84, for 4 piano hands, 1994; The Inner Voice, viola solo and symphony orchestra, 1994–95; All You Are Thirsty, Come To The Waters, small cantata for alto and baritone solo, English horn, piano and percussions, 1995; For Angels, for 2 flutes, 2 clarinets, string quartet and piano, 1996; Yet, Still, the Hallelujah is Sounding, for piano and cello, 1998. *Address:* Na Roktyce 30, 18000 Prague 8, Czech Republic.

**KOŽENÁ, Magdalena;** Czech singer (mezzo-soprano); b. 26 May 1973, Brno; pnr Sir Simon Rattle; one s. *Education:* Conservatoire, Brno, Acad. of Music and Dramatic Art, Bratislava. *Career:* guest singer, Janáček Opera, Brno 1991–; debut as soloist, Vienna Volksoper 1996–97; recent appearances include Bach's B Minor Mass at the QEH, London 2000, Salzburg Festival debut as Zerlina in Don Giovanni 2002, charity concerts following floods in Czech Repub. 2002, Idamante in Idomeneo at Glyndebourne 2003; regular appearances for Czech radio and television; tours in Europe, USA, Japan, Venezuela, Taiwan, Hong Kong, Republic of Korea, Canada; roles include Dorabella in Così fan tutte, Isabella in Italiana in Algeri (Rossini), Venus in Dardanus (Rameau), Mercedes in Carmen, Annius in La Clemenza di Tito, Paris in Paride ed Elena, lead in Orfeo ed Eurydice (both Gluck), lead in Hermia (Britten), Poppea in L'Incoronazione di Poppea (Monteverdi), Mélisande (Debussy). *Recordings include:* Bach Arias (Harmony Magazine Award 1998), Johann Sebastian Bach Cantatas 2000, G. F. Handel Italian Cantatas 2000, G. F. Handel Messiah 2001, Magdalena Kožená – Le belle imagini (Echo Klassik Award 2002, Gold Record of Universal 2003) 2002, Johann Sebastian Bach Arias (Gold Record of Universal 2003, Platinum Record of Universal 2003) 2003, G. F. Handel – Giulio Cesare 2003, Magdalena Kožená – French Arias (Gramophone Award 2003) 2003, Magdalena Kožená – Songs 2004, Magdalena Kožená – Lamento 2004. *Honours:* Chevalier des Arts et des Lettres 2003; First Place in Int. Scheider Competition 1992, First Place in Int. Mozart Competition, Salzburg 1995, George Solti Prize (France), Youngster of Arts, Europe 1996, Orphée d'Or, L'Académie du Disque Lyrique (France) 1999, Diapason d'Or (France) 2000, Echo Klassik Best New Artist (Germany) 2000, Gramophone Awards (London) 2001, Gramophone Artist of the Year 2004, Person of the Year in Culture (Czech Repub.) 2002, 2003. *Current Management:* Central European Music Agency, Kapucínské nám. 14, 602 00 Brno, Czech Republic. *Telephone:* (5) 42213053. *Fax:* (5) 42213056. *E-mail:* david@cema-music.com. *Website:* www .cema-music.com. *Current Management:* Askonas Holt Ltd, Lonsdale Chambers, 27 Chancery Lane, London, WC1A 2PF, England. *Telephone:* (20) 7400-1720. *Fax:* (20) 7400-1723. *E-mail:* peter.bloor@askonasholt.co.uk. *Website:* www.askonasholt.co.uk. *Address:* Národní divadlo, Dvořákova 11, 600 00 Brno, Czech Republic (home). *E-mail:* obchodni.ndb@seznam. *Website:* www .kozena.cz; www.ndbrno.cz.

**KOZMA, Lajos;** Singer (Tenor); b. 1938, Lepesny, Hungary. *Education:* Franz Liszt Academy Budapest; Further study at the Accademia di Santa Cecilia Rome with Giorgio Favaretto and Franco Capuana. *Career:* First success as Debussy's Pelléas, Budapest, 1962; Appearances from 1964 in Florence, Venice, Rome, Milan, London, Philadelphia, New York and

Copenhagen; Amsterdam 1982, as Monteverdi's Orfeo; Teatro San Carlo Naples in Rossellini's La Reine Morte; Further engagements in Paris, Brussels, Aix-en-Provence and Strasbourg; Many concerts in oratorio and Lieder. *Recordings include:* Lucia di Lammermoor; Monteverdi Orfeo; Orlando Furioso by Vivaldi. *Address:* c/o Hungarian State Opera House, Népóztársaság utja 22, 1961 Budapest, Hungary.

**KRAEMER, Nicholas;** Conductor and Harpsichordist; b. 7 March 1945, Edinburgh, Scotland; m. Elizabeth Andreson; three s. (one deceased) two d. *Career:* Harpsichordist with Acad. of St Martin-in-the-Fields and English Baroque Soloists; founded Raglan Baroque Players, 1978, concerts, numerous radio and television broadcasts; first Musical Dir, Opera 80 (now English Touring Opera); conducted Mozart at Glyndebourne, 1980–83, ENO, 1992, Handel and Monteverdi operas, Paris, Lisbon, Amsterdam, Geneva, Marseille; Assoc. Conductor, BBC Scottish Symphony Orchestra, 1983–85; concerts with Polish Chamber Orchestra, Israel Chamber Orchestra, and Frysk Orkest, Netherlands; Artistic Dir, Irish Chamber Orchestra, 1986–92, Handel in Dublin concerts, 1988–89; concerts with Australian Chamber Orchestra, 1991, with Orchestra of the Age of Enlightenment in Mozart in London, 1991; Principal Guest Conductor, Manchester Camerata, 1992–; debuts, ENO, with Magic Flute, 1992, Marseille Opera, with Poppea, 1993; Artistic Dir, London Bach Orchestra; Season 1994–95 included visits to Munster Philharmonic and National Arts Centre Orchestra, Ottawa; with Scottish Chamber Orchestra: Purcell's Fairy Queen, Edinburgh and Glasgow, and two concerts, Orkney Festival; appeared with London Classical Players, Salzburg and Vienna, 1995; Season 1995–96 included concerts with Orchestra of Age of Enlightenment (Purcell series), CBSO and Northern Sinfonia (Purcell's Fairy Queen); Handel's Rodelinda for recording, dir, Jonathan Miller; Handel's Messiah with Scottish Chamber Orchestra; led the Raglan Baroque Players in Rodelinda for Broomhill Opera, 1996; Handel's Tolomeo in 1998; mem., Royal Society of Musicians. *Recordings:* Vivaldi Violin Concertos Op 9 with Monica Huggett, Op 8 including The Four Seasons with Raglan Baroque Players; complete harpsichord concertos of Bach; complete cello concertos of Vivaldi with Raphael Wallfisch; Locatelli Op 1, Op 3, with Raglan Baroque Players; Vivaldi Wind Concertos, La Stravaganza Op 4 with City of London Sinfonia. *Current Management:* Caroline Phillips Management, The Old Brushworks, Pickwick Road, Corsham, Wiltshire, SN13 9BX, England. *Telephone:* (1249) 716716. *Fax:* (1249) 716717. *E-mail:* cphillips@caroline -phillips.co.uk. *Website:* www.caroline-phillips.co.uk/kraemer.

**KRAFT, Jean;** Singer (mezzo-soprano); b. 9 Jan. 1940, Menasha, Wisconsin, USA. *Education:* Studied with Giannini Gregory at the Curtis Institute, Theodore Harrison in Chicago, William Ernst Vedal in Munich and Povla Frijsch in New York. *Career:* Debut: New York City Opera 1960, in Six Characters in Search of an Author by Weisgall; Sang in Houston, Boston, New Orleans, Philadelphia, Santa Fe, Chicago and Dallas; Metropolitan Opera from 1970, as Flora in La Traviata, Emilia (Otello) 1987, Herodias, Ulrica and Suzuki; Maggio Musicale Florence 1988, as Mrs Sedley in Peter Grimes. *Recordings include:* Andrea Chénier and Cavalleria Rusticana (RCA). *Address:* Metropolitan Opera, Lincoln Center, New York, NY 10023, USA.

**KRAFT, Leo (Abraham);** Composer and Teacher; b. 24 July 1922, New York, NY, USA; m. Amy Lager, 16 May 1945, 2 s. *Education:* Pupil in composition of Karol Rathaus, Queens College of the City University of New York, BA, 1945, Randall Thompson, Princeton University, MFA, 1947, and Nadia Boulanger, Paris, 1954–55. *Career:* Faculty Member, Queens College, 1947–. *Compositions:* Orchestral: Concerto for Flute, Clarinet, Trumpet and Strings, 1951; Variations, 1958; 3 Pieces, 1963; Concerto for Cello, Wind Quintet, and Percussion, 1968; Concerto for 12 Instruments, 1966–72; Music, 1975; Concerto for Piano and 14 Instruments, 1978; Chamber Symphony, 1980; Symphony in One Movement, 1985; Ricercare for Strings, 1985; Concerto for Oboe and Strings, 1986; Clarinet Concerto, 1986; Chamber Symphony No. 2, 1996; Chamber: 2 string quartets, 1951, 1959; Sextet, 1952; Partita for Wind Quintet, 1964; Trios and Interludes for Flute, Viola and Piano, 1965; Dialogues for Flute and Tape, 1968; Line Drawings for Flute and Percussion, 1972; Diaphonies for Oboe and Piano, 1975; Dialectica for Flute, Clarinet, Violin, Cello, and Tape, 1976; Conductus Novus for 4 Trombones, 1979; Episodes for Clarinet and Percussion, 1979; Interplay for Trumpet and Percussion, 1983; Strata for 8 Instruments, 1979–84; Washington Square, for 12 players, 1990; 5 Short Pieces for woodwind quintet; Piano pieces; Vocal works including The Vision of Isaiah, for chorus and orchestra, 1998. *Publications:* With S Berkowitz and G Fontrier, A New Approach to Ear Training, 1967; Gradus: An Integrated Approach to Harmony, Counterpoint, and Analysis, 1976, 2nd edition, 1987. *Address:* 9 Dunster Road, Great Neck, NY 11021, USA.

**KRAFT, William;** Composer; b. 6 Sept. 1923, Chicago, Illinois, USA; m. 2 s., 1 d. *Education:* Bachelor's Degree, cum laude, 1951; Master's Degree, 1954; Columbia University; Studied under Jack Beeson, Henry Brant, Henry Cowell, Paul Henry Lang, Otto Luening, Vladimir Ussachevsky. *Career:* Organised and directed Los Angeles Percussion Ensemble; as percussion soloist performed American premiere of Stockhausen's Zyklus and Boulez's Le Marteau sans Maitre; also recorded Histoire du Soldât under Stravinsky's direction; Conductor of contemporary and other music; Assistant Conductor of Los Angeles Philharmonic, 3 years; served as Musical Director and Chief Adviser, Young Musicians Foundation Debut Orchestra, Los Angeles; appeared frequently at Monday Evening Concerts; Visiting Professor in Composition, USC; Guest Lecturer in Composition, California Institute of

Arts, Faculty of Banff Center for Performing Arts; similar residences at University of Western Ontario, Royal Northern College of Music, Manchester, England among others; frequent lecturer at festivals and concert series including Percussive Arts Society International Conference, California State University, Sacramento Festival of New American Music, Res Musica Baltimore concert series; given numerous seminars and master classes at universities and music festivals; Composer-in-Residence, Los Angeles Philharmonic; Founder/Director, Los Angeles Philharmonic New Music group, 1981–85; Composer-in-Residence, Cheltenham International Music Festival, Cheltenham, England, 1986; Visiting Professor in Composition, UCLA, 1988–89. *Compositions include:* Dialogues and Entertainments for soprano solo and wind ensemble, 1980; Double Play for violin, piano and chamber orchestra, 1982; Gallery 83, 1983; Timpani Concerto, 1983; Contextures II: The Final Beast, 1984; Interplay, 1984; Weavings for string quartet, 1984; Gallery 4-5, 1985; Quintessence, 1985; Mélange, 1986; Of Ceremonies, Pageants and Celebrations, 1986; Quartet for the Love of Time, 1987; Interplay, 1984; Episodes, 1987; Horn Concerto, 1988; Kennedy Portrait, 1988; Vintage Rennaissance, for orchestra, 1989; Songs of Flowers, Bells and Death, 1991; Concerto for percussion and chamber ensemble, 1993; Music for String Quartet and Percussion, 1993; Symphony of Sorrows, 1995; Encounters IX, for English horn and percussion, 1999. *Recordings:* Many of his compositions recorded. *Address:* 1437 Crest Drive, Altadena, CA 91001, USA.

**KRAINEV, Vladimir Vsevolodovich;** Russian pianist; b. 1 April 1944, Krasnoyarsk; m. Tatyana Tarasova. *Education:* Moscow State Conservatory with Heinrich Neuhaus and Stanislav Neuhaus. *Career:* début with orchestra as child prodigy in Kharkov 1953, in Moscow 1963; prize winner of several int. competitions; soloist with maj. orchestras in many European cultural centres and festivals; played with Carlo Maria Giulini, Pierre Boulez, John Pritchard, Dmitry Kitayenko; teacher in Moscow Conservatory 1987–91, Hochschule für Musik in Hanover 1991–. *Repertoire includes:* most of classical concertos and all concertos by Mozart and Prokofiev. *Honours:* People's Artist of Russia 1984, USSR State Prize 1986. *Address:* Staatliche Hochschule für Musik und Theater, Walderseestrasse 100, Hanover, Germany. *Telephone:* (3212) 3641485 (Hanover); (095) 158-24-56 (Moscow).

**KRAJNY, Boris;** Pianist; b. 28 Nov. 1945, Kromeriz, Czechoslovakia. *Education:* Conservatory Kromeriz, 1959–63; Academy of Prague, 1963–69. *Career:* Soloist, Prague Chamber Orchestra, 1972–80 and with Czech Philharmonic, 1982–. *Recordings:* Bach's Complete Organ Works, and Busoni's Complete Organ Works, and works by Beethoven, Chopin, Ravel, Debussy, Prokofiev, Bartók, Honegger, Roussel, Poulenc, Martinů. *Honours:* 1st Prize, Piano Competition, Senigallia, 1976; Grand Prix du Disque Charles Gros Paris, 1982. *Address:* Czech Philharmony, Dum umelcu, 11000 Prague, Czech Republic.

**KRÄMER, Gunter;** Stage Director; b. 2 Dec. 1940, Neustadt an der Weinstrasse, Germany. *Education:* Studied at Heidelberg and Freiburg Universities. *Career:* Debut: First opera production, Krenek's Karl V at Darmstadt, 1979; Head of Drama at Bremen and produced Nono's Intelleranza 60 at Hamburg Staatsoper, 1985; Deutsche Oper am Rhein, Düsseldorf, 1986–87, with Die Tote Stadt and Schreker's Die Gezeichneten; Productions at Deutsche Oper Berlin have included The Makropulos Case (seen at Los Angeles, 1992); Die Entführung and Die Zauberflöte, 1991; Intendant of the Theatre Company of Cologne, 1990, producing Weill's Die Dreigroschenoper with it at the Spoleto Festival, 1991; Les Contes d'Hoffmann at Cologne, 1998. *Address:* c/o Opera Köln, Offenbachplatz, 50667 Köln, Germany.

**KRÄMER, Toni;** Singer (Tenor); b. 14 Sept. 1935, Malsch, Germany. *Education:* Studied at the Karlsruhe Musikhochschule. *Career:* Debut: Stuttgart 1965, in Les Contes d'Hoffmann; Sang in Stuttgart as Pinkerton and Alvaro, and other roles in operas by Puccini and Verdi; Sang Florestan and Erik in Klagenfurt, Parsifal and Lohengrin in Saarbrucken; Stuttgart Staatsoper as Walther in Die Meistersinger, Siegfried, and König Hirsch in the opera by Henze; Munich Staatsoper as Dimitri in Boris Godunov; Bayreuth Festival 1985–86, as Siegfried in Der Ring des Nibelungen; Deutsche Oper Berlin 1987, as Siegfried and Froh in the Ring; Metropolitan 1988, as Siegfried in Götterdämmerung; sang Aegisthus in Elektra at Stuttgart, 1989; Stuttgart Staatsoper 1992, as Bacchus in Ariadne auf Naxos. *Recordings include:* Lohengrin; Video of Der Freischütz. *Address:* c/o Staatstheater Stuttgart, Oberer Schlossgarten 6, 7000 Stuttgart 1, Germany.

**KRANTJA, Mustafa;** Composer, Publicist and Conductor; b. 10 April 1921, Kavaje, Albania; m., 3 s. *Education:* Piacenza Conservatory, 1933–40; The Conducting and Composition, The Academy of Music, Prague, 1947–50. *Career:* Debut: Primary conductor, opera house, Tirana; Opera House, Tirana; Bolshoi Theatre, Moscow; Barbiere di Siviglia, Bucharest, 1959–60; The Bartered Bride, Brno, 1960; The Prague Spring Festival, 1950, 1952, 1960; Symphonic concerts, USSR, Romania; mem, Alexander Moislu Foundation; Albanian Association. *Compositions:* Suite for chamber orchestra played in Prague, 1952; Instrumental pieces, songs. *Recordings:* Mozart, flute, harp and orchestra concerto; Mrika, first Albanian opera; Schubert, Symphony no. 8; About 20 major works. *Publications:* Krantja, Ave Musicus, 1998; About 300 symposium research studies, published in Albanian, Italian, Russian and English. *Contributions:* Review, On The Musical Language of the Czech Composer, Janáček. *Honours:* People's Artist, 1985; People's Republic Award, 1956; Dvořák Medal, 1975. *Address:* Pr KongresiLushnjesi, p 41 Sh 3 ap 27, Tirana, Albania.

**KRANZLE, Johannes Martin;** Singer (baritone); b. 1962, Augsburg, Germany. *Education:* Studied at the Frankfurt Musikhochschule. *Career:* Sang in opera at Dortmund, from 1987; Hanover Staatstheater from 1991, notably as Papageno, Guglielmo, Rossini's Figaro and Dandini, 1996; Sang in the premiere of Draussen vor der Tur by F X Thoma, 1994; Guest appearances at the State Operas of Hamburg and Munich, in Henze's Junge Lord, 1994; In Leipzig, as Eisenstein, 1995; Festival engagements at Spoleto and Schleswig Holstein; Season 1998 as Lescaut in Henze's Boulevard Solitude, Frankfurt. *Honours:* Prizewinner at Vercelli, Paris, Perpignan and Rio de Janeiro Competitions.

**KRAPP, Edgar;** Organist, Harpsichordist and University Professor; b. 3 June 1947, Bamberg, Germany; m. Dr Maria-Christine Behrens, 22 July 1978, 2 s. *Education:* Regensburg Cathedral Church Choir, 1956–64; Studied Organ, College of Music, Munich, 1966–71; Pupil of Marie Claire Alain, Paris, 1971–72. *Career:* Concerts in Europe, North and South America, Japan; Radio and television programmes in Germany and Japan; Succeeded Helmut Walcha as Professor of Organ at the Hochschule für Musik, Frankfurt, 1974; Visiting Professor at the Salzburg Mozarteum, 1982–91; Professor of Organ, Hochschule für Musik, Munich, 1993–; Concerts with conductors such as Rafael Kubelik, Colin Davis, Horst Stein, Christoph Eschenbach; Member of Jury of International Organ Competitions at Berlin, Munich, Nuremberg, Linz, Tokyo, Chartres; Member, Bayerische Akademie der Schönen Künste; Member, Board of Directors, Neue Bachgesellschaft, Leipzig; Artistic Director, Organ Series at New Concert Hall Bamberg. *Recordings:* Handel: all organ and harpsichord works; Organ recordings in Haarlem (St Bavo Church), Berlin (St Hedwig's Cathedral), Passau Cathedral, historical instruments in Germany (Brandenburg Cathedral and Benediktbeuern, Ottobeuren Basilica). *Honours:* 1st Prize, ARD Competition, Munich, 1971; Mendelssohn Prize, Berlin, 1971; German Recording Prizes for Organ, 1981; Harpsichord, 1983; Grand Prix du Disque, 1983; Frankfurt Music Prize, 1983. *Address:* Hauptstrasse 15, 82054 Sauerlach-Altkirchen, Germany. *E-mail:* Ekrapp@t-online.de. *Website:* www.edgar-krapp.de.

**KRASSMANN, Jurgen;** Singer (Baritone); b. 6 April 1933, Gorlitz, Germany. *Education:* Studied at the Dresden Musikhochschule and with Rudolf Bockelmann. *Career:* Sang with the Dresden Staatsoper, 1956–64, and appeared there and elsewhere in Germany, notably at Halle in operas by Handel, in roles of Cleontes in Alessandro, Gernando in Faramondo, as Scipio, Phoenix in Deidamia, Garibaldo in Rodelinda and Ottone in Agrippina; Sang in Ariodante at Wiesbaden in 1972 and Floridante at Linz in 1987; Further appearances in Leipzig and elsewhere in Germany as Pizarro, the Dutchman, Rigoletto, Macbeth, Scarpia and Nick Shadow in The Rake's Progress. *Address:* c/o Landestheater, Promenade 39, 4010 Linz, Austria.

**KRAŠTEVA, Neva;** composer and organist; b. 2 Aug. 1946, Sofia, Bulgaria. *Education:* Moscow Conservatory and in Prague and Zürich. *Career:* Lecturer, Sofia State Acad. 1974–; founder of Bulgaria's first organ school. *Compositions include:* Mythological Songs for Soprano and Ensemble 1976, The Old Icon for Low Voice and Organ 1987, Apokriff, cantata 1989, Quantus Tremor, cantata, for mezzo, trumpet, organ and cello 1989, Missa Angelus for female chorus 1991, Oboe Sonatina 1991, Reflections, for low voice and piano 1994, Obretenov's Requiem for contralto, chorus and organ 1995. *Address:* c/o Sofia State Academy, Sofia 1505, Bulgaria.

**KRAUKLIS, Georgij;** Musicologist; b. 12 May 1922, Moscow, Russia; m. Irina Shklaeva, 4 Aug 1946, 1 d. *Education:* Musical College, Conservatory of Moscow, 1946–48; Theoretical Studies, Composition Faculty, 1948–53, Postgraduate course in Musical History, 1953–56, Conservatory of Moscow. *Career:* Consultant to Moscow Philharmonic, 1952–60; Teacher, Choral College, Moscow, 1955–62; Teacher, 1956–67, Docent, 1967–80, Dean, 1978–89, Professor, 1980–, Conservatory of Moscow; Director of Stage, France's Violinists, Sarla, France, 1982; mem, Associate Editor, JALS, USA, 1987–92. *Publications:* Piano Sonatas of Schubert, 1963; Operatic overtures of R Wagner, 1964; Symphonic Poems of R Strauss, 1970; Symphonic Poems of F Liszt, 1974; Conceptions of Orchestral Program Music in The Age of Romanticism, 1999. *Contributions:* Bayreuth Music Festival after 116 years, in Musical Academy, 1993. *Honours:* Prize for article, Ministry of Culture, 1979; Honorary Title of Merited Man (representative) of Russian Art, 1994. *Address:* Kostiakova Street 6/5, Ap 81, 125422 Moscow, Russia.

**KRAUS, Anthony;** conductor and organist; *Chorus Master, Opera North.* *Education:* Univ. of Bristol, GSMD, Nat. Opera Studio, London. *Career:* fmrly Univ. Organ Scholar and conductor, Univ. Chamber Choir and Orchestra, Univ. of Bristol; held positions with English Touring Opera, New Youth Opera; attended Rossini Opera Festival Academia 1999; resident coach on young singers' programme, Opéra du Rhin, Strasbourg 2000; trainee répétiteur, ENO 2000, later full-time music staff mem.; prin. accompanist, London Concert Choir –2003; Chorus Master, Opera North 2003–; coach at music summer schools, including Royal School of Church Music, Finchley Children's Music Group; has performed as pianist and organist throughout UK and Europe. *Honours:* Ricordi Prize for conducting. *Address:* Opera North, Grand Theatre, 46 New Briggate, Leeds, LS1 6NU, England (office). *E-mail:* info@operanorth.co.uk (office). *Website:* www.operanorth.co.uk (office).

**KRAUS, Michael;** Singer (Baritone); b. 17 Jan. 1957, Vienna, Austria. *Education:* Studied in Vienna with Otto Edelmann and Josef Greindl. *Career:* After winning various competitions, including the Hugo Wolf in Vienna, sang at Aachen Opera, 1981–84, Ulm, 1984–87, Vienna Volksoper, 1988–91,

notably as Papageno; US debut in 1991 at San Francisco Opera; Guest appearances in France, Hungary, Netherlands, Greece and Israel, as Mozart's Leporello, Guglielmo and Count, Puccini's Marcello and Lescaut, Janáček's Forester, Monteverdi's Ottone and the Count in Lortzing's Wildschütz. *Recordings include:* Die Zauberflöte; Jonny Spielt auf by Krenek; Der Rosenkavalier; Turandot by Busoni; Krasa's Verlobung im Traum. *Address:* c/o Volksoper, Wahringerstrasse 78, 1090 Vienna, Austria.

**KRAUSE, Tom;** Singer (Baritone); b. 5 July 1934, Helsinki, Finland. *Education:* Studied in Hamburg and Vienna and in Berlin with Margot Skoda, Serjo Nazor and Rudolf Bautz. *Career:* Debut: As Lieder singer in Helsinki, 1957; Stage debut at the Städtische Oper Berlin as Escamillo, 1959; Appearances in Milan, Vienna, Paris, Brussels, Bordeaux, Buenos Aires, Cologne, Munich and Toulouse; Bayreuth 1962, as the Herald in Lohengrin; Glyndebourne and London 1963, as the Count in Capriccio and in Britten's War Requiem; Hamburg Staatsoper from 1962, notably in the premieres of Der Goldene Bock by Krenek, 1964, and Searle's Hamlet, 1967; Metropolitan Opera from 1967, Count Almaviva, Malatesta, Escamillo and Guglielmo; Grand Théâtre Geneva 1983, as Golaud in Pelléas et Mélisande; In Chicago Lyric Opera, San Francisco Opera and Houston Operas; Other roles include Don Giovanni, Renato, Kurwenal, Amonasro, Germont, Pizarro, Amfortas and Mefistopheles; Sang at the 1985 Savonlinna Festival as King Philip in Don Carlo; Active career as Lieder recital singer and Oratorio Singer; Kammersänger in Hamburg; Salzburg Festival 1992, as Frère Bernard in St François d'Assise by Messiaen; Sang the Music Master in Strauss's Ariadne, Fort Lauderdale, 1996; Frère Bernard in St François d'Assise at Salzburg, 1998. *Recordings:* Tristan und Isolde, Le nozze di Figaro, Così fan tutte, Fidelio, Andrea Chénier, La Bohème, Don Pasquale, Turandot, Elektra, Salome, Un Ballo in Maschera and Otello; Carmen; Lohengrin; Oedipus Rex; Euryanthe. *Honours:* Deutsche Schallplatten Prize; Edison Prize; English Gramophone Prize for Sibelius Songs, 1986. *Address:* c/o Finnish National Opera, Bulevardi 23–27, 00180 Helsinki 18, Finland.

**KRAUZE, Zygmunt;** Composer and Pianist; b. 19 Sept. 1938, Warsaw, Poland. *Education:* Studied with Kazimierz Sikorski and Maria Wilkomirska at the Warsaw Conservatory, MA, 1964; Further study with Nadia Boulanger in Paris, 1966–67. *Career:* Soloist in recitals of new music in Europe and the USA; Founded the Warsaw Music Workshop, 1967: group consisting of clarinet, trombone, cello and piano, for which 100 composers have written works; Taught piano at Cleveland State University, 1970–71; Lectures at the International Course for New Music at Darmstadt, in Stockholm, Basle and at US Universities; President of the Polish Section of ISCM from 1980; Resident in Paris from 1982; Has worked for IRCAM (Electronic Music Centre) with Boulez; President of the International Society for Contemporary Music, 1987. *Compositions:* Malay Pantuns for 3 Flutes and Female Voice, 1964; Triptych for Piano, 1964; Esquisse for Piano, 1967; Polychromy, for Clarinet, Trombone, Piano and Cello, 1968; Quatuor pour la Naissance, for Clarinet, Violin, Cello and Piano, 1985; Voices for 15 Instruments, 1968–72; Piece for Orchestra No. 1 and 2, 1969–70; 3 String Quartets, 1960, 1969, 1982; Fallingwater for Piano, 1971; Folk Music for Orchestra, 1972; Aus aller Welt Stammende for 10 Strings, 1973; Automatophone for 14 Plucked Instruments and 7 Mechanical Instruments, 1974; Fete Galante et Pastorale, 1975; Piano Concerto No. 1, 1974–76; Suite de danses et de chansons for Harpsichord and Orchestra, 1977; The Star, Chamber Opera, 1980; Violin Concerto, 1980; Tableva Vivant for Chamber Orchestra, 1982; Piece for Orchestra No. 3, 1982; Arabesque for Piano and Chamber Orchestra, 1983; Double Concerto for Violin, Piano and Orchestra, 1985; Symphonie Parisienne, 1986; Nightmare Tango for Piano, 1987; From Keyboard to Score for Piano, 1987; Sigfried und Zygmunt for Piano and Cello, 1988; Piano Quintet, 1993; Terra Incognita for piano and 10 strings, 1994; Pastorale for wind quintet, 1995; Rapsod, for strings, 1995; Piano Concerto No. 2, 1996; Trois Chansons for 16-voice chorus, 1997. *Honours:* Chevalier dans l'ordre des Arts et des Lettres, 1984. *Address:* c/o Society of Authors ZAiKS, 2 Hipoteczna Street, 00 092 Warsaw, Poland. *Telephone:* (4822) 828 17 05. *Fax:* (4822) 828 13 47. *E-mail:* sekretariat@zaiks .org.pl. *Website:* www.zaiks.org.pl.

**KRAVITZ, Ellen King,** BA, MM, PhD; American musicologist and academic; b. 25 May 1929, Fords, NJ; m. Hilard L. Kravitz 1972; two d. three step-s. *Education:* Georgian Court College, Lakewood, NJ, University of Southern California. *Career:* Full Professor of Music History, California State University, Los Angeles, 1967; researcher in musicology and related arts; Director, Exhibition of Schoenberg's art and music during Schoenberg Centennial Celebration, University of Southern California, 1974; founder, Friends of Music, 1976, Gala; Chair, 1978–1982; participant in Faculty Vocal Extravaganza, California State University, Los Angeles, 1981, 1983, 1985, 1987, 1989, 1991, 1993, 1995, 1997; mem, Pacific Southwest Chapter, American Musicological Society. *Publications:* A Correlation of Concepts Found in German Expressionist Art, Music and Literature, 1970; Editor, Journal of the Arnold Schoenberg Institute, Vol. I, No. 3, Vol. II, No. 3; Catalogue of Schoenberg's Paintings, Drawings and Sketches, 1978; Music in Our Culture, 1996; 3 CDs Edition, 1997; contrib. to Arnold Schoenberg as Artist: Another Look, paper for Musicology Meeting, 1995. *Address:* 526 N Foothill Road, Beverly Hills, CA 90210, USA.

**KREBBERS, Herman Albertus;** Dutch violinist; b. 18 June 1923, Hengelo; m. A. Torlau; one s. one d. *Education:* Amsterdam Musiklyceum with Oscar Back. *Career:* debut concert 1932; soloist with the Concertgebouw Orchestra 1935; leader, Gelderland Orchestra, then the Hague Residentie Orchestra

1950–62; leader, Concertgebouw Orchestra 1962–79; many tours of Europe and the USA as soloist; founded the Guarneri Trio 1963, played in violin duo with Theo Olof; teacher, Amsterdam Musiklyceum. *Recordings:* Bach and Badings Concertos for Two Violins, with Theo Olof and the Hague Philharmonic; Beethoven Concerto with the Hague Philharmonic; Brahms and Bruch Concertos with the Brabant Orchestra; Paganini 1st Concerto with the Vienna Symphony; Haydn Concertos with the Amsterdam Chamber Orchestra. *Honours:* Amsterdam Musiklyceum Prix d'Excellence 1940, Knight Oranje Nassau Order, many int. competition awards. *Address:* Prof Cobbenhagenlaan 724, 5037 DW Tilburg, Netherlands (home). *Telephone:* 4688780 (home).

**KREBS, Helmut;** Singer (Tenor); b. 8 Oct. 1913, Dortmund, Germany. *Education:* Berlin Musikhochschule, 1934–37. *Career:* Began as concert singer; Stage debut, 1937 at the Volksoper, Berlin; Returned to Berlin, 1947; Salzburg Festival, 1949, in the premiere of Orff's Antigonae; Ernesto in Don Pasquale, 1952; Guest appearances in Milan, London, Vienna, Munich, Netherlands and Belgium; Glyndebourne, 1953 as Mozart's Belmonte and Idamantes; Hamburg Radio, 1954 as Aron in the first performance of Schoenberg's Moses und Aron; Berlin, 1956 and 1965, in premieres of Henze's König Hirsch and Der junge Lord; Also heard as the Evangelist in the Passions of Bach; Professor at the Frankfurt Musikhochschule from 1966; Sang at the Deutsche Oper Berlin, 1988 in From the House of the Dead. *Compositions:* Orchestral, Operatic, Chamber, Choral and Vocal works published. *Recordings:* Monteverdi, Orfeo; Henze, Der junge Lord; Bach, Christmas Oratorio; Verdi, Requiem; Stravinsky, Oedipus Rex; Strauss, Ariadne auf Naxos; Schoenberg, Moses und Aron; Wagner, Der fliegende Holländer. *Honours:* Berliner Künstpreis, 1952; Berliner Kammersänger, 1963. *Address:* 11 Im Dol, 14195 Berlin, Germany.

**KREIZBERG, Yakov;** Russian conductor; b. 24 Oct. 1959, St Petersburg; brother of Semyon Bychkov. *Education:* studied with Ilya Musin in St Petersburg, conducting fellowships at Tanglewood and the Los Angeles Philharmonic Inst. *Career:* emigrated to the USA 1976; Music Dir Mannes Coll. Orchestra, New York 1985–88; Music Dir Krefeld Opera and Lower Rhine Symphony 1988–94; led Così fan tutte and Don Giovanni with Canadian Opera 1991–92, Der Rosenkavalier for ENO 1994; Music Dir Komische Oper Berlin 1994–2001; Principal Conductor Bournemouth Symphony Orchestra 1995–2000; Don Giovanni for Chicago Lyric Opera 1996; opera in Berlin includes The Queen of Spades, Goldschmidt's Der gewaltige Hahnrei, Fidelio, Lucia di Lammermoor, Henze's König Hirsch and Die Zauberflöte 1999; Music Dir and Artistic Adviser Jeunesses Musicales (World Youth Orchestra); further engagements with the Chicago Symphony, Los Angeles Philharmonic Orchestra, San Francisco Symphony Orchestra, Detroit Symphony Orchestra, Berlin Philharmonic, Royal Concertgebouw, Leipzig Gewandhaus, Philharmonia, New York Philharmonic, Philadelphia Orchestra, Boston Symphony, Munich Philharmonic; conducted Jenůfa at Glyndebourne 1992, Don Giovanni 1995, Katya Kabanova 1998; Chief Conductor and Artistic Adviser Netherlands Philharmonic and Netherlands Chamber Orchestras 2003–; Principal Guest Conductor Vienna Symphony Orchestra 2003–(08). *Current Management:* Harrison/Parrott Ltd, 12 Penzance Place, London, W11 4PA, England. *Telephone:* (20) 7229-9166. *Fax:* (20) 7221-5042. *Website:* www.harrisonparrott.com.

**KREJCI, Jiri;** Oboist; b. 11 Dec. 1935, Dolni Hbity, Czechoslovakia; 2 s., 1 d. *Education:* Military Music School, Kosice; Conservatory of Music, Prague. *Career:* Debut: Soloist, Haydn Concerto, Radio Symphony Orchestra, Prague, 1960; Solo Oboist of the Theatre Orchestra, Vinohrady, Prague, 1953–56, Karlin, Prague, 1957–59; Principal Oboe, Radio Symphony Orchestra, Prague, 1959–64; Solo Oboist, Prague Chamber Orchestra without Chef, 1965–77; Artistic Leader, Collegium Musicum Pragense, 1965–90; Member, Czech Nonet, 1977–; Member, Prague Wind Quintet, 1982–93; Live Recordings for the BBC in London. *Honours:* Prize, Composers Society, 1984; Honorary Award, Ministry of Culture, Czech Republic. *Address:* Ceskolipska 400/20, 1900 Prague 9, Czech Republic.

**KREK, Uros;** Slovenian composer; *Professor Emeritus of Composition and Theoretical Subjects, Musikethnologischen Instituts;* b. 21 May 1922, Ljubljana; m. Lilijana Pauer 1960. *Education:* Classical Coll., Ljubljana, Music High School, Ljubljana. *Career:* debut, first performance of compositions, Ljubljana 1945; performances of compositions on concert stages, radio and television, film, theatre, records and editions; currently Prof. Emer. of Composition and Theoretical Subjects, Musikethnologischen Instituts, Ljubljana. *Compositions:* Concerto for violin and orchestra; Sinfonietta, Concerto for French horn and orchestra; Concerto for piccolo and orchestra; Rhapsodic Dance for orchestra; Sonata for 2 violins; Five Songs for voice and piano; Movements Concertants, Inventions ferales for violin and strings; Symphony for Strings; Duo for violin and violoncello; La Journée d'un Bouffon for brass quintet; Trio for violin, viola and violoncello; String Quartet; Sur un Melodie for piano; Sonatina for clarinet; Songs for Eva; Concert Diptych for violoncello and orchestra; Sonata for violoncello and piano; 3 Impromptus for violin solo; Sextet for 2 violins, 2 violas and 2 violoncellos; Espressivo and Appassionato for flute and piano; Songs on Folk Tradition for voice and piano; Canticum Resianum, 1988; Vigoroso for violin and piano, 1991; Cantus gratias agentis for soprano, trumpet and organ, 1994; Reflections, 2nd sonata for violin and piano, 1994; Capriccio notturno for violin and harp, 1996; Contrabasso concertante for contrabass and chamber orchestra, 1998 Chamber music, choir music, film and stage music. *Honours:* Preseren Prize 1952, 1992.

*Address:* Na Vrtaci 5, 4248 Lesce, Slovenia (home). *Telephone:* (4) 5318091 (home).

**KREMER, Gidon;** Russian/German violinist; b. 27 Feb. 1947, Riga, Latvia. *Education:* Riga School of Music, Moscow Conservatory (with David Oistrakh). *Career:* recitalist and orchestral soloist worldwide 1965–; has played in most major int. festivals including Berlin, Dubrovnik, Helsinki, London, Moscow, Prague, Salzburg, Tokyo and Zürich; has played with most major int. orchestras including Berlin Philharmonic, Boston Symphony, Concertgebouw, LA Philharmonic, New York Philharmonic, Philadelphia, San Francisco Symphony, Vienna Philharmonic, London Philharmonic, Royal Philharmonic, Philharmonia, NHK Symphony of Japan and all main Soviet orchestras; has worked with Bernstein, von Karajan, Giulini, Jochum, Previn, Abbado, Levine, Maazel, Muti, Harnoncourt, Mehta and Marriner; f. Lockenhaus Chamber Music Festival 1981; plays a Stradivarius; lives in Germany. *Recordings:* has made more than 45 records. *Performances:* first performances include Henze, Stockhausen, Schnittke, Pärt, Astor Piazzola. *Honours:* prizewinner at Queen Elisabeth Competition, Brussels, Montreal Competition and Fourth Int. Tchaikovsky Competition (First Prize) 1970, Paganini Prize, Genoa; Grand Prix du Disque and Deutsche Schallplattenpreis. *Current Management:* ICM Artists, 40 West 57th Street, New York, NY 10023, USA.

**KRENZ, Jan;** Polish conductor and composer; b. 14 July 1926, Włocławek; s. of Otton Krenz and Eleonora Krenz; m. Alina Krenz 1958; one s. *Education:* Higher School of Music. *Career:* conducting debut, Łódź Philharmonic Orchestra 1946; Chief Conductor, State Poznań Philharmonic Orchestra 1947–49; Chief Conductor Polish Nat. Radio Symphony Orchestra of Katowice 1953–67; Chief Conductor Danish Radio Orchestra, Copenhagen 1960s; Leader, Grand Opera House Orchestra (Teatr Wielki), Warsaw 1968–73; conducted Berlin Philharmonic, Staatskapelle Dresden, Leningrad Philharmonic and all the major London orchestras; Gen. Dir of Music, Bonn Orchestra 1979–82; frequent collaboration with Yomiuri Nippon Symphony Orchestra; performing only as guest conductor 1983–; Diploma of Ministry of Foreign Affairs 1980. *Compositions include:* chamber, vocal and symphonic music, orchestral transcriptions of Polish classics, J. S. Bach (including Polyphonic suite on four fragments from Bach's Die Kunst der Fuge) and Szymanowski, film and stage music. *Honours:* Hon. mem. Asscn of Polish Composers; Hon. Conductor Polish Nat. Radio Symphony Orchestra of Katowice; decorations include Order of Banner of Labour (First Class), Commdr's Cross with Star of Polonia Restituta Order; State Prize 1955, 1972, Prize of Asscn of Polish Composers 1968, Grand Prix du Disque, France 1972, Prize of Polish Artists' and Musicians' Asscn (SPAM) Orfeusz 1974. *Address:* al. J. Ch. Szucha 16, 00-582 Warsaw, Poland.

**KRETH, Wolfgang;** Lutenist; b. 29 May 1946, Cologne, Germany. *Education:* Studied Music, 1967–75 at: Musikhochschule, Köln; Musikhochschule, Düsseldorf; Musikhochschule, Frankfurt; Musikhochschule, Aachen; Musiklehrer-Examen; Staatl Diplom for Lute, summa cum laude. *Career:* Several Concerts in Europe (Schwetzinger Festspiele, Musica Bayreuth, Dubrovnik-Festival, Wiener Festwochen, Brühler Barock-Fest; Radio appearances, interviews; mem. Lute Society of England; Lute Society of America; Society Nova Giulianiad, Freiburg; Member of EGTA. *Recordings:* Lute Music of Anthony Holborne and Nicolas Vallet; Lute Concerto of Antonio Vivaldi. *Contributions:* Several articles in Gitarre und Laute, Köln. *Address:* Theophanoplatz Nr 8, 5 Köln 51, Germany.

**KRETSCHMAR, Helmut;** Singer (Tenor); b. 3 Feb. 1928, Kleve, Germany; m. Renate Fischer. *Education:* Studied in Frankfurt with Kurt Thomas and Hans Emge. *Career:* Sang first in concerts and oratorios from 1953; At Hamburg in 1954 sang in the first performance (concert) of Schoenberg's Moses and Aron; Sacred music by Bach at the Berliner Festwochen and the Bach Festivals at Luneberg and Heidelberg, 1960–62; Further appearances at the Handel Festival at Göttingen and in Düsseldorf, Japan, Korea, Paris, Madrid, Bombay, London and Ceylon; Lieder recitals with Renate Fischer, Piano; Repertoire includes sacred music by Handel, Haydn and Mendelssohn; Songs by Wolf, Debussy, Schubert and Schumann; Professor at the Detmold Musikhochschule from 1963. *Recordings include:* Fidelio; Moses und Aron, conducted by Hans Rosbaud; St Matthew Passion, Christmas Oratorio and B Minor Mass by Bach; Beethoven's Missa solemnis; Schubert's Mass in A flat; Die Jahreszeiten by Haydn. *Honours:* First Prize, German Music High Schools, 1953; Kunstpreis of Nordrhein-Westfalen, 1958.

**KREUTER, Melanie;** Singer (Soprano); b. 24 Feb. 1963, Braunschweig, Germany. *Education:* Studied in Hanover and with Ileana Cotrubas. *Career:* Sang at Stuttgart Opera, 1989–91, as Mozart's Susanna, Zerlina and Papagena; Aennchen in Der Freischütz and Lucilla in La Scala di Seta; Komische Oper Berlin from 1989, with guest appearances at Wiesbaden and Hannover; Dortmund Opera from 1992, as Mozart's Susanna, Pamina and Despina; Sophie in Der Rosenkavalier; Sang in local premieres of Argento's The Voyage of Edgar Allan Poe and Casken's The Golem; Many concert and Lieder programmes. *Address:* Dortmund Opera, Kuhstrasse 12, 4600 Dortmund, Germany.

**KRIKORIAN, Mari;** Opera Singer (Soprano); b. 25 May 1946, Varna, Bulgaria. *Education:* Secondary School of Music, Varna, 1964; Graduated, 1971, Master's Class, 1972, Bulgarian State Conservatoire, Sofia; Specialisation course with James King, Vienna, 1977. *Career:* Debut: As Adalgisa in Norma, Varna National Opera, 1976; 1st Soprano, Varna National Opera, in La Bohème, Simon Boccanegra, Fliegende Holländer, Otello, Don Carlo and

Tosca; 1st Soprano, Sofia National Opera, 1983–; Permanent Repertoire includes Norman, Attila, Aida, Il Trovatore, La Forza de Destino, Don Carlos, Otello, La Bohème, Madama Butterfly, Tosca, Liu, Senta, Adriana Lecouvreur, Tatiana in Eugene Onegin, Lisa in Queen of Spades, Yaroslavna in Prince Igor, Verdi's Requiem, Donizetti's Requiem, Bruckner's Requiem, Brahms Deutsches Requiem, Liszt's Christus Oratorio, Rossini's Stabat Mater, Pergolesi's Stabat Mater; Foreign tours, Prague, Budapest, Russia, Armenia, Germany, Italy, France, Spain, Austria, Greece, Egypt, Cyprus, India, Mexico; Film portrait for Bulgarian Television, 1989; Un Ballo in Maschera, 1993; Foreign Tours: Los Angeles (USA) concerts, 1993. *Recordings:* Opera recital, airs from Bellini, Verdi and Puccini, with Sofia Opera Orchestra, conductor Ivan Marinov, State Recording Company Balkanton, 1984; Attila, by Verdi, with Sofia Philharmonic Orchestra, conductor Vladimir Ghiaurov, and with Nicola Guzelev; Chants Liturgieaues Armeniens CD Edition JADE, Paris, France, 1992; Live and studio recordings for Bulgarian radio and television. *Honours:* 1st Prize, Opera Belcanto Competition, Ostende, Belgium, 1980; Honoured Artist of Bulgaria, 1984. *Current Management:* SOFIACONCERT, Bulgaria. *Address:* Druzba 2 bl 213 A, Ap 11, Sofia 1582, Bulgaria.

**KRILOVICI, Marina;** Singer (Soprano); b. 11 June 1942, Bucharest, Romania. *Education:* Studied with Mdme Vrabiescu-Varianu in Bucharest and with Matia Caniglia and Luigi Ricci in Rome. *Career:* Debut: National Opera Bucharest, 1966, as Donna Anna; Sang major roles in the Italian repertory with the Bucharest Opera, Covent Garden debut, 1971, as Aida; Chicago Lyric Opera, 1972, as Mimi; Further appearances in Vienna, Berlin, Munich, Montreal, Lisbon, San Francisco and Strasbourg; Hamburg Staatsoper, 1968–76; Sang Adriana Lecouvreur at Athens, 1998. *Recordings include:* Cavelleria Rusticana; Donizetti's Il Duca d'Alba.

**KRINGELBORN, Solveig;** Singer (Soprano); b. 4 June 1963, Lillestrom, Norway. *Education:* Studied at Stockholm Royal Academy. *Career:* Appearances at the Royal Swedish Opera as Susanna and Papagena, Oslo Opera, 1990–91 as Mimi, Jenůfa and Micaela, with further engagements at the Bolshoi, Moscow, Vienna Staatsoper, Strasbourg, Los Angeles as Mozart's Countess in 1993, Brussels in the premiere of Boesmans' Reigen, Salzburg as Fiordiligi in 1993, Bastille as Antonia in 1993, Geneva as Ilia in 1994 and Mozart's Countess in Salzburg in 1995; Other roles include Musetta, Marguerite, Pamina, Nedda, Serpina in La Serva Padrona, and Drusilla in Poppea; BBC Promenade Concerts in 1991, with the premiere of Lutoslawski's Chantefleurs et Chantefables, conducted by the composer, also televised; Wigmore Hall recital debut in 1992; Other concert repertoire includes Haydn's Jahreszeiten in Paris, Nielsen's 3rd Symphony in London under Simon Rattle, Mahler's 2nd Symphony with the Israel Philharmonic and Cleveland Orchestra, and in Los Angeles in 1993; Sang Mozart's Countess at the 1995 Salzburg Festival and for the San Francisco Opera, 1997–98; Fiordiligi at the 1996 Glyndebourne Festival; Marenka in The Bartered Bride at Glyndebourne and Marie in Wozzeck at the Zürich Opera, 1999; Covent Garden debut as Wagner's Senta, 2000; Engaged as Donna Elvira in Don Giovanni on tour with the Isaeli Philharmonic, and at Bastille Opéra Paris and the Met in New York, 2000. *Recordings include:* Grieg Songs conducted by Rozhdestvensky, a Grieg Solo Song and Tavener Choral Music conducted by David Hill. *Address:* c/o IMG Artists, Lovell House, 616 Chiswick High Road, London W2 5RX, England.

**KRISCAK, Manuela;** Singer (Soprano); b. 1965, Trieste, Italy. *Education:* Studied at the G Tartini Conservatoire, Trieste. *Career:* Debut: Musetta in La Bohème at the Teatro Nuovo, Spoleto, 1990; Appearances as Tisbe in Cenerentola at Spoleto and Rome, Bianca in La Rondine and Zerlina at Catania; Gianetta in L'Elisir d'amore for French television, Un Plaisir in Gluck's Armide at La Scala (1996); Sang Kristina in The Makropulos Case at Glyndebourne (1995–97) and at Strasbourg and Lisbon; Season 1997–98 as Papagena (Die Zauberflöte) and in Paisiello's Il Barbiere di Siviglia at Trieste. *Address:* Teatro Comunale, G Verdi di Trieste, Rive Novembre 1, 34121 Trieste, Italy.

**KRIVINE, Emmanuel;** French violinist and conductor; b. 7 May 1947, Grenoble; s. of Henri Krivine and Rejla Krivine (née Weisbrod); one d. *Education:* Conservatoire Nat. Supérieur de Musique et de Danse, Paris, Conservatoire Royal de Bruxelles. *Career:* pupil of Henryk Szeryng and Yehudi Menuhin; solo violinist, Paris 1964; Brussels 1965–68; Perm. Guest Conductor Radio-France 1976–83; Dir Lorraine-Metz Regional Orchestra 1981–83; Prin. Guest Conductor Orchestra of Lyon 1983; Artistic Dir French Nat. Youth Orchestra 1983–; Musical Dir Nat. Orchestra of Lyon 1987–2000; Conductor French Nat. Orchestra 2001–; Guest Conductor various int. orchestras including Berlin Philharmonic, Concertgebouw and Chamber Orchestra of Europe 1977–. *Honours:* Chevalier, Ordre nat. du Mérite, Officier des Arts et Lettres; Ginette-Neveu Medal 1971 and numerous other awards. *Address:* 2 rue Hotel de Ville, 1800 Vevey, Switzerland.

**KROLL, Mark;** Harpsichordist and Professor of Music; b. 13 Sept. 1946, Brooklyn, New York, USA; m. Carol Lieberman, 9 July 1975, 1 s. *Education:* BA, 1968, Graduate School, Musicology, 1968–69, Brooklyn College, City University of New York; MMus, Harpsichord, Yale University School of Music, 1971. *Career:* Debut: Carnegie Hall, New York City, 1975; Performance in solo recitals, chamber music ensembles and as concerto soloist throughout Europe, South America, USA and Canada; Radio and Television appearances; Numerous television shows for Public broadcasting System and BBC;

Professor of Harpsichord and Theory and Chair of the Department of Historical Performance, Boston University; Conductor, Orchestral works of Rameau, CPE Bach, Vivaldi; Artist-in-Residence, Lafayette College, Conductor and Artistic Director, Opera New England; Visiting Professor: Würzburg Conservatory, Zagreb Music Academy and Belgrade Music Academy; Visiting Professor at the Academies of Music at Warsaw, Cracow and Athens. *Recordings include:* J. S. Bach, complete sonatas for violin and harpsichord; Handel and Scarlatti, harpsichord works; G F Handel, complete works for recorder and harpsichord; Vivaldi's The Seasons, with Boston Symphony Orchestra; Solo Harpsichord works of J. S. Bach; Harpsichord works of JNP Royer; Franz Schubert, 3 Sonatinas for violin and fortepiano; M de Falla, El Retablo de Maese Pedro, with Montreal Symphony; Contemporary American Harpsichord Music; H. von Biber Sonatas of 1681. *Publications:* French Harpsichord Music, 1994; 17th Century Keyboard Music, 1997; Beethoven Violin Sonatas, 2002; Hummel Transcriptions, 2001, 2002; Hummel's Piano Method, 2003; Early Music America Magazine, 2001, 2002. *Contributions:* Numerous articles for Bostonia magazine. *Honours:* Grants from: NEA, 1984; CIES, 1989; Whiting Foundation, 1993; DAAD, 1996; IREX, 1996; NEH, 2002; Copland Fund, 2001,2002; DAAD, 2002. *Address:* Boston University School of Music, 855 Commonwealth Avenue, Boston, MA 02215, USA.

**KROLOPP, Wojciech (Aleksander);** Musician, Manager and Journalist; b. 12 April 1945, Poznań, Poland. *Education:* Academy of Music Poznan, 1973–77; Pedagogy, 1968–70. *Career:* Debut: Soloist Soprano, 1957; Soloist Baritone, 1964; Soloist from 1957 (soprano, bass from 1964); Teacher and Conductor, Polish Choir School, Poznan, 1968–; Managing Director, 1969–, Poznan Boys' Choir, and Director of International Boys' Choir Festival, Poznan, 1980–; 3000 concerts with the Poznan Boys' Choir, 400 conducted concerts in 24 countries; Solo parts in major vocal-instrumental works and songs; Camerata, chamber orchestra, 1980–83; Premiere of Mozart opera, Bastien und Bastienne at the Great Theatre in Poznan also in Taiwan and Hong Kong; By end of 1990 nominated as manager and artistic director of the Polish Nightingales. *Recordings:* Mozart's Coronation Mass and Szymanowski's Stabat Mater, 1991. *Publications include:* The Poznan Choir School, monography, 1989. *Current Management:* Polish Artists' Agency, Warsaw and Penta Promotions, Netherlands. *Address:* Torenstraat 13, 9160 Lokeren, Belgium.

**KROSNICK, Aaron (Burton);** Violinist, Performer-in-Residence and Artist-in-Residence; b. 28 June 1937, New Haven, Connecticut, USA; m. Mary Lou Wesley, 25 Aug 1961, 1 s. *Education:* BA, magna cum laude, Yale College, 1959; MS, Juilliard School of Music, 1961; Fulbright Scholar, Royal Conservatory of Music, Brussels, Belgium, 1961–62; Major teachers, Howard Boatwright, Joseph Fuchs, Ivan Galamian, Arthur Grumiaux. *Career:* Concertmaster (and soloist with orchestras), Springfield, Ohio, Symphony Orchestra, 1962–67; Jacksonville Symphony Orchestra, 1969–80; Sewanee Festival Orchestra, 1969–82; Florida Bicentennial Chamber Orchestra, 1976; Faculty Positions, Wittenberg University, 1962–67; Jacksonville University, 1967–; Summers, Syracuse University, Kneisel Hall Summer School of Ensemble Playing, Sewanee Summer Music Centre, Soloist with extensive concerto repertoire; Appearances with Rome Festival Orchestra, Florida Symphony Chamber Orchestra, Jacksonville University Orchestra and many others; Summers of 1985, 86, Concertmaster and featured Artist, Rome Festival in Italy. *Recordings:* Music of Frederick Delius, Musical Heritage Society. *Honours:* Semi-finalist, Paganini International Competition, Genoa, 1970. *Address:* 13734 Bermuda Cay Court, Jacksonville, FL 32225-5426, USA. *E-mail:* abkmlk@hotmail.com.

**KROSNICK, Joel;** Cellist; b. 3 April 1941, New Haven, Connecticut, USA. *Education:* Studied with William d'Amato, Luigi Silva and Claus Adam; Further study at Columbia University. *Career:* Co-founded and directed the Group for Contemporary Music at Columbia University, 1962; Professor at University of Iowa, 1963–66; Cellist in Uniersity String Quartet; Professor at University of Massachusetts, 1966–70; Performed with New York Chamber Soloists and made solo tours to Belgrade, Hamburg, Berlin, London and Amsterdam; New York solo debut, 1970; Has given first performances of works by Babbitt, Subotnick and Ligeti; Taught at California Institute of Arts, 1970–74; Cellist with the Juilliard Quartet from 1974; World-wide tours in the standard repertoire and contemporary works; Performances in London, 1990 (works by Mozart). *Recordings include:* Albums with the Juilliard Quartet; Carter's Cello Sonata. *Address:* c/o Library of Congress, Washington DC, USA.

**KROSS, Siegfried;** Professor of Musicology; b. 24 Aug. 1930, Wuppertal, Germany; m. Dorothee Brand, 23 Mar 1962, 2 s. *Education:* Studied musicology, German literature, psychology, and experimental physics at Universities of Bonn and Freiburg, Br Gurlitt; DPhil, 1956; Habilitation, 1966. *Career:* Scholar, Deutsche Forschungsgemeinschaft, Vienna, 1959; Assistant, Beethoven Archives, Bonn; Assistant Professor, 1970, Professor, Dean, Faculty of Humanities, 1988, University of Bonn; Vice-President, Landes-Musikrat; mem, American Musicological Society; Gesellschaft für Musikforschung. *Publications:* Die Chorwerke von J Brahms, 1957, 2nd edition, 1963; Das Instrumentalkonzert bei G Ph Telemann, 1969; Dokumentation zur Geschichte des Deutschen Liedes Seit, 1973; Geschichte des Deutschen Liedes, 1989; Briefe Robert und Clara Schumanns, 1978, 2nd edition, 1982; Brahms-Bibliographie, 1983; Johannes Brahms, 2 vols, 1997. *Contributions:* Die Musikforschung, 19th Century Music, 1982; American Choral Review 25, 1983; Brahms, 1983–87; Festschrift: Beitrage zur

Geschichle des Konzerts, 1990. *Address:* Musikwissenschaftliches Seminar der Universitat Bonn, Adenauer Allee 4–6, 53113 Bonn, Germany.

**KRUGER, Anna;** Violist; b. 1965, USA. *Education:* Studies at Manhattan School of Music and at Indiana University with James Buswell. *Career:* Former principal of New Jersey Symphony; Co-Founder, Lark String Quartet, New York; Recent concert tours to Australia, Taiwan, Hong Kong, China, Germany and Netherlands; US appearances at the Lincoln Center, New York, Kennedy Center, Washington DC and in Boston, Los Angeles, Philadelphia, St Louis and San Francisco; Repertoire includes quartets by Haydn, Mozart, Beethoven, Schubert, Dvořák, Brahms, Borodin, Bartók, Debussy and Shostakovich; Concerts at the Wigmore Hall, London, 1994. *Honours:* With Lark Quartet: Gold Medals at 1990 Naumberg and 1991 Shostakovich Competitions; Prizewinner at 1991 London International String Quartet, 1991 Melbourne Chamber Music, 1990 Premio Paulio Borciani, Reggio Emilia and 1990 Karl Klinger Competition, Munich. *Current Management:* Sonata, Glasgow, Scotland. *Address:* c/o Lark Quartet, 11 Northpark Street, Glasgow G20 7AA, Scotland.

**KRUGLOV, Jurij;** Singer (Bass); b. 1960, Sevastopol, Ukraine. *Education:* Studied at Tchaikovsky Academy, Kiev. *Career:* Appearances at the Sevtchenko Opera Theatre, Kiev; National Theatre, Prague and Estates Theatre, 1989, notably as Masetto and the Commendatore in Don Giovanni, conducted by Charles Mackerras; Guest appearances at Odessa, St Petersburg and Ostrava; Festivals of Savonlinna, Wexford and Macerata; Concerts in France, Germany, Russia, the Czech Republic and Slovakia. *Address:* Music Intenational, 13 Ardilaun Road, London N5 2QR, England.

**KRUMM, Philip Edwin;** Composer; b. 7 April 1941, Baltimore, Maryland, USA. *Education:* Studied orchestration and composition with Raymond Moses (student of Casals), 1957–59, with Frank Sturchio (student of Puccini), St Mary's University, with Ross Lee Finney, University of Michigan, 1962–64 and Karlheinz Stockhausen, University of California, Davis, 1966. *Career:* Produced early concert series of major modern works at McNay Art Institute, San Antonio, 1960–61; Performer and Composer at Once Festivals, Ann Arbor, MI, 1962–64; Music Hour, television with Jerry Hunt, 1964; Sampler, television programme with Robert Wilson, 1964 and others. *Compositions:* Paragenesis for 2 Violins and Piano, 1959; Axis; Mumma Mix; Soundtrack score for short film, Angel Of God; Music for Clocks, 1962, Once Festival Chamber Orchestra; Concerto for Saxophone, Phil Rehfeldt, 1964, Bass Clarinet Concerto Performer, Martin Walker, 1972, by Scott Vance and Redlands Ensemble, 1978 and 1986; Farewell To LA, electronic theatre piece, 1975; Sound Machine ('66), 1979; Secret Pleasures, dance suite, 1988–89; No Time At All, electronic-instrumental set, 1989; Short pieces for electronics and instruments: Into The Pines, The Gabrieli Thing; Banshee Fantasia, commissioned by Bay Area Pianists for 100th Anniversary of Henry Cowell's Birth; World Premiere by Blue Gene Tyranny, 3 Day Festival, University of California at Berkeley, 1997. *Recordings:* Sound Machine, by Dallas Chamber Ensemble, Jerry Hunt, 1966; Concerto for bass clarinet, with Scott Vance and Redlands Ensemble, 1996; Music for Clocks (1962) on Music from the Once Festival 1961–1966, 2003; Formations (1962), performed by Blue Gene Tyranny, 2004; Axis and Other Works, 2004. *Publications:* Music Without Notes, 1962. *Address:* 103 Erskine Place, San Antonio, TX 78201-2638, USA. *Telephone:* (210) 733-1008 (home).

**KRUMMACHER, Friedhelm Gustav-Adolf,** DPhil; German academic; b. 22 Jan. 1936, Berlin; m. Aina Maria Landfeldt 1964; one s. one d. *Education:* studied in Berlin, Marburg and Uppsala, Sweden, Free Univ. of Berlin, Univ. of Erlangen-Nürnberg. *Career:* Asst 1965, Private Docent 1973, Erlangen-Nurnberg Univ.; Prof., Musikhochschule Detmold 1975; Prof., Christian Albrechts Univ., Kiel 1976–; Prof., Dir, Musicological Inst., Univ. of Kiel, in charge of Brahms Gesamtausgabe; Leipziger Mendelssohnausgabe; mem. Vetenskapssocietet Lund, Sweden, Jungius-Gesellschaft der Wissenschaften, Hamburg, Norwegian Acad., Royal Swedish Acad. of Music. *Publications:* Die Überlieferung… 1965, Mendelssohn der Komponist 1978, Die Choralbearbeitung… 1978, Mahlers III Symphonie 1991, Bach's Jahrgang der Choralkantoten 1995, Musik im Norden 1996, Bachs Weg in der Arbeit am Werk 2001, Das Streichquartett Vol.I 2001, Vol. II 2003, Festschrift: Rezeption als Innovation 2001, Geschichte des Streichquartetts Vol. I–III 2005, Kieler Schriften zur Musikwissenschaft Vols 22–50 (ed.) 1978–2004; contrib. On Mendelssohn's Oratorios, in The Mendelssohn Companion 2001; contrib. about 170 articles in Archiv für Musikwissenschaft, Die Musikforschung, Kongressberichte, Festschriften. *Address:* Wippen 1, 24107 Kiel 1, Germany.

**KRUSE, Heinz;** Singer (Tenor); b. 1940, Schleswig, Germany. *Education:* Studied at the Hamburg Musikhochschule. *Career:* Sang at the Stuttgart Opera, 1966–68; Hamburg from 1970 in such character roles as Pedrillo and David; Guest appearances in Paris, Toulouse and Bayreuth; Heroic tenor roles from 1987 with Florestan at Mainz, Parsifal at Brunswick, Tristan at Kiel and in concert in London in 1993, and in Hamburg, 1995 and in New York's Carnegie Hall, Siegfried at Hamburg in 1993 and in 1994 in Paris and the Edinburgh Festival; Further engagements as the Emperor in Die Frau ohne Schatten, and Albi in Schreker's Schatzgräber, Hamburg in 1989; Sang Florestan in a concert Fidelio at Edinburgh, 1996; Siegfried in Götterdämmerung for Netherlands Opera, 1998. *Recordings include:* Monostatos in Die Zauberflöte. *Address:* c/o Staatsoper Hamburg, Grosse Theaterstrasse 34, Pf 302448, W-2000 Hamburg 36, Germany.

**KRUSE, Tone;** Singer (Contralto); b. 1958, Oslo, Norway. *Education:* Studied at the Oslo Music High School. *Career:* Sang at the Oslo Opera, 1982–85, then at Cologne Opera; Roles have included Gluck's Orpheus, Magdalene in Die Meistersinger, Margaret in Wozzeck, Suzuki in Madama Butterfly, Zulma in L'Italiana in Algeri, Mother Goose in The Rake's Progress; Sang Erda in Das Rheingold, 1996; Sang Erda in The Ring at Norwich, on tour with the Norwegian National Opera, 1998; Frequent guest appearances in opera and concert throughout Germany. *Recordings:* The Maiden in the Tower, Sibelius. *Address:* c/o Norwegian National Opera, PO Box 8800 Youngstorget, N–0028 Oslo, Norway.

**KRUTIKOV, Mikhail;** Russian singer (bass); b. 23 Aug. 1958, Moscow. *Education:* Moscow State Conservatory and the Opera Studio of Bolshoi Opera, 1982–85; further studies with Evgeni Nesterenko. *Career:* appearances with Bolshoi Opera, 1985–, as Boris Godunov, Pimen, Mephistopheles, Basilio, Mendoza in Prokofiev's The Duenna and Dunua in The Maid of Orleans by Tchaikovsky; Sang in La Straniera and La cena delle Beffe at Wexford Festival, and with the Bolshoi Company on tour to England, 1990; Season 1991–92 as the Inquisitor in Prokofiev's The Fiery Angel at the Prom Concerts, London, The Love for Three Oranges at Florence, the Commendatore in Dargomizshky's Stone Guest at Salzburg and as King Philip in Don Carlos at the Deutsche Oper Berlin; Concert engagements at Queen Elizabeth Hall, London, Shostakovich's 14th Symphony in Vancouver and Lausanne, the Verdi Requiem and Tchaikovsky's Moscow Cantata at the Salle Pleyel, Prokofiev's Ivan the Terrible in Rome and Elijah at Düsseldorf. *Recordings include:* Holofernes in Serov's Judith, Saison Russe; The Gamblers by Shostakovich. *Address:* c/o Bolshoi Opera, Bolshoi Theatre, 1 Teatraknaya Square, 125009 Moscow, Russia.

**KRYSA, Oleh;** Violinist; b. 1 June 1942, Lublin, Poland; m. Tatiana Tchekina 1966, 3 s. *Education:* Lviv Musical School, Ukraine; Moscow Conservatory with David Oistrakh. *Career:* Debut: Lviv, Ukraine, 1958; Professor of Violin, Kiev Conservatory, Moscow Conservatory, Manhattan School of Music; Eastman School of Music; Solo Recital Tours in USSR, Europe, North America, Far East, Australia, New Zealand; First Violin, Beethoven String Quartet, Moscow; Soloist with Symphony Orchestras of Moscow, Leningrad, Kiev, Berlin, Leipzig, Dresden, Stuttgart, Warsaw, Prague, Budapest, Bucharest, Belgrade, Torino, London, Stockholm, Bergen, New York, Chicago, Washington, Wellington, Cape Town. *Recordings:* Mozart Concertos Nos 3 and 5; Bruch Scottish Fantasy; Viotti No. 22; Tchaikovsky; Wieniawski No. 1; Schnittke No's 3 and 4; Shostakovich No. 1; Prokofiev No. 1; Works for Violin and Piano by Beethoven, Brahms, Paganini, Wieniawski, Ravel, Debussy, Poulenc, Franck, Dvořák, Elgar, Delius, Walton, Szymanowski, Prokofiev, Bartók, Schulhoff, Berio, Schnittke; String quartets by Beethoven, Brahms, Arensky; Shostakovich, Berg, Schnittke, String Sextet, Souvenirs de Florence, by Tchaikovsky; Beethoven Violin Concerto; Tchaikovsky Piano Trio. *Honours:* Wieniawski Competition 2nd Prize, 1962; Paganini Competition 1st Prize, 1963; Tchaikovsky Competition 3rd Prize, 1966; Montreal Competition 2nd Prize, 1969; Outstanding Artist of Ukrainian Republic, 1970. *Current Management:* Connaught Artists Management Ltd, 2 Molasses Row, Plantation Wharf, London, SW11 3UX, England. *Telephone:* (20) 7738 0017. *Fax:* (20) 7738 0909. *E-mail:* classicalmusic@connaughtartists.com. *Website:* www.connaughtartists.com. *Address:* 265 Westminster Road, Rochester, NY 14607, USA.

**KRZANOWSKA, Grazyna;** Composer; b. 1 March 1952, Legnica, Poland. *Education:* Studied in Wroclaw. *Career:* Teacher at the Bielsko-Biala Music School. *Compositions include:* Melodies, cantata, 1975; Passacaglia for Orchestra, 1976; Drumroll Symphony, 1978; Bonfires for 2 Voices and Chamber Ensemble, 1979; String Quartet No. 2, 1980; The Little Choral Symphony, 1985; Silver Line for 15 Strings, 1991. *Honours:* Prizewinner at the 1988 Karol Szymanowski Competition. *Address:* c/o Society of Authors ZAiKS, 2 Hipoteczna Street, 00 092 Warsaw, Poland. *Telephone:* (4822) 828 17 05. *Fax:* (4822) 828 13 47. *E-mail:* sekretariat@zaiks.org.pl. *Website:* www .zaiks.org.pl.

**KUBIAK, Teresa;** Soprano; b. 26 Dec. 1937, Łódź, Poland. *Education:* Studied at the Łódź Music Academy with Olga Olgina; BA 1960; MA 1965. *Career:* Debut: Music Festival in Łódź, Amelia in Amelia al Ballo; Grand Opera Theatre Łódź as Michaela in Carmen, 1967; Appeared in the 1969 world premiere of The Story of St John and Herod by Twardowski; Other roles at Łódź, Aida, Tosca, Lohengrin, 1970; US debut at Carnegie Hall in 1970 as Shulamith in Goldmark's Die Königin von Saba; Glyndebourne Festival in 1971 as Lisa in The Queen of Spades and Juno in La Calisto by Cavalli-Leppard; Covent Garden in 1972 as Madama Butterfly and Metropolitan Opera from 1973 as Lisa, Jenůfa, Giorgietta in Il Tabarro, Tosca, Elsa in Lohengrin, Eva in Meistersinger and Elisabeth in Tannhäuser; Appearances in San Francisco, Chicago, Houston, Seattle, Miami, Leipzig, Prague, Warsaw, Venice, Barcelona, Madrid, Lisbon, Munich, Vienna, Paris Opéra, Rome, Canada, Bulgaria, United Arab Emirates, China, Philippines, Soviet Union (Georgia); other roles include Ariadne, Euryanthe, Halka, Senta, Tatiana, Chrysothemis in Elektra, Leonore in Fidelio and Ellen Orford; many recitals and orchestra appearances; Professor of Music/Voice, Indiana University School of Music, Bloomington, Indiana, 1990–; judging national and international vocal competitions. *Recordings include:* Operatic Arias–Muza; 14 Symphonies-Shostakovich; Glagolitic Mass; La Calisto; Eugene Onegin; Euryanthe Elektra, Strauss; Fidelio, Beethoven;. *Honours:* National Opera Competition, Katowice, Poland, 1960; International Music Competition, Toulouse, France, 1963; International Music Competition, Munich, Germany, 1965; Cross of Knight, Polish Government, 1975. *Address:* 2912 Dale Court, Bloomington, IN 47401, USA.

**KUBICKA, Vitazoslav;** Slovak composer, music broadcasting editor and dramaturg; b. 11 Oct. 1953, Bratislava, Czechoslovakia; m. Gabriela Jurolekova 1988; one s. one d. *Education:* Univ. of Music, Bratislava. *Career:* debut, Rostrum of Composers, UNESCO, Paris 1982; mem. Union of Slovak Composers. *Compositions include:* orchestral: Dramatic Overture for Large Orchestra 1980, Concerto for Piano and Orchestra 1984, Maturing, Overture for Orchestra 1984, Fantasy for Violoncello and Large Orchestra 1985; chamber opuses: Fantasy for Flute and Piano 1979, Quintet for Clarinet, Violin, Viola, Violoncello and Piano 1982, Winter, Sonata for Piano 1986; choral: Fugue for Children's Choir 1982; electro-acoustic: Dedicated to Mussorgsky 1981, Satyr and Nymph 1985; for children and youth: Five Stories for Piano 1982, 1985, Harpsichord Concerto 1986, Bass Clarinet Concerto 1989, Autumn Music for violin and strings 1990, Hedge By the Danube for accordion 1990, Way, electro-acoustic 1991, 30 Biblical Songs and Choirs 1990–2003, Gospel according to St Luke, opera to the Biblical text 2000, Born Again, opera to the Biblical text 2003, Danube Requiem for soprano, bass, mixed choir, three trombone, timpani 2004; incidental music for radio (130 pieces), television (20 pieces), film (12 pieces), theatre and video. *Honours:* Slovak Music Fund of Bratislava Jan Levoslav Bella Prize 1988, Prix Critique Radiomagazin Bratislava 1989. *Address:* Drotarska 9, 81102 Bratislava, Slovakia.

**KUBIK, Ladislav;** Composer; b. 26 Aug. 1946, Prague, Czechoslovakia; m. Natalie Bartosevicova, 7 Nov 1974, 1 s., 1 d. *Education:* Composition, 1970, Theory of Music, 1972, PhD, 1981, Prague Academy of Music. *Career:* Music Director, Czechoslovak Radio Prague, 1979–83; General Secretary, Union of Czech Composers and Concert Artists, 1983–. *Compositions:* Symphonic Works: Symphony, 1970; Drammatic Toccata, 1972; Concerto for Piano and Orchestra, 1974; Hommage a Majakowski, 1976; Concerto for Violin and Orchestra, 1980; Choral Works: Songs of Hope, 1982; Chamber-Cantat: Lament of a Warrior's Wife, 1974; Radio Opera: Solaris, 1975; Ballet: Song of Man, 1984; Vocal Symphony Works: February, 1973; Wolkeriana, 1982; To the Earth of Future, 1985; Songs with Orchestra: Words; Chamber Music: 2 String Quartets, 1981, 1986; Trio Concertante, 1983; Duo Concertante; Concerto Grosso, 1987; Divertimento for 8 wind, 1988; Symphony No. 2, 1993; Harpsichord Concerto, 1995; The River in Spring for mezzo and percussion, 1997; In Night for baritone and ensemble, 1997; Piano Concerto, 1999; Sinfonietta, 1999. *Recordings:* 15 titles and numerous recordings in Czechoslovak and foreign radio broadcasts. *Current Management:* Charles University, Prague. *Address:* Na Brezince 6, 150 00 Prague 5, Czech Republic.

**KUBIK, Reinhold;** Musicologist; b. 22 March 1942, Vienna, Austria; 1 s., 1 d. *Education:* Abitur, Humanistic College, Vienna II, 1960; PhD, University Erlangen-Nuremberg, Germany, 1980; Studied Piano, Composition, Conducting wth Hans Swarowsky, Hochschule für Musik, Vienna. *Career:* Conductor, Deutsche Oper am Rhein, Düsseldorf/Duisburg and many European cities including Lille, Barcelona, Ljubljana, 1966–74; Pianist; Composer; Choirmaster; Lecturer, 1980; Proprietor, Hänssler Musik Verlag, Kirchheim, Germany, 1980–90; Visiting Professor, Yale University, USA, 1987; Production Manager, Universal Edition, Vienna, 1992–97; Chief Editor of Gustav Mahler Gesamtausgabe and of Wiener Urtext Edition; Teacher of period acting techniques in Vienna, London, Karlsruhe and Michaelstein; Editor of all Bach Cantatas for J.E Gardiner's project Bach Cantata Pilgrimage; Vice Pres., Int. Gustav Mahler Soc., Vienna. *Publications:* Handel's Rinaldo, 1980; About 120 editions including 80 cantatas by J. S. Bach (Hänssler), EdM 96, 106 and 110, Schubert, Lazarus (Neue Schubert Ausgabe II/10); Handel, Arianna in Creta; Mahler, 5th Symphonie and Das Klagende Lied (3 movement version). *Contributions:* Festschrift Arnold Feil, 1985; KB Stuttgart, 1985; Festschrift Martin Ruhnke, 1986; Veröffentlichungen der International, Handel-Akademie Karlsruhe, vols 2, 3 4 and 7; Handel-Symposium Halle, 1989. *Address:* Liechtenstein Strasse 39/6, 1090 Vienna, Austria. *E-mail:* reinhold.kubik@chello.at.

**KUBO, Yoko;** Composer, Pianist and College Lecturer; b. 5 Dec. 1956, Nishinomiya, Japan. *Education:* BA, 1979, MA, 1981, Osaka College of Music; Diplome d'Etudes Approfondies, University of Paris, France, 1985. *Career:* Debut: 1979; Many concerts of her compositions, Japan and France, 1979–; Lecturer, Osaka College of Music, 1981–; Associate, Instittut Recherche Coordination Acoustique/Musique, Paris, France, 1984–. *Compositions:* La Sensation de Vingtième Siecle, 12 Percussionists, 1977; Collage, Orchestra, 1978; Objet, 2 Pianos and Percussions, 1979; Play, Violin, Violoncello, Piano, 1979; Crossword, Piano, 1980; Mon parc, String Orchestra, 1980; Quatuor à Cordes No. 2, 1980; Concerto pour Violon No. 1, 1981; Puzzle, 3 Marimbas, 1981; On the Tree, Soprano, 8 Voices, Piano, 1981; Chikya ni hajimete yuki ga futta hi no koto, Soprano, 8 Voices, Piano, 1981; Quatuor à Cordes No. 3, 1981; Concerto pour Orgue, 4 Cuivres et Percussions, 1981; Livre Illustré des chats, String Orchestra, 1982;... SONG..., 5 Voices and Piano, 1982; Quatuor à Cordes No. 4, 1982; Paysage, Flute, Percussion, Piano, 1983; Quatuor pour Flute, Hautbois, Violon et Violoncelle, 1983; Quintette pour Piano No. 1, 1983; Marche du roi (extract from Le Roi Nu), String Orchestra, 1984; Espace, 11 Players, 1985; Vision, Piano, 1987; Concerto pour 7 Interprètes, 1987. *Address:* No. 9-25 2-chome, Nigawa-cho Nishinomiya-shi, Hyogo-ken, Japan.

**KUCERA, Vaclav,** PhDr, CSc; Czech composer and musicologist; *Professor of Composition and New Music Technology, Academy of Performing Arts*; b. 29 April 1929, Prague; m. Marie Jerieová 1951; two s. *Education:* Charles University, Prague, Tchaikovsky Conservatory in Moscow with Vissarion Shebalin, L. Mazel, V. Zuckerman, N. Tumanina. *Career:* Music Department of Radio Prague, 1956–59; Cabinet for New Music Studies, 1959–62; Institute of Musicology, 1962–69; General Secretary, Union of Czech Composers and Concert Artists, 1969–83; Teacher of Composition, 1972–, Professor, 1988–, at Music Faculty of Academy for Performing Arts in Prague mem. Union of Czech Composers 1957–69, Union of Czech Composers and Concert Artists, 1969–89, Soc. of Czech Composers 1990–; ISCM, member of Executive Committee, 1978–1982; President of the International Prague Spring Festival, 1988–92; European Association of Conservatoires, Academies de Musique et Musikhochschulen, mem. Exec. Cttee 1992–1998; Member of Supervisor Board for Society for Performance and Mechanical Rights of Composers, Authors and Publishers, 1994–. *Compositions include:* Dramas for 9 Instruments, 1961; Symphony for large Orchestra; Protests, 1963; Blue Planet, male chorus on M. Červanka, 1964; The Pied Piper, 1964; Hic Sunt Homines, a cycle for Piano quartet, 1965; Genesis, 1965; Spectra, for dulcimer, 1965; Diptychon, 1966; Duodrama, 1967; "To be", 1968; Panta rhei, 1969; Invariant, 1969; Tableau, 1970; Scenario, 1970; Argot, 1970; Diario, 1971; Taboo a Due Boemi, 1972; Salut, 1975; Orbis Pictus, 1975; Amoroso, 1975; Consciousness of Continuities, 1976; Aphorisms, 1978; Horizons, 1978; Epigrams, 1978; Catharsis, 1979; Science Fiction, 1980; Rosen für Rosa, 1980; Aquarelles, 1981; Capriccios, 1983; Cardiograms, 1983; Bird, 1983; Nouvelles, 1984; Ballad and Romance, 1984; Eruptions, 1984; Gogh's Self Portrtait, 1985; Bitter and Other Songs, 1985; A Serious Hour, 1986; Prague Ritornelles, 1986; Duettinos, 1988; Consonanza, 1990; Celebrations of Phantasy, 1991; Oraculum, 1992; Tuning, 1994; Concierto Imaginativo, 1994; Guitariana, 1996; Invocation of Joy, 1996; Criterion for orchestra, 1997; Intimate Conversations, 1998; Mimesis, for dulcimer and harp, 1998; Metathesis, 1998; Satiricon De Creatione, 1999; Mysterious Players, 2000; Pax imago vitae, 2000; Cryptoblues, 2000; Two Sonnets on Shakespeare, 2000; When We Two Parted, 2001; Drei Frauenchöre mit Epitaf auf Gedichte von R.M.Rilke, 2002; Cum Grano Lorca, 2001; Saxonata, 2002; Esta noche, 2002; Imagination, 2003, O Leben: Wunderliche Zeit, Liederzylclus on Rilke 2004, When: a Melodrama on Shakespeare 2004, Elegiaco Appassionato, for viola 2005; Electro-acoustic compositions: Kinetic Ballet, 1968; Kinechromia, 1969; Lidice, 1972; Spartacus, 1976. *Publications:* M P Mussorgsky–Music of Life, 1959; Talent, Mastery, World Outlook, 1962; New Trends in Soviet Music, 1967; musicological studies, radio and television lectures. *Honours:* Prize of Queen Marie-José, Geneva, 1970; Prix d'Italia, Rome, 1972; Prize of Czech Radio Prague, 1977; Prize of Czech Trade Unions, Prague, 1977; Prize of Union of Czech Composers and Concert Artists, Prague, 1983; Trentino International Prize, 1994; Prize of Canary Islands, 2002. *Address:* Jizni II, 778, 141 00 Prague 4, Czech Republic. *Telephone:* 272766326. *Fax:* 272766326. *E-mail:* vac .kuc@tiscali.cz. *Website:* www.musica.cz/comp/kucera.htm.

**KUDELA, Irene;** pianist; b. 1965, France. *Education:* studied in Prague and at Paris Conservatoire. *Career:* vocal coach at Glyndebourne Festival from 1997 (The Makropulos Case 2001); other engagements at Philadelphia, New York, Rome, Washington, Helsinki, Budapest, Orange, Salzburg and Paris (Châtelet and Opéra Bastille); Assistant to Mstislav Rostropovich 1985–88, in Europe and USA; Associate Chorus Master at Opéra National de Paris 1999; Season 2001–02 with Dialogues des Carmélites at Gothenberg. *Recordings:* Albums for Erato, Hungaroton and Teldec. *Address:* c/o Göteborgs Operan, Christina Nilssons Gata, 411 04 Göteborg, Sweden.

**KUDRIASCHOV, Vladimir;** Singer (Tenor); b. 1947, Russia. *Education:* Studied at the Gnessin Conservatory, Moscow. *Career:* Sang at the Stanislavsky Theatre in Moscow, 1971–83, then at the Bolshoi Theatre; Roles have included Sobinin in Glinka's Life for the Tsar, Shuisky in Boris Godunov, Count Almaviva, Rodolfo and Sergei in Lady Macbeth of Mtsensk; Guest at Edinburgh in 1991 as Diak in Christmas Eve by Rimsky-Korsakov. *Address:* c/o Bolshoi Theatre, 103009 Moscow, Russia.

**KUDRIAVCHENKO, Katerina;** Russian singer (soprano) b. 2 March 1958, Karpnsk, Sverdlovskaya; m. Paolo Kudriavchenko. *Education:* Tchaikovsky Conservatoire, Moscow. *Career:* member of Bolshoi Opera, 1986–, as Iolanta, Tatiana, Agnes Sorell in The Maid of Orleans, Marfa in The Tsar's Bride, Gilda, Antonida in A Life for the Tsar, Lisa in The Queen of Spades, Prokofiev's The Duenna, Rachmaninov's Francesca, Violetta, Mimi, Liu and Oxsana in Rimsky's Christmas Eve; Western debut as Iolanta at La Scala, 1989; Season 1990–91 with Bolshoi Opera on tour to Spain, Italy, USA (Metropolitan), Japan and Glasgow, Scotland; Freelance Artist debut as Tatiana for New Israel Opera Company at Tel-Aviv, 1992; Season 1992–93 as Mimi with Scottish Opera, Liu and Titania at the Bolshoi; Sang Butterfly at Bologna, 1996. *Honours:* Gold Medallist, Madama Butterfly Competition, Miami, 1990. *Address:* c/o Bolshoi Opera, Bolshoi Theatre, 1 Teatraknaya Square, 125009 Moscow, Russia.

**KUDRIAVCHENKO, Paolo;** Russian singer (tenor); b. 12 Aug. 1952, Odessa, Crimea; m. Katerina Kudriavchenko. *Education:* Tchaikovsky Conservatory, Odessa. *Career:* sang first with Odessa Opera, then Kiev Opera; Bolshoi Opera, Moscow, 1984–, in Rimsky's Invisible City of Kitezh and as Canio, Turiddu, Dimitri in Boris Godunov, Don José and Jéromir in Mlada; Sang Sobinin in A Life for the Tsar with the Bolshoi Company at La Scala and made US debut, 1989, as Manrico for Greater Miami Opera (repeated for Omaha Opera, 1991), as Turiddu and Dimitri; Season 1991–92 as Turiddu at Munich Staatsoper and as Ernani for Welsh National Opera, followed by Manrico for Scottish Opera, Ishmaele in Nabucco at Bregenz Festival, 1993, and Canio at Rouen; season 1993–94 as Calaf and Radames at the Bolshoi; Many concert appearances. *Address:* c/o Bolshoi Opera, Bolshoi Theatre, 1 Teatraknaya Square, 125009 Moscow, Russia.

**KUEBLER, David;** Singer (Tenor); b. 23 July 1947, Detroit, Michigan, USA. *Education:* Studied with Thomas Peck in Chicago and Audrey Field in London. *Career:* Sang in the chorus of the Chicago Opera; Solo career with the Santa Fe Opera from 1972; European debut Berne Opera 1974, as Tamino; Sang Mozart and bel canto roles with Cologne Opera; Glyndebourne Festival, 1976, as Ferrando in Così fan tutte; Metropolitan Opera from 1979; Bayreuth Festival, 1980–82, as the Steersman in Der fliegende Holländer; Santa Fe Opera, 1984, in We Come to the River by Henze; Other roles include Don Ottavio, Rodolfo, Pinkerton, Lionel (Martha), Jacquino in Fidelio, Paolino in Il Matrimonio Segreto and Giannetto in La Gazza Ladra; Donizetti's Ernesto and Nemorino; Glyndebourne, 1987–90, Strauss's Flamand and Matteo; Schwetzingen Festival, 1988, as Rossini's Almaviva, (1989 in La Cambiale di Matrimonio); sang Don Ottavio in Rome and Madrid, 1989; Schwetzingen 1990 as Doric in Rossini's La Scala di Seta; Sang in The Spectre's Bride by Dvořák at the 1991 Promenade Concerts, London; Sang the Berlioz Faust at Wellington and Bregenz, 1992; Rome Opera, 1997 in I Vespri Siciliani; Salzburg Festival 1998, as Boris in Katya Kabanova and for Netherlands Opera, 2000. *Recordings include:* Mitridate re di Ponto by Mozart; Fidelio; Videos of La Scala di Seta and Idomeneo, as Idamante. *Current Management:* Balmer & Dixon Management AG, Kreuzstrasse 82, 8032 Zürich, Switzerland. *Telephone:* (43) 244-8644. *Fax:* (43) 244-8649. *Website:* www.badix.ch.

**KUENTZ, Paul;** Conductor; b. 4 May 1930, Mulhouse, France; m. Monique Frasca-Colombier, 1956. *Education:* Studied at the Paris Conservatoire, 1947–50, with Noel Gallon, Georges Hugon and Eugene Bigot. *Career:* Founded the Paul Kuentz Chamber Orchestra, 1951: many tours of Europe and the USA, including the orchestral works of Bach at Saint-Severin and concert at Carnegie Hall, 1968; Frequent performances of French music, including premieres of works by P M Dubois, J Casterede and J Charpentier; Founded Paul Kuentz Chorus, 1972. *Recordings include:* Bach's Orchestral Suites, Mass in B Minor and Musikalisches Opfer; Vivaldi's Four Seasons, and other concertos; Flute Concertos by Haydn, Blavet, Mozart, Leclair and Pergolesi; Music by Delalande, Mouret, Gabrieli and Gluck; Mozart's Concerto K299, Requiem, Bastien und Bastienne and Church Sonatas; Harp concertos by Handel, Albrechtsberger, Boieldieu, Wagenseil and Dittersdorf; Haydn Symphonies Nos 85 and 101.

**KUERTI, Anton (Emil);** Pianist and Composer; b. Vienna, 1938; m. Kristine Bogyo, 13 Sept 1973, 2 s. *Education:* BM, Cleveland Institute of Music; Diploma, Curtis Institute, 1959; PhD (Hon), York University, 1985, Laurentian University, 1985, Memorial University, 1999, Dalhousie University, 2001. *Career:* Soloist, New York Philharmonic, Cleveland Orchestra, Detroit Symphony, Philadelphia Orchestra, Buffalo Philharmonic, San Francisco Symphony, Denver Symphony, 41 appearances with Toronto Symphony, National Arts Centre Orchestra (Ottawa), Dresden Staatskapelle, Leipzig Gewandhaus, London Symphony; Tours world-wide including Soviet Union, Far East, Australia, Latin America; Numerous television appearances, radio broadcasts; Founder, Festival of Sound, Parry Sound, Ontario; mem, Amnesty International. *Compositions:* Linden Suite for Piano, 1970; String Quartet, 1972; Violin Sonata and Symphony Epomeo, 1975; Piano Man Suite and Piano Concerto, 1985; Clarinet Trio, 1989; Concertino, Jupiter Concerto, 1996. *Recordings:* Recordings include complete cycle of Beethoven Sonatas and Concerti; Brahms and Schumann Concerti; Complete Schubert Sonatas. *Honours:* Leventritt Award, 1957; Honorary Doctorate, Cleveland Institute of Music, 1996; Toronto Arts Award, 1997; Officer, Order of Canada. *Current Management:* Concertmasters Incorporated, 22 Linden Street, Toronto, M4Y 1V6. *Address:* 20 Linden Street, Toronto, Ontario M4Y 1V6, Canada.

**KUHN, Alfred;** Singer (Bass); b. 2 Nov. 1938, Ober-Roden, Germany. *Education:* Studied at the Frankfurt Musikhochschule. *Career:* Debut: Trulove in The Rake's Progress, Darmstadt, 1963; Guest appearances throughout Germany, notably as Wagner's Daland and Landgrave; Rocco in Fidelio; Mozart's Osmin and Sarastro; King Philip in Don Carlos; Donizetti's Dulcamara; Kaspar in Der Freischütz; Düsseldorf, 1986, in the premiere of Belshazzar by Kirchner; Mozart's Antonio at the 1991 Salzburg Festival; La Scala, 1992 as Waldner in Arabella; Sang Varlaam in Boris Godunov at Munich, 1995. *Address:* c/o Bayerische Staatsoper, Max-Josephplatz, 80539 Munich, Germany.

**KUHN, Gustav,** DPhil; Austrian conductor and producer; b. 28 Aug. 1945, Salzburg; s. of Friedrich Kuhn and Hilde Kuhn; m. Andrea Kuhn 1971; one s. one d. *Education:* Acads of Salzburg and Vienna and Univs of Salzburg and Vienna. *Career:* advanced conducting studies under Bruno Maderna and Herbert von Karajan; professional conductor in Istanbul (three years), Enschede (Netherlands), Dortmund (prin. conductor) and Vienna; début at Vienna State Opera (Elektra) 1977, Munich Nat. Theatre (Così fan tutte) 1978, Covent Garden, London 1979, Glyndebourne, Munich Opera Festival and Salzburg Festival 1980, Chicago (Fidelio) 1981, Paris Opéra 1982, La Scala, Milan 1984, Arena di Verona (Masked Ball) 1986, Rossini Opera Festival, Pesaro 1987; Gen. Music Dir in Berne, Bonn and Rome; production début in Trieste (Fliegender Holländer) 1986; other projects include Parsifal,

Naples 1988, Salome, Rome 1988, Don Carlos (French version) and Don Carlo (Italian) for 250th anniversary Teatro Reggio, Turin 1990; Artistic Dir Neue Stimmen (New Voices), Bertelsmann Foundation 1987–, Macerata Festival, Italy (productions of Così fan tutte and Don Giovanni) 1990/91, Marchigiana Philharmonic Orchestra (Dir-Gen. 2003–), Haydn Orchestra 2003–, Conservatorio di Milano Philharmonic Orchestra 2004; Founder and Pres. Accad. di Montegral 1990, Tyrolean Festival, Erl, Austria 1997–; Producer and Conductor Complete Ring Cycle of Richard Wagner, Tyrolean Festival, Erl 2003. *Publication:* Aus Liebe zur Musik 1993. *Honours:* First Prize, Int. Conducting Contest of Austrian TV and Broadcasting Corpn (ORF) 1969, Lilly Lehmann Medal (Mozarteum Foundation), Max Reinhardt Medal (Salzburg), Senator of Honour Award 'Lorenzo il Magnifico' (Florence) 1988. *Address:* Winkl 25, 6343 Erl, Austria (office). *Telephone:* (5373) 8181.

**KUHN, Pamela;** Singer (Soprano); b. 1960, Oregon, USA. *Education:* Bachelor of Music, University of Oregon; Master of Music, University of Southern California with Gwendolyn Koldofsky and Margaret Schaper. *Career:* Debut: London, Wigmore Hall with Graham Johnson, 1984; Recitals at the Purcell Room with Stephen Wilder, Stephen Coombs and Geoffrey Parsons; Isle of Man Festival with Roger Steptoe; Oratorio includes Rossini Petite Messe Solennelle at Queen Elizabeth Hall, Verdi Requiem at Fairfield Halls, Dartington (Diego Masson), Oregon Bach Festival (Helmut Rilling), Penderecki Polish Requiem at Oregon Bach Festival (Penderecki), Brahms Requiem at the Royal Festival Hall and in the USA, Beethoven Missa Solemnis in Lugano, Switzerland, Janáček Glagolitic Mass at Salisbury Cathedral; Opera: Ariadne at Dartington, Aida with Florentine Opera in Milwaukee, Rezia with Scottish Opera at La Fenice, Venice, Soloist in Oberon conducted by Seiji Ozawa at Tanglewood, Edinburgh Festival and Frankfurt Alte Oper, High Priestess with Scottish Opera; Other roles include Micaela, Tosca, Amelia and Sieglinde; Further concert repertory includes operatic evenings with City of Birmingham Symphony Orchestra, Southampton Symphony and Ernest Read Symphony at the Barbican, Shostakovich Symphony 14 with Mark Wigglesworth at St John's Smith Square and Four Last Songs in Nottingham. *Address:* Lombardo Associates, 61 West 62nd, Suite 6F, New York, NY 10023, USA.

**KUIJKEN, Barthold;** Belgian flautist, recorder player and conductor; b. 8 March 1949, Dilbeek, Brussels. *Education:* Conservatoires of Bruges, Brussels and the Hague with Frans Vester and Frans Brueggen; self-taught on the Baroque flute. *Career:* concerts in Europe, North and South America, Japan, Australia, New Zealand, Korea and Israel with his brothers, Lucy van Dael, René Jacobs, Frans Brueggen, Gustav Leonhardt, Bob van Asperen, Luc Devos, Ewald Demeyere. the Parnassus Ensemble, La Petite Bande and the Collegium Aureum; Teacher of Baroque flute at the Hague and Brussels Conservatories; Repertoire includes music by Couperin, Telemann, Handel, Haydn, Bach, Mozart, Schubert and Debussy; Took part in the Towards Bach concert series on the South Bank, London, August 1989. *Recordings:* Solos by J. S. and C. P. E. Bach, Boismortier, Debussy, Fischer, Hotteterre, Telemann, Vivaldi, Weiss; Duos by Boismortier, Hotteterre and W.F. Bach; Suites by Couperin, Hotteterre and Montéclair; Sonatas by Albinoni, J. S. and C. P. E, Bach, Benda, Blavet, Boismortier, Corelli, Friedrich der Grosse, Geminiani, C.H. and J.G. Graun, Guignon, Händel, Kirnberger, Leclair, Locatelli, Müthel, Platti, Quantz, Telemann, Veracini, Vivaldi; A recital of 19th century works for flute and fortepiano (Hummel, F.X. Mozart, Mendelssohn, Schubert); Chamber music by J. S., C. P. E. and J. C. Bach, Boismortier, Couperin, Debussy, Devienne, Dornel, Galuppi, Geminiani, Händel, Haydn, Hotteterre, Janitsch, Mozart, Rameau, Telemann; Concertos by J. S. Bach, Haydn, Mozart, Richter, J. and C. Stamitz, Telemann, and Vivaldi; As a conductor: Mozart's Gran Partita and a program of suites concertantes from the German baroque (J. L. and J. S. Bach, Teleman, Handel). *Publications:* J. S. Bach's flute compositions (ed.). *Address:* Zwartschaapstraat 38, 1755 Gooik, Belgium. *Website:* bartholdkuijken.be.

**KUIJKEN, Sigiswald;** Belgian violinist and conductor; b. 16 Feb. 1944, nr Brussels. *Education:* Bruges Conservatory, Conservatoire Royale Brussels with M. Raskin. *Career:* began to re-establish old technique of violin playing, resting the instrument on the shoulder not under the chin, in 1969, adopted by many players in early 1970s; Played in the Alarius Ensemble (with Wieland Kuijken, Robert Kohnen and Janine Rubinlicht), 1964–72, performances throughout Europe and USA; Founder of the Baroque orchestra, La Petite Bande in 1972; Tours of Europe, Australia, South America, China and Japan with La Petite Bande and in chamber music and solo programmes; Founder, Kuijken String Quartet (with François Fernandez, Marleen Thiers and Wieland Kuijken), specialising in quartets and quintets (with Ryo Terakado, 1st viola) of the Classical period, 1986–; Occasional conductor of modern symphonic orchestras such as Royal Philharmonic Orchestra of Flanders, Cappella Colonienses (WDR Köln), Orchestre Nat. de Bordeaux & Aquitaine, in Romantic programmes (Beethoven, Schumann, Brahms, Mendelssohn), 1998–; Teacher of Baroque violin, Koninklijk Conservatorium, The Hague, 1971–96; Koninklijk Muziekconservatorium, Brussels, 1993–; Guest teacher at many institutions, including Royal College of Music, London, Salamanca Univ. and Accademia Chigiana, Siena. *Recordings include:* Many with La Petite Bande including: Music by Lully, Muffat, Gluck, Haydn's Creation and Symphonies, Mozart's Requiem and Davidde Penitente, Così fan tutte, 1992, J. S. Bach's Passions and Brandenburg Concertos, 1994; Bach Sonatas with Gustav Leonhardt; 20 Haydn Symphonies; Mozart Concert Arias; German Chamber Music; Don Giovanni, 1997; Le nozze di Figaro, 1998, Die

Zauberflöte 2004. *Honours:* Deutsche Schallplattenpreis several times; Grand Prix du Disque, France several times; Deutsche Handel Preis, 1994; Choc de l'année for recording Debussy chamber music, 2000. *Address:* La Petite Bande, Geert Robberechts, Vital Decosterstraat 72, 3000 Leuven, Belgium (office). *Telephone:* (1) 623-08-30 (office). *Fax:* (1) 622-76-10 (office). *E-mail:* info@lapetitebande.be (office). *Website:* www.lapetitebande.be (office).

**KUIJKEN, Wieland;** viola da gamba player, cellist and conductor; b. 31 Aug. 1938, Dilbeek, Brussels, Belgium. *Education:* Bruges Conservatory, Brussels Conservatoire Royale. *Career:* played with the Alarius Ensemble, 1959–72; Played in the avant-garde group Musiques Nouvelles from 1962; Kuijken Early Music Group from 1972; Teacher at the Conservatories of Antwerp, Brussels and the Hague; Masterclasses in the United Kingdom, Innsbruck and the USA; Festival appearances at Flanders, Saintes and the English Bach Festival; Tour of New Zealand and Australia with Gustav Leonhardt, 1979; Cellist with the Kuijken String Quartet from 1986: London debut 1990; Collaborations with his brothers, Frans Brueggen, Alfred Deller and René Jacobs; Repertoire includes music by French, English, Italian and German composers; Performed in the Towards Bach concert series on the South Bank, London, August 1989. *Recordings include:* Leclair Flute Sonatas, Marais Pièces de Viole du Cinquieme Livre and German Chamber Music. *Current Management:* Allied Artists Agency, 42 Montpeiler Square, London, SW7 1JZ, England.

**KUJAWINSKA, Krystyna;** Singer (Soprano); b. 4 April 1938, Kalisz, Poland. *Education:* Studied at the Poznán Academy, 1962–67. *Career:* Debut: Bytom in 1967 as Arabella; Sang at the Poznán Opera from 1970 notably as Elisabeth de Valois, Aida, Desdemona, Micaela, Butterfly, Gioconda and Santuzza; Later roles have included Tosca, the Forza Leonora and Turandot; Guest appearances in France as Electra (Idomeneo), Hamburg as Aida, Parma as Halka, Dresden in Verdi Requiem and Leonora (La Forza del Destino), in Netherlands as Tosca and Santuzza and in Germany and Belgium as Abigaile in Nabucco; Has also appeared at the National Theatre Warsaw as Fidelio, Aida and the Trovatore Leonora. *Address:* c/o Poznán Grand Theatre, Fredry 9, 60-987 Poznán, Poland.

**KULENTY, Hanna,** BMus; Polish composer; b. 18 March 1961, Białystok; one d. *Education:* Acad. of Music, Warsaw and Conservatory, The Hague, studied under Włodzimierz, Kotoński and Louis Andriessen. *Career:* guest performer, Deutscher Akademischer Austauschdienst in Berliner Künstler Programm 1990–91; performances of works by many orchestras in countries including the Netherlands, Latvia, UK, Denmark, Germany. *Works include:* Ad Unum 1985, Symphony No. 1 1986, Perpetuus 1989, Trigon 1989, Concerto for piano and chamber orchestra 1990, Air 1991, A Cradle Song 1993, A Sixth Circle 1995, Drive Blues 2000, Asjaawaa 2001, Hoffmanniana 2003; works for solo instruments and Chamber Orchestras. *Recordings include:* 12½ Musis Sacrum, Chronicles from Warsaw Autumn Festivals, Hanna Kulenty: Ad Unum, Sesto, Arci, Piano Concerto No. 1, Violin Concerto No. 1, Arcs and Circles: Portrait of Hanna Kulenty. *Honours:* Stanisław Wyspiański Award 1987, first prize Composers' Competition, Polish Composers' Union 1986, 1987, first prize Int. Rostrum of Composers 2003, other awards in music competitions. *Address:* c/o Jana Pawła II 69/52, 00-170 Warsaw, Poland.

**KULESHA, Gary (Alan);** Composer, Conductor and Pianist; b. 22 Aug. 1954, Toronto, Canada; m. Larysa Kuzmenko, 30 Dec 1983. *Education:* Associate in Piano, 1973, Associate in Composition, 1978, Royal Conservatory of Music, Toronto; Private Studies with John McCabe, London, England and John Corigliano, New York, USA; L Mus, 1976, Fellow 1978, Trinity College, London, England. *Career:* Composer-in-Residence, Kitchener-Waterloo Symphony, 1989–92; Composer-in-Residence, Candia Opera Company, 1993–95; Composer Adviser, Toronto Symphony Orchestra, 1995–, guest conducting throughout Canada; Principal Conductor, Festival Theatre, Stratford Festival, Canada; Artistic Director and Principal Conductor, Canadian Contemporary Music Workshops and the Composers Orchestra; Works performed throughout North America, Europe, Iceland, Australia and Latin America. *Compositions:* Essay for Orchestra; Second Essay for Orchestra; Chamber Concertos 1–5; Duo for Bass Clarinet and Piano; Second Sonata for Piano; Lifesongs for Alto and String Orchestra, text by composer; Nocturne for Chamber Orchestra; Angels for Marimba and Tape, recorded, 1986; Scores for several Shakespearean plays including All's Well That End's Well, Nimrod, Sydney, Australia 1986 and Henry VIII, Stratford 1986; Shama Songs, 1991; Concerto for Recorder, 1990; 3 Essays for Orchestra, 2nd and 3rd Pico Sonata; Concerto for Viola, 1992; Opera Red Emma, 1995; Symphony, 1998; Partita for piano and strings, 1999; Violin Concerto, 1999. *Recordings:* Recorder Concerto, Michela Petri and ECO conducted by Kamn; Political Implications, Indiana Clarinet Quartet. *Address:* 54 Springbrook Gardens, Toronto, Ontario M8Z 3C1, Canada.

**KULHAN, Jaroslav;** Czech cellist; b. 7 Dec. 1950, Ceske Budejovice; m. Stepanka Kazilova 1978; one s. two d. *Education:* Prague Conservatory; Acad. of Music and Arts, Prague. *Career:* mem., Panocha Quartet 1968–; teacher, Prague Conservatory 1990–. *Recordings:* Haydn Op 51, Op 33, Op 55, Op 76; Smetana Quartets 1 and 2; Dvořák's Chamber Music, Martinů's Quartets; Janáček Quartets No. 1, Schubert Op 29, 125, 161, 163; Fibich Op 8, Quartet A major, Op 11, Op 42; Schumann Op 47. *Honours:* Grand Prix Academy Charles Cros (Martinů's Quartet Nos 4, 6), 1983; Midem Cannes Classical Awards, 1994. *Address:* c/o Prague Conservatory, Na Rejdisti 1, 11000 Prague, Czech Republic (office).

**KULINSKY, Bohumil;** Conductor; b. 5 May 1959, Prague, Czechoslovakia. *Education:* Prague Conservatory, 1978–81; Prague Music Academy, 1981–84; Music Academy of Janáček-Brno, 1984–86. *Career:* Conductor, Czechoslovak Children's Choir Bambini di Praga, 1976–; Concert tours: France; Italy; Democratic Republic of Germany, Federal Republic of Germany, Mongolia, Finland; the United Kingdom; Japan; Appeared on radio and television; Conductor, Prague Symphony Orchestra, appearing at Concerts and Festivals, 1984; Conductor, Czech Chamber Philharmonic Orchestra; Concert Tours: Spain and Germany. *Recordings:* CBS, Sony, Polydor, King Record Japan, Supraphon, Panton; Recordings with Prague Symphony Orchestra. *Address:* Anenska 2, 11000 Prague 1, Czech Republic.

**KULJERIC, Igor;** Composer; b. 1 Feb. 1938, Sibenik, Croatia. *Education:* Studied at Zagreb Academy of Music, graduated 1965 and the Electronic Music Studios in Milan. *Career:* Has conducted various orchestras in Zagreb and elsewhere in Croatia; Art Director, Opera Zagreb and Dubrovnik Festival; Art Director, competition for young conductors, L Matacic, Zagreb; Has conducted various orchestras in Croatia, Europe and the USA; Employs electronic and other advanced techniques in his music. *Compositions include:* The Ballads of Petrica Kerempuh, 1973; Ballets and Incidental Music; Opera: The Power of Virtue, Zagreb, 1977 and Rikard, 2 Acts, after Shakespeare, 1987; Ballad of Petrica Kerempuh, vocal-instrumental, 1973; Canconiere, 1983; Ballet: Ricki Levy, 1991; Croatian Glagolic Requiem, 1996; Chamber music. *Address:* Jagiceva 23, 10000 Zagreb, Croatia.

**KULJUNTAUSTA, Petri;** Composer and Musician; b. 28 Feb. 1961, Tampere, Finland. *Education:* MA, University of Jyväskylä, Finland; Studies in Philosophy, Aesthetics and Pedagogy. *Career:* Electronic compositions and performances as improvisor, 1980s; Music for Petri Kuljuntausta Project, 1989–94; Played with Petri Kuljuntausta Ensemble, string quartet, piano, synthesiser, saxophone, guitar and percussion, 1993–94; Sound/media works and installations in galleries, museums and halls, 1993–; Founder and Chairman, Charm of Sound, 1995–; Member of the Muu, 1995–; Co-Director, Charm of Sound concert series, 1997–; Editor, Charmed Sounds radio programme, Finnish Radio, 1997–; Curator, Sound Box webcast project, Museum of Contemporary Art, Finland, 1998–; mem, DEGEM; WFAE. *Compositions:* Various works for improvisers, 1980s; Chamber Music: Kuun arvet, 1988; Chain, 1994; Ancient Dream, 1994; Pro, 1994; Time, 1994; Enigma, 1994; Big Band: Storm..., 1993; Sound/Media installations: Soundscapes I, 1994; Birdscape Music, 1997; Free Zone, 1998; Transitions, 1998; Formation, 2002; Mixer, 2002; Electronic Film Soundtracks: Texas Scramble, 1995; The Blow, 1997; Days, 2002; Electronic Music: Lux in tenebris, 1995; The Good and Evil, 1995; Flow, 1996; La Mer, 1996; Momentum, 1998; Idea of Proof, 1999; The Waiting Room, 1999; Hysteria, 1999; Aurora Borealis 1, 2002; Four Notes, 2002; Departs/ Arrivals, 2002; VROOM! 2000–2002; Canvas, 2002. *Recordings:* Numerous for various labels throughout Europe and the USA. *Publications:* Several contributions to journals, newspapers and books; On/Off, 2002. *Honours:* Farao Horn Competition Prize, 1995; Luigi Russolo Competition finalist, 1996; Finnish Cultural Foundation, 1998; State's Art Grant, 2000. *Address:* c/o Charm of Sound, PO Box 353, 00131 Helsinki, Finland. *E-mail:* petriear@nic.fi. *Website:* www.nic.fi/~petriear.

**KULKA, Janos;** Conductor; b. 11 Dec. 1929, Budapest, Hungary. *Education:* Studied at the Franz Liszt Academy, Budapest, with Janos Ferencsik and Laszlo Somogyi. *Career:* Repetiteur and Chorus Master at the Budapest Opera from 1950; Conducted Opera in Budapest from 1953 until the 1956 Revolution; Conducted at the Bavarian State Opera, 1957–59, Wurttemberg State Opera, Stuttgart, 1959–61; Principal Conductor of the Hamburg State Opera, 1961–64, Music Director at the Wuppertal Opera, 1964–75; Chief Conductor at Stuttgart from 1976, Nordwestdeutsche Philharmonie, 1976–87; Has worked with leading opera houses in Cologne, Geneva, Paris, Munich, Vienna, Barcelona, Copenhagen, Boston and Buenos Aires; Conducted the premieres of Blacher's Yvonne, Prinzessin von Burgund, 1973, Klebe's Jacobovsky und der Oberst, 1982, and Boehmer's Doktor Faustus, 1985; Has also led operas by Gluck, Mozart, Verdi, Wagner, Schoenberg, Janáček, Dallapiccola and Penderecki; Conducted The Queen of Spades at Berne, 1996. *Recordings include:* Chopin's 2nd Piano Concerto with Tamas Vasary and the Berlin Philharmonic; Opera recital albums with Grace Bumbry, Thomas Tipton, Walter Berry, Sandor Konya, Brigitte Fassbaender and Teresa Stratas; Il Trovatore; Die Abreise by d'Albert with Peter Schreier and Hermann Prey (CPO). *Address:* c/o Staatstheater Stuttgart, Oberer Schlossgarten 6, 70103 Stuttgart, Germany.

**KULKA, Konstanty Andrzej;** Polish violinist; *Professor, Warsaw Academy of Music;* b. 5 March 1947, Gdańsk; m.; two d. *Education:* Higher State School of Music, Gdańsk. *Career:* Prof., Acad. of Music, Warsaw 1994–; participant in two music competitions: Paganini Competition, Genoa 1964, Diploma and Special Prize; Music Competition, Munich 1966 (1st Prize); many gramophone, radio and TV recordings; soloist with Nat. Philharmonic Orchestra, Warsaw 1984–. *Performances:* since 1967 has given some 1,500 concerts all over the world and participates in many int. festivals including Lucerne, Prague, Bordeaux, Berlin, Granada, Barcelona, Brighton; concerts with Berlin Philharmonic Orchestra, Chicago Symphony Orchestra, Minneapolis Orchestra, London Symphony Orchestra, Konzertgebouw Amsterdam Orchestra, English Chamber Orchestra and others. *Recordings include:* Antonio Vivaldi Cztery pory roku (The Four Seasons), Szymanowski: Violin Concertos Nos. 1 & 2 1997, Mozart: Best Of 2000, Karlowicz: Tone Poems/

Violin Concerto 2002, Paderewski: Violin & Piano Works 2003, Penderecki: Violin Concertos Nos. 1 & 2 2003. *Honours:* Gold Cross of Merit, Commdr's Cross, Order of Polonia Restituta; Minister of Culture and Arts Prize 1969, 1973, Minister of Foreign Affairs Prize 1977, Pres. of Radio and TV Cttee Prize 1978, Prize Winner, 33rd Grand Prix du Disque Int. Sound Festival, Paris 1981. *Address:* Filharmonia Narodowa, ul. Jasna 5, 00-950 Warsaw, Poland. *Telephone:* (605) 194753; (22) 5517203. *E-mail:* konstanty.kulka@wp.pl (office).

**KUN, Hu;** Concert Violinist; b. 1963, China. *Education:* Studied at Szechuan and Peking Central Conservatories and at Menuhin International School. *Career:* Debut: Played with Helsinki Radio Symphony and Helsinki Philharmonic Orchestras, 1979; London debut, 1985, followed by concerts with London Symphony Orchestra and the Philharmonic at the Barbican; Further concerts as Wigmore Hall and on tour to Canada, Japan, Singapore, Hong Kong, Brazil, Australia and Europe; Engagements at Concertgebouw Amsterdam and Zürich Tonhalle; Vienna and Berlin debuts, 1987, with the Beethoven and Sibelius Concertos. *Recordings include:* Prokofiev First Concerto with the English String Orchestra and the Sibelius and Khachaturian Concertos, both conducted by Yehudi Menuhin. *Honours:* Winner, City of Paris Menuhin Competition, 1984, Francescatti Competition, 1987, and Lipizer Competition, Italy, 1988.

**KUNDE, Gregory;** Singer (Tenor); b. 1954, Kankakee, Illinois, USA. *Education:* Studied at Illinois State University and the Opera School of Chicago Lyric Opera. *Career:* Sang at Chicago from 1979, Washington Opera, 1983, Dallas, 1986, Seattle, 1987; Metropolitan Opera debut, 1987, as Des Grieux in Manon; European engagements at Nice, Théâtre des Champs Elysées, Paris, 1989, and Geneva, in Guillaume Tell; Montpellier, 1990; as Raoul in Les Huguenots; Detroit, 1989, as Gounod's Roméo; Other roles have included Mozart's Belmonte and Tamino, Ernesto, Alfredo, Montreal 1987, Berlin 1991, San Francisco 1993, Carnegie Hall 1995; sang Arturo in Bellini's Puritani; Other roles include Edgardo in Lucia, Tormo 1993, Leicester in Maria Stuarda, Bologna 1994; Ernesto in Don Pasquale, La Scala 1994, Don Ottavio in Don Giovanni, Geneva 1992, La Scala 1993; Rodrigo in Donna del Lago, La Scala 1993, Rinaldo in Armida, Pesaro 1993; Tonio in Fille du Régiment and Nadir in Les Pêcheurs de Perles; Montpellier and Chicago, 1989, as Des Grieux, and Laertes in Hamlet by Thomas; Sang Lindoro in L'Italiana in Algeri at Berlin, 1992, Idreno in Semiramide at the 1992 Pesaro Festival; Danish Knight in Gluck's Armide to open the 1996–97 season at La Scala. *Recordings:* Bianca e Fernando; Semiramide; Armide; Hamlet. *Address:* c/o Robert Lombardo Associates, 61 West 62nd Street, Suite 6F, NY, NY 10023, USA.

**KUNDLAK, Josef;** Singer (Tenor); b. 1956, Bratislava, Czechoslovakia. *Education:* Studied in Bratislava and the European Opera Centre in Belgium. *Career:* Sang with Bratislava State Opera, 1983–, in works by Janáček and Smetana, in addition to standard repertory; Sang Nemorino in L'Elisir d'amore at Teatro Comunale, Bologna, 1987; Ferrando in Così fan tutte at La Scala Milan, 1989, returning in Die Meistersinger in 1990; Sang at Donizetti Festival at Bergamo in 1991 in Elisabetta al Castello di Kenilworth; Further engagements at Teatro San Carlo, Naples and Bayerische Staatsoper, Munich; Appeared as Belmonte in a new production of Die Entführung at Deutsche Oper Berlin in 1991; Sang Rossini's Almaviva at Genoa in 1992. *Recordings include:* Kudryash in Katya Kabanova, under Charles Mackerras (Supraphon, 1997). *Honours:* Winner, Luciano Pavarotti Competition in Philadelphia, 1985. *Address:* c/e Deutsche Oper Berlin, Richard Wagnerstrasse 10, 1000 Berlin, Germany.

**KUNKEL, Renata;** Polish composer; b. 1 Sept. 1954, Gdańsk. *Education:* Warsaw Acad. of Music. *Career:* Lecturer, Warsaw Acad.; performances of her music in Europe, the USA and Central America. *Compositions include:* orchestral works: Shadows for four instrumental groups 1981, Symphony for symphony orchestra 1983, Inner Landscapes for chamber orchestra 1984, Music for Sirius B for woodwind chamber orchestra 1985, Where Worlds are Naught for string chamber orchestra 1987, The Stream for symphony orchestra 1990; chamber works: three String Quartets 1979–91, Penetrations for flute and percussion 1980, Events for violin and percussion 1980, Idiochrome II for oboe and violin 1986, In A Lit-Up Streak Of Sounds for Ensemble 1989; solo works: Mimesis for violin 1981, Phrases for Piano 1984, Eidos I for flute 1986, Promethidion for violin 1986, Eidos II for clarinet 1987, Intensity for piano 1988, for organ 1990, Ánodos for violin 1990; vocal works: Apogéios for vocal group and orchestra 1984, Idiochromie I for two sopranos and ensemble 1985, Elegy for mixed choir and symphony orchestra 1988, And Give Us Silence to Drink for female choir 1990; other: In Memoriam for magnetic tape 1982. *Honours:* Special Prize, Int. Competition for Women Composers, Mannheim 1989, Prizewinner at the First Lutoslawski International Composers' Competition, 1990. *Address:* c/o Society of Authors ZAiKS, 2 Hipoteczna Street, 00 092 Warsaw, Poland. *Telephone:* (4822) 828 17 05. *Fax:* (4822) 828 13 47. *E-mail:* sekretariat@zaiks.org.pl. *Website:* www.zaiks.org.pl.

**KUNTZSCH, Matthias;** symphony and opera conductor and professor; b. 22 Sept. 1935, Karlsruhe, Germany; m. Sylvia Anderson 1966; one s. one d. *Education:* Hochschule für Musik und Theatre, Hannover, Mozarteum, Salzburg with Lovro von Matacic, Hermann Scherchen, Herbert von Karajan, Zermatt with Pablo Casals, Karl Engel. *Career:* debut conducting Don Pasquale, State Theatre, Braunschweig, 1960; Conductor, Jeunesse Musicale Orchestra, Braunschweig, 1957; Musical Assistant, Hannover Opera, 1958;

Kapellmeister, Opera Braunschweig, 1959; Assistant to Wolfgang and Wieland Wagner, Bayreuth Festival, 1959–64; Principal Conductor, Bonn Opera, 1962–64, Mannheim Opera, 1964–66, Hamburg State Opera, 1966–69, Staatskapellmeister, Munich State Opera, 1969–73; Generalmusikdirektor, Lübeck Opera and Symphony, 1973–77; Generalmusikdirektor and Operndirektor, Saarbrücken State Opera and Symphony, 1977–85; Conductor, International Youth Festival Orchestra, Bayreuth, 1981–86; Principal Guest Conductor and Artistic Adviser, Basque National Symphony, San Sebastian, Spain, 1986–89; Music Dir, Bay Area Summer Opera Theatre Inst. (BASOTI) 1992–; conducted world premieres of operas, Humphrey Searle's Hamlet, Hamburg, 1968 and Gian Carlo Menotti's Help Help the Globolinks, Hamburg, 1968; Günther Bialas's Aucassin et Nicolette, Munich, 1969; Detlev Mueller-Siemens's Genoveva, Germany TV ZDF; Guest Conductor with Utah Opera and Symphony, Colorado Symphony and Vancouver Opera. *Recordings:* With soloists Ruggiero Ricci, Eugene List and others; Conrad Susa's The Blue House with the Colorado Symphony, 2002. *Address:* 123 Nantucket Cove, San Rafael, CA 94901, USA. *E-mail:* operaprof@aol.com.

**KUNZEL, Erich;** Conductor; b. 21 March 1935, New York, USA. *Education:* Studied at Dartmouth College, AB, 1957 and at Harvard and Brown Universities, AM, 1960. *Career:* Assistant to Pierre Monteux, 1963–64; Teacher and Director of Choral Music, Brown University, 1958–65; Conducted the Rhode Island Philharmonic, 1960–65; Assistant to Max Rudolf at the Cincinnati Symphony, 1965, Associate Conductor, 1967, Resident Conductor, 1969–74; Led Pergolesi's La Serva Padrona at Santa Fe, 1957, and the US premiere of The Nose by Shostakovich, 1965; Conducted the Cincinnati Opera, 1966; New Haven Symphony Orchestra, 1974–; Founded the Cincinnati Pops Orchestra, 1977 and toured with it to the Far East, 1990; Has also conducted orchestras in Chicago, Boston, Los Angeles, San Francisco, Montreal, Ottawa and Detroit; Music Director of the Indianapolis Symphony Orchestra; Jazz collaborations with Dave Brubeck, Ella Fitzgerald, Duke Ellington, Benny Goodman, George Shearing and Gerry Mulligan. *Recordings include:* Albums with the Dave Brubeck Trio and the Cincinnati Symphony; Carnaval Roman overture by Berlioz and Pictures at an Exhibition, Hanson's Symphony No. 2 Romania (with Cincinnati Pops Orchestra) 2005. *Address:* c/o Cincinnati Symphony Orchestra, 1241 Elm Street, Cincinnati, OH 45210, USA.

**KUPFER, Harry;** Opera Producer; b. 12 Aug. 1935, Berlin, Germany. *Career:* Worked at theatres in Halle, Stralsund and Karl-Marx-Stadt (now Chemnitz); Director, Deutsches Nationaltheater, Weimar, 1963–72; Chief Producer of Staatsoper Dresden, 1972–81; Chief Producer, Komische Oper Berlin from 1981 and Director from 1994; Has produced for Bayreuth: Der fliegende Holländer, 1978, Der Ring des Nibelungen, 1988; Opera Productions for Welsh National Opera at Cardiff, Covent Garden London, Staatsoper and Volksoper Vienna, Amsterdam, San Francisco, Paris, Hamburg, Cologne, Stuttgart and Frankfurt; Important productions include: Orfeo ed Euridice by Gluck, Mozart Cycle, La Damnation de Faust, Pelléas et Mélisande, Moses und Aron, Lear by A Reimann, premiere production of Die schwarze Maske by Penderecki (Salzburg, 1991), Die Soldaten by B A Zimmermann; Shortened version of The Invisible City of Kitezh by Rimsky-Korsakov at the 1995 Bregenz Festival; Has staged Wagner's Parsifal and the Ring, Berlin Staatsoper, 1995–96; Boris Godunov at the Vienna Volksoper, 1998.

**KUROSAKI, Hiro;** Violinist; b. 1949, Tokyo, Japan. *Education:* Studied at the Vienna Musikhochschule. *Career:* Solo engagements with the Royal Philharmonic, Dresden Staatskapelle, Salzburg Mozarteum and Vienna Symphony Orchestras; Leader of Les Arts Florissants, under William Christie, and has also played in Baroque and early music ensembles with the Clemencic Consort of Vienna and London Baroque; Teacher at the University of Vienna and the Salzburg Mozarteum. *Recordings include:* Mozart's violin sonatas, with Linda Nicholson. *Honours:* Prizewinner at the Wieniawski and Kreisler Competitions, 1977 and 1979. *Address:* c/o Les Arts Florissants, 10 Rue de Florence, 75008 Paris, France.

**KURTÁG, György;** Hungarian composer; b. 19 Feb. 1926, Lugos (Lugoj, Romania). *Education:* Franz Liszt Music Acad., Budapest and in Paris with Marianne Stein. *Career:* Repetiteur, Bela Bartok Music Secondary School, Budapest 1958–63, Nat. Philharmonic 1960–68; Asst to Pal Kadosa, Franz Liszt Acad. of Music, Budapest 1967, Prof. of Chamber Music 1967–86; Composer in Residence, Wissenschaftskolleg zu Berlin 1993–95, Wiener Konzerthaus, Vienna 1995–96; mem. Bayerische Akad. der Schönen Künste, Munich 1987, Akad. der Künste, Berlin 1987. *Compositions include:* Viola Concerto 1954, String Quartet, Op. 1 1959, Wind Quintet 1959, The Sayings of Péter Bornemissza 1963–68, Hommage à Mihály András 1977, Bagatelles 1981, Scenes from a Novel 1981–82, Three Old Inscriptions 1967–86, Kafka-Fragmente 1985–87, Requiem for the Beloved 1982–87, Officium breve in memoriam Andreae Szervánszky 1988–89, Ligatura–Message to Frances-Marie 1989, Hommage à R. Sch. 1990, Transcriptions from Machaut to Bach 1974–91, Attila József Fragments 1981, Three in memoriam 1988–90, Games, two series, Beads 1994, Omaggio a Luigi Nono 1979, eight Choruses 1981–82, Songs of Despondency and Grief 1980–94, Inscriptions on a Grave in Cornwall 1994, Rückblick (Altes und Neues für vier Spieler, Hommage à Stockhausen) 1986, Three Songs to poems by János Pilinszky 1986, Mémoire de Laïka 1990, Curriculum Vitae 1992, Messages of the late Miss R. V. Troussova, Grabstein für Stephan for guitar and Instrumentengruppen, Op. 15c (Prix de Composition Musicale, Fondation Prince Pierre de Monaco 1993) 1989, ...quasi una fantasia..., Double Concerto for piano, cello and 2 chamber ensembles Op. 27.2 (Prix de Composition Musicale, Fondation Prince Pierre de Monaco 1993)

1989–90, Ligature e Versetti for organ 1990, Layka- Emlèk for synthesizer and real sounds (co-composition with his son) 1990, Samuel Beckett: What is the Word for solo voice, voices and chamber ensemble Op. 30b 1991. *Honours:* Merited Artist of Hungarian People's Repub. 1980, Outstanding Artist 1984, Officier des Arts et Lettres 1985; Erkel Prize 1954, 1956, 1969, Kossuth Prize 1973, Bartok-Pasztory Award 1984, Herder Prize, Freiherr vom Stein, Hamburg 1993, Feltrinelli Prize, Accad. dei Lincei, Italy 1993, Austrian State Award for European Composers 1994, Denis de Rougemont Prize 1994, Kossuth Prize 1996, Ernst von Siemens Music Prize, Munich 1998. *Address:* Lihegő v.3, 2621 Verőce; Liszt Ferenc tér 9.I.6, 1061 Budapest, Hungary. *Telephone:* (1) 2735-0177; (91) 121-3994.

**KURTAKOV, Krassimir;** Singer (Bass-baritone); b. 1953, Sofia, Bulgaria. *Education:* Studied in Sofia. *Career:* Sang at the Bulgarian National Opera from 1979; Guest tour of Russia, Cuba, France and Austria, 1980–82; Vienna Kammeroper, 1987–88, as Nicolai's Falstaff and Don Alfonso; Bremerhaven, 1988–90 and Gelsenkirchen Opera, from 1990, including Denisov's L'ecume des jours, 1992; Vienna Staatsoper and elsewhere as Rocco in Fidelio, Mozart's Bartolo, Verdi's Fiesco, King Philip and Ramphis; Colline in La Bohème; Boris, Varlaam and Pimen, in Boris Godunov; Bonn Opera, 1992 in Jakob Lenz by Rihm. *Address:* c/o Bonn Opera, Am Boeselagerhof 1, 5311 Bonn, Germany.

**KURTZ, Eugene (Allen);** Composer; b. 27 Dec. 1923, Atlanta, Georgia, USA. *Education:* BA, Music, University of Rochester, 1947; MA, Music, Eastman School of Music, 1949; Study with Arthur Honegger and Darius Milhaud, Ecole Normale de Musique, Paris, France, 1949–51; Study with Max Deutsch, Paris, 1953–57. *Career:* Guest Professor of Composition, University of Michigan, 1967–68, 1970–71, 1973–74, 1980–81, 1988; Eastman School of Music, 1975; University of Illinois, 1976; University of Texas, 1977–78, 1985–86; Hartt School of Music, 1989; Consultant, Editions Jobert, Paris, 1972–. *Compositions:* The Solitary Walker, 1964; Conversations for 12 Players, 1966; Ca... Diagramme Pour Orchestre, 1972; The Last Contrabass in Las Vegas, 1974; Mécanique, 1975; Logo, 1979; Five-Sixteen, piano, 1982; World Enough and Time, 1982–; String Trio, Time and Again, 1984–85; From Time to Time, violin and piano, 1986–87; The Broken World, for string quartet, 1993–94; Shadows on the Wind, for 17 players, 1995–96; Icare, for solo flute, 1997. Also film scores and incidental music for radio, theatre and television. *Address:* 6 rue Boulitte, 75014 Paris, France.

**KURZ, Ivan;** Czech composer; *Head of Composition, Academy of Performing Arts*; b. 29 Nov. 1947, Prague; m. Zdeňka Sklenářová 1951; two s. one d. *Education:* studied music theory with Karel Risinger, composition with Emil Hlobil, Acad. of Arts and Music, Prague with Václav Dobiáš. *Career:* Dramaturgist for Prague television 1972–74; teacher of music theory, Acad. of Performing Arts, Prague 1976–91, teacher of composition 1991–, Head of Composition 2004–. *Compositions include:* orchestral: Concertino for piano, flute, percussion and strings 1974, Inclined Plane symphonic picture 1979, Emergence symphonic picture 1981, Parable symphonic picture 1982, Symphony No. 3 1986, The Gospel's Folly symphonic picture 1987–89, I Come to Thee symphonic picture 1988, Magnifikace for orchestra 2003, Garden of Life symphonic picture 2004; chamber: Sonata for Piano 1976, Circle of Notes for string quartet 1979, The Touch for piano trio 1982, Litanie for organ and percussion 1984, Expectatio for French horn and piano 1985, Rosae Eglanteriae for string quartet 1999, Song from Bretagne quartet for flute, clarinet, violincello and piano 2003; vocal: Missa Bohemica for children's choir and orchestra 2001, Ave Maria for soprano and orchestra 2001, Song of Divine Lamb for soprano and orchestra 2004; oratorio: At the End of Times cycle of four oratorios for mezzo-soprano, baritone, narrator, mixed choir and orchestra 1992–96; opera: Evening Meeting 1989–90. *Publications:* Expressionism in Music 2002, Teaching of Composition in Middle Europe, Int. Seminar of Middle-European Composition Schools 2002. *Honours:* Ministry of Culture Generation 74 Award 1975, Asscn of Czech Composers Award 1980, 1989, Premium of Czech Music Fund 1990. *Address:* Department of Composition, Malostranské náměstí 13, 118 00 Prague 1; Drtinova 26, 150 00 Prague 5, Czech Republic (home). *Fax:* (2) 57530698 (office). *E-mail:* ivan .kurz@seznam.cz (home). *Website:* www.hamu.cz/skladba (office).

**KUSCHE, Benno;** Singer (Bass-Baritone); b. 30 Jan. 1916, Freiburg, Germany. *Education:* Studied in Karlsruhe and with Fritz Harlan in Freiburg. *Career:* Debut: Koblenz in 1938 as Renato; Sang in Augsburg, 1939–42; Member of the Bayerische Staatsoper Munich from 1946, and Deutsche Oper an Rhein Düsseldorf from 1958; Sang at Salzburg Festival in 1949 in the premiere of Antigonae by Orff, Covent Garden in 1952 as Beckmesser, and in 1953 as La Roche in the first British performance of Capriccio, Glyndebourne Festival in 1954, 1963–64 as Leporello, La Roche and Don Fernando in Fidelio, Komische Oper Berlin in 1958 as Papageno in Die Zauberflöte and Metropolitan Opera, 1971–72 as Beckmesser; Guest appearances in Philadelphia, Amsterdam, Buenos Aires, Zürich, Florence and Bregenz. *Recordings:* Die Meistersinger; Die Kluge and Der Mond by Orff; La Bohème; Lulu. *Address:* c/o Bayerische Staatsoper, Postfach 745, 8000 Munich 1, Germany.

**KUSIEWICZ, Piotr;** Pianist and Singer; b. 30 June 1953, Gdańsk, Poland. *Education:* Pianist Diploma with Professor Zbigniew Sliwinski, 1977; Singer Diploma with Distinction, with Professor Jerzy Szymanski, 1980; Academy of Music, Gdansk. *Career:* Singer, Kraków State Opera, 1981–, Teatr STU, 1983–, Warsaw Opera House, 1984–, Wroclaw State Opera, 1986–; Guest

performances in operas in West Germany, Switzerland, Austria, Netherlands, Luxembourg and Italy; Cooperation with Philharmonic Societies, chamber ensembles and member of vocal ensemble of ancient music, Bornus Consort; As pianist, performances with leading Polish singers as accompanist in Poland and abroad, and accompanist in Geneva International Singer Competition, 1978; As singer and pianist, at Festival of Contemporary Music, Warsaw Autumn, 1981, 1983, 1984, 1987, Krzysztof Penderecki's Festival in Lusawice, Poland on invitation from the composer, 1983, and recordings for Polish Radio; Vocal teacher at Academy of Music in Gdansk, 1986. *Recordings:* GF Handel's Sosarme, Opera Seria in 3 Acts. *Publications:* Co-author, Gdansk Composers, 1980. *Address:* ul Michala Glinki 4–9, 80-271 Gdańsk, Poland.

**KUSNJER, Ivan;** Singer (Baritone); b. 10 Nov. 1951, Rokytancy, Czechoslovakia. *Career:* Sang in operas at Ostrava and Brno from 1977; National Theatre Prague from 1982; Roles have included Mozart's Count, Verdi's Macbeth and Rigoletto, Marcello, Bohus in Dvořák's Jacobin, 1995, and Constantin in Martinů's Greek Passion; Vienna Staatsoper as Germont in La Traviata; Further guest appearances in Paris, Janáček's From the House of the Dead; Berlin, Brussels and Milan; Concerts include Carmina Burana; Zemlinsky's Lyric Symphony and the Spectre's Bride by Dvořák; Season 1998 as Tausendmark in Smetana's Brandenburgers in Bohemia at Prague and Premoyl in Libuše at the Edinburgh Festival. *Recordings:* Dimitri by Dvořák, Smetana's Dalibor and Janáček's Osud. *Address:* c/o National Theatre, PO Box 865, 11230 Prague 1, Czech Republic.

**KÜTHEN, Hans-Werner,** MA, PhD; German musicologist; b. 26 Aug. 1938, Cologne; m. Annette Magdalena Leinen; one s. *Education:* Bonn Univ., studied in Bologna. *Career:* Ed., Beethoven Archives; mem. Gesellschaft für Musikforschung, VG Musikedition; Patron of the Verein Beethoven-Haus Bonn. *Publications:* On Beethoven: Essay, Kammermusik mit Bläsern 1969, Article Beethoven Herder, Das Grosse Lexikon der Musik 1978, Complete edition, Henle, München: Ouverturen und Wellingtons Sieg 1974, Critical Report, separately 1991, Klavierkonzerte I (nos 1–3) 1984, Klavierkonzerte II (nos 4–5) 1996, Klavierkonzerte III (WoO 4, WoO 6, op. 61a) 2004, each with Critical Report; contrib. to int. professional publications, including Beethoven yearbooks, congress reports, scholarly periodicals; journal contribs include: International Congress of the Gesellschaft für Musikforschung, Freiburg i.Br, 1993: Gradus ad partituram; Erscheinungsbild und Funktionen der Solostimme in Beethovens Klavierkonzerten, Congress Report, 1999; Gradus ad Partituram: Appearance and Essence in the Solo Part of Beethoven's Piano Concertos, Beethoven Forum Vol. 9 No. 2, Urbana-Champaign, Ill. 2002; Ein unbekanntes Notierungsblatt Beethovens aus der Entstehungszeit der Mondscheinsonate, Prague, 1996; Rediscovery and reconstruction of an authentic version of Beethoven's Fourth Piano Concerto for pianoforte and 5 strings, see Beethoven Journal Vol. 13 No. 1, San José, 1998 and Bonner Beethoven-Studien Vol. 1, Bonn 1999; On Viadana: Article V in Herder-Lex, 1982, id in Lexikon für Theologie und Kirche, Herder, 2000; Co-Editor, Beethoven im Herzen Europas. Leben und Nachleben in den Böhmischen Ländern, 2000; Ed., Beethoven und die Rezeption der Alten Musik, Report of the Int. Symposium, Bonn 2000, Die hohe Schule der Überlieferung, Bonn 2002; A Lost Sonority: Beethoven's imitation of the Aeolian Harp, Arietta Vol. 4, London 2004; Wer schrieb den Endtext des Violinkonzerts op. 61 von Beethoven? Franz Alexander Pössinger als letze Instanz für den Komponisten, Bonner Beethoven-Studien Vol. 4, Bonn 2005; Coriolanus Overture, conducting score with Preface, Wiesbaden 2005. *Address:* Am Hofgarten 7, 53113 Bonn, Germany.

**KUTTENBAUM, Annette;** Singer (Mezzo-soprano); b. 15 July 1957, Germany. *Career:* Debut: Opernhaus, Zürich, 1981; Sang at Hannover from 1983 and throughout Germany as guest, notably in The Ring and Parsifal at Bayreuth, 1988–92; Dorabella at Nuremberg; Adriano in Rienzi at Berlin and Brangäne in Tristan und Isolde at Weimar, 1996; Octavian in Der Rosenkavalier at Bologna, 1995; Further appearances as Hansel at Amsterdam and Fricka in Walküre at Trieste, 1998; Ortrud in Lohengrin, Braugäne in Tristan, Fricka in Walküre and Kundry in Parsifal, all at Weimar; Concert engagements in Vienna and elsewhere. *Recordings:* Video and CD of Das Rheingold and Götterdämmerung. *Address:* Deutsches Nationaltheater Weimar, Theaterplatz 2, 99423 Weimar, Germany.

**KUUSISTO, Ilkka Taneli,** DipMus; Finnish composer; b. 26 April 1933, Helsinki; m. Marja-Lisa Hanninen 1972; two s. two d. *Education:* Sibelius Acad. with Aarre Merikanto and Nils-Eric Fougstedt, School of Sacred Music and Union Theological Seminary, New York with Seth Bingham, studied in Germany, Vienna. *Career:* debut as conductor 1955, composer 1956; Asst Head of Music Section, Finnish Broadcasting Corporation; Choral Dir, Finnish Nat. Opera; Artistic Dir, Fazer Music Corporation 1982–84; Gen. Dir, Finnish Nat. Opera 1984–92; Pres., Finnish Copyright Asscn 1990–94; Musical Dir, Helsinki City Theatre; Conductor, Radio Symphony Chorus; mem. Composers of Finland, Finnish Light and Film Music Composers. *Compositions:* operas: The Moomin Opera 1974, The Rib of a Man 1978, The War for the Light 1981, Jaeger Stahl 1982, Pierrot or the Secrets of the Night 1991, Mail Maiden 1992, Miss Julia 1994, The Daughters of the Fatherland 1998, Gabriel Come Back 1998, Aino Kallas 2000, Kings Ring 2001, The Shortage 2002, Matilde and Nikolai, Symphony No. 1 2000, Symphony No. 2 2004; ballets: Snow Queen 1978, Robin Hood 1986. *Recordings:* Christmas Carols from Finland with Soile Isokoski (soprano). *Honours:* World Council of Churches Scholarship 1958, Finnish State Scholarship 1968, Pro Finlandia Medal 1990, Prof. hc 1992.

*Address:* Apollonkatu 7, 00100 Helsinki, Finland. *E-mail:* ile.tane@kolumbus .fi.

**KUUSISTO, Jaakko;** Finnish conductor, composer and violinist; b. 1974, brother of Pekka Kuusisto. *Education:* Sibelius Acad. with Géza Szilvay and Tuomas Haapanen, Ind. Univ. with Miriam Fred and Paul Biss, studied composition with Eero Hämeenniemi and David Dzubay. *Career:* apptd concertmaster Lahti Symphony Orchestra 1999, began conducting with the orchestra 2002; has conducted Finnish Radio Symphony, Tapiola Sinfonietta, Savonlinna Festival Opera, BBC Concert Orchestra; Prin. Guest Conductor Oulu Symphony Orchestra 2005–; Jt Artistic Dir (with his brother) Tuusula Lake Chamber Music Festival; compositions have been performed in Scandinavia, Great Britain and USA; first opera The Princess and the Wild Swans premiered Espoo, Finland 2003; has performed as soloist and chamber musician in China, Japan, USA and throughout Europe. *Compositions:* chamber: String Quartet No. 1 1993, Trio 1994, Fantasia 1995, String Quartet No. 2 1997, Play 1998, Loisto 2000; orchestral: Välivuodenajat (Between Seasons) 1996; choral: Tänä aamuna 1995, Leaving 1994, Musiikki 1996, Kolme vuodenaikaa (Three Seasons) 1996; opera: The Princess and the Wild Swans 2002, The Canine Kalevala 2003. *Recordings:* Sibelius, Complete Works for Violin and Orchestra, Sibelius, Rarities, Olli Mustonen, Triple Concerto, Johann Sebastian Bach, Violin Concertos, Tango for Four Vols 1 and 2, Music! 2002, Mussorgsky, Kalevi Aho 2003, Sibelius Soundtrack 2003, Sibelius, Complete Piano Trios Vol. 1 2003, Einojuhani Rautavaara, The Journey 2004, Sibelius, Complete Piano Trios Vol. 2 2004, Sibelius, Complete Piano Quartets 2005. *Current Management:* c/o Niels Veenhuijzen, Harrison-Parrott, 12 Penzance Place, London, W11 4PA, England. *Telephone:* (20) 7229-9166 (office). *Fax:* (20) 7221-5042 (office). *Website:* www.harrisonparrott.com (office).

**KUUSISTO, Pekka Taneli;** Finnish concert violinist; b. 1976, Espoo; brother of Jaakko Kuusisto. *Education:* East Helsinki Music Inst. with Geza Szilvay, Sibelius Acad. with Tuomas Haapanaen, Indiana Univ. School of Music, Bloomington with Miriam Fried and Paul Bliss, Steans Inst. for Young Artists at the Ravinia Festival. *Career:* many concerts with leading Finnish orchestras, including the Finnish Radio Orchestra and the Helsinki Philharmonic Orchestra; tour of Japan season 1996–97; festival engagements at Helsinki, Turku, Ravinia and Schleswig-Holstein; concertos with the Stockholm Sinfonietta and Okku Kamu, Orchestra of St John's Smith Square with John Lubbock, BBC Scottish Symphony Orchestra under Osmo Vänskä and the Malmö Symphony Orchestra under Paavo Berglund; season 1998–99 Australian tour; season 1999–2000 tours to the USA and Japan with the Lahti Symphony and Osmo Vänskä, a tour to S America with Ashkenazy and the Czech Philharmonic and a tour to Germany with the Sibelius Acad. and Lief Segerstam; season 2002–03 Henze's Violin Concerto No. 3 with Orchestra della Toscana, the Beethoven concerto with Beethoven Academie Antwerp, visits to Malaysian Philharmonic, Singapore Symphony, Deutsche Kammerphilharmonie and Australian Chamber Orchestras; season 2003–04 concerts with Zürich Tonhalle Orchestra, Royal Stockholm Philharmonic, Swedish and Australian Chamber Orchestras. *Recordings include:* Sibelius Concerto (with the Helsinki Philharmonic Orchestra under Segerstram), Strings Attached (recital album) 1997, Vivaldi's Four Seasons (with the virtuosi di Kuhmo), Bach Violin Concertos (with Tapiola Sinfonietta and Jaako Kuusisto), album of Olli Mustonen's works conducted by the composer, Folk Trip (Finnish Folk Music with the Luomu Players). *Honours:* winner Int. Jean Sibelius Violin Competition, Helsinki, winner Kuopio Violin Competition 1995. *Current Management:* Harrison/Parrott Ltd, 12 Penzance Place, London, W11 4PA, England. *Telephone:* (20) 7229 9166. *Fax:* (20) 7221 5042. *Website:* www .harrisonparrott.com.

**KUZMENKO, Vladimir;** Tenor; b. 1960, Kiev, Ukraine, Russia. *Education:* Studied in Kiev. *Career:* From 1988 has sung with the National Opera Company of Kiev as Lensky, Rodolfo, Don José, Faust, Dimitri and Count Almaviva; Guest appearances in France, Finland, Austria, Switzerland and Spain; Warsaw Opera in season 1994–95; British debut with the Kiev Opera as Alfredo in La Traviata, on tour in 1995; Hermann in The Queen of Spades for Scottish Opera, 1998. *Address:* c/o Sonata Ltd, 11 Northgate Street, Glasgow G20 7AA, Scotland.

**KUZNETSOV, Fyodor;** Singer (Bass); b. 1960, Sverdlovsk, Ekaterinburg, Russia. *Career:* Many appearances in concerts throughout Russia: Repertoire includes Mahler No.8, Beethoven No.9 and Shostakovich no.14 symphonies, Rossini's Stabat Mater, Bruckner's Missa Solemnis and Handel's Hercules and Samson; Engagements with the Kirov Opera, St Petersburg, from 1994 as Verdi's Philip II, Ferrando, Grand Inquisitor and Sparafucile; Mozart's Figaro and Commendatore, Boris, Pimen and Varlaam in Boris Godunov, Dosifei in Khovanshchina, Prince Gremin and Rimsky-Korsakov's Tsar Saltan; Sang Nikolai Bolkonsky in War and Peace with the Kirov at Covent Garden, 2000; Other roles include Khan Konchak in Prince Igor, Maliuta in The Tsar's Bride and Salieri in Rimsky-Korsakov's Mozart and Salieri; Mussorgsky's Boris Godunov at the London Proms, 2002. *Honours:* Winner, All-Russia Competition, 1987; Laureate Prize of the Mayor of St Petersburg, 1994. *Address:* c/o Kirov Opera, Mariinsky Theatre, Theatre Square, St Petersburg, Russia.

**KUZUMI, Karina;** Violinist; b. 29 April 1973, Tokyo, Japan. *Education:* Study, Toho Gakuen, Tokyo, 1992; Graduated, Pre-College, University of Music and Arts, Tokyo, 1992; Study, Escuela Superior de Musica Reina Sofia, Madrid, 1993; Study, Musikhochschule, Lübeck, 1995; Hochschule für Musik,

Cologne, 1998. *Career:* Debut: Tokyo City Philharmonic Orchestra, Tokyo, 1986; Concert, Nara, 1992; NHK-FM, Japan, 1992; Radio II Classica, Spain, 1994; Recitals at Auditorio Nacional, Madrid and Tokyo, 1994, Burgos, Melilla, Malaga, Valencia and Santander, 1995; Concert at Tokyo, Gronau and Rheine, 1997; Tour of Japan, 1998; La Radio Suisse Romande, 1998; Recital at Tokyo Opera City Recital Hall, 1999; Concert at Alte Oper in Frankfurt, 1999; Concerts with Budapest Symphony Orchestra, Klassiche Philharmonie Bonn, 1999–2000; Leader (Concertmaster) of the Stuttgart Philharmonic in Germany, 2001–. *Honours:* 1st Prize, All-Japan Student Music Competition, 1988; Scholarship, Foundation Isaac Albeniz, 1994; Scholarship, Culture Department, Japan, 1997; 3rd Prize, 33rd Szigeti International Competition, 1997; 3rd Prize, 5th Brahms International Competition, 1998. *Address:* Sanda-cho 4-33-8, Hachioji, 193-0832 Tokyo, Japan; Sodener Str. 31, 70372 Stuttgart, Germany. *E-mail:* kkuzumi@gmx.de.

**KVAPIL, Mgr Jan;** Czech violinist; b. 1943. *Education:* Prague Acad. of Arts. *Career:* mem. Talich String Quartet 1962–94; tours to most European countries and to Egypt, Iraq, North America, Japan and Indonesia; mem. Radio Symphony Orchestra, Prague 1994–97, Czech Philharmonic Orchestra 1997; Trio Mysterium Musicum Prague (sacred music) with Talich Quartet annual visits to France from 1976 and tours of UK 1990–91 with concerts at Wigmore Hall, London, appearances at Bath and Bournemouth Festivals, Queen Elizabeth Hall, London and on BBC 2's Late Show, with Janáček's 2nd Quartet; played Beethoven's Quartet Op. 74, Brahms A minor Quartet, Smetana D minor Quartet and works by Mozart, UK 1991; festival appearances in Vienna, Besançon, Lucerne, Helsinki, Amsterdam, Prague and Salzburg; repertoire also includes works by Debussy, Bartók (complete quartets recorded), Shostakovich, Ravel and Dvořák. *Recordings include:* complete quartets of Beethoven, Mozart and Bartók. *Honours:* Grand Prix Charles Cros, Diapason d'Or, Grand Prix de l' Acad. du Disque Francais, Supraphon Award. *Address:* Hrádková 2169, Újezd Nad Lesy, 19016 Prague 9, Czech Republic (home). *Telephone:* (732) 641268 (Mobile).

**KVAPIL, Radoslav;** Czech pianist; b. 15 March 1934, Brno; s. of Karel Kvapil and Marie Kvapilová; m. Eva Mašlaňová 1960 (died 1993); one s. *Education:* Gymnasium Dr. Kudely, Brno and Janáček Acad. of Musical Arts. *Career:* first piano recital Brno 1954; 1st prize Janáček Competition 1958, Int. Competition, Czechoslovak Radio 1968; Prof. of Piano, Prague Conservatory 1963–73; concerts in countries throughout Europe, in USA and Japan 1963–; performed world premiere of Dvořák's Cypresses 1983; Dir South Bohemia Music Festival 1991–; Pres. Yehudi Menuhin Soc., Prague 1990–, Dvořák Soc., Prague 1997–, Czech Soc. for Music and Arts 1990–. *Recordings include:* complete piano works of Dvořák and Martinů, complete piano and chamber music of Janáček, complete piano works of Jan Hugo Voříšek 1973–74, complete polka cycles of Smetana, Czech contemporary piano music, Piano Concerto by A. Rejcha (first ever recording), Anthology of Czech piano music (for Unicorn-Kanchana label), eight vols, works of Dvořák performed on the composer's piano 1999, Ullman's Sonatas 5–7 2002. *Honours:* Hon. Vice-Pres. Dvořák Soc., London; Chevalier des Arts et des Lettres 2002; Janáček Medal (Cultural Ministry). *Address:* Hradecká 5, 13000 Prague 3, Czech Republic. *Telephone:* (2) 67312430. *Fax:* (2) 67312430 (home). *E-mail:* r.kvapil@ecn.cz (office).

**KVARAN, Gunnar;** Cellist; b. 1960, Reykjavík, Iceland. *Education:* Studied at the Reykjavík College of Music, at the Copenhagen Conservatory and in Basle and Paris. *Career:* Solo concerts, recitals and chamber music throughout Scandinavia, France, Germany, Netherlands and North America; Appearances with the Icelandic Symphony, the Tivoli Orchestra and the Jutland Philharmonic; Professor at the Reykjavík College of Music and member of the Reykjavík Piano Trio. *Address:* c/o World-wide Artists, 6 Petersfield Crescent, Coulsdon, Surrey CR5 2JQ, England.

**KVECH, Otomar;** Czech composer; *Professor, Academy of Arts*; b. 25 May 1950, Prague; m. 1st Miluska Wagnerova 1972 (died 2000); two d.; m. 2nd Dr Jane Smékalová 2003. *Education:* Music Conservatory, Prague, Acad. of Music Arts, Prague with Prof. Pauer. *Career:* debut, Symphony for Organ and Orchestra, Dvořák's Hall, Prague; pianist, Nat. Theatre, Prague 1974–77; Music Prod. 1977–80, Dramaturgist, Ed. 1988–, Radio Prague; Sec., Organization of Czech Composers and Concert Artists 1980–90; Prof. 1990–, Chief of the Composing Section 1998–, Music Conservatory, Prague; Prof., Acad. of Arts, Prague 2002–. *Compositions include:* When the Path Disappeared (song cycle), Three Moments for Accordion, Prague Panorama, six Preludes for flute solo, String Quartet No. 1 1972, String Quartet No. 2 1973, Violin Sonata No. 1 1974, String Quartet No. 3 1974, Symphony for Organ 1974, Methamoforsis for violin solo and strings 1976, Violin Sonata No. 1 1978, String Quartet No. 4 1979, Symphony in E Flat Major 1982, Violin Sonata No. 1 1982, The World Carnival 1983, Symphony in D Major 1984, Cello Sonata 1985, String Quartet No. 5 1985, RUR 1986, Capriccio concerto for piano trio and orchestra 1986, two Sonatas for organ 1986, Symphony in E Minor with string quartet 1987, Piano Quintet 1990, Requiem 1991, three songs for voice and organ 1993–97, Oboe Sonata 1995, Serenata notturna 1996, Nokturnalie 1997, Missa con viola obligata 1998, Sextet for string quartet, oboe and harp 1999, String Quartet No. 6 2000, four Saisons for organ and orchestra 2000–01, String Quartet No. 7 2003, Recitatives and arias for corno inglese and orchestra 2004, Serenade for orchestra, based on Czech Christmas Carols 2004. *Publications:* contrib. to Hudebni Rozhledy (Prague), Opus Musicum (Brno). *Address:* Korunni 67, 130 00 Prague 3, Czech Republic (home). *E-mail:* otomar.kvech@rozhlas.cz.

**KWELLA, Patrizia;** Singer (Soprano); b. 26 April 1953, Mansfield, England. *Education:* Royal College of Music, London. *Career:* Promenade Concert debut in 1979 with John Eliot Gardiner; Concerts and festivals include Ansbach, Bergen, Innsbruck, Aldeburgh, Bologna, Warsaw, Bath, City of London, Edinburgh and Salzburg; Conductors include Richard Hickox, Peter Maag, Christopher Hogwood and Trevor Pinnock; US debut in 1983 with the San Diego Symphony; Further concerts with the San Francisco, Houston and Washington Symphony Orchestras; Sang in many of the Bach, Handel and Scarlatti tercentenary concerts of 1985; Premiere of Night's Mask by Colin Matthews at the 1985 Aldeburgh Festival; Sang Handel's Alcina at the 1985 Spitalfields and Cheltenham Festivals; Repertoire includes Haydn, Mozart, Brahms, Mahler, Stravinsky and Britten. *Recordings:* Handel's L'Allegro, Alcina, Alceste, Resurrezione and Esther; Monteverdi's Orfeo and Il Combattimento; Bach's B minor Mass, Magnificat and St John Passion; Mozart's Coronation Mass, Missa Solemnis and Regina Coeli; Television includes many Man and Music appearances for Channel 4. *Address:* c/o Music and Musicians Artists' Management, 54 Regent's Park Road, London NW1 7SX, England.

**KWIECIEN, Martin;** Polish singer (baritone); b. 1965, Kraków. *Career:* debut, Kraków Opera 1993 as Purcell's Aeneas; appearances as Mozart's Figaro in Luxembourg and Poznan and Papageno at Warsaw; Sang in premiere of Zemlinsky's König Kandaules at Hamburg, 1996; Metropolitan Young Artists Program from 1998; appearing in Katya Kabanova, Rigoletto, Giulio Cesare and l'Italiana in Algeri; Season 2000–01 as Mozart's Count at Glyndebourne, Marcello at Antwerp and Donizetti's Enrico in Buenos Aires. *Honours:* Winner, Breslau International Competition, 1994; Hans Gabor/ Belvedere Competition, Vienna, 1996; Mozart Interpretation Prize, Francisco Viñas Competition, Barcelona, 1998; Represented Poland at 1999 Cardiff Singer of the World Competition.

**KWON, Hellen;** Singer (Soprano); b. 11 Jan. 1961, Seoul, Korea. *Education:* Studied in Cologne. *Career:* Debut: Wiesbaden in 1984 as the Queen of Night; Has sung at Mannheim, 1985–, Paris Opéra, 1986 in Die Zauberflöte, and Hamburg, 1987; Created the role of Alexis de Lechebot in Liebermann's La Forêt at Geneva, 1987; Sang at Bayreuth Festival in 1988 as a Flower Maiden, Glyndebourne Festival in 1990 as the Queen of Night followed by performances at Bonn and Vienna in 1991; Sang Susanna at Hamburg in 1990, Wellgunde in a concert performance of Götterdämmerung at Rome in 1991 and Blondchen in Die Entführung at Salzburg Festival in 1991; Other roles include Strauss's Sophie and Zerbinetta, Rosina, Norina and Musetta; Sang Susanna at the 1992 Israel Festival, Adele in Die Fledermaus at Hamburg, 1996; Constanze in Die Entführung at the Vienna Kammeroper, 1998; Concert tours of USA, France, Italy, Belgium and the Netherlands notably in the B minor Mass and St Matthew Passion of Bach. *Recordings include:* Nightingale in Die Vögel by Braunfels, 1997. *Address:* c/o Hamburgische Staatsoper, Grosse Theaterstrasse 34, 2000 Hamburg 36, Germany.

**KYHLE, Magnus;** Singer (Tenor); b. 1959, Sweden. *Education:* Studied at Stockholm College of Music and the State Opera School in Stockholm. *Career:* Debut: Vadstena Academy in 1983; Engaged at the Royal Opera, Stockholm, 1986–89, Stadttheater Darmstadt, 1989–90 and Landestheater Salzburg, 1990–92; Roles include Mozart's Don Ottavio, Tamino, Monostatos and Ferrando, Pelléas, and Paris in La Belle Hélène; Guest appearances at Tenerife and Tokyo; Season 1990–92 as Tamino and Don Ottavio with the Royal Opera Stockholm, Tamino at Salzburg Landestheater and Ferrando at Semperoper Dresden; Season 1992–93 as Beppe in a new production of Pagliacci at Stockholm, and in a new production of Traviata; Stockholm production of The Phantom of the Opera, 1994–. *Address:* IM Audio and Music HB, Åsögatan 67Vl, 11829 Stockholm, Sweden.

**KYLLONEN, Timo-Juhani;** Finnish composer, accordion player and conductor; b. 1 Dec. 1955, Saloinen. *Education:* Tchaikovsky Conservatoire and Gnesin Music Institute, Moscow. *Career:* debut concert of his works at the Tchaikovsky Conservatory, Moscow, April 1986; biographical programmes, Finnish Television, 1982, 1988; Several concerts and radio and television programmes in Finland, Sweden, USSR, Peru, Ecuador and Norway; Composer-portrait on Netherlands Radio, 1990, also on Argentinian, Brazilian, Cuban, Israeli and Peruvian radio; mem, Finnish Composer's Union. *Compositions include:* Symphony No. 1, op 8, 1985–86; Symphony No. 2 op 29, 1991–95; Suite for String Orchestra op 27, 1991; Awakening op 23b for string orchestra; Two Kalevala Songs for chorus and piano, 1996. *Recordings include:* Compositions by Timo-Juhani Kyllonen, Finlandia Records; Elegia quasi una sonata, op 15, 1987; Trio No. 1, op 9, 1986; Triology for 2 pianos, op 4, 1984; String Quartet No. 1 op 3, 1984, Ondine Records; Ciclo para coro mixto op 5. *Honours:* Pro Musica Award, 1988; Espoo City Arts prize, 1989; Three year Stipendum, Finnish Ministry of Education, 1991–93; 3 different television programmes (personal portraits) on Finnish television. *Current Management:* Finnish Music Information Centre, Lauttasaarentie 1, 00200 Helsinki, Finland. *Address:* Joupinmäki 3C49, 02760 Espoo, Finland.

**KYNASTON, Nicolas,** ARCM; British organist; *Organ Professor, Royal Academy of Music;* b. 10 Dec. 1941, Morebath, Devon; s. of the late Roger Tewkesbury Kynaston and of Jessie Dearn Caecilia Kynaston (née Parkes); m. 1st Judith Felicity Heron 1961 (divorced 1989); two s. two d.; m. 2nd Susan Harwood Styles 1989. *Education:* Westminster Cathedral Choir School, Downside, Accademia Musicale Chigiana, Siena, Conservatorio Santa Cecilia, Rome, Royal Coll. of Music. *Career:* Westminster Cathedral Organist 1961–71; début recital, Royal Festival Hall 1966; recording début 1968; concert career 1971–, travelling throughout Europe, N America, Asia and Africa; Artistic Dir J. W. Walker & Sons Ltd 1978–82, Consultant 1982–83; Organist Athens Concert Hall 1995–; Jury mem. Grand Prix de Chartres 1971, St Albans Int. Organ Festival 1975; Pres. Inc. Asscn of Organists 1983–85; Chair. Nat. Organ Teachers Encouragement Scheme 1993–96; mem. Westminster Abbey Fabric Comm. 2000–; consultant for various new organ projects; recordings include 6 nominated Critic's Choice, The Gramophone 1996 (also Ed.'s Choice); Organ Professor, Royal Academy of Music 2002–. *Publication:* Transcriptions for Organ 1997. *Honours:* Hon. FRCO 1976; EMI/CFP Sales Award 1974; Deutscher Schallplattenpreis 1978. *Address:* 28 High Park Road, Kew Gardens, Richmond-upon-Thames, Surrey, TW9 4BH, England. *Telephone:* (20) 8878-4455. *Fax:* (20) 8392-9314.

**KYR, Robert (Harry);** Composer and Teacher; b. 20 April 1952, Cleveland, Ohio, USA. *Education:* BA, Yale University, 1974; Royal College of Music, London, 1974–76; MA, University of Pennsylvania, 1978; PhD, Harvard University, 1989. *Career:* Composer-in-Residence, New England Philharmonic, 1985–89; Resident Composer of Extension Works, Composers and Performers Consortium, Boston, MA, 1985–; Teacher of Composition and Theory at Harvard University (teaching fellow), 1985–89, Longy School of Music (Director of Compositional Studies), 1986–, Hartt School of Music (visiting lecturer), Fall 1988. *Compositions include:* Commissions: Maelstrom (The Fires Of London), 1981, The Greater Changing, Symphony No. 2 (Mystic Valley Orchestra, Boston), 1986, A Signal In The Land (Johnson City Symphony Orchestra, TN), 1987, The Fifth Season, Symphony No. 3 (Friends Of Music at Yale, Yale Symphony), 1988, Book Of The Hours, Symphony No. 1 (New England Philharmonic), 1988, Toward Eternity (Radcliffe Choral Society, Harvard University), 1988, Symphony No. 4 (New England Philharmonic), 1989, Symphony No. 5 (Pro Arte Orchestra, Boston), 1990; There Is A River for Soprano, Women's Chorus and Orchestra, 1985; Images From Stillness for String Trio, 1986; Images of Reminiscence for Piano, 1987; One for Solo Clarinet. *Publications:* Complete Works published. *Address:* 16 Forest Street No. 41, Cambridge, MA 02140, USA.

# L

**LA BARBARA, Joan Lotz,** BS; American composer, vocalist and writer; b. 8 June 1947, Philadelphia, PA; m. Morton Subotnick 1979; one s. *Education:* Syracuse Univ. School of Music, Berkshire Music Center, Tanglewood, New York Univ. *Career:* debut with Steve Reich and musicians, Town Hall, New York 1971; with Steve Reich 1971–74, Philip Glass 1973–76, John Cage, premiering Solo for Voice 45 with Atlas Eclipticlis, Winter Music with Orchestra of the Hague 1976; in Avignon premiere, Einstein on the Beach (Philip Glass) 1976; premiered Subotnick's Double Life of Amphibians, Los Angeles Olympics Arts Festival 1984; own work, Houston and San Francisco Symphonies 1982, Los Angeles Philharmonic 1983, New York Philharmonic 1984; premiered Subotnick's chamber opera Jacob's Room, American Music Theater Festival and MANCA Festival, Nice 1993–94, quartet of operas Now Eleanor's Idea (R. Ashley), Brooklyn Acad. of Music and Avignon Festival 1994; Balseros (Ashley) for Miami Grand Opera 1997; Dust (Ashley) Yokohama, Japan 1998; Celestial Excursions (Ashley), Berliner Fest Spiele 2003; Messa di Voce (own interactive media work), with Jaap Blonk, Golan Levin and Zachary Lieberman, Ars Electronica, Linz, Austria 2003; vocal soloist on sound score by John Frizzell for the film, I Still Know What You Did Last Summer 1998; film scores include Signing Alphabet 1977, Anima 1991, Immersion 1998, Endless Songs: Artemesia, Egon Schiele, Eva Hesse 2002, Triptych: Buffalo and Maine 2003; many commissions; newborn vocals for film Alien Resurrection 1997; Series Dir and performer, When Morty Met John. . ., a three-year series focussing on the New York School of Composers (John Cage, Morton Feldman, Earle Brown, Christian Wolff) at Carnegie Hall 2001–03; Artistic Dir and Host, Insights, a series of encounters with distinguished composers for The American Music Center 2003–; Curator, EMF@Chelsea Art Museum 2003; mem. ASCAP, The American Music Center, SAG, AFTRA, AEA. *Compositions include:* Angel Voice (for film, Date with an Angel) 1987, To hear the wind roar (choral) 1989–91, In the Dreamtime (self portrait, sound painting) 1989, L'albero dalle foglie azzure for solo oboe with tape 1989, Awakenings for chamber ensemble 1991, Klangbild Köln 1991, Anima (film score) 1991, A Trail of Indeterminate Light for solo cello 1991, 73 Poems to poems by Kenneth Goldsmith 1994, Calligraphy II/Shadows for voice, dizi, erhu, yangqi, Chinese percussion 1995, In the shadow and act of the haunting place for voice and chamber ensemble 1995, de profundis: out of the depths, a sign 1996, A Different Train 1996, Snowbird's Dance, Into the Light for voice, flute and string quartet 2000, Dragons on the Wall, Tianji for voices, instruments and tape collage 2001, Snowbird's Dance: Into the Light and Beyond for voice, flute and string quartet 2004, Woolf Song (an opera in progress) 2004–, Landscape over Zero for voice, string quartet, piano, trombone and sonic atmospheres 2005. *Recordings include:* The Art of Joan La Barbara, Sound Paintings, Joan La Barbara Singing through John Cage, Three Voices for Joan La Barbara (Morton Feldman), Jacob's Room (M. Subotnick), 73 Poems 1994, Awakenings, L'albero dalle Foglie azzurre, Only: Works for Voice and Instruments (Feldman) 1996, ShamanSong 1998, Voice is the Original Instrument 2003. *Exhibition:* 73 Poems, a collaborative work with text artist Kenneth Goldsmith, included in The American Century Part II: Soundworks, The Whitney Museum of American Art. *Publications:* contrib. to Grove's Dictionary, Contemporary Music Journal, Los Angeles Times, Musical America/High Fidelity magazine, Schwann/Opus. *Honours:* DAAD Artist-in-Residency, Berlin, seven NEA Fellowships, Guggenheim Fellowship in Music Composition 2004; ISCM Int. Jury Award, Akustische Int. Competition Award, ASCAP awards. *Address:* 25 Minetta Lane (4B), New York, NY 10012-1253, USA. *Website:* www.joanlabarbara.com.

**LA MONTAINE, John;** Composer; b. 17 March 1920, Chicago, Illinois, USA. *Education:* Studied with Bernard Rogers and Howard Hanson at the Eastman School, with Wagenaar at Juilliard School and with Nadia Boulanger at the American Conservatory, Fontainebleau. *Career:* Pianist with the NBC Symphony conducted by Toscanini, 1950–54; Composer in Residence at American Academy, Rome, 1962; Visiting Professor at the Eastman School, 1964–65; Nixon Chair at Whittier College, California, 1977; President of Fredonia Press. *Compositions include:* Songs of the Rose of Sharon, for soprano and orchestra, 1947; Wonder Tidings for SATB, harp and percussion, 1957; Piano Concerto No.1, 1958; Fragments from the Song of Songs, for soprano and orchestra, 1959; A Trilogy of Medieval Christmas Operas, Novellis, Novellis, The Shephardes Playe and Erode the Greate, 1961–9; Overture: From Sea to Shining Sea (commissioned for the Inauguration of President Kennedy, 1961); Birds of Paradise for piano and orchestra, 1964; Sacred Service, 1964–8; Wilderness Journal, after Thoreau, for bass-baritone, organ and orchestra (commissioned for the opening of the Kennedy Center and the dedication of the Filene Great Organ), 1971; The Nine Lessons of Christmas for SATB, harp and percussion, 1975; Be Glad Then America, a Bicentennial opera (commissioned by Penn State University), 1976; The Lessons of Advent, 1983; Piano Concertos 2, 3, and 4, 1987–9; Arrangement of Bach's Well-Tempered Klavier for Electronic Keyboard, 1991–2; In Praise of Britain's Queen and Elgar's Enigma, a complete solution of Elgar's Enigma, SATB and two orchestras, 1991; Piccolo Sonata, 1993; Passacaglia and Fugue for orchestra, an adaptation of Paul J Siffler's Recitative Passacaglia and Fugue, 2000. *Recordings include:* Piano Concerto No. 1 and No. 4; Piano Sonata; Birds of Paradise; Songs of The Rose of Sharon; Flute Concerto; Wilderness Journal; Incantation for Jazz Band; Conversations for Violin and Piano; Six Shakespeare Sonnets; The Nine Lessons of Christmas; The Well-Tuned Keyboard, 2 CDs, after Bach. *Publications:* Many works published. *Honours:* Guggenheim Fellowships; Pulitzer Prize for Piano Concerto, 1959; American Academy of Arts and Letters Award, 1962. *Address:* 3947 Fredonia Drive, Hollywood, CA 90068, USA.

**LA PIERRE, John;** Singer (Tenor); b. 1961, USA. *Education:* Purchase, New York; St Louis Conservatoire. *Career:* Appearances in opera at Atlanta; St Louis; Omaha; Nevada; Mobile; Cologne Opera as Mozart's Tamino; Ferrando; Ottavio; Belmonte; Belfiore; Glyndebourne as Idamante in Idomeneo; Opéra Comique in La Cambiale di Matrimonio and Il Signor Bruschino by Rossini; Netherlands Opera as Andres in Wozzeck and in Die Meistersinger; Concerts include Bach's B Minor Mass, Washington; Mozart's Requiem, St Louis Symphony Orchestra; Messiah, St Matthew Passion; Haydn's Seasons, Cologne. *Honours:* Finalist, Met Opera National Auditions, 1985. *Address:* Music International, 13 Ardilaun Road, London N5 2QR, England.

**LA RUE, (Adrian) Jan Pieters,** MFA, PhD; academic; b. 31 July 1918, Kisaran, Sumatra; m. 1st Helen Robison 1946 (died 1998); two d.; m. 2nd Marian Green 2000. *Education:* Harvard Univ., Princeton Univ. *Career:* Instructor to Associate Professor and Chairman of Music Department, Wellesley College, 1942–43, 1946–57; Profesor of Music, Graduate School of Arts and Science, New York University, 1957–88; Chairman, 1970–71, Executive Dean, 1963–64; Professor Emeritus, 1988; Visiting Professor, 1947; University of Michigan, 1963; Bar Ilan, Israel, 1980, Tokyo, 1988, Indiana, 1990, Queens, Canada, 1995; Research Professor, Austria, 1954–56; 1st Lieutenant, Transportation Corps, Okinawa Campaign, 16 months in Pacific Theatre, 1943–46; Music Curriculum Project, 1966–67; Councillor, Smithsonian Institute, 1967–73; Musicologist-in-Residence, Kennedy Centre, Washington, 1975; Fellow, American Acad. of Arts and Sciences, 2003. *Compositions:* Concertino, clarinet and orchestra, 1941; Trio, strings, 1942. *Publications:* Guidelines for Style Analysis, 1970 (Sp ed 1988), 2nd ed, 1992; Methods and Models for Musical Style Analysis, with Ohmiya, Makoto, 1988; A Catalogue of 18th Century Symphonies, 1988; Bifocal Tonality in Haydn's Symphonies, 1992. *Contributions:* Die Musik in Geschichte und Gegenwart, 1968; Grove's Dictionary, 6th ed, 1980; Articles in numerous journals and Festschriften, including Festschriften Davison, 1957; Albrecht, 1962; Voetterle, 1968; Geiringer, 1970; Larsen, 1972; Johnson, 1990; Southern, 1992; Ratner, 1992; Editor: Festschriften Reese, 1966; Deutsch, 1968. *Honours:* Ford Foundation Fellow, 1954; Guggenheim Fellow, 1964–65; ACLS Fellow, 1964–65; NEH Research Grant, 1980–84; LaRue Festschrift Studies in Musical Sources and Style (ed Wolf and Roesner), 1990. *Address:* Woods End Road, New Canaan, CT 06840, USA.

**LA SCOLA, Vincenzo;** Italian singer (tenor); b. 1958, Palermo. *Education:* studied with Carlo Bergonzi. *Career:* debut in Parma in 1983 as Ernesto in Don Pasquale; Sang in Genoa and Liège, 1984, as Nemorino in Brussels and Rinuccio in Gianni Schicchi and Tonio in La Fille du Régiment in Paris, 1987–88; La Scala debut in 1988 as Nemorino returning 1991–92 as Alfredo and Edgardo in Lucia di Lammeroor; Other roles include Elvino in La Sonnambula at Venice in 1989, Orombello in Beatrice di Tenda, Mascagni's Amico Fritz, the Duke of Mantua, and Florindo in Mascagni's Le Maschere; Sang Donizetti's Roberto Devereux at Bologna and Edgardo at La Scala in 1992, and Rodolfo in La Bohème at the Verona Arena in 1992; Sang Edgardo in Lucia di Lammermoor at Florence, 1996; Cavaradossi at the Verona Arena, 1998; Season 2000–01 as Nemorino in Chicago, Werther in Palermo and Verdi's Jacopo Foscari at Naples; Gabriele Adorno in Munich, Ernani for the Vienna Staatsoper and the Verdi Requiem in Florence. *Recordings include:* Rossini's Petite Messe Solennelle; Beatrice di Tenda; Rigoletto under Muti; Le Maschere. *Current Management:* Atelier Musicale, Via Caselle 76, San Lazzaro di Savena 40068, Italy. *Telephone:* (051) 19 98 44 44. *Fax:* (051) 19 98 44 20. *E-mail:* info@ateliermusicale.com. *Website:* www.ateliermusicale .com. *E-mail:* vinlas@interfree.it. *Website:* www.vincenzolascola.com.

**LAADE, Wolfgang;** Ethnomusicologist; b. 13 Jan. 1925, Zeitz, Germany; m. Dagmar Diedrich, 15 Aug 1962. *Education:* Musikhochschule Leipzig, 1943; Staatliche Musikhochschule Berlin, 1949–54; PhD, Freie Universität, Berlin, 1954–60. *Career:* Research Fellow, Australian Institute of Aboriginal Studies, 1963–67; Research Fellow, Deutsche Forschungsgemeinschaft, 1968–70; Lecturer in Ethnomusicology, University of Heidelberg, 1969–71; Professor of Ethnomusicology, University of Zürich, Switzerland, 1971–90; Guest lectures at German, Austrian, American and Canadian Universities; Guest professorships: Helsinki, Stockholm, Innsbruck, Moscow; Field research in Lapland, Corsica, Tunisia, Australia, Torres Strait, New Guinea, New Britain, India, Sri Lanka, Taiwan, Zimbabwe. *Recordings:* 17 titles. *Publications:* Books: Die Struktur der korsischen Lamento-Melodik, 1962; Die Situation von Musikleben und Musikforschung in den Laendern Afrikas und Asiens und die neuen Aufgaben der Musikenthnologie, 1969; Neue Musik in Afrika, Asien und Ozeanien; Diskographie und historisch-stilistischer Ueberblick, 1971; Gegenwartsfragen der Musik in Afrika und Asien; eine grundlegende Bibliographie, 1971; Oral traditions and written documents on the history and ethnography of the Northern Torres Strait Islands, Vol. 1, 1971; Klangdokumente historischer Tasteninstrumente, Orgeln, Kiel-und Hammerklaviere eine Diskographie, 1972; Das Geisterkanu; Suedseemaerchen aus der Torres-Strasse, 1974; Musik der Goetter, Geister und Menschen; die Musik in der mythischen, fabulierenden und historischen Ueberlieferung der Voelker Afrikas, Nordasiens, Amerikas und Ozeaniens, 1975; Musikwissenschaft zwischen gestern und morgen; Das korsische Volkslied; ethnographische und historische Fragen, Gattungen und Stil, 3 vols, 1981–87; Musik und Musiker in Maerchen, Sagen und Anekdoten der Voelker Europas, Vol. 1: Mitteleuropa, 1988; Music and Culture in South-East New Britain, 1998; Compact Discs accompanied by books: The Confucius Temple Ceremony, Taiwan, 1991; Taiwan: Music of the Aboriginal Tribes, 1991; Zimbabwe: The Ndebele People, 1991; Papua New Guinea: The Coast of the Western Province, 1993; Music and Culture in Southeast New Britain, 2001. *Address:* Holzmoosrütistrasse 11, 8820 Wädenswil, Switzerland.

**LAAKMAN, Willem;** Singer (Bass-baritone); b. 7 Oct. 1940, Aachen, Germany. *Education:* Studied in Maastricht and Cologne. *Career:* Debut: Lord Tristan in Martha, Amsterdam, 1969; Sang in Netherlands until 1975; Then Krefeld and from 1984 at Coburg; Roles have included Boris Godunov, 1987; Don Giovanni, Macbeth and Papageno; Altenburg from 1992 as Amonasro and Jochanaan in Salome; Dessau Opera from 1995; Other roles elsewhere in Germany have been Strauss's Faninal and Dandini in La Cenerentola; Concerts include Beethoven's Ninth. *Address:* c/o Landestheater Dessau, Fritz-Hesse Platz 1, 4500 Dessau, Germany.

**LABELLE, Dominique;** Singer (soprano); b. 1960, Montréal, Canada. *Education:* Boston Univ. and with Phyllis Curtin. *Career:* concert appearances with Symphony Orchestras of Dallas, Montreal and Boston; Messiah with Pittsburgh Symphony, Mahler's 2nd Symphony in St Louis and Vaughan Williams's Antarctica Symphony at Indianapolis; other repertory includes the Verdi Quattro Pezzi Sacri, the Requiems of Mozart and Frank Martin, Mahler's Fourth, Les Nuits d'Eté and Mozart's Exsultate Jubilate; opera engagements as Donna Anna in the Peter Sellars production of Don Giovanni, Elizabeth Zimmer in Elegy for Young Lovers, Mimi for Glimmerglass Opera, New York, the Countess and Susanna in Le nozze di Figaro at Vancouver 1992; Giulietta in I Capuleti e i Montecchi with Toledo Opera; sang Handel's Rodelinda at Göttingen, Sigismondo in Arminio and Arianna in Vivaldi's Giustino at Solothurn 2000. *Recordings include:* Elektra, with Boston Symphony; Don Giovanni, on video; Masha and Chloe in The Queen of Spades, conducted by Ozawa. *Honours:* Winner, Metropolitan Opera National Council Auditions 1989. *Current Management:* IMG Artists Paris, 54 Avenue Marceau, 75008, Paris, France.

**LABÈQUE, Katia;** French pianist; b. 3 March 1950, Bayonne. *Education:* Paris Conservatoire. *Career:* performs worldwide with sister Marielle Labèque (q.v.); appearances with the Berlin Philharmonic, Bayerischer Rundfunk, Boston Symphony, Chicago Symphony, Cleveland Orchestra, Leipzig Gewandhaus, London Symphony, London Philharmonia, Los Angeles Philharmonic, Filarmonia della Scala, Philadelphia Orchestra, Dresden Staatskapelle and Vienna Philharmonic; has played under direction of Bychkov, Davis, Dutoit, Mehta, Ozawa, Pappano, Rattle, Salonen, Slatkin and Tilson Thomas; festival performances at Berlin, Blossom, Hollywood Bowl, Lucerne, Ludwigsburg, Mostly Mozart New York, BBC Proms, Ravinia, Rheingau, Ruhr, Schleswig Holstein, Tanglewood, Schubertiade in Schwarzenberg and Salzburg Easter Festival; formed new duo with Viktoria Mullova 2001, regular performances throughout Europe at Musikverein, Vienna, Musikhalle Hamburg, Philharmonie Munich, Schwetzinger Festspiele amongst numerous others; performances in 2005 season included recitals at Carnegie Hall, New York, Lucerne, Belgrade, Athens, Essen, throughout Italy as well as at Schubertiade Festival, Schwarzenberg; joined French saxophonist François Jeanneau's Paris Big Band Pandemonium; jazz collaborations with guitarist John McLaughlin; founder, Katia Labèque Band 2001–; first European tour with special guest Gonzalo Rubalcaba 2001; further concerts at Piano Festival Ruhr, Lucerne Festival, Easter Festival Salzburg and during opening ceremony of the new Konzerthaus in Dortmund; Katia Labèque Band and Orchestre Philharmonique de Montpellier performed première of a five-movt concerto (Spellbound by Dave Maric) for piano, keyboards, percussion and orchestra entitled 2004. *Recordings include:* Gershwin's Rhapsody in Blue and Concerto in F, recitals of Brahms, Liszt, Debussy, Ravel and Stravinsky, Rossini's Petite Messe (with the choir of King's College Cambridge), Bartók's Concerto for two pianos and orchestra, Symphonic Dances from West Side Story, España, Encores, Love of Colours, Visions de l'Amen (jtly), Little Girl Blue, Unspoken (with Katia Labèque Band) 2003. *Current Management:* c/o Jilly Clarke, Askonas Holt Ltd, Lonsdale Chambers, 27 Chancery Lane, London, WC2A 1PF, England. *Telephone:* (20) 7400-1740. *E-mail:* Jilly.Clarke@askonasholt.co.uk. *Website:* www.askonasholt.co.uk; www.katialabeque.com; www.labeque.com.

**LABÈQUE, Marielle;** French pianist; b. 6 March 1952, Bayonne; pnr Semyon Bychkov. *Education:* Paris Conservatoire. *Career:* performs worldwide with sister Katia Labèque (q.v.); appearances with the Berlin Philharmonic, Bayerischer Rundfunk, Boston Symphony, Chicago Symphony, Cleveland Orchestra, Leipzig Gewandhaus, London Symphony, London Philharmonia, Los Angeles Philharmonic, Filarmonia della Scala, Philadelphia Orchestra, Dresden Staatskapelle and Vienna Philharmonic; has played under direction of Bychkov, Davis, Dutoit, Mehta, Ozawa, Pappano, Rattle, Salonen, Slatkin and Tilson Thomas; festival performances at Berlin, Blossom, Hollywood Bowl, Lucerne, Ludwigsburg, Mostly Mozart New York, BBC Proms, Ravinia, Rheingau, Ruhr, Schleswig Holstein, Tanglewood, Schubertiade in Schwarzenberg and Salzburg Easter Festival; jazz collabora-

tions with guitarist John McLaughlin. *Recordings:* Mozart's Concertos K242 and K365 (with the Berlin Philharmonic), Carnival of the Animals (with the Israel Philharmonic), Poulenc's Concerto for Two Pianos, recitals of Liszt, Debussy, Brahms and Stravinsky, Dvořák Slavonic Dances, Concertos for two pianos by Bruch and Mendelssohn, Visions de l'Amen (jtly). *Current Management:* c/o Jilly Clarke, Askonas Holt Ltd, Lonsdale Chambers, 27 Chancery Lane, London, WC2A 1PF, England. *Telephone:* (20) 7400-1740. *E-mail:* Jilly.Clarke@askonasholt.co.uk. *Website:* www.askonasholt.co.uk; www.labeque.com.

**LABUDA, Izabela;** Singer (Soprano); b. 1961, Poland. *Career:* Sang Adina in L'Elisir d'amore and other roles in Poland from 1982; Moved to Germany in 1990 singing at the Essen Op•ra as Frau Fluth, Janáček's Vixen, and Hanna Glawari in Die Lustige Witwe; Guest at Mannheim Opera, the Vienna Volksoper and the State Opera of Vienna as First Lady in Die Zauberflöte, 1992; Antonia in Hoffmann at Cologne, 1998; Other repertory includes Lucille in Dantons Tod at Volksoper. *Address:* c/o Staatsoper, Opernring 2, 1010 Vienna, Austria.

**LACHENMANN, Helmut;** Composer; b. 27 Nov. 1935, Stuttgart, Germany. *Education:* Studied at Stuttgart with Jurgen Uhde (piano) and Johann Nepomuk David (composition); Venice with Luigi Nono. *Career:* Teacher of music theory at Stuttgart Hochschule für Musik, 1966–70, Ludwigsburg Hochschule, 1970–76, Hanover Hochschule für Musik, 1976–81 and Musikhochschule Stuttgart, 1981–99; Masterclasses in composition at Basle Music Academy; Instructor at the Ferienkurse in Darmstadt, 1978, 1982, 1998, Cursos Latinamericanos de Musica Contemporanea in Brazil, 1978, and Dominican Republic in 1980; Composition seminars in Blonay 1988, Oslo and Paris, 1989, St Petersburg, 1992, Barcelona and Chicago, 1997, Viitasaari adn Akiyoshidai, 1998; Member of Akademie der Künste, Berlin, Akademie der Schönen Künste, Munich, Freie Akademie der Künste, Hamburg, Leipzig, Mannheim and Academie voor Wetenschapen, Letteren in Schone Kunsten van Belgie, Brussels. *Compositions include:* Souvenir for 41 Instruments, 1959; String Trio, 1966; Les Consolations I and II for voices and percussion, 1967–68, Les Consolations, 1977–78; TemA for flute, voice and cello, 1968; Air for percussion and orchestra, 1968–69; Pression for cello, 1969; Dal Niente for clarinet, 1970; Klaangschattenn mein Seitenspiel, for 48 strings and 3 pianos, 1972; Kontrakaadenz for large orchestra, 1971; Faassade, for large orchestra, 1973; Accanto for clarinet and orchestra, 1975; Tanzsuite mit Deutschlandlied for string quartet and orchestra, 1979–80; Harmonica for tuba and orchestra, 1981–83; Mouvement - vor der Erstarrung, for ensemble, 1983–84; Ausklang for piano and orchestra, 1984–85; Allegro Sostenuto for clarinet, cello and piano, 1986–88; Two string quartets, Gran Torso, 1972, Reigen seligen Geister, 1989; Zwei Gefühlen, Musik mit Leonardo for ensemble, 1992; Das Mädchen mit den Schwefelhölzern, opera, 1990–96; Serynade for piano, 1998; Nun for flute, trombone and orchestra, 1999. *Honours:* Cultural Prize of Music, City of Munich, 1965; Composition Prize, City of Stuttgart, 1968; Bach Prize, Hamburg, 1972; Siemens Prize, 1997. *Address:* c/o Breitkopf and Hartel, Walkmuhlstr 52, 65195 Wiesbaden, Germany.

**LACHMANN, Elisabeth;** Singer (Soprano); b. 20 April 1940, Vienna, Austria. *Education:* Studied in Vienna. *Career:* Debut: Berne in 1961 as Despina, and Cagliari in Wiener Blut; Sang at Karlsruhe, 1962–64 as Micaela, Marenka, Cherubino and Regina in Mathis der Maler, and Graz, 1964–68 as Pamina, Susanna, Frau Fluth and Zdenka in Arabella; Engaged at Dortmund from 1968 as Mimi, Sophie, Sieglinde, Desdemona, Donna Anna, the Trovatore Leonora, Wagner's Elisabeth, Venus and Brünnhilde, Tosca, Amelia in Un Ballo in Maschera, Aida, Senta, Ariadne, Abigaille, Marschallin, Leonore (Fidelio) and Elektra, (R Strauss); These and other roles in guest appearances at Vienna State Opera, Hamburg, Stuttgart, Frankfurt, Cologne, Zürich and Antwerp; Concert and opera tours to the Netherlands, France, Far East, Africa, South America and Switzerland; Professor at Detmold Musikhochschule, 1984–. *Honours:* Kammersängerin, 1994. *Address:* Heiligenpesch 18A, 41069 Mönchengladbach, Germany.

**LACKNER, Christopher;** New Zealand singer (baritone); b. 1951, New Zealand. *Education:* London Opera Centre, and with Otakar Kraus. *Career:* Chorus member of Opera North, then principal roles with Kent Opera, Pavilion Opera and Opera 80; Appearances with the Royal Opera from 1990, in Turandot, Die Zauberflöte (Man in Armour), Les Huguenots, Die Frau ohne Schatten, Rigoletto, Paul Bunyan, Der Freischütz (Kilian), Palestrina, La Bohème (as Benoit), Andrea Chenier and Otello (Herald) 2001, Arabella, Tosca (Sciarrone), Barber of Seville (Officer). *Honours:* Winner, Mobil Song Contest, 1974; Prize of Friends of English National Opera. *Address:* c/o Royal Opera House (contracts), Bow Street, Covent Garden, London, WC2E 9DD, England.

**LADERMAN, Ezra;** Composer; b. 29 June 1924, Brooklyn, New York, USA. *Education:* Studied with Stefan Wolpe, 1946–49; Studied with Miriam Godeon, BA, 1949, Brooklyn College; Columbia University with Douglas Moore and Otto Luening, 1950–52. *Career:* Teacher, Sarah Lawrence College, 1960–61, 1965–66; State University of New York at Binghamton, 1971–82; Director of the Music program, National Endowment for the Arts, 1979–82; Dean, School of Music, 1989–95, Professor of Music, 1995–, Yale University; mem, ASCAP; ACO; AAAL. *Compositions:* 150 works include: Dramatic: Jacob and the Indians, opera, 1954; Goodbye to the Clowns, opera, 1956; The Hunting of the Snark, opera-cantata, 1958; Sarah, television opera, 1959; Ballets Dance Quartet, Esther, Song of Songs, Solos and Chorale, 1965;

Shadows Among Us, opera, 1967; The Black Fox, 1968; Galileo Galilei, opera, 1978; Film and television scores; Orchestral: Piano Concerto, 1939; Leipzig Symphony, 1945; Piano Concerto, 1957; Flute Concerto, 1968; Viola Concerto, 1975; Violin Concerto, 1978; Piano Concerto No. 1, 1978; Concerto for string quartet and orchestra, 1981; Cello Concerto, 1984; Vocal: oratorios The Eagle Stirred, 1961, A Mass for Cain, 1983; Columbus, cantata, 1975; Chamber: Wind Octet, 1957; Clarinet Sonata, 1958; Double Helix for flute, oboe and string quartet, 1968; Partita for violin, 1982; Double String Quartet, 1983; 8 Symphonies, 1963–93; 11 String Quartets, 1959–85, 1997, 2000 (2); Marilyn, opera, 1993; Fantasia for cello, 1997; Cello Ensemble Trilogy, Albo, 1997, Parisot, 1997, Simoes, 1999; Scenes From an Imagined Life I and II, 1997, 1999; Yisrael for orchestra, 1998; Brotherly Love, oratorio, 1999. *Recordings:* Piano Quintet; Quartet No. 6; Concerto for Double Orchestra; Pentimento; Quartet No. 7; June 29th; Chamber Music of Ezra Laderman, vols 1–4, Albany Records. *Honours:* Oscar for film music, The Eleanor Roosevelt Story, 1965. *Address:* 311 Greene Street, New Haven, CT 06051, USA.

**LAFFAGE, Jean-Pierre;** Singer (Baritone); b. 26 June 1926, Paris, France. *Education:* Studied at the Dijon and Paris Conservatories. *Career:* Debut: Paris Opéra 1957, as Valentin in Faust; Sang at the Paris Opéra until 1972 and the Opéra-Comique until 1980; Guest appearances throughout France and Italy; Among his best roles were Don Alvar in Les Indes Galantes, Mozart's Figaro, Escamillo, Sharpless, the Villains in Les Contes d'Hoffmann, Ourrais in Mireille, Scarpia, Ford, Amonasro and Oreste in Iphigénie en Aulide; Professor at the Paris Conservatoire, 1977–87. *Address:* c/o Conservatoire National, 14 Rue de Madrid, 75008 Paris, France.

**LAFITTE, Florence;** Piano Duettist; b. 10 July 1961, France. *Education:* Conservatoire National Superieur de Musique, Lyon, France; Liszt Academy, Budapest, Hungary; Manhattan School of Music, New York, USA. *Career:* Numerous concert appearances in France, Germany, Hungary, USA and Sweden; Tours of Australia, New Caledonia, Indonesia, Brazil, Argentina and Chile. Radio and television appearances at home and abroad. *Recordings:* Concerto for 2 pianos and orchestra by Poulenc, Orchestre Symphonique Francais, Conductor Laurent Petitgirard, VMG; 2 Piano Recital, Mozart, Liszt, Mendelssohn. *Honours:* International Music Video Competition, Fuji television Network, Tokyo, 1987; Honorary Award, Murray Dranoff's Two Piano Competition, Miami, 1990. *Current Management:* Liliane Weinstadt. *Address:* 69 1180 Brussels, Belgium.

**LAFITTE, Isabelle;** Piano Duettist; b. 10 July 1961, France. *Education:* Conservatoire National Superieur de Musique, Lyon, France; Liszt Academy, Budapest, Hungary; Manhattan School of Music, New York, USA. *Career:* Numerous concerts at home and abroad including Germany, Hungary, USA, Sweden; Tours of Australia, New Caledonia, Indonesia, Brazil, Argentina and Chile; Several Radio and Television appearances. *Recordings:* Concerto for Two Pianos and Orchestra by Poulenc, Orchestre Symphonique Francais, Conductor Laurent Petitgirard; Two Piano Recital, Mozart, Liszt, Mendelssohn. *Honours:* International Music Video Competition, Fuji television Network, Tokyo, 1987; Honorary Award, Murray Dranoff's Two Piano Competition, Miami, 1990. *Current Management:* Liliane Weinstadt. *Address:* Rue Langeveld 69, 1180 Brussels, Belgium.

**LAFONT, Jean-Philippe;** Singer (Bass-Baritone); b. 4 Feb. 1951, Toulouse, France. *Education:* Studied in Toulouse with Denise Dupleix and in Paris with Gabriel Bacquier. *Career:* Debut: Toulouse in 1974 as Papageno; Sang at Paris Opéra in 1977 as Nick Shadow in The Rake's Progress, Albi from 1977 as Mozart's Guglielmo and in Grétry's Les Femmes Vengées and Tom Jones, and Paris from 1978 in operas by Gounod, Offenbach, Gluck and Cherubini; Sang in Berlin in the European premiere of Debussy's La Chute de la Maison Usher, at Lyon in 1980 as Choroebus in the French premiere of Les Troyens, and at Aix-en-Provence in 1982 as Boréas in the stage premiere of Rameau's Les Boréades; Guest appearances in Strasbourg, Geneva, Lille, Hamburg, Hanover and Nimes; New York debut in 1983 as Fieramosca in Benvenuto Cellini at Carnegie Hall; Perugia in 1983 in Salieri's Les Danaides, Paris Opéra in 1983 as Rossini's Moise, Brussels and Barcelona in 1984 as Mozart's Count, Rome in 1985 in Cherubini's Demophoon, Aix in 1986 as Leporello in Don Giovanni and sang Amonasro at Bonn in 1989, Debussy's Golaud at Marseilles in 1990, and Alcide in Lully's Alceste at the Théâtre des Champs Elysées, 1991–92; Rigoletto for New Israeli Opera, 1997; Season 1998 with Amfortas at Brussels and Falstaff at the London Prom concerts; Season 2000–01 as Gerard in Nice, Macbeth at Montpellier and Scarpia for Chicago Lyric Opera; Other roles include Thaos in Iphigènie en Tauride and Astor in Cheubini's Démophon. *Recordings include:* Les Boréades; Gounod's Messe Solennelle; La Belle Hélène; Le Postillon de Lonjumeau by Adam; Verdi's Falstaff, conducted by John Eliot Gardiner, 2001. *Address:* c/o Opéra de Marseilles, 2 Rue Molière, 13231 Marseille Cédex 01, France.

**LAGRANGE, Michèle;** French singer (soprano); b. 29 May 1947, Conches, Saone-et-Loire. *Education:* studied in Paris. *Career:* engaged at Lyon Opéra from 1978; sang at Paris Opéra 1984–85 in Jerusalem by Verdi and as Alice in Robert le Diable by Meyerbeer; Opéra Comique 1987 as Donna Anna, at the Teato Colón in Buenos Aires 1982 as Teresa in Benvenuto Cellini, at the Aix-en-Provence Festival 1989 as Fata Morgana in The Love for Three Oranges; sang Marguerite in Faust at Avignon and St Etienne season 1990–91; Montpellier Festival in 1991 in Bizet's Ivan IV, concert performance; sang Fiorella in Offenbach's Les Brigands at Amsterdam and Isabella in Franchetti's Christoforo Colombo at Montpellier in 1992; other roles include

Musette and Elisabeth de Valois. *Recordings include:* Poulenc Salve Regina and Stabat Mater, Guercoeur by Magnard, The Love for Three Oranges. *Address:* c/o Opéra National de Nancy et de Lorraine, 1 rue Sainte Catherine, 54000 Nancy, France.

**LAGZDINA, Vineta;** Composer and Performer; b. 11 Nov. 1945, Oldenberg, Germany; 1 d. *Education:* BMus, University of Adelaide, 1976; Instrumental Teachers' Certificate, 1979; Computer music studies, Adelaide University Conservatorium, 1980–81. *Career:* Sound works included in exhibitions in Australia, New Zealand and Japan; Film music includes electronic, computer generated and instrumental, 1978–; Video art music; Grants for experimental music and movement performances, 1981–82; Composer's grant for radio, 1983; Curated Audio-Eyes, exhibition, 1983; Lecturer, Sydney College of The Arts, Music Across the Arts, 1984–; ABC Radio, 1987; The White Bird Music Theatre, 1987; Shock Of The New, video soundtrack, 1987; Speaking Out, film soundtrack, 1987. *Compositions:* Obstruction, computer sound tape for dance, 1981; Noh-Work, a quadrophonic Percussion Tape, 1982; The Black Snake, tape piece for voice and electronics, 1983; Double-Dream, Triple fate, video soundtracks, 1984–85; Media Massage, spoken song, 1986. *Publications:* 22 Contemporary Australian Composers. *Contributions:* Article in Art Network, 1983 and in New Music Australia 4, 1985. *Address:* Flat 11, 26 Pearson Street, Balmain East 2041, Australia.

**LAHO, Marc;** Belgian singer (tenor); b. 1964, Seraing. *Education:* studied at Liège with Gabriel Bacquier and Luigi Alva. *Career:* appearances at Rennes as Mylio in Le Roi d'Ys, at Marseilles in Thais, I Puritani, L'Africaine, Die Meistersinger and Montségur by Landowski, 1993; Zürich 1994–95 in La Périchole by Offenbach and at Strasbourg as Alfredo in La Traviata; Further appearances in Italy and the USA, Orlando, Florida; Dijon Opera as Don Ottavio, Des Grieux in Manon Lescaut and Paris in La Belle Hélène; Sang Rossini's Comte Ory at Glyndebourne, 1998; Sang Laërte in Hamlet by Thomas in Toulouse and Donizett's Tonio at St Gallen, 2000. *Honours:* Prizewinner, Pavarotti Competition, Philadelphia, 1992. *Address:* c/o Opera Municipal de Marseille, 2 rue Molière, 13001 Marseille, France.

**LAKATOS, Roby;** Hungarian violinist; b. 1965. *Education:* Béla Bartók Conservatory, Budapest. *Career:* resident with his ensemble at Restaurant Les Ateliers de La Grande Ile, Brussels 1986–1996; performances at the Schleswig-Holstein, Ludwigsburg and Helsinki festivals, at the Académies Musicales de Saintes in New York Central Park, and with the Orchestra Nat. de Radio France and Dresden Philharmonic 1996–; 'homecoming' concerts, Thalia Theatre, Budapest 1999; Autumn Strings Music Festival in Prague 2003; concerts with The Lakatos Sextet in the cultural programme of Ireland's presidency of EU 2004. *Compositions include:* On the Waves of the Balaton. *Recordings:* In Gypsy Style 1991, König der Zigeunergeiger 1998, Lakatos Gold 1998–99, Lakatos Best 1998–99, Lakatos: Live from Budapest 1999, With Musical Friends 2001, Kinoshita Meets Lakatos 2002, As Time Goes By (film score from Le Grand Blonde) 2002, The Legend of the Toad 2004. *Honours:* first prize Béla Bartók Conservatory 1984. *Telephone:* 475-76-55-96 (Belgium) (office). *Fax:* (3) 449-02-94 (Belgium) (office). *E-mail:* lakatos@pandora.be (office). *Website:* www.robylakatos.com.

**LAKES, Gary;** Singer (Tenor); b. 26 Sept. 1950, Dallas, Texas, USA. *Education:* Vocal studies with William Eddy at Seattle Opera. *Career:* Debut: Seattle in 1981 as Froh in Das Rheingold; Sang at Mexico City in 1983 as Florestan in Fidelio and Charlotte Opera in 1984 as Samson in Samson et Dalila; Metropolitan Opera debut in 1986 as the High Priest in Idomeneo, returning as Tannhäuser and as Siegmund in a new production of Die Walküre; Sang the Emperor in Die Frau ohne Schatten at the Metropolitan in 1989, Radames at New Orleans, Erik in Der fliegende Holländer at the Metropolitan in 1990 followed by Siegmund in New York (also televised) and San Francisco; Sang in Das Lied Von der Erde at the 1991 Promenade Concerts, London; Season 1991–92 as Lohengrin at Buenos Aires and Erik at the Metropolitan; Sang the Berlioz Faust at the Festival Hall, London, 1994; Florestan at the Lincoln Center Festival, 1996. *Recordings include:* Die Walküre conducted by James Levine. *Address:* c/o Metropolitan Opera, Lincoln Center, New York, NY 10023, USA.

**LAKI, Krisztina;** Singer (Soprano); b. 14 Sept. 1944, Budapest, Hungary. *Education:* Studied at Budapest Conservatory. *Career:* Debut: Berne, 1976 as Gilda in Rigoletto; Sang with the Deutsche Oper am Rhein, Düsseldorf, in Cologne, and at Bregenz and Edinburgh Festivals; Glyndebourne, 1979–80 as Aminta in Die schweigsame Frau and Sophie in Der Rosenkavalier; Salzburg in 1980 as Lucille in Von Einem's Dantons Tod; Tour of Germany in 1984 notably in cantatas by Bach; Paris Opéra in 1984 as Sophie; Other roles include Zdenka in Arabella, Mozart's Queen of Night, Zerlina and Susanna, Carolina in Il Matrimonio Segreto and Nannetta in Falstaff; Sang Marzelline in Fidelio at Hamburg in 1988 and Zdenka at Barcelona in 1989; Sang Marzelline with the company of the Cologne Opera at Hong Kong; Also widely heard in oratorio. *Recordings:* St Matthew Passion by Bach; Handel's Partenope; Masses by Haydn; Dantons Tod; Concert Arias by Mozart; Bach's Christmas Oratorio; Mozart's C minor Mass; Paisiello's Il Barbiere di Siviglia; Mozart's Schauspieldirektor and Myslivecek's Il Bellerofonte. *Address:* Oper der Stadt Köln, Offenbachplatz, 5000 Cologne, Germany.

**LALANDI-EMERY, Lina Madeleine,** OBE; British festival and opera company director; *Founding Director, English Bach Festival Trust;* b. Athens, Greece; m. Ralph Emery (deceased). *Education:* Athens Conservatory, studied privately in England. *Career:* int. career as harpsichordist, London, Paris,

Geneva, Athens; radio and TV broadcasts; founder and Dir, English Bach Festival Trust 1962, specializing in baroque opera, Purcell, Handel, Rameau, Gluck; Handel's Oreste and Oresteia by Xenakis at Covent Garden (Linbury Theatre) 2000; Purcell's Fairy Queen 2001; Gluck, Telemann, Hellenic Festival, Athens and Sadler's Wells, London 2003. *Honours:* Officier, Ordre des Arts et des Lettres 1979, Gold Cross of the Phoenix (Greece) 2004. *Address:* 15 South Eaton Place, London, SW1W 9ER, England. *Telephone:* (20) 7730-5925 (office). *Fax:* (20) 7730-1456 (office). *Website:* www.english -bachfestival.org.uk (office).

**LALE, Peter;** Violist; b. 1960, England. *Career:* Founder Member of the Britten Quartet with debut concert at Wigmore Hall in 1987; Quartet in Residence at the Dartington Summer School in 1987 with quartets by Schnittke; Season 1988–89 includes BBC Lunchtime Series at St John's Smith Square, concerts with the Hermann Prey Schubertiade and collaborations with the Alban Berg Quartet in the Beethoven Plus Series; Season 1989–90 includes debut tours of Netherlands, Germany, Spain, Austria and Finland, festival appearances at Brighton, City of London, Greenwich, Canterbury, Harrogate, Chester, Spitalfields and Aldeburgh; Formerly resident quartet at Liverpool University; Teaching role at Lake District Summer Music, 1989 and Universities of Bristol and Hong Kong in 1990. *Recordings:* Beethoven Op 130 and Schnittke Quartet No. 3; Vaughan Williams On Wenlock Edge and Ravel Quartet; Britten, Prokofiev, Tippett, Elgar and Walton Quartets. *Current Management:* Ingpen & Williams Ltd, 7 St George's Court, 131 Putney Bridge Road, London, SW15 2PA, England.

**LALLOUETTE, Olivier;** Singer (Baritone); b. 1960, Paris, France. *Career:* Appearances with Glyndebourne Festival and Tour, as Dancaïre in Carmen, and Mozart's Guglielmo; Don Giovanni at Rennes, Count Almaviva for Flanders Opera, Simone in La finta Semplice at Versailles and Papageno for Opéra d'Avignon; Geneva Opera as Puccini's Sharpless, La Monnaie Brussels as Giove in Cavalli's La Calisto and Berlin Staatsoper as Passagallo in L'Opera seria, by Gassmann; Further Baroque opera roles with René Jacobs, William Christie, Christophe Rousset and Phillipe Hereweghe; Season 2000–01 as Tusenach in Three sisters by Peter Eövös, at Hamburg, Edinburgh and Vienna; Concerts with Pierre Boulez, Webern Cantata, and Kent Nagano, Carter's opera What Next?; Season 2001–2002 with Massenet's Lescaut at Lyon, Don Giovanni in Avignon, Guglielmo at Liège and Merlin in Chausson's Le Roi Arthus at La Monnaie, Brussels. *Recordings:* Giulio Cesare; Il Ritorno d'Ulisse; Handel's Scipione and Riccardo Primo, Les Fêtes de Paphos by Mondonville; Carmen. *Address:* c/o Musicaglotz, 11, rue le Verrier, 75006 Paris, France.

**LALOR, Stephen;** Composer and Musical Director; b. 11 Jan. 1962, Sydney, New South Wales, Australia. *Education:* MMus, University of New South Wales, 1988; Tchaikovsky Conservatory, Moscow, 1984–85 and 1988–89. *Career:* Freelance Composer and Music Education Writer; Director and Arranger for the Sydney Domra Ensemble, 1978–85; Commissions from Macquarie University (1994), among others. *Compositions include:* Alice: A Musical for Children, 1986; Prelude and Dance for violin and piano, 1988; Six Angels, song cycle for baritone and piano; Three Pieces for piano, 1989; Three Pieces for solo violin, 1989; Damascus, opera, 1990; At the Edhe, for orchestra, 1991; String Quartet, 1991; Maroubra Song Cycle, for soprano, 1991; Capricornia, for string orchestra, 1993; Way Home for soprano or treble, narrator and tape, 1994. *Honours:* USSR Government Ukrainian Society Scholarship, 1988. *Address:* c/o APRA, 1A Eden Street, Crows Nest, NSW 2065, Australia.

**LAMA, Lina;** Concert Violist and Professor of Viola; b. 20 April 1932, Faenza, Italy. *Education:* Diplomas in Violin and Viola, Piano and Composition. *Career:* Debut: Teatro S Carlo, Naples; Professor at Conservatorio di Musica S Cecilia, Rome, 1959; Appearances on BBC and Italian television and radio; Concerts in Germany, Belgium, Italy, Israel, Hungary, Greece, Finland, France, North and South America, Africa, Asia and Japan; Concerts throughout Europe under Italian and foreign Maestri; Sonata per La Gran Viola by Paganini performed at Teatro San Carlo, Naples; Teacher of Viola at Conservatoire of S Cecilia, Roma Festival; International specialisation courses at Festival of Jywaskyla, Finland, Città di Castello, Lanciano, and Mezzolombardo, Italy; Jury Member for international viola competitions: Budapest, 1979, N Paganini, Genova, 1988 and for national viola competition at Vittaorio Veneto, 1986. *Honours:* Concert Prizes in Italy; Accademico of Accademia di S Cecilia, Roma; Cavaliere al Merito della Repubblica Italiana. *Address:* Via Ugo de Carolis 31, 00136 Rome, Italy.

**LAMARCHINA, Robert;** Cellist and Conductor; b. 3 Sept. 1928, New York City, USA. *Education:* Paris Conservatoire; Curtis Institute with Piatigorsky and Feuermann. *Career:* Debut: With St Louis Symphony under Vladimir Golschmann; Played in NBC Symphony Orchestra under Toscanini, 1944; Conductor and Musical Director with Young Musicians Foundation, Los Angeles, 1952–53; Solo Cellist with Chicago Symphony under Fritz Reiner in 1960; Conducted at Metropolitan Opera, La Traviata at Spoleto and Menotti's The Medium at the New York City Opera; Artistic and Musical Director with Honolulu Symphony Society and Hawaii Opera Theatre, 1967–79; Conductor of numerous symphony orchestras and opera companies including New York Philharmonic, St Louis Symphony, Chicago Symphony, Radio Italiana, Zürich Symphony, Vancouver Opera Association and Fujiwara Opera Institute.

**LAMB, Anthony (Stuart);** Clarinettist; b. 4 Jan. 1947, Woodford, England; m. Philippa Carpenter-Jacobs, 1 s., 2 d. *Education:* Royal College of Music;

ARCM. *Career:* Debut: With Chamber Ensemble Capricorn at Wigmore Hall in London, 1974; Principal Clarinet with Royal Ballet Orchestra, 1969–71; Founder member of Capricorn (violin, clarinet, cello and piano), 1973 with many concerts and broadcasts; Co-Principal with English National Opera Orchestra, 1976–; Several BBC broadcasts; Freelance Clarinettist with most major British orchestras; mem, Musicians Union. *Recordings:* With Capricorn: Rimsky-Korsakov's Quintet in B flat for Piano and Wind, Glinka's Grand Sextet in E flat for Piano and Strings, 1985. *Address:* 22 Munster Road, Teddington, Middlesex TW11 9LL, England.

**LAMBERTI, Giorgio;** Singer (Tenor); b. 9 July 1938, Adria, Rovigo, Italy. *Education:* Studied in Mantua. *Career:* Debut: Rome in 1964 as Arrigo in I Vespri Siciliani; US debut at Chicago in 1965 as Radames; Rome in 1965 in the premiere of Wallenstein by Zafred; Metropolitan Opera from 1974 as Enzo, Cavaradossi, Radames and Turiddu; Engagements in Paris, Brussels, Budapest, Baltimore, Amsterdam, Helsinki, Florence and Venice; Covent Garden debut in 1979; Other roles include Pollione, Don José, Jason in Médée, Verdi's Ernani, Alvaro, Manrico and Riccardo, Wagner's Tannhäuser and Lohengrin, Edgardo in Lucia di Lammermoor; Sang Radames at Berlin and Luxor in 1987 and Caracalla Festival, Rome, 1989; Andrea Chénier at Stuttgart in 1988 and appeared as Stiffelio in the first Covent Garden production of Verdi's opera in 1993. *Recordings include:* Ernani; I Lombardi; Il Corsaro; Gemma di Vergy by Donizetti; Bellini's Zaira. *Address:* c/o Stuttgart Staatsoper, Oberer Schlossgarten 6, D–70173 Stuttgart, Germany.

**LAMBERTINI, Marta;** Composer; b. 13 Nov. 1937, San Isidri, Buenos Aires, Argentina. *Education:* Studied at the Catholic University in Argentina and in Buenos Aires. *Compositions include:* Chamber operas: Alice in Wonderland in 1989 and, Oh, Eternidad... Ossia SMR Bach, 1990; Concertino Serenata in 1981 and Galileo Descubre Las Cuatro Lunas De Jupiter, 1985 for orchestra; Instrumental pieces include Assorted Kochels, 1991 and vocal music, Escena De La Falsa Tortuga, 1993; Reunión for string quartet and piano, 1994; La Ribera for speaker and string quartet, 1996; Pathfinder, string trio, 1997. *Address:* c/o Lavalle 1547, Apartado Postal Number 11, Sucursal 44-B, 1048 Buenos Aires, Argentina.

**LAMBRO, Phillip;** American composer, conductor and pianist; b. 2 Sept. 1934, Wellesley, MA. *Education:* studied in Boston, Miami, FL, Music Acad. of the West, CA, studied with Donald Pond and György Sandor. *Career:* debut, Pianists' Fair, Symphony Hall, Boston 1952; composed and conducted music for several motion pictures, including documentaries; major performances in Israel, Europe, S America, Australia and the Orient; compositions performed by Leopold Stokowski, Philippe Entremont, Santiago Rodriguez, Roman Rudnytsky, the Philadelphia Orchestra, the Rochester Philharmonic, Baltimore, Indianapolis, Miami, Denver, Oklahoma and New Orleans Symphonies. *Compositions include:* Miraflores for string orchestra; Dance Barbaro for percussion; Two Pictures for solo percussionist and orchestra; Four Songs for soprano and orchestra; Toccata for piano; Toccata for guitar; Parallelograms for flute quartet and jazz ensemble; Music for wind, brass and percussion; Obelisk for oboist and percussionist; Structures for string orchestra; Fanfare and Tower Music for brass quintet; Night Pieces for piano; Biospheres for 6 percussionists; Trumpet Voluntary; Eight Little Trigrams for Piano. *Address:* 1801 Century Park E, Suite 2400, Los Angeles, CA 90067-2326, USA.

**LAMOREAUX, Rosa (Lea);** Musician and Singer (Soprano); b. 19 Oct. 1955, Farmington, New Mexico, USA; m. James L McHugh, 8 Sept 1991. *Education:* Bachelor of Music, University of Redlands, 1977; ARCM, Royal College of Music, London, England, 1979; Master of Music, University of Redlands, California, 1980. *Career:* Debut: Kennedy Center; Numerous performances at Kennedy Center, Mozart-Requiem, Exultate Jubilate, Bach-B-minor Mass and Magnificat, Coffee Cantata and Peasant Cantata both staged; Carmel Bach Festival in California: Mozart, Bastien Bastienne, Handel, Xerxes, role of Romilda, Bach, B minor Mass, Haydn, Paukenmasse, Lord Nelson Mass, St John Passion, Lieder Recitals; Bach, St Matthew Passion; St Theresa Mass, Pergolesi, La Serva Padrona, Purcell, Dido and Aeneas (the role of Belinda); Bethlehem Bach Festival: B minor Mass, St John Passion and Coffee Cantata, Atlanta Symphony with Robert Shaw, B minor Mass, La demoiselle Elue by Debussy, Cincinnati May Festival; Mozart C minor Mass, Rheingau Music Festival, Germany. *Recordings:* Four Centuries of Song; Spain in the New World; Masters in this Hall; Luminous Spirit, Hildegard von Bingen, chants; I Love Lucette, 15th and 16th century French Theatre music; Berlioz's Messe Solennelle; Gentle Annie, Stephen Foster and Charles Ives; Bach Mass in B minor. *Address:* 4112 Fessenden Street NW, Washington, DC 20016, USA.

**LANCE, Albert;** Singer (Tenor); b. 12 July 1925, Menindie, Australia. *Education:* Studied in Australia and sang minor roles and in operetta. *Career:* Sang Cavaradossi in Sydney in 1952, Offenbach's Hoffmann in 1954 and in Paris from 1956 at Paris Opéra and Opéra-Comique in operas by Puccini, Gounod and Cherubini; Covent Garden debut in 1958 as the Duke of Mantua opposite Joan Sutherland; Bolshoi Theatre Moscow, 1965–66; Guest appearances in Bordeaux, Lyon, Los Angeles, San Francisco, Vienna, Leningrad, Kiev and Buenos Aires; London Coliseum in 1969 in the first British performance of Roussel's Padmâvati; Teacher at Nice Conservatory from 1974. *Recordings include:* Werther; Madama Butterfly; Tosca.

**LANCELOT, James,** MA, MusB, FRCO (CHM), ARCM; British choirmaster and organist; *Master of the Choristers and Organist, Durham Cathedral*; b. 2 Dec. 1952; m.; two d. *Education:* St Paul's Cathedral School, Ardingly Coll., Royal

Coll. of Music, King's Coll., Cambridge. *Career:* sub-organist, Winchester Cathedral 1975–85; Master of the Choristers and Organist, Durham Cathedral 1985–; conductor, Durham Univ. Choral Soc. 1987–; Lay Canon, Durham Cathedral 2002–; mem. Royal Coll. of Organists Council 1988–2000, 2001–, Cathedral Organists' Asscn (Pres. 2001–03). *Recordings:* numerous with King's Coll. Choir, Winchester Cathedral Choir, Durham Cathedral Choir; solo including Complete Organ Works of Hubert Parry. *Publications:* Durham Cathedral Organs (with Richard Hird); contrib. to The Sense of the Sacramental. *Honours:* Turpin Prize (RCO) 1969, Stuart Prize (Royal Coll. of Music) 1971, Hon. FGCM. *Address:* 6 The College, Durham, DH1 3EQ, England (home). *Telephone:* (191) 3864766 (office). *Website:* www .durhamcathedral.co.uk (office).

**LANCERON, Alain;** French record company executive; *President, Virgin Classics*. *Career:* Man. Dir EMI Classics France 1978–96; Pres. Virgin Classics 1996–. *Honours:* Chevalier, Ordre Nat. du Mérite 1993. *Address:* Virgin Classics, EMI, 43 Brook Green, Hammersmith, London, W6 7EF, England (office). *Website:* www.virginclassics.com (office).

**LANDER, Thomas;** Singer (Baritone); b. 1961, Sweden. *Education:* Studied at Stockholm College of Music and the State Opera School. *Career:* Sang with Norrlandsoperan, 1982–83; Engaged at Hamburg Staatsoper, 1986–87, and Vienna Volksoper, 1987–89 as Mozart's Count and Guglielmo; Guest appearances at Aix-en-Provence, Opéra de Lyon and in Italy, Iceland and Israel; Engaged at Hanover, 1990–; Other roles include Mozart's Don Giovanni and Papageno, Malatesta, and Harlequin in Ariadne auf Naxos; Sang Christus in Bach's St John Passion at Lucerne Easter Festival in 1993. *Address:* Nordic Artists Management, Sveavagen 76, 11359 Stockholm, Sweden.

**LANDON, Howard Chandler Robbins,** BMus; American writer, musicologist and academic; *John Bird Professor of Music, University College Cardiff*; b. 6 March 1926, Boston, MA; s. of William G. Landon and Dorothea LeB. Robbins; m. 1st Christa Landon; m. 2nd Else Radant 1977. *Education:* Lenox School, Mass., Swarthmore Coll. and Boston Univ. *Career:* corresp. The Times 1958–61; Hon. Professorial Fellow, Univ. Coll. Cardiff 1971–78, John Bird Prof. of Music 1978–; Prof. of the Humanities, Middlebury Coll., Vt 1980–83. *Publications:* The Symphonies of Joseph Haydn 1955, The Mozart Companion (ed. with Donald Mitchell) 1956, The Collected Correspondence and London Notebooks of Joseph Haydn 1959, Essays on the Viennese Classical Style: Gluck, Haydn, Mozart, Beethoven 1970, Beethoven: A Documentary Study 1970, Joseph Haydn: Chronicle and Works (five vols) 1976–80, Haydn: A Documentary Study 1981, Mozart & the Masons 1983, Handel and his World 1984, 1791: Mozart's Last Year 1987, Haydn: his Life and Music (with D. Jones) 1988, Mozart: The Golden Years 1989, The Mozart Compendium (ed.) 1990, Mozart and Vienna 1991, Five Centuries of Music in Venice (with John Julius Norwich) 1991, Vivaldi: Voice of the Baroque 1992, Une Journée particulière de Mozart 1993, The Mozart Essays 1995, Horns in High C (memoirs) 1999. *Honours:* Verdienstkreuz für Kunst und Wissenschaft (Austria); Hon. DMus (Boston) 1969, (Belfast) 1974, (Bristol) 1982, (Toulouse) 1991. *Address:* Château de Foncoussières, 81800 Rabastens (Tarn), France (home). *Telephone:* 5-63-40-61-45 (home). *Fax:* 5-63-33-76-36 (home). *E-mail:* foncons@aol.com (home).

**LANDOWSKI, Marcel François Paul;** composer; b. 18 Feb. 1915, Pont l'Abbe, France; m. Jacqueline Potier 1941; two s. one d. *Education:* Lycee Janson-de-Sailly, Conservatoire Nationale de Musique de Paris. *Career:* Director, Conservatoire Boulogne-sur-Seine, 1960–65; Director of Music, Comédie Française, Paris, 1962–66; Inspector-General, Musical Studies, 1964, Director of Music Service, Ministry of Cultural Affairs, 1966–70, Music, Lyric and Dance, 1970–74; Founder, Orchestre de Paris, 1967, Honorary President, 1975–; Inspector-General de l'Instruction Publique, 1974–; mem, Institute of France, Academy des Beaux-Arts, 1975. *Compositions:* Operas Rabelais, 1953, La vieille maison, 1983, Montségur, 1985, P'tit Pierre, 1988; Numerous orchestral and choral compositions; Film music and music for Cyrano de Bergerac at Comédie Française; Opera, Galina, premiered at Lyon, 1996. *Honours:* Officer, Légion d'Honneur; Commander des Arts et des Lettres; Croix de Guerre. *Address:* 10 rue Max-Blondat, 92100 Boulogne-sur-Seine, France.

**LANDSMAN, Vladimir;** Violinist; b. 1941, Dushambe, Russia. *Education:* Moscow School of Music; Doctorate, Moscow State Conservatory. *Career:* Soloist, Moscow Philharmonic Society; Toured Soviet Union; Hollywood Bowl, Los Angeles; Concert tours throughout the world; Guest soloist; Bolshoi Hall, Moscow Conservatory; Artistic Director, Seasons Orchestra, Moscow, 1994–95; Teacher, Music Faculty, Université de Montréal; Associate Professor; Teacher, academies all over the world; Teacher, Orford Arts Centre, Quebec; Masterclasses; Served on examination juries. *Recordings:* Over 10 works. *Honours:* Third prize, Jaques Thibaud International Violin Competition, Paris, 1963; First prize, Montreal International Competition, 1966. *Address:* 4039 Grand Blvd, Montreal H4B 2X4, Canada.

**LANE, Gloria;** Singer (Mezzo-Soprano and Soprano); b. 6 June 1930, Trenton, New Jersey, USA; m. Samuel Krachmalnick. *Education:* Studied with Elisabeth Westmoreland in Philadelphia. *Career:* Debut: Philadelphia in 1950 in the premiere of Menotti's The Consul; Broadway in 1954 in the premiere of Menotti's The Saint of Bleecker Street; British debut in 1958 as Baba the Turk in The Rake's Progress, returning in 1972 as Dorabella in Così fan tutte, Strauss's Ariadne and Lady Macbeth; Covent Garden debut in 1960

as Carmen and sang at Florence in 1966 as Federica in Verdi's Luisa Miller; Guest appearances in Vienna, Paris, Venice, Rome, Palermo, Boston, Chicago and San Francisco; New York City Opera, 1971 as Santuzza in Cavalleria Rusticana. *Recordings:* The Consul; Rossini's Mosè in Egitto; The Saint of Bleecker Street. *Address:* c/o New York City Opera, Lincoln Center, New York, NY 10023, USA.

**LANE, Jennifer (Ruth);** Singer (Mezzo-soprano); b. 25 Nov. 1954, Berwyn, Illinois, USA; m. James H Carr, 21 Nov 1987. *Education:* BMus, Chicago Musical College, Roosevelt University, 1977; MA in Performance, City University of New York, 1980. *Career:* Debut: Elsbeth in Strauss's Feuersnot, Santa Fe Opera in 1988; Performances with Santa Fe Opera, New York City Opera, Opera Monte Carlo, L'Opéra Français de New York, Opera Omaha, US stage premiere of Handel's Partenope, Milwaukee's Skylight Opera, Opera Ensemble of New York; Prior to operatic career, toured North and South America with the Waverly Consort; Also tours of the Far East with the Gregg Smith Singers; Many concert performances including appearances with the Atlanta Symphony under Robert Shaw, San Francisco Symphony, The National Symphony, St Louis Symphony, and Harrisburg Symphony in Mahler's 2nd and 3rd Symphonies; Many radio broadcasts including Mahler's 3rd Symphony, personal interviews and Radio Canada recital with countertenor, Alan Fast; Sang Alessandro in Handel's Tolomeo at Halle, 1996; Handel's Serse with New York City Opera, 1997. *Recordings include:* JS Bach's St John Passion, Smithsonian Collection of Recordings; Handel's Theodora with Nicholas McGegan conducting; Bach's Solo Cantata for Alto; John Adams, Grand Pianola Music with composer conducting. *Current Management:* Byers, Schwalbe and Associates Inc, 584 Broadway, Suite 1105, New York, NY 10012, USA. *Address:* 514 West 110th Street, Apt 92, New York, NY 10025, USA.

**LANE, Piers;** British pianist; b. 1958, London, England. *Education:* Queensland Conservatorium with Nancy Weir, in Seattle with Bela Siki, Royal Coll. of Music with Kendall Taylor and Yonty Solomon. *Career:* debut in broadcast recital for ABC aged 12; solo and concert appearances in the USA, France, Germany, Spain, Hungary, Italy, India, the UK, Australia, Greece, Middle East and New Zealand; tour of four Latin American countries 1989; season 1990–91 with visits to Cyprus and Morocco, concerts in the UK, two visits to Australia and engagements in France and S America, and played Bliss Piano Concerto at the Promenade Concerts 1991; has played with such orchestras as the Philharmonia, Royal Philharmonic, BBC Philharmonic, Hallé, City of London Sinfonia and the London Festival Orchestra; frequent recitals on the BBC and chamber concerts with Kathron Sturrock, the New Budapest Quartet, Alexander Baillie and Julian Lloyd Webber; many recitals at Wigmore Hall; contemporary repertory includes Dave Heath's Piano Concerto; Prof. of Piano, Royal Acad. of Music; mem. European Piano Teachers' Asscn, Liszt Soc., Beethoven Pianoforte Soc. of Europe. *Recordings:* Music by Shostakovich, Prokofiev, Schnittke and Rachmaninov with Alexander Baillie; Moskowski and Paderewski Concertos, the Complete Etudes by Scriabin, and Brahms Piano Quintet; Recitals with violinist, Tasmin Little; Mussorgsky's Pictures at an Exhibition, Stravinsky's Petroushka and Balakirev's Islamey. *Honours:* Royal Overseas League Outstanding Musician of the Year 1982. *Current Management:* Patrick Garvey Management, Cedar House, 10 Rutland Street, Filey, North Yorkshire YO14 9JB, England. *Website:* www.patrickgarvey.com.

**LANG, Aidan;** British stage director; *Artistic Director, Buxton Festival*; b. 1959, England. *Education:* Univ. of Birmingham. *Career:* Glyndebourne from 1984, becoming Dir of Productions for the Tour 1991, Principal Assoc. Dir for the Festival; productions with Glyndebourne Touring Opera have included his debut, La Bohème 1991, Matthus's Song of Love and Death and Il Barbiere di Siviglia; premiere of Hamilton's Lancelot at the Arundel Festival, Tamerlano at Göttingen, Carmen for Canadian Opera and La Traviata, Die Zauberflöte (Barcelona) 1990–97; Artistic Dir, Opera Zuid, Netherlands, with productions of Werther, Ariadne, The Cunning Little Vixen and Don Giovanni; further engagements include Le Comte Ory for WNO, Hansel and Gretel in Belfast, Così fan tutte at Cologne, Tosca at Nice, Die Entführung for Istanbul Festival, Il Ritorno d'Ulisse in Lisbon, Mozart's La Finta Semplice at Buxton 1998, Lucio Silla at Garsington; season 1999 directed Magic Fountain by Delius (Scottish Opera) and Don Giovanni (Brazil); season 2000 directed Fierrebras (Buxton) and Cav and Pag (São Páolo); fmr Dir Maastricht Festival, Netherlands eight years; Artistic Dir, Buxton Festival 2000–; other recent productions include La Sonnambula (São Paolo) and Semele (Buxton); directed a new Wagner's Der Ring des Nibelungen at Amazonas Opera Festival, Brazil 2005. *Address:* Buxton Festival, 5 The Square, Buxton, Derbyshire SK17 6AZ, England. *E-mail:* info@buxtonfestival.co.uk. *Website:* www.buxtonfestival.co.uk.

**LANG, David,** PhD; American composer; b. 1 Aug. 1957, LA; m.; three c. *Education:* Stanford Univ., Univ. of Iowa, Yale School of Music. *Career:* studied with Jacob Druckman, Hans Werner Henze (q.v.) and Martin Bresnick; Jr Composer-in-Residence, Horizons Summer Festival 1980s; commissioned by Boston Symphony Orchestra, Cleveland Orchestra, St Paul Chamber Orchestra, BBC Singers, American Composers Orchestra and Santa Fe Opera and Settembre Musica Festival, Turin; co-f. (with Michael Gordon and Julia Wolfe) New York annual music festival Bang on a Can 1987–; composed albums Cheating, Lying, Stealing 1996 and Brian Eno: Music for Airports 1998 for group Bang on a Can All-Stars. *Compositions for orchestra include:* Bonehead, Eating Living Monkeys, Int. Business Machine, for chamber groups include My Very Empty Mouth, My Evil Twin, Hunk of Burnin' Love, I Fought the Law, for solo instruments include The Anvil Chorus. *Other works include:* Illumination Rounds 1982, Frag 1985, Spud 1986, Are You Experienced? 1987–88. *Operas include:* Judith and Holofernes 1989, Modern Painters 1994 (for Santa Fe Opera) and The Carbon Copy Building (with Ben Katchor) 1999. *Honours:* Rome Prize, American Acad., Rome; BMW Prize, Munich Biennale for New Music Theatre; Friedheim Award, Kennedy Center; Revson Fellowship with New York Philharmonic; grants from Guggenheim Foundation, New York Foundation of Arts and Nat. Endowment for the Arts. *Address:* c/o Red Poppy Music, 66 Greene Street, Fifth Floor, New York, NY 10012, USA (office).

**LANG, Edith;** Singer (Soprano); b. 28 April 1927, Chicago, USA. *Education:* Studied in Chicago and Italy. *Career:* Sang in Italy from 1954 with debut as Madama Butterfly, and Hamburg from 1955 as Verdi's Aida, Amelia, Elisabeth de Valois, Leonora and Abigaille, Beethoven's Leonore and Mozart's Donna Anna; Guest appearances in London, Vienna, Milan and Paris; San Francisco in 1959 as the Empress in the US premiere of Die Frau ohne Schatten; Also heard as concert singer; Taught at Lubeck Musikhochschule from 1973. *Address:* Schleswig-Holsteinische Musikakademie, Jerusalemberg 4, Lubeck, Germany.

**LANG, Istvan;** Hungarian composer; b. 1 March 1933, Budapest; m. Csilla Fülöp 1966; one s. *Education:* Acad. of Music, Budapest. *Career:* freelance composer 1958–66; Musical Adviser, State Puppet Theatre 1966–84; Prof. of Chamber Music, Acad. of Music, Budapest 1973–; Sec.-Gen., Asscn of Hungarian Musicians 1978–90; mem. Int. Soc. for Contemporary Music (cttee mem. 1984–87), Int. Music Council (cttee mem. 1989–93), Hungarian Composers' Union. *Compositions:* Dream about the Theatre, Rounded up television operas, In memorian NN, Symphonies Nos 2, 3, 4, 5, 6 and 7, Violin Concerto, Double Concerto for clarinet and harp, Concerto Bucolico, Pezzo Lirico, Rhymes, Constellations, Affetti, Intarsia around a Bartók theme, Music 2-3-4, Sempre in tensione, solo pieces for various instruments, String Quartets Nos 2 and 3, Wind Quintets Nos 1, 2 and 3, Sonata for violin and piano 1990, Cimbiosis 1991, Sonata for cello and piano 1992–93, Off and On for harp and live electronics, Budapest Liaz Terenc Square, Vibrating Object on Parabola Line, Knotes on the Line (chamber music) 1993, Viviofa (chamber music) 1995, The Coward (opera in one act) 1998, Night-fall for trumpet and live electronic music, Meeting a Young Man (electroacustic radio play), Concertino for soprano and live electro-acoustic 1999, No Man is an Island (John Donne), Chamber Cantata No. 3. *Honours:* Erkel Prize 1968, 1975, Merit Artist 1985, Bartók Pásztori Prize 1994. *Address:* Frankel Leo Ut 24, 1027 Budapest, Hungary.

**LANG, Klaus;** Austrian composer and organist; b. 26 April 1971, Graz. *Education:* Univ. of Music, Graz with H. M. Pressl and B. Fürrer, studied with Y. Pagh-Paan in Bremen, Univ. of Graz with O Bruckner. *Career:* performances at Steirischer Herbst 1994–98, Metopher, Stuttgart 1997, Wien modern 1998, 1999, Eclat Stuttgart 1999, Kryptonale '99 Berlin, Lörgange 2000, Vienna, Lucerne Festival, Takefu Festival; compositions performed by Klangforum Wien, Arditti Quartet, Ensemble Intercontemporain, Ensemble die Reihe, SWR Chorus, Studio Percussion Graz, Tehran Symphony Orchestra. *Compositions:* Der Weg des Prizen, Cetus candidus, Die Ewigheitisteine Badehütte mit... cimeinte der Rock wäre aus... Die 3 Spiegel der schönen Karin, Das kaum wahruehmreheib Dostojkis, works for music theatre including Stimme Allein, Königin ók, Handschuh des Immanuel, Die Perser, Fichten. *Recordings:* Klaus Lang Trauermusiken Laubert 1995, Amras Quartett, Dir Uberwinterungder der Mollusken Kurien 1999, Klangforum Wien, Lichtgeschwindigkeit, Sei Jaku für Streichquartett. *Publications:* Auf Wehlklanswellen durch der Töne Meer 1999; contrib. to New Grove Dictionary. *Honours:* Musikförderungspreis der Stadt Graz 1992, Würdigungspreis des Bundesministeriums 1993, Preis der Kompositions-wettbewerbes der Musikpratokolls in steirischentterbst 1993, Kompanistes-seminer des Klompforum 1998. *Address:* Zeitvertrieb Wien Berlin, Zollergasse 5/13, 1070 Vienna, Austria.

**LANG, Petra;** German singer (mezzo-soprano); b. 29 Nov. 1962, Frankfurt. *Education:* studied in Darmstadt and Mainz. *Career:* sang at Basle Opera 1990–91, Karlsruhe 1991–92, Dortmund 1992–95; Brunswick 1995–96: Judith in Bluebeard's Castle, Brangaene in Tristan and Marie in Wozzeck; Salzburg Festival 1993: Virtu in Monteverdi's Poppea; Bregenz 1994: Fenena in Nabucco; La Scala 1995: Die Zauberflöte; other roles include Mozart's Dorabella and Cherubino, Strauss's Octavian and Composer, Suzuki in Butterfly and Gluck's Orpheus; Lieder recitals throughout Germany and at Théâtre du Châtelet, Paris; sang Waltraute in Götterdämmerung with Royal Opera, Birmingham 1998; Brangaene in Tristan und Isolde 2000; Schoenberg's Gurrelieder, London Proms 2000; season 2002–03 as Ariadne at Covent Garden and Brangaene for the Vienna Staatsoper. *Recordings include:* Le nozze di Figaro, Bach Cantatas, Bruckner's Te Deum. *Current Management:* Balmer & Dixon Management AG, Kreuzstrasse 82, 8032 Zürich, Switzerland. *Telephone:* (43) 244-8644. *Fax:* (43) 244-8649. *Website:* www.badix.ch.

**LANG, Rosemarie;** Singer (Mezzo-soprano); b. 1955, Grünstädtel, Schwarzenberg, Germany. *Education:* Studied in Leipzig. *Career:* Sang in opera at Altenburg, then Leipzig; Guest engagements at Dresden as Venus by Wagner, 1988; Berlin Staatsoper as Gluck's Clytemnestra and Wagner's Brangäne, and in premiere of Graf Mirabeau by Siegfried Matthus, 1989 (also televised), and as Azucena by Verdi, 1989; Other roles include Mozart's Dorabella, Cherubino

and Sextus, Bellini's Romeo, Rossini's Cenerentola and Rosina, Strauss's Octavian and Composer in Ariadne; Sang Countess Geschwitz in Lulu, 1997; Many concert appearances. *Recordings include:* Mendelssohn's St Paul; Larina in Eugene Onegin; Schoenberg's Gurre-Lieder; Mozart's Masses; Songs by Schumann and Brahms; Pfitzner's Palestrina as Silla; 8th Symphony by Mahler under Abbado; Rheingold and Walküre (Fricka) by Wagner; Götterdämmerung by Wagner under Barenboim; Guest appearances in Oslo. *Address:* c/o Staatsoper Berlin, Unter den Linden 7, 10117 Berlin, Germany.

**LANG LANG;** Chinese pianist; b. 1982, Shenyang. *Education:* Shenyang Conservatory of Music, Central Music Conservatory, Beijing, Curtis Inst., Philadelphia, USA. *Career:* played the complete Chopin Etudes, Beijing Concert Hall 1995; performed as one of the soloists at the inaugural concert of the China National Symphony 1996; US debut with the Baltimore Symphony Orchestra 1998; last-minute substitution at the Ravinia Festival Gala of the Century, playing the Tchaikovsky Concerto with the Chicago Symphony Orchestra 1999; Carnegie Hall debut playing the Grieg Concerto with the Baltimore Symphony under Yuri Temirkanov, April 2001; joined the Philadelphia Orchestra and Wolfgang Sawallisch for the orchestra's 100th anniversary tour, including a performance in the Great Hall of the People, Beijing, June 2001; BBC Proms debut, playing Rachmaninov's Third Concerto, Aug. 2001; 2001/02 season included recital debuts at London's Wigmore Hall, Washington's Kennedy Center and the Paris Louvre; tour of Europe with the NDR Symphony Orchestra of Hamburg, and performance with the NHK Symphony Orchestra under Charles Dutoit; performed in five concerts at the Ravinia Festival 2002; season 2002/03 included performances with the New York Philharmonic and Lorin Maazel in New York and a tour of Asia, concerts with the Cleveland Orchestra at Severance Hall, a tour of the Midwest with Franz Welser-Möst, appearances with the Los Angeles Philharmonic, the San Francisco Symphony, the Pittsburgh Symphony, the Philadelphia Orchestra); in 2003 he toured China in with concerts and recitals, and festival appearances included the opening concert of the BBC Proms, London, Mostly Mozart, Aspen, Tanglewood, Ravinia, Saratoga, Blossom, Verbier, Schleswig-Holstein and the Ruhr Piano Festival; Carnegie Hall recital debut Nov. 2003; orchestral appearances with the Philadelphia, Los Angeles Philharmonic, London Philharmonic, Orchestre de Paris, Israel Philharmonic, Staatskapelle Berlin, Berliner Philharmoniker. *Recordings:* Peter Tchaikovsky Piano Concerto No. 1 and Mendelssohn Piano Concerto No. 1, with Chicago Symphony Orchestra under Daniel Barenboim, Haydn, Rachmaninov, Brahms, recorded Live at Seiji Ozawa Hall, Tanglewood 2001, Rachmaninov Piano Concerto No. 3 and Scriabin Etudes, with St Petersburg Philharmonic under Yuri Temirkanov 2003, Lang Lang live at Carnegie Hall 2004. *Honours:* first prize in the Shenyang Piano Competition 1987, first prize in the Fifth Xing Hai Cup Piano Competition, Beijing, first prize and outstanding artistic performance in the Fourth International Young Pianists Competition, Germany, first prize at the Second Tchaikovsky International Young Musicians' Competition, Japan 1995, Leonard Bernstein Award 2002. *Address:* c/o Telarc Records, 23307 Commerce Park Road, Cleveland, OH 44122, USA (office). *Website:* www.LangLang.com (office).

**LANGAN, Kevin;** Singer (Bass); b. 1 April 1955, New York, USA; m. Sally Wolf, 16 July 1983. *Education:* New England Conservatory of Music, 1973–75; Indiana University, 1975–80; BM, MM in Voice; Vocal Instruction with Margaret Harshaw. *Career:* Debut: New Jersey State Opera in 1979 in Don Carlos; Principal Bass with San Francisco Opera, 1980–; Appeared with New York City Opera, Houston Grand Opera, Philadelphia Opera, Canadian Opera, Miami, Detroit and Dallas Opera, Geneva, Lyon, Winnipeg and St Louis Opera, Colorado, Santa Fe, Edmonton, Vancouver, Seattle, Tulsa, Pittsburgh, San Diego and Washington DC Opera; Appeared with Chicago Lyric and Metropolitan Opera and sang Astofolo in Vivaldi's Orlando Furioso at San Franciscio in 1989, and Colline at San Diego in 1990; Season 1992 as Donizetti's Raimondo at Seattle followed by Rossini's Basilio, and Leporello at the 1992 Santa Fe Festival; Appears on 1993 video of San Francisco Opera production of Turandot in role of Timur; Appeared as Leporello in 1996 Santa Fe festival production of Don Giovanni; Sparafucile in 1997 as San Francisco Opera's Rigoletto; Timur in Turandot in 1998 with Dallas Opera and Flanders Opera, Antwerp; Season 2000–01 as Sobackini in The Tsar's Bride by Rimsky, at San Franscisco; Pimen in Seattle and Sarastro in San Diego. *Recordings:* Nozze di Figaro with Nicklaus Harnoncourt, conductor, 1994. *Honours:* Finalist, National Metropolitan Opera, 1980; 2nd Place, San Francisco Opera Auditions, 1980; Richard Tucker Foundation Award for Advanced Studies, 1984. *Current Management:* Elizabeth Crittenden. *Address:* Columbia Artists Management Inc, c/o Crittenden Division, 165 West 57th Street, New York, NY 10019, USA.

**LANGDON, Sophie (Catherine);** Concert Violinist and Professor of Violin; b. 26 Aug. 1958, Hemel Hempstead, Hertfordshire, England. *Education:* Royal Academy of Music; Juilliard School, New York, USA; Curtis Institute, Philadelphia, USA; Guildhall School of Music and Drama. *Career:* Debut: As Soloist, 1981 Spitalfields Festival, London in Kurt Weill's Violin Concerto; Violinist of Trio Zingara, 1980–83, winning Munich International Competition, 1981; Recitals, Concertos, Leading, Directing and Chamber Music Performances and Broadcasts in England at Festivals and all London's major venues and throughout Europe and North America; Teacher, Guildhall School of Music and Drama 1981–86, Central Ostrabothnian Conservatoire, Finland 1986–87, Trinity College of Music 1987–, Menuhin School 1991–92,

Chetham's School, Manchester 1988–90, Royal Academy of Music 1990–; Professor of Violin at TCM and RAM; Concerto performances and recordings with the Royal Philharmonic Orchestra, Philharmonia, BBC Symphony Orchestra, BBC National Orchestra of Wales, BBC Scottish Symphony Orchestra, BBC Philharmonic and Berlin Radio Orchestra; Chamber music performances and recordings with, Lontano, Jeux, Aquarius, Music Projects, Langdon Chamber Players and London Sinfonietta; Leader and Director of London Chamber Symphony, Ambache Chamber Orchestra and Academy of London; Guest Leader of City of London Sinfonia, London Mozart Players and Orchestra of St John's Smith Square. *Recordings:* Dame Ethel Smyth Double Concerto for violin and horn on Chandos label; Mozart Chamber Music with Ambache Chamber Ensemble on Pickwick label. *Honours:* Associate of the Royal Academy of Music, 1993. *Address:* 84 North Grove, London N15 5QP, England.

**LANGER, Elena;** Composer; b. 1974, Moscow, Russia. *Education:* Gnessin Music School, Moscow, 1989; Moscow Conservatoire; 1993-98, with Yuri Vorontsov; Royal College of Music, London, from 1998 with Julian Anderson; PhD studies at the Royal Academy, with Simon Bainbridge, from 2001. *Career:* Commissions from Moscow Variety Theatre and Almeida Theatre (first Jerwood Composer in Association). *Compositions:* The Crying, for four clarinets, 1994; Transformations for violin and piano, 1998; Reflection for piano, 1999; Ariadne for voice and ensemble, 2002; Music Theatre commission from the Almeida 2003. *Recordings:* Transformations, and Reflection, 1999. *Address:* c/o Julian Anderson, Royal College of Music, Prince Consort Road, London, SW7 2 BS, England.

**LANGFORD, Roger;** Singer (Baritone); b. 1965, England. *Education:* Studied at the Royal College of Music and Royal Academy of Music. *Career:* Soloist with Yorkshire Bach Choir in the St John Passion, Christmas Oratorio, Bach B minor Mass and Monteverdi Vespers; Concerts in France and Germany including Purcell's Aeneas for Cologne Radio; Music theatre includes Eight Songs For A Mad King by Maxwell Davies, Master Peter's Puppet Show and Monteverdi's Combattimento; Visits to Europe with Nigel Rogers's group, Chiaroscuro, performing English and Italian Baroque music; Sang Elijah at Lincoln Cathedral and The Apostles by Elgar at St Albans Abbey; Season 1989–90 as Papageno for British Youth Opera and in Trouble in Tahiti at Edinburgh Festival; Sang title role of Nicolson's Cat Man's Tale at BOC Covent Garden Festival, 1998.

**LANGHURST, Rebecca;** Singer (soprano); b. 1965, USA. *Education:* Yale Opera Program, Princeton. *Career:* Roles at Yale included Olympia in Les Contes d'Hoffmann, Zdenka in Arabella and Mozart's Despina; Professional debut as Pamina, for Minnesota Opera, followed by appearances in Ariadne auf Naxos at St Louis and Il Trittico for Spoleto Festival, USA; Corinna in Il Viaggio a Reims and Verdi's Nannetta for Wolf Trap Opera; Hero in Béatrice et Bénedict at Alice Tully Hall, New York, and Rossini's Elvria at Kansas City; Other roles include Alexandra in Blitzstein's Regina and Angel More in Thomson's The Mother of us All, for New York City Opera; Staatstheater Mannheim, from 2000, as Mozart's Ilia and Sandrina, Gretel, and Helena in A Midsummer Night's Dream. *Current Management:* Athole Still International Management, Forresters Hall, 25–27 Westow Street, London, SE19 3RY, England. *Telephone:* (20) 8771-5271. *Fax:* (20) 8768-6600. *Website:* www .atholestill.com.

**LANGMAN, Krzysztof (Maria);** Flautist; b. 22 July 1948, Kraków, Poland. *Education:* Academy of Music Kraków, 1970–74; Study under S Gazzeloni at Santa Cecilia Academy of Music, Rome, 1976–77. *Career:* Principal Flautist at State Opera House and Philharmonic Society, Wroclaw; Principal Solo Flute with Baltic Philharmonic Orchestra, Gdansk, 1974–; Assistant Professor of Flute, Academy of Music, Gdansk; Co-operates with Ensemble MW 2 Vanguard Group; Concerts in various countries including Austria, Germany, Greece, Norway, Sweden, Denmark, Netherlands, Belgium, the United Kingdom, Italy, Mexico, Spain, Luxemburg, Switzerland and France. *Recordings:* Numerous for Polish radio and television. *Current Management:* Polish Artists Agency, Warsaw, Poland. *Address:* ul Pawla Gdanca 4a-42, 80-336 Gdańsk, Poland.

**LANGRÉE, Louis;** French conductor; b. 1961, Mulhouse. *Career:* Music Director of the Orchestre de Picardie, 1993–98; Director of Opéra National de Lyon; Music Director of Glyndebourne Touring Opera, with Don Giovanni 1993, La Bohème 1995, Così fan tutte 1998, Pelléas et Mélisande 1999; Carmen and Fidelio, 2000–01; appearances with Netherlands Radio Philharmonic, Monte Carlo Orchestra, Orchestre de Paris, and Orchestre de la Suisse Romande; Netherlands Opera, Opéra National de Paris, Geneva Opera, and festivals at Drottningholm, Orange, Spoleto and New York (Mostly Mozart); London Proms debut 2000, with the Orchestra of the Age of Enlightenment, in Haydn's 44th Symphony and Beethoven's 8th; Season 2001–02 with Manon Lescaut in Geneva, Fidelio and Figaro at Glyndebourne 2001, Hamlet for the Royal Opera and Idomeneo at Glyndebourne 2002. *Recordings include:* Berlioz songs, with Veronique Gens; Mozart Arias with Natalie Dessay and the OAE. *Current Management:* Askonas Holt Ltd, Lonsdale Chambers, 27 Chancery Lane, London, WC2A 1PF, England. *Telephone:* (20) 7400-1700. *Fax:* (20) 7400-1799. *E-mail:* info@askonasholt.co.uk. *Website:* www .askonasholt.co.uk.

**LANGRIDGE, Philip (Gordon);** Singer (Tenor); b. 16 Dec. 1939, Hawkhurst, Kent, England; m. (1) 1 s., 2 d., (2) Ann Murray, 1981, 1 s. *Education:* ARAM, Royal Academy of Music, 1977. *Career:* Debut: Glyndebourne Festival in 1964; Sang at BBC Promenade Concerts, 1970–, Edinburgh Festival, 1970–, Netherlands Opera, Scottish Opera, Handel Opera and major opera houses in the United Kingdom and abroad; Concerts with major international orchestras and conductors including Boston with Previn, Chicago with Solti and Abbado, Los Angeles with Christopher Hogwood, Sydney with Mackerras, Vienna Philharmonic with Previn, Orchestre de Paris with Barenboim and Mehta and with all major British orchestras; Many first performances with some dedicated to or written for him; Has sung in Osud, Turn of the Screw, Mask of Orpheus, Don Giovanni, Fidelio, Idomeneo, The Rake's Progress, Wozzeck, Castor and Pollux, Rigoletto, Poppea, Lucio Silla, Rossini's Otello, La Donna del Lago, and Così fan tutte. Sang in the television production of Tippett's The Midsummer Marriage in 1989, in Mozart's Idomeneo in a new production at Covent Garden in 1989, Berlioz' Benedict for ENO in 1990, Idomeneo at the 1990 Salzburg Festival, Pelegrin in Tippett's New Year at Glyndebourne, Mozart's Titus at Glyndebourne and the Promenade Concerts in 1991; Season 1992–93 included Aschenbach in a new production of Death in Venice at Covent Garden and Nero in Poppea at Salzburg Festival; Sang in Stravinsky's Pulcinella at 1993 London Proms; Jupiter in Semele at Covent Garden, 1996; Captain Vere in Billy Budd at the Met, 1997; Mark in The Midsummer Marriage at Munich, 1998; Title role in Pfitzner's Palestrina, Covent Garden, 2001; Schoenberg's Gurrelieder at the London Proms, 2002; mem, Music Panel, Arts Council of Great Britain. *Recordings:* Over 50 records, including Moses and Aron. *Address:* c/o Allied Artists Agency, 42 Montpelier Square, London SW7 1JZ, England.

**LANKESTER, Michael;** Conductor, Musical Director and Professor of Conducting; b. 12 Nov. 1944, London, England. *Education:* Royal College of Music; ARCM; GRSM. *Career:* Musical Director, National Theatre, 1969–75, composing and conducting numerous items to accompany productions; Conductor, Surrey Philharmonic Orchestra, 1972–, and English Chamber Orchestra; Founder of Contrapuncti; Radio and television broadcasts for BBC and Collaborator with Young Vic Theatre in various productions; Conductor, Cheltenham Festival, Sadler's Wells Theatre and at opening of Royal Northern College of Music, 1973; Made orchestral suite of Britten's The Prince of the Pagodas, and conducted it at the 1979 Promenade Concerts; mem, Noise Abatement Society. *Recordings include:* Gordon Crosse, Purgatory, Ariadne. *Honours:* Watney/Sargent Conducting Scholarship, 1967.

**LANSKY, Paul;** Composer; b. 18 June 1944, New York, USA. *Education:* Studied with George Perle and Hugo Weisgall at Queen's College, New York, BA 1966; Princeton University with Milton Babbitt and Earl Kim, PhD 1969. *Career:* Teacher, Princeton University from 1969; Associate Editor of Perspectives of New Music, 1972. *Compositions:* Modal Fantasy for piano, 1969; String Quartet, 1972–77; Mild Und Leise for tape, 1974; Crossworks for piano and ensemble, 1975; Artifice, on Ferdinand's Reflections, for tape, 1976; Folk Images for tape, 1981; As If for string trio and Electronics, 1982; Folk Images and As It Grew Dark for tape, 1980–83; Electro-acoustic: Night Traffic, 1990; Now and Then, 1991; Word Color, 1992; Memory Pages, 1993; Thinking Back, 1996; For the Moment, 1997; Shadows, 1998. *Publications include:* Affine Music, dissertation, 1969. *Honours:* League of Composers ISCM electronic music award, 1975; Koussevitsky Foundation Award, 1981. *Address:* c/o ASCAP, ASCAP Building, 1 Lincoln Plaza, New York, NY 10023, USA.

**LANTOS, Istvan;** Pianist; b. 1949, Budapest, Hungary. *Education:* Studied piano under Mme Erzsebet Tusa, Budapest Bela Bartók Conservatory; Ferenc Liszt Academy of Music; Graduate with Distinction, Liszt Academy of Music. *Career:* Played solo part in Messiaen's Turangalîla Symphonie, Bayreuth International Youth Festival, 1970, Hitzacker Festival, Germany, and Bratislava International Rostrum of Young Artists; Numerous appearances in Hungarian concert halls and world-wide; Guest performances in eastern Europe and Cuba, Austria, the United Kingdom, Canada, Germany, Netherlands, Ireland, Italy and Switzerland; Has twice toured and held masterclasses in Japan; Soloist with Hungarian State Symphony Orchestra during USA tour; Has toured every 2nd year the major cities in Germany with Hungarian State Symphony Orchestra, 1972–; Also renowned organist; Assistant Professor, Budapest Liszt Academy of Music, 1974–.

**LANZA, Alcides Emigdio;** Canadian composer, pianist, conductor and university professor; b. 2 June 1929, Rosario, Argentina; 2 s., 2 d. *Education:* Centro Latino Americano de Altos Estudios Musicales Instituto Di Tella, Buenos Aires; Postgraduate Courses, Electronic Music, Columbia University, New York, USA; Studied Composition with Julián Bautista and Alberto Ginastera, Piano with Ruwin Erlich, Conducting with Roberto Kinsky; Further Instruction Courses with various noted artists. *Career:* Concert Tours of Europe, North and South America; Artistic Staff, Teatro Colón, Buenos Aires, 1959–65; Pianist, Lecturer and Conductor, Composers/Performers Group, touring Europe; Composer and Teacher, Columbia-Princeton Electronic Music Centre; Dir Emeritus of Electronic Music Studio and Prof. of Composition, McGill University, Montreal, Quebec, Canada, 1971–; Artistic Dir, Group GEMS (Group of the Electronic Music Studio). *Compositions include:* Módulos II, 1982; Módulos III, 1983; Sensors III, for organ and two percussionists, 1982; Eidesis VI, for string orchestra with piano, 1983; Interferences III, for chamber ensemble and electronic sounds, 1983; Acúfenos V, for trumpet, piano and electronic-computer tape, 1980; Ekphonesis VI, actress-singer tape, 1988;... there is a way to sing it... (solo tape), 1988; un mundo imaginario, choir and computer tape, 1989; Vôo, for voice, electro-acoustic music and digital signal processing, 1992; Ontem for voices, tabla, tape and digital signal processing, 1999; aXents, for chamber orchestra and tape, 2003. *Honours:* Hon. Diploma (High Distinction) awarded by OAS and Int. Centre for Music Education, 1996; Victor Martin Lynch-Staunton Award, for exceptional talent and achievements as a composer, 2003. *Current Management:* Shelan Concerts. *Address:* 6351 Trans Island Avenue, Montreal, QC H3W 3B7, Canada. *Telephone:* (514)7337216. *E-mail:* alcides@music.mcgill.ca. *Website:* www.music.mcgill.ca/~alcides.

**LAPERRIERE, Gaétan;** Canadian singer (baritone); b. 1959, Verdun, Montréal; m.; two s. *Education:* St Laurent Coll., studied with Robert Savoie. *Career:* sang in opera at Montréal from 1981, Canadian Opera at Toronto from 1986 as Gounod's Mercutio, Donizetti's Enrico, Mozart's Count 1991, and Raimbaud in Le Comte Ory 1994; performed the title role of Rigoletto at the Calgary Opera, Opéra de Quebec, Opéra-Théâtre de Metz, Opéra-Théâtre de Rennes, Kentucky Opera, New York City Opera; appeared as Renato in Verdi's Un Ballo Maschera at l'Opéra-Bastille de Paris, Opéra d'Avignon, Hong Kong Arts Festival, Opera Lyra at The Nat. Arts Center, Canada; Rodrigo in Don Carlos at Toronto, Montréal, Metz, Boston; US appearances at Washington as Bizet's Zurga, Miami as Hamlet, Boston as Enrico in Lucia di Lamermoor, and Houston (Marcello 1991); San Francisco and New York City 1991, as Germont; Toronto 1993, as Ford in Falstaff, and Montréal 1995, as de Siriex in Fedora; Mercutio at Dallas and Escamillo in Carmen at Metz 1996; sang Debussy's Golo at Bologna; Picariello in Estacio and Murrell's Filumena (world premiere) at Calgary Opera 2002; many concert performances. *Recordings include:* Great Baritone Arias, Les Septs Paroles du Christ, Grandes Voix du Québec, La Bohème (DVD). *Radio:* broadcasts of Romeo and Juliet, Les Dialogues des Carmélites. *Honours:* first prize Nat. Mozart Competition. *Address:* 889 Ninth Avenue, Suite 1, New York, NY 10019, USA (office); c/o Opéra de Montreal, 260 de Maisonneuve Boulevard W, Montréal, QC H2X 1Y9, Canada. *Telephone:* (212) 397-7926 (ext. 14) (office). *E-mail:* laperriere@distributel.net.

**LAPINSKAS, Darius;** Composer and Conductor; b. 9 March 1934, Kaunas, Lithuania; m. Laima Rastenis, 28 Nov 1970, 1 s. *Education:* South Boston High School; BA, Composition, Conducting, New England Conservatory, Boston, 1953–57; Akademie fuer Musik und Darstellende Kunst, Vienna, 1957–58; Musik Hochschule, Stuttgart, 1958–60. *Career:* Musikdirektor, Tuebingen Landestheatre, 1960–65; Kapelmeister, Staatsoper Stuttgart, 1961–65; Schiedsgericht, Composer-Conductor, Mainz television; Guest Conductor with Stuttgart Symphony Orchestra, Stuttgart Philharmonic, South German Radio Orchestra; Mannheim Opera Orchestra; National Symphony Orchestra of Bogotà, and Symphony Orchestra of Antioquia; Artistic Director of New Opera Company of Chicago. *Compositions:* Operas: Lokys, Maras, Amadar, Dux Magnus, Rex Amos; Ballet: Laima; Concerto for piano, strings and percussion; Concerto for violin and orchestra; Haiku, song cycle; Balyvera, song cycle for mezzo-soprano and orchestra; Les Sept Solitudes, aria for mezzo-soprano and orchestra; Ainiu Dainos, song cycle for voice and chamber orchestra. *Recordings:* Les Sept Solitudes; Ainiu Dainos; Mergaites Dalia. *Honours:* BML Prize for Composition, Boston, 1955; Wurttemberg Prize for Composition, 1961; Illinois Arts Council Grant for Composition, 1985, 1986. *Address:* 9368 South Longwood Drive, Chicago, IL 60620, USA.

**LAPLANTE, Bruno;** Singer; b. 1 Aug. 1938, Beauharnois, Quebec, Canada; 2 s. *Education:* 1st Prize in Vocal Art, Conservatoire de Musique du Québec, Montreal. *Career:* Debut: Cimarosa's The Secret Marriage in Germany; Under scholarships from Canada Arts Council, The Government of Quebec, private foundations and from Goethe Institute in Munich; Worked first in Germany, in Paris under the direction of Pierre Bernac and in Montreal with Lina Narducci; Numerous radio and television appearances including Susanna's Secret, Gounod's Romeo and Juliette, and Lehar's Merry Widow; Engagements with major Canadian Symphony Orchestras; Les Noces and Carmina Burana with Grands Ballets Canadiens; 30 concerts in Canada for Les Jeunesse Musicales du Canada; A film dealing with his career in the series, Les Nouveaux Interprètes; Stage appearances include Carmen, Il Trittico, Manon, Don Giovanni and many others; Regular tours throughout Europe for concerts and festivals including Festival du Marais, Paris, 1979 and 2 recitals at Festival International de Musique et d'Art Lyrique, Aix-en-Provence; mem, Union des Artistes de Montreal. *Recordings include:* Integrale des 15 Mélodies de Duparc; Mélodies de Lalo et de Bizet; Mélodies de Berlioz; Works by Offenbach, Jules Massenet, Reynaldo Hahn, Charles Gounod, and César Franck among others. *Honours:* Concours International de Genève, 1966, de Barcelona, 1966, de Montreal, 1967; Grand Prix du Disque, 1977.

**LAPORTE, André;** Composer; b. 12 July 1931, Oplinter, Belgium. *Education:* Studied at Catholic University of Louvain; Organ with Flor Peeters and counterpoint with Marinus de Jong, 1956–58. *Career:* Producer for Belgian Radio, 1963; Brussels Conservatory from 1968; Artistic Director of Belgian Radio Philharmonic Orchestra, 1989–96. *Compositions:* Piano Sonata, 1954; Psalm for 6 voices and brass, 1956; Jubilus for 12 brass instruments and 3 percussionists, 1966; Story for string trio and harpsichord, 1967; Ascension for piano, 1967; De Profundis for mixed choir, 1968; Le Morte Chitarre for tenor, flute and 14 strings, 1969; Night Music for orchestra, 1970; La Vita Non E Sogno for vocalists, chorus and orchestra, 1972; Peripetie for brass sextet; Chamber Music for soprano and ensemble, 1975; Transit for 48 strings, 1978; Das Schloss, opera in 3 acts after Kafka, 1986; Fantasia-Rondino for violin and orchestra, 1988; The Magpie On The Gallows, 1989. *Honours:* Lemmens-Tinel Award, 1958; Koopal Award from the Belgian Ministry of Culture, 1971 and 1976; Prix Italia, 1976. *Address:* c/o SABAM, Rue d'Arlon 75–77, 1040 Brussels, Belgium.

**LAPPALAINEN, Kimmo;** Singer (Tenor); b. 1944, Helsinki, Finland. *Education:* Sibelius Academy, 1966–68; Vocal studies with Fred Hustler in Lugano and Luigi Rici in Rome, 1969–70. *Career:* Finnish National Opera, Helsinki, 1968–72 and Stuttgart Opera from 1972; Sang at Glyndebourne Festival, 1972–74 as Pedrillo in Die Entführung and Idamantes in Idomeneo; Many performances at the Savonlinna Festival in Finland; Sang at Stuttgart in 1983 as Britten's Albert Herring; Also heard in concert. *Address:* c/o Finnish National Opera, Bailevardi 23–27, 00180 Helsinki 18, Finland.

**LAPTEV, Yuri;** Singer (Baritone) and Stage Director; b. 1955, Russia. *Education:* Graduated St Petersburg Conservatoire 1986. *Career:* Stage director at Kirov Opera, St Petersburg, from 1988; Head of Planning, 1991–; Director of the Welcome Back St Petersburg Gala at the Royal Opera House, 1992; Co-productions with the Kirov of Otello, Boris Godunov, The Fiery Angel, Le nozze di Figaro and War and Peace, Opera roles include Mozart's Almaviva, Valentin in Faust, Mathias in The Fiery Angel and Don Carlos in Prokofiev's Betrothal in a Monastery; Sang Captain Jacqueau in War and Peace with the Kirov at Covent Garden, 2000. *Recordings include:* at Covent Garden, 2000. *Recordings include:* The Maid of Pskov, The Fiery Angel, War and Peace, Khovanshchina. *Address:* c/o Kirov Opera, Mariinsky Theatre, Theatre Square, St Petersburg, Russia.

**LARA, Christian;** Singer (Tenor); b. 15 Aug. 1946, Merignac, France. *Education:* Studied in Bordeaux. *Career:* Sang at Lille Opéra, 1976–79 and studied further with Michel Sénéchal in Paris; Sang Juan in Don Quichotte at Venice in 1982, Rodolfo at Nantes, Cavaradossi at Avignon, Faust at Ghent and Antwerp; Theater des Westens, Berlin in 1987 as Sou-Chong in Das Land des Lächelns; Sang Faust at Cologne in 1989 and appeared in La Rondine at Tours in 1991; Concert repertoire includes Mendelssohn's 2nd Symphony; Sang Faust at Vienna in 1991, Ismaele in Nabucco at Karlsruhe, Samson at Besançon, Ruggero in La Rondine at Tours, Cavaradossi in Tosca at Angers, Don José in Carmen at Bregenz and Liège, and Florestan in Fidelio at Tours, all in 1991; In 1992 sang Oedipe Roi by Paul Bastide at Strasbourg, Andrei Khovansky at Strasbourg, Ismaele at Karlsruhe, Florestan at Angers, Don José at the Festival of Bregenz, Jean in Hérodiade at Liège, and in Vestale at Nantes; In 1993 sang Luigi in Il Tabarro at Tours, Jean at Toulon and in 1994 sang Des Grieux in Manon and Don José at Bordeaux. *Address:* 11 Rue Jean Jaurès, 33127 Martignas-sur-Jalle, France.

**LAREDO, Jaime;** Bolivian violinist; b. 7 June 1941, Cochabamba; m. Sharon Robinson. *Education:* studied violin with Antonio de Grassi and Frank Hauser in San Francisco, Josef Gingold and George Szell in Cleveland, and Ivan Galamian at the Curtis Inst., Philadelphia, USA. *Career:* orchestral debut San Francisco 1952; won Queen Elisabeth of the Belgians Competition 1959 and subsequently appeared with most major orchestras in Europe and America; New York debut Carnegie Hall 1960; London debut Albert Hall 1961; frequent visitor to summer festivals at Spoleto, Tanglewood, Hollywood Bowl, Ravinia, Marlboro and Edinburgh; repertoire ranges from Baroque to contemporary works; gave the premiere of Ned Rorem's Concerto; Dir, soloist, works with St Pauls and Scottish Chamber Orchestras; Dir Chamber Music at the 92nd Street NY series in New York; piano concerts worldwide with Joseph Kalichstein and Sharon Robinson as Kalichstein, Laredo, Robinson Trio 1977–. *Recordings include:* Trios by Mendelssohn, Brahms and Beethoven, Brahms Piano Quartets with Emanuel Ax, Isaac Stern, Yo-Yo Ma (Grammy Award). *Honours:* New York City Handel Medallion 1960, Stadium in La Paz named after him, Bolivian stamps with his portrait issued in his honour, Deutsche Schallplatten Prize. *Current Management:* Askonas Holt Ltd, Lonsdale Chambers, 27 Chancery Lane, London, WC2A 1PF, England. *Telephone:* (20) 7400-1700. *Fax:* (20) 7400-1799. *E-mail:* info@askonasholt.co.uk. *Website:* www.askonasholt.co.uk.

**LAREDO, Ruth,** BMus; concert pianist; b. 20 Nov. 1937, Detroit, MI, USA; m. 1960 (divorced 1974), one d. *Education:* Curtis Inst. of Music, under Rudolf Serkin. *Career:* debut, Carnegie Hall with New York Orchestra American Symphony under Leopold Stowkowski; Appeared at Carnegie Hall, the Kennedy Center, Library of Congress and the White House with orchestras the New York Philharmonic, Philadelpha and Cleveland Orchestras, Boston Symphony, St Louis Symphony, Detroit Symphony, National Symphony, the orchestras of Baltimore, Indianapolis, Houston, Buffalo and American Symphony; Participated in The Music from Marlboro Concerts from their inception 1965–; Performed at the Spoleto Festival USA 1983, 1985; Frequent Guest Artist with ensembles, The Tokyo and Shanghai Quartets; Tours with flautist Paula Robison. *Recordings:* Complete Works of Rachmaninov; Complete sonatas of Scriabin and works of Barber. *Contributions:* Columnist, Keyboard Classics Magazine; Editor, C F Peters Publishing Company. *Current Management:* Gutman & Murtha Associates, 450 Seventh Avenue, Suite 603, New York, NY 10123, USA.

**LARGE, Brian;** British musicologist, pianist, writer and television producer; b. 1937, London, England. *Education:* Royal Acad. of Music and London Univ. *Career:* producer of opera on BBC television with many other opera television engagements in Europe and the USA, including La Cenerentola (Houston Opera); TV Dir, La Bohème (Bregenz Festival) (Grand Prix Goldenes Prag Hauptpreis for live performance of opera 2003) 2002. *Publications:* books on Smetana, Martinů and Czech Opera; contrib. entry on Martinů to The New Grove Dictionary of Music and Musicians 1980.

**LARIN, Sergei;** Singer (Tenor); b. 1956, Daugavpils, Latvia. *Education:* Studied at the Vilnius Conservatory. *Career:* Early roles included Alfredo, Hermann and Vladimir in Prince Igor; Sang at Bratislava Opera from 1989 and guested at Dresden same year in Wagner-Régeny's Prometheus; Further appearances in Paris, at Monte Carlo as Don José and the Vienna Staatsoper as Lensky; Frankfurt 1993, as Sergei in Lady Macbeth of the Mtsensk District, La Scala 1993 as Don Carlo; Many appearances with the Kirov Opera, St Petersburg; Season 1996 with Loris in Fedora at La Scala and Don José at the Verona Arena; Sang Dick Johnson at Florence, Lensky at Turin and Don Carlos at the Salzburg Festival, 1998; Season 2000 as Don Carlos in Munich, Don José at the Vienna Staatsoper and Paolo in Francesca da Rimini at Buenos Aires; Engaged as Rienzi at the Vienna Staatsoper, 2003. *Address:* c/o Teatro alla Scala, Via Filodrammatici 2, 2 Milan 1021, Italy.

**LARMORE, Jennifer May,** BMus; American singer (mezzo-soprano); b. 21 June 1958, Atlanta, GA; d. of William C. Larmore and Eloise O. Larmore; m. William Powers 1980. *Education:* Sprayberry High School, Marietta, Ga, Westminster Choir Coll., Princeton, NJ. *Career:* operatic debut with L'Opéra de Nice, France 1985, debut with Metropolitan Opera, New York 1995, Salzburg Festival debut 1993, Tanglewood Festival debut 1998; specializes in music of the Bel Canto and Baroque Periods; Spokesperson and Fundraiser, US Fund for UNICEF 1998–. *Music:* over 40 recordings of operatic and solo repertoire; operatic appearances with most of the world's leading cos; recital appearances include Carnegie Hall, New York, Wigmore Hall, London, Musik Verein, Vienna, Concertgebauw, Amsterdam, Palais Garnier, Paris, L. G. Arts Center, Seoul, Teatro Colón, Buenos Aires, Teatro Liceo, Barcelona, Teatro Monnaie, Brussels, Arts Centre, Melbourne, etc. *Television:* appearances include Star Trek 30th Anniversary broadcast, live Christmas Eve service from St Patrick's Cathedral, numerous live broadcasts from the Metropolitan Opera, etc. *Achievements:* selected by the US Olympic Cttee to sing the Olympic Hymn for the closing of the Atlanta Olympic Summer Games 1996. *Honours:* William M. Sullivan Fellowship 1983, Maria Callas Vocal Competition, Barcelona 1984, McAllister Vocal Competition, Indianapolis 1986, Alumni Merit Award, Westminster Choir Coll. 1991, Gramophone Award for Best Baroque Album 1992, Richard Tucker Foundation Award, New York 1994. *Current Management:* ICM Foster Division, 40 W 57th Street, Floor 16, New York, NY 10019, USA. *Telephone:* (212) 556-5633 (office). *Fax:* (212) 556-6851 (office). *E-mail:* jenniferlarmore@aol.com (home).

**LARNER, Gerald;** Music Critic; b. 9 March 1936, Leeds, England; m. Celia Ruth Mary White, 2 d. *Education:* BA, New College, Oxford. *Career:* Assistant Lecturer, Manchester University, 1960–62; Member of the Guardian staff from 1962; Chief Northern music critic from 1965; Translated Wolf's Der Corregidor into English; Wrote libretto for John McCabe's The Lion, The Witch and The Wardrobe, 1971; Artistic Director, Bowden Festival, 1980–84; mem, Critics Circle. *Contributions:* Musical Times; The Listener. *Address:* 11 Higher Downs, Altrincham, Cheshire WA14 2QL, England.

**LARSEN, Libby (Brown);** Composer; b. 24 Dec. 1950, Wilmington, Delaware, USA. *Education:* Studied at the University of Minnesota with Dominick Argento. *Career:* Co-founded Minnesota (American) Composers Forum, 1973; Resident Composer with the Minnesota Orchestra, 1983–87 and Artistic Director of the Hot Notes series, 1993; Many commissions from leading orchestras and organizations; Has appeared widely as speaker and teacher. *Compositions include:* Operas: Frankenstein, The Modern Prometheus, music drama, 1990; A Wrinkle In Time, 1992; Mrs Dalloway, 1993; Symphony, Water Music, 1985; Piano Concerto, Since Armstrong, 1990; Ghosts Of An Old Ceremony for orchestra, 1991; Sonnets from the Portuguese for soprano and chamber orchestra, 1989; String Quartet: Schoenberg, Schenker and Schillinger, 1991; The Atmosphere As A Fluid System for flute, strings and percussion, 1992; Mary Cassatt form Mezzo, trombone and orchestra, 1994; Eric Hermannson's Soul, opera, 1997; String Symphony, 1998; Songs of Light and Love for soprano and chamber orchestra, 1998; Solo Symphony, 1999. *Recordings:* Missa Gaia, 1994; Dancing Solo, 1997; Water Music, London Symphony Orchestra, 1997. *Honours:* Grammy Award, 1994. *Address:* c/o ASCAP, ASCAP Building, 1 Lincoln Plaza, New York, Ny 10023, USA.

**LARSON, Lisa;** Singer (Soprano); b. 1964, Sweden. *Education:* Vocal studies in Zürich, after a career as flautist. *Career:* Major roles at the Zürich Opera studio followed by Barbarina in Figaro at the Opera in season, 1996–97; Schubert operas at Potsdam, Barbarina at Lausanne, Amor in Gluck's Orfeo at the Cologne Philharmonic and Papagena under Muti at the opening of the season at La Scala; Komische Oper Berlin, as Barbarina and Papagena, 1996; Adele at Ludwigsburg and Frasquita and Tebaldo at Hamburg; Oscar in Un Ballo in Maschera at Basle, 1997; Concerts include Stockholm Festival appearances with Gösta Winbergh and Messiah in Vienna and at the Vatican. *Recordings include:* Schubert operas; Orff's Trionfi, under Franz Welser-Möst; Schumann's Manfred, under Mario Vanzago; Royal Festival Concert, Stockholm, with Gösta Winbergh. *Address:* c/o Opernhaus Zürich, Falkenstrasse 1, 8008 Zürich, Switzerland.

**LARSON, Sophia;** Singer (Soprano); b. 1954, Linz, Austria; m. Hans Sisa. *Education:* Salzburg Mozarteum with Seywald-Baumgartner; Further study with Ettore Campogalliani. *Career:* Sang at St Gallen from 1976 as Verdi's Amelia Boccanegra, Mozart's Ilia, and Silvia in Mascagni's Zanetto; Sang at Ulm, 1979–80 as Fiordiligi, the Marschallin, Beethoven's Leonore and Katya Kabanova; Bremen, 1980–83, and guest at Hamburg, Stuttgart, Trieste and

Rome; Sang at Bologna in 1985 as the Duchess of Parma in Busoni's Doktor Faust, and Turin in 1986 as Puccini's Turandot and in Ghedini's Maria d'Alessandria; Further appearances in South America, Berlin, Berne, Wiesbaden and Bratislava; Bayreuth Festival, 1984–85 as Gutrune in The Ring, and Festival of Verona in 1986 as Minnie in La Fanciulla del West; Studio recordings for French and Italian Radio; Sang Venus in Tannhäuser at Bayreuth Festival in 1987, Gutrune in The Ring at Staatsoper Munich in 1987, Tosca at Turin in 1987, Isolde at Toronto in 1987, War Requiem at Carnegie Hall in 1988, Fedra by Pizzetti at Palermo in 1988, Renata in The Fiery Angel at Grand Théâtre Genève in 1988, Turandot at Zürich in 1988, Senta at Nice and San Francisco in 1988, Sieglinde in Die Walküre at Bayreuth Festival in 1989, Renata at Amsterdam in 1989, Lyrische Symphonie by Zemlinsky at Amsterdam in 1989, Brünnhilde at Linz Brucknerfestival in 1989, Fidelio at Catania in 1989 and Turandot and Tosca at Turin and Zürich in 1990; British debut as Turandot at the London Coliseum, 1995; Sang Leonore in Fidelio at Toronto, 1998. *Address:* c/o Opernhaus Zürich, Falkenstrasse 1, 8008 Zürich, Switzerland.

**LARSSON, Anders;** Swedish singer (baritone); b. 1965. *Education:* Royal Univ. Coll. of Music, Stockholm. *Career:* many appearances in Europe and North America, as Eugene Onegin at Spoleto, Debussy's Pelléas at Brussels, Mozart's Guglielmo and Rossini's don Alvaro at Gothenburg, Papageno for Värmlane Opera, Sweden, and Creon in Haydn's Orfeo at Enschede; Strauss's Harlekin for the Minnesota Symphony Orchestra, Marcello and the Count in Capriccio at Copenhagen; concerts include the Brahms Requiem and Mahler's Des Knaben Wunderhorn; Season 2001–02 with Count Almariva at Glyndebourne, Silvio in Pagliacci at Brussels and Eugene Onegin in Malmö. *Honours:* Christina and Birgit Nilsson Awards. *Current Management:* Ann Braathen Artist Management AB, Folskolegatan 5, 117 35 Stockholm, Sweden. *Telephone:* 8 556 908 50. *Fax:* 8 556 908 51. *E-mail:* info@braathenmanagement.com. *Website:* www.braathenmanagement.com.

**LARSSON, Anna;** Swedish singer (alto). *Education:* Opera Acad., Stockholm. *Career:* oratorio and concert performances include Des Knaben Wunderhorn with the Swedish Radio SO and Okku Kamu, Edin. Festival Orchestra and Esa-Pekka Salonen, Brahms' Alto Rhapsody with the Oslo Philharmonic and Paavo Berglund, Vienna Philharmonic and Seiji Osawa, Los Angeles Philharmonic and Rubin Mehta, Berlin Philharmonic and Claudio Abbado, Mahler's Second Symphony with Lucerne Festival Orchestra and Abbado, Mahler's Third Symphony with the Stockholm Philharmonic, Berlin Philharmonic and Abbado, Das Lied von der Erde with Tonhalle Orchestra and David Zinman, Dream of Gerontius with Chicago Symphony and Daniel Barenboim, Missa Solemnis with Boston SO and Osawa, London Philharmonic and Kurt Masur, Bach's Mass in B Minor with Gewanthaus Orchestra and Herbert Blomstedt, Verdi's Requiem with Munich Philharmonic and Lorin Maazel, St Matthew Passion with London Philharmonic and Masur, Messiah with New York Philharmonic and Sir Neville Marriner; operatic roles include Erda in Das Rheingold, Norn and Waltraute in Götterdämmerung, Orfeo in Orfeo and Euridice, Ottone in L'Incoronazione di Poppea, Andronico in Tamerlano. *Recordings:* Mahler, Second Symphony, Mahler, Third Symphony 1998, Unander-Scharin, Tokfursten 2000, Mahler, Symphony No. 8 2001, Beethoven, Missa Solemnis 2002, Mahler, Des Knaben Wunderhorn, Brahms, Choral Works Vol. 3 2004. *Current Management:* Anna Braathen Artist Management AB, Folskolegatan 5, Stockholm 117 35, Sweden. *Telephone:* (8) 556-908-50 (office). *Fax:* (8) 556-908-51 (office). *E-mail:* info@braathenmanagement.com (office). *Website:* www.braathenmanagement.com (office).

**LARSSON, Charlotte;** Singer (Soprano); b. 1966, Sweden. *Education:* Studied at the State Opera School in Stockholm from 1989. *Career:* Debut: Norrlandsoperan as Signe in Stenhammar's Gillet pa Solhaug; Concert appearances including opening of Århus Festival, 1991; Sang at Karlstad Opera Festival in 1992 and as Liu in Turandot for Stockholm Folkoperan in 1993; Other roles include Mozart's Pamina and Sandrina, Rosalinda and Dvořák's Rusalka; Engaged at Stockholm Royal Opera, 1994. *Address:* Nordic Artists Management, Sveavagen 76, 11359 Stockholm, Sweden.

**LASCARRO, Juanita;** Colombian singer (soprano); b. 1971, Bogotá. *Education:* studied in Bogotá, Cologne Musikhochschule with Hartmut Holl and Mitsuko Shirai. *Career:* British opera debut as Daphne at Garsington 1995; roles include Papagena (Cologne Opera), Peter Grimes (Cologne Opera), Amadis des Gaules (Markgräflichen Theater Bayreuth), Adina and Micaela (all at Teatro Colón Bogotá), Euridice in L'Orfeo (Netherlands Opera) 1996, (Barbican) 1998, Frasquita and First Flower Maiden (Opéra Bastille) 1997, Handel's Cantata Galatea e Polifemo (Beaune) 2000, Cavalli's Dido (Lausanne Opera and Montpellier) 2000, Susanna (Teatro Colón Bogotá, Opéra Bastille, Deutsche Oper Berlin), Janáček's Vixen (WNO) 2002, Mélisande (La Monnaie, Brussels), Weill's Der Kuhhandel (Barbican); season 2002–03 as Emma in Schubert's Fierrabras, Manon, Pamina, Lulu, Corinne (Viaggio), Juliette (Opera Frankfurt) and Leoncavallo's Mimi (Vienna). *Honours:* winner Leipzig Opera, Mendelssohn and Munchner Konzertgesellschaft Competitions 1992–93. *Current Management:* Harrison/Parrott Ltd, 12 Penzance Place, London, W11 4PA, England. *Telephone:* (20) 7229 9166. *Fax:* (20) 7221 5042. *Website:* www.harrisonparrott.com.

**LASKE, Otto,** BMus, MMus, PhD, EdD; composer, poet and musicologist; b. 23 April 1936, Olesnica, Oels, Silesia, Poland. *Education:* Akademie für Tonkunst, Darmstadt, New England Conservatory of Music, Boston, USA,

Goethe University, Frankfurt am Main, Germany, Harvard University, USA, Institute of Sonology, Utrecht, Netherlands. *Career:* debut, Composers' Forum, New York 1969; freelance composer; Prof. of Music; Artistic Dir, Newcomp Inc 1981–91. *Compositions:* 65 works for instrumental, vocal and electro-acoustic music including: Kyrie Eleison, a cappella, 1969, Distances and Proximities for tape, 1973, Perturbations for chamber orchestra, 1979, Terpsichore for tape, 1980, Soliloquy for double bBass, 1984, Furies And Voices, 1989, Treelink for tape, 1992. *Publications:* Music, Memory and Thought 1977, Understanding Music with Al (co-ed.) 1992. *Address:* 83 Appleton Street, Arlington, MA 02174, USA.

**LASSEN, Morten Ernst;** Singer (Baritone); b. 1969, Denmark. *Education:* Diploma, Royal Danish Academy of Music, with Professor Kirsten Buhl-Míller, 1996. *Career:* Debut: Papageno with The Young Operacompagnie, 1993; Sang Bach's B minor Mass, St John and St Matthew Passions, as Jesus and the bass arias; Fauré's Requiem, Handel's Messiah, Mahler's Des Knaben Wunderhorn; Concerts with MDR-Sinfonieorchester, Berliner Symfoniker, Deutsches Symfonie Orchester Berlin, Danish Radio Orchestras; Several radio and television productions; Appearances in festivals of modern music, including Davos Musikfestival with works by Kurt Weill and Ernst Krenek; Season 1996–97, Sang Masetto at Confidencen in Stockholm, and sang at Tiroler Landestheater at Innsbruck as Dandini in Cenerentola and in Willi's Schlafes Bruder; Season 1999–2000 at Deutsche Oper Berlin, Papageno in Die Zauberflöte, Sharpless in Madama Butterfly, Schaunard in La Bohème, Masetto in Don Giovanni, Dancairo in Carmen and Bill in Mahagonny; Concert engagements include appearances with the Danish symphony orchestras and bass part in B minor Mass with Danish Radio Symfony Orchestra conducted by Herbert Blomstedt; Several recitals in Denmark and abroad. *Honours:* Carl Nielsen Travel Scholarship, 1996; EBU Competition Winner, 1997; Prize Winner, VII International Hugo Wolf Lieder Competition, Stuttgart; Aksel Schiotz Prize, 1997. *Current Management:* IMG Artists. *Address:* c/o IMG Artists, Lovell House, 616 Chiswick High Road, London W4 5RX, England.

**LASSMANN, Peep;** Pianist; b. 19 March 1948, Tartu, Estonia; m. Anne Lassmann, 5 Nov 1982, 1 s. *Education:* Tallinn Conservatory, 1966–71; Pianist Diploma, Moscow Conservatory, postgraduate studies, 1971–73. *Career:* Teacher, 1973; Associate Professor, 1985; Head of Piano Department, 1987; Professor and Prorector, 1991; Rector of Tallinn Conservatory, 1992 (since 1993 Estonian Academy of Music); Many Concert Tours in 23 Countries; Recent Recitals, Complete Piano Works of Messiaen; mem, Estonian Piano Teachers Association (President); Music Council of Estonia, (President). *Recordings:* E Tubin Concertino for piano and orchestra, A Rubinstein Sextet for piano and wind instruments; Many recordings in Estonian, Swedish and Moscow Radios. *Contributions:* Numerous articles in various Estonian newspapers and magazines. *Honours:* Various Prizes and Diplomas from The Competitions of Pianists of USSR; The Musician of the Year 1989 of the Estonian Radio Merited Artist of Estonia, 1987. *Address:* Trummi 23–26, Tallinn 200026, Estonia.

**LASZLO, Magda;** Singer (Soprano); b. 1919, Hungary. *Education:* Studied at Franz Liszt Academy, Budapest with Irene Stoasser and Ferenc Szekelyhedi. *Career:* Debut: Budapest in 1943 as Elisabeth in Tannhäuser and Amelia in Simon Boccanegra; Resident in Rome from 1946; Sang in the radio and stage premieres of Dallapiccola's Il Prigioniero in 1949 and 1950; Sang further in modern works by Ghedini, Casella, Lualdi and Malipiero; Guest appearances in Austria, Germany, France, Netherlands and Switzerland; Covent Garden in 1954 as Cressida in the premiere of Walton's Troilus and Cressida; Glyndebourne, 1953–54, 1962–63 as Mozart's Cherubino, Gluck's Alceste and as Monteverdi's Poppea; Other roles were Marie in Wozzeck, Wagner's Isolde and Senta, Strauss's Daphne, Busoni's Turandot, Alfano's Sakuntala, Prokofiev's Renata, Handel's Agrippina, Roxana in King Roger, Gluck's Elena and Bellini's Norma. *Recordings:* Bach Cantatas and St Matthew Passion; L'Incoronazione di Poppea.

**LATARCHE, Vanessa Jayne,** FTCL, LRAM, ARCM; British pianist and teacher; b. 3 April 1959, Isleworth, Middlesex, England. *Education:* Royal College of Music, studied with Kendall Taylor. *Career:* broadcasts for Radio 3, BBC television and Cable television in USA; Piano Teacher at Purcell School and Royal College of Music, Junior Department; Performed at Harrogate International Festival, Battle Festival, various music clubs and concert halls throughout the United Kingdom including Fairfield Halls, Croydon, Purcell Room and Queen Elizabeth Hall and Wigmore Hall, London; Recital and concerto appearances; Director of Latarche Trio. *Address:* 10 Ravenswood Gardens, Isleworth, Middlesex TW7 4JG, England.

**LATCHEM, Malcolm,** ARCM; British violinist; b. 28 Jan. 1931, Salisbury; m. 1964; one s. three d. *Education:* Royal Coll. of Music. *Career:* Philharmonia Orchestra, 1960–65; Sub-Leader, London Philharmonic Orchestra, 1965–69; Dartington String Quartet, 1969–80; Founder Member, 1959, Acad. of St Martin-in-the-Fields. *Recordings:* Chamber music with Acad. of St Martin-in-the-Fields Chamber Ensemble; Handel Trio Sonatas; Mozart's Divertimenti; Spohr's Double Quartets; other chamber music. *Honours:* Hon. MMus (Bristol Univ. 1980). *Address:* Station House, Staverton, Totnes, Devon TQ9 6AG, England. *Telephone:* (1803) 762670.

**LATEINER, Jacob;** Pianist; b. 31 May 1928, Havana, Cuba. *Education:* Studied in Havana with Jascha Fischermann, 1934–40 and Curtis Institute from 1940 with Isabelle Vengerova; Studied chamber music with Piatigorsky

and Primrose. *Career:* Debut: With the Philadelphia Orchestra under Ormandy in 1945; Tanglewood Festival with Koussevitsky in 1947; New York recital debut in 1948; Tours of Europe, USA and Australia from 1954; Premiered the Concerto by Elliott Carter in 1967 and the Third Sonata of Roger Sessions in 1968; Taught at Mannes College, 1963–70, and Juilliard School, NY, from 1966. *Recordings:* Works by Beethoven and other 19th Century repertory; Contemporary American works. *Address:* Juilliard School of Music, Piano Faculty, Lincoln Plaza, New York, NY 10023, USA.

**LATHAM, Alison Mary,** BMus; British editor and writer; b. (Alison Mary Goodall), 13 July 1948, Southsea; m. Richard Latham; three s. *Education:* The Maynard School, Exeter, Birmingham Univ. *Career:* Sr Copy Ed., The New Grove Dictionary of Music and Musicians 1971–77; Asst Ed., The Grove Concise Dictionary of Music 1986–88; Co-Ed., The Musical Times 1977–88; Publications Ed., Royal Opera House, Covent Garden 1989–2000; Ed., Edinburgh Festival programmes 2003–; mem. Royal Soc. of Arts, Royal Musical Asscn, Soc. of Authors, Critics Circle. *Publications:* The Cambridge Music Guide (with Stanley Sadie) 1985, Verdi in Performance (ed. with Roger Parker) 2001, The Oxford Companion to Music (ed.) 2002, Sing Ariel: Essays and Thoughts for Alexander Goehr's Seventieth Birthday (ed.) 2003, The Oxford Dictionary of Musical Terms 2004, The Oxford Dictionary of Musical Works 2004. *Address:* c/o Joanna Harris, Oxford University Press, Walton Street, Oxford, OX2 6DP, England (office). *Telephone:* (1865) 556767 (office). *Fax:* (1865) 354635 (office). *E-mail:* joanna.harris@oup.com (office). *Website:* www.oup.com (office).

**LATHAM, Catherine;** Oboe d'amore player; b. 1965, England. *Education:* Guildhall School of Music, London. *Career:* concerts with the European Baroque Orchestra, 1985–86, under Ton Koopman, William Christie and Roger Norrington: Regular appearances with the London Handel Orchestra (Flavio and Muzio Scevola, 2001); The King's Consort, and the Orchestra of the Age of Enlightenment; Concerto performances in Edinburgh, Dublin, Utrecht and the Wigmore Hall, London; Tour of Europe in John Eliot Gardiner's Bach Cantata Pilgrimage, 2000; Handel's Amadigi with The New Chamber Opera at New College, Oxford, 2001. *Recordings include:* Bach Brandenburg Concertos, Concertos for 2 oboes by Vivaldi and Albinoni. *Address:* c/o The King's Consort, 34 St Mary's Grove, London W4 3LN, England.

**LATHAM-KOENIG, Jan;** British conductor and pianist; *Music Director, Teatro Massimo, Palermo;* b. 15 Dec. 1953, London, England. *Education:* Royal Coll. of Music with Norman del Mar, Kendall Taylor and Lamar Crowson. *Career:* regular appearances as conductor with Royal Philharmonic, Philharmonia, London Philharmonic, BBC Symphony, BBC Philharmonic Orchestra and BBC Nat. Orchestra of Wales; guest conductor Los Angeles Philharmonic and St Paul Chamber Orchestras, the Danish and Swedish Radio Orchestras, Stockholm Philharmonic, Maggio Musicale Orchestras, RAI, Italy, Zürich Tonhalle and the Gulbenkian Orchestra in Lisbon; founded the Koenig Ensemble 1976; concert pianist until 1981; opera engagements include Giulio Cesare with Royal Swedish Opera 1985, La Vestale at Genoa 1984, From the House of the Dead at Venice 1985–86, Tosca for ENO 1987, The Cunning Little Vixen at Vienna Volksoper 1992; festival appearances with La Straniera at Wexford 1987, Manon and Macbeth at Macerata 1987–88, world premiere of L'Ispirazione by Bussotti at Maggio Musicale 1988, and Catalani's Dejanice at Lucca; has conducted Szymanowski's King Roger for Danish Radio and a cycle of Weill operas and cantatas for West German Radio; Rome Opera 1988 with the premiere of Bussotti's Fedra returning with Donizetti's Poliuto to open the 1988–89 season; debut at Vienna Staatsoper 1988 in Macbeth; conducted Leoncavallo's La Bohème at Venice 1990 and Weill's Mahagonny at the 1990 Maggio Musicale Florence; permanent guest conductor Vienna State Opera from 1991; conducted Aida at Covent Garden 1996; Danish premiere of Poulenc's Carmélites 1997 and at the London Prom concerts 1999; Jenůfa at Santiago 1998; Music Dir, Teatro Massimo, Palermo 2005–. *Recordings include:* Weill's Mahagonny with Anja Silja, Der Zar Lässt sich Photographieren, Walton Concertos with London Philharmonic Orchestra. *Current Management:* Askonas Holt Ltd, Lonsdale Chambers, 27 Chancery Lane, London, WC2A 1PF, England. *Telephone:* (20) 7400-1700. *Fax:* (20) 7400-1799. *E-mail:* info@askonasholt.co.uk. *Website:* www.askonasholt.co.uk. *Address:* Teatro Massimo, Piazza G. Verdi, 90138 Palermo, Italy. *Website:* www.teatromassimo.it.

**LATRY, Olivier;** French organist; b. 22 Feb. 1962, Boulogne-sur-Mer; m. Marie-Therese; three c. *Education:* Saint Maur-des-Fossés Conservatoire with Gaston Litaize, Paris Conservatoire with Jean-Claude Raynaud. *Career:* organiste titulaire, Meaux Cathedral 1981–85; organiste titulaire du grand orgue, Cathédrale Notre-Dame de Paris 1985–; teacher of organ, Conservatoire at St Maur-des-Fossés 1990–95; Organ Prof., Paris Conservatoire 1995–; recitals in Europe, Russia, N and S America, Japan and Australia, concentrating on 17th- to 20th-century French organ music; renowned for improvisation. *Recordings include:* music of J S Bach, the complete organ works of Maurice Duruflé, Louis Vierne's Symphonies 2 and 3, Widor's Symphonies 5 and 6, Boëllmann's Suite Gothique, works by Litaize, the complete organ works of Olivier Messiaen, transcriptions for the organ ('Midnight at Notre-Dame'). *Honours:* Prix de la Fondation Cino et Simone del Duca 2000. *Address:* c/o Cathédrale Notre-Dame de Paris, Ile de la Cité 6, Place du Parvis, 75004 Paris, France (office).

**LAUBENTHAL, Horst;** Singer (Tenor); b. 8 March 1939, Duderstadt, Germany; m. Marga Schiml. *Education:* Studied in Munich with Rudolf Laubenthal. *Career:* Debut: Würzburg, 1967, as Mozart's Don Ottavio; Staatsoper Stuttgart from 1968, in operas by Wagner, Mozart and Beethoven; Guest appearances in Vienna, Hamburg and Barcelona; Bayreuth Festival, 1970, as the Steersman in Der fliegende Holländer; Deutsche Oper Berlin, as Lensky in Eugene Onegin and Pfitzner's Palestrina; Glyndebourne, 1972, as Belmonte in Die Entführung; Paris Opéra, 1977; Turin, 1985, as Tamino in Die Zauberflöte (returned 1987, as Don Ottavio); Often heard as the Evangelist in the Passions of Bach. *Recordings:* Tannhäuser, Fidelio, Die Meistersinger; Wozzeck and Lulu; Bach Cantatas and Christmas Oratorio; Trionfi by Orff; Konrgold's Violanta; Schubert's Lazarus.

**LAUBER, Anne (Marianne);** Composer and Conductor; b. 28 July 1943, Zürich, Switzerland. *Education:* Studied at the Lausanne Conservatory and the University of Montreal, 1973–77, with André Prevost. *Career:* Teacher at French-language universities in Canada and president of the Canadian Music Centre from 1987; Commissions from leading orchestras and soloists. *Compositions include:* Au-Dela Du Mur Du Son, symphonic tale, 1983; Concertos for string quartet, 1983, Violin, 1986, and Piano, 1988; Le Songe for flute and string quartet, 1985; Jesus Christus, oratorio, 1986; Piano Quintet, 1989; Requiem, 1989; Canadian Overture, for strings, 1989; Other vocal music. *Address:* c/o Canadian Music Centre, 20 St Joseph Street, Toronto, Ontario M4Y 1J9, Canada.

**LAUFER, Beatrice;** Composer; b. 27 April 1923, New York City, USA. *Education:* Studied at Juilliard School from 1944 with Roger Sessions, Marion Bauer and Vittorio Giannini. *Career:* Performances of her music in Germany, Stockholm, China and USA. *Compositions include:* 2 Symphonies, 1944 and 1961; Opera Ile, after O'Neill's Long Voyage Home, premiered at Stockholm in 1958, revived at Yale School of Music under Phylis Curtin in 1977 and at Shanghai in 1988; Violin Concerto; Concerto for flute, oboe trumpet and strings, 1962; Lyric for string trio, 1966; The Great God Brown, ballet, 1966; My Brother's Keeper, biblical opera, 1968; Adam's Rib for soloists, chorus and orchestra; Concertante for violin, viola and orchestra, 1986; Choral music. *Address:* c/o ASCAP, ASCAP Building, 1 Lincoln Plaza, New York, NY 10023, USA.

**LAUGHLIN, Roy;** conductor and pianist; b. 1954, Belfast, Northern Ireland. *Education:* Edinburgh and Durham Univs. *Career:* conducted Haydn's L'Infedeltà Delusa at Durham; Head of Music with Opera North, conducting The Magic Flute, Orpheus in The Underworld, La Cenerentola and Der Freischütz; Twice Chorus Master at Wexford Festival and conducted Die Schöpfung in 1989; Assistant Conductor of Halifax Choral Society; Recent engagements with Opera North include Fidelio, The Pearl Fishers, Peter Grimes and the British premiere production of Verdi's Jérusalem in 1990, also La Traviata, Attila and Faust; Season 1992–93 with Falstaff for English Touring Opera and Cimarosa's Secret Marriage for the Cheltenham and Buxton Festivals; Led British Youth Opera in La Bohème, 1998. *Current Management:* Robert Gilder & Co., Enterprise House, 59–65 Upper Ground, London, SE1 9PQ, England. *Telephone:* (20) 7928-9008. *Fax:* (20) 7928-9755. *E-mail:* rgilder@robert-gilder.com.

**LAUKKA, Raimo;** Singer (Baritone); b. 1954, Finland. *Education:* Studied in Helsinki. *Career:* Sang with Finnish National Opera from 1989, as Mozart's Figaro, Count, Don Giovanni, Guglielmo and Papageno; Posa in Don Carlos, 1995–96, Germont, Eugene Onegin, Gounod's Valentin in Faust, Donner in Das Rheingold (1996), Escamillo and Marcello; Tampere, 1996, in the title role of Dallapiccola's Il Prigioniero; Savonlinna Festival, 1996, as Wolfram in Tannhäuser and Carlo in La Forza del Destino, 1998; Concert tours include USA, 1988, with Neeme Järvi; London Proms, 2002. *Recordings include:* Kullervo by Sibelius. *Address:* c/o Finnish National Opera, PO Box 176, Helsingkatu 58, 00251 Helsinki, Finland.

**LAUKVIK, Jon;** Norwegian organist, harpsichordist and composer; *Professor of Organ and Historical Keyboard Instruments, University of Music, Stuttgart;* b. 16 Dec. 1952, Oslo. *Education:* Conservatory of Oslo, Musikhochschule, Cologne with Prof. M. Schneider, Prof. H Ruf, studied with M. C. Alain, Paris. *Career:* debut, Oslo 1973; recitals in Western and Eastern Europe, Israel, Japan, Korea and USA; currently Prof. of Organ and Historical Keyboard Instruments, Univ. of Music, Stuttgart, and Prof. of Organ, Norwegian Acad. of Music, Oslo; recordings for several European radio stations; masterclasses; jury mem. for int. competitions. *Compositions:* Via Crucis, Triptychon, Suite for organ, Anrufung for two organs, tape and brass, Euphonie I for organ and five percussionists, Euphonie III for cello and organ, Contre-danse for orchestra. *Recordings:* Neresheim Monastery (works by J. S. and C. P. E. Bach, Raison, Kittel). *Publications:* Orgelschule zur historischen Aufführungspraxis (trans. as Historical Performance Practice in Organ Playing) 1990, G. F. Handel: Organ Concertos op 7 and Nos 13–16 (with W. Jacob) 1990, Orgel und Orgelmusik in der Romantik 2000. *Honours:* first prize and Bach Prize Int. Organ Week, Nuremberg 1977. *Address:* Alte Weinsteige 20, 70180 Stuttgart, Germany. *Website:* www.laukvik.de.

**LAURENCE, Elizabeth;** English/French singer (mezzo-soprano); b. (Elizabeth Scott), 22 Nov. 1949, Harrogate, Yorkshire, England. *Education:* Princess Helena Coll., Herts, Colchester School of Art and Trinity Coll. of Music, London. *Career:* Vienna in Le Marteau sans Maître under Boulez 1983; further concerts with Barenboim, Casadesus, Downes, Myrat, Jordan and Zender; recording for French television, L'Heure Espagnole by Ravel 1985–86;

sang at Madrid Opera as Jocasta in Oedipus Rex 1986, also in Buffalo, USA with M. Valdes 1991, Paris Opéra as Erda in Siegfried and as Cherubino in Le nozze di Figaro, returning for the 1989 world premiere of Der Meister und Margarita by Höller; sang in the world premiere of The Electrification of the Soviet Union by Nigel Osborne, Glyndebourne Festival 1987; tour of Italy and Germany with Ensemble Intercontemporain 1987, in Le Marteau sans maître and Matchavarian ballet music, Pierrot Lunaire, Proms 1987; sang in the premiere of Boulez's revised version of Le Visage Nuptial, La Scala, Milan 1988; sang Fricka in Das Rheingold at Salle Pleyel, Paris 1988, and Schoenberg's Op 22 songs and Mahler's 3rd Symphony in Turin under Lothar Zagrosek and Rudolf Barshai; Covent Garden debut in the British premiere of Berio's Un Re in Ascolto 1989, La Bastille Opéra, Paris 1991; appeared as Judith in a BBC TV production of Bartók's Bluebeard's Castle 1989; contemporary recital of Berio, Bartók, Britten, Reger and Schoenberg at Festival of Montreux; Gurrelieder at Leeds Town Hall 1989; sang Erda in Rheingold at Bonn Opera 1990, Ligeti's Requiem in Belgium and Germany 1991; sang and recorded Le Rossignol, Stravinsky, for the Proms with Boulez; sang Lady de Hautdesert in the premiere of Birtwistle's Gawain at Covent Garden 1991; season 1991–92 as Ravel's Concepcion at Turin and the Duchess of Alba in the premiere of Osborne's Terrible Mouth at the Almeida Theatre; Verdi Requiem, London 1992; season 1993, Die Wuste bat zwolf Ding, Zender, Berlin Opera (concert), Folksongs by Berio, Ulisse by Dallapiccola, Salzburg Festival; season 1994, The Page in Salome, Opéra de Marseille, toured Germany in Pulcinella by Stravinsky, Orchestre de Paris; season 1996, toured France in Pelléas et Mélisande by Debussy, Flora in La Traviata, Marseille Opera, Salzburg Festival with Ravel's Trois Poèmes de S. Mallarmé, L'Enfance du Christ by Berlioz in Malaga, Spain; French premiere of Gurlitt's Wozzeck in Rouen and Caen Opéras; Schoenberg recital, Academia S. Caecilia, Rome; Japanese premiere of Bluebeard's Castle by Bartók in Tokyo conducted by Peter Eötvös; debut at Théâtre Champs Elysées, Paris, with Les Nuits d'été by Berlioz; Stabat Mater by Rossini in Imola; season 1997, Drei Lieder by Stockhausen at Concertgebouw, Amsterdam; Sechs Gesänge by Zemlinsky with Vienna Philharmonic; Second Symphony by L. Bernstein; Das Lied von der Erde Kindertotenlieder; concert of symphonic music 1998, Die Mutter in Lulu, Paris Bastille Opéra; La madre in Nono's Al gran sole carico d'amore, Hamburg Staatsoper; Ommou in Hölszky's Die Wände, Frankfurt Staatsoper; debut as Mère Marie in Les Dialogues des Carmelites at La Scala, Milan; Leucade: L. Martin Toulouse/Nice; premiered Bluebeard's Castle in Tbilisi, Georgia; also Phaedra: Britten; sang Rückert Lieder and Act 3 of Die Walküre in BBC Proms, London 2001; Rihm: Die Eröberung von Mexico under M. Stentz at Frankfurt Staatsoper 2001–02; Geneviève in Pelléas et Mélisande, De Vlaamse Opera, Antwerp 2001; Gertrude in A. Thomas' Hamlet for Chelsea Opera Group; Bluebeard's Castle for Graz Opera 2001; regular recitals in Europe; season 2002, Erwartung SWF Saarbrücken; Rihm's Dies; Henze's The Bassarids, Amsterdam; Henze's We Come to the River, Hamburg Staatsoper; Monleone's Cavelleria Rusticana, Schmidt's Mascagni and Notre Dame at Festival Montpellier; Frau ohne Schatten, Der Rosenkavalier and Lulu at Opéra Bastille; concert of Berio in Milan; recital of Schoenberg with Jay Gottlieb; Falstaff with NSO, UK 2004; has given masterclasses in France and the UK. *Television:* numerous TV recordings, including educational programmes on 20th century music, P. Boulez, D. Masson. *Recordings include:* Le Marteau sans Maître, Le Visage Nuptial, Bartók's Bluebeard's Castle, Gurlitt's Wozzeck, L'Heure Espagnole, Stravinsky's Le Rossignol. *Honours:* Diapason d'or, Prix d'Italia 1988, Grand Prix du Syndicat de la Presse 1997–98. *Current Management:* Robert Gilder & Co., Enterprise House, 59–65 Upper Ground, London, SE1 9PQ, England. *Telephone:* (20) 7928-9008. *Fax:* (20) 7928-9755. *E-mail:* rgilder@robert-gilder.com. *Address:* 123 rue de Grenelle, 75007 Paris, France (home). *Telephone:* 1 47 05 01 27 (home). *Fax:* 1 47 05 57 93 (home). *E-mail:* elizabethlaurence@yahoo.co.uk (home).

**LAURENS, Guillemette;** Singer (Mezzo-soprano); b. 1950, Fontainebleau, France. *Education:* Studied at the Toulouse Conservatoire and the Paris Opéra Studio. *Career:* Debut: Paris Salle Favart as Anne Trulove in The Rake's Progress; Has performed throughout Europe, the USA and South America; Sang Cybele in Lully's Atys at the Paris Opéra with Les Arts Florissants; Repertoire includes German Lieder, French and Italian Baroque chamber music, Pierrot Lunaire by Schoenberg, La Clemenza di Tito, Giulio Cesare, and I Puritani (Paris Opéra); Appeared with Capriccio Stravagante in America in 1989; Engagements with the Ensemble Sequentia in 12th Century Liturgical Drama; Sang at the Festival of Aix-en-Provence in Iphigénie en Aulide, with John Eliot Gardiner, and Towards Bach concert series on London's South Bank in 1989; Monteverdi's Penelope at the 1998 Vienna Festival. *Recordings:* Monteverdi's Vespers with Philippe Herreweghe; Atys and Il Ballo dell'Ingrate, conducted by William Christie; Bach's B minor Mass with Gustav Leonhardt; Charpentier's Le Malade Imaginaire under Marc Minkowski; Diana in Iphigénie en Aulide under John Eliot Gardiner. *Address:* Opéra et Concert, 1 Rue Volney, F–75002, Paris, France.

**LAURIE, Alison Margaret,** MA, BMus, PhD, ARCM; British music librarian and musicologist; b. 5 Jan. 1935, Glossop. *Education:* Beacon School, Bridge of Allan, Stirlingshire, Glasgow Univ., Univ. of Cambridge. *Career:* Sr Asst Librarian, Glasgow Univ. Library 1961–63; Music Librarian, Reading Univ. Library 1963–99; mem. Purcell Soc. Cttee (sec. 1983–88, chair. 1989–), Royal Musical Asscn. *Publications:* Purcell: Dioclesian 1961, Dido and Aeneas (with Thurston Dart) 1961, King Arthur 1971, Secular Songs for Solo Voice 1985, The Indian Queen 1994, The Gresham Autograph (facsimile edn introduction with Robert Thompson) 1995, Dramatic Music, Part 1; contrib. to Musik in Geschichte und Gegenwart 1973, New Grove Dictionary of Music and Musicians 1980, Music and Bibliography: Essays in Honour of Alec Hyatt King 1980, Source Material and the Interpretation of Music: a Memorial Volume to Thurston Dart 1981, Music in Britain: The Seventeenth Century 1992, Henry Purcell, Dido and Aeneas: an Opera 1986, Purcell Studies 1995, contrib. to periodicals, including Brio, Fontes Artis Musicae, Irish Musical Studies, Musical Times, Proceedings of the Royal Musical Association. *Address:* 123 Nightingale Road, Woodley, Reading, RG5 3LZ, England (home). *Telephone:* (118) 9696313 (home).

**LAVENDER, Justin;** Singer (tenor); b. 4 June 1951, Bedford, England. *Career:* Debut: Sang Nadir in Les Pêcheurs de perles at Sydney Opera House, 1982; Has sung Medoro in Haydn's Orlando Paladino at St Gallen, Tamino at Vienna Staatsoper, Pilade (Rossini's Ermione) at Madrid, Le Comte Ory at La Scala, Don Ottavio for Rome Opera and Arnold (Guillaume Tell) and Almaviva at Covent Garden; Appearances in premieres of Il Ritorno di Casanova by Arrigo at the Grand Théâtre Geneva and La Noche Triste by Prodomidès at Théâtre des Champs Elysées, Paris; Further engagements as Fernande in La Favorite at Vichy, Almaviva at Pittsburgh (US debut), Belmonte in Vienna and Berlin, Ferrando (Così fan tutte) at Essen, Lindoro at Buxton Festival and Neocles in Le Siège de Corinthe by Rossini at Madrid and the Festival Hall, London; Season 1993 in Il Pirata at Lausanne, Marzio in Mitridate and Arone in Mosè in Egitto at Covent Garden; Sang Don José in Raymond Gubay's Carmen, Albert Hall, 1997; Gluck's Admeto at Drottningholm, 1998; Concert repertoire includes Bartók's Cantata Profana with Georg Solti, Schubert's Mass in E flat with Giulini and Berlin Philharmonic, Schnittke's Faust Cantata under Claudio Abbado and Oedipus Rex conducted by Bernard Haitink; Mahler's 8th Symphony at the Royal Albert Hall, 2001; Season 2000 as the Duke of Mantua for Florida Opera, the Berlioz Faust in Helsinki and Count Hugo in Spohr's Faust at Cologne; Other conductors have included John Lubbock (Dream of Gerontius), John Pritchard, Menuhin, Alberto Zedda and Leonard Slatkin;. *Contributions:* The Singer, Rhinegold Publications. *Current Management:* Athole Still International Management, Forresters Hall, 25–27 Westow Street, London, SE19 3RY, England. *Telephone:* (20) 8771-5271. *Fax:* (20) 8768-6600. *Website:* www.atholestill.com.

**LAVIRGEN, Pedro;** Singer (Tenor); b. 31 July 1930, Bujalance, Andalusia, Spain. *Education:* Studied with Miguel Barrosa in Madrid. *Career:* Debut: Mexico City in 1964 as Radames; European debut at the Teatro del Liceo, Barcelona as Don José; Sang at Metropolitan in 1969 as Cavaradossi in Tosca, Verona Arena in 1974 and 1976 as Radames, Covent Garden in 1975 and 1978 as Don José and Pollione in Norma, La Scala Milan in 1975 as Don José repeating the role at the 1978 Edinburgh Festival; Other appearances in Hamburg, Munich, Prague, Budapest and Madrid. *Recordings include:* Il Retablo de Maese Pedro by De Falla.

**LAVISTA, Mario;** Composer; b. 3 April 1943, Mexico City. *Education:* Studied composition with Carlos Chávez, musical analysis with Rodolfo Halffter, National Conservatory of Mexico, 1963–67; Studied in Paris with Jean Etienne Marie, in Cologne with K Stockhausen and Henry Pousseaur, 1967–70. *Career:* Professor of Theory and Composition, National Conservatory of Mexico, 1970–; Founder of group, Quanta, 1970–73; Editor of Pauta, Journal of Music, 1982–; mem, International Society of Contemporary Music; Mexican Editions of Music; National College of Mexico; Mexican Academy of Arts. *Compositions include:* Canto Del Alba in C for flute; Nocturno in G for flute; Lamento for bass flute; Ofrenda for alto recorder; Dusk for contrabass; Cante for 2 guitars; Marsias for oboe and crystal cups; Ficciones for orchestra; Simurg for piano; Lacrymosa for orchestra; Missa ad Consolationis Dominam Nostram for choir a capella; Clepsidra for orchestra; Reflections Of The Night for string quartet; Hacia El Comienzo for mezzo-soprano and orchestra, poems by Octavio Paz; Ciucani in B flat for flute and clarinet; Madrigal in B flat for clarinet; Three Nocturnes for mezzo-soprano and orchestra, poems by Alvaro Mutis; Aura, one-act opera based on Aura, a short story by Carlos Fuentes; Music for My Neighbor for string quartet; Danza isorrítmica for four percussionists; Lacrymosa for orchestra, 1994. *Address:* Pirineos 455, Lomas de Chapultepec, 11000, México, DF, Mexico.

**LAWLESS, Stephen;** British stage director; b. 1958, England. *Career:* Dir of Productions, Glyndebourne Touring Opera 1986–91; Death in Venice televised and staged at the 1992 Festival; Dir The Pearl Fishers for Scottish Opera, Falstaff at Glyndebourne and Rameau's Les Boréades at the Royal Acad. 1985; Kirov Opera debut with Boris Godunov 1990, also directed Boris Godunov at the Vienna Staatsoper and La Fenice, Venice 1994; Figaro and Rosenkavalier for Canadian Opera, Ariadne and Ballo in Maschera in Los Angeles, Capriccio in San Francicso and Così fan tutte in Chicago; Hamlet by Thomas at the Vienna Volksoper and a Baroque double bill at Innsbruck: Venus and Adonis, with Dido and Aeneas; season 1996–97 with Wozzeck in Braunschweig, Carmen for New Israeli Opera, Il Trovatore in Los Angeles, The Rake's Progress in Pisa and Mozart's Finta Semplice at Potsdam; L'Elisir d'amore at Madrid 1998; has directed opera worldwide, including Covent Garden, Glyndebourne, Vienna State Opera, Berlin Staatsoper, Nürnberg Opera, Metropolitan Opera (New York), Chicago, New York City Opera, Los Angeles, San Francisco, Washington, and the Hong Kong and New Zealand Festivals; Dir the complete Der Ring des Nibelungen for Beijing Music Festival 2005. *Current Management:* c/o Tim Menah, Askonas Holt Ltd, Lonsdale Chambers, 27 Chancery Lane, London, WC2A 1PF, England.

*Telephone:* (20) 7400-1700. *Fax:* (20) 7400-1799. *E-mail:* info@askonasholt.co .uk. *Website:* www.askonasholt.co.uk.

**LAWLOR, Thomas;** Singer (Bass-Baritone); b. 1938, Dublin, Ireland. *Education:* BA, National University of Ireland; Dublin College of Music; Guildhall School of Music. *Career:* Sang with D'Oyly Carte Company, 1963–71 with tours of North America; Glyndebourne, 1971–, in Eugene Onegin, Ariadne, Così fan tutte, Die Entführung, La Bohème, Le nozze di Figaro, Capriccio, Intermezzo, and The Cunning Little Vixen; Engagements with Opera North in A Village Romeo and Juliet, Tosca, Der Rosenkavalier, Der Freischütz, A Midsummer Night's Dream, Manon Lescaut, the premiere of Rebecca by Wilfred Josephs in 1983, Werther, La Cenerentola, Beatrice and Benedict, Jonny Spielt Auf, Die Meistersinger, The Golden Cockerel and Intermezzo; Further appearances with Kent Opera, English Music Theatre, New Sadler's Wells Opera and Opera Northern Ireland, Royal Opera, Dublin Grand Opera; Sang in Rising of The Moon at Wexford Festival in 1990 and Prokofiev's The Duenna; Regular broadcaster on Radio Telefis Eireann and on BBC radio and television; mem, Faculty Member of Summer Conservatory of Music, Bay View, MI, USA. *Address:* Music International, 13 Ardilaun Road, Highbury. London N5 2QR, England.

**LAWRENCE, Amy;** Singer (soprano); b. 1962, Philadelphia, USA. *Education:* Florida State University, New England Conservatory and Zürich Opera, 1992. *Career:* Sang in La Forza del Destino and Albert Herring at Zürich, Der Schauspieldirektor by Mozart at Basle; Kiel Opera from 1994, as Dianora in Mona Lisa by Schillings, Adele (Fledermaus), Constanze, Susanna, and Speranza in L'Orfeo in Monteverdi's Orfeo; Concerts include Messiah, Die Schöpfung, and Mozart's C minor Mass; Carmina Burana and Barber's Knoxville Summer of 1915 with the Louisiana Philharmonic Orchestra; Season 1997 with the Mozart's Queen of Night for the Norwegian Opera, Oslo, and at Oper Frankfurt in 1998; Constanze with Opera Memphis, 1999; In concert with Brahms Requiem in Basel and Zürich and Bernstein's Symphony No. 3, Kaddish, with London Philharmonic Orchestra. *Recordings:* Beethoven Volkslieder, Weltliche Vokalwerke; Mona Lisa, opera by Max Schillings. *Honours:* National Finalist, Metropolitan Opera Competition; Semi-finalist, Belvedere Opera Competition, New York. *Current Management:* Athole Still International Management, Forresters Hall, 25–27 Westow Street, London, SE19 3RY, England. *Telephone:* (20) 8771-5271. *Fax:* (20) 8768-6600. *Website:* www.atholestill.com.

**LAWRENCE, Helen Ruth,** LRAM ARAM; British singer (mezzo-soprano); b. 22 July 1942, London, England; m. Abraham Marcus, 1969; two c. *Education:* Royal Acad. of Music, London. *Career:* guest artist, Covent Garden, ENO, Handel Opera, Chelsea Opera, Phoenix Opera, Germany, Far East; concerts and recitals with UK music clubs and choral socs, Wigmore Hall, South Bank, Barbican, and in Germany, Italy, Netherlands, Israel; Songmakers' Almanac, SPNM, Lontano, Hallé Orchestra; roles as soprano include Donna Anna, Constanze, Fiordiligi, Médée (Cherubini), Lucrezia Borgia, Lady Macbeth, Violetta, Leonora, Amelia, Abigaille, Tosca, Santuzza, Carmen; mezzo-soprano roles from 1989 include Carmen, Fidalma, Marcellina, Azucena and Mistress Quickly; Artistic Dir and Administrator, New Shakespeare Co. opera season, Regent's Park Open Air Theatre 1983; London masterclasses 1989–92; Chair., Hampstead & Highgate Festival; mem Equity, Incorporated Soc. of Musicians. *Recordings include:* title roles Giordano's Fedora, Berthold Goldschmidt's Beatrice Cenci; Amme Meme in Goldschmidt's Der Gewaltige Hahnrei, Berlin 1992, Ornamente by A. Krein 1997, Portrait of an Artist 1999. *Publications:* Life of Mozart (trans. from Italian), A History of the Camden Festival 2004. *Address:* 38 Glenilla Road, London, NW3 4AN, England. *E-mail:* helen@helenlawrence.co.uk. *Website:* www.helenlawrence.co.uk.

**LAWRENCE-KING, Andrew;** Baroque Harpist and Director; b. 1959, Guernsey, Channel Islands. *Career:* Founder-Member and Director of The Harp Consort, Soloist and Director, appearances with Hilliard Ensemble, Hesperion XX, The King's Singers, Jordi Savall, Paul Hiller. Concerts in Europe, Scandanavia, USA, Canada, Japan, Australia, New Zealand, South America, Russia; Directed Monteverdi's Ulisse at 1992 Swedish Baroque Festival, Malmö; Handel's Almira at Bremen Goethetheatre in 1994, Purcell's Dido and Aeneas in Helsinki in 1995; Ribayaz's Luz y Norte at Sydeny Opera House, Madrid National Auditorium, Berlin & Warsaw Philharmonics, Wigmore Hall, London (1997–1999); Florentine 1589 Intermedi, 2000; Peri's Euridice in Los Angeles, 2000; Padilla's Missa Mexicana at La Scala, Milan 2001 and Queen Elizabeth Hall, London, 2001; Solo recital to open 1992 Utrecht Festival, three concerts within 1995 Boston Early Music Festival, solo tours of USA and Japan; Season 2002–03 on tour in England, Scotalnd, Ireland, Spain and Portugal with Torrejon's la Purpura de la Rosa. *Recordings:* Over 100 titles on Hyperion, EMI, TelDec, Deutsche Harmonia Mundi, Harmonia Mundi USA and others include: The Harp of Luduvico & The Secret of the Semitones (solo harp music), Luz y Norte (Spanish 17th century dances with guitar band), Almira (Handel's first opera), La Purpura de la Rosa (first New World opera), The Italian Concerto (concerto soloist abd director, Bach, Handel, Vivaldi), Carolan's Harp (baroque Irish), Missa Mexicana (17th century polyphony and dances from Puebla Cathedral), The Play of Daniel and Miracles (medival); Concert programmes include: Luz y Norte (with Spanish dance), Missa Mexicana (vocal and instrumental ensemble), Miracles (medival lyrics), His Majesty's Harper (solo recital) as well as orchestral repertoire and operas from medival to 21st century. *Publications:* Der Harpfenschlaeger (Historical harp technique); Luz y Norte (Spanish harp music); Article in Companion to Medieval and Renaissance

Music, Dent 1992. *Honours:* First Winner of the International Award from Cambridge Early Music Society, 1992. Winner Gramophone Award, 1992; Winner German Phonographic Scoiety, Best Early Music CD, Echo Prize, 1998. *Current Management:* Helen Coombs. *Address:* 9 Cliff Street, St Peter Port, Guernsey, GY1 1LH, Channel Islands. *Telephone:* 01481 713037. *Fax:* 01481 700502. *E-mail:* TheHarpConsort@compuserve.com. *Website:* www .TheHarpConsort.com.

**LAWSON, Colin James,** BA, MA, PhD, DMus, ARCM; clarinettist, musicologist and broadcaster; *Director, Royal College of Music;* b. 24 July 1949, Saltburn-by-the-Sea, England; m. Hilary Birch 1982; one s. *Education:* Keble Coll., Oxford, Birmingham Univ., Aberdeen Univ., Univ. of London. *Career:* Lecturer in Music, Univ. of Aberdeen 1973–77; Lecturer, Sr Lecturer and Reader in Music, Sheffield Univ. 1978–97; guest principal clarinet, Orchestra of the Age of Enlightenment 1987–; Prof. of Classical Studies and Early Clarinet, Guildhall School of Music, London 1988–91; principal clarinet, Hanover Band 1987–, London Classical Players 1989–92, English Concert 1991–; Visiting Lecturer, RNCM and RAM 1992; Prof. of Music, Goldsmiths Coll. 1998–2001; Pro Vice-Chancellor/Dean, Thames Valley Univ. 2001–05; Dir, Royal Coll. of Music 2005–; current specialization in historical performance; mem. contemporary ensemble, Lysis; solo, chamber and orchestral appearances throughout the UK, Europe and USA; performed Mozart Concerto on a specially designed basset clarinet. *Recordings:* with Acad. of Ancient Music, Albion Ensemble, Classical Winds, CM90, Cristofori, English Concert, The Parley of Instruments, La Petite Bande, L'Ecole d'Orphée, The King's Consort; concertos by Mahon, Hook, Weber, Spohr. *Publications:* The Chalumeau in Eighteenth-Century Music 1981, The Cambridge Companion to the Clarinet (ed.) 1995, Mozart Clarinet Concerto 1996, Brahms Clarinet Quintet 1998, The Historical Performance of Music: An Introduction (co-author) 1999, The Early Clarinet: A Practical Guide 2000, The Cambridge Companion to the Orchestra (ed.) 2003; contrib. 'Beethoven and the development of wind instruments' (in Beethoven and the Performer) 1994, 'Performing through history' (in Musical Performance: A Guide to Understanding) 2002. *Address:* Royal College of Music, Prince Consort Road, London, SW7 2BS, England. *Website:* www.rcm.ac.uk.

**LAWTON, Jeffrey;** Singer (Tenor); b. 1941, Oldham, Lancashire, England. *Education:* Studied with Patrick McGuigan. *Career:* With Welsh National Opera has sung Tikhon in Katya Kabanova, also televised, various roles in The Greek Passion by Martinů, Florestan, Huon in Oberon, in Janáček's From The House of the Dead and Jenůfa as Laca, Otello, Aeneas in The Trojans and Don José; Sang Siegfried in a new production of The Ring also seen at Covent Garden in 1986, and the Emperor in Die Frau ohne Schatten; Other operatic appearances for Opera North as Erik and Florestan, in Paris, Brussels and Nancy (Otello), and as Siegmund at Cologne; Concert engagements include the Choral Symphony with the Royal Liverpool Philharmonic, Das Lied von der Erde with the BBC Symphony at the Brighton Festival and in Paris, and Mahler's 8th Symphony in Turin; Sang Siegfried in Götterdämmerung in Cologne, Edmund in Lear for English National Opera, Edinburgh Festival in 1990 in Martinů's Greek Passion, Laca in Jenůfa for Welsh National Opera and Tristan, 1992–93, Shuisky in Boris for Opera North, 1993–94, Laca for New Israeli Opera and Tristan for Scottish National Opera; Sang Herod in the final scene from Salome at Promenade Concerts in 1993; Sang Pedro in the premiere of Macmillan's Inès de Castro, Edinburgh, 1996; Wagner concert with the Philhlarmonia, London, 1997; Tristan for Welsh National Opera and at Buenos Aires, 1999–2000. *Recordings include:* The Greek Passion. *Current Management:* Music International. *Address:* Music International, 13 Ardilaun Road, Highbury, London, England.

**LAYTON, Richard;** Violinist; b. 1940, Redditch, Worcestershire, England; m.; four c. *Education:* studied in London. *Career:* freelance musician, then co-leader of the Bournemouth Symphony Orchestra from 1964; leader of the Bournemouth Sinfonietta, 1969; soloist in concertos by Bach, Haydn, Mozart, Prokofiev and in the Brandenburg Concertos; leader of the Silvestri String Quartet, with concerts at Dartington and at Bath Festival; sub-leader of the London Philharmonic Orchestra, 1973, including appearances with the Glyndebourne Festival; guest leader with the BBC National Orchestra of Wales, ENO Orchestra, the Park Lane Players and the Philharmonia; Assoc. Leader of the Royal Philharmonic Orchestra, 1983–98; moved to France 2003. *Address:* Tessé, La Forêt de Tessé, Charente 16240, France. *E-mail:* richard .layton@wanadoo.fr.

**LAYTON, Robert;** Critic, Producer and Writer on Music; b. 2 May 1930, London, England; m. Ingrid Nina Thompson. *Education:* Worcester College, Oxford, 1949–53; Universities of Uppsala and Stockholm, 1953–55; Studied composition with Edmund Rubbra and history of music with Egon Wellesz; Further studies with Professor Carl-Allan Moberg. *Career:* Swedish Film Industry, 1954–55; Teacher in London, 1956–59; BBC Music Division, 1959–90 (music presentation, 1959, music talks, 1960); General Editor, BBC Music Guides, 1973–; Producer of BBC Lunchtime Concerts at St John's Smith Square, 1984–88. *Publications:* Franz Berwald, 1959; Jean Sibelius, 1965; Sibelius and His World, 1970; Dvořák Symphonies and Concertos, 1977; Sibelius, 1981; Companion to The Concerto, 1988; Responsible for Scandinavian music in The New Grove Dictionary of Music and Musicians, 1980; Translated Erik Tawaststjerna's Sibelius, Vol. I, 1976, Vol. II, 1986, Vol. III, 1997; Editor, Companion to The Symphony, 1993; Grieg–A Short Life, 1997. *Contributions:* The Symphony, 1966; The Gramophone; The Listener; The Times; Professional journals in the United Kingdom and Sweden. *Honours:*

Finnish State Literary Prize, 1985; Sibelius Medal, 1987; Knight of the Order of The White Rose of Finland, 1988; Knight of the Order of the Polar Star, Sweden, 2001. *Address:* 112 Goldhurst Terrace, London NW6 3HR, England.

**LAYTON, Stephen;** Choral Director and Organist; b. 1962, England. *Education:* Chorister Winchester Cathedral; Music Scholar Eton College, Organ Scholar King's College, Cambridge. *Career:* appearances with King's College Chapel Choir in Europe, USA and Japan; conducted Messiah and Gluck's Orfeo at Cambridge; Founder and Director of chamber choir Polyphony, making London Proms debut 1995, with Pärt's Passio and Dido and Aeneas; Musical Director of the Holst Singers; Organist and Director of the Choir at Temple Church, London 1996–2006; engagements with the Philharmonic Chorus, London Philharmonic Choir and BBC Symphony Orchestra Chorus; tour of Brazil with Polyphony and Bournemouth Sinfonietta 1995; Bach's Christmas Oratorio and Messiah with the Brandenburg Concert in London 1996; further concerts in Estonia, Hong Kong, France, Spain and Copenhagen; directed Poulenc's Figure Humaine London Proms 1999; conducted BBC Singers London Proms Chamber Music 2002; apptd Dir of Music and Fellow Trinity Coll., Cambridge Oct. 2006–. *Recordings include:* Macmillan's Seven Last Words from the Cross; Folksongs by Holst and Vaughan Williams. *Current Management:* Hazard Chase, Norman House, Cambridge Place, Cambridge CB2 1NS, England. *Telephone:* (1223) 312400. *Fax:* (1223) 460827. *Website:* www.hazardchase.co.uk.

**LAZAR, Hans Jurgen;** Singer (tenor); b. 1958, Bad Salzuflen Germany. *Education:* Studied in Detmold with Sandor Konya. *Career:* Debut: Detmold 1982, as Mozart's Pedrillo; Sang at the Hagen Opera 1985–87, Essen 1988–91, notably as Wagner's David, Janáček's Fox, Alfred in Fledermaus and Nicolai's Fenton; Frankfurt Opera 1988–91, notably as Britten's Flute; Sang Mime at Trieste and Monteverdi's Arnalta in Frankfurt, 2000–01; Many concert appearances, including Mozart masses, and Janáček's Diary of One Who Disappeared.

**LAZAREV, Alexander Nikolayevich;** Russian conductor; b. 5 July 1945; m. Tamara Lazarev; one d. *Education:* Leningrad and Moscow Conservatoires. *Career:* conducting debut at Bolshoi Theatre 1973, conducted numerous ballets and operas of the Bolshoi Theatre's European and Russian repertoires, founder and conductor Ensemble of Soloists of the Bolshoi Theatre 1978–89, Chief Conductor, Artistic Dir, Bolshoi Theatre 1987–95; Chief Conductor Duisburg Symphony Orchestra 1988–93; has conducted numerous orchestras including Berlin Philharmonic, Munich Philharmonic, Orchestra Sinfonica del Teatro alla Scala di Milano, Orchestre Nat. de France and others; UK debut with Royal Liverpool Philharmonic Orchestra 1987; subsequently performed with the City of Birmingham Symphony Orchestra, the Royal Scottish Nat. Orchestra, etc.; Prin. Guest Conductor BBC Symphony Orchestra, 1992–95, Royal Scottish Nat. Orchestra 1994–97, Prin. Conductor 1997–2005. *Honours:* Hon. Prof., Univ. of Glasgow 2005 First Prize USSR Nat. Competition 1971, First Prize and Gold Medal Karajan Competition (Berlin) 1972. *Address:* c/o Tennant Artists, Unit 2, 39 Tadema Road, London, SW10 0PZ, England. *Telephone:* (20) 7376-3758 (London). *Fax:* (20) 7351-0679 (office). *E-mail:* info@tennantartists.com (office). *Website:* www.tennantartists .com (office).

**LAZARIDIS, Stefanos;** stage designer; b. 28 July 1942, Ethiopia. *Education:* studied in Geneva, Central School of Speech and Drama, London. *Career:* designed Le nozze di Figaro at Covent Garden 1972, followed by Idomeneo and Werther 1978–79; collaborated with John Copley at ENO with Die Entführung 1971, Il Trovatore 1972; further designs for ENO have included Katya Kabanova, Dalibor, Euryanthe, Aida, Der fliegende Holländer, Rusalka, Madama Butterfly, Hansel and Gretel and The Mikado; collaborations with Yuri Lyubimov for Tristan und Isolde at Bologna 1983, Rigoletto at Florence 1984 and Fidelio at Stuttgart 1985; British stage premieres of Janáček's Osud 1984, Busoni's Doktor Faust 1986; designed Tosca at Florence and ENO, with Jonathan Miller 1986, Nabucco for Opera North and Oedipus Rex and Bluebeard's Castle for Scottish Opera 1990; Der fliegende Holländer with David Pountney at Bregenz Festival 1989, Carmen at Earl's Court, London 1989, and on tour to Japan and Australia; La Fanciulla del West at La Scala 1991; Pag and Cav at the Berlin Staatsoper 1996; La Fanciulla del West at Zürich 1998; Lohengrin at the Bayreuth Festival 1999; Das Rheingold and Die Walküre for the Royal Opera House, Covent Garden 2005. *Honours:* Prague Quadrennial Int. Exhibition of Stage Design Diploma of Honour 1999.

**LAZARO, Francisco;** Singer (Tenor); b. 13 March 1932, Barcelona, Spain. *Education:* Liceo Conservatory, Barcelona. *Career:* Debut: Barcelona in 1962 as Gaspare in Donizetti's La Favorita; Sang in Macbeth and Der Rosenkavalier at the 1964 Salzburg Festival, under Karajan; Guest appearances in Berlin, Düsseldorf and Frankfurt, San Francisco in 1965, and Barcelona in 1967 as Calaf in Turandot; Frequent performances at the Munich Staatsoper from 1970; Sang at Hamburg in 1984 as Otello; Other roles include Verdi's Manrico and Radames, Des Grieux in Manon Lescaut, Rodolfo and Don José.

**LAZAROF, Henri;** Composer; b. 12 April 1932, Sofia, Bulgaria. *Education:* Studied with Paul Ben-Haim in Jerusalem; Santa Cecilia Academy in Rome with Petrassi, 1955–57; Brandeis University with Harold Shapero, 1957–59. *Career:* Teacher at University of California, Los Angeles, 1962–; Artist in Residence at University of West Berlin, 1970–71. *Compositions include:* Piano Concerto, 1957; Violin Concerto, 1962; Concerto for piano and 20 instruments, 1963; Odes for orchestra, 1963; Double Concerto for violin, viola and chamber orchestra, 1964; Structures Sonores for orchestra, 1966; Mutazione for orchestra, 1967; Cello Concerto, 1968; Events, ballet, 1973; Concertazioni for orchestra, 1973; Spectrum for trumpet, orchestra and tape, 1975; Chamber Symphony, 1977; Mirrors, Mirrors, ballet, 1980; Sinfonietta, 1981; Clarinet Concerto, 1990; Symphony No. 2, 1991, No. 3 (Choral), 1994, No. 4 (Choral), 1995; Oboe Concerto, 1997; Viola Rhapsody, 1997; String Quintet, 1997; Chronicles, string trio, 1997; 3 String Quartets, 1956–80; String Trio, 1957; Wind trio, 1981. *Address:* c/o ASCAP, ASCAP Building, 1 Lincoln Plaza, New York, NY 10023, USA.

**LAZARTE, Julio (Ricardo);** Pianist and Conductor; b. 12 July 1956, Tucuman, Argentina. *Education:* Medico Degree, National University of Tucuman; Piano and Professor of Piano from School of Musical Arts, National University of Tucuman; Dalcroze Certificate, Carnegie Mellon University, Pittsburgh. *Career:* Debut: Pianist, Integral version of sonatas and interludes by John Cage, US Embassy, Argentina, 1985; Conductor, Complete version of church sonatas by Mozart, Santisimo Rosario Basilica, Tucuman, 1990; As pianist has performed complete cycles of works for keyboard or chamber music with piano, by Pachelbel, Zipoli, Marcello, Handel, Haydn, Clementi, Mozart, Brahms, Weber, Debussy, Ravel, Satie, Cage, Ginastera and pioneers of Argentinian and Latin American keyboard music; Tours of USA, Spain, Netherlands and Argentina; As conductor founded and is artistic music director for Camerata Lazarte Chamber Orchestra performing widely; Has taught in many academic and cultural institutions. *Publications:* Author, Lazarte Methodology. *Current Management:* CESI. *Address:* c/o CESI, Marcos Paz 250, Tucuman 250, Argentina.

**LE, Tuan Hung,** BMus, DPhil; composer and musicologist; *Program Director, Australia Asia Foundation*; b. 15 Oct. 1960, Viet Nam. *Education:* Royal Melbourne Inst. of Technology, Univ. of Melbourne, Monash Univ. *Career:* freelance composer, performer and musicologist 1987–; Program Manager, Music, Australia Asia Foundation 1994–, Program Dir 2000–. *Compositions:* Reflections, 1990; Spring, 1991; Prayer for Land, 1991; Longing for Wind, 1996; Calm Water, 1996; Water Ways, 1997; Scent of Memories, 1998; Lotus Pond, 1998; Scent of Time, 2000; Echoes of an Old Festive Song, 2003. *Recordings:* Quivering String, 1992; Musical Transfigurations, 1993; Landscapes of Time, 1996; Echoes of Ancestral Voices, 1997; Scent of Time, 2003, On the Wings of a Butterfly 2005. *Publications:* Dan Tranh Music of Vietnam: Traditions and Innovations 1998; numerous articles in magazines, reviews and journals. *Honours:* Australian Acad. of Humanities Overseas Fellowship 1993. *Address:* PO Box 387, Springvale, Vic. 3171, Australia.

**LE BRIS, Michele;** Singer (Soprano) b. 1938, France. *Education:* Studied at Conservatoire National, Paris. *Career:* Debut: Paris Opéra as Marguerite, 1961; Many appearances at such French opera centres as Marseilles, Nantes, Vichy, Strasbourg, Toulouse and Rouen; Strasbourg in 1965 in local premiere of Mozart's La Finta Giardiniera, Amelia in Un Ballo in Maschera, Tokyo, 1972; Sang Halévy's Rachel in London, 1973 and at Barcelona in 1974; Sang at Barcelona in 1976 as Thais; Other roles have included Rossini's Mathilde, Verdi's Desdemona and Trovatore Leonora, Manon Lescaut, Tosca, Mimi, Minnie and Musetta, Massenet's Salome and Sapho, Regina in Mathis der Maler, Mozart's Countess and Donna, Lisa in The Queen of Spades and Janáček's Jenůfa. *Recordings include:* Highlights from Un Ballo in Maschera and Il Trovatore. *Address:* c/o Theatre National de L'Opéra de Paris, 8 Rue Scribe, 75008 Paris, France.

**LE BROCQ, Mark;** British singer (tenor); b. 1966, England. *Education:* St Catharine's Coll., Cambridge, Royal Acad., Nat. Opera Studio. *Career:* fmr Principal with ENO, roles included Tamino in The Magic Flute, Paris in King Priam, Count Almaviva in The Barber of Seville, Narraboth in Salome, Cassio in Othello, The Schoolmaster in The Cunning Little Vixen, Don Ottavio in Don Giovanni, Cavalli's Egisto, Paolino in Il Matrimonio Segreto, Berlioz's Benedict, Spirit/Autumn in The Fairy Queen, Odoardo in Ariodante, Doctor Maxwell in The Silver Tassie (world premiere), Siward in A Better Place (world premiere); guest appearances include Idomeneo with Opera Northern Ireland, Belmonte in Die Entfuhrung Aus Dem Serail with Garsington Opera, Pinkerton in Madam Butterfly at Royal Albert Hall, Boggart in The Fairy Queen at the Liceu, Barcelona; appearances at Covent Garden and Aix-en-Provence festivals; concerts in the USA, throughout Europe and in the Middle East with Les Arts Florissants, The Gabrieli Consort and others; appeared at BBC Proms 2003. *Recordings include:* Il Trovatore, Carmen, Turandot, Hail Bright Cecilia, Utrecht Te Deum, I Was Glad. *Honours:* RAM Blyth Buesset Opera Prize, RAM Club Prize, Worshipful Co. of Musicians Medal. *Current Management:* Hazard Chase, Norman House, Cambridge Place, Cambridge, CB2 1NS, England. *Telephone:* (1223) 312400. *Fax:* (1223) 460827. *Website:* www.hazardchase.co.uk.

**LE DIZES, Maryvonne;** Violinist and Professor; b. 25 June 1940, Quimper, France; m. 23 May 1964, 3 s., 1 d. *Education:* 1st Prize, Violin, National Conservatory of Music, Paris, 1957; 1st Prize, Chamber Music, National Conservatory of Music, Paris, 1958. *Career:* Debut: Violin Concert; Soloist with Ensemble Intercontemporain, 1978–; Professor at Conservatory of Music, Boulogne Billancourt, France, 1977–. *Recordings:* Works by Berio, Messiaen, Xenakis, Machover, Carter, Brahms. *Honours:* Prize, International Thibaud Competition, Paris, 1961; 1st Prize, N Paganini Competition, Genoa, 1962, and International American Music Competition, NY, 1983; SACEM Paris, 1987. *Address:* CIUP, Maison IAA, 5 Boulevard Jourdan, 75690 Paris Cédex 14, France.

**LE FLEMING, Anthony Ralph,** BA; British composer, organist and conductor; *Director of Music, Holy Trinity Clapham, London*; b. 16 March 1941, Wiltshire, England; m.; three c. *Education:* Salisbury Cathedral School and Queens' Coll., Cambridge. *Career:* organist Bedford School 1965–68; Dir of Music, Abingdon School 1968–73, Holy Trinity Clapham, London 1998–; Music Adviser, Birmingham LEA 1973–81, Devon County 1981–93; freelance composer, organist, conductor 1993–; mem. Incorporated Soc. of Musicians. *Compositions:* works for choir and orchestra, choir unaccompanied and with organ, songs with instrumental or piano accompaniment, instrumental pieces, arrangements in various styles. *Recordings:* Some Shadows of Eternity. *Honours:* first prize English Poetry and Song Soc. *Address:* 64 Park Hall Road, West Dulwich, London, SE21 8BW, England (home). *Telephone:* (20) 8761-4397 (home). *E-mail:* a.lefleming@btinternet (home). *Website:* www.impulse-music.co.uk/lefleming.htm (office).

**LE PAGE, David;** Violinist; b. 1965, England. *Career:* Co-founder and Second Violinist of the Kreutzer Quartet from 1988; South Bank debut in 1989 followed by Amsterdam Concertgebouw and recital at Palazzo Labia in Venice; 1991 Recital at Lancaster House for Queen Elizabeth; Established repertoire and new compositions with improvisations in The Chamber, featuring live film projection and static coloured images within a darkened set. *Honours:* With Kreutzer Quartet: Winner of 1991 Royal Overseas League Competition. *Address:* Manygate Management, Kreutzer Quartet, 13 Cotswold Mews, 30 Battersea Square, London SW11 3 RA, England.

**LE ROUX, Francois;** Singer (Baritone); b. 30 Oct. 1955, Rennes, France. *Education:* Studied with Francois Loup and at Paris Opéra Studio with Vera Rozsa and Elisabeth Grummer. *Career:* Sang at the Opéra de Lyon, 1980–85 as Mozart's Don Giovanni, Papageno, Guglielmo and Count; From 1985 appeared as Debussy's Pelléas at the Paris Opéra, La Scala, Milan, 1986, Vienna Staatsoper, 1988, Barcelona, Helsinki, 1989, Cologne, 1992, Covent Garden, 1994; Glyndebourne Festival debut in 1987 as Ramiro in L'Heure Espagnole; Hamburg in 1987 as Marcello in La Bohème; Sang Lescaut in a new production of Manon at Covent Garden, 1988, returning as Papageno in 1989; Appeared as Hidraot in Armide at Amsterdam in 1988 and Orestes in Iphigénie at Frankfurt, Ulisse in Il Ritorno at Lausanne, 1989; Also sings Valentin in Faust and has sung Don Giovanni at Paris Opéra and in Zürich under Nikolaus Harnoncourt; Created the title role in the world premiere of Birtwistle's Gawain at Covent Garden, 1991; Season 1992 as Maletesta in Don Pasquale at Covent Garden and the title role in Henze's Der Prinz von Homburg at Munich; sang Pelléas at Covent Garden, 1994; Sang Stravinsky's Nick Shadow at Madrid, 1996; Season 1998 with Golaud in Pelléas at the Paris Opéra-Comique and Monteverdi's Orpheus at the Vienna Festival; Sang Monsieur de in Madame de by Damase at Geneva, 2001. *Recordings include:* Pelléas et Mélisande, under Claudio Abbado. *Honours:* Prizewinner at International Maria Casals Competition, Barcelona and the International Competition at Rio de Janeiro. *Address:* c/o Matthias Vogt Management, 1714 Stockton Street, Suite 300, San Francisco, CA 94133-2930, USA.

**LE ROUX, Maurice;** Conductor and Composer; b. 6 Feb. 1923, Paris, France. *Education:* Studied at the Paris Conservatoire, 1944–52, with Messiaen and Fourestier, composition with René Leibowitz and conducting with Dmitri Mitropoulos. *Career:* Worked on musique concrète project with French Radio, 1951; Music Director of the Orchestre National, 1960–68; Artistic Adviser at the Paris Opéra, 1969–73; Inspector General of Music for the Ministry of Culture, 1973–88; Conductor of leading orchestras in guest engagements in France and abroad; Repertoire has included the Monteverdi Vespers and music by Berg, Schoenberg and Xenakis; Music programme Arcana for French television from 1968; Film scores for Truffaut, Godard and others. *Recordings include:* Messiaen Turangalila Symphonie. *Publications:* Introduction a la Musique Contemporaine, 1947; Claudio Monteverdi, 1951; La Musique, 1979; Mussorgsky, Boris Godunov, 1980.

**LE SAGE, Sally,** ARCM; British singer (soprano) and professor of singing; b. 1937, Farnborough, England. *Education:* Royal Coll. of Music and studied with Pierre Bernac on a scholarship in Paris. *Career:* sang with Deller Consort 1964–67; concert appearances throughout the UK, Europe and USA which included the Vienna, Aix, Ghent and Three Choirs Festivals; many BBC concerts and recitals; other concert repertoire included L'Enfant et Les Sortilèges in Leeds with Simon Rattle, Haydn Nelson Mass at Carnegie Hall, NY, USA, Beethoven's 9th for Dutch television in Amsterdam, Mozart's C minor Mass at Royal Festival Hall with Charles Groves, A Child of Our Time in Stockholm under Michael Tippett, Messiah with the Hallé in Manchester, and Mahler's 8th Symphony at the Albert Hall in London; opera appearances with Scottish Opera as The Woodbird in Siegfried, Covent Garden and Glyndebourne, Teofane in Handel's Ottone at Sadler's Wells Theatre and Ann Trulove in The Rake's Progress at Cambridge Arts Theatre. *Honours:* first prize Vocal Concours, 's-Hertogenbosch, Netherlands 1967. *Address:* 24 Eston Avenue, Malvern, Worcestershire WR14 2SR, England. *Telephone:* (1684) 560504.

**LE TEXIER, Vincent;** Singer (Bass-baritone); b. 1957, France. *Education:* Studied privately at the Grenoble Conservatory and at the studio of the Paris Opéra. *Career:* Appearances at the Paris Opéra in Orphée aux Enfers and with the Opéra-Comique in From the House of the Dead; Sang Golaud in Pelléas et Mélisande and appeared at the 1989 Aix Festival, in The Love for Three Oranges; Lyon, as Schaunard in La Bohème, the four devils in Les Contes d'Hoffmann, the King in Debussy's Rodrigue et Chimène (word creation); In

Bordeaux, as Leporello in Don Giovanni, Escamillo in Carmen, the Count in Le nozze di Figaro, Frère Laurent in Roméo et Juliette by Berlioz; In Rouen, as Basilio in Il Barbiere di Siviglia, Kaspar in Freischütz (French version by Berlioz), the Count in Capriccio, the Speaker in Zauberflöte, Mephisto in Faust, Sade in Teresa by Marius Constant, Wozzeck in Wozzeck by Gurlitt (French version); Appearances at the Paris Opéra in Madama Butterfly, and in Pelléas et Mélisande; Golaud in Impressions de Pelléas, by Peter Brook and Marius Constant, in Paris and on tour around Europe, 1991–92; Created the role of Ethnologist in Georges Aperghis's Tristes Tropiques, Strasbourg, 1996; Season 2000–01 as the Berlioz Mephisto at Naples (concert), Eumée in Fauré's Pénélope at Lausanne and Golo for Leipzig Opera. Recordings include: The Love for Three Oranges; Alcyone by Marais; Salome, Strauss; Psalm 129, Guy Ropartz; Messa di Gloria, Donizetti; Platée by Rameau; L'Enfant et les Sortiléges by Ravel; Mélodies by Duparc, Ropartz and Fauré. Honours: Grand Critics' Prize, 1997. Address: 30 rue Darceau, 93100 Montreuil, France.

**LEA, Yvonne;** Singer (Contralto); b. 1960, Cheshire, England. Education: Studied at Royal Northern College of Music with Frederick Cox and at the National Opera Studio, London. Career: Appearances with Glyndebourne Festival in Die Zauberflöte, Hippolyta in A Midsummer Night's Dream, Rosina in Il Barbiere di Siviglia and Linette in The Love for Three Oranges; Royal Opera House, Covent Garden, in Der Rosenkavalier and Third Lady in Die Zauberflöte; Sang Suzuki with Welsh National Opera and appeared at Batignano and Spitalfields Festivals in Cesti's La Dori; Recent engagements in Graham Vick's version of The Ring for the City of Birmingham Touring Opera, as Hippolyta at the 1991–92 Aix Festivals and Grimgerde in Die Walküre for Scottish Opera; Tour of France with A Midsummer Night's Dream, 1994; Sang Mother Goose in The Rake's Progress for Welsh National Opera, 1996; Concert repertoire includes Messiah, Elgar's Sea Pictures, Elijah and Beethoven's Mass in C. Recordings include: Williamson's Six English Lyrics.

**LEA-COX, Graham Russell,** MA, ARCM, ARCO, MTC; conductor; b. 15 Feb. 1957, Bulawayo, Rhodesia. Education: London Univ., Royal Coll. of Music, London, Magdalen Coll., Oxford. Career: debut, Carnegie Hall, New York 1983; Artistic Dir, Texas Boys' Choir, USA 1983–85; freelance conductor, performer 1985–; tours of USA, Canada, Japan, Hong Kong; conducting and solo and chamber recitals in Europe, Scandinavia, Africa; Artistic Dir, English Performing Arts Ensemble 1988–; Conductor and Artistic Dir, Elizabethan Singers of London 1987–97; Conductor, Hanover Band, London; regular tours of Europe and Scandinavia; Artistic Dir and conductor of festivals, including the South Bank, London; guest conductor, WDR Symphony Orchestra, Köln, Germany, Cape Philharmonic Orchestra, South Africa. Compositions: choral and instrumental music, incidental music for stage and recordings of poetical/literary compilations. Recordings: film and television music; chamber music and song from The Court of Queen Victoria; Warchild Festival Highlights, Festival Hall, London; William Boyce Critical Editions and recording series, conducting the Hanover Band, New College Choir, Oxford, Soloists and others, 1998–; Secular Masque; Cantata: David's Lament on the Death of Saul and Jonathan; Odes to St Cecilia; Pindar's Ode, New Year's Ode 1774, The Symphony in Britain, Volume 1: Early British Symphonies, 2001; operas and songs. Publications include: Gluck: The Swedish Opera Mss, Kungliga Teatra 1770–1815 (research for publication), William Boyce Masterworks (critical edn), British Symphonies of the 18th and 19th Centuries (critical edn). Address: c/o Haydn RA Ltd, 36 Station Road, London, SE20 7BQ, England (office). Telephone: (20) 8659-2659 (office). Fax: (20) 8676-9119 (office). E-mail: chefdorch@hotmail.com (office). Website: www.grahamlea-cox.com.

**LEACH, Mary (Jane);** Composer and Performer; b. 12 June 1949, St Johnsbury, Vermont, USA. Education: BA, Theatre, Music, University of Vermont; Postgraduate, Composition, with Mark Zuckerman, Columbia University. Career: Appeared: Experimental Intermedia Foundation (New York), 1982, 1984, 1987, 1992; Relache (Philadelphia), 1984, 1987; Music Gallery (Toronto), Metronome (Barcelona), Newband (New York), 1985; Roulette, New York, 1985, 1995; Charles Ives Center (Connecticut), Logos (Gent, Belgium), 1986, 1987; BACA Downtown (Brooklyn), New Music America (Philadelphia), Palais des Beaux Art (Brussels), Sankt Peter (Cologne), Apollohuis (Eindhoven, Netherlands), 1987; Clock Tower (New York), 1988; Real Ways (Hartford, Connecticut), Franenzeichen Festival (Cologne), Ton Gegen Ton (Vienna), New Music America (New York), 1989; Kunsthalle Bremen, Romanische Summer Festival (Cologne), Music Today (Tokyo), 1990; Experimentelle Music (Munich), 1991; Sound Symposium (Newfoundland), Ijsbreker (Amsterdam), Corn Palace (Minneapolis), 1992; Bang on a Can Festival (New York), 1992, 1993; Interpretations Series (New York), Walker Art Center, 1993; Subtropics Festival (Miami), 1994; Radio: John Schaeffer's New Sounds, 3 MBS Australia, Radio Bremen, WDR-Köln, Earworks; CBC, 1992; Radio Cultura (São Paulo), Radio 2 (Brussels), 1994; First Art, 1995; For television: WDR Köln. Compositions: Note Passing Note, 1981; Solar Spots, 1983; 4BC, Held Held, 1984; 8x4, 1985; Bare Bones, Bruckstück, Pipe Dreams, Sephardic Fragments, 1989; The Upper Room, 1990; Kirchtraum, 1991; Feu de Joie, 1992; Ariadne's Lament, He Got Dictators, Xantippe's Rebuke, 1993; Corrina Ocarina, 1994; Tricky Pan, Windjammer, 1995; Song of Sorrows, 1995; Call of the Dance, 1997; O Magna Vasti Creta, 1997. Recordings: MJL 2, 1986; Celestial Fires, 1993; Aerial No. 6; Ariadne's Lament, 1998. Address: 90 LaSalle Street #13H, New York, NY 10027, USA.

**LEADBETTER, Martin John,** BA, DipMus, DipEurHum; British composer; b. 6 April 1945, London; m. Ivy G. 1969; two s. Education: Trinity Coll. of Music, London, Open Univ., studied with Dr Alan Bush. Career: mem. Performing Right Soc. Compositions include: two symphonies, three string quartets, An English Requiem violin concerto 1972, songs, instrumental and choral works, Marche Tragique for orchestra 1991, Laudate Dominium (performed Fontainebleau, France 1993) 1992, I Hear America Singing 1994, Clarinet Concerto 1999, English Music for strings 2004, Overture in the Classical Style 2004, Overture in the Style of Handel 2004, Jazz Tocata for piano 2004, Symphony in the Style of Mozart 2004, Concertos for flute, oboe, bassoon, horn, trumpet, violin, viola, cello and double bass: Train Music 2005. Publications include: Soliloquy, Little Prelude and Fugue. Address: Ivy Lodge, 2 Priory Lane, Little Wymondley, Herts. SG4 7HE, England. Telephone: (1438) 359292 (home). Fax: (1438) 759113 (home). E-mail: leadzart@btopenworld.com.

**LEAH, Philip,** (J. P. Hale), PGCE, GNSM; British music educator; b. 23 Oct. 1948, Dulwich, London; m. (divorced); two s. Education: Northern School of Music, Manchester, Padgate School of Educ., Warrington. Career: peripatetic music teacher, Glamorgan 1972–73, Birmingham 1973–90; Lecturer, North Worcestershire Coll. of Educ. 1977–80, Univ. . of Wolverhampton 1982–90; founder and Musical Dir, West Birmingham Schools Wind Band 1985–90, Halesowen Symphony Orchestra 1986–89; examiner, Guildhall School of Music and Drama 1988–; flute tutor, Univ. of Wales, Aberystwyth 2000–; mem. Royal Soc. of Musicians of Great Britain, Incorporated Soc. of Musicians, Soc. for the Promotion of New Music, Musicians' Union. Compositions: Concertino for bass tuba and orchestra; Sinfonia for flute and strings; Acme, a suite for chamber orchestra; Sinfonia for chambaer orchestra; Elegy for string sextet. Prelude and Scherzo for string quartet; Three Penny Bit for wind; Wind quintet; Fanfare (1969); Fanfare for a Golden Jubilee; Conversations for flute and piano; Fanfare for a Golden Jubilee; Chorale Prelude on Austria for organ; Wedding Suite for organ; In Annum for tenor solo, SATB choir and string quartet; Winter for SATB choir and string quartet; Song: Meditation for soprano and piano; Psychological Songs for bass voice and piano; Various arrangements for woodwind instruments. Honours: first prize Horatio Albert Lumb Composition Competition 1992. Address: 369 Bromsgrove Road, Hunnington, Halesowen, West Midlands B62 0JL, England (home). Telephone: (07816) 488367 (home). E-mail: philleah@aol.com (home). Website: www.emupublishing.com.

**LEAPER, Adrian;** British conductor; Musical Director, RTVE Symphony Orchestra, Madrid; b. 1953, England. Education: Royal Acad. of Music, studied with George Hurst. Career: Asst Conductor, Halle Orchestra 1986–87, has subsequently worked with all leading British orchestras, the Vienna, Prague and Moscow Symphonies, the Belgian Nat. Orchestra; Music Dir, Orquesta Filarmonica de Gran Canaria 1994, currently guest conductor; Musical Dir, RTVE Symphony Orchestra, Madrid 2001–. Recordings include: albums of Sibelius, Elgar, Holst, Havergal Brian, Tchaikovsky and Nielsen. Current Management: Hazard Chase Limited, 25 City Road, Cambridge, CB1 1DP, England. Telephone: (1223) 312400. Fax: (1223) 460827. E-mail: info@hazardchase.co.uk. Website: www.hazardchase.co.uk.

**LEAR, Evelyn;** American singer (soprano); b. 8 Jan. 1926, Brooklyn, New York; d. of Nina Quartin; m. 2nd Thomas Stewart (q.v.); one s. one d. by previous marriage. Education: New York Univ., Hunter Coll., Juilliard School, Lincoln Teachers Coll. Career: Fulbright Scholarship for study in Germany 1957; joined Berlin Opera, début in Ariadne auf Naxos 1959; début in UK in Four Last Songs with London Symphony Orchestra 1957; début at Metropolitan Opera in Mourning Becomes Electra 1967; début at La Scala, Milan, in Wozzeck 1971; regular performances with leading opera cos and orchestras in Europe and USA; guest appearances with Berlin Opera and Vienna State Opera; soloist with the leading American orchestras including New York Philharmonic, Chicago Symphony, Philadelphia Orchestra, Boston Symphony, San Francisco Symphony and Los Angeles Philharmonic; has given many recitals and orchestral concerts and operatic performances with Thomas Stewart. Film: Buffalo Bill 1976. Major roles include: Marie in Wozzeck, Marschallin in Der Rosenkavalier, Countess in The Marriage of Figaro, Fiordiligi in Così fan tutte, Desdemona, Mimi, Dido in The Trojans, Donna Elvira in Don Giovanni, Marina in Boris Godunov, Tatiana in Eugene Onegin, Lavinia in Mourning Becomes Electra, title role in Lulu. Recordings include: Wozzeck, Lulu, The Flying Dutchman, The Magic Flute, Boris Godunov, Eugene Onegin, Bach's St John Passion, Pergolesi's Stabat Mater, Der Rosenkavalier. Honours: Concert Artists Guild Award 1955, Grammy Award for Best Operatic Performance 1965. Address: 414 Sailboat Circle, Lauderdale, FL 33326; 15101 Rosecroft Road, Rockville, MD 20853, USA (home).

**LEATHERBY, Carol Ann;** Singer (Mezzo-contralto) and Director of Victoriana (Victorian Musical Entertainment); b. 1948, Barking, London, England. Education: Morley College with Ilse Wolf, 1968–69; Guildhall School of Music and Drama, 1969–71; Vienna with Eugenie Ludwig, 1981–82; Private study in London with Lyndon Van der Pump, 1972–. Career: Debut: Purcell Room, London, 1973; Welsh National Opera, 1973–75; Covent Garden Opera, 1975–78; Glyndebourne Festival Opera, 1979–80; New Opera, 1981; Music in Camera, Southern Television, 1980; Delius Talk on Radio London, 1980; Broadcasts for BBC, London and Cardiff; Recitals at Purcell Room, Wigmore Hall; Concerts at Festival Hall and Queen Elizabeth Hall; Memorial concert for Princess Grace of Monaco at Queen Elizabeth Hall, 1983; Specialist in the songs of Frederick Delius; Athens Festival, 1985; Alte Oper, Frankfurt, 1985, 1986; Purcell Room concerts as member of Quintessence founded in 1984, presenting Victorian and Edwardian entertainment in costume and performing music by Gershwin and Cole Porter, 1984, 1985 and 1986; The Vampyr, soap opera for BBC 2 television, music by Heinrich Marschner, 1992; Street Singer (Dance to the Music of Time) BBC television, 1998. *Recordings:* Czech songs by Foerster, Smetana and Dvořák, 1983; Songs of Praise, BBC television; Sita-Mother Earth-Holst recorded at St John's Smith Square in conjunction with the Holst Society. *Current Management:* Pat Nash, Nash International, 135 Epping New Road, Buckhurst Hill, Essex IG9 5TZ. *Address:* 278 Monega Road, Manor Park, London E12 6TS, England.

**LEBARON, Alice Anne;** Composer and Professor of Music; b. 30 May 1953, Baton Rouge, LA, USA; m. Edward J. Eadon 1982; one d. *Education:* BA, music, Univ. of Alabama, 1974; MA, music, State Univ. of New York, Stony Brook, 1978; Darmstadt, 1980; Köln Musikhochschule, 1980–81; National Classical Music Institute, Korea, 1983; DMA, Columbia Univ., 1989. *Career:* Composer-in-Residence (Meet The Composer New Residencies), Washington, DC, 1993–96; Asst Prof. of Music Composition and Theory, Univ. of Pittsburgh, 1997–2001; Prof. of Music, Calif. Inst. of the Arts 2001–. *Compositions:* The E and O Line; Croak (The Last Frog), chamber opera; orchestral: Strange Attractors; Southern Ephemera, 1994; Lasting Impressions, 1995; Mambo, 1995; American Icons, 1996, Traces of Mississippi 2000; chamber music: Pope Joan, Sauger, Inner Voice, Telluris Theoria Sacra, The Sea and the Honeycomb, Noh Reflections, Metamorphosis, Rite of the Black Sea, Planxty Bowerbird, I Am An American... My Government Will Reward You, Lamentation-Invocation, Concerto for Active Frogs, Dish, Waltz for Quintet, Three Motion Atmospheres, Southern Ephemera, Devil in the Belfry, Light Breaks Where No Sun Shines, Story of My Angel, Sachamama 1995, Croak 1997, Solar Music 1997, Sukey 1998; choral: Nightmare 1999. *Recordings include:* Rana, Ritual and Revelations; The Music of Anne LeBaron, 1992; Phantom Orchestra: The Anne LeBaron Quintet, 1992; The Musical Railism of Anne LeBaron, 1995. *Address:* c/o Cal Arts, 24700 McBean Parkway, Valencia, CA 91355, USA.

**LEBHERZ, Louis;** Singer (Bass); b. 14 April 1948, Bethesda, Maryland, USA. *Education:* Studied at Indiana University. *Career:* Debut: Memphis Opera, as Padre Guardiano in La Forza del Destino, 1974; Many appearances at opera houses in North and South America (Caracas, 1981); European engagements at Frankfurt, 1981, Karlsruhe, 1984–85, Berne, 1985–86, Geneva, 1988; Sang Melothal in Guillaume Tell at Covent Garden and the Grand Inquisitor in Don Carlos at Los Angeles, 1990; Appeared in Massenet's La Navarraise with Long Beach Opera, 1990, as Basilio, the Commendatore in Don Giovanni at Los Angeles Music Center, 1991; Sang Rocco at New Orleans, 1992; Grech in Fedora at Los Angeles, 1997; Other roles include Sarastro, King Mark, Fasolt, Baldassare in La Favorita, Verdi's Zaccaria, Nabucco and Fiesco, Colline, and Don Diego in L'Africaine. *Recordings include:* Verdi's Aroldo; Jone by Petrella.

**LEBIC, Lojze;** Composer, Conductor and Professor of Music Theory; b. 23 Aug. 1934, Prevalje, Slovenia; m. Jelena Ukmar 1961, one d. *Education:* Diploma in Archaeology, University of Ljubljana, 1957; Academy of Music, Ljubljana, 1972; studies in Darmstadt. *Career:* Conductor, RTV Ljubljana 1962–72; appeared at Musica Antiqua Europae Orientalis Festival, Bydgozscz, Poland, 1968; Festival van Vlaanderen, 1968; Ohrid Festival, 1968; Jihlava Festival, Czechoslovakia, 1969; Zagreb Biennale, 1969; Dubrovnik Festival, 1969; ISCM Festivals, Brussels, 1981, Zürich, 1991 and Bucharest, 1999; Prof., Univ. of Ljubljana, 1985–. *Compositions include:* Orchestral works: Voices; Korant; Ouverture; Tangram; Cantico I; Nicina, Qeensland Music; Solo instruments with orchestra: Sentences; Symphony with organ, 1993; Voice with orchestra: Myth and Apocrypha, November Song, Burnt Grass; Music About Time, 1996; Chamber Music: Kons a, Kons b; Expressions, String Quartet, Quartet for percussion; Illud tempus; Invisibilia, April vignettes, Chalumeau I–III, Meditation for two; Epicedion; From nearby and far away; Rubato per viola; A taste of time fleeting away; Rej; Impromptus I–IV; Vocal Instrumental: Ajdna for choirs, recorders and percussion instruments; Fauvel 86-vocal instrumental scene; In the Silent Rustle of Time; Eulogy to the World. *Recordings:* various as conductor and composer. *Publications:* The Basis of Music Art, book, 1982; Sound and Silence, Compositional Synthesis of the Eighties, Music Biennale Zagreb, 1985. *Address:* Bratov Ucakar 134, 1000 Ljubljana, Slovenia. *Website:* www2.arnes.si/~hlebic.

**LEBRECHT, Norman;** British writer; b. 11 July 1948, London, England; m. Elbie Spivack 1977; three d. *Education:* Bar Ilan Univ., Israel. *Career:* radio and television producer 1969–78; writer 1978–; Asst Ed., Evening Standard, London 2002–; mem. Soc. of Authors. *Publications:* Discord 1982, Hush! Handel's in a Passion 1985, The Book of Musical Anecdotes 1985, Mahler Remembered 1987, The Book of Musical Days 1987, The Maestro Myth 1991, Music in London 1991, The Companion to Twentieth-Century Music 1992, When the Music Stops 1996, Who Killed Classical Music? 1997, Covent Garden: Dispatches from the English Culture War, 1945–2000 2000, The Song of Names (Whitbread First Novel Award) 2002. *Current Management:* Curtis Brown Ltd, Haymarket House, 28–29 Haymarket, London, SW1Y 4SP, England. *Telephone:* (20) 7393-4400. *Fax:* (20) 7393-4401. *E-mail:* info@curtisbrown.co.uk. *Website:* www.curtisbrown.co.uk. *Address:* 3 Bolton Road, London, NW8 0RJ, England.

**LECHNER, Gabriela;** Austrian singer (soprano); *Professor of Vocal Training and Interpretation, University of Music, Vienna;* b. 8 March 1961. *Education:* Hochschule für Musik und Darstellende Kunst, Vienna. *Career:* sang Sulamith in The Queen of Sheba with the Graz Opera, appeared later in Don Giovanni, Mefistofele (Margarita and Elena), La Forza del Destino, Otello, Don Carlos, Trovatore, Elektra and Cavalleria Rusticana; Amelia in Un Ballo in Maschera at the Vienna Staatsoper (with Pavarotti) followed by such operas as Simon Boccanegra, Trovatore, Otello, Zauberflöte, Rusalka, Elektra, Der Rosenkavalier, Capriccio, Contes d'Hoffmann and Die Walküre (in Vienna); engagements with the Zürich Opera as Elsa in Lohengrin, Der fliegende Holländer (Senta), the Marschallin in Der Rosenkavalier, Capriccio (Gräfin), both Verdi Leonoras, Chrysothemis in Elektra, Elisabetta (Don Carlos) Tosca, the Empress (Die Frau ohne Schatten), Ariadne, Falstaff (Alice Ford), Aida, Amelia in Ballo, Giulietta in Contes d'Hoffmann, Andrea Chénier, (Maddalena); guest appearances at Madrid, Barcelona, Berlin, Paris, Frankfurt, Hamburg, Cologne, Amsterdam, Munich, Prague, Florence, Rome, Edinburgh and Glasgow; conductors have included Abbado, Bernstein, Mehta, Maazel, Barenboim, Dohnányi and Sinopoli; other roles include Valentine (Huguenots), Elettra (Idomeneo), Alceste in Amsterdam, Vitellia (Titus) in Barcelona, Regan (Lear) in Germany, Carlotta in Die Gezeichneten by Schreker (at Zürich and Paris); Guest Prof. for vocal technique and interpretation, Univ. of Music in Vienna 2001–04, Prof. 2004–. *Recordings include:* Un Ballo in Maschera – Amelia with Pavarotti/Abbado (TV), Tosca with Neil Shicoff/Ruggiero Raimondi (TV), Beethoven's Ninth Symphony (album), Humperdinck's Hansel and Gretel (DVD). *Honours:* several major competition awards. *Address:* c/o Theaterplatz 2, 2500 Baden/Vienna, Austria. *E-mail:* lechner@mdw.ac.at (office).

**LEDGER, Sir Philip Stevens,** Kt, CBE, MA, DMus, LLD, FRCM, FRNCM, FRCO; British conductor, organist, pianist/harpsichordist and academy principal; b. 12 Dec. 1937, Bexhill-on-Sea, Sussex; s. of the late Walter Stephen Ledger and Winifred Kathleen Ledger (née Stevens); m. Mary Erryl Wells 1963; one s. one d. *Education:* Bexhill Grammar School, King's Coll. Cambridge. *Career:* Master of the Music, Chelmsford Cathedral 1962–65; Dir of Music, Univ. of East Anglia 1965–73, Dean of School of Fine Arts and Music 1968–71; an Artistic Dir Aldeburgh Festival of Music and Arts 1968–89, Vice-Pres. 1989–; Conductor, Cambridge Univ. Musical Soc. 1973–82; Dir of Music and Organist, King's Coll. Cambridge 1974–82; Prin. Royal Scottish Acad. of Music and Drama 1982–2001; John Stewart of Rannoch Scholar in Sacred Music; Pres. Royal Coll. of Organists 1992–94; Pres. Inc. Soc. of Musicians 1994–95; Chair. Cttee of Prins of Conservatoires 1994–98. *Publications:* (Ed.) Anthems for Choirs 2 and 3 1973, Oxford Book of English Madrigals 1978, edns of Byrd, Handel and Purcell and carol arrangements. *Honours:* Hon. Prof. Univ. of Glasgow 1993–98; Hon. mem. RAM, Guildhall School of Music; Hon. LLD (Strathclyde) 1987, Hon. DUniv (Central England) 1998, Hon. DMus (St Andrews, Glasgow and RSAMD) 2001; Silver Medal of Worshipful Company of Musicians. *Address:* 2 Lancaster Drive, Upper Rissington, Cheltenham, Glos., GL54 2QZ, England (home).

**LEE, Chan-hae,** BM, MM; South Korean composer; b. 8 Oct. 1945, Seoul. *Education:* Yonsei Univ., Catholic Univ. of America, Washington, DC, USA. *Career:* Lecturer, Prof., Yonsei Univ. 1977–; Visiting Prof. Wayne State Univ. 1984, Oakland Univ. 1985, Univ. of Calif., Berkeley 2004–05; Research Assoc., Nationale Conservatoire de Paris, France 1994; Pres., The Korean Soc. of 21st Century Music 1998–; Pres. Korean Women's Soc. of Composition 2001–; Vice-Pres. Korean Women's Asscn for Culture and Arts 2002–; Korean Liaison and mem. Admin. Cttee, Int. Alliance of Women in Music 2002–; mem. bd Korean Music Soc. 1996–; Gen. Sec. Asian Composers' League 1999–, Vice-Pres. (Korea) 2000–; mem. Int. Soc. of Contemporary Music 1990–. *Compositions include:* Hyesang and Chosaeng for voices and ensemble 1980–91, Galpiri for clarinet 1982, The Pilgrim's Progress for chamber ensemble 1990, Glorification for three percussion instruments 1990, The Martyr for string orchestra 1993, From the Point, From the Line for violin solo 1997, Transfiguration for string quartet 1998, Fire Flame for violin and orchestra 1999, Tabernacle for four percussion 1999, Musical He 1999, Be a Light in the Eastern Land for orchestra 2000, Sorickil for taeguem solo 2000, To The Hwangseung for pansori and chamber ensemble 2001, A Total Eclipse of the Sun for flute, clarinet, cello and percussion 2001, The Island under the Full Moon for solo trombone 2001, The Creation (musical) 2001, The Planet Earth for two drummers and orchestra 2001, Be a Light in the Eastern Land 2002, Celebration for wind orchestra 2002, A Beautiful Land for male chorus and orchestra 2002, Ave Maria Stella for mixed chorus 2002, Color in Color for clarinet, violin and cello 2003, Back to the Origin (opera) 2003, The King (musical) 2003, Sin Offering for solo haegeum 2003, Womb of Earth for daegeum, kayageum and traditional orchestra 2004. *Recordings include:* Galpiri 1985, From the Point, From the Line 1998, Musical He 1999, Fire Flame 2000, Sorickil 2000, Back to the Origin 2003, Tabernacle 2003. *Publications:* Music Theory 1978, 16C Counterpoint 1985, Contemporary Music I and II 1991, New Approach to Sightsinging and Ear Training I and II 1995, Introduction to Contemporary Music 1998. *Honours:* Korean Nat. Composition Prize 1999, Int. Rome Choral Music Award 2002. *Address:* Itaewondong Chongwha Apt 2-603, Yongsanku, Seoul, Republic of Korea. *Telephone:* (2) 2123-3080. *Fax:* (2) 313-2821. *E-mail:* chhlee@yonsei.ac.kr.

**LEE, Dennis (Ean Hooi),** BMus, MMus; pianist; b. 2 Dec. 1946, Penang, Malaysia; m. Chee-Hung Toh 1990. *Education:* Univ. of London, Royal Coll. of Music, London with Angus Morrison, Vienna Hochschule with Josef Dichler, studied with Ilonka Deckers in Milan. *Career:* debut, Purcell Room, London, and Kennedy Center, Washington, DC; concerts (recitals, chamber music and orchestral appearances), television and radio recordings, the UK, Europe, USA, Canada, S America, Hong Kong, Japan, China, South-East Asia, Australia, New Zealand; radio broadcasts include live transmissions for BBC Radio 3; festivals include Adelaide, Montreux, Spoleto, Cheltenham, Brighton, Lincoln, Newbury, Warwick, Mananan, Arundel, Singapore Piano Festival; orchestral appearances include BBC Regional, Hallé, Wiener Symphoniker, London Mozart Players, RAI Milan, Polish and Slovak Chamber Orchestras, Warsaw Philharmonic Orchestra, Shanghai Symphony, Singapore Symphony, Malaysian Philharmonic; adjudicator at festivals and competitions; examiner for the Associated Bd of the Royal Schools of Music 1977–. *Recordings:* Szymanowski Piano Pieces, Ravel Duets with Philippe Entremont. *Honours:* BBC Competition prize 1971, Casagrande prize, Italy 1975, 1977, Sydney prize 1977, Busoni prize, Italy 1975. *Address:* Flat 5, 12 St Quintin Avenue, London, W10 6NU, England. *E-mail:* dleepiano@aol.com.

**LEE, Douglas Allen,** BMus, MMus, PhD; American academic; *Emeritus Professor and Chair of Musicology, Vanderbilt University;* b. 3 Nov. 1932, Carmel, IN; m. Beverly Haskell 1961. *Education:* DePauw Univ., Univ. of Michigan, Nat. Endowment for the Humanities Seminar in Editing Early Music, studied with Theodore Lettvin and György Sandor. *Career:* instructor, Mount Union Coll., Alliance, OH 1959–61; Prof. of Music, Wichita State Univ., Kansas 1964–86; Prof. of Musicology, Vanderbilt Univ., Nashville, TN 1986–98, Prof. Emeritus 1998–; Faculty, Mount Union Coll., Univ. of Michigan, Int. Music Camp-Interlochen, Wichita State Univ., Vanderbilt Univ.; Ed., American Music Teacher 1968–70, Sonneck Soc. Newsletter 1988–90. *Publications:* The Works of Christoph Nichelmann 1971, Christoph Nichelmann – Two Concertos 1977, Six Sonatas of Franz Benda, with Embellishments 1981, Franz Benda – A Thematic Catalogue 1984, Chapters in Great Lives in Music – Renaissance to 1800 1989, two chapters in Great Events in History, Arts and Culture 1993, C. P. E. Bach: Six Keyboard Concertos (Collected Works), A Musician at Court: An Autobiography of Franz Benda 1998, Masterworks of Twentieth Century Music 2002, two essays in a reference encyclopedia on The Fifties in America (two vols) 2005; contrib. 23 articles to New Grove Dictionary of Music and Musicians. *Honours:* Outstanding Educators of America award 1973. *Address:* c/o Vanderbilt University, Blair School of Music, 2400 Blakemore Avenue, Nashville, TN 37212 (office); 6517 Cornwall Drive, Nashville, TN 37205, USA (home). *Telephone:* (615) 322-7651 (office).

**LEE, Lynda;** Singer (Soprano); b. 1969, Ireland. *Education:* Studied at the Dublin College of Music. *Career:* Opera engagements with Opera Northern Ireland, Wexford Festival, Musica nel Chiostro and at the Covent Garden Festival as Irene in Tamerlano; Karlsruhe Handelfestspiel, Halle Handelfestspiele; Théâtre de Caen; Expo 98 Lisbon; Covent Garden Festival; On Contract with Opera Leipzig until 2001; Concerts with the Ulster Orchestra, at the Glasgow Mayfest, Bath Festival and in Jonathan Miller's production of the St Matthew Passion; RTE Symphony Orchestra; RIAS Kammerchor, Berlin; Represented Ireland at the 1993 Cardiff Singer of the World Competition; Sang Handel's Agrippina and Zenobia in Radamisto at Halle, 2000–01. *Recordings include:* Bach's, St Matthew Passion, Wallace's Maritana. *Current Management:* Neill Thornborrow at Heissler Remy. *Address:* Drakestrasse 2, 40545 Düsseldorf, Germany.

**LEE, Mi-joo;** South Korean pianist; b. 7 July 1959, Seoul; m. Klaus Hellwig. *Education:* Folkwanghochschule, Essen; Hochschule der Künste, Berlin; New England Conservatory, Boston; Mozarteum, Salzburg. *Career:* stage appearances with orchestra and solo recitals at Berlin Philharmonic Hall, Schauspielhaus, Munich, Dresden, Paris, Milan, Brussels, Tokyo, Seoul, various European countries and many German cities; television and radio appearances on WDR, NDR, RIAS Berlin, Deutschlandfunk, Deutschland Radio Berlin, Radio France, BRT Brussels, Czechoslovak broadcast, Korean broadcast, DeutscheWelle, Südwestfunk 3. *Recordings:* C. Saint-Saëns op 72, 52, 111; Humoresken (Schumann, Reger, Dohnany, Rachmaninov); M. Ravel Concerto G-Major; R. and C. Schumann Op 105, 121, Op 22; Beethoven Op 13, Chopin, Liszt and six Paganini Études; R. Schumann Op 3, 10, 14. *Address:* Mommsenstr 58, 10629 Berlin, Germany.

**LEE, Michelle;** Flautist; b. 31 May 1952, London, England; one d. *Education:* Bartók Conservatory, Budapest, Hungary, 1970–71; Royal College of Music, London, 1971–75; Robert Schumann Institute, Düsseldorf, Germany, 1975–76, 1977–78; Franz Liszt Academy, Budapest, Hungary, 1978–80; ARCM, Flute, Recorder and Piano; Examiner of Music for Trinity College, London; MA in Education and Professional Development. *Career:* Regular solo performances world-wide; Soloist for BBC Radio 3 and given many first performances including the World Premiere of György Kurtág's Seven Bagatelles, Op 14b, 1982 at her Wigmore Hall debut recital; First broadcast performance of Fauré's Morceau de Concours for Flute and Piano on BBC Radio 3, 1985; First British broadcast of György Kurtág's Seven Bagatelles, Op 14B on BBC Radio 3, 1987; First British broadcast of Lászlo Sáry's Pezzo Concerto on BBC Radio 3, 1988; Francisco Estévez, Roland Freisitzer, Philip Grange, Raimund Jülich, György Kurtág and Geoffrey Winters have written specially for her; founded the Charles Cros Festival of Music Fabrezan, France, 2003; mem British Flute Society; FRSA. *Compositions:* Scarlet Runner, for Flute, Percussion, Prerecorded Tape and 5 Synthesizers. *Recordings:* Soloist, Record of Contemporary Music with Live Electronics (Germany); Morton Feldman Flute Concerto with Moscow Philharmonic

Orchestra, 1992; Günther Becker–Drei Inventionen, 1999. *Contributions:* Editor, Trinity College London Woodwind World Flute Albums 4 and 5. *Address:* 4 rue des Tonneliers, 11200 Fabrezan, France.

**LEE, Ming Cho;** Stage Designer; b. 3 Oct. 1930, Shanghai, China. *Education:* Occidental College and University of California at Los Angeles. *Career:* Theatre and ballet designs in New York, 1955–59; Peabody Arts Theater, Baltimore, 1959–63, with designs for Il Turco in Italia, Mahagonny, Werther, Hamlet and Les Pêcheurs de Perles; Designed Tristan und Isolde for Baltimore Civic Opera and Butterfly for the Opera Company of Boston, 1962; Resident Designer at San Francisco Opera from 1961, Juilliard School, New York, 1964–70; Metropolitan Opera, 1965–, with Figaro, Boris Godunov, Lohengrin and Khovanshchina (1985); Premiere of Ginastera's Bomarzo for the Opera Society of Washington, 1967; Giulio Cesare and Lucia di Lammermoor for Hamburg Staatsoper, 1969, 1971; Teacher of set design at Yale Drama School from 1968. *Address:* c/o Metropolitan Opera, Lincoln Center, New York, NY 10023, USA.

**LEE, Noël;** American Composer and Concert Pianist; b. 25 Dec. 1924, Nanking, China. *Education:* BA cum laude, Harvard University, Cambridge, Massachusetts, USA, 1948; Artist's Diploma, New England Conservatory of Music, Boston, 1948. *Career:* Numerous concert tours and appearances in North and South America, Europe, Australia; Engagements on every European State Radio; Vast solo, concerto and chamber repertoire. *Compositions include:* Caprices on the name Schoenberg, piano and orchestra; 8 études, piano; Dialogues, violin and piano; Convergences, flute and harpsichord; Chroniques, piano; Errances, band; 5 songs on Lorca, soprano, flute, guitar; Songs of Calamus, voice, clarinet, cello, percussion; Triptyque, violin, piano and orchestra; Dance Fantasy, orchestra; 5 Preludes prolonged, piano; Partita, quintet piano and winds; Le tombeau d'Aaron Copland, sextet; Azurs, voice and piano 4 hands, plus 13 other song cycles; Variations antiques, flute and piano; 3 Fantasy pieces, flute and guitar. *Recordings include:* 198 solo, piano 4-hand, chamber, and vocal works of Schubert, 19th–century French composers, Debussy, Ravel, Stravinsky, Bartók, Copland, Ives, Carter and other American composers. *Publications:* Critical edition of Debussy's Two Piano works, 1989, and Four-Hand Works, 2001. *Honours:* Commdr des Arts et Lettres, 1998; Grand Prix for Music, City of Paris, 1999. *Address:* 4 Villa Laugier, 75017 Paris, France. *E-mail:* noel.lee@wanadoo.fr.

**LEE, Sung-sook;** South Korean singer (soprano); b. 1948. *Education:* studied in Republic of Korea and at the Juilliard School, New York. *Career:* debut, Premiere of Menotti's Tamu Tamu, Chicago, 1973; sang at Spoleto Festival and San Francisco, 1974; La Scala and Covent Garden 1975; Frankfurt Opera 1976–77; Seattle Opera and Miami from 1978; New York City Opera 1975–76; Concert appearances with the Buffalo Philharmonic, Seattle, Dallas and Pittsburgh Symphonies; Repertoire has included music by Puccini and Rossini (Stabat Mater). *Address:* c/o New York City Opera, Lincoln Center, New York, NY 10023, USA.

**LEE, Young-ja;** South Korean composer; b. 4 June 1936, Wonju. *Education:* studied in Seoul, at the Paris and Brussels Conservatoires and the Manhattan School of Music. *Career:* performances of her work in Europe, Republic of Korea and Central America. *Compositions include:* Suite for orchestra, 1971; Movement symphonique for orchestra, 1972; Piano concerto, 1979; Piano sonata, 1985; Three Love Songs for soprano and harp, 1991; Gae-chun for orchestra, 1991; Quintet for flute, harp and string trio, 1992. *Address:* c/o KOMCA, 2,3/F Samjeon Building, 236-3 Nonhyeon-dong, Kangnam-gu, Seoul, Republic of Korea.

**LEECH, Richard;** Singer (Tenor); b. 1956, Binghamton, California, USA. *Career:* Sang first as baritone, then sang Offenbach's Hoffmann while a student; Many concert and opera appearances from 1980, notably at Cincinnati, Pittsburgh, Baltimore, Houston and Chicago; European debut at the Deutsche Oper Berlin, 1987, as Raoul in Les Huguenots; Chicago Lyric Opera, 1987, and La Scala, 1991, as Rodolfo; Has sung Gounod's Faust at San Diego, 1988, and at the Orange Festival and Metropolitan Opera, 1990; Pinkerton in Washington DC and Florence and La Scala (debut 1990), 1987 and 1989; Donizetti's Edgardo and Nemorino at the Deutsche Oper Berlin, 1988–89, and the Duke of Mantua at the New York City Opera (1988) and Metropolitan Opera, 1990; Season 1991/92 as Raoul in a new production of Les Huguenots at Covent Garden (debut), Pinkerton at Chicago and the Duke of Mantua at the Met; Rodolfo at the Met, 1994; Sang Faust at the Met, 1997; Season 1998 with Gounod's Roméo at San Diego, Werther for Netherlands Opera, 1999; Season 2000–01 as Boito's Faust and Don José at the Met, Rodolfo in Luisa Miller for Palm Beach Opera and Verdi's Riccardo on debut at the Vienna Staatsoper; Concert engagements include Beethoven's Ninth and Verdi Requiem. *Recordings:* Les Huguenots; Fledermaus; Salome; Faust; Rosenkavalier. *Address:* c/o Metropolitan Opera, Lincoln Center, New York, NY 10023, USA.

**LEEDY, Douglas,** BA, MA; American composer, conductor and educator; b. 3 March 1938, Portland, OR. *Education:* Pomona Coll., Univ. of California at Berkeley, studied karnatic vocal music with K. V. Narayanaswamy. *Career:* French horn, Oakland Symphony Orchestra, San Francisco Opera, Ballet Orchestras, Cabrillo Festival Orchestra, 1969–65; mem. music faculty, Univ. of California, Los Angeles 1967–70, Reed Coll. 1973–78; Prof. of Electronic Music, Centro Simon Bolivar, Caracas, Venezuela 1972; Music Dir, Portland Baroque Orchestra 1984–85; complete performances of Handel's Jephtha and Theodora, Portland Handel Festival 1985; mem. Music Library Asscn, Int.

Heinrich Schütz Soc. *Compositions:* Usable Music I for Very Small Instruments with Holes, 1968; The Twenty-Fourth Psalm for chorus and orchestra, 1971; Fantasy on Wie schön leuchtet der Morgenstern for organ and voice; Canti/Music for contrabass and chamber ensemble; Music for Meantone Organ; Hymns from the Rig Veda for chorus and Javanese or American gamelan; Pastorale (Horace) for chorus and just-tuned piano, 4-hands, 1993; This is a Great Country, or What?, multimedia, 1995; 7 symphonies, No. 7 'Selene', 1997; 2 string quartets, 1975, 1995; No More Beethoven! for voices and electric guitar, 1997. *Recordings:* Entropical Paradise: 6 Sonic Environments, Seraphim. *Publications:* Harpsichord Book III (just tuning), Chansons from Petrucci in Original Notation 1983; contrib. to Interval, The Courant, MLA Notes, The New Grove Dictionary of American Music. *Address:* c/o Material Press, Hauke Harder, Holtenauerstr. 80, 24105 Kiel, Germany.

**LEEF, Yinam Arie,** BMus, MA, PhD; Israeli composer; *Professor, Jerusalem Rubin Academy of Music and Dance*; b. 21 Dec. 1953, Jerusalem; m. Tanya Fonarev 1978; one s. one d. *Education:* Rubin Acad. of Music, Jerusalem, Univ. of Pennsylvania, and Tanglewood, USA. *Career:* Visiting Lecturer, Swarthmore Coll., USA 1982–84; Philadelphia Coll. of the Performing Arts 1984; teacher, Univ. of Pennsylvania 1984–85; Lecturer, Sr Lecturer, Assoc. Prof., Jerusalem Rubin Acad. of Music and Dance 1985–; commissions include Fromm Music Foundation at Harvard, Swarthmore Music and Dance Festival, Concerto Soloists Chamber Orchestra of Philadelphia, Penn Contemporary Players, Jerusalem Symphony Orchestra, Israel Sinfonietta Be'er Sheva, Jerusalem Dance Workshop, Rinat Choir, Haifa Symphony Orchestra, Philadelphia Chamber Music Soc., The Verdehr Trio, The Mannheim Series for Contemporary Music; mem. ACUM, League of Composers in Israel. *Compositions:* Gilgulim, woodwind trio, 1976, for string trio, 1980; Three Pieces, piano; Fireflies, soprano, flute, harpsichord, 1977; String Quartet No. 1, 1978; KO, solo oboe, 1978; Ha'Bor, 1978; Laments, chamber orchestra, 1979; Flowers, Insects and a Very Thin Line, flute, oboe, piano trio, 1979; Canaanit Fantasy, piano, 1981; The Invisible Carmel, soprano and 5 players, 1982; Violin concerto, 1983; Octet, 1984; A Place of Fire, mezzo and 11 players, 1985; Fanfares and Whispers, trumpet and string orchestra, 1986; Sounds, Shadows for choir, 1987; How Far East, How Further West?, piano, 1988; Trio for oboe, violin, horn, 1988; Scherzos and Serenades, orchestra, 1989; Elegy, harpsichord, 1990; Tribute, orchestra, 1991; Elegy for string quartet, 1991; Symphony No. 1, 1992; Sea Songs, equal voice choir, 1993; Cantilena, guitar, 1993; Threads of Time and Distance, alto, oboe and string orchestra, 1995; Visions of Stone City, Symphony No. 2, orchestra, 1995; Yizkor, flute, 1995; Said His Lover, alto and clarinet, 1996; Night Light orchestra, 1996; Triptych for clarinet, string trio and piano, 1997; T'filah for three violins, 1997; Viola Concerto, 1998; Thre Lyrical Songs for tenor and string trio, 1999; Bagatelles for flute and piano, 2000; String Quartet No. 2, 2001, Offering, for violin and piano 2001, Reminiscences of Tranquility, for harp 2002, Hallel, for cello, two horns and string orchestra 2002, Soliloquoy, for violin 2003, Serenity Lost, for violin and chamber ensemble 2004, String Quartet No. 3 2005. *Recordings include:* Symphony No. 1, Jerusalem Symphony Orchestra; Violin Concerto, Jerusalem Symphony Orchestra; Yizkor for flute, Noam Buchman, flute; T'filah for Three Violins, 2001, How Far East, How Further West? 2003, Bagatelles, for flute and piano 2005; numerous for Israel Broadcasting Authority. *Honours:* ACUM Prize 1992, 1998, Israel Prime Minister Prize 1993. *Address:* c/o Jerusalem Academy of Music and Dance, Givat-Ram Campus, Jerusalem 91904, Israel (office).

**LEEK, Stephen;** Composer and Conductor; b. 8 Oct. 1959, Sydney, New South Wales, Australia. *Education:* Study with Larry Sitsky, 1979–83; BA (Music), Canberra School of Music, 1983; ABC Young Composers Workshop, 1985. *Career:* Tasmanian Dance Company, 1982–85; Director, Arts Now; Artistic Director, Conductor, The Australian Voices; Commissions from Seymour Group, Chamber Made Opera, Brisbane Biennial Festival, Opera Queensland, The Australian Voices, Gondwana Voices, Centenary of Federation Ceremony, among others; Residencies with St Peters Lutheran College, 1988, 1989, 1996, and Tasmanian Dance Theatre, 1993; Part-time Lecturer, Composition and Improvisation, Queensland Conservatorium. *Compositions include:* At Times... Stillness, for organ, 1985; Thought, for female chorus, flute and piano, 1988; Once on a Mountain, and Songs of Space, Sea and Sky, for choir, 1988–89; Killcallow Catch, music theatre, 1990; Stroke, music theatre in 1 act, 1990; Voyage, for chorus, 1990; Five Songs, for female chorus, 1990; Five Song of the Sun, for orchestra, 1991; As You Like It, for piano, 1992; Great Southern Spirits, for chorus, and vocal soloists, 1993; Island Songs, for chorus, female soloists and piano, 1994; Ancient Cries, 1999; Seeking True South, opera, 2001. *Recordings include:* Sea Children, The Australian Voices; One World, Chanticleer. *Honours:* Sounds Australian Awards, 1991; Churchill Fellowship, 1997. *Address:* PO Box 839, Indooroopilly, Qld 4068, Australia. *E-mail:* artsnow@thehub.com.au. *Website:* www.the australianvoices.com.au.

**LEES, Benjamin;** composer; b. 8 Jan. 1924, Harbin, China. *Education:* Univ. of Southern California with Halsey Stevens, Ingolf Dahl, studied with George Antheil, and in Europe. *Career:* teacher, Peabody Conservatory 1962–64, 1966–68, Queens Coll., New York 1964–66, Manhattan School 1972–74, Juilliard 1976–77; commissions for Tokyo String Quartet, Dallas, Delaware, Wichita and Pittsburgh Symphonies, Philadelphia and Louisville Orchestras, Chamber Music America, Cypress String Quartet, Seattle Symphony Orchestra, Detroit Symphony Orchestra, Orchestre Philharmonique de Monte Carlo, Ford Foundation, Nat. Symphony Orchestra, Pacific Serenades. *Compositions:* five piano sonatas, five string quartets, five symphonies, three

violin sonatas; Sonata for two pianos 1951, Profile for orchestra 1952, Declamations for strings and piano 1953; concertos: Piano 1955, 1966, Violin 1958, Orchestra 1959, Oboe 1963, String Quartet and Orchestra 1965, Chamber Orchestra 1966, Woodwind Quintet and Orchestra 1976, Brass and Orchestra 1983, French Horn and Orchestra 1992; The Oracle (music drama) 1955, Divertimento burlesca for orchestra 1957, Concertante breve 1959, Visions of Poets (cantata after Whitman) 1962, Spectrum for orchestra 1964, The Gilded Cage (opera) 1964, Silhouettes for wind and percussion 1967, Medea of Corinth for vocalists, wind quintet, timpani 1970, Odyssey 1 for piano trio 1971, Odyssey 2 for solo piano 1980, The Trumpet of the Swan for narrator and piano 1972, Collage for string quartet, woodwind quintet, percussion 1973, Etudes for piano and orchestra 1974, Variations for piano and orchestra 1976, Passacaglia for orchestra 1976, Fanfare for a Centennial 1976, Scarlatti Portfolio (ballet) 1979, Mobiles for orchestra 1979, Double Concerto for piano, cello 1982, Fantasy Variations for piano 1984, Portrait of Rodin for orchestra 1984, Mirrors for piano solo 1992–94, Borealis for orchestra 1993, Echoes of Normandy for tenor and orchestra 1994, Celebration for orchestra 1996, Constellations for orchestra 1997, Piano Trio No. 2: Silent Voices 1998, Trio for piano, violin and cello (Silent Voices) 1998, Intermezzo for string orchestra 1998, Concerto for percussion and orchestra 1999, Night Spectres for unaccompanied cello 1999, Mirrors for piano (complete version) 2002, Tableau for two pianos 2003, Tapestry for flute, clarinet, cello, piano 2003, The Nervous Family for SSA chorus and one bassoon 2003. *Recordings:* Symphonies 2, 3, Concerto for orchestra, Louisville Orchestra; Concerto for string quartet and orchestra, Royal Philharmonic; Violin Concerto, American Symphony; 4th Piano; 4th Piano Sonata, Gary Graffman; Complete Violin Works, Ellen Orner violin, Joel Wizansky piano; Concerto for French horn and orchestra, 1997; Symphony No. 4, Memorial Candles, 1998; Symphony Nos 2, 3 and 5, Staatsphilharmonie Rheinland-Pfalz, 2001; Etudes for Piano and Orchestra, Texas Festival Orchestra 2001; Piano Concerto No.2, Albany Symphony Orchestra, withIan Hobson, piano, 2002; Piano Trio No.2 Silent Voices, 2002; Piano Concerto No.1, Nat. Orchestral Asscn, with Joseph Bloch, piano, 2003; Passacaglia for orchestra, Oregon Symphony, 2003. *Honours:* Guggenheim Fellow 1954, 1966, Fulbright Fellow 1956–57, Sir Arnold Bax Medal 1958, Lancaster Symphony Orchestra Composer Award 1985. *Address:* 2451-A Birdie Way, Palm Springs, CA 92264, USA.

**LEFANU, Nicola Frances,** DMus, FRCM; British composer; b. 28 April 1947, Essex; d. of William Richard LeFanu and Elizabeth Violet Maconchy; m. David Newton Lumsdaine 1979; one d. *Education:* St Mary's School, Calne, St Hilda's Coll., Oxford and Royal Coll. of Music. *Career:* Dir of Music St Paul's Girls' School 1975–77; Composer-in-Residence New South Wales Conservatorium of Music, Sydney, Australia 1979; Del. to Moscow Int. New Music Festival 1984; Prof. of Music Univ. of York 1994–; has composed over 60 works including opera, orchestral works, chamber music with and without voice, choral music and solo pieces; Mendelssohn Scholar 1972; Harkness Fellow for composition study Harvard Univ. (MA, USA) 1973–74; Fellow Trinity Coll. of Music, London. *Honours:* Hon. Fellow St Hilda's Coll. (Oxford); Leverhulme Research Award 1989, Cobbett Prize for Chamber Music 1968, First Prize, BBC Composers Competition 1971. *Address:* Department of Music, University of York, Heslington, York, YO10 5DD, England (office). *Telephone:* (1904) 432445 (office). *Fax:* (1904) 432450 (office).

**LEFEBVRE, Claude;** French composer; b. 11 Nov. 1931, Ardres, Calais; m. Ingeborg Giese 1965; two d. *Education:* Paris Conservatory with Darius Milhaud, Musikakademie, Basel, Switzerland with Pierre Boulez. *Career:* teacher of analysis and composition, Conservatory, Metz 1966–96; founder, Artistic Dir, Centre européen pour la recherche musicale, and Int. Meeting of Contemporary Music, Metz 1972–92; Lecturer in Contemporary Music, Univ. of Metz 1976; founder and Artistic Dir, electro-acoustic studio, Lorraine 1978; founder and Artistic Dir, Music Centre, Rendez-vous musique nouvelle, Forbach 1996–2004; freelance composer 2004–. *Compositions include:* Suite, for baritone and ensemble, 1960; D'un arbre de nuit, for flute, cello and piano, 1971; Etwas weiter, for 24 musicians, 1972; Verzweigungen, for organ, 1976; Dérives nocturnes, for choir, 4 horns and organ, 1978; Mémoires souterraines, for flute, clarinet and amplified cello, 1980; Océan de Terre, after a poem by Apollinaire, for soprano, flute, clarinet, trumpet, cello and magnetic band, 1981; Lorraine, for horn and magnetic band, 1983; Oregon, own poem, for soprano and quintet, 1984; Mosella, after a poem by d'Ausone, for organ, 2 trumpets and magnetic band, 1984; Savoure, on a text by Nathalie Méfano, for solo bass, 1984; La Chute, own poem, for bass, piano and magnetic band, 1987; Vallée, Homage to Maurice Ravel, for solo horn, 1987; Virage, on a poem by the composer, 12 mixed voices, 1987; Sur le lac... la main, for children's choir, 1991; L'Insoumise, 2 trumpets, piano and string orchestra, 1991; D'un arbre-océan, for piano, 1992; X..., for baritone and 12 instrumentalists, 1994; Vertigo for soprano and string sextet, 1994; Mort, for baritone, piano and 3 brass instruments, 1996; L'homme et la mer, for organ, 1997; Musique pour René Char, for horn and cello, 1998, Toutes les têtes voltigent dans la nuit, for soundtrack and piano 1999, Luzifer: in den hohen Trompeten der Bäume, for bass singer, clarinet, horn, cello and accordion 2000, Cor(ps) à Cor(ps), for two horns and orchestra 2000, Cinq poèmes pour choeur d'hommes, for male choir 2002, Dans la guele du ciel, for speech and flute orchestra 2004. *Recordings:* three albums. *Publications:* Toutes les têtes voltigent dans la nuit (selected poems). *Honours:* Grand Prix SACEM for chamber music 1980, Officier, Ordre des Arts et des Lettres 1985. *Address:* 9 rue Claude Debussy, 57130 Jouy-aux-Arches, France (home). *Telephone:* 3-87-60-94-20 (home).

**LEFEBVRE, Pierre;** singer (tenor); b. 1959, Drummondville, QC, Canada. *Education:* studied in Montréal and Italy. *Career:* sang at first in such roles as Edgardo and Rodolfo; guest appearances in Lucca, Rome and Montréal; La Scala Milan in Fidelio, Traviata and Don Carlos; Frankfurt Opera Franchetti's Cristoforo Colombo; further Giovanna d'Arco at Bologna, and in Don Zauberflöte at Turin; sang in Les Contes de Hoffmann at the Met 1998. *Recordings include:* Video of Giovanna d'Arco. *Current Management:* Opéra et Concert, 7 rue de Clichy, 75009 Paris, France. *Telephone:* 1 42 96 18 18. *Fax:* 1 42 96 18 00. *E-mail:* agence@opera-concert.com. *Website:* www.opera-concert .com.

**LEFKOWITZ, Mischa;** Concert Violinist; b. 17 March 1954, Riga, Latvia; m. Irini Lefkowitz, 15 June 1980. *Education:* Special School of Music, Riga; Moscow Conservatory of Music; Wayne State University, Detroit, USA; Mozarteum Academy, Salzburg. *Career:* Debut: New York, 1984; Paris, 1985; Radio Show, KPFK; Radio appearances, KPFC, Los Angeles, KCRW, Los Angeles; Television appearances on CBS; Orchestral appearances with major orchestras and recitals; mem, Chamber Music America; College Music Society. *Compositions:* (Recorded) Mozart Concerto A Major; Giardini Concerto A Major; Bloch Concerto; Works by Sarasate, Prokofiev. *Recordings:* Laurel and Sequence Records; Recorded with London Philharmonic and English Chamber Orchestras. *Contributions:* New York Times; Boston Globe; LA Times. *Honours:* City of Paris Prize, 1985; Carnegie Hall American Music Prize, 1983. *Current Management:* ICA Management. *Address:* 3435 Bonnie Hill Drive, Los Angeles, CA 90068, USA.

**LEFTERESCU, Petre;** Violinist and Professor; b. 1 May 1936, Bistrita, Romania; m. Ogneanca Tomici, 27 Sept 1958. *Education:* Bucharest Music Academy, 1953–58 with I. Geanta; Postgraduate courses, Moscow Conservatory, USSR, at D Oistrakh Violin Chair, 1967; Doctor in Musicology, Bucharest, National University of Music, 1999. *Career:* Solo concerts and chamber music, tours as violinist, Romania, 1958–; Violin professor, Cluj Music Academy, 1958–69; Professor of Chamber Music, Bucharest Academy of Music, 1960–; 1st violin, Forum String Quartet, 1985–; Rector of the National University of Music, Bucharest, 1992–96 and 1996–2000; Vicepresident Association Europeanne des Conservatoires, AEC, Paris, 1992–2000; Concert Tours in Germany, Spain, Hungary, China, Singapore. *Recordings:* Romanian and universal music. *Contributions:* Muzica Contemporanul. *Current Management:* ARIA, Romanian Artists' Management Company. *Address:* Calea Victoriei Nr 83, et IX, ap 37, Bucharest 70176, Romania. *Telephone:* 0040 21 6503739.

**LEGA, Luigi;** Singer (Tenor); b. 7 April 1940, Bordighera, Italy. *Education:* Studied in Rome, Basle and Mannheim. *Career:* Debut: Overhausen, as Pinkerton, 1961; Many appearancea at such German opera centres as Munich, Hamburg, Stuttgart, Mannheim, Berlin (Deutsche Oper) and Wuppertal; Further engagements at Amsterdam, Palermo, Barcelona, Rio de Janeiro, Trieste and Vienna as Verdi's Radames, Duke of Mantua, Alvaro, Alfredo, Don Carlos, Manrico and Riccardo; Also a noted interpreter of Don José, Edgardo, Florestan, Andrea Chénier, Turiddu, Rodolfo, Cavaradossi and Des Grieux in Manon Lescaut; Teacher of singing in Wuppertal. *Address:* c/o Wuppertal Buhnen, Spinnstrasse 4, 5600 Wuppertal, Germany.

**LEGANY, Denes;** Composer, Pianist, Conductor and Professor; b. 14 May 1965, Budapest, Hungary; m. Eva Toth 1990; three s. one d. *Education:* BM, Bartók Conservatory of Music; MM, DMA, Liszt Acad. of Music; MD, General Education Management, Budapest Univ. *Career:* Prof., Budapest Univ. School of Music, 1987–94; Prof., Vice-Pres., Budapest Conservatory of Music, 1993–98; specialist, Hungarian Music Council, 1997–; Dir, László Lajtha School of Music and Arts, 1998–99; Artistic and Educational Adviser, Hungarian Music Council, 1999–; Liason Officer, Hungarian Music Information Centre, 1999–; Visiting Prof., several colls and univs; recitals in three continents; lectures on television and radio. *Recordings:* Hommage à Bartók, 1995; works recorded by Hungarian and foreign record companies; Werner Brüggemann series. *Publications:* Easy Piano Pieces for children; Festival Music, for band; Trios for French horn; Suite for trumpet; Trombone Quartets; Saxophone Quartet; Air, for saxophone and piano; Flute Duos; Three Children's Choruses; Fragments, for saxophone solo; Developing Contemporary Art Pedagogical Concepts, 1993. *Address:* Apahida Utca 11, 1112 Budapest, Hungary.

**LEGANY, Dezsö,** LLD, DMusSc; Hungarian musicologist; b. 19 Jan. 1916, Szombathely; m. Erzsébet Hegyi 1961; two s. *Education:* Univ. of Pécs, Liszt Acad. of Music, Budapest, Hungarian Acad. of Sciences, Budapest. *Career:* Prof., Liszt Acad. of Music, Budapest 1951–58; Prof., Bartók Conservatory of Music, Budapest 1958–73; Head of Hungarian Music Dept, Inst. for Musicology, Hungarian Acad. of Sciences 1973–83. *Publications:* Henry Purcell 1959, A Chronicle of Hungarian Music: A Thousand Years of Music History in Documents 1962, Works of F. Erkel 1975, Liszt in Hungary 1869–1873 1976, Letters of Z. Kodály 1982, Liszt and his Country, 1869–1873 1983, F. Liszt Unbekannte Presse und Briefe aus Wien 1822–1886 1984, Liszt in Hungary 1874–86 1986, Liszt and his Country, 1874–1886 1992, Letters of Z. Kodály, Vol. II 2000; contrib. to New Grove Dictionary, New Grove Dictionary of Opera, Sohlmans Musiklexikon, Concise Oxford Dictionary of Opera, Zenei Lexikon, Studia Musicologica, Magyar Zene, New Hungarian Quarterly, Bulletin of the International Kodály Society. *Honours:* Pres.'s Council Labour Decoration, Golden Degree 1987, Honour of the Republic of Hungary 1992, Intermediate Cross of the Hungarian Republic 1993; Artistic

Foundation Grand Prize 1982, American Liszt Soc. Award 1984, Ciffra Foundation Prize 1986, Erkel Ferenc Prize 1988. *Address:* Apahida u 11, 1112 Budapest, Hungary. *Telephone:* (1) 319-5625.

**LEGGATE, Robin,** BA, MA; British singer (tenor); b. 18 April 1946, West Kirby, Cheshire, England. *Education:* Queen's Coll., Oxford, Royal Northern Coll. of Music. *Career:* Royal Opera House, Covent Garden from 1977–2003, as Cassio in Otello (conducted by Zubin Mehta, Christoph von Dohnányi and Colin Davis); Elemer (Arabella), Narraboth (Salome), the Painter in Lulu and Tamino in a new production of Die Zauberflöte, 1979; has also sung in Prince Igor and Il Trovatore at Covent Garden; appearances with the Netherlands Opera and at the Hamburg Staatsoper from 1978; South Australian Opera 1982, as Ferrando in Così fan tutte; Théâtre du Châtelet, Paris, as Tamino 1983; other Mozart roles include Belmonte and Don Ottavio, which he has sung with most of the regional British cos; recent engagements in Le nozze di Figaro in Madrid, Weber's Oberon with Scottish Opera, Eisenstein in a new production of Die Fledermaus for Scottish Opera, and the premiere of André Laporte's Das Schloss, in Brussels; has sung at the Festival Hall from 1976 (debut with the London Symphony in Pulcinella); sang in Mendelssohn's Elijah at Florence 1981, and appeared in Mozart's C minor Mass with the London Philharmonic, conducted by Solti; sang in the stage premiere of Gerhard's Duenna, Madrid 1992; sang in world premiere of Life with an Idiot by Schnittke at Netherlands Opera 1992; Opéra Bastille (St François d'Assise) and at Salzburg Festival (Salome) 1993; sang in first production of Stiffelio (Verdi) at Royal Opera House 1993; Cassio at Covent Garden 1994; The Scribe (Khovanshchina) at La Monnaie, Brussels; Don Basilio in Figaro for the Royal Opera 1998; sang Dr Caius in Falstaff, which opened the new Royal Opera House and Pollux in Die Liebe der Danaë at Garsington 1999; Panait in The Greek Passion by Martinů at Covent Garden 2000, Peter Quint with Chicago Opera Theater 2003; Von Aschenbach with Chicago Opera Theater 2004, Captain Vere with Washington Nat. Opera 2004. *Recordings include:* La Fanciulla del West from Covent Garden, Haydn's Armida, The Light of Life by Elgar. *Address:* 26 Baronsmere Road, London, N2 9QE, England. *Telephone:* (20) 8444-7728 (home). *E-mail:* rleg8@aol.com (home). *Website:* www .robinleggate.com.

**LEGGE, Anthony;** British conductor and chief coach; *Director of Opera, Royal Academy of Music;* b. 1948, England. *Education:* Guildhall School London, Univ. of Oxford, London Opera Centre, studied piano accompaniment with Geoffrey Parsons and Paul Hamburger. *Career:* coach at Glyndebourne from 1993, with Béatrice et Bénédict, Eugene Onegin 1996 and Rodelinda 1998; song recitals with Janet Baker, Thomas Allen, Alan Opie and Robert Tear; Asst, Bayreuth for Die Meistersinger and Barenboim-Kupfer Ring cycle; Head of Music, ENO 1989–2003, part-time music adviser 2003–; Dir of Opera, RAM 2004–; Music Dir, Clonter Opera. *Recordings include:* recital albums with Linda Finnie. *Publication:* The Art of Auditioning. *Address:* c/o Royal Academy of Music, Marleybone Road, London, NW1 5HT, England.

**LEGGE-SCHWARZKOPF, Dame Elisabeth,** DBE; Austrian/British (b. German) singer (soprano); b. 9 Dec. 1915, Jarotschin (now Jarocin), Poznań; d. of Friedrich Schwarzkopf and Elisabeth Schwarzkopf (née Fröhlich); m. Walter Legge 1953 (died 1979). *Education:* Berlin Hochschule für Musik, studied with Prof. Lula Mysz-Gmeiner, Dr Heinrich Egenolf and Maria Ivogün-Raucheisen. *Career:* debut at Deutsches Opernhaus, Berlin 1938; sang at inauguration of post-war Bayreuth Festival 1951; appeared at Vienna State Opera 1943–49, 1958–65, Royal Opera House, Covent Garden 1948–50, La Scala Milan 1948–63, San Francisco Opera 1955–79, Metropolitan Opera, New York 1964–66, Chicago Opera and others; guest singer, Salzburg Festival 1947–64, Reopening of Bayreuth Festival 1951; created Anne Trulove in Stravinsky's Rake's Progress; producer Der Rosenkavalier, Brussels 1981; Corresp. mem. Bayerische Akad. der Künste; Prof. (Baden-Württemberg) 1990. *Recordings include:* 16 complete operas, 6 complete operettas, songs, various symphonies, lieder and arias with orchestra, lieder with piano; key recordings include Bach Cantatas, Brahms's Ein Deutsches Requiem, Mahler's Des Knaben Wunderhorn, Mozart's Don Giovanni, Mozart's Lieder, Schubert's Lieder, R. Strauss's Four Last Songs, R. Strauss's Capriccio, Wagner's Der Meistersinger. *Principal roles include:* Rosina (Barber of Seville), Blondchen, Konstanze (Die Entführung aus dem Serail), Susanna, Contessa (Le Nozze di Figaro), Donna Elvira (Don Giovanni), Fiordiligi (Così fan Tutte), Pamina (Die Zauberflöte), Marzelline (Fidelio), Violeta (Traviata), Gilda (Rigoletto), Alice (Falstaff), Musetta, Mimi (La Bohème), Cio-Cio-San (Madame Butterfly), Liu (Turandot), Manon (Manon), Eva (Meistersinger), Elsa (Lohengrin), Hirtenknabe, Elisabeth (Tannhäuser), Mélisande (Pelléas et Mélisande), Iole (Herakles), Anne (Rake's Progress, world premiere), Margarethe (Faust), Marenka (Bartered Bride), Ännchen, Agatha (Freischütz), Nedda (Pagliacci), Zerbinetta (Ariadne), Sophie und Marschallin (Rosenkavalier), Madeleine (Capriccio), Orff (Trionfo d'Afrodite, world premiere); (concert performances): Leonore (Fidelio), Ilia (Idomeneo), Euridice (Orfeo ed Euridice), Cleopatra (Giulio Cesare). *Film:* Der Rosenkavalier (Salzburg Festival) 1961. *Publication:* On and Off the Record: A Memoir of Walter Legge (ed) 1982. *Honours:* Hon. mem. Acad. di Santa Cecilia, Rome, Acad. of Arts and Letters, Stockholm, RAM, Vienna State Opera; Kammersängerin (Austria); Hon. Senator High School of Music Carl Maria von Weber, Dresden; Goldener Rathaus Mann, Vienna; Grosses Verdienstkreuz 1974; Order of Dannebrog (1st Class) (Denmark); mem. Ordre pour le Mérite (FRG) 1983; Commdr Ordre des Arts et des Lettres 1985; Grosses Bundesverdienstkreuz mit Stern 1995; Hon. DMus (Cambridge) 1976, American Univ. of

Washington DC; Hon. DLit (Glasgow) 1990; Lilli Lehmann Medal, Salzburg 1950, Orfeo d'Oro, Mantua, Hugo Wolf Medal, Vienna, Litteris et Artibus Medal (Sweden), Diapason d'Or, Paris 1984, Premio Viotti 1991, Mozart Medal, Frankfurt, Vercelli, UNESCO Mozart Medal, Paris 1991, Gold Medal, Bundeshauptstadt Vienna. *Address:* Kammersängerin, Rebhusstrasse 29, 8126 Zumikon, Switzerland.

**LEHANE, Maureen,** LRAM; British concert and opera singer (retd); b. London; m. Peter Wishart 1966. *Education:* Queen Elizabeth's Girls Grammar School, Barnet, London and Guildhall School of Music and Drama, London. *Career:* studied under Hermann Weissenborn and John and Aida Dickens; professional debut Glyndebourne 1967; has performed with Handel opera socs in UK, USA, Poland, Sweden, Germany and Holland and at numerous festivals including Stravinsky Festival (Cologne), City of London Festival, Aldeburgh, Cheltenham, Three Choirs Festival, Bath Festival, Oxford Bach Festival, Göttingen Handel Festival (Germany), also appearances in Scandinavia, Netherlands, Berlin, Lisbon and Rome; tours of USA, Australia, Middle East; fmr teacher at Guildhall School of Music, Univ. of Reading and Welsh Coll. of Music and Drama, now teaches privately; mem. jury Int. Singing Competition, Netherlands 1982, Llangollen Int. Eisteddfod 1991–93; Founder and Artistic Dir, Great Elm Music Festival 1987–98, Jackdaws Educational Trust 1993–; numerous TV appearances. *Operas include:* title and leading roles in 13 Handel operas, Ariodante, Clytemnestra 1974, Dido and Aeneas 1976, La Cenerentola, Adriano 1982, The Lady of the Inn 1983, The Falcon 1983, Faust. *Recordings include:* Bach, Haydn, Mozart, Handel, including the first complete recording of Handel's Belshazzar. *Publication:* Songs of Purcell (jt-ed.). *Address:* Jackdaws Educational Trust, Great Elm, Frome, Somerset, BA11 3NY, England. *Telephone:* (1373) 812383. *Fax:* (1373) 812083. *E-mail:* music@jackdaws.org. *Website:* www.jackdaws.org.uk.

**LEHMANN, Charlotte;** German singer (soprano) and academic; *Chair of Voice, Würzburg Academy of Music;* b. 16 Jan. 1938, Zweibrücken; m. Ernst Huber-Contwig 1965; one s. *Education:* Acad. of Music and Univ. of Saarland, Saarbrücken with Sibylle Ursula Fuchs, studied with Paul Lohmann, Wiesbaden. *Career:* sang at concerts in Europe and America; broadcasts, all German radio stations, France Musique, Schweizerischer Rundfunk, RTB Brussels, NL Hilversum, Turkish Radio, others; television performances on ARD and ZDF; started teaching at Hanover Music Acad. 1972; Chair of Voice, Würzburg Acad. of Music 1988–; has taught winners of int. prizes, including Lioba Braun, Thomas Quasthoff and Maria Kowollik; has led int. masterclasses in Brazil, Chile, England, Bulgaria, Japan and Luxembourg; has regularly given courses at the Haus Marteau Music Centre, Lichtenberg-Bayreuth; Ed., Bach and Mozart arias for all voice parts, for publishers Bärenreiter-Verlag; int. jury service; lectures. *Recordings:* Works of Bach, Mozart, Schumann, Wolf, Fauré, Debussy, Hindemith, Schoenberg, other composers. *Honours:* Hon. Pres. Bundesverband Deutscher Gesangspädagogen; prize winner L'Amour du Chant Int. Competition and UFAM, Paris, German Record Critics' Prize for Debussy and Schoenberg recording 1982. *Address:* Gellerstrasse 55, 30175 Hannover, Germany (home). *Telephone:* (11) 852437 (home). *Fax:* (11) 281571 (home). *E-mail:* charlottelehmann@t-online .de (home).

**LEHMANN, Hans Ulrich,** BA, DipMus; Swiss composer and academic; b. 4 May 1937, Biel; m. Ursula Lehmann. *Education:* Univs of Berne, Zürich and Basle, masterclasses in composition with Boulez and Stockhausen. *Career:* Lecturer, Zürich Univs 1969–90; Prof. of Theory and Composition 1972–98, Dir 1976–98, Musikhochschule, Zürich; Pres., SUISA (Swiss Authors' Asscn) 1991–; mem. numerous professional orgs. *Compositions include:* Quanti, 1962; Mosaik, 1964; Noten, 1964–66; Spiele, 1965; Rondo, 1967; Instants, 1968; Konzert, 1969; Régions III, 1970; discantus I and II, 1970; Sonata da chiesa, 1971; Tractus, 1971; zu streichen, 1974; zu blasen, 1975; Tantris, 1976–77; Motetus Paraburi, 1977–78; Kammermusik I, 1978–79; Kammermusik II, 1979; Duette, 1980; Lege mich wie ein Siegel auf dein Herz, 1980–83; Canticum I and II, 1981; Stroking, 1982; Mirlitonnades, 1983; battuto a tre-tratto, 1983; Mon amour, 1983; Triplum, 1984; ludes, 1985; Alleluja, 1985; In Memoriam Nicolai de Flue, 1986–87; Fragmente, 1986–87; Streichquartett, 1987–88; Osculetur me, 1988–89; de profundis, 1988–89; Esercizi, 1989; Wandloser Raum, 1989; ad missam Prolationum, 1989–90; etwas Klang von meiner Oberfläche, 1989–90; Nocturnes, 1990–91; Ut signaculum, 1991–92; El mar, 1993; Prélude à une étendue, 1993–94; Battements, 1994–95; Book of Songs, 1999; Twi-Light, for soprano and ensemble, 1999; Vagues, 1999–2000; Inquiétudes, 2000; Instantanés, 2000; Ritenuto, 2000; Notturno, 2001; Dédales, 2001–02; Der rat der rose, 2002; Annäherungen an HH, 2002–03; Trajets, 2003; Viola in all moods and senses, 2003; Um-risse, 2003, Nachts ist der Himmel näher als am Tag 2004–05. *Honours:* Swiss Musicians' Asscn Composers Prize 1988, City of Zürich Music Prize 1993. *Address:* Haldenstrasse 35, 8615 Wermatswil, Switzerland (home). *Telephone:* (44) 9416214 (home). *E-mail:* h.u.lehmann@freesurf.ch (home). *Website:* www.hu-lehmann .ch (home).

**LEHMANN, Wilfred;** Composer, Violinist and Conductor; b. 1929, Melbourne, Victoria, Australia. *Education:* Studied in Australia and London; Violinist with the Birmingham Orchestra, 1958–60; Conductor, Tokyo Philharmonic Orchestra, 1960–70; Assistant Conductor Queensland Symphony Orchestra, 1972; Nashville Symphony, and Chamber Orchestra, 1976–79; Conductor ABC Sinfonia, Australia, 1982; Member of Sydney String Quartet; Commisions include: Song of Mululu, 1977; Two String Quartets (2nd 1988); Bacchanals, for orchestra, 1988; Concerto for two pianos and percussion, 1991.

*Recordings include:* Bacchanals, and 2nd String Quartet. *Honours:* First Prize, Carl Flesch International Violin Competition (London), 1958; Fellowship in Composition, Tennessee Arts Commission, 1979. *Address:* c/o APRA, 1A Eden Street, Crows Nest, NSW 2065, Australia.

**LEHNHOFF, Nikolaus;** opera producer and stage designer; b. 20 May 1939, Hanover, Germany. *Career:* trained as asst stage dir, Deutsche Oper Berlin and at Bayreuth and the Metropolitan Operas 1963–71; Staged Die Frau ohne Schatten at the Paris Opéra, 1971; Director of several opera productions in Germany and Switzerland; San Francisco, 1985, Der Ring des Nibelungen; Produced Katya Kabanova at Glyndebourne and Der fliegende Holländer at Santa Fe, both in 1988; Returned to Glyndebourne, 1989, Jenůfa; Idomeneo at the Salzburg Festival, 1990; Munich Opera, 1990, Der fliegende Holländer; Elektra at Leipzig, 1991; Season 1991/92 with Lohengrin at Frankfurt and Henze's Der Prinz von Homburg at the Munich Festival; Produced The Makropulos Case by Janáček at Glyndebourne, 1995; Pfitzner's Palestrina at Covent Garden, 1997; Tosca for Netherlands Opera, 1998; Bartered Bride at Glyndebourne, 1999; Henze's Boulevard Solitude at Covent Garden, 2001; Tristan und Isolde at Glyndebourne 2003. *Address:* c/o Glyndebourne Festival Opera, Lewes, Sussex BN8 5UU, England.

**LEHR, Edit;** Singer (Soprano); b. 1954, Budapest, Hungary. *Education:* Studied at the Budapest School of Music and at the Cologne Musikhochschule. *Career:* Sang at Wuppertal Opera, 1980–82, the Freiburg Opera 1982–86, then at Gelsenkirchen; Guest appearances in Heidelberg, Vienna, Basel and Budapest; Among her best roles are Gilda, Violetta, Musetta, Donna Anna, Lauretta, Rosina, Fiordiligi, Susanna, Gretel, the Princess in Der Zwerg by Zemlinsky; Frequent concert appearances throughout Europe. *Address:* c/o Musiktheater im Revier, Kennedyplatz, Pf 101854, 45881 Gelsenkirchen, Germany.

**LEHRBAUMER, Robert;** Pianist, Conductor and Organist; b. 20 July 1960, Vienna, Austria. *Education:* Studied Piano, Organ, Conducting, Composition, Vienna School of Music and Dramatic Art; Diplomas with highest distinction, Organ, Piano, 1987, 1988. *Career:* Played with Vienna Philharmonic Orchestra, Vienna Symphonic Orchestra, Austrian Broadcasting Corporation Orchestra and other major orchestras; Conductors: Claudio Abbado, Yehudi Menuhin, André Previn, Sándor Végh; Appeared with Wolfgang Schneiderhan, Anton Dermota, Walter Berry, Philippe Entremont; Concerts in most European countries, Korea, Japan, Thailand, Indonesia, Malaysia, Mexico, Argentina, USA (including Schubert Festival, Washington, and Carnegie Recital Hall, New York, Kenya, Uganda); International festivals, Vienna, Salzburg, Lucerne, Nurnberg, Prague Spring Festival, Bruckner Festival, Linz Festival and Cervantino, Mexico; Many radio and television performances; Teaching, summer academies, Austria and abroad; World premieres of new works; Specialist, Schubert piano works, Haydn, Mozart, Beethoven piano concertos, A Berg, F Schmidt, E Schulhoff, K Szymanowski. *Recordings:* Baroque, Romantic and contemporary piano music (Liszt, Schumann, Tchaikovsky, Brahms, Schubert, Complete Piano Works by Gottfried von Einem, Albinoni, Pachelbel, Muffat, Kerll). *Current Management:* Freunde der Claviermusik. *Address:* Freunde der Claviermusik, Penkngasse 21, 3150 Wilhelmsburg, Austria.

**LEHRMAN, Leonard Jordan,** BA, MFA, DMA; American conductor, composer, pianist, organist and translator and editor; b. 20 Aug. 1949, Kansas; m. 1st Karen S. Campbell 1978 (divorced 1986); m. 2nd Helene R. Williams (Spierman) 2002. *Education:* studied with Elie Siegmeister, Fontainebleau Conservatoire, Harvard Coll., Ecole Normale de Musique, Paris, Salzburg Mozarteum, Indiana Univ., Cornell Univ., Long Island Univ. *Career:* debut as pianist, Carnegie Recital Hall 1979, as conductor, Bremerhaven and Berlin 1981, 1983; Asst Chorus Master and Asst Conductor, Metropolitan Opera 1977–78; Asst Conductor, Heidelberg Festival 1979, Augsburg Städtische Bühne 1980, and Basler Theater 1980–81; Conductor, Schauspielhaus Wien 1981; Kapellmeister, Stadttheater Bremerhaven 1981–83; Chief Coach, Conductor, Theater des Westens 1983–84; founder, Jewish Music Theatre of Berlin 1983, Laureate Conductor 1986–; Pres., Long Island Composers Alliance 1991–98, Archivist Emeritus 1999–; founder, Dir, Long Island Composers Archive, Long Island Univ. 1994–; librarian, Oyster Bay-East Norwich Public Library 1995–; Ed., The Marc Blitzstein Songbook, Vols 1–3 1999–2003; Dir Oceanside Chorale 2003–; Minister of Music, Christ Church Babylon 2003–; has appeared on numerous television and radio stations, including WHRB (Chief Prod. 1968–70), and WBAI (Prod. 1989–91). *Compositions include:* Flute Concerto; Violin Concerto; 6 musicals: Comic Tragedy of San Po Jo, Growing Up Woman, Let's Change the Woild!, E.G.: A Musical Portrait of Emma Goldman, Superspy!: The S-e-c-r-e-t Musical, The Booby Trap or Off Our Chests; 10 operas: Idiots First (completion of work begun by Marc Blitzstein), Karla, Suppose a Wedding (all part of Tales of Malamud), Sima, Hannah, The Family Man, The Birthday of the Bank, New World: An Opera About What Columbus Did to the "Indians", Sacco and Vanzetti (completion of work begun by Marc Blitzstein), The Wooing. *Address:* 33 Court Street, Valley Stream, NY 11580, USA. *Telephone:* (516) 256-4209. *Fax:* (516) 256-4210. *E-mail:* elehrman@liu.edu. *Website:* ljlehrman.artists-in -residence.com.

**LEIB, Gunther;** Singer (Baritone) and Professor; b. 12 April 1927, Gotha, Thuringen, Germany. *Education:* After violin studies entered vocal class at the Weimar Conservatory. *Career:* First violin in Landeskapelle at Gotha from 1949; Stage debut at Kothen, 1952, as Bartolo in Il Barbiere di Siviglia., Sang at Kothen, Meiningen and Nordhausen; Stadttheater Halle, 1956–57; Staatsoper Dresden from 1957, Berlin from 1961; Sang Christus in Bach's St John Passion in Italy, 1957, conducted by Franz Konwitschny; Annual appearances at the Handel Festivals, Halle; Salzburg Easter Festival, 1974–75, as Beckmesser in Die Meistersinger, conducted by Karajan (also at the Met, 1976); Guest engagements at the Paris Opéra, Moscow Bolshoi, Hamburg Staatsoper, National Operas of Warsaw, Prague and Budapest, Sofia, Stockholm and Helsinki; Other roles were Guglielmo, Raimondo, Papageno, Don Pasquale and Germont; Professor at the Carl Maria von Weber Hochschule, Dresden, 1964–76; Professor at the Musikhochschule Berlin. *Recordings:* Così fan tutte; Die Zauberflöte; Ein Deutsches Requiem; Lucia di Lammermoor; Don Pasquale; La Traviata; St Matthew Passion; Der Dorfjahrmarkt by Benda; La Bohème; Einstein by Dessau. *Address:* Hochschule für Musik Hanns Eisler, Otto-Grotewohlstrase 19, 1008 Berlin, Germany.

**LEIDLAND, Hilde;** Singer (Soprano); b. 1957, Lillestrom, Norway. *Education:* Studied in Oslo, Stockholm and Rome. *Career:* Royal Opera, Stockholm, from 1986, as Mozart's Susanna and Papagena, Gilda in Rigoletto, 1988, and in Monteverdi's Poppea; Other roles in Stockholm include Olympia, Sophie in Rosenkavalier, Zerbinetta, Queen of Night, Constanze, Zerlina and Oscar in Ballo in Maschera; Hanover, 1984, as Mozart's Blondchen; Bayreuth Festival, 1985–92, as the Woodbird, Flower Maiden and Woglinde; Guested at Nice several times, as Oscar in Un Ballo in Maschera and Marcelline in Fidelio; Other guest appearances in Paris, Brussels, Berlin, Stuttgart, Düsseldorf, Wiesbaden, Salzburg and Oslo; Sang Fortuna in Carmina Burana for the Royal Opera, Stockholm, 1998; Regular concert engagements. *Recordings include:* Barbarina in Figaro and Flower Maiden; Parsifal with Barenboim and the Berlin Philharmonic; The Ring and Parsifal from Bayreuth; A live recording made at the Théâtre de la Monnaie of Pascal Dusapin's Opera Medea. *Address:* Royal Opera, PO Box 16094, 10322 Stockholm. Sweden.

**LEIFERKUS, Sergey Petrovich;** Russian singer (baritone); b. 4 April 1946, Leningrad. *Education:* Leningrad Conservatory with Barsov and Shaposhnikov. *Career:* stage debut in Leningrad Theatre of Musical Comedy 1972; soloist Maly Theatre of Opera and Ballet 1972–78, sang in Eugene Onegin, Iolanta, Il Barbiere di Siviglia and Don Giovanni; Kirov (now Mariinsky) Theatre of Opera and Ballet 1977–85, sang Prince Andrei in War and Peace by Prokofiev; Wexford Festival 1982–86, in Griséledis and Le Jongleur de Notre Dame by Massenet, Hans Heiling by Marschner and Königskinder by Humperdinck; Scottish Opera from 1985, as Don Giovanni, Germont and Eugene Onegin 1988; Covent Garden 1987, as Eugene Onegin and Tomsky in The Queen of Spades, with the Kirov Company; ENO 1987, as Zurga in Les Pêcheurs de Perles; US debut 1987, in Symphony No. 13 by Shostakovich, with the Boston Symphony; Wigmore Hall debut recital, sang Luna in a new production of Il Trovatore at Covent Garden and appeared in a concert performance of Giovanna d'Arco at the Festival Hall 1989; concert performance of Mlada by Rimsky-Korsakov, Barbican Hall; US opera debut at San Francisco, as Telramund in Lohengrin, and the title role in Prince Igor at Covent Garden 1989–90; sang Rangoni in Boris Godunov at the Kirov Theatre, St Petersburg 1990; Luna at the Teatro Colón, Buenos Aires, Mazeppa at the Bregenz Festival and Netherlands Opera, Amsterdam, Ruprecht in Prokofiev's Fiery Angel at the BBC Promenade Concerts, London; Tomsky in The Queen of Spades in Boston and New York with the Boston Symphony; Onegin in Montreal, Ruprecht in St Petersburg, Tomsky at Glyndebourne and Vienna State Opera, Rangoni at San Francisco, Iago at Covent Garden and at the Metropolitan 1992; sang Carlo in La Forza del Destino for VARA Radio at the Amsterdam Concertgebouw, Shostakovich 13th Symphony with the New York Philharmonic, Scarpia, Amonasro, Escamillo and Luna 1993; debut at La Scala in The Fiery Angel, further performances as Iago at the Metropolitan, New York, Scarpia at Opéra Bastille, Paris, sang Mephistopheles in La Damnation de Faust with Ozawa and the Berlin Philharmonic in Berlin, the title role in Nabucco at the Bregenz Festival, sang Ruprecht in San Francisco and gave recitals across America, Escamillo at the Teatro Colón, Buenos Aires and Prokofiev's Ivan the Terrible at La Scala 1994; sang Iago at Covent Garden, Mazeppa at Netherlands Opera, Amsterdam, Shostakovich 13th Symphony in Leipzig with the Gewandhaus Orchestra, Gryaznoy in The Tsar's Bride for Opera Orchestra of New York in Carnegie Hall, Escamillo in a gala performance of Carmen in Stuttgart, Iago at the Vienna State Opera, recitals at Cologne and Graz, Amonasro at the Berlin State Opera under Mehta, Scarpia at the Ravinia Festival 1995; Boccanegra in the original version of Verdi's opera and Telramund in Lohengrin at Covent Garden 1997; Klingsor in Parsifal with the Royal Opera, RFH 1998; Klingsor at the Royal Albert Hall (concert), Simon Boccanegra at Melbourne and Prince Igor in Houston 2000–01; season 2001–02 in Pique Dame in Los Angeles and Washington, DC, Simon Boccanegra in Dallas, Aida in Berlin, Lohengrin in Munich, Tosca in London and Munich, solo recitals in Paris and London; season 2002–03 in Otello in Japan (tour), London and San Francisco, Pique Dame in Munich, Fidelio in Dallas, Tosca in Munich, Shostakovich Symphony No. 13 in Prague and Lohengrin in London. *Current Management:* Askonas Holt, Lonsdale Chambers, 27 Chancery Lane, London, WC2A 1PF, England.

**LEIGH, David Anthony,** BA; British harpsichordist and fortepianist; b. 3 April 1953, London, England. *Education:* Reading Univ., Guildhall School of Music. *Career:* debut, Wigmore Hall 1975; recitals all over the UK, Canada, USA, Netherlands, Belgium, Austria; lectures in USA and Austria; master-

classes in USA and the UK; radio broadcasts in the UK, Canada and USA; knowledge of early keyboard instruments and their restoration. *Recordings include:* Harpsichords Historic and Unique (five vols). *Publications:* encyclopaedia articles on harpsichord and clavichord; contrib. to Antique Collector. *Address:* Greystones, The Slade, Charlbury, Oxford OX7 3SJ, England (home). *Telephone:* (1865) 244197 (office); (1608) 810607 (home). *E-mail:* david@laurieleighantiques.com.

**LEISNER, David,** BA; American classical guitarist, composer and teacher; b. 22 Dec. 1953, Los Angeles, CA. *Education:* Wesleyan University and studied with John Duarte, David Starobin, Richard Winslow, Virgil Thomson and David Del Tredici. *Career:* teacher of guitar at Amherst College, 1976–78; New England Conservatory from 1980; Manhattan School of Music from 1993; New York debut at Merkin Hall, 1979; Solo and Chamber Recitals in USA, Canada and Europe; Concerto Soloist with L'Orchestre de la Suisse Romande, Australian Chamber Orchestra, New York Chamber Ensemble and others; Compositions performed by the Fresno Philharmonic, Sanford Sylvan, Eugenia Zukerman, The Saturday Brass Quintet and the Los Angeles Guitar Quartet. *Compositions include:* Embrace of Peace, orchestra, 1991; Dances in the Madhouse, violin (or flute) and guitar, 1982; Orchestrated, 1989; Battlefield Requiem, percussion quartet and solo cello; Ad Majoren Dei Gloriam, brass quintet, 1992; Confiding, for voice and piano, voice and guitar, 1985–86; Candles in Mecca, piano trio, 1988. *Address:* c/o ASCAP, ASCAP Building, One Lincoln Plaza, New York, NY 10023, USA.

**LEIXNER, Vladimir;** Cellist; b. 1953, Czechoslovakia. *Education:* Studied in Prague with members of the Smetana Quartet. *Career:* Cellist in various Czech ensembles from 1970; Co-Founder and Cellist of the Stamic Quartet, Prague, 1977; Performances at the Prague Young Artists and the Bratislava Music Festivals; Tours to Spain, Austria, France, Switzerland, Germany and Eastern Europe; Tour of the USA in 1980 with debut concerts in the United Kingdom at London and Birmingham in 1983; Further British tours in 1985 and 1988 (Warwick Arts Festival) and 20 concerts in 1989; Gave the premiere of Helmut Eder's 3rd Quartet in 1986; Season 1991–92 with visit to the Channel Islands with Festival of Czech Music, to Netherlands, Finland, Austria and France, Edinburgh Festival and debut tours of Canada, Japan and Indonesia. *Recordings:* Shostakovich No. 13; Schnittke No. 4; Mozart's K589 and K370; Dvořák, Martinů and Janáček's Quartets. *Honours:* With Stamic Quartet: Prizewinner, International Festival of Young Soloists, Bordeaux, 1977, Winner ORF Austria International String Quartet Competition, 1986, followed by live broadcast from Salzburg Mozarteum, Academie Charles Cros Grand Prix du Disque, 1991 for Dvořák Quartets.

**LEJET, Edith;** French composer and academic; *Professor of Composition, Ecole Normale de Musique de Paris Alfred Cortot;* b. 19 July 1941, Paris; d. of Donat Lejet and Frida Etheridge. *Education:* Conservatoire National Superieur de Musique de Paris. *Career:* Prof., Dept of Theoretical Studies, Conservatoire National Supérieur de Musique de Paris 1988–; Prof. of Composition, Ecole Normale de Musique de Paris Alfred Cortot 2004–. *Compositions:* Monodrame pour violon et orchestre 1969, Journal d'Anne Frank (oratorio) 1970, Quatuor de saxophones 1974, Harmonie du soir 1977, Espaces nocturnes 1976, Gemeaux for guitar 1978, Triptyque for organ 1979, Volubilis for violoncello 1981, Balance for guitar 1982, Aube Marine 1982, L'Homme qui avait perdu sa voix (musical theatre) 1984, Ressac 1986, Les Rois Mages (oratorio) 1989, Améthyste for 12 strings 1990, Trois eaux-fortes for piano 1992, Trois chants pour un Noël for children's chorus 1994, Océan pathétique for five different instruments 1994, Almost a Song for guitar and viola 1995, Missa Brevis for choir and organ 1996, Des Fleurs en forme de diamants for guitar and seven instruments 1997, Psaume de joie for mixed chorus 1998, Parcours en duo for baritone saxophone and percussion 2001, Diptyque pour orgue et cordes 2003. *Publications:* Pedagogic Books: La Precision Rythmique Dans la Musique (three vols). *Honours:* numerous first prizes at Paris Conservatory, Vocation Foundation 1967, Grand Prix de Rome 1968, Prix Herve Gould 1970, Prix Herve Dugardin 1974, Grand Prix de la Musique de Chambre de la SACEM 1979, Prix Nadia et Lili Boulanger 2003. *Address:* 11–13 rue Cino del Duca, 75017 Paris, France (home). *E-mail:* e.lejet@free.fr (home). *Website:* www.edith-lejet.com (home).

**LEKA, Dhora;** Composer; b. 23 Feb. 1923, Korca, Albania. *Education:* Institute for Women Nena Mbretereshe; Graduated, Conservatory Tchaikovsky, Moscow, 1953. *Career:* Teacher, Korca, 1942–43; Various political activities; Began composing, 1942; Maestro at Lyceum Jordan Misja, Tirana; Secretary General, Artists' League, 1954; Many years of imprisonment; Director, Cultural Foundation Dhora Leka; mem, Society of Women Composers. *Compositions include:* The Clarion Call; Youth; From the Heart of the Youth; Revenge; Those Striped Mountain Peaks that Thunder; Overture on two folk motifs, for symphonic orchestra, 1952; Cantate in four parts, Albania my Homeland to lyrics of Andrea Varti, 1953; Spring Songs, 1957; Opera in Three Acts, Stormy Autumn, 1966–67; Opera song, Zonja Curre, 1971; Three sketches for string orchestra, 1995; Ode for soloist and string orchestra, for 85th birthday of Mother Teresa, 1995; Dance on folk motifs for symphonic orchestra, 1996; In memorium, for string orchestra for Lithuanian violinist Grazhina Fiulipajtes-Lubockij, 1997. *Publications:* Songs in the Storm; My Mother. *Honours:* People's Artist, 1992; Great Master of Labour, 1998. *Address:* RR Durresit, P 240, Sh 8, Ap 66, Tirana, Albania.

**LELEUX, François;** French oboist; b. 1971; m. Lisa Batiashvili. *Education:* Roubaix Conservatory, Conservatoire Nat. Supérieur de Musique, Paris.

*Career:* fmr mem., European Community Youth Orchestra; early experience with French Nat. Opera; first oboe soloist, orchestra of the Paris Opera aged eighteen; currently Prin. Oboist, Chamber Music Orchestra of Europe; co-f., Paris-Bastille Wind Octet 1992; Musical Dir Orchestre de Neuburg; regularly performs with chamber music ensembles, including Mullova Ensemble, Emmanuel Strosser, Katia and Marielle Labèque; extensive int. appearances as soloist, including performances with Deutsche Symphony Orchestra, Tokyo Philharmonic, French Nat. Orchestra, Vienna Chamber Orchestra, Bratislava Chamber Orchestra, Hallé Orchestra, and at the Lincoln Center and Saratoga Chamber Music Festival, USA, Wigmore Hall, London, Tokyo Opera City Concert Hall. *Recordings:* Poulenc, Trio/Britten, Metamorphoses Op49 1995, Beethoven, Octet for Winds/Mozart, Serenades 1996, Telemann, 12 Fantasias for Oboe 1996, Mozart, Concertos pour Hautbois 2000. *Honours:* first prize Int. Competition of Toulon 1990, second prize Prague Spring Int. Music Competition 1991, second prize Int. Music Competition, Munich 1991, European Juventus Prize. *Current Management:* Künstleragentur Dr Raab und Dr Böhm GmbH, Plankengasse 7, Vienna 1010, Austria. *Telephone:* (1) 512-05-01 (office). *Fax:* (1) 512-77-43 (office). *E-mail:* office@rbartists.at (office). *Website:* www.rbartists.at (office).

**LEMALU, Jonathan;** New Zealand singer (bass-baritone); b. 1978. *Education:* Royal Coll. of Music, London. *Career:* concert appearances include the Serenade to Music at the London Proms, Stravinsky's Pulcinella and Symphony no. 14 by Shostakovich with the English CO at the Barbican; season 2001 in Les Troyens at Edinburgh and Messiah in Vienna; festival engagements at King's Lynn, Rávinia (Chicago SO) and Tanglewood (Boston SO) 2002; sang in Falla's Master Peter's Puppet Show at the 2002 London Proms, and as Talbot in Donizetti's Maria Stuarda at the Edinburgh Festival; season 2002–03 as Rossini's Basilio for ENO, Leporello at Sydney, in La Damnation de Faust under Colin Davis and as Neptune in Idomeneo at Glyndebourne; recitals include Schubert's Schwanengesang (Wigmore Hall) and Winterreise (Edinburgh) 2002; Zorastro in Handel's Orlando at Covent Garden 2003. *Recordings:* album: Opera Arias 2005, Love Blows as the Wind Blows 2005. *Current Management:* Askonas Holt, Lonsdale Chambers, 27 Chancery Lane, London, WC2A 1PF, England. *Telephone:* (20) 7400-1700. *Fax:* (20) 7400-1799. *E-mail:* info@askonasholt.co.uk. *Website:* www.askonasholt.co.uk; www.jonathanlemalu.com.

**LEMANN, Jean (Juan);** Composer, Pianist and Professor of Composition; b. 7 Aug. 1928, Vendôme, France; m. Maria Luisa Herreros, 28 Sep 1957, 2 d. *Education:* BA, Mathematics, 1948; Architecture, Catholic University of Chile, 1948–50; Piano studies, 1942–54, Postgraduate, 1955–59, University of Chile, National Conservatory of Music; Composition at University of Chile, Catholic University of Chile, privately; Visiting Fulbright Scholar, Juilliard School of Music, NY, 1970–71. *Career:* Professor of Piano, Music Theory, Choral Conductor, Experimental School of Arts, 1957–61; Professor of Piano, Composition, 1961–91, Vice-Dean, 1981–82, Faculty of Arts, University of Chile; Adviser, cultural and artistic institutions; Pianist, Lecturer, Adjudicator, Composer and Professor of Composition at Faculty of Arts, University of Chile. *Compositions include:* Orchestral, chamber, choral, mime, theatre, ballet, and film music including Leyenda Del Mar; Sonata Para Arpa; El Cuerpo La Sangre; Variaciones Para Piano; Puentes (words, P Neruda); Eolica Para Cello Solo; Akustika for Recorder; Obertura de Concierto for orchestra, 1986; Maestranza de Noche for alto, violin, clarinet, cello and piano, 1987; Fantasia Concertante, piano and orchestra, 1988; Rapsodia for guitar, 1996; Viola da Gamba and Piano, 1992, Barrio Sin Luz for soprano voice and piano, 1992. *Address:* Laura de Noves 460, Las Condes, Santiago, Chile.

**LEMELIN, Stéphane;** Pianist; b. 2 April 1960, Rimouski, Quebec, Canada. *Education:* BM 1982, MM 1983, Peabody Conservatory, USA; Doctor of Musical Arts, Yale University, 1990. *Career:* Performs as soloist and chamber musician across Canada, the USA, Europe and Asia; Frequent CBC and NPR broadcasts; Piano Faculty, Yale University, USA, 1986–90 and University of Alberta, Canada, 1990–2001; Professor of Music, University of Ottawa, 2001–; Visiting Professor, Université de Montréal, 2001–. *Recordings:* Works by Schubert, Schumann, Fauré, Saint-Saëns, Roussel, Poulenc, Debussy, Samazeuilh, Ropartz, and others; Complete Nocturnes by Fauré. *Honours:* Prizewinner, Casadesus International Competition, 1983. *Current Management:* Colwell Arts Management. *Address:* RR #1, New Hamburg, Ontario, N0B 2G0, Canada.

**LEMMING, Christopher;** Singer (Tenor); b. 1965, Camberley, Surrey. *Education:* Guildhall School, London. *Career:* Appearances with Glyndebourne Festival as Dancing Master in Manon Lesccaut, Servant in Capriccio, and Bartholomew in Birtwistle's The Last Supper (2001); Glyndebourne Tour as Lechmere in Britten's Owen Wingrave and Mozart's Titus and Belmonte; Further engagements as Don Ottavio at Cologne and Verona, as Ferrando and Rossini's Almaviva for Opera Holland Park and Molqui in The Death of Klinghoffer by John Adams, for Finnish National Opera (2001); Concerts with the King's Consort, BBC Singers, Royal Liverpool PO, Monteverdi Choir and London PO under Riccardo Muti. *Address:* c/o Glyndebourne Festival Opera, Lewes, Sussex BN8 5UU, England. *Telephone:* 01273 812321. *Fax:* 01273 812 783.

**LEMPER, Ute;** German singer, dancer and actress; b. 4 July 1963, Münster; one s. one d. *Education:* Dance Acad., Cologne, Max Reinhardt Seminar on Dramatic Art, Vienna. *Career:* leading role in Viennese production of Cats 1983; appeared in Peter Pan, Berlin, Cabaret, Düsseldorf and Paris (recipient of Molière Award 1987), Chicago (Laurence Olivier Award) 1997–99 (London and New York), Life's a Swindle tour 1999, Punishing Kiss tour 2000; Die sieben Todsünden (Weill) at Covent Garden Festival, London 2000; collaborations with Michael Nyman include Six Celan Songs 1990, Songbook 1992. *Recordings include:* Ute Lemper Sings Kurt Weill 1988, (Vol. 2) 1993, Threepenny Opera 1988, Mahagonny Songspiel 1989, Illusions 1992, Espace Indécent 1993, City of Strangers 1995, Berlin Cabaret Songs 1996, All that Jazz/The Best of Ute Lemper 1998, Punishing Kiss 2000. *Television appearances include:* L'Affaire Dreyfus (Arte), Tales from the Crypt (HBO), Illusions (Granada) and The Look of Love (Gillian Lynn). *Film appearances include:* L'Autrichienne 1989, Moscou Parade 1992, Coupable d'Innocence 1993, Prêt à Porter 1995, Bogus 1996, Combat de Fauves, A River Made to Drown In, Appetite 1997. *Honours:* French Culture Prize 1993. *Address:* c/o Oliver Gluzman, 40 rue de la Folie Régnault, 75011 Paris, France. *Telephone:* 1-44-93-02-02. *Fax:* 1-44-93-04-40. *E-mail:* info@visiteursdusoir.com (office). *Website:* www.visiteursdusoir.com (office).

**LENDVAY, Kamilló;** Composer and Professor and Head of Music Theory Department; b. 28 Dec. 1928, Budapest, Hungary; m. 6 June 1972, 1 d. *Education:* Ferenc Liszt Academy of Music, Budapest, 1959. *Career:* Musical Leader, State Puppet Theatre, 1960–66; Musical Director, Artistic Ensemble, Hungarian People's Army, 1966–68; Conductor and Artistic Director, Operetta Theatre, Budapest; Musical Lector, Hungarian Radio, 1962–; Composer; Professor and Head of Music Theory Department, Ferenc Liszt Academy of Music, Budapest, 1973–; President, Artisjus, Bureau for Protecting Protecting Authors' Rights; President, Association of the Hungarian Composers. *Compositions include:* Orogenesis, oratorio, 1969–70; Requiem; Cantatas: Cart-Drive into the Night, 1970; Scenes from Thomas Mann's Joseph and His Brothers, 1978–81; Orchestral works: Mauthausen, symphonic poem, 1958; Four Invocations, 1966; Expressions for 11 strings, for chamber orchestra, 1974; The Harmony of Silence, 1980; Chaconne for Orchestra, 1988; Rhapsody for orchestra, 1997; Concertos: Concertino, 1959; Violin Concerto No. 1, 1961–62; Pezzo Concerto, 1975; Violin Concerto No. 2, 1986; Concerto semplice, 1986; Trumpet Concerto, 1990; Concerto for violin, harpsichord and strings, 1991; Concerto for Piano, 2000; Chamber music; Solo pieces; Several works for wind orchestra and choir; Music for films and stage; Stabat Mater. *Recordings:* Numerous. *Honours:* Erkel Musical Prize, 1962, 1964, 1978; Trieste Competition, 1975; Title of Merited Artist, 1981; Grand Prix Inernational du Disque Lyrique for opera The Respectable Street-Walker, 1983; Kossuth Prize, 1988; Bartók-Pasztory Prize, 1989. *Address:* 1137 Szt Istvan Park 23, Budapest, Hungary.

**LENHART, Renate;** Singer (Soprano); b. 1942, Austria. *Education:* Studied at the Vienna Conservatory. *Career:* Concert tour of South America, 1966–67; Subsequent engagement at Zürich Opera: roles there included Micaela, Marzelline in Fidelio, Mozart's Pamina and Zerlina, Constanza in Henze's Il Re Cervo, Julia Farnese in Ginaster's Bomarzo, Miranda in The Tempest by Frank Martin and Lisa in The Queen of Spades; Further roles at Zürich and as guest in Munich, Paris, Amsterdam and Vienna have included Alice Ford, Lyudmila, Glauce in Médée, Sophie, and Frau Fluth in Die Lustigen Weiber von Windsor; Appearances in Monteverdi's Poppea and Ulisse at Bregenz and in the Jean-Pierre Ponnelle cycle at Zürich; Most frequently heard as Pamina, also sang First Lady in the Ponnelle production of Die Zauberflöte. *Address:* c/o Opernhaus Zürich, Flakenstrasse 1, 8008 Zürich, Switzerland.

**LENTZ, Daniel (Kirkland);** Composer; b. 10 March 1942, Latrobe, Pennsylvania, USA; m. Marlene Helen Wasco, 24 Aug 1964, 1 d. *Education:* BS, Music, St Vincent College, 1962; MFA, Ohio University, 1965; Brandeis University, 1965–67; Tanglewood, summer, 1966; Musicology, Stockholm University, Sweden, 1967–68. *Career:* Founder, Director of ensembles, California Time Machine, 1969–73, The San Andreas Fault, 1974 and 1976, The Daniel Lentz Ensemble, 1978–80, Lentz, 1983–85 and Daniel Lentz and Group, 1986–; 10 European tours and major/premiere performances: Gaudeamus Foundation, 1972, New Music America Festivals in 1983 and 1986, LA Olympic Arts Festival, 1984, Wild Turkeys at Carnegie Hall, 1986, The Crack In The Bell, LAPhil New Music Group, 1986. *Compositions include:* Canon And Fugle, 1971; Loverise, 1971; King Speech Song, 1972; Song(s) Of The Sirens, 1973; Missa Umbrarum, 1973; O-Ke-Wa, 1974; Sun Tropes, 1975; Requiem Songs, 1976; Three Pretty Madrigals, 1976; Composition In Contrary And Parallel Motion, 1977; Elysian Nymph, 1978; Wolf Is Dead, 1979, 1982; Uitoto, 1980; Music By Candlelight, 1980; Dancing On The Sun, 1980; Point Conception, 1981; Adieu, 1983; On The Leopold Altar, 1983; Lascaux, 1984; Is It Love, 1984; Bacchus, 1985; Topanga Tango, 1985; Time's Trick, 1985; Wild Turkeys, 1985; The Crack In The Bell, 1986; Apache Wine, for chamber orchestra, 1989; Apologetica for soprano, mezzo chorus and ensemble, 1996; Ze ghosts, for ensemble, 1997. *Recordings:* Several including, Dinner Music, a set of 10 pieces each based on a particular dish at a particular Parisian restaurant, 1999; Self Portrait, 1999. *Address:* Box 311, US Route 30, Latrobe, PA 15650, USA.

**LEON, Tania (Justina);** Composer; b. 14 May 1943, Havana, Cuba. *Education:* Studied in Havana and at New York University. *Career:* Resident in USA from 1967 and creative association with the Dance Theatre of Harlem; Teacher at Brooklyn College, 1985–; Vice Chair, Board of Directors, 1994, Artistic Adviser, New Residencies Program, 1994, Meet the Composer; Professor, Brooklyn College Conservatory of Music, 1994; Visiting Lecturer, Harvard University, 1994; Revson Composer Fellow, New York Philharmonic, 1993–; Visiting Professor, Yale University, 1993; Artistic Adviser, Latin

American Project, American Composers Orchestra, 1992; Numerous conducting engagements include: Savannah Symphony Orchestra, Georgia, 1996; Charlotte Symphony Orchestram North Carolina, 1996; Associate Conductor for The Voyage, Metropolitan Opera, 1996; Residencies include: Composer, Scripps College, Claremont, California, 1996. *Compositions include:* Ballets The Beloved (1972) and Bele (1981); Opera Scourge of Hyacinths, 1994; Kabiosile, piano concerto, 1988; Carabali (1991) and Indigena for orchestra; Son sonore for flute and guitar (1992) and other chamber music; Instrumental and vocal music, including Batey for vocal soloists and 2 percussion, 1989. *Address:* c/o ASCAP, ASCAP Building, 1 Lincoln Plaza, New York, NY 10023, USA.

**LEONARD, Lysiane;** Singer (Soprano); b. 1957, Belgium. *Education:* Studied with Jules Bastin in Brussels, at the Juilliard School and with Hans Hotter in Munich. *Career:* Has sung at the Liège Opera from 1982, notably as Fenena in Nabucco, Elvira (Rossini) Norina, Siebel (Faust), Frasquita (Carmen) and Liu; Guest appearances at Rouen in Les Indes Galantes, the Paris Opéra-Comique in La Belle Hélène and at Montpellier in Schumann's Faust (1985) concert repertory also includes Les Nuits d'été by Berlioz (Aix, 1983); Further concerts in music bv Vivaldi, Bach, Handel, Haydn and Telemann. *Address:* c/o Opera Royale de Wallonie, 1 Rue des Dominicains, 4000 Liège, Belgium.

**LEONARD, Sarah (Jane);** Singer (Soprano); b. 10 April 1953, Winchester, England; m. Michael Parkinson, 5 April 1975, divorced, 1 s., 1 d. *Education:* Music Department, Winchester School of Art, 1969–71; GGSM Diploma, Guildhall School of Music and Drama, London, 1971–76. *Career:* Member, BBC Singers, 1976–81; Member, London Sinfonietta Voices; High Soprano; Broadcasts with BBC Singers, Endymion Ensemble and London Sinfonietta; Television appearances, Video Alice, Channel 4 television, and The Middle of the Road Hour, Channel 4 television; Sang the Mad Boy in Goehr's Sonata about Jerusalem, Aldeburgh Festival, 1990; Sings with Michael Nyman Band; Guest appearances with Hilliard Ensemble; Sang at La Scala, Milan, 1989 and 1992; International Soloist in 20th century repertoire; Sang in the premiere of Lachenmann's Das Mädchen, Hamburg, 1997; Sang Queen Elizabeth in the premiere of Harle's Angel Magick, London Proms, 1998; mem, Incorporated Society of Musicians. *Recordings include:* Drusilla in L'Incoronazione di Poppea; Miserere by Arvo Pärt with Hilliard Ensemble; My Heart is Like a Singing Bird, English Song Company. *Honours:* Susan Longfield Award, Guildhall School of Music and Drama, 1976; Winner, Young Artists and 20th Century Music, Park Lane Group, 1984. *Current Management:* Allied Artists. *Address:* 42 Montpelier Square, London SW7 1JZ, England.

**LEONHARDT, Gustav;** Harpsichordist, Organist and Conductor; b. 30 May 1928, Graveland, Netherlands. *Education:* Schola Cantorum Basle, 1947–50, with Eduard Muller. *Career:* Debut: Vienna in 1950 with Bach's The Art of Fugue on the harpsichord; Professor of Harpsichord at Vienna Academy of Music, 1952–55; Teacher at Amsterdam Conservatory from 1954; Organist at Waalse Kerk, Amsterdam until 1981, since then organist at Nieuwe Kerk, Amsterdam; Founded Leonhardt Consort in 1955; Played the organ and harpsichord and acted the part of JS Bach in a 1967 film, The Chronicle of Anna Magdalena Bach; Visiting Professor at Harvard University, 1969–70; Work as conductor includes Monteverdi's L'Incoronazione di Poppea, Amsterdam in 1972; Extensive tours of USA and Europe as harpsichordist, notably in the works of Bach, Frescobaldi, Sweelinck, Froberger and Louis Couperin; Music by Bach and Böhm at the 1999 London Bach Festival. *Recordings:* About 150 including Bach's Goldberg Variations, as harpsichordist. *Publications:* Editions of The Art of Fugue, 1952 and keyboard music by Sweelinck for the Dutch Critical Edition. *Honours:* Erasmus Prize, 1980; Honorary Doctorates, 1982, 1983 and 1991. *Address:* c/o Allied Artists, 42 Montpelier Square, London, SW7 1JZ, England.

**LEOSON, Markus;** Swedish percussionist, timpanist and cimbalom player; b. 16 Aug. 1970, Linköping. *Education:* Royal Conservatory of Music, Stockholm. *Career:* debut in Stockholm Concert Hall, April 1995; Live radio concert, Stockholm and Reykjavík, Iceland, 1995; Artist in Residence, Swedish Radio, 1996–97; also solo concerts, Norrtelje Festival, Stockholm, Linköping with wind orchestra; Soloist with Tampere Philharmonic Orchestra; Portrait in television programme NIKE, Copenhagen; Solo concert, Gothenburg; Solo, Stockholm, 1997, also soloist with Swedish Radio Symphony Orchestra, Kalmar; Cimbalom Player and Solo Timpanist with Royal Opera orchestra, Stockholm; 1998 engagements with Gothenburg Symphony Orchestra, Helsingborg Symphony Orchestra, St Petersburg, Braunschweig; Concerts in Cologne, Ludwigshafen, 1999; Engaged to play with Norrköping Symphony Orchestra, Malmö Symphony Orchestra and a debut recital with the Philharmonie in Berlin, 2000. *Recordings:* Markus Leoson, Percussion; Numerous for Swedish Radio P2; Chamber music with Ann Sofie von Otter; Percussion and flute. *Honours:* 1st Prize of the Soloist Prize, Sweden, 1995; 2nd Prize, Nordic Soloist Competition, 1995; 2nd Prize, ARD, Munich, 1997; 1st Prize, EBU IFYP Competition, Bratislava, 1997. *Current Management:* H. F. Artists Management, Nibblev 25, 17736 Järfälla, Sweden.

**LEPPARD, Raymond John,** CBE, MA; British conductor and composer; *Music Director, Indianapolis Symphony Orchestra;* b. 11 Aug. 1927, London; s. of A. V. Leppard and B. M. Beck. *Education:* Trinity Coll. Cambridge. *Career:* Fellow of Trinity Coll., Univ. Lecturer in Music 1958–68; Music Dir, BBC Philharmonic (fmrly BBC Northern Symphony) Orchestra 1973–80; Prin.

Guest Conductor, St Louis Symphony Orchestra 1984–93; Music Dir Indianapolis Symphony Orchestra 1987–; has conducted New York Philharmonic, Chicago Symphony, Philadelphia and Pittsburgh Symphony Orchestras and Royal Opera, Covent Garden, English Nat. Opera, Metropolitan Opera, New York, New York City Opera and San Francisco Opera; realizations of Monteverdi's L'Incoronazione di Poppea, Il Ritorno d'Ulisse and L'Orfeo and Cavalli's L'Ormindo, L'Egisto, La Calisto and L'Orione. *Publication:* Authenticity in Music 1989. *Address:* Orchard House, 5040 Buttonwood Crescent, Indianapolis, IN 46228; Indianapolis Symphony Orchestra, 45 Monument Circle, Indianapolis, IN 46204, USA. *Telephone:* (317) 259-9020 (home). *Fax:* (317) 259-0916. *Website:* www.indyorch.org.

**LERDAHL, Fred;** Composer and Music Theorist; b. 10 March 1943, Madison, Wisconsin, USA; m. 29 Nov 1980, 3 d. *Education:* BMus, Lawrence University, 1965; MFA, Princeton University, 1967. *Career:* Professor of Music at University of California at Berkeley, 1969–71, Harvard University, 1971–79, Columbia University, 1979–85, and University of Michigan, 1985–91; Fritz Reiner Professor at Columbia University, 1991; Residency at IRCAM, 1981 and at American Academy in Rome, 1987; Works commissioned by the Fromm Music Foundation, the Koussevitzky Music Foundation, the Juilliard Quartet, the Pro Arte Quartet and the Spoleto Festival. *Compositions:* String trio, 1966; Wake for soprano and chamber ensemble, 1968; Chords for orchestra, 1974–83; Eros for mezzo-soprano and chamber ensemble, 1975; First String Quartet, 1978; Waltzes for chamber ensemble, 1981; Second String Quartet, 1982; Beyond The Realm of Bird for soprano and chamber orchestra, 1984; Fantasy Etudes for chamber ensemble, 1985; Cross-Currents for orchestra, 1987; Waves for chamber orchestra, 1988; Quiet Music, for orchestra, 1994. *Recordings:* Fantasy Etudes; First String Quartet; Second String Quartet; Eros; String Trio. *Publications:* Co-Author, A Generative Theory of Tonal Music, 1983. *Current Management:* Musical Associates of America. *Address:* c/o MAA, 224 King Street, Eaglewood, NJ 01631, USA.

**LERNER, Mimi;** Singer (Mezzo-soprano); b. 1954, Poland. *Education:* Studied at Queen's College, New York and Carnegie-Mellon University. *Career:* Debut: New York City Opera as Sextus in La Clemenza di Tito, 1979; Sang at various American opera houses and at Glyndebourne in 1984 as Marcellina in Le nozze di Figaro; La Scala in 1985 as Alcina, Théâtre Châtelet, Paris, in 1986 as Isabella in L'Italiana in Algeri, and at Amsterdam in 1987 as Eboli in Don Carlos; Sang with New Orleans Opera Association, 1989–90, as Amneris and Adalgisa; Sang Ruggiero in Alcina at Vancouver in 1990, Rosina at Pittsburgh and Despina at Toronto in 1991; Santa Fe Festival in 1991 as Carlotta in Die schweigsame Frau; Sang Marcellina in Figaro at Orchestra Hall, Chicago, 1992; Other roles include Smeton in Anna Bolena, Suzuki, Siebel and Cenerentola; Mistress Quickly in Falstaff at Glimmerglass, 1998. *Recordings include:* Second Lady in a video of Die Zauberflöte, from the Metropolitan. *Address:* c/o New Orleans Opera Association, 333 St Charles Avenue, Suite 907, New Orleans, LA 70130, USA.

**LESCOVAR, Monika;** Cellist; b. 15 March 1981, Kreutztal, Germany. *Education:* Third year pupil, Funktional Musical Pedagogie School, Zagreb; Student, Musikhochschule Lubeck. *Career:* Debut: Second International Tchaikovsky Competition For Young Musicians, Dendai, 1995; Overseas Concert for Children Competition, Japan; Solo performances, Hungarian State Symphony Orchestra, The Eurovision Festival, Budapest, 1993; Philharmonia Hungarica, The UNICEF Concert, 1994; Moscow Philharmonic, Zagreb, 1994; Sendai Philharmonic, Sendai, 1995; Slovenian Philharmonic, Slovenia, 1996; Symphony Orchestra of Sevilla, 1997; Zagreb Philharmonic, the Zagreb soloists, the Croatian Chamber Orchestra, the Dubrovnik Orchestra, Litvania Chamber Orchestra; Recitals all over the world. *Recordings:* Two albums. *Honours:* First prize, Second International Tchaikovsky for Young Musicians Competition, Sendai, 1995; Second prize, Janigro Competition, Zagreb, 1996; Third prize, 6th Rostropovich Competition, Paris, 1997. *Address:* Oboj 20 1, HR 1000 Zagreb, Croatia.

**LESSER, Laurence;** Cellist; b. 28 Oct. 1938, Los Angeles, California, USA; m. Masuko Ushioda, 23 Dec 1971, 1 s., 1 d. *Education:* BA, Harvard University, 1961; Fulbright Scholar, Cologne, with Gaspar Cassadò; Studied with Gregor Piatigorsky in Los Angeles. *Career:* Concert performances in USA, Europe, Japan and South America; Appearances with Boston Symphony, Los Angeles Philharmonic, London Philharmonic and other major orchestras; Assistant to Piatigorsky, University of Southern California, Los Angeles; Teacher at Peabody Institute, Baltimore; Visiting Professor at Toho School of Music, Tokyo; Teacher, appointed President, 1983, New England Conservatory, Boston, Massachusetts, retired 1996; Full-time Cello and Chamber Music Faculty, NEC. *Recordings:* Schoenberg/Monn Concerto; Lazarof Concerto; Chamber Music in Heifetz-Piatigorsky Series. *Address:* New England Conservatory, 290 Huntington Avenue, Boston, MA 02115, USA.

**LESSING, Kolja;** Violinist, Pianist and Composer; b. 15 Oct. 1961, Karlsruhe, Germany. *Education:* Violin lessons, 1964–, piano, 1966–, with mother; Violin studies, Hansheinz Schneeberger masterclasses, Diploma with Distinction, 1982, Basel, Switzerland, 1978–; Piano studies with Peter Efler, Diploma, 1983, Basel, 1979–83. *Career:* Debut: Violin recital at Ettlingen Castle in 1981; Piano, Lausanne in 1982; Concerts throughout Europe; Solo violin recitals and chamber music concerts; Orchestral concerts with Dresdner Philharmonic, Nationaltheaterorchester Mannheim, Radio Sinfonieorchester

Basel and others; Several premieres and numerous recitals, violin solo and piano solo with thematic programmes; Founder Member with Rainer Klaas and Bernhard Schwarz, Trio Alkan, 1988–; Professor, Musikhochschule Würzburg, 1989–. *Compositions:* Mostly recorded, German and Swiss Radio Stations; Various works for solo violin, solo clarinet, 2 clarinets and violin, 1978–. *Recordings include:* Works by Franz Berwald, Walther Geiser, Karl Michael Komma, Isang Yun; Numerous radio recordings, some first recordings, extensive repertoire in Germany, Switzerland and Sweden; Playback recording of Fauré's 2nd Sonata for Violin and Piano, 1989.

**LESTER, Richard;** Cellist; b. 1959, England. *Education:* Studies at the Royal College of Music with Ameryllis Fleming. *Career:* Member of Domus from 1979; Performances in a portable white geodesic dome on informal locations in Europe and Australia; Public workshops, discussion groups and open rehearsals in a wide repertoire; Frequent performances in London at the Wigmore Hall and on the South Bank, throughout the United Kingdom and on Radio 3; Festival engagements at Bath, Cheltenham, Salisbury, Sheffield and the City of London; Tours of South America, Canada, Spain, Italy, Germany, Ireland and Norway; 1991 tours of the Netherlands and New Zealand; Solo concerts and recitals throughout the United Kingdom and tours of Europe, Japan and the Middle East; Concerto performances with the Chamber Orchestra of Europe at Carnegie Hall and in Berlin and Vienna; Salzburg Camerata Academica in Austria, Germany and Italy under Sándor Végh; Cellist with Florestan Trio; Principal Cello, Chamber Orchestra of Europe and Orchestra of the Age of Enlightenment; Member of Hausmusik; Formerly member of Domus; Performs mostly as chamber musician at major festivals and concert venues throughout the world. *Recordings include:* Piano Quartets by Fauré, Dvořák, Brahms, Mozart and Mendelssohn; Schubert's Trout Quintet and Adagio and Rondo Concertante with pianist, Chi-Chi Nwanoku; Works by Martinů, Suk, Kodály and Dohnányi; Complete cello repertoire of Mendelssohn; Boccherini Cello Sonatas; Schumann Trios with the Florestan Trio. *Honours:* Deutsche Schallplattenpreis, 1986 and Gramophone Magazine Award for Best Chamber Music Record of 1986 for Fauré Piano Quartets; Prizewinner at International Scheveninges Cello Competition, 1987; Gramophone Award for Schumann Trios recording, 1999. *Current Management:* Sulivan Sweetland. *Address:* 5 Reynolds Close, London NW11 7EA, England.

**LETHIEC, Michel;** clarinettist; b. 11 Dec. 1946, Poitiers, France. *Education:* studied in Bordeaux and at the Paris Conservatoire. *Career:* concerto engagements with the Monte Carlo Philharmonic, Radio France Philharmonic, Ensemble Orchestre de Paris and the Lausanne Chamber Orchestra; British appearances with the English Chamber Orchestra, Academy of St Martin in the Fields and the Scottish Ensemble; Recitals and chamber concerts with Leonard Rose, Aurèle Nicolet, Karl Engel, Joseph Suk, Elly Ameling, Philippe Entremont and the Talich, Vermeer, Takacs and Sibelius Quartets; Has premiered works by Ballif, Boucourechliev, Marco, Corigliano and Scolari; Festival engagements include Edinburgh and the Eastern Music Festival, USA; Concert repertoire includes music by Copland, Crusell, Hindemith, Krommer, Mercadante, Mozart, Pleyel, Spohr, Stamitz and Weber; Boulez Domaines and Busoni Concertino; Double Concertos by Bruch with viola, Strauss with bassoon, Danzi with flute and Devienne with clarinet; With string quartets plays works by Mozart, Brahms, Weber, Reger, Reicha, Hindemith, Birtwistle, Yun and Bloch; Director of the Pau Casals Festival in Prades. *Honours:* Interpretation Prize at the International Competition in Belgrade; Grand Prix du Disque, 1978 for Asceses by Jolivet; Chevalier de L'Ordre National du Merite, Professeur an Conservatoire de Paris. *Address:* Les Templiers, 06790 Aspremont, France.

**LETNANOVA, Elena;** Concert Pianist, Author and Music Critic; b. 23 Oct. 1942, Bratislava, Slovakia; m. Andrej Mraz 1966 (divorced); one d. *Education:* Faculty of Architecture, Slovak Technical Univ.; VSMU, Music Faculty, Bratislava; postgraduate, PWSM, Acad. of Chopin, Warsaw, Poland, 1968; PhD, Faculty of Philosophy, Comenius Univ., Bratislava, 1979; postgraduate courses in Aesthetics, Comenius Univ., 1983. *Career:* debut, solo pianist with Slovak Philharmonic Orchestra, 1969, recital, Carnegie Hall, New York, 1992; taught at univs of Comenius, Dayton, VSMU and STU, Academia Istropolitana; performed at festivals in Rome, Vienna, San Franciscso, Katowice, Ghent, Munich, Prague, Bratislava and recitals in Madrid, Zaragosa, Zagreb, London, Zürich, Baden, Bordeaux, Bologna, Ljubljana, Warsaw, Bruges, New York, Dallas, Denver, Dayton, Washington DC, Fairfax, Berkeley, Rochester, Cortland, Oxford and other cities in Canada, Israel, Netherlands, Croatia, Belgium, Slovakia, Austria, Italy; Dir, Festival of Flemish Music, Bratislava, 2000. *Recordings:* 30 recordings from Slovak radio, TV, Bratislava and Supraphon Prague: Scarlatti, Liszt, Chopin, Scriabin, Tchaikovsky, Szymanowski, F. Nietzsche to Bartók and J. Cage; Piano Concertos by J. S. Bach, J. Haydn, F. Chopin, H. Górecki, B. Buckinx, J. Hatrik, J. Farkas; 2 CDs with F. Nietzsche Music, Antwerp, 1997, and UNESCO Burgenland, Austria, 2000; performed in three television films (Three Women Artists, 1969, Jan Zelibsky, 1972, Paper's Heads (directed by Hanak), 1996). *Publications:* Books: The Piano Interpretation in 17th, 18th, 19th Centuries, 1991; The Presence of the Past, 1996; Translations: Fundamentals of Musical Thinking by J. Kresanek, Belgium; A.Soljenitsyn's The Message from Exile, 1979; Scenario: Kandinsky-Mussorgsky: Pictures at an Exhibition, multi-media event premiered in Kennedy Union Boll Theatre, Dayton, Ohio, 1990; more than 66 articles in journals in Northfield, Illinois, USA, London, Ghent, Delft, Moscow, Prague, Bratislava. *Honours:* Winner, Special Prize, Chopin Competition, Czech Repub. *Address:* Mudronova 95, 81104 Bratislava, Slovakia. *Telephone:* (2)

6280-4323. *E-mail:* letnanova@ba.telecom.sk. *Website:* elenaletnanova.slke .org.

**LEUCHTMANN, Horst;** Musicologist; b. 26 April 1927, Brunswick, Germany; m. Brita-Angela von Wentzel, 28 Nov 1952, 1 s., 2 d. *Education:* PhD, State Music School, Brunswick, University of Munich, 1957; Honorary Professor, Musikhochschule Munich, 1986. *Career:* Editor, Musikhistorische Kommission, Bayerische Akademie der Wissenschaften; Lecturer, University of Munich and Musikhochschule Munich; Ordentliches Mitglied der Bayerischen Akademie der Schönen Kunst, 1989. *Publications:* Editor, Complete Works of Orlando di Lasso; Editor, Musik in Bayern; Books; Editions; Dictionaries; Translations. *Address:* Markgrafenstrasse 50, 81827 Munich 82, Germany.

**LEVAILLANT, Denis;** Pianist, Composer and Musical Director; b. 3 Aug. 1952, Paris, France; m. Christine Rigaud, 21 Oct 1972, 1 s., 1 d. *Education:* MPhil, 1973; Piano studies since age of 5 years and composition studies since age of 12 years at Nancy, France; Advanced study at Paris, France. *Career:* Debut: As pianist in concert in 1969; First composition record ed, Radio France, 1975; Many occupations as producer and artistic director; mem, SACEM; SACD; SPEDIDAM; ADAMI. *Compositions:* 60 including Le Baigneur, opéra-bouffe, 1976; Douze Mouvements for piano, 1980; Piano Transit, for piano and tape, 1983; Les Pierres Noires, for chamber choir, 1984; OPA MIA, opera, 1987–89; Les Couleurs de la Parole, for orchestra, 1990–91; Tombeau de Gesualdo, for chamber choir, 1994–95; Echo de Narcisse, concerto for piano and orchestra, 1995–96; Le Clair l'Obscur, string quartet #2, 1996–97. *Recordings:* 12 CDs. *Publications:* L'Improvisation Musicale, 1981; Le Piano, 1986. *Contributions:* Le Monde de la Musique, 1981–1983. *Honours:* Villa Medicis, 1983; Prix Italia, 1988. *Current Management:* Bleu 17. *Address:* Bleu 17, 21 Paris-Forêt, 77760 Achères La Forêt, France.

**LEVI, Yoel,** MA; Romanian/American conductor; *Principal Conductor, Orchestre national d'Ile de France;* b. 16 Aug. 1950, Romania; m. *Education:* Tel-Aviv and Jerusalem Acads of Music, Guildhall School of Music, London. *Career:* grew up in Israel; studied under Mendi Rodan, Franco Ferrara, Kiril Kondrashin; won First Prize Conductors' Int. Competition Besançon, France 1978; Asst to Lorin Maazel Cleveland Orchestra for six years, Resident Conductor 1980–84; Music Dir Atlanta Symphony Orchestra (ASO) 1988–2000, extensive European tour 1991, Music Dir Emer. 2000–; Principal Guest Conductor Israel Philharmonic Orchestra, US tour 2004; Music Adviser to Flemish Radio Orchestra; Principal Conductor Orchestre Nat. d'Ile de France 2005–; frequent guest conductor of orchestras throughout N America, Europe and the Far East; conducted Stockholm Philharmonic at Nobel Prize Ceremony 1991; performed at Opening Ceremonies of Centennial Olympic Games 1996; apptd first Music Adviser to Israel Festival for 1997/98 seasons; opera conducting debut La Fanciulla del West at Teatro Comunale, Florence 1997; has also conducted Carmen at Lyric Opera of Chicago, Makropoulos Case by Janacek in Prague, Puccini's Edgar with Orchestra Nat. de France (released as live performance on CD by Radio France), with ASO: Mozart's Magic Flute, The Abduction from the Seraglio, Bartok's Bluebeard's Castle; Distinguished Visiting Prof., Univ. of Georgia School of Music. *Recordings:* more than 40 recordings on different labels with various orchestras, including Cleveland Orchestra, London Philharmonic, Philharmonia Orchestra, Atlanta Symphony Orchestra, of music by Barber, Beethoven, Brahms, Copland, Dohnanyi, Dvorak, Hindemith, Kodaly, Mahler, Mendelssohn, Mussorgsky, Neilsen, Prokofiev, Puccini, Ravel, Rossini, Saint-Saens, Schoenberg, Shostakovich, Sibelius, Stravinsky and Tchaikovsky. *Honours:* Chevalier des Arts et des Lettres 2001; Hon. DFA (Oglethorpe Univ., Atlanta) 1997; Best Orchestra of the Year (awarded to ASO), Int. Classical Music Awards 1991–92. *Address:* La maison de l'Orchestre national d'Ile de France, 19 rue des Ecoles, 94140 Alfortville, France (office). *Telephone:* 1-41-79-03-40 (office). *Fax:* 1-41-79-03-50 (office). *E-mail:* courrier@orchestre-ile.com (office). *Website:* www.orchestre-ile.com (office).

**LEVI MINZI, Carlo;** Pianist; b. 10 Dec. 1954, Milan, Italy. *Education:* Giuseppe Verdi Conservatory, Milan; Piano Diploma, 1974; Piano Certificate, Tchaikovsky Conservatory, Moscow, 1975 and from Curtis Institute of Music, Philadelphia, 1978. *Career:* Recitals and appearances with various orchestras in Europe and USA, 1972–; Television and radio appearances on national stations in Italy, Switzerland, France, Spain, Austria, Germany, Poland, Bulgaria, USA and Mexico; mem, Vice President, Classical Frontiers, NY, USA. *Compositions:* Completion Of Schubert's F Sharp Minor Sonata, 1983, with Quirino Principe; First Performance, Town Hall, NY, 1984; First Radio Recording, WDR, Koln, 1985. *Recordings:* Several. *Contributions:* Various journals.

**LEVIN, Robert D.;** Pianist, Musicologist and Theorist; b. 13 Oct. 1947, Brooklyn, New York, USA; m. (1) Christine Noël Whittlesey, 18 May 1974, divorced 1991, (2) Ya-Fei Chuang, 30 July 1995. *Education:* AB magna cum laude with highest honours, Music, Harvard University, 1968; Private studies with Nadia Boulanger, 1960–64; Conducting with Hans Swarowsky, 1966. *Career:* Solo and chamber appearances throughout Europe, USA, Australia and Japan, 1970–; Pianist, New York Philomusica, 1971–; Head Theory Department, Curtis Institute of Music, Philadelphia, USA, 1968–73; Professor of music, School of the Arts, SUNY Purchase, 1972–86; Professor of Piano, Staatliche Hochschule für Musik, Freiburg, Germany, 1986–93; Professor of Music, Harvard University, 1993–; President, International Johann Sebastian Bach Competition, Leipzig; American Academy of Arts and Sciences.

*Compositions:* Mozart Completions: Requiem, Concerto for piano, violin, orchestra in D; Quintet for clarinet and strings in B flat; Symphonie concertante for flute, oboe, horn, bassoon and orchestra in E flat; Larghetto and Allegro in E flat for 2 pianos; Oboe concerto in F; Horn Concertos in E flat and in D, published and recorded; Sonata Movement in G; Cadenzas to Beethoven Violin Concerto; Hoffmeister Viola Concerto; Mozart Concertos for violin, flute, oboe, horn; Stamitz Viola Concerto (all published). *Recordings:* Mozart Sonatas for piano 4 hands, with Malcolm Bilson; Music for 2 pianos, with Malcolm Bilson; Brahms and Hindemith, Complete Viola/Piano Sonatas, with Kim Kashkashian; Complete Beethoven Piano Concertos with ORR and John Eliot Gardiner; Mozart Concertos, with AAM and Christopher Hogwood; Haydn 4 Piano Trios; Schubert, Sonatas; Schubert 4-hand works with Malcolm Bilson; Complete Bach harpsichord concertos, English Suites, The Well-Tempered Clavier. *Publications:* Who Wrote the Mozart Four Wind Concertante?, 1988; Sightsinging and Ear Training Through Literature (with Louis Martin), 1988; Other texts in harmony and counterpoint published privately. *Contributions:* Mozart-Jahrbuch; Early Music; Various musicological congress reports; Performance Practice; The New Grove; The Mozart Compendium; Eighteenth Century Keyboard Music; The Cambridge Companion to Music. *Address:* Music Department, Harvard University, Cambridge, MA 02138, USA.

**LEVIN, Walter;** Violinist and College Professor; b. 6 Dec. 1924, Berlin, Germany. *Education:* Studied at the Juilliard School with Ivan Galamian. *Career:* Co-founded the La Salle String Quartet at the Juilliard School, 1949, with many concerts featuring modern composers and the quartets of Beethoven, and with European debut in 1954; Composers who have written for the ensemble include Hans Erich Apostel, Earle Brown, Henri Pousseur, Mauricio Kagel, György Ligeti, Penderecki and Witold Lutosławski; Quartet in Residence at Colorado College, 1949–53, then at the Cincinnati College, Conservatory of Music (also Professor there); Quartet disbanded in 1988; Jury Member, International String Quartet Competition, London, 2000. *Recordings include:* Works by Berg, Schoenberg, Webern and Zemlinsky; Beethoven's Late Quartets.

**LEVINE, Gilbert;** Conductor; b. 22 Jan. 1948, New York, NY, USA. *Education:* Reed College, 1965–67; Juilliard School of Music, 1967–68; Studied music history with Arthur Mendel and Louis Lockwood; Conducting with Jacques-Louis Monod; Music Theory with Milton Babbitt and J K Randall; AB, Princeton University, 1971; MA, Music Theory, Yale University, 1972; Conducting with Franco Ferrara, Siena. *Career:* Debut: Nouvel Orchestre Philharmonique de Radio France, Paris, 1973; Guest Conductor with various major North American and European Orchestras including: North German Radio Symphony Orchestra, Hamburg, 1977; Royal Philharmonic Orchestra, London, 1978; (West) Berlin Radio Symphony Orchestra, 1980; Minnesota Orchestra, 1984; Toronto Symphony; New York Philharmonic Orchestra; Dresden State Orchestra; San Francisco Symphony; Philadelphia Orchestra; Baltimore Symphony; Bayerische Staatsorchester; St Paul Chamber Orchestra; L'Orchestre de la Bastille; Montreal Symphony; London Philharmonic; Music Director, Karkow Philharmonic Orchestra, 1987–; TV concerts with Kraków Philharmonic Orchestra, Royal Philharmonic Orchestra, London Philharmonic, Philharmonia Orchestra, Dresden Staatskapelle, Pittsburgh Symphony Orchestra; Artistic Dir and Conductor, Philharmonia Orchestra Creation Series, 2000; Artistic Dir and Conductor, Papal Concerts, RAI Roma, 1988, Royal Philharmonic, 1994, Philharmonia Orchesra, 2000, Pittsburgh Symphony Orchestra, 2004; Dresden Staatskapelle, 2002, Montreal Symphony, 2002, London Philharmonic, 2003. *Recordings:* with RSO Berlin, English Chamber Orchestra, Kraków Philharmonic, Royal Philharmonic, London Philharmonic. *Honours:* Pontifical Kt Commdr, Equestrian Order of St Gregory the Great. *Address:* 1 Gracie Terrace, Apt 2F, New York, NY 10028-7956, USA. *E-mail:* mozart492g@cs.com.

**LEVINE, James;** American musician, conductor and pianist; *Music Director, Metropolitan Opera;* b. 23 June 1943, Cincinnati, OH; s. of Lawrence M. Levine and Helen Levine (née Goldstein). *Education:* Walnut Hills High School, Cincinnati, The Juilliard School, New York. *Career:* Asst Conductor, Cleveland Orchestra 1964–70; Prin. Conductor, Metropolitan Opera, New York 1973–, Music Dir 1976–, Artistic Dir 1986–2004; Music Dir Ravinia Festival 1973–93, Cincinnati May Festival 1974–78; Chief Conductor, Munich Philharmonic 1999–2004; Music Dir UBS Verbier Festival Youth Orchestra 2000–04; Music Dir Boston Symphony Orchestra 2004–; regular appearances as conductor and pianist in Europe and the USA with orchestras including Vienna Philharmonic, Berlin Philharmonic, Chicago Symphony, Philadelphia Orchestra, Philharmonia, Dresden Staatskapelle, Boston Symphony, New York Philharmonic, Israel Philharmonic, Salzburg and Bayreuth Festivals; conducted Metropolitan Opera premieres of I Vespri Siciliani, Stiffelio, I Lombardi (Verdi), The Rise and Fall of the City of Mahagonny (Weill), Lulu (Berg), Porgy and Bess (Gershwin), Oedipus Rex (Stravinsky), Idomeneo, La Clemenza di Tito (Mozart), Erwartung, Moses und Aron (Schönberg), La Cenerentola (Rossini), Benvenuto Cellini (Berlioz), The Ghosts of Versailles (Corigliano) (world premiere), The Great Gatsby (Harbison) (world premiere); conductor Salzburg Festival premieres of Offenbach's Les contes d'Hoffmann 1980 and Schönberg's Moses und Aron 1987; conducted Munich Philharmonic Orchestra at the London Proms 2002, Benvenuto Cellini at the Met 2003. *Recordings:* over 100 albums of symphonic works, chamber music, lieder and song recitals, solo piano music and 36 complete operas. *Honours:* Dr hc (Univ. of Cincinnati, New England Conservatory, Northwestern Univ., State Univ. of

New York, The Juilliard School); Grammy Awards for recordings of Orff's Carmina Burana, Mahler's Symphony No. 7, Brahms' A German Requiem, Verdi's La Traviata, Wagner's Das Rheingold, Die Walküre, Götterdämmerung, Strauss' Ariadne auf Naxos; Cultural Award of New York City 1980, Smetana Medal 1987, Musical America's Musician of the Year Award, Gold Medal, Nat. Inst. of Social Sciences 1996, Nat. Medal of Arts 1997, Anton Seidl Award 1997, Lotus Award 1997, Kennedy Center Honors 2002, World Econs Forum Crystal Award 2003. *Address:* Metropolitan Opera, Lincoln Center, New York, NY 10023, USA. *Telephone:* (212) 799-3100 (office). *Website:* www .metopera.org (office); www.bso.org (office); www.verbierorchestra.com (office).

**LEVINSKY, Ilya;** Singer (Tenor); b. 1965, Baku, Russia. *Education:* Studied at the Baku Academy of Music, until 1989. *Career:* Soloist with the Baku Opera, from 1987; Israel Philharmonic summer opera, from 1991; Member of the Komische Oper Berlin with leading roles in Falstaff, La Traviata, Don Giovanni, Così fan tutte and Die Zauberflöte, until 1998; Season 1996–97 as Dimitri in Boris Gudunov with the Frankfurt Opera, in The Nose by Shostakovich for Netherlands Opera and as Sinodal in Rubinstein's The Demon at the Bregenz Festival; Further engagements include Tamino in Die Zauberflöte at Salzburg Festival, Komische Oper and Frankfurt Opera; Lensky in Eugene Onegin at the Tivoli Festival and Števa in Jenůfa at the Salzburg Festival, 2001. *Recordings include:* Lady Macbeth of Mtsensk and Shostakovich Japanese Songs, Rachmaninov Aleko and Francesca da Rimini; Tchaikovsky Songs; Kalman's Die Herzogin von Chicago, under Richard Bonynge. *Current Management:* Askonas Holt Ltd, Lonsdale Chambers, 27 Chancery Lane, London, WC2A 1PF, England. *Telephone:* (20) 7400-1700. *Fax:* (20) 7400-1799. *E-mail:* info@askonasholt.co.uk. *Website:* www .askonasholt.co.uk.

**LEVY, Edward (Irving);** Composer; b. 2 May 1929, Brooklyn, New York, USA. *Education:* BA, City College New York, 1957; Princeton University with Milton Babbitt; EdD, Columbia University Teachers College, 1967; Further study with Ralf Shapey and Stefan Wolpe. *Career:* Teacher at CW Post College, Long Island University, 1961–67; Professor of Music at Yeshiva University, 1967. *Compositions include:* Duo for violin and cello, 1950; 2 Songs for mezzo and piano, 1951; Clarinet Sonata, 1956; String Trio, 1959; Trio for clarinet, violin and piano, 1961; Images for soprano and piano, 1961; Quintet for flute and ensemble, 1967; Variations On A Theme by Brahms for flute, clarinet and horn, 1979; Concatenations for 2 flutes, clarinet and cello, 1980; Movement for brass quintet, 1980; Works for chorus and for chamber orchestra. *Address:* c/o ASCAP, ASCAP Building, 1 Lincoln Plaza, New York, NY 10023, USA.

**LEVY, Marvin (David);** Composer; b. 2 Aug. 1932, Passaic, New Jersey, USA. *Education:* BA, New York University, 1954; MA, Columbia University, 1956. *Career:* Archivist, American Opera Society, 1952–58; Music Critic for a number of leading publications including Opera News, Musical America, American Record Guide, New York Herald Tribune and Composer; mem, ASCAP. *Compositions include:* Opera: The Tower, 1956, Escorial, 1958, Sobata Electra, 1957, Mourning Becomes Electra, 1967; Vocal: Echoes, 1956, For The Time Being, 1959, One Person, 1962, Sacred Service For The Sabbath Eve: Shir Shel Moshe, 1964, Masada, 1973, In Memoriam WH Auden, 1984; Orchestra: Caramoor Festival Overture, 1958, Symphony, 1960, Kyros, 1961, Piano Concerto, 1970, Trialogus, 1972, Canto De Los Maranos, 1977, Pascua Florida, 1988; Instrumental: String Quartet, 1955, Rhapsody, 1956, Chassidic Suite, 1956, Arrows Of Time, 1988; The Grand Balcony, musical, 1978–92; The Zachary Star, musical, 1996. *Honours:* 2 Prix de Rome Scholarships, 1962, 1965; 2 Guggenheim Fellowships, 1960, 1964; Grants include Ford Foundation, 1965, Damrosch, 1961, National Endowment for The Arts, 1974, 1978; Recipient, Scroll, City of New York. *Current Management:* Sheldon Softer Management. *Address:* c/o Sheldon Softer Management, 130 West 56, New York City, NY 10019, USA.

**LEWIN, David (Benjamin);** Composer and Theorist; b. 2 July 1933, New York, USA. *Education:* Studied with Edouard Steuermann, 1945–50; MFA, Princeton University, 1958, with Milton Babbitt, Roger Sessions and Earl Kim. *Career:* Junior Fellowship at Harvard, 1958–61; Computer music at the Bell Laboratories, Murray Hill, New Jersey; Teacher at the University of California at Berkeley, 1961–67, Stony Brook, New York, 1967–80, Yale University, 1979–85 and Professor at Harvard University, 1985–. *Compositions include:* Viola Sonata, 1958; Essay On A Subject By Webern for chamber orchestra, 1958; Classical Variations On A Theme by Schoenberg for cello and piano, 1960; Fantasia for organ, 1962; Fantasy-Adagio for violin and orchestra, 1963–66; Quarter Piece for string quartet, 1969; Woodwind Trio, 1969; Computer Music, 1971; Fanfare, 1980, for piano, 1982; Generalized Musical Intervals and Transformations, 1987. *Publications include:* Studies of Parsifal, Moses und Aron and Rameau's Traité de l'Harmonie, Some Notes on Pierrot Lunaire, 1997. *Contributions:* Journal of Music Theory; Perspectives of New Music. *Address:* Harvard University, Music Building, Harvard, Cambridge, MA 02138, USA.

**LEWIS, Brenda;** Singer (Soprano); b. 2 March 1921, Harrisburg, Pennsylvania, USA. *Education:* Studied in Philadelphia. *Career:* Sang in The Bartered Bride with the Philadelphia Opera Company; Sang with New York City Opera, 1943–67 with debut as Santuzza in Cavalleria Rusticana, in San Francisco in 1950 as Salome, at Metropolitan Opera from 1952 as Musetta in La Bohème, Marina in Boris Godunov, Barber's Vanessa and Rosalinde in Die

Fledermaus, and at Chicago in 1965 as Marie in Wozzeck; Guest appearances in South America. *Address:* c/o New York City Opera, Lincoln Center, New York, NY 10023, USA.

**LEWIS, Daniel;** Conductor; b. 10 May 1925, Flagstaff, Arizona, USA. *Education:* Studied composition with Nino Marcelli in San Diego, 1939–41; BM, San Diego State College, 1949; Further study with Eugen Jochum in Munich, 1960. *Career:* Leader of the Honolulu Symphony during war service; Assistant Conductor with San Diego Symphony, 1954–56; Leader and Associate Conductor, 1956–59; Music Director of the Pasadena Symphony, 1972–83 notably in neglected 18th century and American music; Guest Conductor with the Los Angeles Philharmonic, Oakland Symphony, Atlanta Symphony, Minnesota Orchestra, Utah Symphony, Seattle Symphony, Los Angeles Chamber Orchestra and the Louisville Orchestra; Chairman of the Conducting Studies Department at the University of Southern California. *Address:* Music Department, UCLA, Los Angeles, California, USA.

**LEWIS, Jeffrey;** Composer; b. 28 Nov. 1942, Port Talbot, South Wales; 1 s., 1 d. *Education:* BMus 1st class honours, 1965, MMus, 1967, University College, Cardiff; PhD, University of Wales, 1977; ARCM Organ Performers; Studied composition with Boguslaw Schaffer, Kraków, Poland, with Don Banks, London, with Stockhausen and Ligeti, Darmstadt, Germany, 1967–68. *Career:* Pianist, Paris Chamber Ensemble, 1967–68; Lecturer in 20th Century Composition Techniques and Experimental Music, City of Leeds College of Music, England, 1969–72; Lecturer, Department of Music, University College of North Wales, Bangor, 1973–; Lecturer, 1973–87, Senior Lecturer, 1987–93, Department of Music, University College of North Wales, Bangor. *Compositions:* Orchestral: Praeludium; Piano Concerto; Mutations I; Antiphony; Fanfares with Variations; Aurora; Memoria; Limina Lucis; Instrumental: Mutations II; Esultante; Momentum for organ; Threnody for piano; Trilogy for piano; Tableau for piano; Fantasy for piano; Two Cadenzas for Piano; Night Fantasy for piano duet; Chamber: Epitaph for Abelard and Heloise; Antiphon; Litania; Stratos; Ritornel; Mobile II; Time-Passage; Wind Quintet: Sonante; Piano Trio; Cantus; Teneritas; Dead Leaves; Choral: Carmen Paschale; Pro Pace; Hymnus Ante Somnum; Westminster Mass; Lux Perpetua; Sequentia de Sancto Michaele; Recordatis. *Recordings:* Commercial CD (Sea of Glass, Lontano Records Ltd); Dreams, Dances and Lullabies for harp; Jeffrey Lewis: Threnody; Cantus; Teneritas; Sonante; Trilogy (ASC CS CD43). *Publications:* Novello; Roberton; Curiad; Article: The Current State of British Cathedral Music, Choir and Organ, 1993. *Address:* Crafnant, Park Crescent, Llanfairfechan, Gwynedd LL33 0AU, Wales. *Telephone:* (1248) 680776.

**LEWIS, Keith;** Singer (Tenor); b. 6 Oct. 1950, Methven, New Zealand. *Education:* Studied in New Zealand and in London from 1976. *Career:* Sang in premiere of Tavener's Thérèse at Covent Garden returning as Rossini's Almaviva and as Bellini's Tebaldo and Tamino in Magic Flute; Appearances world-wide in such operas as Don Giovanni, Armide, La Clemenza di Tito, Eugene Onegin, as Mozart's Ferrando, Belmonte, and Monteverdi's Giove; Concert engagements in Damnation of Faust, Haydn's Creation, Schumann's Paradies und der Peri, The Dream of Gerontius, Bach B minor Mass, and Beethoven's 9th with such conductors as Solti, Giulini and Abbado; Further appearances include Mendelssohn's Elijah with Colin Davis, Verdi's Requiem, Mozart's Requiem and Bach Mass in B minor; Sang in the opening concert of the 1991 Promenade Concerts, in Idomeneo at Glyndebourne in 1991, in Britten's Serenade in London, and Haydn's Creation under Sinopoli; Sang Alwa in Berg's Lulu at the Berlin Staatsoper, 1997; Gregor in The Makropulos Case at Toulouse, 1998; Season 2000–01 as Bizet's Zurga and Verdi's Paolo in Sydney and Posa (Don Carlos) at Melbourne. *Recordings include:* Rossini's Tancredi, Otello and Moses; Gluck's Alceste; Don Giovanni conducted by Haitink; Messiah under Solti; Masses by Haydn under Marriner; Paradies und der Peri under Albrecht; Berlioz Lelio, Te Deum and Requiem under Inbal; Berlioz Requiem under Bertini; Mozart Requiem; Beethoven's 9th, Wand and Giulini; Salome under Mehta. *Current Management:* IMG Artists Europe. *Address:* c/o IMG Artists Europe, Lovell House, 616 Chiswick High Road, London W4 5RX, England.

**LEWIS, Michael;** Australian singer (baritone); b. 1948, Adelaide, SA. *Education:* studied in Adelaide and at the London Opera Centre. *Career:* sang first at Wexford Festival, then with Glyndebourne Festival and Touring Operas, WNO and Scottish Opera, Frankfurt Opera and companies in Australia; resident principal with Opera North and Australian Opera; season 1992–93 as Verdi's Luna, Amonasro, Rigoletto and Renato in Australia, Rigoletto at La Fenice, Venice, Rossini's Figaro for ENO; performances of L'Africaine and Tiefland in Berlin, I Masnadieri and Macbeth in Australia 1998 and Bizet's Zurga in San Diego; performed as Jeronimus Cornelisz in Richard Mills' Batavia (world premiere) 2001; other roles include Mozart's Guglielmo, Alfonso, the Count and Papageno, Malatesta, Lescaut in Manon, Riccardo in I Puritani, Marcello in La Bohème, Germont in La Traviata, Zurga in Les Pecheurs de Perles and Don Carlo in La Forza del Destino; concert repertoire includes Carmina Burana, Belshazzar's Feast, The Messiah and Elijah. *Recording:* Schubert Lieder Orchestrations with Adelaide Symphony Orchestra. *Honours:* Green Room Award (for Rigoletto). *Current Management:* Patrick Togher Artists Management, Suite 25, 450 Elizabeth Street, Surry Hills, 2010 NSW, Australia. *E-mail:* pjtogher@ozemail.com.au.

**LEWIS, Oliver;** Violinist; b. 12 May 1966, London, England. *Education:* Purcell School of Music, London; Konservatorium für Musik, Bern, Switzerland; Studied with Carl Pini, David Takeno, Sándor Végh, Aaron Rosand, Igor

Ozim, Wen Xun Chen. *Career:* Debut: British Concerto debut with National Children's Orchestra of Great Britain, age 12; Solo concert tours, England, France, Spain, Portugal, Switzerland, Germany, Austria, Netherlands, Georgia; Broadcasts world-wide, including German television and radio, Swiss Radio, BBC Radio 3, Classic FM Radio; Swiss Concerto debut with Bern Symphony Orchestra, Casino Berne, 1990; Became Concertmaster and Soloist, Heidelberg Chamber Orchestra, 1991; Gives masterclasses at Dartington International Summer School; Concert performances with the Royal Philharmonic Orchestra, 1999; Leader of Ceruti Ensemble of London. *Recordings:* CDs including world premiere recordings of rare English music; English Romanticism, music by Ferguson, Goossens and Ireland; English Romanticism II, music by Elgar and Goossens; Recorded all the solo violin music of Ennio Morricone for the film The Inverse Cannon, 1999; Malcolm Arnold String Quartets, 2001. *Current Management:* Sessions International (UK). *Address:* 8 Colmans Wharf, 45 Morris Road, London E14 6 PA, England. *E-mail:* sessions.international@virgin.net.

**LEWIS, Richard,** MVO, BEd, MA, FRSA, FTCL; British singer (tenor), educator, counsellor and therapist; b. Trowbridge, Wiltshire, England. *Education:* Metropolitan Univ. of London, Trinity Coll. of Music with John Carol Case, Guildhall School of Music and Drama with Ellis Keeler, studied with Ilse Wolf. *Career:* debut, Wigmore Hall as tenor soloist with Praetorius Consort; sang with BBC Singers and other leading choirs; much work as an oratorio singer; Gentleman in Ordinary of Her Majesty's Chapel Royal, St James's Palace 1976–2002; soloist with Opera for All and in world premieres in St Paul's Cathedral and South Bank; mem. Royal Soc. of Musicians, Equity; accred mem., British Asscn of Counsellors and Psychotherapists. *Recordings include:* numerous as chorister, Music for the Christening of Prince William, Britten's Journey of the Magi (with James Bowman and Graham Trew), Royal Composers with Her Majesty's Chapel Royal Choir, St James's Palace. *Honours:* Queen's Silver Jubilee Medal, Queen's Golden Jubilee Medal, Oriana Madrigal Soc. Prize, Joseph Maas Prize for Tenors, Beryl Searle Scholarship, Vaughan Williams Scholarship, Mitchell City of London Scholarship, Alfred and Catherine Howard Scholarship, Corporation of London Scholarship, Max Hecht Scholarship. *Address:* Melin-y-Grogue, Llanfair Waterdine, Knighton, Powys LD7 1TU, Wales.

**LEWIS, Roger Charles,** BMus, FRWCMD; British broadcasting executive; *Managing Director, ITV Wales;* b. 24 Aug. 1954, s. of the late Griffith Charles Job Lewis and Dorothy Lewis (née Russ); m. Christine Trollope 1980; two s. *Education:* Cynffig Comprehensive School, Bridgend, Univ. of Nottingham. *Career:* freelance musician 1976–80; Music Officer Darlington Arts Centre 1980–82; presenter Radio Tees 1981–84; producer Capital Radio 1984–85; BBC Radio 1 1985–87, Head of Music Radio 1 1987–90; Dir Classical Div. EMI Records 1990–95, Man. Dir 1995, Man. Dir EMI Premier 1995–97; Pres. Decca Record Co. 1997–98; Man. Dir and Programme Controller Classic FM 1998–2004; Dir GWR PLC 1998–2004, The Radio Corpn Ltd 1999–2004; Man. Dir ITV Wales 2004–; Dir Wales Millennium Centre 2004–; Deputy Chair. Boosey & Hawkes 2004–; Chair. Classic FM Charitable Trust 1998–2004, Music and Dance Scheme Advisory Group, Dept for Educ. and Skills 2000–04, Barchester Group 2001–; Trustee Masterprize (Int. Composers' Competition) 1995–, Masterclass Charitable Trust 2000–04; Chair. Trustees Ogmore Centre 1996–; Pres. Bromley Youth Music Trust 2000–05; mem. British Phonographic Inst. (Classical Cttee 1990–98, Chair. 1996–98), WNO (Devt Circle 2001–); Dir Digital One 2003–04; Dir Liverpool Capital of Culture 2003 (mem. of bd Liverpool Culture Co.); Chair. Royal Liverpool Philharmonic 2003; Vice-Pres. London Welsh Male Voice Choir 2004–. *Honours:* Hon. Fellow Royal Welsh Coll. of Music and Drama, hon. mem. Royal Coll. of Music; Sony Radio Award 1987, 1988, 1989, Grand Award Winner and Gold Medal, New York Radio Festival 1987, One World Broadcasting Trust Award 1989, NTL Commercial Radio Programmer of the Year 2002. *Address:* ITV Wales, Television Centre, Culverhouse Cross, Cardiff CF5 6XJ, Wales (office). *Telephone:* (2920) 590191 (office). *E-mail:* roger.lewis@itvwales.com (office). *Website:* www.itv1wales.com (office).

**LEWIS, Anthony (Tony) Robert,** CBE, DL, MA; British sports commentator, journalist, writer and fmr cricketer; *Director, Welsh National Opera;* b. 6 July 1938, Swansea, Wales; s. of Wilfrid Lewis and Florence Lewis (née Flower); m. Joan Pritchard 1962; two d. *Education:* Neath Grammar School, Christ's Coll. Cambridge. *Career:* right-hand batsman; teams: Glamorgan, Cambridge Univ.; double blue and debut at int. level; led Glamorgan to their second Co. Championship title 1969; played in nine Tests (eight as Capt.) scoring 457 runs (average 32.64); 20,495 first-class runs (average 32.4) including 30 hundreds; retd 1974; became cricket commentator and journalist; Pres. Marylebone Cricket Club (MCC) 1998–2000, secured admission of women into MCC Club, Trustee 2002–; fmr Chair. Glamorgan Co. Cricket Club (CCC), Pres. 1987–93, 2003–; Chair. Welsh Tourist Bd 1992–2000; led successful Welsh campaign to host 2010 Ryder Cup; Chair. (non-exec.) World Snooker Ltd 2003–; Dir Welsh Nat. Opera 2003–. *Publications:* A Summer of Cricket 1976, Playing Days 1985, Double Century 1987, Cricket in Many Lands 1991, MCC Masterclass 1994, Taking Fresh Guard 2003. *Honours:* Hon. Fellow, St David's Univ. Coll., Lampeter 1993, Univ. of Glamorgan 1995, Univ. of Wales, Swansea 1996, Univ. of Cardiff 1999. *Address:* Castellau, Near Llantrisant, Mid Glamorgan CF72 8LP, Wales (home); c/o Angie Bainbridge Management, 3 New Cottages, The Holt, Washington, West Sussex, RH20 4AW, England (office). *Telephone:* (1903) 8933748 (office). *Fax:* (1903) 891320 (office). *E-mail:* angie.bainbridge@btopenworld.com (office).

**LEWIS, William;** Singer (Tenor); b. 23 Nov. 1935, Tulsa, Oklahoma, USA. *Education:* Studied at Fort Worth and New York. *Career:* Debut: Fort Worth in 1953 in Gianni Schicchi; Early appearances in Cincinnati, San Francisco and Dallas; New York City Opera in 1957 in Die Fledermaus, Metropolitan Opera from 1958 in Salome, Elektra, Boris Godunov, Jenůfa, The Queen of Spades, La Bohème and Francesca da Rimini; Sang Aeneas in the 1983 New York production of Les Troyens and at Spoleto in 1959 in the premiere of Barber's A Hand of Bridge; Sang at San Francisco, 1984–85 as Loge in The Ring, Wexford Festival and La Scala, 1986–87 in Humperdinck's Königskinder and the title role in the premiere of Testi's Riccardo III; Spoleto Festival in 1989 as Aegisthus in Elektra; Sang Arbace in Idomeneo at San Francisco in 1989 and in the premiere of Blimunda by Azio Corghi at the Teatro Lirico Milan in 1990; Other roles include Pollione in Norma, the Emperor in Die Frau ohne Schatten, Don José, Offenbach's Hoffmann, Radames, Gabriele Adorno in Simon Boccanegra and Strauss's Guntram; Sang Pollux in Die Liebe der Danaë at Avery Fisher Hall, NY, 2000 (concert). *Recordings include:* Adolar in Euryanthe. *Address:* c/o San Francisco Opera, War Memorial Opera House, San Francisco, CA 94102, USA.

**LEWKOVITCH, Bernhard;** Composer and Organist; b. 28 May 1927, Denmark. *Education:* Graduate in Music Theory, 1948, Organ, 1949, Royal Danish Conservatry of Music; Composition teachers were Poul Schierbeck and Jorgen Jersild; Studied in France. *Career:* Organist, 1947–63, Cantor, 1953–63, Sankt Ansgar Catholic Church, Copenhagen; Organist and Cantor, Church of Holy Sacrament, Copenhagen, 1973–; Founder and Leader of Schola Gregoriana Men's Choir, Schola Cantorum Mixed Choir, both now under the name Schola Cantorum. *Compositions include:* Vocal music and instrumental music for orchestra, ensemble, piano and organ including: Mass for 2 corui and mixed choir, Songs of Solomon for tenor and clarinet, horn and bass trombone, Deprecations for tenor, horn and bass trombone, Preacher and Singer for tenor and piano; Six Partitas for 5 brass instruments, vols I–II; Improperia Per Voce (Good Friday); 3 Tasso Madrigali for mixed choir; Responsoria for mixed choir (Good Friday); Helligandskoraler (Holy Ghost Chorales) for 4 brass players, 1980; Il Cantico delle Creature for 8 male voices; Alle meine Kinder, 48 motets, 1996; 5 English Madrigals for tenor, clarinet, horn and bassoon, 1997; Orgelchoräle: Notizen zu den Lübecher-Dialoguen; Ten Songs for baritone and piano. *Honours:* Carl Nielsen Prize, 1997. *Current Management:* Engstrí m & Sídring Musikforlag, Borgergade 17, 1300 Copenhagen K, Denmark. *Address:* Bredgade 69, 1260 K Copenhagen, Denmark.

**LI, Hong-Shen;** Singer (tenor); b. 1960, Beijing, China. *Education:* Studied at the Central Conservatory of Beijing and the Juilliard School with Ellen Faull. *Career:* Joined the San Francisco Opera Merola Program, 1987, performing Rinuccio in Gianni Schicchi and Lindoro in L'Italiana in Algeri; Further appearances as the Duke of Mantua, Aufidio in Mozart's Lucio Silla, the Italian Singer, Alfredo, Tebaldo, Pirro in Ermione and Leukippos in Daphne with the San Francisco Opera; Other roles include Rossini's Count Almaviva, Steuermann in Fliegende Holländer (debut with the Metropolitan Opera), Nadir, Macduff, Nemorino and Idreno in Semiramide; Season 2000–01 as Zerlina at the Met, Handel's Cleopatra for Washington Opera and Manon for Dallas Opera; Concert repertoire includes the Verdi Requiem and Mozart's Requiem, Beethoven's 9th Symphony and Rossini's Stabat Mater. *Honours:* Highest Fellowship Scholarship at Central Conservatory of Beijing; Winner, 1991 Metropolitan Opera Competition Nationals; George London Award; Adler Fellow with the San Francisco Opera, 1989–91. *Address:* c/o San Francisco Opera, War Memorial House, Van Ness Avenue, San Francisco, CA, USA.

**LI, Ming Qiang;** Professor of Piano; b. 1936, Shanghai, China; m. Li Ben Wang, one d. *Education:* studied piano with Alfred Wittenberg and with Prof. Tatiana Petrovna Kravchenko, St Petersburg Conservatory of Music. *Career:* numerous concerts world-wide, performing with many major orchestras; lectures and masterclasses world-wide, including Carnegie Mellon Univ., Rutgers Univ., Univ. of California at Santa Barbara, Univ. of Illinois, Oberlin Coll. Conservatory of Music, Cincinnati Coll. Conservatory of Music, Yale Univ., School of Music, Acad. of Music in Bucharest and National Taiwan Normal Univ.; Vice-Pres., Shanghai Conservatory of Music 1984–89; Artist-in-Residence, Dept of Music and Fine Arts, Hong Kong Baptist Univ. 1993–97; piano masterclasses at other Hong Kong univs; judge in numerous international piano competitions, including International Chopin Piano Competition, Arthur Rubinstein International Piano Master Competition, Van Cliburn International Piano Competition, Sydney International Piano Competition, Montréal International Music Competition and Tchaikovsky Piano Competitions; life mem. American Liszt Soc. *Recordings:* repertoire of works by Bach, Beethoven, Brahms, Chopin, Handel, Liszt, Mozart, Rachmaninov and Schubert; piano music by Chinese composers He Luting, Ding Shande, Wan Jianzhong and Zhe Jainer. *Honours:* Third Prize, Third International Smetana Piano Competition, Prague Spring Festival 1957; First Prize, First George Enescu International Piano Competition, Bucharest 1958; Fourth Prize, Sixth International Chopin Piano Competition, Warsaw 1960. *Address:* 11B Mansion Building, 846 King's Road, Quarry Bay, Hong Kong.

**LI, Yundi;** Chinese pianist; b. 1982, China; s. of Li Chuan. *Education:* Sichuan Music Acad. with Dan Zhao Yi, Shenzhen School of Arts, studied with Arie Vardi in Hanover, Germany. *Career:* originally learned to play accordion, started piano lesson aged seven; concert performances in the USA, Europe and Asia 2004, including New York recital debut, Metropolitan Museum.

*Recordings include:* Chopin Recital 2002, Liszt Piano Sonata in B minor 2003, Liszt Klaviersonate h-moll 2003, Chopin Scherzi Impromptus 2004, Love Moods 2004, Chopin 4 Scherzi 3 Impromptus 2004. *Honours:* prize winner, Stravinsky Int. Youth Piano Competition 1995, South Missouri Int. Youth Piano Competition, USA 1998, Liszt Int. Piano Competition, Netherlands 1999, China Int. Piano Competition 1999; first prize at the Chopin Int. Piano Competition, Warsaw, Poland 2000. *Current Management:* Askonas Holt Ltd, Lonsdale Chambers, 27 Chancery Lane, London, WC2A 1PF, England. *Telephone:* (20) 7400-1700. *Fax:* (20) 7400-1799. *E-mail:* info@askonasholt.co.uk. *Website:* www.askonasholt.co.uk. *Address:* c/o Deutsche Grammophon GmbH, Alte Rabenstrasse 2, 20148 Hamburg, Germany. *Website:* www.deutschegrammophon.com.

**LIANG, Ning;** Singer (mezzo-soprano); b. 1957, Peking, China. *Education:* Studied in Gwangdong and Peking; Further studies at Juilliard School and American Opera Center in New York. *Career:* Debut: Central Conservatory Peking, 1983; Sang at Peking and Shanghai as Carmen and Rosina, Cenerentola at the 1987 Aspen Festival; Philadelphia and Helsinki, 1988 as Dorabella and Carmen; Studied forther at the Juilliard School, 1986–89; Sang Cherubino in London and Hamburg, 1989–91; La Scala, Milan 1990, as Suzuki in Butterfly; Sang Rosina at Toronto and at the Vienna Festiva, 1992; Concert engagements include Beethoven's Ninth in Lisbon and Bellini's Il Pirata in New York; Opera engagements include, Ottavia in L'Incoronazione di Poppea (Marseille and Amsterdam), Stephano in Roméo et Juliette (Hamburg), Octavian (Deutsche Oper Berlin and Hamburg) and Sesto in La Clemenza di Tito (Stuttgart). *Recordings include:* Carmen and Le nozze di Figaro. *Honours:* Numerous Prizes in American Competitions: Metropolitan Opera National Council Competition, Rosa Ponselle International Vocal Competition, Loren L Zachery Competition and the Luciano Pavarotti Competition. *Address:* c/o Hamburgisches Staatsoper, Grosses-Theaterstrasse 34, 2000 Hamburg 36, Germany.

**LIAO, Chang-Yong;** Singer (baritone); b. 1969, China. *Career:* Many engagements in the Far and East and Europe, notably in operas by Mozart (Le nozze di Figaro) and Massenet, with chansons by Duparc, Debussy and Ravel; Contestant at the 1995 Cardiff Singer of the World Competition. *Address:* c/o Mr Wu Xun, Bureau of External Relations, Ministry of Culture, 2 Shatan Beijie, Beijing 100722, People's Republic of China.

**LICARET, Nicolae;** Pianist, Organist and Harpsichordist; b. 24 Sept. 1943, Bucharest; m., 1 s. *Education:* Music School George Enescu, Bucharest; Music Academy, Bucharest. *Career:* Debut: Dalles Hall, Bucharest, 1959; Piano Teacher, Bucharest Hight Music School, 1966–68; Soloist, Bucharest George Enescu Philharmonic Orchestra, 1968–; mem, UNESCO; Union of Romanian Musicians. *Recordings:* Bach's Sonatas; Concertino Ensemble; George Enescu's Pieces; Italian Music; L Alexandra Symphony; Pan Flute and Organ; Phonogram; Handel Organ Concertos; Mozart Piano Quartets; Aurel Stroe Orestia I; Ave Maria; Rameau Harpsichord Pieces; Nicolae Licaret piano, organ, harpsichord; Brahms Piano Quartets; Enescu cello and piano sonatas. *Current Management:* Artexim, Romania. *Address:* Bucharest Philharmonic Orchestra, str Franklin 1, 79741 Bucharest, Romania.

**LICHTENSTEIN, Romelia;** Singer (Soprano); b. 1965, Sofia, Bulgaria. *Education:* Studied in Leipzig. *Career:* Debut: Chemnitz, 1988, as Rossini's Rosina; Appearances at Chemnitz Opera as Pamina, Lortzing's Marie and the soprano roles in Les Contes d'Hoffmann; Leipzig Opera from 1992, notably as Mimi and Fiordiligi; Handel Festival at Halle, 1996, as Elisa in Tolomeo; Cleofide in Handel's Poro, 1998; Guest appearances as concert singer throughout Germany. *Honours:* Winner at Gera, 1990, and Barcelona International Competitions. *Address:* c/o Opernhaus Halle, Universitätsring 24, 4020 Halle an der Salle, Germany.

**LICITRA, Salvatore;** singer (tenor); b. 1967, Berne, Switzerland. *Education:* Accademia Verdiana Parma, studied with Carlo Bergonzi. *Career:* sang Riccardo (Ballo in Maschera) at Parma and Verona Arena 1998; La Scala, Milan 1999–2000, as Alvaro (Forza del Destino) and Manrico in Il Trovatore; season 2001–02 as Alvaro, Pinkerton and Manrico at Verona, and as Manrico at the Vienna Staatsoper; further appearances at Zürich, Rome, Turin and Torre del lago; New York Met debut 2002, as Cavaradossi. *Address:* c/o Metropolitan Opera, Lincoln Center, New York, NY 10023, USA. *Website:* www.salvatorelicitra.com.

**LIDDELL, Nona Patricia,** MBE; British musician; b. 9 June 1927, London; m. Ivor McMahon 1950 (deceased); one d. *Education:* Royal Acad. of Music. *Career:* Leader, English String Quartet, 1957–73; Leader, Richards Piano Quintet, 1964–79; Leader, London Sinfonietta, 1970–94; Currently, London Piano Quartet; Prof., Trinity Coll. of Music; Prof. of Violin, Royal Acad. of Music 1978–94; mem. Inc. Soc. of Musicians; Fellow, Royal Acad. of Music. *Recordings:* Violin Concerto, Kurt Weill; Phantasie by Schoenberg with John Constable; Gemini by Roberto Gerhard with John Constable; Chamber Music by Martinů, Chausson, Herbert Howells; Brahms' Horn Trio and Berkeley Horn Trio with Schiller Trio; Stravinsky's Soldier's Tale; Chamber Music by Schoenberg; Chamber Music by Cyril Scott; Chamber music by Alan Bush. *Honours:* Worshipful Company of Musicians Cobbett Medal 1993. *Address:* 28B Ravenscroft Park, Barnet, Hertfordshire EN5 4NH, England.

**LIDSTRÖM, Mats;** Swedish cellist, teacher and composer; b. Stockholm. *Education:* Gothenburg Univ. with Maja Vogl, The Juilliard School, New York with Leonard Rose and Channing Robbins. *Career:* fmr Prin. Cellist Royal

Swedish Opera, RPO, Norrköping Orchestra; has performed as soloist with orchestras, including LSO, Acad. of St Martin-in-the-Fields, Scottish SO, Royal Nat. Scottish Orchestra, Deutsche SO, Czech Philharmonic, Dallas Symphony, Los Angeles Philharmonic, Oslo Philharmonic; has appeared at festivals, including Aspen, Kinston, Tenerife, Edin., City of London; teacher Gothenburg Univ. 1992–93; Prof. of Cello, RAM 1993–; has given masterclasses at Univ. of Oberlin, San Francisco Conservatory, Cleveland Inst. of Music; transcriptions for cello include works by Stravinsky, Kreisler, Skryabin, J. Strauss, Gershwin, Oscar and Hammerstein. *Compositions:* The Sea of Flowers is Rising Higher for solo cello, Carnival of Venice for violin and two cellos, Christmas Cookies for mezzo-soprano and three cellos, Pastoral and Parody for cello and tuba, No Stopping Now for violin and piano, Maze of Love for voice, piano and symphony orchestra, Interlude for string quartet and orchestra, Suite Tintin for cello and piano. *Recordings:* Musica Sveciae (with Bengt Forsberg) 1994, Kabalevsky, Cello Concerto 1995, Godard and Boëllmann, Cello Sonatas (with Bengt Forsberg) 1996, Swedish Cello Sonatas (with Bengt Forsberg) 1996, Elgar, Cello Concerto (with LSO) 1997, Anne Sofie van Otter, Rendezvous with Korngold 1998, Nadja Salerno-Sonnenburg, Night and Day 1998, Gabriel Pierné/Charles Koechlin, Cello Sonatas 1998, Saint-Saëns, Music for Cello 1999, Schubert, The Trout Quintet 1999, French Cello Music 2001, Smörgasbord 2001, Gunnar de Frumerie, Cello Concerto 2001, Brahms, Clarinet Trio in A minor (with Kjell Fageus) 2003. *Honours:* Hon. ARAM; Palmaer Prize, Sweden 1998. *Telephone:* (20) 8291-3090 (office). *Fax:* (20) 8291-3090 (office). *E-mail:* info@matslidstrom .com (office). *Website:* www.cello.connectfree.co.uk.

**LIDTH DE JEUDE, Philip;** Singer (baritone, tenor); b. 17 June 1952, Voorburg, Netherlands. *Education:* Studied at the Curtis Institute and Manhattan School. *Career:* Sang at Pennsylvania Opera from 1974, Chicago from 1979; Guest appearances elsewhere in USA as Marcello, Enrico (Lucia di Lammermoor), Germont and Gerard in Andrea Chénier; Studied further at Zürich and sang as tenor from 1988, notably at Krefeld Opera as Don José, Riccardo, Radames, Florestan, Bacchus, Peter Grimes and Dimitri in Boris Godunov; Engagements throughout Germany, including Otello at Detmold, 1996; Sang Samson in Netherlands, 1995. *Honours:* Prizewinner at 1981 Geneva Competition. *Address:* c/o Landestheater Detmold, Theaterplatz 1, 4930 Detmold, Germany.

**LIE, Tom Erik;** Singer (baritone); b. 1965, Oslo, Norway. *Education:* Oslo Conservatory, and Oslo Studio, with Ingrid Bjoner; Further study with Theo Adam, Berlin. *Career:* Sang at Gelsenkirchen Opera, as Malatesta, Silvio, and Wagner's Wolfram; Further appearances throughout Germany, and for Norwegian State Opera, as Silvio; Leipzig Opera as Morales in Carmen, Frère Leon in Messiaen's St François, Guglielmo, Papageno, Siegfried in Schumann's Genoveva, and Wolfram; Concerts throughout Norway, and in Germany, the Czech Republic and Spain (National SO); Season 2001–2002 as Donizetti's Belcore in Norway and Robert Storch in Strauss's Intermezzo for Garsington Opera (British debut); Deutsche Oper Berlin from 2002. *Current Management:* Athole Still International Management, Forresters Hall, 25–27 Westow Street, London, SE19 3RY, England. *Telephone:* (20) 8771-5271. *Fax:* (20) 8768-6600. *Website:* www.atholestill.com.

**LIEBERMAN, Carol;** Musician, Violinist and Baroque Violinist; b. 18 Aug. 1943, New York, NY, USA; m. Mark Kroll, 9 July 1975, 1 s. *Education:* BA, City College of New York, 1965; MMus, 1967, DMA, 1974, Yale University School of Music; Violin studies with Raphael Bronstein and Broadus Erle. *Career:* Debut: Carnegie Recital Hall, New York, 1975; Faculty, Boston University School of Music, 1979–; Concertmaster, Masterworks Chorale Orchestra, 1980–; Concerts throughout USA and in Rome, Italy, Antwerp, Caracas, Lisbon and Canada; Broadcasts for WGBH Radio-TV and WBUR Radio, Boston, including 6 part simulcast series for Maine Public Television; Radio and Television Programmes for Canadian Broadcasting Corporation; Former Member, Israel Philharmonic Orchestra and Toronto Symphony; Assistant Professor, College of Holy Cross, 1985–88; Associate Professor, 1989–; Co-Director, Holy Cross Chamber Players, 1985–; Broadcasts for Radio National de Espana, Madrid, 1985; Soloist with Connecticut Early Music Festival, 1985–; mem, Co-Director, Holy Cross Chamber Players; Violinist with Early Music Ensemble of Boston; Violinist of Lieberman/Kroll Duo. *Recordings:* CDs: Schubert Sonatinas for Violin and Fortepiano; Dohnányi Sonata for Violin, Piano and Second Piano Quintet; Numerous recordings for various labels. *Address:* Department of Music, College of the Holy Cross, PO Box 151A, Worcester, MA 01610, USA.

**LIEBERMAN, Janis Joy;** French Hornist; b. 23 Aug. 1950. *Education:* Studied with W. Erol Gomürgen, Ankara, Turkey; BMus, Boston University School of the Arts, principal tutor, Harry Shapiro, 1972; Further studies, American University, Washington DC, with Ted Thayer; MA, San Francisco State University. *Career:* Debut: Soloist, Mozart Concerto No. 2 and No. 4; Schumann Konzertstück for 4 horns and orchestra, San Francisco Concerto Orchestra; Israel Sinfonietta Orchestra, 1975–79, 1993–95, Principal Horn, 1977–79; Jerusalem Symphony, 1975–79; Israel Symphony, 1994–95; Ensemble EnCor, chamber music trio, 2000–; mem, International Horn Society. *Recordings:* With the Israel Sinfonietta and the Women's Philharmonic. *Honours:* Israel America Cultural Foundation Grant, 1977. *Address:* 2001 Santa Clara Street, Richmond, CA 94804, USA.

**LIEBERMANN, Lowell,** BM, MM, DMA; American composer, conductor and pianist; b. 22 Feb. 1961, New York, NY. *Education:* Juilliard School, New York; studied composition with David Diamond and Vincent Persichetti; studied conducting with Laszlo Halasz; studied piano with Jacob Lateiner. *Career:* debut at Carnegie Recital Hall, New York 1978; Composer-in-Residence, Dallas Symphony Orchestra 1999–2002; mem. ASCAP. *Compositions:* Symphony Op. 9, Piano Concerto Op. 11, 2 Piano Sonatas Op. 1, 10 and 82, Sechs Gesänge Nach Gedichten von Nelly Sachs for soprano and orchestra Op. 18, Sonata for viola and piano Op. 13, Missa Brevis for chorus and organ, Song Cycles, Chamber Music, Sonata for flute and piano Op. 24, Quintet for piano, clarinet and string trio Op. 26, Domain of Arnheim Op. 33, Quintet for piano and strings Op. 34, Nocturnes Op. 20, 31, 35, Gargoyles Op. 29, Piano Concerto No. 2 Op. 36 1992, Concerto for flute and orchestra Op. 39 1992, Songs and Piano Pieces, The Picture of Dorian Gray (opera) Op. 45 1995, Sonata for violin and piano Op. 46 1994, Album for the Young for piano Op. 43 1994, Revelry for orchestra, Op. 47 1995, Longfellow Songs Op. 57, Loss of Breath Op. 58, Flute and Harp Concerto Op. 48, Concerto for trumpet and orchestra Op. 64 1999, Nocturne No. 7 Op. 65 for piano 1999, Album Leaf Op. 66 for cello and piano, Symphony No. 2, Op. 67 1999, Three Impromptus Op. 68 for piano 2000, Nocturne Fantasy Op. 69 for two guitars 2000, Dorian Gray: A Symphonic Portrait Op. 70, suite from opera 2000, Pegasus Op. 71 for narrator and orchestra 2000, Rhapsody on a Theme by Paganini Op. 72 for piano and orchestra 2001, The Next Time Op. 73 for baritone and piano 2001, Concerto for violin and orchestra Op. 74 2001. *Recordings:* Piano Music of Lowell Liebermann, Koch International, James Galway plays Lowell Liebermann, BMG, 1998, Symphony No. 2 (Dallas Symphony Orchestra), 2000; numerous recordings on various labels. *Honours:* Grand Prize, Van Cliburn Int. Piano Competition Inaugural Composers' Invitational Competition. *Address:* c/o Theodore Presser Co., 588 North Gulph Road, King of Prussia, PA 19406, USA. *E-mail:* lowell@lowellliebermann.com (office). *Website:* www.lowellliebermann.com.

**LIEBERSON, Peter;** composer; b. 25 Oct. 1946, New York, USA; m. Ellen Kennedy; three d. *Education:* New York University, Columbia University, Brandeis University; composition with Milton Babbitt, Charles Wuorinen, Donald Martino and Martin Boykan. *Career:* mem. BMI. *Compositions include:* Opera, Ashoka's Dream, 1997; Worlds Turning, 1991; Drala; Lalita; Ziji; Raising The Gaze; Variations for violin and piano; Piano Fantasy; Flute Variations; Concerto for 4 groups of instruments; 2 piano concertos, 1983, 1999; Viola Concerto, 1994; Fire, for orchestra, 1995; Horn Concerto, 1999; Cello Concerto, 2000; String Quartet, 1994. *Recordings:* Piano Concerto; Bagatelles; Lalita; Raising The Gaze; Piano Fantasy; Concerto for 4 groups of instruments. *Honours:* Charles Ives Fellowship; National Endowment for The Arts; American Academy of Arts and Letters; Brandeis University Creative Arts Award. *Address:* 47 Anchor Drive, Halifax, Nova Scotia B3N 3E4, Canada.

**LIEBL, Karl;** Singer (Tenor); b. 16 June 1915, Schiltberg, Germany. *Education:* Studied with Paul Bender in Munich and with Albert Meyer in Augsburg. *Career:* Debut: Regensburg in 1950; Sang in Wiesbaden from 1951, Cologne Opera, 1955–59 notably as Huon in Oberon, and Vienna Staatsoper, 1956–59; Sang the Cardinal in Mathis der Maler under Hindemith; Sang at Metropolitan Opera, 1959–68, as Wagner's Lohengrin, Tristan, Loge, Walther, Siegfried, Siegmund and Parsifal; Guest appearances in Munich, Hamburg, Chicago, Baltimore, Brussels, Zürich, Venice and Madrid; Teacher at University of Mainz from 1967. *Recordings:* Der fliegende Holländer; Die Zauberflöte; Lohengrin; Die Meistersinger; Oberon. *Address:* c/o Staatliche Hochschule für Musik, Bingerstrasse 26, 6500 Mainz, Germany.

**LIEBOLD, Angela;** Singer; b. 15 Aug. 1958, Dresden, Germany. *Education:* Studied at Dresden Musikhochschule. *Career:* Appearances at the Dresden Opera from 1985 in the title role of the premiere of Weise Von Liebe und Tod Des Cornets Christopher Rilke by Siegfried Matthus; Lieder recitals in Russia, Hungary, France and Germany; Engagements in opera elsewhere in Germany; Teacher of Singing at the Dresden Musikhochschule from 1983. *Honours:* Prize Winner at the Walter Gruner Lieder Competition, Bach International, Maria Callas Competition, Athens, and Robert Schumann Competition. *Address:* c/o Semper Oper, 8012 Dresden, Germany.

**LIELMANE, Rasma;** Concert Violinist; b. 1958, Latvia, Russia. *Education:* Studied with David Oistrakh at the Moscow Conservatoire. *Career:* Appearances with the leading orchestras of Europe and North America; Collaborations with the Munich Philharmonic, Berlin Symphony and the Dresden Philharmonic; Appearances in London, Hamburg, Toronto, Montreal, Nice and Milan. *Honours:* First Prize, International Violin Competition, Sofia; Prizewinner at the Vianna de Motta Competition in Portugal, Nicola Paganini in Italy, and Maria Canals Competition in Montreal; Tibor Varga Prize in Switzerland.

**LIFCHITZ, Max;** Composer, Conductor and Pianist; b. 11 Nov. 1948, Mexico City, Mexico. *Education:* Studied at the Juilliard School of Music, New York, and Harvard University, Cambridge, Massachusetts, also Berkshire Music Center. *Career:* Debut: Mexico City, 1955; Pianist, Juilliard Ensemble; Lecturer, National Music Camp, Michigan; Faculty, Manhattan School of Music; Assistant Professor in Music, Columbia University; Executive Director, Conductor, North South Consonance Inc; Associate Professor in Music, State University of New York; Chair, Music Department, 1995–98, Chair, Latin American Studies Department, 1996–99, State University of New York at Albany. *Compositions include:* Intervencion for violin and orchestra; Night Voices #13 for cello and orchestra; Kaddish, choir and chamber ensemble, Tiempos; Tientos, Accordion. *Recordings:* Affinities, Piano Solo; Transformation, Cello; Yellow Ribbons No. 2; Canto de Paz; Yellow Ribbons No. 21; Consorte; Winter Counterpoint, flute, oboe, bassoon, viola; Exceptional String Quartet; 5 Albums of American Piano Music; Of Bondage and Freedom. *Publications:* String Quartets and Piano Sonatas by Carlos Chávez for G Schirmer. *Honours:* 1st Prize, Gaudeamus Competition, 1976. *Current Management:* North/South Concerts. *Address:* North/South Concerts, PO Box 5108, Albany, NY 12205-0108, USA.

**LIFSCHITZ, Constantin;** Concert Pianist; b. 1977, Ukraine. *Education:* Gnessin School Moscow, from 1982; Studying with international piano teachers at International Piano Foundation, Lago di Como. *Career:* Concerts in the West from 1990; Collaboration with violinist Vladimir Spivakov, including tour of Japan with the Moscow Virtuosi; Further concerts with the Monte Carlo Philharmonic, Moscow Philharmonic in Munich, Moscow State Symphony Orchestra (concerto debut) and the St Petersburg Philharmonic on tour to Europe, with Yuri Temirkanov, 1997; Chamber music with Lynn Harrell, Gidon Kremer and Mischa Maisky; Contracted to appear at Shostakovich Festival in Tokyo, performing Shostakovich Piano Concerto No. 1, and also for a recital tour of Japan including a performance with the Tokyo Symphony Orchestra; Debut with Chicago Symphony Orchestra, 1999. *Recordings include:* Recitals. *Honours:* Russian Cultural Foundation New Name Scholarship, 1990; Winner, German Echo Classic Record Prize, 1995. *Address:* c/o Chicago Symphony Orchestra (Contracts), Symphony Hall, Chicago, IL, USA.

**LIGENDZA, Catarina;** Singer (Soprano); b. 18 Oct. 1937, Stockholm, Sweden; m. Peter Ligendza. *Education:* Studied in Vienna and Wuerzburg with Henriette Klink, Stuttgart with Trudi Eipperle and Saarbrücken with Josef Greindl. *Career:* Debut: Linz in 1963 as Mozart's Countess; Sang in Brunswick and Saabrücken, 1966–69 as Verdi's Elisabeth de Valois and Desdemona and Strauss' Arabella; Sang at Hamburg Staatsoper from 1967, Deutsche Oper Berlin; Staatsoper Stuttgart from 1970, and Staatsoper Vienna from 1971 with Wagner's Ring, Isolde with Carlos Kleiber, Lisa in The Queen of Spades, and Elsa in Lohengrin with Placido Domingo; Sang at Staatsoper München in Fliegende Holländer, Lohengrin from 1978 and Götterdämmerung; Sang Arabella at La Scala in 1970 and at Salzburg Easter Festival under Karajan; Metropolitan Opera debut in 1971 as Beethoven's Leonore; Bayreuth Festival, 1971–77 as Brünnhilde and Isolde, 1986–87 as Elsa in Lohengrin and Isolde; Covent Garden debut in 1972 as Senta in Der fliegende Holländer; Sang in Wagner's Ring with Deutsche Oper Berlin in 1987 in Japan; Retired from the stage in 1988; Television productions and opera films: Der fliegende Holländer, Lohengrin as Elsa, Freischütz as Agathe, and Elektra as Chrysothemis, with conductors Sawallisch, Russell Davies and Karl Böhm. *Recordings:* Third Norn in Götterdämmerung; Arias by Handel; Eva in Meistersinger von Nürnberg; Lars Erik Larsson, Förkläddgud; Three Songs, Rangström; Tristan und Isolde, conducted by Carlos Kleiber.

**LIGETI, András;** Conductor; b. 1953, Hungary. *Education:* Franz Liszt Academy, Budapest, violin diploma, 1976; Conducting with András Korodi. *Career:* Orchestra Leader, Hungarian State Opera House, 1976–80; Regular concerts as solo violinist in Europe and Canada; Associate Conductor, with György Lehel, of the Budapest Symphony Orchestra, 1985, with tours of the United Kingdom, Europe and America; Regular conductor at the Budapest Opera; British debut in 1989 with the BBC Symphony Orchestra, returning to conduct the BBC Scottish Symphony Orchestra and BBC Philharmonic in 1991, with Bartók's Duke Bluebeard's Castle, Weber's 2nd Piano Concerto and Mahler's 5th Symphony. *Address:* c/o Music Partnership Ltd, 41 Aldebert Terrace, London SW8 1BH, England.

**LIGETI, György Sándor;** Austrian composer; b. 28 May 1923, Dicsöszentmárton (now Târnarveni) in Transylvania, Romania; s. of Dr Sándor Ligeti and Dr Ilona Somogyi; m. Vera Spitz 1957; one s. *Education:* Budapest Acad. of Music (studied with Ferenc Farkas and Sándor Veress). *Career:* taught Budapest Acad. of Music 1950–56; left Hungary 1956; Guest Prof., Stockholm Acad. of Music 1961–71; Composer-in-Residence, Stanford Univ., Calif. 1972; worked in Electronic Studios, Cologne, Fed. Repub. of Germany; active in music composition, Cologne, Vienna, Stockholm, Berlin and Darmstadt; Prof. of Composition, Hamburg Music Acad. 1973–89; mem. Swedish Royal Acad. of Music 1964, Acad. of Arts, Berlin 1968, Free Acad. of Arts, Hamburg 1972, Bavarian Acad. of Fine Arts, Munich 1978, American Acad. and Inst. of Arts and Letters 1984. *Works include:* Artikulation (tape piece) 1958, Apparitions (orchestral) 1958–59, Atmosphères (orchestral) 1960, Volumina (organ) 1961–62, Poème Symphonique for 100 metronomes 1962, Aventures for three singers and seven instrumentalists 1962, Requiem for soprano, mezzo-soprano, two choirs and orchestra 1963–65, Lux Aeterna for 16-part chorus 1966, Concerto for cello and orchestra 1966, Lontano (orchestral) 1967, Continuum (harpsichord), Ten pieces for wind quintet 1968, Ramifications for string orchestra or 12 solo strings 1968–69, String Quartet No. 2 1968, Melodien (orchestral) 1971, San Francisco Polyphonie (orchestarl) 1972, Monument, Selfportrait, Movement (for two pianos) 1976, Le Grand Macabre (opera) 1974–77, Trio (violin, horn, piano) 1982, 3 Phantasien nach Hölderlin (chorus) 1982, Hungarian Etudes (chorus) 1983, 9 Piano Etudes 1985–89, Piano Concerto 1985–88, Nonsense Madrigals for 6 Singers 1988, Violin Concerto 1991, Viola Sonata 1996, Hamburgisches Konzert (horn concerto) 1998–99, Sippla, Dobbal, Nádihegéduvel (for mezzo-soprano and four percussionists) 2000. *Honours:* numerous hon. degrees; Orden pour le Mérite,

Bonn 1975; Commdr, Ordre Nat. des Arts et Lettres, France 1988; Grawemeyer Award 1986, Praemium Imperiale Prize (Japan) 1991, Balzan Award 1991, shared Wolf Prize 1996, Kyoto Prize 2001, Adorno Award 2003, Royal Swedish Acad. of Music Polar Music Prize 2004.

**LIGI, Josella;** Singer (Soprano); b. 10 Jan. 1948, Imperia, Italy. *Education:* Studied in Milan. *Career:* Debut: La Scala, 1972, as a Priestess in Aida; Sang in Milan and appeared as guest in Turin, Valencia and Toulouse, 1974, as Mimi, Desdemona and Aida; Verona Arena, 1983, and Ravenna Festival, 1984, as Amelia in Un Ballo in Maschera; La Scala and Wexford Festival, 1985, in Rossi's Orfeo and as Catalani's Wally; Turin, 1986, as Alice Ford; US debut, 1988, as the Trovatore Leonora for Newark Opera; Concerts include Debussy's Le Martyre de St Sebastian, Salzburg Festival, 1986. *Recordings include:* Sesto in Handel's Giulio Cesare. *Address:* c/o Teatro Regio, Piazza Costello 215, 10124 Turin, Italy.

**LIIMOLA, Heikki Sakari;** Choir Conductor and Teacher; b. 24 March 1958, Tampere, Finland; m. Katri Liimola, 30 July 1983, 3 d. *Education:* MMus, Sibelius Academy, Finland, 1988; Choral Conducting; Studied trumpet, voice, orchestra conducting, with Professor Jorma Panula; Mastercourses and private studies in choir conducting, with Professor Eric Erikson. *Career:* Assistant Conductor and Singer, Finnish Radio Chamber Choir, 1982–87; Conductor, Chorus Cantorum Finlandie; Conductor EOL Chamber Choir, Helsinki; Conductor, Savonlinna Opera Festival Chorus; and others; Teacher of Choir Conducting, Voice Teacher, many courses in Finland and abroad; Conductor, Tampere Philharmonic Choir; Conductor, Harju Chamber Choir; Conductor, Tampere Opera Choir; Conductor, Chamber Choir of Silbelius-Academy; Artistic Director, Tampere International Choir Festival; mem, International Federation of Church Music. *Recordings:* Harju Youth Choir, Christmas Music, 1980; EOL Chamber Choir, Sacred and Profane, 1990; Male Choir of Finnish Church Musicians, 1990; Jaakko Ryhanen and Opera Festival Chorus, 1993; Savonlinna Opera Festival Chorus and Helsinki Philharmonic Orchestra, 1995; Tampere Philharmonic Choir and Tampere Philharmonic Orchestra, 1998, 2000; Harju Chamber Choir, Church Music, 2001. *Publications:* Article in Companion ot Singing. *Honours:* Conductor of the Year, 1998. *Address:* Tohlopinkatu 46G 29, 33310 Tampere, Finland.

**LIKA, Peter;** Singer (Bass-baritone); b. 1949, Germany. *Education:* Studied in Munich. *Career:* Sang with the Augsburg Opera 1972–81 and later joined the Bavarian Chamber Opera for performances of Baroque opera; a noted interpreter of sacred music by Bach and Mozart, appearing in Cologne (1989), Berlin and the Ludwigsburg Festival; Tour of Japan 1987, with Haydn's Die Jahreszeiten; Brussels 1991, in Mozart's Requiem. *Recordings include:* Count Heribert in Die Verschworenen by Schubert (Opus III).

**LIKIN, Jurij;** Oboist; b. 11 Nov. 1967, Minsk, Belarus; m. Anna Jermolowitch, 7 Mar 1987, 1 d. *Education:* Studies with Professor Boris Nitchkov, Music Lyceum, Belarusian State Music Academy, Minsk; 1 year stage in Paris, Class of Maurice Bourgue, Prague Mozart Academy, 1994. *Career:* Debut: Age 16, Stage of Belarusian Philharmonic, Minsk; Ekaterinburg, Moscow, Minsk, Kaliningrad, Prague, Berlin, Brunswick, 1991–94; Trieste, 1993; Stresa, Italy, 1994; Paris Théâtre des Champs-Elysées, 1994; Marseille, 1995; Les Grands Heures de Saint-Emilion, France, 1995; Principal Oboist of State Symphony Orchestra of Belarusian Philharmonic, 1990–94; Soloist of Prague Symphony Orchestra, Prague Chamber Philharmonic and Member of Prague Wind Quintet, 1994–. *Recordings:* (CDs): B Martinŭ; A Reicha; E Bozza; Max Stern; F Poulenc Sonata, Sextet. *Honours:* 1st Prizes in National Competitions of USSR, 1986, 1987. *Address:* Trytova 1120, 19800 Prague 9, Czech Republic.

**LILL, John Richard,** CBE, FRCM, FLCM, FTCM; British pianist; b. 17 March 1944, London; s. of George Lill and the late Margery (née Young) Lill. *Education:* Leyton County High School and Royal Coll. of Music. *Career:* London debut at Royal Festival Hall 1963; plays regularly in European capitals, the USA and the Far East, as recitalist and as soloist with most prin. orchestras; recognized as leading interpreter of Beethoven; Prof., Royal Coll. of Music. *Recordings include:* complete Beethoven piano sonatas, concertos and bagatelles, complete piano works of Rachmaninov (with BBC Nat. Orchestra of Wales/Otaka), Brahms piano concertos, Tchaikovsky Piano Concerto No. 1 (with London Symphony Orchestra), complete Prokofiev sonatas 1991. *Honours:* Hon. DSc (Univ. of Aston), Hon. DMus (Exeter Univ.);Hon. FTCL, FLCM; first prize Royal Overseas League Competition 1963, first prize Int. Tchaikovsky Competition, Moscow 1970, Dinu Lipatti Medal, Chappel Gold Medal. *Current Management:* Askonas Holt Ltd, Lonsdale Chambers, 27 Chancery Lane, London, WC2A 1PF, England. *Telephone:* (20) 7400-1700. *Fax:* (20) 7400-1799. *E-mail:* info@askonasholt.co .uk. *Website:* www.askonasholt.co.uk.

**LILOVA, Margarita;** Singer (Mezzo-soprano); b. 26 July 1935, Tscherwen, Bulgaria. *Education:* Studied in Sofia with Maria Zibulka and Michail Jankov. *Career:* Debut: Varna Opera in 1959 as Maddalena in Rigoletto; Sang in Varna as the Countess in The Queen of Spades and Azucena; Covent Garden and Vienna Staatsoper debuts in 1962 and 1963 as Amneris; Guest appearances at the Paris Opéra, Komische Oper Berlin and the Teatro Colón, Buenos Aires, also at Los Angeles, Berlin, Montreal and Moscow; Member of the Vienna Staatsoper from 1963 including a tour of Japan in 1986, as Marcellina in Le nozze di Figaro and Annina in Der Rosenkavalier; Sang at Salzburg Festival, 1965–67 as the Hostess in Boris Godunov under von Karajan, La Scala Milan in 1973 as Ulrica in Un Ballo in Maschera returning in 1988 as Mary in Der fliegende Holländer; Many concert appearances and song recitals; Professor, Hochschule für Musik und Dorstellende Kunst, Wien, 1993. *Recordings:* Les Contes d'Hoffmann; Boris Godunov; Der Rosenkavalier; Bruckner Te Deum and Mass No. 2; Verdi Messa da Requiem; Video, Maidservant in Elektra conducted by Abbado. *Honours:* Kammersängerin, 1984, Staatsoper Wien. *Address:* c/o Staatsoper, Opernring 2, 1010 Vienna, Austria.

**LILTVED, Oystein;** Singer (Bass); b. 20 Jan. 1934, Arendal, Norway; m. Virginia Oosthuizen. *Education:* Studied with Maria Hittorf in Vienna, Luciano Donaggio in Trieste and Frederick Dalberg in Kapstad, South Africa. *Career:* Debut: Basle in 1959 as Konshak in Prince Igor; Many appearances at the opera houses of Oslo, Stockholm, Düsseldorf, Kassel and Barcelona; Sang in South Africa at Cape Town and at Johannesburg; Sang at Seattle Opera as Hagen in Götterdämmerung; Other roles have been Wagner's Daland, Landgrave and Fafner, Verdi's King Philip and Fiesco, Mozart's Osmin and Sarastro, Mephistopheles, Varlaam in Boris Godunov, Oroveso, Rocco, Raimondo in Lucia di Lammermoor and Swallow in Peter Grimes; Many appearances in concerts and oratorios.

**LIM, Liza;** Composer and Lecturer; b. 30 Aug. 1966, Perth, Western Australia. *Education:* BA, Victoria College of the Arts, 1986; Study with Ton de Leeuw, 1987; MMus, University of Melbourne, 1993. *Career:* Lecturer in Composition, University of Melbourne, 1991; Commissions from Duo Contemporain, The Seymour Group; Intercontemporain (Paris), ABC/BBC, Ensemble Modern (1995) and others. *Compositions include:* Blaze for mezzo and ensemble, 1986; Pompes Funebres for string quartet, 1987; Koan, for alto saxophone and percussion, 1987; Tarocchi, for 3 guitars, double bass and percussion, 1988; Voodoo Child for soprano and ensemble, 1989; Constellations, for violin and string orchestra, 1989; Garden of Earthly Desire, for ensemble, 1989; Diabolical Birds, for ensemble, 1990; Amulet, for viola, 1992; Hell, for string quartet, 1992; The Oresteia, opera for 6 voices, 11 instruments and 1 dancer, 1993; Koto, for ensemble, 1993; Lin Shang Yin for coloratura soprano and 15 instruments, 1993; Cathedral, for orchestra, 1994; Sri Vidya for chorus and orchestra, 1994–95; Street of Crocodiles for ensemble, 1995; Gothic, for 8 strings, 1996; The Alchemical Wedding, for orchestra, 1996; The Cauldron: Fusion of the 5 Elements, for 6 voices and instruments, 1996; The Heart's Ear for flute, clarinet and string quartet, 1997. *Honours:* Sounds Australian Award, 1990. *Address:* c/o APRA, 1A Eden Street, Crows Nest, NSW 2065, Australia.

**LIM, Soon-Lee;** Violist and Conductor; b. 3 Aug. 1957, Singapore; m. 23 June 1983. *Education:* Licentiate, Royal Schools of Music (Violin and Viola); BM with distinction, Eastman School of Music, University of Rochester. *Career:* Debut: Paganini, Grand Viola Sonata, Kilburn Hall, Eastman School of Music; Sub-Principal, Singapore Symphony Orchestra; Assistant Conductor, Singapore Youth Orchestra, 1991–97; Conducted Singapore Symphony Orchestra for the opening and closing ceremonies of the 17th South East Asia Games, 1993; Conducted the Singapore Symphony Orchestra for the World Trade Organisation First Ministerial Conference's Farewell Concert for 4,000 delegates, 1996; Conducted the Asian Youth Orchestra for the National Day Celebration, 1997; Music Director, Resident Conductor, National University of Singapore Symphony Orchestra; mem, American Conductors' Guild; American Viola Society; American String Teachers' Association. *Honours:* 1st Prize, Viola/Cello Open, Singapore National Music Competition, 1981; Jean Frederic Petrenoud Prize with Certificate of Distinction in Orchestra Conducting, 4th Vienna International Music Competition, 1995. *Address:* 58 Toh Tuck Crescent, Singapore 596959.

**LIMA, Luis;** singer (tenor); b. 12 Sept. 1948, Cordoba, Argentina. *Education:* studied voice with Carlos Guicchandut in Buenos Aires and with Gina Cigna in Italy. *Career:* debut in Lisbon in 1974 as Turiddu in Cavalleria Rusticana; Guest appearances in Mainz, Munich, Stuttgart and Hamburg; Sang at La Scala Milan in 1977 as Edgardo in Lucia di Lammermoor; Further appearances in Strasbourg and Spain as Rodolfo, Cavaradossi, and Faust in Mefistofele; US debut in 1976 in a concert performance of Donizetti's Gemma di Vergy at Carnegie Hall; Metropolitan Opera debut in 1978 as Alfredo in La Traviata; Sung at New York City Opera in 1979 in La Bohème and Rigoletto, Salzburg Festival in 1984 as Verdi's Macduff, Maggio Musicale Florence, 1985–86 as Don Carlos and as Riccardo in Un Ballo in Maschera, and Covent Garden in 1985 as Nemorino and Don Carlos, returning to London in 1988 as Edgardo; Salzburg Easter Festival in 1988 as Cavaradossi, and sang Faust at the opening of the season at the Teatro Colón Buenos Aires in 1990; Sang Don José in a new production of Carmen at Covent Garden in 1991 and Verdi's Don Carlos at San Francisco in 1992; Madrid in 1992 as Don José and New York Metropolitan in 1994 as Cilea's Maurizio; Season 1996 with Rodolfo at Covent Garden; Don Carlos at the New York Met, 1997; Season 2000–01 as Rodolfo at the Met, Turiddu for the Vienna Staatsoper, Don José at Zürich and Don Carlos in Madrid. *Recordings include:* Gemma di Vergy; Le Roi de Lahore; Video of Don Carlos and of Carmen, both from Covent Garden. *Current Management:* Stafford Law, Candleway, Broad Street, Sutton Valence, Kent ME17 3AT, England. *Website:* www.stafford-law.com.

**LIMA, Paulo (Costa);** Composer and Professor of Music; b. 26 Sept. 1954, Salvador, Bahia, Brazil; m. Ana Margarida Cerqueira Lima e Lima, 2 s. *Education:* Music School, UFBA, 1969–76; BM, Composition, 1978, MS, 1978, University of Illinois, Urbana, USA; PhD, UFBA, 1998. *Career:* Professor of Music at Universidade Federal da Bahia, 1979; Head of Music Department, UFBa, 1986–88; Director of Music School, UFBA, 1988–92; Participation as composer at many national and international events; Festivals: Campos de Jordao, São Paulo, UFRJ; Director of Music School, Universidade Federal da Bahia, 1988–92; International events at Dresden and Urbana; Assistant President, Universidade Federal da Bahia, 1996–98. *Compositions:* Bundle for Solo Flute, 1977, FCEBa, 1981; Ubaba, O Que Diria Bach, 1983, Funarte for Chamber Orchestra; Atôtô-Balzare, UFBA for Percussion and Piano; Cuncti-Serenata, 1983, Funarte UFBA for Piano Solo; Fantasia, 1984, Funarte UFBA for Piano Solo; Pega Essa Nega e Chera, for piano solo, 1993; Corrente de Xango, for cello, 1995; Ponteio, for piano solo, 1995; Atoto do L'homme armè, for chamber orchestra, 1996; Ibejis, for flute and clarinet, 1996; Frevo, for piano solo, 1997. *Recordings:* Compositores Da Bahia, 5, 7 and 8; Outros Ritmos, 1997; Impressionem, 1997. *Publications:* Editor of Art, Music Periodical, 1981–91. *Contributions:* Musical and academic journals. *Honours:* Composition Prize, Max Feffer, São Paulo 1995; Fellowship in Composition, Vitae Foundation, 1995; Copene Prize, 1996. *Address:* R Sabino Silva 304, ap 401, Chame 40155-250, Salvador, Brazil.

**LIN, Chiu-Ling;** Pianist; b. 13 May 1948, China. *Education:* Licentiate with distinction, Royal School of Music, Singapore, 1964; BMus, New England Conservatory, 1969; MMus, 1972, D.Mus, 1998, Indiana University. *Career:* Debut: Carnegie Recital, 1979; Solo recitals in China, Hong Kong, Singapore, Malaysia, Peru, Argentina, Brazil, England, and Chicago, Minneapolis, Seattle, Atlanta, New York; Soloist with Singapore Orchestra, Des Moines Symphony, Atlanta Symphony, Chicago Civic Orchestra; Artist-in-Residence, Indiana University at South Bend, 1975–76; Professor of Piano, Drake University, Des Moines, 1976–. *Recordings:* Kamran Ince's Cross Scintillation, with Sylvia Wang. *Publications:* Around the World on 88 Keys. *Address:* Music Department, Drake University, 2507 University Avenue, Des Moines, IA 50311, USA.

**LIN, Cho-Liang,** BMus; American violinist; b. 29 Jan. 1960, Taiwan; s. of Kuo-Jing Lin and Kuo-Ling Yu; m. Deborah Lin. *Education:* Juilliard School, New York, Sydney Conservatoire. *Career:* concert tours worldwide; over 100 performances a year; soloist with leading orchestras including London Symphony Orchestra, Philharmonia, Concertgebouw, Orchestre de Paris, Chicago Symphony Orchestra, Philadelphia Orchestra and Boston Symphony Orchestra; played Tchaikovsky's Concerto at London Proms 1999; 20 solo albums; Founder, Dir Taipei Int. Music Festival; mem. Faculty Juilliard School 1991–. *Honours:* Gramophone Record Award 1989, Musical American's Instrumentalist of the Year 2000. *Address:* c/o ICM Artists (London) Ltd, Oxford House, 76 Oxford Street, London, W1N 0AX, England (office); Juilliard School, 60 Lincoln Center Plaza, New York, NY 10023, USA.

**LINCÉ, Janet Isabel,** GGSM; British conductor; b. 4 Feb. 1951, London. *Education:* Guildhall School of Music and Drama. *Career:* guest Chorus Master, BBC Symphony Chorus, London Symphony Chorus, Philharmonia Chorus; Chorus Master, Newbury Spring Festival Chorus; Musical Dir, Royal Lemington Spa Bach Choir; Musical Dir, Reading Festival Chorus; Musical Dir, Choros; performances in Germany and four tours of New Zealand. *Recording:* album: He came all so stille 2004. *Address:* 6 Mill Lane, Upper Heyford, Oxfordshire OX25 5LH, England. *Telephone:* (1869) 232618. *Fax:* (1869) 232618. *E-mail:* info@choros.org.

**LINCOLN, Christopher;** Singer (Tenor); b. 1965, Canberra, Australia. *Education:* Studied with Dame Joan Hammonds. *Career:* Appearances throughout Australia as Tamino, Nadir, Fenton, Rossini's Almaviva, Ferrando (Opera Queensland) and Alfredo (in Perth); Donizetti's Edgardo and Gounod's Faust in Auckland; Cologne Opera from 1990, as Mozart's Pedrillo and Tamino; Rodolfo in Luisa Miller in Sofia and Dessau, Alwa in Lulu and Andrès in Wozzeck (1999) at San Francisco; Števa in Jenůfa for Welsh National Opera; Concerts include Handel's Saul, Samson and Solomon, Haydn's Creation and Seasons and the Verdi Requiem; Solos in music by Bach; Recital at Teatre del Liceu, Barcelona, 1999. *Address:* c/o Harlequin Agency Ltd, 203 Fidlas Road, Cardiff CF4 5NA, Wales.

**LIND, Eva;** Singer (Soprano); b. 14 June 1965, Innsbruck, Austria. *Education:* Studied in Vienna. *Career:* Debut: Landestheater Innsbruck, 1983, as a Flowermaiden in Parsifal; Sang Lucia di Lammermoor at Basle, 1985 and the Queen of Night at Vienna and Paris, 1987; Salzburg Festival 1986 and 1987, as the Italian Singer in Capriccio; Vienna Staatsoper from 1986, as Lucia (Lucia di Lammermoor) and Sophie in Werther; Stuttgart Staatsoper as Adele in Die Fledermaus; British debut as Nannetta in Falstaff, Glyndebourne, 1988; Gounod's Juliette at Zürich, 1990, followed by Sophie in Der Rosenkavalier at Vienna, Brussels and Berne Opera; Concerts with Francisco Araiza at the Teatro Colón, Buenos Aires, 1990; Sang Mozart's Blonde at Catania, 1996; Season 2000–01 as Gounod's Juliette at Karlsruhe and the Primadonna in Donizetti's La Convenienze Teatrali at Stuttgart. *Recordings:* Die Fledermaus, conducted by Placido Domingo; Naiad in Ariadne auf Naxos, with the Leipzig Gewandhaus Orchestra conducted by Kurt Masur; Coloratura arias, including Elisabeth ou La Fille proscrit by Donizetti; Papagena in Die Zauberflöte, conducted by Marriner; Olympia in Tales of Hoffmann, with Jeffrey Tate; Opera duets with Francisco Araiza; Aennchen in Der Freischütz, conductor, Colin Davis.

**LINDBERG, Christian;** Swedish trombonist; b. 15 Feb. 1958, Danderyd, Stockholm; m.; four c. *Education:* studies in Stockholm, London, Los Angeles. *Career:* mem., Royal Stockholm Opera Orchestra 1977–78; Prof., Swedish Royal Acad. 1996–; gives over 100 concerts a year as trombone soloist with world's major symphony orchestras; solo programmes, including music theatre; appearances with Per Lundberg, piano, and with Hakan Hardenberger, trumpet; repertoire includes contemporary music, baroque music played on original instruments, classical and romantic music; works composed for him include concertos by Schnittke, Xenakis, Takemitsu and Arvo Pärt; played at several British festivals and Pitea Festival, North Sweden 1993; season 1993–94 with concerts in Germany, Switzerland, Iceland, Denmark, Sweden, Israel; tours to USA and with Scottish Chamber Orchestra; Schnittke's Dialogue with Nash Ensemble, London; performances with Prague Symphony Orchestra, Czech Republic, and Gothenburg Symphony Orchestra, Sweden; Carnegie Hall debut with Zwilich Trombone Concerto and world premiere of Trombone Concerto by Toru Takemitsu with St Paul Chamber Orchestra, USA; several German festivals and Japan tour 1994; 1994–95 season included performances of Trombone Concerto by Iannis Xenakis, new works by Kalevi Aho and Arvo Pärt, also tours to Australia, France, Japan; season 1998–99 participated at the Israel, Rheingau, Cadaquez and Stavanger Festivals and at the Chamber Unlimited Festival, Stockholm; played with the Singapore Symphony Orchestra and in Brussels and Helsinki; season 1999–2000 with concerts at the Gran Canaria Festival with the Norwegian Chamber Orchestra; premiere of new opera production by Luciano Berio at the Salzburg Festival; premiere of Trombone Concerto by Berio with the Tonnhalle Orchestra in Zürich, Australian premiere with the Sydney Symphony Orchestra; masterclasses; designs instruments and mouthpieces for CONN Instrument Co.; Prince Consort Prof., Royal Coll. of Music, London. *Recordings include:* British Trombone Concerti, American Concerti, Italian repertoire for Trombones, Voice and Chamber Organ, Gemeaux by Takemitsu, Frank Martin's Ballade with Concertgebouw Orchestra and Riccardo Chailly. *Current Management:* Svensk Konsertdirektion, PO Box 5076, 402 22 Goteborg, Sweden.

**LINDBERG, Magnus;** Finnish composer and pianist; b. 27 June 1958, Helsinki. *Education:* Sibelius Acad., Helsinki and studied with Globokar in Paris, Donatoni in Siene and Ferneyhough at Darmstadt. *Career:* founder, EArs Open Soc. 1980. *Compositions include:* Three Pieces for horn and string trio, Arabesques for wind quintet, Quintet for piano and wind, De Tartuffe je Croi for string quartet and piano, Drama for orchestra, Sculpture II for orchestra, Linea d'Ombra for flute and ensemble, Action Situation Signification for horn or clarinets and ensemble 1982, Ritratto for orchestra, Zona for ensemble, Metal Work for accordion and percussion, Kraft for orchestra (Nordic Music Prize) 1985, UR for five players and live electronics, Twine for piano, Trios Sculptures for orchestra, Etwas Zarter, Ohne Audruck, Faust (Prix Italia), Ensemble triptych Kinetics, Marea and Joy 1988–90, (orrente II 1991), Aura 1994, Arena 1995, Cello Concerto 1999, Grand Duo for orchestra 2000, Parada for orchestra 2001, Partia for cello 2001, Clarinet Concerto 2001–02, Jubilees for ensemble 2002, Concerto for orchestra 2002–03. *Address:* c/o Boosey & Hawkes, First Floor, Aldwych House, 71–91 Aldwych, London, WC2B 4HN, England (office). *Website:* www.boosey.com/lindberg (office).

**LINDE, Hans-Martin;** Recorder Player, Flautist and Conductor; b. 24 May 1930, Werne, Germany; m. Gudrun Olshausen, 1 s., 2 d. *Education:* Staatliche Hochschule für Musik, Freiburg, 1947–51, with Konrad Lechner (conducting) and Gustav Scheck (flute). *Career:* Solo flautist of the Cappella Coloniensis of West German Radio, Cologne; Concert tours in Europe, USA, South America, Middle and Far East from 1955; Teacher of Baroque Flute, Recorder and Conducting from 1957; Conductor of Vocal Ensemble, 1965–; Conductor of Chamber Orchestra, 1970–, of the Schola Cantorum Basiliensis, Basle; Co-Editor, Zeitschrift für Spielmusik, 1966–; Concert associations with August Wenzinger and Frans Brueggen; Conducted with Basler-Linde Concert in Keiser's Tomyris and Vivaldi's La Griselda at Ludwigshafen, 1988, 1989. *Recordings include:* Flute Concertos by Leclair, Stamitz, Dittersdorf and Mozart; Recorder Concertos by Sammartini and Vivaldi; English Consort Music and Chamber Music by Bach, Handel, Haydn with the Linde-Consort; Conductor of the Linde-Consort and the Cappella Coloniensis; Guest Conductor of several orchestras and choirs in different European countries and in the USA; Recordings as a conductor include: Bach; Masses, Brandenburg Concertos, Orchestral Suites; Schütz: Exequien; Handel: Water-Music, Music for the Royal Fireworks, Concerti grossi op 6, Keiser's Der Grossmutige Tomyris. *Publications:* Kleine Anleitung zum Verrzieren alter Musik, 1958; Handbuch des Blockflötenspiels, 1962.

**LINDÉN, Magnus;** Singer (Baritone); b. 1 Nov. 1954, Sweden. *Education:* Studied in Stockholm with Erik Saedén and in London with Vera Rozsa. *Career:* Royal Opera, Stockholm, from 1980, notably as Papageno and Guglielmo and in the 1994 premiere of Sctschedrin's Lolita; Drottningholm Festival, 1987, as Don Giovanni, and 1991 as Egisth in Haeffner's Electra; Other roles include Tolomeo in Handel's Giulio Cesare, Zuniga in Carmen and Jovanni in the 1991 premiere of Don Juan Freestyle by Hillerud-Wannefors; Many concert appearances. *Recordings include:* Così fan tutte, from Drottningholm. *Address:* Royal Opera, PO Box 16094, 10322 Stockholm, Sweden.

**LINDENSTRAND, Sylvia;** Singer (Mezzo-Soprano); b. 24 June 1942, Stockholm, Sweden. *Education:* Studied at the Opera School of the Royal Opera, Stockholm. *Career:* Debut: Stockholm 1962, as Olga in Eugene Onegin; Has sung at the Royal Opera, Stockholm as Dorabella, Cherubino, Marina in Boris Godunov, Octavian, Brangäne, Fricka in the Ring and Cenerentola; Sang Tchaikovsky's Maid of Orleans, 1986 and sang in Singoalla by Gunnar de Frumerie 1988; Guest appearances at Bayreuth, 1964, Copenhagen and the

Moscow Bolshoi; Glyndebourne 1975 and 1979, as Dorabella and Amaranta in La Fedeltà Premiata; Aix-en-Provence, 1976, Zerlina in Don Giovanni; Sang Idamante in Idomeneo at Drottningholm; Royal Opera Stockholm, 1991 as Dionysus in the premiere of Backanterna by Daniel Börtz (production by Ingmar Bergman); Many concert engagements. *Recordings include:* Songs by Liszt. *Honours:* Swedish Court Singer, 1982. *Address:* c/o Kungliga Teatern, PO Box 16094, 102 51 Stockholm, Sweden.

**LINDHOLM, Berit Maria;** Opera Singer (soprano); b. (Berit Maria Jonsson), 18 Oct. 1934, Stockholm, Sweden; m. Hans Lindholm, 2 d. *Education:* Stockholm Opera School. *Career:* debut, Countess in Le nozze di Figaro, Stockholm, 1963; Performances all over the world including, New York Met, Carnegie Hall, San Francisco, Chicago, London, Paris, Hamburg, Berlin, Munich, Moscow, Naples, Madrid, Geneva, Zürich, Düsseldorf, Vienna, Barcelona, Bayreuth; Repertoire included: Isolde, Brünnhilde, Kundry, Tosca, Salome, Elektra, Turandot, Fidelio, Dyer's Wife in Die Frau ohne Schatten; Sang in the premiere of Backanterna by Daniel Börtz, Stockholm 1991; Teaches singing; mem, Swedish Royal Academy of Music. *Recordings include:* Les Troyens; Die Walküre; Songs by Swedish Composers. *Honours:* Opera Singer by Appointment of the King of Sweden; Litteris et Artibus, 1988. *Address:* Artistsekretariat Ulf Törnqvist, Sankt Eriksqatan 100, 11331 Stockholm, Sweden.

**LINDNER, Brigitte;** Singer (Soprano); b. 1959, Munich, Germany. *Education:* Studied in Munich. *Career:* Debut: Gärtnerplatz-Theater Munich as a Boy in Die Zauberflöte; Sang Gretel in Humperdinck's opera (also televised) and in Mozart's Bastien and Bastienne; Adult debut at the Ludwigsburg Festival 1980, as Barbarina in Le nozze di Figaro; Bayreuth Festival 1985, as the Shepherd boy in Tannhäuser; Sang Despina in Così fan tutte for Kiel Opera, 1990; Other roles include Papagena and parts in operettas by Lehar and Johann Strauss; Concert appearances in oratorios by Bach, Haydn and Mozart. *Recordings:* Hansel and Gretel, Die Zauberflöte.

**LINDSEY, John Russell;** American professor of violin and violinist; *Professor of Violin, Crane School of Music; Concert Master, Orchestra of Northern New York, Hanover Chamber Orchestra;* b. 26 Aug. 1947, Chicago, IL; divorced; two s., one d. *Career:* Former Concertmaster, Dallas Chamber Players, the Lexington Philharmonic Orchestra, The Warren (Ohio) Chamber Orchestra, The Castle Farm Summer Festival Orchestra (Michigan), the Champlain Valley Symphony Orchestra; Chair. of Strings, Baylor Univ.; The Governor's School of North Carolina; Univ. of Kentucky; Teacher of Strings, Dallas, Texas, Public Schools; Performed and taught violin in the Stage de Musique, Marcillat-en-Combraille, France, 1988, the Incontri di Canna International Chamber Music Festival in southern Italy, 2000 and Ameropa 2004 in Prague; Concert Master, Orchestra of Northern New York and Hanover, NH Chamber Orchestra; Violinist, Ruggieri Chamber Soloists; First Violinist, Aurora Quintet; Prof. of Music and a mem. of the Potsdam Piano Quartet, Crane School of Music, 1981–; mem., violin faculties Ithaca Summer Chamber Music Institute, the Adult Chamber Music Conference at Interlochen, Michigan and the Manitou Music Festival in Glen Arbor, Michigan; Solo recitals at the Carnegie Recital Hall, Museum of the City of New York, St Joseph's Church, Bruno Walter Auditorium, Lincoln Center, New York City; also in Boston, Montreal, Atlanta, and Chicago; mem., Triple Nine Society; Chamber Music America; American String Teachers' Asscn. *Honours:* Mozart Award, 1972; Winner, City of Dayton's Second Annual Allegro Residency for the Arts, 1989; President's Award for Excellence in Teaching (Teacher of the Year Award), Potsdam College, State Univ. of New York, 1993; State Univ. of New York Chancellor's Award for Excellence in Teaching, 2003. *Address:* Crane School of Music, SUNY Potsdam, Potsdam, NY 13676, USA (office). *Telephone:* (315) 267-2431 (office). *Fax:* (315) 267-2413 (office). *E-mail:* lindsejr@potsdam.edu (office).

**LINDSKOG, Par;** Singer (Tenor); b. 1962, Kungelv, Sweden. *Education:* Vocal studies at Gothenburg, from 1981. *Career:* Secondary roles at the Opera Studio and Theatre in Gothenburg; Berlin Staatsoper as Max in Der Freischütz, Narraboth (Salome), Števa (Jenůfa) and the Steersman in Der fliegende Holländer, from 1987; Further engagements in Lisbon, Salzburg, Dresden and Leipzig; Season 1995/96 as Young Man in Moses und Aron under Pierre Boulez at Amsterdam and Salzburg, and under Christoph von Dohnányi with the Philharmonia Orchestra at the Festival Hall, London; Further roles include Tamino, Don Ottavio and Barinkay in Der Zigeunerbaron, Vienna, 1996. *Honours:* Bayreuth Scholarship, 1993. *Address:* c/o Deutsche Staatsoper Berlin, Unter den Linden 7, 1060 Berlin, Germany.

**LINDSLEY, Celina;** Singer (Soprano); b. 1953, USA. *Education:* Studied at the Eastman School of Music. *Career:* Sang at Bielefeld, Kassel and Nuremberg; New York City Opera, 1977, as the Queen of Night; Düsseldorf Opera from 1978, with Autonoe in The Bassarids, 1991; Vienna Staatsoper and Covent Garden, 1985, as Zerbinetta and in Zemlinsky's Der Zwerg; Duisburg, 1985, in the premiere of Goehr's Behold the Sun; Komische Oper Berlin, 1991, as Donna Anna and Essen, 1994, as Violetta; Sang Marie in Gurlitt's Wozzeck at Florence, 1998; Many concerts and Lieder recitals. *Recordings include:* Zemlinsky's Der Kreidekreis and Busoni's Turandot. *Address:* c/o Teatro Comunale, Via Solferino 15, 50123 Florence, Italy.

**LINGE, Ruth;** Opera Singer (Lyrical Soprano); b. 13 Oct. 1927, Porsgrunn, Norway; m. Tormod Linge. *Education:* Private, Oslo, Stockholm, Vienna. *Career:* Debut: As Norina in Don Pasquale, Oslo, 1951; Norsk Operaselskap, 1951–58; Member, Den Norske Opera, 1958–; Main roles include Zerlina,

Donna Elvira, Donna Anna, Cherubino, Papagena, Adina, Gilda, Rosina, Musetta, Olympia; Appearances in television opera productions, radio concerts; Secretary, Board Society of Norwegian Opera Singers; Society of Norwegian Musica Artists.

**LINJAMA, Jouko;** Composer; b. 1934, Finland. *Education:* Sibelius Academy; Musicology and Literature, Helsinki University; Further studies in Composition, Cologne, 1962–64; Staatliche Hochschule für Musik; Kölner Kurse für Neue Musik. *Career:* Organist, St Henrik's Catholic Church, Helsinki, 1958–60; Cantor-Organist, Parish of Tuusula, 1964–97. *Compositions include:* Opera: Finnish Taper, 1998–99 Orchestra: 2 Symphonies from oratorio Homage to Aleksis Kivi, 1972; La Migration d'Oiseaux Sauvages, 1977; Choral Works: How It Is, oratorio, 1968; Homage to Aleksis Kivi, symphonic oratorio, 1970, 1974, 1976; Missa De Angelis, 1969; La Sapienza, oratorio da camera, 1980; Mailman Algusta ia Loomisesta, oratorio, 1983; Requiem, 1998; Chamber Music: String Quartet No. 1, 1978; No. 2, 1979; Concerto for organ, marimba, vibraphone, 2 Wind Quartets, 1981; Concerto for horn and organ, 2001; Quartetto for cornetto, corno and organo, 2002; Duo for piano and organ, 2002; Trio for clarinet, horn and organ, 2003Works for organ: Sonatina supra B-A-C-H, 1968; Magnificat for organ, 1970; Partitasonata Veni Creator Spiritus, 1969; Missa Cum Jubilo for organ, 1977; Organum supra B-A-C-H, 1982; Toccata in D, 1985; Reflections, duet for organ, 1991; Three Liturgical Stained-Glass Paintings, 1993; Cappella Choral Works: Partita per coro, 1979; On The Road to Splendour, 1980; Kalevala Suite, 1981; Toward the Future and Hope, 1984; Has composed numerous solo songs. *Recordings:* Numerous recordings of his work. *Publications:* When My Father Composed the Olympic Hymn, Gummeus, 2002. *Address:* Teosto, Lauttasaarentie 1, 00200 Helsinki 20, Finland.

**LINKE, Fritz;** Singer (Bass); b. 15 May 1923, Claussnitz, Germany. *Career:* Sang in Chemnitz from 1950; Dresden Staatsoper, 1951–56; Staatsoper Stuttgart, 1956–86; Guest appearances in Hamburg, Munich, Paris, Barcelona, Venice, Rome, Bologna, Mannheim, Cologne, Zürich and Karlsruhe; Bayreuth Festival, 1963–70; Roles include Mozart's Osmin and Sarastro, Verdi's Padre Guardiano and King Philip, Wagner's Daland, Fafner, Hunding and Landgrave, Beethoven's Rocco and Baron Ochs in Der Rosenkavalier. *Address:* c/o Staatstheater Stuttgart, Oberer Schlossgarten 6, 7000 Stuttgart 1, Germany.

**LINNENBANK, René;** Singer (Bass); b. 1961, Abcoude, Netherlands. *Education:* Maastricht and Sweelinck Conservatories; Guildhall School, London. *Career:* Debut: Osmin in Die Entführung for Scottish Opera Go Round, 1992; Appearances with Opera-SKON, Netherlands, as Mozart's Sarastro, and Cols (Bastien und Basitienne); Bagheera the Panther in Berkeley's Baa-Baa-Black-Sheep for Opera North; Other roles include Mozart's Figaro, Harasta in The Cunning Little Vixen. Nicolai's Falstaff, and King Tartaglia in Jonathan Dove's The Little Green Bird; Concerts and recitals throughout Europe with such conductors as William Christie, Paul Daniel and Mstislav Rostropovich; Sang Un Turk in the Lully/Molière Bourgeois Gentilhomme, Linbury Theatre, 2001; Season 2001–2002 in Orfeo by Monteverdi at La Monnaie, Brussels, under René Jacobs. *Address:* c/o English Bach Festival, 15 South Eaton Place, London, SW1W 9ER, England.

**LINOS, Glenys;** Singer (Mezzo-soprano); b. 29 Sept. 1941, Cairo, Egypt. *Education:* Athens Conservatory; London Opera Centre. *Career:* Sang in Mainz, Ulm and Wiesbaden from 1970; Guest appearances in most major German opera houses; Bayreuth and Salzburg Festivals; Toulouse, 1983, as Carmen; Festival Hall, London, 1983, in the Verdi Requiem; Ghent, 1984, as Santuzza in Cavalleria Rusticana; Zürich, 1984–85, as Pensithelia in the opera by Schoeck; Paris Opéra-Comique, 1985, in The Stone Guest by Dargomyzhsky; Lausanne and La Scala Milan, 1986, as the Sorceress in Dido and Aeneas and Geneviève in Pelléas et Mélisande; Rome Opera, 1986, as Ermengarda in Agnese di Hohenstaufen by Spontini; Sang Clairon in Capriccio at Bologna, 1987; Auntie in Peter Grimes at the Zürich Opera, 1989; Clytemnestra in Elektra at the Teatro Nuovo, Spoleto, 1990; Television appearances include Adriano in Rienzi, Wiesbaden Opera. *Recordings include:* Monteverdi's Orfeo. *Address:* c/o Opernhaus Zürich, Falkenstrasse 1, 8008 Zürich, Switzerland.

**LIPKIN, Malcolm (Leyland),** ARCM, LRAM, DMus; British composer and lecturer; b. 2 May 1932, Liverpool, England; m. Judith Frankel 1968; one s. *Education:* Liverpool Coll., Royal Coll. of Music; privately with Mátyás Seiber, 1954–57;. *Career:* Debut: Gaudeamus Foundation, Netherlands, 1951; Numerous broadcast and public performances of own compositions of orchestral, choral, vocal, chamber and instrumental music in many countries, 1951–. *Compositions:* Sinfonia di Roma, Symphony No. 1; The Pursuit, Symphony No. 2; Sun, Symphony No. 3; Two Violin Concertos, Piano Concerto, Flute Concerto; Oboe Concerto; Psalm 96 for chorus and orchestra; Four Departures for soprano and violin; Five Shelley Songs; Clifford's Tower for instrumental ensemble; String Trio; Harp Trio; Five Piano sonatas; Violin sonata; Wind Quintet; Metamorphosis for harpsichord; Naboth's Vineyard for recorders, cello and harpsichord; Interplay; Pastorales for horn and strings; Piano Trio; Prelude and Dance for cello and piano; Nocturnes 1–6 for piano, 1987–2002; Bartók Variations for string quartet; Dance Fantasy for solo violin; Five Bagatelles for oboe and piano, 1993; Duo for violin and cello, 1994; Second Violin Sonata, 1997; Pierrot Dances for viola and piano, 1998; From Across La Manche for string orchestra, 1998; Sixth Piano Sonata (Fantasy Sonata), 2002. *Recordings:* Clifford's Tower; Pastorale, string trio recorded by

Nash Ensemble, 1986; Piano Trio recorded by English Piano Trio, 1992; From Across La Manche, recorded by Royal Ballet Sinfonia, 2003. *Contributions:* Musical Times; Musical Opinion; Classical Music. *Address:* Penlan, Crowborough Hill, Crowborough, Sussex, TN6 2EA, England. *Website:* www .malcolmlipkin.co.uk.

**LIPKIN, Seymour;** Pianist and Conductor; b. 14 May 1927, Detroit, Michigan, USA. *Education:* Studied at the Curtis Institute, 1938–47, with David Sapert, Rudolf Serkin and Horsowski; Conducting studies with Koussevitzky at the Berkshire Music Center and as apprentice to George Szell at the Cleveland Orchestra, 1947–48. *Career:* Debut: Conducted the Cleveland Little Symphony, 1948; Soloist with the New York Philharmonic, 1949; Concerts with leading American orchestras; Teacher of conducting at the Berkshire Music Center, 1951–54; Conducted the New York City Opera, 1958, New York Philharmonic, 1959, Long Island Symphony, 1963–79; Joffrey Ballet, 1966–79; Teacher of piano at the Curtis Institute from 1969, Manhattan School from 1972; Resumed solo piano career in New York, 1981. *Honours:* Winner, Rachmaninov Piano Competition, 1948. *Address:* c/o Manhattan School for Music, 120 Claremont Avenue, New York, NY 10027, USA.

**LIPMAN, Michael,** MMus; American cellist and educator; b. 15 March 1954, Meriden, Connecticut, USA; s. of Bruin and Rosalyn Lipman; m. Shirli Nikolsburg, 1999; one d. *Education:* Paul Olefsky, Hartt Coll. of Music; Ronald Leonard and Paul Katz, Eastman School of Music; Leonard Rose, Blossom Music Festival; Eastman School of Music. *Career:* Debut: Recital, Pittsburgh, 1985; Soloist, Aspen Philharmonia Orchestra, 1977; Cello, Rochester Philharmonic, 1977–78; Principal Cello, Aspen Chamber Symphony, 1978–80; Associate Principal Cello, New Haven Symphony, 1978–79; Cello, Pittsburgh Symphony, 1979–; Soloist, Pittsburgh Symphony, 1985, 1993; Recitals and chamber music concerts throughout USA; Participant, Aspen Music Festival, New York String Seminar, Cleveland Chamber Seminar, Grand Teton Music Festival; Cellist and Founding Member, The California University of Pennsylvania String Quartet, 1986; Full-length radio broadcast of Pittsburgh debut recital, WQED, 1986; Solo and chamber music performances in Beijing, China, and Moscow, Russia, 1987, 1989; Faculty, Duquesne University School of Music, 1994–1996; Founding Member, The Dalihapa Ensemble, 1995–; Performing with the Pittsburgh Chamber Music Project. *Recordings:* With Pittsburgh Chamber Music Project, 2002. *Honours:* 1st Prize, Aspen Concerto Competition, 1977; Passamaneck Award, Pittsburgh (Pennsylvania) Y Music Society, 1985. *Address:* 4011 Boulevard Drive, Pittsburgh, PA 15217, USA. *Telephone:* 412 421 8852. *Fax:* 412 421 8852. *E-mail:* niklip@comcast.net.

**LIPOVETSKY, Leonidas;** American pianist, lecturer and educator; b. 2 May 1937, Montevideo, Uruguay; m. Astrid Eir Jonsson 1973; one s. two d. *Education:* Juilliard School of Music, USA, Kolischer Conservatory, Montevideo, Uruguay with Wilhelm Kolischer, studied with Rosina Lhevinne and Martin Canin. *Career:* debut, Nat. Symphony, Montevideo 1959; New York debut 1967; recital, New York 1964; S American premiere of Britten's Piano Concerto in D at Montevideo 1959; concert tours in the UK, Europe, Russia, Scandinavia, USA, Canada, Central and S America, People's Repub. of China; soloist on tour with Czech Philharmonic, Leoš Janáček in Spain and Czechoslovakia and with English Chamber Orchestra in USA, Nat. Symphony Orchestra, Mexico, Nat. Orchestra Asscn, NY, Juilliard Orchestra, NY, Winnipeg Symphony, Canada, Royal Liverpool Philharmonic, Seville Philharmonic, Spain, Nat. Symphony of Iceland, Reykjavík, Chicago Chamber Orchestra, Cedar Rapids Symphony, IA, Nat. Symphony of Colombia, Bogotá, Ossodre, Montevideo, Mexico Nat. Conservatory; numerous broadcasts; Special Guest Artist, UN General Assembly; lectures at Trinity Coll. of Music and Dartington Coll., UK, Juilliard School of Music, New York, Moscow Conservatory, Russia, Shanghai Conservatory, Beijing Conservatory, Shenyang Conservatory, People's Repub. of China, Nat. Museum of Art of Puerto Rico, San Juan; inaugural piano recital, Mexico Nat. Piano Festival, Center for the Arts 2003; retd from Fla State Univ. *Television:* three one-hour programmes for PBS Cincinnati on project 'Music and the Arts' 2003. *Honours:* Commemorative Gold Medal (150 years of Steinway & Sons) 2003. *Address:* Project Music and the Arts, 3523 Ballastone Drive, Land O'Lakes, FL 34638, USA. *Telephone:* (813) 242-2562. *Fax:* (813) 909-0618. *E-mail:* lipovetsky@tampabay.rr.com.

**LIPOVSEK, Marjana;** Slovenian singer (contralto); b. 3 Dec. 1946, Ljubljana. *Education:* in Ljubljana and Graz Music Acad., Austria. *Career:* joined Vienna State Opera, then Hamburg State Opera, FRG; operatic roles include Oktavian in Der Rosenkavalier, Dorabella in Così fan tutte, Marina in Boris Godunov, Ulrica in Un ballo in maschera, Mistress Quickly in Falstaff, Orfeo, Azucena in Il trovatore, Amneris in Aida, Brangäne in Tristan und Isolde, Eboli in Don Carlo, Fricka, Marfa in Khovanshchina, Marina in Boris Godunov, Marie in Wozzeck, Klytemnestra in Elektra, and Amme in Die Frau ohne Schatten; has sung in the leading European opera houses including Berlin, Madrid, Frankfurt, La Scala, Vienna State Opera and Bavarian State Opera, Munich; int. debut as recitalist, Salzburg Festival 1985. *Recordings include:* the Bach Passions, Gluck's Orfeo, Handel's Messiah, Beethoven's Choral Symphony, Wagner's Das Rheingold, Johann Strauss's Die Fledermaus and Frank Martin's Cornet, Marina in Boris Godunov under Claudio Abbado, Mahler's Kindertotenlieder, recital discs of Brahms Lieder and Schumann Lieder. *Television includes:* various concerts and recitals, Carmen, Samson and Delila, Der Ring des Nibelungen, Die Frau ohne Schatten,

Tristan und Isolde. *Honours:* Grand Prix du Disque for Frank Martin's Cornet, Prix Spécial du Jury Nouvelle Académie du Disque Français; Gustav Mahler Gold Medal (Bavaria) 1993, (Vienna) 1996. *Address:* c/o Askonas Holt Ltd, Lonsdale Chambers, 27 Chancery Lane, London, WC2A 1PF, England (office); c/o Artists Management Zürich, Rütistr. 52, 8044 Zürich Gockhausen, Switzerland. *Telephone:* (1) 8218957 (office). *Fax:* (1) 8210127 (office). *E-mail:* schuetz@artistsman.com.

**LIPP, Wilma;** Singer (Soprano); b. 26 April 1925, Vienna, Austria. *Education:* Studied in Vienna and with Toti dal Monte in Milan. *Career:* Debut: Vienna, 1943, as Rosina in Il Barbiere di Siviglia; Member of the Vienna Staatsoper from 1945, notably as Mozart's Queen of Night; Salzburg Festival from 1948, as Mozart's Servilia, Blondchen, Donna Elvira and Queen of Night; Covent Garden, 1951, as Gilda in Rigoletto; La Scala Milan, 1950, and Glyndebourne, 1957, as Constanze in Die Entführung; US debut at San Francisco, 1962, as Nannetta in Falstaff; Guest appearances in London, Hamburg, Munich, Berlin and Paris; Returned to Salzburg, 1983–84, as the Duenna in Der Rosenkavalier (also at Turin, 1986). *Recordings:* Brahms Ein Deutsches Requiem; Die Zauberflöte; Die Entführung; Fra Diavolo; Die Fledermaus; Fidelio; Der Rosenkavalier. *Address:* c/o Staatsoper, Opernring 2, 1010 Vienna, Austria.

**LIPPERT, Herbert;** Singer (Tenor); b. 1963, Germany. *Career:* Sang at the Lubeck Opera 1987–91, in such roles as Pedrillo and Albert Herring; Bregenz Festival 1989, as Ferrando in Così fan tutte, followed by Tamino in Vienna, Munich and Cologne; Salzburg Festival from 1990, in Fidelio, Die Zauberflöte and Die Frau ohne Schatten; Naples and Aix Festival 1992 as Wagner's Steersman and as Don Ottavio; Further engagements at the Stuttgart and Leipzig Operas; Sang Wagner's David at Covent Garden, 1997; Sang Ferrando at Buenos Aires, 1999; Concert repertory includes Bach's St Matthew Passion. *Recordings include:* Don Ottavio in Don Giovanni under Solti. *Address:* c/o Salzburg Festival (Opera). PO Box 140, 5010 Salzburg, Austria.

**LIPTAK, David;** Composer, Pianist and Teacher; b. 18 Dec. 1949, Pittsburgh, Pennsylvania, USA; m. Catherine Tait, 1 d. *Education:* Duquesne University, 1967–71; BM, Eastman School of Music, 1973–76; MM, DMA, Composition. *Career:* Composition and Theory Faculties, Michigan State University, 1976–80; University of Illinois, 1980–87; Eastman School of Music, 1986–, including Chairman of Composition Department, 1993–. *Compositions:* Duo, 1979, 1992; Seven Songs, 1984; Arcs, 1986; Loner, 1989; Trio, 1990; Shadower, 1991; Rhapsodies, 1992; Ancient Songs, 1992. *Recordings:* Seven Songs, 1984; Illusions, 1989. *Publications:* Compositions. *Address:* Composition Department, Eastman School of Music, 26 Gibbs Street, Rochester, NY 14064, USA.

**LIPTON, Daniel B.;** French/American/Canadian conductor and artistic director; *Artistic Director, Opera Ontario;* b. 1950, Paris, France; m. 1st Olga Lucia Gaviria 1983, divorced 1985; m. 2nd Sandra Belitz 2000; one s. one d. *Education:* High School of Music and Art, Manhattan School of Music, Juilliard School, Mannes Coll., Ecole Normale Supérieure, Accademia Chigiana. *Career:* conductor, Settimane Senese, American Ballet Theater, Denver Symphony, Holland Festival (Concertgebouw), Teatro Comunale Bologna, Maggio Musicale Fiorentino (Florence), Zürich Opera, Liceo Barcelona, Madrid Opera, Teatro La Fenice (Venice), Châtelet (Paris), Sadler's Wells (London), Houston Grand Opera, Utah Opera, San Antonio Festival, Hamburg Staatsoper, Opera Royal de Wallonie, Liege, Belgium 1987, Opera di San Carlo, Naples, Italy 1988, Opera de Montreal, Canada 1993, 2003, Teatro Regio di Parma, Italy 1988, 2000, Vlaamse Oper, Antwerp, Belgium, Teatro Real, Madrid, Spain 2001, London Philharmonia, London, England 2002, Macau Festival, China 2002; performances throughout North and South America, Paris Opéra Orchestra and Bayerische Staatsoper (Munich); opera and symphony concerts in Hanover, Hamburg, Dusseldorf, Nuremburg, Kessel, Berlin; gala operas in Mannheim and Karlsruhe; Artistic Dir, Colombia Symphony Orchestra and Opera de Colombia, Bogotà 1975–83, Opera Hamilton, ON, Canada 1986–, San Antonio Festival, San Antonio, TX 1987–; conducted world premiere of Gian Carlo Menotti's The Wedding; season 2003 conducted Rigoletto in Montreal, Die Zauberflote in Avenches, Carmina Burana in Mallorca; season 2004 conducted Rigoletto in Oviedo, Macbeth in Seville, Otello in Hamilton, Don Carlo in Zagreb; Artistic Dir, EurOrchester, Ruhr Valley, Germany 2001–; Prin. Guest Conductor, Philharmonia Hungarica; Guest Conductor, Deutsche Oper, Berlin. *Recordings:* Tosca, Puccini; Recital of Montserrat Caballé and José Carreras at Gran Teatre del Liceo in Barcelona; on video: Donizetti, Don Pasquale; Giordano, Andrea Chénier; Leoncavallo, Pagliacci; Mascagni, Cavalleria Rusticana; Mozart, Nozze di Figaro; Ponchielli, Gioconda; Puccini, La Bohème, Tosca, Turandot; Verdi, Aida, Ballo, Forza, Rigoletto, Trovatore, Hommage a Bernstein, Roy Bias — Machetti, La Belle Epoque; various recordings with Philharmonia Hungarica. *Honours:* Cross of Boyoca (Colombia) Dr hc (McMaster Univ.) 1999. *Current Management:* Harwood Management Group Inc., 509 W 110 Street, New York, NY 10025, USA; Behlerstrasse 26, 14469 Potsdam, Germany (home). *Telephone:* (212) 864-0773. *Fax:* (212) 663-1129 (office); (331) 200-565-26 (home). *E-mail:* jim@harwood-management.com (office); daniellipton@hotmail.com (home). *Website:* www.harwood-management.com (office).

**LIPTON, Martha;** Singer (Mezzo-soprano); b. 6 April 1916, New York, USA. *Education:* Studied at the Juilliard School, New York. *Career:* Debut: New Opera Company, New York, 1941, as Pauline in The Queen of Spades; New York City Opera, 1944, in Martha; Metropolitan Opera from 1944, as Siebel in

Faust, Verdi's Emilia, Amneris and Maddalena, Bizet's Mercedes and Humperdinck's Hansel; 298 performances in 36 parts, Rio de Janeiro, 1950; Carnegie Hall, 1952, in a concert performance of Wolf's Der Corregidor; Chicago, 1956, as Herodias in Salome; Other roles include Verdi's Meg Page and Ulrica, Mozart's Cherubino and Strauss's Octavian; Also heard as Lieder singer and in oratorio. *Recordings:* Mother Goose in The Rake's Progress; Orlofsky in Die Fledermaus; Handel's Messiah. *Address:* c/o Metropolitan Opera, Lincoln Center, New York, NY 10023, USA.

**LISICHENKO, Yuri;** Russian pianist and academic; b. 1 Feb. 1954, Lvov; m. Irina Plotnikova 1974; one s. one d. *Education:* Lvov Special Music School, Moscow Conservatory. *Career:* debut with Philharmonic Orchestra, Hall of Lvov Philharmonia; Professor, Moscow Conservatory; Performed: The Great Hall, 1973, 1975, The Small Hall, 1988, 1989, Moscow Conservatory; Milan, Turin, Verona, Italy, 1991; Basel, Switzerland, with violinist Tatiana Grindenko, 1991; Many television and radio appearances including television film Avantgarde in Music (Company of Musical Programmes), 1989; mem, Union of Musicians, Moscow. *Recordings:* Chopin Sonata, Anton Rubinstein Sonata, Schumann; Melody; Baroque music with Chamber Orchestra under Tatiana Grindenko, 1990; Ondine, Finland. *Honours:* 3rd Prize, Marguerite Long and Jacques Thibaud Competition, Paris, 1975; Honorary Diploma, Tchaikovsky Competitions, 1978. *Address:* Teply Satn styr 25 K1, Apt 244, Moscow 117133, Russia.

**LISOWSKA, Hanna;** Singer (Soprano); b. 15 Sept. 1939, Warsaw, Poland. *Education:* Studied at Warsaw University and Music High School. *Career:* Debut: Teatr Wielki, Warsaw, as Tatiana in Eugene Onegin, 1967; Fidelio as Leonore at Staatsoper Berlin, Deutsche Oper Berlin, Deutsche Oper Düsseldorf, Staatsoper Hamburg, Munich, Stuttgart, Bonn, Zürich, Rome, Wiesbaden, Madrid, Frankfurt am Main, Tokyo, Hanover; Wagnerian repertoire includes Isolde at Leipzig, Senta, Sieglinde, Brünnhilde, Gutrune in Götterdämmerung, Eva in Meistersinger, Elisabeth and Venus from Tannhäuser, all at international venues; Gutrune in Covent Garden; Gutrune und Sieglinde in Metropolitan Opera, New York; German repertoire includes Marschallin, Chrysothemis, Eglantine, Martha; Italian repertoire includes Elisabetta in Don Carlos, Tosca, Minnie, Tatiana, Lisa; Sang Aida and Lady Macbeth and Turandot in Warsaw. *Address:* Teatr Narodowy, Plac Teatralny, 00-950 Warsaw, Poland.

**LISSITSIAN, Rouben;** Singer (Tenor); b. 9 May 1945, Moscow, Russia. *Education:* Central Music School, Moscow, 1953–60; Russian Music Academy, Moscow, 1965–69. *Career:* Debut: Great Hall of Conservatory, Moscow, 1965; Soloist-Vocalist, Cellist, Flautist, Madrigal Ensemble, 1965–69; Part of Evangelist in Mattauspassion by Bach, Great Hall of Philharmonic, St Petersburg, 1973; Samson in Oratorio Samson by Handel, Great Hall of Conservatory, Moscow, 1974; War Requiem by Britten, Wrozlaw-Festival, 1974; Ninth Symphony by Beethoven, Paris Congres de Palais, 1974; Rubajat by Gubaidulina with Schoenberg Ensemble in Amsterdam, 1996; Tours of Germany, Israel, France, Finland, Netherlands, Hungary, USA, Canada, Poland; President, German-Russian Cultural and Educational Academy; Art Director, Russian Dramatic Theatre, Cologne. *Recordings:* P Cornelius, Weihnachtslieder; R Schumann, Lieder; W A Mozart, Requiem; J Brahms, Walzer; S Gubaidulina, Perception; Pärt, Stabat Mater. *Honours:* 1st Prize, Gold Medal, International R Schumann Competition, Germany, 1969. *Address:* Ossendorfer Weg 37, 50827 Cologne, Germany.

**LISSNER, Stéphane Michel;** French theatre director; *Artistic Director, Teatro alla Scala;* b. 23 Jan. 1953, Paris; s. of Georges Lissner and Elisabeth Landenbaum; two s. one d. *Education:* Coll. Stanislas and Lycée Henri IV, Paris. *Career:* Sec.-Gen. Centre dramatique, Aubervilliers 1977–78; Co-Dir Centre dramatique, Nice 1978–83; Dir-Gen. Orchestre de Paris 1994–96; Artistic Dir Teatro Real de Paris 1996–97; Dir Aix-en-Provence Festival 1996–(2009); Co-Dir Théâtre des Bouffes du Nord, Paris 1998–; currently Dir Théâtre de la Madeleine, Paris, and Music Dir Vienna Festival; Superintendent and Artistic Dir Teatro alla Scala 2005–. *Publication:* Métro Chapelle 2000. *Address:* c/o Théâtre de la Madeleine, 19 rue de Surène, 75008 Paris, France; c/o Teatro alla Scala, Via Filodrammatici 2, Milan 20121, Italy. *Website:* www.theatremadeleine.com; www.festwochen.at; www.bouffesdunord.com; www.teatroallascala.org

**LISTER, Marquita,** MMus; American singer (soprano); b. 24 April 1961, Washington, DC. *Education:* New England Conservatory of Music and Oklahoma City Univ. *Career:* Has performed with opera cos in London, Houston (TX), Mexico, Portland (OR), Baltimore (MD), Berlin, San Francisco (CA), Utah, Pittsburgh (PA), Japan, Milan (Italy), Paris; concerts with Plácido Domingo 1991, Sir Neville Marriner and the Acad. of St Martin in the Fields 1994, Keith Lockhart and the Boston Pops 1995–96, Leipzig Radio Orchestra 1995–96; Enid-Phillips Symphony Young Artist Award 1984; Wichita Symphony-Naftzger Young Artist Voice Award 1985; Stewart Awards-Eleanor Steber Music Foundation Award 1988; MacAllister Award 1989; Female Artist of the Year, Pittsburgh Opera 1995–96. *Operas include:* Porgy and Bess 1989, 1993, Carmen 1990, La Clemenza di Tito 1991, 1993, Aïda 1991, 1992, 1993, Falstaff 1992, Turandot 1992, I Pagliacci 1993, Aïda 1997. *Address:* c/o John J. Miller Artist Management, 801 West 181st Street #20, New York, NY 10033, USA.

**LISTOVA, Irene;** Violinist; b. 1960, Moscow, Russia. *Education:* Studied at the Moscow Conservatoire with Leonid Kogan. *Career:* Member of the Prokofiev Quartet (founded at the Moscow Festival of World Youth and the

International Quartet Competition at Budapest); Many concerts in the former Soviet Union and on tour to Czechoslovakia, Germany, Austria, USA, Canada, Spain, Japan and Italy; Repertoire includes works by Haydn, Mozart, Beethoven, Schubert, Debussy, Ravel, Tchaikovsky, Bartók and Shostakovich. *Current Management:* Sonata, Glasgow, Scotland. *Address:* 11 Northpark Street, Glasgow G20 7AA, Scotland.

**LITSCHAUER, Walburga;** Musicologist; b. 15 Oct. 1954, Klagenfurt, Austria. *Education:* Klagenfurt High School; Musicology, Philosophy and Theatre Sciences, University of Vienna; Piano studies, Vienna Conservatory, completed 1979; PhD, thesis The Italian Song in Vienna from 1750 to 1820, University of Vienna, 1980. *Career:* Member of Editorial Board, Director of Vienna Office, Neue Schubert Ausgabe, compendium of all Schubert's compositions; Has edited vols of Schubert's piano music; Director of the Austrian Society of Music, 1998–; mem, Board Member, several national and international Schubert societies. *Publications:* About 100 publications; Neue Dokumente zum Schubert-Kreis, vol. 1, 1986, vol. 2, 1993; Schubert und das Tanzvergnügen, with Walter Deutsch, 1997; About 70 publications on Schubert, Bruckner and music history. *Contributions:* Reclams Musikfuehrer, 1991; Anton Bruckner-Handbuch, 1996; Schubert-Handbuch and Schubert-Lexikon, 1997; Oesterreichisches Musiklexikon, 2001. *Honours:* Franz Schubert Grand Prix, for special achievements in Schubert research. *Address:* Neue Schubert-Ausgabe, Österreichische Akademie der Wissenschaften, Dr Ignaz Seipel-Platz 2, 1010 Vienna, Austria.

**LITTLE, Tasmin E.,** ARCM, FGSM; British violinist; b. 13 May 1965, London; d. of George Little and Gillian Little; m. Michael Hatch 1993; one d. *Education:* Yehudi Menuhin School, Guildhall School of Music. *Career:* studied privately with Lorand Fenyves in Canada; performed with New York Philharmonic, Leipzig Gewandhaus, Berlin Symphony, London Symphony, Philharmonia, Royal Philharmonic, Royal Liverpool Philharmonic, European Community Chamber, Royal Danish and Stavanger Symphony orchestras; has played in orchestras conducted by Kurt Masur, Vladimir Ashkenazy, Leonard Slatkin, Tadaaki Otaka, Sir Charles Groves, Andrew Davis, Jerzy Maksymiuk, Vernon Handley, Yan Pascal Tortelier, Sir Edward Downes, Yehudi Menuhin and Sir Simon Rattle; played at the Proms since 1990; concerto and recital performances in UK, Europe, Scandinavia, South America, Hong Kong, Oman, Zimbabwe, Australia, NZ, USA and Japan; numerous TV appearances including BBC Last Night of the Proms 1995, 1998. *Recordings include:* concertos of Bruch, Dvořák, Brahms, Sibelius, Delius, Rubbra, Saxton, George Lloyd, Ravel, Debussy, Poulenc, Delius, Elgar, Bax, Finzi; Dohnanyi violin sonatas, Bruch Scottish Fantasy, Lalo Symphonie Espagnole, Pärt Spiegel im Spiegel and Fratres. *Publication:* paper on Delius' violin concerto. *Honours:* Hon. DLitt (Bradford) 1996; Hon. DMus (Leicester) 2002. *Address:* c/o Askonas Holt Ltd., 27 Chancery Lane, London, WC2A 1PF, England. *Telephone:* (20) 7400-1700.

**LITTLE, Vera;** Singer (Contralto); b. 10 Dec. 1928, Memphis, Tennesee, USA; m. Professor S Augustithis. *Education:* Studied in Paris, Rome, Copenhagen and Germany. *Career:* Debut: New York City Opera 1950, as Preziosilla in La Forza del Destino; Guest appearances in Israel, Germany and Italy; Deutsche Oper Berlin 1958–85, notably as Carmen and as Melanto in Dallapiccola's Ulisse and in the 1965 premiere of Henze's Der Junge Lord; Vatican Concert 1959, in a Bach Cantata for the Pope; Salzburg Festival 1966 as Beroe, in the premiere of The Bassarids by Henze. *Recordings:* Gaea in Daphne by Strauss and Begonia in Der Junge Lord.

**LITTON, Andrew,** MM; American conductor and pianist; *Music Director, Bergen Philharmonic Orchestra;* b. 16 May 1959, New York. *Education:* Fieldston High School, New York, Mozarteum, Juilliard School. *Career:* Asst Conductor La Scala, Milan 1980–81; Exxon/Arts Endowment Asst Conductor, then Assoc. Conductor, Nat. Symphony Orchestra, Washington, DC 1982–86; Prin. Guest Conductor Bournemouth Symphony Orchestra 1986–88, Prin. Conductor and Artistic Adviser 1988–94, Conductor Laureate 1994–; Prin. Conductor and Music Dir Dallas Symphony Orchestra 1994–2006, Music Dir Emeritus 2006–; guest conductor many leading orchestras worldwide, including Chicago Symphony, Philadelphia, Los Angeles Philharmonic, Pittsburgh Symphony, Toronto Symphony, Montréal Symphony, Vancouver Symphony, London Philharmonic, Royal Philharmonic, London Symphony, English Chamber Orchestra, Leipzig Gewandhaus, Moscow State Symphony, Stockholm Philharmonic, RSO Berlin, RAI Milan, Orchestre Nat. de France, Suisse Romande, Tokyo Philharmonic, Melbourne Symphony and Sydney Symphony orchestras; debut at Metropolitan Opera, New York with Eugene Onegin 1989; also conducted at St Louis Opera, LA Opera, Royal Opera House, Covent Garden and ENO; music consultant to film The Chosen; Prin. Conductor Bergen Philharmonic Orchestra 2002–(09), Music Dir 2005–; Artistic Dir Minnesota Orchestra's Sommerfest –(2008). *Recordings include:* Mahler Symphony No. 1 and Songs of a Wayfarer, Elgar Enigma Variations, complete Tchaikovsky symphony cycle, complete Rachmaninov symphony cycle, Shostakovich Symphony No. 10, Gershwin Rhapsody in Blue, Concerto in F and Ravel Concerto in G (as piano soloist and conductor); Bernstein Symphony No. 2, Brahms Symphony No. 1, Walton's Belshazzar's Feast (with Bryn Terfel and Bournemouth Symphony) (Grammy Award), Rachmaninov Piano Concertos (with Stephen Hough and Dallas Symphony Orchestra) (Classical BRIT Critics' Award 2005) 2004. *Honours:* winner Bruno Walter Conducting Fellowship 1981, Hon. DMus (Bournemouth) 1992; winner William Kapell Memorial US Nat. Piano Competition 1978, BBC/Rupert Foundation Int. Conductors Competition 1982, Yale Univ. Sanford Medal.

*Current Management:* IMG Artists, 616 Chiswick High Road, London, W4 5RX, England. *Telephone:* (20) 8233-5800. *Fax:* (20) 8233-5801. *Website:* www.andrewlitton.com.

**LITZ, Gisela;** Singer (Soprano); b. 14 Dec. 1922, Hamburg, Germany. *Education:* Studied in Hamburg. *Career:* After singing in Wiesbaden joined the Hamburg State Opera: visited Edinburgh with the company, 1952; Sang in the 1954 stage premiere of Martinů's The Marriage; Bayreuth Festival, 1953–54; Often heard in operetta and in Bach's cantatas; Guest engagements in Buenos Aires, Rome, Lisbon, Munich and Brussels; Professor at Hamburg Musikhochschule from 1969. *Recordings:* Lortzing's Der Waffenschmied and Die Opernprobe; Nicolai's Die Lustige Weiber von Windsor; Le nozze di Figaro; Hansel and Gretel; Scenes from operettas. *Address:* Hochschule für Musik und Darstellende Kunst, Harvestehuderweg 12, 2000 Hamburg 13, Germany.

**LIU, Zhuang;** Composer; b. 24 Oct. 1932, Shanghai, China. *Education:* Shanghai Conservatory. *Career:* Teacher at the Peking Central Conservatory and composer with the Central Philharmonic Society; Collaborated with the 'Yellow River' piano concerto, 1971. *Compositions include:* Violin concerto, 1963; Plum Blossom Triptych for orchestra, 1979; Moon Night by the Spring River, woodwind quintet, 1978; Three Trios for flute, cello and harp, 1987; Impressions of Tashgul-Kan for orchestra, 1987. *Address:* c/o Music Copyright Society of China, 85 Dongsi Nan Jajie, Beijing 100703, People's Republic of China.

**LIUBAVIN, Leonid;** Singer (Tenor); b. 1970, Krasnodar, Russia. *Education:* State Tchershakov Theatre and St Petersburg Conservatoire. *Career:* Appearances with the Kirov Opera, St Petersburg, from 1996 as Narraboth in Salome, Tamino, the Prince in The Love for Three Oranges, Antonio in Prokofiev's Betrothal in a Monastery and the Simpleton in Boris Godunov; Further engagements as Iskra in Tchaikovsky's Mazeppa, the Fisherman in Stravinsky's Nightingale and Erik in Der fliegende Holländer; Zinovy in Lady Macbeth of Mtsensk and Tchekalinsky in The Queen of Spades; Sang the Master of Ceremonies in War and Peace with the Kirov Opera at Covent Garden, 2000. *Address:* c/o Kirov Opera, Mariinsky Theatre, Theatre Square, St Petersburg, Russia.

**LIVELY, David;** Pianist; b. 27 June 1953, Ironton, Ohio, USA. *Education:* Ecole Normale de Musique de Paris Licence de Concert, 1970; Studied Privately with Wilhelm Kempff, Claudio Arrau. *Career:* Debut: St Louis Symphony Orchestra, 1968; Soloist with: Cleveland Symphony Orchestra; Baltimore Symphony Orchestra; Kennedy Center, Washington, DC; English Chamber Orchestra; Royal Philharmonic Orchestra; Vienna Symphony Orchestra; Bavarian Radio Orchestra; Berlin Symphony Orchestra; Orchestre National de France; Orchestre National de Monte Carlo; La Scala; Orchestre de la Suisse Romande; Director, St Lizier Festival, France; Guest Professor, University for Music and Performing Arts, Vienna. *Contributions:* Analyse Musicale Masterclasses: Royal Scottish Academy, Glasgow, Hochschule, Vienna. *Honours:* Prizewinner, Queen Elisabeth Competition, Brussels 1972; Tchaikovsky, Moscow 1974, Marguérite Long 1971; Dino Ciani Award, La Scala, 1977. *Current Management:* Liliane Weinstadt Artists Management, 59 avenue de Busleyden, 1020 Brussels, Belgium. *Telephone:* (2) 263-65-65 (office). *Fax:* (2) 263-65-66 (office). *E-mail:* info@concerts-weinstadt.com. *Website:* www.concerts-weinstadt.com.

**LIVENGOOD, Victoria;** Singer (Mezzo-soprano); b. 1961, USA. *Education:* BM, University of North Carolina at Chapel Hill, 1983; MM, Honours, Opera, Boston Conservatory, 1985. *Career:* Sang Gertrude in Hamlet for Miami Opera (1987) followed by Beauty in Beauty and the Beast by Oliver at St Louis; New York Academy of Music 1988, as Juno in Platée; Charlotte in Werther, Seattle Opera, 1989; Meg Page in Falstaff, Calgary Opera, 1991; European debut 1991, as Mozart's Idamante at Nice; Guest appearances as Dorabella for Hawaii Opera (1990) and Carmen at Cologne (1992); Metropolitan Opera debut 1991, as Laura in Luisa Miller; Isolier in Le Comte Ory, Spoleto Festival, Charleston, 1993; Maddalena in Rigoletto, Cologne and Edmonton, 1994; Lola, Cavalleria Rusticana, Metropolitan Opera, 1994; Girl in Mahagonny for Met Opera, 1995; Carmen, Edmonton Opera, 1995; Dalila, Baltimore Opera, 1995; Giulietta in Tales of Hoffmann, Santiago, Chile, 1995; Preziosilla in La Forza del Destino for Met Opera, 1996; Isabella in The Voyage and Maddalena in Rigoletto, for Met Opera, 1996; Hippolyta in A Midsummer Night's Dream, 1996; Waltraute in Die Walküre, 1997; Giulietta in Les Contes d'Hoffmann, 1998; Sonyetka, Lady Macbeth of Mtsensk; Recitalist, Kennedy Center, 1986; Carnegie Hall debut, 1986; Recitalist, Smithsonian Institute, Washington DC, 1986; New York City recital debut, 1987; Soloist with symphonies of Atlanta, Cologne, San Diego, Baltimore, Minnesota and Washington; Cincinnati May Festival, and Lincoln Center Chamber Music Society, 1996; Season 1998–99 Verdi's Requiem Soloist, Carnegie Hall; Sang at the Spoleto Festival and at L'Opéra de Montréal Gala; Sang Marina in Boris Godunov for Washington Opera and Maddalena in Rigoletto at the Met, 2000; Sonyetka, Lady Macbeth of Mtsensk, Met Opera, 2000 as well as Myrtle Wilson in The Great Gatsby; Baba in The Rake's Progress for Vancouver, 2000; Dalila for Cleveland Opera, 2000; Meg Page in Falstaff for San Franscio Opera debut, 2001; Tittle role in the world premiere of La Señorita Cristina by Luis de Pablo in Madrid, 2001; Baba in The Rake's Progress in Buenos Aires, 2002; Madame Flora in The Medium for Spoleto Festival, Italy, 2002; Azucena in Il Trovatore for Portland Opera, 2002; 2002 Met Opera roles include title role of Carmen, Hippolyta in A Midsummer

Night's Dream as well as Helene in War and Peace. *Recordings include:* Puck in Oberon; The Secretary in The Consul; Akrosimova in War and Peace; Abbie in Desire Under The Elms; Soloist on Aid's Requiem; Memento Mori as well as Piercing Eyes; Haydn Canzonettas; Also solo CD: The Secret of Christmas and on Holy Ground. *Address:* c/o Tony Russo, ICM Artists Ltd, 40 W 57th Street, New York, NY 10019, USA. *Telephone:* 212 556 5775. *Website:* www .victorialivengood.com.

**LIVINGSTONE, Laureen,** DipMusEd, RSAMD; Scottish singer (soprano) and teacher; *Professor of Singing, Trinity College of Music, London;* b. 3 Feb. 1946, Dumbarton, Scotland; one s., one d. *Education:* Royal Scottish Acad. of Music and Drama, London Opera Centre. *Career:* wide variety of operatic, concert and television appearances in the United Kingdom and abroad; BBC Proms; recitals including Wigmore Hall and 1st BBC Lunchtime recital in 1976; Guest appearances with London Symphony Orchestra, Hallé, English Sinfonia, Northern Sinfonia, Scottish National and Scottish Chamber Orchestras; Operatic roles include: Zerlina, Pamina, Gretel, Lucia in Rape of Lucretia with Scottish Opera, Susanna, Sophie and Vrenchen in A Village Romeo and Juliet with Opera North, Gilda in Rigoletto and Sophie in Der Rosenkavalier for English National Opera, 1988; Major roles with the New Sadler's Wells Opera, Handel Opera and others; Engagements abroad include Woglinde at Teatro di San Carlo, Naples, 1980 and Gilda for Royal Flemish Opera in Antwerp, 1985; Professor of Singing, Trinity College of Music, London 1993–. *Recordings:* several radio programmes for BBC; Countess Maritza; Gianetta in The Gondoliers, 1st colour production for BBC television; Ninetta in L'Amour des Trois Oranges, BBC television, 1980; Elsie in The Yeomen of the Guard, Channel 5 video; Amore in Il Ritorno d'Ulisse in Patria, Glyndebourne, video 1973. *Honours:* Caird Scholarship, 1967; Winner, Peter Stuyvesant Scholarship, 1969. *Address:* 12 Pymmes Brook Drive, New Barnet, Hertfordshire EN4 9RU, England.

**LLEWELLYN, Grant;** British conductor; *Music Director, North Carolina Symphony Orchestra;* b. 29 Dec. 1960, Tenby, Wales; m. Charlotte Imogen Rose 1984. *Education:* Cheetham's School of Music, Manchester, Gonville and Caius Coll., Cambridge, Royal Coll. of Music, London and Tanglewood Music Center. *Career:* has conducted City of Birmingham Symphony Orchestra, English Chamber Orchestra, Scottish Nat. Orchestra, Royal Liverpool Philharmonic Orchestra, Northern Sinfonia, Scottish Chamber Orchestra, City of London Sinfonia and BBC Symphony, Philharmonic and Welsh Orchestras; took Stockholm Sinfonietta on British tour 1986 and conducted at Spoleto, Charleston and Jeunesse Musicale World Orchestra at Berlin Festival; London Proms debut 1993, with the BBC Nat. Orchestra of Wales in Mendelssohn's Violin Concerto and Beethoven's Seventh Symphony, now Assoc. Guest Conductor with the orchestra; conducted BBC Nat. Orchestra of Wales Opera Gala 1996; American premiere of Goehr's Arianna at Opera Theater of St Louis 1998; Music Dir, Handel and Haydn Soc., Boston 2001–; Music Dir, North Carolina Symphony Orchestra 2004–. *Honours:* Royal Coll. of Music Tagore Gold Medal 1984, Tanglewood Conducting Fellowship and English-Speaking Union Scholar 1985, first prize Leeds Conductors' Competition 1986. *Current Management:* Hazard Chase, 25 City Road, Cambridge CB1 1DP, England. *Telephone:* (1223) 312400. *Fax:* (1223) 460827. *E-mail:* info@hazardchase.co.uk. *Website:* www.hazardchase.co.uk.

**LLEWELLYN, William Benjamin James,** MBE; British composer and conductor; b. 6 May 1925, Farnworth, Widnes, Lancashire; m. Mildred Llewellyn; two s. one d. *Education:* Rydal School, Colwyn Bay, Emanuel Coll. ., Cambridge and Royal Acad. of Music; studied composition under William Alwyn and Eric Thiman. *Career:* Asst Music Master, Charterhouse 1950; f. the Linden Singers; Dir of Music, later Second Master, Charterhouse 1965–87; Music Adviser, Nat. Federation of Women's Insts for six years; Pres., Inc. Soc. of Musicians 1984; Festival Conductor, Leith Hill Music Festival 14 years, Petersfield Festival six years; conductor, Bridgwater Choral Soc. 1995–2004; mem. jury, Great Grimsby Int. Singing Competition 1992, Chair. of Cttee of Adjudicators 1995; adjudicated regularly at competitions and festivals, including Hong Kong; Chair., Royal School of Church Music in Devon 10 years. *Compositions:* compiled and edited the Novello Book of Carols, Sing With All My Soul (52 Worship Songs for choirs) Royal School of Church Music followed by Worship in Song 1997, Lincolnshire Voices for the Grimsby Philharmonic Choir's 140th anniversary, Flying Colours for the Farnham Festival 1987, On Earth in Concert Sing a requiem, Cross and Grave and Glory a passion sequence, The Figure on the Shore 2002. *Address:* Forecourt, Queen's Square, Colyton, Devon EX24 6JX, England (home). *Telephone:* (1297) 552414 (home). *Fax:* (1297) 552414 (home). *E-mail:* wllewellyn@freeuk .com (home).

**LLOYD, Anthony (Stuart);** Singer (Bass-baritone); b. 1970, Cardiff, Wales. *Education:* Welsh College of Music and Drama. *Career:* Don Magnifico in Cenerentola at Ischia, 1993; Welsh National Opera as Mozart's Bartolo; Rossini's Basilio, the Commendatore and High Priest in Nabucco; Freiburg Opera from 1997, as Leporello, Lodovico in Otello; Concerts include Les Troyens under Colin Davis, London and Michel Plasson, Toulouse; Eremit in Der Freischütz for Chelsea Opera; Season 1998–99 as Mephistopheles in Faust and Selim in Il Turco in Italia. *Honours:* Geraint Evans Memorial Prize, Pontypridd. *Address:* Harlequin Agency Ltd, 203 Fidlas Road, Cardiff CF4 5NA.

**LLOYD, David;** Singer (Tenor); b. 29 Feb. 1920, Minneapolis, Minnesota, USA. *Education:* Minneapolis College of Music; Curtis Institute, Philadelphia;

Berkshire Music Center. *Career:* After 1947 debut sang with New York City Opera, then with New England Opera Company; Athens Festival, 1955; Glyndebourne, 1957, as Tamino in Die Zauberflöte and Bacchus in Ariadne auf Naxos; Other roles were Mozart's Belmonte and Idomeneo, Flamand in Capriccio, Rodolfo, Jacquino and Gonsalve in L'Heure Espagnole; Also heard in concert and oratorio; Artistic Director, Hunter College, New York; Director of the Lake George Opera Festival, USA, 1974.

**LLOYD, David (Bellamy);** British piano accompanist; b. 22 Nov. 1937, Stockport, Cheshire. *Education:* ARMCM (Performance and Teaching). *Career:* Debut: Recital with Heddle Nash, Wigmore Hall, 1956; Accompanist to Jan Peerce, Festival Hall, London and tour of France, Germany, Switzerland, Austria and Netherlands; TV appearances with Jack Brymer, Adele Leigh and Charlotte Rimmer; fmr accompanist to Jack Brymer, Leon Goossens and Elizabeth Harwood in recitals and broadcasts, Singapore, Hong Kong, India, New Zealand, Spain, Canada and USA; Sr Lecturer, Royal Northern Coll. of Music and Professional Accompanist, 1967–93; Examiner, Associated Bd of Royal Schools of Music, 1969–2002; mem. Inc. Soc. of Musicians. *Compositions:* Schubert Arpeggione Sonata, arranged by David Lloyd, published. *Recordings:* Brahms Clarinet Sonata Op 120/1, Weber Duo Concertante; Brahms Clarinet Sonata Op 120/2; Schubert Arpeggione Sonata arranged for Clarinet; Schumann Phantasiestücke Op 73; Hurlstone Four Characteristic Pieces; Art of Leon Goossens. *Honours:* Royal Manchester Coll. of Music Hilary Haworth Prize 1958. *Address:* 32 Clarence Court, Bare Lane, Morecambe, Lancashire, LA 4 6 DL, England (home). *Telephone:* (1524) 832894 (home).

**LLOYD, Jonathan;** British composer; b. 30 Sept. 1948, London. *Education:* Composition lessons with Emile Spira; Studied at Royal College of Music, London, with Edwin Roxburgh and John Lambert; Worked with Tristram Cary at Electronic Music Studio. *Career:* Twentieth Century Ensemble, 1968; Awarded Mendelssohn Scholarship and lived in Paris, 1969–70; Occasional work as performer, busker, street musician, 1974–77; Composer-in-Residence, Dartington College Theatre Department, 1978–79. *Compositions include:* Orchestral: Cantique, 1968, 5 Symphonies, 1983–89, Rhapsody for Cello and Orchestra, 1982, Viola Concerto, 1979–80, Everything Returns for Soprano and Orchestra, 1977–78, Mass for 6 Solo Voices, 1983, Missa Brevis, 1984, Toward the Whitening Dawn for Chorus and Chamber Orchestra, 1980, Revelation for 8 Voices, 1990, Marching to a Different Song for Soprano and Chamber Orchestra, 1991, Ballad for The Evening of a Man for Mixed Quartet, 1992; Dramatic: The Adjudicator, community opera, 1985, Music for Alfred Hitchcock's Blackmail, 1993; Edition of the Beggar's Opera, 1999; Tolerance for Orchestra, 1994, People Your Dreams for Voice and Ensemble, 1994, Blessed Days of Blue for Solo Flute and Strings, 1995, Violin Concerto, 1995; Piano Concerto, 1995; And Beyond for chorus and ensemble, 1996; A Dream of a Pass, 1997; Shadows of Our Future Selves for ensemble, 1998. *Recordings:* Mass; Second Symphony, 1992; Largo. *Address:* c/o Boosey and Hawkes Ltd, 1st Floor, Aldwych House, 71–91 Aldwych, London WC2B 4HN, England (office). *Website:* www.boosey.com/lloyd (office).

**LLOYD, Phyllida,** BA; British theatre director and film director; b. 17 June 1957, Bristol; d. of Patrick and Margaret (née Douglas-Pennent) Lloyd. *Education:* Lawnside School (Great Malvern) and Univ. of Birmingham. *Career:* fmr Floor Asst BBC TV; Assoc. Dir Manchester Royal Exchange. *Theatre includes:* Six Degrees of Separation (Royal Court) 1992, Hysteria (Royal Court) 1993, Pericles 1993, The Threepenny Opera 1994, The Way of the World 1995, Dona Rosita (Almeida) 1997, The Prime of Miss Jean Brodie (Royal Nat. Theatre) 1998, Mamma Mia! (London and elsewhere) 1999–, Boston Marriage (Donmar) 2001. *Opera includes:* Gloriana 1993, La Bohème (Opera North at Sheffield Lyceum) 1993, Medea (Opera North) 1996, Carmen 1998, Dialogues of the Carmelites (ENO) 1999, Macbeth (Paris Opera) 1999, Verdi Requiem (English Nat. Opera) 2000, The Handmaid's Tale (Copenhagen) 2000, Fidelio (Glyndebourne) (Royal Philharmonic Soc. opera award) 2001, The Valkyrie (Glastonbury Festival) 2004, Siegfried (ENO) 2004. *Television film:* Gloriana (BBC2) (Emmy Award 2000) 1999. *Current Management:* Annette Stone Associates, Second Floor, 22 Great Marlborough Street, London, W1F 7HU, England. *Telephone:* (20) 7734-0626. *Fax:* (20) 7734-2346.

**LLOYD, Robert Andrew,** CBE; British singer (bass); *Senior Artist, Royal Opera House;* b. 2 March 1940, Southend; s. of William Edward Lloyd and May Lloyd (née Waples); m. 1st Sandra D. Watkins 1964 (divorced 1990); one s. three d.; m. 2nd Lynda A. Hazell (née Powell) 1992. *Education:* Southend High School for Boys, Keble Coll. Oxford, London Opera Centre. *Career:* served as Lt in Royal Navy 1963–66; Lecturer, Bramshill Police Coll. 1966–68; Prin. Bass, Sadler's Wells Opera 1969–72, Royal Opera House 1972–83, Sr Artist, Royal Opera House 2004–; freelance singer with all maj. opera houses and orchestras world-wide, frequent broadcasts as presenter, BBC radio and TV 1983–; film appearances: Parsifal, Bluebeard's Castle; performed title role in Tarkovsky production of Boris Godunov at Kirov Opera, Leningrad 1990; created role of Tyrone in Tower by Alun Hoddinott; Visiting Prof. Royal Coll. of Music, London 1996–; Pres. British Youth Opera 1988–94, Southend Choral Soc. 1996–; mem. Exec. Cttee Musicians' Benevolent Fund 1989–92; mem. Conservatoires Advisory Group 1993–99; Pres. elect Inc. Soc. of Musicians 2005; Hon. Fellow Keble Coll. 1990; Patron Carl Rosa Trust 1994–; Hon. mem. Royal Acad. of Music. *Radio:* regular presenter for BBC Radio 3. *Television:* wrote and presented documentary Six Foot Cinderella 1990, subject of BBC documentary Bob the Bass. *Publications:* numerous contribs to magazines.

*Honours:* Artist of the Year, Teatro Colón, Buenos Aires 1996, Charles Santley Award 1997, Chaliapin Commemoration Medal (St Petersburg) 1998. *Address:* c/o Askonas Holt Ltd, Lonsdale Chambers, 27 Chancery Lane, London, WC2A 1PF, England. *Telephone:* (20) 7400-1713 (office); (20) 8883-0664.

**LLOYD-DAVIES, Mary;** Singer (Soprano); b. 1965, Llanuwchllyn, Wales. *Education:* Studied at the Royal College of Music and in Paris with Pierre Bernac. *Career:* Appearances with Welsh National Opera at Elektra, Turandot, Tosca and Leonore in Fidelio; Isolde, Ortrud and Mrs Grose in The Turn of the Screw for English National Opera; Elisabeth in Tannhäuser and Wagner's Senta for Chelsea Opera Group; Concerts in Germany, South America, USA and Canada; Beethoven's Ninth in Lisbon and Ravel's Schéhérazade in Toulouse; Season 1998–99 with Amelia in Un Ballo in Maschera and Isolde for Welsh national Opera. *Address:* Harlequin Agency Ltd, 203 Fidlas Road, Cardiff CF4 5NA, Wales.

**LLOYD DAVIS, John;** Stage Director, Stage Designer and Lighting Designer; b. 1960, England. *Education:* BA, Philosophy and European Literature Bristol University. *Career:* Staff director, English National Opera, (20 productions, directed 5 revivals) 1984–89; Since 1988 freelance work includes Don Giovanni, Die Zauberflöte, Rigoletto, Death In Venice, Das Schloss, Fall of the House of Usher, Weisse Rose, all in Vienna; Madama Butterfly (Dublin, Ludwigshafen, Royal Danish Opera); Un Ballo in Maschera (Klagenfurt), and other productions throughout Europe and Scandinavia; Also active in theatre in Austria and Germany; Director of Productions for New Sussex Opera; Translations include The Enchantress (Tchaikovsky), and Bluebeard's Castle (Bartók) for English National Opera, Scottish Opera and the BBC. *Publications:* Works on Michael Tippett. *Honours:* Josef Kainz Medal for work at Vienna Volkstheater, 1999. *Current Management:* Athole Still International Management, Forresters Hall, 25–27 Westow Street, London, SE19 3RY, England. *Telephone:* (20) 8771-5271. *Fax:* (20) 8768-6600. *Website:* www.atholestill.com.

**LLOYD-HOWELLS, David;** Composer; b. 11 Jan. 1942, Cardiff, Wales. *Education:* Ealing Music Centre, London, 1960–64; Trinity College of Music, 1967; Pontypridd Technical College 1972–73; South Gwent College 1974; BMus, Honours, Wales, 1977–80; FTCL, FLCM, Diplomas, 1979–80; MMus, Distinction, University of London, 1981–83; York University, 1984–85. *Career:* Tutor in Music, Gwent, 1971–77; Adult Education, 1980–83; Community Musician, 1984; Freelance Composer, Conductor, Artistic Director, Adjudicator; Works mainly with electronic-live media; Music Theatre, Modern Dance Groups, Cedar Dance Theatre Company, London, 1983; D.L.H. Productions, music for film, video and self-therapy, 1990; Artistic Director Sonicity 2000, archive of scores, sonic art works, recordings, essays, poems letters at the National Library of Wales, 1993; Guild for the Promotion of Welsh Music Composers database, Arts Council of Wales. *Compositions include:* Bleak Sleaze; Dark Clowns; Nightcity Pulses; Canticles of Goth; Druidika; The Wrath Conference: (Black Rain, Red Grass, Blue Snow, Green Sand); Digital Weave; Life Music; Surfing the Strobe; Sounds from the Noisebath; Dark Clowns; MEC; Legacy of the Icon Slave; The Insects Convention; Fractosonic Graffiti; NOK; Requiem I-Spy; Youthworks; Rites of War; Mind Songs; Piani Melismata; Freakspeak; Edge of Shadows; Molecular Analysis; Ungrateful Utterance; Everything but Silence; Shadowself Connection; Miscreant Hues 9sound opera in seven cadenzas; *Recordings:* Piano Sonata 2, 1978. *Publications:* Soundgazing: A personal view about the future of music. *Address:* 26, Bevelin Hall, Saundersfoot, Pembrokeshire SA 69 9PG.

**LLOYD-JONES, David Mathias,** BA; Welsh musician and conductor; b. 19 Nov. 1934, London; s. of the late Sir Vincent Lloyd-Jones and Margaret Alwena Mathias; m. Anne Carolyn Whitehead 1964; two s. one d. *Education:* Westminster School, Magdalen Coll. Oxford. *Career:* Repetiteur, Royal Opera 1959–61; Chorus Master, New Opera Co. 1961–64; conducted at Bath Festival 1966, City of London Festival 1966, Wexford Festival 1967–70, Scottish Opera 1968, Welsh Nat. Opera 1968, Royal Opera, Covent Garden 1971, Sadler's Wells Opera Co. (now ENO) 1969; Asst Music Dir ENO 1972–78; Artistic Dir Opera North 1978–90; also conductor for TV operas (Eugene Onegin, The Flying Dutchman, Hansel and Gretel) and has appeared with most British symphony orchestras and conducted worldwide; Chair. Delius Trust 1997–; Gen. Ed. William Walton Edn 1996–. *Music:* many acclaimed recordings of British and Russian music; has edited works by composers, including Mussorgsky, Bizet, Walton, Berlioz, Elgar and Sullivan. *Publications:* Boris Godunov–Translation, Vocal Score, Eugene Onegin–Translation, Vocal Score, Boris Godunov–Critical Edition of Original Full Score, numerous contribs to publs including Grove's Dictionary of Music and Musicians, Musik in Geschichte und Gegenwart, Music and Letters, The Listener. *Honours:* Hon. DMus (Leeds) 1986. *Address:* 94 Whitelands House, Cheltenham Terrace, London, SW3 4RA, England (home). *Telephone:* (20) 7730-8695. *Fax:* (20) 7730-8695.

**LLOYD ROBERTS, Carys;** Singer (Soprano); b. 1969, Wales. *Education:* Studied at the Welsh College of Music and Drama. *Career:* Engagements with the Welsh National Opera, Musica nel Chiostro and City of Birmingham Touring Opera as Papagena, First Lady, Barbarina and Hansel; Purcell's King Arthur with Les Arts Florissants at Covent Garden and The Fairy Queen with the Northern Sinfonia; Concerts include the Jonathan Miller production

of the St Matthew Passion and appearances at Llandaff Cathedral and St Martin-in-the-Fields, London; Sang Lensky for Grange Park Opera, 2000.

**LLOYD-ROBERTS, Jeffrey;** Singer (Tenor); b. 1968, Wales. *Education:* Studied at the Royal Northern College of Music with Barbara Robotham and at Lancaster University. *Career:* Appearances with Welsh National Opera in The Makropulos Case, as Nemorino with English Touring Opera in Le Roi malgré Lui for Chelsea Opera and in Aroldo at the Buxton Festival; Season 1995 as Lindoro in La fedeltà premiata for Garsington Opera and concerts of Korngold's Ring of Polycrates, the B Minor Mass, the Verdi Requiem, Mahler's 8th Symphony and The Dream of Gerontius. *Address:* c/o Musichall Ltd, Vicarage Way, Ringmer, East Sussex, BN8 5 LA, England.

**LLOYD WEBBER,** Baron (Life Peer), cr. 1997, of Sydmonton in the County of Hampshire; **Andrew Lloyd Webber,** FRCM; British composer; *Chairman, The Really Useful Group Ltd;* b. 22 March 1948, s. of the late William Southcombe Lloyd Webber and Jean Hermione Johnstone; brother of Julian Lloyd Webber (q.v.); m. 1st Sarah Jane Tudor (née Hugill) 1971 (divorced 1983); one s. one d.; m. 2nd Sarah Brightman 1984 (divorced 1990); m. 3rd Madeleine Astrid Gurdon 1991; two s. one d. *Education:* Westminster School, Magdalen Coll. Oxford, Royal Coll. of Music. *Career:* Chair. The Really Useful Group Ltd; owner of eight London theatres including the Palace Theatre, Theatre Royal Drury Lane, The London Palladium. *Works:* musicals: Joseph and the Amazing Technicolor Dreamcoat (lyrics by Tim Rice) 1968 (revised 1973, 1991), Jesus Christ Superstar (lyrics by Tim Rice) 1970 (revised 1996), Jeeves (lyrics by Alan Ayckbourn) 1975 (revised as By Jeeves 1996), Evita (lyrics by Tim Rice) 1976 (stage version 1978), Tell Me on a Sunday (lyrics by Don Black) 1980, revised 2003, Cats (based on T. S. Eliot's Old Possum's Book of Practical Cats) (Tony Awards for Best Score and Best Musical 1983) 1981, Song and Dance (lyrics by Don Black) 1982, Starlight Express (lyrics by Richard Stilgoe) 1984, The Phantom of the Opera (Tony Award for Best Musical 1988) (lyrics by Richard Stilgoe and Charles Hart) 1986, Aspects of Love (lyrics by Don Black and Charles Hart) 1989, Sunset Boulevard (Tony Awards for Best Score and Best Musical 1995) (lyrics by Christopher Hampton and Don Black) 1993, Whistle Down the Wind (lyrics by Jim Steinman) 1996, The Beautiful Game (with lyrics by Ben Elton) (London Critics' Circle Best Musical 2000) 2000; other compositions: Variations (based on A minor Caprice No. 24 by Paganini) 1977 (symphonic version 1986), Requiem Mass 1985, Amigos Para Siempre (official theme for 1992 Olympic Games), The Woman in White; film scores: Gumshoe 1971, The Odessa File 1974. *Producer:* Joseph and the Amazing Technicolor Dreamcoat 1973, 1974, 1978, 1980, 1991, Jeeves Takes Charge 1975, Cats 1981, Song & Dance 1982, Daisy Pulls it Off 1983, The Hired Man 1984, Starlight Express 1984, On Your Toes 1984, The Phantom of the Opera 1986, Café Puccini 1986, The Resistible Rise of Arturo Ui 1987, Lend Me a Tenor 1988, Aspects of Love 1989, Shirley Valentine (Broadway) 1989, La Bête 1992, Sunset Boulevard 1993, By Jeeves 1996, Whistle Down the Wind 1996, 1998, Jesus Christ Superstar 1996, 1998, The Beautiful Game 2000, Bombay Dreams 2002, Tell Me On A Sunday, 2003, The Woman in White 2004, and others. *Art Collection:* Pre-Raphaelite and other masters – The Andrew Lloyd Webber Collection, Royal Acad., London 2003. *Film:* The Phantom of the Opera (Dir by Joel Schumacher) 2004. *Publications:* Evita (with Tim Rice) 1978, Cats: the book of the musical 1981, Joseph and the Amazing Technicolor Dreamcoat (with Tim Rice) 1982, The Complete Phantom of the Opera 1987, The Complete Aspects of Love 1989, Sunset Boulevard: from movie to musical 1993; food critic Daily Telegraph 1996–. *Honours:* seven Tony Awards, four Drama Desk Awards, six Laurence Olivier Awards, Triple Play Awards 1996, ASCAP 1988, Praemium Imperiale Award 1995, three Grammy Awards, Golden Globe Award, Academy Award 1996, Richard Rodgers Award for Excellence in Musical Theatre 1996; Commander's Cross of the Order of Merit, Hungary 2005. *Address:* The Really Useful Group Ltd, 22 Tower Street, London, WC2H 9TW, England. *Telephone:* (20) 7240-0880 (office). *Fax:* (20) 7240-1204 (office). *Website:* www.reallyuseful.com (office).

**LLOYD WEBBER, Julian,** FRCM; British cellist; b. 14 April 1951, London; s. of the late William Southcombe Lloyd Webber and of Jean Hermione Johnstone; brother of Lord Lloyd Webber (q.v.); m. 1st Celia M. Ballantyne 1974 (divorced 1989); m. 2nd Zohra Mahmoud Ghazi 1989 (divorced 1999); one s.; m. 3rd Kheira Bourahla 2001. *Education:* Univ. Coll. School and Royal Coll. of Music. *Career:* debut at Queen Elizabeth Hall 1972; debut with Berlin Philharmonic Orchestra 1984; appears at major int. concert halls and has undertaken concert tours throughout Europe, N and S America, S Africa, Australasia, Singapore, Japan, China, Hong Kong and Korea; numerous television appearances and broadcasts in UK, Netherlands, Africa, Germany, Scandinavia, France, Belgium, Spain, Australasia and USA; patron Jacqueline du Pré Charity Concerts 2006–. *Recordings:* world premieres of Britten's 3rd Suite for Solo Cello, Bridge's Oration, Rodrigo's Cello Concerto (Spanish Ministry of Culture Award for world premiere recording 1982), Holst's Invocation, Gavin Bryar's Cello Concerto, Michael Nyman's Cello and Saxophone Concerto, Sullivan's Cello Concerto, Vaughan Williams' Fantasia on Sussex Folk Tunes, Andrew Lloyd Webber's Variations (Gold disc 1978), Elgar's Cello Concerto (British Phonographic Industry Award for Best Classical Recording 1986), Dvořák Concerto, Saint-Saëns Concerto, Lalo Concerto, Walton Concerto, Britten Cello Symphony; Philip Glass Cello Concerto. *Publications:* Classical Cello 1980, Romantic Cello 1981, French Cello 1981, Frank Bridge, Six Pieces 1982, Young Cellist's Repertoire (three vols) 1984, Holst's Invocation 1984, Travels with my Cello 1984, Song of the

Birds 1985, Recital Repertoire for Cellists (four vols) 1986, Short Sharp Shocks 1990, The Great Cello Solos 1992, The Essential Cello 1997, Cello Moods 1999, String Quartets, 2003; Made in England 2003. Contributions to: The Times, The Sunday Times, The Daily Telegraph, USA Today. *Honours:* Suggia Gift 1968, Seymour Whinyates Award 1971, Percy Buck Award 1972, Brit Award for Elgar Cello Concerto recording 1987, Crystal Award, World Economic Forum (Switzerland) 1998, Hon. Doctorate (Univ. of Hull) 2003, (Thames Valley Univ.) 2004. *Current Management:* IMG Artists Europe, Lovell House, 616 Chiswick High Road, London, W4 5RX, England. *Telephone:* (20) 8233-5800. *Fax:* (20) 8233-5801. *E-mail:* vcorley-smith@imgworld.com (office). *Website:* www.julianlloydwebber.com (office).

**LOBANOV, Vassily;** Composer and Pianist; b. 2 Jan. 1947, Moscow, USSR. *Education:* Studied at the Tchaikovsky Conservatoire, Moscow, 1963–69, with Leo Naumov, Sergei Balasanyan and Alfred Schnittke. *Career:* Has accompanied Natalia Gutman and Oleg Kagan individually and as member of trio; Interpreter of modern works at festivals in Moscow, Witten, Vienna and Kuhmo, Finland; Premiered his Second Piano Sonata at the Moscow Autumn Festival, 1980; Has partnered Sviatoslav Richter in duets; December Nights concert in the Pushkin Museum Moscow, 1981; Soloist with the Moscow Philharmonic from 1982; Professor of Piano, Cologne Hochschule, 1997–. *Compositions include:* Oratorio Lieutenant Schmidt, 1979; Opera Antigone, 1985–88; Orchestra: Symphony for chamber orchestra, 1977; Piano Concerto 1981; Cello Concerto, 1985; Sinfonietta, 1986; Concerto for viola and strings, 1989; Piano Concerto No. 2, 1993; Double concerto for violin and clarinet, 1995; Trumpet Concerto; 1998; Viola Concerto No. 2, 1998; Chamber: 5 string quartets, 1966, 1968, 1978, 1987, 1988; Twelve Preludes for piano, 1965; Partita for piano; 1967; 2 Cello Sonatas, 1971, 1989; 2 piano sonatas, 1973, 1980; 3 Suites for piano; Seven Pieces for cello and piano, 1978; Variations for two trumpets, 1979; Seven Slow Pieces for piano, 1978–80; Flute Sonata, 1983; Clarinet Sonata, 1985; Fantasia for solo cello, 1987; Violin Sonata, 1989; Viola Sonata, 1990; Piano Quintet, 1991; Piano Quartet, 1996; String Trio, 1996; Clarinet Quintet, 1999; Vocal: Three Haikus for low voice and piano, 1963; Three Romances (bass), 1965; Five Romances, 1971; Four Poems to texts by Alexei Parin (bass), 1984; Eight Poems (soprano), 1984; Stravinsky's Italian Suite adapted for cello and chamber orchestra, 1985. *Address:* c/o Boosey & Hawkes Ltd, 295 Regent Street, London W1R 8JH, England.

**LOCKHART, Beatriz;** Uruguayan composer; *Professor, University of Montevideo;* b. 17 Jan. 1944, Montevideo; m. Antonio Mastrogiovanni 1969; one d. *Education:* Montevideo Conservatory, studied in Buenos Aires, Argentina. *Career:* teacher, Caracas Conservatory 1974–88, Prof., Univ. of Montevideo 1988–. *Compositions include:* Ecos for orchestra, Concerto Grosso, Masia muju for flute and orchestra 1987, Theme and variations for piano, Ejercio I for tape and other electronic music, Vision de los vencidos for voice and orchestra 1990, Homenaje a Astor Piazzola for piano 1994, Concertino for double bass and orchestra 1999, Concertino for violoncello and orchestra 2004. *Address:* c/o AGADU, Calle canelones 1122, Montevideo, Uruguay (office).

**LOCKHART, James,** BMus, FRCM, FRCO (CHM); British conductor and music director; b. 16 Oct. 1930, Edinburgh; s. of Archibald C. Lockhart and Mary B. Lawrence; m. Sheila Grogan 1954; two s. one d. *Education:* George Watson's Coll., Edin., Univ. of Edin. and Royal Coll. of Music. *Career:* Asst Conductor, Yorkshire Symphony Orchestra 1954–55; Repetiteur and Asst Conductor, Städtische Bühnen Münster 1955–56, Bayerische Staatsoper, Munich 1956–57, Glyndebourne Festival Opera 1957–59; Dir Opera Workshop, Univ. of Texas 1957–59; Repetiteur and Asst Conductor, Royal Opera House, Covent Garden 1959–60, Conductor 1962–68; Asst Conductor, BBC Scottish Orchestra 1960–61; Conductor, Sadler's Wells Opera 1961–62; Prof. Royal Coll. of Music 1962–72; Musical Dir Welsh Nat. Opera 1968–73; General-musikdirektor, Staatstheater Kassel 1972–80, Koblenz and Theater der Stadt, Koblenz 1981–88, Rheinische Philharmonie 1981–91; Prin. Guest Conductor, BBC Concert Orchestra 1982–87; Dir of Opera, Royal Coll. of Music 1986–92, London Royal Schools' Vocal Faculty 1992–96, Opera Consultant 1996–98; Guest Prof. of Conducting, Tokyo Nat. Univ. of Fine Arts and Music (Tokyo Geidai) 1998–2001, Prof. Emer. 2001–; freelance conductor 2001–. *Honours:* Hon. RAM 1993. *Address:* 105 Woodcock Hill, Harrow, Middx, HA3 0JJ, England (home). *Telephone:* (20) 8907-2112 (home). *Fax:* (20) 8907-2112 (home). *E-mail:* Lockgrog@aol.com (home).

**LOCKLEY, Michael Allen;** Singer (Tenor); b. 7 March 1960, Sodus, New York, USA; m. Jennifer Bates, 11 Nov 1989, 1 s. *Education:* BS, Geneseo College; MM, Binghamton University; Resident Artist, Tri-Cities Opera and European Mozart Academies. *Career:* Debut: Tri-Cities Opera, 1983; Performances with New York City Opera, Baltimore Opera, Tulsa Opera, Ash Lawn-Highland Opera Festival and Maggio Musicale, Florence; Has sung Rodolfo in La Bohème, Alfredo in La Traviata, Ferrando in Così fan tutte, Tamino in Die Zauberflöte, Romeo in Roméo et Juliette, and Don José in Carmen; mem, AGMA; Association of Film, Television and Radio Artists. *Recordings:* Arabesque, Greenhays Rivertown. *Honours:* Richard F Gold Grant, Ezio Pinza Council for American Singers. *Current Management:* William R Hendrickson Artists Management. *Address:* 47 Penny Lane, Ithaca, NY 14850, USA.

**LOCKWOOD, Annea (Ferguson);** Composer, Performer and University Lecturer; b. 29 July 1939, Christchurch, New Zealand. *Education:* BMus, University of Canterbury, New Zealand, 1961; Royal College of Music,

London, 1961–63, LRAM, ARCM Piano Performance; Musikhochschule Cologne, 1963–64; Institute for Sound and Vibration Research, psychoacoustical research, postgraduate, Southampton University, England, 1971–73. *Career:* Major performances of own compositions: Cheltenham Festival, United Kingdom, 1965, 1969; Commonwealth Festival, United Kingdom, 1965; Parie Biennale, 1965; Fylkingen Festival, Stockholm, 1970; Queen Elizabeth Hall, London, 1971; Lincoln Center Plaza, New York, 1974; New Music America Festivals, 1979, 1982, 1986; Autunno Musicale a Como, Italy, 1979; Sydney Biennale, 1982; Westdeutscher Rundfunk, Meet the USA Festival, 1982; Asia Pacific Festival, 1984; Westdeutscher Rundfunk, Ives & Co, 1988; New York-Cologne Festival, 1989; New York: Alice Tully Hall, 1992, The Kitchen, 1997, Engine 27, 2000, Hudson River Museum, 2003, Bang on a Can Marathon, 2003; Los Angeles County Museum of Modern Art, 1995; Summergarden Museum of Modern Art, 1997; Whitney Museum of American Art, 2000; Mystic und Maschine festival, Münster, 2000; De Ijsbreker, New Music, New Zealand, Amsterdam, 2001; Other Minds 8 Festival, San Francisco, 2002; mem, BMI Inc; American Music Center. *Compositions include:* Red Mesa, 1989; Thousand Year Dreaming, 1991; Shapeshifter, 1995; Ear-Walking Woman, 1997; Duende, 1998; Floating World, 1999; Piano Transplants; Immersion; Vortex; Ceci n'est pas un piano; A Sound Map of the Danube River. *Recordings:* Glass Concert; World Rhythms; Tiger Balm; A Sound Map of the Hudson River; Thousand Year Dreaming; Red Mesa; Delta Run; Duende; The Angle of Repose; Night and Fog; I Give You Back; Nautilus; Ear-Walking Woman; Monkey Trips. *Publications:* Malaman; Spirit Catchers; Humming; Delta Run; Sound Map of the Hudson River; Glass Concert, World Rhythms, Tiger Balm, Malolo, A Sound Map of the Hudson River; Red Mesa, 1993; I Give You Back, 1995. *Honours:* National Endowment for the Arts Composition Fellow, USA, 1979; CAPS Composition Fellowship, USA, 1979; Arts Council of Great Britain, 1972; Gulbenkian Foundation Grants, 1972; Dr hc Fine Arts, Clark Univ., Worcester (USA), 1999. *Address:* Baron de Hirsch Road, Crompond, NY 10517, USA.

**LOCKWOOD, Lewis Henry,** BA, MFA, PhD; American musicologist, writer, editor and academic; b. 16 Dec. 1930, New York, NY. *Education:* Queens Coll., CUNY, Princeton Univ. *Career:* Faculty 1958–65, Assoc. Prof. 1965–68, Prof. 1968–80, Chair., Dept of Music 1970–73, Princeton Univ.; Ed., Journal of the American Musicological Soc. 1963–66, Beethoven Forum 1991–; Prof. of Music 1980–2002, Chair Dept of Music 1988–90, Harvard Univ.; Gen. Ed., Studies in Musical Genesis and Structure 1984–98; mem. American Acad. of Arts and Sciences, American Musicological Soc. (pres. 1987–88, hon. mem. 1993–). *Publications:* Music in Renaissance Ferrara, 1400–1505 1984, Beethoven Essays: Studies in Honor of Elliot Forbes (co-ed.) 1984, Essays in Musicology: A Tribute to Alvin Johnson (co-ed.) 1990, Beethoven: Studies in the Creative Process 1992, Beethoven: The Music and the Life 2003; contrib. to scholarly books and journals. *Honours:* Dr hc (Università degli Studi, Ferrara) 1991, (New England Conservatory of Music) 1998; Nat. Endowment for the Humanities Sr Fellowships 1973–74, 1984–85, Guggenheim Fellowship 1977–78; ASCAP Deems Taylor Award 1993, Festschrift published in his honour 1997. *Address:* c/o Department of Music, Harvard University, Cambridge, MA 02138, USA. *E-mail:* llockw@fas.harvard.edu.

**LOEBEL, David;** Conductor; b. 7 March 1950, Cleveland, Ohio, USA; m. Jane Cawthorn 1977. *Education:* BS 1972, MMus 1974, Northwestern University. *Career:* Assistant Conductor, Syracuse Symphony Orchestra, 1974–76; Music Director, Binghamton Symphony Orchestra, 1977–82; Music Adviser, Anchorage Symphony Orchestra, 1983–86; Assistant, 1982–86, Associate Conductor, 1986–90, Cincinnati Symphony Orchestra; Associate Conductor, 1990–94, Associate Principal Conductor, St Louis Symphony Orchestra, 1994–2000; Conductor-in-Residence, New World Symphony, 1997–99; Music Director, Memphis Symphony Orchestra, 1999–. *Honours:* 3rd Prize, 1976, Co-winner, 1978, Baltimore Symphony Orchestra Young Conductors' Competition; ASCAP Award, Adventuresome Programming, 1981, 2001, 2002; Seaver NEA Conductors Award, 1992; Northwestern Univ. Alumni Merit Award, 2000. *Address:* c/o Memphis Symphony Orchestra, 3100 Walnut Grove, Suite 501, Memphis, TN 38111, USA. *E-mail:* musdir@memphissymphony.org.

**LOEVAAS-GERBER, Kari;** Singer (Soprano); b. 13 May 1939, Oslo, Norway; m. Manfred Gerber, 1968, 1 d. *Education:* Conservatory Oslo; Musikakademie Wien; Studies with Erna Westenberger, Frankfurt. *Career:* Debut: Nuri, Oslo, 1959; Opera Houses in Dortmund and Mainz; Festivals at Salzburg, Vienna, Lucerne, Bergen, Ludwigsburg, Schwetzingen, Athens, Flanders; Television includes Fischer und seine Fru/Schoeck, 1981 and Peer Gynt, W Egk, 1983; All major radio stations in Germany, Austria, Norway, Switzerland, France and Italy. *Recordings include:* Debut record: Lieder (Grieg, Mussorgsky, Sibelius) with Erik Werba; Petite Messe Solennelle, Rossini; Die Feen, Wagner; War Requiem, Britten; more than 30 records. *Honours:* Deutsche Grammophon Sonderpreis, Vienna, 1960. *Current Management:* Sudwestdeutsche Konzertdirektion Russ, Stuttgart. *Address:* Gugerhalde 10, 8207 Schaffhausen, Switzerland.

**LOGAN, Wendell Morris,** PhD; American composer; b. 24 Nov. 1940, Thomson, GA. *Education:* Fla A&M Univ., Tallahassee, American Conservatory of Music, Chicago, Southern Ill. Univ., Carbondale and Univ. of Iowa. *Career:* Music Dir, Ga Southern Coll. Statesboro 1971–72; Lecturer in Music Theory, arranger for bands, Fla A&M Univ., Tallahassee 1962–63; dir of instrumental music at various public schools, Rudyard, MI 1964–65; Asst Prof. of Music Theory and Composition, Ball State Univ., Muncie, IN 1967–69;

founder, New Music Ensemble 1967; Assoc. Prof. and Chair of Theory Div., Fla A&M Univ. 1969–70; Assoc. Prof. of Music Theory and Composition, Western Ill. Univ., Macomb 1970–73; Dir African-American Music/Jazz Studies Program, Oberlin Coll. Conservatory of Music, Oberlin, OH 1973–, Head Div. of Contemporary Music 1989–90; Visiting Prof., Jamaica School of Music, Kingston 1980, 1983; guest lecturer at numerous univs. *Compositions including:* Woodwind Quintet 1964, Concert Music for orchestra 1964, Stanzas for three players 1967, Polyphony I 1968, Songs of Our Time 1969, Proportions for nine players and conductor 1969, Textures for piano 1972, Memories Of... for jazz ensemble 1972, From Hell To Breakfast 1973, Evocations for harmonica 1973, Three Fragments 1974, Beats For C, D and O 1975, Ice and Fire 1975, Variations on a Motive by Coltrane for jazz ensemble 1975, Song of the Witchdoktor 1976, Music for brass 1976, Electric Time for percussion 1976, Malcolm, Malcolm 1976, Three Pieces for violin and piano 1977, Five Pieces for piano 1977, Duo Exchanges 1978, Eye of the Sparrow 1978, Hughes Set 1978, To Mingus for vibraphone 1979, Dream Boogie 1979, Four Pieces for saxophone 1980, Dance Of The Moors 1980, In the Tradition 1980, Requiem for Charlie Parker 1981, Sing Along 1982, Noah (Built The Ark) 1983, The Drum Major: In Memoriam Dr M. L. King Jr 1983, Praeludium for wind ensemble 1983, Prayer 1983, Listen Lord: A Prayer 1984, Four Miniatures for saxophone 1985, Return of the Collard People 1988, In a Pentamental 1988, Variations On Doo-Wah 1988, Brasstacs I: Sloset 1989, Four Children's Pieces for piano 1989, Two Love Songs 1989, Runagate, Runagate 1990, Roots, Branches, Shapes and Shades (Of Green) for chamber orchestra 1991, Moments 1992, Ibo Landing for orchestra 1994–95, This Little Light of Mine 1995. *Honours:* NEA grants 1973, 1978, 1985, 1995, Martha Baird Rockefeller Fund for Music grant 1979, Oberlin Coll. H.H. Powers Fund for travel 1979, 1990, Nat. Endowment for the Humanities grant 1980, Ohio Arts Council grants 1984, 1985, 1994, 1996, Oberlin Coll. Research Grant 1990, ASCAP Composition Awards 1990–97, Guggenheim Award 1991, Ohio Individual Award 1991, Cleveland Arts Prize 1992, Rockefeller Center Foundation grant as composer-in-residence, Bellagio, Italy 1994. *Address:* 77 W College Street, Oberlin, OH 44074, USA (office). *E-mail:* Wendell .Logan@oberlin.edu. *Website:* www.oberlin.edu.

**LOGIE, Nicholas,** BA; British violist and orchestra manager; *Orchestra Manager, Glyndebourne Touring Orchestra*; b. 12 May 1950, Hemel Hempstead, Hertfordshire, England; m. Marina Orlov 1972; two s. *Education:* Yehudi Menuhin School, 1963–67; Royal Coll. of Music, London; Northwest Deutsche Musikakademie, Detmold, Germany; Santa Cecilia, Rome, Italy. *Career:* Debut: Wigmore Hall, London, 1984; mem. Vienna Symphony Orchestra. 1973–78; Chilingirian String Quartet, 1978–81; Orchestra Man., Glyndebourne Touring Opera 1990–; Baroque Viola, London Baroque, 1985–; Sr Lecturer, Dir of Early Music, Royal Northern Coll. of Music RNCM 1989–2002; Co-Prin. Viola, Orchestra of the Age of Enlightenment 1992–. *Recordings:* Schubert Cello Quintet; 6 Mozart Quartets with Chilingirian Quartet. *Contributions:* 5 Sketches for Solo Viola by Elizabeth Maconchy; Newsletter No. 24, The Viola Society, March 1985. *Address:* Lott's End, Highgate, Forest Row, Sussex RH18 5BE, England. *E-mail:* nick@nlogie.co.uk (office).

**LOH, Lisa;** Pianist; b. 6 Jan. 1967, Hong Kong. *Education:* Diploma, Management Studies; Associate, Licentiate, Guildhall School of Music and Drama; Licentiate, Royal Academy of Music; Associate, Royal College of Music. *Career:* Debut: Purcell Room, South Bank, London, 1993; Appearances in Concerts and Recitals, Fairfield Halls, South Bank and Barbican Centre; Broadcasts on ITV, RTHK Radio Hong Kong; Fellow, Guild of Musicians and Singers. *Honours:* Several Prizes, British Competitions. *Address:* 301 Cromwell Tower, Barbican, London EC 2Y 8 NB, England.

**LOJARRO, Daniela;** Italian/Swiss Singer (soprano); b. 24 June 1964, Rivoli, Turin, Italy. *Education:* studied with Carlo Bergonzi, among others. *Career:* debut, sang Gilda at Bussetto; Performances at major opera houses in Naples, Parma, Trieste, Bari, Covent Garden London, Zürich, Monte Carlo, Turin, Pretoria, Palm Beach, Liège and Opera Ireland; also Rossini Opera Festival, Pesaro and Martina Franca Festival; Repertoire includes main roles in Bellini's La Sonnambula, Bizet's Les Pêcheurs de perles, Delibes' Lakmé, Donizetti's Don Pasquale, l'Elisir d'amore, Lucia di Lammermoor, La Fille du Regiment, Handel's Alcina, Leoncavallo's Pagliacci, Mozart's Don Giovanni, Rossini's Barbiere di Siviglia, La Donna del Lago, Salieri's La Secchia rapita, Verdi's Rigoletto, Falstaff, Un Ballo in maschera, La Traviata; Worked with conductors including Allemandi, Brüggen, Carignani, Kuhn, Oestman, Oren, Paternostro, Rizzi, Viotti and Zedda; Concert and oratorio repertoire includes Bach's Cantata Jauchzet Gott, Corghi/Rossini's Dodo Suite, Mozart's Concert Arias, Pergolesi's Stabat Mater. *Recordings include:* Ermione by Rossini, Nina by Paisiello, Crispino e la Comare by Ricci. *Television:* appeared in Ermione, La Sonnambula and Lakmé. *Film:* sang Lucia and Gilda on soundtrack of Zeffirelli's Toscanini. *Honours:* Winner, Giuseppe Verdi Competition, Parma. *Address:* Gladbachstrasse 48, 8044 Zürich, Switzerland (home). *Telephone:* (1) 3620134 (home). *E-mail:* daniela.lojarro@bluewin.ch.

**LOMBARD, Alain;** Conductor; b. 4 Oct. 1940, Paris, France. *Education:* Studied at the Paris Conservatoire with Line Talleul (Violin) and Gaston Poulet (Conducting). *Career:* Debut: Salle Gaveau, Pais, aged 11 with the Pasdeloup Orchestra; Assistant, the Principal Conductor with Lyon Opéra, 1961–65; American Opera Society, 1963, with Massenet's Hérodiade; Conducted New York Philharmonic and at Salzburg Festival, 1966; Musical Director, Miami Opera, Florida, 1966–74; Metropolitan Opera, 1967,

Gounod's Faust; Director of the Strasbourg Philharmonic, 1972–83; Opéra du Rhin, 1974–80; Guest conductor with Schveningen Festival, Netherlands, Hamburg Opera, L'Orchestre de Paris and other leading orchestras; Conducted Die Zauberflöte at Bordeaux, 1992; Conducted Falstaff at Catania, 1996 and Les Contes d'Hoffmann, 1998. *Recordings include:* Mozart's Così fan tutte, with Strasbourg Ensemble; Berlioz Symphonie Fantastique, Harold in Italy and Roméo et Juliette; Verdi Requiem; Prokofiev Violin Concertos (Amoyal) and Ballet Suites; Bartók Concerto for Orchestra and Miraculous Mandarin; Ravel Piano Concerto, Queffelec, and Daphnis et Chloe No. 2; Gounod Roméo et Juliette. *Honours:* Gold Medal, Dimitri Mitropoulos Competition, 1966.

**LOMBARDO, Bernard;** Singer (Tenor); b. 15 Nov. 1960, Marseille, France. *Education:* Studied in Marseille and Treviso. *Career.* Sang widely in France including Bruno in I Puritani at the Paris Opéra-Comique, 1987; Tour of Australia 1988–89, notably as Turiddu at Sydney and Melbourne; St Gallen in 1988 as Edgardo and Opéra Bastille in France in 1990 as Cassio in Otello; La Scala Milan debut in 1991, as Floreski in Cherubini's Lodoiska; Season 1992 as Hoffmann at Kaiserslautern and Roland in Esclarmonde at St Etienne; Other roles include Jacopo in I Due Foscari, Tybalt in Roméo et Juliette at Zürich, Ismaele in Nabucco and Gabriele Adorno at Geneva. *Recordings include:* Lodoiska and Lucia di Lammermoor. *Address:* c/o Teatro alla Scala, Via Filodrammatici 2, 20121 Milan, Italy.

**LOMON, Ruth;** Composer; b. 7 Nov. 1930, Montreal, Canada; m. Earle Lomon, 4 Aug 1951, 1 s., 2 d. *Education:* McGill University; New England Conservatory. *Career:* Debut: Piano, Montreal, Canada; 2 Piano team with Iris Graffman Wenglin with appearances on radio and television, performing and lecturing on works by women composers, playing contemporary and classical repertoire, 1973–83; Composer/Resident Scholar, Women's Studies Research Center, Brandeis University, Waltham, Massachusetts, 1998–. *Compositions include:* Published: Esquisses for piano solo; Seven Portals of Vision for organ, 5 Songs on poems by William Blake for contralto and violin, Dust Devils for harp, Janus for string quartet, Diptych for woodwind quintet, Metamorphoses for cello and piano, Songs for a Requiem for soprano, piano or woodwinds, Equinox for brass quartet, Celebrations for 2 harps, bassoon concerto, Dialogue for harpsichord and vibraphone, Requiem Mass for full chorus and brass accompaniment; Butterfly Effect for string quartet, 1990, Terra Incognita for orchestra, 1993, and Shadowing for piano quartet, 1993; Oddyssey, trumpet concerto, 1997; Nocturnal Songs for mezzo and harp, 1997; 2 piano quartets, 1993, 1995; Songs of Remembrance, 60-song cycle on poems of the Holocaust for soprano, tenor, mezzo, bass, oboe, English horn and piano, 1996; Odyssey, trumpet concerto, 1997. *Recordings include:* Five Ceremonial Masks for Piano; Soundings and Triptych for two pianos, 1992; Terra Incognita with Warsaw Philharmonic Orchestra under Jerzy Swoboda, 1993; Bassoon Concerto in 3 movements, with bassoonist Grertzer under Gerard Schwarz with Prague Radio Symphony Orchestra; Songs of Remembrance. *Address:* 2A Forest Street, Cambridge, MA 02140, USA.

**LONDON, Edwin;** Composer; b. 16 March 1929, Philadelphia, Pennsylvania, USA. *Education:* Studied at Oberlin College Conservatory and the University of Iowa, PhD, 1961; With Gunter Schullar at Manhattan School of Music and with Milhaud and Dallapicola; Conducting studies with Izler Solomon. *Career:* Teacher at Smith College, Northampton, 1960–68; University of Illinois, 1973–83; Chairman of the Music Department at Cleveland State University, 1978–; Founder and leader of the Cleveland Chamber Orchestra. *Compositions:* Santa Claus, Mime Opera, 1960; 3 Settings of Psalm 23 for Choruses, 1961; Woodwind Quintet, 1958; Sonatina for Viola and Piano, 1962; Brass Quintet, 1965; Portraits of Three Ladies, Theatre Piece, 1967; Four Proverbs, 1968; The Iron Hand, Otarorio, 1975; The Death of Lincoln, Opera, 1976; Psalms of These Days, 1976–80; Metaphysical Vegas, Musical 1981; Bottom Line, for tuba and chamber orchestra, 1997. *Honours:* Guggenheim Foundation Grant; NEA Grants; Hamburg Opera Contemporary Festival Grant. *Address:* c/o ASCAP, ASCAP Building, 1 Lincoln Plaza, New York, NY 10023, USA.

**LONGHI, Daniela;** Soprano; b. 1956, Italy. *Education:* Studied in Verona and Mantua. *Career:* Sang at the Verona Arena from 1981, as the Priestess in Aida and Liu in Turandot; Guest appearances at Turin as Micaela and at Liège as Violetta and Thais; Sang at and Parma as Leonore in the French version of Il Trovatore, 1990; Marseille and Madrid, 1990–91 as Anna Bolena, Montpellier in 1991 as Elizabeth 1 in Roberto Devereux by Donizetti; Other roles include Manon and Mimi; Sang Violetta at Detroit, 1998. *Address:* c/o Opéra de Montpellier, 11 Boulevard Victor Hugo, 34000 Montpellier, France.

**LONSDALE, Michael (James);** Composer; b. 11 Oct. 1961, Newcastle, New South Wales, Australia. *Education:* New South Wales Conservatory, 1985–87; Study with Nigel Butterley 1984–85 and Bozidar Kos, 1986–88. *Career:* Faculty Member, Barker College, Hornsby; Commissions from David Forrest (1986) and Warringah Council, 1989–91. *Compositions include:* Calm Obstables, Mouna, and Pais, all for piano, 1985–86; Celeritas for string trio, piano and wind trio, 1985; Fulgur Arbor for tenor trombone, 1986; I See Past the River... for chorus and orchestra, 1988; Lung Gompa for piano, 1993; It Stirs Beneath, for chorus, 1994; Time is the Loser, for string quartet, 1994; Viper for contra bassoon, 1995. *Honours:* ABC/Department of Education Young Composer of the Year Award, 1979. *Address:* c/o APRA, Locked Bag 3665, St Leonards, NSW 2065, Australia.

**LOOSLI, Arthur;** Concert Singer (Baritone); b. 23 Feb. 1926, La Chaux d'Abel, Berner, Jura, Switzerland; m. Theresia Rothlisberger, 2 s. *Education:* Conservatoire of Berne with Felix Loeffel; Studies with Mariano Stabile, Venice, and Arne Sunnergard, Stockholm, Sweden. *Career:* Debut: Berne, 1958; Performances in Switzerland, Belgium, Sweden, Netherlands, Germany and Italy; Guest Artist at Stadttheater, Berne; mem, Othmar Schoeck Association; Swiss Music Teachers Association. *Recordings:* Elegie, Lieder (Othmar Schoeck); Winterreise (Schubert); Schwanengesang (Schubert); Johannes–Passion (Bach). *Publications:* Illustrations of Franz Hohler's Tschipo and Der Granitblock im Kino. *Honours:* Recipient, 1st Prize, International Singers Competition, Bass Baritone, 's-Hertogenbosch, Netherlands, 1959; Further professional activities. *Address:* Gurtenweg 31A, 3074 Muri, Switzerland.

**LOOTENS, Lena (Helena-Alice);** Singer (Soprano); b. 14 April 1959, Genk, Belgium; 1 d. *Education:* Royal Atheneum of Maasmechelen; Conservatiors of Brussels and Gent; Private studies with Vera Rozsa, London; Margreet Honig, Amsterdam; Kristina Deutekom, Amsterdam. *Career:* Appearances with numerous orchestras; Concert tours to Belgium, Netherlands, Germany, England, Switzerland, Israel and Poland; Appearances on Radio and Television includes, BRT, BBC, WDR, NDR, SDR; Opera engagements in Innsbruck, Monte Carlo, Antwerp, Montpellier, Liège and Versailles, Sang Fulvia in Handel's Ezio at Halle, 1998. *Recordings:* L'Infedeltà Delusa; Concert Arias; Flavio by Handel, Deutsche Schallplattenpreis; L'Incoronazione di Poppea by Monteverdi; Die Israeliten in der Wüste, C P E Bach; Requiem/Mozart; La Guiditta/Almeida; Die Heirat Widerwillen/Humperdinck; CD: Mahler's 4th Symphony. *Honours:* 1st Prize Singing, National Competition for the Youth of Belgium; Alex Devries Scholarship, Roeping Foundation. *Current Management:* Internationaal Concertbureau Arien. *Address:* Platte-Lostr 341, B03010 Kessel-Lo, Belgium.

**LOPARDO, Frank;** American singer (tenor); b. 23 Dec. 1957, New York; m. Carolyn J. Montalbano 1982; two s. *Education:* Queen's Coll. New York and Juilliard School of Music. *Career:* studied with Dr Robert White Jr; professional debut as Tamino in The Magic Flute, St Louis 1984; debut at La Scala, Milan 1987, Glyndebourne Festival 1987, Metropolitan Opera as Almaviva in Il Barbiere di Siviglia 1989–90; now appears regularly at leading opera houses and music festivals around the world; roles include Alfredo in La Traviata, Lensky in Eugene Onegin, Edgardo in Lucia di Lammermoor, The Duke in Rigoletto, Ferrando in Così fan tutte, Don Giovanni; also appears as soloist with leading orchestras and in recordings of such works as Mozart's Requiem, Carl Orff's Carmina Burana, Mozart's Don Giovanni and Così fan tutte, Verdi's Falstaff and La Traviata, as well as Rossini's Il Barbiere di Siviglia, Semiramide and L'Italiana in Algeri. *Honours:* Hon. DMus (Aaron Copland School of Music). *Address:* c/o Royal Opera House, Covent Garden, London, WC2E 9DD, England; 167 Shaw Avenue, Valley Stream, New York, NY 11580; Metropolitan Opera, Lincoln Center, New York, NY 10023, USA. *Telephone:* (516) 568-0355. *Fax:* (516) 568-0355.

**LÓPEZ-COBOS, Jesús,** DPhil; Spanish conductor; *Music Director, Teatro Real, Madrid*; b. 25 Feb. 1940, Toro; s. of Lorenzo López and Gregoria Cobos. *Education:* Madrid Univ. (philosophy), Madrid Conservatory (composition) and Vienna Acad. (conducting). *Career:* worked with major orchestras including London Symphony, Royal Philharmonic, Philharmonia, Concertgebouw, Vienna Philharmonic, Vienna Symphony, Berlin Philharmonic, Hamburg NDR, Munich Philharmonic, Cleveland, Chicago Symphony, New York Philharmonic, Philadelphia, Pittsburgh Symphony; conducted new opera productions at La Scala, Milan, Covent Garden, London and Metropolitan Opera, New York; Gen. Musikdirektor, Deutsche Oper, Berlin 1981–90; Prin. Guest Conductor London Philharmonic Orchestra 1981–86; Prin. Conductor and Artistic Dir, Spanish Nat. Orchestra 1984–89; Music Dir, Cincinnati Symphony Orchestra 1986–2001 (now Music Dir Emer.), Music Dir Lausanne Chamber Orchestra 1990–2000, Orchestre Français des Jeunes 1998–2001, Teatro Real, Madrid 2002–. *Recordings include:* Bruckner symphonies, Haydn symphonies; Donizetti's Lucia di Lammermoor, Rossini's Otello and recital discs with José Carreras; works by Mahler, Respighi, Franck, de Falla, Villa-Lobos and Richard Strauss; Rossini's Il Barbiere di Siviglia and L'Italiana in Algeri; Il Comte Ory, Manon, Les Contes d'Hoffmann, Il Viaggio a Reims. *Honours:* Cross of Merit (1st Class) (FRG) 1989; Officier des Arts et des Lettres 2001; Dr hc (Arts Univ. Cincinnati); First Prize, Besançon Int. Conductors' Competition 1969, Prince of Asturias Award (Spanish Govt) 1981, Founders Award, American Soc. of Composers, Authors and Publrs 1988, Fine Arts Medal (Spain) 2001. *Address:* 8 Chemin de Bellerive, 1007 Lausanne, Switzerland. *Fax:* (21) 6010852 (office). *Website:* www.teatro-real.com (office).

**LOPEZ-YANEZ, Jorge;** singer (tenor); b. 1963, Mexico. *Education:* studied in Mexico City and California. *Career:* debut, Long Beach Opera in 1986 as Rossillon in Die Lustige Witwe; European debut at Hanover in 1988 as the Duke of Mantua; Düsseldorf and Stuttgart, 1988–89 as Ramiro in La Cenerentola; Further engagements as Fenton at Los Angeles and Bordeaux, Oronte in Alcina at the Paris Châtelet, Rossini's Almaviva at Munich, Donizetti's Tonio at Zürich and Alfredo in La Traviata at the Vienna Staatsoper, 1992; Glyndebourne debut in 1995 as Pyrrhus in the British stage premiere of Rossini's Ermione; Sang Nemorino at Santiago and Ernesto at Turin, 1998; Sang Ramiro in Cenerentola at Monte Carlo, 2000; Alfredo for Australian Opera, 2001. *Current Management:* Robert Gilder & Co., Enterprise House, 59–65 Upper Ground, London, SE1 9PQ, England.

*Telephone:* (20) 7928-9008. *Fax:* (20) 7928-9755. *E-mail:* rgilder@robert-gilder.com.

**LORAND, Colette;** Singer (Soprano); b. 7 Jan. 1923, Zürich, Switzerland. *Education:* Musikhochschule Hanover; Zürich with Frau Hirzel. *Career:* Debut: Basle 1946, as Marguerite in Faust; Frankfurt Opera 1951–56, notably as the Queen of Night; Hamburg Opera from 1955, often in operas by Henze, Penderecki and Orff; Edinburgh Festival 1955; Lisbon 1961, as Constanze in Die Entführung; Deutsche Oper Berlin 1972, in the premiere of Fortner's Elisabeth Tudor; Created roles in Orff's De Temporum fine Comoedia, Salzburg Festival, 1973, and Reimann's Lear, Munich 1978 (as Regan, repeated at the Paris Opéra, 1982). *Recordings:* Lear and De Temporum fine Comoedia; Orff's Prometheus. *Address:* c/o Bayerische Staatsoper, Postfach 745, 8000 Munich, Germany.

**LORANGE, Nicole;** Singer (Soprano); b. 28 Nov. 1942, Montreal, Canada. *Education:* Studied with Pierrette Alarie and at the Vienna Music Academy with Erik Werba. *Career:* Sang at first in concert and made stage debut at the Linz Landestheater in 1969 as Desdemona; Further appearances with the Canadian Opera Company as Musetta in 1972, and Opéra Montreal as Tosca in 1980; Metropolitan Opera, 1982–84 as Butterfly, Adriana Lecouvreur and Francesca da Rimini; Other roles include Donna Elvira and Offenbach's Giulietta; Many concert appearances. *Address:* c/o L'Opéra de Montréal, 260 de Maisonneuve Boulevard West Montreal, Province Québec H2H 1Y9, Canada.

**LORD, Bernadette;** Singer (Soprano); b. 1965, Derby, England. *Education:* Studied at the Guildhall School and with Suzanne Danco in Florence; Further study at the European Arts Centre, 1988. *Career:* Joined Opera Wallonie, Liège, and sang Helena in Schubert's Der Häusliche Krieg in Belgium, Netherlands and Paris; Glyndebourne and Covent Garden debuts as Cis in Albert Herring; Other roles include Despina for British Youth Opera at the Cheltenham Festival, Miss Wordsworth in Albert Herring, Lucia in The Rape of Lucretia, Gretel for Opera East, Susanna and Barbarina in Le nozze di Figaro; Sang Jano in Jenůfa at Covent Garden, 1993. *Address:* c/o Opéra Royal de Wallonie, 1 rue des Dominicains, B–4000 Liege, Belgium.

**LORENTZEN, Bent;** Composer; b. 11 Feb. 1935, Stenvad, Denmark; m. Edith Kaerulf Moeller 1958; one s. three d. *Education:* Royal Acad. of Music, Copenhagen, 1960. *Career:* performances throughout Europe of works including Euridice, Die Music kommt mit äusserst bekannt vor!, Eine Wundersame Liebesgeschichte, Stalten Mette, Toto, Fackeltanz, Samba, Pianoconcerto Nordic Music Days, Saxophone Concerto, two choral songs to Enzensberger, 1991, Bill and Julia (opera), The Magic Brilliant, (The Danish National Opera), 1993; The Scatterbrain, Royal Theatre, 1995; Pergolesi's Home Service. *Compositions include:* Purgatorio, choral; Granite; Quartz; Syncretism; Wunderblumen; Flamma; Zauberspiegel; Farbentiegel; Blütenweiss; Colori; Concerto for oboe; Cello Concerto; Hunting Concerto; Double Concerto; Samba; Paradiesvogel; Graffiti; Purgatorio; 3 Madrigals; 5 Motets; Genesis; Stabat Mater; Canon I–V for 2 accordions; New Choral Dramatics; Ammen Dammen Des; Round; 5 easy Piano Pieces, Flood of Paradise; Olof Palme for mixed choir; Comics; 3 Latin Suites; Venezia; Tordenskiold; Der Steppenwolf, opera, 2000. *Recordings include:* The Bottomless Pit; Visions; Cloud-Drift; Mambo, Intersection, Puncti, Triplex, Groppo, Nimbus, Cruor, Goldranken; Abgrund; Die Musik kommt mir äusserst bekannt vor!; Syncretism; A Wonderous Love Story; Sol; Luna; Mars, for organ, 1985; Mercurius; Jupiter; Venus; Saturnus; Umbra, Paesaggio, Dunkelblau, Round, Cyclus I–IV; Piano and oboe concertos; Regenbogen; Comics; Lines; Tears; Orfeo Suite; Intrada; Alpha and Omega; Pergolesi's Home Service, theatre, 1998. *Publications:* Ej Sikkelej, 1967; Recorder System, 1962–64; Musikens AHC, 1969; Mer om Musiken, 1972; Introduction to Electronic Music, 1969. *Current Management:* Edition Wilhelm Hansen, Bornholmsgade 1, 1266 Copenhagen K, Denmark. *Address:* Sotoften 37, 2820 Genofte, Denmark.

**LORENZ, Andrew (Bela);** Australian violinist; *Senior Lecturer in Violin and Viola, University of Southern Queensland*; b. 17 Oct. 1951, Melbourne, Vic.; m. Wendy Joy Lorenz, 1 s. *Education:* DSCM Performers Diploma and Teachers Diploma, Sydney Conservatory of Music, 1970. *Career:* Recitals; Concerto, radio and television performances; Deputy Leader, Melbourne Elizabethen Trust Orchestra, 1972; Led for D'Oyly Carte Opera Company, Sadler's Wells, England, 1973–74; Leader, New England Ensemble (resident piano quartet) and Lecturer, Music Department, University of New England, Armidale, New South Wales, Australia, 1975–82; Founding Member and Leader, New England Sinfonia; World tours with New England Ensemble; Associate Concertmaster, Adelaide Symphony Orchestra, 1983–86; Leader, Australian Piano Trio, 1983–87; Senior Lecturer in Strings, University of Southern Queensland, Toowoomba, Queensland; Leader, Phoenix Ensemble; Director, McGregor Chamber Music School. *Recordings:* Works by Beethoven, Turina, Margaret Sutherland, Mozart, Fauré, John McCabe, Mendelssohn, Goossens; Mary Mageau; Sundry chamber works and Concerto Soloist with many of Australia's leading orchestras and Slovak Radio Symphony; Australian premieres of Benjamin, McCabe and Myslivecek Concertos. *Honours:* Winner, Victorian ABC Concerto Competition, 1972. *Address:* 21 Merlin Court, M/S 852 Toowoomba Mail Servce, Queensland 4352, Australia.

**LORENZ, Gerlinde;** Singer (Soprano); b. 1939, Chemnitz, Germany. *Education:* Studied at the Vienna Music Academy. *Career:* Sang at the Vienna Volksoper from 1967, Staatsoper from 1972; Cologne Opera, 1971–86, with debut as Mimi; Bielefeld, 1985, as Lola in Schreker's Irrelohe and

Oldenburg, 1992, as Ortrud in Lohengrin; Other engagements at Zürich, the Munich Staatsoper, Deutsche Oper Berlin and Frankfurt; Further roles include Mozart's Donna Elvira and Donna Anna, Wagner's Elsa, Eva and Sieglinde, Strauss's Elektra and Elisabeth de Valois; Concerts in Vienna, Salzburg, Paris and elsewhere. *Address:* c/o Oldenburgische Staatstheater, Theaterwall 18, 2900 Oldenburg, Germany.

**LORENZ, Ricardo,** MM, PhD; Venezuelan composer; b. 24 May 1961, Maracaibo. *Education:* Olivares Conservatory, Landaeta Conservatory, Indiana Univ. and Univ. of Chicago. *Career:* Acting Dir, Indiana Univ. Latin American Music Center 1987–92, Visiting Assoc. Dir 2003–04; composer-in-residence, Chicago Symphony Orchestra 1998–2002, Billings Symphony Orchestra, Montana 1998–99. *Compositions include:* Sinfonietta concertante 1987, Concerto for Orchestra 1993, En Tren Vá Changó 2001. *Recordings:* Pataruco: Concerto for Venezuelan Maracas and Orchestra, Está Lloviendo Afuera y No Hay Agua. *Publications:* Scores and Readings at Indiana University Latin American Music Center 1995. *Address:* Latin American Music Center, School of Music, Indiana University, Bloomington, IN 47405, USA (office). *Telephone:* (812) 855-2991 (office). *Fax:* (812) 855-4936 (office). *E-mail:* rieloren@indiana.edu (office). *Website:* www.music.indiana.edu (office).

**LORENZ, Siegfried;** Singer (Baritone); b. 30 Aug. 1945, Berlin, Germany. *Education:* Studied in Berlin. *Career:* Debut: Komische Oper Berlin, 1969, in The Love for Three Oranges; Sang at the Komische Oper and Staatsoper Berlin, notably as Guglielmo, Wolfram, Mozart's Count, Germont, and Posa in Don Carlos; Agamemnon in Gluck's Iphigenia in Aulis, 1987; Soloist at the Leipzig Gewandhaus from 1974, in concert music by Bach, Brahms and Schubert; International appearances in Lieder recitals. *Recordings include:* Winterreise, Die schöne Müllerin and the Brahms Requiem. *Address:* c/o Gewandhausorchester, Augustusplatz 8, 04109 Leipzig, Germany.

**LORIMER, Heather;** Singer (Soprano); b. 1961, Wallasey, Cheshire; m. Gerard Quinn. *Education:* Studied at the Royal Northern College of Music, Manchester with Frederick Cox and now with Iris Dell'Acqua. *Career:* Scottish Opera Go Round, Mimi in La Bohème, 1987; Glyndebourne Festival and Touring Opera, Constanze, Die Entführung aus dem Serail, 1988; Countess, Le nozze di Figaro, 1989; Opera 80, Tatiana in Eugene Onegin in 1989 and Hanna Glawari in The Merry Widow, 1990; Travelling Opera, Mimi; Countess; Donna Elvira; Don Giovanni; Fiordiligi in Così fan tutte; Violetta in La Traviata and Micaela in Carmen; English Touring Opera, Mimi, 1994; Education tours for Glyndebourne, Opera 80 and English National Opera's Lillian Bayliss Programme; Other roles performed include: Giorgetta, Il Tabarro; Liu, Turandot; Norina, Don Pasquale; Rosina, Il Barbiere di Siviglia; Rosalinde, Die Fledermaus; Rosario, Goyescas; Dirce, Medea; Leila, The Pearl Fishers and in 1993 she created the title role in Michael Finnissy's Thérèse Raquin, for the Royal Opera's Garden Venture; Concert repertoire includes, Verdi Requiem; Rossini Stabat Mater; Dvořák Requiem; Elijah; Carmina Burana; Brahms Requiem; Fauré Requiem; Sea Symphony and The Kingdom. *Honours:* International Opera and Bel Canto Duet Competition, Antwerp, Gerard Quinn; Scottish Opera John Noble Competition. *Address:* 92 Sturla Road, Chatham, Kent ME4 5QH, England.

**LORIOD, Yvonne;** French pianist; b. 20 Jan. 1924, Houilles; d. of Gaston Loriod and Simone Loriod (née Bilhaut); m. Olivier Messiaen 1961 (died 1992). *Career:* Prof. of Piano, Conservatoire National de Musique, Paris; specializes in interpretation of complete works including Bach's Well-Tempered Klavier, Beethoven sonatas, Mozart piano concertos, works of Chopin and Debussy and complete works of Olivier Messiaen; first performances in Paris of Bartok's 1st and 2nd concertos, Schoenberg concerto and works by Messiaen, Jolivet, Boulez and other contemporary composers. *Honours:* 7 Grand Prix du Disque, Grand Prix de la Sacem 1986; Commdr Légion d'honneur, Officier des Arts et Lettres, Grand Officier du Mérite. *Address:* c/o Bureau de Concerts Maurice Werner, 17 rue du 4 Septembre, 75002 Paris, France.

**LORTIÉ, Louis;** Concert Pianist; b. 27 April 1959, Quebec, Canada. *Education:* Studied in Quebec with Yvonne Hubert. *Career:* Debut: 1972, Montreal Symphony Orchestra,; World-wide appearances from 1978, with concerts throughout Canada and tours to Europe, USA and Far East; Founded the Lortié-Berick-Lysy Trio, 1995; Engagements as soloist and conductor with Orchestra di Padova e del Veneto; Prokofiev's 1st Concerto at the London Prom Concerts, 2001 Ravel's concerto for the Left Hand at the London Proms, 2002. *Address:* c/o Cramer/Marder Artists, 3436 Springhill Road, Lafayette, CA 94549, USA.

**LOSKUTOVA, Irina;** Singer (Soprano); b. 1965, Salavat, Bashkiria, Russia. *Education:* Graduated State Mussorgsky Conservatoire of Sverdlovsk, 1989. *Career:* Appearances with Mussorgsky Opera and Ballet Theatre, St Petersburg, from 1989; Kirov Opera, Mariinsky Theatre, from 1995, as Tatiana, Yaroslavna in Prince Igor, Mimi, Elisabeth de Valois, Madama Butterfly and Paulina in The Gambler by Prokofiev: Tours of Europe and North America with the Mussorgsky and the Kirov Opera companies; Further roles include Tchaikovsky's Iolanta and Maria (Mazeppa) and Katerina Izmailova: Sang Lyubka in Semyon Kotko by Prokofiev with the Kirov at Covent Garden, 2000 (British premiere). *Recordings include:* Mazeppa. *Honours:* Prizewinner, 1989 Mussorgsky Vocal Competition. *Address:* c/o Kirov Opera, Mariinsky Theatre, Theatre Square, St Petersburg, Russia.

**LOTHIAN, Helen;** Singer (mezzo-soprano); b. 1968, Scotland. *Education:* Studied at the Royal Scottish Academy and the Guildhall School; Further study with Patricia Hay in Scotland. *Career:* Concert appearances throughout the United Kingdom in music by Verdi, Bruckner, Beethoven, Mozart and Haydn; Recitals at the Covent Garden Festival, Clonter Opera Farm and elsewhere; Sang the Lady Artist in Berg's Lulu with the BBC Symphony Orchestra, 1995; Opera engagements include Christoph Rilke's Song of Love and Death by Matthus, for Glyndebourne Touring Opera; Dorabella, Carmen and Cherubino for British Youth Opera, Dardane in Haydn's L'Incontro Improvviso at Garsington and Mozart's Third Lady at the Covent Garden Festival; Romeo in Bellini's I Capuleti e i Montecchi for Castleward Opera, 1995; Royal Opera and Scottish Opera debuts as Flora in La Traviata, 1996. *Current Management:* Askonas Holt Ltd, Lonsdale Chambers, 27 Chancery Lane, London, WC2A 1PF, England. *Telephone:* (20) 7400-1700. *Fax:* (20) 7400-1799. *E-mail:* info@askonasholt.co.uk. *Website:* www.askonasholt.co.uk.

**LOTT, Dame Felicity Ann Emwhyla,** DBE, BA, LRAM, FRAM; British singer (soprano); b. 8 May 1947, Cheltenham; d. of John A. Lott and Whyla Lott (née Williams); m. 1st Robin Golding 1973 (divorced); m. 2nd Gabriel Woolf 1984; one d. *Education:* Pate's Grammar School for Girls, Cheltenham, Royal Holloway Coll., Univ. of London and Royal Acad. of Music. *Career:* debut with ENO as Pamina in Die Zauberflöte 1975; prin. roles at Glyndebourne, Covent Garden, ENO, WNO, New York Metropolitan Opera, Vienna, La Scala, Paris Opéra, Brussels, Hamburg, Munich, Chicago, San Francisco, Dresden; wide recital repertoire; founder mem. Songmakers' Almanac; mem. Equity, Incorporated Soc. of Musicians. *Roles include:* Countess in Le Nozze de Figaro; Ellen Orford in Peter Grimes; Fiordiligi in Così fan Tutti; Elvira in Don Giovanni; Xiphares in Mitridate; Marschallin in Der Rosenkavalier; Countess in Capriccio (Richard Strauss); many recitals with Graham Johnson and duets with Ann Murray; dvd of Offenbach's Hélène in La Belle Hélène and La Grande Duchesse. *Honours:* Hon. Fellow Royal Holloway Coll.; Officier des Arts et des Lettres 2000, Chevalier Légion d'honneur 2001; Dr hc (Sussex) 1990; Hon. DLitt (Loughborough) 1996; Hon. DMus (London) 1997, (Royal Scottish Acad. of Music and Drama) 1998, (Oxford) 2001; Kammersängerin, Bayerische Staatsoper, Munich 2003. *Current Management:* Askonas Holt Ltd, Lonsdale Chambers, 27 Chancery Lane, London, WC2A 1PF, England. *Telephone:* (20) 7400-1700. *Fax:* (20) 7400-0799. *E-mail:* info@askonasholt.co .uk (office). *Website:* www.askonasholt.co.uk (office); www.felicitylott.de.

**LOTT, Maria-Elisabeth;** Concert Violinist; b. 1987, Germany. *Education:* Studies with Josef Rissin at Karlsruhe, 1991–. *Career:* Concert engagements throughout Europe and the USA, including British debut performances Feb 2000 with the Bournemouth Symphony Orchestra and Royal Liverpool Philharmonic Orchestra, playing Paganini's First concerto; Further appearances with the Minnesota Orchestra and Malaysia Philharmonic in Kuala Lumpur; Season 2000–01 with the London Philharmonic, Ensemble Orchestral de Paris, the Ulster Orchestra and NDR Hanover Orchestra. *Recordings include:* Album of Mozart, played on violin used by the composer in 1760's. *Address:* IMG Artists, Lovell House, 616 Chiswick High Rd, London W4 5RX, England.

**LOTTI, Antonio;** Singer (Tenor); b. 1957, Lucca, Italy. *Education:* Studied at São Paulo, Brazil. *Career:* Debut: São Paulo, 1982, as Cavaradossi; Sang in opera throughout South America, Europe from 1987; Verdi's Stiffelio in Amsterdam, Oslo and Copenhagen as Cavaradossi; Paolo in Francesca da Rimini at Bologna, Don Carlos at Catania; Bonn Opera from 1994, as Pery in Il Guaramento by Gomes, Turiddu in Cavalleria Rusticana, and Hoffmann; Other roles include Rodolfo in Luisa Miller. *Address:* c/o Oper der Stadt Bonn, Am Boeselagerlof 1, 53111 Bonn, Germany.

**LOU, Qian-Gui;** Chinese singer (tenor) (retd); b. 1923. *Education:* Aurora Univ. *Career:* Sang roles in opera including Pinkerton in Madama Butterfly, 1958, Lensky in Eugene Onegin, 1962; Soloist, concerts in USSR, Poland, Romania, Czechoslovakia, North Korea, 1953–54; Solo recitals, Beijing, Shanghai, elsewhere in China, 1978–97, and at Redlands Summer Music Festival, USA, 1990; Appearances on Central TV programmes, MTV; Documentary films for stage performances; Artistic Dir, Central Opera House of China, also Savonlinna Opera Festival, Finland (1988); fmr Prof. of Voice, Central Conservatory of Music, Beijing; Mem., Jury for Nat. Vocal Competition, China. *Recordings:* Album released in Moscow, 1954; Album released in Beijing, 1956; Album released in Beijing, 1980; Album released in Guangzhou, 1983; The Treasurable Version of 100 Anthologies of Vocal Music performed by famous Chinese Musicians, 1998. *Honours:* Lifetime Achievement Award, Golden Chime Award 2004. *Address:* 5-102 Building #50, Tian Tong Yuan, East District III, Chang Ping, Beijing 102218, People's Republic of China (home). *Telephone:* (10) 61764939 (home).

**LOUGHRAN, James,** FRNCM, FRSAMD; British conductor; b. 30 June 1931, Glasgow; s. of James Loughran and Agnes (née Fox) Loughran; m. 1st Nancy Coggon 1961 (divorced 1983, died 1996); two s.; m. 2nd Ludmila Navratil 1985. *Education:* Glasgow, Bonn, Amsterdam and Milan. *Career:* Assoc. Conductor, Bournemouth Symphony Orchestra 1962–65; debut Royal Opera House, Covent Garden 1964; Prin. Conductor BBC Scottish Symphony Orchestra 1965–71; Prin. Conductor and Musical Adviser, Hallé Orchestra 1971–83, Conductor Laureate 1983–91; debut New York Philharmonic with Westminster Choir 1972; Prin. Conductor Bamberg Symphony Orchestra 1979–83; Chief Guest Conductor BBC Welsh Symphony Orchestra 1987–90; Guest Conductor of prin. orchestras of Europe, America, Australia and Japan, Guest

Perm. Conductor, Japan Philharmonic Symphony Orchestra 1993; Chief Conductor Århus Symphony Orchestra, Denmark 1996–2003; BBC Proms 1965–89 including The Last Night 5 times 1977–85; recorded complete Beethoven Symphonies with London Symphony Orchestra as contribution to European Broadcasting Union Beethoven Bicentenary Celebrations 1969–70; recordings with Hallé, London Philharmonic, Philharmonia, BBC Symphony, Århus Symphony and Scottish Chamber Orchestras. *Honours:* Liveryman, Worshipful Co. of Musicians 1992; Hon. DMus (Sheffield) 1983; First Prize, Philharmonia Orchestra Conducting Competition 1961, Mancunian of the Year 1981, Gold Disc EMI 1983. *Address:* 34 Cleveden Drive, Glasgow, G12 0RX, Scotland. *Telephone:* (141) 337-2091 (home). *Fax:* (141) 357-0643 (home).

**LOUIE, Alexina Diane,** BMus, MA; Canadian composer; *National Arts Centre Award Composer;* b. 30 July 1949, Vancouver, BC. *Education:* Univ. of British Columbia and Univ. of California at San Diego, USA. *Career:* professional solo pianist, Vancouver, BC 1966–71; music copyist 1970–73; Instructor of Music, Pasadena City Coll., CA, USA 1974–80; Composer-in-Residence, Canadian Opera Co. 1996–2002; Nat. Arts Centre Award Composer 2002–. *Compositions include:* Molly 1972, O Magnum Mysterium: In Memoriam Glenn Gould 1982, Music for a Thousand Autumns for 12 performers 1983, Songs of Paradise, The Eternal Earth, Winter Music, Music for Heaven and Earth, Music From Night's Edge (piano quintet) 1988, Love Songs for a Small Planet for chamber choir and ensemble 1989, Obsessions (Their Own Words) for baritone and orchestra 1993, Neon 1995, Shattered Night, Shivering Stars for orchestra 1997, The Scarlet Princess (mainstage opera for soloists, chorus, orchestra, clarinet, cello and piano) 2004, Imaginary Opera for 12 performers 2005. *Honours:* Order of Ontario 1997; Composition Grantee Canada Council for the Arts 1974, 1980, 1981, Composer of the Year, Canada Music Council 1986, Juno Award 1988, Jules Léger Prize for Chamber Music 1999, Queen's Golden Jubilee Medal 2002. *Address:* c/o 41 Valleybrook Drive, Don Mills, Ontario, M3B 2S6, Canada (office).

**LOUKIANETS, Viktoria,** Ukrainian singer (soprano); b. 1965, Kiev, Russia. *Education:* Kiev Music School and Kiev Conservatoire. *Career:* soloist with Ukrainian Opera, Kiev 1989; guest appearances in France, Portugal, Czech Republic, Italy and Switzerland; principal with the Vienna Staatsoper, singing Adina (L'Elisir d'amore), Elvira (L'Italiana in Algeri), Rosina, the Queen of Night and Olympia (Contes d'Hoffman); other roles include Oscar in Ballo in Maschera, Donna Anna, Wagner's Woglinde; appearances include Violetta at the Salzburg Festival, New York Met debut 1996, Opéra Bastille, Paris 1998, La Scala Milan debut as the Queen of Night 1995, Gilda in Rigoletto at Covent Garden, London 1996–97, Berthe in Le Prophète at the Vienna Staatsoper 1998, Violetta at Covent Garden and the Vienna Volksoper 2000–01. *Honours:* Mozart Bicentennial Competition winner, Italy 1991, Maria Callas Competition winner, Athens 1991. *Current Management:* Opera-Connection Alste & Mödersheim, Leibnizstrasse 94, 10625 Berlin, Germany. *Telephone:* 31996688. *Fax:* 31809739.

**LOUP, François;** singer (bass); b. 4 March 1940, Estavayer-le-lac, Switzerland. *Education:* studied piano organ, composition and singing at Fribourg. *Career:* sang at the Geneva Opera 1964–66, notably in the premiere of Monsieur de Pourceaugnac by Martin; Directed various vocal ensembles for which he harmonised motets, madrigals and Swiss folk songs; Soloist with the Ensemble Vocal de Lausanne, under Michel Corboz; Many performances of Baroque music, notably with the Societa Cameristica di Lugano and with the Opéra de Lyon, in Orfeo by Monteverdi; Oratorio performances in many European countries; Sang in Bizet's Docteur Miracle at the 1975 Spoleto Festival; Sang Bartolo in Le nozze di Figaro at Houston 1988, repeated at Glyndebourne 1989, later at the Albert Hall, London; San Diego and the Opéra de Lyon 1989, as Don Pasquale and as Balducci in Benvenuto Cellini; Season 1992 with Mozart's Bartolo at San Diego, Don Pasquale at Vancouver and the Sacristan in Tosca at San Francisco; Sang in La Bohème at the Met, 1994; Bailiff in Werther at Tel-Aviv, 1996; Debut as Don Pasquale and sang Rossini's Bartolo at Teatro Colón Buenos Aires, 1997; Sang Don Alfonso in Rio de Janeiro and in Florida, 2000; Other roles include Leporello, Figaro, Dulcamara, Masetto, Arkel, Pimen, Frère Laurent in Roméo et Juliette and Sarastro; Dedicatee of several contemporary compositions, and teacher of singing; Pupils include François Le Roux. *Current Management:* Trawick Artists Management, 1926 Broadway, New York, NY 10023, USA.

**LOVE, Shirley;** Singer (Mezzo-soprano); b. 6 Jan. 1940, Detroit, Michigan, USA. *Education:* Studies with Avery Crew in Detroit and Margaret Harshaw in New York; Continued study with Armen Bayajean in New York City. *Career:* Debut: Metropolitan Opera in 1963 in Die Zauberflöte; Remained in New York for 20 seasons, as Carmen, Dalila, Verdi's Maddalena, Amneris and Emilia, Rossini's Angelina and Rosina, Siebel in Faust, Pauline in The Queen of Spades and in operas by Ravel, Menotti and Bernstein; Guest appearances in Cincinnati, Chicago, Miami and Philadelphia; Sang at Baltimore in 1962, in the premiere of Kagen's Hamlet; Concert appearances in Amsterdam, Bologna and Florence; 3 recital tours of South Africa; Three television performances in the Live from the Met series, Otello, Il Barbiere di Seviglia, Der Rosenkavalier; Recent opera performances include: Albert Herring, Cleveland Opera; Cavalleria Rusticana, Milwaukee Florentine Opera; Festival appearances include: Mostly Mozart, New York; Basically Bach, New York; Saratoga festival (Philadelphia Orchestra); Blossom Festival, Cleveland; Madeira Bach Festival, Portugal. *Recordings:* Diary of One Who Vanished, Janáček; The Rake's Progress, Stravinsky. *Honours:* Arts Achievement Award, Wayne State University, 1990; Honorary Doctorate of Music, University of West Virginia, 1999; Listed in several Who's Who publications. *Address:* c/o Metropolitan Opera, Lincoln Center, New York, NY 10023, USA.

**LOVEDAY, Alan (Raymond);** Violinist; b. 29 Feb. 1928, England; m. Ruth Stanfield, 1952, 1 s., 1 d. *Education:* Private study; Royal College of Music, prizewinner. *Career:* Debut: Childhood debut, age 4; Debut in England, 1946; Numerous concerts, broadcasts, television appearances, the United Kingdom and abroad; Played with all leading conductors and orchestras; Ranges from Bach, on un-modernised violin, to contemporary music; Professor, Royal College of Music, 1955–72; Soloist, Academy of St Martin-in-the-Fields. *Address:* c/o Academy of St Martin-in-the-Fields, Raine House, Waine Street, Wapping, London E1 9RG, England.

**LOWENTHAL, Jerome;** Concert Pianist; b. 11 Feb. 1932, Philadelphia, Pennsylvania, USA; m. Ronit Amir, 7 July 1959, 2 d. *Education:* BA, University of Pennsylvania, 1953; MS, Juilliard School of Music, 1956; Premier License de Concert, Ecole Normale de Musique; Piano studies, Olga Samaroff, William Kapell, Eduard Steuermann, Alfred Cortot. *Career:* Debut: Philadelphia Orchestra, 1945; Appearances with orchestras of: New York, Philadelphia, Boston, Cleveland, Israel Philharmonic, Stockholm, Chicago, Los Angeles, Detroit, Pittsburgh; Conductors: Monteux, Stokowski, Bernstein, Ormandy, Giulini, Tennstedt, Mehta, Ozawa, Barenboim, Comissiona; Tours of Southeast Asia, New Zealand, Latin America, Western Europe, USSR, Poland, Romania; Piano Faculty, Juilliard School, 1990–. *Recordings:* Rorem Concerto No. 3, Louisville-Mester; Tchaikovsky Concerti 1, 2 and 3, London Symphony Orchestra Comissiona; Liszt Opera Paraphrases; Gershwin Concerto in F and Rhapsody in Blue, Utah Symphony Orchestra; Sinding, Sonata and short pieces for solo piano; Liszt Concerto No. 1, No. 3, Totentanz, Malediction: Vancouver Symphony, Commissiona. *Honours:* Laureat, Darmstadt Competition 1957; Busoni Competition 1957; Reine Elizabeth 1960. *Current Management:* Herbert Barrett. *Address:* 865 West End Avenue, Apt 11A, NY 10025, USA.

**LOY, Christof;** Stage Director; b. 1950, Essen, Germany. *Education:* Folkwang Hochschule, Essen. *Career:* Staged Falstaff at Maastricht, Die Entführung at Freiburg and La Damnation de Faust at Bremen; Mozart's La finta giardiniera at Mannheim, Le nozze di Figaro in Brussels and Idomeneo at Bonn; Manon, Lucia di Lammermoor, Orfeo and Don Carlos for the Deutsche Oper an Rhein, Dusseldorf; Don Giovanni at Graz, Alcina for Hamburg Opera and Carmen in Cologne; Season 2002 with Gluck's Iphigénie en Aulide at Glyndebourne and Ariadne auf Naxos at Covent Garden, London; Further productions include Der Rosekavalier and Eugene Onegin for the Théâtre de la Monnaie, Brussels, and The Queen of Spades at Bremen. *Address:* c/o Royal Opera House (contracts), Covent Garden, London, WC2, England.

**LOYOLA FERNÁNDEZ, José,** PhD; Cuban composer, teacher and musician (flute); *Professor of Composition, Orchestration and Counterpoint, Instituto Superior de Arte de La Habana;* b. 12 March 1941, Cienfuegos; s. of Efraín Loyola. *Education:* School of Music of the Nat. School of the Arts, Havana, School for Advanced Studies in Music, Warsaw, Poland and Fryderyk Chopin Acad., Warsaw. *Career:* mem., Cienfuegos Nursery Musical Band 1950, Cienfuegos Firemen's Corps Band 1952–59, Loyola Orchestra 1959–62, Central Army Band 1959–60; flautist and composer, Youth and Students Orchestra of the Eighth Festival of Youth and Students, Helsinki, Finland 1962; teacher, Nat. School of the Arts, Havana 1973–75; Dir Amadeo Roldán Conservatory, Havana 1974–75; Nat. Co-ordinator, Gen. Office of Art Schools 1975–76; teacher of composition, Faculty of Music, Higher Inst. for the Arts 1976–, currently Prof. of Composition, Orchestration and Counterpoint, teaching Vice-Rector 1976–78, Dean 1977–78; Lecturer, Second Bambuco Festival, Mexico 1990; mem. Nat. Union of Writers and Artists of Cuba (pres. music bd 1976–77, sec. 1979, deputy pres. 1983–96, pres. 1996–), Cuban Fryderyk Chopin Soc. (pres. 1983–), Union of Writers and Artists of Cuba Golden Boleros Festival (pres. 1987). *Compositions:* Los piroperos 1960–69, Mi rico chachachá 1960–69, Lo sabe Isabel 1960–69, Sinfonietta 1965, Música para flauta y cuerdas 1968, Tres imágenes poéticas 1969, Antipoemas 1970, Música viva No. 1 for percussion 1971, Monzón y el Rey de Koré (opera) 1973, Poética del guerrillero for orchestra 1976, Música viva No. 2 1976, Música viva No. 3 1978, Música viva No. 4 1979, Canto negro 1979, Variaciones folklóricas 1982, Tres piezas cubanas for piano 1985, Tropicalia I 1987, Tropicalia II 1988, Canción del Soy Todo 1990. *Publications:* Música Cabana (ed.); contrib. numerous articles. *Honours:* Eighth Festival of Youth and Students Best Soloist of Popular Music, Helsinki 1962, 26 de Julio Musical Contest Chamber Music Prize, Centenary of Karol Symanowsky medal 1982, winner Union of Writers and Artists of Cuba Nat. Composition Contest 1985, Merit of Polish Culture 1985, winner Cuban Nat. Cultural Award 1988. *Address:* c/o Ana Margarita Cabrera, Instituto Superior de Arte, Calle 120, No. 1110 entre 9na y 13, Cubanacan Playa, Havana 12100, Cuba (office).

**LU, Jia;** Conductor; b. 1964, Shanghai, China. *Career:* Chief Conductor of the National Youth Orchestra of China, 1987; Further engagements with the Leipzig Gewandhaus, Berlin Symphony nd NDR Hamburg Symphony Orchestras; Chief Conductor and Music Director of the Trieste Opera, 1991–95; Principal Conductor of the Orchestra della Toscana, Principal Conductor of Opera di Genova, Carlo Felice, Florence, appearances with the Santa Cecilia Orchestra, Rome, and at the Bologna Opera; Season 1995–96 included debuts with the Bamberg and Chicago Symphonies, English Chamber Orchestra, Deutsch Oper Berlin, Orchestre National de Lyon and

Chamber Orchestra of Europe; Season 1996–97 with the Oslo and St Petersburg Philharmonic Orchestras; Artistic Adviser and Principal Conductor of Norrkoping Symphony Orchestra; Performed with the Stockholm Philharmonic, Hong Kong Philharmonic, Bournemouth Symphony Orchestra, Halle Orchestra and the Malaysian Philharmonic in Kuala Lumpur. *Honours:* Winner, National Chinese Conducting Competition, 1986; First Prize, Pedrotti Competition in Trento, 1990. *Current Management:* IMG Artists, Lovell House, 616 Chiswick High Road, London W4 5RX, England.

**LU, Yen;** Composer; b. 20 Nov. 1930, Nanking, China. *Education:* Department of Music, Taiwan National Normal University; Mannes College of Music, New York; Department of Music, University of Philadelphia, Pennsylvania, USA. *Career:* Musical World of Lu Yen, concert of his music, National Concert Hall, Taipei, 1995; Festival des Compositeurs Taïwanais, Paris, 1996; Composer, Soochow University, Taipei, Taiwan; mem, American Society of Composers, Authors and Publishers. *Compositions:* Fantasy for Orchestra I, Song of the Sea, 1987; Music for Fifteen Strings, 1987; Song, for solo violoncello, 1997. *Recordings:* Piece for Four Hands, played by Rolf-Peter Wille and Lina Yeh, 1988. *Publications:* Piece for Seven Players, 1973; Concert Piece I, Long T'ao Sha, 1976. *Honours:* Taiwan National Jing Din Prize for Recordings, 1988; Taiwan National Prize for Arts, 1992, 1998. *Address:* Department of Music, Soochow University, Shih Lin, Taipei, Taiwan.

**LUBAVIN, Leonid;** Singer (Tenor); b. 1962, Krasnodar, Russia. *Education:* State Academy of Theatre, Music and Cinema, Leningrad, 1980–85; State Rimsky-Korsakov Conservatory of St Petersburg, 1989–94. *Career:* Debut: Narraboth in Salome at the Mariinsky Theatre, 1995; Principal Soloist of the Mariinsky Theatre (Kirov Opera), 1995–; Appearances as Faust, Lohengrin, Tamino, Lensky, Fenton and Hermann in The Queen of Spades; Almaviva in Il Barbiere di Siviglia; Tours with the Kirov to Japan, France, Italy and Germany; Iskra in Mazeppa and Yurodivity in Boris Godunov, New York Met, and tour of Latin America, 1998; With New Israel Opera, Tel-Aviv in Falstaff by Verdi as Fenton, 1998; Performed Das Lied von der Erde by Mahler, Mikkeli Festival, Finland, 1997; Other roles include Benvenuto Cellini by Berlioz at the St Petersburg Opera with the Mariinsky Orchestra, and with the Rotterdam Philharmonic, 1999. *Address:* 12 Krasnoarmeiskaya 23-8, St Petersburg 198103, Russia.

**LUBBOCK, John;** Conductor; b. 18 March 1945, Hertfordshire, England. *Education:* Chorister at St George's Chapel, Windsor then Royal Academy of Music; Conducting studies with Sergiu Celibidache. *Career:* Founder, Camden Chamber Orchestra, 1967 becoming in 1972 the Orchestra of St John's Smith Square; Frequent concerts at St John's Church in Westminster and on tour in the United Kingdom, Europe, USA and Canada; Guest Conductor with City of Birmingham Symphony, London Philharmonic, BBC Scottish Symphony, Bournemouth Symphony and Sinfonietta, London Mozart Players, Irish Chamber Orchestra, Stuttgart Symphony Orchestra and Netherlands Chamber Orchestra; Works regularly with the Ulster Orchestra and as Principal Conductor with Belfast Philharmonic Society and the Oxford University Orchestra; Worked with the Hallé Orchestra in 1992 and again in 1995; Conducted Berio's Sinfonia at Barbican Hall, 1985 and the premiere of Meirion Bowen's orchestration of Tippett's The Heart's Assurance; Schumann's Requiem and Dvořák's Symphonic Variations at St John's, 1997; Conducted Orchestra of St John's at the London Proms, 2002. *Recordings include:* Arnold Guitar Concerto and Rodrigo Concierto de Aranjuez; Haydn Symphonies Nos 44 and 49; Mendelssohn Symphonies Nos 3 and 4; Schubert Symphony No. 5; Stravinsky Apollo and Orpheus; Tchaikovsky Serenade; Vivaldi Concerti op 10, all with the Orchestra of St John's Smith Square. *Current Management:* Owen-White Management. *Address:* c/o Owen-White Management, 14 Nightingale Lane, London N8 7QU, England.

**LUBIN, Steven,** BA, MS, PhD; American pianist; *Adjunct Professor, School of the Arts, Purchase College, State University of New York (SUNY)*; b. 22 Feb. 1942, New York; s. of Jack Lubin and Sophie Lubin; m. Wendy Lubin 1974; two s. *Education:* Harvard Univ., Juilliard School, New York Univ. *Career:* piano studies with Lisa Grad, Nadia Reisenberg, Seymour Lipkin, Rosina Lhevinne, Beveridge Webster; recital and concert tours in USA, Canada, Mexico, England, France, The Netherlands, Spain, Italy, Germany, Austria, Finland, Australia and Ukraine; f. The Mozartean Players 1978–; mem. Faculty Juilliard School 1964–65, Aspen Music School 1967, Vassar Coll. 1970–71, Cornell Univ. 1971–75; Adjunct Prof., School of the Arts, State Univ. of New York (SUNY) Purchase, NY 1975–. *Recordings:* complete Beethoven Piano Concertos, Mozart and Schubert Trios, Six Mozart Concertos as soloist and conductor and other solo and chamber music. *Publications:* articles in The New York Times, Keynote, Ovation, Keyboard Classics and Historical Performance, Brahms Soc. Newsletter 1999; contrib. to The Complete Schwanengesang 2000. *Honours:* Martha Baird Rockefeller Grant 1968, Stereo Review Recording of the Year Award 1988, Kempner Distinguished Professor Award, State Univ. of New York, Purchase, NY 1999–2001. *Address:* Conservatory of Music, School of the Arts, State University of New York, Purchase, NY 10577, USA. *Telephone:* (914) 251-6715 (office). *Website:* www.stevenlubin.com.

**LUBLIN, Eliane;** Singer (Soprano); b. 10 April 1938, Paris, France. *Education:* Studied in Paris then at the Verdi Conservatory in Paris. *Career:* Debut: Aix-en-Provence as Debussy's Mélisande; Paris Opéra-Comique; Monte Carlo Opéra in Menotti's The Medium; Paris Opéra from 1969 in Les

Dialogues des Carmélites, as Massenet's Manon, Marguerite in Faust, Ellen Orford in Peter Grimes and in the 1981 French premiere of Ligeti's Le Grande Macabre. *Recordings include:* Sapho by Gounod. *Address:* c/o Théâtre National de L'Opéra de Paris, 8 Rue Scribe, F75009 Paris, France.

**LUBOTSKY, Mark;** Violinist; b. 18 May 1931, Leningrad, Russia. *Education:* Moscow Conservatory from 1953, with A Yampolsky and D Oistrakh. *Career:* Debut: Bolshoi Hall of Moscow Conservatory, 1950, Tchaikovsky Concerto; Solo recitals and concerts with major orchestras in the United Kingdom, Scandinavia, Germany, Netherlands, Italy, USA, Australia, Japan and Israel; Many television and radio performances; Teacher, Gnessin Institute, Moscow, 1967–76; Professor, Sweelinck Conservatory, Amsterdam, 1976–; Professor, Hochschule für Musik, Hamburg, 1986–; British debut, 1970, Britten's Concerto at the Promenade Concerts. *Recordings:* Concertos from the Baroque by Mozart, Britten, Schnittke, Tubin; Solo Sonatas by Bach; Sonatas by Brahms, Mozart, Shostakovich, Schnittke. *Honours:* Mozart International Competition, Salzburg, 1956; Tchaikovsky International Copetition, Moscow, 1958. *Current Management:* Encore Concerts Ltd. *Address:* Caversham Grange, The Warren, Mapledurham, Berkshire RG4 7TQ, England.

**LUCA, Sergiu;** Violinist and Teacher; b. 4 April 1943, Bucharest, Romania. *Education:* Studied at the Bucharest Conservatory 1948–50, with Max Rostal in London and at the Berne Conservatory; Curtis Institute with Galamian. *Career:* Debut: With the Philadelphia Orchestra conducted by Eugene Ormany, playing the Sibelius Concerto, 1965; Founder and Director, Chamber Music Northwest Festival in Portland, 1971–80; Professor of violin at the University of Illinois 1980–83; Starling Professor of Classical Violin and Violinist-in-Residence at the Shepherd School of Music, Houston, 1983–; Music Director of the Texas Chamber Orchestra, 1983–88; Founder and General Director of Da Camera, in Houston, Texas, an Arts Organisation producing approximately 50 concerts a year of small ensemble repertoir, from Renaissance to Jazz, 1988–; Solo performances in the USA, Europe, and Japan; Recitals of the unaccompanied works of Bach with authentic instrument and bow; Mozart sonatas with Malcolm Bilson. *Recordings:* Bach sonatas and partitas for unaccompanied violin; Bartók works for violin and piano. *Honours:* Finalist, 1965 Leventritt Competition; Winner, 1965 Philadelphia Orchestra Youth Auditions. *Address:* Shepherd School of Music, Rice University, Houston, Texas, USA.

**LUCAS OGDON, Brenda,** ARMCM; British pianist and teacher; b. 23 Nov. 1935, Cheshire, England; m. John Ogdon (deceased); one s. one d. *Education:* Convent of the Nativity, Romiley, Cheshire, Royal Northern Coll. of Music, Manchester, Mozarteum, Salzburg. *Career:* solo career, including debut in Grieg Piano Concerto with Liverpool Philharmonic Orchestra 1956; duo piano career with John Ogdon; appearances in the 1960s included Edinburgh Festival 1962, 1963, 23rd Cheltenham Festival, Aldeburgh Festival, Sintra Festival, the Royal Concert at Royal Festival Hall with Andre Previn and Houston Symphony Orchestra 1969; toured Soviet Union 1985; solo appearances in Hong Kong 1996; recital, Maine, USA 2003; mem. Incorporated Soc. of Musicians. *Recordings:* Bartók: Sonata for 2 Pianos 1968, Mendelssohn: Concerto for 2 Pianos 1970, Rachmaninov: Suites Nos 1 and 2 1975, Saint-Saëns: Carnival of the Animals 1972, Schoenberg: Chamber Symphony 1974, Liszt: Concerto Pathétique, works by Schumann 1972, Brahms: Hungarian Dances, Arensky: Waltz, Bach, Milhaud, Stravinsky, Dvořák 1989, The Piano Music of John Ogdon 1991. *Publications:* 'Virtuoso' The Story of John Ogdon. *Honours:* Gold Medal of Associated Board 1949, Harriet Cohen Silver medal Royal Northern Coll. of Music 1956, ARMCM Teacher's Distinction, ARMCM Performers. *Address:* Flat 3, 8 Edith Grove, London, SW10 0NW, England (home). *Telephone:* (20) 7823-3875 (also fax) (office). *E-mail:* blogdon@aol.com (office).

**LUCHETTI, Veriano;** Singer (Tenor); b. 12 March 1939, Viterbo, Italy; m. Mietta Sighele. *Education:* Studied with Enrico Piazza and in Milan and Rome. *Career:* Debut: Wexford festival 1965, as Alfredo in La Traviata; Spoleto 1967, as Loris in Fedora and in Donizetti's Il Furioso all'isola di San Domingo; Guest appearances in Palermo, Parma, Venice, Vienna, Munich, Paris, Mexico City, Dallas and Houston; Maggio Musicale Florence 1971, 1974, in L'Africaine and Agnes von Hohenstaufen by Spontini; La Scala 1975, in Verdi's Attila; Covent Garden 1973–76, as Rodolfo, Pinkerton and Gabriele Adorno in Simon Boccanegra; Aix-en-Provence 1976, as Jason in Cherubini's Médée, Verona 1984, in Verdi's I Lombardi; Vienna Staatsoper 1988, as Foresto in Attila; Sang Radames at Turin 1990, Don José at the Verona Arena; Also heard in concert, Verdi's Requiem at Covent Garden, 1976. *Recordings:* Médée, Hungaroton; Nabucco and Verdi Requiem; Piccinni's La Cecchina; Griselda by Scarlatti; 2 further recordings of the Verdi Requiem.

**LUCIER, Alvin;** Composer; b. 14 May 1931, Nashua, New Hampshire, USA; m. Wendy Wallbank Stokes, 27 Aug 1979, 1 d. *Education:* The Portsmouth Abbey School; BA, Yale University, 1954; MFA, Brandeis University, 1960; Fulbright Scholarship, Rome, 1960–62. *Career:* Choral Director, Brandeis University, 1962–70; Professor of Music, Wesleyan University, 1970–, Chair of Department, 1979–84; Co-Founder, Sonic Arts Union, 1966–77; Music Director, Viola Farber Dance Company, 1972–77. *Compositions:* Action Music for Piano, 1962, BMI Canada; Music for Solo Performer, 1965 for enormously amplified brain waves and percussion; Vespers, 1967; Chambers, 1968; I Am Sitting in A Room, 1970; Still and Moving Lines of Silence in Families of Hyperbolas, 1972–; Bird and Person Dyning, 1975; Music in A Long Thin Wire 1977; Crossings, 1982–84; Seesaw, 1984; Sound on Paper, 1985; Fideliotrio for viola, cello and piano, 1987; Navigations for string quartet, 1992; Small Waves for piano, trombone and string quartet, 1997; Cassiopeia for orchestra, 1998; Diamonds, for 1, 2 or 3 orchestras, 1999; Electro-acoustic works, including Amplifier and Reflector, 1991; Sound Installations, Empty Vessels, Resonant Objects and Sound on Glass, 1997. *Recordings include:* Bird and Person Dyning; The Duke of York, Cramps Records, Italy. *Publications:* Chambers in collaboration with Douglas Simon, 1980. *Contributions:* Professional publications. *Address:* Music Department, Wesleyan University, Middletown, CT 06457, USA.

**LUCIUK, Juliusz (Mieczyslaw);** Composer; b. 1 Jan. 1927, Brzeznica, Poland; m. Domicela Dabrowska 1956; two d. *Education:* Acad. of Music, Kraków; Studied with Nadia Boulanger and Max Deutsch in Paris, 1958–59. *Career:* Debut: 3 songs performed, 1954; Various works recorded by Polish Radio, BBC, Sender freies Berlin, ORTF France, Italian Palermo, Netherlands Radio. *Compositions:* Numerous including: 3 Passion Songs for soprano and organ; Image, Preludes and Tripticum Paschale for organ; Sonata for bassoon and piano; Variations for cello and piano; Monologues and Dialogues for soprano recorders; Ballets: Niobe; Death of Euridice; Medea; L'Amour d'Orphée, opera-ballet; Demiurgos, chamber opera; Works for solo voice and chamber ensemble: Floral dream; Le Souffle du Vent; Portraits Lyriques; Works for solo voice and chamber orchestra: Tool of the Light; Poéme de Loire; Wings and Hands; Oratorios: St Francis of Assisi; Gesang am Brunnen; Sanctus Adalbertus flos purpureus; Christus Pantocrator; oratorio Divine Stream (text from Roman Triptych by Pope John Paul II) 2004, Polish Litany, The Polish Mass for mezzo-soprano, mixed choir and wind orchestra; Choral works include: 4 Antiphonae and vespera in Assumptione Beatae Mariae Virginis for men's choir; The Mass for men's choir and organ; The Mass, Hymnus de Caritate and Magnificat for mixed choir; Apocalypsis for 4 soloists and mixed choir; Orchestral Works: Four Symphonic Sketches; Symphonic Allegro; Composition for Four Orchestral Ensembles; Speranza Sinfonica; Lamentazioni in memoriam Grazyna Bacewicz; Warsaw Legend (Quasi Cradle Song); Osiers, 5 pieces for string chamber orchestra; Concertino for piano and small symphony orchestra; Concerto for double bass and symphony orchestra; Hommage for strings, 1993. *Address:* Os Kolorowe 6 m 10, 31-938 Kraków, Poland. *Telephone:* (12) 644-16-10 (office).

**LUCKE, Hannfried;** Organist; b. 27 Feb. 1964, Freiburg, Germany. *Education:* Hochschule für Musik, Freiburg; Mozarteum Salzburg and Conservatoire de Musique, Geneva. *Career:* International concert organist with concert performances and broadcasting recordings in numerous countries in Europe, USA, Canada, Japan, Hong Kong and Australia; Professor, University Mozarteum Salzburg, 2000. *Recordings:* Major organ works of JS Bach; Organ works of the romantic period of instruments in Europe, USA and Japan. *Honours:* Prize of honour, Austrian Minister for Cultural Affairs; Premier Prix at Conservatoire de musique, Geneva. *Address:* Meierhofstrasse 44, FL-9495 Triesen, Principality of Liechtenstein.

**LUCKY, Stepán;** Composer; b. 20 Jan. 1919, Zilina, Czechoslovakia. *Education:* Prague Conservatory, 1936–39; Studied with Ridky, 1945–47; Musicology at Prague University, 1945–48; PhD. *Career:* Member of Czech resistance; Committee member of Pritomnost Association for Contemporary Music, 1946–48; Music Critic for Prague papers; Head of Music for Czech television, 1954–58; Taught at Prague Academy, 1956–61; PhD, Charles University Prague, 1990. *Compositions:* Divertimento for 3 Trombones and Strings, 1946; Cello Concerto, 1946; Piano Concerto, 1947; Opera Midnight Surprise, 1959; Violin Concerto, 1965; Octet for strings, 1970; Double Concerto for violin, piano and orchestra, 1971; Nenia for violin, cello and orchestra (dedicated to the victims of the Second World War), 1974; Concerto for orchestra, 1976; Fantasia Concertante for bass clarinet, piano and orchestra, 1983; Wind Quintet, 1985; Sonatina for 2 guitars, 1986; Much film music, 1950–88; Chamber and Instrumental music. *Honours:* State Order for Outstanding Accomplishment, 1969; Artist of Merit, 1972. *Address:* Lomena 24, 162 00 Prague 6, Czech Republic.

**LUDWIG, Christa;** Austrian/French singer (mezzo-soprano); b. 16 March 1928, Berlin, Germany; d. of Anton Ludwig and Eugenie Besalla-Ludwig; m. 1st Walter Berry 1957 (divorced 1970, died 2000); one s.; m. 2nd Paul-Emile Deiber 1972. *Career:* opera debut at 18, guest appearance at the Athens Festival in Epidauros 1965; joined Vienna State Opera 1955, Hon. mem. 1981; appearances at Festivals in Salzburg, Bayreuth, Lucerne, Holland, Prague, Saratoga, Stockholm; guest appearances in season in Vienna, New York, Chicago, Buenos Aires, Milan, Berlin, Munich; numerous recitals and soloist in concerts. *Recordings include:* Lieder and complete operas including Norma (with Maria Callas), Lohengrin, Così fan tutte, Der Rosenkavalier, Carmen, Götterdämmerung, Die Walküre, Bluebeard's Castle, Don Giovanni, Die Zauberflöte, Le Nozze di Figaro, Capriccio, Fidelio. *Publication:* In My Own Voice (biog.) 1994. *Honours:* Hon. mem. Vienna Konzerthaus, Vienna Philharmonic; Hon. Prof.; Commdr des Arts et des Lettres 1989; Chevalier, Légion d'honneur 1989; Grosses Ehrenzeichen 1994; Commdr, Ordre pour le Mérite (France) 1997; Officier de la Légion d'honneur 2003; winner of Bach-Concours, record award for Fricka in Walküre and Des Knaben Wunderhorn, awarded title of Kammersängerin by Austrian Govt 1962, Prix des Affaires Culturelles for recording of Venus in Tannhäuser, Paris 1972, Silver Rose (Vienna Philharmonic) 1980, Golden Ring (Staatsoper, Vienna) 1980, Golden Gustav Mahler Medal 1980, Hugo Wolf Medal 1980, Gold Medal (City of Vienna) 1988. *Address:* 1458 Ter, Chemin des Colles, 06740 Châteauneuf de

Grasse, France; c/o Heidrun Artmüller, Goethegasse 1, 1010 Vienna, Austria. *Telephone:* (4) 97010531 (home). *Fax:* (4) 97010529 (home).

**LUFF, Enid,** MA, LRAM, MMus; British composer; b. 21 Feb. 1935, Ebbw Vale, Glamorgan, Wales; m. Alan Luff 1956; three s. one d. *Education:* Univ. of Wales; studied Advanced Composition with Elisabeth Lutyens and Franco Donatoni. *Career:* Composer, 1971–; runs Primavera self-publishing co. with Julia Usher, 1980–; mem. British Acad. of Composers and Songwriters, Mechanical Copyright Protection Soc., Performing Right Soc., Women in Music, Cyfansoddwyr Cymru/Composers of Wales. *Compositions:* Four piano pieces, Tapestries for chamber group; Symphony No. 1; Mathematical Dream, solo harp; Wind Quintet: The Coastal Road; Sheila NaGig, for soprano and pianoforte; Dream Time for Bells for chamber group; Sky Whispering for solo piano; Sonata: Storm Tide for piano; Come the Morning, for chamber ensemble; Peregrinus, Trilogy for organ, 1991; Listening for the Roar of the Sun, for oboe, speaker, dance and slide projection, 1992; Symphony 2, 1994; The Glass Wall for solo cello, dancers and electronic tape, 1996. *Recordings:* Hierusalem, for chamber ensemble, 2000; Heaven's Bird for chamber ensemble, 2002; Taro Arian/Struck in Silver for sound sculptures and flute 2004; Several works recorded on BBC Recordings and Danish Radio Recordings. *Address:* 12 Heol Tyn y Cae, Cardiff, CF14 6DJ, Wales. *Telephone:* (29) 2061-6023 (also fax) (office). *E-mail:* enidluff@globalnet.co.uk. *Website:* www.primaveramusic.com.

**LUGANSKY, Nikolai L.;** Russian pianist; b. 26 April 1972, Moscow; s. of Lev Borisovich Lugansky and Anna Nikolayevna Luganskaya; m. Lada Borisovna Luganskaya; one s. one d. *Education:* Moscow State Conservatory. *Career:* wide repertoire comprises over 40 piano concertos and music from Bach to modern composers; ensemblist and interpreter of chamber music; performances in Russia and abroad in Australia, Austria, Belgium, Brazil, Canada, England, France, Germany Italy, Japan and elsewhere, including at the Royal Festival Hall and Wigmore Hall in London, the Gaveau and Louvre in Paris, Conservatoria Verdi in Milan, Gasteig in Munich, Concertgebouw in Amsterdam, Alte Oper in Frankfurt. *Recordings include:* some 25 albums. *Honours:* first prize All-Union students' competition Tbilisi Georgia 1988, silver medal Bach Int. Competition, Leipzig, Germany 1988, second prize Rachmaninov Competition, Moscow 1990, first prize Tchaikovsky Int. Competition, Moscow 1994, Terence Judd award for the most promising pianist of a generation 1995. *Address:* Kosygina str. 2, apt 2 Moscow 119334, Russia (home). *Telephone:* (095) 137-18-36 (home).

**LUITZ, Josef;** cellist; b. 2 Aug. 1934, Vienna, Austria; m. Sonja Edelgard Mayerhofer 1962; one s. one d. *Education:* School for Musical Instrument Makers, Vienna, Konservatorium, Vienna with W. Kleinecke; masterclass with N. Hubner in Santiago de Compostella. *Career:* debut at Musikverein, Vienna, 1957; first Cellist, Tonkuenstler Orchestra, 1957–61; Solo Cellist, 1962–; Member, Haydn Quartet, 1965–72, Ensemble Kontrapunkta, 1968–75; Philharmonia Quintet, 1971–77; Professor, Cello, Konservatorium, Vienna, 1972–; Chairman, Tonkuenstler Chamber Orchestra, 1978–; Concordia Trio, 1979–; Chairman, International Chamber Music Festival, Austria, 1978–. *Recordings:* Chamber Music Series for Musical Heritage Society Inc, New York; Spohr Octet with Vienna Octet; With Tonkuenstler Chamber Orchestra; many Radio Productions as Soloist. *Honours:* Professor, Austrian Government, 1985.

**LUKACS, Ervin;** Conductor; b. 1928, Budapest, Hungary. *Education:* Bela Bartók Conservatory, 1950–51; Conductor's Diploma, Ferenc Liszt Academy of Music, 1956. *Career:* Conductor, Hungarian People's Army Artistic Ensemble, 1954–56; Principal Conductor, Miskolc Opera House and Miskolc Symphony Orchestra, 1956–57; Professor, Department of Conducting, Liszt Academy of Music, Budapest, 1956–59; Conductor, Budapest State Opera, 1957–; Masterclass held by Franco Ferrara in Venice and Accademia di Santa Cecilia, Rome, Italy, 1961, 1962; As conductor has made several extensive tours with Hungarian State Symphony Orchestra. *Honours:* 2st Prize, Santa Cecilia International Concours for Conductors, 1962; Liszt Prize; Merited Artist of the Hungarian People's Republic. *Address:* c/o Hungarian State Opera, Budapest, Hungary.

**LUKAS, Laslo;** Singer (Baritone); b. 1964, Budapest, Hungary. *Education:* Franz Liszt Music Academy, Budapest. *Career:* Sang with the Budapest State Opera four seasons, then with the Prague State Opera; Trier Opera from 1991, including Tcherikov in the first production this century of Zemlinsky's first opera, Sarema; Guest appearances in Germany and elsewhere as Rigoletto, Scarpia, Jochanaan in Salome, Macbeth, Posa, Count Luna, Kaspar, Cardillac, and the Man in Hindemith's Mörder, Hoffnung der Frauen; Simone in Zemlinsky's Florentinische Tragödie, at the Prague State Opera. *Recordings include:* Sarema (Koch International). *Address:* c/o Theater der Stadt Trier, Am Augustinerhof, 5500 Trier, Germany.

**LUKAS, Zdenek;** Composer; b. 21 Aug. 1928, Prague, Czechoslovakia. *Education:* Tutorials led by Miloslav Kabelac, 1961–70. *Career:* Worked for Czech Radio 1953–65; Choral conductor in Plzeň 1955–65; Teacher, Prague Conservatoire' Choirmaster, Czechoslovak State Song and Dance Ensemble; Freelance Composer from 1965. *Compositions include:* Radio Opera Long Live the Dead Man 1968; Home Carnival, one-act opera 1968; Orchestral: Piano Concerto 1955; Violin Concerto 1956; Cello Concerto 1957; 6 Symphonies 1960–91; Concerto Grosso for string quartet and orchestra 1964; Symphonietta solemnis 1965; Sonata concertata for piano, winds and percussion 1966; Concerto for violin, viola and orchestra 1969; Variations for piano and orchestra 1970; Postludium for strings 1970; Concertos for Bassoon (1976), Clarinet (1976), Harpsichord (1980), Violin (1980), Flute (1981), Viola (1983), Piano (1984), Cello (1986), Horn (1989); Piano concerto No. 3, 1993; Opera, Revenge for Revenge, 1986; Choral music includes Adam a Eva, oratorio 1969; The Spring is Coming, cycle for male choir and solo violin, 1975; The Message of Music, four-voice girls' choir with piano accompaniment, 1982; Chamber: 3 String Quartets 1960, 1965, 1973; Partita semplice for 4 violins and piano 1964; Wind Quintet 1969; Saxophone Quartet 1970; Electronic work You do not Kill 1971; Trio for Violin, Violoncello and Piano, Op 106, 1974; Prague Pastorale for Organ Solo, Op 158, 1981; Rondo for Bassoon and Piano, Op 168, 1981; 3 Duets for 2 Violins Op 188, 1984; Duo di basso, violoncello and double-bass, op 210, 1987; 4th String Quartet Op 213, 1987. *Address:* Murmanska 13, 100 00 Prague 10, Czech Republic.

**LUKE, Ray;** Composer and Conductor; b. 30 May 1926, Fort Worth, Texas, USA. *Education:* Studied at Texas Christian University and at the Eastman School of Music, Rochester with Bernard Rogers. *Career:* Taught at the East Texas State College 1951–62; Oklahoma City University from 1962; Associate Conductor, Oklahoma City Symphony 1969–73; Principal Guest Conductor 1974–78. *Compositions:* Opera Medea 1979; Ballet Tapestry 1975; 4 Symphonies 1959–70; Bassoon Concerto, 1965; 2 Suites for Orchestra 1958, 1967; Symphonic Dialogues for violin, oboe and orchestra 1965; String Quartet 1966; Piano Concerto 1970; Septet 1979; Operas Drowne's Wooden Image (1994) and Mrs Bullfrog (1994). *Honours:* Grand Prix Gold Medal Queen Elisabeth of the Belgians Competition, for Piano Concerto, 1970. *Address:* c/o ASCAP, ASCAP Building, 1 Lincoln Plaza, NY 10023, USA.

**LUKHANIN, Viacheslav;** Singer (Bass); b. 1960, Maimi-Sai, Russia. *Education:* Graduated Frunze Conservatoire, Kirgizia, 1985. *Career:* Sang at opera houses in Frunze, Novosibirsk and St Petersburg, 1985–94; Mariinsky Theatre, St Petersburg, from 1994 as Mozart's Figaro, Verdi's Grand Inquisitor and King of Egypt, Storm Wind in Kshchei the Immortal by Rimsky-Korsakov and the Priest in Katerina Izmailova; European tours with the Mussorgsky Opera and Kirov Opera companies, St Petersburg; Sang in the British premiere of Prokofiev's Semyon Kotko, with the Kirov at Covent Garden, 2000; other roles include Angelotti in Tosca and the Bonze in Madama Butterfly. *Honours:* Prizewinner, Glinka National vocal and Chaliapin International Competitions, 1987–89. *Address:* c/o Kirov Opera Mariinsky Theatre, Theatre Square, St Petersburg, Russia.

**LUKOMSKA, Halina;** Singer (Soprano); b. 29 May 1929, Suchedniow, Poland. *Education:* State Opera High School, Poznan, 1951–54; Warsaw State Music High School; Further study with Toti dal Monte in Venice. *Career:* Wide appearances as concert singer from 1960, notably in works by Webern, Serocki, Boulez, (Pli selon Pli), Maderna, Schoenberg, Nono and Lutoslawski; Festival engagements at Edinburgh, Perugia, Vienna, Toulouse, and Warsaw; Holland Festival 1967, in Monteverdi's Orfeo; North American tour with Cleveland Orchestra 1973. *Recordings:* Works by Berg (Altenberglieder) and Webern; Pli Selon Pli; Confitebor Domine by JC Bach; Boris Godunov. *Honours:* Winner, 's-Hertogenbosch Competition, 1956.

**LUMSDAINE, David;** Composer; b. 31 Oct. 1931, Sydney, New South Wales, Australia; m. Nicola LeFanu 1 s., 2 d. *Education:* NSW Conservatorium of Music; Sydney University; Studied with Matyas Seiber, Royal Academy of Music, London; D.Mus, 1981. *Career:* Composer; Teacher of Composition and Music Editor, London, England; Lecturer in Music, Durham University, 1970–; Founder, Electronic Music Studio, Durham; Lecturer, King's College, London, 1981–93. *Compositions include:* Orchestral: Episodes, 1969, Looking Glass Music, 1970, Sunflower for chamber orchestra, 1975, Shoalhaven, 1982, Mandela V for symphony orchestra, 1988; Vocal: The Ballad of Perse O'Reilly for tenor, male chorus and 2 pianos, 1953–81, Annotations of Auschwitz for soprano and ensemble, 1964, 1970, Aria for Edward Eyre for soprano and double bass soloists, chamber ensemble, narrators, tape and electronics, 1972, Tides for narrator, 12 voices and percussion, Caliban Impromptu for piano trio, tape and electronica, 1972, Empty Sky, Mootwingee for ensemble, 1986, Round Dance for sitar, table, flute, cello and keyboard, 1989; Piano Works: Canberra, piano solo, 1980, Wild Ride to Heaven, with Nicola LeFanu, for electronics, 1980; Garden of Earthly Delights, 1992; Kalí Dances for ensemble, 1994. *Current Management:* Sounds Australian, PO Box N690, Grosvenor Place, Sydney, NSW 2000, Australia; University of York Music Press, YO10 5 DD. *Address:* 5 Holly Terrace, York YO1 4 DS, England.

**LUMSDEN, Sir David James,** Kt, MusB, MA, DPhil; British musician; b. 19 March 1928, Newcastle-upon-Tyne; s. of Albert Lumsden and Vera May Lumsden (née Tate); m. Sheila Daniels 1951; two s. two d. *Education:* Dame Allan's School, Newcastle-upon-Tyne, Selwyn Coll. Cambridge (organ scholar). *Career:* Asst Organist, St John's Coll. Cambridge 1951–53; Organist and Choirmaster St Mary's, Nottingham and Univ. Organist 1954–56; Founder and Conductor Nottingham Bach Soc. 1954–59; Rector Chori Southwell Minster 1956–59; Dir of Music, Keele 1958–59; Prof. of Harmony, RAM 1959–61; Fellow and Organist New Coll. Oxford and Lecturer, Faculty of Music, Oxford Univ. 1959–76; Prin. Royal Scottish Acad. of Music and Drama, Glasgow 1976–82; Prin. RAM 1982–93; Conductor Oxford Harmonic Soc. 1961–63; Organist Sheldonian Theatre 1964–76; Harpsichordist to the London Virtuosi 1972–75; Pres. Inc. Asscn of Organists 1966–68; Visiting Prof. Yale Univ., USA 1974–75; Conductor Oxford Sinfonia 1967–70; Choragus Oxford Univ. 1968–72; Pres. Inc. Soc. of Musicians 1984–85, Royal Coll. of Organists 1986–88; Chair. Nat. Youth Orchestra 1985–94, Nat. Early

Music Asscn 1986–89; mem. Bd Scottish Opera 1978–83, ENO 1984–89. *Music:* recordings of organ, choral and chamber music. *Publications:* An Anthology of English Lute Music 1954, Thomas Robinson's Schoole of Musicke 1603 1971, Music for the Lute (Gen. Ed.) 1965–82. *Honours:* Hon. Fellow, Selwyn Coll. Cambridge, New Coll. Oxford, King's Coll., London; Hon. RAM; Hon. FRCO; Hon. GSMD; Hon. FRCM; Hon. FRSAMD; Hon. FRNCM; Hon. FTCL; Hon. FLCM; Hon. FRSCM; Hon. FGCM 2005 Hon. DLitt (Reading) 1989. *Address:* 26 Wyke Mark, Dean Lane Winchester, SO22 5DJ, England. *Telephone:* (1963) 877807. *Fax:* (1963) 877891. *E-mail:* lumsdendj@aol.com (home).

**LUMSDEN, Ronald;** Pianist; b. 28 May 1938, Dundee, England; m. (1) Annon Lee Silver, deceased, 1 d., (2) Alison Paice Hill, 1975, 1 s., 1 d. *Education:* Harris Academy, Dundee; Royal College of Music, London; ARCM; LRAM. *Career:* Pianist in Residence, University of Southampton, 1965–68; Henry Wood Promenade Concerts, 1973, 1974; Soloist in Arts Council Contemporary Music Network, 1974–76; Visiting Piano teacher, 1976–; Honorary Director of School of Music, 1984–, Reading University; Frequent broadcasts and recitals in United Kingdom; mem, Executive Committee, Society for Promotion of New Music, 1975–78; Incorporated Society of Music; European Piano Teachers Association. *Recordings:* Messiaen's Canteyodjaya for Gaudeamus Foundation; Open University's Modern Music. *Contributions:* Bartók, in Makers of Modern Culture, 1981. *Honours:* 1st Prize Winner, International Competiton for Interpreters of Contemporary Music, Utrecht, 1968. *Address:* 50 Grosvenor Road, Caversham, Reading, Berkshire, RG4 0EN, England.

**LUND, Tamara;** Singer (Soprano); b. 1941, Finland. *Career:* Sang with Finnish National Opera from 1967, notably in the 1968 local premiere of Berg's Lulu, title role; Member of the Teater am Gärtnerplatz Munich from 1973, with tours to Berlin, Komische Oper and Theater des Westerns; The Theater an der Wien, Vienna; Engaged at the Zürich Opera, 1979–83; Helsinki 1973, as Daphne in the premiere of Apollo and Marsyas by Rautavaara; Other roles have included Carmen, Musetta, Janáček's Vixen and Jenny in Aufsteig und Fall der Stadt Mahagonny; Sang Juno in the incidental music to The Tempest by Sibelius, Savonlinna 1986; Many appearances in operetta.

**LUNDBERG, Gunnar;** Singer (Baritone); b. 1958, Sweden. *Education:* Studied at the State Opera School Stockholm and in Salzburg. *Career:* Debut: Vadstena Accademy, 1984; Member of the Royal Opera Stockholm from 1988, notably as the Herald in Lohengrin, Escamillo, Valentin, Mozart's Count and Figaro, Don Giovanni and Rossini's Figaro; Season 1991 as Barelli in the European premiere of The Aspern Papers by Argento; Engaged for seasons 1992–94 as Silvio in Pagliacci and Marcello in La Bohème; Sang in Carmina Burana at the Stockholm Royal Opera, 1998; Concert repertoire includes Ein Deutsches Requiem, the Bach Passions and B Minor Mass; St John Passion at the 1993 Lucerne Easter Festival.

**LUNDBERG, Mark;** Singer (Tenor); b. 1953, USA. *Education:* Studied with Margaret Harshaw and in New York. *Career:* Santa Fe, 1988, in the American premieres of Die schwarze Maske by Penderecki and Strauss's Friedenstag; Florestan with Cleveland Opera; Nice Opéra as Bacchus in Ariadne auf Naxos, Dortmund, 1995, as Siegmund and Siegfried; Deutsche Oper Berlin, 1995, as Siegmund; Concerts include Das Lied von der Erde, by Mahler. *Honours:* James McCracken Award. *Address:* c/o Deutsche Oper Berlin, Richard Wagnerstrasse 10, 10585 Berlin, Germany.

**LUNDBORG, Charles (Erik);** Composer; b. 31 Jan. 1948, Helena, Montana, USA; m. Zinta Bibelnieks, 14 Nov 1981. *Education:* BM, New England Conservatory of Music, Boston; MA, 1974, DMA, 1985, Columbia University. *Career:* Performances and Commissions by Houston Symphony Orchestra, American Composers Orchestra, Ursula Oppens, Piano, Speculum Musicae, Group for Contemporary Music, Parnassus, New Music Consort, Pittsburgh, New Music Ensemble, Light Fantastic Players, Composers Ensemble, Light Fantastic Players, Composers Ensemble, New Jersey Percussion Ensemble, many others; mem, BMI; American Composers Alliance, Board Member, 1980–82; Board, ISCM, League of Composers, 1975–78. *Compositions:* Passacaglia, Two Symphonies, from Music Forever, No. 2 Piano Concerto; Soundsoup; Solotremolos. *Recordings:* Passacaglia from Music Forever No. 2; Soundsoup. *Contributions:* Milton Babbitt, String Quartet No. 3, Contemporary Music Newsletter, 1974. *Honours:* Guggenheim, 1976–77; NEA Fellowships, 1975, 1981, 1983. *Address:* 2465 Palisade Ave, 8F, Riverdale, NY 10463, USA.

**LUNDGREN, Stefan;** Swedish lutenist and composer; b. 5 May 1949, Hogsby; m. Henrike Brose 1985. *Education:* Music School, Oskarshann, Sweden, Lund University, Schola Cantonum Basiliensis, Basel. *Career:* teacher, performer, composer and publisher; Ed., Lute Music 1979–; Dir, annual lute course, Ried im Zillertal, Austria 1983–; teacher of summer courses, Svenska Gitarr och lutasallskapets 1985. *Compositions:* Sonatas 1–3 for solo lute 1981–84, Sonata No. 4 for solo lute 1986. *Publications:* New School for the Renaissance Lute 1985, 50 English Duets (publisher, four vols), Charles Mouton, Suite in G Minor, J. A. Losy Two Suites, Little Book for Lute 1: Renaissance Lute, Little Book for Lute 2: Baroque Lute, J. S. Bach Complete Works for Lute. *Address:* c/o Lundgren Edition, Postfach 40 11 32, 80711 München, Germany. *Website:* www.luteonline.de.

**LUNDSTEN, Ralph;** Swedish composer, film-maker and artist; b. 6 Oct. 1936, Ersnäs. *Career:* owner, Andromeda picture and electronic music studio 1959–; work for Opera House in Stockholm and Oslo, Modern Museum and Nat. Museum in Stockholm, Louvre and Biennale in Paris, Triennale in Milan, Museum of Contemporary Crafts in New York; has made 12 short films; Cultural Ambassador for Luleå 1999, London Diplomatic Acad. 2000. *Art Exhibitions include:* portrait exhibition at Music Museum, Stockholm 1991–92, 2000. *Achievements:* more than 600 opus, 106 records, 12 short films, as well as art exhibitions. *Compositions include:* Nordic Nature Symphonies: No. 1 The Water Sprite, No. 2 Johannes and the Lady of the Woods, No. 3 A Midwinter Saga, No. 4 A Summer Saga, No. 5 Bewitched, No. 6 Landscape of Dreams, No. 7 The Seasons; Erik XIV (ballet), Gustav III (ballet), Cosmic Love, Ourfather, Nightmare, Horrorscope, Shangri-La, Universe, Discophrenia, Alpha Ralpha Boulevard, Paradise Symphony, The New Age, Pop Age, Music for Relaxation and Meditation, Cosmic Phantazy, The Dream Master, The Gate of Time, The Ages of Man, Sea Symphony, Mindscape Music, Nordic Light, The Symphony of Joy, The Symphony of Light, The Symphony of Love, In Time and Space, Andromedian Tales, Happy Earthday, Inspiration, At the Fountain of Youth, A Vagabond of the Soul, Dreamlight, Suite Andromatique, Joy & Light, Prelude to the Future. *Honours:* Grand Prix Biennale, Paris 1967, Swedish Film Inst. Prize 1964–67, Schwingungen Preis, Germany 1997, 1999; Guinness World Records 2000 'most played muscial composition' (for Out in theWide World), Albert Schweitzer Medal for Science and Peace 2004. *Address:* Frankenburgs väg 1, 132 42 Saltsjö-Boo, Sweden. *E-mail:* ralph .lundsten@andromeda.se. *Website:* www.andromeda.se.

**LUNELL, Hans;** Composer and Computer Scientist; b. 12 April 1944, Skellefteå, Sweden. *Education:* Fil kand, Uppsala University, 1967; Fil dr (PhD), Linköping University, 1983; Musicology, Uppsala University; Music Theory and Composition, Royal College of Music, Stockholm; Piano study with Greta Erikson. *Career:* Assistant Professor, Linköping University, 1971–83; Associate Professor, KTH, Stockholm, 1983–86; Director of Institute for Electro-Acoustic Music in Sweden, 1989–93; mem, Society of Swedish Composers; International Confederation for Electro-Acoustic Music; STIM. *Compositions:* Intensità for piano trio, 1981–82; La notte in Sicilia for soprano, bass clarinet and vibraphone, 1984; Affinities I for piano solo, 1985. *Contributions:* Numerous articles, many to Nutida Musik. *Address:* Teknik-vägen 105, 175 75 Järfälla, Sweden.

**LUNETTA, Stanley,** BA, MA; American composer and timpanist; b. 5 June 1937, Sacramento, CA. *Education:* Sacramento State Coll., Univ. of CA at Davis with Jerome Rosen and Larry Austin, studied with John Cage, David Tudor and Karlheinz Stockhausen. *Career:* founded New Music Ensemble 1963; Ed., Source: Music of the Avant Garde 1971–77; percussionist and teacher in Sacramento. *Compositions:* Many Things for Orchestra 1966; Piano Music 1966; A Piece for Bandoneon and Strings 1966; Free Music 1967; Ta Ta for chorus and mailing tubes 1967; The Wringer, mixed media 1967; Funkart 1967; Twowomanshow, theatre piece 1968; Spider Song with Lartry Austin, 1968; Mr Machine for flute and tape 1969; A Day in the Life of the Mooscak Machines 1972; The Unseen Force theatre piece with dancers 1978; From 1970 much music from a series of self-playing electronic sound sculptures, e.g. Mooscak Machine, Sound Hat and Cosmic Cube. *Address:* 2101 22nd Street, Sacramento, CA 95818, USA. *E-mail:* sTANg@macnexus.org. *Website:* stang .donnerparty.net.

**LUNN, Joanna;** Singer (Soprano); b. 1973, England. *Education:* Royal College of Music, and with Denise Mulholland. *Career:* Engagements with the English Baroque soloists under John Eliot Gardiner, including Bach Cantata Pilgrimage (2000), Gluck and Verdi at the Châtelet, Paris, and Handel's Israel in Egypt at Salzburg and Vienna (2001); Bach's B minor Mass with the New London Consort in New Zealand and Spain; Tour of Japan with the Musicians of the Globe; Debut with English National Opera in The Coronation of Poppea, 2000; St Matthew Passion with the London Handel Festival, 2001; Other appearances with The King's Consort and the Gabrieli Consort. *Honours:* Tagore Gold Medal, RCM. *Address:* c/o Royal College of Music, Prince Consort Road, London SW7, England.

**LUPERI, Mario;** singer (bass); b. 1954, Sardinia, Italy. *Education:* studied in Calgliari, Verona and Siena. *Career:* debut in Perugia 1979, in Olympie by Spontini and in Cherubini's Requiem; Palermo and Florence 1981, as Publio in La Clemenza di Tito and as Thoas in Iphigénie en Tauride; La Scala from 1982, as the Emperor in The Nightingale, Simone in Gianni Schicchi and Pluto in the Monteverdi Orfeo; Macerata Festival 1984–86, as Colline and Timur, Salzburg Easter Festival 1986, as the Grand Inquisitor; Sang Ramphis in Aida at the Munich Staatsoper 1986, Luxor 1987; Season 1986–87 as Verdi's Pistol at Brussels, Oroe in Semiramide and Oroveso in Norma at Naples; North American debut 1988, as Timur at Pittsburgh; Sang Colline at Genoa, 1990, Giorgio in I Puritani at Marseilles, 1991; Mozart's Bartolo in Venice 1991 and in Fra Diavolo at La Scala, 1992; Sang Charon in Monteverdi's Orfeo at Milan, 1998; Season 2000 as the Cardinal in La Juive for New Israeli Opera, Mozart's Commendatore at La Coruña and Pistol in Falstaff in La Monnaie, Brussels; Many concert appearances; including the Commendatore in Don Giovanni at the Festival Hall, London, 1996. *Current Management:* Atelier Musicale, Via Caselle 76, San Lazzaro di Savena 40068, Italy. *Telephone:* (051) 19 98 44 44. *Fax:* (051) 19 98 44 20. *E-mail:* info@ ateliermusicale.com. *Website:* www.ateliermusicale.com.

**LUPTACIK, Jozef;** Musician (clarinet); b. 10 Jan. 1947, Vysoka pri Morave, Czechoslovakia; m. Eva 1972; one s. one d. *Education:* Musical Conservatory, Bratislava, 1962–69; Academy of Music, Bratislava, 1969–73; summer courses with Professor V. Riha, Prague, 1970–71. *Career:* debut, A. Copland, Concerto, Music Festival, Bratislava, 1973; E. Suchon, Concertino (first performance), with Czech Philharmonic, Prague, 1978; Mozart, Weber, Krommer, Concertos with Slovak Philharmonic; mem, Slovak Philharmonic Orchestra, first clarinet Bratislava; Associate Professor, Academy of Music, Bratislava. *Recordings:* E. Suchon, Concertino; Weber/Mozart, Quintets (B Major, A Major); Weber, Concerto in F Minor, E Major; Brahms/Beethoven, Trio; J. Brahms, Sonatas in E Major, F Minor; Mozart, Clarinet Concerto; J. Hummel, Clarinet Quartet. *Honours:* fourth Prize, Belgrade, 1971; member of international juries, international clarinet competitions. *Address:* Hlavna 36, 900 66 Vysoka pri Morave, Slovakia.

**LUPU, Radu,** MA; Romanian pianist; b. 30 Nov. 1945, Galați; s. of Meyer Lupu and Ana Gabor. *Education:* High School, Brașov, Moscow Conservatoire, USSR. *Career:* first piano lessons 1951; won scholarship to Moscow 1961; entered Moscow Conservatoire 1963, graduated 1969; First Prize, Van Cliburn Competition 1966; First Prize, Enescu Int. Competition, Bucharest 1967; First Prize, Leeds Int. Competition 1969; a leading interpreter of the German classical composers; appears frequently with all the major orchestras; has toured Eastern Europe with London Symphony Orchestra; American debut 1972; gave world première of André Tchaikowsky Piano Concerto, London 1975. *Recordings include:* complete Beethoven cycle (with Israel Philharmonic and Zubin Mehta), complete Mozart sonatas for violin and piano with Szymon Goldberg), Brahms piano concerto No. 1 (with Edo de Waart and London Philharmonic Orchestra), Mozart piano concerto K467 (with Uri Segal and English Chamber Orchestra), various Beethoven and Schubert sonatas, Mozart and Beethoven wind quintets in E flat, Mozart concerto for 2 pianos and concerto for 3 pianos transcribed for 2 pianos (with Murray Perahia and English Chamber Orchestra), Schubert Fantasie in F minor and Mozart sonata in D for 2 pianos (with Murray Perahia), Schubert Lieder (with Barbara Hendricks), Schubert Piano Duets (with Daniel Barenboim). *Honours:* Grammy Award for Best Instrumental Record of Year (for Schubert record) 1995, Edison Award for Best Instrumental Record of Year (for Schumann record) 1995. *Address:* c/o Terry Harrison Artists, The Orchard, Market Street, Charlbury, Oxon., OX7 3PJ, England. *Telephone:* (1608) 810330. *Fax:* (1608) 811331. *E-mail:* artists@terryharrison.force9.co.uk (office). *Website:* www.terryharrison.force9.co.uk (office).

**LUTHER, Mark;** singer (tenor); b. 14 Nov. 1961, Bristol, England. *Education:* National Opera Studio, Guildhall School with Noelle Barker. *Career:* debut at St John's Smith Square, 1989, in Elijah; concert appearances include Opera Gala Evening at Covent Garden, Vivaldi's Gloria with the Northern Symphonia and showings at the Purcell Room and the Queen Elizabeth Hall; Opera engagements include touring performances with British Youth Opera as Rodolfo; Other roles include: Idomeneo, Don Ottavio and Remendado (Carmen); Macduff and Arturo in Lucia di Lammermoor for Welsh National Opera, Don José at Rotterdam and the Verdi Requiem in Netherlands; Don Ottavio in Schönbrunn Vienna; Sang Lensky for Opera North at Norwich, 1998; Sang Tamino at Wellington, 1999.

**LUTSIUK, Viktor;** Singer (Tenor); b. 1965, Ivanitchi, Ukraine. *Education:* Kolliarevsky conservatoire, Kharkov. *Career:* Sang at the Dnypropetrov Opera until 1996; Mariinsky Theatre, St Petersburg, from 1996 as Lohengrin, Parsifal, Don Carlos, Lensky in Eugene Onegin, Herman (Queen of Spades), Vladimir in Prince Igor and Dmitiri in Boris Godunov; Andrei in Mazeppa at La Scala (1999), Parsifal at the Royal Albert Hall and Lohengrin in Baden-Baden; Sang the title role in the British premiere of Prokofiev's Semyon Kotko, with the Kirov Opera at Covent Garden, 2000; Sofia Gubaidulina St John Passion at the London Proms, 2002; Other roles include Alfredo, Radames, the Duke of Mantua, Don José, Pinkerton, and Andrei in Khovanshchina. *Recordings include:* Mazeppa and Boris Godunov. *Address:* c/o Kirov Opera Mariinsky Theatre, Theatre Square, St Petersburg, Russia.

**LUTZE, Gert;** Singer (Tenor); b. 30 Sept. 1917, Leipzig, Germany. *Education:* Sang in the choir of St Thomas's Leipzig from 1928. *Career:* Bach's St Matthew Passion conducted by Gunter Ramin; Many appearances as concert and oratorio singer; Opera roles included Puccini's Pinkerton and Rodolfo, Mozart's Ferrando and Rimsky-Korsakov's Sadko; Engagements as Bach singer in Schaffhausen, Zürich, Basle, Berne, Helsinki, Paris, Brussels and Luxembourg; Sang in Prague and China 1955; St Matthew Passion in Bologna and Florence 1957; Further concerts with Karl Richter as conductor.

**LUXON, Benjamin Matthew,** CBE, FGSM; British singer (baritone); b. 24 March 1937, Redruth, Cornwall; s. of Maxwell Luxon and Lucille Grigg; m. Sheila Amit 1969; two s. one d. *Education:* Truro School, Westminster Training Coll., Guildhall School of Music and Drama. *Career:* always a freelance artist; sang with English Opera Group 1963–70; has sung with Royal Opera House, Covent Garden and Glyndebourne Festival Opera 1971–96, Boston Symphony Orchestra 1975–96, Netherlands Opera 1976–96, Frankfurt Opera House 1977–96, Paris Opéra 1980, La Scala, Milan 1986; roles include Monteverdi's Ulisse, Janáček's Forester, Mozart's Don Giovanni and Papageno, Tchaikovsky's Onegin, Verdi's Posa and Falstaff, Wagner's Wolfram, Alban Berg's Wozzeck, Count Almaviva and Sherasmin in Oberon; performs as recitalist with piano accompanist David Willison; folk-singing partnership with Bill Grofut 1976–96; has recorded for all major record cos; retd from professional singing due to severe hearing loss 1996; vocal coach at Tanglewood, USA 1996. *Recordings include:* Mahler's 8th Symphony, Schubert's Song Cycles. *Honours:* Hon. mem. RAM; Bard of Cornish Gorseth; Hon. DMus (Exeter), (RSA of Music and Drama) 1996, (Canterbury Christ Church Coll.) 1997. *Address:* The Mazet, Relubbus Lane, St Hilary, Penzance, Cornwall, TR20 9DS, England.

**LVOV, Boris;** Concert Pianist; b. 1928, Moscow, Russia. *Education:* Studied at the Central School of Music and at the Moscow Conservatoire. *Career:* Debut: First public concert aged nine years; performed at the Moscow Conservatoire in 1946; Many concerts in the former Soviet Union, Eastern Europe and China from 1948; Appearances with David Oistrakh, Rostropovich, Kondrashin and Emil Gilels; Former Professor of Piano, Moscow Conservatoire, then emigrated to Israel and is Professor at the Rubin Academy of Music in Jerusalem; Recent concert tours to Europe, Japan, Scandinavia and USA, both in recital and concert; Repertoire includes music by Haydn, Mozart, Schumann, Liszt, Prokofiev, Bartók and Stravinsky. *Honours:* Winner, Beethoven Cometition for performance of the Hammerklavier Sonata. *Address:* 11 Northpark Street, Glasgow G20 7AA, Scotland.

**LYONS, Graham John,** AGSM; British composer, music publisher and instrument manufacturer; b. 17 July 1936, London. *Education:* Univ. of Oxford, Guildhall School of Music and Drama. *Career:* played saxophone, clarinet and piano in jazz groups and dance bands 1954–58; freelance as a woodwind doubler in many styles and orchestras 1962–80; arranger for BBC light orchestras 1970–80; arranger and session musician for New Zealand TV 1980–81; started own music publishing Co. 1983; launch of the Lyons C clarinet 1991; mem. Incorporated Soc. of Musicians, Musicians' Union, Nat. Secular Soc. *Compositions:* Mixed Bag: series of woodwind ensembles, Take up the Flute, Take up the Clarinet, 60 vols of solo and ensemble compositions for woodwind, Sonata for Clarinet and Piano 1986. *Publications:* numerous collections of short pieces for solo wind instrument and piano 1979–; The Russian Version of the Second World War (compiler and Ed.) 1976, New York: Facts on File 1981. *Honours:* British Design Award for the Lyons C clarinet 1993. *Address:* 11 Tinley Garth, Kirkby Moorside, North Yorkshire, YO62 6AR, England (home). *Telephone:* (1751) 433379 (home). *Fax:* (1751) 430611 (home). *E-mail:* usefulmusic@aol.com (home); composer@clarinet-for-children .com. *Website:* www.firstclarinet.com (home); www.clarinet-for-children.com.

**LYSIGHT, Michel (Thierry);** Belgian composer, conductor, professor and publisher; b. 14 Oct. 1958, Brussels. *Education:* Musicology, Free Univ. of Brussels, 1978; Acad.of Schaerbeek; Conservatoire Royal de Musique, Mons; Conservatoire Royal de Musique, Brussels; Advanced Diplomas, Solfege 1980, Chamber Music 1988, Composition 1989, Conducting, 2002. *Career:* Prof., Academies of Schaerbeek, 1979–, Woluwe Saint-Pierre 1981–90; Prof. of Contemporary Music, Conservatoire Royal de Musique, Brussels, 1980–; Deputy Dir, Acad. of Brussels, 1990–94; Prof., Bikent Univ. of Ankara, Turkey, 2000–01; Founder, Ensemble Nouvelles Consonances, 1995; Founder, Fibonacci Publishing, 1999; Artistic Dir, Kalidisc, 2000–. *Compositions include:* Prelude et Toccata, piano, 1982; Reflexion, clarinet or bassoon and piano 1982; Quatrain, wind quarter 1987; Soleil Bleu, one wind instrument and piano 1989; Onirique, full orchestra, 1989; Trois Croquis 1990; Monochrome, piano 1990; Chronographie I, wind quintet 1990; Sextuor, wind quintet and piano 1990; Quadratura 1991; Quatrain, flute, oboe, clarinet, bassoon, 1990; Chronographie II for string orchestra, 1992–93; Chronographie III 2 instruments and piano, 1993; Trois Instantanés, 1994; Épode, 1997; Piano Concerto, 1995; Chronographie IV for violin and piano, 1996; Hal pot rhythm for wind ensemble, 1999; Couleurs noires for 4 cellos, 1999; Chronographie V, piano, 2001; Anamnèse, choir and string orchestra, 2001; Élémentaires, 3 instruments, 2001; Enigma, 2 instruments and piano or harp, 2001; Alchemy, clarinet quartet or sax quartet, 2001; Random walk, brass quintent or clarinet and string quartet, 2002; Hexagramme, 6 instruments ad lib, 2002; Concerto, clarinet and orchestra, 2002; Trois points, horn, 2002; An awakening, string quartet, 2002; Perseides, recorder, 2002; This is not a bossa, piano, 2003; Initiation, flute and marimba, 2003; Elegy to the memory of Lou Harrison, string orchestra 2004; Homage to Fibonacci, two clarinets or violin and violoncello 2004; Moon Water, string quartet 2004; Runes, violin, clarinet and piano 2004; Chronographie VI-VIII, 2004; Deux Esquisses, piano 2004. *Recordings:* XXth Century Belgian Works for Clarinet and Piano, Ronald Vanspaendonck, clarinet and Leonardo Anglani, piano; Sit Down and Listen, Mireille Gleizes, piano; Oréades; Discoveries; Belgian Sextets; Récital Joseph Grau; Labyrinthes; Serenata for 2000 (Serenata Forlana); XXth Century Belgian Works for Flute and Piano; Thrène, Chronographie IV (Stéphane De May, piano and Damien Paroen, violin); Masterpieces for Horn and Piano (Francis Orval, horn and Jean-Claude Vanden Eynden, piano); Couleurs XXème siècle for trumpet and organ; Soledad; I Musici Brucellensis; Ritual; De l'Art d'Ecouter; Mendelssohn Ensemble (Trois Croquis); Marc Grauwels and Marie-Jose Simard (Initiation). *Publications:* La Transposition, 1982. *Honours:* Irène Fuérison Prize, Belgian Acad. of Fine Arts, 1990; Silver Medal, Acad. of Lutèce, Paris, 1992; Fuga, Belgian Composers Union, 1997. *Address:* 1 rue Vanderlinden, 1030 Brussels, Belgium. *E-mail:* lysight@fibonacci.be. *Website:* www.avk.org/lysight.

**LYSY, Alberto;** Violinist and Teacher; b. 11 Feb. 1935, Buenos Aires, Argentina; Divorced, 4 c. *Education:* Studied with Ljerko Spiller and Yehudi Menuhin. *Career:* Solo recitals and performances with orchestras in Europe, Asia, Israel, North and South America under Adrian Boult, Colin Davis, Pierre Boulez, Mstislav Rostropovich and others. Performed chamber music with Pablo Casals, Yehudi Menuhin, Benjamin Britten, Nadia Boulanger, Gaspar Cassadò and others; Musical Director, International Menuhin Music Academy and Camerata Lysy, Gstaad, Switzerland; Rencontres Musicales Internationales in Blonay, Switzerland and Festival International Lysy in Buenos Aires. *Honours:* Honorary Doctorate, University of Cordoba, Argentina. *Address:* IMMA, Centre d'Etudes, rte de Vevey 7, 1807 Blonay, Switzerland.

**LYSY, Antonio;** Cellist; b. 1963, Rome, Italy. *Education:* Studied with his father, the violinist Alberto Lysy; Menuhin School with Maurice Gendron and William Pleeth; Menuhin Academy with Radu Aldulescu; Royal Northern College of Music with Ralph Kirshbaum. *Career:* Concert engagements in Austria, Argentina, France, Germany, Israel, Italy and Spain; British venues include the Royal Festival Hall, Wigmore Hall, Queen Elizabeth Hall and St John's Smith Square; Chamber concerts with Radu Aldulescu, Gidon Kremer, Lamar Crowson and Yehudi and Jeremy Menuhin; Principal Cellist with the Chamber Orchestra of Europe and appearances with the Manchester-based Goldberg Ensemble; Camerata of Salzburg 1988, with Sándor Végh as conductor; Solo performances of Tchaikovsky's Rococo Variations in Buenos Aires and Italy; Further engagements with the Philharmonia Orchestra and at the Brighton Festival; Artistic Director of Chamber Music Festival in Tuscany, Incontri Musicali in Terra di Siena, from summer 1989. *Recordings:* Bloch's Prayer and Tchaikovsky's Souvenirs de Florence with the Camerata Lysy.

**LYTTELTON, Richard;** record company executive; *President of Classics and Jazz, EMI Music. Career:* joined EMI Music 1974, Pres. of Classics and Jazz 1988–; Chair. English Touring Opera 2003–. *Address:* EMI Classics Group, EMI House, 43 Brook Green, London, W6 7EF (office); English Touring Opera, 52–54 Rosebery Avenue, London, EC1R 4RP, England (office). *Website:* www.englishtouringopera.org.uk (office); www.emiclassics.com (office).

**LYUBIMOV, Yuri Petrovich;** Russian/Israeli/Hungarian theatrical director and actor; *Artistic Director, Moscow Taganka Theatre;* b. 30 Sept. 1917, Yaroslavl'; m. Katalin Lyubimov; one s. *Education:* Vakhtangov Theatre Studio. *Career:* served in Soviet Army 1939–47; Teacher and Dir, Shukin Drama School (Vakhtangov Theatre) 1953–64; Founder and Artistic Dir, Moscow Theatre of Drama and Comedy (Taganka) 1964–84, 1989–; deprived of Soviet citizenship 1983, left Soviet Union 1984, acquired Israeli citizenship 1987, returned 1988, citizenship restored 1989, acquired Hungarian citizenship 1999. *Roles include:* Oleg Koshevoy (The Young Guard, by Fadeyev), Shubin (On the Eve, by Turgenev), Chris (All My Sons, by Arthur Miller), Benedict (Much Ado About Nothing), Mozart (The Little Tragedies, by Pushkin); prominent in Soviet films 1947–, including Busy Stock, Robinson Crusoe, Cuban Cossacks. *Theatre productions include:* The Good Man from Szechuan 1963, Ten Days that Shook the World 1965, Mother (Gorky) 1969, Hamlet 1972, Boris Godunov (Moscow) 1982, Crime and Punishment (London) 1983, The Devils (London, Paris) 1985, Hamlet (London) 1987, Self-Murderer (Moscow) 1990, Electra (Moscow) 1992, Zhivago (Vienna) 1993, The Seagull (Athens) 1993, Creditors (Athens) 1994, Medea (Athens) 1995, The Brothers Karamazov (Moscow) 1997, Marat-Sade (Moscow) 1998, Sharashka (Moscow) 1998, Chronicles (Moscow) 2000, Eugene Onegin (Moscow) 2000, Theatrical Novel (Moscow) 2000, Socrates (Moscow) 2001, Faust (Moscow) 2002, Before and After 2003, Go and Stop the Progress (Moscow) 2004 and others (total of 104). *Opera productions include:* Al gran sole carico d'amore (La Scala) 1975, Boris Godunov (La Scala) 1981, Lulu (Turin, Chicago) 1983, Rigoletto (Florence) 1984, Hovancshina (La Scala) 1985, St Matthew's Passion (La Scala) 1985, Jenufa (London) 1986, Eugene Onegin (Bonn) 1987, The Queen of Spades (Karlsruhe), 1990, Lady Macbeth of Mtsensk (Hamburg) 1990, Nabucco (Bonn) 1997, Love for Three Oranges (Munich) 1991 and others. *Publications:* Le Feu Sacré 1985, Zapiski starego trepacha (Notes from an old Blabbermouth) 2000; several articles in the field of theatre. *Honours:* numerous decorations including Medal for the Defence of Leningrad 1943, for the Defence of Moscow 1944, State Prizes 1952, 1997, Order of the Labour Red Banner 1977, State Prize of Russia 1991, Order of the Great Patriotic War 1996, Services to the Motherland, 1st Class 1997, Golden Medal of Honour of the Pres. of Hungary 1997, Triumph Premium 1998, Nat. Order of the Repub. of Hungary 2002, Kt Commdr of Arts and Literature (France) 2002, Star of Italian Solidarity 2003, Estonian Order of the Cross of Terra Mariana 2003, Royal Order of the Polar Star (Sweden) 2004, Chevalier Cross Order of Honour of Poland 2004 numerous awards including Honoured Artist of the RSFSR 1954, Grand Prix, Int. Theatre Festival, Bonn 1998, Grand Prix, Int. Theatre Festival, Thessalonika 1999, Golden Mask Theatre Prize 2000, Diploma of American Acad. of Arts 2001, K. Stanislavsky Fund Prize 2003. *Address:* Taganka Theatre, Zemlanoy val 76, Moscow 109004 Russia (office). *Telephone:* (095) 915-10-37 (office); (095) 290-19-34 (home). *Fax:* (095) 274-00-33 (office); (095) 290-19-34 (home). *E-mail:* taganka-theatre@mtu-net.ru (office). *Website:* www.taganka-theatre.ru (office).

# M

**MA, Yo-Yo,** BA; American cellist; b. 7 Oct. 1955, Paris, France; of Chinese parentage; m. Jill A. Hornor 1978; one s. one d. *Education:* Harvard Univ. and cello studies with his father, with Leonard Rose and at Juilliard School of Music, New York. *Career:* first public recital at age of five; performed under many distinguished conductors with all the maj. orchestras of the world, including Berlin Philharmonic, Boston Symphony, Chicago Symphony, Israel Philharmonic, London Symphony and New York Philharmonic; regularly participates in festivals of Tanglewood, Ravinia, Blossom, Salzburg and Edinburgh; also appears in chamber music ensembles with artists such as Isaac Stern, Emanuel Ax, Leonard Rose, Pinchas Zukerman, Gidon Kremer and fmrly Yehudi Menuhin; premiered the Concerto by H. K. Gruber, Tanglewood 1989; recital tour with Emanuel Ax celebrating 20th anniversary of their partnership 1995–96; Bach's suites for solo cello at the Barbican Hall, London 1995; established The Silk Road Project to promote study of cultural, artistic and intellectual traditions of the route 2001; Smithsonian Folklife Festival 2002. *Recent recordings include:* John Williams Greatest Hits 1969–1999 1999, My First 79 Years 1999, Solo 1999, Brahms: Piano Concerto No.2, Cello Sonata Op.78 1999, Lulie the Iceberg 1999, Songs and Dances 1999, Franz Joseph Haydn 1999, Simply Baroque 1999, Crouching Tiger, Hidden Dragon (film soundtrack) 2000, Corigliano: Phantasmagoria 2000, Simply Baroque II 2000, Appalachian Journey 2000, Dvorak: Piano Quartet No. 2, Sonatina in G, Romantic Pieces 2000, Classic Yo-Yo 2001, Classical Hits 2001, Heartland: An Appalachian Anthology 2001, Naqoyqatsi (film soundtrack) 2002, Yo-Yo Ma Plays the Music of John Williams 2002, Silk Road Journeys—When Strangers Meet 2002, Obrigado Brazil 2003, Paris—La Belle Époque 2003. *Honours:* Dr hc (Northeastern) 1985 and from 11 other colls or univs, including Harvard, Yale, Tufts and Juilliard, Chinese Univ. of Hong Kong; Avery Fisher Prize 1978; Glenn Gould Prize 1999; 14 Grammy Awards including one for his recording of the six Bach Suites for Unaccompanied Cello 1984, two Emmy Awards, 19 Canadian Gemini Awards. *Current Management:* ICM Artists, 40 W 57th Street, New York, NY 10019, USA. *Website:* www.sonyclassical.com/artists/ma/.

**MAASS-GEIGER, Joachim;** Singer (Bass-baritone); b. 1957, Essen, Germany. *Education:* Studied in Lubeck and Hamburg. *Career:* Sang in opera at Kaiserslautern, 1981–85, Essen from 1986. Appearances at Eutin, Gelsenkirchen and elsewhere as Mozart's Figaro and Leporello, the Grand Inquisitor in Don Carlos, and Alberich in The Ring; Klingsor at Essen, 1993, Don Giovanni and the Doctor in Wozzeck at Saarbrücken and Gelsenkirchen, 1996; Other roles include Curio in Giulio Cesare, Golaud in Pelléas et Mélisande, and Kecal in The Bartered Bride. *Address:* Staatstheater, Schillerplatz, 66111 Saarbrucken, Germany.

**MAAZEL, Lorin,** FRCM; American conductor and musician; *Music Director, New York Philharmonic;* b. 6 March 1930, Neuilly, France; s. of Lincoln Maazel and Marie Varencove Maazel; m. 1st Israela Margalit; four c.; m. 2nd Dietlinde Turban 1986; one s. *Education:* under Vladimir Bakaleinikoff and at Univ. of Pittsburgh. *Career:* début as conductor 1938; Conductor, American Symphony Orchestras 1938–; violin recitalist; European début 1953; festivals include Bayreuth, Salzburg, Edin.; tours include S America, Australia, USSR and Japan; Artistic Dir, Deutsche Oper Berlin 1965–71; Musical Dir Radio Symphony Orchestra, Berlin 1965–75; Assoc. Prin. Conductor, New Philharmonia Orchestra, London 1970–72; Dir Cleveland Orchestra 1971–82, Conductor Emer. 1982–86; Prin. Guest Conductor London Philharmonia 1976–80; Dir Vienna State Opera 1982–84, Music Dir Pittsburgh Symphony Orchestra 1988–96; Music Dir Bavarian Radio Symphony Orchestra 1993–2001, NY Philharmonic 2002–; Palau de les Arts Reina Sofia, Valencia 2005–; Music Dir Orchestre Nat. de France 1988–90. *Composition:* 1984 (premiere Royal Opera House, London) 2005. *Honours:* Officier, Légion d'honneur 1981, Finnish Commdr of the Lion, Portuguese Commdr, Bundesverdienstkreuz (Germany); Hon. DMus (Pittsburgh) 1968, (Royal Coll. of Music) 1984; Hon. DHumLitt (Beaver Coll.) 1973; Hon. DCL (Univ. of S Sewanee) 1988; Dr hc (Ind.) 1988. *Address:* New York Philharmonic, Avery Fisher Hall, 10 Lincoln Center Plaza, New York, NY 10023, USA (office); c/o Z des Aubris, Tal 15 5th Floor, 80331, Munich, Germany. *Website:* www.nyphilharmonic.org (office).

**MACAL, Zdenek;** Conductor; b. 8 Jan. 1936, Brno, Czechoslovakia. *Education:* Brno Conservatory, 1951–56; Janáček Academy 1956–60. *Career:* Debut: Czech Philharmonic Orchestra 1966, at the Prague Spring Festival; British Debut, 1969, with the Bournemouth Symphony; US debut with the Chicago Symphony 1972; Conductor of the Moravian Symphony Orchestra at Olomouc, 1963–67; Tours to Hungary, Bulgaria, West Germany, Austria and Switzerland; Music Director of the Cologne Radio Symphony Orchestra 1970–74; Chief Conductor of the Orchestra of Hanover Radio from 1980; Music Director, Milwaukee Symphony from 1986, Sydney Symphony, 1986–93; Conducted Prince Igor at the Grant Park Concerts, Chicago, 1990. *Recordings:* Dvořák's Cello and Piano Concertos; Brahms Alto Rhapsody, Soukupova; Mozart Piano Concertos K488 and K595; Schoeck's Penthesilea; CD of Dvořák's 9th Symphony and Symphonic Variations, Classic for Pleasure. *Honours:* Winner, International Conductors Competition at Bescançon, 1965; Mitropoulos Competition, NY, 1966. *Address:* c/o Concerto Winderstein GmbH, Leopoldstrasse 25, D–80802 München, Germany.

**McALISTER, Barbara;** singer (mezzo-soprano); b. 1944, Oklahoma, USA. *Education:* Oklahoma University and in Los Angeles. *Career:* sang at Koblenz Opera from 1976, in The Medium, as Stravinskys Mother Goose ad Vercli's Uirica; Sang at Passau 1980–81, Flensburg 1981–83 and Bremerhaven 1983–87; Roles have included Presiosilla, Carmen, Herodias, and Orlofsky; Guest at Monte Carlo 1987, as Meg Page; Concert repertoire includes Messiah, Beethoven's Ninth, the Kindenotenlieder and the Alto Rhapsody. *Address:* c/o Stadttheater Bremerhaven, Theodor-Heuss-Platz, Pf 120541 2850 Bremerhaven, Germany.

**McANDREW, Fiona;** singer (soprano); b. 1967, Ireland. *Education:* University of Western Australia and Guildhall School, London. *Career:* appearances with English Touring Opera; Opera Ireland; Castleward Opera; Covent Garden Festival; Opera Holland Park; Roles include: Poulenc's Blanche, Miss Wordsworth in Albert Herring, Pamina, Donna Elvira, Frasquita and Marie in La Fille du Regiment, Adina, Cilea's Vivetta, Woglinde; Concerts include Reich's Tehillim, Dresden, 1998; Bach's St Matthew Passion and Christmas Oratorio, National Concert Hall, Ireland; Debussy's Le Martyre at St John's Smith Square; 1999 season with La Fée in Cendrillon and Prima Donna in Convenienze Teatrali, Mayfair Festival; Isabella in L'Inganno Felice, Pesaro, Italy and Lady Harriet in Martha for Castleward Opera. *Address:* Music International, 13 Ardilaun Road, London N5 2QR, England.

**MacANN, Rodney;** singer (baritone); b. 1950, New Zealand. *Career:* European debut as The Speaker in The Magic Flute, with Welsh National Opera; Sang with New Zealand Opera before studying singing and theology in London; Appearances with Opera North as Don Alfonso, Sharpless and Jochanaan, and in La Cenerentola and Samson et Dalila; English National Opera as Tchaikovsky's Mazeppa, Ariodates in Xerxes by Handel, Don Alfonso, Klingsor in Parsifal; Scarpia and Escamillo; With the Royal Opera Covent Garden has sung in Andrea Chénier, King Priam, Les Contes d'Hoffmann and Tosca; Engagements in France, Norway and Italy, as Arthur in The Lighthouse by Peter Maxwell Davies; Adelaide Festival, South Australia as Ruprecht in The Fiery Angel; Sang Cuno in Der Freischütz at Covent Garden, 1989, the Music Master in Ariadne for ENO, 1990; Concerts with all the leading British orchestras and frequent performances of Christus in the Bach Passions; Further concerts in Bergen, Florence, NY, and Toulouse; Sang Mozart's Figaro at Wellington, New Zealand, 1995; Sang Sharpless in Butterfly at Wellington, 1999. *Recordings:* Video of Andrea Chénier, Covent Garden, 1984.

**McCABE, John,** CBE, MusB, FRNCM, FLCM, FRCM, RAM, FTCL; British pianist and composer; b. 21 April 1939, Huyton, Lancs. (now Merseyside); s. of Frank McCabe and Elisabeth McCabe (née Herlitzius); m. 1st Hilary Tann 1968 (divorced 1974); m. 2nd Monica Smith 1974. *Education:* Liverpool Inst. High School for Boys, Manchester Univ., Royal Manchester Coll. of Music, Staatliche Hochschule für Musik, Munich. *Career:* pianist-in-residence, University Coll., Cardiff 1965–68; Pres. Inc. Soc. of Musicians 1983–84; Dir London Coll. of Music 1983–90; Chair. Asscn of Professional Composers 1985–86; travels world-wide as pianist-composer. *Compositions include:* The Chagall Windows, Variations on a theme of Hartmann, Notturni ed Alba, Concerto for Orchestra, Cloudcatcher Fells, Fire at Durilgai, Canyons, Edward II (ballet), Arthur, Part I: Arthur Pendragon, Arthur, Part II: Le Morte d'Arthur (ballets), plus other stage works, symphonies, concertos, much orchestral and chamber music, vocal works and keyboard music; numerous piano recordings including complete piano works of Haydn and Nielsen. *Publications:* Rachmaninov, Bartok's Orchestral Music, Haydn's Piano Sonatas, Alan Rawsthorne: Portrait of a Composer and numerous articles on music. *Honours:* Hon. DPhil (Thames Valley) 2001; Royal Manchester Inst. Medal 1962, Royal Philharmonic Prize 1962, Special Citation, Koussevitzky Recording Foundation 1974, Award for service to British music, Composers Guild 1975. *Address:* c/o Novello and Co. Ltd, Music Sales, 8/9 Frith Street, London, W1V 5TZ, England (office).

**McCAFFERTY, Frances;** singer (mezzo-contralto); b. 1965, Edinburgh, Scotland. *Education:* Royal Scottish Academy and Hans Hotter. *Career:* debut, sang in Il Barbiere di Siviglia and Manon Lescaut at Dublin; Appearances as Verdi's Mistress Quickly, with Opera North; Mozart's Third Lady; Ericlea in Monteverdi's Ulisse; Kabanicha in Katya Kabanova; Ulrica in Ballo in Maschera, Neath Opera; First Maid in Elektra, Covent Garden; Wexford Festival in Rimsky's May Night; Sang with ENO as Mistress Quickly; Dorset Opera as Naina in Ruslan and Lyudmila; 1999–2000 Season: Mozart's Marcellina for Opera Holland Park; La Cieca, La Gioconda, Dorset; Concerts with Scottish CO; BBC Scottish Symphony Orchestra; Ulster Orchestra. *Current Management:* Music International, 13 Ardilaun Road, London N5 2QR, England.

**McCALDIN, Denis James,** BMus, BSc, PhD; British conductor, broadcaster and editor; *Emeritus Professor of Performance in Music, Lancaster University;* b. 28 May 1933, Nottingham, England; m. Margaret Anne Smith; one d. one s. *Education:* Birmingham Univ., Nottingham Univ., Mozarteum, Salzburg, Austria. *Career:* Lecturer in Music, Liverpool Univ. 1966–71; Prof. of Performance in Music, Lancaster Univ. 1971–98, Emeritus Prof. 1998–; guest conductor Royal Liverpool Philharmonic Orchestra, Manchester Camerata,

London Mozart Players, Royal Philharmonic Orchestra, Hallé Orchestra; Vice-Chair. Lake District Summer Music 1998–, Artistic Dir 1999–; Dir Haydn Soc. of Great Britain 1979–; mem. Incorporated Soc. of Musicians, Royal Musical Asscn. *Compositions:* Fanfare for a Celebration 1993. *Recordings:* Schubert and Haydn: Church Music 1989, Haydn: Nelson Mass 1998. *Publications:* Stravinsky 1972, Berlioz: Te Deum (ed.) 1973, Mahler 1981, Haydn: Te Deum, Nelson Mass, Little Organ Mass (ed.) 1987–98, Haydn Mass in F 1993, editions of Haydn, Bach and Mozart 1998–; contribs to Beeethoven Companion, Music Review, Music Times, Music and Letters, Music in Education, Times Higher Education Supplement, Soundings. *Honours:* Freeman, City of Lancaster 1990. *Address:* Department of Music, University of Lancaster, Bailrigg, Lancaster, LA1 4YW (office); Heron House, Aldcliffe Mews, Lancaster, LA1 5BT, England (home). *Telephone:* (1524) 61553 (home). *Fax:* (1524) 61553 (home). *E-mail:* d.mccaldin@lancaster.ac.uk (office). *Website:* haydnsocietyofgb.netfirms.com (office).

**McCALLA, Kathleen;** singer (soprano); b. 1957, Iowa, USA. *Education:* Manhattan Institute and with Tito Gobbi and Mario del Monaco in Italy. *Career:* debut, Treviso 1981 in Le nozze di Figaro; Sang throughout Germany from 1983, notably as Traviata, and in the Mozart and Puccini repertory; Bonn Opera from 1992, as Desdemona, Suor Angelica and Leonore in Fidelio; Guest engagements as Alice in Falstaff, Abigaille in Nabucco at Naples and Turandot in Rome, 1996; Other roles include Mozart's Vitelia, Constanze, Countess and Fiordiligi. *Address:* c/o Bonn Opera, Am Boeselageshof 1, 5311 Bonn, Germany.

**McCARTHY, Fionnuala;** singer (soprano); b. 1963, Ireland. *Education:* studied in Johannesburg and at Detmold, Germany. *Career:* debut, Kaiserslautem 1987, as Mimi; Sang at the Mannheim Opera from 1988, debut as Wagner's Woglinde with further appearances as Lauretta, Euridice, Echo, Marzelline, Famine, Zerlina and Mozart's Countess; Sang Marguerite at Giessen (1990) and appeared with the Deutsche Oper am Rhein 1990–92; Sang Donna Elvira with Pimlico Opera at Tullnally, Ireland, 1996; Ighino in Pfitzner's Palestrina at the Deutsche Oper, Berlin, 1996, and Manon there 1998; Season 2000–01 as Sophie, Janáček's Vixen, Pamina and Alice Ford at the Deutsche Oper. *Address:* c/o Deutsche Oper am Rhein, Richard-Wagner-Strasse 10, 10585 Berlin, Germany.

**McCARTHY, John,** OBE; British choral director and director of music; b. 1930, London. *Education:* St Edmund's Coll., Herts. *Career:* Musical Director of the Ambrosian Singers and Ambrosian Opera Chorus and many other famous Choral Groups; Director of Music, Carmelite Priory; Former Chorus Master, Royal Opera House, Covent Garden; Professor, Royal College of Music; Choral Director to nearly all the greatest conductors in the world; Director of many hundreds of very successful recordings and broadcasts. On television has been Choral Director for many operas and music programmes; In London Theatre has been involved in a number of musicals and revivals and several Royal Command Performances; Shows include: Mame; The Great Waltz; Gone With The Wind, Showboat; The King and I; Beyond the Rainbow; Charlie Girl; Hans Anderson; 2 Ronnies; Barnham; I Love My Wife; Plumbers Progress; Phil the Fluter; Joan of Arc; Luther; Biograph Girl; Cats; Choral Director for hundreds of films including the Oscar winning Oliver, Tom Jones, Goodbye My Chips, Scrooge, Cromwell, Fiddler on the Roof, The Great Waltz, Man of la Mancia, Close Encounters; Chariots of Fire; Amadeus. *Recordings include:* Over 150 recordings of operas in French, German, Italian, Russian and English; Conductor of 3 award winning albums for European Grand Prix du Disques; Fauré Requiem; Lucia di Lammermoor; Beethoven's 9th Symphony; Vivaldi's Gloria. *Publications include:* Editor, series of Tudor and Renaissance Music. *Honours:* National Academy of Performing Arts Awards. *Address:* c/o Ambrosian Singers, 4 Reynolds Road, Beaconsfield, Buckinghamshsire HP9 2NJ, England. *Telephone:* (1494) 680873 (office). *Fax:* (1494) 680501 (office).

**McCARTNEY, Sir (James) Paul,** Kt, MBE, FRCM; British songwriter and performer; b. 18 June 1942, Liverpool; s. of James McCartney and Mary McCartney; m. 1st Linda Eastman 1969 (died 1998), one s. two d. one step-d.; m. 2nd Heather Mills 2002, one d. *Education:* Stockton Wood Road Primary School, Speke, Joseph Williams Primary School, Gateacre and Liverpool Inst. *Career:* plays guitar, piano and organ; taught himself to play trumpet at age of 13; wrote first song 1956, wrote numerous songs with John Lennon; joined pop group The Quarrymen 1956; appeared under various titles until formation of The Beatles 1960; appeared with The Beatles for performances in Hamburg 1960, 1961, 1962, The Cavern, Liverpool 1960, 1961; world-wide tours 1963–66; attended Transcendental Meditation Course at Maharishi's Acad., Rishikesh, India Feb. 1968; formed Apple Ltd, parent org. of The Beatles Group of Cos 1968; left The Beatles after collapse of Apple Corpn Ltd 1970; formed MPL Group of Cos 1970; first solo album McCartney 1970; formed own pop group Wings 1971–81, tours of Britain and Europe 1972–73, UK and Australia 1975, Europe and USA 1976, UK 1979, World Tour 1989–90; solo performance at Party at the Palace, Buckingham Palace 2002; Fellow British Acad. of Composers and Songwriters 2000. *Recordings:* albums: with The Beatles: Please Please Me 1963, A Hard Day's Night 1964, Beatles for Sale 1965, Help! 1965, Rubber Soul 1966, Revolver 1966, Sgt Pepper's Lonely Hearts Club Band 1967, Magical Mystery Tour 1967, The Beatles (White Album) 1968, Yellow Submarine 1969, Abbey Road 1969, Let It Be 1970, 1962–1966 (Red Album) 1973, 1967–1970 (Blue Album) 1973, Past Masters Vol. One 1988, Past Masters Vol. Two 1988, The Beatles Anthology: 1 1995, The Beatles Anthology: 2 1996, The Beatles Anthology: 3 1996, 1 2000; with

Wings: Wild Life 1971, Red Rose Speedway 1973, Band On The Run 1973, Venus and Mars 1975, Wings at the Speed of Sound 1976, Wings Over America 1976, London Town 1978, Wings Greatest 1978, Back To The Egg 1979, Wingspan 2001; solo: McCartney 1970, Ram 1971, McCartney II 1980, Tug of War 1982, Pipes of Peace 1983, Give My Regards to Broad Street 1984, Press To Play 1986, All the Best! 1987, CHOBA B CCCP 1988, Flowers in the Dirt 1989, Tripping the Live Fantastic 1990, Unplugged: The Official Bootleg 1991, Paul McCartney's Liverpool Oratorio (with Carl Davis q.v.) 1991, Off The Ground 1993, Paul Is Live 1993, Flaming Pie 1997, Standing Stone (symphonic work) 1997, Run Devil Run 1999, Working Classical 1999, A Garland for Linda (with eight other composers for a capella choir) 2000, Driving Rain 2001, Back In The US: Live 2002, Back in the World 2003, Chaos and Creation in the Back Yard 2005; film soundtracks: The Family Way 1966, James Paul McCartney 1973, Live and Let Die 1973, The Zoo Gang (TV series) 1973. *Radio:* (series) Routes of Rock (BBC) 1999. *Films:* A Hard Day's Night 1964, Help! 1965, Yellow Submarine (animated colour cartoon film) 1968, Let it Be 1970, Magical Mystery Tour (TV film) 1967, Wings Over the World (TV) 1979, Rockshow 1981, Give My Regards to Broad Street (wrote and directed) 1984, Rupert and the Frog Song (wrote and produced) (BAFTA Award Best Animated Film) 1985, Press to Play 1986, Get Back (concert film) 1991. *Publications:* Paintings 2000, The Beatles Anthology (with George Harrison and Ringo Starr) 2000, Sun Prints (with Linda McCartney) 2001, Many Years From Now (autobiog.) 2001, Blackbird Singing: Poems and Lyrics 1965–1999 2001, High in the Clouds (juvenile, with Philip Ardagh and Geoff Dunbar) 2005. *Honours:* Hon. Fellow (Liverpool John Moores Univ.) 1998; Dr hc (Sussex) 1988; two Grammy Awards for Band on the Run (including Best Pop Vocal Performance) 1975, Ivor Novello Award for Best Selling British Record 1977–78 for single Mull of Kintyre, for Int. Hit of the Year 1982 for single Ebony and Ivory, for Outstanding Services to British Music 1989; Guinness Book of Records Triple Superlative Award (43 songs each selling more than 1m copies, holder of 60 gold discs, estimated sales of 100m albums and 100m singles) 1979; Lifetime Achievement Award 1990; Freeman of the City of Liverpool 1984; Lifetime Achievement Award People for the Ethical Treatment of Animals (with Linda McCartney) 1996, Polar Music Prize 1992. *Current Management:* MPL Communications Ltd, 1 Soho Square, London, W1V 6BQ, England. *Website:* www.paulmccartney.com.

**McCARTY, Patricia,** BMus, MMus; viola player, recitalist and chamber musician; b. 16 July 1954, Wichita, Kansas, USA; m. Ronald Wilkison 1982. *Education:* University of Michigan, University of Michigan. *Career:* debut, New York, 1978; Wigmore Hall, London, England, 1986; Beethovenhalle, Bonn, 1991; Japan Tour, 1993; Viola Soloist, Recitalist and Chamber Musician in performances throughout the USA, Europe and Japan; Appearances include Detroit, Houston, Brooklyn, Boston Pops, Beethovenhalle, Suisse Romande, Kyoto and Shinsei Nihon Tokyo orchestras; Recitals in New York, San Francisco, Detroit, Boston and London; Chamber Music performances at Marlboro, Aspen, Tanglewood, Hokkaido and Sarasota festivals; Faculty, Boston Conservatory, Longy School, Meadowmount School of Music. *Recordings:* Viola Works of Rebecca Clarke; Songs of Charles Martin Loeffler; Brahms Viola Quintets; Dvořák String Sextet; Keith Jarrett Concerto; Bach Suites; Schubert Arpeggione Sonata/Beethoven Notturno & Romances; Brahms Sonatas/Schumann Marchenbilder. *Current Management:* c/o Anne Thomas, Ashmont Music, 25 Carruth Street, Boston, MA 02124, USA. *E-mail:* AshmontMus@aol.com.

**McCAULEY, Barry;** singer (tenor); b. 2 June 1950, Altoon, Pennsylvania, USA. *Education:* Eastern Kentucky University and Arizona State University. *Career:* debut, San Francisco Spring Opera 1977, as Don José; San Francisco Opera 1977, as Faust; Further appearances in Houston and San Diego; European debut Frankfurt 1979, as Edgardo in Lucia di Lammermoor; New York City Opera from 1980; Aix-en-Provence Festival, 1980 as Don Ottavio; Paris Opéra from 1982, Teatro Comunale Florence, 1983 (debut as Wilhelm Meister in Mignon); Théâtre de la Monnaie Brussels, 1984 and 1986, as Idamante and Belfiore in La Finta Giardiniera; Glyndebourne Festival, 1985–88, as Don José and Boris in Katya Kabanova; Metropolitan Opera debut 1985, as Jacquino; Vienna Staatsoper, 1984, Don Ottavio; Has sung Offenbach's Hoffmann at the Spoleto Festival, 1989 and Seattle and Geneva, 1990; Other roles include Alfredo at Seattle, 1988, Maurizio in Adriana Lecouvreur, Trieste, 1989, Belmonte, Gluck's Admete, Nemorino, Robert Dudley in Maria Stuarda, the Duke of Mantua, Fenton, Pinkerton, Gerald in Lakmé, Nadir, Lensky and Froh in Das Rheingold; Debut as Parsifal at Amsterdam, 1991. *Address:* Seattle Opera Association, PO Box 9248, Seattle, WA 98109, USA.

**McCAULEY, John J.,** BS, BMus, MSc, MusEd; American pianist, conductor and teacher; b. 16 Nov. 1937, Des Moines, IA. *Education:* Univ. of Illinois at Urbana, Juilliard School of Music, piano with Claire Richards, Carlo Zecchi, Friederich Wuehrer, conducting with Jorge Mester and Jean Morel, piano with Josef Raieff and Beveridge Webster, Tanglewood, Aspen, Mozarteum Summer Acad., Salzburg, Austria, masterclasses in conducting with Herbert von Karajan. *Career:* piano solo debut, Carnegie Recital Hall, New York 1975; Columbia Artists Management Community Concerts recital accompanist throughout USA 1980–84; piano recitals, chamber music concerts throughout USA and Europe, including Lincoln Center and Juilliard 1978–91; New York Radio, The Listening Room with Robert Sherman (WQXR) 1983, 1990; pianist in New York performance of The Night of the Murdered Poets, for narrator and chamber ensemble, by Morris Cotel 1985; American Cathedral's Arts

George V recital series in Paris 2002, 2003; 92nd Street Y Tisch Center for the Performing Arts, Meet the Virtuoso Series of chamber music performances, spring 2003; solo piano recital Nov. 2004; conductor, Bel Canto Opera, New York; east coast tours with Opera Northeast and Eastern Opera Theater 1978–85; Asst Conductor and musical coach, Des Moines Metro Opera 1984–94; Guest Conductor, Bronx Symphony Orchestra 1985, 1997; Asst Conductor, Arizona Opera at Tucson and Phoenix 1984; Music Dir, Nevada Opera Studio 1995; Assoc. Conductor, Brooklyn Philharmonic 1983; founder, Music Dir and Conductor, Chamber Orchestra of Science & Medicine (COSM), New York 2001–, with concerts at Rockefeller Univ., Music at St Paul's Series, Columbia Univ., Advent Lutheran Church, Good Shepherd Church at Lincoln Center; mem. piano faculty, Riverdale Country School and School of Music 1967–80; instructor, Lehman Coll., CUNY 1972–82; instructor in piano, vocal coaching, accompanist for student recitals and masterclasses, 92nd Street Y Music Dept 1997–; adjunct vocal coach, Manhattan School of Music 1997–. *Recording:* The Night of the Murdered Poets, for narrator and chamber ensemble, by Morris Cotel (pianist). *Publications:* contrib. reviews of new music in NOTES (journal of Music Library Asscn). *Honours:* scholarship, Univ. of Illinois, fellowships at Tanglewood, Aspen, graduate teaching fellowship, Juilliard.

**McCAWLEY, Leon,** FRSA; British pianist; b. 12 July 1973, Culcheth, Warrington, England. *Education:* Chetham's School of Music, Curtis Inst. of Music. *Career:* debut, London Philharmonic Orchestra, Bryden Thomson, Royal Festival Hall 1990; works with top orchestras including LPO, CBSO, BBC Nat. Orchestra of Wales, RPO, Philharmonia, BBC Symphony, Royal Scottish Nat., Vienna Symphony, Vienna Chamber, Dallas Symphony, Minnesota Orchestra; recital performances at Wigmore Hall, Queen Elizabeth Hall, Zürich Tonhalle, Vienna Musikverein, Berlin Philharmonie, Washington Kennedy Centre; performances at BBC Proms. *Recordings include:* Schumann: Piano Music; Beethoven: Sonatas and Variations, Complete Piano Works of Samuel Barber, Gál's Complete Works for Solo Piano 2005; frequent broadcasts on BBC Radio 3. *Honours:* BBC Young Musician of the Year, piano section 1990, first prize Beethoven Int. Piano Competition, Vienna 1993, second prize Leeds Int. Piano Competition 1993. *Current Management:* Clarion/Seven Muses, 47 Whitehall Park, London, N19 3TW, England. *Telephone:* (20) 7272 4413. *Website:* www.leonmccawley.com.

**McCOLL, William Duncan;** clarinettist and basset hornist; b. 18 May 1933, Port Huron, MI, USA; m. Sue McColl; one s. *Education:* Oberlin Coll., Manhattan School of Music, State Acad. of Music and Representational Arts, Vienna. *Career:* solo clarinettist with US Seventh Army Symphony Orchestra 1957–58 and Philharmonia Hungarica, Vienna 1959; clarinettist, Festival Casals; solo clarinettist with Puerto Rico Symphony Orchestra and clarinet instructor for Puerto Rico Conservatoire 1960–68; clarinettist, Soni Ventorum Wind Quartet 1963–; Prof., Univ. of Washington 1968–; bass clarinettist, Orquestra Filarmonica de las Americas, Mexico City, summer 1976–78. *Recordings:* Villa-Lobos, Trio for Bassoon, Clarinet, Oboe and quartet ditto with flute; Reicha Quintet in G major; Haydn Clock Organ pieces, arranged for wind quintet; Beethoven, Clock Organ pieces, arranged for wind quintet; Reicha Quintet in E minor; Danzi Quintet in F major; Poulenc Duo for Clarinet and Basson; Villa-Lobos Trio for Clarinet, Bassoon and Piano; Numerous other compositions and arrangements. *Address:* c/o School of Music, University of Washington, Seattle, WA 98195, USA.

**McCORMACK, Elizabeth,** BA; singer (mezzo-soprano); b. 1964, Fife, Scotland; m. Douglas Vipond 1990. *Education:* Glasgow University; Royal Scottish Academy with Duncan Robertson and London Opera Studio. *Career:* Edinburgh Festival debut 1986 with Alan Ramsay's The Gentle Shepherd; Concert performances include Handel's Messiah, Samson and Coronation Anthem; Mozart Requiem, Beethoven Missa Solemnis and CPE Bach Magnificat; Stravinsky's Pulcinella with the English Chamber Orchestra at the Barbican; Sang De Nebra's Requiem and Handel's Dixit Dominus with La Chappelle Royale and Philippe Herreweghe 1989; Haydn's Theresian Mass with the Orchestra of the Age of Enlightenment at the Queen Elizabeth Hall; Has also sung in Elgar's The MusicMakers, Vivaldi's Gloria and the Duruflé Requiem; English National Opera debut, 1989 in The Mikado; Scottish Opera 1990 in the premiere of Judith Weir's The Vanishing Bridegroom; Season 1994–95 as Cenerentola for Castleward Opera and Iolanthe for Scottish Opera; Season 1997 at the Opéra Bastille, Paris, in Parsifal and as Mozart's Annius. *Honours:* Scottish Opera John Noble Bursary, 1987; Decca-Kathleen Ferrier Prize, 1987; Isobel Baillie Performance Award, 1987; Scottish Opera John Noble Award, 1987; Royal Overseas League, 1987; English Speaking Union, 1988; Caird and Munster Scholarships, 1987–89. *Address:* c/o Scottish Opera, 32 Elmbank Crescent, Glasgow, G2 4PT, Scotland.

**McCRAY, James;** singer (tenor); b. 21 Feb. 1939, Warren, Ohio, USA. *Education:* studied with Raymond Buckingham. *Career:* debut, Stratford Festival, Canada, in Weill's Aufstieg und Fall der Stadt Mahagonny; Appearances in Seattle, Kansas City, Miami, San Francisco and the New York City Opera; Guest with Tel-Aviv Opera, Israel; Roles include Verdi's Ismaele, Radames and Manrico, Wagner's Siegmund and Siegfried, Don José, Samson, Ponchielli's Enzo and Puccini's Calaf, Dick Johnson and Cavaradossi; Sang Florestan at Montreal, 1999; Young Siegfried in the first modern Polish production of the Ring, Warsaw, 1989; Wuppertal 1989, as Tristan. *Address:* c/o Wuppertaler Bühnen, Spinnstrasse 4, 5600 Wuppertal, Germany.

**McCREADY, Ivan;** cellist; b. 1963, England. *Education:* Royal Academy of Music with Derek Simpson. *Career:* member of the Borante Piano Trio from 1982; Concerts at the Wigmore Hall and in Dublin and Paris; Beethoven's Triple Concerto at the Festival Wien Klassik, 1989; Season 1990 at the Perth and Bath Festivals and tour of Scandinavia, Russia and the Baltic States; Cellist of the Duke String Quartet from 1985; Performances in the Wigmore Hall, Purcell Room, Conway Hall and throughout England; Tours of Germany, Italy, Austria and the Baltic States; South Bank series 1991, with Mozart's early quartets; Soundtracks for Ingmar Bergman documentary The Magic Lantern, Channel 4 1988; Features for French television 1990–91, playing Mozart, Mendelssohn, Britten and Tippett; Brhams Clarinet Quintet for Dutch Radio with Janet Hilton; Live Music Now series with concerts for disadvantaged people; The Duke Quartet Invites... at the Derngate, Northampton 1991, with Duncan Prescott and Rohan O'Hara; Resident quartet of the Rydale Festival 1991; Residency at Trinity College, Oxford, tours to Scotland and Northern Ireland and concert at the Queen Elizabeth Hall 1991. *Recordings include:* Quartets by Tippett, Shostakovich and Britten (Third) for Factory Classics. *Honours:* Awards include the Harold Craxton at the RAM and the Leche Scholarship. *Address:* c/o Ingrassia, Duke Quartet, Via San Zanobi 7, 50018 Scandicci, Italy.

**McCREDIE, Andrew Dalgarno,** AM, MA, DPhil, FAHA; Australian professor of musicology; b. 3 Sept. 1930, Sydney; s. of Harold A. McCredie and Marjorie C. McCredie (née Dalgarno); m. Xenia Rosner 1965; one d. *Education:* Univ. of Sydney, Royal Acad. of Music, London, Univs of Copenhagen, Stockholm, Hamburg. *Career:* Sr Research Fellow, Univ. of Adelaide 1965–69, Sr Lecturer in Musicology 1970–73, Reader in Musicology 1974–77, Prof. 1978–94, Prof. Emer. 1994–; Adjunct Prof. Monash Univ. 1997–; Hon. Visiting Prof. Univ. of Queensland (Brisbane) 1997–; Visiting Lecturer, Univs of Amsterdam, Utrecht 1964, Western Australia 1970, City Univ. of New York 1974, Yale, Pennsylvania 1977, Ljubljana, Bologna, Marburg, Frankfurt, Kraków, Warsaw 1978, Copenhagen, Belfast (Queen's Univ.), Hamburg, Munich, Zentral Inst. für Musikforschung (Berlin), Berne, Basle, Zurich 1983, Melbourne, Stockholm, Tübingen 1986, Heidelberg, Saarbrücken, Queen's Univ., Kingston, Ont., Brandeis (Boston), City Univ. of New York, NSW (Sydney) 1987, Munich, Braunschweig 1988, Wolfenbüttel, Mainz, Edmonton, Calgary, Saskatoon, London (Ont.), Toronto 1989, Cardiff 1992, Cologne 1994, Zagreb 1994, Dresden (1994, 1996), Cologne Weimar (2001), Louvain (2002); mem. Council Int. Musicological Soc. 1977–87; Mem. Inst. for Advanced Musical Studies, King's Coll. Univ., London 1993; Adviser Musica Antiqua Europae Orientalis 1977–; Advisory Corresp.; appointments with Int. Review of Aesthetics and Sociology of Music 1981–, Current Musicology 1987–, Studies in Music 1980. *Publications:* Musical Composition in Australia (3 vols) 1969, Karl Amadeus Hartmann: Catalogue of all his works with biography 1981 (trans. German), Miscellanea Musicologica, Adelaide (ed.) 1966–94, Paperbacks on Musicology (Gen. Ed.) 1978–, From Colonel Light into the Footlights: The Performing Arts in South Australia from 1836 to the Present 1988, Clemens von Franckenstein 1991, Ludwig Thuille 1993, Karl Amadeus Hartmann 1995, Werner Egle 1997. *Honours:* Edward J. Dent Medal 1974, Paderewski Medal-Bydgoszcz Philharmonia 1982, Australian Centennial Medal 2004. *Address:* Tintorettostrasse 1, 80638 Munich, Germany; 13/18 Lansell Road, Toorak, Vic. 3142, Australia (home). *Telephone:* (89) 178-2325 (Germany); (3) 9826-6348 (Australia) (home).

**McCREESH, Paul D.;** British conductor; b. 24 May 1960, London, England; m. Susan Jones 1983. *Education:* Univ. of Manchester. *Career:* debut, St John Smith's Square 1981; founder and Dir, Gabrieli Consort and Players 1982–; frequent performances and recordings of Baroque and Renaissance in the UK and abroad; guest conducting engagements include Netherlands Philharmonic Orchestra, Stockholm Philharmonic Orchestra, Gothenburg Symphony Orchestra, San Francisco Symphony Orchestra, Orchestre Philharmonique de Radio France. *Recordings include:* Reconstructions, Venetian Easter Mass and Venetian Vespers, Handel's Solomon, Theodora and Messiah, Bach St Matthew Passion, Gluck Paride ed Elena, Mozart C Minor Mass. *Honours:* Gramophone Awards 1990 (for A Venetian Coronation), 1993, ABC Record of the Year 1991, Dutch Edison Awards 1991, 1995, Diapason D'Or, France 1994, 1999, Echo Prize, Germany 1995. *Current Management:* Intermusica Artists' Management Ltd, 16 Duncan Terrace, London, N1 8BZ, England. *Telephone:* (20) 7278-5455 (office). *Fax:* (20) 7278-8434 (office). *E-mail:* mail@intermusica .co.uk (office).

**McCULLOCH, Jenifer Susan,** ARCM; opera singer (lyrico-spinto soprano) and voice teacher; b. 3 Aug. 1957, London, England. *Education:* Royal College of Music, National Opera Studio. *Career:* debut as Countess Almaviva in Mozart's Marriage of Figaro with English National Opera, 1986; Concerts at the major London venues and at festivals in Edinburgh, Cambridge, Henley and Manchester; Appeared in oratorio all over the United Kingdom and Europe; Has sung Brahms' Requiem with David Willcocks and Mendelssohn's Infelice with Solti; Recorded Mozart's Exultate Jubilate and Strauss's Four Last Songs for BBC; American debut in the Four Last Songs, with San Jose Symphony Orchestra; Verdi's Requiem at the Three Choirs Festival and Usher Hall, Edinburgh; Beethoven's Ninth under Laszlo Heltay at 1992 Kenwood Summer Season opening; Appearances in opera include Donna Anna in Don Giovanni for English National Opera; Glyndebourne Festival debut as Vitellia in La Clemenza di Tito, followed by Musetta in La Bohème and Donna Anna for the Touring Opera; Tosca in Dublin, Mozart's Marcellina in Hong Kong, Netherlands (Opera Zuid and Amsterdam), Lisbon, Paris,

Ludwigsburg and London; Various television broadcasts including 2 episodes of Inspector Morse; Professor of Singing, Guildhall School of Music and Trinity College of Music, London; International Adjudicator and Course Director; mem, BVA. *Recordings:* Marriage of Figaro; A Victorian Christmas; Gilbert and Sullivan. *Current Management:* Robert Gilder & Co., Enterprise House, 59–65 Upper Ground, London, SE1 9PQ, England. *Telephone:* (20) 7928-9008. *Fax:* (20) 7928-9755. *E-mail:* rgilder@robert-gilder.com. *Address:* Flat One, 80 Sunnyhill Road, Streatham, London, SW16 2UL, England.

**McDANIEL, Barry;** singer (baritone); b. 18 Oct. 1930, Lyndon, Kansas, USA. *Education:* Juilliard School, New York; Stuttgart Musikhochschule with Alfred Paulus and Hermann Reutter. *Career:* debut sang in recital at Stuttgart in 1953; Mainz Opera, 1954–55; Stuttgart Opera, 1957–59; Karlsruhe, 1960–62; Deutsche Oper Berlin from 1962, notably in Baroque and contemporary works, also Mozart and Wagner; Sang in the premieres of Henze's Der junge Lord, 1965, and Reimann's Melusine, 1971; Salzburg Festival, 1968; Metropolitan Opera, 1972 as Debussy's Pelléas; Other roles include the Barber in Die schweigsame Frau and Olivier in Capriccio; Guest appearances in Schubert Lieder and as Christus in the St Matthew Passion. *Recordings:* Bach, Christmas Oratorio; Ariadne auf Naxos, Dido and Aeneas, La Finta Giardiniera and Der junge Lord, Deutsche Grammophon; Orff's Trionfi, BASF. *Address:* c/o Deutsche Oper Berlin, Richard Wagnerstrasse 10, 1000 Berlin, Germany.

**MACDONALD, Hugh John,** BA, MA, PhD, FRCM; British musicologist and academic; *Avis Blewett Professor of Music, Washington University, St Louis;* b. 31 Jan. 1940, Newbury, Berkshire, England; m. 1st Naomi Butterworth 1963; one s. three d.; m. 2nd Elizabeth Babb 1979; one s. *Education:* Pembroke Coll., Cambridge. *Career:* Lecturer in Music, Univ. of Cambridge 1966–71, Univ. of Oxford 1971–80; Visiting Prof., Indiana Univ. 1979; Gardiner Prof. of Music, Univ. of Glasgow 1980–87; Avis Blewett Prof. of Music, Washington Univ., St Louis 1987–. *Publications:* New Berlioz Edition (gen. ed., complete works) 1965, Berlioz Orchestral Music 1969, Skryabin 1978, Berlioz 1982, Berlioz: Correspondance générale (ed.) Vol. 4 1984, Vol. 5 1989, Vol. 6 1995, Selected Letters of Berlioz 1995, Berlioz: Correspondance générale (ed.) Vol. 7 2001, Vol. 8 2002, Berlioz's Orchestration Treatise 2002; contrib. to The New Grove Dictionary of Music and Musicians, The New Grove Dictionary of Opera, many journals. *Honours:* Szymanowski Medal 1982, Grand Prix de Littérature Musicale Charles Cros 1985, 1996. *Address:* c/o Department of Music, Washington University, St Louis, MO 63130, USA.

**McDONALD, John,** BA, DMA; composer and pianist; b. 27 Oct. 1959, Norfolk, Virginia, USA; m.; two s. one d. *Education:* Yale University, Yale School of Music. *Career:* debut recital, Carnegie Hall, 1995; Associate Professor of Music, Tufts University, 1998–, Chair., Tufts Music Dept, 2000–03; Co-Director of Extension Works, Boston, 1990–2003; Artistic Ambassador, Cultural Specialist in Asia, 1994, 1995; Appearances on NPR, German radio; Premieres in Havana, Shanghai, St Petersburg; Commissions: Fleet Boston Celebrity Series, 1994, 2003; mem, Broadcast Music Inc. *Compositions:* More than 800 works including 20 piano albums, 9 piano sonatas; 2 piano concertos; 2 string quartets; 100 songs; Works for piccolo, flute, early instruments, chamber ensembles, wind ensemble and orchestra; 4 film scores. *Recordings:* Duetto for Piano; Sonatina for Soprano Sax and Piano; As pianist, featured in recordings of music by Donal Fox, John Harbison, Gardner Read, Gunther Schuller, George Walker. *Publications:* Sonatina for Piccolo and Piano, 1997; 2 solo Piccolo albums, 1995 and 1998; Ricercata, for three bass viols, 1999. *Contributions:* Essays, One Composer's Manifesto in the Form of a Wish List; Musings and Minor Writings. *Honours:* First prize, Leo M Traynor Competition for New Viol Music, 1997; Mellon Fellowship, 1996; NEA Grant, 1995. *Address:* Music Department, Tufts University, 48 Professors Row, Medford, MA 02155, USA.

**MacDONALD, Malcolm Calum;** writer on music and journalist; b. 26 Feb. 1948, Nairn, Scotland. *Education:* Downing College, Cambridge. *Career:* freelance writer for musical journals; music copyist; editor; Managing Ed., Tempo Magazine; compiler, Gramophone Classical Catalogue. *Compositions:* Surface Measure and Before Urbino, two songs with orchestra; At the Firth of Lorne and other songs with piano; Piano Pieces; arrangements of various contemporary works. *Publications:* Havergal Brian, Perspective on the Music 1972, John Foulds: His Life in Music 1975, Schoenberg 1976; contrib. to The Listener, Musical Times, Tempo, Musical Events, Records and Recordings. *Address:* 95 King Henry's Road, Swiss Cottage, London NW3, England.

**McDONALD, Margaret;** singer (mezzo-soprano); b. 1964, Grimsby, England. *Education:* Royal Northern College of Music and in Milan. *Career:* early experience with Glyndebourne Festival and Touring Opera; Engagements with Opera North as Carmen, and in Mason's Playing Away, Oberon (1985), Rebecca by Josephs and Gianni Schicchi; Eboli in Don Carlos for Scottish Opera Go Round, Ascanio in Benvenuto Cellini and Bizet's Djamileh for Chelsea Opera Group; Further appearances with English National Opera, English Bach Festival and Buxton Festival; Concerts include the Three Choirs, Quimper, Spitalfields, Saintes and Dublin Contemporary Festivals; Extensive oratorio repertory at concert halls and cathedrals throughout the United Kingdom, including works by Henze and Boulez. *Recordings include:* Isoletta in Bellini's La Straniera, with the Northern Sinfonia; She-Ancient in Tippett's Midsummer Marriage (Nimbus). *Honours:* Curtis Gold Medal, RNCM. *Current Management:* Musicmakers International Artists Representation, Tailor House, 63–65 High Street, Whitwell, Hertfordshire SG4 8AH,

England. *Telephone:* (1438) 871708. *Fax:* (1438) 871777. *E-mail:* musicmakers@compuserve.com. *Website:* www.operauk.com.

**McDONALL, Lois;** singer (soprano); b. 7 Feb. 1939, Larkspur, Alberta, Canada. *Education:* studied in Edmonton, Vancouver and Toronto and with Otakar Kraus in London. *Career:* debut, Toronto 1969 in Wolf-Ferrari's Il Segreto di Susanna; Sang in Ottawa and Toronto, then Flensburg, Germany; Sadler's Wells/English National Opera from 1970, notably as Handel's Semele and in the title role of Hamilton's Anna Karenina (1981); Other roles include Mozart's Countess, Constanze and Fiordiligi, Massenet's Manon and the Marschallin; Sang the Comtesse de Coigny in Andrea Chénier at Toronto, 1988; Teaching at University of Toronto (retired 2001); Freelance singing roles include Fedora, Opera in concert, Anna in Anna Karenina as guest of ENO; mem, National British Equity, ACTRA Canadian Society; Appeared in concert and freelance opera, including at the Miami Festival in Don Sanche, Lizst, with Opera Barrie as the Witch in Hansel and Gretel, The Old Maid in The Old Maid and the Thief; Having retired from the Univ. University of Toronto, she continues to teach privately and adjudicate music festivals; Many appearances for BBC Radio 2 and 3. *Recordings include:* Freia in The Ring (HMV) and Donizetti's Maria Padilla; Kurt Weill's Der Protagonist, Lizst's Don Sanche; Delius's Margot-la-rouge; Wagner's Rienzi. *Address:* c/o Canadian Opera Company, 227 Front Street E, Toronto, ON M5A 1EB, Canada.

**McDONNELL, Thomas Anthony;** singer (baritone); b. 27 April 1940, Melbourne, Australia; m. Mary Jennifer Smith. *Education:* Melba Conservatorium, Melbourne with Lennox Brewer. *Career:* debut, Belcore in L'Elisir d'amore at Brisbane, 1965; Sadler's Wells/English National Opera from 1967, as Mozart's Figaro, Verdi's Germont, Escamillo and in the first British stage performance of Prokofiev's War and Peace (1972) and Henze's The Bassarids (1974); Sang in War and Peace at the opening of the Sydney Opera House, 1973; Created roles in Crosse's The Story of Vasco, 1974, Henze's We Come to the River and Tippett's The Ice Break (both at Covent Garden); Iain Hamilton's The Royal Hunt of the Sun and Nicola LeFanu's Dawnpath (both 1977); London Collegiate Theatre 1977 in the British premiere of Nielsen's Saul and David; Well known as Mozart's Papageno and Tchaikovsky's Onegin; Sang Mozart's Commendatore with Opera Factory, Queen Elizabeth Hall, 1990 and Silva in Ernani for Chelsea Opera Group; Sang Lictor in The Coronation of Poppea for Opera Factory, 1992. *Recordings include:* Israel in Egypt; La Fanciulla del West; Tancredi; Donizetti rarities. *Honours:* Showcase Australia, 1965; Leverhulme Youth and Music Scholarship to Rome.

**MacDOUGALL, Jamie;** Scottish singer (tenor); b. 25 Jan. 1966, Glasgow. *Education:* Royal Scottish Acad. of Music, Guildhall School of Music, studied in Italy with Carlo Bergonzi. *Career:* appeared with Songmakers' Almanac 1988 at the Nottingham Festival, at the Buxton Festival and in London in Handel's Israel in Egypt and Mozart's C minor Mass; Season 1990–91 with Haydn's Creation in Aberdeen and at the Usher Hall, Edinburgh; Bach's Magnificat and Purcell's King Arthur at the Queen Elizabeth Hall; Mozart's C Minor Mass conducted by Frans Brueggen; Handel's Belshazzar; Orlando Paladino by Haydn at Garsington Manor; Bach's Magnificat and B Minor Mass in Belgium; Recital in the Szymanowski series at the Purcell Room; Operatic engagements include the Prologue and Quint in The Turn of the Screw and Gluck's Alceste with the English Bach Festival in Monte Carlo and at Covent Garden; Season 1996 with Septimus in Theodora at Glyndebourne, Fernando in Handel's Almira at Halle, Bach's Magnificat in Manchester and Mozart's Ottavio for GTO. *Recordings:* King Arthur conducted by Trevor Pinnock. *Honours:* Jean Highgate Scholarship and Lieder Prize at RSAM; Finalist in the Kathleen Ferrier Singing Competition, 1986.

**McDOWELL, Kathryn;** British music administrator; *Managing Director, London Symphony Orchestra;* b. 19 Dec. 1959, Belfast; m. Ian Ritchie 1997. *Education:* Edin. Univ. *Career:* began her career working with Welsh Nat. Opera; previous man. and devt positions with Scottish Chamber Orchestra and Ulster Orchestra; Opera and Music Theatre Officer, Arts Council of England 1992–94, apptd Music Dir 1994; fmr Chief Exec. Wales Millennium Centre; Dir City of London Festival 2001–05; Man. Dir LSO 2005–. *Honours:* Hon. FTCL 1996, Hon. RCM 1999. *Address:* London Symphony Orchestra, Barbican Centre, Silk Street, London, EC2Y 8DS, England (office). *Telephone:* (20) 7588-1116 (office). *Fax:* (20) 7374-0127 (office). *E-mail:* admin@lso.co.uk (office). *Website:* www.lso.co.uk (office).

**McELROY, Sam;** singer (baritone); b. 1974, Cork, Ireland. *Education:* Centre de Formation Lyrique, Paris. *Career:* appearances with Opéra National de Paris in Katya Kabanova, Un Maris a la Porte, and Parsifal as Dandini in Cenerentola for English Touring Opera, Nick Shadow in The Rake's Progress, Lockit in The Beggar's Opera and Blazes in Peter Maxwell Davies' The Lighthouse for Opera Theatre Company, Dublin, Rigoletto at Dartington; Concerts include Messiah with the Irish Chamber Orchestra and in Düsseldorf; Season 1999–2000 with Mozart's Count in Dublin; His opera roles for Opera Ireland include Figaro in Il Barbiere di Siviglia, Sharpless in Madame Butterfly, Harry Heegan in Silver Tassie and Cappadocian in Salome;; For Scottish Opera Go Round he has performed Malattesta in Don Pasquale; Japanese debut at the Pacific Music Festival, 1997; He has sung Lescaut in Manon for Opera Monte Carlo. *Honours:* Winner, Lombard and Ulster Music Awards 1992. *Current Management:* Harlequin Agency Ltd, 203

Fidlas Road, Cardiff, CF4 5NA, Wales. *Telephone:* (29) 2075-0821. *Fax:* (29) 2075-5971. *E-mail:* sioned@harlequin-agency.co.uk.

**McFADDEN, Claron;** singer (soprano); b. 1961, Rochester, NY, USA. *Education:* Eastman School, Rochester. *Career:* has sung in concert, opera and oratorio from 1984; Opera debut 1985 in Hasse's L'Eroe Chinese conducted by Ton Koopman; Regular appearances with William Christie in Europe and North and South America, notably as Amour in Rameau's Anacréon at the Opéa Lyrique du Rhin; Netherlands Opera debut 1989, as Zerbinetta in Ariadne auf Naxos; Season 1991 included Mozart's Impresario at the Salzburg Festival and on South Bank, Acis and Galatea with the King's Consort and Rameau's Les Indes Galantes with Les Arts Florissants in Montpellier; Has also worked in concert with the Schoenberg Ensemble and composers Gunther Schuller, Louis Andriessen and Steve Reich; Carmina Burana conducted by Leopold Hager and L'Enfant et les Sortilèges under Sergiu Comissiona; Sang in Purcell's Fairy Queen with Les Arts Florissants at the Barbican Hall, 1992; King Arthur at Covent Garden, 1995; Sang in Bach's B Minor Mass at St John's London, 1997; Lulu at the 1996 Glyndebourne Festival and Controller in the premiere of Jonathan Dove's Flight, 1998; Tippett's The Mask of Time at the 1999 London Proms; Season 2000–01 as Britten's Tytania for Opera North, Musetta for Glyndebourne Touring Opera and Schoenberg's Pierrot Lunaire at the London Proms. *Recordings:* Acis and Galatea and Handel's Ottone with the King's Consort; Haydn's Orfeo with La Stagione Frankfurt; Vocal works by Glenn Gould (Sony Classical); Les Indes Galantes. *Honours:* Prize Winner at the 1988 International Competition, 's-Hertogenbosch. *Current Management:* Phoenix Artists, 6 Windmill Street, London W1P 1HF, England.

**McFARLAND, Robert;** singer (baritone); b. 1958, Canada. *Career:* season 1987 as Donner in Das Rheingold at the Metropolitan and Amonasro at Miami and Houston; European debut Nice 1988, as Jack Rance (repeated for Opera North at Leeds, 1990); Further guest appearances at Miami (Luna in Trovatore), Lisbon (Iago, 1990), Toronto (Escamillo, 1990) and Monte Carlo (Nottingham in Roberto Devereux); Other roles include the villains in Les Contes d'Hoffmann; Renato at Antwerp, 1992 and Tonio (Miami, 1991). *Current Management:* Janet Jarriel, 861 Fair Oaks Drive, Macon, GA 31204, USA.

**McGEGAN, Nicholas,** BA, MA; British conductor; *Music Director, Philharmonia Baroque Orchestra*; b. 14 Jan. 1950, Sawbridgeworth, Hertfordshire, England. *Education:* Corpus Christi Coll., Cambridge, Magdalen Coll. Oxford. *Career:* Prof. of Baroque Flute 1973–79, Prof. of Music History 1975–79, Dir of Early Music 1976–80, Royal Coll. of Music; Artist-in-Residence, Washington Univ., St Louis, MO 1979–85; Music Dir, Philharmonia Baroque Orchestra, San Francisco 1985–; Music Dir, Ojai Music Festival, Ojai, CA 1988; Baroque Artistic Consultant, Santa Fe Chamber Music Festival 1990–92; Music Dir, Gottingen Handel Festival, Gottingen, Germany 1991–; founder and Artistic Dir, Arcadian Acad., San Francisco 1992–; Principal Conductor, Drottningholm Court Theatre, Sweden 1993–96; Principal Guest Conductor, Scottish Opera 1993–98 (new production of Così fan tutte 1998); Baroque Series Dir, St Paul Chamber Orchestra 1999–2003, Artistic Pnr 2003–06; conducted Alcina at Göttingen 2002; Music Dir, Irish Chamber Orchestra 2002–06; Artistic Dir, Killaloe Music Festival 2003–; Artist-in-Residence, Milwaukee Symphony Orchestra 2003–; appearances as guest conductor include San Francisco Symphony, Los Angeles Philharmonic, City of Birmingham Symphony Orchestra, Hallé Orchestra, Sydney Symphony, Melbourne Symphony, Houston Symphony, Nat. Symphony, Atlanta Symphoniy, Minnesota Orchestra, Orchestre de la Suisse Romand, St Louis Symphony, Detroit Symphony, Malaysian Philharmonic, Royal Concertgebouw Orchestra, Aspen Music Festival, Toronto Symphony, Philadelphia Orchestra, New York Philharmonic; mem. advisory bds Maryland Handel Festival and London's Handel House. *Recordings:* as a soloist: C.P.E. Bach's Quartets (flute), J.C. Bach's Sonatas Op1 18 (flute, with Christopher Hogwood), J.S. Bach's Anna Magdalena Notebook (harpsichord), Music for two flutes by the Bach family (with Stephen Preston), Haydn's London Trios (flute), Piano Trios (piano and flute), Vivaldi's Concertos for two flutes; as conductor: J.S. Bach's Cantatas and around 20 operas and oratorios by Handel, of which Susanna and Ariodante have both won Gramophone Awards, and works by Arne, Corelli, P. Humfrey, Matteis, Monteverdi, Mozart, Purcell, Rameau (including three operas), A. Scarlatti, Telemann, Uccellini, Vivaldi. *Publications:* Editions, Philidor's Tom Jones 1978; contrib. articles, including on Handel to Musical Times 1994, on Handel as a practical opera composer (in the collected edn Die Gegenwart der musikalischen Vergangenheit: Meisterwerke der Musik in der Werkstatt des Dirigenten) 1999. *Honours:* two Diapason d'Or Awards (for recordings with the Arcadian Acad.), Halle Handel Festival Handel Prize, Germany, Drottningholmsteaterns Vanners Hederstecken (hon. medal of the Friends of the Drottningholm Theatre). *Current Management:* Schwalbe and Partners, 170 E 61 Street #5N, New York, NY 10021, USA.

**McGIBBON, Roisin;** singer (soprano); b. 1960, Northern Ireland. *Education:* Guildhall School of Music with Margaret Lensky, and at the National Opera Studio. *Career:* represented Northern Ireland in the Cardiff Singer of the World Competition, 1985; Appearances for Radio Telfis Eireann include Lieder by Schumann and Liszt; Wexford Festival 1986, in Humperdinck's Königskinder and Rossini's Tancredi; Has also sung the Composer in Ariadne auf Naxos; Concert engagements in Messiah at Armagh, Britten's War Requiem in Belfast, Savitri by Holst at Aix and Elgar's Apostles in

Nottingham. *Current Management:* Magenta Music International, 64 Highgate High Street, London N6 5HX, England.

**McGILLOWAY, Emer;** singer (mezzo-soprano); b. 1967, Northern Ireland. *Education:* Medecine in Belfast and Dublin, Guildhall School with Laura Sarti. *Career:* Maddalena in Linda di Chamounix, Juno in La Calisto, Der Trommler in Der Kaiser von Atlantis and Veruna in Dvořák's Cunning Peasant at the GSM; Further study at the National Opera Studio, 1997–98; Studying with Robert Dean; Opera North from 1998 as Olga in Eugene Onegin, Lady Essex in Gloriana, also televised, and Mozart's Cherubino; Season 1998–99 in Rusalka and as Hope in Gluck's Orfeo for English National Opera. *Honours:* Herbert Morris Griffen Opera Award; Ann Price Mezzo-soprano Award; Finalist Grimsby International Singing Competition. *Current Management:* Music International, 13 Ardilaun Road, London, N5 2QR, England.

**McGREEVY, Geraldine,** Dip RAM, ARAM; British singer (soprano); b. 1968. *Education:* Univ. of Birmingham; Royal Acad. of Music; National Opera Studio. *Career:* operatic roles include: Contessa Almaviva, Donna Anna, Vitellia, Rosalinde in Fledermaus, Micaela, First Lady and Miss Jessel (WNO); Ellen Orford (Oper Frankfurt); Alice Ford (Aix-en-Provence, 2001 and Paris, 2002); Ghita Der Zwerg, La Monnaie; Fiordiligi (RAM conducted by Sir Colin Davis, 1997 and Opera Zuid, 1999); Female Chorus in Rape of Lucretia (Edinburgh Festival); Alcina, Cleopatra in Giulio Cesare, Angelica in Orlando and Poppea in Agrippina (Early Opera Co); Galatea in Acis and Galatea; Laurette in Le Docteur Miracle; Donna Anna, First Lady, Mistress Page in Sir John in Love, Casilda in Gondoliers (British Youth Opera); concert repertoire includes: Schoenberg's Pierrot Lunaire; Villa Lobos' Bachianas Brasileiras No. 5; Berg's Orchestral Extracts from Wozzeck with Gennadi Rozhdestvensky; Britten's Les Illuminations; Strauss' Vier Letzte Lieder; Wigmore Hall debut, 1997, many appearances there since; Purcell Room debut, 1997; recitals at St John's Smith Square, Frankfurt Opera House, Klavier Festival Ruhr with Graham Johnson, Edinburgh Festival, and in Newcastle with Julius Drake; numerous broadcasts for the BBC and for European radio stations; recent concert engagements include: The English Concert with Trevor Pinnock, The Acad. of St Martin in the Fields with Sir Neville Marriner, the Moscow Tchaikovsky Symphony Orchestra in Zurich with Jane Glover, the London Philharmonic Orchestra with Kurt Masur, the Sharoun Ensemble and Anne Manson in the Cologne Philharmonic and the Royal Liverpool Philharmonic Orchestra with Petr Altrichter and Libor Pesek. *Recordings:* Wolf Goethe Leider (with Graham Johnson); songs by Arthur Bliss (with the Nash Ensemble); contributions to Complete Schubert Edition; music by John Blow (with Red Byrd and the Parley of Instruments); Consort Songs by William Byrd (with Phantasm); Spanish Renaissance Music (with Music Antiqua of London). *Honours:* Worshipful Company of Musicians Silver Medal, 1995; RAM Shinn Fellowship, 1996; Kathleen Ferrier Award, 1996. *Current Management:* Askonas Holt Ltd, Lonsdale Chambers, 27 Chancery Lane, London, WC2A 1PF, England. *Telephone:* (20) 7400-1700. *Fax:* (20) 7400-1799. *E-mail:* info@askonasholt.co.uk. *Website:* www.askonasholt.co.uk; www.geraldinemcgreevy.com (home).

**MacGREGOR, Joanna Clare,** BA, FRAM; British concert pianist; b. 16 July 1959, London; d. of Angela MacGregor and Alfred MacGregor; m. Richard Williams 1986; one d. (deceased). *Education:* South Hampstead High School for Girls, New Hall Coll. Cambridge, Royal Acad. of Music. *Career:* Young Concert Artists Trust concerts and recitals, UK 1985–88; performances of classical, jazz and contemporary music in over 40 countries; has performed with Rotterdam, Oslo and Netherlands Radio and Royal Philharmonic Orchestras, Sydney, Berlin, Chicago, BBC and London Symphony Orchestras, New York Philharmonic, Philharmonia, London Mozart Players, Royal Scottish, Royal Liverpool, English Chamber Orchestras; has worked with Sir Harrison Birtwistle, Pierre Boulez, John Adams, Lou Harrison and jazz artists Django Bates and Andy Sheppard; numerous radio and TV appearances including Last Night of the Proms 1997; established own record label Sound Circus 1998; Prof. of Music, Gresham Coll. 1998–; conducting debut on UK tour with Britten Sinfonia, Assoc. Artistic Dir 2002–; mem. Arts Council of England 1998–. *Recordings:* American Piano Classics, Britten Concerto, Satie, The Gershwin Songbook, and music by Bach, Nancarrow, Scarlatti, Bartók, Debussy, Ravel and Messaien; Memoirs of an Amnesiac (radio play). *Publications:* Music Tuition Book, Joanna MacGregor's Piano World (five vols) 2001. *Honours:* Hon. Fellow Royal Acad. of Music, Trinity Coll. of Music, RSA; European Encouragement Prize for Music 1995, NFMS Sir Charles Grove Award 1998, South Bank Show Award for Classical Music 2000, Royal Philharmonic Soc. Audience Development Award 2003. *Address:* c/o Ingpen and Williams, 7 St George's Court, 131 Putney Bridge Road, London, SW15 2PA, England (office). *Telephone:* (20) 8874-3222 (office). *Fax:* (20) 8877-3113 (office).

**McGUIRE, Edward,** ARCM, ARAM; British composer; b. 15 Feb. 1948, Glasgow, Scotland. *Education:* Royal Acad. of Music with James Iliff, State Acad. of Music, Stockholm, Sweden with Ingvar Lidholm. *Career:* radio broadcasts on BBC Radio 3 include Symphonic Poem, Calgacus 1976, Symphonic Poem, Source 1979; Euphoria performed by The Fires of London 1980, Edinburgh Int. Festival; debut at London Proms 1982; BBC Radio 3 series featured trilogy, Rebirth, Interregnum, Liberation 1990; Wilde Festival commission (String Trio) for performance by The Nash Ensemble 1986; premiere of Guitar Concerto 1988; Peter Pan for Scottish Ballet 1989; mem., Whistlebinkies Folk Music Group 1973–; mem. Scottish Arts Council (music cttee 1980–83), Musicians' Union, Glasgow Branch (chair. 2001–). *Compositions:* A Glasgow Symphony, 1990; The Loving of Etain, 1990 for Paragon Opera; Trombone Concerto, 1991; Viola Concerto, 1998; Accordion Concerto, 1999; Violin Concerto, 2000, Defying Fate (one-act ballet) 2005. *Recordings:* music has featured on albums, including Paragon Premieres, 1993 and Scotland's Music, 1993; The Very Best of the BBC Orchestras, BBC Music Magazine 1997. *Honours:* RAM Hecht Prize 1968, Nat. Young Composers Competition, Liverpool Univ. 1969, Competition for Test Piece for Carl Flesch Int. Violin Competition 1978, Competition for a String Quartet for performance at SPNM 40th Anniversary Gala Concert, Barbican 1983, featured composer Park Lane Group Purcell Room series 1993, BBC Radio 3 Composers of the Week 1995, featured composer Bath Int. Guitar Festival 1996, Int. Viola Congress 1998, Edinburgh Int. Harp Festival 2002, British Composers Award 2003, Creative Scotland Award 2004. *Current Management:* Scottish Music Information Centre, 1 Bowmont Gardens, Glasgow, G12 9LR, Scotland. *Website:* www.scottishmusiccentre.com/edward_mcguire (office).

**MACHL, Tadeusz;** Composer, Organist and Professor; b. 22 Oct. 1922, Lwow, Poland; m. Irena Paszkiewicz-Machl; two c. *Education:* State College of Music, Kraków, 1949–52, under guidance Professor Malawski and Professor Rutkowski. *Career:* Works recorded in Poland, played through Poland and abroad; Professor, Prorector, 1969–72, Academy of Music, Kraków; Director of Chair of Composition, 1966–72; President of Disciplinary Committee of Pedagogical Staff, 1972–77; Leader of Amateur Choirs, 1960–1980; President, Union of Amateur Choirs and Orchestras, 1979–83; mem, Union of Polish Composers and Society of Authors ZAiKS, Warsaw. *Compositions:* For great symphony orchestra: 6 Symphonies: 1947, 1948, 1948, 1954, 1963, 1998; 7 Organ Concertos, 1950, 1952, 1953, 1957, 1979, 1983; Concerto for 3 organs, 1969; 9 Instrumental Concertos: Concerto for voice, 1958; Violin Concerto, 1960; Harpsichord Concerto, 1962; Piano Concerto, 1964; Arpa Concerto, 1965; Concerto for piano and harpsichord, 1966; Violoncello (or Viola) Concerto, 1967; Concerto for 2 pianos and organ, 1969; Concerto for bugle-horn, 1971; 4 Cantatas: Work Day, 1948; Cantata for Youth, 1954; Icar's Flight, 1968; Blue Cross, 1974; Rapsod, 1996; Transcriptions for organ compositions of J. S. Bach: Preludes and Fugues, 1956; Chaconne, 1973; Fantasy G, 1993; Poems: Jubilee Poem, 1979, My Town, 1992, Dirge, 1994; Lyric Suite, 1956; Requiem, 1980; Ouverture Silvery Wings, 1985; Symphonic Scherzo, 1986; Symphonic Poem, 1996; Chamber Music: 4 string quartets, 1950, 1957, 1961, 1972; Lyric Suite, 1955; Herbarium, 1980; Terrarium, 1982; Triptych–Heartiness Landscapes, 1993; Suite for stringed instruments, 1997; Composition for 20 Years of Pontificate of Jan Pawel II, 1998; In Memoriam St Kinga, 1998; Triptych in memoriam Amdrzej Hiolski for chamber orchestra, 2001; Rosary Poems for chamber orchestra, 2001; Organ Music: 5 Virtuoso etudes, 1950; Deux pieces pour grand orgue, 1964; Pièce en cinque mouvements, 1965; Mini Suita, 1967; Triptych, 1968; 10 Compositions pour orgue, 1970; Landscapes I, 1976, II, 1978, III, 1982; Great Fantasy with B-A-C-H Fugue, 1980; Rupicaprae, 1982; 15 Rosary Poems, 1983; Sonate for 3 orgue, 1984; Disonatio, 1989; Poem, 1992; Stained Glass Windows, 1993; 45 Preludes to Polish Church Songs, 1997; Epitafium dédie a Jean Langlais, 1999; Choruses; Songs; Piano Music; Music for cinema, theatre and ballet. *Honours:* Award: Special Mention for String Quartets in Liège, I, 1956, II, 1959; Golden Cross of Merit, 1965; Active Man of Culture, 1970; Bachelors and Officers, Polonia Restituta, 1972, 1988; Merit Teacher of Poland, 1989; 1st Degress Ministry of Culture and Art, 1971 and 1990. *Address:* ul Bol Chrobrego 29/27, 31-428 Kraków, Poland.

**MACHOVER, Tod,** MM; American composer and cellist; b. 24 Nov. 1953, New York; m. June Kinoshita. *Education:* Juilliard School of Music, Univ. of California at Santa Cruz, Columbia Univ. *Career:* Composer-in-Residence, Institut de Recherche et Coordination Acoustique/Musique, Paris 1978–79; Dir, Musical Research 1979–85; faculty mem., Assoc. Prof. of Music and Media, Dir of Experimental Media Facility, Media Laboratory, MIT 1985–, Co-Dir of research consortium 1994–; invented technology named hyperinstruments 1986, began instrument design for this technology 1991–; Brain Opera, first performance, Lincoln Center Festival 1996; tours with his repertoire in the USA, Europe and Asia; music performed by many prominent musicians, such as Yo-Yo Ma, and ensembles. *Compositions include:* Fusione Fugace, 1981–82; Electric Etudes, 1983; Hyperstring Trilogy, 1991–93; Bounce, 1992; Wake-up Music, 1995; Brain Opera, 1995–96; He's Our Dad, 1997; Hypermusic installations at Meteorite Museum, Essen, 1998; Resurrection, premiered at Houston, 1999. *Publications include:* Hyperinstruments: A Progress Report 1992; contrib. book chapters, articles in learned musical journals. *Honours:* Gaudeamus Prize, 1977; Grant, Gulbenkian Foundation, 1980; Grants from National Endowment for the Arts, 1981, 1983, 1985; Prix de la Creation, French Culture Ministry, 1984; Friedheim Award, Kennedy Centre, 1987; Grant, Aaron Copland Fund for music, 1994; Chevalier, Ordre des Arts et des Lettres, 1995. *Address:* MIT Media Laboratory, E15-444, 20 Ames Street, Cambridge, MA 02139, USA. *Website:* www.media.mit.edu/~tod.

**MACIAS, Reinaldo;** singer (tenor); b. 1 Sept. 1956, Cuba. *Education:* studied in the USA and at the Geneva Conservatory. *Career:* sang at first in concert, notably with Messiah, Haydn's Schöpfung and Jahreszeiten and the Requiems of Dvořák, Britten and Mozart; Verdi Requiem in Paris, 1989; Opera roles from 1989, with Almaviva in Vienna and Zürich, Don Ottavio and Ferrando in Netherlands, the Berlioz Iopas at Zürich and Gounod's Roméo in Liège (1993); other roles include the Duke of Mantua, Tamino and Lindoro (all in Zürich, 1991–92). *Current Management:* Stafford Law, Candleway, Broad

Street, Sutton Valence, Kent ME17 3AT, England. *Website:* www.stafford-law .com.

**McINTOSH, Thomas Lee,** MSc, FRSA; British conductor; b. 3 Dec. 1938; m. Miranda Harrison Vincent 1982. *Education:* Juilliard School of Music. *Career:* conductor and Music Dir London City Chamber Orchestra 1973–; Artistic Dir E Anglian Summer Music Festival 1978–, Penang Malaysia Music Festival 1986–87, Opera Anglia 1989–, Artanglia Ltd 1988; principal guest conductor Canton Symphony Orchestra 1994–. *Publications:* Eighteenth-Century Symphonic Music (contributing ed.), arrangements for orchestra of Valentine Waltzes (George Antheil), Rag Suite (various composers), Flower Rag Suite (Scott Joplin), Piano Concerto on Japanese Themes 2005. *Honours:* first prize Int. Kranichstein Competition, prize winner Busoni Competition, Bolanzo, three Sasakawa Foundation awards, UK. *Address:* Cath Anderson, The Old School, Bridge Street, Hadleigh, Suffolk IP7 6BY, England (office). *Telephone:* (1473) 822596 (office). *Fax:* (1473) 824175 (office). *E-mail:* Thomas.McIntosh@ minstrelmusic.co.uk (office). *Website:* www.minstrelmusic.co.uk (office).

**McINTYRE, Sir Donald Conroy,** Kt, CBE, OBE; British singer (bass); b. 22 Oct. 1934, Auckland, NZ; s. of George Douglas and Hermyn McIntyre; m. Jill Redington 1961; three d. *Education:* Mt Albert Grammar School, Auckland, Auckland Teachers' Training Coll. and Guildhall School of Music, London. *Career:* Prin. Bass, Sadler's Wells Opera 1960–67; with Royal Opera House, Covent Garden 1967–; annual appearances at Bayreuth Festival 1967–81; frequent int. guest appearances. *Roles include:* Wotan and Wanderer (Der Ring), Dutchman (Der Fliegende Holländer), Telramund (Lohengrin), Barak (Die Frau ohne Schatten), Pizzaro (Fidelio), Golaud (Pelléas et Mélisande), Kurwenal and King Marke (Tristan and Isolde), Gurnemanz, Klingsor and Amfortas (Parsifal), Heyst (Victory), Jochanaan (Salome), Macbeth, Scarpia (Tosca), the Count (Marriage of Figaro), Nick Shadow (The Rake's Progress), Hans Sachs (Die Meistersinger), Dr. Schöne (Woyzeck), Cardillac (Cardillac by Hindemith), Rocco (Fidelio), The Doctor (Der Freischütz), Prospero (Un Re In Asloto), Sarastro (Magic Flute), Balstrode (Peter Grimes), Telramund (Lohengrin); Prus (The Makropoulos Case), Rheingold, The Ring (video); recordings include Pelléas et Mélisande, Oedipus Rex, Il Trovatore, etc. *Honours:* Hon. DMus (Auckland) 1992; Fidelio Medal, AIDO 1989, NZ Award for Outstanding Contribs, Festival of the Arts 1990. *Current Management:* Ingpen & Williams, 7 St George's Court, 131 Putney Bridge Road, London, SW15 2PA, England. *Address:* Fox Hill Farm, Jackass Lane, Keston, Bromley, Kent BR2 6AN, England (home). *Telephone:* (1689) 855368 (home). *Fax:* (1689) 860724 (home).

**McINTYRE, Joy;** singer (soprano); b. 24 Sept. 1938, Kinsley, Kansas, USA. *Education:* New England Conservatory, Salzburg Mozarteum. *Career:* sang at the Saarbrucken Opera 1964–66, Dortmund 1966–74 and Munich Staatsoper 1976–81; Roles have included Suzuki, Brangaene, Leonore, Venus, Ortrud, the Dyer's Wife, Marie, Abigaille, Santuzza, Turandot, Judith in Bluebeard's Castle and Lady Macbeth; Guest appearances at the Vienna Staatsoper, Lyon, Strasbourg, Brussels, Hamburg and Glasgow (Scottish Opera). *Address:* c/o Bayerische Staatsoper, Max Joseph Platz, Pf 100148, 8000 Munich 1, Germany.

**McKAY, Elizabeth Norman,** BSc, DPhil, LRAM; British musicologist and pianist; b. 21 Nov. 1931, London, England; m. Gilbert Watt McKay 1960; one s. two d. *Education:* Bristol Univ., Somerville Coll., Oxford. *Career:* chamber musician, accompanist, coach, theatre work; teacher; lecturer; broadcaster; founder and hon. mem. Schubert Inst. UK 1992–. *Publications include:* Schubert's Music for the Theatre, Proceedings of The Royal Musical Association, 1966–67; Schubert as a Composer of Operas, Schubert Studies, 1982; The Impact of The New Pianofortes: Mozart, Beethoven and Schubert, 1987; Franz Schubert's Music for the Theatre, 1991; Schuberts Klaviersona-ten von 1815 bis 1825, in Franz Schubert Reliquie-Sonate, 1992; Franz Schubert: A Biography, 1996; Proceedings of the Oxford Schubert Bicentenary Symposium 1997, co-editor; Schubert's String and Piano Duos in context, Schubert Studies, 1998; Schubert and the professional musicians with whom he associated, Schubert und seine Freunde, 1999; contrib. to The New Grove Dictionary of Opera, Pipers Enzyklopadie des Musik Theaters 1994, Schubert Lexikon 1997, The Music Review, The Musical Times, Österreichische Musikzeitschrift, Music and Letters, The Beethoven Newsletter, BBC Music Magazine, Journal of the IFSI, Schubert-Enzyklopädie 2004. *Honours:* hon. bd mem. Int. Franz Schubert Inst. 1992–2005. *Address:* Gamrie, Swan Lane, Long Hanborough, Witney, Oxfordshire OX29 8BT, England.

**McKAY, Marjory Grieve,** GRSM, ARMCM, FTCM, ARCM; British singer (soprano); b. 23 June 1951, Edinburgh, Scotland; m. Frederick Charles McKay 1981. *Education:* Trinity Academy, Edinburgh, Royal Manchester College of Music, Royal Northern College of Music. *Career:* debut as Esmeralda, Scottish Opera, 1980; Scottish opera roles Esmeralda in Bartered Bride, Belleza in L'Egisto and Feklusa in Katya Kabanova; Scottish Opera Go Round, Violetta; Welsh National Opera Workshop, Violetta in La Traviata; Many concerts and recitals in Scotland and the north of England; now living in Sydney, Australia; debut in Australian Opera as Gerhilde in Die Walküre, 1985 and Xenia in Boris Godonuv, 1986; debut with Western Australian Opera as Madama Butterfly, 1987; created the title role in Alan Holley's new opera, Dorothea; Les Huguenots Video (Joan Sutherland's Farewell), 1990; currently with Opera Australia.

**MACKAY, Penelope Judith,** AGSM; British singer (soprano); b. 6 April 1943, Bradford, Yorkshire, England. *Education:* secretarial coll., Lycée Français,

London, Guildhall School of Music and Drama. *Career:* debut, Glyndebourne 1970; sang at Glyndebourne 1970–72, with English Opera Group 1973–75, English Music Theatre 1976–78, ENO 1980–83; freelance work in the UK, Europe and USA; over 20 leading roles; sang in premieres of Lutyens's Time Off 1971, Britten's Death in Venice 1973; British premieres of Hans Werner Henze's La Cubana in the title role 1978, Krenek's Jonny Spielt Auf (Anita) 1984, Ligeti, Le Grand Macabre (Miranda) 1982; Austrian premiere in modern times of Fux's Angelica, Vincitrice di Alcina (Angelica), Graz 1984, and British premiere in modern times of Handel's Rodrigo (Rodrigo) 1985; Prof. of Singing, Royal Acad. of Music, London and Guildhall School of Music and Drama, London; mem. Incorporated Soc. of Musicians, British Voice Asscn, Asscn of Teachers of Singing. *Honours:* Hon. ARAM . *Address:* 30 Fairfield Road, Saxmundham, Suffolk IP17 1BA, England (office). *E-mail:* pennymackay@ gsmd.ac.uk (office).

**MACKAY, Robert Andrew,** BSc, MMus; British composer, actor, singer (baritone), musician (flute, classical guitar, bass) and university lecturer; b. 12 July 1973, London. *Education:* Keele Univ., Bangor Univ. *Career:* session musician in Wales 1997–2001; composer-in-residence, Radio Bratislava, Slovakia 1998–99; bass player, Gyroscope 1998; flute, guitar and bass player, Tystion 1998–2002; collaborator with Pwyll ap Siôn on commission for Nat. Youth Choir of Wales and Opera Heloise 1999; works performed in UK, France, USA and New Zealand; several television appearances and radio broadcasts; mem. PRS, PRC, Equity, Soc. for the Promotion of New Music, BMIC, SAN. *Theatre:* Only Just 1997. *Film appearances:* Merlin, A Beautiful Mistake. *Television appearances:* Idot (S4C), Garej (S4C), 4-Track (S4C), Lois (S4C), Sesiwn Hwyr (S4C). *Radio performances:* Late Junction (BBC Radio 3), Hear and Now (BBC Radio 3), two John Peel sessions (BBC Radio 1). *Compositions include:* Tempestuous Relationships 1995, Environs 1996, Sea Pictures 1997, Voicewind 1998, Postcards from the Summer 1999, Peiriant Gorllewinol, Meddwi Dros Gymru (Radio Cymru Rap Award for Album of the Year 2000) 1999, Flute Melt 2000, Augustine's Message 2001, Need Without Reason 2001, Joyce's Vision 2002, Cain and Abel 2003. *Recordings:* ICMC98 1998, 1er Concurso International de Miniaturas Electroacústicas 2003. *Publications:* Shrug Off Ya Complex 1999, Mr. Blaidd 2000, Hen Gelwydd Prydain Newydd 2000, Y Meistri 2001, Discontact! III 2003,. *Honours:* Bourges Synthése Festival Prix Résidence, France 1997, Hungarian Radio Special Prize (Ear 99) 1999, BBC Radio Cymru Rap Award Album of the Year 2000. *Address:* 239 Earlsfield Road, Earlsfield, London, SW18 3DE, England.

**McKELLAR FERGUSON, Kathleen;** singer (mezzo-soprano); b. 1959, Stirling, Scotland. *Education:* Royal Scottish Academy, Royal College of Music; studied with Margaret Hyde. *Career:* South Bank debut 1987, with the London Bach Orchestra; Beethoven's Ninth at the Gstaad Festival, 1990 and with the Ulster Orchestra; Other repertoire includes Mozart's Requiem, the Brahms Alto Rhapsody, Mahler's 8th, Songs of the Auvergne and A Child of our Time; Season 1990–91 with Haydn's Nelson Mass and the English Chamber Orchestra, Messiah with the Liverpool Philharmonic; Also sings Elgar's Sea Pictures and Music Makers, St Matthew Passion (Fairfields Hall) and Elijah; Concerts with Yehudi Menuhin at Festival Halls; Opera repertoire includes Florence Pike in Albert Herring (Aldeburgh 1986), Maketaten in Aknaten by Philip Glass for ENO 1987, Mozart's Marcellina and Third Lady for Pavillion Opera, Cherubino, and Handel's Bradamante (Alcina) for Flanders Opera 1991, Second Lady (Magic Flute) at Théâtre Royale de la Monnaie, Brussels, 1993, Suzuki (Madama Butterfly) for Opera Forum in Nederlands, 1994–, and Bradamante (Alcina) with Nikolaus Harnoncourt at Zürich Opera; Second Lady at Festival of Aix en Provence. *Address:* c/o Zürich Opera, Falkenstrasse 1, 8008 Zürich, Switzerland.

**McKERRACHER, Colin;** singer (tenor); b. 1960, Falkirk, Scotland. *Education:* Royal Northern College of Music with Joseph Ward, studied with Nicolai Gedda. *Career:* has sung with Glyndebourne Touring Opera and the Festival in Simon Boccanegra and Capriccio, 1986–87; Appearances with Scottish Opera-Go-Round as Števa in Jenůfa, Beppe and Turiddu (Cav and Pag) and Don Carlos; Lensky in Eugene Onegin for Opera 80 followed by Monostatos in The Magic Flute and Ernesto in Don Pasquale; English National Opera and Covent Garden debuts season, 1990–91, as Ferrando and in Così fan tutte. *Honours:* Prizewinner, 1989 Rio de Janeiro International Singing Competition.

**MACKERRAS, Sir Charles,** Kt, CH, AC, CBE; British (b. American) conductor; b. 17 Nov. 1925, Schenectady, NY, USA of Australian parentage; s. of Alan and Catherine Mackerras; m. Judith Wilkins 1947; two d. *Education:* Sydney Grammar School, NSW Conservatoire and Prague Acad. of Music. *Career:* Prin. Oboist Sydney Symphony Orchestra 1943–46; Staff Conductor Sadler's Wells Opera 1948–53; Prin. Conductor BBC Concert Orchestra 1954–56; guest opera conductor at Covent Garden, English Nat. Opera, Berlin State Opera, Hamburg State Opera, Vienna State Opera, etc. 1956–66; First Conductor, Hamburg State Opera 1966–69; Musical Dir, Sadler's Wells Opera, later English Nat. Opera 1970–77, Chief Guest Conductor, BBC Symphony Orchestra 1976–79; Chief Conductor Sydney Symphony Orchestra 1982–85; Prin. Guest Conductor Royal Liverpool Philharmonic Orchestra 1986–88; Musical Dir Welsh Nat. Opera 1987–92, Conductor Emer. 1993–; Prin. Guest Conductor Scottish Chamber Orchestra 1992–95, Conductor Laureate 1995–; Prin. Guest Conductor San Francisco Opera 1993–96 (Conductor Emer. 1996–), Royal Philharmonic Orchestra 1993–96, Czech Philharmonic Orchestra 1997–2003, Philharmonia Orchestra 2002–; Music Dir Orchestra of St Luke's 1998–2001, Music Dir Emer. 2001;

Pres. Trinity Coll. of Music 2000–; guest conductor in Europe, USA, Canada and Australia; 2005 season: Brouček in Prague, Zauberflöte at Glyndebourne, Edinburgh Festival, Fidelio at Barbican, London; 2006: Bartered Bride at Covent Garden, Makropoulos Case at ENO, London. *Arrangements:* Ballets: Pineapple Poll (Sullivan) 1951, Lady and the Fool (Verdi) 1954, Melbourne Cup 1965; reconstruction of Arthur Sullivan's Lost Cello Concerto 1986. *Recordings:* numerous, notably Janáček, Handel, Mozart operas and symphonies, Brahms, Beethoven, Dvořák, Mahler and Schubert; Smetana's Bartered Bride 2005. *Publications:* contributed four appendices to Charles Mackerras: A Musician's Musician by Nancy Phelan 1987, musical articles in various magazines. *Honours:* Hon. RAM 1969, FRCM 1987, FRNCM 1999, FTCL 1999; Hon. Fellow St Peter's Coll. Oxford 1999, Cardiff Univ. 2003; Hon. DMus (Hull) 1990, (Nottingham) 1991, (York, Masaryk, Czech Repub. and Griffith, Australia) 1994, (Oxford) 1997, (Prague Acad. of Music) 1999, (Napier) 2000 (Melbourne) 2003, (Sydney) 2003, (Janáček Acad. of Music, Brno) 2004, Dr hc (RAM) 2005; Evening Standard Award for Most Outstanding Achievement in Opera 1977, Janáček Medal 1978, Gramophone Record of the Year 1977, 1980, 1999, Grammy Award for Best Opera 1981, Gramophone Best Opera Recording 1983, 1984, 1994, 1999, Medal of Merit, Czech Repub. 1996, Prix Caecilia 1999, Preis der Deutschen Schallplattenkritik 1999, Chopin Prize and Lifetime Achievement Award, Midem, Cannes 2000, Asscn of British Orchestras Award 2001, Royal Philharmonic Soc. Gold Medal and BBC Radio 3 Listeners' Award 2005; Queen's Medal for Music 2005. *Address:* 10 Hamilton Terrace, London, NW8 9UG, England. *Telephone:* (20) 7286-4047. *Fax:* (20) 7289-5893.

**MACKIE, David,** MA, BMus, DipMus Ed, RSAM, ARCM; British accompanist, repetiteur and conductor; b. 25 Nov. 1943, Greenock, Scotland. *Education:* Greenock Acad., Royal Scottish Acad. of Music, Glasgow Univ. - Birmingham Univ. *Career:* repetiteur, D'Oyly Carte Opera Co. 1975–76, Chorus Master and Assoc. Conductor 1976–82; freelance accompanist, repetiteur, conductor 1982–. *Publications:* Reconstruction of Sullivan's Cello Concerto (with Sir Charles Mackerras) 1986, Arthur Sullivan and the Royal Society of Musicians of Great Britain 2005. *Address:* 187A Worple Road, Raynes Park, London, SW20 8RE, England (home). *Telephone:* (20) 8946-7892 (home). *Fax:* (20) 8946-7892 (home).

**MACKIE, Neil;** Singer (Tenor); b. 11 Dec. 1946, Aberdeen, Scotland. *Career:* Debut: London with the English Chamber Orchestra under Raymond Leppard; European engagements at the Flanders and Savonlinna Festivals, Concertgebouw Orchestra, in Rome for RAI and in Scandinavia; Tours of Netherlands and Belgium with La Petite Bande conducted by Sigiswald Kuijken; Association with Peter Maxwell Davies includes premieres of The Martyrdom of St Magnus, 1977, The Lighthouse 1980 and Into the Labyrinth 1983; Sang Gomatz in Mozart's Zaide at Wexford, 1981; Premiered Henze's Three Poems of W H Auden at Aldeburgh, 1984; Appeared at Cheltenham and Aldeburgh Festivals; British engagements with the Hallé, Bournemouth Sinfonietta, BBC Symphony and Scottish Chamber Orchestras, and with the London Sinfonietta under Simon Rattle; June 1988, Into the Labyrinth at the Ojai Festival in America; 1988–89 tour of USA with the Scottish Chamber Orchestra and appearances with the Orchestre National de Paris; Professor of Singing, Royal College of Music, London, 1985; Head of Vocal Studies, Royal College of Music, 1993. *Recordings include:* Mozart's Requiem and Haydn's Die Schöpfung with La Petite Bande; Mozart Masses with the King's College Choir; Britten's Serenade, with premiere of Now Sleeps the Crimson Petal and unpublished songs. *Honours:* FRSAMD, 1992; Hon D Mus, Aberdeen, 1993; CStJ, 1996; C.B.E., 1996; FRCM, 1996; FRSE, 1999. *Address:* c/o Royal College of Music (vocal faculty), Prince Consort Road, London, SW7 2 BS.

**MACKIE, William;** Singer (Bass); b. 16 Aug. 1954, Ayr, Scotland. *Education:* Royal Scottish Academy, Glasgow. *Career:* Debut: Scottish Opera, 1980, as Antonio in Le nozze di Figaro; Welsh National Opera, 1982–83, in Cenerentola, A Midsummer Night's Dream and Butterfly; English National Opera, 1989, in Lear by Reimann; Season 1989–90 in Die Zauberflöte at Aix-en-Provence and Hansel and Gretel at Strasbourg; Pocket Opera Nuremberg, 1991, as Assur in Semiramide; Other roles include Rossini's Basilio, Fasolt in Das Rheingold and Lodovico in Otello. *Recordings include:* Parsifal. *Address:* c/o English National Opera, St Martin's Lane, London WC2N 4ES, England.

**McKINNEY, Thomas;** singer (baritone); b. 5 May 1946, Lufkin, TX, USA. *Education:* studied in Houston, Hollywood and New York. *Career:* debut, Houston 1971 as Tchelkalov in Boris Godunov; Sang in opera in Cincinnati, Houston, San Diego and San Francisco; European engagements at the Wexford Festival (Thaïs), the Vienna Volksoper and the Théâtre Royale de la Monnaie, Brussels; Other roles have included Pelléas, Guglielmo, Don Giovanni, Mozart's Count, Papageno, Rossini's Figaro, Eugene Onegin, Hamlet, Belcore, Massenet's Hérode and Athanael (Thais), Verdi's Posa and Ford and Peachum in The Beggar's Opera; San Diego, 1972 in the premiere of Medea by Alva Henderson; Frequent concert appearances. *Address:* c/o Volksoper, Wahringerstrasse 78, 1090 Vienna, Australia.

**MacKINTOSH, Catherine;** violinist; b. 1948, England. *Career:* debut concert at St John's Smith Square, London, 1984; Extensive tours and broadcasts in France, Belgium, Netherlands, Germany, Austria, Switzerland, Italy and Spain. Tours of the USA and Japan, 1991–92; British appearances include four Purcell concerts at the Wigmore Hall, 1987, later broadcast on Radio 3; Repertoire includes music on the La Folia theme by Vivaldi, Corelli, CPE Bach, Marais, A Scarlatti, Vitali and Geminiani; Instrumental works and songs by Purcell, music by Matthew Locke, John Blow and Fantasias and Airs by William Lawes; 17th Century virtuoso Italian music by Marini, Buonamente, Gabrieli, Fontana and Stradella; J. S. Bach and his forerunners, Biber, Scheidt, Schenk, Reincken and Buxtehude; frequent engagements with other ensembles; member of the Purcell Quartet. *Recordings:* six album set on the La Folia theme; Purcell sonatas by Vivaldi and Corelli.

**McKUEN, Rod;** American author and composer; b. 29 April 1933, Oakland, Calif. *Career:* has appeared in numerous films, concerts and on TV, composer of film scores and background music for TV shows; composer-lyricist of many songs; Pres. of numerous record and book cos; mem. Bd of Dirs American Nat. Theater of Ballet, Animal Concern; mem. Bd of Govs Nat. Acad. of Recording Arts and Sciences; mem. American Soc. of Composers, Authors and Publishers (ASCAP), Writers Guild, AFTRA, MPA, NARAS; Pres. of American Guild of Variety Artists (AGVA); mem. Bd of Dirs Calif. Music Theater. *Works include:* Symphony Number One, Concerto for Guitar and Orchestra, Concerto for Four Harpsichords, Seascapes for Piano and Orchestra, Adagio for Harp and Strings, Piano Variations, Concerto Number Three for Piano and Orchestra 1972, The Plains of My Country (ballet) 1972, The City (orchestral suite) 1973, Ballad of Distances (orchestral suite) 1973, Bicentennial Ballet 1975, Symphony Number Three 1975, over 200 record albums. *Film scores:* Joanna 1968, The Prime of Miss Jean Brodie 1969, Me, Natalie 1969, A Boy Named Charlie Brown 1970, Come to Your Senses 1971, Scandalous John 1971, Wildflowers 1971, The Borrowers 1973, Lisa Bright and Dark 1973, Awareness of Emily 1976, The Unknown War 1979, Man to Himself 1980, Portrait of Rod McKuen 1982, Death Rides this Trail 1983, The Living End 1983, The Beach 1984. *Publications:* And Autumn Came 1954, Stanyan Street and Other Sorrows 1966, Listen to the Warm 1967, Twelve Years of Christmas 1968, In Someone's Shadow 1969, With Love 1970, Caught in the Quiet 1970, Fields of Wonder 1971, The Carols of Christmas 1971, And to Each Season 1972, Beyond the Boardwalk 1972, Come to Me in Silence 1973, America–An Affirmation 1974, Seasons in the Sun 1974, Alone, Moment to Moment 1974, The McKuen Omnibus 1975, Celebrations of the Heart 1975, My Country 200 1975, I'm Strong but I Like Roses, Sleep Warm, Beyond the Boardwalk 1976, The Sea Around Me ... The Hills Above 1976, Finding My Father (biographical) 1977, Coming Close to Earth 1977, Hand in Hand... 1977, Love's Been Good to Me 1979, We Touch the Sky 1979, Looking for a Friend 1980, An Outstretched Hand 1980, The Power Bright and Shining 1980, Too Many Midnights 1981, Rod McKuen's Book of Days 1981, The Beautiful Strangers 1981, The Works of Rod McKuen, Vol. 1, Poetry 1982, Watch for the Wind... 1982, Rod McKuen – 1984 Book of Days 1983, The Sound of Solitude 1983, Suspension Bridge 1984, Another Beautiful Day 1985, Valentines 1985, Intervals 1986. *Honours:* Grand Prix du Disque 1966, 1974, 1975, 1982, Golden Globe 1969, Motion Picture Daily Award 1969; LA Shrine Club Award 1975, Freedoms Foundation 1975, Horatio Alger Award 1976; Brandeis Univ. Literary Trust Award 1981, Freedoms Foundation Patriot Medal 1981, Salvation Army Man of the Year 1983, Rose d'Or, Cannes 1986, Myasthenia Gravis Community Service Award 1986. *Address:* P.O. Box 2783, Los Angeles, CA 90028, USA.

**McLACHLAN, Murray,** FRSA; concert pianist; b. 6 Jan. 1965, Dundee, Scotland; m. 1st Mary Russell 1993; m. 2nd Kathryn Page 2001; three c. 2 step-c. *Education:* Chetham's School, Magdalene College, Cambridge with Peter Katin and Norma Fisher. *Career:* debut, Free Trade Hall, Hallé Proms, Manchester, 1983; Performed extensively throughout the United Kingdom as a recitalist and concerto soloist with Royal Philharmonic Orchestra, Scottish Chamber Orchestra, BBC Scottish Orchestra, Manchester Camerata; Toured Belorussia, 1991; Has performed complete cycle of 32 Beethoven sonatas from memory in Glasgow, Dundee and Aberdeen; Head of Keyboard, Chetham's School of Music, Manchester; Tutor, Royal Northern College of Music; Adjudicator, British Federation of Festivals; repertoire also includes complete works of Brahms. *Recordings include:* Complete sonatas of Prokofiev, Myaskovsky Beethoven and Kabalevsky and solo works of Khatchaturian; Piano concerto of Ronald Stevenson; Complete Piano Works of Camilleri; 6 Concertos of Alexander Tcherepnin; 24 Preludes and Fugues of Shchedrin. *Honours:* Piano Prize, Chetham's; Cambridge Instrumental Exhibition; Penguin Rosette Award, for CD of music from Scotland; Knight of the Order of St John of Jerusalem, 1997. *Address:* c/o Chetham's School of Music, Long Millgate, Manchester M3 1SB, England. *E-mail:* info@murraymclachlan.co .uk. *Website:* www.murraymclachlan.com.

**McLAUGHLIN, Marie;** singer (soprano); b. 2 Nov. 1954, Hamilton, Lanarkshire, Scotland. *Education:* London Opera Centre, National Opera Studio. *Career:* sang Susanna and Lauretta while a student; English National Opera from 1978, in The Consul, Dido and Aeneas, A Night in Venice and Rigoletto; Royal Opera Covent Garden from 1980 as Barbarina and Susanna in Le nozze di Figaro, Zerlina, Iris in Semele, Marzelline in Fidelio, Nannetta in Falstaff, Zdenka in Arabella and Tytania in A Midsummer Night's Dream; Glyndebourne Festivals as Micaela (Carmen) and Violetta, 1985, 1987; Salzburg Festival as Susanna, conducted by James Levine; Scottish Opera in Orfeo ed Euridice and Le Nozze di Figaro; Deutsche Oper Berlin as Susanna and Marzelline; Hamburg, Susanna, Marzelline; Chicago Lyric, Zerlina, Despina; Washington, Susanna; Met New York as Marzelline; La Scala, Milan, Adina; Paris Opéra in Roméo et Juliette; Sang Zdenka in Arabella at Covent Garden, 1990; Marzelline in Fidelio at the 1990 Salzburg Festival, Zerlina at the Vienna Festival; Geneva Opera 1992, as Despina, and Jenny in Mahagonny; Sang Jenny at the Opéra Bastille, Paris, 1995; Donna Elvira at

Lausanne, 1996. Concert appearances in London, Edinburgh, New Work, Chicago, Berlin, Spain, France, Belgium and Germany; Conductors worked with include Maazel, Bernstein, Haitink, Barenboim, Davis, Leppard, Celibidache, Harnoncourt, Mehta and Levine; Season 1992–93, as Blanche in the Carmélites at Geneva, Susanna on tour with the Royal Opera to Japan, Ilia in Idomeneo at Barcelona and Ivy in On the Town at the Barbican Hall; Sang Anna Elisa in Lehar's Paganini at the Theater an der Wien, Vienna, 1998; Season 2000–01 as Katerina in Martinů's The Greek Passion at Covent Garden and Weill's Jenny in Geneva. *Recordings include:* Video of Covent Garden Fidelio (Virgin), Handel's L'Allegro, il Pensieroso ed Il Moderato; Die Zauberflöte and Dido and Aeneas, Così fan tutte (Levine), Mozart, Requiem (Bernstein), (Phonogram); Videos of Rigoletto, Carmen, Traviata, Mozart's C Minor Mass and Haydn's Mass in Time of War. *Current Management:* IMG Artists, Lovell House, 616 Chiswick High Road, London W4 5RX, England.

**McLEAN, Barton Keith,** BS, MM, DMus; composer; b. 8 April 1938, Poughkeepsie, NY, USA; m. Priscilla McLean 1967. *Education:* State University College, Potsdam, NY, Eastman School of Music, Indiana University. *Career:* teacher, State University College, Potsdam, 1960–66, Indiana University, South Bend, 1969–76, University of Texas, Austin, 1976–83; Teacher, iEar Studios, 1987–88, 1990–92, Director, iEar Studios, 1987–88, Rensselaer Polytechnic Institute. *Compositions include:* Dimensions I, violin, tape, 1973, II, piano, tape, 1974, III, saxophone, tape, 1978, IV, saxophone, tape, 1979, VIII, piano, tape, 1982; Metamorphosis, orchestra, 1975; Heavy Music, 4 crowbars, electronic, 1979; Ixtlan, 2 pianos, 1982; The Last Ten Minutes, computer generated, 1982; The Electric Sinfonia, 1982; String Quartet, from the Good Earth, 1985; In the Place of Tears, chamber ensemble, voice, 1985; In Wilderness is the Preservation of the World, environmental-electronic, 1986; Voices of the Wild–Primal Spirits, orchestra, 1987; Visions of a Summer Night, computer tape, 1989; Rainforest, 1989; Rainforest Images, computer tape, 1992; Rainforest Reflections, electronic processed soloist and orchestra, 1993; Rainforest Images I and II, video, 1993; Forgotten Shadows, computer tape, 1994; Jambori Rimba, 1996; Desert Spring, 1996; Dawn Chorus, 1996; Forgotten Shadows, 1996; The Ultimate Symphonius 2000, audience interactive sound installation, 1999; Journey on a Long String, for double bass and electronics, 2001; Into the Fire, for stereo sound featuring the voice of Athena Burke, 2003. *Recordings:* Visions of a Summer Night, 1992; Rainforest Images, 1993; Demons of the Night, Fireflies, Earth Music, 1994; The Electric Performer; The McLean Mix and the Golden Age of Electronic Music; Ritual of the Dawn, Forgotten shadows, Rainforest Reflections. *Address:* Coon Brook Road, Petersburgh, NY 12138, USA. *E-mail:* mclmix@aol.com. *Website:* members.aol.com/mclmix2/index.html.

**McLEAN, Priscilla Taylor,** BEd, BMusEd, MM; American composer and video artist; b. 27 May 1942, Fitchburg, MA; m. Barton Keith McLean 1967. *Education:* State Coll., Fitchburg, Mass State Coll. at Lowell, Massachusetts, Indiana Univ. *Career:* concerts, The McLean Mix (husband-wife duo performing own electronic acoustic music), Netherlands, Belgium, Zagreb Muzicki Biennale 1981; Amsterdam, Holland Radio, Oslo, Finland, Sweden 1983; Australia, New Zealand, Hawaii 1990; tours, USA 1983–2005 annually, Canada 1986; guest composer, Kennedy Center for the Performing Arts 1977; Gaudeamus Musiekweek, Netherlands 1979; guest Prof. and composer/performer, Univ. of Hawaii 1985; guest composer, Nat. Orchestral Symposium, Indianapolis Symphony 1985; guest soprano soloist, Cleveland Chamber Orchestra (Wilderness) 1989; guest composer/performer (residency), Univ. of Sarawak, Malaysia 1996; Tunugan Festival of Asian music, Philippines 1997; US Consortium commission 2000; presently touring with music and original videos; mem. BMI, American Music Center, Seamus, SCI, Electronic Music Foundation. *Compositions include:* Variations and Mozaics on a Theme of Stravinsky; Dance of Dawn; Invisible Chariots; The Inner Universe; Fantasies for Adults and Other Children; Beneath the Horizon I, III; Night Images; Messages; Fire and Ice; Elan!; 3 Pieces for In Wilderness is the Preservation of the World; In Celebration; Wilderness; A Magic Dwells, orchestra and tape, 1986; Voices of the Wild, Orchestra and Soloist, electronic music, 1988; The Dance of Shiva, electronic tape and Multiple Slides), 1990; Rainforest, coil with B McLean, 1990; Everything Awakening Alert and Joyful, full orchestra and narrator, 1991; In the Beginning, 1995; Rainforest Images, 1993; Desert Spring with Barton McLean, 1996; Jambori Rimba with Barton McLean, 1997; Desert Voices for midi violin, tape and electronics, 1998; The Ultimate Symphonius 2000, with Barton McLean, 1999; Angels of Delirium for electronic tape, 2001. *Recordings include:* Dance of Dawn 1975; Interplanes, 1978; Variations and Mozaics on a Theme of Stravinsky, 1979; Invisible Chariots, 1979; Electronic Music from the Outside In, 1980; Beneath the Horizon III and Salt Canyons, 1983; In Wilderness is the Preservation of the World, 1987; Rainforest Images II; The Electric Performer; Gods, Demons and the Earth; McLean Mix and the Golden Age of Electronic Music; Fantasies for Adults and Other children: The Vocal music of Priscilla McLean. *Music videos include:* Symphony of Seasons, Jewels of January 2001, The Eye of Spring 2002, Autumn Requiem (with Barton McLean) 2003, July Dance 2003, Xaakalawe/Flowing 2004, Sunburst Songs 2005. *Honours:* winner 17th Sigvald Thompson Composition Award Competition 1988, winning composition IMC Rostrum 1990. *Address:* The McLean Mix/MLC Publications, 55 Coon Brook Road, Petersburgh, New York, NY 12138, USA. *Telephone:* (518) 658-3595 (home). *E-mail:* mclmix@aol.com (home). *Website:* members.aol.com/mclmix2/index.html (office).

**MacLEAN, Susan;** singer (mezzo-soprano); b. 1962, California, USA. *Education:* Minneapolis and Zürich Opera Studio. *Career:* sang at Bielefeld Opera from 1988, notably in Yerma by Villa Lobos and Der Sprung uber den Schatten by Krenek; Zürich, 1989, as Fenena in Nabucco; Wuppertal, 1991, in the premiere of Katharina Blum by Tilo Medek; Heidelberg Festival, 1994–95, as Mignon, by Thomas; Other roles include Carmen, Cenerentola, Strauss's Octavian and Composer, Selika in L'Africaine, and Honegger's Judith. *Recordings include:* Zulma in L'Italiana in Algeri. *Address:* c/o Theater der Stadt Heidelberg, Friedrichstrasse 5, 69117 Heidelberg, Germany.

**McLEAN-MAIR, Kevin;** British singer (tenor); b. 1962, St Albans. *Education:* Royal Acad. of Music, Britten-Pears School, Aldeburgh, masterclasses with Tom Krause. *Career:* performed throughout the UK, including Barbican Hall, St James', Piccadilly, St John's, Smith Square, BBC Friday Night is Music Night and many choral socs; recitals in Lincoln, Bristol and Settle; int. engagements in Canada, Germany, Netherlands (including Concertgebouw) and the USA; opera includes Attendant Spirit, Comus, Benslow Music Trust; Lucano and Nutrice, L'Incoronazione di Poppea, The Cavalli Baroque Ensemble; Ferrando, Così fan tutte, Dartington Hall; Chinese Man, The Fairy Queen, English Bach Festival at the Linbury Studio Theatre, Covent Garden 2001. *Recordings:* Dixit Dominus, The Songs of Ian Venables. *Honours:* Erna Spoorenberg Award for Oratorio, Netherlands 1996. *Current Management:* Helen Sykes Artist's Management, 100 Felsham Road, Putney, London, SW15 1DQ, England; Pollock Management, Postbus 15069, 1001 MB, Amsterdam, The Netherlands (office). *Telephone:* (20) 8780-0060 (agent) (office); (2) 06255599 (Amsterdam) (office). *Fax:* (20) 8780-8772 (agent) (office). *Address:* 50 Frederick Street, Hightown, Luton, Beds., LU2 7QS, England (home). *Telephone:* (1582) 522254 (home).

**McLEOD, John;** composer, conductor and lecturer; b. 8 March 1934, Aberdeen, Scotland; m. Margaret Murray 1961; one s. one d. *Education:* Royal Academy of Music; composition with Lennox Berkeley, conducting with Adrian Boult. *Career:* Director of Music, Merchiston Castle School, Edinburgh, 1974–85; Visiting Lecturer, Royal Scottish Academy of Music and Drama, 1985–89; Visiting Lecturer in Composition and Contemporary Music at Napier University of Edinburgh, 1989–94; Visiting Composer, Lothian Specialist Music Scheme, 1986–92; Ida Carroll Research Fellow, Royal Northern College of Music, 1988–89; Guest Conductor for various Scottish orchestras including Royal Scottish National Orchestra; Director of postgraduate course in composing for film and television at Thames Valley University and London College of Music, 1991–97; Visiting Professor, Royal Academy of Music, 1993–97; Freelance Composer, Conductor and Lecturer, 1997–; Director of The Performing Right Society, 2000–; Director of the British Academy of Composers and Songwriters, 2001–; Member of the Council of the Society for the Promotion of New Music, 2000–. *Compositions include:* The Gokstad Ship for Orchestra, National Youth Orchestra of Scotland Commission, 1982; Stabat Mater for Soloists, Choir and Orchestra, Edinburgh Royal Choral Union Commission, 1986; Percussion Concerto, Evelyn Glennie Soloist, National Youth Orchestra of Scotland Commission; The Song of Dionysius for Percussion and Piano, premiered at the 1989 London Proms with Evelyn Glennie and Philip Smith; Piano Concerto, 1988; A Dramatic Landscape, for clarinet and wind, 1990; The Chronicle of Saint Machar, for baritone, choruses, strings, percussion and organ, 1998; Song of the Concubine for soprano and ensemble, 1998; Film scores for many television and cinema films including, Another Time, Another Place; Works now performed and recorded by leading artists, orchestras and at major international festivals. *Address:* Hill House, 9 Redford Crescent, Colinton, Edinburgh EH13 0BS, Scotland.

**McLEOD, Linda;** singer (soprano); b. 29 Nov. 1952, Indiana, USA. *Education:* Guildhall School, London. *Career:* sang with Opera for All, London, from 1978; English National Opera, as Sonia in War and Peace, as Donna Elvira, and Rusalka and in the premiere of Harvey's Inquest of Love, 1993; Brünnhilde in The Ring with Birmingham Touring Opera; Elisabeth de Valois and Tippett's Andromache for Opera North; Donna Anna for Scottish Opera; Washington Opera, 1992 as Wagne's Santa. *Recordings:* Video of Rusalka; Giovanna in Verdi's Ernani. *Address:* c/o English National Opera, St Martin's Lane, London WC2N 4ES, England.

**MacLEOD, Michael;** British/American music administrator; *General Director, Glimmerglass Opera;* b. Bogotá, Colombia. *Education:* Amherst Coll., Mass. *Career:* Man. Dir John Eliot Gardiner's Monteverdi Choir, English Baroque Soloists, Orchestre Révolutionnaire et Romantique 1984–96; Exec. and Artistic Dir City of London Festival 1996–2001; Exec. Dir New Haven Symphony Orchestra 2001–05; Gen. Dir Glimmerglass Opera 2005–. *Address:* Glimmerglass Opera, POB 191, 7300 State Highway 80, Cooperstown, NY 133326, USA (office). *E-mail:* info@glimmerglass.org (office). *Website:* www .glimmerglass.org (office).

**McLIN, Lena Johnson,** BMus; American composer and teacher; b. 5 Sept. 1928, Chicago, IL. *Education:* Booker T. Washington High School, Atlanta, GA Spelman Coll., Atlanta, American Conservatory of Music, Chicago, Roosevelt Univ., Chicago and Chicago State Univ. *Career:* choral conductor for various community, school and church groups from 1951; accompanist Thomas Dorsey Choir, Pilgrim Baptist Church, Chicago 1952–53; founder and Dir, McLin Ensemble 1957–68; Minister of Music, Trinity Congregational Church, Chicago 1960s; founder and Pastor, Holy Vessel Christian Center, Chicago 1980–; teacher, Julius H. Hess Upper Grade Center, Chicago

1959–60, Gurdon S. Hubbard High School, Chicago 1960–63, John Marshall Harlan Community Acad. High School, Chicago 1963–70; Head of Music Dept, Kenwood Acad., Chicago 1970–91; held choral workshops throughout USA; consultant, Westminster Choir Coll., Princeton, NJ. *Compositions include:* Impressions for piano 1957, And she Took a Ring and Placed it on his Finger 1963, A Summer Day for piano 1970, Free at Last: A Portrait of Martin Luther King Jr 1973, If I Could Give You All I Have 1986, Silence 1987, The Unlucky Apple 1987, My Love 1993, Christmas in Space 1997; choral music: All the Earth Sing Unto the Lord 1967, The Earth is the Lord's 1969, I Want Jesus to Walk With Me 1969, So Stands a College Tall of Higher Learning 1970, In This World 1970, The Colors of the Rainbow 1971, If They Ask You Why He Came 1971, If we Could Exchange Places 1971, I'm Moving Up 1971, We've Just Got to Have Peace All Over This World 1971, What Will You Put Under Your Christmas Tree? 1971, The Torch has been Passed 1971, For Jesus Christ is Born 1971, Psalm 100: Make a Joyful Noise 1971, Sanctus and Benedictus 1971, Psalm 117: Praise the Lord, All Ye Nations 1971, The Little Baby 1971, You and I Together 1971, Friendship 1972, Gwendolyn Brooks: A Musical Portrait 1972, New Born King 1972, Eucharist of the Soul 1972, Let the People Sing Praise Unto the Lord 1973, Winter, Spring, Summer, Autumn 1974, Memory 1976, Since He Came into my Life 1976, Challenge 1976, The Love of God 1976, Te Deum Laudamus 1976, This Land 1976, Christmas Time is Here Again 1978, Now that we are Leaving 1978, Two Introits 1978, Noel 1979, Reach Up! 1987, Introits and Responses for Worship 1990, Take Life's Challenge 1997, Makers of History 1998. *Publications:* Black Music in Church and School 1970, Pulse: A History of Music 1977. *Honours:* Nat. Black Music Caucus Outstanding Achievement Award 1980, Univ. of Chicago Outstanding Teacher Award 1983; scholarship American Conservatory of Music, Chicago 1951. *Address:* 6901 S Oglesby Street, Chicago, IL 60649, USA (office).

**McMASTER, Sir Brian John,** Kt, CBE, LLB; British arts administrator; *Director and CEO, Edinburgh International Festival;* b. 9 May 1943. *Education:* Wellington Coll., Bristol Univ. *Career:* with Int. Artists' Dept, EMI Ltd 1968–73; Controller of Opera Planning, English Nat. Opera 1973–76; Gen. Admin., subsequently Man. Dir Welsh Nat. Opera 1976–91; Festival Dir and CEO Edin. Int. Festival 1991–; Artistic Dir Vancouver Opera 1984–89. *Address:* Edinburgh International Festival, The Hub, Edinburgh's Festival Centre, Castlehill, Royal Mile, Edinburgh, EH1 2NE, Scotland (office). *Telephone:* (131) 473-2032 (office). *Fax:* (131) 473-2002 (office). *E-mail:* eif@ eif.co.uk (office). *Website:* www.eif.co.uk (office).

**McMASTER, Zandra;** singer (mezzo-soprano); b. 1960, Ballymena, Northern Ireland. *Education:* Trinity College of Music, London Opera Centre. *Career:* debut, Purcell Room, London, 1983; Sang Mahler's 4th Symphony at Madrid 1984 and has been resident in Spain singing in concert with most leading Spanish Orchestras; Salzburg Mozarteum 1989–91, Concertgebouw Amsterdam 1990 and US debut 1991, in Bernstein's 1st Symphony at Colorado; Seville World 'Expo concert 1992 and Beethoven's Ninth in Berlin; Concerts in Portugal, Israel, Belgium, Poland, Norway, Canada, Ireland, Germany, Austria, Hungary, USA, Brazil, Greece and Finland. *Current Management:* Conciertos Augusto, 15 calle Viento, 28220 Madrid, Spain.

**MacMILLAN, James Loy,** CBE; British composer, conductor and lecturer in music; b. 16 July 1959, Kilwinning, Ayrshire, Scotland. *Education:* Univs of Edinburgh and Durham. *Career:* formerly lecturer in the music departments of Edinburgh and Manchester Univs; Lecturer at the Royal Scottish Acad. of Music and Drama; performances of his music by the New Music Group of Scotland, Circle, Nomos, Lontano and the Scottish Chamber Orchestra; commissions from the Edinburgh Contemporary Arts Trust, The Traverse Theatre, Scottish Chamber Orchestra, the Paragon Ensemble, Cappela Nova and the Scottish Chamber Choir; Prom Commission, The Confession of Isobel Gowdie, BBC Scottish Symphony Orchestra; featured composer 1990 Musica Nova Festival, Glasgow; Seven Last Words from the Cross premiered on BBC television, Easter 1994; Composer and Conductor, BBC Philharmonic Orchestra 2000–; featured composer at BBC Weekend, The Barbican, London 2005. *Compositions:* Study on Two Planes for cello and piano 1981; Three Dawn Rituals for ensemble 1983; Beatus Vir for chorus and organ 1983; The Road to Ardtalla for ensemble 1983; Songs of a Just War for soprano and ensemble 1984; Piano Sonata 1986; Two Visions of Hoy for oboe and ensemble 1986; The Keening for orchestra 1986; Festival Fanfares for brass band 1986; Litanies of Iron and Stone for ensemble with tape 1987; Untold for ensemble 1987; Visions of a November Spring for string quartet 1988; Busqueda for 8 actors, 3 sopranos, speaker and ensemble 1988; Into the Ferment for Orchestra 1988; Cantos Sagrados for chorus and organ 1989; The Exorcism of Rio Sumpul for Chamber Ensemble 1989; As Mothers See Us, for ensemble 1990; The Berserking, Piano Concerto, 1990; The Confession of Isobel Gowdie for orchestra 1990; Soweton Spring for wind band 1990; Catherine's Lullabies for chorus and ensemble 1990; Scots Song for Soprano and Ensemble 1991; Tuireadh for clarinet and string quartet 1991; Sinfonietta 1991; Tourist Variations, 1 act chamber opera 1992; Visitatio Sepulchri for 7 singers and chamber orchestra, 1993; Trumpet Concerto, 1993; Vs for orchestra, 1993; Seven Last Words from the Cross for choir and strings, 1994; Ines de Castro, opera, 1996; Clarinet Concerto, 1997; Gaudeamus in loci pace for organ, 1998; Quickening for soloists, chorus and orchestra, 1998; Triduum for London Symphony Orchestra, 1996–97; Cello Concerto, 1996; Symphony: Vigil; Raising Sparkes for soprano and chamber ensemble, 1997; 14 Little Pictures for piano trio, 1997; Why is this Night Different?, string quartet, 1997; Magnificat 1999, Cello Sonata No. 2 2000, Mass 2000, Parthenogenesis, scena

2000, Birds of Rhiannon, for orchestra 2001, Nunc Dimittis 2001, A Deep But Dazzling Darkness, violin concerto 2001–02, Symphony No. 3, Silence 2002, Le Tombeau de Georges Rouault for organ 2003, Piano Concerto No. 2 2003, A Scotch Bestiary, organ concerto 2003–04, Lauda alla Vergine Maria, for chorus 2004. *Recordings include:* Confession of Isobel Gowdie, Veni Veni Emmanuel, Cello Concerto. *Honours:* Hon. DUniv (Univ. of Paisley) 1995, Hon. DLitt (Univ. of Strathclyde) 1996; Gramophone Award 1993, Classic CD Award 1993, South Bank Show Award for Classical Music 1997, Evening Standard Classical Music Award for Outstanding Artistic Achievement. *Current Management:* Boosey & Hawkes PLC, First Floor, Aldwych House, 71–91 Aldwych, London, WC2B 4HN, England. *Website:* www.boosey.com/ macmillan. *Address:* c/o BBC Philharmonic, New Broadcasting House, Oxford Road, Manchester, M60 1SJ, England.

**McNAIR, Sylvia;** singer (soprano); b. 23 June 1956, Mansfield, Ohio, USA. *Education:* India University. *Career:* sang in Messiah at Indianapolis, 1980; Euroean debut in the premiere of Kelterborn's Ophelia, Schwetzingen, 1984; Concert appearances in Cleveland, Baltimore, San Francisco, Detroit, Montreal, Indianapolis, Atlanta, St Louis, Washington and Los Angeles; New York at the Carnegie, Avery Fisher and Alice Tully Halls; Season 1991–92 with the Chicago Symphony under Solti, Berlin Philharmonic under Haitink, City of Birmingham Symphony under Rattle, Concentus Musicus under Harnoncourt and London Philharmonic under Masur; Mozart's Ilia and Servilia with the Monteverdi Choir and Orchestra conducted by John Eliot Gardiner; US opera appearances as Pamina at Santa Fe, Ilia; Hero (Béatrice et Bénédict) and Morgana in Alcina at St Louis; Sang Ilia in Lyon and Strasbourg and Susana with Netherlands Opera; Pamina at the Deutsche Oper Berlin and the Vienna Staatsoper; Glyndebourne Festival 1989 as Anne Trulove; Covent Garden and Salzburg debuts as Ilia in Idomeneo; Season 1991–92 with Bastille Opéra (Paris) and Metropolitan Opera (as Marzelline in Fidelio) debuts; Covent Garden 1992, in Rossini's Il Viaggio a Reims; Sang Poppea at the 1993 Salzburg Festival and returned for Pamina in Die Zauberflöte, 1997; The Daughter in the US premiere of Lidholm's A Dream Play, Santa Fe, 1998; Sang Cleopatra in Handel's Giulio Cesare at the New York Met, 1999; Messiah at the 1999 Salzburg Festival. *Recordings:* Albums with Neville Marriner, Roger Norrington, John Eliot Gardiner, Colin Davis, Kurt Masur, James Levine and Bernard Haitink; Idomeneo with John Eliot Gardiner (Deutsche Grammophon). *Current Management:* Askonas Holt Ltd, Lonsdale Chambers, 27 Chancery Lane, London, WC2A 1PF, England. *Telephone:* (20) 7400-1700. *Fax:* (20) 7400-1799. *E-mail:* info@askonasholt.co .uk. *Website:* www.askonasholt.co.uk.

**MacNEIL, Cornell Hill;** American singer (baritone); b. 24 Sept. 1922, Minneapolis, Minn.; s. of Walter Hill and Harriette Belle (née Cornell) MacNeil; m. 1st Margaret Gavan 1947 (divorced 1972); two s. three d.; m. 2nd Tania Rudensky 1972. *Education:* Julius Hartt School of Music, Univ. of Hartford, West Hartford, Conn. *Career:* appeared on Broadway in Sweethearts 1947, Where's Charley 1949; operatic début as John Sorel in world premiere of The Consul (Menotti) 1950; début with New York City Opera as Germont in La Traviata 1953, at La Scala, Milan, as Charles V in Ernani 1959, at Metropolitan Opera, New York in title-role of Rigoletto 1959; has appeared in leading opera houses of Europe, USA, S America; Pres. American Guild of Musical Artists 1971–77, mem. 1971–. *Honours:* Alumnus of Year, Hartt School of Music 1976; Grammy Award for best opera recording (La Traviata) 1984; Medal of Achievement, Acad. of Vocal Arts 1985. *Address:* c/o Columbia Artists Management Ltd, 165 West 57th Street, New York, NY 10019, USA (office).

**MacNEIL, Walter;** singer (tenor); b. 1957, New York, USA; s. of Cornell MacNeil. *Career:* sang at the San Francisco Opera from 1983, as Froh, Rodrigo in Otello and Alfredo; Sang Alfredo at New Orleans 1984, with his father as Germont père; Carnegie Hall 1985, in Semele, and Don Ottavio at Milwaukee 1986; Glyndebourne 1987–88 and Metropolitan 1989, as Alfredo; Sang Aubry in Der Vampyr by Marschner at the 1992 Wexford Festival; Other roles include Tamino (Connecticut Opera, 1991), Ruggiero in La Rondine and Nadir in Les pêcheurs de Perles (Honolulu 1987). *Address:* c/o Metropolitan Opera, Lincoln Center, New York, NY 10023, USA.

**McPHEE, George,** MBE, BMus, DipMusEd, FRCO, FRSCM, FRCO; British organist and composer; b. 10 Nov. 1937, Glasgow, Scotland; m.; one s. two d. *Education:* Royal Scottish Acad. of Music and Drama, Edinburgh Univ., studied organ with Herrick Bunney and Fernando Germani. *Career:* Asst Organist, St Giles Cathedral, Edinburgh 1959–63; Dir of Music, Paisley Abbey 1963–; conducted and played organ with all major Scottish orchestras; numerous recital tours of USA, Canada and Europe; mem. Incorporated Soc. of Musicians, Royal Coll. of Organists. *Compositions:* Magnificat and Nunc Dimittis (Paisley Service), Make we joy, Whence is that goodly fragrance, The New Oxford Song Book (editor), The Saltire Two-Part Song Book. *Honours:* Dr hc (Paisley Univ.) 1997; Limpus Prize 1961. *Address:* 17 Main Road, Castlehead, Paisley, PA2 6AJ, Scotland (home). *Telephone:* (141) 8893528 (home). *E-mail:* profmcphee@ aol.com (home).

**McPHERSON, Gordon,** DMus; Scottish composer and accordion player; b. 27 Aug. 1965, Dundee. *Education:* Univ. of York, Royal Northern Coll. of Music. *Career:* composition teacher, Univ. of Edinburgh; composer-in-residence, Royal Scottish Acad. of Music and Drama; Lecturer in 20th-Century Music and Analysis, Univ. of St Andrews; Head of Composition, Royal Scottish Acad. of Music and Drama 1999–. *Compositions include:* Oh, why should I cry upon

my wedding day? 1985, String Quartet No. 2 'Dead Roses' 1990, Maps and Diagrams of our Pain 1990, Handguns: a Suite 1995, The Baby Bear's Bed 1998, String Quartet No. 3 'The Original Soundtrack' 1999, Upbeat Destroyer (guitar concerto), Born of Funk and the Fear of Failing (guitar concerto) 2000–01, The Waterworks (multi-media), Morning Drunk and Buzzard, The New Black 2005. *Recordings include:* Detours (two-vol. collection) *Honours:* Creative Scotland Award 2003. *Address:* Royal Scottish Academy of Music and Drama, 100 Renfrew Street, Glasgow, G2 3DB, Scotland (office). *E-mail:* g.mcpherson@rsamd.ac.uk (office). *Website:* www.rsamd.ac.uk (office).

**McTIER, Duncan Paul,** BSc, ARCM; double bass player and teacher; b. 21 Nov. 1954, Stourbridge, Worcestershire, England; m. Yuko Inoue 1984. *Education:* King Edward VI Grammar School, Stourbridge, Bristol University. *Career:* Member, BBC Symphony Orchestra, 1975–77; Principal Bass, Netherlands Chamber Orchestra, 1977–84; Senior Double Bass Tutor, Royal Northern College of Music, 1984–; Professor of Double Bass, Royal College of Music, 1987–91; Double Bass Consultant, Royal Scottish Academy of Music and Drama, 1991–; Solo appearances with Netherlands Chamber Orchestra, Concertgebouw Chamber Orchestra, Bournemouth Sinfonietta, Netherlands Philharmonic Orchestra, Orchestre Regional d'Auvergne, Barcelona Municipal Orchestra, Northern Sinfonia Orchestre de Chambre Detmold, Nippon Telemann Ensemble of Osaka, Lausanne Chamber Orchestra, BBC Concert Orchestra, Scottish Chamber Orchestra, Bournemouth Symphony Orchestra; World Premieres of Concertos written by Peter Maxwell Davies, John Casken and Derek Bourgeois; Recitals and master classes throughout Europe and Japan. *Recordings:* Bottesini Grand Duo for Philips; Various pieces with Paganini Ensemble for Denon; Dutch television recordings of Bottesini Grand Duo and 2nd Concerto; Dvořák String Quintet and Waltzes with Chilingirian Quartet (Chandos); Extensive radio recordings. *Honours:* 1st Prize Winner, Isle of Man International Double Bass Competition, 1982. *Current Management:* Music Productions 'J' House, 6 Studland Street, London W6 0JS, England.

**MACURDY, John;** American singer (bass); b. 18 March 1929, Detroit, Mich.; m. Justine May Votypka; one s. one d. *Education:* Wayne State University, Detroit; singing with Avery Crew, Detroit. *Career:* debut, New Orleans, 1952, in Samson et Dalila; Appearances in Baltimore, Houston, Philadelphia, San Francisco and Santa Fe; NYC Opera debut 1959, in Weill's Street Scene; Metropolitan Opera from 1962 as the Commendatore, Crespel in Les Contes d'Hoffmann and Rocco in Fidelio; Sang in the premieres of Antony and Cleopatra, 1966 and Mourning Becomes Elektra, 1967; 1st local Performance of Les Troyens, 1973; Paris Opéra 1973, as Arkel in Pelléas et Mélisande; La Scala Milan 1974, as Rocco in Fidelio; Salzburg Festival 1977–78, as the Commendatore in Don Giovanni; Milan 1984 as the Landgrave in Tannhäuser; Seattle Opera 1986, as Hagen and Hunding in the Ring; Metropolitan 1987, as Fasolt in Das Rheingold; Hunding at San Francisco 1990; Appearances at Aix and Orange Festivals, Hollywood Bowl, Miami Opera and Scottish Opera; Season 1992 in Billy Budd at the Met, as Trulove in The Rake's Progress at Aix-en-Provence, as Fiesco in Simon Boccanegra Montpellier, The Flying Dutchman in Buenos Aires as Daland and L'Africaine in Marseille; 1011 performances as Leading Bass; 1780 operatic performances; Sang Fafner in Das Rheingold at Marseille, 1996; Hunding at the Met, 1996; mem, Bohemian Club. *Recordings:* Don Giovanni; Béatrice et Bénédict; Otello; The Rev Hale in Ward's The Crucible; featured in exclusive 10 CD boxed set of the last 50 years of live recordings from the Archive of Teatro alla Scala. *Honours:* City of Detroit Medal, 1969; Rockefeller Foundation Grant, 1959; Presently only American to be listed in the Wagnerian Annals for singing all the Bass Roles in the Ring Cycle; Inducted into the Academy of Vocal Arts Hall of Fame; Arts Achievement Award, Wayne State Univ., 2003. *Address:* 73 Tall Oaks Court, Stamford, CT 06903, USA.

**McVEAGH, Diana Mary,** ARCM, GRSM; writer on music; b. 6 Sept. 1926, Ipoh, Malaya; m. Dr C. W. Morley 1950 (died 1994). *Education:* Malvern Girls' Coll., Royal Coll. of Music. *Career:* Asst Ed., Musical Times 1965–67; Exec. Cttee of the New Grove 1970–76; contrib. to The Times 1947–69, also to Musical Times, The Listener, Records and Recordings; Exec. Cttee of the GKN English Song Award 1982–89; mem. Royal Musical Asscn Council 1961–76; Vice-Pres., Elgar Soc. *Publications:* Elgar (Dent) 1955, Gerald Finzi: His Life and Music 2005; contrib. to New Grove Dictionary of Music (articles on Elgar and Finzi) 1980 and 2000 edns, Twentieth-Century English Masters (MacMillan) 1986. *Address:* Ladygrove, The Lee, Great Missenden, Bucks HP16 9NA, England.

**McVICAR, David;** stage director; b. 1967, Glasgow, Scotland. *Education:* Royal Scottish Academy of Music and Drama. *Career:* main productions: The Magic Flute, Rigoleteto (Covent Garden); Billy Budd (Chicago Lyric Opera); Agrippina, Don Giovanni (La Monnaie Brussels); Manon, Alcina, Tosca, The Rape of Lucretia (ENO); Hamlet, Sweeney Todd, Don Giovanni, Der Rosenkavalier (Opera North); Idomeneo, Der Rosenkavalier, Madama Butterfly (Scottish Opera); Macbeth (Kirov Opera St Petersburg); Tales of Hoffmann (Salzburg Festival). *Address:* Performing Arts, 6 Windmill Street, London W1P 1HF, England.

**MADDALENA, James;** Singer (Baritone); b. 1954, Lynn, Massachusetts, USA. *Education:* Studied at the New England Conservatory of Music. *Career:* Debut: Rogers and Hammerstein medley with the Boston Pops Orchestra, 1974; From 1974 has appeared in a complete cycle of Bach's cantatas at Emmanuel Church Boston, conducted by Craig Smith; Founder member of the

Liederkreis Ensemble, Naumburg Awad, 1980; Association with director Peter Sellars from 1981 includes the title role in Don Giovanni and Leading roles in Handel's Orlando, American Repertory Theatre, 1982; Così fan tutte, Castle Hill Festival, 1984; Haydn's Armida, New Hampshire Symphony, 1983; Giulio Cesare and the Brecht/Weill Kleine Mahagonny, Pepsico Summerfare, 1985; Soloist in Messiah at Carnegie Hall 1984, with Banchetto Musicale; Sang the title role in the world premiere of Nixon in China by John Adams, Houston, 1987, repeated at Edinburgh 1988 and The Captain in the premiere of Adams's The Death of Klinghoffer, Brussels 1991, and at Lyon, Vienna and NY; Has appeared as Mozart's Count in the Sellars version of Le nozze di Figaro, seen at Purchase, NY and Papageno at Glyndebourne, 1990; Created Merlin in Tippett's New Year at Houston 1989 and in the British premiere at Glyndebourne; Season 1992 in Nixon in China at Adelaide and Frankfurt, Don Alfonso at Glyndebourne; Sang in Susa's Transformations at St Louis, 1997; Frédéric in Lakmé at New Orleans, 1997. Recordings. Brahms Liebeslieder Waltzes, with Liederkreis; Nixon in China and The Death of Klinghoffer. *Address:* c/o Houston Grand Opera Association, 510 Preston Avenue, Houston, TX 77002, USA.

**MADDISON, Dorothy;** Singer (Lyric Coloratura Soprano); b. 12 Jan. 1956, Fergus Falls, Minnesota, USA; m. 29 Dec 1979, Ian Maddison. *Education:* BMus, St Olaf College, Minnesota, 1977; Guildhall School of Music and Drama, London, England, 1977–79; Britten-Pears School, Aldeburgh; Private study with Audrey Langford and Andrew Feidld, Cantica Voice Studio, London. *Career:* Debut: Purcell Room, London, April 1986 with Graham Johnson, piano; Freelance concert and operatic singer; Operatic roles include The Queen of Night in The Magic Flute; Zaide; Madames Herz and Silberklang in The Impressario, Mozart; Norina in Don Pasquale; Adina in Elixir of Love; Rita by Donizetti; Tytania in Midsummer Night's Dream, Britten; Mable, Pirates of Penzance; Zerbinetta, Ariadne auf Naxos, Strauss; The Nightingale, Stravinsky; Oratorio repertoire: includes works by Bach, Handel, Haydn, Mozart, Mendelssohn, Orff; Recital Repertoire: Standard works by European composers, also songs from the American Midwest, a programme featuring works by Minnesota composers Argento, Dougherty, Franklin, Larsen, Paulus, first given in April 1988, Purcell Room, London with Robin Bowman, piano; Recent appearances with: English Bach Festival, New Sadler's Wells Opera Company, Opera Factory, London Opera Players; mem, Equity. *Honours:* Honours and Distinction, St Olaf College, Walter Hyde Memorial Prize, Guildhall School. *Address:* 95 Tanfield Avenue, London NW2 7 SB, England.

**MADER-TODOROVA, Marina;** Singer (Soprano); b. 20 Aug. 1948, Silistra, Bulgaria. *Education:* Studied in Varna, Sofia and Vienna. *Career:* Sang at first in opera at Varna then Mainz and Bremen, 1976–77 as Desdemona and Micaela; Gelsenkirchen 1977–80 as Elisabeth de Valois, Ariadne and Tosca; Further appearances at Dortmund, 1980–83, Hamburg, Stuttgart, Frankfurt and Basle; Engaged at the Deutsche Oper am Rhein, 1984–86, Graz, 1984–89, notably as Eva, Amelia in Ballo in Machera, Leonara in Il Trovatore, Agathe and Ariadne; Further appearances at the Deutsche Oper Berlin, Budapest, Mannheim, Palermo, Zürich, Copenahgen and Liège; Other roles have included Butterfly, Elisabeth in Tannhäuser, Elsa, Mozart's Fiordiligi and Countess, Mimi and Arabella; Many concert appearances. *Address:* Vereinigte Buhnen, Kaiser Josef Platz 10, 8010 Graz, Austria.

**MADGE, Geoffrey Douglas;** Australian concert pianist and academic; *Professor of Classical and Contemporary Piano Repertoire, Royal Conservatorium of Music, The Hague;* b. 3 Oct. 1941, Adelaide; m.; one s. one d. *Education:* Elder Conservatorium Univ. of Adelaide with Clemens Leski, studied with Geza Anda (Lucerne), Peter Solymos (Budapest), Eduardo Del Pueyo (Brussels). *Career:* debut, London 1969; toured Australia as a pianist in a piano trio 1959–63; Prof. of Classical and Contemporary Piano Repertoire and Head of Piano Dept, Royal Conservatorium of Music, The Hague; Int. Soc. for Contemporary Music Festival, Athens 1979, first performance of 32 piano pieces by Skalkottas; annual Holland Festival, Utrecht 1982, second complete performance of Kaikhosru Sorabji's Opus Clavicembalisticum. *Compositions:* Viola Sonata 1963, String Quartet 1965, Violin Sonatina 1966, Monkeys in a Cage (ballet, premiere Sydney Opera house 1977) 1976, Etude for two pianists 1977, Tendrils of the Rock (three movements for piano) 1979, Piano Concerto (premiere Amsterdam 1980) 1979. *Recordings:* first recording of Opus Clavicembalisticum by K. Sorabji 1983, first complete anthology of F. Busoni's music for solo piano 1988, first recording of Skalkottas 1st, 2nd and 3rd Piano Concertos 1999, 2005, 2004. *Honours:* Prix du Président de la République, France 1977, Edison Awards, Netherlands 1977, 1988, Schallplatten Preis, Germany 1984, 1988, 2002, 2004, Caecilia Prize, Belgium 1988. *Address:* Van Beuningenstraat 77, 2582 KL Den Haag, Netherlands (office). *Telephone:* (70) 355-4374 (office). *Fax:* (70) 358-4634 (office). *E-mail:* madge@xs4all.nl (office). *Website:* www.xs4all.nl/~madge (office).

**MADRA, Barbara;** Singer (Soprano); b. 1958, Koszian, Poznan, Poland. *Education:* Studied in Poznan. *Career:* Sang at first with the Poznan Opera then from 1980 at the Brussels Opera, notably as Mimi, Violetta, Fiordiligi, Elisabeth de Valois, Mozart's Vitellia and Arminda, the Trovatore Leonora and Amelia Grimaldi; Guest appearances in Geneva, Lausanne, at the Holland Festival, Buenos Aires, Barcelona and Toulouse (Donna Elvira, 1990); Sang Tatiana at Zürich 1990 and at La Scala in Rimsky's Tale of Tsar Saltan, and as Eva in Die Meistersinger. *Address:* c/o Théâtre Royale, 4 Leopoldstrasse, 1000 Brussels, Belgium.

**MADROSZKIEWICZ, Joanna (Dorota);** Violinist; b. 22 March 1956, Szczecin, Poland; 1 s., 2 d. *Education:* Magister of Art; Akademia Muzyczna Gdansk; Hochschule für Musik, Vienna. *Career:* Engagements at Geneva, Prague, Lublin, Naples; Concerts with Vienna Symphony Orchestra, Polish National Philharmonie, London Mozart Players, Residentre Orkest, Austria Radio Orchestra, Deutsche Kammerakad; Numerous Recitals; Debut at Salzburg Festival as a violin soloist in Weill's Violin Concerto with Vienna Philharmonic Orchestra. *Recordings:* Schubert, Haydn, Beethoven, Wieniawski. *Honours:* Best Young Artist of Poland Award, 1977; Commander of the Order of Polonia Restituta, 1994. *Current Management:* Patricia Garrasi, RESIA, Milan. *Address:* Kielmansegg 26, 2340 Mödling, Austria.

**MADZAR, Aleksandar;** Concert Pianist; b. 1968, Belgrade, Yugoslavia. *Education:* Belgrade Academy of Music, with Eliso Virsaladze in Moscow, at the Strasbourg Conservatory and with Daniel Blumenthal in Brussels. *Career:* Frequent appearances from 1985 with leading orchestras in France, Germany, Italy, Spain, Scandinavia and the United Kingdom; Berlin Philharmonic debut 1990 and further engagements with the Chamber Orchestra of Europe, Royal Philharmonic, Leipzig Gewandhaus, Bremen Philharmonic Orchestra and Czech Philharmonic (1996); Further engagements include visits to the Scottish Chamber Orchestra and the Aldeburgh festival; Chamber Concerts in Munich and Italy; Recitals at Salzburg, Davos, Bad Kissingen and Ivo Pogorelich Festivals and at the Théâtre de la Ville in Paris; Chamber music collaborations in Boston, New York (Carnegie Hall), Milan, Amsterdam Concertgebouw, Vienna Musikverein, and South Africa. *Recordings include:* Prokoviev Violin Sonatas with Kyoko Takezawa; Chopin Concertos and solo works by Ravel; Two concertos by Erwin Schulhoff; Chabrier's music for two pianos. *Honours:* Prizewinner, 1996 Leeds International Piano Competition; Winner, Ferruccio Busoni Competition, 1989; Winner, Barenreiter Prize at the International Mozart Competition, Salzburg, 1985. *Current Management:* Harrison/Parrott Ltd, 12 Penzance Place, London, W11 4PA, England. *Telephone:* (20) 7229 9166. *Fax:* (20) 7221 5042. *Website:* www.harrisonparrott.com.

**MAE, Vanessa;** British violinist; b. 27 Oct. 1978, Singapore. *Education:* Cen. Conservatoire, Beijing, People's Repub. of China, Royal Coll. of Music, London, UK. *Career:* studied with Lin Yao Ji and Felix Andrievsky; concerto debut aged ten, Philharmonic Orchestra 1989; first nat. tour of UK with Tchaikovsky Concerto 1990; first int. tour with London Mozart Players 1990; released three classical recordings with orchestra (youngest artist to record both Tchaikovsky and Beethoven Violin Concertos) 1990–92; over 400 live performances in the Middle East, South Africa, China, SE Asia, Russia, Europe, Baltic States, Cen. Asia, USA, Cen. and S America; The Classical Tour 1997, Int. Red Hot Tour 1995, Storm on World Tour 1998; performed at Hong Kong to China Reunification Ceremony 1996, exclusively for HM The Queen, Buckingham Palace 1998, at 50th Anniversary of Geneva Conventions 1999; opened Classical Brit Awards, Royal Albert Hall 2000; collaborated on soundtrack for Walt Disney film Mulan; catwalk debut with Jean-Paul Gaultier; frequent TV appearances and participant in 'crossover' concerts; involved in work with ICRC, participated in TV Campaign Even Wars Have Limits. *Recordings include:* Tchaikovsky and Beethoven Concertos 1990, The Violin Player (quadruple platinum) 1994, The Classical Album I 1996, China Girl: The Classical Album II 1997, Storm 1998, The Original Four Seasons 2000, Vanessa Mae: The Classical Collection Part I 2000. *Film:* Arabian Nights 2000. *Honours:* BAMBI Top Int. Classical Artist Award, ECHO Klassik Award for Bestselling Album of the Year 1995, World Music Award for Best Selling Classical Artist 1996. *Address:* c/o Trittico Ltd, 34 Philimore Walk, London, W8 7SA, England (office). *Website:* www.vanessamae.com (office).

**MAEGAARD, Jan Carl Christian,** DrPhil, RDI; Danish musicologist and composer; b. 14 April 1926, Copenhagen; s. of the late Johannes H. Maegaard and Gerda Glahnson; m. Kirsten Offer Andersen 1973 (divorced 1993); two d. *Education:* Royal Danish Conservatory and Univ. of Copenhagen. *Career:* freelance musician 1949–56; music critic for various newspapers 1952–60; teacher of theory and music history, Royal Danish Conservatory 1953–58; Asst Prof. Univ. of Copenhagen 1959, Assoc. Prof. 1961–71, Prof. 1971–96; Visiting Prof. State Univ. of New York at Stony Brook 1974; Prof. of Music. UCLA 1978–81; consultant to music Dept Danish State Radio 1962–78, Chief Consultant 1982–96; Chair. Music Cttee State Endowment for the Arts 1968–71; mem. Bd Danish State Radio and Television 1970–74; mem. Danish and Norwegian Acads. *Compositions include:* Elegy of Equinox (for voice, cello and organ), Five Preludes (solo violin), Trio Serenade (piano trio), Chamber Concerto No. 2, Due tempi (for orchestra), Musica riservata I (string quartet), Musica riservata II (for reed quartet), Musica riservata III (for flute, oboe, cello and cembalo), Canon for three flutes, Labirinto I (for viola), Labirinto II (for guitar), Triptykon (for violin, string orchestra), Jeu mosaïque (for harp and chamber orchestra), Partita (for organ), Concerto for cello and orchestra, Partita for cello, Orchestration of Arnold Schoenberg's Variations on a Recitative for organ, Completion of J. S. Bach's Die Kunst der Fuge (for organ), Duo-Phantasy (for two guitars), Pierrot in the Ballroom (for two guitars), Kinderblicke (for two guitars), Progressive Variations (for violin and cello), Die Engel (bass, organ), Intermezzo (organ), Die Verlassenen Liebhaber (bass, organ), Elegia (viola, string orchestra), Fantasia I (organ), Fantasia II (organ), Orchestrations of works by Nielsen, P. Heise, Wagner, J.S. Bach, Schoenberg. *Publications:* Musikalsk Modernisme 1964, Studien zur Entwicklung des dodekaphonen Statzes bei Arnold Schönberg I–III 1972, Praeludier til Musik af Schönberg 1976, Indføring i Romantisk Harmonik I–II 1980, 1986, Kuhlaus Kanons (with Gorm Busk) 1996, Begreber i musikhistorien indbil ca. 1600 1999; numerous articles. *Honours:* Kt of Dannebrog I (First Class). *Address:* Duevej 14, 6, 2000 Frederiksberg, Denmark (home). *Telephone:* 38-88-07-80 (home).

**MAFFEO, Gianni;** singer (baritone); b. 30 March 1939, Vigevano, Milan, Italy. *Education:* Liceo Musiale di Vercelli. *Career:* debut singing Tonion in Pagliacci with the Associazione Lirico Compagnia, 1961; many appearances at such opera centres as La Scala Milan, Genoa, Palermo, Turin and Verona, 1973; sang Schaunard in the Zeffirelli/Karajan Bohème at La Scala, 1963; guest engagements at Vienna, Prague, Rouen, Monte Carlo, Brno, Lisbon, Munich and the NYC Opera; further appearances at Toulouse, Nice, Bordeaux and Frankfurt as Marcello, Sharpless, Germont, Count Luna and Rigoletto. *Recordings:* Madama Butterfly, La Bohème.

**MAGA, Othmar;** Conductor; b. 30 June 1929, Brno, Czechoslovakia. *Education:* Studied at the Stuttgart Hochschule für Musik, 1948–52; Tubingen University, 1952–58; Accademia Chigiana at Siena with Paul van Kempen, 1954–55; Further studies with Sergiu Celibidache, 1960–62. *Career:* Conducted the Göttingen Symphony Orchestra, 1963–67, Nuremberg Symphony, 1968–70; General Music Director at Bochum, 1971–82; Artistic Director of the Odense Symphony Orchestra, Denmark, and Permanent Conductor of the Orchestra of the Pomeriggi Musicali de Milano, 1987–90; Also Professor at the Folkswangschule at Essen; Chief Conductor of the KBS-Symphony Orchestra in Seoul, Korea, 1992–96; Guest Conductor with leading orchestras in Europe, Japan and America. *Current Management:* Musicontact, Egbert Zinner, Hamburg; Svensk Konsertdirektion G. Lodding, Gotenburg; Conciertos Gama, Buenos Aires; Walter Beloch, Milano. *Address:* Merlos 19, 36323 Grebenau, Germany.

**MAGEAU, Mary;** Composer and Harpsichordist; b. 4 Sept. 1934, Milwaukee, Wisconsin, USA. *Education:* BMus, DePaul University, Chicago, 1963; MMus, University of Michigan, 1969. *Career:* Faculty Member, Queensland Conservatory, 1987–91; Queensland University of Technology, 1992–95; Founder Member of the Brisbane Baroque Trio. *Compositions include:* Concerto for harpsichord and strings, 1978; Australia's Animals, for piano, 1978; Concert Pieces for violin, cello and piano, 1984; Indian Summer, for youth orchestra, 1986; Concerto Grosso, 1987; Australis 1788, music drama, 1987; Triple Concerto, for violin, cello, piano and orchestra, 1990; Suite for Strings, 1991; An Early Autumn's Dreaming for orchestra, 1993; Dialogues, for clarinet, viola, cello and piano, 1994; The Furies, for piano and orchestra, 1995. *Honours:* 4th Alienor Harpsichord Composition Awards, 1994. *Address:* c/o APRA, 1A Eden Street, Crows Nest, NSW 2065, Australia.

**MAGEE, Emily;** Singer (Soprano); b. 1968 New York, USA. *Education:* University of Indiana, with Margaret Harshaw. *Career:* Debut: As Mozart's Fiordiligi, Chicago, 1994; As Fiordiligi, European debut, Paris Opéra, 1996; Sang Elsa, Berlin Staatsoper, 1996; Châtelet, Paris, and Bayreuth Festival, 1997 as Eva and Elsa; Further engagements at Portland and San Diego Operas, La Scala, Opéra Bastille, Vienna Staatsoper and Florence; Sang Liu in Turandot and Britten's Ellen Orford at the Chicago Lyric Opera, 1997; Other roles include Mozart's Countess, and Donna Elvira; Marguerite, Poppea, Agathe, Desdemona and Arabella; Covent Garden debut as Jenůfa, 2001. *Recordings:* Lohengrin and Die Meistersinger von Nürnberg under Barenboim. *Honours:* MacAllister Award and Richard F Gold Career Grant. *Address:* c/o Berlin Staatsoper, Unter den Linden 7, 1060 Berlin, Germany.

**MAGEE, Garry;** British singer (baritone); b. 1968, England. *Education:* Guildhall School, Nat. Opera Studio. *Career:* debuts with La Monnaie as Malatesta (Don Pasquale) and Dandini (La Cenerentola), with Vlaamse Opera as Yeletsky (Pique Dame), with Glyndebourne Festival Opera as the Steward (Flight), and title-roles in Don Giovanni for Opera North and Pelléas and Mélisande for English Nat. Opera; recent notable roles include Jean in Julie at La Monnaie, title-roles in Pelléas et Mélisande with Bayerische Staatsoper, Wozzeck with Komische Oper Berlin, Don Giovanni and Eugene Onegin for WNO; concerts include Brahms Requiem with the New Jersey Symphony Orchestra, Mahler's Des Knaben Wunderhorn with the Halle Orchestra, Wozzeck with the Philharmonia; has performed at Wigmore Hall, Théâtre du Châtelet, Stavanger Chamber Music Festival. *Recordings include:* Valentin (Faust) and Donizetti Scenes and Overtures, Don Giovanni, Flight, The Wound Dresser, The Maiden and the Tower (with Estonian Nat. Symphony Orchestra). *Honours:* prizewinner Kathleen Ferrier Awards 1995, Int. Belvedere Competition, Vienna 1996. *Current Management:* Harrison/Parrott Ltd, 12 Penzance Place, London, W11 4PA, England. *Telephone:* (20) 7229-9166. *Fax:* (20) 7221-5042. *E-mail:* info@harrisonparrott.co.uk. *Website:* www .harrisonparrott.com.

**MAGNUSON, Elizabeth;** Singer (Soprano); b. 1968, Chicago, USA. *Education:* Studied in Chicago and with Lucille and Robert Evans in Salzburg. *Career:* Appearances with the Zürich Opera as the Queen of Night, Amanda in Ligeti's Le Grand Macabre, Genio in Haydn's Orfeo and Euridice and Marzelline in Fidelio, from 1992. Concert engagements in the Missa Solemnis, Carmina Burana, Henze's Being Beauteous and Bach's Christmas Oratorio; Concert tours to St Petersburg and South America, with further opera appearances at the Würzburg Festival, the Deutsche Oper Berlin (Queen of Night, 1996), and Zürich, Oberto in Alcina and Mozart's Constanze, season 1996–97; Conductors include Christoph Eschenbach, Rolf Beck, Jesus Lopez Cobos (Messiah in Lausanne) and Ingo Metzmacher (Strauss's Burger als

Edelmann, in Stuttgart); Season 1999–2000 as Constanze in the Deutsche Oper Berlin, Marcelina in Pa êr's Leonora at Winterthur, and Woglinde for Zürich Opera. *Honours:* Winner, Chicago Belcanto Competition, 1991. *Address:* c/o Opernhaus Zürich, Falkenstrasse 1, 8008 Zürich, Switzerland.

**MAGNUSSON, Lars;** Swedish singer (tenor); b. 10 March 1955, Gothenburg. *Education:* University of Gothenburg and the Opera School in Stockholm. *Career:* Principal tenor at the Royal Opera, Stockholm, from 1982; Roles have included, the Italian Tenor in Der Rosenkavalier, Lensky, the Duke of Mantua, Alfredo, David in Die Meistersinger and Rodolfo in La Bohème; Sang Pedrillo in a new production of Die Entführung at Covent Garden in 1987; Further performances in Monte Carlo, Nice, Strasbourg, Vienna, Staatsoper, and San Francisco, 1990; Metropolitan Opera debut 1990 as Pedrillo, returning as David, 1992; Royal Opera Stockholm, Gabriele in Verdi's Simon Boccanegra, 1991; Further engagements as David in Paris, Vienna and Marseilles, and the Steersman in Der fliegende Holländer in Geneva; Sang David in a new production of Die Meistersinger at the Metropolitan, 1993, also San Francisco; Season 1997–98 as the Swan in Carmina Burana at Stockholm, Royal Opera.

**MAGOMEDOVA, Ludmilla;** Singer (Soprano); b. 23 May 1961, Ukraine, Russia. *Education:* Studied in Moscow. *Career:* Made concert tour of Siberia, 1986–87, and made stage debut 1987, as the Trovatore Leonara at Kuibishev; Verdi birthday concert in Moscow (1988) and Staatsoper Berlin from 1989, as Tosca and Leonora; Sang Norma at Graz in 1989, Aida at the Split Festival 1990; Other roles include Violetta, Lisa in The Queen of Spades and Amelia (Un ballo in maschera); Turandot with the Latvian National Opera at the Albert Hall, 1998; Season 2000–01 as Lady Macbeth at the Macerata Festival and Abigaille at the Bolshoi, Moscow. *Address:* c/o Staatsoper Berlin, Unter den Linden 7, 1060 Berlin, Germany.

**MAGUIRE, Hugh;** Violinist and Conductor; b. 2 Aug. 1926, Dublin, Ireland. *Education:* College of Music, Dublin; Royal Academy of Music, London; Studies with George Enescu in Paris, 1949–50. *Career:* Debut: Dublin, 1938; London Debut, Wigmore Hall, 1947; Leader of the Bournemouth Municipal (Symphony) Orchestra, 1953–56, London Symphony Orchestra, 1956–62, BBC Symphony, 1962–67; Leader of the Allegri Quartet, 1968–76; Performances of contemporary British composers including Nicola LeFanu, Sebastian Forbes and Elizabeth Maconchy; Leader of the Melos Ensemble, 1977; Co-Leader of the Orchestra of The Royal Opera House, Covent Garden, 1983–91; Tours of British universities giving concerts and lectures under the auspices of the Radcliffe Trust; Professor at the Royal Academy of Music, London; Director of the Orchestra and Director of String Studies at the Britten-Pears School. *Recordings:* Works by Britten, Sherlaw Johnson, Maconchy, Forbes, Elgar, Alexander Goehr and Frank Bridge with the Allegri Quartet. *Honours:* FRAM, 1960; MMus, The University of Hull, 1975; DLitt, University of Ulster, 1986; D.Mus, The National University of Ireland, 1992. *Address:* Manor Farm, Benhall Green, Saxmundham IP17 1HN, England.

**MAHLER, Hellgart,** ARCM; composer, music teacher and writer; b. 7 May 1931, Vienna, Austria; m. Robert Flitney 1951 (died 1995); three c. *Career:* freelance composer; music teacher 1954–. *Compositions include:* Three Galactic Fragments for piano 1966, 1980, Mira Ceti for violin and orchestra 1973, Albedo 0.43 for symphony orchestra 1965, 1973, Glasscapes 1976, Equations for trumpet and percussion 1980, And the Desert Shall Blossom for small orchestra 1980, The Icknield Quartett II for string quartet and flute 1978, Zero-G for winds, brass, six percussion, harp, piano and violin 1982, Skyscapes for Five Players for percussion orchestra, piano and solo horn 1989, Scherzo and Quatro for violin 1989, Divertimento for guitar 1989, How Beautiful Are Thy Dwelling Places for flute, Quintet 1991, Sonnets for strings (vol. 1) for cello 1991, Isochasm for violin, cello and piano 1991, Sound Sculptures for clarinet, bass clarinet and bassoon 1994, Scherzos for the wholse piano 1994, 1995, The Moon and the Lamp 2 for soprano and clarinet 2000, In Hungarian Mode for violin tubular bells and piano 2003; commissions from Silver Harns 1977, Geoffrey Tozer 1988, Jan Sedivka 1989, John Bussey 1994, Gabriella Smart 1994–95, among others. *Publications:* Three Galactic Fragments, Photons for solo piano, The 1991 Quintet, Sonnets for Strings (vol. 1), Scherzo and Quatro, Divertimenti, Five Caprices and Isochasms 91; contrib. several articles to The Stirng Teacher and a large contribution to Sitzky's book on the piano and its role. *Address:* 108 Stoney Rise road, Devonport, Tasmania 7310 Australia. *Telephone:* (03) 6423 2313.

**MAIER, Franz-Josef;** Violinist and Conductor; b. 27 April 1925, Memmingen, Germany. *Education:* Studied at the Augsburg Conservatory, at the Munich Academy of Music and the Music Gymnasium Frankfurt. *Career:* Debut: Violin recital at Munich, 1942; Soloist with the Reichs Symphony Orchestra on tour of Germany 1942; Studied further at Saarbrucken and after war service at the Hochschule für Musik, Cologne with Philip Jarnach; Played in Schaffer Quartet and the Schubert Trio; Lecturer at the Robert Schumann Conservatory, Düsseldorf, 1949–59; Professor and leader of the violin master classes at the Cologne Musikhochschule 1959; Performances of contemporary, Baroque and early classical music; Co-founded the Collegium Aureum 1964, becoming conductor and leader of the ensemble on violin; Concerts played on original instruments or copies; Leader of the Collegium Aureum Quartet 1970. *Recordings:* Suites from Campra's Les Fêtes Venetiennes and Lully's Amadis; Bach Suites, Brandenburg Concertos; Pergolesi La Serva Padrona; Mozart Serenades, Divertimenti, Piano Concertos and Symphonies, Coronation Mass, Requiem and Solemn Vespers; Beethoven 3rd Symphony, 4th Piano Concerto and Triple Concerto; Handel Concerti Grossi Op 3, Alexander's Feast, Water Music, Music for the Royal Fireworks and Organ Concertos, (Harmonia Mundi and BASF).

**MAISENBERG, Oleg;** Austrian pianist; b. 29 April 1945, Odessa, USSR (now Ukraine); s. of Adel and Josef Maisenberg; two c. *Education:* Moscow Gnessin Inst. of Music (pupil of A. Yokheles). *Career:* winner Franz Schubert Competition in Vienna 1967, 20th Century Music Competition, Vienna 1967; performed Rachmaninov's 1st Piano Concerto with Nat. Orchestra of Moldavia; emigrated to Austria 1981; concert performances world-wide as soloist and chamber musician; recordings of Schubert, Schuman, Liszt, Scriabin, Berg, Stravinsky, R. Strauss, Dvořák, Milhaud, Weber, Schönberg, Bartok, Rachmaninov and Prokofiev; Prof. Stuttgart Conservatory and Vienna Acad. of Music, Hon. mem. Konzerthaus Gesellschaft, Vienna. *Address:* c/o Concerto Winderstein, Leopoldstrasse 25, 80802 Munich; In Der Gugl 7-9, Klosterneuburg 3400, Austria; Agentur Dr Raab/Dr Böhm, Plankengasse 7, 1010 Vienna, Austria. *Telephone:* (22) 432-64-85. *Fax:* (22) 432-64-85.

**MAISKY, Mischa (Michael);** Belgian (b. USSR) concert cellist; b. 10 Jan. 1948, Riga, Latvia; m. Maryanne Kay Lipman 1983; one s. one d. *Education:* Moscow Conservatory (with Mstislav Rostropovich), Univ. of Southern Calif. *Career:* debut with Leningrad Philharmonic Orchestra 1965; emigrated to Israel 1972; debut with Pittsburgh Symphony Orchestra at Carnegie Hall 1973; debut at Royal Festival Hall 1976; debut at Berlin Philharmonic Hall 1978; numerous TV, film and video appearances all over the world; played Walton Concerto, London Festival Hall 1993, Shostakovich Concerto, London Proms. *Recordings include:* Six Suites for Solo Cello (Bach), Three Sonatas for Cello and Piano (Bach), Concerto in A minor Op. 102 for Violin, Cello and Orchestra (Brahms), Concerto for Cello and Orchestra in A Minor (Schumann). *Honours:* All-Soviet prize-winner 1965, Int. Tchaikovsky Competition 1966, winner of Cassada Competition, Florence 1973 and Rostropovich Competition, Paris 1981, Grand Prix du Disque, Paris 1985, Record Acad. Prize, Tokyo 1985. *Address:* 138 Meerlaan, 1900 Overijse, Belgium.

**MAISURADZE, Badry;** Singer (tenor); b. 1967, Georgia, Russia. *Career:* frequent recitals, concerts and opera appearances throughout Europe and in Russia; contestant at the 1995 Cardiff Singer of the World Competition; repertory includes Donizetti's Il Duca d'Alba, Carmen, Tosca, Verdi's Il Corsaro and songs by Rachmaninov; sang Cavaradossi at Covent Garden, 2000. *Current Management:* Askonas Holt Ltd, Lonsdale Chambers, 27 Chancery Lane, London, WC2A 1PF, England. *Telephone:* (20) 7400-1700. *Fax:* (20) 7400-1799. *E-mail:* info@askonasholt.co.uk. *Website:* www .askonasholt.co.uk.

**MAIXNEROVA, Martina,** MMus; Singapore pianist and professor of piano; b. 20 Sept. 1947, Prague, Czechoslovakia; m. Pavel Pranti 1972; two s. *Education:* Conservatory of Music, Prague, Academy of Musical Arts, Prague. *Career:* Professor of Piano in Singapore, 1980; Assistant Professor of Piano at the Academy of Musical Arts, Prague, 1975–80; Professor of Piano at the Music School for Especially Gifted Children in Prague, 1970–73; Adjudicator at the First Rolex Piano Competition in Singapore, 1987; Festival appearances in England, Germany, Czechoslovakia, Austria, Poland, USA and Korea; Solo appearances with orchestras including: Guest soloist with the Prague Chamber Orchestra without a Conductor, 1980; Guest soloist with the Singapore Symphony Orchestra, 1981, England, Sweden, Czechoslovakia and Japan; mem. ARS Cameralis Ensemble, 1976–80; Prague Baroque Ensemble, 1973–80. *Address:* 110 Wishart Road, 03-07 Pender Court, 0409 Singapore.

**MAJOR, Dame Malvina Lorraine,** DBE; New Zealand operatic soprano; b. 28 Jan. 1943, Hamilton; d. of Vincent Major and Eva Major; m. Winston William Richard Fleming 1965; one s. two d. *Education:* Hamilton Tech. Coll. and London Opera Centre. *Career:* debut as Rosina in The Barber of Seville, Salzburg Festival 1968; performances in Europe, UK, USA, Australia, Japan, Jordan, Egypt and NZ; concerts, opera and recording with NZ Symphony Orchestra, Auckland Philharmonia and Southern Symphony Orchestra; Founder Dame Malvina Major Foundation (for excellence in the performing arts) 1991; Amb. for the NZ Year of the Family 1994; Prof. of Singing, Canterbury Univ.; Hon. life mem. NZ Horticultural Soc.; Patron Christchurch City Choir, Canterbury Opera, Nelson School of Music, Waikato Multiple Sclerosis. *Honours:* NZ winner Mobil Song Quest 1963, Kathleen Ferrier Competition winner 1966, Outstanding Achievements in Music Award 1988, NZ Medal 1990, Entertainer and Int. Performer of the Year 1992, NZ Music Award–Classical Disc 1993, 1994 and numerous other awards for services to music. *Address:* P.O. Box 11-175, Manners Street, Wellington, New Zealand. *Telephone:* (4) 495-7483.

**MAJOR, Margaret;** Violist; b. 1932, Coventry, England. *Education:* Royal College of Music. *Career:* Debut: Wigmore Hall, London, 1955 with Gerald Moore; Principal Viola, Netherlands Chamber Orchestra, 1955–59; Oromonte Trio, 1958–65; Principal Viola, Philomusica of London, 1960–65; Viola, Aeolian String Quartet, 1965–81; Professor of Viola, Royal College of Music, London, 1969–97. *Recordings:* Complete String Quartets of Haydn; Late Beethoven Quartets; Ravel and Debussy Quartets; Complete Mozart Viola Quintets. *Honours:* Lionel Tertis Prize, 1951; International Music Association Concert Award, 1955; MA, University of Newcastle upon Tyne, 1970; FRCM, 1992. *Address:* White Barn, 97 North Bersted Street, Bognor Regis, West Sussex PO 22 9 AF, England.

**MAKINO, Yutaka;** Composer; b. 5 July 1930, Tokyo, Japan. *Education:* Studied with Koscak Yamada. *Career:* Freelance composer of operas and instrumental works. *Compositions:* Operas Ayame, Radio Opera, CBS, 1960; Mushrooms, comic opera, Tokyo, 1961; Benkei in the Boat, Tokyo, 1962; Hanjo, Tokyo, 1963; Snow-Woman, Yokohama, 1964; The Origin of the Deer Dance, Tokyo, 1967; The Millionaire Ayaginu, comic opera, Tokyo, 1979; The Tale of Ogetsu, 1990. *Honours:* Argentine Music Festival Prize, 1955; National Arts Festival Grant Prize, 1960; Spanish Radio Prize, 1962. *Address:* c/o JASRAC, Jasrac House 7-13, 1-Chome Nishishimbashi, Minato-ku, Tokyo 105, Japan.

**MAKLAKIEWICZ, Tadeusz (Wojciech);** Composer; b. 20 Oct. 1922, Mszczonow, Poland; m. Maria Pawluskiewicz 1952, 3 d. *Education:* Department of Law, Jagiellonian University, Kraków, 1949; State High School of Music, 1958. *Career:* Debut: Festival of Polish Music, Warsaw, 1951; Dean of Music Education Faculty, 1968–69; Deputy Rector, 1969–71, State High School of Music, Warsaw; Head of Music Education Department, 1973; Rector, 1975–78; President, Authors Agency Ltd, Warsaw, till 1985; Union of Polish Composers; President, Society of Authors ZAiKS, Warsaw, 1993–97; Vice-President, Polish Board of Société Européene de Culture, 1994–. *Compositions:* The Kurpie Suite, for Soprano and Mixed Choir a Cappella, 1957; Cantata: Peace; Friendship; Work; Epitaphium for Symphony Orchestra, 1959; Rondo for Clarinet and Piano or Orchestra; Vienna, Vocalisation for Soprano and Orchestra, 1964; Polonais of the Tank Corps; The Clocks are Ringing; Songs for Children for Voice and Piano; Mazovian Dance for Piano, 1977; Hands Friendly With Hands, for Mixed Choir and Organ, 1977; Quintet for Flute, 2 Clarinets, Bassoon and Harp, 1977; Above Clouds, for Mixed Choir, 1978; March for Brass Band, 1979; Salvum Fac, for Mixed Choir, 1981; The Bible Triptych, for 2 Clarinets and Bassoon, 1982; Suite for Cello, 1983; The Gorals Mass, for Mixed Choir and Organ, 1983; Chryzea Phorminx Ode for 4 Trombones, 1984; Arch of Triumph, for Woodwind Quintet, 1984; Wistful Songs for Baritone and Piano, 1985; Love Letters, Variations for String Orchestra, 1985; Ave Maria, for 3 Violins, 1986; At Zelazowa Wola, 3 Stanzas for Baritone, Flute, Alto, Horn and Harp, 1986; Violin Concerto for Children, 1987; A Memory, for 3 Cellos, 1987; A Flag for Female Choir, 1988; Credo, Motet for Mixed Choir and Organ, 1992; Ave Maria in Honour of Notre Dame of Lourdes, for Soprano and Organ, 1993; Romantic Swans, for Soprano and Piano, 1994; Aria for Soprano and Orchestra, 1995. *Address:* Smolna 8/90, 00-375 Warsaw, Poland.

**MAKRIS, Andreas;** Composer; b. 7 March 1930, Salonika, Greece; m. Margaret Lubbe, 12 June 1959, 2 s. *Education:* Phillips University, Enid, Oklahoma, USA, 1950; Postgraduate studies, Kansas City Conservatory, Missouri, and Mannes College of Music, 1956; Aspen Music Festival; Fontainebleau School, France; Studied with Nadia Boulanger. *Career:* Compositions premiered and performed, USA, Canada, Europe, South America, Japan, USSR; Appeared twice with premieres, national television networks, USA, 1978, 1984; Composer-in-residence, National Symphony Orchestra, 1979–90; Adviser to Matislav Rostropovich for new music, 1979–90; His complete short works performed on Voice of America Radio, 1980, 1982. *Compositions include:* Scherzo for Violins, 1966; Concerto for Strings, 1966; Aegean Festival, 1967; Concertino for Trombone, 1970; Anamnesis, 1970; Viola Concerto, 1970; Efthymia, 1972; Five Miniatures, 1972; Mediterranean Holiday, 1974; Fantasy and Dance for saxophone, 1974; Sirens, 1976; Chromatokinesis, 1978; In Memory, 1979; Variations and Song for orchestra, 1979; Fanfare Alexander, 1980; 4th of July March, 1982; Life-Nature Symphonic Poem, 1983; Concerto Fantasia for Violin and Orchestra, 1983; Caprice Tonatonal, 1986; Intrigues for solo clarinet and wind ensemble, 1987; Concertante for Violin, Cello, French Horn, Clarinet, Percussion and Orchestra, 1988; Sonata for Cello and Piano, 1989; Symphony to Youth, 1989; Trilogy for Orchestra, 1990; Alleluia for mixed chorus and brass quintet, 1990; Concertino for organ, flute and string quartet, 1992; A Symphony for soprano and strings, 1992; Woodwind Quintet, 1993; Decalog–Ten Songs for Young Students, 1995; Antithesis for Orchestra, 1995; TFK Commemorative Fanfare for Strings and Snare Drum, 1995; Concerto for Violin and Strings, 1996; Introduction and Kalamatianos for Solo Trumpet, Strings, Snare and Bass Drum, 1997; Sonatina for Solo Violin, 1997; Sextet for Woodwind Quintet and Piano, 1999; Concertino for Flute or Violin and Piano, 1999; Serenade for Soprano and Violin, 2001; Voyage Caprice for Violin, 2003; Hellenic Odyssey for Orchestra, 2003; Various works for violin, string quartets, voice quintets, duets, arrangements of Paganini and Bach; Compositions for special anniversaries and festival openings. *Address:* 11204 Oak Leaf Drive, Silver Spring, MD 20901, USA.

**MAKRIS, Cynthia;** Singer (Soprano); b. 1956, Sterling, Colorado, USA. *Education:* Studied at the University of Colorado and Adams State College. *Career:* Sang Alice Ford, Donna Elvira and Tosca while a student; European debut at Graz as Violetta; Stadttheater Freiburg, 1980–82 as Constanze, Pamina, Violetta and Saffi in Zigeunerbaron; Sang at Bielefeld from 1982 as Donna Anna, Agathe, Marenka, Lucia di Lammermoor and Manon Lescaut and in revivals of Schreker's Irrelohe and Max Brand's Maschinist Hopkins; Member of the Dortmund Opera from 1986 as Desdemona, Leonora in Il Trovatore, Amelia in Un Ballo in Maschera, and Arabella; Other roles include Marietta in Die Tote Stadt at Düsseldorf and at Antwerp, 1995, Marie in Wozzeck at Karlsruhe, Mozart's Countess, Wagner's Eva and Freia and the Empress in Die Frau ohne Schatten; Has sung the title role in Salome, at Dortmund, Berlin Staatsoper and Deutsche Opér, Tokyo and Scottish Opera at Glasgow, 1990; Verdi's Lady Macbeth at Buenos Aires, 1998 and Norma at Philadelphia; Season 2000 as the Forza Leonora at Savonlinna, Leonora in Trovatore and Beethoven's Leonore in Helsinki; Salome at theWiesbaden festival, Marie in Wozzeck at Santiago and Zandonai's Francesca in Bueons Aires. *Address:* c/o Opernhaus, Kuhstrasse 12, 4600 Dortmund, Germany.

**MAKSYMIUK, Jerzy;** Polish conductor, composer and pianist; *Conductor Laureate, BBC Scottish Symphony Orchestra;* b. 9 April 1936, Grodno, Byelorussia (now Belarus); s. of Roman Maksymiuk and Bronisława Maksymiuk; m. Irena Kirjacka. *Education:* Acad. of Music, Warsaw. *Career:* Conductor, Great Theatre, Warsaw 1970–72; f. Polish Chamber Orchestra 1972–84; Prin. Conductor Polish Nat. Radio Symphony Orchestra, Katowice 1975–77; Prin. Conductor BBC Scottish Symphony Orchestra, Glasgow 1984–93, tours of Greece, Canada and Germany, Conductor Laureate 1993–; Guest Conductor Calgary Symphony, Nat. Arts Centre (Ottawa), BBC Welsh and Philharmonic Orchestras, English Chamber Orchestra, Scottish Chamber Orchestra, City of Birmingham Symphony, London Symphony, London Philharmonic, Philharmonia, Orchestre National de France, Rotterdam Philharmonic, Luxembourg Philharmonic, Hong Kong Philharmonic, Royal Liverpool Philharmonic, Bournemouth Sinfonietta, Ulster Orchestra, Tokyo Metropolitan Symphony, Israeli Chamber Orchestra, Los Angeles Chamber Orchestra, Staatskapelle, Sinfonia Varsovia and other orchestras; has toured Europe, USA, Canada, Japan, Israel and Australia with Polish Chamber Orchestra; collaborated with ENO (Mozart's Don Giovanni) 1990, (Johann Strauss' Die Fledermaus) 1993; regularly performs works of Penderecki, Lutoslawski, Gorecki, Szymanowski, as well as British composers including Peter Maxwell Davies and James MacMillan. *Recordings include:* Paderewski: Symphony 'Polonia', The Romantic Piano Concerto, (Vols 1–4), Vivaldi Violin Concertos, Grieg: Pier Gynt Suites Nos. 1 & 2. *Honours:* Hon. DLitt (Strathclyde ) 1990; First Prize, Paderewski Piano Competition 1964, Gold Medal, Elgar Society 1999. *Current Management:* c/o Kathryn Naish, IMG Artists, Lovell House, 616 Chiswick High Road, London, W4 5RX, England. *Telephone:* (20) 8233-5800. *Fax:* (20) 8233-5801. *E-mail:* knaish@imgworld .com. *Website:* www.imgartists.com. *Address:* Gdańska 2 m. 14, 01-633 Warsaw, Poland. *Telephone:* (22) 8323021.

**MALACHOVSKY, Martin;** Opera Singer (Bass); b. 23 Jan. 1968, Bratislava, Czechoslovakia; m. Iveta Pasková, 1 d. *Education:* Academy of Arts, Bratislava, 1986–92; Hochschule für Musik und darstellende Kunst in Vienna, Masterclasses–E Nesterenko, 1990; Conservatoire National Superieur de Paris (Prof Gottlieb), 1991. *Career:* Debut: Slovak National Theatre, 1991; J Massenet, Don Quixote; Rossini, Il Barbiere di Siviglia (Don Basilio); La Bohème (Colline), Slovak National Theatre, Bratislava; J Offenbach: Les Contes d'Hoffmann (Luther and Crespel), Opéra Comique, Paris, 1996; W A Mozart, Le nozze di Figaro, Bartolo, 1995; Mozart Festival, Madrid, 1992; May Festival, Wiesbaden, 1996; Gounod: Faust (Wagner), National Theatre Prague, 1996; Tour of Japan as Sagristano in Puccini's Tosca with Sherrill Milnes as Scarpia, Peter Dvorsky as Cavaradossi and Shinobu Satoh as Tosca, 1997; mem, Slovak Music Union. *Honours:* 3rd Place, International A Dvořák's Singing Competition in Carlsbad, 1988. *Address:* Interartists, Slovakia. *Address:* Gorkého 13, 811 01 Bratislava, Slovakia.

**MALAGNINI, Mario;** Singer (Tenor); b. 1959, Salo, Italy. *Education:* Studied at the Brescia Conservatory and the Giuseppe Verdi Conservatory, Milan with Piermirando Ferraro; Further study with Tito Gobbi and Giuseppe di Stefano. *Career:* Sang in Frankfurt and Milan, La Scala, 1985, as Radames, and in Il Corsaro; Returned to La Scala 1986–87, as Alfredo and Ismaele in Nabucco; Verona Arena from 1987, as Foresto in Attila, Pinkerton, Riccardo and Radames; Appeared as Don José at Glyndebourne 1987, and in a concert performance of La Battaglia di Legnano at Carnegie Hall, as Arrigo; Further engagements at Florence, as Pinkerton and Gabriele Adorno, Nîmes and Monte Carlo, Pollione in Norma, Vienna, Berlin, Houston, Budapest and Seoul, 1988; Teatro La Fenice Venice, 1990 as Rodolfo in Leoncavallo's Bohème; Sang Radames at Verona and Pinkerton for the Munich Staatsoper, 2000. *Recordings:* Emilia di Liverpool, with the Philharmonia Orchestra, Opera Rara; Norma conducted by Emil Tchakarov. *Honours:* Winner, Tito Gobbi Competition, 1983; Concorso Enrico Caruso and Belvedere Competition, Vienna, 1984. *Address:* c/o Arena di Verona, Piazza Bra 28, 37121 Verona, Italy.

**MALANIUK, Ira;** Singer (Mezzo-Soprano); b. 29 Jan. 1923, Stanislava, Poland. *Education:* Studied with Adam Didur in Lwow and with Anna Bahr-Mildenburg in Vienna; Salzburg Mozarteum. *Career:* Debut: Graz 1945; Sang in Zürich from 1947, notably in The Rake's Progress, 1951; Bayreuth Festival 1951–53, as Brangaene, Magdalena, Fricka and Waltraute, Munich Opera from 1952, as Orpheus, Lady Macbeth and Bartók's Judith; Vienna Opera from 1956; Covent Garden 1953, as Adelaide in Arabella, with the Munich Company; Paris Opéra 1956, in Das Rheingold; Salzburg Festival from 1956, notably in the 1958 local premiere of Barber's Vanessa; Concert performances from 1966; Professor at the Graz Conservatory from 1971. *Recordings:* Die Meistersinger, Arabella, Aida, Così fan tutte, Le nozze di Figaro; Waltraute in Götterdämmerung, conducted by Clemens Krauss, Bayreuth 1953; Brangaene in Tristan und Isolde, under Karajan, Bayreuth, 1952.

**MALAS, Spiro;** Singer (Bass-baritone); b. 28 Jan. 1933, Baltimore, Maryland, USA; m. Marlene Kleinman. *Education:* Studied with E Nagy, Peabody Conservatory of Music, Baltimore; E Baklor and D Ferro, NY; Coached by I Chicagov. *Career:* Debut: Marco, Gianni Schicchi, Baltimore Civic Opera,

1959; NYC Opera debut, Spinellocchio in Gianni Schicchi, 1961; Toured Australia with Sutherland-Williamson International grand Opera Co 1965; Covent Garden debut, London as Sulpice in La fille du Régiment, 1966; Pluto in Haydn's Orfeo ed Euridice, Edinburgh Festival, 1967; Chicago Lyric Opera debut as Assur in Semiramide, 1971; Metropolitan Opera debut NY as Sulpice, 1983; Other roles have been the Sacristan in Tosca, Zuniga, Mozart's Bartolo and Frank in Die Fledermaus; Sang Frank Maurrant in the British premiere of Weill's Street Scene, Glasgow 1989; Don Isaac in Prokofiev's Duenna at the 1989 Wexford Festival; Vancouver 1990, as Baron Zeta in The Merry Widow; Many concert engagements; Teacher, Peabody Conservatory of Music. Recordings. For Decca-London. *Honours:* Winner, Metropolitan Opera Auditions, 1961. *Address:* c/o Columbia Artists Management Inc, 165 West 57th Street, NY 10019, USA.

**MALAS-GODLOEWSKA, Ewa;** Singer (Coloratura Soprano); b. 1955, Warsaw, Poland. *Education:* Studied in warsaw. *Career:* Sang at the Warsaw Opera from 1978 as Zerbinetta, the Queen of Night, Rosina, Norina, and Constanze in Die Entführung; Leading roles at the Vienna Volksoper, Paris Opéra-Comique, Nantes, Olympia, Basle, Berne, Wiesbaden and Dresden; Sang Celia in Mozart's Lucio Silla, at Nanterre and Brussels, 1986; Sang Madeleine in Le Postillon de Longjumeau at the Grand Theatre Geneva, 1990; Queen of Night in new productions of Die Zauberflöte at Houston and Paris, Opéra Bastille, 1991; Théâtre du Châtelet Paris in L'Enfant et les Sortilèges; Concert performances in the United Kingdom, Switzerland, Poland, Germany, Netherlands, Belgium, and France, Gstaad Festival, 1987 in Beethoven's Ninth, conducted by Yehudi Menuhin. *Honours:* Winner, Toulouse International Competition, 1978. *Address:* c/o Opera de la Bastille, 120 Rue de Lyon, 75012 Paris, France.

**MALASPINE, Massimiliano;** Singer (Bass); b. 17 May 1925, Fara Novarese, Italy. *Education:* Studied with Lina Pagliughi. *Career:* Appearances from 1959 at such Italian Opera centres as La Scala Milan, Teatro San Carlo Naples, Teatro Fenice Venice and the Teatro Regio Parma; Further engagements at Genoa, Turin, Brussels, Munich Staatsoper, Montreal, Toulouse, Frankfurt, Rio de Janeiro, Paris, Barcelona and Miami; Roles have included Colline in La Bohème, Oroveso in Norma, Ptolomey in Giulio Cesare; Sarastro and Verdi's Padre Guardiano; Banquo and Ramphis; Teacher of singing in Milan after retiring from stage. *Address:* c/o Teatro alla Scalla, Via Filodrammatici 2, 20121 Milan, Italy.

**MALCOLM, Carlos Edmond;** composer and pianist; b. 24 Nov. 1945, Havana City, Cuba; one s. one d. *Education:* Vedado Institute, Havana, Amadeo Roldan Conservatory, Superior Institute of Arts, Havana. *Career:* debut, National Theatre, Cuba, 1964; Composer and Pianist; National Modern Dance Ensemble, 1964–68; Cuban Institute of Radio, occasionally Cuban Institute of Film, 1968–70; Belongs to The Staff of Composers of The Ministry of Culture of Cuba, 1970–; Toured throughout Mexico, Jamaica, Ecuador, playing own works, teaching and lecutring; Works have been played in New Music Concerts, Warsaw Autumn, Berlin's Biennalle, Japan, Argentina, Hungary. *Compositions:* Quetzalcoat!, Song of the Feathered Serpent, for flute and piano; Beny More redivivo, for string quartet; Adagio for piano, 4 hands; El Remediano; Eclosion; Articulations for piano; 13 studies for piano; Songs set to texts by Caribbean Poets; Rumours, for violin, cello and piano; Meditation for piano, all composed between 1963–90; ACCORDES quartet played, Benny More redivivo; Played with flautist Robert Aitken, Quetzalcoat ! for flute and piano; Other compiositions for piano solo, at Toronto's Premier Grand Theater, Royal Conservatory of Music; Bayreuth Festival of Music; AMBER Trio, Israel, played piano trio, Rumours and first performance of Meditation for piano solo, Germany, 1990; University La Salle of Philadelphia. *Address:* ul Piekna 16, m2, 00-539 Warsaw, Poland.

**MALEK, Viktor;** Conductor; b. 20 Dec. 1922, Velká Polana, Czechoslovakia. *Education:* Conducting and Composition, Conservatoire of Music, Prague, 1946; Musical Sciences, Philosophical-Historical Faculty, Charles University, Prague. *Career:* Assistant Conductor, State Theatre, Ostrava, 1946–48; Conductor, Opera Ustí nad Labem, 1948–62; Opera Conductor, 1962–90; Chief Conductor, 1976–84, National Theatre, Bratislava; Conductor, Wien Volksoper, 1977–81; Teacher, Academy of Music, Bratislava, 1981–; Guest Conductor, Prague, Brno, Budapest, Temisoara, Kiev, Edinburgh, Bilbao, Oviedo and Valladolid; Conducted around 800 performances; Conducted first nights for 20 Czech and 12 Slovak operas, composers including Smetana, Dvořák, Janáček, Martinů, Cikker, Beneš, Verdi, Giordano, Mozart, Gounod, Bizet, Wagner, Borodin, Britten, Puccini, Berg; Recordings for radio and television: Così fan tutte, Ballo in Maschera, Benes' The Emperor's New Clothes, King Oedipus, Hatrik The Lucky Prince and others; Founder, Chamber Orchestra Camerata Slovaca, 1969 and Chamber Opera of Slovak National Theatre, 1973–; Chamber opera tours throughout Europe, especially Spain, Germany, Netherlands, Poland, Yugoslavia, Austria; Founder, Symphony Orchestra of the Academy of Music Bratislava, 1994; Conducted Britten's Albert Herring, Don Carlos, L'Elisir d'amore, Berg's Wozzeck, Beggar's Opera; mem, Slovak Music Association; Slovak Concert Artists' Association. *Recordings:* With chamber orchestra Camerata Slovaca, 1969–: Kusser Meier Erindo, opera; 2 profile records with singers; 3 profile records of Slovak composers Bagin, Malovec and Meier; 300 recordings with instrumental and vocal soloists from Baroque to modern music; 2 CDs. *Honours:* Honoured Artist of Czechoslovakia, 1976. *Address:* Cs Parasutistov 31, 83103 Bratislava, Slovakia.

**MALFITANO, Catherine;** American opera singer (soprano); b. 18 April 1948, New York City; d. of Maria Maslova and Joseph Malfitano; one d. *Education:* Manhattan School of Music. *Career:* has appeared at Lyric Opera, Chicago, Metropolitan Opera, NY, La Scala, Milan, Deutsche Oper, Berlin, Salzburg Festival, Royal Opera House, Covent Garden, London, Paris, Geneva, Vienna, Rome, Marseilles, LA, Florence, Hamburg, Barcelona, Israel. *Operas:* 60 roles in operas including: Madame Butterfly 1995, 1997, Il Trittico, Salome 1995, Wozzeck 1997, Eugene Onegin, Tosca, Don Giovanni, Fidelio, McTeague (world première), Antony and Cleopatra, The Makropoulos Case, Mahagonny 1998, Bolcom 1999, Macbeth 1999. *Honours:* Hon. PhD (De Paul Univ.); received Emmy Award for Tosca. *Address:* c/o CAMT, 165 N 57th Street, New York, NY 10019, USA (office); c/o Rita Schütz, Artists Management, Rütistrasse 52, 8044 Zürich-Gockhausen, Switzerland.

**MALGOIRE, Jean-Claude;** Conductor and Oboist; b. 25 Nov. 1940, Avignon, France. *Education:* Studied in Avignon and at the Paris Conservatory, prizes for oboe and chamber music, 1960. *Career:* 1966 founded La Grande Ecurie et la Chambre du Roy, for the performance of Baroque music; Founded Florilegium Musicum de Paris; Concerts of medieval and Renaissance Music; Handel's Rinaldo at the Festival Hall, London; Rameau's Hippolyte et Aricie for the English Bach Festival at Covent Garden; Campra's Tancrède for the Copenhagen Royal Opera and at the Aix-en-Provence Festival 1986; L'Incoronazione di Poppea at the Stockholm Opera; Rameau's Les Indes Galantes at the Versailles Opéra Royal; Conducted Cephale et Procris by Elisabeth Jacquet de la Guerre at St Etienne, 1989, Kreutzer's Paul et Virginie at Tourcoing; Season 1992 with Lully's Alceste at the Théâtre des Champs-Elysées, Paris, a Vivaldi pastiche, Montezuma, at Monte Carlo and Gnecco's Prova di un'opera seria at Montpellier; Conducted Salieri's Falstaff at Tourcoing, 1996; Polish premiere of Lully's Alceste with the Warsaw Chamber Orchestra, 1998. *Recordings:* Rinaldo; Handel's Xerxes; Hippolyte et Aricie and Les Indes Galantes; Tancrède; Cavalli's Ercole Amante; Handel Concerti Grossi Op 3 and 6, Water and Fireworks Music; Lully Alceste, Psyché and Le Bourgeois gentilhomme; Vivaldi Beatus Vir, Gloria and flute concertos; Charpentier Messe de Minuit; Renaissance music with the Florilegium Musicum de Paris. *Honours:* Prix Internationale de Geneve, Oboe, 1968. *Address:* La Grand Ecurie et la Chambre du Roy, 9 Place des Federées, 93160 Noisy le Grand, France.

**MALIPIERO, Riccardo;** Composer; b. 24 July 1914, Milan, Italy; m. Victoria Schneider, soprano, 21 Dec 1988. *Education:* Studied at the Milan Conservatory, 1930–1937 and with his uncle Gian Francesco Malipiero, at the Venice Conservatory 1937–39. *Career:* Began career as a pianist, interrupted by WWII; After WWII began as Composer and Music Critic; Organized the first International Congress of Dodecaphonic Music, Milan 1949; Lectured in USA 1954 and 1959; Masterclasses at the Di Tella Institute Buenos Aires, 1963 and the University of Maryland, 1969; Director of the Varese Liceo Musicale 1969–, 1984. *Compositions:* Operas Minnie la candida 1942; La Donna e Mobile 1954; Television opera Battono alla Porta 1962; L'Ultima Eva, 1995; Orchestral: Piano Concerto, 1937; 2 Cello Concertos, 1938 and 1959; Balletto 1939; Piccolo Concerto for piano and orchestra, 1945; Antico sole for soprano and orchestra 1947; Cantata sacra for soprano, chorus and orchestra 1947; 3 Symphonies 1949, 1956, 1959; Violin Concerto 1952; Studi 1953; Overture-Divertimento del Ritorno 1953; Concerto for piano and ensemble, 1955; Concerto Breve for ballerina and chamber orchestra 1956; Cantata di Natale for soprano, chorus and orchestra 1959; Concerto per Dimitri for piano and orchestra, 1961; Nyktegersia 1962; Cadencias 1964; Muttermusik 1966; Mirages 1966; Carnet de Notes 1967; Rapsodia for violin and orchestra 1967; Serenata per Alice Tully 1969; Monologo for male voice and strings 1969; Concerto for Piano Trio and orchestra 1976; 2 Piano Concertos 1974; Requiem 1975; Ombre 1986; Go Placidly for baritone and chamber orchestra 1975; Loneliness for soprano and orchestra 1987; Due Arie for soprano and orchestra, 1990; Lieder études for soprano and piano, 1991; Chamber: Musik 1 for cello and 9 instruments 1938; 3 String Quartets 1941, 1954, 1960; Violin Sonata 1956; Piano Quintet 1957; Musica da camera for wind quintet 1959; Oboe Sonata 1959; 6 Poesie di Dylan Thomas 1959 for soprano and 10 instruments; Mosaico for wind and string quartets, 1961; Preludio, Adagio e Finale for soprano, 5 percussionists and piano 1963; In Time of Daffodils, Cummings, for soprano, baritone and 7 instruments 1964; Nuclei for 2 pianos and percussion 1966; Cassazione for string sextet 1967; Piano Trio 1968; Ciaccona di Davide for viola and piano 1970; Giber Folia for clarinet and piano 1973; Memoria for flute and harpsichord 1973; Winter quintet for quintet 1976; Apresmiro for 11 instruments 1982; Voicequintet for soprano and string quartet 1988; Piano Music. *Address:* Via A Stradella 1, 20129, Milano, Italy.

**MALIPONTE, Adriana;** Singer (Soprano); b. 26 Dec. 1938, Brescia, Italy. *Education:* Conservatoire de Mulhouse with Suzanne Stappen Bergmann and with Carmen Melis in Milan; Protegée of Rosa Ponselle, Baltimore. *Career:* Debut: Paris Opéra as Micaela in Carmen, 1962–63; Gran Teatro Liceo, Barcelona with Massenet's Manon, 1964; Sang in San Carlo Naples, Lisbon, Milan, Marseille, Tokyo and in all major operas of the world; Has wide repertoire of some 60 roles; British debut, 1967, at Glyndebourne Festival in Elisir d'amore; La Scala debut in Manon with Pavarotti, Mar 1970, returning in I Masnadieri, 1978, and La Bohème, Elisir d'amore, Carmen, Turandot, (Liu), Luisa Miller; Metropolitan Opera debut in La Bohème with Pavarotti, 1971; Japan, in La Bohème, (Mimi), Traviata and Carmen, 1975, returning in La Bohème, with Carlos Kleiber director, 1981; Pagliacci with Placido Domingo, Covent Garden, 1976; La Bohème and Traviata, Vienna Staatsoper

and at Mozart Festival, director Karl Böhm, 1977; Iris at Newark Symphony Hall; La Traviata with Alfredo Kraus, Pretoria, 1983; Maria Stuarda, director Santi, and Guglielmo Tell, Zürich, 1986–87, 1990; Debut in Adriana Lecouvreur, Tenerife, 1989–90; Recent concerts in Taipei, also Carmen, Turandot and Liu, 1994; Gave recital at Salle Gaveau, Paris, 1994. *Recordings include:* Micaela in Carmen, with Bernstein, 1973; Le Villi (Puccini), RCA; Les Pêcheurs des Perles; Pagliacci with Placido Domingo, video. *Honours:* Winner, Génève International d'Execution Musicale, 1960; Prix Villabella, Grand Prix du Disque, 1965; Grammy, USA, 1973; Maschera d'Argento, Campione d'Italia, 1976; Premio Illica, 1983; Rosa d'Oro, 1984; Vittoria Alata, Brescia, 1985; Chevalier des Arts et des Lettres, Académie de France. *Address:* Via Macchi 75, Milan, Italy.

**MALIS, David;** Singer (Baritone); b. 1961, USA. *Career:* Many appearances in concert and opera in North America and Europe, from 1985; Season 1995 with performances in Athens, Buenos Aires from Pittsburgh; Metropolitan Opera in Peter Grimes and La Bohème; Sang Belcore at San Diego, 1996; Wolfram in Tannhäuser at Palermo, 1998. *Honours:* Winner, 1985 Cardiff Singer of the World Competition. *Address:* c/o Metropolitan Opera, Lincoln Center, New York, NY 10023, USA.

**MALKKI, Susanna;** Finnish conductor and cellist; b. 1977, Helsinki. *Education:* Sibelius Acad. (Helsinki) with Jorma Panula, Eri Klas and Leif Segerstam and Royal Acad. of Music (London). *Career:* co-Prin. cellist, Gothenburg Symphony Orchestra (Sweden) 1995–98; Conductor Musica Nova Festival (Helsinki) 1999; Guest Conductor Birmingham Contemporary Music Group; has also conducted Deutsche Kammerphilharmonie, Aarhus Symphony Orchestra, ASKO Ensemble, Royal Flanders Philharmonic, Royal Stockholm Philharmonic, Finnish Radio Symphony, Northern Sinfonia, Avanti!, Lahti Symphony Orchestra, Helsinki Philharmonic, Rotterdam Philharmonic, BBC Philharmonic, BBC Scottish Symphony, Iceland Symphony Orchestra, Danish Nat. Symphony, WDR Cologne, Stuttgart Philharmonic, Ensemble Intercontemporain, Halle, Munich Philharmonic. *Address:* Amaia Barcena, HarrisonParrott Ltd, Artist and Project Management, 12 Penzance Place, London, W11 4PA, England (office). *Telephone:* (20) 7229-9166 (office). *Fax:* (20) 7221-5042 (office). *E-mail:* amaia.barcena@harrisonparrott.co.uk (office). *Website:* www.harrisonparrott.co.uk (office).

**MALMBERG, Urban;** Singer (Baritone); b. 29 March 1962, Stockholm, Sweden. *Education:* Sang in the Boy's Choir of the Stockholm Opera and appeared as First Boy in the 1974 Bergman film version of Die Zauberflöte; Studied in Stockholm with Helge Brilioth and Erik Saeden. *Career:* Sang at Stockholm in works by Peter Maxwell Davies and Janake Hillerud; Hamburg Staatsoper from 1983, as Malatesta, Don Pasquale, Masetto, Papageno, Schaunard in La Bohème, Harlequin in Ariadne and in Nono's Intolleranza and Die Gespensersonate by Reimann; Guest appearances in Düsseldorf, Las Palmas, London, Moscow, San Francisco and Tokyo; Other roles have included Guglielmo and Donner, Brussels and Bonn, 1990, Belcore, Marcello and Lescaut; Season 1992 with Malatesta at Vancouver and Frère Leon in Messiaen's St François d'Assise at the Salzburg Festival; Concert repertoire includes the St Matthew Passion, Beethoven's Ninth, Ein Deutsches Requiem and Peer Gynt; Sang title role in premiere of Matthias Pintscher's Thomas Chatterton, Dresden 1998. *Recordings:* Ariadne auf Naxos and Les Contes d'Hoffmann; The Count in Schreker's Der Schatzgräber, with Hamburg forces. *Address:* Hamburgische Staatsoper, Grosse-Theaterstrasse 34, 2000 Hamburg 36, Germany.

**MALMBORG, Gunila af;** Swedish singer (soprano); b. 26 Feb. 1933, Lulea; m. Lars af Malmborg. *Education:* Royal Stockholm Acad. of Music. *Career:* debut, Stockholm 1960, as Marzeline in Fidelio; guest appearances in Copenhagen, Oslo, Monte Carlo, Cologne and Kiel; Munich 1968, as Salome and Aida; Glyndebourne 1965, as Lady Macbeth; well-known in Wagner roles and as Verdi's Abigaille and Amelia, Mozart's Donna Anna, Puccini's Tosca and Turandot and Offenbach's Giulietta; mem., Stockholm Opera from 1960. *Address:* c/o Stiftelsen Kungliga Teaterns Solister, PO Box 253, 103 24, Stockholm, Sweden. *E-mail:* info@operasolisterna.se. *Website:* www.operasolisterna.se.

**MALONE, Carol;** Singer (Soprano); b. 16 July 1943, Grayson, Kentucky, USA. *Education:* Studied at the University of Indian at Bloomington, at the Hamburg Musikhochschule and with Joseph Metternich in Cologne. *Career:* Debut: Cologen 1966, as Aennchen in Der Freischütz; Many appearances at such German opera centres as the State Operas of Hamburg, Munich and Stuttgart, Deutsche Oper am Rhein Düsseldorf, Nationaltheater Mannheim and Frankfurt; Further engagements at Brussels, Vienna Volksoper, Salzburg, San Francisco, Amsterdam, Venice and the Edinburgh Festival; Sang with the Deutsche Oper Berlin in the premiere of Love's Labour Lost by Nabokov, Brussels, 1973 and as Zerlina in Don Giovanni, Berlin, 1988; Other roles have included Marzelline, Nannetta, Despina, Susanna, Blondchen, Sophie, Adele in Die Fledermaus and Adelaide in Blacher's Preussisches Märchen; Many concert appearances. *Recordings:* Trionfo d'Afrodite by Orff. *Address:* c/o Deutsche Oper Berlin, Richard Wagnerstrasse 10, 1000 Berlin, Germany.

**MALSBURY, Angela (Mary);** Clarinettist; b. 5 May 1945, Preston, Lancashire, England; m. David Pettit, 24 July 1965, 1 s. *Education:* Beauchamp School, Kibworth, Leicester, 1960–62; Associated Board Scholar, Royal College of Music, London, 1962–66; ARCM, Clarinet Teacher and Piano Teacher; LRAM, Clarinet Performer. *Career:* Debut: Concert debut, Royal

Festival Hall, with London Mozart Players, 1976; Concerto Soloist with major orchestras world-wide; Clarinet Quintets including classical and contemporary repertoire; Member of De Saram Trio, Albion Ensembles and London Winds; Principal Clarinet of London Mozart Players; Clarinet Professor, Royal Academy of Music; mem, Musicians Union. *Recordings:* Richard Baker's Musical Menagerie, Cameristi of London. *Recordings:* Mozart Serenade for 13 Wind Instruments (Academy of St Martins, Albion and LMP); Mozart, Clarinet Quintet with the Coull String Quartet (LDR); Mozart, Clarinet Concerto, London Mozart Players and Jane Glover (ASV); Mississippi Five with Albion Quintet; A Trio of French Styles with De Saran Trio. *Honours:* Philip Cardew Memorial Prize, 1963; Marjorie Whyte Prize, 1964; Mozart Memorial Prize, 1974; Hon. RAM, 1991. *Current Management:* Stephanie Williams Artists. *Address:* 40 Greenford Avenue, Hanwell, London W7 3QP, England.

**MALTA, Alexander;** singer (bass); b. 28 Sept. 1942, Visp, Wallis Canton, Switzerland. *Education:* studied with Desider Kovacz in Zürich, Barra-Carracciolo in Milan and Enzo Mascherini in Florence. *Career:* debut at Stuttgart 1962, as the Monk in Don Carlos. US 1976, with the San Francisco Opera; Sang in Brunswick, Munich, Berlin, Vienna, Frankfurt, Geneva, Paris and Venice from 1966; Chicago Lyric Opera in Ariadne auf Naxos; Seattle Opera as Osmin in Die Entfuhrung; Brussels Opera from 1979, notably in Wozzeck, Lulu and Schubert's Fierrabras; Rome Opera as Orestes in Elektra; Maggio Musicale Florence as Wagner's Fasolt and Landgrave; La Scala Milan in Handel's Ariodante; Hamburg Opera as Golaud in Pelléas et Mélisande, Colline in La Bohème, Die Fledermaus, Munich State Opera, Hoffmann, Adriana Lecouvreur, Deutsche Oper Berlin as Nicolai's Falstaff, Gounod's Mefistophélès and Rocco in Fidelio; Salzburg Festival in Carmen and Don Giovanni, conducted by Karajan; Covent Garden 1985, in Tippett's King Priam, title role; Sang the Voice of Neptune in Idomeneo at the 1990 Salzburg Festival. *Recordings:* Lady Macbeth of the Mtsenk District; Carmen, Don Giovanni and the Bruckner Te Deum; Rigoletto; Zar und Zimmermann; Wozzeck.

**MALTA, Alvaro;** Singer (Bass); b. 19 May 1931, Lisbon, Portugal. *Education:* Studied in Lisbon. *Career:* Has sung at the Teatro San Carlos Lisbon, as Figaro, Papageno, Mephistophélès and Klingsor further appearances until 1984 as the Commendatore, Wurm in Luisa Miller, Ramphis and Trulove in The Rake's Progress; Guest engagements in Italy and France and at the Wexford Festival (1977–79) in Herodiade, Tiefland and L'Amore dei tre Re; Other roles have included Monterone, Colline and Des Grieux. *Address:* c/o Teatro São Carlos, Rua Serpa Pinto 9, 1200 Lisbon, Portugal.

**MALTMAN, Christopher;** British singer (baritone); b. 1970, England. *Education:* Warwick Univ., Royal Acad. of Music, studied with Sesto Bruscantini and Thomas Hampson. *Career:* concert engagements include Haydn's St Nicholas Mass with the English Chamber Orchestra, Elgar's The Apostles, under Vernon Handley, the Fauré Requiem at the Albert Hall and the Vaughan Williams Serenade to Music with the CBSO; created role of Sebastian, world premiere of Thomas Adès's The Tempest at the Royal Opera House, Covent Garden 2004; other opera roles include Silvio in Pagliacci, Haydn's L'Isola Disabitata, Hasse's Solimano, Raimbaud in Le Comte Ory, Guglielmo in Così fan tutte, Figaro in Il barbiere di Siviglia, Tarquinius in The Rape of Lucretia, Laurent in Therese Raquin, and the title role in Billy Budd; appearances at Glyndebourne Festival include Ned Keene in Peter Grimes, Sid in Albert Herring, Figaro in Le nozze di Figaro and Papageno in Die Zauberflöte; recitals at the Châtelet, Paris, Wigmore Hall, the Konzerthaus, Vienna, the Gulbenkian, Lisbon, the Concertgebouw, Amsterdam, the Mozarteum, Salzburg, the Palais des Beaux-Arts, Brussels, the Alte Oper, Frankfurt, the Philharmonie, Köln and at Carnegie Hall and the Lincoln Center, New York, and at the Edinburgh, Brighton, Bath, Buxton, Lichfield, City of London, Harrogate, Arundel, Cheltenham and Schubertiade Festivals. *Recordings include:* Paris in Roméo et Juliette, Serenade to Music, Beethoven Folk Songs, Warlock Songs, Ireland Songs. *Honours:* Queen's Commendation for Excellence at the RAM, Cardiff Singer of the World Competition Lieder Prize 1997. *Current Management:* Askonas Holt Ltd, Lonsdale Chambers, 27 Chancery Lane, London, WC2A 1PF, England. *Telephone:* (20) 7400-1700. *Fax:* (20) 7400-1799. *E-mail:* info@askonasholt.co.uk. *Website:* www .askonasholt.co.uk.

**MAMLOK, Ursula;** Composer; b. 1 Feb. 1928, Berlin, Germany. *Education:* Studied in Berlin and Ecuador, NY with Szell at Mannes College and Manhattan School of Music with Vittorio Viannini; Further study with Wolpe, Steuermann, Shapey and Sessions. *Career:* Teacher, NYU, 1967–76, Kingsborough Community College, 1972–75, Manhattan School, 1976–; Represented USA at the 1984 International Rostrum of Composers. *Compositions:* Concerto for strings, 1950; Grasshoppers: 6 Humoresques, 1957; Oboe Concerto, 1974; Concertino for wind quartet, 2 percussion and string orchestra, 1987; Constellations, for orchestra, 1993; Woodwind Quintet, 1956; 2 string quartets, 1962, 1997; Capriccios for oboe and piano, 1968; Variations and Interlude for percussion quartet 1971; Sextet 1978; String Quintet, 1981; From my Garden for violin or viola, 1983; Akarina for flute and ensemble, 1985; Bagatelles for clarinet, violin and cello, 1988; Rhapsody for clarinet, viola and piano, 1989; Stray Birds for soprano, flute and cello, 1963; Hiku settings for soprano and flute, 1967; Der Andreas Garten for mezzo, flutes and harp, 1987; Sunflowers for ensemble, 1990; Five Intermezzi for guitar, 1992; Piano music and pieces for tape. *Recordings:* Walter Hinrichsen

Award, American Academy and Institute of Arts and Letters, 1989. *Address:* c/o ASCAP, ASCAP Building, 1 Lincoln Plaza, NY 10023, USA.

**MAMMOSER, Carmen;** Singer (Mezzo-soprano); b. 1953, Stuttgart, Germany; m. Ulrich Walddörfer, one s. *Education:* Studied in Stuttgart with Hildegard Dietz and Konrad Richter. *Career:* Sang at Hagen Opera from 1980, Stuttgart Staatsoper from 1985; Roles have included Mozart's Cherubino and Annio, Offenbach's Nicklausse, Eboli in Don Carlos, Suzuki in Butterfly, Adalgisa in Norma, Emilia in Othello (with Plaido Domingo), Carmen; Premiere of Hans Zender's Don Quichote, 1993; Concert tour of South America with the Verdi Requiem; 1999 Concert tour of Australia with Wagner Wesendonck-Lieder; Other concert repertory includes the Passions of J S Bach, Bruch's Achilleus and Orchestral Songs by Manfred Trojahn. *Recording:* Rêve d'Amour, French Songs by Fauré and Duparc. *Address:* Staatsoper Stuttgart, Oberer Schlossgarten 6, 70173 Stuttgart, Germany.

**MANAGER, Richetta;** Singer (Soprano); b. 1952, USA. *Education:* Bachelor, Applied Voice, Washburn University of Topeka, Kansas. *Career:* Leading Artist with Gelsenkirchen Opera from 1982, appeared in the roles of Violetta in La Traviata, Amelia in Un Ballo in Maschera, Alice Ford in Falstaff, Elena in l Vespri Siciliani, Leonora in La Forza del Destino, Nella in Gianni Schicchi, Mimi in La Bohème, Leonore in Fidelio, Tosca, Elsa in Lohengrin, Venus and Elisabeth in Tannhäuser, Agathe in Der Freischütz, The Countess in Le nozze di Figaro, Donna Anna in Don Giovanni, First Lady in Die Zauberflöte, Cleopatra in Handels Giulio Cesare, and Title Role in Alcina, Giulietta in Les Contes d'Hoffmann, Marenka in The Bartered Bride, Rosalinde in Die Fledermaus, Saffi in Der Zigeunerbaron, The Duchess of Parma in Busoni's Dr Faustus, Ariadne, Arabella, the Countess in Capriccio, Denise in Tippett's The Knot Garden; Sang in the premiere of Tippett's New Year, Houston and Glyndebourne, 1989–90; Season 1996 as Elisabeth de Valois at Wuppertal and Isolde at Würzburg; Season 1999–2000 in Leonore at Eutin, and Salome and Alice Ford at Wuppertal; Performed at Numerous Festivals with Several Professional Orchestras. *Honours:* 1st Prize, Metropolitan Opera Guild Auditions; 1st Prize, Federated Music Clubs Competition; Gelsenkirchen's Alfred Weber Prize of Excellence. *Address:* Grenzstr 131, 45881 Gelsenkirchen, Germany.

**MANASSEN, Alex (Jacques);** Composer; b. 6 Sept. 1950, Tiel, Netherlands. *Education:* Studied composition at Sweelinck Conservatory, Amsterdam, with Ton de Leeuw, 1972–79. *Career:* Performances live, on radio and television in the Netherlands; Performances in Italy, France, England, Germany, Israel, Sweden, USA, Poland; Commissions for all important Dutch funds; Teacher of Contemporary and Electronic Music, Sweelinck Conservatory, Amsterdam, 1991; Co-founder, Composer, Manager, Delta Ensemble; Teacher of Music and Informatica, Utrecht Conservatory, 1990; Dean, Director, Teacher of Composition, Swolle Conservatory, 1991–. *Compositions:* Katarsis-Arsis for organ, 1973; Prelude, for strings and harpsichord, 1973/95; Mei, for flute and string quartet, 1974; Citius, Altius, Fortius, Variable instrumentation, 1979; Pandarus Sings, for mezzo soprano, flute, clarinet and piano, 1980; Pandarus Sings, Higher, for soprano, flute, clarinet and piano, 1980; De Waal, for 1 or more instruments, especially for beginners, 1980; Interlude 1, Sextet, for oboe, bassoon, french horn and string trio, 1980; Bass Clarinet Concerto, for bass clarinet and orchestra, 1982; Helix for marimba, 1983; Denkmal an der Grenze des Fruchtlandes, for soprano and chamber ensemble, 1983; Air for Orchestra, 1985; Air for electronic music, 1986; Air-Facilmente, clarinet, violin, cello and piano, 1986; Songs and Interludes, for soprano and chamber ensemble, 1979–88; A Call to La Source Possible, for soprano and chamber ensemble, 1988; Air Conditioned, computer controlled player piano, 1988; Lamento for a landscape, electronic music, 1988; Moordunkel, for soprano, accordion, bass clarinet and percussion, 1990; Two Ears to Hear Two Eyes to See, contralto, tenor and piano, 1990, and for soprano, clarinet and piano, arranged Paul van Ostaijen, 1993; Hallo, Hallo, computer controlled sound generating object on request of the Art Foundation Neerijnen; commissioned by the Amsterdam Fund for the Arts and the Province of Gelderland, 1991; Evening Beach Piano, 1991; Farewell to a Landscape, for high voice and clarinet, 1994; Lamento for the Hanze Towns, 1994; Requiem for a Landscape, based on The Tree Bible by William van Toorn, Gerrit Noordzij and others; Elegy in Memoriam Chris Walraven for 8 celli, 1996; Commissioned by the Fund for the Creation of Music. *Address:* Ankummerdijk 6, NL 7722, XJ Dalfsen, Netherlands.

**MANCA DI NISSA, Bernadette;** Singer (Mezzo-soprano); b. 27 Sept. 1954, Cagliari, Sardinia. *Education:* Studied at the Salzburg Mozarteum. *Career:* Debut: Pesaro Festival, 1982 as Isaura in Rossini's Tancredi; La Scala, 1983 and 1988, as Bradamante in Alcina and Libya in Jommelli's Fetonte; Gluck's Orpheus, 1989; Venice Teatro Fenice, 1991–92, as Farnace in Mitridate and Isabella in L'Italiana in Algeri; Palermo and Chicago, 1996, as Orpheus and the Princess in Suor Angelica by Puccini; Other roles include Otho in Handel's Agrippina; Tolomeo in Giulio Cesare and Meg Page in Falstaff; Sang Gluck's Orfeo at Naples, 1988; and La Scala, Milan, 1989; Covent Garden debut 1999 as Mistress Quickly in Falstaff. *Recordings:* Video of Tancredi. *Address:* c/o Teatro San Carlo, Via S Carlo, 80132 Naples, Italy.

**MANCINELLI, Aldo;** Concert Pianist and Professor of Music; b. 1929, Steubenville, Ohio, USA; m. (1) 1 s., 1 d., (2) Judith Elaine Young, 1 June 1971, 1 s., 1 d. *Education:* Graduated, 1952, Graduate Study, 1953, Oberlin Conservatory of Music; Graduated, Accademia Nazionale di Santa Cecilia, Rome, Italy, 1955; Studied with Claudio Arrau, Rudolf Firkusny and Carlo

Zecchi. *Career:* Debut: Beethoven 1st Piano Concerto, with Wheeling (West Virginia) Symphony, 1941; Recitals throughout Europe, North Africa, Middle East, North America; Appeared as Soloist with major symphony orchestras throughout Europe and USA, including Cleveland Symphony, San Antonio Symphony, La Scala (Milan), Royal Liverpool Philharmonic, Santa Cecilia Orchestra (Rome), NDR Orchestra (Hamburg). *Recordings:* Piano Music of Charles Griffes, Musical Heritage Society; Beethoven's Concerto No. 5 (Emperor). *Recordings:* Many recordings for Radiotelevisione Italiana; French North Africa Radio, Tunis; Romanian Radio, Bucharest; Beethoven 4th Concerto with the Czech National Symphony Orchestra. *Contributions:* Charles Griffes, An American Enigma, in Clavier, 1985. *Honours:* 1st Prize Winner, Ferruccio Busoni, International Piano Competition, Bolzano, Italy, 1954; Laureate, Liverpool International Piano Concerto Competition, 1959; Laureate, Casella, International Piano Competition, Naples, 1953. *Address:* 341 Timber Place, Decatur, IL 62521, USA.

**MANCINI, Caterina;** Singer (Soprano); b. 1920, Italy. *Education:* Studied in Milan and elsewhere in Italy. *Career:* Many appearances from 1948 at such Italian opera centres as Bologna, Venice, Rome, Leonora in Il Trovatore; The Baths at Caracalla; La Scala Milan from 1951, debut as Donizetti's Lucrezia Borgia; Sang Agathe at Rome, 1952, and appeared at the Maggio Musicale Florence and the Verona Arena, 1956; Guest engagements in concert and opera elsewhere in Europe. *Recordings:* La Battaglia di Legnano, Ernani and Il Trovatore; Santuzza in Cavalleria Rusticana and Anaide in Rossini's Mosè in Egitto; Guillaume Tell; Attilia; Il Duca d'Alba by Donizetti. *Address:* c/o Teatro alla Scalla, Via Filodrammatici 2, 20121 Milan, Italy.

**MANDAC, Evelyn;** Singer (Soprano); b. 16 Aug. 1945, Malaybalay, Mindanao, Philippines. *Education:* Oberlin College Conservatory; Juilliard School New York. *Career:* Debut: Mobile, Alabama, 1968 in Orff's Carmina Burana; Santa Fe 1968, in the US premiere of Henze's The Bassarids; Washing DC 1969, as Mimi in La Bohème; Toured with Juilliard Quartet, 1969, in Schoenberg's 2nd Quartet; Seattle Opera 1972, in the premiere of Pasatieri's The Black Widow; Sang in the US premiere of Berio's Passaggio; San Francisco 1972, as Inez in L'Africaine; Glyndebourne 1974–75, as Susanna and Despina; Houston Opera 1975, as Lauretta in Gianni Schicchi; Baltimore Opera 1976, in the premiere of Pasatieri's Inez de Castro; Lisa in The Queen of Spades for US television, 1977; Guest appearances in Toulouse, Turin, Rome, Salzburg Festival and Geneva. *Recordings:* Carmina Burana, conducted by Ozawa.

**MANDANICI, Marcella;** Composer; b. 15 April 1958, Genoa, Italy; m. Giuseppe Venturini, 22 Dec, 1978. *Education:* Piano diploma, Brescia, 1979; Harpsichord Diploma 1984, Composition Diploma 1986, Milan; Composition Diploma, Santa Cecilia Academy, Rome, 1988. *Career:* Autumn Musicale, Como, 1984; Aspekte, Salzburg, 1986; Nuove Musica Italiana, Rome, 1987–88; Settimana di Musica Contemporanea Desenzano, 1987–88; Musica Rave, Milano, 1985; Spazio Musica, Cagliari, 1988; Founded, Nuovi Spazi Sonori, Italian Association for Contemporary Music, Artistic Director, 1987–. *Compositions:* Author of many compositions for solo instruments, chamber ensemble and orchestra including: Invenzione a Cinque, for flute, clarinet, viola, cello and piano, 1982; Edipan Steps for piano, 1983; Rugginenti; Senza Testo, for voice, 1987. *Recordings:* Invenzione a Cinque; Senza Testo. *Honours:* Steirischer Herbst Selection, Graz, 1986; IGNM Selection, Koln, 1987; Antologia Radiotre Selection, Rome, 1988, with Double Path. *Address:* Via Vittorio Emanuele 11-60, 25122 Brescia, Italy.

**MANDEL, Alan (Roger);** Concert Pianist, Professor of Music and Artistic Director; b. 17 July 1935, New York, USA; m. Nancy Siegmeister, 1 June 1963, divorced 1989. *Education:* BS 1956, MS 1957, Juilliard School of Music; Diploma in Piano and composition, Akademie Mozarteum, Salzburg, Austria, 1962; Diploma, Accademia Monteverdi, Bolzano, Italy, 1963. *Career:* Debut: Town Hall, New York City, 1948; Over 305 International Concert Tours in 50 Countries; Noted for his repertoire of esoteric and seldom-played masterpieces; Professor of Music, The American University, Washington DC; Artistic Director, Washington Music Ensemble; Chairman of the Music Division, The American University, Washington DC, 1992. *Compositions:* Symphony, piano concerto, many piano compositions and songs. *Recordings include:* The Complete Piano Works of Charles Ives; Louis Moreau Gottschalk; Forty Works for the Piano; Anthology of American Piano Music 1790–1970; Three Sides of George Rochberg; Carnival Music; Elie Siegmeister; Sonata No. 4 for Violin and Piano; American Piano (CD); Rags and Riches, CD, Premiere Recordings Inc, New York, 1992. *Publications:* Charles Ives: Study No. 5 for Piano, edited by Alan Mandel with Preface Performance notes, Editorial notes and Analytical notes, 1988. *Current Management:* Guy Friedman, 37 Robins Crescent, New Rochelle, NY 10801, USA. *Address:* 3113 Northampton St NW, Washington DC 20015, USA.

**MANDELBAUM, Joel;** Composer; b. 12 Oct. 1932, NY, USA. *Education:* Studied with Walter Piston, Irving Fine, Harold Shapero and Bernhard Heiden; BA, Harvard, 1953; MFA, Brandeis University, 1957; PhD, Indiana University, 1961. *Career:* Teacher, Queen's College, NY, 1961, retired 1999; Director of the Aaron Copeland School of Music, 1981–84; Fellow, MacDowell Colony 1968; mem, American Festival of Microtonal Music; American Society for Jewish Music; Long Island Composers Alliance. *Compositions:* Operas: The Man in the Man-Made Moon 1955; The Four Chaplains, 1957; The Dybbuk, 1971; The Village, 1995; Orchestral: Concovation Overture, 1951; Piano Concerto, 1953; Sursum Corda, 1960; Sinfonia Concertante for oboe,

horn, violin, cello and chamber orchestra, 1962; Memorial for string orchestra, 1965; Trumpet Concerto, 1970; Chamber: 2 wind quintets, 1957, 1991; 2 string quartets, 1959, 1979; Sonatas with piano for flute, 1951, recorder, 1972, second piano, 1980, oboe, 1981, clarinet, 1983, cello, 1986; Duo sonata for violin and cello, 1989; Works for special microtonal instruments, 1961, 1963, 1967, 1977, 1991; Choruses; 11 Song cycles; Musicals and incidental music. *Recordings include:* Three Song Cycles, Erika Sunnegärdh. *Address:* c/o ASCAP, ASCAP Building, 1 Lincoln Plaza, NY 10023, USA.

**MANDUELL, Sir John,** Kt, CBE, FRAM, FRNCM, FRCM, FRSAMD, FWCMD; British composer and music director; b. 2 March 1928, Johannesburg, South Africa; m. Renna Kellaway 1955; three s. one d. *Education:* Haileybury Coll., Jesus Coll., Cambridge, Univ. of Strasbourg, France, Royal Acad. of Music. *Career:* BBC Music Producer 1956–61; Gov. Nat. Youth Orchestra 1964–73, 1978–; Chief Planner, The Music Programme 1964–68; Dir of Music, Univ. of Lancaster 1968–71; Associated Bd of Royal Schools of Music 1971–96; Gov. Chetham's School 1971–; Prin. Royal Northern Coll. of Music 1971–96; Programme Dir Cheltenham Festival 1969–94; Dir Young Concert Artists' Trust 1983–95, Lake District Summer Music Festival 1984–; Pres. European Asscn of Music Acads 1988–96, Opera Bd 1988–95, Bd Royal Opera House 1989–95, Bd Manchester Arts 1991–97; engagements and tours as composer, conductor and lecturer in Canada, Europe, Hong Kong, South Africa and USA; chair. numerous cttees; Chair. or mem. of many int. musical competition juries; European Opera Centre opened with Tosca at Manchester 1998; Mozart's Lucio Silla in London and elsewhere 1999. *Compositions:* Sunderland Point (overture) 1969, Diversions for Orchestra 1970, String Quartet 1976, Prayers from the Ark 1981, Double Concerto 1985, Vistas for Orchestra 1997, Into the Ark (song cycle) 1997, Flutes Concerto 2003, Nonet 2005. *Recordings:* several CDs of own music issued. *Contributions:* The Symphony 1966. *Honours:* Hon. Lecturer in Music, Univ. of Manchester 1976–96; Hon. FTCL 1973; Hon. GSM 1986; Chevalier des Arts et Lettres 1990; Hon. DMus (Lancaster) 1990, (Manchester) 1992, (RSA) 1996; 1st Leslie Boosey Award, Royal Philharmonic Soc. and PRS 1980, 1990. *Address:* Chesham, High Bentham, via Lancaster, LA2 7JY, England. *Telephone:* (1524) 261702. *Fax:* (1524) 261702.

**MANN, Robert;** Violinist, Composer, Conductor and Teacher; b. 19 July 1920, Portland, Oregon, USA; m. Lucy Rowan. *Education:* Juilliard School of Music with Edouard Dethier, Adolfo Beti, Felix Salmond, Edgar Schenkman, Bernard Wagenar and Stefan Wolpe. *Career:* Debut: Violin recital NY 1941; Joined faculty of Juilliard School after wartime service; Founded Juilliard String Quartet 1948; Many concert engagements in Europe and USA; Established 1962 as Quartet-in-Residence under the Whittall Foundation at the Library of Congress, Washington, DC; Quartet-in-Residence at Michigan State University from 1977; First performances of Quartets by Carter, Kirchner, Schuman, Sessions, Piston, Babbitt, Copland and Foss; First US Quartet to visit USSR, 1961; Repertory of 600 wroks; Conductor of contemporary music; Has performed and lectured at the Aspen Music Festival; President of the Naumburg Foundation 1971; Chairman of Chamber Music panel 1980; Coach to Concord, Tokyo, LaSalle and Emerson String Quartets; Formed Duo with s. Nicholas Mann 1980; Visited London with the Juilliard Quartet, 1996 and 2000. *Recordings:* Complete Beethoven Quartets and Mozart's Quartets dedicated to Haydn; Contemporary works. *Address:* c/o Violin Faculty, Juilliard School of Music, Lincoln Plaza, NY 10023, USA.

**MANN, Werner;** Singer (Bass); b. 25 June 1935, Berlin, Germany. *Education:* Studied in Munich and Berne. *Career:* Sang at Aachen Opera, 1980–84; Trier, 1985–90; Pforzheim, from 1993; Roles have included Mozart's Osmin and Sarastro, Pizarro, Don Pasquale, Falstaff, Verdi's Attlia, King Philip and Padre Guardiano; Rossini's Basilio, Wagner's Daland and King Mark; Ochs in Der Rosenkavalier and Trulove in The Rake's Progress; Guest appearances in Geneva, Glasgow and Salzburg; Frequent concert engagements throughout Europe. *Recordings:* Schoenberg's Moses und Aron. *Address:* c/o Stadttheater Pforzheim, Am Weisenhausplatz 5, 3530 Pforzheim, Germany.

**MANNING, Jane,** OBE, FRAM, FRCM, GRSM; British singer (soprano); b. 20 Sept. 1938, Norwich; d. of the late Gerald Manning and Lily Thompson; m. Anthony Payne 1966. *Education:* Norwich High School for Girls, RAM, London and Scuola di Canto, Cureglia, Switzerland. *Career:* London debut concert 1964; since then active world-wide as freelance soprano soloist with special expertise in contemporary music; more than 350 BBC broadcasts; regular tours of USA since 1981 and of Australia since 1978; appearances at all leading European festivals and concert halls; New York début 1983; more than 300 world premières including several operas; Founder/Artistic Dir Jane's Minstrels (ensemble) 1988; many recordings including complete vocal works of Messiaen and Satie; Vice-Pres. Soc. for Promotion of New Music 1996–; Visiting Prof., Mills Coll., Oakland, Calif. 1981, 1982, 1983, 1986, Royal Coll. of Music 1995–; visiting lecturer, univs in UK, USA, Canada, Australia, NZ and Scandinavia; mem. Exec. Cttee Musicians' Benevolent Fund. *Publications:* New Vocal Repertory (Vol. I) 1986, (Vol. II) 1998, A Messiaen Companion 1995. *Honours:* Hon. Prof., Keele Univ. 1996–2002; Hon. DUniv (York) 1988, Dr. hc (Keele Univ.) 2004; Special Award for Services to British Music, Composers' Guild of GB 1973. *Address:* 2 Wilton Square, London, N1, England. *Telephone:* (20) 7359-1593. *Fax:* (20) 7226-4369. *Website:* www .classical-artists/janemanning.com (home).

**MANNING, Peter;** Violinist; b. 17 July 1956, Manchester, England. *Education:* Chathams School 1969–73; Royal Northern College of Music; Indiana University, USA 1973–81. *Career:* Debut: Concert at Wigmore Hall, 1987; Solo appearances with Philharmonia Orchestra, Hallé Orchestre, City of Birmingham Symphony; Co-leader, London Philharmonic Orchestra; Professor, Royal Northern College of Music; Quartet in Residence at the Dartington Summer School, with quartets by Schnittke; Season 1988–89 in the Genius of Prokofiev series at Blackheath and BBC Lunchtime Series at St John's Smith Square; South Bank Concerto conducted by Neville Marriner concerts with the Hermann Prey Schubertiade and collaborations with the Alban Berg Quartet in the Beethoven Plus series; Tour of South America 1988, followed by Scandinavian debut; Season 1989–90 with debut tours of Netherlands, Germany, Spain, Austria and Finland; Tours from 1990 to the Far East, Malta, Sweden and Norway; Schoenberg-Handel Concerto with the Gothenburg Symphony; Festival appearances at Brighton, the City of London, Greenwich, Canterbury, Harrogate, Chester, Spitalfields and Aldeburgh; Collaborations with John Ogdon, Imogen Cooper, Thea King and Lynn Harrell; Formerly resident quartet at Liverpool University; Teaching role at Lake District Summer Music 1989; Universities of Bristol, Hong Kong 1990. *Recordings:* Beethoven Op 130 and Schnittke Quartet No. 3; Vaughan Williams On Wenlock Edge and Ravel Quartet; Britten, Prokofiev, Tippett, Elgar and Walton Quartets; Exclusive contract with EMI from 1990. *Current Management:* Ingpen & Williams Ltd, 7 St George's Court, 131 Putney Bridge Road, London, SW15 2PA, England.

**MANNION, Rosa;** British opera singer (soprano); b. 1962; one c. *Education:* Royal Scottish Acad. of Music. *Career:* Fmr singer with Scottish Opera; Prin. Soprano English Nat. Opera, London 1989–92; appearances in Lisbon, Amsterdam (Netherlands), Berlin, Paris, Salzburg (Austria), Aix-en-Provence (France), Glyndebourne, Royal Opera House, Covent Garden (London). *Operas include:* L'Elisir d'amore, Rigoletto, Der Rosenkavalier, La Traviata, Manon, Show Book, Die Zauberflöte, Le Roi malgré lui, Werther, A Masked Ball, Xerxes, Figaro's Wedding. *Address:* c/o IMG Artists, 616 Chiswick High Rd London, W4 5RX, England.

**MANNOV, Johannes;** Singer (Baritone); b. 1965, Copenhagen, Denmark. *Education:* Studied at the Conservatoires of Freiburg and Karlsruhe. *Career:* Sang with the boys' choir Kobenhauns-Drengekor before adult study; Has sung with the Kassel Opera from 1987 as Mozart's Papageno, Masetto and Figaro; Concert performances under such conductors as Helmuth Rilling, Luigi Nono, George Malcolm, Frans Brüggen, Leif Segerstram and Hans Martin Schneidt; Has performed Mozart's Requiem in Bremen, the Christmas Oratorio in Cologne and Frankfurt and an Italian tour with Bach's St John Passion, 1991–92; Britten's War Requiem in Frankfurt; Sang Mozart's Figaro for Opera Northern Ireland 1991; Season 2000–01 as Christus in the St Matthew Passion, in Berlin, Siegfried in Schumann's Genovea at Garsington and Papageno for San Diego Opera. *Recordings include:* Keresmin in Holger Danske by Kunzen, 1996. *Honours:* Prizewinner, 's-Hertogenbosch Competition, 1986; Helsinki Competition, 1989.

**MANSON, Anne;** Conductor; b. 1961, USA. *Education:* Studied at Harvard University, King's College London, the Royal College of Music with Norman del Mar and James Lockhart and the Royal Northern College of Music. *Career:* As Music Director of Mecklenburgh Opera conducted a wide range of 20th century and contemporary chamber operas; First woman to conduct Vienna Philharmonic Orchestra, in a rehearsal of Boris Godunov in 1997, also first woman to conduct at the Salzburg Festival in 1994; Conducted English Touring Opera in Don Pasquale and Don Giovanni; The Rise and Fall of the City of Mahagonny for Netherlands Touring Opera, 1996; Seven Deadly Sins at the Proms, 1997; Assistant to Claudio Abbado at 1992 Salzburg Festival in From the House of the Dead and in Boris Godunov at Vienna Staatsoper; Conducted at La Monnaie Brussels in 1993 in a triple bill of works by Monteverdi and Judith Weir; Conducted Boris Godunov with the Vienna Philharmonic and Sam Ramey in 1994; US debut at Washington Opera with Samuel Barber's Vanessa in 1995, returned with Dangerous Liaisons in 1998; Conducted Royal Scottish National Orchestra, BBC Scottish, Los Angeles Philharmonic, St Pauls Chamber Orchestra, Scharoun Ensemble; Regular Guest of Ensemble Intercontempoain and Iceland Symphony; Music Director, Kansas City Symphony, 1999–; Conducted Susannah, by Carlisle Floyd, Théâtre de Genève, 2000; Conducted Houston Symphony, 2001. *Recordings:* Tristan Keuris with Residentie Orchestra; Jon Leifs with Iceland Symphony Orchestra. *Honours:* Fellow in Conducting, Royal Northern College of Music; Marshall Scholarship; Prizes at the RCM and RNCM. *Current Management:* ICM Artists Ltd. *Address:* c/o Rachel Bowron, ICM Artists, 40 West 57th Street, New York, NY 10019, USA.

**MANSOURI, Lotfollah (Lotfi);** Opera Stage Director; b. 15 June 1929, Tehran, Iran; m. Marjorie Anne Thompson 1954, 1 d. *Career:* Assistant Professor, University of California, Los Angeles, USA, 1957–60; Dramatic Coach, Music Academy of the West, Santa Barbara, California, 1959; Resident Stage Director, Zürich Opera, Switzerland, 1960–65; Director of Dramatics: Zürich International Opera Studio, 1961–65, Centre Lyrique, Geneva, 1967–72; Chief State Director, Geneva Opera, 1965–75; Artistic Adviser, Tehran Opera, 1973–75; Opera Adviser, National Arts Centre, Ottawa, Canada, 1977; General Director, San Francisco Opera, 1988–99; Guest Director, various opera companies including New York Metropolitan, San Francisco Opera, La Scala, Verona, Vienna Staatsoper, Vienna Volksoper, Salzburg Festival, Covent Garden, Amsterdam Opera, Holland Festival,

L'Opéra de Nice, Festival d'Orange, Australian Opera, Kirov Opera, Lyric Opera Chicago; Dallas Opera; With Surtitles TM initiated above-stage projection of simultaneous opera texts, 1983; Presided over the redevelopment of the War Memorial Open House, gala reopening, Sept 1997; mem, Board of Directors, Opera America, 1979–91, 1993–96; American Guild of Musical Artists; AFTRA; Canadian Actors' Equity Association. *Publications:* An Operatic Life (co-author), 1982. *Address:* War Memorial Opera House, 301 Van Ness Ave, San Francisco, CA 94102-4509, USA.

**MANSUR, Cem,** BSc; Turkish conductor; b. 4 Sept. 1957, Istanbul; m. Lale Mansur 1984. *Education:* The City Univ., London, England, studied conducting at the Guildhall School, London and with Leonard Bernstein at the Los Angeles Philharmonic Inst. *Career:* Conductor, Istanbul State Opera 1981–89, also giving orchestral concerts; London debut 1985, with the English Chamber Orchestra; first performance of Elgar, The Spanish Lady, London 1986; further engagements with orchestras and opera cos in Sweden, Mexico, Spain, Germany, Netherlands, Italy, Romania, Russia, France, Israel and Czechoslovakia; regular appearances at Holland Park Opera and Mid Wales Opera; Kirov Opera at St Petersburg 1993 and 1994 for several operas; Principal Conductor, City of Oxford Orchestra 1989–96, including tours to Vienna, Zürich, Prague and Budapest; led Debussy's Le Martyre de Saint Sebastian at St John's Smith Square; further concerts with the Royal Philharmonic, Georges Enescu Philharmonic, City of London Sinfonia, BBC Concert Orchestra, Mexico City Orchestra, Helikon Opera, Moscow, London Mozart Players and the Hungarian State Orchestra 1989–96; Principal Conductor, Akbank Chamber Orchestra, Istanbul, Turkey 1998–; first performance since its creation of Offenbach's Whittington at the City of London Festival 2000; Pres., Ipswich Choral Soc. 1999–; mem. Conductors' Guild (USA). *Recordings:* works by Turkish composers with the Hungarian State Orchestra. *Honours:* Guildhall School Ricordi Conducting Prize 1981. *Address:* 31 Carlingford Road, London, NW3 1RY, England. *E-mail:* cemmansur@aol.com.

**MANTEL, Gerhard (Friedrich);** Concert Cellist; b. 31 Dec. 1930, Karlsruhe, Germany; m. Renate Mantel, 1 s. *Education:* Music Academies in Mannheim and Paris; Musikhochschule Saarbrucken; Studied with August Eichhorn and Pierre Fournier. *Career:* Solo cellist, Bergen Symphony, Norway; WDR Orchestra, Cologne; World-wide recital tours, mainly with pianist Erika Friesar; Professor, Frankfurt Musikhochschule, 1973–; Assistant Director 1975–; mem, European String Teachers Association. *Recordings:* With Erika Friesar, Sonatas by Mendelssohn, Strauss, Grieg. *Publications:* Cello Technik 1973. *Honours:* Kulturpreis der Stadt Karlsruhe, 1955. *Address:* 6236 Eschborn 2, Felderbergstrasse 44, Germany.

**MANTLE, Neil (Christopher);** Conductor; b. 16 March 1951, Essex, England; m. Inga Wellesley, 17 Oct 1980, 1 s., 1 d. *Education:* Royal Academy of Music, London, 1969–70; Royal Scottish Academy of Music, 1970–73. *Career:* Conducting with Scottish Sinfonia, 1970–, Edinburgh Opera Company, 1975–81, Sinfonia Opera, 1983–84; Guest Conductor, Scottish National Orchestra, 1984; Guest Conductor, BBC Scottish Symphony Orchestra, 1986–; mem, Elgar Society. *Honours:* Hugh S Robertson Conducting Prize, Royal Scottish Academy of Music, 1973; 2nd prize, Leeds Conductors Competition, 1986. *Address:* c/o BBC Scottish SO, Broadcasting House, Queen Margaret Dr, Glasgow, G12 8DG, England.

**MÄNTYNEN, Jaana;** Singer (Soprano); b. 1964, Finland. *Education:* Studied at the Sibelius Academy, Helsinki. *Career:* Represented Finland at 1992 Cardiff Singer of the World Competition; Appearances at Helsinki in Die Zauberflöte, in the title role of Suor Angelica, Gabriel Come Back by Ilkka Kuusisto, The Telephone by Menotti, La Vida Breve, Eugene Onegin (as Tatiana) and The Maiden in the Tower by Sibelius; Savonlinna Festival, 1995, in the premiere of The Palace by Sallinen. *Honours:* Prizewinner at Timo Mustakallio and Lappeenranta Competitions, 1991–92. *Address:* c/o Finnish National Opera, PO Box 176, Helsinginkatu 58, 00251 Helsinki, Finland.

**MANZ, André,** DipMus, MMus; Swiss organist, pianist, harpsichordist and teacher; b. 15 Dec. 1942, Chur; m. Irene Pomey. *Education:* Music Acad. Zürich, Conservatory Winterhur, Hochschule für Musik, Cologne, Germany. *Career:* debut 1964; organ recitals in Switzerland, Germany, Italy, Denmark, Japan, Poland, USA, Canada, Spain and Austria; various radio series; piano duo with Irene Manz-Pomey; mem. Schweizer Tonkunstlerverein (STV), Schweizer Musikpadagogischer Verband (SMPV), Pres., Thurgau Organists' Asscn, Rotary Club. *Compositions:* Play B-A-C-H for six organists and assistants 1971. *Recordings include:* Swiss Baroque Soloists, several organ solo recordings, including the complete organ works by Franz Liszt, Variations on National Anthems, Battles and Thunderstorms for Organ, and Four Hands Organ-Playing Throughout Five Centuries, Festive organ music of the 19th and 20th century 2003. *Publications:* contrib. to various musical journals. *Honours:* many musical prizes and scholarships; Eastern Swiss Radio and Television Asscn Annual Prize 1994, Canton Thurgau Government Annual Cultural Prize 1996;elected hon. Freeman from the City of Amriswil 2004. *Address:* Brunnenfeldstrasse 11, 8580 Amriswil, Switzerland.

**MANZ, Wolfgang;** German pianist; b. 6 Aug. 1960, Düsseldorf; m. Julia Goldstein 1985; two s. one d. *Career:* studied with Drahomir Toman, Prague and Karlheinz Kämmerling, Hanover; teacher, High School of Music, Karlsruhe 1994–98; concert tours UK, Germany, Belgium and Japan; performed Promenade Concerts, London 1984, Gilels Memorial Concert,

Düsseldorf 1986, Karajan Foundation, Paris 1987. *Recordings include:* Chopin Studies, Beethoven Triple Concerto, with English Chamber Orchestra, solo recital Liszt, Schumann and Debussy, Dohnanyi Piano Quintet. *Honours:* First Prize Mendelssohn Competition, Berlin 1981, Second Prize, Leeds Piano Competition 1981, Second Prize Brussels Queen Elizabeth Competition 1983, Van Cliburn Int. Piano Competition Award, Texas 1989. *Address:* Pasteurallee 55, 30655 Hanover, Germany. *Telephone:* (511) 5476025. *Fax:* (511) 5497432.

**MANZE, Andrew (Mark);** Violinist and Conductor; b. 14 Jan. 1965, Beckenham, Kent. *Education:* Cambridge University (Classics), Royal Academy, London, and with Marie Leonhardt, Amsterdam. *Career:* Performances of 17th Century music with La Romanesca, 1987–88; Leader of Amsterdam Baroque Orchestra, under Tom Koopman, 1989–93; Conductor with La Stravaganza, Cologne, Orchestra of the Age of Enlightenment and Philharmonic Baroque Orchestra, San Francisco; Associate conductor, Academy of Ancient Music, 1996–, Concerto debut at the London Proms, 1998; Broadcast programmes with BBC Radio 3. *Recordings include:* 1681 Sonatas of Biber; Bach St Matthew Passion; Tartini solo violin works; Bach Violin Concertos and Handel Concerto Grossi op. 6. *Honours:* Edison Award, 1998. *Address:* c/o Academy of Ancient Music, 10 Brookside, Cambridge, CB 2 1JE, England.

**MANZINO, Leonardo,** DipMus, MMus, PhD; Uruguayan pianist and musicologist; *Adjunct Professor, School of Music, University of Uruguay;* b. 24 Feb. 1962, Montevideo; m. Mercedes Xavier de Mello 2003; one s. *Education:* Kolischer Conservatory, Montevideo, Univ. of Uruguay, Catholic Univ. of America. *Career:* debut, Sala Martins Pena, Brasilia 1983; int. summer music festivals of Brasilia 1983–84; Uruguayan Music Students' Asscn 1983; Jeunesses Musicales of Uruguay Series 1984–85; Argentine Music Foundation Series 1986; Adjunct Prof., School of Music, Univ. of Uruguay 1993–; Dir, Musicanga Classics 1995; Prof. of History of Music, Escuela Municipal de Música de Montevideo 1997. *Publications:* Composers of the Americas, vol. 20 (ed.) 1993, Uruguayan Music in the 1892 celebrations for the IV Centenary of the Encounter of Two Worlds, Latin American Music Review 1993, León Ribeiro: 150th Anniversary of the Romantic Uruguayan Composer 2004. *Honours:* winner Uruguayan Music Students' Piano Competition 1983, winner Jeunesses Musicales of Uruguay Piano Competition 1984. *Address:* Brito del Pino 1423, Montevideo 11600, Uruguay.

**MANZONE, Jacques (Francis);** Violinist and Professor of Music; b. 4 June 1944, Cannes, France. *Education:* Studied at Nice Conservatoire with Henri Mazioux; Paris Conservatoire with Roland Charmy and Jacques Fevrier; Further study with Eugène Bigot and Henryk Szeryng. *Career:* Soloist with the French Radio Orchestra and Société des Concerts du Conservatoire; Cofounded Ensemble Instrumental de France, Paris, 1966; Soloist with Orchestra of Paris, founded by Charles Munch, 1967; Professor, Nice Conservatoire, 1977; Soloist, Nice Philharmonic Orchestra; Professor of Chamber Music, Nice International Summer Academy; Musical Director, Chamber Orchestra of Nice, 1984; Plays a Maggini violin; Musical Director, Chamber Opera of France. *Recordings:* About 30 records as soloist or conductor. *Address:* 7 Avenue des Fleurs, 06000 Nice, France.

**MANZONI, Giacomo,** MusM; Italian composer; b. 26 Sept. 1932, Milan; m. Eugenia Tretti 1960; one s. *Education:* Bocconi Univ., Milan, Univ. of Tübingen and Conservatorio Verdi, Milan. *Career:* Ed. Il Diapason (music review) 1956; music critic, l'Unità 1958–66; music ed. Prisma 1968; mem. editorial staff, Musica/Realtà 1980–; Prof. Conservatorio Verdi 1962–64, 1974–91, Conservatorio Martini, Bologna 1965–68, 1969–74, Scuola di Musica Fiesole 1988–, Accademia Musicale Pescarese 1993–96; mem. Accad. Nazionale di Santa Cecilia, Rome 1994–; has given master courses in composition in Buenos Aires, Granada, Tokyo, Santiago, Beijing, etc. *Compositions include:* La Sentenza 1960, Atomtod 1965, 'Insiemi' 1967, Ombre (alla memoria di Che Guevara) for chorus and orchestra 1968, Per M. Robespierre 1975, Parole da Beckett 1971, Masse: omaggio a E. Varèse 1977, Ode 1982, Scene Sinfoniche per il Dr. Faustus 1984, Dedica (su testi di Maderna) 1985, Dr. Faustus: Scene dal romanzo di T. Mann 1989, 10 versi di E. Dickinson 1989, Malinamusik 1991, Finale e aria (I. Bachmann) 1991, Il deserto cresce (F. Nietzsche) 1992, Moi, Antonin A. (Artaud) 1997, Trame d'Ombre (da Zeami) 1998, O Europa! (A. József) 1999; Sul passaggio del tempo (R. Sanesi) 2001, Sembianti 2003; Musica notturna 1966, Oltre la soglia, for voice and string quartet 2000; Pensiero XX di G. Leopardi for narrator and string quartet 2001 and other chamber music; Una voce chiama, for voice, viola and live electronics (F. Fortini) 1994, Quanto oscura selva trovai (Dante), for trombone, chorus and live electronics 1995; film and incidental music. *Publications:* A. Schoenberg 1975, Scritti 1991, Tradizione e Utopia 1994; translations of Adorno and Schönberg. *Honours:* Dr hc (Udine); Premio Abbiati 1989. *Address:* Viale Papiniano 31, 20123 Milan, Italy. *Telephone:* (02) 4817955. *E-mail:* gmanz-@libero.it (home).

**MARAN, George;** Singer (Tenor); b. 25 July 1926, Massachusetts, USA. *Education:* Studied at Harvard University and New York. *Career:* Sang in sacred music at the Salzburg Festival, 1951–66; European tour 1956 with the Salzburg Festival Company in Mozart's La Finta Semplice, directed by Bernhard Paumgartner; Sang at the Darmstadt Opera 1956–94, notably as Titus by Mozart; Death in Venice by Britten, 1983; Appearances at the Aldeburgh Festival, 1959–60, in The Rape of Lucretia and in the premiere of A Midsummer Night's Dream; Concert and oratorio engagements in Germany,

England and Austria, all European Countries. *Recordings:* La Finta Semplice; Messiah, conducted by Adrian Boult, and Elijah under Josef Krips. *Address:* c/o Staatstheater, Postfach 111432, 64283 Darmstadt, Germany.

**MARANGONI, Bruno;** Singer (Bass); b. 13 April 1935, Rovigo, Italy. *Education:* Studied with Campogalliani and in Venice. *Career:* Debut: Venice 1960, as Anselmo in La Molinarelli by Piccinni; Many apearances at the Teatro Fenice Venice, Teatro San Carlo Naples, Teatro Massimo Palermo and in Turin, Triste and the Caracalla Baths, Rome; Verona Reana, 1973, 1978, 1983–84; Guest engagements at Aix-en-Provence, Lisbon, Barcelona and Chicago; Other roles have included Geronimo in Il Matrimonio Segreto, Mozart's Leporello, Osmin and Sarastro, Marcel in Les Huguenots, Bartolo in Paisiello's Il Barbiere di Siviglia, Uberto in Pergolesi's La Serva Padrona, Alvise in La Gioconda and Wagner's Daland, Pogner and Hunding; Television appearances in La Pietra del Paragone, as Asdrubal, L'Elisir d'amore, Don Carlos, Il Trovatore, Guillaume Tell and Aida. *Address:* c/o Arena di Verona, Piazza Bra 28, 37121 Verona, Italy.

**MARATKA, Kryštof;** Czech composer; b. 1972, Prague; m. *Education:* Acad. of Performing Arts Řehoř, Eben, IRCAM. *Career:* based in Paris from 1994; has received commissions from festivals including Festival Présences, Dresdener Musiktage, Korsholm Music Festival, Caramoor Int. Music Festival; commissioned to write an opera and a symphonic piece for Prague Nat. Opera, the latter was performed at a ceremony to mark Czech entry to EC; works have been performed by musicians including Patrick Gallois, Michel Lethiec, Franz Helmersohn, Gustavo Romero, Raphaël Oleg, Vladimir Mendelssohn, by ensembles including Talich Quartet, Quatuor Ysaye, Quatuor Kandinsky, Mozart Piano Quartet, Ensemble Fa, Grieg Trio, and by orchestras including Orchestre de Radio France, St Petersburg Camerata, Brno State Philharmonic, FOK Prague Symphony Orchestra; composer-in-residence Festival Pablo Casals 2002, Czech Centre, Paris 1993, Caramoor Int. Music Festival 1994; world premieres of his work at Festival Int. de Sully-sur-Loire, Wigmore Hall, Konzerthaus Berlin, Louvre Museum, Prague Spring Festival, Novossibirsk; Czech premiere of his viola concerto performed by the Berg Chamber Orchestra, Dvorák Concert Hall, Prague 2004; world premiere of orchestral work Otisk, Caramoor Int. Music Festival 1994. *Compositions include:* Astrophonia for viola and orchestra, Luminarium for clarinet and orchestra, Exaltum for piano quartet, Otisk for symphony orchestra. *Current Management:* Editions Jobert, 76 rue Quincampoix, Paris 75003, France. *Telephone:* (826) 80-88-80 (office). *Fax:* (1) 42-72-27-67 (office). *E-mail:* info@jobert.fr (office). *Website:* www.jobert.fr (office).

**MARC, Alessandra;** American singer (soprano); b. 29 July 1957, Berlin, Germany. *Education:* studied in the USA. *Career:* Debut: Waterloo Festival 1983, as Mariana in Wagner's Das Liebesverbot; Sang Gluck's Iphigénie (en Aulide) 1984, Tosca at the Connecticut Opera 1987; Wexford Festival 1987, as Lisabetta in La cena delle beffe; Santa Fe 1988, as Maria in Strauss's Friedenstag, followed by Adriadne 1990; Chicago and San Francisco as Aida, which she also sang on her Metropolitan Opera debut; Other roles include the Empress in Die Frau ohne Schatten (Holland Festival, 1990), Sieglinde, and Silvana in La Fiamma by Respighi; Turandot at Philadelphia and Covent Garden (1994); Sang Turandot at the 1996 Macerata Festival and at Turin, 1998 and La Scala, 2001; Sang Königin der Erdgeister in Hans Heiling by Marschner at the Deutsche Oper, 2001; Concert repertoire includes the Verdi Requiem and Beethoven's Ninth; Also a noted recitalist (Wigmore Hall, London, 1990). *Recordings include:* Two versions of Elektra, as Chrysothemis under Barenboim, 1996, and the title role under Sinopoli, 1997. *Current Management:* IMG Artists, 616 Chiswick High Road, London W4 5RX, England.

**MARCELLINO, Raffaele;** Composer; b. 1964, Sydney, New South Wales, Australia. *Education:* BMus, New South Wales Conservatory, 1985; Dip Ed, Sydney College of Advanced Education, 1987. *Career:* Faculty Member, St Vincent's College, Potts Point, 1990–94; University of Tasmania, 1995; Resident Composer, Sydney Youth Orchestra, 1992; Director, Tasmanian Conservatorium, 1996–98; mem, Australian Music Centre (full representation). *Compositions:* Woodwind Quintet, 1983; Cathedrale for 7 brass instruments, 1984; Five Bells for string quartet and percussion, 1984; Five Bells for string quartet and percussion, 1984; Incunabula, for orchestra, 1985; Responsorio for chorus, 1987; Antipodes, for orchestra, 1987; Suite Etuis for orchestra, 1988; Whispers of Fauvel, for clarinet and percussion, 1988; The Remedy, 1 act opera, 1989; Nona for violin, 1991; Prester John, for ensemble, 1991; Don Juan, dance theatre, 1992; Corbaccio, for trombone and orchestra, 1993; Leviathan, for trombone, 1994; Fish Tale, song cycle, 1995; The Lottery in Babylon, chamber work, 1995; On the Passing of Time, triple concerto, 1996; Art of Resonance, tuba concerto, 1998; Maze, ensemble, 1998; Terror Australis, ensemble, 1998. *Recordings:* Don Juan, 1992; Whispers of Fauvel, 1999. *Publications:* Tubaphonics; Tall Poppies; The Crotchet Factory. *Honours:* Australian Composers National Opera Award, 1988; Paul Lowin Prize, Highly Commended, 1997. *Address:* 43 Carawa Street, Mornington, Tasmania, Australia.

**MARCHADIER, Ludmila;** Singer (Soprano); b. 1970, Paris. *Education:* Geneva Conservatoire and Royal Academy, London. *Career:* Appearances in Rigoletto at the Grand Théâtre, Geneva, and King Arthur at the Teatro Arriaga, Bilbao; Despina in Così fan tutte with Garden Opera and Adele in Die Fledermaus for European Chamber Opera; Sang in Purcell's Fairy Queen and the Lully/Molière Bourgeois Gentilhomme for the English Bach Festival at the

Linbury Theatre, Covent Garden, 2001; Other roles include Niece in Peter Grimes; Member of chorus at Glyndebourne Festival Opera. *Address:* c/o English Bach Festival, 15 South Eaton Place, London, SW1W 9ER, England.

**MARCHAND, Jacques;** Composer; b. 1 Dec. 1948, Quebec, Canada. *Education:* BAC in Composition, McGill University, Montreal; BAC in Piano, Vincent D'Indy Music School, Montreal. *Career:* Nearer the Stars, Ballet for Violin Solo (Colorado Ballet Company), 1981; Founder, Orchestre Symphonique Regional d'Abitibi-Temiscamingue, 1986; mem, SOCAN; SODRAC; AOC. *Compositions:* Nearer the Stars, 1981; Suite Pour Orchestre, 1987; Fantaisie Pour Orchestre, 1989; Impromptu Pour Piano et Orchestre, 1993; Un Dimanche A Poznan (Poème Symphonique), 1993. *Recordings include:* Jacques Marchand Compositeur, 1988. *Honours:* Citoyen d'Honneur de la Societe Nationale des Quebecois, 1992; Hommage de la Chambre de Commerce de Rouyn-Noranda, 1993. *Address:* 22, 8 Rue Rouyn-Noranda, Quebec J9X 2A4, Canada.

**MARCHI, Claudia;** Singer (Mezzo-soprano); b. 1967, Bologna, Italy. *Education:* Studied with Elvina Ramella. *Career:* Appearances at Savona from 1992 as Isabella (L'Italiana in Algeri), Verdi's Maddalena and as Sigismonda in the opera by Rossini, under Richard Bonynge, 1992; Australian tour, with Luciano Pavarotti in Verdi's Requiem, 1994; Season 1995 as Fenena in Nabucco and Azucena in Trovatore, at Marseilles; Season 1996–97 as Isabella in Genoa and Isaura in Rossini's Tancredi at the Zürich Opera; Further engagements as Rosina and in works by Jommelli, Bach, Mozart and Pergolesi. *Honours:* Prizewinner at the Verdi Competition in Parma and the Luciano Pavarotti International Voice Competition. *Address:* c/o Opernhaus Zürich, Falkenstrsse 1, 8008 Zürich, Switzerland.

**MARCINGER, Ludovit;** Pianist and Pedagogue; b. 21 Dec. 1932, Malacky, Czechoslovakia; m. Maria Marcingerova, 7 May 1977, 2 d. *Education:* State Conservatoire, Bratislava; Academy of Music and Drama, Bratislava; Ferencz Liszt Academy of Music, Budapest. *Career:* Debut: Recital, Dresden, 1958; Recitals: Prague, 1965; Havana, 1980; With Orchestra, Prague, 1964; J Cikker, Concertino for Piano and Orchestra; Carlsbad, 1966; Grieg, Concerto in A Minor, Bratislava, 1967; A Rubinstein, Concerto No. 5 in D Minor; Piano Accompaniment of the Vocalists: Peter Dvorsky, Tenor, Song Recitals, Oper der Stadt, Bonn, 1983; Grosser Musikvereinssaal, Vienna, Teatro alla Scala, Milano, Brucknerhaus Linz, Slovak National Theatre Bratislava, 1984; Deutsche Oper Berlin, Théâtre de L'Athénée Paris, 1986; Suntory Hall Tokyo, 1989; Peter Mikulas-Bass, Songs Recitals, Mexico City, Caracas, Managua, San Jose, 1992; Bratislava Music Festival, 1994; Prague, 1996; With Other Vocalists, Peking, 1987, Buenos Aires, 1996; mem, Slovak Music Union; Association of Concert Artists of Bratislava. *Recordings include:* A Dvořák, Biblical Songs, Op 99, Tchaikovsky, Songs-Peter Mikulas, Bass, 1990; R Schumann, Frauenliebe und Leben, A Dvořák, 4 Songs, Op 2 V narodnim tonu; F Schubert, Lieder, Peter Mikulas, Bass, 1997. *Honours:* Several Prizes in Music Competitions. *Address:* Vysoka skola muzickych umeni, Zochova 1, 81103 Bratislava, Slovakia.

**MARCO-BUHRMESTER, Alexander;** Singer (Baritone); b. 1963, Basle, Switzerland. *Education:* Studied in Basle and Berne. *Career:* Debut: Berne 1985, as Weber's Abu Hassan; Toured Switzerland as Dandini in La Cenerentola and sang at the Biel Opera 1986 as Marcello in La Bohème; Essen Opera 1989–92, Dortmund from 1992, notably in the premiere of Caspar Hauser by Reinhard Febel; Season 2000–01 in Moses und Aron at the Deutsche Oper Berlin and as Count Luna in Bielefeld. *Address:* c/o St ädtische Buhnen, Kuhstrasse 12, 4600 Dortmund, Germany.

**MARCUSSEN, Kjell;** Composer; b. 19 May 1952, Arendal, Norway. *Education:* Studied at the Agder Music Conservatorium; Diploma in Guitar and Composition, Guildhall School of Music, London with Robert Saxton. *Career:* Debut: Cardiff Festival of Music, 1982; mem, Norwegian Composers' Society. *Compositions:* Cantatas; Orchestral works; Guitar Concerto; Solo and Chamber works; Festival Overture for Symphonic Band, 1994. *Recordings include:* CD, Woodcut for Violin, Flute and Cello; CD, Festival Overture; CD, Tordenskjold Kantate. *Publications:* Guitar Sonata No. 1, 1988; Woodcut for Violin, Flute and Cello, 1988; Partita Jubilante for Brass, 1993; Early Part of Summer for Flute and Harp; Introduction and Allegro for Guitar Duo. *Honours:* Special Mention at 15th Concorso internazionale di composizione originale per banda Corciano, 1994. *Address:* Skoleveien 6, 1380 Heggedal, Norway.

**MARESTIN, Valerie;** Singer (Mezzo-soprano); b. 1962, Pau, France. *Education:* Studied in Lyon with Eric Tappy and in Paris. *Career:* Debut: Théâtre de Paris 1987, as La Belle Hélène; Guest appearances throughout France, including Carmen at Angers (1988); Sang Debussy's Geneviève at Moscow (1987) and Mistress Quickly at Limoges; Other roles include Maddalena, Rossweise, Marcellina in Figaro, Rossini's Isabella (at Rheims and Tours), Massenet's Dulcinée and Fenena in Nabucco; Bregenz Festival 1991, as Carmen; Frequent concert appearances. *Address:* c/o Bregenz Festival, Postfach 311, 6901 Bregenz, Austria.

**MARGGRAF, Wolfgang;** Musicologist; b. 2 Dec. 1933, Leipzig, Germany; m. Anne-Marie Lorz, 4 Jan 1975, 2 s. *Education:* Studied at Universities of Leipzig and Jena, 1952–57; PhD, Leipzig, 1964. *Career:* Professor, 1987; Rector, Musikhochschule Weimar, 1990–93; mem, The Liszt Society, Weimar, 1984–; Gesellschaft für Musikforschung, 1991–. *Publications:* Franz Schubert, 1967, 2nd edition, 1978; Giacomo Puccini, 1977; Franz Liszt, Schriften

zur Tonkunst, 1980; Giuseppe Verdi, 1982; Franz Liszt in Weimar, 1985; Bach in Leipzig, 1985. *Address:* Barfuáerstrasse 12, Eisenach, Germany.

**MARGIONO, Charlotte;** Singer (Soprano); b. 24 March 1955, Amsterdam, Netherlands. *Education:* Studied at the studio of Netherlands Opera. *Career:* Appearances with Netherlands Opera from 1983, as Kate Pinkerton, Fiordiligi, Pamina, Liu and Amelia Grimaldi; Komische Oper Berlin 1985 as Marenka in The Bartered Bride; Berne and the Aix Festival 1988, as Mozart's Countess and Vitellia; Fiordiligi in Così fan tutte at Amsterdam, 1990; repeated Vitellia at Salzburg 1991 and sang Pamina at Bordeaux, 1992; Strauss's Four Last Songs at the 1995 Prom Concerts, London; Beethoven concert with Roger Norrington at Bremen, 1995 (also televised); Season 1995–96, as Agathe at Florence and Desdemona in Amsterdam; Sang Leonore in Fidelio at Glybdebourne, 2001. *Recordings include:* Die Zauberflöte, as First Lady (Erato); Beethoven's Mass in C and Missa Solemnis (DGG); Ein Deutsches Requiem (Philips); Così fan tutte and La Finta giardiniera (Teldec); Countess in Le nozze di Figaro, conducted by Harnoncourt; Donna Elvira in Don Giovanni, under John Eliot Gardiner. *Address:* c/o De Nederlandse Opera, Waterlooplein 22, 1011 PG Amsterdam, Netherlands.

**MARGISON, Richard Charles;** Canadian singer (tenor); b. 16 July 1953, Victoria, BC; m. Valerie Mary Kuinka 1989. *Education:* Univ. of Victoria, Victoria Conservatory of Music, Banff School of Fine Arts, studied singing with Selena James, Leopold Simoneau, Frances Adaskin. *Career:* debut in The Bartered Bride with the Pacific Opera Co., Victoria, BC; has performed with many orchestras, including Vancouver 1989, Toronto 1989, Montréal 1990, London Philharmonic 1991, Chicago 1991, Victoria 1991; regular appearances with opera cos, including ENO 1989 and 1991 as Verdi's Riccardo and as Vakula in Rimsky's Christmas Eve, Montréal Opera 1991, Canadian Opera Co. 1991, Santiago Opera (Teatro Municipal) 1991, Den Norske Opera (Norway) 1991, Calgary Opera 1991 as Nadir in Les Pêcheurs de Perles; other roles include Mozart's Ferrando (Ottawa) and Tito, Pinkerton (Edmonton), Fenton in Falstaff, Faust (at Houston), Don Carlos (San Francisco 1992), Nemorino, Edgardo, Alfredo, Rodolfo and Lensky; season 1992–93 as Riccardo at Antwerp, Don José at Brussels, Don Carlos at Melbourne and Cavaradossi at Covent Garden; many appearances on radio and TV in opera, oratorio and concert; Cavaradossi in Tosca at the reopening of the San Francisco Opera 1997 and at Amsterdam 1998; Boito's Faust at the New York Met 2000, and Manrico in Il Trovatore 2000. *Recordings:* Beethoven 9th with London Philharmonic Orchestra, Yehudi Menuhin conducting 1991, Les Grand Duos D'Amour from French Operas, Quebec Symphony, Simon Streatfield conducting 1988. *Current Management:* Columbia Artists Management LLC, 165 W 57th Street, New York, NY 10019-2276, USA. *Telephone:* (212) 841-9500. *Fax:* (212) 841-9744. *E-mail:* info@cami.com. *Website:* www.cami.com; www .richardmargison.com.

**MARGITA, Stefan;** Singer (Tenor); b. 3 Aug. 1956, Kosice, Czechoslovakia; Studied in Kosice and was member of the National Theatre Prague 1986–91, notably as Hoffmann; Guest appearances in Moscow, Genoa, Stuttgart, Paris and Budapest; Wexford Festival 1991, as Lucentio in The Taming of the Shrew by Goetz; Season 1991–92 as Don Ottavio at the Savonlinna Festival and Bellini's Tebaldo at Budapest; Sang Lensky at Trieste, 1996; and in Smetana's Libuše at Edinburgh, 1998; Season 2000–01 as Laca in Jenůfa at Glyndebourne, Lensky at Montpellier and Anatol in War and Peace for the Opéra Bastille, Paris. *Recordings include:* Bellerofonte by Myslivecek and Mahler's Das klagende Lied (Supraphon). *Address:* c/o National Theatre, PO Box 865, 11230 Prague 1, Czech Republic.

**MARGOLINA, Yelena;** Concert Pianist; b. 1964, Lviv, Ukraine, Russia. *Education:* Studied in Lvov and at the St Petersburg State Conservatoire. *Career:* Debut: Beethoven's Second Concerto, Lvov, 1974; Notable performances at Moscow, Kiev, Khabarovsk, Lvov and Dnepropetrovsk; Western debut playing Prokofiev's Third Concerto, Berlin Schauspielhaus, 1985; Concerts at the Prokofiev Centenary Festival in Scotland, 1991; Performs in chamber concerts and as solo recitalist in a repertoire including works by Haydn, Mozart, Liszt, Beethoven, Debussy and Shostakovich; Concerto repertoire includes: Beethoven 1–4, Schumann, Chopin, Tchaikovsky, Ravel and Prokofiev. *Honours:* Scottish International Piano Competition Winner, 1990; Casals Monferrato in Italy, 1990. *Address:* c/o Sonata, 11 Northpark Street, Glasgow G20 7AA, Scotland.

**MARIANELLI, Dario;** composer; b. Pisa, Italy. *Education:* studied piano and composition in Florence and Guildhall School of Music and Drama, London, Bretton Univ. Coll., Nat. Film and Television School. *Career:* classical composer and composer of film soundtracks. *Compositions:* Canti di Uqbar 1991, Rondo for piano and orchestra 1991, Quintet for Winds No. 1 1992, Six Variations on a theme by S. Prokofiev for chamber group 1993, One Movement for string quartet 1993, Fantasia for oboe and piano 1993, Four Songs for piano and tenor 1993, I Think I Do Remember Him for cello solo 1994, Pagine Di Sinfonie Perdute 1994, Variations on nought for voice, orchestra and live electronics 1994, 3 Madrigals 1994, Two Digressions for violin and piano 1995, String Quartet No. 1 1995, The Art Of Road Crossing 1996, Seeing Things (for text by Seamus Heaney) 1996, No Hot Ashes for violin solo 1996, Sohini and Mahival (cantata in Urdu, in collaboration with B.Shrivastav) 1997, Quintet for Winds No. 2 1998, Small and Neglectable Discrepancies 1998; for dance: Falling Facades 1994, Lock, Stock and Barrel 1995, Shame 1996, Amongst Shadows 1996, Sketches to Portraits 1996, Seeing Things 1996, Spool of Threads 1997, The Brutality of Fact 1998; for theatre: Molecatcher's Daughter

(Production Village, London) 1992, Romeo and Juliet (Pentameters Theatre, London) 1993, Doña Rosita the Spinster (Pentameters Theatre, London) 1993, Antonio's Revenge (Chelsea Centre Theatre, London) 1994, Dr Faustus (RSC) 1997. *Compositions for films:* Models Required 1994, Ailsa 1994, The Sheep Thief 1997, I Went Down 1997, Preserve (TV) 1999, The Funeral of the Last Gypsy King 1999, Southpaw: The Francis Barrett Story 1999, Being Considered 2000, Pandaemonium 2000, The Warrior 2001, The Visitor 2002, Blood Strangers (TV) 2002, In This World 2002, I Capture the Castle 2003, This Little Life (TV) 2003, September 2003, The Bypass 2003, Cheeky 2003, Passer By (TV) 2004, The Brothers Grimm 2005, Shooting Dogs 2005, Pride & Prejudice 2005, Pobby and Dingan 2005, V for Vendetta 2006; also for numerous film and TV documentaries. *Honours:* Gulbenkian Foundation scholarship; Benjamin Britten Int. Composition Prize 1997. *Current Management:* Air-Edel Associates Ltd, 18 Rodmarton Street, London, W1U 8BJ, England. *Telephone:* (20) 7486-6466. *Fax:* (20) 7224-0344. *E-mail:* air-edel@air-edel.co.uk. *Website:* www.air-edel.co.uk.

**MARIANI, Lorenzo;** stage director; *Artistic Director, Teatro Massimo, Palermo;* b. 1950, New York, USA. *Education:* Harvard Univ., Univ. of Florence, Italy. *Career:* debut, Maggio Musicale Florence 1982, Bluebeard's Castle; directed L'Heure Espagnole at Florence, La Traviata, Luisa Miller and Offenbach's Barbe-Bleue 1994 at Bologna; Montepulciano Festival with the Henze-Paisiello Don Chisciotte, Greek by Mark Anthony Turnage and Puccini's Edgar; other productions include La Forza del Destino at Florence, Massenet's Esclarmonde in Turin, I Quattro Rusteghi in Geneva, La Bohème in Chicago and Don Giovanni in Tel-Aviv; revived Antoine Vitez's production of Pelléas et Mélisande for Covent Garden 1993; Aida at Florence 1996; Artistic Dir, Teatro Massimo, Palermo 2005–. *Address:* Teatro Massimo, Piazza G. Verdi, 90138 Palermo, Italy. *Website:* www.teatromassimo.it.

**MARIATEGUI, Suso;** Singer (tenor); b. 1947, Las Palmas. *Education:* studied in Spain, Austria and Italy. *Career:* sang Tamino at the Salzburg Landestheater 1971; Wexford Festival 1973, in Donizetti's L'ajo nell'imbarazzo; Teatro Liceo, Barcelona 1987, in the local premiere of Mozart's Lucio Silla; guest engagements in Spain, Italy, Vienna and Tehran; Madrid concerts in Bach's St Matthew Passion and Haydn's Creation. *Recordings include:* L'ajo nell'imbarazzo.

**MARIMPIETRI, Lydia;** Singer (Soprano); b. 1932, Italy. *Education:* Studied in Italy. *Career:* Sang at La Scala Milan in 1959, at first as Nella in Gianni Schicchi, and as Micaela; Further appearances in Rome, Venice, Parma (Pamina, 1974) and Covent Garden (Nedda and Nannetta, 1973–75); Glyndebourne Festival 1962–65, as Drusilla in Poppea and Susanna; Other roles have included Mimi (at the Vienna Staatsoper), Marguerite, Manon, Bizet's Leila, Donna Elvira, Butterfly (Dallas, 1966) and Rossini's Elvira; Sang Mimi at Rome, 1976. *Recordings include:* L'Incoronazione di Poppea (EMI). *Address:* c/o Teatro dell'Opera di Roma, Piazza B Gigli 8, 00184 Rome, Italy.

**MARIN, Carlos;** singer (baritone); b. 1965, Germany. *Education:* Madrid Conservatoire, and with Montserrat Caballé and Jaime Aragall. *Career:* Appearances at Teatro de la Zarzuela Madrid, as Rossini's Figaro, Sulpice in La Fille du Régiment and Marcello in La Bohème; Sang Marcello at Bologna, 1999, and Taddeo in L'Italiana in Algeri at Garsington (British debut); Other roles include Donizetti's Belcore and Alfonso, Riccardo in I Puritani, Valentin (Faust), Dandini, Guglielmo, and Ford in Falstaff; Concerts include Halfter's Siete Cantos de Espana and Ostasio in Francesca da Rimini, in Amsterdam; Season 2001–02 as Sharpless at Montpellier, Posa in Don Carlos and Enrico in Lucia di Lammermoor for Minnesota Opera and in Parma, Silvio in Pagliacci at Oviedo; Season 2002–03 as Marcello in La Bohème and Don Giglio in La Capricciosa Coretta with Opéra de Lausanne; as Don Giglio also in Bordeaux, Madrid and Konzerthaus Vienna. *Honours:* winner, Francisco Alonso and Julian Gayarre Competitions.

**MARIN, Ion;** Conductor; b. 8 July 1960, Bucharest, Romania. *Education:* Studied at the George Enescu Music School Bucharest, the Mozarteum Salzburg, Accademia Chigiana in Siena and the International Academy, Nice. *Career:* Music Director, Transylvania Philharmonic, 1981, appearing in Romania, East Germany, Czechoslovakia, Greece, Italy and France; Resident Conductor, Vienna Staatsoper, 1987–91, with repertoire from Mozart to Berg; Season 1991–92, in Japan for concerts with Margaret Price and Ruggiero Raimondi, Gala Concert in Prague and Le nozze di Figaro at the Teatro la Fenice, Venice; London debut with the London Symphony Orchestra, 1991, English Chamber Orchestra with Yo-Yo Ma as soloist, 1992; US debut conducting L'Elisir at Dallas 1991, San Francisco, 1992, with Il Barbiere di Siviglia; Led Roman Polanski's production of Les Contes d'Hoffmann at the Opéra Bastille, Paris, 1992; Metropolitan Opera, 1992–93, Semiramide and Ariadne auf Naxos, Magic Flute; Further engagements in L'Italiana in Algeri at Venice, 1992, and with Houston Grand Opera; Concerts with the City of Birmingham Symphony, Philadelphia Orchestra, Santa Cecilia, Rome, BBC Symphony, Rotterdam Philharmonic, Montreal Symphony, 1993; Season 1997 with Scottish Chamber Orchestra, Orchestre National de France and the Yomiuri Nippon Symphony Orchestra, Japan; Tour of Australia with the ABC; Season 1998–99 with Così fan tutte for Nuovo Piccolo, Teatro di Milano, and concerts with the Leipzig, Gewandhaus Orchestra, Dresden Staatskapelle, Swedish Radio Symphony Orchestra; Season 1999–2000 with Orchestre National d'Ile de France, Orchestre Philharmonique de Monte-Carlo and the BBC Scottish Orchestra; Conducted the BBC Scottish Symphony Orchestra at

the London Proms, 2002. *Recordings:* Lucia di Lammermoor, with Studer and Domingo, series of Rossini one-acters starting with Il Signor Bruschino; Semiramide, and sacred music for DGG; Various for other major labels including Mozart arias with Barbara Hendricks and the ECO, 1997; Rodrigo and Khachaturian flute concertos with the Philharmonia Orchestra and Patrick Gallois; Opera Arias with the London Symphony Orchestra and Cheryl Studer. *Honours:* Awards Deutsche Schallplatten; Critics Award, 1992, 1994; Nominations for Grammy award. *Current Management:* Askonas Holt Ltd, Lonsdale Chambers, 27 Chancery Lane, London, WC2A 1PF, England. *Telephone:* (20) 7400-1700. *Fax:* (20) 7400-1799. *E-mail:* info@askonasholt.co.uk. *Website:* www.askonasholt.co.uk.

**MARINOV, Swetoslav;** violinist; b. 21 Sept. 1945, Lom, Bulgaria; m. Elena Maeva 1967; two s. *Education:* Music School of Sofia, Bulgaria, Bulgarian State Conservatoire, Sofia, studied with Vilmoš Tatrai in Budapest, with Mischa Geler in Moscow Conservatoire, with Yfrah Neaman at the Guildhall School of Music and Drama. *Career:* debut as violinist, Orpheus String Quartet, 1969; Performed with the Tilev String Quartet from 1973, and the Bulgarian RT String Quartet, 1975; Leader of Sofia Soloist Chamber Orchestra, 1981 and Leader of Bremerhaven Opera, Germany, 1988; Other concert activity includes violinist and violist of Bulgarian RT String Quartet and Sofia Chamber Orchestra; Concert tours in Europe, Asia, Australia, South America; In duo violin and piano, concerts with Katia Evrova in France, Cycle of Mozart 16 sonatas, 1990, 1991; Cycle of Beethoven 10 sonatas, 1997; In solo viola concert tour with G Tilev, violin, in Sinfonia Concertante by Mozart with Niederheinischen Sinfoniker, Mönchengladbach. *Recordings:* with Radio Sofia, Warsaw, Moscow and Paris. *Honours:* Prizewinner of competition for string quartets in Colmar, 1978 and Evian, France, 1980. *Address:* Rosenweg 5, 27607 Langen, Germany.

**MARIOTTI, Alfredo;** Singer (Bass-baritone); b. 1936, Udine, Italy. *Career:* Sang in opera throughout Italy, notably at La Scala, Rome, La Fenice, Venice, and Florence; Palermo, 1955, in the premiere of Rota's Il Capello; Treviso, 1984, in Wolf-Ferrari's I Quattro Rusteghi; Las Palmas, 1993, as Donizetti's Dulcamara; Sang the Sacristan in Tosca at Verona, 1998. *Recordings include:* Masetto in Don Giovanni and Don Pasquale; Tosca; Rossini's L'Italiana in Algeri, 1976; La Bohème. *Address:* c/o Arena di Verona, Piazza Bra 28, 37121 Verona, Italy.

**MARK, Peter;** Director and Conductor; b. 31 Oct. 1940, New York City, USA; m. Thea Musgrave, 2 Oct 1971. *Education:* BA, Musicology, Columbia University, 1961; Juilliard School of Music, with Jean Morel, Joseph Fuchs, Walter Trampler, MS, 1963. *Career:* Boy soprano soloist, Children's Chorus, New York City Opera and Metropolitan Opera, 1953–55; Principal freelance and string quartet violist, Juilliard Orchestra, Princeton Symphony, Trenton Symphony, Tiemann String Quartet, Beaux Arts and Los Angeles String Quartet, Santa Barbara Symphony, Lyric Opera Chicago, 1960–68; Assistant principal violist, Los Angeles Philharmonic Orchestra, 1968–69; Solo Violist, Europe, South America and US tours, 1965–77; General Director, Conductor, Virginia Opera Association, 1975–; Conductor, Chamber Players, Santa Barbara Chamber Orchestra, 1976–77; Guest Conductor, Wolf Trap Orchestra, 1979, New York City Opera 1981, Los Angeles Opera Repertory Theater 1981, Royal Opera House, London, 1982, Hong Kong Philharmonic Orchestra 1984; Jerusalem Symphony Orchestra, 1988; Tulsa Opera, 1988; Opera Nacional de Mexico, 1989; Conductor, local premiere of Porgy and Bess, Buenos Aires and São Paulo, 1992; Guest Conductor, Opera Nacional de Mexico, 1989, 1992; New York Pops, Carnegie Hall, 1991; Orlando Opera Company, 1993; Richmond Symphony, 1993; Conducted La Bohème at the 1996 Torre del Lago Festival; mem, Phi Beta Kappa; Musicians Union, New York, London, Los Angeles, Norfolk, Virginia. *Recordings:* As conductor: Mary, Queen of Scots, 1979; A Christmas Carol, 1980; Handel's Julius Caesar, 1997; Also numerous recordings as violist. *Honours:* Recipient Elias Lifchey Viola Award Juilliard School of Music, 1963; Rosa Ponselle Gold Medal, 1997. *Address:* c/o Virginia Opera, PO Box 2580, Norfolk, VA 23501-2580, USA.

**MARKAUSKAS, Arvydas;** Singer (Baritone); b. 25 Sept. 1951, Kaunas, Lithuania. *Education:* Studied at the Vilnius Conservatory. *Career:* Sang at the Vilnius Opera from 1979, making his debut as the Count in Lortzing's Der Wildschütz; Guest appearances throughout Russia and eastern Europe and with the Lithuanian Opera in the USA (notably in Chicago); Other roles include Belcore, Posa, Eugene Onegin, Amonasro, Iago, Nabucco and Marcello; Concert repertoire includes Handel's Samson, the War Requiem, Carmina Burana and Kabalevsky's Requiem. *Address:* c/o Lithuania State Opera, Vienuolio 1, 232600 Vilnius, Lithuania.

**MARKERT, Annette;** Singer (Mezzo-soprano); b. 1957, Kaltensundheim, Germany. *Education:* Studied in Leipzig with Helga Forner and with Hannelore Kuhse and Eleanore Elstermann. *Career:* Debut: British Debut, Dec 1989, in the Alto Rhapsody with the BBC Philharmonic under Kurt Sanderling; Has sung with the Landestheater Halle as Handel's Floridante, Rinaldo and Tamerlano, Gluck's Orpheus and Carmen; Bach oratorios on German radio and oratorio performances and Lieder recitals throughout Germany. *Honours:* Second Prize, Maria Canals Competition, Barcelona, 1985; Handel Prize 1989. *Address:* c/o Landestheater Halle, Universitatsring 24–25, 4020 Halle, Germany.

**MARKHAM, Ralph;** pianist; b. 1949, Canada. *Education:* Royal Toronto Conservatory of Music, Cleveland Institute of Music with Vronsky and Babin. *Career:* formed Piano Duo partnership with Kenneth Broadway and has given many recitals and concerts in North America and Europe; BBC debut recital 1979 and further broadcasts on CBC television, Radio France Musique, the Bavarian Radio Hilversum in Netherlands; Stravinsky's Three Dances from Petrushka at the Théâtre des Champs Elysées, Paris, 1984; Season 1987–88, included 40 North American recitals; Concert with the Vancouver Symphony and New York debut on WQXR Radio; Season 1988–89 included the concertos for Two Pianos by Mozart and Bruch in Canada and a recital tour of England and Germany; Recent performances of the Bartók Sonata for two pianos and percussion, with Evelyn Glennie and a 1990–91 tour of North America, Europe and the Far East; Festival appearances include Newport USA 1988. *Recordings:* Duos by Anton Rubinstein; Vaughan Williams Concerto for Two Pianos; Saint-Saëns Carnival of the Animals. *Honours:* Young Artist of the Year, Musical America Magazine, 1980, with Kenneth Broadway. *Current Management:* Robert Gilder & Co., Enterprise House, 59–65 Upper Ground, London, SE1 9PQ, England. *Telephone:* (20) 7928-9008. *Fax:* (20) 7928-9755. *E-mail:* rgilder@robert-gilder.com.

**MARKHAM, Richard,** ARAM, Dip RAM, LRAM, ARCM; British pianist; b. 23 June 1952, Grimsby, England. *Education:* Wintringham Grammar School, piano privately with Shirley Kemp, at RAM with Max Pirani. *Career:* debut, Queen Elizabeth Hall 1974; recitals and concerto performances throughout the UK and abroad; several London appearances at Royal Festival Hall, Royal Albert Hall, Queen Elizabeth Hall, Wigmore Hall, Barbican Hall and Purcell Room; The Henry Wood Promenade Concerts; appearances at festivals in Aldeburgh, Bath, Berlin, Cheltenham, Harrogate, City of London, Schleswig-Holstein and York; regular broadcasts of recitals and concerts for BBC and numerous television and radio stations abroad; has performed with the Philharmonia Orchestra, London Symphony Orchestra, RPO, London Philharmonic Orchestra, ECO, SNO, London Mozart Players, Bournemouth Sinfonietta, Hallé, Ulster and BBC Philharmonic and Scottish Symphony Orchestras; frequent appearances and tours with piano duo partner, David Nettle, in Europe, North America, Australia, Japan, Far East and Middle East. *Recordings:* Kabalevsky, Stravinsky and Rachmaninov with Raphael Wallfisch (cello); Bernstein (Arr. Nettle and Markham), Bennett and Grainger (two pianos); Holst, The Planets (two pianos) and Stravinsky, Petrushka and Le Sacre du Printemps (piano duet) with David Nettle; Elgar, Holst, Grainger and Rossini with CBSO Chorus; Saint-Saëns Carnival of the Animals with Aquarius; South of the Border, a Latin American Collection with Jill Gomez; Nettle and Markham in England; Nettle and Markham in France; Arnold, Concerto for Two Pianos and Concerto for Piano Duet; Complete Two-Piano Works of Brahms; Piano Trio Serenade with Rebecca Hirsch (violin) and Jonathan Williams (cello). *Honours:* Frederick Shinn Fellowship 1975, Gulbenkian Foundation Music Fellowships 1976–78; silver medal Geneva Int. Piano Competition 1972, RAM Chappell Gold Medal 1973, Countess of Munster Musical Trust Award 1973–74, Music Retailers' Assocn Award for Excellence 1985. *Address:* The Old Power House, Atherton Street, London, SW11 2JE, England. *E-mail:* richardpiano@aol.com. *Website:* www.nettleandmarkham.com.

**MÄRKL, Jun;** Conductor, Opera Director and Musical Director; b. 1959, Munich, Germany. *Education:* Studied piano, violin and conducting, with degrees in violin and conducting, Music Academy, Hannover, 1978; Further studies with Kees Bakels, Sergiu Celibidache and Gustav Meier, University of Michigan at Ann Arbor, USA. *Career:* Member, Junge Deutsche Philharmonie, 1980–84; Season 1991–94, Principal Conductor and Music Director, Saarland State Theatre; Since 1994 Opera and Music Director, National Theater Mannheim; Conducted performances of Tosca, Marriage of Figaro, and Dvořák's Dmitrij; Conducted premiere of Detlev Glanert's Der Spiegel des grossen Kaisers, 1995; Season 1995–96, London debut at Royal Opera House, Covent Garden, with Götterdämmerung; Season 1996–97, with Bavarian State Opera in Munich, included new production of Smetana's Bartered Bride, Aida, Madama Butterfly, La Traviata, Peter Grimes; With Berlin State Opera, productions of Lohengrin, Salome, The Flying Dutchman, 1996–97; Also engagements in the same season with La Clemenza di Tito in Stuttgart and Falstaff in Bern, Madama Butterfly, Manon, Tales of Hoffmann, Tosca, Turandot and Hindemith's Cardillac; Premiere of Babylon by Detlef Heusinger, Schwetzinger Festspiele, 1997; Tours to Japan and Australia in 1998 and debut at the Metropolitan Opera, New York; Led Berg's Lulu at Mannheim, 1998, also concerts with the Orchestre de Paris and the RSO Copenhagen; Season 1999 debut at the Metropolitan Opera, New York and the Dallas Symphony Orchestra. *Honours:* Conducting Competition winner, German Music Council, 1986; Scholarship for study at Tanglewood with Leonard Bernstein and Seiji Ozawa, with the Boston Symphony Orchestra. *Address:* c/o Nationaltheater Mannheim, Goetheplatz, 68161 Mannheim, Germany.

**MARKOV, Albert;** Violinist and Composer; b. 8 May 1933, Kharkov, USSR. *Education:* Kharkov Music School; Moscow Gnessin Conservatory; Graduate Master Diploma, 1957; Doctor, 1960. *Career:* Concert Tours in USSR, Eastern and Western Europe, America, Solo with Leningrad Philharmonic, Moscow Philharmonic, major orchestras in Belgium, America, Netherlands, Sweden, England, Denmark, Portugal, Poland, Germany, Yugoslavia and other countries, 1981–; Emigrated to USA 1975, debut with Houston Symphony Orchestra, 1976; Professor, Manhattan School of Music, USA; Artistic Director: Rondo Bennington Music Festival; Founded Albert Markov Music Festival in Nova Scotia, 1995; Art Director, Rondo Bennington Music Festival, Vermont; mem, Rondo Music Society, President; Music Director, Albert Markov Summer Music Festival, Nova Scotia, Canada; NARAS, USA. *Compositions:* Symphony: Kinnor David; Violin Concerto, 1988; Formosa, suite for violin and orchestra; 3 Violin Rhapsodies; 3 Violin Sonatas; Duosonata for two violins; Popular Pieces for violin; Paganini Ostinato (Variations for solo violin); Cadenzas for violin concertos of Mozart, Viotti, Beethoven, Paganini, Brahms; System of violin playing (method); Little Violinist (method); Vocal cycle on A S Pushkin words. *Recordings:* Paganini Concerto No. 2; Other recordings with orchestras and solo compositions by Bach, Veracini, Schubert, Paganini, Prokofiev, Shostakovich. *Publications:* 3 Violin Rhapsodies; Sonata for solo violin; Duo-sonata for two violins; System of Violin Playing; Violin Technique; Little Violinist (method); Violin Caprices; Cadenzas; Edition of the Tchaikovsky Violin Concerto. *Contributions:* Sovetskaya Musica, USSR; Novoye Russkoe Slovo, Russian Daily, USA. *Honours:* Gold Medal, Violin National Competition, Moscow, 1957; Gold Medal, The Queen Elizabeth Violin Competition, 1959; Ysaye Medal, Belgium. *Address:* 3 Farm Creek Road, Rowayton, CT 06853, USA.

**MARKOV, Alexander;** Russian violinist; b. 24 Jan. 1963, Moscow. *Education:* Central Music School, Moscow; Gnessin Music School; Manhattan School of Music. *Career:* Debut: Carnegie Hall, New York, 1979 (recital debut 1983); Many tours in USA and Europe in virtuoso repertoire, notably concertos and Caprices by Paganini; British debut with BBC Philharmonic, 1993; Wigmore Hall, London, 1997, with Paganini's 24 Caprices. *Recordings include:* Paganini's Concertos Nos 1 and 2, 24 Caprices. *Honours:* Gold Medal Paganini Int. Competition 1982, First Prize (jtly) Elena Obraztsova Competition, St Petersburg 2005. *Address:* c/o Albert Markov, 3 Farm Creek Road, Rowayton, CT 06853, USA.

**MARKOVA, Jirina;** Singer (Soprano); b. 9 Sept. 1957, Prague, Czechoslovakia. *Education:* Studied at the Prague Conservatory. *Career:* Prague National Theatre from 1979, notably in operas by Mozart, Donizetti, Smetana, Weber and Janáček; Guest appearances in Germany, Austria, New York and Philadelphia; Sang Zerlina in the bicentenary performance of Don Giovanni, Prague, 1987; National Theatre, 1991, as Rusalka in Dvořák's opera, 1991 and in Puccini's Tabarro; Abigail in Nabucco, 2001 (also at Castle Loket festival, 2002–03); Amneris in Aida, at State Opera Prague, 2003; Dir, Childern oper Prag, 1999–. *Recordings include:* Jitka in Smetana's Dalibor, Rusalka, Janáček's Excursions of Mr Brouček. *Address:* National Theatre Prague, PO Box 865, 11230 Prague 1, Czech Republic.

**MARKOVA, Juliana;** Pianist; b. 8 July 1945, Sofia, Bulgaria; m. Michael Roll, 1 s. *Education:* Sofia Conservatory; Verdi Conservatory Milan with Ilonka Deckers. *Career:* After success in Enescu and Marguérite Long Competitions she performed on both sides of the Atlantic; Berlin Festival, Boston Symphony Orchestra and Andrew Davis and the Los Angeles Philharmonic under Zubin Mehta; Concerto engagements with all major orchestras in the USA and recitals at Lincoln Center NY and in Los Angeles; Recent performances in Atlanta, Cleveland, Chicago, Philadelphia, Detroit, Dallas, Montreal, Toronto and Milwaukee; European tours have included Berlin, Florence and Milan; London concerts with the London Symphony Orchestra, Royal Philharmonic and the Philharmonia, with Claudio Abbado and Simon Rattle; Regional engagements with the City of Birmingham Symphony and Royal Scottish Orchestra; British tour with the Sofia Philharmonic; Season 1991–92 with tour of Japan and debut with the San Francisco Symphony; Repertoire includes concertos by Beethoven, Haydn, Mozart, Prokofiev and Saint-Saëns. *Address:* c/o Lodding, Svensk Konsertdirektia AB, Karfeldsgatan 20, PO Box 5076, S–40222 Göteborg, Sweden.

**MARKOVA-MIKHAILENKO, Olga;** Singer (Mezzo-Soprano); b. 1950, Russia. *Career:* Many appearances throughout Russia in concert and opera; Kirov Opera, St Petersburg, from 1990 as the Mother Superior in The Fiery Angel, Death in Stravinsky's Nightingale, Valsyevna in the Maid of Pskov by Rimsky-Korsakov and Alkonost in Rimsky's Invisible City of Kitezh; Appearances at San Francisco Opera in Boris Godunov and War and Peace; Sang Khivrya in the British premiere of Prokofiev's Semyon Kotko, with the Kirov at Covent Garden, 2000; Other roles include Fillipyevna in Eugene Onegin, Nezhata in Rimsky's Sadko, Vanya in Ivan Susanin, the Duenna in Prokofiev's Betrothal in a Monastery and Naina in Ruslan and Lyudmila. *Address:* c/o Kirov Opera Mariinsky Theatre, Theatre Square, St Petersburg, Russia.

**MARKS, Alan;** Concert Pianist; b. 14 May 1949, Chicago, Illinois, USA. *Education:* Studied Piano with Shirley Parnas Adamas, Juilliard School of Music with Irwin Freundlich; BMus, 1971; Studied at Peabody Conservatory Baltimore with Leon Fleischer, 1971–72. *Career:* New York debut in 1971 followed by tour of US schools, prisons and hospitals with violinist Daniel Heifetz; Tours as soloist throughout USA and in Europe and Japan; British debut in 1979; Chamber music performances at the Marlboro and Santa Fe Festivals; Premiered Seven Pieces and Caprichos by Carlos Chavez, 1975, 1976; Teacher at the 92nd Street 'Y' in New York, 1972–80 and Lincoln Center Institute, 1979–81. *Honours:* Winner of Concert Artists Guild Piano Competition, 1970.

**MARKSON, Gerhard;** German conductor; *Principal Conductor, Radio Telefís Eireann National Symphony Orchestra;* b. Bensheim an der Bergstrasse. *Education:* Frankfurt Acad. of Music, conducting with Igor Markevitch in Monte Carlo, Franco Ferrara in Rome. *Career:* worked as opera and symphony conductor at opera houses in Augsburg, Oldenburg and Freiburg; Music Dir, Hagen Theatre 1991–98; Principal Conductor, Radio Telefís

Éireann (RTÉ) Nat. Symphony Orchestra 2001–; has conducted world-wide, including Bavarian State Opera (Munich), Hamburg State Opera, Norwegian State Opera (Oslo), St Cecilia Orchestra (Rome), RAI (Turin), Monte Carlo Philharmonic, Bournemouth Symphony Orchestra, Norwegian Radio Symphony Orchestra, Swiss Radio Symphony Orchestra (Basle), Polish Radio Symphony Orchestra (Katowice). *Address:* c/o RTÉ National Symphony Orchestra, Radio Telefís Éireann, Donnybrook, Dublin 4, Ireland. *Website:* www.rte.ie/music/nso/index.html.

**MARKUS, Urs;** Singer (Baritone); b. 29 Sept. 1941, Villmergen, Aargau, Switzerland. *Education:* Studied in Zürich, Milan and Fribourg. *Career:* Sang as a bass at the Biel-Solothurn Opera, 1979–81, baritone roles at Trier, 1983–86; Engaged at Brunswick 1986–88, Nationaltheater Mannheim from 1988; Guest engagements at Geneva, Nancy and Metz; Roles have included Pizarro and Gluck's Agamemnon, Mozart's Count and Alfonso, Verdi's Amonasro and Iago, Telramund, the Dutchman and Hans Sachs, Escamillo and Gerster's Enoch Arden; Concert appearances throughout Switzerland in Berlin, Venice and Copenhagen.

**MARKVART, Jan;** Singer (Tenor); b. 30 Aug. 1948, Brno, Czechoslovakia. *Career:* Sang at the Janáček Theatre, Brno, as the Prince in Rusalka, Ismael in Nabucco and Fernando in La Favorita; Turin, 1985, in The Bartered Bride; Buenos Aires, 1986, as Gregor in The Makropulos Case; Prague National Theatre from 1986, notably as Florestan, 1989; Amsterdam, 1988–90, in operas by Janáček; Don José at Bratislava; Theater Luxemburg, 1986–95, as Smetana's Dalibor, Ladislav in The Two Widows and the Prince in Rusalka; Nerone (Nerone, A Boito), State Opera, Prague, 1998; Pinkerton in Madama Butterfly at Tchai-Pei, Taiwan, 1999. *Recordings include:* Stahlav in Smetana's Libuše. *Address:* c/o National Theatre Prague, PO Box 865, 11230 Prague 1, Czech Republic.

**MARLEYN, Paul;** Concert Cellist; b. 1965, England. *Education:* Studied with David Strange at the Royal Academy of Music, from 1981, with Lawrence Lesser in Boston and Aldo Parisot at Yale University. *Career:* Recital and solo appearances from 1988 throughout Europe, Canada and the USA, Jordan Hall Boston, Merkin Hall NY, Chamber Music East and Cape and Island's Music Festivals; Wigmore Hall, London; Tour of Europe 1985 as solo-cellist with the European Community Youth Orchestra under Claudio Abbado; Radio and television engagements in the United Kingdom, the USA and Switzerland; Tours of Japan, South Korea and Switzerland, 1991. *Honours:* Suggia Scholarship, Dove Prize and Thomas Igloi Trust Prize at the RAM; First Prize, Hudson Valley National String Competition, NY, 1988.

**MARLTON, Hilton;** singer (tenor); b. 1970, South Africa. *Education:* Guildhall School, London. *Career:* appearances as Mozart's Tamino and Ottavio, the Mad Woman in Curlew River; Bardolph in Falstaff and Triquet in Eugene Onegin; Alfredo at the Covent Garden Festival, the Serenade to Music at the Festival Hall and The Seven Deadly Sins for the BBC; Further roles include Mozart's Basilio; Rossini's Ramiro, Tonio in La Fille du Régiment and parts in Monteverdi's Ulisse; Ferrando and Don Ottavio for the State Theatre, Pretoria; Recitals at St George's, Bristol (songs by Mendelssohn) and elsewhere; Lechmere in Owen Wingrave for Channel 4 TV; Simon the Canaan in Birtwistle's The Last Supper at Glyndebourne, 2001. *Current Management:* Owen White Management, Top Floor, 59 Lansdowne Place, Hove, East Sussex BN3 1FL, England. *Telephone:* (1273) 727127. *Fax:* (1273) 328128. *E-mail:* info@owenwhitemanagement.com.

**MAROS, Miklós;** composer, teacher and chamber orchestra leader; b. 14 Nov. 1943, Pecs, Hungary; m. Ilona Maros. *Education:* Acad. of Music, Budapest, State Coll. of Music, Stockholm. *Career:* leader, Maros Ensemble; compositions frequently performed in Europe and USA; Composer-in-Residence, West Berlin (DAAD/Berliner Künstler programme); mem. Soc. of Swedish Composers, Int. Soc. for Contemporary Music (Swedish Section), Soc. for Experimental Music and Arts, Royal Swedish Acad. of Music. *Compositions include:* Castratos, opera; Symphonies Nos 1–4; Oolit, chamber orchestra; Divertimento, chamber orchestra; Concerto for Harpsichord and Chamber Orchestra; Concerto for Trombone and Orchestra; Sinfonietta; Concerto for Alto Saxophone and Orchestra; Concerto for Clarinet and Orchestra; Chamber music; Electronic music. *Recordings:* Descort, soprano flute and double bass; Manipulation No. 1, bassoon and live electronics; Divertimento, chamber orchestra; Oolit; Circulation, strings; Dimensions, percussion; Quartet for Saxophones; Symphony No. 1; Stora grusharpan, radio opera; 4 songs from Gitanjali, soprano and chamber ensemble; Concerto for Trombone and Orchestra; Capriccio, guitar; Undulations, alto saxophone and piano; Passacaglia, soprano and organ; Turba, choir; Schattierungen, cello; Praefatio, organ; Concerto for Alto Saxophone and Orchestra; Sinfonia concertante (Symphony No. 3); Trifoglio, harp; Aurora for double wind quintet and windband, 1995; Concerto Grosso for Saxophone Quartet and Orchestra. *Honours:* Lifetime Artists' Award, Swedish Government 1990. *Address:* Krukmakargatan 18, 11851 Stockholm, Sweden.

**MARQUEZ, Marta;** Singer (mezzo-soprano); b. 1955, San Juan, Puerto Rico. *Education:* Juilliard, New York, and with Tito Gobbi in Florence. *Career:* debut, New York City Opera, as Oscar in Un Ballo in Maschera; sang at Saarbrucken from 1979, notably as Constanze, Frau Fluth, Mimi, Violetta, Susanna and Zdenka in Arabella; Spoleto Festival, 1982, as Sylvie in Gounod's La Colombe; Deutsche Oper am Rhein, Düsseldorf, from 1984, with notable roles including Poppea, Hänsel, Cherubino, Idamantes, Cenerentola and Rosina (Barbiere), and further engagements throughout Germany; Puerto

Rico at the Pablo Casals Festival and appearances in Moscow with the Düsseldorf company; other roles include Nedda and Musetta; frequent concert appearances; guest appearances at Royal Opera House, Covent Garden (Zerlina, Musetta), and Bavarian State Opera, Munich (Susanna, Aennchen); sang the title role in the premiere of Klebe's Gervaise Macquart, Düsseldorf, 1996; sang Mascha in Three Sisters by Eötvös at Düsseldorf 1999; Rossini's Isabella 2001. *Address:* Neusserweg 72, 40474 Düsseldorf, Germany.

**MARRINER, Andrew Stephen;** British clarinettist; b. 25 Feb. 1954, London, England; s. of Sir Neville Marriner and Lady Elizabeth Marriner; m. Elizabeth Ann Sparke 1988; one s. *Education:* King's Coll. Choir School, Cambridge, King's School, Canterbury, Univ. of Oxford, Musichochschule, Hannover, Germany. *Career:* debut, solo chamber and orchestral work 1977–; principal clarinet, London Symphony Orchestra 1986–, Acad. of St Martins 1987–; first performances of pieces written for him by John Tavener 1997, Robin Holloway 1997, Dominic Muldowney 1997; mem. Lords Taverner. *Recordings:* Mozart Quintet and Concerto, London Proms 1997, Weber Concerto, Finzi Concerto, Tavener. *Honours:* Hon. RAM 1995. *Current Management:* Ingpen & Williams Ltd, 7 St George's Court, 131 Putney Bridge Road, London, SW15 2PA, England.

**MARRINER, Sir Neville,** Kt, CBE, FRCM, FRAM; British music director and conductor; b. 15 April 1924, Lincoln, England; s. of Herbert H. Marriner and Ethel M. Marriner; m. Elizabeth M. Sims 1955; one s. (Andrew Stephen Marriner) one d. *Education:* Lincoln School, Royal Coll. of Music. *Career:* founder and Dir Acad. of St Martin in the Fields 1956–; Musical Dir LA Chamber Orchestra 1969–78; Dir South Bank Festival of Music 1975–78, Dir Meadowbrook Festival, Detroit 1979–84; Music Dir Minn. Orchestra 1979–86, Stuttgart Radio Symphony Orchestra 1984–89, Barbican Summer Festival 1985–87; Fellow, Trinity Coll. of Music, Hong Kong Acad. for Performing Arts. *Recordings include:* Dvořák Serenades, Haydn Violin Concerto in C, Mozart Serenade K361, Il Barbiere di Siviglia, all Schubert's Symphonies, The English Connection (Vaughan Williams' The Lark Ascending, Elgar Serenade and Tippett Corelli Fantasia), Trumpet Concertos (with Hakan Hardenberger), Mendelssohn Piano Works (with Murray Perahia), Mozart Haffner Serenade, Bach Concertos, Suites and Die Kunst der Fuge, Vivaldi's The Four Seasons, Concerti Grossi by Corelli, Geminiani, Torelli, Locatelli and Manfredini, Mozart Symphonies, Concertos, Serenades and Divertimenti, Handel Messiah, Opera overtures and Water and Fireworks music, Die Zauberflöte 1980, Handel Arias (with Kathleen Battle), Il Turco in Italia and Don Giovanni, Verdi's Oberto 1997, Sylvia McNair: Love's Sweet Surrender 1998, Brahms Symphonies 1–4 1998, Schumann Symphonies 1–4 1998, complete Symphonies of Beethoven, Tchaikovsky, Weber, Gounod, Cantatas of Bach (with Fischer-Dieskau, Janet Baker), Haydn Symphonies. *Honours:* Hon. DMus (Hull) 1998, (Royal Scottish Acad.) 1999; Tagore Gold Medal, an Edison Awards (Netherlands), two Mozart Gemeinde Awards (Austria), three Grand Prix du Disque (France), two Grammy Awards (USA), Shakespeare Prize; Kt of the Polar Star 1984, Officier, Ordre des Arts et Lettres 1995. *Address:* c/o Academy of St Martin-in-the-Fields, Raine House, Raine Street, London, E1 9RG, England.

**MARSALIS, Wynton;** American trumpeter, music administrator and composer; b. 18 Oct. 1961, New Orleans, LA; s. of Ellis Marsalis and Dolores Marsalis; three c. *Education:* Berks. Music Center, Tanglewood, Juilliard School, New York. *Career:* played with New Orleans Philharmonic age 14; joined Art Blakey and the Jazz Messengers 1981; toured with Herbie Hancock 1981; formed own group with brother Branford Marsalis 1982; leader Wynton Marsalis Septet; in addition to regular appearances in many countries with his own jazz quintet, he follows a classical career and has performed with the world's top orchestras; regularly conducts masterclasses in schools and holds private tuition; Artistic Dir Lincoln Center Jazz Dept, New York 1990–. *Compositions:* Soul Gestures in Southern Blues 1988, Blood on the Fields (oratorio) 1994, Jazz/Syncopated Movements 1997. *Recordings include:* All American Hero 1980, Wynton 1980, Wynton Marsalis 1981, Think of One 1983, English Chamber Orchestra 1984, Hot House Flowers 1984, Baroque Music: Wynton Marsalis, Edita Gruberova, Raymond Leppard and the English Chamber 1985, Black Codes (From the Underground) 1985, J Mood 1985, Live at Blues Alley 1986, Tomasi/Jolivet: Trumpet Concertos 1986, Carnaval 1987, Baroque Music for Trumpets 1988, The Majesty of the Blues 1989, Crescent City Christmas Card 1989, Tune in Tomorrow (soundtrack) 1991, Quiet City 1989, 24 1990, Trumpet Concertos 1990, Blue Interlude 1992, Citi Movement 1992, In This House, On This Morning 1992, Hot Licks: Gypsy 1993, On the Twentieth Century 1993, Joe Cool's Blues 1994, Live in Swing Town 1994, In Gabriel's Garden 1996, Jump Start and Jazz 1996, Live at Bubba's 1996, One By One 1998, The Marcial Suite 1998, At the Octoroon Ball: String Quartet No. 1 1999, Big Train 1999, Fiddler's Tale 1999, Reeltime 1999, Sweet Release and Ghost Story 1999, Goin' Down Home 2000, Immortal Concerts: Jody 2000, The London Concert 2000, All Rise 2002, Angel Eyes 2002, The Magic Hour 2004. *Publications:* Sweet Swing Blues on the Road 1994, Marsalis on Music 1995, Requiem 1999. *Honours:* numerous hon. doctorates; Edison Award, Netherlands, Grand Prix du Disque, eight Grammy Awards in both jazz and classical categories, Pulitzer Prize for Music 1997, Algur H. Meadows Award, Southern Methodist Univ. 1997. *Current Management:* Ted Kurland Associates, 173 Brighton Avenue, Boston, MA 02134, USA. *Telephone:* (617) 254-0007. *Fax:* (617) 782-3577. *E-mail:* agents@tedkurland.com.

**MARSCHNER, Wolfgang;** Violinist; b. 23 May 1926, Dresden, Germany. *Education:* Studied violin, piano, composition and conducting, Conservatory Dresden and Mozarteum Salzburg. *Career:* Debut: At age 9 with Tartini's Devil's Trill sonata; Professor, Folkwang-School, Essexn, 1956; Professor, Music Conservatory, Cologne, 1958; Professor, Music Conservatory, Freiburg, 1963–; Regular Mastercourses in Warsaw and Weimar; Director of Pfluger-Foundation for young violinists, freiburg; International soloist career, concerts in Edinburgh Festival and with Berlin Philharmonic and Royal Philharmonic, London; Premiere, Schoenberg's Violin Concerto in many cities including London, Vienna and Zürich; Founder of: International Ludwig Spohr Violin Competition; Jacobus Stainer Violin Maker's Competition; International Youth Violin Competition; German Spohr Academy; Festival Wolfgang Marschner, Hinterzarten. *Compositions:* Various works for orchestra; 2 concerti for violin and orchestra; Sonata for solo violin; Canto notturno for violin and organ; Rhapsody for viola solo. *Honours:* Kranichsteiner prize for contemporary music, 1954; English record prize for interpretation of Schoenberg's Violin Concerto, Bundesverdienstkreuz, 1986. *Address:* Burgunder Strasse 4, 7800 Freiburg, Germany.

**MARSH, David;** British singer (bass); b. 29 May 1947, Middlesborough, England; s. of Alfred Marsh and Dorothy Thompson; m. Susan; two s. *Education:* Royal Northern Coll. of Music, studied with Otakar Kraus. *Career:* sang with ENO, Scottish Opera, Gyndebourne Touring Opera, City of Birmingham Touring Opera, English Touring Opera, Opéra de Lyon, Pfalzbau Theatre Ludwigshafen, Singapore Lyric Theatre, Wexford Festival; roles include Amonasro, Macbeth, Gérard in Andrea Chénier, Don Magnifico, Banquo, Masetto and Commendatore in Don Giovanni, Ramfis, Ferrando in Trovatore, Pantheus in Les Troyens, Dr Grenvil, Pistola in Falstaff, Nourabad in Les Pêcherus de perles, Abimelech in Samson et Delila, Trulove in The Rake's Progress, Quince in A Midsummer Night's Dream, Luther/Crespel in Les Contes d'Hoffmann, Sempronius in Timon of Athens, by Stephen Oliver, The King in Pavel Haas's Sarlatan; also works as commissioned portrait artist. *Address:* Cherrybank, Lands of Loyal, Alyth, Perthshire PH11 8JQ, Scotland.

**MARSH, Jane;** Singer (Soprano); b. 25 June 1944, San Francisco, USA. *Education:* Studied with Ellen Repp at Oberlin College and with Lili Wexburg and Otto Guth in NY, USA. *Career:* Debut: Spoleto Festival 1965, as Desdemona; Sang in Essen, Hamburg, Moscow, Prague, Naples, Trieste and Johannesburg: Further appearances in Pittsburgh, San Antonio and San Francisco, 1968; Deutsche Oper am Rhein, Düsseldorf, from 1968; Salzburg 1973, in the premiere of Orff's De Temporum fine Comoedia; Often heard as Mozart's Donna Anna, Queen of Night and Constanze. *Recordings:* De Temporum fine Comoedia; The Invisible City of Kitezh; Alfonso und Estrella; Penthesilea by Schoeck; Der Vampyr by Marschner, Voce.

**MARSH, Peter (Randall);** Violinist, Violist and Conductor; b. 15 June 1931, Glen Ridge, New Jersey, USA; Studied with Hans Letz, Juilliard School, 1946–50, Scott Willits, American Conservatory, 1952, 1966–67, Emanuel Zetlin, University of Washington, 1955–57. *Career:* Teaching experience includes:California Institute of the Arts, 1985–87; Artist-in-Residence, Lecturer, California State University at Fullerton, 1987–90; Professor, Western Washington University, Bellingham, 1990–97; Lecturer, University of Southern California, 1996–; Director of String Chamber Music, University of Southern California Thornton School of Music; Performing career includes: Chamber Music: 1st Violin, Lenox Quartet, 1957–81; 1st Violin, Philadelphia Quartet, 1981–82; 1st Violin, Berkshire Quartet, 1983–85; 1st Violin, Sequoia Quartet, 1985–87; 1st Violin, Southwest Chamber Music Society, 1988–96; Violin/Viola, Picasso Trio, 1992–95; 1st Violin, Pacific Quartet, 1993–96; Orchestra: 1st Violin, Seattle Symphony, 1955–57; Viola/1st Violin, Pittsburgh Symphony, 1957–61; Concertmaster, Seattle Symphony, Seattle Opera, Pacific Northwest Ballet, 1982–83; California Chamber Symphony, Colorado Festival Orchestra, 1987–89; mem, The Bohemians, New York, 1944–. *Recordings include:* As 1st Violinist with Lenox Quartet and Southwest Chamber Music Society: Milton Babbitt, Composition for 4 instruments, 1948; Beethoven, Sextet for string quartet and 2 horns; Beethoven Violin Sonatas 1–10 2001; Beethoven String Quartet Op.18 No.1 and Op.59 No.3; Berger, String Quartet; Haydn, String Quartets op 20, no's 1–6; L Kirchner String Quartet No. 2; Krenek, op 231 for violin and organ, op 237 for string trio; Prokofiev, Quintet op 39 and Overture on Hebrew Themes; Schoenberg, Concerto for string quartet and orchestra, with the London Symphony, and String Trio. *Contributions:* American String Teachers Magazine, whilst Violin Forum Editor, 1988–90. *Address:* 343 Heather Heights Court, Monrovia, CA 91016, USA.

**MARSH, Roger;** Composer and Lecturer; b. 10 Dec. 1949, Bournemouth, England; m. (1) Christina Rhys, 24 July 1976, 2 s., 2 d., (2) Anna Myatt, 19 Sept 1992, 1 s., 1 d. *Education:* BA, 1971, DPhil, 1975, University of York; Studied with Bernard Rands. *Career:* Harkness Fellow, 1976–78, University of CA, San Diego; Lecturer, Keele University, 1978–88; Lecturer, Senior Lecturer, Professor, University of York; Member of Midland Music Theatre; Director of Black Hair contemporary music ensemble; mem, SPNM Reading Panel, 1991–92; BBC Reading Panel, 1987–. *Compositions:* Not a Soul But Ourselves for 4 Amplified Voices, 1977; The Big Bang, music theatre; Stepping Out for Piano and Orchestra, 1990; Kagura, 1991; Love on The Rocks, music theatre, 1988; Espace for Orchestra, 1994; Heathcote's Inferno for wind orchestra, 1996; Spin for piano and ensemble, 1997; Canto I for string orchestra, 1999; Chaconne for violin, 1999; Sukeruko for percussion quartet,

2000. *Recordings include:* Not a Soul But Ourselves; Numerous radio broadcasts; CDs: Love on The Rocks and Ferry Music; Heathcote's Inferno, 2001. *Publications:* Various. *Honours:* Arts Council Composition Bursary, 1993. *Current Management:* Novello; Maecenas Music. *Address:* The New Rectory, Everingham, York YO2 4JA, England.

**MARSH-EDWARDS, Michael (Richard);** Composer and Conductor; b. 7 April 1928, Westgate-on-Sea, Kent, England; m. (1) Stella K Parrott, 9 April 1952, 1 d., (2) Ann Wardleworth, 11 Nov 1971, (3) Srilnuan Suwan, 9 Jan 1981, 1son. 1 d. *Education:* Trinity College, London University, Associate and Licentiate Diplomas, Hon PhD. *Career:* Conductor Luton Bach Orchestra, 1949–63; conductor 1952–63, Vice President, Luton Symphony Orchestra; Director of Music, Luton Industrial Mission and Luton Community Centre, 1957–62; Conductor, Halton Orpheus Choir, 1973–75; Freelance Conductor and lecturer, Consultant, Bangkok Symphony Orchestra; mem, Lfe Member, Former Vice-Chairman, British Music Society and Havergal Brian Society; Composers' Guild of Great Britain; Performing Right Society. *Compositions:* Toccata for Percussion and Orchestra; Variations, 8 percussionists; 3 Studies, 12 percussionists; Dance Overture; Birthday Overture; Revolutionary Overture, 1956; Chester Overture; Celebration Overture; Music 1, 60 strings; Music 2, strings and percussion; Music 3, strings and Brass; Music 4; Oppositions, 2 orchestras; Structures; Fantasy on the Waltz of Diabelli; Thai Dances; Balinese Dances; Petite Suite pour le Tombeau d'Erik Satie; Treurzang; Suite Guernesiase; Concerto for 11 instruments; Horn Concerto; Devouring Time, high voice and piano; Mischevious Ditties, high voice and piano; Elegy on the Name of Havergal Brian, piano or string orchestra; Peter Goldberg Variations, wind quintet; Concertino for harpsichord and string orchestra; Incantations, for flute, oboe, viola and piano; Toccata on One Note, for piano; Numerous other instrumental, vocal and electronic pieces; Music for children. *Publications:* Author of Concert Notes; Author and Presenter of Radio Scripts. *Honours:* Medal, American Biographical Institute, 1986; Alfred Nobel Medal, 1991. *Address:* 5/2440 Muban Prachachuen, Pakred, Nontaburi 11120, Thailand.

**MARSHALL, Ingram (Douglas);** Composer; b. 10 May 1942, New York, USA. *Education:* BA, Lake Forest College, 1964, Columbia University with Ussachevsky, electronic music, 1964–66, with Morton Subotnick in New York and California, and traditional Indonesian music at the California Institute of the Arts. *Career:* Taught at the California Institute of the Arts until 1974; Performances in Java, Bali and Scandinavia. *Compositions:* Transmogrification for tape, 1966; Three Buchla Studies for synthesizer 1969; Cortez, text-sound piece 1973; Vibrosuperball for 4 amplified percussion 1975; Non Confundar for string sextet, alto flute, clarinet and electronics, 1977; Spiritus for 6 strings, 4 flutes, harpsichord and vibraphone, 1981; Frog Tropes for brass sextet and tape, 1982; Voces resonae for string quartet, 1984. Three Penitential Visions for orchestra, 1987, Raving in the Wind, dance, 1997; Electro-acoustic: Evensongs for string quartet and tape, 1993; Dark Waters, for English horn, tape and electronics, 1995; Sinfonia Kingdom Come for orchestra and tape, 1997; SOE-PA for guitar with digital delay, 1999. *Address:* ASCAP, ASCAP Building, 1 Lincoln Plaza, NY 10023, USA.

**MARSHALL, Margaret Anne,** OBE; British singer (soprano); b. 4 Jan. 1949, Stirling; d. of Robert and Margaret Marshall; m. Dr Graeme G. K. Davidson 1970; two d. *Education:* High School of Stirling and Royal Scottish Acad. of Music and Drama. *Career:* first opera appearance in Orfeo ed Euridice, Florence 1977; has since sung at La Scala, Covent Garden, Glyndebourne, Scottish Opera, Barcelona, Hamburg, Cologne and Salzburg; concert performances in maj. European and US cities and festivals with maj. orchestras; numerous recordings. *Honours:* First Prize, Munich Int. Competition 1974; James Gulliver Award for Performing Arts in Scotland. *Address:* Woodside, Main Street, Gargunnock, Stirling, FK8 3BP, Scotland.

**MARSHALL, Nicholas,** MA; British composer, pianist, conductor and teacher; b. 2 June 1942, Plymouth, Devon, England; m. Angela Marshall 1982; one s. one d. *Education:* Univ. of Cambridge, Royal Coll. of Music. *Career:* Chair. and Artistic Dir, Ashburton Festival 1980–84. *Compositions include:* Section: Partita for Guitar; Three Japanese Fragments for guitar; Seven Folksongs for voice, recorder and piano; Inscriptions for A Peal of Eight Bells for SATB; Suite for Guitar, Flute, Clarinet, Violin and Cello; Four Haiku for Solo Recorder; Trio for Recorders; Sonatina for Solo Flute; Five West Country Folk Songs for SATB; A Playford Garland for SATB; The Young King, Children's Opera; Five Country Dances for orchestra, Cool Winds for Cello and Guitar;, Music in the Wood, song-cycle for high voice and piano; The Birds, song-cycle for mezzo-soprano, recorder and piano; The Willow Pattern Story, children's opera; Concertino for recorder and string quartet; Six Elizabethan Love Songs for male voices; Cat and Mouse, song-cycle for counter-tenor, recorder and harpischord. *Recordings:* Cool Winds: original music for cello and guitar; Three Japanese Fragments: Austin Maruri guitar recital; Here we come a-piping, vocal and intrumental music. *Address:* 2 The Mount, Totnes Down Hill, Totnes, Devon TQ9 5ES, England (home). *Telephone:* (1803) 862118 (home). *E-mail:* nickyangela@tiscali.co.uk (home).

**MARSHALL, Robert (Lewis);** American musicologist; b. 12 Oct. 1939, New York, NY; m. Traute Maass, 9 Sept 1966; one s. one d. *Education:* AB, Columbia University, 1960; MA, 1962, PhD, 1968, Princeton University; French Horn with Gunther Schuller, High School of Music and Art, New York. *Career:* Faculty Member, 1966–83, Chair, 1972–78, Music, University of Chicago; Visiting professor at Princeton University, 1971–72, Columbia

University, 1977; Faculty, 1983–2000, Incumbent Endowed Chair: Louis, Frances and Jeffrey Sachar Professor, Chair, 1985–92, Music, Brandeis University; mem, American Bach Society; Neue Bach-Gesellschaft. *Publications:* The Compositional Process of J. S. Bach, 1972; Studies in Renaissance and Baroque Music in Honour of Arthur Mendel, 1974; Critical Editor, Cantatas for 9th and 10th Sundays after Trinity, 1985; J. S. Bach Cantata Autographs in American Collections, 1985; The Music of J. S. Bach: The Sources, The Style, The Significance, 1989; Mozart Speaks: Views on Music, Musicians and The World, 1991; Eighteenth Century Keyboard Music, 1994, 2nd edn, 2003; Dennis Brain on Record: A Comprehensive Discography, 1996; Bach and Mozart's Artistic Maturity, 1998. *Contributions:* Musical Quarterly; Journal of American Musicological Society. *Honours:* Hon. mem. American Musicological Soc., 2003; Otto Kinkeldey Award, American Musicological Soc. 1974, First Incumbent, Harold Spivacke Consultant to Music Div., Library of Congress 1985, ASCAP-Deems Taylor Award 1990. *Address:* 100 Chestnut Street, West Newton, MA 02465, USA. *E-mail:* rmarshal@brandeis.edu (office).

**MARSHALL, Wayne,** ARCM, FRCO; British organist, conductor and pianist; b. 31 Jan. 1961, Oldham, Lancashire, England. *Education:* Chetham's School Manchester, Royal Coll. of Music, Vienna Hochschule. *Career:* organ scholar at Manchester Cathedral and St George's Chapel Windsor; recitals at St Paul's Cathedral, Westminster Abbey, Festival Hall, Leeds and Birmingham Town Halls, and King's Coll., Cambridge; tours of the USA and Yugoslavia; Windsor and Hong Kong Festivals; worked as repetiteur for Glyndebourne production of Porgy and Bess 1986, appeared as Jasbo Brown the jazz pianist; Asst Chorus Master, Glyndebourne 1987; season 1988–89 included Promenade Concert debut with the Poulenc Concerto and appearances with the City of Birmingham Symphony under Simon Rattle and the BBC Symphony under Paul Daniel; conducted the premiere of Wilfred Joseph's Alice in Wonderland, Harrogate Festival 1990; Carmen Jones in the West End, London 1991; Last Night Proms, London 1997; conductor of Porgy and Bess at the Bregenz Festival 1997–98, London Proms 1998; Duke Ellington Centenary Celebration at the Proms 1999; season 2001–02 with Rotterdam Philharmonic Orchestra, Vienna Symphony Orchestra, Bournemouth Symphony Orchestra and BBC Concert Orchestra; guest conductor with Orchestre National de Lyon, BBC Philharmonic, Orquesta Sinfonica de Euskadi and Bochumer Symphoniker 2002–03; conducted West Side Story at Bregenz Festival 2003; organist-in-residence, Bridgewater Hall, Manchester; featured in major celebrity organ recital series world-wide, including Suntory Hall, Tokyo, Vienna, Berlin, Paris and New Zealand; solo pianist appearances include recitals world-wide, and has duo partnership with Kim Criswell and Tasmin Little; has conducted orchestras, including Dallas, Toronto, Winnipeg Symphony Orchestras, City of Birmingham Symphony Orchestra, London Philharmonic, Bournemouth Symphony, Hallé, Munich Radio and Vienna Symphony Orchestras. *Recordings include:* I Got Rhythm, Gershwin Song Book, Rhapsody in Blue, Saint-Saëns Third (Organ) Symphony with Olso Symphony Orchestra and Mariss Jansons. *Current Management:* Askonas Holt Ltd, Lonsdale Chambers, 27 Chancery Lane, London, WC2A 1PF, England. *Telephone:* (20) 7400-1700. *Fax:* (20) 7400-1799. *E-mail:* info@askonasholt.co.uk. *Website:* www.askonasholt.co.uk.

**MARSONER, Ingrid;** Pianist; b. 1970, Leoben, Austria. *Education:* Hochschule für Musik und Kunst, Graz, 1981; Studied at the Universität für Musik und Darstellende Kunst, Vienna, 1990. *Career:* Teacher at the Universität für Musik, Graz, 1996–; Appearances at the Salzburg Corinthian Summer and Innsbruck Festivals; Peninsula Festival, Los Angeles, Kyoto Chamber Music (Japan) and Mozart Fesivals at Bologna; Repertoire includes J. S. Bach, Partita in C minor; Scarlatti Sonatas; Haydn, Fantasie in C major; Mozart, Fantasie in C minor, Rondo in A minor, Sonatas in A major, C minor and D major; Schubert, Sonatas in A major, A minor, B major, Wanderfantasie in C major, 4 Impromptus; Mendelssohn, Variations sérieuses in D minor op 54; Schumann, Abegg Variations op 1, Papillons, op 2, Kreisleriana op 16, Fantasy in C major op 17, Faschingsschwank aus Wien op 32; Pieces by Chopin, Liszt, Berg and Schoenberg; Mendelssohn Double Concerto in G minor; Chamber music includes Beethoven's Archduke Trio; Fauré Piano Quartet in C minor; Schumann, Dichterliebe; César Franck, Sonata in A major; Messiaen, Quartet for the End of Time. *Address:* Kriemhildplatz 7/7, 1150 Vienna, Austria.

**MARSTON, Nicholas John,** MA, PhD, ARCM, ARCO; British academic and musicologist; *Reader in Music Theory and Analysis and Fellow, King's College, University of Cambridge;* b. 27 Dec. 1958, Penzance, England. *Education:* Humphry Davy Grammar School, Corpus Christi Coll., Cambridge. *Career:* Jr Research Fellow, Selwyn Coll., Cambridge 1984–86; British Acad. Post-doctoral Research Fellow, King's Coll. London 1986–89; Lecturer, Exeter Univ. 1989–94, Bristol Univ. 1994–95; Reader, Univ. of Oxford 1995–2001; Reader in Music Theory and Analysis, Univ. of Cambridge, and Fellow King's Coll. 2001–; Ed.-in-Chief, Beethoven Forum 2006–; mem. Soc. for Music Analysis (vice-pres. 2000–04, (chair. editorial bd 2001–), Royal Musical Asscn, American Musicological Soc. *Publications:* Schumann: Fantasie Op. 17, Beethoven's Piano Sonata in E Op. 109, The Beethoven Companion (co-author); contrib. to The Cambridge Companion to Beethoven, 19th Century Music, Music Analysis, Journal of the American Musicological Association, Beethoven Forum. *Address:* King's College, Cambridge, CB2 1ST, England (office). *Telephone:* (1223) 331331 (office). *Fax:* (1223) 331115 (office). *E-mail:* njm45@cam.ac.uk (office).

**MARTA, Istvan;** Composer; b. 14 June 1952, Budapest, Hungary; 2 d. *Education:* Course in Composition in Yugoslavia led by W Lutoslawski, 1979; Diploma in Composition and Teaching from Ferenc Liszt Academy of Music, Budapest, 1981. *Career:* Folk Music Collecting Tour in Moldavia, Romania, 1973; Over 30 pieces of stage and film music composed; Teacher of History of Classical Music and Analysis of 20th Century Music, Jazz Department, Bela Bartók School of Music, Budapest, 1981–83; Organiser of Planum and Rendezvous, festivals of international contemporary music, 1982 and 1984; Music Director, National Theater, New Theater, Budapest, 1990–95; Director, Art Valley Multicultural Festival, 1995. *Compositions:* Text and Music, stage performance based on Samuel Beckett's radioplay, 1978; King of the Dead, cantata 1979; Christmas Day–24th Lesson, Music for Chamber ensemble, 1980; Our Heats, movements for chamber choir and chamber orchestra, 1983; Visions, ballet performed by the ballet corps of the Hungarian State Opera, 1984; Dolls House Story, composition for percussion instruments, 1985; Workers' Operetta, musical 1985; per quattro tromboni, 1986; Kapolcs Alarm, a videoclip, 1987; Slips and Streams, a ballet for tape, 1989; Doom, A Sigh, string auartet, 1989; The Glassblower's Dream, string quartet, 1990; Anatomy of a Scream, ballet for tape, 1990; Blasting in the Bird Cage for tape, 1990; The Temptation of St Anthony, ballet for tape, 1992; Don't Look Back, ballet for tape, 1995; Faust, ballet for tape, 1995; Liliomfi, musical play, 1997. *Current Management:* Interkoncert, Budapest. *Address:* Ferenciektere 7–8, 1053 Budapest, Hungary.

**MARTIN, Adrian;** singer (tenor); b. 1958, England. *Education:* Studied at the London Opera Centre and the National Opera Studio. *Career:* Debut: With Opera for All as Ramiro and Tonio; Sang small roles at Covent Garden in Parsifal, Salome and Die Zauberflöte, then the Dancing Master in Ariadne and Pong in Turandot; Glyndebourne Festival as Tamino and Idamante; Appearances with English National Opera as Cassio, Alfred, the Steersman, Anatol (War and Peace), Don Ottavio, Vincent (Mireille), Tamino, Ferrando and Rodolfo, Nadir, Jenik in The Makropulos Case and Erik in Fennimore and Gerda; Welsh National Opera as Lensky in Serban's production of Eugene Onegin; Scottish Opera in La Scala di Seta and La Cambiale di Matrimonio by Rossini; Has sung with Opera North as Rodolfo, Alfredo, Camille, Ismaele (Nabucco), Sali in a Village Romeo and Juliet, Tamino, Jacquino, Nadir and Ernesto; Overseas engagements at St Gallen (Hoffmann and Don Ottavio); Hamburg and Zürich (Hoffmann); Paris (Tybalt in Roméo et Juliette at the Opéra) and Queensland (Nadir and Rodolfo at the Lyric Opera); season 1999–2000 at the Erl Festival, Tyrol, as Alberich in The Ring.

**MARTIN, Andrea;** Singer (Baritone); b. 9 March 1949, Klagenfurt, Germany. *Education:* Studied in Vienna and at the Santa Cecilia Academy in Rome; Teachers included Anton Dermota, Hans Hotter, Ettore Campogallian, Mario del Monaco and Giuseppe Taddei. *Career:* Debut: Treviso 1979, as Malatesta in Don Pasquale; Sang with the Wiener Kammeroper and in Klagenfurt, Salzburg, Graz and Munich; Further Italian engagements at Rome, Palermo, Bologna, Venice, Naples and Verona; Ravenna Festival as Michonnet in Adriana Lecouvreur; Has sung in Maria di Rudenz by Donizetti at Venice and Wiesbaden, as Luna in Trovatore at the Dresden Staatsoper; Guest appearances at the Théâtre des Champs-Elysées, Paris, Liège, Barcelona, Lisbon and Vienna; Concert tours of Japan, Korea, the USA and Brazil. *Recordings:* Imelda de Lambertazzi and Alina, Regina di Golconda by Donizetti, Salieri's Axur, and Così fan tutte. *Address:* c/o Teatro La Fenice, Campo S Fantin 2519, 30124 Venice, Italy.

**MARTIN, George Whitney,** BA, LLB; American writer; b. 25 Jan. 1926, New York. *Education:* Harvard Coll., Trinity Coll., Cambridge, Univ. of Virginia Law School. *Career:* practised law 1955–59; writer 1959–. *Publications:* The Damrosch Dynasty, America's First Family of Music 1983, Verdi, His Music, Life and Times (fourth edn) 1992, Aspects of Verdi (second edn) 1993, Verdi at The Golden Gate, Opera and San Francisco in the Gold Rush Years 1993, The Opera Companion (fifth edn) 1997, Twentieth Century Opera, A Guide 1999, CCB: The Life and Century of Charles C. Burlingham, New York's First Citizen 1858–1959 2005; contrib. numerous articles on Verdi and his operas in The Opera Quarterly. *Address:* 53 Crosslands Drive, Kennett Square, PA 19348, USA. *Telephone:* (610) 388-0529 (office). *Fax:* (610) 388-0241 (office). *Website:* www.georgewmartin.com.

**MARTIN, Janis;** Singer (Soprano); b. 16 Aug. 1939, Sacramento, California, USA; m. Gerhard Hellwig. *Education:* Studied with Julia Monroe in Sacramento and Lili Wexberg and Otto Guth in New York. *Career:* Debut: San Francisco, 1960 as Annina in La Traviata; Returned to San Francisco as Marina, Venus and Meg Page; New York City Opera debut 1962, as Mrs Grose in The Turn of the Screw; New York Metropolitan Opera from 1962–66, at first in mezzo roles then from 1973 as Sieglinde, Marie in Wozzeck and Kundry; Bayreuth Festival 1968–73, as Magdalene, Eva, Sieglinde and Kundry; Chicago 1971, as Tosca; Deutsche Oper Berlin 1971–88; Covent Garden 1973, as Marie; La Scala 1980, as The Woman in Erwartung; La Scala, Marie; Geneva Opera 1985 as Isolde; Other roles include Wagner's Senta, Brünnhilde, Isolde, Venus and Kundry; Tosca; Fidelio, Santuzza and Strauss's Ariadne, Dyer's Wife, Salome, Elektra, and Marschallin; Cologne Opera 1988, as the Dyer's Wife; Turin and Bayreuth, 1989, as Brünnhilde; Sang Beethoven's Leonore at Düsseldorf, 1990; Season 1991–92, as the Götterdämmerung Brünnhilde at Brussels and Senta at Naples; Sang Orpheus at the Accademia di Santa Cecilia, Rome, 1996; Elektra at Catania, 1998; Season 2000 as Strauss's Dyer's Wife at the Munich Staatsoper and as Brünnhilde in Die Walküre for the Vienna Staatsoper. *Recordings:* Adriano in

Rienzi; Der fliegende Holländer; Erwartung; Sancta Susanna by Hindemith. *Address:* c/o Deutsche Oper am Rhein, Heinrich-Heine Allee 16, 4000 Düsseldorf, Germany.

**MARTIN, Kathleen;** Singer (Soprano); b. 28 Feb. 1948, Texas, USA. *Education:* studied at UCLA and at California State University Long Beach. *Career:* Debut: San Francisco Opera as Madama Butterfly; England at the Lubeck Opera, 1974–80, as Fiordiligi, Donna Elvira, Nedda, Mimi, Desdemona, the Trovatore Leonora, Elsa, Tatiana and Katya Kabanova; Sang at the Frankfurt Opera 1980–83, guest engagements at the Theater am Gärtnerplatz, Munich; Sang at Toulouse as Jordane in the 1985 premiere of Landowski's Montségur and appeared at the Paris Opéra, 1987. *Address:* c/o Teatre du Capitole, Place du Capitole, 31000 Toulouse, France.

**MARTIN, Marvis;** Singer (Soprano); b. 1956, Tallahassee, Florida. *Education:* University of Miami and Manhattan School. *Career:* Sang the Princess in L'Enfant et les Sortilèges, Metropolitan Opera, 1983; Further New York appearances in Boris Godunov, Ariadne auf Naxos, Porgy and Bess, as Clara; Tchaikovsky's Maid of Orleans; Savonlinna Festival, 1992 as Clara and appearances elsewhere as Pamina and Liu in Turandot; Many concert engagements. *Address:* c/o Metropolitan Opera, Lincoln Center, New York NY 19923, USA.

**MARTIN, Philip (James);** Concert Pianist and Composer; b. 27 Oct. 1947, Dublin, Ireland; m. 22 Aug 1970, 1 s., 1 d. *Education:* St Marys College, Rathmines, Dublin; Patricia Read Pianoforte School, Dublin; Private Studies with Mabel Swainson, Dublin; Royal Academy of Music, London; Private Studies with Louis Kentner, London, and Yvonne Lefèbure, Paris. *Career:* Debut: Wigmore Hall, London, 1970; Regular Performances with major British orchestras; Royal Festival Hall and Royal Albert Hall Debut, 1977; BBC Prom Concerts, 1985, 1987 Recorded live on Omnibus at the Proms, BBC television. *Compositions:* 2 Piano Concertos; Harp Concerto; Beato Angelico, for large orchestra; 3 Piano Trios; Various Chamber Music and over 150 Songs; Symphony, 1999; 2 large choral works. *Address:* Chapel House, Theobalds Green, Calstone Calne, Wiltshire SW11 8QE, England.

**MARTINCEK, Dusan;** Composer; b. 13 June 1936, Presov, Slovakia; m. Magdalena Kockova, 1961, 1 s. *Education:* Piano and Composition, Bratislava Conservatory, 1951–56; Bratislava Academy of Music and Drama, 1956–61. *Career:* Assistant, Music Theory, 1961–72; Associate Professor, Theory, 1973–86; Freelance Artist, 1987–92; University Professor, Composition, Bratislava Academy of Music and Drama, Bratislava, 1993; mem, Numerous musical institutions. *Compositions include:* Dialogues in the Form of Variations for piano and orchestra, 1961; Simple overture for small orchestra, 1961; 8 piano sonatas, 1967–1981; String Quartet, 1982–84; Animation for 35 solo strings, 1983–86; Continuities for large orchestra, 1987–88; Communications for violin and piano, 1988; Interrupted Silence for large orchestra, 1989–90; Coexistences for String Quintet, 1993; 10 Movements for piano, 1992; New Nocturnes for piano, 1993–94; Dedications for piano, 1997; Verso fine...? for violin solo, 1998; Compositions for flute and piano, for solo guitar, and so on. *Honours:* J L Bella Prize, 1981; Certificate of Merit, 1993; Man of the Year, 1993; Great Minds of the 21st Century, USA, 2002; Cetificate of Award, Switzerland, 2002; Living Legends, Cambridge, 2003; Performances throughout Europe and overseas; Best analyses of his works: Tempo, No. 179 (Boosey and Hawkes); Dusan Martincek: An Introduction to His Music (David Babcock); Zuzana Martina Eova in the Slovak Music, 2002; Complete works kept in the Dr Paul Sacher Foundation in Basel, Switzerland. *Address:* Lipskeho 11, 84101 Bratislava, Slovakia.

**MARTINEAU, Malcolm;** Pianist; b. 3 Feb. 1960, Edinburgh, Scotland. *Education:* Studied at St Catharine's College, Cambridge, and at the Royal Academy of Music with Kendall Taylor and Geoffrey Parsons; Further study with Joyce Rathbone. *Career:* Has presented own series (complete songs of Debussy and Poulenc), St John's Smith Square; Britten series broadcast Wolf, Wigmore Hall; complete lieder of Hugo Wolf, Edinburgh Festival; has appeared throughout Europe, N America and Australila and at festivals in Aix-en-Provence, Vienna, Edinburgh, Schubertiade, Munich, Salzburg. *Recordings:* Schubert, Schumann and English song recitals with Bryn Terfel; Schubert and Strauss recitals with Simon Keenlyside; recital records with Angela Gheorghiu and Barbara Bonney; Magdalena Kozena; Della Jones; the complete Fauré songs with Sarah Walker and Tom Krause; the complete Britten Folk Songs; the complete Beethoven Folk Songs; accompaniments for Dame Janet Baker, Sarah Walker, Frederica von Stade, Anne Sofie von Otter, Thomas Hampson, Olaf Bär, Karita Mattila, Solveig Kringelborn, Michael Schade, Ian Bostridge, Amanda Roocroft, Joan Rodgers, Sir Thaomas Allen, Ann Murray, Susan Graham, Dame Felicity Lott, Christopher Maltman and Jonathan Lemalu. *Honours:* Walter Gruener International Lieder Competition, 1984. *Current Management:* Askonas Holt Ltd, Lonsdale Chambers, 27 Chancery Lane, London, WC2A 1PF, England. *Telephone:* (20) 7400-1700. *Fax:* (20) 7400-1799. *E-mail:* info@askonasholt.co.uk. *Website:* www.askonasholt.co.uk.

**MARTINEZ, Odaline de la,** BFA, MMus, FRAM; Cuban composer and conductor; *Artistic Director, Lontano Records Ltd*; b. 31 Oct. 1949, d. of Julian J. and Odaline M. Martinez. *Education:* Tulane Univ., USA, Royal Acad. of Music, Univ. of Surrey, England. *Career:* Founder, Dir European Women's Orchestra (EWO) 1990–, Founder, Music Dir Lontano; performances at Chard Festival of Women in Music 1990, in Abbotsbury (Dorset) and St John's Smith Square (London) 1992; Conductor with EWO of works by female composers including Clara Schumann, Grazyna Bacewicz, Eleanor Alberga, Minna Keal, etc.; first woman to conduct a Promenade Concert, Royal Albert Hall, London 1984; Principal Guest Conductor Camerata of the Americas, Mexico City 1998–; Artistic Dir, Lontano 1976–, Lontano Records Ltd 1992–. *Compositions include:* First String Quartet. *Opera:* Sister Aimée: an American Legend 1984. *Publications include:* Mendelssohn's Sister. *Honours:* Marshall Scholar, Guggenheim Fellow. *Address:* c/o Lontano Trust, 39b Hatherley Mews, Walthamstow, London, E17 4QP, England (office). *Telephone:* (20) 8521-8075 (office). *Fax:* (20) 8531-2764 (office). *E-mail:* odaline@lontano.co.uk. *Website:* www.lontano.co.uk (office).

**MARTINEZ, Ruben;** Singer (Tenor); b. 1962, Argentina. *Career:* Many opera engagements in South America and Europe, notably in Donizetti's L'Elisir d'amore and Gounod's Roméo et Juliette; also sings chansons by Fauré; Contestant at the 1995 Cardiff Singer of the World Competition; Mozart's Lucio Silla with Opera for Europe in London and elsewhere, 1998. *Address:* Street 27 No. 1221 La Plata (CP 1900), Buenos Aires, Argentina.

**MARTINEZ-IZQUIERDO, Ernest;** Spanish conductor and composer; b. 11 June 1962, Barcelona. *Education:* diplomas in composition and orchestral conducting. *Career:* debut, Barcelona 1985 with his Ensemble 'Barcelona 216'; Principal Conductor of the Ensemble Barcelona 216; Assistant Conductor of JONDE (Youth Spanish Orchestra), 1985–87; Assistant Conductor of ONE (Spanish National Orchestra), 1988; Assistant Conductor of the Ensemble Intercontemporain, 1988–90; Concerts with foreign orchestras like Philharmonic Orchestra of Minsk, Ensemble Contemporain de Montreal, Orchestra of The Teatro Comunale di Bolonia or Avanti Orchestra of Helsinki; Concerts with the mainly Spanish orchestras as OBC (Symphonic Orchestra of Barcelona), ONE (Spanish National Orchestra), Cadaqués Orchestra, Symphonic Orchestra of Tenerife, Symphonic Orchestra of Granada; As Guest Conductor or with his own Ensemble, he has conducted in the principal European cities as Paris, Prague, Bordeaux, Amsterdam, Palermo, Luxembourg, Madrid, Rome and in some of the most important festivals, Festival Internacional de Alicante, Festival de Torroella de Montgri, Zagreb's Biennal, Festival Castell de Perelada, Festival de Cadaqués, Holland Festival, Helsinki's Biennal, Barcelona's Festival de Musica del Segle XX, Festival Aujourd'hui Musiques of Perpignan; mem, The Associacio Catalena de Compositors. *Compositions:* Música para orquesta de cuerdas, 1986; Música para 10 vcl y orquesta, 1991; Música per a un festival, 1992; Norte-Sur, 1993; Alternanqa, 1995; Fanfare for chamber ensemble, 1995. *Recordings include:* Album de Colien, Spanish and Portuguese Contemporary Piano Music, 1995; Music for the film Metropolis by Martin Matalon, 1995; Composers of Cercle Manuel de Falla, 1995; Xavier Benguerel: 7 Fables de La Fontaine, 1995. *Address:* Muntaner 511 #6, 08022 Barcelona, Spain.

**MARTINIS, Carla;** Singer (soprano); b. 1921, Danculovice, Yugoslavia. *Education:* Zagreb Conservatory. *Career:* sang first in Zagreb and Prague; New York City Opera, 1950–53, debut as Turandot; Vienna Staatsoper 1951–, debut as Aida, conducted by Karajan; Salzburg Festival, 1951, as Desdemona, conducted by Furtwängler; Paris Opéra, 1951, as Amelia in Un Ballo in Maschera; La Scala Milan, Aix-en-Provence, Naples and Florence, 1952; San Francisco Opera, 1954; sang La Gioconda at Trieste, 1956. *Recordings:* Otello from Salzburg; Donna Anna in Don Giovanni; La Forza del Destino; Tosca.

**MARTINO, Donald (James);** Composer, Clarinettist, Educator and Publisher; b. 16 May 1931, Plainfield, New Jersey, USA. *Education:* BM, Syracuse University, 1952; MFA, Princeton University, 1954; MA, Harvard University (honorary) 1983; Fulbright Grant for study with Luigi Dallapiciola, Florence, Italy, 1954–55, 1955–56. *Career:* Associate Professor of Music, Yale University, 1958–69; Chairman of Composition, New England Conservatory, 1969–79; Irving Fine Professor, Brandeis University, 1979–82; Walter Bigelow Rosen Professor, Harvard University, 1983–93, Professor Emeritus, 1993–; mem, American Academy of Arts and Letters; American Academy of Arts and Sciences; Founder, American Society of Composers; Broadcast Music Inc. *Compositions include:* Published: Contemplations for orchestra, 1956; Concerto for wind quintet, 1964; Concerto for piano and orchestra, 1965; Notturno, flute, clarinet, violin, violoncello, percussion, piano, 1973; Paradiso Choruses, chorus, soloists, orchestra, tape, 1974; Ritorno for orchestra, 1975; Triple Concerto for clarinet, bass clarinet and contrabass clarinet with chamber ensemble, 1977; Fantasies and Inpromptus, piano solo, 1981; Divertissements for youth orchestra, 1981; String Quartet, 1983; The White Island, chorus, chamber orchestra, 1985; Concerto for alto saxophone and chamber orchestra, 1987; From the Other Side, flute, violoncello, percussion, piano, 1988; Twelve Preludes for piano, 1991; Three Sad Songs, viola and piano, 1993; Concerto for violin and orchestra, 1996; Octet, 1998; Serenata Concertante, 1999. *Recordings include:* Donald Martino: Piano Music; Donald Martino: Chamber Music; Donald Martino: Piano and Chamber Music; Donald Martino: A Jazz Set; Paradiso Choruses; Saxophone Concerto. *Publications:* Editor: 178 Chorale Harmonizations for J. S. Bach: A Comparative Edition for Study, 1984. *Contributions:* The Source Set and its Aggregate Formations, Journal of Music Theory, 1961; Notation in General Articulation in Particular, 1966; An Interview by James Boros, 1991; Perspectives of New Music. *Honours:* Pulitzer Prize, 1974; Kennedy Center-Friedheim Award, 1985; Mark M Horblit Award, Boston Symphony, 1987. *Current Management:* Dantalian Inc, USA. *Address:* 11 Pembroke Street, Newton, MA 02158, USA.

**MARTINOTY, Jean-Louis;** French stage director; b. 20 Jan. 1946, Etampes. *Career:* radio producer for ORTF, then critic for L'Humanité; asst to Jean-Pierre Ponnelle, notably in works by Mozart and Monteverdi at Zürich; baroque repertoire includes productions for the Karlsuhe Handel Festival; production of Ariadne auf Naxos seen at the Paris Opéra 1983, Covent Garden 1985; produced three films about renaissance and opera 1985; Gen. Administrator, Paris Opéra at the Palais Garnier 1986–89; productions in season 1994–96 Wagner's Ring at Karlsruhe; Gussmann Opera Seria at Berlin Staatsoper; Cesti's Argia at the Innsbruck Festival. *Recent stage productions include:* Le Petit Prince 2002, Nozze di Figaro 2002. *Honours:* Best Production of the Year 1980, 1981, 1982, 1983, 2002. *Address:* 51310 Joiselle, France.

**MARTINOVIC, Boris;** singer (bass-baritone); b. 1953, Croatia. *Education:* Juilliard School, New York. *Career:* debut, Avery Fisher Hall New York, in Refice's Cecilia; Charleston 1977, in The Queen of Spades; European appearances at Trieste, Rome and Naples; Teatro Regio Parma in Lucia di Lammermoor, Semiramide, Gerusalemme by Verdi and Roméo et Juliette; Pesaro Festival as Rossini's Mosè, Colline at the Paris Opéra, Vienna and Zürich as Escamillo, at Zürich as Onegin and Pesaro 1991 as Orbazzano in Rossini's Tancredi; Bregenz Festival 1992, Escamillo; Sang in Donizetti's Adelia at Genoa, 1998. *Recordings include:* Prince Igor, Ivan Susanin by Glinka and Boris Godunov, as Rangoni; Crespel in Les Contes d'Hoffmann. *Current Management:* Robert Gilder & Co., Enterprise House, 59–65 Upper Ground, London, SE1 9PQ, England. *Telephone:* (20) 7928-9008. *Fax:* (20) 7928-9755. *E-mail:* rgilder@robert-gilder.com.

**MARTINOVIĆ, Sandra;** Croatian singer (mezzo-soprano); b. Doboj, Bosnia and Herzegovina. *Education:* Acad. of Music, Zagreb and RCM. *Career:* fmr soloist with the Croatian Nat. Radio Chorus, touring throughout Europe; operatic roles include Nella in Gianni Schicchi, Tonina in Prima la Musica poi le Parole, Mrs Gobineau in Medium, Marianna in Il Signor Bruschino, Genevieve in Suor Angelica; has performed in opera choruses with Savoy Opera, Holland Park Opera; numerous concert recitals include Schumann's Frauenliebe und Leben; performed charity concert for Adopt-a-Minefield, Wigmore Hall, London 2005; Social and Cultural Events Sec., Croatian Students and Young Professionals Network. *E-mail:* sandra@csypn.org.uk.

**MARTINPELTO, Hillevi;** Singer (Soprano); b. 9 Jan. 1958, Älvalden, Sweden. *Education:* Studied at the Stockholm Opera School. *Career:* Sang Pamina in Die Zauberflöte with the Folksopera in Stockholm and at the Edinburgh Festival; Norrlands Opera from 1987 in Ivar Hallströ m 's Den Bergtagno, also on Swedish television and at the York Festival; Tatiana in Eugene Onegin and Marguerite; Royal Opera Stockholm debut 1987, as Madama Butterfly; Sang the title roles in Gluck's Iphigénie operas at the Drottningholm Festival, 1989–90; Théâtre de la Monnaie, Brussels, from 1990 as Fiordiligi and the Countess in Le nozze di Figaro; Season 1991–92 with Fiordiligi at the Hamburg Staatsoper, Wagner's Eva at Nice, Donna Anna at Aix-en-Provence; Season 1992–93 included: Don Giovanni, Aix-en-Provence Festival, France; Così fan tutte, Hamburg State Opera, Germany; Das Rheingold, Lyric Opera of Chicago, USA; Le nozze di Figaro, Toulouse Opera, France; Châtelet, Monteverdi and Wagner's Eva in Tokyo with Deutsche Oper Berlin; Further engagements include Verdi's Desdemona in Helsinki; Concert engagements with Dvořák's Requiem, Scottish National Orchestra, 1987; Residentie Orchestra of The Hague in Mozart; Belgian Radio Orchestra; Philharmonia of London in The Creation, conducted by Claus Peter Flor; Sang Donna Anna in Don Giovanni, at Glyndebourne, 1994–; Agathe in Der Freischütz for the Royal Danish Opera at Copenhagen, 1997; Further engagements include: Don Giovanni and Clemenza di Tito (Munich) and Idomeneo (Lausanne); Concert appearances with the National Orchestra of Wales, City of Birmingham Symphony Orchestra, the Gesellschaft der Musikfreunde in Vienna and the Vienna Symphony Orchestra amongst others; Alice Page in Falstaff at the 1998 Proms; London Proms 1999, as The Virgin in The Kingdom by Elgar and Schumann's Scenes from Faust; Elsa in Lohengrin at Gothenburg, 2000; Season 2000–01 as Elsa at Gothenburg, Alice Ford at the Paris Châtelet and Agathe for the Berlin Staatsoper; Recital at the 2001 Edinburgh Festival. *Recordings:* Elettra in Idomeneo, conducted by John Eliot Gardiner; Countess in Figaro with Gardiner; Così fan tutte under Simon Rattle; Alice and Oberon in Falstaff. *Address:* Artists Sekretariat Ulf Tornqvist, Sankt Eriksgatan 100, 2 tr S113 31 Stockholm, Sweden.

**MARTINS, Maria de Lourdes;** retd academic; b. 26 May 1926, Lisbon, Portugal. *Education:* National Conservatory of Music, Lisbon, Music High School, Munich, Germany, with H. Genzmer, Orff Institute of the Mozarteum, Salzburg. *Career:* piano concerts on nat. and German radio; television performances in Portugal; debut opera, S Carlos Nat. Theatre, Lisbon 1986; Prof. of Music Education and Composition, Nat. Conservatory in Lisbon 1970–96; founder mem. Portuguese Soc. for Music Education (pres. 1972–77); co-chair. Commission for Music Education; lectures and seminars in Portugal, Argentina, USA, Canada, Japan, Belgium, Germany, Switzerland, Poland and Spain; mem. ISME (mem. of bd), APEM. *Compositions include:* Encoberto de F Pessoa, 1965; O Litoral de A Negreiros, 1971–; Rondó for Wind Orchestra, 1978; Portuguese Christmas Songs for Wind Orchestra, 1978; Portuguese Dances, 1978; Sonatinas 1 and 2 for Piano; Catch, 1981; Ritmite, 1983; Musica de Piano Para Crianças Ed Valentim de Carvalho; Opera: Tres Máscaras, 1983; Simetria for Clarinet Solo, 1984; 4 Poemas de F Pessoa, 1984; Moments of Peace by J Gracen Brown, 1989; II String Quartet, 1989; Concerto de piano, 1990; Divertiment on Mozart Themes, 1991; Kinder Opera 'Donzela Guerreira', 1995; Suite para Quinteto, 1999; Pianoforte and percussion

(commissioned by the International Society for Polyaesthetic Education to be played at their symposium in Austria), 1999. *Recordings:* Wind Quartet; 12 Choral Portuguese Songs; Piano Works, pianist Erzsebet Tusa; Historia de Natal. *Publications:* Pizzicato. *Honours:* Composition Prizes: National Prize Carlos Seixas, 1959; JMP, 1960; C Gulbenkian Foundation, 1965, 1971. *Address:* R. Trindade Coelho 108, 2775-293 Parede, Portugal.

**MARTINSEN, Tom;** Singer (Tenor); b. 1957, Norway. *Education:* Studied in Stockholm with Nicolai Gedda. *Career:* Sang in lyric repertory at Royal Opera, Stockholm, Koblenz Opera, 1985–88; Gelsenkirchen from 1988; Sang Tamino at Dresden, 1992 followed by Hoffmann, 1993; Guest appearances throughout Germany as Mozart's Ferrando; Rossini's Lindoro and Almaviva; Nemorino and Fenton in Falstaff; Modern repertory includes Werle's Drommen om Thérèse; The Two Fiddlers by Maxwell Davies and Norgaard's Siddharta; Sang Hoffmann at Kiel, 1999, Strauss's Narraboth at Dresden, 2001. *Address:* Staatsoper Dresden, Theaterplatz 2, 01067 Dresden, Germany.

**MARTINUCCI, Nicola;** singer (tenor); b. 28 March 1941, Tarent, Italy. *Education:* studied with Sara Sforni in Milan. *Career:* debut, Teatro Nuovo Milan 1966, as Manrico; sang at La Scala and at the Teatro La Fenice, Venice; Deutsche Oper am Rhein Düsseldorf from 1973; Florence 1974 as Filippo in a revival of Spontini's Agnese di Hohenstaufen; Verona Arena 1982–86, as Radames, Calaf and Andrea Chénier; Covent Garden debut 1985, as Dick Johnson in La Fanciulla del West; appearances in Dublin, Tehran, Budapest and Salzburg; Rome Opera 1989, as Poliuto; sang Calaf in London 1990; Pollione at Catania, Manrico at Parma; Season 1992 as Enzo in La Gioconda at Rome and Calaf at the Festival of Caracalla; sang Andrea Chénier there 1996; Calaf at Turin 1998; Season 2000–01 as Calaf in Taiwan and Radames at the Macerata Festival. *Recordings:* Turandot, from Verona (video); Donizetti's Poliuto.

**MARTLAND, Steve;** Composer; b. 10 Oct. 1959, Liverpool, England. *Education:* Graduated from Liverpool University, 1981; Royal Conservatory, The Hague, Netherlands, with Louis Andriessen; Tanglewood USA with Gunther Schuller. *Career:* Works with students and musicians outside the classical tradition; Pieces for informal Dutch ensembles, the Jazz Orchestra Loose Tubes and the band Test Department multimedia project for BBC television; Joint premiere of Babi-Yar with the Royal Liverpool Philharmonic and the St Louis Symphony Orchestra; American Invention performed in the USA and Japan; Performances with the Steve Martland Band, including the 1994 South Bank Meltdown Festival (returned 1997). *Compositions:* Remembering Lennon for 7 players, 1981–85; Lotta Continua for orchestra 1981–84; Duo for trumpet and piano 1982; Canto a la Esperanza for soprano, electric guitar and chamber orchestra 1982; Kgakala for piano 1982; Babi Yar for orchestra 1983; Orc for horn and small orchestra 1984; American Invention for 13 players 1985; Shoulder to Shoulder for 13 players 1986; Dividing the Lines for brass, wind band 1986; Remix for jazz ensemble 1986; Big Mac I, II for 4–8 players 1987; Divisions for electronic tape 1986–87; Drill for 2 pianos 1987; Glad Day for voice and ensemble 1988; Albion for tape and film 1987–88; Terra Firma for 5 voices, with amplification and video 1989; Crossing the Border for Strings, 1991; The Perfect Act for ensemble and voice, 1991; Beat the Retreat, for eleven players, 1997; Kick, for eleven players (1995–96); Eternal Delight for eleven players, 1997; Terminal (1998) and Step by Step for 7/8 instruments; Fairest Isle for Counter-tenor and ensemble, 1999. *Honours:* 1981 Mendelssohn Scholarship; 1985 Government Composition Prize, Netherlands. *Address:* Schott and Co Ltd, 48 Great Marlborough Street, London W1V 2BN, England.

**MARTON, Eva Heinrich;** Hungarian opera singer (soprano); *Professor, Franz Liszt Music University*; b. 18 June 1943, Budapest; d. of Bela and Ilona (née Krammer) Heinrich; m. Zoltan Marton 1965; one s. one d. *Education:* Franz Liszt Acad., Budapest. *Career:* debut, Budapest State Opera, singing there 1968–70; has sung with various opera companies, including Frankfurt Opera 1972–77, Hamburg State Opera 1977–80, Maggio Musicale Fiorentino (Italy), Vienna State Opera, La Scala (Milan, Italy), Rome Opera (Italy), Metropolitan Opera (New York), Lyric Opera (Chicago), Grand Opera (Houston) and San Francisco Opera (USA), Bayreuth and Salzburg Festivals, Teatro Liceo, Barcelona (Spain), Teatro Colón, Buenos Aires, (Argentina), Royal Opera House Covent Garden, London, (UK), Vienna State Opera, Washington Opera; roles include: Empress in Die Frau ohne Schatten, Salome, all three Brünnhildes in Ring Cycle, Elisabeth and Venus in Tannhäuser, Elsa and Ortrud in Lohengrin, Senta in Der fliegende Holländer, title roles of Turandot, Tosca, Manon Lescaut, Fedora, Gioconda, Aida, Amelia in Ballo in Maschera, Leonora in Il Trovatore, Lady Macbeth in Macbeth, Elisabetta in Don Carlo, Leonore in Fidelio, Maddalena in Andrea Chénier, Leonora in La Forza del Destino; Prof., Franz Liszt Music Univ.; mem. Hungarian Nat. Volleyball team. *Films include:* Turandot, Il Trovatore, Lohengrin, Tannhäuser, Elektra, La Gioconda, Tosca. *Recordings include:* Turandot, Andrea Chenier, Fedora, Bluebeard's Castle, Violanta, Tiefland, Mefistofele, Die Walküre, La Wally, Semirama, Götterdämmerung, Siegfried, Tosca, La Gioconda. *Honours:* Gold Star, Repub. of Hungary 1989, Bartók Award 1990, Kossuth Award 1997. *Current Management:* Pf 453/454, Budapest 1537, Hungary. *Telephone:* (30) 9614097 (office). *E-mail:* me2_floria@compuserve.com (office). *Website:* www.martoneva.hu (office). www.evamarton.com (office).

**MARTTINEN, Tauno;** Composer; b. 27 Sept. 1912, Helsinki, Finland. *Education:* Studied Music, Viipuri, 1920s; Studied Music, Helsinki, 1930s.

*Career:* Director, Hameenlinna Music Institute, 1950–75. *Compositions:* The Cloak, 1962–63; The Engagement, 1964; Burnt Orange, 1968; Maitre Patelin, 1969–72; Shaman's Drum, 1974–76; The Earl's Sister, 1977; The Pharoah's Letter, 1978–80; Song of the Great River, 1982–84; Seven Brothers, 1976–86; Mooses Ooppera, 1990; Ballets: A Portrait of Dorian Gray, 1969; Snow Queen, 1970; The Sun Out of the Moon, 1975–77; The Ugly Duckling, 1976, 1982–83; Orchestra: Symphony No. 1, 1958; Symphony No. 2, 1959; Symphony No. 3, 1960–62; Symphony No. 4, 1964; Symphony No. 7, 1977; Panu, God of Fire, 1966; Symphony No. 8, 1983; Symphony No. 9, 1986; The Maid of Pohjola, 1982; Solo Instrument Concerto for piano and orchestra, 1964; Concerto for flute and orchestra, 1972; Concerto for Clarinet and Orchestra, 1974; Concerto for two pianos and orchestra, 1981; Concerto for piano and orchestra No. 4 Op 241, 1984; Chamber Music: Delta, 1962; Alfa op 16, 1963; Visit to the Giant Sage Vipunen, 1969; String Quartet No. 2, 1971; Divertimento, 1977; Intermezzo, 1977–78; Le Commencement, 1979; Trio, 1982; Solo Instrument: Titisee for piano, 1965; Adagio for organ, 1967; Sonatina for piano; Nore dame, 1970; The Cupola, for organ, 1971; Sonata for piano, 1975; Impression for cello, 1978; Prophet for organ, 1984. *Honours:* Honorary Professor conferred by the State, 1972. *Address:* TEOSTO, Lauttasaarentie 1, 00200 Helsinki 20, Finland.

**MARTURET, Eduardo;** Conductor and Composer; b. 19 Sept. 1953, Caracas, Venezuela. *Education:* Music Degree, Anglia University; Further studies in Cambridge, Siena and Rome. *Career:* Debut: Caracas in 1978; Artistic Director, Sinfonietta Caracas, 1986; Music Director with Teatro Teresa Carreño, 1984–76, and Orq Sinfonica Venezuela, 1987–95; Has conducted major orchestras in Germany, Netherlands, USA, Scandinavia and Hungary; SPNM, London; American Symphony Orchestra League; Conductors' Guild, USA. *Compositions include:* Canto Llano; Music For Six And Sax; Tres Tiempos; Casa Bonita; Mantra for Orchestra, 1995. *Recordings:* Brahms Complete Symphonies, Overtures and Concertos; With Berliner Symphoniker, Mozart Symphonies and Complete Violin Concertos; Concertgebouw Chamber Orchestra. *Publications:* Casa Bonita: Catalogue of The Exhibition, 1988; Article, Perspectives of Mozart's Symphonic Music, 1991. *Honours:* Orden Diego De Losada, 1992; Best Conductor, 1992; Best Classical Record, 1992; Orden Andres Bello, 1992. *Current Management:* John Gingrich, New York, USA. *Address:* PO Box 2912, Caracas, Venezuela.

**MARUZIN, Yuri;** Singer (Tenor); b. 8 Dec. 1947, Perm, Russia. *Education:* Studied in Leningrad. *Career:* Debut: Maly Theatre, Leningrad, 1972; Appearances with the Kirov Opera Leningrad, St Petersburg from 1978 notably as Hermann in The Queen of Spades and Dimitri in Boris Godunov and touring to Covent Garden, 1987 as Lensky; Sang the Tsarevich in Rimsky's The Tale of Tsar Saltan at La Scala and Reggio Emilia, 1988; Galitsin in Khovanshchina at the Vienna Staatsoper, 1989; San Francisco Opera as Anatol in War and Peace, Andrei Khovansky in Khovanshchina at Edinburgh, 1991; Bayan in Ruslan and Lyudmila at San Francisco and Palermo, 1995; Other guest engagements at Turin, Nice, Madrid and Toronto; Other roles include Faust, Pinkerton, Rodolfo, Don Carlos, Don Alvaro, Alfredo and the Duke of Mantua; Sang Hermann at Glyndebourne, 1992, 1995; New Israeli Opera, 1997 in Lady Macbeth of the Mtsensk District; Season 2000–01 as Lensky at Miami and Grischa in Rimsky's Invisible City of Kitezh at St Petersburg. *Address:* Kirov Opera and Ballet Theatre, St Petersburg, Russia.

**MARVIN, Frederick;** American pianist and musicologist; b. 11 June 1920, California; s. of Harry and Ann Marvin. *Education:* Curtis Inst. of Music, Philadelphia, Southern California Conservatory, Los Angeles. *Career:* debut, Carnegie Hall 1948; toured USA 1949–54; concerts in every major capital of Europe from 1954, solo recitals, and concert lectures; masterclasses; Prof. of Piano 1968–, Prof. Emeritus and Artist-in-Residence 1990, Syracuse Univ.; retd from performance. *Recordings include:* George Antheil Piano Sonata No. 4, Liszt, Sonatas by Moscheles and L. Berger, Schubert, Sonatas by J.L. Dussek (three vols), Sonatas by Soler (eight vols), Four Villancicos by A. Soler, Lamentacion, Stabat Mater, Salve Regina. *Publications:* 63 sonatas by Soler, four Villancicos and Salve, Lamentation, Soler, edited eight vols Sonatas and seven vols choral works by Padre Soler, two sonatas by J. L. Dussek, Liederabende with Martha Mödl, Gebhardt Musikvertrieb, Stuttgart, 13 Sonatas and Fandango by Padre Antonio Soler 2000; contrib. to music magazines, article on Padre Antonio Soler, New Grove Dictionary of Music and Musicians 2000. *Honours:* Carnegie Hall Award for Most Outstanding Debut in New York City 1948, Schnabel Gold Medal, London 1955, Orden del Mérito Civil (Commander), Spanish Government 1969, Croix de Commandeur, Medille de Vermiel, Arts-Sciences, Lettres, France 1974, Cervantes Medal, Hispanic Soc. of America 2000. *Address:* c/o Ernst Schuh, 246 Houston Avenue, Syracuse, NY 13224, USA. *Telephone:* (345) 472-6066 (office). *Fax:* (345) 472-6066 (office).

**MARVIN, Roberta (Montemorra);** Musicologist; b. 29 July 1953, Massachusetts, USA; m. Conrad A Marvin, 30 June 1973. *Education:* BM, Boston Conservatory of Music, 1975; MA, Tufts University, 1986; PhD, Brandeis University, 1992. *Career:* Lecturer, Tufts University, 1991–92; Visiting Assistant Professor, Boston University, 1992–93; Assistant Professor, University of Alabama, 1993–97; Associate Professor, University of Iowa, 1997–; mem, American Musicological Society; Royal Musical Association; Advisory Board, American Institute of Verdi Studies. *Publications:* Artistic Concerns and Practical Considerations in the Composition of I masnadieri, Studi Verdiani 7, 1992; A Verdi Autograph and the Problem of Authenticity, Studi

Verdiani 9, 1993; Shakespeare and Primo Ottocento Opera: The Case of Rossini's Otello, The Opera and Shakespeare, 1994; Aspects of Tempo in Verdi's Early and Middle Period Italian Operas, Verdi's Middle Period: Source Studies, Analysis and Performance Practice (1849–59), 1997; Giuseppe Verdi's I Masnadieri, critical edition (editor); The Censorship of Verdi's Operas in Victorian London, Music and Letters, 2001; Verdi's Sinfonia in Re maggiore (Ed). *Contributions:* The New Grove Dictionary of Opera, 1992; and The New Grove Dictionary of Music and Musicians, revised edition; Music Quarterly, 2000. *Honours:* Premio Internazionale 'Giuseppe Verdi', 1991; Fulbright Research Fellowships, 1988, 1993; American Philosophical Society, 1992; NEH Summer Stipend, 1993. *Address:* University of Iowa, School of Music, Voxman Music Building, Iowa City, IA 52242, USA.

**MARWOOD, Anthony;** British violinist; *Artistic Director, Irish Chamber Orchestra;* b. 6 July 1965, London. *Education:* RAM Jr Dept, Guildhall School of Music and Drama. *Career:* Wigmore Hall debut 1987; leader, Raphael Ensemble 1989–98; Prom debut, London 1993; founder mem., Florestan Trio 1995–; première of Sally Beamish's violin concerto 1995, and subsequent premières of works by Judith Weir, Rudi van Dijk, Peteris Vasks and Thomas Adès, including Violin Concerto 2005; Prof. of Violin, Guildhall School of Music and Drama 1999–; appearances at Yellow Barn Festival, Vermont, USA July each year; regular appearances as soloist and dir, Acad. of St Martin in the Fields; collaboration with the South Asian dancer, Mayuri Boonham 1999–; Artistic Dir, Irish Chamber Orchestra 2006–. *Recordings:* Schumann Trios (with Florestan Trio), Schumann Sonatas (with Susan Tomes, Coleridge Taylor and Somervell Concertos), Peteris Vasks and Kurt Weill Concertos, Vivaldi's Four Seasons. *Honours:* first prize Shell-LSO competition 1982, Royal Philharmonic Soc. Award (with Florestan Trio). *Current Management:* Owen/White Management, Top Floor, 59 Lansdown Place, Hove, East Sussex BN3 1FL, England. *E-mail:* info@owenwhitemanagement.com (office). *Website:* www.anthonymarwood.com.

**MÄRZENDORFER, Ernst;** Conductor; b. 26 May 1921, Salzburg, Austria. *Education:* Salzburg Mozarteum with Clemens Krauss. *Career:* conducted opera in Salzburg from 1940; Graz Opera 1945–51; Prof., Salzburg Mozarteum 1951; conductor of the Mozarteum orchestra 1953–58, including tour of the USA 1956; has also conducted at the Teatro Colón, Buenos Aires, the Deutsche Oper, Berlin, the Vienna Staatsoper, Vienna Volksoper, Vienna Redoutensaal, concerts world-wide; recent performances include: Bartók violaconcert and Strauss Symphonia domestica in Nice, Dallpiccola and Cherubini Sinfonia in D at the Todi festival, Rosenkavalier in Vienna, Schweigsame Frau in Dresden, Bruckner's 5th in Nantes-Angers 1998; Johann Strauss Konzert, Schweigsame Frau and Rosenkavalier in Vienna, Schweigsame Frau in Dresden 2000; Ariadne auf Naxos in Vienna, Schumann Violoncello Konzert and Strauss Sinfonia domestica in Angers-Nantes, and Wagner Siegfried-Idyll and Bruckner's 6th in Klagenfurt 2001; Symphonieorchester des Bayrischen Rundfunks, Strauss Macbeth in München 2002; Beethoven's 9th in Timisoara, Enescu's Oedipe at Bucharest Festival and R. Strauss 2nd Horn Concerto and Sinfonia domestica in Venice 2003. *Recordings:* Haydn Boccherini Violoncello concerts 1965, Haydn, Complete Symphonies 1970–73, Mozart Symphonies 1968–69, Schubert 5 Deutsche Tänze 1968, Mendelssohn Concerto for violin, piano and strings 1968, Rodrigo Concierto Serenada and Boieldieu Concerto 1969, Ginastera Piano Concerto Solo Hilde Somer 1963, J. Strauss Eine Nact in Venedig 1963, Meyerbeer Les Huguenots 1963, Beethoven Egmont Cavalieri Rappresentazione di anima e di corpo 1963, Schreker Der ferne Klang 1963, Pfitzner Das Christelflein 1963, Schmidt Fredigundis 1963, Josef Strauss Waltzes, Polkas, Dances 2000. *Address:* c/o Vienna Volksoper, Währingerstrasse 78, 1090 Vienna, Austria.

**MASHAYEKHI, Nader;** Composer and Conductor; b. 25 Oct. 1958, Tehran, Iran; m. Gisela Beer, 9 June 1990. *Education:* Studied at Hochschule für Musik, Vienna, Composition, Conducting, Electronic Music. *Career:* Debut: Konzerthaus Festival, Vienna, 1992; Opera performance, Malakut, Vienna Modern, 1997; Pentimento for full orchestra, in Festival Steierische Herbst, 1998; Mise en scène for ensemble in Berlin Philharmonie, mem, Ensemble Wien 2001. *Compositions:* Malakut, opera; Pentimentos, for orchestra; Sonne, for orchestra; Mahler: Das Lied von der Erde, adaptation for ensemble. *Recordings:* Duell for 2 flutes on Tomio and Mari Duo Album; Malakut; Music for flute in the 20th Century; Flute Music, with Gisela Mashayekhi-Beer. *Publications:* Articles in music journals. *Address:* Loudon str 6-8/3, 1140 Vienna, Austria.

**MASHEK, Michal;** Pianist; b. 17 Sept. 1980, Usti Nad Labem, Czechoslovakia. *Education:* Music Conservatory, Teplice; Music Conservatory in Prague. *Career:* Television documentary, Goldberg Variations; Radio Prague recordings, Goldberg Variations and Beethoven Sonata Op 81a. *Recordings:* Fantaisie and Toccata by B Martinů; Goldberg Variations by J. S. Bach. *Honours:* First Prize, International Piano Competition 'Virtuosi Per Musica di Pianoforte'; First Prize in International Beethoven piano competition. *Address:* Vodarska 128, 40331 Usti nad Labem, Czech Republic.

**MASLANKA, David (Henry);** Composer; b. 30 Aug. 1943, Maryland, USA. *Education:* Studied at the New England Conservatory 1959–61, Oberlin College, BMus, 1965, and Michigan State University, PhD, 1965–70. *Career:* Teacher, State University of New York at Geneseo, 1970–74; Sarah Lawrence College, 1974–80; Kingsborough College, City University of New York, 1981–90; Freelance Composer, 1990–. *Compositions include:* Orchestra: Symphony No. 1, 1970; Five songs for soprano, baritone and orchestra,

1976; In Lonely Fields, for percussion and orchestra, 1997; Percussion: Crown of Thorns, 1991; Montana Music: Three Dances for Percussion, 1993; Chamber: Duo for flute and piano, 1972; Quintet No. 1 for wind, 1984; Sonata for alto saxophone and piano, 1988; Sonata for horn and piano, 1996; Wind ensemble: Concerto for piano, winds and percussion, 1976; A Child's Garden of Dreams, 1981; Symphony No. 2, 1987; In Memorium, 1989; Symphony No. 3, 1991; Symphony No. 4, 1993; Mass, 1995; Sea Dreams: Concerto for Two Horns and Wind Orchestra, 1997; Vocal: Anne Sexton Songs for soprano and piano, 1975; The Hungry Heart, for chorus, 1996; Black Dog Songs, for tenor and piano, 1996. *Recordings:* David Maslanka Wind Quintets; Wind Music of David Maslanka; Tears; Mass; Percussion Music of David Maslanka; When Angels Speak; Prevailing Winds. *Honours:* MacDowell Colony Fellowships; Grants from National Endowment for the Arts, Martha Baird Rockefeller, ASCAP, National Symphony Orchestra. *Address:* 2625 Strand Avenue, Missoula, Montana 59804, USA.

**MASON, Andrew,** BMus; British clarinettist; b. 30 Sept. 1977, Kent, England. *Education:* Royal Coll. of Music (Foundation Scholar), studied with Colin Bradbury, Janet Hilton, Robert Hill, Michael Harris. *Career:* solo performances for Park Lane Group at Purcell Room and Wigmore Hall; solo broadcasts for BBC Radio 3; mem. of Aurora Ensemble 1997–; performances St David's Hall, Cardiff, Bridgewater Hall, Manchester, Purcell Room (Park Lane Group), St Martin in the Fields, Cheltenham and Chelmsford Festivals; 'Sounds Exciting' education project 2000–; performs for Live Music Now! with London Clarinet Quartet and the Aurora Ensemble; freelance orchestral musician. *Honours:* prizewinner with Aurora Ensemble, Music d'Ensemble, Paris Conservatoire 2001, Royal Coll. of Music Thurston Clarinet Prize, Royal Coll. of Music Roger Fallows Memorial Prize. *Address:* 40 Westgate Road, Faversham, Kent ME13 8HF, England. *E-mail:* arm1977@btinternet.com. *Website:* www.auroraensemble.com.

**MASON, Anne;** singer (mezzo-soprano); b. 1954, Lincolnshire, England. *Education:* Royal Academy of Music with Marjorie Thomas, National Opera Studio. *Career:* Welsh National Opera Chorus, 1977–79; Opera North from 1982 as Fenena in Nabucco, and in Madama Butterfly; English National Opera 1983, as a Valkyrie in a new production of Die Walküre; Innsbruch Early Music Festival 1983, in Cesti's Il Tito, conducted by Alan Curtis; Kent Opera and Scottish Opera 1984, in new productions of King Priam by Tippett and Edward Harper's Hedda Gabler; Covent Garden appearances in Carmen, as Mercedes; Otello, Emilia; Das Rheingold, Madama Butterfly, Die Walküre, La Clemenza di Tito, Cenerentola, Rosenkavalier, Traviata and Götterdämmerung; Glyndebourne Tour 1987, as Dorabella in Così fan tutte; Recent engagements as Annius in La Clemenza di Tito at Aix, Casoi fan tutte with Welsh National Opera and as Marcellina in Le nozze di Figaro in Madrid; Season 1992 as Donna Clara in the stage premiere of Gerhard's The Duenna, at Madrid, as Henrietta Maria in I Puritani at Covent Garden and Cornelia in Julius Caesar for Scottish Opera; Second Maid in Elektra at the First Night at the 1993 London Proms; Sang Gertrude in Hansel and Gretel for Scottish Opera, 1996; Minsk Woman in the premiere of Jonathan Dove's Flight, Glyndebourne, 1998; Season 2000–01 as Fricka in Das Rheingold at Edinburgh, Verdi's Fenena for ENO and Mozart's Marcellina for WNO; Concerts in the United Kingdom, Germany, France, Austria and Belgium, notably in The Dream of Gerontius and Verdi's Requiem. *Recordings:* Video of HMS Pinafore; Helen in King Priam; Second Bridesmaid in Le nozze di Figaro, conducted by Solti; Marcellina, Figaro, with Haitink; Emilia di Liverpool, Opera Rara. *Honours:* Gerhardt Lieder Prize, the Recital Diploma and the Countess of Munster Award, at the Royal Academy of Music; Finalist in the 1983 Benson and Hedges Gold Award; ARAM of Royal Academy of Music.

**MASON, Barry;** British lutenist, classical guitarist and music director; b. 6 Sept. 1947, Cottingham, Yorkshire, England; m. Glenda Simpson 1983. *Education:* Hull College of Technology, Royal Academy of Music with Anthony Rooley and David Munrow, Royal College of Music with Dian Poulton. *Career:* debut, Purcell Room, 1973; Director, Camerata of London, 1974; Director, 1st Early Music Centre Festival, London, 1977; Director, Progress Instruments Tours, Japan, Europe and USA, 1978; The Wicked Lady film, BBC Shakespeare Films; Director, The Guitarist's Companion, 1986; mem, Council Member, Early Music Centre. *Recordings:* Popular Music From The Time of Elizabeth I; The Muses Garden of Delights; Music For Kings and Courtiers'; The Queens Men; Thomas Companion; Elizabethan Ayres and Duets. *Publications:* contrib. to Guitar International; Early Music News; Early Music Magazine; Music in Education. *Honours:* Peter Latham Award for Musicology, Royal Academy of Music, 1971; 1996 Britten Award for Composition. *Current Management:* Francesca McManus, 71 Priory Road, Kew Gardens, Richmond, Surrey TW9 3PH, England.

**MASON, Benedict;** Composer; b. 21 June 1955, Budleigh, Salterton, England. *Education:* King's College, Cambridge; Study with Peter Maxwell Davies, and with Henri Pousseur in Liège. *Compositions include:* Hinterstoisser Traverse, for 12 players, 1986; Lighthouses of England and Wales, for orchestra, 1987; Oil and Petrol Marks on a Wet Road are Sometimes Held to be Spots where a Rainbow Stood, for 16 voices, 1987; Concerto for the Viola Section, 1990; Self-Referential songs and Realistic Virelais for soprano and 16 players, 1990; Six Rilke songs, 10991; Animals and the origins of Dance, for 21 players, 1992; Music for Concert Halls, Nos 1–10, 1993–97; 2 string quartets, 1987, 1993; Schumann Auftrag: Live Hörspiel ohne Worte, 1994, Opera, Playing Away, 1994; Szene, for female voices, orchestra and sampler, 1998.

*Honours:* Winner, Benjamin Britten Composers Competition, 1998; Siemens Stiftungspreis, 1992. Address c/o 7 Gerard Rd, Harrow, Middx, HAI 2 ND, England.

**MASON, Marilyn;** Organist; b. 29 June 1925, Oklahoma, USA. *Education:* Studied in OK State University, at the University of Michigan, Union Theological Seminary NY, and with Nadia Boulanger, Maurice Duruflé and Arnold Schoenberg. *Career:* Teacher at the University of Michigan, 1947, Chairman of organ department, 1962, Professor 1965; Recital tours of North America, Europe, Australia, Africa and South America; Concerts with the Detroit and Philadelphia Orchestras; 60 Commissions for such composers as Krenek, Cowell, Albright, Ulysses Kay, Sowerby and Ross Lee Finney. *Recordings:* Albums of music by Sessions, Satie, Schoenberg and Virgil Thomson; Recording the music of Pachelbel for the Musical Heritage Society. *Address:* The University of Michigan, School of Music, Ann Arbor, MI 48109, USA.

**MASQUELIN, Martine;** Singer (Soprano); b. 1957, Paris, France. *Education:* Studied at the Paris Conservatoire. *Career:* Debut: Montpellier, 1982 as Lakmé; Düsseldorf, 1983, as Strauss's Sophie and Rossini's Rosina; Liège, 1988–89 as Julietta and Edvige in Offenbach's Robinson Crusoe; Appearances throughout France as Massenet's Thais and Violetta; Saint Care Festival; Concerts in Paris and elsewhere. *Recordings:* Monteverdi's Poppea; Grétry's Zémire et Azor. *Address:* c/o Opéra Royale de Wallome, 1 Rue des Dominicains, 4000 Liège, Belgium.

**MASSARD, Robert;** Singer (Baritone); b. 15 Aug. 1925, Pau, France. *Education:* Conservatories of Pau and Bayonne. *Career:* Sang the High Priest in Samson et Dalila at the Paris Opéra, 1952; Thoas in Iphigénie en Tauride at Aix, 1952; Sang Ashton in Lucia di Lammermoor at the Paris Opéra 1957; Glyndebourne 1958, in Alceste; Orestes in Iphigénie en Tauride with the Covent Garden Company at Edinburgh, 1961; Sang Fieramosca in Benvenuto Cellini with the Royal Opera in London; Bolshoi Theatre Moscow 1962, as Rigoletto; La Scala Milan 1967, as Valentin in Faust; Paris 1974, as Sancho Panza in Massenet's Don Quichotte; Other roles include Nero in L'Incoronazione di Poppea, the Count in Capriccio, Milhaud's Orpheus, Escamillo and Ravel's Ramiro. *Recordings:* Iphigénie en Tauride; Mireille; Thais; Rigoletto; Benvenuto Cellini; Raimbaud in Le Comte Ory, Chant du Monde. *Address:* c/o Philips, Polygram Classics, PO Box 1420, 1 Sussex Place, Hammersmith, London W6 9XS, England.

**MASSET, Francoise;** Singer (Soprano); b. 1970, France. *Education:* Douai Conservatoire; Opera Studio of the Baroque Music Centre, Versailles. *Career:* Appearances throughout France in Chabrier's Une Education manquée, Purcell's Dido and Aeneas and Mozart's Bastien und Bastienne; Chanteuse and Comedienne. *Recordings:* Title role, La Diane de Fontainebleau by Desmarets; Lully's Acis et Galatée; Rameau's Dardanus; Melisse in Gluck's Armide. *Address:* c/o DG Archiv Recordings, 22 St Peter's Square, London W6 9NW, England.

**MASSEY, Andrew (John),** BA, MA; American (b. British) conductor; *Resident Conductor, The Milwaukee Symphony*; b. 1 May 1946, Nottingham, England; m. Sabra A. Todd 29 May 1982; one s. one d. *Education:* Merton College, Oxford 1968, Dartington Summer School with Hans Keller, Witold Lutoslawski and Luciano Berio. *Career:* debut, Cleveland 1978; Asst Conductor Cleveland Orchestra, USA 1978–80; Assoc. Conductor New Orleans Symphony Orchestra 1980–86, San Francisco Symphony Orchestra 1986–; Music Dir Rhode Island Philharmonic 1986–1991, Fresno Philharmonic 1986–93, Music Dir 1987–1992; Music Dir Toledo Symphony, Ohio 1990–2002; guest appearances with Nat. Symphony, Pittsburgh, Vancounver Symphony, Milwaukee Symphony (currently Resident Conductor), San Diego Symphony and others; mem. American Fed. of Musicians; Dreyfus Fellow, Millay Colony for the Arts 2004. *Compositions:* Marina for soprano and chamber ensemble 1973, Cadenza for Winter (solo violin) 2002, Early Morning for orchestra 2003. *Current Management:* John Gingrich Management, PO Box 1515, New York, NY 10023, USA. *Telephone:* (802) 598-7710. *E-mail:* ErsteKappelmeister@gmail.com (office); dom9th@yahoo.com (home). *Website:* www.andrewmassey.com.

**MASSEY, Roy Cyril,** MBE, BMus, FRCO (chm), ADCM, ARCM; British organist and choral conductor; b. 9 May 1934, England; m. Ruth Carol Craddock Grove 1975. *Education:* Univ. of Birmingham, studied with David Willcocks. *Career:* organist, St Alban's, Conybere Street, Birmingham 1953–60, St Augustine's, Edgbaston 1960–65, Croydon Parish Church 1965–68; conductor, Croydon Bach Soc. 1966–68; Special Commissioner, Royal School of Church Music 1964–; organist to the City of Birmingham Choir 1954–; organist, Master of Choristers, Birmingham Cathedral 1968–74; Dir of Music, King Edward's School, Birmingham 1968–74; conductor, Hereford Choral Soc. 1974–2001; organist, Master of Choristers, Hereford Cathedral 1974–2001; Conductor-in-Chief, alternate years Assoc. Conductor, Three Choirs Festival 1975–2001; adviser on organs to Dioceses of Birmingham and Hereford 1974–; led the premieres of Geofrey Burgon's Requiem, Veni Sancte Spiritus by William Mathias, and Te Deum by Paul Patterson; Pres., Royal Coll. of Organists 2003–05; mem. Royal Soc. of Musicians 1991. *Honours:* Hon. FRSCM 1971, Hon. DMus (Cantuar) 1991, Hon. Fellowship of the Guild of Church Musicians 2000. *Address:* 2 King John's Court, Tewkesbury, Gloucestershire, GL20 6EG, England.

**MASSIS, Annick;** Singer (Soprano); b. 1960, France. *Education:* Studied at the Francis Poulenc Conservatoire, Paris. *Career:* Debut: Toulouse, 1991; Engagements include Ophélie in Hamlet and Philéne in Mignon by Thomas at Compiègne; Rosina, Micaela and Anna in The Merry Wives of Windsor at the Opéra-Comique, Paris; Carolina in Il Matrimonio Segreto at Nantes and Aricie (Hippolyte et Aricie by Rameau) at the Paris Opéra Garnier and the Brooklyn Academy of Music; Lucia di Lammermoor at Rouen and as Countess Adèle in Le Comte Ory at the 1997 Glyndebourne Festival; Season 1997–98 as Gluck's Eurydice and Marie in La Fille du Régiment at Geneva; Bizet's Leila at Toulouse and Countess Adèle at Florence and Montpellier; Season 1998 as Ophelia in Hamlet at Washington and Lucia di Lammermoor at the New York Met; Ophelia's Mad Scene from Hamlet by Thomas at the 1999 London Prom concerts; Season 2000–01 as Lucia di Lammermoor at Barcelona, Amina in Madrid and Philine in Mignon at Toulouse; Title role in first modern performance of Meyerbeer's Margherita d'Anjou (concert), Festival Hall 2002; Lucia di Lammermoor at the Met, 2002; Engaged as the Queen of Shemakha in The Golden Cockerel, San Francisco, 2003;. *Address:* c/o Grand Théâtre de Genève, 11 Boulevard du Théâtre, 1211 Geneva 11, Switzerland.

**MASSIS, René;** Singer (Baritone); b. 1946, Lyon, France. *Education:* Studied in Lyon and Milan. *Career:* Debut: Marseille 1976, as Silvio in Pagliacci; Sang in L'Heure Espagnole at La Scala (1978) and has appeared throughout France and Italy; Lucca 1985 in Dejanice by Catalani, Paris Opéra 1988, as Valentin in Faust; Paris Opéra-Comique, 1990, in Auber's Manon Lescaut and at Nice Opéra 1990–91, in Wozzeck and as Guglielmo; Other roles include Rossini's Figaro (Glyndebourne Touring Opera, 1989), Mozart's Count, Belcore, Verdi's Ford and Posa, Fieramosca in Benvenuto Cellini, Eugene Onegin and the Marquis in Massenet's Grisélidis; Sang the title role in the premiere of Goya by Prodromidès, Montpellier, 1996; Season 1999–2000 as Tonio in Pagliacci at Nice, Albert in Werther at Lille and Donizetti's Sulpice for Opéra du Rhin, Strasbourg. *Recordings include:* Chausson's Le Roi Arthus (Erato) Iphigénie en Aulide and La Juive (Philips). *Address:* Théâtre de L'Opéra de Nice, 1a 6 Rue St François de Paule, 06300 Nice, France.

**MASSON, Askell;** Icelandic composer and musician; b. 21 Nov. 1953, Reykjavík. *Education:* Reykjavík Children's School of Music, Reykjavík Coll. of Music, studied with Patrick Savill in London, England, percussion with James Blades. *Career:* debut, Icelandic television playing own music 1969; composer 1967–; composer, instrumentalist, Nat. Theatre of Iceland 1973–75; Prod., Icelandic State Radio 1978–83; Gen. Sec., Icelandic League of Composers 1983–85; Chair., STEF, Iceland Performing Right Soc. 1989–99; working solely on composition. *Compositions include:* The Ice Palace (opera) 1995, Sinfonia Trilogia 1992, Piano Concerto 1985, Concert Piece for snare drum and orchestra 1982, Sonata for violin and piano 1993, Woodwind Quintet 1991, Trio for piano trio 1995, Meditation for organ 1992, Sindur for percussion quartet 1989, Okto November for strings 1982, Run for orchestra 1994, Chamber Symphony 1997, Boreas for tuba 1999. *Recordings:* Marimba Concerto, Clarinet Concerto, Trio, Sonata, Partita, Hrim, Snow, Helfro and others. *Address:* PO Box 821, 121 Reykjavík, Iceland. *E-mail:* askellmasson@hotmail.com. *Website:* www.editions-bim.com.

**MASSON, Diego;** Conductor; b. 21 June 1935, Tossa, Spain. *Education:* Paris Conservatoire, 1953–59; Study with Leibowitz, Maderna and Boulez. *Career:* Worked as percussionist in Paris with the ensemble Domaine Musicale; Founded Musique Vivante, 1966; Conducted premieres of Stockhausen's Stop and Setz die Segel zur Sonne; Early performances of works by Boulez including Domaines and... explosante fixe... and Berio; Musical Director of Marseilles Opéra and Ballet-Theatre Contemporian, Angers; Guest engagements as orchestral conductor in France, Europe, Australia and New Zealand; Conducted La Bohème for Opera North, 1989, premiere of Caritas by Robert Saxton, 1991; Premiere of Il giudizio Universidade by Claudio Ambrosini at Citti dilastelle, 1996; Conducted Turnage's Greek at the Queen Elizabeth Hall, London, 1998; Premiere of Sally Beamish's Monster, Scottish Opera at Glasgow, 2002. *Recordings:* Boulez, Domaine, Globokar, Fluide and Ausstrahlungen; John Woolrich; Stockhausen Aus den sieben tagen, and Liaison; Keuris Alto saxophone concerto. *Current Management:* Ingpen & Williams Ltd, 7 St George's Court, 131 Putney Bridge Road, London, SW15 2PA, England.

**MASTERS, Rachel;** Harpist; b. 9 Sept. 1958, Purley, Surrey, England. *Education:* Junior Student, Guildhall School of Music and Drama, 1971–75; National Youth Orchestra, 1972–76; Scholar, Royal College of Music, 1976–80; ARCM, Honours. *Career:* Debut: Wigmore Hall, 22 June 1982; Joint Winner, SE Arts Young Concert Artists Award, 1979; Joint 2nd Prize, Mobil Oil Harp Competition, 1980; Incorporated Society of Musicians Young Concert Artist, 1981; Principal harp in London Philharmonic Orchestra, since 1989; Professor at Royal College of Music. *Recordings:* Mozart Flute and Harp Concerto, with Phillipa Davies, City of London Sinfonia and Richard Hickox; Chandos: Harp pieces by Debussy, Ravel, Glière, Ginastera and Alwyn; Britten: Ceremony of Carols with King's College, Cambridge. *Honours:* Jack Morrison, Elisabeth Coates, Harp Prizes, Royal College of Music. *Address:* 31 Westfield Road, Surbiton, Surrey KT 6 4EL, England.

**MASTERS, Robert;** Violinist; b. 16 March 1917, Ilford, Essex, England. *Education:* Royal Academy of Music, London. *Career:* Leader, Robert Masters Piano Quartet, 1940–63; Professor of Violin, Royal Academy of Music, London, 1947–64; Leader, Bath Festival Orchestra and Menuhin Festival Orchestra, 1960–75; Leader, London Mozart Players, 1961–78; Director of Music, Yehudi

Menuhin School, England, 1968–80; Co-Director, Menuhin Music Academy, Gstaad, Switzerland, 1980–84; Guest Professor, Taiwan Universities, 1980–; Beijing and Shanghai Conservatories of Music, Banff Arts Centre; Artistic Director, Menuhin International Violin Competition, Folkestone, 1983–95; Artistic Director, New Zealand International Violin Competition, 1992; Director of Music, Hattori Foundation for Music and Art, 1992. *Recordings:* Robert Masters Piano Quartet, Fauré Piano Quartets (Argo); Walton Piano Quartet (Argo); Skalkottas Piano Trio, with Marcel Gazelle and Derek Simpson. *Honours:* FRAM. *Address:* 72d Leopold Road, London SW19 7JQ, England.

**MASTERSON, Valerie,** CBE; British opera and concert singer; b. Birkenhead; d. of Edward Masterson and Rita McGrath; m. Andrew March; one s. one d. *Career:* Prof. of Singing, Royal Acad. of Music, London 1992–; Pres. British Youth Opera 1994–99, Vice-Pres. 2000–; has sung with D'Oyly Carte Opera, Glyndebourne, Royal Opera House, Covent Garden and English Nat. Opera and on TV and radio; also in major opera houses abroad including Paris, Aix-en-Provence, Toulouse, Munich, Geneva, San Francisco and Chicago. *Opera roles include:* La Traviata, Manon, Semele, Merry Widow, Louise, Lucia di Lammermoor, Mireille; other leading roles in Faust, Alcina, Die Entführung aus dem Serail, Le Nozze di Figaro, Così fan Tutte, La Bohème, Magic Flute, Julius Caesar, Rigoletto, Orlando, Der Rosenkavalier, Xerxes, The Pearl Fishers, Die Fledermaus etc. *Recordings include:* Julius Caesar, La Traviata, Elisabetta Regina d'Inghilterra, Bitter Sweet, Ring Cycle, recitals and various Gilbert and Sullivan discs. *Honours:* Hon. FRCM 1992, RAM 1993; Hon. DLitt (South Bank Univ.) 1999; Award for Outstanding Individual Performance of the Year in a New Opera, Soc. of West End Theatre 1983. *Address:* c/o Music International, 13 Ardilaun Road, London, N5 2QR, England.

**MASTILOVIC, Daniza;** Singer (Soprano); b. 7 Nov. 1933, Negotin, Serbia. *Education:* Belgrade Conservatory with Nikola Cvejic. *Career:* Sang operetta in Belgrade, 1955–57; Minor roles at Bayreuth from 1956; Joined Georg Solti at Frankfurt Opera, 1959, debut as Tosca; Guest appearances in Hamburg, Düsseldorf, Zagreb, Vienna and Munich; Teatro Colón Buenos Aires 1972, as Abigaille in Nabucco; Zürich 1973, as Ortrud in Lehengrin; Covent Garden 1973–75, as Elektra; Metropolitan Opera 1975, as Elektra; Commemorated the 50th anniversary of Puccini's death with a performance of Turandot at Torre del Lago, 1974; Landestheater Salzburg 1987, as Clytemnestra in Elektra. *Address:* c/o Landestheater, Schwarzstrasse 22, 5020 Salzburg, Austria.

**MASTROMEI, Giampietro;** Singer (Baritone); b. 1 Nov. 1932, Camoire, Tuscany, Italy. *Education:* Studied in Buenos Aires with Apollo Granforte, Mario Melani and Hilda Spani. *Career:* Sang at the Teatro Colón, Buenos Aires for 13 seasons from 1952; European debut, 1962, appearing in France and Italy, and at the Covent Garden, 1973, as Renato, Un Ballo in Maschera and Amonasro; Verona Arena, 1971–86, as Amonasro and Scarpia; Further appearances at Caracas, Bilbao, Tokyo, Barcelona, Hamburg, Madrid, San Francisco, Dallas and Philadelphia; Also sang Verdi's Iago and Rigoletto and roles in operas by Pergolesi, Scarlatti and Dallapiccola. *Recordings:* Simon Boccanegra; Il Corsaro; Aida.

**MASUR, Kurt;** German conductor; *Principal Conductor, London Philharmonic Orchestra;* b. 18 July 1927, Brieg, Silesia, Poland. *Education:* Nat. Music School, Breslau, Hochschule für Musik, Leipzig. *Career:* theatre conductor in Erfurt and Leipzig 1948–55, conductor, Dresden Philharmonic 1955–58, Chief Conductor 1967–72; Gen. Musical Dir, Mecklenburg State Theatre 1958–60; Prin. Musical Dir, Komische Oper in East Berlin 1960–64; Musical Dir Dresden Philharmonic 1967–72; Conductor, Leipzig Gewandhaus Orchestra 1970–96, Music Dir 1996–; UK début with New Philharmonia Orchestra 1973; début in USA with Cleveland Orchestra 1974; Music Dir Conductor New York Philharmonic 1991–2002; Prin. Conductor London Philharmonic Orchestra 1991–; Music Dir Orchestre nat. de France 2002–; has toured extensively in Europe and the USA. *Honours:* Freeman of City of Leipzig; Hon. Pres. Kulturstiftung, Leipzig Officier, Légion d'honneur, Bundesverdienstkreuz; Hon. Citizen of Brieg (Poland), Commdr Cross of Merit (Poland) 1999 hon. degrees from seven American univs and Univ. of Leipzig. *Address:* Masur Music International Inc., Ansonia PO Box 231478, New York, NY 10023, USA (office). *Telephone:* (646) 623-5803 (office). *Fax:* (212) 414-8276 (office). *E-mail:* stefana@muasurmusic.com (office). *Website:* www.kurtmasur.com (office).

**MASUROK, Yuri;** Ukrainian singer (baritone); b. 18 July 1931, Krasnik, Poland. *Education:* Lvov Institute and Moscow Conservatoire. *Career:* Sang at the Bolshoi, Moscow, from 1963, debut as Eugene Oengin; Vienna Staatsoper as Scarpia, Luna and Escamilio; Aix-en-Provence, 1976, as Germont in La Traviata; Covent Garden debut 1975, as Renato in Un Ballo in Maschera; Returned to London as Posa in Don Carlos, Eugene Onegin and Count di Luna; US debut at Metropolitan Opera 1975, with Bolshoi Company; San Francisco, 1977, as Renato; Metropolitan debut as Germont, 1978; Covent Garden 1983 and 1986, as Luna and Germont; Sang at Wiesbaden 1987 as Scarpia, Budapest as Robert in Iolanta, with the company of the Bolshoi Theatre; Gran Teatre del Liceu Barcelona 1989, as Eugene Onegin; Concerts in the United Kingdom have included Wigmore Hall recitals and Festival Hall concert conducted by Svetlanov; Song repertory includes music by Ravel, Debussy, Schumann and Henze; Other operatic roles include Andrei Bolkonsky in War and Peace, Mazeppa, Rossini's Figaro and Yeletsky in

The Queen of Spades; Sang Onegin at Milwaukee, 1992; Scarpia at Metropolitan, New York, 1993 and at Moscow, 1996. *Recordings:* Eugene Onegin, Tosca, The Queen of Spades and Iolanta on Russian labels; Tosca, Il Trovatore and Boris Godunov. *Address:* c/o Bolshoi Theatre, Ochotnyj Rjad 812, 103009 Moscow, Russia.

**MATAEVA, Irina;** Singer (Soprano); b. 1972, Tumen, Russia. *Education:* St Petersburg Conservatoire, 1995–98. *Career:* Young singers Academy of the Mariinsky Theatre, St Petersburg, from 1998; Roles have included Mozart's Susanna and Barbarina, Tatiana in Eugene Onegin, Natasha in War and Peace, Lisa in la Sonnambula, Zerlina and Sofya in Semyon Kotko by Prokofiev; Appeared with the Kirov Opera in summer season at Covent Garden, 2000; London Proms, 2002. *Honours:* Prizewinner, Gumelev Vocal Competition, 1997. *Address:* c/o Kirov Opera Mariinsky Theatre, Theatre Square, St Petersburg, Russia.

**MATEJ, Daniel;** Slovak composer; b. 9 March 1963, Bratislava. *Education:* Bratislava Acad. of Music and Drama, Conservatoire National Supérior de Musique, Paris, Koninklijk Conservatorium, The Hague, Dartington Summer Music School, Deutscher Akademischer Austauschdienst residency, Berlin. *Career:* founder contemporary music ensemble, Veni 1987; Lecturer in 20th-Century Music History, Bratislava Coll. of Performing Arts 1996–. *Compositions include:* Lament 1988, Video (Billboards) 1992, Memories of You 1 (14 Variations for J. C.) 1993, Wenn wir in höchsten Nöten sein 2000, Vingt Regards 2000, John King (opera) 2001, Machaut 2001. *Recordings:* Wenn wir in höchsten Nöten sein, (with Opera Aperta Ensemble). *Address:* c/o Music Centre Slovakia, Michalská 10, 815 36 Bratislava 1, Slovakia (office). *Website:* www.hc.sk.

**MATHE, Ulrike-Anima;** German violinist; b. 5 March 1964, Freiburg. *Education:* studied in Basel, Juilliard School, Konzertexamen Detmold with Tibor Varga, masterclasses. *Career:* debut in New York 1992; extensive chamber music and solo career, Berlin, Cologne, Munich, USA, Australia, Spain, Italy, Switzerland, Prague, Salzburg, Belgium, Netherlands; Repertory: from Vivaldi to Penderecki, with the whole violin concerto repertoire. *Recordings:* Reger Solo sonatas; Korngold violin concerto; Kreisler Pieces. *Publications:* contrib. to coverage of Strad magazine, Fono Forum, NMZ, Stereoplay. *Honours:* First prize, German Music Competition, 1986; First prize, European Youth Competition, 1985; Young Concert Artists Award, 1988; Fifth prize, Queen Elizabeth Competition, 1989. *Current Management:* SKS Russ, Charlottenplatz 17, 70173 Stuttgart, Germany. *E-mail:* ulrike .mathe@debitel.net.

**MATHER, Bruce;** Composer and Pianist; b. 9 May 1939, Toronto, Canada; m. Pierrette LePage. *Education:* Studied composition at the Royal Conservatory of Music in Toronto, in Paris with Roy Harris, Boulez, Milhaud and Messiaen, Universities of Stanford and Toronto, PhD, 1967. *Career:* Teacher at McGill University Montreal from 1966; Solo piano recitals and piano duet performances with Pierrette LePage. *Compositions:* Five Madrigals for soprano and ensemble, 1967–73; Music for Vancouver, 1969; Musique pour Rouen for string orchestra 1971; Music for Organ, Horn and Gongs, 1973; Eine Kleine Blassermusik, 1975; Au Chateau de Pompariain for Mezzo and Orchestra, 1977; Musique pour Champigny for vocal soloists and ensemble 1976; Ausone for 11 instruments 1979; Musigny for orchestra, 1980; Barbaresco for viola, cello and double bass, 1984; Scherzo for orchestra 1987; Dialogue pour trio basso et orchestre, 1988; Travauz de nuit, for baritone and Chamber orchestra, 1990; Princesse Blanche, opera, 1994; Tallbrem Variations, for 5 percussion and orchestra, 1995. Songs. *Address:* c/o SOCAN, 41 Valleybrook Drive, Don Mills, Ontario M3B 2S6, Canada.

**MATHER, Martin;** Composer; b. 6 Oct. 1927, Harrow, England (Australian National). *Education:* BA (Hons), University of London, 1948; Royal College of Music, with Herbert Howells and Frank Merrick, 1952–55. *Career:* Resident in Australia from 1956; Public Library of New South Wales, 1958–72; Freelance composer; mem, Fellowship of Australian Composers. *Compositions include:* Last Voyage of Matthew Flanders for soprano, tenor, chorus and orchestra, 1965; ANZAC Requiem for soloists, chorus and orchestra, 1967; Sextet, 1975; Fourteen Lieder for baritone and piano, 1986; Homage to Pushkin for baritone and piano, 1988; Twenty Four Preludes for piano, 1994; Entr'actes for piano solo, 1998. *Recordings include:* ANZAC Requiem, with the Adelaide Symphony Orchestra; Sounds Australian, 1976. *Honours:* Patrons Fund Award, RCM, 1954. *Address:* c/o APRA, 1A Eden Street, Crows Nest, NSW 2065, Australia.

**MATHES, Rachel (Clarke);** Opera Singer (Soprano) and College Professor; b. 14 March 1941, Atlanta, Georgia, USA. *Education:* BA, Music, Birmingham-Southern College, 1962; MM, Vocal Performance, 1988, DMA, Vocal Performance, 1991, University of South Carolina; Study at Akademie für Musik und Darstellende Kunst, Vienna, Austria, 1962–63. *Career:* Debut: Aida at Basel, Switzerland, 1965; Deutsche Oper am Rhein, Düsseldorf, Germany, 1965–71; Freelance throughout Europe, 1971–74; Metropolitan Opera, New York, 1974–77, debut as Donna Anna; New York City Opera, 1975, debut as Turandot; Wolf Trap Festival, Verdi's Requiem, 1975; Glasgow Opera, as Donna Anna, 1975. *Recordings:* Highlights from Mozart's Don Giovanni with the Glasgow Opera, 1975. *Address:* c/o Augustana College Music Department, Rock Island, IL 61201, USA.

**MATHIESEN, Thomas James,** BMus, MMus, DMA; American musicologist; *David H. Jacobs Chair in Music, Indiana University*; b. 30 April 1947, Roslyn

Heights, NY; m. Penelope Jay Price 1971. *Education:* Willamette Univ., Univ. of Southern California. *Career:* Lecturer in Musicology, Univ. of Southern California, Los Angeles 1971–72; Prof. of Music and Head Musicology Area 1972–86, Assoc. Dean, Honours and General Education 1986–88, Brigham Young Univ., Provo, UT; Prof. of Music 1988–96, Distinguished Prof. 1996–, Dir of the Center History of Music Theory and Literature 1998–, David H. Jacobs Chair in Music 1998–, Indiana Univ.; mem. American Acad. of Arts and Sciences. *Publications:* as Project Director: Thesaurus Musicarum Latinarum, Doctoral Dissertations in Musicology; A Bibliography of Sources for The Study of Ancient Greek Music, 1974; General Editor, Greek and Latin Music Theory, 1982–2004, 10 vols; Aristides Quintilianus on Music in Three Books: Translation, with Introduction, Commentary and Annotations, 1983; Ancient Greek Music Theory: A Catalogue Raisonné of Manuscripts, 1988 (Duckles Award, 1989); Editor, Festa Musicologica: Essays in Honor of George J Buelow, 1995; Greek Views of Music, 1997; Apollo's Lyre: Greek Music and Music Theory in Antiquity and the Middle Ages, 1999 (Kinkeldey, Berry, and ASCAP-Deems Taylor Awards, 2000); Music in the Mirror: Reflections on the History of Music Theory and Literature for the 21st Century, 2002 (ASCAP-Deems Taylor Award, 2003); Gen. Ed., Studies in the History of Music Theory and Literature 2005–; contrib. to New Grove Dictionary of Music and Musicians, 2nd edn, Die Musik in Geschichte und Gegenwart, 2nd edn. *Honours:* ACLS grant 1977, NEH Fellowship 1985–86, Guggenheim Fellowship 1990–91, NEH grant 1992–96. *Address:* 1800 Valley View Drive, Ellettsville, IN 47429-9487, USA. *Website:* www.music.indiana.edu/chmtl (office).

**MATHIS, Edith;** Swiss singer (soprano); b. 11 Feb. 1938, Lucerne; m. Bernhard Klee. *Education:* Lucerne Conservatoire. *Career:* début Lucerne (in The Magic Flute) 1956; sang with Cologne Opera 1959–62; appeared Salzburg Festival 1960, Deutsche Oper, W Berlin 1963; début Glyndebourne (Cherubino in Le Nozze di Figaro) 1962, Covent Garden (Susanna in Le Nozze di Figaro) 1970, Metropolitan Opera House, New York (Pamina in The Magic Flute) 1970, Berne City Opera 1990; sang to Mendelssohn, Brahms and Schubert, Wigmore Hall, London 1997; mem. Hamburg State Opera 1960–75. *Address:* c/o Ingpen & William Ltd, 26 Wadham Road, London, SW15 2LR, England (office); c/o Bueker-Management, Postfach 1169, Hanover, Germany. *Telephone:* (20) 8874-3222 (office).

**MATORIN, Vladimir Anatolievich;** Russian singer (bass); b. 2 May 1948, Moscow; s. of Anatoly Ivanovich Matorin and Maria Tarasovna Matorina; m. Svetlana Sergeyevna Matorina; one s. *Education:* Gnessin Pedagogical Inst. (now Acad.) of Music. *Career:* soloist, Moscow Stanislavsky and Nemirovich-Danchenko Music Theatre 1974–91, Bolshoi Theatre 1991–; numerous int. tours. *Opera roles include:* Boris Godunov, Ivan Susanin, King René (Iolanthe), Gremin (Eugene Onegin), Dosifei (Khovanshchina), Count Galitsky (Prince Igor), Don Basilio (Barber of Seville), Count (Invisible City of Kitezh) and others. *Honours:* winner, All-Union Glinka Competition of vocalists and Int. Competition of Singers in Geneva, Merited Artist of Russia, People's Artist of Russia. *Address:* Bolshoi Theatre of Russia, Teatralnaya pl. 1, 103009 Moscow (office); Ulansky per. 21, korp. 1 Apt. 53, 103045 Moscow, Russia (home). *Telephone:* (095) 292-38-86 (Bolshoi Opera); (095) 280-44-17 (home).

**MATOUSEK, Bohuslav;** violinist; b. 1949, Czechoslovakia. *Education:* Jaroslav Pekelsky Vaclav Snitil; further study with Arthur Grumiaux, Nathan Milstein and Wolfgang Schniderhan. *Career:* soloist with the Tokyo Symphony Orchestra, 1977–78; Co-founder and leader of the Stamic Quartet of Prague 1980; Performances at the Prague Young Artists and the Bratislava Music Festivals; Tours to Spain, Austria, France, Switzerland, Germany and Eastern Europe; Tour of the USA 1980, debut concerts in the United Kingdom at London and Birmingham, 1983; Further British tours 1985, 1987, 1988, Warwick Arts Festival, and 1989, 20 concerts; Gave the premiere of Helmut Eder's 3rd at the Channel Islands, Festival of Czech Music; Netherlands, Finland, Austria and France; Edinburgh Festival and debut tours of Canada, Japan and Indonesia. *Recordings:* Shostakovich No. 13, Schnittke No. 4, Panton; Dvořák, Martinů and Janáček complete quartets; Haydn Violin Concertos 1–6 Supraphon, Schubet Sonatinas and Grand Duo, Denon; Brahms, Bruch Concertos; Dvořák Concerto; Brahms' Sonatas, Bayuer R E; Dvořák Complete violin and piano; Martinů Duo Concertante; B Martinů Complete violin and piano. *Honours:* with Members of Stamic Quartet: Prizewinner, Winner 1986 ORF, Austrian Radio, International String Quartet Competition followed by live broadcast from the Salzburg Mozarteum; Academie Charles Cros Grand Prix du Disque, 1991, for Dvořák quartets; 1 Prix International Violin Competition Prague, as soloist, 1972. *Current Management:* Robert Gilder & Co., Enterprise House, 59–65 Upper Ground, London, SE1 9PQ, England. *Telephone:* (20) 7928-9008. *Fax:* (20) 7928-9755. *E-mail:* rgilder@robert-gilder.com. *Address:* Dvořákova 311, 25264 Velké Prilepy, Czech Republic.

**MATOUSEK, Lukas;** Composer, Clarinettist and Performer of Medieval Instruments; b. 29 May 1943, Prague, Czechoslovakia; m. (1) Zuzana Matouskova 1966 (deceased), 2 d, (2) Zdenka Kratka 2002. *Education:* Prague Conservatory of Music; Private Study with Mil Kabelac, Composition; Janáček Academy of Music, Brno. *Career:* Artistic Director, Ars Cameralis Ensemble; Many concerts and recordings for broadcasting and television throughout Europe; Recordings as performer with Ars Cameralis, and of own works; Music Director of CD Label, Studio Matous; Dramaturge of Prague Symphony Orchestra. *Compositions include:* For Orchestra: Radices Temporis; Stories; Concerto for percussion and winds; Metamorphoses of Silence for strings; Fanfare of 17th November for 12 brass; Chamber Music: Sonata for violin and piano; Sonata for double-bass and chamber ensemble; Wind-Quintet; Aztecs for percussion, Intimate Music for viola or cello, Recollection of Mr Sudek for brass-sextet, Sonatina for clarinet and piano; Sonnet Sequence for cello and piano; Shadows and Reflections for chamber ensemble; Min-Kaleidoscope for chamber ensemble; Trio for clarinet, violin and Piano; Vocal: Three Cantatas; Colours and Thoughts; Flower of Paradise; Several Children's Choir Pieces. *Recordings:* CD, Gothic Music in Bohemia; Music of Charles University; Machaut-Chansons; L Matousek: Chamber Music. *Address:* Vápencová 10, 147 00 Prague 4, Czech Republic. *E-mail:* cameralis@volny.cz; cameralis@volny.cz. *Website:* www.musica.cz/matousekl/

**MATSUZAWA, Yuki;** Concert Pianist; b. 1960, Tokyo, Japan. *Education:* Studied with: Akiko Iguchi and Hiroshi Tamura at Tokyo University of Fine Arts; Further study with Vladimir Ashkenazy in Europe. *Career:* Concert engagements in Europe, Asia and USA; Radio and television engagements in the United Kingdom, Ireland, Netherlands, Greece, USA, Japan; Irish debut, 1990 with the Berlin Radio Symphony Orchestra; London debut, 1990 at Wigmore Hall; London appearances at: Wigmore Hall, Barbican Hall, St John's Smith Square; Concerto appearances with: Royal Philharmonic Orchestra, BBC Symphony Orchestra, Montreal Symphony Orchestra, Athens Radio Symphony Orchestra, Berlin Radio Symphony Orchestra, NHK Symphony Orchestra, New London Orchestra; Chamber music appearances with Suk Quartet in the United Kingdom and Czechoslovakia and with Martinů Quartet in the United Kingdom; Tours of the United Kingdom and Europe; Concerts with: English Chamber Orchestra, Brno Philharmonic, and Bournemouth Sinfonietta. *Recordings:* Exclusive recording contract with Novalis Records. *Honours:* Prizewinner at such competitions as Queen Elizabeth, Brussels, Maria Canals, Barcelona, and Montreal International, Canada.

**MATTEI, Peter;** Singer (Baritone); b. 1965, Sweden. *Education:* Studied in Framnas and Stockholm. *Career:* Debut: Drottningholm, 1990 as Nardo in Mozart's Finta Giardiniera's Royal Opera Stockholm, 1991 in the premiere of Backanterna by Daniel Bortz; Drottningholm, 1992–93 in Salieri's Falstaff and Haeffner's Electra; Scottish Opera, 1995 as Don Giovanni; Salzburg Festival, 1996 as Minister in Fidelio; Season 1998 as Mozart's Guglielmo for Scottish Opera and Don Giovanni at Aix; Sang Posa in Don Carlos at Stockholm, 1999; Season 2000–01 as Mozart's Figaro at Glyndebourne, Chorèbe in Les Troyens at the Barbican Hall and as Eugene Onegin in Brussels; Mahler's Symphony of a Thousand at the London Proms, 2002. *Recordings:* Electra; Carmina Burana. *Address:* c/o Scottish Opera, 39 Elmbank Crescent, Glasgow G2 4PT, Scotland.

**MATTEUZZI, William;** singer (tenor); b. 1957, Bologna, Italy. *Education:* studied with Paride Venturi. *Career:* debut singing Massenet's Des Grieux in Milan; season 1987 sang Rossini's Ramiro at Bologna, Nemorino at Bergamo and Evander in Alceste at La Scala; Rossini's Comte Ory at Venice, 1988, La Scala, 1991; Pesaro Festival, 1988, in La Scala di Seta, as Roderigo in Rossini's Otello, 1991; Count Almaviva on Metropolitan Opera debut 1988 and at Barcelona, 1991; Sang Lindoro in L'Italiana in Algeri, at Monte Carlo, 1989; Medoro in Orlando Furioso by Vivaldi at San Francisco; Other roles include Flamand in Capriccio and Ernesto in Don Pasquale. *Recordings:* Francesca da Rimini; Borsa in Rigoletto; Edmondo in Manon Lescaut and in Barbiere di Siviglia; Rossini's Zelmira; Tonio in La Fille du Régiment, Carlo and Goffredo in Rossini's Armida; sang Lindoro in L'Italiana in Algeri at Parma, 1998. *Honours:* winner Caruso International Competition, Milan.

**MATTHEW-WALKER, Robert;** Musician; b. 23 July 1939, Lewisham, London, England; m. Lynn Sharon Andrews, 27 Dec 1969, 1 s. *Education:* London College of Printing; Goldsmiths' College; London College of Music; Private Composition study with Darius Milhaud, Paris, 1962–63. *Career:* Composer, Record Company Executive, Author, Critic; mem, Performing Right Society; Critics' Circle. *Compositions:* Symphonies 1–6, 1955, 1958, 1959, 1964, 1968 (2); Violin Concerto, 1962; Piano Sonatas 1–4, 1976 (2), 1980, 1982; Piano Trio, 1978; Horn Concerto, 1980; Cello Sonata, 1980; String Quartet, 1980; Sinfonia Solemnis, 1981. *Recordings:* Le Tombeau de Milhaud; Divertimento on a Theme of Mozart. *Publications:* Rachmaninov: His Life and Times, 1980; Madonna–The Biography, 1989; Havergal Brian, 1995; Heartbreak Hotel–The Life and Music of Elvis Presley, 1995; Editor: The Keller Column, 1990; The Symphonies of Robert Simpson, 1991. *Contributions:* Editor, Music and Musicians, 1984–88; National Dictionary of Biography, Musical Times, other publications. *Address:* 1 Exford Road, London SE12 9HD, England.

**MATTHEWS, Andrea;** Singer (Soprano); b. 6 Nov. 1956, Needham, Massachusetts, USA. *Education:* AB, Princeton University, 1978. *Career:* Debut: Marriage of Figaro as Susanna at Virginia Opera, 1984; Semele in Semele; Gretel in Hansel and Gretel, Virginia Opera; Gilda in Rigoletto, Piedmont Opera; Zerlina in Don Giovanni, Greensboro Opera; Euridice in Orfeo ed Euridice, Violetta in La Traviata, Susanna in Marriage of Figaro, Marie in Bartered Bride and Ilia in Idomeneo at The Stadttheater Aachen, Germany; Other roles include: Musetta, Mimi in La Bohème, Pamina in Magic Flute, Lauretta in Gianni Schicchi, Marzelline in Fidelio, Lucy in The Telephone, Marguerite in Faust, Nannetta in Falstaff; Soloist with many orchestras and companies including: St Louis Symphony; Houston Symphony; Baltimore Symphony; Atlanta Symphony; Stuttgart Philharmonic, Prague Autumn Festival, Philadelphia Orchestra, Puerto Rico Symphony, Honolulu Symphony, National Symphony at Wolf Trap, Los Angeles Master Chorale, Dessoff Choirs, Oratorio Society of New York, Mostly Mozart Festival, New Mexico Symphony, Kalamazoo Symphony, Utah Symphony, St Paul Chamber Orchestra, American Ballet Theater, American Symphony, Raleigh Symphony and Cincinnati Symphony; Art-Song recitals in many American States. *Recordings:* Vaughan Williams's Serenade to Music; Handel's Siroe, Muzio, Berenice, Tolomeo; Christmas Album; Victor Herbert's Thine Alone (songs); Ned Rorem's Three Sisters. *Current Management:* Thea Dispeker Artists Representative. *Address:* c/o Thea Dispeker, 59 East 54th Street, New York, NY 10022, USA.

**MATTHEWS, Colin;** British composer; b. 13 Feb. 1946, London. *Education:* Nottingham University; Composition with Arnold Whittall and Nicholas Maw. *Career:* collaborated with Deryck Cooke on performing version of Mahler's 10th Symphony; taught at Sussex University 1972–73, 1976–77; Administrator Holst Foundation 1983; Assistant to Britten in last years; Trustee Britten-Pears Foundation 1983; Cortège premiered under Bernard Haitink at Covent Garden 1989, Machines and Dreams by the London Symphony Orchestra 1991; Founder NMC Recordings 1989; Associate Composer London Symphony Orchestra 1991–99; Chair Britten Estate 2000; Governor Royal Northern College of Music 2000; Associate Composer Hallé Orchestra 2000, Prince Consort Professor of Composition Royal College of Music 2001. *Compositions:* Ceres for nonet 1972, Sonata No. 4 for orchestra 1975, Partita, violin 1975, Five Sonnets to Orpheus, tenor and harp 1976, Specula for quartet 1976, Night Music for small orchestra 1977, Piano Suite 1979, Rainbow Studies for quintet 1978, Shadows in the Water, tenor and piano 1979, String Quartet No. 1 1979, Sonata No. 5 Landscape for orchestra 1977–81, Oboe Quartet 1981, Secondhand Flames, 5 voices 1982, Divertimento, double string quartet, string orchestra 1982, The Great Journey, baritone and ensemble 1981–86, Toccata Meccanica for orchestra 1984, Triptych for piano quintet 1984, Cello Concerto 1994, Three Enigmas, cello and piano 1985, String Quartet No. 2 1985, Suns Dance, 10 players 1985, Monody for Orchestra 1987, Two Part Invention for chamber orchestra 1987–88, Pursuit, 16 players 1987, Fuga, 8 players 1988, Cortège for orchestra 1989, 2nd Oboe Quartet 1989, Hidden variable, 15 players 1989, Quatrain, wind, brass and percussion 1989, Chiaroscuro for orchestra 1990, Machines and Dreams, full or small orchestra and children 1990, Broken Symmetry for Orchestra 1992, Contraflow, 14 players 1992, Memorial for Orchestra 1993, String Quartet No. 3 1994, Cello Concerto No. 2 1996, Renewal for chorus and orchestra 1996, Elegaic Chaconne, for ensemble 1997, Elegia for 14 players 1998, Aftertones for chorus and orchestra 1999, Pluto for orchestra 1999, Continuum for soprano and ensemble 2000, Horn Concerto 2001, Orchestration of seven Debussy Préludes 2001–03, Estrangements for chorus 2002, Vivo for orchestra 2002, Berceuse for Dresden for cello 2005. *Recordings:* The Great Journey; Cello Concerto, Landscape; Broken Symmetry, 4th Sonata, Suns Dance. *Honours:* Chamber Music Prize BBC 1970; Ian Whyte Award 1975; Park Lane Group Composer Award 1983; Royal Philharmonic Society Prize 1997; Honorary Doctorate University of Nottingam 1999. *Address:* c/o Faber Music Ltd, 3 Queen Square, London WC1N 3AU, England.

**MATTHEWS, David John,** BA; Composer and Writer; b. 9 March 1943, London, England. *Education:* BA Classics, Nottingham University, private study in composition with Anthony Milner. *Career:* Worked with Deryck Cooke on completion of Mahler's 10th Symphony; Assistant to Britten, 1966–70; Artistic Director, Deal Festival, 1989–2003; Artistic Advisor to English Chamber Orchestra; Fifth Symphony premiered at the 1999 London Prom Concerts; mem. British Academy of Composers and Songwriters. *Compositions include:* 5 Symphonies, 1975, 1978, 1983, 1990, 1999; In the Dark Time for orchestra; The Music of Dawn for orchestra; Romanza for cello and small orchestra; Capriccio for two horns and strings; Chaconne for orchestra; From Sea to Sky for small orchestra; Serenade for small orchestra; A Vision and a Journey for orchestra; After Sunrise for orchestra;; Aubade for small orchestra; Oboe Concerto; 2 Violin Concertos; Concerto in Azzurro for cello and orchestra; Variations for strings; Two Pieces for strings; Winter Remembered for viola and strings; Introit for two trumpets and strings; Cantiga for soprano and orchestra; Marina for baritone, basset horn, viola and piano; The Sleeping Lord for soprano, flute, clarinet, harp and string quartet; Winter Passions for baritone, clarinet, string trio and piano; 4 Hymns for chorus; The Company of Lovers for small chorus; The doorway of Dawn for chorus; The Ship of Death for chorus; 10 String Quartets; The Flaying of Marsyas for oboe quintet; Clarinet Quartet; 2 Piano Trios; String Trio; Piano Sonata; Variations for piano; Band of Angels for organ; Three Studies for solo violin; Winter Journey for solo violin; Eight Duos for two violins; 15 Fugues for Violin; Three Roman Miniatures for clarinet; Duet Variations for Flute and Piano; A Little Threnody for cor anglais; The Book of Hours for voice and piano; From Coastal Stations for voice and piano; The Golden Kingdom for voice and piano; Vespers for mezzo soprano and tenor solo, chorus and orchestra; A Congress of Passions for voice, oboe and piano, 1994; Hurrahing in Harvest, for chorus, 1997; Winter Passions for baritone and ensemble, 1999; The Doorway of the Dawn, for chorus, 1999; Aubade for chamber orchestra, 2000; A Congress of Passions for medium voice, oboe and strings, 2000; After Sunrise, for chamber orchestra, 2001; Winter Remembered, for solo viola and strings, 2001; Cello Concerto, Concerto in Azzuro, 2002; Fifteen Fugues for solo violin, 2002. *Recordings:* The Company of Lovers; Romanza; Cantiga; September Music; Introit; The Flaying of Marsyas; A Little Threnody; Winter

Journey; Piano Sonata; Symphony No. 4; Piano Trio 1; The Golden Kingdom; In the Dark Time; Chaconne; Three Studies for solo violin; Britten, 2002. *Publications include:* Editor, Mahler, Symphony No. 10, 1976; Michael Tippett, 1980; Landscape into Sound, 1992; Editor, Beethoven arr Mahler, String Quartet op 95; Mahler: Rückert Lieder; Britten, 2003. *Contributions:* Tempo, TLS, Musical Times. *Honours:* Hon. DMus 1998. *Address:* c/o Faber Music Ltd, 3 Queen Square, London WC1N 3AU, England.

**MATTHEWS, Michael Gough,** ARCM, FRCM, FRNCM, FRSAMD, ARCO; British pianist and teacher; b. 12 July 1931, London, England. *Education:* Royal Coll. of Music. *Career:* debut, Wigmore Hall 1960; pianist recitals; broadcasts and concerts in the UK, Europe and Far East; adjudicator in int. competitions; masterclasses; lecture recitals; piano teacher and supervisor jr studies, RSAMD 1964–71; teacher, Royal Coll. of Music, Dir Jr Dept and Prof. of Piano 1972–75, Registrar 1975, Vice-Dir 1978–84, Dir 1985–93, Vice-Pres. 1994; Dir, Associated Bd of the Royal Schools of Music 1985–93; Dir, Royal Music Foundation Inc., USA from 1985; consultant to HM the Sultan of Oman, Jaguar Cars Sponsored Concerts; piano recitals, lectures and masterclasses in the UK and abroad; mem. Royal Philharmonic Soc., Comité d'Honneur Presence de l'Art, Paris, RCO (vice-pres.), Royal Choral Soc. (hon. vice-pres.), Royal Coll. of Music (vice-pres.) 1997. *Recordings:* two albums of piano music by Fauré, eight nocturnes, nine preludes, two barcarolles, Thème et variations, Mazurka, one album of piano music by Brahms: Op 76 and Op 118. *Honours:* RCM Gold Medal 1953, prize Chopin Int. Piano Competition 1955, Chopin Fellowship 1959, Hon. GSM 1987, Hon. RAM 1979. *Address:* Laurel Cottages, South Street, Mayfield, East Sussex TN20 6DD, England.

**MATTHEWS, Sally;** British singer (soprano); b. 1975, England. *Education:* Guildhall School, London, Young Artist Programme, Covent Garden. *Career:* debut as Nannetta in Falstaff, Covent Garden 2000; season 2000–01 as Mozart's Fiordiligi for Grange Park Opera and Elisa in Il Re Pastore for the Classical Opera Co.; concerts with the Orchestra of St John's, Philharmonia, English Chamber Orchestra and Royal Liverpool Philharmonic Orchestra; first night of 2001 London Proms in Serenade to Music, by Vaughan Williams; season 2001–02 with Debussy's Le Martyre de St Sebastien, with the LSO under Pierre Boulez, and Messiah with the London Philharmonic. *Honours:* Kathleen Ferrier Award 1999. *Current Management:* Van Walsum Management Deutschland GmbH, Königstrasse 36, 30175 Hannover, Germany. *Telephone:* 511 366 07 23. *Fax:* 511 366 07 24. *E-mail:* vwm@kdschmid.de.

**MATTHUS, Siegfried;** German composer; b. 13 April 1934, Mallenuppen, E Prussia; s. of the late Franz Matthus and of Luise Perrey; m. Helga Spitzer 1958; one s. *Education:* Hochschule für Musik, Berlin, Acad. of Arts and Music, Berlin (masterclass with Hanns Eisler). *Career:* composer and consultant, Komische Oper, Berlin 1964–; Prof. 1985–; Artistic Dir Chamber Opera Festival, Rheinsberg; mem. Acad. of Arts of GDR, Acad. of Arts of W Berlin, Acad. of Arts, Munich. *Compositions include:* ten operas, one oratorio, concertos, orchestral and chamber music, etc. *Honours:* Nat. Prize 1972, 1984, Bundesverdienstkreuz (First Class) 2000. *Address:* Elisabethweg 10, 13187 Berlin; Seepromenade 15, 16348 Stolzenhagen, Germany. *Telephone:* (30) 4857362 (Berlin); (33397) 21736 (Stolzenhagen). *Fax:* (30) 48096604 (Berlin); (33397) 71400 (Stolzenhagen). *E-mail:* smatthus@aol.com (home).

**MATTILA, Karita Marjatta;** Finnish singer (soprano); b. 5 Sept. 1960, Somero; d. of Arja Mattila and Erkki Mattila (née Somerikko); m. Tapio Kuneinen 1992. *Education:* Sibelius Acad., Finland and studied with Liisa Linko-Malmio, and Vera Rozsa in London. *Career:* operatic debut at Finnish Nat. Opera as the Countess (Marriage of Figaro) 1983; appeared with Brussels Opera as Countess, Eva, Rosalinde 1984–85; debut at Royal Opera House, Covent Garden as Fiordiligi 1986, subsequent appearances as Pamina, Countess and Agathe 1986–89, Donna Elvira 1992, Musetta 1994, Elisabeth de Valois 1996, Elsa 1997, Chrysothemis 1997; appeared at Barenboim-Ponnelle Festival, Paris 1986, Tel-Aviv 1987, 1990; debut at Metropolitan Opera as Donna Elvira 1990, Eva (Meistersinger) 1993, Lisa 1995, Musetta 1996, Elsa (Lohengrin) 1998, Amelia (Simon Boccanegra) 1999, Fidelio 2000, Chrysothemis 2002, Jenůfa 2003; debut at Opéra Nat. de Paris as Elsa 1996, Hanna Glawari 1997, Lisa 2001; Théâtre du Châtelet: Elisabeth de Valois 1996, Desdemona 2001, Arabella 2002; appearances at Salzburg Festival: Donna Anna 1999, Fiordiligi 2000, Jenůfa 2001; has also appeared in Washington, Houston, Chicago and San Francisco; recitals throughout Europe; has worked under maj. conductors, including Sir Colin Davis, Claudio Abbado, von Dohnanyi, Giulini, Sinopoli, Solti, Haitink, Maazel, Levine. *Recordings:* over 50 solo and opera recordings. *Honours:* first prize Finnish Nat. Singing Competition 1981, first prize BBC Singer of the World, Cardiff 1983, Evening Standard Award 1997, Acad. du Disque Lyrique Award 1997, Grammy Award for Best Opera 1998, Pro Finlandia 2001, Musical America Musician of the Year 2005. *Current Management:* IMG Artists Europe, Lovell House, 616 Chiswick High Road, London, W4 5RX, England. *Telephone:* (20) 8233-5800 (office). *Fax:* (20) 8233-5801 (office). *E-mail:* artistseurope@imgworld.com (office). *Website:* www.imgartists.com (office). *E-mail:* tapio.kuneinen@pp.inet.fi (home).

**MATTINSON, David;** Singer (Bass-baritone); b. 1964, England. *Education:* Choral Scholar, Trinity College, Cambridge; Guildhall School of Music with Thomas Hemsley; Further study with Rudolf Pierney. *Career:* Concert repertoire includes the B minor Mass, Messiah, The Creation, Requiems of Brahms, Verdi and Fauré, The Dream of Gerontius and A Child of Our Time; Appearances with the City of London Sinfonia, the Bournemouth Symphony

and the London Philharmonic Orchestras; Further concerts include Elijah at the Albert Hall; Christus in the St Matthew Passion at the Festival Hall; Mozart's Requiem, and Beethoven's Ninth in Koblenz; Song recitals with the accompanist Clare Toomer in Winterreise, Dichterliebe, La Bonne Chanson and the Songs of Travel by Vaughan Williams: Appearances with the New Songmakers and the Mistry String Quartet and at the Buxton, Malvern and Warwick Festivals; Operatic roles include Gualtiero in Musgrave's The Voice of Ariadne, Mozart's Figaro, Germont, and Glover in La Jollie Fille de Perth; Scottish Opera debut 1991, as Zuniga in Carmen; Debut as Mozart's Figaro, Opera North, 1992; Season 1992 as Villotto in Haydn's La Vera Costanza for Garsington Opera and in Billy Budd for Scottish Opera; Sang Mozart's Figaro for Central Festival Opera, 1996. *Recordings:* Bach St John Passion. *Honours:* Gold Medal Rosebowl and the Worshipful Company of Musicians' Silver Medal, GSM; Gold Medal in the 1988 Royal Overseas League Music Competition; Prizewinner, Walter Gruner International Lieder Competition; Elly Ameling International Lied Concours; 1st prize, 1990 BP Peter Pears Award. *Address:* Kaye Artists Management Ltd, Barratt House, 7 Chertsey Road, Woking, Surrey GU21 5 AG, England.

**MATTIOTTO, Claudia;** Italian pianist; b. 21 Jan. 1959, Torino; m. Guido Scano 1985; one s. *Education:* High School for Training of Primary Teachers, Verdi High Conservatory, Torino, Ecole Internationale de Piano, Lausanne, Switzerland, Mozarteum, Salzburg, Austria, Manhattan School of Music, New York, USA, Instituto Liongueres, Barcelona, Spain. *Career:* solo debut 1981, piano duo debut 1985, with orchestra 1988; concerts in all Italy and in France, Germany, Egypt, India, Slovenia, Romania, Andorra, Greece and Poland; conductor and special teacher in musical courses and seminars; many European broadcasting appearances; collaborator in Caleidoscopio Project 1996–; concert series A Suon Di Musica 2000–; Pres., Int. Centre for Musical Research. *Recordings:* 4 Steps im 4 Hands, series of 15 weekly programmes, Radiokoper, Monte Carlo, Bucharest, Marseille, Trieste radio and television broadcasts; album: Documents (rarities) 2001. *Publications:* In Musica, piano teaching methodology text 1986, Concerto in Famiglia, A Guide for Younger Muscians 2003. *Honours:* Dalcroze Teaching Certificate, Manhattan School of Music 1991, first prize Genova Competition 1986. *Address:* Corso Rosselli 105/10A, 10129 Torino, Italy (office). *E-mail:* info@cirmonline.it (office). *Website:* www.cirmonline.it (office).

**MATTON, Roger;** Composer; b. 18 May 1929, Granby, Quebec, Canada. *Education:* Studied in Arthur Letondal's class, Conservatoire de musique du Quebec, Montreal; Studied composition under Claude Champagne; Studied under Andree Vaurabourg-Honegger and Nadia Boulanger, Ecole normale superieure de musique; Attended Olivier Messiaen's analysis classes, Conservatoire de Paris; Studied ethnomusicology under Marius Barbeau, National Museum of Canada, Ottawa. *Career:* Joined Archives de folklore, Laval, Quebec; Teacher, History Department, Laval, Quebec City; Ethnological Music, 1963–89; Composer of music having received commissions from Canadian Broadcasting Corporation; l'orchestre symphonique de Quebec, Montreal Symphony Orchestra, Le Grand Theatre de Quebec; mem, Canadian League of Composers. *Compositions:* Orchestral: Danse Bresillienne 1946; Danse Lente 1947; L'Horoscope 1958; Mouvement Symphonique 1, 1960, 11 1962, 111 1974, IV 1978; Pax 1950, Soloists with Orchestra: Concerto pur deux pianos et orchestre, 1964; Concerto pour saxophone et orchestre a cordes 1948; Voices with Orchestra: L'escaouette 1957; Te Deum 1967; Chamber Music: Esquisse pour quatuor a cordes 1949; Etude pour clarinette et piano 1946; Piano: Berceuse 1945; Trois Preludes pour piano 1949; Two Pianos: Concerto pour deux pianos et percussion 1955; Danse bresiliene 1946; Organ: Suite de Paques, 1952; Te es Petrus, 1984. *Recordings:* Berceuse; Concerto pour deux pianos et orchestre; Concerto pour deux pianos et percussion; Danse breilienne; l'horoscope; Movement Symphonique 1, 11; Suite de Paques; Te Deum; Trois Preludes pour piano. *Honours:* Awarded distinction at Seventh Gala du Quebec, Montreal for choral suite l'Escaouette 1965; Received Prix du Disque Pierre Mercure for Concerto pour deux pianos et orchestra 1966; Presented with Prix Calixa Lavallee by St Jean Baptiste Society for contribution to French-Canada 1969. *Address:* c/o SOCAN, 41 Valleybrook Drive, Don Mills, Ontario M3B 2S6, Canada.

**MATTSSON, Jack;** Composer and Musician; b. 12 Dec. 1954, Aland, Finland. *Education:* Sibelius Academy, 1974–84. *Career:* Debut: Alandskt Requiem for soloists, chorus and orchestra, 1990; Composer, arranger, conductor since 1980; Finnish radio and television, recordings for various record companies, 1986–; Conductor, Swedish Theatre, Helsinki; mem, Clientship in Finnish Teosto. *Compositions:* Alandskt Requiem, 1991; Serenade for basson and strings, 1990; Carating for violin and piano, 1990; Four bagatelles for flute, violin and viola, 1986; Joy and Thoughts for organ, 1992. *Recordings:* Music theatre Katrina for solo voices chorus and orchestra; Finnish Radio Symphony Orchestra, 1998 s. *Honours:* Alands Culture prize, 1990; Finnish Swedish Culture found, 1987. *Address:* c/o TEOSTO, Lauttasaaventie 1, SF–0020 Helsinki, Finalnd.

**MATUSZCZAK, Bernadetta;** Polish composer; b. 10 March 1931, Thorn; d. of the late Józef Matuszczak and Helena Glowacka. *Education:* Queen Jadwiga Polish Secondary School, Karol Szymanowski Fundamental and Secondary School of Music, studied with Szeligowski and Sitowski at the Poznan Higher Musical School and Warsaw Conservatories, studied in Paris with Nadia Boulanger. *Career:* mem. Asscn of Polish Composers (ZKP), Asscn of Artists and Composers of Polish Stages (ZAiKS). *Compositions include:* Septem Tubae, for mixed choir and symphony orchestra 1965, Julia i Romeo, chamber opera, Warsaw 1970; Humanae Voces, radio oratorio, 1972; Mysterium Heloizy, opera, 1973–74; Elegy about a Polish Boy, symphony composition 1975, The Diary of a Madman, monodrama after Gogol, Warsaw 1978; Apocalypsis, radio oratorio, 1979; Prometheus, chamber opera after Aeschylus, 1981–83; In the Night on the Old Market, symphony for soloists, choir and orchestra, 1988, Wild Swans, ballet fairy-tale 1991, Quo Vadis, opera after H. Sienkiewicz, 1993–94; Canto funebre, for strings, 1995. *Honours:* prize winner Young Polish Composers' Competition 1965, prize winner Grzegorz Fitelberg Composers' Competition for Septem Tubae 1966, prize winner competition organized by Jeunesses Musicales for Musica da camera 1967. *Address:* c/o Society of Authors ZAiKS, 2 Hipoteczna Street, 00 092 Warsaw, Poland (office). *Telephone:* (4822) 828 17 05 (office). *Fax:* (4822) 828 13 47 (office). *E-mail:* sekretariat@zaiks.org.pl (office). *Website:* www .zaiks.org.pl (office).

**MATYS, Jiří,** MgA; Czech composer; b. 27 Oct. 1927, Bakov, Nachod area. *Education:* Brno Conservatory, Janáček Acad. of Music, Brno with Kvapil. *Career:* teacher, Janáček Acad. 1953–57; Head of the School of Music, Kralove Pole in Brno 1957–60; Prof. of the Conservatory, Brno; mem. Asscn of Czech Musicians and Scientists (Prague), Moravian Composers Club (Brno). *Compositions:* Viola Sonata 1954, 5 String Quartets 1957–90, Variations on Death for narrator, horn and string quartet of a poem by Milan Kundera 1959, Morning Music 1962, Solo viola sonata 1963, Music for string quartet and orchestra 1971, Suite for viola and bass clarinet 1973, Symphonic Overture 1974, Dialogue for cello and piano 1976, Sonata for Violin Solo No. 1 1977, Divertimento for Four Horns 1981, Suite for flute and guitar 1981, Music for strings 1982, Suite for Wind Quintet 1984, Music for Piano 1985, I Wish You Knew…, mezzo, cello, piano 1985–86, The Urgency of Time, symphonic picture for viola, orchestra and reciter 1986–87, Poetic Movements V, four compositions for four guitars 1988, Tunning 5 compositions for guitar solo 1990, Sonata for Violin Solo No. 2 1991, No. 3 1993, No. 4 1994, No. 5 1995, No. 6 1996, Night Thoughts, a cycle of piano compositions in five parts 1992, Dedicated to a poet, Fantasy for baritone and string quartet 1995, String Trio for violin, viola and violoncello 1996–97, Friendly Sketches for piano 1998, Duo for violin and cello 1999–2000, Music for contrabass solo 2001, Suite for two contrabass 2002, Leaving…, for flute, violin, cello, piano 2002, String Quartet No. 6 2003, Music for violoncello solo II 2004, While of the Standstill, melodramas for reciter, flute and viola of a poem by Jiří Wolker 2004, Impromptu for flute solo 2004, Call, vocal cycle for baryton and piano 2004. *Recordings:* albums: Tunning for Guitar Solo 1990, Music for string quartet and orchestra 1998, String Quartet No. 3 1999, 5 Impromptus for violin and piano 1999, Suite for viola and bassclarinet 2000, Music for Strings 2001, Written by grief into silence…, vocal cycle for mezzo and orchestra 2001, Strnig trio for violin, viola and violoncello 2004, Lyrical Melodramas for a poem by Josef Kainar for reciter and piano. *Honours:* Int. Award at the Festival of Choral Art, Jihlava 1993, Czech Radio Sacred Music Competition award 1994. *Address:* Milénova 2, 638 00 Brno 38, Czech Republic (home). *Telephone:* 548529482 (home). *Website:* www.musica.cz/comp/matys.htm.

**MAUCERI, John F.;** Conductor and Music Director; b. 12 Sept. 1945, New York, USA; m. Betty Weiss, 15 June 1968, 1 s. *Education:* MPhil, 1971, BA, 1967, Yale University; Tanglewood, 1972. *Career:* Music Director, Yale Symphony, 1968–74; American Symphony Orchestra, 1984–87; Washington Opera, 1979–82; Kennedy Center, 1973–; Scottish Opera, 1987–93; Consultant, Music Theater, Kennedy Center, 1982–; Co-Producer, On Your Toes, Musical Play, Broadway and London's West End, 1982; Lyric Opera of Chicago debut, La Bohème, 1987; Music Director, WNET Gala of Stars, A Musical Toast, 1987; Conducted, the New York Philharmonic Metropolitan Opera Orchestra and Empire Brass, Carnegie Hall, 1987; British premiere of Weill's Street Scene, 1989; Conducted new production of La Forza del Destino for Scottish Opera, 1990, followed by revivals of Salome and Madama Butterfly; Les Troyens in Glasgow and London; Conducted own edition of Blitzstein's Regina at Glasgow, British Premiere, 1991; Madama Butterfly at Turin, 1996; Turandot at Turin, 1998; Premiere of original version of Weill's Der Weg der Verheissung, Chemnitz, 1999. *Recordings:* Original Cast: Candide, 1973, On Your Toes, 1983; New York City Opera, Candid, 1985; Original Cast, Song and Dance, 1985; My Fair Lady, with Kiri Te Kanawa and Jerry Hadley. *Contributions:* Opera Magazine, 1985. *Honours:* Antoinette Perry, Outer Critics Circle, Drama Desk Awards, Best Opera Recording, Candide, 1987. *Current Management:* Columbia Artists Management, 165 West 57th Street, NY 10019, USA.

**MAULTSBY, Nancy;** Singer (Mezzo-Soprano); b. 1970, USA. *Career:* Appearances with Seattle Opera asCharlotte in Werther, Carmen at San Francisco and Erda in Siegfried at Buenos Aires; Further engagements as Carmen for Pittsburgh Opera, Anmeris in Minnesota and Ursula (Béatrice et Benedict) at Santa Fe; Sang The Omniscient Sea-Shell in Die Aegyptische Helena by Strauss for the Royal Opera at the Festival Hall, London, 1998; Concerts include Das Lied von der Erde, the Brahms Alto Rhapsody, Mahler's 2nd symphony (Cleveland Orchestra) and Schoenberg's Gurrelieder, with the Minnesota Orchestra. *Honours:* Marian Anderson and Martin E. Segal Awards, 1993. *Address:* c/o San Francisco Opera, War Memorial House, Van Ness Avenue, San Francisco, CA, USA.

**MAUNDER, Charles (Richard Francis);** Lecturer, Musicologist and Early Music Practitioner; b. 23 Nov. 1937, Portsmouth, England; m.; three s. *Education:* Jesus College, Cambridge, 1955–61; MA, PhD, Cambridge, 1962. *Career:* Fellow of Christ's College, Cambridge, 1964–; Lecturer at Univesities

in Cambridge, London, Reading, Leeds, and in the USA, Philadelphia, Chicago, Northwestern, Northern Illinois, and at musicological conferences, International Mozart Congress, Salzburg, 1991; Performer on the bass viol, Cambridge Consort of Viols, baroque, classical viola, Cambridge Early Music; Violone, concerts in Cambridge and elsewhere include Messiah, St John Passion, Brandenburg Concertos, Bach Christmas Oratorio and Monteverdi Vespers; Has restored early keyboard instruments, including square piano by Johannes Zumpe, London 1766, for Emmanuel College, Cambridge; Instruments built include copies of two-manual harpsichord by Thomas Hitchcock and Mozart's forepiano; Founder of the Cambridge Classical Orchestra, 1990. *Publications:* Mozart's Requiem: On Preparing a New Edition, 1988; Numerous editions of 17th and 189th Century music, including 13 of the 48 vols of J C Bach's Collected Works; Mozart's Requiem K626, C minor Mass K 427 and Vesperae. *Contributions:* Galpin Society Journal, Musical Times, Early Music, Journal of the Royal Musical Association, Music and Letters, Notes, Mozart-Janrbuch. *Address:* 54 High Street, Sawston, Cambridge CB 2 4BG, England.

**MAUNDER, Stuart;** Stage Director; b. 1957, Australia. *Career:* Productions for Australian Opera include Nabucco, Die Fledermaus, Don Pasquale and Romeo et Juliette; Die Entführung and Don Pasquale for Lyric Opera Queensland; Music theatre pieces by Bernstein, Sondheim and Sullivan throughout Australia; Resident in the United Kingdom from 1990; Staff Director at Covent Garden, reviving La Bohème, L'Elisir d'amore and Guillaume Tell at Lisbon, and featuring in ROH/BBC television Top Score presentations; Pirates of Penzance for D'Oyly Carte Opera; Hoffman, Pasquale, Zauberflöte for Opus Festival, France; Mikado, Fille du Regiment for Opera Pacific, USA; Zauberflöte for British Youth Opera and Figaro for Hong Kong Academy. *Address:* 80 Beckwith Road, London SE24 9LG, England.

**MAURER, Elsie;** Singer (Mezzo-soprano); b. 1938, Germany. *Career:* Sang at the Aachen Opera from 1963, Pforzheim 1964–67, Frankfurt Opera from 1968; Among her best roles have been Meg Page, Olga in Eugene Onegin and Mary in Fliegender Holländer; Guest appearances at Brunswick, Oldenburg and elsewhere as Ortrud, Amneris, Herodias and Preziosilla; Sang Countess Geschwitz in Lulu for Essen Opera as guest at Barcelona (1969) and Trieste (1971); Also guested at the Vienna State Opera. *Recordings include:* Die Soldaten by Zimmermann (Teldec).

**MAURO, Ermanno;** Singer (Tenor); b. 20 Jan. 1939, Trieste, Italy. *Education:* Studied at the Toronto Conservatory with Herman Geiger-Torel. *Career:* Debut: Canadian Opera Company 1962, as Tamino in Die Zauberflöte; Sang Manrico in Toronto 1965; Covent Garden from 1967, debut in Manon Lescaut; Guest appearances with Welsh National Opera, Scottish Opera and at Glyndebourne; New York City Opera, 1975 as Calaf in Turandot; BBC television as Paco in La Vida Breve; Metropolitan Opera from 1978, as Canio, Manrico, Ernani, Pinkerton, Paolo in Zandonai's Francesca da Rimini and Des Grieux; La Scala and Rome 1978; San Francisco 1982; Vienna 1983; Brussels 1984, as Manrico; Dallas Opera 1985, as Otello; Other roles include Male Chorus in The Rape of Lucretia; Donizetti's Edgardo, Gounod's Faust, Verdi's Radames, Riccardo, Alfredo and Gabriele Adorno; Don José, Cavaradossi, Dick Johnson and Enzo in La Gioconda; Sang Cavaradossi at the Met 1986, Turiddu 1989; Calaf at the Deutsche Oper Berlin 1987; San Francisco and Barcelona 1989, as Otello and Enzo; Sang Manrico with Zürich Opera 1990, Maurizio in Adriana Lecouvreur at Montreal; Season 1992 at Radames at Dallas, Puccini's Des Grieux at Miami, Calaf at Philadelphia and Turiddu at the Teatro Colón, Buenos Aires; Sang Loris in Fedora at Montreal, 1995. *Address:* c/o Metropolitan Opera, Lincoln Center, NY 10023, USA.

**MAURUS, Elsa;** Singer (Mezzo-Soprano); b. 1968, France. *Education:* Studied with Eugénia Besala-Ludwig, and in Geneva. *Career:* Sang in Le Roi l'a Dit by Delibes at Nantes, then Rossini's Rosina at Rouen, 1994; Opéra d'Aran by Bécaud at the Vienna Konzerthaus, 1994; Concerts include Debussy's Le Martyre, in Rome, Cesar Franck's Les Béatitudes with the Orchesra of Ile de France, Mendelssohn's Erstes Walpurgisnacht at the Théâtre de Champs Elysées and Mozart's Requiem in colmar (1998); Mahler's 2nd and 3rd Symphonies in Japan (1999–2000), the Berlioz Roméo et Juliette in Paris and Poulenc's Carmélites in Italy; Engaged for season 2002 in Ravel's Sheherazade with the Utah symphony, Les Nuites d'été at Lille, as Carmen at Nantes, Nicklausse in Trieste, and Dulcinée in Massenet's Don Quichotte at Marseille. *Address:* c/o Musicaglotz 11, Rue Le Verrier, 75006 Paris, France.

**MAUS, Peter;** Singer (Tenor); b. 1948, Germany. *Career:* Debut: Bayreuth Youth Festival, 1972, in Wagner's Das Liebesverbot; Sang in the 1981 premiere of Kagel's Aus Deutschland; Bayreuth Festival from 1982, with minor roles in Parsifal and Die Meistersinger; Shepherd in Tristan, 1993; Teacher of Singing at the Hochschule für Kunste in Berlin, from 1987. *Recordings:* Das Liebesverbot; Die Meistersinger; Masses by Schubert, Donizetti Mass and Wolf's Der Corregidor; Esquire in Parsifal, conducted by Barenboim;Deutsche Oper Berlin from 1974, in such character roles as Wenzel in The Bartered Bridge, Sparlich in Lustigen Weiber, Peter Ivanov in Zar und Zimmermann, Pong, the Count in Zimmermann's Die Soldaten, Fatty in Mahagonny and Eljeya in From the House of the Dead; Sang M. Triquet in Eugene Onegin and Mozart's Don Curzio at the Deutsche Oper Berlin 2000. *Address:* c/o Deutsche Oper Berlin, Richard Wagnerstrasse 10, 1000 Berlin 10, Germany.

**MAUTI, Nunziata;** Singer (Soprano); b. 28 Aug. 1946, Palma Campania, Italy. *Education:* Studied in Naples and with Gina Cigna. *Career:* Debut: Palermo, 1965 aas Liu in Turandot; Appearances throughout Italy including La Scala and the Verona Arena, 1975–85; US debut Dallas, 1973, as Elvira in I Puritana; Chicago, 1978, as Butterfly and Gilda; Metropolitan Opera, 1977–80 in Traviata and Pagliacci; Wiesbaden, 1986, in Zandonai's Giulietta e Romeo, Turin, 1991 as Sulamith in Goldmark's Königin von Sheba; Other roles include Manon and Mozart's Fiordiligi and Donna Elvira; Verdi's Desdemona and Trovatore Leonora. *Address:* Teatro Regio di Torino, Piazza Castello 215, 10124 Turin, Italy.

**MAVEL, Regina;** Singer (Contralto); b. 1958, Cologne, Germany. *Education:* Cologne Musikhochschule. *Career:* Sang in Die Zauberflöte and Tannhäuser at Dortmund, 1983–84; Essen, 1988 and Munster from 1989 in operas by Bizet, Cornelius and Millöcker; Wiesbaden, 1992–93, in Wagner's Ring; Cologne Opera from 1995; Premiere of Patmos by Schweinitz at Munich, 1990; Other roles include Mary in Der fliegende Holländer and Geneviève in Pelléas et Mélisande; Concerts include Beethoven's Ninth at Bonn, 1994. *Address:* c/o Hessisches Staatstheater, Christian-Zais-Strasse 3–5, Pf. 3247, 6200 Wiesbaden, Germany.

**MAW, (John) Nicholas;** composer; *Composition Faculty Member, Peabody Conservatory;* b. 5 Nov. 1935, Grantham, England; m. Karen Graham 1960; one s. one d. *Education:* Royal Acad. of Music; studies with Nadia Boulanger and Max Deutsch, Paris. *Career:* Composition Teacher RAM 1964–66, Exeter Univ. 1973–75, Yale Univ. 1984, 1985, 1988, Boston Univ. 1986, Bard Coll., New York 1990–99; Fellow Commoner in Creative Arts, Trinity Coll., Cambridge 1966–70; Composition Faculty mem. Peabody Conservatory, Baltimore 1998–. *Compositions include:* operas: One Man Show 1964, The Rising of The Moon 1970, Sophie's Choice 2002; orchestral works: Sinfonia 1966, Sonata for strings and two horns 1967, Serenade for Small Orchestra 1973, 1977, Odyssey 1974–87, Spring Music 1983, The World in the Evening 1988, American Games for Wind Ensemble 1991, Shahnama 1992, Dance Scenes 1995, Voices of Memory, Variations for orchestra 1995, Sophie's Choice: Concert Suite2003; instrumental solos with orchestra: Sonata Notturna for Cello and String Orchestra 1985, Little Concert for oboe, strings and two Horns 1987, Violin Concerto 1993, Cor Anglais Concerto 2004; voice and orchestra: Nocturne 1958, Scenes and Arias 1962, Hymnus, for chorus and orchestra 1995; chamber music: Chamber Music for wind and piano quintet 1962, String Quartet 1965, No. 2 1983, No. 3 1994, No. 4 2005, Ghost Dances 1988, Piano Trio 1991, Intrada to The Art of Fugue, for string quartet 2002; instrumental music: Sonatina for Flute and Piano 1957, Personae for Piano Nos I–III 1973, Nos IV–VI 1985, Music of Memory for Solo Guitar 1989, Sonata for solo violin 1996, Narration for solo cello 2001; vocal music: 5 Epigrams for Chorus 1960, The Voice of Love for mezzo soprano and piano 1966, Reverdie, 5 songs for male voices 1975, Nonsense Rhymes, songs and rounds for children 1975–76, La Vita Nuova for soprano and chamber ensemble 1979, The Ruin, for double choir and solo horn 1980, Five American Folksongs for high voice and piano 1988, Roman Canticle for medium voice and chamber ensemble 1989, Sweté Jesu 1990, The Head of Orpheus, for soprano and 2 clarinets 1992. *Honours:* Midsummer Prize, Corporation of London 1980, Sudler International Wind Band Prize 1991, Stoeger Prize for Chamber Music 1993. *Address:* c/o Faber Music Ltd, 3 Queen Square, London, WC1N 3AU, England.

**MAX, Robert,** GRSM, LRAM, ARAM; British cellist and conductor; b. 7 Feb. 1968, London, England; m. Zoë Solomon 1993; two s. one d. *Education:* Royal Acad. of Music, Royal Northern Coll. of Music, Juilliard School, New York. *Career:* concerts throughout the UK, Europe, North and South America, Russia and the Far East; String Finalist, BBC Young Musician of the Year, 1984; Music Dir for Nonesuch Orchestra, 1993–96, for Zemel Choir, 1994–98, for Pro Corda, 1998–2000; cellist with Barbican Piano Trio. *Recordings include:* Barbican Piano Trio: Mendelssohn D Minor with works by Alan Bush and John Ireland, 1989, Complete Piano Trios of E. Lalo; The Zemel Choir: Liturgical Music of Louis Lewandowski; The English Tradition of Jewish Choral Music Schnittke for ASV; Tchaikovsky and Rachmaninov for Guild. *Address:* 11 Willifield Way, London, NW11 7XU, England.

**MAXWELL, Donald;** British singer (baritone); *Director, National Opera Studio;* b. 12 Dec. 1948, Perth, Scotland; m. Alison Jayne Norman; one d. *Education:* Univ. of Edinburgh. *Career:* debut, Scottish Opera in Musgrave's Mary Queen of Scots 1977; Covent Garden debut in Sallinen's The King Goes Forth to France; performances at La Scala, Paris Opéra, Vienna Staatsoper, Covent Garden, Teatro Colón, Buenos Aires, Edinburgh Festival, Glyndebourne and BBC Proms; major roles include Falstaff, Iago, Wozzeck, Golaud (all for television), Flying Dutchman, Scarpia, Rigoletto, Gunther, Don Alfonso, Bottom in A Midsummer Night's Dream, Tarquinnius in Lucretia; world premieres by Berio, Manoury, Harle, Holt; season 2000 as Don Alfonso for WNO, Faninal in Der Rosenkavalier at Covent Garden, Rossini's Geronimo for ENO and Britten's Balstrode at La Scala; sang Swallow in Peter Grimes in Amsterdam, Don Geronio for the Buxton Festival 2004; sang Swallow in Peter Grimes at the Salzburg Festival, The Bartered Bride at the Royal Opera House 2005; currently Dir, Nat. Opera Studio and Head of Opera Studies, Royal Welsh Coll. of Music and Drama. *Address:* c/o National Opera Studio, The Clore Building, 2 Chapel Yard, Wandsworth High Street, London, SW18 4HZ, England. *Telephone:* (20) 8874-8811. *Fax:* (20) 8875-0404. *E-mail:* info@nationaloperastudio.org.uk. *Website:* www.nationaloperastudio.org.uk.

**MAXWELL DAVIES, Sir Peter,** Kt, CBE, MusB, FRCM, FRSAMD, FRNCM; British composer and conductor; *Master of the Queen's Music;* b. 8 Sept. 1934, Manchester, England; s. of Thomas Davies and Hilda (née Howard) Davies. *Education:* Leigh Grammar School, Royal Manchester Coll. of Music, Manchester Univ.; studied with Goffredo Petrassi, Rome 1957 and with Roger Sessions, Milton Babbitt, Earl Kim, Princeton Univ., NJ, USA (Harkness Fellow) 1962–64. *Career:* Dir of Music, Cirencester Grammar School 1959–62; Harkness Fellowship, Grad. School, Princeton Univ. 1962–64; lecture tours in Europe, Australia, USA, Canada, Brazil; Visiting Composer, Univ. of Adelaide 1966; Prof. of Composition, Royal Northern Coll. of Music, Manchester 1965–80 (Fellow 1978); Pres. Schools Music Asscn 1983–, Composers' Guild of GB 1986–, Nat. Fed. of Music Socs 1989–, Cheltenham Arts Festival 1994–96, Soc. for Promotion of New Music 1995–; Visiting Fromm Prof. of Composition, Harvard Univ. 1985; f. and Co-Dir (with Harrison Birtwistle q.v.) Pierrot Players 1967–71; f. and Artistic Dir The Fires of London 1971–87; f. and Artistic Dir St Magnus Festival, Orkney Islands 1977–86, Pres. 1986–; Artistic Dir Dartington Summer School of Music 1979–84; Assoc. Conductor and Composer Scottish Chamber Orchestra 1985–94, Composer Laureate 1994–; Conductor and Composer, BBC Philharmonic Orchestra (Manchester) 1992–2001; Assoc. Conductor and Composer Royal Philharmonic Orchestra 1992–2001; Master of the Queen's Music 2004–; Fellowship British Acad. of Composers and Songwriters 2005; mem. Accademia Filarmonica Romana 1979, Royal Swedish Acad. of Music 1993, Bayerische Akad. der Schönen Künste 1998; hon. mem. Royal Acad. of Music 1979, Guildhall School of Music and Drama 1981, Royal Philharmonic Soc. 1987, Royal Scottish Acad. 2001. *Compositions include:* Sonata for trumpet and piano 1955, Alma redemptoris mater for ensemble 1957, St Michael sonata for 17 wind instruments 1957, Prolation for orchestra 1958, Five Klee Pictures for percussion, piano and strings 1959, Five Motets for soli, chorus and ensemble 1959, O Magnum Mysterium for chorus, instruments and organ 1960, Te Lucis ante Terminum 1961, String Quartet 1961, Frammenti di Leopardi for soprano, contralto and chamber ensemble 1962, First Fantasia on John Taverner's In Nomine for orchestra 1962, Veni Sancte Spiritus for soli, chorus and orchestra 1963, Second Fantasia on John Taverner's In Nomine 1964, Ecce Manus Tradentis for mixed chorus and instruments 1964, Shepherd's Calendar for young singers and instrumentalists 1965, Notre Dame des Fleurs 1966, Revelation and Fall for soprano and instrumental ensemble 1966, Antechrist for chamber ensemble 1967, Missa super L'Homme Armé for speaker and ensemble 1968, Stedman Caters for instruments 1968, Nocturnal Dances (ballet) 1969, St Thomas Wake-Foxtrot for orchestra 1969, Worldes Blis 1969, Eram quasi Agnus (instrumental motet) 1969, Eight Songs for a Mad King for male singer and ensemble 1969, Vesalii Icones for dancer and ensemble 1969, Taverner (opera) 1970, From Stone to Thorn for mezzo-soprano and instrumental ensemble 1971, Blind Man's Buff (masque) 1972, Hymn to Saint Magnus for chamber ensemble and mezzo-soprano 1972, Renaissance Scottish Dances 1973, Stone Litany for mezzo-soprano and orchestra 1973, Fiddlers at the Wedding 1974, Miss Donnithorne's Maggot for mezzo-soprano and chamber ensemble 1974, The Kestrel Paced Round the Sun 1975, Ave Maris Stella for chamber ensemble 1975, Three Studies for Percussion 1975, The Blind Fiddler for soprano and chamber ensemble 1975, Stevie's Ferry to Hoy (beginner's piano solo) 1975, Three Organ Voluntaries 1976, Kinloche His Fantasie (with Kinloch) 1976, Anakreontika (Greek songs for mezzo-soprano) 1976, Orchestral Symphony No. 1 1976, The Martyrdom of St Magnus (chamber opera) 1976, Runes from a Holy Island 1977, Westerlings (unaccompanied part songs) 1977, A Mirror of Whitening Light for chamber ensemble 1977, Le Jongleur de Notre Dame (Masque) 1978, The Two Fiddlers 1978, Salome (ballet) 1978, Black Pentecost (for voices and orchestra) 1979, Solstice of Light (for Tenor, Chorus and Organ) 1979, The Lighthouse (chamber opera) 1979, Cinderella (pantomime opera for young performers) 1979, A Welcome to Orkney (chamber ensemble) 1980, Orchestral Symphony No. 2 1980, Little Quartet (string quartet) 1980, The Yellow Cake Revue (for voice and piano) 1980, The Medium 1981, The Bairns of Brugh 1981, Piano Sonata 1981, Little Quartet No. 2 (for string quartet) 1981, Lullabye for Lucy 1981, Brass Quintet 1981, Songs of Hoy (Masque for children's voices and instruments) 1981, The Pole Star 1982, Sea Eagle (for horn solo) 1982, Image, Reflection, Shadow (for chamber ensemble) 1982, Sinfonia Concertante (for chamber orchestra) 1982, Into the Labyrinth (tenor and chamber orchestra) 1983, Sinfonietta Accademica (chamber orchestra) 1983, Unbroken Circle 1984, Guitar Sonata 1984, The No. 11 Bus 1984, One Star, At Last (carol) 1984, Orchestral Symphony No. 3 1984, The Peat Cutters 1985, Violin Concerto 1985, First Ferry to Hoy 1985, An Orkney Wedding, with Sunrise 1985, Sea Runes (vocal sextet) 1986, Jimmack the Postie (overture) 1986, Excuse Me 1986, House of Winter 1986, Trumpet Concerto 1987, Resurrection (opera in one act with prologue) 1987, Oboe Concerto 1988, Cello Concerto 1988, Mishkenot (chamber ensemble) 1988, The Great Bank Robbery 1989, Orchestral Symphony No. 4 1989, Hymn to the Word of God (for tenor and chorus) 1990, Concerto No. 4 for clarinet 1990, Caroline Mathilde (ballet) 1990, Tractus 1990, Dangerous Errand (for tenor soli and chorus) 1990, The Spiders' Revenge 1991, First Grace of Light 1991, Strathclyde Concerto No. 5 for violin and viola, No. 6 for flute 1991, Ojai Festival Overture 1991, A Selkie Tale (music-theatre work for performance by children) 1992, The Turn of the Tide (for orchestra and children's chorus and instrumental groups) 1992, Strathclyde Concerto No. 7 for double bass 1992, Sir Charles his Pavan 1992, Strathclyde Concerto No. 8 for bassoon 1993, A Spell for Green Corn: The MacDonald Dances 1993, Orchestral Symphony No. 5 (Royal Philharmonic Soc. Award for Large-Scale Composition 1995) 1994, Cross Lane Fair (for orchestra) 1994, Strathclyde Concerto No. 9 for six woodwind instruments 1994, The Three Kings (for chorus, orchestra and soloists) 1995, The Beltane Fire (choreographic poem) 1995, The Doctor of Myddfai (opera) 1995, Orchestral Symphony No. 6 1996, Strathclyde Concerto No. 10 for orchestra 1996, Piccolo Concerto 1996, Job (oratorio for chorus, orchestra and soloists) 1997, Mavis in Las Vegas–Theme and Variations 1997, Orkney Saga I: Fifteen keels laid in Norway for Jerusalem-farers 1997, The Jacobite Rising (for chorus, orchestra and soloists) 1997, Piano Concerto 1997, Orkney Saga II: In Kirkwall, the first red Saint Magnus stones 1997, Sails in St Magnus I–III 1998, A Reel of Seven Fishermen 1998, Sea Elegy (for chorus, orchestra and soloists) 1998, Swinton Jig 1998, Temenos with Mermaids and Angels (for flute and orchestra) 1998, Spinning Jenny 1999, Sails in Orkney Saga III: An Orkney Wintering (for alto saxophone and orchestra) 1999, Trumpet quintet (for string quartet and trumpet) 1999, Mr Emmet Takes a Walk 1999, Horn Concerto 1999, Orkney Saga IV: Westerly Gale in Biscay, Salt in the Bread Broken 2000, Orchestral Symphony No. 7 2000, Orchestral Symphony No. 8 (Antarctic Symphony) 2000, Canticum Canticorum 2001, De Assumtione Beatae Mariae Virginis 2001, Crossing Kings Reach 2001, Mass 2002, Missa Parvula 2002, Naxos Quartet No. 1 2002, Piano Trio 2002, Naxos Quartet No. 2 2003, No. 3 2003, No. 4 2004, No. 5 2004, Children's Games 2004, Judas Mercator for trombone solo 2004, Fanfare for Carinthia for four trumpets 2004, Tecum Principium for flute and marimba 2004, The Fall of the Leafe for string orchestra 2004, Lullay, my child and weep no more for SATB chorus 2004, Naxos Quartet No. 6 and No. 7 2005, O Verbum Patris for SATB chorus & organ 2005; has written music for films: The Devils, The Boyfriend and many piano pieces, works for choir, instrumental works and realizations of fifteenth and sixteenth-century composers. *Honours:* Hon. Fellow Royal Incorporation of Architects in Scotland 1994, Hon. Fellow Univ. of Highlands and Islands 2004, Freeman of the City of Salford; Officier, Ordre des Arts et des Lettres 1988; several hon. degrees including Hon. DMus (Edin.) 1979, (Manchester) 1981, (Bristol) 1984, (Open Univ.) 1986, (Glasgow) 1993, (Durham) 1994, (Hull) 2001, (Kingston) 2005; Hon. DLitt (Warwick) 1986, (Salford) 1999; Hon. DUniv (Heriot-Watt) 2002; Olivetti Prize 1959, Koussevitsky Award 1964, Koussevitsky Recording Award 1966, Cobbett Medal for services to chamber music 1989, First Award of Asscn of British Orchestras, for contribs to orchestras and orchestral life in UK 1991, Gulliver Award for Performing Arts in Scotland 1991, Nat. Fed. of Music Socs Charles Groves Award for outstanding contrib. to British Music 1995, Royal Philharmonic Soc. Award for Large-scale Composition (for Symphony No. 5) 1995, Inc. Soc. of Musicians Distinguished Musicians Award 2001. *Current Management:* c/o Judy Arnold, 50 Hogarth Road, London, SW5 0PU, England. *Telephone:* (20) 7370-2328. *Fax:* (20) 7373-6730. *E-mail:* j.arnold@maxopus .com. *Website:* www.maxopus.com.

**MAY, Marius;** Cellist; b. 1950, England. *Education:* Studied with Andre Navarra in Paris and with Pierre Fournier in Geneva. *Career:* Debut: Wigmore Hall, 1973, followed by recital and concerto appearances throughout the United Kingdom; Festival Hall 1976, with the Schumann Concerto and the Philharmonia Orchestra; Has played in public from age 10, giving a recital at the Royal College of Music, London, and playing the Saint-Saëns A minor Concerto in Edinburgh; Edinburgh and Bath Festivals, 1976; Soloist with leading orchestras in Europe; Several tours of Germany have included Berlin Philharmonic concert 1980; Concerts with Yehudi Menuhin at the Gstaad Festival, Switzerland. Has recently played the Elgar Concerto with the London Philharmonic and the Finzi Concerto at the Three Choirs Festival with the Royal Philharmonic; Has taught at the University of California in Los Angeles; BBC television concerts include the Tchaikovsky Rococo Variations and a Gala from the Edinburgh Festival. *Current Management:* Ingpen & Williams Ltd, 7 St George's Court, 131 Putney Bridge Road, London, SW15 2PA, England.

**MAYER, Albrecht;** oboist. *Education:* studied oboe with Gerhard Scheuer, Georg Meerwein, Ingo Goritzki, Maurice Bourgue. *Career:* mem. Bamberg Cathedral Choir as a child; solo oboist, Bamberg Symphony Orchestra 1990–92, Berlin Philharmonic 1992–; mem. Sabine Meyer Wind Ensemble; numerous int. performances as soloist; has performed with conductors, including Claudio Abbado, Sir Simon Rattle, Nikolaus Harnoncourt; performs frequently with Berlin Baroque Soloists, Thomas Quasthoff, Matthias Goerne, Leif Ove Andsnes. *Recordings:* with Sabine Meyer Wind Ensemble: Dvořák Serenade/Myslivecek, Octetts 1995, Mozart, Serenades 1997, Beethoven, Octets 1999, Sabine Meyer plays Mozart (two vols); other: Bach Cantatas (with Matthias Goerne, baritone) 1996, G. Müller, Oboen-Quintett (with Bamberger Streichquartett) 1997, Bach, Brandenburg Concert No. 2 (with Michala Petri), Passion Flight (with Kaori Fujii), Kennedy Plays Bach (with Nigel Kennedy) 2000, Telemann, Concerto for Oboe d'Amore 2001, Bach, Reconstructed Concertos 2002, Fauré, Clair de Lune 2002, Romantic Oboe-Concertos in the 20th Century, Schumann/Daelli/Nielsen/Cossart/Yvon/ Koechlin 2003, Bach, Lieder ohne Worte 2003, In Search of Mozart 2004. *E-mail:* mail@albrechtmayer.com (office). *Website:* www.albrechtmayer.com.

**MAYER, Richard;** Composer; b. 9 June 1948, Brno, Czechoslovakia. *Education:* Faculty of Arts, University of Brno; Piano, Composition, Conservatory, Brno; PhD, Musicology, 1975. *Career:* Debut: Brno, 1969, Zlin, 1980; Records of compositions on Czech television and radio; Piano Fantasy, Iceland, the Premiere, USA, 1990; mem, Nordic Society of Prague; Bohemian Music Association; Club of Moravian Composers. *Compositions*

*include:* Sonata for Violin and Piano; Concerto for 2 Pianos and Tromba; Quartet for Clarinet, Violin, Viola and Cello; Variation for Clarinet and Piano; Reykjavík, Sonata for Viola and Cello; Variation for Tromba and Piano, Iceland, Fantasy for Piano Solo; Saga of Northern Night, A Cycle of Compositions for Alto and Bassoon; Drama Musicum Sine Verbis–Chronikon Mundi, 1st Symphony for Chamber Orchestra; Magna Missa Millennia Islandica: Great Magnificent Mass for large orchestra, organ, narrator, solos and choir, dedicated to the forthcoming anniversary of 1000 years of accepting Christianity in Iceland; II Symphony "Icelandic" for Great Orchestra. *Recordings:* Several. *Contributions:* Opus Musicium. *Address:* Cihlarska 14, 602 00 Brno, Czech Republic.

**MAYER, William (Robert);** Composer; b. 18 Nov. 1925, New York, USA. *Education:* BA, Yale University, 1949; Studied with Roger Sessions at Juilliard, 1949 and at the Mannes College of Music, 1949–52. *Career:* Secretary, National Music Council, 1980. *Compositions:* Stage: The Greatest Sound Around, children's opera, 1954; Hell World children's opera, 1956; One Christmas Long Ago, opera in act, 1964; Brief Candle, micro-opera, 1964; A Death in the Family, opera 1983; The Snow Queen, ballet, 1963; Orchestra: Andante for strings, 1955; Hebraic Portrait, 1957; Overture for an American, 1958; Two Pastels, 1960; Octagon for piano and orchestra, 1971; Inner and Outer Strings for string quartet and string orchestra, 1982; Of Rivers and Trains, 1988; String Quartet and other chamber music; Piano Sonata Choruses and song. Honours; Guggenheim Fellowship, 1966; National Institute for Musical Theater Award, 1983. *Address:* ASCAP, ASCAP Building, 1 Lincoln Plaza, NY 10023, USA.

**MAYFORTH, Robin;** Violinist; b. 1965, USA. *Education:* Studied at the Juilliard School, New York. *Career:* Appearances with I Solisti Veneti, under Claudio Scimone; Co-founded the Lark Quartet, USA; Recent concert tours to Australia, Taiwan, Hong Kong, China, Germany, Netherlands; US appearances at the Lincoln Center, New York, Kennedy Center, Washington DC and in Boston, Los Angeles, Phildelphia, St Louis and San Francisco; Repertoire includes quartets by Haydn, Mozart, Beethoven, Schubert, Dvořák, Brahms, Borodin, Bartók, Debussy and Shostakovich. *Honours:* (With Lark Quartet): Gold Medals at the 1990 Naumberg and 1991 Shostakovich Competitions; Prizewinner, 1991 London International String Quartet, 1991 Melbourne Chamber Music, 1990 Premio Paulio Borciani (Reggio Emilia) and 1990 Karl Klinger (Munich) Competitions. *Current Management:* Sonata, Glasgow Scotland. *Address:* c/o The Lark Quartet, 11 Northpark Street, Glasgow G20 7AA, Scotland.

**MAYHEW JONAS, Dame Judith,** DBE, LLM; New Zealand politician, lawyer and academic; *Chairman, Royal Opera House;* b. 18 Oct. 1948, Dunedin; m. 1976 (divorced 1986). *Education:* Otago Girls' High School, Univ. of Otago, NZ. *Career:* barrister and solicitor, NZ 1973, solicitor, England and Wales 1993; Lecturer in Law, Univ. of Otago 1970–73; Lecturer in Law and Sub-Dean, Univ. of Southampton, UK 1973–76; King's Coll., London 1976–89; Dir Anglo-French law degree, Sorbonne, Paris 1976–79; Dir of Training and Employment Law, Titmuss Sainer Dechert 1989–92; mem. Bd London Guildhall Univ. 1992–2002; mem. Court and Council Imperial Coll., London 2001–03; Dir of Educ. and Training, Wilde Sapte 1994–99; City and Business Adviser to Mayor of London 2000–; mem. Court of Common Council Corpn of London 1986–2004, Chair. Policy and Resources Cttee 1997–2003; Special Adviser to Chair. of Clifford Chance 2000–; Dir Gresham Coll. 1990–, London First Centre 1996–, Int. Financial Services London (fmrly British Invisibles) 1996–, London First 1997–, 4Ps 1997–, London Devt Agency 2000 (Chair. Business and Skills Cttee –2004, Vice-Chair. 2003–), Cross River Partnership; Trustee Natural History Museum 1998–; Gov. Birkbeck Coll. London 1993–, Chair. Bd Govs 1999–2003; Chair. Royal Opera House, London 2003–; Provost King's Coll., Cambridge 2003–05; Trustee Natural History Museum. *Honours:* Hon. LLD (Otago) 1998, (City Univ. London) 1999; named New Zealander of the Year in the UK 2004. *Address:* Royal Opera House, Covent Garden, London, WC2E 9DD, England (office). *Telephone:* (20) 7240-1200 (office). *Website:* www .royalopera.org.

**MAYNOR, Kevin (Elliott);** Singer (Bass); b. 24 July 1954, Mt Vernon, New York, USA. *Education:* Diploma, Manhattan School of Music, 1970–72; BME, Bradley University, 1972–76; MM, Northwestern University, 1976–77; MV, Moscow Conservatory, 1979–80; Indiana University, 1980–83; DM, 1988. *Career:* Debut: Carnegie Hall, 1983 in a concert of Strauss's Die Liebe der Danaë; Avery Fisher Hall as Nocco in Fidelio, 1985; New York City Opera, Akhnaten, 1985; Chicago Lyric Opera; Santa Fe Opera; Virginia Opera; Nashville Opera; Long Beach Opera; Chicago Opera Theater; Mobile Opera Theater; Mobile Opera; Apprenticeship, 1st from the West, Bolshoi Opera, 1979–80; Scottish Opera 1987 and Opera Pacific 1994 as Hunding in Die Walküre. *Current Management:* Herbert Barrett Management. *Address:* 201 Egmont Avenue, Mt Vernon, NY 10552, USA.

**MAZURA, Franz;** Singer (Bass-Baritone); b. 22 April 1924, Salzburg, Austria. *Education:* Studied with Fred Husler in Detmold. *Career:* Debut: Kassel 1955; Sang at Mainz and Brunswick until 1964; Mannheim 1964–89; Salzburg 1960, in La Finta Semplice; Pizarro in Fidelio, 1970; Member of Deutsche Oper Berlin 1963; Paris Opéra from 1973, as Wagner's Wotan, Alberich and Gurnemanz; Sang Dr Schön in the 1979 premiere of the three-act version of Berg's Lulu; Bayreuth Festival from 1971, as Biterolf, Alberich, Gunther, Gurnemanz, Klingsor and the Wanderer in the 1988 Ring Cycle directed by Harry Kupfer; Hamburg Opera from 1973; Israel Festival,

Caeserea, as Moses in Schoenberg's Moses und Aron; Guest appearances in Vienna, Buenos Aires, San Francisco, Nice and Strasbourg; Metropolitan Opera debut 1980, as Dr Schön, returned to New York as Klingsor, Alberich, Gurnemanz, Creon in Oedipus Rex, Pizarro, Doctor in Wozzeck, Frank in Die Fledermaus, Rangoni in Boris Godunov and the Messenger in Die Frau ohne Schatten, 1989; Bayreuth Festival, 1988–89 as Klingsor and the Wanderer; Season 1991–92 as Voland (the Devil), in Höller's Meister und Margarita at Cologne and Klingsor at the Met and the Bayreuth Festival; Narrated Henze's Raft of the Medusa, Festival Hall, London, 1997; Schigolch in Lulu at San Francisco, 1998; Sang Schigolch at Bielefeld and the New York Met, 2001. *Recordings include:* Dr Schön, Jack the Ripper in Lulu (Grammy Award 1980) (Deutsche Grammophon); Gunther in Götterdämmerung (Philips); Schoenberg's Moses (Philips). *Current Management:* Ingpen & Williams Ltd, 7 St George's Court, 131 Putney Bridge Road, London, SW15 2PA, England.

**MAZURKEVICH, Yuri (Nicholas);** Professor of Violin and Concert Violinist; b. 6 May 1941, Lvov, USSR; m. Dana Mazurkevich, 4 July 1963, 1 d. *Education:* School of Gifted Children, Lvov, 1948–60; Moscow State Conservatoire, with D Oistrakh, 1960–65, Postgraduate course, Artist Diploma; Masters degree in Performance, 1965–67. *Career:* Concert Violinist appeared all over the world; Recorded for Radio Moscow, France, BBC, ABC (Australia), CBC (Canada), Sender Freies (West Berlin), WGBH (Boston) and many others; Assistant Professor, Violin, Kiev State Conservatory, 1967–73; Associate Professor, Violin, University of Western Ontario, 1975–85; Professor of Violin, Chairman of String Department, 1985–, Boston University; Member of Quartet Canada, 1980–; mem, Music Council of Canada. *Recordings:* Works by Beethoven, Paganini, Tartini, Handel, Spohr, Leclair, Prokofiev, Sarasate, Honegger, Telemann and others in Moscow, Toronto and Montreal, Canada. *Honours:* Prize Winner of 3 International Violin Competitions, Helsinki 1962, Munich 1966 and Montreal 1969. *Address:* 56 Mason Terrace, Brookline, MA 02146, USA.

**MAZZARIA, Lucia;** Singer (Soprano); b. 1964, Gorizia, Poland. *Education:* Studied in Trieste and Rome. *Career:* Debut: Venice 1987, as Mimi; Hamburg Opera 1987, as Mimi, Liu and Micaela; La Scala Milan debut 1988, as Lauretta in Gianni Schicchi, returning as Liu, Euridice and Violetta; Cologne Opera 1991, as Amelia Boccanegra; Further appearances at Monte Carlo, Covent Garden (London), Houston and Vienna; Venice 1990, as Mimi in Leoncavallo's Bohème; Further tours of Russia, Japan and Korea; Sang Desdemona at the 1996 Holland Festival and Micaela in Carmen at Macerata, 1998; Season 2000–01 as Amelia Grimaldi at Macereta, Suor Angelica in Verona and Desdemona in Venice. *Recordings include:* Leoncavallo's Bohème (Nuova Era). *Address:* c/o Opéra et Concert, 1 rue Volney, F–75002 Paris, France.

**MAZZOLA, Denia;** singer (soprano); b. 1956, Bergamo, Italy. *Education:* studied with Corinna Malatrasi. *Career:* sang Amina in La Sonnambula at Brescia, then Lucia di Lammermoor, and Adina at Florence and Milan; Landestheatre Salzburg 1984, as Gilda, St Gallen 1985 as Violetta; Sang at the Zürich Opera 1985–87, notably as Elvira in I Puritani; Appearances as Lucia at Naples, 1988–89, New York City Opera; La Scala Milan, 1987, Sole in Fetonte by Jommelli; Further engagements at Houston, Alice Ford, San Francisco, in Maria Stuarda, Bergamo, Amelia in Elisabetta al Castello di Kenilworth by Donizetti, 1989, Reggio Emilia, Violetta, Barcelona, Elvira, 1990 and the 1990 Montpellier Festival, Palmide in a concert performance of Meyerbeer's Il Crociato in Egitto; Sang Mimi at the 1996 Torre del Lago Festival; Season 2000–01 as Manon Lescaut at Catania, Cherubini's Médée for the Macerata Festival and Hélène in Les Vêpres Siciliennes at Schwerin (concert). *Recordings include:* Lucia di Lammermoor, with forces of the San Carlo, Naples (Nuova Era).

**MAZZOLA, Rudolf;** Singer (Bass); b. 1941, Basle, Switzerland. *Education:* Studied in Basle and Zürich. *Career:* Debut: Commendatore in Don Giovanni at St Gallen; Sang at St Gallen until 1971, Basle, 1971–75; Engaged at the Vienna Volksoper from 1975, debut in Wolpert's version of Molière's Le Malade Imaginaire; Sang Osmin in Die Entführung at the Vienna Staatsoper, 1977, returning as Sarastro, Gremin, Pimen, Padre Guardiano and the Grand Inquisitor; Bregenz Festival 1980 and 1984, as Osmin and the Sacristan in Tosca; Salzburg Festival 1981 in the premiere of Cerha's Baal, Paris Opéra 1983, as Truffaldino in Ariadne auf Naxos; Sang the Doctor in Wozzeck at Barcelona 1984, Rossini's Basilio at Liège 1988; Toronto, Don Alfonso in Così fan tutte, 1992; Nice, La Roche, Capricco, 1993; Created roles in Einem's Tulifant and Krenek's Kehraus um St Stephan, Ronach Theater Vienna, 1990, and sang Mozart's Bartolo at the Theater an der Wien, 1991; Sang the Doctor in Wozzeck at Florence, 1998; Sang Berg's Schigolch and Doctor at the Vienna Staatsoper, 2000. Guest appearances at Frankfurt, Hamburg, Munich, Budapest, Turin and Zürich; Frequent concert and oratorio appearances. *Address:* c/o Staatsoper Opernring 2, 1010 Vienna, Austria.

**MAZZUCATO, Daniela;** Italian singer (soprano); b. 1 Dec. 1946, Venice. *Education:* Venice Conservatory. *Career:* debut, Teatro Fenice Venice, 1966, as Gilda; Appearances throughout Italy, including 1971 at the Verona Arena, as Oscar; Rome 1990, as Valencienne in The Merry Widow and Mozart's Despina, 1995; Palermo, 1996, as Gluck's Euridice; Guest engagements at La Scala, Oscar, 1977, Düsseldorf, Prague and Berlin; Toulouse 1995, as Musetta in La Bohème; Season 1998 as Despina at Glyndebourne; Casparina in Wolf-Ferrari's Il Campiello at Bologna and Pipsi in Lehar's Eva at Naples. *Recordings:* Vivaldi's Serenata a tre; Medea by Cherubini. *Current Manage-*

ment: Stage Door, Via Marconi 71, 40122 Bologna, Italy. *Telephone:* (051) 19984750. *Fax:* (051) 19984779. *E-mail:* info@stagedoor.it. *Website:* www.stagedoor.it.

**MEAD, Philip John,** ARCM, FTCL, LRAM, GRSM; British pianist; *Professor, London College of Music and Media;* b. 8 Sept. 1947, Chadwell St Mary, Essex, England; m. Gillian Mead 1969; three d. *Education:* Royal Acad. of Music, London Coll. of Music and Media. *Career:* debut, Purcell Room 1973; performances at major festivals, England and overseas; specialist in 20th-century piano music; commissioned works include works for piano and electronics by Dennis Smalley, Jonathan Harvey, Tim Souster and others; featured soloist at London South Bank Electric Weekend 1987; soloist, BBC Symphony Orchestra Ives Festival 1996; founder and Artistic Dir, British Contemporary Piano Competition, Cambridge 1988; Prof. and Head of Dept of Contemporary Piano, London Coll. of Music and Media 1998–; repetoire includes Messiaen, Tippett, Stockhausen and George Crumb; commissioned works for brass and piano, Sackman, Poole, Burrell, Ellerby, Wilkins and Emmerson 1999–2003; mem. Sonic Arts, Soc. for the Promotion of New Music (dir), EPTA. *Recordings:* eight albums of electronic music, complete solo piano works of Charles Ives, George Crumb. *Publications:* contrib. to Electro Acoustic Music, Classical Piano. *Honours:* Hon. ARAM 1993, Hon. FLCM 1997; research awards, prizewinner Gaudeamus Int. Competition for Interpreters of Contemporary Music 1978. *Address:* 31 Lingholme Close, Cambridge, CB4 3HW, England (home). *Telephone:* (1223) 357431 (home). *E-mail:* meadpj@hotmail.com (home). *Website:* www.philipmead.com.

**MEALE, Richard,** MBE; composer; b. 24 Aug. 1932, Sydney, Australia. *Education:* New South Wales Conservatorium of Music, University of California at Los Angeles. *Career:* Programme Planning Officer for the Australian Broadcasting Commission, 1962–68; Senior Lecturer in the Department of Music at the University of Adelaide from 1969; Active as Pianist from 1955, notably in the music of Messiaen; mem, Adelaide Festival Centre Trust, 1972; President of the Australian Branch of ISCM, 1977; Chairman of the composition Panel of the Music Board of the Australia Council. *Compositions:* Stage: The Hypnotist Ballet, 1956; Incidental Music to King Lear; Juliet's Memoirs, opera, 1975; Operas Voss, 1986 and Mer de Glace, 1991; Orchestral: Flute Concerto, 1959; Sinfonia for piano and strings, 1959; Homage to Garcia Lorca for double string orchestra, 1964; Images, 1966; Very High Kings, 1968; Clouds Now and Then, 1969; Soon it Will Die, 1969; Evocations, 1973; Viridian, 1979; Symphony, 1994; Instrumental: Divertiemnto for Piano Trio, 1959; Flute Sonata, 1960; Les Alboradas for flute, horn, violin and piano, 1963; Wind Quintet, 1970; Incredible Floridas for flute, clarinet, violin, cello, piano and percussion, 1971; 3 String Quartets, 1974, 1980, 1993; Fanfare for brass ensemble, 1978; Keyboard: Sonatina Patetica, 1957; Orenda, 1959; Coruscations, 1971; Palimpsest, for ensemble, 1998. *Honours:* Composers Fellowship awarded by the South Australian Government 1972–75. *Current Management:* Universal Edition (London) Ltd, 48 Great Marlborough Street, London, W1F 7BB, England. *Telephone:* (20) 7437-6880. *Fax:* (20) 7437-6115.

**MEDCALF, Stephen;** Stage Director; b. 1960, England; m. Susan Gritton, 1 s. *Education:* London Drama Studio. *Career:* Graduated 1983 and became associate director at Glyndebourne 1988, working with Peter Sellars, Peter Hall and Trevor Nunn; Directed in many major international opera houses in France, Portugal, Italy and Australia as well as for Glyndebourne Festival, Opera North, Opera Northern Ireland, The wexford Festival, English Touring Opera, Garsington, Mid Wales Opera (Artistic Adviser) and numerous festivals; Fellow of the Guildhall School of Music and Drama and Resident producer of its opera course; Has directed over 60 opera productions. *Recordings:* Videos: Zauberflöte, Così fan tutte, with John Eliot Gardiner; Le nozze di Figaro, Glyndebourne Festival Opera and Channel 4. *Current Management:* Athole Still International Management, Forresters Hall, 25–27 Westow Street, London, SE19 3RY, England. *Telephone:* (20) 8771-5271. *Fax:* (20) 8768-6600. *Website:* www.atholestill.com.

**MEDEK, Ivo;** Composer; b. 20 July 1956, Brno, Czechoslovakia; m. Zuzana Medková, 11 Aug 1986, 2 s. *Education:* Computers and Structural Mechanics (Dipl ing), Technical University; Master Composition, 1989, PhD, Composition and Theory, 1997, Janáček Academy of Music and Dramatic Art in Brno. *Career:* About 60 compositions of orchestral, chamber, electro-acoustics music, many recorded on television, broadcasts and festivals in the Czech Republic, Europe and USA, 1990, 1994; Docent of Darmstadt courses, lectures in Brno, Austria, Poland, Netherlands, Portugal; Professor of Janáček Academy of Music in Brno; mem, Camerata Brno 'Q' Society, Czech Music Council. *Compositions:* Adledaivan, 1988; Pangea, 1989; Triads, 1989; Cephedidy, 1991; Flow, 1992; Postludio, 1994; Persofonie, 1995; 11 Gestalten des Mondscheins, 1997; Enlargement, for flute, clarinet, piano, violin and cello, 1999; Crossings, multimedia, 1999; Ancient Stories, 1999; Triax, 2001. *Recordings:* Adai; Adeldaivan; Flow; Cepheidy; Postludio; Fests; Pangea; Wandering in Well-known Landscape; Persofonie. *Publications:* Basic General Composing Principles, 1989; Processuality as a Complex Composing Method, 1996. *Contributions:* About 100 articles, Opus Musicum, Czech Music, The Silence. *Honours:* Czech Music Fund Prize, 1993. *Address:* Sirotkova 67, 61600 Brno, Czech Republic.

**MEDEK, Tilo;** German composer; b. 22 Jan. 1940, Jena, Thuringia; s. of Willy Müller-Medek and Rosa Gewehr; m. 2nd Dorothea Medek; three d. one s. *Education:* Humboldt Univ., Berlin with W. Vetter, E. H. Meyer and G.

Knepler, German Acad. of Music, East Berlin with R. Wagner-Régeny. *Career:* moved to West Germany 1977; established music publishing house Edition Tilo Medek 1982; founder mem. Freie Akademie der Künste (Ind. Acad. of Arts), Mannheim. *Compositions include:* opera: Einzug 1969, Icke und die Hexe Yu 1970–71, Appetit auf Frükirschen 1971, Katharina Blum 1984–86, Gritzko und der Pan 1987, Ballet David and Goliath 1972, Der Überfall 2003; orchestral: Triade 1964, Das zögernde Lied 1970, Flute Concerto 1973, Piccolo Concerto 1975, König Johann oder Der Ausstieg for orchestra and organ 1976, Marimba Concerto 1977, Cello Concertos 1978, 1982, 1984, 1992, Organ Concerto 1979–80, Violin Concerto 1980–83, I Sinfonie (Eisenblatter for organ and orchestra) 1983, II Sinfonie (Rheinische) 1986–88, III Sinfonie (Sorbische) 1994–96; chamber: Flute Sonata 1963, six Wind Quintets 1965–99, String Trio 1965, Divertissement for wind quintet and harpsichord 1967, Stadtpfeifer, Schwanengesang for clarinet, trombone, cello and piano 1973, two Nonett 1974, 1996, Tagtraum for seven instruments 1976, Giebichenstein for eight instruments 1976, Reliquienschrein for organ and percussion 1980; vocal: Altägyptische Liebeslieder for two voices and orchestra 1963, Sintflutbestanden for tenor, horn and piano 1967, Gethsemane (cantata) 1980, Der Frieden wird immer gefährlicher for tenor, chorus and orchestra 1996–98; also music for guitar, piano, organ and for other solo instruments. *Publications:* Das Volksliederbuch 1993. *Honours:* Int. Composers' Competition, Gaudeamus Foundation, Netherlands 1967, State Univ. of New York 1968, Opera Competition, GDR 1969, Friedrich-Kuhlau Competition, Uelzen 1970, 22ème Tribune Internationale des Compositeurs, UNESCO, Paris 1975, Prix Folklorique de Radio Bratislava 1975, Prix Danube Bratislava 1977, Ernst-Reuter-Preis (with Dorothea Medek) 1982. *Address:* Edition Tilo Medek, Rheinhöhe, Westerwaldweg 22, 53424 Remagen-Oberwinter, Germany (office). *Telephone:* 02228-8175 (office). *Fax:* 02228-8176 (office). *E-mail:* tilo@medek.net. *Website:* www.medek.net.

**MEDJIMOREC, Heinz;** Pianist; b. 1940, Vienna, Austria. *Education:* Studied in Vienna. *Career:* Performances of Haydn and other composers in Vienna and elsewhere from 1968; Co-founder, Hydn Trio of Vienna, 1968 and has performed in Brussels, Munich, Berlin, Zürich, London, Paris and Rome; New York debut in 1979 and has made frequent North American appearances with concerts in 25 states; Debut tour of Japan 1984, with further travels to the Near East, Russia, Africa, Central and South America; Series at the Vienna Konzerthaus Society from 1976, with performances of more than 100 works; Summer Festivals at Vienna, Salzburg, Aix-en-Provence, Flanders and Montreux; Masterclasses at the Royal College and Royal Academy in London, Stockholm, Bloomington, Tokyo and the Salzburg Mozarteum. *Recordings include:* Complete piano trios of Beethoven and Schubert, Mendelssohn D minor, Brahms B major, Tchaikovsky A minor, Schubert Trout Quintet; Albums of works by Haydn, Schumann, Dvořák and Smetana. *Address:* Haydn Trio, Sue Lubbock Concert Management, 25 Courthorpe Road, London NW3 2LE, England.

**MEDLAM, Charles;** cellist; b. 10 Sept. 1949, Port of Spain, Trinidad. *Education:* studied the cello in London, Paris (with Maurice Gendron at the Conservatoire), Vienna and Salzburg (performance practice with Nikolaus Harnoncourt). *Career:* lectured and played in the resident string quartet at the Chinese Univ. of Hong Kong; founder (with Ingrid Seifert), London Baroque 1978; conducted the first performance of Scarlatti's Une villa di Tuscolo and a revival of Gli Equivoci Sembiante, for the BBC; season 1990–91 included Dido and Aeneas at the Paris Opéra, Blow and Lully at the Opera-Comique, Aci, Galatea e Polifemo in Spain, Netherlands and England, and cantatas by Handel and Rameau in Austria, Sweden and Germany with Emma Kirkby; Salzburg Festival debut 1991, with music by Mozart; further festival engagements at Bath, Beaune, Versailles, Ansbach, Innsbruck and Utrecht and 1993 Proms; frequent tours of Japan and USA. *Recordings:* Marais La Gamme, Theile Matthew Passion, Bach Trio Sonatas, Charpentier Theatre Music, Handel Aci, Galatea e Polifemo, Venus and Adonis, Purcell Chamber Music; Purcell Fantasias, Bach Violin Sonatas, Monteverdi Orfeo, Handel German Arias; A Vauxhall Gardens Entertainment; English Music of the 18th Century; Francois Couperin Chamber Music; The complete trio sonatas of Corelli, Handel, Purcell, Lawes; Gamba sonatas by CPE Bach, harpsichord concertos by JC Bach/WA Mozart; Vivaldi, Trio sonatas Op.1, Christmas Music and Handel Latin Motets with Emma Kirkby, Purcell Fantasias, Couperin's Apotheoses, Rameau Pièces de Clavecin en Concert. *Address:* Brick Kiln Cottage, Hollington, Nr Newbury, Berkshire RG20 9XX, England.

**MEDVECZKY, Adam;** Conductor; b. 1941, Budapest, Hungary. *Education:* Timpanist Graduate, Bela Bartók Conservatory, Department of Conducting, Liszt Academy of Music, Budapest, 1968; Masterclass, Maestro Franco Ferrara, Italy. *Career:* Timpanist, Hungarian State Symphony Orchestra for 9 years; Conductor, Budapest State Opera, 1974; Numerous guest appearances in Bulgaria, Germany, Greece, Netherlands, Poland, Italy, Romania, Russia and USA; Professor, Ferenc Liszt Academy, Budapest, 1981–. *Recordings:* Has made numerous recordings. *Honours:* Liszt Prize, 1976; 2nd Prize, Hungarian Television International Concours for Young Conductors, 1974.

**MEE, Anthony;** Singer (Tenor); b. 9 Sept. 1951, Lancashire, England. *Education:* Studied at the Royal Northern College of Music. *Career:* Debut: Welsh National Opera, 1984 as Ernani; Sang Ernani and Riccardo, 1999–2000 for Welsh National Opera; Gabriele Adorno, Cavaradossi, Nadir and Calaf for English National Opera; Bardolfo in Falstaff at the Berlin Staatsoper;

Concerts include Verdi's Giovanna d'Arco, Boito's Mephistopheles and Verdi's Aroldo in London; Season 1999–2000 with Bardolfo at Ferraa Musica, Italy and in Munich. *Recordings:* Weill's Street Scene and Falstaff, conducted by Abbado (DGG). *Address:* c/o Harlequin Agency Ltd, 203 Fidlas Road, Cardiff CF4 5NA, Wales.

**MEEK, Clarissa;** Singer (Mezzo-soprano); b. 1970, England. *Education:* Guildhall School of Music and Drama. *Career:* Appearances with Scottish Opera in The Merry Widow, Street Scene, Figaro, The Magic Flute, Death in Venice, Jenůfa and Salome; Iolanthe in the opera by Sullivan (also broadcast); Glyndebourne Festival as Madame Larina in Eugene Onegin, Pauline (The Queen of Spades), Glasha (Katya Kabanova) and two roles in the premiere production of Birtwistle's Second Mrs Kong (1994); Season 1996–97 with Haydn's Stabat Mater at Aldeburgh, Thisbe (Cenerentola) in Japan and Maddalena in Rigoletto at Guernsey; Maurya in Hart's Riders to the Sea at Cambridge, 1998; Concerts include Messiah in Hanover and The Dream of Gerontius; Other operas include Les Boréades by Rameau, Tchaikovsky's The Enchantress and Monteverdi's Ulisse (as Penelope). *Honours:* Erich Vietheer Memorial Award at Glyndebourne, 1995. *Address:* c/o C&M Craig Services, 3 Kersley Street, London SW11 4 PR, England.

**MEEK, James;** British singer (baritone); b. 29 July 1957, Winchester, England. *Education:* Guildhall School of Music. *Career:* sang for three seasons at the Buxton Festival and appeared as Owen Wingrave at Aldeburgh; Other roles include Escamillo, Rossini's Figaro, Mozart's Count and Guglielmo, Valentin in Faust and the Doctor in Debussy's posthumous Fall of the House of Usher (Queen Elizabeth Hall 1989); Sang in Haydn's La Vera Costanza in Germany; Concert repertoire includes Elijah, the Petite Messe Solennelle, Handel's Judas Maccabaeus (Flanders Festival) Israel in Egypt and Dixit Dominus; Bach's Christmas Oratorio at the Snape Maltings, St John and St Matthew Passions; Britten's War Requiem in Germany and Yugoslavia and the Requiems of Mozart, Fauré and Brahms; Sang Messiah at the National Concert Hall Dublin, Pulcinella at the Barbican and the Missa Solemnis at Guilford Cathedral; Songs by Henri Dutilleux at Aldeburgh and concerts with the Songmakers' Almanac at the Bath, Nottingham, Buxton and Derby Festivals; Recitals on South Bank in the Schoenberg Reluctant Revolutionary Series, 1989 and Schubert directed by Hermann Prey, accompanied by Iain Burnside; sang Starveling in A Midsummer Night's Dream at Aix-en-Provence, 1992.

**MEHNERT, Thomas;** Singer (Bass); b. 1966, Chemitz, Germany. *Education:* Studied at the Richard Strauss Conservatory, Munich, from 1991, the Munich Singschule. *Career:* Concert performances at the 1995 Rheingau Music Festival, and the Mozart Festival at Würzburg; Engagements at the Cottbus Opera as Colline, Colas in Mozart's Bastien und Bastienne, the Hermit in Der Freischütz Figaro and Banquo, from 1995; Guest appearances with Netherlands Opera as Pluto in Monteverdi's Orfeo and Fifth Solo Voice in Moses und Aron, under Pierre Boulez (also at the Salzburg Festival); Royal Festival Hall, London, in Moses and Aron with the Philharmonia Orchestra under Christoph von Dohnányi, 1996. *Honours:* Deutsche Buhnvereins Grant, 1993. *Address:* c/o Staatsoper Cottbus, Karl Liebnecht Strasse 136, 7500 Cottbus, Germany.

**MEHTA, Zubin;** Indian conductor; *General Music Director, Bavarian State Opera;* b. 29 April 1936, Bombay; s. of the late Mehli Mehta and of Tehmina Daruvala Mehta; m. 1st Carmen Lasky 1958 (divorced); one s. one d.; m. 2nd Nancy Diane Kovack 1969. *Education:* Vienna Acad. of Music, studied under Hans Swarowsky. *Career:* first professional conducting in Belgium, Yugoslavia and UK (Liverpool); Music Dir Montreal Symphony 1961–67, Los Angeles Philharmonic Orchestra 1962–78; Music Dir New York Philharmonic Orchestra 1978–91; Music Dir Israel Philharmonic 1969–, appointed Dir for Life 1981; Gen. Music Dir Bavarian State Opera 1998–; conductor at festivals of Holland, Prague, Vienna, Salzburg and Spoleto; debut at La Scala, Milan 1969; conducts regularly with the Vienna and Berlin Orchestras; winner of Liverpool Int. Conductors' Competition 1958; Music Dir Maggio Musicale, Florence 1969, 1986–. *Honours:* Dr hc Tel Aviv Univ., Weizmann Inst. of Science, The Hebrew Univ. of Jerusalem, Jewish Theological Seminary, Westminster Choir Coll., Princeton, Brooklyn Coll., Colgate Univ.; shared Wolf Prize 1996; Commendatore (Italy), Médaille d'Or Vermeil (City of Paris), Commdr des Arts et des Lettres (France), Great Silver Medal of Service (Austria) 1997, Padma Vibhushan (India) 2001. *Current Management:* Askonas Holt Ltd, Lonsdale Chambers, 27 Chancery Lane, London, WC2A 1PF, England. *Telephone:* (20) 7400-1700. *Fax:* (20) 7400-1799. *E-mail:* info@askonasholt.co.uk. *Website:* www.askonasholt.co.uk. *Address:* Bayerische Staatsoper, Max-Joseph-Platz 2, 80539 München, Germany; Israel Philharmonic Orchestra, 1 Huberman Street, Box 11292, 61112 Tel-Aviv, Israel.

**MEI, Eva;** Singer (Soprano); b. 3 March 1967, Fabriano, Italy. *Education:* Studied at the Luigi Cherubini Conservatory, Florence. *Career:* Debut: Aspasia in Salieri's Axur, re d'Ormus, Siena, 1989; Sang Mozart's Constanze at the Vienna Staatsoper, 1990; Engaged at Zürich as Donna Anna, Alcina, Mozart's Countess and Luitgarde in Schubert's Des Teufels Lustschloss; Covent Garden debut as the Queen of Night, 1993; Berlin Staatsoper as Violetta; La Scala debut as Amenaide in Tancredi, 1993; Rossini Festival at Pesaro as Fanny in La Cambiale di Matrimonio and Berenice in L'Occasione fa il ladro, 1995–96; Vienna Festival as Genio in Haydn's Orfeo ed Euridice, 1995; Norina in Don Pasquale at Genoa, 1998; Season 2000–01 as Violetta for Zürich Opera, Meyerbeer's Dinorah at Parma, Bellini's Amina at Palermo and

Giulietta in Verdi's Un giorno di regno at Bologna; Concert engagements at the Amsterdam Concertgebouw, Queen Elizabeth Hall (London), Academia di Santa Cecilia (Rome) and halls in Buenos Aires, Vienna, St Petersburg and Moscow. *Recordings include:* A Mezzanote, songs by Bellini, Rossini and Donizetti; Rossini's Tancredi and Mozart's Il re Pastore. *Honours:* Caterina Cavalieri Prize at the 1990 Mozart Competition, Vienna. *Address:* c/o Opernhaus Zürich, Falkenstrasse 1, 8008 Zürich, Switzerland.

**MEIER, Jaroslav;** Composer; b. 7 Dec. 1923, Hronov, Czechoslovakia; m. Marta Kurbelova, 1950, 2 s. *Education:* Organ, Academy of Music, Prague, 1939–44; Organ and Composition, Academy of Music, Bratislava, 1947–49. *Career:* Head of Music Department, Radio Bratislava, 1949–56; Head of Music Department, Czechoslovakia television, Bratislava, 1956–; Music Designer (a lot of television and radio plays and films); mem, Union of Czechoslovak Composers; IMZ. *Compositions:* Opera Erindo (rewriting opera by baroque composer J. S. Kusser); Television opera The Night before Immortality (libretto after A Arbuzov); Opera, The Wooden Shoes (libretto after Guy de Maupassant); Orchestral works, Dances from my Country; Songs from my Country; What a Smell (song cycle based on Stefan Zary's poems); Concerto da Camera for organ and orchestra, 1982. *Recordings:* Chamber Music, Trois Impromptus; Prelude and Double Fugue; Divine Love; The Cycle Nocturnal Songs; Toccata et fuga, Fantasia concertante. *Publications:* Obrazovka pina hudby, (The Screen full of Music), 1970; Johann Sigismund Kusser, 1986. *Contributions:* Slovenska hudba (Slovak Music); Hudebni zivot (Music Life); Czeskoslovenska televize (television weekly paper). *Honours:* Prize of Critics at the International Television Festival The Golden Prague, 1976, for television opera The Night before Immortality. *Address:* Palackého 407, 54931 Hronov, Czech Republic.

**MEIER, Johanna;** Singer (Soprano); b. 13 Feb. 1938, Chicago, USA; m. Guido Della Vecchia. *Education:* Studied at the University of Miami with Arturo di Filippi and at the Manhattan School with John Brownlee. *Career:* Debut: New York City Opera 1969, as the Countess in Capriccio; Sang with the City Opera as Donna Anna, Senta, Louise and Tosca; Metropolitan Opera from 1976, as Marguerite, Ariadne, the Marschallin, Ellen Orford, Chrysothemis, Elisabeth, Brünnhilde in Die Walküre and Kaiserin; Guest engagements in Seattle, Washington, Philadelphia, San Diego, Ottawa and Chicago; Other roles include Sieglinde, Musetta, Mozart's Countess, Amelia (Un ballo in Maschera), Agathe and Eva; Bayreuth Festival debut 1981, as Isolde; Vienna Staatsoper from 1983, Fidelio and Senta; Tour of Japan 1986, as Isolde and the Marschallin; Barcelona and Buenos Aires 1987, as Elisabeth in Tannhäuser and Chrysothemis; Sang Turandot at Dallas and New Orleans, 1987–88; Ariadne at Trieste, 1988; Pittsburgh Opera, 1989, as Chrysothemis; The Dyer's Wife in Die Frau ohne Schatten at the 1990 Holland Festival; World premiere Les Liaisons Dangereuses at San Francisco Opera, 1994; Retired, 1994; Director, Producer, Black Hills Passion Play. *Address:* c/o Metropolitan Opera, Lincoln Center, NY 10023, USA.

**MEIER, Jost;** Composer and Conductor; b. 15 March 1939, Solothurn, Switzerland. *Education:* Studied at the Berne Conservatory and with Frank Martin in Netherlands. *Career:* Conducted at the Biel Opera, 1968–79, Basle, 1980–83. *Compositions include:* Sennentuntschi, dramatic legend, Freiburg, 1983; Der Drache, opera in 2 acts, Basle, 1985; Der Zoobar, opera in 4 scenes, Zürich, 1987; Augustin, opera in 4 scenes, Basle, 1988; Dreyfus, opera, Berlin (Deutsche Oper), 1994; Glarus for strings, 1980; Musique for trombone and orchestra, 1986; Musique Concertante, 1989; Esquisses for piano and percussion, 1993; Variations for Viola and Chamber orchestra, 1996; String Quartet, 1988; 2 Clarinet Trios, 1969, 1999; Franz von Assisi for soloists, women's chorus and orchestra, 1996; Galgenlieder for soprano, clarinet, cello and piano, 1996; Music for the Fêtes des Vignerons for soloists, choruses, orchestra and brass bands, 1999. *Address:* c/o Deutsche Oper Berlin, Richard Wagnerstrasse 10, 1000 Berlin, Germany.

**MEIER, Waltraud;** Singer (Mezzo-soprano); b. 9 Jan. 1956, Würzburg, Germany. *Education:* Studied with Anton Theisen in Würzburg and Dietger Jacob in Cologne. *Career:* Sang in Würzburg from 1976 as Cherubino, Dorabella, Nicklaus in Les Contes d'Hoffmann and Concepcion in L'Heure Espagnole, Mannheim 1978–80, as Carmen, Fricka, Waltraute and Octavian; Dortmund 1980–83, as Kundry in Parsifal, Eboli in Don Carlos and as Santuzza in Cavalleria Rusticana; Guest appearances in Cologne, Hamburg, Buenos Aires, Opera de Paris, Staatsoper Wien, Scala di Milano, San Francisco Opera, Munich, Bayreuth from 1983; Sang Kundry in Götz Friedrich's production of Parsifal, Brangäne in Jean-Pierre Ponelle's Tristan und Isolde, and Waltraute in Harry Kupfer's 1988 production of The Ring; Covent Garden debut 1985, as Eboli, returned to London 1988, as Kundry; Made her Metropolitan Opera debut in 1987 as Fricka in Rheingold and Walküre; Other roles include Azucena (Il Trovatore), Venus (Tannhäuser), the Composer (Ariadne auf Naxos); Sang Venus at Hamburg, 1990; Debut at the Teatro San Carlos, Lisbon, 1990 as Ortrud in Lohengrin; Théâtre du Châtelet, Paris, 1990 as Marguerite in La Damnation de Faust; Sang Waltraute at the Bayreuth Festival, 1988–92; Tchaikovsky's Maid of Orleans at Munich; Season 1992–93 as Kundry at La Scala and the Metropolitan, Berg's Marie at the Théâtre du Châtelet, Paris, and 1993–97 and 1999 as Isolde at Bayreuth; Sang Sieglinde at the Vienna Staatsoper and La Scala, Milan, 1994; Carmen at the Metropolitan, 1997; Isolde at Munich, 1998; Sang Leonore at Munich, and La Scala Milan, 1999; Season 2000–01 as Marie in Wozzeck at La Scala, in Salzburg and Vienna as Isolde, Sieglinde at Bayreuth, Amneris at the Berlin Staatsoper and Les Troyens at Munich, 2001; Wagner's Ortrud at Covent

Garden, 2003; Also heard as a concert singer, in Beethoven, Brahms, Mahler and Verdi; New production of Les Contes d'Hoffmann/Giulietta at the Salzburg Festival, 2003; For the season 2003–04 plans to concentrate exclusively on career as lieder and concert singer. *Recordings include:* Opera: Dittersdorf's Doktor and Apotheker; Venus and Kundry; Brahms Alto Rhapsody; Fricka in Bernard Haitink's Die Walküre, Wesendonk and Kindertotenlieder, Missa Solemnis, Mozart Requiem; Wagner recital with the Symphonieorchester des Bayerischen Rundfunks under Lorin Maazel, 1997; Isolde with Barenboim; Leonore with Barenboim; Ortrud with Claudio Abbado; Mahler-Lieder with Maazel, 1998; DVD of Tristan und Isolde, Munich 1998; CD/DVD of Walküre with Zubin Mehta, Munich, 2002. *Honours:* Recipient of several prestigious prizes; Holds titles of Bayerische Kammersängerin at the Bavarian State Opera and Kammersängerin at the Vienna State Opera. *Current Management:* Agentur Dr Hilbert. *Address:* Agentur Dr Germinal Hilbert, Maximilianstr 22, 80539 Munich, Germany. *Website:* www.waltraud-meier.com.

**MEIRON, Rhys;** Singer (Tenor); b. 1970, Wales. *Education:* Guildhall School, London 1997–99. *Career:* Glyndebourne Festival Chorus from 1998; Sang Edmondo in Manon Lescaut at Glyndebourne, 1999; Concert engagements in London, Guilford, Bournemouth, Toronto and Barbados; English National Opera from 1999, as Major Domo in Der Rosenkavalier, First Armed Man in The Magic Flute and Nadir in The Pearl Fishers. *Honours:* Prizewinner, National Eisteddfod, Wales, 1996–97. *Address:* c/o English National Opera, St Martin's Lane, London, WC2, England.

**MEKLER, Mani;** Singer (Soprano); b. 1951, Haifa, Israel. *Education:* Studied in Italy. *Career:* Sang Leonora in ll Trovatore at Stockholm and with Welsh National Opera, 1976, 1977; Glyndebourne debut 1978, as First Lady in Die Zauberflöte; Wexford Festival 1979, as Giulia in Spontini's La Vestale; Deutsche Oper am Rhein, Düsseldorf, from 1979 as Janáček's Jenůfa and Mila (Osud) and Chrysothemis; Further appearances at Drottningholm, Zürich and Milan, La Scala (premiere of Testi's Riccardo III, 1987); Other roles include Puccini's Manon Lescaut, Tosca and Butterfly, Strauss's Salome and Ariadne, and Goneril in Reimann's Lear.

**MELBY, John B.;** Composer; b. 3 Oct. 1941, Wisconsin, USA; m. Jane H. Thompson 1978, 2 s., 1 d. *Education:* Diploma, 1964, BMus, 1966, Curtis Institute of Music; MA, University of Pennsylvania, 1967; MFA, 1971, PhD, 1972, Princeton University. *Career:* Professor of Music, University of Illinois, Urbana. *Compositions include:* ..Of Quiet Desperation for computer-synthesized tape, 1976; Concerto No. 1 for violin and computer-synthesized tape, 1979, No. 2, 1986; Layers for computer-synthesized tape, 1981; Wind, Sand, and Stars for 8 instruments and computer-synthesized tape, 1983; Concerto for violin, English horn and computer-synthesized tape, 1984; Concerto for computer-synthesized tape and orchestra, 1987; Symphony No. 1, 1993; The rest is silence... for organ, 1994; Other concerti, songs and keyboard works. *Recordings include:* 91 Plus 5 for brass quintet and computer-synthesized tape; Forandre: 7 variations for digital computer; Two Stevens Songs for soprano and computer-synthesized tape; Concerto for violin, English horn and computer-synthesized tape; Concerto No. 1 for violin and computer-synthesized tape; Concerto Nos 1 and 2 for flute and computer-synthesized tape; Chor der Steine; Chor der Waisen. *Publications:* Some recent developments in computer-synthesized music, 1973; Proceedings of the 1975 Music Computation Conference (edited with James Beauchamp), 1976; 'Layers': An approach to composition for computer based upon the concept of structural levels, 1983; 'Computer' Music or Computer 'Music', 1989. *Address:* School of Music, 2136 Music Building, 1114 West Nevada, University of Illinois, Urbana, IL 61801, USA.

**MELBYE, Mikael;** Singer (Baritone), Stage Director and Designer; b. 15 March 1955, Frederiksberg, Denmark. *Education:* Royal Danish Conservatory, Copenhagen. *Career:* Debut: Guglielmo in Così fan tutte, Royal Danish Opera, 1976; Vast repertoire of mainly lyric baritone roles including Mozart, Rossini, Donizetti, Verdi and Puccini; International debut as Danilo in The Merry Widow at the Spoleto festival, 1981; Has since appeared in opera houses all over the world including La Scala di Milano, The Paris Opéra, Royal Opera House, Covent Garden, Staatsoper, Munich, Hamburgische Staatsoper, Metropolitan Opera; Debut in 1995 as Stage Director and Designer at the Royal Danish Opera in Così fan tutte; Following this was engaged as the Principal Director and Designer for this house; Directed and designed the premiere performance of Turandot at the Royal Danish Opera, 1996; Director, Arabella, in 1997 (Houston, 1998), Magic Flute, 1998 (Boston Lyric, 2000), La Bohème, Royal Danish Opera, 1999, Rigoletto at Santa Fe Opera, 1999; Sets and Costumes for Giselle at the San Francisco Ballet, 1999, La Sylphide for the Royal Swedish Ballet, 1999, and for the National Ballet of China in 1999; Directed Salome for Jutland Opera, 1999, Royal Danish Opera, 2001 and also Capriccio for Royal Danish Opera, 2001; Designed sets and costumes and directed Nutcracker at Tivoli Gardens, 2001; Costumes and sets for Symphony in C (Balanchine) at Royal Danish Ballet, 2000, and Royal Norwegian Ballet, 2001. *Recordings include:* Carmen (Karajan), Die Zauberflöte (Colin Davis). *Honours:* Oberdörfer Preis, Germany; The Golden Pegasus Award, Italy; Gladsaxe Music Award, Denmark; OV Award for best production (Turandot), Denmark; Knighthood from the Danish Queen, 1996. *Address:* c/o Royal Danish Opera, PO Box 2185, DK –1017 Copenhagen, Denmark.

**MELCHER, Wilhelm;** Violinist; b. 5 April 1940, Hamburg, Germany. *Education:* Studied in Hamburg and Rome. *Career:* Leader of the Hamburg

Symphony Orchestra, 1963; Former Member of Karl Munchinger's Stuttgart Chamber Orchestra, Heilbronn; Co-Founder, Melos Quartet of Stuttgart, 1965; Represented West Germany at the Jeunesse Musicales in Paris, 1966; International concert tours from 1967; Bicentenary concerts in the Beethoven Haus at Bonn, 1970; British concerts and festival appearances from 1974; Cycle of Beethoven quartets at Edinburgh Festival, 1987; Wigmore Hall, St John's Smith Square and Bath Festival, 1990; Associations with Rostropovich in the Schubert Quintet and the Cleveland Quartet in works by Spohr and Mendelssohn; Teacher, Stuttgart Musikhochschule. *Recordings include:* Complete quartets of Beethoven, Schubert, Mozart and Brahms; Quintets by Boccherini with Narciso Ypes and by Mozart with Frank Beyer. *Honours:* Grand Prix du Disque and Prix Caecilia, Academie du Disque, Brussels (with Melos Quartet). *Current Management:* Ingpen & Williams Ltd, 7 St George's Court, 131 Putney Bridge Road, London, SW15 2PA, England.

**MELIS, György;** Singer (Baritone); b. 2 July 1923, Szarvas, Hungary. *Education:* Studied at the Budapest Academy of Music, with Olga Relevhegyi. *Career:* Debut: Budapest Opera 1949, as Morales in Carmen; Many appearances in the major baritone roles of Mozart and Verdi; Sang Don Giovanni at Glyndebourne in 1961, and in Brussels, Berlin and Moscow; Further engagements in Edinburgh, (Bartók's Bluebeard 1973), Vienna and South America; Sang Don Giovanni at Wiesbaden 1987, as guest with the Hungarian State Opera (Bluebeard at Covent Garden 1989); Also heard in concert and oratorio; Song recitals include music by Bartók and Kodály. *Recordings:* Kodály's Háry János and Budavari Te Deum; Don Giovanni; Rigoletto; Szokolay's Samson; Title role in Bluebeard's Castle by Bartók, conducted by Fricasy; Scala Milano, Bartók's Bluebeard, 1978. *Honours:* Kossuth Prize 1962. *Address:* Hungarian State Opera, Népöztarsasag utja 22, 1061 Budapest, Hungary.

**MELKUS, Eduard;** Violinist; b. 1 Sept. 1928, Baden, Austria; m. Marlis Melkus-Selzer, 4 c. *Education:* Studied violin with Ernst Moravec 1942–53, Firmin Touche, Alexander Schaizhet and Peter Rybar; Musicology at Vienna University with Erich Schenk. *Career:* Debut: Vienna 1944; Founded Eduard Melkus Ensemble and Capella Academia, 1965, playing mainly on original instruments of the 18th Century; Professor of Violin and Viola at the Vienna Hochschule für Musik from 1958; Premiered Concerto by Egon Wellesz, 1962; Concerts in all Europe, USA, Australia, Japan, South America; Visiting Professor, University of Georgia, USA, 1973–74, University of Illinois and others; Lectures and master classes in many Universities all over the world; mem, Ex-President, Austria ESTA. *Recordings:* Concertos by Bach, Tartini, Vivaldi, Haydn; sonatas by Biber, Corelli, Bach, Mozart and Handel; Solo violin music by Bach, Haydn's La Vera Costanza at the Schönbrunn Palace, Vienna, 1984 (television). *Publications:* Die Violine, Schott, many articles on interpretation. *Honours:* Kornerpreis 1967; Edison Prize, Prix Academia Charles C Gross; Great Cross of Honour of the Republic of Austria. *Address:* Obere Donaustrasse 57/14, 1020 Vienna 2, Austria.

**MELLERS, Wilfrid Howard,** OBE, MA, DMus, DPhil; British composer, writer and academic; *Professor Emeritus of Music, University of York*; b. 26 April 1914, Leamington; s. of Percy Wilfrid Mellers and Hilda Maria Lawrence; m. 1st Vera Hobbs 1940; m. 2nd Peggy Pauline Lewis 1950 (divorced 1975); two d.; m. 3rd Robin Hildyard 1987. *Education:* Leamington Coll. and Downing Coll. Cambridge. *Career:* Supervisor in English Studies and Lecturer in Music, Downing Coll. Cambridge 1945–48; Staff Tutor in Music, Extramural Dept, Univ. of Birmingham 1948–60; Distinguished Andrew Mellon Visiting Prof. of Music, Univ. of Pittsburgh, USA 1960–63; Prof. and Head of Dept of Music, Univ. of York 1964–81, now Emer.; Part-time Prof., Guildhall School of Music, London, City Univ., London and Keele Univ. 1981–; many compositions and books published. *Music:* one full-scale opera, two chamber operas. *Publications:* François Couperin and the French Classical Tradition 1950, Man and His Music 1957, Music in a New Found Land (themes and developments in American music) 1964, Harmonious Meeting 1964, Twilight of the Gods: The Beatles in Retrospect 1973, Bach and the Dance of God 1981, Beethoven and the Voice of God 1984, A Darker Shade of Pale: A Backdrop to Bob Dylan 1984, Angels of the Night: Women Jazz and Pop Singers in the Twentieth Century 1986, The Masks of Orpheus 1986, Vaughan Williams and the Vision of Albion 1988, Le Jardin Retrouvé: Homage to Federico Mompou 1989, The Music of Percy Grainger 1992, The Music of Francis Poulenc 1993, Between Old Worlds and New 1997, Singing in the Wilderness 2001, Celestial Music 2002. *Honours:* Hon. DPhil (City Univ.) 1981. *Address:* Oliver Sheldon House, 17 Aldwark, York, YO1 7BX, England (office). *Telephone:* (1904) 638686. *Fax:* (1904) 638686 (home).

**MELLES, Carl;** Austrian conductor; b. 15 July 1926, Budapest; s. of György Melles and Maria Lazar; m. Gertrude Dertnig 1963; one s. one d. *Education:* Gymnasium and Acad. of Music, Budapest. *Career:* conducts all the maj. orchestras of Europe including Vienna and Berlin Philharmonic, New Philharmonia London, Scala Milan; guest appearances at Flanders, Salzburg and Bayreuth Festivals and Vienna State Opera; concert tours in Europe, Japan, S. Africa; Hon. Conductor Brunswick State Orchestra 1996–. *Recordings:* Classical Excellence, Hollywood, Florida with the Austrian Broadcast Symphony Orchestra, Beethoven symphonies I–IX. *Honours:* Hon. mem. Vienna Singakademie 1978; Franz Liszt Prize, Budapest 1954, Prize of Italian Record Critic Asscn for Dallapiccola's Il Prigioniero 1974; Brahms Medal, Vienna Singverein 1983, Hon. Gold Medal, City of Vienna 1986, Great Silver Badge of Honour, Austria. *Address:* Grünbergstrasse 4, 1130 Vienna, Austria. *Telephone:* (1) 813-52-06. *Fax:* (1) 813-52-06.

**MELLON, Agnès;** Singer (Soprano); b. 17 Jan. 1958, Epinay-sur-Seine, France; m. Dominique Visse. *Education:* Studied in Paris and San Francisco. *Career:* Sang with the Paris Opéra and the Opéra-Comique; Later appearances in the Baroque repertoire, notably as Tibrino in Cesti's Orontea at the 1986 Innsbruck Early Music Festival, Eryxene in Hasse's Cleofide, 1987 and Telaire in Rameau's Castor et Pollux at the 1991 Aix-en-Provence Festival; Sang the title role in Rossi's Orfeo at the Queen Elizabeth Hall, London, with Les Arts Florissants, 1990; Sang in Mondonville's Les Fêstes de Paphos at Versailles, 1996. *Recordings include:* Rossi's Orfeo, Cavalli's Xerxes, Lully's Atys, Charpentier's Médée and David et Jonathas, Hasse's Cleofide, Rameau's Anacréon and Zoroastre; Labels include Erato and Harmonia Mundi.

**MELLOR, Alwyn;** Singer (Soprano); b. 1968, Rawtenstall, Lancashire, England. *Education:* Royal Northern College of Music, with further study in Italy and St Petersburg. *Career:* Roles with Welsh National Opera (from 1992) have included Tatiana, Ginevra in Ariodante, Liu, Fiordiligi, Marguerite; Anne Trulove, and Micaela; Donna Elvira for WNO and Glyndebourne Touring Opera, Fiordiligi at Sante Fe (1997); Concerts include Edinburgh Festival with the Scottish Chamber Orchestra; Die Schöpfung in Amsterdam with the Bach Soloists under Marc Minkowski, 1993; US debut with the Kansas City Camerata, 1996; Season 1997 with Britten's Spring Symphony (Rotterdam Philharmonic Orchestra under Donald Runnicles); Sang Marenka in new production of The Bartered Bride for Opera North, 1998. *Recordings include:* Elsie in Yeomen of the Guard, with WNO. *Honours:* Awards from the Peter Moores Foundation. *Current Management:* Ingpen & Williams Ltd, 7 St George's Court, 131 Putney Bridge Road, London, SW15 2PA, England.

**MELNIKOV, Alexander;** Concert Pianist; b. 1973, Russia. *Education:* Moscow Tchaikovsky Conservatory, with Lev Naumov, from 1991. *Career:* Regular guest at international festivals, including the Schleswig-Holstein (Germany), Yehudi Menuhin (Switzerland), Styrian Festival (Austria) and the Bashmet Festival at Bonn; Recitals throughout Europe, America and the Far East, concertos with such conductors as Gergiev, Lazarev and Fedoseyev; Chamber music with Vadim Repin, Boris Pergemenschikov and the Shostakovich Quartet; Performs regularly in Japan in recitals and concertos with the Japan Philharmonic, recitals in Toronto with Vodim Repin (violin); Solo recitals in the USA, Luxembourg, London, Paris and Moscow; Repertoire includes Beethoven, Grieg, Schumann and Schubert. *Honours:* Laureate of the Robert Schumann Competition, Zwickau, 1989; Queen Elisabeth of Belgium Competition, Brussels, 1991. *Address:* c/o IMG Artists, Lovell House, 616 Chiswick High Road, London W4 5RX, England.

**MELROSE, Leigh;** Singer (Baritone); b. 1972, New York, USA. *Education:* St John's College, Cambridge; Royal Academy of Music. *Career:* Debut: Dancairo in Carmen, for English National Opera; Other roles with ENO Mozart's Count, Papageno, Ned Keene, Junius and Leoncavallo's Rodolfo; roles elsewhere include Rossini's Figaro for New York City Opera; Silvio for Welsh Nat. Opera; Birtwistle's Punch in Porto; Rambo in John Adam's The Death of Klinghoffer (Channel 4 film); Concerts include various BBC Proms; Carmina Burana; Belshazzar's Feast; Friar Lawrence in Berlioz's Romeo et Juliette. *Address:* c/o IMG Artists, Lovell House, 616 Chiswick High Road, London W4 5RX, England.

**MENARD, Pierre;** Violinist; b. 1945, Quebec, Canada. *Education:* Studied at Quebec Conservatory and at Juilliard with Dorothy DeLay, Ivan Galamian and the Juilliard Quartet. *Career:* Solo appearances in Canada and the USA; Former Concertmaster of the Aspen Festival Orchestra and the Nashville Symphony; Co-Founder and Second Violinist of the Vermeer Quartet from 1970; Performances in most North American centres, Europe, Israel and Australia; Festival engagements at Tanglewood, Aspen, Spoleto, Berlin, Edinburgh, mostly Mozart (New York), Aldeburgh, South Bank, Santa Fe Chamber Music West, and the Casals Festival; Resident Quartet for Chamber Music Chicago; Masterclasses at the Royal Northern College of Music, Manchester; Member of the Resident Artists Faculty of Northern Illinois University. *Recordings:* Quartets by Beethoven, Dvořák, Verdi and Schubert (Teldec); Brahms Clarinet Quintet with Karl Leister (Orfeo). *Honours:* 1st Prize in Chamber Music, Quebec Conservatory; Winner, National Festival of Music Competition; Prix d'Europe from the Quebec Government. *Address:* Allied Artists, 42 Montpelier Square, London SW7 1JZ, England.

**MENESES, Antonio;** cellist; *member, Beaux Arts Trio*; b. 23 Aug. 1957, Refice, Brazil. *Education:* studied with Antonio Janigro in Düsseldorf and Stuttgart. *Career:* appeared widely in Europe and America from 1977; appearances with the Berlin Philharmonic conducted by Karajan, with the London Symphony Orchestra in London and the USA, and with the Israel Philharmonic, Vienna Philharmonic and Concertgebouw Orchestras; other conductors include Abbado, Previn, Maazel and Muti; tours of Australia 1984, 1987; engagements at the Lucerne and the Salzburg Easter Festivals, with the Berlin Philharmonic; mem., Beaux Arts Trio 1998–. *Recordings include:* Brahms Double Concerto (with Anne-Sophie Mutter), Strauss Don Quixote (conducted by Karajan). *Honours:* second prize int. competitions in Barcelona and Rio de Janeiro, first prize ARD Competition, Munich 1977, gold medal Tchaikovsky Int. Competition, Moscow 1982. *Current Management:* Encore Arts Management, USA. *Telephone:* (812) 320-4389. *E-mail:* info@ encoreartsmanagement.com. *Website:* www.encoreartsmanagement.com; www.beauxartstrio.org.

**MENKOVA, Irina;** Violinist; b. 1960, Moscow, Russia. *Career:* Co-founder, Glazunov Quartet, 1985; Concerts in the former Soviet Union and recent appearances in Greece, Belgium, Poland, Germany and Italy; Works by Beethoven and Schumann at the Beethoven Haus in Bonn; Further engagements in Canada and Netherlands; Teacher, Moscow State Conservatoire and Resident at the Tchaikovsky Conservatoire; repertoire includes works by Borodin, Shostakovich and Tchaikovsky, in addition to the standard works. *Recordings:* Tchaikovsky on Olympia label. *Honours:* Prizewinner, Borodin Quartet and Shostakovich Chamber Music Competitions, with the Glazunov Quartet. *Current Management:* Sonata, Glasgow, Scotland. *Address:* 11 Northpark Street, Glasgow G20 7AA, Scotland.

**MENOTTI, Gian Carlo;** Italian composer; b. 7 July 1911, Cadegliano; one s. *Education:* Curtis Inst. of Music, Philadelphia, Pa. *Career:* went to USA 1928; mem. teaching staff, Curtis Inst. of Music 1941–45; Hon. Assoc. Nat. Inst. of Arts and Letters 1953; Founder and Pres. Festival of Two Worlds, Spoleto, Italy. *Compositions include:* operas: Amelia Goes to the Ball, The Old Maid and the Thief, The Island God, The Telephone, The Medium, The Consul, Amahl and the Night Visitors, The Labyrinth (own libretti), The Saint of Bleecker Street 1954, The Last Savage 1963, Martin's Lie 1964, Help, Help, The Glotolinks (space opera for children) 1968, The Most Important Man in the World 1971, Tamu Tamu 1973, Arrival 1973, La Loca 1979, St Teresa 1982, The Boy Who Grew Too Fast 1982, Goya 1986, Giorno di Nozze 1988; Song of Hope (cantata) 1980; ballet: Sebastian; film: The Medium (producer); Vanessa (libretto) 1958, The Unicorn, The Gorgon and the Manticore – A Madrigal Fable, Maria Golovin 1959, The Last Superman 1961, The Death of a Bishop of Brindisi (cantata) 1963; chamber music, songs, etc. *Honours:* Hon. BM (Curtis Inst. of Music); Guggenheim Award 1946, 1947; Pulitzer Prize 1950, 1955; Kennedy Center Award 1984. *Address:* ASCAP Building, 1 Lincoln Plaza, New York, NY 10023, USA; Yester House, Gifford, East Lothian, EH41 4JF, Scotland.

**MENTZER, Susanne;** Singer (Mezzo-soprano); b. 21 Jan. 1957, Philadelphia, USA. *Education:* Juilliard School, New York and with Norma Newton. *Career:* Debut: Houston Opera 1981, as Albina in La Donna del Lago; Appeared with Dallas Opera 1982, in Gianni Schicchi and Das Rheingold; Washington Opera as Cherubino; Chicago Lyric Opera, Phladelpha Opera and New York City Opera as Rosina in Il Barbiere di Siviglia; Houston Opera as Rossini's Isolier, and at Rossini Festival Pesaro, Italy, the Composer in Ariadne auf Naxos and Giovanna Seymour in Anna Bolena; European debut with Cologne Opera 1983, as Cherubino, later Massenet's Cendrillon; La Scala Milan as Zerlina in Don Giovanni; Vienna Staatsoper as Cherubino; Covent Garden debut 1985, as Rosina, returned as Giovanna Seymour 1988, and Dorabella in Così fan tutte 1989; Metropolitan Opera debut 1989, as Cherubino; Monte Carlo 1988, as Adalgisa in Norma; Sang Octavian at the Théâtre des Champs-Elysées, Paris 1989; Annius in La Clemenza di Tito at La Scala, 1990 and Sesto in the Chicago premiere of Mozart's opera, 1991; Salzburg Festival, Cherubino and Zerlina, Metropolitan Opera, Idamante, 1991; In Les Contes d'Hoffmann as Nicklausse, Octavian in Der Rosenkavalier, Composer in Ariadne auf Naxos, Metropolitan Opera, 1992–93; Geneviève in Pelléas et Mélisande at the Palais Garnier, Paris, 1997; Roméo at the Opéra Bastille; Nicklausse at the Met, 1998; Season 2000–01 as Octavian and Mélisande at the Met, Adalgisa at Covent Garden and Mozart's Idamante at the Dresden Staatsoper. *Recordings include:* Anna Bolena with Sutherland and Bonynge and Bruckner Te Deum on Philips label, Mozart Masses with King's College Choir; Barber of Seville, EMI, (Rosina); Idomeneo, Philips, (Idamante); Don Giovanni, EMI (Zerlina). *Address:* J.M. Poilvé, 16 avenue Franklin D.Roosevelt, F–75008 Paris, France.

**MENUHIN, Jeremy;** pianist; b. 2 Nov. 1951, San Francisco, CA, USA. *Education:* studied in Paris with Nadia Boulanger, Israel with Mindru Katz (piano), Vienna with Hans Swarowsky (conducting). *Career:* public performances from 1965; New York recital debut 1984; Berlin Philharmonic 1984; Dame Myra Hess series, Chicago 1985; regular recitals, Kennedy Center (Washington, DC), Berlin Philharmonie, Amsterdam Concertgebouw, La Salle Pleyel; US tours with Czech Philharmonic and Prague Chamber Orchestra 1989; guest appearances, San Francisco and Houston Symphonies; European orchestras include BBC, Royal and Amsterdam Philharmonics, Salzburg Mozarteum, Orchestre Nat. de France; 1987–88 season included Windsor Festival concert with English Chamber Orchestra; Beethoven's 1st concerto with Leningrad Philharmonic conducted by Yehudi Menuhin; 1989 European concert tour with Toulouse Chamber Orchestra; chamber music with cellists Colin Carr, Steven Isserlis, Marius May; recitals with sopranos Edith Mahis and Arleen Auger, Aldeburgh 1987; with Hallé Orchestra, Zürich Tonhalle Orchestra, Sinfonia Varsovia 1994; tour of Germany, Czech Republic and Poland with Philharmonia Hungarica (Schumann, Bartók's 3rd Piano Concerto); Bath Festival with English Symphony Orchestra; Beethoven's 5th Piano Concerto with Orchestra of St John's Smith Square; tour of Russia and further concerts throughout Europe 1995; St Nazaire Festival, Wigmore Hall, and other festivals; season 1998–99 toured Germany, Lithuania, Netherlands and France; solo recitals at the Ubeda Festival, Spain and the Ravello Festival in Italy; recent performances include concerts in Brazil and Mexico and recitals in Netherlands, Switzerland and the UK and tours with the Sinfonia Varsovia in Germany. *Recordings include:* works by Schubert, Mozart, Debussy, Beethoven; Bartók's two violin sonatas with father, Yehudi Menuhin; Dvořák Quartets and Quintet with Chilingirian Quartet; Schubert's Late Piano Works 1998. *Honours:* Grand Prix de Disque 1981. *Current Management:* Upbeat Classical Management, PO Box 479, Uxbridge, UB8

2ZH, England. *Telephone:* (1895) 259441. *Fax:* (1895) 259341. *E-mail:* info@upbeatclassical.co.uk. *Website:* www.upbeatclassical.co.uk.

**MENZEL, Peter;** Singer (Tenor); b. 31 Jan. 1943, Dresden, Germany. *Education:* Studied at the Dresden Muskihochschule. *Career:* Sang with the Dresden Opera from 1968; Berlin Staatsoper from 1977, notably in the 1979 premiere of Leonce und Lena by Dessau; Other roles have included Monostatos, Oronte in Alcina, Jacquino, Mime, Pang in Turandot, the Captain in Wozzeck, and Bardolph; Many concert appearances, notably with the Thomas Choir Leipzig on tour to Switzerland, Italy and Japan. *Address:* c/o Oper Berlin, Unter den Linden 7, 1060 Berlin, Germany.

**MERCER, Alexandra;** British singer (mezzo-soprano) and artists' manager; b. 12 May 1944, Gravesend, Kent, England; m. Philip Mercer 1965; two d. (twins). *Education:* studied with Maestro Antonio and Lina Riccaboni Narducci in Milan, Royal Scottish Acad. of Music. *Career:* debut, Barga Festival 1970; has appeared in opera throughout the UK and Europe, with cos such as English Bach Festival Trust, Kent Opera, Royal Opera House Covent Garden, Opera Rara, and Barber Inst.; roles include Poppea, Despina, Dorabella, Rosina, Hansel, Ascanius, Smeton, Isabella, Mrs Sedley, The Sorceress and Samson; festival appearances include Barga 1970, Edinburgh 1978, 1979, Bath 1981, Wexford 1984; regular appearances in concert, oratorio and recital; BBC soloist for Radio 3 and 2 with BBC debut in 1984; artists' man. *Recordings:* Opera Rara, 100 Years of Italian Opera 1800–1910. *Honours:* Vaughan Williams Trust Award 1972, 1973. *Address:* 25E Frognal, London, NW3 6AR, England (office).

**MERCER, Gregory;** Singer (Tenor); b. 1960, USA. *Career:* Opera appearances at the Metropolitan, New York, Chicago, Sarasota Opera and Dalls; Lawrenceville, NJ, 1988 as Ferrando in Così fan tutte; Monadnock Festival, New York, from 1987; Graz Opera, from 1992, notably as Raffaele in Stiffelio by Verdi, 1994; Concert and broadcast appearances. *Recordings:* Lord Byron by Virgil Thomson. *Address:* Opera Graz, Kaiser Joseph Platz 10, 8010 Graz, Austria.

**MERCHANT, Jan;** Singer (Mezzo); b. 1960 South Carolina, USA. *Education:* Metropolitan Opera Studio; University of South Carolina. *Career:* Opera engagements in Switzerland, Germany, Netherlands and USA: 1989 with Hannover Opera, Venus in Offenbach's Orpheus in the Underworld; Independent productions: Mephisto in Hervé's Le Petit Faust in Hamburg, Fildama in Cimarosa's Matrimonio Segreto, Countess in Le nozze di Figaro, Maddelena in Rigoletto, Second Dame in Zauberflöte; Concert Soloist with Nord Deutsche Rundfunk in Hamburg, most notably Stabat Mater (Dvořák), Requiem (Mozart); Elijah in Maryland; 1995–98, Director of Choral Music, and member of Vocal Staff, Vienna Musical School in addition to guesting. *Address:* c/o Vocal Department, Vienna Musical School, Quellenstr. 102, 1101, Vienna, Austria.

**MERIGHI, Giorgio;** Singer (Tenor); b. 20 Feb. 1939, Ferrara, Italy. *Education:* Studied at the Rossini Conservatory, Pesaro. *Career:* Debut: Spoleto Festival 1962, as Riccardo in Un Ballo in Maschera; Many appearances on Italian stages, including the Verona Arena and at the Florence Festival (Meyerbeer's Robert le Diable 1968); Covent Garden 1971 and 1974; Metropolitan Opera debut 1978, as Manrico in Il Trovatore; Guest engagements in Berlin, Monte Carlo, Barcelona, Marseilles and Brussels; Geneva 1984, as Pollione in Norma; Wiesbaden Festival 1985, as the Duke of Mantua; Italian television as Pinkerton in Madama Butterfly; Munich and Palermo 1987–88 as Maurizio in Adriana Lecouvreur; Sang Luigi in Il Tabarro at the Met 1989, Maurizio at Bonn; Season 1992 with Don José at Genoa, Andrea Chénier at Turin and concert in memory of Mario del Monaco at the Torre del Lago Festival; Sang Ismaele in Nabucco at Verona, 1996; Gabriele Adorno in Simon Boccanegro at Monte Carlo, 1998; Sang Loris in Fedora at Genoa, 2000. *Address:* c/o L'Opera de Monte Carlo, BP 139, Place du Casino, Monte Carlo, Monaco.

**MERILÄINEN, Usko;** Composer; b. 27 Jan. 1930, Tampere, Finland. *Education:* Diploma in Composition, Sibelius Academy, 1955. *Career:* Mem, Chairman, Association of Finnish Composers, 1981–92. *Compositions include:* Epyllion for orchestra, 1963; Piano Sonata No. 2, 1966; Papillons for 2 Pianos, 1969; Concerto for Piano and Orchestra No. 2, 1969; Symphony No. 3, 1971; Concerto for 13 Instruments, 1971; Piano Sonata No. 3, 1972; Concerto for Double Bass and Percussion, 1973; Psyche, ballet in 2 acts, (tape), 1973; Piano Sonata No. 4, 1974; Concerto for Cello and Orchestra, 1975; Dialogues for Piano and Orchestra, 1977; Mobile, ein Spiel for Orchestra, 1977; Simultus for 4 Instruments, 1979; (Suvisoitto) Summer Sounds for Flute and Grasshoppers, 1979; Kyma for String Quartet, 1979; Paripeli for Cello and Piano, 1980; Quattro notturni per Arpa, 1984–85;... but this is a landscape, Monsieur Dali!, 1986; Exodus for Choir and Orchestra, 1988; Concerto No. 2, Aikaviiva (Timeline) for Orchestra, 1989; Letter to a Cellist for Cello Solo and Ensembles, 1990; Concerto for Guitar and Orchestra, 1991; Piano Sonata No. 5, 1992; String Quartet No. 3, 1992; Geasseija niehku, summer concert for Chamber Orchestra, 1993–94; Fetes d'Henriette for Flute, Cello and Piano, 1995; Kehrä, for orchestra, 1996; Sona, for piano, 1997. *Recordings include:* Visions and Whispers with Mikael Helasvuo on flute; Ku-Gu-Ku, electroacoustic works; Timeline, Concerto No. 2 under Leif Segerstram; Papillons, Piano Sonatas 2, 4 and 5 with Jaana Kärkkäinen and Ilmo Ranta. *Honours:* Wihuri Foundation International Sibelius Prize, 1965; Prof hc, Doctor hc, Sibelius Academy, 1997. *Address:* Nokiantie 102, 33300 Tampere, Finland.

**MERKA, Ivan;** Cellist and Musicologist; b. 15 May 1926, Kosice, Czechoslovakia; m., 1 s., 1 d. *Education:* Violoncello, Masaryk Institute of Music and Singing, Ostrava; State Exam for Violoncello teaching, Brno; Musical science and philosophy, Masaryk University, Brno, 1952; Cello, Janáček Academy of Musical Arts, Brno, 1953. *Career:* Deputy Lead Cello, Radio orchestra, Ostrava, 1945–47; Lead violoncello, Opera orchestra of National Moravian-Silesian Theatre, Ostrava, 1953–60; Lead violoncello, Janáček Philharmonic Orchestra, Ostrava, 1960–68; Teacher of violoncello, Janáček Conservatoire, Ostrava, 1953–; Director, Janáček Conservatorie, Ostrava, 1990–92; Lecturer, Janáček Academy of musical arts in Brno, 1970–80; Assistant Professor, Janáček academy of musical Arts, Brno, 1992–; Soloist, concert halls, broadcasting, performed 16 cello concerts; 48 sonatas and suites; 205 other compositions for cello and piano; 884 radio performances; 223 public concerts; Brno quartet, 1948–50; Silesia piano trio, 1946–56; Ostrava string quartet, 1953–88; State ensemble of Janáček Philharmonic Orchestra, 1960–; 509 broadcast transmissions; 2281 public concerts; 200 string quartets; 62 trips abroad; mem, Beethoven Society of the Czech Republic; Board of Directors, Leoš Janáček Foundation. *Publications:* Articles, studies, papers, broadcast transmissions, television scripts with a musical theme, annual reports; Monograph, Violoncello: History, literature, personalities, 1995. *Honours:* Ostrava string quartet Haydn Prize, Budapest, 1959; Zdenka Podhajská Foundation Award, 1997; Senior Prix, 2000; European Gustav Mahler Prize, European Union of the Arts, 2001. *Address:* Mexica 5, 712 00 Ostrava, Czech Republic.

**MERRILL, Nathaniel;** Stage Director; b. 8 Feb. 1927, Massachusetts, USA. *Education:* Trained with Boris Goldovsky at New England Conservatory of Music and with Gunther Rennert, Herbert Graf and Carl Ebert in Europe. *Career:* Debut: Boston 1952, with the US premiere of Lully's Amadis; Metropolitan Opera New York from 1955, resident stage director from 1960, with productions of Turandot, Meistersinger, Les Troyens, Aida, Rosenkavalier, Adriana Lecouvreur, Luisa Miller, Parsifal, Porgy and Bess, 1985, Il Trovatore, Samson et Dalila and L'Elisir d'amore (collaborations with designer Robert O'Hearn); Other stagings at Strasbourg, Vancouver, Verona, San Francisco, New York City Opera and the Vienna Staatsoper. *Address:* c/o Metropolitan Opera, Lincoln Center, New York 10023, USA.

**MERRIMAN, Nan;** Singer (Mezzo-soprano); b. 28 April 1920, Pittsburgh, USA; m. Tom Brand. *Education:* Studied with Alexia Bassian in Los Angeles and with Lotte Lehmann. *Career:* Debut in concert, 1940; Opera debut as La Cieca in La Gioconda, Cincinnati, 1942; Sang in Toscanini's NBC broadcasts as Maddalena in Rigoletto, Gluck's Orpheus and Meg Page in Falstaff; Glyndebourne 1953, 1956, as Baba the Turk in The Rake's Progress and Dorabella in Così fan tutte; Sang at Aix-en-Provence as Dorabella, at the Holland Festival and La Scala Milan (1955), Piccola Scala 1958, in the local premiere of Dargomyzhsky's The Stone Guest; Guest engagements in Paris, Geneva, Amsterdam, Chicago and San Francisco. Many appearances in concert. *Recordings include:* Così fan tutte conducted by Karajan (Columbia). *Honours:* 1st Prize, National Federation of Music Clubs, 1943.

**MERRITT, Chris;** singer (tenor); b. 27 Sept. 1952, Oklahoma City, USA. *Education:* Oklahoma City University, apprentice artist at the Santa Fe Opera. *Career:* Sang in Augsburg as Idomeneo, Rossini's Otello, Rodolfo and Julien in Louise; New York City Opera debut 1981, as Arturo in I Puritani; Appeared in Rossini's Tancredi at Carnegie Hall, Il Viaggio a Reims at the Vienna Staatsoper, Ermione in Naples and Maometto II at San Francisco Opera; Paris Opéra debut 1983, in Rossini's Moise; Sang Uberto in La Donna del Lago at Covent Garden; Season 1985–86 in Il Viaggio a Reims at La Scala, as Rodrigo (La Donna del Lago) in Paris, Idreno in a concert performance of Semiramide at Covent Garden; Leukippos in Daphne at Carnegie Hall; Maggio Musicale Florence 1986, as Benvenuto Cellini; Aeneas in Les Troyens in Amsterdam; Nemorino in L'Elisir d'amore at Orlando, Florida; Opened the 1988–89 season at La Scala in Guillaume Tell by Rossini; Title role in Robert le Diable at Carnegie Hall; Sang in I Puritani at the Rome Opera, 1990; Arnold in a new production of Guillaume Tell at Covent Garden, 1990; Sang Admète in Alceste at the opening of the 1990–91 season at Chicago; Benvenuto Cellini at Geneva, 1992; Season 1992–93 as Leicester in Rossini's Elisabetta at Naples, Arnold at Covent Garden and San Francisco, Rodrigo in La Donna del Lago at La Scala and Conte di Libenskof in Il Viaggio a Reims at Pesaro; Season 1996–97 as Schoenberg's Aron in Amsterdam and Paris and in the premiere of Henze's Venus and Adonis at Munich; Featured Artists (People No. 183) Opera Magazine Festival issue, 1992; Concert engagements in Verdi's Requiem; Haydn's Creation and the Choral Symphony in Israel; Rossini's Petite Messe Solennelle in Amsterdam; Benvenuto Cellini by Berlioz at the Festival Hall, London under Valery Gergiev, 1999; Sang Lilaque in Henze's Boulevard Solitude at Covent Garden, 2001. *Recordings:* Rossini's Stabat Mater, Ermione and Il Viaggio a Reims; Donizetti's Emilia di Liverpool; I Puritani; Faust, conducted by Michel Plasson. *Current Management:* Askonas Holt Ltd, Lonsdale Chambers, 27 Chancery Lane, London, WC2A 1PF, England. *Telephone:* (20) 7400-1700. *Fax:* (20) 7400-1799. *E-mail:* info@askonasholt.co.uk. *Website:* www.askonasholt.co.uk; www.onatech.com/chris-merritt.

**MERTENS, Klaus;** Singer (Tenor); b. 25 March 1949, Kleve, Germany; m. Ingrid Mertens, 14 May 1986, 1 s., 3 d. *Education:* Diploma, 1976. *Career:* Numerous radio recordings and television productions; Oratorio Work and Song Recitals, 1976–; mem, Bach-Gesellschaft. *Recordings:* Ranging from Renaissance to 20th Century Composers including Bach complete recordings of all Cantatas, St Matthew Passion, St John Passion and all other major vocal works; Sang the title role in Handel's Riccardo Primo at Magdeburg, 1996. *Address:* Buschhovener Strasse 2, 53347 Alfter, Germany.

**MESHIBOVSKY, Alexander;** Concert Violinist and Associate Professor; b. 15 April 1949, Kharkov, Russia. *Education:* Special School of Music for Gifted Children, Kharkov, 1955–65; Kharkov Conservatory, 1965–70; Masterclasses with Boris Goldstein, Moscow, 1971–74. *Career:* Concertmaster, Soloist, Moscow Chamber Orchestra, Russian Concert Agency, 1971–72; Soloist, Moscow Concert Agency, 1972–74; Dozent, Innsbruck Conservatory, 1975–76; Concerts in many European Countries, USA; Associate Professor, East Tennessee State University, 1984–; Associate Professor, West Virginia University, 1988. *Compositions:* Paganini Variations; Transcriptions of works by Debussy, Gershwin, Rachmaninov and many others. *Current Management:* Alpha Attractions Inc, New York, USA. *Address:* 82-46 Lefferts Blvd, Apt 2D, Kew Gardens, NY 11415, USA.

**MESPLÉ, Magdeleine (Mady);** French singer (coloratura soprano) and teacher; b. 7 March 1931, Toulouse; d. of Pierre and Yvonne (née Sesquière) Mesplé; m. 1st René Guedon 1957; one d.; m. 2nd Raymond Dawalibi 1983 (divorced). *Education:* Institut Sainte-Elisabeth and Conservatoire Nat. de Musique, Toulouse. *Career:* made debut Liège, Belgium 1952; has appeared at major opera houses including Théâtre de la Monnaie, Brussels 1954, Opéra de Paris 1956–, Bolshoi Theatre, Moscow, USSR (now Russian Fed.), Palais Royal 1972, Metropolitan Opera, New York, USA 1973, Aix en Provence festival; teacher Conservatoire Nat. de Région de St-Maur-des-Fossés, Bordeaux, Lyon, Conservatoire Européen, Paris; has taught masterclasses in Toronto, Beijing, Shanghai, Taipei, Hong Kong, La Réunion etc.; mem. jury for numerous int. competitions including Washington, Bucharest, Paris, Cologne, Bilbao, Toronto; has had works written for her by Betsy Jolas, Maurice Ohana, Charles Chaynes. *Performances include:* Lakmé 1952, Lucia di Lammermoor 1960, Il était une fois l'opérette 1972, 1974, Les Dialogues des Carmélites, Guillaume Tell, Le Barbier de Séville, Rigoletto, Les contes d'Hoffman, Elégie pour jeunes amants, Cloches de Corneville, Vie Parisienne, Les Saltimbanques. *Recordings include:* Lakmé, Werther, Véronique, Valses de Vienne, Le maître de chapelle, Les Saltimbanques, Art de la coloratura (No 1 Airs français, No 2 Airs italiens). *TV includes:* Château des Carpathes. *Honours:* Officier de la Légion d'honneur; Commdr de l'Ordre nat. du Mérite; Commdr des Arts et Lettres. *Address:* 9 bis rue Girardon, 75018 Paris, France. *Telephone:* (1) 42-23-67-49. *Fax:* (1) 42-23-67-49.

**MESSIEREUR, Petr;** Violinist; b. 1937, Czechoslovakia. *Education:* Studied at Prague Academy of Art. *Career:* Leader of the Talich String Quartet from 1972; Tours to most European countries, Egypt Iraq, North America, Japan, Indonesia; Chamber Ensemble of the Czech Philharmonnic from 1975; Annual visits to France from 1976; Tours of the United Kingdom 1990–91, with concerts at the Wigmore Hall, appearances at the Bath and Bournemouth Festivals, Queen Elizabeth Hall and on BBC 2's Late Show, with Janáček's 2nd Quartet; Also played Beethoven's Quartet Op 74, the Brahms A minor, Smetana's D minor and works by Mozart in England; Festival appearances in Vienna, Besançon, Dijon, Helsinki, Amsterdam, Prague and Salzburg; Repertoire also includes works by Debussy, Bartók (complete works recorded by Supraphon), Shostakovich, Ravel and Dvořák. *Recordings include:* For the French companies Sarastro and Calliope, with the complete quartets of Beethoven; Albums for Collins Classics. *Honours:* Grand Prix Charles Cros.

**MESSITER, Malcolm;** Oboist; b. 1 April 1944, Kingston, Surrey, England; m. Christine Messiter. *Education:* Paris Conservatoire 1967; Royal College of Music, London; ARCM. *Career:* Debut: Purcell Room, London, 1971; Principal Oboe, BBC Concert Orchestra, 1972–77; Solo concert engagements; Many appearances as chamber music player. *Honours:* Royal College of Music Oboe Prize, 1970. *Address:* 67 Crescent Way, Hadley Wood, Herts EN4 0EQ, England.

**MESTER, Jorge;** Conductor; b. 10 April 1935, Mexico City, Mexico. *Education:* MA, Juilliard School of Music, New York, 1958; Studied with Leonard Bernstein, Berkshire Music Center, Tanglewood, summer 1955; Albert Wolff, the Netherlands. *Career:* Teacher of Conducting, Juilliard School of Music, 1955–67; Music Director, Louisville Orchestra, 1967–79; Music Director, Aspen (Colorado) Music Festival, 1970–; Musical Adviser and Principal Conductor, kansas City (Missouri) Philharmonic Orchestra, 1971–74; Music Director, Casals Festival, Puerto Rico, 1979–; Teacher of Conducting, Conductor of School Ensembles, 1980–; Chairman, Conducting Department 1984–87, Juilliard School; Music Director, Pasadena (California) Symphony Orchestra, 1984–; Guest Conductor in North America and overseas; Chief Conductor of the West Australia Symphony and Principal Guest conductor of the Adelaide Symphony Orchestra; Conducted Der Rosenkavalier at Sydney, 1992. *Recordings:* For Cambridge; Columbia; Composers Recordings Inc; Desto; Louisville; Mercury; Vanguard including Dallapiccola Piccola musica notturna, Hindemith Concert Music for viola and Kammermusik No. 2; Bruch's 2nd Symphony; Penderecki De Natura Sonoris; Shostakovich Hamlet Music; Strauss's Six Songs Op 68; Milhaud Symphony No. 6; Martin Cello Cencerto. *Honours:* Naumburg Award, 1968; Alice M Distwon Award for Conductors, 1985. *Address:* c/o The Juilliard School, Lincoln Center, New York, NY 10023, USA.

**MESZOLY, Katalin;** Singer (Contralto); b. 1950, Hungary. *Education:* Studied singing under Professor Jenö Sipos, Budapest; Professor Paula Lindberg, Salzburg, Austria. *Career:* Budapest State Opera, 1976–, from debut, leading contralto of Budapest Opera; Performed title role of Carmen 129 times at Budapest and overseas; Azucena, Il Trovatore; Amneris, Aida; Ulrica, Un Ballo in Maschera; Preziosilla, La Forza del Destino, Marfa in Khovanshchina; Judith, Bluebeard's Castle, at La Scala 1981; Sang Britten's Mrs Herring at Budapest, 1988, Herodias in Salome, 1989; Ulrica (Un Ballo in Maschera) for Opéra de Montréal, 1990; Sang in Kodály's Spinning Room at Budapest, 1998; Has appeared in oratorios including Verdi's Requiem, Mozart's Requiem; Gives song recitals; Guest performer in numerous countries and Operas including Milan Scala, Austria, West Germany, Spain, France, Mexico, Egypt and others. *Honours:* Liszt Prize. *Address:* Hungarian State Opera House, Népötarsasag utja 22, 0161 Budapest, Hungary.

**METCALF, John Philip,** BMus; British composer; b. 13 Aug. 1946, Swansea, Wales; m. Gillian Alexander 1972; two s. one d. *Education:* Univ. of Cardiff. *Career:* commissions from festivals of Cardiff, Swansea and North Wales, Bath and Cheltenham, England and Frankfurt, Germany, also from BBC, Gulbenkian Foundation, London Sinfonietta and WNO; opera, Kafka's Chimp, premiered at Banff 1996; Artistic Dir, Vale of Glamorgan Festival and Artistic Dir, Swansea Festival. *Compositions:* Horn Concerto 1972, PTOC 1973, Auden Songs 1973–77, Five Rags for Charlotte 1975, Ave Maria (choral) 1977, The Journey (opera) 1981, Music of Changes for orchestra 1981, Two Carols 1981, Clarinet Concerto 1982, The Crossing (music theatre) 1984, The Boundaries of Time (cantata) 1985, Piano Trio 1988, Tornrak (opera) 1989, Orchestra Variations 1990, Kafka's Chimp (opera) 1996, Paradise Haunts for violin and orchestra 1995, Dances from Forgotten Places for strings 1999, The Garden of Wales for chorus 1999, Endless Song for piano 1999; four other operas, also music for dance, film and television. *Honours:* Gulbenkian Dance Fellow 1973, UK–USA Bicentennial Arts Fellow 1977–78, Univ. of Wales Creative Arts Fellow 1984, Hon. Fellow (Univ. of Wales, Lampeter, Royal Welsh Coll. of Music and Drama). *Address:* Ty Yfory, Llanfair Road, Lampeter, Ceredigion SA48 8JZ, Wales. *E-mail:* john@metcalf.demon.co.uk. *Website:* www.johnmetcalf.co.uk.

**METCALFE, John;** Violist; b. 1964, England. *Education:* Studied at the Royal Northern College of Music with Simon Rowland-Jones, at the Guildhall School of Music, and with Bruno Giuranna at Berlin Hochschule. *Career:* Concerts, Europe, USA, Japan, and on Channel 4 and Canadian television; Principal viola with the Kreisler String Orchestra; Member of Durutti Column, 1984–88; Violist with Duke String Quartet from 1985; Performances in the Wigmore Hall, Purcell Room, Conway Hall and throughout the United Kingdom; With Duke Quartet, tours with Rosas throughout Europe and to Brazil; South Bank series, 1991, with Mozart's early quartets; Soundtrack for Ingmar Bergman documentary The Magic Lantern, Channel 4, 1988; BBC debut feature; Features for French television, 1990–91, playing Mozart, Mendelssohn, Britten and Tippett; Brahms Clarinet Quintet for Dutch Radio with Janet Hilton; Live Music Now series with concerts for disadvantaged people; The Duke Quartet invites... at the Derngate, Northampton, 1991, with Duncan Prescott and Rohan O'Hara; Resident quartet, Rydale Festival, 1991; Residency, Trinity College, Oxford, tours to Scotland and Northern Ireland and concert at the Queen Elizabeth Hall, 1991; Season 1993/94 with Duke Quartet at Casa Manilva Festival, Spain, and tour of the United Kingdom; Founded Factory Classical Label, 1988. *Compositions:* Arranger for Pretenders, Blur, Cranberries, Morrissey, Lloyd Cole; Compositions for television; With Duke Quartet, composing music for Union Dance Co. *Recordings include:* Quartets by Tippett, Shostakovich and Britten (Third); Other albums including music by Dvořák, Barber and Glass; 3 world premieres by Kevin Volans. *Honours:* Martin Musical Trust Award; South East Arts Scholarships. *Address:* 81b Sarsfield Road, London SW12, England.

**METTERS, Colin (Raynor);** Conductor; b. 22 Jan. 1948, Plymouth, Devon, England; m. Susan Furlong, 28 June 1980, 2 d. *Education:* ARCM, Violin and Conducting, Royal College of Music, 1966–71; Studied Conducting under Vernon Handley and George Hurst, 1966–71; Liverpool Seminar under Charles Groves, 1969; Masterclasses with Nadia Boulanger, 1968. *Career:* Musical Director, Ballet Rambert, 1972–74; Conductor, Sadler's Wells Royal Ballet, 1974–82; Teacher of Conducting, Canford Summer School of Music, 1973–83; Musical Director, East Sussex Youth Orchestra, 1979–; Guest Conductor with London Schools Symphony Orchestra, British Youth Symphony Orchestra, National Centre for Orchestral Studies; Freelance Conductor, 1982–; Director of Conducting, Royal Academy of Music, 1983–; Conducted major British, Provincial and BBC Orchestras; Conducted extensively abroad. *Recordings:* BBC radio and television and various. *Honours:* Honorary RAM conferred at RAM Graduation, 1995. *Current Management:* Helen Sykes Artists Management, 100 Felsham Road, Putney, London SW15 1DQ, England. *Address:* c/o Royal Academy of Music, Marylebone Road, London, NW1 5HT, England.

**METTRAUX, Laurent;** Swiss composer; b. 27 May 1970, Fribourg. *Education:* St Michael's Coll., Conservatoire de Fribourg with Prof. René Oberson, studied composition with Prof. Eric Gaudibert, conducting with Prof. S.-L. Chen, Geneva. *Career:* first compositions aged 12; Symphonie pour orchestre de chambre first performed by Orchestre de Chambre de Lausanne, conductor Jesus Lopez-Cobos; directed first performance of his composition, Lysistrata; first performance of Concerto for 15 solo strings under Tibor Varga at opening concert, Tibor Varga Festival 1994; numerous commissions; mem. Swiss Musicians' Asscn 1995–. *Compositions include:* Symphonie pour orchestre de chambre (first prize and public prize Competition for Young Composers) 1993, Concerto for 15 solo strings 1994, Vers le Soleil Couchant

(oratorio) 1995–96, Trio No. 2 for piano, violin and cello 1995–96, three Concertos for Violin 1996, 1998, 1999, Elògio della Nòtte (after Michelangelo) for bass voice and piano 1997, Ombre for orchestra 1995–98, String Trio 1998, Crucifixion for mixed choir 1998, Le Cocyte for orchestra 1999, String Quartet (first performed by Talich Quartet) 1998–99, La Plus belle des Lumières for a cappella mixed choir 2000, Wind Quintet 2000, String Quintet 2001–02, Le Nom Caché (oratorio for the Nat. Swiss Exposition of 2002) 2001–02, Concerto for organ and orchestra (for inauguration of new great organ, Lausanne Cathedral) 2002–03, Complainte for solo violin (written at request of Shlomo Mintz as set piece for Int. Violin Competition of Sion) 2003, Double-Concerto for violin, pi'pa and orchestra 2002–04, Trio for clarinet, cello and piano 2003. *Honours:* Donauschinger Musiktage Prize 1998. *Address:* Route Principale 160, 1791 Courtaman, Switzerland (office). *E-mail:* laurent.mettraux@bluewin.ch. *Website:* www.isuisse.com/mettraux (office).

**METTRE, Raimundo;** Singer (Tenor); b. 1949, Brazil. *Education:* Studied in Berlin and Milan. *Career:* Sang at the Piccola Scala Milan 1982, in Ariodante; Appearances at Zürich as Almaviva and the Duke of Mantua (1985–86), Basle (Rodolfo, 1987), at Rio de Janeiro as Werther and Don José and at Barcelona as Mozart's Ferrando and Don Ottavio; Other roles include Percy in Anna Bolena (at Lisbon), Belmonte (at Tel-Aviv); US debut at Philadelphia, as Ernesto in Don Pasquale; Concert repertoire includes the Verdi Requiem, Puccini's Messa di Gloria, Rossini's Stabat Mater and oratorios by Handel. *Address:* Opernhaus Zürich, Falkenstrasse 1, 8008 Zürich, Switzerland.

**METZ, Catherine;** Violinist; b. 1965, USA. *Education:* Studied in New York. *Career:* Recitalist, Lincoln Center's Alice Tully Hall, 92nd Street 'Y' and appearances with major orchestras; Chamber Musician at the Santa Fe Festival, Spoleto Festival and Lockenhaus Kammermusikfest and the International Musicians Seminar in Prussia Cove; Co-Founder, Orion Quartet and has given concerts at Washington DC 's Kennedy Center, at Boston Gardner Museum and throughout the USA; Carnegie Hall recital, 1991 and as part of the Centenial Celebration tribute; Concerts as Turku Festival in Finland. *Current Management:* Ingpen & Williams Ltd, 7 St George's Court, 131 Putney Bridge Road, London, SW15 2PA, England.

**METZMACHER, Ingo;** German conductor; *Chief Conductor, Netherlands Opera;* b. 1957, Hannover. *Education:* studied piano, theory and conducting in Hannover, Salzburg and Cologne. *Career:* joined Ensemble Modern contemporary music ensemble as pianist 1981, began conducting the ensemble 1985; apptd solo répétiteur at Frankfurt Opera 1985, made conducting debut at Frankfurt with The Marriage of Figaro 1987; apptd Music Dir Musiktheater im Revier, Gelsenkirchen 1987; debut at Brussels Opera with Franz Schreker's Der Ferne Klang 1988; Prin. Guest Conductor Bamberger Symphony Orchestra 1995–99; Gen. Music Dir Hamburg State Opera, Hamburg Philharmonic Orchestra and Hamburg Music Festival 1997–2005; works conducted in Hamburg include Richard Strauss's Der Rosenkavalier, Verdi's Macbeth and Don Carlos, Wagner's Lohengrin, Von Weber's Der Freischütz, Debussy's Pelleas et Melisande, Berg's Wozzeck and Lulu, Poulenc's Dialogue des Carmelites, Beethoven's Fidelio, Maderna's Hyperion, Nono's Al Gran Sole Carico d'Amore; tours with Hamburg Philharmonic include Lucerne Festival and BBC Proms; performances as guest conductor include opera houses throughout Germany, Vienna Philharmonic, London Philharmonic, Berlin Philharmonic, Munich Philharmonic, Boston Symphony, Orchestre Nat. de France, Vienna Symphony, San Francisco SO, Los Angeles SO, Montréal SO; toured Europe with Gustav Mahler Jugendorchester 2004, 2005; Chief Conductor Netherlands Opera, Amsterdam 2005–; works conducted in Amsterdam include Korngold's Die Tote Stadt, Henze's The Bassarids, Verdi's Simon Boccanegra, Janáček's The Cunning Little Vixen, Richard Strauss's Elektra; Chief Conductor Deutsches Symphonie-Orchester, Berlin (2007–). *Recordings:* A Portrait of Charles Ives (with Ensemble Modern) (Académie Charles Gros Grand Prix) 1992, Conlon Nancarrow, Studies (with Ensemble Modern) 1993, Hans Werner Henze, Requiem (with Ensemble Modern) 1994, A Tribute to Benny Goodman 1998, Henze, Symphony No. 9 (with Berlin PO) 1998, Britten, Serenade (with Bamberger SO) 1999, Karl Amadeus Hartmann Symphonies Nos 1–8 (with Bamberger SO) (Preis der Deutschen Schallplattenkritik) 2000, Who is Afraid of 20th Century Music? (with Hamburg Philharmonic) 2001–05. *Publications:* Keine Angst vor Neuen Tönen (Opernwelt Book of the Year) 2005. *Honours:* Echo Preis Conductor of the Year 1998, Opernwelt magazine Opera Conductor of the Year 1998, Opernwelt Opera House of the Year 2005. *Current Management:* Intermusica Artists' Management Ltd, 16 Duncan Terrace, London, N1 8BZ, England. *Telephone:* (20) 7278-5455 (office). *Fax:* (20) 7278-8434 (office). *E-mail:* mail@intermusica.co.uk (office). *Website:* www.intermusica.co.uk (office).

**MEVEN, Peter;** Singer (Bass); b. 1 Oct. 1929, Cologne, Germany. *Education:* Studied at the Cologne Musikhochschule with Robert Blasius. *Career:* Debut: Hagen, Westfalen, 1957, as Ferrando in IL Trovatore; Sang in Mainz, Wiesbaden and Oldenburg from 1959; Deutsche Oper Berlin from 1964; Many guest appearances in Germany and engagements in Amsterdam, Basle, Lisbon, Stockholm, Moscow and San Francisco; Covent Garden London, Gurnemanz in Parsifal; Bayreuth 1971, as Fafner; Salzburg 1974, as Sarastro in Die Zauberflöte; Paris Opéra as Daland in Der fliegende Holländer, 1981; Brussels 1983–85, as Kaspar in Der Freischütz and Pogner in Die Meistersinger (also at the Metropolitan 1976–77); Sang Lodovico in Schreker's Die Gezeichneten for Austrian Radio; Sang Hagen and Hunding in the Ring at Geneva, 1988; King Heinrich in Lohengrin at Santiago, 1988, Hagen at the

1989 Holland Festival; Sang Rocco in Fidelio at Düsseldorf, 1990. *Recordings:* Sacred music by Bruckner; Der Freischütz; Mathis der Maler by Hindemith; Fidelio. *Address:* Deutsche Oper am Rhein, Heinrich Heine Allee 16, 4000 Düsseldorf, Germany.

**MEWES, Karsten;** Singer (Baritone); b. 18 March 1959, Pirna, Saxony, Germany. *Education:* Studied at the Hanns Eisler Musikhochschule Berlin. *Career:* Sang at the Potsdam Opera and the Komische Oper Berlin, 1985–88; Berlin Staatsoper from 1985, notably in the 1989 premiere of Graf Mirabeau by Siegfried Matthus; Season 2000–01 as Iago at Halle and as Schtschelkalov in Boris Godunov at the Komische Oper, Berlin; Guest appearances in Dresden and elsewhere as Mozart's Count, Masetto, Guglielmo and Papageno, Lortzing's Zar, Silvio, Escamillo and Hans Scholl in Udo Zimmermann's Die weisse Rose; Concert repertoire includes works by Bach, Handel, Brahms and Fauré; Lieder recitals in Germany, Finland, Norway, Czechoslovakia, Poland and France. *Honours:* Competition Prize Winner at Zwickau, Verona, Hamburg, Rio de Janeiro, 1985–87.

**MEYER, Edgar,** BMus; American composer and double bassist; b. 24 Nov. 1960, Tulsa, Okla; s. of Edgar A. Meyer and Anna Mary Metzel; m. Cornelia (Connie) Heard 1988; one s. *Education:* Georgia Inst. of Tech., Atlanta, Indiana School of Music, Bloomington. *Career:* began playing bass aged five under tutelage of father; began composing pop songs and classical pieces as a child; studied with Stuart Stanley at univ.; formed 'bluegrass' band Strength in Numbers, Nashville, Tenn. 1984; signed to MCA label; regular bass player, Santa Fe Chamber Music Festival 1985–93; appeared with concert artists Emanuel Ax (piano) and Yo-yo Ma (cello); collaborated with Katty Mattea on album Where Have You Been (Grammy Award, Country Music Award, Acad. of Country Music Asscn Award) 1990; premiere of Concerto for Bass 1993; joined Chamber Music Soc., Lincoln Center, New York 1994; formed band Quintet for Bass and String Quartet, soloist debut performance 1995; premiere of Double Concerto for Bass and Cello 1995; premiere of Violin Concerto 2000; recitals with Amy Dorfman, Bela Flack and Mike Marshall; performed at Aspen, Caramoor and Marlboro Festivals; debuted with Boston Symphony Orchestra, Tanglewood, Mass 2000; Visiting Prof., RAM, London, UK. *Music includes:* albums: Unfolding 1986, The Telluride Sessions (Strength in Numbers) 1989, Dreams of Flight 1987, Love of a Lifetime 1988, Appalachia Waltz 1996, Uncommon Ritual 1997, Short Trip Record 1999, Bach Unaccompanied Cello Suites Performed on a Double Bass 1999, Appalachian Journey (Grammy Award 2001) 2000, Perpetual Motion 2000. *Honours:* Winner, Zimmerman-Mingus Competition, Int. Soc. of Bassists 1981, Avery Fisher Prize 2000, Grammy Award for the Best Crossover Album 2001. *Address:* c/o Sony Classical, 550 Madison Avenue, New York, NY 10022-3211, USA (office); c/o IMG Artists, Lovell House, 616 Chiswick High Road, London, W4 5RX, England (office).

**MEYER, Felix,** PhD; Swiss musicologist; b. 24 May 1957, St Gallen; m. Rosmarie Anzenberger 1986; one s. one d. *Education:* Univ. of Zürich, studied violin in St Gallen, piano with Hans Steinbrecher in St Gallen, Werner Bärtschi in Zürich, Ian Lake in London. *Career:* Sec., Swiss Youth Music Competition 1984–85; Curator of Music Manuscripts, Paul Sacher Foundation, Basel 1986, duties including curator of concert series Klassizistische Moderne, Basel 1996, and curator of exhibition of music manuscripts at Pierpont Morgan Library, New York 1998; Dir, Paul Sacher Foundation 1999–; mem. Swiss Musicological Soc., German Musicological Soc., American Musicological Soc. *Publications:* A Study of Charles Ives's Concord Sonata 1991, Quellenstudien II: Zwölf Komponisten des 20. Jahrhunderts (ed., contrib.) 1993, Klassizistische Moderne (ed., contrib.) 1996, Settling New Scores (ed., contrib.) 1998, Béla Bartók's Music for Strings (facsimile edn, ed.) 2000; co-ed., contributor two facsimile edns of works by Igor Stravinsky; contrib. to journals, including Music Analysis, Archiv für Musikwissenschaft, Revista de musicología, Neue Zürcher Zeitung. *Address:* Sevogelstrasse 85, 4052 Basel, Switzerland.

**MEYER, Henry;** Violinist and College Professor; b. 29 June 1923, Dresden, Germany. *Education:* Studied at Prague Music Academy in Paris with George Enescu and at the Juilliard School with Ivan Galamian. *Career:* Co-Founded the Lasalle String Quartet at the Juilliard School, 1949; Many concerts featuring modern composers and the quartets of Beethoven; European debut 1954; Composers who wrote for the ensemble include Hans Erich Apostel, Earle Brown, Henri Pousseur, Mauricio Kagel, György Ligeti, Penderecki and Witold Lutoslawski; Quartet-in-Residence and Professor, Cincinnati College-Conservatory of Music; Quartet disbanded 1988; Has since given masterclasses in the USA, Europe, Israel, Australia and Japan. *Recordings include:* Works by Berg, Schoenberg, Webern and Zemlinsky; Beethoven's Late Quartets; Brahms; Wolf. *Address:* c/o Cincinnati College-Conservatory of Music, Cincinnati, OH 45221, USA.

**MEYER, Kerstin,** CBE; singer (mezzo-soprano) and rector emerita; b. 3 April 1928, Stockholm, Sweden; m. Björn G. Bexelius 1974 (died 1997). *Education:* Royal Swedish Conservatory, Stockholm, Swedish University College of Opera, Accademia Chigiana, Italy, Mozarteum, Austria. *Career:* debut, Royal Opera, Stockholm, 1952, as Azucena in Il Trovatore; Orchestra appearances with the Hallé Orchestra; London Philharmonic, Berlin and Vienna Philharmonics, Suisse Romande, Santa Cecilia, Chicago, ABC, BBC, NZBC television; Leading roles in most of the important Houses and Festivals in Europe, North and South America, Far East, such as Royal Opera House Covent Garden, Welsh and Scottish Operas, Glyndebourne and Edinburgh Festivals; La Scala, Milan, La Fenice and Santa Cecilia, Italy, Vienna and Salzburg, Austria; Munich, Berlin, Cologne and Hamburg, Germany; Paris, Marseilles, France, Moscow, Tashkent, Tallinn, Riga, USSR, Metropolitan Opera House, San Francisco, Santa Fe, Tulsa, USA; Teatro Colón, Argentina; Mexico City, Tokyo, Hong Kong; Sang in first British performances of operas by Henze and Einem at Glyndebourne and in the world premieres of operas by Goehr and Searle (Hamburg), Henze's The Bassarids at Salzburg, 1966, and Ligeti's Le Grand Macabre at Stockholm, 1978; President, Swedish University College of Opera, 1984–94; Advisory Director, European Mozart Academy, Kraków and New York, 1994–98; Since retirement teaching vocal interpretation; Giving Masterclasses at the Summer school of Music, Mozarteum, Salzburg; mem, Board Member, STIM; Assessor, HEFCE, London, 1994–95. *Recordings:* Operas, recitals with von Karajan, Barbirolli, Solti, Hans Schmidt-Isserstedt and Sixten Ehrling. *Honours:* Royal Swedish Court Singer, 1963; Swedish Vasa Order; Swedish Litteris et Arbitus; Swedish Illis Quorum, 1994; German Cross of Honour 1st Class; Italian Order of Merit. *Address:* Porsvaegen 48, 16570 Haesselby, Sweden.

**MEYER, Krzysztof;** Composer, Music Theorist and Pianist; b. 11 Aug. 1943, Kraków, Poland; 1 s., 1 d. *Education:* High School of Music, Kraków; American Conservatory, Fontainebleau. *Career:* Debut: Warsaw in 1965; Professor: High School of Music, Kraków, 1966–87 and High School of Music, Cologne, 1987–; President of Union of Polish Composers, 1985–89. *Compositions include:* Stage Works: Cyberiada, opera, premiere in 1986, The Gamblers, completion of Shostakovich's opera, premiere 1983, The Maple Brothers, children's opera, premiere 1990; Orchestral: 4 Symphonies, Hommage à Johannes Brahms; Musica incrostate; Concertos for: Piano, Violin, Violoncello, 2 for Oboe, Trumpet, Saxophone, 2 for flute, Double concerto for Harp and Cello, Symphony in Mozartean style, Caro Luigi for 4 Cellos and Orchestra; For Choir and Orchestra: Epitaphium Stanislaw Wiechowicz in memoriam, (Symphony No. 2), Symphonie d'Orphée (Symphony No. 3), Farewell Music for Orchestra, 1997; Lyric Triptych for Tenor and Chamber Orchestra, Mass for Choir and Organ; Chamber Works: Clarinet Quintet, Piano Quintet, 10 String Quartets, 1963–94; Piano Trio, String Trio; For Various Ensembles: Concerto Retro; Hommage à Nadia Boulanger, Capriccio, Canzona and Sonata for Cello and Piano; For Piano: 5 Sonatas, 24 Preludes; Solo Sonatas for: Cello, Cembalo, Violin, Flute, Fantasy for Organ. *Recordings include:* String Quartets Nos 1–9; Hommage à Brahms; Symphonies 1–6; Clarinet Quintet; The Gamblers, and others. *Publications:* Dimitri Shostakovich, 1973; Shostakovich, 1995. *Contributions:* Various Journals. *Honours:* Grand Prix, Prince Pierre de Monaco, 1970; Award, Minister of Culture and Art, Poland, 1973, 1976; Medal, Government of Brazil, 1975; Gottfried von Herder Preis, Wien, 1984; Award, Polish Composers Union, 1992; Jurzykowski Foundation, New York, 1993. *Address:* Kurt Schumacher Str 10 W-51, 51427 Bergisch Gladbach, Germany.

**MEYER, Paul;** Clarinettist and Conductor; b. 5 March 1965, Mulhouse, France. *Education:* Studied at the Paris Conservatoire and the Basle Musikhochschule. *Career:* Debut: Orchestre Symphonique du Rhin, 1978; Concerts in New York, 1984; Formed association with Benny Goodman; Engagements with the Orchestre National de France, BBC Symphony Orchestra, Royal Philharmonic, Tokyo Symphony Orchestra, Salzburg Mozarteum, Suisse Romade, Zürich Tonhalle and ABC Australia; Modern repertory includes works by Boulez (Domains), Gould and Henze; Premiere of Concerto by Gerd Kuhr at the Sinfonia Varsovia, 1994; Premiered Penderecki's arrangement of Viola Concerto, 1996, and the Concerto by Berio, with the Concertgebouw Orchestra, 1997; Tour of the USA with Yo-Yo Ma, Emmanuel Ax and Pamela Frank, playing Brahms and Schoenberg, 1995; Further partnerships with Eric Le Sage, Barbara Hendricks, Gidon Kremer, Maria João Pires, Jean-Pierre Rampal, Rostropovich, Heinrich Schiff and Isaac Stern; Quintet with the Carmina, Cleveland, Emerson and Takacs String Quartets; Concerts as conductor with the Munich CO, English CO and with Carmen in the South of France, 1997. *Recordings include:* Concertos by Mozart, Copland and Busoni, with the English CO; Weber and Fuchs wth the Carmina Quartet; Mendelssohn and Reinecke, with Eric Le Sage. *Honours:* Winner, French Young Artists Competition, 1982; USA Young Artists Competition, 1984. *Address:* Bureau des Concerts Jaques Thelen, Théâtre des Champs Elysées, 15 Avenue Montaigne, 75008 Paris, France.

**MEYER, Sabine;** Clarinettist; b. 30 March 1959, Crailsheim, Germany. *Education:* Studied with her father, Karl Meyer, with Otto Hermann in Stuttgart and Hans Deinzer in Hanover. *Career:* Joined the Bavarian Radio Symphony Orchestra from 1983, at first under Herbert von Karajan then Claudio Abbado; Trio partnership with her brother Wolfgang, and Reiner Behle, notably in the Trios with Clarinet by Beethoven and Brahms; Further Collaborations with Pianist Rudolf Buchbinder, Cellist Heinrich Schiff and the Cleveland and Brandis Quartets; Regular concerts in the Divertimenti and Serenades of Mozart with members of the BerlinPhilharmonic; Premieres of Octet for Winds by Edison Denisov, 1991 and the Romance for clarinet and orchestra by Richard Strauss, 1991. *Honours:* Winner, ARD competition at Munich. *Address:* c/o Berlin Philharmonic Orchestra, Philharmonie, Matthäukirchstrasse 1, 1000 Berlin 30, Germany.

**MEYER-TOPSOE, Elisabeth;** Singer (soprano); b. Copenhagen, Denmark. *Education:* studied in Copenhagen and with Birgit Nilsson in Stockholm. *Career:* debut, Augsburg 1989 as Oxana in Tchaikovsky's Cherevichki; sang the Trovatore Leonora and Arabella at Augsburg; Nuremburg Opera from 1990, as Wagner's Elisabeth and Senta; Weber's Euryanthe, also at Aix en

Provence 1993; Copenhagen from 1992 as Ariadne, the Marschallin, Desdemona and Senta; Vienna Staatsoper debut 1995 as Third Norn in Götterdämmerung; US debut 1996 in Strauss's Vier Letzte Lieder at Monterey; sang Ariadne at Maggio Musicale, Firenze, Vienna Staatsoper, Toulouse, Lausanne and Nancy; sang Senta in Vienna Staatsoper, Zürich, Mannheim, Stockholm, Savonlinna, Staatsoper, Berlin, Copenhagen, Verona, Wiesbaden Mai-Festspiele, Santiago de Compostella, Bonn, Malaga; sang Marschallin at the Teatro Colón, Buenos Aires, Trieste, Leipzig, Unter den Linden, Berlin and Sevilla; sang Ingeborg in Heise's Drot og Maske at Århus 2000; sang Elsa at Torino, Essen; sang Chysothemis at Rome, Verona, Paris in concert; engaged to sing Senta in Rome 2004, Governess in Turn of the Screw in Naples 2005. *Address:* Rosenvangets Sideallé 3, 2100 Copenhagen, Denmark.

**MEYER-WOLFF, Frido;** Singer (Bass-baritone); b. 22 April 1934, Potsdam, Germany. *Education:* Studied in Berlin, Paris and Hamburg. *Career:* Debut: Stralsund 1955, as Mozart's Figaro; Appearances at Trier, Hamburg, Kassel, Kiel and the Deutsche Oper Berlin; Opéra Comique Paris, 1963, in the premiere of Menotti's The Last Savage; Spoleto Festival, 1964; As Ochs in Der Rosenkavalier; Aix en Provence Festival, 1963, 1964, Marseilles from 1961, Brussels, 1965, Monte Carlo 1967–94, Nice 1962–89, Lausanne 1987; Decorated Chevalier des Arts et Lettres by the French Government, 1985; Direction of open-air theatre Jean Cocteau Cap d'All near Monaco, created and conducted a new chamber orchestra from 1989; Other roles include parts in operas by Verdi, Wagner, Puccini, Strauss, Rossini, Smetana and Moussorgsky; Sang in Wozzeck, Samson et Dalila, and Das Schloss by Reimann, first performance, 1992 at Deutsche Oper Berlin; Frequent concert appearances. *Honours:* Chevalier dans l'Ordre des Palmes Academiques, 1997. *Current Management:* Boris Orlob. *Address:* c/o Boris Orlob, Jägerstr. 70, 10117 Berlin, Germany. *Website:* www.meyer-wolff.com.

**MEYERS, Anne Akiko;** Violinist; b. 1970, San Diego, California, USA. *Education:* Indiana University with Josef Gingold; Colburn School of Performing Arts with Alice and Eleanor Schoenfeld; Dorothy DeLay and Masao Kawasaki at Juilliard School, New York. *Career:* Debut as concerto soloist, age 7; Later appeared with Los Angeles Philharmonic, New York Philharmonic conducted by Mehta and New York String Orchestra at Carnegie Hall; Far East engagements with Japan Philharmonic and NHK Symphony Orchestra; Summer festivals include Aspen, Ravinia, Tanglewood, Hollywood Bowl; Tours: St Louis Symphony with Leonard Slatkin, Australian Chamber Orchestra, Baltimore Symphony with David Zinman, Moscow Philharmonic; Appeared on television with John Williams and Boston Pops; Played with Minnesota Orchestra, Prague Symphony Orchestra, Hallé Orchestra, Orchestre de Paris and Jerusalem Symphony; Appearances in Montreal Symphony, Boston Symphony, St Louis Symphony, Philadelphia Orchestra, Toronto Symphony, Swedish Radio Orchestra, Moscow Philharmonic, Belgian Radio Orchestra; Berlin Radio Symphony. *Recordings include:* Concertos by Barber and Bruch with Royal Philharmonic Orchestra and Christopher Seaman; Lalo Symphonie Espagnole and Bruch Scottish Fantasy with Royal Philharmonic Orchestra, Lopez-Cobos, César Franck and Richard Strauss Sonatas; Mendelssohn with Philharmonia and Andrew Litton; Salût d'Amour for RCA. *Contributions:* Featured, Strad Magazine. *Honours:* Youngest to sign with Young Concert Artists; Sole recipient of Avery Fisher Career Grant, 1993. *Current Management:* ICM Artists, 40 W 57th St, New York, NY 10019; Jasper Parrott, London; Japan Arts, Tokyo. *Address:* Harrison/Parrott Ltd, 12 Penzance Place, London, W11 4PA, England. *Telephone:* (20) 7229 9166. *Fax:* (20) 7221 5042. . *Website:* www .harrisonparrott.com.

**MEYERSON, Janice,** BA, MM; American singer (mezzo-soprano); b. 12 March 1951, Omaha, NE; m. Raymond Scheindlin 1986. *Education:* Washington Univ., St Louis, Missouri, New England Conservatory. *Career:* Fellowship, Berkshire Music Center (Tanglewood) 1976–77; Carmen (title role), New York City Opera and Théâtre Royal de la Monnaie, Brussels; Amneris in Aida, Teatro Colón, Buenos Aires and Frankfurt Opera; Santuzza in Cavalleria Rusticana, New York City Opera; Judith in Bluebeard's Castle, New York Philharmonic and Palacio de Bellas Artes, Mexico City; Brangaene in Tristan and Isolde, Leonard Bernstein conducting Philadelphia Orchestra; soloist, Mahler's 3rd Symphony, American Symphony, Carnegie Hall; soloist, Boston Symphony, Milwaukee Symphony, Minnesota Orchestra, New Orleans Symphony, National Symphony, Dallas Symphony, Washington Opera, Houston Grand Opera, Montreal Opera, Opera Co. of Philadelphia, Aspen Festival, Spoleto USA, Marlboro, Tanglewood, Wolf Trap, Schleswig-Holstein Music Festival, Deutsche Oper Berlin, Moscow State Symphony Orchestra; Teatro São Carlo, Lisbon and Vlaamse Opera; Adriano in Rienzi in London 1999; Kabanicha in Katya Kabanova in Dublin 2000; Herodias in Salome, Florida Grand Opera 2003; Barcelona Liceu 2004. *Recordings:* For the Night to Wear (with Boston Musica Viva) 1994. *Address:* 420 Riverside Drive, Apt GC, New York, NY 10025, USA. *E-mail:* Jcmeyerson@aol.com (home). *Website:* www.janicemeyerson.com.

**MEYFARTH, Jutta;** Singer (Soprano); b. 1933, Germany. *Career:* Sang at Basle in 1955; Aachen Opera 1956–59; Member of Frankfurt Opera from 1959; La Scala Milan debut 1960; Maggio Musicale Florence 1961, as Elsa in Lohengrin; Bayreuth Festival 1962–64, as Freia, Gutrune and Sieglinde; Munich Opera 1965, as Donna Anna; Guest appearances in Buenos Aires, Brussels, Rome, London, Lisbon, Athens, Lyon and Antwerp; Other roles

included Wagner's Isolde, The Empress in Die Frau ohne Schatten, Aida, and Martha in Tiefland.

**MEYLAN, Raymond,** DLitt; flautist and musicologist; b. 22 Sept. 1924, Genava; m. Anne-Marie Bersot 1959; one d. *Education:* Univ. of Lausanne, Univ. of Zürich, Conservatoire of Genava, studied in Paris with Marcel Moyse, Accademia Chigiana, Sienna, with Ruggero Gerlin. *Career:* Debut: 1944; Solo Flute, Orchestra Alessandro Scarlatti, Naples, 1951–54; Pomerriggi Musicali, Milan, 1954–58; Orchestra of Radio Beromünster, Zürich, 1958–70; Basler Orchesten Gesellschaft, Basle, 1971–89; Lecturer in Musicology, University of Zürich, 1969–77; Conductor, Orchestre Académique de Zürich, 1969–77, Orchesterverein Liestal, 1977–91; Studies in archaeology of flutes, 1972–; mem, Swiss Association of Musicians, Swiss Musicological Society; French Society of Musicology. *Compositions:* Le Choix, for voice, choir, flute, vibraphone and marimba, 1979; Notre Dame de Lausanne, for wind, 1986; Bourrasque, for large orchestra in ampitheatre, 1987; Cinq Miniatures, for flute and guitar, 1987; Assonances, for scattered orchestra, 1988. *Recordings:* Flute Concertos by Danzi, Widor and Reinecke; Salieri, in Virtuoso Oboe; Bernard Reichel, VDE Gallo; Beethoven, 10 themes and variations, op 107; Telemann, triple concerto, with Zagreber Solisten, A. Janigro, Amadeo and The Bach Guild. *Publications:* L'énigme de la musique de basses danses du quinzième siècle (The Puzzle of the Music of the Low Dances of the 15th Century), 1969; La Flûte, 1974; Publications on Attaingnant, Mazzocchi, A and D Scarlatti, Sarri, Bach, Nardini, Fischer, Schwindl, Kozeluh, Bellini, Donizetti, other works forthcoming. *Contributions:* Musical and scholarly journals; Musical dictionaries. *Address:* Buchenstr 58, 4142 Münchenstein, Switzerland. *Telephone:* (61) 411-5633 (home).

**MEZÖ, Laszlo;** Cellist; b. 1940, Hungary. *Education:* Franz Liszt Academy, Budapest. *Career:* Cellist of the Bartók Quartet from 1977; Performances in nearly every European country and tours of Australia, Canada, Japan, New Zealand and the USA; Festival appearances at Adelaide, Ascona, Aix, Venice, Dubrovnik, Edinburgh, Helsinki, Lucerne, Menton, Prague, Vienna, Spoleto and Schwetzingen; Tour of the United Kingdom 1986 including concerts at Cheltenham, Dartington, Philharmonic Hall, Liverpool, RNCM, Manchester and the Wigmore Hall; Tours of the United Kingdom 1988 and 1990 featuring visits to the Sheldonian Theatre, Oxford, Wigmore Hall, Harewood House and Birmingham; Repertoire includes standard classics and Hungarian works by Bartók, Durkó, Bozay, Kadosa, Soproni, Farkas, Szabo and Lang. *Recordings include:* Complete quartets of Mozart, Beethoven and Brahms; Major works of Haydn and Schubert (Hungaraton); Complete quartets of Bartók (Erato). *Honours:* With Members of Bartók Quartet, Kossuth Prize, Outstanding Artists of the Hungarian People's Republic 1981; UNESCO/IMC Prize 1981. *Current Management:* Ingpen & Williams Ltd, 7 St George's Court, 131 Putney Bridge Road, London, SW15 2PA, England.

**MICHAEL, Audrey;** Singer (Soprano); b. 11 Nov. 1949, Geneva, Switzerland. *Education:* Studied with father, Jean-Marie Auberson, and in Milan and Hamburg. *Career:* Sang with the Hamburg Staatsoper, 1976–81, Deutsche Oper am Rhein Düsseldorf, 1981–86; Guest appearances throughout Europe; Roles have included Gluck's Amor in Orpheus, Ilia (Idomeneo), Mozart's Pamina, Susanna, Countess and Papagena, Elvira (L'Italiana in Algeri), Adina, Lauretta, Zdenka, Mélisande and Elisabeth Zimmer in Elegy for Young Lovers by Henze; Sang at Hamburg in the premieres of Kommen und gehen by Heinz Holliger, 1978, William Ratcliff by Ostendorf, 1982 and Jakob Lenz by Wolfgang Rihm, 1979; Théâtre Municipal Lausanne, 1991 as Sextus in Gluck's La Clemenza di Tito; Sang Sextus at the Théâtre des Champs Elysées, Paris, 1996; Concert engagements in the Baroque and modern repertory throughout Switzerland and in Berlin, Stuttgart, Paris, Lisbon and Buenos Aires. *Recordings include:* Monteverdi Orfeo, L'Enfant et les Sortilèges, Masses by Schubert and Beethoven; Rigoletto, Luisa Miller and Parsifal; Monteverdi Ballo delle Ingrate and Vespers of 1610. *Address:* c/o Opéra de Lausanne, PO Box 3972, 1002 Lausanne, Switzerland.

**MICHAEL, Beth;** Singer (Soprano); b. 1962, Gwent, Wales. *Education:* Studied at the Welsh College of Music and Drama and the RAM, London. *Career:* Debut: Pheadra in Cavalli's L'Egisto for Scottish Opera, 1982; Roles with Opera 80/English Touring Opera include Cenerentola, Carmen, Gretel, Frasquita, the Merry Widow and Lucia; Further engagements as Manon Lescaut, Butterfly (Surrey Opera), Tosca (Regency Opera) and at Wexford, Bayreuth and London (English National Opera); Appearances with the Royal Opera, Covent Garden, in Death in Venice, The Cunning Little Vixen, Turandot, Der Rosenkavalier, La Traviata and Die Walküre; Countess Ceprano in Rigoletto, 1997; Many concert appearances, and engagements on radio and television. *Address:* c/o English National Opera (contracts), St Martin's Lane, London WC2N 4ES, England.

**MICHAEL, Nadja;** German singer (mezzo-soprano); b. 1969, Leipzig. *Education:* studied in Stuttgart and in the USA with Carlos Montane. *Career:* debut, Ludiwgsburg Festival 1993, as Third Lady in Die Zauberflöte; appearances at Wiesbaden as Amastris (Xerxes) and Eustazio (Rinaldo), Dulcinée in Don Quixote at St Gallen and Tchaikovsky's Olga at Glynde-bourne; Strauss's Dryad at the Dresden Semper Oper and Handel at the Berlin Staatsoper; season 1997–98 as Varvara in Katya Kabanova at Covent Garden (debut), Ottavia in Poppea at Munich, Wagner's Venus at Naples and Mahler's Rückert Lieder and Second Symphony; further concerts include Elijah, Messiah, Berio's Folk Songs and Mahler's Das Lied von der Erde (Swiss television); appearances in Carmen in Italy and at St Gallen and

Tokyo; sang in Tippett's Midsummer Marriage at Munich 1998; sang Hansel in Hansel and Gretel at the Staatsoper in Berlin; engaged to sing Charlotte in Werther and Carmen at the New Nat. Theatre in Tokyo and at La Monnaie in Brussels; Delilah in Samson and Delilah in Venice; Venus in Tannhäuser in Toulouse and at the Bavarian Staatsoper, Munich 2000; season 2000–01 as Carmen in Vienna, Naples and Berlin (Deutsche Oper), Eboli in Don Carlos at Munich and Amneris in Verona. *Current Management:* c/o Elizabeth Gottmann, Arts und Promotion GmbH, Duesseldorter Street 40A, 65760, Eschborn-Frankfurt, Germany. *Telephone:* 6196768520 (office). *Fax:* 61967685220 (office). *E-mail:* gottmann@artsundpromotion.de (office). *Website:* www.nadja-michael.de.

**MICHAELS-MOORE, Anthony,** BA; British singer (baritone); b. 8 April 1957, Grays, Essex; s. of John Frederick Moore and Isabel Shephard; m. Ewa Bozena Migocki 1980; one d. *Education:* Gravesend School for Boys, Univ. of Newcastle, Fenham Teacher Training Coll. *Career:* prin. baritone, Royal Opera House, Covent Garden 1987–97; roles in all British opera cos; debut La Scala, Milan (Licinius in La Vestale) 1993, New York Metropolitan Opera (Marcello in La Bohème) 1996, Vienna Staatsoper (Lescaut in Manon) 1997, San Francisco Opera (Eugene Onegin) 1997, Paris Bastille (Sharpless in Madama Butterfly) 1995; specializes in 19th-century baritone repertoire. *Television appearances include:* BBC Proms (Beethoven's Missa Solemnis, Mahler's Symphony No. 8), Carmina Burana recorded at La Scala, Milan 1996. *Music:* major recordings include: Carmina Burana, Lucia di Lammermoor, La Vestale, La Favorite, Falstaff and Il Tabarro, Aroldo. *Radio:* regular BBC Radio 3 broadcasts, Verdi operas from Royal Opera House, Met Opera relays from New York. *Honours:* winner Luciano Pavarotti/Opera Co. of Phila Prize 1985, Royal Philharmonic Soc. Award Winner 1997. *Address:* c/o IMG Artists, Media House, 3 Burlington Lane, Chiswick, London, W4 2TH, England (office). *Telephone:* (20) 8233-5868 (office).

**MICHAILOV, Maxim;** Singer (Bass); b. 1961, Moscow, Russia. *Education:* Studied at the Gnessin Conservatory, Moscow. *Career:* Sang with the Bolshoi company, Moscow, from 1987 as Sarastro, Ivan Khovansky in Khovanshchina, Tsar Dodon in The Golden Cockerel and Zaccaria in Nabucco; Edinburgh Festival 1991 on tour with the Bolshoi in Eugene Onegin and Rimsky's Christmas Eve; Guest appearances in opera and concert throughout Russia; Sang Sarastro at Schönbrunn, Vienna, 1996. *Address:* c/o Bolskoi Theatre, 103009 Moscow, C1S, Russia.

**MICHALOWSKA, Krystyna;** Singer (Mezzo-soprano); b. 13 July 1946, Vilnius, Poland. *Education:* Studied in Gdansk. *Career:* Debut: Bydgoszcz 1970, as Azucena; Engagements in Szczecin, Poznan and Gdansk; Guest appearances in Germany, Bulgaria, Romania, Russia and Czechkoslovakia. Appearances at Bielfeld and elsewhere in Germany from 1980, as Leonora in La Favorita, Carmen, Eboli, Lady Macbeth, Ulrica, Fides, Rosina, Konchakovna, Olga and Larina in Eugene Onegin, Dalila, Laura in La Gioconda, Sara in Roberto Devereux and the Nurse in Die Frau ohne Schatten; Bielefeld 1991, in Yerma by Villa-Lobos, as Ortrud and in the premiere of Katharin Blum by Tilo Medek; Frequent concert appearances. *Address:* c/o Stadtisches Buhnen, Brunnenstrasse 3, 4800 Bielefeld 1, Germany.

**MICHELI, Lorenzo;** Italian classical guitarist; b. 13 June 1975, Milan; m. Giulia Ichino 2002. *Education:* Accademia Chigiana, Siena, Conservatory of Trieste, Musik-Akademie der Stadt Basel, studied with Paola Coppi in Milan, F. Zigante in Lausanne, with O. Ghiglia. *Career:* debut recital, Milan, 1994; has performed worldwide, as soloist and with orchestra; has given over 250 concerts in Italy, Austria, Spain, Switzerland, the UK, France, Ireland, Croatia, Poland, Germany, Slovenia, Greece, Canada and more than 30 US states, plus Africa and Latin America. *Compositions:* two film and TV soundtracks, including Viaggio Verso Casa (film) 1998. *Recordings:* works by M. Castelnuovo-Tedesco; complete M. Llobet guitar works; Guitar Music by Dionisio Aguado; Three Quartets, op 19 by F. de Rossa; Lorenzo Micheli in Concert at Texas Tech Univ. (video). *Publications:* In Memoriam Michael Tippett, Il Fronimo, 1998; Mauro Giuliani's Guitar Technique and Early Nineteenth-Century Pedagogy (essay, Guitar Forum II), 2004; Miguel Llobet (book), 2004. *Honours:* Guitar competitions worldwide including Alessandria, 1997; Guitar Foundation of America Competition, 1999. *Address:* Via Breguzzo 5, 20148 Milan, Italy. *E-mail:* lorenzo.micheli@libero.it (home). *Website:* www.lorenzomicheli.it (home).

**MICHELOW, Sybil;** Singer (Contralto) and Voice Coach; b. 12 Aug. 1925, Johannesburg, S. Africa; m. Derek Goldfoot 1950. *Education:* Music Diploma, Witwatersrand Univ., S. Africa; Private studies with Franz Reizensten (Piano) and Mary Jarred (Singing); LTCL, 1995. *Career:* Debut: London, 1958; Concert performances in the UK and abroad, especially of Handel's Messiah; Frequent radio and TV appearances, notably in Rule Britannia at the Last Night of the Proms; Singing Instructor, Royal Acad. of Dramatic Art, 1956–; mem, Royal Soc. of Musicians of GB (Gov. 1982–85, 1988–93); mem. Inc. Soc. of Musicians. *Compositions include:* Incidental music for Royal Academy of Dramatic Art production of Brecht plays Chalk Circle and Mother Courage; Children's stories with music, South African Broadcasting Corporation. *Recordings include:* Music of Court Homes, vol. 4, and Bach Cantatas 78 and 106; Bliss Pastoral; Dallapiccola Sicut Umbra; Dido and Aeneas; Esparanto Songs by Frank Merrick. *Address:* 50 Chatsworth Road, London, NW2 4DD, England. *E-mail:* sybelowgold@amstrad.com.

**MICHELS, Maria;** Singer (Soprano); b. 1931, Germany. *Career:* Sang at the St ädtische Oper Berlin from 1955 and appeared further in opera at Kiel,

Mannheim and Frankfurt; Essen 1963–66, Munich Staatsoper 1966–69, then the Hanover Opera; roles have included Cherubini's Médée, the Queen of Night, Strauss's Sophie and Zerbinetta, Lulu, Lucia di Lammermoor, Musetta and Olympia; Guest appearances at the Vienna and Stuttgart State Operas, Florence and Brussels (in Arabella), Paris Opéra and Barcelona (as Lulu, 1969).

**MICHIELS, Jan Prosper;** Belgian pianist; b. 10 Oct. 1966, Izegem; m. Inge Spinette 1991. *Education:* Royal Conservatory, Brussels, Hochschule der Künste, Berlin with Hans Leygraf. *Career:* Professor of Piano, Royal Conservatory, Brussels; worked with conductors as Peter Eötvös, Hans Zender, Serge Baudo, Lothar Zagrosek. *Recordings:* Several CDs with works of Brahms, Beethoven, Mendelssohn, Debussy, Ligeti, Huybrechts, Poulenc, Weber, Benjamin, Bartók and Liszt; Ligeti, Etudes I–XIV; Brahms, op 116–119; Debussy, Préludes, Images. *Honours:* Prizewinner, several competitions including Queen Elizabeth Competition, Brussels, 1991. *Address:* Achterstraat 22B, 9310 Meldert (Aalst), Belgium. *E-mail:* janinge@pi.be.

**MICHNIEWSKI, Wojciech;** Conductor and Composer; b. 4 April 1947, Łódź, Poland. *Education:* Conducting, Theory of Music, Composition, Warsaw Academy of Music, 1966–72; Honours degree with distinction, 1972. *Career:* Assistant Conductor 1973–76, Conductor 1976–79, Warsaw National Philharmonic Orchestra; Artistic Director, The Grand Opera Theatre, Łódź, 1979–81; Musical Director, Modern Stage, Warsaw Chamber Opera, 1979–83; Principal Guest Conductor, Polish Chamber Orchestra and Sinfonia Varsovia, 1984–; Conductor, concerts in most European countries, South America, Asia; Appeared West Berlin Philharmonic Hall, La Scala, Milan, Teatro Colón in Buenos Aires; Participant in numerous international festivals including Steyrischer Herbst, Graz, Austria; International May Festival, Barcelona, Spain; Rencontres Musicales, Metz, France; International May Festival, Wiesbaden, Germany; Bemus Festival, Belgrade, Yugoslavia; Dimitria Festival, Thessaloniki, Greece; Warsaw Autumn Festival; Wratisalvia Cantans Music Festival; International Biennale, East Berlin; Polish Chamber Orchestra and Sinfonia Varsovia, 1984–86; General and Artistic Director, The Poznan Philharmonic Orchestra, 1987–; Others. *Recordings:* Gramophone Records; CBS Japan; EMI; Pavane Olympia; Polskie Nagrania Muza; Polton; Tonpress; Radio and television recordings. *Current Management:* Polish Artists Agency PAGART. *Address:* ul Braci Zauskich 3/77, 01 773 Warsaw, Poland.

**MICHNO, Alexander;** Double Bass Player; b. 29 Nov. 1947, Moscow, Russia; m. Elena Stoliarenko, 18 Oct 1991, 2 d. *Education:* Graduated: Gnesin School of Music, Moscow, 1963; Gnesin College of Music, Moscow, 1966; Gnesin Institute of Music, Moscow, 1971. *Career:* Debut: Moscow, 1969; Teaching at Gnessin College of Music, 1966–, at Gnessin Institute of Music (Academy of Music, 1991–), 1977–; Bassist in Moscow Philharmonic Symphonic Orchestra under K Kondrashin, 1973–80, as Co-Principal Bassist in USSR State Academy Symphony Orchestra under E Svetlanov, 1980–94, as Principal Double Bass in Asturias Symphony Orchestra, Northern Spain, 1994–; Performed as Soloist on Moscow radio and television, giving many recitals and concerts with symphony and chamber orchestras and appearing at International Bass Week in Michaelstein, 1996, 1997, 1998, 1999, Bass Festival 1998 in Reading, England, and Dresden 1999, Germany; Served on Jury for Bass Competitions, USSR, 1980, 1984, Russia, 1988, Kishinev (as Jury Chairman), 1989, Munich, 1991, Kromeriz, 1997; Has given courses in Spain and Germany; mem, British Double Bass Society. *Compositions:* Study for Double Bass, as editor, 1983, 1998. *Recordings include:* Bottesini–Grand Duo, for Violin and Double Bass, 1975; Ivanov–Concerto in the Romantic Style, 1977; Respighi–Concerto a Cinque, 1988; Eccles, Bottesini, Glier and others, with Galina Schastnaja, piano, CD, 1997. *Publications include:* Development of Playing Skills, 1988; History of the Art of Playing the Double Bass, 1988; Musical Heritage of G Bottesini, 1989; Giovanni Bottesini, 1997. *Contributions:* Italian Influences in St Petersburg, in The BIBF Journal, 1999. *Honours:* 1st Prize, International Markneukirchen Double Bass Competition, 1975. *Address:* Ramon y Cajal 2-2-A, 33205 Gijon, Spain.

**MIDDENWAY, Ralph,** BA; Australian composer, writer and editor; b. 9 Sept. 1932, Sydney, NSW; m., three d. *Education:* Univ. of Sydney, NSW Conservatory. *Career:* music and drama teacher Tudor House School, Moss Vale 1958–64; Theatre Consultant, Sec., Warden Adelaide Univ. Union 1965–77; Theatre Consultant, Gen. Man. The Parks Comomounity Centre 1977–82; mem. Faculty of Music, University of Adelaide 1977–82; music and opera critic 1970–86; freelance writer 1970–; editor 1982–; horticulturist 1989–; Founding Chair. Richard Wagner Soc. of S Australia 1988–2002; Pres. Town and Country Planning Asscn 1973–74; Vice-Pres. S Australian Flowergrowers Asscn 1999–2001; mem. Adelaide Univ. Union, Australian Music Centre, Australasian Performing Right Asscn, Soc. of Editors, Australian Arts Media Alliance, Richard Wagner Soc. of S Australia, S Australian Farmers Fed. *Compositions include:* Missa Omnibus Sanctis, for chorous 1960, Mosaics for 13 brass and two percussion 1970, The Child of Heaven, for chorus, brass sextete and two percussion 1971; Two arias for The Tempest, baritone and orchestra 1980, Stone River, for medium voice and 4 percussion 1984; Stream of Time, for bass clarinet and piano 1984; Sinfonia Concertante for brass quintet and orchestra 1985; Sonata Capricciosa, for piano 1986; Mosaics for orchestra and saxophone ensemble 1986; The Letters of Amalie Dietrich, 1 act opera 1986, Barossa, Singspiel in 2 acts 1988; Stone River, for mezzo-soprano and piano 1989, The Lamentations of Jeremiah, for chorus 1990; The Eye of Heaven, for baritone and string quartet 1991; East River, sonata for piano

1995, The Eye of Heaven, for chorus 2000, Sång Sångars, for 7 solo voices, flute, cello and organ 2002, music for Sure and Certain Hope, epic theatre piece (with playwright Chris Tugwell) 2003; commissions from Univ. of Adelaide Foundation and Adelaide Chamber Orchestra, among others; many recordings. *Publications:* The Enigma of Parsifal, essays (co-ed. and contrib.) 2001, What is Love? (3 one-act plays for young actors) 2004 contrib. to journals, magazines and newspapers in Australia, Canada, UK and USA. *Address:* POB 753, Victor Harbor, S Australia 5211, Australia. *Telephone:* (8) 8558-8325. *E-mail:* venteman@comstech.com. *Website:* www.comstech.com/~venteman/.

**MIDORI;** Japanese violinist; b. 25 Oct. 1971, Osaka; d. of Setsu Goto. *Education:* Professional Children's School, Juilliard School of Music, NY Univ. *Career:* began violin studies with mother aged four; moved to USA 1982; début with New York Philharmonic 1982; recording début 1986 aged 14; now makes worldwide concert appearances; founder and Pres. Midori and Friends (foundation) 1992. *Honours:* Dorothy B. Chandler Performing Arts Award, New York State Asian-American Heritage Month Award, Crystal Award (Japan), Suntory Award 1994. *Current Management:* ICM Artists Ltd, Oxford House, 76 Oxford Street, London, W1N 0AX, England. *Address:* c/o Midori and Friends, 850 Seventh Avenue, Suite 1103, New York, NY 10019 (office); c/o Byron Gustafson, ICM Artists, Ltd., 40 West 57th Street, New York, NY 10019, USA. *E-mail:* violin@gotomidori.com. *Website:* www.midoriandfriends.org; www.gotomidori.com.

**MIGENES, Julia;** American singer (soprano); b. 1948, New York; m. 4th Peter Medak. *Education:* Juilliard School of Music (New York). *Career:* Opera debut at 3½ years; has appeared in operas, on Broadway, on TV and in films; performances include Royal Opera House, Covent Garden, London 1987, Earl's Court, London, UK 1991. *Operas include:* Madam Butterfly, Manon Lescaut 1987, Tosca 1991. *Film:* Carmen. *TV series:* Magnum, The Twilight Zone. *Theatre includes:* West Side Story. *Recordings include:* Carmen, Kismet, Rags.

**MIHALIČ, Alexander;** Slovak composer; b. 7 Aug. 1963, Medzilaborce. *Education:* Košice Conservatory, Bratislava Acad. of Music and Drama, Ecole Normale de Musique, Paris, Conservatoire Nat. de Région, Boulogne, Université de Paris VIII and Ecole de Sciences Sociales, Paris. *Career:* mem. of teaching staff, Institut de Recherche et Coordination Acoustique/Musique, Paris 1992–. *Compositions include:* six prelúdii 1982–83, Forlana 1983, Hudba 1986, Skladba 1987, Music for String Quartet 1988, Kompozicia 1990, Encyclopaedia musicalis (multiple work in progress) 1991–. *Honours:* Prix de Résidence int. electro-acoustic competition, Bourges 1988. *Address:* 8 Résidence les Aigles, 3 rue Adolf Wersand, 93440 Dugny, France. *Telephone:* 1-48-37-79-28. *E-mail:* mihalic@club-internet.fr.

**MIHELCIC, Pavel;** Composer; b. 8 Nov. 1937, Novo Mesto, Yugoslavia; m. Majda Lovse, 10 April 1965, 2 d. *Education:* Diploma, 1963, Special Class 1967, Academy of Music, Ljubljana. *Career:* Professor, Conservatory of Music, 1982–; Manager, Department of Smyphonic Music, Ljubljana Broadcasting Corporation, 1982–; President, Slovenian Composers Society, 1984–. *Compositions include:* Orchestral works: Bridge for strings; Asphalt ballet; Concerto for horn and orchestra; Sinfonietta; Musique Funèbre for violin and orchestra; Chamber works: Limite; Blow Up; Take-off for piano; Sonatine; Sonata 80; Chorus, 1, 2, 3, 4, 5, 10, 13; Games and Reflections; Double Break; Published by Edition DSS, Ljubljana and Edition Peters, Leipzig; Recorded: Quinta Essentia for brass quintet; Timber-line for chamber orchestra; Exposition and Reflections for 9 horns; Stop-time for horn and chamber orchestra; Team for woodwind quintet; Introduction and Sequences for orchestra; Scenes From Bela Krajina; Fading Pictures; Snow of First Youth for orchestra; Glittering Dusk for Orchestra, 1993; Return to Silence, for Orchestra, 1995; Concerto Grosso, 1997. *Contributions:* Standing Music Critic, Delo, Ljubljana; Zvuk, Sarajevo. *Honours:* Preseren Prize, 1979; Zupancic Prize, 1984. *Address:* Melikova ul 10, 61108 Ljubljana, Slovenia.

**MIHEVC, Marko;** University Professor; b. 30 April 1957, Ljubljana, Slovenia; m., 1 d. *Education:* Diploma, Academy for Music, University of Ljubljana; Diploma, Hochschule für Musik, Vienna; Master's Degree, Hochschule für Musik, Vienna. *Career:* Debut: Concert for violin and orchestra with Zagreb Philharmonic Orchestra, Ljubljana, 1989; Symphonic poem Equi, Slovene Philharmonic Orchestra, Ljubljana, 1991; Initiator and Organiser of the Night of Slovene Composers, 1991; Symphonic poem In Signo Tauri, Slovene Philharmonic Orchestra, Ljubljana, 1992; Capricios for Violin and Piano, Vienna, 1993; University career, Professor of Composition and Head of Composition Department, 1994; Symphonic poem Miracula, Slovene Philharmonic Orchestra, Ljubljana, 1994; Cantata Proverbia, Slovene Philharmonic Orchestra, Ljubljana and RTS Choir, 1995; Symphonic poem Alibaba, Slovene Philharmonic Orchestra, Ljubljana, 1995; Cantata Enigmata, Orchestra of Camerata Labacensis and academic choir, 1998; Symphonic poem The Planets, Symphonic Orchestra of RTS, Slovenia, 1998; Concerto for Violin and Orchestra, 1989; Childrens' Opera Aladin and his Wonder Lamp; 5 symphonic poems; 2 cantatas; Symphonic poem Mar Saba, Slovene Philharmonic Orchestra, Ljubljana, 2000. *Address:* Groharjeva 18, 1000 Ljubljana, Slovenia.

**MIKHAILOV, Maxim;** Singer (Bass-baritone); b. 1956, Moscow. *Education:* Gnessin Institute, Moscow, until 1988. *Career:* Soloist at the Bolshoi Theatre from 1987; Recitalist and guest opera appearances in Italy, Germany, Denmark, Hungary and elsewhere; Season 1993–94 in Rossini's La Scala di

Seta and Massenet's Chérubin at the Wiener Kammeroper, in the Mozart Festival at Schönbrunn and in Rachmaninov's Miserly Knight at the Bolshoi; Seaso 1995 with Orlik in Mazeppa at Amsterdam, concert performance of Prokoviev's War and Peace at the Vienna Konzerthaus, and Rimsky's May Night at the Wexford Festival; Season 1996–97 with Prince Khovansky in Khovanshchina at Nantes and Mozart's Masetto at Covent Garden; Sang Giove in Cavalli's Calisto at the Vienna Kammeroper, 1998; Season 2000–01 as Banquo in Oslo and the Mayor in Rimsky's May Night, at Bologna. *Address:* Allied Artists, 42 Montpelier Square, London SW7 1JZ, England.

**MIKI, Minoru;** Composer; b. 16 March 1930, Tokushima, Shikoku, Japan. *Education:* Studied composition with Ikenouchi and Ifukube at the Toyko National University of Fine Arts and Music, 1951–55. *Career:* Founder and Artistic Director, Ensemble Nipponia, later Pro Musica Nipponia, ensemble of traditional Japanese instruments, 1964; Foreign tours with the Ensemble from 1972; Founded the opera theatre Utaza, 1986; Founded the multi-culture ensemble YUI Ensemble, 1990; Founded the Orchestra Asia, 1993; Founded the Asia Ensemble, 2002; Director, Japan Federation of Composers; Director, Yonden Cultural Foundation. *Compositions include:* Eurasian Triology including Symphony for Two Worlds, 1969–81; Shunkin-Sho, opera in 3 acts, Tokyo, 1975; Ada (An Actor's Revenge), opera in 2 acts, English Music Theatre at the Old Vic, London, 1979; The Monkey Poet, folk opera, 1983; Joruri, opera in 3 acts, St Louis. 1985; Yomigaeru, folk-opera, Tokyo, 1989; Wakahime, opera in 3 acts, Okayama, 1991; Shizuka and Yoshitsune, opera in 3 acts, Kamakura, 1993; The River Sumida/Kusabira, a twin opera, 1995; Pipa Concerto, 1997; The Tale of Geuji, opera in 3 acts, Saint Louis, 2000; Memory of the Eart for Asian soloists and orchestra, 2000. *Recordings:* Works Selections I–VI of Minoru Miki including Eurasian Triology, Camerata Records. *Publications:* The Method of Japanese Instruments, 1995; An Actor's Revenge, 1989. *Honours:* Grand Prize of the National Art Festival, 1970; Giraud Opera Prize for composition of Shunkin-sho, 1976; National Purple Ribbon, 1994; The Order of the Rising Sun, 2000. *Current Management:* Japan Arts Corporation, Tokyo. *Address:* 1-11-6 Higashi Nogawa, Komae-shi, Tokyo 201–002, Japan. *Fax:* 334899341. *E-mail:* m-miki@mtb.biglobe.ne.jp. *Website:* www.m-miki.com. *E-mail:* m-miki@mtb.biglobe.ne.jp. *Website:* www.m-miki.com.

**MIKLOSA, Erika;** Singer (Soprano); b. 1970, Hungary. *Education:* Studied in Budapest, Philadelphia, USA and Milan, Italy. *Career:* Sang Papagena and Adele in Die Fledermaus and Donizetti's Lucia di Lammermoor at the Opera House, Budapest; Mozart's Queen of Night at Vienna, Berlin, Stuttgart, Cologne, Leipzig and Wiesbaden, 1993–; Other roles include Donizetti's Linda di Chamounix, Stravinsky's Le Rossignol and Oscar in Verdi's Un Ballo in Mascera; Sang the Fiakermilli in Arabella at Zürich, 2000. *Honours:* Winner, International Mozart Competition, Budapest, 1993; European Culture Prize, Zürich, 1995. *Address:* Hungarian National Opera, Andrassy ut 22, 1061 Budapest, Hungary.

**MIKULAS, Peter;** Singer (Bass); b. 1954, Slovakia. *Education:* Studied at the University of Music and Drama in Bratislava with Viktoria Stracenská. *Career:* Soloist with the Slovak National Theatre in Bratislava, 1978–; Roles have included Kecal, Dulcamara, Gremin, Raimondo, Fiesco, Don Alfonso, Sarastro, Lodovico, Lindorf, Coppelius, Dr Miracle and Dapertutto, Mephisto, Don Pasquale, Banquo, Philip, Don Quichotte, Zaccaria and Golaud; Extensive concert repertoire. Guest appearances in leading European theatres, National Theatre Prague, Berlin Staatsoper, De Nederlandse Opera in Amsterdam; Has sung in Vienna, Salzburg, Paris, London, Liverpool, Birmingham, Madrid, Barcelona, Granada, Rome, Milan, Genoa, Frankfurt, Stuttgart, Hamburg, Copenhagen, Ankara, Budapest, Tokyo, Dallas, Ottowa, Buenos Aires, Rio de Janeiro and at the Prague Spring, Carinthian Summer and Edinburgh Festivals; Sang Lutobor in Smetana's Libuše at Edinburgh, 1998; Season 2000–01 as Dulcamara at Bratislava and Kolenati in The Makropulos Case at the Met; Collaborated with conductors Ceccato, Bychkov, Pesek, Belohlavek, Solti, Mackerras, Giulini and Altrichter. *Current Management:* Art Agency Ltd, Bratislava; Exclusively in England, Music International, London. *Address:* Art Agency Ltd, Dom novinárov, Zupné ná m 7, 811 03 Bratislava, Slovakia.

**MILAN, Susan,** ARCM, FRCM; British flautist; *Professor of flute, Royal College of Music;* b. 1947; m.; two s. *Education:* Junior Exhibitioner, Royal College of Music; Studied with John Francis at the Royal College of Music and Geoffrey Gilbert at the Guildhall School of Music; Attended the Marcel Moyse Masterclasses in Switzerland; Graduated from the Royal College of Music with Honours. *Career:* Principal Flute of the Bournemouth Sinfonietta, 1968–1972; Principal Flute and first woman member of the Royal Philharmonic Orchestra, 1974–82; Developed Solo Career; Recording contracts with Hyperion, ASV, Chandos Records, DaCapo, Cala, Omega, Nippon Columbia, Upbeat Records; Many Commissions and first performances from composers including: Nareshe Sohal 1967, Peter Lamb 1970, Robert Saxton 1973, David Morgan 1974, Jindrich Feld 1975, Antal Dorati 1980, Richard Rodney Bennett 1981, 1982, Ole Schmidt 1984, Robert Walker 1987, Carl Davis 1989, Robert Simpson 1991, Roger Steptoe 1995, Edward Cowie 1997, Edwin Roxburgh 2000, Jean Sichler 2001, Cecilia McDowall 2003; Tours world-wide as Soloist and Recitalist; Lady Chairman British Flute Society, 1990–94; Runs two annual masterclass courses; Professor of Flute, Royal College of Music, London 1984–; Ensembles: The London Chamber Music Group — Flute, Oboe, Violin, Viola, Cello, Harp, Piano. *Recordings:* Include: Flute Concerto by Ole Schmidt; Saint-Saëns Taratelle; Mozart concertos K313/314 with the English

Chamber Orchestra conducted by Raymond Leppard for Chandos; Mozart flute and harp concerto K299, Salieri flute and oboe concerto with the City of London Sinfonia conducted by Richard Hickix for Chandos; La Flute Enchante, French pieces for flute and orchestra, City of London Sinfonia conducted by Richard Hickox; Beethoven Trios with Sergio Azzolini, Ian Brown, Levon Chilingirian and Louise Williams; Saint-Saens Romancevand Prokofiev Sonata in D with Clifford Benson; The Chamber Music of Eugene Goossens, London Chamber Music Group 2004. *Publications:* Flute Technique- Quadruplets; Cadenzas for Mozart Concertos in D/G, and Andante in C; Cadenzas for Salieri Concerto for Flute and Oboe. *Honours:* Fellowship, Royal College of Music, 1999. *Current Management:* Master Classics Artists, 13 Rodney House, Pembridge Crescent, London, W11 3DY. *Address:* Oakcombe, Marley Common, Haslemere, Surrey, GU27 3PP, England (home). *Telephone:* (1428) 641457 (home). *Fax:* (20) 7229-3931 (office); (1428) 654826 (home). *E-mail:* smilan3805@aol.com (home). *Website:* www.susanmilan.com (home).

**MILANOV, Michail;** Singer (Bass); b. 1949, Sofia, Bulgaria. *Education:* Studied in Sofia. *Career:* Sang in Bulgaria from 1974; Throughout Germany from 1977, notably at the Theater am Gärtnerplatz, Munich, from 1988 (Dosifey in Khovanshchina, 1992); Other roles have included Mefistofele, King Philip, Rocco, Hagen, King Mark, and Colline in La Bohème (Verona Arena, 1982); Season 1993 as Sparafucile at Macerata and Dosifey in Munich; Sang the Duc d'Arco in Salvator Rosa for Dorset Opera, 2000; Many concert appearances and lieder recitals. *Address:* c/o Staatstheater am Gärtnerplatz, Gärtnerplatz, W-8000 Munich 5, Germany.

**MILANOVA, Stoika;** Bulgarian concert violinist; b. 5 Aug. 1945, Plovdiv. *Education:* Studied with father Trendafil Milanova and with David Oistrakh at the Moscow Conservatory. *Career:* Appearances with principal British orchestras from 1970; Engagements in most European countries; Yomiuri Nippon Symphony Orchestra, Japan, 1975; Concerts with the Hallé Orchestra and at the Hong Kong Festival; Tour for Australian Broadcasting Commission, 1976; US and Canadian debuts 1978; Tours of Eastern Europe 1985–86; Duo recitals with Radu Lupu and Malcolm Frager. *Recordings:* Balkanton (Bulgaria), including the complete Brandenburg Concertos with Karl Munchinger and Prokofiev's Violin Concertos; Sonatas with Malcolm Frager. *Honours:* 2nd Prize, Queen Elisabeth Competition, Belgium, 1967; 1st Prize, City of London Int. Competition (Carl Flesch), 1970; Grand Prix du Disque, 1972. *Current Management:* Terry Harrison Artists Management, The Orchard, Market Street, Charlbury, Oxfordshire OX7 3PJ, England. *Telephone:* (1608) 810330. *Fax:* (1608) 811331. *E-mail:* artists@terryharrison .force9.co.uk.

**MILASHKINA, Tamara (Andreyevna);** Singer (Soprano); b. 13 Sept. 1934, Astrakhan, USSR. *Education:* Studied with Elena Katul'skaya at the Moscow Conservatory. *Career:* Debut: Bolshoi Theatre 1957, as Titania in Eugene Onegin; Has sung Lisa in The Queen of Spades, Zarina in The Legend of Tsar Saltan, Yaroslavna in Prince Igor and Natasha (War and Peace) with the Bolshoi Company; Guest appearances at La Scala (Lida in La battaglia di Legnano, 1962), Helsinki, Paris, Wuppertal and in North America; Vienna Staatsoper 1971, as Lisa; Deutsche Oper Berlin 1974, as Tosca; Other roles include Fevronia (The Invisible City of Kitezh), Maria (Tchaikovsky's Mazeppa) and Lyuba (Prokofiev's Semyon Kotko) and Verdi's Elisabeth de Valois and Leonora (Il Trovatore). *Recordings include:* Mazeppa, Tosca, The Queen of Spades and The Stone Guest. *Address:* c/o Bolshoi Theatre, Pr Marxa 8/2, 103009 Moscow, Russia.

**MILBURN, Ellsworth;** Composer; b. 6 Feb. 1938, Greensburg, Pennsylvania, USA. *Education:* Studied with Scot Huston at the University of Cincinnati College-Conservatory of Music, 1956–58, with Roy Travis and Henri Lazarof at the University of California at Los Angeles, 1959–62, and with Milhaud at Mills College in Oakland, 1966–68. *Career:* Teacher, University of Cincinnati College-Conservatory of Music, 1970–75; Rice University, Houston, from 1975. *Contributions:* Opera Gesualdo 1973; 5 Inventions for 2 flutes, 1965; Massacre of the Innocents, chorus, 1965; Concerto, piano and chamber orchestra, 1967; String Trio, 1968; Soli, 5 players on 10 instruments, 1968; String Quintet, 1969; Soli II for 2 players on flutes and double bass, 1970; Voussoirs for orchestra, 1970; Soli III for clarinet, cello and piano, 1971; Soli IV, flute, oboe, double bass and harpsichord, 1972; Violin Sonata, 1972; Lament, harp, 1972; Spiritus mundi for high voice and 5 instruments, 1974. *Address:* Rice University, Shepherd School of Music, PO Box 1892, Houston, TX 77251, USA.

**MILCHEVA-NONOVA, Alexandrina;** Singer (Mezzo-soprano); b. 27 Nov. 1936, Shoumen, Bulgaria. *Education:* Studied with G Cherkin at the Sofia Conservatory. *Career:* Debut: Warna 1961, as Dorabella in Così fan tutte; Sang at the Bulgarian National Opera in Sofia from 1968; Guest appearances in Vienna, Brussels, Paris, Amsterdam, Berlin (Komische Oper), London and Zürich; Munich 1979 and 1984; Verona Arena 1980 and 1984; Maggio Musicale Florence 1983, in Suor Angelica, Teatro Liceo Barcelona 1983, as Preziosilla in La Forza del Destino; La Scala Milan as Marfa in Khovanshchina, repeated at the Paris Opéra 1984; Geneva 1984, as Adalgisa in Norma; Other roles include Azucena, the Princess in Adriana Lecouvreur, Dalila, Carmen and Cenerentola. *Recordings include:* Carmen, Boris Godunov and Khovanshchina (Balkanton); Aida and songs by Mussorgsky (Harmonia Mundi); Leoncavallo's La Bohème (Orfeo). *Address:* c/o Bulgarian National Opera, Sofia, Bulgaria.

**MILES, Alastair;** Singer (bass); b. 1961, England. *Education:* flute and voice, Guildhall School and National Opera Studio. *Career:* debut, sang Trulove, in The Rake's Progress, for Opera 80, 1985; appearances from 1986 with Glyndebourne Festival and Touring Opera in Capriccio, Katya Kabanova, The Rake's Progress and Die Zauberflöte; Welsh National Opera as Basilio, Sparafucile, Raimondo and Silva, in Ernani; Royal Opera, Covent Garden in Parsifal, Viaggio a Reims, I Capuleti, Fidelio, Rigoletto, La Cenerentola and La Bohème; other engagements in Vancouver, Amsterdam, San Francisco, Lyon and Deutsche Oper Berlin; concert appearances under Gardiner in Beethoven's Missa Solemnis, Mozart's Requiem, Handel's Saul and Agrippina and Verdi Requiem; under Harnoncourt in Handel's Samson and Bach Cantatas; with Kurt Masur in Elijah and the St Matthew Passion; Berlioz, La Damnation de Faust and Romeo and Juliette under Colin Davis; Bartolo in Figaro with Simon Rattle and the CBSO; Messiah under Helmut Rilling; Damnation of Faust with Myung Whun Chung; Season 1993 in the Choral Symphony under Giulini and title role in Le nozze di Figaro under Harnoncourt for Netherlands Opera; sang Sir George Walton in I Puritani, Met, 1997; sang Philip II in Don Carlos for Opera North 1998; Season 2000 as Gounod's Frère Laurent at Covent Garden, Bellini's Giorgio in Munich, Alvise in La Gioconda for ENO (concert) and in Beethoven's Ninth at the Ravenna Festival; Mendelssohn's Elijah at the London Proms, 2002. *Recordings include:* Lucia di Lammermoor; Saul and Agrippina; Elijah; La Traviata; Rigoletto; Verdi Requiem; Die Zauberflöte; Don Giovanni; Berlioz Roméo et Juliette; Le nozze di Figaro; La Cenerentola. *Current Management:* AOR Management Inc., 6910 Roosevelt Way NE, PMB 221, Seattle, WA 98115, USA.

**MILES-JOHNSON, Deborah;** Singer (Mezzo-soprano); b. 1965, England. *Career:* Concerts include: Handel's Israel in Egypt on tour to Spain, Elijah in Toronto, St Matthew Passion under Andrew Parrott, Mozart's C Minor Mass at the Barbican and Elgar's Music Makers at Peterborough Cathedral; Opera roles include: Bianca in The Rape of Lucretia, Mrs Peachum in The Beggar's Opera, Madame Popova in Walton's Bear (Thaxted Festival), Orlofsky in Fledermaus (Haddo House) and Mrs Sedley in Peter Grimes; Royal Opera Covent Garden in Birtwistle's Gawain; Dido and Aeneas with the English Bach Festival; Season 1997 with Schubert and Haydn in Switzerland, Handel's Il Parnasso in Festa and Stravinsky's Requiem Canticles with the CBSO under Simon Rattle; Further concerts with Klangforum at the Vienna Konzerthaus (Barraqué's au dela du hasard...) and at the Wigmore Hall with Fretwork: debut there in Upon Silence by George Benjamin. *Recordings include:* Resurrection by Peter Maxwell Davies; Rutti's Magnificat; Pärt's Stabat Mater, with Fretwork, under Parrott. *Address:* 19 Gorham Drive, St Albans AL 1 2HU, England.

**MILKINA, Nina;** British concert pianist; b. 27 Jan. 1919, Moscow, USSR (now Russian Federation); d. of Jacques and Sophie Milkine; m. Alastair Robert Masson Sedgwick 1943; one s. one d. *Education:* studied under Leon Conus and Profs Harold Craxton and Tobias Matthay, studied composition with Glazunov and Sabaniev; Moscow and Paris Conservatoires. *Career:* debut aged 11 with Lamourex Orchestra, Paris; noted as interpreter of Mozart's piano works; chosen by BBC to broadcast all Mozart's piano sonatas; gave Mozart Bicentennial recital at Edinburgh Int. Festival 1991; int. adjudicator; Hon. Fellow RAM. *Recordings include:* Mozart piano concertos and recitals, Chopin Mazurkas, Scarlatti Sonatas, Mozart and Haydn Sonatas, Brahms piano trios, works by Rachmaninov, Prokofiev, Scriabin, Bach. *Publications:* Works for Piano, Early Compositions. *Address:* 17 Montagu Square, London, W1H 2LE, England. *Telephone:* (20) 7487-4588.

**MILLER, Clement A.;** Musicologist; b. 29 Jan. 1915, Cleveland, Ohio, USA; m. (1) Jean Miller (deceased), 2 s., 1 d., (2) Nancy Voigt 1983. *Education:* BM, Piano, 1936, MM, Music Theory, 1937, Cleveland Institute of Music; MA, Western Reserve University, 1942; PhD, Musicology, University of Michigan, 1951. *Career:* Instructor, Head of Music Department (History), Dean of Faculty, Acting Director, Cleveland Institute of Music, Ohio, 1937–65; Professor of Music, Fine Arts Department, John Carroll University, 1967–79; mem, American Musicological Society; Renaissance Society of America; Music Library Association; Musica Disciplina. *Publications:* Heinrich Glarean: Dodecachordon, 1965; Franchinus Gaffurius: Musica Practica, 1968; Johannes Cochlaeus: Tetrachordum Musices, 1970; Sebald Heyden: De Arte Canendi, 1972; Hieronymus Cardanus: Writings on Music, 1973; Le Gendre, Maille, Morpain: Collected Chansons, 1981; Nicolaus Burtius: Musices Opusculum, 1983; Co-editor: A Correspondence of Renaissance Musicians, 1990; Commentary and Translation: Musica Practica by Bartolomeo Ramis de Pareia, 1993. *Contributions:* The Musical Quarterly; Journal of the American Musicological Society; Die Musik in Geschichte und Gegenwart; New Grove Dictionary of Music and Musicians. *Honours:* Guggenheim Fellowship, 1974–75; Outstanding Educator of America, 1975. *Address:* 7922 Bremen Avenue, Parma, OH 44129, USA.

**MILLER, Sir Jonathan Wolfe,** Kt, CBE, MB, BCh, FRA; British stage director, film director, physician and writer; b. 21 July 1934, London; s. of the late Emanuel Miller; m. Helen Rachel Collet 1956; two s. one d. *Education:* St Paul's School, St John's Coll., Cambridge and Univ. Coll. Hosp. Medical School, London. *Career:* co-author of and appeared in Beyond the Fringe 1961–64; Dir John Osborne's Under Plain Cover, Royal Court Theatre 1962, Robert Lowell's The Old Glory, New York 1964 and Prometheus Bound, Yale Drama School 1967; Dir at Nottingham Playhouse 1968–69; Dir Oxford and Cambridge Shakespeare Co. production of Twelfth Night on tour in USA 1969;

Research Fellow in the History of Medicine, Univ. Coll., London 1970–73; Assoc. Dir Nat. Theatre 1973–75; mem. Arts Council 1975–76; Visiting Prof. in Drama, Westfield Coll., Univ. of London 1977–; Exec. Producer Shakespeare TV series 1979–81; Artistic Dir Old Vic 1988–90; Research Fellow in Neuropsychology, Univ. of Sussex; Fellow, Univ. Coll. London 1981–; mem. American Acad. of Arts and Sciences. *Productions:* for Nat. Theatre, London: The Merchant of Venice 1970, Danton's Death 1971, The School for Scandal 1972, The Marriage of Figaro 1974, The Wind in the Willows 1990; other productions The Tempest, London 1970, Prometheus Bound, London 1971, The Taming of the Shrew, Chichester 1972, The Seagull, Chichester 1973, The Malcontent, Nottingham 1973, Arden Must Die (opera) 1973, The Family in Love, Greenwich Season 1974, The Importance of Being Earnest 1975, The Cunning Little Vixen (opera) 1975, All's Well That Ends Well, Measure For Measure, Greenwich Season 1975, Three Sisters 1977, The Marriage of Figaro (ENO) 1978, Arabella (opera) 1980, Falstaff (opera) 1980, 1981, Otello (opera) 1982, Rigoletto (opera) 1982, 1984, Fidelio (opera) 1982, 1983, Don Giovanni (opera) 1985, The Mikado (opera) 1986, Tosca (opera) 1986, Long Day's Journey into Night 1986, Taming of the Shrew 1987, The Tempest 1988, Turn of the Screw 1989, King Lear 1989, The Liar 1989, La Fanciulla del West (opera) 1991, Marriage of Figaro (opera), Manon Lescaut (opera), Die Gezeichneten (opera) 1992, Maria Stuarda (opera), Capriccio (opera), Fedora (opera), Bach's St Matthew Passion 1993, Der Rosenkavalier (opera), Anna Bolena (opera), Falstaff (opera), L'Incoronazione di Poppea (opera), La Bohème (opera) 1994, Così fan Tutte (opera) 1995, Carmen (opera) 1995, Pelléas et Mélisande (opera) 1995, She Stoops to Conquer, London 1995, A Midsummer Night's Dream, London 1996, The Rake's Progress, New York 1997, Ariadne auf Naxos, Maggio Musicale, Florence 1997, Falstaff, Berlin State Opera 1998, The Beggar's Opera 1999, Tamerlano, Sadler's Wells, Paris and Halle 2001, Acis and Galatea, Holland Park Opera, London 2003. *Films:* Take a Girl Like You 1969 and several films for television including Whistle and I'll Come to You 1967, Alice in Wonderland 1966, The Body in Question (series) 1978, Henry the Sixth, part one 1983, States of Mind (series) 1983, Subsequent Performances 1986, The Emperor 1987, Jonathan Miller's Opera Works (series) 1997. *Art exhibition:* Mirror Image, National Gallery, London 1998. *Publications:* McLuhan 1971, Freud: The Man, his World, his Influence (ed.) 1972, The Body in Question 1978, Subsequent Performances 1986, The Don Giovanni Book: Myths of Seduction and Betrayal (ed.) 1990, On Reflection 1998. *Honours:* Hon. Fellow, St John's Coll. Cambridge, Royal Coll. of Physicians 1997, Royal Coll. of Physicians (Edin.) 1998; Dr hc (Open Univ.) 1983, Hon. DLitt (Leicester) 1981, (Kent) 1985, (Leeds) 1996, (Cambridge) 1996; Dir of the Year, Soc. of West End Theatre Awards 1976, Royal Television Soc. Silver Medal 1981, Royal Soc. of Arts Albert Medal 1992. *Current Management:* IMG Artists, 616 Chiswick High Road, London, W4 5RX, England. *E-mail:* jford@imgworld.com. *Website:* www.imgartists.com.

**MILLER, Kevin;** Singer (Tenor); b. 1929, Adelaide, Australia. *Education:* Studied at Elder Conservatory, Adelaide. *Career:* Sang with the Australian National Theatre Company, Melbourne in operas by Mozart, Rossini and Vaughan Williams; Studied further in London, and in Rome with Dino Borgiloi and toured with the Australian Opera, 1955; Glyndebourne Festival, 1955–57, as Pedrillo, Monostatos and Scaramuccio in Ariadne auf Naxos; Welsh National Opera from 1958, notably as Rossini's Ramiro, Vanja in Katya Kabanova, Sellem in The Rake's Progress and Offenbach's Orpheus; Toured West Germany and Australia, 1962 with Orpheus in the Underworld and The Rake's Progress. *Recordings:* The Rake's Progress, conducted by the composer.

**MILLER, Lajos;** Hungarian singer (baritone); b. 23 Jan. 1940, Szombathely; s. of Lajos Miller and Teréz Sebestyén; m. Zsuzsa Dobránszky; one s. *Career:* studied at Music Acad. of Budapest under Jenő Sipos; mem. Hungarian State Opera 1968–; has sung with major cos in France, Germany, Italy, Monaco, Switzerland, Austria, UK, USA, Belgium, Venezuela, Canada, Chile, Japan, Argentina, Russia. *Operatic roles include:* (Verdi) Renato, Rodrigo, Simon Boccanegra, Don Carlos, Rolando (Battaglia di Legnano), Iago, Nabucco, Conte di Luna, Miller, Germont, (Gluck) Orpheus, Orestes, (Mozart) Don Giovanni, Guglielmo, (Giordano) Carlo Gérard, (Leoncavallo) Silvio, (Rossini) Figaro, Guglielmo Tell, (Tchaikovsky) Eugene Onegin, Yeletsky, (Puccini) Scarpia, (Bizet) Escamillo, (Berio) Commandant Ivo, (Donizetti) Enrico, (Rimsky-Korsakov) Grasnoi, (Puccini) Sharpless. *Recorded roles:* Don Carlos (Ernani), Simon Boccanegra, Lycidas, Sharpless (Madame Butterfly), Fanuel, Valentin (Faust), Andrei (War and Peace), Manfredo (Il Giuramento), Chelkalov (Boris Godunov), Belfagor, Zosimo (Maria Egiziaca), Falásar (Semirama), Arias by Verdi. *TV films:* Orfeusz Es Eurydike (Rainieri de Calzabigi and Christoph Willibald Gluck) 1985, Enrico (Lucia di Lammermoor), Marcello (Tabarro), Silvio (Pagliacci), Loth (Madarasz Loth), two portrait films 1995, Angelica (Ibert), L'elisir d'amore (Donizetti), Rigoletto (Verdi), Bank Ban 2002. *Honours:* Grand Prix, Fauré singing contest, Paris 1974, First Prize, Toti dal Monte singing contest, Treviso, Italy 1975, Liszt Prize 1975, Kossuth Prize 1980. *Address:* Hegyalja u. 32, 3232 Mátrafüred; State Opera, Andrássy ut 22, 1061 Budapest, Hungary. *Telephone:* (61) 331-2550.

**MILLER, Leta (Ellen),** BA, PhD, MM; American musicologist, flautist and professor; b. 30 Sept. 1947, Burbank, CA; m. Alan K. Miller 1969, 1 s, 1 d. *Education:* Stanford Univ., Hartt Coll. of Music. *Career:* Prof., Univ. of Calif., Santa Cruz; Recitalist of baroque and modern flute. *Recordings:* Modern Flute: The Prismatic Flute, by Lou Harrison, David Cope and Gordon Mumma, with Ensemble Nova, 1988; Solstice, Canticle No. 3 Ariadne by Lou

Harrison, with A Summerfield Set, 1990; Music of Germaine Tailleferre, 1993; Birthday Celebration by Lou Harrison, 1994; Chansons de Bilitis and other French Chamber Works, by Debussy, 1995; Lou Harrison: Rapunzel and other Works, 1997; La Musique de Germaine Tailleferre, 1999; Baroque Flute: 6 Sonatas for Flute and Continuo and Flute Unaccompanied by CPE Bach, 1988; 6 Sonatas for Flute and Continuo, The Earlier Sonatas, 1990; 4 Sonatas for Flute and Keyboard, 1992; New Music for Early Instruments, 1995; Josef Bodin de Boismortier, Music for 1–4 Flutes, 1996; Antonio Vivaldi: Soprano Cantatas, 1997; Renaissance Flute: Les Plaisirs d'amour–Sixteenth Century Chansons from the French Provinces, 1993; Instant Breath for Solo Flute, Music by Hi Kyung Kim, Centaur Records, 2000; Dancing with Henry: New Discoveries in the Music of Henry Cowell, Mode Records, 2001; Drums Along the Pacific, New Albion Records, 2003; Lou Harrison: works: 1939–2000, Mode Records, 2003. *Publications:* Music in the Paris Academy of Sciences 1666–1793, with A Cohen, 1979; Music in the Royal Society of London 1660–1806, with A Cohen, 1987; Lou Harrison: Composing a World, 1998; Editor: Chansons from The French Provinces 1530–1550, vol. 1, 1980, vol. 2, 1983; Thirty Six Chansons by French Provincial Composers 1529–1550, 1981; Gioseppe Caimo: Madrigali and Canzoni for Four and Five Voices, 1990; Lou Harrison: Selected Keyboard and Chamber Music 1937–1994 (editor), 1998; Lou Harrison in New Grove Dictionary, 2001; Lou Harrison in Musik in Geschichte und Gregenwart, 2002. *Contributions:* Music and Letters, 1985; Journal of The Royal Musical Association, 1990; Studies in the History of Music, 1992; Journal of Musicology, 1993; Early Music, 1995; Current Musicology, 1995; American Music, 1999; Opera Journal, 1999; Musical Quarterly, 2001; John Cage: Music, Intention and Philosophy, 2002; American Music, 2002; Cambridge Companion to John Cage, 2002; Journal of Musicology 2002. *Address:* Music Center, University of California, Santa Cruz, CA 95064, USA.

**MILLER, Margaret;** Violist; b. 1960, Indiana, USA. *Education:* Studied at Indiana and Wisconsin Universities. *Career:* Principal Violist with the Colorado Springs Orchestra and Co-founded the Da Vinci Quartet, 1980, under the sponsorship of the Fine Arts Quartet; Many concerts in the USA and elsewhere in a repertoire including works by Mozart, Beethoven, Brahms, Dvořák, Shostakovich and Bartók. *Honours:* (with the Da Vinci Quartet): Awards and grants from the National Endowment for the Arts, The Western States Arts Foundation and the Colorado Council for the Humanities; Artist in Residence, University of Colorado. *Current Management:* Sonata, Glasgow, Scotland. *Address:* 11 Northpark Street, Glasgow G20 7AA, Scotland.

**MILLER, Mildred;** Opera Singer Recitalist, Impresario and Teacher; b. 16 Dec. 1924, Cleveland, Ohio, USA; m. Wesley W Posvar, 30 April 1950, 1 s., 2 d. *Education:* BMus Cleveland Institute of Music, 1946; Artist's Diploma, New England Conservatory, 1948. *Career:* Debut: Metropolitan Opera, 1951; Metropolitan Opera, 1951–74 as Cherubino, Marriage of Figaro; Octavian, Der Rosenkavalier; Siebel, Faust; Nicklausse, Les Contes d'Hoffman; Suzuki, Butterfly; others: 253 performances in 21 parts; Radio debut, 1952, Telephone Hour; Television debut, 1952, Voice of Firestone; Appearances with all major US opera companies and in Vienna, Berlin, Munich, Stuttgart, Frankfurt, 1959–73; Film, Merry Wives of Windsor; Musical comedy with Pittsburgh Civic Light Opera; Founder Opera Theater of Pittsburgh, 1978; Faculty Carnegie Mellon University, 1990–. *Recordings:* Many recordings with major record labels. *Honours:* 4 Honorary degrees; Distinguished Daughter of Pennsylvania; Grand Prix du Disque; Solo Recital, Nixon White House. *Address:* Opera Theater of Pittsburgh, PO Box 110108, Pittsburgh, PA 15232, USA.

**MILLET, Gilles;** Violinist; b. 1965, England. *Education:* Studied in London and with Feodor Droujinin, violist of the Beethoven Quartet. *Career:* Many concerts throughout the United Kingdom in works by Shostakovich, Fauré and English composers; Venues include Aldeburgh Festival (Quartet in Residence), Middle Temple (London), Huddersfield and Andover. *Honours:* with members of the Danel Quartet) Prizewinner in competitions at Florence, St Petersburg, Evian and London, 1991–94. *Address:* Manygate Management, 13 Cotswold Mews, 30 Battersea Square, London SW11 3 RA, England.

**MILLGRAMM, Wolfgang;** Singer (tenor); b. 16 April 1954, Ostseebad Kuhlungsborn, Germany. *Education:* Studied with Gunter Leib in Berlin; Musikhochschule, Berlin. *Career:* Debut: Semperoper in Dresden, 1992 as Graf Elemer in Arabella; Deutsche Staatsoper, Berlin, singing the Steersman in Fliegender Holländer, Walther in Tannhäuser and Alfred in Die Fledermaus; Visited Japan, Hungary and Switzerland with Deutsche Staatsoper; Solo appearances in Yugoslavia, Romania and the former Soviet Union; Chamber Singer in 1988; Sang the Steersman at Bregenz Festival, 1988, 1989, and in concert for Radio France, 1990; Season 1992–93 was engaged at the City of Nuremberg Theatre where he made guest appearance in 1991 as Adolar in Euryanthe; Other roles include: Erik in Holländer, José in Carmen; During that period also sang the Drum Major in Wozzeck and Max in Freischütz; Further appearances: Frankfurt am Main as Alfred in Fledermaus; Parsifal in Nuremberg and Hoffmann at Gärtnerplatz in Munich, 1995; Eleazar in La Juive, Aegisth in Elektra, Florestan in Fidelio at Dortmund in season 1995–96; Season 1998 with Max in Jonny Spielt auf by Krenek at Karlsruhe and Assad in Goldmark's Die Königin von Saba at Dortmund; Season 2000–01 as Manrico at Dortmund, Tristan in Prague and Bacchus at the Theater am Gärtnerplatz, Munich. *Recordings include:* Ariadne auf Naxos and First Prisoner in Fidelio, conducted by Haitink. *Current Management:*

Buhnen und Konzertagentur, Sigrid Roslock. *Address:* Eugen-Schonhaar-Strasse 1, 10407 Berlin, Germany.

**MILLING, Stephen;** Singer (Bass); b. 1965, Denmark. *Career:* Many appearances with the Royal Danish Opera, Copenhagen, and elsewhere in Scandinavia; Repertory includes Die Zauberflöte (Sarastro) and Don Carlos (King Philip); Also sings Lieder by Brahms; Contestant in the 1995 Cardiff Singer of the World Competition; Guest at Covent Garden, London, with the Royal Danish Opera in Prokofiev's Love for Three Oranges; Season 2000–01 as Fasolt and Hunding in The Ring, for Seattle Opera, Landgrave in Tannhäuser at the Deutsche Oper Berlin and as soloist in The Dream of Gerontius with the London SO. *Address:* Sundevedsgade 2, st tv, 1751 Copenhagen V, Denmark.

**MILLINGTON, Barry John,** BA; British music journalist and writer; b. 1 Nov. 1951, Hadleigh, England; m. Deborah Jane Calland 1996. *Education:* Clare Coll., Cambridge. *Career:* editorial staff mem., The New Grove Dictionary of Music and Musicians 1975–76; criticism for Musical Times and newspapers, notably The Times 1977–82, 1988–2001; Reviews Ed. for BBC Music Magazine 1992–2002; Chief Music Critic, Evening Standard 2002–; founder and Artistic Dir, Hampstead and Highgate Festival 1999–2003; dramaturgical adviser on new production of Lohengrin at Bayreuth Festival 1999; mem. Royal Musical Asscn, Critics Circle. *Publications:* Wagner 1984, Selected Letters of Richard Wagner (trans. and ed. with S. Spencer) 1987, The Wagner Compendium: A Guide to Wagner's Life and Music (ed.) 1992, Wagner in Performance (ed. with S. Spencer) 1992, Wagner's Ring of the Nibelung: A Companion (ed. with S. Spencer) 1993, The New Grove Wagner 2002; contrib. to Oxford Illustrated History of Opera 1994, The New Grove Dictionary of Opera 1992, The New Grove Dictionary of Music and Musicians (revised edn) 2001, numerous other publications in newspapers and periodicals. *Address:* 50 Denman Drive South, London, NW11 6 RH, England (home). *E-mail:* bmillin397@aol.com (office).

**MILLIOT, Sylvette,** DMus; French violoncellist and musicologist; b. 6 June 1927, Paris. *Education:* Studied Violoncello, National Conservatory of Music, Paris. *Career:* Research Assistant, Museum of the National Conservatory of Music, Paris; Soloist, Radio France; Various concert tours; Head of Research, CNRS, French National Centre for Scientific Research in Musicology and Musical Iconography; mem. French Musicology Society; French Society of 18th Century Studies. *Publications:* Documents inédits sur les Luthiers parisiens du XVIIIe siécle, 1970; La Sonate, 1978; Le Violoncelle en France au XVIIIe Siécle, 1981; Le Quatuor, 1986; Marin Marais, 1991; Entretiens Avec André Navarra, 1991; Catalogue descriptif des instruments de Stradivarius et de Guarnerius del Gesù de Charles-Eugène Gand, 1994; History of Parisian Violin Making from the XVIIIth Century to 1960, Vol. I, The Family Chanot-Chardon, 1994, vol. II, The Violin Makers of the XVIIIth Century, 1997; The Vuillaume Family 2005. *Contributions:* Revue Française de Musicologie; Recherches sur la Musique française classique; The STRAD; Articles on Lutherie Française, 1992, 1993, 1995, 1998; The Grove Dictionary of Music and Musicians; Die Musik in Geschichte und Gegenwart. *Honours:* 1st Prize for Violoncello, National Conservatory of Music; Héléne Victor Lyon Prize; Solo Artist's Guild Prize. *Address:* 6 Villa de la Reunion, 75016 Paris, France.

**MILLO, Aprile;** Singer (Soprano); b. 14 April 1958, NY, USA. *Education:* Studied with her parents and with Rita Patané. *Career:* Debut: Salt Lake City 1980, as Aida; Gave concert performances in Los Angeles and made La Scala Milan and Welsh National Opera debuts at Elvira in Ernani; Metropolitan Opera debut 1984, as Amelia Boccanegra; returned to NY as Elvira, Elisabeth de Valois and Aida; Guest appearances in Hamburg and Vienna; Other roles include Leonara in Il Trovatore and La Forza del Destino; Sang Aida and Liu at the Metropolitan 1987, followed by Elvira in Ernani, Elisabeth de Valois and Imogene in Il Pirata; Carnegie Hall 1987, Il Battaglia di Legnano, as Lida, Verona Arena and Caracalla festival 1988–90; Sang Aida at Washington 1990, Luisa Miller at Rome; Season 1991–92, as Marguerite at Chicago, debut, Elisabeth de Valois at the Met and Verona and Aida at the Festival of Caracalla; Sang Maddalena in Andrea Chénier at Rome, 1996; Amelia (Ballo in Maschera) at Palma de Mallorca, 1998 and for Palm Beach Opera, 2001. *Recordings:* Luisa Miller and Don Carlos conducted by James Levine; Met production of Aida on video and DVD; Un Ballo in Maschera. *Address:* c/o S A Gorlinsky Ltd, 33 Dover Street, London W1X 4 NJ, England.

**MILLOT, Valerie;** Singer (Soprano); b. 1963, France. *Education:* Studied at the Paris Conservatoire. *Career:* Lyon Opéra, 1990–91 in The Three Wishes by Martinů and as Puccini's Musetta; Season 1992 as Gounod's Mireille at Avignon and Sacchini's Antigone at Montpellier; Nancy Opéra 1994, as Elsa in Lohengrin; Montpellier 1993–94, as Offenbach's Giulietta and Brunehild in Reyer's Sigurd; Mme Lidone in Poulenc's Carmélites, Nantes, 1996; Poulenc's La Voix Humaine at Nancy, 1998; Sang Elisabeth de Valois at Dusseldorf, 2000; Frequent concert engagements. *Recordings:* Les Brigands by Offenbach. *Address:* Opéra de Nancy, Rue St Catherine, 54000 Nancy, France.

**MILLS, Alan;** Composer and Pianist; b. 21 July 1964, Belfast, Northern Ireland. *Education:* Ulster College of Music, 1978–81; Music, Churchill College, Cambridge University, 1983–86; MA (Cantab); Advanced Composition, Guildhall School of Music and Drama, London, 1986–87. *Career:* As Pianist and Accompanist for BBC Northern Ireland, Dutch Television and Radio France, 1987–; Director of Music, Anna Scher Theatre Company 1989–. *Compositions include:* 25 songs for voice and piano, 1986–; Daybreak over Newgrange for large orchestra and chorus, 1987; Three Irish poems for baritone and small orchestra, 1991; Sonatina for piano, 1993, published 1995; Incantation for

trombone and piano, 1993, published 1993; Hymn to the Aten for chamber choir and harp, 1993, published 1994; Capriccio for harpsichord, 1993, published, 1995; Romanza for horn and piano, 1994, published 1995; Epitaph for a cappella double choir, 1995; Psalm 137, for a cappella choir, 1996; Memorial for cello and piano, 1998, published 1999; Three Pieces forpiano solo, 1997–99; Hymn to Inana for a cappella choir, 2000; Three Studies for piano solo, 2001; O Magnum Mysterium for a cappella choir, 2001; In Nomine for String Trio, 2002; Marsyas for solo Flute, 2002. *Recordings:* Hymn to the Aten, by Concert de L'Hostel-Dieu, Lyon. *Address:* 87 Palmerston Road, Wood Green, London N22 4QS, England.

**MILLS, Beverly;** Singer (Mezzo-soprano); b. 1957, Kent, England. *Education:* Trinity College, and London Opera Studio, with Nancy Evans. *Career:* Debut: Batignano Festival, 1980, as Alessandro in Handel's Tolomeo; Aldeburgh from 1981, as Britten's Nancy and Lucretia; Glyndebourne Touring Opera, 1981, as Cherubino; Sang in Cavalli's L'Egisto for Scottish Opera, 1982, and on tour to Venice and Schwetzingen; Further appearances with Welsh National Opera, and City of Birmingham Touring Opera (Smetana's Two Widows, 1999 and as Debussy's Geneviève, 2000); Other roles include Dorabella, Suzuki in Butterfly, Rosina, Siebel and Cenerentola; Operetta and concert engagements. *Address:* c/o Music International, 13 Ardilaun Rd, London N5 2QR, England.

**MILLS, Bronwen;** Singer (Soprano); b. 1960, England. *Education:* Studied at London University, The Guildhall School of Music and with Joy Mammon. *Career:* Opera engagements include Dido and Aeneas with Opera Restor'd at the 1986 Edinburgh Festival; Queen Elizabeth Hall 1989 in The Death of Dido by Pepusch and Dibdin's Ephesian Matron; Season 1989–90, with Traviata for New Israeli Opera and Dublin Grand Opera; Elizabeth Zimmer in Henze's Elegy for Young Lovers in London; Norina in Don Pasquale and Madeline in Fall of the House of Usher by Glass in Wales; Donna Anna in Don Giovanni for Opera North, 1992; Man Who Mistook his Wife for a Hat, Michael Nyman, for Music Theatre Wales, 1992–93; Other roles include Mozart's Countess and Fiordiligi, Opera 80, the Governess and Miss Jessel in the Turn of the Screw, and Micaela; Opera North as the Queen of Shemakah in The Golden Cockerel, Strauss's Daphne and Blondchen in Die Entführung; Concert engagements with the Scottish Chamber Orchestra in Handel's Dixit Dominus and Bach's B minor Mass; St Matthew Passion in Stratford and Haydn's Stabat Mater at St John's Smith Square; Mozart's C minor Mass with the Northern Sinfonia, Beethoven's Missa Solemnis at Canterbury Cathedral and the Christmas Oratorio in Belgium; Wexford Festival, 1990, in Handel's L'Allegro, il Penseroso ed il Moderato; Tour of English Cathedrals with London Festival Orchestra in 1991, Messiahs in Germany, Norway in 1992 also Messiahs in Lithuania and Moscow, Kremlin, with Yehudi Menuhin; Further appearances at the Malvern, Music at Oxford, Cambridge and Sully-sur-Loire Festivals. *Recordings:* Solomon by John Blow, Hyperion; Beggar's Opera, Polly Peachum, Hyperion; Dibdin Operas, Hyperion; 100 years of Italian Opera, Opera Rara; Emilia di Liverpool, Opera Rara.

**MILLS, Erie;** Singer (Soprano); b. 22 June 1953, Granite City, IL, USA. *Education:* National Music Camp, Interlochen, MI; BMus, MA, University of IL; Studied with Karl Trump, Grace Wilson and Elena Nikolai. *Career:* Debut: St Louis 1978, in the US premiere of Martin y Soler's L'Arbore di Diana; Ninette in Love for Three Oranges, Chicago Lyric Opera, 1979; Sang New York City Opera debut as Cunegonde, Candide, 1982; Metropolitan Opera debut, New York as Blondchen, Die Entführung aus dem Serail, 1987; New York recital debut, 1989; Guest appearances with Cincinnati Opera; Cleveland Opera; San Francisco Opera; Minnesota Opera; Opera Society of Washington DC; Santa Fe Opera; Houston Grand Opera; Hamburg State Opera; Teatro alla Scala, Milan; Vienna State Opera; Sang Marie in La Fille du Régiment at New Orleans, 1989, Blondchen in Die Entführung for Opéra de Montréal, 1990; Sang Zerlina at Milwaukee, 1996 and the Queen of Night at New Orleans, 1997; Soloist with many leading orchestras; Numerous recitals; Television appearances; Roles include Rossini's Rosina; Offenbach's Olympia; Donizetti's Lucia; J Strauss's Adele; R Strauss's Zerbinetta. *Recordings:* For New World Records. *Address:* c/o Metropolitan Opera, Lincoln Center, New York, NY 10023, USA.

**MILLS, John,** ARCM, ARAM, FCLCM; British classical guitarist; *Head of Guitar, Royal Welsh College of Music and Drama*; b. 13 Sept. 1947, Kingston-upon-Thames, England; m. Jacoba Cornelia; one s. one d. *Education:* Royal Coll. of Music. *Career:* recitalist throughout British Isles 1965–; international debut, Canada 1972; has performed widely overseas, including USA, Australia, New Zealand, Japan, Singapore, Scandinavia, Holland, France, Greece, Italy; work in the chamber music field; specialist teaching areas early guitar (particularly 19th century) and postural difficulties; Prof. at the Royal Acad. of Music; Head of Guitar, Royal Welsh Coll. of Music and Drama 1991–; mem. Musicians' Union, Incorporated Soc. of Musicians, Delius Soc. *Compositions:* Hommage to Frederick Delius, Suite for Five Guitars, Idyll for Violin and Guitar. *Recordings:* Guitar Music of Five Centuries 1972, Music from the Student Repertoire 1973, 20th Century Guitar Music 1977, John Mills and Raymond Burley 1983, The John Mills Guitar Trio 1981. *Publications:* John Mills Guitar Tutor; contrib. to Classical Guitar Magazine. *Current Management:* Sympathetic Developments, 5 Greenclose Lane, Wimborne, BH21 2AL, England. *Telephone:* (1202) 880331 (office). *Fax:* (1202) 888037 (office). *E-mail:* Graham@symdev.co.uk (office). *Website:* www .pitchperfect.org/johnmills.

**MILLS, Richard (John);** Composer and Conductor; b. 14 Nov. 1949, Toowoomba, Queensland, Australia. *Education:* University of Queensland; Queensland Conservatorium; Guildhall School of Music, London, England. *Career:* Regular Guest Conductor of all major Australian Orchestras; Artist-in-Residence, Australian Ballet, 1987–88; Artist-in-Residence, Australian Broadcasting Corporation, 1989–90; Artistic Director, Adelaide Chamber Orchestra, 1991–97; Artistic Adviser, Queensland Symphony Orchestra, 1991–94; Artistic Adviser, Brisbane Biennial International Music Festivals, 1995–97; Artistic Director, West Australian Opera, 1997–. *Compositions:* Principal Works: Music for Strings, Concerti for Trumpet and Percussion; Bamaga Diptych; Fantastic Pantomines; Flute Concerto (written for James Galway); Concerto for Violoncello and Orchestra; Violin Concerto (for Carl Pini, 1992); Summer of the Seventeenth Doll, Opera, 1994; Requiem Diptych for brass quintet, 1997; The Code of Tupsichore, for orchestra, 1997; A Symphony, 1998. *Honours:* National Critics Awards, 1988, 1991; Sir Bernard Heinze Award, 1997. *Current Management:* Arts Management, 180 Goulburn Street, Darlinghurst, New South Wales 2010, Australia. *Address:* 22 Gray Road, Hill End, Queensland 4101, Australia.

**MILNE, Hamish;** Pianist; b. 27 April 1939, Salisbury, England; m. Margot Gray, 1 s., 2 d. *Education:* Royal Academy of Music, London; Guido Agosti, Rome, Siena. *Career:* Debut: 1963; Concerto, Recital, Chamber Music in the United Kingdom, Europe, USA and USSR; Over 100 BBC Broadcasts; Proms Debut, 1978; Professor, Piano, Royal Academy of Music, London. *Recordings:* Piano works by Chopin, Liszt, Haydn, Medtner, Mozart, Reubke, Schumann, Weber. *Publications:* Bartók, 1981; Heritage of Music, Contributor, 1982. *Contributions:* Medtner-Centenary Appraisal, 1981. *Honours:* Collard Fellowship, 1977; FRAM, 1978. *Address:* 111 Dora Road, London SW19 7JT, England.

**MILNE, Lisa,** MBE; British singer (soprano); b. 1971, Scotland. *Education:* Royal Scottish Acad. of Music. *Career:* from 1994 appearances throughout Scotland in concert and recital; mem. of Scottish Opera from 1994, as Gianetta in L'Elisir d'amore (debut role), Mozart's Susanna, Zerlina and Ilia, the Dew Fairy in Hansel and Gretel and Coryphée in Alceste; season 1996 in recitals at Covent Garden and Aix en Provence and City of London Festivals; concerts with the Nat. Youth Orchestra of Scotland, Scottish Chamber, Royal Philharmonic, London Philharmonic and Royal Liverpool Philharmonic Orchestras; season 1997–98 as Servilia in La Clemenza di Tito for WNO, Atalanta in Xerxes at Göttingen and Handel's Rodelinda at Glyndebourne; Nielsen's Springtime on Funen at the 1999 London Proms; with ENO as Aennchen in Der Freischütz and Morgana in Alcina 1999; season 2000–01 with Marzelline in Fidelio at Glyndebourne and Stravinsky's Anne Trulove for ENO; Handel's Samson at the London Proms 2002; Micaela in Carmen for GTO and Marzelline in Fidelio at Dallas Opera. *Recordings include:* Handel and Vivaldi with the King's Consort, Vaughan Williams Serenade to Music, Land of Heart's Desire, Idomeneo (role of Ilia), Songs of John Ireland, Songs of Roger Quilter. *Honours:* Maggie Teyte Prize 1993, John Christie Award 1996, Royal Philharmonic Soc. Young Artist Award 1998. *Current Management:* Askonas Holt Ltd, Lonsdale Chambers, 27 Chancery Lane, London, WC2A 1PF, England. *Telephone:* (20) 7400-1700. *Fax:* (20) 7400-1799. *E-mail:* info@askonasholt.co.uk. *Website:* www.askonasholt.co.uk.

**MILNES, Sherrill,** MMusEd; American opera singer; b. 10 Jan. 1935, Hinsdale, Ill.; s. of James Knowlton and Thelma Roe Milnes; m. 2nd Nancy Stokes 1969; one s.; one s. one d. by first marriage; m. 3rd Maria Zouves 1996. *Education:* Drake Univ., Northwestern Univ. *Career:* studied with Boris Goldovsky, Rosa Ponselle, Andrew White, Hermanes Baer; with Goldovsky Opera Co. 1960–65, New York City Opera Co. 1964–67, debut with Metropolitan Opera Co., New York 1965, leading baritone 1965–; has performed with all American city opera cos and major American orchestras 1962–73; performed in Don Giovanni, Vespri Siciliani and all standard Italian repertory baritone roles, Metropolitan Opera and at San Francisco Opera, Hamburg Opera, Frankfurt Opera, La Scala, Milan, Covent Garden, London, Teatro Colón, Buenos Aires, Vienna State Opera, Paris Opera and Chicago Lyric Opera; recordings for RCA Victor, London Decca, EMI Angel, Phillips, Deutsche Grammophon, 60 albums 1967–; most recorded American opera singer 1978; Chair. of Bd Affiliate Artists Inc. *Honours:* three hon. degrees, Order of Merit (Italy) 1984, three Grammy Awards. *Address:* c/o Herbert Barrett, 1776 Broadway, Suite 1610, New York, NY 10019, USA.

**MILVEDEN, J. Ingmar G.,** LPh, PhD; Composer and Assistant Professor; b. 15 Feb. 1920, Gothenburg, Sweden; m. Ulla Milveden; one s. one d. *Education:* musical theory, counterpoint, composition with Dr S. E. Svensson, Uppsala, musicology with Prof. C. A. Moberg; Schola Cantorum Basiliensis, Basel. *Career:* debut, Serenade for Strings, Philharmonic Orchestra of Gothenburg, conductor Issay Dobrowen 1942; Asst Prof. of Musicology, Univ. of Uppsala. *Compositions:* Great Mass for Uppsala Cathedral 1969, Pezzo Concertante for orchestra and soloists 1971, Clarinet Concerto 1972, Now, cantata to Linnean texts for choir and orchestra, Gaudeat Upsalia, cantata for 500th anniversary of University of Uppsala 1977, Musica in honorem Sanctae Eugeniae 1982, Pentatyk for mixed choir 1993, Sonata for violoncello solo 1998, Toccata celebrativa for organ 1999. *Publications:* Zu den liturgischen Hystorie in Schweden. Liturgie und choralgeschichtliche Untersuchungen 1972. *Address:* Torkelsgatan 16B, 753 29 Uppsala, Sweden.

**MILYAEVA, Olga;** Violist; b. 1967, Moscow, Russia. *Education:* Studied at the Central Music School, Moscow. *Career:* Co-Founder, Quartet Veronique,

1989; Many concerts in the former Soviet Union and Russia, notably in the Russian Chamber Music Series and the 150th Birthday Celebrations for Tchaikovsky, 1990; Masterclasses at the Aldeburgh Festival, 1991; Concert tour of the United Kingdom in season 1992–93; repertoire includes works by Beethoven, Brahms, Tchaikovsky, Bartók, Shostakovich and Schnittke; Resident Quartet, Wilwaukee University, USA. *Honours:* (With Quartet Veronique): Winner, All-Union String Quartet Competition, St Petersburg, 1990–91; Third Place, International Shostakovich Competition, St Petersburg, 1991. *Current Management:* Sonata, Glasgow, Scotland. *Address:* c/o Sonata (Quartet Veronique), 11 Northpark Street, Glasgow G20 7AA, Scotland.

**MIMS, Marilyn;** Singer (Soprano); b. 1962, USA. *Education:* Studied at Indiana University with Virginia Zeani. *Career:* Sang at Kentucky Opera from 1987 as Lucia and Violetta, New Orleans Opera from 1990 and at the Metropolitan Opera in 1990 as Donna Anna and Fiordiligi; Guest appearances with Hawaii Opera as Constanze in 1988, and Fiordiligi at Santa Fe; Sang at San Francisco Opera, 1990–92 as Donna Anna and Anna Bolena. *Recordings include:* Ortlinde in Die Walküre, conducted by James Levine. *Address:* San Francisco Opera, War Memorial Opera House, San Francisco, CA 94102, USA.

**MIN, Lee Huei;** Concert Violinist; b. 1982, Singapore. *Education:* University of Michigan, 1991-1995; Yale University School of Music, from 1996, with Erick Friedman. *Career:* Appearances with Washington Symphony and Prague Chamber Orchestras; Inaugurated Singapore Symphony young audience programmes, 2000; Wigmore Hall, London, debut October 2001; Season 2001–2002 with tours of China and elsewhere in Asia; Plays Giuseppe Guarneri Violin, 1704; Resident in London. *Honours:* Winner, Singapore National Music Competition, 1990; Kocian International Violin competition, 1993. *Address:* c/o Wigmore Hall (contracts), Wigmore St, London, W1, England.

**MINCH, John;** music publishing executive; *CEO, Boosey & Hawkes Group.* *Career:* fmr Man. Dir Boosey & Hawkes publishing div., formed Regent Street Music Ltd, purchasing Boosey & Hawkes 2003, currently CEO. *Address:* Boosey & Hawkes Music Publishers Ltd, Aldwych House, 71–91 Aldwych, London, WC2B 4HN, England (office). *E-mail:* john.minch@boosey.com (office). *Website:* www.boosey.com.

**MINDE, Stefan P.;** Conductor; b. 12 April 1936, Leipzig, Germany; m. Edith Halla 1961; two s. *Education:* Member of Thomanerchor, Leipzig, 1947–54; MA, Mozarteum, Salzburg, Austria, 1958. *Career:* Debut: State Theatre, Wiesbaden, Germany, Krenek: Life of Orestes; Civic Opera Frankfurt am Main under Sir Georg Solti; Hessisches Staatstheater Wiesbaden under Sawallisch; Principal Conductor at Civic Theatre Trier, Mosel; Berkshire Music Festival at Tanglewood, Massachusetts, USA with Eric Leinsdorf; Chorusmaster and Conductor, San Francisco Opera; General Director and Conductor at Portland Opera Association, Oregon, 1970–84; Founder, Music Director and Conductor of Sinfonia Concertante, Chamber Orchestra, Portland, Oregon; Guest appearances with New York City Opera, Philadelphia, Pittsburgh, Cincinnati, San Diego, Phoenix, Los Angeles, Seattle, Vancouver, British Columbia, Toronto, Edmonton, Calgary, Lisbon, Portugal, Saarbrucken, Cologne, Nuremberg, Hawaii Opera, Eugene Opera, Utah Opera, Sapporo, Japan and others; Guest Professor at Portland State University, Pacific Lutheran University, Tacoma, Washington and Florida State University; Conducted Wagner's Ring at Flagstaff, Arizona, 1996, engaged to repeat in 1998. *Address:* 1640 SE Holly Street, Portland, OR 97214; c/o Anthony George, 250 West 77th Street, New York, NY 10024, USA. *Telephone:* (212) 580-1306 (office). *Fax:* (212) 721-9144 (office).

**MINDEL, Meir;** Composer; b. 25 Dec. 1946, Lvov, Russia; m. Tzippi Bozian 1968; four d. *Education:* harmony, counterpoint, electronic music with Itzhak Saday, 1970–71; Rubin Music Acad., Tel-Aviv, 1971–75; composition with Abel Ehrlich, 1975–77. *Career:* debut, concert in Rubin Acad., Agony for Flute, 1974; radio broadcasts, Israeli Young Composer, The Blue and the White, 1982, Circle, A Maya Prophecy, 1987, Together with... Meir Mindel, An Hour of M. M. Compositions, 1988, Israel Broadcasting Authority; represented Israel at World Festival of Jewish Music, Montréal, Canada, 1983; Genesis with Morli Consort, Israel Defence Forces Army Broadcasting, 1984; attempted to develop a new musical 'language' for recorders; music performed in Israel and abroad; mem., Kibbutz Composers' Organisation (Gen. Dir, Sec.), Israel Composers' League (Sec. of Management and board mem.), Open-Air Museum Project, Kibbutz Negba (founder). *Compositions include:* The Tie, strings, 1980; Grotesque, piano, 1983, recorders, 1985; Genesis, recorders, 1983; A Maya Prophecy, mixed choir a cappella, 1985; Agony, flute, 1986; The Courting Muse, trombone, 1986; Tamar, flute, horn, piano, 1988; Poem, horn, 1988; My City, 2 choirs; The Family Tree, singers ensemble, 1989; Iri, 2 choirs, 1989; Koli, songs, 1989; The Shadow, children's choir, 1989; Murmurs, trumpet, flugelhorn, 1989; Between Rosh Pina and Safed, song; Music for Michal Gretz-Mindel's poem A White Lie, for children's choir, 1994; Symbiosis, for clarinet, bass clarinet and magnetic tape; Circles; The Catch; Where Are You All?; SugiHara, for shakuhachi Japanese bamboo flute, eastern percussion instruments and orchestra, 1995; Sounds of Strings, 18 arrangements for string quartet, 1996. *Recordings:* Negba 40; Bereshit (Genesis), 1987; Song of Songs 85-Duo Beersheba; A Maya Prophecy, Tel-Aviv Philharmonic Choir; Murmurs, A Courting Muse, in Composers in search of their roots; Iri (Acum Prize), 1989; Tamar; Israeli Sounds of Strings,

18 arrangements of folk songs, 1998. *Address:* The Open-Air Museum, Negba, Kibbutz Negba, D.N. Lachish 79408, Israel.

**MINEVA, Stefka;** Singer, (Mezzo-Soprano); b. 1949, Stara Zagora, Bulgaria. *Education:* Studied in Sofia. *Career:* Debut: Staga Zora 1972, as Berta in Il Barbiere di Siviglia; Sang Suzuki, Olga and Amneris at Stara at Zagora; Sofia Opera from 1977, notably as Marfa in Khovanshchina. Guest appearances throughout Europe; Metropolitan Opera, 1986–88, as Marfa; Sang Koncha-kovna in Prince Igor at Perugia, 1987, Liubasha in The Tsar's Bride at Rome and Kabanicha in Katya Kabanova at Florence, 1989; Other roles include Marina in Boris Godunov, Eboli, Adalgisa and Leonora in La Favorita; Sang Fenena in Nabucco at the 1991 Verona Arena. *Recordings:* Rimsky-Korsakov's Vera Sheloga and Prokofiev's War and Peace; Madama Butterfly. *Honours:* Prize Winner, 1976 Sofia and 1977 Osten International Competitions. *Address:* c/o Arena di Verona, Piazza Bra 28, 37121 Verona, Italy.

**MINGARDO, Sara;** Singer (Contralto); b. 1970, Venice, Italy. *Education:* Academia Chigiana of Siena. *Career:* Many performances at leading Italian opera houses, including Teatro Comunale of Bologna, La Scala Milan, Teatro Comunale Florence, Teatro Regio Turin and Teatro San Carlo, Naples; Further engagements in Puccini's Trittico under Riccardo Chailly, as Emilia in Otello under Claudio Abbado in Berlin and Salzburg (1996); Sang title role in revival of Handel's Riccardo Primo with Les Talens Lyriques under Christophe Rousset at Fontevraud, France, 1995. *Recordings include:* Riccardo Primo (Decca/L'Oiseau Lyre). *Address:* c/o Deutsche Oper Berlin, Bismarckstrasse 35, 1000 Berlin 10, Germany.

**MINICH, Peter;** Singer, (Tenor); b. 1928, St Polten, Switzerland. *Education:* Studied at the Horak Conservatory, Vienna. *Career:* Debut: St Polten 1951, in Millöcker's Bettelstudent; Engaged at St Gallen 1951–55, Graz, 1955–60; Vienna Volksoper from 1960, notably as Eisenstein in Fledermaus on tour to Japan, 1985; Salzburg Festival 1962–63, in Die Entführung: Other roles have included the Baron in La Vie Parisienne, Paquilo in La Périchole, René in Graf vom Luxembourg by Lehar and Jim Mahoney in Mahagonny; Frequent concert and television appearances. *Address:* c/o Volksoper, Wahringerstrasse 78, 1090 Vienna, Austria.

**MINJILKIEV, Bulat;** Singer (Bass); b. 1941, Russia. *Education:* Studied in Tashkent and Milan. *Career:* Tashkent Opera in works by local composers, and as Pimen in Boris Godunov, and Gremin; Kirov Opera, St Petersburg from 1987, as Konchak in Prince Igor, Ivan Khovansky in Khovanshchina, and the Inquisitor in The Fiery Angel; Edinburgh Festival, 1991, as Mato in Mussorgsky's Salammbô, Palermo, 1994, as Glinka's Ruslan; Season 1994–95 in Rimsky's Invisible City of Kitezh at the Champs Elysées theatre, Paris, and as Boris in Lady Macbeth by Shostakovich; Sang Kotchubei in Tchaikovsky's Mazeppa at Savonlinna, 1996. *Recordings include:* Khovansh-china, Prince Igor and Sadko. *Address:* Kirov Opera, Mariinsky Theatre, 1 Theatre Square, St Petersburg, Russia.

**MINKOFSKI-GARRIGUES, Horst;** Concert Pianist, Composer and Profes-sor; b. 23 July 1925, Dresden, Germany; m. Edeltraud Peschke, 1 s., 2 d. *Education:* Music Academy and Conservatory, Dresden; Studies with Professor Herbert Wuesthoff, Romana Lowenstein, Karl Knochenhauer, Hermann Werner Finke, Schneider-Marfels. *Career:* Debut: State Orchestra, Dresden; Numerous appearances, concerts and radio broadcasts throughout the world. *Compositions:* For Orchestra: Klaviermusik, op 15, Piano Concerto, Variations over a theme by Tchaikovsky, op 8, Expo '67 to 2 pianos and orchestra; For piano solo; Impromptus, Preludes, Sonatinas, Sonata op 23 and Scherzo, op 37; For piano, four hands; Eight Miniatures, op 27, Introduction, Theme and Variations for 2 Pianos and Cello, op 14, Andante for 2 pianos, Expo '67 for 2 Pianos op 28, Pictures of a Child for 2 Pianos op 30; Chamber Music includes: Song Cycle; Love and Deception, op 41, works for flute and piano, organ, op 38. *Recordings:* World Premiere Recording of the Complete works for Piano, four hands by Schubert, 11 albums, in collobration with former student, Lothar Kilian; Also compositions for 4 hands by Beethoven, Brahms, Tchaikovsky, Saint-Saëns, Dvořák and Smetana; With Orchestra: Concerto for 2 pianos by Bach; Concerto in D-Major by Haydn, Klaviermusik, op 15 by Minkofski-Garrigues; Numerous solo and chamber music recordings including Schubert's Sonatas for Violin and Piano with Wolfgang Marschner. *Address:* 205 Edison Ave, St Lambert, Montreal, Quebec J4R 2P6, Canada.

**MINKOWSKI, Marc;** Conductor; b. 4 Oct. 1962, Paris, France. *Education:* Studied at the Hague Conservatory and at the Pierre Monteux Memorial School, USA. *Career:* Founder of and has performed with, Les Musiciens du Louvre, 1984; Has conducted works by Handel including Riccardo Primo, 1991, for the English Bach Festival and Gluck's Iphigénie en Tauride at Covent Garden; French repertoire includes Charpentier's Malade Imaginaire, Alcyone by Marin Marais, Mouret's Les Amours de Ragonde and Titon et l'Aurore by Mondonville, Rameau's Hippolyte et Aricie, Gluck's Armide; Lully's Phaëton, Opéra de Lyon, 1993; Ariodante by Handel, Welsh National Opera, 1994; Agrippina by Handel, Semper Oper, Dresden, 1994; Dido and Aeneas by Purcell, Houston Grand Opera, 1995; Orchestre de Chambre de Genève, 1995; Amsterdamse Bach Solisten, 1995; Rotterdam Philharmonic, 1995; Idomeneo by Mozart, Opéra de Paris-Bastille, 1996; Orfeo ed Euridice by Gluck, National Opera, Netherlands, 1996; Armide by Gluck, Opéra de Nice, 1996; L'Inganno Felice by Rossini, Poissy, France, 1996; Acis et Galatée, summer tour, 1996; Die Entführung at the 1998 Salzburg Festival; Music Director of the Flanders Opera, from 1997; Le nozze di Figaro at Aix, 2000. *Recordings:* Les Amours de Ragonde by Mouret; Mondonville's Titon et

l'Aurore; Stradella's San Giovanni Battista; Grétry's La Caravane du Caire; Alcyone by Marin Marais; Le Malade Imaginaire by Charpentier; Platée by Rameau; Rebel's Les Elemens; Handel's Amadigi; Handel's Teseo; Il Trionfo del Tempo by Handel; Concerti Grossi op 3, by Handel; Rameau's Hippolyte et Aricie, 1994; La Resurrezione by Handel, 1995; Gluck's Armide, 1999. *Honours:* 1st prize, 1st International Concert of Ancient Music, Bruges, 1984. *Address:* c/o VWM, 4 Addison Bridge Place, London, W14 8XP, England.

**MINTER, Drew;** Singer, (Countertenor); b. 11 Jan. 1955, Washington DC, USA. *Education:* Studied at Indiana University and with Rita Streich, Erik Werba and Marcy Lindheimer. *Career:* Performed in concert with various early music ensembles, including the Waverly Consort of New York; Stage debut as Handel's Orlando at the St Paul's Baroque Festival, 1983; Further appearances in early opera at Boston, Brussels and Los Angeles; Omaha and Milwaukee 1988, as Arsace in Handel's Partenope and Otho in L'Incorona-zione di Poppea; Santa Fe 1989, in the US premiere of Judith Weir's A Night at the Chinese Opera and as Endimione in La Calisto by Cavalli; Television appearances include Ptolemeo in Handel's Giulio Cesare, directed by Peter Sellars; Sang the title role in Handel's Ottone, Göttingen, 1992; Endymion in Cavalli's Calisto at Glimmerglass, 1996. *Recordings:* Ottone in Handel's Agrippina and the title role in Floridante, conducted by Nicholas McGegan. *Address:* c/o Glimmerglass Opera, PO Box 191, Copperstown, New York, NY 13326, USA.

**MINTON, Yvonne Fay,** CBE; Australian singer (mezzo-soprano); b. 4 Dec. 1938, Sydney; d. of R. T. Minton; m. William Barclay 1965; one s. one d. *Education:* Sydney Conservatorium of Music and studied in London with H. Cummings and Joan Cross. *Career:* sang with several opera groups in London; début Covent Garden 1965, Prin. Mezzo-soprano 1965–71; US debut, Lyric Opera, Chicago (Octavian in Der Rosenkavalier) 1972; Guest Artist, Cologne Opera 1969–, Australian Opera 1972–73, also with Hamburg State Opera and at Bayreuth, Paris, Salzburg, Metropolitan Opera, New York, Munich and San Francisco; recordings include Der Rosenkavalier, Figaro, La Clemenza di Tito, Mozart's Requiem, Elgar's The Kingdom; many concert appearances; created role of Thea in Tippett's The Knot Garden 1970. *Honours:* Hon. ARAM . *Address:* c/o Ingpen and Williams, 26 Wadham Road, London, SW15 2LR, England. *Telephone:* (20) 8874-3222. *Fax:* (20) 8877-3113.

**MINTZ, Shlomo;** Israeli violinist; b. 30 Oct. 1957, Moscow, USSR; s. of Abraham Mintz and Eve (née Labko) Mintz; m. Corina Ciacci; two s. *Education:* Juilliard School of Music, New York, USA. *Career:* went to Israel when very young; many concert tours; Premio Accad. Musicale Chigiana, Siena, Italy 1984; Music Dir, conductor, soloist Israel Chamber Orchestra 1989–93; Artistic Adviser Limburg Symphony Orchestra, Netherlands 1994; guest conductor and soloist for numerous orchestras world-wide. *Recordings include:* Violin Concertos by Mendelssohn and Bruch (Grand Prix du Disque, Diapason d'Or) 1981, J. S. Bach Complete Sonatas and Partitas for Solo Violin, The Miraculous Mandarin by Bartok (with Chicago Symphony Orchestra, conducted by Abbado), Compositions and Arrangements by Kreisler (with Clifford Benson, piano), Twenty-four Caprices by Paganini, Two Violin Concertos by Prokofiev (with London Symphony Orchestra, conducted by Abbado), The Four Seasons by Vivaldi (with Stern, Perlman, Mehta). *Address:* ICM Artists Ltd, 40 West 57th Street, Floor 16, New York, NY 10019, USA.

**MINUTILLO, Hana;** Singer (Mezzo-soprano); b. 1963, Jihlava, Czechoslo-vakia. *Education:* Studied at the Pardubice Conservatory. *Career:* Sang at Liberec in Nabucco, Manon and Rusalka; Opera Studio of the National Theatre Prague from 1989, as Carmen, Rosina and Arsamene in Handel's Serse; Further study in Belgium and with Svatava Subrtova, followed by Mozart's Clemenza di Tito in Darmstadt (1993–94 season) and concert performances of Les Troyens under Michel Plasson in Toulouse and Arhens; Bregenz Festival in Francesca da Rimini and Nabucco; Season 1994–95 as Carmen and The Fox in The Cunning Little Vixen, under Mackerras, at the Théâtre du Châtelet, Paris; Further engagements as the Witch in Rusalka at Essen, The Diary of One who Disappeared, by Janáček, with Peter Schreier in Leipzig, Olga in Eugene Onegin at Amsterdam and Mozart's Annio (Clemenza di Tito) at Wiesbaden; Flowermaiden at Zürich, 1997. *Recordings include:* Rusalka, conducted by Charles Mackerras. *Address:* c/o Opernhaus Zürich, Falkenstrasse 1, 8008 Zürich, Switzerland.

**MIRAGEAS, Evans,** BA; American artistic director and casting director; *Artistic Director, Cincinnati Opera*; b. Ann Arbour, MI. *Education:* Univ. of Mich. *Career:* joined WFMT radio station, Chicago 1982, became prod. of classical music programmes; produced radio broadcasts for Lyric Opera of Chicago 1983–89; Artistic Admin. Boston Symphony Orchestra, worked with Seiji Ozawa 1989–94; Sr Vice-Pres. of A&R, Decca Record Co., London 1994–2000; ind. consultant and casting dir to institutions, including Brooklyn Philharmonic, Brooklyn Acad. of Music, Handel and Haydn Soc. of Boston, Milwaukee Symphony Orchestra, WDR Symphony Orchestra of Cologne, Pasadena Pops, Los Angeles Opera, Lincoln Center Festival 2000–; Artistic Dir Cincinnati Opera 2005–. *Address:* Cincinnati Opera, Music Hall, 1243 Elm Street, Cincinnati, OH 45202, USA (office). *Telephone:* (513) 768-5500 (office). *Fax:* (513) 768-5552 (office). *E-mail:* info@cincinnatiopera.org (office). *Website:* www.cincinnatiopera.org.

**MIREA, Marina;** Singer (soprano); b. 1941, Bucharest, Romania; m. *Education:* Bucharest Conservatory. *Career:* sang at the Bucharest National Opera, 1969–, notably as Violetta, Constanze, Pamina, Lucia di Lammermoor, Olympia, Lakmé, Gilda, Norina, Rosina, Rosalinde, Anchen, Caroline, Miss

Wordswoord (A. Hering); guest engagements at the Berlin and Budapest State Operas, at Tel-Aviv and in France, Russia, Germany, Greece, Czechoslovakia and Yugoslavia; teacher, Bucharest Music Univ., 1992–, Constanta Ovidius Univ., 1997–. *Address:* Garoafei str., bl. 6, Bucharest, Romania.

**MIRFIN, Timothy (Tim);** Singer (Bass); b. 1974, England. *Education:* Gonville & Caius College, Cambridge; Royal Academy, and National Opera Studio, London. *Career:* Early roles included Mozart's Figaro (RAM) and Clodomiro in Lotario, for the London Handel Festival; Other roles include Argante in Rinaldo, for Grange Park Opera, Britten's Bottom, and Don Pedro in Beatrice and Benedict; Wigmore Hall debut Nov. 2000, singing Russian songs; Season 2001–2002 with Welsh National Opera, as Publio in La Clemenza di Tito, Fernando in Beethoven's Leonore, and Parson in The Cunning Little Vixen; Also sings Mozart's Masetto and Figaro, Simone in Puccini's Gianni Schicchi; Leporello and Basilio in Barbiere di Siviglia; performances for Edinburgh Int. Festival, 2001, 2002, 2003; Season 2002–03: Engelotti in Tosca and Colline in La Bohème, Welsh Nat. Opera; Sarastro in Magic Flute for Scottish Opera; Collatinus in Rape of Lucretia for Opera East;. *Honours:* Friends of Covent Garden and Countess of Munster Trust Award; Winner, Royal Overseas League Competition, Nat. Mozart Singing Competition. *Current Management:* c/o Askonas Holt, Lonsdale Chambers, 27 Chancery Lane, London WC2A 1PF, England.

**MIRICIOIU, Nelly;** Romanian singer (soprano); b. 31 March 1952, Adjud; d. of Voicu Miricioiu and Maria Miricioiu. *Education:* Conservatoire G. Enesco, Iassy. *Career:* professional debut as Queen of the Night in The Magic Flute in Romania 1970; western European debut as Violetta in Scottish Opera production of La Traviata 1981; debut at Covent Garden as Nedda in Pagliacci 1982, at La Scala as Lucia in Lucia di Lammermoor 1983; has since appeared at many of the other opera houses of the world including Verona, San Francisco, Vienna, Berlin, Hamburg, Madrid, Florence and in recitals and concerts; repertoire includes Mimi (La Bohème), Julietta (I Capuleti e I Montecchi), Gilda (Rigoletto), Marguerite and Elena (Mefistofele), Michaela (Carmen), Marguerite (Faust), Violetta (La Traviata), Manon Lescaut; repertoire also includes Anna Bolena and Lucrezia Borgia (by Donizetti), Norma (Bellini), Tancredi (Rossini), Elisabeth (Don Carlos) 1996, Il Pirata (Bellini), Emma d'Antiochia (Mercadante), Tosca (Puccini), I Vespri Siciliani (Verdi), Jerusalem (Verdi), Giovanna d'Arco (Verdi), Semiramide (Rossini); made first recording, recital Wigmore Hall, London 1986; master classes in London; numerous recordings. *Honours:* winner of 10 int. competitions. *Current Management:* c/o Bruce Zemsky/Alan Green, Columbia Artists Management, Inc., Zemsky/Green Division, 165 West 57th Street, New York, NY 10019-2276, USA. *Telephone:* (212) 841-9648. *Fax:* (212) 841-9742. *E-mail:* musicami@aol.com. *Address:* c/o Royal Opera House (Contracts), Covent Garden, London, WC2E 9DD (office); 53 Midhurst Avenue, Muswell Hill, London, N10, England. *Telephone:* (20) 8883-8596.

**MIROGLIO, Thierry (Jean-Michael);** Percussionist; b. 1 Sept. 1963, Paris, France. *Education:* Baccalaureate; Studied Musical Acoustics with Iannis Xenakis, Paris University, Sorbonne; Percussion with J P Drouet and Sylvie Gualda, National Conservatory, Versailles; Harmony and Counterpoint, Chamber Music, National Conservatory of Boulogne, Billancourt. *Career:* Researcher and Soloist with ensembles: Musique Vivante; Atelier Ville d'Avray; Orchestra Opera de Paris; Orchestre Radio France; Musica Insieme, Soloist, concerts in Festivals of Radio France, Angers, Besancon, Orleans, Nice, Salzburg, Athens, Paris, Würzburg, Venice, Bamberg, Rouen, Munich, Trento, Cremona also in South America; Artistic Director, Percussion Season of the French Society of Contemporary Music; Radio broadcasts; Masterclasses, lectures, seminars on the volution of Percussion style from the origin until our time, numerous countries; Masterclasses, South America, 1990; World or Grand Premieres of works of Cage, Ohana, Boucourechiev, Ballif, Pousseur, Denisov, Donatoni, Kelemen, Henze, several dedicated to him; currently Prof. Darius Milhaud Conservatory, Paris; He has recently premiered the latest work of Xenakis for solo percussion and ensemble and the percussion concerti of Marlos Nobre; Recent tours have taken him throughout Europe, Asia, South America ant the USA. *Recordings:* For French, German, Austrian, Italian, Canadian and Greek radio; Has recorded a disc of Saariaho's pieces. *Honours:* 1st prize, Percussion, National Conservatory, Versailles; Prize for Chamber Music, National Conservatory of Boulogne. *Address:* 215 ave Henri Ravera, 92220 Bagneux, France. *Telephone:* 1-46-56-61-00. *Fax:* 1-46-56-61-00. *E-mail:* miroglio@club-internet.fr. *Website:* www.thierrymiroglio-percussion.com.

**MIRSHAKAR, Zarrina;** composer and teacher; b. 19 March 1947, Dushanbe, Tajikstan. *Education:* Moscow State Conservatory. *Career:* mem. Union of Composers of Tajikistan, 1992; Union of Soviet Composers, 1974–92. *Compositions include:* String Quartet; 24 music pieces for piano; Three Frescos of Pamir for violin and piano, published 1979; Sonata for clarinet solo, published 1982; Sonata for oboe solo; Respiro for violin, chamber orchestra and timpani; Six pieces for piano, published 1987; Music for documentary film, Our Baki; Colours of Sunny Pamir, symphonic poem, published 1989; Sonata for oboe solo; Symphonietta for string orchestra; Symphony for chamber orchestra; Three Inventions for piano quintet. *Recordings include:* 24 music pieces for piano; Sonata for clarinet solo; Sonata for oboe solo; Cycle of songs for children on M. Mirshaker's poems; Six Pieces for flute and clarinet, 1995. *Honours:* Lenin Komsomol Prize Laureate, 1985. *Address:* Pionersky St proezd I 12, 734003 Dushanbe, Tajikstan.

**MIRTOVA, Elena;** Russian singer (soprano); b. 1962, South West Siberia. *Education:* Leningrad Conservatory. *Career:* debut, sang at the Musical Academy and Philharmonic Hall in Prague while a student; Sang Maria in Rimsky-Korsakov's The Tsar's Bride in Moscow and Leningrad; Series of concerts in Moscow and Leningrad, 1984; Principal soloist at the Kirov Theatre in Leningrad, St Petersburg, from 1988; Rimsky's Olga and Maria, Tchaikovsky's Tatiana and Iolanta and Violetta; Sang in the 14th Symphony of Shostakovich with the Chamber Orchestra of the Lithuanian Philharmonic at the Berliner Philharmonie, 1989; sang Iolanta at Frankfurt 1990 and Leonora in Il Trovatore with Omaha Opera 1991. *Honours:* Winner, Glinka Competition, 1984; First prize, Dvořák Voice Competition, Karlovi Vari, 1987; Winner, Fidenza, Parma Verdi Competition, 1990. *Address:* c/o Marinksky Theatre, 1 Teatralnaya Square, St Petersburg, 190000, Russia. *Website:* www.mariinsky.ru.

**MIRZOYAN, Edvard Mikhailovich;** Armenian composer; b. 12 May 1921, Gori, Georgian SSR; s. of Mikhail Mirzoyan and Luciné Mirzoyan; m. Elena M. Stepanyan 1951; two c. *Education:* Yerevan Conservatory, Moscow Conservatory. *Career:* teacher Komitas Conservatory, Yerevan, Armenia 1948–, Prof. 1965–; mem. CPSU 1952–90; Pres. Union of Composers of Armenian SSR 1957–91; Sec. USSR Union of Composers 1962–90; mem. Cen. Cttee of Armenian CP 1964–90; Deputy of Supreme Soviet of Armenian SSRCP 1959–90; People's Deputy of USSR 1989–91; mem. USSR Supreme Soviet 1990–91; Pres. Armenian Peace Fund 1978–. *Compositions include:* Symphonic Dances 1946, Soviet Armenia (cantata), To the Heroes of the War (Symphonic poem), Symphony of Light (ballet), Symphony for strings and timpani 1962, Sonata for cello and piano 1967, Poem for Piano, Lyrical Picture Shushanik 1973, In Memory of Aram Khachaturyan 1988, Album for my Granddaughter 1988, Poem for Cello and Piano 1995, Circle Seasons based on the words of Chinese poets 1997; string quartet, romances, instrumental pieces, songs, film-music. *Honours:* Armenian Meritorious Artist 1958; Armenian People's Artist 1963; USSR People's Artist 1981; Order of Cyril and Methodius, Bulgaria 1981. *Address:* c/o Armenian Composers' Union, Demirchyan Street 25, Apt 9, 375002 Yerevan, Armenia. *Telephone:* (10) 52-92-59. *Fax:* (10) 72-36-39.

**MISHENKINE, Arkadij;** Singer (Tenor); b. 1961, Russia. *Education:* Studied in Kazan, at the Moscow Conservatory and the Bolshoi Opera Studio. *Career:* Sang at the Bolshoi Theatre, Moscow, from 1989, Tchaikovsky's Lenski and Jaromir, Rossini's Almaviva, Paolo in Francesca de Rimini by Rachmaninov, Vladimir in Prince Igor, Lykov in The Tsar's Bride by Rimsky, Alfredo, and Antonio in Prokofiev's Betrothal in a Monastery; Guest appearances in France, North America and Japan; Many concert engagements. *Address:* Bolshoi Theatre, 103009 Moscow, Russia.

**MISHURA, Irina;** Singer (Mezzo-Soprano); b. 1965, Krasnodar, Russia. *Education:* Gnessin Institute, Moscow. *Career:* Appearances with the Moldovan State Opera as Carmen, Amneris, Azucena, Adalgisa in Norma, Ulrica and Princess Eboli (Don Carlos); Mussorgsky's Marina and Marfa, Olga (Eugene Onegin) and Lyubasha in The Tsar's Bride, by Rimsky-Korsakov; European engagements 1998–99, as Carmen and Amneris at the Vienna Staatsoper, and appearances in Munich, Brussels and Tel-Aviv (New Israeli Opera); Rimsky's The Snow Maiden with the Detroit Symphony, Carmen for San Francisco Opera, Dalila at Michigan and Adalgisa for Baltimore Opera; Concerts include Los Angeles Philharmonic under Valery Gergiev and Verdi Gala in Israel; Season 1999–2000 with Carmen in Vienna and Munich, Fricka in Die Walküre for Dallas Opera and Principessa in Adriana Lecouvreur at Trieste; Season 2001–2002 with Carmen, Dalila, Azucena and Amneris at the New York Met, and for Opera Pacific, Washington Opera and Cologne Opera. *Address:* IMG Artists Lovell House, 616 Chiswick High Road, London W4 5RX, England.

**MISKELL, Austin;** Singer (Tenor) and Professor of Voice; b. 14 Oct. 1925, Shawnee, Oklahoma, USA; m. 2 s. *Education:* Oklahoma City University, 1946–47; Hochschule für Musik, Zürich, 1955–65; Mozarteum of Salzburg, 1955–65; LRAM, Royal Academy of Music, London. *Career:* Featured soloist with Elizabethan Consort of Viols, London, Anglian Chamber Soloists London, Ricecare, Ensemble for Ancient Music, Zürich, Arte Antica Zürich; Musinger Players, New York, 1986–; Sang in 25 countries, 1950–86; Performances with Tonhalle Orchestra, Zürich, Orchestra de la Academia Santa Cecilia Rome, London Symphony Orchestra, Pro Arte, London, Stuttgarter Synfoniker and others; Participant at music festivals including: Sagra Musicale, Perugia, Italy, Settimane Musicali, Ascona, Switzerland, Salzburger Festspiel, Britten, Purcell Festival, Buenos Aires, Mozart Festival, Munich, Bergen Festival, Norway, 1970–80; Assistant Professor of Voice at National University of Columbia, Bogota, 1976–82; Head of Voice at Conservatory of Tolima, Ibague, Columbia, 1978–82; Teacher of Voice, Italian Opera, Teatro Colón, National Opera Company, Bogota, 1978–82; Lecturer in Voice, University of New Mexico, 1982–84; Professor of Voice, College of Santa Fe, 1982–96. *Address:* c/o College of Santa Fe, Vocal Faculty, Santa Fe, New Mexico, USA.

**MISKIMMON, Annilese;** Northern Irish stage director; *Artistic Director, Opera Theatre Company;* b. 1968, Belfast. *Education:* Christ's Coll., Cambridge, City Univ., London. *Career:* WNO from 1997, assisting Richard Jones, David Alden and Peter Stein; Asst to Graham Vick, Glyndebourne for Manon Lescaut and Così fan tutte, to Peter Hall for Simon Boccanegra; production of La Traviata for WNO subject of TV series (HTV) 2000; further stagings include La Clemenza di Tito for Opera Bordeaux and Figaro at the Peking

Conservatory, for WNO; Goehr's Arianna at Cambridge, J. C. Bach's Endimione for Cambridge Classical Opera and Weill operas for the BBC Symphony Orchestra; season 2000–01 with Hansel and Gretel for San Francisco Opera and Bernstein's On the Town with the BBC Concert Orchestra; Artistic Consultant, Castleward Opera, Ireland; Artistic Dir, Opera Theatre Company, Dublin 2003. Honours: Margot Simon Award, Glyndebourne 2000. Address: Opera Theatre Company, Temple Bar Music Centre, Curve Street, Dublin 2, Ireland. Website: www.opera.ie.

**MISSENHARDT, Gunter;** Singer (Bass); b. 29 March 1938, Augsburg, Germany; m. Agnes Baltsa, 1974. Education: Studied at the Augsburg Conservatory and with Helge Roswaenge. Career: Sang at the Bayerische Staatsoper Munich, 1965–68; Frankfurt, 1968–72; Berne, 1973–78; Appearances from 1978 at Aachen, Bremen and Brussels, 1986; Since 1984, State Opera Vienna (Ochs, Osmin, Varlaam, Colline); 1984, Grand Opéra Paris (Ochs); Covent Garden, London, since 1985, Bartolo, Varlaam, Ochs, Rocco; 1994 Scala di Milano (Osmin); Düsseldorf, 1988; Théâtre des Champs Elysées Paris, 1989, as Ochs in Der Rosenkavalier; Season 1987–88 as the Doctor in Wozzeck at Strasbourg and Schigolch in Lulu at Brussels; Other roles have included Kecal, Osmin, Bett in Zar und Zimmerman, Masetto, Mozart's Figaro and Varlaam in Boris Godunov; Sang Osmin in Die Entführung at Geneva, 1996; Simon in Lortzing's Regina at Karsruhe, 1998; Season 2000 as Osmin at Dresden and Baron Ochs for the Teatre Real, Madrid. Address: c/o Deutsche Oper am Rhein, Heinrich Heine Allee 16, 4000 Duseeldorf, Germany.

**MITCHELL, Clare;** British costume designer and stage designer; b. 1960, England. Education: Bristol Old Vic Theatre School. Career: Assistant Costume Designer, Royal Shakespeare Company, Stratford; Costumes for premiere of Rebecca by Wilfred Josephs at Leeds, 1983; English National Oper for Madama Butterfly, Scottish Opera Don Giovanni, and Jenůfa in production by Yuri Lyubimov at Zürich and Covent Garden, 1986–93; Costumes and sets for Ulisse by Monteverdi and Handel's Flavio at the Batignano Festival, Rigoletto for Opera 80 and Donizetti's Tudor trilogy for Monte Carlo Opera; Costumes for Traviata at English National Opera, 1996. Address: c/o English National Opera, St Martin's Lane, London WC2N 4ES, England.

**MITCHELL, Donald Charles Peter,** PhD, CBE, FRCM; British writer on music and critic; Life President, Britten Estate Ltd; b. 6 Feb. 1925, London; m. Kathleen Livingston; two foster s. Education: Durham Univ., with Arthur Hutchings and A. E. F. Dickinson, Southampton Univ. Career: founder, Music Survey 1947; Ed. (with Hans Keller), Music Survey series 1949–52; music critic, The Musical Times 1953–57; Ed., Tempo 1958–62; Head of Music Dept, Faber and Faber 1958, Man. Dir Faber Music 1965–76, Vice-Chair. 1976–77, Chair. 1977–88, Pres. 1988–95; music staff, Daily Telegraph 1959–64; founding Prof. of Music, Sussex Univ. 1971–76, Visiting Prof. 1977–; Chair., Britten Estate Ltd 1986–2000, Life Pres. 2000–; Trustee, Britten-Pears Foundation 1986–2000, Trustee Emer. 2000–; Gov., Royal Acad. of Music 1988–, Council of Honour 2000–; Chair., Performing Right Soc. 1989–92; Vice-Pres., CISAC 1992–94; Dir of study courses, Britten-Pears School, Snape; Visiting Prof., York Univ. 1991, King's Coll., London 1995–99. Television: music adviser for film, Owen Wingrave (Channel 4) 2001. Publications include: Benjamin Britten (ed. with Hans Keller) 1952, The Mozart Companion (ed. with H. C. Robbins Landon) 1956, The Life and Music of Mahler 1958–85 (three vols), The Language of Modern Music 1963, Benjamin Britten 1913–76: Pictures from a Life (with John Evans) 1978, Britten and Auden in the Thirties 1981, Benjamin Britten: Death in Venice 1987, Letters from a Life: Selected Letters and Diaries of Benjamin Britten Vols 1–2 1923–45 (ed. with Philip Reed) 1991, Vol. 3 1946–51 (ed. with Philip Reed and Mervyn Cooke) 2004, Cradles of the New: Writings on Music 1951–1991 1995, The Mahler Companion (with Andrew Nicholson) 1999; contrib. to magazines and journals, including Music Survey, The Chesterian, Tempo, TLS, Musical Times, Music and Letters, Opera; contrib. articles and broadcasts on Berg, Britten, Hindemith, Mahler, Malcolm Arnold, Mozart, Prokofiev, Reger, Schoenberg, Stravinsky and Weill. Honours: Hon. MA (Sussex), Hon. DUniv (York), Hon. DMus (Srinakhavinvirot Univ., Bangkok) 2001;Hon. RAM 1992, Hon. Research Fellow Royal Coll. of Music 2000; Royal Philharmonic Soc. Award 1992, Gustav Mahler Soc. Mahler Medal of Honour, Vienna 1987, Univ. of Toronto Dist. Visitor Award 1999, Charles Flint Kellogg Award 2002. Address: 83 Ridgmount Gardens, London, WC1E 7AY, England. Fax: (20) 7436-7964 (office). E-mail: mahler@mitchelld.demon.co.uk.

**MITCHELL, Geoffrey Roger;** British singer (countertenor), conductor and choir manager; b. 6 June 1936, Upminster, Essex. Education: studied with Alfred Deller and Lucy Manen. Career: countertenor, lay clerk, Ely Cathedral, 1957–60; Westminster Cathedral, 1960–61; Vicar-choral, St Paul's Cathedral, 1961–66; Founder and conductor, Surrey Univ. Choir, 1966; Man., John Alldis Choir, 1966–; Cantores in Ecclesia, 1967–77; Conductor, New London Singers, 1970–86; Prof., Royal Acad. of Music, 1974–95; Singing Teacher, King's Coll., and St John's Coll., Cambridge, 1975–85; Conductor, Geoffrey Mitchell Choir, 1976–; Conductor, London Festival Singers, 1987–; BBC Choral Manager, 1977–92; Guest Conductor, Camerata Antigua of Curitiba, Brazil. Recordings: Various with: John Alldis Choir; Cantores in Ecclesia; Pro Cantione Antigua; 53 recordings with Opera Rara Geoffrey Mitchell Choir; 19 complete operas for Chandos Opera in English Series. Honours: Hon. ARAM 1975; Hon. FTCL 1990. Address: 49 Chelmsford Road, Woodford, London, E18 2PW, England (home). Telephone: (20) 8491-0962 (home). Fax: (20) 8491-0956 (home). E-mail: geoffreymitchell@compuserve.com.

**MITCHELL, Ian,** BMus, GRSM, ARAM; British clarinettist; b. 14 Feb. 1948, S Yorkshire, England; m. Vanessa Noel-Tod 1970; one s. one d. Education: Royal Acad. of Music, London Univ., Goldsmiths' Coll. Career: debut in Purcell Room, London 1971; solo appearances throughout the UK, Europe, Middle East, USA, Australia, Democratic People's Republic of Korea and Taiwan; chamber concert performances in Europe; solo broadcasts on BBC and for Swedish, American, Belgian, Austrian and German radio stations; soloist on British television and in films of composers Cornelius Cardew and John Cage; numerous first performances, many works written for him; Dir Gemini leading chamber ensemble, which is a pioneer in music educ.; mem. Dreamtiger, Eisler Ensemble of London, Entertainers Clarinet Quartet, AMM, Critical Band, Mitchell Ryan Duo; part-time Lecturer in Performance, Exeter Univ., Univ. Dir of Music 1996–2005, Warden ISM Performers and Composers Section 2005–06; mem. ISM, Clarinet and Saxophone Soc. of Great Britain (Chair. 2000–02). Recordings: works of Nicola LeFanu (with Gemini), works of Oliver Knussen (with London Sinfonietta), Draughtman's Contract, The Masterwork and others (with Michael Nyman Band), Eisler (with Dagmar Krauze), works by David Lumsdaine, John White, Lindsay Cooper, Philip Grange, Xenakis, Janáček, solo album of music for bass clarinet, music by Geoffrey Poole, numerous chamber ensemble recordings. Publications: Structure and Content of Lessons, Preparing for Performance; contrib. to Musical Times, Clarinet and Saxophone, Contact, New Grove Dictionary of Music and Musicians, Music Teacher, Musical Performance. Honours: Hon. ARAM 1997. Address: 137 Upland Road, East Dulwich, London, SE22 0DF, England. Telephone: (20) 8693-4694 (office). Fax: (20) 8693-4426 (office). E-mail: mitchells@dulwich1.demon.co.uk. Website: www.dulwich1.demon.co.uk/gemini.

**MITCHELL, Lee;** Composer, Pianist and Educator; b. 27 April 1951, Wilmington, Delaware, USA. Education: BMus, Peabody Institute, Johns Hopkins University, 1970; Studies, University of California, Santa Barbara; PhD, University of Berne, Switzerland, 1976. Career: Debut: Wilmington, Delaware; Professor, Music Theory and History, Academy of Music, Biel, Switzerland, 1973–76; Professor of Music Theory and History, Peabody Institute, Johns Hopkins University, Baltimore, 1976–86; Chairman, Theory, Hopkins, 1984–86; Adjunct Professor of Music, Goucher College, Towson, Maryland, 1980–83; Lecturer, University of Esztergom, Hungary, 1980, 1981, 1983; Profesor of Music, Johns Hopkins University, School of Continuing Studies, 1986–; Television appearances, Baltimore, 1969; Radio broadcasts, Budapest, 1981, Switzerland, 1993; Piano Concerts, USA, Switzerland, Germany, Netherlands, Greece, Hungary; Compositions performed in the USA, Peru, Europe; mem, Sonneck Society; American Musicological Society. Compositions include: Baltimore Reflections for flute and piano, 1989; Variations and Toccata for organ; Fantasy Allegro for flute and organ, 1993; Ballade for violin, viola and piano, 1994; Four Jewish Melodies for clarinet and piano, 1995. Honours: Rockefeller Grant in Composition, 1965; Winner, Dame Myra Hess Memorial Concert Series Award, Chicago, 1987; Artist Fellow in Musical Composition, State of Delaware, 1991; Meet the Composer Grants, 1992, 1993, 1994, 1996. Address: Comanche Circle/Warwick Park, Millsboro, DE 19966, USA.

**MITCHELL, Leona;** Singer, (Soprano); b. 13 Oct. 1949, Enid, OK, USA. Education: Studied at University of Oklahoma and in Santa Fe and San Francisco; With Ernest St John Metz in Los Angeles. Career: Debut: San Francisco, 1972, as Micaela in Carmen; Metropolitan Opera from 1975, as Micaela, Pamina, Puccini's Manon, Liu and Mini, Elvira in Ernani and Leonora in La Forza del Destino; Barcelona 1975, as Mathilde in Guillaume Tell; Guest appearances in Houston, Washington, Stuttgart and Geneva; Covent Garden debut 1980, as Liu in Turandot; Sydney Opera, 1985, as Leonora in Il Trovatore; Nice Opera, 1987 as Salome in Massenet's Hérodiade; Paris Opéra-Comique in Puccini's Trittico, all 3 soprano leads; Verona 1988, Aida; Sang Elvira in Ernani at Parma, 1990, the Trovatore Leonora at the Teatro Colón Buenos Aires; Season 1992 as Aida for New Israeli Opera; Sang Strauss's Ariadne at the Sydney Opera House, 1997 and Aida at Santiago; Season 1999–2000 as Turandot at Sydney and Elisabeth de Valois in Melbourne. Recordings: Gershwin's Bess. Address: c/o Teatro Regio, Via Garibaldi 16, 43100 Parma, Italy.

**MITCHELL, Madeleine Louise,** MMus, GRSM, ARCM, FRSA; British concert violinist; Professor of Violin, Royal College of Music; b. 1957; single; one d. Education: Royal Coll. of Music Foundation Scholar, Eastman and Juilliard Schools, New York. Career: BBC TV Music Time 1979; debut recital, South Bank, London 1984; South Bank recitals include awards by Worshipful Company of Musicians, Kirckman Soc., Park Lane Group; numerous solo tours in concertos and recitals in the UK, Germany, Czechoslovakia, Spain, Italy, USA, Canada; world tour, British Council 1989, 1990; Violinist Fires of London 1985–87; numerous int. festival appearances, including Aspen, Athens, Belfast, Brazil – Articulacouns, Cardiff, Dartington, ISCM Masters of 20th Century Music, Warsaw, Kiev, Lincoln Center, Malta, Malvern, St Magnus, Schwetzingen, Toronto, Warwick, York; soloist on tour with Wurttemberg, Munich Chamber Orchestras, Ulster, Czech Radio Symphony (Plzen), Malaga Symphony, Karlovarsky Symphony, London Festival Orchestra; Wigmore Hall debut recital 1989; solo tour, South America 1991; concertos with City of London Orchestra, QEH, London 1992, Royal Philharmonic Orchestra, London 1993 under Sir Alexander Gibson, Polish Radio Symphony 1994, Kiev Radio/TV Orchestra 1994, Ulster Orchestra; tours also include Poland, Ukraine, South Bank recitals 1993, 1994, 1995, 1996, 2005; recitals in

New York 1994, 1997, 2001; Wigmore Hall recitals 1995, 1997, 2001, 2003; Prof. of Violin, Royal Coll. of Music 1994–; numerous masterclasses worldwide; Artistic Dir, London Chamber Ensemble, BBC Proms 1996, Red Violin Festival, Cardiff 1997 with Lord Menuhin; Patron, Music in Quiet Places 1993–97; radio and TV broadcasts, Spain 2001; tour of Australia, Canberra Int. Chamber Music Festival, Artist-in-Residence, and Brazil 1999; apptd Leader, Bridge String Quartet 2001; recital, Lincoln Center, New York, for UK in NY Festival 2001; concerto, Queen Elizabeth Hall, London 2004; festivals France, Spain, Italy 2004; works written for her by Brian Elias, Stuart Jones, Piers Hellawell, Anthony Powers, Vladimir Runshak, James MacMillan, John Woolrich, Michael Nyman, Jonathan Harvey, Thierry Pecou, Roxanna Panufnik, Stephen Montague, Nigel Osborne, Tarik O'Regan. *Television:* broadcasts in Poland, Ukraine, Hong Kong, Colombia, Australia (ABC and Channel 7 television), Germany, UK (including BBC radio and TV), Singapore, Spain, Italy, Canada, Colombia, Czechoslovakia. *Recordings:* Messiaen Quartet for the End of Time 1994; British Treasures (violin sonatas by Goossens, Hurlstone and Turnbull) (with Andrew Ball) 2003; Hummel violin sonatas 2003; Bridge 2004; In Sunlight: Pieces written for Madeleine Mitchell 2005. *Publications:* Tribute to Dorothy DeLay, in The Strad 2002, Perspectives in Muso Magazine 2004. *Honours:* Cosmopolitan Performance Arts Achievement Award (jtly with Darcey Bussell) 1991. *Address:* 41 Queen's Gardens, London, W2 3AA, England. *E-mail:* mlmfrsa@aol.com. *Website:* www.classical-artists.com/madeleinemitchell (office).

**MITCHELL, Scott;** Pianist; b. 1964, Perth, Scotland. *Education:* Studied at the Royal Academy of Music with Alexander Kelly and John Streets; Further study with members of the Amadeus Quartet. *Career:* Member of the Borante Piano Trio, 1982–; London Performances at the Purcell Room and Wigmore Hall in the trios of Beethoven; Tours to Dublin, Paris and Vienna, Beethoven's Triple Concerto at the 1989 Festival Wiener Klassik; Concerts in Tel-Aviv and Jerusalem and association with the Israel Piano Trio at the 1988 Dartington Summer School; Season 1990 at the Perth and Bath Festivals, tour of Scandinavia, Russia and the Baltic States; Television appearances on Channel 4 and BSB; Duo partnerships with Laurence Jackson (violin) and Duncan Prescott (clarinet) with concerts at the Wigmore and Purcell Room; Accompanist to Yvonne Howard (mezzo soprano) and Barry Banks (tenor), including tour of France, Spain and Portugal, 1989. *Recordings:* Albums for Chandos with Duncan Prescott and Collins Classics with Jennifer Stinton (flute). *Honours:* Leverhulme Scholarship; English Speaking Union Scholarship; Lisa Fuchsova Prize, Royal Overseas League Competition, 1990. *Current Management:* Scott Mitchell Management. *Address:* The Old Stable, Shudy Camps Park, Shudy Camps, Cambs CB 1 6RD, England.

**MITCHINSON, John Leslie,** ARMCM, FRMCM; British opera and concert singer (tenor) and administrator; b. 31 March 1932, Blackrod, Lancashire, England; m. Maureen Guy 1958; two s. *Education:* Royal Manchester College of Music, singing with Frederick Cox, Heddle Nash and Boriska Gerab. *Career:* debut in TV series with Eric Robinson, Music for You; Stage debut as Jupiter in Handel's Semele at Sadler's Wells Theatre, 1959; Senior Lecturer, Royal Norther College of Music, 1987–92; Head of Vocal Studies, Welsh College of Music and Drama, 1992–; Many radio, television, concert and opera appearances world-wide, ENO, WNO, Scottish Opera, Basle Opera, Prague Opera; Most of the world's Music Festival; Roles included: Idomeneo, Aegisthus, Luca in From the House of the Dead, Manolios in The Greek Passion; Dalibor, Florestan, Siegmund; Sang Svatopluk Cech in the first British production of Janáček's The Excursions of Mr Brouček, ENO, 1978; Wagner's Tristan and Peter Grimes for Welsh National Opera; Opera North and Buxton Festival, 1983 as Max in Der Freischütz and Gualtiero in Vivaldi's Griselda; Menelaus in Belle Hélène, Scottish Opera, 1995; Banff Arts Centre, Canada, performances of The Raven King (Opera in 2 Parts) by Mervyn Burtch, 1999; Director of Vocal Studies at the Welsh College of Music and Drama, Cardiff. *Recordings:* Mahler 8th Symphony, Bernstein; Mahler 8th Symphony, Wyn Morris; Das Lied von der Erde, Alexander Gibson, Béatrice et Bénédict, Berlioz (Colin Davis); Lelio, Berlioz (Pierre Boulez); Tristan und Isolde, Wagner (Reginald Goodall); Glagolitic Mass, Janáček (Simon Rattle); Glagolitic Mass (Kurt Masur), Gewandhaus Orchestra, 1990; Das Lied von der Erde, Raymond Leppard; Das Lied von der Erde, Horenstein; Dream of Gerontius, Simon Rattle and CBSO. *Honours:* Queen's Prize and Royal Philharmonic Kathleen Ferrier Prize 1956–57; Curtis Gold Medal, RMCM, 1953; Ricordi Opera Prize 1952. *Address:* The Verzons Granary, Munsley, Ledbury, Herefordshire, England.

**MITIC, Nikola;** Singer, (Bass-Baritone); b. 27 Nov. 1938, Nis, Serbia. *Education:* Studied in Belgrade and with V Badiali in Milan. *Career:* Many appearances at the Belgrade National Opera from 1965; Guest engagements with the company at Copenhagen, 1968, Barcelona, 1972. Further appearances at the Vienna Staatsoper, Philadelphia, 1970; Düsseldorf, Perugia Festival, 1973, Rome 1975 and Dublin; Roles have included Rigoletto, Mozart's Figaro, Eugene Onegin, Mazeppa, Riccardo in I Puritani, Posa in Don Carlos and Enrico in Lucia di Lammermoor. *Address:* c/o Teatro dell'Opera di Roma, Piazza B, Gigli 8, 00184 Rome, Italy.

**MITO, Motoko;** Violinist; b. 13 June 1957, Kyoto, Japan; m. Yoske Otawa, 17 Mar 1989. *Education:* Toho School of Music, Tokyo; Hochschule Mozarteum, Salzburg, Austria. *Career:* Debut: Salzburg; Concertmaster, International Music Art Society Orchestra, Tokyo, 1980–81; Soloist, International Mozart Week, Salzburg, 1984; Many recitals and appearances with Professor Erika Frieser, Piano, throughout Europe and Japan, 1984–; Member, Salzburger

Streichquartett, 1987–. *Recordings:* Preiser Record, 1 Salzburger Streichquartett; Preiser Record, 2 Salzburger Streichquartet. *Current Management:* Sound Gazely, Tokyo, Japan. *Address:* Kamiyasumatsu 11, Tokorozawa, Japan.

**MITTELMANN, Norman;** Singer (Opera, Baritone); b. 25 May 1932, Winnipeg, Manitoba, Canada; m. 24 Feb 1979, 2 d. *Education:* Curtis Institute of Music, with Martial Singher, Ernzo Mascherini, diploma, 1959. *Career:* Debut: Toronto Opera Company; Opera houses, Germany; Italy; Austria; Puerto Rico; Canada; USA; Poland; Switzerland; Roles include: Amonasro, (Aida), Zürich, 1967; William Tell, May Festival, Florence, 1969; Rigoletto, Chicago Opera Theatre, 1977; Scarpia, (Tosca), Venice, 1979; John Falstaff, Hamburg and Berlin, 1979; Nelusko, (L'Africaine), San Francisco Opera; Mandryka, (Arabella), La Scala; Sang at Zürich until 1982. *Recordings:* Video of La Gioconda, from San Francisco, 1979. *Honours:* Gellow, Rockefeller Foundation, 1956–59; Award, Fischer Foundation, 1959. *Current Management:* Robert Lombardo Associates, 61 West 62nd Street, Suite F, New York, NY 10023, USA.

**MIZELLE, Dary John;** Composer; b. 14 June 1940, Stillwater, OK, USA; m. 5 c. *Education:* Studied at the California State University and University of California at Davis, PhD, 1977. *Career:* Professor, University of South Florida, 1973–75, Oberlin College, 1975–79, State University at Purchase, New York, 1990. *Compositions:* Polyphonies, I–III, 1975–78; Polytempus I for trumpet and tape, 1976; Primavera-Heterphony for 24 celli, 1977; Samadhi for quadrophonic tape, 1978; Polytempus II for marimba and tape, 1979; Quanta II and Hymn of the World for 2 choruses and ensemble, 1979; Lake Mountain Thunder for cor anglais and percussion ensemble, 1981; Thunderclap of time, music for a planetarium, 1982; Requiem Mass for chorus, soloists and orchestra, 1982–2002; Sonic Adventures, 1982; Quintet for Woodwinds 1983; Contrabass Quartet, 1983; Indian Summer for string quartet and oboe, 1983; Sounds for orchestra, 1984; Concerto for contrabass and orchestra, 1974–8; Genesis for orchestra, 1985; Blue for orchestra 1986; Percussion Concerto 1987; Parameters for percussion solo and chamber orchestra, 1974–87; Earth Mountain Fire, 1987–; Fossy: A Passion Play, music theatre, 1987; Chance Gives me What I Want, dance, 1988; SPANDA complex of 198 compositions lasting over 13 days, including Transmutations and Metamorphoses, 1989; Silverwind for solo flute, 1990; Polytempus IV Quartet for mallet instruments, 1991; Metacontrasts for clarinet, violin, piano, 1993; Transforms for piano, 1995; Amore for two violins, 1995; Summer Vision a concerto for violin and orchestra, 1996; Endless Melody for orchsestra, 1996; Niagara for large orchestra, 1999; Iguanas for Brass, Percussion and Theatre, 2001; Forbidden Colours for soloistic flute and chamber orchestra, 2000; Illuminations for computer and Chamber Orchestra, 2002; Dream of the Vacationers, chamber opera, 2002. *Address:* ASCAP, ASCAP Building, 1 Lincoln Plaza, NY 10023, USA.

**MIZZI, Alfred (Freddie Paul);** Musician, Clarinettist; b. 12 Oct. 1934, Valletta, Malta; m. 24 June 1953, 2 d. *Education:* ALCM, 1966. *Career:* Debut: As soloist with the Malta National Orchestra, 1961; Belfast Arts Festival, 1967; Member, World Symphony Orchestra performances in New York, Washington and Florida, 1971; Soloist in concerts in Bucharest, Mannheim, Mozart Castle, Darmstadt, Wigmore Hall and Barbican Centre, London, 1973–83; Concerts in France and Greece as part of the Mediterranean Arts Festival, 1985; Concerts at the Czechoslovakia Arts Festival, 1986; Soloist with: Stamitz Symphony Orchestra, West Germany; Watford Chamber Orchestra, England; Zapadocesky Symphony Orchester, Czechoslovakia and others; Soloist with string quartets: The Brevis String Quartet, Malta; Salzburg String Quartet, Austria; Sinnhoffer String Quartet, West Germany; Quartetto Academica, Romania; The Rasumovsky String Quartet, Great Britain and others; Television appearances and radio broadcasts in Malta, Romania, BBC Germany, USA, France, Greece, Italy; mem, Performing Right Society, London. *Honours:* Phoenicia International Culture Award, 1985; Malta Society of Arts Award, 1986. *Current Management:* Corinthia Group of Companies. *Address:* II Klarinett, Ursuline Sisters Street, G'Mangia, Malta.

**MOBBS, Kenneth William,** MusB, MA, FRCO, LRAM; British keyboard player, tutor and historian; b. 4 Aug. 1925, Northamptonshire; s. of George William and Grace Elsie Mobbs (née Pack); m. 1st Joyce McNeill 1950; three d.; m. 2nd Mary J. Randall 1979. *Education:* Kettering Grammar School, Clare Coll., Cambridge, Royal Coll. of Music (studied with Greville Cooke, M. P. Conway, Frank Merrick, Harold Darke, Gordon Jacob). *Career:* debut organ recital, King's Coll., Cambridge 1949; Lecturer, then Sr Lecturer in Music, Univ. of Bristol 1950–83; Musical Dir, Bristol Opera School 1954–64; Musical Dir, Bristol Intimate Opera 1982–83; freelance keyboard performer, including harpsichord concerto, solo piano, fortepiano recitals and numerous accompaniments on BBC radio; Dir, Mobbs Keyboard Collection. *Compositions include:* Engaged! (comic opera) 1963. *Recordings include:* Mobbs Keyboard Collection Vol. 1, Golden Age of the Clarinet, Twenty Early Keyboard Instruments (Kensound 01); Four English Early Grands (Kensound 02); Die Schöne Müllerin, with Niall Hoskin (Kensound 03); Piano Recitals (Kensound 04); Organ Recitals (Kensound 05). *Publications:* contrib. to Encyclopaedia of Keyboard Instruments 1993, Early Music, Galpin Society Journal, English Harpsichord Magazine. *Address:* 16 All Saints Road, Bristol BS8 2JJ, England. *Telephone:* (117) 9733613 (also fax). *E-mail:* kenneth@ mobbsearlykeyboard.co.uk (office). *Website:* www.mobbsearlykeyboard.co.uk (office).

**MOE, Bjorn (Kare);** Concert Organist; b. 10 Aug. 1946, Hegra, Norway; m. Kristine Kaasa, 21 June 1975. *Education:* Trondheim School of Music, 1963–67; Musik-Akademie der Stadt Basel Abteilung Konservatorium and Schola Cantorum Basiliensis 1968–73, Eduard Muller and Wolfgang Neininger; Paris, Gaston Litaize and Praha, Jiri Reinberger. *Career:* Professor at Trondelag Musik-konservatorium, Trondheim 1973–84; Full-time Concert Organist 1985–; Concerts with the complete works of Olivier Messiaen, the main works of Max Reger and other organ music from all periods though mainly the 20th Century; World premiere of several new works from Switzerland, Iceland and Norway; Co-operates with other arts as theatre, dance and poetry; Organ Expert; Counsellor; Arranged Te Deum by Ludvig Nielsen for choir, soloists, strings, brass, percussion and organ, premiere, Ratzenburg, Germany 1971; Transcribed among others Ferruccio Busoni's Fantasia Contrappuntistica for organ, premiere Trondhein, Norway, 1986, and George Gershwin's Rhapsody in Blue for organ, premiere Basle, Switzerland, 1988. *Recordings:* CD with works of Torsten Nilsson, 1999. *Publications:* The Steinmeyer-organ, Trondheim Cathedral, 1996. *Honours:* Numerous scholarships and prizes from many countries; Since 1990 paticipant in the Norwegian government's income guarantee programme for artists. *Address:* Postboks 16, 7221 Melhus, Norway.

**MOENNE-LOCCOZ, Philippe;** French musician and composer; *Artistic Director, Musiques Inventives d'Annecy (MIA)*; b. 21 March 1953, Annecy; m. 30 Aug 1986; three s. *Education:* Studies in electro-acoustic Composition, 20th century analysis, string bass, contemporary, classical and popular music. *Career:* Debut: At age 10; Teaches aspects of music through animation at special children's centre; Teacher of electro-acoustic Music; Dir, Collectif et Compagnie, now known as Musiques Inventives d'Annecy (MIA) (studio for research, creative work and music education, renamed ), Annecy; Artistic Dir, Festival Concert d'Hiver et d'Aujourd'hui, Annecy; Int. career with Trio Collectif and Solstice ensembles, Canada, Hungary, Netherlands, Switzerland, Spain and the USA; mem, Asscn for Electro-acoustic Music, Geneva. *Compositions:* Electro-acoustic works: Boucles; Réves opaques; Oscillation; Petit musique du Soir; Mixed works, electro-acoustic and traditional instruments; Le cri des idées sur l'eau; Recontre; Mixage 4; Oscillation No. 1, 2, 6; Inventions, 1991; Chaos for tape only; Aspérites (CDO2), 1992; Fermez la porte, 1992; Limites Extrêmes, 1999; music for theatre: Franz ou les changements profonds, 1997; Les Cris, 2004;. *Recordings:* Réves opaques, cassete C1; Le cri des idées sur l'eau, Radio Suisse Romanda, CDs, Trola, Chutts, 1989; Super Trio with Trio Collectif and Canadian Electronic Ensemble of Toronto, CD; Limites, CD, 2000. *Address:* 24 bis Avenue Marechal Leclerc, 38300 Bourgoin-Jallieu (home); 1 rue Jean Jaurès, 74000 Annecy, France (office). *E-mail:* miannecy@wanadoo.fr (office); philippe .moenne-loccoz@wanadoo.fr (home). *Website:* www.miannecy.fr.fm (office); (home).

**MOEVS, Robert (Walter),** MA; American composer and professor; *Professor Emeritus, Rutgers University*; b. 2 Dec. 1920, La Crosse, Wisconsin; m. Maria Teresa Marabini 1953; one s., one d. *Education:* Harvard Coll.; Conservatoire Nat.l, Paris, France; Harvard Univ. *Career:* Fellow, American Acad. in Rome; Prof., Harvard Univ. 1955–63; Prof., Rutgers Univ., 1964–91, Prof. Emer. 1991; mem., Founding Mem., American Soc. of Univ. Composers; mem. Exec. Cttee, Int. Soc. for Contemporary Music. *Compositions:* Numerous works for solo instruments, chorus, orchestra, chamber music; 6 Symphonic Pieces, 1955–86; 3 String Quartets, 1957, 1989, 1995; Musica da Camera, IV, 1965–97. *Recordings:* Numerous works recorded. *Publications:* Numerous works published in Paris, Italy and USA. *Contributions:* Musical Quarterly; Perspectives of New Music; Journal of Music Theory. *Honours:* Award, Nat. Inst. of Arts and Letters, 1956; Recipient, Guggenheim Fellowship, 1963–64; Several ASCAP awards. *Address:* 1728 Millstone River Road, Hillsborough, NJ 08844, USA.

**MOFFAT, Anthony;** Violinist; b. 1995, Hexham, Northumberland. *Education:* Royal Academy of Music, with Manoug Parikian. *Career:* Founder member of the Borante Trio, with recitals throughout Europe and Beethoven's Triple Concerto in Vienna; London concerts at the Wigmore Hall and Purcell Room; Solo performances for BBC Radio; Engagements as leader of the BBC Concert Orchestra, Royal Liverpool Philharmonic and National Symphony Orchestra of Ireland; Former Associate Leader of the Hallé Orchestra, Manchester; Leader of the Orchestra of Scottish Opera, from 2000. *Honours:* Marjorie Hayward Prize, RAM. *Address:* c/o Scottish Opera, 39 Elmbank Crescent, Glasgow, G2 4PT, Scotland.

**MOFFAT, Julie;** Singer (Soprano); b. 1966, Leicester, England. *Education:* Studied at the Royal College of Music, 1984–88, with Marion Studholme; Further study with Pamela Cook and Paul Hamburger. *Career:* Debut: London 1987, in Elliott Carter's A Mirror on Which to Dwell; British premiere of Jonathan Harvey's From Silence, 1989; Appearances with such contemporary music groups as Klangforum Wien, Ensemble Inter Contemporain, Ensemble Moderne of Frankfurt and the BBC Singers; Repertoire has included works by Zender, Barraqué, Webern, Zimmerman, Nono, Beat Furrer and Varèse; Requiem for Reconciliation with Helmuth Rilling at the 1995 Stuttgart Music Festival; Frequent engagements in oratorios by Bach, Beethoven, Haydn, Mozart, Rossini, Mendelssohn and Schubert; Season 1996–97 at the Vienna Konzerthaus, the Bregenz, Salzburg and Schleswig-Holstein Festivals, with the Geneva Chamber Orchestra, at the Berlin Festival and with London Sinfonietta. *Recordings:* Albums with Klangforum Wien, Stuttgarter Bach Akademie and Ensemble Intercontemporain; Music

by Zimmermann and Dallapiccola. *Honours:* Foundation Scholarship to the RCM, 1984. *Address:* Owen/White Management, 39 Hillfield Avenue, London N8 7 DS, England.

**MOFFO, Anna;** American singer (soprano); b. 27 June 1932, Wayne, Pa; d. of Nicholas Moffo and Regina (Cinti) Moffo; m. Robert Sarnoff 1974. *Education:* Curtis Inst. *Career:* appeared in TV opera Madame Butterfly, Italy 1956; singer opera houses in Paris, London, Salzburg, Vienna, Milan, numerous others abroad; American debut at Lyric Opera Co., Chicago 1957, Metropolitan Opera Co., New York 1959; appeared Voice of Firestone telecast 1957; recital tours, US; numerous recordings. *Roles include:* soprano Norma, La Bohème, Mignon, Rigoletto, Falstaff, Madame Butterfly, The Barber of Seville, La Traviata, Thaïs, The Daughter of the Regiment, Stiffelio, Tosca, Hansel and Gretel, Faust, Don Pasquale, Romeo and Juliet, The Magic Flute, Turandot, La Juive, The Marriage of Figaro, Otello, Il Trovatore, Luisa Miller, La Belle Hélène, The Gypsy Baron. *Honours:* Order of Merit (Italy); Young Artists award, Philadelphia Orchestra; Fulbright Award for study in Europe; Liebe Augustin Award. *Address:* c/o Metropolitan Opera, Lincoln Center, New York, NY 10023, USA (office).

**MOHLER, Hubert;** Singer (Tenor); b. 1922, Augsburg, Germany. *Education:* Studied in Augsburg. *Career:* Sang in the choir of the Augsburg Stadttheater, 1946–52; Appeared in solo roles at Gelsenkirchen, 1952–57; Oberhausen, 1957–61; Augsburg, 1961–64; Many appearances at the Cologne Opera, 1964–89, as Mozart's Pedrillo, Monostatos and Basilio, Mime in the Ring, David in Die Meistersinger, Valzacchi, Rosenkavalier, the Captain in Wozzeck, the character roles in Les Contes d'Hoffmann and Adam in The Devils of Loudun; Many appearances in Germany and abroad as concert singer. *Recordings:* Mozart Masses; Les Brigands by Offenbach. *Address:* c/o Oper der Stadt Köln, Offenbachplatz, 5000 Cologne, Germany.

**MOHR, Thomas;** Singer (Baritone); b. 17 Oct. 1961, Neumunster, Holstein, Germany. *Education:* Studied in Lubeck, graduating in 1985, and in Hamburg. *Career:* Debut: Lubeck 1984, as Silvio in Pagliacci; Sang at Lubeck and Detmold, 1984–85, Bremen, 1985–87, Nationaltheater, Mannheim, from 1987; Guest appearances at the Schleswig-Holstein Festival, 1987, and at Cologne, Hamburg and Ludwigsburg; Other roles include Mozart's Count and Papageno, Rossini's Figaro, Lortzing'z Zar and Count in Der Wildschütz, Wolfram and Billy Budd; Many concerts and Lieder recitals; Season 2000–01 as Spohr's Faust for Cologne Opera, Moses in the US premiere of Weill's The Eternal Road (Brooklyn Academy, NY) and Mauregato in Schubert's Alfonso and Estrella, at Zürich. *Honours:* Winner, 1984 's-Hertogenbosch Competition; 1985 German Lied Competition, London. *Address:* Nationaltheater, Am Goetheplatz, 6800 Mannheim, Germany.

**MOK, Warren;** Singer (Tenor); b. 1960, Hawaii. *Education:* University of Hawaii; Manhattan School of Music. *Career:* Appearances at the Deutsche Oper, Berlin, 1988–, as the Duke of Mantuo, Alfredo, Rodolfo, Don Carlos, Ferrando, Count Almaviva, Nemorino and Prince Cou-Chong in Das Land des Lächelns; Premieres of Henze's Das verratene Meer and Reimann's Das Scholss; Further engagements at the Vienna and Athens Festivals, Leipzig, Copenhagen and Lisbon Operas; Many companies in the USA; Season 1999–2000 with Calaf in Lithuania, Gabriele Adorno at Martina Franca, Don José in Hong Kong, Alfredo at Shanghai, Verdi's Alvaro at Copenhagen and Manrico for Opéra de Monte Carlo. *Address:* Music International, 13 Ardilaun Road, London N5 2QR, England.

**MOLDOVEANU, Eugenia;** Singer (Soprano); b. 19 March 1944, Bursteni, Romania. *Education:* Studied at the Ciprian Porumbescu Conservatory and in Bucharest with Arta Florescu. *Career:* Debut: Bucharest 1968 as Donna Anna in Don Giovanni; Guest appearances in Belgrade, Sofia, Athens, Amsterdam, Trieste, Stuttgart, Dresden and Berlin; Repertoire includes roles in operas by Mozart, Verdi and Puccini; Sang Mozart's Countess while on tour to Japan with Vienna Staatsoper, 1986; Season 1987 sang Mozart's Countess at La Scala Milan, Butterfly at Verona and Donna Anna at Turin, Countess, 1989. *Address:* Teatro Regio di Torino, Piazza Castello 215, 10124 Turin, Italy.

**MOLDOVEANU, Nicolae;** Conductor; b. 20 July 1962. *Education:* Musikhochschule in Zürich, Basel and Bern, Switzerland; Royal Academy of Music, London. *Career:* Violinist, 1982; Repetiteur, conductor, Altmarkt Theatre, former E Germany; worked with orchestras in Switzerland, Germany, UK, South Africa and Romania; Resident Conductor, Bournemouth Orchestra, 1996; Principal Conductor, English Sinfonia, 1998–; Assoc. Guest Conductor, London Mozart Players, 2002–; Associate, Royal Academy of Music, London, 1997. *Honours:* Edwin Samuel Dove Prize and Ricordi Conducting Prize, Royal Academy of Music, London, 1993. *Current Management:* Clarion/Seven Muses, 47 Whitehall Park, London N19 3TW, England.

**MOLDOVEANU, Vasile;** Singer, (Tenor); b. 6 Oct. 1935, Konstanza, Romania. *Education:* Studied in Bucharest with Constantin Badescu. *Career:* Debut: Bucharest 1966, as Rinuccio in Gianni Schicchi; Stuttgart debut 1972, as Donizetti's Edgardo; Munich Opera from 1976, as Rodolfo and the Duke of Mantua; Deutsche Oper Belin and Chicago Lyric Oper 1977; Hamburg Opera 1978, as Don Carlos; Metropolitan Opera from 1979, as Pinkerton, Turiddu, Gabriele Adorno, Luigi in IL Tabarro and Henri in Les Vêpres Siciliennes; Covent Garden 1979, as Don Carlos; Zürich Opera 1980, in Verdi's Attila; Monte Carlo 1982, in Lucia di Lammermoor; Guest appearances in Helsinki, Brussels, Barcelona, Dresden, Cologne, Frankfurt and Athens; Other roles include Mozart's Don Ottavio, Pedrillo and Tamino; Stuttgart Staatsoper and

Nice 1988, as Cavaradossi and as Puccini's Dick Johnson; Sang Pinkerton at Rome, 1990. *Address:* c/o Teatro dell Opera di Roma, Piazza B. Gigli 8, 00184 Rome, Italy.

**MOLEDA, Krzysztof;** Singer (Tenor); b. 6 April 1955, Poznan, Poland. *Education:* Music High School, Lodz, 1972–75. *Career:* Debut: Sang Wenzel in The Bartered Bride, Lodz, 1975; Sang with Warsaw Chamber Opera, 1978–80, Stettin 1980–82 and Freiberg 1982–83; Dresden Staatsoper from 1983, as Nemorino, the Duke of Mantua, Alfredo, Cassio, Riccardo (Un ballo in Maschera), Fenton, Rodolfo, Pinkerton and Cavaradossi; Guest engagements at Leipzig, Schwerin, Frankfurt an der Oder, Lille and Bratislava; Prague State Opera from 1990; Other roles include Strauss's Elemer (Arabella), Italian Singer (Rosenkavalier) and Narraboth in Salome. *Recordings include:* Rossini's Il Signor Bruschino (Eterna). *Address:* c/o Prague State Opera, Legerova 75, CR-110 00 Praha 1, Czech Republic.

**MOLINO, Pippo;** Composer; b. 10 June 1947, Milan, Italy; m. Giovanna Stucchi, 22 July 1972, 1 s., 2 d. *Education:* Degree, Composition and Choral Music. *Career:* Debut: Venezia Opera Prima Festival Competition, 1981; mem, SIMC; Societa Italiana Musica Contemporanes. *Compositions:* Replay 1, 11, piano, 1978; Tres, violin and viola, 1978; Litanie, orchestra, 1979; Il Canto Ritrovato, orchestra, 1980; Il Cavalier Selvatico, oratorio, 1981; Cantabile, flute piano, 1983; Jeu, oboe, 1984; Da Lontan, harp, 1985; Per la Festa Della Dedicazione, organ, 1986; Harmonien, wind quintet, 1989; Radici, clarinet, 1991; Ricordando, twelve instruments, 1992; Quintetto, clarinet, string quartet, 1993; Itinerari, string orchestra, 1994; Angelus, soprano, alto and string orchestra, 1997. *Recordings:* Il Pensiero Dominante; Nel Tempo. *Publications:* Articles in La Musica, Musica e Realta, Reggio Emilia, Il Giornale della musica. *Honours:* Rimini Aterforum, 1979; Venezia Opera Prima, 1981; Roodeport International Eisteddfod of South Africa, 1983. *Current Management:* BMG Ariola, Rugginenti. *Address:* Via Pistrucci 23, 20137 Milano, Italy.

**MOLL, Kurt;** German singer (bass); b. 11 April 1938, Buir; m. Ursula Pade 1968; one s. two d. *Education:* Staatliche Hochschule für Musik, Cologne. *Career:* operatic debut Cologne; subsequently sang operatic roles at Aachen, Mainz, Wuppertal, Hamburg; appeared Bayreuth 1968, Salzburg 1970, La Scala, Milan 1972, Covent Garden, London 1975, Metropolitan Opera, New York 1978; Prof. Staatliche Hochschule für Musik, Cologne 1991–; mem. Hamburg, Bavarian and Vienna State Operas. *Address:* Grosse Theaterstrasse 34, 20354 Hamburg (office); Voigtelstr. 22, 50933 Cologne, Germany.

**MOLLER, Niels;** Singer (Tenor) and Administrator; b. 4 Sept. 1922, Gorlev, Denmark. *Education:* Studied in Copenhagen, latterly at the Opera School of the Royal Opera. *Career:* Debut: Sang Rossini's Figaro in Copenhagen, 1953; Changed to tenor roles 1959 and sang in Copenhagen until 1975 as Florestan, Tannhäuser, Don José, Aegisthus, Shuisky, the Drum Major in Wozzeck and Zeus in Monteverdi's Ulisse; Bayreuth Festival, 1962–65, as Melot and Erik; Guest appearances at Brussels, Vienna, Oslo, Geneva, Venice, Barcelona, 1968, Lisbon, 1972 and Bordeaux; Baritone roles included Renato in Un Ballo in Maschera, Dandini, and Tarquinius in The Rape of Lucretia; Sang the title role in the premiere of Macbeth by H Koppel and retired as singer, 1975 after appearing as Aegisthus; Director of the Royal Opera Copenhagen 1978–83; Frequent concert engagements. *Recordings:* Schoenberg Gurrelieder; Parsifal, Bayreuth, 1962; Saul and David by Nielsen. *Address:* c/o Det Kongelige Teater, Box 2185, 1017 Copenhagen, Denmark.

**MOLLET, Pierre;** Singer (Baritone); b. 23 March 1920, Neuchâtel, Switzerland. *Education:* Studied in Neuchâtel, Lausanne and Basle. *Career:* Performed as concert singer in France and Switzerland from 1948; Opéra-Comique, Paris from 1952, notably as Debussy's Pelléas; Aix-en-Provence 1952, in Iphigénie en Tauride by Gluck; Paris Opéra, 1954, in Gounod's Roméo et Juliette; Geneva 1963, in the premiere of Martin's Monsieur de Pourceaugnac, repeated at the Holland Festival; As a concert singer often appeared in the cantatas of Bach and in music by Honegger, which he studied with the composer. *Recordings:* Pelléas et Mélisande, Roméo et Juliette and L'Enfant et les Sortilèges; La Damnation de Faust; Iphigénie en Tauride.

**MOLLOVA, Milena;** Concert Pianist and Professor of Piano; b. 19 Feb. 1940, Razgrad, Bulgaria; 1 s., 2 d. *Education:* Studied piano with Pavla Jekova; Studied with composer and pianist Dimitar Nenov, 1947; Studied with Professor Panka Pelisheck from 1949; Studied at the Bulgarian Music Academy with Professor Pelischeck from age 14; Studied in the class of Professor Emil Gilels at the Moscow State Conservatory, 1960–61. *Career:* Debut: First piano concert at age 6; Soloist in Sofia State Orchestra with the Beethoven third piano concerto, directed by Professor Sasha Popov; During her education gave numerous concerts in Bulgaria and successful participation in international competitions in Moscow, Paris and Munich; Concert tours in USSR, 1958, 1959, 1960, in Czechoslovakia, Poland, Belgium and Yugoslavia; Appointed Assistant to Professor Pelisheck at the Bulgarian Music Academy, Sofia 1963 and as a concert pianist to the Bulgarian Concert Agency; Conducted own class of young piano students, 1969–; Tour of Japan and Cuba, 1973; Appointed Reader 1976 and Professor 1989 in the Bulgarian Music Academy; To celebrate 40 years on stage, played in Sofia and Varna the whole 32 Beethoven sonatas in 9 concerts; During last few years has conducted Masterclasses in Essen, Germany and Manfredony, Foggia, Italy. *Recordings:* Numerous recordings of piano works from Bach to modern composers.

**MOLNAR, András;** Singer (Tenor); b. 1948, Hungary. *Education:* Hungarian Radio Children's Choir; Studied singing, 1976. *Career:* Member, Choir of The Hungarian Radio and Television, 1977–78; Soloist at Budapest State Opera, 1979–; Appeared in title roles in Erkel's László Hunyadi, Mozart's Magic Flute, Verdi's Ernani and in La Forza del Destino, Don José in Carmen, 1981–82, Title role in Lohengrin, 1981–82; Invited to sing title role in Theo Adam's new production of Wagner's Lohengrin at Berlin State Opera, 1983; Regular appearances with Budapest State Opera including the premiere of Ecce Homo by Szokolay, 1987; Sang at Teatro Colón Buenos Aires, 1987 as Donello in La Fiamma by Respighi; Budapest 1988–90, in Erkel's Hunyadi László and as Tannhäuser; Frequently participates in oratorio performances; Other performances in: Florestan in Fidelio, Budapest, 1984, Zürich and Graz in 1994; Wagner's Meistersinger at Budapest, 1985, Der fliegende Holländer at Bonn 1986, Zürich, 1987 and Liège in 1995; Tristan at Budapest in 1988, Parsifal in Budapest, 1982 and Antwerp in 1987; Tannhäuser in Rouen, 1992, Limoges in 1994; Radames in Aida, Budapest in 1994; Die Walküre, Budapest with Yuri Simonow, 1995; Sang Siegfried in Götterdämmerung at Budapest, 1998; Lohengrin at Trier, 2001. *Honours:* 1st Prize, Treviso Toti dal Monte International Vocal Competition, 1980; Kossuth Prize–First Hungarian Cultural Prize, 1994. *Address:* c/o Valmalète Concerts, 7 rue Hoche, F–92300 Levallois Perret, France.

**MOLNAR, Nicolette;** Stage director; b. 1959, London, England. *Education:* Columbia University, New York, USA; Hochschüle für Musik, Hamburg, with Götz Friedrich. *Career:* Staff Director at ENO, 1987–1994; Directed for: Stadttheater Luzern (Elisir d'Amore, 1991); Dublin Grand Opera (Lakmé, 1993); Castleward Opera, Belfast (I Capuleti e I Montecchi, 1995 and Ariadne auf Naxos, 1996); Royal Academy/Royal College of Music, London (Midsummer Night's Dream, 1996); Santa Fe Opera (Così fan tutte, 1997); Orlando Opera (Tosca, 1997, Turandot, 1998 and Fliegende Holländer, 1999); Opera Ontario (Tosca, 1998 and Eugene Onegin, 2001); University of Michigan (Turn of the Screw, 1998 and Cenerentola, 2002); Lyric Opera of Kansas City (Così fan tutte, 1999); Wolf Trap Opera (Don Giovanni, 2000); Atlanta Opera (Così fan tutte, 2000 and Fliegende Hollander, 2002); Co-Opera/Opera Ireland (Madama Butterfly, 2001); Lake George Opera (Entführung aus dem Serail, 2002). *Address:* c/o Pinnacle Arts Management, 889 Ninth Avenue, Suite No. 1, New York, NY 10019, USA.

**MOLNAR-TALAJIC, Liljana;** Singer (soprano); b. 30 Dec. 1938, Bronsanski, Brod, Yugoslavia. *Education:* Studied in Sarajevo. *Career:* Debut: Sarajevo, 1959, as Mozart's Countess; Sang at Sarajevo and Zagreb, 1959–75; Guest appearances at the Vienna Staatsoper, Florence and San Francisco, 1969; Philadelphia from 1970, Naples 1971; Verona Arena, 1972–73, as Aida and the Forza Leonora; Sang at Covent Garden, 1975, 1977, Metropolitan Opera, 1976, Aida; Further appearandces at Barcelona, Nice and the Deutsche Oper Berlin, 1977–78, Milan, Rome and Marseilles; Other roles have included the Trovatore Leonora, Amelia in Ballo in Maschera, Desdemona and Norma. *Recordings:* Verdi Requiem. *Address:* c/o Arena di Verona, Piazza Bra 28, 37121 Verona, Italy.

**MONELLE, Raymond (John),** BMus, PhD; British critic and university lecturer; b. 19 Aug. 1937, Bristol; m. Hannelore E M Schultz 1964 (divorced 1983); two d. *Education:* Pembroke Coll., Oxford, Royal Coll. of Music, London, Univ. of Edinburgh. *Career:* Sr Lecturer, Bedford Coll. of Physical Educ. 1966–69; Lecturer in Music, Univ. of Edinburgh, 1969–, Reader 1999–; Music Critic, The Scotsman, 1972–88; Music Critic, The Independent, 1986–; Critic, Opera Magazine, 1984–. *Compositions:* Much educational choral music published; Several commissioned works, e.g. Missa Brevis 1979; Cantata, Ballattis of Luve, 1983. *Contributions:* Music Review; Music and Letters; British Journal of Aesthetics; Music Analysis, Comparative Literature, International Review of the Aesthetics and Sociology of Music. *Publications:* Books: Linguistics and Semantics in Music, 1992; The Sense of Music, 2000; The Musical Topic, 2005. *Address:* c/o Opera Magazine, 36 Black Lion Lane, London, W6 9BE, England; 80 Marchmont Road, Edinburgh, EH9 1HR, Scotland (home). *Telephone:* (131) 447-0477 (home). *E-mail:* r.monelle@music.ed.ac.uk (home).

**MONETTI, Mariaclara;** Concert Pianist; b. 1965, Italy. *Education:* Studied in Turin, at the Salzburg Mozarteum and at the Conservatories of Venice and Lucerne; Teachers include Geza Anda and Vladimir Ashkenazy. *Career:* Many appearances in 18th Century repertoire throughout Europe; British appearances with the London Symphony at the Barbican and London recitals in the Purcell Room and St John's, Smith Square. *Recordings include:* Mozart concertos K466 and K595, with the Royal Philharmonic; The complete Paisiello Piano Concertos, with the English Chamber Orchestra and a solo CD of the complete piano works of Dallapiccola. *Honours:* Gold Medal, Viotti International Competition. *Address:* Manygate Management, 13 Cotswold Mews, 30 Battersea Square, London SW11 3 RA, England.

**MONK, Allan,** OC; Canadian singer (bass-baritone); b. 19 Aug. 1942, Mission City, BC. *Education:* studied in Calgary with Elgar Higgin and in NY with Boris Goldovsky. *Career:* debut, Western Opera, San Francisco 1967 in Menotti's The Old Maid and The Thief; has sung in Portland, St Louis, Chicago, Hawaii and Vancouver; Canadian Nat. Opera, Toronto 1973 in premiere of Wilson's Abelard and Heloise; Metropolitan Opera from 1976 as Schaunard in La Bohème, The Speaker in Die Zauberflöte, Berg's Wozzeck, Wagner's Wolfram and Verdi's Posa and Ford; sang Macbeth at Toronto 1986, followed by Carlo in La Forza del Destino; Opéra de Montréal 1988 as Don

Giovanni; sang Nick Shadow in The Rake's Progress for Vancouver Opera 1989; Wozzeck and Iago at Toronto in 1990; sang Simon Boccanegra for Long Beach Opera 1992; owner of private singing studio in Alberta. *Recordings include:* Andrea Chénier, La Traviata, Allan Monk with Calgary Philharmonic Orchestra. *Honours:* Artist of the Year 1983. *Address:* c/o Tryptych, 583 Durie Street, Toronto, ON M6S 3H2, Canada.

**MONK, Meredith Jane;** American composer, director and choreographer; b. 20 Nov. 1942, d. of Theodore G. Monk and Audrey Lois (Zellman). *Education:* Sarah Lawrence Coll. *Career:* Founder and Artistic Dir House Foundation for the Arts 1968–; formed Meredith Monk & Vocal Ensemble 1978–. *Works include:* Break 1964, 16 Millimeter Earrings 1966, Juice: A Theatre Cantata 1969, Key 1971, Vessel: An Opera Epic 1971, Paris 1972, Education of the Girlchild 1973, Quarry 1976, Songs from the Hill 1976, Dolmen Music 1979, Specimen Days: A Civil War Opera 1981, Ellis Island 1981, Turtle Dreams Cabaret 1983, The Games 1983, Acts from Under and Above 1986, Book of Days 1988, Facing North 1990, Three Heavens and Hells 1992, Atlas: An Opera in Three Parts 1991, New York Requiem 1993, Volcano Songs 1994, American Archaeology 1994, The Politics of Quiet 1996, Steppe Music 1997, Magic Frequencies 1998, Micki Suite 2000, Eclipse Variations 2000, Mercy 2001, Possible Sky 2003, Last Song 2003. *Honours:* Dr hc (Bard Coll.) 1988, (Univ. of the Arts) 1989, (Juilliard School of Music) 1998, (San Francisco Art Inst.) 1999, (Boston Conservatory) 2001; Golden Eagle Award 1981, Nat. Music Theatre Award 1986, German Critics' Award for Best Recording of the Year 1981, 1986, MacArthur "Genius" Award 1995, Samuel Scripps Award 1996 and many other awards. *Address:* 228 West Broadway, New York, NY 10013, USA (office). *Website:* www.meredithmonk.org (office).

**MONNARD, Jean-François,** LLM; Swiss artistic director; *Artistic Director, Deutsche Oper Berlin;* b. 4 Nov. 1941, Lausanne; m. Lia Rottier. *Education:* Univ. of Lausanne, Music Acad., Lausanne, Folkwang Hochschule, Essen, Germany. *Career:* resident conductor, Kaiserslautern, Graz, Austria, Trier, Aachen and Wuppertal; Music Dir in Osnabruck; orchestral and opera performances throughout Europe; Artistic Dir Deutsche Oper Berlin 1998–. *Contributions:* articles to professional journals. *Address:* Richard-Wagner-Str. 10 10585 Berlin, Germany. *Telephone:* (30) 34384214. *Fax:* (30) 34384457. *E-mail:* straub@deutscheoperberlin.de (office).

**MONOSOFF, Sonya;** Violinist and Professor Emerita; b. 11 June 1927, Ohio, USA; m. Carl Eugene Pancaldo, 8 Dec 1950, 4 d. *Education:* Artists Diploma, Juilliard Graduate School, 1948. *Career:* Debut: New York City, USA; Concerts and Masterclasses: USA, Canada, Europe, Israel, Australia and New Zealand; Professor, Professor Emerita of Music, Cornell University; mem, Early Music America, Steering Committee; American Musical Instrument Society, Editorial Board. *Recordings:* Heinrich Biber, Mystery Sonatas and 1681 Sonatas; JS Bach, Sonatas for Violin and Harpsichord; Mozart, Sonatas. *Contributions:* Notes: Early Music; The New Grove; The Musical Times. *Honours:* Stereo Review, Best Record of the Year (Bach), 1970; Fulbright Lectureship, New Zealand, 1988; Bunting Institute, 1967–68; Smithsonian Institute, 1971. *Address:* 101 Devon Road, Ithaca, New York, NY 14850, USA.

**MONOSZON, Boris;** Violinist and Conductor; b. 1955, Kiev, Russia. *Education:* Graduate, Moscow Conservatoire, 1979. *Career:* Made several concert tours of European and Latin American countries as concert master, Prague Symphony; Interpreted Concerto for Violin and Orchestra by Sibelius, Royal Festival Hall, London, England. Soloist, Teplice State Philharmonic Orchestra, 1982–. *Honours:* Laureate, Tibor Varga International Competition, Switzerland, 1981.

**MONOT, Pierre-Alain;** Trumpeter; b. 7 March 1961, Switzerland. *Education:* Diplôme de virtuosité de trompette; Etudes de direction d'orchestre. *Career:* Solo trumpet, Stadtorchester, Winterthur; Chief Conductor, Nouvel Ensemble Contemporain; Guest Conductor, Rousse Philharmonic; Bieler Sinfonieorchester; Orchester des Musikkollegium, Winterthur; mem, Association Suisse des Musiciens. *Compositions:* Stèles for Strings, 1998; Trois Airs de cour for brass quartet and orchestra; Concertino for double bassoon; Concerto for bass trombone. *Recordings:* with the Novus Brass Quartett. *Honours:* First prize, Competition of Union Bank of Switzerland, 1987. *Current Management:* Mrs Esther Herrmann. *Address:* Weinbergstrasse 18, 8001, Zürich.

**MONOYIOS, Ann;** Singer (Soprano); b. 28 Oct. 1949, Middletown, CT, USA. *Education:* Studied at Princeton University and with Oren Brown. *Career:* Concert performances in Baroque music with the Folger Consort, Washington DC; Stage debut with the Concert Royal of New York, in Rameau's Les Fêtes d'Hébé; European debut at the 1986 Göttingen Festival, in Handel's Terpsichore with the English Baroque Soloists conducted by John Eliot Gardiner, Opéra Comique Paris and Aix-en-Provence Festival, 1987, as Lully's Sangaride (Atys) and Psyché; Sang Elisa in Mozart's Il Re Pastore at the Nakamichi Festival in Los Angeles, 1990; Further engagements at Salzburg, Spoleto and Frankfurt; Season 1999 as Nice in J.C. Bach's Serenata Endimione at Duisburg, and Handel's Theodora at Göttingen. *Recordings:* Iphigénie en Aulide with the Opéra de Lyon; Purcell's Dioclesian and Timon of Athens, 1996.

**MONTAGNIER, Jean-Paul C.;** MA, PhD; French musicologist; b. 28 Sept. 1965, Lyon. *Education:* Univ. of Lyon, Conservatoire National Supérieur de Musique, Paris, Duke Univ., Durham, NC, USA. *Career:* Asst Prof. Music Dept, Nancy 2 Univ. 1992–96, later Prof. of Musicology; Assoc. Prof. Music Dept, Metz Univ. 1996–2000, Dir of Graduate Studies 1996–2000, Chair of Dept 1999–2000; mem. of bd, Société Française de Musicologie 1994–99; Sec. to the Ed., Revue de Musicologie 1994–; Mem., Scientific Cttee, CMBV 'Atelier d'étude sur le petit motet'; Assoc. Mem., CNRS team 'atelier d'étude sur la musique baroque française' 1996; Mem. Editorial Bd, new critical edition of the works of Jean-Baptiste Lully 1997–; Sec., European Science Foundation research programme, 'Musical Life in Europe 1600–1900: Circulation Institutions, Representations' 1998–92; Sec., Lully Asscn 1998–; Assoc. Mem., CNRS team 'Patrimoine musical en France'; Mem. Scientific Cttee, programme Musica Gallica 2001–; Mem. Advisory Panel, Eighteenth-Century Music 2002–; Artistic Dir, Ensemble Vocal de la Chartreuse de Bonlieu; mem. Société Française de Musicologie, Int. Musicological Soc., Royal Musical Soc., American Musicological Soc. *Publications:* La Vie l'œuvre de Louis-Claude Daquin 1694–1772, Un Mécène musicien. Philippe d'Orléans Régent 1674–1723, Charles-Hubert Gervais. Un Musicien au service du Régent et de Louis XV; contrib. many articles to journals, conference reviews and programme notes; edns of Marcello's Le Théâtre à la mode, Charpentier's Te Deum, Charpentier's Messe de Minuit, de Mondonville's Jubilate Deo, Gervais' Super flumina Babilonis, Œuvres complètes, Campra's Messe de mort, Du Mont's Magnificat, Madin's Les Messes; contrib. to New Grove Dictionary of Music and Musicians, Die Neue Musik in Geschichte und Gegenwart. *Address:* Université Nancy 2, 23 blvd Albert 1er, 54000 Nancy, France (office). *Telephone:* 3-83-96-71-40 (office). *E-mail:* Jean-Paul .Montagnier@univ-nancy2.fr (office).

**MONTAGUE, Diana,** ARCM; British singer (mezzo-soprano); b. 8 April 1953, Winchester; d. of Mr and Mrs N. H. Montague; m. Philip Doghan 1978; one s. *Education:* Testwood School, Totton, Hants., Winchester School of Art and Royal Northern Coll. of Music. *Career:* professional début at Glyndebourne 1977; prin. mezzo-soprano, Royal Opera House, Covent Garden 1978; freelance artist 1984–; has toured throughout Europe and USA appearing at Metropolitan Opera and Bayreuth, Aix-en-Provence, Salzburg and Glyndebourne festivals; sang at Promenade Concerts, London 1991; Ariadne auf Naxos for Opera North 1998. *Address:* c/o IMG Artists, Lovell House, 616 Chiswick High Road, London, W4 5RX, England (office).

**MONTAGUE, Stephen (Rowley),** AA, MM, DMA, IRCAM, CCRMA; British/American composer and pianist; b. 10 March 1943, Syracuse, New York, USA; m. Patricia Mattin 1986; one s. one d. *Education:* St Petersburg Junior Coll., Florida, Florida State Univ., Ohio State Univ.; Postgraduate work, Conducting, Mozarteum, Salzburg, 1966; Fulbright, Warsaw, Poland, 1972–74; Computer Music, IRCAM, Paris, France; Stanford Univ. *Career:* Debut: Wigmore Hall, London, England. 1975; Warsaw Autumn Festivals, 1974, 1980, 1989, 1991, 1995; Metz Festival, 1976; New Music America, 1987, 1988, 1990; Montague/Mead Piano Plus first tour of the USA, 1986; Frequent European and N. American tours to present; Chair., Sonic Arts Network, UK, 1987–88; Almeida Festival, London, 1988; Guest Prof., Univ. of Texas at Austin, 1992, 1995, 2000; Featured Composer, Speculum Festival, Norway, 1992; World tours with Maurice Agis' inflatable sculpture, Dreamspace, 1987–2005; Centre Pompidou premiere, 1995; Composer-in-Association with the Orchestra of St John's Smith Square, London, 1995–97; Cheltenham Festival, 1995, 1997, 2001; Ultima 95 Festival, Oslo; Featured Composer at Cambridge Festival, 2000 and at Making New Waves Festival, Budapest, 2001, 2002; Chair, 1993–98, Artistic Dir, 1998–99, Soc. for the Promotion of New Music, 1993–95; British Acad. of Composers and Songwriters; Artistic Dir, Open Score Project UK 2004–05; Artistic Consultant, BBC John Cage Uncaged Festival, London, 2004. *Compositions include:* Eyes of Ambush, 1973; Sound Round, 1973; Paramell Va, 1981; At the White Edge of Phrygia, 1983; String Quartet No. 1, 1989–93; Behold a Pale Horse, 1990; Wild Nights, 1993; Silence: John, Yvar and Tim, 1994; Varshavian Autumn, 1995; Snakebite, 1995; Dark Sun, 1995; Piano Concerto, 1997; Southern Lament, 1997; A Toy Symphony, 1999; Black 'n' Blues, 2000; Bright Interiors III, 2000; When Dreams Collide, 2001; Disparate Dances, 2002; The Hammer Hawk, 2002; Intrada 1631, 2003; Toccare Incandescent, 2003; Autumn Leaves, 2003; Five Easy Pieces, 2003. *Recordings include:* CDs: Stephen Montague Orchestra and Chamber Works, 1994; Snakebite, 1997; Silence: John, Yvar and Tim, 1997, Montague Piano Works 2005. *Honours:* Ernst von Dohnányi Award, 1995; 1st Prize, Bourges Electronic Music Competition, 1994; Hon. Fellow, Trinity Coll. of Music, London, 2001; Fellow, Leeds Coll. of Music 2004; runner up, British Acad. of Composers Songwriters Award 2004. *Address:* 2 Ryland Road, London, NW5 3EA (home); United Music Publishers, 33a Lea Road, Waltham Abbey, Essex, EN9 1ES England (office). *Telephone:* (1992) 703110 (office); (20) 7267-5416 (home). *Fax:* (1992) 703189 (office). *E-mail:* info@ump.co.uk (office); srmontague@aol.com (home). *Website:* www .ump.co.uk (office).

**MONTAL, Andre;** Singer (Tenor); b. 18 Nov. 1940, Baltimore, USA. *Education:* Studied at the Eastman School, The Music Academy of the West at Santa Barbara and the Curtis Institute. *Career:* Debut: American Opera Society New York, 1964, as Tebaldo in I Capuleti e i Montecchi; Has sung at opera houses in Boston, Chicago, Philadelphia, San Francisco and Vancouver; Metropolitan Opera fro m 1974; Further engagements with Australian Opera at Sydney; Other roles have included Donizetti's Ernesto, Nemorino, Tonio and Edgardo, Oronte in Alcina, Gounod's Roméo, Rossini's Almaviva, Lindoro, and Idreno in Semiramide, Mozart's Ferrando, Belmonte and Don Ottavio;

Mephistopheles in Prokofiev's Fiery Angel, Verdi's Duke, Pinkerton and the Italian Singer in Rosenkavalier.

**MONTALVO, Marisol;** American singer (soprano); b. 1970. *Education:* Zürich Opera Studio, Manreo College of Music. *Career:* appearances with Dortmund Opera as Euridice, Flowermaiden in Parsifal and Sulamith in Goldmark's Königin von Saba; Sang Rossini's Elvira at Chautauqua, Mozart's Barbarina at Sarasto and Musetta in La Bohème for Castel Vocal Arts; Bizet's Frasquita and Nannetta in Falstaff for Regina Opera; Echo in Ariadne auf Naxos and Mozart's Despina in Brooklyn; Susanna for New Rochelle Opera; Season 1999–2000 with Esmeralda in The Bartered Bride at Glyndebourne, Marie in Lortzing's Zar and Zimmermann, Gretel, Micaela in Carmen, and Suzel in Mascagni's L'Amico Fritz. *Address:* c/o Théâtre du Châtelet, 2 rue Edouard Colonne, 75001 Paris, France.

**MONTARSOLO, Paolo;** singer (bass) and producer; b. 16 March 1925, Portici, Naples, Italy. *Education:* studied with Enrico Conti in Naples and at La Scala Opera School. *Career:* debut, La Scala 1954; Guest appearances in Italy in operas by Rossini, Donizetti, Wolf-Ferrari and Mozart; Bergamo 1955, in a revival of Donizetti's Rita; Verona 1956; Glyndebourne Festival from 1957, as Mustafà in L'Italiana in Algeri, Selim in Il Turco in Italia, and Mozart's Osmin, Leporello and Don Alfonso; Florence, 1966, in Luisa Miller; Deutsche Oper am Rhein, Düsseldorf, 1973; Paris Opéra 1977, as Don Magnifico in La Cenerentola; Geneva Opera 1984, in L'Italiana in Algeri; Engagements in Moscow, Lisbon, New York, Naples and Rio de Janeiro; Sang Don Magnifico at the Berlin Staatsoper, 1987; Mustafà at Covent Garden, debut 1988; Salzburg Festival 1988–89, as Mozart's Bartolo and Don Magnifico; Staged and sang Don Pasquale at the Dallas Opera, 1989, Covent Garden, 1990; Sang Donizetti's Dulcamara at the Royal Opera, 1992; Engaged in Manon Lescaut at the 1997 Glyndebourne Festival. *Recordings:* La Cenerentola; Il Barbiere di Siviglia; Rita and Viva La Mamma; La Serva Padrona; Madama Butterfly.

**MONTÉ, Ruth;** Concert Harpsichordist, Organist and Pianist; b. 3 Dec. 1958, Galatzi, Romania; m. Noel Monté, 26 Oct 1986. *Education:* Summa cum laude, Academy of Music, Bucharest; Juilliard School of Music, New York; Studies with Rozalyn Tureck, Trevor Pinnock, John Weaver, Peter Husford, Frederick Neemann, Peter Williams, Lukas Foss. *Career:* Debut: Bucharest, Romania, 1973; Bucharest, Romania, 1977, Weimar, Germany, 1978; Television and radio appearances in Romania; Lecturer, Performer, Bach on Harpsichord, Piano, Organ in North America; Lecturer, Performance, 50th Anniversary of the UN, New York Academy of Sciences; mem, Chamber Music America; Early Music and Gramophone. *Recordings:* Integral of Bach's Keyboard Music on Harpsichord, Piano and Organ. *Honours:* Laureate, National Youth Music Festival, Romania, 1973. *Address:* 923 Fifth Avenue #17B, New York, NY 10021, USA.

**MONTEBELLO, Benedetto;** Conductor; b. 20 May 1964, Rome, Italy; m. Lorena Palumbo, 5 April 1997. *Education:* 1st class degree as Music Historian, La Sapienza University, Rome; Graduated as Guitarist, Bandmaster, Composer and Conductor, 1st class degree, S Cecilia Musical Conservatory, Rome; Specialist courses in Conducting with G Kuhn and D Gatti. *Career:* Debut: Conducted Beethoven's 1st Piano Concerto and 2nd Symphony, Anzio International Festival, 1989; Has conducted major orchestras including Radio Sofia Symphony Orchestra, Burgas National Orchestra, Oradea National Philharmonic Orchestra, Oltenia Philharmonic Orchestra, Craiova, S Cecilia National Academy Symphonic Orchestra, in Italy and abroad; Conducted premiere of G Guaccero's Salmo Metropolitano for large orchestra, based on P P Pasolini's texts, on 20th anniversary of Pasolini's death; Recent performances include Stravinsky's Histoire du Soldât, Ibert's Flute Concerto, Brahms' 1st Symphony, Chopin's 1st and 2nd Piano Concertos, Mussorgsky's Pictures at an Exhibition; Teacher of Conducting, U Giordano Conservatory of Music, Foggia. *Recordings:* Conductor, complete works of G Guaccero; Ennio Morricone's 3rd Concerto for Guitar, Marimba and Orchestra, with S Cecilia National Academy Symphonic Orchestra. *Contributions:* Musical articles in national newspapers; Encyclopaedic items on Treccani. *Honours:* Winner, Rinaldi Prize for Conductors, 1995. *Address:* Via Segesta No. 51, 00179 Rome, Italy.

**MONTEFUSCO, Licinio;** Singer (baritone); b. 30 Oct. 1936, Milan, Italy. *Education:* studied in Milan. *Career:* debut, Teatro Nuovo, Milan, 1961 as Zurga in Les Pêcheurs de Perles; sang Renato in Un Ballo in Maschera at Florence, 1963, followed by appearances throughout Italy, notably at the Teatro Regio Turin; guest appearances at the Vienna Staatsoper, 1964–, Deutsch Oper Berlin, 1966–; US debut, Philadelphia, 1965; La Scala, Milan, 1970 as Montfort in I Vespri Siciliani; sang at Monte Carlo, 1967–68, Brussels and Strasbourg, 1972–74, Verona, 1972 as Amonasro, Marseilles, 1979; sang Francesco Foscari in I Due Foscari at Turin, 1984 and Posa in Don Carlos, 1985; other roles have included Verdi's Germont, Luna, Rigoletto, Macbeth, Carlos and Ford, Enrico in Lucia di Lammermoor, Alfonso in La Favorita, Marcello, Gérard and Valentin. *Address:* İstanbul Devlet Opera ve Balesi, Atatürk Kültür Merkezi, Taksim, 80124 Istanbul, Turkey.

**MONTENEGRO, Roberto;** Uruguayan conductor; *Musical Director, Symphony Orchestra of Uruguay State Radio;* b. 18 Sept. 1956, Montevideo. *Education:* Hamburg Musikhochschule, studied with Guido Santorsola, Gerhard Markson, Aldo Ceccato and Sergiu Celibidache. *Career:* debut, Santa Barbara Festival Symphony Orchestra, California 1985; conducted the world premiere of Francisco Rodrico's Guitar Concerto with the Venezuelan Nat.

Orchestra 1992, and world premiere of Cesar Cano's Piano Concerto with the Spanish Nat. Orchestra 1993; teacher of masterclasses in Uruguay and Argentina, Italy (European Community Music High School) and Spain (Santiago de Compostela's Int. Conducting Masterclasses); Asst to Aldo Ceccato in Hamburg and Hannover; jury mem., Young Concert Artists, New York, USA; Artistic and Musical Dir, SODRE, Uruguay 1991–95; guest conductor in Spain, France, Argentina, Venezuela, Czech Republic, USA, Canada, Israel; Shira Int. Symphony Orchestra in Jerusalem Classical Winter Festival; Musical Dir, OSSODRE (Symphony Orchestra of Uruguay State Radio) 2004–, performance at the Prague Spring Festival, centenary of Dvořák's death. *Honours:* hon. mem. Young Concert Artists 1994, Baron, Royal Order of the Bohemian Crown 1995, Jerusalem Prize 2004. *Address:* Avenida del Libertador 1684, Apt 1202, PO Box 1552, Montevideo, Uruguay. *Telephone:* (598-2) 900-5725 (office). *Fax:* (598-2) 900-5725 (office). *E-mail:* montenegrouy@yahoo.com.ur (office).

**MONTGOMERY, Kathryn;** Singer, (Soprano); b. 23 Sept. 1952, Canton, Ohio, USA. *Education:* Studied at the University of Bloomington, Indiana. *Career:* Debut: Bloomington 1972, as Elvira in Ernani; Sang at Norfolk from 1978 as Frasquita, and in the premiere of Musgrave's Christmas Carol; European debut at Cologne 1980, as Leonore in Fidelio; Sang at Cologne and Zürich 1980–82, Mannheim 1981–85; Guest engagements at Venice, Edinburgh, Barcelona and Brussels; Metropolitan Opera debut 1985, as Chrysothemis; Pretoria, South Africa, 1984 as Salome; Other roles include Wagner's Elsa, Senta and Sieglinde, Tosca, Donna Anna, Berg's Marie, Donna Elvira and the Empress in Die Frau ohne Schatten; Sang Aksinya in Lady Macbeth of Mtsensk at the Deutsche Oper Berlin, 1988; Frequent concert appearances. *Address:* c/o Deutsche Oper Berlin, Richard Wagner-strasse 10, 1000 Berlin 1, Germany.

**MONTGOMERY, Kenneth;** Conductor; b. 28 Oct. 1943, Belfast, Ireland. *Education:* Royal Belfast Academical Institution; Royal College of Music, London. *Career:* Debut: Glyndebourne Festival 1967; Staff Conductor, Sadler's Wells, English National Opera 1967–70; Assistant Conductor, Bournemouth Symphony Orchestra and Sinfonietta from 1970; Conducted Weber's Oberon at Wexford, 1972; Strauss's Ariadne and Capriccio for Netherlands Opera, 1972, 1975; Director, Bournemouth Sinfonietta, 1974–76; Covent Garden debut 1975, Le nozze di Figaro; Principal Conductor, Dutch Radio Orchestra from 1976; Musical Director, Glyndebourne Touring Opera 1975–76; Guest appearances with Welsh National Opera, Canadian Opera; Concert performance of Donizetti's Anna Bolena at Amsterdam, 1989; Hansel and Gretel for Netherlands Opera, 1990; Conducted Tosca and The Magic Flute for Opera Northern Ireland at Belfast, 1990; Season 1991 with Alcina for Vancouver Opera, Figaro in Belfast and The Passion of Jonathan Wade for the Monte Carlo Royal Opera (repeated at San Diego, 1996). *Honours:* Silver Medal, Worshipful Company of Musicians, 1963; Tagore Gold Medal, Royal College of Music, 1964. *Address:* c/o Robert Gilders Co, Enterprise House, 59–65 Upper Ground, London SE1 9 PQ, England.

**MONTVIDAS, Edgaras;** Lithuanian singer (tenor); b. 1975, Vilnius. *Education:* Kaunas Music School, Conservatory of Juozas Gruodis, Lithuanian Music Acad., Young Artists' Programme, Covent Garden. *Career:* Alfredo and Donizetti's Arturo for Lithuanian Nat. Opera; Nemorino on tour to Chicago; concerts include Berlioz Te Deum, Mozart C Minor Mass and Liszt Coronation Mass; Covent Garden debut as Ruiz in Il Trovatore; sang in Falla's La Vida Breve, London Proms 2002 and as Alfredo at Covent Garden; sang Alfredo for GTO 2003. *Honours:* scholarships and awards in Lithuania and elsewhere. *Current Management:* Van Walsum Management Deutschland GmbH, Königstrasse 36, 30175 Hannover, Germany. *Telephone:* (511) 366 07 23. *Fax:* (511) 366 07 24. *E-mail:* vwm@kdschmid.de.

**MOODY, Howard,** MA, FRCO; British conductor, pianist and composer; b. 7 May 1964, Salisbury, Wiltshire, England; m. Emily Blows; two d. one s. *Education:* Salisbury Cathedral School, Canford School, New Coll., Oxford, Guildhall School of Music and Drama. *Career:* Artistic Dir, Sarum Chamber Orchestra 1986–; worked as conductor with many of the major British orchestras, Netherlands Radio Chorus, Opera Factory, Icelandic Opera, Orchestra della Toscana, Romanian State Chorus, Salisbury Festival Chorus and as a music dir in London's West End; as keyboard player established duo partnerships with cellist David Watkin using modern piano and fortepiano; plays harpsichord; organ continuo player with English Baroque Soloists, Acad. of St Martin-in-the-Fields, Orchestra of St John's, for John Eliot Gardiner's Bach 2000 pilgrimage; collaborations with saxophonist John Surman, including appearances at European jazz festivals as improviser and conductor; projects for Children's Music Workshop; work with the deaf. *Compositions:* commissions include dramatic, instrumental and choral works for Station House Opera (funded by the Arts Council of Great Britain) 1997, Weigh Me The Fire (choral work commissioned by Southern Cathedrals Festival) 1997, stage works for Bangladesh Festival 1998, for ENO 2000, works for Children's Music Workshop (including oratorio Songs of the Forest 2005), Jack de Johnette, The Anvil, Salisbury Festival; collaborations include Requiem with Paco Pena, musical with poet Ian McMillan and orchestral transcriptions for John Surman, Marc Almond and Marianne Faithfull. *Recordings:* as pianist: Beethoven Cello Sonatas (with David Watkin, cello, recorded on original fortepianos) 1996, Francis Pott Cello Sonata (with David Watkin) 1997; as conductor: John Surman's Proverbs and Songs, numerous choral recordings with Radio Chorus, live recordings for BBC. *Address:* The

Song House, Ashdown Road, Forest Row, East Sussex RH18 5BW, England. *Telephone:* (1342) 825705 (office). *E-mail:* howard.moody@lineone.net (office).

**MOODY, Ivan (William George),** BMus; British composer; b. 11 June 1964, London; m. Susanna Simoes Diniz 1989. *Education:* Royal Holloway Coll., London Univ.; Studies with John Tavener, 1984–86. *Career:* Works performed and broadcast in the UK, Austria, Denmark, Portugal, Italy, Germany, Finland, Estonia, Netherlands, Brazil and USA; Lecturing for music festivals in the UK, Netherlands and Finland and courses in the UK and Portugal; Conducting of various choirs in Europe in Orthodox and Renaissance sacred repertoire; Works performed throughout E. and W. Europe, Brazil and USA. *Compositions include:* Lithuanian Songs, 1986; Cantigas de Amigo; Canticle at The Parting of The Soul; Burial Prayer; Miserere, 1988; Hymn of The Transfiguration; Lament for Christ, 1989; Liturgy of St John Chrysostom, 1991; Cantigas do Mar, 1991; Anamnisis; Hymn of Joseph of Arimathea; Hymn to Christ the Saviour, 1991; Vigil of the Angels, 1991; Passion and Resurrection, 1992; Fables, chamber opera, 1994; Elegia for baritone and ensemble, 1998; Apok-athilosis, Orthodox Vespers of Good Friday, 1999. *Recordings:* As Conductor: Ippolitov–Ivanov, Divine Liturgy, Ikon, Tavener, various works, Ikon. *Publications:* Editions of Renaissance polyphony for Mapa Mundi, 1989, 1991, Chester Music, 1990–, Fundacao Calouste Gulbenkian, 1991. *Address:* c/o Vanderbeek and Imrie Ltd, 15 Marvig, Lochs, Isle of Lewis HS2 9QP, Scotland. *E-mail:* vanderbeek@madasafish.com (office).

**MOORE, Carman (Leroy),** MS; American composer, conductor and music critic; b. 8 Oct. 1936, Lorain, Ohio; divorced; two s. *Education:* Ohio State Univ.; Music, Composition, Juilliard School of Music, 1966; Studied composition with Hall Overton, Luciano Berio, Vincent Persichetti. *Career:* Commissioned performances by New York Philharmonic, San Francisco Symphony, Rochester Philharmonic, The Chamber Music Soc. of Lincoln Center; Performances by Cleveland Orchestra, Nexus Ensemble, Aeolian Chamber Players; Founder, Composer, Conductor, Skymusic Ensemble, 1978; Taught at Yale School of Music, Queens and Brooklyn Colls, Manhattanville; Music Critic, Columnist, The Village Voice, 1966–76; Master Composer, Young Choreographers and Composers Project, American Dance Festival, 1986–. *Compositions:* Wildfires and Field Songs; Gospel Fuse; Hit: A Concerto for Percussion and Orchestra; Mass for the 21st Century; Concertos, The Theme is Freedom, for Skymusic Ensemble; Wild Gardens of the Loup Garou, and The Last Chance Planet opera; Paradise Lost, musical; Four Movements for A Five Toed Dragon for Orchestra and Chinese Instruments; Berenice Variations, for clarinet, piano, violin and violoncello; Love Notes to Central Park, mixed media for Skymusic Ensemble, 1996; Journey to Benares, musical, 1999; Gethsemane Park, opera, 1998; Mystery of Tao, chamber music, 2001; Rasur, God of Peace, music theatre, 2002; The Sorcerer's Apprentice, 2005. *Recordings:* Youth in a Merciful House, Sextet, Folkways; Berenice: Variations on A Theme of G F Handel; Four Movements for A Fashionable 5-Toed Dragon, Hong Kong Trade Development Council; Lyrics to all songs on Felix Cavaliere, Bearsville; Home, Interfaith Meditations; Spirit of Krishna. *Publications:* Somebody's Angel Child: The Story of Bessie Smith, 1970; Rockit. *Contributions:* Frequently to New York Times, The Village Voice, Vogue, others. *Honours:* numerous awards. *Address:* 152 Columbus Avenue, 4R, NewYork, NY 10023, USA. *Telephone:* (212) 580-0825 (home). *E-mail:* skycarmuse@mindspring.com (home). *Website:* www .carmanmoore.com (home).

**MOORE, Diana;** Singer (Soprano); b. 1965, England. *Education:* University of Birmingham; Royal Academy of Music. *Career:* Concert appearances in the Saint Matthew Passion and Rossini's Petite Messe at St John's Smith Square; Fauré's La naissance de Venus with The Sixteen, Bach's B minor Mass at the Brighton Festival and La Resurrezione by Handel at Oslo (2001); Psalm 4 by Alexander Goehr with the New London Chamber Choir and Still Life at the Penguin Café with the Royal Ballet; Janáček's The Diary of One Who Disappeared for English National Opera and in the Netherlands; Season 2001 with Armindo in Handel's Partenope at the Covent Garden Festival (Linbury Theatre) and Purcell's Dido under Trevor Pinnock; Bach's St Matthew Passion at the London Proms, 2002. *Address:* c/o English National Opera, St Martin's Lane, London WC2, England.

**MOORE, Dorothy Rudd,** BMus; American composer, teacher and singer; b. 4 June 1940, Wilmington, DE. *Education:* Howard High School, Wilmington School of Music, Howard Univ., Washington, DC, American Conservatory, Fontainebleau, France. *Career:* teacher, Harlem School of the Arts, New York 1965–66, New York Univ. 1969, Bronx Community Coll. 1971; private piano, voice, sight singing and ear training instructor, New York 1968–; founding mem., Soc. of Black Composers 1968–75; mem., New York State Council for the Arts 1988–90; Lucy Moten Fellowship 1963; American Music Center grant 1972; New York State Council on the Arts grant 1985; mem. Nat. Endowment for the Arts, Recording and Composers (panel mem. 1986–88), New York Women Composers, New York Singing Teachers' Asscn, American Composers' Alliance, BMI. *Compositions include:* Flight for piano 1956, Symphony No. 1 1962, Songs from the Rubaiyat 1962, Reflections for concert band 1962, Baroque Suite for unaccompanied violoncello 1964, Three Pieces for Violin and piano 1966, Modes for ensemble 1968, Moods for ensemble 1969, Lament for nine instruments 1969, Trio No. 1 1969, From the Dark Tower 1970, Dirge and Deliverance for cello 1970, Weary Blues 1972, Dream and Variations for piano 1974, Sonnets on Love, Rosebuds and Death 1975, In Celebration for chorus 1977, Night Fantasy for clarinet 1978, A Little Whimsy for piano 1978,

Frederick Douglass (opera) 1981, Transcension (I Have Been to the Mountaintop) for chamber orchestra 1985, Flowers of Darkness 1988, Voices From The Light for chorus 1997. *Address:* 33 Riverside Drive, 16A, New York, NY 10023, USA.

**MOORE, Gillian,** MBE, BMus, MA, FRCM; British music administrator; *Artistic Director, London Sinfonietta;* b. 20 Feb. 1959, Glasgow; d. of Charles Moore and Sara Queen; partner Bruce Nockles; one s. *Education:* Univ. of Glasgow, Royal Scottish Acad. of Music and Drama, Univ. of York, Harvard Univ. *Career:* Educ. Dir London Sinfonietta 1983–93, Artistic Dir 1998–; Head of Educ. Royal Festival Hall 1993–96, Music Audience Devt Man. 1996–; Artistic Dir ISCM World Music Days, Manchester 1997–98; Visiting Prof. Royal Coll. of Music 1996–; Gov. Nat. Youth Orchestra of GB; mem. British Govt Nat. Curriculum Working Group on Music; freelance work as broadcaster, lecturer and writer in music, consultant on music and educ. *Honours:* Hon. Mem. Guildhall School of Music 1993; Sir Charles Grove Award for Outstanding Contrib. to British Music 1992, Asscn of British Orchestras Award for Contrib. of Most Benefit to Orchestral Life in the UK 1999. *Address:* London Sinfonietta, 4 Maguire Street, London SE1 (office); 108 Waller Road, London, SE14 5LU, England (home). *Telephone:* (20) 7928-0828 (office); (20) 7639-6680 (home). *Fax:* (20) 7928-8557 (office); (20) 7639-6675 (home).

**MOORE, Jonathan;** Actor, Writer and Stage Director; b. 1960, England. *Career:* Worked in the Theatre and for Television; Co-librettist and Director of Greek by Mark-Anthony Turnage, premiered at the 1988 Munich Biennale and seen later at the Edinburgh Festival, at the London Coliseum, 1990, directed the version on BBC television; Directed Henze's Elegy for Young Lovers, La Fenice, Venice; Wrote the Libretto for Horse Opera, a television film opera for Channel Four, Music by Stewart Copeland; Staged the premiere of Hans Jürgen von Bose's 63 Dream Palace at Munich, 1990 and the premiere of Michael Berkeley's Baa Baa Black Sheep, Opera North, 1993; British Premiere of Schnitke's Life With an Idiot, ENO London Coliseum, 1995; Further Projects: Libretto and Direction of premiere East and West, by Ian McQueen (Almeida 1995); Libretto and Direction of premiere Mottke the Thief by Bernd Franke, Bonn Opera, 1998; The Nose (Shostakovich), ENO London Coliseum, 1996; Staged the premiere of Macmillan's Inès de Castro, Edinburgh, 1996 and subsequent revivals including a filming by BBS TV and Porto Festival;Directed world premieres of Die Versicherung by Jan Muller-Wieland, Darmstadt, 1999, and Facing Goya by Michael Nyman, Santiago del Compostella and Valencia, 2000; Directed and translated The Magic Flute for Scottish Opera 2002/03 and Three Ways of Dying with Daniel Hope and Uri Caine at the Feldkirch Festival;. *Honours:* Best Libretto Award, Munich, for Greek, 1988; Best Director Award, for 63 Dream Palace, Munich, 1990; Royal Philharmonic Society Award and the Midem Award, Cannes, 1991; Nominated for Olivier Award, for Greek, ENO Coliseum, 1991; BMW Award, for Die Vier Himmelsrichtungen, Munich, 1994. *Current Management:* Ingpen & Williams Ltd, 7 St George's Court, 131 Putney Bridge Road, London, SW15 2PA, England.

**MOORE, Kermit;** Cellist, Conductor and Composer; b. 11 March 1929, Akron, Ohio, USA; m. Dorothy Rudd, 20 Dec 1964. *Education:* BMus, Cleveland Institute of Music, 1951; MA, New York University, 1952; Paris Conservatory, 1953–56. *Career:* Debut: New York Town Hall, 1949; Cello recitals in Paris, Brussels, Vienna, Cologne, Hamburg, Munich, Geneva, Basel, Amsterdam, Tokyo, Seoul, New York, Boston, Chicago and San Francisco; Guest Conductor of Detroit Symphony, Brooklyn Philharmonic, Symphony of New World; Festival Orchestra at the United Nations; Berkeley (California) Symphony; Dance Theater of Harlem; Opera Ebony. *Compositions:* Music for cello and piano; Music for Viola, percussion and piano; Many Thousand Gone, strings, chorus and percussion; Music for timpani and orchestra; Music for flute and piano; Five Songs for DRM. *Recordings:* Brahms: Sonata in E Minor, Dorothy Rudd Moore; Dirge and Deliverance, Performance Records; Mendelssohn, Sonata in D Major, Kermit Moore: Music for Cello and Piano, Performance Records; Karl Weigl Sonata, Love Song and Wild Dance, Orion records. *Publications:* Chapter in The Music Makers, 1979. *Current Management:* Rud/Mor Corporation. *Address:* 33 Riverside Drive, New York, NY 10023, USA.

**MOORE, Latonia;** American singer (soprano); b. Houston, TX. *Education:* Univ. of North Tex., Acad. of Vocal Arts, Philadelphia, studied with Bill Schumann. *Career:* began professional career with performances for Acad. of Vocal Arts and the Opera Co. of Philadelphia; has also performed with Dallas Opera, Palm Beach Opera, Semperoper Dresden, Deutsche Oper Berlin; operatic roles include Mimi in La Bohème, Donna Elvira in Don Giovanni, Despina in Così fan tutte, Marguerite in Faust, title role in Lucrezia Borgia, Countess in Le Nozze di Figaro, Fidelia in Edgar, Micaela in Carmen, Liu in Turandot; concert recitals include Mahler's Second Symphony with Nat. Symphony in Washington, Mahler's Fourth Symphony and Berg Lieder at Festival de Paques de Deauville, France, Mozart's Coronation Mass, Mendelssohn's Second Symphony, Verdi's Requiem. *Recording:* Mahler, Second Symphony 2002. *Honours:* first prize and public prize Competizione dell'Opera, Dresden 2002, first prize Licia Albanese Puccini Foundation Competition, New York 2002, first prize Palm Beach Opera Competition 2003, first prize Dallas Opera Competition 2003, first prize Marseilles Opera Competition 2003, second prize Int. Belvedere Competition, Vienna 2003, Dallas Opera Maria Callas Debut Artist of the Year 2005. *Current Management:* Matthew Laifer Artists Management, 410 W 24th Street, Suite 2i, New

York, NY 10011, USA. *Telephone:* (212) 929-7429 (office). *Fax:* (212) 633-2628 (office). *E-mail:* laiferart@aol.com (office). *Website:* www.laiferart.com (office).

**MORA, Barry;** Singer (Baritone); b. 1944, New Zealand. *Education:* Studied in London with Otakar Kraus and John Matheson. *Career:* Sang in Gelsenkirchen, 1977–79 as: Verdi's Posa and Luna; Mozart's Speaker and Figaro; Sang at Frankfurt from 1979 as Tamare, in Die Gezeichneten, and Ford, in Falstaff; Festival Hall debut, 1979 as Schumann's Faust; Covent Garden Debut 1980 as Donner, in Das Rheingold; Scottish Opera in 1983 as the Traveller, in Death in Venice; Welsh National Opera from 1986 as Donner, Gunther, The Forester in The Cunning Little Vixen and Frank in Die Fledermaus, 1991; Netherlands Opera, 1991; Engagements at Deutsche Oper Berlin, Zürich Opera, Aachen, Düsseldorf, Barcelona, Wellington and Canterbury, New Zealand; Also sang in 1992: Rosenkavalier, Sydney; La Traviata, Barcelona; Parsifal, Frankfurt; Così fan tutte, Wellington; Un Ballo in Maschera, Brussels; Concert repertoire includes, Puccini's Messa di Gloria, Bach's B minor Mass and St John Passion; Carmina Burana, Stravinsky's Canticum Sacrum, Lieder eines fahrenden Gesellen by Mahler, Lulu at Buenos Aires, Così fan tutte at Barcelona Opera, La Cenerentola, Australian Opera, 1994 and for Opera New Zealand; Current roles with Australian Opera as Dr Schön, in Lulu, Alidoro, in La Cenerentola; Tales of Hoffmann, 1995; Wellington Opera: Ping, in Turandot, 1994; Balstrode, in Peter Grimes, 1995; Father, in Hansel and Gretel, 1995; Season 1999 at Sydney as the Doctor in Wozzeck and in Auckland as Puccini's Sharpless. *Address:* c/o Jennifer Eddy Management, Suite 11, The Clivedon, 596 St Kilda Road, Melbourne, Vicotira 3004, Australia.

**MORAL, Antonio;** Spanish artistic director and critic; *Artistic Director, Teatro Real, Madrid;* b. 1956, Puebla de Almenara, Cuenca. *Career:* music critic for newspapers and other media 1984–91; f. Scherzo music magazine 1985, Dir –2001; f. and Dir Mozarti Festival of Madrid 1988–97; Musical and Artistic Dir, Music Programme of the Foundation of the Caja Madrid Savings Bank 1990–2005; Artistic Dir Liceo de Cámara, Madrid 1992–2005, Lied Cycle, Teatro de la Zarzuela 1994–2005; f. and Artistic Dir Mozart Festival of La Coruña 1998–2002; Artistic Dir Teatro Real, Madrid 2005–; founding mem. int. jury, Cannes Classical Awards 1995–2001; mem. Int. Piano Competition Umberto Micheli, Milan (mem. int. cttee 1998–). *Address:* Teatro Real, Plaza de Oriente s/n, Madrid 28013, Spain (office). *Telephone:* (91) 516-0660 (office). *E-mail:* info@teatro-real.com (office). *Website:* www.teatro-real.com (office).

**MORAN, Robert;** American composer; b. 8 Jan. 1937, Denver, Colorado. *Education:* Studied with Hans Erich Apostel and Roman Haubenstock Ramati in Vienna, Luciano Berio and Darius Milhaud at Mills Coll. *Career:* Founded and co-directed the New Music Ensemble, San Francisco Conservatory; Performances throughout USA and Europe as Pianist; Lecturer on contemporary music. *Compositions:* Silver and The Circle of Messages, for chamber orchestra, 1970; Emblems of Passage for 2 orchestras, 1974; Angels of Silence for viola and chamber orchestra, 1975; The Last Station of the Albatross, for 1–8 instruments, 1978; Survivor from Darmstadt, 1984; Mixed media works and stage works including Let's Build a Nut House, chamber opera, 1969; Erlösung dem Erlöser, music drama, 1982; LeipzigerKerzenspiel, 1985; The Juniper Tree, 1985; Desert of Roses, 1992; From the Towers of the Moon, 1992; Dracula Diary, 1994; Night Passage, opera, 1995; Remember Him to Me: an Opera, 1996; Entretien Mysterieux, for orchestra, 1996; 4 Partitions for violin and orchestra, 1997; Voce della Fontana, for soprano and ensemble, 1998. *Address:* Box 54202, Philadelphia, PA 19105 (home); c/o BMI, 320 West 57th Street, New York, NY 10019, USA (office). *Telephone:* (215) 546-0582 (home). *E-mail:* rbtmoran@macconnect.com. *Website:* members.macconnect .com/users/r/rbtmoran/index.htm (office).

**MORAVEC, Antonín;** Czech violinist and composer; b. 29 April 1928, Brno; m. Karla Moravcova 15 July 1950. *Education:* Conservatory of Brno, Janáček Acad. of Musical Art, Brno, Moscow Tchaikovsky Conservatory. *Career:* Prof., Janáček Acad., Brno, Music Acad., Prague; mastercourses at Kunitachi Music Acad., Tokyo, Japan, Tchaikovsky Conservatory, Moscow, Mozarteum, Salzburg, Basel-Muttenz, Switzerland, courses of the Warsaw Acad. organized in Castle Lanzut, Castle of Pommersfelden, Germany; mem. 35 juries of int. violin competitions; has performed solo violin concertos world-wide; recitals on radio and TV. *Compositions:* several compositions for violin and piano including Snowdrop for Leni Bernstein, Violin Concerto 2003, Cadenzas for 18 Violin Concertos by Viotti, Haydn, Mozart, Paganini, Beethoven, Brahms, Slavik and Szymanowski, new rev. L. Janáček Violin Sonata. *Recordings:* Violin Sonatas by Martinů, Shostakovich, Prokofiev, Piano Trio by M. Istvan. *Honours:* Hon. Prof, Kumitachi Music Acad, Tokyo 1961; prizewinner, violin competitions in Brno 1940, 1958, Prague 1950, 1951, Berlin 1951, L. Janáček Medal, Ministry of Culture 1978, Merited Artist of Czech Repub. 1979, Prize, Union of Czech Composers 1982, Medal of Janáček Acad. of Music, Brno 1997, Sr Prize of Intergram and Foundation 'Life of Artist', Prague 1998, Commemorative Medal, The American Biographical Inst. 1999. *Address:* Taussigova 1152, 182 00 Prague 8, Czech Republic.

**MORAVEC, Paul,** BA, MMus, DMA; American composer, academic, electronic music synthesist and conductor; b. 2 Nov. 1957, Buffalo, NY. *Education:* Harvard Univ., Cambridge, MA, Columbia Univ., New York. *Career:* Asst Prof. of Music, Dartmouth Coll., Hanover, NH. *Compositions:* Missa Miserere 1981, Ave Verum Corpus 1981, Pater Noster 1981, Sacred Songs 1982, Three Anthems 1983, Songs for violin and piano 1983, Music for chamber ensemble 1983, Wings 1983, Spiritdance 1984, Innocent Dreamers 1985, Four

Transcendent Love Songs 1986, Prayers and Praise 1986, Whispers 1986, The Kingdom Within 1987, three string quartets 1986, 1990, 1992, Aubade for strings 1990, Piano Concerto 1992, Violin Concerto 1994, Cello Concerto 1998, Mood Swings for piano trio 1998, Fire/Ice/Air dramatic cantata 1998, Tempest Fantasy for solo clarinet and piano trio (Pulitzer Prize) 2004, Protean Fantasy 2005, Ariel Fantasy 2005, The Time Gallery 2005. *Current Management:* JL Music Productions, 250 W 100th Street, Suite 104, New York, NY 10025, USA. *Address:* c/o Music Department, Dartmouth College, Hanover, NH 03755, USA.

**MORAWETZ, Oskar;** Composer and Professor; b. 17 Jan. 1917, Czechoslovakia; m. 1958, 1 s., 1 d. *Career:* Professor of Music, University of Toronto; Orchestral compositions performed frequently by Canadian Orchestras, Canadian Broadcasting Corporation and in USA, Europe and Australia; Among major orchestras abroad, his compositions have been performed by the Philadelphia, Chicago, Detroit, Minneapolis, Indianapolis, Washington and Aspen Festival Orchestras in USA and major orchestras in France, Sweden, Norway, Belgium, Netherlands, Italy, Czechoslovakia and Greece; Conductors who have programmed his works include, William Steinberg, Zubin Mehta, Karel Ancerl, Kubelik, Walter Susskind, Seiji Ozawa, Adrian Boult, Izler Solomon, Sixten Ehrling and Ernest MacMillan; Artists such as Glenn Gould, Rudolf Firkusny and Anton Kuerti have premiered his piano compositions and Maureen Forrester, Jon Vickers, Louis Marshall, Dorothy Maynor, Louis Quilico and Lillian Sukis have included compositions in programmes in Canada, USA, Europe and Australia. *Compositions:* Memorial to Martin Luther King for cello and orchestra; Sinfonietta For Winds and Percussion, From The Diary of Anne Frank; Fantasy in D; Piano Concerto; Clarinet Concerto, 1989; Tribute to W.A. Mozart, string quartet, 1990; Improvisations of Inventions by J. S. Bach, string quartet, 1992; The Whale's Lament, for piano, 1993. *Recordings:* Many of his compositions have been recorded by various record companies. *Address:* c/o OSA, Cs armady 20, 160-56 Prague 6, Bubenec, Czech Republic.

**MORAWSKI, Jerzy,** MA, PhD, D.habil; Polish musicologist; b. 9 Sept. 1932, Warsaw; m. Katarzyna. *Education:* Warsaw Conservatory, Inst. of Musicology, Warsaw Univ., Inst. of Arts, Polish Acad. of Sciences, Jagiellonian Univ., Kraków. *Career:* Asst, Dept of Theory and History of Music, 1956–70, Dr, Head, History Music Section, 1970–79, Vice-Dir, Inst of Arts and Polish Acad. of Sciences, 1979–81; Lecturer, Warsaw Univ. 1968–70, Acad. of Catholic Theology, Warsaw, 1970–73, Jagiellonian Univ. Kraków, 1971–82, 1999–2000; mem, fmr Vice-Sec. and Pres., Polish Composers' Union, Musicological Section. *Publications include:* Research on Liturgical Recitative in Poland, 1973, 1986, 1992, 1995; The Problems of the Tropes Techniques, 1976, 1979; Polish Hymns, 1991; Sursum Corda: Presentation of a Motif, 1999; Two Unfamiliar Tonaria from Silesian Antiphonaries dating from the Thirteenth and Fourteenth Centuries, 2002; Editor-in-Chief of serial publications: Monumenta Musicae in Polonia and Musica Medii Aevi; Books: Musical Lyric Poetry in Medieval Poland, 1973; Theory of Music in the Middle Ages, 1979; Liturgical Recitative in Medieval Poland, 1996; The History of Music in Poland, Vol. I The Middle Ages 2003; Ed., Musica Antiqua Polonica: Anthology, The Middle Ages, 1972; The Rhymed History of St Jadwiga, 1977; The Rhymed History of St Adalbert, 1979; The Polish Cistercian Sequences, 1984; Jan Stefani's Six Partitas for Wind Instruments, 1993;. *Contributions:* numerous professional publications. *Address:* ul Dluga 24m 43, 00–238 Warsaw, Poland.

**MORDKOVITCH, Lydia,** PhD, FRNCM; British (b. Russian) violinist; *Professor of Violin, Royal Academy of Music;* b. 30 April 1944, Saratov, Russia. *Education:* School for Talented Children, Kishinev, Stoliarski School, Odessa, Nejdanova Conservatoire, Odessa, Tchaikovsky Conservatoire, Moscow and studied with David Oistrakh. *Career:* went to Israel 1974; has lived in UK since 1980; Sr Lecturer, Kishinev Inst. of Art 1970–73; Sr Lecturer, Rubin Acad. of Music, Jerusalem 1974–80; Prof. of Violin, Royal Northern Coll. of Music, Manchester, England 1980–, RAM, London 1995–; soloist in recitals, concerts, on radio and TV, USSR, then Europe, USA, S and Cen. America 1974–; Hon. ARAM. *Recordings:* over fifty records and CDs for RCA, Chandos, Collins and Carlton. *Honours:* Prizewinner Young Musicians Competition, Kiev 1967, Long-Thibaud Competition, Paris 1969, Gramophone Award (for Shostakovich concertos) 1990, three Diapason d'Or Awards, Woman of the Year Award, American Biog. Inst. 1996, 1997, 1998, 1999, 2000, Outstanding Woman of the 20th Century, Outstanding Woman of the 21st Century, American Biog. Inst. *Address:* Royal Academy of Music, Marylebone Road, London, NW1 5HT, England (office). *Telephone:* (20) 7873-7373 (office). *Website:* www.ram.ac.uk (office).

**MORDLER, John;** opera house director; *Director, Opéra de Monte-Carlo.* *Career:* Dir Opéra de Monte-Carlo 1984–(2007); mem. Comité d'Honneur, Les Azuriales Opera Festival; mem. Bd Opera Europa. *Address:* Opéra de Monte-Carlo, Casino de Monte-Carlo, Place du Casino, BP 139, Monte-Carlo 98007, Monaco (office). *Telephone:* 98-06-28-00 (office). *Fax:* 98-06-28-10 (office). *E-mail:* contact@opera.mc (office). *Website:* www.opera.mc (office).

**MOREHEN, John Manley,** JP, MA, PhD, DLitt, FRCO (Chm), FRCCO, FRSA; British musicologist, organist and conductor; b. 3 Sept. 1941, Gloucester, England; m. Marie Catherine Jacobus 1969; one s. one d. *Education:* Clifton Coll., Bristol, Royal School of Church Music, Croydon, New Coll., Oxford, Coll. of Church Musicians, Washington, DC, USA and King's Coll. Cambridge. *Career:* Asst Dir of Music, St Clement Danes Church, Strand, Hampstead

Parish Church, London; keyboard player, Hampstead Choral Soc., Martin Sidwell Choir, London Bach Orchestra 1964–67; Lecturer, Coll. of Church Musicians, Washington Cathedral, American Univ., Washington, DC 1967–68; sub-organist, St George's Chapel, Windsor Castle 1968–72; Lecturer in Music, Univ. of Nottingham 1973–82, Sr Lecturer 1982–89, Prof. of Music 1989–2002, Head of the School of Humanities 1998–2001, Emer. Prof. of Music 2002–; numerous broadcasts as organist, speaker and conductor 1964–; recital tours of Europe and N America; many presentations on computer applications in music at conferences in the UK, USA, Canada, France and the Netherlands; Freeman of the City of London and Liveryman of the Worshipful Company of Musicians 1991; Justice of the Peace, Nottinghamshire 1991; Pres., E Midlands Choirs Charitable Trust 1993–2000; panel mem., Humanitites Research Board 1994–97; HEFCE Subject Assessor, Music 1994–95; Music Adviser to the Commonwealth Scholarship Commission 1996–2000; Pres., Incorporated Soc. of Musicians 2003–04. *Recordings:* with choirs of New Coll., Oxford and Hampstead Parish Church. *Publications:* numerous critical edns of 16th- and 17th-century English and Italian choral and instrumental music, including vols in the series Early English Church Music, The Byrd Edition, The English Madrigalists, Recent Researches in the Music of the Renaissance; contrib. to most major British and American musical journals and to New Grove Dictionary of Music 1980, 2002, Die Musik in Geschichte und Gegenwart, New Dictionary of Nat. Biography 2004. *Honours:* Hon. FGCM. *Address:* Chestnut Barn, Syerston Hall Park, Newark, Nottinghamshire NG23 5NL, England (home). *Telephone:* (1636) 525068 (office). *E-mail:* John@ Morehen.fsworld.co.uk (home); John.Morehen@Nottingham.ac.uk (office). *Website:* www.nottingham.ac.uk/music/staff-homepages/morehen.html (office).

**MOREL, Francois;** Composer; b. 14 March 1926, Montreal, Canada. *Education:* Studied piano with private teacher; Studied composition with Clude Champagne, Conservatoire de Muique, Montreal. *Career:* Working for Radio-Canada writing background music for theatre, radio and television, 1956–81; Professor of composition, orchestration and analysis; l'Ecole de musique, Universite Laval, Quebec City; President of publishing firm, Les Editions Quebec-Musique, Montreal; Received commissions for compositions from Canadian Broadcasting Corporation, First International Festival of Contemporary Music for Wind Symphony Orchestra, Edmonton Symphony Orchestra; McGill Chamber Orchestra, Societe de Musique Contemporaine du Quebec, Guitar Society of Toronto 1976; Olympic Games Committee; Montreal International Competition among others. *Compositions:* Orchestral: Antiphonie 1953; Boreal 1959; Departs 1968–69, Diptyque 1948, revised 1955–56; Esquisse 1947–47; L'Etoile noire 1961–62; Iikkii 1971; Jeux 1976; Litanies 1955–56, revised 1970; Melisma 1980; Le mythe de la roche percee 1960–61; Neumes despace et reliefs 1967; Prismes-anamorphoses 1967; Radiance 1970–72; Requiem for Winds 1962–63; Rituel de l'espace 1958–59; Sinfonia 1963; Spirale 1956; Trajectoire 1967; Instrumental Ensemble: Cassation 1954; Etude en forme de toccate 1965; Quatuor No. 1, 1952, No. 2, 1962–63; Quintette pour cuivres 1962; Rhythmologue 1970; Lumières sculptèes, for wind and 3 percussion, 1992; Les éphemères, for 4 horns and tuba, 1995; Et le crepuscule se trouva libre, for orchestra, 1996; Metamporphoses, for orchestra, 1998; Symphonie pur cuivres 1956. Instrumental Solo and Vocal Solos. *Address:* c/o CAPAC Canada, PRS Ltd, Berners Street, London W1, England.

**MORELLI, Adriana;** Italian singer (soprano); b. 1954. *Education:* Regiio Calabria. *Career:* debut in Spoleto 1978, as Musetta; sang Sophie in Werther at Bergamo 1979, Lauretta in Gianni Schicchi at Lucca, 1981; further engagements as Butterfly and Mimi at Spoleto and Lille, Elisabeth de Valois at Dijon, Amsterdam, Amelia, Un Ballo in Maschera, at Trieste; sang Margherita in Mefistofele and Tosca at Genoa, 1987–88, Giorgetta in Il Tabarro at Florence 1988 and Maria Stuarda at Piacenza, 1990; La Scala debut, 1990, as Nedda in Pagliacci; sang Silvia in Mascagni's Zanetta at Florence, 1996; sang Puccini's Giorgetta at Verona, 2000; stage and concert appearances in South America. *Current Management:* Melos Konzerte Wien, Salesianergasse 12/11, 1030 Vienna, Austria. *Telephone:* (1) 714 91 96. *Fax:* (1) 714 91 91. *E-mail:* info@melos.at. *Website:* www.melos.at.

**MORETTI, Isabelle Cécile Andrée;** French harpist; b. 5 May 1964, Lyons. *Education:* studied with Germaine Lorenzini. *Career:* teacher, Conservatoire Nat. Supérieur de Paris 1995–; recital and masterclass tours of USA and Republic of Korea 2004, Estonia and Latvia 2005. *Recordings include:* concertos by Boieldieu, Parish Alvars, Rodrigo, and Ginastera, Debussy: Sonata for flute, viola and harp, Chansons de Bilitis, Prélude à l'après-midi d'un faune. *Honours:* Conservatoire National Supérieur de Paris Premier Prix 1983, first prize in Munich 1983, Bordeaux 1984, Geneva 1986, winner Israel Harp Contest 1988, Nouvelle Académie du Disque Grand Prix 1995, Victoire de la Musique Classique 1996. *Address:* La Hillière, 44470 Thouaré sur Loire, France. *Telephone:* 2-40-77-58-46. *Fax:* 2-40-77-58-46.

**MORGAN, Arwel Huw;** Singer (Bass); b. 1950, Ystalyfera, Swansea, Wales. *Career:* Joined the chorus of Welsh National Opera in 1978; Solo roles in Wales have included Don Fernando, Fidelio; Ladas in The Greek Passion; Angelotti in Tosca; Hobson, Peter Grimes; The Parson in The Cunning Little Vixen; Created the role of Maskull for New Celtic Opera's Voyage to Arcturus; English National Opera from 1987 in Lady Macbeth of Mtsensk and The Cunning Little Vixen; Toured the United Kingdom 1988, as Osmin in Opera 80s Die Entführung aus dem Serail; Season 1992 as Leporello, and as Carl Olsen, in Weill's Street Scene for ENO; Fabrizio in The Thieving Magpie for

Opera North; Sang Leporello in a new production of Don Giovanni for Welsh National Opera, 1996; Zuniga in Carmen at the London Coliseum, 1998; Sang Britten's Snug at the Teatro Nazionale, Rome, 1999. *Recordings:* Polonius in Hamlet by Ambroise Thomas, conducted by Richard Bonynge. *Current Management:* Ingpen & Williams Ltd, 7 St George's Court, 131 Putney Bridge Road, London, SW15 2PA, England.

**MORGAN, Beverly;** Singer (Soprano); b. 17 March 1952, Hanover, New Hampshire, USA. *Education:* Mt Holyoke College, 1969–71; BMus, Honours, New England Conservatory of Music, 1971–73; MMus, Honours, 1973–75, New York. *Career:* Debut: Recital debut as winner of Concert Artists Guild Award, 1978; Operatic Appearances with Wiener Staatsoper, San Francisco Opera, Opera Company of Boston, Pittsburgh, Omaha and Philadelphia Operas, Kennedy Center in Washington and Scottish National Opera; Sang in the premiere of Glass's Satyagraha at Amsterdam, 1980, and in the US Premiere of Zimmermann's Die Soldaten, Boston, 1982; Other appearances in Bernstein's A Quiet Place at La Scala and in Vienna at Santa Fe in the US Premieres of Henze's English Cat and Penderecki's Die schwarze Maske, 1985, 1988; Scottish Opera as Berg's Lulu, 1987; Other roles include Tatiana and Violetta at Seattle and Fusako in Henze's Das Verratene Meer, Berlin and Milan; Concert appearances with Boston Symphony, San Francisco Symphony, Chamber Society of Lincoln Center, American String Quartet, Marlboro Music Festival, American Composers Orchestra; Performances under Leonard Bernstein, Seiji Ozawa and Herbert Blomstedt. *Recordings:* DGG. *Current Management:* Columbia Artists Management Incorporated, NY, USA. *Address:* c/o Crittenden Division, Columbia Artists Management Incorporated, 165 West 57th Street, NY 10019, USA.

**MORGAN, David S.;** Composer and Conductor; b. 18 May 1932, Ewell, Surrey, England; m. Crisetta Macleod (divorced), one s. two d.; m. 2nd Una Grimshaw. *Education:* Sydney Grammar School, Sydney Conservatorium, 1946–52; Study in London with Norman Del Mar and Matyas Seiber, 1955–56; BMus, University of Durham, 1970. *Career:* Cor anglais player in the Sydney Symphony Orchestra; Composer and Arranger with the South Australian Department of Education, 1975–93; Commissions from the Adelaide Chamber Orchestra and Musica da Camera, among others. *Compositions include:* 6 Symphonies (1949–99); Mass in B Major, 1948; Horn Concerto, 1957; Violin Concerto, 1957; Concerto for Viola and Strings, 1958; Concerto Grosso No. 2 for string trio and string orchestra, 1978; Sinfonia for 11 string players, 1978; Loss for 4 percussion, 1982; Suite for String Orchestra, Percussion and Piano, 1985; Fun and Games for 4 percussion, 1986; Jubilee Overture, 1986; Harpsichord Sonata, 1992; Concerto for Orchestra No. 1, 1993, No. 2, 1994; Trumpet Concerto, 1995; 2 Harpsichord Concertos. *Address:* 31 Forth Street, Nuriootpa, South Australia, 5355, Australia.

**MORGAN, Michael (DeVard);** Conductor; b. 17 Sept. 1957, Washington, DC, USA. *Education:* Oberlin College Conservatory of Music; Berkshire Music Centre, Tanglewood, 1977. *Career:* Debut: Operatic, Vienna State Opera, 1982; Apprentice Conductor, Buffalo Philharmonic, 1979–80; Assistant Conductor, St Louis Symphony, 1980–81; Assistant Conductor, Chicago Symphony, 1986–; Guest Conductor: New York and Warsaw Philharmonics, Vienna, Baltimore, Houston, New Orleans Symphony Orchestras; National Symphony, Washington; Deutsche Staatsoper, Berlin; Summer Opera Theater, Washington, DC; Orchestras in Italy, Denmark and Netherlands. *Honours:* 1st prize, Hans Swarowsky International Conductors Competition Vienna, 1980; Prizes in Conducting Competitions at Baltimore, 1974; San Remo, 1975; Copenhagen, 1980. *Current Management:* Sheldon Soffer Management Inc, NY; Alex Saron, Blaricum, Netherlands, Europe. *Address:* 1220 Decatur Street, NW, Washington, DC 20011, USA.

**MORGAN, Morris;** Singer (Baritone); b. 26 Sept. 1940, Berlin, Germany. *Education:* Studied in Düsseldorf, Cologne and Wiesbaden, 1955–71. *Career:* Sang at Cologne in the 1965 premiere of Die Soldaten by Zimmermann; Kiel Opera 1965–68, notably in the 1965 premiere of Reimann's Traumspiel; Wiesbaden 1968–71, Bern 1971–79, Freiburg 1978–81; Further engagements at Düsseldorf, Mannheim, Stuttgart, Bremen, Saarbrucken, Lubeck and Klagenfurt; Returned to Berne 1985, as Marcello in La Bohème; Concert appearances in baroque music and as Lieder singer. *Recordings include:* Die Soldaten; Zemlinsky's Kleider Machen Leute; Israel in Egypt and Carmina Burana. *Address:* Stadttheater Bern, Nageligasse 1, 3011 Bern, Switzerland.

**MORGNY, Bengt-Ola;** Singer (Tenor); b. 1959, Sweden. *Education:* Studied in Gothenburg and Berlin. *Career:* Soloist with the Deutsche Oper Berlin from 1986, including premiere of Das Schloss by Reimann, Deutsche Oper Berlin, 1992; Oper de Stadt Köln from 1993 as Mozart's Basilio and Curzio, Jacquino in Fidelio and Wenzel in The Bartered Bride; Royal Opera House, Copenhagen since 1996 as Goro (Butterfly), Pong (Turandot) Brighella (Ariadne), Dr Cajus (Falstaff), Pict von Piels (Le Grand Macabre), Arbace (Idomeneo); Festival at Drottningholm from 1989, as Pedrillo in Die Entführung, Azor in Zémire et Azor by Grétry, and in Soliman II by J M Kraus; Guest appearances at Oslo, Stockholm, Hamburg, Munich, Paris, Monte Carlo and Geneva as Pong (Turandot), Der Bucklige (Frau ohne Schatten), Brussels, Liège, Tel-Aviv and Sarajevo as Harlequin and Soldier (Der Kaiser von Atlantis); Sang Mozart's Pedrillo at Spoleto, 1998; The Scourge of Hyacinth, production of Robert Wilson and Tania Leon, Geneva, Nancy, St Polten (Austria), Teatro Bellas Artes, Mexico City, 2001. *Recordings include:* Zemlinsky's Der Kreidekreis; Mörder, Hoffnung der Frauen, Hindemith; Das Schloss, Reimann; Video of Die Entführung; Turandot, as Pong, Copenhagen, G Sinopoli; The Handmaid's Tale, P Rouders, The Doctor, CD. *Address:* Det Konglige Teater, Postboks 2185, 1017 Copenhagen, Denmark. *E-mail:* morgny@home.se.

**MORINO, Giuseppe;** Singer (Tenor); b. 18 Aug. 1950, Assisi, Italy. *Career:* Debut: Spoleto, 1981, as Gounod's Faust; Festival of Martina Franca, 1986, as Idreno in Semiramide; Season 1987 as Admète in Gluck's Alceste at La Scala, Pylades in Rossini's Ermione at Pesaro and the Duke of Mantua at the Vienna Staatsoper; Donizetti's Edgardo at Naples, 1989, Meyerbeer's Raoul at Novara, 1993; Astrologer in Rimsky's Golden Cockerel at Rome, 1995; Other roles include Tebaldo in Bellini's Capuleti, Rossini's Almaviva, Donizetti's Gianni di Parigi and Gounod's Romeo. *Address:* c/o Teatro dell'Opera, Piazza B Gigli 8, 00184 Rome, Italy.

**MØRK, Truls;** Norwegian cellist; b. 25 April 1961, Bergen; s. of John Mørk and Turid Otterbech; two s. one d. *Education:* studied under his father, with Frans Helmerson at Swedish Radio Music School, in Austria with Heinrich Schiff and in Moscow with Natalia Shakovskaya. *Career:* debut, BBC Promenade Concerts 1989; has since appeared with leading European, American and Australian orchestras, including the Berlin Philharmonic, New York Philharmonic, Philadelphia Symphony, Cincinnati Philharmonic, Rotterdam Philharmonic, London Philharmonic, Pittsburgh Symphony, City of Birmingham Symphony, Orchestre de Paris, NHK Symphony, Royal Concertgebouw and Cleveland, Los Angeles and Gewandhaus Symphony Orchestras; regular appearances at int. chamber music festivals; founder Int. Chamber Music Festival in Stavanger, Artistic Dir –2003. *Recordings include:* Schumann, Elgar and Saint-Saëns concertos, Tchaikovsky Rococo Variations, recitals of cello works by Grieg, Sibelius, Brahms, Rachmaninov and Myaskovksy, Dvořák and Shostakovich cello concertos, Haydn cello concertos with Norwegian Chamber Orchestra, Britten Cello Symphony and Elgar Cello Concerto with Sir Simon Rattle and the City of Birmingham Symphony Orchestra, Britten Cello Suites (Grammy Award 2002), Schumann Cello Concerto with Paavo Jarvi and Orchestre Philharmonique de Radio France 2005. *Honours:* prizewinner Moscow Tchaikovsky Competititon 1982, first prize Cassado Cello Competition, Florence 1983, W Naumburg Competition, New York 1986, UNESCO Prize European Radio-Union Competition, Bratislava 1983. *Current Management:* Harrison/Parrott Ltd, 12 Penzance Place, London, W11 4PA, England. *Telephone:* (20) 7229-9166. *Fax:* (20) 7221-5042. *Website:* www.harrisonparrott.com.

**MOROZ, Vladimir;** Singer (Baritone); b. 1974, Rechitsa, Ghornel District, Russia. *Education:* Graduated Minsk Academy of Music, 1999. *Career:* Debut: Byelourussian National Opera, 1997, as Eugene Onegin; Young Singers Academy of the Mariinsky Theatre, St Petersburg, from 1999; Repertoire includes Robert in Tchaikovsky's Iolanta, Rossini's Figaro, Enrico (Lucia di Lammermoor), Yeletzky in The Queen of Spades and Andrei Bolkonsky in War and Peace; Sang Andrei, and Mizgir in The Snow Maiden by Rimsky-Korsakov, with the Kirov Opera at Covent Garden, 2000. *Honours:* Prizewinner, International Lysienko Competition, 1997. *Address:* c/o Kirov Opera, Mariinsky Theatre, 1 Theatre Square, St Petersburg, Russia.

**MOROZOV, Alexander;** Singer (Bass); b. 1950, USSR. *Education:* Studied at the Leningrad Conservatory. *Career:* Joined the Kirov Opera, Leningrad, 1983 and has sung Don Basilio, Mephistopheles, Pimen, Boris Godunov and Surin in The Queen of Spades; Sang at Covent Garden 1987 with the Kirov, as Surin, Pimen and Boris; Tours to Zürich and France; Sang Zemfira's father in a concert performance of Rachmaninov's Aleko at the Santa Cecilia, Rome, 1989; Amsterdam 1989, as Pimen; Dolokhov in War and Peace for Seattle Opera, 1990; Scottish Opera 1990 as Padre Guardiano in La Forza del Destino; Covent Garden company as Basilio, and Fiesco in a new production of Simon Boccanegra conducted by Georg Solti, 1991; Sang in Gala celebrating 125th Anniversary of Feodor Chaliapin's birth in St Petersburg, 1998; Mussorgsky's Boris Godunov at the London Proms, 2002. *Recordings include:* Lord Rochefort in Anna Bolena, 1996. *Honours:* First Prize at competitions in Rio de Janeiro and Moscow, Tchaikovsky International. *Address:* Allied Artists, 42 Montpelier Square, London, SW7 1JZ, England.

**MOROZOV, Igor;** Singer (Baritone); b. 1948, Moscow, USSR. *Education:* Studied at the Moscow Conservatory. *Career:* First engagement at the Kirov Theatre Leningrad, then sang at the Bolshoi, Moscow, from 1976 as Eugene Onegin, Count Luna, Germont, Yeletzky, The Queen of Spades; Robert in Tchaikovsky's Iolanta; Sang in Shchedrin's Dead Souls at Boston, 1988; Guest engagements in Finland and Hungary as concert and opera atrist; British debut at Covent Garden, 1988; Season 2000–01 at the Deutsche Oper Berlin as Scarpia, Verdi's Miller and Renato, and Rochefort in Anna Bolena; Dubois in Tchaikovsky's Maid of Orleans and Kadoor in Si j'étais Roi at Wexford; Ferdinand in Prokofiev's Duenna at the Bolshoi, Moscow. *Address:* Allied Artists, 42 Montpelier Square, London SW7 1JZ, England.

**MOROZOV, Vladimir Mikhailovich;** Russian singer (bass); *Head of Vocal Training Department, Herzen State Pedagogical University;* b. 12 Feb. 1933, Leningrad; m.; one s. *Education:* Leningrad State Conservatory. *Career:* soloist with Kirov (now Mariinsky) Opera 1959–; Prof. and Head of Vocal Training Dept, Herzen State Pedagogical Univ. of Russia; mem. CPSU 1965–91. *Roles include:* Varlaam (Boris Godunov), Ivan the Terrible (The Women from Pskov), Grigory (Quiet Flows the Don), Peter the Great (Peter I), Dosifey (Khovanshchina). *Honours:* Glinka Prize 1974, USSR State Prize 1976, RSFSR People's Artist 1976, USSR People's Artist 1981. *Address:* Herzen State Pedagogical University of Russia, St Petersburg, 48 Moika Emb., St Petersburg 191186, Russia.

**MORRICONE, Ennio;** Italian film score composer; b. 10 Nov. 1928, Rome; s. of Mario Morricone and Libera Morricone; m. Maria Travia; two s. two d. *Education:* Acad. of Santa Cecilia, Rome. *Film scores:* Il Federale 1961, La Voglia matta 1962, Diciottenni al sole 1962, La Cuccagna 1962, Il Successo 1963, Le Monachine 1963, I Basilischi 1963, Duello nel Texas (as Dan Savio) 1963, La Scoperta dell'America 1964, I Motorizzati 1964, ...e la donna creò l'uomo 1964, I Maniaci 1964, Prima della rivoluzione 1964, I Due evasi di Sing Sing 1964, Per un pugno di dollari (as Leo Nichols) 1964, Le Pistole non discutono 1964, I Malamondo 1964, Thrilling 1965, Slalom 1965, Non son degno di te 1965, Menage all'italiana 1965, Idoli controluce 1965, La Battaglia di Algeri 1965, Una Pistola per Ringo 1965, Gli Amanti d'oltretomba 1965, Altissima pressione 1965, I Pugni in tasca 1965, Centomila dollari per Ringo 1965, Il Ritorno di Ringo 1965, Per qualche dollaro in più 1965, La Ragazza del bersagliere 1966, Per Firenze 1966, Navajo Joe (as Leo Nichols) 1966, Mi vedrai tornare 1966, Matchless 1966, I Lunghi giorni della vendetta 1966, Un Fiume di dollari 1966, Sette pistole per i MacGregor 1966, Agent 505 - Todesfalle Beirut 1966, Uccellacci e uccellini 1966, El Greco 1966, Un Uomo a metà 1966, Das Gewisse Etwas der Frauen 1966, La Resa dei conti 1966, Il Buono, il brutto, il cattivo 1966, Sette donne per i MacGregor 1967, Scusi, facciamo l'amore? 1967, Pedro Páramo 1967, Il Giardino delle delizie 1967, Dalle Ardenne all'inferno 1967, L'Avventuriero 1967, Le Streghe 1967, OK Connery 1967, I Crudeli (as Leo Nichols) 1967, Per pochi dollari ancora (theme) 1967, La Cina è vicina 1967, L'Harem 1967, La Ragazza e il generale 1967, Faccia a faccia 1967, Arabella 1967, Tepepa 1968, Il Mercenario 1968, Mangiala 1968, Italia vista dal cielo 1968, Grazie, zia 1968, Il Grande silenzio 1968, ...e per tetto un cielo di stelle 1968, Ecce Homo 1968, Diabolik 1968, Escalation 1968, Da uomo a uomo 1968, La Bataille de San Sebastian 1968, Comandamenti per un gangster 1968, Teorema 1968, Partner 1968, Roma come Chicago 1968, Gli Intoccabili 1968, C'era una volta il West 1968, Vergogna schifosi 1969, Senza sapere niente di lei 1969, Queimada 1969, Giotto 1969, La Donna invisibile 1969, Dio è con noi 1969, L'Assoluto naturale 1969, Fräulein Doktor 1969, Cuore di mamma 1969, L'Alibi 1969, Galileo 1969, Gentleman Jo... uccidi 1969, La Monaca di Monza 1969, Metti una sera a cena 1969, Un Bellissimo novembre 1969, Ruba al prossimo tuo 1969, Un Tranquillo posto di campagna 1969, I Marziani hanno dodici mani 1969, H2S 1969, Sai cosa faceva Stalin alle donne? 1969, Un Esercito di cinque uomini 1969, La Stagione dei sensi 1969, Una Breve stagione 1969, Le Clan des Siciliens 1969, Zenabel 1969, Uccidete il vitello grasso e arrostitelo 1970, Metello 1970, Giochi particolari 1970, La Califfa 1970, Two Mules for Sister Sara 1970, L'Uccello dalle piume di cristallo 1970, La Moglie più bella 1970, Indagine su un cittadino al di sopra di ogni sospetto 1970, Hornets' Nest 1970, Città violenta 1970, I Cannibali 1970, Quando le donne avevano la coda 1970, Le Foto proibite di una signora per bene 1970, Vamos a matar, compañeros 1970, Oceano 1971, Gli Occhi freddi della paura 1971, Incontro 1971, Forza 'G' 1971, La Classe operaia va in paradiso 1971, Tre nel mille 1971, Il Gatto a nove code 1971, Una Lucertola con la pelle di donna 1971, Veruschka 1971, Krasnaya palatka 1971, Il Decameron 1971, La Tarantola dal ventre nero 1971, Giornata nera per l'ariete 1971, Il Giorno del giudizio 1971, Sans mobile apparent 1971, Addio, fratello crudele 1971, Sacco e Vanzetti 1971, L'Istruttoria è chiusa: dimentichi 1971, Malastrana 1971, Giù la testa 1971, Maddalena 1971, Le Casse 1971, 4 mosche di velluto grigio 1971, ¡Viva la muerte... tua! 1971, La Violenza: Quinto potere 1972, Questa specie d'amore 1972, Quando la preda è l'uomo 1972, Perché? 1972, Il Maestro e Margherita 1972, Lui per lei 1972, Guttoso e il 'Marat morto' di David 1972, Fiorina la vacca 1972, Il Diavolo nel cervello 1972, Les Deux saisons de la vie 1972, D'amore si muore 1972, Crescete e moltiplicatevi 1972, La Cosa buffa 1972, Chi l'ha vista morire? 1972, Bianchi bandinelli e la Colonna Traiana 1972, Anche se volessi lavorare, che faccio? 1972, Mio caro assassino 1972, Le Tueur 1972, Cosa avete fatto a Solange? 1972, Bluebeard 1972, J. and S. - storia criminale del far west 1972, L'Attentat 1972, Sbatti il mostro in prima pagina 1972, Un Uomo da rispettare 1972, Il Ritorno di Clint il solitario 1972, Quando le donne persero la coda 1972, La Vita, a volte, è molto dura, vero Provvidenza? 1972, Vaarwel 1973, Sepolta viva 1973, Quando l'amore è sensualità 1973, Libera, amore mio... 1973, Che c'entriamo noi con la rivoluzione? 1973, Allonsanfan 1973, Le Serpent 1973, Le Moine 1973, La Proprietà non è più un furto 1973, Revolver 1973, Rappresaglia 1973, Ci risiamo, vero Provvidenza? 1973, Giordano Bruno 1973, Il Mio nome è Nessuno 1973, Il Giro del mondo degli innamorati di Peynet 1974, Fatti di gente per bene 1974, La Cugina 1974, L'Anticristo 1974, Spasmo 1974, Mussolini: Ultimo atto 1974, Sesso in confessionale 1974, Il Fiore delle mille e una notte 1974, Le Trio infernal 1974, Milano odia: la polizia non può sparare 1974, Le Secret 1974, Storie di vita e malavita 1975, Il Sorriso del grande tentatore 1975, Labbra di lurido blu 1975, Gente di rispetto 1975, Macchie solari 1975, L'Ultimo treno della notte 1975, Peur sur la ville 1975, Leonor 1975, Der Richter und sein Henker 1975, Per le antiche scale 1975, The Human Factor 1975, Una Vita venduta 1976, Todo modo 1976, San Babila ore 20 un delitto inutile 1976, René la canne 1976, Per amore 1976, Film 1976, La Donna della domenica 1976, Il Deserto dei Tartari 1976, Attenti al buffone 1976, L'Arriviste 1976, Ariel Limon 1976, L'Agnese va a morire 1976, Salò o le 120 giornate di Sodoma 1976, Der Dritte Grad 1976, Divina creatura 1976, 1900 1976, L'Eredità Ferramonti 1976, Stato interessante 1977, Il Prefetto di ferro 1977, Il Mostro 1977, The Dragon, the Odds 1977, Corleone 1977, Le Ricain 1977, Exorcist II: The Heretic 1977, Orca 1977, Holocaust 2000 1977, Autostop rosso sangue 1977, L'Immoralità 1978, Forza Italia! 1978, Il Gatto 1978, One, Two, Two: 122, rue de Provence 1978, Pedro Páramo 1978, Così come sei 1978, La Cage aux folles 1978, Ten to Survive 1979, Il Prato 1979, Il Ladrone 1979, Dedicato al mare Egeo 1979, Le

Buone notizie 1979, Il Giocattolo 1979, Viaggio con Anita 1979, L'Umanoide 1979, Bloodline 1979, La Luna 1979, I... comme Icare 1979, Uomini e no 1980, Si salvi chi vuole 1980, The Fantastic World of M.C. Escher 1980, Bugie bianche 1980, Windows 1980, Un Sacco bello 1980, Stark System 1980, Ogro 1980, Nouvelles rencontres 1980, The Island 1980, L'Oeil 1980, La Banquière 1980, La Cage aux folles II 1980, La Dame aux camélias 1980, Il Pianeta azzurro 1981, Bianco, rosso e Verdone 1981, Occhio alla penna 1981, La Disubbidienza 1981, So Fine 1981, Le Professionnel 1981, La Tragedia di un uomo ridicolo 1981, Porca vacca 1982, Nana 1982, Il Bandito dagli occhi azzurri 1982, Espion, lève-toi 1982, A Time to Die 1982, The Thing 1982, White Dog 1982, Blood Link 1982, Maja Plisetskaja 1982, Hundra 1983, Le Ruffian 1983, El Tesoro de las cuatro coronas 1983, Copkiller 1983, La Chiave 1983, Le Marginal 1983, Sahara 1983, Pelota 1984, Once Upon a Time in America 1984, Les Voleurs de la nuit 1984, Code Name: Wild Geese 1984, Red Sonja 1985, Kommando Leopard 1985, Il Pentito 1985, La Cage aux folles 3 - 'Elles' se marient 1985, La Venexiana 1986, La Gabbia 1986, The Mission 1986, Quartiere 1987, Mosca addio 1987, Il Giorno prima 1987, The Untouchables 1987, Gli Occhiali d'oro 1987, Il Cuore di mamma 1988, Frantic 1988, A Time of Destiny 1988, Rampage 1988, Nuovo cinema Paradiso 1989, Casualties of War 1989, Fat Man and Little Boy 1989, Tre colonne in cronaca 1990, Tempo di uccidere 1990, ¡Átame! 1990, Dimenticare Palermo 1990, Stanno tutti bene 1990, The Big Man 1990, Tracce di vita amorosa 1990, State of Grace 1990, Hamlet 1990, Mio caro dottor Gräsler 1991, Ilona und Kurti 1991, Money 1991, La Domenica specialmente 1991, Bugsy 1991, A Csalás gyönyöre 1992, Beyond Justice 1992, City of Joy 1992, La Villa del venerdì 1992, Love Potion No. 9 1992, Roma imago urbis 1993, In the Line of Fire 1993, Il Lungo silenzio 1993, La Scorta 1993, Jona che visse nella balena 1994, Una Pura formalità 1994, Wolf 1994, Love Affair 1994, Disclosure 1994, L'Uomo proiettile 1995, The Night and the Moment 1995, Pasolini, un delitto italiano 1995, L'Uomo delle stelle 1995, Ninfa plebea 1996, I Magi randagi 1996, Tashunga 1996, La Sindrome di Stendhal 1996, Vite strozzate 1996, Sostiene Pereira 1996, La Lupa 1996, Naissance des stéréoscopages 1997, Con rabbia e con amore 1997, Cartoni animati 1997, Marianna Ucria 1997, U Turn 1997, Lolita 1997, The Thing: Terror Takes Shape 1998, Bulworth 1998, La Leggenda del pianista sull'oceano 1998, Il Fantasma dell'opera 1998, Lucignolo 1999, In the Line of Fire: The Ultimate Sacrifice 2000, Canone inverso - making love 2000, Mission to Mars 2000, Vatel 2000, Sensitive New-Age Killer 2000, Malèna 2000, La Ragion pura 2001, Cowboys Don't Kiss in Public 2001, Un Altro mondo è possibile 2001, Aida degli alberi 2001, Threnody 2002, Senso '45 2002, Ripley's Game 2002, Il Diario di Matilde Manzoni 2002, L'Ultimo pistolero 2002, Arena Concerto 2003, Al cuore si comanda 2003, La Luz prodigiosa 2003, The Wages of Sin 2003, 72 metra 2004, Kill Bill: Vol. 2 2004, Guardiani delle nuvole 2004, Sorstalanság 2005, Karol, un uomo diventato papa 2005, Eridendo l'uccise 2005, Libertas 2005. *Television scores:* The Virginian (series theme) 1962, Lo Squarciagola 1966, 1943: un incontro 1969, La Sciantosa 1970, Nessuno deve sapere (series) 1971, Correva l'anno di grazia 1870 1971, L'Uomo e la magia 1972, L'Automobile 1972, Moses the Lawgiver 1975, Diamanti gotichi 1976, Noi lazzaroni (series) 1978, Le Mani sporche 1978, Invito allo sport (series) 1978, Orient-Express (series) 1979, The Life and Times of David Lloyd George (series) 1981, Marco Polo (series) 1982, The Scarlet and the Black 1983, Wer war Edgar Allan? 1984, Die Försterbuben 1984, Via Mala (series) 1985, C.A.T. Squad 1986, I Promessi sposi (series) 1988, Gli Indifferenti (series) 1988, Camillo Castiglioni oder die Moral der Haifische 1988, Gli Angeli del potere 1988, C.A.T. Squad: Python Wolf 1988, Il Principe del deserto (series) 1989, The Endless Game 1990, Voyage of Terror: The Achille Lauro Affair 1990, Cacciatori di navi 1990, Una Storia italiana 1992, Piazza di Spagna (series) 1993, Missus 1993, La Piovra series 1-10 1984-99, Genesi: La creazione e il diluvio 1994, Abraham 1994, Jacob 1994, Joseph 1995, Moses (title music) 1996, Il Barone (series) 1996, Samson and Delilah 1996, In fondo al cuore 1997, Nostromo (series) 1997, David (theme) 1997, Solomon 1997, Ultimo 1998, I Guardiani del cielo 1998, Il Quarto re 1998, La Casa bruciata 1998, Ultimo 2 - La sfida 1999, Nanà 1999, Esther 1999, Padre Pio - Tra cielo e terra 2000, Perlasca, un eroe italiano 2002, Un Difetto di famiglia 2002, Il Papa buono 2003, Musashi (series) 2003, Maria Goretti 2003, Charlie Chaplin - Les années suisses 2003, Il Cuore nel pozzo 2005. *Current Management:* Gorfaine/Schwartz Agency Inc, 13245 Riverside Drive, Suite 450, Sherman Oakes, CA 91423, USA.

**MORRIS, Colin;** Singer (Baritone); b. 17 Nov. 1952, Sheerness, Kent, England. *Education:* BA, 1974, PhD, 1978, Geography, Exeter University; ARCM Performers, 1977; Private Study with Derek Hammond-Stroud. *Career:* Debut: Edinburgh Festival with Kent Opera, 1979; Many concert and recital appearances in the United Kingdom and Netherlands; Lieder repertoire of over 300 songs; Toured the United Kingdom and USA with Pavilion Opera, London Opera Players, Regency Opera, D'Oyly Carte, Crystal Clear Opera; Castleward Opera; Central Festival Opera, Holland Park; Penang Festival; Overseas opera debut, as Bartolo (Rossini), Singapore, 1992; Main roles are Don Alfonso, Leporello, Magnifico, Bartolo, Pasquale, Dulcamara; Falstaff, Rigoletto, Sharpless, Scarpia, Tonio and Alberich; Operetta, especially 'patter' roles in Gilbert and Sullivan. *Recordings:* Several song recitals on BBC, Radio Kent. *Address:* 49 Winstanley Road, Sheerness, Kent ME12 2PW, England. *Telephone:* 1795 664694.

**MORRIS, Gareth (Charles Walter),** FRSA; British flautist; b. 13 May 1920, Clevedon, Somerset; m. 1st 1954; one d.; m. 2nd Patricia Mary Murray 1975; one s., two d. *Education:* Bristol Cathedral School and privately; Royal Acad. of Music, London. *Career:* Soloist; Prof., Royal Acad. of Music, 1945-85;

Principal Flautist, Philharmonia Orchestra, London, 1948-72; Fellow Royal Soc. of Arts, also Mem. of Council and Chair., Music Cttee; Gov. Royal Soc. of Musicians. *Recordings:* Numerous. *Publications:* Flute Technique, 1991; Numerous articles in journals. *Honours:* ARAM, 1945; FRAM, 1949;. *Address:* 4 West Mall, Clifton, Bristol, BS8 4BH, England (home). *Telephone:* (117) 9734966 (home).

**MORRIS, James Peppler;** American singer (bass-baritone); b. 10 Jan. 1947, s. of James Morris and Geraldine Peppler; m. 1st Joanne F. Vitali 1971; one d.; m. 2nd Susan Quittmeyer 1987; one s. one d. (twins). *Education:* Univ. of Maryland, Peabody Conservatory and Acad. of Vocal Arts. *Career:* debut at Metropolitan Opera, New York 1970; opera and concert appearances throughout USA, Canada, S. America, Europe, Japan and Australia. *Recordings include:* Wotan in the New Ring Cycles, The Flying Dutchman, operas by Wagner, Offenbach, Mozart, Verdi, Donizetti, Bellini. *Title roles include:* The Flying Dutchman, Don Giovanni, Le Nozze di Figaro, Macbeth, Boris Godunov, Faust, Billy Budd, Otello. *Address:* c/o Colbert Artists Management Inc., 111 West 57th Street, New York, NY 10019, USA.

**MORRIS, Joan (Clair);** Singer and Teacher; b. 10 Feb. 1943, Portland, Oregon, USA; m. William Bolcom, 28 Nov 1975. *Education:* Gonzaga University, 1963-65; Diploma, American Academy of Dramatic Arts, 1968. *Career:* Debut: Wigmore Hall, 1993; Performed at the Boston Pops, 1976; Polly Peachum in The Beggar's Opera, Guthrie Theatre, Minneapolis, 1979; Soloist, World Premiere of William Bolcom's Songs of Innocence and Experience, Stuttgart Opera, 1984 and at New York Premiere, 1987; Weill Recital Hall, Carnegie Hall, 1987; Soloist, world premiere of William Bolcom's 4th Symphony with the St Louis Symphony 1987; Played the Nurse in world premiere of William Bolcom's Casino Paradise, 1990; Alice Tully Hall, Lincoln Center, 1976, 1977, 1978, 1980, 1983, 1995; Ewart Hall, American University in Cairo, 1988; 20th Anniversary Concert with guest Max Morath at Hunter College, 1993; Church of Santo Spirito, Florence, 1989; Since 1981, Adjunct Associate Professor of Musical Theater at University of Michigan; Azazels, University of Michigan. *Compositions include:* Songs: Carol, 1981; Tears at the Happy Hour, 1983, both with William Bolcom. *Recordings include:* After The Ball: A Treasury of Turn-of-the-Century Popular Songs, 1974; Songs by Ira and George Gershwin, 1978; Blue Skies, 1985; Let's Do It: Bolcom and Morris Live at Aspen, 1989; Orchids in the Moonlight, with tenor Robert White, 1996; 20 albums recorded to date, including Songs of Rodgers and Hart, Jerome Kern and Leiber and Stoller. *Publications:* Contributor to the New Grove Dictionary of American Music. *Honours:* Grammy Nomination, After the Ball, 1975. *Current Management:* ICM Artists, 40 W 57th Street, New York, NY 10019, USA. *Address:* 3080 Whitmore Lake Road, Ann Arbor, MI 48105, USA.

**MORRIS, Robert (Daniel);** Composer, Music Theorist and Professor; b. 19 Oct. 1943, Cheltenham, England; m. Ellen Koskoff, 10 June 1979, 1 s., 2 d. *Education:* BM, with distinction, Eastman School of Music; MM 1966; DMA 1969; University of Michigan. *Career:* Instructor, University of Hawaii, 1968-69; Assistant Professor, 1969-75, Director, Yale Electronic Music Studio, 1973-78; Associate Professor, 1975-78; Chairman, Composition Department, 1974-78, Yale University; Associate Professor, 1977-80, Director, Electronic and Computer Music Studio, 1977-80, University of Pittsburgh; Associate Professor, 1980-85; Professor, 1986-, Eastman School of Music. *Compositions:* Continua for Orchestra, 1969; Thunders of Spring Over Distant Mountains, Electronic Music, 1973; In Different Voices for 5 Wind Ensembles, 1975-76; Plexus for Woodwinds, 1977; Passim, 1982; Echanges, piano and computer-generated tape, 1983; Cuts, wind ensemble, 1984; Concerto for piano and strings, 1994. *Recordings:* Phases for two-pianos and electronics; Motet On Doo-dah; Hamiltonian Cycle; Inter Alia; Karuna. *Publications:* Composition with Pitch-Classes: A Theory of Compositional Design, 1986. *Contributions:* Reviews and Articles in Journal of Music Theory, Perspectives of New Music; Musical Quarterly; JAMS; In Theory Only.

**MORRIS, Stephen;** Violinist; b. 1970, Bridlington, Yorkshire, England. *Education:* Studied with Yfrah Neaman in London and with Manoug Parikian and Maurice Hasson at the Royal Academy of Music. *Career:* Leader of the RAM symphony orchestra 1988; Further study with Howard Davis; Leader of the Pegasus and Thames Chamber Orchestra; As soloist plays Bruch, Bach, Mendelssohn and Lalo; 2nd violin of the Duke String Quartet from 1985; Performances in the Wigmore Hall, Purcel; Room, Conway Hall and throughout the United Kingdom; Tours to Germany, Italy, Austria and the Baltic States; South Bank series 1991, with Mozart's early quartets; Soundtrack from Ingmar Berman documentary and The Magic Lantern, Channel 4 1988; BBC Debut feature; Features for French television 1990-91, playing Mozart, Mendelssohn, Britten and Tippett; Brahms Clarinet Quintet for Dutch Radio with Janet Hilton; Live Music Now series with concerts for disadvantaged people; The Duke Quartet invites... at the Derngate, Northampton, 1991, with Duncan Prescott and Rohan O'Hara; Resident quartet of the Rydale Festival 1991; Residency at Trinity College, Oxford, tours of Scotland and Northern Ireland and concert at the Queen Elizabeth Hall 1991. *Recordings:* Quartets by Tippett, Shostakovich and Britten 3rd for Factory Classics. *Honours:* Awards at the RAM include the John Waterhouse Prize; London Orchestral Society Prize; Poulet Award; Inter-collegiate Quartet Prize. *Address:* c/o Ingrassia, Duke Quartet, Via San Zanobi 7, 1-50018 Scandicci (Fi), Italy.

**MORRIS, Wyn;** Conductor and Musical Director; b. 14 Feb. 1929, Wales; m. Ruth Marie McDowell 1962; one s. one d. *Education:* Royal Academy of Music; Mozarteum, Salzburg, Austria. *Career:* Apprentice conductor, Yorkshire Symphony Orchestra, 1950–51; Musical Director, 17th Training Regiment, Royal Artillery Band, 1951–53; Founder and conductor, Welsh Symphony Orchestra, 1954–57; Koussevitsky Memorial Prize, Boston Symphony Orchestra, 1957; Observer, on invitation George Szell, Cleveland Symphony Orchestra, 1957–60; Conductor, Ohio Bell Chorus, Cleveland Orpheus Choir, Cleveland Chamber Orchestra, 1958–60; Choir of Royal National Eisteddfod, Wales, 1960–62; London Debut, Royal Festival Hall with Royal Philharmonic Orchestra, 1963; Conductor to Royal Choral Society, 1968–70, Huddersfield Choral Society, 1969–74; Ceremony of Investiture for Prince Charles as Prince of Wales, 1969, Royal Choral Society tour of USA, 1969; Chief Conductor, Musical Director, Symphonica of London, Current: Specialist, conducting works of Mahler. *Recordings:* Des Knaben Wunderhorn, with Janet Baker and Geraint Evans; Das klagende Lied; Symphonies 1, 2, 5, 8; No. 10 in Deryck Cooke's final performing version. *Honours:* August Mann's Prize, 1950; Fellow, Royal Academy of Music, 1964; Mahler Memorial Medal, Bruckner and Mahler Society of America, 1968. *Address:* c/o Manygate Management, 1 Summerhouse Lane, Harmondsworth, Middlesex UB7 OAW, England.

**MORRISON, Bryce,** MA, MMus; British teacher, pianist, critic and lecturer; *Guest Professor, Royal Academy of Music;* b. 27 Nov. 1938, Leeds, Yorkshire. *Education:* Music Scholar, Kings School, Canterbury 1952; studied with Ronald Smith, Iso Elinson and Alexander Unisky. *Career:* has published interviews with most of the world's great pianists including Horowitz, Rubinstein and Clifford Curzon; Jury Mem. of over 40 int. piano competitions; Chair. First Terence Judd Int. Award 1982 and of the Scottish Int. Piano Competition 1998; his students have been int. prizewinners including first prizes at Santander, Pozzoli and finalist status at Leeds; has lectured and given Masterclasses world with TV appearances in the UK, USA, Canada and Australia; extensive broadcasts for BBC, ABC and CBC; also in Poland, USA, and New Zealand; Guest Prof. Royal Acad. of Music, Birmingham Conservatoire, Chetham's School of Music, Manchester; Visiting Prof. Texas Conservatory for Artists; Trustee John Ogdon Foundation 2002. *Publications:* published extensively in: The Times, The Times Literary Supplement, Observer, Telegraph, Independent, Gramophone and others; also in America and Australia; major contrib. to Phaidon Book of The Piano; two BBC Talks published by Oxford University Press; short biography of Liszt; written over 300 annotations for Decca, EMI, Sony, DG and others; personal adviser for testament Records for whom he has weitten perdonal tributes to Schnabel, Edwin Fisher, Solomon, Arrau and others. *Honours:* held the Corina Frada Pick Chair of Advanced Piano Studies, Ravinia Festival, Chicago 1988, Hon. ARAM 1995. *Address:* Flat 19, 11 Hinde Street, London, W1M 5AQ, England (home). *Telephone:* (20) 9735-1440 (also fax).

**MORTIER, Gérard;** Belgian music director; *Director-General, Paris Opéra;* b. 25 Nov. 1943, Ghent. *Education:* Univ. of Ghent. *Career:* engaged in journalism and communications 1966–67; Admin. Asst Flanders Festival 1968–72; Artistic Planner, Deutsche Oper am Rhein, Düsseldorf 1972–73; Asst Admin. Frankfurt Opera 1973–77; Dir of Artistic Production, Hamburg Staatsoper 1977–79; Tech. Programme Consultant, Théâtre Nat. de l'Opéra, Paris 1979–81; Dir-Gen. Belgian Nat. Opera, Brussels 1981–91; Dir Salzburg Music Festival 1992–2001; Fellow, Wissenschaftskolleg (Inst. for Advanced Study), Berlin 2001–02; Dir. Kultur Ruhr triennial arts festival 2002; Dir-Gen. Paris Opéra 2004–; mem. Acad. of Arts, Berlin. *Honours:* Dr hc (Univ. of Antwerp), (Univ. of Salzburg); Commdr, Ordre des Arts et des Lettres 2000, Chevalier, Légion d'honneur. *Address:* c/o Opéra National de Paris, 120 rue de Lyon, 75012 Paris, France (office). *Website:* www.opera-de-paris.fr (office).

**MORYL, Richard;** Composer and Conductor; b. 23 Feb. 1929, Newark, NJ, USA. *Education:* Studied at Montclair State College, New Jersey and Columbia University, MA 1959; Further study with Boris Blacher and Arthur Berger. *Career:* Teacher, 1960–72; Founder, New England Contemporary Music Ensemble, 1970; Director, Charles Ives Center for American Music, 1979. *Compositions:* Ballons for percussion, orchestra, radios and audience, 1971; Vols for piano, organ and orchestra, 1971; Chroma, 1972; Loops for large orchestra with any instruments, 1974; Strobe for large orchestra with any instruments, 1974; The untuning of the Skies, 1981; The Pond, flute and chamber orchestra, 1984; Instrumental music including Rainbows, I and II, 1982–83 and The Golden Phoenix for string quartet and percussion, 1984; Vocal: Flourescents for 2 choruses, 2 percussion and organ, 1970; Illuminations for soprano, 43 choruses and chamber orchestra, 1970; De morte cantoris for soprano, mezzo and ensemble, 1973; Das Lied for soprano and ensemble, 1975; Stabat Mater, 1982; Come, Sweet Death, chorus and piano, 1983; Mixed media works including Passio avium, 1974; Atlantis, 1976; Visiones mortis, 1977; Music of the Spheres, 1977; An Island on the Moon, 1978; A Sunflower for Maggie, 1979; Music for tape, electronics. *Address:* ASCAP, ASCAP Building, 1 Lincoln Plaza, NY 10023, USA.

**MOSCA, Silvia;** Singer (Soprano); b. 1958, Italy. *Education:* Studied in Naples. *Career:* Debut: Mantua Teatro Sociale as the Trovatore Leonara; Has sung at opera houses throughout Italy and appeared as Luisa Miller at the Metropolitan 1988; Leonora at Liège and Miami 1988–89; Sang Aida at Buenos Aires and the Savonlinna Festival, 1989; Elvira in Ernani at Rome and Venice, 1989–90. *Address:* c/o Teatro La Fenice, Campo S Fantin 1965, 30124, Venice, Italy.

**MOSCATO, Jacques;** Conductor and Clarinettist; b. 1945, France. *Career:* Debut: Municipal Orchestra as Clarinettist, 1955; Director, Public concert, Switzerland, 1962; In charge, Music Department, International University, City of Paris from 1968; Director, Charleville Mezières Conservatorium from 1969; Conductor, Concerts in West Germany, Belgium and France, 1971; Guest Conductor, Australian Broadcasting Commission, 1976, 1978; Conductor, Monte Carlo Symphony, the Salle Garnier of Monte Carlo, 1979–94; Guest Conductor, Istanbul Symphonic Orchestra, Symphony Orchestra, Pays Loire, France, 1984, 1989. *Compositions:* Music for film, Symphonic Interdite, 1983; A Music Ballet, Resonances, 1989. *Recordings:* Albums, Symphony No. 2, plus eleven Viennese Dances (Beethoven), 1977, Les Musiciens Monegasquesm, 1981. *Address:* Academie de Musique, Prince Rainier III de Monaco, 1 Boulevard Albert 1er, Monaco.

**MOSER, Edda;** German singer (soprano); b. 27 Oct. 1942, Berlin; d. of the late Hans-Joachim and of Dorothea Moser. *Education:* Conservatory of Berlin. *Career:* Has performed with numerous opera cos, including Vienna, Munich, Hamburg, Cologne and Metropolitan Opera, New York, USA; specializes in Mozart operas; own show on TV; title of Kammersängerin Wien conferred 1982; awarded Grand Prix du Disque three times. *Film:* Don Giovanni. *Publication:* Mehr als Worte (contrib). *Address:* Oper der Stadt Bonn, Am Boeselagerhof 1, 5300 Bonn 1, Germany.

**MOSER, Thomas;** Singer (Tenor); b. 27 May 1945, Richmond, Virginia, USA. *Education:* Richmond Professional Institute; Curtis Institute Philadelphia; California with Martial Singher, Gerard Souzay and Lotte Lehmann. *Career:* After success at the 1974 Metropolitan Auditions sang in Graz from 1975; Munich Opera, 1976, as Mozart's Belmonte; Vienna State Opera from 1977, as Mozart's Tamino, Ottavio, Titus and Idomeneo, Strauss's Flamand and Henry; Achilles in Iphigénie en Aulide, conducted by Charles Mackerras; New York City Opera 1979, as Titus; Salzburg Festival 1983, in La Finta Semplice; La Scala Milan, 1985, as Tamino; Rome Opera, 1986, as Achilles; Paris Opéra Comique, 1987 as Mozart's Idomeneo and Tito; Sang the Tenor in the premiere of Berio's Un Re in Ascolto, Salzburg, 1984; Vienna Staatsoper, 1987, as Achilles in Iphigénie en Aulide, Schubert's Fierrabras at the Theater an der Wien, 1988; Sang Florestan in Fidelio at La Scala and Salzburg, 1990; New production of Lucio Silla at Vienna, 1991, the Emperor in Die Frau ohne Schatten at Geneva, 1992; Season 1992–93, with Florestan at Zürich and the Emperor at Salzburg; Sang title role in Pfitzner's Palestrina at Covent Garden, 1997; As concert singer in Beethoven's Choral Symphony and Missa Solemnis, Britten's War Requiem, the Bach Passions, Schmidt's Das Buch mit Sieben Siegeln and Mozart's Requiem; Max in Der Freischütz with the Royal Opera at the Barbican, 1998; Sang Nielsen's David at Ludwigsbug (concert) 1999; Season 2000–01 as Strauss's Emperor at Barcelona and Florestan at the Teatre Real Madrid; Parsifal under Abbado at Edinburgh, 2002; Sang Strauss's Emperor at the Opéra Bastille, 2002. Conductors include Giulini, Colin Davis, Mehta, Leinsdorf, Leopold Hager and Horst Stein. *Recordings:* Roles in Stiffelio, Verdi; Mozart and Salieri, Rimsky-Korsakov; Zaide; La Finta Giardiniera and Don Giovanni, Mozart; Die Freunde von Salamanka, Schubert; Genoveva, Schumann; Oedipus Rex, Stravinsky; Handel's Utrecht Te Deum and Dvořák's Requiem. *Address:* c/o IMG Artists Paris, 54 Avenue Mareau, F–75008 Paris, France.

**MOSES, Geoffrey;** singer (bass); b. 24 Sept. 1952, Abercynon, Wales. *Education:* Emmanuelle College, Cambridge, Guildhall School of Music and with Otakar Kraus and Peter Harrison. *Career:* debut with Welsh National Opera, 1977, as Basilio in Il Barbiere di Siviglia; Other roles include Seneca, L'Incoronazione di Poppea, Sarastro and Padre Guardiani in La Forza del Destino; Covent Garden debut 1981, in Les Contes d'Hoffmann; Returned in a new production of Otello; Glyndebourne Festival debut 1984; Sang Fiesco in Simon Boccanegra 1986; Brussels Opera in Hoffmann and Boccanegra; Welsh National Opera in Peter Stein's production of Falstaff; Season 1990–91, with WNO in Figaro, Carmen and Falstaff, also on tour to Japan; Sang Professor Millar in the premiere of Friend of the People by David Horne, Glasgow 1999; Created Petrus in The Last Supper, by Birtwistle, Berlin Staatsoper 2000; Concert engagements include: La Damnation de Faust in Frankfurt and the Choral Symphony with the Scottish National Orchestra; Sang in Strauss's Die Liebe der Danaë for BBC Radio 3, conducted by Charles Mackerras. *Recordings:* Rigoletto. *Current Management:* The Old Brushworks, 56 Pickwick Road, Corsham, Wiltshire, England. *Telephone:* (1249) 716716. *Fax:* (1249) 716717. *E-mail:* cphillips@caroline-phillips.co.uk. *Website:* www .caroline-phillips.co.uk.

**MOSHINSKY, Elijah,** BA; British opera director; b. 8 Jan. 1946, s. of Abraham Moshinsky and Eva Moshinsky; m. Ruth Dyttman 1970; two s. *Education:* Melbourne Univ. and St Antony's Coll. Oxford. *Career:* apptd to Royal Opera House 1973, Assoc. Producer 1979–; work for Royal Opera includes original productions of Peter Grimes 1975, Lohengrin 1978, The Rake's Progress 1979, Un Ballo in Maschera 1980; Macbeth 1981, Samson et Dalila 1981, Tannhäuser 1984, Otello 1987, Die Entführung aus dem Serail 1987, Attila 1990, Simon Boccanegra 1991, Stiffelio 1993, Aida 1994, Otello 1994, The Makropoulos Case 1996, The Queen of Spades 1998; has also produced work for ENO, Australian Opera, Metropolitan Opera, New York, Holland Festival, Maggio Musicale, Florence etc. *Theatre productions include:* Troilus and Cressida (Nat. Theatre) 1976, The Force of Habit (Nat. Theatre) 1976, Three Sisters (Albery) 1987, Light Up the Sky (Globe) 1987, Ivanov (Strand) 1989, Much Ado About Nothing (Strand) 1989, Another Time (Wyndham's) 1989, Shadowlands (Queen's) 1989, Cyrano de Bergerac 1992,

Genghis Cohn 1993, Danton 1994; Dir Matador (Queen's) 1991, Becket (Haymarket) 1991, Reflected Glory (Vaudeville) 1992, Richard III 1998, The Female Odd Couple (Apollo) 2001; productions for BBC TV of works by Shakespeare, Ibsen and Sheridan. *Address:* 28 Kidbrooke Grove, London, SE3 0LG, England. *Telephone:* (20) 8858-4179.

**MOSLEY, George;** singer (baritone); b. 1960, England. *Education:* Studied with Laura Sarti at the Guildhall School, at the Academia Chigiana in Siena, the Munich Hochschule für Musik and the National Opera Studio, London. *Career:* Performed in many operas including: Dandini in La Cenerentola, 1987, and Onegin in Tchaikovsky's Eugene Onegin, 1989, both for Opera 80; Orlofsky in Strauss's Die Fledermaus, Scottish Opera, 1990; Marco in Puccini's Gianni Schicchi, 1990, The Sportsman in Delius's Fennimore and Gerda, 1990 and the Duke of Albany in Reimann's Lear, 1991, all for the English National Opera; Patroclus in King Priam, Opera North, 1991; Malatesta in Don Pasquale and Guglielmo in Così fan tutte, 1991 and Dandini in La Cenerentola in 1992, all for Teatro Verdi, Pisa, Italy; Schaunard in La Bohème for Scottish opera, 1993; Ottone in Incoronazione di Poppea and Count in Le nozze di Figaro, both for Teatro Verdi, Pisa, Italy, 1993; Father in Baa Baa Black Sheep for Opera North and BBC television, 1993; Count in Le nozze di Figaro for Concert Hall, Athens, 1993; Papageno in The Magic Flute for Scottish Opera, 1994; Sang Berardo in Riccardo Primo at the 1996 Handel Festival at Göttingen; Schaunard in La Bohème at Hong Kong, 1998; Season 2000–01 with Albert in Werther at Peking, Bellini's Rodolfo in Athens and Thomas' Hamlet at the Teatro Regio, Turin; Josef K in Il Processo for Reggio Emilia and La Piccola Scala, Milan, 2002; Sharpless in Butterfly, Hong Kong, 2002; Don Pedro in Maria Padilla, Buxton Festival, 2003. *Recordings include:* Schumann's Dichterliebe and Liederkreis Op 39; Aeneas in Dido and Aeneas conducted by John Eliot Gardiner; Tavener's Eternity's Sunrise, 2000. *Honours:* First Prize, International Mozart Competition, Salzburg, 1998. *Current Management:* Robert Gilder & Co., Enterprise House, 59–65 Upper Ground, London, SE1 9PQ, England. *Telephone:* (20) 7928-9008. *Fax:* (20) 7928-9755. *E-mail:* rgilder@robert-gilder.com.

**MOSUC, Elena;** Singer (Soprano); b. 18 Jan. 1964, Iasi, Romania. *Education:* Studied at the George Enescu Conservatory, Bucharest. *Career:* Debut: Tasi Opera 1990, as Mozart's Queen of Night; Further appearances as Lucia di Lammermoor, Gilda and Violetta; Concerts with the Moldau Philharmonic and in Mozart masses at Bucharest; Theater am Gärtnerplatz Munich, Vienna Staatsoper and Deutsche am Rhein 1990, as the Queen of Night; Zürich Opera from 1991, as Lucia and Donna Anna; Season 2000–01 as Luisa Miller and Micaela for Zürich Opera; Offenbach's Olympia in Vienna, Donna Anna for Bonn Opera, Gilda in Warsaw, Violetta for Finnish National Opera and Constanze in Rome. *Address:* Zürich Opera, Falkenstrasse 1, 8008 Zürich, Switzerland.

**MOTHERWAY, Fiona;** Singer (Soprano); b. 1967, Western Australia. *Education:* Studied in Australia and at the Royal Academy of Music (graduated 1994). *Career:* Performances with British Youth Opera and elsewhere as Fiordiligi; Cambridge Handel Opera Group as Melissa in Amadigi di Gaula; other Handel roles include Semele, Atalanta (Xerxes), Cleopatra and Ginevra (Ariodante); Also sings Mozart's Countess, Susanna and Pamina, Musetta, Gilda and Purcell's Dido; Season 1996–97 with Olympia in Contes d'Hoffman for Stowe Opera and Naiade in Ariadne for Castleward Opera; Concerts include Strauss Four Last Songs, Haydn's Creation and Nelson Mass, Messiah, Bach B minor Mass, Mozart's C minor Mass and Requiem; Mahler's 4th Symphony under Colin Davis; Concert tour of Australia, 1996–97. *Address:* C&M Craig Services Ltd, 3 Kersley Street, London SW11 4 PR, England.

**MOTT, Louise;** Singer (mezzo-soprano); b. 1971, Barnet, Hertfordshire, England; Graduated 1996, Royal College of Music Opera Department; also studied at Guildhall School of Music and Drama and National Opera Studio, London. *Career:* Opera roles include Bradamante in Alcina, ENO; Annio in La Clemenza di Tito, Welsh Nat. Opera; Edith in Alfred, Agrippina, Ariodante, Sesto in Giulio Cesare, Orlando, Rosmira in Partenope, Serse and Dido in Dido and Aeneas, for The Early Opera Co.; Marlinchen in Roderick Watkins' The Juniper Tree at Munich Bienale; Marguerite in Deirdre Gribbin's Hey Persephone! for Almeida Opera; Emerald in Robin Holloway's Boys and Girls Come Out to Play, and Blind Mary in The Martyrdom of St Magnus, for The Opera Group; Wife/Sphinx/Doreen in Mark Anthony Turnage's Greek, with the London Sinfonietta; Concerts include Mozart's Requiem at the Albert Hall, Messiah at St John's Smith Square, Elgar's Dream of Gerontius and The Music Makers, Dvořák Requiem, Elijah, and the Stabat Maters of Haydn and Rossini; Wigmore Hall debut 1996, with the Young Songmakers' Almanac series; Mozart's Requiem at Bath Abbey, 1997; 2003–04 season: Fidalma in The Secret Marriage and Annina in Der Rosenkavalier for Opera North; Ariodante for English Touring Opera; Madame Larina in Eugene Onegin for Scottish Opera on Tour; Vivaldi Gloria with the Bach Choir, Royal Festival Hall and Royal Albert Hall; Messiah at The Lighthouse, Poole with Bournemouth Symphony Orchestra; UK premiere of Caldara's Amarilli vezzosa with the Orchestra of St John's Smith Square; performances of Mahler Kindertotenlieder and Mussorgsky Nursery Songs with Hebrides Ensemble. *Honours:* Lies Askonas Singing Prize, Peter Pears Exhibition and Keith Falkner Prize for Bach and Handel, at RCM. *Current Management:* c/o Helen Sykes Artists Management, 100 Felsham Road, Putney, London, SW15 1DQ, England.

**MOULDS, Christopher;** Conductor and Keyboard Player; b. 1967, Halifax, England. *Education:* Studied at City University, the Guildhall School and Royal College of Music. *Career:* Conducted Figaro and The Rake's Progress at the RCM; Member of Music Staff, English National Opera, 1991–95, working with productions of Billy Rudd, Carmen, Wozzeck, Orfeo, Lohengrin and Street Scene; Harpsichord continuo for ENO's Xerxes and Ariodante; Chorus Master at Glyndebourne Festival from 1995, conducting Figaro 1997; Further engagements with British Youth Opera, Opera Company Tunbridge Wells (Barber and Figaro), European Community Youth Orchestra and London Sinfonietta (as orchestral keyboard player); Conducted The Magic Flute for ENO, 1996, 1997–98. *Address:* Flat 549, Manhattan Buildings, Fairfield Road, London E3 2UL, England.

**MOULSON, John;** Singer, (Tenor); b. 25 July 1928, Kansas City, Missouri, USA. *Education:* Studied in Atlanta. *Career:* Debut: Berlin Komische Oper 1961 as Cavaradossi; Sang at the Komische Oper until 1982 as Alfredo, Traviata, Hoffmann, the Steersman in Fliegende Holländer, 1969–72, and as Lensky, Gabriele Adorno and Oedipus Rex; Sang at Boston 1988, in the US premiere of Dead Souls by Shchedrin; Further guest engagements in Germany, England, Italy, Poland, Russia and the USA.

**MOULT, Daniel Adam Ashbrook,** MA, FRCO; British organist; b. 13 Dec. 1973, Manchester; m. Melanie Evans 2004. *Education:* Manchester Grammar School, St John's Coll., Oxford, Sweelinck Conservatorium, Amsterdam. *Career:* organist and Asst Dir of Music, Coventry Cathedral 1995–2002; visiting organ tutor, Birmingham Conservatoire 2003–; organ tutor on Oundle, Salisbury and Amsterdam courses; organ animateur, Bridgewater Hall, Manchester; tutor, Royal Coll. of Music Junior Dept, St Giles Int. Organ School, London; concert organist throughout UK and Europe (with repertoire from 14th century to present day); mem. Editorial Panel Organists' Review; mem. Royal Coll. of Organists, Incorporated Soc. of Musicians, Incorporated Asscn of Organists, British Inst. of Organ Studies. *Recordings:* various recordings for BBC TV and radio 2, 3 and 4, and Dutch radio; organist for four albums from Coventry Cathedral; producer for two albums. *Publications:* contrib. to Choir and Organ, Organists Review, British Institute of Organ Studies Journal. *Honours:* Univ. of Oxford John Betts Organ Scholarship 1994, Durrant, Turpin and Dixon prizes (FRCO) 1993. *Address:* 34 Wilkie House, Cureton Street, London SW1P 4EH, England (office). *Telephone:* (20) 7233-6682 (home). *E-mail:* music@dmoult.freeserve.co.uk (home).

**MOUND, Vernon;** Opera Director; b. 1954, England. *Education:* Studied at London University. *Career:* Has worked with the Royal Opera, the Scottish Ballet, the Swan Theatre, Opera North and the Black Theatre of Prague as Stage Manager; Administrator; Company Manager; Assistant Director; Staff producer at Opera North 1983–88, assisting on new productions and directing revivals; Workshops for children and adults, including community piece Quest of the Hidden Moon; Directed small-scale touring version of Carmen; The Gondoliers for New Sadler's Wells Opera, 1988; Directed the Opera Informal and the Sondheim Workshop at the Royal College of Music, 1989–91; Directed Handel's Ariodante for the Birmingham Conservatoire, 1990, and The Marriage Contract and Le Pauvre Matelot for Morley Opera; Productions of Amahl and the Night Visitors at the Barbican Centre and Alice, the Musical at St Martin-in-the-Fields; La Finta Giardiniera for the Opera Hogskolan in Stockholm, Mar 1991, and Pedrotti's Tutti in Maschera at the Britten Theatre; La Fille du Régiment, 1992; Associate Director Carmen Jones at The Old Vic.

**MOUNTAIN, Peter;** Violinist; b. 3 Oct. 1923, Shipley, Yorkshire, England; 1 s. 2 d. *Education:* Royal Academy of Music, London. *Career:* Debut: Wigmore Hall, London, 1942; Leader, Soloist, Symphony Orchestra, Tours of Europe and Far East; Member, Boyd Neel Orchestra, Philharmonia Orchestra; Leader, Royal Liverpool Philharmonic Orchestra, 1955–66; Concertmaster, BBC Training Orchestra, 1968–75; Head of Strings, Royal Scottish Academy of Music and Drama, 1975–90; Soloist, Guest Leader, Many British Orchestras; Coach, Youth Orchestras; Adjudicator and Examiner; Committee, Scottish Arts Council; Chairman, Scottish Society of Composers; Incorporated Society of Musicians; Musicians' Union, European String Teachers Association. *Honours:* Fellow, Royal Academy of Music, London, 1963; Fellow, Royal Scottish Academy of Music and Drama, 1988; Honorary LLD, University of Bradford, 1995. *Address:* 93 Park Road, Bingley, West Yorkshire BD 16 4BY, England. *Telephone:* 01274 568762. *Fax:* 01274 220884. *E-mail:* pwmount@blueyonder.co.uk.

**MÖWES, Thomas;** Singer (Baritone); b. 7 Sept. 1951, Halle, Germany. *Education:* Studied at the Weimar Hochschule. *Career:* Sang as Bass-Baritone at the Magdeburg Opera from 1977, and Baritone roles at Halle from 1988, Leipzig and Dresden from 1990; Roles have included Busoni's Doktor Faust, Nekrotzar in Le Grand Macabre and Orestes in Elektra; Guest engagements as Basle as Verdi's Posa, and at Frankfurt as Faninal in Der Rosenkavalier; Other roles include Handel's Polyphemus, Don Alfonso, Ottokar in Der Freischütz, Luna, Nabucco, Rigoletto, Wolfram and Escamillo; Season 2000–01 as Kurwenal for Nederlandse Reisopera, Strauss's Faninal at Frankfurt and Reimann's Lear for Essen Opera; Many concert appearances. *Address:* Frankfurt Opera, Frankfurt am Main, Germany.

**MOYER, Frederick;** Pianist; b. 1957, . *Education:* Curtis Institute of Music; BMus, Indiana University. *Career:* Debut: New York, 1982; Performed in nearly all the states of USA; Frequent tours of Europe, Asia and South America; Solo Appearances with Orchestras include: Philadelphia, Houston, Milwaukee, Boston, Cleveland, Baltimore, Minnesota, St Louis, Dallas,

Indianapolis, Pittsburgh, Utrecht, London, Rio di Janeiro, Montevideo, Singapore, Hong Kong, Tokyo and the major orchestras of Australia; Participant in numerous Music Festivals. *Recordings:* 18 commercial recordings for major labels. *Address:* c/o Betsy M Green Associates, Artists Management, 36 Hampshire Road, Wayland, MA 01778, USA.

**MOYLAN, William (David);** Professor, Composer and Recording Producer; b. 23 April 1956, Virginia, Minnesota, USA; m. Vicki Lee Peterlin, 18 Dec 1976. *Education:* BMus, Composition, Peabody Conservatory, Johns Hopkins University, 1979; MMus, Composition, University of Toronto, Canada, 1980; Doctor of Arts in Theory and Composition, Ball State University, USA, 1983. *Career:* Chairperson, Department of Music, University of Massachusetts, Lowell. *Compositions:* Published works include: On Time–On Age, for soprano, flute, trumpet, piano and four-channel tape, 1978; Concerto for Bass Trombone and Orchestra, 1979; Brass Quintet, for brass quintet and tape, 1979; Two Movements for String Orchestra, 1980; Duo for Flute and Tape, 1980; Seven Soliloquies, for trumpet, 1981; Metamorphic Variations, for clarinet, 1983; The Now, for high voice, horn and piano; Trio for Trombones, for alto, tenor and bass trombones, 1984; Three Interplays for Trumpet Duo, 1984; Wind Quintet No. 2, 1985; Stilled Moments for solo violin, 1988; Evocations for Guitar, 1988; La Liberté, for soprano and piano, 1989; Eroica, a Piano Sonata, 1989; Two Suspended Images, for wind controller, 1990; Ask Your Mama, 1990; The Dream Deferred, for two-channel tape, 1990; Mother Earth and Her Whales, 1993; The Stolen Child, 1995; For a Sleeping Child, 1996. *Publications:* The Art of Recording: The Creative Resources of Music Production and Audio, 1992. *Address:* Department of Music, University of Massachusetts at Lowell, 35 Wilder Street, Suite 3, Lowell, MA 01854, USA.

**MOYLE, Richard Michael,** MA, PhD; Ethnomusicologist; b. 23 Aug. 1944, Paeroa, New Zealand; m. Linden Averil Evelyn Duncan, 1 s., 2 d. *Education:* Trinity Coll., London, Univ. of Auckland. *Career:* Visiting Lecturer in Anthropology, Indiana University, USA, 1971–72; Assistant Professor in Music, University of Hawaii, 1972–73; Research Fellow, Ethnomusicology, 1974–77, Research Grantee, 1977–82, Australian Institute of Aboriginal Studies; Senior Research Fellow, Faculty of Arts, University of Auckland, New Zealand, 1983–86; Associate Professor of Ethnomusicology and Director of Archive of Maori and Pacific Music, University of Auckland, 1986–. *Recordings:* The Music of Samoa; Traditional Music of Tonga; Compiler, Tonga Today. *Publications:* Fagogo: Fables from Samoa, 1979; Songs of the Pintupi, 1981; Alyawarra Music, 1985; Tongan Music, 1987; Traditional Samoan Music, 1988; Sounds of Oceania, 1989; Polynesian Song and Dance, 1991; Fananga: Fables from Tonga in Tongan and English, Vol. I, 1996, Vol. II, 1998; Balgo: The Musical Life of an Aboriginal Community, 1997. *Contributions:* numerous professional journals. *Address:* Department of Anthropology, University of Auckland, Private Bag 92019, Auckland, New Zealand.

**MOYSEOWICZ, Gabriela (Maria);** Composer, Pianist and Choir Director; b. 4 May 1944, Lwow, Poland. *Education:* Lyceum of Music, Kraków, Poland, 1962; Academies of Music, Kraków and Katowice, Poland; MA, 1967. *Career:* Debut: Playing own piano concerto, Kraków, 1957; Piano recitals; Public performances of own compositions throughout Poland; Radio appearances, discussions and interviews. *Compositions:* Over 60 works include: Media vita, for 2 violins, cello, soprano and bass recitativ; 9 Moments Musicaux, for piano and strings; Rhapsody No. 1 for piano; Marche Funébre, for cello and piano; Deux Caprices, for violin solo; Ave Maria, for 2 mixed choirs a capella; Sonata No. 1, for cello and piano; Two Canzonas, for viola de gamba solo; Piano Sonata numbers 3 to 8 including the 6th Noumenon and 8th Concatenatio; Sonata Polska, for violin and piano; Alleuja for choir; Credo for 4 voice choir, 1991; Trio for piano, violin and violoncello, 1992, 1993; Discours, ave Mdme H Steingroever, for flute and piano, 1993; Passacaglia for violin, 1994; Shadow symphony for large orchestra; Violin Sonata No. 2; Cello Sonata No. 2; Norwidiana for piano; Churchmusic: Media Vita, Dies irae, Ave Maria, Pater noster, Kyrie, Alleluja, Amen Credo; Memento Mori I and II; Stabat Mater. *Recordings:* Piano recitals and chamber music on German broadcasting. *Address:* Stallupöner Allee 37, 14055 Berlin, Germany.

**MOZES, Robert;** Violist; b. 1950, Romania. *Education:* Studied at the Cluj Academy of Music and the Tel-Aviv Rubin Music Academy. *Career:* Member of and solo appearances with the Israel Philharmonic; Chamber music concerts in Israel, the USA, Canada and Japan; Co-Founder, Jerusalem String Trio, 1977, performing in Israel and in Europe from 1981; Repertoire includes string trios by Beethoven, Dohnányi, Mozart, Reger, Schubert and Taneyev; Piano Quartets by Beethoven, Brahms, Dvořák, Mozart and Schumann; Concerts with Radu Lupu and Daniel Adni. *Recordings:* Albums for Meridian, Channel Classics Studio, Holland and CDI, Israel. *Address:* c/o Ariën Artists, Jerusalem Trio, de Boeystraat 6, B–2018 Antwerp, Belgium.

**MOZHAYEV, Fyodor;** Singer (Baritone); b. 1958, Voroshilovgrad, Ukraine. *Education:* Studied at the Kharkov Conservatoire. *Career:* Sang first at the Moldavian State Opera and at the Perm Opera 1982–93; Member of the Bolshoi Opera from 1994, with Mozart's Figaro, 1995; Guest engagements with the Kirov Opera, Kharkov Opera and in Kiev; Has also sung widely in France and in Poland, Budapest and Malta; Other roles include Verdi's Iago, Renato, Luna and Germont, Scarpia, Ruprecht in The Fiery Angel, Lionel in The Maid of Orleans, Escamillo and Rubinstein's Demon; Sang Napoleon in War and Peace at La Scala and Donner in Das Rheingold at St Petersburg, 2000. *Honours:* Prizewinner at 1979 Riga Song Competition. *Address:* Sonata Ltd, 11 North Park Street, Glasgow G20 7AA, Scotland.

**MRACEK, Jaroslav (John Stephen),** BMus, MA, PhD; academic; *Professor of Music and Musicology Emeritus, San Diego State University;* b. 5 June 1928, Montreal, Canada; m. 1963; two s. *Education:* Royal Conservatory of Music, Toronto, University of Toronto, Indiana University; harpsichord with Willi Apel, John R. White, Paul Nettl, Walter Kaufmann, Bernard Heiden, Marie Zorn; piano with Alberto Guerrero. *Career:* taught instrumental, vocal music English and History at Lisgar Collegiate Institute, Ottawa, Canada, 1953–59; Lecturer: University of Illinois, Urbana 1964–65; Assistant Prof., Associate Prof., Prof., San Diego State University, 1965–91; General Director, the Smetana Centennial, International Conference and Festival of Czechoslovak Music, San Diego State University, 1987; Conducted at Canadian Music Festival, San Diego State University, 1987. *Publications:* Seventeenth-Century Instrumental Dance Music, 1976; 5 articles, New Grove Dictionary of Music and Musicians, 1980; Papers published in proceedings: International Musicological Congress-Bach, Handel, Schütz-Stuttgart, 1985; Musica Antiqua Congress, Bydgoszcz, 1985; Rudolf Firkusny at 75, Musical America, 1987; Smetana Centennial, Musical America, 1985. *Honours:* Rudolf Firkusny Medal 1992. *Address:* 5307 W Falls View Drive, San Diego, CA 92115, USA.

**MUCZYNSKI, Robert;** Composer and Professor of Music; b. 19 March 1929, Chicago, Illinois, USA. *Education:* BM, 1950, MM, 1952, DePaul University, Chicago; Academy of Music, Nice, France, 1961. *Career:* Visiting Lecturer, DePaul University, Chicago, summers 1954–56; Head of Piano Department, Loras College, Dubuque, Iowa, 1956–58; Visiting Lecturer, Roosevelt University, Chicago, 1964–65; Professor, Head of Composition, University of Arizona, Tucson, 1965–87; Professor Emeritus, 1988–. *Compositions:* Over 40 published works including: Concerto for piano and orchestra; First Symphony; Suite for orchestra; Concerto for alto saxophone and chamber orchestra; 3 Piano Sonatas; 3 piano trios; String trio; Sonatas for cello, for alto saxophone, for flute and piano; Time pieces, for clarinet, piano; Scores for 9 documentary films; Commission: Dream Cycle, for solo piano, 1983; Quintet for winds, 1985; Third Piano Trio, 1986–87; Moments, for flute and piano; Desperate Measures (Paginini Variations for piano). *Recordings:* In release: Compact Disc recordings of Concerto No. 1 for piano and orchestra; A Serenade for Summer; The Three Piano Trios; Trio for violin, viola, cello; Alto Saxophone Concerto; Sonata for flute and piano; Time Pieces for clarinet and piano; Sonata for cello and piano; Symphonic Dialogues for orchestra; Sonata for alto saxophone and piano; Fantasy Trio for clarinet, cello and piano; Complete works for flute. *Honours:* Nominated for Pulizer Prize in Music, 1982. *Address:* 2760 N Wentworth, Tucson, AZ 85749, USA.

**MUFF, Alfred;** Singer (Bass-Baritone); b. 31 May 1949, Lucerne, Switzerland. *Education:* Studied with Werner Ernst in Lucerne, Elisabeth Grümmer and Irmgard Hartmann-Dressler in Berlin. *Career:* Debut: Don Ferrando in Fidelio, Lucerne, 1974; Member of the opera companies in Lucerne, Linz, Mannheim and since 1986 Zürich; Opera roles include, Philippo II and Grand Inquisitor, Don Carlo; Boris Godunov; Falstaff; Der fliegende Holländer; Barak in Die Frau ohne Schatten; Hans Sachs in Die Meistersinger von Nuernberg; King Marke and Kurwenal in Tristan und Isolde; Appeared as Wotan and Wanderer in Ring des Nibelungen; King Heinrich in Lohengrin; Jochanaan in Salome; Orestes in Elektra; Musiklehrer in Ariadne auf Naxos; Ochs in Der Rosenkavalier; Morosus in Die scweigsame Frau; Waldner in Arabella; Osmin in Die Entführungl; Albert in Werther; Kezal in Die verkaufte Braut; Dr Schön in Lulu und Dokter in Wozzeck; Pizarro in Fidelio and Scarpia in Tosca at the Opernhaus Zürich, since 1986; Appearances also include: Barak at Milan's La Scala, Munich Festival; Title part of Der fliegende Holländer and Landgraf, Tannhäuser in Barcelona's Teatro del Liceu, Bruckner Festival, Linz, and at the Deutsche Oper Berlin and for a recording; Philip II in the original (French) version of Don Carlo at the Paris Opéra, in the Italian version at the Théâtre de la Monnaie in Brussels and at the Munich State Opera; Stravinsky's Oedipus Rex under Erich Leinsdorf in Geneva; Beethoven's Ninth Symphony at Geneva, Vienna and Basel; Jochanaan, Salome at the Vienna State Opera, at the Semper Oper in Dresden, in Barcelona and at the Festival of Taormina (under Giuseppe Sinopoli); Dvořák's Te Deum, in Vienna and at the Prague Spring Festival; Beethoven's Missa Solemnis on a tour of Switzerland, in Turin, Cologne and Vienna; Mahler's Eighth Symphony in Bonn; Schoenberg's Gurrelieder in Barcelona and Torino; Schnittke's Faust Kantate under Claudio Abbado in Vienna; Haydn's Paukenmesse with the Israel Philharmonic Orchestra under Zubin Mehta; Wotan, Die Walküre at the Munich Opera Festival, at the Vienna State Opera and in a new production at the Cologne Opera; Gurnemanz in Parsifal at the Brucknerfest in Linz; Wanderer in a new production of Siegfried and Wotan in a revival of Rheingold at the Hamburg State Opera; Die Schöpfung under Wolfgang Sawallisch for a television concert and under Nikolaus Harnoncourt for a radio concert; Pizarro, Fidelio under Peter Schneider at the RAI Torino; Barak in a new production of Die Frau ohne Schatten and Morosus in Die schweigsame Frau at the Zürich Opera; Opera roles in the 2003/04 season: Uraufführung L'Upupa by Hans Wwerner Nenze, Salzburger Festspiele; Musiklehrer, Ariadne; Grand Inquisitore; Landgraf; Osmin; Kezal (tschechisch); and Baron Ochs von Lerchenau at Zürich; under Wolfgang Sawallisch; Die Zauberflöte under Armin Jordan; Der fliegende Holländer under Pinchas Steinberg; Die Walküre under Christoph von Dohnanyi, Adorno in Schreker's Die Gezeichneten; Paul Dessau, Hagadah, Lulu Dr Schön for Television under Franz Welser Möst. *Recordings include:* First complete version of Die Frau ohne Schatten under Wolfgang Sawallisch; Die Zauberflöte under Armin Jordan; Der fliegende Holländer under Pinchas Steinberg; Die Walküre under

Christoph von Dohnányi; Adorno in Schreker's Die Gezeichneten; Paul Dessau, Hagadah. *Honours:* Kunstpreis of the City of Lucerne. *Address:* c/o Opernhaus Zürich, Falkenstrasse 1, 8008 Zürich, Switzerland.

**MUKERIA, Shalva;** singer (tenor); b. 1965, Georgia, Russia. *Education:* Graduated Odessa Conservatoire, 1991. *Career:* Appearances from 1994 with Odessa Opera as Nemorino, Alfredo, Edgardo, Rodolfo and Werther; From 1996 sang Cassio in Otello as Las Palmas, and Rodolfo for Besançon Opera; Rodolfo and Alfredo on tour in Britain; Sang Bellini's Elvino at Florence, 2000; Season 2000–2001 with Millennium Gala in Dusseldorf, Alfredo for the Royal Opera Copenhagen and the Verdi Requiem in Helsinki; Other concerts include Rossini's Stabat Mater. *Honours:* winner, Song Competitions at Prague and Tbilisi. *Current Management:* Athole Still International Management, Foresters Hall, 25–27 Westow Street, London, SE19 3RY, England. *Telephone:* (20) 8771-5271. *Fax:* (20) 8768-6600. *E-mail:* enquiries@atholestill.co.uk. *Website:* www.atholestill.com.

**MULA, Inva;** Singer (Soprano); b. 1967, Albania. *Career:* Sang in concert with Placido Domingo at Brussels, Munich and Olso, 1994; Appearances at the Opéra Bastille as Frasquita in Carmen and as Donizetti's Adina and Norina at Los Angeles (1995); Season 1995 as Offenbach's Antonia and Lisette in Puccini's La Rondine at Bonn; Dirce in Cherubini's Médée at Compiègne, 1996; Sang Gilda in Rigoletto at the Verona Arena, 2001. *Honours:* Winner, Georg Enescu Competition, Bucharest, 1991; Grand Prix Madama Butterfly, Barcelona, 1992; Prizewinner, Concours International de Voix d'Opéra Placido Domingo, Paris, 1993. *Address:* c/o Arena di Verona (Festival di Opera), Piazza Bra 28, 37121 Verona, Italy.

**MULDOWNEY, Dominic John,** BPhil; British composer; b. 19 July 1952, Southampton; s. of William Muldowney and Barbara Muldowney (née Lavender); m. Diane Ellen Trevis 1986; one d. *Education:* Taunton's Grammar School, Southampton and Univ. of York. *Career:* Composer-in-Residence, Southern Arts Asscn 1974–76; Music Dir Royal Nat. Theatre 1976–; Prof. of Composition, RAM 1999–; has composed music for British and int. festivals, for many films and TV and over 50 scores for the theatre. *Publications:* Piano Concerto 1983, Saxophone Concerto 1984, Sinfonietta 1986, Ars Subtilior 1987, Lonely Hearts 1988, Violin Concerto 1989, Three Pieces for Orchestra 1990, Percussion Concerto 1991, Oboe Concerto 1992, Trumpet Concerto 1993, Concerto for 4 Violins 1994 The Brontës (ballet) 1995, Trombone Concerto 1996, Clarinet Concerto 1997, The Fall of Jerusalem (oratorio) 1998, God's Plenty (ballet) 1999. *Honours:* Prix Italia 1993, 1997. *Address:* c/o Carlin Music, 3 Bridge Approach, Chalk Farm, London, NW1 8BD, England. *Telephone:* (20) 7734-3251 (office).

**MÜLLER, Barbel;** German singer (mezzo-soprano); b. 1968, Duisburg. *Education:* Frankfurt Musikhochschule and studied with Laura Sarti and Elsa Cavelti. *Career:* sang in concert from 1987 and made opera debut at Linz 1991, singing the Composer (Ariadne), Dorabella and Carmen; Further appearances as Sesto (Clemenza di Tito), Orlofsky, Charlotte and Octavian (Strasbourg, 1995); Concert repertoire includes Mozart's Requiem (at Stuttgart), the Christmas Oratorio (Ulm and Amsterdam), St Matthew Passion (Tubingen), Elijah (Zürich) and Bach's B Minor Mass (Frankfurt).

**MULLER, Markus;** Singer (Tenor); b. 1958, Saulgau, Germany. *Education:* Studied in Stuttgart with Helmuth Rilling. *Career:* Sang at Dortmund Opera from 1987, Deutsche Oper am Rhein at Düsseldorf from 1991; Roles have included Belmonde and Mozart's Arsace (Idomeneo), Nicolai's Fenton, Tamino, and the Astrologer in Rimsky's Golden Cockerel; Guest appearances at Dresden from 1991, including Belmonte in Die Entführung and Rossini's Almaviva; Premiere of Klebe's Gervaise Macquart at Düsseldorf, 1995; Sang Oronte in Alcina at Dusseldorf, 1999; Many concert appearances. *Address:* Deutsche Oper am Rhein, Heinrich-Heine Alle 16a, 40213 Düsseldorf, Germany.

**MÜLLER, Rufus;** Singer (Tenor); b. 5 Feb. 1959, Kent, England. *Education:* Choral Scholar, New College, Oxford; Studying with Thomas LoMonaco, New York. *Career:* Worked with many established conductors including: Ivor Bolton, Richard Hickox, Joshua Rifkin, Andrew Parrott and Ivan Fischer; Opera and concert appearances throughout Europe, Japan and the USA; Roles performed include: Bastien in Mozart's Bastien und Bastienne; Aminta in Peri's Euridice; Tersandre in Lully's Roland; Giuliano in Handel's Rodrigo; Lurcanio in Handel's Ariodante; Recitals in Wigmore Hall and Barbican, London, and on radio for BBC, in Munich, Tokyo, Madrid, Utrecht, Salzburg and New York; Recent engagements include Schubert's Die schöne Müllerin, Munich; Jonathan Miller production of St Matthew Passion at Brooklyn Academy of Music; Mendelssohn's St Paul with the Leipzig Gewandhaus Choir; Beethoven's Ninth Symphony and Handel's Messiah with the Swedish Chamber Orchestra; Televised tour of Messiah in Spain with Trevor Pinnock and the English Concert; World première, Rorem's Song Cycle Evidence of Things Not Seen, Carnegie Hall, New York, and Washington DC; St Matthew Passion in Sweden, Germany and Switzerland; Castor in Rameau's Castor et Pollux; Mendelssohn's Elijah in New York; Monteverdi's Il Ritorno d'Ulisse in Athens and Florence; Recital, Musée d'Orsay, Paris; Sang Alessando in Handel's Poro at the 1998 Halle Festival; Further engagements include: Title role in Rameau's Pygmalian, Opera Atelier, Toronto; Evangelist in Bach's St Matthew's passion with the CBSO; Recital, New York New Festival of Song, Carnegie Hall. *Recordings include:* Bach's St John Passion; Die Zauberflöte; Beethoven's Choral Fantasia; Dowland's First Book of Airs; Haydn's O Tuneful Voice; 19th Century Songs; The Evangelist in Bach's St Matthew

Passion; Telemann's Admiraltätsmusik and Solo Cantatas; Rorem: Evidence of Things Not Seen. *Honours:* GKN English Song Award, 1985; 2nd Prize, Oratorio Society of New York, 1999. *Address:* The Garden Flat, 26 Oliver Grove, London SE25 6EJ, England.

**MÜLLER-BRACHMANN, Hanno;** German singer (bass-baritone); b. 20 Aug. 1970, Cologne. *Education:* Basle Acad. of Music, Staatliche Hochschule für Musik Freiburg, Staatliche Hochschule für Musik Mannheim with Rudolf Piernay. *Career:* debut, Theater Freiburg 1992; with Deutsche Staatsoper, Berlin 1996–, as Donner, Kothner, Biterolf, Mozart's Figaro, Papageno, Leporello, Guglielmo, Orest, Golaud, Tomski, Escamillo; with Bayerische Staatsoper 1999–, as Fernando, Orest, Guglielmo, Papageno; with Vienna Staatsoper as Guglielmo; with Elliott Carter's opera What Next? under Daniel Barenboim in Berlin, Chicago and New York 1999–2000, Amfortas, Berlin 2005, Leporallo, Vienna 2005; concert performances under conductors including Kurt Masur, Sir Neville Marriner, Christoph Eschenbach, Sir John Eliott Gardiner, András Schiff, Christoph V. Dohnányi, Philippe Herreweghe, René Jacobs, Fabio Luisi, Myung-Wun Chung, Riccardo Chailly, Herbert Blomstedt, Michael Gielen and Nikolaus Harnoncourt; has performed with orchestras, including Berlin, London and New York Philharmonics, Concertgebouw Amsterdam, Gewandhaus Leipzig, Acad. of St Martin-in-the-Fields, Chicago Symphony Orchestra and Staatskapelle Berlin; Lieder recitals in Germany, Switzerland, France, Japan and Austria. *Recordings include:* Bach's bass solo cantatas, Salieri's La Passione, Schubert recital, Bach's Mass in B minor, Mozart's Requiem, Rossini's Petite Messe Solonnelle, Schumann's Der Rose Pilgerfahrt, Telemann's Orpheus, Haydn's Creation, Bach's Christmas Oratorio, Schoenberg's Jakobsleiter (Hänssler), Bach's Cantatas 213 and 214, Wagner's Tannhäuser with Daniel Barenboim), Bach's Matthäus-Passion, Die Zauberflöte (conducted by C. Abbado) 2005. *Film:* Cosi fan tutte 2003. *Television:* La Bohème 2002. *Honours:* first prize Bundeswettbewerb Gesang, Berlin 1992, 1994, Meistersingerwettbewerb Nürnberg 1995, Prix Davidoff 1995, Int. Brahms-Soc. Schleswig-Holstein Brahms Prize 1995. *Current Management:* Askonas Holt Ltd, Lonsdale Chambers, 27 Chancery Lane, London, WC2A 1PF, England. *Telephone:* (20) 7400-1700. *Fax:* (20) 7400-1799. *E-mail:* info@askonasholt.co.uk. *Website:* www.askonasholt.co.uk.

**MÜLLER-LORENZ, Wolfgang;** Singer (Tenor); b. 24 Nov. 1946, Cologne, Germany. *Education:* Studied in Cologne. *Career:* Sang as Baritone, at the Mannheim Opera, 1972; Engagements at Munich, Nuremburg, Karlsruhe, Frankfurt and Mannheim as Papageno, Rossini's Figaro and Dvořák's Jacobin; Studied further with Hans Hopf and sang at the Graz Opera from 1980 as Lohengrin, Cavardossi, Calaf and Loge; Siegmund and Siegfried in a Ring cycle, 1989; Sang with the Deutsche Oper Berlin on tour to Washington, 1989, and as Bacchus in the original version of Ariadne auf Naxos at the Landestheater, Salzburg, 1991; Other roles have included Otello, Dimitri in Boris Godunov, Parsifal, The Marquis in Lulu, Erik, Herman and Fra Diavolo, Zürich Opera, 1989; Season 2000–01 as Tannhäuser at the Munich Staatsoper and Tristan at Covent Garden; Frequent concert appearances notably in contemporary works. *Address:* c/o Landestheater, Schwarstrasse 22, 5020 Salzburg, Austria.

**MULLER-MOLINARI, Helga;** Singer (Mezzo-soprano); b. 28 March 1948, Pfaffenhofen, Bavaria, Germany. *Education:* Studied with Felicie Huni-Mihaczek in Munich and with Giulietta Simionato in Rome. *Career:* Sang at Saarbrucken, 1972–73; La Scala Milan, 1975 in L'Enfant et Les Sortilèges, Piccola Scala 1979 in Vivaldi's Tito Manlio; Further appearances at the Salzburg Festival, as Annina, 1983, Barcelona, as Cherubino 1984, Turin as Carmen, 1988 and Monte Carlo, Portrait de Manon by Massenet, 1989; Roles in operas by Rossini, Mozart and other composers at Nancy, Dublin, Pesaro and elsewhere; Trieste 1991 as Werther. *Recordings include:* Der Rosenkavalier, Ariadne auf Naxos, Mozart Requiem, Bruckner Te Deum, Oronte by Cesti, Monteverdi Madrigals; Handel Partenope; L'Arcadia in Brenta by Galuppi, Rossini's Aureliano in Palmira and La Gazza Ladra. *Address:* Teatro Comunale di Trieste, Riva Novembre 1, 34121 Trieste, Italy.

**MULLOVA, Viktoria;** Russian violinist; b. 27 Nov. 1959, Moscow; d. of Yuri Mullov and Raissa Mullova; one s. two d. *Education:* studied in Moscow at Cen. Music School and Moscow Conservatory under Leonid Kogan. *Career:* left USSR 1983; has appeared with most maj. orchestras and conductors and at int. festivals. *Recordings include:* Tchaikovsky and Sibelius Violin Concertos with Boston Symphony under Seiji Ozawa (Grand Prix du disque), Bartok, Bach and Paganini solo works, Shostakovich Concerto No. 1, Prokofiev Concerto No. 2, Brahms Violin Sonatas, J.S. Bach Partitas for violin and piano, Mendelssohn Concertos, J. S. Bach Partitas for Solo Violin, Brahms Violin Concerto, Janáček, Prokofiev and Debussy Sonatas, J. S. Bach Violin Concertos, Concerto for Violin and Oboe, Stravinsky Concerto, Bartok Concerto No. 2, Through the Looking Glass (incl. works by Miles Davis and Yousso N'Dour), Mozart Concertos Nos 1, 3 and 4. *Honours:* first prize at Sibelius Competition, Helsinki 1980, Gold Medal, Tchaikovsky Competition, Moscow 1982. *Current Management:* Askonas Holt, Lonsdale Chambers, 27 Chancery Lane, London, WC2A 1PF, England. *Telephone:* (20) 7400-1700. *Fax:* (20) 7400-1799.

**MUMELTER, Martin;** Violinist; b. 12 May 1948, Innsbruck, Austria; m. Magdalena Pattis, 2 s., 2 d. *Education:* Konservatorium Innsbruck; Philadelphia College of Performing Arts. *Career:* Mainly with 20th Century Music and Wiener Symphoniker, Staatskapelle Berlin, RSO Vienna, Symphony Orchestra des Bayerischen Rundfunks, Bamberger Symphoniker, RTL-Luxemburg, Mozarteum Orchestra Salzburg; Appearances at Musikbiennale Berlin, Bregenzer Festspiele, Sagra musicale Umbra, Edinburgh Fringe Festival, Festwochen der Alten Musik Innsbruck; Recitals: New York at Merkin Hall and Carnegie Recital Hall, 1983 and 1987; Professor of Violin and Director of Orchestra, Konservatorium Innsbruck, 1971–75; Professor of Violin at University Mozarteum, Salzburg, 1986–. Recordings: 200 Radio recordings; CDs including complete Ives Sonatas (with Herbert Henck, piano), concerto by Schnittke (Nr 3) Chamber music by Ives, Cage, Bartók. Publications: Ums Leben spielen (book), 1994; Several radio plays for Austrian Radio and SRG Zürich. Honours: Finalist, Gaudeamus Competition, Rotterdam, 1971; Preis der Kritik Musikbiennale Berlin, 1979; Berlanda Preis des Landes Tirol, 1985. Current Management: Hans Adler, Auguste-Viktoria-Straáe 64, 14199, Berlin, Germany. Address: Pizachw. 31, 6073 Sistrans, Austria.

**MUMFORD, Jeffrey;** Composer; b. 22 June 1955, Washington, USA. Education: University of California, at Irvine and San Diego; New York, with Elliott Carter. Career: Commissions from, Robert Evett Fund of Washington, DC, 1977, Cellist Fred Sherry, 1981, Aspen Wind Quintet, 1983, McKi m Fund, Library of Congress, 1986, New York New Music Ensemble, 1987, Violist Marcus Thompson, 1989, Amphion Foundation for the Da Capo Chamber Players, 1989, Fromm Music Foundation, 1990, Roanoke Symphony Orchestra, 1991; Walter W Naumburg Foundation, 1991, Abel/Steinberg/Winant Trio, 1991, Roanoke Symphony Orchestra, 1992, Cellist Joshua Gordon, 1994, Cincinnati Radio Station WGUC, 1994, National Symphony Orchestra, 1995; Works Extensively Performed in the USA and abroad, including Performances at the Library of Congress, Aspen Music Festival, Bang On A Can Music Festival, Seattle Chamber Music Festival, London's Purcell Room, Helsinki Festival, Musica Nel Nostro Tempo Festival, Milan and by Saint Paul Chamber Orchestra; Meet the Composer/Arts Endowment Commissioning US Program, 1996; Sonia and louis Rothschild for the Opus 3 Trio, 1998; The Contemporary Music Forum and Philip Berlin, 1999; Artist-in-Residence, Bowling Green State University, 1999–2000; mem, NARAS; Recent commissions include: Radio Station WCLV, Cleveland, 2002; Sharan Leventhal, Violinist, 2001; Rhonda Taylor and David Reminick, saxophonists, 2001; Wendy Richman, violist, 2001; Nncy Ruyle Dodge Charitable Trust, for the Corigliano Quartet, 2000; Cleveland Chamber Symphony, 2000; Phillips Collection (D.C.), Miller Theatre (N.Y.C.), Schubert Club (St. Paul, MN.), for Margaret Kampmeier, 1999. Compositions include: Fragments From the Surrounding Evening; A Flower in Folding Shadows, for piano and four hands; Linear Cycles VII, for solo violin; Echoes in a Cloud Box, for violin and cello; Jewels Beyond the Mist; Diamonds Suspended in a Galaxy of Clouds, Soprano Solo; Lullaby, for soprano and piano; In Forests of Evaporating Dawns; A Pond Within the Drifting Dusk; A still radiance within dark air, for piano solo, flute, clarinet, violin, viloncello, 1996; A layer of vivid stillness for cello solo and 12 cellos, 1996; Ringing fields enveloping blue for cello and piano; A window of resonant light, cello piano percussion, 1997; In afternoons of deep and amplified air, string quartet, 1998; Amid the Light of Quickening Memory for orchestra, 2002; The Promise of the Far Hoizon, string quartet, 2002; A Precious Continuity is a day expanding, 2001; Through the Filtering Dawn of Spreading Daybright, 2001; Wending, solo viola, 2001; A Landscape of interior resonances, solo piano, 2001; Revisiting variazioni elegiaci, solo viola, 2001; A Distance of unfolding light, orchestra, 2000; Billowing Pockets brightly layered, cello and chamber orchestra, 2000; As a spray of reflected meadowlight informs the air, alto sax, violin and percussion, 2000; Undiluted days, piano trio, 2000. Recordings: A pond within the drifting dusk; The focus of blue light; Fragments from the surrounding evening. Contributions: Quadrivium Music Press; Perspectives of New Music. Honours: Guggenheim Fellowship; Awards from, Minnesota Composers Forum, American Music Center, Alice M Ditson Fund; Ohio Arts Council Individual Artist Fellowship, 2002; American Academy of Arts and Letters: Academy Award in Music, 2003. Address: c/o Theodore Presser Co., 588 North Gulph Road, King of Prussia, PA. 19406, USA.

**MUMMA, Gordon;** Composer, Performer, Author and Professor of Music; b. 30 March 1935, Framingham, Massachusetts, USA. Career: Composer and Performer of electro-acoustic and instrumental music with performances and recordings in North and South America, Europe and Japan; Television and film performances, Germany and USA; Visiting Lecturer, various colleges and universities; Composer and Performing Musician, Sonic Arts Union, New York City, and Merce Cunningham Dance Company, 1966–74; Professor of Music, 1975–95, Professor Emeritus, 1995–, University of California, Santa Cruz; Visiting Professor of Music, University of California, San Diego, 1985–87; mem, Society for Ethnomusicology; Broadcast Music Inc. Compositions include: Music from The Venezia Space Theatre; Dresden Interleaf 13 Feb 1945; Mesa; Hornpipe; Schoolwork; Cybersonic Cantilevers; Pontpoint; Than Particle, for percussion and digital computer, 1985; Epifont, for tape, 1985, Begault Meadow Sketches, tape, 1987; Songs Without Words, 1995. Recordings: All listed compositions plus performance of music by Robert Ashley, David Behrman, George Cacioppo, John Cage, Mauricio Kagel and Christian Wolff. Contributions: Numerous books and journals including: James Klosty's Merce Cunningham; Appleton and Perera's Development and Practice of Electronic Music; Gilbert Chase's Roger Reynolds: A Portrait; Journal of Audio Engineering Society; Darmstadt Beitrage zur neue Musik; Neuland I; Sound Recording, major article to The New Grove Dictionary of American Music, 1986. Current Management: Artservices, 325 Spring Street,

New York, NY 10013, USA. Address: Porter College, University of California, Santa Cruz, CA 95064, USA.

**MUNDT, Richard;** Singer (Bass); b. 8 Sept. 1936, Illinois, USA. Education: Studied in New York and Vienna. Career: Debut: Saarbrucken 1962, as the Commendatore in Don Giovanni; Appearances at Kiel, Dortmund, Darmstadt, Graz, Liège and the Spoleto Festival; American engagements at the New York City Opera, San Francisco, Portland, Chicago and Cincinnati; Other roles have included Mozart's Osmin, Don Giovanni, Figaro and Sarastro, Rocco, Arkel in Pelléas et Mélisande, Ramphis, King Philip, Padre Guardiano and Wagner's Marke, Daland, Fasolt, Pogner, Hunding and Landgrave.

**MUNI, Nicholas;** American stage director; b. 1960. Career: Artistic Dir, Tulsa Opera, 1988–97; has directed over 150 opera productions with leading US companies; Season 1989–90, with Il Trovatore at Seattle, transferring to Houston, Toronto and Vancouver; French version of Verdi's opera at Tulsa, with new production of The Juniper Tree by Philip Glass and Robert Moran; New York City Opera debut with La Traviata, 1991; world premiere of Frankenstein the Modern Prometheus, by Libby Larsen, for Minnesota Opera; US premiere of Rossini's Armida at Tulsa, 1992; complete version of Lulu for Canadian Opera and Ariadne auf Naxos at Opera Theater of St Louis; world premiere of Moran's The Shining Princess at Minnesota, 1993; staging of Norma for Seattle and Houston, Los Angeles, 1996; Artistic Dir, Cincinnati Opera 1997–2005, produced Jenůfa there 1998. Address: c/o Cincinnati Opera, Music Hall, 1243 Elm Street, Cincinnati, OH 45202, USA.

**MUNKITTRICK, Mark;** Singer (Bass); b. 1951, Boston, Massachusetts, USA. Education: Studied at Fresno State College, California. Career: Sang in Carnegie Hall concert performances of Donizetti's Gemma di Vergy and Puccini's Edgar, 1976–77; New York City Opera 1977, as Daland and Pogner; Guest appearances in Washington, Baltimore, Los Angeles and Atlanta, as Leporello, Alfonso, Raimondo and Monteverdi's Seneca; Sang at Karlsruhe, 1978–87, as Mephistopheles, Rocco, Basilio, Kecal, Banquo, King Philip, Ramphis, the Landgrave in Tannhäuser and Fafner; Madrid, 1984, as Handel's Giulio Cesare; Dresden Staatsoper 1989 as Morosus in Die schweigsame Frau; Member of the Stuttgart Staatsoper from 1985; Guest engagements throughout Germany and Europe; Other roles include Arthur in The Lighthouse by Maxwell Davies, Kaspar and Henry VIII in Anna Bolena; Sang Taddeo in L'Italiana in Algeri at Stuttgart, 1996; Sang Angelotti in Tosca at Stuttgart, 1998; Poet in Donizetti's Le Convenienze Teatrali, 2001; Wide concert repertory including bass solo in the Missa Solemnis. Recordings include: Gemma di Vergy and Edgar. Address: c/o Stuttgart Staatsoper, Oberer Schlossgarten 6, 7000 Stuttgart, Germany.

**MUNOZ, Daniel;** Singer (Tenor); b. 1951, Buenos Aires, Argentina. Education: Studied in Buenos Aires. Career: Sang at the Teatro Colón Buenos Aires from 1979, Teatro de la Zarzuela Madrid from 1980; Studied further in Milan and sang from 1982 at opera houses in Spain, Portugal and South America; Nancy Opera 1983, as Cavaradossi, Liège 1986 as Pinkerton and the Berne Stadtheater, 1988; Sang Cornil Schut in Pittore Fiamminghi at Trieste and Calaf at the Szeged Festival, Hungary, 1991; Other roles include Don José, Faust, Werther, Don Carlos and Des Grieux in Manon Lescaut; Sang Andrea Chénier at Buenos Aires, 1996; Canio in Pagliacci at Cape Town, 1998; Sang Verdi's Riccardo at Budapest, 2000; Frequent concert appearances. Address: Teatro Comunale, Riva Novembre 1, 34121 Trieste, Italy.

**MUNSEL, Patrice;** Singer (Soprano); b. 14 May 1925, Spokane, Washington, USA. Education: Studied with Charlotte Lange, William Herman and Renato Bellini in New York. Career: Debut: Metropolitan Opera 1943, as Philine in Mignon; Sang in New York until 1958, as Adele in Die Fledermaus, Offenbach's Périchole, Lucia di Lammermoor, Rosina, Olympia in Les Contes d'Hoffmann, the Queen of Shemakha, Zerlina, Despina and Gilda; European Tour 1948; Starred in 1953 film Melba; Appeared in musical comedy after leaving the Metropolitan.

**MURA, Peter;** Hungarian conductor; b. 21 June 1924, Budapest; m. Rose Tóth; one d. Education: High School of Music, Budapest. Career: debut, Hungarian State Opera House 1948; solo repetiteur 1945–, Conductor of the Stagione 1950–53, Hungarian State Opera House; Dir and Chief Conductor, Miskolc Nat. Theatre Opera Co. 1953–57; State Opera Conductor, Warsaw, Poland 1957–58; Conductor, Silesian Opera, Bytom, Poland 1958–61; Dir and Chief Conductor, Miskolc Symphony Orchestra, Hungary 1961–84; Conductor, Hungarian State Opera 1984–87; Prof., High School of Music, Budapest 1986–; Conductor, Wiener Kammeroper 1990–91. Recordings: Mozart: Idomeneo Overture and Ballet, Symphony in A 1974. Honours: Ferenc Liszt Prize 1966, Merited Artist of the Hungarian Republic 1972. Address: Podmaniczky U 63, 1064 Budapest, Hungary (home). Telephone: 1-311-8978 (home). Fax: 1-311-8978 (home). E-mail: mura76@freewail.hu (home).

**MURGATROYD, Andrew;** Singer (Tenor); b. 1955, Halifax, Yorkshire, England. Education: Studied singing with Barbara Robotham at Lancaster University and with Rudolf Pierney; Lay-Clerk at Christ Church Cathedral, Oxford. Career: Concert engagements include Israel in Egypt for John Eliot Gardiner in Stuttgart, Milan, Paris, Rome, East Berlin and Turin; Handel's Esther for WDR in Cologne and Acis and Galatea for Swiss television; Monteverdi Vespers and Alexander's Feast at Aix-en-Provence; Performances of Bach's St John Passion in London, Cambridge and Spain, and the St Matthew Passion at the Festival Hall, 1990; Debussy's Rodrigue et Chimène in London and Manchester; Beethoven's Ninth with the Hanover Band in

London and Germany; Contemporary Music Network Tour with Richard Bernas, 1990; Sang in Haydn's St Nicholas Mass and Stabat Mater at St John's, London, 1997. *Recordings include:* Beethoven's Missa Solemnis and Ninth Symphony (Nimbus); Monteverdi Vespers with The Sixteen (Hyperion); Campra's Tancrède (Erato); Leclair Scylla et Glaucus; John Tavener, We Shall See Him As He Is, (Chandos); Antonio Teixeira, Te Deum (Collins Classics). *Address:* c/o CDI, Lyndhurst, Denton Road, Ben Rhydding, Ilkley, W Yorks, LS29 8QR, England.

**MURGU, Corneliu;** Romanian singer (tenor); *Director-General, Opera Naţională Timişoara*; b. 1948, Timişoara. *Education:* studied in Romania, in Florence and with Marcello del Monaco in Treviso. *Career:* debut, Wiener Staatsoper with Cavalleria Rusticana (Turiddu) 1978; other appearances include Deutsche Oper Berlin, Munich, Hamburg, Stuttgart, Düsseldorf, Zürich and Graz until 1982; Met debut with Ballo in Maschera (Riccardo) 1982; appearances in Naples, Rome and Andrea Chénier in Bonn 1982; Norma (Pollione) in Lyon, Carmen and Turandot in Caracalla, Rome 1983–85; La Scala debut with Aida (Radames) 1986; Andrea Chénier and Samson in Rio de Janeiro and Cavalleria Rusticana in Barcelona 1987–89; Otello at Opéra Bastille in Paris 1990; Cavalleria Rusticana/Pagliacci and Carmen in Rotterdam 1994–95; debut in Verona with Otello 1994; Covent Garden debut with Calaf in Turandot; currently Dir-Gen., Opera Naţională Timişoara. *Recordings include:* Otello with Renato Bruson, Fanciulla del West with Gwyneth Jones, Cavalleria Rusticana/Pagliacci, Carmen. *Address:* Opera Naţională Timişoara, Strada Marasesti nr. 2, 300080 Timişoara, Romania. *Telephone:* (256) 433020. *Fax:* (256) 201283. *E-mail:* murgule@hotmail.com. *Website:* www.ort.ro.

**MURPHY, Aubrey;** Violinist; b. 1960, Dublin, Ireland. *Education:* Royal Irish Academy, Yehudi Menuhin School and Indiana University. *Career:* Guest leader from 1992 with Scottish Chamber Orchestra, BBC Ulster Orchestra and Orchestra of the Royal Opera House, Covent Garden (currently a principal); Frequent chamber concerts and member of chamber group playing at country houses and stately homes; Concert Master of the Estonian-Finnish Symphony Orchestra. *Address:* c/o Royal Opera House (orchestra), Covent Garden, London. WC2, England. *Telephone:* (20) 7240 1200. *Fax:* (20) 7212 9502.

**MURPHY, Emma,** MMus, FTCL; British recorder player and soprano. *Education:* Univ. of Birmingham, Trinity Coll. of Music. *Career:* performances with early music ensembles, including The King's Consort, Ex Cathedra, New London Consort and New Trinity Baroque, and with her own ensemble Da Camera; performances of contemporary music, including Park Lane Group and a duo with marimba; annual recital tours of Japan; Musical Dir, The City Carollers; Countess of Munster Musical Trust Award. *Recordings:* with The King's Consort, Ex Cathedra and Sprezzatura; A Celtic Celebration (with Da Camera). *Publications:* An Introduction to Fontegara and the Art of Divisions. *E-mail:* emma@emmamurphy.co.uk. *Website:* www.emmamurphy.co.uk.

**MURPHY, Heidi Grant;** Singer (soprano); b. 1962, USA. *Education:* Studied in New York. *Career:* Member of the Met Opera's Young Artist Development Program, from 1988; Met debut in Die Frau ohne Schatten (1989) followed by Xenia (Boris Godunov), Papagena, Oscar, Nannetta, Sophie in Der Rosenkavalier, Soeur Constance (Carmélites), Ilia; Servilia (La Clemenza di Tito), Pamina and Susanna in season 1997–98; Santa Fe debut 1991, as Susanna; European debut at Brussels 1991, in La Favorita, followed by Monteverdi's Drusilla with Netherlands Opera, Mozart's Celia (Lucio Silla) and Ismene (Mitridate) at Salzburg, Servilia at the Paris Opéra and Ilia at Frankfurt; Concerts include Mozart's C Minor Mass (Houston Symphony), Mahler's Eighth Symphony (Atlanta Symphony and Vienna Philharmonic); New York Philharmonic debut 1996, in Honegger's Jeanne d'Arc au Bûcher; Semire in Les Boréades by Rameau at the 1999 London Prom concerts; Sang Strauss's Sophie at the New York Met, 2000; Conductors have included Levine, Ozawa, Robert Shaw, Masur, Michael Tilson Thomas and Charles Dutoit. *Recordings include:* Idomeneo, from the Met (DGG); Haydn's Die Schöpfung (Teldec). *Honours:* Winner, 1988 Metropolitan National Council Auditions. *Current Management:* Askonas Holt Ltd, Lonsdale Chambers, 27 Chancery Lane, London, WC2A 1PF, England. *Telephone:* (20) 7400-1700. *Fax:* (20) 7400-1799. *E-mail:* info@askonasholt.co.uk. *Website:* www.askonasholt.co.uk.

**MURPHY, Suzanne;** Singer (Soprano); b. 15 Oct. 1941, Limerick, Ireland. *Education:* Studied with Veronica Dunne at the College of Music in Dublin, 1973–76. *Career:* Has sung with Welsh National Opera from 1976 as Constanze, Amelia (I Masnadieri and Un Ballo in Maschera), Elisabeth de Valois, Leonora (Il Trovatore), Elvira (Ernani and I Puritani), Violetta, Norma, Lucia di Lammermoor and Musetta; Has sung Constanze and Donna Anna for English National Opera; Donna Anna and the soprano roles in Les Contes d'Hoffmann for Opera North and Constanze for Scottish Opera; German debut 1985, as Norma in a concert performance of Bellini's opera in Munich; Returned 1988 for Amelia (Un Ballo in Maschera); Vienna Staatsoper debut 1987, as Electra in Idomeneo; Invited to return 1988–89 (Armenian Gala Benefit Concert); Has sung Reiza in Oberon at Lyon and Donna Anna at the Aix-en-Provence Festival; North American engagements include Norma at the New York City Opera, Amelia (Ballo), Elvira (Puritani) and Lucia in Vancouver, Fiordiligi, Ophelia (Hamlet) and Violetta in Pittsburgh; Sang Alice Ford in the Peter Stein production of Falstaff for Welsh National Opera (repeated in New York and Milan 1989); Sang Norma for the Dublin Grand Opera Society 1989, Hanna Glawari in The Merry Widow for Scottish Opera;

Title role in La Fanciulla del West for Welsh National Opera, 1991; Electra in Idomeneo at the Albert Hall (Proms) and in Wales with WNO, 1991; Season 1992 with Elvira in Ernani and Tosca, in new productions for WNO; Concert appearances in Austria, Sweden, Denmark, Belgium and Portugal; Sang Leonore in Fidelio on South Bank, London, 1989 and at Belfast, 1996; Sang the Kostelnička in Jenůfa at Geneva, 2001. *Current Management:* Ingpen & Williams Ltd, 7 St George's Court, 131 Putney Bridge Road, London, SW15 2PA, England.

**MURRAY, Ann;** Irish singer (mezzo-soprano); b. 27 Aug. 1949, Dublin; m. Philip Langridge 1981; one s. *Education:* Royal Northern Coll. of Music, London Opera Centre with Frederick Cox. *Career:* debut at Aldeburgh with Scottish Opera as Alceste in the opera by Gluck 1974; US debut with the New York City Opera as Sextus in La Clemenza di Tito 1979; fmrly performed with ENO, Royal Opera; many concert appearances, including the London Proms, European recital tours, and has performed in festivals at Aldeburgh, Edin., Munich, Salzburg, Wexford, Glyndebourne, Vienna; roles in opera include Idamante, Octavian, Beatrice, Xerxes, Brangaene, Myrtale (Thaïs), Queen Laodicea (Eritrea), Siebel (Faust), Tebaldo (I Capuleti e i Montecchi), the Child (L'Enfant et les Sortilèges), Dorabella (Così fan tutte), Cecilio (Lucio Silla), the Composer (Ariadne auf Naxos), Sifare (Mitridate), Nicklausse (Les Contes d'Hoffmann), Minerva (Il Ritorno d'Ulisse), Ruggiero (Alcina), title role in Giulio Cesare, and roles in Mary Stuart, Le Comte Ory, Cenerentola, Ascanio, Cherubino, The Beggar's Opera, Alceste, Ariodante. *Honours:* Bavarian Order of Merit 2005. *Current Management:* Askonas Holt Ltd., Lonsdale Chambers, 27 Chancery Lane, London, WC2A 1PF, England.

**MURRAY, John Horton;** Singer (Tenor); b. 1961, Braunschweig, Germany (of American parents); m. Louise Sweet, 3 c. *Education:* Studied at Curtis Institute in Philadelphia and the MET Lindemann Young Artist Devt. *Career:* Debut as David in Meistersinger at Spoleto Festival, 1992; Performances of Stolzing, Don Jose, The Emperor in Frau Ohne Schatten and Aeneas in Les Troyens at the Metropolitan Opera, 1995–; Don Jose, Verona Arena, 1996; Stolzing and Bacchus, Lyric Opera of Chicago, 1998; Menelaus in Strauss's Ägyptische Helena, Royal Opera, Festival Hall, London, 1998; Tichon in Katya Kabanova, 2000; Bacchus in Santa Fe, 1999 and Menelaus, 2001; Apollo and Menelaus at Deutsche Oper Berlin, Parisfal in Edinburgh, Lohengrin at the Liceo, and La Scala debut as Bacchus in 2000; 2001–02 season: as Laca in Jenůfa for Geneva Opera, Paul in Tote Stadt for New York City Opera and Stolzing at Rai Orchestra Sinfonica Naz.; 2002–03 season: Bacchus at Liceo and Rienzi at Antiken Festspiele, Trier; 2003–04 season: Emperor for Metropolitan Opera, Bacchus at Seattle Opera. *Recordings:* The Magician in Menotti's Medium; Wagner: Scenes from Lohengrin and Siegfried. *Honours:* National Institute for Music Theater Prizes; George London Award, 1988; Finalist in 1989 Metropolitan National Council Auditions; Musician's Emergency Fund Winner, 1990. *Address:* c/o IMG Artists, Lovell House, 616 Chiswick High Road, London W4 5RX, England. *E-mail:* Johnhortonmurray@aol.com. *Website:* JohnHortonMurray.com.

**MURRAY, Niall;** Opera Singer (Baritone); b. 22 April 1948, Dublin, Ireland; m. Barbara F M Murray, 1 d. *Education:* Royal Academy of Music, Dublin. *Career:* Debut: Boy Soprano in Pantomime, Dublin; Appearances as Curly in Oklahoma, Dublin, 1970; Opera debut, Bomarzo, Coliseum, London, 1976; Baritone Lead in over 52 musicals including, English National Opera, London; Television and radio appearances, England and Ireland frequently; Also appeared in Cabarets and Musicals, major opera appearances include Papageno, Schaunard, Figaro (Barber of Seville), and Lescaut (Manon); Sang Iago at the Basle City Theatre 1988 (under the name Mario di Mario); Sang Falstaff at Lübeck, 1999. *Recordings:* Niall Murray Sings (Irish Songs); Danilo; The Merry Widow; Robert in La Fille du Régiment. *Address:* c/o English National Opera, London Coliseum, St Martin's Lane, London WC2N 4ES, England.

**MURRAY, William;** Singer (Baritone); b. 13 March 1935, Schenectady, New York, USA. *Education:* Studied at Adelphi University and in Rome. *Career:* Debut: Spoleto 1957, in Il segreto di Susanna by Wolf-Ferrari; Appearances in Munich, Salzburg, Amsterdam and Frankfurt; Member of the Deutsche Oper Berlin from 1969; Sang Dallapiccola's Ulisse at La Scala in 1970, and took part in the premiere of Nabokov's Love Labour's Lost, Brussels 1973; Other roles include Don Giovanni, Verdi's Macbeth, Luna, Rigoletto and Germont, Puccini's Scarpia and Lescaut, Wagner's Wolfram and parts in We Come to the River by Henze, Orff's Antigonae and Paisiello's Re Theodoro in Venezia. *Honours:* Fulbright Scholarship, 1956; Kammersänger of the Deutsche Oper Berlin. *Address:* c/o Deutsche Oper Berlin, Richard Wagnerstrasse 10, 1000 Berlin, Germany.

**MURTO, Matti;** Composer, Lecturer and Teacher; b. 12 July 1947, Finland; m., 1 s., 1 d. *Education:* Diploma of Music Theory, Sibelius Academy, 1973; Studied Musicology, University of Helsinki, 1989–91. *Career:* Headmaster of Music Conservatory, Ostro Bothnia, 1980–85; General Manager, Tampere Philharmonic Orchestra, 1985–87; Music Teacher, Hameenlinna Music Schools and Tampere, 1988–90; Headmaster, Savolinna Music School, 1991–; mem, Finnish Composers. *Compositions:* Reel Fantasies for strings, 1980; Aurora Borealis, Prelude for orchestra, 1983; The Fiddlers for Strings, 1988; Concertino for violin and strings, chamber music, solo pieces. *Recordings:* Concertino for violin and strings; Savonlinna Music School SAMCD, 1996; Reel fantasies for strings, Ostro Bothma's Chamber orchestra, 1984; Quartet for flute, clarinet, bassoon, cello and piano, 1997; Many works for accordion. *Publications:* Soivat soinnut, Introduction for harmony, 1994. *Current Management:* Modus Musiikki Ov. *Address:* c/o TEOSTO, Lauttasaarentie 1, SF–00200, Helsinki, Finland.

**MUSACCHIO, Martina;** Singer (Soprano); b. 11 Feb. 1956, Aosta, Italy. *Education:* Studied in Geneva with Ursula Buckel and in Florence, Munich and Zürich. *Career:* Sang at Zürich Opera 1981–82, Lucerne 1982–85; Guest appearances at Geneva, Düsseldorf, Venice, Mantua, Lausanne and Ravenna; Roles have included Mozart's Susanna, Zerlina, Despina, Pamina and Papagena, Donizetti's Norina and Adina, Martha, Micaela, Euridice, Orff's Die Kluge and Ismene in Honegger's Antigone; Sang Lisetta in La Rondine at Monte Carlo, 1991; Concert appearances throughout Switzerland and in Hamburg, Munich, Stuttgart, Paris, Venice and Madrid, notably in Baroque repertoire. *Address:* c/o Opéra de Monte Carlo, Place du Casino, Monte Carlo.

**MUSGRAVE, Thea,** CBE, MusDoc; British composer; b. 27 May 1928, Edinburgh; d. of James Musgrave and Joan Musgrave (née Hacking); m. Peter Mark 1971. *Education:* Edinburgh Univ. and Paris Conservatoire (under Nadia Boulanger). *Career:* Lecturer, Extra-Mural Dept, Univ. of London 1958–65; Visiting Prof., Univ. of California, Santa Barbara 1970; Guggenheim Fellow 1974–75, 1982–83; Distinguished Prof., Queen's Coll., City Univ. of New York 1987–2002. *Works include:* Chamber Concertos 1, 2 & 3 1966, Concerto for Orchestra 1967, Clarinet Concerto 1968, Beauty and the Beast (ballet) 1969, Night Music 1969, Horn Concerto 1971, The Voice of Ariadne (chamber opera) 1972–73, Viola Concerto 1973, Space Play 1974, Mary, Queen of Scots (opera) 1976–77, A Christmas Carol (opera) 1978–79, An Occurrence at Owl Creek Bridge (radio opera) 1981, Harriet, A Woman Called Moses 1980–84, Black Tambourine for women's chorus and piano 1985, Pierrot 1985, For the Time Being for chorus 1986, The Golden Echo 1987, Narcissus 1988, The Seasons (orchestral) 1988, Rainbow (orchestral) 1990, Simón Bolívar (opera) 1993, Autumn Sonata 1993, Journey through a Japanese Landscape (marimba concerto) 1993, On the Underground (vocal) 1994, Helios (oboe concerto) 1995, Phoenix Rising (orchestral) 1997, Canta, Canta (clarinet and ensemble) 1997, Lamenting with Ariadne 1999, The Mocking Bird (baritone and ensemble) 2000, Pontalba (opera) 2003, Turbulent Landscapes for orchestra 2004, Wood, Metal, Skin (concerto for percussion and orchestra) 2004, Journey into Light (soprano and orchestra) 2005; chamber music, songs, choral music, orchestral music. *Honours:* Hon. DMus (CNAA, Smith Coll., Old Dominion Univ.); Koussevitzky Award 1972, 2000. *Current Management:* c/o Novello & Co., 14–15 Berners Street, London, W1T 3LJ, England.

**MUSOLENO, Rosemary;** Singer (Soprano); b. 1965, USA. *Education:* Studied at the Juilliard School, New York, and with Renata Scotto. *Career:* Debut: Opéra de Lyon, as Drusilla in Monteverdi's Poppea; Sang at Lyon as Mozart's Susanna, Cherubino, Servilia and Zerlina; Season 1991 as Poppea at St Etienne and Spoleto, USA; Colorado Opera and Los Angeles, 1994, as Liu in Turandot; Alice Ford in Falstaff for Long Beach Opera; Frequent concert appearances. *Recordings include:* Applausus by Haydn. *Address:* c/o Long Beach Opera, 6372 Pacific Coast Highway, Long Beach, CA 90803, USA.

**MUSTONEN, Olli;** Finnish pianist, composer and conductor; b. 7 June 1967, Helsinki; s. of Seppo Mustonen and Marja-Liisa Mustonen; m. Raija Kerppo 1989. *Career:* began studies with harpsichord, studied piano with Ralf Gothóni and Eero Heinonen, composition with Einojuhani Rautavaara; has played with many of the world's leading orchestras; has appeared at festivals including Berlin, Hollywood Bowl, BBC Proms and Salzburg; Artistic Dir Turku Music Festival 1990–92, Ludus Mustonalis concert series, Helsinki Festival Orchestra. *Major compositions:* Fantasia (for piano and strings) 1985, Toccata (for piano, string quartet and double bass) 1989, two Nonets (for two string quartets and double bass) 1995, 2000, Triple Concerto (for three violins and orchestra) 1998. *Honours:* Edison Award 1992, Gramophone Award for Best Instrumental Recording 1992. *Current Management:* Van Walsum Management Ltd, 4 Addison Bridge Place, London, W14 8XP, England. *Telephone:* (20) 7371-4343. *Fax:* (20) 7371-4344. *Website:* www.vanwalsum.co .uk.

**MUTI, Riccardo;** Italian conductor; b. 28 July 1941, Naples; s. of Domenico Muti and Gilda Mazzavillani 1969; two s. one d. *Education:* San Pietro Conservatory, Majella, Naples and Milan Conservatory of Music. *Career:* Prin. Conductor, Maggio Musicale, Florence 1969–81; Prin. Conductor, Philharmonia Orchestra, London 1973–82, Music Dir 1979–82, Conductor Laureate 1982–; Prin. Guest Conductor Philadelphia Orchestra 1977–80, Prin. Conductor and Music Dir 1980–92, Conductor Laureate 1992–; Music Dir La Scala, Milan 1986–2005; Prin. Conductor Filarmonica della Scala 1988–2005; concert tours in USA with Boston, Chicago and Philadilphia Orchestras; concerts at Salzburg, Edinburgh, Lucerne, Flanders and Vienna festivals; also conducted Berlin Philharmonic, Bayerische Rundfunk Sinfonie Orchester, Vienna Philharmonic, New York Philharmonic and Concertgebouw Amsterdam; opera: Florence, Munich, Covent Garden, La Scala, Ravenna, Vienna, Accad. di Santa Cecilia (Rome), Accademico Dell'Accademia Cherubini (Florence). *Honours:* Hon. PhD (Weizmann Inst. of Science), Dr hc (Pennsylvania, Philadelphia, Bologna, Urbino, Milan, Cremona, Lecce); Guido Cantelli Award 1967, Diapason d'Oro, Premio Critica Discografia Italiana, Prix Académie nat. du disque 1977, Deutscher Schallplatten Preis, 'Bellini d'Oro', Abbiati Prize, Grand Prix du disque for La Traviata (Verdi), Requiem in C minor (Cherubini) 1982, Disco d' Oro for Music for Films, Wolf Prize 2000; Grand Golden Medal of the City of Monaco, Grand Silver Ehrenkreuz Medal (Austria), Officer Order of Merit (Germany), Verdienstkreuz (First Class, Germany) 1976, Cavaliere Gran Croce (Italy) 1991, Légion d'honneur (France), Hon. KBE 2000, Russian Order of Friendship 2001, Silver Medal of the Salzburg Mozarteum 2001. *Current Management:* Columbia Artists Management, 165 W 57th Street, New York, NY 10019, USA. *Address:* c/o Teatro alla Scala, Via Filodrammatici 2, Milan 20121, Italy. *Telephone:* (02) 88791 (office).

**MUTTER, Anne-Sophie;** German violinist; b. 29 June 1963, Rheinfelden/ Baden; m. 1st Dithelf Wunderlich 1989 (deceased); m. 2nd André Previn 2002. *Career:* studied with Prof. Aida Stucki, Winterthur, Switzerland; began musical career playing piano and violin 1969; played in the Int. Music Festival, Lucerne 1976; début with Herbert von Karajan at Pfingstfestspiele, Salzburg 1977; soloist with major orchestras of the world; also plays with string trio and quartet; Guest Teacher RAM, London 1985; est. foundation promoting gifted young string players throughout the world; Hon. Pres. Mozart Soc., Univ. of Oxford 1983. *Recordings include:* Mozart: Five Violin Concertos 2005. *Honours:* Youth Music Prize (FRG) for violin 1970, for piano 1970, for violin 1974; Artist of the Year, 'Deutscher Schallplattenpreis', Grand Prix Int. du Disque, Record Acad. Prize, Tokyo 1982, Internationaler Schallplattenpreis 1993; Order of Merit (of Germany, of Bavaria), Herbert von Karajan Award 2003. *Current Management:* Kaye Artists Management, Barratt House, 7 Chertsey Road, Woking, GU21 5AB, England. *Address:* Effnerstrasse 48, 81925 Munich, Germany; c/o London Symphony Orchestra, Barbican Hall, London, EC1, England. *Telephone:* (89) 984418 (Germany). *Fax:* (89) 9827186 (Germany).

**MYERS, Michael;** Singer (Tenor); b. 1955, USA. *Education:* Studied at Curtis Institute, Philadelphia. *Career:* Debut: Central City Opera 1977, in The Bartered Bride; US appearances in Minnesota, Tulsa, Cleveland, San Francisco, Los Angeles and Des Moines; Season 1981–82 as Belmonte in Ottawa, Alfred in Die Fledermaus for Charlotte Opera, Faust for Providence and Virginia Operas and Jenik in Kentucky and Augusta; Highlights of 1982–83 were debuts at the New York City Opera, as Rodolfo, Santa Fe Opera as Quint (Turn of the Screw), Monteverdi's Nerone with Canadian Opera and the Duke of Mantua for Hawaii Opera Theatre; Sang Nick in the premiere of The Postman Always Rings Twice for St Louis Opera (1982) and repeated the role at the 1983 Edinburgh Festival; Scottish Opera debut 1984, as Idomeneo, returning as the Duke in Rigoletto and Cavalli's Orione; Season 1984–85 included Percy to Joan Sutherland's Anna Bolena for Canadian Opera, Flotow's Lionel in Portland and Lord Puff in the US premiere of Henze's The English Cat, at Santa Fe; Season 1985–86 featured debuts with Seattle Opera (Des Grieux in Manon), in Toulouse (Gounod's Roméo), Long Beach Grand Opera (Belmonte), Montpellier (Rimsky's Mozart) and with the Mostly Mozart Festival (Belfiore in La Finta Giardiniera); Active during 1986–87 at Philadelphia (Wagner's Steersman), Pittsburgh (Edgardo in Lucia di Lammermoor) with the Canadian Opera as Dimitri in Boris Godunov and the Mostly Mozart Festival as Agenore in Il Re Pastore; From 1987 has sung Berg's Painter with the Chicago Opera, the Berlioz Faust with Lyon Opéra, Sergei in Lady Macbeth of Mtsensk with Canadian Opera, Boris in Katya Kabanova at Glyndebourne and Ismael in Nabucco in Philadelphia and New York; Season 1992 as Tom Rakewell at Brussels and Percy in Anna Bolena at Santiago; Tom Rakewell at Madrid, 1996; Donizetti's Edgardo for New Israeli Opera, 1999; Concert engagements include Rossini's Stabat Mater (Cincinnati May Festival) and Huon in Oberon for Radio France. *Honours:* First Prize 1979 Merola Program of the San Francisco Opera. *Address:* c/o Columbia Artists Inc, 165 West 57th Street, New York, NY 10019, USA.

**MYERS, Pamela;** Singer (Soprano); b. 1952, Baltimore, USA. *Career:* Debut: San Francisco Western Opera, 1977 as Mozart's Countess; Sang the title role in Stephen Oliver's The Duchess of Malfi, Santa Fe 1978; Appearances at New York City Opera from 1979, Scottish Opera 1980–81, as Lucia; Giessen 1981 in the title role of Menotti's La Loca, Amsterdam 1983 as Mozart's Constanze, Innsbruck Early Music Festival 1984 in Handel's Rodrigo; Sang at Marseille 1988 and 1991 as Desdemona and Ellen Orford; Other roles have included Aennchen in Der Freischütz, Zerlina, Zerbinetta, Micaela, Luisa Miller, Violetta, Liu and Lady Macbeth; Noted concert artist. *Address:* c/o Opera de Marseille, 2 Rue Molière, 1321 Marseille, France.

**MYERS, Peter (Joseph);** Composer; b. 3 Feb. 1962, Werribee, Victoria, Australia. *Education:* BA (Hons), 1984, MA, 1990, La Trobe University. *Career:* Faculty Member, La Trobe University, 1984–90; Pascoe Vale Girls' Secondary College, 1993–. *Compositions include:* Transformations, for oboe, 1983; Aftermath for concert band Octet for Winds, 1984; Scintilla, for orchestra, 1986; Of Minds and Minds for Ensemble, 1987; Antipathy for mezzo and ensemble, 1988; Towards the Equinox for chamber ensemble, 1986; Vex for violin, 1988; Homage to the Ancient, for trombone, percussion, and piano; Pasar, for piano, 1991; Bilanx for violin, cello, piccolo, clarinet and piano, 1991; Demons Within, for orchestra, 1993; Paroxysms, for string quartet, 1993. *Address:* APRA, 1A Eden Street, Crows Nest, NSW 2065, Australia.

**MYERSCOUGH, Clarence,** FRAM; violinist; b. 27 Oct. 1930, London, England; m. Marliese Scherer, one s. one d. *Education:* Royal Academy of Music, London, Paris Conservatoire. *Career:* Prof. of Violin, Royal Academy of Music 1964–; soloist, recitalist and chamber music player; appeared in many int. music festivals, including Ascona, Segovia, Madrid, Badajoz and Cardiff; several tours in USA and Far East; broadcasts for BBC, ITV, RTE, HK TV and major European stations; founder mem., Fidelio Quartet; mem. Incorporated Soc. of Musicians, Royal Soc. of Musicians of Great Britain. *Recordings:* String Quartets of Britten, Tippett, Delius, Arriaga; Violin Sonata by Hoddinott with Martin Jones. *Honours:* Winner, All England Violin Competition, National Federation of Music Festivals and Albert Sammons Prize, 1951; 2nd Prize, Carl Flesch International Violin Competition, 1952. *Address:* 17 Salterton Road, London, N7 6BB, England.

**MYERSCOUGH, Nadia,** LRAM, ARAM, Artist Dip.; British/Swiss violinist; b. 29 July 1967, London, England; d. of Clarence Myerscough. *Education:* Royal Acad. of Music, London, Indiana Univ., Bloomington, USA, studied with Clarence Myerscough, Franco Gulli, Rostislav Dubinsky, Luba Edlina, Shigeo Neriki. *Career:* soloist, recitalist and chamber music player; broadcasts on BBC Radio 3, Classic FM, France Music, Radio MEC Brazil, Polish radio and TV; appearances at South Bank, Wigmore Hall, City of London Festival, Wexford Festival; soloist with the Lucerne Festival Strings, London Soloists, Kent Concert Orchestra, Bangkok Philharmonic; mem New Helvetic Soc., Royal Soc. of Musicians RAM Club. *Recordings:* Dvořák, Suk, Smetana; The Festival Strings Lucerne Vivaldi Concerto; Chamber Music Works by Alan Rawsthorne. *Honours:* B. J. Dale Prize, Countess of Munster Award, several scholarships, English Speaking Union Fellowship. *Current Management:* M&M Management, 17 Salterton Road, London, N7 6BB, England. *Telephone:* (20) 7272-2547 (office). *Fax:* (20) 7272-2547 (office). *E-mail:* myerscough@ waitrose.com (office).

# N

**NAAF, Dagmar;** Singer (Mezzo-soprano); b. 1934, Munich, Germany. *Education:* Studied in Munich. *Career:* Sang in Opera at Freiburg, 1958–63, Munich, 1963–66, Wiesbaden, 1963–66 and Hanover, 1966–70; Engaged at Cologne, 1967–69, Graz, 1970–72, Staatsoper Munich 1974–76; Guest appearances at Brussels, Berne, Marseilles, Rio de Janeiro, (Amsterdam, Octavian, 1965), Barcelona and Vienna, 1972; Other roles have included Monteverdi's Ottavia, Handel's Cornelia, Gluck's Paride, Dorabella, Brangaene; Strauss's Composer and Clairon; Verdi's Preziosilla, Azucena, Amneris and Eboli; Noted concert artist. *Address:* c/o Bayerische Staatsoper, Postfach 100148, 8000 Munich, Germany.

**NADAREISHVILI, Zurab;** Composer; b. 4 Jan. 1957, Poti, Georgia; m. Niho Shawdia, 23 November 1985, 1 s., 1 d. *Education:* Theoretical Department, Music School, Poti; Tbilisi State Conservatoire. *Career:* Debut: Tbilisi, 1985; Performed in St Petersburg, 1987, Moscow, 1988, Amsterdam, 1992, USA, 1993; mem, Georgian Composers Union. *Compositions:* 2 String Quartets; Brass Quintet; Orchestral Minatures; Symphonic Poem; Hymns, for chamber orchestra; Variations, for piano; Variations, for piano and orchestra; Instrumental Pieces. *Recordings:* Hymns, for chamber orchestra, 1988. *Publications:* The Way to Music, 1987; Musical Georgia, 1997. *Honours:* Moscow Composers International Competition, 1987; Georgian Composers Union Award, 1992; 3rd Place, Moscow Prokofiev Competition, 1997. *Address:* Street No. 20, fl 41, Tbilisi 380071, Georgia.

**NADELMANN, Noëmi;** Singer (Soprano); b. 1966, Zürich, Switzerland. *Education:* Studied at Bloomington, Indiana. *Career:* Sang at Lucerne Opera, 1988–89, Zürich and Augsburg (as Norina in Don Pasquale); Theater am Gärtnerplatz, Munich, from 1990, as Zerlina, Blondchen, Aennchen in Der Freischütz, Manon and Zerbinetta; Komische Oper Berlin, 1994–95, as Traviata, Lucia di Lammermoor, Nedda and Musetta; Munich, 1996, as Rosalinde in Die Fledermaus and the title role in Orffs Die Kluge; Further appearances at Venice, Geneva and the Metropolitan, New York debut 2000, as Musetta; Sang Rosalinde for Zürich Opera and Armida in Handel's Rinaldo at the Prinzregententheater, Munich, 2000; Wiener Blut and Die lustige Witwe at Zürich, 2002. *Address:* Theater am Gärtnerplatz 3, 8000 Munich 5, Germany.

**NADLER, Sheila;** Singer (mezzo-soprano); b. 1945, New York, NY, USA. *Education:* studied at the Manhattan School of Music, at the Opera Studio of the Metropolitan Opera and Juilliard School. *Career:* sang at San Francisco and New York City Opera 1970–72, Baltimore 1972–, notably in 1975 in the premiere of Inez de Castro by Pasatieri, Metropolitan Opera 1976–; sang Anna in Les Troyens at La Scala, 1982, and Clytemnestra in Elektra at Santiago, 1984; further appearances as Fricka and Waltraute in The Ring, at Marseilles, Lyon and Brussels and as Erda, Herodias, Jocasta in Oedipus Rex, Azucena, Ulrica, Mistress Quickly, Cornelia in Giulio Cesare and La Cieca in La Gioconda; sang Clytemnestra in Elektra at Seattle, 1996; as Poulenc's Mme de Croissy, Santa Fe, 1999. *Address:* c/o Baltimore Opera Company, 527 North Charles Street, Baltimore, MD 21201, USA.

**NADOR, Magda;** Singer (Soprano); b. 16 Dec. 1955, Dorog, Hungary. *Education:* Studied at the Budapest Music Academy. *Career:* Debut: Budapest National Opera, 1979, as Mozart's Constanze; Komische Oper Berlin from 1982, as Mozart's Fiordiligi and Queen of Night, and Gilda in Rigoletto; Guest appearances at Amsterdam (as Adele), Zürich, Düsseldorf and Munich; Vienna Staatsoper, 1986, as Oscar in Un Ballo in Maschera; Queen of Night at Stuttgart and Graz, 1987; Berlin and Wiesbaden, 1991–91, as Isotta in Strauss's Die Schweigsame Frau; Concerts include Salzburg Festival, 1986. *Address:* National Opera House, Nepoztarsarag utja 22, 1061 Budapest, Hungary.

**NAEF, Yvonne;** Singer (Mezzo-soprano); b. 1965, Switzerland. *Education:* Studied in Zürich, Basle and Mannheim. *Career:* Concert and recital appearances from 1987; Opera debut as Rossini's Cenerentola, followed by an engagement at St Gallen, as Ulrica, Ariodante, Gluck's Orfeo and Sara in Roberto Devereux, from 1992; Wiesbaden from 1993, as Preziosilla, Rosina, Suzuki, Fricka, Brangaene and Adalgisa; Monte Carlo 1994, as Giovanna Seymour in Anna Bolena, and La Scala Milan as Offenbach's Giulietta; Invalid Woman in Schoenberg's Moses and Aron at Amsterdam, Salzburg and the Festival Hall, London (1996); Appearances as Verdi's Amneris at St Gallen, Wiesbaden and the Deutsche Oper Berlin; Concert engagements in Prokofiev's Alexander Nevsky (at Naples), Mahler's Second Symphony (Venice), Bach's B Minor Mass (Lausanne) and Das Lied von der Erde (Toulouse); Bayreuth Festival 1997, as Waltraute and Second Norn, in The Ring; Season 2000–01 as Wagner's Venus at Hamburg, Stravinsky's Anna in Les Troyens at Salzburg and Eboli at the Vienna Staatsoper (debut); Azucena at Covent Garden, and returned to Hamburg for Marina in Boris Godunov. *Honours:* Second Prize, Lieder and Oratorio section, 1987 Maria Callas Competition, at Athens. *Address:* c/o Opernhaus Zürich, Falkenstrasse 1, 8008 Zürich, Switzerland.

**NAEGELE, Philipp (Otto);** American/German violinist, violist and professor; b. 22 Jan. 1928, Stuttgart, Germany; one s. *Education:* BA, Queens College, New York, USA, 1949; MA 1950, PhD 1955, Princeton University, New Jersey. *Career:* Violinist and Violist, Marlboro Music Festival, Marlboro, Vermont, 1950–; Violinist, Cleveland Orchestra, 1956–64; Member, Resident String Quartet, Kent State University, Kent Ohio, 1960–64; Violin Faculty, Cleveland Institute of Music, 1961–64; Assistant Professor, 1964–68, Associate Professor, 1968–72, Professor, 1972–78, William R. Kenan Jr Professor of Music, 1978–2000, Professor Emeritus, 2000–, Smith College, Northampton, Massachusetts; Member, Végh String Quartet, 1977–79; Violist, Cantilena Piano Quartet, concerts USA and abroad, 1980–96; Numerous concerts: Music from Marlboro series, USA, independently, Europe; Residences: National Arts Center, Ottawa; Yehudi Menuhin School, England; Freiburg Hochschule für Musik; Banff Center for the Arts; Rubin Academy, Tel-Aviv University; Teacher, Chamber Music Ensembles, Musicorda Summer School, Mount Holyoke College, 1987–94. *Recordings:* Numerous recordings of violin/viola solos and chamber music, including part of complete recorded edition of chamber works of Max Reger for his centennial, Da Camera, 1973. *Publications:* Gustav Mahler and Johann Sebastian Bach; August Wilhelm Ambros in Grove's Dictionary of Music and Musicians, A Marlboro Book of Texts in Translation: A Resource. *Address:* 57 Prospect Street, Northampton, MA 01060, USA. *Telephone:* (413) 586-1757 (home). *Fax:* (413) 586-1757 (home). *E-mail:* pnaegele@smith.edu (office).

**NAFE, Alicia;** Singer (Mezzo-soprano); b. 4 Aug. 1947, Buenos Aires, Argentina. *Education:* Studied in Buenos Aires with Ferruccio Calusio and in Europe with Luigi Ricci and Teresa Berganza. *Career:* Sang in Barcelona after winning competition there, debut in Verdi's Requiem; Sang in Toledo and at the Bayreuth Festival, 1975; Member of the Hamburg Opera, 1977–81; Geneva Opera, 1981, in La Cenerentola; Lyon 1981, in Beatrice et Benedict by Berlioz; Sang Rosina with the Cologne Opera at the 1981 Edinburgh Festival; La Scala 1984, as Idamante in Idomeneo; Covent Garden 1985, as Rosina; Guest engagements in Spain, South America, France, Germany and China; Other roles include Carmen and Dorabella; Sang Adalgisa at Covent Garden, 1987; Metropolitan Opera debut 1988, as Sextus in La Clemenza di Tito and Ramiro in La Finta Giardiniera; Sang Massenet's Charlotte at the Teatro Regio Parma, 1990; Grandmother in La Vida Breve at Madrid, 1998; Also heard in oratorios and as song recitalist. *Recordings:* Mercedes in Carmen and La Vida Breve; Monteverdi Madrigals; Così fan tutte. *Address:* c/o Teatro Regio, Via Garibaldi 16, 43100 Parma, Italy.

**NAGANO, Kent;** American conductor; *Music Director, Berkeley Symphony Orchestra;* b. 22 Nov. 1951, Berkeley, CA. *Education:* studied under Ozawa, Boulez and Bernstein. *Career:* first achieved int. recognition when he conducted Boston Symphony Orchestra in performance of Mahler's Symphony No. 9 1984; conducted US premiere of Messiaen's The Transfiguration; debut at Paris Opera conducting world premiere of Messiaen's St François d'Assise; debut, Metropolitan Opera, New York conducting Poulenc's Dialogues de Carmelites 1994; Music Dir Berkeley Symphony Orchestra, CA 1978–; Music Dir Opera de Lyon 1989; Assoc. Prin. Guest Conductor, London Symphony Orchestra 1990, Music Dir 1994–99; Music Dir Hallé Orchestra 1992–2000; Artistic Dir Deutsches Symphonie-Orchester Berlin 2000–(07); Prin. Conductor and Music Dir Los Angeles Opera 2001–06; Music Dir Montréal Symphony Orchestra 2005–. *Honours:* several awards for operatic recording. *Current Management:* Van Walsum Management Ltd, 4 Addison Bridge Place, London, W14 8XP, England. *Telephone:* (20) 7371-4343. *Fax:* (20) 7371-4344. *Website:* www.vanwalsum.co.uk.

**NÄGELE, Barbara;** Recorder Player; b. 16 March 1973, Lustenau, Austria. *Education:* Studied at the Hochschule für Musik und Theater in Zürich, Switzerland, with Kees Boeke and Matthias Weilenmann. *Career:* Member of 'Trio O'Henry' together with Claudia Geraeur and Martina Joos; Appearances (among others) at Bludenzer Tage für Zeitgemässe Musik, Austria, 1997; Festival of Ancient Music, Stary Sacz, Poland, 2000; Festival Musica Nova, Sofia, Bulgaria, 2001; Festival Bohemia-Saxony, Czech Republic, 2001; Cycle of premieres with works of Swiss composers, Zürich, 2000–01; Radio appearances (live recordings): St Peter's Church, Zürich, 1996; Great Hall of the HFMT, Zürich; Radio features: Austrian Radio ORF 1, 1998; Swiss Radio DRS 2, 2000; Bulgarian radio and television, Sofia, 2001; Premieres: Kees Boeke's The Unfolding, 1997; Martin Derungs's A Set of Pieces, 2000; Thomas Müller's Erste Etappe in Richtung farbiger Eindrücke, 2000; Giorgio Tedde's Medio Aevo, 2000; Andreas Nick's Trio pour flûtes à bec, 2000; Annette Schmucki's tatsache. eisschollen. Der unzertrennliche anstoss abweichender labialität, 2001; Gerald Bennett's Textures of Time, 2001. *Honours:* Kiwanis Kammermusik-Wettbewerb, Zürich, 1995; International Recorder Competition, Calw, Germany, 1995; Orpheus Förderpreis, Zürich, 1997; Premio Bonporti, Rovereto, Italy, 1997; Migros Kammermusik-Wettbewerb, Zürich, 1999. *Address:* Neustadt 22, A 6800 Feldkirch, Austria.

**NAGELSTAD, Catherine;** Singer (Soprano); b. 1967, California. *Education:* San Francisco Conservatory and in Rome. *Career:* As Zdenka in Arabella and Magda in La Rondine, Southern California Festival; European debut as Mozart's Constanze, Hamburg, 1993; Concerts with Placido Domingo in USA and Europe; Staatsoper Stuttgart as Musetta and Mozart's Vitellia; Venus in King Arthur; Tosca and Alcina, 1998–99; Season 1999–2000 with Constanze, Fiordiligi and Poppea, Elisabeth de Valois and Violetta at Stuttgart; Musetta at Covent Garden. *Honours:* Winner, Palm Springs; Pasalena Opera Guild

Competitions, 1991–92. *Address:* Music International, 13 Ardilaun Road, London N5 2QR, England.

**NAGY, Janos B.;** Singer (tenor); b. 1943, Debrecen, Hungary. *Education:* Bartók Conservatory, Budapest. *Career:* Sang with Hungarian Territorial Army choir on tour, 1967–70; Stage debut at Budapest, 1971, as Don José in Carmen; Many performances in operas by Verdi and Puccini; Berlin 1978, in the Verdi Requiem; Warsaw national Opera 1979; Member of Deutsche Oper am Rhein, Düsseldorf from 1981; Other roles include Puccini's Des Grieux, Cavaradossi and Calaf, Verdi's Manrico, Duke of Mantua, and Macduff, Nemorino in L'Elisir d'amore and Pollione in Norma; Guest appearances at opera houses in Germany and Switzerland; Sang Radames with the Deutsche Oper am Rhein, Düsseldorf, 1989. *Recordings:* Boito's Nerone (Hungaroton); Kodály's Te Deum; Psalmus Hungaricus and Missa Brevis; Christus by Liszt; Mosè in Egitto; Szokolay's Blood Wedding; Simon Boccanegra. *Address:* c/o Hungarian State Opera House, Nepöztarsasay utja 22, 1061 Budapest, Hungary.

**NAGY, Robert;** Singer (Tenor); b. 3 March 1929, Lorain, Ohio, USA. *Education:* Cleveland Institute of Music. *Career:* Metropolitan Opera from 1957, as Canio in Pagliacci, Beethoven's Florestan, Herod in Salome and the Emperor in Die Frau ohne Schatten; With the Met and the New York City Opera (from 1969) has sung in 1000 opera performances; Guest appearances in Chicago, Baltimore, San Diego, Seattle, Montreal and New Orleans; Repertoire includes roles by Wagner, Verdi, Barber, Bizet and Puccini.

**NAKAMURA, Tomoko;** Singer (Soprano); b. 1961, Japan; m. Uwe Heilmann. *Education:* Studied at Detmold and with Elisabeth Schwarzkopf. *Career:* Debut: Detmold Opera, 1983, as Madama Butterfly; Sang at the Stuttgart Staatsoper from 1986, notably as Mozart's Constanze (also at the Vienna Staatsoper, 1992), Queen of Night and Donna Anna, Olympia in Les contes d'Hoffmann, and Gilda; Numerous concert appearances. *Honours:* Prize Winner, Mozart Competition, Salzburg, 1985. *Address:* Stuttgart Staatsoper, Oberer Schlossgarten 6, 7013 Stuttgart, Germany.

**NAKARIAKOV, Sergei;** Russian trumpeter; b. 10 May 1977, Gorky. *Career:* acclaimed performance at Korsholm Festival, Finland aged 12; debut at Salzburg Festival with Lithuanian Chamber Orchestra 1991; appeared at Schleswig-Holstein Musikfestival 1992; began recording career aged 15; numerous int. performances, including Royal Festival Hall and Royal Albert Hall, London, Hollywood Bowl in Los Angeles, Lincoln Center in New York; has performed with Tchaikovsky Orchestra, Munich Chamber Orchestra, Berliner Sinfonie Orchester, Bremen Philharmoniker, Toronto Symphony Orchestra, English Chamber Orchestra, Rotterdam Philharmonic; has collaborated with conductors, including Kent Nagano, Valery Gergiev, Vladimir Spivakov, Vladimir Ashkenazy, Emmanuel Krevine, Jesus Lopez-Cobos; festival appearances include Colmar, Menton, Salzburg, Montreux, Lucerne, Strasbourg, Cannes; frequent tours in Japan, USA, Canada, Germany. *Recordings:* Trumpet Works 1992, Trumpet Concertos 1993, Carmen Fantasy 1994, Baroque Trumpet Concertos 1996, Élégie 1997, Concertos for Trumpet 1999, No Limit 2000, From Moscow with Love 2001, Echoes from the Past 2002. *Honours:* Prix Davidoff, Schleswig-Holstein 1992, ECHO Klassik Award 2002. *Current Management:* c/o Ingeborg Hossmann, Box 125, Gstaad 3780, Switzerland. *Telephone:* (33) 744-8820 (office). *Fax:* (33) 744-8830 (office). *E-mail:* artpro@datacomm.ch (office). *Website:* www .nakariakov.com.

**NALL, Cecily;** Singer (Soprano); b. 1960, Georgia, USA. *Education:* Studied in USA and Graz, Austria. *Career:* Debut: Spoleto Festival, 1985, as Zerbinetta in Ariadne and Naxos; Season 1986 as Blondchen in Die Entführung at Santiago and Offenbach's Olympia for Miami Opera; Aachen Opera, 1987–91, Darmstadt, 1991–93; Many guest appearances elsewhere in Europe; Cleveland, 1988, as Mozart's Constanze; Cincinnati Opera from 1992, as Olympia, Sophie in Der Rosenkavalier, and Mozart's Susanna (1995). *Address:* Cincinnati Opera Association, Music Hall, 1241 Elm Street, Cincinnati, OH 42510, USA.

**NAOURI, Laurent;** Singer (Baritone); b. 1964, Paris. *Education:* Studied at Marseille; Guildhall School, London. *Career:* Debut: Guglielmo in Così fan tutte; Lully's Phaeton and Roland at Lyon and Montpellier; Les Contes d'Hoffmann, Metz; Massenet's Des Grieux and Mozart's Figaro, Opéra Bastille, Paris; 1997–98 Season: Jupiter in Orphée aux Enfers, Geneva; Antenor in Rameau's Dardanus; Bottom in A Midsummer Night's Dream, Lyons; Many appearances at Aix-en-Provence Festival; Season 1999–2000 as Melisso in Alcina at the Palais Garnier, Paris, and as Hucscar in Les Indes Galantes by Rameau; the Villains in Les Contes d'Hoffmann at Antwerp. *Recordings:* Hidraot in Gluck's Armide. *Address:* c/o Geneva Opera, Grand Théâtre de Genéve, 11 Boulevard du Théâtre, 1211 Geneva 11, Switzerland.

**NASEDKIN, Alexei;** Concert Pianist; b. 20 Dec. 1942, Moscow, Russia. *Education:* Studied at Central Music School and the Conservatoire, Moscow. *Career:* Debut: Public concerts from 1951, aged 9; Has toured extensively in Russia and throughout the world, playing works by Haydn, Scarlatti, Mozart, Beethoven, Schubert, Chopin, Prokofiev and Shostakovich; Professor in Piano at Moscow Conservatoire from 1968; Vladimir Ovchinikov has been among his pupils. *Compositions:* Works for piano and orchestra. *Recordings:* Many. *Honours:* Gold Medal at competitions in Vienna and Munich, 1967; Prizewinner at Leeds, 1966, and Moscow, 1962. *Address:* c/o Sonata, 11 Northpark Street, Glasgow G20 7AA, Scotland.

**NASH, Graham (Thomas);** Conductor; b. 21 June 1952, London, England; Divorced, 1 s. *Education:* LRAM, Royal Academy of Music, 1970–74. *Career:* Debut: Conducting, Royal Albert Hall, 1980, Kraków Radio Symphony Orchestra, Poland, 1988 and London Philharmonic Orchestra, 1985; Conducting, Victor Hochhauser, Opera Gala Nights at Royal Albert Hall, Royal Festival Hall, Barbican, 1980–89; Guest Conductor, London Festival Ballet; Music Director, London City Ballet, 1986–88; Kuopio Orchestra debut in Finland, 1987; mem, Incorporated Society of Musicians. *Compositions:* In Memoriam, Lord Mountbatten for large orchestra, 1979. *Honours:* North London Orchestral Society Prize for Conducting, 1974; Blake Memorial Prize for Flute, Ensemble Prize, 1974. *Address:* 53 Faraday Avenue, Sidcup, Kent DA14 4JB, England.

**NASH, Peter Paul;** Composer; b. 1950, Leighton Buzzard, Bedfordshire, England. *Education:* Cambridge University, with Robin Holloway. *Career:* Composition Fellow at Leeds University, 1976–78; Composer in Residence at the National Centre for Orchestral Studies, 1983; Producer, BBC Radio 3, 1985–87; Critic and Broadcaster, (presenter of Music Week on Radio 3); Symphony premiered at the 1991 Promenade Concerts, London. *Compositions:* String Trio, 1982; Wind Quintet; Insomnia for chamber ensemble; Etudes for orchestra (On the Beach, Percussion Study, Parting) 1983–84; Figures for harp; Earthquake, scena for narrator and six players, quintet, 1987; Symphony, 1991. *Address:* c/o Faber Music Ltd, 3 Queen Street, London WC1N 3AU, England.

**NASH, Rebecca Errington,** BA, GradDipEd, PGDip(opera); Australian singer (soprano); b. 1971, Melbourne. *Education:* Studied with Dame Joan Hammond in Melbourne; Royal College of Music, London, until 1999. *Career:* Appearances throughout Australia as Pamina, Donna Elvira, Marguerite in Faust, Gilda, Micaela and Nedda (Pagliacci); Mozart's Countess for Opera Australia at Sydney Opera House, 2000; Concerts include Strauss Vier letzte Lieder, under Daniel Harding; Beethoven's Ninth and Egmont under Frans Bruggen with Scottish Chamber Orchestra and The Orchestra of the 19th Century; Mendelssohn's Elijah under Kurt Masur; Verdi Requiem; Ein Deutsches Requiem; Mozart C Minor Mass; Mahler 4; The Creation; Messiah; Handel's Jephtha; Madama Butterfly for Scottish Opera; Barena in Jenůfa; Fifth Maid in Elektra; First Maid in Daphne for Royal Opera Covent Garden; Season 2003–04 included Marschallin in Der Rosenkavalier with ENO; Fifth Maid in Elektra under Donald Runnicles at BBC Proms; concerts with The Orchestra of the 18th Century, Mozart's Coronation Mass (RTVE Madrid), Dvořák Requiem (Danish Radio); Season 2004–05 includes Beethoven's Ninth Symphony in Hong Kong with Frans Brüggen and the Orchestra of the 18th Century, Vier letze Lieder with Sir Richard Armstrong and the Scottish Opera Orchestra; other roles include Desdemona, Arabella, Katya Kabanova, Jenůfa and Magda in La Rondine. *Current Management:* Askonas Holt Ltd, Lonsdale Chambers, 27 Chancery Lane, London, WC2A 1PF, England. *Telephone:* (20) 7400-1700. *Fax:* (20) 7400-1799. *E-mail:* info@askonasholt.co.uk. *Website:* www.askonasholt.co.uk.

**NASIDZE, Sulkhan;** Composer; b. 17 March 1927, Tbilisi, Georgia; m. Lali Surguladze, 20 July 1963, 1 s., 1 d. *Education:* Tbilisi Conservatory. *Career:* Debut: Concerto for Piano and Symphony Orchestra, Tbilisi, 1954; Chamber, Symphony, Chamber-Instrumental, Chamber-Vocal, Choral, Ballet, Film Music Interpreted in Concert Halls and Opera Houses; Television and radio, 1954–97; mem, Union of Composers, Georgia. *Compositions:* Chamber Symphony, 1969; Symphony, Pirosmani, 1977; Symphony, Dalai, 1979; Concerto for violin, cello and chamber orchestra, 1982; Ballet, King Lear, 1988; Concerto for cello and symphony orchestra, 1990; Stringed quartet No. 2, No. 3, Epitaph No. 4, No. 5; Con sordino; Piano concerto No. 3, Autumn Music; Piano Quintet; Piano Quartet, Metamorphosis; Piano Trio, Antiphonia. *Recordings:* Chamber Symphony, Melodia Panton; Symphony, Pirosmani Melodia; Symphony, Passione Melodia; Symphony, Dalai Melodia. *Publications:* Particularities of Gurian Folk Polyphony Songs, 1970; Polyphonic Processes in Z Paliachvifiil Opera, 1971; Some Words About Modern Music, 1974. *Honours:* Shota Rustaveli Prize, Georgia, 1978; State Prize, Russia, 1986. *Address:* Kazbegi Avenue 20, Apt 6, Tbilisi 380077, Georgia.

**NASRAWI, Douglas;** Singer (Tenor); b. 1960, California, USA. *Career:* Resident in Paris, 1982–; Appearances under conductors William Christie, Kent Nagano, John Eliot Gardiner and Jean-Claude Malgoire; Leading roles in La Clemenza di Tito; Pulcinella by Stravinsky and Lully's Alceste; 1993–94 Season: Ecclitco in Haydn's Il mondo della luna; Premiere Jocaste by Charles Chayne at Rouen; Germanico in Biber's Chi la dura, la vince, Innsbruck and Salzburg; 1998 Season with Hindemith, Toch, Weill, Milhaud bill at Karlsruhe and as Flamingo in Montemezzi's L'Amore dei tre Re at Bregenz. *Recordings:* Osman in Handel's Almira, CPO; Alecton and Apollon in Lully's Alceste; Schütz Symphoniae sacrae; Purcell Songs of Welcome and Farewell. *Address:* c/o Karlsruhe Opera, Baumeisterstrasse 11, 7500 Karlsruhe, Germany.

**NASU, Teruhiko,** BA, MA, MPhil; University Lecturer; b. 23 Dec. 1960, Tokyo, Japan; m. Machiko; one d. *Education:* Rikkyo Univ., Tokyo, Japan, Univ. of Cambridge. *Career:* part-time lecturer in music, St Gregory's Institute for Religious Music 1991– Toho Gakuen Junior Coll. 1993–97, Japan Lutheran Theological Coll. 1995–96, Rikkyo Univ. 1996–2000; Lecturer in Music, Senzoku Gakuen Coll. 1996–2000; Assoc. Prof. of Music, Aoyama Gakuin Univ.; mem. Musicological Soc. of Japan, Royal Musical Asscn, Plainsong and Mediaeval Music Soc., Japan Soc. of Liturgical Musicology. *Publications:* The

Publication of Byrd's Gradualia Reconsidered, Brio xxxii 1995, On Versus and Versiclus, Grocheio's De Musica: A Japanese Translation 2001. *Honours:* Kan Memorial Scholarship 1984. *Address:* Aoyama Gakuin University 4–4–25 Shibuya, Shibuya-Ku, Tokyo, 150–8366 Japan (office). *Telephone:* (3) 3409-7921 (office). *Fax:* (3) 3409-5414 (office). *E-mail:* tnasu@cl.aoyama.ac.jp (office). *Website:* www.aoyama.ac.jp (office).

**NATANEK, Adam (Tadewsa);** Conductor; b. 23 July 1933, Kraków, Poland; m. Danuta Daniecka, 27 July 1966. *Education:* Department of Pedagogy, 1957; Department of Composition and Conducting, 1960; Academy of Music, Kraków, 1960. *Career:* Debut: Kraków Philharmonic Orchestra, 1960; Conductor, Lublin Philharmonic Orchestra, 1961–69; Head, Artistic Director, Chief Conductor, 1969–90; First Guest Conductor, Symphonic Orchestra, Valladolid, Spain, 1984–, Artistic Director, Chief Conductor, 1990; Artistic Director Rzeszów Philharmonic and Music Festival in Iancur, Poland; Professor, Marie Curie-Skiodowska University, Lublin, –1992; Member of Jury, numerous music competitions; Appearances throughout Europe, South Korea, Africa, Cuba and Latin America. *Recordings:* Numerous radio and television recordings with orchestras including National Warsaw Philharmonic, Great Symphony Orchestra of Polish Radio and Television, Katowice, Polish Radio and Television Orchestra, Kraków; First world-wide CD recording of Ignacy Feliks Dobrzynski's Piano Concerto with the New Polish Symphony Orchestra. *Contributions:* Promoter and Reviewer, Maria Sklodowska-Curie University, Lublin and Academy of Music, Warsaw and Poznan. *Honours:* Numerous prizes including Commander's Cross of the Order of Polish Revival. *Address:* ul Szczerbowskiego 13/10, 20-012 Lublin, Poland.

**NATRA, Sergiu;** Composer; b. 12 April 1924, Bucharest, Romania. *Education:* MA, National Music Academy, Bucharest, 1952; Studied Composition with Leo Klepper. *Career:* Commissions of Symphony Works, Chamber Music, Stage and Film Music in Romania; Major commissions in Israel by the Israel Festival, Israel Philharmonic Orchestra, Israel Radio, Israel Composers Fund; Resident in Tel-Aviv from 1961; Professor, Composition; Examiner for higher musical education, Israel Ministry of Education and Culture, 1964–71; Commission for Testimonium, 1968; mem, Honorary Director, World Harp Congress. *Compositions:* 3 Corteges in the Street, 1945; Suite for orchestra, 1948; Sinfonia for strings; Music for violin and harp, Music for harpsichord and 6 instruments, 1964; Music for oboe and strings, 1965; Sonatina for harp, 1965; Song of Deborah, 1967; Variations for piano and orchestra, 1966; Prayer for harp, 1972; Sonatina for trumpet solo, 1973; Sonatina for trombone solo, 1973; Sacred Service, 1976; From the Diary of a Composer, 1978; Variations for harpsichord, 1978; Hours for mezzo-soprano, violin, clarinet and piano, 1981; Music for harp and three brass instruments, 1982; Divertimento for harp and strings, 1983; Ness Amim, Cantata for solo voices, choir, chamber orchestra with harpsichord, 1984; Music for violin and piano, 1986; Sonatina for piano, 1987; Music for NICANOR for harp solo and chamber ensemble, 1988; Developments for viola solo and chamber orchestra, 1988; Sonata for four harps, 1993; Sonata for harp and string quartet, 1997; Sound Picture, two pianos, 1998. *Recordings:* Suite for orchestra, 1948; Music for harpsichord and 6 instruments; Song of Deborah; Sonatina for harp; Trio for violin, violoncello and piano; Developments, for viola and chamber orchestra. *Address:* 10 Barth St, Tel-Aviv 69104, Israel.

**NAUHAUS, Gerd (Ernst Hermann);** Musicologist; b. 28 July 1942, Erfurt, Germany; m. Ursula Karsdorf, 15 Aug 1965, 2 s., 1 deceased, 1 d. *Education:* Matriculation, 1961; Diploma, Musical Education, 1965, Diploma, Musicology, 1969, PhD, 1980, Martin Luther University, Halle-Wittenberg. *Career:* Dramaturg at Zwickau Opera House, 1967; Musicologist, 1970–, Vice-Director, 1980–, Robert Schumann House, Zwickau; Director, 1993; mem, Vice-Chairman, Scientific Secretary, Robert Schumann Society, Zwickau; German Musicological Society; Saxon Cultural Council, 1993–2002. *Publications:* Robert Schumann, Diaries and Household Books, complete scholarly edition, vol. III, 1982, vol. II, 1987; Clara Schumann 3 part Songs After Poems by Geibel, 1989; Piano Sonata in G minor, 1991; March in E Flat Major, 1997 (first editions). *Honours:* Schumann Prize, Zwickau Town Council, 1986. *Address:* Robert-Schumann-Haus, Hauptmarkt 5, 08056 Zwickau/Saxony, Germany.

**NAYLOR, Peter Russell,** MA, BMus, ARCM; British composer; b. 5 Oct. 1933, London; s. of Alfred Douglas Naylor and Rebecca Kate Naylor. *Education:* Univ. of Cambridge, London Univ.; Fellow, Royal Coll. of Organists, London, 1961. *Career:* Lecturer, City Literary Inst., London, 1963–65; Lecturer, Harmony and Counterpoint, History, Royal Scottish Acad. of Music and Drama, 1965–71; Organist, Ashwell Festival, Herts., 1964–69; Assoc. Organist, Glasgow Cathedral, 1972–85; Music Assoc., Scottish Opera for Youth, 1975–80; Repetiteur, Shepway Youth Opera, Kent, 1982–85; mem., British Acad. of Composers and Songwriters, Scottish Soc. of Composers. *Compositions:* Symphony in One Movement, Tides and Islands; Organ Concerto; Beowulf for symphonic wind band; Odysseus Returning, three act opera; Pied Piper, one-act opera; The Mountain People, workshop opera; Earth was Waiting, cantata; Wassail Sing We for SA chorus, piano and percussion; A Hero Dies for 22 voices and clarsach; Movement for organ; Air and Variations for 2 pianos; Clarinet Quintet; Love and Life (5 songs); Carols and Anthems; Daybreak to Starlight, 16 pieces for organ, The Oak Tree and the Cypress (for speaker, mezzo-soprano, harp and organ) 1998, Tides of Summer (5 pieces for organ) 2001, Echoes and Reflections (4 pieces for organ) 2002, Trumpet in 3 (for organ) 2004 Three Hymn Preludes (for organ) 2005.

*Recordings:* Eastern Monarchs, Elizabethan Singers, Louis Halsey and the Choir of St John's College, Cambridge, George Guest; Now the Green Blade Riseth, SATB Choir of Glasgow Cathedral, John R Turner; Clarinet Quintet, Colin Bradbury and the Georgian Quartet; Movement and Stillness (four songs), Stephen Pusey (baritone), Peter Naylor (piano). *Publications:* The Oak Tree and the Cypress 1998; Movement and Stillness: Four Songs for Baritone and Piano 1998; Tides of Summer 2001; Echoes and Reflections 2002; Trumpet in 3 2004; Three Hymn Preludes 2005; Gabriel's Message; The Bell Carol; Three Wordless Songs for Organ 2006. *Honours:* London Univ. Convocation Trust Prize, 1959; Aschenberg Composition Prize, 1959. *Address:* Greenacres, Brady Road, Lyminge, Folkestone, Kent, CT18 8HA, England. *Telephone:* (1303) 863284.

**NAYLOR, Steven,** BMus, FRAM; British pianist, accompanist, vocal coach and opera administrator; *Director of Artistic Administration, Glyndebourne Festival;* b. 1956, Gwent, Wales. *Education:* Univ. Coll., Cardiff, at the Nat. Opera Studio and the Royal Acad., London; further piano studies with Geoffrey Parsons. *Career:* Accompanist and opera coach at many venues in the UK and abroad; Joined Glyndebourne, 1989, Head of Music, 1998–, Dir of Artistic Administration, 1999–; BBC Radio 3 broadcasts; further engagements at the Wexford and Buxton Festivals, the Munich Festival and the Hans Werner Henze Summer Acad., Germany; Canadian Opera, Singapore Arts Festival, Royal Opera House Covent Garden, English Nat. Opera and Paris (Opéra and Châtelet); Netherlands Opera, Amsterdam. *Honours:* prizes for piano accompaniment at RAM, and Countess of Munster Musical Trust Scholarship; Jani Strasser Award, Glyndebourne 1993. *Address:* Glyndebourne Festival Opera, Glyndebourne, Lewes, East Sussex, BN8 5UU, England (office). *Telephone:* (1273) 812321 (office). *Fax:* (1273) 815016 (office). *E-mail:* steven.naylor@glyndebourne.com (office). *Website:* www .glyndebourne.com (office).

**NEARY, Alice;** British cellist; b. 15 Dec. 1972, London, England; d. of Martin Gerard James Neary and Penelope Neary (née Warren). *Education:* Chetham's School of Music, RNCM with Ralph Kirshbaum, SUNY, Stonybrook with Timothy Eddy. *Career:* debut playing Haydn's C major concerto with the London Symphony Orchestra at the Barbican, 1994; South Bank Show (ITV) appearance in programme on John Tavener, 1995; Wigmore Hall, London, debut, 1999; Recitals for the Park Lane Group Series at the Purcell Room, for BBC Radio 3 and at Bridgewater Hall, Manchester; Concertos with the English CO, in Canada with the Israel Symphony Orchestra (Season 2000), Orchestra of St John's, London, and Royal Liverpool Philharmonic Orchestra; Bach's Solo Suites at St John's 2000; Performances at the International Musicians Seminar, Prussia Cove, with National Tour 2000; Festival engagements at the Manchester International Cello Festival, Santa Fe Chamber Music Festival and Presteigne Festival (Artist-in-Residence, 1999); Recitals with pianist Gretel Dowdeswell and the Ovid Ensemble, Wigmore Hall recital April 2000. *Recordings include:* Innocence by John Tavener. *Honours:* Pierre Fournier Award, 1988; Silver Medal, 1994 Shell/London Symphony Orchestra Competition; Prize Winner, Adam International Cello Competition, New Zealand, 1997; Countess of Munster Musical Trust. *Address:* 7 Cornwall Avenue, Finchley N3 1LH, England.

**NEARY, Martin Gerard James,** LVO, MA, FRCO; British conductor and organist; b. 28 March 1940, s. of the late Leonard W. Neary and of Jeanne M. Thébault; m. Penelope J. Warren 1967; one s. two d. *Education:* City of London School and Gonville & Caius Coll. Cambridge. *Career:* Asst Organist, St Margaret's Westminster 1963–65, Organist and Master of Music 1965–71; Prof. of Organ, Trinity Coll. London 1963–72; Organist and Master of Music, Winchester Cathedral 1972–87; Organist and Master of Choristers, Westminster Abbey 1988–98; has led Westminster Abbey Choir on tours to France, Germany, Switzerland, Hungary, USA, Russia, Ukraine; Founder and Conductor Martin Neary Singers 1972–; Chair. Church Services Cttee, Musicians Benevolent Fund 1993–; Herbert Howells Soc. 1993–; Conductor Waynflete Singers 1972–87; Pres. Cathedral Organists Asscn 1985–88; Pres. Royal Coll. of Organists 1988–90, 1996–98; Guest Conductor Australian Youth Choir 1999–; Visiting Artistic Dir Paulist Boy Choristers of Calif. 1999–2000; many organ recitals and broadcasts in UK, Europe, USA, Canada, the Far East and Australia; many choral premières; guest conductor English Chamber Orchestra, London Symphony Orchestra; numerous recordings. *Publications:* editions of early organ music, contribs to organ journals. *Honours:* Hon. RAM; Hon. F.T.C.L.; Hon. Fellow Royal School of Church Music. *Address:* 71 Clancarty Road, Fulham, London, SW6 3BB, England. *Telephone:* (20) 7736-5268. *Fax:* (20) 7610-6995.

**NEBE, Michael;** Cellist and Conductor; b. 28 July 1947, Nordenbeck, Waldeck, Germany. *Education:* Educational Diploma and Teaching Qualifications, Dortmund Conservatorium; MMus, King's College, University of London, England, studied under Thurston Dart, Brian Trowell, Antony Milner, Geoffrey Bush; Licentiate, Royal Academy of Music, studying with Florence Hooton and Colin Hampton; Conducting, private studies in Germany and at Morley College, London under Lawrence Leonard; International Conductors' Seminar, Zlin, Czech Republic, 1991 and 1993 under Kirk Trevor, Jiri Belohlavek and Zdenek Bilek. *Career:* Debut: Wigmore Hall, London, 1977; Member, London Piace Consort, London Piace Duo, both until 1987, Plaegan Piano Quartet; Numerous performances as soloist and chamber music player throughout the United Kingdom; Tours in Germany, Netherlands, USA, Canada, Australia; Conductor and Musical Director of Whitehall Orchestra (The Orchestra of the British Civil Service), 1990–; Associated

Conductor, Surrey Sinfonietta until 1994; Founder and Musical Director, Fine Arts Sinfonia of London, 1994–; Appearances as conductor in the United Kingdom, Germany Spain, Turkey; Teacher, conductor, freelance musician, soloist, translator, writer, lecturer and adjudicator; Made numerous live and recorded radio and television appearances, CD recordings; Conducted over 100 British and world Premieres; mem, Dvořák Society; Incorporated Society of Musicians; Musicians' Union. *Publications:* Translation into German, Eta Cohen's Violin Tutor, 1979; Cello Tutor, 1984; Articles for British newspapers and magazines. *Current Management:* Thornton Management. *Address:* c/o Thornton Management, 24 Thornton Avenue, London SW2 4HG, England.

**NEBLETT, Carol;** singer (soprano); b. 1 Feb. 1946, Modesto, CA, USA. *Education:* studied with Lotte Lehmann and Pierre Bernac. *Career:* sang with Roger Wagner Chorale from 1965; Stage debut as Musetta, New York City Opera 1969; Returned as Marietta in Die Tote Stadt, Poppea, and Margherita and Elena in Boito's Mefistofele; Chicago 1975, as Chrysothemis in Elektra; Veinna Staatsoper debut 1976 as Minnie in La Fanciulla del West, Covent Garden 1977; Metropolitan Opera debut 1979, as Senta in Der fliegende Holländer; Returned as Tosca, Amelia (Un Ballo in Maschera), Manon Lescaut and Alice Ford in Falstaff; Appearances in Dallas, Turin, Leningrad, Pittsburgh, Baltimore and San Francisco; Other roles include Violetta, Minnie in La Fanciulla del West, Mozart's Countess, Charpentier's Louise and Antonia in Les Contes d'Hoffmann; Salzburg Festival as Vitelia in La Clemenza di Tito (has also appeared as Vitelia in Jean-Pierre Ponnelle's film of the opera); Teatro Regio Turin 1987, in Respighi's Semirama; Sang Mme Lidoine in Les Dialogues des Carmélites at San Diego, 1990; Debut as Norma for Greater Miami Opera 1990; Aida for Cincinnati Opera; Season 1992 as Tosca for Opera Pacific at Costa Mesa, Queen Isabella in Franchetti's Cristoforo Colombo at Miami and as Amelia in Un Ballo in Maschera at Dublin; Sang the title role in Blitzstein's Regina at Costa Mesa, 1990. *Recordings include:* Die Tote Stadt (RCA); La Fanciulla del West (Deutsche Grammophon); La Bohème (HMV).

**NEBOLSIN, Eloar;** Pianist; b. 24 Dec. 1974, Tashkent, Uzbekistan. *Education:* Tashkent Uspensky School of Music, 1980–91; Lscuela Superior de Musica, Reina, Sofia, 1991–95. *Career:* Wigmore Hall, London, 1993; New York–92nd Str Y, 1994; Ravina Festival with Riccardo Chailly, Chicago Symphony, 1994; Berlin Philharmonie with V L Ashkenazy, Deutsche Symphony Orchestra, 1995; Avery Fisher Hall with New York Philharmonic and Leonard Slatkin Cleaveland Orchestra, 1996. *Recordings:* Chopin and Liszt Recital; Chopin Piano Concerto No.1, Vladimir Ashkenazy conducting, Deutsche Symphony Orchestra. *Honours:* Concertino Praga Radio Competition; Santander Piano Competition Paloma O'Shea. *Current Management:* Konzertdirection Hans Ulrich Schmid. *Address:* 136-40, 62nd Avn, Flushing, NY 11367, USA.

**NEGRIN, Francisco (Miguel);** Opera Director; b. 5 June 1963, Mexico City, Mexico. *Education:* Studied cinematography in France notably at Aix-en-Provence. *Career:* Staff Producer at Théâtre Royal de la Monnaie, Brussels; Has assisted directors such as Patrice Chereau, K E Herrmann and Graham Vick; Associations with many opera houses including: Paris Châtelet, Salzburg Landestheater and Seattle Opera; Directed the premiere of his version of Debussy's The Fall of the House of Usher, Christ Church, Spitalfields, 1986, and at London International Opera Festival and Lisbon Opera, 1989; Has produced Werther at Opera de Nice, 1990, Orlando Paladino at Garsington Manor, 1990, La Traviata and the Mozart pasticcio The Jewel Box at Opera North, 1991 being the first outside production to be invited by Glyndebourne to be performed there, 1991, Così fan tutte at Seattle Opera, Don Carlos at Victoria State Opera, Melbourne, L'Heure Espagnole and La Colombe at the Guildhall School of Music, 1993, and Handel's Julius Caesar at Australian Opera in Sydney, 1994 and Melbourne, 1995; World premieres of Tourist Variations and Visitatio Sepulchri by James Macmillan at Glasgow's Tramway and at the Edinburgh Festival, Una Cosa Rara by Martin y Soler at the Drottningholm Festival; Schoeck's Venus at Geneva, 1997; Handel's Partenope for Glimmerglass Opera, New York, 1998. *Recordings:* Julius Caesar on CD and Video. *Current Management:* IMG Artists. *Address:* c/o Diana Mulgan, IMG Artists, Lovell House, 616 Chiswick High Road, London W4 5RX, England.

**NÉGYESY, János;** Violinist; b. 13 Sept. 1938, Budapest, Hungary. *Education:* Franz Liszt Music Acad., Budapest. *Career:* concert master, Berlin Radio Orchestra, Germany 1970–74; Prof. of Music, Univ. of California San Diego, USA 1979–; soloist in all major European festivals, including Berliner Festwochen, Royan Festival, Donaueschingen, Paris, Witten Chamber Music Festival, Meta Music Festival Berlin, Metz Festival, festivals in New York, San Francisco, Washington, DC, Baltimore, Vancouver, Tokyo, Buenos Aires, Mexico City, Tehran, Helsinki, Stockholm, Zürich, Paris, Torino, Ferrara and Budapest; mem. New York Acad. of Sciences, American Asscn for the Advancement of Science, International Platform Asscn. *Compositions:* latest multimedia works for Electronic Violin System: Digitales 1993, Igitur 1993, en route 1995, Kaleidoscope 3 and 4 (with Adam Findley) 2001, 2003. *Recordings:* All Violin Sonatas by Charles Ives 1975, Dedications to János Négyesy 1978, John Cage: Freeman Etudes I–XVI for solo violin 1984, Personae, Violin Concerto by Roger Reynolds 1992, The Complete Violin Duos by Béla Bartók (with Päivikki Nykter) 1993, The Complete Freeman Etudes for Solo Violin by John Cage 1995, Dedications 2, Solo Violin works written for and dedicated to János Négyesy 1995, Dedications to János Négyesy and Päivikki Nykter, New Works for 2 violins 2000. *Publications:* New Violin Technique 1978. *Address:*

University of California San Diego, Department of Music, 9500 Gilman Drive, La Jolla, CA 92093, USA. *E-mail:* jhegyesy@ucsd.edu. *Website:* felix.ucsd.edu/~jnegyesy.

**NEIDHART, Elke;** stage director; b. 1940, Germany. *Education:* Stuttgart Drama and Opera School. *Career:* Assistant at the Zürich Stage Opera, 1964; Resident Director of Australian Opera from 1977, staging Fidelio, Cav and Pag, Lohengrin and Salome; Has also staged Fidelio for Lyric Opera of Queensland, Puritani and Flying Dutchman for Victorian State Opera; From 1990, Director of Productions at Cologne Opera, assisting on and restaging The Ring, From the House of the Dead, Don Giovanni, Der Prinz von Homburg and La Finta Semplice; Il Trovatore at Sydney, 1996; Tannhäuser for Opera Australia, 1998. *Address:* c/o State Opera South Australia, 216 Marion Road, Netley, SA 5037, Australia.

**NEIGHBOUR, Oliver Wray,** BA, FBA; British fmr music librarian; b. 1 April 1923. *Education:* Eastbourne Coll., Birbeck Coll., London. *Career:* Entered Dept of Printed Books, British Museum 1946, Asst Keeper in Music Room 1951, Deputy Keeper 1976, Music Librarian, Reference Div., British Library 1976–85. *Publications:* (with Alan Tyson) English Music Publishers' Plate Numbers, 1965; The Consort and Keyboard Music of William Byrd, 1978; (ed), Music and Bibliography: Essays in Honour of Alec Hyatt King, 1980; Article on Schoenberg in New Grove Dictionary of Music and Musicians, 1980 and 2001; Editor of First Publications of Works by Schumann, Schoenberg and Byrd. *Address:* 12 Treborough House, 1 Nottingham Place, London, W1U 5LA, England (home). *Telephone:* (20) 7935-1772 (home).

**NEIKRUG, Marc (Edward);** Composer and Pianist; b. 24 Sept. 1946, New York City, USA. *Education:* Studied with Giselher Klebe in Detmold 1964–68; Stony Brook State University of New York; MM in Composition 1971. *Career:* Commissions from the Houston Symphony and the St Paul Chamber Orchestra (Consultant on Contemporary Music 1978); Los Alamos premiere at the Deutsche Oper Berlin, 1988; Duo partnership with Pinchas Zukerman; Visited London, 1989; British premiere of Violin Concerto at South Bank and duo recital at the Barbican Hall. *Compositions:* Piano Concerto 1966; Solo Cello sonata 1967; Clarinet Concerto 1967; 2 String Quartets 1969, 1972; Viola Concerto 1974; Suite for cello and piano 1974; Rituals for flute and harp 1976; Concertino for ensemble 1977; Fantasies for violin and piano 1977; Continuum for cello and piano 1978; Cycle for 7 pianos 1978; Kaleidoscope for flute and piano 1979; Eternity's Sunrise for orchestra 1979–80; Through Roses, theatre piece 1979–80; Mobile for orchestra 1981; Violin Concerto 1982; Duo for violin and piano 1983; Los Alamos opera, 1988; Chettro Ketl, for chamber orchestra, 1994; Sonata Concertante for violin and piano, 1994; String Quintet, 1995; Pueblo children's Songs for soprano and piano, 1995; Piano Concerto, 1996. *Honours:* NEA Awards 1972 and 1974; Prizes for Through Roses at the Besancon Film Festival 1981, and the International Film and Television Festival, New York, 1982. *Address:* c/o ASCAP, ASCAP Building, 1 Lincoln Plaza, NY 10023, USA.

**NEILL, Stuart;** Singer (Tenor); b. 1965, Atlanta, Georgia, USA. *Career:* Sang Rodolfo in La Bohème at San Francisco, 1993 (also at Venice and the Deutsche Oper Berlin); Season 1994–95 as Arturo in I Puritani at Santiago, Geneva, Venice and the Vienna Staatsoper; Dallas Opera, 1996, as Don Ottavio; Other roles include Arnoldo in Guillaume Tell at Amsterdam, 1995, Gualtiero in Bellini's Pirata, Fernando in La Favorita, and Alfredo; Further appearances at the Lyric Opera Chicago, Naples and Nice; Season 1998 as Donizetti's Tonio at Philadelphia and Arnold in Guillaume Tell for Washington Opera; Sang the Italian Tenor in Der Rosenkavalier at the Met, 2000. *Address:* Washington Concert Opera, 1690 36th Street North West, Suite 411, Washington, DC 20007, USA.

**NEJCEVA, Liljana;** Singer (Mezzo-soprano); b. 1945, Silistra, Bulgaria. *Education:* Studied at the music schools in Ruse and Sofia. *Career:* Sang at the Leipzig Opera 1969, as Amastris in Xerxes, Ulrica, Lady Pamela in Fra Diavolo, Fidalma in Il Matrimonio Segreto and Konchakovna in Prince Igor; Member of Bayerische Staatsoper Munich, 1973–78, as Azucena, Maddalena, Marina in Boris Godunov and Cherubino; Has sung with Nationaltheater Mannheim, 1981–; Guest appearances include Hamburg (as Eboli), Berlin Staatsoper (Dorabella), Vienna Volksoper (Carmen) and Cologne (Suzuki); Also sings Luisa Miller; Travelled to Japan and Cuba; Concert engagements in Munich, Prague, Rome, Frankfurt and Paris. *Address:* Music International, 13 Ardilaun Road, London N5 2QR, England.

**NEL, Anton;** Pianist and Professor of Piano; b. 29 Dec. 1961, Johannesburg, South Africa. *Education:* BMus, University of the Witwatersand, South Africa, 1983; Performers Diploma, MMus 1984, D.Mus 1986, University of Cincinnati, USA. *Career:* Debut: Carnegie Recital Hall, New York, 1986; Performances with major orchestras including Chicago, Seattle, Cincinnati, Brooklyn; Recitals and chamber music concerts throughout USA, Canada, Europe, Parts of Africa; Recitals in Alice Tully Hall, New York; Barbican Centre and Queen Elizabeth Hall, London; Many appearances at summer festivals including Aspen, Ravinia; Professor of Piano, Eastman School of Music, Rochester, New York; mem, Pi Kappa Lambda. *Recordings:* Saint-Saëns, Carnival of the Animals; Haydn-4 Sonatas. *Honours:* 1st Prize, Walter W Naumburg International Piano Competition; 1st Prize, Joanna Hodges International Piano Competition; Prizes at Leeds and Pretoria International Piano Competition. *Current Management:* Walter W Naumburg Foundation.

**NELSON, John;** Conductor; b. 6 Dec. 1941, San José, Costa Rica. *Education:* Studies at Juilliard School, New York. *Career:* Conductor, Berlioz's Les Troyens, New York, 1972; Conductor, New York City Opera, 1972–; From 1973 at Metropolitan Opera, conducting Cavalleria Rusticana, Pagliacci, Jenůfa, Il Barbiere di Siviglia, Carmen and L'Incoronazione di Poppea; Conducted US premiere of Britten's Owen Wingrave, Santa Fe Opera; Music Director, Indianapolis Symphony Orchestra, 1977–88; Music Director St Louis Opera, 1981–91, continuing as Principal Guest Conductor; Caramoor Festival, New York; Tour of Europe, 1987; Guest engagements with leading orchestras in North America and Europe; Debut with Lyon Opéra, 1991 conducting Béatrice and Bénédict; Conducted Benvenuto Cellini at Geneva Opera, 1992; Offenbach's The Tales of Hoffmann at the Bastille; Recent productions include Handel's Xerxes, Massenet's Don Quichotte with Chicago Lyric Opera, Béatrice and Bénédict with Welsh National Opera, Faust at Geneva Opera, Benvenuto Cellini with Rome Opera, Don Carlos at Lyon Opéra and A new opera at Lyon Opéra by Marcel Landowski; Verdi's Vespri Siciliani at Rome, 1997 and Handel's Giulio Cesare, 1998. *Recordings:* Béatrice and Bénédict; CD, Bach Arias with Kathleen Battle; Gorecki's Beatus Vir with Czech Philharmonic; Handel's Semele with English Chamber Orchestra and Kathleen Battle, awarded Grammy Award, Best Operatic Recording of 1993; CD of Works of Paul Schönfield, 1994; Gorecki's Miserere with Chicago Symphony and Chicago Lyric Opera Choruses. *Honours:* Diapason d'Or Award for Erato recording of Béatrice and Bénédict, 1992. *Address:* c/o IMG Artists Europe, Lovell House, 616 Chiswick High Road, London, W4 5RX, England.

**NELSON, Judith,** BA; American singer (soprano); b. 10 Sept. 1939, d. of Virgil D. Nelson and Genevieve W. Manes; m. Alan H. Nelson 1961; one s. one d. *Education:* St Olaf Coll., Northfield, Minn. *Career:* Alfred Hertz Memorial Fellowship, Univ. of Calif., Berkeley 1972–73; European debut 1972; specializes in baroque repertoire; has appeared with most of the major baroque orchestras in USA and Europe including Acad. of Ancient Music, Tafelmusik, Toronto, Philharmonia, San Francisco; has performed with San Francisco, St Louis, Baltimore and Washington Nat. Symphony Orchestras and Los Angeles Philharmonic; has appeared in opera in Boston, LA, Brussels, Innsbruck, Venice, Turin and Rome and at Maryland Handel Festival; masterclasses at UCLA, Univ. of Chicago, Bath Summer School, Bruges Festival, Jerusalem Music Center. *Honours:* Hon. DFA (St Olaf Coll.) 1979. *Address:* 2600 Buena Vista Way, Berkeley, CA 94708, USA. *Telephone:* (415) 848-1992.

**NELSON, Richard Lawrence,** BA, MD; American French horn player, tenor horn player, professor of surgery and epidemiologist; b. 11 Oct. 1946, Evanston, IL; m. Susan Jane Berryman 1972; three s. two d. *Education:* Stanford Univ., Univ. of Chicago, studied French horn with Paul Navarro, Liss van Pechman, Arnold Jacobs. *Career:* Prof. of Surgery, Univ. of Illinois at Chicago 1995–; mem. Illinois Brass Band 1993–2001, North American Brass Band Assn, Int. Horn Soc., Historic Brass Soc., Chicago Brass Band 2002, Prairie Brass Band 2004–; mem. American Coll. of Surgeons. *Recordings:* Christmas Fantasy, Illinois Brass Band Live, Championship Brass, Shakin' not Stirred. *Publications:* contrib. to Wind and Song – Arnold Jacobs by Brian Frederickson 1996. *Honours:* North American Brass Band Champions 1996, 1997, 1998, 2000, 2001, Order of Brass Band World 2001. *Address:* 1740 W Taylor, M/C 957, Chiacgo, IL 60612 (office); 2224 Lincolnwood Drive, Evanston, IL 60201, USA (home). *Telephone:* (312) 996-5162 (office). *Fax:* (312) 996-2704 (office). *E-mail:* altohorn@uic.edu (office); shadow881@aol.com (home).

**NELSON, Ron;** Composer and Professor of Music; b. 14 Dec. 1929, Joliet, Illinois, USA; m. Helen Mitchell, deceased, 1 s., 1 d. *Education:* BM, 1952, MM, 1953, DMA, 1956, Eastman School of Music, Rochester; Ecole Normale de Musique, Paris, France, 1955–56. *Career:* Professor Emeritus, 1993. *Compositions:* Opera, The Birthday of the Infanta, 1956; The Christmas Story, 1958; Toccata for Orchestra, 1963; What is Man?, 1964; Rocky Point Holiday, 1969; This is the Orchestra, 1969; Prayer for an Emperor of China, 1973; Five Pieces for Orchestra after Paintings of Frank Wyeth, 1975; Four Pieces after the Seasons, 1978; Three Autumnal Sketches, 1979; Mass of LaSalle, 1981; Nocturnal Pieces, 1982; Three Settings of the Moon, 1982; Medieval Suite, 1983; Aspen Jubilee, 1984; Te Deum Laudamus, 1985; Danza Capriccio for saxophone, 1988; Three pieces after Tennyson, 1989; Fanfare for the Hour of Sunlight, 1989; Morning Alleluias, 1989; The Deum Laudamus, 1991; To the Airborne, 1991; Passacaglin (Homage on B-A-C-H), 1992; Lauds (Praise High Day), 1992; Epiphanies, fanfares and chorales, 1994; Chaconne (In memoriam. . .), 1994. *Address:* Sonoran Highlands, 28412 N 97th Way, Scottsdale, AZ 85262, USA.

**NELSONS, Andris;** Latvian conductor; *Principal Conductor, Latvian National Opera*; b. Riga. *Education:* Emils Darzins Music Coll., Latvian Acad. of Music, studied conducting with Alexander Titov in St Petersburg, pvt study with Mariss Jansons, masterclasses with Neeme Järvi and Jorma Panula. *Career:* began career as trumpeter with Latvian Nat. Opera Orchestra; Asst Conductor Latvian Nat. Opera 2001–03, Prin. Conductor 2003–; performances with Latvian Nat. Opera include Tosca, La Bohème, Un Ballo in Maschera, Romeo and Juliet, Petruschka, Firebird, Sheherazade, Barber of Seville, Rites of Spring, Eugene Onegin; regular guest with Latvian Nat. Symphony Orchestra, performances include Beethoven's Symphony No. 5, Mahler's Symphony No. 3, Rachmaninov's Symphony No. 2; guest appearances with Nordwest Deutsche Philharmonie, Brandenburgisches

Staatsorchester, Tapiola Sinfonietta, Rundfunk Sinfonieorchester Berlin, Umea Symphony Orchestra, Tampere Philharmonic Orchestra, and at the Interlaken Festival, Savolinna Opera Festival. *Honours:* Latvian Grand Music Award 2001. *Address:* Latvian National Opera, Aspazijas bulvaris 3, Riga 1050, Latvia (office). *E-mail:* info@opera.lv (office). *Website:* www.opera .lv (office).

**NELSSON, Woldemar;** Conductor; b. 4 April 1938, Kiev, Ukraine. *Education:* Studied with his father in Kiev, then at the Novosibirsk Conservatory and in Moscow and Leningrad. *Career:* Assistant to Kyrill Kondrashin at the Moscow Philharmonic, 1972; Conducted leading orchestras in the USSR, with such soloists as Rostropovich, David Oistrakh and Gidon Kremer; Emigrated to West Germany 1977 and conducted major orchestras in Hamburg, Munich, Berlin, Frankfurt, Vienna, London, Geneva, Amsterdam, Tel-Aviv, Jerusalem and Montreal; Directed the premiere of Henze's ballet Orpheus, Stuttgart 1979, and took the production to Washington and the Metropolitan Opera New York; Guest Conductor with Stuttgart Opera from 1980; General Music Director of the State Theatre in Kassel; Has conducted opera productions in Paris, Philadelphia, Japan, Vienna and Barcelona; Bayreuth Festival, 1980–85, Lohnegrin and Der fliegende Holländer; Conducted the world premiere of Penderecki's opera Die schwarze Maske, Salzburg 1986; Music Director of the Royal Opera, Copenhagen. *Recordings include:* Lohengrin (CBS); Der fliegende Holländer (Philips). *Honours:* Max Reger Prize. *Address:* c/o Staatstheater Stuttgart, Oberer Schlossgarten 6, 7000 Stuttgart 1, Germany.

**NEMETH, Geza;** Violist; b. 1930, Hungary. *Education:* Franz Liszt Academy, Budapest. *Career:* Violist of the Bartók Quartet from 1957; Performances in nearly every European country and tours to Australia, Canada, Japan, New Zealand and the USA; Festival appearances at Adelaide, Ascona, Aix, Venice, Dubrovnik, Edinburgh, Helsinki, Lucerne, Menton, Prague, Veinna, Spoleto and Schwetzingen; Tour of the United Kingdom 1986 including concerts at Cheltenham, Dartington, Philharmonic Hall Liverpool, RNCM Manchester and the Wigmore Hall; Tours of the United Kingdom 1988 and 1990, featuring visits to the Sheldonian Theatre Oxford, Wigmore Hall, Harewood House and Birmingham; Repertoire includes standard classics and Hungarian works by Bartók, Durko, Bozay, Kadosa, Soproni, Farkas, Szabo and Lang. *Recordings include:* Complete quartets of Mozart, Beethoven and Brahms; Major works of Haydn and Schubert (Hungaroton); Complete quartets of Bartók (Erato). *Honours:* (with members of Bartók Quartet) Kossuth Prize, Outstanding Artist of the Hungarian People's Republic, 1981; UNESCO/IMC Prize 1981. *Current Management:* Ingpen & Williams Ltd, 7 St George's Court, 131 Putney Bridge Road, London, SW15 2PA, England.

**NENDICK, Josephine;** Singer (Soprano); b. 1940, Kent, England. *Education:* Studied at the Royal College of Music, the Guildhall School of Music with Audrey Langford. *Career:* Sang first at the Aldeburgh Festival, then premiered works by Boulez and Bo Nilsson at Darmstadt; Has sung with such ensembles as Capricorn, Domaine Musical, Ensemble Musique Nouvelles, Music Group of London, Les Percussions de Strasbourg; Festival engagements at Avignon, Berlin, Cheltenham, London (English Bach), Edinburgh, Prades, Royaun, Warsaw; Conductors include Pierre Boulez, Ernest Bour, Charles Bruck, Colin Davis, Michael Gielen, Norman Del Mar, Bruno Maderna, Manuel Rosenthal; Repertoire includes Berg, Der Wein; Berio Magnificat, Chamber Music, Circles; Four Popular Songs, Sequenza; Boulez Improvisations sur Mallarmé, Le Marteau sans Maitre, Le Soleil des Eaux; Birtwistle Entractes and Sappho Fragments; Bussotti Le Passion selon Sade; Ravel Chansons Medécasses and 3 Poemes de Stephane Mallarmé; Schoenberg Pierrot Lunaire and Das Buch der Hängenden Gärten; Webern Songs Op 8 and Op 13; Bartók Village Scenes; Works by Barraqué, Smith Brindle, Finnissy, Dillon, Cage, Crumb, Dallapiccola, Stravinsky, Babbitt, Ives and Satie; Sang in Bach's Christmas Oratorio, Berlioz Les Troyens (Ascanius), Delius A Mass of Life; Mahler Das Lied von der Erde, Monteverdi L'Incoronazione di Poppea (Drusilla, at Bremen) and Mozart's Requiem and C minor Mass. *Recordings include:* Boulez Le Soleil des Eaux; Lutyens Quincunx, with the BBC Symphony Orchestra; Barraqué Sequence and Chant après Chant.

**NENTWIG, Franz Ferdinand;** Singer (Bass-Baritone); b. 23 Aug. 1929, Duisburg, Germany. *Career:* Debut: Bielefeld 1962, as Ottokar in Der Freischütz; Sang in Darmstadt and Hanover and at the Vienna Volksoper, Vience 1983, as Amfortas in Parsifal; Wagner performances in Munich, Berlin and Hamburg; Tour of Japan 1984 with the Hamburg Company; Metropolitan Opera 1984 as Telramund in Lohengrin; Barcelona 1986 also in Lohengrin; Further appearances in Cologne, Frankfurt, Karlsruhe, Stuttgart and Mannheim; Other roles include Pizarro in Fidelio, Escamillo, Strauss's Jochanaan and Mandryka, Mozart's Count and Don Alfonso, Verdi's Rigoletto and Amonasro and Wagner's Dutchman, Wotan and Gunther; Sang Hans Sachs with the Berlin Staatsoper on tour to Japan, 1987; Salzburg Festival and Turin 1987, as Schoenberg's Moses and as Wotan; Sang Dr Schön in Lulu and Dr Vigilius in Schreker's Der ferne Klang, 1988; Wotan in the first Polish production of the Ring, 1989; Brussels 1990, as Shishkov in From the House of the Dead; Sang La Roche in a new production of Capriccio at Covent Garden, 1991; Season 1991–92 as Wotan at Brussels and Beckmesser at Spoleto. *Recordings include:* Schreker's Der Schatzgräber. *Address:* c/o Théâtre Royal de la Monnaie, 4 Leopolstrasse, 1000 Brussels, Belgium.

**NERDRUM, Sonja;** Opera Singer (Mezzo-soprano); b. 1 Oct. 1953, Bern, Switzerland. *Education:* West London Institute of Higher Education: Singing studies with Eduardo Asquez, Jeffrey Talbot, and subsequently with Françoise Garner. *Career:* Debut: Abbaye de Flaran, Gascogne, as Dorabella in Così fan tutte directed by Jean-Claude Auvray, 1978; Dorabella in Angers, conductor Sylvain Cambreling; Apollo/Mirtillo in Handel's Il pastor fido at Den Norske Opera, in the Drottningholm production; Giacinta in Mozart's La finta semplice in Batignano, conductor David Parry; Zweite Dame in Die Zauberflöte at Opéra de Montpellier; Dorabella in Oslo Summer Opera, returning as Hermia in A Midsummer Night's Dream; La Baronne in La vie parisienne for English National Opera; Donizetti's Maria Stuarda in Kristiansund; Marcellina in Le nozze di Figaro at Versailles and for Jean-Claude Malgoire at Tourcoing; Puccini's Tosca, touring Middle and Far East; Concert repertoire includes Norwegian, French, Italian, German, English and Russian songs. *Honours:* Honorary RCM, Royal College of Music, 1988. *Address:* c/o K Berg, 39 Avenue Road, London NW8 6 BS, England.

**NERSESSIAN, Pavel;** Concert Pianist; b. 26 Aug. 1968, Ramenskoye, Moscow, Russia. *Education:* Central Music School, Moscow and Tchaikovsky Conservatory. *Career:* Concert tours of Russia from 1972 and more recent appearances in Spain, Hungary, Italy, France and Ireland; Season 1992–93 in Cannes and Dublin, tour of Japan and appearances in Austria, England, Ireland, Canada, and the USA; Professor of Piano at Moscow Conservatory. *Honours:* 2nd Prize, Beethoven Competition in Vienna, 1985. *Current Management:* Ingpen & Williams Ltd, 7 St George's Court, 131 Putney Bridge Road, London, SW15 2PA, England.

**NESCHLING, John;** Conductor; b. 1945, Rio de Janeiro, Brazil. *Education:* Studied in Vienna with Hans Swarowsky; Further study with Leonard Bernstein in the USA. *Career:* Engagements with the London, Vienna and Berlin Radio Symphony Orchestras, New York and Israel Philharmonic, the Tonhalle, Zürich and the Italian Radio at Naples and Milan; Opera appearances at Berlin (Deutsche Oper and Staatsoper), Stuttgart, Hamburg and Stockholm; Principal Conductor of the San Carlo Lisbon 1981–88; Music Director of the Teatro São Paulo and at St Gallen in Switzerland (Die Zauberflöte 1989); Engaged for Trovatore, Figaro, Pagliacci and Gianni Schicchi at St Gallen; Lucia di Lammermoor, Butterfly, Andrea Chénier and Il Barbiere di Siviglia as guest conductor at the Vienna Staatsoper; Conducted Il Guarany by Gomes at Bonn, 1994 and Der Rosenkavalier at Palermo, 1998. *Recordings include:* Il Guarany, 1996. *Honours:* Winner, International Competition for young conductors in Florence, London Symphony Orchestra International Competition. *Address:* Walter Beloch srl, Artists Management, Via Melzi D'Eril, 26 20154 Milan, Italy.

**NESS, Arthur J.;** American musicologist; b. 27 Jan. 1936, Chicago, Ill.; m. Charlotte A. Kolczynski 1982. *Education:* BMus, Music Theory, University of Southern California, 1958; AM, Music, Harvard University, 1963; PhD, Musicology, New York University, 1984. *Career:* Assistant Professor, University of Southern California, 1964–76; Associate Professor, Daemen College, 1976–83; Visiting Lecturer, State University of New York, Buffalo, 1983–87; Editor and Music Engraver, 1990–; Former General Editor, Monuments of the Lutenist Art, 1992–94; Fulbright Fellow, University of Munich, Germany. *Compositions:* Three Poems by Kenneth Patchen, for alto and piano. *Publications:* Lute Works of Francesco Canova da Milano (1497–1543), 1970; The Herwarth Lute Tablatures, 1984; The Königsberg Manuscript (with John M Ward), 1989; The Lute Works of Marco dall'Aguila, 2003. *Contributions:* Major contributor, New Grove Dictionary of Music, 1980, New Harvard Dictionary of Music, 1986; Journal of American Musicological Society; Le Luth et sa Musique II, 1985; Music in Context: Essays for John M Ward, 1985; New Grove Dictionary of American Music, 1986. *Honours:* Healey Award 1984. *Address:* 2039 Commonwealth Avenue, Suite 10, Boston, MA 02135, USA. *Telephone:* (617) 254-6509. *E-mail:* 71162.751@compuserve.com.

**NESTERENKO, Evgeni,** DipEng; Russian/Austrian singer (bass); b. 8 Jan. 1938, Moscow; s. of Evgeni Nesterenko and Velta Baumann; m. Ekaterina Alexeyeva 1963; one s. *Education:* Leningrad Eng Inst. and Leningrad Conservatory with V. Lukanin. *Career:* debut as General Ermolov in War and Peace, Maly Theatre, Leningrad 1963; soloist with Leningrad Maly Opera and Ballet Theatre 1963–67; soloist with Kirov Opera 1967–71; teacher of solo singing, Leningrad Conservatory 1967–71, Moscow Conservatory 1972–93, Konservatorium der Stadt Wien 1993–2003; soloist with Bolshoi 1971–; mem. CPSU 1974–91; mem. staff, Moscow Musical Pedagogical Inst. 1972–74; Chair. of Singing at Moscow Conservatory 1975–93, Prof. 1981–93; Prof. Vienna Acad. of Music 1993–; USSR People's Deputy 1989–91; roles include Boris Godunov, Dosifey (Khovanshchina), Khan Konchak (Prince Igor), Mephistopheles (Faust), Grigori (Quiet Flows the Don), General Ermolov (War and Peace), Kutuzov (War and Peace), Filippo II (Don Carlo), Attila, Zaccaria (Nabucco), Don Pasquale, Sarastro (Magic Flute), Bluebeard, Gremin (Eugene Onegin), Ivan Susanin, Old Convict (Lady Macbeth), Don Basilio, Enrico VIII, Moses, Ivan Khovansky, Water-Sprite (Rusalka), Don Bartolo; mem. Int. Acad. of Creative Endeavours, Moscow 1991. *Recordings:* Glinka's Ruslan and Lyudmila and Ivan Susanin, Tchaikovsky's Mazeppa, Iolanta and Eugene Onegin, Rachmaninov's Francesca da Rimini and Aleko, Songs by Shostakovich and Mussorgsky, Suite on Poems of | Michelangelo and 14th Symphony by Shostakovich, Verdi Requiem, Nabucco, Attila and Trovatore, Gounod's Faust, Dvořák's Rusalka, Donizetti's Don Pasquale and L'Elisir d'amore, Bela Bartók's Bluebeard's Castle; videos: Verdi's Attila, Rachmaninov's Aleko, Mussorgsky's Boris Godunov and Khovanshtchina,

Glinka's A Life for the Tsar. *Publication:* Evgeni Nesterenko, Thoughts on my Profession 1985. *Honours:* People's Artist of the USSR 1976, Lenin Prize 1982, Viotti d'Oro Prize, City of Vercelli (Italy) 1981, Melodia Golden Disc, USSR 1984, Giovanni Zenatello Prize, Verona (Italy) 1986, Chaliapin Prize 1992, Wilhelm Furtwängler Prize, Germany 1992, Austrian Kammersänger 1992, Casta Diva Prize, Russia 2001, Golden Pegasus Theatre Prize, Poland 2004.

**NETHSINGHA, Andrew Mark,** MA, FRCO, ARCM; British conductor and organist; *Director of Music, Gloucester Cathedral;* b. 16 May 1968, Worcs.; s. of Lucian Nethsingha and Jane Nethsingha; m. Lucy; one s. one d. *Education:* Royal Coll. of Music, Univ. of Cambridge. *Career:* Asst Organist, Wells Cathedral 1990–94; Master of the Choristers and Organist, Truro Cathedral 1994–2002; Musical Dir Three Spires Singers and Orchestra 1994–2002; Dir of Music, Gloucester Cathedral 2002–; Musical Dir Gloucester Choral Soc. 2002–; Artistic Dir Three Choirs Festival 2002–; conducted Philharmonia, Royal Philharmonic Orchestra, BBC Concert Orchestra; conducted in China, South Africa, Canada, USA and Europe; organ recitals include at Nôtre-Dame de Paris, Washington Nat. Cathedral; mem. Inc. Soc. of Musicians, Royal Coll. of Organists. *Recordings:* Magnificat and Nunc Dimittis Vol. 10, Popular Choral Music from Truro, Popular organ music series Vol. 6, The Complete New English Hymnal Vol. 10, Music for a Cathedral's Year. *Address:* 7 Miller's Green, Gloucester, GL1 2BN, England (home). *Telephone:* (1452) 524764 (office). *Fax:* (1452) 300469 (office). *E-mail:* andrew@nethsingha.freeserve.co .uk (office).

**NETREBKO, Anna;** Russian singer (soprano); b. 1971, Krasnodar. *Education:* Rimsky-Korsakov Conservatory. *Career:* debut, Mariinsky Opera Theatre, St Petersburg 1994, as Susanna; roles include Glinka's Ludmila with Kirov Opera, Gilda in Rigoletto and Kundry in Parsifal at St Petersburg; appearance at Salzburg Festival 1998; tours with Kirov Opera as Pamina and Bizet's Micaela; sang Gilda at Washington 1999, Mimi at San Francisco 1999–2000; concerts with Rotterdam Philharmonic Orchestra include London Proms and Teresa in Benvenuto Cellini, Royal Festival Hall 1999; sang Natasha in War and Peace at St Petersburg and London 2000; other roles include Zerlina and Louisa in Prokofiev's Betrothal in a Monastery at San Francisco, Rosina, Pamina and Xenia in Boris Godunov, Donna Anna at Salzburg and Mozart's Servilia at Covent Garden 2002. *Recordings:* Glinka's Ruslan and Ludmila. *Honours:* first prize All-Russian Glinka Vocal Competition, Moscow 1993, third prize Rimsky-Korsakov Int. Competition of young opera singers St Petersburg 1996, Costa Diva prize 1998, Golden Sophit prize St Petersburg 1999. *Address:* State Academic Mariinsky Theatre, Teatralnaya pl. 1, St Petersburg, Russia. *Telephone:* 812-114 4004; 812-314 1744.

**NETTL, Bruno,** BA, MA, PhD; musicologist and writer; *Professor of Music and Anthropology Emeritus, University of Illinois;* b. 14 March 1930, Prague, Czechoslovakia; m. Wanda Maria White 1952; two d. *Education:* Indiana Univ., Univ. of Michigan Ann Arbor. *Career:* instructor in music 1953–54, Asst Prof. of Music 1954–56, 1959–64, Music Librarian 1958–64, Wayne State Univ., Detroit; Ed., Ethnomusicology 1961–65, 1988–2002, Yearbook of the Int. Folk Music Council 1975–77; Assoc. Prof. of Music 1965–67, Prof. of Music and Anthropology 1967–92, Prof. Emeritus 1992–, Chair Division of Musicology 1967–72, 1975–77, 1982–85, Univ. of Illinois, Urbana; numerous visiting lectureships and professorships, including Visiting Prof. of Music Harvard Univ. 1990, Distinguished Albert Seay Prof. of Music Colorado Coll. 1992, Visiting Hill Prof. of Music Univ. of Minnesota 1995, Benedict Distinguished Visiting Prof. of Music Carleton Coll. 1996; mem. American Acad. of Arts and Sciences, Coll. Music Soc., Int. Council for Traditional Music, Int. Musicological Soc., Soc. of Ethnomusicology (pres. 1969–71, hon. mem. 2001). *Publications:* North American Indian Musical Styles 1954, Music in Primitive Culture 1956, An Introduction to Folk Music in the United States (third edn, revised by H. Myers, as Folk Music in the United States: An Introduction 1976) 1960, Cheremis Musical Styles 1960, Reference Materials in Ethnomusicology 1961, Theory and Method in Ethnomusicology 1964, Folk and Traditional Music of the Western Continents 1965, Daramad of Chahargah: A Study in the Performance Practice of Persian Music (with B. Foltin Jr) 1972, Contemporary Music and Music Cultures (with C. Hamm and R. Byrnside) 1975, Eight Urban Musical Cultures: Tradition and Change (ed.) 1978, The Study of Ethnomusicology: 29 Issues and Concepts 1983, The Western Impact on World Music: Change, Adaptation, and Survival 1985, The Radif of Persian Music: Studies of Structure and Cultural Context 1987, Blackfoot Musical Thought: Comparative Perspectives 1989, Comparative Musicology and Anthropology in Music: Essays on the History of Ethnomusicology (ed. with P. Bohlman) 1991, Excursions in World Music (with others) 1992, Community of Music: An Ethnographical Seminar in Champaign-Urbana (ed. with others) 1993, Heartland Excursions: Ethnomusicological Reflections on Schools of Music 1995, In the Course of Performance: Studies in the World of Musical Improvisation (ed. with M. Russell) 1998, Encounters in Ethnomusicology 2002. *Honours:* Hon. LHD (Univ. of Chicago) 1993, (Univ. of Illinois) 1996, (Carleton Coll.) 2000, (Kenyon Coll.) 2002;hon. mem. American Musicological Soc. 1995; Koizumi Prize in Ethnomusicology, Tokyo 1994. *Address:* c/o University of Illinois, Department for Performing Arts, EPASW Bldg, 1040 W Harrison Street, MC-255, Chicago, IL 60607; 1423 Cambridge Drive, Champaign, IL 61821, USA.

**NEUBAUER, Margit;** Singer (Mezzo-soprano); b. 1950, Austria. *Education:* Studied in Vienna. *Career:* Sang at Linz Landestheater, 1975–77, notably in 1976 premiere of Der Aufstand by Helmut Eder; Engagements at Frankfurt Opera from 1977, Zürich, 1978–79, Hamburg, 1980–83, Deutsche Oper Berlin,

1982–85; Bayreuth Festival 1981–86, as Sigrune in Die Walküre and a Flowermaiden in Parsifal; US tour with Deutsche Oper, 1985; Roles have included Cherubino, Flosshilde, Brigitte in Korngold's Tote Stadt, Annina, Rosenkavalier and the title role in Miss Jule by Bibalo; Many concert appearances, notably in Baroque music. *Recordings:* Parsifal, Bayreuth, 1985; Bach B minor Mass and Handel Utrecht Te Deum.

**NEUENFELS, Hans;** Stage Director; b. 1941, Krefeld, Germany. *Career:* Debut: Produced Il Trovatore at Nuremberg, 1974; Frankfurt Opera, 1976–80, with Macbeth, Aida, Die Gezeichneten by Schreker and Busoni's Doktor Faust; Productions at Deutsche Oper Berlin, 1982–86 have included La Forza del Destino, Rigoletto and Zimmermann's Die Soldaten; Paris Opéra 1989 with the premiere of York Höller's Der Meister und Margarita, the last production at the Palais Garnier before the opening of the Opéra Bastille; Il Trovatore at the Deutsche Oper, 1996; Le Prophète by Meyerbeer at the Vienna State Opera, 1998. *Address:* c/o Deutsche Oper Berlin, Bismarckstrasse 35, 1000 Berlin 10, Germany.

**NEUGEBAUER, Hans;** Singer (Bass) and Stage Director; b. 17 Nov. 1916, Karlsruhe, Germany. *Education:* Studied in Mannheim and Hamburg. *Career:* Debut: Karlsruhe 1946, as Bett in Zar und Zimmermann; Sang Buffo and other roles at Karlsruhe until 1951, Frankfurt Opera, 1951–60, notably as the King in Aida and Mozart's Figaro; Producer of opera from 1955, first at Frankfurt and Heidelberg, then Kassel, 1962–64; Staged premiere of Zimmermann's Die Soldaten at Cologne, Der Rosenkavalier at Glyndebourne, 1965; Guest engagements as Producer at Düsseldorf, Kassel, Mannheim, Basle, Trieste and Chicago. *Address:* c/o Oper der Stadt Koln, Offenbachplatz 5000 Cologne, Germany.

**NEUHOLD, Günter;** Austrian conductor; b. 2 Nov. 1947, Graz; m. Emma Schmidt; one s. *Education:* Master's degree, 1970; Advanced courses with Franco Ferrara in Rome, Hans Swarowski in Vienna. *Career:* Engaged at various German opera houses, 1972–80, ending as First Kapellmeister in Hanover and Dortmund; Music Dir, Teatro Regio di Parma, 1981–86, devoted mainly to Verdi operas and as Chief Conductor, Arturo Toscanini Symphonic Orchestra of Emilia Romagna; Chief Conductor, Musical Dir, Flanders Royal Philharmonic Orchestra, Antwerp, 1986–90, with tours, Germany, Italy, UK, France; Gen. Music Dir, Badisches Staatstheater Karlsruhe, 1989–95, conducting a Richard Strauss cycle and Ring des Nibelungen; Gen. Music Dir, Artistic Dir, Theater der Freien Hansestadt Bremen and Philharmonische Orchester Bremen, 1995–2002; Concerts with Wiener Philharmoniker, Staatskapelle Dresden, Philharmonic Orchestra Monte Carlo, Tokyo Philharmonic Orchestra, Tokyo Metropolitan Opera, radio orchestras of several German stations, also ORF, RAI, BBC, Radio-Television Moscow, CBC Canada, ABC Australia, Nat. Orchestra of Capitol Toulouse; Operas at Wiener Staatsoper, La Scala, Staatsoper Dresden, Nationaltheater München, Berliner Staatsoper, Deutsche Oper Berlin, Komische Oper Berlin, Oper Leipzig, Staatsoper Hamburg, Grand Théatre Genève, Opéra de Monte Carlo, Capitol Toulouse, Real Madrid, Philadelphia Opera, Teatro Colon, Buenos Aires, Teatro San Carlos, Naples; tours of USA, Japan, Russia; Appeared Salzburg Festival, 1978, 1980, 1983, 1986, Radio France Festival-Montpellier, Flanders Festival, Musikfestspiele Dresden. *Recordings:* Bach St Matthew Passion; Bartók's Bluebeard's Castle and Concerto for Orchestra; Brahms Symphony No. 1; Berlioz Damnation de Faust; Rolf Liebermann orchestral and vocal works; Mahler Symphonies Nos 1, 2, 3, 5; Puccini Madama Butterfly (vers 1904); Strauss's Dynastie; Wagner: Rheingold, Walküre, Siegfried, Götterdämmerung; and many more. *Honours:* Grand Decoration of Honour in Silver for Services to the Repub. of Austria 1999; 1st Prize, Contest in Florence, Marinuzzi Contest, San Remo, 1976, Böhm Contest, Salzburg, 1977; 2nd Prize, Swarowski Contest, Vienna, 3rd Prize, Cantelli Contest, Milan, 1977. *Address:* Scheibengasse 14, 1190 Vienna, Austria. *Website:* www.dirigent.at (home).

**NEUMANN, Gunther;** Singer (Tenor); b. 22 Aug. 1938, Stablack, Germany. *Career:* Debut: Potsdam, 1965, as Belmonte; Komische Oper Berlin from 1969, notably as Idomeneo, Lohengrin, Verdi's Riccardo and Alvaro, Pinkerton and Rodolfo; Modern repertory includes Alwa in Lulu, Sergei in Lady Macbeth and Schoenberg's Aron (Cologne, 1995); Guest engagements at the Vienna Staatsoper as Tannhäuser and Volksoper as Vitalino in Handel's Giustino, 1995, Hamburg as Walther von Stolzing, Verona and Tel-Aviv (Handel's Belshazzar, 1995); Other roles include Offenbach's Bluebeard at Covent Garden, 1989, and Grischka in Rimsky's Kitezh at Komische Oper, 1996; Sang Calaf in Berlin, 1998; Season 2000–01 as Herod in Salome at Trier, Shuisky in Boris Godunov at the Komische Oper, Berlin, and Wagner's Loge at Meiningen. *Address:* Komische Oper Berlin, Behrenstrasse 55–57, 10117 Berlin, Germany.

**NEUMANN, Veroslav;** composer; b. 27 May 1931, Czechoslovakia; m. 1st Jana Hoskova 1958; m. 2nd Hana Kapinusova 1989. *Education:* Acad. of Musical Arts, Prague. *Career:* Prof., Popular Conservatory, Prague 1969–91; co-owner, Edit Records and Publishing Ltd, Prague 1990–2001; Dir, Prague Conservatoire 1991–2004. *Compositions:* The Chimney Opera, 1965; Story of the Old Armchair, full-length lyrical comedy opera after Dickens, 1987; Panorama of Prague, 1962; Symphonic Dances for full orchestra, 1984; Little Singers Christmas, 1976; String Quartet, 1969; 5 Dramatic Sequences for cello and piano, 1978; Portraits of a Man, for violin and piano, 1987; The Lament of Ariadne Abandoned (for women's choir), 1970; Atlantis (for mixed choir), 1985; Rhymes, 5 Ditties for soprano, flute and piano, 1980; When Birds

Fall Silent, 4 Songs for medium-range voice and piano or piano quartet, 1985; Farewell Amadeus!, Sonatina for soprano, flute and piano, 1987. *Honours:* Prize, International Choral Competition, Tours, 1982; Award, Panton Publishing House, Prague, 1987; Czech Composers and Concert Artists Prize, 1987. *Address:* Na Petrinach 1896/31, 162 00 Prague 6, Czech Republic. *E-mail:* velovat@volny.cz.

**NEUMANN, Wolfgang;** Singer (Tenor); b. 20 June 1945, Waiern, Austria. *Education:* Vocal studies in Essen and Duisburg. *Career:* Debut: Bielefeld 1973, as Max in Der Freischütz; Sang at Augsburg from 1978, Mannheim from 1980; Maggio Musicale Florence 1983, as Tannhäuser; Appearances in Zürich, Bologna, Munich and Hamburg; Other roles include Wagner's Erik, Rienzi, Schoenberg's Aron (at Barcelona), Tristan, Lohengrin and Siegfried, Verdi's Otelo, the Emperor in Die Frau ohne Schatten, Turiddu in Cavalleria Rusticana, Puccini's Calaf and Edgar in Reimann's Lear; Concert repertoire includes Schoenberg's Gurrelieder and Das Lied von der Erde by Mahler; Metropolitan opera debut as Siegfried in the Met's new production of Siegfried by Otto Schenk/James Levine, 1988; Sang the Cardinal in Mathis der Maler at Munich, 1989; Teatro Colón Buenos Aires 1990, as Rienzi in a concert performance of Wagner's opera; Sang Wagner's Erik at the Deutsche Oper Berlin, 2001; Siegfried in Götterdämmerung at Mannheim, 2002. *Current Management:* Ingpen & Williams Ltd, 7 St George's Court, 131 Putney Bridge Road, London, SW15 2PA, England.

**NEUWIRTH, Olga,** MA; Austrian composer; b. 4 Aug. 1968, Graz. *Education:* Conservatory of Music, San Francisco, USA, Vienna Acad. of Music and Performing Arts, Electroacoustic Inst., studied composition under Erich Urbanner, Elinor Armer, Adriana Hölszky, Tristan Murail and Luigi Nono. *Career:* participant, 'Stage d'Informatique Musicale', IRCAM, Paris; jury mem., Munich Biennale 1994; mem. Composers' Forum, Darmstadt Summer School; composer-in-residence with Koninklijk Philharmonic Orchestra of Flanders, Antwerp, Belgium 2000, Luzerner Festwochen 2002. *Radio music:* Punch & Judy 1994. *Theatre music:* Ein Sportstück 1997, Abenteuer in Sachen Haut 2000, Virus 2000, Ein Sommernachtstraum 2000, Totenauberg 2001, Philoktet 2002, Lost Highway 2003, Der jüngste Tag 2004. *Film score:* The Long Rain 1999. *Compositions include:* Locus... doublure... solos 2001, Ecstaloop 2001, Torsion: transparent variation 2001, Verfremdung/Entfremdung 2002, Lost Highway 2003. *Recordings include:* Vexierbilder 1993, Loncera Caprifolium 1993, Sans Soleil 1994, Five Daily Miniatures 1994, Spleen 1994, Vampyrotheone 1995, Akroate Hadal 1995, Risonanze! 1996, Pallas/Construction 1996, Hooloomooloo 1996, Bählamms Fest 1997, Photophorus 1997, Todesraten 1997, Nova/Minraud 1998, Hommage à Klaus Nomi 1998, Ad auras... in memoriam H 1999, Settori 1999, Morphologische Fragmente 1999, Clinamen/Nodus 1999, The Long Rain 2000, Construction in Space 2000, Inciendo/fluido 2000, Settori, Quasare/Pulsare. *Honours:* Publicitiy Preis, austro mechana 1994, Ernst von Siemens-Stiftung Förderpreis, Munich, Schleswig-Holstein-Musik-Festival Hindemith-Preis 1999, Ernst Krenek-Preis 1999. *Current Management:* c/o Andrew Rosner, Allied Artists, 42 Montepelier Square, London, SW7 1JZ, England. *Telephone:* (20) 7589-6243 (office). *Fax:* (20) 7581-5269 (office). *Website:* www.olganeuwirth .com.

**NEVILLE, Margaret;** Singer (Soprano); b. 3 April 1939, Southampton, Hampshire, England. *Education:* Studied with Ruth Packer and Olive Groves in London, Maria Carpi in Geneva. *Career:* Debut: Covent Garden in 1961 in Die Zauberflöte; Appearances at Sadler's Wells, Scottish Opera, Welsh National Opera, Barcelona, Aix, Berlin and Hamburg; Glyndebourne, 1963–64 in Die Zauberflöte and L'Incoronazione di Poppea; Roles included Mozart's Zerlina, Despina and Susanna, Verdi's Gilda, Donizetti's Norina and Humperdinck's Gretel; Sang in the 1967 BBC production of Cavalli's L'Erismena. *Recordings:* Hansel and Gretel. *Honours:* Mozart Memorial Prize, 1962. *Address:* 74 Orchards Way, Highfield, Southampton SO17 1RE, England.

**NEVSKAYA, Marina;** Organist and Composer; b. 1 Oct. 1965, Moscow, Russia. *Education:* Central Music School, 1984; Moscow Tchaikovsky State Conservatory, 1989; Postgraduate, Moscow Conservatory, 1989–91; Studies, Royal Carillon School, Mechelen, Belgium, 1993–94. *Career:* Debut: Organ Concert, Moscow, 1986; Festival of Young Composers, Moscow, 1985; Recitals, Moscow Conservatory, 1987, 1988, Dnipropetrovsk and Yalta, Ukraine, 1989, Festival of Young Organists, Polotsk, Byelorussia, 1989; Participation, Organ Forum, Kazan, 1990, International Summer Organ Course, The Organ Art of Flor Peeters, Mechelen, 1990, 1991; International Organ Week, Vlaardingen, Netherlands, 1991, 1993; Recitals, Vlaardingen, 1991, Belaya Tserkov, Ukraine, 1991, 1992, Dnepropetrovsk and Yalta, 1992, Krasnoyarsk, 1993; Concert tours, Belgium and Netherlands, 1993, 1994, Italy, 1993, Siberia, 1994; Recitals, St Petersburg, 1994, Yalta, 1995, 1996, 1999; Organ Soloist Tver Philharmonic, 1992–; Teacher of harmony, polyphony, analysis of musical form and piano, Academy of Fine Arts, Moscow, 1995–; Participation, Yearly Music Festivals, Tver and Moscow; Concert tour in Belgium with choir, 1998; Recitals at the State Big Concert Hall of the Republic of Tatarstan in Kazan, 1998, 1999; Recital at the Organ Festival in Brno, Czech Republic, 1999; Participation in the Days of Russian Culture in Armenia in Yerevan, 1999. *Compositions:* Symphoniette; String Quartet; 2 Piano Sonatas; Sonata for Trumpet and Piano; Sonata for Violin and Organ; Suite for Organ; Poem for Viola and Piano; Vocal and Piano Cycles; Pieces for Wind Instruments; Pieces for Carillon and Other Chamber Works. *Recordings:* Italian, French and German Organ Music of the 17th–18th Centuries; Organ Recital, 5th

International Bach Festival, Tver, 1997; Playing in the British Bach Film, 1993. *Address:* Tver Academic Philharmonic, Sovetskaya str 18/43, 170000 Tver, Russia.

**NEWAY, Patricia;** Singer (Soprano); b. 30 Sept. 1919, Brooklyn, New York, USA; m. Morris Gesell. *Education:* Studied at Mannes College of Music and with Morris Gesell. *Career:* Debut: Chautauqua in 1946 as Fiordiligi in Così fan tutte; New York City Center Opera from 1948 notably as Berg's Marie, in Britten's The Rape of Lucretia and in the 1954 premiere of Copland's The Tender Land; Created roles in Menotti's The Consul in 1950 and Maria Golovin in 1958; Sang at Aix-en-Provence Festival in 1952 in Iphigénie en Tauride, Paris Opéra-Comique, 1952–54 notably as Tosca and Katiusha in Alfano's Risurrezione and with American companies in works by Poulenc, Hoiby and Weisgall; Formed Neway Opera Company in 1960. *Recordings:* The Consul; Cantatas by Buxtehude; Iphigénie en Tauride.

**NEWBOULD, Brian Raby,** BA, BMus, MA; British writer and academic; *Professor Emeritus of Music, University of Hull;* b. 26 Feb. 1936, Kettering, Northants.; m. 1st Anne Leicester 1960; one s. one d.; m. 2nd Ann Airton 1976; one d. *Education:* Univ. of Bristol. *Career:* Lecturer, Royal Scottish Acad. of Music, Glasgow 1960–65, Univ. of Leeds 1965–79; Prof. of Music, Univ. of Hull 1979–2001, Prof. Emeritus 2001–; numerous talks/discussions on nat. radio, lectures with live illustrations by Allegri String Quartet, Chilingirian String Quartet, the Lindsays, London Mozart Trio, Jyväskylä Sinfonia. *Artistic achievements:* realizations of Schubert's Symphonies No. 7 in E 1979, No. 10 in D 1981, completion of Schubert's Symphony No. 8 in B minor 1982, orchestration of Schubert's other symphonic fragments, completions of Schubert's String Trio String Trio in B flat 2000, Piano Sonata in C 2003; Patrick for narrator and small orchestra, completion of fragmentary Klavierstück 1995, transcription for clarinet and string quartet of Arpeggione Sonata 1996. *Publications:* Musical Analysis in the Sixth Form, Music to an Unpurged Ear 1981, Schubert and the Symphony: A New Perspective 1992, Schubert: The Music and the Man 1997, Schubert Studies (ed.) 1998, Schubert the Progressive (ed.) 2003; contrib. to Musical Times, Music & Letters, 19th-Century Music, Current Musicology Music Review, Musiktheorie, Schubert-Jahrbuch, Schubert durch die Brille, The Schubertian, BBC Music Magazine, The Guardian, The Scotsman, Glasgow Herald, Daily Telegraph, Radio Times, Jewish Echo, Classic CD, Classical Music, Ovation, Journal of the Conductors' Guild, Beethoven Newsletter, Nieuwsbrief Franz-Schubert Stichting, Meddelelse Franz Schubert Selskabet Danmark, Music Teacher. *Honours:* Hon. Vice-Pres. Schubert Inst. (UK), Hon. Pres. Sheffield Gramophone Soc. *Address:* c/o Department of Music, University of Hull, Hull, HU6 7RX, England (office). *E-mail:* B.R.Newbould@hull.ac.uk (office). *Website:* www .briannewbould.co.uk.

**NEWLAND, Larry;** Conductor; b. 24 Jan. 1935, Winfield, Kansas, USA; m. Paula Kahn, 18 Feb 1977, 2 d. *Education:* BM, Oberlin Conservatory, 1955; MM, Manhattan School of Music, 1957. *Career:* Violist and keyboard player with New York Philharmonic, 1960–74; Assistant Conductor, New York Philharmonic, 1974–85; Music Director, Harrisburg, Pennsylvania Symphony, 1978–94; Guest Conductor with New York City Ballet and orchestras world-wide, 1974–; Chair, Music Department and Director of Ensembles, Adelphi University, Garden City, New York, 1990–; Faculty, International Opera Workshop, Czech Republic, 1997, Associate Artistic Director, 1998–. *Recordings:* Numerous broadcasts with New York Philharmonic and other orchestras. *Contributions:* Articles in Apprise. *Honours:* Harold Bauer Award, 1957; Koussevitzky Conducting Prize, 1961; Leonard Bernstein Conducting Fellowship, 1962. *Address:* 300 West End Avenue G-B, New York, NY 10023, USA.

**NEWLIN, Dika;** Musicologist and Composer; b. 22 Nov. 1923, Portland, Oregon, USA. *Education:* BA, Michigan State University, 1939; MA, UCLA, 1941; PhD, Columbia University, 1945; Composition studies with Schoenberg and Sessions. *Career:* Teacher at Western Maryland College, 1945–49, Syracuse University, 1949–51, Drew University, 1952–65, North Texas State University, 1963–75, and Virginia Commonwealth University, 1978–. *Compositions:* Sinfonia for Piano, 1947; Piano Trio, 1948; Chamber Symphony, 1949; Fantasy On A Row for Piano, 1958; Study In Twelve Tones for Viola D'Amore and Piano, 1959; Atone for Chamber Ensemble, 1976; Second-Hand Rows for Voice and Piano, 1978; Three Operas; Piano Concerto; Symphony for Chorus and Orchestra. *Publications:* Bruckner–Mahler–Schoenberg, 1947, 1978; Schoenberg Remembered 1938–76, 1980; Translations of Leibowitz's Schoenberg et s. Ecole, 1949, Schoenberg's Style and Idea, 1951, and Rufer's Das Werk Arnold Schoenberg, 1962. *Address:* Music Dept, Virginia Commonwealth University, 922 Park Avenue, Richmond, VA 23284, USA.

**NEWMAN, Anthony;** Harpsichordist, Organist, Composer, Fortepianist and Conductor; b. 12 May 1941, Los Angeles, California, USA; m. Mary Jane Flagler, 10 Sept 1968, 3 s. *Education:* BS, Mannes College; MA, Harvard University; DMA, Boston University; Diplome Superieure, Ecole Normale de Musique, Paris. *Career:* Debut: Carnegie Recital Hall; Performing artist in USA and Europe from 1967 with Detroit Symphony, Boston Symphony, Los Angeles Symphony, New York Philharmonic and as conductor with Los Angeles Chamber, Y Chamber, New York, Scottish Chamber, and St Paul Chamber Orchestras; Appearances with Israel Symphony, Calgary Symphony, Colorado Symphony, New Jersey Symphony, Youth Chamber Orchestra and Vienna Boys Choir, and St Stephens Cathedral, Vienna, Kraków Festival, 1991, 1992. *Compositions include:* Concertino for piano and winds; Concerto

for viola and strings; Symphony for string orchestra; Grand Hymns Of Awakening for chorus, orchestra and bagpipes; Works for organ solo, piano quintet, quartets for flutes and various smaller works; On Fallen Heroes, sinfonia for orchestra, 1988; Symphony for strings and percussion, 1987; 12 Preludes and Fugues for piano; Symphony No. 1 and 2 for organ solo. *Recordings:* Over 100 including Bach, Baroque and Classical repertoire; On Fallen Heroes, Brandenburg Concerti. *Publications:* Bach and The Baroque, 1985; Symphony No. 1 for Organ and No. 2 for Organ; Three Preludes and Fugues for Organ, 1990; Variations on Bach; 12 Preludes and Fugues for Piano; Sonata for Piano, 1992. *Current Management:* ICM, 40 West 57th Street, New York, NY 10019, USA. *Address:* State University of New York, Purchase, NY 10577, USA.

**NEWMAN, Henry;** singer (baritone); b. 1950, England. *Career:* roles with Welsh National Opera include Zurga in Les Pêcheurs de Perles, Mozart's Count, Papageno, Don Alfonso and Don Giovanni, Marcello, Germont, Britten's Demetrius, Don Pasquale, Tomsky, Scarpia and Sharpless: Further appearances with English National Opera, Opera North and Scottish Opera. Season 1999–2000 as Foreman of the Mill in Jenůfa at Glyndebourne, Scarpia for Mid Wales Opera, the Forester in The Cunning Little Vixen for City of Birmingham Touring Opera and the Speaker in Die Zauberflöte for London City Opera; radio and television broadcasts.

**NEWMAN, Leslie;** Flautist; b. 1969, Canada. *Education:* BMus, University of Toronto; MMus, Yale University, with Thomas Nyfenger; Studies with Julius Baker at Juilliard School of Music; Also studied at Mozarteum in Salzburg; Scholarship student with András Adorján, Peter Lukas-Graf and Wolfgang Schulz. *Career:* Debut: Performed Carl Nielsen's Flute Concerto with the Toronto Symphony Orchestra, aged 18; Performances at Lincoln Center's Alice Tully Hall, New York; Salzburg Festival, Wigmore Hall, London; Taiwan's National Concert Hall; Soloist, Toronto Symphony Orchestra Tour to 1988 Winter Olympics Arts Festival at Calgary; Performed major flute concerti with orchestras throughout Canada; Recitalist on BBC Radio 3, England, and CBC Radio in Canada; Duo with pianist John Lenehan, debuted at Wigmore Hall, London, with live BBC broadcast; Appearances at Canadian National Competitive Festival of Music. *Recordings include:* 2 solo CDs; Four concerti with CBC Vancouver Orchestra. *Honours:* Winner, Canadian National Competitive Festival of Music, aged 17; Canada Council Grants; Outstanding Performance Major, Yale University; Top Prizewinner, CBC National Young Performer's Competition; Finalist, New York's Pro Musicis International Competition. *Address:* c/o Latitude 45/Arts Promotion Inc, 109 St Joseph Blvd West, Montreal, Quebec H2T 2P7, Canada.

**NEWMAN, Thomas Montgomery,** MMus; American composer; b. 29 Oct. 1955, Los Angeles, CA; s. of Alfred Newman; m. Ann Marie Zirbes; three c. *Education:* Univ. of Southern California, Yale Univ. *Career:* mem. BMI. *Compositions for film:* Summer's End 1984, Reckless 1984, Revenge of the Nerds 1984, Grandview, USA 1984, Desperately Seeking Susan 1985, Girls Just Want to Have Fun 1985, The Man with One Red Shoe 1985, Real Genius 1985, Gung Ho 1986, Jumpin' Jack Flash 1986, Light of Day 1987, The Lost Boys 1987, Less Than Zero 1987, The Great Outdoors 1988, The Prince of Pennsylvania 1988, Cookie 1989, Men Don't Leave 1990, Welcome Home, Roxy Carmichael 1990, Career Opportunities 1991, Naked Tango 1991, The Rapture 1991, Deceived 1991, The Linguini Incident 1991, Fried Green Tomatoes 1991, The Player 1992, Whispers in the Dark 1992, Scent of a Woman 1992, Flesh and Bone 1993, Josh and S.A.M. 1993, Threesome 1994, The Favor 1994, Corrina, Corrina 1994, The Shawshank Redemption 1994, The War 1994, Little Women 1994, Unstrung Heroes 1995, How to Make an American Quilt 1995, Up Close & Personal 1996, Phenomenon 1996, American Buffalo 1996, The People vs Larry Flynt 1996, Mad City 1997, Red Corner 1997, Oscar and Lucinda 1997, The Horse Whisperer 1998, Meet Joe Black 1998, American Beauty 1999, The Green Mile 1999, Erin Brockovich 2000, My Khmer Heart 2000, Pay It Forward 2000, In the Bedroom 2001, The Execution of Wanda Jean 2002, The Salton Sea 2002, Road to Perdition 2002, White Oleander 2002, Finding Nemo 2003, Lemony Snicket's A Series of Unfortunate Events 2004, Cinderella Man 2005, Jarhead 2005. *Compositions for television:* The Paper Chase (series) 1978, The Seduction of Gina (film) 1984, Amazing Stories (episode 'Santa '85) 1985, Heat Wave (film) 1990, Against the Law (series) 1990, Those Secrets (film) 1992, Citizen Cohn (film) 1992, Arli$$ (series) 1996, Boston Public (series theme) 2000, Six Feet Under (series theme) 2001, Angels in America (mini series) 2003, Katedralen 1.z 2004. *Honours:* BAFTA, American Beauty; Grammy Award, American Beauty. *Current Management:* Gorfaine/Schwartz Agency Inc, 13245 Riverside Drive, Suite 450, Sherman Oaks, CA 91423, USA. *Website:* www.gsamusic.com.

**NEWSTONE, Harry;** conductor; b. 21 June 1921, Winnipeg, Canada; one s. *Education:* With Dr Herbert Howells, 1943–45; Guildhall School of Music and Drama, 1945–49; Accademia di Santa Cecilia, Rome, 1954–1956. *Career:* Debut: Chamber Orchestra with Haydn Orchestra at Conway Hall, London, 1949; Full orchestra at Royal Festival Hall Philharmonia Orchestra, 1959; Formed Haydn Orchestra in 1949; BBC broadcasts from 1951 with Haydn Orchestra, London Philharmonic Orchestra, London Symphony Orchestra, Philharmonia, RPO, BBC Symphony and other BBC orchestras; Guest appearances in Berlin, Copenhagen, Hamburg, Budapest, Prague, Jerusalem, Toronto, Vancouver, Victoria BC, Mexico City, Liverpool Philharmonic, London Mozart Players, Jacques Orchestra and Bournemouth Symphony Orchestra; Musical Dir, Sacramento Symphony Orchestra, CA 1965–78; Dir of

Music, Univ. of Kent 1979–86; Prof. of Conducting, Guildhall School of Music 1979–87; Visiting Lecturer, Univ. of the Pacific, Stockton, CA 1988–89. *Recordings:* Bach Brandenburg Concertos; Clavier Concertos with Mindru Katz; Haydn Symphonies, 49, 73, 46, 52; Haydn and Mozart Arias with Jennifer Vyvyan and Peter Wallfisch; Mozart Symphony 41 and Serenata Notturna; Stravinsky Dumbarton Oaks Concerto; Mozart Opera Overtures; Clarinet and Orchestra works by Copland, Arnold, Lutoslawski and Rossini with Gary Gray and Royal Philharmonic Orchestra. *Publications:* Editions of works by Bach, Mozart and Haydn for Eulenburg Edition Miniature Scores, including new edition of Haydn's 12 London Symphonies from 1983–. *Address:* 4 Selborne Road, Ilford, Essex IG1 3AJ, England.

**NEWTON, Norma;** Singer (Soprano); b. 20 March 1936, Dolgeville, New York, USA. *Education:* Studied in Austin (Texas) and Paris. *Career:* Sang at the Dallas Civic Opera 1962–63, City Opera New York 1964 and 1966 as Donna Elvira and Mozart's Countess; Member of the Kiel Opera, Germany, 1966–72, Graz 1972–73; Sang Butterfly with Welsh National Opera 1973 and appeared widely as guest as Mozart's Pamina, Fiordiligi and Susanna, Eurydice, Katya Kabanova and Berg's Marie; Teacher in Houston from 1980.

**NICHITEANU, Liliana;** Singer (Mezzo-Soprano); b. 1962, Bucharest, Romania. *Education:* Studied at the Bucharest Academy. *Career:* Numerous engagements including Oslo as Rosina, 1989; Berliner Philharmonie, Fjodor in Boris Godunov, concerts and recordings (CD) with Claudio Abbado, 1993; Vienna, Rossini, Messa di Gloria, 1995; Seasons 1995–97, sang Octavian at Frankfurt; Zerlina at the Mozart Festival, Madrid; Cherubino and Despina with Harnoncourt in Zürich; Sang Te Deum, Bruckner, in Edinburgh Festival concert; Sang at Salzburg Festival with Valery Gergiev; Fatima in Oberon at Zürich, 1998; Der Rosenkavalier as Octavian in Opéra Bastille Paris and in Vienna, 1998, 2000, 2001; Così fan tutte as Dorabella, Munich, 2001 and 2002; Concert repertory: Bach: Magnificat; St John Passion; Brahms Alto Rhapsody; Mahler; Concert appearances world-wide in Bach B minor Mass; Mozart, Requiem and C minor Mass; Mahler, Des Knaben Wunderhorn; Mahler, 8th Symphony; Rossini, Stabat Mater and Messa di Gloria; Hindemith, Die junge Magd, Sieben Lieder for orchestra and alto. *Recordings:* Moussorgsky, Boris Godunov with Claudio Abbado; Mozart's Don Giovanni as Zerlina and in Così fan tutte as Dorabella, both with Alain Lombard. *Honours:* Belvedere Contest, 2 prizes and 6 special prizes, Vienna, 1989; Geneva CIEM contest, 2 prizes and Suisse Prize, 1991. *Current Management:* Rita Schütz, Rütistr 52, 8077 Zürich, Switzerland. *Address:* c/o Zürich Opera, Falkenstrasse 1, 8008 Zürich, Switzerland.

**NICHOLAS, James;** Cellist; b. 25 Jan. 1957, Valley Stream, New York, USA. *Education:* BM in Cello Performance, 1979, MM, Cello Performance, 1982, Master of Early Music, 1988, D.Mus, 1988, Indiana University. *Career:* Freelance Cellist and Baroque Cellist; Announcer and Producer, Connecticut Public Radio WPKT Meriden, WNPR Norwich and WEDW Stamford and Greenwich. *Compositions:* Concerto for natural horn (Romantic), 1984; Panikhida (Mnemosynon) for Unaccompanied natural horn, 1987; 3 Sonatas for Natural Horn and Piano, 1985, 1993, 1995; Son of Horn Concerto, 1988; Corni Duos, 1991; Grande fantaisie en forme de potpourri, pour cor à pistons en fa et pianoforte (ca 1838), 1991; Psalsima (Chants) for natural horn and small orchestra, 1991; Return of The Shoe Quintet: The Sequel for horn and strings, 1994; Mozart: Horn Concerto in Eb, K370b and 371, a reconstruction, 1994; Mozart: Horn Concerto in E, K494a, a reconstruction, 1995. *Publications:* J. S. Bach–Six Sonatas and Partitas, An Urtext edition for viola, 1986; J. S. Bach–Six suites for Cello, an attempt at an Urtext for viola, 1986; J. S. Bach–Suite No. 6 S1012, a performing version for the 4 stringed cello, 1986; Edition of Horn Concerti from the Lund Manuscript, 1989. *Contributions:* The Horn Call. *Honours:* Performer's Certificate, Indiana University, 1978. *Address:* c/o Birdalone Books, 9245 East Woodview Drive, Bloomington, IN 47401-9101, USA.

**NICHOLLS, David Roy,** MA, PhD, FRSA; British musicologist and composer; *Professor of Music, University of Southampton*; b. 19 Nov. 1955, Birmingham; m. Tamar Hodes 1984; one s. one d. *Education:* St John's Coll. ., Cambridge with Hugh Wood. *Career:* Keasbey Fellow in American Studies, Selwyn Coll. ., Cambridge 1984–87; Lecturer in Music, Keele Univ. 1987, Sr Lecturer in Music 1992, Prof. . of Music 1995–2000; Prof. of Music, Univ. of Southampton 2000–. *Compositions include:* Pleiades for 3 groups of instruments, 1979–80; The Giant's Heart for singers and instrumentalists, 1983; 2 Japanese Miniatures for 8 instruments, 1988–89; Winter Landscape with skaters and birdtrap, string quartet, 1989–90; Cantata: Jerusalem, soprano, double choir, double wind band, 1990–91; String Quartet, NMC D006, 1992, Bingham String Quartet. *Publications:* American Experimental Music, 1890–1940, 1990; new edition of Henry Cowell's New Musical Resources, 1995; Contributing Editor, The Whole World of Music: A Henry Cowell Symposium, 1997; Contributing Editor, The Cambridge History of American Music, 1998; Contributing Editor, The Cambridge Companion to John Cage, 2002; John Cage, 2006. *Address:* Department of Music, University of Southampton, Southampton, SO17 1BJ, England (office).

**NICHOLLS, Hyacinth;** Singer (Mezzo-soprano); b. 10 Sept. 1956, Trinidad. *Education:* Studied at the Guildhall School of Music and the National Opera Studio. *Career:* Sang Cherubino, Octavian, Dorabella, Carmen and Dalilah while a student; Professional debut in 1985 at Wigmore Hall; Sang in the European premiere of Virgil Thomson's Four Saints in Three Acts, Belgium, 1983; Glyndebourne Festival from 1986 in Porgy and Bess, Sang Purcell's

Sorceress at Battersea Arts Centre, 1995; L'Enfant et les Sortilèges, Die Entführung, La Traviata, The Electrification of the Soviet Union as Natasha in the premiere, and as Varvara in Katya Kabanova; Tour of Italy in 1989 with Albert Herring; Other roles include Fenina in Nabucco and Humperdinck's Gretel; Sang in the Royal Opera's Garden Venture in 1989; Has performed the role of Carmen for several opera companies including English National Opera's Baylis Programme and the Royal Opera House's Education Programme; Other roles include the title role in Gluck's Orfeo, Dalila, Third Lady (Magic Flute) and Suzuki (Madama Butterfly); Has recently returned from Syria where she sang the role of Dido in a production of Syria's first ever opera; Further roles include Carmen and Serena (Porgy and Bess); Concert repertoire includes Schumann Lieder with recital at St John's with Iain Burnside, Beethoven's Mass in C, the B minor Mass and the St Matthew Passion. *Honours:* Ricordi Opera Prize; Susan Longfield Award; Winner, Maggie Teyte International Competition, 1985. *Current Management:* Helen Sykes Artists Management. *Address:* c/o Helen Sykes Artists Management, 100 Felsham Road, Putney, London SW15 1DQ, England.

**NICHOLLS, Rachel;** Singer (Soprano); b. 1965, Bedford, England. *Education:* Trinity College of Music; Royal College of Music; London Royal Schools Opera. *Career:* Concerts include Bach's B minor Mass, Mozart's Requiem and Nielsen's 3rd Symphony; Bach's St Matthew Passion and Handel's Apollo e Dafne, with the London Handel Orchestra; Choral Symphony, with the Hanover Band, Dixit Dominus in Birmingham and Messiah at the Albert Hall; Mozart's Mass in C minor (St John Smith's Square); Bach's Magnificat and Saint John Passion, the Brahms and Fauré Requiems, Elgar's Coronation Ode and Poulenc's Gloria; Season 2001 with Handel's L'Allegro for the London Handel Festival, Messiah in Halle, and the Vaughan Williams Sea Symphony at the Brighton Festival; Royal Opera Covent Garden from 2001, as a Flowermaiden in Parsifal and Echo in Ariadne auf Naxos; Other roles include Donna Elvira, Puccini's Lauretta, Maria in Mazeppa, Micaela, Marenka and Mozart's Countess. *Recordings* include Metella in Handel's Silla (Somm). *Address:* c/o Royal Opera House (contracts) Covent Garden, London, WC2.

**NICHOLLS, Simon;** Pianist; b. 8 Oct. 1951, London, England; m. Lorraine Wood 1976. *Education:* Junior Exhibitioner, 1963–69, Foundation Scholar, 1969–74, Royal College of Music; Diplomas: GRSM, ARCM and LRAM. *Career:* Performances in London, St John's Smith Square, Wigmore Hall, South Bank, Snape Maltings, Aldeburgh and at music clubs throughout the United Kingdom; Broadcasts on BBC and ITV and Radio; Tours and broadcasts in France, Netherlands, Germany, Ireland, Greece and USA; Piano Teacher at Yehudi Menuhin School, 1976–86 and Professor at Royal College of Music, 1985–Teacher at Birmingham Conservatorie, 2000–; mem, IS M. *Recordings:* Simon Nicholls Plays Scriabin. *Publications:* The Young Cellist's Repertoire, Recital Repertoire for Cellists with Julian Lloyd Webber. *Contributions:* Piano Journal; Music and Musicians; Tempo; Music Teacher, International Piano Quarterly. *Address:* 49 Grove Road, London N12, England.

**NICHOLSON, George Thomas Frederick,** BA, DPhil; British composer, pianist and conductor; *Senior Lecturer in Music, University of Sheffield*; b. 24 Sept. 1949, Great Lumley, Co. Durham; m. Jane Ginsborg 1984; one s. one d. *Education:* Univ. of York. *Career:* freelance teacher, Guildhall School of Music and Drama, Morley Coll. ., London 1978–88; recitals with Jane Ginsborg, soprano and with Philip Edwards, clarinet, Triple Echo and with John Kenny, trombone; Lecturer, Keele Univ. 1988–96; Sr Lecturer, Univ. of Sheffield 1996–, Head of Music 2003–05; mem. British Acad. of Composers and Songwriters. *Compositions:* Triple Echo (Trio Award, Gaudeamus Competition, Rotterdam) 1982, Orchestral Works: 1132, The Convergence of the Twain, Blisworth Tunnel Blues for soprano and orchestra, Chamber Concerto, Cello Concerto, Flute Concerto, Fenestrae, Concerto for orchestra; chamber works: Winter Music, Ancient Lights, Movements, Stilleven, three Nocturnes, Piano Sonata, Brass Quintet, The Arrival of the Poet in the City (melodrama) for actor and seven musicians, Muybridge Frames for trombone and piano 1992, Mots Justes for piano solo 1988–97, Catch, Shailing and Wambling 2001, Umbra/ Penumbra for trombone and piano, Mister Biberian his Dompe for guitar solo 2002, Autumn Journey; vocal: Aubade, Vignette, Peripheral Visions, Alla Luna for soprano, clarinet and piano, Letters to the World 1997–99, Idyll, Embers. *Recordings:* String Quartet No. 3, Peripheral Visions, Letters to the World, Spring Songs, Nodus, Mots Justes, Muybridge Frames, Umbra/Penumbra, The Arrival of the Poet in the City. *Publications:* contrib. articles to Composer Magazine 1983–87. *Honours:* Yorkshire Arts Composers' Award 1977, Greater London Arts Asscn Young Composer 1979–80. *Address:* c/o Department of Music, University of Sheffield, 38 Taptonville Road, Sheffield S10 2TN, England. *Telephone:* (114) 222-0479 (office). *Fax:* (114) 222-0469 (office). *E-mail:* g.nicholson@shef.ac.uk. *Website:* www.shef.ac.uk/music/staff/gn/gnhomepage.html.

**NICHOLSON, Linda;** Fortepiano Player; b. 1955, England. *Career:* Member of the London Foretpiano Trio from 1978; Duo with Violinist, Hiro Kurosaki; Solo recitals and concertos, performances of the Viennese classics on original instruments at major festivals and concert series throughout Europe including Italy, Belgium, France, Germany, the United Kingdom and the Netherlands; 12 Concert series of the complete piano trios of Haydn in London 1982, to mark the composer's 250th anniversary; Complete piano trios of Beethoven at the Wigmore Hall in 1987; Season 1991 with Mozart Trios and quartets in London, tour on the early Music Network and lunchtime recitals at the Queen Elizabeth Hall; Played Mozart in Barcelona, Lisbon and Germany;

Frequent radio broadcasts. *Recordings:* Complete Trios by Mozart; Trios by Haydn and Beethoven; Mozart Concertos; Complete Violin Sonatas by Mozart, with Hio Kuoselui. *Address:* 21 Clapham Common Northside, London SW4 0RG, England.

**NICKLIN, Celia (Mhry);** Musician and Oboist; b. 28 Nov. 1941, Malmesbury, Wiltshire, England; m. Howard Gough, 8 Feb 1964, 3 d. *Education:* Royal Academy of Music, London; Hochschule für Musik Detmold, Germany. *Career:* Principal Oboe, City of Birmingham Symphony Orchestra 1962–63; London Mozart Players 1970, Academy of St Martin in the Fields 1970; Professor, Royal Academy of Music, London. *Recordings:* Vaughan Williams, Handel, Vivaldi Oboe Concertos with Academy of St Martin, Mozart with London Mozart Players; Many hundred more. *Honours:* FRAM. *Address:* 19 Park Hill, Carshalton, Surrey SM 5 3 SA, England.

**NICOLAI, Claudio;** Singer (Baritone); b. 7 March 1929, Kiel, Germany. *Education:* Vocal studies with Clemens Kaiser-Breme in Essen and Serge Radamsky in Vienna. *Career:* Debut: Theater am Gärtnerplatz, Munich, 1954; Early engagements as a tenor then as baritone from 1956; Appearances at Bregenz Festival, Vienna Volksoper and in Stuttgart, Hamburg, Brussels, Munich, Berlin, Paris, London, Stockholm, Oslo, Prague, Bucharest, Budapest, Zürich and Amsterdam; Member of the Cologne Opera from 1964; Sang in the 1965 premiere of Zimmermann's Die Soldaten and visited London in 1969 for the British premiere of Henze's Der Junge Lord; Sang with Oper der Stadt Köln from 1966; Roles include Giovanni, Count, Papageno and Guglielmo; Tel-Aviv in 1984 in Die Zauberflöte, Metropolitan Opera in 1988, sang Don Alfonso at Brussels and Barcelona in 1990 and Don Alfonso under John Eliot Gardiner at Amsterdam in 1992; Professor at the Musikhochschule Cologne; Salzburg Festival, 1976–79; Nozze di Figaro, Giovanni, Vienna Staatsoper; 15 years guest at the Berlin Staatsoper and three times in Japan; Così fan tutte in Paris with J E Gardiner. *Recordings:* Der Freischütz; Die Fledermaus; Die Kluge; Highlights from Die Soldaten. *Address:* c/o Staatliche Hochschule für Musik, Degobertstrasse 38, 5000 Köln 1, Germany.

**NICOLESCO, Mariana;** Singer (Soprano); b. 28 Nov. 1948, Brasov, Romania. *Education:* Music and Violin in Romania, age 6–18, graduating with Bruch Concerto; Voice with Jolanda Magnoni, Conservatorio Santa Cecilia, Rome; Later with Elisabeth Schwarzkopf and Rodolfo Celletti. *Career:* Debut: Television concert, Voci Rossiniane International Award, Milan, 1972; Sang Violetta in La Traviata, Teatro Comunale, Florence, 1976, Gran Teatro del Liceu, Barcelona, 1976, 1978, 1981, also San Francisco Opera, 1991; Violetta at Metropolitan Opera, 1978, where she also appeared as Gilda in Rigoletto, 1978, and Nedda in Pagliacci, 1979, 1986, Donna Elvira in Don Giovanni, Teatro dell'Opera, Rome, 1984, Munich Staatsoper and Munich Festival, 1986–93, Tokyo, 1988, La Scala, Milan, 1987, 1988, 1993; Also at La Scala, world premiere of Berio's La Vera Storia, 1982, and Un Re in Ascolto, 1986; Dargomishky's Stone Guest, 1983, Mozart's Lucio Silla, 1984, Luigi Rossi's L'Orfeo, 1985, Jommelli's Fetonte, 1988, 3 recitals, 1988–93; Elettra in Idomeneo, Salzburg Festival, 1990, 1991, Japan, 1990, Dresden Semper Oper, 1991; A true dramatic coloratura: Bellini's Beatrice di Tenda, La Fenice, Venice, 1975, Donizetti's Maria di Rohan, Martina Franca Festival, 1988, Elisabeth Queen of England in Roberto Devereux, Monte Carlo, 1992, 1997; Sang at First Christmas Concert in the Vatican, televised world-wide, 1993; Anna Bolena, Munich, 1995; World premiere, Krzysztof Penderecki's Seven Gates of Jerusalem of the Holy City, 1997; Performed at leading opera houses world-wide; Concerts at Royal Festival Hall London, Carnegie Hall New York, Musikverein Vienna, Boston Symphony Hall, Concertgebouw Amsterdam, Teatro Real Madrid, Cleveland Symphony Hall, Teatro alla Scala; Great Conservatory Hall, Moscow. *Recordings:* Bellini: Beatrice di Tenda; Donizetti: Maria di Rohan; Verdi: Simon Boccanegra; Puccini: La Rondine; Mozart: Le nozze di Figaro; World premiere: Meyerbeer cantata Gli Amori di Teolinda, Ravel cantatas Alcyone, Alyssa. *Address:* c/o Wolfgang Stoll, Martius Str 3, 80802 Munich, Germany.

**NICOLESCU, Antonius;** Singer (Tenor); b. 17 Aug. 1946, Bucharest, Romania. *Career:* Debut: Romanian National Opera, Bucharest, 1971, as Vladimir in Prince Igor; Guest appearances at Athens, Berlin Staatsoper, and Heidelberg; Opéra Bastille, Paris, 1992, as Hoffmann; Berne, 1995, in Zandonai's I Cavalieri di Ekebu, Hamburg, 1996, as Don José; Other roles include Alfredo (Essen, 1994), Pinkerton, Ernesto, Faust, Gerald in Lakmé, Lenky and Don Ottavio. *Address:* c/o Hamburg Staatsoper, Theaterstrasse 34, 20354 Hamburg, Germany.

**NICOLET, Aurèle;** Swiss flautist and music teacher; b. 1926, Neuchâtel. *Education:* Univ. of Zurich and Conservatory of Music (Paris). *Career:* Solo flautist with Winterthur City Orchestra and Berlin Philharmonic; teacher Musikhochschule, Berlin and Staatlische Hochschule für Musik, Freiburg, Germany; numerous concert appearances and recordings; Music Prize, Verband der Deutschen Kritiker 1964.

**NICOLL, Harry;** Singer (tenor); b. 1970, Coupar Angus, Perthshire, Scotland. *Education:* Studied at the Royal Scottish Academy of Music and Drama. *Career:* Sang with Scottish Opera Go Round from 1979 as Nemorino, Ferrando, Alfredo and Ramiro; Appearances with Welsh National Opera as Valetto in L'Incoronazion di Poppea, Vasek, the Idiot in Wozzeck and Brighella and the Dancing Master in Ariadne; Sang with English National Opera in Pacific Overtures, Street Scene and The Mikado and with Scottish Opera in their Rossini double bill, as The Lover in the premiere of Judith Weir's The Vanishing Bridegroom in 1990, as Bardolph and as Almaviva;

Other engagements with Opera North in Acis and Galatea and L'Heure Espagnole, Park Lane Group in La Finta Semplice, Glyndebourne Touring Opera as Pedrillo in Die Entführung, English Bach Festival in Versailles as Thespis in Rameau's Platée, Kammeroper Berlin in The Lighthouse, Il Re Pastore and Il Matrimonio Segreto; La Fenice Venice in Zaide, Frankfurt and Jerusalem as Roderigo in Otello, Cologne Opera as Vasek, The Bartered Bride, Opera Voor Vlaanderen, Pedrillo in Die Entführung, New Israeli Opera, Tel-Aviv, Idiot in Boris, Vasek in Bartered Bride, and as Almaviva, Barbiere; Théâtre des Champs Elysées as Medor in Roland by Lully; Has sung in several operas at the Batignano Festival; Concert appearances in the United Kingdom and abroad. *Current Management:* Musicmakers International Artists Representation, Tailor House, 63–65 High Street, Whitwell, Hertfordshire SG4 8AH, England. *Telephone:* (1438) 871708. *Fax:* (1438) 871777. *E-mail:* musicmakers@compuserve.com. *Website:* www.operauk.com. *Address:* c/o Ron Gonsalves, 10 Dagnan Road, London SW12 9LQ, England.

**NICOLLS, Sarah,** LRAM, ARCM, LGSM, LTCL; British pianist; b. 1 April 1974, Newcastle upon Tyne. *Education:* Chetham's School of Music, King's Coll., London, RAM, Guildhall School of Music and Drama. *Career:* debut recital Purcell Room, London (Park Lane Group Young Artists concert) 2001; recitals at Cheltenham Contemporary Concerts Series, British Music Information Centre, Anglia Polytechnic Univ. 2001; recitals at Aldeburgh Festival, Steinway Launch Week (London Coll. of Music), Nat. Portrait Gallery, BBC Broadcasting House, London Sinfonietta State of the Nation weekend, Purcell Room 2002; multimedia concert 'Cinesthesia', Purcell Room, Bath Int. Festival Rising Stars recital, Wigmore Hall and St John's Smith Square debuts, festival performances in Austria, Holland and Aveiro Int. Piano Festival (Portugal), gave British premiere of Berio's Piano Sonata 2003; soloist with Britten-Pears Contemporary Ensemble, pianist in the Tate Ensemble; teacher, RAM Jr Dept; UK tour, Berio recital at Italian Cultural Inst., London, recitals at Bath and Cheltenham festivals, 'Cinesthesia II' 2004. *Recordings:* complete piano music of Niccolo Castiglioni. *Honours:* winner British Contemporary Piano Competition 2000. *Current Management:* Margaret Murphy Management, 7 Grove Park, London, E11 2DN, England. *E-mail:* info@sarahnicolls.com. *Website:* www.sarahnicolls.com.

**NICULESCU, Ștefan;** Romanian composer; b. 31 July 1927, Moreni, Dîmbovița Co.; s. of Lazar Niculescu and Maria Niculescu; m. Colette Demetrescu 1952. *Education:* Acad. of Music and Theatrical Art, Bucharest Coll. of Eng, Bucharest, C. Porumbescu Conservatory of Music, Bucharest. *Career:* studies in electronic music Munich 1966; researcher, Inst. for Art History of the Romanian Acad., Bucharest 1960–63; Prof., Acad. of Music, Bucharest 1963–87, 1992–; Sec. for Symphonic, Chamber and Opera Music Romanian Composers' Union 1990–93; Guest, Deutscher Akademischer Austauschdienst, West Berlin 1971–72, Internationale Frienkurse für Neu Musik, Darmstadt 1992; Corresp. mem. Romanian Acad. 1993–, mem. 1996–. *Works include:* orchestral: Scènes for small orchestra (7 winds, trumpet, trombone, piano, celesta, xylophone, percussion, double bass) 1962, Symphonies for 15 Soloists 1963, Hétérophony 1967, Formanti 1968, Unisonos I 1970, Unisonos II 1971, Ison Ia for small orchestra (14 players) 1973, Ison Ib 1973, Symphony No. 1 1975, Ison II for small orchestra (4 flutes, 4 French horns, 4 trumpets, 4 trombones, 6 percussion) 1977, Symphony No. 2 'Opus Dacicum' 1980, Synchrony II 'Omaggio a Enescu e Bartók' 1981, Symphony No. 3 'Cantos' 1984, Symphony No. 4 'Deisis' 1995, Symphony No. 5 'Litanies' 1997, Umdecimum for small orchestra (11 players) 1998, Prohodiri – A Romanian Requiem for mixed chorus and orchestra 2000–03; chamber music: Sonata for clarinet, piano 1955, String Trio for violin, viola, cello 1957, Inventions for clarinet and piano 1965, Sextet for flute, oboe, English horn, 2 clarinets, alto saxophone 1969, Triplum I for flute, cello, piano 1971, Triplum II for clarinet, cello, piano 1973, Echos I for violin 1977, Synchrony I for any 2–12 players 1979, Echos II for violin and synthesizer 1984, Ricercare in uno for clarinet, violin, synthesizer 1984, Duplum for cello, piano (and synthesizer) 1984, Synchrony III for flute, oboe, bassoon 1985, Hétérophonies for Montreux for flute, oboe, clarinet, French horn, bassoon 1986, Synchrony IV for clarinet, piano, percussion 1987, Incantations, 6 percussion 1991, revised 2000 (also version as Incantations II for solo percussion 2000), Sextuplum for oboe, clarinet, bassoon, violin, cello, percussion 1993, Sequentia for flute, clarinet, violin, viola, cello, percussion 1994; choral: Cantata I (text by Nina Cassian) for children's/female chorus and orchestra 1959, Cantata II (text by Gellu Naum) for tenor, mixed chorus and orchestra 1960, Cantata III, 'Rascrucee' (text by Tudor Arghezi) for mezzo-soprano, flute, 2 oboes (2nd + English horn), 2 clarinets (2nd + bass clarinet) 1965, Heraclit's Aphorisms for 20 mixed voices 1969, Invocatio for 12 mixed voices 1989, Axion for female chorus, sopranino saxophone (+ alto saxophone, tenor saxophone) 1992, Psalm XII for 6 male voices 1993; piano: Tastenspiel 1968; stage and film music. *Recordings:* Symphony No. 2, Symphony No. 3, Ison II, Sonata for Clarinet and Piano. *Publications:* Reflectii despre Musică (Reflections about Music) 1980, Un Nouvel "Esprit de Temps" en Musique 1987, Global Language in Music 2000. *Honours:* Romanian Acad. Prize 1962, French Acad. Prize 1972, Prizes of the Romanian Composers' Union 1972, 1975, 1977, 1979, 1981, 1982, 1984, 1985, 1986, 1988, 1994, Festival Montreux Prize, Int. Record Critics' Award 1985, Herder Prize, Vienna 1994, George Apostu Grand Award 1994. *Address:* Intr. Sublocotenent Stăniloiu 4, 73228 Bucharest 39, Romania (home); Calea Victoriei 141, 70149 Bucharest (office). *Telephone:* (21) 6424370 (home); *Fax:* (21) 2527945 (home).

**NIEHAUS, Manfred;** German composer and stage director; b. 18 Sept. 1933, Cologne. *Education:* Studied with Zimmermann at Cologne. *Career:* Dramaturg and Director at Wurttemberg Landesbuhne, Esslingen am Neckar, 1963–65; Editor for Westdeutsche Rundfunk, Cologne from 1967 and freelance composer from 1989; mem, Vice President, DKIV Section, NRW. *Compositions:* Music theatre works Bartleby, Cologne and Berlin, 1967; Die Pataphysiker, Kiel, 1969; Maldoror, Kiel, 1970; Die Badewanne, Bonn, 1973; It Happens, Bonn, 1973; Sylvester, Stuttgart, 1973; Tartarin Von Tarascon, Hamburg, 1977; Die Komponiermaschine, Nuremberg, 1980; Das Verlorene Gewissen, Gelsenkirchen, 1981; Das Christbaumbrettl, Cologne, 1983; Die Geschichte vom Riesen und dem Kleinen Mann im Ohr, Emmerich, 1984; Wie es Klingt, Essen, 1993; Narcissus und Echo, 1993; Hermione, 1996; Leda, Cologne 1998; Onkel Peters Geschichten, 1997, Das Weiberdorf 2004. *Honours:* Cologne Forderpreis 1966. *Address:* Simrockstr. 18, 50823 Köln, Germany. *Telephone:* (221) 525401. *Fax:* (221) 5892742.

**NIEHOFF, Beatrice;** Singer (Soprano); b. 1952, Mannheim, Germany. *Career:* Sang at Karlsruhe and Darmstadt, 1977–82; Later appearances in Hamburg, Zürich, Berlin and Vienna notably as Mozart's Constanze, Countess, Pamina and Fiordiligi, Dvořák's Rusalka, Weber's Agathe and Wagner's Elsa; Modern repertory includes operatic roles in Fortner's Bluthochzeit, Zemlinsky's Der Kreidekreis, Hindemith's Mathis der Maler and Schoeck's Massimilia Doni; In 1988 sang Eva in a new production of Die Meistersinger at Essen and the Protagonist in the German premiere of Berio's Un Re in Ascolto at Düsseldorf; Returned to Düsseldorf in 1989 as Cleopatra in Giulio Cesare by Handel; Sang Strauss's Chrysothemis at Aachen, 1999. *Address:* c/o Deutsche Oper am Rhein, Dusseldorf, Heinrich Heine Allee 16a, D–40213, Dusseldorf, Germany.

**NIELSEN, Inga;** Danish singer (soprano); b. Holbaek, Seeland; m. Robert Hale. *Education:* Vienna Music Acad. and Musikhochschule Stuttgart. *Career:* performs at Vienna State Opera, La Scala Milan, Covent Garden London, and the opera houses of Munich, Düsseldorf, Hamburg, Stuttgart, Berlin, Paris, Zürich, New York and Buenos Aires; has performed at the festivals of Bayreuth, Munich, Aix-en-Provence, Edinburgh, Holland, Athens, Ludwigsburg, Wexford, Vienna and at the Mostly Mozart Festival in New York; has performed at numerous concerts and recitals and made many TV and radio broadcasts; debut, Gelsenkirchen, Germany 1973; sang in Munster 1974–75, Bern 1975–77; mem., Frankfurt Opera 1978–83, singing Konstanze in Mozart's Die Entführung aus dem Serail, later at the Salzburg Festival and Covent Garden, 1987–89; roles include Schwetzingen in the premiere of Hans Werner Henze's Die Englische Katze, 1983, Donizetti's Lucia in Pittsburgh, Oslo and Hamburg 1984–87, Marguerite in Palermo 1987, Ilia and Fiodiligi in Cologne and Strasbourg 1989, Christine in the Italian premiere of Strauss's Intermezzo in Bologna 1990, Marzelline at Zürich and Gilda at Oslo 1992; Zürich debut as Agathe in Der Freischütz and later as Leonore in Fidelio; sang Salome in Leipzig 1994, Ursula in Hindemith's Mathis der Maler at Covent Garden 1995, Chrysothemis in Elektra in Japan, Feldmarschallin in Der Rosenkavalier at the Royal Opera in Copenhagen 1994, Elsa in Lohengrin and Jenny in Aufstieg und Fall der Stadt Mahagonny at the Hamburg State Opera 1998, Elisabeth in Tannhäuser at the Zürich Opera 1999, the Empress in Die Frau ohne Schatten for the Vienna Staatsoper 2001, Die Frau in Arnold Schönberg's Erwartung at Covent Garden, Senta in Der Fliegende Holländer at the Hamburg State Opera 2003. *Recordings include:* Oberon, Zemlinsky's Geburtstag der Infantin, Schumann's Der Rose Pilgerfahrt, Parsifal, Salome, Don Giovanni, Mozart's Il Re Pastore, Haydn's The Seven Last Words on the Cross; Song of Love (with Robert Hale) 1997, Fidelio 2000, recitals and oratorios. *Honours:* Order of the Dannebrog 1992, Königliche Kammersängerin 1998. *Current Management:* Theateragentur Dr Germinal Hilbert, Maximilianstrasse 22, 80539 Munich, Germany. *Telephone:* (89) 2907470. *Fax:* (89) 29074790. *E-mail:* agentur@hilbert.de. *Website:* www.hilbert.de.

**NIELSEN, Svend;** Composer; b. 20 April 1937, Copenhagen, Denmark. *Education:* Studied Music, University of Copenhagen; Music Theory, Royal Academy of Music, Copenhagen. *Career:* Debut: Copenhagen, 1962; Teacher, Royal Academy of Music, Århus, 1967–. *Compositions:* Orchestral: Metamorphoses, 1968; Nuages, 1972; Symphony, 1978–79; Nocturne, 1981; Concerto for violin and orchestra, 1985; Nightfall for chamber orchestra, 1989; Symphony No. 2, 1997; Voice and Instruments: Three of Nineteen Poems, 1962; Duets, 1964; Romances, 1970–74; Chamber Cantata, 1975; Sonnets of Time, 1978; Ascent Towards Akseki, 1979; Choral Music: Motets, 1982; Imperia, 1982; Jorden, 1983; Sommerfugledalen for 12 solo singers, 1999; Piano Music: Romantic Piano Pieces, 1974; 5 Inventions, 1983; Chamber: Rondo for flute quintet, 1986; String Quartet, 1987; Black Velvet, Clarinet Quintet, 1988; Variations for double quintet, 1989; Windscapes for brass quintet, 1990; Aria for orchestra, 1991; Aubade for orchestra, 1994; Sinfonia Concertante for cello and chamber orchestra, 1994; Shadowgraphs for 10 instruments, 1995; The Colour Blue, for 3 ensembles, 1998. *Recordings:* Carillons; Sinfonia Concertante; Nightfall. *Honours:* Carl Nielsen Prize, 1981; Lifelong Grant, Danish State, 1982–; Schierbeck Prize, 1995. *Address:* Royal Academy of Music, 8210 Århus V, Denmark.

**NIELSEN, Tage;** Professor and Composer; b. 16 Jan. 1929, Frederiksberg, Denmark; m. Aase Grue-Sorensen, 14 Oct 1950, 1 s., 2 d. *Education:* Musicology, University of Copenhagen, 1947–55; Additional studies in Israel 1972, Italy 1974, USA 1975. *Career:* Debut: As Composer, 23 October 1949, UNM Festival, Stockholm; Deputy Head of Music Department, Radio Denmark, 1957–63; Director, Professor, Royal Academy of Music, Århus,

1963–83; Chair of Board, Danish State Art Foundation, 1971–74; Director, Accademia di Danimarca, Rome, 1983–89; Managing Director, The Society for Publication of Danish Music, 1989–93; mem, Danish Composers Society. *Compositions:* Two Nocturnes, piano, 1961; Il gardino magico, orchestra, 1968; Three Character Pieces and an Epilogue, piano, 1972–74; Passacaglia, orchestra, 1981; Laughter in the Dark, opera, 1987–91; Paesaggi, 2 pianos, 1985; Five Opera Fragments, 13 instruments, 1986; The Frosty Silence in the Gardens, guitar, 1990; Lamento and Chorale Fantasy, organ, 1993–95; Laughter in the Dark, opera after V. Nabokov, Arus 1995. *Recordings:* Il giardino magico; Five Opera Fragments. *Publications:* Fra on Langgaard, Alban Berg's Lulu and Lutoslawski and others in Dansk Musiktidsskrift. *Honours:* The Anker Prize, 1975; The Schierbeck Prize, 1992; Wilhelm Hansen Prize, 1998. *Address:* Peter Bangsvej 153, 2000 Frederiksberg, Denmark.

**NIEMAN, Alfred (Abbe);** Composer and Pianist; b. 25 Jan. 1913, London, England; m. Aileen Steeper, 2 s. *Education:* RAM; RAM; ARAM; FGSM. *Career:* Concert appearances in a two piano team and performances with BBC for 5 years; Professor of Composition and Piano and Lecturer at Guildhall School of Music; mem, CGGB; British Association of Music Therapy; Consultant, National Association for Gifted Children. *Compositions include:* 2nd Piano Sonata; 9 Israeli Folksongs; Paradise Regained for cello, piano and Chinese cymbals; Symphony No. 2; Variations and Finale for piano; Adam, cantata for tenor, 4 trombones, 5 percussion and piano; Various songs; Sonata for guitar, commissioned from Gilbert Biberian through The Arts Council and first performed at Purcell Room in 1986; Soliloquy for solo cello, commissioned by Stefan Popov and first performed at St John's Smith Square in 1986 and a further 6 times in Bulgaria; Suite for piano; Three Expressions for unaccompanied chorus; Chromotempera, concerto for cello and piano. *Recordings:* Canzona for quintet, flute, oboe, clarinet, violin and piano. *Publications:* Schumann; Tension In Music; The Earth It Is Your Shoe for solo guitar. *Contributions:* A Fresh Look at Webern, in The Composer, No. 30. *Honours:* McFarren Gold Medal. *Address:* 21 Well Walk, London, NW3, England.

**NIEMELA, Hannu;** Singer (Baritone); b. 17 April 1954, Lohtaja, Finland. *Education:* Graduated from Sibelius Academy, Helsinki, 1983; Further study with Kim Borg and Hans Hotter. *Career:* Debut: Zürich Opera in 1985 as Marullo in Rigoletto; Member of Karlsruhe Opera, 1985–89 and Staatstheater Mainz from 1989; Guest engagements at Savonlinna and Schwetzingen Festivals and at Berne, Basle, Mannheim, Dresden, Prague, Leningrad and Strasbourg; Karlsruhe in 1986 in the premiere of Der Meister und Margarita by Rainer Kunad; Other roles have included Mozart's Count, Papageno and Don Giovanni, Gluck's Orestes, Escamillo, Wozzeck and Demetrius in A Midsummer Night's Dream, and Verdi's Macbeth and Falstaff; Sang the title role in the German premiere of Le Roi Arthus by Chausson, Cologne, 1996; Willy Brand in the premiere of Kniefall in Warschau by G Rosenfeld, Dortmund, 1998; Season 2000–01 as Kurwenal and Count Luna at Dortmund and the title role in the premiere of Tüür's Wallenberg; Iago and title tole in The Death of Klinghoffer at Helsinki; Noted concert artist. *Address:* c/o Staatstheater, Gutenbergplatz 7, 6500 Mainz, Germany.

**NIES, Otfrid;** Violinist and Writer on Music; b. 5 May 1937, Giessen, Germany; m. Christel Nies-Fermor, 7 Sept 1961, 2 s., 2 d. *Education:* Violin studies with Max Rostal, 1960–64, and chamber music with Rudolf Kolisch. *Career:* Member of National Theatre Orchestra, Mannheim, 1964–66; Leader, Stadttheaterorchester Hagen, 1966–71 and leader for Staatstheaterorchester Kassel, 1971–; Presentation of music for player piano by Conlon Nancarrow at Documenta 7, Kassel, 1982; Founder of Archiv Charles Koechlin, 1984; mem, Association Charles Koechlin, Paris; Internationale Schoenberg-Gesellschaft, Vienna. *Recordings:* Quintets, Op 80 for piano and strings, Op 156 for flute and harp, by Charles Koechlin; Music for violin and player piano by Conlon Nancarrow. *Publications:* Orchestration of Quartre Interludes, Op 214 for The Ballet Voyages, Op 222, 1947, by Charles Koechlin, 1986. *Contributions:* Many articles on Charles Koechlin in Das Orchester, Neue Zeitschrift fuer Musik, Fonoforum. *Address:* Saengerweg 3, 3500 Kassel, Germany.

**NIGG, Serge;** French composer; b. 6 June 1924, Paris; m. Micheline Nourrit, 1950, 1 d. *Education:* Paris Conservatory with Messiaen, 1941–46; Studied with Leibowitz, 1945–48. *Career:* Freelance Composer; Professor of Orchestration at the Paris Conservatory; President, Societe Nationale de Musique, 1989; Elu membre de l'Academie des Beaux-Arts, 1989; President de l'Academie and President de l'Institut de France, 1995. *Compositions include:* 3 Sonatas for piano; 1 sonata for violin solo; 1 sonata for violin and piano; 4 Mélodies on poems of Paul Eluard; Concerto for viola and orchestra, 1988; 2 Piano Concertos; Concerto for flute and strings; Mirrors for William Blake for orchestra, 1978; Fulgur for orchestra; Million d'Oiseaux d'Or for orchestra; Du Clair au Sombre song-cycle for soprano and orchestra to poems by Paul Eluard; Symphony poems Timour and Pour un poéte captif; 2 Violin concertos, 1957, 1998; Jérome Bosch-Symphony; String quartet, 1982; Du clair au sombre, for orchestra, 1986; Violin Sonata, 1994; Poéme Pour Orchestre. *Recordings:* 1st Piano Concerto (Orchestre National de France); Violin Concerto (Christian Ferras); Visages d'Axel; Le Chant du Dépossédé; Arioso for violin and piano; Poéme for orchestra; Million d'Oiseaux d'Or, Orchestre de Paris; Four Sonatas: No. 1, for piano, No. 2, for piano, No. 3 for solo violin, and No. 4 for violin and piano, Deux Images de huit for piano. *Contributions:* Discours de réception a l'Academie des Beaux Arts, 1990; Revue 'Diapason': Les Quatuors de Bela Bartók, 1991; Communication a l'Academie des Beaux-

Arts: Peut-on encore, en 1992, enseigner la composition musicale?; 4 Sonatas. *Publications:* Published discourses from academic seminars and symposia. *Honours:* Officer de l'Ordre du Mérite, Président de l'Académie des Beaux Arts, 1995; Chevalier de la Légion d'honneur; Officier de l'Ordre des Arts et des Lettres; Grand Prix du Disque 1957, 1967, 1973, 1981 (twice), 1989, 1996, three Prix de l'Académie Des Beaux-Arts 1976, 1983,Médaille de vermeil de la Ville de Paris. *Address:* 15 bis rue Darcel, 92100 Boulogne-sur-Seine, France.

**NIIMI, Tokuhide;** Composer; b. 5 Aug. 1947, Nagoya, Japan. *Education:* Graduated University of Tokyo 1970 and studied at the Tokyo National University of Fine Arts and Music, 1971–78. *Career:* Faculty Member, Toho Gauden School of Music, Tokyo; Board Member, Directors of the Japanese Composers Society; mem, Japanese Federation of Composers. *Compositions include:* Percussion Concerto, 1973; Enlacage I for chorus and orchestra, 1977; Enlacage II for 3 percussionists (1978) and III for 2 marimbas and 2 percussionists (1980); 2 Symphonies, 1981, 1986; Three Valses for piano duet, 1986; 2 Piano Concertos, 1984 and 1993 (Eyes of the Creator); Under Blue Skies, for children's chorus, mixed chorus and orchestra, 1986; Ohju for cello, 1987; Kazane, for clarinet, violin and cello, 1989; Au-Mi for soprano, violin, cello and piano, 1989; Heteorhthmix for orchestra, 1991; Chain of Life for chamber orchestra, 1993; Planets Dance for 6 percussionists, 1993; String Quartet, 1994; Fusui, for small orchestra, 1994; The Cosmic Tree for koto and orchestra, 1996; Soul Bird for flute and piano, 1996; Spiral of the Fire, for orchestra, 1997; Fujin, Raijin, for Japanese big drum, organ and orchestra, 1997; Garden in the Light, for piano quintet, 1997; Towards the Silence, for string orchestra, 1998; Fairy Ring, for clarinet and piano, 1998. *Recordings:* Eye of the Creator; Garden in the Light. *Honours:* Grand Prix of Composition, 8th International Competition of Ballet Music, Suisse Roman, Geneva. *Current Management:* Akira Tanaka, Zen-On Music Co Ltd. *Address:* 1-26-6-303, Chuo, Nakano-ku, Tokyo, Japan.

**NIKITIN, Yevgeny;** Singer (Bass); b. 1970, Murmansk, Russia. *Education:* St Petersburg Conservatoire. *Career:* Appearances at the Kirov Opera from 1996 (Young Singers' Academy of the Mariinsky Theatre, 1999); Roles have included Mozart's Figaro, Don Giovanni, Rossini's Basilio, Glinka's Ruslan and the Viking Merchant in Sadko by Rimsky-Korsakov; Wagner's Fasolt and Dutchman, Rangoni in Boris Godunov, Rodolfo in La Sonnambula, the Bonze in Madama Butterfly and Ramphis in Aida: Sang Dolokhov in War and Peace and Remeniuk in the British premiere of Prokofiev's Semyon Kotko, with the Kirov Opera at Covent Garden, 2000. *Recordings include:* Boris Godunov. *Honours:* Prizewinner, Pechovsky, Rimsky-Korsakov and Tchaikovsky Competitions, 1996–98. *Address:* c/o Kirov Opera, Mariinsky Theatre, 1 Theatre Square, St Petersburg, Russia.

**NIKKANEN, Kurt;** Concert Violinist; b. Dec. 1965, Hartford, Connecticut, USA. *Education:* Began violin studies aged 3; Boston University Prep Division with Roman Totenberg; Juilliard School, New York, with Dorothy DeLay, graduated 1986. *Career:* Won first competition, 1976; Carnegie Hall debut, 1978, playing the Saint-Saëns Introduction and Rondo Capriccioso; 1980, played the Paganini 1st Concerto with the New York Philharmonic; Bruch 1st Concerto with the Boston Pops; Appearances with the Hartford Symphony, Colorado Philharmonic, New Jersey Chamber Orchestra and Aspen Chamber Symphony; European debut, 1981, with recital tour of Finland; Cleveland Orchestra debut in the Glazunov Concerto, July 1988; British debut playing the Elgar Concerto with the Royal Liverpool Philharmonic conducted by Libor Pesek, Sept 1988; Toured in Venezuela; Debuted at the Kennedy Center in Washington DC; Further engagements with the Helsinki Philharmonic under James DePreist, and an orchestral/recital tour of Japan; Season 1990–91, made debuts in London, Munich and Barcelona; Season 1991–92, engagements with the San Francisco, New Orleans and Portland Symphonies; Recital debuts in Vancouver, Berlin and Paris; Played the Glazunov Concerto at the 1991 Promenade Concerts, London; 1995, BBC Scottish Symphony, Bergen Philharmonic, Seattle International Festival, Hallé Orchestra, Khumo Festival, Resedentie Orchestra of Holland; Premiered John Adams Concerto in Sweden with the Stockholm Philharmonic, John Adams conducting, January 1995; Season 1996–97 included the Adams Concerto with the Hallé Orchestra, the New Zealand Symphony Orchestra and the Cincinnati Symphony, Dvořák and Brahms on Far East tour; Performed Aaron Jay Kernis' Concerto for violin and guitar at the 1998 Aspen Festival, conducted by Hugh Wolff, and HK Gruber's Violin Concerto, Nebelsteinmusik performed with the Swedish Chamber Orchestra under the composer's direction in 1999; Gave a recital at Wigmore Hall, London performing Violin Dance, pieces inspired by dance forms; Meditations for flute and strings, 1997; Via Crucis for solo voices, chorus and orchestra, 1997; A Polish Folksong for soprano and orchestra, 1998; Season 2001–02 with New York City Ballet, concerts with Auckland Philharmonic, Eugene Symphony Orchestra and return to Hong Kong Symphony Orchestra. *Recordings include:* Tchaikovsky and Glazunov Concertos. *Current Management:* Harrison/Parrott Ltd, 12 Penzance Place, London, W11 4PA, England. *Telephone:* (20) 7229 9166. *Fax:* (20) 7221 5042. *Website:* www.harrisonparrott.com.

**NIKODEMOWICZ, Andrzej;** Polish composer and pianist; b. 2 Jan. 1925, Lvov; s. of Marian and Helena; m. Kazimiera Maria Grabowska 1952; one s. one d. *Education:* Conservatory of Lvov with Adam Soltys, studied with Tadeusz Majerski. *Career:* Prof. of Composition and Piano, Conservatory of Lvov 1951–73; Prof. of Faculty of Music, Univ. of Maria Curie-Sklodowska in Lublin 1980–; Prof., Faculty of Church Musicology, Catholic Univ., Lublin; mem. Polish Composers' Soc., Soc. of Authors ZAiKS. *Compositions include:*

Ekspresje 66 miniatures for piano solo 1959–60, violin works, Songs for voice and piano, Chamber Concerto 1968, Composizione sonoristica for violin, violoncello and piano 1966–71, Musica concertante per tre for flute, viola and piano 1966–67, three nocturnes for trumpet and piano 1964, Symphonic music 1974–75, Concerto for violin and symphony orchestra 1973, choir music including 500 Polish Christmas carols, Glass Mountain (pantomime) 1969, 35 religious cantatas including Magnificat for choir of women and orchestra 1977–78, Evening Offering 1980, Hear My Cry, O God 1981, five lullabies for violin and piano 1991, four songs for soprano, trumpet and organ, George Herbert 1992, Variations, Ave maris Stella for organ 1993, Concerto for piano and symphony orchestra 1994; Laudate Dominum (cantata) 1985–87, Via Crucis (cantata) 1996, Concerto No. 2 for piano and symphony orchestra 2002, Concerto No. 3 for piano and symphony orchestra 2002, Concerto-meditazione for violoncello and symphony orchestra 2003, Concerto No. 4 for piano and symphony orchestra 2003, Concerto No. 5 for piano and symphony orchestra 2004. *Recordings:* two cantatas, cycle of songs. *Publications:* contrib. several reviews in Ruch Muzyczny. *Honours:* Dr hc (Lwów Musical Acad.) 2003; Prize of Saint Friar Albert 1981, Mayor of Lublin City Award 1998, Asscn of Polish Composers Award 2000, Ministry of Culture Award 2000, Artistic Award of the City of Lublin 2002, Diploma and Medal of His Holiness Pope John II Pro Ecclesia et Pontifice 2003. *Address:* ul Paryska 4/37, 20-854 Lublin, Poland. *Telephone:* (4881) 7415629.

**NIKOLOV, Nikola;** Singer (Tenor); b. 1924, Sofia, Bulgaria. *Education:* Studied in Sofia. *Career:* Debut: Varna in 1947 as Pinkerton; Sang at Varna until 1953 then studied further in Moscow and sang at Sofia National Opera from 1955; Appearances in Moscow and Leningrad in the 1950s, La Scala Milan in 1958 as Jenik in The Bartered Bride; Season 1958–60 at Wexford Festival, Vienna Staatsoper and Covent Garden as Radames; New York Metropolitan in 1960 as Don José, State Operas of Berlin and Hamburg and Naples in 1963 as Vasco da Gama in L'Africaine. Sang further in Munich, Barcelona, Geneva, Belgrade, Budapest and Bucharest; Other roles included Manrico, Turiddu, Cavaradossi, Calaf and Don Carlos; *Recordings:* Aida; Carmen; Boris Godunov; L'Africaine. *Address:* c/o Bayerische Staatsoper, Postfach 100148, 8000 Munich 1, Germany.

**NIKOLOVA, Zistomira;** Singer (mezzo-soprano); b. 10 March 1949, Svilengrad, Bulgaria. *Career:* Sang in opera houses throughout Yugoslavia, as Verdi's Azucena, Eboli and Amneris, Marina in Boris Godunov, Adalgisa in Norma, Carmen, Dalila, Marfa (Khovanshchina) and Clytemnestra; Staatstheater Karlsruhe, 1995–96, notably as Fricka and Waltraute in The Ring; Guest appearances in Moscow, St Petersburg, Mannheim, Leipzig and Marseilles; Numerous concert appearances; Sang Fortunata in Makernas's Satyricon at Zagreb, 1998. *Address:* Karlsruhe Opera, Baumeisterstrasse 11, 7500 Karlsruhe, Germany.

**NIKOLSKY, Gleb;** Singer (Bass); b. 1959, Moscow, Russia. *Education:* Studied at the Moscow conservatory and at La Scala, Milan. *Career:* Soloist at the Bolshoi Theatre, Moscow, as Verdi's King Philip, Ramphis, Fiesco and Padre Guardiano, Boris, Dosifey, Ivan Susanin and Gounod's Mephistopheles; Guest appearances in Italy, the USA and Zürich (Gremin in Eugene Onegin, 1990); Carnegie Hall 1990, as the Archbishop in Tchaikovsky's The Maid of Orleans; Metropolitan Opera from 1991. *Address:* Bolshoi Theatre, 103009 Moscow, Russia.

**NILON, Paul;** Singer (Tenor); b. 1961, Keighley, Yorkshire. *Education:* Studied with Frederic Cox at the Royal Northern College of Music. *Career:* Appearances with Opera 80 as Don Ottavio, the Duke of Mantua and Sellem in The Rake's Progress; La Fenice, Venice, as Sellem; Musica nel Chiostro in Batignano, Italy, as Jacquino in Beethoven's Leonora; Has sung Strauss's Scaramucchio and Mozart's Belmonte for Opera Northern Ireland, 1987–88; Mario and the Magician, Stephen Oliver, world premiere Batignano, 1988; With City of Birmingham Touring Opera has sung Fenton in Falstaff and Mozart's Tamino; Has sung with Opera North from 1988 as Hylas in The Trojans, Kudras (Katya Kabanova), Belfiore (La Finta Giardiniera), Leander in Nielsen's Maskarade (British premiere), Ferrando and Don Ottavio; Engagements with New Israel Opera and English National Opera, 1990–92 as Ferrando, Narraboth (Salome) and Telemachus in The Return of Ulysses; Tamino ENO, 1992–93, Duel of Tancredi and Clorinda; Tamino Scottish Opera, 1992, ENO, 1993; In Ariodante ENO, as Lurcanio, 1993; Many concert appearances; Almaviva, Barbiere, ENO and New Israeli Opera; King Ouf in L'Etoile; Paolino in Secret Marriage; Benedict in Beatrice and Benedict, Welsh National Opera; Pirro in Rossini's Ermione at Glyndebourne 1996; Alfredo for GTO and Grimoaldo in Rodelina (GTO, 1998); Sang Monteverdi's Ulysses at Florence, 1999; Season 2000–01 as Lurcanio in Ariodante at the Munich Staatsoper, with Opera North in Prague as Michel in Martinů's Julietta, Golo in Schumann's Genoveva at Edinburgh and Don Ottavio for ENO. *Recordings include:* L'Assedio di Calais by Donizetti and Vol. II and III in One Hundred Years of Italian Opera (Opera Rara); Medea in Corinta by Mayr; Orazi e Curiazi, Mercadante (Opera Rara). *Current Management:* Ingpen & Williams Ltd, 7 St George's Court, 131 Putney Bridge Road, London, SW15 2PA, England.

**NILSON, Göran W.;** Conductor and Pianist; b. 5 Jan. 1941, Halmstad, Sweden; m. Catharina Ericson 1965, 1 s., 1 d. *Education:* Royal High School of Music, Stockholm; Further studies in Paris, London and New York. *Career:* Debut: As Pianist at age 15, Stockholm Concert Hall, 1956; As Pianist, tours in Europe and USA; Conductor, Royal Opera, Stockholm, 1963–69; Chief

Conductor, Örebro and Gävle, 1974–93; Guest Conductor, Europe, USA, Asia, Mexico and South Africa; mem, Royal Swedish Academy of Music, 1986–. *Recordings:* Many recordings of as Pianist/Conductor, especially Swedish music with several Scandinavian orchestras. *Honours:* Jeton Reward from Royal High School of Music, Stockholm, 1956. *Address:* Tantogatan 47-I, 11842 Stockholm, Sweden.

**NILSSON, Anders;** Composer; b. 6 July 1954, Stockholm, Sweden; m. Elzbieta Mysliwiec, 11 Feb 1989, 2 d. *Education:* Private musical studies; Music High School, Stockholm, 1971–73; Birkagården Folk High School, Stockholm, 1973–75, 1977–78; Composition, State College of Music, Stockholm, 1979–83. *Career:* Debut: 1st of Trois Pièces pour grand orchestre, with Danish Radio Symphony Orchestra, Copenhagen, 15th Jan 1981; Composer, Conductor, Swedish National Theatre Centre and Stockholm City Theatre, 1975–78; Full-time Composer, 1983–; Represented at International Society for Contemporary Music World Music Days, 1990, 1993, and elsewhere; mem, Swedish Composers' League; International Society for Contemporary Music. *Compositions include:* Trois Pièces pour grand orchestre, 1980–88; Ariel for oboe, tape and string orchestra, 1985; Reflections for soprano and chamber ensemble, 1982; Cadenze for chamber orchestra, 1987; Concerto for organ and orchestra, 1987; Sinfonietta for orchestra, 1992; Divertimento for chamber ensemble, 1991; KRASCH for saxophone quartet and percussion-ensemble, 1993; Concerto Grosso for saxophone quartet and orchestra, 1995; Symphony No. 1, 1996; Mind the Gap, for orchestra, piano concerto, 1997; Concerto for marimba and orchestra, 1998. *Recordings:* Ariel; Cadenze; Concerto for organ and orchestra; Five Orchestral Pieces for piano; Reflections; KRASCH; Divertimento; Aria. *Publications:* Scores: Resonance for piano, 1985; Reflections, 1986; Ariel, 1990; Five Orchestral Pieces for piano, 1993; Mountains for organ, 1994; Divertimento for chamber ensemble, 1995; concerto Grosso for saxophone quartet and orchestra, 1995; Piano Concerto, 1997; Symphony, 1997; Marimba Concerto, 1988. *Contributions:* Numerous articles to Nutida Musik, Swedish magazine for contemporary music. *Honours:* Rosenborg Prize, Gehrmans Music Publishers, 1988; 1st Prize, Grand Prix de Saint-Rèmy-de-Provence, for Mountains, 1992. *Address:* Fyrskeppsvägen 128, 121 54 Johanneshov, Sweden.

**NILSSON, Bo;** Composer; b. 1 May 1937, Skelleftehamn, Sweden; Divorced, 2 d. *Education:* Piano under Micha Pedersen, 1945–50; Audiology under K G St Clair Renard, 1951–54; Counterpoint and instrumentation under Karl Birger Blomdahl, 1955–57. *Career:* Debut: Composer, Cologne, 1956; Free-lance Artist, 1976–; Compositions played world-wide; Author. *Compositions include:* Brief an Gösta Oswald, 1958–59; Drei Szenen, 1960–61; Swedenborg Dreaming for electronic music, 1969; Déjà Vu for woodwind quartet, 1967; Déjà connu, Déjà entendu for wind quintet, 1976; We'll Be Meeting Tomorrow for mixed choir, soprano, celesta and triangles, 1970; Fatumeh for speaker, soloists, mixed choir, electronics and large orchestra, 1973; La Bran for soprano, saxophone, mixed choir, orchestra and electronics, 1975; Fragments for marimba, 5 Thai-gongs, 1975; Floten aus der Einsamkelt for soprano, 9 players, 1976; Bass, bass, tuba solo, 8 Javanian tuned gongs, Chinese gong, 1977; Plexus for brass instruments, piano and percussion, 1979; Wendepunkt-Infrastruktur-Endepunkt, brass quintet, 1981; Autumn Song for baritone and orchestra, 1984; My Summerwind is Yours, for baritone and orchestra, 1984; Brief an Gösta Oswald; Arctic Romance, 1995; A Spirit's Whisper in Swedenborg's Gazebo, 1996; Arctic Air, for orchestra, 2001; Film music; Songs; Jazz. *Recordings:* Introduction and Midsummer Tune; Quantitaten, Raga Rena Rama; Rendez-vous; You; Illness; Walz in Marjoram; Blue-Black Samba; The Last Lass; To Love; Lidingo Airport; Forward Waltz; The Swinging World of Bo Nilsson; The Missile; In The Loneliness of The Night; Ravaillac; A Spirit's Whisper, 1997; Many Others. *Publications:* Spaderboken, 1962; Missilen eller Livet i en mossa, 1994. *Honours:* Christopher Johnson Grand Prize, 1975; Hilding Rosenberg Prize, 1993; Honoré Causa 2000 at the University of Lulea; State Artist's Salary, 1974–. *Address:* Kocksgatan 48, 4 tr, 116 29 Stockholm, Sweden.

**NILSSON, Pia-Marie;** Singer (Soprano); b. 1961, Sweden. *Education:* Studied at Stockholm College of Music and the State Opera School. *Career:* Debut: Stockholm Folkoperan in 1985 as the Queen of Night; Sang at Royal Opera Stockholm and the Drottningholm Theatre, 1986–88 and Frankfurt Opera from 1989 as Sandrina in La Finta Giardiniera, Servilia in La Clemenza di Tito, Pamina, Oscar in Ballo in Maschera, Gilda and Sophie; French debut in 1991 as Donna Anna at Nancy; Concert engagements in Scandinavia, Italy, Switzerland, Germany and Austria; Engaged as Oscar for the Théâtre de la Monnaie, Brussels, 1995; Season 1994–95, Ring Cycle, Frankfurt; Season 1995–96 as Susanna at Frankfurt; Broadcasting commitments in Scandinavia.

**NILSSON, Raymond;** Singer (Tenor); b. 26 May 1920, Mosman, Sydney, Australia. *Education:* Studied at the New South Wales Conservatorium and at the Royal College of Music in London. *Career:* After early experience in Australia sang with the Carl Rosa Company, the English Opera Group and Sadler's Wells; Royal Opera House Covent Garden from 1952 as Don José, Alfredo, Germont and Pandarus in Troilus and Cressida; Guest appearances in Wiesbaden and elsewhere in Germany as concert artist, with further tours to USA and Netherlands; Australian tours with the Elizabethan Opera Company in 1958 and Sadler's Wells in 1960; Other roles included Turiddu, Rodolfo, Narraboth in Salome and Luigi in Il Tabarro; BBC performances of Schoenberg's Gurrelieder, Hindemith's Mathis der Maler, Oedipus Rex and Kodály's Psalmus Hungaricus; Sang in Janáček's Glagolitic Mass with ABC,

Australia. *Recordings:* Bob Boles in Peter Grimes; Psalmus Hungaricus. *Address:* c/o Australian Opera, PO Box 291, Strawberry Hills, New South Wales 2012, Australia.

**NIMSGERN, Siegmund;** Singer (Baritone); b. 14 Jan. 1940, St Wendel, Germany. *Education:* Vocal studies with Paul Lohmann and Jakob Staempfli. *Career:* Debut: Lionel in Tchaikovsky's Maid of Orleans, Saarbrucken, 1967; Sang in Saarbrucken until 1971 then Deutsche Oper am Rhein, Düsseldorf, 1971–74; London Promenade Concerts in 1972 as Mephistopheles in La Damnation de Faust; La Scala Milan and Paris Opéra in 1973, Covent Garden in 1973 as Amfortas in Parsifal; Paris, 1977–82 as the Speaker in Die Zauberflöte, Creon in Oedipus Rex, Telramund in Lohengrin and Beethoven's Pizarro; Metropolitan Opera in 1978 as Pizarro and Bayreuth Festival, 1983–85 as Wotan in the Peter Hall production of Der Ring des Nibelungen; Often heard as concert singer; Chicago Lyric Opera in 1988 as Scarpia and sang Wotan in Das Rheingold at Bonn in 1990, Don Pizarro in Fidelio at La Scala and Telramund at Frankfurt in 1991; Sang Creon in Cherubini's Médée at Trier, 1999. *Recordings:* St John Passion by Bach; Masses by Haydn and Hummel; Pergolesi's La Serva Padrona; Cantatas by Bach and Telemann; Bach's Magnificat; St Matthew Passion and Bach B minor Mass; Alberich in Das Rheingold; Mosè in Egitto; Die Schöpfung; Marschner's Der Vampyr. *Current Management:* Ingpen & Williams Ltd, 7 St George's Court, 131 Putney Bridge Road, London, SW15 2PA, England.

**NIRQUET, Jean;** Singer (Countertenor), Conductor and Musicologist; b. 15 Aug. 1958, Paris, France. *Education:* Baccalauréat of Sciences; Licence, History, Sorbonne University, Paris; Flute, bassoon, piano and theory studies at Strasbourg Music High School and Conservatory until 1964; Harmony and conducting with Claude-Henry Joubert, singing with Jacqueline Bonnardot at Conservatory of Orléans until 1978; Music analysis with Betsy Jolas, singing with Christiane Eda-Pierre at Conservatory of Paris. *Career:* Engagements at opera houses of Paris, Lyon, Nice, Strasbourg, Karlsruhe and Helsinki; Radio appearances in France, Germany and Netherlands and at numerous festivals; Film for Südwestfunk 2, Pasticcio of Handel-Martinoty, 1985. *Recordings:* Handel's Alessandro; Cavalli's Serse; Charpentier's Vespers of the Annunciation, Te Deum and David et Jonathas; Gilles' Requiem; Prodomidès' H H Ulysse. *Publications:* Rose et Colas de Monsigny, 1982; L'Irato de Méhul, 1984; La Dramaturgie des Opéras de Lully Dans L'Etude des Tempi; Analyse d'Epiphanie d'André Caplet. *Current Management:* Anglo Swiss, London, England; Rainer-Poilvé, Paris, France; Kempf, Munich, Germany. *Address:* c/o Poilvé, 16 avenue Franklin D. Roosevelt, F–7500 Paris, France.

**NISHIDA, Hiroko;** Singer (Soprano); b. 17 Jan. 1952, Oita, Japan. *Education:* Studied in Tokyo. *Career:* Sang with the Bonn Opera, 1979–81; Appearances at Zürich Opera as Butterfly, Berne, Mimi, St Gallen, Micaela and the Forza Leonora at Berlin, Munich, Cologne, Frankfurt, Düsseldorf, Stuttgart and Mannheim; Sang Butterfly with Opéra de Lyon in 1990; Further guest appearances at San Diego, Enschede and Amsterdam, Vienna Staatsoper; Hamburg; Prague; Sofia; Vancouver; Tokyo; Other roles include Arminda in La Finta Giardiniera, Pamina, Manon Lescaut, Lauretta, Elisabeth de Valois and Kunigunde in Lortzing's Hans Sachs; Concert repertoire includes works by Bach, Handel, Mozart, Schubert, Beethoven, Bruckner and Mahler. *Address:* Magnihalde 11, 9000 St Gallen, Switzerland.

**NISHIKAZE, Makiko;** Composer and Pianist; b. 22 April 1968, Wakayama, Japan. *Education:* Studied at Aichi University of Fine Arts and Music, 1987–91; Mills College, California, USA, 1991–93; Studies, graduating as MA, Hochschule der Künste, Berlin, Germany, 1994–99. *Career:* Finalist, Forum '93 International Composition Competition, Montreal, 1993; Participant, Darmstadt Summer Course, 1994; Piano solo recitals, Berlin, 1996, 1999; Appeared at Chamber Music Festival in Kanagawa, Japan, 1997; Concerts in New York, Israel, Brazil, and Barcelona, Spain, 1998. *Compositions:* Haiku, for sextet, CD, 1994; Celestial Fruits, for ensemble, 1995; Shades I–V, for piano, 1995–96; Chant I–III, for voice, 1997–98; North Piano I–V, for piano, 1997; Lux, for string quartet 1999; Oratorio for vocal ensemble 2000; Garden, Nocturnal, for ensemble 2001. *Recordings:* Radio recordings, Canada and Germany. *Honours:* Grants from Berlin Senate, 1994; Composition Prize, Stuttgart, 1995; Fellowship, Akademie Schloss Solitude, 1999; State Schleswig-Holstein Prize 2000; State Niedersachsen Prize 2001. *Current Management:* Edition Wandelweiser, Berlin. *Address:* Sophie-Charlotten Strasse 112, 14059 Berlin, Germany.

**NISHIYAMA, Ikuko;** Japanese pianist; b. 28 Dec. 1976, Tokyo. *Education:* Purcell School, London, UK, Hochschule für Musik und Darstellende Kunst, Vienna, Austria. *Career:* performed Shostakovich Piano Concerto No. 1 with London Gala Orchestra, Royal Festival Hall, London 1991; piano recital, Casals Hall, Tokyo, Japan 1998; Beethoven Piano Concerto No. 3 with Tokyo New City Orchestra 2003. *Recordings:* CD of works by Mozart, Beethoven and Schumann. *Honours:* Third Prize, 10th Int. Beethoven Piano Competition 1997, First Prize, 10th Int. Chamber Music Competition, Greece 2000. *Address:* 3-30-18 Ozenji-nishi, Asao-ku, Kawasaki-shi, Kanagawa 215-0017, Japan (home).

**NISKA, Maralin;** Singer (Soprano); b. 16 Nov. 1930, San Pedro, California, USA. *Education:* Studied with Lotte Lehmann. *Career:* Sang widely in California from 1955; Sang at San Diego Opera in 1965 as Mimi in La Bohème, sang Floyd's Susannah with the Met National Company, at New York City Opera in 1967 as Mozart's Countess returning as Turandot, Tosca, Salome and Janáček's Emilia Marty, and at Metropolitan Opera, 1970–77 as Tosca,

Musetta and Hélène in Les Vêpres Siciliennes; Italian debut as Marie in Wozzeck at Maggio Musicale Florence, 1978; Other roles have included Violetta, Madama Butterfly, Donna Elvira, Manon Lescaut and Marguerite in Faust.

**NISKANEN, Jyrki;** Singer (Tenor); b. 12 Feb. 1956, Finland. *Education:* Studied at the Helsinki Sibelius Academy and with Vera Rozsa in London. *Career:* Debut: Tampere, 1986, as Tonio in La Fille du régiment; Sang Alfredo at Helsinki, 1989; Savonlinna Festival, 1992–96, as Florestan and Verdi's Macduff; Théâtre du Châtelet, Paris, 1994, as Siegmund; Florence, 1995, in Zemlinsky's Eine Florentinische Tragödie; Season 1996 as Siegmund at the Vienna Staatsoper, Tristan at Barcelona and Florestan in Rio de Janeiro; Concerts, in Europe and USA, include Requiems of Mozart and Verdi; Season 1998 as Shostakovich's Sergei at Florence, Alvaro in La Forza del Destino at Savonlinna; Sang Wagner's Lohengrin at Nice, 1998 and Seville, 1999; Tristan in Nice, Washington, Munich and Florence, 2001; Loge and Siegmund at Catania; Beethoven's Ninth at la Scala, 1999, and Gabriele Adorno at Catania. *Address:* c/o Savonlinna Opera Festival, Olavinkatu 35, 57130 Savonlinna, Finland. *E-mail:* sirkka.kuula-niskanen@pp.inet.fi.

**NISSEL, Siegmund Walter,** OBE; British violinist; b. 3 Jan. 1922, Munich, Germany; s. of Isidor Nissel and Malvine Nissel; m. Muriel Nissel 1957; one s. one d. *Education:* Mittelschule Vienna, London Univ. and violin tuition privately with Prof. Max Weissgärber, Vienna and Prof. Max Rostal, London. *Career:* Leader, London Int. Orchestra 1947; Founder mem. Second Violin, Amadeus Quartet 1948–87; Prof. of Chamber Music, Musikhochschule, Cologne, FRG 1978–, RAM, London 1986– (Dir for Chamber Music). *Honours:* Hon. mem. RAM; Hon. DMus (York, London); Grosses Verdienstkreuz, Germany; Ehrenkreuz für Wissenschaft und Kunst, Austria, 1. Klasse. *Address:* 11 Highgrove Point, Mount Vernon, Frognal Rise, London, NW3 6PZ, England. *Telephone:* (20) 7681-7078 (office). *Fax:* (20) 7681-7269 (home).

**NISSMAN, Barbara;** Concert Pianist; b. 31 Dec. 1944, Philadelphia, Pennsylvania, USA. *Education:* BMus, 1966, MMus, 1966, D.Mus Arts, 1969, University of Michigan; Studied with Pianist, György Sandor. *Career:* Debut: American Orchestral Debut with Philadelphia Orchestra, Ormandy, 1971; Appearances with London Philharmonic, Royal Philharmonic, Rotterdam Philharmonic, L'Orchestre de la Suisse Romande, BBC Symphony, Netherlands Chamber, Munich Philharmonic, Bavarian Radio Orchestra; USA; Philadelphia, Pittsburgh, Minnesota, Chicago, Cleveland, St Louis, National, New York Philharmonic Orchestras; With Ormandy, Muti, Mata, Skrowaczewski, Zinman, Slatkin; Concert tours of the Far East, Latin America and Soviet Union; Presented Dutch Premiere of Ginastera Piano Concerto, 1978 in Concertgebouw; Soloist at Gala 60th birthday concert for Ginastera with Suisse Romande, 1976; Third Piano Sonata, 1982, of Ginastera, dedicated to Ms Nissman; Masterclasses given at Moscow, St Petersburg Conservatories, Federal University of Brazil and throughout USA. *Recordings:* Complete Solo and Chamber Music of Alberto Ginastera, 2 vols; Music of Franz Liszt; Complete piano sonatas of Prokofiev, 3 vols; Chopin by Nissman, Beethoven by Nissman, Bartók by Nissman (includes first performance of unpublished 1898 Sonata). *Publications:* Alberto Ginastera – Piano Sonata No. 3, 1982; Bartók and the Piano: A Performer's View (includes CD), 2002. *Address:* Rte 2, Box 260, Lewisburg, WV 24901, USA. *Website:* www.barbaranissman.com.

**NITESCU, Adina;** Singer (Soprano); b. 1965, Romania. *Education:* Studied at the George Enescu Conservatoire, Bucharest, and in Munich; Stipendium from Georg Solti, 1991–92. *Career:* Roles with the Opera Studio of the Bavarian State Opera included Mozart's Countess and Fiordiligi; Bucharest Opera debut as Mimi in La Bohème, 1993; Further engagements as Donna Anna at Leipzig, Saarbrucken and Essen; Mimi at Cologne and Wiesbaden, Marzelline in Fidelio at the 1996 Bregenz Festival and Gounod's Marguerite at the Deutsche Oper, Berlin, First Lady in Die Zauberflöte, and in Gluck's Armide to open the 1996 season at La Scala, Milan; Glyndebourne Festival 1997, as Manon Lescaut in a new production of Puccini's opera. *Address:* Planie 7, 72764 Reutlingen, Germany.

**NITSCHE, Horst;** Singer (Tenor); b. 22 March 1939, Vienna, Austria. *Education:* Studied at the Bruckner Conservatory, Linz. *Career:* Sang at the Landestheater Salzburg from 1970, Vienna Staatsoper 1972; Appearances in Vienna (also at Volksoper) as Monostatos, Don Curzio, Jacquino, Zorn in Meistersinger, Flavio in Norma and Missail in Boris Godunov; Sang in the 1976 premiere of Kabale und Liebe by Einem; Salzburg Festival from 1977, in Salome, Don Carlos, Die Zauberflöte and Le nozze di Figaro. *Recordings:* Character roles in Il Trovatore, Der Rosenkavalier, Die Zauberflöte and Don Carlos. *Address:* Vienna Staatsoper, Opernring 2, 1010 Vienna, Austria.

**NIXON, Marni;** Singer (Soprano) and Teacher; b. 22 Feb. 1930, Altadena, California, USA. *Education:* Studied at the University of Southern California with Carl Ebert, Stanford University with Jan Popper and the Berkshire Music Center with Boris Goldovsky and Sarah Caldwell. *Career:* Has sung in musical comedy, programmes for children's television, concerts, opera and film soundtracks; Provided the singing voices for Deborah Kerr in The King and I, Natalie Wood in West Side Story and Audrey Hepburn in My Fair Lady; Has appeared in Los Angeles, San Francisco, Tanglewood and Seattle as Mozart's Blondchen, Constanze and Susanna, Philine in Thomas' Mignon, and Strauss's Zerbinetta and Violetta; Concert engagements in Cleveland, Toronto, Los Angeles, Israel and London; Modern repertory includes works by Webern, Ives, Hindemith and Stravinsky; Teacher at California Institute of Arts, 1969–71 and Music Academy of The West, Santa Barbara, from 1980; Appears as Cabaret Artist. *Recordings include:* Webern Complete Works, conducted by Robert Craft. *Address:* c/o Music Academy of The West, 1070 Fairway Road, CA 93109, USA.

**NIXON, Roger;** Composer; b. 8 Aug. 1921, Tulane, California, USA. *Education:* Studied at University of California, Berkeley, PhD in 1952, notably with Roger Sessions, Arthur Bliss, Bloch and Schoenberg. *Career:* Teacher at Modesto Junior College, 1951–59 and San Francisco State University from 1960. *Compositions:* Opera: The Bride Comes To Yellow Sky, 1968; Orchestral: Air for Strings, 1953, Violin Concerto, 1956, Elegaic Rhapsody for Viola and Orchestra, 1962, Viola Concerto, 1969, San Joaquin Sketches, 1982, California Jubilee, 1982, Golden Jubilee, 1985; Chamber: String Quartet No. 1, 1949, Conversations for Violin and Clarinet, 1981, Music for Clarinet and Piano, 1986; Vocal: Christmas Perspectives for Chorus, 1980, Festival Mass for Chorus, 1980, Chaunticleer for Male Chorus, 1984, The Canterbury Tales for Chorus, 1986, The Daisy for Chorus, 1987; Song Cycles include, A Narative Of Tides for Soprano, Flute and Piano, 1984. *Honours:* Grants and commissions from the San Francisco Festival of The Masses and American Bandmasters Association. *Address:* c/o ASCAP, ASCAP Building, 1 Lincoln Plaza, New York, NY 10023, USA.

**NKETIA, Joseph Hanson Kwabena;** Ghanaian composer, academic and writer; *Director International Centre for African Music and Dance, University of Ghana*; b. 22 June 1921, Mampong, Ashanti Region. *Education:* Presbyterian Training Coll. and Theological Seminary, Akropong, School of Oriental and African Studies, London, Trinity Coll. of Music, London, Birkbeck Coll., London, Columbia Univ. and Juilliard School of Music, New York, Northwestern Univ., Evnaston, IL. *Career:* composer from 1940; teacher, Presbyterian Training Coll. 1941–44, 1949–52, acting Principal 1954; Asst, SOAS, Univ. of London 1946–49; Research Fellow, Univ. Coll. of Ghana 1952–59, Sr Research Fellow 1959–61; Assoc. Prof., Univ. of Ghana, Legon 1962, Prof. 1963–65, Dir Inst. of African Studies 1965–79, Prof. Emeritus 1990–; Dir Int. Centre for African Music and Dance 1993–; Dir musical ensemble for Ghana Dance Troupe 1963–70; Prof., Univ. of Calif. at Los Angeles 1969–82, Prof. Emeritus 1982–; Horatio Appleton Lamb Visiting Prof. of Music, Harvard Univ. 1971; Visiting Prof. of Music, Univ. of Queensland, Brisbane, Australia 1979; Andrew Mellon Prof. of Music, Univ. of Pittsburgh, PA 1982–91, Chair. Dept of Music 1986–89, Andrew Mellon Prof. Emeritus 1992; Visiting Prof., China Conservatory of Music, Beijing; Langston Hughes Visiting Prof., Univ. of Kansas-Lawrence 1992; Cornell Visiting Prof. Dept of Music and Dance, Swarthmore Coll., PA 1995; Distinguished Hannah Prof. of Integrative Studies, Mich. State Univ., East Lansing 1997; Fellow, Ghana Acad. of Arts and Sciences 1959; mem. Exec Bd, Int. Folk Music Council 1959–70; mem. Int. Music Council 1962–66, 1978, exec. mem. 1971–77, mem. of honour 1980; mem. Scientific Bd, Int. Inst. for Comparative Music Studies and Documentation (Berlin) 1964; mem. Soc. for Ethnomusicology Council (dir at large 1968, vice-pres. 1972–73); mem. Int. Soc. for Music Educ. (bd dirs 1967–74, vice-pres. 1968–74); Chair. African Regional Secretariat, Int. Music Council (UNESCO) 1972; Regional Coordinator for Africa, Bd Dirs Universe of Music: A World History (UNESCO) 1980; mem. Int. Comm. for a Scientific and Cultural History of Mankind, UNESCO 1980–; mem. Scientific Cttee, Institut des Peuples Noir, Burkina Faso 1986; mem. Bd Dirs, African Studies Asscn 1986–90; mem. Int. Semiotic Inst. 1987; mem. African Music Soc., Historical Soc. of Ghana, Int. Council for Traditional Music, Nat. Music Asscn of Ghana (pres.). *Compositions include:* Adanse Kronkron (Divine Testimony) 1940, African Pianism: Twelve Pedagogical Pieces 1946–75, Suite for flute and piano 1959, Four Akan Solo Songs 1962, Canzona 1963, Antubam (Dirge for cello and piano) 1965, For Violin 1967, Four Flute Pieces 1969, Quartet No. 1 for Atenteben 1969, Quartet No. 2 for Ateneben 1969, Chamber Music in the African Idiom 1976. *Publications:* Akanfoo Anansesem 1949, Akanfoo Nnwom Bi 1949, Ananwoma 1951, Anwonsem 1952, Kwabena Amoa 1952, Akwansosem Bi 1952, Adae 1953, Semode 1954, Funeral Dirges of the Akan People 1955, The Writing of Twi: Asante Spelling 1955, Possession Dances in African Societies 1956, Kookoo ho Mpanisem 1959, African Music in Ghana: A Survey of Traditional Forms 1962, Drumming in Akan Communities of Ghana 1963, Folk Songs of Ghana 1963, Ghana: Music, Dance and Drama: A Review of the Performing Arts of Ghana 1965, Music in African Cultures: A Review of the Meaning and Significance of Traditional African Music 1966, Adowa Songs 1966, The Place of Authentic Folk Music in Music Education 1966, Our Drums and Drummers 1968, Creating a Wider Interest in Traditional Music: The Place of Traditional Music in the Musical Life of Ghana 1969, Ethnomusicology in Ghana 1970, Kokofu Ayan: Drum Language of Kokofu (Ashanti) 1973, The Music of Africa 1974, Ayan 1975, Collating and Disseminating Oral Sources of Musical Information 1977, Amoma 1978, Selected Reports in Ethnomusicology: Studies in African Music (ed., with Jacqueline C. DjeDje) 1984. *Honours:* elected to Ghana Acad. of Arts and Sciences 1959, hon. mem. Royal Anthropological Inst. of Great Britain and Ireland 1972; African Music Soc. Cowell Award 1958, Rockefeller Foundation Fellowship 1958–59;; Ford Foundation Fellowship 1961, Grand Medal of Ghana 1968, Ghana Arts Award 1972, ASCAP Deems Taylor Award 1975, Int. Music Council-UNESCO Music Prize for Distinguished Service to Music 1981, Nat. Entertainment Critics and Reviewers Asscn of Ghana Flagstar Award 1993. *Address:* Internatinoal Centre for African Music and Dance, University of Ghana, PO Box 25, Legon, Accra, Ghana (office). *Telephone:* (233) 21-500381 (office). *Website:* www.ug.edu.gh.

**NOBLE, Jeremy;** Musicologist, Critic and Broadcaster; b. 27 March 1930, London, England. *Education:* Worcester College, Oxford, 1949–53; Private music studies. *Career:* Music Critic for The Times, 1960–63, and The Sunday Telegraph, 1972–76; Research Fellow, Barber Institute Birmingham, 1964–65; Associate Professor at State University of New York, Buffalo, 1966–70 and from 1976; Fellow, Harvard Institute for Renaissance Studies, Florence, 1967–68; Leverhulme Research Fellow, 1975–76; Many broadcasts for BBC Radio 3. *Publications:* Articles on Josquin, Debussy and Stravinsky for the Musical Times; Purcell and The Chapel Royal, in Essays on Music, 1959; Mozart: A Documentary Biography, translation of O Deutsch with E Blom and P Branscombe, 1965; Entries on Josquin and, jointly with EW White, Stravinsky for The New Grove Dictionary of Music and Musicians, 1980. *Address:* Department of Music, State University of New York, Buffalo, NY 14260, USA.

**NOBLE, John,** MA; British singer (baritone); b. 2 Jan. 1931, Southampton. *Education:* Univ. of Cambridge; privately with Clive Carey and Boriska Gereb. *Career:* Concerts and Oratorio with major orchestras throughout the United Kingdom; tours in Europe and USA; Guest Artist in opera with Covent Garden and other companies; Many broadcasts for BBC in wide range of music including several first performances; Prof. of Singing and Hon. Fellow, Trinity Coll. of Music, London; mem. and fmr Chair., Solo Performers, Inc. Soc. of Musicians. *Recordings:* Vaughan Williams, The Pilgrim's Progress, title role, conductor Boult; Britten, Albert Herring (Vicar), conductor Britten; Delius, Sea Drift, conductor Groves. *Address:* 185 Syon Lane, Isleworth, Middx, TW7 5PU, England (office). *Telephone:* (20) 8560-5988 (office). *Fax:* (20) 8560-5988 (office).

**NOBLE, Timothy;** Singer (Baritone); b. 22 Feb. 1945, Indianapolis, Indiana, USA. *Career:* Sang supporting roles in Carmen, Turandot and Wozzeck with San Francisco Opera in 1981; Houston Opera from 1982 as Ping, Leporello and Falstaff; Colorado Springs Festival in 1982 as Rigoletto and Fort Worth and Opéra-Comique Paris in 1983 as Sharpless and Germont; Season 1985–86 at Santa Fe in the premiere of John Eaton's The Tempest, as Falstaff in Amsterdam and as Simon Boccanegra at Glyndebourne returning in 1988 as Germont; San Francisco in 1987 as Tomsky in The Queen of Spades, Venice in 1988 in Verdi's Stiffelio; Sang Shaklovity in Khovanshchina at the Metropolitan in 1988 and San Francisco in 1990, returning to New York in 1991 as Leporello; Opera Pacific at Costa Mesa and the Santa Fe Festival in 1991 as Renato and as Jack Rance in La Fanciulla del West; Other roles include William Tell, Amonasro, Macbeth, Iago, Tonio, Alfio, Di Luna and Scarpia; Sang Columbus in the premiere of The Voyage by Philip Glass at New York Metropolitan in 1992; Iago at the 1996 Holland Festival and Rigoletto for Flanders Opera, 1998; Sang Rigoletto, Antwerp and Gent, 1998, and Flying Dutchman at Indianapolis Opera; Iago at Amsterdam, 1999; Sang in Henze's Venus and Adonis at Toronto, 2001; Further engagements in musicals and as concert artist; Professor of Voice, Indiana University, 1999–. *Address:* c/o Caroline Woodfield, ICM, 40W 57th Street, New York, NY 10019, USA.

**NOCENTINI, Maria Costanza;** Italian singer (soprano); b. 1970. *Education:* Bologna Conservatory. *Career:* appearances as Tebaldo in Don Carlos at Salzburg, Giulia in La Scala di Seta at Reggio Emilia, Berenice in L'Occasione fa il ladro, by Rossini, Donizetti's Adina at Naples, Lisa in La Sonnambula at Rome, Handel's Galatea at Messina, Armida in Rinaldo at Beaume, Clorinda in La Cenerentola at Genoa and Musetta in Munich, Vienna and Santiago; La Scala Milan as Pamina, Nannetta in Falstaff, Bergère in Gluck's Armide, and Mozart's Barbarina; Sophie in Werther at Naples, Modena and Parma; Handel's Semele at Spoleto and Mozart's Countess at Glyndebourne, 2000; Concerts include Haydn's Die Schöfung, in Santiago. *Honours:* Toti Dal Monte Prize; International Viotti Competition; Miguel Cervantes Prize at Francesco Viñas Competition, Barcelona. *Current Management:* Atelier Musicale Srl, via Caselle 76, 40068 San Lazzaro di Savena, Italy. *Telephone:* (051) 199844 44. *Fax:* (051) 199844 20. *E-mail:* info@ateliermusicale.it. *Website:* www.ateliermusicale.it.

**NÖCKER, Hans Gunter;** Singer (Bass-Baritone); b. 22 Jan. 1927, Hagen, Germany. *Education:* Studied in Brunswick and with Hans-Hermann Nissen and Willi Domgraf-Fassbaender in Munich. *Career:* Debut: Munster in 1952 as Alfio in Cavalleria Rusticana; Many appearances in Germany particularly at Hamburg, Munich and Stuttgart; Bayreuth Festival, 1958–60, Munich 1963 in the premiere of Egk's Die Verlobung in San Domingo and Schwetzingen 1966 in Gluck's Armide; Sang at Deutsche Oper Berlin in the 1972 premiere of Fortner's Elisabeth Tudor, La Fenice Venice in 1983 as Klingsor in Parsifal, and Berlin in 1984 in the premiere of Reimann's Gespenstersonate; Guest appearances in Florence, Brussels, Palermo, London and Edinburgh; Sang at Munich in the 1986 premiere of D Kirchner's Belshazzar; Sang in Orff's Trionfo di Afrodite at Munich Festival in 1990; Sang in the premiere of Bose's Schlachthof 5, Munich, 1996. *Recordings:* Orff's Trionfo di Afrodite; Oedipus der Tyrann; Götterdämmerung. *Address:* c/o Bayerische Staatsoper, Postfach 745, 8000 Munich 1, Germany.

**NODA, Ken;** Concert Pianist and Musical Assistant to Artistic Director, Artistic Administration, Metropolitan Opera; b. 5 Oct. 1962, New York, USA. *Education:* Private studies with Daniel Barenboim. *Career:* London debut in 1979 with the English Chamber Orchestra and Daniel Barenboim; Later engagements with the Philharmonia, Berlin Philharmonic, Orchestre de Paris, Rotterdam Philharmonic, New York Philharmonic and Chicago Symphony; Conductors include Abbado, Chailly, Andrew Davis, Kubelik,

Leinsdorf, Levine, Mehta, Ozawa and Previn; Recitals in London, Toronto, Chicago, Lincoln Center New York, Hamburg and La Fenice, Venice; Festival appearances at Mostly Mozart, New York, Ravinia and Tanglewood; 1986 debut with the Vienna Philharmonic in Salzburg; Season 1986–87 in concerts with the Berlin Philharmonic, the Hallé and the Philharmonia; 1988 concerts with the Rotterdam Philharmonic playing Mozart under James Conlon, Beethoven's Triple Concerto with Pinchas Zukerman and Lynn Harrell at Ravinia; Toured Japan with Ozawa and the New Japan Philharmonic; Resumed concert career in New York with solo recitals at Metropolitan Museum of Art, 1998, 92nd Street, New York, 1999; Lieder recitals with Jessye Norman in 1998 and Hildegard Behrens, 1999, both at Salzburg Festival. *Address:* c/o Metropolitan Opera, Lincoln Center, New York, NY 10023, USA.

**NOEL, Rita;** Singer (Mezzo Soprano); b. 21 Nov. 1943, Lancaster, South Carolina, USA. *Education:* Studied at Eastman School, at Queens College, Charlotte, South Carolina and in New York and Vienna. *Career:* Played violin and viola with the Vienna Chamber Orchestra and the Berlin Symphony; Stage debut with the Metropolitan National Opera Company, 1966, as Flora in Traviata; Further appearances at the Theater am Gärtnerplatz Munich, Bielefeld, Amsterdam and Miami; Other roles have included Mozart's Cherubino and Sextus, Cornelia in Giulio Cesare, Carmen, Rosina, Octavian, Nickausse, Azucena and Santuzza; Frequent concert engagements. *Address:* c/o Staatsheater am Gärtnerplatz, Gärtnerplatz 3, 8000 Munich, Germany.

**NOLAN, David;** Violinist; b. 1949, Liverpool, England. *Education:* Studied with Yossi Zivoni and Alexander Moskowski at the Royal Manchester College of Music; Studied in Russia, 1973–74. *Career:* Debut: Played the Mendelssohn Concerto, 1965; Joined the London Philharmonic Orchestra, 1972, Leader 1976–92; Many appearances with the London Philharmonic Orchestra and other orchestras in concertos by Bach, Beethoven, Brahms, Bruch, Glazunov, Korngold, Mozart, Paganini, Saint-Saëns, Stravinsky, Tchaikovsky and Walton; Leader, Philharmonia Orchestra, 1992–94; Leader, Bournemouth Symphony Orchestra, 1997–2001; Solo Concertmaster, Yomiuri Nippon Symphony Orchestra, Tokyo, 1999–. *Recordings:* The Lark Ascending by Vaughan Williams; The Four Seasons by Vivaldi; Mozart Rondo in C for violin and orchestra with the BBC Philharmonic. *Honours:* RMCM performances, diploma, distinction. *Address:* Flat 1, 34 Craven Street, London WC2N 5NP, England; 5-21-8-2F Nishi-Shinjuku, Shinjuku-ku, Tokyo 160-0023, Japan.

**NOLEN, Timothy;** Singer (Baritone); b. 9 July 1941, Rotan, Texas, USA. *Education:* Studied at the Manhattan School of Music and with Richard Fredericks and Walter Fredericks. *Career:* Debut: New Jersey Opera Newark as Rossini's Figaro; Sang Marcello in La Bohème with San Francisco Opera in 1968; Appearances in Chicago, Houston, Boston and Minneapolis; European debut at Rouen in 1974 as Pelléas; Sang at Amsterdam in 1974 in the premiere of The Picture of Dorian Gray by Kox, at Cologne, 1974–78 and Paris, Bordeaux, Aix and Nantes as Mozart's Count, Figaro and Guglielmo, Donizetti's Malatesta and Belcore, Monteverdi's Orpheus, and Dandini in La Cenerentola, Puccini's Gianni Schicchi, the Emperor in The Nightingale by Stravinsky and Ford in Falstaff; Sang in the premieres of Carlisle Floyd's Willie Stark and Bernstein's A Quiet Place, Houston in 1981 and 1983; Further engagements at Florence, Geneva, Miami, New York, City Opera and Philadelphia; Santa Fe Festival in 1992 as Mr Peachum in The Beggar's Opera and Frank in Die Fledermaus; Sang Malatesta at Chicago, 1995; Season 1998 as Somarone in Béatrice and Bénédict at Santa Fe and Don Pasquale at St Louis; Season 2001–02 as Rossini's Don Magnifico at Cincinnati and Trinity Moses in Mahagonny at Genoa.

**NONI, Alda;** Singer (soprano); b. 30 April 1916, Trieste, Italy. *Education:* Studied in Trieste and Vienna. *Career:* Debut: Ljubljana in 1937 as Rosina in Il Barbiere di Siviglia; Sang first in Yugoslavia then joined the Vienna Staatsoper in 1942; Sang Mozart's Despina and Verdi's Gilda and Oscar; Appeared as Zerbinetta in a 1944 performance of Ariadne auf Naxos to celebrate the 80th birthday of Richard Strauss; Sang in Milan, Rome, Venice and Turin from 1945 and at Cambridge Theatre London in 1946 as Norina in Don Pasquale opposite Marino Stabile; La Scala from 1949 in Cimarosa's Il Matrimonio Segreto and Piccinni's La Buona Figliuola; Sang Zerlina, Nannetta and Papagena with the company of La Scala during its 1950 visit to London; Glyndebourne, 1950–54 as Blondchen, Despina and Clorinda in La Cenerentola; Guest appearances in Berlin, Paris at the Opéra-Comique, Lisbon, Madrid and Rio de Janeiro. *Recordings include:* Ariadne auf Naxos; Don Pasquale; L'Elisir d'amore; Lucia di Lammermoor; Il Matrimonio Segreto; Le nozze di Figaro; La Cenerentola.

**NORBERG-SCHULZ, Elisabeth;** singer (soprano); b. Jan. 1959, Norway. *Education:* Accademia di Santa Cecilia, Rome, Pears-Britten School, Snape and studied with Elisabeth Schwarzkopf in Zürich. *Career:* gave lieder recitals and sang Britten's Les Illuminations at Snape in 1981; sang supporting roles in Italy and elsewhere at first, then sang Gilda and Lucia di Lammermoor; Has appeared under such conductors as Georg Solti, Riccardo Muti and Claudio Abbado, notably at La Scala Milan; Sang Musetta in La Bohème with La Scala on a visit to Japan in 1988 and at Rome Opera in 1989 as Barbarina in Le nozze di Figaro; Maggio Musicale Fiorentino in 1989 as Ilia in Idomeneo and sang Pamina in Die Zauberflöte at the Salzburg Landestheater in 1991 as part of the Mozart bicentenary celebrations; Season 1992 as Norina at Naples, Guardian of the Threshold in Die Frau ohne Schatten and Servilia in La Clemenza di Tito at Salzburg; Covent Garden debut 1995, as Liu in Turandot;

Sang Cimarosa's Carolina at Rome, 1996; Season 1997–98 as Liu in Turandot at Bologna and in Rota's Italian Straw Hat at La Scala; Adalgisa in Norma at Rome, 1999; Season 2001 on tour to London and in Europe with Handel's Tamerlano. *Current Management:* Owen/White Management, 59 Lansdowne Place, Hove, East Sussex BN3 1FL, England. *Telephone:* (1273) 727127. *Fax:* (1273) 328128. *E-mail:* info@owenwhitemanagement.com. *Website:* www .owenwhitemanagement.com.

**NORBY, Erik;** Composer; b. 9 Jan. 1936, Copenhagen, Denmark. *Education:* Copenhagen Boys' Choir and Tivoli Band; Copenhagen Conservatory; Diploma in Composition, 1966. *Career:* Teacher, North Jutland Conservatory until 1975 then freelance composer. *Compositions include:* Orchestra: Folk Song Suite, 1962, Music for 6 sextets, 1966, The Rainbow Snake, 1975, Illuminations, Capriccio, 1978, 3 Dances, 1983; Chamber: Illustrations, 1965, Schubert Variations, 1974, Partita, 1981, Tivoli Collage, 1983, Ravel: Le Tombeau De Couperin, 1984; Solo Instrument: 12 Danish Folk Songs for piano, 1961, Chromaticon, partita in 8 movements, 1971, Five Organ Chorales, 1976–78; Choral: March, 1972, Winter Twilight, 1973, Nightingale, 1973, Song Near The Depth Of Spring, 1973, Festival Cantata, on the occasion of the 150th anniversary of Copenhagen Cathedral, 1979, Edvard Munch Triptych, 1978–79; Solo Voice: Two Songs, 1963, Six Shakespeare Sonnets, 1981, 13 Elizabethan Love Songs, The Ballad About My Life, 1984; Music for educational use: Three Suites, 1961, Three Small Suites, 1962, Little Sonatina, Three Humoresques, Evening Song, Suite No. 2, 1963. *Recordings:* Numerous recordings of his work. *Current Management:* Koda, Maltegårdsvej 24, 2820 Gentofte, Denmark. *Address:* Kochsvej 13, 3tv, 1812 Frederiksberg C, Denmark.

**NORDAL, Jon;** Composer and President, Reykjavík College of Music; b. 1926, Iceland. *Education:* Studied with Arni Kristjansson, Jon Thorarinsson and Dr V Urbancic at Reykjavík College of Music, Iceland; Studies with W Frey and W Burkhard at Zürich, Switzerland, 1949–51 and in Paris and Rome; Darmstadt summer courses, 1956–57. *Career:* President, Reykjavík College of Music. *Compositions:* Orchestral: Concerto Lirico for harp and strings, Concerto for orchestra, 1949, Concerto for piano and orchestra, 1956, Sinfonietta Seriosa, 1956, A Play Of Fragments, 1962, Adagio for flute, harp, piano and strings, 1965, Stiklur, 1970, Canto Elegiaco, 1971, Leidsla, 1973, Epitaphio, 1974, The Winter Night, 1975, Twin Song for violin, viola and orchestra, 1979, Dedication, 1981, Choralis, 1982, Concerto for cello and orchestra, 1983; Chamber: Sonata for violin and piano, Fairy Tale Sisters for violin and piano, Chorale Prelude for organ, 1980, Duo for violin and cello, 1983; Requiem, 1995; From Dream to Dream, string quartet, 1997; Dreaming on a Dormant String, for violin, cello and piano, 1998; My Faith is but a Flicker, for chorus, 1999; Choir Music: Seven Songs for male chorus, 1955. *Address:* STEF, Laufasveji 40, Reykjavík, Iceland.

**NORDEN, Betsy;** Singer (Soprano); b. 17 Oct. 1945, Cincinnati, Ohio, USA. *Education:* Studied at Boston University. *Career:* Member of Metropolitan Opera Chorus from 1969; Solo appearances at the Metropolitan from 1972 in Le nozze di Figaro and as Papagena, Elvira in L'Italiana in Algeri, Constance in the Carmélites, Oscar and Despina in Così fan tutte, 1990; Sang in The Cunning Little Vixen at Philadelphia season, 1980–81, Constance at San Francisco in 1983 and Gretel at San Diego, 1985; Many concert appearances. *Address:* c/o Metropolitan Opera, Lincoln Center, New York, NY 10023, USA.

**NORDGREN, Pehr (Henrik);** Composer; b. 19 Jan. 1944, Saltvik, Finland. *Education:* Studied composition under Professor Joonas Kokkonen, musicology at Helsinki University and composition and traditional Japanese music at Tokyo University of Arts and Music, 1970–73. *Career:* Assistant at Helsinki University. *Compositions include:* Euphonie 1 Op 1, 1967; 7 String Quartets, 1967–92; Ten Ballades To Japanese Ghost Stories By Lafcadio Hearn, 1972–77; As In A Dream, Op 21, 1974; Symphony Op 20, 1974; Autumnal Concerto for traditional japanese instruments and orchestra, 1974; Wind Quintet No. 2, Op 22, 1975; Butterflies, 1977; Summer Music Op 34, 1977; Symphony for strings Op 43, 1978; In Patches, 1978; Piano Quintet Op 44, 1978; In The Palm Of The King's Head for soprano, baritone, chams and orchestra, 1979; Three Cello Concertos, 1980–92; The Lights Of Heaven for soprano, tenor, chorus and ensemble, 1985; Symphony No. 2, 1989; Cronaca for strings, 1991; Concerto for viola, double bass and chamber orchestra, 1994; Violin Concerto, 1994. *Recordings:* Hoichi Earless Op 17; Ballades. *Address:* TEOSTO, Lauttasaarentie 1, 0020 Helsinki 20, Finland.

**NORDHEIM, Arne;** Norwegian composer; b. 20 June 1931, Larvik; m. 1st 1956; m. 2nd 1981; two c. *Education:* Oslo Conservatory of Music and electronic music studies in Paris, Utrecht, Warsaw and Stockholm. *Career:* began to compose 1950; first maj. work Stringquartett 1956; since composed several works for orchestra and solo instruments and symphonic music, voice or electronic sound and one ballet score; worked as music critic for several daily newspapers 1959–67; critic Dagbladet, Oslo 1960–68; fmr Prof. of Electronic Music; mem. Royal Swedish Acad. of Music; Hon. mem. Int. Soc. for Contemporary Music 1996–. *Music:* approx. 180 works including Epitaffio, Canzona, Floating, Wirklicher Wald, The Tempest (ballet) and solo concertos for cello, oboe and accordion. *Honours:* Nordic Council Music Prize 1972, Prix Italia 1980, awarded Norwegian State Residence of Honour 1982, Steffens Prize 1993; Commdr Order of St Olav 1997, Commdr Order al Merito (Italy) 1998, Commdr Orderu Zasługi Rzeczy pos Politej Polskie (Poland) 1999. *Address:* Wergelandsveien 2, 0167 Oslo, Norway. *Telephone:* 22-11-28-27. *Fax:* 22-11-38-47.

**NORDIN, Birgit;** Singer (Soprano); b. 22 Feb. 1934, Sangis, Norrbotten, Sweden. *Education:* Studied at the Stockholm Opera School and with Lina Pagliughi in Italy. *Career:* Debut: Stockholm in 1957 as Oscar in Un Ballo in Maschera; Annual visits to the Drottningholm Opera from 1960 notably in operas by Mozart; Sang at Wexford Festival in 1963 and 1965, and Glyndebourne Festival in 1968 as Blondchen in Die Entführung; Sang Jenny in Weill's Mahagonny at Copenhagen in 1970, Berlin in 1970 as soloist in Bach's St Matthew Passion and Christmas Oratorio; Television appearance as Berg's Lulu and sang the Queen of Night in Bergman's film version of The Magic Flute in 1974; Oratorio engagements in Scandinavia, Germany, England and Austria; Has sung with the Royal Opera Stockholm on tour to Covent Garden in 1990 and the Edinburgh Festival; Other roles include Mozart's Susanna and Pamina, Gilda, Rosina, Sophie in Der Rosenkavalier and Mélisande; Sang Angelica in Handel's Orlando at Stockholm, 2000. *Recordings:* Die Zauberflöte; Madrigals by Monteverdi; Video of Don Giovanni, as Donna Elvira. *Honours:* Swedish Court Singer, 1973. *Address:* c/o Kungliga Teatern, PO Box 16094, 10322 Stockholm, Sweden.

**NORDIN, Lena;** Singer (Soprano); b. 18 Feb. 1956, Visby, Sweden. *Education:* Studied voice and piano at the College of Music in Malmö and Stockholm, and in Salzburg, Florence and Siena. *Career:* Debut: Verdi's Luisa Miller; Member of soloist ensemble of the Royal Opera in Stockholm, 1987; Has performed numerous roles including: Cleopatra, Donna Anna, Antonia, Lauretta, Marguerite, Constanze, Violetta, Maria Stuarda, Contessa, Nedda, Norma and Sophie; Has also sung at the Drottningholm Court Theatre (Dido, and Regina in Soler's Cosa Rara); Sang Strauss's Daphne in Salzburg and Marguerite at Savonlinna Festival; Has guested Wexford Opera Festival twice, including as Aspasia in Mozart's Mitridate, 1989; Other roles include Adele, Countessa di Folleville in Rossini's Il viaggio a Reims and Donna Elvira; Has sung as a regular guest in Copenhagen, and also in Dresden, London, Moscow and Seville; Has sung Violetta at the National Opera of Helsinki and Elena in Vespri Siciliani in Darmstadt; Odabella in Verdi's Attila and Die Prinzessin in Schreker's opera Das Spielwerk in Darmstadt, 2003; Concert engagements include performances in USA, France, Germany and in Scandinavia. *Recordings:* Title roles in Berwald's Estrella di Soria, Hallman's Solitär and in Naumann's Gustav Wasa; Carmina Burana; Arias by Mozart, Verdi and Gounod; Mary Stuart, Queen of Scots; CD of Mozart Concert Arias, 1996. *Honours:* Christina Nilsson Prize, 1959; Birgit Nilsson Prize, 1987; Svenska Dagblacket, Prize, 1987; Jussi Björling Prize, 1997; Royal Court Singer, King Carl Gustaf; Litteris et Artibus, King Carl Gustaf, 2003. *Current Management:* Eberhard Gross, Künsteragentur, Germany. *Address:* Östermalmsg 3, 11424 Stockholm, Sweden. *Website:* lenanordinsoprano.homestead .com.

**NORDMO-LOVBERG, Aase;** Singer (Soprano) and Administrator; b. 10 June 1923, Malselv, Norway. *Education:* Studied with Hjaldis Ingebjart in Oslo. *Career:* Debut: Concert debut in 1948, and operatic debut in 1952 as Imogen in Cymbeline by Arne Eggens; Member of the Royal Opera Stockholm, 1953–69 with debut as Elisabeth in Tannhäuser; Vienna Staatsoper in 1957 as Sieglinde in Die Walküre; Concert appearances in London, Philadelphia and Paris, 1957; Metropolitan Opera, 1959–61 as Elsa in Lohengrin, Eva, Sieglinde and Leonore; Bayreuth Festival, 1960 as Elsa and Sieglinde; Sang at the Stora Theatre Gothenburg in 1963 and 1967 as Elisabeth and Tosca; Engagements at the Drottningholm Court Theatre included Angelica in Handel's Orlando; Professor at the Oslo Music School from 1970 and Director of The Oslo Opera, 1978–81. *Recordings include:* Excerpts from the 1960 Bayreuth Festival. *Honours:* Gold Medal for Singing, Harriet Cohen International Music Award, 1958; Orde Van Oranje-Nassau, 1963; Officer of L'Ordre de Leopold II, 1964; Commander, St Olavs Orden, 1981; Commander, Kungl Nordstjerne Orden, 1986.

**NORDSTRÖM, Hans-Henrik;** Danish composer; b. 26 June 1947, Nakskov; m. Anne Kristine Smith, 1 s. *Education:* Royal Danish Academy of Music, Copenhagen, 1965–70. *Career:* Debut: Copenhagen, 1990; mem, Danish Composers Society. *Compositions:* Kybikos (wind band), 1989–90; That Autumn, (orchestra) 1990–91; The Mountains in Monestiés (sinfonietta), 1988; Triptychos (3 double basses and sinfonietta), 1989–90; Dialogue (tuba and percusion), 1991; Srebrenica (organ), 1993; Tympanon (3 percussion), 1993; Reflections I, (sextet), 1992; Reflections II (violin and harp), 1992; Reflections III (flugelhorn and piano), 1993; Night (choir), 1992; Clockwork and Raindrops (sextet), 1991; Room/Space, String Quartet I, 1991–92, Seven Vignettes from Susaa (sinfonietta), 1994; Andalusian Reflections (piano trio), 1995, Sonata per l'Inverno (piano), 1994–95; String Quartet II (Faroese), 1994; M 31 (clarinet trio), 1995–96; Songlines (sinfonietta), 1995; Carnac (sextet), 1995; Images d'automne (flute, clarinet, bassoon), 1996; Icelandic Suite (reed quartet), 1996; Fara fram vid (clarinet), 1996; To Winter (saxophone quartet), 1996–97; Sketches from Hirsholmene (sinfonietta), 1997; La Primavera (flute, oboe, bassoon, harpsichord), 1997; La rosa, la noche y el tiempo, 1997; String Quartet III (Norwegian), 1998; Il Quadrato magico (reed quartet), 1998–99; Abstractions (saxophone, percussion), 1998; Entwicklungen (2 accordions), 1998; Flows, 1998 (3 flutes); Fantasy, (bass flute) 1998; Tres Poemas de Federico García Lorca (mezzo, clarinet, cello, harp and percussion), 1998; Birds of Susaa Are Dreaming New Songs (saxophone quartet), 1999; A Dream (flute and harpsichord), 1998–99; Gravures en taille-douce (harpsichord), 1998–99; String Quartet No. 4 (Hebredian), 1999; Asterion (violin), 1999; Mykines (sinfonietta), 2000; Limbo (violin, cello and piano), 2000; Mouvements (piano trio), 2000; Land of Shadows (bass clarinet and percussion),

2000; Light (flute and guitar), 2000; Fluctuations (4 guitars), 2000; Night Glow and Dawn Frosting (soprano and guitar), 2000; Chac (organ), 2001; Lost Traces (saxophone and percussion), 2001; The Twelve Bens (string trio), 2001; In the Woods (violin and sinfonietta), 2001; Nada y todo (recorder quartet), 2001; Imaginations (harpsichord) 2002; "..if a Tone in the Night" (recorder and accordian) 2002; Growth (brass quintet) 2002; Fair Isle (cello, 12 woodwinds and 4 french horns) 2002; Riverrun (Sinfonietta) 2002; Quarks (String Trio) 2002; Tingsomingenting (guitar) 2003; A.L.P. (fl, cl, gt, perc and vl) 2003; Following the Wake (piano trio) 2003; Sketches from Iceland (pno quartet) 2003; Morning Knight (Mezzo, rec., sax and perc) 2003; A.L.P. Too (viola and guitar) 2003; Nuages d'automne (trombone and sinfonietta) 2003–4; Nuvele Italiane (piano) 2004; Nuages Elégique (trombone) 2004, Triskele (wind quintet) 2004, Roest (alto, bassoon and piano) 2004, Ante Discum Solis (saxophone and harp) 2004, Infinite Water (clarinet and tape) 2004, Dieciséis Fragmentos (mezzo, guitar and percussion) 2004, Sjúrdur (soprano and saxophone) 2004, Anna Livia (mezzo and guitar) 2004. *Recordings:* Many CDs including Hans-Henrik Nordström 1 (Portrait CD), 1997; Hans-Henrik Nordström 2 (Portrait CD), 1999; Hans Henrik Nordström 3 (Portrait CD), 2001; Hans-Henrik Nordstrøm 4, "In the Woods" (Portrait CD) 2003, Hans-Henrik Nordström 5, "North West" (Portrait CD) 2005. *Honours:* Grant, Danish Art Foundation, 1990–; Artistic Director, Contemporary Music in Susaa Festivals, held in August every year since 1993–; Danish Composers' Society's Grant 2001; Wilhelm Hansen Foundation's Grant 2003, 2004; Composer of the Year 2003 in Bornholm Music Festival; Composer of the Year in Birkeroed, 2004. *Address:* Skovmarksvej 52, Vetterslev, 4100 Ringsted, Denmark. *E-mail:* hans-henrik@nordstroem.dk (office). *Website:* www .nordstroem.dk.

**NOREJKA, Virgilius;** Singer (Tenor) and Administrator; b. 22 Sept. 1935, Siaulai, Lithuania. *Education:* Studied in Vilnius. *Career:* Debut: State Opera of Vilnius, 1957 as Lensky in Eugene Onegin; Sang in Lithuania as Alfredo, the Duke in Rigoletto, Werther, Don José, Almaviva and The Prince in The Love For Three Oranges; Guest appearances in Moscow, Leningrad, Kiev and Kharkov; Gave recitals and sang Russian folksongs, in addition to operatic repertoire; Further engagements at the Berlin Staatsoper and in Poland, Bulgaria, Denmark, Finland, Italy, Austria, Hungary, USA and Canada; Sang Radames at Hamburg Staatsoper and also appeared in operas by Lithuanian composers; Director of the Vilnius Opera, 1975–. *Recordings:* Various. *Address:* Av Rómulo Gallegos, Edf Residencias, Santa Rosa, Apt 4-B, Sebucan, Caracas 1071, Venezuela.

**NORGÅRD, Per;** Composer; b. 13 July 1932, Gentofte, Denmark. *Education:* Degrees in Music History, Music Theory and Composition, Royal Danish Academy of Music, 1952–55; Studied with Nadia Boulanger, Paris, France, 1956–57. *Career:* Teaching positions at Odense Conservatoire, 1958–61, Royal Academy of Music, 1960–69, Royal Academy of Music, Århus, 1965; Terrains Vagues premiered by the BBC Symphony Orchestra, 2001. *Compositions include:* Operas: Gilgamesh, 1971–72, Siddharta, 1974–79, The Divine Circus, 1982; Nuit des Hommes, 1995; Orchestral: Symphony No. 1, 1953–55, Voyage Into The Golden Screen, 1968–69, Twilight, 1976–77, Symphony No. 3 in 2 Movements, 1972–75, No. 4, 1981, No. 5, 1990, Spaces Of Time, 1991; Symphony No. 6, 1999; String and Wind orchestras: Metamorphosis, 1953, Modlys, 1970; Chamber: 8 String Quartets, 1952–97; Fragment V, 1961, Prelude And Ant Fugue (With A Crab Cannon), 1982, Lin for clarinet, cello and piano, 1986; Solo keyboard: Sonata in One Movement, 1953, Canon, 1971; Choral: Evening Land, 1954, Frost Psalm, 1975–76, Interrupted Hymn, Scream, Drinking Song; Piano Concerto, 1995; Terrains Vagues for orchestra, 2001; Solo instruments and orchestra: Between, 3 movements for cello and orchestra, 1985, Helle Nacht, violin concerto, 1987, King, Queen and Ace for harp and 13 instruments, 1989; Percussion: Iching, solo, 1982; 9 Symphonies, 1958–90; Violin Concerto No. 2, 1993; Viola Concerto, 1995; Organ Concerto No. 2, 1996; Elf's Mirror for solo voices, chorus and orchestra, 1996; 9 string quartets, 1955–94. *Recordings:* Much of his work recorded and available on CD. *Honours:* Numerous honours including Nordic Council Prize for Music for opera Gilgamesh, 1974; Sonning Music Prize; Holds several Honorary posts. *Address:* Koda, Maltegårdsvej 24, 2820 Gentofte, Denmark.

**NORHOLM, Ib;** Composer; b. 24 Jan. 1931, Copenhagen, Denmark. *Education:* The Royal Danish Academy of Music, Copenhagen. *Career:* Music Critic with several major Copenhagen Newspapers; Professor of Composition, The Royal Danish Academy of Music; Organist in Copenhagen. *Compositions include:* Stanzas And Fields; Strofer Og Marker; Trio Op 22; Fluctuations, The Unseen Pan; Exile, Music For A Composition for Large Orchestra; From My Green Herbarium; September-October-November; After Icarus; Tavole Per Orfeo; Invitation To A Beheading, 1965; Isola Bella, 1968–70; Den Unge Park, 1969–70; Day's Nightmare, 1973; Violin Concerto, 1974; Heretic Hymn, 1975; The Garden Wall, 1976; The Funen Cataracts, 1976; Essai Prismatique, 1979; Lys, 1979; Decreation, 1979; The Elements; Moralities–Or There May Be Several Miles To The Nearest Spider; Ecliptic Instincts; Apocalyptic Idylls, 1980; Before Silence, 1980; Haven Med Steir Der Deler Sig, 1982. *Recordings:* Much of his work recorded. *Current Management:* Koda, Maltegårdsvej 24, 2820 Gentofte, Denmark. *Address:* Henningsens Allé 30B, 2900 Hellerup, Denmark.

**NORMAN, Daniel,** BA, MEng (Oxon.), DipRAM; British singer (tenor); b. 1970; m. Sarah Norman (née Moore); one s. *Education:* Lichfield Cathedral School, Shrewbury School, New Coll, Oxford, Banff Centre for the Arts, Canada, Tanglewood Music Center, USA, Royal Acad. of Music. *Career:* concerts and song recitals in all the major venues in UK and Europe; prin. roles with Paris Opera, Bavarian State opera, New Israeli Opera, Opera Zuid, Nationale Reis Opera (Netherlands), New Kent Opera, Tete a Tete, Early Opera Company, Opera Boston, Almeida Opera. *Recordings include:* Billy Budd (Richard Hickox), Hyperion Schubert Edition (Graham Johnson), Hugh Wood's Comus (Sir Andrew Davies), Brett Dean's Winter Songs (Berlin Phil. Wind Quintet), A Child of Our Time (CBSO), Britten War Requiem (Warsaw), Arabella (Garsington), Turn of the Screw (Glyndebourne), Midsummer Night's Dream (Madrid). *Current Management:* Askonas Holt Ltd, Lonsdale Chambers, 27 Chancery Lane, London, WC2A 1PF, England. *Telephone:* (20) 7400-1700. *Fax:* (20) 7400-1799. *E-mail:* info@askonasholt.co.uk. *Website:* www .askonasholt.co.uk.

**NORMAN, Jessye,** MMus; American singer (soprano); b. 15 Sept. 1945, Augusta, Ga; d. of Silas Norman and Janie Norman (née King). *Education:* Howard Univ., Washington, DC, Peabody Conservatory, Univ. of Michigan. *Career:* Vocal Winner, Int. Musikwettbewerb, Bayerischer Rundfunk, Munich, Fed. Repub. of Germany 1968; operatic début Deutsche Oper Berlin 1969; début La Scala, Milan 1972, Royal Opera House, Covent Garden 1972; American operatic début, Hollywood Bowl 1972; performer Lincoln Centre 1973–; tours in N and S America, Europe, Middle East, Australia; int. festivals including Aix-en-Provence, Aldeburgh, Berliner Festwochen, Edin., Flanders, Helsinki, Lucerne, Salzburg, Tanglewood, Spoleto, Hollywood Bowl, Ravinia; with leading orchestras from USA, UK, Israel, Australia; recent performances include La Voix Humaine, Orchestre nat. de Lyon 2002. *Honours:* Hon. MusDoc (Howard) 1982, (Univ. of the South, Sewance) 1984, (Univ. of Mich.) 1987, (Edin.) 1989; Hon. DMus (Cambridge) 1989; Grand Prix du Disque (Acad. du Disque Français) 1973, 1976, 1977, 1982; Deutsche Schallplatten Preis für Euryanthe 1975; Cigale d'Or (Aix-en-Provence Festival) 1977; Grammy Award 1980, 1982, 1985, Musician of the Year (Musical America) 1982, IRCAM Record Award 1982, Alumna Award (Univ. of Michigan) 1982; Commdr, Ordre des Arts et des Lettres 1984. *Address:* L'Orchidee, PO Box South, Crugers, NY 10521; Philips Records Polygram, 825 8th Avenue, New York, NY 10019, USA.

**NORRINGTON, Sir Roger Arthur Carver,** Kt, OBE; British conductor; b. 16 March 1934, s. of Sir Arthur Norrington and Edith Joyce Carver; m. 1st Susan Elizabeth McLean May 1964 (divorced 1982); one s. one d.; m. 2nd Karalyn Mary Lawrence 1986; one s. *Education:* Dragon School, Oxford, Westminster School, Clare Coll. Cambridge, Royal Coll. of Music. *Career:* freelance singer 1962–72; Prin. Conductor, Kent Opera 1966–84; Guest Conductor with many British and European orchestras, appearances BBC Promenade Concerts and City of London, Bath, Aldeburgh, Edin. and Harrogate festivals; regular broadcasts UK, Europe, USA; Prin. Conductor Bournemouth Sinfonietta 1985–89; Assoc. Chief Guest Conductor London Philharmonic Orchestra 1993–; Chief Conductor South German Radio Orchestra 1997–, Camerata Academica Salzburg 1997–; conductor Radio Sinfonie Orchester, Stuttgart 1998–; Musical Dir London Classical Players 1978–97, London Baroque Players 1975–, Schütz Choir of London 1962, Orchestra of St Lukes, NY 1990–94; Co.-Dir Early Opera Project 1984–, Historic Arts 1986–; many gramophone recordings. *Honours:* Hon. DMus (Kent) 1994; Cavaliere, Ordine al Merito della Repubblica Italiana, Ehrenkreuz Erster Klasse (Austia) 1999.

**NORRIS, David Owen,** MA, FRCO, FRAM; British pianist and broadcaster; *Professor, Royal College of Music;* b. 16 June 1953, Northampton; s. of Albert Norris and Margaret Norris; two s. *Education:* Keble Coll. Oxford, Royal Acad. of Music, and privately in Paris. *Career:* Prof., RAM 1977–89; Dir Petworth Festival 1986–92; Artistic Dir Cardiff Festival 1992–95; Chair. Steans Inst. for Singers, Chicago 1992–98; Gresham Prof. of Music, Cardiff School of Music 1993–97; Prof., Royal Coll. of Music 2000–; Prof. of Music, Univ. of Southampton 2000–; Fellow, Worshipful Co. of Musicians 2005. *Recordings:* Complete piano music of Elgar, Dyson, Quilter and the World's First Piano Concertos. *Achievements:* gave world premières of Schubert's First Song Cycle and Elgar's Piano Concerto (also on CD). *Honours:* First Gilmore Artist Award 1991. *Address:* 17 Manor Road, Andover, Hants., SP10 3JS, England. *Telephone:* (1264) 355409. *E-mail:* don@soton.ac.uk (office). *Website:* davidowennorris.co.uk.

**NORRIS, Geoffrey;** Critic and Musicologist; b. 19 Sept. 1947, London, England. *Education:* ARCM, 1967; BA, University of Durham, 1969; University of Liverpool, 1969–70, 1972–73; Institute of Theatre, Music and Cinematography, Leningrad, 1971. *Career:* Music Critic for The Times, Daily Telegraph; Lecturer in Music History, Royal Northern College of Music, 1975–77; Commissioning Editor, New Oxford Companion to Music, 1977–83; Music Critic, The Daily Telegraph, 1983; Chief Music Critic, 1995–, Daily Telegraph; mem Royal Musical Association; The Critics' Circle. *Publications include:* Encyclopedia of Opera, co-author, 1976; Rachmaninov, 1976, 2nd edition, 1993; Shostakovich: The Man and His Music, co-author, 1982; A Catalogue of the Compositions of S Rachmaninov, co-author, 1982. *Contributions:* New Grove Dictionary of Music and Musicians, 1980, 2001; Musical Times; Music Quarterly; Tempo; Music and Letters; BBC Broadcasts. *Address:* The Daily Telegraph 1 Canada Square, Canary Wharf, London E14 5DT, England.

**NORTH, Nigel;** British lutenist, classical guitarist and professor of lute; b. 5 June 1954, London, England. *Education:* Guildhall School of Music, Royal College of Music, studied with John Williams, Carlos Bonell, Francis Baines,

Michael Schaffer in Germany. *Career:* performances from 1973 with the Early Music Consort of London, Academy of Ancient Music, Schütz Choir of London and Early Opera Project with Roger Norrington, Kent Opera, English Concert with Pinnock, Taverner Players, London Baroque, Trio Sonnerie, Raglan Baroque Players, and The Sixteen Choir and Orchestra; Professor of Lute at the Guildhall School from 1976; Solo debut at Wigmore Hall in 1977 with Bach recital on lute and played at Bach 300th anniversary concerts in London, 1985 with Maggie Cole; Solo recitals and tours from 1977 world-wide; Accompanist to such singers as Alfred Deller and Emma Kirkby; Summer Academies include The Lute Society of America, 1980–88 and Trio Sonnerie Summer School, 1989; Masterclasses, lectures and workshops in Sardinia, Rome, Venice, Vancouver, New York and San Francisco. *Recordings:* As soloist, music by Robert de Visée, Dowland, Bach and Vivaldi; Albums of Monteverdi, Handel, Purcell, Corelli and Vivaldi with London Baroque, Taverner Players, The English Concert, Academy of Ancient Music, Raglan Baroque Players, Trio Sonnerie and The Sixteen Choir and Orchestra (Monteverdi Vespers, 1988); Music by Bach, 1990s. *Publications:* Lute Music By William Byrd, 1976; Lute Music by Alfonso Ferrabosco, 1979; Continuo Playing on Lute, Archlute and Theorbo, 1987.

**NORTH, Roger (Dudley)**, LRAM; British composer, writer and tutor; b. 1 Aug. 1926, Warblington, Hampshire; m. Rosamund Shreeves 1965; two d. *Education:* Oxford Univ.; Royal Acad. of Music. *Career:* Various small choir and orchestra conductorship posts, 1950–56; Evening Institute teaching, 1951–; Morley Coll. 1963–91; approx. 100 broadcast talks for BBC, 1960–70; mem. British Acad. of Composers and Songwriters. *Compositions:* Sonata for clarinet and piano, published around 1956; Salle d'Attente Suite, 1977; Film Music: Music for Dance and Theatre; 1 Act Opera (performed but not published). *Recordings:* Salle d'Attente, ballet suite, 1977. *Publications:* The Musical Companion, Book I, 1977; ABC of Music (Musical Companion), 1979; Wagner's Most Subtle Art, 1996. *Contributions:* Thematic Unity in Parsifal to Wagner Society Magazine; The Rhinegold–The Music to English National Opera Guide, 1985. *Honours:* William Wallace Exhibition, Royal Acad. of Music, 1949; Battison Haynes Prize for Composition, Royal Acad. of Music, 1949; Oliviera Prescott Gift for Composition, Royal Acad. of Music, 1950. *Address:* 24 Strand on the Green, London W4 3PH, England. *Telephone:* (20) 8995-9174 (office). *E-mail:* roger.north@btinternet.com (office). *Website:* www .roger.north.btinternet.co.uk (office).

**NORTHCOTT, Bayan (Peter)**; Music Critic and Composer; b. 24 April 1940, Harrow-on-the-Hill, Middlesex, England. *Education:* BA, Dip ED, University College, Oxford; BMus, University of Southampton. *Career:* Music Critic for the New Statesman, 1973–76, Sunday Telegraph, 1976–86 and The Independent, 1986–; mem, Music Section, Critics Circle, 1974–92. *Compositions include:* Hymn to Cybele, 1983; Sextet, 1985; Concerto for horn and ensemble, 1996; Instrumental music and songs. *Contributions:* New Grove Dictionary of Music and Musicians, 1980; Music and Musicians; The Listener; Musical Times; Daily Telegraph; Guardian; Tempo; Dansk Musiktidsskrift; BBC Music Magazine, including articles on Goehr, Tippett, Maw, Davies, Carter, Jonathon Harvey and Poulenc. *Address:* 52 Upper Mall, London, W6, England.

**NORUP, Bent**; Danish singer (baritone); b. 7 Dec. 1936, Hobro. *Education:* studied with Kristian Rils in Copenhagen, with Karl Schmitt-Walter in Munich and with Herta Sperber in New York. *Career:* debut: Copenhagen in 1970 as Kurwenal in Tristan und Isolde; sang at Royal Theatre of Copenhagen, 1970–73, Brunswick, 1973–78, Nuremburg, 1978–, Hannover, 1981–, Bayreuth Festival, 1983, San Antonio Festival, 1985 and guest appearances in leading roles world-wide including Vienna, London, Paris, Hamberg, Berlin, Düsseldorf, Hannover, France, Spain, Netherlands, Poland, Ireland and USA; roles include Holländer, Telramund, Amfortas, Klingsor, Wotan, Sachs, Pizarro, Jochanaan, Iago, Scarpia, and Borromeo; Sang Telramund in Lohengrin at Venice in 1990, and Klingsor at Århus in 1992; Sang Telramund in Logengrin at Naples, 1995; Ludwigsburg Festival 2000, as Abner in Nielsen's Saul and David (concert); well known as concert singer. *Recordings include:* Orestes in Elektra.

**NOSEDA, Gianandrea**; Conductor; b. 1965, Milan, Italy. *Education:* Milan Conservatoire, and with Myung-Wha Chung in Siena. *Career:* Principal Conductor of the Orchestra Sinfonica di Milano, from 1994; Principal Guest Conductor at the Mariinsky Theatre, St Petersburg, 1997; Principal Conductor of the Orquesta de Cadaques and Principal Guest of the Rotterdam Philharmonic, 1999; Repertoire includes La Sonnambula, Der fliegende Holländer, Le nozze di Figaro, Don Carlos and Sleeping Beauty; Conducted the Kirov Ballet at Covent Garden, 2000; Complete Prokofiev Piano Concertos with the Orchestra Sinfonica di Milano; Guest at the Cheltenham Festival, 2000, with the BBC Symphony, at the Teatro Real, Madrid, and the Salle Pleyel, Paris; Principal Conductor, BBC Philharmonic Orchestra, July 2002–; Conducted the BBC Philharmonic at the London Proms, 2002. *Address:* c/o Kirov Opera, Mariinsky Theatre, 1 Theatre Square, St Petersburg, Russia.

**NOSEK, Václav**; Conductor; b. 5 April 1921, Stary Plzenec, Czechoslovakia; m. 15 July 1950, 1 d. *Education:* Composition and Conducting, Conservatory; International course with Clemens Krauss, Salzburg. *Career:* debut, Plzeň Theatre; Conductor, Playwright, theatre and opera, Plzeň, Ústí n/L, Brno, Prague National Theatre Ceske Budejovice (South Bohemia); Appeared on radio in operas and concerts, especially 20th music by A. Berg, Schonberg, Prokofiev, Shostakovich, Honegger, Britten, Dessau and other composers;

Many premieres of contemporary operas, including Martinů's Les Larmes du Couteau and Les Trois Souhaits, also ballet Le Raid de Veilleux; mem, Societas Janáček. *Recordings:* B. Martinů: Les Trois Souhaits, The Marriage, The Ballets. *Contributions:* Many articles on B. Martinů and L. Janáček to specialist music reviews. *Honours:* Honorary Member, Societas Martinů. *Address:* c/o Prague National Theatre, PO Box 865, 11230 Prague, Czech Republic.

**NOSSEK, Carola**; Singer (Soprano); b. 10 Feb. 1949, Schwerin, Germany. *Education:* Studied in Dresden and Schwerin. *Career:* Debut: Dresden Staatsoper, 1972, as Nanette in Lortzing's Der Wildschütz; Berlin Staatsoper from 1975, as Marenka in The Bartered Bride, Mozart's Servilia and Despino, Marzelline in Fidelio and Echo in Ariadne; Orff's Die Kluge, 1990, Susanna, 1991, and Nuri in Tiefland, 1995; Guest at Las Palmas Festival and elsewhere; Concert repertory includes songs by Hanns Eisler and Schubert's Lazarus. *Address:* c/o Berlin Staatsoper, Unter den Linden 7, 1060 Berlin, Germany.

**NOTARE, Karen**; American singer (soprano); b. 1961. *Education:* Manhattan School of Music, New York. *Career:* debut in Madama Butterfly for New York City Opera, 1987; European debut as Leoncavallo's Zaza, at the 1990 Wexford Festival; Tosca with Greater Miami Opera and the Royal Danish Opera, Mimi at Nice, Desdemona in Hong Kong and Mariella in Mascagni's Piccola Marat at the 1992 Wexford Festival; Bonn Opera from 1994, as Manon Lescaut, Donna Elvira, and Lisa in The Queen of Spades; Concerts with the Pittsburgh and Cincinnati Symphonies, Verdi Requiem with the Eastern Connecticut Symphony Orchestra; Season 1996 with the Trovatore Leonora for Fort Worth Opera, and Tosca with Opera Zuid, Netherlands; Season 1999 as Salome in Dublin and as Santuzza in Auckland. *Current Management:* Pinnacle Arts Management, 889 Ninth Avenue, Second Floor, New York, NY 10019, USA. *Telephone:* 212-397-7915. *Fax:* 212-397-7920. *Website:* www .pinnaclearts.com.

**NOTT, Jonathan**; British conductor; *Music Director, Bamberger Symphoniker*; b. 1962, Solihull, England. *Education:* choral scholar St John's Coll., Cambridge, Royal Northern Coll. of Music, Nat. Opera Studio. *Career:* Repetiteur then Conductor, Frankfurt Opera 1988–; First Kapellmeister, Wiesbaden Opera and Symphony Orchestra 1991–96, covering all main opera repertoire, including complete Ring Cycle of Wagner as part of Centenary Maifestspiele; Music Dir, Luzern Opera and Symphony Orchestra 1997–2003; Chief Conductor, Ensemble Intercontemporain 2000; Chief Conductor and Music Dir, Bamberger Symphoniker 2000–; guest appearances with WDR Cologne, Leipzig Gewandhaus, Tonhalle, NDR Hamburg. NHK Symphony, Concertgebouw, London Philharmonic, Munich Philharmonic and Berlin Philharmonic; world premieres of work by Ferneyhough Rihm, Lachenmann. *Recordings:* with ASKO Ensemble, Moscow Philharmonic, orchestral works including the Requiem of Gyorgy Ligeti with Berlin Philharmonic, Complete Schubert Symphonies with Bamberger Symphoniker. *Address:* Bamberger Symphoniker, Postfach 11 01 46, 96029 Bamberg, Germany (office). *E-mail:* intendanz@bamberger-symphoniker.de (office). *Website:* www.bamberger -symphoniker.de.

**NOVIKOV, Leo**; Violinist and Violin Teacher; b. 11 July 1964, Moscow, Russia; m. Tanya Novikov, 1 April 1989, 3 s. *Education:* Moscow State Institute of Music; Music College, Moscow Conservatoire; Special Secondary Music School, Moscow Conservatoire. *Career:* Debut: Solo Recital, Tbilisy Conservatoire, Georgia, with State Chamber Orchestra, 1989; Many solo performances in Moscow, Georgia, Latvia, 1989–92; Solo Performance in television link-up broadcast from Moscow, 1990; Rank and file violinist, Moscow Philharmonic Orchestra, Solo performer with Solo Performers Chamber Orchestra of Moscow Philharmonic, 1990–93; Senior Teacher, Australian Institute of Music, 1993–; Solo performances in Concert Hall of Sydney Opera House, 1996, 1997, and on national television; Conducted first experimental masterclasses on television; mem, Musicians' Union of Australia; Australian String Teachers Association. *Recordings:* First solo CD recording, 1997. *Address:* 915 Anzac Parade, Naroubra, Sydney, NSW 2035, Australia.

**NOVOA, Salvador**; American singer (tenor) and voice teacher; b. 30 Oct. 1937, Mexico City, Mexico; m. 16 Aug 1968, 3 s., 1 d. *Education:* School of Music, The University of Mexico, 1957–62; Voice with Felipe Aquilera Ruiz, 1957–66; Kurt Baum, 1972–80. *Career:* Debut: As Pinkerton in Madama Butterfly, Mexico Opera Company, 1960; Erik in Der fliegende Holländer with the Philadelphia Lyric Opera; Several roles in various operas with the New York City Opera including: Don José and Cavaradossi, the title roles in Bomarzo and Don Rodrigo, Faust in Mefistofele and Edgardo in Lucia di Lammermoor; He has appeared with opera companies widely including San Diego Opera, Houston Grand Opera, Boston Opera, Cincinnati Opera, Teatro Colón, Argentina, Opera Municipal de Marseille, Stuttgart Opera Company, Tehran; His repertoire includes: Radames, Andrea Chénier; Bomarzo (Pier Francesco), Carmen (Don José), Cavalleria Rusticana (Turiddu); Don Rodrigo, Faust, Macbeth, Macduff, Faust in Mefistofele; Pollione in Norma; Samson in Samson and Delilah; Numerous other roles in various operas; Symphonic repertoire includes, Beethoven's Ninth Symphony and Verdi's Messa da requiem. *Recordings:* Bomarzo by Alberto Ginastera, CBS Records. *Honours:* 2nd Prize, Metropolitan Opera Regional Auditions, Mexico City, 1959. *Address:* 4 Cedargate Lane, Westport, CT 06880-3759, USA. *E-mail:* snovoa@aol.com (home). *Website:* www.learn2sing.net (home).

**NOVOHRADSKY, Thomas;** artistic director; *Artistic Director (Opera), New National Theatre, Tokyo. Education:* Univ. of Music and Dramatic Arts, Vienna. *Career:* Asst Stage Dir St Gallen Theatre, Switzerland 1980–82; apptd Asst Stage Dir Wiener Staatsoper 1982, Production Man. 1993–2001; has also worked for Teatro alla Scala, Salzburg Festival, Bregenz Festival; researcher New Nat. Theatre, Tokyo 1999–2001, Artistic Consultant (Opera) 2001–03; Artistic Dir (Opera) 2005–(07). *Address:* New National Theatre Tokyo, 1-1-1 Hon-machi, Shibuya-ku, Tokyo 151, Japan (office). *Website:* www .nntt.jac.go.jp (office).

**NOVOTNY, Jan;** Czech pianist; *Professor of Piano, Prague Conservatory*; b. 15 Dec. 1935, Prague; m. 26 April 1985, 2 d. *Education:* Prague Conservatory, 1950–55; Academy of Music Arts, Prague, 1955–59. *Career:* Debut: Prague, 1954; Concert performances world-wide with frequent appearances at Prague Spring Festival, Festival de Bonaguil, France and on Radio Prague, Bern, Gothenburg, Brussels, Paris and TV Prague; jury mem., Rudolf Firkusny Int. Competition, Prague; Prof. of Piano, Prague Conservatory 1961–, and Head, Piano Classes Dept 1988–95; President, Smetana Society, 1991. *Recordings:* Beethoven's Sonatas Op 10 No3, Op 22, Op 28, Op 31 No. 1; Smetana's Complete Piano Works, 10 records, 7 CDs; Schumann's Phantasie C major Op 17; FX Dussek's Piano Concertos; st Piano Sonatas; Jaroslav Jezek's Complete Piano Works; Ignaz Moscheles' Concerto No. 5 Op 87 in C minor; JL Dussek's Last Piano Sonatas and Piano Concertos with Prague Chamber Philharmonic Orchestra. *Publications:* Smetana: Piano Compositions, in 7 vols, complete edition 1st time in history. *Contributions:* Gramorevue, Prague. *Honours:* State Prize 1984, Annual Prize of Panton Ed., Prague 1987. *Address:* Prague Conservatory, Na Rejdisti 1, Prague (office); Achátová 18, Prague 5, 153 00, Czech Republic (home). *Telephone:* (2) 57911263 (home). *E-mail:* novotny .piano@quick.cz (home).

**NOWACK, Hans;** Singer (Bass); b. 1930, Waldenburg, Germany. *Education:* Completed vocal studies 1956. *Career:* Sang at Heidelberg Opera from 1959, Bielefeld 1961 and Bremen Opera 1963–66; Essen Opera from 1967, with guest engagements at Vienna, Barcelona, Mexico, Venice, Lisbon and New Orleans; Roles have included Osmin, Sarastro, Kaspar in Der Freischütz, Gurnemanz, Hunding, Rocco and Ochs; Further visits to Hamburg, Munich, Berlin and Warsaw, as Jupiter in Rameau's Platée, Marke, the Commendatore, Daland, Boris Godunov and Hindemith's Cardillac. *Address:* Theater Essen, Rolandstrasse 10, W-4300 Essen 1, Germany.

**NOWAK, Grzegorz;** conductor; b. 1951, Poland. *Education:* Poznan Academy of Music, Eastman School of Music, Rochester, Tanglewood with Bernstein, Ozawa, Leinsdorf and Markevitch. *Career:* Music Director for Slupsk Symphony Orchestra, 1976–80; Won first prize in 1984 at Ansermet Conducting Competition, Geneva; Engagements followed with London Symphony, Montreal Symphony and Orchestre National de France; Has also appeared with orchestras of Rome, Oslo, Stockholm, Copenhagen, Helsinki, Monte Carlo, Jerusalem, Madrid, Lisbon, Baltimore, Cincinnati, San Diego, Vancouver, Ottawa, Tokyo, Hong Kong, Geneva, Zürich, Baden-Baden, Milan, Saarbrücken, Rotterdam, Florence, Göteborg, Malmö, Birmingham, Liverpool, Bournemouth, Manchester, Belfast and Glasgow; Music Director of the Biel Symphony Orchestra, Switzerland; Led the Polish premiere of Simon Boccanegra, Warsaw, 1997. *Recordings:* Ravel's Daphnis et Chloe and Bartók's Dance Suite with the London Symphony Orchestra. *Honours:* American Patronage Prize, 1984; Europaischen Förderpreis für Musik, 1985.

**NUCCI, Leo;** Singer (Baritone); b. 16 April 1942, Castiglione dei Pepoli, Bologna, Italy; m. Adriana Anelli. *Education:* Studied with Giuseppe Marchesi and Ottaviano Bizzarri. *Career:* Debut: Spoleto in 1967 as Rossini's Figaro; Sang Puccini's Schaunard at Venice in 1975, at La Scala Milan in 1976 as Figaro, at Covent Garden in 1978 as Miller in Luisa Miller and Metropolitan Opera from 1980 as Renato in Un Ballo in Maschera, Eugene Onegin, Germont, Amonasro and Posa in Don Carlos; Sang at Paris Opéra in 1981 as Renato and at Pesaro in 1984 in a revival of Rossini's Il Viaggio a Reims; Wiesbaden in 1985 as Rigoletto, at Salzburg Festival, 1989–90 as Renato, Turin in 1990 as Silvio in Pagliacci and Parma as Di Luna in Il Trovatore; Sang Iago in concert performances of Otello at Chicago and New York in 1991; Season 1992 as Luna at Turin, Tonio at Rome, Iago at Reggio Emilia, the Forza Don Carlo at Florence and Rossini's Figaro at the Festival of Caracalla; Sang Dulcamara at Turin, 1994; Sang Rossini's Figaro at the Verona Arena, 1996; Sang Macbeth at Buenos Aires, 1998; Season 2000–01 as Germont at Verona, Count Luna at La Scala, Verdi's Franesco Foscari for the San Carlo Opera, Naples, and Nabucco at the Vienna Staatsoper. *Recordings:* Donizetti's Maria di Rudenz; Ford in Falstaff; Il Viaggio a Reims; Aida; Simon Boccanegra; Otello; Rigoletto; Michonnet in Adriana Lecouvreur; Video of Il Barbiere di Siviglia, from the Metropolitan;. *Address:* c/o Allied Artists Agency, 42 Montpelier Square, London SW7 1JZ, England.

**NUNEMAKER, Richard E.,** BS, MM; American clarinettist and saxophonist; b. 30 Nov. 1942, Buffalo, NY; m. Lynda Perkins 1964; one s. one d. *Education:* Performer's Certificate in clarinet, State Univ. of New York Coll. at Fredonia, Univ. of Louisville; studied with Clark Brody, Jerome Stowell, James Livingston, Allen Sigel, William Willett. *Career:* bass clarinet, saxophone, Houston Symphony Orchestra 1967–; clarinet, saxophone, Houston Pops 1970–85; Cambiata Soloists 1970–84; Faculty, clarinet, saxophone, Asst Dir, Wind Ensemble, Univ. of St Thomas, Houston 1970–92; clarinet, saxophone, Music America Chamber Ensemble 1977–92; clarinet, saxophone, Pierrot Plus

Ensemble, Rice Univ. 1987–92; clarinet and saxophone concertos with Lawrence Foster, Jorge Mester, Sergiu Comissiona, other conductors; frequent recitalist and soloist with chamber music ensembles on radio and TV, including new music; principal clarinet, Orquesta Filarmonica de la Ciudad de México 1987; Clarinet and Saxophone Opus 90, New Directions in American Chamber Music 1990; Carnegie debut, New and Improvised Music Concert, music of Willian Thomas McKinley 1994; European debut, tour with Camerata Bregenz, conductor Christoph Eberle, Austria 1994; mem. Int. Conference of Symphony and Opera Musicians, American Federation of Musicians, Int. Clarinet Assn, Houston Composers' Alliance. *Recordings:* From The Great Land, Logo I, America Swings, Stompin' At The Savoy; as exec. producer: Multiplicities, Golden Petals, Magical Place of My Dreams Between Silence and Darkness, The Louisville Project (all contain music for clarinet and saxophone commissioned by Richard Nunemaker). *Publications:* If the Shoe Fits, Scales and Chords (A New Approach for all Instruments). *Honours:* Distinguished Alumni Fellow, Univ. of Louisville 2002. *Current Management:* Lyn-Rich Management, 4114 Leeshire Drive, Houston, TX 77025, USA. *Telephone:* (713) 665-8877. *Fax:* (713) 667-0283. *Address:* 4114 Leeshire Drive, Houston, TX 77025, USA (home). *E-mail:* Rnunemaker@aol .com (home).

**NUSSBAUMER, Georg;** Composer; b. 24 Aug. 1964, Linz, Austria; m., 1 d. *Education:* Bruckner Conservatory; Sweelinck Conservatory, Amsterdam; Studied recorder with W v Hauwe. *Career:* Work performed at Konzerthaus, Vienna, 1991, 1992, Ciurlionis Museum Kaunas, 1992, Zur Kunst der Klangzucht, Linz, 1993, Unerhörte musik, Berlin, 1996, Ars electronica, Linz, 1996, Atlas mapping, Bregenz, 1997, Melos Ethos, Bratislava, 1997, Insel Musik, Berlin, 1997, Schaubühne Berlin, 1999. *Compositions:* Für einen Klavierzyklus, piano, 1994; Organ O Agie, organ, 1991; Introibo ad altare dei, installation, action, ensemble, 1995; AnArmorica, ensemble, 1996; 4 String Quartets, 1997, 1998; Icarusetude/Chopinyonnaise, piano, 1999; Der Hebel des Lichts, installation, 1999. *Recordings:* Lebenssee/3 Männer, with poet Walter Pilar. *Honours:* Prizes and Scholarships from Austrian Government; Casinos Austria Competition, recommendation. *Address:* Ottensheimer-strasse 42, 4111, Walding, Austria.

**NYIKOS, Markus Andreas;** cellist; b. 9 Dec. 1948, Basel, Switzerland; m. Verena Kamber 1982, one d. *Education:* Musik Akademie, Basel with Paul Szabo; Konservatorium Luzern with Stanislav Apolin; Masterclasses with Zara Nelsova, Pierre Fournier, Sándor Végh and Janáček Quartet. *Career:* cello solo at Festival of Strings Lucerne, 1974–79 and with Philharmonische Virtuosen Berlin, 1983–; Professor, Hochschule der Kunste Berlin, 1979–; Guest Professor at Shanghai Conservatory; Numerous concerts and radio appearances world-wide. *Recordings:* Vivaldi; Cello Concertos with Radio Sinfonie Orchestra Berlin; Brahms Sonatas in E minor and F major, with pianist, Gerard Wyss; Schubert's Arpeggione-Sonata in A minor with Gerard Wyss; With La Groupe Des Six, compositions by Auric, Poulenc, Honegger, and Milhaud, with pianist, Jaroslav Smykal. *Current Management:* Robert Gilder & Co., Enterprise House, 59–65 Upper Ground, London, SE1 9PQ, England. *Telephone:* (20) 7928-9008. *Fax:* (20) 7928-9755. *E-mail:* rgilder@ robert-gilder.com.

**NYMAN, Michael;** British composer; b. 23 March 1944, London. *Education:* Royal Acad. of Music, King's Coll. London. *Career:* composer, writer and music critic 1968–78; lecturer 1976–80; established MN Records label 2005–. *Film and television soundtracks:* Peter Greenaway films: 5 Postcards from Capital Cities 1967, Vertical Features Remake 1976, Goole by Numbers 1976, A Walk Through H: The Reincarnation of an Ornithologist 1978, 1–100 1978, The Falls 1980, Act of God 1980, Terence Conran 1981, The Draughtsman's Contract 1982, The Coastline 1983, Making a Splash 1984, A Zed and Two Noughts 1985, Inside Rooms: 26 Bathrooms, London & Oxfordshire 1985, Drowning by Numbers 1988, Fear of Drowning 1988, Death in the Seine 1988, The Cook, The Thief, His Wife and Her Lover 1989, Hubert Bals Handshake 1989, Prospero's Books 1991; other films: Keep it Downstairs 1976, Tom Phillips 1977, Brimstone and Treacle 1982, Nelly's Version 1983, Frozen Music 1983, The Cold Room 1984, Fairly Secret Army 1984, The Kiss 1985, L'Ange frénétique 1985, I'll Stake My Cremona to a Jew's Trump 1985, The Disputation 1986, Ballet Méchanique 1986, Le Miraculé 1987, The Man Who Mistook His Wife for a Hat 1987, Monsieur Hire 1989, Out of the Ruins 1989, Le Mari de la coiffeuse 1990, Men of Steel 1990, Les Enfants Volants 1990, Not Mozart: Letters, Riddles and Writs 1991, The Final Score 1992, The Fall of Icarus 1992, The Piano 1993, Ryori no tetsujin 1993, Mesmer 1994, A La Folie (Six Days, Six Nights) 1994, Carrington 1995, Anne no nikki (The Diary of Anne Frank) 1995, Der Unhold (The Ogre) 1996, Enemy Zero 1996, Gattaca 1997, Titch 1998, Ravenous 1999, How to Make Dhyrak: A Dramatic Work for Three Players and Camera, Truncated with Only Two Players 1999, Wonderland 1999, Nabbie no koi (Nabbie's Love) 1999, The End of the Affair 1999, The Claim 2000, Act Without Words I 2000, That Sinking Feeling 2000, La Stanza del figlio 2001, Subterrain 2001, 24 heures de la vie d'une femme 2002, The Man with a Movie Camera 2002, The Actors 2003, Nathalie... 2003, Charged 2003, Ident (Channel 5) 2004. *Other compositions:* orchestral: A Handsom, Smooth, Sweet, Smart, Clear Stroke: Or Else Play Not At All 1983, Taking a Line for a Second Walk 1986, L'Orgie Parisienne 1989, Six Celan Songs 1990, Where the Bee Dances 1991, Self Laudatory Hymn of Inanna and Her Omnipotence 1992, The Upside-Down Violin 1992, MGV (Musique à Grande Vitesse) 1993, On the Fiddle 1993, Concerto for Harpsichord and Strings 1995, Concerto for Trombone 1995, Double Concerto 1996, Strong on

Oaks, Strong on the Causes of Oaks 1997, Cycle of Disquietude 1998, a dance he little thinks of 2001, The Draughtsman's Contract for Orchestra 2001, Dance of the Engines 2002, Gattaca for Orchestra 2003, The Claim for Orchestra 2003, The Piano: Concert Suite 2003, Violin Concerto 2003; chamber music: First Waltz in D, Bell Set No. 1 1974, 1–100 1976, Waltz in F 1976, Think Slow, Act Fast 1981, 2 Violins 1981, Four Saxes (Real Slow Drag) 1982, I'll Stake My Cremona to a Jew's Crump 1983, Time's Up 1983, Child's Play 1985, String Quartet No. 1 1985, Taking a Line for a Second Walk 1986, String Quartet No. 2 1988, String Quartet No. 3 1990, In Re Don Giovanni 1991, Masque Arias 1991, Time Will Pronounce 1992, Songs for Tony 1993, Three Quartets 1994, H.R.T. 1995, String Quartet No. 4 1995, Free for All 2001, Five who Figured Four Years Ago 2002, Mapping 2002, Yellow Beach 2002, 24 Hour Sax Quartet 2004, For John Peel 2004; instrumental: Shaping the Curve 1990, Six Celan Songs 1990, Flugelhorn and Piano 1991, For John Cage 1992, The Convertibility of Lute Strings 1992, Here to There 1993, Yamamoto Perpetuo 1993, On the Fiddle 1993, To Morrow 1994, Tango for Tim 1994, Elisabeth Gets her Way 1995, Viola and Piano 1995, Titch 1997, Fourths, Mostly (for organ) 2001; dramatic works: Strange Attractors, The Princess of Milan, A Broken Set of Rules 1984, Basic Black 1984, Portraits in Reflection 1985, And Do They Do 1986, The Man Who Mistook His Wife for a Hat 1986, Miniatures/Configurations 1988, Letters, Riddles and Writs 1991, Noises, Sounds and Sweet Airs 1994, Facing Goya 2000, Man and Boy: Dada (opera) 2003, Love Counts 2004; vocal: A Neat Slice of Time 1980, The Abbess of Andouillets 1984, Out of the Ruins 1989, Polish Love Song 1990, Shaping the Curve 1991, Anne de Lucy Songs 1992, Mozart on Mortality 1992, Grounded 1995, The Waltz Song 1995, The Ballad of Kastriot Rexhepi 2001, Mosè 2001, A Child's View of Colour 2003, Acts of Beauty 2004; with Michael Nyman Band: In Re Don Giovanni 1977, The Masterwork/Award-Winning Fishknife 1979, Bird List Song 1979, Five Orchestral Pieces Opus Tree 1981, Bird Anthem 1981, M-Work 1981, Love is Certainly, at Least Alphabetically Speaking 1983, Bird Work 1984, The Fall of Icarus 1989, La Traversée de Paris 1989, The Final Score 1992, AET (After Extra Time) 1996, De Granada a la Luna 1998, Orfeu 1998, The Commissar Vanishes 1999, Man with a Movie Camera 2001, Compiling the Colours (Samhitha) 2003, Three Ways of Describing Rain (Sawan; Rang; Dhyan) 2003, Zeit und Ziel 1814–2002, Manhatta 2003; dance: Flicker 2005. *Recordings include:* film soundtracks, The Piano Sings 2005. *Publications:* Libretto for Birtwistle's Dramatic Pastoral, Down by the Greenwood Side 1968–69, Experimental Music: Cage and Beyond 1974; contrib. critical articles to journals, including The Spectator. *Address:* Michael Nyman Ltd, 83 Pulborough Road, London, SW18 5UL, England (office). *Telephone:* (20) 8870-8961 (office). *Fax:* (20) 8875-9377 (office). *E-mail:* info@michaelnyman.com (office); m.n.ltd@dial.pipex.com (office). *Website:* www.michaelnyman.com (office).

**NYQUIST, Kristian (Benedikt);** German harpsichordist and fortepianist; b. 16 Oct. 1964, Los Angeles, Calif.; m. Judith Nyquist,1991; two s. one d. *Education:* Staatliche Musikhochschule, Karlsruhe, 1983–88; Conservatoire National de Région Rueil-Malmaison, 1988–92. *Career:* Debut: Ernst Toch Saal, Mannheim, Germany, 1986; Concerts as Recitalist, Continuo Player, Duo Partner and Soloist in Germany, France, Belgium, Netherlands, Poland, Czech Republic, Switzerland, Russia, USA, Brazil; Lecturer, Univ. of Music, Mannheim 1989–, Univ. of Karlsruhe 1995–; mem. Deutscher Tonkunstler-Verband, Stuttgart Section, France Action Musique. *Radio:* (for SWR Stuttgart): F. Devienne, 6 sonatas for oboe and continuo 2004; C.P.E. Bach Solo pieces for fortepiano 2004. *Recordings:* Beethoven Violin Sonatas op. 30, 2001; Hans Werner Henze Complete Works for Harpsichord, 2001, 2004; J.S. Bach Goldberg Variations, 2003; C.P.E. Bach, 5 Sonatas for harpsichord and flute, 1996; J.S. Bach, 5 Flute Sonatas, 1997; D'Anglebert Harpsichord Music, 1998. *Publications:* Realisations of Figured-Bass Parts; Trio-Sonatas by Tartini; Sonata Pastorale by Campioni, Zimmermann, Verlag. *Honours:* 1st Prize, Concours Musical de Region d'Ile de France, 1991; Prague Spring Competition, Honorary Mention, 1994, Prix de Virtuosité. *Address:* Soon-waldstrasse 27, 55566 Bad Sobernheim, Germany. *Telephone:* 67516577. *Fax:* 67516577. *E-mail:* kristian.nyquist@arcor.de.

**NYSTEDT, Knut;** composer, conductor and organist; b. 3 Sept. 1915, Oslo, Norway; m. Brigit Nystedt 1942; one s. one d. *Education:* Artium, organ with Arild Sandvold, Oslo Conservatory of Music, Ernest White, New York, composition with Bjarne Brustad, Oslo, Aaron Copland, New York. *Career:* debut organist 1938; Guest-Conductor, Oslo Philharmonic, 1945; Organist, Torshov Church, Oslo, 1946–82; Conductor, Norwegian Soloist Choir, 1950–90, performances world-wide; Professor of Choral Conducting, Oslo University, 1964–85. *Compositions:* 5 String Quartets, 1938, 1948, 1955, 1966, 1988; Piano variations, 1948; Symphony for strings, 1950; Lucis Creator Optime, soli, chorus, orchestra, 1968; With Crown and Star, Christmas opera, 1971; Pia memoria, 9 brass instruments, 1971; Music for 6 trombones, 1980; Exsultate, 1980; Mountain Scenes, concert band, 1981; A Hymn of Human Rights, chorus, organ and percussion, 1982; For a Small Planet, chorus, recitation, harp, string quartet, 1982; Sinfonia del Mare, 1983; Ave Maria, chorus, violin solo, 1986; Songs of Soloman, church opera, 1989; Ave Christe, women's chorus, orchestra, 1991; Messa per Percussione, 1991; Concerto Arctandriae, strings, 1991; 4 Grieg Romances, chorus a capella, 1992; The Conch, male quartet with countertenor, 1993; Concerto Sacro, violin, organ, 1993; Miserere, 16-part chorus of mixed voices, 1994; One Mighty Flowering Tree, chorus, brass, 1994; Gebete für Mitgefangene (Bonhoeffer), soprano, organ, 1994; Kristnikvede, 1000th anniversary of Christianity in Norway, chorus, orchestra, 1994; Libertas Vincit, 50th anniversary of liberation from German occupation, recitation, chorus, orchestra, 1994; A Song as in The Night (Esaiah), soprano and baritone solo, chorus and string orchestra, 1996; Magnificat for a New Millennium, chorus, four trombones and percussion, 1997; Apocalysis Joannis, solos, chorus and orchestra, commissioned for Oslo Philharmonic, 1998; Prayers of Kierkegaard, mixed chorus, 1999; The World Became Flesh, chorus, 2000; Reach Out for Peace (Fred Kaan), chorus, 2001; The Shakespeare sonnets, tenor solo, 2002; Psalmus 138, violin solo, chorus and orchestra, 2002; Jesu Sieben Worte, chorus, 2002. *Address:* Vestbrynet 25 B, 1160 Oslo, Norway.

# O

**OAK, Kilsung;** Composer; b. 7 May 1942, Tong Yung, Korea; m., 1 s., 2 d. *Education:* MA, Long Island University; DMA, Columbia University. *Career:* The Group for Contemporary Music, 1972; Riverside Dance Festival, 1976; Seoul Symphony orchestra, 1994; mem, ASCAP; The Korean Society of the I-Ching; The Korean Composers Association. *Compositions:* Symphony; Amorphosis; String quartet; Sonata for piano; Duo for violin and piano; Dahn for violin and piano; GHI for violin and piano; The Days of Indong for orchestra. *Recordings:* Amorphosis for soprano and 12 percussionists. *Publications:* Symphony, 1997; Amorphosis, 1997; String quartet, 1995; Sonata for piano, 1998; Duo for violin and piano, 1992; Dahn for violin and piano, 1992; GHI for violin and piano, 1993. *Contributions:* Rappaport Prize, 1971; The Korea Arts and Culture Foundation Award, 1995 and 1998; The Best Film Award by the Korean Film Critics Society, 1996. *Address:* Jong-Gu, Piloon-Dong 32-1, Seoul, Republic of Korea.

**OAKLEY-TUCKER, John;** Singer (baritone); b. 1959, Canada. *Education:* Guildhall School of Music, Britten-Pears School, Ravel Acad. with Peter Pears, Gerard Souzay, Elisabeth Schwarzkopf and Thomas Hampson; continues to study with David Pollard. *Career:* operatic debut in the title role of Britten's Owen Wingrave, conducted by Steuart Bedford, Aldeburgh, 1984; sang in Glyndebourne Opera Festival Chorus in Jenůfa, Arabella, Le nozze di Figaro and Falstaff, 1988–90; operatic roles include lead role, Tom in Hans Werner Henze's The English Cat, conducted by the composer, Berlin, 1989, Italy, 1990 and Barbican, London, 1991 as part of the Henze BBC Festival; title role in Eugene Onegin, Co-Opera, London, 1993; lead role of Pluto in the world premiere of Hilda Paredes' chamber opera, The Seventh Pip, Mexico City, 1993; Belcore with Island Opera, 1994; English tour with Camberwell Opera as Il Conte, 1994–95, both directed by Mark Tinkler; Pluto in The Seventh Pip, San Diego, 1995; further roles include Don Giovanni, Guglielmo, Papageno, Sid (Albert Herring) and Billy Budd; concert performances include Bach's St John's and St Matthew's Passion, Duruflé's Requiem, Dvořák's Requiem, Elgar's Apostles, Fauré's Requiem, Handel's Messiah, Mozart's Requiem, Orff's Carmina Burana, Rossini's Petite Messe Solennelle and Vaughan Williams Sea Symphony; toured UK, Spain, Portugal, singing Mahler's Kindertotenlieder for the Ballet Rambert, 1988–89; recital debut with Graham Johnson, Schumann's Dichterliebe and English Song, Purcell Room, 1987; performances with the Songmakers' Almanac; Schubert's Winterreise with Nicholas Bosworth, Purcell Room, 1992; recital tour of the Middle East with Iwan Llewelyn-Jones, 1993; Schubert's Die schöne Müllerin with Iwan Llewelyn-Jones, Purcell Room, 1994; other recitals in the UK and abroad; formed duo, Tucker and Rohr, 1996, with pianist Alard von Rohr, performances include Carnegie Hall in New York, 1998 and Konzerthaus, Berlin, 1999. *Recordings:* Tom in Hans Werner Henze's The English Cat (German television), 1991; Pluto in Hilda Paredes' The Seventh Pip (with Arditti String Quartet), 1995; Baritone Solo, Symphony No. 5, Alexander Lokshin conducted by Rudolf Barschai, 1997. *Honours:* AGSM; Countess of Munster Musical Trust Scholarship. *Current Management:* Judith Newton, 75 Aberdare Gardens, London, NW6 3AN, England. *Address:* Sonnenallee 152, 12059 Berlin, Germany.

**OBATA, Machiko;** Singer (Soprano); b. 23 Feb. 1948, Sapporo, Japan. *Education:* Studied in Tokyo and Cologne. *Career:* Appearances with the Cologne Opera as Mozart's Pamina and Servila, Marzelline in Fidelio, Gretel, Liu and Flora in The Turn of The Screw; Sang the Woodbird in Siegfried in 1991; Guest engagements at Strasbourg, Munich and the Opéra Comique in Paris; Salburg Easter and Summer Festivals in 1991 as Barbarina in Le nozze di Figaro; Sang the Princess in Les Brigands by Offenbach at Colgone, 2001; Frequent concert appearances. *Address:* c/o Oper der Stadt Köln, Offenbach-platz, 5000 Cologne, Germany.

**OBERHOLTZER, William;** Singer (Baritone); b. 1947, Bloomington, Indiana, USA. *Education:* Studied at Indiana State University. *Career:* Debut: Indiana in 1972 in Herakles by John Eaton; Sang Marcello at St Gallen in 1976 then at Saarbrucken, 1978–81, Gelsenkirchen, 1981–86, and Kassel from 1986, St John in Wolfgang von Schweinitz' Patmos in 1990; Engaged at Munster, 1986–88 and made guest appearances at Düsseldorf as Marcello, Linz, Krefeld and Hannover; Other roles include Mozart's Count and Don Giovanni, Valentin, Renato, Rigoletto, Ford, Paolo, Wagner's Wolfram and Amfortas, Strauss's Jochanaan and Mandryka, and Wozzeck; Season 1998 as Matthes in Weill's Die Burgschaft, at Bielefeld; Sang Dallapiccola's Prigio-niero at Bielefeld, 1999; Concert engagements include Bach's St John Passion in Berlin and Carmina Burana. *Address:* c/o Bühnen der Stadt Bielefeld, Brunhenstrasse 3–9, Pf 220, 4800 Bielefeld, Germany.

**OBERLIN, Russell;** American college lecturer and singer (countertenor); b. 11 Oct. 1928, Akron, OH. *Education:* Juilliard School. *Career:* founding member of New York Pro Musica Antiqua and soloist with many orchestras including New York Philharmonic, Chicago Symphony and Buffalo Philharmonic; Little Orchestra Society, Clarion Concerts, Smithsonian Institute Concert Series, CBS Radio Orchestra; Masterclasses throughout USA; Opera appearances in major roles at Covent Garden in Midsummer Night's Dream, San Francisco Opera, at Edinburgh and Vancouver Festivals and American Opera Society; Solo recitalist throughout USA; Radio and television appearances; Thomas Hunter Professor of Music, Hunter College and The Graduate Center of the City University of New York, 1966–; mem, National Association of Teachers of Singing; Academia Monteverdiana; Founding Board Member, Waverly Consort, Berkshire (Mass) Concert Series, Soho Baroque Opera Company; American Academy of Teachers of Singing. *Recordings include:* A Russell Oberlin Recital; Russell Oberlin, Handel Arias; Russell Oberlin, Baroque Cantatas; Soloist with New York Philharmonic, Handel's Messiah; Bach's Magnificat in D; Soloist with New York Pro Musica, The Play of Daniel; Thomas Tallis's Sacred Music; Josquin des Pres' Missa Pange Lingua; Walton's Façade with Hermione Gingold; Numerous other recordings including recently reissued CDs including: Troubadour and Trouvére Songs. English Polyphony of the 13th and Early 14th Centuries, The French Ars Antiqua and William Byrd Music for Voice and Viols. *Address:* c/o Hunter College, City University of New York, 695 Park Avenue, New York, NY 10021, USA.

**OBERMAYR, Christine;** Singer (Mezzo-Soprano); b. 30 May 1959, Wiesba-den, Germany. *Education:* Studied in Mainz with Josef Metternich. *Career:* Debut: Theater am Gärtnerplatz Munich in 1983 as Cherubino; Sang a Flowermaiden at Bayreuth Festival in 1984; Roles in Munich have included Hansel, Flotow's Nancy, Nicklausse and Orlofsky; Engagements at Wiesba-den, 1984–89 as Carmen, Emilia, Otello, Olga, Janáček's Fox, the Composer in Ariadne and Ottavio in L'Incoronazione di Poppea; Further appearances at the Theater an der Wien, the Paris Opéra and the Teatro Regio Turin; Sang Lyubasha in Rimsky's Tsar's Bride in 1985 and Mary in Der fliegende Holländer at Naples in 1992; Many concert and lieder performances. *Honours:* Prizewinner in competitions at Vienna, Wiesbaden and Berlin.

**OBERSON, René;** Composer, Organist and Professor; b. 27 June 1945, La Tour-de-Treme, Fribourg, Switzerland; m. 2 s., 1 d. *Education:* Teachers' Training College, Schools of Music in Fribourg, Berne and Geneva. *Career:* Organist at concerts in Switzerland and abroad notably at Notre-Dame, Paris, France and Symphony Hall, Osaka, Japan; Professor, School of Music, Fribourg. *Compositions include:* L'Exilée (The Exiled Woman), 1983; Concerto for Pan Pipes, 1984; Le Grand Cercle (The Great Circle), 1985; Homo Somniens, 1988; Au Seuil De L'Ere Du Verseau (On The Threshold Of The Era Of Aquarius), 1988; Jumière Divine, Omniprésente, Invulnerable for Organ, 1990; Espoirs for 2 Trumpets, 2 Trombones and Organ, 1990. *Recordings include:* Numerous works have been recorded by the Lausanne Chamber Orchestra, the Berne Symphony Orchestra, Netherlands National of Jeunesses Musicales Orchestra; Also radio recordings. *Contributions:* Has reconstructed the Fourth Concerto for Organ or Harpsichord and String Orchestra by the Swiss composer, Meyer von Schauensee, 1720–1798. *Address:* Pavillon Trobère Miraval, 1756 Lovens, Switzerland.

**OBRADOVICH, Aleksandar;** Composer and Professor of Composition; b. 22 Aug. 1927, Bled, Yugoslavia; m. Biljana, 2 Aug 1953, 1 s. *Education:* Academy of Music, 1952; Grants to spec. in London and New York. *Career:* Assistant Professor, Associate Professor, Professor, Faculty of Music Art, Belgrade, 1954–91; General Secretary of Union of Composers of Yugoslavia, 1962–66; Rector, University of Arts, Belgrade, 1978–83; President of Senate, 1981–82, President, 1982–83, of Union of Yugoslavian Universities; mem, Society of Serbian Composers. *Compositions:* 8 Symphonies, 5 concertos, 5 cantatas; Wind Of Flame, Green Knight, Stradum, cycles of songs; A Springtime Picnic At Dawn, ballet; Many other symphonic works, 15 vocal, instrumental and chamber works, music for 7 films and for 9 radio dramas; Electronic music and chorale works; Compositions have been performed in 32 different countries. *Recordings:* Radio-Televizja Belgrade. *Publications:* Orchestration I–II, 1978, III in preparation; Electronic Music and Electronic Instruments, 1978. *Contributions:* Over 350 articles and music critiques. *Honours:* 25 Prizes including October Prize of Belgrade in 1959 for Symphonic Epitaph, 4th July Prize in 1972 for lV Symphony and 7th July Prize in 1980 for his whole work. *Address:* Branka Djonovica 8, Belgrade 11 040, Serbia and Montenegro.

**OBRAZTSOVA, Elena Vasilyevna;** Russian singer (mezzo-soprano); *Director, Elena Obraztsova Cultural Centre, St Petersburg;* b. 7 July 1939, Leningrad (now St Petersburg); d. of Vasily Alekseevich Obraztsov and Nataliya Ivanovna Obraztsova (née Bychkova); m. 1st Vyacheslav Makarov (divorced 1983); one d.; m. 2nd Algis Žiuraitis 1983 (died 1998). *Education:* Leningrad Conservatoire (under tuition of Prof. Grigorievna). *Career:* Prof., Moscow Conservatoire 1973–94; mem. and Prin. Soloist Bolshoi Theatre, Moscow 1964–; Dir St Petersburg Elena Obraztsova Cultural Center 1999–; has appeared at most leading opera houses of Europe and America, including Vienna State Opera 1975, Metropolitan Opera New York 1976, La Scala Milan 1976, Salzburg 1978, Covent Garden, London 1981 and has toured extensively in Russia and throughout world; gives masterclasses in Europe and Japan; judge of int. vocal competitions; est. Int. Yelena Obraztsova Competition for young opera singers, St Petersburg 1999 and for chamber music singers, Moscow 2000; Academician Acad. of Russian Art 1999–. *Roles include:* Marina Mniszek in Boris Godunov (debut, Bolshoi 1963), Countess in Queen of Spades, Konchakovna in Prince Igor, Marfa in Khovanshchina, Lyubasha in The Tsar's Bride, Helene Bezukhova in War and Peace, Frosia in Semionkotko, Princess de Bouillon in Adriana Lecouvreur, Jocasta in Oedipus Rex, Oberon in A Midsummer Night's Dream, Silvana in La Fiamma, Giovanna Seymour in Anna Bolena, Herodiade, Amneris in Aida, Azucena in

Il Trovatore, Eboli in Don Carlos, Santuzza in Cavelleria Rusticana, Ulrica in Un Ballo in Maschera, Adalgiza in Norma, Orfeo in Orfeo ed Euridice, Neris in Medea, Leonora in La Favorita, Aunt Princess in Suor Angelica, Frederica in Louise Miller, Carmen, Charlotte in Werther, Delilah in Samson and Delilah, Judith in Duke Bluebeard's Castle, Granny in The Gambler and others; recital repertoire includes works by more than 100 composers; staged Werther at Bolshoi Theatre 1986. *Film:* Cavalleria Rusticana 1981. *Recordings:* over 50 recordings for Melodia, Polydor, DG, EMI, CBS, Philips etc. including operas, oratorios, cantatas, solo discs of arias and chamber music. *Play:* Amalia in Antonia von Elba 1999. *Television includes:* My Carmen 1977, And My Image Will Rise Before You 1979, The Merry Widow 1984, Higher Than The Love 1991, Elena The Great 1995. *Publication:* Bolshoi (poetry) 2001. *Honours:* Hon. mem. Pushkin Acad. 1995–, Russian Acad. of Art Critics and Musical Performance 1999–; Order for Services to the Fatherland 1999 and other decorations; gold medals at competitions Helsinki 1962, Moscow 1962, 1970, Barcelona 1970, Medal of Granados 1971, Gold Pen of Critics, Wiesbaden 1972, Award of Merit, San Francisco 1977, Gold Verdi, Italy 1978, Bartók Memorial Medal, Hungary 1982, State Prize of Russia 1974, Lenin Prize 1976, People's Artist of USSR 1976, Gold Star-Hero of Labour 1990. *Address:* c/o Bolshoi Theatre, Teatralnaya pl. 1, 125009 Moscow (office); Ermolaevsky per. 9-6, 125001 Moscow, Russia. *Telephone:* (095) 292-31-08 (office); (095) 292-06-58 (office); (095) 292-66-90 (office); (095) 209-17-67 (home). *Fax:* (095) 292-66-90 (office); (095) 292-66-32 (office); (095) 292-16-74 (home). *E-mail:* pr@bolshoi .ru (office).

**O'BRIEN, Eugene;** Composer and Teacher; b. 24 April 1945, Paterson, New Jersey, USA. *Education:* Studied at University of Nebraska, MM 1969, with Bernd Alois Zimmermann at Cologne, Indiana University with John Eaton and Iannis Xenakis, and Donald Erb at the Cleveland Institute of Music, DMA, 1983. *Career:* Teacher, 1973–81, Composer-in-Residence, 1981–85, Cleveland Institute; Associate Professor at Catholic University of America in Washington DC, 1985–87, and at Indiana University School of Music, 1987–. *Compositions:* Orchestral: Symphony, 1969, Cello Concerto, 1972, Dedales for Soprano and Orchestra, 1973, Rites Of Passage, 1978, Dreams And Secrets Of Origin for Soprano and Orchestra, 1983, Alto Saxophone Concerto, 1989; Chamber: Intessitura for Cello and Piano, 1975, Embarking For Cythera for 8 Instruments, 1978, Tristan's Lament for Cello, Allures for Percussion Trio, 1979, Psalms and Nocturnes for Flute, Viola da Gamba and Harpsichord, 1985, Mysteries of the Horizon for 11 Instruments, 1987; Vocal: Requiem Mass for Soprano, Chorus and Wind Ensemble, 1966, Nocturne for Soprano and 10 Instruments, 1968, Elegy for Bernd Alois Zimmermann for Soprano and Ensemble, 1970, Lingual for Soprano, Flute and Cello, 1972; Taking Measures, ballet, 1984. *Honours:* Guggenheim Fellowship, 1984–85. *Address:* c/o ASCAP, ASCAP Building, 1 Lincoln Plaza, New York, NY 10023, USA.

**OCHMAN, Wiesław;** Polish tenor, producer and painter; b. 6 Feb. 1937, Warsaw; s. of Jan Ochman and Bronisława Ochman; m. Krystyna Ochman 1963; one s. one d. *Education:* Acad. of Mining and Metallurgy, Kraków 1960, studied with Prof. Gustaw Serafin, Kraków and with Prof. Maria Szłapak, Jerzy Gaczek and Sergiusz Nadgryzowski. *Career:* début Silesian Opera, Bytom 1960; soloist: Silesian Opera, Bytom 1960–63, Opera in Kraków 1963–64, Great Theatre, Warsaw 1964–75, Deutsche Staatsoper 1967, Hamburgische Staatsoper 1967–, Metropolitan Opera, New York 1975–, La Scala, Milan 1981; Festivals at Glyndebourne, Salzburg, Orange; guest performances in operas in Paris, Munich, Frankfurt am Main, San Francisco, Miami, Chicago, Geneva, Budapest, Washington, Staatsoper in Vienna, Grand Theatre in Moscow, Staatsoper and Deutsche Oper in W Berlin, Teatro Colón in Buenos Aires, Gran Teatre del Liceu in Barcelona, Accademia Santa Cecila in Rome, Carnegie Hall in New York, Teatro de la Maestranza in Seville; participation in TV films including Eugene Onegin, Tcharevitch, Salome, Don Giovanni; numerous recordings; mem. Pres. Council for Culture 1992–95; Goodwill Amb. for UNICEF 1996. *Exhibitions:* 75 one-man exhibns of paintings. *Operatic roles include:* Faust, Don Carlos, Tosca (Cavaradossi), Carmen (Don José), Boris Godunov (Dimitri), Lucia di Lammermoor (Edgardo), I vespri siciliani (Arrigo), La Traviata (Alfredo), Don Carlos (Don Carlos), The Hunted Manor (Stefan), Cavalleria Rusticana (Turiddu), Eugene Onegin (Lensky), Pique Dame (Herman), Der Zauberflöte (Tamino), Idomeneo (Idomeneo), La clemenza di Tito (Titus), Der Fliegende Holländer (Eric), Fidelio (Florestan), King Roger (Shepherd), Les pêcheurs de perles (Bizet), Salome (Herod), Khovanshchina (Prince Golitsyn), Halka (Jontek), Jenůfa (Laca), Rigoletto (Prince), Don Giovanni (Don Ottavio). *Operas directed:* Don Giovanni (Mozart), Traviata (Verdi) 2000, Tcharevitch (Lehar) 2001, Eugene Onegin (Tchaikovsky) 2002. *Recordings:* Jenůfa (Janacek) 1995, 2002, Halka (Moniuszko) 1995, Bruckner Masses 1996, Armida (Dvorák) 1996, Stabat Mater/Legends (Dvorák) 1997, Rusalka (Dvorák) 1998, King Roger (Szzymanowski) 1999, Great Operas of Richard Strauss 2001, Orchestral & Choral Works (Penderecki) 2002, Te Deum/Lachrimosa (Penderecki) 2003, Prokofiev: 50th Anniversary Edn – Limited Edn 2003, Cantatas (Gasieniec) 2004. *Honours:* Commdr's Cross with Star, Order of Polonia Restituta 2001; Minister of Culture and Art Prize 1973, The City of Warsaw Prize 1976, Pres. of Radio and TV Cttee Prize (1st Class) 1976, Prime Minister Prize (1st Class) 1979, Minister of Foreign Affairs Diploma 1977, 1986, Medal Maecenas of Art 1976, The City of Kraków Gold Award, Medal of Merit for Nat. Culture 1986. *Address:* ul. Miączyńska 46B, 02-637 Warsaw, Poland. *Telephone:* 603-640-845 (office).

**OCHOTNIKOV, Nikolai;** Singer (Bass); b. 1948, Russia. *Career:* Principal with the Kirov Opera, St Petersburg; Season 1990–91, with Kutuzov in War and Peace for the BBC and in Seattle; Edinburgh Festival, 1991, as Dosifey in Khovanshchina; Sang Boris Godunov at Helsinki and the New York Metropolitan, 1992; Season 1995 as the King in Iolanta at Birmingham and the Prince in Rimsky's Invisible City of Kitezh with the Kirov at Edinburgh; Other roles include Verdi's King Philip and Glinka's Ivan Susannin. *Recordings:* Khovanshchina and War and Peace.

**O'CONNOR, Gerard;** Singer (Bass); b. Co Galway, Ireland. *Education:* University College, Cork; National Opera Studio, London. *Career:* Appearances in: Butterfly; Bohème; Figaro; Macbeth for Opera Ireland; Sparafucile in Rigoletto and Cieco in Mascagni's Iris at Holland Park; Il Barbiere di Siliglia by Paisiello, Wexford; Mamirov, Tchaikovsky Enchantress, Brighton; Chelsea Opera in Tannhäuser and Der Freischütz; Britten's Snug at Singapore; Season 1999: with Les Contes d'Hoffmann for Central Festival Opera; Rossini's Basilio for Castleward Opera; Varlaam in Boris Godunov for Opera Ireland; Company House Principal, English National Opera, 2001–; Boris in Lady Macbeth of Mtsensk, ENO and Dublin; Dikoy in Katya Kabanova for Opera Ireland; Croucher in the Silver Tassie, ENO and Dublin. *Honours:* Guiness Bursary, National Opera Studio, 1994–95. *Address:* Music International, 13 Ardilaun Road, London N5 2QR, England.

**OCTORS, Georges;** Conductor; b. 1940, Zaire, Africa. *Education:* Studied violin at first, then composition with Francis de Bourguignon at the Brussels Conservatory; Conducting studies with André Cluytens. *Career:* Founded and conducted the Antwerp Bach Society Chamber Orchestra; Assistant to Cluytens at the National Orchestra of Belgium, 1967; Music Director, 1975–83, Resident Conductor, 1983–86, Conductor and Musical Adviser of Gelders Orchestra in Arnhem, 1986–; Musical Director of the Chamber Orchestra of Wallonia, 1990; Guest appearances in Amsterdam, Leningrad, London with London Symphony Orchestra at the Barbican Hall in 1990, and elsewhere; Featured soloists have included Jessye Norman, Yehudi Menuhin, Igor Oistrakh, Uto Ughi, Paul Tortelier, Kyung Wha Chung and Vladimir Ashkenazy. *Honours:* Winner of various competitions as violinist.

**ODINIUS, Lother;** Singer (Tenor); b. 1970, Aachen, Germany. *Education:* Berlin Musikhockschule, 1991–95; Masterclasses with Bernd Weikl and Dietrich Fischer, Dieskau. *Career:* Debut: Schubertiade at Feldkirch, 1995 in the oratorio Lazarus; Mozart's Pedrillo, Bad Hersfeld Festival, 1995; Brunswick Staatstheater, 1996; Salzburg Festival, 1997; Mozarteum concerts; Further appearances at Stuttgart, Bonn, Vienna Volksoper; Lieder recitals at Paris, Cologne, Hamburg and Frankfurt; Concert tours with Philippe Herreweghe. *Recordings:* Lucio Vero in Jommelli's Il Vologeso.

**ODNOPOSOFF, Ricardo;** Violinist and Educator; b. 24 Feb. 1914, Buenos Aires, Argentina; m. (2) Irmtraut Baum, 20 Mar 1965. *Education:* MMus, High School Music, Berlin, 1932. *Career:* Violinist, playing in concerts throughout the world, 1932–; Teacher, University of Caracas, Venezuela, 1943–47; Taught summer courses Mozarteum, Salzburg, 1955–60; International Summer Academy, Nice, France, 1959–73; Professor, High School for Music, Vienna, 1956–, Professor Emeritus 1975–; Teacher, High School for Music, Stuttgart, Germany, 1964–94; Music High School, Zürich, 1975–84; mem, Freemason. *Honours:* Decorated Chevalier des Arts et Lettres, France; Chevalier de l'Ordre Rose Blanche, Finland; Comdr Order of Leopold II, Belgium; Grosses Verdienstkreuz des Verdienstordens, Germany; Mun Hwa Po Chang, South Korea; Medal for Merit, Argentina; Medal of Honor in Silver, City of Vienna, 1979; Ehrenkreuz für Wissenshaft und Kunst i Klasse, Austria; Medal of Merit in Gold, Government Baden-Wurttemberg, West Germany; Gold Ring of Honor by the Wiener Philharmoniker; Honour Member, Academie of Music, Stuttgart. *Address:* 27 Singerstrasse, 1010 Vienna, Austria.

**OEHRING, Helmut;** German composer and guitarist; b. 16 July 1961, Berlin. *Education:* masterclasses at Berlin Akademie der Künste. *Compositions include:* Coma 1 1991, Documentation 1 (chamber opera) 1993–96, Dokumentaroper (music theatre) 1994–95, Das D'Amato System (dance opera) 1996, Requiem 1998, Silence Moves It 1 and 2, 6ECHS, 7IEBEN and 8CHT, Dramma in Musica: Furcht und Begierde (for deaf soloists, soprano and ensemble) 2002. *Recordings include:* Dokumentaroper, Requiem. *Honours:* Deutschlandsender Kultur Hans Eisler prize 1990, WDR Cologne Young Composer's Award 1992, Orpheus Prize, Italy 1996, Hindemith Prize 1997, Schneider-Schott Music Prize 1998. *Address:* c/o Boosey & Hawkes, Komponisten Abteilung, Lützowufer 26, 10787 Berlin, Germany (office). *Website:* www.helmutoehring.de.

**OELZE, Christiane;** German singer (soprano); b. 9 Oct. 1963, Cologne; m. Bodo Primus; one d. *Career:* studied with Klesie Kelly-Moog and Erna Westenberger; won several Lieder competitions including Hugo-Wolf-Wettbewerb 1987, Hochschule Wettbewerb für Lied-Duo 1988; recital tours USA, S. America, Japan; has worked with many maj. int. conductors and has appeared on all important European concert stages and at int. festivals, including Salzburg Festival; began singing in opera 1990. *Roles include:* Despina (Ottawa), Pamina (Leipzig, Lyon, Hamburg, Munich), Konstanze (Salzburg, Zürich), Anne Trulove (Glyndebourne), Regina (in Mathis der Maler, Covent Garden), Zdenka (Covent Garden), Zerlina (Covent Garden), Ännchen (in Der Freischütz, Covent Garden), Mélisande (Glyndebourne), Servilia (in La Clemenza di Tito, Covent Garden), Susanna (Salzburg), Ilia (in Idomeneo, Glyndebourne), Igluno (Palestina, Covent Garden), Sophie (in

Rosenkavalier, Hamburg). *Recordings include:* several solo recitals, concert arias, Mass in C minor (Mozart), Christmas Oratorio, St John and St Matthew Passions, Webern songs and cantatas, Le Nozze di Figaro and many others. *Television:* Pelléas et Mélisande, Glyndebourne 1999. *Address:* c/o Artists Management HRA, Sebostiensplatz 3, 80331 Munich, Germany. *Telephone:* (89) 2602 4333 (office); (172) 6423344 (Mobile). *Fax:* (89) 2602 4344 (office). *E-mail:* AgenturHRA@aol.com (office).

**OERTEL, Christiane;** Singer (Mezzo-Soprano); b. 22 Dec. 1958, Potsdam, Germany. *Education:* Studied at the Leipzig Hochschule, 1975–82. *Career:* Member of the Komische Oper Berlin from 1988 as Cherubino, Olga, Dorabella and Carlotta in Die schweigsame Frau; Debuts at Covent Garden, Hamburg and in 1991 as Cherubino; Hamburg Cherubino; Japan visit with Covent Garden as Cherubino, 1992; Engagement Theater Erfurt, 1982–88; Debut as La Cenerentola, G Rossini, Komische Oper, 1994; Concert with Gewandhaus Leipzig under Kurt Masur; Season 2000–01 at the Komische Oper as Mozart's Annio and Meg Page in Falstaff; Siebel in Faust at the Landestheater, Salzburg; Many concert appearances. *Address:* c/o Komische Oper Berlin, Behrenstrasse 55–57, 10117 Berlin, Germany.

**OFENBAUER, Christian,** MA; Austrian organist and composer; b. 24 March 1961, Graz. *Education:* Klagenfurt Conservatory, Vienna Musikhochschule. *Career:* organist at Votivkirche, Vienna 1982–87; composer, TheaterAngelus-Novus 1982–87; mem. ensemble, Die Reihe 1983–92; freelance ed., Universal Edition 1985–; Visiting Prof. Vienna Musikhochschule 1991–92; Guest Prof. of Composition Univ. Mozarteum Salzburg 1994–97. *Compositions include:* Tod des Hektor 1987, Medea 1990–94, unordentliche inseln/de la motte fouqué-vertonung 1995, Streichquartettsatz 1997, fancies/fancy papers (violin concerto) 1997. *Address:* Burggasse 119/15, 1070 Vienna, Austria.

**OGAWA, Noriko;** pianist; b. 28 Jan. 1962, Kawasaki, Japan. *Education:* Tokyo Coll. of Music High School, Juilliard School, New York, studie piano with Benjamin Kaplan. *Career:* concerto soloist from 1976 playing works by Mendelssohn, Tchaikovsky, Liszt, Schumann and Chopin; New York recital debut in 1982, London Wigmore Hall debut in 1988 playing Schumann's Fantasy and Liszt's Sonata; recitals throughout England and Ireland, Germany, Spain, France, Scandinavia, USA; major appearances worldwide include the Harrogate Festival and the Tokyo and Yokohama Festivals; several recordings for the BBC, including Tchaikovsky B flat minor and Prokofiev No. 3 Concertos with Rozhdestvensky and the State Symphony Orchestra of the Russian Ministry of Culture; has appeared with Tokyo Symphony and Philharmonic, the Yomiuri Nippon Symphony Orchestra (with Jan Pascal Tortelier) and the Singapore Symphony; formed a duo with clarinettist, Michael Collins in 1988, performing at Wigmore Hall and various festivals; 1991 included performances with Philharmonia Orchestra at the Festival Hall, the Ulster Orchestra and Bournemouth Symphony; gave world premiere of a work by Lyn Davies at Lower Machen Festival and live BBC solo broadcast; duo with pianist Kathryn Stott 2001, gave premiere of double concerto 'Circuit' by Filkin with BBC Philharmonic, Piano 2003; adjudicated piano finals of BBC Young Musician 2000, 2002, 2004; appointed adviser for the new concert hall MUZA Kawasaki Symphony Hall 2004. *Recordings:* Czerny Etudes, Liszt, Prokofiev, Finzi Bagatelles, Rachmaninov Piano Concertos 2 and 3, Mussorgsky's Pictures at an Exhibition, Takemitsu complete solo piano works, Beethoven's Ninth (arranged by Wagner), Debussy complete solo piano works. *Honours:* second prize Int. Music Competition of Japan 1983, Gina Bachauer Memorial Scholarship, Juilliard 1984, third prize Leeds Int. Piano Competition 1987, Japanese Ministry of Educ. Art Prize 1999. *Current Management:* c/o Libby Sutton, Hazard Chase, 25 City Road, Cambridge, CB1 1DP, England. *Telephone:* (1223) 312400 (office). *Fax:* (1223) 460827 (office). *E-mail:* libby.sutton@hazardchase.co.uk. *Website:* www .hazardchase.co.uk (office).

**OGDON, Wilbur L.;** Composer and Professor of Music Theory, Literature and Composition; b. 19 April 1921, USA; m. Beverly Jean Porter 1958, 1 s., 2 d. *Education:* BM, University of Wisconsin, 1942; MA, Hamline University, St Paul, Minnesota, 1947; PhD, Indiana University, 1955; Further study, University of California, Berkeley, 1949–50, Ecole Normale de Musique, 1952–53; Studied composition with Ernst Krenek, Roger Sessions, Rene Leibowitz. *Career:* Professional positions and teaching: University of Texas, 1947–50; College of St Catherine, St Paul, 1956–57; Illinois Wesleyan University, 1957–65; Music Director, Pacifica Foundation, Berkeley, 1962–64; University of Illinois, 1965–66; University of California, San Diego, 1966–; Founding Chair, Music Department, 1966–71; Emeritus, UCSD, 1991–. *Compositions:* 3 Piano Pieces, 1950; Capriccio for Piano, 1952; Seven Piano Pieces, 1987; Voice: 3 Baritone Songs, 1950–56; Two Ketchwa Songs, 1955; Le Tombeau de Jean Cocteau, I, II and III, 1964, 1972, 1976; By the ISAR, 1969; Winter Images, 1981; Summer Images, 1985; The Awakening of Sappho (chamber opera), 1980; Chorus: Statements; 3 Sea Songs; Instrumental: 7 Pieces and a Capriccio for violin and piano, 1988–89; 6 Small Trios, trumpet, marimba, piano, 1980; 5 Preludes, violin, piano, 1982; 5 Preludes, violin, chamber orchestra, 1985; Capriccio and 5 Comments, symphony orchestra, 1979; Serenade No. 1 for Wind Quintet, 1987; Serenade No. 2 for Wind Quintet, 1990; Palindrome and Variations, string quartet, 1962; 3 Trifles, cello, piano, 1958; Two Sea Chanteys, soprano, baritone and two percussionists, 1988; Four Chamber Songs, soprano with viola, cello, flute, oboe and harp, 1989; Four Tonal Songs, 1988–90; A Modern Fable, 2 soprano, baritone with violin, cello, clarinet, bass clarinet and percussion; 13 Expressions, solo violin and six instruments, 1993;Variation Suite, for violin

and viola, 1995–96; Violin Suite, 1998; Three Moon Songs, for baritone and piano, 1998; Five Movements for string quartet, 1999. *Recordings:* The Music of Will Ogdon I, II. *Publications:* Series and Structure, 1955; Horizons Circled (with Ernst Krenek and John Stewart), 1974; How Tonality Functions in Webern's Opus 9, Extempore, 1990; On Webern's Op 27, II, in Journal of Music Theory; An Unpublished Treaties by Rene Leibowitz and How Tonality Functions in Schoenberg's op 11, No. 1, Journal of Schoenberg Institute. *Address:* 482 15th Street, Del Mar, CA 92014, USA.

**OGNIVTSEV, Alexander (Pavlovich);** Singer (Bass); b. 27 Aug. 1920, Petrovoskoy, Russia. *Education:* Studied at the Kishinev Conservatory. *Career:* Debut: Bolshoi Theatre, Moscow, 1949 as Dosifey in Khovanshchina; Has sung major roles in the Russian bass repertory such as Rimsky Korsakov's Ivan the Terrible and Tchaikovsky's Prince Gremin and Renée in Iolanta; Has also performed Philip II in Don Carlos, Mephistopheles, Don Basilio and the General in Prokofiev's The Gambler (also on the Bolshoi's visit to the Metropolitan in 1975); Sang in the premieres of Shaporin's The Decembrists in 1953 and Kholminov's An Optimistic Tragedy in 1967; Guest appearances in Italy at La Scala, Austria, France, Romania, Canada, Poland, India, Turkey, Hungary and Japan; Appeared in 1953 film version of the life of Shalyapin and sang Aleko in a film of Rachmaninov's opera. *Honours:* People's Artist of Russia, 1965.

**OGNOVENKO, Vladimir;** Singer (Bass); b. 1957, Russia. *Education:* Studied at the Urals Conservatory. *Career:* Sang at the Sverdlovsk Opera until 1984, then principal at the Kirov Opera, St Petersburg; Season 1991–92 as Bolkonsky in War and Peace at San Francisco, Boris Godunov at Helsinki and Varlaam in Boris Godunov at the New York Metropolitan (as guest with the Kirov); Palermo, 1993, in Rimsky's Sadko, San Francisco, 1995, as Farlaf in Ruslan and Lyudmila; Other roles in Lady Macbeth by Shostakovich, Ivan the Terrible by Rimsky, Prince Igor (as Galitsky) and Il Barbiere di Siviglia; Sang the Grand Inquisitor in Kirov Gala Concert, St Petersburg, 1998; Season 2000–01 in Shostakovich's Lady Macbeth at the Met, as Maljuta in The Tsar's Bride by Rimsky at San Francisco, Chub in Tchaikovsky's Cherevicihi at Cagliari and Galitzky in Price Igor for Houston Opera; Mussorgsky's Boris Godunov at the London Proms, 2002. *Recordings include:* Videos of Prince Igor and Sadko. *Address:* Kirov Opera, Mariinsky Theatre, 1 Theatre Square, St Petersburg, Russia.

**OHANESIAN, David;** Singer (Baritone); b. 6 Jan. 1927, Bucharest, Romania. *Education:* Studied in Budapest with Aurel Costescu-Duca and in Cluj with Dinu Badescu. *Career:* Debut: Cluj in 1950 in Pagliacci; Sang Tonio at Bucharest in 1952 and remained at the National Opera until 1977 as Verdi's Iago, Rigoletto, Amonasro and Luna, Eugene Onegin, Telramund, Scarpia, Escamillo and Rossini's Figaro, in Meyerbeer's Margherita d'Anjou and Tchaikovsky's Mazeppa; Noted as Enesco's Oedipe, which he sang in Bucharest and as guest abroad; Engagements in Hamburg, Moscow, Prague, Lyon, Paris, Barcelona, Budapest, Leningrad, Warsaw and Tel-Aviv. *Recordings include:* Oedipe and Cavalleria Rusticana. *Publications:* Passion of Music, with I Sava, Bucharest, 1986.

**OHANESSIAN, Beatrice,** LRAM; Iraqi pianist and composer; b. 1930, Baghdad. *Education:* Inst. of Fine Arts, Baghdad, RAM, London, Juilliard School of Music, NY. *Career:* prin. concert pianist with Iraqi Nat. Symphony Orchestra 1961–95; Head of Piano Dept, Inst. of Fine Arts, Baghdad 1961; teacher, Univ. of Minnesota, Macalester Coll., St Paul 1969–72; taught and performed in Geneva 1972–74; soloist, Minneapolis Symphony Orchestra; resident in USA 1996–. *Compositions:* Fantasy on Iraqi There, Hamurabi Overture, Spring Ballade, Variations on an Armenian Folk Tune, The Door. *Honours:* Frederick Westlake memorial prize, Fulbright scholarship. *Address:* c/o Minnesota Orchestra, Orchestra Hall, 1111 Nicollet Mall, Minneapolis, MN 55403, USA.

**OHLSSON, Garrick;** American pianist; b. 3 April 1948, White Plains, NY. *Education:* Westchester Conservatory, Juilliard School with Sascha Gorodnitsky, studied with Olga Barabini and Rhosa Lhevinne. *Career:* appears regularly with major orchestras, including New York Philharmonic, Chicago Symphony, Boston Symphony, Philadelphia Orchestra, Los Angeles Philharmonic and with orchestras in recital series throughout the world. *Recordings include:* Complete Solo Works of Chopin and numerous other recordings. *Honours:* prizewinner at Busoni Piano Competition, Italy 1966, Chopin Int. Piano Competition, Warsaw 1970, Montreal Int. Piano Competition 1970. *Current Management:* ICM Artists Ltd, 8942 Wilshire blvd, Beverly Hills, CA 90211, USA. *Telephone:* (310) 550-4477 (office). *Fax:* (310) 550-4460 (office).

**O'HORA, Ronan,** FRNCM, FGSM; British pianist; *Head of Keyboard Studies, Guildhall School of Music and Drama;* b. 9 Jan. 1964, Manchester; m. Hannah Alice Bell 1991. *Education:* Royal Northern Coll. of Music. *Career:* recitals and concerts in the United Kingdom, USA, Australia, New Zealand, Germany, France, Italy, Austria, Switzerland, Spain, Denmark, Norway, Sweden, Belgium, Netherlands, Portugal, Ireland, Yugoslavia and Czechoslovakia; concerts with Philharmonia, Royal Philharmonic, BBC Symphony, Hallé, Bournemouth Symphony, Royal Liverpool Philharmonic, BBC Philharmonic, BBC Scottish, Zürich Tonhalle Orchestra, Netherlands Radio Symphony and Chamber Orchestras, Philharmonia Hungaria, Indianapolis Symphony, and Florida Philharmonic; Sr Tutor, Royal Northern Coll. of Music; Head of Keyboard Studies, Guildhall School of Music and Drama 1999–. *Recordings:* Concertos by Tchaikovsky, Grieg and Mozart with the Royal Philharmonic Orchestra; Britten complete music for two pianos with

Stephen Hough; Numerous radio recordings in the United Kingdom, USA, France, Netherlands, Poland, Czechoslovakia, Portugal and Ireland. *Recordings:* more than 30 recordings including music of Chopin, Schubert, Brahms and Beethoven. *Honours:* Freeman of The City of London 2000; Silver Medal, Worshipful Company of Musicians 1984, Dayas Gold Medal 1985, Stefania Niedrasz Prize 1985. *Address:* 183 Honor Oak Road, Forest Hill, London, SE23 3RP, England (home). *E-mail:* ronanohora@tiscali.co.uk (home).

**ÖHRN, Per-Erik,** BA; Swedish artistic director, opera singer, translator and librettist; *Artistic Director, Drottningholms Slottsteater;* b. 18 Oct. 1946, Malmö. *Education:* Opera Acad. Göteborg, Univ. of Göteborg. *Career:* opera singer 1972–82; Stage Dir 1973–; Artistic Dir, NorrlandsOperan, Umeå, Sweden 1988–96, Drottningholms Slottsteater 1996–; Sr Prof., Opera Acad., Göteborg, Univ. 2004–. *Address:* Drottningholms Slottsteater, Box 15417, Stockholm, 10765, Sweden (office). *Telephone:* (08) 55693100 (office). *Fax:* (08) 55693101 (office). *E-mail:* dst@dtm.se (office). *Website:* www.dtm.se (office).

**OHYAMA, Heiichiro;** Violinist, Violist and Conductor; b. 31 July 1947, Kyoto, Japan; m. Gail J Ohyama, 1 s. *Education:* Toho Music High School; Toho College of Music; Guildhall School of Music and Drama; AGSM, Indiana University, USA. *Career:* Debut: New York City, USA; Professor of Music at University of California, Santa Barbara; Assistant Conductor and Principal Violist with Los Angeles Philharmonic; Music Director, Santa Barbara Chamber Orchestra and Crossroads Chamber Ensemble; Music Director and Artistic Director with La Jolla Chamber Music Festival; mem, Musicians Union, England. *Recordings:* Various. *Contributions:* Marlboro Music Festivals; Santa Fe Chamber Music festivals; Round Top Music Festivals. *Honours:* Carl Flesch International Competition, 1968; Indiana University, 1971; Winner, Young Concert Artist, 1975. *Address:* c/o Konsertbolaget AB, Vasagatan 52, 5–11120, Stockholm, Sweden.

**OISTRAKH, Igor Davidovich,** FRCM; Russian violinist; b. 27 April 1931, Odessa; s. of late David Oistrakh; m. Natalia Zertsalova 1960; one s. *Education:* State Conservatoire, Moscow. *Career:* many foreign tours, several concerts with father David Oistrakh; appears with maj. orchestras throughout the world as soloist and conductor; Prof. Brussels Conservatoire; teaches int. master classes; Pres. Russian br. of ESTA, César Franck Foundation; Hon. mem. Beethoven Soc., Bonn, E Ysaÿe Soc., Brussels, H. Wieniawski Soc., Poznań, J. Heifetz Soc., California; winner of numerous competitions; over 100 recordings. *Honours:* numerous awards. *Address:* c/o Conservatoire Royal de Musique, 30 rue de la Régence, Brussels, Belgium (office).

**OKADA, Yoshiko;** Pianist; b. 5 Oct. 1961, Japan; m. Grzegorz Cimoszko, 1 s. *Education:* Ecole Normale de Musique, Paris, 1976–80; Studied in Paris with Yvonne Loriod, 1980–82, in London with Maria Curcio and in Switzerland with Nikita Magaloff. *Career:* Debut: Carnegie Hall, New York in 1991; Touring in recital and as soloist with orchestras throughout USA, Canada, Poland, Denmark, Belgium, Switzerland and France. *Recordings:* Japan: CDs of Mozart Sonatas and Concertos with Warsaw Chamber Orchestra. *Current Management:* Albert Kay Associates Inc. *Address:* Albert Kay Associates Inc, Concert Artists Management, 58 West 58th Street, New York, NY 10019-2510, USA.

**OKE, Alan;** Singer (Tenor); b. 1954, London, England. *Education:* Studied at Royal Academy of Music, Glasgow and in Munich with Hans Hotter. *Career:* Sang first in concert and in oratorios; Stage debut with Scottish Opera; Roles include: Papageno in Die Zauberflöte, Schaunard in La Bohème, and Olivier in Capriccio; Sang in Cavalli's L'Egisto in Frankfurt, Venice and Schwetzingen, 1983; Covent Garden, 1984 in Taverner by Maxwell Davies; Took part in British premiere of Weill's Street Scene, Glasgow, 1989; Guest appearances with English National Opera and Opera North; Sang Malatesta, in Don Pasquale, Stratford-Upon-Avon, 1990; Sang Macheath in The Threepenny Opera, Leeds, 1990; Season 1992 with Pluto in Orpheus in the Underworld, for Opera North; Tenor roles include Alfredo in La Traviata for Opera North; Gaston in La Traviata for GTO at Glyndebourne, 1996; Season 1998 as Ravel's Gonsalve and Puccini's Rinuccio at Auckland, Shuisky for New Sussex Opera, and in Caterina Cornaro at the Queen Elizabeth Hall, London; Season 2000 as Boris in Katya Kabanova for Opera North and Pinkerton for Castleward Opera. *Recordings include:* Giuseppe in The Gondoliers. *Current Management:* Musichall. *Address:* Vicarage Way, Ringmer, West Sussex BN8 5 LA, England.

**OKERLUND, David;** Singer (Baritone); b. 1965, Kearney, Nebraska, USA. *Education:* Merola Opera Program, San Francisco. *Career:* Appearances with San Francisco Opera as Don Giovanni, the Herald in Lohengrin, Eugene Onegin and Mozart's Count; Puccini's Sharpless in Tokyo and Guglielmo for Opera Carolina; Season 1998–99 as Stanley in the San Francisco premiere of A Streetcar Named Desire, and Gunther in Götterdämmerung; Germont in La Traviata for Vancouver Opera; Concerts include Carmina Burana, Die Schöpfung by Haydn and the Brahms Requiem. *Honours:* Adler Fellow, 1995. *Address:* Harlequin Agency Ltd, 203 Fidlas Road, Cardiff CF4 5NA, Wales.

**OLAFIMIHAN, Tinuke;** singer (soprano); b. 1961, London, England. *Education:* Colchester Institute, Morley College, National Opera Studio, London, studied with Elisabeth Schwarzkopf. *Career:* debut as Despina at the Queen Elizabeth Hall in 1989 with the National Opera Studio; Has sung Zerlina in Don Giovanni at the Snape Maltings, Messiah with The Sixteen under Harry Christophers and appearances with the Vivaldi Concertante at

St John's Smith Square and in the St John Passion at Belfast; Sang Susanna in a production of Figaro by Colin Graham and Barbarina for Opera Northern Ireland and in Aix-en-Provence; Sang Carmina Burana at the Queen Elizabeth Hall in 1990 and Clara in the Covent Garden premiere of Porgy and Bess in 1992. *Honours:* Peter Stuyvesant Foundation Scholarship; Walter Legge/Elisabeth Schwarzkopf Society Award; Finalist, 1988 Richard Tauber Competition. *Current Management:* Stafford Law, Candleway, Broad Street, Sutton Valence, Kent ME17 3AT, England. *Website:* www.stafford-law.com.

**OLAFSSON, Kjartan;** Composer; b. 18 Nov. 1958, Reykjavík, Iceland; 2 d. *Education:* BM, Reykjavic College of Music, 1984; Institute in Sonology, Netherlands, 1984–86; Licentiate of Music, PhD, Sibelius Academy, 1995. *Career:* Debut: Reykjavík, 1985; mem, Society of Composers in Iceland. *Compositions:* Reflex for Orchestra, 1988; Bribraut for Clarinet Trio, 1993; Summary for tape, 1994; Utstrok for Orchestra, 1995. *Recordings:* Reflex for Orchestra; Utstrok for Orchestra; Bribraut for Clarinet Trio; Dimma for Viola and Piano; Summary for Tape; Dark Days for electronics and live performance. *Publications:* Calmus Theory Books, 1, 2, 3, 4. *Contributions:* CALMUS (Calculated Music). *Honours:* Prize, Competition for Young Composers; Grants, Ministries of Iceland and Finland. *Address:* c/o STEF, Laufasvegi 40, 101 Reykjavík, Iceland.

**OLAH, Tiberiu;** Composer; b. 2 Jan. 1928, Arpasel, Transylvania, Romania; m. Yvonne Olah, 28 Mar 1959. *Education:* Academia de Musica, Cluj, 1946–49; Tchaikovsky Conservatory, Moscow, 1949–54; Composition Diploma, magna cum laude. *Career:* Debut: Trio, Cluj, 1955; Performance of Cantata for Female Choir and Ensemble at Prague in 1962, Warsaw and Budapest in 1963, Warsaw in 1966, West Berlin STB Orchestra in 1967, Darmstadter Ferienkurse in 1968; Performance of Columna by Infinita Orchestra; World's first performance and commissioned works: West Berlin, 1971, Perspectives, Paris, 1971, Ed Salabert's ORTF Orchestra, Translations for 16 Strings, New York Lincoln Center, Washington Kennedy Center, 1974; Time Of Memory to the memory of N and S Koussevitsky, Berlin Festwochen, 1988; Concerto Delle Coppie; Bucharest: The International Week of New Music, 1991; Obelisque For Wolfgang Amadeus for Saxophone and Orchestra, Karlsruhe, Germany, 1992; Concertante commissioned by Land Baden, Wurttemberg. *Recordings:* Numerous. *Publications:* Editor: Muzicale, Bucharest, Salabert, Paris, Schott, Germany, Muzyka, Moscow. *Address:* c/o GEMA, Rosenheimer Str. 11, 81667 Munich, Germany.

**OLANO, Miguel;** Singer (Tenor); b. 1962, Cenicero, La Rioja, Spain. *Education:* Madrid Conservatory; Florence, with Gino Bechi and at Siena with Carlo Bergonzi. *Career:* Debut: Wels, Austria, 1991, as Rodolfo; Appearances as Puccini's Edgar at Torre del Lago and as Cavaradossi at Vercelli, Bregenz and Salzburg; Season 1995 with Don Carlos at the Paris Châtelet; Further engagements as Puccini's Des Grieux at Livorno and Pisa, Manrico, Pollione (Norma) and Don Carlos at the Amsterdam Concertgebouw; Other roles include Andrea Chénier, Turiddu and Calaf in Turandot; Sang Don Juan in Margarita la Tornera by R. Chapi, opposite Placido Domingo, at Madrid (2000); US debut Washington Opera 2000, as Cavaradossi; Season 2000–01 as Don Carlos and Calaf at Washington; Des Grieux at L'Opéra de Genève. *Address:* c/o Musicaglotz, 11, Rue le Verrier, 75006 Paris, France.

**OLCZAK, Krzysztof Robert;** Polish composer and accordionist; b. 26 May 1956, Łódź; m. 1980; one s. one d. *Education:* Fr Chopin Academy of Music, Warsaw, Academy of Music, Gdansk. *Career:* solo and chamber concerts in Poland from 1978; Played with National Philharmonic, 1985, 1986 and Bialystok, Gdansk, Koszalin, Łódź, Opole, Poznan, Wroclaw, Austria, Finland, Germany, Italy, Norway, Sweden and Russian Philharmonic Orchestras; Appearances at contemporary music festivals include Styrian Autumn, Austria, Warsaw Autumn, Poznan Spring, Gdansk Encounters of Young Composers; Conservatorium Legnica, 1987, 1991, Musik Biennale, Berlin in 1987, Musica Polonica Nova, Wroclaw in 1988, and Internationale Studienwoche, Bonn in 1991; Tour of Scandinavia with American Waterways Wind Orchestra in 1990; Lecturer at Gdansk Academy of Music. *Compositions include:* Accordion Solos: Manualiter, 1977, Phantasmagorien, 1978, Winter Suite, 1980, Fine Pluie, 1980, Berceuse, 1984, Rondino, 1985, Pozymk for 4 performers, 1982, Sea Spaces for Soprano and Prepared Piano, 1982, Cantata for Soprano, 2 Accordions, 1984, Sinfonietta Concertante for Percussion and Orchestra, 1985–86, Belt The Bellow for Tuba and Accordion, 1986, Trio, Homage to Karol Szymanowski, 1987, Intervals for Organ and 2 Accordions, 1987, Concerto for Accordion and Orchestra, 1989, Concerto Grosso for Wind Orchestra, 1990. *Address:* 11 Listopada 79, 80-180 Gdańsk, Poland.

**OLDFIELD, Mark;** singer (baritone); b. 1957, Sheffield, England. *Education:* School of Music, Colchester with Rae Woodland, Royal College of Music; further study with Kenneth Woollam. *Career:* operatic work has included Metcalf's Tornrak at Banff Centre in Canada, and Papageno for London Opera Players; London International Opera Festival in 1989 in The Fisherman by Paul Max Edlin; Sang Purcell's Aeneas and Eugene Onegin at the Royal College of Music; Concert repertoire includes the Brahms Requiem, Snape Maltings, Bach's Magnificat, Las Palmas, and Cantata No. 11, Handel's Chandos Anthems with the English Chamber Orchestra under Charles Mackerras, Vaughan Williams's Five Mystical Songs, Carmina Burana, Monteverdi Madrigals and the Brahms Liebeslieder in Northern Italy; Sang Mercurio in Cavalli's La Calisto in Provence; Eiriksdottir's I Have Seen Someone, at the Riverside Studios, London, 1996. *Current Management:* Robert Gilder & Co., Enterprise House, 59–65 Upper Ground, London, SE1

9PQ, England. *Telephone:* (20) 7928-9008. *Fax:* (20) 7928-9755. *E-mail:* rgilder@robert-gilder.com.

**O'LEARY, Thomas;** Singer (Bass); b. 3 Sept. 1924, Punxsutawney, Pennsylvania, USA. *Education:* Studied with Alexander Kipnis in New York. *Career:* Debut: San Jose in 1947 as Kecal in The Bartered Bride; Sang at Nuremberg, 1960–65, Vienna Volksoper, 1962–75 with further engagements at Munich, Hamburg, Rome, Bologna, Berlin, Barcelona, Zürich, Marseilles and Frankfurt; Appearances at Boston, Baltimore and New Orleans from 1967, Chicago in 1977, and San Francisco, Houston and San Diego; Other roles have included Sarastro, Rocco, King Philip, Zaccaria, Mephistopheles, Arkel, Boris and Pimen in Boris Godunov, Wagner's Mark, Daland, Pogner, Hunding, Hagen and Gurnemanz; Frequent concert performances. *Address:* c/o Volksoper, Wahringerstrasse 78, 1090 Vienna, Austria.

**OLEDZKI, Bogdan;** Conductor; b. 25 June 1949, Stupsk, Poland; m. Ewa Gtowacka, 12 Aug 1981. *Education:* Warsaw Music Academy, 1974. *Career:* Debut: National Philharmonic Orchestra, Warsaw in 1974; Conductor in Warsaw, Radom and Poznan, 1974–82; Principal Conductor for Rzeszow Philharmonic Orchestra, 1982–84; Conductor for Great Opera, Warsaw, 1984–; Guest Conductor with Philharmonic Orchestra, Poland and Salzburg-Aspecte, Edinburgh and Skopje Festivals. *Current Management:* Polish Artistic Agency (PAGART), Warsaw, Poland. *Address:* Bandrowskiego 8m 60, 01-496 Warsaw, Poland.

**OLEFSKY, Paul;** Cellist and Professor; b. 4 Jan. 1926, Chicago, Illinois, USA. *Education:* Studied at Curtis Institute with Gregor Piatigorsky, 1943–47, with Pablo Casals and with Karajan and Monteux (conducting). *Career:* Former First Cellist of Philadelphia Orchestra and Detroit Symphony Orchestra; Concert soloist with leading orchestras in USA and abroad; Recitalist in North America and Europe with solo works by Kodály and Bach and the premieres of works by Milhaud, Tcherepnin, Virgil Thomson and Shapleigh; Professor of Cello and Chamber Music at University of Texas, Austin, 1974–; Concert cellist; Conductor; University Professor; President, Amatius Classics Productions; President, Amatius Classics Foundation; mem, Littlefield Society, University of Texas at Austin. *Recordings:* Complete Beethoven Sonatas; Complete Brahms Trios; Tchaikovsky and Arensky Trios; 4 Vivaldi and Boccherini Concertos with English Chamber Orchestra; Complete Bach Suites and Chaconne; Complete Kodály, Op 4, 7, 8; Shapleigh Sonatas and Quartet; Bartók Concerto; Romanian Dances; Duos; Virgil Thomson Concerto, Ormandy and Philadelphia Orchestras. *Honours:* Naumberg Award, 1948; Michaels Memorial Award of the Young Concert Artists, 1953. *Current Management:* Amatius Classics Foundation. *Address:* 7603 Yaupon Drive, Austin, TX 78759, USA.

**OLEG, Raphaël;** French violinist; b. 8 Sept. 1959, Paris. *Education:* Paris Conservatoire. *Career:* international reputation as recitalist and with Europe's major symphony orchestras; Lucerne Festival in 1986 with the Czech Philharmonic and Vaclav Neumann; First Prize in Tchaikovsky International Competition in 1986; British debut in 1987 playing the Brahms Concerto with the London Symphony Orchestra under Jeffrey Tate; 1987 tour of European Festivals with the Orchestre National de France and Lorin Maazel; Engagements with the Concertgebouw under Chailly, Orchestre de Paris under Bychov, the Philadelphia Orchestra under Maazel and the Munich Staatsorchester under Sawallisch; British appearances with the Philharmonia, English Chamber Orchestra, Northern Sinfonia, Scottish Chamber Orchestra and City of London Sinfonia; Japanese debut in 1989 at Suntory Hall; Engagements in 1989–90 season included a tour of Italy with ECO and Tate, and a tour of France and Switzerland with the Academy of St Martin-in-the-Fields and Marriner; Gave recitals at Prague Spring Festival and Paris, concerts with the Orchestre National de France, and Polish Chamber Orchestra; 1990–91 toured Germany with Chamber Orchestra of Europe and Berglund, and Japan with the Nouvel Orchestre Philharmonique. *Current Management:* Van Walsum Management Ltd, 4 Addison Bridge Place, London, W14 8XP, England. *Telephone:* (20) 7371-4343. *Fax:* (20) 7371-4344. *Website:* www.vanwalsum.co.uk.

**OLEJNICEK, Jiri;** Singer (Tenor); b. 11 Feb. 1937, Brno, Czechoslovakia. *Education:* Studied at the Brno Conservatory from 1954. *Career:* Sang at Opava Opera from 1962, and Janáček Opera in Brno from 1964; Roles have included Tamino, Alvaro, Rodolfo, the Prince in Rusalka, Stahlav in Smetana's Libuše and Dmitri in Boris Godunov; Guest appearances in Florence in 1967 and Barcelona as Lensky in 1976; Frequent concert engagements. *Address:* c/o Janáček Opera, Dvořákova 11, 657-70 Brno, Czech Republic.

**OLESCH, Peter (Otto);** Singer (Bass-Baritone); b. 10 Sept. 1938, Andreashutte, Oberschlesien, Germany. *Education:* Studied in Dresden with Rudolf Bockelmann. *Career:* Debut: Berlin Staatsoper in 1963 as a Flemish Deputy in Don Carlos; Sang at the Berlin Staatsoper until 1982 in such roles as Masetto, Monterone, Bartolo, Pistol, Falstaff, Alberich, Alfio in Cavalleria Rusticana, Vaarlam and Rangier in Penderecki's The Devils of Loudun; Sang at Leipzig Opera in 1989 as Don Pasquale; Many concert performances. *Recordings:* Puntila by Dessau. *Address:* c/o St ädtische Theater, 7010 Leipzig, Germany.

**OLIVEIRA, Elmar;** Violinist; b. 28 June 1950, Waterbury, Connectuicut, USA. *Education:* Hart College of Music, Hartford, CT; Manhattan School of Music. *Career:* Appearances with orchestras including New York Philharmonic, Cleveland, Baltimore, Chicago Symphony, Dallas, Montreal and Moscow

Philharmonic. *Recordings include:* Sonata by Husa. *Honours:* First Prize, Naumburg Competition, 1975; Gold Medal, Tchaikovsky International Competition, 1978.

**OLIVER, Alexander;** Singer (tenor); b. 27 June 1944, Scotland. *Education:* Royal Scottish Acad.; further studies in Vienna and with Rupert Bruce-Lockhart. *Career:* Netherlands Opera from 1971 in The Love For Three Oranges, Intermezzo, Peter Grimes, L'Ormindo and The Turn of the Screw; Scottish Opera in A Midsummer Night's Dream, Wozzeck, The Bartered Bride, Eugene Onegin and Mahagonny; Opera North as Nemorino in L'Elisir d'amore; Glyndebourne Opera in Il Ritorno d'Ulisse, Ariadne auf Naxos and Albert Herring in 1985; Covent Garden in Eugene Onegin, Le nozze di Figaro, Andrea Chénier, Manon and Albert Herring, 1989; Zürich Opera from 1978 in L'Incoronazione di Poppea and Les Contes d'Hoffmann; Brussels Opera in 1982 as Arbace in Idomeneo, returning for the world premiere of Le Passion de Gilles by Boesmans; Antwerp Opera and Canadian Opera debuts in 1983 in Death in Venice and Poppea; La Fenice Venice in Curlew River, La Scala Milan in the premiere of Riccardo III by Flavio Testi and sang Mime in a new production of Siegfried at Covent Garden in 1990; sang Shapkin in From the House of the Dead at Brussels in 1990, and at Salzburg in 1991 in Le nozze di Figaro; sang Schmidt in Werther for Netherlands Opera, 1996; concert engagements with the Concertgebouw Orchestra in the St John and St Matthew Passions of Bach and Stravinsky's Pulcinella; Houston Symphony and Chicago Symphony and frequent appearances with the Songmakers' Almanac. *Recordings include:* Videos of Gilbert and Sullivan's The Sorcerer and Pirates of Penzance.

**OLIVER, John (Edward);** Composer; b. 21 Sept. 1959, Vancouver, Canada. *Education:* MMus, 1984, D.Mus, 1992, Composition, McGill University, Montreal; BMus Composition, University of British Columbia; Studies: Composition, Guitar, Piano, Voice, San Francisco Conservatory of Music, 1977–79. *Career:* Works performed by: New Music Concerto, Toronto 1982, 87, Vancouver New Music, 1982, 1990, Societé de Musique Contemporaine de Quebec, 1989, Canadian Opera Company, 1991; Composer-in-Residence, Banff Centre, Leighton Artist Colony, 1989, 1990 and Music Department, 1990, 1991, Canadian Opera Company, 1989, 1991, Vancouver Opera, 1992–; mem, Society of Composers, Authors and Music Publishers of Canada; American Federation of Musicians; Canadian Electro-acoustic Community. *Compositions:* Gugcamayo's Old Song and Dance, Canadian Opera Company, 1991; El Reposo del Fuego, 1987; Aller Retour, 1988; Marimba Dismembered, 1990; Before the Freeze, 1984. *Recordings:* El Reposo del Fuego; Marimba Dismembered; Before the Freeze. *Publications:* New Music in British Columbia in Soundnotes, Fall, 1992. *Honours:* Canada Council Arts Awards, 1984–87, 1991; 8th CBC National Radio Competition for Young Composers, 1988; Two prizes, 1989 PROCAN Young Composers Competition.

**OLIVER, Lisi;** American stage director and translator; b. 13 Dec. 1951, Frankfurt am Main, Germany. *Education:* BA, Smith College, 1973; ALM Harvard University, 1988; PhD in Linguistics, Harvard University, 1995. *Career:* Stage Manager, Bolshoi Opera US Tour, 1974; Inaugural Gala for President Carter, 1978; Production Stage Manager, Assistant Director, Opera Company of Boston, 1975–78; Assistant Director, Komische Oper Berlin, 1979–80; Director, Opera Company of Boston, Opera New England, Skylight Comic Opera, Des Moines Metro Opera, Atlanta Opera, Baldwin-Wallace Conservatory, Opera Company of the Philippines, Massachusetts Institute of Technology, Wolftrap Farm Park, City of Boston First Night, 1980–90; Director of Opera Studio, New England Conservatory, 1988–90; First projected titles at Bolshoi Opera, 1991; Director, Atlanta Opera Studio, 1989–95; Title Supervisor, Atlanta Opera, Director of Raymond Street Translations, Translation and Titles Rental Company; Professor of Mediaeval Studies and Linguistics, Louisiana State University. *Publications:* Translations of Surtitles used by many American Companies; The Beginnings of English Law, University of Toronto Press, 2002. *Honours:* Yvonne Burger Award, Smith College, 1973; Merit Award, Komische Oper, 1980; National Opera Institute Grant, 1978–80; Whiting Fellowship, Harvard University, 1994–95; Outstanding Graduate Faculty in English, LSU, 1997; Phi Beta Phi Award, LSU, 1998; BP Amoco Award for outstanding undergraduate teaching, 2001. *Address:* 2021 Cedardale Avenue, Baton Rouge, LA 70808, USA. *E-mail:* lolive1@lsu.edu (office).

**OLIVERO, Magda;** Italian singer (soprano); b. 25 March 1910, Saluzzo, Turin. *Education:* studied in Turin with Luigi Gerussi, Luigi Ricci and Ghedini. *Career:* debut, Turin 1933, as Lauretta in Gianni Schicchi; La Scala 1933, in Nabucco; sang widely in Italy as Adriana Lecouvreur, Puccini's Liu, Suor Angelica and Minnie, Violetta, Zerlina, Poppea and Sophie in Der Rosenkavalier; retired in 1941 but returned to stage in 1951 to sing Adriana at the composer's request; sang at Stoll Theatre in London as Mimi 1952, with further appearances in Edinburgh, Paris, Brussels, Amsterdam and Buenos Aires; other roles included Fedora, Mascagni's Iris, Zandonai's Francesca, Puccini's Giorgetta and Tosca and parts in operas by Poulenc and Menotti; US debut at Dallas 1967 as Médée, Metropolitan Opera 1975 as Tosca. *Recordings:* Turandot, Fedora, Francesca da Rimini, La Fanciulla del West, Il Tabarro, Risurrezione by Alfano, Médée, Madama Butterfly.

**OLIVEROS, Pauline;** Composer and Performer; b. 30 May 1932, Houston, Texas, USA. *Education:* BA, San Francisco State College, 1957. *Career:* Director, San Francisco Tape Music Center, 1966, Expo '67 Montreal, Canada, 1967, and Expo '70 Osaka, Japan, 1970; Professor of Music, University of

California, San Diego, 1970; Summer Olympics, Los Angeles, 1984; Works performed and solo performances world-wide and with numerous orchestras. *Compositions:* Roots For The Moment; Tara's Room; The Well And The Gentle; Tashi Gomang; Rose Moon; Sonic Meditations; Horse Sings From Cloud; Rattlesnake Mountain; Lullaby For Daisy Pauline; Spiral Madala; Bonn Feier; Double Basses At 20 Paces; 3 Songs for Soprano and Piano; To Valerie Solanas and Marilyn Monroe; Jar Piece; Sound Patterns; Njinga the Queen King, music theatre, 1993; From Unknown Silences for ensemble, 1996; Cicada Song, for accordion, 1996; Beyond the Mysterious Silence for low voice and ensemble, 1996. *Recordings:* The Well And The Gentle; The Wanderer; Accordion And Voice; Vor Der Flüt. *Publications:* Software for People, 1984. *Contributions:* Numerous. *Address:* c/o ASCAP, ASCAP Building, 1 Lincoln Plaza, New York, NY 10023, USA.

**OLLESON, (Donald) Edward,** BA, MA, DPhil; academic and writer on music; *University Lecturer in Music, University of Oxford;* b. 11 April 1937, South Shields, England; m. Eileen Gotto; two s. one d. *Education:* Hertford College, Oxford. *Career:* Assistant Lecturer, Univ. of Hull 1962–63; Research Lecturer, Christ Church, Oxford 1963–66; Faculty Lecturer, Univ. of Oxford 1966–72; Fellow, Merton Coll. 1970–; University Lecturer in Music, 1972–. *Publications:* Editor, Proceedings of The Royal Musical Association, vols 94–100; Essays, with Nigel Fortune and FW Sternfeld, on Opera and English Music in honour of Sir Jack Westrup, 1975; Participation in Everyman Dictionary of Music, 5th edition, 1975; Modern Musical Scholarship, 1978; Co-editor, Music and Letters, 1976–86. *Address:* Faculty of Music, St Aldate's, Oxford OX1 1DB, England.

**OLLI, Kalevi;** Singer (Bass-Baritone); b. 1951, Finland. *Education:* Studied at the Sibelius Academy in Helsinki, including Composition with Eino-Johani Rautavaan, 1971–78. *Career:* Sang Silvano in Un Ballo in Maschera at Helsinki in 1977 and sang at the Frankfurt Opera, 1978–84; Appearances at the Savonlinna Festival as the Dutchman and concert engagements, including Lieder recitals, in Germany, Switzerland and elsewhere; mem, Finnish Composers; Finnish Drama Authors. *Recordings:* Complete songs by Rachmaninov; Schumann's Dichterliebe with Toiva Kuula, and Schwanengesang with Ulrich Koneftke. *Honours:* Prizewinner in competitions at Savonlinna, Lappeenranta and Geneva, 1977–81; Sang in Boris Godunov at Royal Opera Stockholm Warlaan, 1997, and at Deutsche Oper Berlin Alberich in Rheingold; Sang whole Ring Cycle in Helsinki, 1996–99; Season 1998 as Alberich in Siegfried at Helsinki; Sang in Sapporo, Japan with Tan Dum and Orchestra Theatre II, 1999. *Address:* c/o Finnish National Opera, PO Box 176, Helsingkatu 58, 00251 Helsinki, Finland.

**OLLMANN, Kurt;** Singer (Baritone); b. 19 Jan. 1957, Racine, Wisconsin, USA. *Education:* Studied with Gerard Souzay, among others. *Career:* Sang with the Milwaukee Skylight Opera, 1979–82; Engagements in Santa Fe, Washington DC, Milan and Brussels in operas by Debussy and Mozart; Pepsico Summerfare New York in 1987 as Don Giovanni, in the Peter Sellars version of Mozart's opera; Sang under Bernstein in the Viennese premiere of A Quiet Place in 1986 and as Maximilian in a concert performance of Candide at the Barbican in London, 1989; Seattle Opera in 1988 as Mercutio in Gounod's Roméo et Juliette; St Louis Opera, 1989–90, as Purcell's King Arthur and Mozart's Count; Many concert appearances; Season 1992 in On The Town at the Barbican Hall and the title role in the US premiere of Bose's The Sorrows of Young Werther at Santa Fe; Season 1999–2000 for Seattle Opera as the Speaker in Die Zauberflöte and Frédéric in Lakmé. *Recordings:* Count Paris in Roméo et Juliette, conducted by Michel Plasson; Candide and West Side Story conducted by the composer; Mercutio in Roméo et Juliette, under Leonard Slatkin, 1996. *Address:* Opera Theater of St Louis, PO Box 13148, St Louis, MO 63119, USA.

**OLMI, Paolo;** Conductor; b. 1953, Italy. *Education:* Studied with Massimo Pradella and Franco Ferrara in Rome. *Career:* Frequent appearances with major orchestras in Italy and abroad from 1979; Opera debut at Teatro Communale di Bologna, 1986; Conducted Rossini's Mosè in Egitto at Rome 1988, later at the Bayerische Staatsoper, Munich; Deutsche Oper am Rhein, Düsseldorf, with Traviata, Théâtre des Champs Elysées with Rossini's Guillaume Tell; British debut 1991, with Royal Philharmonic in a concert performance of Nabucco; Bellini's Zaira at Catania, 1990; Concerts at the Schleswig-Holstein Festival, the Philharmonic Berlin, the Frankfurt Alte Oper and the Philharmonie in Munich; English Chamber Orchestra with Rostropovich as soloist; Appointed Principal Conductor of the RAI Rome 1991; Deutsche Oper Berlin 1992 with La Forza del Destino, tour of Italy with the Royal Philharmonic 1993, Verdi Requiem at the Festival Hall 1994; Conducted Mosè at Covent Garden 1994; Madama Butterfly at Copenhagen, 1996; Season 1998 with L'Elisir d'amore at Madrid; Toured Italy with Royal Philharmonic Orchestra, London Philharmonic Orchestra and BBC Symphony Orchestra, 1998–2001; Verdi Requiem with the London Philharmonic Orchestra at the Festival Hall, 2001, Rigoletto in Rotterdam; Ballo in Maschera and Nabucco at Tokyo, 2000–01. *Address:* c/o IMG Artists, Lovell House, 616 Chiswick High Road, London W4 5RX, England.

**OLMSTEAD, Andrea Louise,** BM, MA; American musicologist; b. 5 Sept. 1948, Dayton, OH; m. Larry Thomas Bell 1982. *Education:* Hartt Coll. of Music, New York Univ. *Career:* faculty, The Juilliard School 1972–80, Boston Conservatory 1981–2004. *Publications:* Roger Sessions and His Music 1985, Conversations with Roger Sessions 1987, The New Grove 20th Century American Masters 1987, The Correspondence of Roger Sessions 1992,

Juilliard: A History 1999; contrib. to Journal of the Arnold Schoenberg Institute, American Music, Musical Quarterly, Tempo, Musical America, Perspectives of New Music, Music Library Association Notes, Journal of Musicology. *Honours:* three Nat. Endowment for the Humanities grants 1989, 1992, 2000, Outstanding Academic Book, Choice 1986. *Address:* 73 Hemenway Street, Apt 501, Boston, MA 02115, USA. *E-mail:* LBell10276@aol.com. *Website:* www.AndreaOlmstead.com.

**OLOF, Theo;** Violinist; b. 5 May 1924, Bonn, Germany. *Education:* Studied with Oskar Back in Amsterdam. *Career:* Debut: Amsterdam in 1935; Tours of Europe, the USA and Russia from 1945 as soloist; Leader of the Hague Residentie Orchestra, 1951–71; Duo partnership with Hermann Krebbers included premieres of concertos written for them by Geza Frid, 1952, Henk Badings in 1954 and Hans Kox in 1964; Leader of the Concertgebouw Orchestra, 1974–85; Recitals with pianist, Janine Dacosta, and Gérard van Blerk until 1985 and teacher at the Hague Conservatory; Has given first performances of works by Bruno Maderna and Hans Henkemans. *Address:* de Lairessestraat 12 B, 1071 PA Amsterdam, Netherlands.

**OLSEN, Derrick;** Singer (Bass-Baritone) and Administrator; b. 30 March 1923, Berne, Switzerland. *Education:* Studied in Berne, Geneva and Lucerne. *Career:* Sang at Grand Théâtre Geneva, 1944–69, Basle, 1950–55, with guest engagements at Holland and Schwetzingen Festivals, Buenos Aires, Milan, Berlin Staatsoper, Zürich, Lucerne and Marseilles; Roles included Mozart's Count, Masetto and Alfonso, Pizarro, Rossini's Basilio and Bartolo, Iago, Germont and Melitone, Wagner's Dutchman, Telramund and Klingsor, Jochanaan, Malatesta and Achilles in Penthesilea by Schoeck; Sang at Basle Opera in 1952 and 1958 in the premieres of Leonore by Liebermann and Titus Feuerfuchs by Sutermeister; Concert premieres of oratorios by Honegger, Cantate de Noel, 1953, Kelterborn and Frank Martin, Mystère de la Nativité, 1958 and Martinů, Gilgamesh, 1958; Sang in the British premiere of Schoenberg's Von Heute auf Morgen, Festival Hall, 1963; Member of the Quatuor Vocale de Genève and Artistic Director of the Radio Orchestra Beromunster at Zürich, 1958–70. *Recordings:* Pelléas et Mélisande; Monteverdi's Combattimento; Sutermeister's Schwarze Spinne; Martin's Le Vin Herbé; Handel's Apollo e Dafne. *Address:* c/o Opernhaus Zürich, Falkenstrasse 1, 8008 Zürich, Switzerland.

**OLSEN, Frode;** Singer (bass); b. 10 April 1952, Oslo, Norway. *Education:* Studied at Opera State Conservatory in Oslo and Düsseldorf. *Career:* Debut: Düsseldorf, 1982; Sang at Deutsche Oper am Rhein Düsseldorf, 1982–86, notably as Mozart's Masetto and Don Alfonso; Badisches Staatstheater Karlsruhe from 1986, as Sarastro, Pimen, Gremin, Zaccaria, Wagner's Pogner, King Mark and Landgrave, Orestes and Basilio; Guest engagements at: Dresden, Leipzig, Strasbourg, Dortmund, Berne, Vienna, Volksoper, Oslo; Fasolt, in The Ring at Brussels, 1991; Salzburg Festival debut 1992, as a Soldier in Salome; Further appearances as: Sarastro at Brussels, 1992, King Ludwig in Euryanthe at Music Festival in Aix-en-Provence, 1993, Doctor, in Wozzeck at Frankfurt, Gremin, in Eugene Onegin at the reopened Glyndebourne Opera House, 1994; Other roles include: Raimondo, the Commendatore in Don Giovanni, Colline, Timur, Elmiro in Rossini's Otello; Concert repertoire includes: Verdi's Requiem, Rossini's Petite Messe Solennelle, Stabat Mater, Messiah, Bach's Christmas Oratorio, St Matthew Passion, Elijah, Die Schöpfung; Melchtal in Guillaume Tell in Pesaro-Rossini Festival, 1995; Sang Gurnemanz, in Parsifal for first time, Rouen, France; For 1996 at Glyndebourne, Valens in Handel's Theodora, and Gremin in Onegin; Astradamors in Ligeti's Le grand Macabre with Salonen, and Doktor in Wozzeck with Abbado at Salzburger Festspiele, 1997; Season 1998 with Gurnemann at Brussels, Doktor in Hamburg, 1998; François in first German performance of Messiaen's St François of Assisi, Leipzig; Sang in the premiere of Berio's Cronaco del Luogo 1999; Season 2000–01 as King Mark at Strasbourg, followed by the Dutchman, and Dikoy in Katya Kabanova at Amsterdam. *Recordings:* Astradamors in Le grand Macabre with Salonen; Doktor in Wozzeck with Metzmacher. *Current Management:* Athole Still International Management, Forresters Hall, 25–27 Westow Street, London, SE19 3RY, England. *Telephone:* (20) 8771-5271. *Fax:* (20) 8768-6600. *Website:* www.atholestill.com.

**OLSEN, Keith,** BM, MM; American singer (tenor); b. 1957, Denver, CO. *Education:* San Francisco Conservatory, University of Tennessee, Juilliard School of Music. *Career:* US debut with New York City Opera, 1982, in Die Lustige Witwe; European: Staatstheater Karlsruhe as Rodolfo in 1987; Sang at San Francisco as Capriccio, Helsinki, Los Angeles, Barcelona as Alfredo, Pretoria as Rodolfo and as Rodolfo in Hamburg, London, Arena di Verona, Frankfurt, Düsseldorf, Wiesbaden, Hannover and Toronto, with Manrico in Berlin and Leipzig, Hans in Stuttgart and Macduff in Bologna; Other guest appearances include Radames in Rome and Radio France with Dick Johnson, Turiddu and Hoffmann in Bonn; Film credits include Puccini's Des Grieux, 100th anniversary performance, RAI, Turiddu, South African Broadcasting Corporation and Beethoven's Ninth Symphony with Kurt Masur, Mittel Deutsche Rundfunk; Sang for three years at the Royal Opera House, Covent Garden, with debut as Rodolfo and subsequently as Pinkerton and Boris in Katya Kabanova; (Boris, 1997); Season 1997–98 as Don José at Toulouse and Calaf at Turin. *Recordings:* Giuliano in Handel's Rodrigo; Sang at Palermo Opera as Lensky (1999) and Cavaradossi (2001). *Address:* c/o San Francisco Opera, War Memorial Opera House, San Francisco, CA 94102, USA.

**OLSEN, Stanford;** Singer (tenor); b. 1959, Salt Lake City, Utah, USA. *Education:* Studied with the Metropolitan Opera Development Program. *Career:* For the Metropolitan Opera in New York has sung Arturo in Puritani, Don Ottavio, Ferrando, Belmonte, Idreno (Semiramide), Count Almaviva, Ernesto and Fenton; European career includes Don Ottavio at the Deutsche Oper Berlin, Rossini's Comte Ory for Netherlands Opera and Belmonte under John Eliot Gardiner; Concert at the Mostly Mozart Festival New York, in Boston and elsewhere for the Handel and Haydn Society (Messiah and The Creation), for the Berlin Philharmonic (Berlioz Requiem, 1989) and at the Salzburg Festival with the International Bach Academy; New York recital debut at Alice Tully Hall 1990, with Die schöne Müllerin; Season 1993–94 at the Ravinia Festival in Fidelio, with the Houston Symphony in Britten's War Requiem and a tour of Spain with Messiah, conducted by Helmuth Rilling; Sang Iopas in Les Troyens at La Scala, 1996. *Current Management:* Athole Still International Management, Forresters Hall, 25–27 Westow Street, London, SE19 3RY, England. *Telephone:* (20) 8771-5271. *Fax:* (20) 8768-6600. *Website:* www.atholestill.com.

**OMACHI, Yoichiro;** Conductor; b. 22 Aug. 1931, Tokyo, Japan. *Education:* Studied at Tokyo Academy of Music, 1948–54, with Akeo Watanabe and Kurt Woss; Academy of Music, Vienna with Karl Bohm, Franco Ferrara, and Herbert von Karajan. *Career:* Toured Japan in 1957 with Karajan and the Berlin Philharmonic; Guest conductor with the Berlin Philharmonic, Tonkunstler Orchestra, Vienna, 1959; Chief Conductor, Tokyo Philharmonic Orchestra, 1961; Founded Tokyo Metropolitan Symphony, 1964; Guest conductor with Vienna Symphony Orchestra, 1964–67; Permanent Conductor of the Dortmund Opera, 1968–73; East Asian tour with the Tokyo Philharmonic, 1973; Season 1976–77 conducted Aida at Mannheim, Fidelio in Prague, Madama Butterfly at the Berlin Staatsoper and The Merry Widow in Tokyo; Concerts in Japan, South America, 1978–79; Madama Butterfly at the Vienna Staatsoper in 1980, Permanent Conductor, 1982–84, including Attila on Austrian television and ballet performances; Professor in Opera Faculty at the Tokyo Academy of Music. *Recordings:* Various with the Tokyo Philharmonic.

**O'MARA, Stephen;** Singer (Tenor); b. 1962, Brooklyn, New York, USA. *Career:* Sang widely in North America, including Turiddu and Radames at the New York City Opera; Vienna Staatsoper from 1991, as Don José and Pinkerton; Deutsche Oper Berlin, 1993, as José; Season 1994–95 as Tom Rakewell at Glyndebourne and Luigi in Il Tabarro at Cologne; Royal Opera, Copenhagen, 1996, as Alvaro in La Forza del Destino; Further appearances at Oslo, and the Bregenz Festival; Season 1998 as Samson at Montpellier and Narr' Havas in the premiere of Fénélon's Salammbô, at the Paris Opéra Bastille; Season 2000–01 as Verdi's Riccardo at Bregenz, Gabriele Adorno at Strasbourg, Radames for Houston Opera and Menelaus in Strauss's Die Aegyptische Helena at Cagliari. *Address:* c/o Opéra de la Bastille, 120 Rue de Lyon, 75012 Paris, France.

**OMBUENA, Vicente;** Tenor; b. 1949, Valencia, Spain. *Education:* Studied in Valencia. *Career:* Sang at first in concert then with Mainz Opera, 1989–91 as Don José, Erik, Cassio and Lysander in A Midsummer Night's Dream; Sang at Hamburg Staatsoper from 1991 notably as Ernesto in Don Pasquale; Season 2000–01 for New Israeli Opera at Savonlinna as Nemorino and in Tel-Aviv as Macduff; Verdi Requiem in Karlsruhe. *Recordings include:* Franchetti's Cristoforo Colombo. *Address:* Staatsoper Hamburg, Grosse Theaterstrasse 34, Pf 302448, W-2000 Hamburg 36, Germany.

**OMILIAN, Jolanta;** Singer (Soprano); b. 1956, Warsaw, Poland. *Education:* Studied at the Chopin Academy in Warsaw. *Career:* Debut: Venice in 1979 as Violetta; Sang widely in Germany including Bonn and Dortmund and at the 1985 Macerata Festival as Elisabetta in Roberto Devereux; Sang in Maria Stuarda at Palermo in 1989, Donizetti's Parisina at Basle in 1990 and Norma at Rio de Janeiro; Other roles include Dorabella and Leonora in Trovatore, Amenaide in Tancredi, Fiorilla in Il Turco in Italia, and Anaide in Mosè in Egitto. *Recordings include:* Adriano in Siria by Pergolesi; Il Bravo by Mercadante. *Address:* Montpellier Opéra, 11 Boulevard Victor Hugo, 34000 Montpellier, France.

**ONAY, Gülsün;** Turkish pianist; b. 12 Sept. 1954, Istanbul; d. of Jochen and Gülen Reusch; m. 1st Ersin Onay 1975 (divorced 1986); one s.; m. 2nd Norbert Schappacher 1987. *Education:* Conservatoire Nat. Supérieure de Musique, Paris and under Nadia Boulanger, Monique Haas, Pierre Sancan and Bernhard Ebert. *Career:* first concert aged six; appearances with Warsaw Philharmonic, Staatskapelle Dresden and Berlin Radio Symphony Orchestra, (Germany), Salzburg Mozarteum Orchestra (Austria), Tokyo Symphony, Japan Philharmonic and the Bavarian, Danish, Austrian and Finnish Radio Symphony Orchestras; winner numerous int. competitions; Turkish State Artist since 1986. *Recordings include:* Chopin—Debussy—Saygun 1990, Bartok—Saygun 1991. *Honours:* Dr hc (Bosphorus) 1988. *Address:* c/o Schlossgasse 20, 7800 Freiburg, Germany.

**ONCINA, Juan;** Singer (Tenor); b. 15 April 1925, Barcelona, Spain. *Education:* Studied in Oran, Barcelona with Mercedes Caspir and in Milan with Augusta Oltrabella. *Career:* Debut: Barcelona 1946, as Des Grieux in Manon; Sang opposite Tito Gobbi in Il Barbiere di Siviglia at Barcelona; Paris 1949 in Il Matrimonio Segreto; Florence 1949–50, in Cherubini's Osteria Portoghese and Lully's Armide; Glyndebourne 1952–65, as Don Ramiro in Cenerentola, Ferrando, Comte Ory, Scaramuccio in Ariadne auf Naxos, Rossini's Almaviva, Fenton in Falstaff, Don Ottavio, Lindoro in L'Italiana in

Algeri and in Anna Bolena; Palermo 1959, in Belini's Beatrice di Tenda; Verdi and Puccini roles from 1963; Guest appearances in Monte Carlo, Venice, Triste and Florence; Vienna Staatsoper 1965; Hamburg 1971–74; Last major role as Cavaradossi, in Vienna, 1976. *Recordings:* Le Comte Ory and La Cenerentola from Glyndebourne; Don Pasquale; L'Arlesiana by Cilea; Un Giorno di Regno by Verdi; Donizetti's Roberto Devereux; Sacchini's Oedipe a Colonne. *Address:* c/o Hamburgische Staatsoper, Gross-Theaterstrasse 34, 2000 Hamburg 36, Germany.

**O'NEIL, James;** Singer (Tenor); b. 1954, Shawnee, Oklahoma, USA. *Career:* Debut: Santa Fe, 1978, in Salome; Sang at St Gallen and Berne, 1979–82; Bielefeld Opera from 1982, in Fennimore and Gerda by Delius, Schreker's Der singende Teufel and as Eleazar in La Juive; Staatsoper Berlin from 1985, as Arrigo in Les Vêpres Siciliennes, Turiddu and Lohengrin; Rome Opera, 1991, as Leukippos in Daphne by Strauss; Parsifal at Chemnitz, 1992, and Siegfried and Siegmund for Oslo Opera, 1993–96; Los Angeles, 1993, as Strauss's Emperor; Season 1996 as Oedipus Rex, Théâtre du Châtelet, Paris, and the title role in the premiere of Zemlinsky's Der König Kandaules, at Hamburg. *Address:* Hamburg Staatsoper, Grosse Theaterstrasse 34, 20354 Hamburg, Germany.

**O'NEILL, Charles;** Singer (Tenor); b. 22 Sept. 1930, Ridgefield Park, New Jersey, USA. *Education:* Studied in New York. *Career:* Debut: Fort Worth Opera in 1958 as Radames; Appearances at opera houses in Santa Fe, Cincinnati, Hamburg, Stuttgart, Berlin, Cologne, Frankfurt, Düsseldorf and Zürich; Member of the Theater am Gärtnerplatz Munich, with guest engagements to Toronto, Vancouver, Belgrade and Basle; Other roles have been Florestan, Don José, Don Carlos, Alvaro, Manrico, Otello, Turiddu, Samson, Cavaradossi, Rodolfo, Calaf, Andrea Chénier, Oedipus Rex by Stravinsky, Bacchus and Siegmund.

**O'NEILL, Dennis;** Singer (Tenor); b. 25 Feb. 1948, Pontarddulais, Wales. *Education:* Studied privately with Frederick Cox, Campogalliani and Ricci. *Career:* State Opera of South Australia, 1975–77, then principal tenor for Scottish Opera; Debuts with Covent Garden in Norma in 1979, Glyndebourne at the Italian Singer in Der Rosenkavalier in 1980, USA at Dallas in Lucia di Lammermoor in 1983, and Vienna Staatsoper as Alfredo in La Traviata in 1983; Has sung internationally including Hamburg, Berlin, Paris, Brussels, Marseilles, Nice, Munich, Cologne, Oslo, Barcelona, Zürich, Chicago, San Francisco, Metropolitan Opera, Vancouver, San Diego and Copenhagen; Long association with the Royal Opera House, Covent Garden in many roles including Rodolfo in La Bohème, the Duke in Rigoletto, Edgardo in Lucia di Lammermoor, Riccardo in Un Ballo in Maschera, and Foresto in Attila; Season 1992 with British Youth Opera Gala at Covent Garden, as Manrico in Munich, Riccardo at the Opéra Bastille and Radames at Tel-Aviv; Covent Garden 1994–95, as Radames in Aida; Season 1998 with Alfredo for the Royal Opera and Macduff at Geneva; Sang Radames at the Met, 1999 and Otello at Hamburg, 2000; Enzo in La Gioconda at ENO (concert) 2000; Season 2000–01 as Calaf at Covent Garden and Manrico for Australian Opera at Sydney. *Recordings include:* Opera Gala Recital, 1991. *Current Management:* Ingpen & Williams Ltd, 7 St George's Court, 131 Putney Bridge Road, London, SW15 2PA, England.

**O'NEILL, Fiona;** Singer (Soprano); b. 1958, England. *Education:* Studied at the Royal Northern College of Music; Masterclasses at Aldeburgh. *Career:* Solo roles have included Musetta, Norina and Donna Anna for Travelling Opera, Mabel in The Pirates of Penzance for New D'Oyly Carte, Serpetta in La Serva Padrona at the Northcutt Theatre in Exeter, and Salome for the Stockholm Folkopera at the Edinburgh Festival; English National Opera, 1990–91 as Papagena and as Gerda in Fennimore and Gerda; Sang the title role in Lakmé and Louise at the Bloomsbury Theatre and Pedrotti's Tutti in Maschera at the Britten Theatre; Concert engagements include Kurt Weill songs at the Cheltenham and Edinburgh Festivals; Premiere of Goehr's Sing Ariel, at the 1990 Aldeburgh Festival and Handel's Solomon at Birmingham in 1990; Festival Hall debut with the Philharmonia Orchestra in 1990 and debut at the Barbican with the RPO in 1991; Sang Mimi for Castleward Opera, 1996.

**ONO, Kazushi;** Conductor; b. 1961, Tokyo, Japan. *Education:* National Univ., Tokyo and in Munich with Wolfgang Sawallisch and Giuseppe Patanè. *Career:* Chief Conductor of the Tokyo Philharmonic, 1988, tour of England and Germany, 1994; Chief Conductor of the Zagreb Philharmonic Orchestra, 1988; Music Director, 1990–96; Hamburg Opera debut 1995 with Rigoletto; Music Director of the Karlsruhe Opera from 1996 with Symphonic concerts in charge of the Badisches Staatskapelle; Repertory includes La Traviata, La Bohème; Henze's Junge Lord and The Ring; Norma, Der fliegende Holländer and Schreker's Der Schatzgräber, 2000; Season 1999–2000 with the NDR Symphony in Hamburg and concerts in Frankfurt, Lyon and Bordeaux; British debut with Mahler 8 at Belfast; Further concerts with the BBC and Bournemouth Symphony Orchestra; Boston Symphony Orchestra debut, 1999 with Bartók and Prokofiev; Music Dir of La Monnaie, the Royal Opera House of Belgium, 2002–, producing Elektra by Strauss, I Due Foscari by Verdi, Ballata by Francesconi and Khovanshchina by Mussorgsky; He made his symphonic debut with a performance of Mahler 7. *Address:* c/o IMG Artists, Lovell House, 616 Chiswick High Road, London W4 5RX, England.

**OOI, Chean See;** Conductor; b. 1965, Malaysia. *Education:* Studied with Volker Wangenheim in Cologne and with W F Hausschild and Dennis Russell Davies. *Career:* Principal Conductor of the Classic Philharmonic Orchestra, Bonn, 1991–94; Guest conductor with German orchestras; Performances of

Fidelio and Die Zauberflöte at Bahia, Brazil, 1998, 2000; Resident Conductor of the Malaysian Philharmonic Orchestra, 1997–; Conducting Workshops in Malaysia, Germany and France and with the Jeunesses Musicales World Orchestra; Season 1999–2000 with the Czech Virtuosi and Czech Philharmonic Choir. *Honours:* First Prize, Conductors Competition at Halle, Germany. *Address:* c/o IMG Artists, Lovell House, 616 Chiswick High Road, London W4 5RX, England.

**OOSTWOUD, Roelof;** Singer (Tenor); b. 16 Jan. 1946, Leeuwarden, Netherlands. *Education:* Studied at University of Toronto and with Louis Quilico. *Career:* Guest appearances in opera throughout North America and in London, Vienna, Paris and Amsterdam; Theater am Gärtnerplatz, Munich, from 1978; North American premiere of Verdi's Stiffelio (title role) with the Opera Company of Boston, 1978; Premiere of Berio's Vera Storia at La Scala, Milan, 1982; Düsseldorf from 1982, notably in Schreker's Die Gezeichneten, Henze's Bassarids (as Dionysus) and as Strauss's Bacchus (1995); Berne, 1992, as Sergei in Lady Macbeth, Coburg, 1996, as Verdi's Otello; Concert and oratorio performances; Sang Oreste in Gluck's Iphigénie en Tauride, Rio de Janeiro, 1997. *Address:* c/o Deutsche Oper am Rhein, Heinrich-Heine Alle 16a, 40213 Düsseldorf, Germany.

**OPALACH, Jan;** Singer (Bass-Baritone); b. 2 Sept. 1950, Hackensack, New Jersey, USA. *Education:* Studied at Indiana State University. *Career:* Sang at various regional USA operatic centres, New York City Opera from 1980 as Bartolo, Papageno, Schaunard, Kingfisher (Midsummer Marriage) and Leporello; Caramoor Festival, 1980, as Viltotta in the USA premiere of Haydn's La Vera Costanza; St Louis 1986 in USA premiere of Rossini's Il Viaggio a Reims; Sang at Seattle Opera, 1991–92, as the Music Master in Ariadne auf Naxos and Guglielmo in Così fan tutte; New York City Opera, 1991 as the Forester in The Cunning Little Vixen, Mozart's Figaro at Toronto; Sang in Rossini Gala Opera at New York's Fisher Hall, 29 February 1992; New York Premiere, B A Zimmerman's Die Soldaten, Wesener, NYCO, 1992; New York Premiere, Tippett's Midsummer Marriage, King Fisher, 1993; World Premiere, Glass's The Voyage, Metropolitan Opera, 1992; American Premiere, Schnittke's Faust Cantata, American Symphony Orchestra with Botstein; Rossini's Italiana in Algeri, Taddeo, Netherlands Opera; Season 1997–98 in Handel's Serse at the New York City Opera. *Recordings:* Solo Bach Cantatas and Bach Ensemble; 2 world premiere recordings R Beaser's Seven Deadly Sins, D Russell, American Composers' Orchestra (ARGO); Syringa, Elliott Carter; Speculum Musicae (Bridge). *Honours:* NEA Recital Grant, 1986; W M Naumburg Vocalist Award, 1989; Metropolitan Opera Nationals Award; Hertogenbosch Vocalisten Concours, 1981. *Current Management:* Janice Mayer and Associates. *Address:* 201 West 54 Street, Suite 1c, New York, NY 10019, USA.

**OPIE, Alan;** Singer (Baritone); b. 22 March 1945, Redruth, Cornwall, England. *Education:* Guildhall School of Music, London; London Opera Centre with Vera Rosza. *Career:* Debut: Sadler's Wells Opera 1969, as Papageno in Die Zauberflöte; Appearances with English National Opera, Welsh National Opera, Aldeburgh Festival and Santa Fe Opera; Other roles include Mozart's Guglielmo, Rossini's Figaro, Verdi's Germont, Britten's Demetrius and Charles Blount (Gloriana) and Massenet's Lescaut; Sang Wagner's Beckmesser with English National Opera 1984 and at Bayreuth, 1987, 1988, Berlin, 1990, Munich, 1994; Sang Germont with ENO, 1990 and the title role in Busoni's Doctor Faust; Glyndebourne Festival 1990, as Sid in Albert Herring; Season 1992 as The Fiddler in Königskinder for ENO, Balstrode in Peter Grimes at Glyndebourne, Melitone in The Force of Destiny and Papageno at the Coliseum; Balstrode at New York Metropolitan, 1994; Panza in Don Quichotte, Paolo in Munich, 1995; Title Role in World premiere of Berio's Outis at Las Scala, Milan in 1996 and again in 1999 and Châtelet, Paris, 1999. Sang Rossini's Taddeo for ENO, 1997; Balstrode in Peter Grimes at the New York Met, 1998; Season 1998 as Don Alfonso at Glyndebourne, Janáček's Gamekeeper at Spoleto and Sharpless in Madama Butterfly at the New York Met; Has sung Beckmesser in Meistersinger at Munich in 1994, 1996, 1997 and 1998 and Vienna, 1999; Season 2000–01 as Britten's Balstrode at the Vienna Staatsoper, Don Carlo in Ernani for ENO, Don Alfonso at Glyndebourne, Strauss's Faninal at the Met and Germont for the Royal Opera, Covent Garden. *Recordings include:* Maria Stuarda by Donizetti (EMI); The Bear, Rape of Lucretia, Troilus and Cressida, Barber of Seville; Hugh the Drover; Beckmesser in Meistersinger; Balstrode in Peter Grimes; Tonio in Pagliacci; Marcello in La Bohème. *Honours:* Grammies for Balstrode in Peter Grimes, 1996 and Beckmesser in Die Meistersinger, 1997; Nominated for an Olivier Award, Outstanding Achievement in Opera for Falstaff, 1998. *Address:* c/o Allied Artists Agency, 42 Montpelier Square, London SW17 1JZ, England.

**OPPENHEIM, David J.;** Clarinettist and University Dean (Emeritus); b. 13 April 1922, Detroit, Michigan, USA; m. (1) Judy Holiday, 1948, 1 s., (2) Ellen Adler, 1957, 1 s., 1 d., (3) Patricia Jaffe, 1987. *Education:* Interlochen National Music Camp, Michigan; Juilliard School of Music, New York, 1939–40; University of Rochester Eastman School of Music, 1940–43. *Career:* Director, Masterworks Division, Columbia Records, 1950–59; Producer, Director, Writer, Network News, CBS Television, 1962–68; Executive Producer, Public Broadcasting Laboratory, 1968–69; Co-Producer of Saul Bellow's Last Analysis, Broadway, New York, 1962; Producer of documentary films on Stravinsky and Casals, CBS; Executive Producer, Cultural Programming, Public Broadcasting Laboratory; Clarinet soloist, Prades, France, 1957, San Juan, Puerto Rico, 1959; Performed under Koussevitsky, Toscanini, Leins-

dorf, Steinberg, Bernstein, Stokowski, Stravinsky; Performed chamber music with Casals, Serkin and Casadesus; Tony Awards Nominating Committee, 1983–87; Artist-in-Residence, New Mexico, Music Festival; Chamber music performer with Istomin Horzowski. *Recordings:* Brahms Clarinet Quintet with Budapest Quartet; Mozart Clarinet Quintet in A Major with Budapest Quartet; L'histoire du Soldàt, Octet, Septet (premiere), conducted by Stravinsky; Bernstein Sonata, clarinet and Leonard Bernstein, piano (dedicated to David Oppenheim); Copland Sextet with Juilliard Quartet; Douglas Moore Quintet with New Music Quartet. *Address:* 1225 Park Avenue 6A, New York, NY 10128, USA.

**OPPENS, Ursula;** Concert Pianist; b. 2 Feb. 1944, New York City, USA. *Education:* BA, Radcliffe College, 1965; Juilliard School 1966–69, with Rosina Lhevinne, Guido Agosti and Leonard Shure. *Career:* Debut: New York, 1969; Performances with Boston Symphony, New York Philharmonic and other leading American orchestras; Recitals at Tully Hall, Kennedy Center; Appearances at Aspen, Berkshire and Marlboro Festivals; Tours of Europe and US as soloist and as member of Speculum Musicae; Performances of contemporary music; Engagements with the Chamber Music Society of Lincoln Center and the Group for Contemporary Music; Conposers who have written for her include Rzeweski, Wolff, Carter and Wuorinen; Teacher at Brooklyn College, City University of New York. *Recordings include:* Busoni, Mozart and Rzewski. *Honours:* Winner, Busoni International Piano Competition, 1969; Avery Fisher Prize, 1976. *Current Management:* Colbert Artists Management, 111 West 57, New York, NY 10019, USA. *Address:* c/o Witmer Management, Leidsegracht 42, NL–1016 CM Amsterdam, Netherlands.

**OPRISANU, Carmen;** Singer (Mezzo-soprano); b. 1964, Brasov, Romania. *Education:* Studied at the Cluj Music Academy. *Career:* Sang with the Romanian Opera at Cluj, 1986–93, and gave concerts with the Bucharest Radio Symphony Orchestra and the Georges Enescu Philharmonic (tours of Italy and Spain); Bucharest State Opera 1993, as Carmen and Rosina; Lucerne Theatre 1993–96, as Carmen, Suzuki, Isabella in L'Italiana in Algeri, the Composer (Ariadne auf Naxos), Sesto in La Clemenza di Tito and Adalgisa; Season 1995 as Isabella at the Deutsche Oper Berlin and Sigismondo in the German premiere of Rossini's opera, at Wildbad; Charlotte in Werther, Rosina and Maddalena with the Zürich Opera; Season 1997–98, Rosina in Covent Garden and Barcelona, Cenerentola at Hamburg, Pierotto in Linda di Chamonix with La Scala, in Zürich as Fenena in Nabucco and Hänsel; Season 1998–99, Carmen and Charlotte in Amsterdam and Charlotte in Madrid; Season 2000 as Orlofsky for Zürich Opera, Rossini's Isabella for New Israeli Opera and Dulcinée in Don Quichotte at the Opéra Bastille, Paris. *Recordings:* Title role in Sigismondo; Orlofsky in Fledermaus and Elisabetta in Maria Stuerda (Nightingale Classics). *Honours:* Prizewinner at the 1992 Vienna Belvedere Competition and the 1995 Placido Domingo Operalia Competition, in Madrid; Winner, Leonard Bernstein International Oratorio and Song Competition, Jerusalem, 1996. *Address:* c/o Opernhaus Zürich, Falkenstrasse 1, 8008 Zürich, Switzerland.

**ORAMO, Sakari;** Finnish conductor and violinist; *Music Director, City of Birmingham Symphony Orchestra;* b. 1966, Helsinki; m. Anu Komsi. *Education:* Sibelius Acad., Utrecht Conservatoire. *Career:* founder-mem. Avanti Chamber Orchestra 1982–89; violin leader Finnish Radio Symphony Orchestra 1991, Assoc. Prin. Conductor 1994–2003, Chief Conductor 2003–; further engagements with major Scandinavian orchestras, City of Birmingham Symphony, BBC Symphony and Philharmonic, London Sinfonietta and Rotterdam Philharmonic; Danish Radio Symphony 1994–, tour of Australia; Music Dir City of Birmingham Symphony Orchestra (CBSO) 1997–, conducting the Sibelius Violin Concerto and Nielsen's Fifth at BBC Promenade Concerts, London 1999, and conducting at London Proms 2002, 2003; 2003–04 season included Artistic Directorship of CBSO's musical festival 'Floof'; also concerts with NDR Hamburg, Los Angeles Philharmonic, Orchestre de Paris, New York Philharmonic, Berlin Philharmonic. *Honours:* Hon. DUniv (Univ. of Cen. England) 2003. *Current Management:* Harrison-Parrott Ltd, 12 Penzance Place, London, W11 4PA, England. *Telephone:* (20) 7229 9166. *Fax:* (20) 7221 5042. *Website:* www.harrisonparrott.com. *Address:* City of Birmingham Symphony Orchestra, CBSO Centre, Berkley Street, Birmingham, B1 2LF, England. *Website:* www.cbso.co.uk.

**ORBAN, György;** Hungarian composer; b. 12 July 1947, Tirgu-Mures, Romania. *Education:* Cluj Conservatory. *Career:* teacher of theory, Cluj Conservatory –1979; moved to Hungary; Ed., Editio Musica Budapest; teacher of composition, Music Acad., Budapest. *Compositions:* orchestra: Five Canons to Poems by Attile Joszef for soprano and chamber ensemble 1977, Triple Sextet 1980, two Serenades 1984, 1985, four Duos with soprano and clarinet 1979, soprano and double bass 1987, soprano and violoncello 1989, soprano and violin 1992, Sonata Concertante for clarinet and piano 1987, Wind Quintet 1984, Brass Music for Quintet No. 1 1987, Sonata for bassoon and piano 1987, Sonata for violin 1970, three Sonatas for violin and piano 1989, 1991, three Suites for piano 1986, 1997, 1998, four Piano Sonatas 1987, 1988, 1989; chorus and orchestra: Rorarte Coeli (oratorio) 1992, Regina Martyrum (oratorio) 1993, Missa No. 2 1990, No. 4 1991, No. 10 1993, Requiem 2003; chorus and chamber ensemble: Missa No. 7 1993, Flower Songs for female choir 1978, Chorus Book in Memory of S. A. No. 1 1984, Chorus Book No. 2, Book of Medallions (cycle of nine choruses) 1987, Stabat Mater 1987, Passion (oratorio) 1997, Christmas Oratorio 1998, Sketches from Verona for orchestra 1998, three string quartets 1994, 1994, 1998, about 40 Latin motets for mixed and female chorus; operas: Pikkó hertzeg 2000, Büvölet 2004. *Address:* 1016

Budapest, Mészáros u. 15–17 (office); 1121 Budapest, Adorján út 4, Hungary (home). *Telephone:* (1) 246-3136 (home).

**ORCIANI, Patrizia;** Singer (Soprano); b. 1959, Fano, Urbino, Italy. *Education:* Studied at the Bologna Conservatory. *Career:* Debut: Fano in 1983 as Mimi in La Bohème; Has sung widely in Italy notably as Liu at the 1991 Verona Festival and as Handel's Cleopatra at the Valle d'Istria Festival; Sang at the Bonn Opera, 1991–92; Other roles include Donizetti's Adina and Norina, Rossini's Elvira, Micaela and Giulietta in Les Contes d'Hoffmann; Season 1998 as Lucieta in Wolf Ferrari's Il campiello at Bologna and Venus in Tannhäuser at Palermo. *Recordings include:* Cimarosa's L'Italiana in Londra; Nina by Paisiello; Il Signor Bruschino. *Address:* c/o Bonn Opera, Am Boeselagerhof 1, Pf 2440, W-5300 Bonn, Germany.

**ORDONEZ, Antonio;** Singer (Tenor); b. 27 Oct. 1948, Madrid, Spain. *Education:* Studied in Madrid with Miguel Garcia Barrosa. *Career:* Concert appearances in Spain and USA from 1980; Opera debut at Teatro Zarzuela Madrid 1982, as Pinkerton; Sang Don Carlos at Liège 1986 and at Deutsche Oper Berlin 1988; Teatro Liceo Barcelona 1986, in Pacini's Saffo, with Montserrat Caballé; Further guest appearances as Cavaradossi at Dallas 1987, Calaf at Ravenna Festival 1988 and as Alvaro in La Forza del Destino at Washington 1989; San Francisco Opera 1991 as Foresto in Attila; Other roles include Rodolfo, Deutsche Oper 1989, Alfredo, Riccardo, Gabriele Adorno and Edgardo in Lucia di Lammermoor, Liège 1987; Sang Don José in Carmen at Earl's Court, London 1991. *Address:* c/o San Francisco Opera, War Memorial Opera House, San Francisco, CA 94102, USA.

**ORE, Cecilie;** Composer; b. 19 July 1954, Oslo, Norway. *Education:* Piano studies at Norwegian State Academy of Music and in Paris; Studied Composition with Ton de Leeuw at Sweelinck Conservatory, Amsterdam, and at Institute of Sonology in Utrecht. *Career:* Frequent performances at Nordic and international festivals; Commissioned by BBC Symphony Orchestra; mem, Society of Norwegian Composers. *Compositions:* Orchestral music: Porphyre, 1986; Nunc et Nunc, 1994; Chamber music: Helices, for wind quintet, 1984; Preasems Subitus, for string quartet, 1989; Erat Erit Est, for ensemble, 1991; Futurum exactum, for string ensemble, 1992; Lex Temporis, for string quartet, 1992; Ictus, for 6 percussionists, 1997; Semper Semper, for saxophone quartet, 1998; Nunquam Non, for ensemble, 1999; Non Nunquam, for string trio, 1999; Cirrus, for string quartet, 2002; Cumulus, for wind trio, 2002; Schwirren for vocal ensemble, 2003; Music for dramatic work: A. – a shadow opera, 2001. *Recordings:* Codex Temporis, 1996; Tempora Mutantur, 2002; A. – a shadow opera, 2003. *Honours:* 1st and 2nd Prize, International Rostrum for Electro-acoustic Music, 1988. *Address:* Ullevålsvn 61 B, 0171 Oslo, Norway.

**O'REILLY, Brendan;** Violinist; b. 1935, Dublin, Ireland. *Education:* Studied at Belvedere College Dublin, with David Martin at the Royal Academy of Music and with Andre Gertler in Brussels. *Career:* Played with the Radio Eireann String Quartet in Cork, then freelanced with the Royal Philharmonic and the English Chamber Orchestra; Co-founded the Gabrieli Quartet in 1967 touring Europe, North America, the Far East and Australia; Festival engagements in the United Kingdom, including Aldeburgh, City of London and Cheltenham; Concerts every season in London, participation in the Barbican Centre's Mostly Mozart Festival and resident artist at the University of Essex from 1971; Has co-premiered works by William Alwyn, Britten, Alan Bush, Daniel Jones and Gordon Crosse, 3rd Quartet of John McCabe in 1979 and the 2nd Quartets of Nicholas Maw and Panufnik, 1983–80; British premiere of the Piano Quintet by Sibelius in 1990. *Recordings:* 5 CDs including early pieces by Britten, Dohnányi's Piano Quintet with Wolfgang Manz, Walton's Quartets and the Sibelius Quartet and Quintet, with Anthony Goldstone. *Address:* c/o GRMAM, 8 Wren Crescent, Bushey Heath, Herts, WD23 1AN, England.

**O'REILLY, Graham (Henry Meredith);** Singer, Conductor and Musicologist; b. 4 Sept. 1947, Parkes, New South Wales, Australia; m. (1) Jill Barralet, 2 Sept 1972, divorced, 1 s., 1 d., (2) Brigitte Vinson, 27 Dec 1986, 2 d. *Education:* BA, Honours, University of Sydney, 1968; Associate, Sydney Conservatorium of Music, 1966; Licentiate, Trinity College, London, 1969. *Career:* Debut: Messiah at Sydney Town Hall in 1971; Music Teacher in Sydney, 1970–73; Researcher of late Restoration stage music, 1973–, and pitch in Renaissance vocal music, 1979–; Concert and session singer in London, 1973–82; Director for early music ensembles, 1976–, and for The Restoration Musick, 1980–81, Psallite, 1981–86 and Ensemble européen William Byrd, 1983–; Singing Teacher, 1980–93; Member of Groupe Vocal de France, 1982–86; Solo oratorio and ensemble singer specialising in early music. *Recordings:* With Psallite: Music by Tallis, Byrd and Gibbons and Collected Works of Jon Dixon; With Groupe Vocal de France: Sacred Music of Giacinto Scelsi; With Ensemble William Byrd: English Music of The Seventeenth Century, Vol. 1: Orlando Gibbons, Vol. 2: Welcome Vicegerent, music of Henry Purcell; Palestrina: Canticum Canticorum; Handel: Music for Cannons, Vol. 1; 3 Chandos anthems; Handel: Dixit Dominus, Nisi Dominus; Scarlatti: Musica Sacra; Miserere, (Allegri/Bai, F Scarlatti, Leo); The Last Judgement, Charpentier. *Publications:* Editor, Eccles: Music to Macbeth, Cathedral Music, 1978. *Honours:* Frank Busby Musical Scholarship, Sydney University, 1967. *Address:* 10 rue Massenet, 93600 Aulnay-Sous-Bois, France. *E-mail:* Grabyrdy@aol.com.

**ORGONASOVA, Luba;** Singer (Soprano); b. 22 Jan. 1961, Bratislava, Czechoslovakia. *Education:* Studied at Bratislava Conservatory. *Career:* Concert and operatic engagements in Czechoslovakia 1979–83; Hagen Opera, West Germany, 1983–88 as Mozart's Ilia and Pamina, Gilda and Violetta, Lauretta and Sophie in Der Rosenkavalier; Guest appearances in Nuremberg, Essen, Hamburg and Zürich; Vienna Volksoper 1988–89; Sang Pamina and Donna Anna at Aix-en-Provence Festival, 1988–89; Opéra de Lyon 1988 as Madame Silberklang in Der Schauspieldirektor; Sang Constanze at Deutsche Oper Berlin and in Lisbon 1991, with concert performances of Die Entführung under John Eliot Gardiner in London and Amsterdam; Other roles include Susanna, Atalanta in Handel's Serse, Marzelline, Cendrillon and Antonia, Les Contes d'Hoffmann; Sang Donna Anna at Chicago, 1995; Season 1999–2000 as Donna Anna at the Opéra Bastille, Gluck's Euridice at Zürich and Elettra in Idomeneo at Salzburg; Concert repertoire includes Janáček's Glagoltic Mass, Bruckner's Te Deum and the Missa Solemnis, all at Zürich, Haydn's Harmonie Mass at Bremen and Oratorios by Bach, Handel and Dvořák. *Recordings:* Die Zauberflöte. *Address:* c/o Chicago Light Opera, 20 North Wacker Drive, Chicago, IL 60604, USA.

**ORKIS, Lambert Thomas,** BM, MM; American pianist, fortepianist and educator; b. 20 April 1946, Philadelphia, PA; m. Janice Barbara Kretschmann 1972. *Education:* Curtis Institute of Music, Temple Univ. *Career:* world-wide performances; premiered solo works of George Crumb, Richard Wernick, Maurice Wright and James Primosch, including Wernick's Piano Concerto, Washington, DC and Carnegie Hall, New York, with National Symphony Orchestra, conducted by Mstislav Rostropovich 1991; recitals with cellist Mstislav Rostropovich 1981–, with violinist Anne-Sophie Mutter 1988–, with soprano Arleen Augér 1987–90, with soprano Lucy Shelton 1981–, with cellist Han-Na Chang 2001, with violinist Julian Rachlin 2000; founding mem., fortepianist, Castle Trio 1988–; pianist, Smithsonian Chamber Music Soc. 1983–; Honoured Artist, New Aspect International Arts Festival, Taipei, Taiwan 1996; pianist, Library of Congress Summer Chamber Festival 1986–89, American Chamber Players 1986–89, 20th Century Consort 1976–87; soloist with National Symphony Orchestra, Great Performances (PBS) 1983; soloist-in-residence 1983; principal keyboard, National Symphony Orchestra, Washington, DC 1982–; Faculty mem., Temple Univ., Philadelphia; Prof. of Piano, Co-ordinator of Master of Music programme in piano accompanying and Chamber Music 1968–; soloist, National Symphony Orchestra Piano 2000 Festival; trios with Anne-Sophie Mutter and Lynn Harrell 2001–2002; pianist, Bay Chamber Concerts Summer Music Festival 2002–; Kennedy Center Chamber Players 2003–; judge at Carnegie Hall Int. American Music Competition for Pianists 1985, Kennedy Center Friedheim Awards 1991, Trondheim Int. Chamber Music Competition 2003. *Recordings:* solo: Music of Louis Moreau Gottschalk, 1988; Schubert Impromptus, 1990; Schubert Moment Musicaux and 3 Klavierstücke, 1993; George Crumb, A Little Suite for Christmas, Richard Wernick, Sonata for Piano, 1986; Richard Wernick, Piano Concerto, with Symphony II, composer conducting, 1998; with Anne-Sophie Mutter: Berlin Recital, 1996, Beethoven Cycle of 10 Sonatas for Piano and Violin, 1998; Bartók Sonata No. 2, 1998; with Anner Bylsma: Works by Franchomme and Chopin, 1994, works by Brahms and Schumann, 1995; with Arleen Augér: Schubert Lieder, 1991; with Castle Trio: Beethoven Cycle of Piano Trios, 1989–92; Recital 2000, 2000; A Life With Beethoven (DVD), 2000; The Complete Violin Sonatas (DVD), 2001; Tango, Song and Dance, 2003; Keys to the Future, works of Richard Wernick and James Primosch, 2003. *Publications:* A Journey Back to Beethoven (article) 1998. *Honours:* Grammy Award, Best Chamber Music Performance 1999, Best Classical Album 1999, National Public Radio Critic's Choice Award 1999, Temple University Faculty Award for Creative Achievement 1982. *Address:* PO Box 6023, Arlington, VA 22206-0023, USA. *Telephone:* (703) 998-0791. *Fax:* (703) 998-6531. *E-mail:* orkispiano@lambertorkis.com. *Website:* www.lambertorkis.com.

**ORLANDI MALASPINA, Rita;** Singer (Soprano); b. 28 Dec. 1937, Bologna, Italy; m. Massimiliano Malaspina. *Education:* Studied with Carmen Melis in Milan. *Career:* Debut: Teatro Nuovo Milan, 1963 as Verdi's Giovanna d'Arco; Sang widely in Italy, and at Covent Garden, London, Munich, Hamburg, Paris, Nice, Barcelona, Vienna and Buenos Aires; Metropolitan Opera debut 1968; Other roles included Puccini's Tosca and Suor Angelica, Wagner's Elsa, Giordano's Maddalena and Verdi's Aida, Odabella, Leonora, Amelia, Abigaille, Desdemona, Luisa Miller, Elisabeth and Lucrezia (I Due Foscari); Also heard in concert. *Address:* c/o Teatro alla Scala, Via Filodrammatici 2, Milan, Italy.

**ORLOFF, Claudine;** Pianist; b. 6 Jan. 1961, Brussels, Belgium; m. Burkard Spinnier, 1 Oct 1983, 2 s. *Education:* Diplome superieur, Piano, class of J C Vanden Eunden, 1985, Diplome superieur, Chamber Music, class of A Siwy, 1987, Conservatoire Royal de Musique, Brussels; Private studies with B Lemmens, 1985–88. *Career:* Recording for RTB, 1978; Regular appearances as soloist and in chamber music; Often includes contemporary works in recital programmes, including Van Rossum's 12 preludes, 1986; Many concerts on 2 pianos (with Bukard Spinnier), Belgium, France, Germany, including Musique en Sorbonne, Paris, July 1991; Radio engagement, Hommage a Milhaud, live, RTB Brussels, Oct 1992. *Honours:* Ella Olin Prize, Brussels, 1985. *Current Management:* F E de Wasswige Music Management. *Address:* c/o Conservatoire Royale de Musique, 30 Rue de la Régence, B–1000 Brussels, Belgium.

**ORMAI, Gabor;** Violist; b. 1950, Hungary. *Education:* Studied with Andras Mihaly at the Franz Liszt Academy, Budapest, with members of the Amadeus Quartet and Zoltán Szekely. *Career:* Founder member of the Takacs Quartet,

1975; Many concert appearances in all major centres of Europe and the USA; Tours of Australia, New Zealand, Japan, South America, England, Norway, Sweden, Greece, Belgium and Ireland; Bartók Cycle for the Bartók-Solti Festival at South Bank, 1990; Great Performers Series at Lincoln Center and Mostly Mozart Festival at Alice Tully Hall, New York; Visits to Japan 1989 and 1992; Mozart Festivals at South Bank, Wigmore Hall and Barbican Centre, 1991; Bartók Cycle at the Théâtre des Champs Elysées, 1991; Beethoven Cycles at the Zürich Tonhalle, in Dublin, at the Wigmore Hall and in Paris, 1991–92; Resident at the University of Colorado, Resident at the London Barbican, 1988–91, with masterclasses at the Guildhall School of Music; Plays Amati instrument made for the French Royal Family and loaned by the Corcoran Gallery, Gallery of Art, Washington DC. *Recordings:* Schumann Quartets Op 41, Mozart String Quintets (with Denes Koromzay), Bartók 6 Quartets, Schubert Trout Quintet (with Zoltán Kocsis) Hungaroton; Haydn Op 76, Brahms Op 51, Nos 1 and 2, Chausson Concerto (with Joshua Bell and Jean-Yves Thibaudet); Works by Schubert, Mozart, Dvořák and Bartók. *Honours:* Winner, International Quartet Competition, Evian, 1977; Winner, Portsmouth International Quartet Competition, 1979. *Address:* c/o Phelps, Takaes Quartet, 6 Malvern Road, London, E8 3LT, England.

**ORREGO-SALAS, Juan A.;** Composer, Professor of Music and Architect; b. 18 Jan. 1919, Santiago, Chile; m. Carmen Benavente 1943, 4 s., 1 d. *Education:* BA 1938, MA 1943, State Uniersity of Chile. *Career:* Conductor, Catholic University Choir, 1938–44; Professor of Musicology, Faculty of Music, State University of Chile, 1942–61; Editor, Revista Musical Chilena, 1949–53; Music Critic, El Mercurio, 1950–61; Director, Instituto de Extension Musical, Chile, 1957–59; Chairman, Music Department, Catholic University, Chile, 1951–61; Professor of Music, Director of Latin American Music Centre, Indiana University, USA, 1961–. *Compositions include:* Orchestral: Variaciones serenas for strings, 1971; Volte for chamber orchestra, 1971; Symphony No. 4, 1966; Violin Concerto, 1983; Second Piano Concerto, 1985; Cello Concerto, 1992; Symphony No. 5, 1995; Sinfonia in One Movement, 1997; Chamber Music: Trio No. 2, 1977; Presencias, 1972; Tangos, 1982; Balada for cello and piano, 1983; Partita, 1988; 2 string quartets, 1957, 1996; Piano Quintetm 1997; Vocal Music: Missa in tempore discordige, 1969; The Days of God, 1974–76; Bolivar for narrator, chorus and orchestra, 1982; The Celestial City, 1992; Stage Music: The Tumbler's Prayer (ballet), 1960; Widows (opera), 1989; Introduction and Allegro Concertante for one piano, four hands and chamber orchestra, 1999. *Publications include:* Latin American Literary Review, 1975; Music of the Americas (co-editor), 1967; Encyclopedia Americana, 1970. *Contributions:* Musical Quarterly; Tempo; Revista Musical. *Address:* 490 S Serena Lane, Bloomington, IN 47401, USA.

**ORSANIC, Vlatka;** Singer (Soprano); b. 29 Jan. 1958, Zabok, Croatia. *Career:* Sang at Ljubiana Opera from 1979, as Lucia, Gilda, Elvira in I Puritani and Rossini's Rosina; Belgrade, 1981, as Lucia, and guest appearances elsewhere in Yugoslavia; Darmstadt Opera from 1992, as Jenůfa, Rosalinde, Mimi, Mozart's Vitellia and Donna Anna, Tatiana and Traviata; Essen, 1995, as Shostakovich's Lady Macbeth, and Rusalka; Katya Kabanova at Darmstadt, 1996; Vienna Konzerthaus in War and Peace, Janáček's Mr Brouček and Schumann's Genoveva; Komische Oper, Berlin, 1998, as Verdi's Lady Macbeth; As Mozart's Elettra at Salzburg Festspielhaus and as Verdi's Leonora (Trovatore) in Bonn; Sang Shostakovich's Lady Macbeth at Meiningen, 1999 and Verdi's at Leipzig. *Address:* Komische Oper, Behrenstrasse 55–57, 10117 Berlin, Germany.

**ORTH, Norbert;** Singer (Tenor); b. 1939, Dortmund, Germany. *Education:* Studied in Hamburg and Cologne and at the Dortmund Opera House School. *Career:* Sang in Enschede, Netherlands, then at opera houses in Düsseldorf, Nuremburg, Munich, Paris, Berlin and Stuttgart; Metropolitan Opera 1979, as Pedrillo in Die Entführung; Augsburg 1981, as Max in Der Freischütz; Appearances at the Salzburg and Bayreuth Festivals; Loge in Das Rheingold 1984; Sang Walther in Die Meistersinger at Hanover 1986; Sang Tannhäuser at Kassel 1988, Lohengrin at Hanover and Wiesbaden; Walther in Die Meistersinger at the rebuilt Essen Opera, 1988; Théâtre du Châtelet, Paris 1990, as Walther; Season 1992 as Berg's Alwa at Dresden and Parsifal at Turin; Also heard in the concert hall, as Lieder and oratorio singer. *Recordings:* Die Entführung; Schubert's Die Freunde von Salamanka; Augustin Moser in Die Meistersinger, Bayreuth 1974. *Address:* c/o Niedersächsische Staatstheater, Opernplatz 1, 300 Hannover 1, Germany.

**ORTIZ, Cristina;** Brazilian concert pianist; b. 17 April 1950, Bahia; d. of Silverio M. Ortiz and Moema F. Ortiz; m. Jasper W. Parrott 1974; two d. *Education:* Conservatório Brasileiro de Música, Rio de Janeiro, Acad. Int. de Piano (with Magda Tagliaferro), Paris and Curtis Inst. of Music, Philadelphia (with Rudolph Serkin). *Career:* New York recital debut 1971; has appeared in concerts with the Vienna Philharmonic, Berlin Philharmonic, the Concertgebouw, Chicago Symphony, New York Philharmonic, Israel Philharmonic, Los Angeles Philharmonic, leading British orchestras and has undertaken many tours of North and South America, the Far East, New Zealand and Japan; appeared with NHK Symphony, the Bergen Philharmonic and Philharmonia under Janowski 1997; has recorded extensively for EMI, Decca, Pantheon, Collins Classics and Pickwick Records; played with conductors including Previn, Mehta, Kondrashin, Ashkenazy, Leinsdorf, Chailly, Masur, Salonen, Colin Davis, Janssons, Fedoseyev, Zinman, Rattle, Järvi and Fürst. *Honours:* First Prize Van Cliburn Int. Competition, Texas 1969. *Current Management:* Harrison-Parrott Ltd, 12 Penzance Road, London, W11 4PA, England. *Telephone:* (20) 7229-9166.

**ORTIZ, Francisco;** Singer (Tenor); b. 1948, Spain. *Education:* Studied in Barcelona and Madrid. *Career:* Debut: Barcelona 1973, as Foresto in Attila; Further appearances as Foresto in London, Paris, 1974, Madrid and Venice, 1976, Toulouse, 1979; New York City Opera 1973, as Turiddu, Nice 1974, as Radames, Geneva 1975, as Puccini's Des Grieux; Sang Pollione in Norma at Amsterdam, Barcelona and Vienna 1978–80; Théâtre de la Monnaie Brussels 1981, as Cavaradossi, Sydney Opera 1982, as Manrico; Further engagements at Hamburg, Santiago, Ernani 1979, Paris, Rio de Janeiro and the Vienna Staatsoper, Alvaro in La Forza del Destino; Appeared with Canadian Opera Company at Toronto as Pollione 1991; Performances in Zarzuela and as concert artist. *Address:* c/o Canadian Opera Company, 227 Front Street East, Toronto, Ontario MFA 1E8, Canada.

**ORTIZ, William;** Composer; b. 30 March 1947, Salinas, Puerto Rico; m. Candida Ortiz, 26 Mar 1988, 3 d. *Education:* Puerto Rico Conservatory of Music; MA, PhD, State University of New York, Stony Brook; State University of New York at Buffalo. *Career:* About 100 works for orchestra, chamber ensembles, solo works, songs, opera and electronic music; Composer-in-Residence, Atlantic Center for the Arts; mem, Society of Composers; American Composers Alliance; American Music Center; Composers Forum. *Compositions include:* Tropicalización, 1999; Trio Concertante en 3 Realidades; Unknown Poets from the Full-Time Jungle for soprano and piano, 1992; Loaisai; Nueva York Tropical; Caribe Urbano, for Violin, Viola, Violoncello, 1995; Garabato; A Sensitive Mambo in Transformation; Suspension de Soledad en 3 Tiempos 1990; Rican, street opera, 1991; 2 string quartets 1976, 1987; Graffiti Nuvorican, 1988; Cantilena for guitar, 1996; Montage para sueño for orchestra, 2001; Fotografia de Héctor, for guitar, 1997; Esta es la tierra de los que aguantan callados y pacientes por un nuevo despertar, Guitar Concierto, 2001; Elogio a la Plena, for Band, 2002. *Recordings:* 1245 E 107th Street; Amor, Cristal y Piedra; William Ortiz Chamber Music; Abrazo; New Music for Four Guitars; Freedom Flight: Guitar Music of Ortiz and Piorkowski. *Publications:* Du-Wop and Dialectics, in Perspectives of New Music, 1988; Musical Snobbism, Latin American Music Conference; Music Critic to San Juan Star. *Honours:* Music Composition Prize, Ateneo Puertorriqueno, 1989; Guest Composer, Latin American Music Festival, Caracas, Venezuela, 1991–92; Premiered Composer, 1995 Casals Festival; Grammy nomination Tropicalización, 2001. *Address:* Plaza de la Fuente, 1275 Calle España, Toa Alta, Puerto Rico 00953. *E-mail:* williamortizupr@yahoo .com. *Website:* www.geocities.com/williamortiz00953.

**ORVAL, Francis,** DipMus; American horn player and academic; b. 8 Sept. 1944, Liège, Belgium; m. Julie Roy; two s. one d. *Education:* Conservatoire Royal de Musique de Liège, Belgium. *Career:* debut as first solo horn, aged 16, National Orchestra of Belgium, André Clutyens, Conductor; 20 years experience as Principal Horn with major orchestras in Belgium and Luxembourg; Professor, Music Conservatories, Liège and Luxembourg; Co-Director Grétry Music Academy, Liège; Artistic Music Director, Académie Internationale d'Eté de Wallonie; Founder, Organiser, 2 International Horn Competitions, 1977; University Professor, USA, 1983; Has performed as soloist and recitalist around the world; Adjudicator for several competitions; Professor of Horn, Musikhochschule, Trossingen, Germany; mem. International Horn Soc. (fmr officer). *Compositions:* Libre/Free/Frei for horn solo; Champaign for horn and piano; Method for natural horn; Triptych for horn alone; Transcription for horn of Bach's 6 suites for cello. *Recordings include:* Haydn's Concerto for 2 horns; Belgian Contemporary Music; Schumann's Konzertstück; Weber's Concertino; The Berwald and Beethoven Septets with the Uppsala Chamber Soloists; Brahms Horn Trio, with A. Grumiaux and G. Sebok; Bach, 6 Suites for Cello, arrangement for horn; Masterpieces for Horn and Piano with Jean-Claude Vanden Eynden. *Publications:* contrib. articles to Brass Bulletin, Horn Call, Historic Brass Society Journal. *Honours:* First Prize, International music Competition, Louise MacMahon, Lawton, Oklahoma, USA, 1987. *Address:* Boulevard Piercot 14/052, 4000 Liège, Belgium.

**OSBORNE, Charles Thomas,** FRSL; Australian/British writer, critic and poet; b. 24 Nov. 1927, Brisbane, Qld; civil union with Kenneth Thomson 2006. *Education:* Griffith Univ., studied piano with Archie Day and Irene Fletcher, voice with Vido Luppi and Browning Mummery. *Career:* Asst Ed. London Magazine 1957–66; Asst Literary Dir Arts Council of Great Britain 1966–71; Literary Dir 1971–86; Opera Critic, Jewish Chronicle 1985–; Chief Theatre Critic, Daily Telegraph 1986–92; mem. Editorial Bd Opera magazine; mem. Critics' Circle, PEN. *Publications:* The Gentle Planet 1957, Opera 66 1966, Swansong 1968, The Complete Operas of Verdi 1969, Letters of Giuseppe Verdi (ed.) 1971, The Concert Song Companion 1974, Wagner and his World 1977, The Complete Operas of Mozart 1978, W. H. Auden: The Life of a Poet 1980, The Dictionary of Opera 1983, Letter to W. H. Auden and Other Poems 1984, Giving It Way 1986, The Operas of Richard Strauss 1988, The Complete Operas of Richard Wagner 1990, The Bel Canto Operas of Rossini, Donizetti and Verdi 1994, The Pink Danube 1998, The Opera Lover's Companion 2004; contribs to anthologies, newspapers and journals, including Opera, London Magazine, Spectator, Times Literary Supplement, Encounter, New Statesman, Observer, Sunday Times. *Honours:* Hon. DUniv; Gold Medal 1993. *Address:* 125 St George's Road, London, SE1 6HY, England (home). *Telephone:* (20) 7928-1534 (home). *Fax:* (20) 7401-9099 (home).

**OSBORNE, Nigel,** BA, BMus; British composer; *Reid Professor of Music, University of Edinburgh;* b. 23 June 1948, Manchester, England. *Education:* Univ. of Oxford with Kenneth Leighton and Egon Wellesz, and at Polish Radio Experimental Studio, Warsaw. *Career:* fmr Lecturer Univ. of Nottingham

1978; conducted the premiere of The Sun of Venice, Royal Festival Hall, London 1992; reworking of the Electrification of the Soviet Union on tour with Music Theatre Wales, including Linbury Theatre, Covent Garden, 2002; The Piano Tuner (Linbury Studio, Royal Opera House, London) 2004; currently Reid Prof. of Music, Univ. of Edinburgh; extensive composition for theatre, including Glyndebourne, ENO, Opera Factory, Wuppertal, Hebbel Theatre (Berlin), Shakespeare's Globe (London), the Ulysses Theatre (Istria), BBC Radio 3 and BBC2. *Compositions include:* Seven Last Words cantata (Radio Suisse Romande and Ville de Geneve Opera Prize) 1971, Heaventree for chorus 1973, Remembering Esenin for cello and piano 1974, The Sickle for soprano and orchestra 1975, Chansonier for chorus and ensemble 1975, Prelude and Fugue for ensemble 1975, Passers By for trio and synthesizer 1978, Cello Concerto 1977, I Am Goya for baritone and quartet 1977, Vienna, Zürich, Constance for soprano and quintet 1977, Figure/Ground for piano 1978, Kerenza at the Dawn for oboe and tape 1978, Orlando Furioso for chorus and ensemble 1978, Songs from a Bare Mountain for women's chorus 1979, In Camera for ensemble 1979, Under the Eyes for voice and quartet 1979, Quasi una fantasia for cello 1979, Flute Concerto 1980, Gnostic Passion for chorus 1980, Poem without a Hero for four voices and electronics 1980, Mythologies for sextet 1980, The Cage for tenor and ensemble 1981, Piano Sonata 1981, Choralis I–III for six voices 1981, Sinfonia I 1982, Sinfonia II 1983, Cantata piccola for soprano and string quartet, Fantasia for ensemble 1983, Wildlife for ensemble 1984, Alba for mezzo-soprano, ensemble and tape 1984, Zansa for ensemble 1985, Hell's Angles chamber opera 1985, Pornography for mezzo-soprano and ensemble, The Electrification of the Soviet Union opera after Pasternak 1986, Lumiere for string quartet and four groups of children 1986, The Black Leg Miner for ensemble 1987, Esquisse I and II for strings 1987, Stone Garden for Chamber Orchestra 1988, Zone for oboe, clarinet and string trio 1989, Tracks for two choirs, orchestra and wind band 1990, Eulogy (for Michael Vyner) 1990, Canzona for brass 1990, Violin Concerto 1990, The Sun of Venice (after Turner's visions of Venice) 1991, Terrible Mouth opera 1992, Sarajevo opera 1994, Forest-River-Ocean for carnyx, string quartet and electronics 2002. *Honours:* Netherlands Gaudeamus Prize, Radcliffe Award, Koussevitzky Award of the Library of Congress, Washington. *Address:* c/o Department of Music, Alison House, 12 Nicolson Square, Edinburgh, EH8 9DF, Scotland. *Telephone:* (131) 650-2424. *Fax:* (131) 650-2425. *E-mail:* n.osborne@music.ed.ac.uk.

**OSKARSSON, Gudjon;** Singer (Bass); b. 1965, Reykjavík, Iceland. *Education:* Studied in Iceland and Italy (Osimo and Milan). *Career:* Member of the Norwegian Opera from 1990, as Colline, Zuniga, Sparafucile and Raimondo (Lucia di Lammermoor); Fafner, Hunding and Hagen in The Ring, 1993–96 (also at Norwich, 1997); Further appearances at Mozart's Commendatore at Glyndebourne and Covent Garden (1996–97), as Raimondo at Munich and Fafner in Das Rheingold at La Scala (1996); Season 1998 with Titurel in Parsifal at Brussels, the Commendatore at Aix and King Mark for Scottish Opera; Concerts include: Tosca and Otello with the Israel Philharmonic Orchestra (1995–97), Act I of Die Walküre with the London Symphony Orchestra, Rocco in Fidelio under Carlo Rizzi and the Berlioz Messe Solennelle with the Gothenburg Symphony Orchestra; Further concerts with the Oslo and Bergen Philharmonics and the Trondheim Symphony Orchestra; Season 2000–01 as Priam in Les Troyens at Salzburg and Fafner in Das Rheingold at Toulouse. *Address:* c/o Norwegian Opera, PO Box 8800, Youngstorget, 0028 Oslo, Norway.

**OSKOLKOV, Sergei (Alexandrovich);** Composer and Pianist; b. 9 March 1952, Donetsk, Ukraine; m. Natalia Semionovna Oskolkova, 23 April 1986, 2 s. *Education:* Poetry and Painting lessons; Piano class of Galina Sladkovskaya, Donetsk Music College, 1967–71; Piano class of Pavel Serebryakov, 1971–77, Composition class with Vjacheslav Nagovitsin and Yuri Falik, 1976–81, Leningrad Conservatory. *Career:* Debut: As Pianist with Donetsk Philharmonic Orchestra, October 1972; Performance of vocal compositions, Leningrad, 1975; Publishing poetry and selling paintings and graphics, 1972–; Participant as Composer and Pianist at international festivals in Berlin, Kazan, St Petersburg and Kalingrad, 1985; Concert tours, Germany, France, Belgium, Ukraine, Kazakhstan, Latvia; mem, Union of Composers of Russia, 1988. *Compositions:* 2 String Quartets, recorded 1976, 1979; Sinfonietta for string orchestra, recorded 1979; 2 Concertos for piano and orchestra, recorded 1981, 1988; Count Nulin, opera, recorded Leningrad Radio, 1983; Set of Pieces and 2 Sonatas for piano, recorded 1994, published; Music for Russian folk instruments; Music for theatre and film. *Recordings:* Offenbach, Liszt, as pianist with St Petersburg Quartet, CD, 1994; 2nd Piano Sonata and cycle of songs by Oskolkov, 1996; Mussorgsky and Tchaikovsky, as pianist, Radio St Petersburg, 1996. *Address:* St Petersburgsky Prosp 51, ap 5, Petrodvorets, St Petersburg 198903, Russia.

**OSOSTOWICZ, Krysia;** Violinist; b. 1960, England. *Education:* studied with Yehudi Menuhin and Sándor Végh. *Career:* founder mem. of Chamber Ensemble Domus and leader of the Endymion Ensemble; founder and leader of the Dante String Quartet; many performances as soloist and chamber musician, with repertoire from Baroque to Bartók. *Recordings include:* Les Vendredis, with Dante Quartet. *Current Management:* Connaught Artists Management Ltd, 2 Molasses Row, Plantation Wharf, London, SW11 3UX, England. *Telephone:* (20) 7738 0017. *Fax:* (20) 7738 0909. *E-mail:* classicalmusic@connaughtartists.com. *Website:* www.connaughtartists.com.

**OSTENDORF, John;** Singer (Bass-baritone); b. 1 Nov. 1945, New York, USA. *Education:* Studied at Oberlin College with Margaret Harshaw. *Career:*

Debut: Chautauqua Opera 1969, as the Commendatore in Don Giovanni; Appearances at San Francisco, Houston, Baltimore, Toronto and Philadelphia; Amsterdam 1979 in the premiere of Winter Cruise by Henkeman; Repertoire includes Don Alfonso, Basilio, Escamillo, Ramphis in Aida and Handel's Julius Caesar; Many concert performances, notably in the Baroque repertoire. *Recordings:* Bach's St John Passion and Handel's Imeneo, Joshua and Acis and Galatea. *Address:* c/o San Francisco Opera, War Memorial Opera House, San Francisco, CA 84102, USA.

**OSTHOFF, Wolfgang;** German musicologist; b. 17 March 1927, Halle Saale; m. Renate Götz, three s. *Education:* Frankfurt Conservatory with Kurt Hessenburg and others; Universities of Frankfurt and Heidelberg with H. Osthoff, T. Georgiades and others. *Career:* Assistant Lecturer, Munich University, 1957–68; Professor, 1968–, Emeritus, 1995, Würzburg University; mem, International Musicology Society and others. *Publications:* Das dramatische Spätwerk Claudio Monteverdis, 1960; Beethoven Klavier Konzert c-moll, 1965; Theatergesang und darstellende Musik in der Italienischen Renaissance, 2 vols, 1969; Heinrich Schütz, 1974; Stefan George und 'les deux Musiques', 1989; Briefwechsel Hans Pfitzner-Gerhard Frommel, 1990; Editions: Claudio Monteverdi, 12 Composizioni vocali profane e sacre (inedite) 1958, Hans Pfitzner, Concerto for Violoncello and Orchestra Op. posth. (1888) 1978, Claudio Monteverdi, L'Orfeo 1998, Hans Pfitzner, Von deutscher Seele Op. 28 2004, Gerhard Frommel, Sämtliche Lieder mit Klavierbegleitung I 2004. *Contributions:* musicology journals. *Honours:* Dr hc (University of Rome 'La Sapienza') 1999. *Address:* Institut für Musikwissenschaft, University of Würzburg, Residenzplatz 2, 97070 Würzburg, Germany.

**ÖSTMAN, Arnold;** Swedish conductor; b. 1939, Malmö; m. Kristina Modig. *Education:* Univs of Paris and Stockholm. *Career:* fmr Lecturer, State Acad. of Music and Drama, Stockholm; Artistic Dir Vadstena Acad. 1969, f. Norrlands Operan 1974, Gen. Admin. and Artistic Dir Drottningholm Court Theatre 1979–92; has conducted at opera houses including Covent Garden, Parma, Paris Bastille, Paris Garnier, Trieste, Cologne, Bonn, Toulouse, Nice, Vienna Staatsoper, Vienna Volksoper, Wexford, Washington, Lausanne, Gothenburg Opera, Graz Opera; symphonic conductor with orchestras including German radio orchestras of Hamburg, Cologne, Stuttgart and Baden-Baden, Stuttgart Philharmonic, Orchestre nat. de France, de Lille, orchestra of La Fenice, Venice, Adelaide Symphony Orchestra, Orchestra Sinfonia Siciliana, Scottish Chamber Orchestra, Acad. of Ancient Music, London, Royal Concertgebouw Orchestra, Amsterdam, Oslo Philharmonic Orchestra, Minneapolis Symphony Orchestra, Sydney Symphony Orchestra, Melbourne Symphony Orchestra, Rotterdam Philharmonic, Gothenburg Symphony Orchestra, Swedish Radio Orchestra; works regularly with Netherlands Radio Chamber Orchestra (symphonic and operatic); mem. Royal Swedish Acad. of Music. *Recordings include:* Così fan tutte, Le Nozze di Figaro, Don Giovanni, Die Zauberflöte (Diapason d'Or and Deutsche Schallplattenpreis), Gluck's Alceste for Naxos; co-producer two TV films: Christina the Winter Queen, Gustav III (both winners of Prix d'Italia). *Honours:* Chevalier, Légion d'honneur; Hon. PhD. *Current Management:* Haydn Rawstron Ltd, 36 Station Road, London, SE20 7BQ, England. *Telephone:* (20) 8659-2659. *Fax:* (20) 8676-9119.

**O'SULLIVAN, Cara;** Singer (Soprano); b. 1970, Cork, Ireland. *Career:* Engagements with Welsh National Opera as Donna Anna and Violetta; At Garsington for Mozart's Fiordiligi and Constanze; The Queen of Night for Opéra de Nantes, 1999–2000; Helmwige in Die Walküre for the Royal Opera, 1998–99; Concerts include the Verdi Requiem at the Albert Hall; Beethoven's Ninth; Elijah; Messiah in Barcelona with Paul McCreesh; Brahms Requiem; Poulenc's Gloria. *Honours:* Winner, Stanislav Moniuszko Vocal Competition, Warsaw, 1996. *Address:* Harlequin Agency Ltd, 203 Fidlas Road, Cardiff CF4 5NA, Wales.

**OTAKA, Tadaaki;** Japanese conductor; b. 8 Nov. 1947, Kamakura; s. of Hisatada Otaka and Misaoko Otaka; m. Yukiko Otaka 1978. *Education:* Toho Music School, Toho Music Acad., Vienna Acad., Austria. *Career:* began studying violin 1951; apptd. Chief Conductor Tokyo Philharmonic Orchestra 1971–, Conductor Laureate 1991–; Chief Conductor Sapporo Symphony 1981–86, Prin. Conductor 1998–; Prin. Conductor BBC Welsh Symphony Orchestra (now BBC Nat. Orchestra of Wales) 1987–95, Conductor Laureate 1996–; Chief Conductor Yomiuri Nippon Symphony Orchestra 1992–98; Music Adviser and Prin. Conductor Kioi Sinfonietta (Tokyo) 1995–; Dir Britten Pears Orchestra 1998–2001; has conducted BBC Proms, and orchestras including City of Birmingham Symphony, Royal Liverpool Philharmonic, Royal Scottish National, Bournemouth Symphony, BBC Symphony, London Symphony, London Philharmonic, Rotterdam Philharmonic, Bamberg Symphony and Strasbourg Philharmonic. *Music:* many recordings with BBC Nat. Orchestra of Wales including works by Takemitsu and Franck, and Britten's Peter Grimes with Yomiuri Nippon. *Honours:* Hon. Fellowship (Welsh Coll. of Music and Drama) 1993; Hon. CBE 1997; Dr hc (Univ. of Wales) 1993; 2nd Prize Min-On Conductors' Competition 1969, Suntory Music Award 1992, Elgar Medal 2000. *Current Management:* c/o Askonas Holt, Lonsdale Chambers, 27 Chancery Lane, London, WC2A 1PF, England. *Telephone:* (20) 7400-1700. *Fax:* (20) 7400-1799. *E-mail:* info@askonasholt.co.uk.

**OTELLI, Claudio;** Singer (Bass-baritone); b. 1959, Vienna, Austria. *Education:* Studied at the Vienna Musikhochschule. *Career:* Bregenz Festival, 1986, Vienna Staatsoper, 1989–94; Salzburg Festival, 1986, in Elektra; Rome

Opera, 1994, as Alfio and Tonio in Cav and Pag; Season 1996 as Escamillo at Hamburg and Donner in Das Rheingold at La Scala, Milan; Canadian Opera Company, Toronto, 1996, as Orestes in Elektra; Other roles include Wagner's Dutchman and Klingsor, and Carlo in La Forza del Destino; Further appearances at Frankfurt, Berlin, Tokyo and Barcelona; Sang Jochanaan in Salome at Santa Fe, 1998; Season 2000–01 as Ford in Falstaff for the Vienna Staatsoper, Hindemith's Cardillac at Frankfurt, Orestes in Elektra for new Israeli Opera at Savonlinna, Telramund in Essen and Pizarro for Frankfurt Opera (Alfio and Tonio, 2001). *Address:* Santa Fe Opera, PO Box 2408, Santa Fe, NM 87504, USA.

**OTEY, Louis;** Singer (Baritone); b. 1957, USA. *Career:* Sang in The Rape of Lucretia and La Bohème at Dallas, 1985; Season 1985 with Menotti's The Medium and as Don Giovanni for Victoria State Opera; Sang Sharpless in Butterfly at Chicago and Covent Garden, 1990; Miami Opera from 1992, as Enrico in Lucia di Lammermoor and the Villains in Les contes d'Hoffmann; Season 1994 as Mozart's Count at Costa Mesa and Germont for New York City Opera; Monte Carlo and Cincinnati, 1996, as the Philosopher in Massenet's Chérubin, and Iago in Otello; Sorel in Menotti's The Consul, at the 1998 Spoleto Festival; Season 2000–01 as Francesco in the European premiere of Ginastera's Beatrix Cenci, at Geneva; Pinkerton for Dallas Opera and in the premiere of La Señorita Cristina by Luis de Pablo, at Madrid. *Address:* Cincinnati Opera Association, Music Hall, 1241 Elm Street, Cincinnati, OH 45210, USA.

**OTT, Karin;** Singer (Soprano); b. 13 Dec. 1945, Wädenswil, Zürich, Switzerland. *Education:* Studied in Zürich and Germany. *Career:* Sang first with the opera house of Biel-Solothurn; Appeared in Mussorgsky's Sorochintsy Fair at Brunswick 1970; Zürich 1970, as Tove in Schoenberg's Gurrelieder; Paris Opéra as the Queen of Night in Die Zauberflöte; Salzburg Festival 1979–81; Venice 1981, in the premiere of Sinopoli's Lou Salomé; Engagements at Stuttgart, Berlin, Zürich, Amsterdam and Vienna; Sang Scoltarella in the premiere of the original version of Henze's König Hirsch, 1985, as Kassel. *Recordings include:* Die Zauberflöte, conducted by Karajan (Deutsche Grammophon). *Address:* c/o Opernhaus Zürich, Falkenstrasse 1, 8008 Zürich, Switzerland.

**OTTENTHAL, Gertrud;** Singer; b. 1957, Bad Oldesloe, Schleswig-Holstein, Germany. *Education:* Studied in Lubeck. *Career:* Sang at Wiesbaden Opera 1980, Hamburg 1981–82; Engagements at Vienna Volksoper 1982, Salzburg Festival 1984, Vienna Festival 1986–88; Sang Mozart's Countess at Klagenfurt 1984, Komische Oper Berlin 1986, returned to Berlin 1990 as Mimi; Further appearances at Theater am Gärtnerplatz Munich, Barcelona and the Schwetzingen Festival; Other roles include Agathe, Fiordiligi, Sandrina in La Finta Giardiniera, Rosalinde, Antonio and Arianna in Giustino by Handel; Concert repertoire includes works by Bach, Handel, Mozart, Bruckner and Schubert; Sang Elisabeth de Valois at the Komische Oper, Berlin, 1999; Season 2000 as the Queen in Zemlinsky's Der König Kandaules, at the Vienna Volksoper, and Wagner's Gutrune at the Erl Festival, Tyrol. *Recordings:* Werther, Der Rosenkavalier and Der Wildschütz; Mrs Ma in Der Kreidekreis by Zemlinsky; Donna Elvira in Don Giovanni, conducted by Neeme Järvi. *Address:* c/o Komische Oper Berlin, Behrenstrasse 55–57, 1086 Berlin, Germany.

**OTTO, Lisa;** Singer (Soprano); b. 14 Nov. 1919, Dresden, Germany; m. Albert Blind. *Education:* Dresden Musikhochschukle, with Susane Steinmetz-Pree. *Career:* Debut: Beuthen 1941, as Sophie in Der Rosenkavalier; Sang in Beuthen 1941–44; Nuremburg 1945–46; Dresden 1946–51; St ädtische (later Deutsche) Oper Berlin from 1951; Took part in the 1965 premiere of Henze's Der junge Lord; Salzburg 1953–57, as Blondchen and Despina; Glyndebourne 1956, as Blondchen in Die Entführung; Guest appearances in Vienna, Milan and Paris; Other roles include Mozart's Papagena and Susanna, Beethoven's Marzelline, and Ighino in Palestrina; Sang at the Deutsche Oper Berlin until 1983; Many engagements as concert singer. *Recordings:* St John Passion by Bach; Der junge Lord; Die Zauberflöte; Così fan tutte.

**ÖTVÖS, Csilla;** Opera Singer; b. 23 June 1947, Budapest, Hungary; m. Antal Szabados, 23 Aug 1975. *Education:* Liszt Ferenc Academy of Music. *Career:* Debut: Ariadne auf Naxos, Zerbinetta, 1974; More than 48 roles in the Hungarian State Opera include Despina in Mozart's Così fan tutte, Rosina in Rossini's Il Barbiere di Sivigla, Norina in Don Pasquale, Adina in Elisir d'amore; Appearances on Hungarian television, including Lehár's Die Lustige Witwe. *Recordings:* Szép Alom: Hungarian operettas and folk music; Operettcsillogás; International operettas. *Publications:* Contributions to several magazines; Photograph on cover page of Till Géza's Big Book of Operas. *Honours:* Pro Kultúra Hungarica, 1985; Bartók-Pásztory Prizez, 1992. *Address:* Szt István Krt 13 III, 1955 Budapest, Hungary.

**OUE, Eiji;** Conductor; b. 1959, Hiroshima, Japan. *Education:* Studied at Toho School of Music and with Bernstein and Ozawa at Tanglewood, from 1978. *Career:* Assistant to Bernstein at concerts in Paris, Vienna and Milan; Music Director of the Erie Philharmonic, Pennysylvania, 1991–95; Associate conductor of the Buffalo Philharmonic Orchestra, 1987–91; Music Director of the Minnesota Orchestra, 1995; Tours through USA and to Europe, 1997–98; Director of the Grand Teton Music Festival in Wyoming, 1995; Further engagements with the New York Philharmonic Orchestra, Philadelphia Orchestra, Oslo Philharmonic Orchestra, Santa Cecilia, Rome, Los Angeles Philharmonic Orchestra; Chief conductor of the NDR SO, Hannover from 1998. *Recordings:* The Rite of Spring and The Firebird by Stravinsky;

Strauss Ein Heldenleben and Mussorgsky. *Honours:* Koussevitzky prize, 1980; Hans Haring Gold Medal at the Salzburg Mozarteum, 1981. *Address:* c/o IMG Artists, Lovell House, 616 Chiswick High Road, London W4 5RX, England.

**OUNDJIAN, Peter;** Violinist; b. 21 Dec. 1955, Toronto, Ontario, Canada. *Education:* Studied at the Juilliard School with Ivan Galamian and Dorothy DeLay. *Career:* Leader of the Tokyo Quartet from 1981; Regular concerts in the USA and abroad; First cycle of the complete quartets of Beethoven at the Yale at Norfolk Chamber Music Festival, 1986; Repeated cycles at the 92nd Street Y (New York), Ravinia and Israel Festivals and Yale and Princeton Universities; Season 1990–91 at Alice Tully Hall and the Metropolitan Museum of Art, New York, Boston, Washington DC, Los Angeles, Cleveland, Detroit, Chicago, Miami, Seattle, San Francisco, Toronto; Tour of South America, two tours of Europe including Paris, Amsterdam, Bonn, Milan, Munich, Dublin, London, Berlin; Quartet-in-Residence at Yale University, University of Cincinnati College-Conservatory of Music. *Recordings:* Schubert's major Quartets; Mozart Flute Quartets with James Galway and Clarinet Quintet with Richard Stolzman; Quartets by Bartók, Brahms, Debussy, Haydn, Mozart and Ravel; Beethoven Middle Period Quartets (RCA). *Honours:* Grand Prix du Disque du Montreux; Best Chamber Music Recording of the Year from Stereo Review and the Gramophone; Four Grammy nominations. *Address:* Intermusica Artists Management, 16 Duncan Terrace, London N1 8BZ, England.

**OUSSET, Cécile;** French pianist; b. 23 Jan. 1936, Tarbes. *Education:* Paris Conservatoire. *Career:* French début with Orchestre de Paris; British début, Edin. Festival 1980; U.S. début with LA Philharmonic 1984; first recital at Théâtre des Champs-Elysées 1987–88; played Debussy's Preludes on BBC TV 1988. *Recordings include:* concertos by Rachmaninov, Liszt, Saint-Saëns, Ravel, Grieg and Mendelssohn and recitals of Chopin, Debussy and Liszt. *Honours:* prizewinner, Van Cliburn, Queen Elisabeth of Belgium, Busoni and Marguerite Long-Jacques Thibaud competitions; Grand Prix du Disque for recording of Brahms 2nd Piano Concerto. *Address:* c/o Intermusica Artists' Management, 16 Duncan Terrace, London, N1 8B7, England (office).

**OUZIEL, Dalia;** Pianist; b. 28 Sept. 1947, Tel-Aviv, Israel; m. Jerrold Rubenstein, 1 July 1969, 1 s., 1 d. *Education:* Rubin Academy, Tel-Aviv; Royal Conservatories, Mons and Brussels, Belgium. *Career:* Soloist and Chamber Artist; Performs at festivals and is known through her numerous recordings. *Recordings include:* Beethoven Variations, Piano Solo; Mozart Concerti, Double Piano Concerto, Sonatas for Violin and Piano, complete Piano Duos; Violin-Piano Sonatas of Mozart, Brahms, Fauré, Copland, Ives, Mendelssohn, Ravel, Grieg, Villa-Lobos, others; Piano Trios of Fauré, Schubert, Brahms, Mendelssohn, others; Fauré Piano Quartets; Chausson Concerto; Schubert Trout; Mendelssohn Sextet; Beethoven Lieder. *Address:* Avenue de la Rose des Vents 4, 1410 Waterloo, Belgium.

**OVCHINIKOV, Vladimir Pavlovich;** Russian pianist; b. 1 Jan. 1958, Beleby, Urals. *Education:* privately under Anna Artobolevskaya and Moscow Conservatoire (under Alexey Nasedkin). *Career:* London debut, Barbican Hall 1987; has since given recitals in UK, Europe, USA, Canada and Japan and appeared with BBC Symphony, Royal Liverpool Philharmonic, Netherlands Philharmonic, Moscow Philharmonic and other major orchestras; lecturer, Keyboard Studies, Royal Northern Coll. of Music 1994–; Silver Medal (jtly with Peter Donohoe), Moscow Tchaikovsky Competition 1982; First Prize, Leeds Int. Piano Competition 1987. *Address:* c/o Manygate Management, 13 Cotswold Mews, 30 Battersea Square, London, SW11 3RA, England. *Telephone:* (20) 7223-7265. *Fax:* (20) 7585-2830.

**OVENS, Raymond;** Violinist; b. 14 Oct. 1932, Bristol, England; m. Sheila Margaret Vaughan Williams, 1 s., 1 d. *Education:* Royal Academy of Music; ARAM. *Career:* Debut: Wigmore Hall, London, 1950; Leader, London Symphony Orchestra, 1951; Principal 2nd Violin, Royal Philharmonic Orchestra, 1956; Assistant Leader, 1972; Leader until 1980, BBC Scottish Symphony Orchertra; Leader, Philharmonia Orchestra 1980–85, Orchestra of the English National Opera from 1985; Has played concertos with the BBC Scottish Symphony, the Vancouver Symphony and the Philharmonia Orchestra; Concerts and Recitals for BBC; Leader, Lyra String Quartet; Leader, Ceol Rosh Chamber Group. *Honours:* FRAM.

**OVERMAN, Robert;** Singer (Baritone); b. 1957, North Carolina, USA. *Career:* Sang at the Landestheater, Salzburg, from 1984; Karlsruhe Opera, 1986–91; Guest appearances at Mannheim, Stuttgart and Zürich; Salzburg Festival, 1987; Leipzig Opera, 1990, as Count Luna; Bonn Opera from 1992, in Le Villi and La Rondine by Puccini, and as Iago; Sang Carlo in La Forza del Destino at Karlsruhe, 1993, and Jack Rance in La Fanciulla del West at Catania, 1995; Other roles include Germont, and Alfio in Cavalleria Rusticana. *Address:* Bonn Opera, Am Boeselagerhof 1, 5311 Bonn, Germany.

**OWEN, Barbara,** BMus, MMus; American organist and musicologist; *Organist, St Anne's Episcopal Church, Lowell, Massachusetts;* b. 25 Jan. 1933, Utica, NY. *Education:* Westminster Choir Coll., Boston Univ., North German Organ Acad., Acad. of Italian Organ Music. *Career:* Music Dir First Religious Soc., Newburyport 1963–2002; Curator AGO Organ Library, Boston Univ. 1985–; Organist, St Anne's Episcopal Church, Lowell, Mass 2002–; Ed. of Publs, Westfield Center for Early Keyboard Studies 2001–; freelance researcher, lecturer, recitalist, teacher and organ consultant; mem. American Guild of Organists, Organ Historical Soc. (Pres. 1997–99), American Musical

Instrument Soc., British Inst. of Organ Studies, Reed Organ Soc. *Publications include:* Editions of Music: A Century of American Organ Music (four vols) 1975, 1976, 1983, 1991, A Century of English Organ Music 1979, A Handel Album 1981, The Candlelight Carol Book 1981, 4 Centuries of Italian Organ Music 1994, A Pachelbel Album 1994; books written: The Organs and Music of King's Chapel 1965, 1993, The Organ in New England 1979, E. Power Biggs, Concert Organist 1987; Co-ed.: Charles Brenton Fisk, Organ Builder 1986, The Registration of Baroque Organ Music 1997; contrib. to Grove's Dictionary (7th edn), Grove's Dictionary of Musical Instruments, New Grove Dictionary of American Music, Harvard Dictionary of Music. *Honours:* Alumni Merit Award, Westminster Choir Coll. 1988, OHS Distinguished Service Award 1988, AMIS Curt Sachs Award 1994. *Address:* 28 Jefferson Street, New-buryport, MA 01950, USA; (978) 465-2068 (home). *Fax:* (978) 465-2068 (home).

**OWEN, Lynn,** BS, MS; American singer (soprano) and voice teacher; *Voice Teacher, Manhattan School of Music;* b. Kenosha, WI; m. Richard Owen 1960; three s. *Education:* Northwestern University, Juilliard School of Music, Vienna Academy of Music, Austria. *Career:* debut Constanze in Abduction from the Seraglio, New Orleans Opera, USA; La Fanciulla del West (Minnie), Fliegende Holländer (Senta), Metropolitan Opera, New York; Don Carlos (Elisabetta), Forza del Destino (Leonora), Il Trovatore (Leonore), Prince Igor (Jaroslavna), Zürich, Switzerland; Il Trovatore, Turandot, Fidelio (Leonora), Krefeld Opera, Hamburg and Frankfurt, Germany; Fanciulla del West, Central City, Fliegende Holländer, Aspen, USA; Ballo in Maschera, Othello, Calgary, Canada; Il Trovatore, Caracas, Venezuela; Siegfried (Brünnhilde), Art Park, New York; Isolde, Mexico City Opera; Concerts and recitals throughout USA and Europe; US premiere, Strauss, Aegyptische Helena, NY (title role); Frau Ohne Shatten (Dyer's wife); Die Walkuere (Sieglinde) NY; world premieres, US (Owen) Mary Dyer, The Death of the Virgin, Abigail Adams, Rain,(Alice Tully, New York); Voice Teacher, Columbia Univ./ Barnard Coll., New York 1983–, Manhattan School of Music 1993–; mem. Nat. Asscn of Teachers of Singing, New York Singing Teachers' Asscn. *Recordings:* Serenus Records, Vanguard Records, Vienna to Broadway, Aurora, Rain, Albany Records. *Publications:* contribs to music journals. *Honours:* Fulbright Scholar. *Address:* 21 Claremont Avenue, New York, NY 10027, USA. *Telephone:* (212) 864-4968 (office). *E-mail:* operaowen@aol.com (office).

**OWEN, Stephen;** Singer (bass-baritone); b. 1961, USA. *Career:* Concert appearances at Carnegie Hall and in Seattle and Honolulu; Dallas, Philadelphia and Cleveland Operas; European debut as Gunther in Götterdämmerung at Salzburg, 1990; Further appearances as Wagner's Dutchman at Kassel, Aachen and Graz; Don Pizarro, Escamillo and Jochanaan; Roles at Aachen Opera have included The Villains in Les Contes d'Hoffmann and Scarpia; Graz Opera as Kurwenal, Amonasro, Orest and Sharpless; Teatro Colón, Buenos Aires, 1993, as the Ring Master in Lulu. *Current Management:* Athole Still International Management, Forresters Hall, 25–27 Westow Street, London, SE19 3RY, England. *Telephone:* (20) 8771-5271. *Fax:* (20) 8768-6600. *Website:* www.atholestill.com.

**OWENS, Anne-Marie;** Singer (mezzo-soprano). b. 15 Aug. 1955, Jarrow, Tyne and Wear, England. *Education:* Newcastle School of Music, the Guildhall School and the National Opera Studio. *Career:* Sang Gluck's Orpheus, Dido, Dalila and Angelina (La Cenerentola) while student; Professional debut as Mistress Quickly on the Glyndebourne Tour; For English National Opera has sung Charlotte, Rosina, Maddalena, Suzuki (Madama Butterfly), Bianca (The Rape of Lucretia), Solokha in the British premiere of Rimsky-Korsakov's Christmas Eve, 1988, and Magdalene; Covent Garden 1989, as Third Lady in Die Zauberflöte and Rossweise in a new production of Die Walküre; Visit to the Vienna Staatsoper with the company of the Royal Opera, 1992; Sang Jocasta in Oedipus Rex for Opera North, followed by the title role in Ariane and Bluebeard by Dukas, 1990; Season 1992 in Les Contes d'Hoffmann at Covent Garden, as Baba the Turk in The Rake's Progress at Brussels and Preziosilla in The Force of Destiny for ENO; Other roles include Arnalta in Monteverdi's Poppea (Glyndebourne Festival); Clotilde in Norma and the Hostess in Boris Godunov (Royal Opera); Baba the Turk (Brussels); Fidalma in Il Matrimonio Segreto (Lausanne); Sang Venus in a new production of Tannhäuser for Opera North; T Picker's Emmeline at the New York City Opera, 1998; Kundry in Parsifal for Scottish Opera, 2000; Concert appearances with the City of Birmingham Symphony, BBC Symphony, London Mozart Players, Royal Liverpool Philharmonic; Has sung at the London Proms, Aix-en-Provence, San Sebastien, Rouen and Detroit (US debut with Messiah); Season 2000–01 as Kundry for Scottish Opera, Laura in La Gioconda (concert) and Arnalta in Poppea for ENO; Brangaene for Opera North and Azucena in Glasgow. *Current Management:* Hazard Chase, Norman House, Cambridge Place, Cambridge CB2 1NS, England. *Telephone:* (1223) 312400. *Fax:* (1223) 460827. *Website:* www .hazardchase.co.uk.

**OWENS, David Bruce;** composer; b. 16 Oct. 1950, USA; m. 1974, one s. two d. *Education:* Eastman School, Rochester, NY, Manhattan School, New York. *Career:* mem. ASCAP. *Compositions:* Sonatina for Percussion Solo, 1969; Quartet for Strings, 1969; Encounter for Orchestra, 1970; Gentle Horizon for Chamber Ensemble, 1972; Ricercar for Band, 1978; Concerto for Viola and Orchestra, 1982; The Shores of Peace for Chorus and Chamber Orchestra, 1984; Fantasy on a Celtic Carol for Viola and Piano, 1985; Jonah, opera in 3 acts, 1986–89; One in Heart, processional for Organ or Orchestra or Band, 1988; My Frozen Well for SATB Chorus, 1991; Echoes of Edo for Piano Solo,

1993; Trio for Violin, Horn and Piano, 1995; Double Concerto for euphonium, tuba and orchestra, 1997; Choral, piano, organ pieces and songs. *Contributions:* columns and articles on 20th Century music, also reviews of many books in music; The Christian Science Monitor; Ovation; Musical America. *Honours:* ASCAP/Deems Taylor Award for Distinguished Criticism, for Christian Science Monitor column, Inside 20th Century Music, 1983. *Address:* 75 Travis Road, Holliston, MA 01746, USA.

**OXENBOULD, Moffatt;** Artistic Director; b. 18 Nov. 1943, Sydney, Australia. *Education:* Studied at the National Institute for Dramatic Art. *Career:* Stage Manager with Elizabethan Trust Opera, 1963–65, Sutherland Williamson Opera, and at Sadler's Wells, London, 1966–67; Planning Co-ordinator with Elizabethan Trust Opera-Australian Opera, 1967–73; Artistic Administrator, Australian Opera, 1974–84, Artistic Director 1984–2000; Productions include: The Rape of Lucretia, 1971, Il Trittico, 1978, La Clemenza di Tito, 1991, Idomeneo, 1994, and Madama Butterfly, 1997; La Bohème, 1999. *Publications:* Joan Sutherland: A Tribute, 1989. *Contributions:* Various Australian publications. *Honours:* Order of Australia, 1985; Dame Joan Hammond Award, 1986. *Address:* c/o Opera Australia, PO Box 291, Strawberry Hills, New South Wales 2012, Australia.

**OXLEY, James;** Singer (tenor); b. 1964, England. *Education:* Royal College of Music (as Cellist), Oxford University, and with Rudolf Piernay. *Career:* Debut: Royal Albert Hall 1991, under David Willcocks; Concerts include Les Illuminations, and the Brahms Experience on South Bank (1992) and Edinburgh Festival, 1993; Season 1995–96 with Messiah (CBSO and Ulster Orchestras), and Alexander's Feast by Handel with the Brandenburg Consort; A Child of our Time in Oxford and Sweden, L'Enfance du Christ in Spain, and Britten's War Requiem; Bach's B Minor Mass on tour to France with Le Concert Sprituel; Opera roles include Tamino (at Durham), Ottavio, Rodolfo and Alfredo; Title roles in Britten's Prodigal Son, with Kent Opera; Season 1996–97 with Purcell's King Arthur in France and The Fairy Queen at Schlossbruhl; Werther at Wexford, the Christmas Oratorio under Marc Minkowski, the Missa solemnis at the Festival Hall, London, and Messiah with the CBSO. *Honours:* First Prize at the 1994 International Vocalisten Councours/Hertogenbosch. *Current Management:* Hazard Chase Ltd, Norman House, Cambridge Place, Cambridge, CB2 1NS, England. *Telephone:* (1223) 312400. *Fax:* (1223) 460827. *Website:* www.hazardchase.co.uk.

**OZAWA, Seiji;** Japanese conductor; *Artistic Director, Tokyo Opera Nomori;* b. 1 Sept. 1935, Shenyang, China; m. 1st Kyoko Edo; m. 2nd Vera Ilyan; one s. one d. *Education:* Toho School of Music, Tokyo with Prof. Hideo Saito, Tanglewood, USA and in West Berlin under Herbert von Karajan. *Career:* Asst Conductor (under Leonard Bernstein), New York Philharmonic 1961–62 (including tour of Japan 1961); Guest Conductor, San Francisco Symphony, Detroit Symphony, Montréal, Minneapolis, Toronto and London Symphony Orchestras 1961–65; Music Dir Ravinia Festival, Chicago 1964–68; Music Dir Toronto Symphony Orchestra 1965–69, San Francisco Symphony Orchestra 1970–76, Boston Symphony Orchestra 1973–2002, Vienna State Opera 2002– (10); co-founder and Artistic Dir Tokyo Opera Nomori 2005–; toured Europe conducting many of the major orchestras 1966–67; Salzburg Festival 1969; toured USA, France, FRG, China 1979, Austria, UK 1981, Japan 1981, 1986, toured England, Netherlands, France, Germany, Austria and Belgium 1988; opened music acad., Geneva 2005–; makes frequent guest appearances with leading orchestras of America, Europe and Japan; has conducted opera at Salzburg, Covent Garden, La Scala, Vienna Staatsoper and Paris Opera; conducted world premiere, Messiaen's St Francis of Assisi, Paris 1983; many recordings. *Honours:* Hon. DMus (Univ. of Mass., New England Conservatory, Wheaton Coll., Norton, Mass.); First Prize, Int. Competition of Orchestra Conductors, France 1959, Koussevitsky Prize for outstanding student conductor 1960, Laureate, Fondation du Japon 1988. *Current Management:* ESTA Central Committee, Alter Markt 2, 5020 Salzburg; Breibergstrasse 6, 50939 Cologne 41, Germany. *E-mail:* estainternational@wanadoo.fr (office). *Website:* www.esta-int.com (office).

**OZOLINS, Arthur Marcelo,** BSc; Canadian concert pianist; b. 7 Feb. 1946, Lübeck, Germany. *Education:* University of Toronto, Canada, Mannes College of Music, New York, USA; studies with Pablo Casals, Jacques Abram, Nadia Boulanger, Nadia Reisenberg, Vlado Perlemuter. *Career:* debut, Toronto Symphony Orchestra, Toronto, 1961; Soloist with Royal Philharmonic, Hallé Orchestra, Stockholm and Oslo Philharmonic, Leningrad Philharmonic, Montreal Symphony, Toronto Symphony; Recitals, New York, London, Paris, Moscow, Leningrad, Buenos Aires, Sydney, San Paulo; 7 Tours, USSR; Television and radio performances, CBC, BBC, Swedish Radio; Concerto repertoire included works by Bach, Brahms, Beethoven, Mozart (K414, K466 and K503), Rachmaninov, Prokofiev, Tchaikovsky and Tippett (Handel Fantasy); mem, AFM; English Speaking Union. *Recordings:* The Complete Piano Concerti and Paganini Rhapsody of Rachmaninov with Mario Bernardi and the Toronto Symphony plus Dohnányi's Variations on a Nursery Song, Healey Willan's Piano Concerto and Strauss Burleske; Numerous Solo recordings. *Honours:* 1st Prizes, Edmonton Competition, 1968, CBC Talent Festival, 1968; Juno Award, Best Classical Record, 1981; 7 Canada Council Awards. *Current Management:* Robert Gilder & Co., Enterprise House, 59–65 Upper Ground, London, SE1 9PQ, England. *Telephone:* (20) 7928-9008. *Fax:* (20) 7928-9755. *E-mail:* rgilder@robert-gilder.com. *Address:* 159 Colin Avenue, Toronto, Ont. M5P 2C5, Canada (home). *Telephone:* (416) 489-2762 (home).

**OZOLINS, Janis (Alfreds);** Violoncellist, Concert Singer and Orchestral Conductor; b. 29 Sept. 1919, Riga, Latvia; m. Adine Uggla, 15 May 1951, 2 s., 1 d. *Education:* Diploma, Solo Violoncello, Conservatory of Latvia, 1944; Studied with Professor E Mainardi, Rome, 1947–48; Studied Composition, Riga, and Royal Academy of Music, Stockholm, Singing Teachers Examination, Stockholm, 1958; Examinations in Musicology, University of Uppsala, 1962. *Career:* Debut: Violoncello, Riga, 1933; Concert radio recitals, solo performances with orchestra, Latvia, Sweden, Denmark, the United King-

dom, Italy, Switzerland; Music Master, 1956–; Conductor, Landskrona Symphony Orchestra, Sweden, 1957; Bass Soloist, Beethoven's 9th Symphony with H Blomstedt, Norrköping, Sweden, 1961; Director, Växjö Municipal School of Music and Municipal Music Dor, Växjö, Sweden, 1964–84; Conductor, operas and ballets, Växjö. *Contributions:* Sohlmans Musiklexicon. *Honours:* National Prize of Latvia, 1944; Culture Prize, Växjö Lions Club, 1976; Royal Gold Medal, Swedish Orchestra National Federation, 1977, 1984. *Address:* Via Sicilia 1, 63039 San Benedetto del Tronto (AP), Italy.

# P

**PAASIKIVI, Lilli;** Singer (mezzo-soprano); b. 1970, Finland. *Education:* Royal Academy, Stockholm, and Royal College of Music, London; with Neil Mackie; Further studies with Janet Baker, 1990–94. *Career:* Debut: Noorland Opera 1993, as Ottone in Poppea; appearances at Paris Châtelet (Pilgrim in Saariaho's L'amour de loin 2001); Finnish National Opera from 1998 as Cenerentola, Suzuki, Dorabella, Marguerite (Berlioz Faust) and Rosina; Cordelia in the premiere of Sallinen's King Lear; Jitsuko Honda in premiere of Hosokawa's Hanjo at Aix Festival 2004. *Recordings:* Kullervo Symphony, The Tempest, The Maiden in the Tower, by Sibelius, Complete Alma Mahler Songs. *Current Management:* Harrison/Parrott Ltd, 12 Penzance Place, London, W11 4PA, England. *Telephone:* (20) 7229 9166. *Fax:* (20) 7221 5042. *Website:* www.harrisonparrott.com.

**PABST, Michael;** Singer (tenor); b. 1955, Graz, Austria. *Education:* Studied in Graz and Vienna. *Career:* Principal Tenor at Vienna Volksoper, 1978–84, singing operetta and lyric opera roles; Dramatic repertoire from 1985, including: Max, in Der Freichütz, Munich; Bacchus, at Philadelphia, Stuttgart, Frankfurt and Houston; Lohengrin, at Hamburg and Zürich; Walther, at Cape Town and Trieste; Erik, at La Scala and Buenos Aires; Huon in Oberon, at La Scala; Florestan at the Savonlinna Festival and Siegmund at Liège; Guest appearances at Vienna Staatsoper from 1991, with Florestan, The Drum Major in Wozzeck, Max, Jenik in The Bartered Bride, Erik; Other roles include Hoffmann, Pedro in Tiefland, Luigi in Il Tabarro; Schubert's Fierrabras; Sergei, in Lady Macbeth; Strauss's Matteo, Aegisthus, Burgomaster in Friedenstag and Apollo. *Recordings include:* Heinrich in Schreker's Irrelohe, 1995; Season 1998 in Henze's Venus and Adonis at Genoa and as Bacchus in Ariadne at Toulouse. *Current Management:* Athole Still International Management, Forresters Hall, 25–27 Westow Street, London, SE19 3RY, England. *Telephone:* (20) 8771-5271. *Fax:* (20) 8768-6600. *Website:* www .atholestill.com.

**PACE, Patrizia;** Singer (Soprano); b. 1963, Turin, Italy. *Education:* Studied at Turin Conservatory. *Career:* Debut: La Scala 1984 as Celia in Mozart's Lucio Silla; Has appeared in Milan as Micaela, Mozart's Despina, Susanna and Zerlina, Oscar, Lisa in La Sonnambula and in premiere Il Principe Felice by Mannino, 1987; Guest appearances at Deutsche Oper Berlin, Spoleto Festival and the Vienna Staatsoper as Oscar and Rossini's Elvira, 1986 and 1988, Gilda, Nannetta in Falstaff and Yniold; Further engagements at Hamburg Staatsoper as Liu, Florence, Genoa, Palermo and Covent Garden 1991 and 1993 as Gilda, and Yniold in Pelléas et Mélisande; Other roles include Rosina, and Sofia in Il Signor Bruschino; Season 1998 at Catania as Gilda and Marzelline; Engaged as Nannetta in Falstaff for the Royal Opera, 1999; Sang Zobeida in Donizetti's Alahor in Granata at Palermo, 1999, Zerlina at La Coruña, 2000. *Recordings:* Barbarina in Le nozze di Figaro and Mozart's Requiem; Mozart's C minor Mass. *Address:* c/o Teatro alla Scala, Via Filodrammatici 2, Milan, Italy.

**PACIOREK, Grazyna;** Composer; b. 11 Dec. 1967, Zyrardow, Poland. *Education:* Degree in Violin, State School of Music, Warsaw, 1987; Studying Composition under Professor M Borkowski, Academy of Music, Warsaw; International courses for young composers, Polish Section, ISCM, Kazimierz Dolny, Poland, 1989, 1990, 1991; Computer course and workshops, Studio of Electro-acoustic Music, Academy of Music, Kraków, 1991. *Career:* Many performances at the composers concerts in Warsaw (Academy of Music, Royal Castle) and in Kraków, 1987–91; Composed music for film aired on Polish television, 1991; Works presented in radio programme at Gdansk Meeting of Young Composers, Oct 1991 and 5th Laboratory of Contemporary Chamber Music, 1991; mem, Polish Society for Contemporary Music; Polish Composers' Union Youth Circle. *Compositions include:* Monologue for Oboe Solo; Te-qui-la for 6 percussion group; Toccata for violin, cello and piano, string quartet; Muzyka Mapothana for oboe and accordion; Concert for viola and orchestra; Electronic Music, film music. *Honours:* June 1991, Academy of Music in Warsaw applied to Minister of Culture and Fine Arts for her artistic scholarship in 1991. *Address:* ul Sienkiewicza 28/4, 05-825 Grodzisk Maz, Poland.

**PADMORE, Elaine Marguirite,** BMus, MA, LTCL; British artistic director and broadcaster; b. 3 Feb. 1947, Haworth, Yorks.; d. of Alfred and Florence Padmore. *Education:* Newland High School, Hull, Arnold School, Blackpool, Univ. of Birmingham and Guildhall School of Music, London. *Career:* Lecturer in Liberal Studies, Coll. of Art, Croydon and Kingston 1968–70; Books Ed., Music Dept, Oxford Univ. Press 1970–71; Producer Music Div., BBC 1971–76, Presenter Festival Comment 1973–81, Chief Producer Opera, BBC Radio 1976–83, Announcer Radio Three 1982–90, Programmes include Parade, Music of Tchaikovsky's Russia, England's Pleasant Land; opera singer; Lecturer in Opera, RAM 1979–86; Artistic Dir Wexford Festival Opera 1982–94, Dublin Grand Opera Soc. 1989–90; Artistic Dir Royal Danish Opera 1993–2000; Dir of Opera, Covent Garden 2000–; contrib. to musical books and journals. *Honours:* Hon. ARAM; Kt of the Dannebrog, Denmark 1994; Hungarian Pro Musica Award for Summertime on Bredon 1973, Prix Musical de Radio Brno for The English Renaissance 1974, Sunday Independent Award for Services to Music in Ireland 1985. *Address:* Royal Opera House, Covent Garden, London, WC2E 9DD, England (office).

**PADMORE, Mark Joseph;** British singer (tenor); b. 8 March 1961, London, England; m. Josette Simon 1996. *Education:* Kings Coll., Cambridge, studied with Erich Vietheer, Gita Denise, Janice Chapman and Diane Forlano. *Career:* singer at Major Festivals including Aix-en-Provence, Edinburgh, BBC Proms, Salzburg, Spoleto, Tanglewood, New York; Opera House debuts: Teatro Comunale, Florence, 1992; Opéra Comique, Paris, 1993; Théâtre du Châtelet, 1995; Royal Opera House, Covent Garden, 1995; Scottish Opera, 1996; Opéra de Paris, 1996; Rameau's Zoroatre at the 1998 London Proms; Season 1999–2000 at ENO as Apollo in Monteverdi's Orfeo and the Evangelist in the St John Passion; Jonathan in Saul with the Gabrieli Consort, 2002; London Proms Chamber Music, 2002; Engaged as Handel's Jephtha for WNO, and Iopas in Les Troyens in Paris, under John Eliot Gardiner, 2003. *Recordings:* Chabrier Briseis; Charpentier, Médée; Handel, Messiah; Esther, Samson; Haydn, Masses; Purcell, Fairy Queen and King Arthur; Rameau, Hippolyte et Aricie. *Current Management:* Van Walsum Management Ltd, 4 Addison Bridge Place, London, W14 8XP, England. *Telephone:* (20) 7371-4343. *Fax:* (20) 7371-4344. *Website:* www.vanwalsum.co.uk.

**PADOUROVA-HAVLAKOVA, Lydie;** Singer (Mezzo-Soprano); b. 30 Aug. 1957, Prague, Czechoslovakia; m. Jan Padour, 1 June 1979, 1 s. *Education:* Conservatoire of Prague; University of Music in Prague. *Career:* Debut: National Theatre in Prague, 1986; Prague National Theatre: Janáček's Kata Kabanova (Varvara), Prokofiev's Betrothal in a Monastery (Klara), Tchaikovsky's Queen of Spades (Pavlina and Dafnis), 1987, Mozart's Le nozze di Figaro, as Cherubino, 1988 and Purcell's Dido and Aeneas (Dido). *Recordings:* Arias by Mascagni: Santuzza; Bizet's Carmen; Mozart's Dorabella; Thomas' Mignon; Purcell's Dido; Donizetti's Orsini (Lucrezia Borgia); Complete Opera: Prokofiev's Betrothal in a Monastery. *Current Management:* Na Lysinach 461/30, 14700 Prague, Czech Republic.

**PADRÓS, David;** Composer and Pianist; b. 22 March 1942, Igualada, Barcelona, Spain. *Education:* Municipal Music School, Barcelona, 1966; Musikhochscule Trossingen, Germany, 1966–69; Konservatorium, Basel, 1969–72; Zürich, Switzerland, 1972–75; Freiburg, Germany, 1976–82. *Career:* Commissions and performances in European Music Festivals; mem, Associacio Catalana de Compositors. *Compositions:* Styx, Chamber Ensemble; Heptagonal, piano; Crna Gora, Chamber Ensemble; Khorva, orchestra; Cal Ligrama (F1 in G, piano); 2 Legendes, organ; Batalla, piano, harpsichord and strings; Musik im Raum, chamber ensemble; Jo-Ha-Kyu, orchestra; Arachne, Chamber ensemble; Maqam, piano; Trajectories, violin; Confluences, brass ensemble, percussion, tape; Chaconne, string quartet, harpsichord; El Sermo de R Muntaner, 4 mixed voices, 4 old wind instruments, organ; Ketjak, pianists quartet; Recordant W A M, clarinet and organ; La Sala de la Suprema Harmonia, chamber ensemble, 1991; Jdeb, recorder quartet, 1992; 6 Differencies, organ, 1992; Ghiza-i-ruh, flute, clartinet, piano, 1993; Nocturne, flute, viola, clarinet, 1992; Gjatams, piano quartet, 1993; Xucla el silenci nocturn, flute, clarinet, violin, cello, 1994; Qawwali, recorder quartet, 1994; Klagelied, piano, 1994; Manas, piano, percussion, wind quintet, 1996; 5 Tankas, mezzo, flute, clarinet, guitar, 1996, Cheops, chamber orchestra, 1997; Sunyata, flute, guitar, 1997;17 Cançons populars catalanes, piano, 1998; Verwandlung, flute quartet, 1999; 3 Poemas sonores, mixed chorus, 1999; El temps segons Rama, orchestra, 1999; Piano Concerto, 2000–01; Acciones y reacciones, flute, piano, 2000; Degung, recorder, vibraphon, 2000; Projeccions, chamber orchestra, 2001. *Recordings:* Musik in Raum, Association of Catalan Composers; Arachne; Confluencies; Chamber Music, 6 works on CD; La Sala de la Suprema Harmonia; Materials; Klagelied; Verwandlung; Complete piano works; 5 Tankas. *Contributions:* Revista Musical Catalana; Revista Quodlibet. *Honours:* Hans-Lenz-Preis, Germany, 1969; Komposition-Preis der Stiftung Landis and Gyr, Switzerland, 1976. *Address:* Rossello 213, 1-1, 08008 Barcelona, Spain. *Telephone:* 93 2170943.

**PADROS, Jaime;** Composer and Pianist; b. 26 Aug. 1926, Igualada, Spain; m. Eva Marie Wolff, 1962, 1 s., 2 d. *Education:* Baccalaureate, Monastery of Montserrat, Barcelona; Formation, Escolania de Montserrat, 1939–; Piano, organ and musical studies with Dom David Pujol; Piano studies with Frank Marshall and Alicia de Larrocha, Academia Marshall, 1941; Composition with Josep Barbera, Cristobal Taltabull, Barcelona, Darius Milhaud, Paris. *Career:* Debut: As Composer, Ballet Fantasia de circo, 1954; Concerts in all major cities and radio stations in Spain, Paris, Prague and many German cities; First pianist to rediscover several of the works of the 18th Century Spanish Composers Antonio Soler and Narcis Casanoves; First to play complete piano works of Arnold Schoenberg, Alban Berg, Anton Webern and other contemporary composers in Spain; Piano Teacher, Academy of Music, Trossingen, West Germany, 1964–94; Numerous commissioned works, 1954–. *Compositions:* Chamber music for different casts of instruments: Tannkas del somni 1950; Sonata para piano, 1954; Quintet per a quartet d'arc i piano, 1962; Planctus, 1977; Cancionero del lugar, 1978; Policromies, 1980; Several settings of folk songs for choir; Poemas de fragua, 1984; Musica cambiante (piano solo and string orchestra), 1986. *Recordings:* Contrapuntos sobre canciones populares castellanas, 1962; Sternverdunkelung, 1960; Llibre d'alquimies I, 1967; Serenata, 1978; Trama concentrica, 1982; Paseo y contradanza, 1985. *Honours:* Premio Juventudes musicales, 1954; Premi Orfeo catala, 1962. *Address:* Seelengraben 30, 89073 Ulm, Germany.

**PAGE, Anne,** BMus, DipEd; Organist; b. 2 Dec. 1955, Perth, Australia. *Education:* Univ. of Western Australia, with Maire-Claire Alain at Conservatoire Nationale de Musique, Rueuil-Malmaison, France, with Peter Hurford in Cambridge, and with Jacques van Oortmerssen at the Sweelinck Conservatory, Amsterdam. *Career:* organ recitalist in the UK, Europe, USA and Australia; teacher and course dir; debut Royal Festival Hall, London 1988; directed Cambridge Summer Recitals 1987–94; pioneered revival of serious interest in the harmonium; Prof. of Harmonium at the Royal Acad. of Music, London 2003; mem. Incorporated Soc. of Musicians, British Institute of Organ Studies. *Recordings:* French Music for Harmonium (two vols) 1988, 1990, Sigfrid Karg-Elert: Music for Harmonium 1990, Two Mander Organs 1990, Veni Creator Spiritus: choral and orgam music of Carl Rütti (with Cambridge Voices) 1998, J. S. Bach's Orgelbüchlein 1999, The Willis Organ of Emmanuel United Reform Church 2001, Olivier Messiaen: Livre du Saint Sacrement 2002. *Honours:* Prix d'excellence à l'unanimité, Conservatoire Nationale de Musique 1981.

**PAGE, Charlotte;** Singer (Soprano); b. 1972, England. *Education:* Royal College of Music, London. *Career:* First niece in Peter Grimes for Covent Garden, Welsh National Opera, 1999; Gretel for Opera Northern Ireland; Frasquita for Central Festival Opera; Zerlina for Pimlico Opera and Offenbach's Hélène, Holland Park; Other roles include Mozart's Despina; Pamina, Second Lady and Cherubino; Clinene in Cavalli's L'Egisto; Mélisande for Atelier Lyrique, Orleans; On tour to France; Further concerts in Tokyo and throughout the United Kingdom. *Address:* Music International, 13 Ardilaun Road, London N5 2QR, England.

**PAGE, Christopher (Howard);** Medievalist; b. 8 April 1952, London, England; m. Régine Fourcade, 15 Sept 1975. *Education:* BA, English, Oxford University; DPhl, York University. *Career:* University Lecturer in Medieval English, University of Cambridge; Frequent Broadcaster on BBC Radio 3, both as Lecturer and as Director of his Ensemble, Gothic Voices; Presenter of Radio 4 Arts programme, Kaleidoscope. *Recordings:* Directed Gothic Voices in Sequences and Hymns by Abbess Hildegard of Bingen; The Mirror of Narcissus; Songs by Guillaume de Machaut; The Garden of Zephirus; Courtly Songs of the Early 15C; The Castle of Fair Welcome; Courtly Songs of the late 15th Century; The Service of Venus and Mars; A Song for Francesca; Music for the Lionhearted King. *Publications:* (Book) Voices and Instruments of the Middle Ages; Sequences and Hymns by Abbess Hildegard of Bingen; The Owl and the Nightingale: Musical Life and Ideas in France, 1100–1300, 1989; Latin Poetry and Conductors Rhythm in Medieval France, 1997; Music and Instruments of the Middle Ages: Studies in Text and Performance, 1997. *Contributions:* Many academic and scholarly contributions to Early Music; Galpin Society Journal; Proceedings of the Royal Musical Association; New Oxford History of Music; Cambridge Guide to the Arts in Britain; Early Music History; The Historical Harpsichord. *Honours:* British Entrant and Prizewinner, Innsbruck International Radio Prize, 1981; Several Awards for Record of Hildegard; Gramophone Awards for three records; Fellow, Fellowship of Makers and Restorers of Historical Instruments; senior Research Fellow in Music, Sydney Sussex College, Cambridge. *Address:* Sidney Sussex College, Cambridge University, Cambridge, England.

**PAGE, Paula;** Singer (Soprano); b. 24 Sept. 1942, Corinth, Mississippi, USA. *Education:* Studied at Indiana University, Bloomington and on a Fulbright Scholarship in Europe. *Career:* Debut: Inez in Il Trovatore, Hamburg, Staatsoper, 1968; Hamburg Staatsoper 1968–72; Appearances at Wuppertal, Aachen, Bremen, Santa Fe, Norfolk, Antwerp, Liège, Bordeaux, Lison, Venice, Düsseldorf; Berlin, Frankfurt am Main Opera from 1983; Repertory includes lyric roles and parts in modern operas, including Staatstheater by Maurizio Kagel; Presently Professor of Voice, Staatliche Hochschule für Musik. *Honours:* Prizewinner, New York Metropolitan Auditions of the Air, 1967; WGN Auditions of the Air, 1967; Geneva International Competition, 1968; s-Hertogenbush Holland, 1968; Martha B Rockefeller Grant, 1977. *Address:* Königsberger Strabe 25, 6239, Germany.

**PAGE, Steven;** singer (baritone); b. 1950, England. *Education:* Opera Studio, London with Margaret Hyde. *Career:* sang Don Alfonso and Nick Shadow with Opera 80, (now English Touring Opera); For English National Opera he has sung the title role in Mozart's Don Giovanni, Tarquinius in The Rape of Lucretia, Albert in Werther, Paolo in Simone Boccanegra, Valentine in Faust and the Count in Marriage of Figaro and most recently the role of Figaro; For Scottish Opera he has appeared as Guglielmo in Così fan tutte, Marcello in La Bohème, Chorèbe in Les Troyens, Ford in Falstaff and the title role of Don Giovanni and the Count in Marriage of Figaro; He has also taken part in four seasons at the Buxton Festival in leading roles and has appeared with Opera Factory as Don Giovanni at the Queen Elizabeth Hall; For Glyndebeourne Touring Opera has sung Nick Shadow in The Rake's Progress, Leporello in Don Giovanni, Anubis in Harrison Birtwistle's The Second Mrs Kong and Coyle in a new production by Robin Philips of Britten's Owen Wingrave; Made his debut Glyndebourne Festival as Nick Shadow in 1994 and returned as Leporello in Don Giovanni and Anubis; Sang Geronio in Rossini's Il Turco in Italia, Garsington, 1996; Season 1999 in Tippett's The Mask of Time at the London Prom concerts.

**PAGLIARANI, Mario;** Swiss composer; b. 27 June 1963, Mendrisio, Ticino canton. *Education:* Conservatorio di Milano, studied with Salvatore Sciarrino. *Compositions include:* Alcuni particolari oscuri 1983, Vie d'uscita 1986, Lucciole o imperi? 1989–90, Paesaggio-Madrigale 1991, Pierrot lunatique

1993, Cappuccetto rosso 1994, Bergweg 1995, Canzone fantasma 1996, Apparizione di Franz Schubert fra le onde 1997, Trio pozzanghera 1998, Rarefatto cantabile 1999. *Recordings:* Alcuni particolari oscuri, Paesaggio-Madrigale, Pierrot lunatique. *Honours:* Musica Ticinensis prize 1987, VI Concurso de obras musicales para Radio prize, Madrid 1995. *Address:* c/o Schweizer Musikedition, Postfach 7851, 6000 Lucerne 7, Switzerland (office). *E-mail:* mail@musicedition.ch (office). *Website:* www.musicedition.ch (office).

**PAGLIAZZI, Franco;** Singer (baritone, dramatic tenor); b. 8 April 1937, Florence, Italy; m. Denise Serghieva 4 July 1965, 1 s. *Education:* Studied at Centro Lirico del Teatro Comunale, Florence; Studied with Ettore Campogalliani. *Career:* Debut: Cherubini's Elisa, Maggio Musicale Fiorentino, Florence, 1960; As baritone, sang numerous Verdi roles including Rigoletto, Conte di Luna, Amonasro, Iago, Posa, Carlo V; Sang in theatres including Firenze Teatro Comunale, Naples San Carlo, Milan La Scala, Wien Staatsoper, Dublin, Orange Festival, Sofia, Lugano, Brussels, Bielefeld, Amsterdam, Ostrava, Catania, and other venues until 1974; From 1976, singing as dramatic tenor under name Marc Alexander; Sang roles including Enzo, Gabriele, Macduff, Manrico, Don Alvaro, Calaf; Appearances include Barcelona, Teatro del Liceo, Valencia, Rouen, Bordeaux, Braunschweig, Como, Mantova; Recitals in Italy, Switzerland, Japan, until 1998; Sang with conductors such as Muti, Gavazzeni, Bartoletti, G Patanè, Savini, Rivoli, Morelli, Wung Chung. *Recordings:* Conte di Luna in Il Trovatore, 1968; Nello in Donizetti's Pia de Tolomei, 1968; Arias from Il Trovatore, Ernani, Ballo in Maschera, 1963; Un Converso in Cherubini's Elisa, 1960. *Honours:* Competitions, Milan, AS LI CO, 1960; Busseto Voci Verdiane, 1962 Sofia Competition, 1963; First Prize, Vercelli Viotti, 1964. *Address:* Via del Ghirlandaio 24, 50121 Florence, Italy.

**PAHUD, Emmanuel;** Flautist; b. 1970, France. *Education:* Premier Prix at the Paris Conservatoire, 1990; Further study with Aurèle Nicolet. *Career:* Principal Flute of the Berlin Philharmonic, and many concerts as solo artist appearances at leading international festivals and chamber music societies throughout Europe and Japan; Season 1997–98, Nielsen Concerto with Zürich Tonhalle Orchestra and David Zimman; Recital tour of USA; Mozart Flute and Harp Concerto with Berlin Philharmonic; Tour of Japan including Suntory Hall; Ligeti's Flute and Oboe Concerto with Philharmonia under Heinz Holliger; Season 1998–99, Recital in USA and Japan with Eric le Sage; Mozart Concerto K313 with Danish National Radio; CPE Bach and Jolivet concertos with the Orchestra d'Auvergne; Wigmore Hall recital with Stephen Kovacevitch; New York Mostly Mozart festival; Salzburg Festival, Mozart Concerto with Berlin Philharmonic and Abbado; Recitalist in International Rising Stars Series in season 1997–98, with concerts at Carnegie Hall and in Europe; Season 1998–99, included concerto appearances with the Vienna Chamber, Zürich Chamber, Budapest Festival, Mostly Mozart Festival, New York and chamber concerts to celebrate the 1999 Poulenc centenary; Season 1999–2000 included concerto performances with the Berlin Philharmonic under Claudio Abbado; The Baltimore Symphony, the London Philharmonic and return recital tours with Eric Le Sage in North America and the Far East. *Recordings include:* Mozart Concertos with the Berlin Philharmonic and Abbado; French repertory with pianist Eric Le Sage. *Honours:* Prize Winner at several international competitions. *Current Management:* Askonas Holt Ltd, Lonsdale Chambers, 27 Chancery Lane, London, WC2A 1PF, England. *Telephone:* (20) 7400-1700. *Fax:* (20) 7400-1799. *E-mail:* info@askonasholt.co .uk. *Website:* www.askonasholt.co.uk.

**PAIK, Byung-dong;** South Korean academic; b. 26 Jan. 1936, Seoul; m. Woo Wha-ja 1969. *Education:* Shin-Heung High School, Jeon-joo; Coll. of Music, Seoul National Univ.; Stadtliche Hochschule für Musik, Hanover, Germany. *Career:* debut, Annual Korean New Composers Prize with Three Symphonic Chapters 1962; six composition recitals since first recital 1960–; has presented his works several times with National Symphony Orchestra, Seoul Philharmonic Orchestra and other ensembles; Prof., Personnel Management mem., Coll. of Music, Seoul National Univ.; Pres., Perspective Composers Group. *Compositions:* Major works, Symphonic Three Chapters, 1962; Un I, II, III, IV, V, VI for Instrumental Ensemble; Drei Bagetellen für Klavier, 1973; Concerto for Piano and Orchestra, 1974; Veranderte Ehepaar, 1986; In September for Orchestra, 1987; Contra, 1988. *Recordings:* Ein kleine Nachtheil für Violine und Klavier, SEM, Seoul, 1978; Guitariana for two Guitars, SEM, 1984; Byul-Gok 87, Jigu Record Corporation, Seoul, 1987. *Publications:* Musical Theory, 1977; Essays: Seven Fermatas 1979; Essays: Sound or Whispering, 1981; Harmony, 1984; Music for Culture, 1985; College Musical Theory, 1989; The Streams of Modern Music, 1990. *Address:* 214-1 Sangdo 1 dong, Dongjakgu, A-202 Sangdo Villa, Seoul, Republic of Korea.

**PAIK, Kun-woo;** South Korean pianist; b. 10 March 1946. *Education:* Juilliard School, New York and in London and Italy. *Career:* interpreter of piano works of Ravel, Liszt, Scriabin and Prokofiev; has played with orchestras throughout N America and Europe, notably Indianapolis Symphony, Rotterdam Philharmonic, Royal Philharmonic, London Symphony, BBC Symphony (soloist, Last Night of the Proms 1987), Orchestre Nat. de France, Polish Radio Nat. Symphony; lives in Paris; recitals at all maj. European music festivals. *Honours:* three Diapason d'Or awards.

**PAIK, Nam June;** South Korean/American kinetic artist; b. 1932, South Korea. *Education:* Univ. of Tokyo, Japan. *Career:* left S. Korea 1949, moved permanently to NY 1964; mem. Fluxus (anarchic, neo-dadaist Movt) 1961. *Major works include:* Urmusik 1961, Opera Sextronique, performed NY 1967,

The K-456 Robot. *Exhibitions include:* Galerie Parnassus, Wuppertal, Germany 1963, Video Works 1963–68, Hayward Gallery, London 1988.

**PAILLARD, Jean-François;** conductor and musicologist; b. 28 April 1928, Vitry-le-Francois, France; m. Anne Marie Beckensteiner; three s. *Education:* First Prize in Music History, Paris Conservatoire; Studied conducting with Igor Markevitch, Salzburg; Graduated from the Sorbonne in mathematics. *Career:* Founded the Jean-Marie Leclair Instrumental Ensemble, 1953; Many tours of Europe, USA and the Far East with the Jean-François Paillard Chamber Orchestra, notably in French music of the 17th and 18th centuries; Organiser and Teacher of Conducting Courses, Spring and Summer, France; mem, French Musicological Society; French Society of the 18th Century. *Recordings include:* Bach, Brandenburg Concertos, Suites for Orchestra, Harpsichord Concertos and Musical Offering; Handel Alexander's Feast, Water and Fireworks Music, Dettingen Te Deum, Concertos for oboe, organ and harp; Couperin Les Nations; Delalande Symphonies; Charpentier Te Deum, Magnificat and Messe de Minuit, Baroque trumpet concertos (Maurice André); Rameau Les Indes Galantes; Mozart Divertimenti; Flute and Violin concertos, concerto K 299. *Publications:* La Musique Francaise Classique, 1960, 1973; Archives de la Musique Instrumentale; Archives de la Musique Religieuse. *Honours:* Many Grand Prix du Disque (Academie Charles Cros, Disque Francais Disque Lyrique); Prix Edison, Netherlands; German Record Prize; Gold Record, Japan. *Address:* 23 rue de Marly, 7860 Etang la Ville, France.

**PAITA, Carlos;** Conductor; b. 10 March 1932, Buenos Aires, Argentina; m. Elisabeth de Quartbarbes, 7 c. *Education:* Studied with Juan Neuchoff and Jacobo Fischer. *Career:* Debut: Teatro Colón, Buenos Aires; Conducted the National Radio Orchestra in Argentina; Verdi Requiem, 1964, Mahler's 2nd Symphony, 1965; Stuttgart Radio Symphony from 1966; Appearances in London, Paris, Edinburgh and the USA (debut 1979, with the Houston Symphony Orchestra); He has guest conducted orchestras all over the world, including the Washington National Orchestra, the Russian State Orchestra, at the Prague Festival, in Poland, Romania, Bratislava, Slovakia and at the Enesco Festival in Bulgaria and the Flanders Festival in Belgium. *Recordings:* Festival Wagner; Grands Overtures; Verdi Requiem; Beethoven's Eroica Symphony; Rossini Overtures; Mahler's 1st Symphony; Symphonie Fantastique by Berlioz. *Honours:* Grand Prix, Academie Charles Cros, Paris, 1969; Grand Prix de L'Academie Francaise, 1978. *Address:* 15 Chemin du Champ d'Anier, 1209 Geneva, Switzerland.

**PAL, Támás;** Conductor; b. 16 Sept. 1937, Gyula, Hungary. *Education:* Studied with Janos Viski and Andréas Korody at the Franz Liszt Academy Budapest. *Career:* Conducted the Budapest State Opera 1960–75, notably at the Edinburgh Festival (1973) and the Wiesbaden May Festival (1974); Principal Conductor of the Szeged Symphony Orchestra and Opera, 1975–83; Permanent Conductor of the Budapest Opera, 1983–85; Artistic Director of the open air summer music festival at Budapest, 1987; Has conducted operatic rarities such as Salieri's Falstaff, Liszt's Don Sanche and Il Pittor Parigino by Cimarosa; Directed Aida at Szeged, 1997. *Recordings include:* Liszt Piano Concerto No. 2 with the Hungarian State Orchestra; Brahms Symphony No. 3 and Academic Festival Overture with the Budapest Symphony Orchestra; Il Pittor Parigino (premiere recording). *Address:* c/o Hungarian State Opera House, Nepoztarsasag uta 22, 1061 Budapest, Hungary.

**PALACIO, Ernesto;** Singer (Tenor); b. 19 Oct. 1946, Lima, Peru. *Education:* Studied in Peru and Milan, Italy. *Career:* Debut: Sang Almaviva in San Remo, Italy, 1972; Sang lyric roles in Milan, Rome, Venice, Trieste, Bologne, Turin, Genoa, Palermo, Naples, Parma, Catania; Guest appearances in London (Covent Garden), New York (Metropolitan and Carnegie Hall), Buenos Aires (Colon), Berlin (Philharmonic), Edinburgh, Marseilles, Bordeaux, Lille, Nancy, Lyon, Strasbourg, Houston, Dallas, Zürich, Düsseldorf, Munich, Caracas, Chile; Other roles include 18 operas of Rossini, Don Giovanni, Così fan tutte, Re Pastore, Die Zauberflöte, Finta giardiniera, Finta Semplice (Mozart); Elisir d'amore, Don Pasquale, La fille du Régiment, Esule di Roma, Torquato Tasso (Donizetti); Sang in a revival of Ciro in Babilonia by Rossini at Savona, 1988; Appeared as Argirio in Tancredi opposite Marilyn Horne at Barcelona, May 1989, Bilbao, Jan 1991; Bonn Opera 1990, as Almaviva. *Recordings:* Mosè in Egitto; Il Turco in Italia; Miserere by Donizetti; Adelaide di Borgogna by Rossini; Vivaldi's Serenata a Tre; Torquato Tasso; Catone in Utica by Vivaldi; Unpublished arias by Rossini, conducted by Carlo Rizzi; Prince Giovanni in Una Cosa Rara.

**PALACIO, Pedro (Antonio);** Composer; b. 15 April 1961, La Rioja, Argentina; 1 s., 1 d. *Education:* Diplomas: Master of Guitar, 1979, Master of Musical Composition, 1985, Cordoba, Argentina; Master of Composition and Musical Analysis, France, 1987. *Career:* Debut: Variations for Piano performed at National Festival for Contemporary Music, Argentina, 1984; Performance of works: Teatro Colón, Argentina; Festival Antidogma Musica, Italy; Mengano Quartett and WNC Ensemble, Cologne, and Turmheim Ensemble, Palermo, Germany; Ensemble Stringendo, Ensemble Aleph at Festival of Evreux, BMA Ensemble at Nantes, Wozzeck Trio, ENMD-Montreuil Ensemble, France; World Music Days Festival, Zürich, Switzerland; Poland Broadcasting Symphony Orchestra; Symphony Orchestra of Cordoba; SACEM, France. *Compositions:* Axis; Triolaid; Quintolaid; Latidos; Yugoslavia Burning; Omphalo; Dämmerung; Laughs of Tokyo; Histoire d'Oiseaux Mathématiques; Quateur à Cordes No. 1, 1998; Cuerdas Vocales, 1998; El tiempo suspendido resonante II, 2000. *Recordings:* Albums: Dämmerung; Laughs of

Tokyo; Histoire d'oiseaux mathématiques, Ensemble Aleph; El tiempo suspendido resonante II. *Publications include:* Roman-B for guitar, 1987; Herejía for solo violin, 1998. *Honours:* Essec-Invention, France, 1986; Icons, Italy, 1988; Trinac, Argentina, 1989; André Jolivet, France, 1991; Kazimierz Serocki, Poland, 1996; Alberto Ginastera, Argentina, 1996. *Address:* 56 avenue Jean-Jaurès, 75019 Paris, France.

**PALAY, Elliot;** Singer (Tenor); b. 18 Dec. 1948, Milwaukee, Wisconsin, USA. *Education:* Studied at Indiana University, Bloomington with Charles Kullmann; Further study with Clemens Kaiser-Breme in Essen. *Career:* Debut: Lubeck 1972, as Matteo in Arabella; Sang in Freiburg, Düsseldorf, Munich and Stuttgart; Komische Oper Berlin 1977, in Aufstieg und Fall der Stadt Mahagonny; Returned to USA and sang at the New York City Opera; Santa Fe and Seattle 1983, as Siegfried in Der Ring des Nibelungen; Antwerp and Ghent 1983, as Siegmund in Die Walküre; Dresden 1984, in Wozzeck; Other roles include Wagner's Tristan and Walther, Verdi's Radames and Ismaele, the Emperor in Die Frau ohne Schatten and Boris in Katya Kabanova; Sang Siegfried with the Jutland Opera at Århus, 1987; Opera roles in Munich from 2000. *Address:* c/o Den Jydske Opera, Musikhuset Arkus, Thomas Jensens Alle, 8000 Århus, Denmark.

**PALECZNY, Piotr;** Polish pianist and academic; b. 10 May 1946, Rybnik; m.; one s. *Education:* State Higher School of Music, Warsaw (studied under Prof. Jan Ekier). *Career:* winner pianist competitions in Sofia 1968, Munich 1969, Warsaw 1970, Pleven 1971, Bordeaux 1972; f. master courses in music, Bordeaux, Amsterdam, Paris, Buenos Aires, Tokyo, Lugano, Warsaw; soloist with orchestras including Warsaw Nat. Philharmonic Orchestra, Polish Radio Nat. Symphony Orchestra, Chicago Symphony, American Symphony, Royal Philharmonic, Concertgebouw, BBC London Orchestra, Yomiuri Nippon, Tonhalle Zurich, RAI Roma, Santa Cecilia, Mexico Nat., Buenos Aires Nat., Gewandhaus, Nat. Orchestra Madrid; has performed major concert halls, including Carnegie Hall, Avery Fisher Hall and Alice Tully Hall, New York, Orchestra Hall, Chicago, Suntory Hall, Tokyo, Teatro Colon, Buenos Aires, Gewandhaus, Leipzig, Concertgebouw, Amsterdam, Royal Festival Hall, London; Artistic Dir Chopin Int. Festival, Duszniki Zdrój; Prof. of Piano Performance, Frederick Chopin Acad. of Music, Warsaw; Grand Prix VIII Chopin Competition 1970; judge, int. music competitions in Warsaw, Paris, Santander, Tokyo, Hamamatsu, Prague, Taipei, Cleveland, London. *Recordings include:* K. Szymanowski Concert Symphony No. 4, complete Ballads, Sonatas, and Concertos by Chopin, The Best of Fryderyk Chopin ('Fryderyk 1999' Award, Polish Phonographic Acad.), works by Paderewski, Szymanowski, Lutosławski. *Honours:* Kt's Cross, Order of Polonia Restituta, Gold Cross of Merit; granted title of Prof. by Pres. of Poland 1998. *Address:* Frederick Chopin Academy of Music, ul. Okólnik 2, 00-368 Warsaw, Poland (office). *Telephone:* (22) 8277241 (office).

**PALEY, Alexander;** Concert Pianist; b. 9 Jan. 1956, Kishinev, USSR; m. 29 July 1978, 1 d. *Education:* Master's Degree, PhD, Moscow Conservatory. *Career:* Debut: Kishinev, 2 April 1969; Performed with Moscow Virtuosi (V Spivakov), 1985–90; Bolshoi Theatre Orchestra, 1986; With Monte Carlo Philharmonic, 1989; With Colorado Symphony, 1991; Recitals, Châtelet, Paris, 1990, Auditorium de Halles, 1991, Strasbourg, Moscow, Prague, Berlin, Sofia; Appeared with National Symphony Orchestra, Wolf Trap Festival, 1991 and Boston Pops, 1991; Chamber music with Fine Arts Quartet, New York Chamber Soloists also with V Spivakov, Bella Davidovich, Oleg Krysa, D Sitkovetsky and B Pergamentshikov; Musical Director, Cannes-sur-Mer Festival, France. *Recordings:* Talent, Belgium; Liszt, all 4 Mephisto valses, other pieces; National Public Radio, USA; Radio France; Melodia, Moscow, 1990. *Address:* 850 West 176th Street, Apt 4 D, New York, NY 10033, USA.

**PALM, Mati-Johannes;** Estonian singer (bass); *Opera Soloist, Estonian National Opera; Professor of Singing, Estonian Academy of Music;* b. 13 Jan. 1942, Tallinn; two c. *Education:* Tallinn Conservatoire, studied in Moscow and at La Scala. *Career:* sang with the Estonian State Opera from 1967, notably as Boris, Basilio, King Philip, Ivan Khovansky, the Dutchman, Silva, Zaccaria, Raimondo, Colline and Gremin; guest appearances from 1980 in Helsinki as Attila, the Savonlinna Festival as the Dutchman, Paris Opéra in 1988 as Pimen, at Karlsruhe in 1992 in Khovanshchina as Dosifei, Buenos Aires from 1991 in Iolanta and Lohengrin; sang King Philip in Don Carlos at Tallinn 1971, 2000; sang Mephistopheles in Boito's Mefistofele and Banquo in Verdi's Macbeth; further appearances in Moscow, St Petersburg, Prague and Berlin, with many concerts, including 55 cantatas and oratorios, including Bach's St John Passion, Handel's Messiah, Mozart's Requiem, Beethoven's Missa Solemnis, Rossini's Stabat Mater, Verdi's Requiem; judge at int. singing competitions; currently soloist, Estonian Nat. Opera and Prof. of Singing, Estonian Acad. of Music. *Recordings:* M. Palm 1972, Aries of Verdi, Romances of A. Kapp and G. Sviridov, Mussorgski's Boris Godunov (Pimen), Two Cantatas of J. S. Bach BWV 78 140, Estonian opera singer Mati Palm, Mati Palm sings Estonian and Italian Songs, A. Kapp's Oratorio Hiob, R. Tobias Oratorio Des Jona Sendung, Verdi's Nabucco (Zaccaria), E. Tubin Barbara von Tiesenhusen (Konguta). *Film recording:* Mati Palm is Singing 1972. *Honours:* State Order of White Star; Gold Medal Classical Singing Competition, Sofia, First Prize Baltic States Young Singers Competition 1971, Silver Medal F. Vinase Int. Competition, Barcelona 1972, Soviet Union State Prize 1983, G. Ots Prize. *Address:* c/o Estonian National Opera, Estonia Boulevard 4, 10148 Tallinn, Estonia (office). *Telephone:* (372) 683-1230 (office); (372) 51 13 703 (mobile). *Fax:* (372) 631-3080 (office). *E-mail:* mati.palm.001@mail.ee.

**PALMER, Felicity Joan,** CBE, FGSM; British singer (mezzo-soprano); b. 6 April 1944, Cheltenham; d. of Sylvia and Marshall Palmer. *Education:* Erith Grammar School and Guildhall School of Music and Drama. *Career:* soprano, then mezzo-soprano; has performed at all major int. opera houses, including La Scala, Milan, Royal Opera House, Covent Garden, Opéra de Paris, Netherlands Opera and Glyndebourne. *Operas include:* Elektra, Semele, Mahagonny, Pelléas et Mélisande, The Ring Cycle, Falstaff, Un Ballo in Maschera. *Recordings include:* Poèmes pour mi, Holst Choral Symphony, The Music Makers, Sea Pictures, Phaedra, songs by Poulenc, Ravel and Fauré, Victorian ballads. *Honours:* Kathleen Ferrier Memorial Prize 1970. *Current Management:* Askonas Holt Ltd, Lonsdale Chambers, 27 Chancery Lane, London, WC2A 1PF, England. *Telephone:* (20) 7400-1700. *Fax:* (20) 7400-1799. *E-mail:* info@askonasholt.co.uk. *Website:* www.askonasholt.co.uk.

**PALMER, Larry;** Harpsichordist and Organist; b. 13 Nov. 1938, Warren, Ohio, USA. *Education:* Studied at Oberlin College Conservatory and Eastman School at Rochester, DMA 1963; Harpsichord with Isolde Ahlgrimm at Salzburg Mozarteum and with Gustav Leonhardt at Haarlem. *Career:* Recitalist on Harpsichord and Organ throughout the USA and Europe, with premieres of works by such composers as Vincent Persichetti and Ross Lee Finney; Harpsichord Editor of The Diapason from 1969; Professor of Harpsichord and Organ at Southern Methodist University in Dallas, 1970. *Recordings:* Organ works of Distler and harpsichord pieces from the 17th to the 20th centuries. *Publications:* Hugo Distler and his Church Music, 1967; Harpsichord in America: A 20th Century Revival, 1989 (2nd Ed 1992). *Address:* c/o Southern Methodist University, Meadows School of the Arts, Dallas, TX 75275, USA.

**PALMER, Peter (Rodney),** MA; British writer on music and translator; b. 7 March 1945, West Bridgford, Notts. *Education:* Exhibitioner in Modern Languages, Gonville and Caius Coll., Cambridge. *Career:* apprentice stage Dir, Int. Opera Studio, Zürich 1967–69; Founder and Artistic Dir East Midlands Music Theatre; first British stage productions of works by Janáček, Krenek, John Ogdon, Schoeck; Founding Ed. Bruckner Journal 1997; Visiting Lecturer, Romantic and Modern Swiss Music, Pro Helvetia Foundation 1998–99; Symposium Speaker, Lucerne Festival 1999. *Publications:* trans include: From the Mattress Grave, song cycle by David Blake, 1980, Essays on the Philosophy of Music by Ernst Bloch 1985, Wagner and Beethoven by Klaus Kropfinger 1991, Late Idyll: The Second Symphony of Johannes Brahms by Reinhold Brinkmann 1995, Johann Faustus, libretto by Hanns Eisler in: Hanns Eisler: A Miscellany 1995. *Contributions:* Die Tat, Zürich, Music and Letters, Organists' Review, German Life and Letters, Tempo, The Musical Times, New Grove Dictionary of Music and Musicians, Musik in Geschichte und Gegenwart, Perspectives on Anton Bruckner 2001, Ivor Gurney Society Journal 2003, Reger-Studien 7 2004; talks for BBC Radio 3. *Address:* 2 Rivergreen Close, Bramcote, Nottingham, NG9 3ES, England. *Telephone:* (115) 928-8300 (office). *Fax:* (115) 928-8300 (office). *E-mail:* peter@peterpalmer.wanadoo.co.uk (office).

**PALMER, Rudolph (Alexis);** Conductor, Composer and Pianist; b. 5 Aug. 1952, New York City, USA; m. Madeline Rogers, 21 June 1981. *Education:* BA, Russian, French, Bucknell University, 1973; BS, Composition, Mannes College of Music, 1975; MM, Juilliard, Composition, 1977; DMA, Juilliard, Composition, 1982. *Career:* Conducting and Composition Faculty, Mannes College of Music, 1982–; Director, Great Neck Choral Society, 1983–84; Orchestra Director, Horace Mann School, 1988–93; Associate Conductor, Amor Artis Chamber Choir, Fairfield County Chorale; Conductor, North Jersey Music Educators Orchestra, Brewer Chamber Orchestra; Palmer Chamber Orchestra; Palmer Singers; Queen's Chamber Band. *Compositions:* Contrasts for Four Bassoons; O Magnum Mysterium; Commissions: Songs of Reflection; The Vision of Herod; The Immortal Shield; Orchestration of Leonard Bernstein's Touches; Numerous other works for chamber groups, chorus and orchestra, including 2 string quartets, 1 symphony, Dance-Music (a ballet), orchestral overtures and several dramatic cantatas. *Recordings:* Accompanist: Lieder, (by women composers); The Unknown Dvořák; Conductor: Baroque Cantatas of Versailles; The Romantic Handel; Handel's Imeneo; Telemann's Pimpinone; Handel's Berenice; Handel's Siroe; Pergolesi's La Serva Padrona; Handel's Joshua; Handel's Muzio; A Scarlatti's Ishmael; Haydn's La Canterina; Handel Arias, with various artists; Handel's Muzio Scevola; Handel's Alexander Balus; Handel's Deidamia; Handel's Faramondo; Gluck's Il Parnaso Confuso; Chorusmaster, Bach, St John Passion; Handel, Alexander Balus. *Address:* 215 West 88th Street, Apt 7E, New York, NY 10024, USA.

**PALOLA, Juhani;** Finnish violinist; *Teacher, Lahti Conservatory*; b. 25 Nov. 1952, Helsinki; m. Liisa-Maria Lampela, 27 Sept 1977, 2 d. *Education:* Oulu Music Institute, Sibelius Academy; privately in Munich with Takaya Urakawa and in London with Eli Goren. *Career:* Debut: Soloist, Oulu Symphony Orchestra, 1968; Concerts as Soloist and Chamber Musician, Finland, Sweden, 1968–, Norway, Ukraine, Romania, Albania, Germany, Switzerland, USA, Austria; Professor of Violin, Teachers Training College, Rorschach, Switzerland; First Violin in Arioso Quartet, St Gallen 1986–97, Weimar Trio 1998–2004; teacher Lahti Conservatory 2003–. *Recordings:* Classic 2000, Relief. *Address:* Lummekatu 12, 15240 Lahti, Finland. *Telephone:* (40) 5955607 (home). *E-mail:* juhani.palola@phnet.fi. *Website:* www.phnet.fi.koti/paloj.

**PALOMBI, Antonello;** Singer (Tenor); b. 1965, Umbria, Italy. *Education:* Studied in Italy. *Career:* Debut: Sang Pinkerton in Germany, 1990; Appearances as Dourmont in La Scala di Seta at Pistoia and as the Duke of Mantua in Austria; Edoardo in La Cambiale di Matrimonio by Rossini at Macerata, Ferrando at Ravenna, Macduff at Livorno and Attalo in Rossini's Ermione in Berlin; Teatro Comunale, Pisa, as Alfredo, Ramiro (La Cenerentola), Don José and Monteverdi's Telemaco (Ritorno d'Ulisse); Nemorino at San Gimmingano, the Duke of Mantua in Tokyo and Sou Chong in Das Land des Lächelns at Florence; Sang Edmondo in a new production of Manon Lescaut at Glyndebourne, 1997; Concerts include Pulcinella, at Pisa and Modena; Fenton in Falstaff at the 1999 London Proms. *Address:* Teatro Comunale G Verdi, Via Palestro 40, 56200 Pisa, Italy.

**PÅLSSON, Hans;** Swedish, pianist and academic; b. 1 Oct. 1949, Helsingborg; m. Eva Pålsson 1980; three s. one d. *Education:* Staatliche Hochschule für Musik und Theater, Hanover, Germany. *Career:* debut, Stockholm 1972; concerts in some 20 countries; performed in 30-part TV series, Dead Masters, Live Music 1994–99; dedicatee of 60 solo pieces and piano concertos; Prof., Lund Univ. 1987; juror at int. piano competitions, masterclasses; mem. Royal Swedish Acad. of Music. *Recordings:* some 25 albums. *Honours:* Swedish first prize Nordic Music Prizes Competition 1972, Swedish Phonogram Award 1987, Royal Medal Litteris et Artibus 1997. *Current Management:* Svensk Konsertdirektion, Danska Vägen 25B, 41274 Gothenburg, Sweden. *Address:* Gotlandsvägen 4, 22225 Lund, Sweden (home). *Telephone:* (31) 830095 (office). *E-mail:* hanspalsson@telia.com (home).

**PAMPUCH, Helmut;** Singer (Tenor); b. 1939, Grossmahlendorf, Oberschlesien, Germany. *Education:* Studied at Nuremberg with Willi Domgraf-Fassbaender, 1957–62. *Career:* Sang at Regensburg from 1963; Appearances in Brunswick, Wiesbaden and Saarbrucken; Member of the Deutsche Oper am Rhein, Düsseldorf, 1973–, notably in character and buffo roles; Bayreuth debut 1978, later appeared as Mime in Das Rheingold, 1990; Paris Opéra 1979, in the premiere of the full version of Berg's Lulu, conducted by Pierre Boulez; Has sung Mozart's Monostatos at La Scala 1985, and Mime in Ring cycles at San Francisco 1984–90 and Zürich 1989; Further engagements at the State Operas of Hamburg, Munich and Stuttgart; Deutsche Oper Berlin and the Grand Théâtre Geneva; Sang Mime in Das Rheingold at Bayreuth, 1992 and at Buenos Aires, 1995; Many concert appearances. *Recordings include:* Lulu (Deutsche Grammophon); Das Rheingold (Philips). *Address:* c/o Deutsche Oper am Rhein, Heinrich-Heine Allee 16, 4000 Düsseldorf, Germany.

**PAN, Yiming;** Pianist and Educator; b. 9 July 1937, Shanghai, China; m. Ying Shi-Zhen 1960, 2 s. *Education:* Piano Department, Central Conservatory of Music, Beijing, 1954–59; Bachelor's degree, 1959; Studied Piano with Li Chang-Sun, C. Stevenska (Poland), D. Klavchenko (USSR), others. *Career:* Teaching Piano, 1959–91, Associate Professor, 1983–90, Deputy Director. Piano Department, 1983–91, Professor of Piano, 1990–91, Central Conservatory of Music; Came to Singapore, 1991; Piano Professor, LaSalle-SIA, College of Arts; Recitals and concerto concerts, main Chinese cities such as Beijing, Tianjin, Chengdu, Xian; Recital on radio, Central People's Broadcasting, 1984; Joint recitals, Beijing, with Professor Jacob Latiener of Juilliard School of Music and with Professor Razits of Indiana University; Jury Member, National Piano Competitions, China, formerly, and National Music Competitions, Singapore, 1991, 1993, 1995; mem, Resources Panel, National Arts Council of Singapore; Chinese Musicians Association. *Compositions include:* The Youth Piano Concerto, co-composer. *Recordings:* Major works of Beethoven, Chopin, Granados, and many Chinese composers. *Publications:* Author, more than 10 articles about piano performing and teaching; Editor: The Album of 45 Piano Sonatas by Scarlatti, 1st Chinese edition; Foreign Piano Pieces for the Young, vols 1–6. *Honours:* 1st Prize, Piano Competition, Central Conservatory of Music, 1957. *Address:* Blk 38, #14-2406, Upper Boon Keng Road, Singapore 380038, Singapore.

**PANAGULIAS, Ann;** Singer (Soprano); b. 1963, USA. *Career:* Sang Berg's Lulu at San Francisco, 1989, returned as Natasha in War and Peace; Marzelline in Fidelio and Musetta; Wexford Festival, 1991 as Eleanora in Donizetti's Assedio di Calais; Vancouver, 1992 as Norina, Los Angeles, 1992 as Pamina and Dallas, 1994 as Poppea; Washington Opera, 1995 as Marenka in The Bartered Bride; Guest appearances at Geneva and Bordeaux, as Fiordiligi, and Paris, in Lully's Roland; Santa Fe Opera from 1992, notably in the US premiere of Bose's Werther and the world premiere of D Lang's Modern Painters; Sang Poulenc's Blanche for Portland Opera, 2000. *Address:* c/o Santa Fe Opera, PO Box 2408 Santa Fe, NM 87504, USA.

**PANERAI, Rolando;** Singer (baritone); b. 17 Oct. 1924, Campi Bisensizo, Florence, Italy. *Education:* studied in Florence with Raoul Frazzi and in Milan with Armani and Giulia Tess. *Career:* debut, Naples in 1947 as Faraone in Rossini's Moses; sang at La Scala from 1951, debut in Samson et Dalila; Venice 1955 in the stage premiere of Prokofiev's The Fiery Angel; Aix in 1955 as Mozart's Figaro; Salzburg from 1957 as Ford in Falstaff, Masetto in Don Giovanni, Guglielmo in Così fan tutte and Paolo in Simon Boccanegra; sang in the Italian premiere of Hindemith's Mathis der Maler, Milan 1957; Covent Garden debut 1960 as Figaro; other roles include Verdi's Luna and Giorgio Germont, Henry Ashton in Lucia di Lammermoor and Marcello in La Bohème; appearances in Verona, Florence, Rome, San Francisco 1958, Moscow, Rio de Janeiro, Athens, Berlin, Munich and Johannesburg; returned to Covent Garden in 1985 as Dulcamara in L'Elisir d'amore; Maggio Musicale Florence

1988 as Puccini's Gianni Schicchi; sang Michonnet in Adriana Lecouvreur at the 1989 Munich Festival; Douglas in Mascagni's Guglielmo Ratcliff at Catania, 1990; returned to Covent Garden 1990, and to Barcelona 1998, as Dulcamara; season 2000–01 with Don Alfonso at the Opéra Bastille and Dulcamara at Frankfurt. *Recordings:* I Puritani; Così fan tutte; Il Trovatore; Falstaff; Il Barbiere di Siviglia; La Bohème; Aida; Verdi's Oberto; Parsifal with Maria Callas.

**PANHOFER, Wolfgang;** Cellist; b. 6 June 1965, Vienna, Austria. *Education:* Music and Psychology, University; Hochschule Vienna with Benesch and Herzer; Royal Northern College of Music with Ralph Kirschbaum, courses with B Pergamenshikov, W Pleeth, A Schiff, Paul Tortelier. *Career:* Debut: Dvořák Concerto, Grosser Wiener Musik-Vereinssaal; Youngest freelancing member, Vienna Philharmonic; Soloist, most European countries, Japan, USA, Egypt, Korea, Turkey, India, Iran; Concertos with Vienna Symphony Orchestra, Vienna Chamber Orchestra, almost all the Polish orchestras, Bombay Chamber Orchestra, Hamburg Symphony Orchestra, BBC Chamber Ensemble, Cairo Symphony Orchestra; Appearances on BBC television with Paul Tortelier, Polish television with Philharmony Katowice, Austrian television with Franz Welser-Möst; Played with Josef Suk at the 150th Birthday Concert of Dvořák, Wiener Konzerthaus; Schleswig-Holstein Music Festival with Pergamenshikov; Held masterclasses in Europe, USA, Japan, Korea, Egypt, Turkey and Iran; Debut at Carnegie Hall, New York 2000; mem, ESTA; Former President, WUT, Society for Modern Music and Literature. *Recordings:* Contemporary Austrian music, with Vienna J. S. Chamber Orchestra. *Honours:* Sir John Barbirolli Prize, 1984; Anerkennungspreis der Alban Berg Stiftung. *Address:* Gaertnergasse 13, A 2100 Korneuburg, Austria.

**PANKRATOV, Vladimir;** Singer (bass); b. 1958, St Petersburg, Russia. *Education:* Studied at the St Petersburg Conservatoire. *Career:* Sang with the Kirov Opera in St Petersburg and on tour to Edinburgh, Italy, Sweden, France and Japan in Prince Igor, War and Peace and Khovanshchina; Italian roles include Sparafucile, Philip II, Fiesco, Dulcamara and Basilio; Sarastro, Leporello and Mozart's Commendatore; Guest engagements with Heidelberg Opera until 1995; Debut with Théâtre du Capitole Toulouse, 1996; Concert repertoire includes songs by Borodin, Glinka and Tchaikovsky, and the Requiems of Fauré, Mozart and Verdi; Frequent concerts in Israel, where he also teaches at the Rubin Academy. *Current Management:* Athole Still International Management, Forresters Hall, 25–27 Westow Street, London, SE19 3RY, England. *Telephone:* (20) 8771-5271. *Fax:* (20) 8768-6600. *Website:* www.atholestill.com.

**PANNELL, Raymond;** Composer and Pianist; b. 25 Jan. 1935, London, Ontario, Canada. *Education:* Studied piano with Steuermann and composition with Wagenaar and Giannini at Juilliard. *Career:* Taught at Toronto Royal Conservatory from 1959, Directed opera workshops at Stratford Festival, Ontario, 1966; Assistant Director and Resident Conductor at Atlanta Municipal Theater, 1960 and Director of Youth Experimental Opera Workshop, 1969; Co-founder and General Director of Co-Opera Theatre in Toronto, 1975. *Compositions:* Stage works: Aria da Capo, opera in 1 act, Toronto 1963; The Luck of Giner Coffey, opera in 3 acts; Go, children's opera, 1975; Midway 1975; Push, developmental opera in 1 act, Toronto 1976; Circe, masque, Toronto 1977; Aberfan, video opera, CBC 1977; N-E-U-S, radio opera 1977; Souvenirs, opera in 1 act, Toronto 1979; Refugees, vaudeville, Little Rock, Arkansas, 1986 (revised version); The Downsview Anniversary Song-Spectacle Celebration Pageant 1979; Harvest, television opera, CBC 1980; The Forbidden Christmas, musical 1990. *Honours:* Salzburg Television Opera Prize for Aberfan, 1977. *Address:* c/o SOCAN, 41 Valleybrook Drive, Don Mills, Ontario M3B 2S6, Canada.

**PANNI, Marcello;** Italian conductor and composer; b. 24 Jan. 1940, Rome; s. of Arnaldo Panni and Adriana Cortini; m. Jeanne Colombier 1970; one d. *Education:* Accad. di Santa Cecilia, Rome under Goffredo Petrassi and Conservatoire Nat. Supérieur, Paris. *Career:* conducting debut, Festival of Contemporary Music, Venice 1969; has since achieved renown in field of avant-garde music conducting first performances of works by Berio, Bussotti, Cage, Feldman, Donatoni, Clementi, Sciarrino, and others at all major European festivals and for Italian Radio; regular guest conductor for Accademia di Santa Cecilia, the Italian radio orchestras and other European orchestras performing full range of baroque, classical and modern works; Musical Dir Bonn Opera House 1994–97, Nice Opera House 1997–2001; Artistic Dir San Carlo Opera House, Naples 2001–02; opera début with The Barber of Seville, Hamburg 1977 and has since conducted opera in all the principal opera houses in Europe; American debut with Elisir d'amore, Metropolitan Opera, New York 1988; conducted world premiere of Bussotti's Cristallo di Rocca (opera) at La Scala 1983; Milhaud Prof. of Composition and Conducting, Mills Coll., Oakland, Calif. 1980–84; Bolshoi debut with Macbeth, Moscow 2003. *Works include* symphonic and chamber music and music for experimental theatrical works; operas: Hanjo (one act) 1994, Il giudizio di Paride (one act) 1996, The Banquet 1998, Garibaldi en Sicile (two acts) 2005. *Address:* 3 Piazza Borghese, 00186 Rome, Italy. *Telephone:* (06) 6873617.

**PANOCHA, Jiri;** Violinist; b. 1940, Czechoslovakia. *Education:* Studied at the Prague Academy of Arts. *Career:* Leader of International Student Orchestra in Berlin, under Karajan; Co-founded the Panocha Quartet, 1968; Many concert appearances in Europe, the USA, Canada, Iraq, Mexico, Cuba and other countries; Repertoire includes works by Smetana, Janáček, Dvořák,

Martinů, Haydn, Mozart, Beethoven, Schubert, Bartók and Ravel. *Recordings include:* Dvořák late quartets and Terzetto; Haydn Op 33, Nos 1–6, D Major Op 64; Martinů Complete Quartets; Mendelssohn Octet (with Smetana Quartet); Mozart Oboe Quartet, Clarinet Quintet and Horn Quintet; Schubert Quartettsatz D703 (Supraphon). *Honours:* Prizewinner (with members of Panocha Quartet) at Kromeriž, 1971; Weimar 1974; Prague 1975; Bordeaux 1976; Grand Prix du Disque, Paris, 1983 for Martinů recordings. *Address:* Panocha Quartet, Bureau de Concerts J. Mauroy, 19 rue des Primereres, L-2351, Luxembourg.

**PANTILLON, Christopher (David);** Cellist; b. 26 Jan. 1965, Neuchatel, Switzerland. *Education:* Baccalaureat es Lettres, Humanities, Neuchatel, Switzerland, 1983; Studied with Heinrich Schiff, Conservatory, Basle, 1984–88; Diploma of Cello, 1988; Studied with Valentin Erben, Hochschule für Musik, Vienna. *Career:* Numerous appearances as soloist or chamber player; Member, Trio Pantillon (with 2 brothers); Concerts in Geneva, Zürich, Bern, Vienna, Paris, Rome, England, France, Germany, Netherlands; Appeared on Swiss television and radio; mem, ESTA. *Recordings:* Kabalevsky: Cello-Concerto No. 1 in G Minor. *Honours:* 2nd Prize, Swiss Youth Competition, Lucerne, 1983. *Current Management:* Music Management International. *Address:* La Chanterelle, 2022 Bevaix, Switzerland.

**PANUFNIK, Roxanna,** FRSA; Composer; b. 1968, London, England. *Education:* Studied at the Royal Academy, with Paul Patterson and Henze. *Career:* BBC Researcher and Presenter; Visiting teacher of composition at various schools in England and Barbados; First ever Composer-in-Residence for the Royal County of Berkshire; Performances of her music at all London's main concert venues and throughout the United Kingdom, Europe, Asia, Antipodes and USA; mem, British Academy of Composers and Songwriters; PRS; MCPS. *Compositions include:* Westminster Mass for Westminster Cathedral Choir; Olivia, string quartet; The Music Programme, chamber opera; Leda, ballet; Beastly Tales (words Vikram Seth) for voices and orchestra; Powers & Dominions, harp concertino; Orchestrated Samuel Arnold's opera Inkle and Yarico (1787) for its first modern performance, Barbados, 1997; The Upside Down Sailor, commissioned by Collegiate Wind Ensemble, for narrator and wind nonet, words by Richard Stilgoe. *Recordings:* Angels Sing (all Roxanna Panufnik's religious choral works), The Joyful Company of Singers, Westminster Cathedral Choir; The Upside Down Sailor (for narrator and wind nonet) with Richard Stilgoe & David Campbell's Soundwood Ensemble. *Honours:* ARAM, 1998. *Current Management:* Helen Sykes Artists Management. *Telephone:* (20) 8780-0060. *E-mail:* helen@hsam .unet.com. *Website:* www.roxannapanufnik.com.

**PANULA, Jorma;** Finnish conductor, composer and academic; b. 10 Aug. 1930, Kauhajoki. *Education:* Sibelius Acad., Helsinki. *Career:* Artistic Dir Turku Philharmonic Orchestra, Finland Aarhus Symphony, Denmark 1963–97; Prin. Conductor Helsinki Philharmonic 1965–72; Prof. of Orchestral Conducting, Sibelius Acad., Helsinki 1973–93; trains conductors in USA, Russia, Sweden, Italy and Australia; fmr Visiting Prof. Music Acads of Stockholm and Copenhagen, Yale Univ., Bartók Seminar, Hungary. *Music:* (operas) Jaakko Ilkka, The River Opera; musicals, church music, a violin concerto, a jazz capriccio and vocal music. *Honours:* Music Prize, Royal Swedish Acad. of Science 1997. *Address:* c/o Sibelius Academy, P. Rautatie-katu 9, 00100 Helsinki 10, Finland (office).

**PANZARELLA, Anna Maria;** Singer (Soprano); b. 1970, France. *Education:* Studied in Grenoble and Geneva, at the Royal College of Music and at the National Opera Studio. *Career:* Debut: Sang Fransquita in Carmen with Geneva Opera; Appeared in La Rondine for Opera North, as Frasquita in Lisbon, and Stephano in Roméo et Juliette at Covent Garden; Season 1995–96 as Puccini's Lauretta in Brussels, First Lady (Die Zauberflöte) at Aix and Amore in the world premiere of Goehr's Arianna at Covent Garden; Season 1996–97 as Donna Elvira for Opera Zürich, Balkis in Haydn's L'Incontro Improvviso at Lausanne and Rameau's Aricie in Paris and New York; Season 1997 as Adèle in Le Comte Ory for GTO and Despina at the Bastille, Paris; Sang Erinice in Rameau's Zoroastre at the Brooklyn Academy of Music and Lyon Opéra, 1998. *Recordings include:* Mozart's Requiem with Les Arts Florissants and William Christie (Erato). *Address:* c/o PG & PM, 7 Whitehorse Close, Royal Mile, Edinburgh, EH8 8BU, Scotland.

**PAPAVRAMI, Tedi;** Violinist; b. 1971, Tirana Albania. *Education:* Paris Conservatoire, with Pierre Amoyal. *Career:* Many appearances from 1988 in Europe and South Africa; Festival engagements at Montreux, Newport and Schleswig-Holstein; Season 1998–99 in Paris, Monaco, Germany, Italy and Spain; Conductors have included Kurt Sanderling and Zdenek Macal; Season 2000–01 with the Orchestre Philharmonique de Nice, Stuttgart Chamber Orchestra and Istanbul State Symphony; Chamber music partners include Emanuel Pahud (flute), Raphael Oleg (violin) and Gary Hoffman (cello); Debut tour of Japan 2001; with Paganini's 24 Caprices; South American tour with Mozart's Sinfonia Concertante, K364; Trans. of works of Ismail Kadare (into French) 2000–. *Publications:* as trans. (into French) for Ismail Kadare: L'Envoi du Migrateur, Vie, Jeu et Mort de Lul Mazrek, Le Successeur, La Fille d'Agamemnon. *Honours:* Rodolpho Lipizzer Prize Gorrizia 1985, First Prize, Paris Conservatoire, 1986; Georges Enescu Prize, SACEM, 1992; Winner, Sarasate Competition, Pamplona, 1993. *Current Management:* c/o Musicaglotz, 11, Rue Le Verrier, 75006, Paris, France. *Address:* 166 avenue du Maine, 75014 Paris, France (home).

**PAPE, Gerard (Joseph);** Composer; b. 22 April 1955, Brooklyn, New York, USA; m. Janet Smarr Pape, 23 Aug 1981, 2 s. *Education:* BA, Columbia, University, 1976; MA, 1978, PhD, 1982, University of Michigan; Studied composition with George Cacioppo and William Albright. *Career:* Director, Composer-in-Residence, Sinewave Studios, 1980–91; Music presented in over 25 Sinewave Studios concerts in Ann Arbor, Michigan; Produced the annual Festival of Contemporary Orchestral, Ensemble and Electronic Music, Ann Arbor, twice, 1986–91; Since 1991, Director, Les Ateliers, UPIC Paris, France (Electronic Music Studio); mem, ASCAP. *Compositions include:* Ivan and Rena for 4 Vocal Soloists and Orchestra, 1984; Cosmos for Large Orchestra, 1985; The Sorrows of The Moon for Baritone and Tape, 1986; Folie à Deux for Violin and Piano, 1986; Exorcism for Baritone and Orchestra, 1986; Catechresis for Soprano and Orchestra, 1987; Cerberus for Organ and Tape, 1987; Vortex (String Quartet No. 2), 1988; Three Faces of Death for Orchestra, 1988; Piano Concerto, 1988; Xstasis for Ensemble and Tape, 1992; 2 Electro-Accoustic Songs for Voice, Flute and Tape, 1993; Le Fleuve du Désir (String Quartet No. 3), 1994; Monologue for bass voice and tape, 1995; Battle for 4 solo voices and tape, 1996; Makbenach for saxophone, ensemble and tape, 1996; Feu Toujours Vivant, for large orchestra and live electronics, 1997; Funeral Sentence, for 2 sopranos and percussion, 1998; Makbenach IV, for trombone and tape, 1998; Fabula for soprano and tape, 1999; Aquarelles for clarinet and tape, 1999; Mon Autre Peau for tape 1999; Les Cenci, opera, 2000–. *Recordings:* Mode 26, 6 pieces of Music by Gerard Pape, 1992; Electro-Acoustic Chamber Works, 1998. *Contributions:* Complexity, Composition, Perception, published in Currents in Musical Thought, 1994; Luigi Nono and his Fellow Travellers in Contemporary Music Review. *Honours:* Various grants to produce the Sinewave series of concerts, Michigan Council for The Arts; Meet The Composer, 1989; 8 ASCAP Standard Awards, 1992–99. *Address:* 62 Rue Michel Ange, 75016 Paris, France.

**PAPE, René;** Singer (Bass-baritone); b. 4 Sept. 1964, Dresden, Germany. *Education:* Member of Dresden Kreuzchor 1974–81, tours to Japan and Europe; Dresden Musikhochschule from 1981. *Career:* Debut: Berlin Staatsoper 1987, as the Speaker in Die Zauberflöte; Sang in 1989 premiere of Siegfried Matthus's Graf Mirabeau at Berlin Staatsoper and has appeared there and elsewhere in Germany as Mozart's Figaro and Alfonso, Verdi's Banquo, Procida and King in Aida, Gremin in Eugene Onegin and Galitzky in Prince Igor; Guest engagements at Frankfurt and Vienna Staatsoper; Salzburg Festival 1991, as Sarastro in Die Zauberflöte; Many concert appearances, notably in Mozart's Requiem for the bi-centenary performances in 1991; Sang the Speaker in Die Zauberflöte at the Met, 1995; Appeared as King Henry in Lohengrin at Covent Garden, 1997; Season 1998 with Pogner in Die Meistersinger at the Berlin Staatsoper and Verdi's Philip II at Salzburg; Season 2000–01 as King Mark at the Met, Pogner at the Berlin Staatsoper, Leporello for the Salzburg Festival and King Philip in Don Carlos at the Vienna Staatsoper; Season 2002–03 as Massimiliano in I Masnadieri and Heinrich in Lohengrin at Covent Garden. *Address:* c/o Allied Artists Agency, 42 Montpelier Square, London SW7 1JZ, England.

**PAPERNO, Dmitry;** Concert Pianist and Professor of Piano; b. 18 Feb. 1929, Kiev, USSR; m. Ludmila Gritsay, 21 May 1966, 2 d. *Education:* Honours degree, Moscow Tchaikovsky Conservatory, 1951; Postgraduate, 1955. *Career:* Debut: Recital, Moscow, 1955; Pianist-Soloist, Mosconcert; About 1500 solo recitals and performances in the former Soviet Union, Eastern and Western Europe and Cuba including The USSR State Orchestra, (Moscow, Leningrad and Brussels, Belgium EXPO 1958), Gewandhaus Orchestra, (Leipzig, 1960), Hallé Orchestra, (Manchester, 1967), and many others 1955–76; Numerous concerts in USA, 1977–2001, also Netherlands, France, Belgium, Majorca and Portugal, 1985–2001; Sonata recital with Mstislav Rostropovich, Pasadena, California, USA, 1989; Teaching: Moscow State Gnesin Institute, 1967–73; DePaul University, Chicago, USA, 1977–2001; Full Professor of Piano, 1985, now Emer.; Many masterclasses in the USA and Europe including Tchaikovsky Conservatory, Moscow. *Recordings include:* Melodia, USSR; Works by Chopin, Liszt, Grieg, Schumann, Bach-Busoni, Debussy, Medtner; 2 videotapes for Moscow television: piano recital and Chopin F minor concerto with Moscow Radio and Television Orchestra under Gennady Rozhdest-venski; Selected Works of Scriabin, 1978, and Tchaikovsky's The Seasons, 1982; 7 CDs, USA; Russian Piano Music, 1989; Works of Bach-Busoni, Beethoven, Schubert, Brahms, 1990; Uncommon Encores, 1992; Chopin Live, including the 5th Chopin Competition, Warsaw, 195, 1997; Paperno Live: Selected works from the 1960s and 1970s 1998, Through the Years: Recordings of a Moscow Pianist 2004. *Publications:* 2 books in Russian; Notes of a Moscow Pianist, 1983; Post Scriptum, 1987, 2 pieces for piano: A Little Poem, Waltz-Scherzo 2003; Articles and reviews in USSR and USA. *Address:* 3410 N Lake Shore Drive, Apt 15N, Chicago, IL 60657, USA (home). *Telephone:* (773) 472-7359 (home). *E-mail:* dpaperno@juno.com (home).

**PAPIAN, Vag;** Conductor and Pianist; b. 1960, Russia. *Education:* Moscow and St Petersburg Conservatories. *Career:* Performances as piano soloist throughout Russia from 1979; Conducting studies, with Ilia Musin, led to Associate status with the Armenian SO, from 1987 (chief conductor, 1990); Associate Conductor, Been Sheva SO, Israel, from 1990; Music director; Israel Camerata; Soloist and Conductor with the Jerusalem Symphony; Season 2000–2001 with English Chamber orchestra and a tour to Far East; Further conducting engagements with New Japan Philharmonic and Malmö, Trondheim, Lucerne and Valencia Symphonies; Armenian PO, Israel CO, Belgrade SO and Bucharest Virtuosi; Productions of Don Giovanni, Carmen and Nielsen's Saul and David in Israel; Norma for Armenian Opera, 2001; Concerts as pianist in Europe, North and South America and Far East; Accompanist for Maxim Vengerov, violin. *Recordings include:* recitals.

**PAPINEAU-COUTURE, Jean;** Composer; b. 12 Nov. 1916, Outremont, Québec, Canada; m. Isabelle Baudoin (deceased 1987). *Education:* Conducting with Francis Findley, Composition with Quincy Porter, Piano with Beveridge Webster; BMus, New England Conservatory of Music, Boston, 1941; Composition and Harmony under Nadia Boulanger at Madison, Wisconsin, Lake Arrowhead and Santa Barbara, California. *Career:* Teaching Piano, Jean-de-Brebeuf College, Montreal, 1943–44; Teacher of Music, Conservatoire de Musique et d'Art Dramatique de la Province de Québec, Montreal, 1946–52; Professor, 1951–, Faculty Secretary, 1952–67, Vice Dean, 1967, Dean, 1968–73, Faculty of Music, University of Montreal; Commissions from Canadian Broadcasting Corporation, Montreal Symphony Orchestra, others. *Compositions include:* Suite Lapitsky, orchestra, 1965; Dialogues, 1967; Sectuor, 1967; Nocturne, 7 instruments, 1969; Oscillations, orchestra, 1969; Chanson de rahit, voice, ensemble, 1972; Obsession, 1973; Trio in 4 movements, 1974; Slano, 1975; Le débat du coeur et du corps de villon, voice, ensemble, 1977; Prouesse, viola, 1986; Nuit Polaire, contralto, 10 instruments, 1986; Vers l'Extinction, organ, 1987; Thrène, violin, piano, 1988; Courbes, organ, 1988; Les arabesques d'Isabelle, flute, cor-d'anglais, clarinet, bassoon, piano, 1989; Celebrations, woodwinds, 5 brass percussions, piano, strings, 1990; Quasipassacaille, C'est bref, organ, 1991; Tournants, organ, 1992; Automne, flute oboe, clarinet, bassoon, horn, string quintet, 1992; Vents capricieux sur le clavier, flute, oboe, clarinet, bassoon, piano, 1993; Chocs sonores, marimba, cymbal and tom; Glanures, soprano, chamber orchestra, 1994; Fantastique, violoncello solo, 1995; Quartet for oboe, violin, cello and piano, 1998. *Recordings:* Many on various labels. *Honours:* Canadian Governor-General's Prize, 1994. *Address:* 4694 Lacombe, Montreal, Quebec H3W 1R3, Canada.

**PAPIS, Christian;** French singer (tenor); b. 1960, Algrange. *Education:* Paris Conservatoire. *Career:* Glyndebourne Festival Opera from 1992 as Boris in Katya Kababova (1998, also on Tour), Lensky in Eugene Onegin and Gregor in The Makropulos Case (1997); Further engagements as Don Ottavio in Dublin, Massenet's Des Grieux at Lausanne, Tamino throughout France and Berlioz's Bénédict in Toulouse; Werther in France and Netherlands, Alfredo for Opera Zuid, Don José in Bordeaux, Rodolfo in Amsterdam and Vincent in Gounod's Mireille at the Opéra Comique; the Berlioz Faust in Madrid, Matteo in Arabella and Gounod's Roméo at Geneva Opera; Season 1998–99 as Idomeneo in Nantes, Števa in Jenůfa and Berg's Alva in Liège; Wagner's Froh in Geneva and Alim in Massenet's Le Roi de Lahore at St Etienne and Bordeaux.

**PAPOULIAS, Althea-Maria;** Singer (Soprano); b. 1968, Montreal, Canada. *Education:* Studied at Metill University, Montreal. *Career:* Sang at Cologne Opera from 1993, as Pamina, Gretel and Elvira in L'Italiana in Algeri; Vienna Staatsoper, 1996 as Liu in Turandot; Guest appearances as Agathe in Der Freischütz, Musetta, Puccini's Suor Angelica, Drusilla in Monteverdi's Poppea and Purcell's Dido; Sang Mozart's Fiordiligi for Glyndebourne Touring Opera, 1998; Sang Verdi's Alice Ford at the Vienna Volksoper, 2000; Concerts include songs by Debussy, Ravel and Duparc. *Honours:* Prizewinner, Belvedere Competition, Vienna, 1993. *Address:* c/o Glyndebourne Touring Opera, Glyndebourne, Lewes, East Sussex BN8 5UU, England.

**PAPP, Christine;** Singer (Mezzo-soprano); b. 1959, Sonneberg, Germany. *Education:* Studied in Weimar, Berlin and Milan. *Career:* Sang at Meiningen Opera, 1983–86; Further appearances at Magdeburg, Potsdam and the Berlin Staatsoper; Frankfurt Opera from 1991 as Verdi's Azucena and Ulrica, Fidalma in Il Matrimonio Segreto, Mozart's Marcellina, Annina in Der Rosenkavalier and Santuzza; Concert repertory includes Beethoven's Ninth; Lieder recital in New York. *Address:* c/o Berlin Staatsoper, Unter den linden 7, 1060 Berlin, Germany.

**PAPPANO, Antonio;** American conductor and pianist; *Music Director, The Royal Opera, Covent Garden;* b. 30 Dec. 1959, Epping, London; m. Pam Bullock 1995. *Education:* studied in USA with Norma Verrilli, Arnold Franchetti and Gustav Meier. *Career:* Répétiteur and Asst Conductor New York City Opera, Gran Teatro del Liceo, Barcelona, Frankfurt Opera, Lyric Opera of Chicago early to mid-1980s; asst to Daniel Barenboim for Tristan und Isolde, Parsifal and the Ring cycle at Bayreuth Festival 1986; opera conducting debut with Norwegian Opera, Oslo 1987; Music Dir, Norwegian Opera 1990–92; Covent Garden debut conducting La Bohème 1990; Vienna Staatsoper debut conducting new production of Wagner's Siegfried 1993; season 1996 included the original Don Carlos in Brussels and at the Paris Théâtre du Châtelet; season 1997 Salome at Chicago and Eugene Onegin at the Metropolitan; Prin. Guest Conductor Israel Philharmonic Orchestra 1997–2000; seasons 1999–2001 Lohengrin at Bayreuth; has conducted many world-class orchestras, including Berlin Philharmonic Orchestra, Boston Symphony Orchestra, Chicago Symphony Orchestra, Cleveland Orchestra, London Symphony Orchestra, Los Angeles Philharmonic Orchestra, Orchestre de Paris, Oslo Philharmonic Orchestra, Munich Philharmonic Orchestra; Music Dir Théâtre Royal de la Monnaie, Brussels 1992–2002, conducting a wide variety of titles; Music Dir Royal Opera, Covent Garden 2002–; new productions of Ariadne auf Naxos, Wozzeck, Madama Butterfly and Pagliacci, revival of Falstaff 2002–03; Don Giovanni, Aida, Lady Macbeth of Mtsensk, Faust and Peter Grimes in 2003–04; Das Rheingold and Die Walküre 2005;

Music Dir Orchestra of the Nat. Acad. of Santa Cecilia, Rome 2005–. *Recordings include:* Puccini's La Rondine (Gramophone Award for Best Opera Recording and Record of the Year 1997), Il Trittico 1999, Britten's The Turn of the Screw (Théâtre Royal de la Monnaie production) (Choc du Monde de la Musique, Prix de l'Acad. du Disque Lyrique Grand Prix Int., Orphée d'Or) 1999, Werther 1999, Manon Gramophone Award for Best Opera Recording 2001; many recordings as conductor including Rachmaninov's Piano Concertos 1 & 2 2005; recordings as pianist with Rockwell Blake, Barbara Bonney and Han-Na Chang. *Honours:* Royal Philharmonic Soc. Award for best conductor 2005. *Current Management:* IMG Artists Paris, 54 avenue Marceau, 75008 Paris, France. *Address:* c/o Royal Opera House, Covent Garden, London, WC2E 9DD, England. *Website:* www.roh.org.uk.

**PAQUETTE, Daniel;** Professor Emeritus of History of Music; b. 1930, Morteau, Doubs, France; m. Madeleine Mougel 1957, one s. one d. *Education:* National Conservatoire of Dijon, National Conservatoire of Saint Etienne. *Career:* Teacher of Musical Education, Lycées in Angiers, 1952, Dijon, 1953–64; Assistant, Institute of Musicology, University of Strasbourg, 1964–69; Lecturer, University of Dijon, 1970–72; Professor, University of Lyon, 1972–; Head, Musicology Section, Universities of Besançon and Dijon (Audio-visual education), St Etienne; Leader, Philharmonic Choirs of Dijon and Voix Amies Dijon, 1953–64; Leader, University Orchestra, Strasbourg, 1964–69. *Compositions:* Les Dames des Entreportes, symphonic poem; Operetta for children; Les Fantomes du Val au Faon; A cappella choral music based on ancient music of 16th–18th century; Film and chamber music; Films, J J Rousseau et la musique; J Ph Rameau, musicien sensible et savant rigoureux; Oratorio, for 2 choruses, 4 singers, string orchestra, piano, trumpet, based on verses by Lamartine, A Hymn of Peace. *Publications:* L'Instrument de musique dans la Grece Antique, 1984; Jean Philippe Rameau musicien bourguignon, 1983; Musique baroque, Aspects de la musique en France et à Lyon au XVIII, since 1990; Articles in Dictionaire de la Musique, 1976–86 and Die Musik in Geschichte und Gegenwart, 1999. *Address:* Les Furtins, 71960 Berzé-la-Ville, France.

**PARATORE, Anthony;** Concert Pianist; b. 17 June 1946, Boston, MA, USA. *Education:* BM, Boston Univ., 1966; BM, MS, Juilliard School, New York, 1970. *Career:* debut, Metropolitan Museum, 1973; guest appearances with New York Philharmonic, Chicago, San Francisco, Detroit, Washington National, Denver, Boston, Indianapolis, Atlanta, San Diego, BBC London, Vienna Philharmonic, Berlin Philharmonic, Vienna Symphony, RAI Orchestra, Nouvel Philharmonique, Warsaw Philharmonic, Amsterdam Philharmonic, Rotterdam Philharmonic, Norwegian Chamber Orchestra, English Chamber Orchestra, Prague Chamber Orchestra, Bavarian Radio Orchestra, London Symphony Orchestra, Munich Chamber Orchestra; festival appearances, mostly Mozart, Salzburg, Berlin, Strauss Tage, Lucerne, Istanbul, Adelaide Festival in Australia, and Spoleto; PBS television special, The Paratores, Two Brothers, Four Hands; NPR radio, All Things Considered and A Note To You; mem., Boston Musicians' Asscn, Dante Alighieri Society. *Compositions:* premieres of new compositions; Wolfgang Rihm, Maskes; Manfred Trojan, Folia; William Bolcom, Sonata for two pianos in one movement. *Recordings:* Pictures at an Exhibition, Mussorgsky; Opera Festival for Four Hands; Mendelssohn Concerti for two pianos and orchestra; Variations for Four Hands; Schoenberg Chamber Symphony op 9; Stravinsky, Sacre du Printemps; Ravel; Bolero, Ma Mère L'Oye, Rapsodie Espagnole; Gershwin; Rhapsody in Blue, Concerto in F; Brahms Liebeslieder Waltzes, opus 52 and 65, Waltzes opus 39; Saint-Saëns, Carnival of the Animals; Variations on a Theme by Haydn Sonata in F minor, opus 34; Points on Jazz, by Dave Brubeck. *Contributions:* Keyboard Classics; Clavier magazine. *Honours:* First Prize, Munich International Music Competition, Duo-Piano Category, 1974; George Washington Honor Medal, 1998. *Current Management:* Konzert-Direktion Hans Adler, Auguste-Viktoria-Strasse 64, 14199 Berlin, Germany. *Telephone:* (30) 825–6333. *Fax:* (30) 826–3520. *Website:* www.musikadler.de.

**PARATORE, Joseph D.;** Concert Pianist; b. 19 March 1948, Boston, MA, USA. *Education:* BM, Boston Univ., 1970; MS, Juilliard School, 1972. *Career:* debut, Metropolitan Museum of Art, 1973; guest appearances with New York Philharmonic, Chicago Symphony, San Francisco, Detroit, Indianapolis, Atlanta, Washington National, Boston, Denver, San Diego, BBC London, Vienna Philharmonic, Berlin Philharmonic, Vienna Symphony, RAI, Nouvel Philharmonique, Warsaw Philharmonic, Amsterdam Philharmonic, Rotterdam Philharmonic, Norwegian Chamber Orchestra, English Chamber Orchestra, Prague Chamber Orchestra, Bavarian Radio Orchestra, London Symphony, Munich Chamber Orchestra; festival appearances, Lucerne, Istanbul, Adelaide Festival in Australia, Salzburg, Berlin, Strauss Tage, Spoleto, mostly Mozart; television appearances include: WGBH-PBS television special The Paratores, Two Brothers/Four Hands; radio: NPR All Things Considered and A Note to You; mem., Boston Musicians' Asscn, Dante Alighieri Society. *Compositions:* Wolfgang Rihm, Maskes; Manfred Trojan, Folia; William Bolcom, Sonata for two pianos in one movement. *Recordings:* Mussorgsky–Pictures at an Exhibition and Opera Festival for Four Hands; Mendelssohn Concerti for Two Pianos and Orchestra; Variations for Four Hands; Schoenberg, Chamber Symphony op 9; Stravinsky, Sacre du Printemps; Ravel: Bolero, Ma Mère L'Oye, Rapsodie Espagnole; Gershwin: Rhapsody in Blue, Concerto in F; Brahms: Variations on a Theme by Haydn and Sonata in F minor, Liebeslieder Waltzes Op 52 and 65, Waltzes Op 39; Saint-Saëns, Carnival of the Animals; Points on Jazz, by Dave Brubeck.

*Contributions:* Keyboard Classics–The Art of Transcribing Mussorgsky; Clavier magazine–Master Class–Ravel Ma Mère L'Oye. *Honours:* First Prize, Munich International Music Competition, Duo-Piano Category, 1974; George Washington Honor Medal, 1998. *Current Management:* Konzert-Direktion Hans Adler, Auguste-Viktoria-Strasse 64, 14199 Berlin, Germany. *Telephone:* (30) 825–6333. *Fax:* (30) 826–3520. *Website:* www.musikadler.de.

**PARDEE, Margaret;** American violinist, violist and teacher of violin and viola; b. 10 May 1920, Valdosta, GA; m. Daniel R. Butterly 1944. *Education:* Institute of Musical Art, Juilliard School; studied with Sascha Jacobsen, Albert Spalding, Louis Persinger, Ivan Galamian. *Career:* debut at New York Town Hall, 1952; toured as Soloist and in String Quartet and Duo Recitals as Violinist and Violist, USA; Soloist with Symphony Orchestra; Faculty Member, Juilliard School, 1942–; Concert Master, Great Neck Symphony, New York, 1954–85; Faculty Member and Director, Meadowmount School of Music, 1956–85, 1988–92; Adjunct Professor, Queens College, New York, 1978–, State University of New York, Purchase, 1980–; Jury Member, National and International Competitions; Faculty Member, Estherwood Festival and School, Dobbs Ferry, New York, 1984–85, Estherwood Festival and Summer School, Oneonta State University, 1986; Faculty, Bowdoin Summer Music Festival, Bowdoin College, Brunswick, Maine, 1987; Taught in Conservatory of Music of the Simon Bolivar Orchestra in Caracas, Venezuela, 1988, 1989; Invited to teach in Caracas, Venezuela for Municipal Orchestra and Symphonica, 1991–; On Faculty at Killington Chamber Music Festival, Killington, 1993–. *Address:* c/o Juilliard School, Lincoln Center Plaza, New York, NY 10023, USA.

**PARIK, Ivan;** Slovak composer and teacher; b. 17 Aug. 1936, Bratislava; m. Magdalena Barancoková 1970; one d. *Education:* Bratislava Conservatory, Acad. of Music and Dramatic Arts, Bratislava. *Career:* debut composition Music for four strings; Lecturer Acad. of Music and Dramatic Arts, Bratislava 1962–, Pro-Rector 1990–94, Rector 1994–97, Rector Emer.; currently teacher Univ. of Konstantin the Philosopher; Chair. Music Foundation; mem. Slovak Music Union. *Compositions:* Orchestral including: Music for Ballet, 4 scenes for large orchestra, 1968; Fragments, suite for ballet, 1969; Musica pastoralis for large orchestra, 1984; Music for Flute, Viola and Orchestra, 1987; Two Arias on text fragments of Stabat mater for higher voice and orchestra; Chamber including: Sonata for flute, 1962; Songs about Falling Leaves for piano, 1962; Time of Departures, diptych for soprano and piano, 1976; Seen Closely Above the Lake for reciter, wind quintet, piano and string quartet, also version for orchestra, 1979; Pastorale for Organ, 1979; Music for Milos Urbásek for string quartet, 1981; Duet for Violas, 1981; How to Drink from a Well, music to poem by Milan Rúfus for reciter and chamber orchestra, 1990; Meditacia, for flute and organ, 1997; Choral including Among the Mountains, ballad for mixed choir, 1973; Electro-acoustic music including: Music to Opening II for flute solo and tape, 1970; In memoriam Ockeghem, 1971; Homage to Hummel, 1980; Scenic and film music including: Fragment, ballet in 1 act on motifs of Kobo Abbe's novel Sand Woman, 1969; King Lear, 1969; Three Sisters, 1981; Medea, 1983; Macbeth, 1982; St Francis of Assisi, 1992; Triptych for soprano and orchestra (music for Jacopone da Todi's Stabat Mater) 2003. *Publications:* How to Read a Score (co-author) 1986, How to Conduct (co-author); contrib. many articles. *Honours:* Slovák Philharmonic Orchestra Hon. Medal 1986, Academy of Music Gold Medal, Prague 1997. *Address:* Gajova 17, 81109 Bratislava, Slovakia. *Telephone:* (97) 670240 (office); (903) 226004 (home). *E-mail:* mparikova@hotmail.com (home).

**PARIK, Ivan;** Czech conductor; b. 1955. *Education:* Munich Staatsoper with Wolfgang Sawallisch, studied with Hans Swarowsky in Vienna, Arvid Jansons and Kurt Masur in Weimar. *Career:* has appeared while leading orchestras in Czechoslovakia and elsewhere in Eastern Europe; Conductor, Ostrava Opera from 1980, leading works by Mozart, Verdi, Puccini, Weber, Gounod, Wagner, Bizet, Strauss, Shostakovich and Czech composers; Guest Conductor, Vienna Volksoper, notably with The Bartered Bride, Die Entführung, Die Zauberflöte and Dvořák's Jacobin; guest appearances in Dresden with Rusalka and Lohengrin, Bilbao and Prague with Così fan tutte; conducted Rigoletto at Gars am Kamp, Austria 1992; Musical Dir, Klagenfurt Opera from 1992; concert engagements in works by Mozart, Schubert, Berlioz, Brahms, Dvořák, Janáček, Debussy, Stravinsky and Strauss; mem. Slovak Music Union, ISCM. *Address:* c/o Czech National Symphony Orchestra, Weilova 2/114, 102 00 Prague 10, Czech Republic.

**PÂRIS, Alain;** Conductor; b. 22 Nov. 1947, Paris, France; m. Marie-Stella Abdul Ahad, 23 June 1973. *Education:* Licence in Law, Paris, 1969; Studied Piano with Bernadette Alexandre-Georges, Ecriture with Georges Dandelot; Conducting with Pierre Dervaux (Licence de concert, Ecole Normale de Musique, 1967), Louis Fourestier, Paul Paray. *Career:* Debut: 1969; Guest Conductor, with major French orchestras including, Orchestre de Paris, Orchestre National, Orchestre de Lyon, Toulouse, Strasbourg; Performed with various orchestras abroad including, Dresdner Philharmonic, Slovak Philharmonic, Orchestre de la Suisse Romande, Philharmonia Hungarica, Philharmonie George Enesco (Bucharest), Orchestra de la BRT (Brussels), Milan, Saint Petersburg, Germany, Luxembourg, Greece, Iraq, Hong Kong, Granada, Ankara; Assistant Conductor, Orchestre du Capitole de Toulouse, 1976–77; Associate Conductor, 1983–84, Permanent Conductor, 1984–87, Opéra du Rhin, Strasbourg; Producer, Musical Broadcasts for Radio France, 1971–; Professor of Conducting, Strasbourg Conservatory, 1986–89; Regular Conductor, French Season Concerts, Capella Symphony Orchestra and Chorus, St Petersburg, 1996–; mem, Société Française de Musicologie.

*Publications:* Dictionnaire des interprètes et de l'interprétation musicale, Paris, Robert Laffont, 1982, 4th edition 1995; Spanish Translation, Turner, Madrid, 1989; German Translation, dtv, Munich, 2nd edition, 1997; Les Livrets d'opéra, Paris, Robert Laffont, 1991; Editor, French Edition of the New Oxford Companion to Music (Dictionnaire encyclopédique de la musique, Robert Laffont 1988) and Baker's Biographical Dictionary of Musicians (Dictionnaire biographique des musiciens, Robert Laffont 1995). *Contributions:* Encyclopaedia Universalis; Retz; Quid; Scherzo; Courrier musical de France; Diapason; La Lettre du Musicien. *Honours:* Licence de concert, Ecole Normale de Musique, Paris, 1967; 1st Prize, concours international de Besançon, 1968. *Address:* 33 Rue de Constantinople, 75008 Paris, France.

**PARISOT, Aldo Simoes;** Brazilian cellist and teacher; *Samuel Sanford Professor of Music, Yale University;* b. 30 Sept. 1920, Natal; m. Elizabeth Sawyer-Parisot; one s. *Education:* Yale Univ. and private studies with Thomazzo Babini and Ibere Gomes Grosso. *Career:* debut with the Boston Symphony, Berkshire Music Center 1947; principal cellist Pittsburgh Symphony 1949–50; tours of Europe, Asia, Africa, South America and throughout the USA from 1948; plays solo works by Bach and the sonatas of Brahms and Beethoven in recital; joined faculty of Peabody Conservatory 1956–58, Mannes Coll. 1962–66, New England Conservatory 1966–70; Prof. in School of Music, Yale Univ. 1958–, currently Samuel Sanford Prof. of Music; Music Dir Aldo Parisot Int. Cello Course and Competition, Brazil 1977; artist-in-residence, Banff Center for the Arts, Canada 1981–83; has given the premieres of works by Quincy Porter, Villa-Lobos (concerto No. 2 1955), Claudio Santoro (concerto 1963), Leon Kirchner (concerto for violin, cello and orchestra 1960), Alvin Etler (concerto 1971), Yehudi Wyner (De novo 1971) and Donald Martino; formed students at Yale Univ. into the 'Yale Cellos' ensemble. *Address:* The School of Music, Yale University, PO Box 208246, New Haven, CT 06520-8246, USA.

**PARKER, Jon Kimura;** Concert Pianist; b. 25 Dec. 1959, Vancouver, Canada. *Education:* Masters in Music, 1983 and Doctor of Musical Arts, 1989, Juilliard School; Teachers: Adele Marcus, Lee Kum-Sing, Edward Parker and Marek Jablonski. *Career:* Debut: New York, 1984 and London 1984; Performed with London Symphony, London Philharmonic, Toronto Symphony, Cleveland Orchestra, Minnesota Orchestra, Los Angeles Philharmonic, Philadelphia Orchestra, Scottish National Orchestra, Berlin Radio Symphony, NHK Orchestra, Japan, and all Canadian Orchestras; Recital tours in Europe, Canada, North and South America, Far East and Australia; Command performance for Queen Elizabeth II and Prime Minster of Canada, 1984; Featured on CBC television documentary show The Journal, Local Boy Makes Great in 1985; Benefit performance of Beethoven's Emperor Concerto at Sarajevo, New Year's Eve, 1995; Host of television series, Whole Notes, 1999–. *Recordings:* Tchaikovsky Piano Concerto No. 1; Prokofiev Piano Concerto No. 3 with André Previn and Royal Philharmonic Orchestra, 1986; Solo Piano Music of Chopin, 1987; Two Pianists are Better Than One, with Peter Schickele, 1994; Barber Piano Concerto with Yoel Levi and Atlanta Symphony, 1997. *Honours:* 1st Prize and Princess Mary Gold Medal, Leeds International Piano Competition, 1984; Canadian Governor General's Performing Arts Award, 1996; Officer of the Order of Canada, 1999. Numerous other first prizes in international competitions. *Address:* c/o ICM Artists Ltd, 40 West 57th Street, New York, NY 10019, USA.

**PARKER, Moises;** Singer (Tenor); b. 1945, Las Villas, Cuba. *Education:* Studied in Munich, at Juilliard School and Verdi Conservatory Milan; Teachers included Tito Gobbi, Richard Holm and Hermann Reutter. *Career:* Debut: New York City Opera 1976 as Don José; Sang at Strasbourg Opera 1978–80 as Tamino, Hoffmann and Ratansen in Roussel's Padmâvatî; Season 1981–82 with Welsh National Opera and Scottish Opera as Rodolfo and Alvaro; Brunswick and Augsburg 1982–83 as Don José and Alvaro; Deutsche Oper Berlin as Pinkerton; Sang Otello at Coburg 1984 and at Stuttgart and Klagenfurt 1989; Theater des Westens Berlin 1988–89, as Gershwin's Porgy, Würzburg 1990 as Bacchus; Member of Kiel Opera from 1988, notably as Turiddu in Cavalleria Rusticana and Win-San-Lui in Leoni's L'Oracolo, 1990; Sang Tannhäuser at Passau 2000; Concert repertoire includes Messiah, Beethoven's Ninth and the Missa Solemnis, Elijah, Rossini's Stabat Mater and Messe Solennelle, Verdi's Requiem. *Honours:* Prize Winner at 1974 Voci Verdiane Competition at Bussetto, 1975 Francisco Vinas at Barcelona. *Address:* c/o Buhnen des Landeshaupt, Rathausplatz, 2300 Kiel, Germany.

**PARKER, Roger;** Writer on Music; b. 2 Aug. 1951, London, England. *Education:* Studied at London University with Margaret Bent and Pierluigi Petrobelli. *Career:* Professor at Cornell University, USA, 1982–94; Co-ordinating Editor of Donizetti Critical Edition, 1988; Founding Co-Editor, Cambridge Opera Journal, 1989–98; University Lecturer in Music and Fellow of St Hugh's College, Oxford, 1994–99; Professor of Music and Fellow, St John's College, Cambridge, 1999. *Publications:* Critical Edition of Verdi's Nabucco, 1987; (with A Groos) Giacomo Puccini; La Bohème, 1986, and Reading Opera, 1989; Studies in Early Verdi, 1989; Analyzing Opera: Verdi and Wagner (with C Abbate), 1989; Articles on Verdi and his operas in The New Grove Dictionary of Opera, 4 vols, 1992; Oxford Illustrated History of Opera, editor, 1994; Leonora's Last Act: Essays in Verdian Discourse, 1997. *Honours:* Dent Medal, 1991. *Address:* Faculty of Music, West Road, Cambridge CB 3 9DP, England.

**PARKER-SMITH, Jane (Caroline Rebecca);** Concert Organist; b. 20 May 1950, Northampton, England; m. John Gadney, 24 October 1996. *Education:*

Barton Peveril Grammar School, Eastleigh, Hants, 1959–67; Royal College of Music, 1967–71; Postgraduate Study with Nicolas Kynaston and Jean Langlais, Paris. *Career:* Westminster Cathedral, 1970; Royal Festival Hall, 1975; BBC Promenade Concert, 1972; Solo Recitals, Jyvasklya Festival, Finland, 1977, Stockholm Concert Hall, 1980, Hong Kong Arts Festival, 1988, Roy Thomson Hall, Toronto, 1989, City of London Festival, 1992, Festival Paris Quartier D'Été, 1995, American Guild of Organists Centennial Convention, New York, 1996; Festival Internazionale de musica organistica, Magadino, Switzerland, 1999; Athens Concert Hall, 1999; Cube Concert Hall, Shiroishi, 2000; Lapua Organ Festival, Finland, 2003; American Guild of Organists National COnvention, Philadelphia, 2002, Royal Festival Hall, 2003; Severance Haqll, Cleveland, USA, 2003; mem, Incorporated Society of Musicians; Royal College of Organists; Incorporated Association of Organists. *Recordings:* Widor Symphonies, Music for Trumpet and Organ with Maurice Andre; Liszt Organ Works, Saint-Saëns Organ Symphony No. 3, Janáèek Glagolitic Mass with the City of Birmingham Symphony Orchestra, conductor Simon Rattle; Baroque Organ Concertos with Prague Chamber Orchestra, conductor Steuart Bedford; Popular French Romantics, Armagh Cathedral; Lefébure-Wély Romantische Orgelmusik; Romantic and Virtuoso Organ Works. *Honours:* ARCM, 1966; Winner, National Organ Competition, 1970; LTCL, 1971; Hon FGMS, 1996, Hon FNMSM, 1997. *Current Management:* Karen McFarlane Artists Inc, Cleveland, USA. *Address:* 141 The Quadrangle Tower, Cambridge Square, London W2 2PL, England. *Telephone:* (20) 7262 9259. *Fax:* (20) 7262 9259. *E-mail:* jane@parker-smith.demon.co.uk. *Website:* www. impulse-misic.co.uk/parker-smith.htm.

**PARKIN, Simon;** Composer, Pianist and Teacher; b. 3 Nov. 1956, Manchester, England. *Education:* Yehudi Menuhin School, 1967–74; BMus, University of Manchester, 1977; Graduate, Royal College of Music, 1978; Associate, Royal College of Music, 1973. *Career:* Performances in St John's, Smith Square, London, Wigmore Hall and Queen Elizabeth Hall, London; Performances as duo-partner in Budapest, Liszt Academy and Berlin (Otto Braun Saal); Resident Pianist at ISM, LDSM and Lenk courses; Compositions performed in London, New York, Frankfurt, Germany; Broadcasts on German radio; Teaching Posts: Royal Northern College of Music; Yehudi Menuhin School. *Compositions:* Ted Spiggot and the Killer Beans (Opera); Le Chant des Oiseaux (choral work); Laughter and Tears (Requiem, choir and orchestra) Piano trio, string quartet, chamber concerto; Composer of several sonatas for solo instruments and piano. *Honours:* Recipient various university and college prizes; Morley College Centenary Concerto Prize for chamber concerto. *Address:* 39 Crompton Road, Burnage, Manchester M19 2QT, England.

**PARKINSON, Del R.;** Pianist and University Professor; b. 6 Aug. 1948, Blackfoot, Idaho, USA; m. Glenna M Christensen, 6 Aug 1986. *Education:* BM, 1971, MM, 1972, Performers Certificate, 1972, DM, 1975, Indiana University; Postgraduate Diploma, The Juilliard School 1977; Fulbright Hays Grant for graduate study in London, England, 1974–75. *Career:* Debut: Wigmore Hall, London, 1976; Carnegie Recital Hall, New York, 1981; Concerto appearances with Chicago Civic Orchestra, Utah Symphony, Boise Philharmonic and Guadalajara Symphony; Solo recitals in USA, England and Mexico; Chamber Music in USA and aboard Royal Viking Cruise Line; Performer in American Piano Duo, 1984–; Performed with American Piano Quartet throughout USA, Asia and Europe, 1989–95; Teaching Career: Assistant Professor at Furman University, 1975–76, Piano Co-ordinator at Ricks College, 1977–85, Professor at Boise State University, 1985–. *Recordings:* American Piano Quartet, 1992; American Piano Duo, Celebrating Gershwin, 1998; Mendelssohn Concerto, American Piano Duo, 2004. *Publications:* Selected Works for Piano and Orchestra in One Movement, 1821–53, Indiana University Doctoral Dissertation, 1975. *Contributions:* Record review for Journal of American Liszt Society of Charles Koechlin piano music, 1984. *Honours:* Idaho Governor's Award for Excellence in the Arts, 1988; Idaho Commission on the Arts Career Fellowship, 1997; Boise Mayor's Award for Artistic Excellence, 2001; Boise State Univ. Foundation Scholar Award for Research and Creative Activity, 2003. *Address:* Music Department, Boise State University, Boise, ID 83725, USA.

**PARKMAN, Stefan;** Choral Conductor and Professor; b. 22 June 1952, Uppsala, Sweden; m. Karin Axelsson; one d. one s. *Education:* Musicology, Uppsala Univ., 1972–74; Royal Coll. of Music, Stockholm, 1978–83; Professorship in Choral Conducting, Uppsala Univ. *Career:* Conductor, Boys' Choir, Uppsala Cathedral 1974–89, Royal Philharmonic Chorus, Stockholm 1985–93, Acad. Chamber Choir of Uppsala 1983–; Chief Conductor, Danish National Radio Choir 1989–2002, Swedish Radio Choir 2002–; freelance appearances with numerous symphony orchestras and ensembles throughout Scandinavia, including the Royal Philharmonic Orchestra and the Royal Opera, Stockholm; regular guest conductor of the BBC Singers (London), Nederlands Kamerkoor (Amsterdam), Rundfunkchor (Berlin); regular teacher of masterclasses and seminars in Sweden and overseas; appearances as a tenor soloist (mainly Evangelist parts) in baroque oratorios and passions. *Recordings:* numerous recordings, particularly for the Chandos label. *Honours:* made Knight of the Dannebrog by Queen Margrethe II, Denmark 1997; Royal Swedish Academy of Music (elected mem.) 1998. *Address:* Uppsala University Choral Centre, PO Box 638, 75126 Uppsala, Sweden. *E-mail:* stefan.parkman@musik.uu.se.

**PARMEGIANI, Bernard;** Composer; b. 27 Oct. 1927, Paris, France; m., one s. *Career:* Groupe Recherches Musicales from 1959, composer of music for fixed sounds. *Compositions include:* Violostries for violin and tape, 1965;

Jazzex, with jazz instrumentalist J.L. Chautemps, 1966; Et Après, with Michel Portal, 1967; electro-acoustic music: 65 works including Capture Ephémère, 1968; L'oeil ecoute, 1970; Pour en finir avec le pouvoir d'Orphée I, 1971–73; Enfer, from Dante, 1972; De natura sonorum, 1974–76; L'écho du miroir, 1980; La création du monde, 1981–1984; Exercisme I, II, III, IV 1985–89; cycle Plain-temps, 1991–93; Sonare, 1996; La Mémoire des Sons, 2000–01; Espèce d'Espace, 2002–03; Numerous scores for film, TV, radio and stage. *Recordings:* La Création du monde; Violostries; La Divine Comédie (Bayle/Parmegiani); Sonare; Questions de temps; Pop Eclectic, Plate Lunch. *Publications:* L'Envers d'une oeuvre/de natura sonorum, 1982; Portrait Polychrome: Bernard Parmegiani. *Honours:* Grand Prix de l Acad. du Disque, 1979; Prix de la Sacem, 1981; Golden Nica, Ars Electronica of Linz (Austria), 1993. *Address:* c/o GRM/INA, Maison de Radio France, 116 Avenue du Pt Kennedy, 75220 Paris Cédex, France. *E-mail:* parme@free.fr.

**PARMERUD, Ake;** Swedish composer; b. 24 July 1953, Lidköping; s. of Harald Parmerud and Ing-Brit Parmerud; m. Mireille Leblanc; two s. *Education:* Gothenburg Conservatory, from 1978. *Career:* Lecturer in Computer Music and Composition Gothenburg Conservatory 1987; Lindblad-Studio of University of Gothenburg; mem. RAM 1998. *Compositions:* Time's Imaginary Eye, for soprano, tape and slides, 1980; Floden av glas, multimedia, 1978–82; Remaim, orchestra and tape, 1982; Yttringer, soprano and ensemble, 1983; Kren, 1984; Maze, 1985; Yàn, percussion, ensemble and tape, 1985; Isola for chamber orchestra and tape, 1986; Inori, harpsichord and synthesizer, 1987; Les objects obscurs, 1991; Inside Looking Out, computer and ensemble, 1992; Jeux imaginaires, 1993; Stings and Shadows, harp and computer, 1993; Renaissance, 1994; Grains of Voices, 1995; Mirage 1996; Efterbild, computer and orchestra, 1998; The Heart of Silence, multimedia, 1998, Les Flûtes en feu 2000, The Fire Inside, sound/video installation 2000, Substring Bridge for guitar and computer 2002, Bows, Arcs and the Arrow of Time for string orchestra, computer and video 2004, La Vie Mécanique tape 2004. *Honours:* 1st Prize Festival de Bourges 1978, 1980, 1984, 1986, 1991, Prix Ars Electronica 1990, 1994, 1st Prize Stockholm Electronic Arts Awards 1993, The Rosenberg Prize 1997, 1st Prize Metamorphosis Festival 1999. *Address:* Klostergången 3, S–41318, Göteborg, Sweden. *Telephone:* (31) 494942 (office). *E-mail:* ake.parmerud@musik.gu.se (office). *Website:* www .parmerud.com.

**PARNAS, Leslie;** Concert Cellist and Professor of Music; b. 22 Nov. 1932, St Louis, Missouri, USA; m. Ingeburge Parnas, 2 s. *Education:* Curtis Institute of Music, Philadelphia, with Piatigorsky. *Career:* Debut: New York Town Hall, 1959; Solo Cellist, annual world-wide concert tours with leading orchestras; Director, Kneisal Hall Summer Music School, Blue Hill, Maine; Teacher at the St Louis Conservatory of Music, from 1982; mem, Chamber Music Society of Lincoln Center, New York. *Recordings:* Has recorded for Columbia and Pathé-Marconi Records. *Honours:* Pablo Casals Prize, Paris, 1957; Primavera Trophy, Rome, 1959; Prizewinner, International Tchaikovsky Competition, Moscow, 1962. *Address:* c/o Columbia Artists Management, 165 West 57th Street, New York, NY 10019, USA.

**PARR, Patricia (Ann);** Pianist and Educator; b. 10 June 1937, Toronto, Canada; two s. *Education:* Curtis Institute of Music, Philadelphia, Pennsylvania, USA; Studied Piano with Isabelle Vengerova; Composition with Gian-Carlo Menotti; Diploma, 1957; Postgraduate studies with Rudolf Serkin. *Career:* Debut: Toronto Symphony age 9; Soloist with Philadelphia, Cleveland, Pittsburgh, Toronto Orchestras and others; New York Town Hall debut; Soloist and Chamber Musician appeared extensively in Canada and USA; In Trio Concertante toured Australia, 1975 and 1978; Festival appearances include Marlboro, Stratford, Fontana, Marin County, Festival of the Sound; Founding Member, Amici Chamber Ensemble; Faculty, Duquesne University, 1967–74, University of Toronto, 1974–; Royal Conservatory of Music, 1982–90; 16th Season with AMICI, series in Toronto, tours of Mexico, Jamaica, Eastern Europe, Eastern Canada. *Recordings:* Musica Viva Series with Clarinettist Joaquin Valdepenas; With Violinist Lorand Fenyves; With Hornist Eugene Rittich; With Marc Dubois, tenor; 8 CD's as a member of the Amici Chamber Ensemble. *Address:* 1702–71 Charles St E, Toronto, Ontario M4Y 2T3, Canada.

**PARRIS, Robert,** BS, MS; American composer; b. 21 May 1924, Philadelphia, PA. *Education:* University of Pennsylvania with Peter Mennin and William Bergsma, Juilliard with Ibert and Copland, Berkshire Music Center, Ecole Normale in Paris with Honegger. *Career:* has taught at Washington State College and University of Maryland; George Washington University 1963, Professor, 1976–; commissions from Detroit Symphony Orchestra and the Contemporary Music Forum. *Compositions include:* Orchestra: Symphony, 1952; Piano Concerto, 1953; Concerto for 5 kettledrums and orchestra, 1955; Viola Concerto, 1958; Violin Concerto, 1958; Flute Concerto, 1964; Concerto for trombone and chamber orchestra, 1964; Concerto for percussion, violin, cello and piano, 1967; The Phoenix, 1969; The Messengers, 1974; Rite of Passage, 1978; The Unquiet Heart for violin and orchestra, 1981; Chamber Music for orchestra, 1984; Vocal: Night for baritone string quartet and clarinet, 1951; Alas for the Day, cantata, 1954; Hymn for the Nativity for chorus and brass ensemble, 1962; Dreams for soprano and chamber orchestra; Cynthia's Revell's for baritone and piano, 1979; Chamber: 2 String Trios, 1948, 1951; 2 String Quartets, 1951, 1952; Sonata for solo violin, 1965; The Book of Imaginary Dreams, Parts I and II for ensemble, 1972, 1983; Three Duets for electric guitar and amplified harpsichord, 1984. *Honours:* NEA

grants 1974, 1975. *Address:* c/o ASCAP, ASCAP Building, 1 Lincoln Plaza, NY 10023, USA.

**PARRISH, Cheryl;** Singer (Soprano); b. 6 Nov. 1954, Pasadena, Texas, USA. *Education:* Graduated Baylor University, 1977 and studied at Vienna Musikhochschule, 1978–79. *Career:* Has sung at San Francisco Opera from 1983, as Sophie in Rosenkavalier and Werther and Mozart's Blondchen and Susanna (season 1990–91); Miami Opera, 1987 and 1991, as Ophelia in Hamlet and as Despina; Sang Adele in Die Fledermaus at Toronto, 1987 and San Diego, 1991; Sophie in Der Rosenkavalier at Zürich Opera, 1988 and has guested further at Florence and Santa Fe; Shepherd in Tannhäuser at Austin, Texas, 1996; Frequent concert appearances. *Address:* c/o San Francisco Opera, War Memorial Opera House, San Francisco, CA 94192, USA.

**PARROTT, Andrew Haden,** BA; British conductor and scholar; b. 10 March 1947, Walsall; s. of R. C. Parrott and E. D. Parrott; m. 1st Emma Kirkby 1971; m. 2nd Emily Van Evera 1986; one d. *Education:* Queen Mary's Grammar School, Walsall, Merton Coll., Oxford. *Career:* Dir of Music Merton Coll., Oxford 1969–71; Founder, Conductor and Dir, Taverner Choir, Taverner Consort and Taverner Players 1973–; Music Dir and Prin. Conductor London Mozart Players 2000–; Music Dir New York Collegium 2002–; BBC Promenade Concerts début 1977; fmr musical asst to Sir Michael Tippett; freelance orchestral and operatic conductor; occasional writer, lecturer and continuo player; Open Postmastership, Merton Coll. 1966–69; Leverhulme Fellowship 1984–85; Hon. Research Fellow, Royal Holloway, Univ. of London 1995–; Hon. Sr Research Fellow, Univ. of Birmingham 2000–. *Recordings include:* medieval, renaissance and 20th-century music, Monteverdi, Purcell, Vivaldi, Bach, Handel, Mozart. *Publications include:* New Oxford Book of Carols 1992, The Essential Bach Choir 2000 (German edn. 2003). *Current Management:* Allied Artists, 42 Montpelier Square, London, SW7 1JZ, England. *Telephone:* (20) 7589-6243. *E-mail:* name@alliedartists.co.uk.

**PARROTT, Ian,** MA, DMus (Oxon.), FTCL, FLCM, ARCO; British composer; *Professor Emeritus, Univ of Wales, Aberystwyth;* b. 5 March 1916, London, England; two s. *Education:* Royal Coll. of Music 1932–34. *Career:* Lecturer, Univ. of Birmingham 1946–50; Gregynog Prof. of Music, Univ. of Wales, Aberystwyth 1950–83, Prof. Emer. 1983–; Examiner, Trinity Coll. of Music, London 1949–; Fellow, Welsh Music Guild 2003; Vice-Pres. Elgar Soc., P. Warlock Soc. *Compositions:* five symphonies, 1946, 1960, 1966, 1978, 1979; five string quartets, 1946, 1956, 1957, 1963, 1994; four operas, The Sergeant-Major's Daughter 1943, The Black Ram 1953, Once Upon a Time 1959, The Lady of Flowers 1981; Sinfonia Concertante 2003. *Recordings:* String Quartet No. 4 in Contemporary Welsh Chamber Music, Lyrita, 1971, The Music of Ian Parrott, Tab. 1 1997, Fanfare Overture 1998, Prelude and Waltz 1999, Fantasising 2005, Sinfonia Concertante included in British Recorder Concertos 2005. *Publications:* Master Musician Elgar 1971, Music of Rosemary Brown 1978, Cyril Scott and His Piano Music 1992, The Crying Curlew, P. Warlock 1994. *Contributions:* Elgar and P. Warlock Soc. journals and Welsh Music. *Honours:* First Prize, Luxor, Royal Philharmonic Soc. 1949, Harriet Cohen Award 1966, J. Edwards Award 1977, J. Rooper Prize for String Quartet No. 2 1983, Glyndwr Award 1996. *Address:* Henblas Abermad, Aberystwyth, Ceredigion, SY23 4ES, Wales (home). *Telephone:* (1974) 241660 (home).

**PARRY, Susan;** Singer (Mezzo-soprano); b. 13 Feb. 1963, Luton, Bedfordshire, England. *Education:* Studied at Birmingham University and the Royal Academy of Music. *Career:* Welsh National Opera from 1987, as the Witch in Hansel and Gretel, and Kate Pinkerton; English National Opera debut 1992, in the premiere of John Buller's The Bacchae; Company Principal with ENO from 1995, as the Kitchen Boy in Rusalka, Brangaene (first major role, 1996), Janáček's Fox, Strauss's Octavian and Composer, and Dorabella, (1997); Concerts include the Brahms Liebeslieder Waltzes under Antal Dorati, Messiah at the Albert Hall and Beethoven's Ninth at the Festival Hall; Season 1996 included concert of Gluck's Iphigénie en Tauride with the Orchestra of the Age of Enlightenment, Covent Garden debut in Alzira, and Tebaldo in Don Carlos at the London Proms; Falla's El Amor Brujo with the BBC Philharmonic Orchestra, Henze's La Cubana with the Ballet Rambert and an orchestration of Alma Mahler Lieder at Maastricht; Imelda in Verdi's Oberto at Covent Garden, 1997, Pierotto in Donizetti's Linda di Chamounix with the OAE and Hansel in concert with the CBSO under Mark Elder; Elizabeth I in new production of Mary Stuart, ENO 1998; Miss Jessel in The Turn of the Screw, Cincinnati (US debut); London Proms, 2002. *Address:* c/o English National Opera, St Martin's Lane, London, WC2, England.

**PARSCH, Arnost;** Composer; b. 12 Feb. 1936, Bucovice, Moravia, Czechoslovakia. *Education:* Brno Academy, with Miloslav Istvan. *Career:* Founder member of Brno Composers' Group, 1967; Assistant Professor 1971–73, Professor 1990, Janáček Academy of Performing Arts; President of Brno International Music Festival, 1993–. *Compositions:* Sonata, chamber orchestra, 1966; Two symphonies, 1967, 1970; A Sign of Longing, cantata, 1972; Three string quartets, 1969, 1981, 1994; Electric-acoustical; Poetica no. 3, 1967; Transposizioni II, 1969; Polyfonie no. 1, 1979; Metamorphozes of Time, 1989; The King's Ride, cantata, 1984; The Welcoming of Spring, for vocal soloists, chorus and orchestra, 1990; Rapsotietta for 11 strings, 1992; Loneliness for orchestra, 1993; Voice of the River, for nine players, 1994; Hillside for violin and percussion, 1993; Executions and Resurrections, five songs for female voice and piano, 1996; Bridge, orchestra, 1996; Happy Water for cor anglais and cello, 1998. *Address:* c/o OSA, Cs armady 20, 160–56 Praha 6–Buberec, Czech Republic.

**PARSONS, Brian Geoffrey,** GRSM, ARCM; Singer (tenor); b. 6 Aug. 1952, Luton, England. *Education:* Boston County Music School, Lincolnshire, Royal Coll. of Music, Royal Coll. of Music Opera School. *Career:* Vicar choral, St Paul's Cathedral 1977–79; BBC Singers 1981–83; Groupe Vocal De France 1983–84; Opera 80 (now English Touring Opera) Count Almaviva, Il barbiere di Siviglia 1980; Lindoro, L'italiana in Algeri 1985; Prof. of Singing, Conservatoire National Supérieur de Musique, Lyon 1998–, Guildhall School of Music and Drama 2000–; mem. Incorporated Soc. of Musicians, Asscn of English Singers and Speakers. *Recordings:* Rameau: Castor et Pollux (English Bach Festival, conductor Charles Farncombe) 1983, Rameau: Naïs (English Bach Festival, conductor Nicolas McGegan) 1982. *Honours:* Finalist, National Federation of Music Societies Award 1977, Finalist, Richard Tauber Competition 1982. *Address:* 5 Montrose Avenue, London, NW6 6LE, England (home). *Telephone:* (20) 8969-4880 (home). *E-mail:* bgparsons@aol.com (home).

**PÄRT, Arvo;** Estonian composer; b. 11 Sept. 1935, Paide. *Education:* Tallinn Conservatory with Heino Eller. *Career:* worked as sound producer for Estonian radio 1957–67; teacher at Tallinn Conservatory 1967–78; emigrated to Berlin 1980. *Compositions include:* orchestral music: 3 symphonies 1963, 1966, 1971, Collage über B-A-C-H 1964, Cantus in Memory of Benjamin Britten 1977, Tabula Rasa 1977, Psalom, 1985, 1991, 1995, Festina lente 1988, Trisagion 1992, 1994, Orient and Occident 1999, Lamentate 2002; vocal music: Our Garden 1959 (rev. 2003), Credo 1968, An den Wassern zu Babel sassen wir und weinten... 1976, 1984 and other versions, Summa 1977, several other versions, Missa Syllabica 1977, 1995, 1996, Passio 1982, Te Deum 1984–85, 1992, Stabat Mater 1985, Magnificat 1989, Miserere 1989, Berliner Messe 1990, 1997, Litany 1994, Kanon Pokajanen 1997, Triodion 1998, Como anhela la cierva 1999, Cecilia 2000, Littlemore Tractus 2001, Most Holy Mother of God 2003, In principio 2003; chamber music: Für Alina 1976, Pari intervallo 1976, Fratres 1977 (several other versions), Passacaglia 2003. *Honours:* Hon. DMus (Sydney) 1996; Hon. Dr (Tartu) 1998, (Durham) 2002; Triumph Award (Russia) 1997, Culture Prize 1998, Herder Award (Germany) 2000, Commandeur de l'Ordre des Arts et des Lettres de la République Française (France) 2001, C. A. Segizzi Composition Trophy (Italy) 2003, Musical America Composer of the Year 2005. *Current Management:* c/o Universal Edition Ltd, POB 3, A-1015 Vienna, Austria. *Telephone:* (1) 337-23-143 (office). *Fax:* (1) 337-23-400 (office). *E-mail:* office@universaledition.com (office). *Website:* www.universaledition.com (office).

**PARTRIDGE, Ian H.,** CBE; Singer (tenor) and Teacher; b. 12 June 1938, London, England; m. Ann Glover 1959, 2 s. *Education:* Clifton College, 1952–56; Royal College of Music, 1956–58; Guildhall School of Music, 1961–63. *Career:* Debut: Bexhill, 1958; Concerts and Recitals World-wide; Covent Garden debut, 1969; Numerous Broadcasts for BBC and World-wide Television; Appearances include, St Nicolas for Thames Television; mem, Garrick Club; Governor, RSM; Director, PAMRA. *Recordings:* Schöne Müllerin, Schubert; Dichterliebe and Liederkreis op 39-Schumann; On Wenlock Edge and Other Songs, V Williams; The Curlew, Peter Warlock; Songs by Fauré, Duparc, Delius, Gurney. *Honours:* Harriet Cohen Award, 1967; Prix Italia, 1977; Hon RAM, 1996. *Address:* 127 Pepys Road, London SW20 8NP, England.

**PASATIERI, Thomas;** American composer; b. 20 Oct. 1945, New York. *Education:* Juilliard with Giannini and Persichetti, Aspen Music School with Darius Milhaud. *Career:* freelance composer 1965–; commissions from Nat. Educational Television, Houston Grand Opera, Baltimore Opera, Michigan Opera Theater, Univ. of Arizona, Evelyn Lear and Thomas Stewart. *Compositions:* operas: The Trysting Place 1964, Flowers of Ice 1964, The Women 1965, La Divina 1965, Padrevia 1966, The Penitentes 1967, Calvary 1971, Black Widow 1972, The Seagull 1972, The Trial of Mary Lincoln 1972, Signor Deluso 1974, Inés de Castro 1976, Washington Square 1976, Three Sisters 1979, Before Breakfast 1980, The Goose Girl 1981, Maria Elena 1983, Frau Margot 2007; vocal: Selected Songs 1971, Heloïse and Abelard for soprano, baritone and piano 1973, Rites of Passage for voice and chamber orchestra or string quartet 1974, Three Poems of James Agee 1974, Permit Me Voyage for soprano, mixed chorus and orchestra 1976, Far from Love for soprano, clarinet, violin, cello and piano 1976, Songs Vol. One 1977, Songs Vol. Two 1980, Day of Love 1983, Mass for soprano, alto, tenor and bass soloists, mixed chorus and orchestra 1983, Three Sonnets from the Portuguese 1984, A Joyful Noise for mixed chorus, brass sextet, organ, percussion 1985, Sieben Lehmannlieder for voice and orchestra 1988, Windsongs 1989, Alleluia for voice and orchestra 1991, Three Mysteries for mixed chorus 1991, The Harvest Frost for mixed chorus and chamber ensemble 1993, Canciones del barrio for voice and string quartet 1993, Bang the Drum Loudly for mixed chorus and piano or two-part treble chorus and piano 1994, Canticle of Praise for mixed chorus and organ 1995, Mornings Innocent for men's chorus, oboe, cello, harp and piano 1995, Three Poems of Oscar Wilde 1998, A Rustling of Angels 2003, Letter to Warsaw for voice and chamber orchestra 2003; instrumental: Piano Sonata No. 1 1966, Invocation 1968, Piano Sonata No. 2 1969, Cameos for solo piano 1969, Theatrepieces for clarinet, violin and piano 1987, Serenade for violin and chamber orchestra 1992, Concerto for piano and orchestra 1993, Concerto for two pianos and strings 1994, Quartet for flute and strings 1995, Sonata for viola and piano 1995, Sonata for flute and piano 1997, Piano Sonata No. 3 1999. *Address:* c/o Theodore Presser Company, 588

N Gulph Road, King of Prussia, PA 19406, USA. *E-mail:* thomas@ thomaspasatieri.com. *Website:* www.thomaspasatieri.com.

**PASCAL, Michel;** French electro-acoustic composer and academic; b. 12 Oct. 1958, Avignon; m. Maxime Pascal; two d. *Education:* CNSM Paris, CNR Marseille, INA-GRM and IRCAM, Paris with I. Xenakis, H. Dutilleux, W. Lutoslawski and L. Berio. *Career:* debut as asst of Jean Etienne Marie, CIRM, Nice, 1985–87, for studio and Festival of Contemporary Music; Composer in many fields, including acoustic, choir, instrumental, dance music, music for theatre, film, video and television production; as synthesist, performer and creator of the Studio Instrumental, works played on hyperinstruments with live electronics; Prof. of Electro-acoustic Composition, Conservatoire de Nice; mem., SACEM, SACD, Rainbow Across Europe. *Compositions:* Falaises et Emergences, for tape, 1981; Voiles, for choir and synthesizers, 1987; Protos, for symphonic orchestra, 1989; Puissance 3, for string trio, 1997; Puzzle, instrumental acousmatics, 1995–99. *Recordings:* Albums: Contribution to Nausicaa, Centre de la Mer, Boulogne, 1990; Sonic Waters, with Michel Redolfi-Berceuse/Albin Michel, 1990; Repertoires Polychromes, 1999; Puzzle, 1999. Videos: Mille Mêtres sous la Jungle, 1995; Les Grottes ornées de Borneo, 1996. Other: music for Luc Henri Fage's film, French national television. *Publications:* Les Nouveaux Gestes de la Musique 1999. *Address:* Aix en Musique, 3 Place John Rewald, Espace Forbin, 13100 Aix en Provence; rue Sainte Croix, 13480 Cabries, France.

**PASCHER, Hartmut;** violist; b. 1956, Vienna, Austria. *Education:* Vienna Acad. of Music. *Career:* member of the Franz Schubert Quartet from 1979; Many concert appearances in Europe, the USA and Australia, including the Amsterdam Concertgebouw, the Vienna Musikverein and Konzerthaus, the Salle Gaveau Paris and the Sydney Opera House; Visits to Zürich, Geneva, Basle, Berlin, Hamburg, London, Rome, Rotterdam, Madrid and Copenhagen; Festival engagements include Salzburg, Wiener Festwochen, Prague Spring, Schubertiade at Hohenems, the Schubert Festival at Washington DC and the Belfast and Istanbul Festivals; Tours of Australasia, USA; Frequent concert tours of the United Kingdom: Frequent appearances at the Wigmore Hall and Cheltenham Festival; Teacher of the Graz Musikhochschule; Masterclasses at the Royal Northern College of Music at Lake District Summer Music. *Recordings include:* Schubert's Quartet in G, D877; Complete Quartets of Dittersdorf; Mozart: String Quartet in D, K575, String Quartet in B Flat, K589, Tchaikovsky String Quartets No. 1 and 3 op. 11 D major and op. 30 E flat minor. *Address:* Roatanskygasse 41, 1170 Vienna, Austria.

**PASCOE, John;** British artistic director; b. 1949, Bath, England. *Career:* debut designed Julius Caesar for English National Opera, also seen in San Francisco, Geneva, the Metropolitan and on television, 1979; Designed Lucrezia Borgia at Covent Garden and Alcina at Sydney, both with Joan Sutherland, Tosca for Welsh National Opera, 1980; Producer and Designer: La Bohème in Belfast, Solomon at the Göttingen Festival, 1984; Producer and Designer: Rameau's Platée in Spoleto Festival, also seen in BAM, New York; Designer: Orlando in San Francisco and Chicago; Così fan tutte in Dallas; Anna Bolena, with Joan Sutherland, in Toronto, Chicago, Detroit, Houston and San Francisco, 1985–86; Designer: Amahl and the Night Visitors; Norma, in Santiago, 1987; Producer and Designer: Anna Bolena at Covent Garden; Norma in Los Angeles and Detroit, both with Joan Sutherland, 1988; Producer and Designer: La Bohème in Bath; Designed: Tosca in Nice; Apollo and Hyacinthus at Cannes Festival, Madrid, Paris, 1991, 1992; Producer and Designer: La Traviata in Bath; Designer: Anna Bolena in Washington, DC, 1993; Founder, Bath and Wessex Opera. *Honours:* Evening Standard Award for Julius Caesar, 1979. *Current Management:* Athole Still International Management, Forresters Hall, 25–27 Westow Street, London, SE19 3RY, England. *Telephone:* (20) 8771-5271. *Fax:* (20) 8768-6600. *Website:* www .atholestill.com.

**PASCOE, Keith;** Violinist; b. 1959, England. *Career:* Founder Member of the Britten Quartet, debut concert at the Wigmore Hall, 1987; Quartet in Residence at the Dartington Summer School, 1987, with quartets by Schnittke; Season 1988–89 in the Genius of Prokofiev series at Blackheath and BBC Lunchtime Series at St John's Smith Square; South Bank appearances with the Schoenberg/Handel Quartet Concerto conducted by Neville Marriner, concerts with the Hermann Prey Schubertiade and collaborations with the Alban Berg Quartet in the Beethoven Plus series; Tour of South America 1988, followed by Scandinavian debut; Season 1989–90 with debut tours of Netherlands, Germany, Spain, Austria, Finland; Tours from 1990 to the Far East, Malta, Sweden, Norway; Schoenberg/Handel Concerto with the Gothenburg Symphony; Festival appearances at Brighton, the City of London, Greenwich, Canterbury, Harrogate, Chester, Spitalfields and Aldeburg; Collaborations with John Ogdon, Imogen Cooper, Thea King and Lynn Harrell; Formerly resident quartet at Liverpool University; Teaching role at Lake District Summer Music 1989; Universities of Bristol, Hong Kong 1990. *Recordings:* Beethoven Op 130 and Schnittke Quartet No. 3 (Collins Classics); Vaughan Williams On Wenlock Edge and Ravel Quartet (EMI); Britten, Prokofiev, Tippett, Elgar and Walton Quartets (Collins Classics); Exclusive Contract with EMI from 1991. *Current Management:* Ingpen & Williams Ltd, 7 St George's Court, 131 Putney Bridge Road, London, SW15 2PA, England.

**PASHLEY, Anne;** Singer (Soprano); b. 5 June 1937, Skegness, England; m. Jack Irons, 1 s., 1 d. *Education:* Guildhall School of Music, London. *Career:* Took part as sprinter in 1956 Olympic Games, at Melbourne; Stage debut in

Semele, with Handel Opera Society, 1959; Glyndebourne debut 1962, in Die Zauberflöte; Covent Garden debut 1965, as Barbarina in Le nozze di Figaro; Guest appearances with English National Opera, Scottish Opera, Welsh National Opera and at Edinburgh and Aldeburg Festivals; Foreign engagements in France, Germany, Portugal, Spain, Belgium, Italy, Israel; Leading roles in 8 BBC television operas and numerous radio braodcasts; New Opera Company, London, in the British premiere of Hindemith's Cardillac, 1970; mem, Equity. *Recordings include:* La Morte de Cléopâtre, Berlioz; Magnificat, Bach; Albert Herring and Peter Grimes, Britten. *Contributions:* The Listener. *Address:* 289 Goldhawk Road, London W12, England.

**PASINO, Gisella;** Singer (Mezzo-soprano); b. 1965, Genoa, Italy. *Education:* Studied at Genoa with Maggia Olivero. *Career:* Debut: Padua, 1987 as the Princess in Suor Angelica; Rome, 1987 as Amneris in Aida; Sang Verdi's Preziosilla at Piacenza, 1989; Anacoana in Franchetti's Cristoforo Colombo at Frankfurt, 1991; Season 1995–96 as Carmen at Rotterdam and the Princess in Adriana Lecouvreur at Livorno. *Honours:* Cristoforo Colombo. *Honours:* Prizewinner, Competitions in Genoa and Milan. *Address:* c/o Netherlands Opera, Waterlooplein 22, 1011 PG Amsterdam, Netherlands.

**PASKALIS, Kostas;** Singer (Baritone); b. 1 Sept. 1929, Levadia, Boeotia, Greece; m. Marina Krilovici. *Education:* Studied at the National Conservatory Athens. *Career:* Debut: Athens 1954, as Rigoletto; Vienna Staatsoper from 1958, debut as Renato in Un Ballo in Maschera; Tour of North America 1960; Glyndebourne 1964–72, as Macbeth and Don Giovanni; Metropolitan Opera debut 1965, as Don Carlos in La Forza el Destino; Rome Opera 1965–66 as Rigoletto and Posa, in Don Carlos; Salzburg Festival 1966, as Pentheus in the premiere of Henze's The Bassarids; La Scala Milan 1967, as Valentin in Faust; Guest appearances in Leningrad, Kiev, Berlin and Moscow; Sang Nabucco at Brussels 1987; New Jersey Opera 1988, as Don Giovanni; Director of the National Opera of Greece from 1988; Sang Simon Boccanegra for Athens Opera, 1995; Teacher with the European Opera Centre, 1998–. *Recordings:* Escamillo in Carmen (HMV); Alfonso in Donizetti's Lucrezia Borgia. *Address:* National Union of Greece, 18-A Harilaou Trikoupi Street, 106 79 Athens, Greece.

**PASKUDA, Georg;** Singer (Tenor); b. 7 Jan. 1926, Ratibor, Germany. *Career:* Sang small roles in various German theatres from 1951; Bayreuth Festival from 1959, notably as Froh and Mime; Paris Opéra 1960; Bavarian State Opera Munich from 1960, notably in operas by Strauss, Puccini, Lortzing, Wagner, Verdi and Mozart; Munich 1967, as Don Carlos and 1986 in the premiere of V.D Kirchner's Belshazzar; Sang at the Munich Staatsoper until season 1994–95. *Recordings:* Parsifal, Tannhäuser and Arabella; Die Frau ohne Schatten; Das Rheingold and Der fliegende Holländer, from Bayreuth. *Address:* c/o Bayerische Staatsoper, Postfach 745, 8000 Munich 1, Germany.

**PASQUETTO, Giancarlo;** Italian singer (baritone); b. 1959, Verona. *Career:* sang widely in Italy from 1984 as Alfio in Cavalleria Rusticana, Count Luna, Marcello, Verdi's Miller and Carlo in La Forza del Destino; Metropolitan Opera, New Yok, 1989 as Miller; Season 1993 as Nabucco at Bregenz, Germont at Verona and for New Israeli Opera, 1998; Rigoletto at the Berlin Staatsoper and Tonio in Pagliacci at La Scala, Milan; Further appearances as Guzman in Verdi's Alzira at Parma and at Covent Garden as Rigoletto, 1994; Other roles include Amonasro, Simon Boccanegra, Glyndebourne, 1987; Riccardo in I Puritani; Sang Boccanegra at Munich, 2000. *Recordings include:* Simon Boccanegra, from Glyndebourne 1998. *Current Management:* Il Trittico, Via Rocche 4, 37121 Verona, Italy. *Telephone:* 045 8001500. *Fax:* 045 8046801. *Website:* www.iltrittico.net.

**PASQUIER, Bruno;** Violist; b. 10 Dec. 1943, Neuilly-sur-Seine, France. *Education:* Studied at the Paris Conservatoire 1957–63 with Etienne Ginot and his father, Pierre Pasquier. *Career:* Mix à Munich, 1965; Queteur à cadas, string quartet, 1972–83; Leader, viola section in the orchestra of the Paris Opéra, 1972; Soloist with the Orchestre National de France, 1984–89; With Regis Pasquier and Roland Pidoux founded the New Pasquier Trio, 1970; Solo performances with leading orchestras in France and abroad; Professor of Viola and of Chamber Music at the Paris Conservatoire, 1983; Plays a Maggilli viola, ca 1620. *Honours:* Chevalier de l'Ordre des Arts et Lettres, 1991. *Address:* c/o Agence Cazeneuve, 5–7 avenue Mac-Mahon, F 75017 Paris, France.

**PASQUIER, Regis;** Violinist; b. 10 Oct. 1945, Fontainebleau, France. *Education:* Studied at the Paris Conservatoire, gaining first prize in violin and chamber music aged 12; Further study with Isaac Stern. *Career:* Concert tours of Belgium, Netherlands and Luxembourg 1958; New York recital 1960; Many concerts with leading orchestras in Europe and America; Soloist with the Orchestre National de France, 1977–86; With Bruno Pasquier and Roland Pidoux formed the New Pasquier Trio, 1970; Sonata recitals with pianist Jean-Claude Pennetier; Concerto repertoire ranges from standard classics to works by Xenakis and Gilbert Amy (Trajectoires); Plays a Montagnana instrument; Professor of Violin and of Chamber Music at the Paris Conservatoire, 1985. *Honours:* Chevalier, Légion d'honneur. *Address:* Conservatoire National Superieur de Musique, 14 Rue de Madrid, 75008 Paris, France.

**PASSOW, Sabine;** Singer (Soprano); b. 1960, Essen, Germany. *Education:* Studied in Essen and Hannover. *Career:* Sang in opera at Oldenburg from 1987; Komische Oper Berlin from 1991, as Mozart's Countess, Handel's Cleopatra, Marenka in The Bartered Bride, Micaela and Agathe; Arianna in

Handel's Giustino, 1995; Alice Ford in Falstaff, 1996; Guest at the Munich Staatsoper from 1986, notably in Strauss's Daphne and as Ismene in Mozart's Mitridate, 1990; Guest with Komische Oper at Covent Garden, 1989; Tours of Japan, 1991 and 1994; Cleopatra at the Schwetzingen Festival, 1993; Sang Elisabeth in Tannhäuser at Darmstadt, 1994 and at Cottbus in 1999; Sang Anna in Seven Deadly Sins by Brecht/Weill; Concerts of music by Bach; Season 2000–01 as Butterfly at Cottbus, Elisabeth at Saarbrücken, Alice Ford for the Komische Oper and Agathe at the Eutin Festival. *Address:* Komische Oper Berlin, Behrenstrasse 55–57, 10117 Berlin, Germany.

**PATAKI, Eva;** Pianist; b. 19 Oct. 1941, Budapest, Hungary; m. T Bantay, 27 Aug 1971. *Education:* Diploma, Concert Performance, Pedagogy, Franz Liszt Music Academy, Budapest; Studied with Carlo Zecchi in Salzburg. *Career:* Debut: Recital, Budapest, 1965; Assistant, Mozarteum, Salzburg, 5 years; Coach, Royal Opera, Stockholm, 1967–; Concerts, radio and television, with Helena Doese, Catarina Ligendza, C-H Ahnsjö, Nicolai Gedda, Gösta Winbergh, others, all over Europe and in Moscow, St Petersburg and other venues, 1967–; Teacher of Masterclasses; Producer, concerts at Royal Opera, Stockholm, 1985–. *Recordings:* Several. *Current Management:* Artistsekretariat Ulf Tornqvist, Sankt Eriksgatan 100 2 tr, 113 31 Stockholm, Sweden.

**PATCHELL, Sue;** Singer (Soprano); b. 1948, Montana, USA. *Education:* Studied in Montana and at University of California at Los Angeles. *Career:* Engaged at Graz Opera, 1974, Gelsenkirchen, 1979–86; Wiesbaden, 1986–, notably as Elsa in Lohengrin, 1988, and Elisabetta in Don Carlos at Wiesbaden Festival, 1990; Hamburg Staatsoper as Tatiana in Eugene Oengin, Barcelona, 1989 and 1990, as Eva and Chrysothemis, Antwerp Opera as Elisabeth in Tannhäuser and Ariadne; Other roles include Marguerite, Mozart's Countess and Donna Elvira, Frau Fluth and Rosalinde; Sang Isolde at Trieste, 1996; Marietta in Die Tote Stadt at Wiesbaden, 1997; New York Met debut 1999, as Isolde; Sang Leonore at Bonn, 2001, and Isolde at Barcelona, 2002; Concert repertoire includes Das Buch mit Sieben Siegeln by Franz Schmidt. *Recordings:* Das Dunkle Reich by Pfitzner. *Address:* c/o Atholle Still Management, Foresters Hall, 25–27 Westow Street, London, SE19 3RY.

**PATON, Iain;** Singer (tenor); b. 1960, Scotland. *Education:* Studied at Royal Scottish Academy and with David Keren in London. *Career:* Appearances with Glyndebourne Festival and touring Opera in Capriccio, Death in Venice and Le nozze di Figaro, Don Curzio; Sang in Judith Weir's The Vanishing Bridegroom for Scottish Opera at Glasgow and Covent Garden; Season 1992–93, as Pedrillo in Die Entführung and in The Makropulos Case, season 1993–94, as Vanya in Katya Kabanova, Tamino and the Shepherd in Tristan und Isolde; Sang Leicester in Maria Stuarda for Scottish Opera-Go-Round, 1992; City of Birmingham Touring Opera in Mozart's Zaide; Concert repertoire includes Liszt's Faust Symphony and appearances with Scottish Early Music Consort in Northern Ireland, Germany and Poland; Sang Eurimachos in Dallapiccola's Ulisse for BBC, 1993; Season 1995–96 in Purcell's King Arthur and as Mozart's Pedrillo with Les Arts Florissants and Boris in Katya Kabanova at Dublin; Season 1997 with Ferrando for Flanders Opera and Scottish Opera; Sang Vasek in The Bartered Bride for Opera North, 1998; Sang Don Carlos in Les Indes Galantes by Rameau at the Palais Garnier, Paris, 1999; Season 2000–01 as Grimoaldo in Rodelinda at Göttingen and Lensky for Opera North; Almaviva in Il Barbiere di Siviglia, Vlaamse Opera, Ghent 2005. *Honours:* Eric Vertier Award, at Glyndebourne. *Current Management:* Askonas Holt Ltd, Lonsdale Chambers, 27 Chancery Lane, London, WC2A 1PF, England. *Telephone:* (20) 7400-1700. *Fax:* (20) 7400-1799. *E-mail:* info@askonasholt.co.uk. *Website:* www.askonasholt.co.uk.

**PATRIARCO, Earle;** Singer (baritone); b. 1965, USA. *Career:* many concert and recital engagements in Europe and the USA, with songs by Poulenc and Strauss; Opera repertory includes Così fan tutte and The Queen of Spades; Contestant at the 1994 Cardiff Singer of the World Competition. *Current Management:* Askonas Holt Ltd, Lonsdale Chambers, 27 Chancery Lane, London, WC2A 1PF, England. *Telephone:* (20) 7400-1700. *Fax:* (20) 7400-1799. *E-mail:* info@askonasholt.co.uk. *Website:* www.askonasholt.co.uk.

**PATTERSON, Paul (Leslie);** Composer and Educator; b. 15 June 1947, Chesterfield, England; m. Hazel Wilson, 1981, 1 s., 1 d. *Education:* Royal Academy of Music; FRAM, FRSA, 1980, Hon FLCM, 1997. *Career:* Freelance Composer, 1968–; Art Council Composer-in-Association, English Sinfonia, 1969–70; Director, Contemporary Music, Warwick University, 1974–80; Composer-in-Residence, SE Arts Association, 1980–82, Bedford School, 1984–85; Professor of Composition, 1970–, Head of Composition/20th Century Music, 1985–97, Royal Academy of Music; Artistic Director, Exeter Festival, 1991–97; Composer-in-Residence, 1990–91; Manson Chair of Composition, 1997–; Composer-in-Residence, National Youth Orchestra, 1997–; Visiting Professor of Composition, Christchurch University; mem, RSA. *Compositions:* Te Deum, 1988; Symphony, 1990; The Mighty Voice, 1991; Songs of the West, 1995; Rustic Sketches, 1996; Hell's Angels, 1998; Gloria, 1999; Millennium Mass, 2000; Orchestraland, 2000; Performances world-wide by leading orchestras, soloists, ensembles, also film and television music. *Recordings:* Concerto for Orchestra; Little Red Riding Hood; Mass of Sea; Magnificat, with Bach Choir. *Publications:* Rebecca, 1968; Trumpet Concerto, 1969; Time Piece, 1972; Kyrie, 1972; Requiem, 1973; Comedy for 5 Winds, 1973; Requiem, 1974; Fluorescences, 1974; Clarinet Concerto, 1976; Cracowian Counterpoints, 1977; Voices of Sleep, 1979; Concerto for Orchestra, 1981; Canterbury Psalms, 1981; Sinfonia, 1982; Mass of the Sea, 1983; Deception Pass, 1983;

Duologue, 1984; Mean Time, 1984; Europhony, 1985; Missa Brevis, 1985; Stabat Mater, 1986; String Quartet, Harmonica Concerto, Magnificat and Nunc Dimitus, 1986; Te Deum, 1988; Tunnell of Time, 1988; The End, 1989; Violin Concerto, 1992; Little Red Riding Hood, 1993; Magnificat, 1994; Royal Eurostar for the opening Channel Tunnel, 1994; Songs of the West, overture, 1995; Deviations, for String Octet, 2001; City Within, 2000; Cello Concerto, 2002; Jubilee Dances, 2002; Bug for solo harp, 2003; Three Little Pigs, 2004. *Honours:* Medal of Honour, Polish Ministry of Culture, 1986; Leslie Boosey Award, 1996. *Address:* 31 Cromwell Avenue, Highgate, London N6 5HN, England. *E-mail:* musicpp@hotmail.com. *Website:* www.paulpatterson.co.uk.

**PATTERSON, Susan;** Singer (Soprano); b. 1962, USA. *Career:* Sang widely in USA and made European debut in 1988 with the Welsh National Opera as Violetta; Sang at San Francisco in 1988 and 1991 as Anne Trulove and Constanze; Sang Gilda at Vancouver in 1989 and in Cherubini's Lodoiska at La Scala, 1990–91; Sang at Rome Opera in 1991 as Adèle in Le Comte Ory, Fiordiligi at Cologne and Berenice in Rossini's L'Occasione fa il Ladro at Schwetzingen and Paris; Sang Aspasia in Mozart's Mitridate at Amsterdam in 1992; Magda in La Rondine at St Louis, 1996; Rusalka for ENO, 1998; Frequent concert appearances. *Address:* c/o San Francisco Opera, War Memorial Opera House, San Francisco, CA 94102, USA.

**PATTON, Chester;** Singer (Bass); b. 1965, Columbia, MS, USA. *Education:* Studied at the San Francisco Conservatory of Music. *Career:* Appearances with San Francisco Opera from 1993, as Don Basilio, the King of Egypt in Aida, First Nazarene in Salome, Colline, Raimondo and Lord Walton in I Puriatni; Bay Area credits include further appearances with West Bay Opera, Opera San José, Pocket Opera and Berkeley Contemporary Opera; Title role in the US premiere of Tippett's King Priam, San Francisco Opera Center; Debut with Opera Pacific as Basilio, Beethoven's Pizarro at Lyon, High Priest in Nabucco at the Opéra Bastille and Timur in Turandot (1997); Hawaii Opera Theater as Ferrando in Trovatore, Sparafucile and Colline. *Recordings include:* Mandarin in San Francisco Opera production of Turandot. *Address:* c/o San Francisco Opera, War Memorial House, Van Ness Avenue, CA 94102, USA.

**PAUER, Jiri;** Composer and Administrator; b. 22 Feb. 1919, Libusin, Kladno, Czechoslovakia. *Education:* Studied with Alois Haba at Prague Conservatory, 1943–46, and at Academy of Musical Arts. *Career:* Professor of Composition at Prague Academy, 1965–89; Head of Opera at Prague National Theatre, 1951–55, 1965–67; Director 1979–89; Director of Czech Philharmonic, 1958–79. *Compositions include:* Operas: Prattling Slug, for children, 1958; Zuzana Vijirova, 1958; Little Red Riding Hood, Olomouc, 1960; Matrimonial Counterpoints, Ostrava, 1962; The Hypochondriac (after Moliere), Prague, 1970 revised version, Prague, 1988; Swan-Song, monodrama, Prague, 1974; Ballet: Ferdy the Ant, 1975; Orchestral: Comedy Suite, 1949; Bassoon Concerto, 1949; Rhapsody, 1953; Oboe Concerto, 1954; Horn Concerto, 1958; Symphony, 1963; Commemoration, 1969; Trumpet Concerto, 1972; Initials, 1974; Symphony for Strings, 1978; Marimba Concerto, 1984; Suite, 1987; Symphonic Probes, 1990; Chamber: Divertimento for 3 clarinets, 1949; Violin Sonatina, 1953; Cello Sonata, 1954; 4 String Quartets, 1960, 1969, 1970, 1976; Divertimento for Monet, 1961; Wind Quintet, 1961; Piano Trio, 1963; Characters for brass quintet, 1978; Episodes for string quartet, 1980; Trio for 3 horns, 1986; Violin Sonata, 1987; Nonet No. 2, 1989; Green Pieces for trumpet, horn and trombone, 1997; Piano music, cantatas and songs. *Address:* c/o National Theatre, PO Box 865, 11230 Prague 1, Czech Republic.

**PAUK, György;** British violinist; b. 26 Oct. 1936, Budapest, Hungary; m. Susan Mautner 1959; one s. one d. *Education:* Franz Liszt Acad. of Music, Budapest under Zathureczky, Leo Weiner and Zoltán Kodály. *Career:* concerts all over East Europe 1952–58 and the rest of the world; settled in Western Europe 1958, The Netherlands 1958–61, England 1961–; Prof. of Violin, Royal Acad. of Music 1987–; Artistic Dir Mozart Bicentenary Festival, London 1991; Prof. of violin, Winterthur-Zürich Konservatorium of Music 1994–; jury mem. Int. violin competitions. *Recordings include:* numerous concertos, the complete violin/piano music of Mozart and Schubert, Handel and Brahms sonatas, Mozart string quintets, all Bartok's music for solo, duo and sonatas; first performances of Penderecki's violin concerto, UK, Japan, Sir Michael Tippett's Triple Concerto, London 1980, Lutoslawski's Chain 2, UK, Netherlands, Hungary, with composer conducting, Sir Peter Maxwell Davies' violin concerto, Switzerland, Germany, William Mathias violin concerto, England. *Honours:* Hon. mem. and Prof. Guildhall School of Music and Drama, London 1987; Hon. RAM 1990; Paganini Prize 1956, Sonata Competition Prize, Munich 1957, Jacques Thibaud Prize 1959, Grand Prix for Bartók Records (Ovation Magazine, USA) 1982, Best Record of 1983 (Gramophone Magazine), Grammy nomination for most recent Bartók records 1995; highest civilian award, Hungarian Govt 1998. *Address:* c/o Royal Academy of Music, Marylebone Road, London, NW1 5HT.

**PAUL, Thomas;** Singer (Bass); b. 22 Feb. 1934, Chicago, Illinois, USA. *Education:* Studied at the Juilliard School with Beverly Johnson and Cornelius Reid. *Career:* Debut: New York City Opera 1962, as Sparafucile in Rigoletto; Sang in New York, Pittsburgh, Washington, Vancouver, San Francisco and Montreal as Mozart's Figaro and Sarastro, Pogner in Die Meistersinger, Bartók's Duke Bluebeard, Padre Guardiano, La Forza del Destino; Ptolemy in Giulio Cesare by Handel; Sang at Central City Colorado in the premiere of Robert Ward's Lady from Colorado, 1964; Many concert performances; Teacher at the Eastman School, Rochester, and the Aspen School, Colorado. *Recordings:* Brander in La Damnation de Faust.

**PAULSEN, Melinda;** Singer (Mezzo-soprano); b. 1970, USA. *Education:* Swarthmore College; Munich Hochschule; Lieder with Helmut Deutsche. *Career:* Opera Studio of the Bavarian State Theatre, Munich; Appearances at Bregenz Festival, Wratislava Cantans, Poland; Conductors include Helmuth Rilling, Marek Janowski and Roberto Abbado; Ramiro in Mozart's La Finta Giardiniera at Klagenfurt, 1998; Many recital and concert engagements. *Recordings:* Puck in Oberon. *Honours:* Winner, International ARD Competition, Munich, 1992. *Address:* c/o BMG Classic Artists, 69–79 Fulham High Street, London SW6 3JW, England.

**PAULUS, Stephen Harrison;** Composer; b. 24 Aug. 1949, Summit, New Jersey, USA; m. Patricia Ann Stutzman, 18 July 1975, 1 s. *Education:* Alexander Ramsey High School, 1967; BA, 1971, MA, Music Theory and Composition, 1974; PhD, Music Theory and Composition, 1978, University of Minnesota. *Career:* Co-Founder, Minnesota Composer's Forum, 1973–85; Composer-in-Residence, Minnesota Orchestra, 1983–87; Vice-President, Minnesota Composer's Forum, 1983–; mem, American Society of Composers, Authors and Publishers; Minnesota Composers' Forum. *Compositions:* Operas: The Village Singer; The Postman Always Rings Twice; The Woodlanders, 1984; Harmoonia, opera, 1990; The Woman at Otowi Crossing, 1995; Summer, 1999; Orchestral, Suite from The Postman Always Rings Twice; Symphony in Three Movements; Reflections; Ordway Overture; Concerto for Orchestra; Spectra; Chorus and Orchestra: So Hallow'd Is The Time; Letter For The Times; Canticles; North Shore; Chorus: Too Many Waltzes; Jesn Carols; Echoes Between the Silent Peaks; Chamber Ensembles: Partita for Violin and Piano; Music for Contrasts, String Quartet; Courtship Songs, Flute, Oboe, Cello, Piano; Wind Suite, WW Quartet; Voice, Letters from Colette, Soprano and Chamber Ensemble; All My Pretty Ones, Soprano and Piano; Artsongs, Tenor and Piano; Mad Book; Shadow Book, Tenor and Pianoforte; Three Elizabethan Songs, Soprano and Pianoforte; Visions from Hildegard III for chorus and ensemble, 1996; Toccata for organ, 1996. *Recordings:* So Hallow'd Is The Time, for Chorus, Orchestra and Soloists; Symphony in Three Movements, Neville Marriner/Minnesota Orchestra. *Address:* c/o Opera Theater of St Louis, PO Box 13148, St Louis, MO 63119, USA.

**PAUSTIAN, Inger;** Singer (Mezzo-Soprano); b. 1937, Denmark. *Education:* Studied in Copenhagen. *Career:* Engaged at Kiel Opera, 1965–67, Hanover, 1967–69, Frankfurt, 1969–78; Guest appearances at Hamburg, 1970, Munich, 1971, and Valencia, 1976, as Ortrud in Lohengrin; Bayreuth Festival, 1968–71, as Siegrune, Wellgunde and a Flowermaiden; Sang at Zürich Opera, 1976–77; Other roles included Monteverdi's Penelope, Mozart's Marcellina, Magdalene, Brangaene, Herodias and the Nurse in Die Frau ohne Schatten; Verdi's Azucena, Amneris and Eboli, Guilietta in Les Contes d'Hoffmann, Larina in Eugene Onegin and Agave (The Bassarids by Henze); Frequent concert performances. *Address:* c/o Opernhaus Zürich, Falkenstrasse 1, 8008 Zürich, Switzerland.

**PAUTZA, Sabin;** Composer and Conductor; b. 8 Feb. 1943, Calnic, Romania; m. Corina Popa, 2 Oct 1974, 2 d. *Education:* Conducting, Bucharest Academy of Music, 1964; Composition, Accademia Musicale Chigiana, Siena, Italy, 1970. *Career:* Debut: Romanian Athenee, Romania, 1964; Professor of Harmony and Conducting, Iassy Academy of Music, 1965–84; Conductor, Iassy Academy of Music Orchestra, 1969–84; Appearances, Bayreuth Wagner Youth Festival, 1974, 1977, 1978, Carnegie Hall, New York, 1984; Extensively performed as a Conductor in Europe, Australia and North America; Music Director, Conductor, Plainfield Symphony Orchestra, New Jersey, USA, 1987–. *Compositions:* Symphony No. 1, In Memoriam; Symphony No. 2, Sinfonia Sacra; Offering to the Children of the World for double choir; Games I, II, III, IV, V, and VI, for orchestra; 3 String Quartets, 1976, 1977, 1979; Double Concerto for viola, piano and orchestra; Ebony Mass for choir, organ and orchestra; Another Love Story, opera for children; Laudae for chamber orchestra; Five pieces for large orchestra; Nocturnes for soprano and orchestra; Haiku for soprano and chamber orchestra; Simfonietta, 1994; Rita Dove Triptych, 1994; Chimes for percussion instruments, 1995; String Quartet No. 4: Ludus Modalis, 1998; Mood Swings, microcantata for mezzo-soprano and piano on verses by Tristan Tzara; Ode to Hope, cantata for soprano solo, choir and orchestra, dedicated to the New Millennium; Antiphonon Melos–Dramatic oratorio, 1969, revised 1999; Saxophone Concerto 1996, revised 2001; Sonata a Quatro, for strings, 1969 revised 2000. *Recordings:* On Opera Omnia, Vols 1–9, on CD. *Honours:* George Enesco Prize for Composition, Romanian Academy, 1974; Romanian Union of Composers Prize, 1977; Martin Luther King Jr Prize for 'Chimes', 1995; Honorary Doctorate, London Institute for Applied Research. *Address:* 240 Locust Avenue, Locust, NJ 07760, USA.

**PAVAROTTI, Luciano,** DMus; Italian singer (tenor); b. 12 Oct. 1935, Modena; s. of Fernando Pavarotti and Adele (née Venturi) Pavarotti; m. 1st Adua Veroni 1961 (divorced); three d.; m. 2nd Nicoletta Mantovani 2003; one d. *Education:* Istituto Magistrale. *Career:* debut as Rodolfo in La Bohème at Reggio nell'Emilia 1961; appearances include Staatsoper Vienna, Royal Opera House, London 1963, La Scala 1965, Edgardo in Lucia di Lammermoor in Miami, USA 1965, Metropolitan Opera House, New York 1968, Paris Opera and Lyric Opera of Chicago 1973, Manrico at the Met 1988, the Duke in Rigoletto 1989, Nemorino in L'Elisir d'amore at Covent Garden 1990, Otello and Nemorino in New York 1991–92, Verdi's Don Carlos at La Scala 1992–93, Cavaradossi at Covent Garden 1992, at the Met 1999, Arvino in I Lombardi at Metropolitan Opera 1994, Gustavus in Ballo in Maschera at Covent Garden 1995, at the Met 1997, Radames at the Met 2001, Tosca at Covent Garden 2002, at the Met 2004; recitals and concerts abroad, including the USA, Europe and fmr USSR, appeared with two other tenors at World Cup Concert, Caracalla, Pavarotti in the Park, London 1991; retd 2004. *Film:* Yes, Giorgio 1981. *Recordings include:* La Bohème, Madama Butterfly, Beatrice di Tenda, Lucia di Lammermoor, La Fille du Régiment, Maria Stuarda, Un Ballo in Maschera, Luisa Miller, Macbeth, Mefistofele, Idomeneo, Aida, Norma, Tosca, Otello, Ti Adoro 2003. *Publications:* Pavarotti: My Own Story (with William Wright), Grandissimo Pavarotti 1986. *Honours:* hon. degree (PA) 1979; Noce d'Oro Nat. Prize, Luigi Illica int. prize, first prize Gold Orfeo (Acad. du Disque Lyrique de France), Grammy Award for best classical vocal soloist 1981, Kennedy Center Honor 2001, Freedom of the City of London 2005; Grand Officer, Italian Repub., Légion d'honneur. *Current Management:* Herbert Breslin, 119 West 57th Street, New York, NY 10019, USA; Via Giardini 941, 41040 Saliceta, Modena, Italy (home).

**PAVIOUR, Sir Paul,** Kt, AM, MMus; composer and musician (organ); b. 14 April 1931, Birmingham, England. *Education:* studied in London with Herbert Howells, Vaughan Williams and Adrian Boult, University of London. *Career:* Faculty Member, All Saints College, Bathurst, 1969–75; Conductor, Goulburn Consort of Voices, 1975–; commissions from Goulburn Festival of the Arts, Australian Government, and others; Goulburn College of Advanced Education, 1975–84; Organist and Conductor with Argyle Operatic Society, 1977–. *Compositions include:* Horn Concerto, 1970; Missa Australis, 1971; Take Kissing as a Natural Law, for female voices and flute, 1971; Four Carols, 1972; A New Australian Mass, 1973; All Systems Go for chorus and orchestra, 1980; An Urban Symphony (No. 2), 1982; This Endris Nyghte, Christmas Cantata, 1982; Concerto for Oboe, Strings and Percussion, 1983; Symphony No. 5, 1985. *Honours:* Centenary Medal 2000. *Address:* 4 Beppo Street, Goulburn, NSW 2580, Australia (home). *Telephone:* 4821 2450 (home).

**PAVLOVSKAYA, Tatiana;** Singer (Soprano); b. 1970, Murmansk, Russia. *Education:* Graduated St Petersburg Conservatoire, 1994. *Career:* Engaged with the Kirov Opera, St Petersburg, from 1995; Roles have included Madama Butterfly, Tatiana in Eugene Onegin, Yaroslavna (Prince Igor); Mozart's Countess and Clara in Prokofiev's Betrothal in a Monastery; Further apearances as Paulina in The Gambler by Prokofiev, Natasha in War and Peace, Wagner's Elsa and Maria in Mazeppa; San Francisco Opera debut in Betrothal in a Monastery, under Gergiev; British debut as Maria at Glasgow, with the Kirov, 1999; Sang Sofya in the British premiere of Prokofiev's Semyon Kotko, with the Kirov Opera at Covent Garden, 2000. *Honours:* Winner, International Pechkovsky Vocal Competition; International Competition for Young Singers, Wrocław, Poland. *Address:* c/o Kirov Opera, Mariinsky Theatre, 1 Theatre Square, St Petersburg, Russia.

**PAY, Anthony;** Clarinettist; b. 21 Feb. 1945, London. *Education:* Studied with John Davies and Wilfred Kealey. *Career:* Debut: Mozart's Concerto with National Youth Orchestra on tour to Europe, 1961; Principal Clarinet of the Royal Philharmonic, 1968–78; London Sinfonietta 1968–83, including the premiere of Henze's The Miracle of the Rose, 1982; Principal with the Academy of St Martin-in-the-Fields (1976–86), Academy of Ancient Music (1983–94) and the Orchestra of the Age of Enlightenment, 1986–; Member of the Nash Ensemble, 1986–93; Teacher at the Guildhall School, London, 1982–90; Frequent concerts as conductor and clarinettist. *Recordings include:* Berio Concertino; Concertos by Weber, Crusell and Mozart; Chamber works by Beethoven (Septet), Schubert (Octet), Mozart and Brahms (Quintets) and others. *Address:* c/o Orchestra of the Age of Enlightenment, 5th Floor, Westcombe House, 56–58 Whitcombe St, London, WC2H 7RW, England.

**PAYER-TUCCI, Elisabeth;** Singer (Soprano); b. 1944, Germany. *Career:* Sang at the Berne Opera, 1968–70 and at the Cologne Opera until 1976; New York in 1980 as Irene in a concert rendition of Rienzi; Sang the Siegfried Brünnhilde at the Metropolitan, Isolde at Rome and Ariadne at Lisbon; Sang at Verona Festival as Turandot, Brünnhilde at Barcelona and Senta at Rio de Janeiro (1987); Other roles have included Verdi's Amelia in Un Ballo in Maschera, the Forza Leonora, and Santuzza in Cavalleria Rusticana.

**PAYNE, Anthony Edward,** BA, FRCM; British composer; b. 2 Aug. 1936, London; s. of the late Edward Alexander Payne and (Muriel) Margaret Payne; m. Jane Manning (q.v.) 1966. *Education:* Dulwich Coll., London and Durham Univ. *Career:* freelance musical journalist, musicologist, lecturer, etc. with various publs and BBC Radio, active in promoting "new music", serving on Cttee of Macnaghten Concerts (Chair. 1967) and Soc. for the Promotion of New Music (Chair. 1969–71), composed part-time 1962–73; full-time composer 1973–; tutor in Composition, London Coll. of Music 1983–85, Sydney Conservatorium 1986, Univ. of W Australia 1996; Milhaud Prof., Mills Coll., Oakland, Calif. 1983; Artistic Dir Spitalfields Festival; Composition Tutor Univ. of Western Australia 1996; Contrib. Daily Telegraph 1964–, The Times 1964–, The Independent 1986–, Country Life 1995–; mem. Cttee Asscn Frank Bridge Trust, RVW Trust, MBF Awards and Trusts. *Compositions:* Paraphrases and Cadenzas 1969, Paean for solo piano 1971, Phoenix Mass 1972, The Spirits Harvest for full orchestra 1972, Concerto for Orchestra (Int. Jury Choice for Int. Soc. for Contemporary Music Festival 1976) 1974, The World's Winter for soprano and ensemble 1976, String Quartet 1978, The Stones and Lonely Places Sing (septet) 1979, Song of the Clouds for oboe and orchestra

1980, A Day in the Life of a Mayfly (sextet) 1981, Evening Land for soprano and piano 1981, Spring's Shining Wake for orchestra 1981, Songs and Seascapes for strings 1984, The Song Streams in the Firmament (sextet) 1986, Fanfares and Processional 1986, Half Heard in the Stillness for orchestra 1987, Consort Music for string quintet 1987, Sea Change (septet) 1988, Time's Arrow for orchestra 1990, The Enchantress Plays bassoon and piano 1990, Symphonies of Wind and Rain for chamber ensemble 1991, A Hidden Music 1992, Orchestral Variations: The Seeds Long Hidden 1993, Empty Landscape–Heart's Ease (sextet) 1995, Break, Break, Break for unaccompanied chorus 1996, Elgar's Third Symphony (commissioned by Elgar Trust to complete Elgar's sketches) 1997, Piano Trio 1998, Scenes from The Woodlanders for soprano and ensemble 1999, Of Knots and Skeins for violin and piano 2000, Betwixt Heaven and Charing Cross for unaccompanied chorus 2001, Visions and Journeys for orchestra (British Composers Award 2003) 2001, Poems of Edward Thomas for soprano and piano quartet 2003, Horn Trio 2005. *Recordings include:* The Music of Anthony Payne (Gramophone Critics' Choice) 1977. *Publications:* Schoenberg 1968, The Music of Frank Bridge 1984, Elgar's Third Symphony: The Story of the Reconstruction 1998; contrib. to Musical Times, Tempo, Music and Musicians, The Listener, Daily Telegraph, The Times, The Independent, Country Life. *Honours:* Hon. DMus (Birmingham) 2000, (Kingston) 2002; Radcliffe Award 1975, South Bank Show Award 1998, Evening Standard Classical Music Award 1998, New York Critics' Circle Nat. Public Radio Award 1999, Classical CD Award 1999. *Address:* 2 Wilton Square, London, N1 3DL; c/o Boosey & Hawkes, 295 Regent Street, London, W1B 2JH, England. *Telephone:* (20) 7359-1593. *Fax:* (20) 7226-4369.

**PAYNE, Nicholas;** British opera company director; *Director, Opera Europa*; b. 4 Jan. 1945, Bromley, Kent, England; m. Linda Jane Adamson 1986; two s. *Education:* Eton Coll. and Trinity Coll. Cambridge. *Career:* worked for Paterson Concert Management 1967; Arts Council administration course 1967–68; joined finance dept Royal Opera House, Covent Garden 1968–70; Subsidy Officer, Arts Council 1970–76; Financial Controller, Welsh Nat. Opera 1976–82; Gen. Admin. Opera North 1982–93; Dir of Opera, Royal Opera House 1993–98; Gen. Dir ENO 1998–2002; Dir Opera Europa 2003–. *Honours:* Hon. mem. Guildhall School of Music and Drama, Royal Northern College of Music; Dr hc (Metropolitan Univ.). *Address:* Opera Europa, 23 rue Léopold, 1000 Brussels, Belgium (office). *Telephone:* (20) 7713-9055 (office). *E-mail:* nicholas.payne@opera-europa.org (office). *Website:* www.opera-europa.org (office).

**PAYNE, Patricia;** singer (mezzo-soprano); b. 1942, Dunedin, New Zealand. *Education:* studied in Sydney and London. *Career:* debut at Covent Garden, 1974, as Schwertleite in Die Walküre: returned as Ulrica in Un Ballo in Maschera, Azucena, Erda in Das Rheingold, First Norn in Götterdämmerug and Filippyevna in Eugene Onegin, 1989; Barcelona, 1974–75, as La Cieca in La Gioconda and as Erda; Bayreuth Festival and San Francisco Opera, 1977; La Scala, Milan, 1978 as Ulrica; Verona Festival, 1980; Guest appearances at Frankfurt Opera and the Metropolitan, New York (debut 1980 as Ulrica, sang in La Gioconda, 1983); Has sung Gaea in the British premiere of Strauss's Daphne, Opera North, 1987; Appearances with English National Opera in The Love for Three Oranges, Salome and The Magic Flute; Sang Prokofiev's Princess Clarissa with Opera North at the 1989 Edinburgh Festival; Season 1992 as Herodias in Salome at Wellington; Sang the Witch in Hansel and Gretel and Auntie in Peter Grimes at Wellington, 1996; Concert repertoire includes the Wesendonck Lieder, Bach's St John Passion (in Paris), the Alto Rhapsody and Beethoven's 9th (Spain), Alexander Nevsky and the Mozart Requiem (London, Festival Hall). *Recordings include:* Un Ballo in Maschera and Peter Grimes; Beethoven's Missa Solemnis. *Honours:* Sidney Sun Aria Winner, 1966; Prize Winner, 's-Hertogenbosch Competition, 1972.

**PAYNTER, John Frederick,** OBE, GTCL, DPhil; British academic; *Professor Emeritus of Music, University of York*; b. 17 July 1931, England; m. 1st Elizabeth Hill 1956 (died 1998); one d.; m. 2nd Joan Minetta Burrows 2003. *Education:* Trinity Coll. of Music, London and Univ. of York. *Career:* teacher, primary and secondary schools 1954–62; Lecturer in Music, CF Mott Coll. of Educ., Liverpool 1962–65; Prin. Lecturer and Head, Dept of Music, Bishop Otter Coll., Chichester 1965–69; Lecturer, Univ. of York 1969, Sr Lecturer 1974–82, Prof. of Music and Head, Dept of Music 1982–94, Prof. Emer. 1994–. *Compositions:* choral and instrumental works, including Landscapes 1972, The Windhover 1972, May Magnificat 1973, God's Grandeur 1975, Sacraments of Summer 1975, Galaxies for Orchestra 1977, The Voyage of St Brendan 1978, The Visionary Hermit 1979, The Inviolable Voice 1980, String Quartet No. 1 1981, Cantata for the Waking of Lazarus 1981, The Laughing Stone 1982, Contrasts for Orchestra 1982, Variations for Orchestra and Audience 1983, Conclaves 1984, Piano Sonata 1987, Four Sculptures of Austin Wright for Orchestra 1991, 1994, String Quartet No. 2, Time After Time 1991, Breakthrough, for two pianos 2002, Ouverture d'Urgence, for two pianos 2003, Of Time and Place (song cycle) for soprano, recorder and piano 2004, Sequela for recorder solo 2004, Inscape 2005. *Publications include:* Sound and Silence (with P. Aston) 1970, Hear and Now 1972, The Dance and The Drum (with E. Paynter) 1974, All Kinds of Music (Vols 1–3 1976, Vol. 4 1979), Sound Tracks 1978, Music in the Secondary School Curriculum 1982, Sound and Structure 1992, Resources of Music series (ed.) 1965–89: Jt Ed.: British Journal of Music Education 1984–97, Companion to Contemporary Musical Thought 1992, Between Old Words and New: writings on music by W. Mellers 1997. *Honours:* Hon. mem. Guildhall School of Music and Drama 1986; Leslie Boosey Award

1998. *Address:* Department of Music, University of York, Heslington, York, YO10 5DD, England (office).

**PAZDERA, Jindrich;** Violinist and Conductor; b. 25 July 1954, Zilina, Czechoslovakia; m. 23 Jan 1982, one s. *Education:* Moscow State Conservatory, 1974–79; Violin Class by Leonid Kogan, graduated with honours, 1979. *Career:* Debut: Bratislava, Violin Concerto No. 2, by Karol Szymanowski, with the Slovak Philharmonic Orchestra, 1974; Concerts in 24 countries in Europe, America and Asia, as soloist with orchestras and as a chamber musician (violin and piano, Bohemia Piano Trio); Teacher: Bratislava Secondary Music School, 1983–94; Prague Academy of Arts, 1991–; Reader of Violin, 1995–; Repertoire: 25 violin concertos and many recital programmes; Numerous first performances of contemporary Slovak and Czech works; mem, Slovak Music Association; Czech Association of Music Artists and Scientists; Stamic Quartet (string) 1st Violin 2001–. *Broadcast:* Schubert Complete Works for Violin and Piano 2000–03. *Recordings:* CD: Violin Concertos, Vivaldi 1990, Le Quattro Stagioni, Vivaldi 1992, Chamber Orchestra works by Suk, Barber, Bruckner and Shostakovich 1993, Piano Trio works by Beethoven, Dvořák 1995, Violin works by W A Mozart 1997, Dvořák, Serenade and Sextet in A major, live recording violin/piano recital in Kioi Hall Tokyo, Beethoven, Janáček, Martinů, Smetana 2003, Stamic Quartet, Smetana, Dvořák, Mozart, Schubert, Janáček 2002–03, Phantasies for violin/piano b Schubert, Suk, Milhaud 2004. *Publications:* A Reconstruction of a W A Mozart's Sinfonia Concertante in A, for Violin, Viola and Cello (K104-320e), A World Premiere, 1991, CD Rec, 1997; Translations of Methodical and Muspsychological Works of Russian Authors (V P Bronin, G Kogan); Selected Chapters from the Method of Violin Playing, 1999. *Honours:* A Frico Kafenda Slovak National Music Award, 1985. *Address:* Luzická 8, 120 00 Prague, Czech Republic. *E-mail:* jindrich@pazdera.biz. *Website:* www.pazdera.biz.

**PEACOCK, Lucy;** Singer (Soprano); b. 21 June 1947, Jacksonville, Florida, USA. *Education:* North West University, USA, and at the Opera Studio of the Deutsche Oper Berlin. *Career:* Debut: Berlin 1969, as the Milliner in Der Rosenkavalier; Sang in Berlin as Flotow's Martha, Mozart's Pamina, Countess and Servilia, Cavalli's Calisto, Micaela in Carmen and Rosina in Il Barbiere di Siviglia; Guest appearances in Düsseldorf, Vienna, Munich, Hamburg, Turin, Geneva, Paris and London; Bayreuth 1985, as Freia in Das Rheingold and in Die Walküre and Götterdämmerung; Sang Eva in Die Meistersinger at the 1988 Festival; Sang Mathilde in Guillaume Tell at Catania, 1987; Deutsche Oper Berlin as Marenka in The Bartered Bride and as Myrtocle in Die Toten Augen by d'Albert; Created the title role in Desdemona und ihre Schwestern by Siegfried Matthus, Schwetzingen 1992; Princesse de Bouillon in Adriana Lecouvreur at Adelaide, 1994; Gertrud in Hansel and Gretel at the Berlin Deutsche Oper, 1998; Season 2000 at the Deutsche Oper in Die Frau ohne Schatten and Der Rosenkavalier; Television appearances include Martha, in Flotow's opera. *Current Management:* Ingpen & Williams Ltd, 7 St George's Court, 131 Putney Bridge Road, London, SW15 2PA, England.

**PEARCE, Alison (Margaret);** Singer (soprano); b. 5 Aug. 1953, Bath, England. *Education:* Dartington College of Arts, 1971–72; AGSM, distinction in Performance, Guildhall School of Music and Drama, 1972–77; Certificate of Advanced Musical Studies, 1975–77; With Pierre Bernac, Paris, 1977–78, Gerhard Husch, Munich, 1980–81. *Career:* Debut: Wigmore Hall, London; International soloist, oratorio, concert, opera, recital; Regular performances, all major choirs, orchestras and conductors including Colin Davis, Charles Groves, David Willcocks, James Lockhart, Steuart Bedford, Sylvain Cambreling, Libor Pesek; Major festivals: Three Choirs, Cheltenham, Llandaff, St Davids, Brighton, Flanders, France, Netherlands, Germany, Spain, Norway, Philippines, Poland, Israel; Soloist, world premieres: Sinfonia Fidei (A. Hoddinott), Six Psalms (D. Muldowney), Music's Empire (J. McCabe); Hell's Angels (P. Patterson), Requiem (J. Bartley); Regular international television and radio appearances include 1995–96 BBC Fairest Isles series, Eugenie (The Rising of the Moon, N. Maw), Diana (The Olympians, A. Bliss), Bronwen, (Bronwen, J. Holbrooke); Television debut, 1982, Hallé Orchestra; British Opera debut, title role in Lucia di Lammermoor, 1982; Other roles include Violetta (La Traviata), Abigaille (Nabucco), Manon (Manon Lescaut), Elisabeth (Tannhäuser), Tosca, Fidelio; Season 2003–04: numerous recitals and opera galas, Mahler 8th, Verdi Requiem, Vaughan-Williams Sea Symphony, Tosca, R. Strauss Four Last Songs, Finzi Dies Natalis, Handel Messiah, Gounod Faust in UK, Italy, Belgium, Netherlands, Germany, Poland, China. *Current Management:* Ariette Drost, Netherlands. *Address:* PO Box 223, Covent Garden, London WC2H 9BY, England. *E-mail:* divapearce@hotmail.com.

**PEARCE, Michael;** Composer; b. 25 March 1954, Windsor, New South Wales, Australia. *Education:* BA, 1978, BMus (Hons), 1979 (study with Peter Sculthorpe), University of Sydney; Sussex University, with Jonathan Harvey, 1980. *Career:* Faculty Member, New South Wales Conservatory, 1981–; University of Sydney, 1990; Active interest in urban aboriginal music. *Compositions include:* Kynesis, for string quartet, flute, guitar and harpsichord, 1978; Eulogy, for flute, percussion and piano, 1979; Interiors, for violin, cello, flute, carinet and percussion, 1981; Deserts I for 4 percussion, 1982; Deserts II and III for ensembles, 1982–83; Chamber Symphony, 1987; Canciones, for soprano and 7 instruments, 1990; Oh Tierra, Esperame for soprano and piano, 1991; Chamber Symphony No. 2, 1991; Commissions from Synergy and Seymour Group. *Honours:* Sarah Makinson Prize for Composi-

tion, 1979. *Address:* c/o APRA, 1a Eden Street, Crows Nest, NSW 2065, Australia.

**PEARCE, Michael;** Singer (Baritone); b. 1945, Chelmsford, Essex, England. *Education:* Choral Scholar at St John's College, Cambridge; Study with Otakar Kraus and Elizabeth Fleming. *Career:* Concert appearances in China, Canada, Brazil and throughout Europe; Repertory includes Mozart Requiem (at Bruges), Monteverdi Vespers (Maastricht), Bach B Minor Mass (Turin and Edinburgh), Messiah (London and Brighton) and Brahms Requiem (Royal Festival Hall); Haydn's Theresienmesse at Windsor, The Creation at the London Barbican and Schöpfungsmesse at the Queen Elizabeth Hall; Opera roles include Ortel in Meistersinger and 5th Jew in Salome, both at the Royal Opera House, Claudius in Handel's Agrippina with Midsummer Opera, Lysiart in Weber's Euryanthe with New Sussex Opera and Beethoven's Rocco; Season 1996–97 with A Child of our Time by Tippett, the Berlioz Messe Solennelle and Elijah in Norway; Mozart's Requiem and Carmina Burana in Spain; Verdi Requiem at Canterbury Cathedral and Messiah with David Willcocks; Christus in Bach's St John Passion in London, St Matthew Passion at Salisbury and the B Minor Mass at Beverley Minster; Season 1998–99 with Germont for Opera Brava, Mozart's Count for Kentish Opera, Dundas in the premiere of David Horne's Friend of the People; Concerts include Missa Solemnis, B minor Mass, the Dream of Gerontius and A Child of Our Time. *Recordings include:* Handel Coronation Anthems under Simon Preston; Bach B Minor Mass, Edinburgh 1990. *Honours:* Winner, first English Song Award at the Brighton Festival. *Address:* 1 Homelands Copse, Fernhurst, Haslemere, Surrey GU27 3JQ, England.

**PEARCE, Richard;** Conductor, Organist and Pianist; b. 1965, England. *Education:* Organ Scholar at Trinity College, Cambridge; Guildhall School, London. *Career:* Tours with Trinity College Choir to North America and Far East; Conductor, accompanist and organist throughout Britain, including Purcell Room, Wigmore Hall, and BBC and commercial broadcasts; Accompanist at 1997 Cardiff Singer of the World Competition; Conductor of Whitehall Choir at St John's Smith Square (Handel's Israel in Egypt, 2000), engagements with BBC Singers; Season 1999–2000 with recitals at the Louvre, Paris, and Tokyo; Performances at the London Prom Concerts and in France. *Recordings include:* Stanford, Fauré and Christmas Music, with BBC Singers; Mahler 4th Symphony, with Northern Sinfonia. *Address:* c/o BBC Singers, BBC Broadcasting House, Portland Place, London, W1 1AA, England.

**PEARLMAN, Martin;** Conductor, Harpsichordist and Composer; b. 21 May 1945, Chicago, USA. *Education:* Studied with Karel Husa at Cornell University (BA 1967) and with Gustav Leonhardt, harpsichord, in the Netherlands, 1967–68; MM in composition with Yehudi Wyner at Yale University (1971) and further harpsichord study with Ralph Kirkpatrick. *Career:* Founder and director of early music group, Banchetto Musicale, 1973 (named Boston Baroque from 1992); Faculty member at University of Massachusetts at Boston, 1976–81; Many tours as harpsichordist in repertory which includes D Scarlatti and Couperin family; US premieres of works by Handel, Rameau and other Baroque composers, as conductor; Handel's Semele at the Kennedy Center, Washington DC, 1995. *Publications include:* Performing editions of Monteverdi's L'Incoronazione di Poppea, Purcell's Comical History of Don Quixote, and Mozart's fragment, Lo Sposo Deluso; Complete edition of the harpsichord music of Armand-Louis Couperin. *Honours:* Erwin Bodky Award, 1972; Prize-winner at 1974 Bruges Competition. *Address:* c/o Washington Opera (Artists Contracts), John F Kennedy Center for the Arts, Washington DC 20566, USA.

**PEARSON, Gail;** Singer (Soprano); b. 1970, Neath, Wales. *Education:* Studied at Royal Northern College of Music. *Career:* With Welsh National Opera has sung Gilda, Despina, Oscar (Un Ballo in Maschera), Clorinda (Cenerentola) and Musetta (1999); Jano in Jenůfa at Glyndebourne, Mozart's Barbarina for Scottish Opera and Ninette in La Finta Semplice for the Buxton Festival; Oberto in Handel's Alcina at Zürich and for English National Opera, 1999; Other roles include Mimi, Micaela and Susanna; Concerts at Bournemouth, Aix-en-Provence Festival and Wigmore Hall, London. *Address:* c/o Harlequin Agency Ltd, 203 Fidlas Road, Cardiff CF4 5NA, Wales.

**PECCHIOLI, Benedetta;** Singer (Mezzo-Soprano); b. 1949, Italy. *Career:* Debut: Piccola Scala, as Clarina in La Cambiale di Matrimonio, 1973; Appearances at Monte Carlo from 1974, Rouen, 1974–75, Maggio Musicale, Florence, 1976–77, in Henze's Il Re Cervo and as Fenena in Nabucco; Spoleto Festival, 1976, as Cenerentola, Geneva, 1980 and 1986, Brussels, 1982 and 1987; Metropolitan Opera debut, 1983, as Rosina; Further engagements at Teatro Regio Turin, Bilbao Festival, Teatro Massimo Palermo and Aix-en-Provence Festival (Meg Page, 1971); Concert appearances in the Ring at Paris, and at Carnegie Hall, New York; La Scala, Milan, 1989, in Rossi's Orfeo; Other roles include Fidalma in Il Matrimonio Segreto, Liseta in Il Mondo della Luna, Erilda in Le Pescatrici by Haydn, Maddalena, Federica in Luisa Miller, Donizetti's Smeton in Anna Bolena and Orsini in Lucrezia Borgia, and Geneviève in Pelléas et Mélisande. *Recordings include:* Il Guiramento by Mercadante; Demetrio e Polibio by Rossini; Donizetti's Pia de Tolomei. *Address:* c/o Teatro alla Scala, Via Filodrammatici 2, Milan, Italy.

**PECI, Aleksandër;** Composer; b. 24 April 1951, Tirana, Albania. *Education:* Jordan Misja Art Lyceum, Tirana, 1965–69; Tirana Conservatory, 1969–74. *Career:* Musical Director at Përmeti, 1974–77; Composer-in-residence, Tirana Reuve Theatre, 1977–99; Amsterdam International Composers Workshop,

1992. *Compositions:* Sonata, violin and piano, 1972; Suite for flute and strings, 1974; Two cello concertos, 1974, 1982; Variations, horn and orchestra, 1975; The Kids and the Wolf, ballet, 1979; 1st Symphony, vocal soloists and orchestra, 1984; Piano concerto, 1980; Symphony no. 2, 1985–88; Four Rhapsodies for orchestra, 1977–87; Land of the Sun, low voice and orchestra, 1989; Suite for string quartet, 1990; Dialogue Liturgique, 1993; Epic of Gilgamesh for narrator, solo female voices and tape, 1997; Raindrops on Glass, soprano and tape, 1997; Broken Dream, bassoon, 1998; Remodelage piano, 1998; Le paradis des enfants for children's chorus, piano, percussion and ensemble, 1998; Polycentrum for strings, 1999. *Address:* c/o Vereniging Buma, PO Box 725, 1180 AS Amstelveen, Netherlands.

**PECKOVÁ, Dagmar;** Czech singer (mezzo-soprano); b. 4 April 1961, Chrudim; m. 1st J. Vejvoda; m. Aleš Kasprík 1997; one s.; m. 2nd Klaus Schiesser; one d. *Education:* Prague Conservatory. *Career:* soloist at Karlín Musical Theatre, Prague 1982–85; soloist with numerous cos including Czech Philharmonic 1985–, with Semper Opera, Dresden 1985–88, with State Opera Berlin 1989–92; guest appearances in Tokyo, Paris 1992, Bregenz Festival, Austria 1992, 1993, Hamburg 1993, Salzburg Festival 1993, 1995, 1996, Basel 1994, Zürich 1994, London 1995, Tel-Aviv 1996, La Corona Festival, Spain 1996, San Sebastien Festival, Spain 1996, Prague Spring Festival 1996, Frankfurt 1996; concert tours Austria, Switzerland, Germany, UK 1993, France, Japan 1990, 1994, USA 1997–99; charity concerts after floods in Czech Repub. 2002; lives in Germany 2002–. *Recent roles include:* Leonora (Basel), Cherubino in The Marriage of Figaro (London), Rosina in The Barber of Seville (Berlin, Dresden), Carmen (Prague), Varvara in Katya Kabanova (Salzburg, Barcelona). *Recordings include:* Martinů—Nipponari 1991, Mozart—Che Bella 1994, Janáček—Moravian Folk Poetry in Song 1994, Mahler—Adagietto, Kindertotenlieder 1996, Songs of Mahler and Berio 1997, Janáček—Kátá Kabanová 1997, Janáček—Diary of One Who Disappeared 1999, recital of music by Wagner, Schoenberg, Zemlinsky and Brahms 2000, Lieder by Strauss, Schoeck, Berg 2001, Lieder by Dvořák 2001, Arias (live) 2002. *Honours:* First Prize, Antonin Dvořák Competition 1982, Second Prize, Brno Vocal Competition 1985, Czech Music Fund Award (for role of Liza Doolittle in My Fair Lady) 1985, First Prize, Prague Spring Vocal Competition 1986, Berlin Critics' Prize (for role of Dorabella in Così fan tutte) 1989, European Foundation for Music Prize 1993, Thalia Prize (for Carmen) 2000. *Address:* Okrouhlo 45, 254 01, Czech Republic (office). *E-mail:* yaga@telecom.cz (office). *Website:* www.peckova.cz (office).

**PECORARO, Herwig;** Tenor; b. 1959, Bludenz, Switzerland. *Education:* Studied at the Bregenz Conservatory. *Career:* Sang at the Graz Opera, 1985–90 and Bregenz Festival from 1985 as a Priest in Die Zauberflöte and the Steuermann in Fliegende Holländer; Sang at Vienna Staatsoper from 1991 notably as Pedrillo and Steuermann; Other engagements at Nice and the Smetana Theatre in Prague; Appeared at the Vienna Volksoper in 1992 in Dantons Tod; Season 2000–01 as Mozart's Pedrillo at the Vienna Staatsoper and Rosillon in Die Lustige Witwe at Leipzig. *Address:* c/o Vienna Staatsoper, Opernring 2, 1010 Vienna, Austria.

**PEDANI, Paolo;** Singer (Bass); b. 1930, Italy. *Education:* Studied in Milan. *Career:* Sang in Cherubini's L'Osteria Portoghese and Falla's Vida Breve at La Scala, 1950–51; Appearances at Bologna, Genoa, Trieste and Venice from 1954, Wexford Festival, 1956–59, Spoleto, 1961; Aix-en-Provence Festival from 1959, in Haydn's Mondo della Luna and as Masetto; Venice, 1966, in premiere of La Metamorfosi di Bonaventura by Malipiero; Florence, 1976, in the Italian premiere of Henze's Il Re Cervo; Guest appearances at Barcelona, Catania, Mexico City and Antwerp; Other roles included Rossini's Alidoro, Don Magnifico, Taddeo and Basilio, Don Pasquale, Don Alfonso, Melitone in La Forza del Destino and Paisiello's Basilio; Character roles from 1970.

**PEDERSEN, Laura;** Opera singer (Soprano); b. 1969, Sioux City, Iowa, USA. *Career:* Debut: Donna Elvira in Don Giovanni for Tirana Opera, Albania, this production was a cultural gift from the Austrian Government to the Albanian people in 1996; Theatre engagements, Lyric Opera, Cleveland, 1991–94, educational outreach programs, apprenticeships and main stage and leading roles; Cleveland opera, 1990–97, educational outreach programs, mini-residencies, leading roles; Tirana Opera, 1996, mainstage leading role; Tulsa Opera, mainstage role; Bremen Theater, Bremen, Germany, leading roles; Norina, Don Pasquale; Maria, West Side Story; Oscar, The Masked Ball; Amour, Orphée; Susanna, Marriage of Figaro; Adele, Die Fledermaus. *Address:* 347 Morewood PKW, Rocky River, Ohio 44116, USA.

**PEDERSON, Monte;** Singer (Bass-Baritone); b. 1960, Sunnyside, Washington, USA. *Education:* Studied in USA and with Hans Hotter in Munich. *Career:* Debut: San Francisco Opera, as M Gobineau in Menotti's The Medium, 1986; Engaged at various opera houses in USA and at Bremen, 1987–88, notably as Szymanowski's King Roger; Montpellier and Bregenz, 1988–89, as Wagner's Dutchman; Minister in Fidelio at Orange, Deutsche Oper Berlin and Stuttgart, 1989–90; Sang Pizarro in a new production of Fidelio at Covent Garden, 1990, followed by concert performance at the Festival Hall, conducted by Lorin Maazel; Season 1990–91 as Shishkov in From the House of the Dead at Cologne, Orestes in Elektra at San Francisco and Amfortas at La Scala; Salzburg Festival, 1992, as Shishkov, Houston Opera, 1992, as Amfortas in a production of Parsifal by Robert Wilson; Other roles include Jochanaan in Salome, Basle, 1989, and Angelotti; Sang Nick Shadow at the 1996 Salzburg Festival; Golaud in Pelléas at Brussels, Scarpia at Stuttgart, 1998; Sang Kurwenal at the NY Met, 1999; Season 2000 as

Debussy's Golo at Toronto, Orestes in Elektra at the Munich Staatsoper and Britten's Claggart at Cagliari. *Recordings include:* Video of Covent Garden Fidelio. Address Théâtre Royale de la Monnaie, 4 Léopoldstrasse, 1000 Brussels, Belgium.

**PEDICONI, Fiorella;** Singer (Soprano); b. 1950, Italy. *Education:* Studied at Conservatorio Giuseppe Verdi, Milan. *Career:* Appeared at first in Il Barbiere di Siviglia and I Puritani at opera houses in Italy; Sang Violetta at Glyndebourne, 1988, Gilda at Covent Garden, 1989; Appeared in Bussotti's L'Ispirazione at Turin, 1991, as Sandrina in La Finta Giardiniera at Alessandria; Has also sung in operas by Haydn, Pergolesi, Rossini, Respighi, Cimarosa and Donizetti at such opera centres as La Scala, Milan; San Carlo, Naples; La Fenice, Venice; Teatro dell'Opera, Rome; Grand Théâtre, Geneva; Théâtre des Champs Elysées, Paris, and the Gran Liceo, Barcelona.

**PEDUZZI, Richard;** stage designer and costume designer; b. 28 Jan. 1943, Argentan, France. *Education:* Academie de Dessin, Paris. *Career:* collaborations with producer Patrice Chéreau have included L'Italiana at Spoleto, 1969, and Les Contes d'Hoffman and Lulu at the Paris Opéra, 1974, 1979; Der Ring des Nibelungen at Bayreuth, 1976; Lucio Silla for La Scala, Théâtre des Amandiers in Nanterre and Théâtre de la Monnaie, Brussels, 1984–85; Co-Artistic Director with Chéreau of Théâtre des Amandiers, 1982–89; Stage designs for Tony Palmer's production of Les Troyens at Zürich, 1990, Don Giovanni at Rome, 1991; Costume designs for War and Peace at San Francisco, 1991, Le nozze di Figaro (designs), Salzburg, 1995. *Address:* c/o Teatro dell'Opera, Piazza B Gigli 8, 00184 Rome, Italy.

**PEEBLES, Antony (Gavin Ian);** Concert Pianist; b. 26 Feb. 1946, Southborough, England; m. Frances Clark, 1982, divorced 1999, 2 s., 2 d. *Education:* BMus, Trinity College, Cambridge (1968); Piano with Peter Katin. *Career:* Debut: Wigmore Hall, London, 1969; Has given concerts in 125countries; Soloist with London Symphony, Royal Philharmonic, Philharmonia, Hallé, Royal Liverpool Philharmonic, City of Birmingham Symphony, BBC Philharmonic Orchestras and BBC National Orchestra of Wales. *Recordings:* Copland Fantasy; Bartók Studies; Dallapiccola Quaderno Musicale di Anna Libera; Ravel Gaspard de la Nuit, Miroirs, Sonatine, Pavane; Recital of Liszt operatic transcriptions; Schubert Lieder transcribed by Liszt. *Honours:* 1st Prize, BBC Piano Competition, 1971; 1st Prize, Debussy Competition, 1972. *Current Management:* Allegro Artists, Conifers, Roselands Avenue, Mayfield, East Sussex TN 20 6EB, England. *Address:* 130 Roehampton Vale, London SW15 3RX, England.

**PEEBLES, Charles Ross,** MA, ARCM; British conductor; b. 31 Aug. 1959, Hereford, England. *Education:* Trinity Coll., Cambridge, Guildhall School of Music and Drama, Tanglewood. *Career:* orchestras worked with include City of London Sinfonia, City of Birmingham Symphony, Bournemouth Sinfonietta, European Community Chamber Orchestra, London Mozart Players, English Chamber Orchestra, BBC Symphony Orchestra, Scottish Chamber Orchestra, Nash Ensemble, Composers Ensemble, London Sinfonietta, Vienna Chamber Orchestra; from 1992 all major orchestras of Spain, including Orquesta Nacional de España; opera work includes Opera 80/English Touring Opera, Garsington Opera, Glyndebourne, Broomhill Opera. *Recordings:* Orchestral Works by M. Berkeley and Leighton, also Honegger's Amphion, Andrew Toovey's The Juniper Tree (opera). *Honours:* first prize Cadaques Int. Conducting Competition, Spain 1992. *Current Management:* The Music Partnership Ltd, 41 Aldebert Terrace, London, SW8 1BH, England. *Address:* 71 Bartholomew Road, London, NW5 2AH, England.

**PEEL, Ruth;** Singer (Mezzo-soprano); b. 29 March 1966, Rinteln, Germany. *Education:* Royal Northern College of Music. *Career:* Opera roles have included Third Lady in Die Zauberflöte at Geneva and the 1994 Aix Festival, Kate Pinkerton at Antwerp and the Page in Salome at Covent Garden; Kate in Britten's Owen Wingrave for Glyndebourne Touring Opera, the title role in The Rape of Lucretia, under Stuart Bedford, and the Countess of Essex in Gloriana for Opera North; Concerts include recitals in the Covent Garden Festival, Wigmore Hall, Glasgow, Manchester and St John's Smith Square, (Young Songmakers' Almanac, with Graham Johnson); Concerts include Pergolesi's Stabat Mater at the Barbican Hall, Mahler's 2nd Symphony in Lithuania, Beethoven's 9th in Japan under Ozawa and Holst Songs for the BBC; Beethoven's 9th under Osawa for opening of Winter Olympics, 1998; Mahler 2 in Brisbane, Holst and Brahms recitals for BBC Radio 3. *Recordings:* Brahms recital. *Honours:* Claire Croiza French Song Prize, at the RNCM; Kathleen Ferrier Decca Prize, 1993; Lieder Prize, RNCM. *Address:* 141 King Henry's Road, London NW3 3RD, England.

**PEETERS, Harry;** Singer (Bass); b. 7 Aug. 1959, Roermond, Netherlands. *Education:* Studied in Maastricht. *Career:* Debut: Vienna Volksoper, 1984 as Rossini's Basilio; Paris Opéra, 1985 in Rossini's Le Siège de Corinthe; Deutsche Oper am Rhein, Düsseldorf, from 1987; Geneva from 1987 as Bluebeard, by Dukas; Seneca in Poppea and the villains in Les Contes d'Hoffmann; San Francisco and Houston, 1992 as Gurnemanz in Parsifal; Season 1994 as Sarastro at Los Angeles and in the premiere of P Schat's Symposium at Amsterdam; Cologne Opera as Escamillo; Orestes in Elektra, 1995; Ariodate in Handel's Xerxes; Other repertory includes Idomeneo, Oedipus Rex, Poliuto by Donizetti and Monteverdi's Orfeo; Season 1998 as Kaspar in Der Freischütz at Cologne; Wagner's Amfortas for Netherlands Opera and Orestes at Catania; Sang Wotan at Münster, 1999; Season 2000–01 at Cologne as Prus in The Makropoulas Case and Alberich in Das Rheingold. *Address:* Cologne Opera, Offenbachplatz, 50505 Cologne, Germany.

**PEHRSON, Joseph Ralph,** BA, MM, DMA; American composer and pianist; b. 14 Aug. 1950, Detroit, MI; m. Linda Past 1985. *Education:* Univ. of Michigan, Eastman School of Music. *Career:* Harmonic Etude for Solo Horn at Merkin Concert Hall, New York 1988 performed by Francis Orval; Hornucopia by the Francis Orval Horn Ensemble, Budapest, Hungary 1989; several works at Greenwich House, New York 1992 including Tonreiter, Lewis Carroll Songs, Etheroscape and Windwork; several works performed by Goliard Concerts at their Warwick Music Festival, New York 1992 and on tour in USA 1992–93; guest composer, Univ. of Akron 1993; Exhilarations for Clarinet, Cello and Piano was performed by Composers Concordance 1993; Thanatopsis was performed by Long Island Composers Alliance 1994; commission by St Luke's Chamber Ensemble for a piece for trumpet and strings, entitled Trumpet in a New Surrounding, performed 1997 at the Dia Center for the Arts, Manhattan; commission by the Archaeus Ensemble, Romania, for a new piece for nine players, Wild, Wild, West, performed 1997, Bacau, Romania; Three Piano Pieces by Jeffrey Jacob, in Rees, Germany 1998; performance of Lustspiel at Univ. of Colorado 1998; performed Exhilarations at Univ. of Chicago 1998, and Three Arts Club, Chicago 1998; tour of Russia 2001. *Compositions include:* for orchestra: Chromakkordion, 1995; chamber ensemble: Concerto for Horn and 8 Instruments, 1987; Confessions of the Goliards for Tenor Voice, Flute, Violin and Cello, 1992; Hornorarium for Four Horns, 1994; Forest of Winds, for Wind Ensemble, 1994; trios and duos include: Arecibo for Piano and Percussion, 1976; Exhilarations for Clarinet, Cello and Piano, 1993; Jollity for Violin and Harp, 1994; for solo instruments: Three Pianopieces, 1991; Panoply for Solo Flute, 1992; Lake Fantasy for Solo Oboe, 1993; Spectral Harmony, alto sax, horn, 1997; Stringing, violin and piano, 1999; Electronic Pieces, Unheard Verklärte Neunzehn, 2000. *Recordings:* Thanatopsis; Trumpet in a New Surrounding, trumpet and string quartet, 1996; Wild, Wild West, for 7 instruments, 1997; The Nature of the Universe II, for baroque flutes. *Address:* c/o Composers Concordance, PO Box 36 – 20548 (PABT), New York, NY 10129, USA. *E-mail:* joseph@composersconcordance.org. *Website:* www .composersconcordance.org.

**PEINEMANN, Edith;** German concert violinist; b. 3 March 1939, Mainz; d. of Robert Peinemann and Hildegard (née Rohde) Peinemann. *Education:* Guildhall School of Music, London. *Career:* studied under her father and later with Heinz Stauske and Max Rostal; since then has performed with leading orchestras and conductors worldwide; Carnegie Hall debut 1965; performed at Salzburg, Lucerne and Mamboro Chamber Music Festivals; Prof. of Music, Frankfurt. *Honours:* First Prize, ARD competition, Munich 1956. *Address:* c/o Pro Musicis, Ruetistrasse 38, 8032 Zurich, Switzerland.

**PELINKA, Werner,** MA, DPhil; Austrian composer and pianist; b. 21 Jan. 1952, Vienna; m. Liliane Flühler 1976; two d. *Education:* Hochschule für Welthandel, Vienna, Univ. of Michigan, USA, Konservatorium der Stadt Wien, Hochschule für Musik und darstellende Kunst, Vienna, Univ. of Vienna. *Career:* concerts with horn player Roland Horvath (member of Vienna Philharmonic) as Ensemble Wiener Horn; teaching, Konservatorium Wien, Toho-Vienna Music Acad. 1991–2000; Man. Viennese Children's Music Festival, Kinderklang 1992–2003; Formation of a Tomatis Institute in Vienna (training in Paris) 1994–95; concerts with Ensemble Imago (Founding mem.) 2004–. *Compositions:* Op. 1–45 e.g. Op. 1: Pater Noster, Op. 5: Sinfonietta con Corale, Op. 9: Trio Reflexionen, Op. 14: Passio Silvae, Op. 24: Concerto for Jon, Op. 28: Die Erbsenprinzessin, Opera after Hans Christian Andersen (libretto, Martin Auer) 1995, Op. 33: In adventu, Op. 39: Cantata brevis. *Recordings:* Horn and Klavier 4 (with Op. 2, Op. 5 and Op. 8), with Werner Pelinka (piano) and Roland Horvath (horn); Österreichische Komponisten der Gegenwart (with Op. 12), with Brigitte Hübner (contralto) and Werner Pelinka (piano), Passio Silvae (with Op. 14), with Johannes Jokel (bass voice), Roland Horvath (horn) and Werner Pelinka (piano), Horn und Klavier 5 (with Op. 24), New Music for Orchestra VMM (with Op. 5), with ORF Symphonic Orchestra conducted by Christo Stanischeff, Soloist, Erwin Sükar, Horn, Trio Arabesque Op. 26 (oboe, bassoon, piano—Tonkünstler Ensemble), Diagonal, concert pieces for strings, Op. 27, Ruse Philharmonic conducted by Tsanko Delibozov (CD), CD, Musik-Sprache-Dichtung-Musik (with Op. 9), J'aime le son du cor (with Op. 14), with Walter Fink (bass voice). *Publications:* Die Vertonungen des lateinischen Paternoster der nachklassischen Zeit (Diss 1985, Vienna). *Address:* Gusenleithnergasse 30, 1140 Vienna, Austria. *Telephone:* (1) 9148674. *Fax:* (1) 9124290 (office).

**PELLEGRINI, Maria;** Singer (Soprano); b. 15 July 1943, Pescara, Italy. *Education:* Studied at the Opera School of the Royal Conservatory in Toronto. *Career:* Debut: With the Canadian Opera Company as the Priestess in Aida, 1963; Sang Gilda 1965; Appearances in Montreal, Toronto and Vancouver; Sadler's Wells Opera from 1967, Covent Garden from 1968, notably as Violetta, Micaela in Carmen and Madama Butterfly; Guest appearances in Genoa, Bologna, Parma and Trieste and with the Welsh National Opera; US debut Pittsburgh, 1975; Sang Musetta in Ottawa, 1980. *Recordings include:* Carmen.

**PELLEGRINO, Ronald (Ron) Anthony,** BM, PhD; American composer and musician; b. 11 May 1940, Kenosha, WI. *Education:* Lawrence Univ., Univ. of Wisconsin with Rene Leibowitz and Rudolph Kolisch. *Career:* electronic music studio at Univ. of Wisconsin from 1967; Dir of the electronic music studios, Ohio State Univ. 1968–70, Oberlin Conservatory 1970–73; Assoc. Prof., Texas Tech Univ., Lubbock 1978–81; founded electronic music performance ensembles Real Electric Symphony and Sonoma Electro-Acoustic Music Soc. *Compositions include:* Electronic and Mixed Media; S&H Explorations, 1972;

Metabiosis, 1972; Figured, 1972; Cries, 1973; Kaleidoscope, Electric Rags, 1976; Setting Suns and Spinning Daughters, 1978; Words and Phrases, 1980; Siberian News Release, 1981; Spring Suite, 1982; Laser Seraphim and Cymatic Music, 1982; Tape and Instruments: The End of the Affair, 1967; Dance Drama, 1967; Passage, 1968; Markings, 1969; Leda and the Swan, 1970; Phil's Float, 1974; Wavesong, 1975; Issue of the Silver Hatch, 1979. *Publications include:* An Electronic Music Studios Manual 1969. *Honours:* National Endowment for the Arts and National Endowment for the Humanities grants for founding the Leading Edge contemporary music series. *Address:* c/o University of Wisconsin, Madison, WI 53706, USA. *E-mail:* ronpell@microweb.com.

**PELLEKOORNE, Anne;** Singer (Contralto); b. 1957, Amsterdam, Netherlands. *Education:* Studied at the Hamburg Musikhochschule. *Career:* Concerts for German television and at Rome under Gerd Albrecht, Hindemith programme; Appearances at Wiesbaden and Zürich in Die Zauberflöte and Die Walküre; Wagner's Ring at Rome; Bavarian State Opera from 1989 in Salome and Der Rosenkavalier and the premiere of Bose's Schlachthof 5, 1996; Concert tour of Brazil, 1996; Sang Angustias in the premiere of Reimann's Bernarda Albas Haus, Munich 2000. *Address:* Bavarian State Opera, Max-Joseph Platz, 80539 Munich, Germany.

**PELLETIER, Louis-Philippe;** Pianist and Professor; b. 1945, Montreal, Canada. *Education:* Studies with Lubka Kolessa, Claude Helffer, Harald Boje, Aloys Kontarsky. *Career:* Professor of Piano, Chair, Department of Piano, McGill University. *Recordings:* Piano Works, Bach, Beethoven, Schumann, Brahms, Debussy, Boulez, Messiaen, Stockhausen, Xenakis, Schoenberg, Berg, Webern, Vivier, Papineau-Couture, Garant. *Honours:* 1st Prize, Arnold Schoenberg Piano Competition, Rotterdam, 1979; Artist of the Year, Canadian Music Council, 1980. *Address:* Latitude 45, Arts Promotion Inc, 109 St Joseph Blvd West, Montreal, Quebec H2T 2P7, Canada.

**PEČMAN, Rudolf;** Czech academic; *Professor, Institute of Musicology, Masaryk University, Brno;* b. 12 April 1931, Staré Město u Frýdku-Místek). *Education:* Masaryk University, Brno. *Career:* Asst 1955, Docent 1984, Prof. of Musicology 1990–, Philosophy Faculty, Masaryk Univ., Nummo Memoriali Ateneo Rector 1995–; Czech Music Counsel UNESCO 1997; mem. Czech Music Soc., G-F-Händel-Gesellschaft, Halle (Saale). *Publications:* Josef Myslivecek und sein Opernepilog, Brno, 1970; Beethoven dramatik (Beethoven the Dramatic Composer), Hradec Králové, 1978; Beethovens Opernpläne, Brno, 1981; Josef Mysliveček, Prague, 1981; Georg Friedrich Händel, Prague, 1985; Eseje o Martinů (Essays about Martinů), Brno, 1988; F X Richter und seine 'Harmonischen Belehrungen', Michaelstein/Blankenburg, 1991; Style and Music 1600–1900 (in Czech), Brno 2nd Ed, 1996; The Attack on Antonín Dvořák (in Czech), Brno, 1992; The Stage Works of Ludwig van Beethoven (in Czech), Brno, 1999; Vladimír Helfert (in Czech), Brno, 2003, F.X. Šalda and Music (in Czech), Prague 2004. *Honours:* Smetana Prize 1974, Janáček Prize 1984, Mozart Prize 1987. *Address:* Arna Nováka 1, 66088 Brno (office); Loosova 12, 638 00 Brno, Czech Republic (home). *Telephone:* 549 494 623 (office); 548 520 261 (home). *Fax:* 549 497 478 (office). *E-mail:* music@phil .muni.cz (office).

**PEMBERTON JOHNSON, Anne;** Singer (Soprano); b. 3 Sept. 1958, New York, NY, USA. *Education:* New England Conservatory and Peabody Institute. *Career:* Sang in Heinz Holliger's Not I at Frankfurt, Paris and Almeida Festival, London; Appearances at Munich in George Crumb's Star Child conducted by Paul Daniel and at Salzburg Festival with the Ensemble Modern under Hans Zender; Premieres of works at Library of Congress and Kennedy Center, Washington DC; Recent engagements of Pli selon Pli by Boulez and Berg's Altenberg Lieder with RAI Milan and BBC Philharmonic Orchestras; Season 1992–93 with Stravinsky's Rossignol in The Hague, conducted by Edward Downes, and opening concert of Luigi Nono Festival of the Venice Biennale, 1993; Other conductors include Matthias Bamert and Peter Eötvös. *Current Management:* Ingpen & Williams Ltd, 7 St George's Court, 131 Putney Bridge Road, London, SW15 2PA, England.

**PEÑA, Paco;** Spanish flamenco guitarist; b. 1 June 1942, Córdoba; s. of Antonio Peña and Rosario Pérez; m. Karin Vaessen 1982; two d. *Career:* int. concert artist since 1968; f. Paco Peña Flamenco Co. 1970, Centro Flamenco Paco Peña, Córdoba 1981; Prof. of Flamenco, Rotterdam Conservatory, Netherlands 1985; composed Misa Flamenca 1991; produced Musa Gitana 1999, Voces y Ecos 2002; composed Flamenco Requiem 2004. *Honours:* Ramón Montoya Prize 1983, Oficial de la Cruz de la Orden del Mérito Civil, Spain. *Address:* c/o MPM London, 4 Boscastle Road, London, NW5 1EG, England. *Telephone:* (20) 7681-7475 (office). *Fax:* (20) 7681-7476 (office); (20) 7485-2320. *E-mail:* info@mpmlondon.com (office). *Website:* www.pacopena.com (office).

**PENCARREG, Wyn;** singer (baritone); b. 1965, Wales. *Education:* Royal Northern College of Music; masterclasses with Geraint Evans, Brigitte Fassbaender and Sherrill Milnes. *Career:* roles at RNCM included Britten's Bottom and John Bunyan in The Pilgrim's Progress, Glyndebourne Chorus from 1993; Sang Masetto with Glyndebourne Tour (1995), Mozart's Don Alfonso with Goldberg Festival Opera, Count for Mid Wales Opera, and Figaro for English Touring Opera; Sang Malcotent in premiere of Jonathan Dove's In Seach of Angels, for Mecklenburg Opera at the Covent Garden Festival, 1996; Season 1998 at the Glyndebourne Festival as Kuligin in Katya Kabanova and Servant in Capriccio. *Honours:* Erich Viether Memorial Award 1995. *Current Management:* Musichall, Vicarage Way, Ringmer, BN8 5LA, England.

*Telephone:* (1273) 814240. *Fax:* (1273) 813637. *E-mail:* info@musichall.uk .com. *Website:* www.musichall.uk.com.

**PENDACHANSKA, Alexandrina;** Singer (Soprano); b. 1970, Bulgaria. *Education:* Studied with her mother, Valeri Popova. *Career:* Debut: Sang in concert at Sofia, 1987, with Violetta's Act 1 aria; Concert tour of West Germany, 1989; Performances of Traviata in Sofia and Bilbao; Performances of Lucia in Cairo and Sofia; Performances of Gilda in a new production of Rigoletto for Welsh National Opera, 1991; Concert engagements with the Sofia Philharmonic and other orchestras in Bulgaria, Moscow and Kiev; Lucia di Lammermoor (title role) in Dublin, Ophelia in Hamlet with Monte Carlo Opera, 1991–92; Sang Marie in La Fille du Régiment at Monte Carlo, 1996; Elisabetta in Donizetti's Roberto Devereux, Naples, 1998; Season 2000 as Donna Anna at Houston, Rossini's Ermione for Santa Fe Opera, Adalgisa in Florence and Lucrezia in Verdi's I Due Foscari at Naples. *Recordings:* Antonida in A Life for the Tsar by Glinka. *Honours:* Second Prize, International Competition, Bilbao, 1988; Winner, 23rd International Dvořák Competition in Prague, 1988; Pretoria Music Competition, 1st Prize, 1990. *Address:* c/o PG & PM, 7 Whitehorse Close, Royal Mile, Edinburgh, EH8 8BU, Scotland.

**PENDERECKI, Krzysztof;** Polish composer and conductor; b. 23 Nov. 1933, Dębica, Cracow Prov.; s. of Tadeusz Penderecki and Zofia Penderecka; m. Elżbieta Solecka 1965; one s. one d. *Education:* Jagiellonian Univ., Cracow and State Higher Music School, Cracow. *Career:* studied composition first with Skołyszewski, later with Malawski and Wiechowicz, Cracow; graduated from State Higher Music School, Cracow 1958; Lecturer in Composition, State Higher Music School (now Music Acad.), Cracow 1958–66, Prof. Extraordinary 1972–75, Prof. 1975–; Rector Cracow Conservatory 1972–87; Prof. of Composition, Folkwang Hochschule für Musik, Essen 1966–68; Musical Adviser, Vienna Radio 1970–71; Prof. of Composition, Yale Univ., USA 1973–78; Music Dir, Casals Festival, Puerto Rico 1992–2002; Music Man. Sinfonia Varsovia Orchestra 1997–; Guest Conductor China Philharmonic Orchestra 2000–; mem. Presidential Council of Culture 1992–; Hon. mem. RAM, London 1974; Corresp. mem. Arts Acad. of GDR, Berlin 1975; Extraordinary mem. Arts Acad. of W Berlin 1975; mem. Royal Acad. of Music, Stockholm 1976, Acad. Nat. de Sciences, Belles-Lettres et Arts, Bordeaux, American Acad. of Arts and Letters 1999, Hong Kong Acad. for the Performing Arts 2001, etc. *Works include:* Psalms of David (for choir and percussion) 1958, Emanations (for 2 string orchestras) 1958, Strophes (for soprano, speaker and ten instruments) 1959, Anaklasis (for strings and percussion) 1959–60, Dimensions of Time and Silence (for 40-part mixed choir and chamber ensemble) 1959–60, String Quartet no. 1 1960, no. 2 1968, Threnody for the Victims of Hiroshima (for 52 strings) 1960, Polymorphia (for strings) 1961, Psalms (for tape) 1961, Fluorescences (for large orchestra) 1961, Sonata for Cello and Orchestra 1964, St Luke's Passion 1965–66, Capriccio per oboe e 11 archi 1965, De natura sonoris (for large orchestra) 1966, Dies irae (for soprano, tenor, bass, chorus and large orchestra) 1967, The Devils of Loudun (opera) 1968–69, Cosmogony 1970, De natura sonoris II (for wind instruments, percussion and strings) 1970, Russian Mass Utrenja 1971, Partita (for harpsichord, guitars, harp, double bass and chamber orchestra) 1972, Symphony no. 1 1972–73, Canticum Canticorum Salomonis (for 16 voices and chamber orchestra) 1970–73, Magnificat (for bass solo, voice ensemble, double choir, boys' voices and orchestra) 1973–74, When Jacob Awoke (for orchestra) 1974, Violin Concerto 1967–77, Paradise Lost (opera) 1976–78, Christmas Symphony No. 2 1979–80, Te Deum 1979–80, Lacrimosa 1980, Cello Concerto no. 2 1982, Viola Concerto 1983, Polish Requiem 1980–84, Black Mask (opera) 1984–86, Der unterbrochene Gedanke (for string quartet) 1988, Adagio (for orchestra) 1989, Symphony No. 4 (Adagio for orchestra) 1989, Sinfonietta (for orchestra) 1990–91, Symphony No. 5 (for orchestra) 1991–92, Partita (for orchestra, rev. ed.) 1991, Ubu Rex (opera) 1991, Benedicamus Domine 1992, Benedictus 1992, Flute Concerto 1992–93, Quartet for Clarinet and String Trio 1993, Violin Concerto No. 2 1992–95, Divertimento (for cello solo) 1994, Symphony No. 3 1995, Agnus Dei from Versöhnung Messe (a cappella choir) 1995, Seven Gates of Jerusalem (oratorio) 1995–96, Passacaglia (chamber music) 1995–96, Larghetto (chamber music) 1997, Sonata for Violin and Piano 2000, Sextet for Violin, Viola, Cello, Piano, Clarinet and French Horn 2000, Concerto Grosso for Three Cellos 2001, Benedictus 2002, Resurrection Piano Concerto 2002. *Honours:* Hon. mem. Accad. Nazionale di Santa Cecilia, Rome 1976, Acad. Int. de Philosophie et de l'Art, Berne 1987, Musikkreis der Stadt, Duisburg 1999, Gesellschaft der Musikfreunds, Vienna 2000; Corresp. mem. Academia Nacional de Bellas Artes, Buenos Aires 1982; Fellow Royal Irish Acad. of Music; Hon. Prof. Moscow Conservatory 1997, Cen. Beijing Conservatory 1998, St Petersburg Conservatory 2003; Dr hc (Univ. of Rochester, NY) 1972, (St Olaf Coll., Northfield, Minn.) 1977, (Katholieke Univ., Leuven) 1979, (Univ. of Bordeaux) 1979, (Georgetown Univ., Washington, DC) 1984, (Univ. of Belgrade) 1985, (Univ. Autónoma, Madrid) 1987; Hon. DMus (Glasgow) 1995, (Jagiellonian Univ., Cracow) 1998, (Ukrainian Nat. Tchaikovsky Acad. of Music) 1999, (Pittsburgh) 1999, (Lucerne) 2000, Univ. of St Petersburg, Yale Univ., Univ. of Leipzig 2003, and many others; Fitelberg Prize for Threnody for the Victims of Hiroshima 1960, also UNESCO award 1959, Polish Minister of Culture and Art Prize 1961, (First Class) 1981, Cracow Composition Prize for Canon 1962, North Rhine-Westphalia Grand Prize for St Luke's Passion 1966, also Pax Prize (Poland) 1966, Alfred Jurzykowski Foundation Award, Polish Inst. of Arts and Sciences in America 1966, Prix Italia 1967/68, State Prize (1st Class) 1968, Gustav Charpentier Prize 1971,

Gottfried von Herder Prize 1977, Prix Arthur Honegger for Magnificat 1978, Grand Medal of Paris 1981, Sibelius Prize (Wihouri Foundation, Finland) 1983, Order of Banner of Labour (1st Class) 1983, Premio Lorenzo il Magnifico (Italy) 1985, Wolf Foundation Award 1987, Grammy Award Nat. Acad. of Recording Arts and Sciences (for Best Contemporary Composition) 1988 (for Best Instrumental Soloist Performance with Orchestra) 1999, (for Best Choral Composition) 2001, Officier, Ordre de Saint-Georges de Bourgogne (Belgium) 1990, Grawemeyer Award for Music Composition 1992, Grand Cross Order of Merit (Fed. Repub. of Germany) 1990, City of Strasbourg Medal 1995, Commdr Ordre des Arts et des Lettres 1996, Crystal Award, World Econ. Forum, Davos 1997, Business Center Club Award, Warsaw 1998, AFIM Indie Award 1999, Köhler-Osbahr-Siftung Music Award 1999, Ordine al Merito della Repub. Italiana 2000, Best Living Composer Award, Midem Classic Cannes 2000, Príncipe de Asturias Award 2001, Roman Guardini Prize, Catholic Acad. of Music 2002, North Rhine-Westphalia Award 2003, Praemium Imperiale 2004. *Current Management:* Schott Musik International, Weihergarten 5, 55116 Mainz, Germany. *Telephone:* (6131) 246250. *E-mail:* katja.riepl@schott-musik.de. *Address:* ul. Cisowa 22, 30-229 Cracow, Poland. *Fax:* (12) 4251660. *E-mail:* biuro@elzbietapenderecka.org. *Website:* www.penderecki.de.

**PENDLEBURY, Sally;** Cellist; b. 1960, England. *Education:* Studied at Chetham's Schhol of Music, in Düsseldorf and at New England Conservatory. *Career:* Led Cello Section of the European Community Youth Orchestra, 1982–85; Member of the Chamber Orchestra of Europe; Recitals with Natalia Gutman and Yuri Bashmet; Co-founded Vellinger String Quartet, 1990; Participated in master classes with Borodin Quartet at Pears-Britten School, 1991; Concerts at Ferrara Musica Festival, Italy and debut on South Bank with London premiere of Robert Simpson's 13th Quartet; BBC Radio 3 Debut, December 1991; Season 1992–93 with concerts in London, Glasgow, Cambridge, at Davos Festival, Switzerland and Crickdale Festival, Wiltshire; Wigmore Hall with Haydn (Op 54, No. 2), Gubaidulina and Beethoven (Op 59, No. 2), Purcell Room with Haydn's Seven Last Words. *Address:* c/o Georgina Ivor Associates (Vellinger Quartet), 66 Alderbrook Road, London SW12 8 AB, England.

**PENHERSKI, Zbigniew;** Composer; b. 26 Jan. 1935, Warsaw, Poland; m. Malgorzata, 1 s. *Education:* Composers Diploma, Warsaw Conservatory of Music, 1959. *Compositions include:* Musica Humana for baritone, choir and symphony orchestra, 1963; Missa Abstracta for tenor, reciting voice, choir and symphony orchestra, 1966; Street Music, chamber ensemble, 1966; Samson Put on Trial, radio opera, 1968; 3 Recitativi for soprano, piano and percussion, 1968; 3M-H1, electronic piece, 1969; Instrumental Quartet, 1970; Incantationi 1 Sextet for Percussion Instruments, 1972; The Twilight of Peryn, opera in 3 parts, 1972; Masurian Chronicles 2, for symphony orchestra and magnetic tape, 1973; Radio Symphony for 2, 1975; Anamnesis for symphony orchestra, 1975; String Play for string orchestra, 1980; Edgar: The Son of Walpor, opera in 3 parts, 1982; Jeux Partis for saxophone and percussion, 1984; 3 impressions for soprano, piano and four percussions, 1985; Scottish Chronicles for symphony orchestra, 1987; The Island of the Roses, chamber opera, 1989; Signals for Symphony orchestra 1992; Cantus for mixed choir, 1992; Signals No.2, 1995; Genesis for bass solo, vocal ensembles, reciting voices, selected instruments and electronic sounds, 1995; Introduction and Toccata for clarinet, trombone, cello and piano, 1998; Little Music for the End of Century for recorder, two percussions, organ and tape, 1999; Cantus II for mixed choir, 2000; Little String Litany for string orchestra, 2002; Lamentations for baritone and string quartet, 2003. *Honours:* Hon. Citizen Kragujevac (Yugoslavia), Russe (Bulgaria), Ho-Chi-Minh (Vietnam), Hon. mem. Scottish Soc. of Composers 1987; Silver Cross of Merit 1975, Prime Minster's Award for works for children and youth 1982. *Address:* ul. Krucza 24A, 05–120 Legionowo by Warsaw, Poland (home). *Telephone:* (22) 7844163 (home). *E-mail:* zpenherski@wp.pl (home). *Website:* www.zaiks.org.pl (office); www .polmic.pl (home).

**PENICKA, Miloslav;** Australian (b. Czech) composer; b. 16 April 1935, Ostrava, Czechoslovakia; s. of Judr Soběslav and Jasmila Rybáková; m. Sandra Parton; two d. one s. *Education:* Prague Conservatorium and Prague Academy of Music and Arts, 1964, studied with František Pícha and Emil Hlobil. *Career:* Percussionist with the Sydney Symphony Orchestra 1965–69; Abbotsleigh School, Wahroonga 1969–75; mem. Full Member, Australian Music Centre; Writer Member, Australian Performing Right Association. *Compositions include:* Symphony, 1964; 4 Overtures, 1972, 1975, 1989, 2003; 2 Orchestral Suites, 1994, 1995; 2 Serenades for small orchestra, 1958, 1961; 2 Piano Concertos, 1963, 1996; Clarinet Concerto, 1977; Divertimento for Violin, Wind, Timpani and Bass, 1963; 3 String Quartets, 1962, 1969, 2002; Clarinet Quintet, 1967; Piano Quartet, 1973; Mosaics for Cor Anglais Quartet, 2003, Pargamyshky for brass quintet 2005, Piano Trio 2005; 2 Piano Sonatas 1958, 1979; Sonatinas for Violin and Piano, 1978, Cello and Piano, 1991, Piano, 1978; Four Pieces for Flute and Piano, 1977, Oboe and Piano, 1995, Partita for cello 1991; Music for String Orchestra: Divertimento, 1972, Sonatina, 1980, Partita, 1987, and Dance Suite, 1991; 3 Piano Cycles, 1990, 1996/2000; Piano pieces, vocal, and theatre music. *Current Management:* Australian Music Centre, POB N690, Grosvenor Place 1220, Asutralia. *Website:* www.amcoz .com.au. *Address:* 9 Warraroon Road, Lane Cove 2066, Australia (home).

**PENKOVA, Reni;** Singer (Mezzo-soprano); b. 28 Oct. 1935, Tarnovo, Bulgaria. *Education:* Studied with Nadia Aladjem and Elena Doskova-Ricardi in Sofia. *Career:* Debut: Burgas 1960, as Olga in Eugene Onegin;

Member of the National Opera Sofia from 1964; Guest appearances in Netherlands and England; Glyndebourne Festival 1971–77 as Olga, Pauline in The Queen of Spades, Dorabella in Così fan tutte and Meg Page in Falstaff; Other roles include Gluck's Orpheus, Cherubino, Octavian in Der Rosenkavalier, Amneris, and Angelina in La Cenerentola; Also heard in concert and oratorio; Member of the Bulgarian National Opera, Sofia, until 1991; Presently, Vocal Professor, State Musical Academie, Sofia; Further roles include Bartók, (Bluebeard's Castle), Judith, 1975; Britten, (Midsummer Night's Dream), Oberon, 1982; Verdi (Nabucco), Fenena, 1976; Bellini, (Norma), Adalgisa, 1984; Donizetti, (La Favorita), Leonora, 1985; Cilea, (Adriana Lecouvreur), La Princesse de Bouillon, 1987. Recordings include: Prince Igor by Borodin (HMV). Address: 1202 Bulgaria Blvd, Slivnitza 212-A, Sofia, Bulgaria.

**PENN, William (Albert);** Composer; b. 11 Jan. 1943, Long Branch, New Jersey, USA. Education: Studied with Henri Pousseur and Maurico Kagel at the State University of New York at Buffalo, MA, 1967, and at Michigan State University, PhD, 1971; Further Study at Eastman School with Wayne Barlow. Career: Faculty member of Eastman School, 1971–78; Staff Composer at New York Shakespeare Festival, 1974–76; Folger Shakespeare Theatre and Sounds Reasonable Records in Washington from 1975. Compositions include: String Quartet, 1968; At Last Olympus, Musical, 1969; Spectrums, Confusions and Sometime for Orchestra, 1969; The Pied Piper of Hamelin, Musical, 1969; Chamber Music No. 1 for Violin and Piano, 1971, for Cello and Piano, 1972; Symphony, 1971; The Boy Who Cried Wolf is Dead, Musical, 1971; Ultra Mensuram 3 Brass Quintets, 1971; The Canticle, Musical, 1972; Inner Loop for Band, 1973; Niagura 1678 for Band, 1973; Night Music for Flute and Chorus, 1973; Miriors sur le Rubaiyat for Piano and Narrator, 1974; Mr.Toad's Wild Adventure for orchestra, 1993; Saxophone Concerto, 1995; The Revelations of St John the Divine, wind ensemble, 1995; Incidental Music and Songs. Honours: American Society for Composers, Authors and Publishers Awards and National Endowment for the Arts Fellowship. Address: c/o ASCAP, ASCAP Building, 1 Lincoln Plaza, New York, NY 10023, USA.

**PENNARIO, Leonard;** Concert Pianist; b. 9 July 1924, Buffalo, New York, USA. Education: Studied with Guy Maier, Olga Steeb and Ernest Toch. Career: Debut: With the Dallas Symphony Orchestra, 1936, playing the Grieg Concerto; Soloist with the Los Angeles Philharmonic, 1939; Played Liszt's E flat Concerto with the New York Philharmonic under Artur Rodzinski, 1943; Tour of Europe, 1952, in the popular Romantic repertory; Chamber Concerts with Jascha Heifetz and Gregor Piatigosky in Los Angeles; Premiered the Concerto by Miklos Rozsa with the LA Philharmonic under Zubin Mehta, 1966.

**PENNETIER, Jean-Claude;** Pianist and Conductor; b. 16 May 1942, Chatellerault, France. Education: Studied at Paris Conservatoire. Career: Numerous Solo appearances in Europe and elsewhere, 1968–; Chamber Musician with Regis Pasquier (Violin) and Trio with E Krivine and F Lodeon; Recitals with Piano Four Hands; Duo with Clarinettist Michel Portal 1979–80; Member of such ensembles as Domaine Musical, Musique Vivante, Ars Nova, Itineraire and Musique Plus; Performer of Contemporary Music at the Roayn and La Rochelle Festivals; Has conducted the Ensemble Intercontemporain and the orchestras of French Radio; Premiered Maurice Ohana's 24 Preludes (1973) and Piano Concerto, 1981; Nikiprovetski's Piano Concerto, 1979; Professor of Chamber Music at the Paris Conservatoire, 1985–. Honours: Winner, Prix Gabriel Fauré and International Competition Montreal, 2nd Prize, Long-Triubaud Competition; Winner, Geneva International Competition, 1968. Address: Conservatoire National Superieur de Musique, 14 Rue de Madrid, 75008 Paris, France.

**PENNISI, Francesco;** Composer; b. 11 Feb. 1934, Acireale, Italy. Education: University Faculty of Arts, Rome, 1954–55; Further study with Robert W. Mann, 1954–59. Career: Co-founder of new music society at Rome, Nuova Consonanza, 1960; Participation in Palermo International New Music Week, 1960–. Compositions: A Cantata on Melancholy, 1967; Sylvia Simplex, music theatre, 1972; Fantasia, cello and orchestra, 1997; La vigne di Samaria, chorus and orchestra, 1974; Gläserner Tag, orchestra, 1978; La partenza di Tisies viola and orchestra, 1979; Descrizione dell Isola Ferdinandea, chamber opera, 1983; Per Agamemnone, orchestra, 1983; I mandolini e le chitarre for soprano and ensemble, 1986; Aci il fume, radio opera, 1986; Tre Pezzi, clarinet, viola and piano, 1987–90; Purpureass rosas for two sopranos, baritone and clarinet quartet, 1990; L esequie della luna, music theatre, 1991; Una cartolina da selim (omaggio a Mozart), 1991; The Wild Swans, soprano and ensemble, and Medea dixit, for soprano and ensemble, 1992–93, Tristan, music theatre after Ezra Pound, 1995; Altro efetto di luna, soprano and ensemble, 1996; Scena, flute and orchestra, 1997; Chamber and solo instrumental music. Address: c/o SIAE (Sezione Musica), Viale della Letteratum n:30, 00144 Rome, Italy.

**PENNY, Andrew Jonathan;** Conductor; b. 4 Dec. 1952, Hull, Yorkshire, England; m. Helga Robinson, 3 Sept 1988, 1 s., 1 d. Education: ARNCM, GRNCM, Royal Northern College of Music, Manchester, after Clarinet and Conducting studies; Studied Conducting on Rothschild Scholarship with Charles Groves and Timothy Reynish; Studied with Edward Downes on courses in Netherlands and later at BBC Conductors' Seminar; Clarinet studies with Sydney Fell. Career: Conductor Sheffield Philharmonic Orchestra 1979–89; Musical Director, Hull Philharmonic Orchestra 1982–; broadcasts with the BBC. Recordings: 30 CDs including premiere recordings of

Sullivan's ballet and theatre music, symphonies by C.Armstrong Gibbs, Edward German and film music by Vaughan Williams and William Walton; Cycle of Malcolm Arnold Symphonies for Naxos with the National Symphony Orchestra, Dublin. Honours: Ricordi Prize, Royal Northern College of Music, 1976. Address: 14 South Lane, Hessle, East Yorkshire, England.

**PENRI-EVANS, David,** BMus, MMus, DMA, PGCE, FTCL; British composer; b. 18 Jan. 1956, Wrexham, Wales. Education: Centenary Coll. of Louisiana, Univ. of Wales, Louisiana State Univ., USA, Trinity Coll., London; composition with Dinos Constantinides. Career: teacher, Victoria Coll., Jersey 1979–81, Portsmouth Grammar School 1987–92; Dir of Music, Elmhurst Ballet School 1992–94, John Lyon School 1995–96, Brooklands Coll., Weybridge 1996–; Asst Prof., American Univ. in London 1987; Founder-Dir Tempo New Music Festival 1987–94; Guest Composer, Louisiana Festival of Contemporary Music 1990, 1995, Conservatoire Nat. de Région de Rouen 2000; Chair. Portsmouth Dist Composers' Alliance; mem. BMI, British Acad. of Composers and Songwriters. Compositions: many comms in UK and USA; Violin Prologue 1982, Brown Studies 1983, Symphony 1983, String Quartet, Dinas Brân 1984, Night Music 1985, Study in Grey, Opera 1985, Death in the Surf 1987, Textures 1990, Sunrise with Sea Monsters 1990, Aurelia 1993, Sift 1994, Five Haiku for Peace 1995, Four Ways of Having Sex in Zero Gravity 2000, Rain Journal 2001. Honours: . Address: 5 Royston Avenue, Byfleet, Surrey KT14 7PR, England (home). E-mail: dpenrievans@brooklands.ac.uk (office). Website: www.penrievans.free-online.co.uk/DPE_Web_01.

**PENROSE, Timothy (Nicholas);** Singer; b. 7 April 1949, Farnham, Surrey, England; m. (1) Shirley Margaret Bignell, (2) Carol Heather Oake, 15 Nov 1986. Education: Licentiate and Fellow, Trinity College, London. Career: Debut: Opera–Holland Festival, 1974; Numerous solo concert appearances throughout the United Kingdom and most European countries; Visits to North and South America; Tours with Pro Cantione Antique of London, Solo Recitals for BBC and European Radio Stations; Concerts with Medieval Ensemble of London and London Music Players; mem, Gentlemen-in-Ordinary, Her Majesty's Chapel Royal, 1972–75; City Glee Club, London. Recordings: Handel's Semele; Purcell's The Fairy Queen, with John Eliot Gardiner; Others with Pro Cantione Antiqua, Medieval Ensemble of London, London Music Players and London Early Music Group. Honours: Recipient, Greater London Arts Association, Young Musicians Award, 1975. Address: c/o Pro Cantione Antiqua, Concert Directory International, Lyndhurst, Denton Road, Ben Rhydding, Ilkley W Yorks, LS29 8QR, England.

**PEPER, Uwe;** Singer (Tenor); b. 20 May 1939, Hamburg, Germany. Career: Debut: Halberstadt, 1966 as Mozart's Pedrillo; Komische Oper Berlin from 1969 as Monostatos and Jacquino in Fidelio, Zürich, Frankfurt and Paris as Jacquino; Pedrillo at the Salzburg Festival, 1990–91; Mime in The Ring at the Salle Pleyel, Paris, 1992; Deutsche Oper Berlin, 1995–96 in Boris Godunov and Andrea Chénier; Sang Guillot in Massenet's Manon, 1998; Sang Jacquino in Fidelio, Strauss's Valzacchi and the Emperor in Turandot at the Deutsche Oper, 1999–2001. Recordings: Salome, Die Entführung, Die Zauberflöte. Address: Deutsche Oper Berlin, Richard Wagnerstrasse 10, 1058 Berlin, Germany.

**PEPI ALÓS, Jorge;** Argentine pianist and composer; b. 28 March 1962, Cordoba. Education: Acad. Menuhin, Gstaad and studied with Edith Fischer. Career: concerto soloist and chamber musician (notably in two-piano duo with Edith Fischer) in Europe, USA and S America; organizer, Festival Int. de Piano de Blonay; teacher, Conservatoire de la Chaux-de-Fonds. Compositions include: Septet 1983, Metamorfosis I 1989, La Caccia al tesoro (chamber opera) 1990–92, Extravagario 1993–94, Amalgama 1995, Metamorfosis IV 1995, Amalgama 1995–96, Nachtstücke 1998, Vie Merveilleuse et Burlesque du Café 1999–2000. Honours: Orpheus Prize 1987, Association des Musiciens Suisses Prix d'étude 1988, Edition Musicale Suisse composition prize 1991, Soc. Suisse des Auteurs composition prize 1993, first prize Gerona Int. Competition 1995, Grand Prix Gilson 1995. Address: 9 rue des Granges, 2300 La Chaux-de-Fonds, Switzerland. Telephone: 21 943 31 22. E-mail: edith .jorge@tiscalinet.es.

**PERAHIA, Murray;** American pianist and conductor; b. 19 April 1947, New York, NY; s. of David Perahia and Flora Perahia; m. Naomi (Ninette) Shohet 1980; two s. Education: High School of Performing Arts, Mannes Coll. of Music, studied with Jeanette Haien, Arthur Balsam, Mieczyslaw Horszowski. Career: debut, Carnegie Hall 1968; won Leeds Int. Piano Competition 1972; has appeared with many of world's leading orchestras and with Amadeus, Budapest, Guarneri and Galimir string quartets; regular recital tours N America, Europe, Japan; Co-Artistic Dir Aldeburgh Festival 1983–89; numerous recordings including complete Mozart Piano Concertos; prin. guest conductor, Acad. of St Martin-in-the-Fields. Honours: Dr hc (Univ. of Leeds), Hon. FRCM, FRAM; Kosciusko Chopin Prize 1965, Avery Fisher Award 1975, Gramophone Record Award 1997, Grammy Award 1999; Hon. KBE 2004. Current Management: IMG Artists, 22 East 71 Street, New York, NY 10021, USA. E-mail: info@imgartists.com. Website: www.imgartists.com.

**PERDIGAO, Maria Madalena Azeredo;** artistic director; b. 28 April 1923, Figueira Da Foz, Portugal; m. Dr José De Azeredo Perdigao; one s. Education: Coimbra University, Conservatorio Nacional, Lisbon; studied with Marcel Ciampi, National Conservatory of Paris. Career: lectures on musical subjects; Head of Music Department, Calouste Gulbenkian Foundation, 1958–74; created the Gulbenkian Orchestra, 1962, The Gulbenkian Choir, 1964, The Gulbenkian Ballet, 1965 and organized the Gulbenkian Music Festivals,

1958–70; President, International Music Festival of Lisbon, 1983; Piano Recitals and Concert Performances; Assessor to the Ministry of Education for Artistic Education, Lisbon, Portugal, 1978–84; Director of the Department of Artistic Creation and Art Education of The Calouste Gulbenkian Foundation. *Address:* R. Marques de Fronteira, 8, 2ø D, 1000 Lisbon, Portugal.

**PEREIRA, Clovis;** Composer; b. 14 May 1932, Caruaru, Brazil; m. Rizomar Pereira, 18 Feb 1955, 2 s., 2 d. *Education:* Studies with Guerra Peixe, 1951; School of Arts, Boston University, 1991. *Career:* Debut: Conductor, Lamento e Dansa Brasileira, 1968; Arranger, Radio Jornal do Commercio, 1950; Head, Music Department, Television, 1960; Chairman, Conservatorio Pernambucano de Musica, 1983; Tour of USA as Brazilian Representative and Conductor of University of Paraiba Chorus, 4th International Choir Festival, 1974; Teacher, University da Paraiba, Rio Grande do Norte e Pernambuco, 1994. *Compositions:* Grande Missa Nordestina para Coro, Solistas e Orquestra; 3 Peças Nordestinas; Terno de Pifes; Cantiga; Velame; Cantata de Natal; Poetas Nordestinos, Songs for Voice and Piano; Concertino para Violino e Orquestra de Camara, 1994. *Honours:* 1st Prize, Primeiro Concurso Nacional de e Orq de Camara, 1964; Trofeu Cultural Cidade do Recife, 1997. *Address:* Rua Pe, Bernardino Pessoa, 395 Apt 102, Recife 51020-210, Brazil.

**PERÉNYI, Miklós;** Hungarian cellist and composer; b. 5 Jan. 1948, Budapest; s. of László Perényi and Erzsébet Seeger; m. Tünde Angermayer; one s. *Education:* Music Acad. of Budapest; studied with Enrico Meinardi in Rome and Ede Bande in Budapest. *Career:* started playing cello aged five, first public recital aged nine, Budapest; Prof. of Violoncello, Franz Liszt Acad. of Music, Budapest 1974–; appearances at int. music festivals including Edinburgh, Lucerne, Prague, Salzburg, Vienna, Hohenems, Warschau, Berlin, Cello Festivals in Kronberg, Wintherthur and Manchester, UK, Festival Pablo Casals, Prades, France, as well as in Japan, China and USA. *Recordings include:* works of Ernö Dohnányi, Ferenc Farkas, Zoltán Kodály, György Ligeti, András Mihály and Sàndor Veress (with Dénes Várjon), complete Beethoven Sonatas (with András Schiff), Hungarian Cello Music, Beethoven – Complete Music for Piano and Violoncello. *Honours:* prizewinner, Int. Cello Competition Pablo Casals, Budapest 1963, Liszt Prize 1970, Kossuth Prize 1980, Bartòk-Pasztory Prize 1987. *Current Management:* Sonia Simmenauer Impresariat, Bornstrasse 12, 20146 Hamburg, Germany. *Telephone:* (40) 42313111. *Fax:* (40) 42313113. *E-mail:* Sonia.Simmenauer@ impresariat-simmenauer.de. *Website:* www.impresariat-simmenauer.de/ perenyi.html. *Address:* Ferenc Liszt Academy of Music, PO Box 206, Liszt Ferenc tér 8, 1391 Budapest, Hungary.

**PERERA, Ronald (Christopher);** Composer; b. 25 Dec. 1941, Boston, Massachusetts, USA. *Education:* Studied with Leon Kirchner at Harvard, MA 1967, and at the electronic studios of Utrecht University. *Career:* Teacher at Syracuse University, 1968–70, Dartmouth College, 1970, Smith College, Northampton, 1971–2002; Elsie Irwin Sweeney Professor of Music Emeritus at Smith College; mem, ASCAP; College Music Society, National Opera Association. *Compositions include:* Instrumental: Piano Suite 1966; Alternate Routes for Electronics, 1971; Fantasy Variations for piano and electronics, 1976; Tolling for 2 pianos and tape, 1979; Choral: Mass, 1967; Three Night Pieces, 1974; Earthsongs, 1983; Songs: Dove sta amore for soprano and tape, 1969; Apollo Circling, 1972; Three Poems of Günther Grass for mezzo, chamber ensemble and tape, 1974; The White Whale for baritone and orchestra, 1981; The Canticle of the Sun for chorus, 1984; The Yellow Wallpaper, chamber opera, 1989; Music for flute and orchestra, 1990; The Saints for orchestra, 1990; The Outermost House, cantata for mixed chorus, narrator, solo soprano and chamber orchestra, 1991; S, opera based on novel by John Updike, 1995. *Recordings include:* Earthsongs; Crossing the Meridian: Chamber Works with Voice; The Outermost House and The Canticle of the Sun; Music for flute and orchestra; Five Summer Songs; The Golden 1 Door. *Publications include:* Co-editor, Development and Practice of Electronic Music, 1975; Sleep Now for High Voice and Piano, 1994 and a further 30 pieces published; The Golden Door, cantata for speaker, mixed chorus and ensemble, 1998; The Araboolies of Liberty Street, opera in one act, 2001. *Honours:* ASCAP Awards for Composition since 1972; Artists Foundation of Massachusetts Fellowship, 1978; Four MacDowell Colony Fellowships, 1974–88; National Endowment for the Arts Grants, 1976, 1988. *Current Management:* Music Associates of America. *Address:* 21 Franklin Street, Northampton, MA 01060, USA. *Website:* www.ronaldperera.com.

**PERESS, Maurice;** American conductor and trumpeter; b. 18 March 1930, New York. *Education:* New York Univ., Mannes Coll., studied conducting with Philip James and Carl Bamberger. *Career:* played trumpet before appointed by Bernstein as Asst Conductor of the New York Philharmonic 1961; conducted revivals of Candide, Los Angeles 1966, West Side Story, New York 1968; Music Dir, Corpus Christi Symphony Orchestra 1962–75, Austin Symphony 1970–73, Kansas City Philharmonic 1974–80; guest conductor in Brussels, Hong Kong, Vienna, Jerusalem and Mexico City; conducted the premiere of Bernstein's Mass at the opening of the Kennedy Center, Washington, DC 1971, and at the Vienna Staatsoper 1981; led the US premiere of Einem's Der Besuch der alten Dame at the San Francisco Opera 1972; has orchestrated, edited and conducted jazz music by Duke Ellington, Eubie Blake and Gershwin (60th anniversary concert of the Rhapsody in Blue, New York 1984); has taught at New York Univ., Univ. of Texas at Austin, Queens Coll., New York; Pres. Conductors' Guild of the American Symphony Orchestra League. *Recordings include:* Bernstein's Mass (musical dir), Organ Concertos 1 and 2 by Rheinberger (with E. Power Biggs and the Columbia

Symphony Orchestra). *Publication:* Dvořák to Duke Ellington: A Conductor Explores America's Music and its African-American Roots 2005. *Current Management:* Gershunoff Artists LLC, 2731 NE 14 Street, Suite 3, Fort Lauderdale, FL 33304-1650, USA. *Telephone:* (954) 769-9105. *Fax:* (954) 769-9107.

**PEREIZ, Jose-Maria;** Tenor; b. 1934, Spain. *Education:* Studied in Spain and Switzerland. *Career:* Sang at the Lucerne Opera, 1959–60, then at Innsbruck and Basle; Sang at Graz Opera, 1963–84 in such roles as the Duke of Mantua, Don Carlos, Rodolfo, Calaf, Radames, Cavaradossi, Andrea Chénier, Alfredo and Turiddu; Guest appearances in Switzerland and elsewhere as Vasco da Gamain L'Africaine, by Meyerbeer, Faust, Pelléas, Sergei in Lady Macbeth of Mtensk and Albert Gregor in The Makropulos Case; Also active in operetta at Berlin, Barcelona and Vienna. *Address:* c/o Graz Opera, Vereingte Buhnen, Kaiser Josef Platz 10, 8010 Graz, Austria.

**PÉRISSON, Jean-Marie;** Conductor; b. 6 Sept. 1924, Arcachon, France. *Education:* Studied with Jean Fournet in Paris and with Igor Markevitch in Salzburg. *Career:* Conducted the orchestra of the Salzburg Mozarteum in Austria and Germany then led the French Radio Orchestra at Strasbourg, 1955–56; Permanent Conductor at the Orchestre Philharmonique of Nice and Musical Director of the Nice Opera; Conducted cycles of The Ring and the French premieres of Katerina Izmailova by Shostakovich in 1964, Elegy for Young Lovers by Henze in 1965 and Prokofiev's The Gambler in 1966; Gave Janáček's Katya Kabanova at the Salle Favart, Paris, and conducted the Monte Carlo Opera, 1969–71; Directed the Presidential Symphony Orchestra, 1972–76, and worked in the French repertory at the San Francisco Opera; Conducted Carmen at Peking in 1982. *Address:* c/o San Francisco Opera, War Memorial Opera House, San Francisco, CA 94102, USA.

**PERL, Alfredo;** Concert Pianist; b. 1965, Santiago, Chile. *Education:* studied at the Universidad de Chile with Carlos Botto; Cologne Musikhochschule with Günter Ludwig; with Maria Curcio in London. *Career:* concerts throughout South America and Europe, with the Filarmonica de Santiago and the Zagreb Symphony; Liszt Années de Pèlerinage for the BBC 1990; recitals at the Herkulessaal, Munich, May 1991; recital, Queen Elizabeth Hall, London 1992; concerts with the Royal Philharmonic and the Noord-Nederlands Orchestra 1992; Leipzig Gewandhaus recital and in Prague 1993, also US debut with the Florida Philharmonic, a recital at Ravinia; 1993–94 season, recitals in Hamburg, Hannover, Moscow Conservatoire, with the Medici Quartet in London and the Lebanon; 1994–95 season, recitals in Prague, London's Queen Elizabeth and Wigmore Halls, Moscow Conservatoire, Düsseldorf, Bologna; Beethoven sonata series at the Wigmore Hall 1996–97; recital tour of Germany 1997; debut at Royal Albert Hall with BBC Philharmonic Orchestra 1997; Season 1999–2000: recitals at the Wigmore Hall, London, Sudwestrundfunk, Mainz, a Beethoven Sonata cycle in Dortmund, tour of South America with the Deutsche Kammerphilharmonie and Netherlands with the Prokofiev Orchestra; Season 2002–03: debut with Leipzig Gewandhausorchestra at the Barbican; tour of Australia, concerts with the Netherlands Philharmonic Orchestra, Vienna Symphony Orchestra, BBC Welsh, recitals at Sydney Opera House, Wigmore Hall, Teatro Municipal de Santiago de Chile; Season 2003–04: tour of Germany with Orquesta de Málaga, performances at Stuttgart Philharmonic, Munster Symphony; recitals at Wigmore Hall, Bath Festival, Leicester Festival, Rheingau Festival, Schwetzingen Festspiele. *Recordings:* Fantasias by Schumann, Liszt and Busoni; Brahms Sonatas for clarinet and piano, with Ralph Manno; Complete Beethoven sonatas and Diabelli Variations; Grieg Concerto and Szymanowski, Symphonie Concertante; CD, Beethoven Cello Sonatas, with Guido Schieffen; Liszt's 2 piano concertos and Totentanz with BBC Symphony Orchestra under Yakov Kreizberg. *Honours:* Prizewinner at such competitions as Vina del Mar (Tokyo), Ferruccio Busoni at Bolzano and the Beethoven in Vienna; 1st Prize, International Piano Competition in Montevideo. *Current Management:* c/o Harrison Parrott Ltd, 12 Penzance Place, London, W11 4PA, England. *Telephone:* (20) 7229-9166. *Fax:* (20) 7221-5042. *E-mail:* sabine .frank@harrisonparrott.co.uk. *Website:* www.harrisonparrott.co.uk.

**PERLE, George,** BMus, MMus, PhD; American composer and author; b. 6 May 1915, Bayonne, NJ; m. 1st Laura Slobe 1940; m. 2nd Barbara Phillips 1958; two d.; m. 3rd Shirley Gabis Rhoads 1982. *Education:* DePaul Univ., American Conservatory of Music, New York Univ. *Career:* Prof. Emer., City Univ. of New York; major compositions performed by Chicago Symphony, Boston Symphony, BBC Symphony, Royal Philharmonic Orchestra, Philadelphia Symphony, San Francisco Symphony, Juilliard Quartet, New York Philharmonic, Bavarian State Radio Orchestra, Da Capo Chamber Players, Cleveland Quartet, Dorian Wind Quintet, Goldman Band; mem. various professional organizations including American Acad. and Inst. of Arts and Letters 1978–, American Acad. of Arts and Sciences 1985–. *Compositions include:* Quintet for strings 1958, Concerto for cello and orchestra 1966, Songs of Praise and Lamentation for soloists, chorus and orchestra 1974, Sonata for cello and piano 1985, Sonata a Cinque 1986, Dance Fantasy for orchestra 1986, Concerto for piano and orchestra 1990, Sinfonietta II 1990, Transcendental Modulations for orchestra 1993, Phantasyplay for piano 1994, Duos for horn and string quartet 1995, Musical Offerings for piano left hand 1998, Nine Bagatelles for piano 1999. *Recordings include:* Concerto No. 2 for piano and orchestra, Two Rilke Songs 1941, Four Wind Quintets 1967–84, Fantasy Variations for piano 1971, Dickinson Songs 1978, Concertino for piano, winds and timpani 1979, Ballade for piano 1980, Six New Etudes for piano 1984, Concerto No. 1 for piano and orchestra 1990, Sinfonietta II 1990. *Publications:*

Serial Composition and Atonality 1962, Twelve-Tone Tonality 1977, The Operas of Alban Berg, Vol. I, Wozzeck 1980, Vol. II, Lulu 1985, New Grove Second Viennese School (co-author) 1983, The Listening Composer 1990, The Right Notes 1995, Style and Idea in the Lyric Suite of Alban Berg 1995. *Contributions:* professional journals. *Honours:* Guggenheim Fellowships 1966, 1974, Pulitzer Prize for Wind Quintet IV 1986, MacArthur Fellowship 1986. *Address:* 138 Ipswich Street, Boston, MA 02215, USA.

**PERLMAN, Itzhak;** Israeli violinist; b. 31 Aug. 1945, Tel-Aviv; s. of Chaim Perlman and Shoshana Perlman; m. Toby Lynn Friedlander 1967; two s. three d. *Education:* Shulamit High School, Tel-Aviv, Tel-Aviv Acad. of Music and Juilliard School, USA, studied with Ivan Galamian and Dorothy De Lay. *Career:* gave recitals on radio at the age of 10; went to USA 1958; first recital at Carnegie Hall 1963; has played with maj. American orchestras 1964–; has toured Europe regularly and played with maj. European orchestras 1966–; debut in UK with London Symphony Orchestra 1968; toured Poland, Hungary, Far East; played with Israel Philharmonic Orchestra in fmr Soviet Union; appearances at Israel Festival and most European Festivals; Prin. Guest Conductor Detroit Symphony Orchestra 2001–; numerous recordings. *Honours:* Hon. DMus (Univ. of S Carolina) 1982, Dr hc (Yale, Harvard and Yeshivah Univs); several Grammy awards, EMI Artist of the Year 1995, Royal Philharmonic Soc. gold medal 1996; Medal of Liberty 1986, Nat. Medal of Arts 2001. *Current Management:* Askonas Holt Ltd, Lonsdale Chambers, 27 Chancery Lane, London, WC2A 1PF, England; IMG Artists, 22 825 Seventh Avenue, New York, NY 10019, USA.

**PERLMAN, Navah;** Concert Pianist; b. 1970, USA. *Education:* Studied with Ronit Lowenthal, and with Dorothy DeLay at Juilliard; Graduated Brown University. *Career:* Season 1999–2000 with St Paul Chamber Orchestra, Nashville SO, Philadelphia Orchestra, Pittsburgh SO and Fort Worth Chamber Orchestras; European debut at Ruhr Festival, Bochum, 1999; Further engagements with the Barcelona Symphony, Israel Philharmonic, New Japan PO, and National Orchestra of Mexico; Recital and concerto appearances with Kurt Nikkainen (violin) and Zuill Bailey (cello), including Kennedy Center, Metropolitan Museum, and Ravinia Festival; Beethoven's Triple Concerto throughout USA. *Current Management:* Askonas Holt Ltd, Lonsdale Chambers, 27 Chancery Lane, London, WC2A 1PF, England. *Telephone:* (20) 7400-1700. *Fax:* (20) 7400-1799. *E-mail:* info@askonasholt.co .uk. *Website:* www.askonasholt.co.uk.

**PERLONGO, Daniel;** Composer; b. 23 Sept. 1942, Gaastra, Michigan, USA. *Education:* Studied with Leslie Bassett and Ross Lee Finney at the University of Michigan (MM 1966) and with Goffredo Petrassi at the Academia di Santa Cecilia, Rome, 1966–68. *Career:* Resident at the American Academy in Rome, 1970–72; Professor of composition and theory at Indiana University of Pennsylvania, 1980–. *Compositions include:* Piano Sonata, 1966; Myriad for orchestra, 1968; Intervals, for string trio, 1968; Missa Brevis, 1968; Movement in Brass, for 12 instruments, 1969; Changes for wind ensemble, 1970; Ephemeron, for orchestra, 1972; Variations for chamber orchestra, 1973; Voyage for chamber orchestra, 1975; 2 String Quartets, 1973, 1983; Ricercar, for oboe, clarinet and bassoon, 1978; A Day at Xochimiloo, for wind quintet and piano, 1987; Lake Breezes, for chamber orchestra, 1990; Piano Concerto, 1992; Arcadian Suite for horn and harp, 1993; Three Songs for chorus, 1994; Shortcut from Bratislava for orchestra, 1994; Two Movements for orchestra, 1995; Sunburst, for clarinet and orchestra, 1995. *Honours:* NEA Fellowships, 1980 and 1995. *Address:* c/o ASCAP, ASCAP Building, 1 Lincoln Plaza, New York, NY 10023, USA.

**PERRAGUIN, Hélène;** Singer (Mezzo-soprano); b. 7 Sept. 1963, Tours, France. *Career:* Paris Opéra-Comique from 1986 in Die Zauberflöte and Suor Angelica; Season 1988–89 in Massenet's Amadis at St Etienne; Wagner's Ring at the Théâtre du Châtelet, Paris and The Love for Three Oranges at Aix-en-Provence; Opéra Bastille, Paris, 1991 as Pauline in The Queen of Spades; Sang Carmen for Opéra de Lyon, 1996; Leonore in La Favorite at Metz, 1993; Other roles include Mozart's Cherubino and Dorabella; Siebel in Faust and Ursula in Béatrice et Bénédict by Berlioz. *Address:* Opéra de Lyon, 1 Place de la Comédie, 69001 Lyon, France.

**PERRETT, Danielle Gillian,** MMus, ILTM; Musician and Teacher; b. 2 July 1958, London, England; m. *Education:* RCM Junior Department, Exeter Univ., London Univ. *Career:* musicianship and harp teacher, RCM Junior Department 1980–; debut, Purcell Room 1983; asst examiner, Trinity Coll. London 1988–; harp coach, Kent County Youth Orchestra 1985–; head of harp studies, London Coll. of Music 1996–; Mozart flute and harp concerto with Halstead, Brown, Hanover Band, Wigmore Hall 2001; performances at World Harp Congress, Prague 1999, Geneva 2002; broadcast for BBC World Service 2003; mem. Musicians' Union, Incorporated Soc. of Musicians, FITPRO, United Kingdom Harp Assćn, Clarsach Soc. *Compositions:* After Debussy, House Music, Lever Harp 2000, A Patchwork Suite, Technical Development for Harpists, Lift off for Harp (with David Gough). *Recordings:* Dussek and the Harp 1993, The Complete Chamber Music and Songs 1996, The Alabaster Box, Elis Pehkonen 2001, Tranquil Haven 2003. *Publications:* harp articles in UK Harp Association Magazine, reviews for BBC Music Magazine, features for World Harp Congress Review, magazines of Victorian Harp Society, South Australian Harp Society, Trinity College, London, Harp Syllabuses; contrib. to Incorporated Society of Musicians Music Journal, Clarsach Society London Branch Publications. *Honours:* Associated Board Sheila Mossman Prize 1974, Clothworkers Company Thomas Aitchison Trust Fund Award 1975, Henry

and Lily Davis Trust, Arts Council Award 1982, Royal Overseas Harp Prize 1983, Music for small groups, Arts Council Award 1991, Freedom of Worshipful Company of Musicians 2003. *Current Management:* International Artists' Management, 135 Stevenage Road, Fulham, London, SW6 6PB, England. *Telephone:* (20) 7381-9751 (office). *Fax:* (20) 7381-2406 (office). *Website:* danielleperrett.co.uk (home).

**PERRIERS, Danièle;** Singer (Soprano); b. 24 June 1945, Beaumont-le-Roger, Eure, France. *Education:* Studied in Paris with Janine Micheau, Roger Bourdin and Fanelu Revoil. *Career:* Debut: Marseille, 1968, as Sophie in Werther; Has appeared in France at the Paris Opéra and the Opéra-Comique, and in Nice, Bordeaux, Lyon, Rouen, Toulouse and Strasbourg; Also engaged at the Grand Théâtre de la Monnaie, Brussels, and in Liège and Monte Carlo; Glyndebourne Festival 1972–73 and 1976, as Despina and Blondchen; Widely known in the Coloratura and light lyrical repertory and in operettas; Sang also in works by Bizet, Boieldieu, Lecocq, Offenbach, Rossini and Richard Strauss. *Recordings:* Les Brigands by Offenbach; Die Entführung, Glyndebourne 1972; L'Amant jaloux by Grétry.

**PERRY, Douglas R.;** Singer (tenor); b. 19 Jan. 1945, Buffalo, New York, USA. *Career:* Sang at the New York City Opera from 1970 with his debut as Mozart's Basilio, and at Santa Fe Festival from 1971, notably in the US premieres of Reimann's Melusine in 1972 and Weir's A Night at the Chinese Opera in 1989; Sang in the premieres of Glass's Satyagraha at Stuttgart in 1980 and The Voyage at the Metropolitan in 1992; Other modern repertory has included Menotti's Tamu Tamu at Chicago in 1973 and Bernstein's A Quiet Place at Houston in 1983; Has also sung Rameau's Platée, M. Triquet in Eugene Onegin and Scaramuccio in Ariadne auf Naxos; Sang Quint in The Turn of the Screw at Montreal, 1996; Orlofsky in Die Fledermaus at Miami, 1998. *Recordings:* Satyagraha; A Quiet Place. *Address:* c/o Santa Fe Opera, PO Box 2408, Santa Fe, NM 87504, USA.

**PERRY, Elisabeth;** Concert Violinist; b. 1955, England. *Education:* Graduated, Menuhin School, 1972 and studied further with Dorothy DeLay and Oscar Shumsky at Juilliard. *Career:* Debut: South Bank, London, 1978; Concerts in Cincinnati, Florida, Chicago, Colorado and San Francisco and showings at Carnegie Hall with Alexander Schneider; Bartók's Second Concerto in Chicago; Further engagements in France, Switzerland, Italy and Germany; Leader of Deutsche Kammerakademie, 1987; Concerts in Sviatoslav Richter's Festival of British Music at Moscow and Leningrad, 1987; US championship of Schnittke's Quasi una Fantasia at Alice Tully Hall and the Berg Chamber Concerto at Queen Elizabeth Hall under Lionel Friend; Recital tour of New Zealand, 1990, and the Berg Violin Concerto in London; Plays a Giovanni Grancini Violin on loan from Yehudi Menuhin. *Recordings include:* Bach's Double Concerto, with Menuhin; Kirschner's Duo for Violin and Piano. *Honours:* Winner, Concert Artists Guild Competition, New York.

**PERRY, Eugene;** Singer (Baritone); b. 1955, Nashville, Tennessee, USA. *Education:* Studied in New York. *Career:* Debut: Sang St Ignatius in Four Saints in Three Acts by Virgil Thomson, with the Opera Ensemble of New York, 1986; Sang Tarj in premiere of Under the Double Moon, by Anthony Davis, St Louis, 1989; Don Giovanni in the Peter Sellars production of Mozart's opera at Purchase and elsewhere; European debut as Alidoro in La Cenerentola at Nice, 1989; Season 1990–91 at New York City Opera, as Shiskov in US stage premiere of From the House of the Dead and as Stolzius in Die Soldaten by Zimmermann; Appeared as the Devil in Dvořák's Devil and Kate at St Louis, 1990; Théâtre de la Monnaie, Brussels, 1991, as Mamoud in premiere of The Death of Klinghoffer by John Adams (repeated at Brooklyn Academy of Music, New York); Sang Mercutio in Cavalli's Calisto at Glimmerglass Opera, 1996. *Recordings include:* Video of Don Giovanni; The Death of Klinghoffer. *Honours:* George London Award from National Institute of Music Theater, 1986. *Address:* c/o New York City Opera, Lincoln Center, New York, NY 10023, USA.

**PERRY, Herbert;** Singer (Baritone); b. 1955, Nashville, Tennessee, USA. *Education:* Studied with his twin brother, Eugene, in Texas and Arizona. *Career:* Sang at the Houston and St Louis Operas from 1984; Sang at the Spoleto Festival at Charleston in 1987 as Citheron in Rameau's Platée, at Pepsico Summerfare in 1989 as Leporello in Don Giovanni, at Chicago Opera, Nice and Santa Fe in 1991 in I Puritani, as Mozart's Figaro and as Masetto, and sang Leporello at Toronto in 1992; Sang Mozart's Don Alfonso at Toronto, 1995; Season 1999–2000 in Weill's Die Burgschaft, at Charleston, and the premiere of In the Penal Colony by Philip Glass, for Seattle Opera. *Recordings include:* Video of Don Giovanni, in the production by Peter Sellars. *Address:* Lyric Opera Chicago, 20 North Wacker Drive, Chicago, IL 60606, USA.

**PERRY, Janet;** singer (soprano); b. 27 Dec. 1947, Minneapolis, Minnesota, USA; m. Alexander Malta. *Education:* Curtis Institute, Philadelphia, with Euphemia Gregory. *Career:* debut Linz 1969, as Zerlina in Don Giovanni; Appearances in Munich and Cologne as Norina (Don Pasquale), Adina (L'Elisir d'amore), Blondchen (Die Entführung), Zerbinetta (Ariadne auf Naxos) and Olympia (Les Contes d'Hoffmann); Guest engagements in Vienna, Frankfurt, Stuttgart and at the Aix-en-Provence Festival; Glyndebourne 1977, as Aminta in Die schweigsame Frau; Numerous opera and operetta films for German television; Salzburg Festival; Sang Zerbinetta in Ariadne auf Naxos, RAI Turin, 1989; Violetta at the 1990 Martina Franca Festival; Season 1992 as Gluck's Eurydice at Bonn and Cleopatra in Giulio Cesare at the Halle Handel Festival. *Recordings:* Papagena in Die Zauberflöte, conducted by Karajan; Falstaff, Der Rosenkavalier, Beethoven's Ninth,

Bruckner Te Deum; Nannetta in Falstaff; Egk's Peer Gynt. *E-mail:* janetperry@canada.com. *Website:* www.janetperry.com.

**PERRY, Jennifer;** Singer (Soprano); b. 1969, Rotterdam, Netherlands. *Education:* Studied at the Royal Academy and the Guildhall School of Music. *Career:* Concerts include Handel's Dixit Dominus on tour with the Tallis Scholars and regular appearances with other leading choral societies; Other repertoire includes Mozart's C minor Mass and songs by Schubert and Duparc; Operatic roles include Despina, Susanna and First Lady. *Address:* c/o Ron Gonsalves Management, 7 Old Town, Clapham, London SW4 0JT, England.

**PERRY, Ross;** Stage Director and Choreographer; b. 1954, Montreal, Canada. *Education:* Studied in Atlanta and Jacksonville. *Career:* Resident Assistant Director for Houston Grand Opera from 1986, working with such operas as Boris Godunov, Così fan tutte, Turandot, Figaro, Salome and Faust; Assistant at the Los Angeles Music Center with Idomeneo and at Santa Fe and Spoleto; Has worked further as Director and/or Choreographer at Houston, with Hansel and Gretel, The Mikado, Mefistofele and Desert of Roses by Robert Moran; Further engagements with Australian Opera (Così fan tutte, 1992), Victoria State Opera (Carmen) and Washington Opera (Mefistofele, 1995). *Current Management:* Athole Still International Management, Forresters Hall, 25–27 Westow Street, London, SE19 3RY, England. *Telephone:* (20) 8771-5271. *Fax:* (20) 8768-6600. *Website:* www.atholestill.com.

**PERTIS, Attila;** Pianist; b. 5 March 1966, Budapest, Hungary; m. Monika Egri, 28 June 1991. *Education:* Bartók Conservatory, Budapest; Liszt Music Academy, Budapest; Music Academy, Vienna. *Career:* Performances, Hungarian Days, London, 1989, and Musikverein, Vienna, 1991; Appeared at Budapest Spring Festival and Carinthian Summer Festival, Austria; With Monika Egri founded Egri and Pertis Piano Duo, 1980s; Television and radio recordings, Hungary, Austria, Italy. *Recordings:* For Hungarian radio and television, Austrian radio and television (ORF); CD, Journey Around the World, 1995; Liszt: Opera Fantasies and Transcriptions for two pianos, 1997–98. *Contributions:* Die Presse; Kronen Zeitung; Piano Journal. *Current Management:* Annart Artists Management, Barkács utca 7, 1221 Budapest, Hungary; J A Ellison, International Artists Management, 135 Stevenage Road, Fulham, London SW6 6PB, England; Künstlermanagement Till Dönch, Weimarer Strasse 48, 1180, Vienna. *Address:* Kaltwasserstrasse 1, 3413 Unterkirchbach, Austria.

**PERTUSI, Michele;** Singer (Bass); b. 1965, Parma, Italy. *Education:* Studied in Parma with Carlo Bergonzi. *Career:* Debut: Modena, as Silva in Ernani, 1984; Appearances at Teatro Donizetti, Bergamo, Ravenna Festival and Teatro Comunale, Bologna; Teatro Regio, Parma, 1987–, notably as Dulcamara, 1992; Season 1992 as Mozart's Count at Orchestra Hall, Chicago, and Figaro at Florence; Sang Talbot in Maria Stuarda at Barcelona, Assur in Semiramide at Pesaro; Other roles include Raimondo in Lucia di Lammermoor, Pagano in I Lombardi, and Rossini's Maometto; Sang Don Giovanni at Lausanne, 1996; Sang in Lucrezia Borgia at La Scala, 1998; Season 2000–01 as Rossini's Selim and Alidoro at Monte Carlo, Mahomet in Le Siège de Corinthe at Pesaro and Don Giovanni at Coruña; the Villiains in Hoffmann, and Alidoro, at Covent Garden, and the Berlioz Mephisto on London's South Bank; Don Alfonso at the Met and Guillaune Tell for the Vienna Staatsoper; London Proms, 2002. *Recordings include:* Mozart's Figaro, Assur, Alidoro, Silva, Lodovico in Otello; La Wally by Catalani. *Address:* c/o Teatro Regio, Via Garibaldi 16, 43100 Parma, Italy.

**PERUSKA, Jan;** violist; b. 1954, Czechoslovakia. *Education:* studied in Prague with members of the Smetana Quartet. *Career:* co-Founder and Violist of the Stamic Quartet of Prague, 1977; Performances at the Prague Young Artists and the Bratislava Music Festivals; Tours to Spain, Austria, France, Switzerland, Germany and Eastern Europe; Tour of the USA 1980, debut concerts in the United Kingdom at London and Birmingham, 1983; Further British tours, 1985, 1987, 1988 (Warwick Arts Festival) and 1989 (20 concerts); Gave the premiere of Helmut Eder's 3rd Quartet, 1986; Season 1991–92 with visit to the Channel Islands (Festival of Czech Music), Netherlands, Finland, Austria and France, Edinburgh Festival and debut tours of Canada, Japan and Indonesia. *Recordings:* Shostakovich No. 13, Schnittke No. 4; Mozart K589 and K370; Dvořák, Martinů and Janáček complete quartets. *Honours:* (with members of Stamic Quartet): Prize Winner, International Festival of Young Soloists, Bordeaux, 1977; Winner, 1986 ORF (Austrian Radio) International String Quartet Competition (followed by live broadcast from the Salzburg Mozarteum); Academie Charles Cros Grand Prix du Disque, 1991, for Dvořák Quartets. *Current Management:* Robert Gilder & Co., Enterprise House, 59–65 Upper Ground, London, SE1 9PQ, England. *Telephone:* (20) 7928-9008. *Fax:* (20) 7928-9755. *E-mail:* rgilder@robert-gilder .com.

**PERUSSO, Mario;** Conductor and Composer; b. 16 Sept. 1936, Buenos Aires, Argentina. *Career:* Deputy Conductor at Teatro Colón, Buenos Aires, giving his own opera Escorial in 1989 and Puccini's La Rondine, 1990; Conducted Otello and Turandot at La Plata, season 1990–91. *Compositions include:* Operas: La Voz del Silencio, 1 act, Buenos Aires, 1969; Escorial, 1 act, Buenos Aires, 1989; Sor Juana Ines de la Cruz, 1991–92, premiered, 1993; Guayaquil, lyric drama, 1993; Conducted Tosca at La Plata, 1995. *Recordings include:* La Voz del Silencio. *Address:* c/o Teatro Colón, Buenos Aires, Cerrito 618, 1010 Buenos Aires, Argentina.

**PERUZZI, Elio;** Clarinettist and Conservatory Teacher; b. 14 Oct. 1927, Malcesine, Verona, Italy. *Education:* Canetti Institute, Vicenza; B Marcello Conservatory, Venice. *Career:* Debut: Olympic Theatre, Vicenza; Soloist with Virtuosi di Roma, Solisti Veneti, Solisti di Milano, 1950–; String Quartets of Milan, Ostrava, Brno, Prague and Zagreb, and with Brno Philharmonic Orchestra, Bozen Orchestra, Padua Chamber Orchestra, Filarmonico di Bologna, 1960–; Founder, Bartók Trio (clarinet, violin, piano), 1958, Piccola Camerata Italian (mediaeval, renaissance and baroque instruments), 1967; Performances, Europe, USA, South America, USSR, Canada, 1960–. *Recordings:* Mozart Clarinet Quintet with Moravian Quartet, 18th and 19th century music with Virtuosi di Roma. *Publications:* Esercizi e Studi Method for Recorder, 1972; Editor, various works including: Sonatas by Robert Valentine for 2 Recorders, 1973; G Rossini Variations for Clarinet and Orchestra, 1978; A Ponchielli's Il Convegno for 2 Clarinets and Piano, 1988. *Honours:* Accademia Tiberina, Rome. *Current Management:* Francesca Diano, Via Vallisnieri 13, 35100 Padova, Italy. *Address:* Via Monte Solarolo 9, 35100 Padova, Italy.

**PEŠEK, Libor;** Czech conductor; b. 22 June 1933, Prague. *Education:* Prague Acad. of Musical Arts. *Career:* studied conducting with Karel Ancerl, Vaclav Neumann and Václav Smetáček; f. Prague Chamber Harmony 1958; Chief Conductor Slovak Philharmonic 1980–81; Conductor-in-Residence Czech Philharmonic Orchestra 1982–, Germany tour 1998; Prin. Conductor and Artistic Adviser Royal Liverpool Philharmonic Orchestra 1982–97, Hon. Conductor 1997–; Visiting Conductor Prague Symphony Orchestra 1989–; Pres. Prague Spring Festival 1994–; mem. Bd of Supervisors OPS Prague European City of Culture 1999–; conducted Royal Liverpool Philharmonic Orchestra, Prague Spring Festival 2000; has conducted Philharmonia, London Symphony, Royal Philharmonic, BBC Philharmonic, Hallé, Oslo Philharmonic, Danish Radio, Los Angeles Philharmonic and Cincinnati, Dallas, Minnesota, Pittsburgh, Cleveland, Montreal, Indianapolis and Philadelphia orchestras, Orchestra of La Scala, Milan and Orchestre de Paris; charity concerts after floods in Czech Repub. 2002. *Recordings include:* works by Dvořák, Suk, Janáček, Martinů and Britten. *Honours:* Hon. mem. Preston Univ. 1997; Hon. Fellow, Univ. of Cen. Lancashire 1997; Hon. KBE; Classic Prize for Extraordinary Merit in Musical Culture (Czech Repub.) 1997, Journal Harmonie Lifelong Contrib. to Czech Culture 2002. *Current Management:* IMG Artists (Europe), Lovell House 616 Chiswick High Road, London, W4 5RX, England. *Telephone:* (20) 8233-5800. *Fax:* (20) 8233-5801. *E-mail:* cdennes@imgworld.com.

**PESKO, Zoltan;** Composer and Conductor; b. 15 Feb. 1937, Budapest, Hungary. *Education:* Diploma, Liszt Ferenc Music Academy, Budapest, 1962; Master Courses in Composing with Goffredo Petrassi, Accademia di S Cecilia, Rome, Italy and in Conducting, Pierre Boulez, Basel, Switzerland and Franco Ferrara, Rome, Italy, 1963–66. *Career:* Debut: As Composer and Conductor, Hungarian television, 1960; Work with Hungarian television, 1960–63; Assistant Conductor to Lorin Maazel, West Berlin Opera and Radio Orchestra, West Berlin, 1969–73; Performances at Teatro alla Scala, 1970; Professor, Hochschule, West Berlin, 1971–74; Chief Conductor, Teatro Communale, Bologna, Italy, 1974–; Conducted Wagner's Ring at Turin, 1988; Concert performance of Mussogsky's Salammbô at the 1989 Holland Festival; Teatro Lirico Milan 1990, premiere of Blimunda by Azio Corghi; Has also led the premieres of Bussotti's Il Catalogo è questo, 1960; Donatoni's Voci, 1974, In Cauda, 1982, Tema 1982, Atem 1985; Jolivet's Bogomile suite 1982; Dies by Wolfgang Rihm, 1985; Fünf Geistliche Lieder von Bach by Dieter Schnebel, 1985; Season 1992 with Der fliegende Holländer at Naples and Le Grand Macabre at Zürich; Conducted Fidelio at Rome, 1996. *Compositions:* Tension, String Quartet, 1967; Trasformazioni, 1968; Bildinis einer Heligen, Soprano and Children's Choir, Chamber Ensemble, 1969; Jelek, 1974. *Recordings:* Various for CBS Italiana. *Contributions:* Melos. *Honours:* Prize for Composition, Academia di S Cecilia, Rome, Italy, 1966; Premio Discografico, for recording debut as Conductor, Italian Critics, 1973. *Current Management:* Musart, 20121 Milan, Via Manzoni 31, Italy. *Address:* 40125 Bologna, Teatro Communale, Largo Respighi, Italy.

**PESKOVA, Inna;** Violist; b. 1960, Moscow, Russia. *Education:* Studied at Moscow Conservatoire with Alexei Shislov. *Career:* Co-founder, Glazunov Quartet, 1985; Many concerts in Russia and recent appearances in: Greece; Poland; Belgium; Germany; Italy; Works by Beethoven and Schumann at Beethoven Haus in Bonn; Further engagements in Canada and Netherlands; Teacher at Moscow State Conservatoire and Resident at Tchaikovsky Conservatoire; Repertoire includes works by: Borodin; Shostakovich; Tchaikovsky in addition to standard works. *Recordings include:* CDs of the six quartets of Glazunov. *Honours:* With Glazunov Quartet: Prizewinner of Borodin Quartet and Shostakovich Chamber Music Competitions. *Address:* c/o Sonata (Glazunov Quartet), 11 Northpark Street, Glasgow G20 7AA, Scotland.

**PETCHERSKY, Alma;** Concert Pianist; b. 1950, Argentina. *Education:* Studied with Roberto Caamano in Buenos Aires; Maria Curcio in London and with Magda Tagliaferro and Bruno Seidlhofer of the Vienna Academy. *Career:* Debut: Teatro Colón Buenos Aires with Bartók's 3rd Concerto; Concert and broadcasting engagements in Russia, USA, Canada, Spain, Germany, Brazil, Czechoslovakia, Mexico and the Far East; London appearances at the Wigmore Hall. *Recordings:* Works of the German, French and Russian schools, Latin-American and Spanish Romantic Composers; Complete piano music by Ginastera; Recordings for the BBC, London and CBC, Canada.

*Current Management:* M Gilbert Management. *Address:* 516 Wadsworth Avenue, Philadelphia, PA 19119, USA.

**PETER, Fritz;** Singer (Tenor); b. 7 Nov. 1925, Camorino, Switzerland. *Education:* Studied in Winterthur, Zürich and Stuttgart, 1945–55. *Career:* Sang at Ulm Stadttheater, 1955–61, Zürich Opera from 1961, notably in premieres of Martinů's Greek Passion, 1961, Sutermeister's Madame Bovary, 1967, and Kelterborn's Ein Engel kommt nach Babylon, 1977; Guest appearances at Geneva, Lucerne, Munich, Hamburg, Frankfurt, Cologne, Nice, Milan, Helsinki, Vienna and Edinburgh, as Ernesto, Max and Tristan; Many concert performances. *Recordings include:* Monteverdi's Poppea and Ulisse conducted by Nikolaus Harnoncourt. *Address:* Opernhaus Zürich, Falkenstrasse 1, 8008 Zürich, Switzerland.

**PETERS, Roberta,** DLitt, DMus; American singer (soprano); b. 4 May 1930, New York; d. of Sol and Ruth (née Hirsch) Peters; m. Bertram Fields 1955; two s. *Education:* Elmira and Ithaca Colls. *Career:* Debut in Don Giovanni, Metropolitan Opera, New York 1950; has performed at numerous opera houses and festivals including Royal Opera House, Covent Garden, London, Vienna State Opera, Munich Opera and West Berlin Opera, Germany, Vienna and Salzburg, Austria, and Munich festivals, Bolshoi Theatre and Kirov Opera, USSR, now Russian Fed.; tours include USA, Russian Fed., Israel, People's Repub. of China, Japan, Repub. of China (Taiwan), S. Korea and Scandinavia; Chair. Nat. Inst. Music Theater 1991–; mem. Nat. Council of Arts 1992; Hon. LHD (Westminster) 1974, (Lerigh) 1977; Hon. D MUS (Colby) 1980; Hon. DFA (St John's) 1982; Hon. D LITT (New Rochelle) 1989; first American recipient of Bolshoi Medal; named Woman of the Year by Fed. of Women's Clubs 1964, Nat. Medal for Arts 1998. *Publication:* Début at the Met. *Address:* ICM Artists Ltd, 40 W 57th St, New York, NY 10019, USA (office); Scarsdale, New York, NY 10583, USA (home).

**PETERSEN, Dennis;** Singer (Tenor); b. 11 May 1954, Iowa, USA. *Education:* Studied at University of Iowa and with San Francisco Opera's Merola Programme. *Career:* Concert appearances in Mozart's Requiem, Messiah and Bach's Magnificat with St Paul Chamber Orchestra; Haydn's Theresienmesse at Spoleto Festival in Charleston; Sang in Tippett's A Child of Our Time at Carnegie Hall and concerts with New Jersey and Baltimore Symphonies under David Zinman and Calgary Philharmonic under Mario Bernadi; Engagements with San Francisco Opera, 1985–, including: Don Quichotte, Captain in Wozzeck, Mime in Der Ring des Nibelungen, Die Meistersinger, and Tybald in Roméo et Juliette; Lyric Opera of Chicago debut in season 1992–93 as Mime in Das Rheingold under Zubin Mehta; Sang Carlo in Donizetti's Il Duca d'Alba at Spoleto Festival; Season 1994–95 at Chicago Lyric Opera in Boris Godunov, and Mime in Siegfried; Metropolitan Opera in Lady Macbeth of Mtsensk (debut) and as Bob Boles in Peter Grimes; Season 1995–96 at San Francisco Opera in Anna Bolena and Madama Butterfly, Chicago Lyric Opera, Andrea Chénier–The Ring Cycle and Miami Opera in Ariadne auf Naxos; Leo in Antheil's Transatlantic for Minnesota Opera, 1998; Sang Monostatos at the Met, 2000. *Address:* c/o San Francisco Opera, War Memorial House, Van Ness Avenue, San Francisco, CA, USA.

**PETERSEN, Marlis;** Singer (Soprano); b. 1969, Sindelfingen, nr Stuttgart, Germany. *Education:* Studied with Sylvia Geszty and at the NY City Dance School, Stuttgart. *Career:* Appearances at Nuremberg Opera from 1991, as Aennchen in Der Freischütz, Mozart's Blondchen, Oscar, Adele (Die Fledermaus), Rosina and The Queen of Night; Concert engagements in Porto, Madrid, Milan, Brussels and Amsterdam; Deutsche Oper am Rhein from 1998, as Mozart's Serpetta and Susanna, Marie in La Fille du Régiment and Norina (Don Pasquale); Season 2000–01 as Lulu at Kassel, Oscar at Bregenz, and Adele at the Opéra Bastille; Covent Garden debut 2002, as Zerbinetta in Ariadne auf Naxos; Sang Lulu at the Vienna Staatsoper, 2002. *Honours:* Prizewinner at Berlin and J. Offenbach Competitions, 1990–91. *Address:* c/o Deutsche Oper am Rhein, Heinrich Heine Allee 16 a, D–40213 Dusseldorf, Germany.

**PETERSEN, Nils (Holger);** Composer and Minister of the Danish Church; b. 27 April 1946, Copenhagen, Denmark; m. Frances Ellen Hopenwasser, 11 Sept 1971, divorced 1989, 1 s., 1 d. *Education:* Degree in Mathematics, University of Copenhagen, 1969; Postgraduate studies in Mathematics, Universities of Copenhagen and Oslo; Studies in Theology, Copenhagen University; Piano studies with Elisabeth Klein, composition with Ib Norholm; PhD in Theology, University of Copenhagen, 1994. *Career:* Minister of The Danish Church, 1974–; Research Fellow, 1990–, Research Lecturer, 1995, University of Copenhagen; External Professor of Gregorian Studies, University of Trondheim, Norway, 1997–; Freelance Composer with compositions performed on Danish, Swedish, Norwegian and Dutch Radio and on Danish television, at Nordic Music Days and various concerts in many countries; mem, Danish Composers Society; Board of the Nordic Society for Interart Studies. *Compositions:* Piano and Guitar solo works, published and recorded; Fools Play, opera, 1970 first performed in 1985; Vigil for Thomas Beckett, liturgical opera, 1989; Church Cantatas, 1971, 1974 and 1976; Antiphony for Good Friday for 9 Instruments and Voice; 2 Wind Quintets; Solo works for violin, piano and organ; The Lauds of Queen Ingeborg, liturgical opera, 1991; Fragments of a Distant Voice, Electrophonic work for the Danish State Radio, 1992; Concerto for Clarinet in B and Octet, 1994; A Plain Song, piano. *Recordings:* Various instrumental works on major labels. *Publications:* Kristendom i Musikken, 1987; Liturgy and the Arts in the Middle Ages, 1996. *Contributions:* Various articles on Theologico-musical aspects of the

western culture in musical and theological papers. *Honours:* Hakon Borresen Memorial Prize, 1993. *Address:* Mimersgade 56, 1 tv, 2200 Copenhagen N, Denmark.

**PETERSON, Claudette;** Singer (Soprano); b. 15 July 1953, Lakewood, Ohio, USA. *Education:* Studied at San Francisco Conservatory. *Career:* Sang at San Francisco Opera from 1975; Washington Opera, 1979, as Blondchen in Die Entführung, Boston, 1980, as Dunyasha in War and Peace, Chicago, 1982, as Adele in Fledermaus; New York City Opera, 1985–86, as Manon and Lisette in La Rondine; Sang Yum-Yum in The Mikado for Canadian Opera at Toronto, 1986; Other roles have included Lucia (Arizona Opera) and Gilda (Shreveport); Further engagements at Buffalo, Houston, Geneva and Honolulu; Frequent concert appearances. *Recordings include:* Musgrave's A Christmas Carol. *Address:* c/o New York City Opera, Lincoln Center, New York, NY 10023, USA.

**PETERSON, John (Murray);** Composer; b. 14 Jan. 1957, Wollongong, New South Wales, Australia. *Education:* BMus, honours, 1990, MMus, 1994, Sydney University; PhD, Sydney University. *Career:* Orchestral works performed by Queensland Philharmonic Orchestra, Tasmanian Symphony Orchestra, West Australian Symphony Orchestra, New Zealand Symphony Orchestra and the National Orchestra of Wales; Broadcasts on ABC, Classic FM and BBC Radio 3; Participant, Australian Composers' Orchestral Forum, 1998, 2001; mem, Australian Music Centre; Musicological Society of Australia; Fellowship of Australian Composers. *Compositions:* Ex Tenebris Lux, orchestra, 1989; At The Hawk's Well, music theatre piece, 1990; Walking On Glass, piano solo, 1992; A Voice From The City, voice and small ensemble, 1994; Cyberia, orchestra, 1996; The Still Point, cello and piano, 1997; Diabolic Dance, violin and cello, 1997; Rituals in Transfigured Time, orchestra, 1997; Of Quiet Places, voice and guitar, 1998; Port Kembla, orchestra, 1998; Staring at the Sun, large mixed ensemble, 1998; Drive, alto saxophone and piano, 1998; WiredLife, mandolin duo, 1999; Spike, cello duo, 1999; At the Still Point, viola and piano, 1999; Landmarks, brass quartet, 1999; From Mountains to Sea, mixed sextet, 1999; Moving Fast Through Autumn Light, solo mandolin, 2000; Tallawarra, string quartet, 2000; Encomium, clarinet and cello, 2000; Three Ritual Dances, solo piano, 2000; Illawarra Music, large orchestra, 2000; The Earth That Fire Touches, orchestra, soprano soloist and SATB chorus, 2000; Five Islands, solo piano, 2001; Nocturnalia, orchestra, 2001; New England Dances, Orchestra, 2002; Liquid Steel, String quartet, 2002; Woollungah Dances, three solo clarinets and orchestra, 2002; The velocity of Celebration, mixed ensemble, 2003; Shadows and Light, soprano and tenor solo, SATB chorus, string orchestra and percussion, 2004. *Recordings:* Greenbaum Hindson Peterson, 1995; Drive, 2000; Spike, 2001. *Honours:* Semi-finalist, Masterprize, London, 1997, 2001. *Address:* 67 Kingsclear Road, Alexandria, NSW 2015, Australia.

**PETERSONS, Ingus;** Latvian singer (tenor); b. 12 Feb. 1959, Gulbene. *Education:* Riga Acad. *Career:* debut in Riga 1985 as Lensky in Eugene Onegin; sang at the Riga Opera as the Duke of Mantua, Alfredo, Don Carlo and Nemorino; sang at Wexford Festival as Arturo in La Straniera by Bellini 1987, Opera North, Leeds as Edgardo in Lucia di Lammermoor 1988; sang Hoffmann at the Folksoperan Stockholm 1991; other roles have included Des Grieux in Massenet's Manon and the Italian Singer in Der Rosenkavalier; sang Rodolfo in La Bohème and Riccardo in Un ballo in maschera at Riga Opera 2004. *Address:* c/o Latvian National Opera, Aspazijas Blvd 3, 1050 Riga, Latvia. *Telephone:* 371 707 3715. *Fax:* 371 722 8930. *E-mail:* info@opera .lv. *Website:* www.opera.lv.

**PETIBON, Patricia;** Singer (Soprano); b. 1969, France. *Education:* Studied in Paris. *Career:* Appearances with Les Arts Florissants and at the Beaune Festival as Dano in Armida abbandonata by Jommelli and as Argene in L'Olimpiade by Pergolesi; Season 1996-97 as Rameau's Aricie at the Paris Palais Garnier and as Mozart's Blondchen at Strasbourg and Montpellier; Paris Châtelet as Landi's Sant' Alessio; Guest appearances at Aix-en-Provence, La Scala Milan, Buenos Aires and the Wigmore Hall, London; Season 1999 as Zerbinetta at Strasbourg, Lakmé at Toulouse and Gluck's Amor at the Châtelet; Season 2000-01 as Offenbach's Olympia at the Vienna Staatsoper and Zelmira in Haydn's Armida at the Theater an der Wien; Ophélie in Hamlet at Toulouse and Dalinda in Handel's Ariodante in Paris; Frequent concert appearances. *Recordings include:* Stratonice by Méhul; Sant'Alessio by Landi, Die Entführung, Acis and Galatea (Erato); Werther, Haydn's Armida (EMI). *Address:* c/o Opéra et Concert, 1 rue Volney, F-75002 Paris, France.

**PETIT, Jean-Louis;** Conductor, Harpsichordist and Composer; b. 20 Aug. 1937, Favrolles, France. *Education:* Studied in Paris with Igor Markevitch, Pierre Boulez and Olivier Messiaen. *Career:* Organised and conducted various ensembles in the regions of Champagne, 1958–63 and Picardy, 1964–70; Performances on Radio and Television, tours of Europe and the USA; Co-directed the Paris Summer Festival, 1972–77; Founder member of the contemporary music group Musique Plus; Director of the Association musicale international d'echange (AMIE); Director of the Ecole Nationale de Musique of Ville d'Avray. *Compositions include:* Au-delà du signe for Orchestra; De Quelque Part Effondrée de l'homme for Quartet; Continuelles discontinués for Percussion; (82 Opus) Transcriptions of early music. *Recordings include:* Works by Boismortier, Leclair, Marais, Rameau, Lully, Mouret, Devienne, Campra, Francoeur, Couperin and Mondonville; Roussel's Sinfonietta; Les

Troqueurs by d'Auvergne; 2nd Symphonie of Gounod; Chamber Music by Saint-Saëns.

**PETKOV, Dimiter;** Singer (Bass); b. 5 March 1939, Sofia, Bulgaria; m. Anne-Lise Petkov. *Education:* Sofia Music Academy with Christo Brambarov. *Career:* Debut: Sofia as Ramfis and Zaccaria, 1964; Guest appearances, Glyndebourne Festival, 1968, 1970, as Osmin and Gremin; Rostropovich Festival, Aldeburgh, 1983; Earl's Court, London, 1988; Birmingham Arena, 1991; Daytona Festival with London Symphony Orchestra, 1993; Arena di Verona as Philipp II, 1969, As Zaccaria, 1981, as Ramfis, 1986, 1987; Appearances: Vienna State Opera, 1972–86, 1990, as Philip II, Ramfis, Boris, Khovansky, Mephisto; Madrid, Barcelona, 1978–86, 1990; Chicago, 1980; Bologna, 1980–83, 1988; Catania, Palermo, Lecce, 1981, 1984, 1986; La Scala, Milan, 1981, 1984, 1989; Washington DC, 1982, 1984; Carnegie Hall, New York City, 1982, 1984, 1989; Zürich, Hamburg, Bonn, 1984–85, 1990; Naples, 1984, 1991; Rome, 1987, 1992; Florence, 1986–89, 1991; Monte Carlo, 1986, 1989; Paris, 1986, 1988; Deutsche Oper Berlin, 1988–93; Dallas, 1989, 1993; Opéra Bastille, Paris, 1990–93; Appeared with Berlin Philharmonic, London Symphony Orchestra, National Symphony Washington DC, Boston Symphony Orchestra at Tanglewood, Israel Philharmonic (Zubin Mehta) at Tel-Aviv, Montreal Symphony Orchestra, RAI Orchestras in Milan, Rome, Naples, Orchestre de Paris, Orchestre National de France, Concertgebouw Amsterdam, St Petersburg Philharmonic Jerusalem Symphony, San Francisco Symphony; In demand for all the Verdi bass roles: Philipp, Zaccaria, Fiesco; Bellini, Rossini, Donizetti; Mephisto by Gounod in French repertoire; All main roles in Russian repertoire: Boris Godunov, Ivan Khovansky, Ivan Susanin, others; Sang Shishkov in From the House of the Dead, Opéra du Rhin, 1996; Old Prisoner in Lady Macbeth at Florence, 1998. *Recordings:* EMI, Lady Macbeth of Mtsensk; EMI, Shostkovich 13th Symphony with London Symphony Orchestra; Aleko by Rachmaninov; Khovanshchina by Mussorgsky; Erato, Yolanta by Tchaikovsky, Mussorgsky cycles and Boris arias, 1989; Koch, Shostakovich cycles, 1993; Sony, Boris Godunov, 1992; Verdi Requiem at Eckphrasis Records, New York, 1994; Has sung with such conductors as Abbado, Mehta, Bartoletti, Previn, Molinari-Pradelli, Rostropovich, Ozawa, Rozdestvensky, Prêtre, Bernstein, Pritchard, Maazel and Giulini; Appeared in Werner Herzog's film Fitzcarraldo and sang Ernani at Manaus. *Address:* Rue du Conseil-Général 6, 1205 Geneva, Switzerland.

**PETRE, Leonardus (Josephus);** Professor of Trumpet; b. 27 Jan. 1943, Saint Triniden, Belgium; m. Maes Arlette, 24 July 1965, 2 s. *Education:* Bachelor of Medicine, University of Leuven, 1962; Music schools of St Trinden en Hasselt, First prizes in Music-Reading and Trumpet; Royal Music Academy (Conservatoire Royal) Brussels, First Prizes in Music Reading, Transposition, Trumpet and Musical History. *Career:* Teacher of trumpet and several other brass instruments in several music schools; Professor of Trumpet at the Lemmens Institute, Leuven; Many appearances as member of orchestra or soloist on the Belgian and German radio and television; Soloist at many classical concerts in Belgium, France, Netherlands and Germany; Trumpet-Soloist with The New Music Group, and Collegium Instrumentale Brugense; Member of the Xenakis Ensemble, Netherlands; Creator and leader of The Belgian Brass Quintet 2, 1973–79; Conductor of brassband and fanfare; Specialist in playing Bach-trumpet (piccolo) and copies of very old trumpets; mem, International Trumpet Guild. *Recordings:* Several cantatas of J. S. Bach with La Chapelle des Minimes, Brussels. *Contributions:* Several articles concerning the trumpet and brass playing in local music magazines. *Address:* Smoldersstraat 44, 3910 Herk de Stad, Belgium.

**PETRENKO, Mikhail;** Singer (bass); b. 1976, St Petersburg, Russia. *Education:* St Petersburg Conservatoire. *Career:* Debut: Kirov Opera 1998, as Ivasenko in Prokofiev's Semyon Kotko; Young Singers' Academy of the Mariinsky Theatre, St Petersburg, from 1998; Other roles have included Svetozar in Ruslan and Lyudmila, Mozart's Masetto, Fafner in Das Rheingold and the King of Egypt in Aida; Sang Bermyata in Rimsky-Korsakov's The Snow Maiden, Amsterdam and London (concert performances), 1999–2000; Ivasenko in the British premiere of Semyon Kotko, with the Kirov Opera at Covent Garden, 2000. *Address:* c/o Kirov Opera, Mariinsky Theatre, 1 Theatre Square, St Petersburg, Russia.

**PETRENKO, Vasily;** Russian conductor; *Principal Conductor, Royal Liverpool Philharmonic Orchestra;* b. 1976. *Education:* St Petersburg Capella Boys Music School, St Petersburg Conservatory, masterclasses with Ilya Musin, Mariss Jansons, Yuri Temirkanov, Esa-Pekka Salonen. *Career:* Resident Conductor St Petersburg State Opera and Ballet Theatre 1994–97; Prin. Guest Conductor St Petersburg State Orchestra of Classical and Contemporary Music 1998–; Chief Conductor State Acad. Orchestra of St Petersburg 2005–06; Prin. Conductor Royal Liverpool Philharmonic Orchestra 2006–; has also conducted St Petersburg Symphony and Chamber Orchestras, Royal Orchestra of Flanders, Barcelona SO, Norrköping Symphony, BBC Nat. Orchestra of Wales, BBC Philharmonic, Swedish Radio Symphony, Netherlands Symphony, Spanish Nat. Orchestra, City of Birmingham SO, Moscow Philharmonic, Rotterdam Philharmonic, Orchestre National de Capitole de Toulouse. *Honours:* first prize Shostakovich Choral Conducting Competition, St Petersburg 1997, second prize Prokoviev Conducting Competition, St Petersburg 2003, first prize Cadaques Int. Conducting Competition, Spain 2004. *Current Management:* c/o Nicholas Mathias, IMG Artists, Lovell House, 616 Chiswick High Road, London, W4 5RX, England. *Address:* Royal Liverpool Philharmonic Orchestra, Philharmonic Hall, Hope Street, Liverpool, L1 9BP, England (office). *Telephone:* (151) 210-2895 (office). *Fax:* (151) 210-2902 (office). . *Website:* www.liverpoolphil.com (office).

**PETRI, Michala;** Danish musician (recorder player); b. 7 July 1958, Copenhagen; d. of Kanny Sambleben and Hanne Petri; m. Lars Hannibal 1992; two d. *Education:* Staatliche Hochschule für Musik und Theater, Hanover. *Career:* debut aged five, Danish Radio 1964; soloist with Orchestra Tivoli, Copenhagen 1969; over 3,000 concerts in Europe, USA, Japan, Australia and the Far East; numerous appearances at festivals, performances on TV and radio; performs frequently world-wide with lutenist and guitarist, Lars Hannibal; hon. artist, Soro Int. Organ Festival 1992; has inspired and initiated various contemporary compositions by Malcolm Arnold, Vagn Holmboe, Per Norgaard, Thomas Koppel, Daniel Boertz, Gary Kulesha and others; mem. of presidium, UNICEF Denmark; bd mem., Wilhelm Hansen Foundation; Vice-Pres., Cancer Asscn, Denmark. *Recordings:* more than 50 albums, including 12 with the Acad. of St Martin-in-the-Fields, Bach Sonatas and Handel Sonatas with Keith Jarrett, Vivaldi Concertos with Heinz Holliger, Henryk Szeryng, contemporary concerts with English Chamber Orchestra, three albums with Lars Hannibal. *Publications:* ed. of several works for Wilhelm Hansen and Moeck. *Honours:* Jacob Gade Prize 1969, 1975, Critics' Prize of Honour 1976, Nording Radio Prize 1977, Niels Prize 1980, Tagea Brandts Prize 1980, Maarum Prize 1981, Schroder Prize 1982, Deutsche Schallplattenpreis 1997, 2002, Sonning Music Prize 2000, H. C. Lumbye Prize; Knight of Dannebrog 1995. *Address:* Nordskraenten 3, 2980 Kokkedal, Denmark. *Telephone:* 45-86-25-77. *Fax:* 45-86-56-77. *E-mail:* mail@michalapetri.com. *Website:* www.michalapetri.com.

**PETRIC, Ivo;** Musician, Composer and Conductor; b. 16 June 1931, Ljubljana, Slovenia. *Education:* Music Acad., Ljubljana. *Career:* debut, Piano Trio, 1952; Conductor of Slavko Osterc Ensemble (for contemporary music), 1962–82; Ed.-in-Chief of Composers Editions, 1970–2002; Artistic Dir, Slovenian Philharmonic, 1979–95; mem., Asscn of Slovenian Composers. *Compositions:* orchestral music; concertos for various instruments; chamber music; sonatas for various instruments with piano, three symphonies 1954, 1957, 1960, six string quartets 1956–2004, Trumpet Concerto, 1986; Dresden Concerto for Strings, 1987; Trois Images, 1973; Dialogues Entre Deux Violons, 1975; Jeux Concertants for Flute and Orchestra, 1978, Toccata Concertante for 4 Percussionists and Orchestra, 1979, Gallus Metamorphoses, 1992; Scottish Impressions, 1994; The Song of Life, 1995; The Four Seasons, 1995; The Autumn Symphony, 1996; Two MacPhadraig's Scottish Diaries for piano, 1996, 2002; Grohar's Impressions II, 1998; Three Places in Scotland, 2002; Autumn Concerto for violin and orchestra, 2003. *Recordings:* 11 CDs of orchestral, chamber and solo music. *Honours:* Slovene State Preseren Foundation Prize, 1971; First Prize, Wieniawski International Composition Competition for Violin, 1975; Ljubljana Prize for Artists, 1977; Oscar Espla International Competition, First Prize, 1984; Kozina Award for six string quartets, 2001. *Address:* Bilecanska 4, 11000 Ljubljana, Slovenia (home). *Telephone:* (1) 548-1194 (home). *E-mail:* ivopetricc@siol.net (home). *Website:* www.ivopetric.com (home).

**PETRINSKY, Natascha;** Singer (mezzo-soprano); b. 1966, Vienna, Austria. *Education:* Studied in Israel. *Career:* Sang Carmen with New Israeli Opera; Appearances from 1995 with Giuseppe Sinopoli (conductor) in the Verdi Requiem, Beethoven's Ninth and Missa Solemnis, in Rome, Mahler's Third (Israel Philharmonic) and Wellgunde in Das Rheingold; Bayreuth Festival 2000, as Kundry in Parsifal; Engagements at Operahaus Halle as Amneris, Azucena and Marie in Wozzeck; Medea in Cavalli's Giasone at Spoleto USA and Carmen for Finnish Opera; Season 2001–2002 as Britten's Lucretia in Lausanne, Mahler's Second in Singapore, Das Lied von der Erde with the Royal Ballet, Covent Garden, Tchaikovsky's Pauline for Geneva Opera and Janáček's Fox in Paris, Châtelet; Other concerts include Mendelssohn's Elijah, at the Dresden Festival and Mahler's Third in Hong Kong; Further opera roles include Mozart's Donna Elvira and Countess Almaviva. *Current Management:* Athole Still International Management, Forresters Hall, 25–27 Westow Street, London, SE19 3RY, England. *Telephone:* (20) 8771-5271. *Fax:* (20) 8768-6600. *Website:* www.atholestill.com.

**PETRO, Janos;** Conductor and Chief Music Director; b. 5 March 1937, Repceszemere, Hungary; m. 27 Aug 1959, 1 s., 1 d. *Education:* Conductor and Composer, Academy of Music, Budapest, 1959. *Career:* Debut: As Composer, Vienna, 1959; Opera and Concerts in Budapest, Vienna, Berlin, Dublin, Bratislava, Frankfurt, Hamburg, Graz; Radio Budapest; Vienna Symphonic Record Register; Television Budapest and Vienna; mem, Musicians Alliance, Budapest, President and Member. *Recordings include:* Goldmark: Concerto for Violin and Orchestra; Mendelssohn: Concerto for Violin and Orchestra; Haydn: Scena di Berenice and Concert Arias; P Karolyi; Epilogus; P Karolyi: Consolatio; Bizet: Symphony C-major; Bizet: Suite L'Arlesienne; Beethoven: Egmont Overture; Liszt: Les Préludes; Haydn: Symphony No. 104. *Honours:* F Liszt Prize, Conductor, Budapest, 1983; World Young Composer Prize, Vienna, 1959; State Prize, Budapest, 1982. *Current Management:* Interkoncert Budapest, Vorosmarty ter 1, Austrokonzert, Vienna. *Address:* c/o Austroconcert International, Gluckgasse 1, A–1010 Vienna, Austria.

**PETROBELLI, Pierluigi,** BLitt, MFA; Italian musicologist and writer; b. 18 Oct. 1932, Padua; s. of Giuseppe Petrobelli and Carolina Talpo. *Education:* Univ. of Rome, Princeton Univ., Harvard Univ. and Summer School, Univ. of California at Berkeley, USA. *Career:* Ed. Rivista Italiana di Musicologia 1968–71, Studi verdiani 1981–; teaching asst, Univ. of Parma 1968–70, Assoc.

Prof. of Music History 1970–72; librarian and teacher of music history, Rossini Conservatory, Pesaro 1970–73; Lecturer in Music, King's Coll., London, UK 1973–77; Reader in Musicology, Univ. of London 1978–80; Dir Istituto di Studi Verdiani, Parma 1980–89, Istituto Nazionale di Studi Verdiani, Parma 1989–; Prof. of Music History, Univ. of Perugia 1981–83, Univ. of Rome 'La Sapienza' 1983–2005; Chair of Italian Culture, Univ. of California at Berkeley 1988; Lauro de Bosis Lecturer in the History of Italian Civilization, Harvard Univ. 1996; Visitante distinguido, Univ. of Cordoba, Argentina; mem. External Advisory Bd, Faculty of Music, Univ. of Oxford, UK, Advisory Bd, Forschungsinstitut für Musiktheater, Univ. of Bayreuth, Thurn, Germany; mem. Accad. Nazionale dei Lincei, Academia Europaea; Corresp. mem. American Musicological Soc.; Foreign Hon. mem. Royal Musical Asscn, UK. *Publications:* Thematic Catalog of an 18th-Century Collection of Italian Instrumental Music (held in the Music Library, Univ. of California at Berkeley, with V. Duckles and M. Elmer) 1963, Giuseppe Tartini: le fonti biografiche 1968, Mozart's Il re pastore (critical edn, with Wolfgang Rehm) 1984, Carteggio Verdi-Ricordi 1880–1881 (co-ed.) 1988, Tartini, le sue idee e il suo tempo 1992, Music in the Theater: Essays on Verdi and Other Composers 1994, Italian edn 1998; contribs to scholarly books and professional journals. *Honours:* Hon. mem. Akad. der Mozartforschung, Salzburg. *Address:* 34 via di San Anselmo, 00153 Rome, Italy (home). *Telephone:* (0521) 286044 (office); (06) 5750433 (home). *Fax:* (0521) 287949 (office). *E-mail:* petrobel@rmcisadu.let.uniromat.it (office); direzione@studioerdiani.it (office).

**PETROFF-BEVIE, Barbara;** singer (soprano) and professor of music; b. 2 June 1934, Hamburg, Germany; m. Joseph Petroff, 17 May 1973, 1 s., 1 d. *Education:* University; Masterclasses, Hochschule für Musik, Hamburg; Opera classes, Bern and Geneva Conservatories; Diploma. *Career:* debut as Constanze in Entführung aus dem Serail, Stadttheater Luneberg 1959, and as Clarice in Haydn's Il mondo della luna, Stadttheater Bern 1960; main appearances include Århus (Denmark), Bern and Geneva (Switzerland), The Hague (Netherlands), Royal Opera Ghent (Belgium), Linz (Austria), Kiel (Germany), Grand Theatre, Geneva; sang as Carolina in Il matrimonio segreto, Gilda in Rigoletto, Blondchen and Constanze in Entführung, Musetta, Sophie in Der Rosenkavalier, Ännchen in Freischütz, Susanna in Figaro, Despina in Così fan tutte, Adele in Die Fledermaus, Rosina in Barbiere di Siviglia and Adina in L'Elisir d'amore; operettas: Maritza in Gräfin Maritza and Evelyne in Graf von Luxemburg. *Address:* 12 rue de Chêne-Bougeries, 1224 Geneva, Switzerland.

**PETRONI, Luigi;** Singer (Tenor); b. 1970, Italy. *Career:* Debut: Cimarosa's Il Matrimonio segreto, Turin; Appearances in The Civil Wars by Philip Glass; Rossini's Ricciardo e Zoraide and Mavra by Stravinsky; Wexford Festival 1997 as Boemondo in Mercadante's Elena da Fetre; Concerts include Rossini's Stabat Mater with the Oslo Radio Symphony Orchestra, 1997. *Recordings:* Elena da Feltre. *Honours:* Winner, International Enrico Caruso Competition; International Voice Contest, Turin. *Current Management:* Prima International. *Address:* c/o Prima International, Palazzo Zambeccari, Piazza de Calderini 2/2, 40124 Bologna, Italy.

**PETROV, Andrei Pavlovich;** Russian composer; b. 2 Sept. 1930, Leningrad; s. of Pavel Platonovich Petrov and Olga Petrovna Vaulina; m. Natalia Fishkova 1954; one d. *Education:* Leningrad Conservatory. *Career:* Chair. Leningrad (now St Petersburg) Composers' Union 1964–; mem. CPSU 1957–90; Dir-Gen. Spring Music Festival, St Petersburg. *Compositions include:* Radda and Loiko (Symphonic poem), Violin Concerto, Piano Concerto, Symphonies Nos 1, 2, 3, 4, The Creation of the World (ballet), Peter the Great (opera), Mayakovsky Begins (opera), Pushkin (choral dance work), The Master and Margarita (ballet music), God-children of Katherine the Great (musical) 1995–96; also operettas, songs, music for over 80 films including The Promised Heaven 1992 (Nika Prize). *Honours:* State Prize 1967, 1976, 1996, USSR People's Artist 1980. *Address:* Petrovskaya nab. 4, Apt 75, 197046 St Petersburg, Russia. *Telephone:* (812) 232-29-63. *Fax:* (812) 311-35-48. *E-mail:* peterbass@mail.ru (office).

**PETROV, Ivan;** Singer (Bass); b. 23 Feb. 1920, Irkutsk, USSR. *Education:* Glazunov Music College Moscow, 1938–39, with a Mineyev. *Career:* Sang with Ivan Kozlovsky's opera group from 1939; Concert engagements with the Moscow Philharmonic, 1941; Bolshoi Theatre, Moscow, from 1943; Sang there in the 1953 premiere of Shaporin's The Decembrists; Paris Opéra, 1954, as Boris Godunov; Concert tour of Europe, 1954–55; Other operatic roles include Glinka's Ruslan, Dosifey in Khovanshchina, Mepistopheles in Faust, Verdi's King Philip and Basilio in Il Barbiere di Siviglia. *Recordings:* Eugene Onegin; Rachmaninov's Aleko; Prince Igor; Ruslan and Lyudmila; Boris Godunov; Verdi Requiem; The Tale of Tsar Saltan by Rimsky-Korsakov, Tchaikovsky's Mazeppa and Romeo and Juliette. *Recordings include:* Title role in Prince Igor, conducted by Mark Ermler. *Address:* c/o Bolshoi Theatre, Pr Marxa 8/2, 103009 Moscow, Russia.

**PETROV, Marina,** MA; Recital Pianist and Piano Lecturer; b. 27 Dec. 1960, Kiev, Russia. *Education:* Central Music School for Gifted Children, Belgrade, Central Music School for Gifted Children, Kiev, College of Music, Belgrade, Moscow Conservatoire, Belgrade Academy of Music. *Career:* debut in Belgrade 1969; recital pianist 1969–; first appearance on television and radio in Belgrade in 1969; subsequently played in Kiev and Moscow; tours in Yugoslavia; has also played in Norway and in the United Kingdom at venues including London, Dartington Hall and Bristol 1990–; lecturer in piano.

*Contributions:* The Times. *Address:* 28B Caedmon Road, London N7 6DH, England.

**PETROV, Nikolai Arnoldovich;** Russian pianist and professor; *President, Academy of Russian Art*; b. 14 April 1943, Moscow; m. Larisa Petrova; one d. *Education:* Moscow Conservatory (pupil of Yakov Zak). *Career:* debut in Moscow 1962; soloist of Moscow Philharmonic 1966–; toured many countries of Europe and America as soloist and with maj. conductors and orchestras; took part in music festivals; first performer of music by contemporary Russian composers, including Rodion Shchedrin, first performances in Russia of works by Bach, Beethoven, Mozart, Debussy, Ravel, Liszt; Prof. Moscow Conservatoire 1994–; Founder and Pres. Acad. of Russian Art 1995–; Vice-Pres. Int. Asscn The World of Culture 1993. *Honours:* State Prize of Russia 1993; People's Artist of Russia, Musician of the Year (Musikalnaya Zhizn journal) 1994. *Address:* c/o Sovinart, Murmansky proezd 18, apt 77, 129075 Moscow; Ostozhenka 22, apt 2, 119034 Moscow, Russia (home). *Telephone:* (095) 215-7571 (office); (095) 992-8333 (home). *Fax:* (095) 215-2274 (office). *E-mail:* soninart.mos@g23.relcom.ru (office); npetrov@mail.ru (home). *Website:* www.nbcf.ru.

**PETROV, Petar Konstantinov;** Bulgarian composer and pianist; b. 23 June 1961, Stara Zagora. *Education:* Musical School, St Zagora, State Musical Academy, Sofia. *Career:* debut in New Bulgarian Music, 1984; Manager and Pianist in Chilorch-choire, Sofia, 1988–91; Honorary Professor of Contrapunct in Bulgarian State Academy, 1990–93; Professor of Counterpoint and Composition in Music School, St Zagora; Composition Masterclass of Profesor Anatol Vieru-Rumenia, 1993–95; many appearances as Chamber Pianist with Rosed Idealov–Clarinet, 1990–97. *Compositions:* Sonata, partita for violin solo, 1986; Concerto Piccolo for flute, violin and piano, 1987; The Christian Convert, for organ, 1989; Studies Nos 1–19, for various solo instruments, 1989–99; Ricercare, for three instruments, 1990; Symphony No. 5, alla bulgarese, for electronic instruments, 1998; Dialogues with Mr Galiley, for chamber ensemble, 1997; In Memorium, for piano, 1997; Dewy concerto for clarinet and 3 key instruments, 1997; 6 Mediations for chamber ensemble, 1997; Symphony No. 6 'Because these we are', 1998; Second concerto for Violin (Viola) and Orchestra, 1998; Phantoms in Viennese Forest, six commentaries for piano, 1998; Concerto for Piano and Orchestra, 'In memory of Eric Satie', 1999. *Recordings:* Concerto for Violin and Orchestra No. 1, 1987; Symphony No. 1, Lamento, 1987; Symphony No. 2, Katarsis, 1990; Concerto Piccolo IV, 1994; Dialogues with the Silence, 1994; Estampie, 1994; Symphony No. 3, Momento, 1994; Symphony No. 4, Dona nobis pacem, 1995; Bach Studies for Clarinet, Viola and Piano, 1995; CD, Messages I, 1997; Toccata for Piano, 1997; Messages II, 1999. *Address:* c/o MUSICAUTOR, 63 Tzar Assen Str, 1463 Sofia, Bulgaria.

**PETROVA, Petia;** Singer (Mezzo-soprano); b. 1970, Sofia, Bulgaria. *Career:* Many appearances in Bulgaria and Germany; In Operas by Rossini, Il Barbiere di Siviglia, La Donna del lago and L'Italiana in Algeri; Engagements with the Hamburg State Opera include Rossini's Rosina, Suzuki in Madama Butterfly and Mercédès in Carmen. *Honours:* Winner of competitions in Sofia and Barcelona; Finalist, Cardiff Singer of the World Competition, 1999. *Address:* c/o Hamburg State Opera, Grosse Theaterstrasse 34, 20354 Hamburg, Germany.

**PETROVICS, Emil;** Hungarian composer; b. 9 Feb. 1930, Nagybecskerek (now Zrenjanin, Yugoslavia); s. of Jovan Petrovics and Erzsébet Weninger; one d. *Career:* studied at Conservatory, graduated from Music Acad. of Budapest; Musical Dir Petöfi Theatre 1960–64; Lecturer Coll. of Dramatic and Cinematographic Arts 1964–; Prof. of Composition Music Acad., Budapest; Dir Hungarian State Opera 1986–90; mem. Hungarian Parl. 1967–85; mem. Széchenyi Acad. of Arts, Budapest 1991–, Serbian Acad. of Sciences and Arts, Belgrade 1993–. *Compositions for musical stage:* C'est la guerre (single act) 1961; Crime and Punishment 1969; Book of Jonah (oratorio) 1965; Lysistrate (comic opera for concert performance) 1962 (all performed in Czechoslovakia, Finland, France, FRG, Hungary and Yugoslavia); Salome (ballet) 1984; 2nd to 5th Cantatas: There Let Me Die 1972, Fanny's Posthumous Papers 1978, We All Must Go 1980, Letters from Turkey 1981, 6th Cantata: We Take a Rest. *Instrumental music:* Concerto for Flute 1957; String Quartet 1958; Symphony for Strings 1964; Quintet for Winds 1966; Rhapsody No. 1 and No. 2 for Violin and Viola Solo 1982, 1983; Concertino for Trumpet and Orchestra 1990; 2nd String Quartet 1991; Rhapsody No. 2 for Violoncello Solo 1991; Vörösmarty – Overture for Orchestra 1993; Cantata No. 7: Pygmalion, for Mixed Chorus, Narrator and Orchestra 1994–95; Lament and Consolation (three poems for tenor voice and piano) 1996; Piangendo e Meditando, for String Orchestra 1997; Cantata No. 9: By the Danube 1998; Concerto for Piano and Orchestra 1999, Symphony No. 2 for Orchestra 2001; other works for chorus, incidental film and stage music. *Publication:* Ravel 1959. *Honours:* Erkel Prize 1960, 1963, Kossuth Prize 1966, holder of titles Merited Artist 1975, Eminent Artist 1982. *Address:* Attila utca 39, 1013 Budapest, Hungary. *Telephone:* (1) 375-6032. *Fax:* (1) 212-75-02 (home).

**PETRUSHANSKY, Boris;** Concert Pianist; b. 3 June 1949, Moscow, Russia. *Education:* Studies at Central School of Music and Moscow Conservatoire. *Career:* Many concert tours of Russia and appearances in Italy, Hungary, the United Kingdom, Germany, France, Japan and Australasia; Repertoire includes works by: Beethoven; Brahms; Liszt; Prokoviev; Shostakovich; Schnittke; Gubaidulina; Professor at Academica Pianistica in Italy. *Recordings include:* Works by: Schnikkte; Gubaidulina. *Honours:* Prizewinner in competitions at: Leeds, 1969; Moscow, 1970; Munich, 1971; Casagrande, 1975. *Address:* c/o Sonata, 11 Northpark Street, Glasgow G20 7AA, Scotland.

**PETRUTSHENKO, Natalia;** Pianist; b. 21 Aug. 1963, Ulan-Ude, Russia. *Education:* Basic Musical Education, Kemerovo; Completed High Music School, Nikolayev, Ukraine, 1983; Diploma with highest honours, graduating from class of Professor Dorenski, 1991, PhD, 1993, Tchaikovsky Moscow Conservatoire. *Career:* Comprehensive repertoire with orchestra and solo; Participant, 1st Rachmaninov International Competition for Pianists, Moscow and International Competition for Young Performers, Japan, 1993; Guest performance tour to Japanese towns; Numerous concerts in major cities in Russia, Ukraine, Belarus, the Baltic States, Bulgaria and Romania; Professor, High Music School, Kurgan, Russia, 1994; Soloist, District Philharmonic Society, Nikolayev, Ukraine, 1995; Living in Varna, Bulgaria, 1996–; European tour in preparation. *Address:* Jen Skobelov str block 19, ap 37, Varna 9000, Bulgaria.

**PETUKHOV, Mikhail;** Concert Pianist; b. 24 April 1954, Varna, Bulgaria. *Education:* Studied in Kiev and at Moscow Conservatoire with Tatiana Nikolayeva. *Career:* Many concerts in Russia, Italy, Belgium, Netherlands, Czechoslovakia and Germany; Played with Royal Scottish Orchestra, 1992, followed by Tchaikovsky First Concerto with City of Birmingham Symphony under Yuri Simonov; Repertoire has also included works by Purcell, Ravel, Handel, Stravinsky, Mendelssohn, Schumann, Schoenberg and Ives; Professor in Piano at Moscow Conservatoire. *Honours:* 3rd Prize at J. S. Bach Competition, Leipzig, 1972; Queen Elizabeth Competition at Brussels, 1975. *Address:* c/o Sonata, 11 Northpark Street, Glasgow G20 7AA, Scotland.

**PEYSER, Joan Gilbert,** BA, MA; American musicologist and writer; b. 12 June 1931, New York, NY. *Education:* Barnard Coll., Columbia Univ. *Career:* Ed., The Musical Quarterly 1977–84; regular contrib. to the Sunday New York Times 1966–85; mem. American Musicological Soc., Music Critics Asscn, PEN. *Publications:* The New Music: The Sense Behind the Sound 1970, revised second edn as Twentieth Century Music: The Sense Behind the Sound 1980, Boulez: Composer, Conductor, Enigma 1976, The Orchestra: Origins and Transformations (Ed., First Prize Humanities Category, Prof. and Scholarly Publ. Div. Asscn of American Publishers) 1986, Bernstein: A Biography 1987, The Memory of All That: The Life of George Gershwin 1993, The Music of My Time (essays) 1995, To Boulez and Beyond: Music in Europe Since the Rite of Spring 1999; contrib. to periodicals and journals. *Honours:* five ASCAP/Deems Taylor Awards. *Address:* 19 Charlton Street, New York, NY 10014, USA. *Telephone:* (212) 675-5066. *Fax:* (212) 675-9544.

**PFAFF, Luca;** Conductor; b. 25 Aug. 1948, Olivone, Switzerland; m. Dominique Chanet, 1986, 2 s. *Education:* Basel University; Conservatorio G Verdi, Milan; Musikakademie, Vienna; Accademia Santa Ceàlia, Rome. *Career:* Director, Orchestre Symphonique du Rhin, France; Director, Carme, Milan; Founder, Ensemble Alternance, Paris; Guest Conductor, major orchestras, Europe. *Recordings:* Scelsi; Donatoni; Dusapin, Opera Roméo et Juliette; Mozart, Gran Partita. *Contributions:* Monde de la Musique; Harmonie; Rivista Musicale; Diapason d'Or, 1985; Best CD of 1988; Donatoni, CHOC, Monde de la Musique. *Current Management:* Valmalete, Paris, France. *Address:* c/o Ariën Arts & music, de Boeystraat 6, B–2018 Antwerp, Belgium.

**PFISTER, Daniel;** Composer; b. 6 Nov. 1952, St Gallen, Switzerland. *Education:* Teachers' Training College, 1970–74; Konservatorium Winterthur (Conservatoire), 1974–78; Teachers' Diploma piano, 1978; Musikhochschule Zürich, music theory with Hans Ulrich Lehmann, 1977–78; Hochschule für Musik und darstellende Kunst in Wien, composition with Prof Alfred Uhl, 1978–84; Diploma composition, 1984; Hochschule für Musik und darstellende Kunst in Wien, conducting with Otmar Suitner, 1984–87. *Career:* Freelance Composer; Private teacher for music theory composition and piano, 1982–; mem, SMPV Schweizerischer Musikpaedagogischer Verband. *Compositions:* Saitenspiel, 1982 for 2 guitars; Concerto for string orchestra, 1982–87; Aeon for soprano and piano, 1983; Aeon for soprano and orchestra, 1983–84; Canto for soprano or flute or saxophone, 1985–88; Canto for soprano (flute), clarinet and vibraphone, 1986; Neun und Zehne auf einen Streich, for guitar, 1988; Touches for flute, oboe, clarinet, bassoon, horn, trumpet, snare drum, gong, xilorimba, vibraphone, guitar, piano, violin, viola, cello, 1988–89; Bruchstuecke aus Touches, 1988, 880 un satiesme, instrument is free, 1988; 12 kleine Odien for flute and guitar, 1987–89; Max and Moritz for reciter and guitar, 1990–91. *Address:* Lehnstrasse 33 9014, St Gallen, Switzerland.

**PHARR, Rachel (Elizabeth Caroline);** Harpsichordist; b. 15 April 1957, Picayune, Mississippi, USA; m. Bernard Gerard Kolle, 1 Jan 1989. *Education:* BMus Summa Cum Laude, Piano Performance major, 1978, MMus, Piano Performance major, 1980, University of Southwestern Louisiana, Lafayette; Aspen Music School, Aspen Festival, 1980, 1981; MMus, Harpsichord Performace major, Arizona State University, Tempe, 1982; Banff Centre School of Fine Arts, Canada, 1987–89. *Career:* Harpsichordist with Houston Baroque Ensemble, 1983–87, with Texas Chamber Orchestra in Houston, Texas, 1985–87; Numerous concerts, Banff Centre, Banff, Alberta, Canada, 1987–89; Performed at Aspen Music Festival, 1981, Breckenridge Music Institute, 1982, 1983; Featured Soloist in Houston Harpsichord Society's presentation of the entire J. S. Bach Well-Tempered Klavier for Bach Tercentenary, 1985; New Music America concerts, 1986; Tours as Solo Harpsichord, 1986, with Liedermusik Ensemble, 1987; Harpsichord Accompanist, Banff Centre, 1988–89; Radio performances, KLEF, Houston and

WWNO, New Orleans; Television performance, NBC-Channel 4, Denver. *Address:* c/o Newton T Pharr, 314 Dodson Street, New Iberia, LA 70560, USA.

**PHIBBS, Joseph,** MMus, DMA; Composer; b. 1974, London. *Education:* The Purcell School, Harrow, King's Coll., London, Cornell Univ., New York, Britten-Pears Contemporary Music course, Aldeburgh. *Career:* Asst Lecturer in Composition, King's Coll. 1995–96; teaching asst, Cornell Univ.; musical dir and composer for productions at the Wolsey Theatre, Ipswich, of Robinson's Walk 1995, The Devil's Cardinal 1996, Watership Down 1996, Romeo and Juliet 1997, Animal Farm 1997. *Compositions:* orchestral works: Soiree (winner BBC Young Composer's Forum) 1996, Dreams of a Summer Night 2000, In Camera 2001, Lumina (for BBC Last Night of the Proms) 2003; chamber orchestra works: Cayuga (for Faber Millennium Series) 2000; chamber works: Broken Sequence 1996, Char Fragments 1999, Trio Semplice (for Schubert Ensemble Chamber Music 2000 project) 2000, Ritual Songs and Blessings (for London Spitalfields Festival) 2002, La noche arrolladora (for BBC Proms) 2002, Rainland 2004. *Honours:* British Acad. Award, London Univ. 1995; Sage Fellowship 1997, Robbins Composition Prize 1998, Blackmore Prize in Composition 2001, all at Cornell Univ. *Address:* c/o Faber Music, 3 Queen Square, London, WC1N 3AU, England. *E-mail:* josephphibbs@yahoo .co.uk.

**PHILIP, Robert Marshall,** MA, PhD, ARCM; British writer and lecturer; *Senior Lecturer, The Open University;* b. 22 July 1945, Witney, Oxfordshire; m. Susan Tomes 2004; two d. (from previous marriage). *Education:* Royal College of Music, Peterhouse, Cambridge, University (now Wolfson) College, Cambridge. *Career:* Junior Research Fellow at University Wolfson College, Cambridge, 1972–74; Producer, BBC television, Open University Department, 1976–99; Lecturer in Music, Open University, 2000–; Freelance Music Critic and Broadcast Talks; Early Recordings and Musical Style, 1992; mem, Royal Musical Association. *Radio:* contrib. to broadcast series: The Long Playing Era (Radio 3); The Developing Musician (Radio 3); Composer and Interpreter (BBC World Service); Musical Yearbook (BBC World Service); Vintage Years (Radio 3). *Publications:* Early Recordings and the Musical lStyle 1992, Performing Music in the Age of Recording 2004; contrib. to Records and Recording; BBC Record Review. *Honours:* Organ Scholarship, Peterhouse, Cambridge, 1964; Visiting Research Fellowship, Open University, 1995–98; ASCAP Deems Taylor Award, 1992. *Address:* The Open University, Walton Hall, Milton Keynes, MK7 6AA, England. *E-mail:* robert .philip@lineone.net (home).

**PHILIPPE, Michel;** Singer (Bass-baritone); b. 1943, Pau, France. *Education:* Studied at the Paris Conservatoire. *Career:* Sang at the Paris Opéra from 1971; Appearances at the Orange and Aix-en-Provence Festivals, Hamburg Staatsoper, Royal Opera Stockholm, Geneva, Madrid and Rio de Janeiro; Chorèbe and Panthée in Les Troyens at Montreal, 1993; Other roles have included Rossini's Figaro, Marcello, Scarpia, Mozart's Count, Don Giovanni, Valentin in Faust and Iago. *Honours:* Winner, Voix et Musique Concours, Paris, 1971. *Address:* c/o L'Opéra de Montréal, 260 de Maisonneuve Boulevard West, Montreal, Quebec H2X 1Y9, Canada.

**PHILIPS, Daniel;** Violinist; b. 1960, USA. *Career:* Winner of Young Concert Artists International Auditions and recitalist at Lincoln Center's Alice Tully Hall, 92nd Street 'Y' and appearances with major orchestras; Chamber musician at Santa Fe Festival, Spoleto Festival, Lockenhaus Kammermusikfest and the International Musicians Seminar in Prussia Cove; Co-founded the Orion Quartet and has given concerts at Kennedy Center, Washington DC, at Gardner Museum, Boston and throughout USA; Carnegie Hall recital, 1991 as part of the Centennial Celebration tribute to next 100 years of music making; Concerts at Turku Festival in Finland; Professor of Violin at State University of New York and Faculty member at Aaron Copland School of Music. *Current Management:* Ingpen & Williams Ltd, 7 St George's Court, 131 Putney Bridge Road, London, SW15 2PA, England.

**PHILIPS, Leo;** Violinist; b. 1960, England. *Education:* Studied at Yehudi Menuhin School and with Sándor Végh, Dorothy DeLay and Shmuel Ashkenasi. *Career:* Concerts as Chamber Musician and Soloist; Former member of the Chamber Orchestra of Europe; Leader and Principal Director of East of England Orchestra; Co-founder Vellinger String Quartet, 1990; Participated in master classes with Borodin Quartet at Pears-Britten School, 1991; Concerts as Ferrara Musica Festival, Italy and debut on South Bank with London premiere of Robert Simpson's 13th Quartet; BBC Radio 3 debut, December 1991; Season 1992–93 with concerts in London, Glasgow, Cambridge, at Davos Festival, Switzerland and Crickdale Festival, Wiltshire; Wigmore Hall with Haydn (Op 54, No. 2), Gubaidulina and Beethoven (Op 59, No. 2), Purcell Room with Haydn's Seven Last Words. *Recordings include:* Elgar's Quartet and Quintet, with Piers Lane. *Address:* c/o Georgina Ivor Associates (Vellinger Quartet), 66 Alderbrook Road, London SW12 8 AB, England.

**PHILLIPS, John (Alan);** Musicologist; b. 14 April 1960, Adelaide, South Australia, Australia. *Education:* BMus (Hons), 1983, PhD, Musicology, in progress, University of Adelaide; Conducting, Composition, Vienna Konservatorium and Hochschule, 1983–85. *Career:* Active Choral Conductor, Adelaide; Involved on major research project on Bruckner's 9th symphony finale, 1989–, its new performing version completed with Nicola Samale, Rome, May 1991, first performed, Linz, Austria, by Bruckner Orchestra, Dec 1991, first recorded by same orchestra, 1993; Lectures, conference papers, Australia, Europe; Press conferences, Australian, German, Austrian, US newspapers; Interviews, Australian, German, Austrian Radio. *Compositions:* Many unpublished works; Choral arrangements. *Recordings:* Two-piano recording, Bruckner 9th Symphony Finale with Edward Kriek, ABC Radio, Dec 1990. *Publications:* Bruckner's 9th Symphony Revisited. Towards the re-evaluation of a four-movement symphony, dissertation, 1995; Editor: Anton Bruckner: 9th Symphony in D Minor: Finale: Reconstruction of the Autograph Score from the Surviving Manuscripts: Performing Version by Nicola Samale, John A Phillips and Giuseppe Mazzuca, with the assistance of Gunnar Cohrs, 1992; Anton Bruckner Gesamtausgabe: Zu Band IX; Finale: Rekonstruktion der Autograph-Partitur nach den erhaltenen Quellen. a) aller dem Finale der IX Symphonie zugehörigen Manuskripte, 1994. *Address:* 107 Fourth Avenue, Joslin, SA 5070, Australia.

**PHILLIPS, Margaret Corinna;** British concert organist and harpsichordist; *Professor of Organ, Royal College of Music;* b. 16 Nov. 1950, Exeter, Devon, England. *Education:* Royal College of Music, 1968–72; FRCO; GRSM; ARCM, organ performing with honours; Studied privately with Marie-Claire Alain in Paris, France, 1972–73. *Career:* Debut: Royal Festival Hall, 1972; Director of Music, St Lawrence Jewry next Guildhall, London, 1976–85; Professor of Organ and Harpsichord, London College of Music, 1985–91; Tutor in Organ Studies, Royal Northern College of Music, 1993–97, Visiting Tutor, 1997–; Prof. of Organ Royal College of Music 1996–, Prof. in Charge of Organ 1998–2003; President, Incorporated Association of Organists, 1997–99; Recitals throughout: Europe, USA, Mexico, Australia; Radio broadcasts in: the United Kingdom, Sweden, Denmark, Netherlands, Australia; Performances with: London Choral Society, BBC Singers, The Sixteen and London Mozart Players; Lecturer, English Church and Organ Music; mem, Incorporated Society of Musicians; Royal College of Organists (Council Member 1982–2003). *Recordings:* Festliche Orgelmusik; English Organ Music from Queen Elizabeth I to Queen Elizabeth II; D Buxtehude; Orgelmusik i Karlskoga kyrka; Klosters Orgel; Organ Music of Saint-Saëns; 18th Century English Organ Music; 19th Century English Organ Music; Wesley, Music for Organ; Dances for Organ; Voluntaries and Variations; The Young Bach, John Stanley – the Complete Voluntaries for Organ. *Address:* The Manse, Chapel Lane, Milborne Port, Sherborne DT9 5 DL, England. *Telephone:* (1963) 250899. *E-mail:* phillips.eos@lineone.net.

**PHILLIPS, Paul Schuyler,** BA, MA, MM; American conductor and composer; *Director of Orchestras and Chamber Music, Brown University;* b. 28 April 1956, New Jersey, USA; m. Kathryne Jennings 1986; two d. *Education:* Columbia Coll., Columbia Univ., New York, Coll.-Conservatory of Music, Univ. of Cincinnati, Eastman School, Mozarteum, Salzburg, Austria, Los Angeles Philharmonic Inst., Aspen and Tanglewood. *Career:* Conducting Asst, Frankfurt Opera, Germany 1982–83; First Kapellmeister, Stadttheater Luneburg, Germany 1983–84; Assoc. Conductor Greensboro Symphony and Asst Conductor Greensboro Opera 1984–86; Youth Concert Conductor Maryland Symphony 1985–99; Assoc. Conductor Savannah Symphony 1986–89; Dir Savannah Symphony Chorale 1987–89; Assoc. Conductor Rhode Island Philharmonic 1989–92; Music Dir Brown Univ. Orchestra 1989–; guest conductor with more than 50 orchestras, choirs, opera and ballet cos worldwide; orchestras include San Francisco Symphony, Dallas Symphony, Detroit Symphony, Louisville Orchestra, Rochester Philharmonic and Netherlands Radio Chamber Orchestra; opera: Boston Acad. of Music, Opera Providence and Commonwealth Opera; ballet: Savannah Ballet, Wisconsin Dance Ensemble and Festival Ballet of Rhode Island; choirs: Masterworks Chorale, Boston, Hampshire Choral Soc., McGill Chamber Singers and Wellesley Coll. Choir. *Compositions:* concert works and music for theatre and film. *Recordings:* conductor with Iceland Symphony Orchestra. *Publication:* A Clockwork Counterpoint: The Music and Literature of Anthony Burgess 2006. *Honours:* eight ASCAP Awards for Programming of Contemporary Music 1986–2005, First Prize, Wiener Meisterkurse and NOS Int. Conducting. *Address:* Brown University, Box 1924, Providence, RI 02912, USA (office). *Telephone:* (401) 863-1472 (office). *Fax:* (401) 863-1256 (office). *E-mail:* Paul_Phillips@brown.edu (office). *Website:* www.brown.edu (office).

**PHILLIPS, Peter;** Choral Director; b. 15 Oct. 1953, Southampton, England. *Education:* Studied at Winchester College and an Organ Scholar at St John's College, Oxford. *Career:* Has taught at Oxford University and Trinity College of Music and the Royal College of Music; Founded the Tallis Scholars, 1973 and Gimell Records, 1981; Regular concerts in the United Kingdom and abroad, including USA from 1988 and Australia from 1985; From 1989 the Far East and Promenade Concert debut with Victoria's Requiem; United Kingdom concerts include Bath Festival, 1995; BBC Proms, 1988, 2001, 2003; Three Choirs Festival, 2002; Also conducted BBC Singers, 2003; Collegium Vocale of Ghent, 2003; Documentary features on TV, 1990, 2002; mem, Chelsea Arts Club; MCC. *Recordings include:* Lassus Music for Double Choir; Sarum Chant; John Sheppard Media Vita; Gesualdo Tenebrae Responsories; Cornysh Stabat Mater, Salve Regina and Magnificat; Clemens non Papa Missa Pastores Quidnam vidistis; Victoria Requiem and Tenebrae Responsories; Cardoso Requiem; Josquin Masses; Byrd The Great Service and Three Masses; Medieval Christmas Carols and Motets; Palestrina Masses, 4 CDs; Tallis Complete English Anthems and Spem in Alium; Allegri Miserere and Mundy Vox Patris Caelestis; Taverner Missa Gloria Tibi Trinitas; Russian Orthodox Music; Ikon of Light by John Tavener; CD based on South Bank Show feature; Isaac Missa de Apostolis; Tomkins The Great Service; Tallis Lamentations of Jeremiah; Tallis, Missa Puer Natus; Obrecht, Missa Maria Zart; Live in Rome; Live in Oxford. *Contributions:* The New Republic; Music

and Letters; The Listener; The Spectator; The Guardian; Proprietor, The Musical Times, 1995–. *Honours:* (with Tallis Scholars): Record of the Year, Gramophone Magazine, 1987; Gramophone Award for Early Music Record of the Year, 1987, 1991, 1994. *Current Management:* Tallis Scholars, Hazard Chase Ltd, Norman House, Cambridge Place, Cambridge, CB2 1NS, England. *Telephone:* (1223) 312400. *Fax:* (1223) 460827. *Website:* www.hazardchase.co.uk; www.PeterPhillips.info.

**PHILLIPS, Richard,** BA; Festival Director; b. 15 Sept. 1940, Warwick, England; m. Veronica; two d. *Education:* Oundle School, Univ. of Oxford. *Career:* Sadler's Wells Opera 1966–70; York Arts Asscn 1970–80; Festival Director, Warwick Arts Soc. 1982–, Charlecote Park Festival 1983–98, Norfolk and Norwich Festival 1986–91, Solihull Arts Festival 1990–92, King's Lynn Festival 1997. *Honours:* Hon. Fellow Birmingham Conservatoire 2002. *Address:* Warwick Arts Society, Pageant House, 2 Jury Street, Warwick, CV34 4EW, England (office). *Telephone:* (1926) 497000 (office). *Fax:* (1926) 407606 (office). *E-mail:* richardp@warwickarts.org.uk (office). *Website:* www.warwickarts.org.uk (office).

**PHILLIPS, Todd;** Violinist; b. 1968, USA. *Education:* Juilliard School with Sally Thomas and at the Salzburg Mozarteum with Sándor Végh. *Career:* Leader with the Orpheus Chamber Orchestra and solo performances with the Pittsburgh Symphony Orchestra (debut aged 13), the Brandenburg Ensemble, Camerata Academica of Salzburg, and leading American orchestras; Chamber music at the Santa Fe, Marlboro and Mostly Mozart festivals; Joint leader of the Orion String Quartet, with concert tours throughout North America and to London, Vienna and Amsterdam; 'Fourteen Musicians from Marlboro' tours; Season 1996–97 with Chamber Music Society of Lincoln Center, including premiere of George Perle's Quintet for horn and strings; Member of the violin and chamber music faculties at the Mannes School of Music. *Recordings include:* Mozart's Sinfonia Concertante K364, with the Orpheus Chamber Orchestra (DGG). *Current Management:* Ingpen & Williams Ltd, 7 St George's Court, 131 Putney Bridge Road, London, SW15 2PA, England.

**PHILOGENE, Ruby Catherine,** MBE; British singer (mezzo-soprano); b. 14 July 1965, London, England. *Education:* Curtis Institute, Philadelphia; Guildhall School of Music and Drama. *Career:* Concert engagements with the San Francisco Symphony Orchestra, London Philharmonic and City of London Sinfonia; Season 1994–95 included Mahler 2 with the Liverpool Philharmonic, Messiah under Yehudi Menuhin, Bach B Minor Mass and Schumann's Scenes from Faust with the London Philharmonic Orchestra, Janáček's Glagolitic Mass and Les Nuits d'Eté by Berlioz; Opera appearances as Britten's Hermia (with the London Symphony Orchestra under Colin Davis), in Biber's Arminio at Innsbruck, the Page in Salome (Covent Garden 1997), in Handel's Orlando with the Gabrieli Consort and as Goehr's Arianna; Season 1997–98 as Dorabella in Così fan tutte for Opera North and a new production of Parsifal in Brussels; Other repertory includes the Sorceress in Dido and Aeneas (Staatsoper Berlin) and Smeraldine in The Love for Three Oranges, at Lyon and San Francisco; Carmen for Opera North, 1998; Tokyo debut, with Bach Collegium, 2003; World premiere of Pierre Bartholomé's Oedipe sur la Route, La Monnaie, Paris, 2003; Britten's Midsummer Night's Dream, La Monnaie, 2004; Regular concerts and opera with Rotterdam Philharmonic. *Recordings include:* A Midsummer Night's Dream; Arianna. *Honours:* Winner, Anna Instone Memorial Award, 1990; 1993 Kathleen Ferrier Memorial Prize. *Current Management:* Askonas Holt Ltd, Lonsdale Chambers, 27 Chancery Lane, London, WC2A 1PF, England. *Telephone:* (20) 7400-1700. *Fax:* (20) 7400-1799. *E-mail:* info@askonasholt.co.uk. *Website:* www.askonasholt.co.uk. *Address:* Impulse Art Management, O. Z. Voorburgwal 72–74, 1012 GE, Amsterdam. *Address:* Jacob Marisstraat 97-1, HX1058 Amsterdam, Netherlands; 22 Pine House, Avenue Gardens, Droop Street, London, W10 4EJ, England. *Telephone:* (20) 8400-1721. *Website:* www.philogene.net.

**PIA, Claude;** Singer (Tenor); b. 1968, Berne, Switzerland. *Education:* Studies with Gina Cigna (Milan), Nicola Gedda (Switzerland) and Edita Gruberova. *Career:* Appearances in Berne, Lucerne and Basle, 1993–96, as Belfiore in Il Viaggio a Reims, the Painter in Lulu, Rossini's Almaviva, Tamino, and Dinna in La Vestale; Season 1996–97 as Ramiro in La Cenerentola at Lille and Mozart's Belmonte at Biel; Season 1997–98 as Rodolfo at Biel, Nikolai's Fenton at Visp, Painter and Negro in Lulu at the Opéra Bastille, Hoffmann at Klagenfurt and Narraboth in Salome at Barcelona; Season 1999–2000 as Lensky in St Etienne, Don Ottavio in Frankfurt, Arbace in Idomeneo at Toulouse and Belmonte for Nice Opéra; Further engagements as Verdi's Fenton in Frankfurt, Belfiore in La Finta giardiniera, and in concerts throughout Europe. *Address:* c/o Theateragentur Dr G. Hilbert, Maximilianstrasse 22, 80539 Munich, Germany.

**PIANA, Dominique;** harpist, teacher, performer, composer and arranger and writer; b. 5 July 1956, Eupen, Belgium; m. Will Joel Friedman 1985; one s. *Education:* Royal Conservatory of Music, Brussels, Claremont Graduate University, CA. *Career:* Professor of Harp, La Sierra University, Riverside, California, USA, 1982–2001; Professor of Harp, University of Redlands, California, 1985–2001; Holy Names College, Oakland, California, 2001–; As performer: Solo and lecture recitals, Chamber Music, Concerti; California Arts Council Touring Roster, 2000–01; Founder, Pleasanton Chamber Players; mem, American Harp Society, Programme Chairman, 1992 National Conference; American String Teachers Association; World Harp Congress; American Liszt Society; OPERA America. *Compositions:* Mélodies imaginaires, for solo harp, 1995. *Recordings:* Harpiana Productions: Fancy, entertaining music for harp, 1984; Lulling the Soul, Carols of Love and Wonder, 1992; The Harp of King David, Songs of Longing and Hope, 1994; Beyond Dreams, the Spirit of Romanticism, 1996. *Publications:* Contributions to Revue Musicale Belge, Belgium; Lumière, France; Contemplation, The Franz Liszt Anthology for Harp. *Address:* 3078 Camino del Cino, Pleasanton, CA 94566, USA. *Fax:* (925) 600-1441. *E-mail:* dominiquepiana@comcast.net. *Website:* www.dominiquepiana.com.

**PIAU, Sandrine;** French singer (soprano); b. 1969. *Education:* studied with Julius Rudel in Paris, with Rachel Yakar and René Jacobs at Versailles. *Career:* concert appearances in Bach's Passions and Magnificat under Philippe Herrweghe and Mozart's Exultate Jubilate with Jean-Claude Malgoire; has also appeared under William Christie in Rossi's Orfeo, Mozart's Davidde Penitente, Campra's Idoménée and Purcell's King Arthur (Covent Garden and Paris 1995); has also sung in Purcell's Fairy Queen, Rameau's Les Indes Galantes and Castor et Pollux (at Aix), Handel's Scipione (as Berenice) and Pergolesi's Stabat Mater; sang Almirena in Handel's Rinaldo under Christophe Rousset, Beaune 1996; season 1998 as Antigona in Handel's Admeto on tour to Australia and in Montpellier and Beaune; season 2000 as Atalanta in Handel's Serse at Dresden, Ismene in Mozart's Mitridate at the Paris Châtelet, and in Handel's Tamerlano at Drottningholm, Stockholm. *Current Management:* Ornello Cogliolo, Via del Babuino 76, 00187 Rome, Italy. *Telephone:* (06) 3207627. *Fax:* (06) 3207628. *E-mail:* cogliolo@cogliolo.it. *Website:* www.cogliolo.it.

**PICCONI, Maurizio;** Singer (Bass-Baritone); b. 1957, Italy. *Education:* Studied at Osimo. *Career:* After winning competitions such as the Concours Bellini in 1983 and the Philadelphia International in 1985, sang widely in Italy; Roles have included Rossini's Taddeo, Gianni Schicchi, Bartolo, Dulcamara, Belcore and Malatesta; Sang at Zürich in 1988 as Sulpice in La Fille du Régiment, at Bonn in 1992 as Leporello and further appearances at Dublin, Bilbao, Amsterdam, Strasbourg and Philadelphia; Sang Rossini's Bartolo at Pavia, 1995; Sang Sulpice in La Fille du régiment at St Gallen, 2000. *Recordings include:* Il Furioso all'Isola di San Domingo by Donizetti. *Address:* c/o Bonn Opera, Am Boeselagerhof 1, Pf 2440 Bonn, Germany.

**PICHLER, Guenter;** Violinist and Conductor; b. 9 Sept. 1940, Austria. *Education:* Studied in Vienna. *Career:* Leader of the Vienna Symphony Orchestra, 1958; Leader of Vienna Philharmonic, 1961; Professor, University for Music, Vienna, 1963–; Guest Professor, University for Music, Cologne, 1993–; Founder, leader of the Alban Berg Quartet from 1971; Annual concert series at the Vienna Konzerthaus, the QEH London, Théâtre des Champs Elysées, Paris, Opera Zürich, Philharmonie Cologne, Alte Oper Frankfurt, Madrid, and festival and concert engagements world-wide; Associate Artists at the South Bank Centre, London; Conducting engagements include Vienna, Israel, Irish and Norwegian Chamber Orchestras; London Mozart Players, Ensemble Orchestral de Paris, Orchestre della Toscana, Hallé Orchestra, Deutsche Kammerphilharmonie, Tokyo Osaka and Sendai Philharmonic Orchestras and NHK Orchestra; Principal Guest Conductor Orchestra Kanazawa; US appearances: Washington DC, Chicago, Boston, Philadelphia, Los Angeles, San Francisco and New York (Carnegie Hall). *Recordings include:* Complete quartets of Beethoven, Brahms, Berg, Webern and Bartók; Late quartets of Mozart, Schubert, Haydn and Dvořák; Ravel, Debussy and Schumann Quartets; Live recordings from Carnegie Hall (Mozart, Schumann); Konzerthaus in Vienna, Mozart; Complete Beethoven; Brahms, Dvořák, Smetana, Rihm, Schnittke, Berio, Janáček; Opéra-Comique Paris, (Brahms). *Honours:* Grand Prix du Disque; Deutscher Schallplatenpreis; Edison Prize; Japan Grand Prix; Gramophone Magazine Award; International Classical Music Award, 1992; Honorary Member of the Vienna Konzerthaus. *Address:* Intermusica Artists' Management, 16 Duncan Terrace, London N1 8BZ, England.

**PICK-HIERONIMI, Monica Maria Anna;** German singer (soprano); *Professor, Staatliche Hochschule für Musik, Cologne;* b. 14 Dec. , Olpe; d. of Jacob Pick and Helene Schäfer; m. Otto Hieronimi 1968; one s. *Education:* Rheinische Musikschule, Cologne. *Career:* numerous nat. and int. opera and concert appearances including performances in Munich, Mannheim, Frankfurt, Stuttgart, Vienna Staatsoper, Hamburg, Barcelona Theatre del Liceu, Spain, Rome, Deutsche Staatsoper Berlin, Paris, Milan, Italy, Zurich, Switzerland, Brussels, Prague, Verona (first German Aida), Italy 1992, Carnegie Hall, New York 1992; has performed at many festivals, including Buxton, UK, Würzburg Mozartfest, Schleswig-Holstein, Karlsruhe Händelsfestspiele, Prague Spring Festival, Arena di Verona Int. Festival, Vienna Festival Weeks, Festival di Caracalla, Rome 1991, Oslo, Helsinki, Luxor; Prof. Staatliche Hochschule für Musik, Cologne 1992–. *Operas include:* Don Giovanni, Norma, Elektra (Idomeneo, Chrysothemis), La Forza del Destino, Ariadne, La Clemenza di Tito, Otello, Il Trovatore, Un Ballo in Maschera, Aida, Der Rosenkavalier, Die Frau ohne Schatten (Kaiserin). *Recordings:* Christ on the Mount of Olives 1987, Verdi's Requiem 1989, Don Giovanni 1991, Nabucco, under Guadagno with Arena di Verona 1996. *Honours:* Carpine d'Oro, Brescia 1990. *Address:* Steinackerweg 25, 64658 Fürth-Steinbach (office); Ankerstrasse 11, 50676 Cologne, Germany (home). *Telephone:* (6253) 3906 (office); (221) 3319261 (home). *Fax:* (360) 3510204 (office). *E-mail:* pickhieronimi@aol.com (home).

**PICKENS, Jo Ann;** American singer (soprano); b. 4 Aug. 1950, Robstown, Tex.; d. of Anne Belle Sanders. *Career:* started singing career in Chicago Lyric

Opera; has perfomed in recital and concerts around the world and appeared with conductors including Solti, Dorati, Rattle, Norrington, Pesek and Sanderling; also appears in opera, notably Berlioz's The Trojans 1987 and Armide 1988. *Honours:* Award, Int. Competition for Singers, Paris 1980; Metropolitan Opera Regional Auditions 1981; Benson & Hedges Gold Award 1981. *Address:* c/o Norman McCann International Artists Ltd, The Coach House, 56 Lawrie Park Gardens, London, SE26 6XJ, England.

**PICKER, Martin;** American fmr professor and musicologist; b. 3 April 1929, Chicago, Illinois; m. Ruth Gross, 21 June 1956, 1 s., 2 d. *Education:* PhB, 1947, MA, 1951, University of Chicago; PhD, University of California, Berkeley, 1960. *Career:* Instructor, University of Illinois, 1959–61; Assistant Professor, 1961–65; Associate Professor, 1965–68; Professor, 1968–97, Emeritus Professor, 1997–, Rutgers University; Chairman, Music Department, Rutgers College, 1973–79; mem, American Musicological Society; International Musicological Society. *Publications:* The Chanson Albums of Marguerite of Austria, 1965; Introduction to Music, with Martin Bernstein, 3rd edition, 1966, 4th edition, 1972; Fors Seulement: 30 Compositions, 1981; The Motet Books of Andrea Antico, 1987; Johannes Ockeghem and Jacob Obrecht: A Guide to Research, 1988; Henricus Isaac, A Guide to Research, 1991; New Josquin Edition, vol. 16, 2000; Editor-in-Chief, Journal of the American Musicological Society, 1969–71. *Honours:* I Tatti Fellow, Harvard University, 1966–67; NEH Fellow, 1972–73. *Address:* 3069 Chimney Ridge, Charlottesville, VA 22911, USA (home).

**PICKER, Tobias;** Composer; b. 18 July 1954, New York. *Education:* Studied with Charles Wuorinen at the Manhattan School of Music (BM 1976) and with Elliott Carter at Juilliard (MM 1978). *Career:* Composer-in-Residence with the Houston Symphony Orchestra, 1985–87; Commissions from the American Composers Orchestra, San Francisco Symphony Orchestra, St Paul Chamber Orchestra, and Ursula Oppens; Operas, Emmeline, premiered at the Santa Fe Festival, 1996 and Fantastic Mr. Fox, Los Angeles, 1998; Cello Concerto premiered at the London Proms, 2001. *Compositions include:* 4 Sextets for various instruments, 1973, 1973, 1977, 1981; Rhapsody for violin and piano, 1979; 3 Piano Concertos, 1980, 1983, 1986; Violin Concerto, 1981; 3 Symphonies, 1982, 1986, 1989; Serenade for piano and wind quintet, 1983; Piano-o-rama, for 2 pianos, 1984; Encantadas, for narrator and orchestra, 1984; Dedication Anthem for band, 1984; Old and Lost Rivers, for orchestra, 1986; String Quartet, New Memories, 1987; Piano Quintet, 1988; Romances and Interludes, after Schumann, for oboe and orchestra, 1990; Two Fantasies, for orchestra, 1991; Bang, for piano and orchestra, 1992; Violin Sonata, Invisible Lilacs, 1992; And Suddenly it's Evening, for orchestra, 1994; Suite for cello and piano, 1998; Cello Concerto, 2001. *Honours:* Charles Ives Scholarship, 1978; Guggenheim Fellowship, 1981. *Address:* c/o ASCAP, ASCAP Building, 1 Lincoln Plaza, New York, NY 10023, USA.

**PICKETT, Philip;** Director and Performer of Early Wind Instruments; b. 17 Nov. 1950, London, England. *Education:* Introduced to variety of early wind instruments by Anthony Baines and David Munrow: experienced on recorder, crumhorn, shawm, rackett and others; Professor of Recorder at the Guildhall School of Music, 1972, helping to organise the School's early music department; Fellow of the GSM, 1985; Soloist with leading ensembles, including the Academy of St Martin in the Fields, Polish Chamber Orchestra, London Mozart Players, City of London Sinfonia, London Bach Orchestra and the English Concert; As Director of the New London Consort has appeared at major festivals and concert halls in Finland, France, Germany, Greece, Netherlands, Hong Kong, Israel, Belgium, Spain, Italy, Latin America, Switzerland, USSR and Yugoslavia; British appearances include five Early Music Network tours; Medieval Christmas Extravaganza on the South Bank and concerts for the 21st anniversary of the Queen Elizabeth Hall; Director of the South Bank Summerscope Festival of Medieval and Renaissance Music (Pickett's Pageant), 1988; Regular engagements at the Bath, Edinburgh, King's Lynn, Edinburgh and City of London Festivals; BBC Programmes include music for half the complete Shakespeare play series, BBC 2; Music in Camera showings and regular concerts on Radio 3; Composed music for A Meeting in Vallodolid (Shakespeare and Cervantes) for Radio 3, 1991; Promenade Concerts include Bonfire of the Vanities (Medici Wedding Celebrations of 1539), 1990; Oswald von Wolkenstein concert at the Purcell Room, London, 1997 and Miracles of Mary at the QEH; Engaged to conduct Acis and Galatea for Holland Park Opera, London, 2003. *Recordings include:* Dances from Terpsichore by Michael Praetorius; Medieval Carmina Burana; The Delights of Posilipo (Neopolitan Dances); Instrumental music by Biber and Schmelzer; Monteverdi Vespers and Orfeo; Cantatas and concertos by Telemann and Vivaldi; Medieval pilgrimage to Santiago; CD of Virtuoso Italian Vocal Music with Catherine Bott: de Rore, Cavalieri, Luzzaschi, G Caccini, Rasi, Gagliano, Marini, Frescobaldi, Monteverdi, F Caccini, Bernardi, Rossi and Carissimi (Il lamento in morte di Maria Stuarda); Biber Requiem. *Address:* c/o Jessica Atkinson, Polygram Classics (Publicity), PO Box 1420, 1 Sussex Place, Hammersmith, London W6 9XS, England.

**PIDOUX, Roland;** Cellist; b. 29 Oct. 1946, Paris, France. *Education:* Studied at the Paris Conservatoire from 1960, with André Navarra, Jean Hubeau and Joseph Calvet. *Career:* Co-founded the Ensemble Instrumental de France; Played with the orchestra of the Paris Opéra from 1968; Member of the Via Nova Quartet, 1970–78; Joined Regis and Bruno Pasquier, 1972, to form the Pasquier Trio; Directed the record collection Les Musiciens for Harmonia Mundi, 1979; Soloist with the Orchestra National of France, 1979–87; Professor of Cello at the Paris Conservatoire, 1987; Plays a Stradivarius of

1692. *Address:* Conservatoire National Superieur de Musique, 14 Rue de Madrid, 75008 Paris, France.

**PIECZONKA, Adrianne,** BMus; Canadian singer (soprano); b. 2 March 1963, Poughkeepsie, New York, USA. *Education:* Univ. of Western Ontario; Univ. of Toronto, Opera Division. *Career:* Began European career in 1989 at Vienna Volksoper; mem., Vienna State Opera 1991, sang Countess in Marriage of Figaro; Donna Elvira and Donna Anna in Don Giovanni; Desdemona in Otello; Agathe in Der Freischütz; Eva in Die Meistersinger von Nürnberg; Tatyana in Eugene Onegin; Antonia in Les Contes d'Hoffmann; Die Tochter in Cardillac; Micaela in Carmen; UK operatic debut, Glyndebourne Festival, 1995, Arabella, 1996; Sang Elsa in Lohengrin at Munich State Opera and in Los Angeles and Dresden; Debut at La Scala as Donna Anna, 1999, later as Marschallin in Der Rosenkavalier; Debut Covent Garden as Donna Anna, 2002; Debut at Metropolitan Opera as Lisa in Pique Dame, 2004; Sang Elisabetta in Don Carlo at Salzburg Festival, 2003; Has worked with Riccardo Muti, Claludio Abbado, Sir Colin Davis; Christian Thielemann, Sir Georg Solti; Lorin Maazel, Zubin Mehta; Appears frequently on BBC Radio, CBC and Austrian radio ORF. *Recordings include:* First Lady in Die Zauberflöte conducted by Solti, 1989; Die Fledermaus (Rosalinde), 1997; Complete Richard Strauss Orchestral Songs, 1998; Don Giovanni (Donna Anna), 1999; Millennium Opera Gala, 2000; Aids Gala Berlin, 2003; Don Giovanni (Donna Elvira) for television, video and DVD, 1995. *Honours:* Winner, 's-Hertogenbosch Singing Competition, Netherlands, 1988; Pleine-sur-Mer Singing Competition, France, 1988; Dora Award for best operatic performance (Canada) 2004. *Website:* www.adriannepieczonka.com.

**PIERARD, Catherine;** Soprano; b. 1960, England. *Career:* Many appearances in the United Kingdom and Europe, with the Jerusalem Symphony Orchestra, City of London Sinfonia, Scottish Chamber Orchestra and Concertgebouw; Opera roles have included Tatiana in Eugene Onegin, Fiordiligi and Donna Elvira with English Touring Opera (1994), Papagena in Die Zauberflöte at the 1990 London Proms, Purcell's Dido (Spitalfields Festival 1993), Gluck's Alceste, Iphigénie and Euridice; Engagements with Roger Norrington in Orfeo at the Bath Festival and Purcell's Fairy Queen in Florence; Drusilla and Fortune in Monteverdi's Poppea under Richard Hickox; Season 1995–96 in Mozart's C Minor Mass, Messiah with the Ulster and London Bach Orchestras and Ravel's Shéhérazade with the Bournemouth Symphony Orchestra; Biber's Arminio at the Salzburg and Innsbruck Festivals, Bach's Magnificat at Ottawa and Handel's Belshazzar with Nicholas Kraemer. *Recordings include:* Monteverdi Arias (Hyperion) Dioclesian and The Fairy Queen (EMI); Britten's Rape of Lucretia (Chandos). *Telephone:* (20) 8995-3226. *Fax:* (20) 8742-7476. *E-mail:* catherinepierard@aol.com.

**PIKE, Jeremy,** MA, PhD, LRAM; British composer; *Head of Composition, Chetham's School of Music*; b. 20 Nov. 1955, London; m. Teresa Majcher, 15 Aug 1981, 1 d. *Education:* MA, King's College, Cambridge, 1973–76; Junior Exhibitioner, Royal Academy of Music, 1969–73; Postgraduate Composition and Conducting, Royal Academy of Music, 1976–77; LRAM, Piano, 1979. *Career:* British Council Scholarship to study composition with Henryk Gorecki in Poland, Katowice Academy of Music, 1978–79, and with Tadeusz Baird at the Warsaw Academy, 1979; Director of Contemporary Music, University of Warwick, 1981–87; Dir of Electroacoustic Music Royal Acad. of Music 1987–92; Head of Composition Chetham's School of Music 1989–. *Compositions include:* Time and Tide for Chorus and Orchestra, Bassoon Concerto, 2 Piano Concertos, A Street Under Siege for orchestra, Stamford Overture, 6 String Quartets, Oboe Quartet, Clarinet Quartet, Aphelion and Praesagium for violin and piano, 6 Piano Sonatas and other Piano works; vocal works. *Honours:* Hon. ARAM; Churchill Fellowship in the Application of New Tech. to the Arts 1998. *Address:* Chetham's School of Music, Long Millgate, Manchester M3 1SB, England (office). *E-mail:* jeremypike@chethams.com (office).

**PIKE, Julian;** Singer (Tenor); b. 1948, England. *Education:* Studied at the Royal College of Music and with Pierre Bernac in France. *Career:* Sang Don José in Peter Brook's version of Carmen in Paris, Zürich, Stockholm, Copenhagen and New York, 1982–84; Sang Michael in productions of Stockhausen's Donnerstag aus Licht in Netherlands, Germany, Italy and London (Covent Garden, 1985); Tour with the European Community Youth Orchestra under Matthias Bamert, 1985; Wexford Festival, 1985, in Mahagonny; Appearances with Kent Opera in Poppea and Rameau's Pygmalion; Has sung in Henze's English Cat in Frankfurt, at the Edinburgh Festival and for the BBC; Premiere productions of Montag aus Licht in Milan, Amsterdam, Frankfurt and Paris, from 1988; Sang Roderick in The Fall of the House of Usher by Glass with Music Theatre Wales, 1989; Ligeti Festival at the South Bank, 1989; Other roles include the Dancing Master in Ariadne and Piet the Pot in Le Grand Macabre; Season 1992 as Michael in the premiere of Stockhausen's Dienstag aus Licht at Lisbon and later at Amsterdam; Recitals at the Bath, City of London, Camden and Aldeburgh Festivals: repertoire includes, Bach, Monteverdi and contemporary music; Tours of France, Germany, Belgium, Netherlands, Poland, Finland and Austria (Salzburg); Appearances with the Songmakers' Almanac and Fortune's Fire Lute Song Ensemble; Head of Vocal Studies, Birmingham Conservatoire, 1999. *Address:* Birmingham Conservatoire, Paradise Place, Birmingham B3 3HG, England.

**PIKE, Lionel John,** BMus, MA, DPhil, FRCO, ARCM; British organist and academic; *Professor Emeritus of Music, Royal Holloway College*; b. 7 Nov.

1939, Bristol; m. Jennifer Parker; two d. *Education:* Bristol Cathedral School, Pembroke Coll., Oxford. *Career:* Asst Organist, Bristol Cathedral 1957–59; Asst Organist, Royal Holloway Coll., London 1965, Organist and Dir of the Chapel Choir 1969–2005, Sr Lecturer in Music, later Prof. of Music –2005; Dean, Faculty of Music, Univ. of London; mem. Purcell Soc. (Cttee mem.), Vaughan Williams Soc., Robert Simpson Soc. (fmr Chair.), Havergal Brian Soc., Royal Musical Soc., Royal Coll. of Organists. *Compositions:* Monkey Music, The Pilgrim Way, Encircled by Sea, The Lyra Davidica Motets. *Recordings:* with the Chapel Choir of Royal Holloway Coll. 1993–2005. *Publications:* Beethoven, Sibelius and the Profound Logic, Hexachords in late Renaissance Music, Vaughan Williams and the Symphony, Pills to Purge Melancholy: the evolution of the English Ballett, Purcell: Symphony Anthems for in The Works of Henry Purcell (ed.); contrib. to Tempo, Music and Letters. *Honours:* Limpus Prize, Royal Coll. of Organists. *Address:* 34 Alderside Walk, Englefield Green, Egham, Surrey, TW20 0LY, England (home). *Telephone:* (1784) 435863 (home).

**PILAND, Jeanne;** Singer (Mezzo-Soprano); b. 3 Dec. 1945, Raleigh, North Carolina, USA. *Education:* Bachelor's Degree, University of North Carolina; Further studies in New York with Gladys White and Professor Carolyn Grant. *Career:* Debut: New York City Opera, 1972; New York City Opera, 1974–77; Sang at the Deutsche Oper am Rhein from 1977 as Cherubino, Composer, Ariadne, Octavian in Der Rosenkavalier, Silla in Palestrina and the Child in L'Enfant et les Sortilèges; Hamburg from 1981, Munich from 1985; Ludwigsburg Festival 1984, as Dorabella, Vienna Staatsoper, 1984, 1987, 1991 as Composer and Dorabella; Sang the Composer in Paris, Dresden, Hamburg, Vienna, Nice, Monte Carlo, Amsterdam, 1987, Ariadne auf Naxos at Covent Garden and Aix-en-Province, 1985; Returned to Aix 1986 and 1988, as Mozart's Idamante and Sextus, Composer and Octavian; Has appeared as Octavian at Dresden 1986 for 75th Anniversary of World premiere, Cologne, Zürich, Nice 1986, and Monte Carlo 1987, Santa Fe, 1988; Aix-en-Province, Munich, Hamburg 1988, as Idamante and Octavian; Sang Octavia in L'Incoronazione di Poppea Annius, La Clemenza di Tito, at Geneva, 1989; Other roles include Rosina and Cenerentola, Preziosilla, Smeaton (Anna Bolena), Zerlina and Massenet's Charlotte, Rosina, Concepcion, (L'Heure Espagnole), Elena (La Donna del Lago), Marguerite (Damnation de Faust), Clytemnestra, Iphigenia in Aulis, La Scala Milan, Cherubino, 1981; Houston and Los Angeles, Dorabella; Vancouver, Adalgisa, Norma, 1991–Carmen; Sang Charlotte in Werther for Florida Grand Opera, 1996; Olivia in the premiere of Trojahn's Was ihr wollt (Twelfth Night), Munich, 1998; Season 2000 as Neris in Cherubini's Médée at Montpellier (concert) and Eboli in Don Carlos at Dusseldorf; Repertoire includes, Berlioz, Les Nuits d'Eté, Shéhérazade, Mahler's Symphonies and Lied-Cycles. *Address:* c/o Grand Théâtre de Genève, 11 Boulevard de Théâtre, 1211 Geneva 11, Switzerland.

**PILARCZYK, Helga;** Singer (Soprano); b. 12 March 1925, Schoningen, Brunswick, Germany. *Education:* Studied in Brunswick and Hamburg. *Career:* Brunswick, 1951–54, debut as Irmentraud in Lortzing's Der Waffenschmied; Hamburg Staatsoper, 1954–68, notably as Berg's Marie and Lulu, the Mother in Dallapiccola's Il Prigioniero, Jocasta in Oedipus Rex, Renata in The Fiery Angel; St ädtische Oper Berlin, 1956, in the premiere of Henze's Il Re Cervo; Glyndebourne, 1958, 1960, as the Composer in Ariadne auf Naxos and Columbina in Arlecchino; Covent Garden, 1959, as Salome; US debut Washington, 1960, as the Woman in Erwartung; Metropolitan Opera, 1965, as Marie in Wozzeck. *Recordings:* Erwartung; Pierrot Luniare. *Publications:* Kann Man die Moderne Opern Singen?, 1964. *Address:* c/o Hamburgische Staatsoper, Grosse-Theaterstrasse 34, 2000 Hamburg 36, Germany.

**PILAVACHI, Anthony;** Irish stage director; b. 1962, Cyprus. *Education:* Guildhall School of Music and Drama, 1984–86. *Career:* Debut: Pergolesi's La Serva Padrona at Monte Carlo, 1983; Director and Assistant at the Bonn Opera, 1987–92, notably with Falstaff (1991); Director and Assistant, Cologne Opera, 1992–95, notably with Peter Grimes, 1994; Carmen at Bergen (1992); Il Barbiere di Siviglia and Traviata at Bogota (1994); Season 1995 with Un Ballo in Maschera at Freiburg, Carmina Burana at Dresden in the Zwinger Courtyard, Handel's Tolomeo with the Hallé and Lulu at Lubeck, 1996; Season 1997–98 in Freiburg with Orpheus in the Underworld and The Love of Three Oranges, for the reopening of theatre at Freiburg; Tales of Hoffmann at Lubeck; La Traviata at Gothenburg; Madama Butterfly at Lubeck; Engaged for 1998–99 season with Saul at Komische Oper Berlin; Daphne at Deutsche Oper Berlin; Faust at Freiburg; Season 1999–2000, Fliegende Holländer at Frankfurt; Dialogues of Carmelites and The Magic Flute at Freiburg; Seasons 2000–02 directed Cendrillon at Lubeck, Boris Godunov at Hanover, Così fan tutte at Bremen, Onegin at Freiburg, La Bohème at St Gallen, Fanciulla del West at Dessau and Figaro at Oldenburg; Season 2002–03, world premiere of Verdi, Gustavo III at Gothenburg, Sweden, Il Tabarro and Gianni Schicchi at Lübeck, Lohengrin at Bremen, Cavalleria Rusticana and Pagliacci at Dessau; Season 2003–04, Rigoletto at Cottbus, German premiere of Verdi, Gustavo III at Darmstadt, Idomeneo at Oldenburg; Season 2004–05: Entführung aus dem Serail at Oldenburg, Eugene Onegin at St Gallen, and Don Giovanni at Cottbus; Season 2005–06: Freischütz at Krefeld, Clemenza di Titus at Oldenburg, Zar und Zimmermann at Bremen. *Honours:* Princess Grace of Monaco Scholarship, 1983. *Address:* c/o Siemensstrasse 02, 50825 Köln, Germany. *Telephone:* 221 554284. *E-mail:* AnthonyPilavachi@gmx.de.

**PILGRIM, Shirley;** British singer (soprano) and teacher; *Singing Teacher, Queenswood and Chancellors Schools*; b. 1957, London; m. 1980. *Education:*

Studied at the Royal Academy of Music with Ilse Wolf and Patricia Clark; Further study at the National Opera Studio. *Career:* Sang with the Glyndebourne Festival and Touring Opera choruses; Solo debut as Helena with the Touring Opera, in A Midsummer Night's Dream; Appearances in Hong Kong, and at the Buxton and Wexford Festivals; With Opera East has sung Mimi, and the Female Chorus in The Rape of Lucretia; Scottish Opera as Despina, and cover for various roles; New D'Oyly Carte Opera Co., Elsie in Yeomen of the Guard and Phyllis in Iolanthe; Oratorio and concert engagements, notably at the Barbican Hall, London, and recitals including lighter American music; Sang in Born Again directed by Peter Hall at the Chichester Festival; Other recent roles include: Countess in The Marriage of Figaro, Fiordiligi in Così fan tutte, Tosca in Tosca, Mimi in La Bohème. *Recordings include:* Solo album: Shirley Pilgrim with Attitude; Duet album–Lloyd Weber. *Honours:* ARCM, 1979; Dip RAM, 1981. *Address:* 85 Chichester Road, Edmonton Green, London N9 9 DH, England.

**PILOU, Jeannette;** Singer (Soprano); b. July 1931, Alexandria, Egypt. *Education:* Studied with Carla Castellani in Milan. *Career:* Debut: Milan in 1958 as Violetta; Sang widely in Italy as Mélisande, Mimi, Liu, Susanna, Manon, Nedda, Micaela, Marguerite and Nannetta; Appearances in Barcelona, Buenos Aires, Hanover, Hamburg and Wexford; Vienna in 1965 as Mimi; With Metropolitan Opera from 1967–86 with debut as Gounod's Juliette; Covent Garden, 1971 as Madama Butterfly; Sang at Monte Carlo 1973 in the premiere of Rossellini's La Reine Morte; Other roles have included the female leads in Von Einem's Der Prozess, Gluck's Euridice, Marzeline in Fidelio and Magda in La Rondine; US appearances in Houston, Chicago, San Francisco, New Orleans and Philadelphia; Sang Mélisande in Athens, 1998. *Recordings include:* Micaela in Carmen.

**PILZ, Gottfried;** stage designer and costume designer; b. 1944, Salzburg, Austria; m. Isabel Ines Glathar; one s. *Education:* Academy of Arts, Vienna. *Career:* Assistant at the Vienna State Opera to Wieland Wagner, Luchino Visconti, Teo Otto, Luciano Damiani, Rudolf Heinrich and others, 1965–69; Assistant to Filippo Sanjust, 1969–72; debut in Reimann's Melusine world premiere at Berlin, Edinburgh and Schwetzingen Festival, staged by Gustav Rudolf Sellner; Operas, Dramatic Theatre and Ballets in Austria, Belgium, the United Kingdom, Netherlands, USA and Switzerland, principal in Germany; Exhibitions in Berlin, Kunsthalle Bielefeld, Düsseldorf, Kunsthalle Kiel and Wuppertal (Reflexe I–III, Aus-Grenzen I–III); debut as a producer with Rameau's Hippolyte et Aricie at Oper Leipzig, 1993; collaborations with John Dew, 1979–92 (Wagner's Ring, Krefeld, 1981–85, The Unknown Repertory at Bielefeld, 1983–91, Les Huguenots Deutsche Oper Berlin, 1987 as well as Royal Opera House, Covent Garden, 1991 and others); With Götz Friedrich (Der Rosenkavalier, Un Ballo in Maschera, Deutsche Oper Berlin, 1993) with Gunther Krämer since 1990 at Kölner Schauspiel, with Nikolaus Lehnhoff at Oper Frankfurt and Leipzig; Munich and Zürich, Henze's new version of Der Prinz von Homburg, 1992 and 1993; With Christine Mielitz, Rienzi at Komische Oper Berlin, 1992, engaged for Henze's The Bassarids at Hamburg State Opera, 1994 and also for 1994 at Oper Leipzig, Moses and Aron staged by George Tabori; Designs for the premiere production of Bose's Schlachthof 5, at the 1996 Munich Festival; Wagner's Ring at Helsinki, 1996–99. *Address:* Leipzig Opera, Augustusplatz 12, 7010 Leipzig, Germany.

**PILZ, Janos;** Violinist; b. 1960, Hungary. *Education:* Studied at the Franz Liszt Academy of Budapest and with Sándor Devich, György Kurtág and András Mihaly. *Career:* Member of the Keller String Quartet from 1986, debut concert at Budapest, March 1987; Played Beethoven's Grosse Fuge and Schubert's Death and the Maiden Quartet at Interforum 87; Series of concerts in Budapest with Zoltan Kocsis and Deszö Ranki (piano) and Kalman Berkes (clarinet); Further appearances in Nurembourg at the Chamber Music Festival La Baule and tours of Bulgaria, Austria, Switzerland, Italy (Ateforum 88 Ferrara), Belgium and Ireland; Concerts for Hungarian Radio and Television. *Recordings:* Albums for Hungaroton from 1989. *Honours:* 2nd Prize, Evian International String Quartet Competition, May 1988. *Address:* c/o Kunstter-Management T. Dönch, Weimarer Strasse 48, A–1180 Wien, Ausrtia.

**PIMLOTT, Steven,** MA; British theatre and opera director; b. 18 April 1953, Manchester; m. Daniela Bechly 1991; two s. one d. *Education:* Univ. of Cambridge. *Career:* began career in regional theatre and opera; work directed includes: The Park 1984, Twelfth Night (Crucible Theatre, Sheffield) 1986, Samson et Delila (Bregenz) 1988, Carmen (Earl's Court, London) 1990, Sunday in the Park with George (Nat. Theatre) 1990, Molière's The Miser (Nat. Theatre) 1991, Joseph and the Amazing Technicolour Dreamcoat (Palladium, London) 1991, (Broadway) 1993, Julius Caesar (RSC, Stratford) 1991, Murder in the Cathedral (RSC, Stratford) 1993, La Bohème (ENO) 1993, Unfinished Business (RSC, Barbican) 1994, Butterfly Kiss (Almeida) 1994, Measure for Measure (RSC, Stratford) 1994, The Strip (Royal Court) 1995, Macbeth (Hamburg-Staatsoper) 1997, Camino Real (RSC), Never Land (Royal Court), Bad Weather (RSC), musical staging of Doctor Doolittle (Triumph Apollo) 1998, Hamlet (RSC) 2001; Dir 1996/97 RSC Season, including productions of As You Like It and The Learned Ladies, 1998/99 RSC Antony and Cleopatra, 2000 RSC Richard II, 2001 RSC Hamlet; world premiere of Ion Almeida opera L'incoronazione di Poppea, ENO; Assoc. Dir RSC 1996–2002, Assoc. Artist 2002–; Artistic Dir The Other Place RSC 1999–2001; world première of Bombay Dreams (Apollo Victoria, London) 2002; Artistic Dir Chichester Festival Theatre 2003–, Nathan the Wise and The Seagull (Chichester) 2003; Artistic Dir Savoy Opera (London) 2004–, Bombay Dreams,

Broadway (NY) 2004, The Master and Margarita (Chichester) 2004. *Address:* c/o Harriet Cruickshank, 97 Old South Lambeth Road, London, SW8 1XU; Old House, Old House Road, Great Horkesley, Colchester, Essex CO6 4EQ, England.

**PINI, Carl;** Violinist; b. 2 Jan. 1934, London, England. *Education:* Studied with his father, cellist Anthony Pini (1902–89) and in London. *Career:* Former leader of the Philomusica of London, English Chamber Orchestra and Philharmonia Orchestras (1974–); Leader of the London String Quartet from 1968 and the Melbourne Symphony Orchestra from 1975; Many chamber recitals in English works and the established repertory. *Address:* c/o Melbourne SO, PO Box 9994, Melbourne, VIC 3001, Australia.

**PINKHAM, Daniel,** AB, MA; American composer; *Professor, New England Conservatory;* b. 5 June 1923, Lynn, Mass. *Education:* Harvard Univ.; pvt. studies with Nadia Boulanger. *Career:* Faculty mem., New England Conservatory 1957–, later Prof.; Music Dir King's Chapel, Boston 1958–2000; Fellow, American Acad. of Arts and Sciences. *Compositions:* four symphonies 1961, 1962, 1986, 1990, concertos for trumpet, violin, organ, piano, piccolo, theatre works and operas, chamber music, songs, electronic music, TV film scores, The Creation of the World (oratorio) 1994, String Trio 1998. *Recordings:* Christmas Cantata, Signs of the Zodiac, Symphonies 2, 3 and 4, Angels are everywhere, Serenades, Miracles, Epiphanies, Magnificat, Proverbs, Diversions, Concertante for violin and harpsichord soli, strings and celesta, Inter alia, Advent Cantata, Wedding Cantata, String Quartet, Versets, Holland Waltzes. *Honours:* Hon. LittD (Nebraska Wesleyan Univ.) 1976; Hon. MusD (Adrian Coll.) 1977, (Westminster Choir Coll.) 1979, (New England Conservatory) 1993, Ithaca Coll.) 1994, (Boston Conservatory) 1998; Fulbright Fellowship 1950, Ford Foundation Fellowship 1962, Composer of the Year American Guild of Organists 1990, Alfred Nash Patterson Foundation Lifetime Achievement Award 1996. *Address:* 150 Chilton Street, Cambridge, MA 02138-1227, USA (home). *Telephone:* (617) 876-8375 (home). *Fax:* (617) 876-2412 (home). *E-mail:* pinkham150@comcast.net (home). *Website:* www.danielpinkham.net (home).

**PINNOCK, Trevor David,** CBE, ARCM, FRAM; British harpsichordist and conductor; b. 16 Dec. 1946, Canterbury; s. of Kenneth and Joyce Pinnock. *Education:* Canterbury Cathedral School, Royal Coll. of Music, London. *Career:* Jt F. Galliard Harpsichord Trio, début, London 1966, solo début, London 1968, Dir The English Concert 1973–2003; Artistic Dir, Prin. Conductor Nat. Arts Centre Orchestra, Ottawa 1991–96, Artistic Adviser 1996–; has toured Western Europe, USA, South America, Canada, Australia, Japan with The English Concert, as solo harpsichordist and as orchestral/opera conductor; début Metropolitan Opera, New York 1988. *Recordings include:* Handel, J. S. Bach, C. P. E. Bach, Rameau, Vivaldi, Scarlatti, 16th-, 17th- and 18th-century harpsichord music and most of the standard baroque orchestral/concerto/choral repertoire. *Honours:* Gramophone Award for Bach Partitas BWV 825-30 2001. *Current Management:* Askonas Holt Ltd, Lonsdale Chambers, 27 Chancery Lane, London, WC2A 1PF, England. *Telephone:* (20) 7400-1700. *Fax:* (20) 7400-1799. *E-mail:* info@askonasholt.co.uk. *Website:* www.askonasholt.co.uk.

**PINSCHOF, Thomas;** Flautist; b. 14 Feb. 1948, Vienna, Austria. *Education:* Artist and Teacher Diploma, Conservatorium of Vienna with Camillo Wanausek; Studies with Aurèle Nicolet; Masterclasses with Karl-Heinz Zöller, Jean-Pierre Rampal, Severino Gazzelloni; Postgraduate Studies, Indiana University, USA. *Career:* Debut: Wiener Musikverein, Brahms-Saal, 1965; Member, Vienna Symphony Orchestra, 1971–72; Berkshire Music Festival, Tanglewood, USA (with Scholarship Boston Symphony Orchestra), 1969; Founder, ENSEMBLE I, 1971–; Artist-in-Residence, with ENSEMBLE I, Victorian College of the Arts, Melbourne, Australia, 1976; Acting Head, Woodwind Department, Lecturer in Flute and Chamber Music, Victorian College of Arts, Melbourne, until 1988; Lecturer, Canberra School of Music, Melbourne University. *Recordings:* Deutsche Grammophon, Adel-Cord, Philips. *Publications:* Music editions for various publishers including, own series, Pinschofon, with Zimmermann. *Contributions:* The Flautist; Flutenotes; Musikerzeihung; Österreichishce Musikzeitschrift; Kunst und Freie Berufe. *Honours:* 2nd Prize, International Flute Competition, Severino Gazzelloni, 1975; Alban Berg Foundation Award, 1971; Australia Council Music Board Grantee, 1984–85 for project with Prof Nikolaus Harnoncourt. *Address:* Mozart Circle, Donvale, VIC 3111, Australia.

**PINTSCHER, Matthias;** German composer; b. 29 Jan. 1971, Marl. *Education:* Detmold Musikhochschule, Robert Schumann Hochschule, Düsseldorf. *Career:* commissions from Berlin Philharmonic, NDR Symphony Orchestra, Cleveland Orchestra; composer-in-residence to the Nationaltheater, Mannheim 1999–2000; composer-in-residence, Konzerthaus Dortmund 2002–03; première of Thomas Chatterton, opera in two acts, Dresden Oper 1998, L'Espace Dernier, Opéra de Paris 2003. *Compositions:* Choc (Monumento IV) 1996, Fünf Orchesterstücke 1997, a twilight's song 1997, Musik aus Thomas Chatteron 1998, Hérodiade-Fragmente 1999, Sur depart 1999, with lilies white 2000–01, 1 tenebrae 2000–01, en sourdine 2002. *Recordings:* Fünf Orchesterstücke, Musik aus Thomas Chatteron, Choc, Hérodiade-Fragmente, dernier espace avec introspecteur, Départ (Monument III), Figura I und II, Lieder und Schneebilder (Nr 1–4), Janusgesicht, a twilight's song. *Honours:* Foundation Prince Pierre de Monaco 1999, Kompositionspreis der Osterfestspiele Salzburg 2000, Hindemith-Preis from the Schleswig-Holstein Music Festival 2000, Hans Werner Henze Prize (Westfälischer Musikpreis)

2002. *Current Management:* Van Walsum Management, 4 Addison Bridge Place, London, W14 8XP, England. *Telephone:* (20) 7371-4343 (office). *Fax:* (20) 7371-4344 (office). *E-mail:* vwm@vanwalsum.com (office). *Website:* www.vanwalsum.com (office).

**PIRES, Filipe;** Composer; b. 26 June 1934, Lisbon, Portugal; m. Ligia Falcao, 29 Mar 1958. *Education:* Piano Superior Course, 1952; Composition Superior Course, 1953, National Conservatory, Lisbon; Piano and Composition, Hannover Music High School, 1957–60. *Career:* Prof. of Composition, Porto National Conservatory, 1960–70; Prof. of Composition, Lisbon National Conservatory, 1972–75; Music Specialist, UNESCO, Paris, 1975–79; Concert tours in Europe (Pianist and Composer); Professor of Composition, Porto High School of Music, 1993–; Artistic Dir Director, National Orchestra, Porto, 1997–99; mem, Vice-President, Portuguese Authors Society. *Compositions:* Figurations I, flute; Sonatine, violin and piano; Piano Trio; Figurations II, piano; Figurations III, 2 pianos; 3 Poems by Fernando Pessoa, high voice and piano; String Quartet; Ostinati, 6 percussionists; Zoocratas, music theatre; Disimulation, for guitar; Brass septet; Epos, orchestra; Ricercare, orchestra; Playing Ludwig, orchestra; Babel, speaker, tenor, baritone, bass, male choir, orchestra; 3 Bagatelles, piano; Partita, piano; Varied song, piano; Stretto, 2 pianos. *Recordings:* Piano Trio; Figurations I; Figurations IV; Ostinati; Figurations III; String Quartet; Canto Ecumenico, tape music; Litania, tape music; Homo Sapiens, tape music; 20 Choral Songs; Portugaliae Genesis, baritone, mixed choir and orchestra; Sintra; Akronos, orchestra; Sonata, piano; Sonorities Studies, piano; Figurations I, flute; Figurations II, piano; Figurations III, 2 pianos; Figurations IV, harp; Sonatine, cello and piano. *Publications:* Theory of Counterpoint and Canon, 1981; Oscar da Silva-Analytical and biographical study; Helena Costa- tradition and renewal. *Honours:* Concours Quatour, Liège 1959; German Industry, Colonia 1959; Alfredo Casella, Naples 1960; Calouste Gulbenkian, Lisbon 1968. *Address:* R Costa Cabral, 2219-4D, 4200 Porto, Portugal.

**PIRES, Maria João;** Portuguese pianist; b. 23 July 1944, Lisbon; m.; four c. *Education:* Lisbon Acad. of Music. *Career:* debut recital aged four; early concert tours of Portugal, Spain and Germany; int. career from 1970, with performances in Europe, Africa and Japan; British debut 1986; debut tour of N America 1988; appearances with numerous famous orchestras and conductors world-wide; repertoire includes Mozart, Schubert, Schumann, Beethoven and Chopin. *Recordings include:* Complete Mozart Piano Sonatas (Edison Prize, Prix de l' Acad. du Disque Français, Prix de l' Acad. Charles Cros), Debussy Etudes (Grammy Award) 1990, Concertos by Mozart (Grammy Award) 1991. *Honours:* First Prize, Beethoven Int. Competition, Brussels 1970. *Address:* c/o Herzberger Artists, 't Woud 1, 3862 PM Nijkerk, Netherlands (office).

**PIRONKOFF, Simeon (Angelov);** Composer; b. 18 June 1927, Lom, Bulgaria. *Education:* Graduated from State Music Academy at Sofia, 1953. *Career:* Violinist at National Youth Theatre, Sofia, 1947–51, later working as Conductor, Bulgarian Film Studios from 1961, Vice-President of Union of Bulgarian Composers, 1980. *Compositions include:* Opera: Socrates' Real Apology, Monodrama, Sofia, 1967; The Good Person of Szechwan (after Brecht), Stara Zagora, 1972; The Life and Suffering of Sinful Sophronius, Oratorio, Sofia, 1977; The Motley Bird, Ruse, 1980; Oh, My Dream, Ruse, 1987; Orchestral: Symphony for Strings, 1960; Movements for Strings, 1967; Night Music, 1968; Requiem for an Unknown Young Man, 1968; A Big Game for little orchestra, 1970; Ballet Music in Memory of Igor Stravinsky, 1987; Music for Two Pianos and Orchestra, 1973; Concerto Rustico for Cello and Orchestra, 1982; Entrata and Bulgarian Folk Dance, 1983; Lyric Suite for Strings, 1983; In the Eye of the Storm for Tenor and Orchestra, 1986; Symphonic Sketch on a Popular Melody, 1986; Flute Concerto, 1987; Passaglia for Symphonic Orchestra, 1991; Chamber: 3 Trios, 1949, 1950, 1987; 3 String Quartets, 1951, 1966, 1985; Sonata for Solo Violin, 1955; Berceuse for Clarinet and Piano, 1983; Theme and Variations for Violin and Piano, 1985; Symphony for 11 Soloists, 1990; Songs of Life and Death, Poetry of Emily Dickinson for Woman's Voice and Chamber Assembly, 1988; Tree Movements for Harp Solo, 1992; Piano Music, Choruses and Songs; Bosnian Lullaby, 1993; The Green Rain for mixed choir, 1994; Fantanziya for baritone, cello and piano, 1997; Four capriccios by Paganini transcribed for string ensemble; The Memory of a Piano, symphonic music for piano and orchestra; El Tango, variations for symphonic orchestra; Fantasy, on poetry of Heinrich Heine for baritone, piano and cello; The Flight of the Bumblebee, Rimsky-Korsakov, transcription for four saxophones; Film and Theatre Music. *Address:* Vitoscha Blvd 56, 1463 Sofia, Bulgaria.

**PISCHNER, Hans;** Teacher, Harpsichordist, Musicologist, Intendant and Retired; b. 20 Feb. 1914, Breslau, Germany. *Education:* Musicology studies at University of Breslau; Keyboard studies with Bronislav von Pozniac and Getrud Wertheim; Professor, 1949, PhD, 1961. *Career:* Head of Radio Music Department, 1950–54, Head of Music Department, 1954–56, Ministry of Culture; Representative, Ministry of Culture, 1956–62; Intendant, Deutsche Staatsoper, Berlin, 1963–89; Numerous appearances as soloist and accompanist in Europe, America and Japan, now retired; Chairman, Neue Bach-Gesellschaft, Leipzig. *Recordings:* Numerous works by Bach, both as soloist and continuo player; Bach Sonatas with David Oistrakh; Senior President, International Society for Young Artists, 'Bünneu Reif', 1995–' Bundesverdienstkreuz, 1999. *Publications:* Music in China, 1955; Die Harmonielehre Jean-Philippe Rameaus, 1967; Premier en eines Lebens, autobiography, 1986. *Contributions:* Several articles for professional journals. *Honours:* Handel Prize, Halle, 1961; National Prize, 3rd class, 1961; Johannes R Becher, 1962;

National Prize, 1st Class; Bundesverdienstkreuz der Bundesrepublik Deutschland, 1999. *Address:* Friedrichstrasse 105C, 10117 Berlin, Germany.

**PITTMAN, Richard (Harding);** Conductor; b. 3 June 1935, Baltimore, Maryland, USA; m. 10 Sept 1965, 1 s. *Education:* BMus, Peabody Conservatory, 1957; Private study in conducting with Laszlo Halasz, NY, 1960–63, Sergiu Celibidache, Accademia Musicale Chigiana, Siena, Italy, 1962, W Brueckner Ruggeberg, Hamburg, 1963–65 and Pierre Boulez, Basel, Switzerland, 1970. *Career:* Instructor, of Conducting and Opera, Eastman School of Music, 1965–68; Teacher of Orchestral Conducting and Orchestra Conductor, New England Conservatory, 1968–85; Guest Conductor of National Symphony, Washington DC, BBC Orchestras, London Sinfonietta, Frankfurt Radio Symphony, Germany, Hamburg Symphony, BBC Concert Orchestra, City of London Symphonia, Ulster Orchestra, Belfast, Nebraska Chamber Orchestra, Lincoln, Dutch Ballet Orchestra, Amsterdam, and Kirov Opera Orchestra, St Petersburg, Russia; Additional Guest Conductor, Banff Arts Festival, Canada; BBC Singers; American Repertory Theatre, Cambridge, Massachusetts; Symphony Orchestra of Ireland, Dublin, 1999; Seattle Symphony, Washington, 2000; Music Director, Boston Musica Viva, 1969–; The Concord Orchestra, 1969–, New England Philharmonic, Boston, 1997–; Guest Conductor, Canadian Opera Co., Toronto, 2000–02. *Recordings:* Music by Ives, Berio, Davidovsky, Harris, Schwantner, Henry Brant, Wilson, Lieberson, Rands, Ellen Taaffe Zwilich, Shifrin, Musgrave, Crawford and Seeger; William Kraft; John Harbison; Ezra Sims. *Honours:* Laurel Leaf Award from American Composers Alliance, New York, 1989; Peabody Conservatory Distinguished Alumni Award, 1996; ASCAP Award for Adventurous Programming (New Zealand Philharmonic), 2003; Chamber Music America/ASCAP Award for Adventurous Programming (Boston Musica Viva), 2004. *Current Management:* Tornay Management, New York. *Address:* 41 Bothfeld Road, Newton Center, MA 02459, USA.

**PITTMAN-JENNINGS, David;** Baritone; b. 1949, Oklahoma, USA. *Career:* Studied in America., Sang Lensky at Graz Opera in 1977 and was engaged at Bremen, 1981–85; Sang at Paris Opéra, 1982–83, as Don Fernando in Fidelio and Schaunard in La Bohème; Sang Germont at Tel-Aviv in 1988, and Wozzeck at Reggio Emilia in 1989; Member of the Karlsruhe Opera from 1990, singing Amfortas in Parsifal at Strasbourg in 1991; Season 1992 in Dallapiccola's Il Prigioniero, and as Mandryka in Arabella at the Vienna Staatsoper; Other roles have included Guglielmo, the Count in Capriccio, Mozart's Count and Figaro, Lescaut, Chorèbe in Les Troyens, Marcello and Gluck's Orestes; Sang in Schoeck's Venus at Geneva, 1997; Genoa 1998 in Peter Grimes; Season 2000–01 as Wozzeck at Santiago, Scarpia at Buenos Aires and Klingsor for the Edinburgh Festival; Cortez in Die Eroberung von Mexico, by Rihm, at Frankfurt, Orestes at Antwerp and Janáček's Forester in Ghent; Concerts include Beethoven's Ninth, Elijah, Ein Deutsches Requiem and L'Enfance du Christ. *Address:* c/o Staatstheater Karlsruhe, Baumeisterstrasse 11, Pf 1449, W-7500 Karlsruhe, Germany.

**PITTSINGER, David;** Singer (Bass-Baritone); b. 1962, USA. *Career:* Sang with San Francisco Opera from 1987; Brussels from 1988, as Verdi's Fiesco; Mephistopheles in Faust; Nick Shadow in Stravinsky's Rakes Progress; Shrecker's Der Ferne Klang; Mozart's Figaro and Don Giovanni at Nice, 1991, and Cologne, 1995; Salzburg, 1992, as Orbazzano in Rossini's Tancredi; Vienna Festival as Nick Shadow, 1993, and Lausanne, 1999; Season 1996–97, debuted as Olin Blitch in Carlisle Floyd's Susannah with Vancouver Opera; Performance of Bach's Christmas Oratorio with Amsterdamse Bach Solisten, Netherlands; Season 1997–98, debut at L'Opéra de Montréal, and also Maccerata Festival as Mephistopheles in Gounod's Faust; Boito's Mefistofele for Pittsburgh Opera, 1997, and St Louis, 1998; Season 1998–99, duo-recital with soprano Patricia Schuman including works by Mozart, Verdi, Tchaikovsky, Dvořák, Bowles and Copland; Debut as Four Villains in Offenbach's Les Contes d'Hoffmann for Opera Company of Philadelphia; Sang Publio in La Clemenza di Tito in Paris; Metropolitan Opera in Don Carlo, Rake's Progress, 1998, and as Colline in La Bohème, 1999; Season 2000–01 as Rossini's Alidoro in Brussels, Rossini's Selim in Buenos Aires and Tiresias in Oedipus Rex at Naples; Massenet's Don Quichotte, Buenos Aires 2005. *Recordings:* Simon Boccanegra by Verdi; La Calisto by Cavalli; Susannah by Floyd; Alfonso in Donizetti's Lucrezia Borgia. *Honours:* Grammy Award for Susannah. *Address:* Columbia Artists Management Inc, 165 W 57th St, New York, NY 10019, USA.

**PIZARRO, Artur;** Concert Pianist; b. 17 Aug. 1968, Lisbon, Portugal. *Education:* Studied with Sequeira Costa in Lisbon and at the University of Kansas; National Conservatory of Music in Lisbon. *Career:* Numerous concert performances in Europe from 1987; London debut 1989, at the Wigmore Hall, followed by concerts with the London Mozart Players at the Queen Elizabeth Hall; Has also played with the RAI-Torino Symphony, the Gulbenkian Orchestra and the Moscow Philharmonic; Rachmaninov's 3rd Concerto with the City of Birmingham Symphony in Leeds and the BBC Symphony under Andrew Davis in London, 1990; Further engagements with the London Symphony (de Burgos), Royal Liverpool Philharmonic (Pesek), Los Angeles Philharmonic at Hollywood Bowl, English Chamber Orchestra, City of London Sinfonia, Hallé and BBC Symphony (Proms 1991); Recitals in the United Kingdom, Japan, Australia and the USA; Played the Ravel Concerto in G at the 1991 Promenade Concerts, London; Recital in International Piano Series at South Bank, 1997. *Honours:* Winner 1987 International Vianna de Motta Competition, Lisbon; Greater Palm Beach Symphony Invitational Piano Competition, Florida, 1988; First Prize, Harvey Leeds International Pianoforte Competition 1990. *Current Management:* Hazard Chase Ltd, Norman House, Cambridge Place, Cambridge, CB2 1NS, England. *Telephone:* (1223) 312400. *Fax:* (1223) 460827. *Website:* www.hazardchase.co.uk.

**PIZER, Elizabeth (Faw Hayden);** Composer and Musician; b. 1 Sept. 1954, Watertown, New York, USA; m. Charles Ronald Pizer, 10 July 1974. *Education:* High School Diploma, New York State Regents Diploma, Watertown High School, 1972; Boston Conservatory of Music, Boston, Massachusetts, 1972–75. *Career:* Numerous major concert performances of her compositions internationally including, San Jose State University Symphonic Band, 1979; Members of Honolulu Symphony Orchestra, String Quartet, 1980; Lincoln Center, New York, Charleston, South Carolina; Jacksonville, Florida, Donne in Musica Festival, Rome, 1982; San Francisco Chamber Singers, Nevada City, San Francisco, Berkeley and Ross, California, 1982; Piccolo Spoleto Festival, 1983; University of Michigan, 1983; Mexico City, 1984; Heidelberg, West Germany, 1985; Oakland, California, 1986; Many major broadcasts of compositions, throughout the USA, 1979–86 and a live concert broadcast including pre-recorded material in Australia, 1986. *Compositions:* Expressions Intimes, for Solo Piano, 1975, recorded by pianist Max Lifchitz, 1992; Quilisoly, for Flute and Piano, or Violin and Piano, 1976; Look down, Fair Moon, for Voice and Piano, 1976; Elegy, (formerly known as Interfuguelude) for String Orchestra, or String Quartet or Wind Quartet, 1977; Fanfare Overture, Symphonic Band, 1977–79; Five Haiku, for Soprano and Chamber Ensemble, 1978; Five Haiku II, for Mezzo-Soprano and Piano, 1979; Madrigals Anon, A Capella Choir, 1979; Sunken Flutes, Electronic Tape, 1979; String Quartet, 1981; Lyric Fancies, Solo Piano, 1983; Kyrie Eleison, A Capella Chorus, 1983; Strains and Restraints, solo piano, 1984, recorded by Max Lifchitz, 1992; Nightsongs, voice and piano, 1986; Arlington, electronic tape, 1989; Embryonic Climactus, electronic tape, 1989; Aquasphere, electronic tape, 1990; Elegy in Amber (In Memoriam Leonard Bernstein) string orchestra, 1993, recorded by the Slovak Radio Symphony Orchestra conducted by Robert Stankovsky, 1996. *Address:* 19458 Southshore Road, Point Peninsula, Three Mile Bay, New York, NY 13693, USA.

**PIZZARO, Artur;** pianist. *Career:* Prof. Guildhall School of Music and Drama, London; has appeared with numerous orchestras, including Philadelphia Orchestra, LA Philharmonic, Baltimore Symphony, NHK Symphony (Tokyo), Montréal Symphony, Toronto Symphony, Hong Kong Philharmonic, Leipzig Chamber Orchestra, Rotterdam Philharmonic, Vienna Symphony, Royal Philharmonic, BBC Symphony Orchestra; has recorded nine solo albums of works by Liszt, Bach-Liszt, Kabalevsky, Rodrigo, Vorisek, Mompou, Shostakovich, Scriabin, Milhaud. *Honours:* winner, Leeds Int. Piano Competition 1990. *Current Management:* Linn Records, Floors Road, Waterfoot, Glasgow G76 0EP, Scotland. *Telephone:* (141) 3035027. *Fax:* (141) 3035007. *E-mail:* info@linnrecords.co.uk. *Website:* www.linnrecords.com.

**PIZZI, Pier Luigi;** stage director and designer; b. 15 June 1930, Milan, Italy. *Education:* Milan Polytechnic. *Career:* debut designing Don Giovanni at Genoa, 1952; Designs and productions for such Baroque operas as Handel's Ariodante, La Scala, 1982, and Rinaldo (seen at Reggio Emilia, Paris, Madrid and Lisbon); Rameau's Hippolyte et Aricie and Castor et Pollux, Aix-en-Provence, 1983, 1991; Gluck's Alceste for La Scala, 1987; Other work has included Les Troyens, to open the Opéra Bastille at Paris in 1990, followed by Samson et Dalila, 1991; I Capuleti e i Montecchi at Covent Garden, 1984, (revived, 2001); Don Carlos at Vienna, 1989; La Traviata seen at Monte Carlo, Venice and Lausanne; Rossini productions at Pesaro include Otello and Tancredi, 1991; Staged Gluck's Armide at La Scala to open the 1996–97 season; Rossini, Guillaume Tell, Rossini Opera Festival, 1995; Verdi, Macbeth, Arena di Verona, 1997, Britten's Death in Venice, Genoa 2001, La Traviata, Teatro Real, Madrid 2003, Massenet's Thaïs, Venice 2003, Salieri's Europa riconosciuta, La Scala Milan 2004. *Honours:* Légion d'Honneur, Officier des Arts et des Lettres. *Address:* c/o Opéra de Monte Carlo, MC 98000, Monaco.

**PLA GARRIGOS, Adolf;** Musician and Pianist; b. 4 Oct. 1960, Sabadell, Spain; m. Roser Farriol. *Education:* Superior Diploma, Public Conservatoire of Barcelona, 1984; Postgraduate, Franz Liszt Academy, Budapest, 1988; Meisterklassen Diploma, Würzburg, Germany, 1992. *Career:* Invited to the International Festivals of Barcelona, Madrid, Havana and St Petersburg, also at Pau Casals Festival in Spain, El Salvador and Prades, France; Appeared in concerts in Italy, Germany and Hungary and on Spanish National Radio, Russian National Radio and Catalan television; mem, Director of Professional Conservatoire of Sabadell, 1989–93, 1996–97; Council Member, Catalan Association of Performance, 1994–. *Recordings:* CD of music by Schumann, Granados and Ravel as soloist, Ma De Guido, 1995. *Current Management:* Felip Pedrell. *Address:* c/o Felip Pedrell 24, E 08208 Sabadell, Spain.

**PLACIDI, Tommaso;** Conductor; b. 29 March 1964, Rome, Italy. *Education:* Geneva Conservatory; Vienna Academy of Music; Academia Musicale Chigiana, Siena, Italy. *Career:* Assistant Conductor, London Symphony Orchestra; Guest conductor, in Europe, of the London Symphony Orchestra, Orchestre National du Capitole de Toulouse, Orchestre Philharmonique de Strasbourg, Orchestre Philharmonique des Pays de Loire, Orchestre de la Suisse Romande, Orchestre de Chambre de Lausanne, Wiener Kammerorchester, Orchestra Sinfonica RAI, Turin, Orchestra del Teatro Regio, Turin, Orchestra della Toscana, Florence, Orchestra Sinfonica Haydn Bolzano, Trento, Orchestra of Bratislava Opera House, Philharmonisches Staatorchester Halle, Radio Philharmonie Hannover des NDR, Orchestre Philharmoni-

que de Liège, Orchestre Philharmonique du Luxembourg, Norddeutsche Philharmonie Rostock. *Recordings:* Tchaikovsky's Violin Concerto, Piano Concerto No. 1; Weber's Clarinet Concertos, Münchner Rundfunkorchester, Germany, 1997; Bruch Concerto for Clarinet and Viola, Hannover Radio Philharmonic, 2002. *Honours:* 1st Prize, Besançon Conducting Competition, 1992; 1st Prize, Donatella Flick Conducting Competition, London, 1966. *Current Management:* IMG Artists, London, Konzert-Direktion Hans Adler, Berlin. *Address:* 5 Chemin Taverney, 1218 Geneva, Switzerland.

**PLAGGE, Wolfgang (Antoine Marie);** Composer and Pianist; b. 23 Aug. 1960, Oslo, Norway; m. Lena Rist-Larsen, 25 June 1993. *Education:* Began Piano, age 5; Piano with Robert Riefling and Jens Harald Bratlie, Norway, Composition with Oistein Sommerfeldt and Johan Kvandal; Piano with Evgenij Koroliev, Composition with Werner Krützfeld, Musikhochschule, Hamburg, graduated 1983. *Career:* Debut: Pianist, Oslo, 1972; 1st published work at age 12; Commissions. *Compositions include:* Music for 2 Pianos, 1982–89; Piano Sonata V, 1985–86, VI, 1988–91; Vesaas-Sange: Baryton og Piano, 1989–90; A Litany for the 21st Century: Sonata for Horn and Piano, 1989; Festival Music, symphonic band, 1989, 1994 Version, symphonic orchestra; Concerto: Horn and Orchestra, 1990; Canzona: Brass Quintet and Pianoforte, 1990; Concerto: Violin and Orchestra, 1991; Concerto: 2 Pianos and Orchestra, 1991; Solarljod: Solsanger fra Norron Middelalder, 1992; Sonata II, Bassoon and Pianoforte, 1993; Hogge i Stein, A Portrait of Trondenes Church and Her People, narrator, choir, 3 soli, orchestra, 1994; Concerto for Trumpet and Orchestra, 1994. *Recordings:* Canzona, Wolfgang Plagge, piano, and Arctic Brass; Bassoon sonata, Robert Ronnes, bassoon, Eva Knardahl, piano; Concerto for Horn and Orchestra, Froydis Reed Wekre, horn, Trondheim Symphony Orchestra, conductor Ole Kristian Ruud; Contemporary Music for Brass: Canzona, Wolfgang Plagge, piano, and Arctic Brass; Eivind Groven; Piano Concerto, Wolfgang Plagge, piano, Trondheim Symphony Orchestra, conductor Ole Kristian Ruud. *Address:* Seljeflouten 39, 1346 Gjettum, Norway.

**PLAISTOW, Stephen,** ARCM; pianist, critic, broadcaster and radio producer; b. 24 Jan. 1937, Welwyn Garden City, England. *Education:* Clare College, Cambridge. *Career:* freelance journalist 1961–; BBC Music Producer, 1962–74; Chairman British Section of ISCM and Music Section of ICA, 1967–71; Member, Music Panel, Arts Council of Great Britain, 1972–79; Chief Assistant to Controller of Music, BBC, 1974–79; Chairman, British section of ISCM and Arts Council Contemporary Music Network, 1976–79; Editor, Contemporary Music, BBC, 1979–92; Deputy Head of Radio 3 Music Department, BBC, 1989–92; mem. Royal Society of Musicians. *Contributions:* The Gramophone, Guardian, Musical Times, Tempo, BBC Music, Independent, Revista de libros. *Honours:* Lesley Boosey Award, 1994; Hon. RAM. *Address:* 5 Gloucester Court, 33 Gloucester Avenue, London NW1 7TJ, England. *Telephone:* (20) 7485-2693. *E-mail:* stephen.plaistow@ecosse.net. *Website:* sites.ecosse.net/stephen.plaistow.

**PLANCHART, Alejandro (Enrique);** Music Historian and Composer; b. 29 July 1935, Caracas, Venezuela; Divorced, 1 d. *Education:* BMus, 1958, MMus, 1960, Yale University School of Music; PhD, Harvard University, 1971. *Career:* Freelance Arranger, Composer, New York and New Haven, 1960–64; Instructor/Assistance Professor, Yale, 1967–75; Associate Professor, University of Victoria, 1975–76; Associate Professor, University of California at Santa Barbara, 1976–; Visiting Professor, Brandeis, 1982–83. *Compositions:* Divertimento for Percussion Trio; Five Poems of James Joyce for Soprano and Piano. *Recordings:* 20 recordings of medieval and renaissance music with the Cappella Cordina, Lyrichord and Musical Heritage Society. *Publications:* The Repertory of Tropes at Winchester, 2 vols, Princeton, 1977; Beneventanum Troporum Corpus, with John Boe co-editor, 10 vols in press. *Contributions:* Guillaume Dufay's Masses: Notes and Revisions, in Musical Quarterly, 1972; Fifteenth Century, Masses: Notes on Chronology and Performance, in Study Musicali 10, 1983; About 50 other titles. *Address:* 1070 Via Regina, Santa Barbara, CA 93111, USA.

**PLASSON, Michel;** Conductor; b. 2 Oct. 1933, Paris, France. *Education:* Studied at the Paris Conservatoire and in the USA with Leinsdorf, Monteux and Stokowski. *Career:* Musical Director in Metz, 1966–68; Director of the Orchestra and of the Théâtre du Capitole de Toulouse, 1968–83; Operatic performances in Toulouse include Salome, Aida, Die Meistersinger, Faust, Parsifal, Carmen and Montségur by Landowski (world premiere, 1985); Conductor of the Orchestre National du Capitole de Toulouse from 1983; At the Palais Omnisport de Paris-Bercy has conducted Aida, Turandot, the Verdi Requiem and Nabucco, 1984–87; Guest engagements with the Berlin Philharmonic Orchestra, London Philharmonic, Orchestre de la Suisse Romande, and the Gewandhaus Orchestra Leipzig; Paris Opéra, Geneva Opera, State Operas of Vienna, Hamburg and Munich, Zürich Opera, Covent Garden, Metropolitan Opera, Chicago and San Francisco; Principal Guest Conductor of the Zürich Tonhalle Orchestra from 1987; Conducted new production of Guillaume Tell at Covent Garden, 1990; Il Trovatore at the Halle aux Grains, Toulouse, 1990; Faust at the 1990 Orange Festival; Returned to Covent Garden, 1991, Tosca; Season 1991–92 with Lucia di Lammermoor at Munich, Guillaume Tell at Covent Garden, Don Quichotte at Toulouse and Carmen at Orange; Conducted La Forza del Destino at Orange, 1996; Original version of Boris Godunov at Toulouse, 1998; Honorary Conductor for Life of the Orchestre National du Capitole de Toulouse. *Recordings include:* La Vie Parisienne; La Grande Duchesse de Gérolstein; Chausson's Symphony; Saint-Saëns Piano Concertos; Premiere pressings of Roussel's Padmâvati, Magnard's Symphonies and Guercoeur, Symphonic poems by Chausson; Les Pêcheurs de Perles; Faust. *Address:* c/o Orchestre National du Capitole de Toulouse, Halle aux Grains, Place Dupuy, 31000, Toulouse, France.

**PLATT, Ian;** singer (baritone); b. 1959, Fleetwood, England. *Education:* studied with John Cameron at Royal Northern College of Music. *Career:* sang Rossini's Figaro, Guglielmo, Papageno and Junius in The Rape of Lucretia for Royal Northern College of Music; Professional debut for Kent Opera, in La Traviata and Il Barbiere di Siviglia; Engagements with Opera 80 as Don Magnifico in La Cenerentola and Baron Zeta in The Merry Widow; New Sadler's Wells Opera as Agamemnon in La Belle Hélène; Sang Tom in Henze's The English Cat at Hebbel Theatre, Berlin and toured with Travelling Opera as Schaunard and Mozart's Figaro; Welsh National Opera and Scottish Opera, 1991, in La Traviata; Alcindoro in La Bohème for Glyndebourne Touring Opera, 1991; Pirate King, D'Oyly Carte, 1993; Don Magnifico, Welsh National Opera, 1993–94. *Recordings include:* Il Crociato in Egitto by Meyerbeer, Opera Rara. *Current Management:* Robert Gilder & Co., Enterprise House, 59–65 Upper Ground, London, SE1 9PQ, England. *Telephone:* (20) 7928-9008. *Fax:* (20) 7928-9755. *E-mail:* rgilder@robert-gilder.com.

**PLATT, Richard (Swaby);** Musicologist; b. 14 May 1928, London, England; m. (1) 2 s., 1 d., (2) Diane Ibbotson, 3 Dec 1977, 1 s., 1 d. *Education:* Associate, Royal College of Art, 1953; Studied privately with Walter Bergmann, 1965–, Hugh Wood, 1966–68. *Career:* Painter, Printmaker, exhibiting at Royal Academy, London Group and others, 1953–61; One man show of works, Leicester Galleries, 1956; Musicologist, specialising in 18th Century English Music, 1969. Editions, William Boyce, 12 Overtures; Thomas Arne, 4 Symphonies; Works by Croft, Roseingrave, Mudge, Fisher; Gli Equivoci, by Stephen Storace; Peleus and Thetis by William Boyce; mem, Royal Musical Association. *Recordings:* Editions of music Boyce (Solomon), Arne and Roseingrave. *Publications:* Contributor of chapters, New Grove, 1980, 2001 and Grove Opera 1992; Theatre Music 1700–1760 in Blackwell's History of Music in Britain vol. 4; The Symphony, 1720–1840, 1983; Semele by John Eccles, Judgement of Paris, 1984, 2000. *Contributions:* BIOS 17, on Gerard Smith Organ Contract; Early Music, Nov. 2000, on Richard Mudge. *Address:* 3 Stratton Place, Falmouth, Cornwall TR11 2ST, England.

**PLATT, Theodore,** DMus; Russian conductor, composer, double bassist and harpsichordist; b. 8 Sept. 1937, Moscow. *Education:* Ippolitov-Ivanov Conservatory of Music, Moscow Conservatory of Music. *Career:* founder and Dir, four chamber ensembles, including first baroque and classical ensembles in USSR (Moscow) 1968–81, New York Concertino Ensemble 1981; live concerts on major classical music radio stations in USA; eight years as double bass soloist, Moscow Chamber Orchestra; discovered and premiered lost Baroque works; teacher of string instruments and voice; mem. Conductors Guild, Coll. Music Soc. *Compositions:* two symphony concertos, cycles of vocal compositions, one quartet. *Address:* c/o Conductors Guild, PO Box 18398, Richmond, VA 23226, USA.

**PLATZ, Robert H. P.;** Composer and Conductor; b. 16 Aug. 1951, Baden-Baden, Germany. *Education:* Studies with Wolfgang Fortner, Karlheinz Stockhausen, Francis Travis; IRCAM computer workshop for Composers. *Career:* Founded new music group Ensemble Köln, 1980; Own concert series with Ensemble Köln, 1982; Appeared in new music festivals such as Musik der Zeit WDR and Musica Viva series of Munich, Donaueschingen and La Rochelle; Performed at Salzburg Festival, Metz; All works recorded by Radio Stations in Germany. *Compositions:* Schwelle, Full Orchestra and Tape; Chlebnicov, Ensemble and Tape; Maro and Stille, Soprano, Violin and Piano Solos, plus Ensembles and Choirs; Raumform, Clarinet Solo; Flotenstücke–Seven Pieces for Flute and Ensemble; Requiem for Tape; Pianoforte 2; Closed Loop, Guitar; Verkommenes ufer, opera (texts Heiner Müller); Quartett (Zeitstrahl) for String Quartet, 1986; Dunkles Haus, music theatre, 1991; Grenzgänge Steine, for soprano, 2 pianos and orchestra, 1993; Echo I–V, for ensemble 1994–98. *Publications:* Musikalische Prozesse, 1979; Uber Schwelle, 1980; Uber Schwelle II, 1981; Uber Tasten, 1983; Versuch einer Asthetik des Kleinen, 1984; Blumroder, Nicht Einfach, Aber Neu, 1980; Formpolyphone Musik, 1981; Stegen: Robert HP Platz, 1982; Van den Hoogen: Komplizierte Horbarkeit, 1982; Blumröder: Maro, 1984; Van den Hoogen: Raumform, 1984; Allende-Blin: Uber Chielnicov, 1984; Record Maro, Irvine Arditi, Violin.

**PLAVIN, Zecharia;** Pianist; b. 7 June 1956, Vilnius (Vilna), Lithuania; m. 12 June 1984, 1 s., 1 d. *Education:* BMus, MMus, Ciurlionis School of Arts, S Rubin Academy of Music, University of Tel-Aviv, Israel. *Career:* Concerts with Israel Philharmonic Orchestra, Jerusalem Symphony Orchestra, Symphonietta of Beer-Sheva, Haifa Symphony Orchestra, others; Recitals on all major stages in Israel; Concerts in Western Europe from 1988; Numerous recordings for Israel Broadcasting Authorities; Work for Israel Concert Bureau Omanuth Laam. *Recordings:* Various. *Publications:* The Metamorphoses by O Partos. *Honours:* 1st Prize, S Rubin Academy of Music Competition, 1978; National François Shapira Prize, 1980; Diploma, Israel Broadcasting Competition, 1985. *Current Management:* International Music Consultants.

**PLAZAS, Mary;** Singer (Soprano); b. 9 Sept. 1966, Wallingford, England. *Education:* Studied at Royal Northern College of Music with Ava June and at National Opera Studio. *Career:* Solo recitals at Wigmore Hall, Purcell Room, Birmingham Town Hall and Royal Exchange Theatre, Manchester; Concerts at Cheltenham and Aldeburgh Festivals; Opera engagements include Poulenc's La Voix Humaine at Aix-en-Provence, Nannetta at Aldeburgh and Despina for Mid-Wales Opera; English National Opera debut, 1992, as

Heavenly Voice in Don Carlos; Opera North, 1992–, as the Gypsy in British premiere of Gerhard's The Duenna, Barbarina and Susanna in Figaro and Tebaldo in Don Carlos; Sang in Opera Factory's Nozze di Figaro for Channel 4 Television and appeared as Echo in Ariadne auf Naxos for Garsington Opera; Joined English National Opera as Company Principal, Aug 1995 and sang Echo in Ariadne auf Naxos, 1997; Tina in premiere of Dove's Flight for GTO at Glyndebourne, 1998; Season 2000–01 as Donna Elvira for GTO and Lauretta in Gianni Schicchi for ENO. *Honours:* Winner, Kathleen Ferrier Memorial Scholarship, 1991. *Address:* c/o Owen-White Management, 14 Nightingale Lane, London N8 7QU, England.

**PLECH, Linda;** Singer (Soprano); b. 1951, Vienna, Austria. *Education:* Studied in Vienna and at Salzburg Mozarteum. *Career:* Sang as Mezzo at Klagenfurt Opera, 1976–77; Oldenburg, 1980–84; Soprano roles at Kaiserslautern, 1985–86, Hamburg Staatsoper, 1987–88 as Donna Anna and Elisabeth de Valois; Cologne, 1989, as Jenůfa; Bregenz Festival, 1988–89, as Senta in Der fliegende Holländer; Sang the Trovatore Leonora at Deutsche Oper Berlin, 1989, Ariadne auf Naxos at Antwerp; Season 1991–92 as Senta at Geneva, Elisabeth in Tannhäuser at Barcelona; Other roles include Marenka in The Bartered Bride and Giulietta in Les Contes d'Hoffmann. *Address:* c/o Grand Théâtre de Genève, 11 Boulevard du Théâtre, 1211 Geneva, Switzerland.

**PLESHAK, Victor (Vasilievich);** Composer; b. 13 Nov. 1946, Leningrad, Russia; 2 s. *Education:* Choral College of Chapel; Choir Conductors Department, Composers Department, St Petersburg Conservatoire (with B Tischenko). *Career:* Debut: Many-coloured Balls, song cycle for children, verses by Akimya, Leningrad Radio. *Compositions:* Over 17 musicals and operas including: The Red Imp, musical, 1980; The Knight's Passions, 1981; The Glass Menagerie, opera, 1987; A Tale of a Blot, New Year operetta, 1988; Caution Baba-Yaga, ecological opera; Inspector, an opera after Gogol, 1993; Choral Cycle, About Friendship, Love and Brotherhood, to verses by R Burns, 1983; Over 100 published songs including: V Pleshak, Songs for voice and piano (guitar, accordion), in Soviet Composer, 1988. *Recordings:* The Tale of a Dead Tsarevna and Seven Epic Heroes, opera in 2 acts; The Widow of Valencia, musical after the play by Lope de Vega; Oh These Pretty Sinners, musical farces after Lasage and Rabelais; Puss in Boots, musical after the play by Pierrot; Author of over 150 theatre performances including 30 musicals, and over 400 songs. *Compositions include:* The Turnip, opera after Russian folk tale, 1992; The Canterville Ghost, musical after story, 1994; Ruslan and Ludmila, after Russian fairy-tale, Pushkin, 1999. *Recordings:* Hymn of St Petersburg Region, 1997; Hymn of St Petersburg University, 1999. *Address:* Gorokhovaya St (formerly Dzerzhinskaya) 53 kv 29, 190031 St Petersburg, Russia.

**PLETNEV, Mikhail Vasilievich;** Russian pianist, conductor and composer; *Founder, Russian National Orchestra;* b. 14 April 1957, Arkhangelsk. *Education:* Moscow State Conservatory with Yakov Flier and Lev Vlasenko (piano), Albert Leman (composition). *Career:* gave recitals and played with orchestras in major cities of Russia, Europe, Japan and America; gained reputation as Russian music interpreter; Founder and Chief Conductor Russian Nat. Orchestra 1990–99, Hon. Conductor 1999–, and head of the Conductor Collegium 2006–; tours with orchestra and as piano soloist in various countries; has performed with Haitink, Maazel, Chailly, Tennstedt, Sanderling, Blomstedt, Järvi, Thielemann; also conducted Philharmonia Orchestra, Deutsche Kammerphilharmonie, Norddeutsche Rundfunk Symphony Orchestra, London Symphony Orchestra, Berlin Philharmonic, Bayerische Rundfunk Symphony, Orchestre Nat. de France, Israel Philharmonic, San Francisco Symphony and Pittsburgh Symphony; teacher in Moscow Conservatory 1981–1992. *Honours:* First Prize Int. Tchaikovsky competition, Moscow 1978, People's Artist of Russia 1990, State Prize of Russia 1993. *Current Management:* Columbia Artists Management Ltd, 28 Cheverton Road, London, N19 3AY, England. *Telephone:* (20) 7272-8020. *Fax:* (20) 7272 8991. *E-mail:* info@cami.co.uk. *Address:* Starokonyushenny per. 33, Apt 16, Moscow, Russia. *Telephone:* (095) 241-43-39 (home).

**PLISHKA, Paul;** Singer (Bass); b. 28 Aug. 1941, Old Forge, Pennsylvania, USA. *Education:* Studied at Montclair State College and with Armen Boyazjian. *Career:* Debut: Paterson Lyric Opera, 1961; Metropolitan Opera from 1967, as King Marke in Tristan, Procida in Les vêpres Siciliennes, Varlaam and Pimen in Boris Godunov, Oroveso in Norman, Leporello and the Commendatore in Don Giovanni, Banquo in the Peter Hall production of Macbeth, and Philip II in Don Carlos; La Scala, 1974, in La Damnation de Faust; San Francisco, 1984, as Silva in Ernani; Teatro Liceo Barcelona, 1985; Orange Festival, 1987, as Phanüel in Massenet's Hérodiade; Sang Daland in Der fliegende Holländer at the Metropolitan, 1989; Procida at Carnegie Hall, 1990; Opera Company of Philadelphia, 1990, as the Mayor in La Gazza Ladra, Fiesco in Simon Boccanegra at the Metropolitan; Grand Park concerts Chicago, in Prince Igor; Season 1991–92 as Giorgio in Puritani at Chicago, the Pope in Benvenuto Cellini at Geneva and Zaccaria at Montreal; Sang Mozart's Bartolo at the Met, 1997; Grand Inquisitor in Don Carlos at Salzburg, 1998; Sang Des Grieux in Manon at the Met, 2001. *Recordings:* Crespel in Les Contes d'Hoffmann and Henry VIII in Anna Bolena; Norma; Le Cid and Donizetti's Gemma di Vergy; Faust; Wurm in Luisa Miller. *Current Management:* Ingpen & Williams Ltd, 7 St George's Court, 131 Putney Bridge Road, London, SW15 2PA, England.

**PLOWRIGHT, Jonathan Daniel;** British pianist; b. 24 Sept. 1959, Doncaster, S Yorkshire; s. of Cyril James Plowright and Molly Plowright; m. Diane Rosemary Shaw 1990. *Education:* Stonyhurst Coll., Birmingham Univ., Royal Acad. of Music, London, Peabody Conservatory of Music, Baltimore, USA. *Career:* debut Carnegie Recital Hall, New York 1984, Purcell Room, London 1985; has performed with all maj. UK orchestras and numerous int. orchestras; solo recitals throughout UK and many int. tours; regular BBC broadcasts; performed world premiere Constant Lambert's piano concerto, St John's Smith Square 1988; eight commercial recordings. *Honours:* Hon. ARAM; McFarren Gold Medal (RAM) 1983, Fulbright Scholarship 1983, Countess of Munster Scholarship, Commonwealth Musician of the Year 1983, winner European Piano Competition 1989.

**PLOWRIGHT, Rosalind Anne,** LRAM; British singer (mezzo-soprano); b. 21 May 1949, d. of Robert Arthur Plowright and Celia Adelaide Plowright; m. James Anthony Kaye 1984; one s. one d. *Education:* Notre Dame High School, Wigan, Royal Northern Coll. of Music, Manchester. *Career:* began career at London Opera Centre 1973–75; Glyndebourne Chorus and Touring Co. 1974–77; debut with ENO as Page in Salome 1975, Miss Jessel in Turn of the Screw 1979 (Soc. of West End Theatre Award), at Covent Garden as Ortlinde in Die Walküre 1980; has sung also in Switzerland, Germany, France, Spain, Portugal, Italy, Netherlands, Denmark, Austria, Greece, USA, Argentina, Chile, Israel; has sung mezzo repertoire 1999–; Metropolitan Opera debut 2003. *Television:* House of Elliot 1992, The Man Who Made Husbands Jealous 1997. *Principal roles include:* Ariadne, Alceste, Médée, Norma, Tosca; title role and Elizabeth I in Mary Stuart, Maddalena in Andrea Chénier, Antonia in The Tales of Hoffman, Donna Anna in Don Giovanni, Vitellia in La Clemenza di Tito, Madame Butterfly, Manon Lescaut, Suor Angelica, Giorgetta in Il Tabarro, Aida, Abigaille in Nabucco, Desdemona in Otello, Elena in I Vespri Siciliani, Leonora in Il Trovatore, Amelia in Un Ballo in Maschera, Leonora in La Forza del Destino, Violetta in La Traviata, Kundry in Parsifal, Kostelnička in Katya Kabanova, Amneris in Aida, Cassandra in Les Troyens, Eboli in Don Carlos, Fricka in Rheingold and Walküre. *Honours:* First Prize, 7th Int. Competition for Opera Singers, Sofia 1979, Prix Fondation Fanny Heldy, Acad. Nat. du Disque Lyrique 1985. *Address:* c/o Raffaella Coletti, Firenze Musicale, Via Maggio 35, 50125 Florence, Italy; 83 St Mark's Avenue, Salisbury, Wilts., SP1 3DW, England (home).

**PLOYHAROVA-PREISLEROVA, Vlasta;** Singer (soprano); b. 25 Jan. 1928, Zbynice, Klatovy, Czechoslovakia; m. Frantisek Preisler Senior 1972; one s. one d. *Education:* Conservatory of Prague; Corso Academia Musicale Siena, Italy (Gina Cigna), 1960, 1961, 1962, 1963. *Career:* Debut: In Smetana's Bartered Bride at Janáček Theatre, Brno, 1958; Appeared at Theatre Olomouc, 1956–84, Theatre Brno, 1960–64, Theatre Ostrava, 1967–77; Operatic repertoire included: Puccini's Turandot and Madama Butterfly, Strauss's Rosenkavalier (as Sophie), Tchaikovsky's Eugene Onegin, Iolanta, Massenet's Manon, Verdi's Gilda, Bizet's Carmen, Gounod's Marguerite, Gluck's Orfeo and Euridice, Beethoven's Fidelio, Mozart's Don Giovanni, Così fan tutte, Offenbach's Les Contes d'Hoffmann and Janáček's Cunning Little Vixen and From the House of the Dead; also operas by Skroup, Dvořák, Fibich, V. Novak, V. Blodek, B. Martinů, Smetana, Pergolesi, Weber, Rossini, Flotow, J. F. Halévy, Lortzing, Rimsky-Korsakov, Leoncavallo, N. Zajc, A. Honegger; concert repertoire included: Bach's Magnificat, Beethoven's 9th Symphony, Mahler's 4th Symphony. *Honours:* International Competition, Toulouse, France, Silver Medal, 1957. *Address:* Brno, Jánska 16, 60200, Czech Republic.

**PLUDERMACHER, Georges;** Pianist and Professor of Piano; b. 26 July 1944, Guéret, France. *Education:* Studied with Geneviève Joy and Jacques Fevrier at the Paris Conservatoire; Further study with Geza Anda at Lucerne, 1963–64. *Career:* Many appearances throughout Europe from 1965; Contemporary repertory has included the premieres of Archipel I by Boucourechliev (1967) and Synaphai by Xenakis (1971); Engagements with the Domaine Musical, Musique Vivante and the Orchestra of Paris Opéra; Duos with Yvonne Loriod and chamber music with the Nouveau Trio Pasquier; Professor at the Paris Conservatoire from 1993. *Recordings include:* Complete Sonatas by Mozart; Estampes and Images by Debussy. *Honours:* Second Prize, Leeds International Competition, 1969; First Prize Geza Anda Competition, 1979. *Address:* c/o Dept. Piano, 14 Rue de Madrid, 75008 Paris, France.

**PLUISTER, Simon;** Dutch composer, conductor and organ and piano teacher; b. 12 Nov. 1913, Obdam; m. Jacoba Maria Leentvaar 1943; one s. one d. *Education:* Amsterdam Conservatory with Hendrik Andriessen and Ernest W. Mulder, studied composition with Daniel Ruyneman, pianoforte with André Jurres. *Career:* debut as composer, Amsterdam, 1936; Composer for Dutch Broadcasting, NCRV, 1950–57; Conductor, The Harold Shamrock Concert Orchestra, Radio Tivoli Orchestra and Vocal Ensemble with instruments, 1955–66; Organ Teacher, Music School, Emmeloord, 1969–79; mem, GENECO (Society of Dutch Composers). *Compositions:* For Orchestra: 15 Psalms and Hymns, 3 Suites, Punch-and-Judy Show, 3 Cascades, Rhapsody in Beer-tonality; For Solo, Choir and Orchestra: Psalm 65, 121, 137, 138, Cantata St Luke 24, Concerto da chiesa The Acts II; 3 Operettas; 2 Works, Voice with Orchestra; 3 Works for String-Orchestra; 75 Works for Small-Orchestra (Short pieces and suites); Concertino for Piano and Orchestra, Ricercare and Ciga for Organ and String-Orchestra; Chamber Music, Donemus, Amsterdam, Netherlands; Music for Pianoforte 2 hds, 4 hds and for 2 Pianofortes; Calvinus Sinfonia for Strings 1987; Commission NCRV; To Silvestre Revueltas, from Mexico, at his death, for Choir (mixed voices) and

Orchestra, 1987, (choir singing and speaking); Five Brown Songs, for Soprano, Flute, Alto Saxophone and Pianoforte, 1988; Larghetto for Strings, 1988; The Days after the Crucifixion, Prologue from the Opera, Bar Abbas, for Soli, Female-Choir and Orchestra, 1986, (also as Cantata); Opera Bar Abbas, for Soli Choir and Orchestra, 1986–88; Concerto da Chiesa for 2 Recorders, V-Cello and Organ, 1990; Ant Brothers (fruit nursery) Musical for Soli Choir and Orchestra, 1990–91; Chronicle of an Eyewitness, Electronic Music for a Broadcast-Play; Super Flumina Babylonis for Soprano-Solo, Male-Choir and Pianoforte, 1992; Ave Verum Corpus and Gloria for Baritone-Solo, Male Choir and Organ, 1992; Duo Facile for Violin, V-Cello; Fantasia for Trio (Violin, Viola and V-Cello), 1993; Requiem for strings, flute, clarinet, sax, trumpet, trombone, organ and choir, 1995. *Address:* Zwartemeerweg 23, 8317 PA Oud-Kraggenburg, Nop, Netherlands.

**PLUJNIKOV, Konstantin;** Singer (Tenor); b. 1946, Russia. *Education:* St Petersburg Conservatory. *Career:* Sang with the Kirov Opera, St Petersburg from 1971; Roles have included Lensky, Vladimir in Prince Igor, Don Ottavio, the Duke of Mantua, Alfredo, Edgardo, Lucia di Lammermoor, Ernesto, Faust and Lohengrin; Guest appearances with the Kirov Opera at San Francisco, 1993 and La Scala, Milan, as Agrippa in The Fiery Angel by Prokofiev, 1995; Season 1998 as Shuisky in Boris Godunov with the Kirov Opera at Drury Lane, London and the New York Met. *Honours:* Prizewinner at Glinka, Geneva and Bucharest Competitions. *Address:* Kirov Opera, 1 Theatre Square, Mariinsky Theatre, St Petersburg, Russia.

**PLUSH, Vincent;** Composer; b. 18 April 1950, Adelaide, South Australia. *Education:* BM, University of Adelaide; Studied computer music, University of California, San Diego, USA. *Career:* Staff, Music Department, Australian Broadcasting Commission; Teacher, NSW State Conservatorium of Music, 1973–80; Tutor, Music Department, University of NSW, 1979; Founder, The Seymour Group, University of Sydney, 1976; Consultant for many arts bodies on Federal, State and Municipal levels; Composer-in-Residence, Musica Viva, 1985; Artistic Director, The Braidwood Festival, 1989 and 1991; Composer-in-Residence, ABC Radio, 1987. *Compositions:* Work for Orchestra, Pacifica, 1986, rev 1987; Works for Ensemble: On Shooting Stars-Homage to Victor Jara, 1981; Facing the Danger, 1982; The Wakefield Convocation, 1985; Helices, from The Wakefield Chronicles, 1985; The Love Songs of Herbert Hoover, 1987; Works for Solo Instrument and Ensemble; Aurores, from O Paraguay!, 1979; Bakery Hill Rising, 1980; Gallipoli Sunrise, 1984; Fire-Raisers, 1984; Works for Brass Band: The Wakefield Chorales, 1985–86; March of the Dalmations, 1987; Works for Narrator and Accompaniment: The Wakefield Chronicles, 1985–86; The Maitland and Morpeth String Quartet, 1979–85; The Muse of Fire, 1986–87; Instrumental Works: Chu no mai, 1974–76; Encompassings, 1975; Chrysalis, 1977–78; Stevie Wonder's Music, 1979; The Wakefield Invocation, 1986; The Wakefield Intrada, 1986; Works for Tape: Vocal Works; Choral Works; Music Theatre Works and Arrangements. *Address:* c/o Australian Music Centre, PO Box 49, Broadway 2007, Australia.

**PLUYGERS, Catherine,** MMus, ARCM; oboist and artistic director; b. 20 Nov. 1955, Colchester, Essex, England. *Education:* Univ. of London, Royal Coll. of Music, Banff Centre School of Fine Arts, Canada, Goldsmiths Coll. *Career:* freelance orchestral player with BBC, Royal Ballet Orchestra, Ulster Orchestra; Founder Member, Thomas Arne Players, with Purcell Room debut, 1985, Wigmore Hall debut, 1986; Recital tour, oboe and organ music, South Norway, sponsored by Norwegian Arts Council, 1982; Formed New Wind Orchestra (NEWO), 1985 and New Wind Summer School, 1988; Premiered Sonata No. 2, opus 64, oboe and piano, dedicated to self by Dr Ruth Gipps, 1986; BBC World Service broadcast, 1986; NEWO South Bank Premiere, Queen Elizabeth Hall, 1986; Formed London New Wind Music Festival, annual festival (Sept. to Nov.) of contemporary wind music 1998–; invited to North Korea as part of promotion of Music by Women Composers; also performed in USA and Far East. *Compositions:* Gloryland, Mixed Media one woman show on subject of War and The Square, A Mixed Media piece performed in Purcell Room, 1990, by the Group Interartes and Hong Kong City Hall, 1990. *Recordings:* English Music for Oboe and Piano, with accompanist Matthew Stanley, 1984. *Current Management:* New Wind Management Ltd, 119 Woolstone Road, Forest Hill, London, SE23 2TQ, England.

**PODLEŚ, Ewa;** Polish singer (contralto); b. 26 April 1952, Warsaw. *Education:* Warsaw Music Acad. *Career:* debut, Warsaw Chamber Opera as Dorabella 1975; after winning prizes at Athens and Geneva 1977, Moscow 1978 and Toulouse 1979, sang widely in Europe as Rosina, Cenerentola and Carmen; sang at the Metropolitan Opera as Handel's Rinaldo 1984, at Trieste and Warsaw as Jaroslavna in Prince Igor, at Covent Garden as Edvige in Guillaume Tell 1991, and at the Opéra Bastille, Paris as Dalila in Samson et Dalila; other noted roles have been Rossini's Arsace and Isabella, Leonora in La Favorita, Ragonde in Comte Ory, and Tancredi at Antwerp 1991; sang the Marquis in La Fille du Régiment at La Scala 1996; Ulrica at Madrid 1998; premiere of Phèdre by Penderecki, New York 2000; season 2000–01 as Rossini's Tancredi in Warsaw, Countess Melibea in Il Viaggio a Reims at La Coruña, and Arsace in Semiramide at Liège; Eboli at Philadelphia 2004. *Recordings include:* Verdi Requiem; Penderecki's Te Deum. *Honours:* Seattle Opera Artist of the Year 2003. *Current Management:* Matthew Sprizzo, 477 Durant Avenue, Staten Island, NY 10308, USA. *Telephone:* (718) 948-5402. *Fax:* (718) 984-8996. *E-mail:* MSprizzo@aol.com. *Website:* www.podles.pl.

**POGAČNIK, Miha;** violinist and music director; b. 31 May 1949, Kranj, Yugoslavia; m. Judith Csik 1974; one s. one d. *Education:* Cologne Conservatory of Music (Musikhochschule), Indiana University School of Music, studied with Veronek, Ozim, Gingold, Rostal, Szeryng. *Career:* over 100 Concerts per season 1977–, in USA, Canada, Mexico, South America, Australia, New Zealand, China, Scandinavia, Western and Eastern Europe; Music Dir Chartres Festival d'Ete 1981–; Pres. and founder, IDRIART International, Geneva (Institute for the Development of Intercultural Relations Through the Arts) now represented in 30 countries 1983–; Music Dir of some 20 IDRIART Festivals on five continents. *Address:* IDRIART, c/o Grad Borl, Ustanova Gandin Fundacija, Dolane 1, 2282 Cirkulane, Slovenia. *E-mail:* miha@mihavision.com. *Website:* www.idriart.org.

**POGORELICH, Ivo;** Croatian concert pianist; b. 20 Oct. 1958, Belgrade; s. of I. Pogorelich and D. Pogorelich; m. Aliza Kezeradze 1980 (died 1996). *Education:* Tchaikovsky Conservatoire of Moscow, then studied with Aliza Kezeradze. *Career:* debut recital in Carnegie Hall, New York, USA 1981; has appeared in major concert halls throughout the world; f. Bad Wörishofen Festival (Germany) 1988; inaugurated Ivo Pogorelich Int. Solo Piano Competition, Pasadena, CA 1993; UNESCO Goodwill Amb. 1988; f. Sarajevo Charitable Foundation (to raise funds for people of Bosnia in fields of medicine and health) 1994; Fellow-Commoner, Balliol Coll. Oxford 1993. *Recordings:* numerous recordings for Deutsche Grammophon, starting with a Chopin recital in 1981 and including works by Bach, Beethoven, Brahms, Chopin, Haydn, Liszt, Mozart, Mussorgsky, Prokofiev, Ravel, Scarlatti, Schumann and the Tchaikovsky Piano Concerto No. 1. *Honours:* First Prize, Casagrande Competition, Terni, Italy 1978, First Prize, Montréal Int. Music Competition, Canada 1980, Special Prize, Int. Chopin Competition, Warsaw 1980. *Current Management:* c/o Kantor Concert Management, 67 Teignmouth Road, London, NW2 4EA, England. *Telephone:* (20) 8208-2480. *Fax:* (20) 8208-2490.

**POGSON, Geoffrey;** Tenor; b. 1966, England. *Education:* Studied at Cambridge and Trinity College of Music. *Career:* Appearances with Glyndebourne Festival in The Queen of Spades in 1995, English National Opera, Scottish Opera and Opera North; Roles include Monostatos, Augustin Moser, Vere in Billy Budd, Quint in The Turn of the Screw and Cornwall in Lear. *Recordings include:* Remendado in Carmen conducted by Abbado.

**POHJANNORO, Hannu,** MMus; Finnish composer; b. 4 July 1963, Savonlinna. *Education:* Helsinki Conservatory, Sibelius Acad. *Career:* teacher, Sibelius Acad. 1992–93, 1998, Helsinki Conservatory 1992–95, Helsinki Univ. Dept of Musicology 1994–98, Espoo Music Inst. 1996–, Sibelius Acad. electronic music studio 1997–. *Compositions include:* Matkalla 1991, Kuvia, heijastuksia 1992, Eilisen linnut 1994, Saari, rannaton 1994, Korkeina aamujen kaaret 1996, Syksyn huoneet 1997, Kuun kiertoa kohti 1998, Paluu 2000, Ajan reuna 2003, XL 2003–04. *Recordings:* Eilisen linnut, Kuun kiertoa kohti, Ajan reuna. *Address:* c/o Finnish Musici Information Centre, Lauttasaarentie 1, 00200 Helsinki, Finland (office). *E-mail:* hpohjann@siba.fi. *Website:* www.uusinta.com/pohjannoroE.html (office).

**POHJOLA, Seppo;** Finnish composer; b. 4 May 1965, Espoo. *Education:* Espoo Coll. of Music and Sibelius Acad., Helsinki. *Compositions include:* String Quartet No. 1 1989–91, Pixilated 1992, Daimonion 1994, String Quartet No. 2 1995, Game Over 1996, Vae victis 1997, Taika 1999, Vinha 1999, String Quartet No. 3 2000, Oravan laulu 2000, Tralala 2000, Liebelei 2001, New York New York 2001, Elämän Kevät 2002, Wedding March 2002, Symphony No. 1 2002, Tapiolandia 2003, Ukri 2003. *Honours:* winner Soc. of Finnish Composers New Tone Competition, Kuhmo Chamber Music Festival 2002. *Address:* Esankuja 9, 01400 Vantaa, Finland. *E-mail:* sjpohjola@luukku.com.

**POHL, Carla;** Singer (Soprano); b. 1942, Johannesburg, South Africa. *Education:* Studied in South Africa and at the Wiesbaden Conservatory. *Career:* Sang at Pforzheim from 1970; Freiburg from 1979, notably as Tosca, Maddalena in Andrea Chénier, Marenka in The Bartered Bride and Stauss's Chrysothemis; Wiesbaden, 1979–81; Deutsche Oper am Rhein, Düsseldorf, from 1981, as Wagner's Elisabeth, Eva and Sieglinde, the Empress in Die Frau ohne Schatten, Strauss's Ariadne and Marschallin, and Leonore in Fidelio; Guest appearances in Mannheim, Berlin, Nancy, Karlsruhe, Stuttgart, Vienna State Opera, Munich State Opera, Milan, Rome and Brunswick; Tour of South Africa, 1985; Deutsche Oper am Rhein 1987, as Rezia in Oberon; Deutsche Oper Berlin and Santiago Chile 1988, as Chrysothemis and Elsa; Sang Wagner's Venus at Cape Town, 2000. *Address:* c/o Deutsche Oper am Rhein, Heinrich-Heine Allee 16, 4000 Düsseldorf, Germany.

**POKA, Balazs;** Singer (Baritone); b. 1947, Eger, Hungary. *Career:* Soloist with the Hungarian National Opera from 1976 as Rossini's Figaro and Dandini, Valentin, Eugene Onegin, and Carlo in La Forza del Destino; Bregenz Festival 1991 as Escamillo; Season 1993 as Don Giovanni at Madrid and Lisbon, Busoni's Turandot at Opéra de Lyon; Other roles include Germont, Marcello, Renato, Rodrigo and Puccini's Lescaut; Sang Ping in Turandot; Concert appearances at La Scala, Milan, Palermo, Bergamo, Hamburg, Amsterdam, Antwerp and Rome. *Recordings:* Kodály's Háry János; From Blues to Opera; La Bohème, Puccini; L'Arlesiana, Cilea; Judgement in Jerusalem, Szehely; Petroviks, Crime and Punishment. *Address:* Hungarian National Opera, Audrassy ut 22, 1061 Budapest, Hungary.

**POLA, Bruno;** Singer (Baritone); b. 1945, Rovereto, Trento, Italy. *Education:* Berlin Conservatory, 1963–68. *Career:* Engaged at Kaiserslautern Opera 1968–71, Kiel 1972–73, Cologne 1974–77, Zürich Opera 1978–81; Recitals and concerts throughout Germany, Netherlands, Switzerland and Austria; From 1982 engagements at such major opera centres as Milan, Rome, Lisbon, Vienna, Munich and Hamburg; Metropolitan Opera from 1988, in Cavalleria Rusticana, Il Barbiere di Siviglia, Gianni Schicci, Rigoletto, Don Giovanni, La Fanciulla del West, Falstaff, Simon Boccanegra, and L'Elisir d'amore; Season 1995–97 in Cavalleria Rusticana and La Forza del Destino at the Met; Aida and Dulcamara at Vienna and Covent Garden; Amonasro in Aida at Santiago, Arena di Verona and Covent Garden; Further opera appearances at Turin, Ascona, Montreal, Pittsburgh, Florence, Geneva and Houston; Melitone in La Forza del Destino at Savonlinna, 1998; Sang Falstaff at the Deutsche Oper, 2000–01. *Address:* Via al Ronco 7, 6933 Muzzano, Switzerland.

**POLASKI, Deborah;** American singer (soprano); b. 26 Sept. 1949, Richmond Centre, WI. *Education:* Conservatory of Music, Ohio and American Inst. of Music, Graz. *Career:* sang at Gelsenkirchen, Karlsruhe and Ulm from 1976; further appearances at opera houses in Hanover, Munich, Hamburg and Freiburg; Festival of Waiblingen 1983, in a revival of Croesus by Reinhard Keiser; Oslo 1986, as Elektra; other roles include Leonore in Fidelio, Wagner's Isolde and Sieglinde and Marie in Wozzeck; Bayreuth Festival 1988, as Brünnhilde in the Ring cycle directed by Harry Kupfer; sang Brünnhilde in Rotterdam 1988, Cologne 1990; Stuttgart Staatsoper 1989, as Elektra (also at the Teatro Nuovo Spoleto 1990); season 1992 as the Dyer's Wife in Die Frau ohne Schatten at Amsterdam and Brünnhilde at Bayreuth; sang Brünnhilde in new Ring Cycle at Covent Garden 1994–95, returned 1997 as Elektra; sang Isolde under Abbado at Salzburg 1999; sang Cassandra and Dido in Les Troyens at Salzburg 2000; Brünnhilde in Ring Cycles at the Berlin Staatsoper 2001–02. *Recordings:* Wolf-Ferrari's Sly, Brünnhilde's Immolation with the Chicago Symphony, R. Strauss's Elektra (with Chorus and Symphony Orchestra of Westdeutscher Rundfunk, Cologne) 2005. *Honours:* Kammersänger (Austria) 2003. *Address:* Oper der Stadt Köln, Offenbachplatz, 5000 Cologne, Germany.

**POLAY, Bruce;** American conductor and composer; *Music Director and Conductor, Knox-Galesburg Symphony*; *Professor of Music and Choir, Knox College Illinois*; b. 22 March 1949, Brooklyn, New York; m. Louise Phillips, 17 Dec 1983, 2 s., 3 d. *Education:* BM, Composition, University of Southern California, 1971; MA, Composition, California State University, 1977; DMA, Instrumental Music, Arizona State University, 1989; Conducting studies with Herbert Blomstedt, Jon Robertson, Murray Sidlin, Alberto Bolet. *Career:* Debut: Conducting: US, Lakewood (California) Chamber Orchestra, 1972; Europe, Filarmonica de Stat Sibiu, Romania, 1993; Music Director and Conductor, Knox-Galesburg (Illinois) Symphony, 1983–; Professor of Music and Choir, Knox College; Recent guest conducting in USA, Belarus, Mexico, Italy, Romania, Russia, Spain, UK and Ukraine. *Compositions:* Encomium for three-part children's chorus, narrator and orchestra, 1987; Concerto for Tenor Trombone, 1991; Three Word Paintings for a cappella chorus, 1991; Cathedral Images for orchestra, 1993; Concerto-Fantasie for piano and orchestra, 1997; Anniversary Mourning, for a cappella choir, 1996; Sound Images: Pictures for an Exhibition, for solo piano, 1995; Bondi's Journey: An Orchestral Rhapsody after Jewish Themes, 1994; Sinfonia Concertante, 1998; Y'Urning, cycle for soprano, clarinet and piano, 1998. *Recordings:* Cathedral Images, CD, 1996; Y'Urning, 1999; Elegy for solo violin and small orchestra, 2001; Suite of Preludes for Organ, 2002; Illumination for orchestra, 2003, Suite on Catalonian Folksongs for String Orchestra 2004, 3 Duets for 2 Violins on Catalonian Folksongs 2005. *Publications:* Encomium 1987, Consolation for Organ 1998, Amazing Grace for Violin & Piano 2001, Prelude for Kingsfold for Organ 2001, Elegy for Violin Solo & Small Orchestra 2004, Suite of Preludes for Organ 2005. *Honours:* Illinois Orchestra of the Year (Knox-Galesburg Symphony), 1986, 1998; Illinois Conductor of the Year, 1997; Exceptional Achievement Award, Knox College, 1998. *Address:* Knox College, Campus Box 5, Galesburg, IL 61401 (office); 1577 N Cherry Street, Galesburg, IL 61401, USA (home). *Telephone:* (309) 341-7208 (office). *Fax:* (309) 341-7019 (office). *E-mail:* bpolay@knox.edu (office).

**POLEGATO, Brett;** Singer (Baritone); b. 9 May 1968, Niagara Falls, Ontario, Canada. *Career:* Opera appearances in North America: As Don Pasquale, Papageno, Rossini's Dandini, 1998 and Mozart's Count; European debut at Avignon in title role of Monteverdi's Orfeo; Savonlinna Festival as Silvio in Pagliacci; Engagements with L'Opéra de Montréal, season 1998; Season 2000–01 with Pelléas at Strasbourg and Leipzig, Britten's Ned Keene at La Scala; Concert repertory includes songs by Schubert and Schumann. *Recordings:* Ulbalde in Gluck's Armide; Messiah (Arabesque); Kalman's Die Herzogin von Chicago (Decca); To a Poet, solo recital; Bach Coffee and Peasant Cantates. *Honours:* Finalist, Singer of the World Competition, Cardiff, 1995. *Address:* c/o IMG Artists, Lovell House, 616 Chiswick High Road, London W4 5RX, England.

**POLGÁR, László;** Hungarian singer (bass); b. 1 Jan. 1947, Somogyszentpál; s. of Lajos Polgár and Anna Kántor; m. Ágnes Gergely; three d. *Education:* Liszt Ferenc Music Acad., Budapest 1967–72. *Career:* scholarship holder 1972–73; soloist, Hungarian State Opera, Budapest 1972–; postgraduate study under Hans Hotter, Hochschule für Musik und Darstellende Kunst, Vienna 1979–81; Lieder recitalist; also sings Oratorio (Verdi's Requiem, etc.). *Performances:* début in Seneca (Monteverdi: L'Incoronazione di Poppea); appearances in Staatsoper, Vienna; Royal Opera House, Covent Garden, Salzburg Festival, Zürich, Munich, Hamburg, Hannover, Paris, Madrid, Venice, Bologna, Florence, Rome, Moscow, Prague, Dresden, Berlin, Stockholm, Buenos Aires, Metropolitan Opera, New York, Philadelphia, Los Angeles, Pittsburgh, Pa. *Operatic roles include:* Osmin, Sarastro, Leporello, Figaro, Publius (La Clemenza di Tito), Bellini: Oroveso (Norma), Rodolfo (La Sonnambula), Basilio (Il Barbiere di Sevilla), Don Geronio (Il Turco in Italia), Philippo II (Don Carlo), Il Guardiano (La Forza del Destino), Conte Walter (Luisa Miller), Fiesco (Simone Boccanegra), Ramphis (Aida), Gurnemanz (Parsifal), Marke (Tristan), Collin (La Bohème), Timur (Turandot), Bluebeard (Duke Bluebeard's Castle), Rocco (Fidelio), Gremin (Eugene Onegin), Boris Godunov. *Recordings include:* Balassa: The Door Outside, Lendvay: La p... respectueuse, Mozart Mass No. 6, Vesperae K. 339, Don Giovanni, La Clemenza di Tito, Petrovic: Crime and Punishment, Handel: Atalanta, Beethoven Fidelio, Die Gezeichneten, Poliuto, Fierrabras, Duke Bluebeard's Castle (Grammy Award 1999), Il Rè (Aida). *Honours:* First Prizes at competitions: Dvořák, Karlovy Vary 1971, Schumann, Zwickau 1974, Erkel, Budapest 1975, Ostende 1977, Budapest (Hungarian Radio) 1977, Vienna (Hugo Wolf) 1980, Philadelphia (Luciano Pavarotti) 1981, Liszt Prize 1985, Merited Artist 1986. *Address:* Ábel Jenő utca 12, 1113 Budapest, Hungary. *Telephone:* (1) 668-285.

**POLIANICHKO, Alexander;** Russian conductor and violinist; b. 26 March 1953. *Education:* St Petersburg Conservatoire with Prof. Ilya Musin. *Career:* fmr violinist with the Leningrad Philharmonic Orchestra, under Evgeny Mravinsky; apptd House Conductor Mariinsky (Kirov) Theatre 1989; fmr Artistic Dir St Petersburg Orchestra; Dir of the Opera Kirov Theatre; Artistic Dir Belorussian CO, Minsk from 1987; fmr Principal Conductor Bournemouth Sinfonietta 1997; conducted the Mariinsky (Kirov) Opera and Ballet Theatre at the Edinburgh Festival (The Marriage) 1991, Los Angeles (The Nutcracker) 1993, Tel-Aviv (Khovanshchina) 1996; London debut conducting ENO's production of Eugene Onegin 1994, returning to ENO to conduct Eugene Onegin and Carmen 1997, 1998; season 1994–95 conducted La Bohème with Norwegian Opera in Oslo, The Fiery Angel with San Francisco Opera, and toured Australia for ABC; season 1995–96 with La Bayadère at the Opéra Nat. de Paris, later touring with this production to the New York Met; debut at La Scala conducting the Mariinsky Opera's production of Mussorgsky's Khovanschina 1998; conducted Lady Macbeth of Mtsensk for Stuttgart Opera 1998, returning in subsequent years to conduct The Queen of Spades, Tosca, Boris Godunov, Turandot, and La Traviata; Covent Garden debut 1999, conducting for the Royal Ballet, returning in 2000–01; seasons 1999–2000 and 2000–01 conducting La traviata at Deutsche Oper Berlin; conducted Paris Opéra in Stravinsky's Mavra, Prokofiev's The Prodigal Son and Weill's Seven Deadly Sins 2001; recent appearances at San Francisco Opera, conducting Turandot, La Bohème and The Cunning Little Vixen, at the Bolshoi Theatre, Moscow, conducting La Bohème, Tosca, The Queen of Spades), at the Royal Danish Opera, conducting The Queen of Spades, The Love of Three Oranges, and at the Royal Opera House, Covent Garden, conducting The Queen of Spades; conducted The Queen of Spades at Gothenburg Opera 2003, returning to conduct a new production of Boris Godunov 2005; conducted Hansel and Gretel for WNO 2004; conducted Roméo et Juliette for Opéra de Lyon and Carmen for Australian Opera 2005; many guest appearances with leading Russian orchestras; has taken part in many int. festivals, including Aldeburgh, Bergen, Edinburgh, Mikkele and Savonlinna, the Golden Mask Festival (Moscow), The Avantgarde to the Contemporary Festival (St Petersburg), the Shaliapin Festival (Kazan, Russia), and the Bulat Mizhilkiev Festival in Bishkek (Kyrgystan). *Honours:* first prize All-Union Conductors' Competition 1988. *Current Management:* Ingpen & Williams Ltd, 7 St George's Court, 131 Putney Bridge Road, London, SW15 2PA, England. *Address:* c/o kanal Griboedova 74-33, 190068 St Petersburg, Russia (home). *E-mail:* a_polyanichko@mail.ru.

**POLIANSKY, Valerig K.;** Russian conductor; *Chief Conductor and Artistic Director, State Academic Symphony Capella;* b. 19 April 1949, Moscow; m. Olga P Lapuso, 1 s., 1 d. *Education:* State Conservatoire Tchaikovsky, Moscow, graduated in Choir Conducting, 1971, Orchestra Conducting, 1974. *Career:* Debut: Moscow Operetta; Conducted, Shostakovich's Katerina Izmailova at Bolshoi Theatre; Conductor Chamber Choir of the Ministry of Culture 1980; Conductor State Chamber Choir 1990; Chief Conductor and Artistic Dir State Acad. Symphony Capella of Russia 1992–. *Recordings:* Rachmaninov Vespers, Liturgia of St John Chrysostom, A Schnittke, Choir Concert; A Bruckner, Geistliche motetten, L Cherubini, Requiem in C minor, P Tchaikovsky, Liturgia of St John Chrysostom, Various choruses; Orchestral Serenade. *Contributions:* Soviet Music; Music Life; Music in the USSR. *Honours:* Arezzo Prize for best conductor, 1975; Honoured Artist of the People of Russia until 1996. *Address:* Pyatnitskaya str. 2, Moscow 115035 (home); Begovay 4 alleya 3-40, 125040 Moscow, Russia (home). *Telephone:* (095) 953-51-94. *Fax:* (095) 953-89-96. *E-mail:* gaskros@rambler.ru.

**POLISI, Joseph W.,** MA, MMus, DMA; American bassoon player; *President, The Juilliard School;* b. 1947. *Education:* Univ. of Connecticut, Tufts Univ., Yale Univ., Conservatoire Nat. de Paris with Maurice Allard. *Career:* Pres., The Juilliard School, New York; extensive solo and chamber bassoon performances throughout USA; Chair., Seaver Inst., Nat. Endowment for the Arts Conductors' Program; mem. Nat. Cttee on Standards in the Arts; fmr accreditation evaluator for Nat. Asscn of Schools of Music. *Recordings:* A Harvest of 20th Century Bassoon Music 1979. *Honours:* Hon. DMus (Curtis Inst. of Music, Philadelphia) 1990, Dr hc (New England Conservatory) 2001; Hon. mem. Royal Acad. of Music, London, England 1992. *Address:* The Juilliard School, 60 Lincoln Center Plaza, New York, NY 10023, USA.

**POLIVNICK, Paul,** BM; American conductor; b. 7 July 1947, Atlantic City, NJ; m. Marsha Hooks 1980. *Education:* Juilliard School of Music, New York, Aspen Music School, Colorado (summers), Berkshire Music Center, Tanglewood, MA (summers), Accademia Musicale Chigiana, Siena, Italy (summer). *Career:* Conductor, Debut Orchestra, Los Angeles 1969–73; Assoc. Conductor, Indianapolis Symphony Orchestra 1977–80; Assoc. Principal Conductor, Milwaukee Symphony Orchestra 1981–85; Music Dir, Alabama Symphony Orchestra, Birmingham 1985–; mem. American Symphony Orchestra League. *Honours:* Dr hc (Montevallo Univ.) 1986. *Address:* c/o Alabama Symphony Orchestra, 1814 First Avenue N, Birmingham, AL 35209, USA.

**POLLARD, Mark;** Composer and Music Director; b. 14 Feb. 1957, Melbourne, Victoria, Australia. *Education:* BA (Hons) 1981, MA 1984, La Trobe University. *Career:* Senior Tutor, La Trobe University, 1983–85; Lecturer, Victoria College of the Arts, 1986–; Music Director of various contemporary ensembles; Commissions from Seymour Group, Australian Chamber Soloists, New Audience, and others. *Compositions include:* Quinque II for tape, 1979; Krebs for piano, 1983; A Sympathetic Resonance for guitar, 1989; Bass Lines for amplified double bass, 1990; Carillon for Sacha for piano, 1991; Two Drummings for Joe, for choir, 1991; The Quick or the Dead, for string quartet, 1992; A View from the Beach, for orchestra, 1994; The Art of Flirting for clarinet, 1994; Inherit the Wind, for English horn, 1994. *Honours:* Spivakovsky Awards, 1993. *Address:* c/o APRA, 1A Eden Street, Crows Nest, NSW 2065, Australia.

**POLLASTRI, Paolo;** Oboist; b. 12 July 1960, Bologna, Italy; m. Christine Dechaux 1988, 2 d. *Education:* Scientific Diploma, Bologna, 1979; Oboe Diploma, Bologna, 1977; Oboe Diploma 1982, Baroque Oboe Diploma 1982, Brussels; Diploma D'Onore (Accademia Chigiana, Siena), 1977. *Career:* 1st Oboe, Orchestra Giovanile Italiana, 1977; Genova, 1979; Rai Roma, 1981; Orchestra Regionale Toscana-Firenze, 1982–89; Accademia di S Cecilia, Roma, 1989; Solisti Veneti, 1984–89; Television and radio appearances with RAI 1, 2, 3 (Solisti Veneti); Television Australiana (Solisti Veneti); Radio Israeliana (Accademia Bizantina); BBC (Solisti Veneti); Played at Festivals in Montreux, Salzburg, Zagreb and Belgrade, Martigny and Vevey, Toulouse, Paris, Stuttgart, Edinburgh, Sydney, Melbourne and Canberra; Winner of Italian competition to teach in conservatories, 1993; Teacher, Studea di Musica, Fiesole, 1993–. *Recordings:* Numerous recording include: Respighi, Solisti Veneti, Erato; Vivaldi, Oboe concertos, Accademia Bizantina, Frequenz; Malipiero, Respighi, Ghedini, Rota, Woodwind Quintet, Fonè. *Publications:* IDRS, 1998; I Fiati, 1999. *Contributions:* II Dopo Concerto, 1980–81; The Italian Academy of Woodwinds, 1988–89. *Current Management:* Studio Musica, Viale Caduti in Guerra, 194, 41100 Modena, Italy. *Address:* Via di Mugnana 3, 50027 Strada in Chianti, Florence, Italy.

**POLLEI, Paul,** BM, MM, PhD; Pianist and Administrator; b. 9 May 1936, Salt Lake City, UT, USA; m., two c. *Education:* Univ. of Utah, Eastman School of Music, Florida State Univ. *Career:* Prof. of Piano, Brigham Young Univ. 1963–2001; founder of Gina Bachauer International Piano Competition 1976–; creator of American Piano Quartet (2pianos/8hands) 1984–; teacher; soloist; lecturer; speaker; mem. Music Teachers' Nat. Asscn, European Piano Teachers' Asscn, World Federation of Int. Music Competitions. *Recordings:* American Piano Quartet. *Publications:* Essential Technique for the Pianist. *Honours:* The Madeleine Award 2002. *Address:* 138 W Broadway, Salt Lake City, UT, 84101, USA (office). *Telephone:* (801) 2974250 (office). *Fax:* (801) 5219202 (office). *E-mail:* paul@bachauer.com (office). *Website:* www.bachauer.com (office).

**POLLET, Françoise;** singer (soprano); b. 10 Sept. 1949, Boulogne Billancourt, near Paris, France. *Education:* Versailles Conservatory and in Munich. *Career:* debut, Lubeck, as the Marschallin, 1983; Sang at Lubeck until 1986, as Santuzza, Fiordiligi, Donna Anna, Elisabeth in Tannhäuser, Amelia in Ballo in Maschera, Alice Ford, Giulietta, Ariadne and Arabella; Appearances as Agathe at Marseilles, Vitellia in La Clemenza di Tito at Opéra-Comique, Paris, and Dukas' Ariadne at Théâtre du Châtelet in a production by Ruth Berghaus, 1991; At Montpellier has sung Reizia in Oberon, Meyerbeer's Valentine, Catherine of Aragon in Saint-Saëns's Henry VIII, Elisabeth, and Magnard's Berenice; Hamburg, 1990, in premiere of Liebermann's Freispruch für Medea; Covent Garden, 1991, as Valentine; Sang Ariadne auf Naxos at Toulouse, 1998; Other roles include Cassandra in Les Troyens, at Brussels, and Mozart's Countess; Concert repertoire includes Schumann's Liederkreis and Les Nuits d'Eté by Berlioz; Sang Amelia (Ballo in Maschera) at Venice, 1999, and Geneviève in Chausson's Le Roi Arthus at the 2000 Edinburgh Festival (concert); London Proms, 2002. *Recordings include:* 4th Symphony by Guy Ropartz; La Vièrge in Jeanne d' Arc au Bûcher by Honegger, conducted by Ozawa. *Current Management:* TransArt (UK) Ltd, Cedar House, 10 Rutland Street, Filey, North Yorkshire YO14 9JB, England. *Telephone:* (1723) 515819. *Fax:* (1723) 514678. *E-mail:* transartuk@transartuk.com. *Website:* www.transartuk.com.

**POLLETT, Patricia (Engeline Maria);** Violist and Associate Professor, University of Queensland; b. 13 Oct. 1958, Utrecht, Netherlands; m. Dr Philip Keith Pollett, 28 Jan 1978, 1 s. *Education:* BMus, Honours, University of Adelaide, 1979; ARCM, Royal College of Music, 1980; Hochschule der Kunst, West Berlin, 1988; Teachers: Beryl Kimber, Peter Schidlof, Margaret Major, Bruno Giuranna. *Career:* Member of I Solisti Veneti, 1983–84; Founder Member of Perihelion, contemporary ensemble; Resident at University of Queensland, 1988–; Concerto Soloist with Gulbenkian Orchestra, Lisbon,

1984, Queensland Philharmonic Orchestra, 1989 and 1995, Queensland Symphony Orchestra, 1990, 1991 and 1994, Sydney Symphony Orchestra, 1991, and Mozart Symposium at University of Otago, New Zealand, 1991. Commissioned new works for viola by Colin Spiers, Andrew Schultz, Nigel Sabin, Philip Bracanin, Ross Edwards, Colin Brumby (world premiere performances of these works), Robert Davidson, Stephen Cronin, Mary Mageau, Andrew Ford and Elena Kats-Chernin. *Recordings:* Tapestry; Points of Departure; Chamber Music of Andrew Schultz; Anthology of Australian Music; Evocations; Patricia Pollett: Viola Concerti; Solo: Viola Power, Australian works for viola. *Address:* 21 Almay Street, Kenmore, Queensland 4069, Australia.

**POLLINI, Maurizio;** Italian pianist; b. 5 Jan. 1942, Milan; s. of Gino Pollini and Renata Melotti; m. Maria Elisabetta Marzotto 1968; one s. *Career:* has played with Berlin and Vienna Philharmonic Orchestras, Bayerischer Rundfunk Orchestra, London Symphony Orchestra, Boston, New York, Philadelphia, LA and San Francisco Orchestras; has played at Salzburg, Vienna, Berlin, Prague Festivals; recordings for Polydor Int. *Honours:* First Prize Int. Chopin Competition, Warsaw 1960; Ernst von Siemens Music Prize, Munich 1996. *Current Management:* Harrison/Parrott Ltd, 12 Penzance Place, London, W11 4PA, England. *Telephone:* (20) 7229 9166. *Fax:* (20) 7221 5042. *Website:* www.harrisonparrott.com.

**POLOLANIK, Zdenek,** MgA; Czech (Moravian) composer; b. 25 Oct. 1935, Brno; m. Jarmila Linka; one d. one s. *Education:* Brno Conservatoire, Janáček Acad. of Performing Arts, Brno. *Career:* freelance composer from 1961–; composed 600 works including concert music and ballet, spiritual music for liturgical purposes and musical scores for film, radio, incidental music, etc; mem. Prítomnost composers' consortium, Prague. *Compositions include:* Variations for organ and piano, 1956; Sinfonietta, 1958; String Quartet, 1958; Divertimento for 4 horns and strings, 1960; 5 Symphonies, 1961, 1962, 1963, 1969; Concentus resonabilis for 19 soloists and tape, 1963; Musica Spingenta I–III, 1961–63; Mechanism, ballet, 1964; Horn sonata, 1965; Piano Concerto, 1966; Concerto Grosso I and II, 1966, 1988; Missa Brevis, 1969; Song of Songs, oratorio, 1970; Snow Queen, ballet, 1978; Lady Among Shadows, ballet, 1984; Summer Festivities for chorus and 2 pianos, 1985; Christmas Message, 1987; March for wind orchestra, 1990; Easter Way, 14 songs for soprano and ensemble, 1990; Small Mythological Exercises, melodrama, 1991; Ballad for cello and piano, 1992; Christmas Triptych for bugle and 4 trombones, 1993; First One Must Carry the Cross, chamber oratorio for medium voice and synthesizer, 1993; Eulogies, Psalms for chorus, 1993; Psalms for women's chorus, 1993; Cisařuv mim (Emperor's Mime), 1993; Chválozpevy, 1994; Spor duše s tělem (Dispute of Soul with Body), 1994; Two Ballads for lower voice, 1995; Prazská legenda (Prague Legend), 1995; Winterballad, 1996; Sexton, 1996; Horka blahoslavenství (Bitter Hallow), 1996; Citadella, 1997; Cycles of Noels for organ, piano, large symphony orchestra, 1997; Dulces cantilenae, 1997; Cantus laetitiae, 1997; Setkání (Ordinario and Proprio), 1997; Musica sacra, 1999; Slavnostní konická mše (Solemn Konical mass), 2000; Baletní epizody (Ballettic episodes), 2001; Interludium, 2001; Missa solemnis, 2001; Capriccio for cello and orchestra, 2002;. *Recordings:* Missa Brevis 1994, Pastorale for Organ, Liturgical mass, Te Deum, Ave Maria 1996, Time and Joy of Merrymaking 1997, Ballad 1997, What's New 1997, Snow Queen 1998, Pierot 1999, Noel's Adventní (Advent) 1999, The Angel's Message to the World, Capriccio for cello and orchestra. *Publications:* contrib. to journals and books. *Honours:* Holyś Cyril and Method Decoration; Josef Blaha Prize for Music Composition, Hon. Freeman Ostrovacice. *Address:* Osvobození 67, 66481 Ostrovačice, Czech Republic (home). *Telephone:* (546) 427417. *E-mail:* zdenek.pololanik@tiscali.cz. *Website:* www.volny.cz/pololanik.

**POLOZOV, Vyacheslav M.;** Singer (tenor); b. 1950, Mariupol, Ukraine, USSR. *Education:* Studied at the Kiev Conservatory. *Career:* Debut: Kiev Opera 1977, as Alfredo in La Traviata; Leading tenor at the Saratov Opera 1978; Leading tenor at Minsk Opera 1980; Bolshoi Opera Moscow, 1982, Alfredo and Turiddu; Sang Pinkerton at La Scala 1986; US debut with Pittsburgh Symphony Orchestra 1986, as Cavaradossi; US stage debut the Chicago Lyric Opera 1986, as Rodolfo in La Bohème; Further appearances at Washington DC (1986, as Lykov, in The Tsar's Bride), New York (Met 1987, as Pinkerton); Palm Springs, as Cavaradossi; San Antonio (as Cavaradossi); Met (as Rodolfo, 1987, summer park concerts); Washington DC, as Dimitri in Boris Godunov; Season 1987/88 with Calaf in New City Opera, repeated at the Bayerische Staatsoper Munich; Rome Opera as Lykov and the Metropolitan as Verdi's Macduff; Michigan Opera Theatre as Rodolfo in La Bohème, (1988 debut); Further debuts at the San Francisco Opera (1988 as Enzo, in La Gioconda), Carnegie Hall (1988, as Andrea Chénier), Canadian Opera Company (1989 as Cavaradossi), Greater Miami Opera (1989, as Alvaro in La Forza); Sang Pinkerton in San Francisco, 1989, Lyon Opéra (debut 1990), as Pinkerton, repeated in the Greater Miami Opera; appearance, at the 1990 Caracalla Festival, Rome, and Turiddu and Lensky with the Chicago Lyric Opera, 1990; Calaf with the Greater Miami Opera; Cavaradossi in the Houston Grand Opera, 1991; as Lensky in Hamburg; as Don Carlo in Denver at the Opera Colorado. *Recordings include:* Aleko by Rachmaninov (Melodia); Boris Godunov (Erato, under M. Rostropovich), TY broadcast Canadian Opera Company, Tosca. *Honours:* Winner, All-Russia Glinka Competition 1981; Sofia Competition, Bulgaria, 1984 (for the Duke of Mantua); Madama Butterfly Competition, Tokyo, 1987. *Address:* 367 Columbus PKWY, Mineola, NY 11501, USA.

**POLSTER, Hermann Christian;** Singer; b. 8 April 1937, Leipzig, Germany. *Education:* Univ. of Leipzig. *Career:* Sang with the Dresden Kreuzchor while a boy; Many engagements with the Leipzig Bach Soloists, the chorus of St Thomas's Leipzig and the Leipzig Gewandhaus Orchestra; Guest appearances Berlin; Munich, Frankfurt, Hamburg, Roma, Milano, Torino, Amsterdam (St Matthew Passion); Halle (Shostakovich 14th Symphony); Tokyo, Osaka (Bach: St Matthew and St John Passion, Beethoven's Ninth); Paris (Fidelio), Moscow, Buenos Aires, Rio de Janerio, Aix-en-Provence, Venice, Dubrovnik, Prague (Beethoven's Ninth); Other repertoire includes Monteverdi's Vespers; Buxtehude Cantatas, Telemann Cantatas, Psalms, Serenades; Handel Saul, Acis and Galatea, Samson, Belshazzar, Judas Maccabaeus, Solomon, Jephtha, Hercules and Messiah; Bach Cantatas and Oratorios; Haydn Oratorios; Mozart Masses, Requiem, Solemn Vespers and Die Zauberflöte (Sarastro); Beethoven Missa Solomnis, Mass in C and Christus am Olberg; Mendelssohn Elijah, St Paul, Erste Walpurgisnacht; Schumann Paradies und die Peri; Verdi Requiem; Brahms Ein Deutsches Requiem; Mahler 8th Symphony; Janáček Glagolitic Mass; Stravinsky Oedipus Rex; Wagner Die Meistersinger (Pogner); Tchaikovsky Eugene Onegin (Gremin); Blacher The Grand Inquisitor; Shostakovich 13th Symphony, Songs of Michelangelo; Professur für Gesang Musikhochschule Leipzig, International Masterclasses, Juror in international competitions (Brussels, Moscow, Berlin, Leipzig); mem. Deutscher Musikrat, Bundesverband Deutscher Gesangspädagogen (Vize-präsident); Neue Detusche Bachesellschaft. *Recordings:* St Matthew Passion and Bach Cantatas; Elijah and Orff's Die Kluge; Beethoven: Fidelio (1804 version), Missa solemnis; Shostakovich Michelangelo Songs; Mozart Litaneien; Concert works conducted by Karl Böhm, Karajan, Herbert Kegel, Neville Marriner, Wolfgang Sawallisch and Kurt Masur. *Honours:* Kammersänger, Kunstpreisträger. *Address:* c/o Gewandhausorchester, Augustusplatz 8, 4109 Leipzig, Germany.

**POLVERELLI, Laura;** Italian singer (mezzo-soprano); b. 1964, Siena. *Education:* Florence and Verona Conservatories. *Career:* appearances at Seattle Opera, Liceu Barcelona, La Scala Milan, Florence, Hamburg, Pesaro and Théâtre des Champs-Elysées, Paris; roles have included Mozart's Sesto, Donna Elvira and Dorabella (Glyndebourne, 2000); Gluck's Orfeo, Verdi's Abigaille and parts in Il Turco in Italia, Le Comte Ory, La Cenerentola, Lucia di Lammermoor, La Traviata and Le nozze di Figaro; Concerts include Rossini and Pergolesi Stabat Mater, Bach's St Matthew Passion and B minor Mass; Season 2000–01 as Dorabella in Così fan tutte, at Glyndebourne, Rossini's Isabella at Venice and Rosina in Paris; La Clemenza di Tito in Munich and Handel's Tamerlano in Florence. *Recordings include:* Le nozze di Figaro and Così fan tutte; Zaida in Il Turco in Italia and Hemon in Traetta's Antigone. *Current Management:* Opéra et Concert, 7 rue de Clichy, 75009 Paris, France. *Website:* www.opera-concert.com.

**POMERANTS-MAZURKEVICH, Dana;** Concert Violinist and Professor of Violin; b. 11 Oct. 1944, Kaunas, USSR; m. Yuri Mazurekvich, 4 July 1963, 1 d. *Education:* MMus, 1961–65, Artist Diploma 1965–68, Moscow State Conservatory. *Career:* Performed as the Mazurekvich Violin Duo member and also as a soloist in: USSR, Poland, USA, Canada, Australia, England, France, Belgium, East and West Germany, Hong Kong, Taiwan, Switzerland, Italy, Roumania, Mexico and other countries; Recorded for Radio Moscow, France, ABC (Australia), WGGH (Boston); CBC (Canada); BBC (England); Sender Freies (W Berlin), and others. *Recordings:* Works by Telemann, Prokofiev, Honegger, Sarasate, Spohr, Rawsthorne, Wieniawski, Shostakovich, Leclair, Handel and others; Masters of the Bow, Toronto, Canada; SNE, Montreal, Canada. *Current Management:* Robert M Gewald Management. *Address:* School of Music, Boston University, 855 Commonwealth Avenue, Boston, MA 02215, USA.

**POMMIER, Jean-Bernard;** French pianist and conductor; b. 17 Aug. 1944, Beziers; two d. by Irena Podleska. *Education:* Conservatoire de Paris. *Career:* as pianist has appeared with conductors including: Herbert von Karajan, Bernard Haitink, Pierre Boulez, Riccardo Muti, Gennadi Rozhdestvensky, Leonard Slatkin, Zubin Mehta and Daniel Barenboim; has conducted numerous orchestras including Chamber Orchestra of Europe, Orchestre de Paris; debut with Royal Liverpool Philharmonic Orchestra 1991; Artistic Dir Northern Sinfonia, Newcastle-upon-Tyne 1996–; performances world-wide; masterclasses in Chicago, London, Lausanne and Melbourne. *Recordings include:* Mozart Piano Concerti (with Sinfonia Varsovia), Poulenc Piano Concerti (with City of London Sinfonia), Brahms Cello Sonatas and Violin Sonatas, Complete Beethoven Piano Sonatas, complete Mozart Sonatas. *Honours:* Officier, Ordre nat. du mérite; awards include Int. Competition of Young Musicians, Berlin, Prix de la Guilde des artistes solistes Français, Diapason d'Or, Tchaikovsky Prize, Moscow. *Address:* Musiké Académies Productions, Route Praz Gilliard 12, 1000 Lausanne, Switzerland. *Telephone:* (21) 7841141 (home). *Fax:* (21) 7841148 (office); (21) 7841148 (home).

**POMPILI, Claudio;** Composer; b. 12 May 1949, Gorizia, Italy. *Education:* BMus, University of Adelaide, 1983; Study with Richard Meale and Tristram Cary in Australia (1980–82) and with Franco Donatoni and Salvatore Sciarrino in Italy (1984–85); IRCAM studios, Paris, 1984. *Career:* Faculty Member, University of Adelaide, 1983–84, University of New England, 1987–97; Associate Professor and Director, Conservatorium of Music, University of Wollongong, 1998–; Commissions from Duo Contemporain, Perihelion and others. *Compositions include:* Medieval Purity in a Bed of Thorns, for tape, 1981–84; The Star Shoots a Dart, for flute, clarinet, violin and cello, 1985; Polymnia Triptych for soprano and large ensemble, 1986;

Songs for Ophelia for soprano, 1989; Scherzo alla Francescana, for double bass, 1990; Trio for violin, guitar and double bass, 1990; Zeitfluss: Teuflicher kontrapunkt, for wind quintet, 1990; Lo spazio stellato si riflette in suoni, for baroque flute, 1990; Ah, amore che se n'ando nell'aria, for clarinet, viola and cello, 1991; String Quartet, 1992; El viento lucha a obscura con tu sueno, 1993; Fra l'urlo e il tacere, for bass clarinet, 1993. *Honours:* Adolf Spivakovsky Scholarship, 1990. *Address:* c/o SIAE (Sezione Musica), Viale della Letteratura n. 30, 00144 Rome, Italy.

**PONCE DE LEÓN, Griselda;** classical guitarist; b. 1 May 1934, Rosario, Argentina. *Education:* Accademia Musicale Chigiana, Italy, Musica en Compostela, Spain, Fine Arts School, Rosario, studied with Nelly Ezcaray, Maria Luisa Anido, Andres Segovia, Sila Godoy and Narciso Yepes. *Career:* debut in Rosario, 1944; Many concerts for radio and television in Argentina before 1958; First performance of Giuliani's Concerto op 30, with conductor José Rodríguez Fauré, Argentina, 1963; Performances for Radio Televisione Italiana and others, Italy, 1983–93; Concert recording for Cracovia's television, Poland, 1992; Performed in: Teatro Colón, Buenos Aires; El Circolo, Rosario; Municipal, São Paolo, Brazil; Rudaki Opera, Tehran, Iran; Ghione, Rome, Italy; and others; Teacher, Cordoba Conservatory, Argentina; Teacher, Instituto Superior de Musica de la Universidad de Rosario, Argentina; Teacher, Italian Conservatories, Pescara, Potenza and Bologna; Masterclasses and lectures. *Address:* Via le Ballarin 153–int 7, 00142 Rome, Italy. *E-mail:* griselponcedeleon@tiscalinet.it.

**POND, Celia (Frances Sophia);** Cellist; b. 5 Jan. 1956, London, England; m. Ambrose Miller, 4 April 1981. *Education:* BA 1974–77, MA 1981, Girton College, Cambridge University; LRAM, Royal Academy of Music, London, 1977–78; Staatliche Hochschule für Musik, Rheinland, 1978–81. *Career:* Principal Cello, Artistic Adviser, European Union Chamber Orchestra, 1981–; Many recitals throughout Europe with Trio Gardellino, 1983–86; Cello and Piano Duo, Celia and Mary Pond; Recitals in the United Kingdom and Far East including Hong Kong and Peking; mem, Incorporated Society of Musicians. *Recordings:* Antonio Duni; Cantate da Camera Dedicate Alla Maesta di Giovanni V. *Contributions:* Early Music, 1978; Solo Bass Viol Music in France. *Honours:* Edith Helen Major Prize, Cambridge, 1976; West German Government Scholarship, 1978. *Address:* Hollick, Yarnscombe, N Devon EX31 3LQ, England.

**PONDJICLIS, Sophie;** Singer (Mezzo-soprano); b. 1968, France. *Career:* Appearances at Florence, the Paris Opéra Bastille, La Scala Milan, Palais Garnier, Hamburg Opera and Marseille; Paris Châtelet in Stravinsky's Les Noces, repeated in Rome; Sang title role in Esther de Carpentras by Milhaud, 1992; Recitals at the Châtelet, Studio Bastille, Mannheim and Villa Medici in Rome; Further enagements as Carmen, Ruggiero in Alcina and Rossini's Rosina; Season 2000–01 at the Berlin Konzerthaus as Ravel's Enfant, Mozart's Marcellina in Paris, Madrid and Barcelona, Isaura in Rossini's Tancredi at Marseille and Olga in Eugene Onegin at Geneva. *Recordings include:* Stabat Mater by Gouvy. *Honours:* Winner, Toti dal Monte Competition, Treviso. *Address:* c/o Musicaglotz, 11, Rue le Verrier, 75006 Paris, France.

**PONIATOWSKA, Irena,** PhD; Polish musicologist; b. 5 July 1933, Góra Kalwaria; m. Andrzej Poniatowski, 14 Nov. 1953 (died 1994); one d. *Education:* Warsaw Univ. *Career:* tutor, Inst. of Musicology, Warsaw Univ. 1970, Vice-Dir 1974–79, Asst Prof. 1984, Extraordinary Prof. 1991, Ordinary Prof. 1996–2004, Vice-Dean Faculty of History 1988–90, 1993–99; Pres. Council, Chopin Soc. 1976–84, Vice-Pres. 1986–91; Pres. Congress, Musica Antique Europae Orientalis, Poland 1988, 1991, 1994, 1997, 2000, 2003, Polish Chopin Acad. 1994, Congress Chopin, Warsaw, 1999, Council of Inst. of Fryderyk Chopin, 2001–; Ed. of many encyclopaedias including Polish Encyclopaedia of Music, Vols 1–5 1979–1997. *Publications:* Beethoven Piano Texture 1972, The Chronicle of the Important Musical Events in Poland 1945–72 1974, Piano Music and Playing in XIX Century Artistic and Social Aspects 1991, Dictionary of Music for Schools 1991, 1997, History and Interpretation of Music 1993, 1995, Musical Work: Theory History, Interpretation (ed.) 1984, Maria Szymanowska 25 Mazurkas 1993, Chopin in the Circle of his Friends, Vols I–V (ed.) 1995–99, J.A. Hasse und Polen (co-ed.) 1995, 24 Préludes by Fryderyk Chopin (facsimile edn with commentary) (ed.) 1999, Henryk Wieniawski Polonaise Brillante pour le violon avec accompagnement de piano op. 4, urtext and critical edn 2000, Musica antique Europae Orientalis X Acta Musicologica (co-ed.) 1994, Bydgoszcz 1997, Bydgoszcz XI 1999, Bydgoszcz XII 2003, Bydgoszcz XIII 2004, Chopin and His Works in the Context of Culture, Vols 1–2 (ed.) 2003; numerous articles in collective works. *Contributions:* Muzyka; Ruch Muzyczny; Rocznik Chopinowski; Chopin Studies; Hudobny Život; Quadrivium. *Honours:* Hon. mem. Accad. Filarmonica di Bologna 1998; Officer's Cross, Order of Polonia Restituta 2000; Medal of Nat. Educ. Cttee 2004, Medal of Merits for Polish Culture 2004, Prize of Polish Composers' Union 2004. *Address:* Filtrowa 63-38, 02-056 Warsaw, Poland (home). *Telephone:* (22) 8252850 (home).

**PONKIN, Vladimir;** Conductor; b. 1951, Irkutsk, Siberia, Russia. *Education:* Studied at Gorky Conservatoire and with Rozhdestvensky in Moscow. *Career:* Assistant conductor at Bolshoi Theatre and at Moscow Chamber Theatre; Conductor with Yaroslavl Philharmonic Orchestra, later with Russian State Cinema Orchestra; Guest engagements with St Petersburg Philharmonic and Russian State Academic Symphony Orchestra; Chief Conductor and Music Director of Russian State Maly Symphony from 1991; Music Director of New

Moscow State Symphony Orchestra; Has toured to Italy, Hungary, Germany, Austria, Spain and Denmark; Repertoire has included much contemporary music as well as standard works. *Recordings include:* CDs on the Chant du Monde. *Honours:* Winner, 1990 Rupert Foundation Conducting Competition, London. *Address:* c/o Sonata, 11 Northpark Street, Glasgow G20 7AA, Scotland.

**PONOMARENKO, Ivan;** Baritone; b. 1955, Ukraine, Russia. *Education:* Studied at the Odessa Conservatory and with Irina Arkhipova. *Career:* Sang first with Odessa State Opera Theatre as Escamillo, Don Giovanni, Renato in Un Ballo in Maschera, Germont and Amonasro; Member of the Kiev Opera from 1981 touring with company to Germany, Spain, Netherlands, Hungary, France and Spain; Sang at Strasbourg Festival in 1993 as Nabucco; British debut on tour in 1995; Recitalist with a wide repertoire. *Address:* c/o Sonata Ltd, 11 Northpark Street, Glasgow G20 7AA, Scotland.

**PONS, Juan;** Singer (Baritone); b. 8 Aug. 1946, Ciutadella, Menorca. *Education:* Studied in Barcelona. *Career:* Sang at the Teatro Liceo Barcelona, at first as a tenor; Covent Garden 1979, as Alfio in Cavalleria Rusticana; Barcelona 1983, Herod in Massenet's Hérodiade; Paris Opéra 1983, as Tonio in Pagliacci; Guest appearances in Munich, Madrid and at the Orange Festival; Verona Arena 1984–85, Amonasro; La Scala Milan 1985, as Rigoletto and as Sharpless in Madama Butterfly; Metropolitan Opera 1986, as Scarpia in Tosca; Well known as Verdi's Falstaff; (Munich Staatsoper 1987), San Francisco and Rome 1989; Also sings Renato in Un Ballo in Maschera and roles in operas by Donizetti; sang Verdi's Germont at Chicago 1988; Sharpless in Madama Butterfly at La Scala, 1990; Barcelona 1989, as Basilio in Respighi's La Fiamma (also at Madrid); Season 1992 as Tonio in Pagliacci at Philadelphia, Scarpia at San Francisco and Luna at Madrid; Sang Amonasro at the Verona Arena, 1994; Tonio at Los Angeles, 1996; Season 1998 as Count of Westmorland in Wolf-Ferrari's Sly at Zürich, and Renato at Milan; Season 2000–01 as Germont in Florence, Amonasro at the Verona Arena, Rigoletto for the Opéra Bastille and Nabucco at the Met. *Recordings:* Aroldo by Verdi; Pagliacci. *Address:* c/o Teatra alla Scala, Via Filodrammatici 2, Milan, Italy.

**PONSFORD, David Stewart,** MA, PhD, FRCO, ARCM; British organist, harpsichordist and musicologist; *Publications Officer, British Institute of Organ Studies;* b. 18 Jan. 1948, Cardiff, Wales. *Education:* Queen's Coll., Taunton, Royal Manchester Coll. of Music, Emmanuel Coll., Cambridge, Univ. of Cardiff. *Career:* Asst Organist, Wells Cathedral 1971–76; Organist, St Matthew's, Northampton; Conductor, Northampton Bach Choir 1977–79, Cheltenham Bach Choir 1981–88; organ, harpsichord and academic tutor, Birmingham Conservatoire 1982–91; harpsichord and organ tutor, Wells Cathedral School 1986–; Assoc. Lecturer in Performance Practice, Univ. of Cardiff 2000–; Ed. and contrib., Bios Journal 2003; Publs Officer, British Inst. of Organ Studies 2005–. *Recordings:* Annus Mirabilis 1685, Harpsichord music by Bach, Handel, Scarlatti and Sandoni 1999, Vive Le Roy, organ music by Bach, Couperin, Gringy from Greyfriars Kirk, Edinburgh 1999, Complete J.S. Bach Violin Sonatas (with Jacquelline Ross) 2002, J.S. Bach Clavier-übung Part 3 2003, Parthenia 2005. *Publications:* The Organ of Gottfried Silbermann, in Choir and Organ 1997, Inégalité and Recits: Genre Studies in 17th century French Organ Music, in The Organ Yearbook 1998–99, J.S. Bach and the Nature of French Influence, in The Organ Yearbook 2000, edn of Biber: Rosary Sonatas 2006; contrib. to The Musical Times, Choir and Organ, Organist's Review, The Organ Yearbook. *Honours:* Leverhulme Research Fellowship 2004. *Address:* Ford Cottage, Middle Duntisbourne, Cirencester, Glos., GL7 7AR, England (home). *Telephone:* (1285) 651995 (home). *Fax:* (1285) 651995 (home). *E-mail:* dsponsford@aol.com (home). *Website:* www .davidponsford.org (office).

**PONSONBY, Robert (Noel),** CBE, MA, FRSA; British arts administrator; b. 19 Dec. 1926, Oxford, England; m. Lesley Black 1977. *Education:* Trinity Coll., Oxford. *Career:* staff mem., Glyndebourne Opera 1951–55; Artistic Dir Edinburgh Festival 1956–60; Gen. Admin. Scottish Nat. Orchestra 1964–72; Controller of Music, BBC 1972–85; Artistic Dir Canterbury Festival 1986–88; Admin. Friends of Musicians Benevolent Fund 1987–93. *Publication:* Short History of Oxford University Opera Club 1950; contribs to numerous magazines and journals; obituaries for The Times, The Independent and The Guardian. *Honours:* Hon. RAM 1975; Janáček Medal, Czech Govt 1980. *Address:* 11 St Cuthbert's Road, London, NW2 3QJ, England (home).

**PÖNTINEN, Roland;** Swedish pianist and composer; b. 1963, Stockholm; m. Camilla Wiklund, one d. one s. *Education:* Stockholm Royal Music Acad. and with Menahem Pressler, György Sébok and Elisabeth Leonskaya. *Career:* debut, Royal Stockholm Philharmonic Orchestra, playing Franck's Symphonic Variations 1981; many appearances with leading orchestras, including all major Swedish ensembles, Oslo Philharmonic, Los Angeles Philharmonic (Hollywood Bowl), Jerusalem Symphony, BBC Symphony, Tonhalle Orchestra, Zurich, Accademia Santa Cecilia, Rome, Philharmonia Orchestra, Scottish Chamber Orchestra; festival engagements include Bergen, Schleswig-Holstein, Ludwigsburg, Edinburgh, La Roque d'Anthéron Piano Festival, Promenade Concerts, London (playing Grieg Piano Concerto, Ligeti Piano Concerto), Aldeburgh Festival, Berliner Festwochen, Maggio Musicale Fiorentino, Kuhmo Chamber Music Festival; recitals throughout Scandinavia, Western Europe, Japan, Korea, Australia and New Zealand; premiere of composition Blue Winter played by Philadelphia Orchestra and Wolfgang Sawallisch, Carnegie Hall 1998; mem. Royal Swedish Acad. of Music. *Compositions:* Blue Winter 1998. *Recordings include:* over 70 albums of solo and chamber music, playing works by Busoni, Chopin, Janáček, Scriabin Piano Concerto (with Royal Stockholm Philharmonic Orchestra), Rachmaninov's Etudes-Tableaux. *Honours:* Litteris et Artibus medal, for skills in the arts 2001. *Current Management:* Svensk Konsertdirektion, Danska Vägen 25 B, 412 74 Göteborg, Sweden. *Telephone:* (31) 830095. *Website:* www .loddingkonsert.se; www.rolandpontinen.com.

**PONTVIK, Peter;** Swedish composer, ensemble leader, Musicologist and Music producer; b. 29 April 1963, Copenhagen, Denmark; Grew up in Uruguay; 2 s. *Education:* Composition with Marino Rivero, 1983–86; Musicology, Choir Conducting with Sara Herrera at the National Conservatory, Montevideo, 1984–86; Composition with Sven-David Sandström, Royal Academy of Music, Stockholm, 1989–92, and with Wolfgang Rihm, Academy of Music, Karlsruhe, Germany, as well as early music with Hans-Georg Renner, 1992–94; Ferienkurse für Neue Musik, Darmstadt, 1994. *Career:* Debut: 1st performance of Reencuentro con Misiones for bandoneon at Taller de Música Contemporánea, Montevideo, 1985; Scandinavian UNM Festival: selected works 1990, 1993 and 1994; Founder and Artistic Leader of Ensemble Villancico, Stockholm, 1994–; Radio appearances, several works, Swedish and German Broadcasting, 1994–; mem, FST (Society of Swedish Composers); ISCM; Founder and Artistic Dir Stockholm Early Music Festival 2002–. *Compositions:* Amen for mixed choir, 1989; Three Images for Three Recorders, 1990; Candombe for wind orchestra, 1990–91; Yeikó for bandoneon, percussion and dancer, 1992–93; Allelu for mixed choir, 1993; En kort mässa-Missa brevis for choir and brass quintet, 1994; Sagitra, for choir and percussion, 1996–2002; Norr om himlen, song cycle, 2002. *Recordings:* with Ensemble Villancico: Cancionero de Upsala 1556 and Music from a Pack of Cards; ¡A la xácara! — the Jungle Book of the Baroque; Hyhyhyhyhyhyhyhy, the New Jungle Book of the Baroque (Latin American Baroque Music; Radio and TV productions; Research in early music. *Contributions:* articles: Codex kellungensis gåtfullt gotländskt musikfynd, 2003. *Honours:* 1st Prize, International Competition for Choir Composition, Tolosa, Spain, 1989; Ivan Lukacic Prize, Varazdin, Croatia with Ensemble Villancico, 2001, Swedish Music Festivals Driving Force of the Year 2004. *Address:* Tångvägen 9, 1 tr, 126 38 Hägersten, Sweden. *Telephone:* +46 8 30 43 29. *E-mail:* peter.pontvik@zeta.telenordia.se.

**POOK, Jocelyn;** British composer and viola player; b. 14 Feb. 1960, Birmingham; d. of Wilfred Pook and Mary Cecil Williams. *Education:* King Edward VI School, Bury St Edmunds and Guildhall School of Music and Drama. *Career:* composes music for film, TV, theatre, dance and the concert platform; has toured and recorded with many leading names in pop, rock and classical music including The Communards (three-year tour), Laurie Anderson, Massive Attack, Ryuichi Sakamoto and Peter Gabriel; Assoc. Guildhall School of Music and Drama. *Musical scores include:* films: Strange Fish (Prix Italia 1994) 1994, Mothers and Daughters (Mention Speciale at Grand Prix Int. Video-Danse 1994) 1994, Blight (Golden Plaque Award, Chicago Int. Film Festival 1997) 1996, Eyes Wide Shut (Chicago Film Critics' Award 2000) 1999, Comment j'ai tué mon père 2000, Time Out/L'emploi du Temps 2001, La Repentie 2002, Gangs of New York (featuring her track Dionysus from Untold Things album) 2003, Wild Side 2004, The Merchant of Venice 2004; TV: People's Century/Half the People (BBC) 1996, Saints and Sinners (S4C documentary series) 1997, The Lost Supper (Channel 4) 1998, Just Enough Distance (BBC 2) 1998, Trouble at the House (BBC 2) 1998, The Establishment (Channel 4 documentary series) 1999, Dancing Inside (BBC 2) 1999, Butterfly Collectors (Granada) 1999, In a Land of Plenty (BBC 2, co-written with Harvey Brough) 2001, Death on the Staircase 2004. *Dance includes:* Phantasmata (Shobana Jeyasingh Dance Co.), Requiem (Darshan Singh Bhuller, performed by the Phoenix Dance Co. *Television commercials include:* Blow the Wind/Pie Jesu (Orange Mobile Phone TV advert) (Designers and Art Dirs Asscn Silver Award 1997) 1997, Ode to Why (Enron advertising campaign) 2000–01. *Recordings include:* Deluge 1997, Flood 1999, Untold Things 2001, Wild Side 2004, The Merchant of Venice 2004. *Honours:* American Soc. of Authors Composers and Publrs' Prize 1999. *Address:* c/o First Name, Suite 302, 43 Lancaster Gate, London, W2 3NA, England (office). *Telephone:* (20) 7706-8484 (office). *Fax:* (20) 7706-3434 (office). *E-mail:* aston@ mailbox.co.uk (office). *Website:* www.jocelynpook.com (office).

**POOLE, John;** Choral Director; b. 1934, Birmingham, England; m. Laura McKirahan, 22 July 1987, 3 s. *Education:* Studied at Oxford University. *Career:* Former Organist of London University Church and Music Director at University College, London; Founded the Bloomsbury Singers and Players; Director of the BBC Singers, 1972–90 and has directed the BBC Symphony Chorus and Singers in many concerts throughout the United Kingdom and abroad; Music Director of the Groupe Vocal de France, 1990–95 and Chief Guest Conductor of the BBC Singers, with frequent performances of modern repertory; Guest Director, world-wide; mem, FRCO. *Recordings:* Giles Swayne, Cry, with BBC Singers; Martin Mass, Britten, A Boy Was Born, BBC Singers, Westminster Cathedral Choristers; Chants d'Eglise with Groupe Vocal de France. *Address:* Le Logis de Thoiré, 79200 La Peyratte, France.

**POOT, Sonja;** Singer (Soprano); b. 3 Dec. 1936, Gravenzande, Netherlands. *Education:* Studied in Salisbury (Rhodesia), Amsterdam and Vienna. *Career:* Sang at Bonn Opera, 1964–71, notably as Constanze in Entführung, and Donizetti's Lucia and Maria di Rohan; Nuremberg, 1971–73, Stuttgart Staatsoper, 1973–78; Guest engagements at Basle, Amsterdam (Elsa 1978), Vienna Volksoper, Rome, Geneva (Elettra in Idomeneo, 1973), Barcelona and Ottawa; Other roles have included Mozart's Donna Anna, Queen of Night and

Pamina, Anna Bolena, Lucrezia Borgia, Violetta, Amelia in Ballo in Maschera and Norina in Don Pasquale; Many concert performances. *Address:* c/o Staatsoper Stuttgart, Oberer Schlossgarten 6, 7000 Stuttgart, Germany.

**POPE, Cathryn;** Singer (Soprano); b. 1960, England. *Education:* Studied with Ruth Packer at the Royal College of Music; Further study at the National Opera Studio. *Career:* With English National Opera has sung Papagena and Pamina in The Magic Flute, Anna (Moses), Susanna, Zerlina, Sophie (Werther), Leila (The Perl Fishers), Gretel and Werther; Sang Oksana in the first British production of Christmas Eve by Rimsky-Korsakov, 1988; Sang Amor in Orpheus and Euridice for Opera North; Royal Opera Covent Garden as Gianetta (L'Elisir d'Amor), Frasquita (Carmen) and a Naiad (Ariadne auf Naxos). *Recordings include:* Anne Trulove in The Rake's Progress; Barbarina in Le nozze di Figaro; Sang Gretel with Netherlands Opera 1990, Pamina at the London Coliseum; Sang in new productiions of The Marriage of Figaro and Königskinder at the Coliseum, 1991–92; Gilda in a revival of Rigoletto, 1992/93; Featured Artist, Opera Now magazine, Feb 1992. *Recordings include:* Video of Rusalka (as Wood Nymph). *Address:* c/o English National Opera, St Martin's Lane, London WC2, England.

**POPE, Michael Douglas,** FRSA; British musician, producer, choral conductor and writer; b. 25 Feb. 1927, London, England; m. 1st Margaret Jean Blakeney 1954, one s.; m. 2nd Gillian Victoria Peck 1967, one s. one d. *Education:* Guildhall School of Music and Drama. *Career:* served in Army 1945–48; joined BBC 1954, Asst. Music Division 1960, Producer, music programmes and music talks 1966–80; planned and produced many programmes and series with BBC Chorus, subsequently BBC Singers; productions include revivals of works by Elgar, Stanford, Bantock (Omar Khayyám trilogy 1979), Bennett, Rootham, Hurlstone, Boyce (Solomon 1979), Parry (Prometheus Unbound 1980) and other composers; premiere of Everyman, music drama by Kennedy Scott 1977; Missing Music 1972; The Direction of Modern Music 1980; Musical Dir, London Motet and Madrigal Club 1954–93; Guest Conductor, RTE; Hon. Sec., Royal Philharmonic Soc. 1983–85; mem. Royal Musical Asscn, Incorporated Soc. of Musicians (chair. Wiltshire Centre 2005–), Elgar Soc. (chair. 1978–88, vice-pres. 1988). *Publications include:* King Olaf and the English Choral Tradition in Elgar Studies 1990; contributions to DNB, Royal College of Music Magazine. *Address:* Quarry Farm House, Chicksgrove, Salisbury, Wiltshire SP3 6LY, England.

**POPKEN, Ralph;** German singer (countertenor); b. 1962, Wilhelmshaven. *Education:* studied in Hanover with Emma Kirkby. *Career:* sang in concerts and oratorios from 1984, in Europe and the USA; Opera debut, Hanover 1989 in Enrico Leone by Steffani; Handel Festival at Göttingen from 1992 in Agrippina, Ottone and Radamisto; Deutsche Staatsoper Berlin, 1992–95 in Graun's Cesare e Cleopatra, Gassmann's L'opera seria; Theater an der Wien, 1998 and 1999–2000; Theater des Westens, Berlin in Chicago (musical); Sang Narciso in Handel's Agrippina at Halle, 1999–2000. *Recordings:* Radamisto, Cesare e Cleopatra; Bach-Cantatas. *Address:* c/o Heide Stock, Ferdinand-Wallbrecht-Str. 13, 30163 Hannover, Germany.

**POPLE, Ross;** Conductor and Cellist; b. 11 May 1945, Auckland, New Zealand; m. (1) Anne Storrs, 25 June 1965, divorced, 3 s., 1 d., (2) Charlotte Fairbairn, July 1992, 1 s. *Education:* Royal Academy of Music, London; Recital Medal, Honorary RAM; Paris Conservatoire. *Career:* Debut: London, 1965; Principal Cello, Menuhin Festival Orchestra; BBC Symphony Orchestra, 1976–86; Director of London Festival Orchestra, 1980–; Founder, Cathedral Classics, Festival of Music in Cathedrals, United Kingdom, 1986–; London South Bank series, Birthday Honours, 1988–; Founder and Developer of The Warehouse, Waterloo (home to London Festival Orchestra and recording studio), 1993. *Recordings:* Haydn, Boccherini, Mozart, Mendelssohn, Schoenberg, Vaughan Williams, Holst, Strauss, Arnold, Franck, Bach and others, for various labels. *Address:* Sellet Hall, Stainton, Kendal LA 8 0LE, England.

**POPOV, Stefan;** Cellist; b. 1940, Bulgaria. *Education:* Studied in Sofia, the Moscow Conservatory with Sviatoslav Knushevitsky and Mstislav Rostropovich, 1961–66. *Career:* Debut: Sofia 1955; Many concert appearances in Europe, North America, Asia notably at London, Moscow, Boston, Florence, Geneva, Dublin, Genoa, Milan, Budapest; Concerto repertoire includes works by Vivaldi, Haydn, Boccherini, Beethoven, Schumann, Dvořák, Brahms, Elgar, Hindemith, Milhaud, Honegger, Kabalevsky and Shostakovich; Don Quixote by Strauss; Respighi Adagio with Variations; Prokofiev Symphonie Concertante; Bloch Schelomo; Sonata collaborations with the pianist Allan Schiller; Has taught at Boston University, the New England Conservatory of Music. *Honours:* Winner of competitions in Moscow 1957, Geneva 1964, Vienna 1967, Florence 1969; 1966 Techaikovsky International Competition, Moscow. *Address:* Sofia-concert, Bulgarian Artistic Agency, 3 Volov Street, Sofia, Bulgaria.

**POPOV, Valery;** Singer (Tenor); b. 1965, Kharkiv, Ukraine. *Education:* Studied at the Kharkov Institute of Arts. *Career:* Has sung at the Kiev and Kharkov Opera Houses and from 1994 as Principal at the Brno Opera Theatre, Czechoslovakia; Roles have included Cavaradossi, Don Alvaro, Don Ottavio, Don Carlos, Turriddu, Samson and Alfredo; Sang Don José on tour to France in 1992; Further appearances throughout Europe and North America; Jenik in The Bartered Bride at Ostrava, 1998; Sang Meyerbeer's Robert le Diable at Prague, 1999; Robert in Tchaikovsky's Iolanta at Monte Carlo, 2001. *Honours:* Prizewinner, Belvedere International Competition, Vienna. *Address:* c/o Sonata Ltd, 11 North Park Street, Glasgow G20 7AA, Scotland.

**POPOV, Vladimir;** Singer (Tenor); b. 29 April 1947, Moscow, Russia. *Education:* Studied at Tchaikovsky Conservatory, Moscow. *Career:* Sang at Bolshoi Opera, Moscow, 1977–81; Studied further in Milan and emigrated to USA, 1982, singing Ramirez in La Fanciulla del West at Portland; Metropolitan Opera debut, 1984, as Lensky in Eugene Onegin; Further engagements as Calaf at Houston, 1987, as Cavaradossi at Philadelphia, 1987, as Dimitri in Boris Godunov at Covent Garden, 1988, and Hermann in The Queen of Spades at Washington, 1989; Sang Calaf with Covent Garden Company at Wembley Arena, 1991, Samson at Detroit and Canio in Pagliacci at Buenos Aires, 1992; Other roles include Ernani, Gabriele Adorno, Don José and Radames (San Francisco, 1989).

**POPOVA, Valeria;** Singer (Soprano); b. 1945, Bulgaria. *Education:* Studied with father Sacha Popov, in Sofia and with Gina Cigna. *Career:* Debut: Sang Lauretta in Gianni Schicchi at National Theatre, Belgrade; Sang at Plovdiv Opera, 1971–76, Sofia from 1976; Guest engagements in former Soviet Union, Germany, Romania and Cuba; Other roles include Violetta, Manon, Mozart's Countess, Jenůfa, Fiordiligi, Marguerite, Donna Anna, Pamina and Leonora in La Forza del Destino; Sang Amelia in Ballo in Maschera at Milwaukee, 1990; Also teacher of singers: d. Alexandrina Pendachanska has been among her pupils. *Recordings include:* Arias by Puccini, Verdi, Massenet and Bellini. *Address:* c/o PG & PM, 7 Whitehorse Close, Royal Mile, Edinburgh, EH8 8BU, Scotland.

**POPOVICI, Dorum;** Composer; b. 17 Feb. 1932, Resita, Romania. *Education:* Studied in Timosoara, 1944–50, at Bucharest Conservatory, 1950–55, and Darmstadt, 1968. *Career:* Editor of Romanian Radio and Television, 1968. *Compositions:* Operas: Promethu, Bucharest, 1964; Mariana Pineda, Iasi, 1969; Interrogation at Daybreak, Galati, 1979; The Longest Night, Bucharest, 1983; Firmness, composed 1989; Orchestral: Triptyque, 1955; 2 Symphonic Sketches, 1955; Concertino for strings, 1956; Concerto for orchestra, 1960; 4 Symphonies, 1962, 1966, 1968, 1973; Poem Bizantin, 1968; Pastorale Suite, 1982; Chamber: Cello sonata, 1952; Violin Sonata, 1953; String Quartet, 1954; Fantasy for String Trio, 1955; Sonata for 2 cellos, 1960; Sonata for 2 violas, 1965; Quintet for piano, violin, viola, cello, clarinet, 1967; Piano Trio, 1970; Madrigal for flute, clarinet, string trio and trombone; Cantatas, piano music, choruses, songs. *Publications include:* Elizabethan Music, 1978: Italian Renaissance Music, 1978. *Address:* Vaselor 3A sect 2, Bucharest, Romania.

**PORTELLA, Nelson;** Singer (Baritone); b. 1945, Brazil. *Education:* Studied in Rio de Janeiro. *Career:* Sang widely in South America opera houses from 1970, Teatro Liceo Barcelona from 1980, Naples from 1983 and Venice from 1985; Caracalla Festival, 1986, Ravenna, 1988; Roles have included Don Giovanni, Leporello, Masetto, Germont, Iago, Sharpless, the Count in Capriccio and Wozzeck. *Recordings include:* Scarpia, in Tosca (Balkanton); Mascagni's Le Maschere (Cetra).

**PORTER, Andrew Brian,** MA; British music critic; b. 26 Aug. 1928, Cape Town, South Africa; s. of Andrew Ferdinand and Vera Sybil (née Bloxham) Porter. *Education:* Diocesan Coll., Rondebosch, Cape Town, Univ. Coll. Oxford. *Career:* music critic The Financial Times 1950–74; Ed. The Musical Times 1960–67; music critic The New Yorker 1972–92, The Observer 1992–97, Times Literary Supplement 1997–; Visiting Fellow All Souls Coll. Oxford 1973–74; Bloch Prof., Univ. of Calif. at Berkeley 1981. *Opera:* librettos for The Tempest 1985, The Song of Majnun 1991 and numerous translations. *Publications:* A Musical Season 1974, Wagner's Ring 1976, Music of Three Seasons 1974–77 1978, Music of Three More Seasons 1977–80 1981, Musical Events: A Chronicle 1980–1983 1987, Musical Events: A Chronicle 1983–1986 1989, Verdi's Macbeth: A Sourcebook (ed. with David Rosen) 1984, A Music Critic Remembers 2000; contrib. to Music and Letters, Musical Quarterly, Musical Times, Proceedings of the Royal Musical Association, Atti del Congresso Internazionale di Studi Verdiani. *Honours:* Corresp. mem. American Musicological Soc. 1993; ASCAP–Deems Taylor Award 1975, 1978, 1982, Nat. Music Theater Award 1988. *Address:* 9 Pembroke Walk, London, W8 6PQ, England.

**PORTER, David Hugh,** BA, PhD; American pianist, harpsichordist and educator; b. 29 Oct. 1935, New York, NY; m. 1st Laudie E. Dimmette 1958 (deceased); three s. one d.; m. 2nd Helen L. Nelson 1987. *Education:* Swarthmore College, Princeton University, Philadelphia Conservatory of Music, studied piano with Edward Steuermann, harpsichord with Gustav Leonhardt. *Career:* debut in Philadelphia, 1955; Piano and Harpsichord Recitals and Lecture-Recitals throughout USA, 1966–; in London and Edinburgh, 1977; Performances on radio and television, 1967–; Professor of Classics and Music, Carleton College, 1962–; President, Carleton College, 1986–87; President, Skidmore College, 1987–98; Visiting Professor of Liberal Arts, Williams College, 1999–; Author: Only Connect: Three Studies in Greek Tragedy, Horace's Poetic Journey, The Not Quite Innocent Bystander: Writings of Eduard Steuermann, Virginia Woolf and Logan Pearsall Smith: an Exquisitely Flattering Duet; Virginia Woolf and the Hogarth Press: Riding a Great Horse. *Publications:* contrib. articles to Music Review and Perspectives of New Music; Numerous articles in classical journals. *Honours:* Steuermann Scholarship, Philadelphia Conservatory of Music, 1955–. *Address:* 5 Birch Run Drive, Saratoga Springs, NY 12866, USA. *E-mail:* ddodger@skidmore.edu.

**PORTMAN, Rachel Mary Berkeley;** British composer; b. 11 Dec. 1960, Haslemere; m. Uberto Pasolini; three d. *Education:* Worcester Coll., Oxford. *Career:* composer of film and TV scores, for US productions 1992–.

*Compositions for film and television:* Experience Preferred... But Not Essential 1982, The Storyteller (TV series) 1986–88, 1990, Life is Sweet 1990, Oranges Are Not the Only Fruit (TV drama) 1990, Antonia and Jane 1991, Where Angels Fear to Tread 1991, Used People 1992, The Joy Luck Club 1993, Benny and Joon 1993, Friends 1993, Sirens 1994, Only You 1994, War of the Buttons 1994, To Wong Foo – Thanks for Everything! 1995, A Pyromaniac's Love Story 1995, Smoke 1995, The Adventures of Pinocchio 1996, Marvin's Room 1996, Emma (Acad. Award 1997) 1996, Addicted to Love 1997, The Cider House Rules 1999, Chocolat 2000, The Emperor's New Clothes 2001, Hart's War 2002, The Truth About Charlie 2002, Nicholas Nickleby 2002, The Human Stain 2003, The Little Prince 2003, The Manchurian Candidate 2004, Because of Winn-Dixie 2005, Flightplan 2005. *Recordings include:* Rachel Portman Soundtracks (compilation album), numerous soundtrack recordings. *Honours:* British Film Inst. Young Composer of the Year Award 1988. *Address:* c/o Bucks Music, Onward House, 11 Uxbridge House, London, W8 7TQ, England (office).

**POSCHNER-KLEBEL, Brigitte;** Singer (Soprano); b. 1957, Vienna, Austria. *Education:* Studied in Vienna with Gerda Scheyrer and Gottfried Hornik. *Career:* Sang with Vienna Staatsoper, 1982–, Volksoper, 1983–; Guest appearances at Aix-en-Provence Festival, 1988–89, Fiordiligi, La Scala, Milan as Pamina, 1986, Venice, Amsterdam and Tokyo; Sang Susanna in Khovanshchina at Vienna Staatsoper, 1989; Other roles include Hansel, Rosalinde, Esmerelda, Sophie in Der Rosenkavalier, Xenia in Boris Godunov and Lucy in The Beggar's Opera; Frequent concert appearances. *Recordings:* Khovanshchina; Video of Elektra conducted by Abbado, as a Maidservant. *Address:* c/o Staatsoper, Opernring 2, 1010 Vienna, Austria.

**POSPISIL, Juraj;** Composer; b. 14 Jan. 1931, Olomouc, Czechoslovakia. *Education:* Studied at the Olomouc School of Music (1949–50), Janáček Academy, Brno (1950–52) and with Cikker at the Bratislava Academy (1952–55). *Career:* Lecturer in theory and composition at the Bratislava Academy of Music and Drama, 1955–91. *Compositions include:* The Mountains and the People, symphonic poem, 1954; Symphonies, 1958, 1963, 1967, 1978, 1986, 1996, 1999; Sonata for strings, 1961; Song About a Man, symphonic variations, 1961; Trombone Concerto, 1962; 4 String Quartets, 1970, 1979, 1985, 1990; Inter Arna, cycle of 3 operas, 1970; Violin Concerto, 1968; Clarinet Concerto, 1972; To Bratislava, for baritone and orchestra, 1973; Symphonic Frescoes I–III, 1972, 1976, 1981; Concerto Eroico, for horn and orchestra, 1973; Chamber Sinfonietta, 1974; November Triptych, for chamber chorus, wind and piano, 1977; 2 Trios for piano, violin and cello, 1977, 1987; Concerto for soprano and orchestra, 1984; Dulcimer Concerto, 1989; Sonata for alto trombone and strings, 1991; Bass Quintet, 1991; The Lord's Prayer of the Hussites, sacred cantata, 1991; Manon Lescaut, scenic drama, 1993; Bass Tuba concerto, 1994; Autumn Bottling, for bass voice and string quartet, 1994. *Address:* c/o SOZA, Rastislavova 3, 821 08 Bratislava, Slovakia.

**POSSEMEYER, Berthold;** Singer (Baritone); b. 1950, Gladbeck, Westfalen, Germany. *Education:* Studied in Cologne with Josef Metternich. *Career:* Sang at first in concert and gave Lieder recitals, notably at Paris, New York, Jerusalem, Hamburg, Turin and Venice; Stage career from 1978, at first at Oldenburg, then from 1979 at Essen, as Rossini's Figaro, Papageno, Guglielmo, Eugene Onegin and Silvio in Pagliacci; Sang at Gelsenkirchen Opera, 1984–86, then returned to concerts; Repertoire includes works by Bach, Mozart, Mendelssohn and Distler. *Address:* c/o Musiktheater im Rivier, Kennedyplatz, 4650 Gelsenkirchen, Germany.

**POSTNIKOVA, Viktoria;** Concert Pianist; b. 12 Jan. 1944, Moscow, USSR; m. Gennadi Rozhdestvensky 1969. *Education:* Studied at the Moscow Central School of Music with E B Musaelian, 1950–62; Further study with Yakov Flier at the Moscow Conservatoire. *Career:* Many concert appearances in Europe, Russia and the USA from 1966; Repertoire includes music by Bach, Handel, Scarlatti, Haydn, Mozart, Liszt, Chopin, Mendelssohn, Schumann, Brahms and Rachmaninov; Modern repertoire includes music by Busoni, Ives, Britten and Shostakovich; Played in the British premiere of Schnittke's Concerto for piano duet and orchestra in London 1991. *Recordings:* Tchaikovsky Concertos (Decca); Busoni Concerto and complete piano works by Janáček and Tchaikovsky (Erato); Violin sonatas by Busoni and Strauss (Chandos); Complete piano concertos of Brahms, Chopin and Prokofiev (Melodiya). *Honours:* Prizewinner at competitions in Warsaw (1965), Leeds (1966), Lisbon (1968) and Moscow (1970). *Address:* Allied Artists, 42 Montpelier Square, London SW7 1JZ, England.

**POTOCNIK, Tone;** Slovenian pianist, organist and ; b. 13 Jan. 1951, Bukovica, Skofja Loka. *Education:* Academy of Music, Ljubljana, Academy of Music, Zagreb, Croatia, Academy of Santa Cecilia, Rome, Conservatoire of Santa Cecilia, Rome, Rome Papal Institute for Church Music, Licenza in Canto Gregoriano, Licenza in Musica Sacra. *Career:* specialised in the piano music of G. Gurdieff and T. de Hartmann, Institute for the Harmonious Development of Man; performances in Italy and the other countries in Europe; Prof. of Gregorian Chant, Piano and Score Play at the Academy of Music in Ljubljana, Slovenia; Founded the 1st School of Gregorian Chant in Slovenia and Shola Cantorum, Cantate Domino; Recording for RTV Slovenia–Cerkveno leto v Gregorijanskem koralu (Church year in Gregorian Chant); Tonus psalmorum; Performs at independent recitals as an organist; Premiere performances of contemporary Slovene composers (L. Lebic, P. Ramovs, L. Vrhunc, M. Gabrijelcic); Soloist and with RTV and Philharmonic orchestra of Ljubljana; Organ and piano accompaniment of instrumental and vocal soloists and chorus. *Recordings:* Eno je dete rojeno, with Komorni zbor Ave (The Child was born, with The Chamber Choir Ave); Ave Maria, with Branko Robinsak–tenor; Music highlights of Baroque, with Norina Radovan, soprano and Tibor Kerekes, trumpet; Hugolin Sattner with Komorni Zbor Ave, Ch. Gounold – J.G.Rheinberger with Ljubljanski oktet. *Address:* Zabrdo 1, 4229 Sorica, Slovenia (home). *Telephone:* (41) 977282 (home).

**POTOURLIAN, Artin Bedros;** Bulgarian composer and teacher; *Associate Professor, State Musical Academy, Sofia*; b. 4 May 1943, Kharmanli; s. of Bedros Michael Potourlian and Siranouch Artin Papazian; m. Akopjan Anahid Aram, 28 June 1974, 2 s. *Education:* Theoretical Faculty with speciality in Musical Pedagogy, State Academy of Music, Sofia, 1967; Composition at Yerevan State Conservatoire Komitas, 1974. *Career:* First public performance of compositions in Yerevan, Moscow and Tbilisi, 1970–74; Performances of Symphonies Nos 1 and 2 in Sofia, 1976 and 1978; Member of Bulgarian Composers Union, 1978; Regular appearances in New Bulgarian Music Festival, 1980–04; Authorial recitals of chamber compositions at Yerevan, Armenia in 1987 and Sofia in 1991, 2003; Performances of Four Spiritual Songs (on themes by Nerses Shnorhali) for organ in Austria at Vienna, Klagenfurt, Anif, 1991, and Friedrichshafen am Bodensee, 1997; Participation in Holland-Bulgarian Music Festival, Sofia, 1992; Teacher of Polyphony State Musical Academy, Sofia 1990–2000, Assoc. Prof. 2000–; Performances at Salzburg of Arabesques Confessions and Fantasia, Worlds, for two pianos, and participant in symposium West ruft Ost, 1995; Performance of Improvisations for clarinet and piano, Bratislava, Slovakia, 1998; mem, Society for Contemporary Music in Bulgaria, 1992–. *Compositions:* Sonata for violin and piano, 1972; Music for 3 Flutes, 2 Pianos, Tam-Tam and Strings, 1977–78; Klavier Quartet, 2001, Opera, Women's Cry, in one act, 1979; Poem for organ and symphony orchestra, 1980; Chamber Concerto, for piano and strings, 1981; Concerto for violin and symphony orchestra, 1983; Music in memory of Evariste Galois for symphony orchestra 1984, Four Spiritual Songs on themes by Nerses Shnorhali, 1988; Klavier Quintet, 1989; Fantasia for piano and symphony orchestra, 1990; Mosaici for symphony orchestra, 1993; Diverti-mento for Wind Quintet, Harp, Harpsichord and Percussion 1994, Piano Trio, 1995; L'infinito for mezzo soprano solo, baritone solo, chorus and symphony orchestra, poetry by Giacomo Leopardi, 1998; Songs; Concerto for cello and chamber orchestra, 1999; Concerto Grosso '87, 2000; Elegia for symphony orchestra 2002, Melomonologue for viola solo, 2003, Epigraph, Epistrophes, Epilogue for violin and viola 2004. *Recordings:* Arabesques for piano; The Confession for piano; Kaissa's Temple for piano; Fantasia, Worlds for 2 pianos; Symphony No. 2, documentary; Others on Bulgarian radio; Mosaici, 1994. *Publications:* Metrorythmic tempo modulation 1992, Geometric Transforma-tions of the Plane and the Space and Invention Polyphony, 1999, Crab counterpoint 2004. *Honours:* 1st Prize in Composition Competition, Pazardjik, 1985; Prizes of Bulgarian Composers Union for Arabesques, 1983 and Violin Concerto, 1989. *Address:* Tsarigradskoshosse Bl 4, Vch B, 1113 Sofia, Bulgaria (home). *Telephone:* 872-1007 (home). *E-mail:* art_b_pot@hotmail.com (home).

**POTT, Francis John Dolben,** FLCM; English composer, pianist and university lecturer; *Head of Composition & Research Development, London College of Music & Media*; b. 25 Aug. 1957, Oxfordshire, England; m. Virginia Straker, 19 Sept 1992, 1 s, 1 d. *Education:* Chorister, New College, Oxford; Music Scholar, Winchester College and Magdalene College, Cambridge; Composition with Robin Holloway, Hugh Wood; Piano with Hamish Milne, London; MA, BMus, University of Cambridge. *Career:* Freelance composition/performance; Tutor in Compositional Techniques, Oxford University, 1987–89; Lecturer in Music, St Hugh's College, 1988; Lecturer in Music, Director of Foundation Studies, West London Institute, 1989–91; John Bennett Lecturer in Music, St Hilda's College, Oxford, 1991–; Visiting Tutor in Composition, Winchester College, 1991–96; Piano recitalist and accom-panist; Administrative Head of Music, London College of Music and Media, Thames Valley University, London 2001–2002; Head of Research Develop-ment and Composition, London College of Music and Media, 2002–. *Compositions:* Organ: Mosaici di Ravenna, 1981; Empyrean, 1982; Fenix, Music for Lincoln Minster, Organ, Brass, Percussion, Timpani, 1985; Passion Symphony, Christus, 1986–90, premiered Westminster Cathedral, 1991; Toccata for Organ, 1991; choral (church) and other works; Piano Quintet, premiered by The Twentieth Century Consort, Smithsonian Institute, USA, 1993; Solo piano works, Sonata for cello and piano, premiered Wigmore Hall, London, 1996,; A Song on the End of the World, 1999 Elgar Commission, Three Choirs Festival, chorus, orchestra, soloists, organ, texts by Czeslaw Milosz and others, premiere, Worcester Cathedral, 1999; Many television and radio broadcasts; Works performed in 15 countries world-wide; Many sacred choral works and compositions for piano solo. *Recordings:* Christus, organ symphony, 1992; Cello Sonata, David Watkin, 1997, Sacred Choral: My Song is Love Unkown, The Souls of the Righteous, Tenebrae (conductor Nigel Short) 2003. *Publications:* Organ Works, 1989; Christus, organ symphony, 3 vols, 1994–99; Toccata for piano solo, 1999; Cello Sonata, 2000. *Honours:* Gerald Finzi Trust Memorial Award for Composition, 1981; Lloyd's Bank National Composing Competition, 1982; Barclaycard National Composing Competition, 1983; First Prize, 2nd S.S.Prokofiev International Compsing Competition, Moscow, 1997. *Address:* London College of Music and Media, Thames Valley University, St Mary's Road, Ealing, London, W5 5RF (office); Thurlows, Main Road, Littleton, Winchester, Hampshire SO22 6PS, England (home). *Telephone:* 020 8231 2569 (office); (1962) 885874 (home). *E-mail:* francis.pott@tvu.ac.uk (office); francis.pott@britishacademy.net (home). *Website:* www .britishacademy.com/members/pott.htm.

**POULENARD, Isabelle;** Singer (Soprano); b. 5 July 1961, Paris, France. *Education:* Studied at L'Ecole de l'Opera de Paris. *Career:* Sang at Tourcoing in operas by Mozart, Paisiello, Monteverdi, Scarlatti and Vivaldi, conducted by Jean-Claude Malgoire; Has performed in operas at the festivals of Carpentras and Avignon; Hippolyte et Aricie under William Christie at the Opéra-Comique; Les Dialogues des Carmélites at the Opéra du Rhin; Cesti's Orontea at the Innsbruck Festival, under René Jacobs; Sang Gluck's Iphigénie en Aulide with the City of London Sinfonia at the Spitalfields Festival; Other repertoire includes Paisiello's ll Re Teodoro in Venezia, Handel's Alessandro and Massenet's Grisélidis; Concert appearances throughout France and in Venice, Flanders, Innsbruck and Stuttgart; British engagements at the Barbican, London and for Music at Oxford; Season 1992 as Teutile in the Vivaldi pastiche Montezuma at Monte Carlo and in Conti's Don Chisciotte at the Innsbruck Festival of Early Music; Sang Bita in Cimarosa's Il Mercato di Malmantile, Opéra du Rhin, 1996. *Recordings:* Music by Cesti, Rameau, Couperin, Schütz, Cavalli, Bach and Vivaldi; Monteverdi's ll Combattimento di Tancredi e Clorinda; Lully's Armide, La Malade imaginaire by Charpentier and Die Zauberflöte (Erato); Handel's Tamerlano (CBS); Le Cinesi by Gluck and Les Indes Galantes by Rameau, (Harmonia Mundi). *Address:* c/o Opéra du Rhin, 19 Place Broglie, 07008 Strasbourg, France.

**POULET, Michel;** Cellist; b. 1960, France. *Education:* Studied at the Paris Conservatoire with Jean-Claude Pennetier and with members of the Amadeua and Alban Berg Quartets. *Career:* Member of the Ysaÿe String Quartet from 1986; Many concert performances in France, Europe, America and the Far East; Festival engagements at Salzburg, Tivoli (Copenhagen), Bergen, Lockenhaus, Barcelona and Stresa; Many appearances in Italy, notably with the Haydn Quartets of Mozart; Tours of Japan and the USA 1990 and 1992. *Recordings:* Mozart Quartet K421 and Quintet K516 (Harmonia Mundi); Ravel, Debussy and Mendelssohn Quartets (Decca). *Honours:* Grand Prix Evian International String Quartet Competition, May 1988; special prizes for best performances of a Mozart quartet, the Debussy quartet and a contemporary work; 2nd Prize, Portsmouth International String Quartet Competition, 1988. *Address:* c/o Phelps, Ysaÿe Quartet, 6 Malvern Road, London, E8 3LT, England.

**POULSON, Lani;** American singer (mezzo-soprano); b. 7 March 1953, Tremonton, Utah. *Career:* freelance singer throughout Europe since 1984; sang as Charlotte, Ramiro, Carmen, Octavian and The Composer, Countess Geschwitz in Lulu at Théâtre Royal de la Monnaie, Brussels, Cherubino at Hamburg Staatsoper, Sextus in La Clemenza di Tito at Court Theatre, Drottningholm, as Dorabella at Montpellier 1988, as Andromeda in world premiere of Perseo ed Andromeda by Sciarrino in Stuttgart 1991, in world premiere of Das Schweigen der Sirenen by Riehm also in Stuttgart; appearances at Amsterdam, Antwerp, Berlin (Staatsoper), Budapest, Drott-ningholm, Düsseldorf, Frankfurt, Graz, Hamburg, Lisbon, Madrid, Man-nheim, Montpellier, Munich, Strasbourg, Tel-Aviv, Trieste, Verona; concert repertory includes: St Matthew Passion, Mozart's Requiem and Beethoven's Mass in C; Season 1993–94, sang performances of Sesto in Dresden, also as part of the Dresden Musikfestspiele; Season 1994–95 included world premiere of Rihm's Das Schweigen der Sirenen at Staatstheater, Stuttgart returning to Dresden for further performances of La Clemenza di Tito; world premiere concert performance of L'Icone Paradoxale by Gerard Grisey 1996, and also in Strasbourg, Frankfurt and Reggio Emilia; Season 1997–98, Ottavia in L'Incoronazione di Poppea, Utah Opera, and debut as Magdalene in Meister-singer in Lisbon; Season 1998–99, new production of Al gran sole carico d'amore by Luigi Nono at Stuttgart, Mahagonny and Mamma Lucia in Cavalleria Rusticana in Stuttgart, Third Lady in Zauberflöte in Trieste, La Clemenza di Tito and Le Nozze di Figaro in Dresden, debut as Magdalene in Meistersinger in Lisbon, Der Rosenkavalier in Frankfurt and Ottavia L'Incoronazione di Poppea for Utah Opera; Season 1999–2000 included Poppea for Columbus Opera and Al gran sole carico d'amore at Staatstheater in Stuttgart; recent and forthcoming engagements include Charlotte in a production of Zimmermann's Die Soldaten, Brigitta in Die tote Stadt, lead role in Vivier's Kopemikus in Amsterdam, world premiere of Breitscheid's Im Spiegel Wohnen in Stuttgart, Jakobsleiter and Der feme Klang at Con-certgebouw, Amsterdam, Beethoven's Ninth Symphony in Berlin, 2ndNorn in Madrid, Grisey's L'icone paradoxale in Vienna, Freiburg, Amsterdam, Berlin, Düsseldorf and Brussels, Dvořák's Requiem in Leipzig and Beethoven's Missa Solemnis in Maastricht. *Honours:* Prizewinner, Concours the de Chant de la Ville de Toulouse, 1984; Grand Prizewinner, First Prize Mezzo and Winner of Elly Ameling Prize for Lieder at the 's-Hertogenbosch the Vocal Competition. *Address:* c/o Haydn Rawstron Ltd, 36 Station Road, London, SE20 7BQ, England.

**POULTON, Robert;** Singer (baritone); b. 1960, Brighton, England. *Educa-tion:* Studied with Rudolf Piernay, Guildhall School of Music and Drama; Further study, European Opera Centre, Belgium and National Opera Studio, London. *Career:* Sang The Ferryman in Britten's Curlew River for Nexus Opera at the 1986 Bath Festival; Repeated at the Promenade Concerts; With Glyndebourne Touring Opera has appeared in L'Heure Espagnole, L'Enfant et Les Sortilèges, La Traviata, Le nozze di Figaro, Katya Kabanova and Jenůfa, (last two also televised); Oratorio repertoire includes Purcell's, Haydn's Creation, Vaughan Williams', Bach's St John Passion, Handel's Messiah, Elgar's The Kingdom and Finzi; Concerts in Singapore, Italy, Belgium and Israel; Created roles of Doctor, Policeman and Stranger in Judith Weir's The

Vanishing Bridegroom, Scottish Opera, 1990; Created title role in Gassir the Hero by Theo Loevendie for Netherlands Opera, 1991; ENO Debut, Leander in Love for Three Oranges, 1991; Engaged as Figaro (Mozart) Scottish Opera; Ned Keene, Peter Grimes, Glyndebourne Festival Opera, 1992; Sang Punch in Birtwistle's Punch and Judy for Netherlands Opera, 1993; Count Almaviva in The Marriage of Figaro for ENO, 1994, 1996; Ned Keene, 1992, 1994; (Grimes), ENO, Nantes, Cologne and Copenhagen; Created Mr Dollarama in Birtwistle's The Second Mrs Kong, Glyndebourne Tour 1994 and festival, 1995, and Marcello, 1995; Douphol in Traviata for GTO at Glyndebourne, 1996; Germont Père, 1996, Prus in Makropolus Case, 1997, Glyndebourne Touring Opera; Enrico in Lucia di Lammermoor for Stowe Opera, 1998; Season 1998–99, Father in Hansel and Gretel for Welsh National Opera, also televised for Opera Northern Ireland; Falstaff for Garsington Opera; Season 2000–01 as Eugene Onegin for Grange Park Opera and in the premiere of From Morning to Midnight by David Sawer for ENO. *Recordings:* Baron Zeta in Die Lustige Witwe, 1993; Hugh the Drover; L'Enfance du Christ. *Honours:* Silver Medal for Singing and Lord Mayor's Prize, Guildhall School of Music. *Current Management:* Musicmakers International Artists Representation, Tailor House, 63–65 High Street, Whitwell, Hertfordshire SG4 8AH, England. *Telephone:* (1438) 871708. *Fax:* (1438) 871777. *E-mail:* musicmakers@compuserve.com. *Website:* www.operauk.com.

**POUNTNEY, David Willoughby,** CBE, MA; British opera director; *Intendant and Artistic Director, Bregenzer Festspiele*; b. 10 Sept. 1947, Oxford; s. of E. W. Pountney and D. L. Byrt; m. Jane R. Henderson 1980; one s. one d. *Education:* St John's Coll. Choir School, Cambridge, Radley Coll. and St John's Coll. Cambridge. *Career:* first opera production, Scarlatti's Trionfo dell'Onore, Cambridge 1967; Katya Kabanova at Wexford Festival 1972; Dir of Productions, Scottish Opera 1975–80, notably with Die Meistersinger, Eugene Onegin, Jenůfa, The Cunning Little Vixen, Die Entführung and Don Giovanni; Australian debut in Die Meistersinger 1978; world premiere of Philip Glass' Satyagraha, Netherlands Opera 1980; Prin. Prod. and Dir of Productions, ENO 1982–93, notably with The Flying Dutchman, The Queen of Spades, Rusalka, The Valkyrie and Lady Macbeth of Mtsensk; American debut with Houston Opera, Verdi's Macbeth, returning for the world premiere of Bilby's Doll by Carlisle Floyd, Katya Kabanova and Jenůfa; produced Weill's Street Scene for Scottish Opera 1989; other productions include From the House of the Dead in Vancouver, Dr Faust in Berlin and Paris, The Fiery Angel at the State Opera of S Australia, Adelaide, The Flying Dutchman, Nabucco and Fidelio for the Bregenz Festival, The Excursions of Mr Brouček for the Munich State Opera, the world premiere of Philip Glass' The Voyage at the Met, The Fairy Queen for ENO, Der Kamkasianische Kreidekreis in Zürich, A Midsummer Night's Dream in Venice, Jenůfa for the Vienna Staatsoper 2002, Turandot at Salzburg 2002; recent engagements include Lulu for the new Nat. Opera of Japan, Cav/Pag for Deutsche Oper Berlin and the '8 Little Greats' season at Opera North; Intendant and Artistic Dir Bregenzer Festspiele 2003–. *Publications:* Powerhouse; The Doctor of Mydffai (libretto for Peter Maxwell Davies), Mr Emmett Takes a Walk (libretto for Peter Maxwell Davies); several trans. from German, Italian, Russian and Czech. *Honours:* Janáček Medal, SWET Award, Martinu Medal, Olivier Award; Chevalier, Ordre des Arts et des Lettres. *Current Management:* IMG Artists, Lovell House, 616 Chiswick High Road, London, W4 5RX, England. *Address:* c/o Bregenzer Festspiele, Postfach 311, 6901 Bregenz, Austria. *E-mail:* info@bregenzerfestspiele.com. *Website:* www.bregenzerfestspiele .com.

**POUSSEUR, Henri;** Composer; b. 23 June 1929, Malmedy, Belgium. *Education:* Studied at the Liège Conservatory, 1947–52; Brussels Conservatory, 1952–53. *Career:* Worked at the Cologne and Milan electronic music studios, notably with Stockhausen and Berio; Taught music in Belgian schools, 1950–59; Founded in 1958 and directed the Studio Musique Electronique APELAC in Brussels; Lecturer in courses of new music, Darmstadt, 1957–67, Cologne, 1962–68, Basle, 1963–64, and the State University of New York at Buffalo, USA, 1966–69; Lecturer at the Liège Conservatory; Professor of Composition, 1971, Director of the Institution, 1975–94; Teacher at Liège University, 1970–94; Directed the organisation of the New Institut de Pedagogie Musicale in Paris; Resident Composer and Lecturer at Leuven Catholic University, 1993–99. *Compositions:* Symphonies, for 15 soloists, 1954; Mobile, for 2 pianos, 1958; Trois visages de Liège, electronic, 1961; Votre Faust, fantasy in the opera genre, with Michel Butor, 1960–68; Petrus Hebraicus, chamber music/theatre, for Schoenberg's centenary, 1973–74; La Rose de Voix, for 4 speakers, 16 solo voices, 4 choirs, 8 instruments, 1982; Traverser la forêt, for speaker, 2 solo voices, chamber choir and 12 instruments, 1987; Dichterliebesreigentraum, for 2 solo voices, 2 solo pianos, choir and orchestra, 1993; Aquarius-Memorial, cycle for solo piano and chamber orchestra, 1994–99; Le village planétaire vol de Nivelles, electro-acoustic programme of 16 hours duration, 2001; Don Juan à Gnide, music theatre, 1996; Suite du Massacre des Innocents, Wind band, 1997;. *Recordings:* CDs: Electronic Works, Traverser la Forêt; Dichterliebesreigentraum; La Guirlande de Pierre; Liège à Paris; Aquarius Memorial; Paraboliques (voltage-controlled electronic music), 1972. *Publications include:* Books: Ecrits d'Alban Berg, selected and translated with commentary, 1956; Fragments théoriques l Sur la musique experimentale, 1970; Musique Sémantique Societe, 1972; Die Apotheose Rameaus (Versuch zum Problem der Harmonik), 1987; Schumann le Poète (25 Moments d'une lecture de Dichterliebe), 1993; Musiques Croisées, 1997. *Honours:* Doctor Honoris Causa, Universities of Metz and Lille. *Current Management:* Cebedem, rue

d'Arlon 75/77, B01040 Brussels, Belgium; Edizioni Sovini Zerboni, Galleria del Corso 4, I–20722 Milan Italy. *Address:* 38 Avenue Wellington, 1410 Waterloo, Belgium.

**POWELL, Christopher (Kit) Bolland,** BMus, MSc; New Zealand composer and academic; b. 2 Dec. 1937, Wellington; m. Brigitte Bänninger 1966; one s. one d. *Career:* teacher of Math. and Music, New Zealand High School 1962–75; Lecturer, Christchurch Teachers' Colls 1975–84; studied in Europe 1980–81; has written experimental music for choruses and percussion and five song cycle settings of poems by Michael Harlow and three major works of experimental music, theatre; Computer Music, Swiss Computer Music Centre 1985; Atelier UPIC, Paris 1987; mem. Composers Asscn of New Zealand, Swiss Tonkünstlerverein. *Compositions:* The Evercircling Light for Choir SATB and Percussion 1980, Galgenlieder 1980, Christophorus for Children's Choir and Orchestra 1981, Les Episodes for Soprano, Bass Soloists and Orchestra 1987, Chinese Songs for Soprano and Tape 1988, Concerto for 2 Violins, String and Percussion 1989, Hauptsache man geht Zusammen hin, chamber opera for SATB, Speaker and Instrumental Ensemble 1989–93, Gargantua for Wind Orchestra 1990, Whale for Solo Trombone and Tape 1993, Piano Poems 1994, Dies irae for Men's Choir, Soprano and Instrumental Ensemble 1995, Clara Schumann, for Soprano, Piano and Tape 1996, Concerto for Five Percussionists and Orchestra 1997, Koauau for 8 Flautists with 16 Flutes (Contrabass Flute to Piccolo) 1998, Salmagundi – Entertainment for Brass Ensemble 1998, Home Thoughts from Abroad for Symphony Orchestra 1999, Concerto for Trombone, Tuba and Orchestra 2001, Rothko Variations for Orchestra 2004. *Recordings:* Devotion to The Small 1980, The Evercircling Light 1982, Hubert The Clockmaker 1982, Whale 1994, Chinese Songs 1995. *Publications:* Workbook for University Entrance Prescription 1973, Musical Design 1975, Musik mit gefundenen Gegenständen 1982, Suite for Solo Trombone. *Address:* Promenadenstrasse 24, 8193 Eglisau, Switzerland. *E-mail:* kit.powell@solnet.ch. *Website:* www.sounz.org.nz/composer; www .musicedition.ch/sme/index_e.htm.

**POWELL, Claire;** Singer (Mezzo-Soprano); b. 1954, Tavistock, Devon, England. *Education:* Royal Academy of Music; London Opera Centre. *Career:* Sang Alceste and Cherubino at Sadler's Wells while with London Opera Centre; London debut recital Wigmore Hall, 1979; Early appearances with Glyndebourne Festival Opera: has sung in Il Ritorno d'Ulisse, Falstaff, La Fedeltà Premiata and A Midsummer Night's Dream; Appearances with Welsh National Opera, Scottish Opera, Opera North and English National Opera, roles include, Berlioz, Didon, Beatrice and Marguerite, Carmen, Verdi's Ulrica and Preziosilla, Mussorgsky's Marina, Mozart's Cherubino and Idamante, Gluck's Alceste and Orfeo, Handel's Cornelia and Cyrus, Ponchielli's Laura, Saint-Saëns's Dalila, Ravel's Concepcion and Tchaikovsky's Pauline; Covent Garden from 1980, Les Contes d'Hoffmann, Midsummer Night's Dream, Otello, Lulu, Rigoletto, Die Zauberflöte, Ariadne auf Naxos, A Florentine Tragedy, Don Carlos (Eboli 1989); Médée (Neris), Rigoletto (Maddalena), Orlofsky, in Die Fledermaus and Samson et Dalila; US debut 1990, as Maddalena at San Francisco; Sang Pauline in The Queen of Spades at Madrid, 1990; Guest appearances in Frankfurt, San Francisco, Barcelona, Madrid, Toronto, Paris, Rome, Brussels, Liège and Lisbon; Sang Eboli in a new production of Don Carlos for Opera North, 1993; April 1995, role of Auntie, Peter Grimes, Royal Opera House; Guest appearances in Munich and Hamburg as Carmen and Eboli, and Lausanne as Mistress Quickly; Title role in Gerhard's The Duenna, Leeds, 1996; Sang Mistress Quickly in new production of Falstaff in Cologne with Conlon and Carsen, 1997; Emilia in new production of Otello in Brussels with Pappano and Decker, 1997; Auntie in Peter Grimes at Tokyo with Otaka, and at Savonlinna with Royal Opera House, new production, San Francisco with Runnicles and Alder, 1998; Mistress Quickly in Hamburg, 1999; Sang Margret in a new production of Wozzeck at Covent Garden, 2002; Concert repertoire includes St Matthew Passion, Verdi Requiem, Das Lied von Erde, La Mort de Cléopâtre, Stabat Mater, Petite Messe Solennelle by Rossini, Messiah and Elijah. *Recordings include:* Title role in The Duenna; Rosenkavalier conducted by Bernard Haitink; Video of Les Contes d'Hoffmann (as Nicklause) and A Midsummer Night's Dream; El amor Brujo, Der Rosenkavalier, Il Ritorno d'Ulisse in Patria; Video of Otello with Solti, Royal Opera House. *Honours:* Richard Tauber Memorial Prize, 1978; FRAM; ARAM. *Address:* c/o Penelope Marland Artists' Management, 10 Roseneath Road, London SW11 6AH, England.

**POWELL, Mel;** Composer; b. 12 Feb. 1923, New York, USA; m. Martha Scott, 23 July 1946, 1 s., 2 d. *Education:* BMus, MA, Yale University, 1952; Studied piano with Sara Barg and Nadia Reisenberg; Composition with Paul Hindemith. *Career:* Chairman, Yale University Composition Faculty, 1954–69; Dean, California Institute of The Arts School of Music, 1969–72; Provost (CalArts), 1972–76; Professor and Fellow of The Institute, 1976–; President, American Music Center, 1957–60; Consultant, National Endowment for The Arts, 1970–73; Awarded Honorary Life Membership in Arnold Schoenberg Institute. *Compositions:* Filigree Setting for String Quartet; Haiku Settings for Voice and Piano; String Quartet, 1982; Woodwind Quintet; Modules for Chamber Orchestra; Strand Settings for Mezzo Soprano and Electronics; Duplicates, a concerto for Two Pianos and Orchestra, 1990; Many other orchestral pieces, vocal, chamber music and electronic works including Computer Prelude, 1988; Settings, for chamber orchestra, 1992; Piano Trio, 1994; Sextet, 1996; Six Miniatures for soprano and harp, 1998. *Recordings:* The Music of Arnold Schoenberg and Mel Powell; The Music of Milton Babbitt and Mel Powell; The Chamber Music of Mel Powell; Mel Powell: Six Recent

Works. *Publications:* Compositions, essays and articles. *Contributions:* Perspectives of New Music; Journal of Music Theory; American Scholar. *Honours:* Guggenheim Fellowship, 1960; National Institute of Arts and Letters Grant Award, 1964; Works chosen to represent USA in International Society for Contemporary Music Festivals, 1960 and 1984; Pulitzer Prize, 1990. *Address:* c/o California Institute of The Arts, Valencia, CA 91355, USA.

**POWER, Patrick;** Singer (tenor); b. 6 June 1947, Wellington, New Zealand. *Education:* Studied at Universities of Otago and Auckland, New Zealand; Studied at University of Perugia, Italy. *Career:* Principal lyric tenor with: The Norwegian Opera in Oslo; Gärtnerplatz, Munich and Krefeld; Covent Garden debut, 1983, as the Simpleton in Boris Godunov, followed by Britten's Serenade for the Royal Ballet; Has Sung Alfredo for Kent Opera, Rodolfo and Almaviva for Scottish Opera; Glyndebourne Festival as Flute and Des Grieux in Manon for Opera North; Wexford Festival in title role of Massenet's Le Jongleur de Notre Dame; Overseas engagements as The Italian Tenor in Rosenkavalier and Fenton for Royal Danish Opera; Don Ottavio, Tamino and Rodolfo in Cologne; Belmonte in New Zealand and at Drottningholm; Le Comte Ory and Huon in Oberon at Lyon and Alceste in Paris; Alfredo, Tamino and Don Ottavio in Canada; Almaviva in San Francisco; Season 1988–89, as Nadir in Les Pêcheurs de Perles in Pisa; Faust with Victorian State Opera; Returned to Australia as Pinkerton, Hoffmann, Rodolfo and the Duke of Mantua; Sang Nadir at Adelaide, 1996; Don José for Welsh National Opera. *Recordings include:* Beethoven's 9th Symphony conducted by Roger Norrington; Balfe's Bohemian Girl conducted by Richard Bonynge; Nadir for Tulsa Opera, 1997; Canio in Pagliacci for Opera Ireland, 1998; Radames in Aida at Nantes, Angers and Rennes, France, Cavalleria rusticana and Pagliacci for Opera New Zealand, Pinkerton in Madama Butterfly for Wellington Opera, 1999. *Current Management:* Athole Still International Management, Forresters Hall, 25–27 Westow Street, London, SE19 3RY, England. *Telephone:* (20) 8771-5271. *Fax:* (20) 8768-6600. *Website:* www.atholestill.com.

**POWERS, Anthony;** Composer; b. 13 March 1953, London, England. *Education:* Studied with Nadia Boulanger in Paris and with David Blake and Bernard Rands at York. *Career:* Composer-in-Residence, Southern Arts; Composer-in-Residence, University of Wales, Cardiff College. *Compositions include:* Piano Sonata No. 2, 1985–86; Stone, Water, Stars, 1987; Horn Concerto, 1989; Cello Concerto, 1990; String Quartet No. 2, 1991; Terrain for orchestra, 1992; In Sunlight for violin and piano, 1993; Symphony 1994–6; Fast Colours, for ensemble, 1997; Memorials of Sleep, for tenor and chamber orchestra, 1998. *Current Management:* Oxford University Press, London, England. *Address:* Oxford University Press, Music Department, 70 Baker St, London W1M 1DJ, England.

**POWTER, Adrian;** British singer (baritone); b. 1970, Cambridge, England. *Education:* Royal Northern Coll. of Music with Neil Howlett. *Career:* joined Glyndebourne Festival Opera where he sang the Naval Captain in Manon Lescaut; cr. Philip in Harrison Birtwistle's The Last Supper at Deutsche Staatsoper, Berlin 2000 (later at Glyndebourne Festival and Touring Operas); other roles have included The Abbot in Curlew River for the Aldeburgh Foundation in Japan, Jupiter in Peleus and Thetis and The Lion in Pyramus and Thisbe for Opera Restor'd, The Forester in The Cunning Little Vixen for Surrey Opera, Guglielmo in Così fan tutte, Figaro in Figaro's Wedding and Baron Douphol in La Traviata for Opera Project, title-role in Don Giovanni for London Opera Players, Figaro in Figaro's Wedding and Orsini in Rienzi for Palace Opera, Dr Falke in Die Fledermaus, Giuseppe in The Gondoliers and Pish-Tush in The Mikado for Carl Rosa Opera and Marullo in Rigoletto for Mid-Wales Opera; concerts throughout UK as well as in Germany, Ireland, Italy, Netherlands, Portugal, and Singapore singing with Acad. of Music, Apollo Chamber Orchestra, Darmstadt Hofkapelle, English Symphony Orchestra, Halle Orchestra, London Soloists' Chamber Orchestra, Orchestra of the Age of Enlightenment and Royal Liverpool Philharmonic Orchestra under conductors including William Boughton, David Chernaik, Edward Higginbottom, Libor Pešek and Kent Nagano; sang Mahler Lieder eines fahrenden Gesellen on tour with Rambert Dance Co. and with London Soloists' Chamber Orchestra at the Purcetl Room; recent engagements have included The Abbot in Curlew River at Opéra de Rouen, Peter in Hansel and Gretel for Cork Opera Works, Guglielmo in Così fan tutte for Stowe Opera, Schaunard in La bohème for Longborough Festival Opera and Dandini in La cenerentola for Garden Opera; current engagements include Zurga in Les pecheurs de penes for Swansea City Opera, Guglielmo Così fan tutte for Garden Opera, Schaunard in La bohème for Castleward Opera, Dandini in La cenerentola at Kijani Kenya Festival, Bonario in La capricciosa corretta for Bampton Classical Opera, Brahms Requiem and Szymanowski Stabat Mater in Chester Cathedral, Dvořák Te Deum for Brighton Orpheus Choir, Fauré Requiem for Watford Philharmonic Soc., The Kingdom for Folkestone Choral Soc., Messiah for Raymond Gubbay Ltd at Bridgewater Hall, Manchester, Mozart Requiem for Aberystwyth Choral Soc., A Sea Symphony in Chichester Cathedral and Belshazzar's Feast in Arundel Cathedral. *Radio:* Friday Night is Music Night with Catherine Bott and the BBC Concert Orchestra (BBC Radio 2). *Television:* Opera Works (series of opera master-classes with Jonathan Miller for BBC 2) 1998. *Current Management:* James Black Management, The Old Grammar School, High Street, Rye, East Sussex, TN31 7JF, England. *Telephone:* (1797) 224668. *Fax:* (1797) 224668. *E-mail:* james@jamesblackmanagement.com. *Website:* www.jamesblackmanagement .com.

**PRAESENT, Gerhard;** Composer and Conductor; b. 21 June 1957, Graz, Austria; m. Sigrid Praesent-Koenig, 2 s. *Education:* Composition and Conducting, University of Music, Graz, 1982 and 1985. *Career:* Debut: Composer, Weiz, 1978; Assistant, 1986–92; Professor, University of Music and Dramatic Arts, Graz, 1992–; over 500 performances of works in 20 countries; Several commissioned compositions for the Vienna Concert Hall, The Austrian Chamber Symphony and the University of Graz among others; Numerous concerts including festivals in Graz, Hong Kong, Vienna; Vice-Pres., Styrian Tone Arts Asscn; mem, ISCM; OEKB; OEGZM. *Compositions:* Oeuvre of over 50 compositions including Symphonic Music: Symphonic Fragment; Hermitage; Configurations; Chaconne; Works for strings: La Tâche, Sonata Regina per SF; Sounds of Wood; Missa for string quartet, A Rayas; Chamber Music: Trio intricato; Sonata del Gesù; Sonata al dente; Marcia funebre, Encore Piece; Vocal music: Song; Fantasy on a Bach-Choral; Missa minima. *Recordings:* 4 dozen radio recordings, Austria; Two CDs, La Tâche, 1997; Sounds of Wood, 1999. *Honours:* Austrian State scholarship; CA Prize; Composition Prize, Berlin; Federal Music Award for Symphonic Fragment, 1992; Reinl prize for La Tâche; Prize of the City of Vienna, 1996; Theodor Koerner prize, 1997. *Address:* Badstr 58, 8063 Eggersdorf, Graz, Austria. *E-mail:* praesent@telering.at.

**PRANTL, Pavel,** MA; Czech concertmaster and professor of violin; b. 21 April 1945, Susice; m. Martina Maixnerova 1972; two s. *Education:* Conservatory of Music, Kromeriz, Acad. of Musical Arts, Prague, masterclasses with David Oistrakh. *Career:* debut with Czechoslovak Broadcasting Coroporation 1956; mem. first violin group, Czech Philharmonic Orchestra 1967–76, Asst Concertmaster 1976–78; Concertmaster, Artistic Dir, Prague Chamber Orchestra Without a Conductor 1978–80; founder, Artistic Leader, Prague Baroque Ensemble 1973–80; Concertmaster, Singapore Symphony Orchestra 1980–93; guest soloist with Prague Symphony Orchestra 1968, Moravian Philharmonic Orchestra 1975, Radio Plzeň Symphony Orchestra 1977, Singapore Symphony Orchestra 1981–87; numerous tours abroad, including festivals in Salzburg, Montreux, Edinburgh, Würzburg, Japan (Tokyo, Hokkaido), Republic of Korea (Seoul), USA (Cornell Univ., Univ. of California at Los Angeles, San Diego); Head of String Dept, Hong Kong Acad. for Performing Arts 1993–95; Dir, Singapore Professional String Centre 1995; Concertmaster, Prague Radio Symphony Orchestra 1996, Prague Radio Chamber Orchestra 1996–2000; Artistic Dir and Concertmaster, Czech Philharmonic Chamber Orchestra 1996–. *Recordings:* Ivo Blaha's Violin Concerto 1970, Czech Chamber Music, Czech Classical Violin Concertos 1991. *Honours:* Hon. DFA (London Inst. of Applied Research), Hon. Professorships, Univ. of Bruxelles, Haute Ecole de Recherche, Paris. *Address:* Stanton Management, 45-05 Newtown Road, Astoria, NY 11103, USA. *Telephone:* (718) 956-6092. *Fax:* (718) 956-5385. *E-mail:* TDStanton@StantonMgt.com.

**PRATICO, Bruno;** Singer (Bass-Baritone); b. 1962, Aosta, Switzerland. *Education:* Studied at the opera school of La Scala. *Career:* Sang Rossini's Mustafà and Bartolo under Abbado at La Scala; Bologna in 1987 as Belcore, Reggio Emilia in 1988 as Gaudenzio in Il Signor Bruschino; Has sung widely in Italy and guest appearances elsewhere include Opéra de Lyon in 1989, in Salieri's Prima La Musica poi le Parole, and Marseille in 1990 as Leporello; Other repertory includes The Mikado (Macerata Festival), Zurga in Les Pêcheurs de Perles and Geronimo in Cimarosa's Il Matrimonio Segreto; Season 1998 in Don Pasquale at Genoa, La Rocca in Un Giorno di Regno at Parma and Don Magnifico in La Cenerentola at Pesaro. *Recordings include:* Leoncavallo's La Bohème; Lakmé and Paisiello's Don Chisciotte; Cimarosa's I Due Baroni di Rocca Azzurra. *Address:* c/o La Scala Milan, Via Filodrammatici 2, 20121 Milan, Italy.

**PRATLEY, Geoffrey Charles;** Accompanist; *Professor, Trinity College of Music;* b. 23 March 1940, Woodford, Essex, England; m. (1) Wendy Eathorne, 27 Mar 1965, 1 d., (2) Vija Rapa, 20 June 1987, 1 d. *Education:* Royal Academy of Music, 1958–63; LRAM, ARCM, 1960; GRSM, 1961; BMus, Dunelm, 1969. *Career:* numerous concerts throughout the world with many international artists including Baker, Domingo, Tortelier, Goossens, Brymer, Holmes, Streich and Milanova; Professor, Royal Academy of Music, from 1965–; Professor, Trinity College of Music, 1990–; mem, Incorporated Society of Musicians; Royal Society of Musicians. *Compositions:* Dorothy Parker Poems for female voice and piano, 2000; Six Irish Folk-Songs, for voice and piano; Six English Folk-Songs, for voice and piano. *Recordings:* Ivor Gurney Songs with C Keyte; numerous BBC Recordings for radio and television. *Publications:* Handel Operatic Repertory Bk2: Arias for tenor and piano; Concert Master Series: Book 1–Tchaikovsky Violin Solos with Piano; William Walton's Viola Concerto, new viola/piano score; Great Orchestral Cello Solos, for cello and piano (2 books); Great Orchestral Violin Solos, for violin and piano; Great Operatic Melodies, arranged for piano duet. *Honours:* ARAM, 1967; FRAM, 1977, Pres. RAM Club 2004–05. *Address:* The Willows, Bambers Green, Bishops Stortford CM 22 6PE, England (home). *Telephone:* (1279) 870907 (home). *Fax:* (1279) 870991 (home).

**PRATSCHKE, Sinead,** MMus; Singer (soprano); b. 1971, Canada. *Education:* Royal Coll. of Music, National Opera Studio. *Career:* operatic roles as Susanna, Poulenc's Thérèse, Handel's Dorinda, Tytania, Euridice, Cunegonde, Valencienne, Barbarina, Despina, Gretel, Musetta; recital appearances at Jubilee Hall, Aldeburgh Festival 1997, Songmakers' Almanac; oratorio performances include Apollo e Daphne, The English Concert at Queen Elizabeth Hall, Mozart's C Minor Mass, Switzerland, Magnificat, National Concert Hall in Dublin, Ireland, St Matthew Passion, National

Orchestra of Wales at Brangwyn Hall, Aldeburgh Early Music Festival. *Recordings include:* Handel's Samson and Judas Maccabaeus (Maulbronn Handel Festival, Germany), Rodrigo Centenary Recording, Royal Philharmonic Orchestra, Zélide (Musikfestspiele Sanssouci, Berlin). *Honours:* Canada Council, Countess of Munster, Madeleine Finden, Ian Fleming Trust. *Address:* 70A Stondon Park, Forest Hill, London, SE23 1JZ, England. *Telephone:* (20) 8699-8060. *E-mail:* spratschke@hotmail.com.

**PRATT, Stephen Philip;** British, composer, lecturer, broadcaster and conductor; *Professor of Music, Liverpool Hope University College;* b. 15 June 1947, Liverpool; m. Monica Mullins, 14 Oct 1972, 1 s., 3 d. *Education:* Certificate of Education, Christ's College, Liverpool, 1965–68; Royal Manchester College of Music, 1968–69; BA, Honours, University of Reading, 1969–71; BMus, University of Liverpool, 1971–72. *Career:* Broadcaster, BBC Radio Merseyside, 1971–; Senior Lecturer in Music, 1972–, Head of Music, 1991–, Liverpool Hope University College; Freelance Conductor, 1975–; Part time Lecturer, Open University, 1976–78; Part time Lecturer, Lancashire Polytechnic, 1983–; Part time Lecturer, Liverpool University, 1984–86; Fellow, University of Liverpool, 1993–; Broadcaster, BBC Radio 3, 1994–; Professor of Music, Gresham College, London, 1997–2000, Prof. of Music Liverpool Hope Univ. 2003–. *Compositions include:* Star and Dead Leaves; Winter's Fancy, 1978; Some of Their Number for orchestra, 1980; Fruits of The Ground for horn trio, 1982; The Judgement of Paris for orchestra, 1985; Strong Winds, Gentle Airs for concert band, 1987; String Trio, 1988; Uneasy Vespers for mixed choir, soloists and orchestra, 1991; At The Turn of The Year for piano, 1993; About Time for small ensemble with tape, 1995; The Song Within, 1997; Violin Concerto, 1997; Undulations and Other Movements, 1998; Four Studies after John Cage, 1998; Aphrodite's Rock 2001, Lovebytes for soprano and ensemble 2003. *Recordings:* Star and Dead Leaves, 1977; 2 of 4 Studies after John Cage, 1998; At the Turn of the Year, 1999; Undulations and Other Movements, 1999. *Publications:* Violin Concerto, Aphrodite's Rock, Lovebytes 2005; contrib. to Arts Alive, 1972–; Reviewer, 1976–78, The Guardian; Classical Music, 1975–78. *Honours:* Chandos Composition Prize, Musica Nova, Glasgow, 1981. *Current Management:* Edition HH, 68 West End, Launton, Bicester, Oxon OX26 5DG, England. *Address:* 9 Wellington Avenue, Liverpool L15 0EH, England. *Website:* hope.ac.uk.

**PRECHT, Ulrika;** Singer (Mezzo-soprano); b. 1959, Sweden. *Education:* Studied in Opera Studio 67 and Stockholm State Opera, Stockholm. *Career:* Debut: Royal Opera, Stockholm, as Cherubino, 1990; Sang Dalila with Folkoperan Stockholm, 1991, and Nancy in Martha for Dublin Opera, 1992; Season 1992–93 in Rossini's Il Signor Bruschino at Frankfurt, Eboli in Don Carlos at Stockholm and title role of Carmen at Sodertaleoperan; Concert engagements throughout Scandinavia. *Address:* Nordic Artists Management, Svervagen 76, 11359 Stockholm, Sweden.

**PREECE, Dane Richard,** BA, ARCM, LGSM; British pianist, music director and repetiteur; b. 12 Feb. 1960, Hereford, England. *Education:* Univ. of Nottingham, Birmingham Conservatoire with Frank Wibaut. *Career:* concerto and recital appearances in major British venues and Huddersfield, Buxton and Warwick Festivals; pianist with Melachrino Strings and Orchestra 1987–93; accompanist, BBC radio and TV; repetiteur with D'Oyly Carte Opera Co., CBTO, Birmingham Music Theatre, Mid Wales Opera and Opera International; Guest Music Dir for RSC, Nat. Theatre, Chichester Festival Theatre, Theatre Royal Plymouth, West Yorkshire Playhouse, Crucible Theatre, Sheffield, Birmingham Repertory Theatre, RAM and West End theatres; piano tutor and vocal coach, Birmingham Conservatoire 1988–; repertoire coach, RAM 2000–. *Recordings:* Spend Spend Spend, Serenade and Dance – The Music of Paul Lewis, James Moody – Music for Harmonica and Piano (with James Hughes), The Snowman – The Stage Show. *Honours:* Hon. BC; Univ. of Nottingham Barber Organ Scholarship 1978, First Prize, Robert William and Florence Amy Brant Pianoforte Competition 1982. *Address:* 23 Oakwood Road, Smethwick, Warley, West Midlands, B67 6BX, England (home). *E-mail:* dane@anytimenow.com (home).

**PREECE, Margaret;** Singer (Soprano); b. 1965, England. *Career:* Appearances with English National Opera as Zerlina, Janáček's Vixen, Ninetta (Love for Three Oranges) and Nymph in Monteverdi's Orfeo; Elisabeth de Valois for Opera-Go-Round, in The Ring Saga for City of Birmingham Touring Opera and Oriana in Handel's Amadigi with Opera Theatre Dublin (also on tour to France); Alice Ford, Fiordiligi and Adina for English Touring Opera; Donizetti's L'Ajo nel Imbarazzo and Provenzale's Lo Schiavo di sua Moglie at Musica nel Chiostro, Batignano; Season 1997 with the Queen of Night for Opera Theatre Dublin and Despina and Papagena for Opera North; British premieres of Kurt Weill's Love Life and Gershwin's Of These I Sing, both recorded for BBC Radio 3; Concerts include Mozart's Davidde Penitente (at Seville), Beethoven's Missa solemnis, Dvořák Requiem and Paul Patterson's Mass of the Sea; Further opera roles include Oscar (Ballo in Maschera), Cordelia in Reimann's Lear, Susanna, Mozart's Countess, Anne Trulove, and Gilda. *Address:* C&M Craig Services Ltd, 3 Kersley Street, London SW11 4 PR, England.

**PREGARDIEN, Christoph;** Singer (Tenor); b. 18 Jan. 1956, Limburg, Germany. *Education:* Studied at the Frankfurt Hochschule für Musik and in Milan and Stuttgart. *Career:* Sang first with the Limburg Cathedral Choir; Operatic engagements in Frankfurt, Gelsenkirchen, Stuttgart, Ludwigshafen, Hamburg, Antwerp and Karlsruhe; parts include Almaviva, Tamino, Fenton and Don Ottavio; Concert appearances in the festivals of Flanders,

Netherlands, Israel, Paris, Aix, Ansbach, Innsbruck and Göttingen; Conductors include Sigiswald Kuijken, Gustav Leonhardt, Ton Koopman, Philippe Herreweghe, Roger Norrington, Ivan Fischer, Hans-Martin Linde, Wolfgang Gönnenwein, Frans Brueggen, Helmuth Rilling, Ferdinand Leitner and Michael Gielen; Sang in production of the St Matthew Passion for Belgian television; Towards Bach and Haydn concert series on London's South Bank, 1989; Sang in L'Infedeltà Delusa by Haydn for Flanders Opera 1990; Debut recital at the Wigmore Hall, London, 1993, returned in Schubert's Winterreise, 1997; Sang in the premiere of Rihm's St Luke Passion, Stuttgart 2000. *Recordings:* Over 100 including St John and St Matthew Passion conducted by Leonhardt; St John Passion, Bach's Magnificat; L'Infedeltà Delusa by Haydn; Mozart Concert Arias conducted by Kuijken; Buxtehude Cantatas and Mozart Requiem under Ton Koopman; Bach Lutheran Masses under Herreweghe; Symphoniae Sacrae by Schütz; Grimoaldo in Rodelinda (Harmonia Mundi); Die schöne Müllerin and Schiller texts by Schubert; Schubert CD: Lieder von Abschied und Reise; Killmayer's Hölderlin cycles; Winterreise, with Andreas Staier; Lieder von Liebe und Tod, with Tilman Hoppstock. *Honours:* Preis der Deutschen Schallplattenkritik; Edison Awards 1995, 1998; Cannes Classical Award, 1995; Diapason d'Or de l'Année, 1996, 1997; Choc de la Musique, 1997; Caecilia-Preis, Belgium, 1998; Orphée d'Or, Academie du Disque Lyrique, Prix Georg Solti, 1998; Preis der Deutschen Schallplettenkritik, Viertekjahresliste, 1999. *Address:* c/o Claudia Nitsche, Gierather Mühlenweg 15, 51469 Bergisch Gladbach, Germany.

**PREIN, Johann (Werner);** Singer (Bass-baritone); b. 3 Jan. 1954, Trofaiach, Leoben, Austria. *Education:* Studied with Herma Handl-Wiedenhofer in Graz. *Career:* Sang in concerts and recitals from 1979; Stage career from 1984, notably at Graz and Vienna; Bayreuth Festival, 1984–85, as Donner in Das Rheingold; Engaged at Gelsenkirchen from 1986; Guest appearances at the Vienna Staatsoper, Düsseldorf and Barcelona; Wiesbaden 1988, as King Henry in Lohengrin; At Gelsenkirchen in 1989 sang Wagner in the first German production of Busoni's Doktor Faust, in the completion by Antony Beaumont; Other roles include: Mephistopheles (Faust); 4 villains in Les Contes d'Hoffmann; The Speaker in Die Zauberflöte; Biterolf and the Landgrave in Tannhäuser; Wotan in Der Ring des Nibelungen; Achilles in Penthesilea by Schoeck; Season 1998 with the Doctor in Wozzeck at Trieste and Weber's Kuno in Rome; Season 1999 as Strauss's Jochanaan and Faninal at Wiesbaden, followed by Talbot in Maria Stuarda. *Recordings include:* Lieder by Joseph Mathias Hauer (Preiser); Der Konthur in Schulhoff's Flammen, 1995. *Address:* Musiktheater im Revier, Kennedyplatz, 4650 Gelsenkirchen, Germany.

**PREISLER, Frantisek, Sr;** Czech opera stage manager and producer; b. 29 April 1948, Opava; m. Vlastimila Plosharova Preislerova 1972; one s. *Education:* Janáček Acad., Brno. *Career:* debut, Smetana's Two Widows at the Theatre Olomouc 1973; Producer, Theatre Olomouc 1973–80, Theatre Maribor, Ljubljana 1980–83; Coll. Lecturer, Janáček Acad., Brno 1982–92; Producer, Janáček Theatre, Brno 1983–92; Dir, Janáček Opera, Brno 1985–92; productions of over 60 operas from the Slav repertoire (Smetana's Bartered Bride, Two Widows and The Secret, Dvořák's Rusalka, Janáček's Jenůfa, Cunning Little Vixen and Kata Kabanova, Mussorgsky's Boris Gudunov and Khovanshchina, Tchaikovsky's Eugene Onegin, Borodin's Prince Igor) and also Bizet's Carmen, Puccini's Madama Butterfly, La Bohème, Gershwin's Porgy and Bess, and Strauss's Rosenkavalier, Mozart's Le nozze di Figaro and Don Giovanni, Gounod's Faust, Rossini's Il Barbiere di Siviglia, Donizetti's L'Elisir d'amore; Verdi's La Traviata; Massenet's Werther and numerous others; mem. Free Artist.

**PREISLER, Frantisek, Jr;** Czech conductor; b. 23 Oct. 1973, Olomuc. *Education:* Janáček Conservatory, Brno, Janáček Acad., Brno, studied in Vienna, Austria. *Career:* debut, Janáček's Katya Kabanova at Janáček Theatre, Brno 1993; Chief Conductor, Musical Theatre Karlin, Prague; Conductor, Nat. Theatre, Prague; Chief Conductor, Janáček Symphony Orchestra, Prague 1997–; conducted operas and musicals including Smetana's The Kiss and the Two Widows, Mozart's Così fan tutte, Die Zauberflöte, Don Giovanni, Beethoven's Fidelio, Rossini's Il Barbiere di Seviglia, Verdi's Nabucco, Aida, La Traviata, Rigoletto, Macbeth, Otello and La Forza del Destino, Puccini's Turandot, La Bohème and Tosca, Leoncavallo's Pagliacci, Mascagni's Cavalleria rusticana, Dvořák's Rusalka, Meyerbeer's Les Huguenots, Die Fledermaus. *Recordings include:* B. Smetana's Two Widows (for radio and television). *Address:* Novákonych 19, 180 00 Prague 8, Czech Republic. *E-mail:* preislerfr@volny.cz. *Website:* www.preisler.cz.

**PREMRU, Raymond (Eugene);** Composer and Trombonist; b. 6 June 1934, Elmira, New York, USA; Divorced, 2 d. *Education:* BMus, Composition (Performers), Certificate of Trombone, Eastman School of Music, University of Rochester, New York, 1956. *Career:* Member, Phillip Jones Brass Ensemble, 1960–; Commissions from Cleveland Orchestra (Lorin Maazel), Pittsburgh Symphony (André Previn), Philadelphia Orchestra (Riccardo Muti), Philharmonia Orchestra (Lorin Maazel), London Symphony Orchestra (Previn), Royal Choral Society (Meredith Davies), International Trumpet Guild, York Festival, Cheltenham Festival, Camden Festival, Philip Jones Brass Ensemble; Visiting Professor, Trombone, Guildhall School of Music, Eastman School of Music, Rochester, 1987. *Compositions:* Music from Harter Fell; Quartet for 2 Trumpets, horn and Trombone; Divertimento for Ten Brass; Concertino for Trombone, flute, oboe, clarinet and bassoon; Tissington variations. *Recordings:* Easy Winner, Argo/Decca Records; Modern Brass, Philip Jones Brass Ensemble. *Contributions:* International Trombone Association Journal;

Instrumentalist Magazine. *Address:* Eastman School of Music, University of Rochester, 26 Gibbs Street, Rochester, NY 14604, USA.

**PRESCOTT, Duncan;** Clarinettist; b. 1964, England. *Education:* Studied at the Royal Academy of Music with Anthony Pay, and with Karl Leister. *Career:* Recitals at the Wigmore Hall and on the South Bank; Member of the Nash Ensemble, with whom he has broadcast the Brahms, Reger and Weber Clarinet Quintets; Mozart Clarinet Concerto with the London Sinfonietta and the English String Orchestra; Performances at many jazz venues, including Ronnie Scott's; Member of the Boronte Ensemble and duo partnership with pianist Scott Mitchell; Further engagements in Germany, America, Israel, Russia, Japan, Hong Kong and Italy. *Recordings:* Virtuoso pieces with Scott Mitchell (Chandos). *Honours:* Capitol Radio Music Prize; Lambeth Music Award; Frank Britton Award; Malcolm Sargent Music Award; Scholarships from the Myra Hess Trust, Countess of Munster Trust and the English Speaking Union.

**PRESSLER, Menahem;** pianist and academic; *Member, Beaux Arts Trio*; b. 16 Dec. 1923, Magdeburg, Germany; m. Sara Szerzen; one s. one d. *Education:* educated in Israel, studied with Petri and Steuermann. *Career:* Distinguished Prof. of Music, Indiana Univ., USA 1955–; soloist under Stokowski, Dorati, Ormandy, Mitropoulos; co-founder, Beaux Arts Trio 1955–, which performs annually in the capitals of Europe and Americas, in residence at the Library of Congress, Washington, DC 1984–; appearances at festivals in Edinburgh, Salzburg, Paris; subscription concerts in New York, Metropolitan Museum and at Harvard Univ. *Recordings:* most of the Trio repertoire, more than 50 records. *Honours:* Deutsche Bundesverdienstkreuz First Class 2005; winner Debussy Prize, San Francisco, three Grand Prix du Disque, Gramophone Record of the Year Award, Prix d'honneur Montreux Prix Mondial du Disques, Musical America Ensemble of the Year (with Beaux Arts Trio) 1997. *Current Management:* Encore Arts Management, USA. *Telephone:* (812) 320-4389. *E-mail:* info@encoreartsmanagement.com. *Website:* www .encoreartsmanagement.com. *E-mail:* info@menahempressler.org. *Website:* www.menahempressler.org; www.beauxartstrio.org.

**PRESTON, Katherine Keenan,** BA, MA, PhD; American music historian; *Associate Professor of Music, College of William and Mary*; b. 7 Dec. 1950, Hamilton, OH; m. Daniel F. Preston 1971; one s. *Education:* University of Cincinnati, Evergreen State College, Olympia, WA, University of Maryland, Graduate Center of CUNY. *Career:* taught at University of Maryland, Catholic University, and Smithsonian Institution; Associate Professor, College of William and Mary, Williamsburg, Virginia, 1989–; mem. American Musicological Society; Sonneck Society for American Music. *Publications:* Books: Scott Joplin, Juvenile Biography, 1987; Music for Hire: The Work of Journeymen Musicians in Washington DC 1875–1900, 1992; Opera on the Road: Traveling Opera Troupes in the USA, 1820–1860, 1993; The Music of Toga Plays (Introduction) in Playing Out The Empire: Ben Hur and other Toga Plays and Films, 1883–1908, edited by David Mayer, 1994; Editor of Irish American Theater, Vol. 10 in Series Nineteenth-Century American Musical Theater, 1994. *Contributions:* Various Articles including: The 1838–40 American Concert Tour of Jane Shirreff and John Wilson, British Vocal Stars in Studies in American Music, 1994; Popular Music in the Gilded Age: Musicians' Gigs in Late Nineteenth-Century Washington DC, in Popular Music, 1985; Music and Musicians at the Mountain Resorts of Western Virginia, 1820–1900, in A Celebration of American Music, 1989; Numerous articles in The New Grove Dictionary of American Music, 1986 and The New Grove Dictionary of Opera, 1992. *Address:* 137 Pintail Trace, Williamsburg, VA 23188, USA.

**PRESTON, Simon John,** OBE, MusB, MA, FRAM, FRCM, FRCO, FRCCO, FRSA; British organist and conductor; b. 4 Aug. 1938, Bournemouth. *Education:* Canford School, King's Coll., Cambridge. *Career:* Sub-Organist, Westminster Abbey 1962–67; Acting Organist, St Albans Abbey 1967–68; Organist and Lecturer in Music, Christ Church, Oxford 1970–81; Organist and Master of the Choristers, Westminster Abbey 1981–87; Conductor, Oxford Bach Choir 1971–74; Artistic Dir, Calgary Int. Organ Festival; Patron, Univ. of Buckingham; mem. Royal Soc. of Musicians, Council of Friends of St John's Smith Square; over 30 recordings. *Honours:* Edison Award 1971; Grand Prix du Disque 1979, Performer of the Year Award, American Guild of Organists 1987. *Address:* Little Hardwick, Langton Green, Tunbridge Wells, Kent TN3 0EY, England. *Telephone:* (1892) 862042.

**PRESTON, Stephen;** Flautist and Choreographer; b. 24 May, 1945, Skipton, Yorkshire, England. *Education:* Studied at the Guildhall School of Music, London (1963–66) with Geoffrey Gilbert; Further study with Wieland Kuijken in Amsterdam. *Career:* Leading flautist with the Academy of Ancient Music, English Baroque Soloists and London Classical Players; Founder members of the English Concert, under Trevor Pinnock; Artistic Director of the MZT Dance Company; Choreographer for many early operas, including works by Gluck and Purcell. *Recordings include:* Concertos by Vivaldi; Trio Sonatas by J. S. Bach. *Address:* c/o MZT, 1 Oast Cottage, Great Maxfield, Three Oaks, Nr. Hastings, East Sussex, TN 35 4NU, England.

**PRÊTRE, Georges;** French conductor; b. 14 Aug. 1924, Waziers; s. of Emile Prêtre and Jeanne (née Dérin) Prêtre; m. Gina Marny 1950; one s. one d. *Education:* Lycée and Conservatoire de Douai, Conservatoire national supérieur de musique de Paris and Ecole des chefs d'orchestre. *Career:* Dir of Music, Opera Houses of Marseilles, Lille and Toulouse 1946–55; Dir of Music, Opéra-comique, Paris 1955–59; Dir of Music, l'Opéra de Paris 1959,

Artistic Dir 1966, Dir-Gen. of Music 1970–71; conductor of the symphonic asscns of Paris and of principal festivals throughout the world; also conducted at La Scala, Milan and major American orchestras; Conductor Metropolitan Opera House, New York 1964–65, La Scala, Milan 1965–66, Salzburg 1966; First Visiting Conductor, Vienna Symphony Orchestra 1985–, Opéra Bastille (Turandot) 1997, Opéra-Comique (Pelleas et Melisande) 1998; Turandot at La Scala 2001; concert to celebrate 80th birthday, l'Opéra-Bastille 2004. *Honours:* Officier, Légion d'honneur 1971, Haute Distinction République Italienne 1975, Commdr République Italienne 1980; Europa Prize 1982, Victoire de la musique Award for Best Conductor 1997. *Address:* c/o Marcel de Valmalete, 7 rue Hoche, 92300 Levallois-Perret (office); Château de Vaudricourt, à Naves, par Castres 81100, France.

**PREVIN, André George;** American conductor, pianist and composer; b. (Andreas Ludwig Priwin), 6 April 1929, Berlin, Germany; s. of Jack Previn and Charlotte (née Epstein) Previn; m. 1st Betty Bennett (divorced); two d.; m. 2nd Dory Langan 1959 (divorced 1970); m. 3rd Mia Farrow 1970 (divorced 1979); three s. three d.; m. 4th Heather Hales 1982 (divorced); one s.; m. 5th Anne-Sophie Mutter 2003. *Education:* Berlin and Paris Conservatories. *Career:* Music Dir Houston Symphony, US 1967–69; Music Dir and Principal Conductor, London Symphony Orchestra 1968–79, Conductor Laureate 1979–; composed and conducted approx. 50 film scores 1950–65; guest conductor of most major world orchestras, also Royal Opera House, Covent Garden, Salzburg, Edin., Osaka, Flanders Festivals; Music Dir, London South Bank Summer Music Festival 1972–74, Pittsburgh Symphony Orchestra 1976–84, LA Philharmonic Orchestra 1984–89; Music Dir Royal Philharmonic Orchestra 1985–86, Prin. Conductor 1987–92; Chief Conductor and Music Dir Oslo Philharmonic Orchestra 2004–06, Conductor Laureate 2006–. *Television:* series of television specials for BBC and for American Public Broadcasting Service. *Major works:* Symphony for Strings 1965, Overture to a Comedy 1966, Suite for Piano 1967, Cello Concerto 1968, Four Songs (for soprano and orchestra) 1968, Two Serenades for Violin 1969, Guitar Concerto 1970, Piano Preludes 1972, Good Companions (musical) 1974, Song Cycle on Poems by Philip Larkin 1977, Every Good Boy Deserves Favour (music, drama, text by Tom Stoppard, 1977, Pages from the Calendar (for solo piano) 1977, Peaches (for flute and strings) 1978, Principals 1980, Outings (for brass quintet) 1980, Reflections 1981, Piano Concerto 1984, Triolet for Brass 1987, Variations for Solo Piano 1991, Six Songs for Soprano and Orchestra on texts by Toni Morrison 1991, Sonata for Cello and Piano 1992, The Magic Number (for soprano and orchestra) 1995, Trio for Bassoon, Oboe and Piano 1995, Sonata for Violin 1996, Sonata for Bassoon and Piano 1997, Streetcar Named Desire (opera) 1998, The Giraffes Go to Hamburg (for soprano, alto, flute and piano), Three Dickinson Songs (for soprano and piano), Diversions (for orchestra). *Publications:* Music Face to Face 1971, Orchestra (ed.) 1977, Guide to Music 1983, No Minor Chords: My Days in Hollywood 1992. *Honours:* Television Critics' Award 1972, Acad. Award for Best Film Score 1959, 1960, 1964, 1965, Glenn Gould Prize 2005; Hon. KBE 1996. *Current Management:* c/o Ronald Wilford/Jonathan Brill, Columbia Artists Management, 165 W 57th Street, New York, NY 10019, USA.

**PREVITALI, Fabio;** Baritone; b. 1961, Venice, Italy. *Education:* Studied at the Venice Conservatory. *Career:* Debut: Luca in 1987 in Salieri's Falstaff; Sang at Treviso in 1987 as Albert in Werther, Frank in Die Fledermaus and in Linda di Chamounix; Season 1988 at opera houses in Paris, Verona and Reggio Emilia; Other roles in Don Giovanni, Maria Stuarda, La Bohème, Eugene Onegin and Semele. *Recordings include:* Franchetti's Cristoforo Colombo, taped at Frankfurt in 1991. *Address:* Reggio Emilia Opera, Teatro Municipale, Piazzo Martini 7 Luglio, 42100 Reggio Emilia, Italy.

**PREVOST, André;** Composer; b. 30 July 1934, Hawkesbury, ON, Canada. *Education:* Conservatoire de Musique de Montréal; Studied under Olivier Messiaen at Paris Conservatoire and Henri Dutilleux at Ecole Normale, Paris; Studied electronic music under Michel Philippot, ORTF; Studied under Aaron Copland, Zoltán Kodály, Gunther Schuller and Elliott Carter at Berkshire Music Center, Tanglewood, Massachusetts. *Career:* Professor of composition and analysis, Faculty of Music, University of Montreal; composed music played throughout Canada and also France, USA, England, Yugoslavia, India and New Zealand; commissions have been received from Jeunesse Musicales du Canada, Quintette de Cuivres de Montreal, Charlottetown Festival, Ten Centuries Concerts, Canadian Broadcasting, McGill Chamber Orchestra, l'Orchestre symphonique de Quebec, Communaute Radiophonique des Pays de Langue Francaise, London (Ontario) Symphony Orchestra, Société de Musique Contemporaine du Québec, Canadian Music Centre among others. *Compositions include:* Orchestral: Célébration 1966; Chorégraphie I, 1972, II 1976, III 1976, IV 1978; Cosmophonie 1985; Diallele 1968; Evanescence 1970; Fantasmes 1963; Hommage 1970–71; Ouverture 1975; Scherzo 1960; Soloists with Orchestra: Concerto pour Violoncelle et Orchestre 1976; Le Conte de l'Oiseau 1979; Hiver dans l'Ame 1978; Paraphase 1980; Oboe Concerto, 1993; Chamber Music: Improvisation Pour Violon Seul 1976; Improvisation pour Violoncelle Seul 1976; Improvisation pour Alto Seul 1976; Mobiles 1959–60; Mouvement pour Quintette de Cuivres 1963; Musique pour l'Ode au St Laurent 1965; Mutations 1981; Quatuor 1958, No. 2 1972; Sonate pour Alto et Piano 1978; Sonate No. 1 pour Violoncelle et Piano 1962; No. 2 Pour Violoncelle et Piano 1985; Suite pour Quotuor a Cordes 1968; Triptyque 1962; Trois Pieces Irlandaises 1961; Solo Voice: Geoles 1963; Improvisation pour Voix et Piano 1976; Musique Peintes 1955; Chorus: Ahimsa 1984; Missa de Profundis 1973; Psalm 148 1971; Images d'un Festival for baritone, chorus and orchestra, 1993; Keyboard: Cinq Variations sur un Thème Grégorien 1956; Improvisation pour piano 1976; Variations en passacaille 1984. *Address:* c/o SOCAN, 41 Valleybroo Drive, Don Mills, Ontario M3B 2S6, Canada.

**PREY, Florian;** Singer (Baritone); b. 1959, Hamburg, Germany. *Education:* Studied with father, Hermann Prey, and at Munich Musikhochschule. *Career:* Gave Lieder recitals and appeared in concert from 1982; Opera debut as the Count in Schreker's Der ferne Klang, Venice, 1984; Sang in a staged version of St Matthew Passion at Teatro La Fenice, 1984; Silvio for Vienna Kammeroper, 1986; Stadttheater Aachen, 1988–, as Harlekin in Ariadne auf Naxos, Falke and Papageno; Writer of stage pieces and film scripts (Montag eine Parodis, 1985). *Address:* c/o Stadttheater, Theaterstrasse 1–3, 5100 Aachen, Germany.

**PRIBYL, Luboš;** Pianist; b. 29 Oct. 1975, Prague, Czechoslovakia. *Education:* Conservatoire in Prague with Professor Radomír Melmuka, 1990–96; Academy of Music in Prague with Professor Emil Leichner, 1997–. *Career:* Debut: Zlín, performance in the concert of the Zlín Symphony orchestra, 1989–; Recital in the Beethoven festival in Teplice, 1992–; Concerts in Bolzano, Brixen, Italy, 1994; Concert tour in Japan (Tokyo, Sapporo, Obihiro, Asahikava), 1996; Played Tchaikovsky's Concert No. 1, with orchestra of the Prague Conservatoire, 1997; Short portrait on Czech television, 1997. *Recordings:* A few recordings in Czech Radio (Chopin, Tchaikovsky, Rachmaninov, Martinů, Jezek); CD, piano recital (Haydn, Liszt, Semtana, Rachmaninov, Martinů, Jezek). *Honours:* Competition, Virtuosi per musica di pianoforte, Czech Republic, 1st Prize, 1988; Competition 'Citta di Senigallia', Italy, 5th prize, 1991; Beethoven Competition in Hradec nad Moravicí, Czech Republic, 1st Prize, 1992; F P Neglia Competition in Enna, Italy, 2nd Prize, 1993; Dr Václav Holzknecht Competition in Prague, 1st Prize, 1995; Mavi Marcoz Competition in Aosta, Italy, 5th Prize, 1995. *Address:* Smeralova 34, 170 00 Prague 7, Czech Republic.

**PRICE, Curtis Alexander,** AM, PhD, FRCM, FRNCM; American musicologist; *Principal, Royal Academy of Music;* b. 7 Sept. 1945, Springfield, MO. *Education:* Southern Illinois Univ., Harvard Univ. with John Ward and Nino Pirotta. *Career:* teacher, Washington Univ., St Louis, MO 1974–81; teacher, King's Coll. London 1981, Reader 1985, Prof. 1988; Prin. RAM, London 1995–; Prof., Univ. of London 2000–; mem. Royal Musical Asscn (Pres. 1999–2002); Trustee Musica Britannica and the Handel House Museum; Fellow, King's Coll. London. *Publications include:* The Critical Decade for English Music Drama 1700–1710 1978, Music in the Restoration Theater: with a Catalogue of Instrumental Music in the Plays 1665–1713 1979, Henry Purcell and the London Stage 1984, H. Purcell: Dido and Aeneas (ed.) 1986, Italian Opera and Arson in Late Eighteenth-Century London 1989, The Impresario's Ten Commandments: Continental Recruitment for Italian Opera in London 1763–4 (with J. Milhous and R. D. Hume) 1992, Man and Music: The Early Baroque Era (ed.) 1993, Purcell Studies (ed.) 1995. *Honours:* Hon. RAM; Hon. KBE 2005. *Address:* Royal Academy of Music, Marylebone Road, London, NW1 5HT, England (office). *Telephone:* (20) 7873-7373 (office). *Fax:* (20) 7873-7374 (office). *E-mail:* go@ram.ac.uk (office). *Website:* www.ram.ac.uk (office).

**PRICE, Eileen,** BEd, ARCM; British singer (mezzo soprano); b. Cardigan, Wales; m. Iain McWilliam (deceased); two s. *Education:* Homerton Coll., Cambridge, Royal Coll. of Music, London. *Career:* has performed with all major British orchestras and conductors including Sir Malcolm Sergent, Sir Adrian Bolt, Sworowsky, Bryden Thomson and Sir John Barbirolli; own radio and TV series; appeared at Citizens Theatre, Glasgow and Royal Court Theatre, London; retd Head of Vocal Studies, Welsh Coll. of Music and Drama; Teacher of Voice, Royal Holloway, Univ. of London 1991–, Jr Guildhall School of Music and Drama, London 1996–; Dir and Creator Teachers of Singing Training Course for AOTOS; mem. and Past Chair. Asscn of Teachers of Singing, Asscn of Teachers of Singing (USA). *Honours:* Jenny Lind Prize, Royal College of Music, Henry Leslie Prize, Clara Butt Prize, Tagore Medal for Most Distinguished Student of the Year. *Address:* 2A Byron Hill Road, Harrow on the Hill, Middx, HA2 0HY, England (home). *Telephone:* (20) 8426-5698 (home).

**PRICE, Gwynneth Patricia;** British singer (soprano); b. 1945, Bath, England. *Education:* studied in London with E. Herbert-Caesari, and with Parry Jones at Trinity Coll. of Music. *Career:* has sung at opera houses throughout the world, including the Royal Opera House, Covent Garden, as the Priestess in Aida, Fortune Teller in Arabella, Milliner and Duenna in Rosenkavalier, Villager in Jenůfa 1993; sang title role in Menotti's The Old Maid and The Thief at Norfolk Festival 1992, Alice in Verdi's Falstaff; concert repertoire includes Verdi's Requiem, conducted by Colin Davis, Tosca, Santuzza in Cavalleria Rusticana; fmr mem. Council of the Friends of Covent Garden; Founder and Dir Floriale Singers and Covent Garden Singers; now one of the Britain's leading voice coaches and pronunciation specialists; has made guest appearances on BBC radio. *Honours:* Long Service Silver Medallist, 35 Years with Royal Opera. *Address:* 65 Lancaster Grove, Hampstead, London, NW3 4HD, England (home). *Telephone:* (20) 7794-6455 (home).

**PRICE, Henry;** Tenor; b. 18 Oct. 1945, Oakland, California, USA. *Career:* Many seasons at the New York City Opera where he sang Telemaco in Monteverdi's Ulisse, Tamino, Almaviva, Narciso in Il Turco in Italia, Gennaro in Lucrezia Borgia and operetta roles; Other appearances in Philadelphia and Miami, at the US Spoleto Festival and from 1983 in Europe, notably at the

Mainz and Linz Operas. *Address:* c/o New York City Opera, Lincoln Center, New York, NY 10023, USA.

**PRICE, Janet,** BMus, MMus, LRAM, ARCM; British singer (soprano); b. 1938, Abersychan, Pontypool, Gwent, S Wales; m. Adrian Beaumont 1963. *Education:* Univ. of Wales Cardiff; special study of French Music with Nadia Boulanger, Paris; studied Singing with Olive Groves, Isobel Baillie and Hervey Alan. *Career:* singer in concerts with leading orchestras and conductors throughout UK and Western Europe; numerous premieres, including Belgian premiere of Tippett's Third Symphony, Festival of Flanders 1975; has sung opera with Glyndebourne Festival Opera, Welsh Nat. Opera Co., Kent Opera Co., Opera Rara, Handel Opera Soc., Northern Ireland Opera Trust, San Antonio Grand Opera, Tex., USA, BBC TV; has made a speciality of resurrecting neglected heroines of Bel Canto period, being the first person to sing a number of these roles in the modern era; highlights include: live commercial recording of Beethoven's 9th Symphony with Bernard Haitink and Concertgebouw Orchestra and Chorus, Tippett's 3rd Symphony with Haitink and London Philharmonic Orchestra, Stravinsky's Les Noces with Rozhdestvensky and BBC Symphony Orchestra and Chorus; sang role of Hecuba in Kent Opera's production of Tippett's King Priam (video); Prof. of Singing, RAM 1997–; Fellow, Royal Welsh Coll. of Music and Drama 2004. *Recordings:* for several labels. *Publications:* Haydn's Songs from a Singer's Viewpoint (article to The Haydn Yearbook) 1983. *Honours:* Hon. ARAM 2000; Winner, British Art Council First Young Welsh Singers' Award 1964. *Address:* 73 Kings Drive, Bishopston, Bristol, BS7 8JQ, England (home).

**PRICE, Leontyne;** American singer (soprano); b. 10 Feb. 1927, Laurel, Miss.; d. of James A. Price and Kate (née Baker) Price; m. William Warfield 1952 (divorced 1973). *Education:* Central State Coll., Wilberforce, Ohio and Juilliard School of Music. *Career:* appeared as Bess (Porgy and Bess), Vienna, Berlin, Paris, London, New York 1952–54; recitalist, soloist 1954–; soloist Hollywood Bowl 1955–59, 1966; opera singer NBC-TV 1955–58, San Francisco Opera Co. 1957–59, 1960–61, Vienna Staatsoper 1958, 1959–60, 1961; recording artist RCA-Victor 1958–; appeared Covent Garden 1958–59, 1970, Chicago 1959, 1960, 1965, Milan 1960–61, 1963, 1967, Metropolitan Opera, New York 1961–62, 1963–70, 1972, Paris Opéra as Aida 1968, Metropolitan Opera as Aida 1985 (retd); numerous recordings; Hon. Vice-Chair. US Cttee UNESCO; Fellow American Acad. of Arts and Sciences; Trustee Int. House. *Honours:* Hon. DMus (Howard Univ., Cen. State Coll., Ohio); Hon. DHL (Dartmouth); Hon. Dr of Humanities (Rust Coll., Miss.); Hon. DHumLitt (Fordham); Presidential Medal of Freedom, Order of Merit (Italy), Nat. Medal of Arts 1985, Essence Award 1991, 20 Grammy Awards for classical recordings. *Address:* c/o Columbia Artists Management Inc., 165 West 57th Street, New York, NY 10019; Price Enterprises, Room 920, 1133 Broadway, New York, NY 10010, USA.

**PRICE, Luke;** Singer (Tenor); b. 1968, Germany. *Education:* Chorister, Westminster Cathedral; Trinity College, London. *Career:* Appearances at Batignano Festival as Eufemio in Storace's Gli Equivoci; Apprentice in Die Meistersinger for Netherlands Opera and at Covent Garden; Engagements at Opéra de Lyon, Paris Châtelet, Salzburg and Glyndebourne (Festival and Touring); Other roles include Tchaikovsky's Lensky, Arturo in I Puritani and Camille in Die Lustige Witwe; Member of Covent Garden chorus from season 2000–2001; Sang Janissary in revival of Mozart's Die Entführung, 2000. *Address:* c/o Royal Opera House (chorus), Covent Garden, London, WC2, England.

**PRICE, Dame Margaret Berenice,** DBE; British singer (soprano); b. 13 April 1941, Tredegar, Wales; d. of the late Thomas Glyn Price and of Lilian Myfanwy Richards. *Education:* Pontllanfraith Grammar School and Trinity Coll. of Music, London. *Career:* operatic debut with Welsh Nat. Opera in Marriage of Figaro; renowned for Mozart operatic roles; has sung in world's leading opera houses and festivals; has made many recordings of opera, oratorio, concert works and recitals and many radio broadcasts and TV appearances; fmr performer with Bavarian State Opera, Munich; Fellow Coll. of Wales 1991. *Major roles include:* Countess in Marriage of Figaro, Pamina in The Magic Flute, Fiordiligi in Così fan tutte, Donna Anna in Don Giovanni, Konstanze in Die Entführung, Amelia in Simon Boccanegra, Agathe in Freischütz, Desdemona in Otello, Elisabetta in Don Carlo, Aida and Norma, Amelia in Ballo in Maschera. *Honours:* Hon. Fellow, Trinity Coll. of Music; Hon. DMus (Wales) 1983; Elisabeth Schumann Prize for Lieder, Ricordi Prize for Opera, Silver Medal of the Worshipful Co. of Musicians, Bayerische Kammersängerin. *Address:* c/o Stefan Hahn, Agentur Augstein, Eduard-Schmid-Str. 30, D-81541 Munich, Germany.

**PRICE, Perry;** Singer (Tenor); b. 13 Oct. 1942, New York, Pennsylvania, USA; m. Heather Thomson. *Education:* Studied at University of Houston, in London with Otakar Kraus and in New York. *Career:* Debut: San Francisco, as Des Grieux in Manon, 1964; New York (City Opera), Houston, Philadelphia, San Diego and Portland; Sang further at Montreal, Vancouver, Toronto, Lisbon and Stadttheater Augsburg; Other roles have included Mozart's Ferrando, Don Ottavio and Tamino, Rossini's Almaviva and Lindoro, the Duke of Mantua, Edgardo, Nemorino, Faust and Hoffmann; Active in concert and as teacher.

**PRICK, Christoph;** Conductor; b. 23 Oct. 1946, Hamburg, Germany. *Education:* Studied in Hamburg with Wilhelm Bruckner-Ruggebourg. *Career:* Assistant at the Hamburg Staatsoper; Permanent conductor at Trier Opera, 1970–72, Darmstadt, 1972–74; Musical Director at Saarbrucken, 1974–77,

Karlsruhe, 1977–84; Staatskapellmeister at the Deutsche Oper Berlin, 1977–84 (returned to conduct the premiere of Wolfgang Rihm's Oedipus, 1987); Conducted Così fan tutte at Los Angeles 1988 and Arabella at Barcelona, 1989; Music Director, Los Angeles Chamber Orchestra, 1992–95; Conducted Fidelio and Tannhäuser at the Metropolitan, 1992; Music Director City of Hannover, Germany, as of 1993–94 Season; Led Die schweigsame Frau at Dresden, 1998.

**PRIDAY, Elisabeth;** Singer (Soprano); b. 1955, Buckingham, England. *Education:* Studied at the Royal Academy of Music. *Career:* Joined the Monteverdi Choir 1975: concerts at the Aix Festival, and BBC Promenade; Sang in Handel Opera's Giustino 1983 and Hasse's L'Eroe Cinese at the 1985 Holland Festival; Appearances with Roger Norrington for the Maggio Musicale Florence (Speranza in Orfeo) and Amor in Gluck's Orfeo with the Scottish Chamber Orchestra; Dido and Aeneas with the English Concert in Germany, London and the Brighton Festival Concert performances of Bach's B minor Mass in King's College, Cambridge, Handel's Carmelite Vespers with the European Baroque Orchestra, Alexander's Feast for RAI in Italy and Messiah at the Festival de Beaune in France and also QEH; Monteverdi Vespers in St John's Smith Square, Bristol, St Albans; Concerts in France and England with Chiaroscuro and Climene in Gluck's La Corona at the City of London Festival; Paris 1991 with the Deller Consort. *Recordings:* Bach Motets with the Monteverdi Choir; Purcell's King Arthur, Music for the Chapels Royal and the Fairy Queen; Handel's Israel in Egypt, Semele and Dixit Dominus with the Winchester Cathedral Choir; Motets by Schütz and Monteverdi; Rameau's Les Boréades; Vivaldi Glorias (Nimbus); Dido and Aeneas with Trevor Pinnock and also with John Eliot Gardiner.

**PRIESTMAN, Brian;** Conductor, Music Director and Professor; b. 10 Feb. 1927, Birmingham, England; m. Ford McClave, 2 Mar 1972, 1 d. *Education:* BMus, 1950, MA, 1952, University of Birmingham; Dipl Sup, Brussels Conservatoire, 1952. *Career:* Has held Musical Directorships of Royal Shakespeare Theatre and with Symphony Orchestras in Edmonton, Canada, Baltimore, Denver and Miami; Principal Conductor, New Zealand and Malmö Symphony Orchestras; Former, Dean and Professor, University of Cape Town; Artist-in-Residence, University of Kansas, USA; mem, Board Member, Conductors' Guild. *Recordings:* For major recording companies. *Honours:* DHL, University of Colorado, 1972. *Current Management:* Mariedi Anders Artists Management, San Francisco, USA. *Address:* c/o Impresario A/S, Tollbugaten 3, N–0152 Oslo, Norway.

**PRIETO, Carlos;** Concert Cellist; b. 1 Jan. 1937, Mexico City, Mexico; m. Maria Isabel, 28 Dec 1964, 2 s., 1 d. *Education:* Mexico City Conservatory of Music, under Imre Hartman, 1942–54; Studied with: Pierre Fournier, Geneva, 1978; Leonard Rose, New York, USA, 1981, 1982. *Career:* Member of Trio Mexico, 1978–81; International career as Concert Cellist; Many world tours, USA, Canada, Western and Eastern Europe, USSR, Latin America, China, Japan, India, 1981–; Performances in Carnegie Hall and Lincoln Center, New York; Kennedy Center, Washington; Salle Pleyel and Salle Gaveau, Paris; Philharmonic Hall, Leningrad; Concertgebouw, Amsterdam; Has performed at International Music Festivals; Played at world premieres of many cello concerti including those of Carlos Chavez, Joaquin Rodrigo. *Recordings include:* Complete Bach Suites for Cello Solo, 1985; Works by Paganini, Ponce, Rachmaninov, Fauré, Mendelssohn, Tchaikovsky. *Publications:* Alrededor del Mundo con el Violonchelo (Around the World with the Cello), autobiography, 1987; Russian Letters, 1965. *Current Management:* Gurtman & Murtha Associates Inc, New York City, USA; Choveaux Management, Mancroft Towers, Oulton Broad, Lowestoft, Suffolk, England. *Address:* c/o Gurtman and Murtha Associates Inc, 450 7th Floor #603, New York, NY 10123-0101, USA.

**PRIEW, Uta;** Singer (Mezzo-soprano); b. 3 Aug. 1944, Karlovy, Varg, Czechoslovakia. *Education:* Studied at Halle and Leipzig. *Career:* Sang in opera at Weimar from 1970; Staatsoper Berlin from 1975 as Cenerentola; Selika in L'Africane, 1992; Clytemnestra, 1994; Fricka in Wagner's Ring, 1996; Bayreuth Festival, 1988–96 in The Ring and as Ortrud, Venus and Brangaene; Dresden Staatsoper, 1988 as Kundry; Deutsche Oper Berlin, 1990 as Amneris; Sang Clytemnestra at the Théâtre du Châtelet, Paris, 1996; Brangaene at Monte Carlo, 1998; Berlin Staatsoper 2000–01, as the Kostelnička in Jenůfa, Wagner's Mary and Herodias in Salome. *Recordings:* Video of Götterdämmerung. *Address:* Staatsoper Berlin, Unter den Linden 7, 1060 Berlin, Germany.

**PRIMROSE, Claire;** Singer (mezzo-soprano); b. 2 Oct. 1957, Melbourne, Victoria, Australia. *Education:* Graduate, Victorian College of Arts; Studied voice with Joan Hammond, Melbourne; Studied interpretation of French Song with Gerard Souzay, Paris. *Career:* Debut: As Mezzo Soprano in Australia; As Soprano from 1990, as the sister in Holloway's Clarissa, English National Opera; Mezzo Soprano: Krista in The Makropolous Case; Meg Page in Falstaff; Mercédès in Carmen, Cornelia, in Giulio Cesare; Title role in Cendrillon at Wexford Festival; Charlotte in Werther at Montpellier; Giulietta in Les Contes d'Hoffmann at Lille; Salud in La Vida Breve at Liège; Suzuki in Madama Butterfly for Opera North; Orlofsky in Die Fledermaus at the Hong Kong Festival; Dorabella in Così fan tutte; Sesto in La Clemenza di Tito for Opera Forum, Holland; Soprano: Leonore in Fidelio, Medea in Teseo, Athens Festival and Sadler's Wells; Dido in Dido and Aeneas at Bologna; Title role in Alceste, Monte Carlo Festival and Covent Garden; Elettra, in Idomeneo, Valencia Festival, 1991; Chrysothemis, State Opera of South Australia and

Festival of Melbourne; Leonore, in Fidelio, Australian Opera, 1992–93; Paris debut as Alceste, at Châtelet; Scandinavian debut as Elettra, in Idomeneo, Helsinki, and with the New Israeli Opera in Tel-Aviv, 1992; Fiordiligi, Lyric Opera of Queensland; Santuzza, Australian Opera, 1994 and 1996; Numerous concert appearances include a Wigmore Hall recital with Roger Vignoles in Berlioz's Roméo et Juliette, Salle Pleyel, Paris, and Leonara, in La Forza del Destino, Scottish Opera.; Sang Verdi's Lady Macbeth at Sydney, 1998; Season 2000–01 as Sieglinde at Brunswick and Senta in Dublin. *Honours:* Winner, Metropolitan Opera Competition; Winner, Pavarotti International Competition, Philadelphia. *Current Management:* Athole Still International Management, Forresters Hall, 25–27 Westow Street, London, SE19 3RY, England. *Telephone:* (20) 8771-5271. *Fax:* (20) 8768-6600. *Website:* www.atholestill.com.

**PRINCE-JOSEPH, Bruce;** Conductor, Composer, Organist, Harpsichordist and Pianist; b. 30 Aug. 1925, Beaver Falls, Pennsylvania, USA. *Education:* BMusA, Yale University, 1946; MMusA, University of Southern California, 1952; Conservatoire Nationale de Musique, Paris, France, 1953. *Career:* Staff Pianist, Organist, Harpsichordist, New York Philharmonic, 1955–74; Professor, Chairman, Department of Music, Hunter College of the City University of New York, 1955–78. *Recordings:* 6 Sonatas for Violin and Harpsichord, RCA, 1965; Glagolitic Mass, Janáček, 1967, Ode to St Cecilia, Handel, 1958, Columbia Records. *Honours:* Grammy Nomination, 1965, for 6 Sonatas for Violin and Harpsichord; Associate Fellow, Berkeley College, Yale University, 1978–83. *Address:* 6540 Pennsylvania Avenue, Kansas City, MO 64113, USA.

**PRING, Katherine;** Singer (Mezzo-Soprano); b. 4 June 1940, Brighton, England. *Education:* Studied at the Royal College of Music with Ruth Packer; Further study with Maria Carpi in Geneva and Luigi Ricci in Rome. *Career:* Debut: Geneva 1966, as Flora in La Traviata; Sang at Sadler's Wells from 1968, notably as Carmen, Dorabella, Poppea, Eboli, Azucena and Waltraute; Sang in the 1974 British stage premiere of Henze's The Bassarids; Covent Garden debut 1972, as Thea in The Knot Garden; Bayreuth 1972–73, as Schwertleite in Die Walküre; Glyndebourne 1978, as Baba the Turk in The Rake's Progress; Other modern roles included Kate in Owen Wingrave and Jocasta in Oedipus Rex; Retired 1982. *Recordings:* Fricka and Waltraute in The Ring conducted by Reginald Goodall; The Magic Fountain by Delius. *Address:* c/o Trafalgar Perry Ltd, 4 Goodwin's Court, St Martin's Lane, London WC2N 4LL, England.

**PRING, Sarah;** Singer (soprano); b. 1962, England. *Education:* Studied at Guildhall School, in Florence with Suzanne Danco, and with Johanna Peters. *Career:* Sang Norina, Susanna, Concepcion and Martinů's Julietta while a student in London, the Trovatore Leonora in Belgium; Professional debut at Glyndebourne, 1988, as Alice in Falstaff, returning as Barena in Jenůfa; Glyndebourne Touring Opera as Glasha in Katya Kabanova, First Lady in Die Zauberflöte and Dorabella; Opera North debut, 1989, as Concepcion, Scottish Opera, 1991, as Mimi; Concert appearances at Festival Hall (Jenůfa), Greenwich Festival (Judas Maccabeus), Belfast (Beethoven's Ninth) and Purcell Room; Sang Gluck's Euridice for Opera West, 1991; English National Opera debut, 1993, Princess Ida, Don Pasquale; ENO, 1993, Norina, Don Pasquale; ENO, 1994, Nannetta, Falstaff, also Glyndebourne Touring Opera, Second Niece, Peter Grimes. 1995, Second Niece, Paris Châtelet; Covent Garden debut 1996 as a Rhinemaiden in Götterdämmerung; Berta in Il Barbiere di Siviglia, 1997–98. *Honours:* Joint winner, 1990 John Christie Award. *Current Management:* Musicmakers International Artists Representation, Tailor House, 63–65 High Street, Whitwell, Hertfordshire SG4 8AH, England. *Telephone:* (1438) 871708. *Fax:* (1438) 871777. *E-mail:* musicmakers@compuserve.com. *Website:* www.operauk.com.

**PRINGLE, John;** Singer (Baritone); b. 17 Oct. 1938, Melbourne, Victoria, Australia. *Education:* Studied Singing in Melbourne and with Luigi Ricci in Rome. *Career:* Debut: Australian Opera, as Frank in Die Fledermaus, 1967; Many appearances with Australian Opera as Mozart's Don Giovanni and Leporello, Count and Papageno, Verdi's Posa, Ford, the Lescauts of Puccini and Massenet, Rossini's Barber, Britten's Death in Venice, Mozart's Figaro, Don Alfonso, Debussy's Golaud; Nick Shadow in The Rake's Progress, Andrei in War and Peace, Janáček's Forester and Robert Storch in Intermezzo (Glyndebourne, 1983); Also sings Olivier in Capriccio and appeared at Paris, Brussels and Cologne, 1980–85; Sang Beckmesser in Meistersinger for Australian Opera, 1988–89, Comte de Nevers in Les Huguenots, 1990; Appeared in Los Angeles and San Diego, 1992; Gianni Schicchi at Sydney, 1995 and sang Prus in The Makropulos Case at Sydney, 1996; Don Alfonso at Sydney, 1997–98; Teatro Regio, Turin, as Musiklehrer, 1998; Conjoint Professor of Vocal Studies, Newcastle University Conservatorium, 1998–; Sang Don Alfonso at Sydney, 2001. *Recordings include:* Video of Les Huguenots; Videos of Intermezzo and Love for Three Oranges (both Glyndebourne); Die Meistersinger (Australian Opera). *Honours:* Member, Order of Australia, 1988. *Address:* c/o Australian Opera, PO Box 291, Strawberry Hills, New South Wales 2012, Australia.

**PRIOR, Benjamin;** Singer (Tenor); b. 1943, Venice, Italy. *Career:* Sang widely in Italy from 1967, with Edgardo at La Fenice Venice in 1969; Wexford Festival, 1971, in La Rondine and Vienna Staatsoper, 1972, as Verdi's Riccardo; Barcelona 1971, as Percy in Anna Bolena, San Francisco 1980 (Alfredo), Buenos Aires 1981 (Pinkerton) and New Orleans Opera 1981–88; Sang Pinkerton at Verona (1983) and has also sung Verdi's Rodolfo (Luisa Miller) and Foresto, Nemorino, Faust, Macduff, the Duke of Mantua and Des Grieux. *Address:* Opera di Verona, Piazza Bra 28, 37121 Verona, Italy.

**PRITCHARD, Edith;** Singer (Soprano); b. 1962, Edmonton, Canada. *Education:* Studied at University of Toronto and Royal Northern College of Music. *Career:* Represented Canada at the 1991 Cardiff Singer of the World Competition; Sang Fiordiligi at the 1991 Glyndebourne Festival and the Countess in Cornet Rilke by Siegfried Matthus with the 1993 Glyndebourne Tour; Other roles include First Lady in Die Zauberflöte at Covent Garden, 1992–93, Licenza in Mozart's Sogno di Scipione at Buxton Festival and the Heavenly Voice in Don Carlos for Opera North. *Honours:* Brigitte Fassbaender Prize for Lieder, Royal Northern College of Music, and 1992 John Christie Award, Glyndebourne. *Address:* c/o 'Glen Craig', Llangollen Road, Trevor, Llangollen LL20 7 TN, Wales.

**PRITCHARD, Gwyn (Charles);** Composer, Conductor and Cellist; b. 29 Jan. 1948, Richmond, Yorkshire, England; m. Claudia Klasicka, 23 June 1967, 2 d. *Education:* Royal Scottish Academy of Music and Drama, 1966–69; Studied cello with Joan Dickson, Composition with Dr Frank Spedding; DRSAM. *Career:* Director of Music, Salisbury Cathedral School, 1969–70; BBC contract for documentary Young Composer, 1972–73; Freelance cellist and member of various chamber ensembles 1973–78; Artistic Director and Conductor, Uroboros Ensemble, 1981–; Founded Reggello International Festival of Music, Italy, 2003; Compositions performed world-wide including Warsaw Autumn Festival, Mexico Festival, Huddersfield Contemporary Music Festival, International Composers Forum, USA, Eastern and Western Europe, and Australia; Featured Composer at Southampton International New Music Week, 1989; mem, Society for the Promotion of New Music. *Compositions:* Concerto for Viola and Orchestra, 1967, revised 1984; Tangents, 1970; Spring Music for Chamber Orchestra, 1972; Enitharmon, 1973; Becoming, 1974; Five pieces for Piano, 1975; Ensemble Music for Six, 1976; Nephalauxis, 1977; Strata, 1977; Jardenia, 1978; Objects in Space, 1978; Mercurius, 1979; Duo, 1980; Earthcrust, 1980; Visions of Zosimos, 1981; Sonata for Guitar, 1982; Moondance, 1982; Lollay, 1983; Dramalogue, 1984; Chamber Concerto, 1985; Madrigal, 1987; La Settima Bolgia, 1989; Eidos, 1990; Janus, 1991; Wayang, 1993; Demise, 1994; Break Apart, 1995; Raum Greift Aus, 1996; Forse Mi Stai Chiamando, 1997; From Time to Time, 2000; Features and Formations, 2003. *Current Management:* Camerata Artists. *Address:* 40 Woolstone Road, London SE23 2SG, England.

**PROBST, Dominique (Henri);** Percussionist, Composer and Conductor; b. 19 Feb. 1954, Paris, France. *Education:* Baccalaureate, Philosophy Studies, La Sorbone, Paris, 1971; Paris Conservatoire National Superieur de Musique, 1st Prize Percussion, 198; Prize, Composition, Lili and Naida Boulanger Foundation, 1979. *Career:* As Musician at La Comédie Francaise, and many other great Parisian theatres, 1974–; Titulary Member, Concert Colonne and Ensemble Percussion 4; Assistant, CNSM, Paris, 1978–; Professor, Levallois Conservatory of Music, 1984–. *Compositions:* Numerous pieces for Theatre: King Lear, 1978; Dom Juan, Berenice, 1979; Macbeth; Les Caprices de Marianne, Les Plaisirs de L'Ile Enchantée, 1980; Les Cenci, 1981; Marie Tudor, 1982; L'Esprit des Bois; Dialogues des Carmélites, 1984; La Mouette, L'Arbre des Tropiques, Le Cid, 1985; L'Hote et le Renegat; Thomas More' Richard de Gloucester' Bacchus, 1987; Ascese-A-Seize, 16 percussion players; Les Plaisirs de l'Ile Enchantee, for recorder, violin, guitar and percussion; Coda and Variation IV, guitar. *Contributions:* Professional journals including La Revue Musicale. *Honours:* Prize Marcel Samuel Rousseau, Académie des Beaux-Arts of Paris, 1986, for Opera, Maximilien Kolbe. *Address:* 39 Rue Durantin, 75018 Paris, France.

**PROBST, Wolfgang;** Singer (Bass-baritone); b. 16 Nov. 1945, Neuhausen, Germany. *Education:* Studied in Munich with Marianne Scheck. *Career:* Staatsoper Stuttgart from 1971 as King Philip in Don Carlos, Wotan in The Ring, in the premiere of Glass's Akhnaten (1984), and as Bartók's Bluebeard (1996); Guest at Munich as Wotan, Jochanaan and Wagner's Dutchman; Orange Festival, 1979, as Klingsor, Dallas, 1980, as Wotan (US debut); Sang Orestes in Elektra at Buenos Aires, 1987, and Boris Godunov at Basle, 1990; Trieste, 1992–94, as Hans Sachs and Kaspar in Der Freischütz; Sang Pizarro in Fidelio at Stuttgart, 1998; Season 2000–01 at Stuttgart in the premiere of Adriana Hölszky's Giuseppe e Sylvia, and in Donizetti's La Convenienze Teatrali and I Pazzi per progetto. *Recordings include:* Video of Der Freischütz, from Stuttgart. *Address:* Staatsoper Stuttgart, Oberer Schlossgarten 6, 70173 Stuttgart, Germany.

**PROCHAZKOVA, Jarmila;** Musicologist; b. 27 Feb. 1961, Trebic, Czechoslovakia. *Education:* Piano, Conservatoire in Brno; Mašaryk University in Brno; Faculty of Musicology. *Career:* Scholarship-holder of the Leoš Janáček Fund, practice at Janáček Archives; Custodian, Janáček Archive of the Music History Department of Moravian Museum in Brno; mem, Commission to edit Janáček's Musical Works. *Publications:* Leoš Janáček, Album for Kamila Stösslova, in Czech and German, 1994, in English, 1996; Jarmil Prochazkova, Bohumir Volny, Leoš Janáček, born in Hukvaldy, Czech and English versions, 1995. *Contributions:* About 20 on Janáček's composition method, folk inspirations, sociological aspects; On The Genesis of Janáček Symphony Dunaj, 1993; Leoš Janáček and the Czech National Band, 1995. *Address:* Foltynova 6, 635 00, Brno, Czech Republic.

**PROCTER, (Mary) Norma;** British concert singer (contralto, retd); b. 15 Feb. 1928, Cleethorpes, Lincs.; d. of John Procter and Clarice Procter. *Education:* Wintringham Secondary School, Grimsby, vocal and music studies in London with Roy Henderson, Alec Redshaw, Hans Oppenheim and Paul Hamburger. *Career:* London debut at Southwark Cathedral 1948; operatic debut at Aldeburgh Festival in Britten's Rape of Lucretia 1959, 1960; first appearance at Royal Opera House, Covent Garden in Gluck's Orpheus 1961; specialist in concert works, oratorios and recitals; has performed at festivals and with major orchestras in Germany, France, Netherlands, Belgium, Spain, Italy, Portugal, Norway, Denmark, Sweden, Finland, Austria, Luxembourg, Israel and S America and with conductors including Bruno Walter, Leonard Bernstein, Jascha Horenstein, Bernard Haitink, Rafael Kubelik, Karl Richter, Pablo Casals, Malcom Sargent, Charles Groves, David Willcocks, Alexander Gibson, Charles Mackerras and Norman del Mar; Pres. Grimsby Philharmonic Soc. *Recordings include:* The Messiah, Elijah, Samson, Second, Third and Eighth Symphonies and Das Klagende Lied (Mahler), First Symphony (Hartmann), Scenes and Arias (Nicholas Maw), Le Laudi (Hermann Suter), Brahms and Mahler Ballads (with Paul Hamburger), Songs of England with Jennifer Vyvyan 1999, The Rarities (Britten) including world premiere release of 1957 recording of Canticle II – Abraham and Isaac (with Peter Pears and Benjamin Britten) 2001. *Honours:* Hon. RAM 1974. *Address:* 194 Clee Road, Grimsby, Lincs., DN32 8NG, England (home). *Telephone:* (1472) 691210 (home).

**PROKINA, Elena;** Soprano; b. 16 Jan. 1964, Odessa, Russia. *Education:* Studied in Odessa and at the Leningrad Theatre Institute and Leningrad Conservatory. *Career:* Kirov Theatre Leningrad from 1988 as Emma in Khovanshchina, Violetta, Marguerite, Natasha in War and Peace (seen on BBC television), Tatyana, Desdemona, Pauline in The Gambler, Jaroslavna in Prince Igor, Iolanta and Maria in Mazeppa; Tours with the Kirov Company in Europe and Kirov Gala at Covent Garden, 1992–; Appearances in Los Angeles as Donna Anna, and Lina in Stiffelio; Lisbon and Sydney as Tatiana; Shostakovich No. 14 with the London Symphony Orchestra under Rostropovich, 1993; Covent Garden debut in 1994 as Katya Kabanova in a production by Trevor Nunn, returning 1995 as Desdemona; Katya at Covent Garden in 1997; Verdi's Amelia Grimaldi at Glyndebourne, 1998; Sang in Rachmaninov's Aleko at the 1999 London Prom concerts; Season 1999–2000 for Zürich Opera as Tatiana in Eugene Onegin, Giselda in I Lombardi, Lucrezia (I Due Foscari) and Tosca; Elisabeth de Valois, 2001; Amelia Grimaldi at Sydney and Marie in Wozzeck for Dallas Opera, 2000. *Current Management:* Askonas Holt Ltd, Lonsdale Chambers, 27 Chancery Lane, London, WC2A 1PF, England. *Telephone:* (20) 7400-1700. *Fax:* (20) 7400-1799. *E-mail:* info@askonasholt.co.uk. *Website:* www.askonasholt.co.uk.

**PROMONTI, Elisabeth;** Opera Singer (soprano); b. 9 July 1942, Budapest, Hungary; one s. *Education:* diploma, Choir Conducting Faculty, Franz Liszt Music Acad., Budapest; diploma, Opera, Lied, Oratorio, Akad. Mozarteum, Salzburg; studied with Zoltan Zavodsky, Viorica Ursuleac, Friederike Baumgartner, Elisabeth Grümmer International Opera Studio, Opera Zürich, 1970–71. *Career:* debut, as Aida, Bielefeld Municipal Theatre, 1967; sang such roles as Aida, Amelia, Desdemona, Elisabeth, Donna Anna, Pamina, Countess, Elsa and Marie at opera houses of Bielefeld, Oberhausen, Kiel, Bremen, Heidelberg, Bordeaux, Vienna, Zürich, 1967–75; Concert Singer, 1975–; appearances on radio and television; tours in Europe, USA and Canada; Dir, Swiss Kodály Institute, 1983–95; Pres., Swiss Kodály Society, 1991–96; Dir, Concorde Opera Management Ltd, Vienna, 1998–. *Recordings:* Zoltán Kodály, Epigrammes, 1991; Folk Songs Arranged by Great Composers, 1993. *Address:* Hagenberggasse 25/4, 1130 Vienna, Austria.

**PROSTITOV, Oleg;** Composer; b. 7 Sept. 1955, Stavropol, Russia; m. Grishina Lyudmila, 22 May 1976, 1 s., 1 d. *Education:* Rimsky-Korsakov State Conservatoire, Leningrad (Petersburg), 1979; Postgraduate courses with Professor Mnatsakanyan, pupil of Shostakovich, Leningrad (St Petersburg) Conservatoire, 1983. *Career:* Debut: Stavropol, 1972; Participant of 3 international music festivals, Baku, 1987; Sofia, 1990; St Petersburg, 1991; Sonata-fantasy, Amadeus; mem, Union of the Composers of Russia, since 1979. *Compositions:* 5 symphonies, 2 piano concertos, a violin concerto, 5 children's musicals, a great number of chamber and vocal instrumental works (sonatas, suites, string quartets, cantatas, romances), about 100 songs. *Recordings:* Sonata-fantasy, Amadeus; Sonata for trombone, violin and piano performed in Moscow, St Petersburg, Florida, Stuttgart, Paris, A Black Man, monopera for baritone, mixed choir, large symphony orchestra based on the poem by S Esenin. *Honours:* 1st Prize for vocal cycle on the poems by S Esenin for baritone and piano, Young Musicians' Competition, Leningrad (St Petersburg), 1978. *Current Management:* Chairman, Krasnoyarsk Department, Union of the Composers of Russia. *Address:* Krasnoyarsky Rabochy, 124-A Apt 25, 660095 Krasnoyarsk, Russia.

**PROTSCHKA, Josef;** German singer (tenor); *Rector, Hochschule für Musik Cologne*; b. 5 Feb. 1946, Prague, Czechoslovakia. *Education:* Philology and Philosophy at Universities of Tubingen and Bonn; Cologne Musikhochschule with Erika Köth and Peter Witsch. *Career:* Giessen, 1977–78, Saarbrücken, 1978–80, leading tenor at Cologne Opera from 1980, singing all main tenor parts in Ponnelle's Mozart cycle, Lionel (Martha), Tom Rakewell, Faust, Max, Lensky, Jenik in The Bartered Bride, José, Hermann (Queen of Spades), Loge, Erik, Eisenstein; Freelance from 1987; Important debuts: Salzburg Festival and Vienna State Opera (Hans), 1985; La Scala and Semperopera Dresden (José), 1986; Bregenz Festival (Hoffmann), Maggio Musicale, Florence (Flamand) and Zürich Opera, 1987; Wiener Festwochen (Fierrabras-Schubert), 1988; Hamburg State Opera as Florestan and Elis in Schreker's Schatzgräber, 1989, Idomeneo, 1990; Royal Opera, Brussels, 1989, as Florestan and Lohengrin, 1990; Florestan at Covent Garden and Tokyo NHK, 1990; US debut, Houston (Song of the Earth), 1991; Now appears regularly on stage at festivals and opera houses with leading conductors and producers; Also lieder recitals, concerts, radio and television productions; Professor, Hochschule für Musik Köln 2002–, Det Kongelige Danske Musikkonservatoriet, Copenhagen 1993–. *Recordings include:* Haydn Die Schöpfung; Schubert Fierrabras; Schubert Schöne Müllerin; Mendelssohn Lieder, complete; Fidelio (Florestan) and Flying Dutchman (Erik) with Vienna Philharmonic and Dohnányi; Mozart Lieder, complete; Videos: Fidelio, Covent Garden; Tales of Hoffmann, Bregenz Festival; Fierrabras, Theater an der Wien; Schatzgräber, Hamburg Opera; Missa solemnis, Uracher Musiktage; Lieder recital, Urach. *Address:* Ringstrasse 17B, 50765 Köln, Germany. *Telephone:* (221) 912818100 (office). *Fax:* (221) 912818108 (office). *E-mail:* josef.protschka@gu.x.de (office).

**PROUVOST, Gaetane;** Violinist; b. 21 July 1954, Lille, France; m. Charles de Couessin, 6 July 1985, 2 s. *Education:* Baccalaureate; 1st Prize, Violin and Chamber Music, Cycle de Perfectionnement, Conservatoire National Superieur, Paris; Studied: With Ivan Galamian, Juilliard School of Music, New York; Chigiana, Siena, Italy; With D Markevitch, Institut des hautes etudes musicales, Montreux; Pupil of Zino Francescatti. *Career:* Debut: Carnegie Hall, 1974; Soloist with Radio-France Orchestra, Orchestre Lamoureux, Bucharest Philharmonic; Gdansk Philharmonic, Ensemble Intercontemporain, Ensemble Forum; Performed under conductors J Conlon, K Nagano, G Bertini, P Boulez, A Tamayo, S Baudo, R Kempe; Recitals with M Dalberto, N Lee, P Barbizet, B Rigutto, A Queffelec; Premiered: Olivier Greif's Sonate; M Rateau's Offrande lyrique, Paris, 1984; Participated in Etienne Perrier's film Rouge Venitien; Professor, Conservatoire National Superieur de Musique, Paris; mem, Alumni Association of Conservatoire National Superieur de Musique, Paris. *Recordings:* Prokofiev, Sonatas op 80 and 94 for violin and piano (with A R el Bacha); Szymanowski, Complete works for violin and piano; Zino Francescatti's Works. *Publications:* Biography of Zino Francescati. *Honours:* Prizewinner, Carl Flesch International Competition, London; Award for Best Record, France, 1987. *Current Management:* Ch de Covessin, France. *Address:* 7 rue des Volontaires, 75015 Paris, France.

**PROUZA, Zdenek;** Cellist; b. 3 Aug. 1955, Prague, Czechoslovakia; m. Katherine H Allen, 25 April 1987. *Education:* Conservatory of Music, Prague; Academy of Performing Arts, Prague; Hochschule für Musik, Wien; Mozarteum, Salzburg; Accademia Musicale Chigiana, Siena. *Career:* Debut: Recital debut in Prague, 1973; Principal Cellist with Czech Chamber Orchestra and Nurnberg Symphony Orchestra; Co-Principal with Vienna Chamber Orchestra and Munich Chamber Orchestra; Solo appearances in Czechoslovakia, West Germany, Belgium, France, Italy, Austria, USA and Canada; mem, American Cello Society. *Recordings:* Pauer, Radio Prague; Suk, Czech television; Suk, ORTF; Vivaldi, RAI; Saint-Saëns, Colosseum; Musical Heritage Society. *Honours:* Concertino Praga, 1970; Beethoven Cello Competition, 1972; Czech Cello Competition, 1976; Contemporary Performance Award, Czech Music Foundation, 1977, 1978. *Current Management:* The Added Staff. *Address:* 820 West End Avenue, Suite 3C, New York, NY 10025, USA.

**PROVOST, Serge;** Composer, Performer and Professor; b. 1952, Saint-Timothée de Beauharnois, Quebec, Canada. *Education:* Studied composition and analysis with Gilles Tremblay, organ with Bernard Lagacé; Studied writing, electracoustics, orchestration, piano and harpsichord, Conservatoire de Musique, Montréal 1970–79; Studied composition and analysis under Claude Ballif, Paris 1979–81. *Career:* Professor of analysis, Trois-Rivières and Hull Conservatories; Took part in Banff Centre's Composers Workshop 1979 and Rencontres Internationales de la Jeunesse at Bayreuth Festival; given organ recitals in France, Germany and Canada. *Compositions include:* Les Isles du Songe, for choir, orchestra and percussion; Cretes, a piece for 2 harpsichords which Swiss duo Esterman-Gallet commissioned and played in 1980; Tetrarys, 1988, saxophone, harp, flute, piano; Les Jardins Suspendus, 1989, 4 ondes martenots, piano. *Honours:* Won 1st Prize in composition for choir, orchestra and percussion with Les Isles du Songe, 1979; Won First Prize in analysis at Conservatoire de Paris 1981. *Address:* c/o SOCAN, 41 Valleybrook Drive, Don Mills, Ontario M3B 2S6, Canada.

**PROWSE, Philip;** British stage director and stage designer; b. 29 Dec. 1937, Worcestershire, England. *Education:* Slade School of Fine Art, London. *Career:* teacher at Birmingham College of Art; teacher Slade School of Fine Art 1995–99, Prof. 1999–03, now Emer.; Designed ballets for Covent Garden, followed by Orfeo ed Euridice, 1969, and Ariadne auf Naxos, 1976; Director of Citizens Theatre, Glasgow, 1970–; Produced and Designed Handel's Tamerlano for Welsh National Opera, 1982, and Les Pêcheurs de Perles for English National Opera, 1987; Designs for Jonathan Miller's production of Don Giovanni at English National Opera, 1985 and The Magic Flute for Scottish Opera; Work as Producer and Designer for Opera North includes Orfeo ed Euridice, Die Dreigroschenoper and Aida, 1986, British premiere of Strauss's Daphne, 1987, and La Gioconda, 1993; Staged the house premiere of Verdi's Giovanna d'Arco, Covent Garden, 1996 (also at Opera North, 1998); Professor, Slade School, University College London, 1999–; Dir Citizens 1970–2004. *Current Management:* c/o Cruickshank Cazenove, 97 Old South Lambeth Road, London SW8 1XU, England. *Telephone:* (20)7735-2933.

**PRUETT, Jerome;** singer (tenor); b. 22 Nov. 1941, Poplar Bluff, Missouri, USA. *Education:* Studied with Thorwald Olsen in St Louis and with Boris Goldovsky in West Virginia. *Career:* Debut: Carnegie Hall New York 1974, in a concert performance of Donizetti's Parisina d'Este; Sang with New York City

Opera then followed a career in Europe: Vienna Volksoper, 1975, in the premiere of Wolpert's Le Malade Imaginaire; Théâtre de la Monnaie Brussels, 1983, as Julien in Louise and as Boris in Katya Kabanova; Geneva Opera, 1984, as Debussy's Pelléas; Sang at Nancy, 1984, in Henze's Boulevard Solitude; Other roles include Mozart's Belmonte and Tamino, Nicolai's Fenton, Tonio in La Fille du Régiment and Ernesto in Don Pasquale; Amsterdam and Paris, 1988, as Boris in Katya Kabanova and Faust; Sang Ferrando in Così fan tutte at the Gran Teatre del Liceu Barcelona 1990; Sang Alfredo and Gounod's Faust for Opera North, 1996. *Recordings:* Louise (Erato).

**PRUNELL-FRIEND, Agustin;** Spanish singer (tenor); b. 1969, Tenerife, Canary Islands. *Education:* Guildhall School of Music and Drama, London, UK. *Career:* debut as Ramiro in Cenerentola at Madrid 1996; appearances at Teatro La Fenice (Nettuno in world premiere of Cavalli's Orione with Venice Baroque Orchestra, Maderna's Venetian Journal), Teatro Real, Madrid (Cefalo in new Pizzi production of Hidalgo's Celos Aun del Ayre Matan, conducted by Malgoire), Royal Opera House, Covent Garden (Acis in Acis and Galatea and M. de la Grille in EBF's production of Lully's Le Bourgeois Gentilhomme with Malgoire); sings regularly with Rafael Fruhbeck de Burgos and orchestras including Akademie Alte Musick Berlin, Rundfunk Berlin, Dresdner Philarmonie, Nacional de Espana, Sinfonica de Mexico, RAI Torino, Barroca di Venezia, Bergen Philharmonie, Sinfonica de Tenerife; future engagements include the Evangelist in Matthaus-Passion with Fruhbeck de Burgos, Jephtha for Collegium Gent, Berlioz Requiem in Dresden, Britten's War Requiem with Lorin Maazel, Sartorio's Orfeo with Alberto Zedda; lieder recitals with Graham Johnson. *Recordings:* Rossini's Turco in Italia (Kicco Classics), Handel's Ode to St Cecilia and Carmina Burana (Sello RTVE), Beethoven's Fidelio and Cavalli's Orione (Teatro La Fenice). *Address:* c/o Musiespaña, Humberto Orán. C/José Marañón 10, 4 Izda., 28010 Madrid, Spain. *Telephone:* (91) 591-3290. *Fax:* (91) 591-3291. *E-mail:* prunellfriend@hotmail.com. *Website:* www.prunell-friend.com.

**PRUSLIN, Stephen Lawrence,** BA, MFA; pianist and writer on music; b. 16 April 1940, Brooklyn, NY, USA. *Education:* Brandeis Univ., Princeton Univ., studied piano with Eduard Steuermann. *Career:* Taught at Princeton until 1964, then moved to London; Recital debut as pianist at Purcell Room, South Bank, 1970; Concert appearances with BBC Symphony and Royal Philharmonic; Recital accompanist to Bethany Beardslee, Elisabeth Söderström and Jan DeGaetani; Appearances with London Sinfonietta and the Fires of London (Co-founder), 1970–87; Repertoire has included works by Elliott Carter, Maxwell Davies (premiere of Piano Sonata), late Beethoven, Bach and John Bull; Collaborated with Davies on music for Ken Russell's film The Devils and has written other film and theatre music, including Derek Jarman's The Tempest; Articles on contemporary music, translation of Schoenberg's Pierrot Lunaire and librettos for Birtwistle's Monodrama, 1967, and Punch and Judy, 1968; Libretto for Craig's Progress by Martin Butler. *Recordings include:* albums as solo and ensemble pianist. *Publications include:* Peter Maxwell Davies: Studies from Two Decades (editor), London, 1979. *Current Management:* Universal Edition (London) Ltd, 48 Great Marlborough Street, London, W1F 7BB, England. *Telephone:* (20) 7437-6880. *Fax:* (20) 7437-6115.

**PRYCE-JONES, John;** Conductor; b. 1946, Wales. *Education:* Studied in Penarth and Worcester and at Corpus Christi College, Cambridge (Organ Scholar). *Career:* Assistant Chorus Master and Conductor at Welsh National Opera, 1970–; Freelance conductor in the United Kingdom and abroad until 1978; Chorus Master and Conductor with Opera North, 1978–; Head of Music, Scottish Opera, 1987; Debut with English National Opera in The Mikado; Music Director of The New D'Oyly Carte Opera, 1990–92; First US visit of the Company with The Mikado and The Pirates of Penzance; Artistic Director of the Halifax Choral Society; Has conducted the Oslo Philharmonic, the Bergen Symphony and the Norwegian Broadcasting Orchestra; Debut with Icelandic Opera, 1991, with Rigoletto; Principal Conductor and Musical Director, with Northern Ballet Theatre, 1992; Rigoletto, with Opera North, 1992; La Bohème with Welsh National Opera, 1993; Conducted CBSO, BBC National Orchestra of Wales. *Recordings:* Pirates of Penzance; Mikado; Iolanthe; Gondoliers. *Honours:* ARCO; MA. *Address:* 4 Croft Way, Menston, West Yorkshire CS29 6LT, England.

**PRYOR, Gwenneth;** Concert Pianist; b. 7 April 1941, Sydney, New South Wales, Australia; m. Roger Stone, 10 Dec 1972, 1 s., 1 d. *Education:* Diploma, New South Wales Conservatorium of Music; ARCM, Royal College of Music. *Career:* Debut: Wigmore Hall, London; recitals and concerts in major cities in United Kingdom, Europe, North and South America and Australia; Many records and radio broadcasts, both solo and chamber music; Teaching, Morley College; mem, Incorporated Society of Musicians; Royal Society of Musicians. *Recordings:* Moussorgsky's Pictures at an Exhibition; Schumann's Carnaval and Papillons; Gershwin's Rhapsody in Blue and Concerto; With clarinettist Gervase de Peyer; Malcolm Williamson Concertos. *Honours:* Prize for Most Outstanding Student, New South Wales Conservatorium, 1960; 1st Prize, Australia House, 1963; Gold Medal, Royal College of Music, 1963. *Current Management:* Michael Harrold Artist Management. *Address:* c/o 13 Clinton Road, Leatherhead, Surrey, KT 22 8NU, England.

**PRZYBYLSKI, Bronislaw Kazimierz;** Composer; b. 11 Dec. 1941, Łódź, Poland. *Education:* Studied at the Łódź Stage College of Music, 1964–69, with Boleslaw Szabelski in Katowice, and with Roman Haubenstock-Ramati at the

Vienna Hochschule für Musik, 1975–76. *Career:* Faculty Member, Łódź State College of Music, from 1964. *Compositions include:* Wind Quintet, 1967; String Quartet, 1969; Quattro Studi for orchestra, 1970; Suite of Polish Dances, 1971; Scherzi musicali for strings, 1973; Midnight, monodrama for actor and chamber ensemble, 1973; Concerto Polacco for accordion and orchestra, 1973; Voices for 3 actors and chamber ensemble, 1974; Requiem for soprano, 2 reciters, boys' chorus and orchestra, 1976; Sinfonia da Requiem, 1976; Arnold Schoenberg In Memoriam for string quartet, 1977; Sinfonia Polacca, 1974–78; The City of Hope, for bass, chorus and 2 orchestras, 1979; Sinfonia-Affresco, 1982; Concerto for harpsichord and strings, 1983; Return, quasi symphonic poem, 1984; Miriam, ballet, 1985; Concerto Classico for accordion and orchestra, 1986; The Dragon of Wawel, ballet, 1987; Lacrimosa 2000 for strings, 1991; Autumn Multiplay for 6 instruments, 1994; Sinfonia-Anniversario, 1995; Missa Papae Joannis Pauli Secundi, 1998; Solo songs; Choruses. *Address:* c/o Society of Authors ZAiKS, 2 Hipoteczna Street, 00 092 Warsaw, Poland. *Telephone:* (4822) 828 17 05. *Fax:* (4822) 828 13 47. *E-mail:* sekretariat@zaiks.org.pl. *Website:* www.zaiks.org.pl.

**PTASZYNSKA, Marta;** Polish composer and percussionist; b. 29 July 1943, Warsaw; m. Andrew Rafalski, 9 Nov 1974, 1 d. *Education:* Acad. of Music, Warsaw; Acad. of Music, Poznań; Studied composition with Nadia Boulanger and Olivier Messiaen in Paris and electronic music at Centre Bourdan, ORTF; Cleveland Institute of Music. *Career:* Performances at international festivals including ISCM World Music Days, and international conventions; Radio and television appearances in Poland and USA; Teacher of Composition and Percussion at Warsaw Higher School of Music and Prof. of Composition in USA, including Indiana University in Bloomington, Northwestern Univ., Cincinnati College Conservatory, Univ. of California in Berkeley and Santa Barbara; Prof. of Composition, Univ. of Chicago, 1998–; Commissions from American and European orchestras, chamber groups and major institutions including Chicago Symphony Orchestra, Cincinnati Symphony Orchestra, Polish Chamber Orchestra, Sinfonia Varsovia, Polish TV, BBC, Nat. Opera in Warsaw; and for musicians including Yehudi Menuhin, Ewa Podles, Keiko Abe, Evelyn Glennie. *Compositions:* Spectri Sonori for Orchestra, 1973; Siderals for 10 Percussionists, 1974; Un Grand Sommeil Noir, 1977; Dream Lands, Magic Spaces, 1978; Die Sonette an Orpheus, 1981; Winter's Tale, 1984 (Int. Rostrum of Composers at UNESCO Award, 1985); Marimba Concerto, 1985; Moon Flowers, 1986; Oscar of Alva, opera on G.G.Byron's poem, 1972 (revised 1986; Polish Radio and TV Award); Songs of Despair and Loneliness, 1988–89; Saxophone Concerto, 1988; Poetic Impressions, 1991; Holocaust Memorial Cantata, 1992; Spider Walk, 1993; Mister Marimba, opera for children, 1993–96; Liquid Light for mezzosoprano, piano and percussion, 1995; Concerto Grosso, 1996; Letter to the Sun, 1998; Inverted Mountain for orchestra, 2001; Mosaics for string quartet, 2002; The Drum of Orfeo for percussion and orchestra, 2003. *Recordings:* Polskie Nagrania; Un Grand Sommeil Noir, 1979, La Novella D'Inverno, 1985, Concerto for Marimba 1985, Moon Flowers 1986, Songs of Despair and Loneliness 1989; CD Accord-Universal: Holocaust Memorial Cantata 1992, Mister Marimba (opera) 1996; Dux Records: Poetic Impressions 1991, Mancala 1996; Pro Viva: Space Model 1975; Epigrams 1977; Bayer Records: Graffito 1988; many archive recordings at Polish Radio and also Moon Flowers at BBC in 1986. *Publications:* Many works published. *Contributions:* Cum Notis Variorum. *Honours:* Officer Cross of Repub. of Poland, 1995; Alfred Jurzykowski Award, New York, 1997; Polish Government Award, 2000. *Address:* c/o University of Chicago, Department of Music, 1010 East 59th Street, Chicago, IL 60637 (office); c/o ASCAP, ASCAP Building, On Lincoln Plaza, New York, NY 10023, USA. *Telephone:* (773) 702-8663 (office). *Fax:* (773) 753-0558 (office). *E-mail:* mptaszyn@uchicago.edu (office). *Website:* www.music.uchicago.edu (office); www.pwm.com.pl/ptaszynska (office); www.ptaszynska.art.pl (home).

**PUDDY, Keith;** Music Professor, Clarinettist and Researcher; b. 27 Feb. 1935, Wedmore, England; m. Marilyn Johnston, 14 Feb 1970, 1 s. *Education:* Studied at Royal Academy of Music, London. *Career:* Principal Clarinet for Hallé Orchestra under Barbirolli, at age 23; Returned to London for solo and chamber music; Former member of The Gabrieli Ensemble, The Music Group of London, The New London Wind Ensemble; Now plays with The London Wind Trio and London Music Phoenix; Awarded Leverhulme Trust Fellowships in 1983 and 1988 to study and research clarinets; Principal Clarinet and Wind Adviser on period instruments to the New Queen's Hall Orchestra, London; Performs and records on both modern and period instruments; Professor at the Royal Academy of Music and Trinity College of Music, London; Member of the London Wind Trio and NSW Queen's Hall Orchestra; Freelance Clarinettist, playing solo and chamber and also performing on early period instruments. *Recordings:* Major chamber repertoire on various labels; Brahms Sonatas; Brahms Quintet; Mozart Concerto; Mozart Quintet; Beethoven Septet; Numerous solo period recordings. *Honours:* Honorary FTCL, 1970; FRAM, 1995. *Address:* 20 Courtnell Street, London W2 5BX, England.

**PUGH, William;** Singer (Tenor); b. 1 July 1949, Scotland. *Education:* Studied at Oxford and St Andrew's Universities and the London Opera Centre; A pupil of the Spanish tenor, Eduardo Asquez. *Career:* Appearances in opera throughout Germany from 1981: Hildesheim, 1981–84; Oberhausen, 1984–86, Oldenburg, 1986–91, Saarbrücken, 1991–94 (as Werther, Mozart's Titus, Eisenstein, Danilo and Libenskof in the German premiere of Il Viaggio a Reims by Rossini); Subsequently as guest artist in Mannheim: 1994, Schaum der Tage (Denisov); 1995, Il Viaggio a Reims; 1998–2000, the Painter in Lulu

(Berg); Essen: 2000, Faust (Gounod); Bielefeld, 1993–94: Faust (Spohr) (recording) and the German premiere of The Duenna by Gerhard; Other roles have included Belmonte, Ferrando, Don Ottavio, Almaviva, Hoffmann, Don José, Alfredo, the Duke of Mantua, Edgardo and Rodolfo. *Address:* Lupinenstrasse 3a, 26125 Oldenburg, Germany.

**PUHLMANN, Albrecht;** opera house director; *Director, Staatsoper Stuttgart.* *Career:* fmr Dir Basel Opera for 13 years; Intendant, Staatsoper Hannover 2001–06, producing controversial avant-garde productions; Dir Staatsoper Stuttgart 2006–(11). *Address:* Staatstheater Stuttgart, Oberer Schlossgarten 6, Stuttgart 70173, Germany (office). *Telephone:* (711) 2032 (office). *Fax:* (711) 2032-389 (office). *E-mail:* info.verwaltung@staatstheater -stuttgart.de (office). *Website:* www.staatstheater.stuttgart.de (office).

**PULIEV, Michael;** Singer (Bass-baritone); b. 27 March 1958, Sofia, Bulgaria. *Education:* Studied in Sofia with Boris Christoff. *Career:* Sang at the National Opera, Sofia, 1984–86, then gave concerts in Bulgaria, China, Korea, Germany and Switzerland; Sang at Stadttheater Bern, 1986–87 and at Liège-, as Mars in Orphée aux Enfers, Frère Laurent in Roméo et Juliette and roles in Mascagni's Nerone, Die Zauberflöte, Le nozze di Figaro, La Traviata and Andrea Chénier. *Honours:* Winner, Bulgarian young singers competitions; Prizewinner, Maria Callas Competition at Athens, 1984, Geneva International, 1987.

**PURCELL, Kevin (John);** Composer, Author and Conductor; b. 9 Sept. 1959, Melbourne, Victoria, Australia. *Education:* BA (Music), La Trobe University, 1980; MMus, University of Melbourne, 1991; GradDipMus, New South Wales Conservatory, 1993; Janáček Academy, Brno, 1994; Composition with Brenton Broadstock, 1989–91; Conducting with Myer Fredman, 1993. *Career:* Conductor in Australia and England; Faculty Member, University of Melbourne, 1990–92; Resident in London. *Compositions include:* Symphony No.1 The Monk of St Evroul, 1990; Three Brass Monkeys, for trumpet, horn and bass trombone, 1990; An Umbrella for Inclement Weather, for flute, oboe and clarinet, 1991; Kite Songs for a Crescent Moon, for mezzo and large ensemble, 1992; Symphony No. 2 The Enchanter of Caer-Myrddin, 1992; The Thirty-Nine Steps, one-act chamber opera, 1993–95. *Honours:* Charles Mackerras Conducting Award, 1995. *Address:* c/o APRA, 1A Eden Street, Crows Nest, NSW 2065, Australia.

**PURVES, Christopher;** Singer (bass-baritone); b. 1960, England. *Education:* Choral scholar at King's College, Cambridge. *Career:* Appearances with English and Welsh National Operas and Opera Northern Ireland as Mozart's Figaro, Leporello, Masetto, the Speaker and Papageno; Other roles include Don Pasquale, the Sacristan in Tosca, Dandini in La Cenerentola, Janáček's Forester and Melibeo in La Fedeltà Premiata (Garsington, 1995); Melot in Tristan and Isolde for Scottish Opera, 1998; Concerts with such conductors as Colin Davis, Pesek, Rattle, Hickox, Christophers and Herreweghe. *Recordings include:* Israel in Egypt, with Gardiner; Purcell and Charpentier albums. *Current Management:* Hazard Chase, Norman House, Cambridge Place, Cambridge CB2 1NS, England. *Telephone:* (1223) 312400. *Fax:* (1223) 460827. *Website:* www.hazardchase.co.uk.

**PURVS, Arvids;** Latvian conductor, composer and music critic; b. 22 March 1926, Mengele; m Marija Falkenburgs 1952; one d. *Education:* violin, conducting and composition at private lessons; attended music seminars at Univs of Waterloo and Halifax, Canada. *Career:* Music Dir, St Andrew's Latvian Lutheran Church Choir, Toronto, Canada, 1958–; Conductor, Women's Choir, Zile, Toronto, 1974–; conductor at over 40 Latvian Song Festivals in the USA, Canada, Australia and Europe, leading orchestras and massed choirs of up to 4,000 voices, as in the Festival at the Royal Albert Hall, London, 1977 and in the XXth National Song Festival, Riga, Latvia, 1990; mem. Toronto Latvian Concert Asscn (pres. 1967–), Latvian Song Festival Asscn in Canada (chair. 1977–). *Compositions include:* Cantata of Psalms for soloists, chorus, orchestra and organ, 1956; Calling of the Bells for chorus and orchestra 1972, Toward the Light for chorus, speaker, orchestra and organ, 1975; Time, cantata for chorus, string orchestra, timpani and organ, 1980, Thus Said the Lord for chorus, orchestra and organ 1990. *Publications:* Pa skanosu vasaru (My Musical Summers) 2000. *Honours:* Music Award, The Arts Foundation of the Asscn of Latvians in the Free World, 1977, 2001; Order of Three Stars, Latvian Republic, 1997. *Address:* 65 Rivercove Drive, Etobicoke, ON M9B 4Y8, Canada (home). *Telephone:* (416) 621-1751 (home). *Fax:* (416) 621-8385 (home).

**PUSAR, Ana;** Singer (soprano); b. 1954, Celje, Yugoslavia. *Education:* Studied in Celje and at School of Music, Ljubljana. *Career:* Sang in Ljubljana from 1975 as Rosina, Manon, Tatiana, Dido, Nedda, Micaela, Desdemona and Poppea; Berlin Komische Oper, 1979–85; Appearances at the State Operas of Berlin and Dresden; Guest appearances in Japan, Prague, Moscow, Leningrad, Edinburgh, Venice and Madrid; Roles have included: Mozart's Fiordiligi and Countess, Agathe, Ariadne, Elsa, Madama Butterfly and Ellen Orford; Sang the Marschallin at reopening of Dresden Semper Oper, 1985, Vienna Staatsoper from 1986 as Donna Anna, Arabella, Agathe and the Marschallin, Munich Staatsoper in Daphne, as the Countess in Figaro and Capriccio and Donna Anna; Has also sung in Barcelona, Venice, Hamburg, Montreal, Geneva, Stuttgart, Lisbon, Toulouse, Graz and Cologne; Season 1992 with Sieglinde in Die Walküre at Bonn; Concert appearances in most major European centres; Has worked with such conductors as Peter Schneider, Gerd Albrecht, John Pritchard, Nikolaus Harnoncourt and Lorin Maazel; From 1992 sang: Tatiana at Venice, 1993, Katya Kabanova at Zürich,

1994 and Graz, 1994 in Stiffelio, as Lina; Gertrud at Palermo, 1995; Sang Mozart's Countess at Ljubljana, 2000. *Recordings include:* Der Rosenkavalier, Semper Opera; Bontempi Requiem; Dvořák Stabat Mater; Così fan tutte; Hugo Wolf, Lieder, 1990; Rachmaninov Lieder and Romances; Orfeo, 1994. *Honours:* Winner, Toti dal Monte Competition and Mario del Monaco Competition, 1978; National Award of Slovenia, 1979. *Current Management:* Music International. *Address:* c/o Music International, 13 Ardilaun Road, London N5 2QR, England.

**PUSHEE, Graham;** Australian singer (countertenor); b. 1954, Sydney. *Education:* studied in London with Paul Esswood, Schola Cantorum Basiliensis, Basel, Switzerland. *Career:* debut, Sydney, 1973, as Oberon in A Midsummer Night's Dream; Concerts in Australia, 1973–77; Handel Festivals at Karlsruhe in Orlando, Poro, Scipione, Belshazzar and Admeto; Paris Opéra, 1987, as Giulio Cesare; Australian Opera at Sydney as Ruggiero in Alcina, 1990, Opera North, 1993, as Andronico in Handel's Tamerlano; Turin, 1995, as Oberon and Staatsoper Berlin, 1996, as Endimione in Cavalli's La Calisto; Further appearances in operas by Gluck (as Orpheus), Cesti (Orindo in L'Orontea at Basle, 1990), Monteverdi and Stradella; Handel's Giulio Cesare for Opera Australia, 1997, and for Houston Grand Opera and at Karlsruhe; Rinaldo for Opera Australia; Semele for Berlin Staatsoper and Innsbruck Festival; In La Calisto at the Salzburg Festival, Barcelona, Brussels (La Monnaie) and Lyon; Season 2000–01 as Giulio Cesare at Sydney, in the premiere of Tatiana by Azio Corghi for La Scala Milan, and in Handel's Tamerlano at Halle. *Recordings include:* La Calisto; Handel Arias; Vivaldi, Solo Sacred Works. *Address:* c/o Australian Opera, PO Box 291, Strawberry Hills, NSW 2012, Australia.

**PUSZ, Ryszard;** Percussionist and Teacher; b. 5 Feb. 1948, Frille, Germany; m., 1 s., 3 d. *Education:* Studied with Richard Smith, Elder Conservatorium, and with George Gaber, Indiana University. *Career:* Music teacher 1970–73; Worked in Education Department of South Australia Music Branch 1974–86; Head of Percussion, School of Music, ACTAFE 1986–; Commissioned and premiered over 50 works for Percussion, and performed Australian premieres of numerous works of prominent overseas composers; Arranged many pieces for Percussion Solo and Ensemble; Orchestral Percussionist with Australian Youth Orchestra, 1964–70, Adelaide Symphony Orchestra, Adelaide Chamber Orchestra, 1964–90; Performed as Soloist with many orchestras and ensembles including Hungarian Youth Orchestra, Adelaide Symphony Orchestra, Prague Conservatory Percussion Ensemble, Stuttgart Musikhochschule Percussion Ensemble, Corpus Christi Percussion Ensemble (USA) at numerous festivals including International Percussion Festival, Bydgoszcz (Poland), Adelaide Festival of Arts, Banff Festival (Canada), International Barossa Music Festival, Perkusja 2001, Warsaw (Poland), as well as at major music academies and concert halls throughout Europe, USA, the Far East, and Australia; Has conducted various percussion ensembles and other performing groups; Discovered and developed a new, one-handed tremolo technique, applied in existing and new commissioned pieces; Has worked with filmmakers, theatre directors, and visual artists to produce performance projects for educational puproses and other productions; Music Director COME OUT '93 Festival; Pioneered the teaching of instrumental music by Distance Mode in Australia; Founded The Percussion Society of Australia, Adelaide Percussions, Sonitus, Drumworks and Percusson (a double father-son percussion quartet). *Compositions include:* Baltika (Steelband); Drumworks Quintet for 75 Players; Keep on Drummin!; Three Camps Thrice; ForE (multiple perscussion solo); Tsunami (Taiko ensemble). *Publications:* Percussion: A Comprehensive Approach; Time and Again: Essentials of Percussion Practice. *Honours:* Sounds Australian Awards for Most Significant Contribution by a South Australian to the Presentation of Australian Music, and Australia Council Fellowship to present Australian compositions overseas. *Address:* School of Music, Adelaide Institute of TAFE, 279 Flinders Street, Adelaide, SA 5000, Australia. *E-mail:* rpusz@camtech.net.au.

**PUTILIN, Nikolai Georgiyevich;** Russian singer (baritone); b. 1954. *Education:* Krasnoyarsk Inst. of Arts. *Career:* lessons with Nikola Nikolov in Bulgaria; started as singer of Variety Theatre; soloist of Syktyvkar Musical Theatre, Komi Repub. 1983–85; Kazan Opera Theatre 1985–92; Kirov (Mariinsky) Theatre in St Petersburg 1992–; Prizewinner Int. Chaliapin Competition 1989. *Repertoire includes:* over 40 leading roles toured Metropolitan Opera, La Scala, Teatro Comunale di Firenze, Covent Garden, Bolshoi Theatre and others. *Address:* Mariinsky Theatre, Teatralnaya pl. 1, St Petersburg, Russia (office). *Telephone:* (812) 114-44-41 (office).

**PUTKONEN, Marko;** Singer (Bass); b. 1947, Finland. *Education:* Studied at the Sibelius Academy, Helsinki. *Career:* At the Finnish National Opera has sung Mozart's Bartolo, Nicolai's Falstaff, in Katerina Izmailova, Sallinen's Red Line and the 1990 premiere of Rautavaara's Vincent (as Gauguin); Guested at Los Angeles, 1992, in the premiere of Kullervo by Sallinen; Further guest appearances at the Savonlinna Festival (Rocco, 1992), Zürich and Geneva. *Address:* Finnish National Opera, 23–27 Bulevardi, 00180 Helsinki, Finland.

**PUTNAM, Ashley;** Singer (Soprano); b. 10 Aug. 1952, New York, USA. *Education:* University of Michigan, with Elizabeth Mosher and Willis Patterson. *Career:* Norfolk Opera, Virginia, from 1976 as Donizetti's Lucia and the title role in the US premiere of Musgrave's Mary Queen of Scots; NYC Opera debut, 1978, as Violetta; Later sang Bellini's Elvira, Verdi's Giselda, Thomas' Ophelia and Donizetti's Maria Stuarda; European debut 1978 as

Musetta at Glyndebourne; Returned for Arabella 1984; Lucia with Scottish Opera; Mozart's Fiordiligi at Venice and for BBC television, Sifare in Mitridate at Aix, Donna Anna in Brussels and Countess Almaviva in Cologne; Covent Garden debut 1986, as Janáček's Jenůfa; Appearances at Santa Fe in Thomson's The Mother of us All and in the title role of Die Liebe der Danaë, 1985; Metropolitan Opera debut 1990, as Donna Elvira; Florence 1990, as Katya Kabanova; Sang Ellen Orford in Peter Grimes at the Geneva Opera and Vitellia in La Clemenza di Tito at the 1991 Glyndebourne Festival; Season 1991–92 as Fusako in the US premiere of Henze's Das Verratere Meer, at San Francisco, and the Marshallin at Santa Fe; Eva in Die Meistersinger at Cleveland, 1995; Sang St Teresa I in Thomson's Four Saints in Three Acts, Houston and Edinburgh, 1996; Concert engagements with the Los Angeles Philharmonic, New York Philharmonic and Concertgebouw Orchestras; Regular concerts at Carnegie Hall. *Recordings:* The Mother of us All; Mary Queen of Scots; Musetta in La Bohème. *Address:* c/o Los Angeles Opera, 135 N. Grand Ave, Los Angeles, CA 90012, USA.

**PÜTZ, Ruth-Margret;** German singer (soprano); b. 26 Feb. 1932, Krefeld; m. 1966; two d. *Education:* singing studies in Cologne and Hanover. *Career:* mem. Württemberg State Opera, Stuttgart 1959–, Vienna State Opera 1960–64, Hamburg Opera 1963–; guest appearances in Milan and Rome, Italy, London, Paris, Madrid, Lisbon, Moscow and Leningrad (now St Petersburg), USSR (now Russian Fed.), Stockholm, Helsinki and Buenos Aires; has performed at many festivals including Bayreuth, Salzburg, Austria and Edinburgh, UK; numerous recordings for Columbus, Electrola, CBS and Decca. *Honours:* title of Kammersängerin conferred 1962; Soviet Culture Prize. *Address:* Herderstr. 5, 71229 Leonberg, Germany.

**PUUMALA, Veli-Matti;** Finnish composer; b. 18 July 1965, Kaustinen. *Education:* Sibelius Acad., Helsinki, Accademia Musicale Chigiana summer course with Franco Donatoni, Siena. *Compositions include:* Scroscio 1989, Verso 1991, Ghirlande 1992, Line to Clash 1993, Tutta via 1993, String Quartet 1994, Chant Chains 1995, Chains of Camenae 1996, Soira 1996, Chainsprings 1997, Umstrichen vom Schreienden 1997–98, Taon concerto for double bass 1998–2000, Hommages Fugitives 2000–01, Seeds of Time piano concerto 2004, Credenza 2005. *Current Management:* c/o Fennica Gehrman, PO Box 158, 00121 Helsinki, Finland. *E-mail:* info@fennicagehrman.fi (office). *Website:* www.fennicagehrman.fi (office).

**PUYANA, Rafael;** Colombian harpsichordist; b. 14 Oct. 1931, Bogotá; s. of Ernesto Puyana and Alicia de Puyana. *Career:* studied under Wanda Landowska; lives in Spain and Paris; Colombia's Amb. to UNESCO, Paris; Teacher of harpsichord Cursos Manuel de Falla, Granada and Summer Acad. Musica en Compostela, Santiago de Compostela 1976–; gives performances throughout the world; works written for and dedicated to him by several composers including Federico Mompou, Xavier Montsalvatge, Julian Orbón, Alain Louvier and Stephen Dodgson; appeared in two films about life of Domenico Scarlatti (BBC TV and Televisión Española). *Honours:* Grand Prix du Disque (twice), Deutsche Schallplatten Preis for recording of works by François Couperin; Orden de Isabel la Católica (for his contrib. to study and performances of Spanish baroque and contemporary harpsichord music) 1996. *Address:* 8 rue de Cirque, 75008 Paris, France; Hacienda La Chucua, Carrera 4 No 87-21, Santa Fe de Bogotá, Colombia.

**PY, Gilbert;** Singer (Tenor); b. 9 Dec. 1933, Sete, France. *Career:* Debut: Verviers, Belgium, 1964 as Pinkerton in Madama Butterfly; Paris Opéra from 1969, notably as Manrico, Don José, Samson, Florestan, Tannhäuser, Lohengrin and in La Damnation de Faust; Paris Opéra-Comique 1969, in the title role of Les Contes d'Hoffmann; Nice Opéra in the local premiere of Sutermeister's Raskolnikov; Toulouse 1970, in Gounod's La Reine de Saba; Guest appearances in Vienna, Munich, Verona, Florence, Barcelona, New Orleans and Budapest; Turin 1973, as Lohengrin; Sang at the 1987 Orange Festival as Jean in Massenet's Hérodiade; Aeneas in Les Troyens at Marseilles 1989. *Recordings include:* Carmen (RCA); La Vestale by Spontini. *Address:* c/o Opéra de Marseille, 2 rue Moliére, 1323 Marseille Cédex 01, France.

**PYATT, David;** British horn player; *Principal Horn, London Symphony Orchestra;* b. 26 Sept. 1973, St Albans; m.; two c. *Education:* Selwyn Coll., Cambridge. *Career:* fmr Principal Horn, Nat. Youth Orchestra and Nat. Youth Chamber Orchestra of Great Britain; from 1988 performed with the London Symphony and Hallé Orchestras, English Chamber Orchestra and London Mozart Players; tours of Germany and Japan with the BBC Nat. Orchestra of Wales; played the Second Concerto by Strauss at the London Proms 1993; repertoire ranges from Telemann, Haydn and Mozart to contemporary composers; broadcast on BBC and independent television and radio; season 1998–99 included debut at Salzburg Festival, concert with Deutsche Symphonie Orchestre, Berlin, and Promenade Concerts with BBC Symphony Orchestra; season 2001–02 with concerts in London and Europe, as soloist in Britten's Serenade; has performed with Columbus Symphony Orchestra, Salzburg Mozarteum Orchestra, Norrkoping Symphony Orchestra, Istanbul State Symphony Orchestra, Gulbenkian Orchestra, Lisbon, Orquestra Sinfonica do Estado de Sao Paulo, Netherlands Radio Chamber Orchestra, BBC Nat. Orchestra of Wales, Orchestre Philharmonique de Radio France; soloist Last Night of the Proms Strauss No. 1 with BBC Symphony Orchestra under Leonard Slatkin 2004, soloist Edinburgh Int. Festival Weber Concertino with Northern Sinfonia under Thomas Zehetmair 2004; Principal Horn, London Symphony Orchestra 1998–. *Recordings include:* Strauss

Concerti, Britten Serenade, Mozart Concerti, Horn and Piano Works with Martin Jones, English Music with Anthony Rolfe Johnson, Peter Donohoe and Levon Chilingirian, Schubert's Auf der Strom with Michael Schade and Graham Johnson. *Honours:* BBC Young Musician of the Year Award 1987, Gramophone Magazine Young Artist of the Year 1996. *Current Management:*

c/o Mrs Caroline Oakes, Clarion/Seven Muses, 47 Whitehall Park, London, N19 3TW, England. *Telephone:* (20) 7272-4413/5125. *Fax:* (20) 7281-9687. *E-mail:* admin@c7m.co.uk. *Website:* www.c7m.co.uk. *Address:* London Symphony Orchestra, St Luke's, 161 Old Street, London, EC1V 9NG, England. *Website:* www.lso.co.uk.

# Q

**QUARTARARO, Florence;** American singer (soprano); b. 31 May 1922, San Francisco. *Education:* studied with Elizabeth Wells in San Francisco, Pietro Cimini in Los Angeles. *Career:* debut at Hollywood Bowl 1945, as Leonora in Il Trovatore; Metropolitan Opera from 1946 as Micaela (Carmen), Pamina, Verdi's Violetta and Desdemona and Nedda (Pagliacci); San Francisco 1947, as Donna Elvira in Don Giovanni; guest appearances at Philadelphia and elsewhere in the USA; Arena Flagrea, Naples 1953 as Margherita in Mefistofele; many concert appearances.

**QUASTHOFF, Thomas,** BL; Germany singer (bass-baritone); b. Nov. 1959, Hildesheim. *Education:* Univ. of Hanover, studied with Charlotte Lehmann in Hanover and with Carol Richardson. *Career:* many appearances at the world's leading concert halls in Oratorio and Lieder; season 1995 with US debut at the Oregon-Bach Festival and Japan debut with the Internationale Bachakademie under Helmuth Rilling; season 1995–96 at the Schleswig-Holstein Festival, the Herkulessaal in Munich and in Paris and Madrid; Britten's War Requiem at the Edinburgh Festival under Donald Runnicles; season 1996–97 with the English Chamber Orchestra, Berlin Philharmonic under Rattle and the Chamber Orchestra of Europe under Abbado; Schubert Bicentenary concerts 1997, including Wigmore Hall recital and Winterreise for television; sang in Mahler's Des Knaben Wunderhorn at the Edinburgh Festival 2002; sang Don Fernando in Fidelio, Salzburg 2003. *Recordings include:* Bach Cantatas, St John Passion and Schumann Lieder (Grand Prix Gabriel Fauré, Paris), Schubert Goethe-Lieder, Fidelio under Colin Davis and Mozart Arias, Des Knaben Wunderhorn by Mahler, with Anne Sofie von Otter 2001. *Current Management:* Ingpen & Williams Ltd, 7 St George's Court, 131 Putney Bridge Road, London, SW15 2PA, England.

**QUEFFÉLEC, Anne;** French concert pianist; b. 17 Jan. 1948, Paris; d. of Henri Queffélec and Yvonne Pénau; m. Luc Dehaene 1983; two s. *Education:* Conservatoire National, Paris (First Prize for Piano 1965, for Chamber Music 1966). *Career:* since 1968 has played all over Europe, Japan (seven tours), Israel, Africa, Canada and USA; has played with BBC Symphony, London Symphony, Royal Philharmonic, Bournemouth Symphony, Hallé, Scottish Chamber, City of Birmingham Symphony, Miami Symphony, NHK Tokyo, Tokyo Symphony orchestras, Nouvel orchestre philharmonique de Radio-France, Orchestre nat. de Radio-France, Orchestre de Strasbourg, Ensemble Intercontemporain, etc., under conductors including Zinman, Groves, Leppard, Marriner, Boulez, Semkow, Skrowaczewski, Eschenbach, Gardiner, Pritchard, Atherton, etc.; has played at numerous festivals including Strasbourg, Dijon, Besançon, La Roque-d'Anthéron, La Grange de Meslay, Bordeaux, Paris, King's Lynn, Bath, Cheltenham, London Proms; judge in several int. piano competitions; Masterclasses in France (including Ecole normale de musique, Paris), England and Japan; Pres. Asscn des amis d'Henri Queffélec, Asscn musicale 'Ballades'. *Recordings:* has made about 30 records for Erato-RCA, Virgin Classics and Mirare of music by Scarlatti, Chopin, Schubert, Fauré, Ravel (all his piano works), Debussy, Liszt, Hummel, Beethoven, Mendelssohn, Bach, Satie, complete piano works of Henri Dutilleux 1996 and Mozart and Haydn recitals. *Radio:* many appearances on BBC Radio 3, France Musique and Japanese radio. *Television:* many appearances on musical programmes but has also appeared on literary and religious programmes. *Honours:* First Prize, Munich Int. Piano Competition 1968, Prizewinner, Leeds Int. Piano Competition 1969; Best Interpreter of the Year, Victoires de la Musique 1990; Chevalier Légion d'honneur 1998, Officier, Ordre nat. du mérite 2001. *Address:* 15 avenue Corneille, 78600 Maisons-Laffitte, France. *Telephone:* 39-62-25-64. *Fax:* 39-62-25-64.

**QUELER, Eve;** American conductor; b. 1 Jan. 1936, New York. *Education:* Mannes Coll. of Music, New York, City Coll. of New York, piano with Isabella Vengerov, conducting with Carl Bamberger, Joseph Rosenstock, Walter Susskind and Igor Markevich. *Career:* began as pianist, asst conductor New York City Opera 1958 and 1965–70; later became a conductor; guest-conducted Philadelphia, Cleveland, Montréal Symphony, New Philharmonia, Australian Opera, Opéra de Nice, Opera de Barcelona, San Diego Opera, Edmonton Symphony, Nat. Opera of Czechoslovakia, Hungarian State, Hungarian Operahaz, Hamburg Opera, Pretoria, Hamilton, Ont., Opei Bonn and various other orchestras; Music Dir and Conductor Opera Orchestra of New York 1968–. *Recordings:* Puccini's Edgar, Verdi's Aroldo, Massenet's Le Cid, Boito's Nerone, Strauss' Guntram, Wagner's Tristan und Isolde, Janacek's Jenufa. *Publications:* articles in Musical America and Orpheus magazines. *Honours:* Dr hc (Russell Sage Coll., Colby Coll.); Chevalier des Arts et des Lettres, Musician of the Month, Musical American Magazine, Martha Baird Rockefeller Fund for Music Award. *Address:* c/o Alix Barthelmes, Manager Opera Orchestra, 239 W 72nd Street, New York, NY 10023, USA.

**QUILICO, Gino;** Singer (Baritone); b. 29 April 1955, New York, USA. *Education:* Graduated University of Toronto 1978; Vocal studies with Lina Pizzolongo and his father. *Career:* Canadian debut 1978, in a television performance of The Medium; Member of the Paris Opera from 1980, in operas by Rossini, Britten, Poulenc, Puccini, Gounod, Massenet, and Gluck; British debut with Scottish Opera at the 1982 Edinburgh Festival, as Puccini's Lescaut; Covent Garden debut 1983, as Valentin in Faust; later London appearances as Puccini's Marcello, Donizetti's Belcore, Rossini's Figaro,

Escamillo and Posa in Don Carlos (1989); Aix-en-Provence Festival 1985 and 1986, as Monteverdi's Orfeo and Mozart's Don Giovanni; Metropolitan Opera debut 1987, as Massenet's Lescaut; Malatesta in Don Pasquale at Lyon; Sang Dandini in La Cenerentola at the 1988 and 1989 Salzburg Festivals; Rome Opera 1990, as Riccardo in I Puritani; Sang Gluck's Oreste at the 1994 Vienna Festival; Sang Iago at Cologne, 1996; Sang Escamillo at Metropolitan Opera and Munich Festival, 1997; Zurga in Les Pêcheurs de Perles at Chicago and Barber of Seville in Seville, 1998; Season 1999–2000 as Donizetti's Enrico at Los Angeles, Massenet's Lescaut for La Scala, Iago in Montreal and Escamillo at the Munich Staatsoper. *Recordings include:* Lescaut in Manon (EMI); Dancairo in Carmen (Deutsche Grammophon); Mercutio in Roméo et Juliette (EMI); Marcello in La Bohème and Malatesta in Don Pasquale (Erato); Video of 1988 Salzburg Cenerentola. *Address:* c/o IMG Artists, Lovell House, 616 Chiswick High Road, London W4 5RX, England.

**QUILLA CROFT, Howard;** Singer (Baritone); b. 1966, Huddersfield, England. *Education:* Royal College of Music, London; National Opera Studio. *Career:* Debut: Mozart's Count, for the Opera Company, 1993; Appearances with Glyndebourne Touring Opera 1993–4, as Don Giovanni, A Captain in Eugene Onegin and Fiorello in Il Barbiere di Siviglia; Glyndebourne Festival 1994, in Eugene Onegin; Further engagements as Escamillo in Carmen for British Youth Opera, and Fiorello for Opera Northern Ireland. *Honours:* Cuthbert Smith and Agnes Nicholls Trophy; Kirkless Young Musician of the Year. *Address:* c/o Glyndebourne Touring Opera, Glyndebourne, Lewes, Sussex BN8 5UU, England.

**QUING, Miao;** Singer (mezzo-soprano); b. 1955, China. *Education:* Peking Conservatory. *Career:* Sang Carmen under the direction of Jacqueline Brumaire at Peking, 1982; Studied further at the Nancy Conservatoire and sang Butterfly from 1986 at Basle, Berlin, Lausanne, Toulon and Covent Garden; Guested with the Peking Opera at Savonlinna as Carmen, sang Donna Elvira at Brunswick (1991) and in Ariadne and Zauberflöte at the Bonn Opera; Many concert engagements. *Address:* Oper der Stadt Bonn, Am Boeselagerhof 1, Pf 2440, 5300 Bonn, Germany.

**QUINN, Andrea,** BA; British conductor and music director; b. 22 Dec. 1964; m. Roderick Champ 1991; one s. two d. *Education:* Royal Acad. of Music, London, Nottingham Univ.; Bartók Int. Seminar, Hungary. *Career:* Music Dir London Philharmonic Youth Orchestra 1994–97, Royal Ballet 1998–2001; Music Dir New York City Ballet 2001–; has conducted London Symphony Orchestra, London Philharmonic, Philharmonia, Royal Philharmonic, Hallé, Scottish Chamber, Northern Sinfonia, London Mozart Players and other leading orchestras in UK, Australia, Hong Kong, Sweden, Norway, Italy, Singapore; operas and music theatre pieces conducted include Misper (Glyndebourne), Four Saints in Three Acts (ENO), Harrison Birtwistle's Pulse Shadows (UK tour), Royal Opera House debut conducting Royal Ballet's Anastasia and on tour Cinderella in Turin and Frankfurt and Swan Lake in Japan, China and N America; Fellow Trinity Coll. of Music 2000, Assoc. Royal Acad. of Music 2001. *Dance:* conducted world premiere of Saint-Saens's Carnival of the Animals (choreography Christopher Wheeldon) 2003, Double Feature ( Susan Stroman) 2004. *Current Management:* Nicholas Curry, Clarion/Seven Muses, 47 Whitehall Park, London, N19 3TW, England. *Address:* New York City Ballet, New York State Theater, New York City, NY (office); 325 North Broadway, Nyack, NY 10960, USA (home). *Telephone:* (212) 870-5570 (office); (20) 7272-4413. *E-mail:* nick@c7m.co.uk (office). *Website:* www.nycballet.com (office).

**QUINN, Gerard;** Singer (Baritone); b. 1962, Irvine, Scotland; m. Heather Lorimer, 1 d. *Education:* Studied flute at Napier College, Edinburgh; Singing at The Royal Northern College of Music, Manchester with Patrick McGuigan; The National Opera Studio, London; In Vienna with Otto Edelmann and presently with Iris Dell'Acqua. *Career:* Early appearances as Golaud in Pelléas et Mélisande, Escamillo, Mozart's Count and Junius in The Rape of Lucretia; Buxton Festival Opera 1985; Glyndebourne Festival debut 1987, in Capriccio; Glyndebourne Tour, 1988, in La Traviata; Scottish Opera debut 1989, Donner, (Das Rheingold); English National Opera debut 1990, as Pantaloon, (The Love for Three Oranges), also for New Israeli Opera; Royal Opera, Covent Garden debut Flemish Deputy, (Don Carlo), 1989; Meru, (Les Huguenots), 1991 and in 1994 Le Comte in the British premiere of Massenet's Chérubin; Welsh National Opera debut, 1993, Enrico, (Lucia di Lammermoor), 1995, Father, Hansel and Gretel, Germont, (La Traviata); Bath and Wessex Opera, title role Rigoletto, 1994; English Touring Opera, 1994, Marcello, La Bohème; European Chamber Opera 1993, Count di Luna, Il Trovatore (also recorded), 1994 Count Alamaviva, Le nozze di Figaro and Rigoletto; Crystal Clear Opera, Sharpless, Madama Butterfly, 1995; Other roles performed include Nabucco, Germont, Ford, Michele in Il Tabarro, Tonio, Pagliacci, Zurga in The Pearl Fishers, Malatesta, Don Pasquale, Danilo in The Merry Widow, Don Giovanni and Eugene Onegin; Sang Rolla in I Masnadieri for the Royal Opera in Savonlinna, 1997; Concert repertoire includes Elijah, Carmina Burana, Sea Symphony, Dream of Gerontius, Brahms Requiem and Britten's War Requiem. *Address:* c/o International Opera and Concert Artists, 75 Aberdare Gardens, London NW6 3AN, England.

**QUITTMEYER, Susan;** Singer (Mezzo-soprano); b. 1955, USA; m. James Morris. *Education:* Studied at Wesleyan University, Illinois, and at the Manhattan School of Music. *Career:* Sang with the America Opera Project, notably in the premiere of John Harbison's A Winter's Tale, at San Francisco, 1979; Guested at St Louis (debut in a revival of Martin y Soler's L'Arbore di Diana, 1978), and sang further at San Francisco from 1981; Sang in Montreal from 1983, Los Angeles 1984; Santa Fe 1984–88, notably in the US premiere of Henze's We Come to the River; Further US appearances in Philadelphia, Cincinnati and San Diego; Sang the Messenger in Monteverdi's Orfeo at Geneva (1986) and Sesto in Giulio Cesare at the Paris Opéra, 1987; Further European engagements as Octavian for Netherlands Opera, Cherubino and Annius at Munich and Zerlina at the Vienna Staatsoper; Salzburg Festival debut 1991, as Idamantes in Idomeneo; Concerts with the Los Angeles Philharmonic and the Symphony Orchestras of Oakland, Sacramento and San Francisco; Metropolitan Opera from 1987 as Nicklausse in Les Contes d'Hoffmann and Dorabella; Sang Varvara in Katya Kabanova and Siebel with James Morris, 1991; Other roles include Meg Page, Cherubino, the Composer in Ariadne, Carmen, Pauline (The Queen of Spades) and Zerlina (Miami 1988); Engaged as Siebel at San Francisco, 1995; Many concert appearances. *Address:* c/o Metropolitan Opera, Lincoln Center, New York, NY 10023, USA.

**QUIVAR, Florence;** Singer (Mezzo-Soprano); b. 3 March 1944, Philadelphia, USA. *Education:* Philadelphia Academy of Music; Juilliard School New York. *Career:* Concert appearances with the New York, Los Angeles and Israel Philharmonics, the Cleveland, Philadelphia and Mostly Mozart Festival Orchestras and the Boston Symphony; Conductors include Mehta, Bernstein, Leinsdorf, Boulez, Muti and Colin Davis; Metropolitan Opera debut 1977, as Marina in Boris Godunov: returned to New York for Jocasta (Oedipus Rex): Isabella (L'Italiana in Algeri), Fides (Le Prophète) and Serena in Porgy and Bess; Guest appearances in Berlin, Florence, Geneva, Montreal and San Francisco; Recent engagements includeLaDamnation de Faust in Geneva, the Wesendonk Lieder in Madrid and London, the Verdi Requiem with the Philharmonia Orchestra, Mahler's 3rd Symphony with the New York Philharmonic and performances with the Berlin Philharmonic under Giulini; Festival appearances with the Israel Philharmonic in Salzburg, London, Lucerne, Florence and Edinburgh; Sang Ulrica in Un ballo in maschera at the 1990 Salzburg Festival (also televised); Season 1990/91 with Mahler's 2nd and 3rd symphonies (LaScala and New York, and in Japan); Met Opera as Federica in Luisa Miller; Gurrelieder under Zubin Mehta; London Proms 1991, in The Dream of Gerontius; Sang in the Met Opera Gala concert, 1996; Goddess in the premiere ofLaAmistad by A Davis, Chicago, 1998; Sang Brangaene at Houston, 2000. *Recordings:* Rossini's Stabat Mater (Vox); Mahler's 8th Symphony under Seiji Ozawa (Philips); Mendelssohn's Midsummer Night's Dream (Deutsche Grammophon); Berlioz's Romeo and Juliet (Erato); Virgil Thomson's Four Saints in Three Acts (Nonesuch); Verdi Requiem; Un ballo in maschera conducted by Karajan (Deutsche Grammophon); Luisa Miller (Sony); Schoenberg's Gurrelieder. *Address:* Kaye Artists Management, Barratt House, 7 Chertsey Road, Woking, Surrey GU21 3 AB, England.

# R

**RÄÄTS, Jaan;** Estonian composer and teacher; *Professor Emeritus of Composition, Estonian Academy of Music*; b. 15 Oct. 1932, Tartu; s. of Peeter Rääts and Linda Rääts; m. 1st Marianne Rääts 1958; m. 2nd Ebba Rääts 1983; three c. *Education:* Tartu Music School with Aleksandra Sarv, Tallinn Conservatory with Mart Saar, Heino Eller. *Career:* mem. CPSU 1964–90; recording engineer, Estonian Radio 1955–66, Chief Dir Music Programmes, Estonian TV 1966–74; Teacher of composition, Tallinn Conservatory (later Estonian Acad. of Music) 1968–70, 1974–, Prof. 1990–2003, Prof. Emer. 2003–; initiated Estonian Music Days 1979; Vice-Chair. Estonian Composers' Union 1964–74, Chair. 1974–93. *Compositions include:* Symphony No. 1 1957, Symphony No. 2 1958, Symphony No. 3 1959, Symphony No. 4 Cosmic 1959, Concerto for chamber orchestra No. 1 1961, Violin Concerto No. 1 1963, Symphony No. 5 1966, Symphony No. 6 1967, Piano Concerto No. 1 1968, 24 Preludes 1968, Toccata 1970, Symphony No. 7 1973, 24 Estonian Preludes 1977, Violin Concerto No. 2 1979, 24 Marginalia 1979, 24 Marginalia for two pianos 1982, Piano Concerto No. 2 1983, Symphony No. 8 1985, Concerto for two pianos and symphony orchestra 1986, Concerto for chamber orchestra No. 2 1987, Piano Concerto No. 3 1990, Concerto for guitar and orchestra 1992, Concerto for trumpet and piano 1994, Concerto for violin and chamber orchestra 1995, Violin Concerto No. 3 1995, Five Sketches for Requiem for symphony orchestra 1999, Concerto for flute, guitar and symphony orchestra 2001, Symphony No. 9, Symphony No. 10, 10 piano sonatas, seven piano trios –2004, six string quartets. *Film scores:* Roosa kübar 1963, Null kolm 1965, Tütarlaps mustas 1966, Supernova 1966, Viini postmark 1967, Gladiaator 1969, Tuulevaikus 1971, Väike reekviem suupillile 1972, Ohtlikud mängud 1974, Aeg elada, aeg armastada 1976, Pihlakaväravad 1982. *Honours:* People's Artist of the Estonian SSR 1977, 3rd Class Order of the White Star 2002. *Address:* c/o Estonian Composers' Union, A. Lauteri Street 7c, 10145 Tallinn, Estonia. *Telephone:* 646-6536 (office); 645-4395 (office); 648-5744 (home); 520-3339 (home). *E-mail:* heliloojatelüt@mail.ee (office); emie@emie .ee; ebba@hot.ee (home). *Website:* www.zzz.ee/edition49 (office).

**RABES, C.-A. Lennart;** Pianist, Harpsichordist, Organist and Conductor, Lecturer, Editor and Examiner; b. 1938, Eskilstuna, Sweden. *Education:* Music Academy, Zürich; Accademia Chigiana, Siena; ARCM, London; Studied Piano with Professor S Sundell, Stockholm, E Cavallo, Milan, B Siki, Zürich, M Tagliaferro, Paris; J von Karolyi, Munich; Studied Conducting with Paul von Kempen, Siena, Adrian Boult, London; BA, Music, Pacific Western University, Los Angeles, California, 1992. *Career:* Debut: As Pianist and Conductor, Stockholm, 1951; Performances in major cities of Europe, Canada and USA; Many recordings for Swedish, Austrian, French, Swiss and German broadcasting companies; Director, International Liszt Centre, Stockholm; Organist, various churches, Munich, 1960–66, Swiss Church, London, 1966–78; Founder, Musical Director, Deal Summer Music Festival, Deal, Kent, England, 1981–83, Sabylund Festival, Sweden, 1985–; Repetiteur at Norrlandsopera, Umea, 1985–88; Has given concerts at historical places including on Wagner's Erard at the Wagner Museum, Tribschen, Lucerne, Switzerland, 1985; Lecturer for research associations, universities radio and conservatories; Examiner, Associated Board, Royal Schools of Music, London; Working at Operastudio 67, Stockholm. *Recordings:* Piano works by Liszt. *Publications:* Liszt's Scandinavian Reputation, in Liszt and His World, 1998. *Address:* Synalsvagen 5, 16149 Bromma, Stockholm, Sweden.

**RABIN, Shira;** Violinist; b. 1 April 1970, Tel-Aviv, Israel. *Education:* Studied at the Juilliard School with Dorothy DeLay. *Career:* Debut: Played with the Israel Philharmonic 1979; Appeared in the International Huberman Week with Isaac Stern and the Israel Philharmonic 1983; Toured Europe 1983, Canada coast-to-coast tour 1985; Played with Henryk Szeryng during Israel Philharmonic Jubilee Season 1987; Soloist in the Stradivarius Year in Cremona; Israel representative in Italian Nights of Music with Zubin Mehta; Gala concert at Carnegie Hall with Isaac Stern; Musical Discovery of 1989 in Italy, after recital debut in Milan; German debut Feb 1991, with the Bavarian Radio Symphony Orchestra; US debut 1992 with the Philadelphia Orchestra under Riccardo Muti; Further concerts with the Pittsburgh Orchestra under Lorin Maazel. *Address:* c/o Israel Philharmonic Orchestra, PO Box 11292, 1 Huberman St, 61112 Tel-Aviv, Israel.

**RABSILBER, Michael;** Singer (Tenor); b. 8 Sept. 1953, Stassfurt, Magdeburg, Germany. *Education:* Studied at Leipzig Musikhochschule. *Career:* Debut: Stadttheater Halle 1980 in Wagner-Régeny's Die Burger von Calais; Sang at Halle until 1984 then joined the Komische Oper Berlin, with guest appearances in Leipzig and Dresden; Roles have included Mozart's Belmonte and Don Ottavio, Lensky, Ferrando Tamino, Max in Der Freischütz, Nicolai's Fenton and Pinkerton; Sang Zhivny in a production by Joachim Herz of Janáček's Osud, Dresden 1991; Florestan in Fidelio at the Komische Oper, 1997; Season 2000 as Fenton in Berlin and Tamino at the Loreley Festival; Frequent concert engagements. *Address:* c/o Komische Oper Berlin, Behrenstrasse 55–57, 1086 Berlin, Germany.

**RACETTE, Patricia;** Singer (Soprano); b. 1967, San Francisco, USA. *Education:* Studied with the Merola Opera Program, San Francisco. *Career:* Has sung with the San Francisco Opera from 1990, as Alice Ford, Rosalinde, Freia, Micaela, Mimi, Antonia and Mathilde in Guillaume Tell, 1997; Other roles include Musetta for Netherlands Opera and at the Metropolitan (1994), Ellen Orford for Vancouver Opera and Gluck's Iphigénie en Tauride at Saint Louis; Further appearances with the New York City and Vienna State Operas; Concerts include the Messa per Rossini and Stephen Albert's Flower in the Mountain, at San Francisco; Sang Emmeline Mostover in the premiere of Tobias Picker's Emmeline, Santa Fe, 1996, Mathilde at Washington, 1998; Sang Violetta and Offenbach's Antonia at the Met, 1999; Season 2000–01 as Ellen Orford at La Scala, Luisa Miller for San Francisco Opera and Jenůfa in Washington; Poulenc's Blanche at the Met, 2003. *Address:* c/o IMG Artists, Lovell House, 616 Chiswick High Road, London W4 5RX, England.

**RADETA, Zdenko;** Composer and Conductor; b. 16 Sept. 1955, Kragujevac, Yugoslavia; m. Miroslava Jankovic, 28 Sept. 1980, 2 s., 1 d. *Education:* Department of Composition and Orchestration and Department of Conducting, Faculty of Music, Belgrade; Advanced studies at Tchaikovsky Conservatoire, Moscow, 1991–92. *Career:* Debut: Four Sketches for chamber ensemble, 1974; Singer in Choir, Radio Television Belgrade; Producer, Radio Belgrade; Professor of Harmony and Counterpoint, Mokranjac Intermediate School, Belgrade; mem, Association of Composers of Serbia; SOKOJ. *Compositions:* 9 Piano pieces, 1972–90; Solo songs, 1974–84; 12 works for choirs, 1974–87; 1st String Quartet, 1980; Caleidoscope for 15 strings, 1985; Caleidoscope 2 for symphony orchestra, 1988; Gloomy Songs, Cyclus songs for voice, cor anglais and piano, 1998. *Recordings:* Permanent recordings for Radio Television Belgrade including Caleidoscope 2, 1st String Quartet, Remembrance for flute and piano, Wedding for mixed choir, and ballet Verities; Gloomy Songs, 1999. *Honours:* October Prize, City of Belgrade, 1974; SOKOJ Awards, 1983, 1984; 6 Awards from Association of Composers of Serbia. *Address:* Jurija Gagarina 186/4, 11070 Belgrade, Serbia and Montenegro.

**RADIGUE, Eliane;** Composer; b. 24 Jan. 1932, Paris, France; m. Arman, 17 Feb 1953, divorced 1971, 1 s., 2 d. *Education:* Studied with Pierre Schaeffer, Pierre Henry; School of the Arts, New York University, University of Iowa, California Institute of the Arts, USA. *Career:* Work with electronic sounds on tape; Recent performances: Salon des Artistes Decorateurs, Paris; Foundation Maeght, St Paul de Vence; Albany Museum of the Arts, New York; Gallery Rive Droite, Paris; Gallery Sonnabend, New York; Gallery Yvon Lambert, Paris; etc; Festivals including: Como, Italy; Paris Autumn; Festival Estival, Paris; International Festival of Music, Bourges, France; New York Cultural Center; Experimental Intermedia Foundation, New York; Vanguard Theater, Los Angeles; Mills College, Oakland, California; University of Iowa; Wesleyan University; San Francisco Art Institute. *Compositions include:* Environmental Music, 1969; OHMNT-Record Object, 1971; Labyrinthe Sonore, tape music, 1971; Chry-ptus, 1971; Geelriandre, 1972; Biogenesis, 1974; Adnos, 1975; Adnos II, 1980; Adnos III, 1982; Prelude a Milarepa, 1982; 5 songs of Milarepa, 1984; Jetsun Mila, 1986. *Recordings:* Songs of Milarepa, New York; Mila's Journey Inspired by a Dream; Jetsun Mila, New York. *Contributions:* Musique en Jeu, 1973; Art Press, 1974; Guide Musical, 1975. *Address:* 22 rue Liancourt, 75014 Paris, France.

**RADNOFSKY, Kenneth (Alan);** Saxophonist; b. 31 July 1953, Bryn Mawr, Pennsylvania, USA; m. Nancy Abramchuk, 1 May 1977, 2 d. *Education:* BM cum laude, University of Houston, Texas; MM, with honours, New England Conservatory of Music, Boston. *Career:* Carnegie Hall debut, 1985 Performance of Gunther Schuller Saxophone Concerto written for Radnofsky; European debut, 1987 with Leipzig Gewandhaus Orchestra as first ever Saxophone Soloist under direction of Kurt Masur; First ever saxophone soloist with Dresden Staatskapelle Orchestra and Pittsburgh Symphony Orchestra; Solo works premiered or dedicated to Radnofsky by Milton Babbitt, Donald Martino, Gunther Schuller, Morton Subotnick, Lee Hoiby, David Amram, Alan Hovhaness and John Harbison; Saxophonist with Boston Symphony, 1977–; Soloist with BBC, Boston Pops and numerous USA orchestras. *Recordings:* Soloist with New York Philharmonic in Debussy Rhapsody with Masur on Teldec, 1996; Bass clarinet in Schoenberg Kammersymphonie with Felix Galimir. *Contributions:* Numerous articles in Saxophone Journal. *Honours:* Appointed youngest member of Faculty, New England Conservatory, 1976. *Address:* PO Box 1016, E Arlington, MA 02174, USA.

**RADOVAN, Ferdinand;** Singer (baritone); b. 26 Jan. 1938, Rijeka, Yugoslavia. *Education:* Studied in Belgrade. *Career:* Debut: Belgrade National Opera 1964 as Germont; Sang at Ljubljana 1965–67, Graz 1967–74, Dortmund 1974–77; Guest appearances at Vienna Volksoper, Düsseldorf, Essen, Bordeaux and Prague and the State Operas of Hamburg and Munich; Returned to Yugoslavia 1977; Other roles have included Escamillo, Mozart's Count and Don Giovanni, Verdi's Rigoletto, Nabucco, Amonasro, Renato, Luna and Iago; Prince Igor, Scarpia, Barnaba in La Gioconda, Nélusko in L'Africaine, Jochanaan, Enrico, Gérard and Milhaud's Christophe Colombe; Concert and oratorio engagements. *Address:* Slovensko Narodno Gledalisce, Zupancicava 1, 61000 Ljubljana, Slovenia.

**RAE, Caroline (Anne);** Pianist and Musicologist; b. 7 Jan. 1961, Leeds, England; m. Peter Whittaker, 20 Aug 1993, two s. *Education:* BA, 1982, MA, 1986, DPhil, 1990, Somerville College, Oxford; Hochschule für Musik und Theater, Hannover, Germany, 1985–88; DiplMus (Distinction), 1988; Piano studies with Fanny Waterman, David Wilde, Yvonne Loriod-Messiaen, masterclasses with Karl-Heinz Kämmerling; French Government Scholarship, 1982–83; ARCM, 1984. *Career:* Debut: 1982; As pianist: Recitals, lecture-recitals, chamber music, masterclasses in the United Kingdom, Germany and France; Two-piano duo with Robert Sherlaw Johnson; Appearances for BBC television and Channel 4; As musicologist: College Tutor, Oxford University, 1984–88; Lecturer in Piano, Oxford Polytechnic, 1984, 1988; Lecturer, Department of Music, University of Wales, Cardiff, 1989–; Radio France Broadcast, 1992; Visiting Lecturer, University of Rouen, France, 1993; University of Köln, 2000; mem, Royal Musical Association. *Publications:* The Music of Maurice Ohana, Aldershot, 2000; Articles on 20th Century French music published in English, French and German. *Contributions:* New Grove Dictionaries; Musical Times; Cahiers Debussy; Les Cahiers du CIREM; NZM; Revista Musica; Contemporary Composers. *Address:* School of Music, Corbett Road, Cardiff University, CF10 3EB, Wales. *Telephone:* (29) 2087 4391. *Fax:* (29) 2087 4379. *E-mail:* rae@cardiff.ac.uk.

**RAE, (John) Charles Bodman,** MA, PhD, DMus, ARCM, FCLCM, FRSA; composer; b. 10 Aug. 1955, Catterick, England; m. Dorota Kwiatkowska 1984. *Education:* Cambridge University, Chopin Academy of Music, Warsaw; piano with Fanny Waterman; composition with Edward Cowie, Robert Sherlaw Johnson and Robin Holloway. *Career:* Broadcaster: Contributions as Writer, Presenter for BBC Radio 3 including Glocken, Cloches, Kolokola (six-hour series on European Bells); An Affair with Romanticism, features on Penderecki and Lutoslawski; Lecturer, Composition and Analysis, 1979–81, 1983–92, Head of School of Creative Studies, 1992–97, City of Leeds College of Music; Visiting Composer, University of Cincinnati College-Conservatory of Music, Ohio, USA, 1993; Director of Studies, Royal Northern College of Music, Manchester, 1997–2001; Elder Professor of Music, and Director/Dean of the Elder Conservatorium of Music, University of Adelaide, 2001–; mem, Royal Musical Association; Fellow, Royal Society of Arts; British Academy of Composers and Songwriters. *Compositions:* Six Verses of Vision, 1976; String Quartet, 1981; Jede Irdische Venus, 1982; Fulgura Frango, 1986; Donaxis Quartet, 1987. *Publications:* The Music of Lutoslawski, 1994, rev. 1999; Muzyka Lutoslawskiego, 1996; Bells in European Music. *Honours:* Fellowship, Leeds College of Music, 1999. *Address:* c/o Elder Conservatorium of Music, Elder Hall, University of Adelaide, SA 5005, Australia.

**RAEKALLIO, Matti Juhani,** DMus; pianist and professor; b. 14 Oct. 1954, Helsinki, Finland; m. 1st Sinikka Alstela 1977 (divorced 1996); m. 2nd Lara Lev 1998; one s. one d. *Education:* Turku Inst. of Music, private lessons with Maria Diamond Curcio, London, and with Dieter Weber, Vienna Music Acad., Austria, Leningrad Conservatory, Sibelius Acad., Finland. *Career:* debut as orchestra soloist, Turku 1971; solo, Helsinki 1975; extensive tours with all professional Finnish symphony orchestras, 1971–; recitals in Nordic countries 1971–, in Finland 1975–, in Central Europe 1979–; Recitals in USA, 1981–, in Japan, 1990–; First American tour as orchestra soloist with Helsinki Philharmonic Orchestra, 1983; Visiting Professor, Western MI University, 1984–85; Recitals in Helsinki Festival, 1981–97, Savonlinna Opera Festival, 1988–2000; Various Other Finnish and central European Festivals; Beethoven Complete Sonatas in 8 Finnish cities, 1989–91; Concerto repertoire includes over 60 works for Piano and Orchestra; Professor, Royal Swedish College of Music, Stockholm, 1994–1995; Associate Professor, Sibelius Academy, Helsinki, 1994–2001, full Professor, 2001; Member, commission for research of culture and society (Academy of Finland), 1998–2000; Board of Directors, Society for Finnish Concert Soloists. *Recordings include:* Complete Prokofiev Sonatas; about 20 albums; numerous for the archives of the Finnish Broadcasting Company. *Contributions:* several Finnish journals of music. *Address:* c/o Sibelius Academy, Pl 86, 00251, Helsinki, Finland.

**RAFFAELLI, Piero;** Italian violinist and violin teacher; b. 8 April 1949, Cesena; m. Santarelli Mariangela 1975; two d. *Education:* G. B. Martini Conservatory of Music, Bologna, masterclasses with various teachers. *Career:* debut 1968, Italy; radio appearances in Italy and Norway; Italian and European Concerts with Ensemble l Cameristi di Venezia; Solo Concerts with Capella Academica of Vienna, Italy; Chamber Music Group Layer and Soloist, Italy; Europe, North America with Italian Ensembles, 1971–73; Leader, Guitar Trio Paganini (also a viola player); Duo Recitals, Barcelona, Vienna, Berlin, Olso, Trondheim, Greece, Italy; Violin Teacher, Conservatory of Music, Bologna, 1978–. *Recordings:* With Ensemble E Melkus; Wien; Solo Violin Works by M Kich (Yugoton) dedicated to him, 1981; Contemporary Violin Chamber Music Recording, 1982. *Publications:* Revisions of Violin Works in First Printing for Zanibon and Violoncelo, 1979; A Vivaldi Concerto F 1 n 237 in D for violin, strings, cembalo, 1980; N Paganini 3 Duetti Concertanti for Violin and Violoncello, 1982. *Address:* Via Filli Latini 112, 47020, S. Giorgio di Cesena, Italy.

**RAFFALLI, Tibère;** Singer (Tenor); b. 1954, Corsica. *Career:* Sang Gabriele Adorno in Simon Boccanegra at Glyndebourne, 1986 (Gonzalve in L'Heure Espagnole, 1987); Bologna, 1987, as the Berlioz Faust, Montpellier, 1989, as Floresky in Cherubini's Lodoiska; Season 1990–91 as La ërte in Hamlet by A Thomas at Turin, Julien in Louise at Liège and Berlioz's Bénédict for Opéra de Lyon; Strasbourg, 1991, as Manalois in Martinů's Greek Passion; Other roles include Edgardo in Lucia di Lammermoor and Massenet's Werther. *Recordings include:* L'Heure Espagnole. *Address:* Opéra de Lyon, 1 Place de la Comédie, 69001 Lyon, France.

**RAFFANTI, Dano;** singer (tenor); b. 5 April 1948, Lucca, Italy. *Education:* La Scala School. *Career:* debut at La Scala School 1976, in Bussotti's Nottetempo; Verona 1978, in Orlando Furioso: Dallas 1980, in the US

premiere of Vivaldi's opera; San Francisco 1980, as Almaviva in Il Barbiere di Siviglia; Houston 1981–82, as Giacomo in La Donna del Lago by Rossini; Metropolitan Opera from 1981, as Alfredo, Rodolfo, the Duke of Mantua, Edgardo, Goffredo in Handel's Rinaldo and the Italian Singer in Der Rosenkavalier; Teatro San Carlos Naples and Covent Garden, 1983 and 1984, as Tebaldo in I Capuleti e i Montecchi by Bellini; Guest appearances in Hamburg, Berlin, Santiago, Bilbao and at the Landestheater Salzburg; Maggio Musicale Florence 1989, as Idomeneo; Sang the Duke of Mantua at Turin, Dec 1989; Florence 1990, as Ugo in Donizetti's Parisina; Season 1992 as Cléomène in Le Siège de Corinthe by Rossini at Genoa. *Recordings include:* Fra Diavolo (Cetra); I Capuleti e i Montecchi; La Donna del Lago.

**RAFFEINER, Walter;** Singer (Tenor); b. 8 April 1947, Wolfsberg, Germany. *Education:* Studied in Vienna and Cologne. *Career:* Debut: Sang at Hagen in Germany as a Baritone; Sang at Darmstadt as a Tenor, 1979 and appeared at Frankfurt from 1980 as Max, Parsifal, Florestan, Stolzius in Die Soldaten and the Painter and Negro in Lulu; Sang at Rouen and the Paris Opéra 1982, as Siegmund and Lohengrin; Guest appearances in Hamburg, Freiburg, Vienna, Düsseldorf and Munich; Salzburg Festival 1986, as Silvanus Schuller in the premiere of Penderecki's Schwarze Maske; Appeared as Siegmund with the Kassel Opera at the restored Amsterdam Opera House; Other roles have included Tristan, Pedro in Tiefland, Ivanovich in The Gambler, Sergei in Katerina Izmailova, Shuisky, Herod, Yannakos in Martinů's Greek Passion and Tichon in Katya Kabanova; Sang in the premiere of Lampersberg's Einöde der Welt, Bonn, 1995; Sang in the premiere of Gute Meine böses spiel by Karl-Wieland Kurz, Schwetzingen 2000. *Recordings:* Drum Major in Wozzeck.

**RAFFELL, Anthony;** Singer (Baritone); b. 1940, London, England. *Career:* Sang first with a touring company with the works of Gilbert and Sullivan; Opera debut at Glyndebourne 1966, in Werther by Massenet; Sang at Gelsenkirchen, Karlsruhe and Bremen; Debut, Covent Garden as Pantheus in The Trojans, 1969; Member of the Stuttgart Opera from 1985; Metropolitan Opera debut 1983, as Kurwenal, in Tristan und Isolde, returning as Hans Sachs, 1985; Appearances in Ring Cycles with the English National Opera and in Seattle; Further appearances as Klingsor in Turin, Wotan in Genoa, Jochanaan in Rio de Janeiro, Falstaff in Lisbon and at Parma, Trieste and Nancy; Metropolitan Opera 1989, as Gunther, in Götterdämmerung; Sang Telramund at Buenos Aires, 1991; Regularly at Vienna State Opera, Hamburg, Berlin and Stuttgart; More recently in Buenos Aires in Tales of Hoffmann, as a guest, 1993; Sang Wotan/Wanderer at Wiesbaden, 1994, Jochanaan in Switzerland, 1996 and Telramund and Wotan in Prague, 1997. *Recordings:* Video of Der Ring des Nibelungen, conducted by James Levine. *Current Management:* SK Management, 5 Meadscroft, 15 St John's Road, Eastbourne, BN20 7NQ, England.

**RAFTERY, J. Patrick;** Singer (baritone); b. 4 April 1951, Washington DC, USA. *Education:* Studied with Armen Boyajian. *Career:* Debut: Chicago Lyric Opera 1980, as Shchelkalov in Boris Godunov; European debut 1982, at the Théâtre du Châtelet, Paris, as Zurga in Les Pêcheurs de Perles; Glyndebourne 1984, as Guglielmo; Santa Fe, New Mexico, 1984 in Verdi's Il Corsaro and Gwendoline by Chabrier; Covent Garden debut 1985, as Mozart's Count; Further appearances with the New York City Opera and in Hamburg, Brussels, and Cologne; Santiago 1988, as Luna in Il Trovatore; Rome Opera 1988, as Puccini's Lescaut; Sang Belcore in L'Elisir d'amore at Genoa in 1989; Other roles include Escamillo, Mercutio (Roméo et Juliette), Eugene Onegin, Valentin (Faust), Yeletsky in The Queen of Spades and Rossini's Figaro; Sang Rossini's Figaro at Vancouver, 1991; Matho in the premiere of Fénélon's Salammbô, Paris Opéra Bastille, 1998; Sang Mozart's Lucio Silla at Lausanne, 2001.

**RAGACCI, Susanna;** Singer (Soprano); b. 1959, Stockholm, Sweden. *Education:* Studied in Florence. *Career:* Sang first at Rome as Rossini's Rosina, then appeared at Florence, Venice, Palermo, Turin and La Scala Milan; Sang Gilda in Dublin and at the Wexford Festival in Cimarosa's Astuzie Femminili; Opera di Wallonie in Liège 1987–88 as Rosina and as Egloge in Mascagni's Nerone; Sang at Bologna in the 1987 Italian premiere of Henze's English Cat and at Florence as the Italian Singer in Capriccio; Théâtre du Châtelet, Paris, 1992 as Sofia in Il Signor Bruschino. *Recordings:* Vivaldi's Catone in Utica and La Caduta di Adamo by Galuppi; I Pazzi per Progresso by Donizetti; L'Elisir d'amore.

**RAGATZU, Rosella;** Singer (Soprano); b. 1964, Cagliari, Sardinia. *Education:* Studied at the Cagliari Conservatory and with Magda Olivero and Claudio Desderi. *Career:* Sang Fiordiligi at Spoleto (1987) and Donna Anna at Treviso, 1989; Toured Italy, 1990, as Mozart's Countess and sang this role with Donna Anna at the 1991 Macerata Festival; Further guest appearances at the Leipzig Opera, Teatro Regio Turin (in Don Carlos) and at Frankfurt in a concert of Franchetti's Cristoforo Colombo (1991), as Queen Isabella; Mozart's Countess at Turin, 1998; Season 2000 as Mme Cortese in Il Viaggio a Reims at Liège and Rossini's Mathilde at the Vienna Staatsoper. *Honours:* Winner, 1987 Concorso Sperimento di Spoleto and 1989 Concorso Toti dal Monte, Treviso.

**RAGIN, Derek Lee,** BMus, MMT; American singer (countertenor); b. 17 June 1958, West Point, NY. *Education:* Arts High School, Newark, NJ, Newark Boys' Chorus School, Newark Community Center of Arts, Oberlin Conservatory of Music. *Career:* debut with Opera-Festwoche der Alten Musik, Innsbruck, Austria 1983; recital debut, Wigmore Hall, London 1984; recital

Aldeburgh Festival 1984; sang title role in Handel's Tamerlano at Lyon Opéra, France, at Göttingen Handel Festival; BBC debut recital 1984; debut at the Metropolitan Opera in Handel's Giulio Cesare 1988; recitals and oratorio in Frankfurt, Munich, Stuttgart, Cologne, Venice, Milan, Bologna, New York, Amsterdam, Maryland Handel Festival, London, Washington, Atlanta, Boston, San Francisco; made Salzburg debut in Gluck's Orfeo 1990; Gluck's Orfeo in Budapest 1991; season 1992 in Conti's Don Chisciotte at Innsbruck and as Britten's Oberon at Saint Louis; sang in Ligeti's Le Grand Macabre at the Paris Châtelet and the Salzburg Festival 1997; Hasse's Attilio regolo at Dresden 1997; sang in Legrenzi's La divisione del mondo at Innsbruck 2000. *Recordings:* Purcell's Dido and Aeneas (role of Spirit) 1985, Handel's Tamerlano (title role) 1985, Handel's Giulio Cesare (roles of Flavio and Tolomeo), Handel's Saul, Vivaldi Cantatas. *Current Management:* Colbert Artists Management Inc, 111 W 57th Street, New York, NY 10019, USA. *Telephone:* (212) 757-0782. *Fax:* (212) 541-5179. *E-mail:* nycolbert@colbertartists.com. *Website:* www.colbertartists.com.

**RAGNARSSON, Hjalmar (Helgi);** Composer; b. 23 Sept. 1952, Isafjordur, Iceland; m. Sigridur Asa Richardsdottir, 2 s., 1 d. *Education:* Isafjordur School of Music, 1959–69; Reykjavík College of Music, 1969–72; BA, Brandeis University, USA, 1974; Rijksuniversiteit Utrecht-Instituut voor Sonologie, Netherlands, 1976–77; MFA, Cornell University, USA, 1980. *Career:* Rector, Iceland Academy of the Arts, 1999–; mem, Composers Society of Iceland, President 1988–92; President, Federation of Icelandic Artists, 1991–98. *Compositions include:* Six songs to Icelandic Poems for voice and chamber ensemble, 1978–79; Romanza for flute, clarinet and piano, 1981; Canto for mixed choirs and synthesizer, 1982; Mass for mixed choir, 1982–89; Trio for clarinet, cello and piano, 1983–84; Five Preludes for piano, 1983–85; Tengsl for voice and string quartet, 1988; Spjotalög for orchestra, 1989; Raudur Thradur, ballet music for orchestra, 1989; Rhodymenia Palmata, chamber opera, 1992; Concerto for organ and orchestra, 1997; Music for theatre including Icelandic National Theatre and Reykjavík Municipal Theatre; Music for films: Tears of Stone, 1995; No Trace, 1998; Music for television films, Iceland State Television Service and Swedish State Television. *Recordings:* Conductor, Icelandic Choral works with the University Choir of Iceland; Own choral works for Hljomeyki Chamber Choir. *Publications:* Jon Leifs, Icelandic Composer: Historical Background, Biography, Analysis of Selected Works, MFA thesis, 1980; A Short History of Icelandic Music to the Beginning of the Twentieth Century, 1985; Film script: Tears of Stone, co-author, 1995. *Address:* Laekjarhjalli 22, 200 Kopavogur, Iceland.

**RAGUNATHAN, Sudha,** MA; Indian singer; d. of Smt. Choodamani. *Career:* studied under Padmavibushan Sangeetha Kalanidhi, Dr M.L. Vasanthakumari. *Recordings include:* albums: San Marga 1994 Kaleeya Krishna 1994, Classical Vocal 1994, Padmashri 2004, Om Meditation 2004, Shakti 2005. *Honours:* Amutha Isai Vani by Ikankai Thamil Sangam, USA 1988. *Current Management:* c/o Accords Croisés, 23 rue des Fontaines du Temple, 75003 Paris, France. *Telephone:* (1) 47-53-68-68 (office). *Fax:* (1) 47-53-68-69 (office). *E-mail:* info@accords-croises.com (office). *Website:* www.accords-croises.com (office). *E-mail:* sudaragu@vsnl.com. *Website:* www.sudharagunathan.com.

**RAICHEV, Rouslan;** Conductor; b. 2 May 1924, Milan, Italy. *Education:* Studied the piano in Milan, then with Leopold Reichwein, Emil Sauer and Karl Böhm in Vienna (until 1944). *Career:* Assistant at the Vienna Staatsoper 1942–43; Chief Conductor at the Königsberg Opera 1943–44; Conductor of the Varna Opera, Bulgaria, 1946–48; Conductor of the Sofia Opera 1948–89 (Musical Director 1981–89); Conducted the State Orchestra of Plovdiv 1968 and directed stage works at the Schleswig-Holstein Festival 1974–78; Guest conductor at the Vienna Staatsoper, La Scala Milan and the Paris Opéra. *Recordings include:* Rachmaninov Aleko.

**RAIMONDI, Gianni;** Singer (Tenor); b. 13 April 1923, Bologna, Italy. *Education:* Studied with Gennaro Barra-Caracciolo and with Ettore Campogalliani in Milan. *Career:* Debut: Bologna 1947, as the Duke of Mantua; Sang Pinkerton at Budrio, 1947; Bologna 1948, as Ernesto in Don Pasquale; Florence 1952, in Rossini's Armida, with Callas; London, Stoll Theatre, 1953; Naples 1955, in the premiere of Madame Bovary by Pannain; La Scala Milan from 1956, notably as Alfredo and as Lord Percy in Anna Bolena, opposite Callas, and in Mosè and Semiramide (1958, 1962); US debut San Francisco 1957; Verona Arena from 1957; Guest appearances in Vienna from 1959, Munich from 1960; Metropolitan Opera from 1965, as Rodolfo, Cavaradossi and Faust; Hamburg Staatsoper 1969–77; Other appearances in Paris 1953, Chicago, Dallas, Lisbon, Edinburgh, Geneva, Zürich and Helsinki; Other roles included Gabriele Adorno, Ismaele (Nabucco), Arrigo in Les Vêpres Siciliennes, Pollione, and Edgardo. *Recordings:* La Favorita (Cetra); La Traviata (Deutsche Grammophon); Linda di Chamounix; Maria Stuarda, with Callas; I Puritani; Armida. *Address:* c/o Teatro alla Scala, Via Filodrammtatici 2, Milan, Italy.

**RAIMONDI, Ruggero;** Monegasque singer (bass) and director; b. 3 Oct. 1941, Bologna, Italy; m. Isabel Maier 1987. *Career:* operatic début in La Bohème, Spoleto Festival 1964; début at Metropolitan Opera, New York in Ernani 1970; engagements include Don Giovanni, Le Nozze di Figaro, Faust, Attila, Nabucco, Don Carlos, Boris Godunov, Don Quichotte, Don Pasquale, Otello, Contes d'Hoffmann, Carmen, Il Viaggio a Rheims, Falstaff, I Vespri Siciliani, I Lombardi, L'Italiana in Algieri, Il Turco in Italia, Tosca, Assassinio nella Cattedrale, Cosi fan' Tutte and others. *Films:* Don Giovanni 1979, Six Characters in Search of an Author 1981, La Vie est un Roman 1982, Carmen

1985, Tosca 2001. *Opera productions include:* Don Giovanni, The Barber of Seville, Don Carlos. *Honours:* Commdr Ordre des Arts et Lettres, Officier de la Légion d'Honneur, Kt Order of Malta, Grand Ufficiale della Repubblica Italiana, Citizen of Honour (Athens), Commdr Ordre du Mérite Culturel (Monaco). *Address:* 140 bis rue Lecourbe, 75015 Paris, France.

**RAIMONDO, Ildiko;** Singer (Soprano); b. 11 Nov. 1962, Arad, Romania. *Education:* Studied at the Arad Conservatory. *Career:* Sang at Chemnitz from 1983 and from 1988 at the Vienna Kammeroper, in Dresden and at the Landestheater Linz; Bregenz Festival 1991 (as Micaela) and further appearances at the Vienna Volksoper and Staatsoper; Other roles have included Mozart's Zerlina, Susanna, Despina and Pamina, Sophie in Der Rosenkavalier and Walter in La Wally; Concerts include Masses by Mozart and Rossini, Die Schöpfung, the Verdi Requiem and Ein Deutsches Requiem; Marzelline in Fidelio at the 1996 Edinburgh Festival; Eurydice in Leopold I's Il figliol prodigo, Vienna, 1997. *Address:* c/o Staatsoper Vienna, Opernring 2, 1010 Vienna, Austria.

**RAITIO, Pentti;** Composer and Music Educator; b. 4 June 1930, Pieksamaki, Finland. *Education:* Studied composition with Joonas Kokkonen, 1961–63; Erik Bergman, 1963–66; Diploma, Sibelius Academy, Helsinki, 1966. *Career:* Director, Hyvinkaa School of Music, 1967–; Chairman, Lahti Organ Festival, 1981–85; Association of Finnish Music Schools, 1986–. *Compositions:* Orchestral: 13, 1964; Audiendum, 1967; 5 Pieces for String Orchestra, 1975; Petandrie, 1977; Noharmus, 1978; Noharmus II, 1980; Canzone d'autunno, 1982; Flute Concerto, 1983; Due figure, 1985; Yoldia arctica, 1987; Chamber: Small Pieces for brass instruments, 1984; Wind Quintet, 1975; Nocturne for violin and piano, 1977; Vocal: 3 Songs for soprano, 1962; The River, 7 Songs for soprano and 7 instruments, 1965; Along the Moonlit Path, 3 songs for soprano and 4 instruments, 1965; Orphean Chorus, 3 songs for baritone and men's chorus, 1966; 3 Songs for baritone and string quartet, 1970; One Summer Evening for men's chorus, 1971; Song for men's chorus, 1972; Song for a Rain Bird for baritone and piano, 1974; I'm Looking at the River, 6 songs for women's or youth chorus, 1986. *Address:* c/o Hyvinkaa School of Music, 05800 Hyvinkaa, Finland.

**RAJNA, Thomas,** DMus, ARCM; British composer and pianist (retd); b. 21 Dec. 1928, Budapest; s. of the late Dr Nandor Rajna and Hella Eisen; m. Anthea Valentine Campion 1967; one s. two d. *Education:* Nat. Musical School, Budapest, Franz Liszt Acad. of Music, Budapest and Royal Coll. of Music, London. *Career:* freelance composer, pianist and teacher, London 1951–63; Prof. of Piano, Guildhall School of Music 1963–70; Lecturer, Univ. of Surrey 1967–70; Sr Lecturer in Piano, Faculty of Music, Univ. of Cape Town 1970–89, Assoc. Prof. 1989–93; launched own record label Amarantha Records 2001; Fellow, Univ. of Cape Town 1981. *Compositions include:* film and ballet music, orchestral and chamber music, two piano concertos, Harp Concerto 1990, Amarantha (opera in 11 scenes) 1991–94, Video Games (for orchestra) 1994, Rhapsody for clarinet and orchestra 1995, Fantasy for violin and orchestra 1996, Suite for violin and harp 1997, Stop All the Clocks (four songs on poems by W. H. Auden) 1998, The Creation – A Negro Sermon for unaccompanied choir 2000, Valley Song (opera) 2002–04, Tarantula for violin and piano 2001. *Recordings include:* works by Stravinsky, Messiaen, Scriabin, Granados, Liszt, Schumann, Dohnanyi and own compositions: Amarantha, Suite for violin and harp, Rhapsody for clarinet and orchestra. *Publications:* Dialogues for clarinet and piano 1970, Concerto for harp and orchestra, Suite for violin and piano, Tarantulla for violin and piano 2001. *Honours:* DMus (Cape Town) 1985 Liszt Prize, Budapest 1947, Artes Award (SABC) 1981, UCT Book Award 1996, Cape Tercentenary Foundation Merit Award 1997. *Address:* 10 Wyndover Road, Claremont, Cape Town, West Cape 7708, South Africa (home). *Telephone:* (21) 671 3937 (home). *Fax:* (21) 671 3937 (home). *E-mail:* trajna@telkomsa.net (home). *Website:* www.cama.org.za.

**RAKOWSKI, Andrzej,** MA, MSc, PhD, DSc; Polish musicologist and acoustician; *Chair of Musicology, A. Mickiewicz University;* b. 16 June 1931, Warsaw; m. Magdalena Jakobczyk 1972; one s. two d. *Education:* Univ. of Durham, UK, Warsaw Univ. of Technology, Warsaw Univ., State Coll. of Music in Warsaw. *Career:* Prof. of Musical Acoustics 1963–2001, Prof. Emer. 2001–; Pres. 1981–87, Chopin Acad. of Music, Warsaw; part-time Prof., Inst. of Musicology, Warsaw Univ. 1987–2003; Chair. of Musicology, A. Mickiewicz Univ. 1997–; Visiting Prof., McGill Univ., Montreal, Canada 1985, Hebrew Univ., Jerusalem, Israel 1991, Central Inst. for the Deaf, St Louis, Mo., USA 1997–98, Univ. Nova de Lisboa, Portugal 2004; mem. Polish Music Council (Vice-Pres. 1984–89), Union of Polish Composers, Polish Acad. of Sciences (Pres. Acoustical Cttee 1996–), European Soc. for Cognitive Sciences of Music (Pres. 2000–03); Fellow, Acoustical Soc. of America 2001–. *Publications:* Categorical Perception of Pitch in Music 1978, The Access of Children and Youth to Musical Culture 1984, Studies on Pitch and Timbre of Sound in Music (ed.) 1999, Creation and Perception of Sound Sequences in Music (ed.) 2002; contrib. over 100 articles on music perception and music acoustics to int. journals. *Honours:* Golden Cross of Merit 1973, Bachelor's Cross (Order of Polonia Restituta) 1983, Officer's Cross 2002. *Address:* Fryderyk Chopin Academy of Music, Okolnik 2, 00-368 Warsaw (office); Pogonowskiego 20, 01-564 Warsaw, Poland (home). *Telephone:* (22) 827-8303 (office); (22) 839-9456 (home). *Fax:* (22) 827-8310 (office). *E-mail:* rakowski@chopin.edu.pl. *Website:* www.chopin.edu.pl/angielskie/osobowe/rakowski.html (office).

**RAMEY, Phillip,** BA, MA; American composer; b. 12 Sept. 1939, Elmhurst, IL. *Education:* Int. Acad. of Music, Nice with A. Tcherepnin, De Paul Univ.,

Chicago, Columbia Univ., New York with Jack Beeson. *Career:* programme ed., New York Philharmonic 1977–93; freelance composer, with premieres in New York, Boston, Sacramento, Chicago, London, Aldeburgh Festival, Tangier, Vilnius, Montreux; Vice-Pres. USA, The Tcherepnin Soc. 2002–. *Compositions include:* five piano sonatas 1961, 1966, 1968, 1988, 1989 (for left hand), Concert Suite for piano and small orchestra 1962 (revised, reorchestrated and expanded 1984 as Concert Suite for piano and orchestra), Music for brass and percussion 1964, Orchestral Discourse 1967, Night Music for percussion 1967, Suite for violin and piano 1971, three piano concertos 1971, 1976, 1994, La Citadelle, Rhapsody for oboe and piano 1979, A William Blake Trilogy for soprano and piano 1980, Moroccan Songs to Words of Paul Bowles for high voice and piano 1982–86, Proclamation for orchestra (orchestration of Aaron Copland's Proclamation for piano) 1985, Concerto for horn and strings 1987, Rhapsody for cello 1992, Trio Concertant for violin, horn and piano 1993, Tangier Portraits for piano 1991–99, La Citadelle for horn and piano 1994, Praeludium for five horns 1994, Color Etudes for piano 1994, Gargoyles for horn 1995, Elegy for horn and piano 1995, Nightfall aria for flute and piano 1996, Concertino for four horns, timpani and percussion 1996, Sonata-Ballade for two horns and piano 1997, Dialogue for two horns 1997, Phantoms (Ostinato Etude) for piano 1997, Sonata for harpsichord 1998, Effigies for viola and piano 1998, Lyric Fragment for flute and harpsichord (or piano) 1998, Lament for Richard III for piano 2001, Color Etudes for piano and orchestra (arranged from Color Etudes for piano) 2002, Orchestral Epigrams 2002, Winter Nocturne for piano 2003, Ode for FDR for piano 2004. *Publications:* Irving Fine: An American Composer in his Time 2005. *Address:* 825 West End Avenue, Penthouse F, New York, NY 10025, USA (office). *Telephone:* (212) 866-1063 (office). *Fax:* (212) 866-2550 (office). *E-mail:* bklisenbee@aol.com.

**RAMEY, Samuel;** American singer (bass-baritone); b. 28 March 1942, Kolby, KS. *Education:* Wichita State Univ. with Arthur Newman, studied in New York with Armen Boyajian. *Career:* debut, New York City Opera as Zuniga in Carmen 1973, returned as Mephistopheles (Gounod and Boito), Attila, Don Giovanni, Henry VIII (Anna Bolena) and Massenet's Don Quichotte; Glyndebourne debut as Mozart's Figaro 1976; Nick Shadow in The Rake's Progress 1977; guest appearances in Hamburg, San Francisco, Chicago and Vienna, as Colline in La Bohème, Figaro, and Arkel in Pelléas et Mélisande; Covent Garden debut 1982, returned to London for a concert performance of Semiramide 1986 and as Philip II in Don Carlos 1989; Metropolitan Opera debut 1984, as Argante in Rinaldo 1986–87 as Walton in I Puritani and Escamillo; Pesaro 1984, in a revival of Rossini's Il Viaggio a Reims; Bartók's Bluebeard at the Met 1989; Pesaro Festival 1986 (Maometto II) and 1989 (La Gazza Ladra); Munich as Mephistopheles 1988; Don Giovanni at Salzburg from 1987, Metropolitan and Maggio Musicale, Florence 1990; season 1992–93 as Attila at San Francisco and Geneva, Rossini's Basilio at the Met, Philip II in Venice and New York, the Hoffmann Villains and Berlioz Mephistopheles at Covent Garden, and Nick Shadow at Aix-en-Provence; sang Mephistopheles in a new production of Faust at the Vienna Staatsoper 1997; other roles include the villains in Les Contes d'Hoffmann, Verdi's Renato and Banquo, and Mozart's Leporello; Covent Garden 1997, as Verdi's Fiesco and Oberto; Philippe in Don Carlo at the Paris Opéra Bastille 1998; season 2000–01 as Verdi's Zaccaria at Houston; Attila for the Chicago Lyric Opera and Rossini's Mustafà at the Met; Don Quichotte 2001. *Recordings:* Bach B Minor Mass, I Due Foscari, Un Ballo in Maschera, Ariodante, Lucia di Lammermoor, Maometto II, Petite Messe solenelle, Haydn's Armida, Le nozze di Figaro, The Rake's Progress, Il Turco in Italia, La Donna del Lago, Il Viaggio a Reims, Don Giovanni. *Current Management:* IMG Artists, Lovell House, 616 Chiswick High Road, London, W4 5RX, England. *Telephone:* (20) 8233-5800. *Fax:* (20) 8233-5801. *E-mail:* artistseurope@imgworld.com. *Website:* www.imgartists.com.

**RAMICOVA, Dunya;** Costume Designer; b. 1950, Czechoslovakia. *Education:* Studied at Yale School of Drama. *Career:* Has collaborated with Director Stephen Wadsworth on Jenůfa and Fliegende Holländer for Seattle Opera, Fidelio for Scottish Opera and La Clemenza di Tito for Houston Grand Opera; Costume designs for Peter Sellars production of Die Zauberflöte and The Electrification of the Soviet Union at Glyndebourne, Tannhäuser at Chicago, Nixon in China for Houston and St François d'Assise at Salzburg, 1992; Premiere of The Voyage by Philip Glass at the Metropolitan, 1992, production by David Pountney; Covent Garden, 1992, costumes for Alcina; Costumes for the house premiere of Mathis der Maler, Covent Garden, 1995, Tan Dun/Peter Sellars Peony Pavilion, Vienna, 1998. *Address:* c/o Metropolitan Opera, Lincoln Center, New York, NY 10023, USA.

**RAMIREZ, Alejandro;** Singer (Tenor); b. 2 Sept. 1946, Bogota, Columbia. *Education:* Qualified as Doctor of Medicine, then studied singing at Conservatory of Bogota; Further study at the Musikhochschule Freiburg, 1973–75; Completed studies with Annelies Kupper in Munich and Gunther Reich in Stuttgart. *Career:* Sang in Pforzheim, 1975–77, Kaiserslautern, 1977–80; Member of Mannheim Opera, 1980–82, Frankfurt from 1982; Covent Garden, London, 1984 as Nemorino in L'Elisir d'amore; Vienna Staatsoper, 1985 as Alfredo; Salzburg Festival in 1985 in the Henze/Monteverdi Il Ritorno d'Ulisse; Other roles include Belmonte, Don Ottavio, Tamino, Ferrando, Jacquino in Berlin 1984, Elvino in La Sonnambula, Rossini's Almaviva and Lindoro, Strauss's Narraboth and Flamand, Rodolfo and Edgardo; Concert repertoire includes the Evangelist in the Bach Passions, and works by Handel, Bruckner, Schumann, Dvořák, Beethoven and Verdi; Bavarian State Opera as Don Ottavio, Frankfurt, 1980–85; La Scala Milan in 1988 as Henry Morosus in

R Strauss's Schweigsame Frau, 1990; Season 1992 as Rodolfo at Bonn and Tamino at Düsseldorf; Professor of Singing at the Musikhochschule of Mannheim, Germany; Sang Pollione in Norma at Karlsrune, 2000. *Recordings include:* Schumann's Manfred; St John Passion and Christmas Oratorio by Bach; Sacred Music by Schubert, Mendelssohn and Charpentier; The Seven Last Words by Schütz; Mozart's Nozze di Figaro under Riccardo Muti. *Address:* Andersenstrasse 55, 68259 Mannheim, Germany.

**RAMIRO, Yordi;** Singer (Tenor); b. 1948, Acapulco, Mexico. *Career:* Debut: Mexico City, 1977, as Pinkerton; Sang at the Vienna Staatsoper from 1978 and guested at the San Francisco Opera, 1979, as Rinuccio in Gianni Schicchi; Further appearances at Seattle as Alfredo, Barcelona as Rodolfo (1980) and Mexico City as Edgardo; Strasbourg, 1983, as Gounod's Roméo; Covent Garden, 1984, in Der Rosenkavalier and Arturo in I Puritani at the 1985 Bregenz Festival; Metropolitan Opera debut, 1985, as Paco in La Vida Breve; Other roles include Ernesto in Don Pasquale, Nemorino, the Duke of Mantua and Tebaldo in I Capuleti by Bellini. *Recordings include:* Rigoletto and La Traviata (Naxos). *Address:* c/o Staatsoper Vienna, Opernring 2, 1010 Vienna, Austria.

**RAMSAY, Dervla;** Northern Irish singer (mezzo-soprano); b. 25 Aug. 1970, Derry, N Ireland. *Education:* Guildhall School of Music and Drama, London; Studies with Renata Scotto and Margarita Rinaldi. *Career:* debut, sang Volpino in Haydn's Lo Speziale, Bagno di Lucca, 1994; Janissary in Mozart's Die Entführung at Covent Garden, 2000; Countess Ceprano in Rigoletto; Page in Wagner's Lohengrin; Train bearer in Strauss' Elektra, Royal Opera House, Covent Garden; mem. Royal Opera Chorus, 1999–. *Honours:* Winner, Ulster Bank's Music Foundation Award for Young Musicians, 1993; Concorso Intermazionale di Bagna di Lucca, 1994. *Address:* c/o Royal Opera House (chorus), Covent Garden, London, WC2, England.

**RAN, Shulamit,** PhD; American/Israeli composer; b. 21 Oct. 1949, Tel-Aviv, Israel; d. of Zvi and Berta Ran; m. Abraham N. Lotan 1986; one s. *Education:* Mannes Coll. of Music (New York). *Career:* Moved to USA 1963; William H. Colvin Prof. of Composition Univ. of Chicago, IL 1973–; Visiting Prof. Princeton Univ., NJ 1987; Composer-in-Residence Chicago Symphony Orchestra 1990–; Brena and Lee Freeman, Sr Composer-in-Residence Lyric Opera of Chicago 1994; Visiting Prof. Princeton Univ. 1987; works performed by New York Philharmonic Orchestra 1963, Israel Philharmonic Orchestra 1971, Chamber Music Soc. (Lincoln Center, New York) 1987, Chicago Symphony Orchestra 1988, 1991, 1993, 1995, Philadelphia Orchestra 1990, Cleveland Orchestra 1991, 1993, Orchestre de la Suisse Romande, Amsterdam Philharmonic; piano performances in the USA, Europe and Israel; numerous comms; Fellow American Acad. of Arts and Sciences; Dr hc (Mount Holyoke Coll) 1988, (Spertus Inst) 1994, (Beloit Coll) 1996; Guggenheim Foundation Awards 1977, 1990; American Acad. and Inst. of Arts and Letters Award 1989. *Works include:* O the Chimneys 1969, Concert Piece for Piano and Orchestra 1970, Hyperbolae 1977, Verticals 1983, Sonata-Waltzer 1983, String Quartet No 1 1984, Concerto da Camera I 1985, Concerto for Orchestra 1986, Concerto for Orchestra 1986, East Wind (for solo flute) 1987, Concerto da Camera II 1987, String Quartet No 2 (Vistas) 1988–89, Mirage for 5 Players 1990, Symphony (Pulitzer Prize in Music) 1991, Legends for Orchestra 1993, Between Two Worlds: The Dybbuk, Opera 1994–95 (premiered at Chicago 1997). *Address:* University of Chicago, Dept of Music, 5801 S Ellis Ave, Chicago, IL 60637, USA.

**RANACHER, Christa;** Singer (Soprano); b. 12 Dec. 1953, Dollach in Kärnten, Austria. *Education:* Studied in Vienna and attended master classes by Mario del Monaco and Elisabeth Schwarzkopf. *Career:* Sang at Regensburg, 1984–85, Monchengladbach from 1985, Leonore in Fidelio, 1989; Further appearances at Gelsenkirchen, Mannheim, Munster, Hannover, the Deutsche Oper Berlin, Staatsoper Munich and Zürich; Season, 1992, as Salome at Dusseldorf and Shostakovich's Katerina Izmailova at Berne; Other roles include Mozart's Countess and Donna Anna, Agathe, Marenka in The Bartered Bride, Senta, and Ada in Wagner's Die Feen, Tosca, Santuzza, Zdenka, Arabella, Judith in the opera by Siegfried Matthus, Sophie in Cerha's Baal and Andromache in Troades by Reimann; Sang Stella in Goldschmidt's Der Gewaltige Hahnrei, Bonn, 1995; Noted concert performer; Season 2000 as Andromache in Troades, at Berlin, and Amélia in Clara by Hans Gefors, for Berne Opera. *Address:* c/o Stadttheater Bern, Nägeligasse 1, CH –3011 Berne, Switzerland.

**RANCATORE, Desirée;** Singer (Soprano); b. 1972, Sicily. *Education:* Studied with Margaret Baker-Genovesi. *Career:* Debut: Mozart's Barbarina at the 1996 Salzburg Festival; Appearances at Bologna in Figaro, at Parma in L'Arlesiana and as Frasquita in Carmen at Genoa; Flowermaiden in Parsifal at Florence and the Opéra Bastille, Paris; Sophie in Der Rosenkavalier at Palermo and Gilda at the San Francisco Opera, 2000–01; Covent Garden debut as Nannetta in Falstaff, repeated at the Vienna Staatsoper; Further engagements in Don Carlos at Salzburg and Die Zauberflöte at the Bastille; Blonde in Die Entführung at Salzburg and in film conducted by Charles Mackerras. *Recordings:* DVD of Nannetta in Falstaff, Covent Garden. *Honours:* Winner, 1996 Maria Caniglia Competition. *Address:* c/o Opéra Bastille, 120 Rue de Lyon, 75012 Paris, France.

**RANDLE, Thomas;** Singer (Tenor); b. 21 Dec. 1958, Hollywood, California, USA. *Education:* Studied at the University of Southern California. *Career:* Concert appearances in the USA and Europe with the London Philharmonic Orchestra, Boston Symphony Orchestra and the Leipzig Radio Symphony

Orchestra; Conductors include Helmuth Rilling, Gennadi Rozhdestvensky, Michael Tilson Thomas and André Previn; Has sung Berg and Stravinsky, and the US and world premieres of works by Tippett, Heinz Holliger and William Kraft, with the Los Angeles Philharmonic; Often heard in Bach, Handel and Mozart; Bach's Christmas Oratorio in Leipzig; Operatic repertoire includes all the major tenor roles of Mozart, Rossini and Donizetti, and French roles of Massenet and Thomas; British debut as Tamino in Nicholas Hytner's production of The Magic Flute (English National Opera, 1988, returned, 1989); European opera debut at the Aix-en-Provence Festival, France, in Purcell's The Fairy Queen; Sang Monteverdi's Orfeo at Valencia, 1989; Ferrando in Brussels and with Scottish Opera; Sang Tamino at Glyndebourne, 1991; Sang Dionysius in the premiere of John Buller's The Bacchae and as Pelléas, English National Opera, 1992; Sang title role in reduced version of Pelléas et Mélisande with Peter Brook in Paris and European tour, Netherlands Opera in world premiere of Peter Schaat's opera Symposion, based on Life of Tchaikovsky, in 1994; Season 1994 returned to English National Opera to sing Tippett's King Priam and appeared in Britten's Gloriana at Covent Garden; Fairy Queen at ENO, 1995; Sang Idomeneo for Scottish Opera, 1996 and Mozart's Lucio Silla at Garsington, 1998; Recent engagements include: Tom Rakewell in The Rake's Progress with Netherlands Opera; Title role in Hasse's Solimano at the Staatsoper, Berlin, and Alfredo in La Traviata for Opera North; Sang in the premiere of The Last Supper by Birtwistle, Berlin Staatsoper, 2000; Season 2000–01 as Schubert's Fierrabras at Buxton, Loge in The Rheingold for ENO, Berlioz's Bénédict for WNO and in Handel's Tamerlano at Halle; Handel's Samson at the London Proms, 2002. *Recordings:* Purcell's Fairy Queen with Les Arts Florissants; Tippett's The Ice Break with London Sinfonietta; Britten's War Requiem with BBC Scottish Symphony Orchestra; Luigi Nono, Canti di Vita e d'Amore with Bamberg Symphony Orchestra; Mozart's Requiem with German National Youth Orchestra; Handel's Esther with Harry Christophers and The Sixteen; Requiem of Reconciliation with Helmuth Rilling and the Israel Philharmonic Orchestra; Handel's Messiah with the Royal Philharmonic Orchestra; Handel's Samson with Harry Christophers and the Symphony of Harmony and Invention. *Address:* c/o IMG Artists Europe, Lovell House, 616 Chiswick High Road, London W4 5RX, England.

**RANDOLPH, David,** BS, MA; American conductor, writer, lecturer and broadcaster; *Conductor, The St Cecilia Chorus and Orchestra;* b. 21 Dec. 1914, New York, NY; m. Mildred Greenberg 1948. *Education:* City Coll. of New York, Teachers Coll., Columbia Univ. *Career:* Conductor, The Masterwork Chorus and Orchestra, The St Cecilia Chorus and Orchestra 1965–, at Carnegie Hall, Avery Fisher Hall, Kennedy Center, Washington, DC; numerous choral works, including Bach's B Minor Mass, St Matthew Passion, St John Passion, Magnificat, Christmas Oratorio, Brahms' Requiem, Schickelslied, Nänie, Gesang der Parzen, Mozart's Requiem, Vaughan Williams's Sea Symphony and Hodie, Dona Nobis Pacem, and Mass in G Minor, Haydn's Mass in Time of War, Orff's Carmina Burana, Beethoven's Mass in C and Missa Solemnis, Mozart's Mass in C Minor, Mendelssohn's Symphony No. 2, Elijah and Die erste Walpurgisnacht, Poulenc's Gloria, Rutter's Gloria, Kodály's Te Deum, 171 complete performances of Handel's Messiah, Haydn's St Cecilia Mass, Theresienmesse, Lord Nelson Mass, Dvořák's Requiem; guest conductor with The Philharmonia Orchestra (Barbican Centre, London), with Brahms' Requiem 1988; pre-concert lecturer, New York Philharmonic, Cleveland Orchestra, Vienna Symphony Orchestra; Conductor, David Randolph Singers; season 2000–01 with Beethoven's Ninth and The Music Makers by Elgar; season 2001–02 with Rachmaninoff's The Bells; season 2002–03 with Puccini's Messa di Gloria. *Compositions:* A Song for Humanity (Edward) 1936, Andante for Strings 1937. *Recordings:* works by Monteverdi, Schütz, Handel's Messiah, writer and narrator The Instruments of the Orchestra 1995, Madrigals of Weelkes, Bateson, Wilbye, Gesualdo, 13 Modern American Madrigals, The Triumphs of Oriana. *Publication:* This is Music: A Guide to the Pleasures of Listening 1964. *Honours:* Columbia Univ. Distinguished Alumni Award, Coll. of the City of New York Townsend Harris Medal. *Address:* 420 E 86th Street, Apt 4C, New York, NY 10028-6456, USA. *Telephone:* (212) 744-1444. *E-mail:* schapin@nyc.tt.com. *Website:* www .stceciliachorus.org.

**RANDOVÁ, Eva;** Singer (mezzo-soprano); b. 31 Dec. 1936, Kolin, Czechoslovakia. *Education:* Studied with J. Svanova at Usti nad Labem, and at the Prague Conservatory. *Career:* Sang first at Ostrava, as Eboli, Carmen, Amneris, the Princess in Rusalka, and Ortrud; Prague National Opera from 1969; Nuremberg and Stuttgart from 1971; Bayreuth Festival from 1973, as Gutrune, Fricka and Kundry; Salzburg Festival, 1975, Eboli in Don Carlos, conducted by Karajan; Covent Garden debut, 1977, as Ortrud; Returned to London as Marina, Venus, the Kostelnicka in Jenůfa, 1986, and Azucena in a new production of Il Trovatore, 1989; Metropolitan Opera, 1981, 1987, as Fricka and Venus; Orange Festival, 1985, as Marina in Boris Godunov; Vienna, 1987, in Rusalka; Sang Ortrud at San Francisco, 1989, Stuttgart, 1990; Sang Marina in Boris Godunov at Barcelona, 1990; Season 1992 as Clytemnestra at Athens; Covent Garden, 1994, as Kabanicha in Katya Kabanova (returned 1997); Sang Erda in Siegfried at Stuttgart, 1999; Grandmother in Jenůfa at Covent Garden, 2001; Frequent concert engagements; Jury Member, 1999 Cardiff Singer of the World Competition. *Recordings:* Bach cantatas; Santuzza in Cavalleria Rusticana; Mahler's Resurrection Symphony; Glagolitic Mass by Janáček; Šarka by Fibich; The Cunning Little Vixen and Jenůfa, conducted by Charles Mackerras. *Current Management:* Askonas Holt Ltd, Lonsdale Chambers, 27 Chancery Lane,

London, WC2A 1PF, England. *Telephone:* (20) 7400-1700. *Fax:* (20) 7400-1799. *E-mail:* info@askonasholt.co.uk. *Website:* www.askonasholt.co.uk.

**RANDS, Bernard,** MMus; British composer and conductor; b. 2 March 1935, Sheffield, Yorkshire, England. *Education:* Univ. of Wales, Bangor; studied in Italy with Dallapiccola, Boulez, Maderna and Berio. *Career:* instructor in the music dept, York Univ. 1968–74; Fellowship in Creative Arts, Brasenose Coll., Oxford 1972–73; Prof. of Music, Univ. of California, San Diego 1976; Visiting Prof., California Inst. of the Arts, Valencia 1984–85; worked at electronic music studios in Milan, Berlin, Albany (New York), Urbana; appearances as conductor of new music, notably with the London Sonor ensemble; founder mem., music theatre ensemble CLAP. *Compositions:* Serena, music theatre, 1972–78; Orchestral: Per Esempio, 1968; Wildtrack I–III, 1969–75; Agenda, 1970; Mesalliance, 1972; Ology for jazz group, 1973; Aum, 1974; Serenata 75b, flute, chamber orchestra, 1976; Hirath, cello, orchestra, 1987;... Body and Shadow..., 1988; Instrumental: Espressioni, series of piano pieces, 1960–70; Actions for Six, 1962; Formants I, II, 1965–70; Tableau, 1970; Memo 1–5, solo pieces, 1971–75; Dejà I, 1972; As all get out, 1972; Etendre, 1972; Response, double bass, tape, 1973; Scherzi, 1974; Cuaderna for string quartet, 1975; Madrigali, 1977; Obbligato, string quartet, trombone, 1980;... In the Receding Mist..., flute, harp, string trio, 1988; 2 String Quartets, 1974, 1994; Vocal: Ballad 103, 1970–73; Metalepsis 2 for mezzo, 1971; Lunatici, soprano, ensemble, 1980; Dejà 2, soprano, ensemble, 1980; Sound Patterns, various combinations with voices; Canti del Sole, tenor, orchestra, 1983; London Serenade, 1984; Le Tambourin, suite 1, 2, 1984; Ceremonial, 1, 2, 1985–86; Serenata 85, 1985; Requiescat, soprano, chorus, ensemble, 1985–86;... Among the Voices..., chorus, harp, 1988; Canzoni per Orchestra, 1995; Symphony, 1995; Cello Concerto, 1996; Triple Concerto, 1997; Requiescant for soprano, chorus and orchestra, 1997; Opera commission for the Aspen Festival, 1999. *Honours:* Hon. Fellow, Univ. of Wales, Bangor 2003; Pulitzer Prize for Canti del Sole 1984. *Current Management:* Universal Edition (London) Ltd, 48 Great Marlborough Street, London, W1F 7BB, England. *Telephone:* (20) 7437-6880. *Fax:* (20) 7437-6115. *Website:* www.bernardrands.com.

**RANGEL(-LATOUCHE), César,** Concert Pianist and Pedagogue; b. 3 April 1950, Caracas, Venezuela; m. María Cristina Graterol, 1 April 1995, 1 s. *Education:* Bachelor of Music, Juilliard School of Music, New York; Master of Music, Doctor of Music, Piano Performance, Indiana University; Diploma in Performance, Conservatory Juan Manuel Olivares. *Career:* Debut: Carnegie Recital Hall, New York; Extensive performances throughout USA; Invited by President of Venezuela to recital tour throughout the country; Repertoire includes: Bach's Goldberg Variations; Complete cycle, Beethoven Sonatas; Chopin, 24 Preludes and Etudes; Ravel's Gaspard de la Nuit; Stravinsky's Petrouchka; Performed Bartók's Second Piano Concerto, International Festival, Caracas; Television and radio appearances include Spain Radio and Television TVE, BBC; Performed Beethoven's Fifth Concerto with the Venezuelan Symphony Orchestra under Irwin Hoffmann; Recent engagements include concert at Konzerthaus in Berlin with Beethoven's Fifth Piano Concerto, with Berliner Symphoniker under Eduardo Marturet; Teacher, Piano Performance, Master's Programme, Simón Bolívar University, Caracas. *Recordings:* Chopin Etudes op 10, 25; Schubert Sonatas in G major and B Flat major; Beethoven Sonatas op 109, 110, 111; Beethoven's Emperor Concerto. *Address:* Calle Loma Larga 30, Los Guayalitos, Baruta, Caracas 1081, Venezuela.

**RANGELOV, Svetozar;** Singer (Bass); b. 1967, Bulgaria. *Education:* Graduated, State Musical Academy, Sofia, 1994. *Career:* Many concert and opera engagements in Bularia and elsewhere in Europe; Opera debut as Ferrando in Il Trovatore with the Bulgarian National Opera, 1995; Repertory also includes Le nozze di Figaro, Verdi's Vespri Siciliani and songs by Glière, Cui and Borodin; Contestant at the 1995 Cardiff Singer of the World Competition. *Address:* j.k. Druzba, bl.43, entr 7, ap 114, Sofia 1592, Bulgaria.

**RÁNKI, Dezső;** Hungarian pianist; b. 8 Sept. 1951, Budapest; s. of József Ránki and Edith Jecsmen; m. Edit Klukon 1979; two c. *Education:* Ferenc Liszt Music Acad., Budapest (under Pál Kadosa). *Career:* has given recitals and appeared with several leading orchestras throughout Europe, including Berlin Philharmonic, Concertgebouw and London Philharmonic; regular concert tours N America and Japan; four-hands piano recitals with Edit Klukon in many European cities 1982–; has taught piano at Budapest Music Acad. since 1973. *Recordings include:* works by Bartók, Brahms, Haydn, Kadosa, Mozart, Ravel and Schumann. *Honours:* First Prize, Int. Schumann Competition, Zwickau, GDR 1969, Grand Prix Int. du Disque (Paris) 1972, Liszt Prize 2nd Degree 1973, Kossuth Prize 1978. *Current Management:* Caecilia, 29 rue de la Coulouvrenière 1204 Geneva, Switzerland. *Telephone:* (22) 8091526. *Address:* Ördögorom Lejtő 11/B, 1112 Budapest, Hungary (home). *Telephone:* (1) 246-4403 (home).

**RANKINE, Peter (John);** Composer and Conductor; b. 11 March 1960, Queensland, Australia. *Education:* BMus, Queensland Conservatory, 1984; GradDipMus, 1985; MMus, University of Queensland, 1996. *Career:* Faculty Member, University of Queensland, 1987; Queenland University of Technology, 1988–94; Commissions from Queensland Wind Soloists, Australian Broadcasting Commission, Dance North, Opera Queensland, Canticum and others. *Compositions include:* Bunyip!, chamber opera, 1985; Three Movements for Orchestra, 1986; Eulogy for wind quintet, 1987; Symphonia Dialectica, 1988; From Fire by Fire for Wind octet, 1989; Celtic Cross for violin and chamber orchestra, 1990; Time and the Bell: Clarinet Concerto,

1990; John Brown, Rose, and the Midnight Cat, for ensemble, 1992; Surya Namaskar, Chaand Namaskar, for horn and percussion, 1993; Please No More Psalms, ballet score, for oboe, clarinet, percussion, violin and cello, 1994; Media Vita, for choir, clarinet, trombone and percussion, 1997. *Honours:* Sounds Australian Awards, 1990–91. *Address:* 3/15 Bellewe Terrace, St Lucia, Qld 4067, Australia.

**RAPER, Marion Eileen,** MA, LRAM; British pianist, vocal coach, teacher and accompanist; *Lecturer in Accompaniment, Italian for Singers and Piano, Leeds College of Music;* b. 18 Feb. 1938, Birmingham, England; m. 1962 (divorced 1979). *Education:* Royal Acad. of Music, Univ. of London, Gold-smiths' Coll., London, Open Univ., Univ. of Manchester. *Career:* recitals throughout England with singers and instrumentalists; broadcasts for BBC and Capital Radio; Lecturer in Accompaniment, Italian for Singers and Piano, Leeds Coll. of Music 1985–; master-classes; piano duo tours of Canada with Jennifer Hillman 1987, 1989; TV appearances (ITV and Channel 4); vocal coach, accompanist and teacher; mem. Incorporated Soc. of Musicians, Royal Soc. of Musicians. *Address:* 3 Cavendish Drive, Guiseley, Leeds, LS20 8DR, England (home). *Telephone:* (1943) 873060 (home). *E-mail:* Marion.Raper@btinternet.com.

**RAPF, Kurt;** Austrian conductor, musician, composer and academic; b. 15 Feb. 1922, Vienna; s. of Rudof Rapf and Anna Rapf; m. Ellen Rapf 1961; one d. *Education:* Music Acad., Vienna. *Career:* Founder and Conductor, Collegium Musicum Wien (Vienna String Symphony) 1945–56; Asst Conductor to Hans Knappertsbusch, Opera House Zürich, Switzerland 1948–49; accompanist for singers and instrumentalists; Dir of Music, Innsbruck 1953–60; broadcast and TV activities; numerous tours in Europe, USA, Canada, Middle and Far East; many appearances at festivals in Europe, Asia and America; Prof. and Chief of Music Dept, City of Vienna 1970–87; Head of Austrian Composers' Guild 1970–83; Founder and Music Dir Vienna Sinfonietta 1986; lecturer and jury participations. *Compositions:* more than 200 works for orchestra, choir, chamber orchestra, organ and piano solo, chamber music and vocal works include six symphonies 1976–2001, two operas, Passio Aeterna 1979, Poem Symphonic 1981, Requiem 2000. *Recordings:* more than 70 records as conductor, harpsichordist, organist, pianist and composer.

**RAPHANEL, Ghilaine;** Singer (Soprano); b. 19 April 1952, Rouen, France. *Education:* Studied at the Rouen Conservatory and at the Paris Conservatoire with Janine Micheau. *Career:* Sang Rosina in Il Barbiere di Siviglia at the Opera Studio of the Paris Opéra; Stadttheater Basle from 1980 as Gilda, Constanze, Juliette, Manon, and Titania in A Midsummer Night's Dream; Guest appearances in Lyon and Nantes; Hamburg Staatsoper, 1985, as the Queen of Night and Zerbinetta; Aix-en-Provence Festival, 1985, Zerbinetta; Sang at Mézières, 1988, as Amor in Orfeo ed Euridice; At Nancy, 1989, as Susanna. *Recordings include:* Pousette in Manon, L'Etoile by Chabrier; Fiorella in Les Brigands by Offenbach; Marguérite de Valois in Les Huguenots; Sang Nicolai's Frau Fluth at the Paris Opéra-Comique, 1995–96. *Address:* c/o Opéra de Nancy et de Lorraine, Rue Ste Catherine, 54000 Nancy, France.

**RAPPE, Jadwiga;** Singer (Contralto); b. 1957, Poland. *Education:* Studied in Warsaw and Breslau. *Career:* Sang at first in concert and made stage debut at Warsaw in 1983; Has sung throughout Europe in concert, notably with masses by Mozart, Bach and Beethoven and Szymanowski's Stabat Mater; Perform-mances of Erda in Wagner's Ring at the Deutsche Oper Berlin, Warsaw and Covent Garden from 1988; Concerts of La Gioconda in Amsterdam and Strauss's Daphne (as Gaea) in Geneva, 1990–91; Other roles include Ulrica, Orpheus and Juno in Semele; Countess in The Queen of Spades for Scottish Opera, 1998; Season 2000–01 as Gaea in Daphne for the Deutsche Oper Berlin and Erda in Siegfried for Geneva Opera. *Address:* Warsaw National Opera, Grand Theatre, Place Teatrainy 1, 00-950 Warsaw, Poland.

**RASILAINEN, Jukka;** Singer (Bass-baritone); b. 1959, Helsinki, Finland. *Education:* Studied in Rome and Helsinki. *Career:* Debut: Savonlinna Festival, 1983, as Leporello; Lahti, 1984, as Rossini's Basilio; Dortmund Opera from 1986, as Verdi's Zaccaria and Ferrando, Galitzky in Prince Igor and Wozzeck; Karlsruhe, 1990, as Masetto and the Commendatore, in Don Giovanni; Vienna Staatsoper, 1991, as Wagner's Dutchman, Dresden, 1992–95, as Kaspar in Der Freischütz, Pizarro and Kurwenal; Finnish National Opera, 1996, as Wotan in Das Rheingold; Other roles include the Villains in Les contes d'Hoffmann, Scarpia, Amonasro and Jochanaan; Sang Strauss's Mandryka and Orestes at the Dresden Staatsoper, 1999; Season 2000–01 as Wagner's Wanderer at Mannheim, Wotan for the Zürich Opera and Jochanaan in Salome at Dresden. *Address:* c/o Finnish National Opera, PO Box 176, Helsingkatu 58, 00251 Helsinki, Finland.

**RASKATOV, Alexander;** Russian composer; b. 1953, Moscow. *Education:* Moscow Conservatory. *Career:* has received commissions from Gidon Kremer, Sabine Meyer Wind Ensemble, Netherlands Wind Ensemble, Hilliard Ensemble, Schoenberg Ensemble; composer-in-residence Stetson Univ., USA 1990; mem. Asscn for Contemporary Music. *Compositions:* 66 for soprano and 12 instruments 1990, Dolce far niente for cello and piano 1991, Xenia for chamber orchestra 1991, Commentary on a Vision for solo percussion and orchestra 1991, Kyrie eleison for solo cello 1992, Miserere for viola, violin, cello and orchestra 1992, Misteria brevis for piano and percussion 1992, Concerto for oboe and 15 strings 1993, Madrigal in Metal for five percussionists 1993, Eco perpetuo for solo bassoon, bass clarinet, trombone, percussion, harp, piano, cello and double bass 1993, Seven Stages of Hallelujah for soprano

(with the use of percussion) and piano 1993, I will see a rose at the end of the path... for string quartet 1994, Litany for 15 musicians 1994, Xcos for cello and accordion 1994, Pas de deux for soprano (with tubular bells), soprano and tenor saxophones 1994, Farewell from the Birds of Passage for alto saxophone, percussion and strings 1994, Primal Song for viola and 15 string instruments 1995, Credo in Byzantinum for harpsichord or piano 1995, Songs of Sunset for mezzo-soprano, viola and piano 1995, Gebet for soprano and string quartet 1996, Resurrexit for soprano, mezzo-soprano and chamber orchestra 1996–97, Blissful Music for cello and chamber orchestra 1997, Quasi Hamlet for soprano and chamber ensemble 1997, Swinging the Dream Pendulum for violin and instrumental ensemble 1998, Ritual for voice and percussion 1997, Ritual II for four saxophones, percussion, piano and strings 1998–99, Paradise Lost? for wind ensemble 1999, Pro-Kofiev et Contra-Kofiev for wind instruments and percussion 1999, Before Thy Throne... for violin and percussion 1999, Circle of Singing-2 for baritone and piano 2000, Praise for four male voices and church bells 2000, In nomine for eight voices, wind instruments and percussion 2001, Voices of Frozen Land for seven voices, wind instruments and percussion 2001, Put-Path-Chemin-Weg for viola and orchestra 2003, Five Minutes from the life of W. A. Mozart. *Honours:* Salzburg Easter Festival composition prize 1998.

**RASMUSSEN, Karl Aage;** Composer, Conductor and Professor of Music; b. 14 Dec. 1947, Kolding, Denmark; m. Charlotte Schiotz. 7 May 1975. *Education:* Composition with Per Norgaard, degrees in Music History, Theory and Composition, Academy of Music, Århus. *Career:* Teacher: Academy of Music, Århus, 1970–, Royal Academy, Copenhagen, 1980–; Director, Conductor, Chamber Ensemble, The Elsinore Players, 1975–; Numerous duties at the New Music Department, Danish Radio, co-editing The Danish Music Magazine; Lectures, many European countries, USA; Artistic Director, NUMUS Festival, Århus, also Esbjerg Ensemble (1991–); mem, Danish Music Council; Danish Arts Foundation. *Compositions include:* Stage: Jephta, two-act opera, 1976–77; Majakovskij, two-act scenic concert piece, 1977–78; Jonas, musical play for radio, 1978–80; 'Our Hoffmann', opera, 1986; The Sinking of the Titanic, opera, 1994; Orchestral: Symphony Anfang und Ende, 1973; Contrafactum, concerto for cello and orchestra, 1980; A Symphony in Time, 1982; Movements on a Moving Line, 1985; Phantom Movements, 1989; Litania, 1994; Cosmology According to Chagall, piano and chamber orchestra, 1996; Blissful Music for violin and orchestra, 1997; Chamber: Protocol and Myth, 1971; Genklang, 1972; A Ballad of Game and Dream, 1974; Lullaby, 1976; Berio Mask, 1977; Le Tombeau de Père Igor, 1977; Parts Apart, 1978; Capricci e Dance, 1979; Italiensk Koncert, 1981; Ballo in Maschera, 1981; Pianissimo Furioso, 1982; A Quartet of Five, 1982; Solos and Shadows, 1983; Fugue/Fuga (Encore VIII), 1984; Surrounded by Sales, 1985; Still, string quartet, 1988; Solo instrument: Invention, 1972; Antifoni, 1973; Paganini Variations, 1976; Fugue/Fuga, 1984; Triple Tango, 1984; Etudes and Postludes, piano, 1990; I Will See a Rose at the end of the Path, string quartet, 1994; Vocal: Love Is In The World, 1974–75; One And All, 1976; Encore Series I–XI, 1977–85; Gebet for soprano and string quartet, 1996; Resurrexi...... for soprano, mezzo and chamber orchestra, 1997; Praise, for 4 voices, 1998. *Recordings:* String Quartets, Arditti String Quartet; A Symphony in Time, Danish Radio Symphony Orchestra; Movements on a Moving Line, Speculum Musicae. *Honours:* Carl Nielsen Prize, 1991. *Address:* Brokbjerggaard, 8752 Oestbirk, Denmark.

**RASMUSSEN, Paula;** Singer (Mezzo-soprano); b. 1965, California, USA. *Career:* Concert appearances with San Francisco Symphony under Nicholas McGegan in Bach Cantatas, the Los Angeles Master Chorale in Messiah, Bruckner's Te Deum and Pergolesi's Magnifict and with José Carreras in Dublin, 1992; Opera engagements as Nancy T'ang in the Peter Sellars production of Nixon in China at Los Angeles, Paris and Frankfurt; Lola in Cavalleria Rusticana with Long Beach Opera; Nancy in Albert Herring, Hansel, Anna in Les Troyens, Hippolyta in Midsummer Night's Dream and the Composer in Ariadne auf Naxos with the Los Angeles Music Center Opera; Sang Handel's Serse at Cologne, 1996 and Geneva, 1998; Season 2000 as Carmen at Cologne, Handel's Serse in Dresden and Cherubino for the New York City Opera. *Honours:* Regional Winner, 1992 Metropolitan Opera Competition. *Address:* c/o IMG Artists, Lovell House, 616 Chiswick High Road, London W4 5RX, England.

**RASMUSSEN, Sunleif;** Faroese composer; b. 19 March 1961, Sandur. *Education:* Norges Musikkhøgskole, studied in Denmark with Bent Sørensen, Royal Danish Acad. of Music. *Compositions include:* Sig mær hví er foldin føgur (Tell Me Why the World is Pretty) 1982, Kvøldvísa um summarmála (Evening Tune in April) for choir 1983, Vár (Spring) for choir 1983, Sóljurnar og náttin (Marsh Marigolds and the Night) 1984, Blátt (Blue) for choir 1985, Skærur vindur (Pure Winds) for choir 1988, String Quartet No. 1 1989–90, Vetrarmyndir (Winter Pictures) for wind quintet and piano 1991, Tid, Ild, Baglæns (Time, Fire, Backwards) for choir and pre-recorded tape 1991–92, Syngjandi grót (Singing Rocks) 1992, Landid (The Land) 1992–93, Sum hin gylta sól (Like the Golden Sun) for piano and electronics 1993, Til Syvstjernen (To the Pleiades) for violin, flute, clarinet and piano 1993, Eitt ljós er kveikt (A Light has been Lit) for organ and tape 1993, The Song of the Sea (orchestra and tape) 1994–95, Tilegnelse (Dedication) for mezzo-soprano and ensemble 1995, Symphony No. 1 (Oceanic Days) (Nordic Council Music Award 2002) 1995–97, Cantus Borealis (wind quintet) 1996, Vox humana (electronic score) 1997, Pictures from the Sea's Garden for saxophone and percussion 1998, Arktis for mezzo-soprano and ensemble 1998, Trauer und Freude for 10 instruments 1999, Surrounded (chamber orchestra) 2000. *Recordings include:* Symphony No. 1 Oceanic Days, Dem Licht Entgegen, Surrounded, Arktis, Mozaik / Miniature, Tilegnelse, Trauer und Freude. *Honours:* Hon. Pres. Faroese Arts Festival 2003. *Address:* c/o Arts Festival, Norðurlandahúsið, Postboks 1260, 110 Tórshavn, Faroe Islands (office).

**RATH, John Frédéric,** BA; British opera and concert singer (bass); b. 10 June 1946, Manchester, England. *Education:* Manchester University, RNCM, Opera School at Basle; studied with Elsa Cavelti, Max Lorenz and Otakar Kraus. *Career:* debut as Ramphis in Aida, RNCM; Appearances with: English Music Theatre Company, Glyndebourne Festival, Touring Company Royal Opera House, Covent Garden, La Fenice, Venice, Maggio Musicale in Florence; Roles include: Masetto in Don Giovanni, Argante in Handel's Rinaldo, Sparafucile in Rigoletto, Escamillo and Zuniga in Carmen; Recently in Peter Brook's La Tragèdie de Carmen in Paris, its European tour and New York as Escamillo; Kent Opera: Rocco in Fidelio; Nexus Opera: The Traveller in Britten's Curlew River at Wells Cathedral and filmed by BBC 2; Edinburgh Festival: Jochanaan in Salome; English Bach Festival: Charon in Handel's Alceste; Appearances at various festivals; Principal Bass with D'Oyly Carte Opera; Concert and oratorio work throughout Europe including notable performances of Handel's Theodora in London, Spain and Italy, Bach Cantatas in NY and concert performances including Wotan in Das Rheingold and Die Walküre; Opera North: The Doctor in Berg's Wozzeck, 1993; Sarastro in Mozart's The Magic Flute, 1994; Nourabad in Bizet's Les Pêcheurs de Perles, 1995; Created a new English version of Schubert's Winter Journey with the poet Miriam Scott and performed it; Sang Herod in Stradella's San Giovanni Batista, Batignano, 1996; Satyr and Cythéron in Rameau's Platée in Berkeley, California, and Ferrando in Il Trovatore for Opera South in Cork, Ireland, 1998; Sang 2nd Soldier in Salome and the Poet in Salieri's Prima la musica poi le parole for Oper Frankfurt, 1999; Ashby in La Fanciulla de l'West for Opera Zuid, Maastricht; King Philip, Don Carlos; Pizarro, Fidelio; Goalud, Pelléas et Mélisande for Stadtsoper Bremerhaven, 2002–03; Sebastiano d'Alberts Tiefland; Wicks Booth, Sondheim Assassins; Iago, Otello and bass-baritone roles in Contes de Hoffman, also for Bremerhaven, 2003–04. *Recordings:* The Gondoliers and Iolanthe with the D'Oyly Carte. *Address:* Cwmilechwedd Fawr, Llanbister, Powys LD1 6UH, Wales.

**RATJU, Adrian;** Composer and Musicologist; b. 28 July 1928, Bucharest, Romania. *Education:* Studied harmony, counterpoint and compositions at the Bucharest Conservatory, 1950–56; Summer course at Darmstadt, Germany, 1969. *Career:* Professor at the Bucharest Conservatory from 1962; Executive Committee of the Union of Composers and Musicologists, Bucharest, from 1968. *Compositions include:* 2 String Quartets, 1956, 1988; 2 Symphonies, 1961, 1977; Concerto for oboe, bassoon and orchestra, 1963; Three Madrigals for chorus, after Shakespeare, 1964; Diptych for orchestra, 1965; Partita for wind quartet, 1966; Impressions for ensemble, 1969; Fragment of a Triumphal Arch for Beethoven for soprano, clarinet and piano, 1970; Six Images for orchestra, 1971; Transfigurations, for piano, clarinet and spring trio, 1975; Trio for flute and oboe and clarinet, 1980; Sonata a Cinque, for brass quintet, 1984; Sonata for solo violin, 1985; Trio for piano, clarinet and guitar, 1987; Piano Concerto, 1988; Echoes, for vibraphone and marimba, 1989; Violin Sonata, 1991; Convergences, for piano, clarinet and percussion, 1994; Hommage a Erik Satie, for voice and piano, 1994. *Honours:* Six composition prizes from the Union of Composers and Musicologists, 1967–93. *Address:* c/o UCMR, Calea Victoriei 141, Sector 1, Bucharest, Romania. *Telephone:* 0040212127966. *Fax:* 0040212107211. *E-mail:* ucmr@itcnet.ro.

**RATTAY, Evzen;** Cellist; b. 1945, Czechoslovakia. *Education:* Studied at the Prague Academy of Arts. *Career:* Cellist of the Talich String Quartet from 1962; Tours to most European countries, Egypt, Iraq, North America, Japan, Indonesia; Chamber Ensemble of the Czech Philharmonic from 1975; Annual visits to France from 1976; Tours of the United Kingdom, 1990–91, with concerts at the Wigmore Hall, appearances at the Bath and Bournemouth Festivals, Queen Elizabeth Hall and on BBC 2's Late Show, with Janáček's 2nd quartet; Also played Beethoven's Quartet Opus 74, the Brahms A minor, Smetana D minor and works by Mozart in England; Festival appearances in Vienna, Besançon, Lucerne, Helsinki, Amsterdam, Prague and Salzburg; Repertoire also includes works by Debussy, Bartók (complete quartets recorded), Shostakovich, Ravel and Dvořák. *Recordings include:* Complete quartets of Beethoven; Albums. *Honours:* Grand Prix Charles Cros. *Address:* c/o Clarion/Seven Muses, 64 Whitehall Park, London N19 3 TN, England.

**RATTI, Eugenia;** singer (soprano); b. 5 April 1933, Genoa, Italy. *Education:* studied with her mother. *Career:* concert tour with Tito Schipa, 1952; stage debut, 1954, in Sestri Levante; La Scala Milan from 1955, as Lisa in La Sonnambula, and in the premiere of Milhaud's David, 1955, and Dialogues des Carmélites, 1957; Holland Festival, 1955, 1961, as Nannetta and Adina; Edinburgh Festival, 1957, Il Matrimonio Segreto; Holland Festival, 1970, in Haydn's La Fedeltà Premiata; returned to Glyndebourne, 1973 and 1976, as the Italian Singer in Capriccio; Other roles include Zerlina in Don Giovanni, Susanna, Rosina, Musetta and Oscar. *Recordings:* Un Ballo in Maschera; Il Matrimonio Segreto; Aida; La Sonnambula; Don Giovanni, conducted by Leinsdorf.

**RATTLE, Sir Simon,** Kt, CBE; British conductor; *Artistic Director and Chief Conductor, Berlin Philharmonic Orchestra*; b. 19 Jan. 1955, Liverpool; m. 1st Elise Ross 1980 (divorced 1995); two s.; m. 2nd Candace Allen 1996; pnr Magdalena Kožená; one s. *Education:* Royal Acad. of Music. *Career:* won John

Player Int. Conducting Competition 1973; has conducted Bournemouth Symphony, Northern Sinfonia, London Philharmonic, London Sinfonietta, Berlin Philharmonic, LA Philharmonic, Stockholm Philharmonic, Vienna Philharmonic, Philadelphia Orchestra, Boston Symphony orchestras, etc.; debut at Queen Elizabeth Hall, London 1974, Royal Festival Hall, London 1976, Royal Albert Hall, London 1976; Asst Conductor, BBC Symphony Orchestra 1977–80; Assoc. Conductor, Royal Liverpool Philharmonic Soc. 1977–80; Glyndebourne debut 1977, Royal Opera, Covent Garden debut 1990; Artistic Dir, London Choral Soc. 1979–84; Prin. Conductor and Artistic Adviser, City of Birmingham Symphony Orchestra (CBSO) 1980–90, Music Dir 1990–98; Artistic Dir South Bank Summer Music 1981–83; Jt Artistic Dir Aldeburgh Festival 1982–93; Prin. Guest Conductor, LA Philharmonic 1981–94, Rotterdam Philharmonic 1981–84; Prin. Guest Conductor Orchestra of the Age of Enlightenment 1992–; Artistic Dir and Chief Conductor Berlin Philharmonic Orchestra 2002–; Hon. Fellow St Anne's Coll. Oxford 1991. *Honours:* Hon. DMus (Liverpool) 1991, (Leeds) 1993; Edison Award (for recording of Shostakovich's Symphony No. 10) 1987, Grand Prix du Disque (Turangalîla Symphony) 1988, Grand Prix Caecilia (Turangalîla Symphony, Jazz Album) 1988, Gramophone Record of the Year Award (Mahler's Symphony No. 2) 1988, Gramophone Opera Award (Porgy and Bess) 1989, Int. Record Critics' Award (Porgy and Bess) 1990, Grand Prix de l' Acad. Charles Cros 1990, Gramophone Artist of the Year 1993, Montblanc de la Culture Award 1993, Toepfer Foundation Shakespeare Prize (Hamburg) 1996, Gramophone Award for Best Concerto recording (Szymanowski Violin Concertos Nos 1 and 2), Albert Medal (RSA) 1997, Choc de l'Année Award (for recording of Brahms Piano Concerto Op. 15) 1998, Outstanding Achievement Award, South Bank Show 1999, Diapason Recording of the Year Award (complete Beethoven Piano Concertos) 1999, Gramophone Award for Best Opera Recording (Szymanowski's King Roger) 2000, Gramophone Awards for Best Orchestral Recording and Record of the Year (Mahler's Symphony No. 10) 2000, Comenius Prize (Germany) 2004, Classical BRIT Award (for Beethoven Symphonies) 2004; Officier, Ordre des Arts et des Lettres 1995. *Current Management:* c/o Lisa Perry, Askonas Holt Ltd, Lonsdale Chambers, 27 Chancery Lane, London, WC2A 1PF, England. *Telephone:* (20) 7400-1706. *Fax:* (20) 7400-1799. *E-mail:* info@askonasholt.co.uk. *Website:* www.askonasholt.co.uk. *Address:* Berlin Philharmonie Orchestra, Philharmonie, Matthäckirchstrasse 1, 14057 Berlin, Germany (office).

**RAUCH, Wolfgang;** singer (baritone); b. 27 Jan. 1957, Cologne, Germany. *Education:* Studied in Cologne with Josef Metternich and in Italy with Mario del Monaco. *Career:* Sang with the Deutsche Oper am Rhein Düsseldorf from 1984, member of the Bayerische Staatsoper Munich from 1987; Guest appearances at La Scala Milan, the State Operas of Vienna and Hamburg and the Deutsche Oper Berlin; Sang Papageno in Mozart bicentenary performances of Die Zauberflöte at Barcelona and Bonn, 1991; Other roles include Lortzing's Tsar, Marcello, Mozart's Guglielmo and Figaro, Count Perruchetto in Haydn's La Fedeltà Premiata, Silvio, Lionel in Tchaikovsky's The Maid of Orleans, Strauss's Count in Capriccio and Harlekin and the Herald in Lohengrin (Hamburg, 1998); Season 2000–01 as Puccini's Marcello at Hamburg, Strauss's Spirit Messenger at Barcelona and Lescaut in Henze's Boulevard Solitude for Covent Garden; Frequent concert and broadcasting engagements. *Address:* c/o Hamburgische Staatsoper, Grosse Theaterstrasse 34, 20354 Hamberg, Germany.

**RAUNIG, Arno;** German singer (countertenor); b. 1956, Klagenfurt. *Education:* Vienna Boys' Choir, Linz Conservatoire, studied with Kurt Equiluz in Vienna. *Career:* many appearances in Baroque music throughout Europe, notably in works by Bach, Handel and Mozart in Vienna, Berlin and Hamburg; repertoire includes Mozart's Ascanio in Alba and Idomeneo, Handel's Radamisto and Xerxes, Cesti's Pomo d'Oro and The Fairy Queen; Wiesbaden Festival, 1992, in the premiere of Der Park by Hans Gefors; sang Creon in the premiere of Medea by Osca Strasnoy, Spoleto 2000. *Current Management:* Agentur Schimanski, Syker Straße 8, 28307 Bremen, Germany. *Telephone:* (421) 48 44 713. *Fax:* (421) 498 98 60. *Website:* www.scarpia.de.

**RAUTAVAARA, Einojuhani,** MA; Finnish composer; b. 9 Oct. 1928, Helsinki; m. Sini Koivisto 1984. *Education:* Univ. of Helsinki, Sibelius Acad., Juilliard School of Music with Vincent Persichetti, New York, USA, Tanglewood Music Center with Aaron Copland and Roger Sessions, studied with Vladimir Vogel in Ascona, Switzerland, Kölner Musikhochschule with Rudolf Petzold, Germany. *Career:* Lecturer in Music Theory, Sibelius Acad. 1966–76; Art Prof., Finland 1971–76; Prof. of Composition, Sibelius Acad. 1976–90. *Compositions include:* operas: Kaivos 1957, Thomas 1983, Vincent 1986, House of the Sun 1990, Gift of the Magi 1993, Aleksis Kivi 1995, Rasputin 2001; other: Cantus Arcticus concerto for birds and orchestra, Angel of Dusk concerto for double bass and orchestra, concerti for cello, flute, piano, violin, organ, double bass, clarinet and harp, Vigilia (Orthodox Mass), two choir-operas, eight symphonies, cantatas, String Quintet 1997, four string quartets. *Publication:* Omakuva (memoirs) 1989. *Current Management:* Boosey & Hawkes, Aldwych House, 71–91 Aldwych, London, WC2B 4HN, England. *Website:* www.boosey.com.

**RAUTIO, Nina;** Singer (soprano); b. 21 Sept. 1957, Bryansk, Russia. *Education:* Studied at Leningrad Conservatoire. *Career:* Sang first at the Leningrad State Theatre, 1981–87; Bolshoi Opera from 1987; Western debut with Bolshoi Company at Metropolitan and the Edinburgh Festival 1991, as Tatiana and as Oksana in Rimsky's Christmas Eve; Season 1992, as Manon Lescaut at La Scala, conducted by Lorin Maazel, Verdi Requiem at Rome, Aida at the Savonlinna Festival and in concert performances conducted by Zubin Mehta; Sang with the Pittsburgh Symphony on tour to Seville Expo 92 and as Elisabetta in Don Carlo to open the season at La Scala; Season 1993–94, as Lisa in The Queen of Spades at the Opéra Bastille Paris, Ballo in Maschera and Aida at Covent Garden, Verdi Requiem at Florence and the Festival Hall, Beethoven and Mahler in Pittsburgh, Desdemona at the Orange Festival, the Glagolitic Mass at La Scala and Amelia Boccanegra at Florence; Season 1994–95, as Aida at the Staatsoper Berlin and Amelia Boccanegra at Florence and Turin; Season 1995–96 Metropolitan Opera debut as Aida; Sang Aida at the Verona Arena, 1996, and the Trovatore Leonora at Geneva, 1998; Sang Tosca at Glasgow, 2000. *Recordings:* Manon Lescaut; Verdi Requiem; Guillaume Tell; Norma. *Current Management:* Athole Still International Management, Forresters Hall, 25–27 Westow Street, London, SE19 3RY, England. *Telephone:* (20) 8771-5271. *Fax:* (20) 8768-6600. *Website:* www .atholestill.com.

**RAWLINS, Emily,** BMus; opera and concert singer; b. 25 Sept. 1950, Lancaster, OH, USA; m. 1982. *Education:* Indiana University, Curtis Institute of Music, Hochschule für Musik, Vienna. *Career:* debut in Basel, Switzerland; Basel Stadttheater, 1973–77; Deutsche Oper am Rhein, 1977–82; Debuts, Theater der Stadt Bonn, 1975, National Theater, Mannheim, 1976, Theater der Stadt Köln, 1977, Städtische Bühnen, Dortmund, 1979, Städtische Bühnen, Augsburg; San Francisco Opera, 1980; American premiere, Lear, Salzburg Festival, world premiere of Baal, 1981; Vienna Staatsoper, 1981; Teatro Nacional de São Carlos, Lisbon, 1982; Grand Théâtre de Genève, 1982; Houston Grand Opera, 1983; American premiere of Anna Karenina, Los Angeles Opera Theater, 1983; Appeared on television, ZDF Germany, 1981, 1982, ORF, Austria, 1981; Film appearances in Bartered Bride and Fra Diavolo, 1983, and Baal, 1984; Vienna State Opera, 1985; ORF with Wiener Symphoniker; Concert Opera Association, 1986; World premiere of Das Schloss, Opera National, Brussels, 1986; Sang Third Norn in Götterdämmerung at Cologne, 2000. *Recordings:* Baal (singing part of Sophie) 1985. *Address:* c/o Alferink, Appololaan 181, 1077 AT Amsterdam, Netherlands.

**RAWNSLEY, John;** Singer (Baritone); b. 14 Dec. 1949, England. *Education:* Royal Northern College of Music. *Career:* Debut: Glyndebourne Touring Opera, 1975; Later sang Verdi's Ford and Stravinsky's Nick Shadow on tour, Mozart's Masetto, Rossini's Figaro and Puccini's Marcello at Glyndebourne; Covent Garden debut, 1979, as Schaunard in La Bohème; French debut at Nancy in 1980, as Tonio in Pagliacci; English National Opera from 1982, as Amonasro and as Rigoletto in Jonathan Miller's production of Verdi's opera; Tour to the USA, 1984; Italian debut, 1985, as Verdi's Renato in Trieste; La Scala Milan, 1987, as Tonio; Guest engagements at the Vienna Staatsoper, San Diego, Barcelona, Bilbao, Brussels and Geneva: Roles include Paolo Albiani (Simon Boccanegra), Macbeth, Papageno, Don Alfonso and Taddeo in L'Italiana in Algeri; Sang Rigoletto at Turin, 1989; Simon Boccanegra in a concert performance at the Festival Hall, 1990; Season 1992 as Rigoletto at Oslo and the Coliseum, and in The Beggar's Opera at the Aldeburgh Festival; Sang Falstaff for Opera Zuid, Netherlands, 1994. *Recordings:* Rigoletto; Masetto in Don Giovanni; Videos of Così fan tutte, Il Barbiere di Siviglia, La Bohème and Rigoletto. *Address:* c/o Kaye Artists Management, Barratt House, 7 Chertsey Road, Woking, Surrey GU21 5 AB, England.

**RAXACH, Enrique;** Dutch composer; b. 15 Jan. 1932, Barcelona, Spain. *Education:* studied in Darmstadt with Messiaen, Boulez, Stockhausen and Maderna, 1959–66. *Compositions include:* Estudis for strings, 1952; Six Movements for orchestra, 1955; Polifonias, for strings, 1956; Metamorphose I–II for orchestra, 1956–58; Metamorphose III for 15 solo instruments, 1959; Columna de fuego for orchestra 1958; Fluxion, for 17 players, 1963; Syntagma, for orchestra, 1965; Fragmento II for soprano, flute and 2 percussionists, 1966; Textures for orchestra, 1966; Inside Outside for orchestra and tape, 1969; Paraphrase for mezzo-soprano and 11 players, 1969; 2 String Quartets, 1961, 1971; Rite of Perception, electronic tape music, 1971; Interface for chorus and orchestra, 1972; Scattertime for 6 players, 1972; Sine Nomine for soprano and orchestra, 1973; Figuren in einer Landschaft for orchestra, 1974; Chimaera for bass clarinet and tape, 1974; Erdenlicht for orchestra, 1975; Aubade for percussion quartet, 1979; The Hunting in Winter for horn and piano, 1979; Am Ende des Regenbogens, for orchestra, 1980; Careful with that... for clarinet and percussionist, 1982; Chalumeau for clarinet quartet, 1982; Ode for flute and string trio, 1982; Vortice for 9 clarinets, 1983;... hub of ambiguity, for soprano and 8 players, 1984; Opus Incertum for chamber orchestra, 1985; Calles y sueños, for chamber orchestra, 1986; Obsessum for bassoon and 9 accordions, 1988; Nocturno del hueco for chorus, large ensemble and tape, 1990; Danses Pythiques for harp, 1992; Decade for bass clarinet and accordion, 1992; 12 Preludes for piano, 1993; Reflections inside, electronic tape music, 1994; Piano Concertino, 1995; Neumes for percussion sextet, 1996; Nocturnal Stroll for flute orchestra, 1996; Chapter Three for orchestra, 1997. *Address:* c/o Vereniging BUMA, PO Box 725, 1180 AS Amstelveen, Netherlands.

**RAYAM, Curtis;** Singer (Tenor); b. 4 Feb. 1951, Belleville, Florida, USA. *Education:* Studied at the University of Miami with Mary Henderson Buckeley. *Career:* Debut: Miami, 1971, in Manon Lescaut; Appearances in Dallas, Houston and Jackson Opera South; European debut at the Wexford Festival, 1976, in Giovanni d'Arco by Verdi, returning as the Sultan in Mozart's Zaide and as Wilhelm Meister in Thomas' Mignon; Boston, 1979, as Olympion in the US premiere of Tippett's The Ice Break, conducted by Sarah

Caldwell; Amsterdam, 1981, as Massenet's Werther; Further engagements at Salzburg, Paris, Frankfurt and Venice; La Scala, 1985, in Handel's Alcina, returning 1988 as Orcane in Fetonte by Jommelli; Spoleto, 1988, as Creon in Traetta's Antigone; Other roles include Rossini's Otello and Cleomene (L'Assedio di Corinto), Mozart's Idomeneo, Belmonte and Mitridate, Irus in Il Ritorno d'Ulisse, Nemorino and Puccini's Pinkerton and Rodolfo; Sang Titus April in the premiere of Buchuland by Roelof Temmingh, Pretoria, 1998. *Recordings include:* Treemonisha by Scott Joplin; Da-ud in Die Aegyptische Helena by Strauss. *Honours:* Finalist, Metropolitan Auditions, 1972; Winner, Dallas Competition, 1974.

**RAYMOND, Deborah;** Soprano; b. 26 Nov. 1951, Chicago, Illinois, USA; m. Nando Schellen, 19 June 1991. *Education:* BMus, School of Music, University of Iowa; Private studies with Jean Kraft, Bill and Dixie Neill, Pauline Tinsley, Virginia Zeani. *Career:* Debut: Netherlands Opera, Amsterdam, 1983; Leading roles: Salome at Staatsoper Dresden, 1988, at Aachen, 1989, at Salt Lake City, Utah, 1993, at Charlotte, North Carolina, 1994, with Arizona Opera at Tucson and Phoenix, 1995; Marie in Wozzeck, at Coburg, 1989, at Spoleto Festival, USA, 1997; Woman in Erwartung, with Netherlands Radio Symphony Orchestra, 1988, in Indianapolis, 1994; Zoë in Stephen Climax (Hans Zender), La Monnaie Opera, Brussels, 1990; Eine Diene in Reigen (Ph Boesmans/Luc Bondy), La Monnaie, Brussels, 1991–93 (Strasbourg and Paris); Tatiana in Eugene Onegin, with the Bolshoi Opera of Belorus at Minsk, 1993; Mimi in La Bohème, USA, 1994, 1996, 1997; Title role in Tosca, USA, 1996, 1998, 2000; Nedda in Pagliacci, USA, 1997–98; Cio-Cio San in Madama Butterfly, USA, 1997–99; Appears often in concerts and recitals, in USA 1996, 1997, 1999, 2000, 2001; Voice teacher at Northern Arizona University, Flagstaff AZ as of 2001. *Recordings include:* Reigen (Philippe Boesmans-Bondy). *Current Management:* Sara Tornay and Blythe de Blasis. *Address:* c/o Sara Tornay, 155 W 72nd Street, New York, NY 10023, USA.

**REA, John;** Composer; b. 14 Jan. 1944, Toronto, Ontario, Canada. *Education:* Studied with John Weinzweg at University of Toronto and Milton Babbitt at Princeton. *Career:* Teacher at McGill University, 1973, Dean of the Faculty of Music, 1986–91; Composer-in-Residence at Mannheim, 1984; Founder Member of the Montreal music society Les Evénements du Neuf. *Compositions:* Music theatre pieces: Les Jours, ballet, 1969; The Prisoner's Play, opera, 1973; Hommage à Richard Wagner, 1988; Com-possession, 1980; Le Petit Livre des Ravalet, opera, 1983; Offenes Lied, operatic scenes, 1986; Operatic scenes based on Dante's Inferno and Poe's Morella, 1990–93; Orchestral: Hommage à Vasarely, 1977; Vanishing Points, 1983; Over Time, 1987; Time and Again, 1987; Chamber: Clarinet Sonatina, 1965; Sestina, 1968; Prologue, Scene and Movement for soprano, viola and 2 pianos, 1968; Tempest, 1969; What You Will for piano, 1969; La Dernière Sirène for ondes martenot, piano and percussion, 1981; Les Raison des Forces Mouvantes for flute and string quartet, 1984; Some Time Later for amplified string quartet, 1986; Vocal: Litaneia for chorus and orchestra, 1984. *Address:* c/o McGill University, Faculty of Music, Strathcona Music Building, 555 Sherbrooke Street West, Montreal, Quebec H3A 1E3, Canada.

**REANEY, Gilbert;** Professor; b. 11 Jan. 1924, Sheffield, England. *Education:* Licentiate, Royal Academy of Music, 1946; BA 1948, BMus 1950, MA 1951, Sheffield University; Sorbonne University, Paris, France, 1950–53. *Career:* Performer, BBC and tours of the United Kingdom and the continent, 1952–88; Research Fellow, Reading University, 1953–56, Birmingham, 1956–59; Director of London Medieval Group, 1958–; Visiting Professor, Hamburg University, Germany, 1960; Associate Professor, University of California, Los Angeles, 1960–62, Full Professor, 1963–97; mem, Royal Musical Association; American Musicological Society; Plainsong and Medieval Music Society. *Publications:* Early 15th Century Music, 7 vols, (10 vols for Corpus Scriptorum de Musica), 1955–83; Catalogue, Medieval Polyphonic Manuscripts to 1400, 2 vols, 1966, 1969; The Music Theory of John Hothby, 1989. *Contributions:* Assistant and Co-editor of numerous articles in Musica Disciplina, 1956–97; General Editor of Corpus Scriptorum de Musica. *Address:* 1001 Third Street, Santa Monica, CA 90403, USA.

**REARICK, Barbara;** Singer (Mezzo-soprano); b. 1960, USA. *Education:* Studied at Manhattan School of Music and at Britten-Pears School with Nancy Evans and Anthony Rolfe Johnson. *Career:* Concert and opera performances in the United Kingdom and USA; British debut, 1987, at Aldeburgh Festival as Britten's Lucretia; Sang Copland's Old American Songs with Lukas Foss, piano, at the Snape Concert Hall; Other repertoire includes Messiah, Lieder eines fahrenden Gesellen, L'Enfance du Christ and Britten's Charm of Lullabies orchestrated by Colin Matthews, all at Snape; Ravel's Chansons Madécasses, Haydn Masses with the Orchestra of St John's Smith Square and Handel's Dixit Dominus at the Norfolk and Norwich Festival, American popular songs there, 1992, with Richard Rodney Bennett; Operatic repertoire includes Meg Page, Chautauqua Opera, Suzuki in Opera Delaware and Annina in Rosenkavalier in New York City Opera; Member of the Britten-Pears Ensemble, with performances throughout the United Kingdom and USA. *Address:* c/o Owen-White Management, 14 Nightingale Road, London N8 7QU, England.

**REAUX, Angelina;** Singer (Soprano); b. 1959, Houston, Texas, USA. *Career:* Sang in various New York night clubs and was discovered by Leonard Bernstein; Sang Mimi in La Bohème at Rome, 1987, and recorded the role with Bernstein; New York Academy of Music, 1989, as Dido by Purcell, Musetta at Boston and Despina at the Kentucky Opera, 1993; Other roles include

Pamina, Nedda and the Woman in La Voix Humaine; Sang The Queen of Sparta in La Belle Hélène for L'Opéra Français de New York, 1996. *Recordings include:* La Bohème; Street Scene by Weill and Blitzstein's Regina. *Address:* c/o Kentucky Opera, 631 South Fifth Street, Louisville, KY 40202, USA.

**REAVILLE, Richard;** Singer (Tenor); b. 1954, England. *Career:* Appearances with English National Opera, Welsh National Opera, Scottish Opera and Mid Wales Opera; Glyndebourne Festival and Tour, London Opera Players and festivals in the United Kingdom, France and Germany; Roles have included Jacquino in Fidelio, Mozart's Monostatos and Arbace, Britten's Peter Grimes and Albert Herring and Herod in Salome; Wagner's Loge, Froh and David, and Don José on tour to the Far East (1996); Concerts throughout Europe, including engagements with the BBC Philharmonic Orchestra, Danish Radio Symphony Orchestra, Belgian State Orchestra, Odense Philharmonic, Weimar Staatskapelle and various chamber ensembles; Mahler's Das Lied von der Erde with the Rander Orchestra (Denmark), Puccini's Messa di Gloria with the Ostrava Philharmonic Orchestra and Ligeti's Le Grand Macabre with the Odense Symphony Orchestra (1996–97); Sang Second Judge in Param Vir's Broken Strings, Glasgow, 1998. *Address:* c/o Tivoli Artists, 3 Vesterbrogade, DK –1630 Copenhagen, Denmark.

**RECHBERGER, Herman;** Finnish composer and performer; b. 14 Feb. 1947, Linz, Austria; m. (1) Ilse Maier, 1966, 1 s., 1 d., (2) Soile Jaatinen, 1972, 1 s., 2 d. *Education:* Graphic Arts, Linz, 1967; Teaching degree, Classical Guitar, Recorder, 1973, Diploma, Composition, 1976, Sibelius Academy, Helsinki. *Career:* Music Teacher, Choir Conductor, 1975–79; Producer of Contemporary Music, Artistic Director of Experimental Studio, Finnish Broadcasting, 1979–84; State Grant, 1985–; Recitals of new recorder music, most European countries, Russia, Cuba, USA; Performed own works, ISCM Music Days, Helsinki and Stockholm, 1978, Athens, 1979, Warsaw, 1992, and Helsinki Biennale, 1981, 1983; Frequent performances and tours with ensembles Poor Knights; Guest Composer for Hungarofilm at Hungarian Broadcasting Company's Electronic Music Studio, 1985, and Slovak Radio (Rustle of Spring), 1986; Composer-in-Residence. *Compositions include:* Orchestral: Consort Music 1, 2, 4, 5; The Garden of Delights; Venezia; 3 guitar concertos; Goya; Cello Concerto, 1999; Operas: The Nuns; Laurentius nunc and semper, 1998; The Night of Wishes, 2000; Ballet, The Changeling Princess, 1997; Radiophonic works: The Rise of Mr Jonathan Smith; Magnus Cordius, entries in a diary; Vocal music: Vanha Linna; Hades; Dunk; Notturno inamorata; Seis Canciones de anochecer; Musica Picta for small children; Tape music: Cordamix; Narod; KV-622bis; Moldavia; Rustle of Spring; Multimedia: Zin Kibaru; Firenze 1582; Survol; La Folia; Chamber music: Consort Music 3 for brass nonet; El Palacio del Sonido for 3 guitars; Consort Music 6 for 12 recorders; Musical graphics and pictographic scores for educational purposes; Many arrangements and reconstructions of early music and Ancient Greek music, e.g. the world's first opera, Jacopo Peri's Euridice. *Recordings include:* The King's Hunt, Esa-Pekka Salonen, French horn; Cordamix; Rasenie järi, Rustle of Spring; The Garden of Delights, Austrian RSO, conductor Leif Segerstam; Consort Music I, Clas Pehrson, recorders, Swedish RSO, conductor Leif Segerstam. *Address:* Laajavuorenkuja 5 B 11, 01620 Vantaa, Finland.

**RECHNAGEL, Axel;** Organist and Cantor; b. 27 March 1936, Århus; m. 2 d. *Education:* Århus Cathedral School, 1954; University of Århus, 1955–59; State Academy of Music, Århus, 1960; Vienna, Austria, 1959; USA, 1969. *Career:* Organist, Ringkobing, 1961; Organist and Kantor, Nyborg, Denmark, 1965; Retired 1999; mem, Dansk Organist og Kantor Samfund; Det danske Orgelselskab. *Compositions:* Koncert for Orgel, 1968. *Recordings:* Concerto for Organ, 1993. *Publications:* Concerto For Organ, The Society for the Publication of Danish Music, 1998; Co-author, Nyborg Vor Frue Kirke 1388–1988. *Honours:* Toccata for Organ, Odense, Denmark, 1996. *Address:* Grejsdalen 5, 5800, Nyborg, Denmark.

**RECTANUS, L. Hans;** Professor of Music; b. 18 Feb. 1935, Worms, Germany; m. Elisabeth Zilbauer, 1 s., 1 d. *Education:* Civic Music Academy and University, Frankfurt/Main; Academy of Music and Interpretive Art, University of Vienna; School for Protestant Church Music, Schlüchtern/ Hesse; PhD, University of Frankfurt, 1966. *Career:* Teacher (Music, German Literature) for Gymnasium, 1960–63; Lecturer and Assistant, University of Frankfurt/Main, 1963–66; Lecturer, 1966–71, Professor, 1971–, Teachers' College, Heidelberg; mem, Präsidium, Hans Pfitzner Society, Munich; Society for Music Research, Cassel; Society of Professional Choirmasters. *Compositions:* Edited: Hans Pfitzner String Quartet in D minor; Trio for violin, violoncello and piano. *Publications:* Leitmotiv und Form in den Musikdramatischen Werken Hans Pfitzners, 1967; Neue Ansätze im Musikunterricht, 1972; Hans Pfitzner, Sämtliche Lieder mit Klavierbegleitung, vol. I, 1980, vol. II, 1983. *Contributions:* Die Musikforschung; Riemannmusiklexikon; Studien zur Musikgeschichte des 19 Jahrhundert; Mitteilungen der Hans Pfitzner-Gesellschaft; Festschrift H. Osthoff; Renaissance-Studien; Zeitschrift für Musik-Pädagogik; Lexikon der Musikpädagogik; Pfitzner-Studien. *Honours:* Kritiker-Preis, 1956; Recipient, Music Director, Organist Prizes. *Address:* Schlittweg 31, 6905 Schriesheim/Bergstr, Germany.

**REDEL, Kurt;** Conductor and Flautist; b. 8 Oct. 1918, Breslau, Germany. *Education:* Studied flute, conducting and composition at the Breslau Hochschule für Musik. *Career:* Conductor and flute soloist from 1938; Professor at Salzburg Mozarteum, 1938; Professor at the Music Academy

Detmold, 1943; Debut as flautist outside Germany at Menton, 1950; Founded the Munich Pro Arte Orchestra, 1952; Conducted at Festival de Royaumont and the Semaines Musicales in Paris, 1953; Founder and Artistic Director of the Easter Festival at Lourdes; Conductor of the Mozart Chamber Orchestra of Salzburg. *Recordings include:* Bach's Brandenburg Concertos, Orchestral Suites, Die Kunst der Fuge, Musikalisches Opfer, Harpsichord and Violin Concertos, Magnificat, Masses and Cantatas; Telemann Concertos for flute, oboe, trumpet, viola and violin, St Mark Passion and St Matthew Passion; Vivaldi Four Seasons and other concertos; Concerti Grossi by Handel, Torelli, Corelli, Scarlatti, Stölzel; Music by Marais, Couperin, Caldara, Carissimi and Marcello; Mozart Symphonies, Divertimenti, and Concertante K364; Solo flautist in Mozart Sonatas, Quartets and Concertos; Schubert 4th Symphony with the Czech Philharmonic.

**REDEL, Martin Christoph;** German composer; b. 30 Jan. 1947, Detmold. *Education:* studied with Kelterborn and Gishele Klebe at Detmold, and with Isang Yun in Hanover. *Career:* Faculty, Detmold Hochschule from 1971, Professor of Composition 1979, Rector 1993; President of Jeunesses Musicales 1992. *Compositions include:* String Quartet, 1967; Strophen, for orchestra, 1970; Epilog for baritone, flute and guitar, 1971; Dispersion, for ensemble, 1972; Kammersinfonie II, 1972; Konfrontationen, for orchestra, 1974; Correspondences, for 2 percussion, 1975; Interplay for ensemble, 1975; Mobile, for oboe, clarinet and bassoon, 1976; Concerto for Orchestra, 1978; Espressioni, for woodwind quintet, 1980; Traumtanz for percussion and strings, 1981; Bruckner Essay for orchestra, 1982; Clarinet Quintet, 1988; Visions Fugitives for accordion and percussion, 1993; Teamwork, for 17 instruments, 1997; Vivo, for 4 percussion, 1997. *Publications:* Grundlagen des Kadenzspiels im Tonsatzunterricht 1975. *Honours:* Arthur Honegger Prize. *Website:* www.martin-redel.info.

**REDGATE, Christopher (Frederick);** Oboist and Lecturer; b. 17 Sept. 1956, Bolton, Lancashire, England; m. Celia Jane Pilstow, 3 Oct 1981, 2 s. *Education:* Chetham's School of Music, Manchester; Royal Academy of Music, London. *Career:* Solo and chamber performances, England, Europe, USA; Many performer-in-residence courses for composersl; Artist-in-Residence, Victorian College of the Arts, Melbourne, Australia, including recitals, lectures, recordings, 1983; Toured Canada, 1985; American debut, Pittsburgh International Festival of New Music, 1986–92; Professor of Oboe, Darmstadt International School for Contemporary Music, 1978–2003; Performed regularly with the Phoenix Wind Quintet, Krosta Trio, Exposé, Lontano; Broadcasts, radio in the United Kingdom and Netherlands; Television; Many works written or commissioned for him by Michael Finnissy, James Clarke, Roger Redgate and others. *Recordings:* Pascillli for oboe; Platinium Fiction by Luca Francescin; Lost Lard, oboe music of Michael Finnissy; Quintets by Redgate, Fox and Clarke; Ferneyhough's Allegebrah and Coloratura. *Address:* 1 Batten Place, Sandford-on-Thames, Oxfordshire OX4 4SZ, England.

**REDGATE, Roger;** Composer; b. 3 June 1958, Bolton, England. *Education:* Chetham's School of Music, Manchester; RCM, London, with Edwin Roxburgh; Freiburg Hochschule, with Brian Ferneyhough. *Career:* Co-founder, with Richard Barrett, Ensemble Exposé, 1984; Northern Arts Fellow in Composition; Universities of Durham and Newcastle, 1989–92; Lecturer in Composition Goldsmiths' College, London, 1997–. *Compositions include:* 2 String Quartets, 1983, 1985; Eidos for piano, 1985; Eperons for oboe and percussion, 1988; Vers-Glas for 14 amplified voices, 1990; Inventio, for ensemble, 1990; Celan Songs, for soprano and ensemble, 1991–4; Beuys for piano, 1992; Feu la Cendre, for cello, 1992; Scribble for ensemble, 1992; Eurydice, multimedia, 1993; Iro/ku, for prepared piano, 1994,... still... for bass flute, violin, viola and cello, 1995. *Honours:* Darmstadt Kranich-Steiner Prize for composition, 1988. *Address:* c/o Music Department, Goldsmiths' College, University of London, New Cross, London SE14 6NW, England.

**REDOLFI, Michel;** Composer; b. 8 Dec. 1951, Marseilles, France. *Education:* Studied I Marseilles and at the University of San Diego, 1973–84. *Career:* Co-founder, Groupe de Musique Electroacoustique, Marseilles, 1969; Director, Centre International de Recherche Musical, Nice, 1986–; Development of concept of sub-aquatic concerts, in California and France; Also sound installations for public buildings in Austria, Germany, Netherlands and France. *Compositions include:* Pacific Tubular Waves (1978), Immersion (1979), Too Much Sky (1986), Volare (1987) and Desert Tracks (1988), all for tape; Sub-aquatic works: Sonic Waters (1981–91), Crysallis (1992) and Virtual Lagoon (1997); Multi-media: L'ecume de la nuit (1984), La Galaxie du Caiman (1990) and Matu Pan (1993); Sound Installations Les murs ont la parole (Paris, 1984), Phoenix, jardin de s. (Nice, 1990), Hurricane (Paris, Disneyland, 1991), Pavillon de Monaco (Seville, 1992) and Atlanticum (Bremerhaven, 1996); Electronic, with tape; Nausicaa (1991), Jungle (1991), Portrait (1993), Songes drolatiques (1994), and Millennium (1995). *Honours:* Prix Luigi Russolo, 1978; Prix Ars Electronica, 1994, 1996. *Address:* Centre de la Musique Contemporain, 16 Place de la Fontaine auz Lions, 75019, Paris, France.

**REEDER, Haydn (Brett);** Composer, Pianist and Conductor; b. 27 Feb. 1944, Melbourne, Victoria, Australia. *Education:* BMus, University of Melbourne, 1965; MA, La Trobe University, 1991. *Career:* Editor for Universal Edition, Schott and Chester, music publishers, 1970–82; Lecturer, La Trobe University, 1984–88; Commissions from Elision and Melbourne Windpower, 1987–88. *Compositions include:* Mandala Rite for clarinet and guitar, 1982;

Strad Evarie, for cello and piano, 1984; Temi Distratti for trombone, cello and percussion, 1985; Sirens' Hotel, chamber opera, 1986; Masks for piano, 1986; Clashing Auras for wind octet, 1989; Dance in a Mirror of Time, for 7 instruments, 1989; Chants at Play with Solid Background, 1990; Glances Repose, for violin, 1990; Draw neat to the Bell for guitar, 1990; Piano Pieces 1–3. *Honours:* Primo, Citta di Trieste Orchestral Competition. *Address:* c/o APRA, 1A Eden Street, Crows Nest, NSW 2065, Australia.

**REEKIE, Jonathan;** British music administrator; *Chief Executive, Aldeburgh Productions;* m.; two c. *Career:* co. co-ordinator, Glyndebourne Opera 1988–91; Musica nel Chiostra, Batignano; founder Almeida Opera 1992; Chief Exec., Aldeburgh Productions 1997–; trustee of Arts Foundation. *Address:* Aldeburgh Productions, Snape Maltings Concert Hall, Snape, Suffolk IP17 1SP, England (office). *Telephone:* (1728) 687100 (office). *Fax:* (1728) 687120 (office). *E-mail:* enquiries@aldeburgh.co.uk (office). *Website:* www.aldeburgh .co.uk (office).

**REES, Jonathan;** Violinist and Director; b. 1963, England. *Education:* Studied at the Yehudi Menuhin School and with Dorothy DeLay at Juilliard. *Career:* Student engagements at the Windsor, Gstaad and Llandaff Festivals and three tours of the Netherlands; Later recitals at the Bath, City of London, Brighton, Henley and Salisbury Festivals; Concerto soloist with the Bournemouth Sinfonietta, Philharmonia, London Soloists Chamber Orchestra and the Royal Philharmonic; Concerts with the Academy of St Martin in the Fields at Carnegie Hall, the Festival Hall and at St Martin's Church; Beethoven's Concerto with the Bournemouth Sinfonietta, 1990; Director of the Scottish Ensemble: concerts in Edinburgh, elsewhere in Scotland and in Austria, Belgium, France, Germany, the Netherlands, Norway and North and Central America; Festivals include Berlin, Guelph, Prague, Sofia, Cheltenham and Edinburgh; Royal Command Performances at the Palace of Holyrood House and at Balmoral. *Honours:* Prizewinner, 1978, BBC Young Musician of the Year Competition; 1st Prize, Royal Overseas League Competition, 1979.

**REEVE, Stephen;** British composer; b. 15 March 1948, London, England. *Education:* Liège Conservatoire with Henri Pousseur. *Career:* major comms for BBC South 1975, Inst. for Research and Co-ordination in Acoustics and Music 1980, Inst. of Contemporary Arts, London 1985; mem. PRS. *Compositions:* The Kite's Feathers 1969–70, Japanese Haikai for mezzo and ensemble, Colour Music for woodwind quartet 1970, Poème: Couleurs du Spectre for orchestra with optional light projection 1972–73, Summer Morning by a lake full of colors, an expansion of Schoenberg's Farben for large orchestra 1974, Aux régions éthérées for three chamber groups 1975–76, Grande thèse de la petite-fille de Téthys, an ethnic encyclopaedia for solo cello 1980–87, L'Oracle de Delphes music-theatre for brass quintet 1985, Strophe for solo rock and four classical guitars 1985–86, Les Fées dansent selon la mode double scene for three to five dancer-percussionists and six to ten or more actor extras 1988–89, O que Zeus apparaisse à l'horizon for gamelan ensemble and tape 1989–90, Volontaires d'Icare for harpsichord trio 1995. *Address:* 73 Knightsfield, Welwyn Garden City, Herts., AL8 7JE, England (home).

**REEVES, Paul;** Singer (Bass); b. 1970, England. *Education:* Guildhall School, London, with Rudolf Piernay; National Opera Studio. *Career:* Roles at GSMD included Budd in Albert Herring, Pasquale in The Aspern Papers by Argento and Rossini's Basilio; Appearances at Mozart's Publio for the Glyndebourne Tour, Colline in La Bohème and Speaker in The Magic Flute for British Youth Opera; Ramphis in Aida for Ashleyan Opera, Mozart's Bartolo for Opera Box and Sarastro in Die Zauberflöte for Kentish Opera; Season 2001 with the King in Raymond Gubay's Aida at the Albert Hall, and Matthew in Birtwistle's The Last Supper at Glyndebourne; Recitals at the Wigmore, Fairfield and Blackheath Halls. *Honours:* Richard Lewis-Jean Shanks Award; Tillett Trust Award. *Address:* c/o Glyndebourne Festival Opera, Lewes, Sussex BN8 5UU, England. *Telephone:* 01273 812321. *Fax:* 01273 812783.

**REGAZZO, Lorenzo;** Singer (Bass); b. 1968, Venice, Italy. *Education:* Studied with Regina Resnik and Sesto Bruscantini. *Career:* Many appearances at the Rossini Festival, Pesaro, in La Scala di Seta, La Cenerentola and L'Ingano felice; Salzburg Festival as Publio in La Clemenza di Tito and in Les Boréades by Rameau, conducted by Simon Rattle; Further engagements in L'Italiana in Algeri at Munich and Venice, La Gazza Ladra, Rossini's Zelmira (Lyon) and Il Viaggio a Reims (Bologna); Royal Opera House 2000–01, as Publio, Alidoro in La Cenerentola and Lorenzo in I Capuleti e i Montecchi; Performances in Don Giovanni at Vienna, Milan and Brussels, Handel's Agrippina in Paris and as Mozart's Figaro at the 2001 Salzburg Festival; Concerts with the Berlin Philharmonic, under Claudio Abbado. *Address:* c/o Opéra Bastille, 120 Rue de Lyon, 75012 Paris, France.

**ŘEHÁNEK, František,** PhDr; Czech philologist, musicologist and teacher; b. 13 Sept. 1921, Mistek; m. Marie Řehánková-Motáčková 1954; one s. *Education:* Charles Univ., Prague, Music School, Mistek, Univ. of Brno, studied violin with Gabriel Štefánek and Josef Muzika. *Career:* mem. Czech Soc. of Musicology. *Publications include:* Janáček's Teaching of Harmony (dissertation) 1965, Leoš Janáček's Sonata for Violin and Piano 1988, Harmonic Thinking of Leoš Janáček 1993, Leoš Janáček and the Whole-Tone System 1998; contrib. Modality in Janáček's Music Theory (in Colloquium Probleme der Modalität, Leoš Janáček heute und morgen) 1988, Modality in the Works of Vitezslav Novák (in Zprávy Spolecnosti Vitezslava Nováka 17) 1990, To the Problem of Modality with Bohuslav Martinů (in Colloquium Bohuslav Martinů, his Pupils, Friends and Contemporaries) 1990,

Alois Hába's Wallachian Suite (in Zpávy Spolecnosti Vitězslava Nováka 25, 26) 1995, On Harmonic Thinking of Leoš Janáček (in Hudebni věda) 2001, Fourth Chords of Leoš Janáček (in Miscellanea, Czech Soc. of Musicology) 2001, The Diatonic Modes with Leoš Janáček (in Hudebni věda) 2003. *Address:* Vlnařská 692, 460 01 Liberec VI, Czech Republic (home).

**REHNQVIST, Karin;** Composer; b. 21 Aug. 1957, Stockholm, Sweden; m. Hans Persson 1982, one d., two s. *Education:* Swedish Royal Academy of Music, Stockholm, with Gunnar Bucht, Pär Lindgren and Brian Ferneyhough. *Career:* Conductor, Stans Kör choir, 1976–; mem., Society of Swedish Composers, 1985–; Royal Acad. of Music, Sweden. *Compositions include:* Stråk for strings, 1982; Dance for piano, 1984; Davids nimm, 3 female voices, 1984; Kast, for strings, 1986; Songs from the Saga of Fatumeh, for male chours, 1988; Here I am, Where are you? for girls' voices, 1989; Violin Concerto, Skrin, 1990; The Triumph of Being for girls' voices, 1990; Lamento for orchestra, 1993; Sun Song, for female voice, speakers and chamber orchestra, 1994; Visletens lov for mixed chorus, 1996; Arktis Arktis! for orchestra, 2000–01; On the Far Side, concerto for clarinet and orchestra, 2002; Teile dich Nacht for mixed choir and solo female voice, 2002; Ljus av ljus (Lumière source de lumière) for children's choir and symphony orchestra, 2003. *Publications:* Young People – New Music, an introduction to composition. *Honours:* Läkerol Arts Award, 1996; Expressen's Spelmannen Prize, 1996; Christ Johnsson Prize, 1997; City of Stockholm Honour Prize, 1999; Kurt Atterberg Prize, 2001; Litteris et Artibus, 2002. *Address:* Swedish Music Information Centre, 79 Sandhamnsgatan, 10254 Stockholm, Sweden. *Website:* www.editionreimers.se/tt/kr; www.mic.stim.se.

**REIBEL, Guy;** Composer; b. 19 July 1936, Strasbourg, France. *Education:* Studied with Messiaen and Serge Wigg. *Career:* Groupe de recherches musicales, 1963–; Lecturer in electro-acoustic music at the Paris Conservatoire; Founded Atelier des Choeurs, Radio France, 1976; Director, Groupe Vocal de France, 1986–90, with many premieres; Adviser to Cité De la Musique, La Villette, 1983–89; Professor of Composition, Paris Conservatoire, 1976; Collaborations with Pierre Schaeffer. *Compositions include:* Musaiques for 2 voices, percussion and orchestra, 1987; Fugitivement à la surface de l'eau, for ensemble, 1989; Variations cinétiques, ensemble, 1989; Etudes de flux, for orchestra, 1990; Métaphores, for soprano and two guitars, 1991; Le coq et le renard, for flute and chorus, 1991; La Marseillaise des Mille, for 500 voices and orchestra, 1992; Calliphores, for 12 voices, 1995; Musique en Liesse, for 12 brass and 2 percussion, 1995; Trois Epigrammes de Clément Marot, chorus, 1996; Surface Légèrement spérique, for tape, 1996; Mamemimomusiques, for orchestra, 1997. *Publications include:* Essais sur l'idée musicale, 1997. *Address:* Centre de Musique Contemporain, 16 Place de la Fontaine, 75019 Paris, France.

**REICH, Steve,** MA; American composer; b. 3 Oct. 1936, New York; s. of Leonard Reich and June Carroll; m. Beryl Korot 1976; two s. *Education:* Cornell Univ., Juilliard School of Music, Mills Coll. *Career:* studied composition with Berio and Milhaud; also studied at the American Soc. for Eastern Arts and in Accra and Jerusalem; f. own ensemble 1966; Steve Reich and Musicians have completed numerous tours world-wide 1971–; his music performed by maj. orchestras and ensembles in United States and Europe; recipient of three Rockefeller Foundation Grants 1975–81 and a Guggenheim Fellowship; mem. American Acad. of Arts and Letters 1994; Bavarian Acad. of Fine Arts 1995; Regent Lectureship, Univ. of Calif. at Berkeley 2000; Montgomery Fellowship, Dartmouth Coll. *Major works include:* It's Gonna Rain (tape) 1965, Come Out (tape) 1966, Melodica (tape) 1966, Piano Phase for two pianos or two marimbas 1967, Violin Phase for violin and tape or four violins 1967, My Name Is for three tapes recorders and performers (manuscript only) 1967, Pendulum Music for 3 or 4 microphones, amplifiers and loudspeakers 1968, Four Organs for four electric organs and maracas 1970, Phase Patterns for four electric organs 1970, Drumming for 4 pairs of tuned bongo drums, 3 marimbas, 3 glockenspiels, 2 female voices, whistling and piccolo 1970–71, Clapping Music for two musicians clapping 1972, Music for Pieces of Wood for five pair of tuned claves 1973, Music for Mallet Instruments, Voices, and Organ 1973, Six Pianos 1973, Music for 18 Musicians (Grammy Award for Best Contemporary Composition 1995) 1974–76, Music for a Large Ensemble 1978, Variations for Winds, Strings, and Keyboards 1979, Octet 1979, Tehillim for voices and ensemble 1981, Vermont Counterpoint for amplified flute and tape 1982, The Desert Music for 10 singers (amplified) and reduced orchestra 1984, Eight Lines for ensemble 1983, Sextet for percussion and keyboards 1984, New York Counterpoint for amplified clarinet and tape, or 11 clarinets 1985, Six Marimbas (transcription of Six Pianos 1973) for 6 marimbas 1986, Three Movements for orchestra 1986, Electric Counterpoint for electric guitar or amplified acoustic guitar and tape, amplified guitar soloist and tape, or guitar ensemble 1987, The Four Sections for orchestra 1987, Different Trains for string quartet and tape (orchestrated 2000) (Grammy Award for Best Contemporary Composition 1990) 1988, The Cave (with Beryl Korot) for amplified voices and ensemble 1993/2003, Duet for two solo violins and string ensemble 1993, Typing Music 1993, Nagoya Marimbas for two marimbas 1994, City Life for amplified ensemble 1995, Proverb for voices and ensemble 1995, Triple Quartet for amplified string quartet (with pre-recorded tape), or three string quartets, or string orchestra 1998, Know What Is Above You for four women's voices and 2 percussion 1999, Electric Guitar Phase for electric guitar and pre-recorded tape (arrangement of Violin Phase 1967) 2000, Tokyo/Vermont Counterpoint for KAT MIDI mallet and pre-recorded tape (arrangement of Vermont Counterpoint 1981)

2000, Three Tales (video opera, video by Beryl Korot) 2002, Dance Patterns for 2 xylophones, 2 vibraphones, 2 pianofortes 2002, Cello Counterpoint for amplified cello and multi-channel tape 2003, You Are (Variations) (text by Rabbi Nachman of Breslov (English), Psalms (Hebrew), Wittgenstein (English) and Pirke Avot (Hebrew) for amplified ensemble and voices, no brass, 2 marimbas, 2 vibraphones, 4 pianofortes, strings, and voices 2004. *Recordings include:* Come Out, Violin Phase, It's Gonna Rain, Four Organs, Drumming, Six Pianos, Music for Mallet Instruments, Voices and Organ, Music for a Large Ensemble, Octet and Variations for Winds, Strings and Keyboards, Music for 18 Musicians, The Desert Music, Electric Counterpoint, Different Trains, The Four Sections, Nagoya Marimbas, City Life, Proverb, Hindenburg (in collaboration with Beryl Korot). *Honours:* Commdr des Arts et Lettres 1999; Dr hc (Calif. Inst. of the Arts) 2000; Koussevitzky Foundation Award 1981, Schumann Prize, Columbia Univ. 2000. *Current Management:* c/o Elizabeth Sobol, IMG Artists, 825 Seventh Avenue, New York, NY 10019, USA; c/o Andrew Rosner, Allied Artists 42, Montpelier Square, London, SW7 1JZ, England. *Telephone:* (212) 774-6721 (New York); (20) 7589-6243 (London). *Fax:* (212) 246-1596 (New York); (20) 7581-5269 (London). *E-mail:* artistsny@imgworld.com. *Website:* www.imgartists.com; www.alliedartists.co .uk; www.stevereich.com.

**REICHERT, Manfred;** Conductor; b. 5 May 1942, Karlsruhe, Germany. *Education:* Studied at the Karlsruhe Hochschule, 1961–65; Musicology at the University of Fribourg/Breisgau, 1966–67. *Career:* Producer at South West German Radio, Baden-Baden, 1967–83; Founded the chamber group Ensemble 13, 1973; Directed the festivals Wintermusik and Musik auf den 49ten at Karlsruhe, 1980 and 1983; Artistic Director of the Festival of European Culture at Karlsruhe, 1983–87; Teacher at the Hochschule für Musik at Karlsruhe from 1984; Conducted the premieres of Hans-Jürgen von Bose's Variations for Strings, 1981, Wolfgang Rihm's Chiffre-Zyklus, 1988, and Gejagte Form, 1989.

**REID-SMITH, Randall;** Singer (Tenor); b. 1959, Barboursville, West Virginia, USA. *Education:* Studied in Cincinnati and New York. *Career:* Sang in concert and opera at Santa Fe, Dayton and Michigan; Roles have included Don José, Rodolfo and Pinkerton; Brunswick Opera from 1990, as Don Ottavio, Rossini's Almaviva, Fenton in Falstaff and Nemorino; Dortmund Opera from 1993, as Tamino, Ferrando and the Duke of Mantua; Sang Don Ottavio at Aachen, 1995; Guest appearances at Leipzig, Madrid, Vienna and Bregenz. *Address:* c/o Dortmund Opera, Kuhstrasse 12, 4600 Dortmund, Germany.

**REIMANN, Aribert;** Composer and Pianist; b. 4 March 1936, Berlin, Germany. *Education:* Berlin Hochschule für Musik with Boris Blacher (composition), Ernst Pepping (counterpoint) and Rausch (piano), 1955–59; Studied musicology at the University of Vienna, 1958. *Career:* Professor of the Contemporary Lied at the Hamburg Musikhochschule, 1974–83, Berlin Hochschule der Künste, 1983; Freelance composer, notably of operas; Accompanist to Dietrich Fischer-Dieskau in Lieder recitals; London premieres, Lear and The Ghost Sonata, 1989; Opera Das Schloß premiered at the Deutsche Oper Berlin, 1992, Bernarda Albas Haus premiered at the Bavarian State Opera, Munich, 2000; mem, Berlin Akademie der Künste, 1971; Bayerische Akademie der Schönen Künste, 1976; Freie Akademie der Künste, Hamburg, 1985; Order 'Pour le Mérite' for Science and Art, 1993; Grand Cross with Star for Distinguished Service of the Order of Merit, 1995; Commander of the Ordre du Mérite Culturel, Monaco, 1999; 'Goldene Nadel' of the German Association of Playwrights, 1999. *Compositions:* Operas: Ein Traumspiel (Strindberg), 1964; Melusine, 1970; Lear (Shakespeare), 1978; Die Gespenstersonate (Strindberg), 1983; Troades (Euripides), 1985; Das Schloß (Kafka), 1992; Bernarda Albas Haus, 2000; Ballet: Stoffreste, 1958, revised as Die Vogelscheuchen, 1970; Orchestral: Elegie for orchestra, 1957; Cello Concerto, 1959; Monumenta for wind and percussion, 1960; Piano Concerto No. 1, 1961, No. 2, 1972; Sinfonie (from the opera Ein Traumspiel), 1964; Rondes for string orchestra, 1967; Loqui, for orchestra, 1969; Music from the ballet Die Vogelscheuchen, 1970; Variations for orchestra, 1975; Sieben Fragmente, 1988; Concerto for violin, cello and orchestra, 1988–89; Violin Concerto, 1995–96; 9 Stücke, 1993; Violin Concerto, 1997; Vocal: Ein Totentanz, baritone, chamber orchestra, 1960; Hölderlin-Fragments, soprano, orchestra, 1963; 3 Shakespeare Sonnets, baritone, piano, 1964; Epitaph, tenor, 7 instruments, 1965; Verra la Morte, cantata, 1966; Inane, soprano, orchestra, 1968; Zyklus, baritone, orchestra, 1971; Lines, soprano, strings, 1973; Wolkenloses Christmas, Requiem for baritone, cello, orchestra, 1974; Lear, symphony for baritone, orchestra, 1980; Unrevealed, baritone, string quartet, 1980; Tre Poemi di Michelangelo, 1985; Neun Sonette der Louize Labé; Chacun sa Chimère, for tenor and orchestra, 1981; Three Songs (poems by Edgar Allan Poe), 1982; Requiem, soprano, mezzo, baritone, orchestra, 1982; Ein apokalyptisches Fragment, for mezzo, piano and orchestra, 1987; Orchestration of Schumann's Gedichte der Maria Stuart, 1988; Lady Lazarus, for soprano solo, 1992; Eingedunkelt, for alto solo, 1992; Nightpiece (James Joyce) for soprano and piano, 1992; Schubert's Mignon Lieder, for soprano and string quartet, 1995; Kumi Ori, for baritone and orchestra, 1999; Drei Gedichte der Sappho, for soprano and 9 instruments, 2000; Chamber: Piano Sonata, 1958; Canzoni e Ricercare for flute, viola and cello, 1961; Cello Sonata, 1963; Nocturnos, for cello and harp, 1965; Reflexionen, for 7 instruments, 1966; Spektren, for piano, 1967; Variationen, for piano, 1979; Invenzioni, for 12 players, 1979; Solo for cello, 1981; String Trio, 1987; Auf dem Weg, for piano, 1989–93; Solo for viola, 1996; Metamorphosen, for 10 instruments,

1997; Solo for clarinet, 2000. *Honours:* Berlins Arts Award for Music (Young Generation), 1962; Rome Prize, 1963; Schumann Prize, Düsseldorf, 1964; Stuttgart Award for Young Composers, 1966; Critics Award for Music, Berlin, 1970; Grand Cross for Distinguished Service of the Order of Merit, 1985; Ludwig Spohr Prize of Braunschweig, 1985; Prix de composition musicale, Fondation Prince Pierre de Monaco, 1986; Bach Prize of the Free Hanseatic City of Hamburg, 1987; Order of Merit of the state of Berlin, 1988; Frankfurt Music Award, 1991. *Current Management:* Schott Musik International GmbH & Co KG. *Address:* c/o Yvonne Stern, Schott Musik International GmbH & Co KG, Weihergarten 5, 55116 Mainz, Germany.

**REINEMANN, Udo;** Singer (Baritone); b. 6 Aug. 1942, Lubeck, Germany. *Education:* Studied at Krefeld, the Vienna Academy of Music and with Erik Werba and W Steinbruck at the Salzburg Mozarteum, 1962–67. *Career:* Debut: Song recital at Bordeaux, 1967; Gave more recitals, then studied further with Germaine Lubin in Paris and with Otakar Kraus in London; Many performances in Lieder, opera and oratorio; Founded a vocal quartet, 1975, with Ana-Maria Miranda, Clara Wirtz and Jean-Claude Orliac (Lieder Quartet); Sang in the premiere of Adrienne Clostre's opera Nietzsche, 1978; My Chau Trong Thuy by Dao, 1979. *Recordings include:* Vocal quartets by Haydn; Lieder by Clara Schumann and Richard Strauss; Posthumous Lieder by Hugo Wolf. *Honours:* 1st Prize for concert singing, Vienna Academy of Music, 1967.

**REINER, Thomas;** Composer; b. 12 Aug. 1959, Bad Homburg, Germany (Australian resident from 1979). *Education:* BA, La Trobe University, 1983; Study with Hans Werner Henze, 1984–86, Barry Conyngham and Peter Tahourdin, 1987–89; MMus, University of Melbourne, 1990; PhD, University of Melbourne, 1996; Electronic and computer music studies, 1997–. *Career:* Staff Member, University of Melbourne, 1990–91, and Monash University, 1993–98. *Compositions include:* Journey and Contemplation for guitar and ensemble, 1987; Moth and Spider for alto saxophone and percussion, 1988; Paraphrase, Surge and Response, for orchestra, 1988; Bali Suite, for ensemble, 1989; Fantasy and Fugue for trombone, 1989; Kalorama Prelude for piano, 1989; Schumannianna: An Orchestration of Robert Schumann's Mondnacht, 1991; Baby Orang Utan for piano, 1991; Words for 6 solo voices, 1992; Three Sketches for cello, 1993; Construction in Time for guitar and piano, 1993; Oblique for flute, 1994; Flexious for flute and guitar, 1995–96; Septet for chamber ensemble, 1996; Grace Notes for B flat clarinet, 1997. *Publications:* Author of articles on musical time and electronic dance music. *Honours:* Prizes in the International Witold Lutoslawski Composers Competition, 1992; Dorian Le Gallienne Composition Award, 1994; Albert H Maggs Composition Award, 1995; International Borwil Composer's Competition, 1997. *Address:* c/o APRA, 1A Eden Street, Crows Nest, NSW 2065, Australia.

**REINHARDT, Rolf;** Conductor; b. 3 Feb. 1927, Heidelberg, Germany. *Education:* Studied piano with Frieda Kwast-Hodapp and composition with Wolfgang Fortner. *Career:* Conducted Opera in the Heidelborg, Stuttgart, Darmstadt 1948–1957; GMD Oper und Konzerte in Trier (1959–1968) Assistant Bayreuth 1954–57; 1968–1992 Leiter der Opernabteilung Hochschule für Musik und Darstellende Kunst Frankfurt/M; 1973–1983 Leiter das Hachchores Köln; Zahlreiche Schallplatten und Kundfunkautnahmen. *Recordings:* Bach's Magnificant, Cantatas and Concertos for harpsichord and violin; Haydn Sinfonia Concertante and Concertos for trumpet, Horn and oboe; Mozart Violin Concertos, Concertante K297b, Thamos King of Egypt and Litaniae Lauretanae; Handel Organ Concertos and Silete Venti; Stamitz Viola Concerto, Sinfonia Concertante; Bartók 1 and Brahms 2 Piano Concertos, with György Sandor; Mozart Bastien and Bastienne, La Finta Giardiniera; Bartók Music for Strings, Percussion and Celesta, Wooden Prince and Miraculous Mandarin; Beethoven Egmont; Schumann Cello Concerto, Violin Fantasia, Konzertstück for four horns and D minor Introduction and Allegro; Dvořák and Goldmark Violin Concertos, with Bronislav Gimpel; Lieder accompanist for Fritz Wunderlich. *Honours:* Two Grand Prix du disque by Durante (6 Concerto grossi) and Bartok (Wooden Prince/ Miraculous Mandarin); Lieder accompnist u.a. for Fritz Wunderlich. *Address:* Staatliche Hochschule für Musik, Escherheimer Landstrasse 33, Postfach 2326 Frankfurt, Germany.

**REINHARDT-KISS, Ursula;** Singer (Soprano); b. 3 Nov. 1938, Letmathe, Sauerland, Germany. *Education:* Studied with Ellen Bosenius in Cologne and Irma Beilke in Berlin. *Career:* Debut: Saarbrücken, 1967 as Marie in Der Waffenschmied; Sang in Saarbrücken until 1969 then Aachen, 1969–71; Guest appearances in Lubeck, Cologne, Zürich, Antwerp, Milan, Copenhagen and Rome; Drottningholm in 1983 in Il Fanatico Burlato by Cimarosa; Komische Oper Berlin as Susanna and Lulu, and Dresden Staatsoper as Aminta in Die schweigsame Frau; Sang at Graz in 1985, in Angelica Vincitrice di Alcina by Fux, returning in 1987 in the premiere of Der Rattenfänger by Cerha; Also sings Salomé in Hérodiade by Massenet. *Recordings:* Sacred Music by Mozart; Lazarus by Schubert; Epitaph for Garcia Lorca, by Nono. *Address:* c/o Vereinigte Bühnen, Kaiser Josef Platz 10, 8010 Graz, Austria.

**REINHART, Gregory;** Singer (Bass); b. 1955, USA. *Career:* Sang at Tourcoing, 1981, in Paisiello's Il Re Teodoro, Innsbruck, 1982 and 1987, in Cesti's Oronte and Semiramide; King of Scotland in Ariodante at Nancy (1983) and in Henze's English Cat at the Paris Opéra-Comique, 1984; Nice, 1986, as Henry VIII in Anna Bolena and at Aix-en-Provence as Ismenor in Campra's Tancrède; London concert performances of Poppea and Moses und Aron, 1988; Opéra-Bastille Paris, 1990, as Panthé in Les Troyens and Santa Fe, 1992, as Mozart's Commendatore; Sang Basil Hallward in the premiere of Lowell

Liebermann's The Picture of Dorian Gray, Monte Carlo, 1996; Other roles include Lord Robinson in Il Matrimonio Segreto, Monteverdi's Seneca, Huascar in Les Indes Galantes and Douglas in Rossini's Donna del Lago; Sang Claudio in Handel's Agrippina at Halle, 1999; Premiere of K.... by Philippe Manouri at the Opéra Bastille, Paris, 2001. *Recordings:* Handel's Tamerlano; Tancrède by Campra; Rameau's Zoroastre; Messiah. *Address:* c/o Cédelle, 78 Boulevard Malesherbes, F–75008 Paris, France.

**REISSIG, Heiko Christian;** German singer (tenor), actor and stage director; b. 19 Feb. 1966, Wittenberge. *Education:* Univ. of Music and Theatre, Leipzig, Berlin and Munich. *Career:* opera singer and actor, Komische Oper, Berlin; Oper Leipzig; Theater Hof, Görlitz and other venues in Germany; actor, film and TV; singer, numerous festivals and concert tours abroad including Japan, Mexico and Austria; mem. Int. Yehudi Menuhin Soc., London, Int. Soc. Supporting Young Stage Artists (pres.), BühnenReif. *Address:* c/o BR - Künstlerskretariat, Postfach 67 02 34, 10207 Berlin, Germany. *Telephone:* 4 22 74 87. *E-mail:* heikoreissig@gmx.de. *Website:* www.heikoreissig.de.

**REITER, Alfred;** Singer (Bass); b. Dec. 1965, Augsburg, Germany. *Education:* Studied at Munich Music Academy and with Astrid Varnay and Hans Hotter. *Career:* Debut: Wiesbaden State Theatre, 1995 as Lefort in Lortzing's Zar und Zimmermann; Performances of Mozart's Sarastro at the Deutsche Oper Berlin, Ludwigsburg Festival, Vienna and Lisbon; Monteverdi's Seneca at Nuremberg and Stuttgart; Hans Schwarz and Titurel in Parsifal at the Bayreuth Festival, Pogner in Meistersinger at Nuremberg, Fafner in Siegfried at Geneva and in Das Rheingold at the Vienna Staatsoper; Royal Opera Covent Garden 2001–02 as Titurel and as Peneios in Strauss's Daphne (concert); Season 2002–03 as Sarastro in Salzburg, Paris and London, Timur in Turandot at San Francisco and Gurnemanz in Cardiff, Geneva and Bologna; Concerts include Haydn's Die Schöpfung (Ludwigsburg 2000) and Beethoven's Missa Solemnis (Philadelphia, 2001). *Current Management:* Balmer & Dixon Management AG, Kreuzstrasse 82, 8032 Zürich, Switzerland. *Telephone:* (43) 244-8644. *Fax:* (43) 244-8649. *Website:* www.badix.ch.

**RELYEA, John;** singer (baritone); b. 1970, Canada. *Education:* studied with Jerome Hines. *Career:* appearances from 1995 with San Francisco Opera as Colline, and Mozart's Figaro; Metropolitan Opera as Alidoro in La Cenerentola and in Die Meistersinger and Lucia di Lammermoor; Escamillo at the Paris, Hamburg and Munich Operas; concerts include Elijah in San Francisco, Bach's B minor Mass with the Cleveland Orchestra and Magnificat in Philadelphia; Beethoven's 9th and Messiah with the Pittsburgh SO; Verdi Requiem under Antonio Pappano in Brussels and Frankfurt; Mozart's C minor Mass with the Boston SO, and Requiem in Pittsburgh 2001–02; further engagements at Covent Garden in La Bohème, Semele and Lucia di Lammermoor. *Honours:* winner Merola Grand Finals, San Francisco 1995, Richard Tucker Award 2004. *Current Management:* Askonas Holt Ltd, Lonsdale Chambers, 27 Chancery Lane, London, WC2A 1PF, England. *Telephone:* (20) 7400-1700. *Fax:* (20) 7400-1799. *E-mail:* info@askonasholt.co .uk. *Website:* www.askonasholt.co.uk.

**REMEDIOS, Alberto Telisforo,** CBE; British singer (tenor); b. 27 Feb. 1935, Liverpool; s. of Albert Remedios and Ida Remedios; m. 1st Shirley Swindells 1958; one s.; m. 2nd Judith Hosken 1965; one s. one d. *Career:* studied with Edwin Francis, Liverpool; joined Sadler's Wells Opera Co. 1955; now sings regularly with ENO and Royal Opera House, Covent Garden; has made numerous appearances in USA, Canada, Argentina, Germany, France and Spain and appeared in concert with major British orchestras. *Recordings include:* Wagner's Der Ring des Nibelungen and Tippett's A Midsummer Marriage. *Honours:* Queen's Prize, Royal Coll. of Music; First Prize, Int. Singing Competition, Sofia, Bulgaria; Sir Reginald Goodall Award Wagner Soc. 1995. *Address:* c/o Stuart Trotter, 21 Lanhill Road, London, W9 2BS, England. *Telephone:* (20) 7289-6315.

**REMEDIOS, Ramon;** Singer (Tenor); b. 9 May 1940, Liverpool, England. *Education:* Studied at the Guildhall School of Music, the National School of Opera and the London Opera Centre. *Career:* Has sung with Opera For All, Scottish Opera, Welsh National Opera and European companies; Notably as Alfredo, Macduff, Ismaele in Nabucco, Grigory/Dimitri, Don Ottavio, the Duke of Mantua, the Painter in Lulu, Skuratov (From the House of the Dead), Tamino and Almaviva; English National Opera: Alfredo, Rodolfo, Don José, Pinkerton, Paris in La Belle Hélène, Smith in the British premiere production of Christmas Eve (1988) and Lensky in Eugene Onegin; Covent Garden, 1990, as Uldino in a new production of Attila; Television appearances in Top C's and Tiaras, and The Word by Rick Wakeman; Season 1992 as Sir Bruno Robertson in I Puritani at Covent Garden; Concert engagements include operatic arias in Glasgow, a Viennese Evening at the Festival Hall and Verdi's Requiem (Royal Festival Hall, Mar 1991). *Recordings include:* The Word, with the Eton College Choir; Kalman's Countess Maritza with New Sadler's Wells Opera; A Suite of Gods, songs by Rick Wakeman. *Honours:* School Tenor Prize, Ricordi Prize and Countess of Munster Trust, Guildhall School of Music; Finalist, Kathleen Ferrier Competition. *Address:* c/o The Master-singers, 15 David Avenue, Wickford, Essex SS11 7BG.

**REMENIKOVA, Tanya;** cellist and cello teacher; b. 31 Jan. 1946, Moscow, USSR; m. Alexander Braginsky. *Education:* Moscow Conservatoire, studied with Prof. Rostropovich. *Career:* regular appearances in recitals and with various orchestras, including Israel Philharmonic, Orchestra National de Belgique; Foreign tours: Europe, Taiwan, People's Republic of China; New York debut, 1979; Radio: BBC, RTB (Belgium), WFMT (Chicago), WQXR (New York); North American tours: Chicago, New York, Washington, DC, Minneapolis, Los Angeles, elsewhere; Professor of Cello, School of Music, University of Minnesota; Artist-in-Residence, Churchill College, Cambridge, 1981, 1986; Premieres of Stephen Paulus, American Vignettes, 1988; mem, College Music Society; American String Teachers' Association. *Recordings:* Stravinsky, Suite Italienne; Shostakovich, Sonata op 40; Britten, Sonata in C; Rachmaninov, Sonata Op 19; Grieg, Sonata Op 36. *Honours:* Gold Medal, Gaspar Cassado Cello Competition, 1969; Eugene Ysaye Award for Musical Contribution, Brussels, 1979. *Address:* 4141 Dupont Avenue South, Minneapolis, MN 55409, USA.

**REMEŠ, Vaclav;** violinist; b. 1950, Czechoslovakia. *Education:* Prague Conservatory. *Career:* founder mem., Prazak String Quartet 1972; tour of Finland 1973, followed by appearances at competitions in Prague and Evian; concerts in Salzburg, Munich, Paris, Rome, Berlin, Cologne and Amsterdam; tour of the UK 1985, including Wigmore Hall debut; tours of Japan, the USA, Australia and New Zealand; tour of the UK 1988, and concert at the Huddersfield Contemporary Music Festival 1989; recitals for the BBC, Radio France, Dutch Radio, the WDR in Cologne and Radio Prague; appearances with the Smetana and LaSalle Quartets in Mendelssohn's Octet. *Honours:* 1st Prize, Chamber Music Competition of the Prague Conservatory, 1974; Grand Prix, International String Quartet Competition, Evian Music Festival, 1978; 1st Prize, National Competition of String Quartets in Czechoslovakia, 1978; Winner, String Quartet of the Prague Spring Festival, 1978.

**REMMERT, Birgit;** Singer (Alto); b. 1966, Germany. *Education:* Studied at the Detmold Musikhochschule with Helmut Kretschmar. *Career:* Sang in Beethoven's Ninth under Nikolaus Harnoncourt in London, 1991, and again under Giulini in Stockholm, 1994; Further concerts include Mendelssohn's Walpurgisnacht in Graz, Biber's Requiem and Vespers under Harnoncourt in Vienna, the song cycle Sunless by Mussorgsky, in Amsterdam, and Das Lied von der Erde under Philippe Herreweghe at the Théâtre des Champs-Elysées, Paris; Holland Festival 1992, as Martha in Tchaikovsky's Iolantha, Hamburg, 1993 as Erda in the Ring and Ulrica at Dresden; Zürich Opera, 1994, as Dalila, Suzuki and Third Lady in Die Zauberflöte; Other repertory includes Mahler's Eighth and Das klagende Lied (with Chailly at the Concertgebouw), Mahler 3rd Symphony with Simon Rattle in Birmingham and the Nurse in Monteverdi's Poppea at Salzburg Festival; Mahler's Second with the CBSO under Rattle at the 1999 London Proms; Sang Fricka in Das Rheingold and Die Walküre at the Bayreuth Festival, 2000; Mahler's Symphony of a Thousand at the London Proms, 2002. *Recordings include:* Beethoven's Ninth; Lieder by Brahms, Clara Schumann and Tchaikovsky; Bach Cantatas with Peter Schreier; Bruckner, Te Deum and F Minor Mass with Welser-Möst. *Honours:* Lieder Prize at the Palma d'oro Competition, Ligure.

**RENDALL, David;** Singer (Tenor); b. 11 Oct. 1948, London, England. *Education:* Studied at the Royal Academy of Music and at the Salzburg Mozarteum. *Career:* Debut: Glyndebourne Touring Company, 1975, as Ferrando in Così fan tutte; Covent Garden from 1975, as the Italian Tenor in Der Rosenkavalier, Almaviva, Matteo, Rodolfo, Des Grieux in Manon and Rodrigo in a new production of La Donna del Lago by Rossini (1985); Glyndebourne Festival, 1976, Ferrando, returned as Belmonte and Tom Rakewell (1989); English National Opera from 1976, as Leicester in Mary Stuart, Rodolfo, Alfredo, Tamino and Pinkerton; European debut at Angers, 1975, as the High Priest in Idomeneo; North American debut, Ottawa, 1977, as Tamino; New York City Opera, 1978, Rodolfo and Alfredo; San Francisco debut, 1978, Don Ottavio; Metropolitan Opera from 1980, as Ottavio, Ernesto, Belmonte, Idomeneo, Lenski, Ferrando, Alfred in Die Fledermaus and Mozart's Titus; Lyon Opéra, 1983, in the title role of La Damnation de Faust by Berlioz; Further engagements in Amsterdam, Berlin, Paris, Milan, Hamburg, Tel-Aviv, Turin, Washington, Vienna, Dresden, Chicago, Santa Fe and Munich; Other operatic roles include Gounod's Faust (Palermo) and the Duke of Mantua; Many concert appearances in Europe and the USA; Sang the Duke of Mantua and Matteo at Covent Garden, 1989/90; Cavaradossi with English National Opera, 1990; Season 1992 as Don Antonio in the stage premiere of Gerhard's The Duenna (Madrid), Pinkerton at the Coliseum and for Welsh National Opera; Genoa 1996–97, as Hoffmann and Don José; Otello for ENO, 1998; Sang Wagner's Erik at Toronto and Cavaradossi for Covent Garden, 2000. *Recordings:* Maria Stuarda; Così fan tutte; Ariodante; Mozart's Requiem; Beethoven's Missa solemnis; Madama Butterfly; Bruckner's Te Deum. *Honours:* Young Musician of the Year Award, 1973; Gulbenkian Fellowship, 1975. *Address:* c/o IMG Artists, Lovell House, 616 Chiswick High Road, London W4 5RX, England.

**RENICK, Therese;** Singer (Mezzo-soprano); b. 1963, St Louis, Missouri, USA. *Education:* Studied in Vienna with Hilde Zadek. *Career:* Debut: Würzburg, 1985, in Der Barbier von Bagdad by Cornelius; Krefeld Opera, 1985–88, as Carmen and Azucena; Essen from 1989, as Verdi's Eboli and Amneris, and Mozart's Dorabella; Salzburg, 1987–88, in Schoenberg's Moses und Aron; Season 1995–96 as Ortrud in Lohengrin at Dessau and in the premiere of Bose's Schlachthof 5 at Munich; Other roles include Santuzza, Venus in Tannhäuser and Fenena in Nabucco (Munich, 1996); Concerts include the Requiems of Mozart and Verdi, and Beethoven's Ninth. *Address:* Bayerische Staatsoper, Max-Joseph Platz, 80539 Munich, Germany.

**RENICKE, Volker;** Conductor and Professor; b. 3 July 1929, Bremen, Germany; m. Rey Nishiuchi, 5 April 1975. *Education:* Nordwestdeutsche Musikakademie, Detmold, 1950–54; Accademia Chigiana, Siena, with Paul van Kempen. *Career:* In Korea, 1991, with Korean Symphony Orchestra in the Korean Orchestral Festival; Tokyo Mozart 200 Anniversary of Death, Idomeneo, 1991; In Seoul Opera Favorita and Fidelio at National Theatre, 1992; International Festival in Tsuyama, Japan, Mozart Tito, 1993; Salzburg Mozart Requiem, 1993; Guest conducting and concerts in England, France, Germany, Netherlands, Luxembourg, Switzerland, Italy, Yugoslavia and Korea; Concerts with all major Japanese orchestras; In Korea with Seoul Philharmonic Orchestra and Korean Symphony Orchestra; Zauberflöte and Traviata in Opernhaus Köln, 1995; mem, Kojimachi Rotary Club, Tokyo. *Recordings:* With Jörg Demus and NHK Orchestra members; Piano concertos of Bach, Haydn, Mozart, Debussy, Franck, Fauré; With Karl Suske, violin, and NHK Orchestra members; Recordings of Vivaldi and Bach; Humperdinck's Hansel and Gretel, in Japanese, with Yomiuri Orchestra. *Current Management:* Christoph Schellbach, Representation of Classical Musicians in Europa, Lutherstrasse 7, D 34117 Kassel, Germany. *Address:* 5-26-15 Okuzawa, Setagaya-ku, 158 Tokyo, Japan.

**RENNERT, Jonathan,** MA, FRCO, ARCM, LRAM; British organist, harpsichord continuo player, conductor and writer; b. 17 March 1952, London, England; m. Sheralyn Ivil 1992; one d. *Education:* St Paul's School, London, Foundation Scholar, Royal Coll. of Music, Organ Scholar, St John's Coll., Cambridge, Stuart of Rannoch Scholar in Sacred Music, Univ. of Cambridge. *Career:* numerous recitals, concerts, recordings, radio and TV appearances world-wide as conductor, solo organist, accompanist or continuo player; Dir of Music, Holy Trinity Church, Barnes, London 1969–71; Musical Dir Cambridge Opera 1972–74; Dir of Music, St Jude's, Courtfield Gardens, London; conductor American community choirs in London 1975–76; Acting Dir of Music, St Matthew's, Ottawa, Canada 1976–78; Dir of Music, St Michael's, Cornhill, London, Musical Dir St Michael's Singers 1979–; Musician-in-Residence, Grace Cathedral, San Francisco, USA 1982; Conductor Elizabethan Singers 1983–88; Festival Dir Cornhill Festival of British Music 1982–88; Admin. Int. Congress of Organists, Cambridge 1987; Course Dir and Chair. Cen. London Dist Cttee, Royal School of Church Music 1995–; Musical Dir London Motet and Madrigal Club 1994–; Dir of Music, St Mary-at-Hill, London, and Dir St Mary-at-Hill Baroque Chamber Orchestra and Bach Cantata Series 1996–; Master of the Reigate Choristers (from St Mary's Choir School) 1997–2000; moderating and training examiner, Associated Bd of the Royal Schools of Music; Examiner and fmr Council mem. Royal Coll. of Organists; mem. Incorporated Soc. of Musicians (Warden, Performers' and Composers' Section 2002–03), Worshipful Co. of Musicians (Master 2003–04). *Publications:* William Crotch (1775–1847): Composer, Teacher, Artist 1975, George Thalben-Ball: A Biography 1979; contrib. of articles to New Grove Dictionary of Music and Musicians, Die Musik in Geschichte und Gegenwart (DGG). *Honours:* Hon. Fellow, Royal Canadian Coll. of Organists. *Address:* 46 Doods Road, Reigate, Surrey, RH2 0NL, England (home). *Telephone:* (1737) 244604 (home). *E-mail:* jonathanrennert@hotmail.com (home).

**RENNERT, Wolfgang;** German conductor and music and opera director; *Principal Guest Conductor, Semperoper, Dresden;* b. 1 April 1922, Cologne; s. of Dr Alfred Rennert and Adelheid (née Nettesheim) Rennert; m. 1st Anny Schlemm 1957 (divorced 1968); m. 2nd Ulla Berkéwicz 1971 (divorced 1975); one s.; m. 3rd Simone Kaempf 2004. *Education:* Mozarteum Salzburg. *Career:* Chief Conductor and Deputy Dir of Music, Frankfurt 1953–67; Head of Opera, Staatstheater am Gärtnerplatz 1967–71; Dir of Music and Dir of Opera, Nat. Theatre, Mannheim 1980–85; Perm. Guest Conductor, State Opera, Berlin 1970–2000; Guest Conductor, Royal Opera, Copenhagen 1975–79; Prin. Guest Conductor, Semperoper, Dresden 1991–; Prin. Guest Conductor, Portuguese Symphony Orchestra, Lisbon 1998–2002; guest appearances with Vienna State Opera, Munich and Hamburg Operas, Royal Opera House Covent Garden, San Francisco Opera, Dallas Opera, Salzburg Festival, Munich Festival and Venice, Rome and Palermo opera houses. *Address:* Holbeinstrasse 58, 12203 Berlin, Germany. *Telephone:* (30) 8333094.

**RENTOWSKI, Wieslaw (Stanislaw Vivian);** Composer and Organist; b. 23 Nov. 1953, Bydgoszcz, Poland; m. Magdalena Kubiak, 5 Sept 1985, 1 s. *Education:* MA, Psychology, University of Łódź, 1978; MA, Organ, Academy of Music, Łódź, 1985; MA, Composition, Fr Chopin Academy of Music, Warsaw, 1987; MMus, Composition, Louisiana State University School of Music, 1991. *Career:* Debut: Carnegie Hall, Lagniappe for 8 instruments, 1991; Compositions performed at: International Festival of Contemporary Music, Warsaw Autumn, 1984, 1986, 1987, 1989; Internationale Sinziger Orgelwoche, Bonn, 1989, 1990; Festival International de Lanaudière, Canada, 1989; International Festival of Contemporary Music, Baton Rouge, USA, 1990, 1991; Organist, many performances and recordings including solo recitals and chamber concerts in Warsaw, Banff, Toronto, Bayreuth, Baton Rouge and New Orleans. *Compositions:* Por dia de anos, published in 1987 and 1989; Chorea minor, published 1989. *Recordings:* Anagram, 1986; Wayang, 1989; Por dia de anos, 1990; Anagram, 1986; Wayang, 1989. *Contributions:* Intellectual music harmony, article to Ruch Muzyczny national musical magazine, Poland, 1989. *Address:* Louisiana State University School of Music, Baton Rouge, LA 70803, USA.

**RENZETTI, Donato;** Conductor; b. 30 Jan. 1950, Milan, Italy. *Education:* Studied at the Conservatorio Giuseppe Verdi, Milan. *Career:* Assisted Claudio Abbado in Milan, then conducted the Verdi Requiem in Salzburg; Gave Rigoletto at Verona in 1981 and has since worked at most Italian opera houses; Conducted the premiere of Corghi's Gargantua at Turin, 1984; Paris Théâtre Musical, Macbeth; Conducted La Sonnambula at the Chicago Lyric

Opera, 1988, and Le nozze di Figaro at Rome, 1989; Bonn Opera and Teatro Fenice, Venice, 1990, with Il Barbiere di Siviglia and Ernani; Has given orchestral concerts in Italy and elsewhere; Conducted Turandot at the 1996 Macerata Festival and at Dallas, 1998. *Honours:* Prizewinner at the Gino Marinuzzi International Competition, 1976; Bronze Medal, Ernest Ansermet Competition at Geneva, 1978; Guido Cantelli Prize at Milan, 1980. *Address:* c/o Teatro dell'Opera, Piazza Beniamino Gigli 8, 00184 Rome, Italy.

**RENZI, Emma;** South African singer (soprano); b. 8 April 1926, Heidelberg, Transvaal. *Education:* Coll. of Music, Kapstad, London Opera Centre, studied with Santo Santonocito in Catania, with Virginia Borroni in Milan. *Career:* debut, Karlsruhe as Sieglinde 1961; has sung in major cities world-wide, including Milan, Genoa, Lisbon, Buenos Aires, Barcelona, Edinburgh, Mexico City, Johannesburg, Naples, Rome and Munich; Italian Radio in Parisina by Mascagni 1977; Verona Arena 1989; other roles include Norma, Aida, Amelia (Un Ballo in Maschera), Tosca, Leonora (Il Trovatore), Turandot, the Duchess of Parma (Doktor Faust), Abigail, Lady Macbeth, Elisabeth, and Countess Almaviva; Head, Pretoria Technikon Opera School 1981–91; Sr Lecturer in Singing, Witwatersrand Univ. 1992–2003. *Recording:* Emma Renzi: A Tribute. *Honours:* Hon. DMus; Vita Award 1986, OMSS 1987, Nederburg Special Award 1993, ATKV Award 1995. *Address:* 39 Auckland Avenue, Auckland Park, Johannesburg 2092, Gauteng, South Africa (home). *Telephone:* (11) 726-3974 (home). *Fax:* (11) 726-3974 (home).

**REPIN, Vadim Viktorovich;** Russian violinist; b. 31 Aug. 1971, Novosibirsk, Siberia; s. of Viktor Antonovich Repin and Galina Georgievna Repina; m. Nato Gabunia (divorced). *Education:* Novosibirsk Music School with Zakhar Bron. *Career:* toured Europe since 1985; debut in London (Barbican) 1988, in USA 1990; performances with the Royal Concertgebouw, Suddeutscher Rundfunk, Royal, Israel and St Petersburg Philharmonic Orchestras, NHK, Tokyo Metropolitan, Hallé, and Kirov Orchestras, Berlin and Sydney Symphony Orchestras; USA appearances with the Cleveland, Chicago, Minnesota Symphonies and Los Angeles Philharmonic; season 1996–97 with New York Philharmonic; worked with conductors including Menuhin, Bychkov, Gergiev, Prêtre, Rozhdestvensky, Jansons and Boulez; chamber music partners include Boris Berezovsky, Bella Davidovich and Alexander Melnikov; lives in Switzerland. *Recordings include:* Shostakovich No. 1 and Prokofiev No. 2 with the Hallé Orchestra under Nagano 1995, Prokofiev Violin Sonatas and Five Melodies with Berezovsky 1995, Tchaikovsky and Sibelius Concertos with the London Symphony under Krivine 1996, Tchikovsky and Shostakovich piano trios with Berezovsky and Yablonsky 1997, Lalo Symphonie Espagnole with the London Symphony Orchestra under Nagano 1998, Tutta Bravura (with Markovich) 1999, Vadim Repin au Louvre (with Berezovsky, Barachovsky, Lakatos, Gothoni) 1999, Tchaikovsky and Myaskovsky violin concertos with the Kirov Orchestra under Gergiev 2002, A Night of Encores (recorded live with the Berlin Philharmonic under Jansons) 2004. *Honours:* Wieniawski competition winner, Poznan 1982, Tibor Varga competition winner, Sion 1985, Queen Elizabeth competition winner, Brussels 1990. *Current Management:* Interclassica Music Management, Schönburgstrasse 4, 1040 Vienna, Austria. *Telephone:* (1) 5853980 (office). *Website:* www.vadimrepin.com.

**REPPA, David;** Set Designer; b. 2 Nov. 1926, Hammond, Indiana, USA. *Education:* Professional training at the Metropolitan Opera, 1957–58. *Career:* Debut: Designed Le nozze di Figaro for North Shore Opera, New York, 1960; Has worked with Sarah Caldwell's Opera Company of Boston and in Miami and San Francisco; Debut with the Metropolitan Opera, 1974, Duke Bluebeard's Castle and Gianni Schicchi; Other designs include Aida, 1976, Dialogues des Carmélites, 1977, and Don Carlos, 1979; As staff scenic designer has worked with most Metropolitan Opera scenic designers, supervising painting and construction of sets and adapting productions for the company's former spring tours. *Address:* c/o Metropolitan Opera, Lincoln Center, New York, NY 10023, USA.

**REPPEL, Carmen;** Singer (Soprano); b. 27 April 1941, Gummersbach, Germany. *Education:* Studied at the Hamburg Musikhochschule with Erna Berger. *Career:* Debut: Flensburg, 1968, as Elisabeth de Valois; Has sung in Hanover, Hamburg, Frankfurt, Cologne, Mannheim, Wiesbaden and Kassel; Bayreuth Festival, 1977–80, as Freia and Gutrune, and in Die Walküre and Parsifal; Wuppertal, 1983, in a concert performance of Schwarzschwanenreich by Siegfried Wagner; San Francisco, 1983, as Ariadne auf Naxos; Sang Mozart's Electra at Stuttgart, 1985; Hamburg and Vienna, 1985, as Leonore and Chrysothemis; Munich Opera, 1986, as Andromache in the premiere of Troades by Reimann; Zürich Opera, 1986, Salome; Further appearances in Berlin, Zürich, Barcelona, Milan and Tokyo; Other roles include Fiordiligi, Donna Anna, Mélisande, Mimi, Liu, Marenka in The Bartered Bride, Violetta, Desdemona, Leonora in Il Trovatore, Ariadne, Salome, Elsa and Sieglinde; Sang in Flavio Testi's Ricardo III at La Scala, 1987; Sieglinde in Die Walküre at Bologna, 1988; Strauss's Ariadne and Salome, Turin, 1989; Salome at the Torre del Lago festival, 1989. *Recordings include:* Freia and Gerhilde in Der Ring des Nibelungen, from Bayreuth; Les Troyens by Berlioz; Chrysothemis in Götz Friedrich's film version of Elektra.

**RESA, Neithard;** Violist; b. 1950, Berlin, Germany. *Education:* Studied in Berlin with Michel Schwalbe, Cologne with Max Rostal, USA with Michael Tree. *Career:* Prizewinner of German Music Foundation, 1978; Principal Viola of Berlin Philharmonic, 1978; Co-founded the Philharmonia Quartet, Berlin, giving concerts throughout Europe, USA and Japan; British debut, 1987, playing Haydn, Szymanowski and Beethoven at Wigmore Hall; Bath Festival, 1987, playing Mozart, Schumann and Beethoven; Other repertoire includes quartets by Bartók, Mendelssohn, Nicolai, Ravel and Schubert; Quintets by Brahms, Weber, Reger and Schumann. *Address:* Cimbernstr 34A, 14129 Berlin, Germany.

**RESCIGNO, Nicola;** Opera Conductor and Artistic Director; b. 28 May 1916, New York City, USA. *Education:* Italian Jurisprudence Degree, Rome. *Career:* Debut: Brooklyn New York Academy of Music, 1943; Co-Founder, Artistic Director, Chicago Lyric Opera, 1954–56; Presented American Debut of Maria Callas; Co-Founder/Artistic Director, Dallas Civic Opera (The Dallas Opera), 1957–; Regularly presents American debuts; past debuts include, Sutherland, Vickers, Berganza, Montarsolo, Caballé, Knie, Domingo, Olivero, Dimitrova, W Meier; Instrumental in presenting baroque opera including American professional stage premieres of Handel's Alcina, Monteverdi's L'Incoronazione di Poppea, Samson, Giulio Cesare, and Vivaldi's Orlando Furioso; Guest Conductor: San Francisco, Metropolitan (debut 1978, Don Pasquale)Chicago Lyric, Cincinnati, Philadelphia, Washington, Tulsa, Houston, at the Metropolitan Opera has conducted Donizetti's Don Pasquale and L'Elisir d'amore, Rossini's Italiana in Algeri and Verdi's La Traviata; Guest Conductor in Canada, South America, Italy, Portugal, the United Kingdom, Switzerland, Austria and France; Conducted the premiere of Argento's The Aspern Papers, Dallas, 1988; Werther at Rome, 1990; Aida at the 1990 Caracalla Festival, Rome; Season 1991 with Il Barbiere di Siviglia at Philadelphia. *Current Management:* CAMI Conductors Division.

**RESICK, Georgine;** Singer (Soprano); b. 1953, USA. *Education:* Studied with George London. *Career:* Sang Sophie in Werther at Washington; Cologne Opera from 1981 as Marzelline in Fidelio, Oscar, Adina (L'Elisir d'amore) and Anne Trulove; Chicago Opera, 1984, as Blondchen in Die Entführung; Drottningholm Festival, 1985, as Mozart's Susanna and Constanze; Carolina in Il Matrimonio Segreto at Paris and Edinburgh; US appearances from 1986, including Hilde Mack in Henze's Elegy for Young Lovers at Long Beach Opera, 1996. *Recordings include:* Così fan tutte; Video of Le nozze di Figaro. *Address:* Long Beach Opera, 6372 Pacific Coast Highway, Long Beach, CA 90803, USA.

**RESNIK, Regina;** American singer (mezzo-soprano); b. 30 Aug. 1924, d. of Samuel Resnik and Ruth Resnik; m. 1st Harry W. Davis 1947; one s.; m. 2nd Arbit Blatas 1975. *Education:* Hunter Coll., New York. *Career:* opera début as Lady Macbeth, New Opera Co. 1942; Mexico City 1943; New York City Opera 1943–44; Metropolitan Opera 1944–1983; sang 80 roles, soprano and mezzo-soprano, became regular mem. Royal Opera, London, Vienna State Opera, Bayreuth, Salzburg, San Francisco, Chicago, La Scala, Milan, Paris, Buenos Aires, Berlin, Brussels, etc.; Stage Dir for maj. productions Hamburg, Venice, Sydney, Vancouver, Strasbourg, Warsaw, Lisbon, Madrid, Wiesbaden; appeared on Broadway in Cabaret 1987, in A Little Night Music 1990, New York City Opera, 50th anniversary celebrations Danny Kaye Playhouse; Trustee Hunter Foundation, Metropolitan Opera Guild Bd. *Honours:* Dr hc (Hunter) 1991; Lincoln Center and Vienna State Opera awards; Pres.'s Medal, Commdr, Ordre des Arts et des Lettres. *Address:* American Guild of Musical Artists, 1727 Broadway, New York, NY 10019, USA.

**RESS, Ulrich;** Singer (Tenor); b. 29 Oct. 1958, Augsburg, Germany. *Education:* Studied at Augsburg Conservatory, 1975–78, with Leonore Kirchstein from 1979. *Career:* Sang at Stadttheater Augsburg, 1979–84, notably as Idamante and Rossini's Almaviva; Engaged at Bayerische Staatsoper from 1984, as Mozart's Pedrillo and Monostatos, Verdi's Bardolph and Macduff, Beppe in Pagliacci and Pong in Turandot; Sang the Steersman and Strauss's Truffaldino at Munich, 1991; Guest appearances at Bayreuth and Barcelona, 1988–89, as David in Meistersinger, Strasbourg and Nice, Jacquino, 1989; Munich Staatsoper 2000–01 in Carmen, Tannhäuser, Katya Kabanova, Falstaff and Arabella. *Recordings:* Young Servant in video of Elektra conducted by Abbado; Bardolph in Falstaff conducted by Colin Davis; Massimilia Doni by Schoeck. *Address:* c/o Bayerische Staatsoper, Postfach 100184, 8000 Munich 1, Germany.

**REUTER, Rolf;** Conductor; b. 7 Oct. 1926, Leipzig, Germany. *Education:* Studied at the Dresden Hochschule für Musik, 1958–61. *Career:* Repetiteur and conductor at Eisenach, 1951–55; Musical Director at Meiningen, 1955–61; Leipzig Opera, 1961–73 (Generalmusikdirektor from 1963); Music Director at Weimar, 1979–80, Komische Oper Berlin, 1981–94; Professor of Music and Conductor of the orchestra at the Hanns Eisler Hochschule, Berlin; Guest conductor in Cuba, France, Germany, Yugoslavia, Czechoslovakia, Tokyo, Houston, Rome, Buenos Aires, Copenhagen, Moscow and Prague; Gave Der Ring des Nibelungen at the Paris Opéra, 1978, and Tristan und Isolde at the Berlin Staatsoper; Gave the premieres of Guayana Johnny by Alan Bush (1966) and Judith by Siegfried Matthus (1975); Visited Covent Garden and Wiesbaden, 1989, with the company of the Komische Oper, conducting The Bartered Bride and Judith; Conducted a new production of Der Freischütz at the Komische Oper, 1989; Le nozze di Figaro for New Israeli Opera, 1992. *Recordings include:* Beethoven's incidental music for Egmont; Handel: Oratorio L'Allegro, il Moderato ed il Penseroso; Hans Pfitzner: Das Herz and Das Dunkle Reich; Siegfried Matthus: Judith and Hyperion Fragmente; Berlioz: Lélio and Symphonie Fantastique; Mozart: Divertimenti and Oboe Concerto; Festliche Weihnachtskonzerte (Corelli, Telemann, Tartini, Locatelli). *Honours:* Honorary Member, Oper Leipzig; Honorary Member, Komische Oper Berlin. *Current Management:* Berliner Konzertagentur.

*Address:* c/o Berliner Konzertagentur, Dramburgerstrasse 46, 12683 Berlin, Germany.

**REVERDY, Michèle;** Composer; b. 12 Dec. 1943, Alexandria, Egypt; 1 d. *Education:* Literature, Sorbonne, Paris; Counterpoint with Alain Weber, Analysis with Claude Ballif, Composition with Olivier Messiaen, Paris Conservatory; Casa de Velazquez, Madrid. *Career:* Teaching, lycées, 1965–74; Professor of Analysis, regional and municipal conservatories, 1974–83; Producer, Radio-France, 1978–80; Professor, Class of Analysis, Paris Conservatory, 1983–. *Compositions include:* Kaleidoscope for harpsichord and flute, 1975; Number One for guitar, 1977; Météores for 17 instruments, 1978; L'Ile aux Lumières for solo violin and string orchestra, 1983; Scenic Railway for 16 instruments, 1983; La Nuit Qui Suivit Notre Dernier Dîner, chamber opera, 1984; Triade for guitar, 1986; Trois Fantaisies de Gaspard de la Nuit for choir or 12-voice ensemble, 1987; Sept Enluminures for soprano, clarinet, piano and percussion, 1987; Propos Félins for string orchestra and children's choir, 1988; Le Cercle du Vent for orchestra, 1988; Vincent, opera based on the life of Vincent Van Gogh, 1984–89; Le Précepteur, opera (Jakob Lenz) for coloratura soprano, soprano, mezzo-soprano, contralto, 3 tenors, 2 baritones, 3 basses and 20 instruments. *Recordings:* CD, Michèle Reverdy (Scenic Railway, Sept Enluminures, Météores, Fugure, Kaleidoscope); Triade, CD Rafael Andia, guitar; Le Château, 1980–86, Opera for 9 soloists, 2 choirs (men and children), orchestra, text from Franz Kafka. *Publications:* L'oeuvre pour piano d'Olivier Messiaen, 1978; Histoire de la Musique Occidentale, 1985; L'oeuvre pour orchestra d'Olivier Messiaen, 1988. *Address:* 75 rue des Gravilliers, 75003 Paris, France.

**REVZEN, Joel,** BMus, MMus; conductor and pianist; *Artistic Director, Arizona Opera. Education:* The Juilliard School. *Career:* Asst Conductor, St Paul Chamber Orchestra 1986–90; founding Dean, St Louis Conservatory 12 years; Artistic Dir, Berkshire Opera, Mass 1991–; Music Dir, Fargo-Moorhead Symphony –2000; Artistic Dir and Prin. Conductor, Western New York Chamber Orchestra 2000–03; Artistic Dir, Arizona Opera 2003–, also Gen. Dir 2004–; on conducting roster Metropolitan Opera 1999–; guest conductor with Kirov Opera, Prague Symphony Orchestra, Prague Chamber Orchestra, Janáček Philharmonic, Sinfonia of Antwerp, Orchestre Nat. de Lyon, Norwegian Opera, Nat. Theatre Mannheim, Augsburg Symphony, Washington Opera, Minnesota Opera, Tucson Symphony, Dallas Symphony, Florida Philharmonic, Kennedy Center Chamber Players, Minnesota Orchestra, Nat. Symphony, Orchestra of St Luke's, Kansas City Symphony, Utah Symphony, San Antonio Symphony, Symphony of Southwest Florida, Seattle Symphony; as chamber musician has performed with Jaime Laredo, Sharon Robinson, Michael Tree, Arlene Augér. *Recordings:* The Art of Arleen Augér 1994, Haydn, The Seasons 1995, Haydn, Die Schöpfung 1995, Larsen, Water Music 1997, Larsen, Symphony No. 4 2000, Mendelssohn, Concerto for piano and violin 2000, Feminine Escapes 2002, Music by Russell Peterson (composer and conductor) 2002. *Honours:* Dr hc (St Louis Conservatory of Music); Frank Damrosch Prize in Conducting. *Current Management:* Janice Mayer and Associates LLC, 250 W 57th Street, Suite 2214, New York, NY 10107, USA. *Telephone:* (212) 541-5511 (office). *Fax:* (212) 541-7303 (office). *E-mail:* jmayer@janicemayer.com (office). *Website:* www.janicemayer.com (office). *Address:* Arizona Opera, 4600 N 12th Street, Phoenix, AZ 85014, USA (office). *E-mail:* info@azopera.com. *Website:* www.azopera.com.

**REX, Christopher;** Cellist; b. 2 Jan. 1951, Orlando, Florida, USA; m. Martha Anne Wilkins, 30 Nov 1985, 1 s., 1 d. *Education:* Bachelor of Music, Curtis Institute of Music, Philadelphia, Pennsylvania, 1972; Graduate studies with Leonard Rose, Juilliard School, New York. *Career:* Debut: Premiered Stephen Paul's Double Concerto with brother Charles, Lincoln Center, New York; 7 years with Philadelphia Orchestra, 1972–79; Principal Cello, Atlanta Symphony, 1979–; Principal Cello, New York Philharmonic, 1988 European tour; Founding Member, Georgian Chamber Players; mem, NARAS; AFM. *Recordings:* Saint-Saëns, Muse and Poet with Martium Philharmonic. *Publications:* Editor, Mussorgsky's Pictures at an Exhibition; Art work for Choral Journal. *Honours:* First cellist to win Young Artist Competition, American Federation of Music Clubs, 1979. *Address:* 1237 Woods Circle NE, Atlanta, GA 30324, USA.

**REY, Isabel;** Singer (Soprano); b. 1966, Valencia, Spain. *Education:* Studied at the Valencia Conservatory with Ana Luisa Chova and in Barcelona with Juan Oncina and Tatiana Menotti. *Career:* Debut: Bilbao, 1987, as Amina in La Sonnambula; Madrid as Ilia in Idomeneo and Vienna in concerts of Mozart's Exultate Jubilate; Ascanio in Alba (Fauno); Handel's Saul and Beethoven's Ninth; Zürich Opera, 1991–, as Susanna in Le nozze di Figaro, Gilda in Rigoletto, Adina in L'Elisir d'amore; Juliette in Roméo et Juliette, Marie in La Fille du Régiment; Susanna with Harnoncourt, Nederlandse Opera, 1993, 1994; Concerts with José Carreras world-wide, 1993–; Sang Susanna in a new production of Figaro at Zürich, 1996 and at Madrid, 1998; Sang Gilda and Lucia di Lammermoor at Zürich, Susanna at La Coruña, 2000. *Recordings:* Nozze di Figaro (Erato); With José Carreras, Zarzuela Arias and duets. *Address:* Opernhaus Zürich, Falkenstrasse 1, 8008 Zürich, Switzerland.

**REYMOND, Valentin;** Conductor; b. 1954, Neuchâtel, Switzerland. *Education:* Studied at Conservatories of Bienne and Zürich. *Career:* Assistant at the Grand Théâtre Geneva; Has assisted such conductors as Jean-Marie Auberson, Horst Stein, Armin Jordan and Roderick Brydon; Music Director of Opéra Décentralisé; Concert and broadcast appearances with Orchestre de la Suisse Romande and Orchestre de la Radio Suisse Italienne, Orchestre de Chambre de Toulouse, Krasnoyarsk Symphony Orchestra (Siberia), Russian State Symphony Orchestra; Operatic appearances: Traviata (Opéra de Lucerne); Rape of Lucretia (Opéra Décentralisé and Opéra de Lausanne); Albert Herring (Bern Opera, Opéra de Lausanne and Opéra de Nantes); Les Pêcheurs de Perles (Dublin Opera); Les Mamelles de Tirésias, Das Rheingold, Die Walküre, Le Roi Malgré Lui (Opéra de Nantes); L'Etoile (Opera North); Iphigénie en Aulide for Opera North, 1996. *Address:* Music International, 13 Ardilaun Road, London N5 2QR, England.

**REYNOLDS, Anna,** FRAM; British singer (mezzo-soprano); b. 5 June 1931, Canterbury; d. of Paul Grey Reynolds and Vera Cicely Turner; m. Jean Cox 1994. *Education:* Benenden School, Royal Acad. of Music. *Career:* studied with Prof. Debora Fambri, Rome; has appeared at many int. festivals including Spoleto, Edin., Aix-en-Provence, Salzburg Easter Festival, Vienna, Bayreuth, Tanglewood; has sung with leading orchestras all over the world including Chicago Symphony, New York Philharmonic, Berlin Philharmonic, London Symphony, etc.; has appeared in opera performances in New York Metropolitan, La Scala, Milan, Covent Garden, Bayreuth, Rome, Chicago Lyric Opera, Teatro Colón, Buenos Aires, Teatro Fenice, Venice and many others. *Address:* Peesten 9, 95359 Kasendorf, Germany. *Telephone:* (9228) 1661. *Fax:* (9228) 8468 (home). *E-mail:* jean.cox@t-online.de (home).

**REYNOLDS, Julian;** Conductor and Pianist; b. 1962, London, England. *Education:* Vienna Hochschule für Musik and with Albert Ferber. *Career:* Debut: Wigmore Hall recital, 1981; Pianist with European Community Youth Orchestra, 1980–85; Assistant musical director at Netherlands Opera, 1986–94, conducting Bluebeard's Castle by Bartók, Luisa Miller and Mozart's Mitridate; A Midsummer Night's Dream, 1993; Kirov Opera, St Petersburg, with La Traviata and Le nozze di Figaro; Otello at Stuttgart and The Cunning Little Vixen at Maastricht; Concerts throughout the United Kingdom and the Netherlands; Season 1998–99 with Haydn's Seasons at Melbourne and Luisa Miller at Mainz; Associate Conductor of Netherlands Opera from 1999, with L'italiana in Algeri, Figaro and L'Elisir d'amore; Recital appearances with Barbara Bonney and Kiri Te Kanawa; Ravel's Ma Mère l'Oye, and own orchestrations of Alma Mahler Songs. *Address:* c/o IMG Artists, Lovell House, 616 Chiswick High Road, London W4 5RX, England.

**REYNOLDS, Roger (Lee);** Composer; b. 18 July 1934, Detroit, Michigan, USA; m. Karen Jeanne Hill, 11 April 1964, two d. *Education:* BSE, Physics, University of Michigan; BM, Music Literature, MM, Composition, University of Michigan. *Career:* Faculty member, University of California at San Diego, 1969–; George Miller Visiting Professor, University of Illinois, 1971; Founding Director, Center for Music Experiment, University of California at San Diego, 1972–77; Visiting Professor, Yale University, 1981; Senior Research Fellow, ISAM, Brooklyn College, 1985; Valentine Professor of Music, Amherst College, 1988; Rothschild Composer-in-Residence, Peabody Conservatory of Music, Baltimore, 1992–93. *Compositions:* Some 100 compositions including: Dreaming, 1992; Symphony (The Stages of Life), 1991–92; The Emperor of Ice Cream, 1961–62; Visions, 1991; Transfigured Wind, I–IV, 1984–85; Voicespace I–V, 1975–86; Odyssey, 1989–93; last things I think, to think about, 1994; Watershed I, III, IV, 1995; The Red Act Arias, 1997; Justice, 1999–2001. *Recordings:* About 60 on CD or DVD including: Whispers Out of Time; Transfigured Wind IV; Coconino. . . a shattered landscape; The Ivanov Suite; Versions/Stages I–V; Voicespace I, III, IV, V; Variation; Archipelago, Personae; Odyssey; First Custom Designed Classical DVD, Watershed, 1998. *Publications:* 4 books: Mind Models: New Forms of Musical Experience, 1975; A Searcher's Path: A Composer's Ways, 1987; A Jostled Silence: Contemporary Japanese Musical Thought, 1992–93; Form and Method: Composing Music,2002. *Honours:* Pulitzer Prize in Music, 1989, National Institute of Arts and Letters Award, 1971. *Current Management:* Graham Hayter, Contemporary Music Promotions. *Address:* 624 Serpentine Drive, Del Mar, CA 92014, USA. *Website:* www.rogerreynolds.com.

**REYNOLDS, Verne Becker;** Composer and Horn Player; b. 18 July 1926, Lyons, Kansas, USA. *Education:* BM, 1950, Cincinnati Conservatory of Music; MM 1951, University of Wisconsin; Further study with Herbert Howells at the Royal College of Music, London. *Career:* Horn player with the Cincinnati Symphony Orchestra, 1947–50, and first horn of the Rochester Philharmonic, 1959–68; Faculty Member, University of Wisconsin, 1950–53, Indiana University School of Music at Bloomington, 1954–59, and Eastman School of Music at Rochester, 1959–95. *Compositions include:* Violin Concerto, 1951; Saturday with Venus, overture, 1953; Serenade for 13 wind instruments, 1958; Flute sonata, 1962; String Quartet, 1967; Concertare I–V, for various instrumental combinations, 1968–76; Horn sonata, 1970; Violin Sonata, 1970; Ventures for orchestra, 1975; Events for trombone choir, 1977; Scenes Revisited for wind ensemble, 1977; Festival and Memorial Music, for orchestra, 1977; Trio for horn, trombone and tuba, 1978; Fantasy-Etudes I–V for various wind instruments, 1979–92; Concerto for band, 1980; Cello Sonata, 1983; Quintet for piano and winds, 1986; Brass Quintet, 1987; Songs of the Season for soprano, horn and piano, 1988; Trio for oboe, horn and piano, 1990; Clarinet sonata, 1994; Letter to the World for soprano and percussion, 1994; Concerto for piano and wind ensemble, 1996; Concerto for orchestra, 1997; String Quartet, 1998; Sonata for viola and piano, 1998. *Publications:* Horn handbook, 1997. *Address:* 102 Southern Parkway, Rochester, NY 14618, USA.

**RHODES, Cherry;** Educator, Concert Organist and Adjunct Professor; b. 28 June 1943, Brooklyn, New York, USA; m. Ladd Thomas. *Education:* BMus, Curtis Institute of Music, Philadelphia, Pennsylvania, 1964; HS Music, Munich, studied with Karl Richter, 1964–67; Private Study with Marie-Claire Alain and Jean Guillou, Paris, 1967–69; Summer schools, Harvard and University of Pennsylvania, 1961, 1962, 1963. *Career:* Soloist, Philadelphia Orchestra, South German Radio Orchestra, Chamber Orchestra of French National Radio, Pasadena Chamber Orchestra, Phoenix Symphony Orchestra; Los Angeles Philharmonic; First American to win an international organ competition, Munich; Recitals, Lincoln Center, New York City, Notre Dame, Paris, Royal Festival Hall, London, Los Angeles Music Center, Milwaukee Performing Arts Center, Orchestra Hall, Chicago, Meyerson Symphony Center, Dallas; Numerous appearances at national and regional conventions of AGO; Performances, several Bach festivals; International festivals Bratislava, Nuremberg, Paris, St Albans, Luxembourg, Vienna and throughout Poland; Gave opening recital on new organ at John F Kennedy Center in Washington DC; Broadcast performances in USA, Canada and Europe; Adjudicator for national and international organ-playing competitions. *Publications:* Editor, Ascent for Organ by Joan Tower; Co-editor, Prelude and Variations on Old Hundredth by Calvin Hampton. *Address:* Thornton School of Music, University of Southern California, Los Angeles, CA 90089-0851, USA.

**RHODES, Jane;** Singer (Soprano); b. 13 March 1929, Paris, France; m. Roberto Benzi, 1966. *Career:* Debut: Marguerite in La Damnation de Faust, Nancy, 1953; Sang Renata in the first (concert) performance of The Fiery Angel by Prokofiev; Sang in the 1956 premiere of Le Fou by Landowski; Paris Opéra from 1958, as Marguerite, Carmen, Salome, and Kundry, 1974; Metropolitan Opera, 1960, Carmen; Aix-en-Provence, 1961, in L'Incoronazione di Poppea; Paris Opéra-Comique, 1968, in L'Heure Espagnole and La Voix Humaine; Also sang in Duke Bluebeard's Castle by Bartók. *Recordings:* Carmen; La Juive by Halévy; Mireille by Gounod; Margared in Le Roi d'Ys by Lalo; The Fiery Angel; Public Opinion in Orphée aux Enfers.

**RHODES, Michael;** Singer (baritone), Actor and Teacher; b. 13 Aug. 1923, Brooklyn, New York, USA; m Anne Foegen. *Education:* BA, Dartmouth College; Juilliard School of Music; Mannes School; New York College of Music; Actors Studio; Private Study, Voice with Robert Weede, Guiseppe De Luca, Apollo Granforte. *Career:* Debut: New York City Opera, Jochanaan, Salome, 1947; Concert Debut: Carnegie Hall, New York Philharmonic, Stokowski, Boris and Elektra with Mitropoulis; New York City Opera; Berlin Staatsoper; Deutsche Oper, Berlin; Opera National, Paris; La Scala, Milan; Royal Opera Amsterdam; Royal Opera, Copenhagen; Théâtre de la Monnaie, Brussels; Monte Carlo Opera; Rome Opera; Australian Opera, Sydney; Theatre Liceu, Barcelona; Bolshoi, Moscow; Broadway: Carousel, Oklahoma, Most Happy Fella; Radio: NBC Concerts with Toscanini; RAI Wozzeck with Karajan; Masterclasses: Milan, Paris, Barcelona; mem, American Guild of Musical Artists; Deutsche Bühnen Genossenschaft. *Honours:* Commander Italian Republic, 1955, Commander Legion of Honor, 1958; Bellas Artes, Spain, 1960. *Address:* Januarius-Zickstr 1, 54296 Trier, Germany.

**RHODES, Phillip Carl;** Composer; b. 6 June 1940, Forest City, North Carolina, USA. *Education:* Studied with Iain Hamilton at Duke University (BA 1962); Composition with Donald Martino and Mel Powell, theory with Gunther Schuller and George Perle at Yale University (MM 1963). *Career:* Composer-in-Residence and faculty member at Louisville, 1969–72; Composer-in-Residence and Andrew W Mellon Professor of the Humanities at Carleton College, Northfield, Minnesota, from 1974; President of Carleton College Music Society, 1985–87. *Compositions include:* Four Movements for chamber orchestra, 1962; Remembrance for symphonic wind ensemble, 1967; About Faces, ballet, 1970; Divertimento for small orchestra, 1971; String Trio, 1973; Museum Pieces, for clarinet and string quartet, 1973; Quartet, for flute harp, violin and cello, 1975; On the Morning of Christ's Nativity, cantata, 1976; Ceremonial Fanfare and Chorale, for 2 brass choirs, 1977; Wind Songs for children's chorus and Orff instruments, 1979; In Praise of Wisdom, for chorus and brass choir, 1982; Nets to Catch the Wind, for chorus and percussion, 1986; The Gentle Boy, opera, premiered 1987; The Magic Pipe, opera, 1989; Wedding Song, for soprano, violin and organ, 1990; Reels and Reveries, variations for orchestra, 1991; Mary's Lullaby, for soprano, violin and organ, 1993; Chorale and Mediatationa (O Sacred Head Now Wounded) for women's voices and organ, 1995; Fiddle Tunes, for violin and synthesized strings, 1995, Three Appalachian Settings for SATB and Violin 2000, Two Appalachian Settings for String Quartet 2001, Shakespeare in Song for High Voice, Clarinet in B flat and Piano 2001, March Parody (With Variations) for Concert Band 2002, Meditation Upon Lactantius' De Ave Phoenice for Bassoon and Harp 2002; solo instrumental pieces. *Address:* c/o BMI, 320 West 57th Street, New York, NY 10019, USA. *Website:* www.prhodescomposer.com.

**RHODES, Samuel;** Violist; b. 13 Feb. 1941, Long Beach, New York, USA; m. 30 Dec 1968, 2 d. *Education:* BA, Queens College, New York City; MFA, Princeton University. *Career:* Debut: Carnegie Recital Hall, 1966; Faculty of Tanglewood and participant of Marlboro Festival, 1960–; Member of Juilliard String Quartet, 1969–; Faculty Juilliard School, 1969 Appeared: Great Performances, PBS television, 1977; Hindemith: The Viola Legacy 3 Concert Series, Carnegie Recital Hall, 1985; CBS Sunday Morning, 1986; Rcitals: Library of Congress, Washington DC, Juilliard School, Participant in International Hinemith Viola Festival, New York Chapter, 1996–. *Composi-*

*tions:* Quintet for string quartet and viola. *Recordings:* Schoenberg Quartets; Complete Beethoven Quartets; Mozart-Haydn Quartets; Complete Bartók Quartets; Schubert and Dvořák Quartets; Guest Artist with Beaux Arts Trio; 4 Carter Quartets; Berg Lyric Suite; Complete Hindemith Quartets; Mendelssohn Op 12, Op 13; Hindemith Four Viola Solo Sonatas. *Honours:* 3 Grammy Awards, 1971, 1976, 1985. *Address:* c/o The Juilliard School, Lincoln Center, 144 West 66th St, New York, NY 10023, USA.

**RHODES, Teddy Tahu;** New Zealand singer (baritone); b. 1965. *Education:* Guildhall School, London with Ruldoph Piernay and David Harper, also studied with Maud Adams Taylor. *Career:* debut as Dandini in La Cenerentola with Opera Australia 1998; represented New Zealand at Cardiff Singer of the World Competition 1999; season 1999 with Sharples for Canterbury Opera, Marcello and Silvio (Pagliacci) for Opera New Zealand; season 2000–01 as Mozart's Count and Britten's Demetrius for Opera Australia; US debut as Joe in the premiere of Jake Heggie's Dead Man Walking, San Francisco; season 2001–02 as Guglielmo, Belcore and the Herald in Lohengrin for Opera Australia, Escamillo and Marcello for Dallas Opera; Stanley in Previn's A Streetcar Named Desire for Austin Opera; sang Escamillo in Carmen at Dallas 2004, at Sydney Opera House 2005; sang Leander in The Love for Three Oranges and the title role in Don Giovanni at Sydney Opera House, Papageno in Die Zauberflote for WNO, Il conte Almaviva in Le nozze di Figaro at Houston Grand Opera 2005. *Recordings include:* The Voice (Australian Record Asscn Best Classical Album) 2004, Mozart 2005, Vagabond 2005. *Current Management:* Askonas Holt Ltd, Lonsdale Chambers, 27 Chancery Lane, London, WC2A 1PF, England. *Telephone:* (20) 7400-1700. *Fax:* (20) 7400-1799. *E-mail:* info@askonasholt.co.uk. *Website:* www.askonasholt.co.uk.

**RHYS-DAVIES, Jennifer;** Singer (Soprano); b. 8 May 1953, Panteg, Gwent, Wales. *Education:* Studied at Trinity College of Music, London. *Career:* Appearances with Welsh National Opera as the Forester's Wife in The Cunning Little Vixen, Fortune in Poppea, Miss Jessel in Turn of The Screw, also in Dresden and Leipzig, First Lady in Die Zauberflöte and Donna Elvira; Further appearances as Constanze for Opera 80 and Donna Anna for Kent Opera on tour to Valencia; Opera North as Sandrina in La Finta Giardiniera, Aloysia in the Mozart-Griffiths pastiche; Sang Semiramide and Sieglinde at Nuremberg, Queen of Night for Dublin Grand Opera and Scottish Opera, 1993; Covent Garden and English Nationa Opera debut in 1993 as Berta in Barbiere di Siviglia and Mrs Fiorentino in Street Scene; Concert engagements in Beethoven's Mount of Olives and Haydn's Seasons at Dublin, Handel's Dixit Dominus and Poulenc's Gloria for Stuttgart Radio, Haydn's Orlando Paladino at Garsington; Sang Clorinda in Cenerentola at Royal Opera House, The Duenna in Der Rosenkavalier, Amaltea in Moses, Queen of Night in Stuttgart, Lady Macbeth for WNO and Nuremberg; Italian Singer in Capriccio at Glyndebourne, 1998; Season 2000–01 as Mozart's Marcellina at Garsington and Elettra at Basle. *Recordings:* As Berta in Barber of Seville; Various recordings for Opera Rara. *Honours:* Kennedy Scott Prize and Rowland Jones Memorial Award, Trinity College. *Address:* c/o Glyndebourne Festival Opera, Glyndebourne, Lewes, Sussex BN8 5UU, England.

**RHYS-EVANS, Huw;** Singer (Tenor); b. 1959, Tregaron, Ceredigion, Wales. *Education:* Studied, Royal Academy of Music; Studied, National Opera Centre. *Career:* Wide range of operatic engagements; Sang Ferrando in Così fan tutte, America, France, the Netherlands and Majorca; Pedrillo in Die Entfuhrung aus dem Serail, France; Tamino, Die Zauberflote, North Netherlands Philharmonic Orchestra; Ernesto, Don Pasquale; Ismaele Nabucco, Welsh National Opera; Vivaldi Mendelssohn's Die Hochzeit des Camacho, Flanders Festival; First Jew, Salome, Bastille Opéra; Celebrated singer of oratorio; Evangelist in Bach's passions, Netherlands, Leith Hill Music Festival; B Minor Mass, Besançon; Messiah, St Martin-in-the-Fields; The Royal Albert Hall; Singapore Symphony Orchestra; Nelson Mass, Teatro La Fenice, Venice; Elijah, Singapore; Amsterdam Baroque Orchestra; Les Musiciens du Louvre; Evangelist in Bach's St John Passion, Leith Musical Festival, Southwark Cathedral; Evangelist in Bach's St Matthew Passion; Arias, St Matthew Passion, Zupthen, Netherlands; The Seasons, Rochester Cathedral; Elijah, St Paul's Festival Choir; Messiah, Harrogate; Jonathan Saul, Darmstadt, Germany; Pang, Turandot, Mid-Wales Opera; Count Almaviva, The Barber of Seville, Opera North; Idreno in Semiramide, Chelsea Opera Group; Monteverdi Vespers, Mozart Requiem; Belfiore Il viaggio a Reims, Amiens and Versailles; Ottavio in Don Giovanni, 1999 Perth Festival of the Arts; Belmonte in Seraglio, The Opera Project. *Recordings:* Stabat Mater; Ferrando; Pedrillo; Orff. *Address:* 609A Kenton Lane, Harrow Weald, Middlesex HA3 7HJ, England.

**RIBARY, Antal;** Composer; b. 8 Jan. 1924, Budapest, Hungary. *Education:* Diploma in Art History, Pazmany Peter University of Budapest; Diploma in Composition, Academy of Music, Budapest. *Career:* Debut: 2 Michelangelo songs, 1947; The Divorce of King Louis (one-act opera) performed at the Hungarian State Opera House, 1959. *Compositions include:* Pantomime Suite; Hellas Cantata; Requiem for the Lover; Six Lines from the Satyricon; Concerto Grosso; Five Quartets; Four Violin and Piano Sonatas; King Louis Divorces, opera; Two Michelangelo Songs; Five Shakespeare Sonnets; Five Villon Songs; Symphonies I–VII, 1960–84; De Profundis/Motetta; Two Poems for choirs; Rest C G Rossetti; Chant pour 8 Ligne/Baudelaire; Two Piano Concertos, 1979–80; In manuscript: Symphonies V–XII; In Memoriam Charles Beaudelaire; Six portraits imaginaires de Charles Moreas; Four Piano Concertos; Masks and Churches in Spain, suite for orchestra; Two Spanish Songs for voice and piano. *Recordings:* The Music of Antal Ribary,

vols 1, 2 and 3; Sonata for Alto and Piano; Six Staves from Satyricon, 1980. *Publications:* Music Criticism 1960–70. *Address:* Felka 3, 1136 Budapest, Hungary.

**RICCARDI, Franco;** singer (tenor); b. 1921, Italy. *Career:* debut in Naples, 1947, as Pinkerton; has sung widely in Italy, and notably at La Scala Milan from 1954, as Monostatos, Missail, Goro, Pang, and Bardolph; Rome Opera, 1963, as David in Die Meistersinger; Caracalla Festival and Verona Arena, 1968–69; sang at Dallas Opera, 1970, Martina Franca Festival, 1982; other roles have included Borsa in Rigoletto, Arturo in Lucia di Lammermoor, Cassio and Shuisky.

**RICCI, Ruggiero;** American violinist; b. 24 July 1918, San Francisco; s. of Pietro Ricci and Emma Bacigalupi; m. 1st Ruth Rink 1942; m. 2nd Valma Rodriguez 1957; m. 3rd Julia Whitehurst Clemenceau 1978; two s. three d. *Education:* under Louis Persinger, Mischel Piastro, Paul Stassévitch and Georg Kulenkampff. *Career:* début with Manhattan Symphony Orchestra, New York 1929; first tour of Europe 1932; served USAF 1942–45; Prof. of Violin, Indiana Univ. 1970–73, The Juillard School 1975–78, Univ. of Mich. 1982–87, Hochschule für Musik, Mozarteum, Salzburg, Austria 1989–2002; played first performances of the violin concertos of Ginastera, Von Einem and Veerhoff; specializes in violin solo literature. *Recordings:* over 500 recordings, including the first complete recording of Paganini Caprices. *Publications:* Left Hand Violin Technique 1987. *Honours:* Cavaliere Order of Merit (Italy); Officier de l'Ordre des Arts et Lettres (France) 2004. *Current Management:* Intermusica, 16 Duncan Terrace, London, N1 8BZ, England. *Telephone:* (20) 7278-5455 (office). *Address:* 1099 West Chino Canyon Road, Palm Springs, CA 92262, USA (home). *Telephone:* (760) 320-9785 (home). *Fax:* (760) 320-4768 (home). *E-mail:* jricci1@dc.rr.com (home). *Website:* www.ruggieroricci.com.

**RICCIARELLI, Katia;** Italian opera singer; b. 18 Jan. 1946, Rovigo; m. Pippo Baudo 1986. *Education:* Benedetto Marcello Conservatory (Venice). *Career:* Debut at Mantua 1969; appearances include Lyric Opera, Chicago, USA 1972, Royal Opera House, Covent Garden, London 1974, La Scala, Milan 1976, Metropolitan Opera Co., New York, USA 1975, San Francisco Opera, USA, Paris Opera, Verona Festival, Palermo 1997, Lecce 1998. *Operas include:* La Bohème 1969, 1974, I Due Foscari 1972, Suor Angelica 1976, Anna Bolena, Lucrezia Borgia, Imogene, Don Carlos 1989. *Recordings include:* I Due Foscari, Turandot, Carmen, Aida, Un Ballo in Maschera, Falstaff, Il Trovatore, La Bohème, Tosca. *Address:* c/o John Coast Ltd, Manfield House, 376-9 Strand, London WC2R 0LR, England (office).

**RICH, Alan,** AB, MA; American music critic, editor and writer; b. 17 June 1924, Boston, MA. *Education:* Harvard Univ., Univ. of California, Berkeley, studied in Vienna, Austria. *Career:* Asst Music Critic, Boston Herald 1944–45, New York Sun 1947–48; contrib., American Record Guide 1947–61, Saturday Review 1952–53, Musical America 1955–61; music teacher, Univ. of California, Berkeley 1950–58; Programme and Music Dir, Pacifica Foundation FM Radio 1953–61; Asst Music Critic, New York Times 1961–63; Chief Music Critic and Ed., New York-Herald Tribune 1963–66; Music Critic and Ed., New York World-Journal-Tribune 1966–67; Contributing Ed., Time magazine 1967–68; Music and Drama Critic and Arts Ed., California magazine 1979–83, Contributing Ed. 1983–85; Gen. Ed., Newsweek magazine 1983–87; Music Critic, Los Angeles Herald-Examiner 1987–; teacher, New School for Social Research 1972–75, 1977–79, Univ. of Southern California School of Journalism 1980–82, California Inst. of the Arts 1982–; artist-in-residence, Davis Center for the Performing Arts, CUNY 1975–76. *Publications:* Careers and Opportunities in Music 1964, Music: Mirror of the Arts 1969, Simon and Schuster Listener's Guide to Music (three vols) 1980, The Lincoln Center Story 1984; contrib. numerous articles and reviews to various journals. *Address:* c/o Los Angeles Herald-Examiner, 1111 S Broadway, Los Angeles, CA 90015, USA.

**RICH, Elizabeth;** Concert Pianist; b. 8 Feb. 1931, New York City, USA; m. Joel Markowitz, 30 June 1952, 2 s., 1 d. *Education:* Juilliard School of Music; Scholarships at ages 7–18. *Career:* Debut: New York Philharmonic Auditions, Young People's Concert, Carnegie Hall, 1949; English premiere of Clara Schumann Piano Concerto, Beethoven Choral Fantasy, Queen Elizabeth Hall, London, 1985; Complete Cycle, Mozart Piano Sonatas, NY, 1984–85; Guest artist at Mt Desert Festival of Chamber Music, 1987–91, 1993, 1994 and 1995; 4th Recital, Alice Tully Hall, Lincoln Center, 1993; Mozart Concerto and Bach Concerto, St Martin's in the Field, London Chamber Soloists Orchestra, 1993; Opened Mozart Days at the Prague Festival in the Dvořák Hall, Prague, 1997; Schumann Concerto, Bridgeport Symphony, January 25th, 1997; Mozart recital at Weill Hall, Carnegie Hall, 2000; Weill Hall Recital, April 15th, 2004; 'In Their Own Words', Bach, Schumann, Weber, Beethoven; Mozart Piano Concerto, K271, Purcell Room, London Chamber Soloists Orchestra, October 12th, 2001; Schumann Concerto, Kalamazoo Symphony, February 18th, 2001. *Contributions:* Article in Piano Today, Winter 2001, Playing Late Mozart. *Recordings:* For Dutch radio; Schumann CD for Connoisseur Society, 6 Noveletten and Carnaval, 1992; 2 Piano Concerti of Carl Maria von Weber, Clara Schumann Concerto, Janáček Philharmonic Orchestra, 1995; Haydn and CPE Bach, 1998; Complete Mozart Sonatas, vols I–III, 2000–01, vol IV, 2004;. *Current Management:* Liegner Management. *Address:* c/o Liegner Management, PO Box 884, New York, NY 10023, USA.

**RICHARD, André;** Composer and Conductor; b. 18 April 1944, Berne, Switzerland. *Education:* Studied in Geneva, and in Freiburg with Klaus Huber and Brian Ferneyhough, 1975–78. *Career:* Director, Freiburg Institute for New Music, 1980–; Horizonte Concert Series, Freiburg, until 1989; co-founder, Freiburger Solistenchor, 1983, with concerts of works by Luigi Nono, and others; Director of experimental studio at Heinrich Strobel Foundation, from 1989. *Compositions include:* Ritornelle, for 3 precussion instruments, 1976; Cinque, for piano, 1979; Trilogie, for flute, oboe and harpsichord, 1981; String Quartet, 1982; Etude sur la carré rouge, for chamber ensemble, 1984–6; Echanges, for orchestra and live electronics, 1986; Musique de rue (Street Music) for 6 instruments and tape, 1987; Glidif for bassoon, clarinet, 2 doublebasses and live electronics, 1990. *Publications include:* Articles on the music of Luigi Nono, 1991, 1993. *Address:* c/o SUISA, Rue de l'Hopitâl 22, Case Postele 409, 2001 Neuchâtel, Switzerland.

**RICHARDS, Denby;** British music critic, author and lecturer; b. 7 Nov. 1924, London; m. Rhondda Gillespie 29 May 1973. *Education:* Regent Street Polytechnic, London; self-taught piano and 50 years attending concerts and studying scores. *Career:* early writing on Kensington News, then Music Critic to Hampstead and Highgate Express for 30 years; contrib. to Music and Musicians from first issue 1952, Ed. 1981–84, Opera Ed. 1984–; Ed. Musical Opinion 1987–; numerous radio and TV appearances in UK, USA, Scandinavia, Australia; Lecturer, including Seminar Course on History and Function of Western Musical Criticism, at Yale Univ., USA; mem. The Critics' Circle, Royal Overseas League, Zoological Soc. of London. *Publications:* The Music of Finland 1966; numerous programme notes and record sleeves. *Contributions to:* Music and Musicians, Records and Recording, Musical Opinion, New Film Review, Parade, other journals in UK and internationally. *Address:* 2 Princes Road, St Leonards-on-Sea, East Sussex, TN37 6EL, England. *Telephone:* (1424) 715167 (office). *Fax:* (1424) 712214 (office). *E-mail:* musicalopinion2@aol.com (office). *Website:* www.musicalopinion.com (office).

**RICHARDS, Timothy;** Singer (Tenor); b. 1970, Wales. *Education:* Royal Northern College of Music and with Dennis O'Neill. *Career:* Concerts throughout the United Kingdom and Europe including Messiah, the Mozart and Verdi Requiems, The Creation and Rossini's Stabat Mater; Opera roles include Alfredo for Welsh National Opera, The Duke of Mantua at Innsbruck and Cassio in Otello at Basle; Season 1999–2000 with Macduff in Leipzig and Rodolfo, Nemorino and Fenton for Dresden Opera; Other roles include Tamino, British Youth Opera, Belmonte and Verdi's Ismaele. *Address:* Harlequin Agency Ltd, 203 Fidlas Road, Cardiff CF4 5NA, Wales.

**RICHARDSON, Carol;** Singer (Mezzo-soprano); b. 1948, California, USA. *Education:* Studied at Occidental College, Los Angeles, with Martial Singher in Philadelphia and in New York. *Career:* Debut: Klagenfurt, 1973, as Nicklausse in Hoffmann; Sang at Kiel from 1975, Bayreuth Festival, 1976–81, in Parsifal; Engagements at Bern Stadttheater until 1984, Cenerentola at Bielefeld, 1988; Other roles have included Dorabella and Cherubino, Rosina, Orlofsky, Nancy in Martha, Lola and Zerlina; Further guest appearances at Hamburg, Gelsenkirchen, Karlsruhe and Hanover; Noted concert performer; Season 1998 at ENO in Purcell's Fairy Queen and the premiere of Dr Ox's Experiment by Gavin Bryars. *Address:* c/o English National Opera, St Martin's Lane, London WC2N 4ES, England.

**RICHARDSON, Marilyn;** Singer (Soprano) and Stage Director; b. 1936, Sydney, New South Wales, Australia; m. (1) Peter Richardson, 1954, 3 c., (2) James Christiansen, 1974, 3 step-c. *Education:* Diploma, New South Wales Conservatorium of Music. *Career:* Australian premiere of Schoenberg's Pierrot Lunaire, ISCM concert, Sydney, 1958; Debut with Basler Theater, Switzerland, 1972, Lulu; Salome, debut with The Australian Opera, 1975, Aida; Roles and operas include Four Sopranos in Tales of Hoffmann, Marschallin, Countess, Donna Anna, Katya Kabanova, Queen of Spades, Otello, Eva, Sieglinde, Elsa, Mimi, Rosalinda, Merry Widow, Laura in Voss, Leonore (Fidelio), Isolde, 1990, and Tosca, 1992; Emilia Marty in The Makropulos Case, 1996; Has appeared with all State Companies; The Excursions of Mr Brouček, Fiordiligi, La Traviata, Madama Butterfly, Midsummer Marriage; Desdemona, Marguerite, Mistress Ford, Senta, Alcina, Cleopatra; Soloist in a huge range of concert music, including Australian premieres of about 400 songs and vocal works; Directed Les Pêcheurs de Perles at Adelaide, 1996. *Honours:* Churchill Fellowship, 1969; Australian Council Creative Fellowship, 1991; Joan Hammond Award, 1993; Honorary D.Mus, University of Queensland, 1993. *Address:* Australian Opera, PO Box 291, Strawberry Hills, NSW 2012, Australia.

**RICHARDSON, Mark;** singer (bass-baritone); b. 1966, England. *Education:* Royal Manchester College of Music. *Career:* English National Opera Company Principal as Lamoral in Arabella, Masetto, Colline in La Bohème and France in Reimann's Lear, Varlaam in Boris Godunov, Leporello; Other roles in War and Peace, Der Rosenkavalier, Rimsky's Christmas Eve and The Pearl Fishers, Ariodate in Xerxes, Donald in Billy Budd, Hobson in Peter Grimes, Parson in The Cunning Little Vixen, Niklausse in Dr Ox's Experiment; Season 1995–96 as Bizet's Zuniga and Nourabad; Guest appearances at Buxton, as Mustafà in L'Italiana in Algeri, Welsh National Opera (Angelotti and Rossini's Basilio) and the Bergen Festival (Sparafucile in Rigoletto); Sang Frank Maurrant in the Italian premiere of Street Scene, in Turin. *Current Management:* Robert Gilder & Co., Enterprise House, 59–65 Upper Ground, London, SE1 9PQ, England. *Telephone:* (20) 7928-9008. *Fax:* (20) 7928-9755. *E-mail:* rgilder@robert-gilder.com.

**RICHARDSON, Meryl;** Singer (soprano); b. 1965, England. *Education:* Royal Northern College of Music, with Neil Howlett; Further study with Philip Thomas and Jeffrey Talbot. *Career:* Appearances with English National

Opera as Musetta, and as Helmwige in Die Walküre, 2001–2002; Title role in British premiere of Barber's Vanessa and Brünnhilde in Die Walküre (chamber version) for the Covent Garden Festival; Other roles include Lady Macbeth (Buxton Festival), Leonora in La Forza del Destino, Anna Bolena and Elvira in Ernani; Concerts include Vier letzte Lieder, Mozart's C minor Mass, Tippett's A Child of our Time and the Verdi Requiem; Aksinya in Lady Macbeth of Mtsensk for ENO, 2002. *Current Management:* Athole Still International Management, Forresters Hall, 25–27 Westow Street, London, SE19 3RY, England. *Telephone:* (20) 8771-5271. *Fax:* (20) 8768-6600. *Website:* www.atholestill.com.

**RICHARDSON, Stephen;** Singer (bass); b. 1965, Liverpool, England. *Education:* Studied at the Royal Northern College of Music. *Career:* Has sung at Glyndebourne and with GTO, English and Welsh National Opera, Scottish Opera and Kent Opera; Roles have included Mozart's Osmin, Sarastro and Commendatore, Colline, Sparafucile, Silva in Ernani and Rossini's Basilio; US debut with Messiah at Carnegie Hall and other concerts with leading British orchestras Montreal Philharmonic Orchestra and Prague Symphony Orchestra; Premieres of Tavener's Eis Thanaton, Resurrection and Apocalypse, with other works by Gerald Barry, Birtwistle (Punch and Judy), Knussen, Mason and Casken; Festival appearances at Aldeburgh, BBC Proms, Vienna, Hong Kong, Boston and Brussels; Season 1996–97 with Colline and Sparafucile for Welsh National Opera, Daland with Chelsea Opera Group and Tiresias in Oedipus Rex for the BBC; Baron Ochs for ENO, 1999; Season 2000–01 as Casken's The Golem at the Aspen Festival, Mr. Flint in Billy Budd at Covent Garden and Fafner in The Rhinegold for ENO; Oliver Knussen's Where the Wild Things Are and Higglety, Pigglety, Pop! at the London Proms, 2002. *Current Management:* Harrison/Parrott Ltd, 12 Penzance Place, London, W11 4PA, England. *Telephone:* (20) 7229 9166. *Fax:* (20) 7221 5042. *Website:* www.harrisonparrott.com.

**RICHTER, Marga;** Composer; b. 21 Oct. 1926, Reedsburg, Wisconsin, USA. *Education:* Juilliard School, New York, from 1945, with Rosalyn Tureck, William Bergsma and Vincent Persichetti (MS 1951). *Career:* Freelance Composer, with premieres of her music at Salzburg, Chicago, Cannes, Cologne, Tucson, Atlanta, Brookville and New York. *Compositions include:* Clarinet sonata, 1948; Piano Sonata, 1954; 2 Piano Concertos, 1955, 1974; Aria and Toccata for viola and strings, 1957; String Quartet, 1958; Abyss, ballet, 1964; Bird of Yearning, ballet, 1967; Requiem for piano, 1978; Blackberry Vines and Winter Fruit for orchestra, 1976; Spectral Chimes/Enshrouded Hills for three contrapuntal quintets and orchestra, 1980; Düsseldorf Concerto for flute, viola, harp, percussion and strings, 1982; Seacliff Variations for piano, violin, viola, cello, 1984; Lament for Art O'Leary for soprano voice, 1984; Out of Shadows and Solitude for orchestra, 1985; Qhanri-Tibetan Variations for cello and piano, 1988; Quantum Quirks of a Quick Quaint Quark, I–III for orchestra, organ and piano, 1992–93; Variations and Interludes on Themes from Monteverdi and Bach, concerto for piano, violin, cello and orchestra, 1993; Riders to the Sea, opera in one act, 1996; Choruses and songs. *Recordings include:* Qhanri; Lament for Strings; Sonata for Piano; Seacliff Variations; Out of Shadows and Solitude; Spectral Chimes/Enshrouded Hills; Landscapes of the Mind II; Sonora for 2 clarinets and piano; Variations and Interludes on Themes from Monteverdi and Bach. *Honours:* Annual ASCAP Awards, 1966–2002; NEA Fellowships, 1978, 1980. *Address:* 3 Bayview Lane, Huntington, NY 11743, USA.

**RICHTER DE VROE, Nicolaus;** German composer and violinist; b. 1 Feb. 1955, Halle. *Education:* Moscow Conservatory, Berlin Akademie der Künste with Goldmann. *Career:* violinist with the Bavarian Radio Symphony 1988–; co-founder of XSEMBLE, Munich 1990. *Compositions include:* Tetra, series I–III, for differentiated quartets, 1984–91; Durchlässige Zonen I, for 13 instruments, 1985; String Quartet, 1986. Zu Fuss nach Island, graphic music, 1986; Isole de Rumore, for orchestra, 1988; Frag In Memorian Luigi Nono, for ensemble, 1990; Decemberhelft, for alto flute, guitar, cello and percussion, 1990; Naiss' orchestr' ance, 1992; Engfernt: Tänze, for ensemble, 1993; Shibuya movements for orchestra, 1993; Air't'rance, for ensemble, 1997; Éraflures, violin concerto, 1997. *E-mail:* n.devroe@web.de. *Website:* www .nicolaus-richter-de-vroe.kulturserver.de.

**RICKARDS, Steven,** BMusEd, MM, DM; American singer (countertenor), composer and music educator; b. 1955. *Education:* Florida State University, Tallahassee, Indiana University, Bloomington, Oberlin College Baroque Performance Institute, Indiana University, Bloomington, Guildhall School of Music and Drama, London. *Career:* concert engagements with the Waverly Consort (New York), Chicago's Music of the Baroque, Concert Royal, New York, Arts Musica and Chanticleer; British appearances with the Ipswich Bach Choir and at the East Cornwall Bach Festival; Tour of Ireland with the Gabrieli Consort and world-wide recitals with lutenist Dorothy Linell; Has toured France and Michigan with Messiah 1981–82; Carnegie Hall debut 1987, with the Oratorio Society of New York; Boston Early Music Festival in Handel's Teseo and Santa Fe Opera as Ariel in the premiere of John Eaton's The Tempest (1985); Sang with the Opera Company of Philadelphia as Apollo in Death in Venice; Recent revivals of Handel's Siroe in New York, Locke's Psyche in London, Hasse's L'Olimpiade in Dresden and Mondonville's De Profundis at Harvard; Sang in John Adams' El Niño at the Châtelet Theatre in Paris, 2000; Teaches singing at University of Indianapolis and Butler University, USA. *Compositions:* A Christmas Vision; All Good Gifts; Calm on the List'ning Ear of Night; Come Let Us Sing To The Lord; Come Thou Long Expected Jesus; Little Lamb; As the Lyre to the Singer; Behold the Tabernacle of God; Breathe on Me, Breath of God; Angels Did Sing. *Recordings include:* Bach cantatas 106 and 131 with Joshua Rifkin; St John Passion by Bach; Gradualia by Byrd with Chanticleer; Medarse in Siroe by Handel; Mass in B Minor by Bach; Buxtehude Project Vol. I Sacred Cantatas; T Campion Songs; J Dowland Songs. *Current Management:* John Gingrich Management, PO Box 1515, New York, NY 10023, USA.

**RICKENBACHER, Karl Anton;** Conductor; b. 20 May 1940, Basle, Switzerland; m. Gaye Fulton, 21 July 1973. *Education:* Opera and Concert Conducting Degree, Konservatorium Berlin; Studies with von Karajan and Pierre Boulez. *Career:* Debut: RIAS Berlin; Assistant Conductor, Zürich Opera, 1966–69; 1st Kapellmeister St ädt Bühnen Freiburg, 1969–75; Music Director of Westphalian Symphony, 1976–85; Principal Conductor of BBC Scottish Symphony, 1978–80; Featured in, Karl Anton Rickenbacher Conducts, BBC Scotland and appeared in Olivier Messiaen–Chronochromie, on Bavarian television; Concerts for ZDF Germany and Swiss, Belgian and French television; Since 1985, Freelance Guest Conductor in Europe, North America, Japan, Australia and Israel in opera and concert repertoire. *Recordings:* Over 50 titles with London Philharmonic, Bavarian Radio Symphony, Bamberg Symphony, Berlin Radio Symphony RSB, Budapest Radio Symphony. *Honours:* Grand Prix du Disque, for Milhaud CD, 1993; Diapason d'Or, for Messiaen CD, 1994; Cannes Classical Award, for Hartmann CD, 1994; Echo Award for R. Strauss CD, 1999; Echo Award for O. Messiaen CD, 2000. *Current Management:* TransArt (UK) Ltd, Cedar House, 10 Rutland Street, Filey, YO14 9JB, North Yorkshire, England. *Telephone:* (1723) 515819. *Fax:* (1723) 514678. *E-mail:* transartuk@ transartuk.com. *Website:* www.transartuk.com. *Address:* Oriole, 1822 Chernex-Montreux, Switzerland.

**RIDDELL, Alistair (Matthew);** Composer and Computer Technologist; b. 22 June 1955, Melbourne, Victoria, Australia. *Education:* BA (Hons), 1981, MA, 1989, La Trobe University (PhD 1993); Graduate Studies, Princeton University, 1989–93. *Career:* Fellowships at Princeton and La Trobe Universities, 1989–95. *Compositions include:* (Most with Computer-Processed Sound) Ligeti-Continuum, 1982; Studies in Perception, Context and Paradox: Three-Existential Constellations: Canon in 6 Voices, 1982; Bach-Inventio No. 4, 1982; Atlantic Fears, 1983; Core Image (four 4), 1983; Atmisfearia, 1989; Entering 2–12, 1990; Third Hand, 1991; Idyll Moment, 1991; Heavy Mouse, 1992; Z Says, 1993; Triptychos, 1995. *Recordings:* CD, 42, 1997. *Honours:* AC Artists and New Technology Program Grant, 1987. *Address:* 12 Napier Street, Fitzroy, Victoria 3065, Australia.

**RIDDELL, David;** Conductor; b. 1960, Elgin, Scotland. *Education:* St Andrew's University; Guildhall School, London. *Career:* Engagements for Den Jyske Opera, Denmark, in La Périchole, Butterfly, Cenerentola, The Pirates of Penzance, Paganini and Reesen's Farinelli (1992); Don Giovanni for Århus Summer Opera, 1989–90, followed by Il Barbiere di Siviglia, 1991; Die Fledermaus for Odense Symphony Orchestra, 1992; British appearances with La Forza del Destino for Scottish Opera, Eugene Onegin for Opera 80 and Rimsky's Mozart and Salieri at the Royal Scottish Academy of Music; Regular concerts at the Guildhall School; Season 1996 with Bach's Christmas Oratorio for the Randers Chamber Orchestra, and Burns International Festival Concert with the Northern Sinfonia in Scotland.

**RIEBL, Thomas;** Violist; b. 1956, Vienna, Austria. *Education:* Studied at the Vienna Academy of Music and with Peter Schidlof and Sándor Végh. *Career:* Led the violas of the World Youth Orchestra, 1972; Solo debut at the Vienna Konzerthaus in 1972 and has since appeared with leading orchestras in Europe and North America including the Chicago Symphony, Helsinki Radio, Bournemouth Symphony, Los Angeles and Vienna Chamber Orchestras; Conductors include Abbado, Walter Weller, Andrew Davis, Horst Stein, Erich Bergel and Edo de Waart; Festival appearances at Salzburg, Vienna, Aspen, Ravinia, New York, Munich, Lockenhaus and Carinthian Summer Festival; Concerts with the Juilliard Quartet, Gidon Kremer and Jessye Norman (Brahms Lieder Op 91); Founder Member of the Vienna Sextet; Professor of Viola at the Musikhochschule, Mozarteum, at Salzburg from 1983. *Recordings include:* Brahms Lieder Op 91 with Brigitte Fassbaender and Irwin Gage. *Honours:* Prizewinner at international competitions at Budapest in 1975 and Munich in 1976; Ernst Wallfisch Memorial Award at the International Naumberg Viola Competition in New York, 1982.

**RIEDEL, Deborah;** Singer (Soprano); b. 31 July 1958, Sydney, New South Wales, Australia. *Education:* Studied at the Sydney Conservatorium and in London. *Career:* Sang Hansel with Western Australian Opera, 1986, followed by Meg Page and Thomas' Mignon, Mimi and Countess Maritza; The Australian Opera from 1988, as Zerlina, Micaela, Juliette, Susanna, Elvira and Violetta; Appearances with the Victorian State Opera as the Drummer in Ullmann's Emperor of Atlantis, Nayad in Ariadne auf Naxos, Leila (Les Pêcheurs de Perles), Marguerite in Faust; London engagements as Freia in Das Rheingold, Mimi and Elvira at Covent Garden; Teresa in Benvenuto Cellini at Geneva Opera, Bastille (Paris), and Rome; Sang Elvira at Bordeaux, Violetta in the Netherlands, Amina in La Sonnambula at San Diego, California 1994, the Countess at Montpellier, Adina in L'Elisir d'amoreGounod's Marguerite in Faust at Geneva; Donna Anna in Munich and Vienna; Concert engagements as Mariana in Il Signor Bruschino at the Festival of Flanders; Mozart Coronation Mass, Bordeaux, Child of Our Time with London Symphony Orchestra NY Philharmonic; War Requiem (Britten) in London and Prague; Miss Solemnis, Beethoven in Prague, Beethoven in Tenerife,

Royal Albert Hall, London; Rossini's Petite Messe Solennelle; Scarlatti's St Cecilia Mass and frequent appearances with the Australian Pops Orchestra; Mozart's Vespers for the Rantos Collegium and Messiah for the ABC in Melbourne and Sydney; Mendelssohn's Midsummer Night's Dream and Mozart Exultate Jubilate with the Sydney Symphony Orchestra and Strauss's Four Last Songs for the Australian Ballet and ABC Perth and Adelaide; Season 1997 with Maria Stuarda in Sydney and Donna Anna at the Met; Alice Ford in Falstaff at San Diego, 1998; at Sydney as the Trovatore Leonora, Donna Anna and Elettra in Idomeneo for Welsh Nat. Opera and Opera Australia; the Marschallin for WNO and Tosca in Adelaide; Fidelio in Tours and Reims; Margerite in Faust for Opera Australia; In concert in Barcelona and Bergen (Messiaen's Poème pour Mi) and Sydney; in recital with Richard Bonynge. *Recordings include:* Paganini and Giuditta, Die Herzogm von Chicago, Requiem Embriaco, Power of Love, Gypsy Princess (video). *Honours:* Winner, Australian regional final of the Metropolitan Opera Auditions; Dame Sister Mary Leo Scholarship; Dame Mabel Brookes Fellowship; Aria Award, Sydney Sun, 1986. *Address:* c/o Harlequin Agency Ltd, 203 Fidlas Road, Cardiff, CF14 5NA, England.

**RIEDLBAUCH, Václav;** Czech composer; *Professor, Academy of Performing Arts;* b. 1 April 1947, Dýšina; m.; two s. *Education:* Prague Conservatoire. *Career:* Lecturer, Prague Acad. of Performing Arts, Sr Lecturer, Sec. Dept of Composition 1984–; Chief Composer Nat. Theatre Opera 1987–89; Dir Gen. Czech Philharmonic Orchestra 2000–; Prof., Acad. of Performing Arts, Prague 2000–; Chair. Young Composers Section, Czech Composers' and Performing Artists' Union 1982–. *Compositions include:* musical dramatic works: Macbeth (ballet for soloist and group dancers and large orchestra) 1979–82; symphonic works: The Rozmberk Sonata for Winds and Percussion Instruments 1971, Symphony 1972, Symphony with Refrain 1973, Concerto-Battle for Organ and Orchestra 1973, Deadly Rondo for Orchestra 1975, The Story – Symhonic narration 1983; chamber instrumental music: Sonatina for James for Violin and Piano 1971, Cathedrals – Organ toccata 1972, The Picture (Still Life with a Dead Nightingale) for flute and piano 1974, Tale for Flute, Violin, Violoncello and Piano 1974, Lamento for Clarinet and Piano 1975, Ballads for Violin and Piano 1975, Stories for Bass-clarinet and Piano 1975, Allegri e Pastorali for wind quintet 1976, Luring for Flute and Piano 1977, Canons for Piano 1977, Parade for Organ 1978, Pastorali e Concerti for brass quintet 1978, Concertie Trenodi for wind octet 1979, The Curtain – Movement for organ 1982, Conjunction – Game for two organs or other keyboard instruments 1983; vocal works: Touzenec pisni – Songs for Tenor and Piano After Verses by R. Tagore 1975, Songs from Rejdova for Soprano, Contralto, Violin and Piano 1976, Tesknice (nostalgic songs) – Three folk songs for two flutes-a-bec and three-part children's choir 1976, Wedding Singing for girls, female or male choirs after Sappho 1978, Rather-Or Cycle for Children – Seven children's choirs to words by R. Steindl 1978, Songs and Games to Excerpts from Shakespeare for six singers, two violins, oboe and violoncello 1979, Teachers Song (celebration of Bohemian baroque) for organ and children's choir to words by V. Fischer 1980, The Primer – Excerpts from beginnings at school – Four polyphonic pieces for children's choir 1980, Daidalos the Creator, for male choir with barytone solo after Ovid 1982; instructive works: Special Book of Prague – A book of polyphonic compositions for accordion 1972, Pastorale for Three Flutes-a-bec 1973, The Wizard – Accordion school for children 1973–76, SU South Bohemian Nocturnes, for two violins, violoncello, accordion and trumpet 1979, Reversals for children's accordion 1980, SU 2' Povidacky (talks) – Eight polyphonic pieces for two violins 1982. *Honours:* Artist of Merit 1987. *Address:* Academy of Performing Arts, Malostranské nám. 12, 110 00 Prague 1 (office); Revoluční 6, 110 00 Prague 1, Czech Republic (home). *Telephone:* (2) 57533956 (office); (2) 22310710 (home). *Fax:* (2) 57530405 (office).

**RIEGEL, Kenneth;** Singer (Tenor); b. 19 April 1938, Womelsdorf, Pennsylvania, USA. *Education:* Manhattan School of Music; Berkshire Music Center; Metropolitan Opera Studio. *Career:* Debut: Santa Fe Festival in 1965 as the Alchemist in the US premiee of Henze's König Hirsch; San Francisco Opera, 1971, Metropolitan Opera, NY, 1973, Vienna State Opera, 1977, Paris Opéra, 1979 as the Painter in the premiere of the three-act version of Lulu, La Scala, 1979, Hamburg State Opera, 1981, Geneva Opera, 1981, Deutsche Oper, West Berlin, 1983, and Bonn Opera, 1983; Sang the Leper in the premiere of Messiaen's St François d'Assise, Paris, 1983, at Brussels Opera, 1984, and at Royal Opera Covent Garden, 1985 in Der Zwerg by Zemlinsky; Appeared in film, Don Giovanni, directed by Joseph Losey, 1988, and at Stuttgart in 1989 as Dionysos in The Bassarids by Henze; Season 1992 as Herod in Salome at Covent Garden and Salzburg; Season 1996 with Aegisthus at Salzburg and the Inquisitor in Dallapiccola's Prigioniero at Florence; Herod in Salome at Santa Fe, 1998; Title role in the premiere of K. ... by Philippe Manouri at the Opéra Bastille, Paris, 2001. *Recordings:* Der Zwerg; Damnation of Faust; Florentinische Tragoedie; Don Giovanni; Lulu; Mahler Symphony No. 8; Berlioz's Requiem. *Honours:* Nominated for Olivier Award for Best Individual Performance in an Opera, 1985. *Current Management:* SAFIMM Corporation. *Address:* c/o SAFIMM Corporation, 250 West 57th Street, Suite 1018, New York, NY 10107, USA.

**RIFKIN, Joshua,** BS, MFA; American conductor, musicologist and composer; b. 22 April 1944, New York; s. of Harry H. Rifkin and Dorothy Helsh; m. Helen Palmer 1995; one d. *Education:* Juilliard School and New York, Göttingen and Princeton Univs. *Career:* Musical Adviser, Assoc. Dir Nonesuch Records 1963–75; Asst, Assoc. Prof. of Music, Brandeis Univ. 1970–82; Dir The Bach

Ensemble 1978–; Visiting Prof. New York Univ. 1978, 1983, 2000, Yale Univ. 1982–83, Princeton Univ. 1988, Stanford Univ. 1989, King's Coll. London 1991, Univ. of Basel 1993, 1997, Ohio State Univ. 1994, Univ. of Dortmund 1996, Schola Cantorum Basiliensis 1997, 2001, Univ. of Munich 2000; Fellow, Inst. for Advanced Study, Berlin 1984–86; guest conductor English Chamber Orchestra, Los Angeles Chamber Orchestra, St Louis Symphony Orchestra, St Paul Chamber Orchestra, Scottish Chamber Orchestra, BBC Symphony Orchestra, Bayerische Staatsoper, San Francisco Symphony Orchestra, City of Glasgow Symphony Orchestra, Jerusalem Symphony Orchestra, Prague Chamber Orchestra; contributed to the revival of interest in the ragtime music of Scott Joplin; as a musicologist has researched Renaissance and Baroque music; recreated J. S. Bach's Wedding Cantata BWV 216 (fragment, originally 1728) 2005. *Recordings:* Bach Mass in B minor 1982, Bach Magnificat 1983, numerous Bach cantatas 1986–2001, Rags and Tangos 1990, Haydn Symphonies 1994, Silvestre Revueltas 1999, rags by Scott Joplin, Mozart Posthorn Serenade, fanfares and sonatas by Pezel and Hammerschmidt, sonatas by Biber, vocal music by Busnois, Josquin. *Publications:* articles on Haydn, Schütz, Bach and Josquin in The Musical Times, Musical Quarterly and other journals, and in the New Grove Dictionary of Music and Musicians. *Honours:* Dr hc (Univ. of Dortmund) 1999; Gramophone Award 1983. *Address:* 61 Dana Street, Cambridge, MA 02138, USA. *Telephone:* (617) 876-4017 (office). *Fax:* (617) 441-5572 (office). *E-mail:* jrifkin@compuserve.com.

**RIGACCI, Susanna;** Singer (Soprano); b. 1959, Stockholm, Sweden. *Education:* Studied in Florence. *Career:* Debut: Rome Opera, as Rossini's Rosina; Appearances in opera throughout Italy, and guest at Dublin as Gilda in Rigoletto; Wexford Festival in Cimarosa's Astuzie Femminili; Season 1987 in the Italian premiere of Henze's English Cat, at Bologna, and in Capriccio at Florence; Season 1991–92 as Weber's Aennchen at Liège and Sofia in Rossini's Il Signo Bruschino at the Paris Théâtre du Châtelet. *Recordings include:* Vivaldi's Catone in Utica; L'Elisir d'amore. *Address:* c/o Via Giambologna 3a, 50132 Florence, Italy.

**RIGAL, Joel;** French pianist and fortepianist; b. 17 Aug. 1950, Castres. *Education:* Master Degree, Musicology, University of Paris-Sorbonne; Graduate, Aix en Provence and Marseilles Conservatories; Piano and Fortepiano Studies with Pierre Barbizet and Paul Badura-Skoda, Vienna. *Career:* Debut: Vienna Theatre, 1979; Performances in Paris: Châtelet, 1983, Gaveau, 1987, Musée de la Villette, 1997–; Purcell Room, London, 1981–; Opera, Cairo, 1989–; Bibliotek Theatre, Rotterdam, 1991–; Budapest Strings Orchestra, Budapest, 1995; several television and radio appearances. *Recordings:* with Nadine Palmier: Mozart, Complete Works for Piano Duet and 2 Keyboards; French Music, The Golden Age; Schubert, The Final Masterpieces. *Publications:* Le clavier bien partagé (teaching manual), 1993; contrib. to Marsyas. *Current Management:* c/o Bureau de Concerts Maurice Werner, 17 rue du Quatre Septembre, 75002, Paris, France.

**RIGBY, Jean Prescott,** ARAM, ARCM, ABSM; British opera singer; b. Fleetwood, Lancs.; d. of Thomas Boulton Rigby and Margaret Annie Rigby; m. James Hayes 1987; three s. *Education:* Elmslie Girls' School, Blackpool, Birmingham School of Music, RAM and Opera Studio. *Career:* studied piano and viola at Birmingham then singing at RAM with Patricia Clark, with whom she continues to study; Prin. Mezzo-Soprano, English Nat. Opera 1982–90, roles include Mercedes, Marina, Lucretia, Dorabella, Octavian, Penelope, Jocasta, Helen (King Priam), Rosina; début Covent Garden 1983, roles have included Tebaldo, Mercedes, Hippolyta, second Lady, Magic Flute and Olga, Eugene Onegin, Cenerentola, Nicklausse (Hoffman); Glyndebourne début 1984, sang Nancy in Albert Herring and Mercedes in Carmen 1985; American début 1993; TV appearances in Così fan tutte and film on Handel; videos of Xerxes, Rigoletto, Lucretia, Carmen, Albert Herring; also sings concert repertoire and has made recordings with Giuseppe Sinopoli. *Honours:* Hon. FRAM 1989; Hon. Assoc. Birmingham Conservatoire 1996; numerous prizes and scholarships at RAM including Countess of Munster, Leverhulme, Peter Stuyvesant, RSA scholarships and the Prin.'s Prize; Royal Overseas League and Young Artists' Competition 1981. *Address:* c/o Askonas Holt, Lonsdale Chambers, 27 Chancery Lane, London, WC2A 1PF, England.

**RIHM, Wolfgang;** composer; b. 13 March 1952, Karlsruhe, Germany. *Education:* Hochschule für Musik Karlsruhe, with Eugen W Velte, studied with Stockhausen in Cologne and Klaus Huber in Freiburg. *Career:* Teacher at the Karlsruhe Hochschule für Musik, 1973–78; Freelance Composer; From 1985 Professor of Composition at Musikhochschule Karlsruhe, British premiere of Jakob Lenz in London in 1987, Die Eroberung von Mexiko premiered at the Hamburg Staatsoper, 1992. *Compositions include:* Operas: Deploration, 1974, Jakob Lenz, 1978, Oedipus, 1987; Die Eroberung von Mexico, 1992; Orchestral: Three Symphonies, 1969–76, Sub-Kontar, 1975–76, La Musique Creuse Le Ciel for 2 pianos and orchestra, 1979, Monodram for cello and orchestra, 1983, Medea-Spiel, 1988, Passion, 1989, Schwebende Begegnung, 1989, Dunkles Spiel, 1990; La lugubre gondola for orchestra, 1992; Vers une symphonie fleuve, I–IV, 1994–8; Musik für oboe und orchester, 1994; Styx und Lethe for cello and orchestra, 1998; Marsyas, for trumpet and orchestra, 1998; Musick für Klarinette und orchester, 1999; Vocal: Hervorgedunkelt for mezzo and ensemble, 1974, Umhergetrieben Aufgewirbelt, Nietzsche Fragments for baritone and mezzo, chorus and flute, 1981, Lowry-Lieder (Wondratschek), 1987, Song Cycles for soprano and orchestra, Frau, Stimme for soprano and orchestra, 1989, Mein Tod, Requiem In Memoriam Jane S, 1990; Abschiedsstücke for female voice and 15 instruments, 1993; Raumauge for chorus and 5 percussion, 1994; Deutsches Stück

mit Hamlet, for mezzo, baritone and orchestra, 1997; In doppelter Tiefe for mezzo, alto and orchestra, 1999; Chamber: Paraphrase for cello, percussion and piano, 1972, Ländler for 13 strings, 1979, 10 string quartets, 1970–97, Gebild for trumpet, strings and percussion, 1983, Duomonolog for violin and cello, 1989; Music for voice and piano, organ and piano. *Current Management:* Universal Edition (London) Ltd, 48 Great Marlborough Street, London, W1F 7BB, England. *Telephone:* (20) 7437-6880. *Fax:* (20) 7437-6115.

**RILEY, Dennis,** PhD; American composer; b. 28 May 1943, Los Angeles. *Education:* Univs of Colorado, Illinois and Iowa with George Crumb and Ben Johnston. *Career:* Lecturer, California State Univ. at Fresno, 1971–74, Columbia, New York 1974–78. *Compositions include:* Concertante music 1–4, for ensembles, 1970, 1972, 1974, 1978; 4 Choral Cantatas, 1966–80; Wedding Canticle for baritone and viola, 1968; Elegy: in Memoriam David Bates for cello and strings, 1975; Seven Songs on Poems of Emily Dickinson for soprano and orchestra, 1982; Noon Dances for chamber orchestra, 1983; Symphony, 1984: Operas Rappaccini's Daughter, and Cats' Concert, 1984; Five Poems of Marilyn Hacker for soprano and ensemble, 1986. *Honours:* Guggenheim Fellowship, NEA grants, Forum Foundation Commission.

**RILEY, Howard,** BA, MA, MMus, MPh; British musician (piano) and composer; b. 16 Feb. 1943, Huddersfield, Yorks., England. *Education:* Univ. of Wales, Indiana Univ., USA, York Univ. *Career:* festival, club, TV and radio appearances as solo and group pianist, throughout Europe and N America 1967–; Creative Assoc., Centre of the Creative and Performing Arts, Buffalo, NY, USA 1976–77. *Recordings include:* albums: Facets 1983, For Four On Two Two 1984, In Focus 1985, Live At The Royal Festival Hall 1985, Feathers 1988, Procession 1990, The Heat Of Moments 1991, Beyond Category 1993, The Bern Concert 1993, Inner Mirror 1996, Making Moves 1997, Short Stories 1998, One to One 1999, Synopsis 2000, Overground 2001, Airplay 2001, Consequences 2005. *Publications:* The Contemporary Piano Folio 1982. *Honours:* Bicentennial Arts Fellowship 1976. *Address:* Flat 2, 53 Tweedy Road, Bromley, Kent, BR1 3NH, England (home). *Telephone:* (20) 8290-5917 (home).

**RILEY, Terry Mitchell,** MA; American composer, pianist and raga singer; b. 24 June 1935, Colfax, CA; s. of Wilma Ridlofi and Charles Riley; m. Ann Yvonne Smith 1958; three c. *Education:* San Francisco State Univ., Univ. of California, studied with Duane Hampton, Adolf Baller and Pandit Pran Nath. *Career:* Creative Assoc., Center for Creative and Performing Arts, Buffalo 1967; taught music composition and N Indian raga at Mills Coll. 1971–83; freelance composer and performer 1961–; launched Minimal Music Movt with composition and first performance of In C 1964; Guggenheim Fellowship 1980. *Compositions include:* The Harp of New Albion for solo piano in just intonation, Sunrise of the Planetary Dream Collector, Sri Camel, The Ten Voices of the Two Prophets, Chorale of the Blessed Day, Eastern Man, Embroidery, Song from the Old Country, G-Song, Remember This Oh Mind, The Ethereal Time Shadow, Offering to Chief Crazy Horse, Rites of the Imitators, The Medicine Wheel, Song of the Emerald Runner, Cycle of five string quartets, Trio for violin, clarinet and cello 1957, Concert for two pianos and tape 1960, String Trio 1961, Keyboard Studies 1963, Dorian Reeds for ensemble 1964, In C 1964, A Rainbow in the Curved Air 1968, Persian Surgery Dervishes for electronic keyboard 1971, Descending Moonshine Dervishes 1975, Do You Know How it Sounds? for low voice, piano and tabla 1983, Cadenza on the Night Plain for string quartet 1984, Salome Dances for Peace string quartet 1988, Jade Palace for orchestra and synthesiser 1989, Cactus Rosary for synthesiser and ensemble 1990, June Buddhas for chorus and orchestra 1991, The Sands for string quartet and orchestra 1991, Four Woelfi Portraits for ensemble 1992, The Saint Adolf Ring chamber opera 1993, Ritmos and Melos 1993, El Hombre string quartet 1993, Ascension for solo guitar 1993, The Heaven Ladder for piano four hands 1996, Three Requiem Quartets 1997, Autodreamographical Tales for narrator and instruments 1997. *Address:* 13699 Moonshine Road, Camptonville, CA 95922, USA. *Telephone:* (916) 288-3522. *Fax:* (916) 288-3468.

**RILLING, Helmuth;** German conductor, chorus master, organist and academic; b. 29 May 1933, Stuttgart; m. Martina Greiner 1967; two d. *Education:* Staatliche Hochschule für Musik, Stuttgart with Johann Nepomuk David, Conservatorio di Santa Cecilia, Rome with Fernando Germani, studied conducting with Leonard Bernstein in New York. *Career:* founder and Dir, Gächinger Kantorei, Stuttgart 1954–; organist and choirmaster, Gedächtniskirche, Stuttgart 1957–98; London debut as organist 1963, as conductor 1972; taught organ and conducting, Berliner Kirchenmusikschule, Berlin-Spandau; Dir, Spandauer Kantorei 1963–66; founder, Bach-Collegium Stuttgart 1965–; Prof. of Conducting, Staatliche Hochschule für Musik, Frankfurt 1966–85; Dir, Frankfurter Kantorei 1969–81; co-founder and Artistic Dir, Summer Festival (now Oregon Bach Festival), Eugene, USA 1970–; teacher, Indiana Univ., Bloomington, USA 1976–77; founder and Dir, Sommer Acad. Johann Sebastian Bach Stuttgart 1979–99, Internationale Bachakademie Stuttgart 1981–, Bach Acads in Tokyo, Buenos Aires 1983, Santiago de Compostela, Spain, Prague, Kraków, Moscow, Budapest, Caracas; Chief Conductor, Real Filarmonía de Galicia, Santiago de Compostela, Spain 1996–2000; founder, Stuttgart Festival Choir and Orchestra 2001–; world wide int. appearances with own ensembles and as guest conductor and guest prof.; regular co-operation with Israel Philharmonic Orchestra, Cleveland Orchestra, Boston Symphony Orchestra, Minnesota Orchestra, LA Philharmonic, Toronto Symphony Orchestra, New York Philharmonic, Vienna Philharmonic Orchestra, Münchner Philharmoniker, Radio-

Sinfonieorchester Munich; mem. Kungl. Musikaliska Akad., Stockholm 1993. *Recordings:* Cycle of Bach Cantatas with the Frankfurter Kantorei, the Gächinger Kantorei and the Figuralchor of Stuttgart 1970–84, Motets, Lutheran Masses, Choral Preludes and Orgelbüchlein by Bach, Magnificats by Schütz, Bach, Monteverdi and Buxtehude, Carissimi's Jephte and Judicum Salomonis, Handel's Belshazzar, Telemann's Ino and Pimpinone, Mozart's Concertos K364 and K190, Mass K317 and Vesperae Solennes de Confessore, Geistliche Chormusik, St Matthew Passion, Symphoniae Sacrae and Cantiones Sacrae by Schütz, Messiaen's Cinq Rechants, Edition Bachakademie: The Complete Works of Bach (172 albums) 1998–2000, Credo by Penderecki and Wolfgang Rihm's Deus Passus 2001–02. *Publications:* Johann Sebastian Bach, Matthäus-Passion, Einführung und Studienanleitung 1975, Johann Sebastian Bachs h-moll-Messe 1975. *Honours:* Hon. DFA (Concordia Coll.) 1990, Dr hc (Univ. of Oregon) 1999; Grand Prix du Disque 1985, UNESCO/IMC Music Prize 1994, Theodor Heuss Prize 1995, Int. Prize Compostela 1999, Cannes Classic Award 1999, Grammy Award for Best Choral Performance 2000, Hanns Martin Schleyer Prize 2001. *Current Management:* c/o Kristina Pauli, Internationale Bachakademie Stuttgart, Presse- und Öffentlichkeitsarbeit, Johann-Sebastian-Bach-Platz (Hasenbergsteige 3), 70178 Stuttgart, Germany. *Telephone:* (711) 6192117 (office). *Fax:* (711) 6192151 (office). *E-mail:* pr@bachakademie.de (office). *Website:* www .bachakademie.de (office).

**RIMMER, John Francis;** Composer; b. 5 Feb. 1939, Auckland, New Zealand. *Education:* University of Auckland; Further study with John Weinzweig in Toronto. *Career:* Lecturer at University of Auckland 1974–99; Founder of electro-acoustic music studio; Chair in Music 1995. *Compositions include:* Symphony, 1968; Electro-acoustic: Composition nos 1–10, 1968–77; Seaswell, 1978; Projections at Dawn, 1985; Fleeting images, 1985; Beyond the Saying, 1990; A Vocalise for Einstein, 1991; La Voci di Galileo, 1995; Pacific Soundscapes with Dancing, 1995; Viola Concerto, 1980; Meeting Place for orchestra, 1984; Gossamer for 12 strings, 1984; With the Current, for ensemble, 1986; Symphony, the Feeling of Sound, 1989; Cloud Fanfares for orchestra, 1990; Millennia for brass ensemble, 1991; Bowed Insights, string quartet, 1993; The Ripple Effect, for ensemble, 1995; Flashes of Iridescence for piano, 1995; A Dialogue of Opposites, for cello, 1997; Memories, for youth orchestra, 1998; Galileo, chamber opera, 1998, Europa, Concerto for Brass Band and Orchestra 2002, Transcend, Concerto for Orchestra 2003, Thermal Labyrinths for Brass Band 2004. *Address:* 67 Marlborough Avenue, Glenfield, Auckland 1310, New Zealand (home). *Telephone:* (9) 444-8419 (home).

**RINALDI, Alberto;** Singer (Baritone); b. 6 June 1939, Rome, Italy. *Education:* Studied at the Accademia di Santa Cecilia, Rome. *Career:* Debut: Spoleto in 1963 as Simon Boccanegra; Teatro Fenice Venice in 1970 as Rossini's Figaro; Appearances in Milan, Rome, Naples, Paris, Rio de Janeiro, Ghent, Florence and Aix-en-Provence; Edinburgh Festival in 1973; Glyndebourne Festival in 1980 as Ford in Falstaff; Sang Mozart's Count on tour to Japan with the company of the Vienna Staatsoper, 1986; Sang at the Berlin Staatsoper in 1987 as Dandini in La Cenerentola; Pesaro and Cologne, 1988–89 in Il Signor Bruschino and Il Cambiale di Matrimonio; Bonn Opera in 1990 as Rossini's Figaro; Sang Blansac in La Scala di Seta at the 1990 Schwetzingen Festival; Season 1992 as Blansac at Cologne and Paris; Sang Geronio in Rossini's Il Turco in Italia, Brussels, 1996; Don Pasquale at Brussels, 1998; Season 2000–01 as Belcore at the Vienna Staatsoper and Rambaldo in Puccini's La Rondine at Rome. *Recordings:* Masetto in Don Giovanni; Il Matrimonio Segreto; Il Campanello; Pagliacci; Video of La Scala di Seta. *Address:* c/o Oper der Stadt Köln, Offenbachplatz, 5000 Cologne, Germany.

**RINALDI, Margarita;** Singer (Soprano); b. 12 Jan. 1933, Turin, Italy. *Education:* Studied in Rovigo. *Career:* Debut: Spoleto in 1958 as Lucia di Lammermoor; La Scala Milan in 1959 as Sinaide in Mosè by Rossini; Dublin in 1961 as Carolina in Il Matrimonio Segreto and Gilda; Verona Arena in 1962 and 1969; US debut at Dallas in 1966 as Gilda; Glyndebourne Festival in 1966 as Carolina; Bregenz Festival in 1974 and 1980 in Un Girono di Regno and as Alice Ford; Further appearances in Barcelona, Chicago, San Francisco, Wexford, Rome, Naples and Turin; Other roles include Amina, Norina, Linda di Chamounix, Marie in La Fille du Régiment, Bertha in La Prophète, Sophie, Ilia, Fiordiligi, Violetta, Oscar and the Marschallin; Maggio Musicale Florence, 1977–78 as Amenaide in Tancredi and Helena in A Midsummer Night's Dream; Retired from stage in 1981; Many concert engagements. *Recordings:* Lucia di Lammermoor; Rigoletto; Le Prophète; La Scala di Seta; L'Africaine; Ilia in Idomeneo.

**RINGART, Anna;** Singer (Mezzo-Soprano); b. 15 Jan. 1937, Paris, France. *Education:* Studied with Irene Joachim and Marguerite Liszt in Paris; Hamburg Musikhochschule with Frau Anders-Mysz-Gmeiner. *Career:* Sang at such German opera centres as Lubeck, Koblenz, Düsseldorf and Hamburg; Sang at the Paris Opéra from 1973 under Karl Böhm, Pierre Boulez, Seiji Ozawa and Georg Solti, in a repertoire extending from Mozart to Schoenberg's Moses und Aron; Appeared in the 1985 premiere of Docteur Faustus by Konrad Boehmer; Opéra-Comique in 1988 as the Nurse in Boris Godunov; Has sung at many festivals of contemporary music notably with the group Contrasts. *Address:* c/o Théâtre National de Paris, 8 Rue Scribe, 75009 Paris, France.

**RINGBORG, (Hans) Patrik Erland;** conductor; b. 1 Nov. 1965, Stockholm, Sweden. *Education:* Stockholm Institute of Music, Royal College of Music, Stockholm, further studies in Vienna and London. *Career:* debut Ystad Summer Opera, Akhnaten by Glass, 1989; Städtische Bühnen, Freiburg, Bizet's Carmen, 1992; Royal Opera, Stockholm, triple bill with Scheherazade, 1993; Conductor and Coach since 1987, Swedish Radio Choir, 1988, Sächsische Staatsoper, Dresden, 1988, Royal Opera, Stockholm, 1989–93 (including television), Canadian Opera Company, 1992, 2nd Kapellmeister and Studienleiter, Städtische Bühnen Freiburg, 1993–95; Co 1st Kapellmeister, Städtische Bühnen Freiburg, 1995–. *Honours:* British Council Fellow, 1987; Major Scholarship, Royal Academy of Music, Stockholm, 1987; Music Fellowship, Swedish-American Foundation, 1990; 1st R-U, First Competition for Opera Conductors, Royal Opera, Stockholm, 1997. *Current Management:* Nordic Artist, Stockholm, Sweden, Künstleragentur Markow, München, Germany. *Address:* Hindenburgstrasse 28, 79102 Freiburg in Breisgau, Germany.

**RINGBORG, Tobias;** violinist and conductor; b. 2 Nov. 1973, Stockholm, Sweden. *Education:* Royal Univ. Coll. of Music, Stockholm with Harald Thedéen, Juilliard School, New York. *Career:* debut, Tchaikovsky Concerto, with Royal Stockholm Philharmonic Orchestra, 1994; Appearances with every Swedish Symphony and Chamber Orchestra; Recitals throughout Europe and USA, including Concertgebouw, Amsterdam; National Gallery of Art, Washington DC; Several appearances and concerts for Swedish Television and Radio; Solo performances in Germany, Hungary and the USA; Brahms Concerto with Orchestre Nationale de Belgique, Brussels, 1995; Tour with Polish Radio Chamber Orchestra, Beethoven Concerto; Plays 18th Century Gagliano violin on loan from Swedish Academy of Music; engagements as conductor in Sweden 1999–. *Recordings:* Joseph Marx: Sonata in A major; Romantic Swedish Violin Concertos; Strindberg and Music; Numerous recordings for Swedish Broadcasting Corporation. *Honours:* Soloist Prize, Royal Swedish Academy of Music, 1994; First Prize, Concourt International de Musique de Chimay, Belgium, 1995. *Address:* c/o Svenska Konsertbyrån AB, Jungfrugatan 45, 11444 Stockholm, Sweden.

**RINGHOLZ, Teresa;** Singer (Soprano); b. 30 Dec. 1958, Rochester, New York, USA. *Education:* Studied at the Eastman School, Rochester and in San Francisco. *Career:* Debut: Western Opera Theatre, San Francisco in 1982 as Gilda; Toured in the USA then sang in Europe from 1985 with debut at Strasbourg as Zerbinetta; Cologne Opera from 1985 as Liu, Sophie, Susanna, Despina, Pamina and Sandrina in La Finta Giardiniera; Sang at the Salzburg Festival, 1987–88 and at Tel-Aviv with the Cologne Opera Company; Further appearances in opera and concert throughout Germany, France and Switzerland; Other roles include Gretel, Oscar, Lauretta, Micaela, Marzelline and Adele in Die Fledermaus; Season 1992 as the Wife in the premiere of Schnittke's Life With an Idiot, Amsterdam, and as Fanny in Rossini's La Cambiale di Matrimonio, Paris; Most recently sang at the Kennedy Center with the Washington Opera in 1994 as Susanna in Le nozze di Figaro; Violetta in Bogota and Fiordiligi in Barcelona, Seville and the Hamburg Staatsoper; Sang Gluck's Alceste at Drottningholm, 1998; Tatiana in Eugene Onegin at Osnabrück, 2000. *Address:* St Apernstrasse 20, 50667 Cologne, Germany.

**RINGO, Jennifer;** Singer (Soprano); b. 1965, USA. *Education:* University of Iowa; Juilliard School, New York; Merola Opera Program; Houston Grand Opera Studio. *Career:* Appearances with San Francisco Opera, Houston Opera, Maggio Musicale (Florence) Grand Théâtre de Genève and Canadian Opera Company; Poulenc's La Voix Humaine in New York and Cologne; Other repertory includes Der Zwerg by Zemlinsky, Wozzeck and Enescu's Oedipe; Concerts in Vienna, Berlin, Nice, Barcelona and Rotterdam; Festival engagements at Aspen, Caramoor, Ravina, Tanglewood and Hollyowood Bowl; Season 2000–01 with Britten's Ellen Orford at Tours, Berg's Lulu Symphonie at Aspen, Donna Elvira and Mozart's Countess at Lisbon and Ullmann's Kaiser von Atlantis at Cincinnati. *Address:* c/o Musicaglotz, 11 rue Le Verrier, 75006 Paris, France.

**RINKEVICIUS, Gintaras;** Conductor; b. 20 Jan. 1960, Vilnius, Lithuania. *Education:* Studies at St Petersburg and Moscow Conservatoires. *Career:* Assistant conductor of Lithuanian Philharmonic Orchestra, 1979; Music Director of Lithuanian State Symphony Orchestra from 1988; Tours with Moscow Radio Orchestra to: Italy; Spain; Austria; Finland; Yugoslavia; Worked with such soloists as Natalia Gutman, Peter Donohoe, Oleg Kagan and Vladimir Ovchinikov; Repertoire includes music by Dvořák, Mahler, Poulenc, Orff, Honegger, Prokoviev, Elgar and John Adams, in addition to standard works; Appearances with Lithuanian State Opera, notably conducting Nabucco in Paris, 1992; Guest engagements with Russian State Symphony, Moscow Philharmonic and St Petersburg Philharmonic Orchestras; Performed Wagner's Flying Dutchman, in Vilnius, 1995; Turandot with the Latvian National Opera at the Albert Hall, London, 1998. *Honours:* Winner, All-Union Conducting Competition at St Petersburg Conservatoire; Third Prize, Herbert von Karajan Conducting Competition, 1985; Second Prize, in Janos Ferencsik Competition, Budapest, 1986. *Address:* c/o Sonata, 11 Northpark Street, Glasgow G20 7AA, Scotland.

**RINTZLER, Marius Adrian;** German opera and concert singer; b. 14 March 1932, Bucharest, Romania; m. Sanda Dragomir 1964. *Education:* Acad. of Music, Bucharest. *Career:* soloist with Bucharest Philharmonic 1959; début in opera in Bucharest as Don Basilio in Il Barbiere di Siviglia 1964; went to Germany 1966; leading bass at Düsseldorf's Deutsche Oper am Rhein 1968–; guest singer with major opera cos, including Metropolitan, San Francisco, Glyndebourne, Paris, Brussels, Munich; repertoire includes various roles in

Richard Strauss' Rosenkavalier (Ochs), Capriccio (La Roche), Schweigsame Frau (Morosus), in Rossini's La Cenerentola (Don Magnifico), Il Barbiere (Bartolo), in Richard Wagner's Ring (Alberich), in Mozart's Don Giovanni (Leporello), Die Entführung (Osmin); appears with major symphony orchestras in Europe and USA, including Philharmonia (London), Berlin Philharmonic, Cleveland Symphony; also gives recitals, TV appearances in England, Germany and France. *Honours:* Kammersänger. *Address:* Friedingstrasse 18, 40625 Düsseldorf, Germany (home). *Telephone:* (211) 297083 (home).

**RIPPON, Michael (George);** Singer (Bass-Baritone); b. 10 Dec. 1938, Coventry, Warwickshire, England. *Education:* MA, St John's College, Cambridge, 1957–60; Royal Academy of Music, 1960–63; ARAM. *Career:* Debut: Handel Opera Society in 1963 as Nireno in Giulio Cesare; Sang in the 1967 London premiere of Puccini's Edgar; Covent Garden Opera in 1969; Sang Leporello with Welsh National Opera in 1969; Glyndebourne Festival, 1970–73 in Die Zauberflöte, Le nozze di Figaro, The Queen of Spades and The Visit of The Old Lady; Has also sung with English National Opera, Scottish Opera, Handel Opera, Boston Opera, New York City Opera and PACT, Johannesburg, and at most leading music festivals and societies in the United Kingdom and abroad; Sang in the premieres of Maxwell Davies's The Martyrdom of St Magnus in 1977, Le Jongleur de Notre Dame in 1978, The Lighthouse in 1980 and Black Pentecost in 1982, and as Merlin in Hamilton's Lancelot in 1985; Benoit in La Bohème at Hong Kong, 1998. *Recordings:* Belshazzar's Feast; Bach Cantatas and B minor Mass; Mozart's Requiem; Purcell's Ode to St Cecilia; Handel's Israel in Egypt; Schoenberg's Moses and Aron; Vaughan Williams's Hugh The Drover; Holst's The Wandering Scholar; Mathias' This Worlds Joie; Salome.

**RISHTON, Timothy (John);** Organist and Musicologist; b. 14 Aug. 1960, Lancashire, England; m. Tracy Jane Hogg, 11 July 1987, 2 s., 1 d. *Education:* BA Music, University of Reading; Certificate in Welsh; MMus, University of Manchester, England; PhD University of Wales; Associate, Royal College of Organists. *Career:* Numerous recitals world-wide including complete Stanley series, London, 1981 and complete Bach Trio Sonatas, London and Salford, 1983; Complete Bach organ works, Norway, 1988–89; Concert tours in Central Europe, the Arctic, Scandinavia, the Far East and USA; 1st performance of Smethergell Harpsichord Concerto, Tadley, 1983; Dedicatee of new compositions by Henning Somevvo and Hans-Olav Lien; Lectures, Boxhill Summer School annually 1985–90, University of Oxford 1986 and 1987; University of Reading, 1988; Norwegian Music Conservatoire, Trondheim, 1993–; Many public lectures in English, Welsh and Norwegian (some broadcast); Many radio and television broadcasts for HTV, S4C, NRK (Norway) and BBC, 1984–; University of Wales, Bangor, Wales, 1984–87, 1989–91; Organist and Master of Choristers, Collegiate Church of St Cybi, Holyhead and Parish Churches of Holy Island, Anglesey, 1984–87; University of Tromso, 1998–; Reader in Performance Practice at Tromso, 2001. *Compositions:* Organ Works. *Recordings:* with Aled Jones, 1985; Organ Works of the Eighteenth-Century, 1986; From Many Lands, 1991; Walther and Bach arrangements of Albinoni and Vivaldi, 2001; Contemporary Norwegian Organ Music, 2001. *Compositions:* Organ works published in Norway, Sweden and Germany. *Publications:* Aspects of Keyboard Music; Essays in Honour of Susi Jeans, 1986; Organist in Norway, 1989; Liturgisk orgelspill, (various editions) 1995; Voll Kyryje, 1996. *Address:* 6315 Innfjorden, Norway.

**RISLEY, Patricia;** Singer (Mezzo-soprano); b. 12 Jan. 1968, South Carolina, USA. *Education:* Indiana University and Chicago Lyric Opera Center for American Artists. *Career:* Chicago Lyric Opera from 1995, as Siebel in Faust and in Berio's Un re in ascolto, Die Walküre, Die Zauberflöte and Norma; Metropolitan Opera from 1998 as Tebaldo in Don Carlo, Thisbe in Cenerentola and Mercédès in Carmen; European debut 1997 in Die Sieben Todsünden by Weill at Florence; Further roles include Mozart's Dorabella at St Louis, Farnace in Mitridate for Wolf Trap Opera and Cherubino at the Deutsche Oper, Berlin; Diana in La Calisto and Cesti's Orontea for Music of the Baroque; Gounod's Stephano and Meg Page in Falstaff at Chicago and Munich. *Current Management:* Balmer & Dixon Management AG, Kreuzstrasse 82, 8032 Zürich, Switzerland. *Telephone:* (43) 244-8644. *Fax:* (43) 244-8649. *Website:* www.badix.ch.

**RISSET, Jean-Claude;** Composer and Researcher; b. 13 March 1938, Le Puy, France; m. Rozenn Cornic, 2 children. *Education:* Ecole Normale Supérieure; studied composition with André Jolivet. *Career:* Bell Laboratories, USA, 1964–69; Centre National de la Recherche Scientifique, 1979–72 (Dir of Research, 1985–); head of computer dept at IRCAM, Paris, 1975–79, with Pierre Boulez; fmr Composer-in-Residence, MIT and Stanford, USA. *Compositions include:* Little Boy, tape, 1968; Mutations I, tape, 1969; Dialogues, for 4 instruments and tape, 1975; Inharmonique, soprano and tape, 1977; Moments Newtoniens, for 7 instruments and tape, 1977; Mirages, 16 instruments and tape, 1978; Filtres, for 2 pianos, 1984; Sud, 1985; Dérives, for chorus and tape, 1985–87; Phases, for orchestra, 1988; Electron Positron, 1989; Duet for One Pianist, 1989; Lurai, for celtic harp and computer, 1991; Triptyque for clarinet and orchestra, 1991; Une aube sans soleil, soprano and percussion, 1991; Invisibles/Invisible soprano and computer, 1994; Mokee, for bass, piano and tape, 1996; Contre Nature, percussion and tape, 1996; Elementa, for tape, 1998; Escalas, for orchestra, 2001; Resonant Sound Spaces, 2002. *Recordings:* Works appear on 24 Cds. *Publications:* in Science, Musique en jeu, Esprit, Critique, Contemporary Music Review, Perspectives of New Music, Pour la Science, etc. *Honours:* Grand Prix National de la Musique, France, 1991; Médaille d'Or du CNRS, 1999; Hon. DMus Univ. of Edinburgh 1994, Univ. of Cordoba, Argentina 2000. *Address:* Laboratoire de Mécanique et d'Acoustique, CNRS, 31 chemin Joseph Aiguier, 13402 Marseille Cédex 20, France. *E-mail:* jcrisset@lma.cnrs-mrs.fr.

**RITCHIE, Anthony Damian,** PhD; New Zealand composer; b. 18 Sept. 1960, Christchurch. *Education:* Canterbury Univ., Liszt Acad., Budapest, studied composition with Attila Bozay. *Career:* Lecturer, Canterbury Univ. 1985–87; Composer-in-Schools, Christchurch 1987; Mozart Fellowship at Otago Univ. 1988–89; Composer-in-Residence, Southern Sinfonia 1993–94; Lecturer in Composition, Otago Univ. 2001–05. *Compositions include:* Concertino for piano and strings 1981, Autumn piano concerto 1985, Shintaro San for brass band 1986, Beginnings for orchestra 1987, Music for Tristan for piano 1988, The Hanging Bulb for orchestra 1989, To Face the Night Alone for baritone, chorus and orchestra 1990, As Long as Time for unaccompanied choir 1991, Berlin Fragments for soprano and piano 1992, Flute Concerto 1993, Symphony No.1 'Boum' 1993, Viola Concerto 1994, Star Fire (opera) 1995, A Bugle Will Do for orchestra 1995, Then I Understood for choir and orchestra 1996, Guitar Concerto 1996, The Eagle has Landed (one-act opera) 1997, From the Southern Marches for choir and orchestra 1997, Revelations for orchestra 1998, Symphony No. 2 'The Widening Gyre' 1999, Ahua for choir and orchestra 2000, 24 Preludes for piano 2002, String Quartet No.2 2002, 'Quartet' (chamber opera) 2003, Timeless Land for orchestra and film 2003, The God Boy (two-act opera) 2004. *Recordings:* Music for Tristan, The Hanging Bulb for orchestra, Flute Concerto, Viola Concerto, As Long as Time, 24 Preludes for Piano, Tui for flute solo, Widow's Songs. *Address:* c/o Music Department, University of Otago, Box 56, Dunedin, New Zealand (office). *E-mail:* anthony.ritchie@xtra.co.nz. *Website:* www.anthonyritchie.co.nz.

**RITTERMAN, Dame Janet Elizabeth,** DBE, PhD, MMus, FRNCM, FRSA; music college director; b. 1 Dec. 1941, Sydney, Australia; d. of Charles Eric Palmer and Laurie Helen Palmer; m. Gerrard Peter Ritterman 1970. *Education:* North Sydney Girls' High School and New South Wales State Conservatorium of Music, Australia, Univ. of Durham and King's Coll. London, UK. *Career:* pianist; accompanist, chamber music player; Sr Lecturer in Music, Middx Polytechnic 1975–79, Goldsmiths' Coll. Univ. of London 1980–87; Head of Music, Dartington Coll. of Arts 1987–90, Dean Academic Affairs 1988–90, Acting Prin. 1990–91, Prin. 1991–93; Visiting Prof. of Music Educ., Univ. of Plymouth 1993–; Dir Royal Coll. of Music 1993–2005; Chair. Assoc. Bd Royal Schools of Music (Publishing) Ltd 1993–2005, The Mendelssohn and Boise Foundations 1996–98, 2002–04, Advisory Council, Arts Research Ltd 1997–, Fed. of British Conservatoires 1998–2003; Vice-Pres. Nat. Asscn of Youth Orchestras 1993–; mem. Music Panel, Arts Council of England 1992–98, Council Royal Musical Asscn 1994–2004 (Vice-Pres. 1998–2004), Bd English Nat. Opera 1996–2004, Exec. Cttee Inc. Soc. of Musicians 1996–99, Arts and Humanities Research Bd 1998–2004 (Post grad. Panel 1998–2002, Chair. Post grad. Cttee 2002–04), Steering Cttee, London Higher Educ. Consortium 1999–2005, Arts Council of England 2000–02, Dept for Educ. and Skills Advisory Group, Music and Dance Scheme 2000–2005, Council of Goldsmith's Coll., Univ. of London 2002–, Arts and Humanities Research; Trustee, Countess of Munster Musical Trust 1993–, Prince Consort Foundation 1993–; Fellow Univ. Coll., Northampton 1997, Dartington Coll. of Arts 1997 Gov. Associated Bd Royal Schools of Music 1993–2005, Purcell School 1996–2000, Heythrop Coll. Univ. of London 1996–; mem. Österreichischer Wossemscjaftsrat 2002–; Gov. Dartington Coll. of Arts 2005–; mem. Bd, Nat. Campaign for the Arts 2005–; Sr Fellow, RCA 2004. *Publications:* articles in learned journals, France, Germany, Australia and UK. *Honours:* Hon. RAM 1995, Hon. mem. GSMD (Guildhall School of Music and Drama) 2000; Hon. DUniv (Univ. of Cen. England) 1996, Hon. DLitt (Univ. of Ulster) 2004.

**RIVA, Ambroglio;** Singer (Bass); b. 1951, Ignazio, Milan, Italy. *Career:* Debut: Teatro Nuovo Milan, 1975, in Lucia di Lammermoor; Has appeared widely in Italy, notably in La Bohème at Verona (1980) and at the Verona Arena in Aida and Carmen; Sang in Donizetti's Martyrs at Bergamo, in Anna Bolena at Brescia and Sparafucile in Rigoletto at Ferrara; Valle d'Istria Festival, 1985, as Polyphemus in Acis and Galatea; Maggio Musicale Florence, 1990, as Angelotti in Tosca; Further appearances at Salzburg, Würzburg and Berlin. *Address:* c/o Teatro Comunale, Via Solferino 15, 50123 Florence, Italy.

**RIVENQ, Nicolas;** Singer (Baritone); b. 1958, London, England. *Education:* Studied with Madame Bonnardo in Paris, at the Orléans Conservatory and with Michel Sénéchal at the School of The Paris Opéra; Further study with Nicola Rossi-Lemeni at Indiana University. *Career:* Sang major roles in such operas as Boris Godunov, La Traviata and Don Giovanni at Indiana; 1984–85 season as Sulpice in La Fille du Régiment, Guglielmo, Marcello and Jupiter in Orphée aux Enfers, and Christus in Bach's St Matthew Passion; Recitals in Moscow and Leningrad in 1984 and sang Bach Cantatas with English Chamber Orchestra in London and Edinburgh; Sang in Lully's Atys under William Christie at the Paris Opéra in 1986 and on tour to Tourcoing, Versailles and New York, 1988; Schwetzingen and Karlsruhe Festivals in 1988 with Tarare by Salieri under Jean-Claude Malgoire, Paris Opéra, 1989; Season 1989 with Rameau's Platée at Montpellier and Don Giovanni for Opera Northern Ireland; 1990–91 included Osman and Adario in Les Indes Galantes at Aix, Mozart's Count in Toulouse and performances of La Clemenza di Tito by Gluck at Tourcoing; Cherubini's Anacréon with The Orchestra of The Age of Enlightenment, 1992; Sang Sallustia in Pacini's L'Ultimo giorno di Pompei, Martina Franca, 1996; Turin 1998 in Bernstein's Candide; Sang Ambassadeur in Madame de, by Damase, at Geneva, 2001. *Address:* c/o Opéra et Concert, 1 rue Volney, F–75002 Paris, France.

**RIVERS, Malcolm;** Singer (baritone); b. 1940, England. *Education:* Royal College of Music. *Career:* Appearances with English National Opera in various roles including Alberich in The Ring, Escamillo in Carmen, and Marullo in Rigoletto; Sang in Troilus and Cressida and La Fanciulla del West at Covent Garden, Germont in La Traviata and Alberich in Seattle, numerous other appearances; Sang Sullivan's Pirate King and Pooh-Bah with the D'Oyly Carte Company, 1989; Alberich in The Ring at Falstaff, Arizona, 1996; mem., RSC. *Current Management:* Athole Still International Management, Forresters Hall, 25–27 Westow Street, London, SE19 3RY, England. *Telephone:* (20) 8771-5271. *Fax:* (20) 8768-6600. *Website:* www.atholestill.com.

**RIZZI, Carlo;** Italian conductor; *Music Director, Welsh National Opera;* b. 19 July 1960, Milan. *Education:* Milan Conservatoire, studied with Vladimir Delman in Bologna, Accademia Chigiana with Franco Ferrara. *Career:* debut, Milan Angelicum in Donizetti's L'Aio nell'Imbarrazzo 1982; conducted Falstaff, Parma 1985 and widely in Italy with Rigoletto, La Traviata, Tancredi, Donizetti's Torquato Tasso, Beatrice di Tenda, La Voix Humaine, Don Giovanni, L'Italiana in Algeri and Salieri's Falstaff; British debut at Buxton Festival with Torquato Tasso 1988; Netherlands Opera debut with Don Pasquale and productions of Fra Diavolo and Norma at Palermo 1989; Royal Philharmonic debut 1989, London Philharmonic debut 1990, Philharmonia debut 1991; Australian Opera with Il Barbiere di Siviglia and Lucrezia Borgia 1989–90; Tosca for Opera North and La Cenerentola at Covent Garden 1990; concert repertoire includes symphonies by Tchaikovsky and works by Haydn, Mozart, Beethoven and French composers; regular guest in Italy and Netherlands; US opera debut with Il Barbiere di Siviglia 1994; Don Giovanni and La Bohème for WNO 1996; Tristan and Isolde at Oxford and Bristol 1999; conducted Semiramide in Pesaro 2003; conducted Nabucco at the Met, I vespri siciliani in Zurich, Un ballo in maschera in Turin, Ariadne auf Naxos for WNO, Mefistofele in Amersterdam, Falstaff in Strasburg and Madama Butterfuly in Seville 2004; Music Dir, WNO 1992–2001, 2004–(08). *Recordings:* L'Italiana in Algeri, Donizetti's Il Furioso sull'Isola di San Domingo, Rossini's Ciro in Babilonia, Paisiello's La Scuffiara, Piccinni's La Pescatrice, Arias for tenor and orchestra by Rossini (with Ernesto Palacio), Schubert, Liszt and Debussy with the London Philharmonic and Philharmonia. *Current Management:* Allied Artists, 42 Montpelier Square, London, SW7 1JZ, England; Prima International Artists Management, Piazza de' Calderini 2/2, 40124 Bologna, Italy. *Address:* c/o Welsh National Opera, Wales Millennium Centre, Bay Chambers, West Bute Street, Cardiff, CF10 5GG, Wales. *Website:* www.wno.org.uk.

**RIZZI, Lucia;** Singer (Mezzo-soprano); b. 1965, Turin, Italy. *Education:* Studied architecture and music in Turin. *Career:* Appearances throughout Italy, in Tokyo and at the Aldeburgh Festival, under such conductors as Myung Wha Chung, Gianandrea Gavazzeni and Semyon Bychkov; Operas include Monteverdi's Poppea, Pergolesi's Frate 'nnamorato and Vivaldi's Farnace; Roles include Mozart's Fiordiligi, Dorabella and Sesto, Clarice in La Pietra del Paragone and Rossini's Roggiero (Tancredi) and Cenerentola (both at Zürich, 1996–97); Further engagements in Luisa Miller, Falstaff, Boris Godunov, Lady Macbeth of the Mtsensk District (in Florence), Stravinsky's Rossignol and Les Noces (Monte Carlo) and the Italian premiere of Tchaikovsky's Cantata Moscow, at Genoa; Other concerts in music by Vivaldi, Mahler and Schoenberg, at most Italian music centres; Sang Rosmene in a revival of Pergolesi's Il prigionero superbo, Jesi, 1998. *Recordings include:* Rossini Rarities. *Address:* c/o Opernhaus Zürich, Falkenstrasse 1, 8008 Zürich, Switzerland.

**RIZZO, Francis;** Stage Director and Administrator; b. 8 Nov. 1936, New York, NY, USA. *Education:* BA, Hamilton College, 1958; Yale University School of Drama, 1958–60. *Career:* American Director, Spoleto Festival of Two Worlds, 1968–71; Artistic Administrator, Wolf Trap Farm Park for The Performing Arts, 1972–78; Artistic Director, the Washington Opera, 1977–87; As director staged productions for New York City Opera, Houston Grand Opera, Washington Opera, Wolf Trap, Opera Theater of St Louis, Santa Fe Opera, Baltimore Opera, Teatro Verdi, Trieste, Michigan Opera Theater, Théâtre Municipal, Marseilles; mem, American Guild of Musical Artists. *Contributions:* Opera News. *Address:* 590 West End Avenue, New York, NY 10024, USA.

**ROARK-STRUMMER, Linda;** American singer (soprano); *Associate Professor of Voice, University of Tulsa;* b. 1952, Tulsa, OK. *Education:* Univ. of Tulsa. *Career:* sang Dorabella at St Louis 1977; engaged at Hannover 1979–80, Linz 1980–86 as Regina in the 1983 Austrian premiere of Lortzing's opera and in the premiere of In Seinem Garten Liebt Don Perlimpin Belinda by B. Sulzer; New York City Opera 1985 as Giselda in I Lombardi; over 150 performances of Verdi's Abigaille, notably at the Deutsche Oper Berlin 1987, Ravenna 1988 and Montréal and Verona 1992; La Scala Milan 1988 as Lucrezia in I Due Foscari; sang Krasava in a concert performance of Smetana's Libuce in New York; other roles include Lina in Stiffelio, the Forza and Trovatore Leonoras, Arabella, Jenůfa and Antonia; guest engagements at Hamburg, Krefeld, Milwaukee and Venice; sang Norma for Opera Hamilton at Toronto 1991; Turandot at Portland 1996; Poulenc's Mère Marie at Portland 2001; Assoc. Prof. of Voice and Dir of Opera Workshop, Univ. of Tulsa. *Address:* School of Music, Tyrrell Hall 103, University of Tulsa, 600 South College, Tulsa, OK 74104, USA. *E-mail:* linda-strummer@utulsa.edu. *Website:* www.lindaroark-strummer.com.

**ROBBIN, Catherine;** Singer (mezzo-soprano); b. 28 Sept. 1950, Toronto, Canada. *Career:* many appearances in Baroque music; sang in Messiah with English Baroque Soloists under Gardiner, Bach's B minor Mass with Monteverdi Choir and Handel's Orlando at the 1989 Promenade Concerts; opera performances include Olga in Eugene Onegin at Opéra de Lyon, Purcell's Dido and Handel's Orlando, (role of Medoro) with Acad. of Ancient Music and Handel's Xerxes at Carmel Bach Festival; collaborations with Trevor Pinnock, Hogwood, Andrew Davis, John Nelson, Jukka-Peka Saraste and Charles Dutoit; repertoire includes Les Nuits d'Été by Berlioz, Mahler's Lieder eines Fahrenden Gesellen and Rückert Lieder, Elgar's Sea Pictures and the Brahms Alto Rhapsody; many recitals in Canada and the USA and appearances at Aldeburgh Festival and with the Songmakers' Almanac; sang the title role in the North American premiere of Handel's Floridante in Toronto, 1990; Annius in La Clemenza di Tito at the Queen Elizabeth Hall, London, 1990; sang in Handel's Rinaldo at Blackheath and Bromsgrove, 1996. *Recordings include:* Beethoven's Mass in C and Missa Solemnis; Messiah under Gardiner; Berlioz Songs, also Gardiner; Haydn's Stabat Mater with Trevor Pinnock and the English Concert; Orlando under Hogwood; Mahler Song Cycles. *Honours:* Gold Award at the International Benson and Hedges Competition, Aldeburgh, England. *Current Management:* Caroline Phillips Management, The Old Brushworks, Pickwick Road, Corsham, Wiltshire, SN13 9BX, England. *Telephone:* (1249) 716716. *Fax:* (1249) 716717. *E-mail:* cphillips@caroline-phillips.co.uk. *Website:* www.caroline-phillips.co.uk/robbin.

**ROBBINS, Julien;** Singer (Bass); b. 14 Nov. 1950, Harrisburg, Pennsylvania, USA. *Education:* Studied, Philadelphia Academy of Vocal Arts, and with Nicola Moscona in New York. *Career:* Debut: Philadelphia 1976, in Un Ballo in Maschera; Engagements at Santa Fe, Miami, Washington and Chicago; Metropolitan Opera from 1979, as Ramphis, Colline, Gremin and Don Fernando in Fidelio; Deutsche Oper Berlin 1990, as Abimelech in Samson et Dalila; Sang Masetto at the Metropolitan, 1990; World premiere, The Voyage, by Philip Glass, Metropolitan Opera (Second Mate and Space Twin), Nightwatchman in Meistersinger, 1993; Deutsche Oper, Berlin, Don Giovanni, 1992, 1993, Escamillo, 1993, Turandot, (Timur) 1992; Staatsoper Berlin, Barber of Seville, Basilio, 1992; 1993 Deutsche Oper, Berlin, Figaro in The Marriage of Figaro; Season 1994 at San Diego as Count Rodolfo in La Sonnambala at Lisbon as Escamillo in Carmen and the Dresdner Festival, Messiah; Le Comte Ory, Le Gouverneur, Glyndebourne, 1997–98; Alidoro in La Cenerentola, Achilles in Giulio Cesare for Metropolitan, 2000; Don Alfonso in Così fan tutte for Metropolitan Opera, 2001. *Recordings:* Salome, First Soldier, Berlin Philharmonic, 1991; Doctor, La Traviata, Metropolitan Opera, 1992. *Current Management:* c/o Martha Munro, Munro Artist Management, 786 Dartmouth Street, South Dartmouth, MA 02748, USA. *Address:* 2805 Windy Hill Road, Allentown, PA 18103-4663, USA.

**ROBERTI, Margherita;** Singer (Soprano); b. 1930, Davenport, Iowa, USA. *Education:* Studied at Hunter College and the Mannes School of Music, New York; Further study in Italy, 1956. *Career:* Debut: Teatro Alfieri Turin, 1957, as Leonore in Il Trovatore; Appeared at Covent Garden in 1959 as Tosca; La Scala debut in 1959 as Abigaille in Nabucco; Engagements at the Verona Arena from 1959; Metropolitan Opera debut in 1962 as Tosca; Edinburgh Festival in 1963 as Luisa Miller and Glyndebourne Festival in 1964 as Lady Macbeth; Other roles include Elisabeth de Valois, Amelia in Un Ballo in Maschera, Hélène in Les Vêpres Siciliennes and Odabella in Atilla; Guest appearances as concert artist in England and North America. *Recordings include:* Elena in Donizetti's Marino Faliero.

**ROBERTS, Brenda;** Singer (Soprano); b. 16 March 1945, Lowell, Indiana, USA. *Education:* Studied at Northwestern University, Evanstown with Hermann Baer; Further study with Lotte Lehmann, Gerald Moore and Josef Metternich in Germany. *Career:* Debut: Staatstheater Saarbrucken, 1968 as Sieglinde in Die Walküre; German appearances at Düsseldorf, Essen, Frankfurt, Nuremberg, Wiesbaden and Wuppertal; Member of the Hamburg Staatsoper; Bayreuth Festival in 1974 as Brünnhilde in Siegfried; Sang Isolde at Kassel in 1983; American engagements in Baltimore, Chicago, Baltimore and San Francisco; Metropolitan Opera debut in 1982 as the Dyer's Wife in Die Frau ohne Schatten; Other roles include Salome at Vienna in 1984 and Salome at Bremen in 1986, Wagner's Senta and Elsa, Verdi's Elisabeth de Valois, Aida, Lady Macbeth, Leonora and Violetta, Mozart's Donna Elvira and Countess, Puccini's Tosca, Giorgetta and Turandot, Santuzza and Lulu; Sang in a concert performance of Die Bakchantinnen by Egon Wellesz at Vienna in 1985; Kiel Opera in 1990 as Elektra and the title role in the premiere of Medea by Friedhelm Dohl; Sang Schoenberg's Erwartung at Palermo, 2000. *Address:* Buhnen Landeshaupstadt, Rathausplatz, 2300 Kiel, Germany.

**ROBERTS, Deborah;** Singer (Soprano); b. 1952, England. *Education:* Studied at Nottingham University, editing and interpreting Renaissance Baroque music; Further study with Andrea von Ramm in Basle. *Career:* Has sung with the Tallis Scholars on tours to Europe, Australia and the USA, appearing at most major festivals; Guest concerts with the Deller Consort and the Consort of Musicke; Frequent engagements with Musica Secreta notably in the Early Music Centre Festival, the Lufthansa Festival of Baroque Music and at the National Gallery; Early Music Network tour of Britain with programme Filiae Jerusalem, sacred music for women's voices by Monteverdi,

Carissimi, Cavalli, Viadana, Grandi and Marco da Gagliano; Other repertoire includes works by Marenzio, Wert, Luzzaschi, Luigi Rossi and the women composers Francesca Cacini and Barbara Strozzi; Participation in lecture-recitals and workshops on performance practice and ornamentation. *Recordings:* With Musica Secreta, as musical director, Luzzaschi Madrigals for 1–3 Sopranos; Ensemble Music of Barbara Strozzi, 1994; Over 30 recordings with Tallis Scholars. *Honours:* Prizewinner, Bruges Early Music Competition, 1981. *Address:* 84 Devonshire Road, London SE23 3SX, England.

**ROBERTS, Dorothy (Elizabeth);** Concert Pianist; b. 1930, Brisbane, Queensland, Australia; Divorced, 1 s. *Education:* Studies at Sydney Conservatorium of Music, including Piano, Harmony, History of Music, Form of Music, Chamber Music; Clara Schumann technique with Adelina de Lara, London. *Career:* Music concerts at Balliol College, Oxford, Purcell Room, South Bank, London; Performed Liszt's Piano Concerto in E Flat with London Symphony Orchestra at Royal Albert Hall, London; Other concerto performances with the Hallé Orchestra, Northern Sinfonia Orchestra and London Bach Players; Recitals in London, the United Kingdom provinces, Glasgow, Germany, Australia, France, Netherlands, Canada; Television appearance with the Hallé Orchestra; Other television appearances with Richard Bonynge, 2 pianos, including playing with the BBC Orchestra. *Honours:* AMusA; LMus; Honorary DLit, Bradford University, 1995; Recently confirmed as the only Grand Pupil of the Clara Schumann piano-playing tradition. *Current Management:* Lee Reid Concerts. *Address:* Alveley House, 17 Lindum Road, Lincoln LN 2 1 NS, England.

**ROBERTS, Eric;** Singer (baritone); b. 16 Oct. 1944, Conway, North Wales. *Career:* Debut: Opera debut as Papageno with Welsh National Opera; Has sung with various British companies as: Guglielmo; Falke; Mozart's Figaro, Count and Trinity Moses, in Mahagonny, Scottish Opera; English National Opera in Pacific Overtures and the British premiere of Rimsky's Christmas Eve, 1988; D'Oyly Carte Opera Company, 1988–90; Further appearances as: Don Alfonso for Opera North; Bartolo and Britten's Redburn for Scottish Opera; Don Isaac in the British premiere of Gerhard's The Duenna; Haly, in L'Italiana in Algeri at Dublin; Eugene Onegin, for Opera Omaha, Nebraska, 1993; Australian debut as Bartolo, Lyric Opera of Queensland, 1992; Sang Don Isaac in Gerhard's The Duenna, Leeds, 1996; Concert engagements in Britten's War Requiem at Belgrade and L'Enfant et les Sortilèges at Rotterdam. *Current Management:* Athole Still International Management, Forresters Hall, 25–27 Westow Street, London, SE19 3RY, England. *Telephone:* (20) 8771-5271. *Fax:* (20) 8768-6600. *Website:* www.atholestill.com.

**ROBERTS, Kathleen;** Singer (Soprano); b. 9 Oct. 1941, Hattiesburg, Mississippi, USA. *Education:* Studied at Mississippi College, at Texas Christian University and in Zürich and Darmstadt. *Career:* Debut: St Gallen in 1967 as Violetta; Appearances at opera houses in Zürich, Geneva, Cologne and Frankfurt; Member of the Darmstadt Opera as Marzelline in Fidelio, Micaela, Aennchen in Der Freischütz, Mozart's Pamina, Susanna and Constanze, Gretel, Martha and Mimi; Modern repertoire has included Luise in Henze's Der Junge Lord and Laetita in The Old Maid and The Thief by Menotti; Many concert appearances; Teacher of Singing in Darmstadt and elsewhere.

**ROBERTS, Paul (Anthony);** Concert Pianist; b. 2 June 1949, Beaconsfield, England; 2 s. *Education:* BA, Honours, University of York, 1970; Royal Academy of Music, London. *Career:* Juror, International Debussy Piano Competition, France, 1982, 1984; Cycle of Complete Debussy Piano Music at Purcell Room, London in 1984; World premiere of Maurice Ohana's piano etudes in a live broadcast for Radio France, 1986; Premieres of Ohana work for BBC in 1984, 1986 and 1988; World premiere of original piano score of an unpublished opera by Debussy, Rodrigue et Chimène, BBC Radio 3 in 1988; Lecturer, Professor of Piano at Guildhall School of Music, 1985–; Director, International Piano Summer School, SW France; Music at Ladevie. *Publications:* Book reviews for Times Educational Supplement, Composer, and Revue Musicale, Paris. *Current Management:* Management USA, Pat Zagelow, 3420 NE 21st Avenue, OR 97212, USA. *Address:* 10 Montague Road, London E8 2HW, England.

**ROBERTS, Stephen Pritchard;** Singer (Baritone); b. 8 Feb. 1949. *Education:* Scholar, Associate, 1969, Royal College of Music; Graduate, Royal Schools of Music, 1971. *Career:* Professional Lay-Cleric, Westminster Cathedral Choir, 1972–76; Sings regularly in London, the United Kingdom and Europe, with all major orchestras and choral societies; Has sung in USA, Canada, Israel, Italy, Hong Kong, Paris, Poland, Spain, Singapore and South America; Opera roles include: Count in Marriage of Figaro, Falke in Die Fledermaus, Ubalde in Armide, Ramiro in Ravel's L'Heure Espagnole, Aeneas in Dido and Aeneas, Don Quixote in Master Peter's Puppet Show, Mittenhofer in Elegy for Young Lovers by Henze; Television appearances include Britten's War Requiem, Weill's Seven Deadly Sins, Delius's Sea Drift, Handel's Jephtha and Judas Maccabaeus, Penderecki's St Luke Passion at 1983 Proms, Walton's Belshazzar's Feast at 1984 Proms; Has worked with many orchestras specializing in authentic Baroque; Concert and oratorio performer singing all major baritone roles by JS Bach, Mozart, Handel, Elgar and Britten, also the choral symphonies by Mahler and Beethoven; Sang in Bach's St Matthew Passion at the Festival Hall, 1997; Professor at Royal Schools of Music, Vocal Faculty, 1993–. *Recordings include:* Numerous, many with King's College and St John's College, Cambridge, and Bach Choir of London including: St Matthew Passion, Punch and Judy with London Sinfonietta, The Apostles

with London Symphony Orchestra, Caractacus with London Symphony Orchestra, Requiem with RPO, Messiah, Alexander's Feast, Carmina Burana with Berlin RSO, St Luke Passion, King Priam with London Sinfonietta, and A Sea Symphony; Dyson Canterbury Pilgrims; 2 CDs of English Songs. *Address:* 144 Gleneagle Road, London SW16 6 BA, England. *E-mail:* SRobertsBaritone@aol.com. *Website:* www.StephenRoberts.uk.com.

**ROBERTS, Susan;** Singer (Lyric-Coloratura Soprano); b. 1960, USA; m. Dimitry Sitkovetsky (qv), 26 July 1983. *Career:* Sang at first at the Bielefeld Opera then in Wiesbaden and Frankfurt; Has sung Blonchen in productions of Die Entführung by Ruth Berghaus in Frankfurt, Giorgio Strehler in Bologna, Jean-Pierre Ponnelle in Cologne and Giancarlo del Monaco in Bonn; Sang Minette in the premiere of Henze's English Cat at Frankfurt and again in Edinburgh and for the BBC; Further appearances at the Bayreuth and Orange Festivals and other German theatres; Paris Opéra in 1988 in the premiere of La Celestina by Maurice Ohana; Season 1990–91 as Blondchen for Netherlands Opera and Zan in Blitzstein's Regina for Scottish Opera; Concert engagements with radio orchestras in Vienna, Turin and Berlin, the National Orchestra of Spain, Orchestre Philharmonique Paris, Orchestre de Lyon and the Düsseldorf Symphonic; Recitals at the Vassa, Lockenhaus and Schleswig-Holstein Festivals; Season 1992 as Handel's Agrippina at the Buxton Festival; Sang in Param Vir's Snatched by the Gods at the Almeida Theatre, 1996; Sang Poulenc's Thérèse for Grange Park Opera, 1999. *Honours:* Martha Baird Rockefeller Foundation Grant; Laureate Winner, Concours International Musicale, Geneva. *Address:* Music International, 13 Ardilaun Road, London N5 2QR, England.

**ROBERTS, Winifred;** British violinist; b. 1930, Lismore, NSW, Australia; m. Geraint Jones (died 1998). *Education:* Royal Coll. of Music, studied with Antonio Brosa, Albert Sammons and Herbert Howells. *Career:* performances include Nat. Gallery Concerts, England, Promenade Concerts, three Choirs Festival, Lake District Festival, Salisbury Festival, Manchester Festival; soloist, Festival Hall and QEH; tours of Italy, Spain, USA; BBC radio and television broadcasts; Prof. of Violin, Royal Acad. of Music, now retd; teacher of advanced performers class, Morley Coll., London, now retd; private teaching; adjudicating and acting as outside examiner at music colls and schools. *Recordings:* History of Music, Biber Sonata, Vivaldi Double Concerto, Harpsichord and Violin Sonatas (with Geraint Jones). *Honours:* Royal Coll. of Music Tagore Gold Medal and first prize in violin playing, Hon. RAM 1983. *Address:* Flat 25, Circus Lodge, Circus Road, London, NW8 9JL, England. *Telephone:* (20) 7289-5391. *Fax:* (20) 7289-5391.

**ROBERTSON, Christopher;** Singer (Baritone); b. 1964, USA. *Education:* Studied in San Francisco (member of the 1987 Merola Opera Program). *Career:* Many appearances at Leading Opera Houses in North America and Europe; Metropolitan Opera, season 1992–93, as Marcello and Sharpless in Butterfly; Don Giovanni, 1995–96; European debut as Guglielmo at Frankfurt Opera, followed by Mozart's Count at Munich, Egberto in Verdi's Aroldo at Covent Garden, and Oreste in Gluck's Iphigénie en Tauride at the Berlin Staatsoper; Prus in The Makropulos Case at Vancouver, Germont for English National Opera (1996) and Amonasro for San Francisco Opera (1997); Further engagements as Donner in Das Rheingold at Valencia, Count Luna with Florida Grand Opera, 1997 and Rigoletto with San Francisco Opera, also in 1997, Renato in Un Ballo in Maschera at Seattle and for Flanders Opera, and in Belgium, New Orleans, Montreal, Rio de Janeiro, Madrid and Santiago. *Honours:* Robert Jackson Memorial Grant, Richard Tucker Music Foundation. *Address:* c/o Metropolitan Opera, Lincoln Center, NY 10023, USA.

**ROBERTSON, David;** American conductor; *Music Director, St Louis Symphony Orchestra;* b. Santa Monica, CA. *Education:* RAM. *Career:* Conductor Jerusalem Symphony Orchestra 1985–87; Music Dir Ensemble Intercontemporain, Paris 1992–2000; Music Dir Orchestre Nat. de Lyon and Artistic Dir Lyon Auditorium 2000–04; Music Dir St Louis Symphony Orchestra 2005–; Prin. Guest Conductor BBC Symphony Orchestra 2005–; has conducted orchestras, including LSO, Hallé, Royal Concertgebouw, Orchestre de Paris, NHK Symphony, Hamburg NDR Symphony, Bayerisches Staatsorchester, Staatskapelle Berlin, Orchestra del Maggio Musicale Fiorentino, Santa Cecilia Orchestra, Rome, Tonhalle Zürich, Berlin Philharmonic, New York Philharmonic and the symphony orchestras of Atlanta, Dallas, Detroit, Cleveland, San Francisco; conducted US premiere of Berio's Stanze with Pittsburgh Symphony 2005, world premiere of Danielpour's Songs of Solitude with Philadelphia Orchestra and Thomas Hampson 2005, French premiere of Birtwistle's Theseus Games with the Ensemble Intercontemporain 2005; opera engagements have included Metropolitan Opera, Opera de Lyon, La Scala, Bayerische Staatsoper, Paris Châtelet, Hamburg State Opera, San Francisco Opera; has given masterclasses at Paris Conservatory, The Juilliard School, Tanglewood, Aspen Music Festival. *Recordings:* Milhaud, Works for Piano and Orchestra 1993, Edouard Lalo, Namoura, Musique de Ballet 1995, Silvestrov, Symphony No. 5 1996, Jessye Norman, In the Spirit 1996, American Clarinet 1999, Manoury, 60th Parallel 1999, Dusapin, Extenso 2000, Ginastera, Estacia 2001, Bartók, The Miraculous Mandarin 2002, Boulez, Rituel in memoriam Bruno Maderna 2003, Steve Reich, Different Trains 2004. *Honours:* Musical America Conductor of the Year 1999. *Address:* St Louis Symphony Orchestra, 718 North Grand Boulevard, St Louis, MO 63103, USA (office). *E-mail:* artistic@slso.org (office). *Website:* www.slso.org (office).

**ROBERTSON, Duncan,** LRAM, FGSM; British singer (tenor); b. 1 Dec. 1924, Hamilton, Scotland; m. Mary Dawson 1950; one s. one d. *Education:* Scottish Nat. Acad. of Music, Royal Coll. of Music, London. *Career:* varied career in Oratorio including appearances in most European countries; opera performances mostly at Glyndebourne and with Scottish Opera, also Covent Garden, Sadler's Wells, English Opera Group, Welsh Opera, Handel Opera; many broadcasts ranging from light music to BBC Radio 3; some TV, recordings and recital work; sang in Canticum Sacrum by Stravinsky, first performance in UK conducted by Robert Craft 1956; appeared in Oedipus Rex by Stravinsky, with Jean Cocteau as narrator and conducted by Stravinsky 1959; sang in Benjamin Britten's 50th Birthday Concert 1963; sang with Giulini conducting, performance of Schubert's Mass in E Flat, televised from the Edinburgh Festival 1968; Prof. of Singing, Guildhall School of Music and Drama, London, 1966–77; Lecturer in Singing, Royal Scottish Acad. of Music and Drama, Glasgow, 1977–88; Fellow Emer., Guildhall School of Music 1979. *Honours:* Gold Medal, Scottish Nat. Acad. of Music 1945. *Address:* Heathers, 5 The Driftway, Upper Beeding, West Sussex, BN44 3JX, England (home).

**ROBERTSON, John;** Scottish singer (tenor); b. 20 Sept. 1938, Galashiels. *Education:* Sedburgh and Edinburgh Univs. *Career:* regular appearances with Scottish Opera; 850 performances in 50 roles, including Ferrando, Tamino, Ottavio, Albert Herring and Almaviva; has toured with the co. to Austria, Germany, Switzerland, Yugoslavia, Poland, Portugal and Iceland in The Turn of the Screw, The Rape of Lucretia and A Midsummer Night's Dream; appearances at Edinburgh as Tannhäuser and in Le nozze di Figaro; has directed the Edinburgh Opera in La Traviata, L'Elisir d'amore and La Sonnambula; oratorio and concert work throughout Scotland and on BBC and Scottish television; teaches voice in Glasgow and Edinburgh and at the School of Vocal Studies at the Royal Northern Coll. of Music, Manchester. *Recordings include:* Le nozze di Figaro. *Address:* 1746 Great Western Road, Glasgow, G13 2TQ, Scotland.

**ROBERTSON, Stewart (John);** Conductor, Pianist and Music Director; b. 22 May 1948, Glasgow, Scotland. *Education:* Royal Scottish Academy of Music, 1965–69; Bristol University, 1969–70; Vienna Academy, 1975; Salzburg Mozarteum, 1977; Teachers: Otmar Suitner and Hans Swarowsky for conducting, and Denis Matthews for piano. *Career:* Assistant Chorus Master, Scottish Opera, Edinburgh Festival Chorus, 1968–69; Chorus Master, London City Singers, 1970–72; Conductor for Cologne Opera, 1972–75; Music Director, Tanz Forum, Zürich Opera, 1975–76, Scottish Opera Touring Company, 1976–79; Assistant Conductor, Oakland Symphony Orchestra, 1985–86; Music Director and Principal Conductor, Glimmerglass Opera, NY, 1987–; Guest Conductor for SNO, and BBC Scottish Symphony Orchestra, CBSO Swiss-Italian Radio Symphony Orchestra, San Jose Symphony Orchestra, Utah Symphony Orchestra, Britt Festival, Long Beach, Portland, Sacramento, Kentucky Opera, Arkansas Opera and Montreal Opera; Season 1998 with L'Elisir d'amore for Florida Grand Opera and Thomson's The Mother of us All for Glimmerglass Opera; Artistic Dir, Opera Omaha 2005–. *Current Management:* John Miller, Robert Lombardo Associates, NY, USA. *Address:* 81 Poppy Road, Carmel Valley, CA 93924, USA.

**ROBINS, Brian Martin;** British writer, lecturer and broadcaster; b. 2 Jan. 1940, Cheltenham, England; pnr Anne Young; one d. *Education:* Univ. of London. *Career:* classical record retailer 1957–90; adult educ. lecturer 1984–87; freelance writer and lecturer 2001–; broadcaster for BBC; mem. Royal Musical Assccn. *Publications:* The John Marsh Journals 1998, Catch and Glee Culture in Eighteenth Century England, The Catch and Glee in 18th Century Provincial England (in Concert Life in Eighteenth-Century Britain) 2004, Catch and Glee Culture in Eighteenth-Century England 2006; contrib. to New Grove Dictionary of Music and Musicians 2000, New Dictionary of National Biography 2004, Early Music, The Journal of the Royal Musical Association, Fanfare (USA), Goldberg Early Music Magazine (Spain). *Honours:* Andrew W. Mellon Fellowship 1994, British Acad. Exchange Fellowship to Huntington Library, San Marino, USA 2000. *Address:* Bière, 71190 Broye, France (home). *Telephone:* (385) 543163 (home). *E-mail:* brian.robins4@tiscali.fr (home).

**ROBINSON, Christopher John,** CVO, CBE, BMus, MA, FRCO; British conductor and organist; b. 20 April 1936, Peterborough; s. of the late John Robinson; m. Shirley Ann Churchman 1962; one s. one d. *Education:* St Michael's Coll., Tenbury, Rugby and Christ Church, Oxford. *Career:* asst organist Christ Church, Oxford 1955–58, New Coll., Oxford 1957–58; Music Master Oundle School 1959–62; asst organist Worcester Cathedral 1962–63, organist and master of choristers 1963–74; organist and Choirmaster St George's Chapel, Windsor Castle 1975–91; Conductor City of Birmingham Choir 1964–2002, Oxford Bach Choir 1977–97, Leith Hill Musical Festival 1977–80; organist and Dir of Music St John's Coll., Cambridge 1991–2003 (fmr conductor Choir of St John's Coll.); Fellow St John's Coll., Cambridge 1991–; Pres. RCO 1982–84. *Recordings:* Parry, Cathedral Music 1994, Tavener, Sacred Works 1994, Mendelssohn, Church Music 1998, Howells, Requiem 1999, Tavener, Christmas Proclamation 2000, Britten, Rejoice in the Lamb 2000, Rubbra, Magnificat and Nunc dimittis in A-flat 2001, Walton, English Choral Music 2002, Finzi, Lo, the full, final sacrifice Op. 26 2002, Leighton, Sacred Choral Music 2004, Elgar, Sacred Choral Music 2004, Durufle, Requiem, Berkeley, Crux fidelis Op. 43 No. 1, Stanford, Anthems and Services. *Honours:* Hon. MMus (Birmingham) 1987, Hon. MusD (Lambeth) 2002;Hon. Fellow Univ. of Central England 1990, Hon. RAM, Hon. FGCM 2002. *Address:* St John's College, Cambridge, CB2 1TP, England (office).

**ROBINSON, Dean;** Singer (Bass); b. 20 Aug. 1968, Bathurst, Australia. *Education:* Studied in Australia and Royal Northern College of Music. *Career:* Opera engagements at Covent Garden in Don Carlos, Die Meistersinger, Lohengrin, Palestrina (also at Metropolitan Opera) and Ariadne auf Naxos; for English National Opera Colline in La Bohème, 2nd Soldier in Salome, Pluto in Orfeo and created role of Passauf in Gavin Bryers' Dr Ox's Experiment; Colline, Mr Ratcliffe in Billy Budd and Angelotti for Welsh Nat. Opera; Sparafucile and Sarastro for Scottish Opera; Colline, Sparafucile and Don Giovanni with Mid Wales Opera; Claudio in Agrippina, Polyphemus in Acis and Galataea, and King of Scotland in Ariodante, for The Early Opera Company; Death in The Emperor of Atlantis for Mecklenburgh Opera; with English Touring Opera Sarastro, and Comte de Grieux in Manon; Concerts include St John Passion at Westminster Abbey, Mozart Requiem with Eric Ericsson, Messiah with Sir John Eliot Gardiner and the English Baroque Soloists, L'enfance du Christ with Kent Nagano, Verdi's Requiem with Sir David Willcocks. *Recordings:* Don Pedro in Beatrice et Benedict with Sir Colin Davis and the London Symphony Orchestra; Masetto in Don Giovanni; Duca d'Argile in La Prigione di Edimburgo for Opera Rara and appearances on several Opera Rara recital discs. *Film:* First Officer in The Death of Klinghoffer for Channel 4 TV. *Address:* c/o Harlequin Agency Limited, 203 Fidlas Road, Cardiff, CF14 5NA, Wales. *E-mail:* deanrobinson@orange.net.

**ROBINSON, Ethna;** Singer (mezzo-soprano); b. 20 June 1956, Dublin, Ireland. *Education:* Studied in Birmingham and at the Guildhall School, London. *Career:* English National Opera from 1984, as Rosette in Manon and in the British premiere of Akhnaten by Glass; Premieres of Birtwistle's The Mask of Orpheus, 1986, and Harvey's Inquest of Love, 1993; Other roles have included Mozart's Dorabella and Cherubino, Hansel, Olga in Eugene Onegin, Berlioz's Béatrice, Margret in Wozzeck, and Pauline in The Queen of Spades; Tour of Russia with ENO, 1990; Season 1998 as The Prioress in Suor Angelica for ENO, and Third Lady in The Magic Flute; Season 2000–01 as St Theresa III in Thomson's Four Saints in Three Acts, for ENO, and Larina in Eugene Onegin for Opera North. *Recordings include:* Video of ENO Mikado. *Current Management:* Owen/White Management, Top Floor, 59 Lansdowne Place, Hove, East Sussex, BN3 1FL, England.

**ROBINSON, Faye;** Singer (Soprano); b. 2 Nov. 1943, Houston, Texas, USA. *Education:* Studied with Ruth Stewart at Texas Southern University and with Ellen Faull in New York. *Career:* Debut: New York City Opera, 1972, as Micaela; Has sung Violetta, the Queen of Shemakha and Liu in New York; Washington Civic Opera in 1973 as Violetta and Juliette; Jackson, FL, 1974–75 as Desdemona and Adina; Aix-en-Provence in 1975 in Der Schauspieldirektor and La Serva Padrona; Engagements in Houston, Barcelona and Frankfurt; Buenos Aires in 1980 in Les Contes d'Hoffmann; Schwetzingen Festival in 1981 as Elektra in Idomeneo; Paris Opéra and Bordeaux in 1982 as Juliette and Luisa Miller; Other roles include Constanze, Norina and Oscar; Sang in the premiere of The Mask of Time in Boston, 1984 and in the first British performance of Tippett's oratorio; Cologne in 1988 as Constanze. *Recordings:* Mahler's 8th Symphony; The Mask of Time. *Address:* c/o Houston Grand Opera, 510 Preston Avenue, Houston, TX 77002, USA.

**ROBINSON, Gail;** Singer (Soprano); b. 7 Aug. 1946, Meridian, Mississippi, USA. *Education:* Studied at Memphis State University and with Robley Lawson. *Career:* Debut: Memphis, 1967 as Lucia in Lammermoor; Appearances in Berlin, Munich and Hamburg; Sang with Metropolitan Opera from 1970, in Die Zauberflöte and as Gilda, Adina, Oscar, Marie in La Fille du Régiment, Rosina and Gretel; Director, Metropolitan National Council Auditions and now Director, Metropolitan Young Artist Development Program. *Honours:* Winner of Metropolitan's National Council Auditions, 1966. *Address:* c/o Metropolitan Opera, Lincoln Center, New York, NY 10023, USA.

**ROBINSON, Michael Finlay,** BA, BMus, MA, DPhil; British academic (retd); *Professor Emeritus of Music, University of Wales, Cardiff;* b. 3 March 1933, Gloucester, England; m. Ann James 1961; two s. *Education:* Univ. of Oxford. *Career:* teacher, Royal Scottish Acad. of Music 1960–61; Music Lecturer, Univ. of Durham 1961–65; Asst Prof., McGill Univ., Montreal, Canada 1965–67, Assoc. Prof. 1967–70; Music Lecturer, Univ. of Wales, Cardiff 1970–75, Sr Lecturer in Music 1975–91, Head of Music Dept 1987–94, Prof. of Music 1991–94, Prof. Emer. of Music 1995–. *Compositions:* two String Quartets 1972, 1974, A Pretty How Town for baritone and eight instrumentalists 1983, Fantasy for unaccompanied cello 1997, other chamber music and songs. *Publications:* Opera Before Mozart 1966, Naples and Neapolitan Opera 1972, Giovanni Paisiello: a thematic catalogue of his works Vol. 1 1991, Vol. 2 1993; contrib. to Proceedings of the Royal Musical Association, New Grove, Chigiana, Studi Musicali, Soundings, Early Music, Music and Letters, The Alternative Endings of Mozart's Don Giovanni (in Opera Buffa in Mozart's Vienna) 1997. *Address:* Northridge House, Usk Road, Shirenewton, Monmouthshire, NP16 6RZ, Wales (home). *Telephone:* (1292) 641538 (home). *E-mail:* northridge33@tiscali.co.uk (home).

**ROBINSON, Paul;** Singer (Baritone); b. 1970, England. *Education:* Chorister and Choral Scholar, Kings College, Cambridge; Royal College of Music. *Career:* Concerts include St John Passion at the London Bach Festival, Bach's Magnificat at Bristol Cathedral, Monteverdi Vespers in Vancouver, St Matthew Passion for Italian Radio and Schubertiade Recital at the Wigmore Hall; Mozart's Coronation Mass with the Royal Flanders Philharmonic Orchestra, Purcell's Indian Queen with the Academy of Ancient Music,

Messiah with the CBSO and Haydn's Mariazeller Mass at Canterbury Cathedral; Opera Roles include The Speaker in The Magic Flute for Opera West, Mangus in Tippett's Knot Garden and Janáček's Poacher and Britten's Demetrius for the RAM; Season 1997–98 with the Brahms Requiem in London, Bach's Christmas Oratorio in Oxford, St John Passion with the Royal Liverpool Philharmonic Orchestra, Carmina Burana at Bristol and Handel's Joshua with the Academy of Ancient Music. *Recordings:* Many Albums with King's College Choir; Robert in Hugh the Drover by Vaughan Williams.

**ROBINSON, Peter;** Conductor; b. 1949, England. *Education:* Studied music at Oxford. *Career:* Assistant Organist, Durham Cathedral; Associated with the Glyndebourne Festival Opera, 1971–73; Head of Music Staff and Resident Conductor, Australian Opera, 1973–80; Assistant Music Director, English National Opera, 1981–89, conducting Le nozze di Figaro, Don Giovanni, Die Zauberflöte, Così fan tutte, Otello, Rigoletto, The Mastersingers, Madama Butterfly, Orfeo, Maria Stuarda, The Mikado, Carmen, Werther, Hansel and Gretel, Simon Boccanegra and The Turn of the Screw; Appearances for Kent Opera with The Beggar's Opera and Don Giovanni, and the Scottish Opera with The Pearl Fishers; Conducted Così fan tutte in a production for BBC television; Has conducted in Australia; Le nozze di Figaro, Victoria State Opera, 1987; Die Entführung VSO, 1989; Così fan tutte, The Australian Opera, 1990; Don Giovanni, State Opera of South Australia, 1991; Engagements with Opera Factory (Marriage of Figaro also for television), 1991; Figaro at Adelaide, 1997; Symphony concerts with the London Symphony, London Mozart Players and London Sinfonietta; Concerts with the Melbourne and Sydney Symphony Orchestras, 1988–90; Sound and Video recordings with Lesley Garrett for Silva Screen Records and BBC television; Conducted The Magic Flute for British Youth Opera, 1996. *Current Management:* Marks Management Ltd. *Address:* c/o 14 New Burlington Street, London W1X 1FF, England.

**ROBINSON, Sharon;** Concert Cellist; b. 2 Dec. 1949, Houston, Texas, USA; m. Jaime Laredo 1976. *Education:* North Carolina School of the Arts, 1968; University of Southern California, 1968–70; BM, Peabody Conservatory of Music, 1972. *Career:* Debut: New York in 1974; Member of Kalichstein-Laredo-Robinson Trio from 1976; Soloist at Marlboro Music Festival, Mostly Mozart Festival and South Bank Festival in London, Edinburgh Festival, Madeira Bach Festival, Helsinki Festival and Tivoli Gardens; Commissioned and premiered Ned Rorem's After Reading Shakespeare, for solo cello and premiered Alan Shulman's Kol Nidrei for cello and piano, William Bland's Rhapsody for cello and piano, and Robert Blake's Cello Sonata; mem, Violoncello Society of America. *Recordings:* Vivaldi Sonatas; Fauré's Elegy; Debussy Sonata; Rorem's After Reading Shakespeare; Beethoven's Triple Concerto; With Kalichstein-Laredo-Robinson Trio, Mendelssohn and Brahms Trios; Duos for Violin and Cello with Jaime Laredo. *Honours:* Avery Fisher Award, 1979; Levintritt Award, 1975; Pro Musicis Foundation Award, 1974. *Current Management:* Askonas Holt Ltd, Lonsdale Chambers, 27 Chancery Lane, London, WC2A 1PF, England. *Telephone:* (20) 7400-1700. *Fax:* (20) 7400-1799. *E-mail:* info@askonasholt.co.uk. *Website:* www.askonasholt.co.uk.

**ROBINSON, Timothy;** Singer (Tenor); b. 1968, England. *Education:* Studied at New College Oxford (Choral Scholar) and with William McAlpine at the Guildhall School. *Career:* 1996 concerts include Mozart's Davidde Penitente at Seville, Messiah in Singapore, Weber's Euryanthe at the Queen Elizabeth Hall, South Bank, and Proms debut as Jupiter in Semele, under William Christie; Opera roles include Kudrjash in Katya Kabanova for Glyndebourne Touring Opera, Fenton and Scaramuccio (Ariadne auf Naxos) for English National Opera and Jupiter at the Aix-en-Provence Festival (French premiere, 1996); Member of the Royal Opera, in such operas as Nabucco, Traviata and Fedora; Sang in the British premiere of Pfitzner's Palestrina, 1997; Season 1997–98 in Katya Kabanova at Glyndebourne and in Turandot at the Paris Opéra; Other roles include Don Ottavio, Tamino and Alfredo, with Travelling Opera; Arminio in Verdi's Masnadieri for the Royal Opera, 1998; Sang St John in The Kingdom by Elgar at the 1999 London Prom concerts; London Proms, 2002. *Recordings include:* Bach's Magnificat; Vaughan Williams Serenade to Music; Beethoven Cantatas. *Address:* 11 Gilmore Road, Lewisham, SE13 5AD.

**ROBISON, Paula;** Flautist; b. 8 June 1941, Nashville, Tennessee, USA; m. Scott Nickrenz, 1 d. *Career:* Founding Artist Member, Chamber Music Society of Lincoln Center; Joint Recitalist with pianist Ruth Laredo and Guitarist Eliot Fisk; Soloist, New York Philharmonic, Atlanta, American and San Francisco Symphony Orchestra; Recitalist at numerous venues including Carnegie Hall and Kennedy Center and Wigmore Hall in January 1990; Commissioned and premiered Kirchner's Music for Flute and Orchestra with the Indianapolis Symphony, Toru Takemitsu's I Hear the Water Dreaming, Robert Beaser's Song of the Bells; Numerous television appearances including Live from Lincoln Center, 1984–85; Christmas at the Kennedy Center; Sunday Morning, CBS Television; For 10 years (1978–1988) Co-Director of Chamber Music, Spoleto Festival at Charleston, South Carolina, and Spoleto, Italy; Blue Ridge Airs II, flute and orchestra, Kenneth Frazelle, 1991; Soloist, London Symphony Orchestra, Michael Tilson Thomas, 1995; I Solisti Veneti, Claudio Scimone, 1995. *Recordings:* Has made many recordings including, Flute Music of the Romantic Era; The Sonatas for Flute and Harpsichord by J. S. Bach (complete) and G F Handel (complete) with Kenneth Cooper; Release for Music Masters: American Masterworks for flute and piano. *Current Management:* Shaw Concerts. *Address:* c/o London Symphony Orchestra, Barbican Centre, Silk Street, London, EC 2, England.

**ROBLES, Marisa,** HRCM, FRCM; British concert harpist; b. 4 May 1937, Madrid, Spain; d. of Cristóbal Robles and María Bonilla; m. 3rd David Bean 1985; two s. one d. from previous marriages. *Education:* Madrid Royal Conservatoire of Music. *Career:* Prof. of Harp, Madrid Royal Conservatoire of Music 1958–63; Harp Tutor, Nat. Youth Orchestra of GB 1964–85; Prof. of Harp, Royal Coll. of Music, London 1969–94; Artistic Dir World Harp Festival, Cardiff, Wales 1991, World Harp Festival II 1994; appearances as soloist with all maj. orchestras in GB and throughout the world, including New York Philharmonic; chamber music performances with Marisa Robles and Friends, Marisa Robles Harp Ensemble, Marisa Robles Trio and other chamber groups; solo recitals in Australia, Canada, Europe, Japan, NZ, S America and the USA; many TV appearances and radio performances; masterclasses in GB and abroad; four recordings of Mozart's Flute and Harp Concerto with James Galway (q.v.) and more than 20 other recordings. *Publications:* several harp pieces and arrangements. *Address:* 38 Luttrell Avenue, London, SW15 6PE, England. *Telephone:* (20) 8785-2204.

**ROBLOU, David,** ARAM, Dip RAM, LRAM, ARCM, ARCO; British conductor, harpsichordist, organist, pianist and vocal coach; b. 23 Dec. 1949, London, England. *Education:* Royal Acad. of Music, masterclasses with Nadia Boulanger (London) and Kenneth Gilbert (Antwerp). *Career:* Artistic and Musical Dir, Midsummer Opera; Prof., Guildhall School of Music and Drama 1974; mem. Musicians' Union, Incorporated Soc. of Musicians. *Recordings:* numerous chamber music recordings with New London Consort, including harpsichord solo, J. S. Bach: Brandenburg Concerto No. 5. *Current Management:* Sounds Lyrical Artists Management, 109 Algernon Road, London, SE13 7AP, England. *Telephone:* (20) 8244-5789 (office). *Fax:* (20) 7652-0070 (office). *E-mail:* sounds.lyrical@ntlworld.com (office).

**ROBOTHAM, Barbara;** Musician and Singer; b. 15 Jan. 1936, Blackpool, England; m. Eric Waite, 30 Aug 1958, 1 s. *Education:* ARMCM Teachers Diploma with distinction, 1957, Performers Diploma with distinction, 1959, Royal Manchester College of Music. *Career:* Appearances with all major British Orchestras; Festival appearances include Three Choirs Festival, Cheltenham, Haydn-Mozart Festival, Gulbenkian Lisbon, and Bordeaux France; Concerts include Paris, Madrid, Barcelona, Prague, and Frankfurt; Principal Lecturer at Royal Northern College of Music and Professor of Voice at Lancaster University; mem, Incorporated Society of Musicians. *Recordings:* Stravinsky's Cantata on Old English Texts; Walton's Gloria. *Honours:* Imperial League of Opera Prize and Curtis Gold Medal, 1958; 1st Prize, Liverpool Philharmonic International Singers Competition, 1960; 2nd Prize, Concours International de Geneva, 1961; Honorary Fellowship, Royal Manchester College of Music, 1967; Honorary Fellowship, Royal Northern College of Music, 1992; Honorary Fellowship, University of Central Lancashire, 1998. *Address:* 49 Blackpool Road North, St Annes on Sea, Lancashire, England.

**ROBSON, Christopher;** British singer (countertenor); b. 9 Dec. 1953, Falkirk, Scotland; m. Laura Carin Snelling 1974 (divorced 1984); one s. (with Samantha Lambourne). *Education:* Cambridge Coll. of Arts and Technology, Trinity Coll. of Music, London with James Gaddarn, studied with Paul Esswood and Helga Mott. *Career:* debut in Handel's Samson, Queen Elizabeth Hall, London, 1976; Opera debut, Handel's Sosarme, Barber Institute, Birmingham, 1979; Principal roles, Kent Opera, Phoenix Opera, Handel Opera Society, Royal Opera Covent Garden (Semele), 1988–; English National Opera (Orfeo, Xerxes, title role in Julius Caesar and Akhnaten, Lear), Frankfurt State Opera, Berliner Kammeroper (Orlando title role), Houston Grand Opera, New York City Opera, Opera Factory Zürich, Opera Factory-London Sinfonietta, Nancy Opera, Innsbruck Tirolertheater; Sang at major festivals, the United Kingdom, France, Spain, Austria, Netherlands, USA, Switzerland, Germany, Poland, and BBC Proms; Concerts throughout the United Kingdom and Europe; Broadcasts, BBC, SFB, WDR, ORF, DRS, Radio France Musique; Monteverdi Choir, 1974–84; London Oratory Choir, 1974–80; The Spieglers, 1976–82; St George's Theatre Company, 1976; Westminster Cathedral Choir, 1980–85; Kings Consort, 1981–86; New London Consort, 1986–; Sang in Xerxes on ENO Russian tour, 1990; Season 1992–93, Ptolemy (Julius Caesar) for Scottish Opera, Polinesso (Ariodante) for ENO, Andronicus (Tamerlano) for Karlsruhe, Ezio title role, Berliner Kammeroper; Season 1993–94, Tamerlano title role, Opera North, Arsamenes (Xerxes), ENO, Apollo (Death in Venice), Liège, Oberon (Midsummer Night's Dream), Covent Garden Festival, Tolomeo (Giulio Cesare); Season 1994–95, Oberon, ENO; Season 1995–96, Arsamenes, Chicago Lyric Opera, Vlaamse Oper Antwerp, Bayerische Staatsoper Munich, Oberon, Ravenna Festival; Season 1966–97, Didimus (Theodora), Glyndebourne Touring Opera; Season 1997–98, Orlofsky (Fledermaus), Munich; Season 1998–99 World premieres of Lunn's The Maids, Lyric Theatre, London and Dove's Flight at Glyndebourne Opera; Season 1999–2000, Polinesso (Ariodante), Munich; Engaged for season 2001–2002 as Baba the Turk in The Rake's Progress, Munich; film Hell for Leather directed by Dominik Scherrer; World premier of Hans Jurgen von Bose K-Projekt 12/14, a one-man opera commissioned by the Bavarian State Opera to open the 2003 Opernfestspiel. *Television appearances include:* A Night with Handel (Channel 4/NVC/Warner Music), Xerxes (ThamesTV/Channel 4/RM Arts/Arthaus), Hail Bright Cecilia (Channel 4/EMI), The Rake's Progress and Rodelinda (both Bayerische Rundfunk), Flight (Channel 4). *Recordings include:* Resurrection, Maxwell Davies; Psyche, Locke; Ezio, Handel; Artaxerxes, Arne; Magnificat, Bach; Xerxes, Handel; Vivaldi Gloria, Decca; Jonathan Dove, Flight, Chandos. *Honours:* Opernfestspiel Preis, Munich, 1997; Bayerische Kammersaenger, 2003. *Address:* c/o Music International, 13 Ardilaun Road, London N5 2QR, England. *E-mail:* chrisopera@lineone.net.

**ROBSON, Elizabeth;** Singer (Soprano); b. 1938, Dundee, Scotland; m. Neil Howlett. *Education:* Studied at Royal Scottish Academy of Music and in Florence. *Career:* Debut: Sadler's Wells in 1961 as Micaela; Appearances at Covent Garden throughout the 1960s as Musetta, Zdenka, Sophie, Susanna, Pamina, Marzelline and Nannetta in Falstaff; Guest appearances with Scottish Opera as Zerlina and at the 1967 Edinburgh Festival as Anne Trulove in The Rake's Progress; Sang also at Aix-en-Provence and La Scala Milan; Noted concert artist. *Recordings:* Marzelline in Fidelio.

**ROBSON, Nigel;** Singer (Tenor); b. 1955, Argyllshire, Scotland. *Education:* Royal Northern College of Music with Alexander Young. *Career:* Sang with the Glyndebourne Festival Chorus and English National Opera from 1981 as Monteverdi's Orfeo and in the premiere of Birtwistle's The Mask of Orpheus, 1986; British stage premiere of Weill's Der Protagonist; Sang Ferrando in Così fan tutte and in David Freeman's production of Falstaff, in the premiere of Michael Finnissy's The Undivine Comedy and in Tippett's Songs for Dov conducted by Tippett, La Finta Giardiniera for Opera North and Don Ottavio in Don Giovanni for Opera Factory; Idomeneo at Munich (1996) and sang in new production of Monteverdi's Ulysses for Opera North, 1997 Appearances with the Monteverdi Choir and Orchestra including tours of Italy, Germany and France; Performances of Monteverdi's Vespers in Venice and Orfeo in Spain as well as Idomeneo in Lisbon, Paris, Amsterdam and London; Sang Handel's Jephtha at the Handel Festival in Göttingen and the Holland Festival; Sang the Anonymous Voice in the British premiere of Tippett's New Year at Glyndebourne in 1990; Concerts at the Festival Hall with Janáček's Glagolitic Mass, with the Ensemble Intercontemporain in Paris and with the London Sinfonietta in Henze's Voices in 1991; Season 1992 as Claggart in Billy Budd for Scottish Opera and Nero in The Coronation of Poppea for Opera Factory; Other recent roles have included the title role in Idomeneo at the Bayerische Staatsoper; Ulisse in Il Ritorno d'Ulisse in Patria and Pandarus in Walton's Troilus and Cressida for Opera North; Laca in Jenůfa for WNO, 1998; Season 2000–01 as Peter Grimes at Maastricht, Golo in Schumann's Genoveva at Garsington and Britten's Captian Vere for Canadian Opera at Toronto. *Recordings include:* Handel's Tamerlano; Alexander's Feast and Jephtha; Tippett's Songs for Dov; Stravinsky's Renard; Arbace in Idomeneo; Britten's The Rape of Lucretia; Walton's Troilus and Cressida. *Current Management:* Ingpen & Williams Ltd, 7 St George's Court, 131 Putney Bridge Road, London, SW15 2PA, England.

**ROBSON, Richard;** Singer (Bass); b. 1964, County Durham, England. *Education:* Guildhall School with Otakar Kraus; Further Study with Arlene Randazzo. *Career:* Debut: Badger in The Cunning Little Vixen and Antonio in Figaro, at Glyndebourne; Speaker in The Magic Flute and Gremin in Eugene Onegin, for Kent Opera; Debut with Wiener Kammeroper as Rossini's Basilio, 1990; Festival Engagements at Vienna Schonbrunn, Barcelona, Brighton, Hong Kong and Edinburgh; Colline and Sparafucile in Rigoletto for Bath and Essex Opera; Wexford Festival, 1994–95, in Rubinstein's The Demon and as Il Cieco in Mascagni's Iris; Further Appearances in Iris at Rome and Munich and with the Chelsea Opera Group; Season 1996–97 with Ramfis in Aida for Norwegian Opera and return to Wexford; Concerts include Elgar's Apostles at Canterbury Cathedral, Rossini's Petite Messe in Strasbourg, Verdi Requiem in Croydon and Mozart's Requiem on Tour to Germany; Creon in Cherubini's Médée and Frederico in Verdi's Battaglia di Legnano (St John's Smith Square and Chelsea Opera Group).

**ROCHAIX, François;** stage director; b. 2 Aug. 1942, Geneva, Switzerland. *Education:* University of Geneva, Berliner Ensemble, East Berlin. *Career:* founded the Atelier de Genève, 1963, actor and director; Director of the Théâtre de Carouge, 1975–81; Produced The Turn of The Screw and Death in Venice at Geneva in 1981 and 1983, La Traviata for Opera North in 1985, Cardillac and Parsifal at Berne, 1988–89, Der Ring des Nibelungen, 1985–87, and Die Meistersinger in 1989 at Seattle; Production of Tristan und Isolde for Opéra Lyon in 1990; Dialogues des Carmélites at Geneva, 1993. *Address:* 7 Vy aux Vergnes, 1295 Mies, Switzerland.

**ROCHAT, Michel,** MMus; Swiss conductor; b. 29 Jan. 1931; m. Josette-Marie Rochat 1959; two d. *Education:* Conservatoires of Lausanne, Geneva and Paris with Maestro Cahuzac, Basel Musikakademie. *Career:* taught clarinet, Switzerland 1952, conducting, Switzerland 1960; played clarinet, Basel Contemporary Music Group 1968–72; Prof. and Dir, Conservatoire Supérieur, Lausanne 1963–83; guest conductor, Belgium, Bulgaria, Italy, Greece, Romania, Russia, Switzerland, Venezuela 1976–85; Gen. Music Dir and Conductor, Izmir Nat. Symphony Orchestra 1982–85; guest conductor, Nat. Symphony Orchestra, Istanbul 1982–85; Prof., Nat. Inst. of Arts and Nat. Acad. of Arts, Taiwan 1985–; conductor in Taiwan, in Taipei City and Kaohsiung Symphony Orchestras, Taipei Bach Orchestra, Artist's Ensemble 1985–, Hwa Shing Children's Chorus 1989–90, Rong Shing Chorus 1993–96, Asia Int. Festival for Contemporary Music 1994, Dan Tie Orchestra 1995–, Music Camp for Chinese Music, Ilan 1996, Lan Yang Chinese Ensemble, performing at Int. Children's Festival and Taipei Chinese Music Festival 1996, Lan Yan Chinese Ensemble, Taiwanese Opera Ilan 1996–; guest conductor, Taipei Municipal Chinese Orchestra 1993–, Experimental Chinese Orchestra, Taipei, Taichung and Kaohsiung tours 1997, Festival I-Lan Taiwan 2003–04; mem. Swiss Musicians' Asscn. *Compositions:* Taiwanese

operas: Seven Words 1996, Kavalan Story 1997, Kavalan Princess 1998, Ataya Song 1999, The Mouse Bride Children 2000; arranged Taiwanese songs; hymns for Taoist Association 2000, Music, Dance and Theater (opera ballet) 2001, Improvisation and Dance for flute and piano, Christmas Songs for choir, brass and organ 2002, Avis for soprano and piano 2003, Alleluia for choir and brass ensemble 2003, Amen for choir and brass ensemble 2003, Treasures of I-Lan concerto for two violins and Chinese orchestra 2004. *Recordings:* Masterpieces of Chinese Music 1995, Chinese Contemporary Music 1995, Chinese Music for the Young 1996, Dan Tie Chinese Ensemble 1996, Concert for Dragon Boat Festival 1996, Religious Music, Christmas Songs, Chinese and Taiwanese Pieces 1999, Commemoration of Centenary 1999, Kamalan Princess 1999, Dao Anthems 2000, Flowers Listen 2000, Taipei Chinese Orchestra: Works from Lu Liang Whei 2002, Works of Wang, Chen, Guh and Rochat 2004. *Publications:* To Know Tonality 1995, Clarinet for Beginners 1996, Introduction to Conducting 1996, Rudiments of Intervals and Notation 1996. *Honours:* Rio de Janeiro Int. Competition first prize, Gold Medal and Villa-Lobos Prize 1975, Medal of St-Laurent du Var (France) 1980, Lion's Club Best Music Teacher in Taiwan 1993. *Address:* Route de la Vuy 8, 1305 Penthalaz, Switzerland (home). *Telephone:* (21) 861-29-30 (home). *Fax:* (21) 681-31-23 (home). *E-mail:* rochat31@freesurf.ch. *Website:* www.michelrochat.ch.

**ROCHE, Elizabeth Barbara Winifred,** BA; Musicologist and Music Critic; b. 12 March 1948, Southport, England; m. Jerome Roche (deceased), one d. *Education:* Univ. of Durham. *Career:* research on 18th-century German Catholic Church Music with Denis Arnold; research on rise of interest in early music in Britain from 1870 onwards; assisted Jerome Roche's work on 17th-century north Italian church music; mem. Royal Musical Asscn. *Publications:* A Dictionary of Early Music (with Jerome Roche); contrib. to New Grove Dictionary of Music and Musicians, New Oxford Companion to Music, The Musical Times, Early Music. *Address:* 31 Sideling Fields, Tiverton, EX16 4AG, England (home). *Telephone:* (1884) 254051 (home).

**ROCHESTER, Marc;** Music Journalist, Organist, Conductor and Adjudicator; b. 28 April 1954, London, England; m Magdelene Teresa de Rozario, 1998. *Education:* BMus, MA, PhD, University of Wales, 1972–77; FTCL; ARCM; LRAM. *Career:* Music Critic, Western Mail, 1975–80; Correspondent, Organists review, Musical Times, 1980–89, Independent, 1987–, Gramophone, 1989; Sub-organist, Bangor Cathedral, 1978–80; Organist and Master of Choristers, Londonderry Cathedral, 1980–82; Music Tutor, New University of Ulster, Northern Ireland, 1980–84; Solo Recitalist; Choral Conductor; Examiner, Associated Board, Royal Schools of Music, Trinity College London, Northern Ireland Schools Examinations Council; University of London; Lecturer, Putra University, Malaysia, 1997–99; Programme Co-ordinator and Organist, Dewan Filharmonik Petronas, Kuala Lumpur. *Compositions:* Hymn tunes; Various church music. *Recordings:* Soloist, 20th Century British Organ Music, 1983; Conductor, Hymns of C F Alexander, Derry Cathedral Choir, 1981; Accompanist, Beaufort Male Voice Choir, 1977, 1978, Leila Carewe (soprano), 1980; A European Organ Tour. *Publications:* Frank Martin at Golgotha, 1977; Editor, catalogue, Traditional Welsh Musical Instruments. *Contributions:* Articles on 20th century music. *Address:* 48 Jalan Bayan 4, 47100 Puchong Jaya, Malaysia.

**ROCKWELL, John Sargent,** PhD; American journalist, arts administrator, music critic and author; b. 16 Sept. 1940, Washington, DC; s. of Alvin John and Anne Hayward; m. Linda Mevorach; one d. *Education:* Harvard Univ., Univ. of Munich, FRG and Univ. of Calif., Berkeley. *Career:* music and dance critic, Oakland (Calif.) Tribune 1969; Asst Music and Dance Critic, Los Angeles Times 1970–72; freelance music critic, New York Times 1972–74, staff music critic 1974–91, Ed. Arts and Leisure section 1998–; European Cultural Corresp. and Prin. Classical Recordings Critic, New York Times, Paris 1992–94; Dir Lincoln Center Festival, Lincoln Center for the Performing Arts, New York 1994–98. *Publications:* All American Music: Composition in the Late 20th Century 1983, Sinatra: An American Classic 1984. *Address:* New York Times, 229 West 43rd Street, New York, NY 10036, USA.

**RODAN, Mendi;** Conductor and Professor; b. 17 April 1929, Jassy, Romania; m. Judith Calmanovici, 2 c. *Education:* BMus, MA, Academy of Music, Arts Institute. *Career:* Permanent Conductor for Radio and Television Orchestra, Bucharest, 1953–58; Founder and Permanent Conductor of Jerusalem Chamber Orchestra; Chief Conductor, Music Director, Jerusalem Symphony, 1963–72; Music Director for Israel Sinfonietta, 1977–91; Music Director and Permanent Conductor of Orchestre National Belge, 1983–89; Music Director, IDF Educational Corp Chamber Orchestra, 1990–92; Laureate Conductor of Israel Sinfonietta, 1991–; Associate Conductor, Israel Philharmonic Orchestra, 1993–97; Guest Conductor for Israel Chamber Ensemble, Jerusalem Symphony, Israeli New Opera, Haifa Symphony; Concert tours world-wide with orchestras including Oslo Philharmonic, Vienna Symphony, Berlin Radio Symphony, London Symphony, London Philharmonia, Frankfurt Radio, Stockholm Philharmonic and Berlin Radio Symphony; Adviser at Jerusalem International Music Centre and Head of Jerusalem Academy of Music and Dance, 1985–94; Music Director and Chief Conductor, Israel Symphony Orchestra, 1997–; Member of the International Jury for Composition and Conducting, Poland, Israel, Italy; Professor for Orchestra Conducting and Ensembles at Rochester University, Eastman School of Music Guest appearance in Europe, USA and South America; With the China National Symphony Orchestra and with orchestras in the USA (Toledo, Passadena, Oklahoma, Bloomington and Rochester) and in Mexico, Venezuela, the Far

East and Australia. *Honours:* Order of Distinction, The Republic of Italy; Fr Peleg Prize 1997 Musician of the Year, Israel; Honorary Citizenship of Tuscon Arizona, USA. *Address:* Israel Symphony Orchestra, 16 Jabotinsky, Jerusalem 75229, Israel.

**RODDE, Anne-Marie;** Singer (Soprano); b. 21 Nov. 1946, Clermont-Ferrand, France. *Education:* Studied at the Conservatory of Clermont-Ferrand and at the Paris Conservatoire with Irene Joachim and Louis Nougera. *Career:* Sang at Aix-en-Provence in 1971 as Amor in Orfeo ed Euridice, Yniold in Pelléas et Mélisande at Paris in 1972, in Cantate Nuptial by Milhaud and The Nightingale by Stravinsky; Sang in Hyppolite et Aricie at Covent Garden, Falstaff, Cherubini's Médée, and Rosenkavalier at Paris Opéra House, Pelléas et Mélisande at Rome Opera House, Pearl Fishers at Stockholm Opera, Magic Flute debut in 1991 at La Bastille Opéra, Magic Flute at Montreal and Bonn Opera; Appearances in Amsterdam in Le nozze di Figaro and at Zürich and Barcelona; Many appearances in the Baroque repertory including London Bach Festival in Les Boréades by Rameau; Other roles include Zerbinetta, Oscar, Nannetta, Ravel's Child and Dirce in Médée, Paris Opéra in 1986; Sang Frasquita in Carmen at Florence, 1993. *Recordings:* Les Indes Galantes by Rameau; Handel's Xerxes; Lully's Le Triomphe d'Alcide; Les Boréades; Honegger's Jeanne d'Arc au Bûcher; Messiah; Songs by Debussy; Avietta di Camera by Rossini; Songs by Widor; Works by Bellini, Donizetti and Gluck.

**RODEN, Anthony;** Singer (Tenor); b. 19 March 1937, Adelaide, Australia; m. Doreen Roden. *Education:* Associated Australian Insurance Institute; Licenciate, Adelaide Conservatory. *Career:* Debut: Glyndebourne, England; Appearances at Glyndebourne and Netherlands Festivals, English, Welsh and Scottish National Operas, Opera North, Prague National Opera, Krefeld Opera, Victorian State Opera, Covent Garden in Peter Grimes, Freiburg Opera, Hamburg, Madrid and Barcelona; Numerous concerts for BBC, British, Italian and Dutch Orchestras; Sang Samson and Tannhäuser in Melbourne in 1992, Mahler's 8th Symphony, Royal Liverpool Philharmonic Orchestra, and Florestan for Glyndebourne; Mahler, Das Lied von der Erde, Taiwan; Vitek in The Makropulos Case at Glyndebourne, 1995; Sang Vitek at Hamburg, 2000; Principal Tutor, Royal Northern College of Music. *Recordings include:* Britten War Requiem, Dresden Philharmonic Orchestra under Herbert Kegel. *Honours:* John Christie Award, 1971; Opera Prize, Adelaide Conservatory. *Current Management:* Patricia Greenan. *Address:* 33 Castlebar Road, Ealing, London W5 2DJ, England.

**RODERICK JONES, Richard Trevor,** GRSM, ARCM, MMus, FRSA; British composer, conductor, pianist and musicologist; *Composer-in-Residence, Alcester Grammar School;* b. 14 Nov. 1947, Newport, Gwent, Wales; m. Susan Ann Thomason 1992. *Education:* Royal Coll. of Music and Univ. of Bristol. *Career:* Head of Music, South Warwickshire Coll., Stratford-upon-Avon 1970–79; Extramural Tutor, Univ. of Birmingham 1971–79; Musical Dir Nat. Youth Theatre of Wales 1978–87; Tutor, Welsh Coll. of Music and Drama 1979–93; Extramural Tutor, Univ. Coll. Cardiff 1980–93, 1997–; External Tutor, Univ. of Oxford 1993–95; Visiting Lecturer, Birmingham Conservatoire 2001–02; Composer-in-Residence, Alcester Grammar School 2002–. *Compositions:* piano concerto, three symphonies, three chamber concertos, three sinfoniettas, numerous choral works, including oratorio Altus Prosator, Missa Sarum, numerous chamber works, including two piano trios, piano quartet, stage works, including Me and My Bike (opera, BBC comm.), Chanticleer (church opera), Altar Fire (scenic celebration), Game Circle (scenic cantata), Sun Kingdom (opera), more than 30 scores for TV and stage. *Honours:* Royal Coll. of Music Cobbett Prize 1970. *Address:* The Limes, 7 Manor Barns, Middle Street, Ilmington, Shipston-on-Stour, Warwicks., CV36 4LS, England (home). *Telephone:* (1608) 682209 (home). *E-mail:* rroderickjones@aol.com (home).

**RODESCU, Julian;** Singer (Bass); b. 1 May 1953, Bucharest, Romania; m. Barbara Govatos, 4 June 1983. *Education:* BMus, MMus, Juilliard School; Teachers: Giorgio Tozzi, William Glazier, Jerome Hines, Hans Hotter and Daniel Ferro. *Career:* Debut: Plutone in Monteverdi's Il Ballo delle Ingrate with Brooklyn Opera, 1980; Carnegie Hall debut in 1989 with Rostropovich in world premiere of Shostakovich's Rayok; Teatro alla Scala with Riccardo Muti in 1991, Boston Symphony with Seiji Ozawa in Boston Symphony Hall, Carnegie Hall and Tanglewood; Appearances with Miami Opera, New York City Opera, Knoxville Opera, Aachen Stadttheater, Kennedy Center in Washington DC, Alice Tully Hall, WHYY-TV Philadelphia, WQXR, WNCN New York, Central City Opera and Opera Delaware. *Recordings:* Shostakovich's Rayok; Tchaikovsky's Queen of Spades; Bortniansky's Complete Vocal Concerti. *Honours:* Winner of Luciano Pavarotti Competition, 1988. *Current Management:* Ann Summers International. *Address:* 1420 Locust Street, Philadelphia, PA 19102, USA.

**RODGERS, Joan,** CBE, BA; British soprano opera and concert singer; b. 4 Nov. 1956, Whitehaven, Cumbria; d. of late Thomas Rodgers and of Julia Rodgers; m. Paul Daniel (q.v.) 1988; two d. *Education:* Whitehaven Grammar School, Univ. of Liverpool and Royal Northern Coll. of Music, Manchester. *Career:* first maj. professional engagement as Pamina (The Magic Flute), Aix-en-Provence Festival 1982; début at Metropolitan Opera House, New York, in same role 1995; other appearances include title role (Theodora) at Glyndebourne, The Governess (Turn of the Screw) for Royal Opera House, Blanche (Dialogues des Carmélites) for English Nat. Opera and in Amsterdam, Marschallin (Der Rosenkavalier) for Scottish Opera and title role (Alcina) for English Nat. Opera; regular appearances at Royal Opera House, English Nat. Opera, Glyndebourne, Promenade Concerts and with leading British and

European cos; concert engagements in London, Europe and USA with conductors including Solti, Barenboim, Mehta, Rattle, Harnoncourt and Salonen; numerous recordings; Kathleen Ferrier Memorial Scholarship 1981. *Honours:* Royal Philharmonic Soc. Award as Singer of the Year 1997, Evening Standard Award for Outstanding Individual Performance in Opera 1997. *Address:* c/o Ingpen and Williams Ltd, 26 Wadham Road, London, SW15 2LR, England.

**RODGERS, Sarah Louise,** BA, FRSA; British composer; b. 15 April 1953, Aylesbury, England. *Education:* Walthamstow Hall, Sevenoaks, Univ. of Nottingham. *Career:* composer 1982–; Chair. Composers' Guild of GB 1992–95; Dir MCPS 1996–; Founding Dir British Acad. of Composers and Songwriters 1999–; Concert Chair. British Acad. of Composers and Songwriters 1999–, British Composer Awards 2003–; Dir tutti.co.uk Ltd 2000–; Trustee British Music Information Centre 1997–. *Compositions:* Spanish Sonata 1990, The Roaring Whirl 1992, Saigyo 1995, The King of the Golden River 2000, The Fire will Blaze Again 2003. *Recordings:* The Roaring Whirl 1995, The King of the Golden River 2000. *Publications:* contrib. to Music Journal (Incorporated Soc. of Musicians), The Works (British Acad. of Composers and Songwriters), scripts for BBC Radio 3. *Current Management:* Impulse Music Consultants, 18 Hillfield Park, London, N10 3QS, England. *Telephone:* (20) 8444-8587 (office). *Fax:* (20) 8245-0358 (office). *E-mail:* impulse@impulse-music.co.uk (office). *Website:* www.impulse-music.co.uk (office).

**RODRIGUEZ, Robert Xavier;** Composer; b. 28 June 1946, San Antonio, TX, USA. *Education:* MM, Univ. of Texas, Austin, 1969; DMA, Univ. of California, Los Angeles, 1975; further study with Jakob Druckman at Tanglewood and Nadia Boulanger in Fontainebleau/Paris; masterclasses with Elliott Carter and Bruno Maderna at Tanglewood. *Career:* faculty mem., Univ. of Southern California, 1973–75, Univ. of Texas, Dallas, 1975–; Composer-in-Residence, Dallas Symphony Orchestra, 1982–85, San Antonio Symphony Orchestra, 1996–98. *Compositions include:* 2 Piano Trios, 1970, 1971; Canto for soprano, tenor and chamber orchestra, 1973; Favola Concertante for violin, cello and strings, 1975 (revised 1977); Variations for violin and piano, 1975; Transfigurationis Mysteria for soloists, narrator, chorus and orchestra, 1978; Favola Boccaccesca, 1979; Estampie, ballet for orchestra, 1981; Semi-Suite for violin and orchestra, 1981; Suor Isabella, Opera, 1982; Trunks for narrator and orchestra, 1983; Oktoechoes for orchestra, 1983; Seven Deadly Sins for wind ensemble, 1984; Tango, chamber opera, 1985; Varmi'ts! for narrator, chorus and orchestra, 1985; Monkey See, Monkey Do, children's opera, 1986; The Ransoms of Red Chief, children's opera, 1986; A Colorful Symphony for narrator and orchestra, 1987 We the People for narrator, chorus and orchestra, 1987; The old Majestic, opera, 1988; Invocations of Orpheus, trumpet concerto, 1989; A Gathering of Angels for orchestra, 1989; Les Niais Amoureux for chamber ensemble, 1989; Fantasia Lussuriosa for piano, 1989; Ursa: Four Seasons for double bass and orchestra, 1990; Frida, opera, 1991; Pinata for orchestra, 1991; Tango di Tango for orchestra, 1992; The Song of Songs for actor, soprano and chamber ensemble, 1992; Meta 4 for string quartet, 1994; Hot Buttered Rumba for orchestra, 1993; Mascaras for cello and orchestra, 1994; Adoracion Ambulante (Con Flor y Canto), folk celebration for soloists, mariachis, percussion ensemble, chorus and orchestra, 1994; Scrooge for bass-baritone, chorus and orchestra, 1994; Concerto Grosso, 1997; Forbidden Fire for bass-baritone, chorus and orchestra, 1998; Sinfonia à la Mariachi for double orchestra, 1998; Bachanale for orchestra, 1999; The Last Night of Don Juan for actors, singers, dancers, puppets and orchestra, 2000; The Tempest for actors and orchestra, 2001; Incidental Music for A Midsummer Night's Dream, 2001; Decem Perfectum for wind ensemble, 2002; Flight for narrator and orchestra, 2003. *Honours:* Guggenheim Fellowship, 1976; Prix de Composition Prince Pierre de Monaco, 1971; Prix Lili Boulanger, 1973; Goddard Lieberson Award, American Acad. and Inst. of Arts and Letters, 1980. *Address:* c/o ASCAP, ASCAP Building, 1 Lincoln Plaza, New York, NY 10023; c/o G. Schirmer, 257 Park Avenue South, New York, NY 10010, USA.

**ROE, Betty,** LRAM, ARCM, ARAM, LTCL, FTCL, FRSA; composer, singer (soprano) and pianist; b. 30 July 1930, London, England; m. John Bishop (deceased); one s. two d. *Education:* Royal Acad. of Music. *Career:* organist and choirmaster, including Kensington 1958–68, 1978–88; Music Dir, London Acad. of Music and Dramatic Art 1968–78; professional soprano 1962–; John Aldiss Singers, St Clement Dane Chorale; founded NorthKen Chorale; Musical Dir NorthKen Concerts 1980–; founded Thames Publishing, specializing in English vocal music and books about British composers; festival adjudicator 1960–; Associated Bd examiner; founder, Robish Music 2003; mem. Equity, Incorporated Soc. of Musicians, Asscn of Teachers of Singing, Performing Artists' Media Rights Assocn, Assocn of English Singers and Speakers, Royal Soc. of Musicians. *Compositions:* four chamber operas, musicals, cantatas, organ music, music theatre entertainments, choral music, piano, flute and other instrumental music, much of it for schools and young people. *Recordings:* Music's Empire, The Music Tree, The Family Tree. *Publications include:* Songs from the Betty Roe Shows (five vols), Pubs are People Places, Serious: Noble Numbers, Music's Empire, Conversation Piece for Horn and Piano, Soliloquy and Dialogue for Horn and Piano, Two Garden Songs for Soprano, Violin and Piano 2004. *Address:* 14 Barlby Road, Kensington, London, W10 6AR, England (home). *Telephone:* (20) 8969-3579 (home). *E-mail:* br@robish.fsnet.co.uk (home). *Website:* www.bettyroe.com.

**ROEBUCK, Janine Lorraine Spence;** British singer (mezzo-soprano); b. 1954, Barnsley; d. of Kenneth and Edna Roebuck. *Education:* Royal Northern Coll. of Music, Paris Conservatoire with Regine Crespin, Nat. Opera School, London, studied with Arwel Treharne Morgan. *Career:* appearances in La Buona Figliola, Buxton; as Rossini's Isabella for Opera 80; Lucille in The Silken Ladder and Clarina in The Marriage Contract for Scottish Opera; Mozart's Dorabella and Maddalena in Rigoletto for Pavilion Opera; Eduige in Handel's Rodelinda at Batignano; English Bach Festival in Dido and Aeneas and Gluck's Alceste, Monte Carlo and Covent Garden; operetta with D'Oyly Carte –1982, New Sadler's Wells Opera; shows with Richard Baker and Marilyn Hill Smith and BBC broadcasts; Mahler's Rückertlieder with Scottish Ballet; concerts in Coventry and Peterborough Cathedrals; Carmen in Middle East and Far East; opera recital at the Opera House in Manaus, Brazil; Thiske in Rossini's Cerentola at the Linbury Theatre, Royal Opera House, Covent Garden; devised a tribute to Joyce Grenfell, Stately as a Galleon. *Recordings:* Rodgers and Hammerstein Love Songs, Kiss Me Kate, The King and I. *Address:* 55A Thorparch Road, London, SW8 4SX, England (office). *Telephone:* (20) 7978-1397 (office). *E-mail:* janine.roebuck@hotmail.com (office).

**ROGÉ, Pascal;** French pianist; b. 6 April 1951, Paris; two s. *Education:* Paris Conservatoire, private studies with Lucette Descaves, Pierre Pasquier and Julius Katchen. *Career:* début Paris 1969, London 1969; specialist in Ravel, Poulenc, Debussy, Satie; soloist with leading orchestras; exclusive recording contract with Decca. *Honours:* Premiers Prix for Piano and Chamber Music at the Paris Conservatoire 1966, First Prize Marguerite Long-Jacques Thibaud Int. Competition 1971, Grand Prix du Disque and Edison Award 1984, Gramophone Award for Best Instrumental Recording 1988, Best Chamber Music Recording 1997. *Current Management:* Clarion/Seven Muses, 47 Whitehall Park, London, N19 3TW, England. *Website:* www.c7m.co.uk. *Address:* Lorentz Concerts, 3 rue de la Boétie, 75008 Paris, France; 17 avenue des Cavaliers, 1224 Geneva, Switzerland.

**ROGER, David;** Stage Designer; b. 1950, England. *Career:* For Opera Factory in London designed La Calisto, The Knot Garden, Osborne premiere of Hell's Angels, Birtwistle premiere of Yan Tan Tethera in 1986, a conflation of Gluck's Iphigenia operas, Ligeti's Adventures and Nouvelles Adventures, Mahagonny Songspiel, Così fan tutte, Don Giovanni, Reimann's The Ghost Sonata and The Marriage of Figaro in 1991; Other work has included Le Grand Macabre by Ligeti at Freiburg, Akhnaten by Philip Glass and The Return of Ulysses at English National Opera, La Bohème for Opera North and Manon Lescaut for Opéra-Comique in Paris; Madama Butterfly at the Albert Hall, 1998. *Address:* c/o English National Opera, St Martin's Lane, London WC2, England.

**ROGERS, Lesley-Jane,** ARAM; Singer (soprano); b. 25 April 1962, Bristol, England; m. Robin Daniel 1988, 1 step-s., 1 step-d. *Education:* Royal Academy of Music, 1981–85; Harry Farjeon Prize, Harmony, 1982; LRAM (Pianoforte Teachers), 1983; Ella Mary Jacob Prize, Singing, 1983; GRSM Honours, 1984; Greta G M Parkinson Prize, Piano, 1984; LRAM (Singing Teachers), 1985. *Career:* Performed extensively in the fields of oratorio and solo cantatas and is also a contemporary music specialist; Particularly wide oratorio repertoire incorporating standard and unusual works; Hundreds of solo cantatas, especially Bach and Telemann; Performances of contemporary music such as Ligeti's Aventures and Nouvelles Aventures; Several world premieres, including Fédélé's La chute de la maison Usher with Ensemble Intercontemporain; mem, Life Member, National Early Music Association; British Actors' Equity Association. *Recordings:* Handel Tamerlano (highlights), role of Asteria, European Community Baroque Orchestra, director Roy Goodman, TéléDiffusion de France, live recording, 1990; Caldara Madrigals and Cantatas, Wren Baroque Soloists, 1992; Caldara Motets, Wren Baroque Soloists, 1994; Peter Maxwell Davies Resurrection, role of electronic soprano, BBC Philharmonic Orchestra, conductor Davies, 1994; Peerson Private Musicke, Wren Baroque Soloists, 1994; Carl Rütti Choral Music, conductor Stephen Jackson, BBC Symphony Chorus, 1995; Percy Grainger, Jungle Book, The Love Song of Har Dyal, Choir and Orchestra of Polyphony, Hyperion, 1996; Sadie Harrison, Taking Flight, 2000; The Soprano Sings Schubert Lieder, piano Christopher Ross, 2002; Julia Usher Sacred Physic, 2002; Celtic Magic, recorders John Turner, piano Keith Swallow, 2003. *Address:* The Old Rectory Coach House, High Street, Bourton-on-the-Water, Gloucestershire GL54 2AP, England. *Telephone:* (1451) 821481. *E-mail:* info@lesleyjanerogers.demon.co.uk. *Website:* www.lesleyjanerogers.demon.co.uk.

**ROGERS, Nigel David,** BA, MA; British singer (tenor), conductor and teacher; b. 21 March 1935, Wellington, Shropshire, England. *Education:* King's Coll., Cambridge, private musical tuition in Rome and Milan, Hochschule für Musik, Munich. *Career:* began professional career with quartet, Studio der Frühen Musik, 1961; operatic debut at Amsterdam in 1969; sang in Monteverdi's Ulisse and Orfeo under Harnoncourt at Vienna and Amsterdam, 1971, 1976, Poppea at Amsterdam under Leonhardt in 1972 and Il Combattimento at Milan under Berio in 1973; sang in British premiere of Arden Must Die by Goehr at Sadler's Wells in 1974 and the title role in Handel's Teseo at Warsaw in 1977; Prof. of Singing, Royal Coll. of Music 1979–2000; conducting from 1985; directed and sang in the serenata La Gloria di Primavera by Alessandro Scarlatti (BBC invitation concert) 1996. *Recordings include:* Monteverdi's 1610 Vespers and Orfeo, John Dowland Lute Songs 1988, Sigismondo d'India 1991, Florentine Intermedi of 1589, Dido and Aeneas, Songs of Henry Lawes 1994, Symphonie Sacrae of Schütz 1995, Monteverdi, Vespers of 1610 1996. *Publications:* contrib. to various magazines

and academic publications, including a chapter on voice, in Companion to Baroque Music 1991. *Honours:* Hon. RCM 1980. *Address:* Wellington House, 13 Victoria Road, Deal, Kent CT14 7AS, England (home).

**ROGG, Lionel;** Organist and Composer; b. 21 April 1936, Geneva, Switzerland; m. Claudine Effront, 1957, 3 s. *Education:* Geneva Conservatory; Piano with Nikita Magaloff; Organ with Pierre Segond. *Career:* Complete Bach organ works in 10 recitals, Victoria Hall, Geneva, 1961; Concerts (organ, harpsichord) world-wide; Interpretative courses, USA, the United Kingdom, Switzerland, Austria, Japan, Italy. *Compositions include:* Organ: 12 chorales; Variations, Psalm 91, 1983; Introduction, ricercare, toccata; Cantata, Geburt der Venus; Also: Face à face, 2 pianos; Missa Brevis, chorus and orchestra; Concerto for organ and orchestra, 1992. *Recordings:* Complete Bach organ works; Art of Fugue; Complete Buxtehude organ works; Rogg Plays Reger; Rogg Plays Rogg (organ compositions); Du Mage, Clérambault. *Publications:* Improvisation Course for Organists. *Honours:* Grand Prix du Disque, 1970; Deutscher Schallplatten Preis, 1980; Doctor honoris causa, University of Geneva. *Address:* 38A route de Troinex, 1234 Vessy, Geneva, Switzerland.

**ROGLIANO, Marco;** Violinist; b. 26 Nov. 1967, Rome, Italy; m. Ciccozzi Antonella, 1 s. *Education:* Conservatory Santa Cecilia, Rome; Mozarteum of Salzburg; Academy W Stauffer. *Career:* Debut: Helsingborg Concert Hall Playing Sibelius Violin Concerto fo 47 with the Helsingborg Symphony Orchestra, 1989; Casals Hall, Tokyo, 1991, Paris, 1993, Moscow, 1993; With the Radio Symphonic Orchestra of Moscow, 1994; Milan, 1995; Rome, 1996; Munich, 1997; Numerous Radio and Television Appearances in France, Bulgaria, Sweden. *Recordings:* Salvatore Sciarrino, 1947; 6 Caprieei for Solo Violin, 1976; Angelo Ragazzi; 3 Violin Concertos; Franz Adolf Berwald; The Violin Concerto. *Contributions:* Musical Journals and Magazines. *Address:* Lorenzo il Mgnifico 15, 06162 Rome, Italy.

**ROGNER, Heinz;** Conductor; b. 1929, Leipzig, Germany. *Education:* Studied composition and piano with Egon Boelsche and Hugo Steuer in Leipzig. *Career:* Repetiteur and Conductor at the German National Theatre in Weimar; Teacher, Leipzig Musikhochschule, 1954–58; Principal Conductor for Great Leipzig Radio Orchestra, 1959–63; General Musical Director, Deutsche Staatsoper Berlin, 1962–73; Chief Conductor of the Berlin Radio Symphony Orchestra, 1973 with tours to Eastern Europe, Austria, Sweden, France, Belgium, Switzerland, Germany and Japan; Regular Guest Conductor for Yomiuri Nippon Symphony Orchestra from 1978, Principal Conductor, 1984. *Recordings:* Strauss Horn Concertos; Weber's Abu Hassan and Eine Nacht in Venedig, with the Dresden Staatskapelle; Trumpet Concertos by Torelli, Grossi, Fasch and Albinoni; Schubert's 7th Symphony, arranged by Weingartner, and 9th Symphony; Reger's Romantic Suite and Symphonic Prologue; Beethoven's Cantata on the Accession of Leopold II, Die Glorreiche Augenblick and Vestas Feuer; Strauss's Duet Concertino and Preludes to Palestrina by Pfitzner. *Honours:* National Prize, 1975; Gerhardt Eusler Gold Plakette, 1979; Professor, 1981.

**ROGOFF, Ilan;** Israeli concert pianist and conductor; b. 26 July 1943, s. of Boris Rogoff and Sofija Rogoff; m. Vesna Zorka Mimiça 1985; two d. *Education:* Israel Acad. of Music, Royal Conservatoire, Brussels, Mannes Coll., Juilliard School, New York. *Career:* has played all over Israel, Europe, N. America, Latin America, S. Africa, Japan and Far East with Israel Philharmonic Orchestra and many other orchestras; plays mostly works by Romantic composers including Beethoven, Schumann, Brahms, Chopin, Liszt, César Franck, Rachmaninov, Tchaikovsky, Piazzolla; has performed twentieth-century and contemporary works including world premiere of concerti by John McCabe and by Ivan Erod; has performed with various chamber music groups including Enesco Quartet, Orpheus Quartet, Amati Trio, Festival Ensemble, Matrix Quintet, Shron Trio and Quartet, soloists of Vienna Chamber Orchestra and Vienna Philharmonic Orchestra; conducting début 1985, with Israel Philharmonic 1988; radio performances and TV appearances in UK, Spain, Austria, Germany, Israel, Canada, USA, SA, Colombia, Ecuador, Venezuela and Argentina; lectures and recital/lectures, masterclasses; Trustee Tel-Aviv Museum. *Recordings include:* Chopin in Mallorca, Chopin Concerti (version for piano and string quintet), Portraits by Schumann, numerous works by Bach–Busoni, César Franck, Schumann, Schubert, Chopin, Beethoven and Liszt, transcriptions for piano solo of works by Astor Piazzolla. *Publications:* Transcriptions for Piano Solo of Works by Astor Piazzolla, Ed Two Chopin Concerti for Piano and String Quartet; articles on music published in Scherzo magazine (Madrid). *Honours:* various int. awards. *Address:* Estudio/Taller, Calle Bartomeu Fons 13, 07015 Palma de, Spain. *Telephone:* (71) 707016. *Fax:* (71) 707703. *E-mail:* ilanrogoff@telefonica.net. *Website:* www.infonegocio.com/ilanrogoff.

**ROGOSIC, Marko;** Composer and University Professor of Music; b. 6 April 1941, Podgorica, Yugoslavia. *Education:* History of Arts and Philosophy; BA, MA in Music, Musical Academy in Belgrade; Specialisations and study tours throughout Europe including London, Paris and Moscow. *Career:* Professor of Music; Chief Editor, first Montenegrin Musical Herald; President, Association of Composers of Montenegro; mem, League of Composers' Association of Yugoslavia; President, Montenegrin Association of Composers. *Compositions:* Seashore Water-Colour for clarinet and piano; Sonata in C-minor for piano; Sonata Fantasy for violin and piano; Concerto for contrabass and orchestra; Shepperds' Game for oboe or violin and piano; Suite for flute and fiddlers; Music for ballet Vladimir and Kosara. *Recordings:* Sonata for Piano; Concerto for Contrabass and Orchestra; Seashore Water-Colour. *Publications:* Methodics of Music Education, reader for students, 1981; Monograph of Association of Composers, 1996; Anthology of Soloist and Chamber Music of Montenegrin Composers, 1998. *Contributions:* Numerous in professional journals. *Address:* Dahna 15, 81000 Podgorica, Serbia and Montenegro.

**ROHAN, Jiri;** Double Bass Player; b. 11 Jan. 1965, Prague, Czechoslovakia; m. Dana Skrovankova, 13 June 1992, 1 d. *Education:* Conservatory, Prague; Academy of Music, Prague; 10 years Piano Studies, Art Academy, Prague; 6 years Double Bass Study, Prague Conservatory; 4 years Double Bass Studies, Academy of Music, Prague. *Career:* Debut: Solo Concert with Symphony Orchestra, Prague, 1985; Czech Philharmonic Orchestra, 1983–85; Suk Chamber Orchestra, 1988–91; Munich Philharmonic Orchestra, 1990; Czech String Ensemble, 1992; Prague String Quintet, 1993–97; Osaka Symphonic, 1994. *Recordings:* Over 40 CDs with Several Symphonic Orchestras; Over 10 CDs with Suk Chamber Orchestra; 2 CDs with Czech String Ensemble; 3 CDs with Prague String Quintet; CD with Czech Chamber Orchestra. *Publications:* Psychological Aspects of Music Listening, 1993. *Address:* Mahenova 168/7, 150 00 Prague 5, Czech Republic.

**ROHNER, Ruth;** Singer (Soprano); b. 18 Sept. 1935, Zürich, Switzerland. *Education:* Studied in Winterhur and Amsterdam. *Career:* Sang at the Opera of Biel-Solothurn, 1960–61, Vienna Kammeroper, 1960–62 and engaged at Zürich opera from 1962 notably in the premieres of Sutermeister's Madame Bovary in 1967 and Kelterborn's Ein Engel Kommt Nach Babylon in 1977; Many performances in the lyric and coloratura repertory and in the first local performances of Burkhard's Ein Stern Geht auf Jakob and Krenek's Karl V; Guest engagements at Berne, Basle, the State Operas of Hamburg and Munich, Düsseldorf, Strasbourg, Helsinki and Châtelet Paris; Festival appearances at Lausanne, Wiesbaden and Athens; Noted concert artist in oratorio and lieder. *Address:* c/o Zürich Opera, 8008 Zürich, Switzerland.

**ROHRL, Manfred;** Singer (Bass); b. 12 Sept. 1935, Augsburg, Germany. *Education:* Studied at the Augsburg Conservatory and with Franz Kelch and Margarethe von Winterfeld. *Career:* Debut: Augsburg in 1958 as Masetto; Member of the Deutsche Oper Berlin notably in the 1965 premiere of Der Junge Lord by Henze; Guest appearances in Brussels, Nancy, Düsseldorf, Geneva, Zürich, Zagreb and Edinburgh; Netherlands Opera in 1984 as Leporello; Sang Waldner in Arabella at the Deutsche Oper Berlin in 1988, and Dr Kolenaty in The Makropulos Case in 1989; Many performances in the buffo repertory; Sang Taddeo in L'Italiana in Algeri with the Deutsche Oper in 1992; Mozart's Bartolo at Glyndebourne, 1994; Sang Bartolo at the Deutsche Oper, 2000. *Recordings:* Various. *Address:* c/o Deutsche Oper Berlin, Richard Wagnerstrasse 10, 1000 Berlin 1, Germany.

**ROJAS, Rafael;** Singer (Tenor); b. 15 Sept. 1962, Guadalaja, Mexico. *Education:* University of Guadalajara, Royal Scottish Academy and Northern College of Music. *Career:* Student roles included the Duke of Mantua, Manrico, Tamino, Rodolfo, Roberto Devereux and Ernani; Engagements in Guadalajara City and Mexico City; US Debut as Alfredo in Traviata, Seattle, followed by Rafael Ruiz in El Gato Montes for Washington Opera; Concerts include the Verdi Requiem with the Jerusalem Symphony Orchestra and the Hallé Orchestra; Lambeth Palace, London, Monmouth Cathedral, and the Glasgow Mayfest; Season 1997–98 as Paco in La Vida Breve at Nice, Pinkerton for Glimmerglass Opera, USA, Werther at Boston, Rodolfo and Nemorino at Seattle and Verdi's Macduff for Houston Opera; Season 2002–02 as Alfredo at Boston, Riccardo at Bregenz, Dick Johnson for Opera Zuid and Rodolfo at Melbourne; Don Carlos in Leipzig and Cavaradossi for Opera North. *Honours:* Domingo Prize at 1995 Placido Domingo Competition. *Address:* c/o IMG Artists, Lovell House, 616 Chiswick High Road, London W4 5RX, England.

**ROLAND, Claude-Robert;** Conductor, Organist and Composer; b. 19 Dec. 1935, Pont-de-Loup, Belgium; m. Anne-Marie Girardot, 6 Sept 1963, 1 s. *Education:* Athénée Royal; Academy of Music, Châtelet; Conservatories in Liège, Paris, Brussels, with Messiaen and Defossez. *Career:* Organist, Notre Dame Church, Wasmes, 1955–63, and Basilica Charleroi, 1963–67; Professor, Brussels Conservatory, 1972–; *Current:* Works of Hoyoul, Lohet, Dumont, Buston, Schlick, Froidebise, Guillaume, Quatrefages; Conductor: Satie, Prokofiev, Guillaume, RTBF. *Compositions:* Over 100 works including Demain seulement, on poems by Alain Grandbois; Preludes, piano, 1962; Rossignolet du bois, orchestra, 1971; Rondeau, organ, 1979; Thriller, trumpet and piano, 1984; Datura 281, piano, 1987; Ricordanza, bass-clarinet and piano, 1989; Music for Molière, Labiche, Turgenev and Ghelderode. *Recordings:* Compositeurs Liegeois, organ; Alpha; Musique Au Chateau, organ and brass; Musica Magna. *Publications:* Orgues en Hainaut, 1966. *Contributions:* Musique Vivante; Feuillets du Spantole; Hainaut-Tourisme, UWO. *Address:* 59 Rue Lebeau, 1000 Brussels, Belgium.

**ROLANDI, Gianna;** Singer (Soprano); b. 16 Aug. 1952, New York, USA; m. Andrew Davis. *Education:* Studied with her mother and with Ellen Faull and Max Rudolf. *Career:* Debut: Sang Offenbach's Olympia in Les Contes d'Hoffmann at the New York City Opera in 1975; Metropolitan Opera in 1979 as Sophie, later singing Olympia, Stravinsky's Nightingale and Zerbinetta; Glyndebourne debut in 1981 as Zerbinetta returning in 1984 as Zdenka in Arabella and Susanna; English National Opera in 1983 as Cleopatra in Giulio Cesare; San Diego in 1984 as Ophelia in Hamlet by Thomas; Sang Lucia di Lammermoor at San Francisco in 1986, and Curiazio in a performance of Cimarosa's Gli Orazi e i Curizai, to mark the 200th anniversary of the French Revolution, at Rome Opera in 1989; Other roles

include Gilda, the Queen of Night and parts in operas by Donizetti at the New York City Opera; Sang Despina at Chicago, 1993; Concert tour of the USA with the BBC Symphony Orchestra, 1996. *Address:* c/o Teatro dell'Opera, Piazzo Beniamino Gigli 8, 00184 Rome, Italy.

**ROLFE JOHNSON, Anthony,** CBE; British singer; b. 5 Nov. 1940, Tackley, Oxon.; m. Elisabeth Jones Evans; one s. two d. and two s. from previous m. *Career:* has appeared with all major UK opera cos and with Netherlands Opera, Hamburg State Opera, Zürich Opera, at the Monnaie Theatre, Brussels, La Scala Milan, Metropolitan Opera New York and at Aix-en-Provence and Salzburg Festivals; concerts with all major UK orchestras and with Chicago Symphony, Boston Symphony, New York Philharmonic and Cleveland orchestras in USA. *Recordings include:* Acis and Galatea, Saul, Hercules, Jephtha, Alexander's Feast, Esther, Solomon, Semele, Messiah, J. S. Bach's St Matthew Passion and St John Passion, Peter Grimes, Samson, Oedipus Rex, Orfeo, War Requiem. *Roles include:* Fenton (Falstaff), Albert Herring, Don Ottavio (Don Giovanni), Tamino (Magic Flute), Essex (Gloriana), Ferrando (Così fan tutte), Male Chorus (Rape of Lucretia), Orfeo (Monteverdi's Orfeo), Jupiter (Semele) and Aschenbach (Death in Venice). *Address:* c/o Askonas Holt, Lonsdale Chambers, 27 Chancery Lane, London, WC2A 1PF, England.

**ROLL, Michael;** British pianist; b. 17 July 1946, Leeds, England; m. Juliana Markova; one s. *Education:* studied piano with Fanny Waterman. *Career:* debut, Royal Festival Hall 1958, playing Schumann Concerto with Malcolm Sargent; regular appearances with major British orchestras; played at Hong Kong Festival with London Philharmonic and toured Japan with the BBC Symphony; also toured Netherlands, Germany, Switzerland, Spain and Eastern Europe; tours of Russia and Scandinavia in recital and with orchestra; conductors include Boulez, Giulini, Leinsdorf and Previn; visits to Aldeburgh, Bath, Edinburgh, Granada and Vienna Festivals; US debut 1974, with Boston Symphony Orchestra conducted by Colin Davis; 1987–88 season with recitals in Milan, East Berlin, Dresden, Leipzig and London; Prof., Folkwang Hochschule, Essen, Germany 1987; 1988–89 season with London Symphony, Scottish Nat. Orchestra, Hallé, Bournemouth Symphony, Helsinki Philharmonic and Hong Kong Philharmonic Orchestras; recitals in London, Milan, Leipzig, Berlin and Dresden; played concertos in the 1990 Promenade Concerts, with Kurt Masur in Leipzig and London and Valery Gergiev in Leningrad and UK; 1991–92 season played concertos with Skrowaczewski and the Hallé, BBC Philharmonic, BBC Scottish Orchestras and Leipzig Gewandhaus, recitals in the Int. Piano Series at the Queen Elizabeth Hall and at the Klavierfestival Ruhr in Germany with Helsinki Philharmonic under Comissiona, for the English Chamber Orchestra at the Barbican and New York debut recital 1992; performed complete cycle of Beethoven piano concertos with London Mozart Players, Barbican 1995; Cologne Philharmonic Orchestra (debut) 2002; major Australian tour 2002. *Recordings include:* Beethoven Piano Concertos (complete cycle). *Honours:* First Prize, Leeds Int. Piano Competition 1963. *Current Management:* Terry Harrison Artists Management, The Orchard, Market Street, Charlbury, Oxon., OX7 3PJ, England. *Telephone:* (1608) 810330. *Fax:* (1608) 811331. *E-mail:* artists@terryharrison.force9.co.uk.

**ROLLAND, Sophie;** cellist; b. 18 July 1963, Montreal, Canada. *Education:* Conservatoire de Musique du Quebéc, Montreal with Walter Joachim, studied with Nathaniel Rosen in New York, Pierre Fournier in Geneva and William Pleeth in London. *Career:* debut with Montreal Symphony Orchestra under Charles Dutoit, 1982; regular appearances throughout Canada with all major orchestras including the Montreal, Toronto and Vancouver Symphony Orchestras; Toured in USA, France, Spain, England, Wales, Germany, Switzerland, Bulgaria, Hungary, Yugoslavia, Finland and China; Frequent guest at international chamber music festivals including Kuhmo, Dubrovnik and Parry Sound; Duo partnership with pianist, Marc-André Hamelin since 1988; 1990–91 season includes Beethoven cycle in New York at Carnegie Hall in 1991, Washington DC, Montreal with broadcast for CBC, and in London at Wigmore Hall in 1991 and broadcast for BBC; Plays a 1674 cello by Petrus Ranta of Brescia. *Honours:* Premier Prix à l'Unamanité Montreal; Study awards from the Canadian and Quebec Governments; Prix d'Europe, Canada; 1st Prize, Du Maurier Competition; Virginia P Moore Prize, Canada Arts Council, 1985. *Address:* 27 Cleveland Avenue, London W4 1SN, England.

**ROLOFF, Elisabeth,** BA, MA; concert organist; b. 18 Feb. 1937, Bielefeld, Germany. *Education:* Berlin High School of Music, Bremen Conservatory of Music, Cologne High School of Music, Royal College of Music. *Career:* Organist and Choirmaster, Christ Church, Hannover, Germany, 1968–74; Titular Organist, German Church, Paris, France, 1974–82; Concerts throughout Europe, Israel and USA; Faculty, Rubin Academy of Music, Jerusalem, Israel, 1983–; Titular Organist, Redeemer Church, Jerusalem, 1983–; Main Appearances: Europe: Alte Oper, Frankfurt; Royal Festival Hall, London; King's College Chapel, Cambridge, England; St Ouen, Rouen; Notre Dame, La Madeleine, Chartres Cathedral, France; Switzerland, Italy, Hungary, Romania; USA; Boston, Salt Lake City, Philadelphia; Russia: St Petersburg; Volgograd; International Organ Festivals: Bach Organ Festival, Jerusalem; Sorø, Denmark; Orléans, France; Tallinn, Estonia; Riga, Latvia; Prague, Kiev, São Paulo, Montevideo, Buenos Aires; Mexico; Radio appearances: Germany, Israel, Norway; mem, Association Jehan Alain; Internationale Mendelssohn-Stiftung, eV. *Recordings:* Organ works by Pachelbel, Buxtehude, J. S. Bach and Mozart; Organ Landscape Jerusalem. *Honours:* Decree of International Letters for Cultural Achievement, 1996. *Current*

*Management:* International Music Consultants, PO Box 45401, Tel-Aviv 61453, Israel. *Address:* 28, Ha-Palmah Street, Jerusalem 92542, Israel.

**ROLOFF, Roger (Raymond);** Singer (Baritone); b. 22 Feb. 1947, Peoria, Illinois, USA; m. Barbara A Petersen, 19 Mar 1982. *Education:* BA, magna cum laude, English, IL Wesleyan University, 1969; MA, Illinois State University, 1972; Graduate study in English, SUNY, Stony Brook; Private voice study with Sam Sakarian, New York City, 1975–; Vocal and Dramatic coaching with teachers including Hans Hotter. *Career:* Debut: Deertrees Opera Theatre, Maine, 1975; Operatic roles include Wotan and Wanderer in The Ring, Jochanaan in Salome, and Ruprecht in Prokofiev's Fiery Angel; Appearances with English National Opera, Deutsche Oper Berlin, Seattle, Kentucky, Dallas, San Diego and New York City Operas, Niederschsische Staatsoper Hannover, Hawaii Opera Theater, Houston Grand Opera and major orchestras in USA and Canada; Concert appearances in Milwaukee, Boston, Los Angeles, Germany and Switzerland; Sang the Dutchman in a concert performance of Der fliegende Holländer at Boston in 1990, and Telramund in Lohengrin at Nice in 1990. *Address:* International Music Consultants, PO Box 45401, Tel-Aviv 61453, Israel.

**ROLTON, Julian;** Pianist; b. 1965, England. *Career:* Co-founded the Chagall Piano Trio at the Banff Centre for The Arts in Canada, resident artist; Debut concert at the Blackheath Concert Halls in London, 1991; Further appearances at Barbican's Prokofiev Centenary Festival, Warwick Festival and the South Place Sunday Concerts at Conway Hall in London; Purcell Room recitals in 1993 with the London premiere of Piano Trios by Tristan Keuris, Nicholas Maw and Dame Ethel Smyth, composed 1880; Premiere of Piano Trio No. 2 by David Matthews at Norfolk and Norwich Festival in 1993; Engaged for Malvern Festival in 1994. *Address:* South Bank Centre, c/o Press Office (Pamela Chowhan Management), London SE1, England.

**ROMANENKO, Yelena;** Singer (Mezzo-Soprano); b. 1951, Kharkov, Russia. *Education:* Studied at the Institute of Arts at Kharkov. *Career:* Participated in the foundation of an opera programme with the State Opera Company of Kharkov; Many performances in Russia and on tour in Europe and America, as Santuzza, Azucena, Eboli, Carmen, Dalila and Marfa in Khovanshchina; British debut on tour with the National Opera of the Ukraine in 1995, as Marina in Boris Godunov and Fenena in Nabucco; Concert recitalist in German, Czech and Russian works. *Address:* c/o Sonata Ltd, 11 North Park Street, Glasgow G20 7AA, Scotland.

**ROMANOVA, Nina;** Mezzo-Soprano; b. 1946, Leningrad, Russia. *Education:* Studied with Vera Sopina at Leningrad Academy of Music. *Career:* Performed at Pushkin Theatre in Kishinov then from 1976 member of the Maly Theatre Leningrad, now St Petersburg; Roles have included Rosina in Barber of Seville, Azucena in Il Trovatore, Eboli in Don Carlo, Lady Macbeth, Carmen, Olga in Eugene Onegin, The Countess and Polina in The Queen of Spades, Marina in Boris Godunov and Marfa in Mussorgsky's Khovanshchina; Concerts include Alexander Nevsky by Prokofiev in Verona, St Matthew Passion, St John Passion, Mass in B minor by Bach, Mozart's Requiem, Verdi's Requiem, and Mahler's 2nd and 8th Symphonies; Guest performances with St Petersburg Mussorgsky State Academic Opera and Ballet Theatre, formerly Leningrad Maly Theatre, as member of the Opera Company; Sang in Italy at Palermo, Modena, Reggio Emilia, Parma, Ferrara, Ravenna and Catania, in France at Paris, Cannes and Nantes, New York and in Japan at Tokyo, Osaka, Hiroshima and Iokogama, Greece, Portugal and Netherlands; Sang in Rimsky's Invisible City of Kitezh at Bregenz, 1995. *Address:* Maly Opera and Ballet Theatre, St Petersburg, Russia.

**ROMBOUT, Ernest;** Dutch oboist; *Professor of Oboe, Conservatory of Music, Utrecht;* b. 30 Aug. 1959; m. Anne-Lou Langendyk 1995; one s. one d. *Education:* Staatliche Hochschule für Musik, Freiburg, Germany and studied with Heinz Holliger. *Career:* debut at Concertgebouw, Amsterdam 1983; soloist in major halls in Amsterdam, Berlin, Moscow, Munich, Lisbon, Paris, Zürich; festivals include Biennale of Venice, Donaueschinger Musiktage, Ludwigsburger Festspiele, Festival of New Music Middelburg, Takefu Festival, Japan, Summer Festival, Avignon, Summer Festival, Los Angeles; Prof. of Oboe, Conservatory of Music, Utrecht 1985–; masterclasses and workshops in Netherlands, Russia, Austria and Liechtenstein 1993–; mem. of jury, Int. Oboe Competition (CIEM), Geneva 1998. *Recordings:* solo: Oboe Concertos, Haydn, Mozart, Theme and Variations by J N Hummel with the Concertgebouw Chamber Orchestra; Oboe Concertos by L Francesconi, D del Puerto; Omaggio all'Opera Lirica, arrangements of works by Rossini, Bellini, Donizetti, Verdi and others for oboe and harp with harpist Erika Waardenburg. *Honours:* Prize Winner Ancona Competition of Winds, Italy 1979. *Address:* Oude Eemnesserstraat 34, 1221 HL Hilversum, Netherlands. *E-mail:* erombout@tiscali.nl.

**ROMERO, Angel;** classical guitarist and conductor; b. 17 Aug. 1946, Malaga, Spain; one s. two d. *Education:* studied guitar with Celedonio Romero, conducting with Soltan Rushnia, Eugene Ormandy, Morton Gould, Ather Fiedler. *Career:* debut, Lobero Theatre, Santa Barbara, California, 1958; First classical guitarist to perform at the Hollywood Bowl at West Coast premiere of Joaquin Rodrigo's Concerto de Aranjuez with the Los Angeles Philharmonic; Performances with the Boston Symphony, Chicago Symphony, Philadelphia Orchestra, New York Philharmonic, Cleveland Orchestra, Orquesta National de Espana, Berlin Philharmonic, Concertgebouw-Amsterdam; Halls include Carnegie Hall, Musikverein-Vienna, Orchestra Hall, Chicago; Performed for both Presidents Jimmy Carter and Richard Nixon, also the Pope at the

Vatican; Television appearances include the celebration of the 500th anniversary of Columbus' discovery at the United Nations with the Orquesta National de Espana, 1992; Also with Arther Fiedler and the Boston Pops; Performed with conductors including Eugene Ormandy, Raymond Leppard, Neville Mariner, Jesús López Cobos, Rafael Frühbeck de Burgos, Eduardo Mata, Giuseppe Patanè, Morton Gould, André Previn; Conducted the Academy of St Martin-in-the-Fields, Pittsburgh Symphony Orchestra, San Diego Symphony Orchestra. *Compositions:* movie score for Bienvenido-Welcome. *Recordings:* Guitar Concertos; Concerto de Aranjuez; Giuliani Guitar Concertos; Vivaldi Concertos; Villa Lobos and Schifrin Guitar Concertos; Touch of Class; Angel Romero plays Bach; Granados 12 Spanish Dances. *Honours:* Mexican Academy Award (Ariel) for best original score. *Address:* c/o Konzertveranstaltungen Andreas Schlessl, Postfach 810952, 81909, Munich, Germany.

**ROMERO, Angelo;** Singer (Bass-baritone); b. 30 May 1940, Cagliari, Sardinia. *Education:* Studied in Rome. *Career:* Debut: Opera di Camera, Rome, as Monteverdi's Orfeo, 1966; Appearances throughout Italy, including Rome, Milan and Verona Arena (1982); Raimbaud in Le Comte Ory at Venice, 1988, Dandini in Cenerentola at Parma, 1990, and Geronimo in Il Matrimonio Segreto at Lausanne, 1993; Further guest appearances at Buenos Aires, Cincinnati, Geneva and Aix-en-Provence; Sang Cimarosa's Maestro di Capella for Rome Opera, 2001. *Recordings include:* Le Maschere by Mascagni; Donizetti's Gianni di Parigi. *Address:* c/o Opera de Lausanne, PO Box 3972, 1002 Lausanne, Switzerland.

**ROMERO, Patricia,** DipCNM, LCNM, LTCL; pianist and teacher; b. 20 Sept. 1953, Mexico City, Mexico; m. David Hanesworth; one s. *Education:* Conservatorio Nacional de Música, Mexico City, Trinity Coll., London, studied with Louis Kentner. *Career:* debut, Wigmore Hall, London 1976; performed widely in the UK, Spain, Switzerland, Italy, France, Greece and the Middle East; London appearances include Purcell Room, Wigmore Hall, Fairfield Halls, St John's Smith Square, Leighton House; performances with Orquesta Sinfonia del Bajio, Orquesta de la Universidad de Guadalajara, Orquesta Sinfonica de Coyoacan; radio broadcasts in Mexico City, Guadalajara and for the BBC; performed complete piano works of Maurice Ravel at the Purcell Room, London 1994; tours of Australia, New Zealand, Scandinavia and Russia 1998, of Argentina and Brazil 1999; concert with the Philharmonic of the Univ. of Hertfordshire 1999; tour of Turkey, Greece, Italy, France and Spain 2000, Spain and the Canary Islands 2001; concerts in the Arcadia and Oriana 2002; tours of Spain, Switzerland and Mexico 2004, concerts in the UK 2004; mem. European Piano Teachers Asscn (UK), Incorporated Soc. of Musicians (Performers Section), ILAMS. *Honours:* First Prize Yamaha 1971, Maud Seton Pianist Prize, London 1975, Herbert Skead Competition 1975. *Current Management:* Pro-Musas Concert Management, 114 Woodcote Grove Road, Coulsdon, Surrey CR5 2AF, England. *Telephone:* (20) 8660-9262 (office). *Fax:* (20) 8660-9262 (office). *Telephone:* (20) 8660-4096 (home). *E-mail:* patricia .romero@btopenworld.com.

**ROMERO, Pepe;** American (naturalized) classical guitarist; b. 3 Aug. 1944, Málaga, Spain; s. of Celedonio Romero and Angelita (née Gallego) Romero; m. 1st Kristine Eddy 1965; m. 2nd Carissa Sugg 1987; one s. three d. *Education:* various music acads in USA, including Music Acad. of the West. *Career:* began career in Seville, Spain, as part of Romero Quartet 1951, re-formed in USA 1960; averages 200–250 concerts a year world-wide; recordings number more than 50 solos, plus others with the Romero Quartet and various orchestras; artist-in-residence Univ. of Southern Calif. 1972, Univ. of Calif., San Diego 1984. *Publications:* Guitar Method, Guitar Transcriptions for 1, 2 and 4 guitars.

**ROMIG, James,** MA, PhD; Composer; b. 5 Aug. 1971, Long Beach, CA, USA. *Education:* University of Iowa; Rutgers University. *Career:* Teacher, University of Iowa; Teacher, Rutgers University; Conductor and Music Director, Society of Chromatic Art; Conductor of new-music ensembles, Luna Nova and Frankenstein's Monster; Assistant Music Director and Conductor of Helix, Rutgers University new-music ensemble; Played percussion with the Joffrey Ballet, the Handel and Haydn Society of Boston and the Symphony Orchestra, Percussion Ensemble and Center for New Music at the University of Iowa; commissions/works performed by many US ensembles and orchestras; Prof., Bucknell Univ., 2001–02; Western Illinios Univ., 2002–; lectures at several US univs; mem, ASCAP; American Music Center; Society for Music Theory; Pi Kappa Lambda National Music Honor Society. *Compositions:* Trio for orchestra, 1998; Spin, for flute, violin, violoncello, percussion, 1999; Variations for string quartet, 1999; Piano trio for violin, violoncello, piano, 1997; Six Pieces, for string orchestra, 1996. *Publications:* How to Listen to a New Pice of Music, A Conversation with Milton Babbitt, Parametric Counterpoint: Babbittonian Ideals in Composition and Performance. *Honours:* Finalist, Civic Orchestra of Chicago, First Hearing, 1998; ASCAP Standard Award, 1998–2003; Finalist, Rudolph Nissim Award, ASCAP Foundation, 2002; Meet the Composer grant, 2003. *Address:* Western Illinois University, Dept of Music, Macomb IL 61455, USA. *Telephone:* (309) 298-1338 (office). *E-mail:* jromig@jamesromig.com (home). *Website:* www.jamesromig (office).

**RONCO, Claudio;** Cellist and Composer; b. 16 Sept. 1955, Torino, Italy; m. Lone K Loëll, 17 Sept 1983, 2 s. *Education:* MA in Music, Student of Anner Bylsma and Christophe Coin, Conservatorio Music, Torino. *Career:* Debut: Como with the Clemencic Consort of Vienna, 1982; Soloist with the Clemencic Consort, Vienna, 1982–; Hesperion XX, Ensemble 14, for ZDF, 1991;

Television programme on Jewish music and Solo recital for Radio Canada, Montreal. *Compositions:* Tombeau de Mr Farinelli for violin, violoncello and harpsichord, 1994; Serenata Pastorale for 3 voices, violin, violoncello, harpsichord. *Recordings:* Several recordings with Hesperion XX, Clemencic Consort; First recording of Veracini, Bonporti, Lanzetti; Paganini; Gade, Heise trios. *Address:* Cannaregio 3023, Venice 30121, Italy.

**RONCONI, Luca;** Stage Director; b. 8 March 1933, Susah, Tunisia. *Education:* Graduated, Accademia d'Arte Drammatica, Rome, 1953. *Career:* Began as an actor then directed plays; Opera debut in 1967 with Jeanne d'Arc au Bûcher by Honegger and Busoni's Arlecchino at Turin; Later work has included revivals of neglected operas by Purcell, Jommelli, Cimarosa and Rimsky-Korsakov, The Tsar's Bride; Founding Director of theatre laboratory at the Teatro Metastasio, Prato, 1977; Produced Così fan tutte at Teatro La Fenice, 1983, Piccinni's Iphigénie en Tauride at Bari, 1985, seen also in Paris and Rome; Teatro alla Scala with Rossi's Orfeo in 1985 and Cherubini's Lodoiska in 1990; Productions of Don Giovanni in 1990 and I Vespri Siciliani at Bologna, Rossini's Ricciardo e Zoraide at the 1990 Pesaro Festival; Staged Rossini's Otello at Brussels, 1994 and Cenerentola at Pesaro, 1998; Modern repertory includes stagings of works by Stockhausen, Berio and Globokar; Director of the Teatro Stabile at Turin from 1989. *Address:* c/o Teatro alla Scala, Via Filodrammatici 2, Milan, Italy.

**RONGE, Gabriela Marie;** singer (soprano); b. 3 July 1957, Hanover, Germany. *Career:* Sang in opera at Heidelberg from 1982, and Osnabruck from 1983 notably as Fiordiligi and Hanna Glawari; Further engagements at Hanover, 1985–87, Cologne, 1989, Frankfurt, Bonn, the Deutsche Oper Berlin and Brunswick; Bayerische Staatsoper Munich from 1987 as the Marschallin, Elsa, Eva and Agathe; Frankfurt in 1987 as Gluck's Iphigénie en Tauride, Paris Opéra in 1989 as Eva, and Isabella in Wagner's Das Liebesverbot at Palermo in 1991; Sang Aida at Schwerin, 1999; Brünnhilde in the Ring at Graz and Senta at the Deutsche Oper Berlin; Noted interpreter of Lieder. *Address:* c/o Teatro Massimo Bellini, via Perrotta 12, 95131 Catania, Italy.

**RONI, Luigi;** Singer (Bass); b. 22 Feb. 1942, Vergemoli, Lucca, Italy. *Education:* Studied with Sara Sforni Corti in Milan. *Career:* Debut: Spoleto in 1965 as Mephistopheles in Faust; Sang in Milan, Rome, Turin, Venice, Palermo, Florence and Naples; Moscow in 1973 with La Scala Company; Guest appearances in Vienna, Munich, Berlin, London, Paris, New York, Chicago, Dallas and Houston; Orange Festival in 1984 as the Grand Inquisitor in Don Carlos; Other roles include Mozart's Commendatore and Mussorgsky's Dosifey; La Scala in 1987 as Lodovico in Otello; Sang MacGregor in Mascagni's Guglielmo Ratcliff at Catania, 1990, Rossini's Basilio at Bonn, and Festival d'Orange in 1990 as the Grand Inquisitor in Don Carlos. *Recordings include:* Aida; Don Giovanni; Fernand Cortez by Spontini; Zaira by Bellini; Otello. *Address:* c/o Teatro Massimo Bellini, 95100 Catania, Italy.

**ROOCROFT, Amanda,** FRNCM; British singer (soprano); b. 9 Feb. 1966, Coppull; d. of Roger Roocroft and Valerie Roocroft (née Metcalfe); m. 2nd David Gowland 1999; two s. *Education:* Royal Northern Coll. of Music. *Career:* appearances include Sophie in Der Rosenkavalier, Welsh Nat. Opera 1990, Pamina in The Magic Flute, Covent Garden 1991, 1993, Fiordiligi in Così fan tutte, Glyndebourne 1991, European tour with John Eliot Gardiner 1992, Bavarian State Opera 1993, 1994, Covent Garden 1995, Giulietta in I Capuleti e I Montecchi, Covent Garden 1993, Ginevra in Ariodante, ENO 1993, Donna Elvira in Don Giovanni, Glyndebourne 1994, New York Metropolitan Opera 1997, Amelia in Simon Boccanegra, Bavarian State Opera 1995, Mimi in La Bohème, Covent Garden 1996, Countess in Marriage of Figaro, Bavarian State Opera 1997, New York Metropolitan Opera 1999, Cleopatra in Giulio Cesare, Covent Garden 1997, Desdemona in Otello, Bavarian State Opera 1999, Covent Garden 2001, Jenůfa, Glyndebourne 2000, Berlin 2002, Katya Kabanova, Glyndebourne 1998, Covent Garden 2000, Meistersinger, Royal Opera House 2002; debut at BBC Promenade Concert and Edin. Festival 1993; regular concert engagements and recitals; Fellow, Univ. of Cen. Lancs. 1992. *Recordings include:* Amanda Roocroft (solo album) 1994, Mozart and his Contemporaries 1996, Vaughan Williams Serenade to Music (with Matthew Best) 1990, Così fan tutte (with John Eliot Gardiner) 1993, Schoenberg String Quartet No. 2 (with Britten Quartet) 1994, Vaughan Williams Sea Symphony (with Andrew Davies), Mahler Symphony No. 4 (with Simon Rattle), Vaughan Williams Pastoral Symphony (with Bernard Haitink). *Television documentaries include:* The Girl from Coppull, The Debut (Granada TV), Hard Pressed for Signals (Channel 4), Jenufa (BBC Wales). *Honours:* Hon. DMus (Manchester) 2003; Kathleen Ferrier Prize 1988; Silver Medal, Worshipful Co. of Musicians 1988, Royal Philharmonic Soc./Charles Heidsieck Award 1990, Barclay Opera Award 2000. *Current Management:* c/o Ingpen & Williams Ltd, 26 Wadham Road, London, SW15 2LR, England. *Telephone:* (20) 8874-3222. *Fax:* (20) 8877-3113.

**ROOLEY, Anthony;** British lutenist, director and lecturer; b. 10 June 1944, Leeds, Yorkshire, England; one s. with Emma Kirkby. *Education:* Royal Acad. of Music. *Career:* teacher of guitar, lute, Royal Acad. of Music 1968–71; founder (with James Tyler), Consort of Musicke 1969–; dir and lutenist, many early music concerts, Europe, Middle East, USA; dir 1971–, often giving concerts of Renaissance theme; appearances, BBC, French and German television and radio; int. festivals, Europe, Scandinavia, USA; concerts with sopranos Emma Kirkby, Evelyn Tubb, alto Mary Nichols, tenor Andrew King, Simon Grant, Joseph Cornwell (Consort of Musicke mems), bass David Thomas, tenor Paul Agnew, other early music specialists; music-theatre

includes staging of Le Veglie di Siena (music by Orazio Vecchi), Copenhagen, London 1988; collaboration with Italian commedia dell'arte actors La Famiglia Carrara in Marriage of Pantelone; Promenade Concert 1988, based on settings of poet Torquato Tasso; concerts in Tel-Aviv, New York 1988; co-dir (with Arjen Terpstra) record label, Musica Oscura; teacher, Japan, Padova, Basle, Dartington, promoting Renaissance attitudes to performance; co-dir (with Don Taylor), video Banquet of the Senses: Monteverdi's Madrigali Erotici; mem. Viola da Gamba Soc., Galpin Soc., Wine Soc., Royal Soc. of Arts. *Recordings include:* Madrigals by Monteverdi, de Rore, Marini, Porter, Pallavicino, Marenzio, d'India; L'anime del Purgatorio (Stradella); Madrigals and Fantasias, Psalms and Anthems (John Ward); Arie Antiche, The Mad Lover (The Orpheus Circle); The Dark is my Delight (Women in Song); Maurice Greene: Songs and Keyboard works (The Handel Circle); The Mistress, The Mantle, Orpheus, Sound the Trumpets from Shore to Shore (Purcell). *Publications include:* A New Varietie of Lute Lessons (album and book) 1975, The Penguin Book of Early Music (album and book) 1979, Performance: Revealing the Orpeus Within 1990; contrib. to Lute Society Journal, Early Music, Guitar. *Address:* c/o Consort of Musicke, 13 Pages Lane, London, N10 1PU, England. *E-mail:* consort@musicke.net.

**ROOSENSCHOON, Hans;** South African composer; b. 17 Dec. 1952, The Hague, Netherlands. *Education:* Pretoria Conservatory, 1969–71, 1974–75; Royal Academy of Music, London, with Paul Patterson, 1977–78; D.Mus, University of Cape Town, 1991. *Career:* Production Manager, South African Broadcasting Corporation, Johannesburg, 1980–95. *Compositions:* Suite for oboe and piano, 1973; Ekstase for chorus and orchestra, 1975; Cantata on Psalm 8, 1976; Tablo for orchestra, 1976; Sinfonietta, 1976; Katutura for orchestra, 1977; Palette for strings, 1977; Mosaiek for orchestra, 1978; Ars Poetica for baritone, chorus and orchestra, 1979; Psalm 23 for choirs, 1979; Firebowl for chorus, 1980; Ikonografie, Anagram and Architectura, all for orchestra, 1983–86; Horizon, Night-Sky and Landscape for strings, 1987; Chronicles for orchestra, 1987; Clouds Clearing for strings, 1987; Mantis, Ballet Suite, 1988; Circle of Light for orchestra, 1989; Die Sonnevanger, for orchestra, 1990; The Magic Marimba, 1991; Mbira for chorus, 1994; Trombone Concerto, 1995; String Quartet, 1995; Keyboard, Organ and Electronic Music. *Address:* c/o SAMRO, PO Box 31609, Braamfontein 2017, Johannesburg, South Africa.

**ROOT, Deane Leslie;** American musicologist, museum curator, teacher, librarian and editor; b. 9 Aug. 1947, Wausau, WI; m. Doris J. Dyen 1972; two d. *Education:* New Coll., Sarasota, FL, Univ. of Illinois. *Career:* faculty, Univ. of Wisconsin 1973; editorial staff, New Grove Dictionary of Music and Musicians 1974–76; Research Assoc., Univ. of Illinois 1976–80; Visiting Research Assoc., Florida State Univ. 1981–82; Curator, Stephen Foster Memorial and Adjunct Asst Prof. in Music, Univ. of Pittsburgh 1982–96, Chair of Music Dept 2002–05; Heinz Chapel Administrator 1983–95; Dir of Cultural Resources 1990–94, Adjunct Assoc. Prof. 1992–96, Prof. of Music, Dir of Center for American Music 1998–, Univ. of Pittsburgh; Pres., Sonneck Soc. for American Music 1989–93; Delegate American Council of Learned Socs 1996–99. *Recordings:* Proud Traditions, Musical Tribute to Pitt. *Publications:* American Popular Stage Music 1860–1880, Music of Florida Historic Sites, Resources of American Music History (co-author), Music of Stephen C. Foster (co-ed.), Nineteenth Century American Musical Theater (series ed., 16 vols) 1994, Voices Across Time: American History Through Song 2004; contrib. to New Grove Dictionary of Music and New Grove Dictionary of American Music, American National Biography, various journals, yearbooks, conference proceedings. *Telephone:* (412) 624-4126. *Fax:* (412) 624-4186. *E-mail:* dlr@pitt.edu *Address:* Department of Music, University of Pittsburgh, Pittsburgh, PA 15260, USA.

**ROOTERING, Jan-Hendrik;** Singer (Bass); b. 18 March 1950, Wedingfeld, Nr Flensburg, Germany. *Education:* Studies with his father, Hendrikus Rootering, a voice teacher; Further education at Musikhochschule Hamburg. *Career:* Debut: Colline in La Bohème, 1980; Engagements include Concerts, Opera Performances and Lieder Recitals as well as numerous recordings with such conductors as Sawallisch, Muti, Levine, Abbado, Marriner, Davis and others; Appearances at Munich State Opera, Vienna State Opera, Berlin Deutsche Oper, Amsterdam, Geneva, Hamburg State Opera, London's Covent Garden, New York's Metropolitan Opera, Chicago's Lyric Opera, San Francisco Opera and Milan's La Scala. *Recordings:* Beethoven Ninth Symphony conducted by Bernstein, 1989; Fasolt in Das Rheingold; Sang Gurnemanz in Parsifal at the Opéra Bastille, Paris, 1997; La Roche in Capriccio at the Metropolitan, 1998 New York Met 2000, as Sarastro and Daland; Hans Sachs at Covent Garden, 2002. *Honours:* Honorary Title of Bavarian Kammersänger, 1989; Honorary Title of Professor with the Hochschule für Musik in Munich, 1994. *Address:* 45 West 67th Street, Apt 26C, New York, NY 10023, USA.

**ROREM, Ned,** MA; American composer; b. 23 Oct. 1923, Richmond, IN. *Education:* American Conservatory, Chicago with Leo Sowerby, Northwestern Univ., Curtis Inst., Philadelphia, Juilliard School, New York, studied with Thomson and Copland. *Career:* lived in Morocco 1949–51, in France 1951–57; Composer-in-Residence Univ. of Buffalo 1959–61, Univ. of Utah 1966–67, Curtis Inst. 1980–, Manhattan School of Music 1985–, Yale Univ. 1998–; Pres., American Acad. of Arts and Letters 2000–03. *Compositions:* three symphonies 1951, 1956, 1959, four string quartets 1948, 1950, 1990, 1994, Design for orchestra 1953, A Childhood Miracle (opera) 1955, The Poets' Requiem 1955, The Robbers (opera) 1958, Eleven Studies for Eleven Players

1960, Ideas for orchestra 1961, Lift up your Heads for chorus and wind 1963, Lions (A Dream) for orchestra 1963, Miss Julie (opera) 1965, Letters from Paris for chorus and orchestra 1966, Sun eight poems for high voice and orchestra 1966, Water Music for clarinet, violin and orchestra 1966, Bertha (one-act opera) 1968, War Scenes for voice and piano 1969, three piano concertos 1950, 1951, 1969, Little Prayers for soprano, baritone and orchestra 1973, Air Music variations for orchestra (Pulitzer Prize 1976) 1974, Serenade on Five English Poems 1975, Hearing five scenes for singers and seven instruments 1976, Sunday Morning for orchestra 1977, The Nantucket Songs 1979, Remembering Tommy concerto for piano, cello and orchestra 1979, After Reading Shakespeare for solo cello 1980, The Santa Fe Songs for voice and piano quartet 1980, After Long Silence for soprano, oboe and strings 1982, An American Oratorio 1983, Winter Pages for five instruments 1982, Whitman Cantata 1983, Violin Concerto 1984, Septet, Scenes from Childhood 1985, Organ Concerto 1985, End of Summer for violin, clarinet and piano 1985, String Symphony 1985, Homer (Three Scenes from the Iliad) for chorus and eight instruments 1986, Goodbye My Fancy for chorus, soloists, orchestra 1988–89, The Auden Poems for tenor and piano trio 1989, Swords and Plowshares for four vocal soloists and orchestra 1991, Piano Concerto for left hand and orchestra 1992, Cor anglais concerto 1995, String Quartet No. 4 1995, Evidence of Things not Seen (365 songs to texts by 24 authors) 1997, Double Concerto for violin, cello and orchestra 1998, Evidence of Things Not Seen (36 songs for four voices and piano) 1999, Aftermath for voice and trio 2002, Cello Concerto 2002, Flute Concerto 2002, Mallet Concerto 2003, Our Town (opera) 2004–05; 100s of songs and 12 song cycles. *Publications:* Paris Diary 1966, Music from Inside Out 1966, New York Diary 1967, Music and People 1968, Critical Affairs 1970, The Later Diaries 1974, Pure Contraption 1974, Setting the Tone 1980, The Nantucket Diary 1985, Settling the Score 1988, Knowing When to Stop 1994, Other Entertainment (essays) 1995, Dear Paul, Dear Ned, Lies, A Diary (1986–99) 2001, A Ned Rorem Reader 2002. *Honours:* ASCAP Foundation Lifetime Achievement Award. *Address:* c/o ASCAP, ASCAP Building, 1 Lincoln Plaza, New York, NY 10023, USA.

**RORHOLM, Marianne;** Singer (Mezzo-Soprano); b. 1960, Denmark. *Education:* Opera Academy at Copenhagen. *Career:* Debut: Royal Opera, Copenhagen as Cherubino; Season 1984–85 sang Olga, Lola and Rosina at Copenhagen and as the Sorceress in Dido and Aeneas at Paris Opéra; Frankfurt Opera, 1985–88 as Rosina, Dorabella, Sextus in La Clemenza di Tito, Nicklausse and Octavian; Sang Cherubino with the Israel Philharmonic under Daniel Barenboim and at the 1987 Ludwigsburg Festival; Bayreuth Festival in 1988 as a Flowermaiden in Parsifal; Season 1988–89 included US debut with the Indianapolis Symphony under Raymond Leppard, a concert at Carnegie Hall, Cherubino and Isolier in Le Comte Ory for Netherlands Opera; Regular appearances with the Deutsche Oper am Rhein, Düsseldorf, and Basle Operas; Season 1992 as Annius in La Clemenza di Tito at Toulouse, Varvara in Katya Kabanova at Bonn, Purcell's Dido at Brussels and the Berlioz Marguerite at Amsterdam; Season 2000 as Offred in the premiere of The Handmaid's Tale by Paul Ruders, at Copenhagen, and Carlotta in Die schweigsame Frau, at Århus; Concert repertory includes Mahler's Das Lied von der Erde. *Recordings include:* Kate Pinkerton in Madama Butterfly; Salome under Giuseppe Sinopoli; Dryad in Ariadne auf Naxos; Sang Verdi's Preziosilla at Copenhagen, 1996 and Nicklausse in Les Contes d'Hoffmann at Dublin, 1998. *Honours:* Carl Nielsen Scholarship, 1984; Elisabeth Dons Memorial Prize, 1985. *Current Management:* Ingpen & Williams Ltd, 7 St George's Court, 131 Putney Bridge Road, London, SW15 2PA, England.

**ROS MARBA, Antoni;** Conductor; b. 2 April 1937, Barcelona, Spain. *Education:* Barcelona Conservatory; Studied orchestral conducting with Eduard Toldra, Celibidache at Accademia Chigiana, and Jean Martinon at Düsseldorf. *Career:* Debut: Barcelona in 1962; Principal Conductor, 1965–68, and later as Principal Guest Conductor and Artistic Consultant for Spanish Radio and Television Orchestras, for City of Barcelona Orchestra, 1967–77, Spanish National Orchestra, 1978–81, and Netherlands Chamber Orchestra, 1979–86; Principal Guest Conductor for Netherlands Chamber Orchestra since it joined with Netherlands Philharmonic Orchestra, 1986–; Further appearances and tours world-wide including Europe, North and South America, Japan, and China and with orchestras such as Berlin Philharmonic Orchestra; Recently developed international career as an opera conductor with special success at Teatro de la Zarzuela, Madrid, and Gran Teatro del Liceu, Barcelona; Appointed Musical Director at National Opera Theatre Real, Madrid, 1989; Season 1992 with the stage premiere of Gerhard's The Duenna at Madrid, repeated for Opera North; Idomeneo for Scottish Opera, 1996. *Recordings include:* Haydn's Seven Last Words on the Cross; Others with Victoria de Los Angeles, Teresa Berganza, English Chamber Orchestra and Netherlands Chamber Orchestra. *Honours:* National Music Prize of Spain, Ministry of Culture, 1989; Arthur Honegger International Recording Prize for Seven Last Words on the Cross; Cross of St Jordi Generalitat de Cataluna. *Address:* c/o Teatro Real, Plaza de Isabel II s/n, 28013 Madrid, Spain.

**ROSAND, Aaron;** Violinist and Teacher; b. 15 March 1927, Hammond, Indiana, USA. *Education:* Studied with Marinus Paulsen, 1935–39, Leon Samenti, 1940–44, and Efrem Zimbalist, 1944–48. *Career:* Debut: With the Chicago Symphony under Frederick Stock playing the Mendelssohn Concerto, 1937; Played at New York Town Hall in 1948; European debut at Copenhagen in 1955; Tours of Europe, the Far East and Russia; Appearances with leading orchestras in the USA; Repertoire includes concertos by Lalo, Ries, Vieuxtemps, Joachim, Hubay and Wieniawski; Taught at the Academie Internationale d'Été in Nice from 1971, Peabody Conservatory, Baltimore and Mannes College, NY, and Curtis Institute, Philadelphia, 1981–; Plays a Guarneri del Gesu of 1741. *Recordings:* 15 CD recordings. *Honours:* Chevalier Pour Mérite Cultural et Artistique, 1965; Gold Medal of the Foundation Ysaÿe, Belgium, 1967. *Current Management:* Jacques Leiser Artist Management. *Address:* c/o Jacques Leiser Artist Management, The Del Prado, 666 L/Pas Street, Suite 602, San Diego, CA 92103, USA.

**ROSCA, Andreaiana;** Pianist and Professor; b. 19 Nov. 1961, Bucharest, Romania; m. Alexandru-Ioan Geamana, 14 July 1984. *Education:* Music High School Dinu Lipatti, 1968–80; Bucharest University of Music, 1982–86; Masterclasses with Bernard Ringeissen and Roger Vignoles. *Career:* Debut: At age 16 with Philharmonic Orchestra Ploiesti, Romania, playing Mozart's C minor concerto; Concerts in Romania with major orchestras including The Radio and Television Orchestra; Numerous recordings for radio and television; Recitals in Romania, Belgium; Played at Verbier Festival, and in Poland and Japan; Repertoire includes Beethoven Piano Concertos; Liszt; Mozart; Schumann; Brahms; Cycles of lieder and Romanian music such as Enesun; Accompanist for International Singing Competition for Radio Cologne, Germany; EPTA, Romania; Dinu Lipatti Foundation. *Recordings:* For Radio Cologne, Lieder and Romanian piano repertoire. *Honours:* National Prizes, 1979, 1980, 1982, 1986; Accompaniment Prize, Bianca, 1993. *Address:* 23 Principatele Unite, Sector 4, 7051 Bucharest, Romania.

**ROSCA, Marcel;** Romanian singer (bass); b. 1948, Bucharest. *Career:* sang at the Nat. Opera, Bucharest from 1980; guest appearances at the Bolshoi Theatre, Moscow and in Poland, China and Korea; Gelsenkirchen Opera from 1985, Essen 1986; roles include King Philip in Don Carlos, Boris Godunov, Gremin, Wagner's Hunding and Fafner, Osmin and Mozart's Commendatore, Arkel in Pelléas, Sparafucile in Rigoletto, Sarastro, Mephistophele, Rocco, Pagno in I Lombardi; sang Rocco in the 1806 version of Fidelio, Amsterdam 1997; sang at Essen 1998–2000 as Peneios in Daphne, Waldner in Arabella, Rocco, King Heinrich in Lohengrin, Don Pasquale and Gounod's Mephisto; Walter in Luisa Miller 2001; concerts throughout Europe and S America in the Verdi Requiem and Beethoven's Ninth; many television appearances and recordings. *Honours:* Star of Romania 1970. *Address:* c/o Essen Opera, Rolandstrasse 10, 4300 Essen 1 (office); Hagenauerstrasse 13B, 45138 Essen, Germany (home). *Telephone:* (201) 88120 (office). *E-mail:* mrosca@cityweb.de.

**RÖSCHMANN, Dorothea;** Singer (soprano); b. 1969, Flensburg, Germany. *Education:* Studied in Germany and with Vera Rozsa in London. *Career:* Member of the Deutsche Staatsoper Berlin, appearing as Papagena, Iris (Semele) and Sophie in Der Rosenkavalier (1997); Salzburg Festival from 1995, as Susanna and in concert; Further engagements as Zerlina at Tel-Aviv, Handel's Dorinda (Orlando) at Halle, Monteverdi's Drusilla (at Munich) and Dorina in Caldara's I Disingannati at the Early Music Festival Innsbruck; Other roles include Weber's Ännchen (at Berlin and Munich), Handel's Arianna (Giustino) at Göttingen and Servilia in La Clemenza di Tito, at the 1997 Salzburg Festival; Season 1998 with Susanna at Salzburg and Donizetti's Norina at Brussels; Sang Nannetta in Falstaff at Salzburg, 2001; Season 2001–02 as Anne Trulove at the Munich Festival, Elmire in Keiser's Croesus, Staatsoper Berlin, Griselda (Scarlatti), Nannetta, Pamina, Zerlina and Fiordiligi; Covent Garden debut as Pamina, 2003; Concerts at Carnegie Hall, the Vienna Musikverein, Leipzig Gewandhaus, Hamburg Musikhalle and Semperoper, Dresden. *Recordings include:* Pergolesi's Stabat Mater and Keiser's Masaniello Furioso; Messiah with Paul McCreesh and Bach's Secular Cantatas with Reinhard Goebbel (DGG); Bach's Weihnachtsoratorium and Telemann's Orpheus with René Jacobs (Harmonia Mundi). *Current Management:* Askonas Holt Ltd, Lonsdale Chambers, 27 Chancery Lane, London, WC2A 1PF, England. *Telephone:* (20) 7400-1700. *Fax:* (20) 7400-1799. *E-mail:* info@askonasholt.co.uk. *Website:* www.askonasholt.co.uk.

**ROSCOE, Martin;** Pianist; b. 3 Aug. 1952, Halton, Cheshire, England. *Education:* Royal Manchester College of Music with Marjorie Clementi and Gordon Green. *Career:* Appearances at Cheltenham, Bath, Leeds, and South Bank Music Festivals; Performances at Royal Festival Hall, Queen Elizabeth Hall, Royal Albert Hall, and Wigmore Hall in London with Hallé, City of Birmingham, Royal Philharmonic, Royal Liverpool Philharmonic, Northern Sinfonia, London Mozart Players, and BBC Philharmonic Orchestras; Tours of Australia, Middle East and South America; Further appearances at Harrogate Festival with Scottish National Orchestra, BBC, and Welsh Symphony Orchestras; Played at the Promenade Concerts with BBC Symphony Orchestra in 1987, and with French Philharmonic Orchestra in 1989; Recitals with violinist Tasmin Little, notably in the Kreutzer Sonata; mem, Incorporated Society of Musicians; Musicians Union. *Recordings:* Many for BBC Radio 3 including Piano Concertos of Berwald, Liszt, Beethoven, Stravinsky, Fauré, Vaughan Williams, and Shostakovich; Solo works by Beethoven; Complete Sonatas of Schubert, Debussy, Liszt and Bartók; Concertos by Strauss and Szymanowski; Solo commercial recordings with music by Liszt. *Honours:* Davas Gold Medal, 1973; Silver Medal, Worshipful Company of Musicians, 1974; British Liszt Piano Competition, 1976; Sydney International Piano Competition, 1981. *Current Management:* Hazard Chase, Norman House, Cambridge Place, Cambridge CB2 1NS, England. *Telephone:* (1223) 312400. *Fax:* (1223) 460827. *Website:* www.hazardchase.co.uk.

**ROSE, Gregory;** Conductor; b. 18 April 1948, Beaconsfield, England. *Education:* BA, Magdalen College, Oxford University, 1967–70; Trained Violinist, Pianist and Singer. *Career:* Conductor, Founder of Singcircle, Circle, 1977–; Music Director, London Jupiter Orchestra, 1986–; Conductor, Reading Festival Chorus, 1984–88; Conductor, London Concert Choir, 1988–96; Conductor, Reading Symphony Orchestra, 1986–91; Conductor, National Youth Choir of Wales, 1986–89; Conducted BBC Concert Orchestra, Ulster Orchestra, Estonian National Symphony Orchestra, Netherlands Radio Chamber Orchestra, BBC Singers, Nederlands Kamerkoor, Groupe Vocal de France, WDR Choir, Steve Reich and Musicians, London Philharmonic, Odense Symfonieorkester and Latvian Filharmonia; Series Director, Cage at 70, Almeida Festival, 1982 and Reich at 50, Almeida Festival, 1986; Conducted Thomson's Four Saints in Three Acts, Spitalfields, 1996 and the British stage premiere of Goldschmidt's Beatrice Cenci, 1998. *Recordings:* Hyperion, Mouth Music, Stockhausen's Stimmung; Wergo, Son Entero by Alejandro Viñao; Continuum, music by Simon Emmerson; October Music, music by Trevor Wishart; Chandos, music by Janáček; Numerous recordings for BBC radio and television, Channel 4, ITV and European radio stations. *Publications:* Various compositions. *Current Management:* Connaught Artists Management Ltd, 2 Molasses Row, Plantation Wharf, London, SW11 3UX, England. *Telephone:* (20) 7738 0017. *Fax:* (20) 7738 0909. *E-mail:* classicalmusic@connaughtartists.com. *Website:* www.connaughtartists.com. *Address:* 57 White Horse Road, London E1 0ND, England.

**ROSE, John Luke,** BMus, LMusTCL, PhD; British composer, pianist, lecturer, teacher and writer and conductor; b. 19 July 1933, Northwood Hills, Middx, England. *Education:* Univ. of London, Trinity Coll. of Music. *Career:* debut, Univ. of Oxford 1958; Extension Lecturer in Music, Univ. of Oxford 1958–66; lecturer, teacher and examiner in UK, USA, Canada, Fiji, New Zealand, Australia, India; lecturer, teacher and examiner, Trinity Coll. of Music 1960–; part-time teacher, St Marylebone Grammar School 1963–66; staff tutor, Dept of Extra-Mural Studies, Univ. of London 1966–84; mem. Asscn of Univ. Teachers, British Acad. of Composers. *Compositions:* Symphony No. 1 The Mystic (Royal Philharmonic Soc. Prize) 1982, Piano Concerto 1977, Overture Macbeth 1977, Symphony No. 2 (Royal Philharmonic Soc. Prize) 1985, Symphonic Dances, String Quartet, Part-songs, two piano sonatas, various piano works, Blake's Songs of Innocence, The Pleasures of Youth (cantata), Hymns and Anthems, Apocalyptic Visions for piano, St Francis (musical play) 1985, Violin Concerto 1987, Odysseus (opera) 1987. *Publications:* Wagner's Tristan and Isolde: A Landmark in Musical History (introductory essay to libretto book) 1981, Ludwig, Wagner and the Romantic View (essay and lecture, V&A Museum exhibition). *Honours:* Hon. Fellow, Trinity Coll. London 1961. *Address:* Kalon, 113 Farnham Road, Guildford, Surrey, GU2 7PF, England (home).

**ROSE, Jürgen;** Stage Designer; b. 25 Aug. 1937, Bernburg, Germany. *Education:* Studied acting and painting in Berlin. *Career:* Ballet designs for the Stuttgart Ballet, 1962–73; Collaborations with director, Otto Schenk for Don Carlos and Die Meistersinger in Vienna, Simon Boccanegra and Der Rosenkavalier at Munich and Così fan tutte in Berlin; Bayreuth Festival in 1972 and 1990 with Tannhäuser and Der fliegende Holländer, in productions by Götz Friedrich and Dieter Dorn; Salome and Die Entführung in Vienna, Lucia di Lammermoor and Lohengrin in Hamburg; Premiere of Isang Yun's Sim Tjong at Munich in 1972; Designed Die Zauberflöte for the Munich Opera and the 1981 Ludwigsburg Festival; Le nozze di Figaro for the 1997 Munich Festival; Bayreuth Festival, Tristan und Isolde (1999), Met New York, Premiere of H.W. Henze's L'Upupa, Salzburg Festival, 2003; Own direction in own stage-and costume designs: La Traviata (1994), Die Zauberflöte (1996), Bonn Opera/Don Carlo (2000) and The Cunning Little Vixen (2002) Munich Opera. *Recordings include:* Video of Munich production of Die Zauberflöte. *Address:* c/o Bayerische Staatsoper, Postfach 100148, 8000 Munich 1, Germany.

**ROSE, Peter;** Singer (bass); b. 1961, Canterbury, Kent, England. *Education:* University of East Anglia; Guildhall School of Music with Ellis Keeler; National Opera Studio. *Career:* Debut: As Commendatore in Don Giovanni with Glyndebourne Opera in Hong Kong, 1986 and on tour; Welsh National Opera, 1986–89 as Bartolo, Basilio, Prince Gremin in Eugene Onegin, Angelotti in Tosca, Osmin, Tutor in Count Ory and Marke in Tristan; Glyndebourne Touring Opera as Don Inigo in L'Heure Espagnole, Osmin and Basilio; Maggio Musicale Florence as Commendatore; Scottish Opera as Narbal in Les Troyens; Sang in La Damnation de Faust in Chicago, BBC Proms and Salzburg Festival with Chicago Symphony under Solti; English National Opera as Angelotti and Bottom; Covent Garden debut 1988 as Lord Rochefort in Anna Bolena then Cadmus in Semele, Bonze in Madama Butterfly, Lodovico in Otello, Nightwatchman in Meistersinger; Kecal in The Bartered Bride, Chicago Lyric Opera, Commendatore, Gessler in Guillaume Tell and Basilio at San Francisco, 1991–92; Also sang Walther in Luisa Miller, Amsterdam, 1st Nazarene in Salome, Salzburg, Bottom at Aix-en-Provence, Commendatore at Covent Garden in 1993, Mustafà (Italiana), Amsterdam, Pimen in Boris Godunov at New Israeli Opera, Ramfis in Aida, Hunding in Walküre, Berlin Staatsoper, in 1994 and Dosifei in Khovanshchina, Hamburg; Other roles include Fasolt in Rheingold; Bottom at the Met; Sang in Pfitzner's Palestrina at Covent Garden, 1997; Engaged for Rachmaninov's Aleko at the 1999 London Prom concerts; Season 2000 as Silva in Ernani for ENO and King Mark in Tristan at Covent Garden; Britten's Claggart at Cologne, 2001; Ravel's Le Heure espagnole at the London Proms, 2002. *Recordings include:*

Nozze di Figaro with Barenboim and the Berlin Philharmonic; Video of Clemenza di Tito for Glyndebourne; Salome with Dohnányi, Seven Deadly Sins (also on video); Barber of Seville (with Peter Moores); Beatrice Cenci, Goldschmidt; Ballo in Maschera, Teldec. *Current Management:* Askonas Holt Ltd, Lonsdale Chambers, 27 Chancery Lane, London, WC2A 1PF, England. *Telephone:* (20) 7400-1700. *Fax:* (20) 7400-1799. *E-mail:* info@askonasholt.co.uk. *Website:* www.askonasholt.co.uk.

**ROSEBERRY, Eric Norman,** BA, BMus, PhD, FRCO; British musician and writer; b. 18 July 1930, Sunderland, England; m. 1st Elspeth Mary Campbell 1952; four d.; m. 2nd Frances Jill Sharp 1969. *Education:* Univs of Durham and Bristol. *Career:* Dir of Music, Stand Grammar School for Boys, Manchester 1953–58; Co. Music Organiser, Huntingdonshire, 1958–64; Music Assistant, BBC London 1964–69; Radcliffe Lecturer in Music, Univ. of Sussex 1969–72; Lecturer, Extra-Mural Dept, Univ. of Bristol 1972–; Sr Lecturer in Music, Bath Coll. of Higher Educ. 1972–85; Dir of Music, Bath Symphony Orchestra 1977–89; Founder-Dir Apollo Ensemble of Bath 1989. *Publications:* Faber Book of Christmas Carols and Songs 1969, Dmitri Shostakovich: His Life and Times 1982, essays appearing in, Of German Music 1976, The Britten Companion 1984, Benjamin Britten Death in Venice, Cambridge Opera Handbooks 1987, Shostakovich's Musical Style, USA 1990, Shostakovich and Britten in Shostakovich Studies 1995, On Mahler and Britten 1995, essays in The Cambridge Companion to Britten 1999. *Contributions:* articles and reviews in Tempo, The Listener, Music and Musicians, Music and Letters, Musical Times, CD Review, programme notes for BBC Symphony Concerts, Aldeburgh Festival and the Proms, sleeve notes for Chandos Records, broadcast talks on BBC Radio 3. *Honours:* Classic FM Red Award for outstanding contrib. to classical music 2002. *Address:* The Toll House, Marshfield, Chippenham, Wilts., SN14 8JN, England (home).

**RÖSEL, Peter;** German pianist; *Professor, University of Music, Dresden;* b. 2 Feb. 1945, Dresden; m. Heidrun Bergmann; one s. one d. *Education:* Tchaikovsky Conservatory, Moscow with Dmitri Bashkirov and Lev Oborin. *Career:* debut with Berlin Symphony 1964; performances at int. festivals, including Dresden, Salzburg, La Roque d'Anthéron, Edinburgh, BBC London Proms, Perth, Hollywood Bowl, Hong Kong; frequent guest with New York Symphony, Los Angeles Symphony, Montreal Symphony, Toronto Symphony and Detroit Symphony Orchestras, Philharmonia, Royal Philharmonic, Berlin Philharmonic, Deutsches Symphonie-Orchester Berlin, Radio Symphony Orchestra Berlin, Staatskapelle Dresden and Dresdner Philharmonie, Gewandhausorchester Leipzig, MDR-Sinfonieorchester, Mozarteum Orchester Salzburg as well Netherland Philharmonic; has played with conductor incuding Blomstedt, Boreyko, Dutoit, Fedossejew, Haenchen, Haitink, Hording, Herbig, Janowski, Kempe, Kitajenko, Kondrashin, Masur, Kurt Sanderling, Stefan Sanderling, van Steen, Stein, Temirkanov, Tennstedt and Vonk; performed Rachmaninov's Piano Concero No. 3 under Kurt Masur at 150th Anniversary of New York Philharmonic; Season 2003–04 performed among others with Dresdner Philharmonie, Brandenburgisches Staatsorchester Frankfurt, Bern Symphony Orchestra, Radio Symphony Orchestra Seoul and gave several concerts in USA; Season 2004–05 gave concerts among others with Philharmonisches Orchester Freiburg, Göttinger Symphonie Orchester, Orchester des Opernhauses Halle and MDR-Sinfonieorchester; guest of Dresdner Philharmonie, Gewandhaus Leipzig and on occasion of Strauss Festival, playing the Burleske with Sächsische Staatskapelle 2005; played all five Beethoven piano concerts with Kioi Sinfonietta Tokyo at Semperoper and gave a recital with works by Mozart, Debussy, J.S. Bach/ Busoni and Brahms also at the Semperoper Dresden as part of Dresdner Musikfesfspiele 2005; guest of Schubertiade in Roskilde 2005; Season 2005–06 concerts with MDR-Sinfonieorchester under Kurt Masur, Philharmonisches Staatsorchester Halle under Heribert Esser, Toledo Symphony Orchestra under Stefan Sanderling, Dresdner Philharmonie under Dmitrij Kitajenko and performance of Britten's Piano Concerto with Mozarteum Orchester Salzbur; Prof., Univ. of Music, Dresden 1985–; mem. Saxon Acad. of the Arts. *Recordings include:* complete concerti by Weber, Beethoven, Schumann and Rachmaninov, complete piano works by Brahms, major piano sonatas by Mozart, Beethoven, Schubert and Schumann, various chamber music works. *Honours:* Prizewinner, Moscow Tchaikovsky Competition and Montreal Piano Competition. *Current Management:* Berliner Konzertagentur Monika Ott, Dramburgerstrasse 46, 12683 Berlin, Germany. *Telephone:* (30) 5144858. *Fax:* (30) 5142659. *E-mail:* berlinkonzert.ott@t-online.de. *Website:* www .berlinkonzert-ott.de.

**ROSELL, Lars-Erik;** Composer and Organist; b. 9 Aug. 1944, Nybro, Sweden. *Education:* Organ Student, 1963–69; Composition with Ingvar Lidholm, Stockholm Royal College of Music, 1968–71. *Career:* Teacher, Counterpoint, Composition, Stockholm Royal College of Music, 1972–, Professor from 2001; Freelance Organist, Performances of Contemporary Music. *Compositions include:* Terry Riley for 3 Pianos, 1970; Poem in the Dark for mezzo and ensemble, 1972; After the Fall, Dramatic Scene Based on Arthur Miller, for vocal soloists and ensemble, 1973; Visiones Prophetae, Biblical Scene, 1974; Musik for cello and string orchestra, 1975; Ordens källa, Scenic Cantata, 1980; Tillfälligt avbrott, chamber opera, 1981; Organ Concerto, 1982; Amédée, chamber opera, 1987; Five Aphorisms, cello solo, 1990; Fantasia Concertante for cello and orchestra, 1992; The Illusionist, chamber opera, 1996; Three Orchestral Songs for soprano and baritone, 1999; Out of the Shadows, chamber opera, 2001; Choir music, chamber music and other stage music. *Recordings:* Lars-Erik Rosell, In Between. *Address:* Gnejsstigen 2, 19633 Kungsängen, Sweden. *E-mail:* lars-erik.rosell@kmh.se.

**ROSEN, Charles,** PhD; American pianist and writer; b. 5 May 1927, New York, NY; s. of Irwin Rosen and Anita Gerber. *Education:* Juilliard School of Music, Princeton Univ., Univ. of S. California. *Career:* studied piano with Moriz Rosenthal and Hedwig Kanner-Rosenthal 1938–45; recital début, New York 1951; first complete recording of Debussy Etudes 1951; première of Double Concerto by Elliott Carter, New York 1961; has played recitals and as soloist with orchestras throughout America and Europe; has made over 35 recordings including Stravinsky: Movements with composer conducting 1962, Bach: Art of Fugue, Two Ricercares, Goldberg Variations 1971, Beethoven: Last Six Sonatas 1972, Boulez: Piano Music, Vol. I, Diabelli Variations, Beethoven Concerto No. 4, 1979, Schumann: The Revolutionary Masterpieces, Chopin: 24 Mazurkas 1991; Prof. of Music, State Univ. of NY 1972–90; Guggenheim Fellowship 1974; Messenger Lectures, Cornell Univ. 1975, Bloch Lectures, Univ. of Calif., Berkeley 1977, Gauss Seminars, Princeton Univ. 1978; Norton Prof. of Poetry, Harvard Univ. 1980–81; George Eastman Prof., Balliol Coll., Oxford 1987–88, Prof. of Music and Social Thought, Univ. of Chicago 1988–96. *Publications:* The Classical Style: Haydn, Mozart, Beethoven 1971, Beethoven's Last Six Sonatas 1972, Schoenberg 1975, Sonata Forms 1980, Romanticism and Realism: The Mythology of Nineteenth-Century Art (with Henri Zerner) 1984, The Musical Language of Elliott Carter 1984, Paisir de jouer, plaiser de penser 1993, The Frontiers of Meaning: Three Informal Lectures on Music 1994, The Romantic Generation 1995, Romantic Poets, Critics and Other Madmen 1998, Critical Entertainment: Music Old and New 2000, Beethoven's Piano Sonatas: A Short Companion 2001, Piano Notes 2003; contrib. to books, newspapers and journals. *Honours:* Hon. DMus (Trinity Coll., Dublin 1976, Leeds Univ. 1976, Durham Univ.); Dr hc (Cambridge) 1992; Nat. Book Award 1972, Edison Prize, Netherlands 1974. *Current Management:* John Gingrich Management Inc, PO Box 1515, New York, NY 10023, USA.

**ROSEN, Jerome (William);** Composer, Clarinettist and Professor of Music; b. 23 July 1921, Boston, Massachusetts, USA; m. Sylvia T Rosen, 1 s., 3 d. *Education:* MA, University of California, Berkeley, 1948; Special student at National Conservatory of Paris; Studied with Darius Milhaud, 1949–50. *Career:* Professor of Music and Director of Electronic Studio at University of California, Davis, 1963–; mem, American Composers' Alliance; Musicological Society. *Compositions include:* Sonata for Clarinet and Cello, 1954; 2 String Quartets, 1953 and 1965; Suite for 4 Clarinets, 1962; Three Songs for Chorus and Piano, 1968; Clarinet Concerto, 1973; Serenade for Clarinet and Violin, 1977; Calisto And Melibea, chamber opera, 1978; Campus Doorways for Chorus and Orchestra, 1978; Music for 2 Clarinets, 1980; Fantasy for Violin, 1983; Concertpiece for Clarinet and Piano, 1984; Sextet Sine Nomine, 1996; Emperor Norton of the USA, 1997;. *Contributions:* Various musical journals and articles in Grove's Dictionary of Music and Musicians. *Honours:* George Ladd Prix de Paris, 1949–51; Fromm Foundation, 1952; Guggenheim Fellowship, 1958. *Address:* Department of Music, University of California, Davis, CA 95616, USA.

**ROSEN, Nathaniel (Kent);** Cellist; b. 9 June 1948, Altadena, California, USA; m. Margo Shohl. *Education:* Studied with Eleonore Schoenfeld in Pasadena and with Piatigorsky at the University of Southern California, Los Angeles. *Career:* Assistant to Piatigorsky, 1966–76; Solo debut with the Los Angeles Philharmonic, 1969; New York debut, 1970, Carnegie Hall; Principal Cellist, Los Angeles Chamber Orchestra, 1972–76; Pittsburgh Symphony Orchestra, 1977–79; Professor, University of Illinois at Champaign-Urbana, 1988–94; Professor, Manhattan School of Music, 1981–88, 1994–; Appearances with leading American and European Orchestras and as Recitalist and in Chamber Music. *Recordings:* Complete music for Cello and Piano by Chopin; Shostakovich Cello Concerto No. 1; Brahms Sonatas; Bach Suites. *Address:* c/o Manhattan School of Music, Cello Faculty, 120 Claremont Ave, New York, NY 10027, USA.

**ROSEN, Robert (Joseph);** Composer and Performer; b. 20 May 1956, Melfort, Saskatchewan, Canada; m. Deborah Alpaugh, 18 Aug 1979, 2 s., 1 d. *Education:* BMus, Distinction, University of Alberta, 1977; Advanced Music Studies Programme of Banff Centre, 1979–81; Darmstadt Summer Course, 1982; Studied composition with Violet Archer and Bruce Mather; Worked for short periods with John Cage, R Murray Schafer, Witold Lutoslawski, Iannis Xenakis and Morton Feldman; National Choreographic Workshop, Vancouver, 1985. *Career:* Broadcasts as performer on CBC National Radio; Compositions performed in Canada, Sweden, Germany, Netherlands, France, Spain, USA, Italy and Australia by such notable performers as Robert Aitken, Jean-Pierre Drouet and Alan Hacker; Founding Member of performing ensemble, Fusion 5; Created film scores for documentaries produced by Helios Pictures for the National Film Board of Canada; Assistant Director of Music Programs at the Banff centre for The Arts from 1991; Musical Director of Kokoro Dance. *Compositions:* From Silence for Piano and Orchestra; String Quartet, 1979; Krikos, l, 1980, ll, 1982; Enigmas From The Muse; Meditation No. 1 for Flute, Violin and Cello, No. 2 for Small Orchestra, No. 4 for 2 Pianos, No. 5, Mosaic for Flute and Piano, No. 6 for Piano, No. 7, Coro for 24 Voices; In Anticipation Of Beautiful Shadows for 7 Cellos; Mi Istakistsi for Flute, Percussion and String Quartet; Zero To The Power for Violin, Cello, Taiko Percussion and Electronics; Stones for 2 Sopranos, Tuba and Percussion; Canyon Shadows: Stones; Animals for 2 Sopranos, Alpenhorn and Tuba, 1993. *Publications:* Canadian Composers at Banff, Celebration, Canadian Music

Centre. *Address:* c/o SOCAN, 41 Valleybrook Drive, Don Mills, Ontario M3B 2S6, Canada.

**ROSEN, Rudolf;** Singer (Baritone); b. 1960, Switzerland. *Education:* Berne Academy of Music, with Jakob St ämpfli. *Career:* Many concert engagements in Oslo, Stuttgart, Leipzig, Munich, Zürich and Geneva; conductors have included Neeme Järvi, John Nelson, Helmuth Rilling and Michel Corboz; Further engagements at Tel-Aviv and Mexico City; Heilbronn and Salzburg Festivals, 1996–97; concert repertoire from Lieder to Oratorios; Stuttgart State Opera from 2001, including engagement as Don Giovanni, 2002. *Honours:* Prizewinner, Internaional Music Competition, Geneva (1997), ARD Music Competition Munich (1998) and Belvedere Song Competition, Vienna. *Address:* c/o Theateragentur Dr G. Hilbert, Maximilianstrasse 22, Munich, Germany.

**ROSENBAUM, Victor,** BA (Hons), MFA; American pianist, conductor and administrator; b. 19 Dec. 1941, Philadelphia, Pa; two d. *Education:* Brandeis and Princeton Univs, Aspen Music School; studied piano with Leonard Shure and Rosina Lhevinne, composition with Roger Sessions, Earl Kim and Edward T. Cone. *Career:* solo performances in USA, Japan, Brazil, Israel and Russia; chamber performances with Leonard Rose, Roman Totenberg, Arnold Steinhardt, Cleveland Quartet, Vermeer Quartet, Brentano Quartet, New World Quartet, at Tully Hall, Town Hall, New York, Jordan Hall, Boston; Conductor, Concerto Company chamber orchestra; fmr Faculty mem. Eastman School of Music, Brandeis Univ.; Faculty mem. New England Conservatory, Mannes Coll. of Music, Longy School of Music, Cambridge, Mass (Dir and Pres. 1985–2001). *Compositions:* For voice, piano, chorus, chamber ensemble and theatre pieces. *Recordings:* Beethoven: The Last Three Sonatas (Bridge), Schubert: Sonata, D959, Moments Musicaux (Bridge), John Harbison Trio. *Address:* Longy School of Music, 1 Follen Street, Cambridge, MA 02138 (office); 160 Lake Street, Brighton, MA 02135, USA (home). *E-mail:* vrosenbaum@aol.com (home).

**ROSENBERG, Pamela;** American music administrator; *Intendant, Berlin Philharmonic Orchestra*; b. Los Angeles, CA; m. Wolf Rosenberg (deceased); two c. *Education:* Univ. of Calif. at Berkeley, Ohio State Univ., Guildhall School of Music, London. *Career:* previous positions at Netherlands Opera, Amsterdam, Deutschen Schauspielhaus, Hamburg; Scenic Supervisor, subsequently Artistic Admin. Frankfurt Opera; Co-Dir Stuttgart Opera 1991–2000; Gen. Dir San Francisco Opera 2001–06; Intendant Berlin Philharmonic Orchestra 2006–. *Address:* Stiftung Berliner Philharmoniker, Herbert-von-Karajan-Str. 1, Berlin 10785, Germany (office). *Telephone:* (30) 254-88-0 (office). *Website:* www.berlin-philharmonic.com (office).

**ROSENBOOM, David;** American composer, performer and academic; *Dean, School of Music, California Institute of the Arts*; b. 9 Sept. 1947, Fairfield, Ia. *Education:* studied with Salvatore Martirano, Lejaren Hiller, Kenneth Gaburo, Gordon Binkerd, Bernard Goodman, Paul Roland, Jack McKenzie, Soulima Stravinsky and John Garvey, Univ. of Illinois, Urbana. *Career:* worked in commercial broadcast media; independent performer, composer and producer; special studies in physics, computer science, experimental psychology, and multi-media, New York Univ., and independently; has composed extensively for both instrumental and technological media; organized numerous performing groups, including the performance art group, Maple Sugar, Toronto (with Jacqueline Humbert and George Manupelli) and the open instrumental ensemble, Challenge, Oakland (with Braxton and Winant); has collaborated with many leading composers and musicians; Creative Assoc., Center for Creative and Performing Arts, State Univ. of NY, Buffalo 1960s; Artistic Coordinator New York's Electric Circus 1960s; Co-Founder and Pres. Neurona Co., New York 1969–71; Prof. and Founder Dept of Music and Interdisciplinary Grad. Studies Programme, York Univ., Toronto 1972–79, Coordinator of Interdisciplinary Studies, Faculty of Fine Arts, Founding Dir Electronic Media Studios and Lab. of Experimental Aesthetics; teacher, Mills Coll., Oakland 1979–88, Darius Milhaud Prof. of Music, Head of Music Dept and Dir Center for Contemporary Music 1988; Head, Music Dept, California Inst. of the Arts 1984–90, fmr Co-Dir Center for Experiments in Art, Information and Tech. and Conductor of the New Century Players, Dean of School of Music 1990–; taught interdisciplinary subjects at San Francisco Art Inst. and California Coll. of Arts and Crafts; guest faculty mem. at numerous insts. including George A. Miller Visiting Prof., Univ. of Illinois 1995, Banff Centre for the Arts, Simon Fraser Univ.; has served as adviser, bd mem. and professional affiliate with nat. arts orgs in USA and Canada; has developed computer software for music, was co-designer of a computerized keyboard instrument with Donald Buchia, the Touché, and is co-author (with L. Polansky and P. Burk) of HMSL (Hierarchical Music Specification Language), a widely used music programming language. *Compositions include:* The Brandy of the Damned, music theatre 1967, How Much Better if Plymouth Rock Had Landed on the Pilgrims 1972, On Being Invisible 1976, In the Beginning I–IV, for Various Instrumental Combinations 1978–80, Future Travel for Piano, Violin and Computer Music System 1982, Champ Vital 1987, Systems of Judgement 1987, Predictions, Confirmations and Disconfirmations 1991, Extended Trio 1992, It Is About To... Sound, Interactive Computer Music Installation 1993, It Is About To ... Vexations 1993, On Being Invisible II: Hypatia Speaks to Jefferson in a Dream (self-organizing opera with brain-evoked responses and interactive media) 1995, Brave New World: Music for the Play 1995, Seeing the Small In the Large (Six Movements for Orchestra) 1998, Bell Solaris (Twelve Movements for Piano) 1998, Naked Curvature for six instruments, whispering voices, sound effects, and HMSL software 2000,

Four Lines for two to four instruments and electronic tracks 2001. *Recordings include:* A Precipice In Time (quintet with computer processing) 1966, How Much Better If Plymouth Rock Had Landed On The Pilgrims for unspecified instruments 1969, The Seduction of Sapientia for viola da gamba and electronics 1974, Suitable for Framing for two pianos 1975, South Indian Mrdangam, Brainwave Music 1976, On Being Invisible for brainwaves and computer music system 1977, And Out Come the Night Ears for piano and electronics 1978, In The Beginning (series of nine works for soloists, chamber ensembles, orchestra and electronics) 1978–81, Future Travel for computer and acoustic instruments 1982, Zones of Influence for percussion soloist and computer instrument 1984–85, Roundup (anthology of live electro-acoustic works) 1987, Systems of Judgment for computer music systems and various instruments 1988, Extended Trio for instruments and HMSL 1992, Two Lines (duets in collaboration with Anthony Braxton) 1995, On Being Invisible II 2000. *Publications include:* Biofeedback and the Arts: Results of Early Experiments 1975, The J. Jasmine Songbook (jtly) 1978, Collected Articles (1968–1982) 1984, In the Beginning – A Collection of Works, 1978–1981 1987, Music for Keyboard Instruments and Improvisation Groups, 1964–1981 1987, Collected Scores 1965–1973 1987, Extended Musical Interface with the Human Nervous System: Assessment and Prospectus 1990; contribs to Perspectives of New Music, Leonardo, Musicworks, Computer Music Journal, Performing Arts Journal, and others. *Address:* CalArts-School of Music, 24700 McBean Parkway, Santa Clarita, CA 91355-2397, USA (office). *Telephone:* (661) 253-7816 (office). *Fax:* (661) 255-0938 (office). *E-mail:* david@music .calarts.edu (office). *Website:* music.calarts.edu/~david (office).

**ROSENKRANZ, Helge;** violinist; b. 1962, Austria. *Career:* member of Franz Schubert Quartet, Vienna, 1989–; many concert engagements in Europe, USA, and Australia including Amsterdam Concertgebouw, Vienna Musikverein and Kozerthaus, Salle Gaveau, Paris and Sydney Opera House; Visits to Zürich, Geneva, Basle, Hamburg, Rome, Rotterdam, Madrid and Copenhagen; Festival engagements include Salzburg, Wiener Festwochen, Prague Spring, Schubertiade at Hohenems, Schubert Festival in Washington DC, Belfast and Istanbul; tours of Australasia, Russia and USA; Frequent concert tours to the United Kingdom; Featured in Concerto by Spohr with Royal Liverpool Philharmonic, Liverpool and Festival Hall, London; many appearances at Wigmore Hall and at Cheltenham Festival; Masterclasses at Royal Northern College of Music and Lake District Summer Music. *Recordings include:* Schubert's Quartet in G, D877; Complete Quartets by Dittersdorf. *Address:* Steingasse 27, 5020 Salzburg, Austria.

**ROSENSHEIN, Neil;** Singer (Tenor); b. 27 Nov. 1947, New York, USA. *Education:* Studied in New York. *Career:* Debut: Florida Opera in 1972 as Almaviva in Il Barbiere di Siviglia; Sang in Washington, Dallas, Boston and Santa Fe; European debut at Vaison-la-Romaine in 1980 as Almaviva; Further appearances in Geneva, Zürich and Paris; Covent Garden debut in 1986 as Lensky in Eugene Onegin; Chicago Lyric Opera in 1988 as Alfredo in La Traviata; Sang in the premiere of The Aspern Papers by Dominick Argento, Dallas, 1988; Berlioz Festival at Lyon in 1989 as Benvenuto Cellini; Other roles include Mozart's Tamino and Belmonte, Verdi's Fenton and Don Carlos, Massenet's Des Grieux and Werther at Turin, Sydney and Metropolitan in 1989, and Števa in Jenůfa; Season 1992–93 at the Metropolitan as Faust, Werther, Alfredo in Traviata and Léon in the premiere of Corigliano's The Ghosts of Versailles; Sang the Berlioz Faust at Turin in 1992 and Peter Grimes at Sydney; Sang Cavaradossi at Santa Fe, 1994. *Recordings:* Eugene Onegin. *Address:* c/o Metropolitan Opera, Lincoln Center, New York, NY 10023, USA.

**ROSEWELL, Michael;** conductor; *Associate Conductor, English Touring Opera. Career:* began his career working at Staatstheater Kassel, Staatstheater Wiesbaden, Nationaltheater Mannheim in Germany; joined staff Vienna State Opera; Artistic Dir London Phoenix Ensemble; Dir of Opera, Benjamin Britten Int. Opera School, RCM; guest conductor English Touring Opera, then apptd Assoc. Conductor 2005–; works conducted with English Touring Opera include Così fan tutte, Mary, Queen of Scots, Marriage of Figaro, Janáček's Jenufa; has also conducted at Clonter Opera Theatre, Aldeburgh Festival, ENO, Kent Opera, London Handel Festival, Bath Festival; numerous performances of works by Benjamin Britten, including A Midsummer Night's Dream, The Rape of Lucretia, world premiere of Plymouth Town (with RCM Sinfonietta) 2004; has also conducted Die Zauberflöte, Barber of Seville, La Bohème, Handel's Alessandro Severo, Gazzaniga's Don Giovanni. *Address:* English Touring Opera, 52–54 Rosebery Avenue, London, EC1R 4RP, England (office). *E-mail:* admin@englishtouringopera.org.uk (office). *Website:* www.englishtouringopera.org.uk (office).

**ROSKELL, Penelope;** Pianist; b. 1960, Oxford, England; m. Richard Griffiths, 26 Oct 1985. *Education:* GMus (RNCM) Honours, PPRNCM, Royal Northern College of Music; Private study with Guido Agosti in Rome. *Career:* Solo pianist with tours world-wide at invitation of the British Council; Concerts regularly in Europe, Scandinavia, USA, Africa, Asia, Middle and Far East; Broadcasts on BBC Radio 3, WFMT Radio Chicago and British and Polish television; Professor of Piano at London College of Music; Recitals at Wigmore Hall and Purcell Room; Concerto engagements include recording with Oxford Pro Musica; Tours with Manchester Camerata and the Bournemouth Sinfonietta under Simon Rattle. *Honours:* Winner of British Contemporary Piano Competition. *Current Management:* Helen Sykes Artists Management. *Address:* c/o Helen Sykes Artists Management, 100 Felsham Road, Putney, London SW15 1DQ, England.

**ROSS, Christopher;** Pianist (accompanist and chamber musician) and Conductor; b. 1961, England. *Career:* Has worked with such musicians as soprano Jennifer Smith, cellist Raphael Wallfisch, violinist Dona Lee Croft (tour of the USA) and José Carreras (2 albums); Many performances in France, Germany, Switzerland, Portugal, Namibia, Japan, Korea, India, Malaysia and all London's concert halls; Conducted Le Nozze di Figaro in Switzerland and Mozart's Requiem Mass in London, 2003. *Honours:* Accompanist's Prize, Richard Tauber Competition; Accompanist's Prize, NFMS competition (twice). *E-mail:* chris_ross@ntlworld.com.

**ROSS, Elinor;** Singer (Soprano); b. 1 Aug. 1932, Tampa, Florida, USA. *Education:* Studied with Zinka Milanov in New York. *Career:* Debut: Cincinnati Opera in 1958 as Leonora in Il Trovatore; Guest appearances in Boston, Chicago, Baltimore and Philadelphia; Sang at Carnegie Hall in the 1968 US premiere of Verdi's Alzira; Metropolitan Opera from 1970 with debut as Turandot; European engagements at La Scala, Bologna, Palermo, Vienna, Budapest, Zagreb, Verona and Florence; Other roles include Bellini's Norma, Verdi's Aida, Elisabetta, Amelia, Lady Macbeth and Abigaille, Mozart's Donna Anna, Puccini's Tosca and Giordano's Maddalena; Sang Tosca at the Metropolitan in 1973, and the Trovatore, Leonora at Buenos Aires in 1974; Frequent concert appearances. *Address:* c/o Metropolitan Opera, Lincoln Center, New York, NY 10023, USA.

**ROSS, Elise;** Singer (soprano); b. 28 April 1947, New York, USA; m. Simon Rattle (divorced). *Career:* Sang with the Juilliard Ensemble, New York and the Los Angeles Philharmonic Orchestra from 1970; Performances of music by Berio in USA and Europe (Passagio in Rome); Tour of Europe with the London Sinfonietta and appearances at Royan and Bath Festivals and in Venice and Warsaw; Sang in Bussotti's Passion Selon Sade and Le Racine at La Scala in 1991; Concerts with the Ensemble Intercontemporain, Paris from 1976; Repertoire includes Berlin Cabaret songs, lieder by composers of the Second Viennese School, Chansons by Ravel and Debussy and lieder by Mozart, Schumann and Strauss; Shostakovich Symphony 14 with the Los Angeles Philharmonic and Ensemble Intercontemporain; Has sung Cherubino for Opera North and for Long Beach Opera; Sang Marie in Wozzeck at Los Angeles in 1989, Mélisande with Netherlands Opera and Berlioz's Romeo and Juliette, Rotterdam, 1993.

**ROSS, Walter;** Composer; b. 3 Oct. 1936, Lincoln, Nebraska, USA. *Education:* MMus, University of Nebraska, 1962; DMA, Cornell University, 1966, with Robert Palmer. *Career:* Music Faculty, University of Virginia, 1967–. *Compositions:* Concerto for brass quintet and orchestra, 1966; Five Dream Sequences for percussion quartet and piano, 1968; 2 Trombone Concertos, 1970, 1982; Canzona I and II for brass instruments, 1969, 1979; In the Penal Colony, Opera, 1972; 3 Wind Quintets, 1974, 1985, 1989; A Jefferson Symphony, for tenor, chorus and orchestra, 1976; Concerto for wind quintet and strings, 1977; String Trio, 1978; Nocturne for strings, 1980; Violin Sonata, 1981; Concerto for bassoon and strings, 1983; Suite No. 1 for chamber ensemble, 1983; Concerto for oboe, harp and strings, 1984; 3 Brass Trios, 1985, 1986, 1986; Concerto for flute, guitar and orchestra, 1987; Sinfonia Concertante for strings, 1987; Oil of Dog, for brass quintet and actor, 1988; Concerto for euphonium, brass and timpani, 1988; Scherzo Festivo, for orchestra, 1992; Summer Dances for oboe and marimba, 1992; Clarinet Concerto, 1994; Harlequinade for 5 wind instruments and piano, 1994; Vocal Music, including Songs and Choruses. *Address:* c/o ASCAP, ASCAP Building, 1 Lincoln Plaza, New York, NY 10023, USA.

**ROSSBERG, Dieter;** Conductor; b. 1952, Hamburg, Germany. *Education:* Studied at the Hamburg Academy, with Horst Stein, György Ligeti, Götz Friedrich and August Everding. *Career:* Principal Conductor/Kapellmeister and Deputy General Music Director in various opera houses in Germany and Austria, 1975–92; Since 1973 has appeared as a guest conductor for opera concert and radio productions (NHK-Tokyo, Bayerische Rundfunk-München, Radio Hilversum, NDR, Danish and Norwegian Broadcasting Corporation) and festivals in Germany: Berlin, Bonn, Cologne, Essen, Hamburg, Hannover, Frankfurt and Munich and abroad: Austria, Canada, Denmark, Estonia, France, Finland, Hungary, Italy, Japan, Tokyo, Monaco, Netherlands, Norway, Slovenia, Sweden, Switzerland, Turkey; Has worked with many noted instrumentalists and singers including René Kollo, Gegam Grigorian, Ingvar Wixell, Peter Mattei and stage directors and choreographers such as John Neumier; Performed as a freelance conductor, 1992–; More than 90 different operas in 1000 performances with a wide concert repertoire; Has conducted many world premieres. *Address:* Lottbeker Platz 4, 22359 Hamburg, Germany.

**RÖSSEL-MAJDAN, Hildegard;** Singer (Contralto); b. 30 Jan. 1921, Moosbierbaum, Austria; m. Karl Rossel-Majdan, 1 d. *Education:* HS for Music and Dramatic Art, Vienna. *Career:* Concert and oratorio singer under leading Austrian and foreign conductors, 1948–; Member of Vienna State Opera, 1951–71; Professor, University for Music and Dramatic Art, Vienna, 1971–91; Concerts, opera and oratorio in Europe, USA and Japan; Lecturer in Austrian seminaries and in Japan; President of Goetheanistic Konservatory and Waldorfpedagogical Akademy. *Recordings:* Various. *Address:* Agnesgasse 13, Vienna, Austria.

**RÖSSLER, Almut;** German organist and conductor; b. 12 June 1932, Beveringen; d. of Helmut Rößler; one s. *Education:* Secondary educ. in Düsseldorf, studied the organ, church music and composition in Detmold and Paris. *Career:* Has performed at numerous concerts and music festivals in

Germany and abroad; numerous TV and radio appearances; conductor Johannes-Kantorei; Chevalier de l'Ordre des Palmes Académiques (France) 1981; Förderpreis für junge Künstler, Fed. State of N Rhine-Westphalia 1960; Organist of the Year, Univ. of Michigan, USA 1986. *Publications include:* Beiträge zur geistigen Welt Olivier Messiaens (trans. to English 1986) 1984, Ur- und Erstaufführungen von Werken von Jolivet, David, Baur, Leitner, und andere (essays), Konzert für Orgel und Orchestra von Klebe 1980, Livre du Saint Sacrement von Olivier Messiaen 1986. *Address:* c/o Martin-Luther-Platz 39, 40212 Düsseldorf, Germany.

**ROST, Andrea;** Hungarian operatic soprano; b. 1962, Budapest; d. of Ferenc Rost and Erzsébet Privoda. *Education:* Ferenc Liszt Acad. of Music, Budapest. *Career:* operatic debut as Juliette in Gounod's Romeo et Juliette, Budapest 1989; solo artist at Wiener Staatsoper 1991; La Scala debut as Gilda in Rigoletto 1994; debut, Metropolitan Opera, New York as Adina in L'Elisir d'amore 1996; took part in Superconcert with José Carreras and Plácido Domingo, Budapest 1996; appeared as Elisabeth in Donizetti's opera, London 1997; debut, Tokyo Opera, as Violetta 1998; took part in concert in memory of Lehár with José Carreras and Plácido Domingo, Bad Ischl, Austria 1998; has also appeared at Staatsoper, Vienna, Salzburg Festival, Opéra Bastille, Paris, Royal Opera House, Covent Garden and Chicago Opera; Lammermoori Lucia debut, Munchen, Wigmore Hall recital, London, Valencia recital 2002; Traviata debut, Deutsche Oper, Berlin, Desdemona, Otello, Tokyo, Lammermoori Lucia premier, Covent Garden, London 2003, Gilda, Rigoletto, Metropolitan, New York 2004. *Recordings include:* Mozart – Le nozze di Figaro (Susanna) 1994, Mahler – Symphony No. 8 1995, Verdi – Rigoletto (Gilda) 1995, Mendelssohn – Elias (die Witwe/ein Engel) 1996, Andrea Rost – Le delizie dell'amor 1997, Gaetano Donizetti – Lucia Di Lammermoori (Lucia) 1998, A Tribute to Operetta 1999, Amore II 2000, Escape Through Opera 2001, Erkel: Bánk bán (Melinda) 2003, ...che cosa è amor... [Mozart Arias] 2004. *DVDvideos include:* Johann Strauss Gala 2000, Wolfgang Amadeus Mozart: Don Giovanni (Zerlina) 2000, A Verdi Gala from Berlin 2002, Erkel: Bánk bán (Melinda) (opera film) 2003. *Honours:* First Prize, Helsinki Competition 1989, Bartók Béla – Pásztory Ditta Award, Ferenc Liszt Artistic Merit of Honour 1997, Nat. Artistic Merit of Honour 1999, Medal Obersovszky, Prima Primissima Award 2003, Kossuth Prize 2004. *Current Management:* Theateragentur Dr Hilbert, attn z.Hd.: Christine Sienel, Maximilianstrasse 22, 80539 Munich, Germany. *Telephone:* (89) 290747-0. *Fax:* (89) 290747-90. *E-mail:* agentur@hilbert.de. *Website:* www.hilbert.de. *Address:* c/o Katalin Zsigo, Pf. 190, 1276 Budapest (office); Nefelejes u. 27, 2040 Budaörs, Hungary (home). *Fax:* (23) 416-583 (home). *E-mail:* info@andrearost.com (home). *Website:* www.andrearost.com (home).

**ROSTROPOVICH, Mstislav Leopoldovich;** Russian cellist, conductor and pianist; b. 27 March 1927, Baku, Azerbaijan; s. of Leopold Rostropovich and Sofia Fedotova; m. Galina Vishnevskaya (q.v.) 1955; two d. *Education:* Moscow Conservatoire. *Career:* cello début (USSR) 1940; numerous concert tours in USSR and abroad as soloist and cellist in trio with Emil Gilels and Leonid Kogan and later with David Oistrakh and Sviatoslav Richter and as pianist with Galina Vishnevskaya; début in USA as cellist 1955, as conductor 1975; Music Dir Nat. Symphony Orchestra (Washington, DC) 1977–94; Conductor Laureate 1991–; expelled from Soviet Union 1974, deprived of Soviet citizenship 1978, citizenship restored 1990; Joint Artistic Dir Aldeburgh Festival (UK) 1977–; Founder and Pres. Rencontres Musicales d'Evian festival (France); mem. Union of Soviet Composers 1950–78, 1989–; Prof. Moscow and Leningrad Conservatoires 1960–78; among composers who have written works for him are Prokofiev, Shostakovich, Miaskovsky, Khachaturian, Kabalevsky, Britten, Piston, Shchedrin, Schnittke, Bernstein, Penderecki; f. Int. Competition for Young Cellists. *Honours:* Hon. mem. Acad. of St Cecilia (Rome), Guildhall School of Music and Drama 1991, AAAS; Hon. FRAM; Commdr, Ordre des Arts et des Lettres, Légion d'honneur; Hon. KBE 1987; Hon. DMus (Oxford) 1980; hon. degrees (including Humanities, Law, Letters, Music) from over 20 univs; First Prize at All-Union Competition of Musicians 1945, Int.'Cellist Competitions, Prague 1947, 1950, Budapest 1949, USSR State Prize 1951, People's Artist of the USSR, Lenin Prize 1964, Gold Medal, Royal Philharmonic Soc. (UK), Siemens Prize (FRG), Sonning Prize (Denmark), Albert Schweitzer Music Award 1985, Presidential Medal of Freedom 1987, Four Freedoms Award 1992, Kennedy Center Honor 1992, Freedom of Speech and Expression Award (Franklin Delano Roosevelt) 1992, Imperial Award 1993, Wolf Foundation Prize in Arts, 2004. *Address:* c/o National Symphony Orchestra, John F. Kennedy Center for the Performing Arts, Washington, DC 20566, USA; Gazetny per. 13, Apt 79, 103009 Moscow, Russia. *Telephone:* (095) 229-04-96 (Moscow) (home); 1-45-53-69-16 (Paris) (home); (202) 785-8100 (USA).

**ROTH, Daniel;** French organist and composer; *Organist, Église Saint-Sulpice, Paris; Professor of Organ, Musikhochschüle, Frankfurt-am-Main;* b. 31 Oct. 1942, Mulhouse; m. Odile Mangin 1968; one d. three s. *Education:* Paris Conservatoire with Maurice Duruflé, Rolande Falcinelli, Henriette Puig-Roget and Marcel Bitsch, also studied with Marie-Claire Alain. *Career:* organist at Sacre-Coeur, Paris 1963–85, Église Saint-Sulpice 1985–; Prof. of Organ, Marseille Conservatoire 1973–79, later at Strasbourg Conservatoire; Visiting Prof., Summer Acad. at Haarlem, Netherlands; Prof., Catholic Univ. 1974–76; resident artist, Nat. Shrine, Washington, DC 1974–76; Prof., Saarbrücken Musikhochschule 1988; Prof. of Organ, Musikhochschule, Frankfurt am Main 1995–. *Compositions include:* several works for organ published by Leduc, Bärenreiter, Schott (Mainz), Novello, and for flute and organ, choir and organ (Missa Brevis) published by Schott. *Recordings include:* works by Bach, Liszt, Franck, Guilmant, Boëly, Saint-Saëns, Widor, Vierne, Dupré and Jolivet. *Honours:* Hon. Fellow Royal Coll. of Organists; Officier des Arts et Lettres; Acad. des Beaux Arts (Institut de France) Florent Schmitt Prize for composition 2000. *Current Management:* Denny Lyster Artists Management. *E-mail:* dennylyster@dennylyster.free-online.co.uk. *Address:* Église Saint Sulpice, 75006 Paris, France. *Website:* www.danielrothsaintsulpice.org.

**ROTH, David (Robert),** LRAM, ARAM, MMus, DMus; British violinist; b. 9 March 1936, Stockton-on-Tees, Co. Durham, England; m. Ruth Elaine West 1963; two s. *Education:* Univ. of Edinburgh, Royal Acad. of Music. *Career:* debut at West Linton, Peebles, Scotland 1954; with Netherlands Chamber Orchestra, Amsterdam 1960–64; played Bloch Sonata No. 1, Kol Israel Radio, Tel-Aviv 1962; Deputy Leader Northern Sinfonia Orchestra, Newcastle upon Tyne 1966–68; Second Violin, Allegri String Quartet 1969–99; teaching at Univ. of Southampton; mem. Incorporated Soc. of Musicians, Musicians' Union. *Recordings:* with Allegri String Quartet for Open Univ.; many recordings for various labels. *Address:* 16 Oman Avenue, London, NW2 6BG, England (home).

**ROTHENBERGER, Anneliese;** German opera singer (soprano) and painter; b. 19 June 1926, Mannheim; d. of Josef Rothenberger and Sophie Häffner; m. Gerd W. Dieberitz 1954 (deceased). *Education:* Real- und Musikhochschule, Mannheim. *Career:* debut, Coblenz Theatre 1947; with State Opera Hamburg, Munich, Vienna 1958–70; guest singer at La Scala, Milan, Metropolitan Opera, New York and Salzburg, Glyndebourne and Munich Festivals, etc.; TV Special 1969–; several exhbns as painter, Germany and Switzerland; recital tours to Russia, Japan, Iceland, Germany and USA. *Exhibitions include:* Haus Engelhardt, Mannheim, Alte Schule CH-8268 Salenstein, Schloss Mainan. *Films:* Oh, Rosalinda 1955, Der Rosenkavalier 1960. *Television:* many appearances on Zweites Deutsches Fernsehen. *Publication:* Melody of My Life 1973. *Honours:* Distinguished Service Cross 1st Class, Great Cross. *Address:* Quellenhof, 8268 Salenstein am Untersee, Switzerland.

**ROTZSCH, Hans-Joachim;** Singer (Tenor); b. 25 April 1929, Leipzig, Germany; Educator. *Education:* Institute for Church Music at the Musikhochschule Leipzig, 1949–53; Organ study with Gunter Ramin; Vocal studies with P Losse and P Polster in Leipzig. *Career:* Many concerts and recordings of sacred music in Germany, Switzerland, Austria, Poland, Russia and Czechoslovakia; Appearances at the Leipzig Opera from 1961 and Kantor at St Thomas's School, Leipzig, from 1972; President of the Bach Committee, East Germany, 1983. *Recordings:* Bach Cantatas; St Luke Passion by Schütz; Dessau's Das Verhör des Lukullus; Mendelssohn's Elijah.

**ROUILLON, Philippe;** Singer (Baritone); b. 1955, Paris, France. *Education:* Studied at the Conservatoire National Supérieur de Paris; Ecole d'Art Lyrique de l'Opéra de Paris. *Career:* Performed Golaud in Pelléas et Mélisande and High Priest of Dagon in Samson et Dalila, Vienna; Chorèbe in Les Troyens, Ruprecht in The Fiery Angel, Orest in Elektra, Renato in Un Ballo in Maschera, the High Priest of Dagon, The High Priest in Alceste and Thoas in Iphigénie en Tauride in Paris; Ruprecht, High Priest of Dagon, Gellner in La Wally and Escamillo in Carmen at Amsterdam; Jochanaan in Salome, Lisbon and Strasbourg; Guillaume Tell in Liège; Samson et Dalila and Les Contes d'Hoffmann in Zürich; Frequent appearances in Germany in a variety of leading baritone roles; Close collaborations with Festival of Bregenz, Austria; Further engagements include: Rigoletto in Leipzig, Tel-Aviv and Hamburg, Pagliacci in Hamburg, Macbeth and Guillaume Tell in Liège, Tosca in Amsterdam and Ballo in Maschera in Bregenz; Season 2000–01 as Macbeth at the Munich Staatsoper, Thaos in Iphigénie en Tauride at Salzburg and Scarpia for Bonn Opera. *Recordings include:* Thaïs by Massenet; Saint François d'Assise by Messiaen with Kent Nagano; Chant de Paix by Landowski; Henry VIII by Saint-Saëns; Le Déluge by Saint-Saëns; Lélio and La Damnation de Faust by Berlioz. *Honours:* First Place, Prix Opéra and Prix de Public, international competition in Verviers, 1979; First Prize, Rio de Janeiro Competition, 1983.

**ROULEAU, Joseph-Alfred,** OC; Canadian singer (bass); *President, Jeunesses Musicales du Canada;* b. 28 Feb. 1929, Matane, QC; s. of Joseph-Alfred Rouleau and Florence Bouchard; m. 1st Barbara Whittaker 1952; one d.; m. 2nd Jill Renée Moreau; one s. one d. *Education:* Coll. Jean de Brebeuf, Montreal, Univ. of Montreal, Conservatoire of Music, Province of Québec. *Career:* debut at Montréal Opera Guild in Un Ballo in Maschera 1951; Royal Opera House, Covent Garden 1957–87, singing over 40 roles; guest artist at prin. opera houses all over the world; tours of Canada 1960, Australia (with Joan Sutherland) 1965, Russia 1966, 1969, Romania, S Africa 1974, 1975, 1976; Paris Opera 1975, Metropolitan Opera, New York 1984, 1985, 1986, San Francisco 1986, 1987; roles include Boris Godunov (Boris Godunov), Philip II and Inquisitore (Don Carlos), Basilio (Barber of Seville), Mephistopheles (Faust), Dosifei (Khovanshchina), Don Quixote (Don Quixote), Ramfis (Aida), Prince Gremin (Onegin), Father Lawrence (Roméo et Juliette), Colline (La Bohème), Raimondo (Lucia di Lammermoor), Titurel (Parsifal), Abimelech (Samson et Dalila), Crespel (Contes d'Hoffmann), Arkel (Pelléas et Mélisande), Sarastro, Osmin (Die Entführung), Daland (Der fliegende Holländer), Oroveso (Norma), Don Marco (The Saint of Bleecker Street), Trulove (The Rake's Progress), The Prince (Adriana Lecouvreur), Bartolo; Prof. of Voice, Univ. of Québec 1980–98, mem. Admin. Bd, Prof. Emeritus 2004–; mem. Bd

Corpn of Montreal Opéra Co. 1980–; Pres., Jeunesses Musicales du Canada 1989– (Prix Joseph Rouleau for Vocal Art named after him 1995); founder and mem. of bd Concours Musical Int. de Montréal 2002–. *Recordings include:* scenes from Anna Bolena, Ruddigore, Roméo et Juliette (Gounod), L'Enfance du Christ (Berlioz), Sémiramide, Lucia di Lammermoor, Don Carlos, Aida, Il Trovatore, Renard (Stravinsky), F. Leclerc's Songs, Les habitués du rêve de Jacques Hêtu (song cycle), French operatic arias (with Royal Opera House Orchestra), Boris Godunov (Prix Félix 2000). *Honours:* Dr hc (Québec à Rimouski); Prix Archambault 1967, La Société St Jean Baptiste Prix Calixa-Lavallée, Montreal 1967, Royal Opera House, Covent Garden Silver Medal 1983, Felix Award for Best Classical Artist of the Year 1989, Prix du Québec pour les Arts d'interprétation 1990, Panthéon de l'art lyrique du Canada 1992, Jeunesses Musicales du Canada Médaille du mérite exceptionnel 1995, Conseil québecois de la musique Prix Opus Hommage 2003, Prix du Gov. Gen. de Canada 2004, Opéra Canada Prix Ruby 2003; Officier, Ordre du Canada 1977, Grand Officier, Ordre Nat. du Québec 2004. *Address:* c/o Jeunesses Musicales, 305 avenue du Mont-Royal Est, Montréal, PQ H2T 1P8 (office); 7 Roosevelt, Suite 20, Ville Mont-Royal, PQ H3R 1Z3, Canada (home). *Telephone:* (514) 739-3238 (home); (819) 688-3676 (home); (514) 845-4108 (office). *Fax:* (514) 739-9135 (home); (514) 845-8241 (office). *E-mail:* reuee_rouleau@hotmail.com (home). *Website:* www.jeunessesmusicales.com.

**ROUSE, Christopher (Chapman);** Composer; b. 15 Feb. 1949, Baltimore, Maryland, USA; m. Ann Jensen, 28 Aug 1983, 1 s., 2 d. *Education:* BMus, Oberlin Conservatory, 1971; Private study with George Crumb, 1971–73; MFA, DMA, Cornell University, 1977. *Career:* Assistant Professor, University of Michigan, 1978–81; Assistant Professor, 1981–85, Associate Professor, 1985–91, Professor, 1991–, Eastman School of Music; Composer-in-Residence, Indianapolis Symphony Orchestra, 1985–86; Composer-in-Residence, Baltimore Symphony Orchestra, 1986–88. *Compositions:* Ogoun Badagris, 1976; Ku-Ka-Ilimoku, 1978; Mitternachtslieder, 1979; Liber Daemonum, 1980; The Infernal Machine, 1981; String Quartet, 1982; Rotae Passionis, 1982; Lares Hercii, 1983; The Surma Ritornelli, 1983; Gorgon, 1984; Contrabass Concerto, 1985; Phantasmata, 1985; Phaethon, 1986; Symphony No. 1, 1986; Jagannath, 1987; String Quartet No. 2, 1988; Bonham, 1988; Iscariot, 1989; Concerto per corde, 1990; Karolju, 1990; Violin Concerto, 1991; Trombone Concerto, 1991; Violoncello Concerto, 1992; Flute Concerto, 1993; Symphony No. 2, 1994; Envoi, 1995; Compline, 1996; Guitar Concerto, 1999. *Honours:* Friedheim Award, Kennedy Center, 1988; Guggenheim Fellowship, 1990; Academy of of Arts and Letters Award, 1993; Pulitzer Prize, 1993.

**ROUSSET, Christophe;** French harpsichordist and conductor; b. 12 April 1961, Avignon. *Education:* studied with Huguette Dreyfus, Kenneth Gilbert, Bob van Asperen and Gustav Leonhardt, chamber music with the brothers Kuijken and Lucy van Dael. *Career:* frequent solo appearances in France and throughout Europe; concertos with La Petite Bande, Musica Antiqua Köln, Acad. of Ancient Music; Asst for Les Arts Florissants; collaborations with artists, including William Christie, Agnès Mellon, Wieland Kuijken and Christopher Hogwood; conducts Les Arts Florissants, Il Seminario Musicale and other ensembles; founded Les Talens Lyriques (title from Rameau's Les Fêtes d'Hébé) 1991–, giving many performances of Baroque Opera; revival of Handel's Riccardo Primo at Fontevraud, France 1995; Handel's Admeto at Beaune and Montpellier and in Australia 1998; Wigmore Hall concerts 1999; Mozart's Mitridate at Le Châtelet, Paris 2000; Cavalli's La Didone, Lausanne 2000; Monteverdi's l'Incoronazione di Poppea, Amsterdam 2002; V. Martin y Soler's La Capricciosa Corretta, Lausanne 2003; Lulli's Roland, Lausanne 2004; Mozart's Entführung aus dem Serail 2005; Salieri's La Grotta di Trofonio 2005; Handel's Alcina and Tamerlano, Drottningholm 2000, 2002, 2005, Rameau's Zoroastre at Drottningholm 2005. *Recordings include:* Harpsichord Music by Bach, Rameau and Gaspard le Roux, Handel's Scipione and Riccardo Primo, Jommelli's Armida Abbandonata, Les Fêtes de Paphos by Mondonville, Mozart's Mitridate, Antigona by Traetta, complete keyboard works of Couperin, Rameau Overtures, Lulli's Persée, Lulli's Roland complete keyboard works of D'Anglebert, Handel Arias, Baroque Zarzuelas, Miserere by Leo, complete keyboard works of Forqueray. *Honours:* Officier, Ordre des Arts et des Lettres, Chevalier, Ordre Nationale du Mérite; first prize Bruges Competition 1983, Gramophone Award 1998, Académie Charles Cros Grand Prix du Disque 2004. *Address:* c/o Lorraine Villermaux, Les Talens Lyriques, 11 passage de la Boule Blanche, 750128 Paris; 30 rue du Dragon, 75006 Paris, France (home). *Telephone:* 1-53-46-64-64 (office). *Fax:* 1-53-46-64-69 (office). *E-mail:* contact@lestalenslyriques.com (office). *Website:* www .lestalenslyriques.com (office).

**ROUTH, Francis John,** BA, MA, ARAM, FRCO; British composer, pianist and writer; b. 15 Jan. 1927, Kidderminster, England; m. 1st Virginia Anne Raphael 1956; m. 2nd Diana Florence Elizabeth Cardell Oliver 1991; two s. two d. *Education:* King's Coll., Cambridge, Royal Acad. of Music, studied with Matyas Seiber. *Career:* appeared as pianist, occasionally conducted in London and elsewhere, South Bank, radio broadcasts; founder and Dir Redcliffe Concerts 1963–64; Ed., Composer 1980–88; Dir British Musical Heritage 2000–. *Compositions:* A Sacred Tetralogy 1959–74, Dialogue for violin and orchestra 1968, Double Concerto 1970, Sonata for solo cello 1971, Spring Night 1971, Symphony I 1972, Cello Concerto 1973, Mosaics 1976, Oboe Quartet 1977, Fantasy for violin and pianoforte 1978, Scenes for orchestra 1978, Vocalise 1979, Concerto for ensemble I 1982, Concerto for ensemble II 1983, Tragic Interludes for oboe 1984, Celebration for piano 1984, Elegy for piano 1986, Oboe Concerto 1986, Poème Fantastique for piano and orchestra

1986–88, Four Marian Antiphons for organ 1988, Romance 1989, Woefully Arranyed for soloists, choir and orchestra 1990, Fantasy Duo for violin and piano 1990, Romanian Dance 1990, Concerto for ensemble III 1991, Suite for string orchestra 1992, Clarinet Quintet 1994, Capriccio 1995, Scenes for orchestra II 1997, Triumphal March 1997, Suite for Tbilisi concerto for ensemble IV 1997, Divertimento for string quartet 1998, Angels of Albion scenes for piano III 1998, Bretagne scenes for piano IV 1998, Sonata Festiva scenes for piano V 1999, Agnus Dei 2002, Symphonic Variations 2003, Symphony II 2004. *Recordings:* A Sacred Tetralogy (organ Christopher Bowers-Broadbent) 1984, Celebration, Elegy (piano Jeffrey Jacob) 1986, Oboe Quartet, Tragic Interlude (oboe Robin Canter with Redcliffe Ensemble) 1992, A Woman Young and Old (soprano Margaret Field) 1995, Clarinet Quintet (clarinet Nicholas Cox with Redcliffe Ensemble) 1995, On a Deserted Shore 1996, Four Marian Antiphons, Exultet Coelum Laudibus 1998, Divertimento for string quartet (Bochmann Quartet) 1998, Scenes for piano III and IV 1999, Symphonic Variations 2003. *Publications:* The Organ 1958, Contemporary Music 1968, The Patronage and Presentation of Contemporary Music 1970, Contemporary British Music 1972, Early English Organ Music 1973, Stravinsky 1974; contrib. to various journals and The Annual Register 1980–. *Address:* 68 Barrowgate Road, Chiswick, London, W4 4QU, England (office). *Telephone:* (20) 8995-1223 (office). *Fax:* (20) 8995-1223 (office). *E-mail:* redcliffe@frouth.freeserve.co.uk (office). *Website:* www.redcliffe-edition.com (office).

**ROUTLEY, Nicholas;** Conductor, Composer and University Lecturer; b. 26 June 1947, England; m. Margo Adelson, m. 26 May 1982, 1 s., 2 d. *Education:* George Heriot's, Edinburgh; St John's College, Cambridge; Piano studies with Peter Feuchtwanger; Conducting with Hans Heimler, Franco Ferrara. *Career:* Debut: Pianist, Wigmore Hall, 1979; Conductor, Taiwan Symphony Orchestra, 1984; University of Cambridge, 1973–75; University of Sydney, 1975–; University of Hong Kong, 1982–85, 1990–93; mem, Musicological Society of Australia. *Compositions:* Sicut Lilium, for choir and vibraphone, 1996; Sanctus, for choir and percussion, 1996; Like Snow, 5 songs for voice and piano, 1997; Icarus For Orchestra, 1997; Mycenae Lookout for baritone solo, choir, 2 pianos and percussion, 1998. *Recordings:* The Hermit of Green Light (Australian vocal music), 1983; Monteverdi Vespers of 1610, 1989; Josquin, 1994; Clare MacLean, The Complete Choral Music, 1995; Josquin, Secular Music, 1996. *Publications:* A Practical Guide to Musica Ficta, 1985; Arianna Thrice Betrayed (Gordon Athol Anderson Memorial Lecture), 1998; Symphony, 2000. *Contributions:* 2 articles on Debussy's Preludes in Musicology Australia, 1992, 1993. *Address:* Department of Music, University of Sydney, NSW 2006, Australia.

**ROWLAND, Christopher (Selwyn);** Violinist, Teacher and Quartet Leader; b. 21 Dec. 1946, Barnet, Hertfordshire, England; m. Elizabeth Attwood, 18 Dec 1982, 1 s. *Education:* BA, MA, Trinity College, Cambridge, 1965–68; Associate, Royal Academy of Music, 1980; D.Mus, Bucknell University, PA, 1981. *Career:* Performed live on radio throughout the United Kingdom and Europe and regularly in North America; Supervisor of Chamber Music, Tutor in Violin, Royal Northern College of Music, Manchester; Violinist for contemporary music group, Lumina; Leader of Sartori Quartet, 1970–74 and Fitzwilliam Quartet, 1974–84, with tours to Russia in 1976 and 1978. *Recordings:* Many. *Publications:* Shostakovich–Man and Music, 1982. *Contributions:* Music Times; Soviet Music; Berlioz Bulletin. *Honours:* Numerous prizes at Royal Acadey of Music and Cambridge University; Grammy Awards and Grand Prix du Disque. *Address:* Fountain House, Low Street, Burton-in-Lonsdale, Via Carnforth, Lancashire, England.

**ROWLAND, Gilbert;** Harpsichordist and Organist; b. 8 Oct. 1946, Glasgow. *Education:* Harpsichord and Organ, Royal College of Music, 1965–69; Masterclasses, Dartington. *Career:* Debut: Wigmore Hall, 1973; Harpsichordist, Wigmore Hall, 1973, 1975; Harpsichordist, Purcell Room, 1979, 1982, 1983, 1985; Harpsichordist, Greenwich Festival, 1975–84; Berlin, 1985; Many recitals in North England; Radio performances at BBC Concert Halls, 1977–78; Broadcasts, French harpsichord Music, 1984; Scarlatti Sonatas, 1986; Soler Sonatas, 1983; mem, ARCO; ARCM. *Recordings:* Scarlatti Sonatas; Rameau keyboard works; Soler Sonatas; Complete Handel Suites, forthcoming. *Contributions:* Article on Scarlatti for NEMA, 1985. *Address:* 418 Brockley Road, Brockley, London SE4 2 DH, England.

**ROWLAND, Joan (Charlotte);** Pianist and Teacher; b. 7 May 1930, Toronto, Canada; m. John Michael Thornton, 5 May 1956, 3 s., 1 d. *Education:* BA, English, Columbia University, 1970; Piano study with Mona Bates in Toronto, 1938–48, theoretical studies at Royal Conservatory of Music, 1940–46 and piano study with Eduard Steuermann at Juilliard School, NY, 1952–56. *Career:* Debut: With the Toronto Symphony under Ernest MacMillan in 1942; Recital debut in New York in 1948; Solo recitals in Canada, USA and Europe and for Canadian Broadcasting Corporation since 1942; 2 Tours of USA and London with Columbia Canadian Trio and toured with Reginald Kell Players; Soloist for various orchestras including Toronto Symphony, Wiesbaden Orchestra, Mozarteum Orchestra, Mozart Festival Orchestra, and San Francisco and Buffalo Symphonies; Toured with Piano Duo Schnabel in USA and Europe, 1981–95. *Recordings:* Schubert Grand Duo and B flat Variations, Mozart Sonata in F major, Schubert E minor Sonata, Schubert Fantasy in F minor and Variations in A flat, all with Piano Duo Schnabel; Solo recording of Schumann Fantasy and Carnaval. *Publications:* Playing Four-Hands: A Pilgrim's Progress, The Piano Quarterly, 1986–87. *Honours:* 1st Prize, Kranichsteiner Modern Music Competition, Darmstadt, Germany, 1954; 1st

Prize, Mozarteum Piano Competition, Salzburg, 1955. *Address:* 285 Riverside Drive No. 4A, New York, NY 10025, USA.

**ROWLAND-JONES, (Simon) Christopher;** violist and composer; b. 8 Sept. 1950, Colchester, England. *Education:* Royal College of Music. *Career:* debut Carnegie Hall, 1979; Chilingirian String Quartet, 1971–78, 1992–; Nash Ensemble, Villiers Piano Quartet; Chameleon; Arenski Ensemble; Professor and Chamber Music Co-ordinator, Royal College of Music; mem, Musicians Union; Performing Right Society. *Compositions:* 2 String Quartets; Piano Quartet; String Trio; Rivers Gods; Seven pieces for Solo Viola; String Quintet (Painting by Numbers), 1998. *Recordings include:* Dale, Phantasy and Suite; Bloch, Suites; Schubert, Schumann and Beethoven; Bach Solo Cello Suites, vol. 1, suites 1–3, after own edition/transcription. *Publications:* Transcription of Bach Cello Suites, 1998. *Address:* 77 The Vineyard, Richmond, Surrey TW10 6AS, England.

**ROWLANDS, Carol;** British singer (mezzo-soprano); b. 1951, Newcastle upon Tyne, England; d. of Edward Rowlands and Roma Rowlands. *Education:* Univ. of Hull, Royal Northern Coll. of Music with Andrew Field and Peter Alexander Wilson. *Career:* appeared with Scottish Opera 1982–90 in L'Egisto, The Magic Flute, Le nozze di Figaro, Rigoletto, Il Trovatore, Lulu, Madama Butterfly and Salome; has also understudied Mozart's Cherubino, Puck in Oberon, Wellgunde in Das Rheingold, Clairon in Capriccio, Judith in Bluebeard's Castle 1990, and Didon in Berlioz's The Trojans for Scottish Opera; performed Santuzza in Scottish Opera Go Round's autumn tour of Pagliacci and Cavalleria Rusticana 1989; for Univ. Coll. sang Tigrana in Edgar by Puccini; also performed the title role of Regina by Blitzstein for Scottish Opera, Santuzza in Cavalleria Rusticana for Opera South, the Mother in Amahl and the Night Visitors for Opera West, Suzuki in Madama Butterfly at Isle of Man, and concert performances in the title role of Orfeo with John Currie Singers; season 1992–93 as Cherubino in Marriage of Figaro in Malta, Waltraute in Die Walküre for Scottish Opera, Marcellina in Marriage of Figaro for Scottish Opera, Second Lady in The Magic Flute for Scottish Opera, Marcellina in Opera Factory and the title role in Carmen for Regency Opera; sang Mrs Grose in The Turn of the Screw for Broomhill Opera 1996; Birtwistle's Judy for Theatre Wales at Queen Elizabeth Hall, London 1998; Judy in Punch and Judy for Music Theatre Wales 1998; Mother Jeanne in Les Dialogues des Carmelites for Welsh Nat. Opera 1999; Baba the Turk in The Rake's Progress for English Touring Opera 2000; Throttlethumper in The Wondrous Tale of Fanferlizzy Sunnyfeet by Schwertsik for Broomhill Opera 2001; Berta in The Barber of Seville, Holland Park 2001; Tisbe in La Cenerentola for Opera Northern Ireland; Mrs Grose in The Turn of The Screw for Broomhill Opera 2001 and Nationale Reisopera, Netherlands 2002; Suzuki in Madama Butterfly for London City Opera US tour 2003; Despina in Così fan tutte for Longborough Opera 2003; Mrs Sedley in Peter Grimes for Nationale Reisopera, Netherlands 2004. *Honours:* John Scott Award for contrib. to Scottish opera 1989. *Address:* Flat A, 3 The Boundary, Seaford, East Sussex BN25 1DG, England (office). *Telephone:* (1323) 491082 (office). *E-mail:* carol@carolrowlands.com (office). *Website:* www.carolrowlands.com (office); www.impetuousportraits.com.

**ROXBURGH, Edwin;** Conductor, Composer and Oboist; b. 6 Oct. 1937, Liverpool, England. *Education:* RCM 1957–60, with Herbert Howells and Terence McDonagh; Further study with Nadia Boulanger and Luigi Dallapiccola and at St John's College, Cambridge. *Career:* Principal oboe of Sadler's Wells Opera, 1964–67, and soloist in contemporary music (Berio's Sequenza VII); Teacher of composition at RCM, 1968–; Founded 20th Century Ensemble of London, 1969. *Compositions include:* Night Music for soprano and orchestra, 1969; How Pleasant to Know Mr. Lear, for narrator and chamber orchestra, 1971; A Mosaic for Cummings, for 2 narrators and orchestra; Montage for orchestra, 1977; At the Still Point of the Turning World for amplified oboe and electronics, 1978; Voyager, for wind instruments, 1989. *Honours:* Cobbett Medal, 1970. *Address:* British Music Information Centre, 11 Stratford Place, London W1, England.

**ROZARIO, Patricia;** singer (soprano); b. 1960, Bombay, India; m. Mark Troop; one d. *Education:* Guildhall School of Music. *Career:* concerts with Songmakers' Almanac, including tour to USA; solo recitals, South Bank, London and elsewhere; frequent performances of Bach, Handel, Mozart; Vaughan Williams' Serenade to Music, BBC Proms 1988; Schumann's Paradies und der Peri, Madrid with Gerd Albrecht; appearances at Bath and Edin. Festivals; season 1993–94 included Wexford Festival appearance, tour of Germany with BBC Nat. Orchestra of Wales/Otaka, Hong Kong Philharmonic, world premiere of Taverner's Apocalypse, BBC Proms; season 1994–95 included recital in Lebanon, Purcell Room with Nash Ensemble; sang Les illuminations at St John's Smith Square, London 1997; performed in Handel's Triumph of Time and Truth, BBC Proms 1999. *Operatic roles include:* Giulietta (Jommelli's La schiava liberata) for Netherlands Opera, Gluck's Euridice for Opera North, Mozart's Bastienne and Pamina for Kent Opera, Ilia on Glyndebourne tour, Ismene in Lyon production of Mithridate and Zerlina at Aix, Statue in Rameau's Pygmalion and Purcell's Belinda for Kent Opera; Florinda in Handel's Rodrigo at Innsbruck, Nero in L'incoronazione di Poppea and Massenet's Sophie; concert performance of Il re pastore, Queen Elizabeth Hall, London, world premiere of John Casken's Golem, as Miriam, Almeida Festival, London, Ismene at Wexford Festival 1989, cr. title role in premiere of Taverner's Mary of Egypt, Aldeburgh Festival 1992, season 1992–93 in Monteverdi's Il combattimento, ENO and Haydn's L'infedeltà delusa, Garsington Opera, Romilda in Serse, Brussels

1996. *Recordings include:* Mahler Symphony No. 4, London Symphony Orchestra, Songs of the Auvergne with John Pritchard (conductor), Haydn Stabat Mater with Trevor Pinnock (conductor), Golem (Gramophone Award 1991), Taverner: We Shall See Him As He Is, Mary of Egypt, To a Child Dancing in the Wind; Spanish Songs, Britten's Rape of Lucretia. *Honours:* British Song Prize, Barcelona, Maggie Teyte Prize, Sängerforderungspreis, Salzburg Mozarteum, Guildhall School of Music Gold Medal, Asian Women of Achievement Arts and Culture Award 2002. *Current Management:* Stafford Law, Candleway, Broad Street, Sutton Valence, Kent ME17 3AT, England. *Website:* www.stafford-law.com.

**ROZE, Jeanine Michèle;** French music promoter; b. 19 Aug. 1943, Aurillac (Cantal); d. of Henri Roze and Chana Roze (née Bernholc). *Education:* Lycée Lamartine, Paris, Univ. of Paris-IV Sorbonne. *Career:* Publicity Ed. Maillard agency 1962–63, Artistic Sec. 1964–75; artistic agent 1975–88; promoter of concerts etc. 1998–; creator and organizer Sunday morning concerts at Théâtre de Châtelet 1975, of Alban Berg quartet 1988–, of piano on the Champs-Elysées 1991–, at Théâtre de Champs-Elysées, in La Comédie des Champs-Elysées, of recitals by Jessye Norman at Pleyel 1990, 1991. *Publications include:* Schubert, album de famille (co-ed.) 1992, Musique en têtes (series of 16 musical post cards, ed.) 1992. *Honours:* Chevalier, Ordre des Arts et des Lettres. *Address:* 17 rue du Colisée, 75008 Paris, France. *Website:* www.jeanine-roze-production.com.

**ROZHDESTVENSKY, Gennadiy Nikolayevich;** Russian conductor; b. 4 May 1931, Moscow; s. of Nikolai Anosov and Natalia Rozhdestvenskaya; m. Viktoria Postnikova; one s. *Education:* Moscow State Conservatoire. *Career:* Asst Conductor, Bolshoi Theatre 1951, Conductor 1956–60, Prin. Conductor 1965–70, Artistic Dir 2000–01; Chief Conductor of USSR Radio and TV Symphony Orchestra 1961–74; Chief Conductor Stockholm Philharmonia 1974–77, 1992–95, Moscow Chamber Opera 1974–83; Founder, Artistic Dir, Chief Conductor, State Symphony Orchestra of Ministry of Culture 1983–92; Prin. Conductor BBC Symphony Orchestra 1978–82, Vienna Symphony Orchestra 1980–83; has been guest conductor of numerous orchestras throughout Europe, America and Asia; Prof. of Conducting, Moscow State Conservatoire 1965–. *Publications:* The Fingering of Conducting 1974, Thoughts about Music 1975; numerous articles. *Honours:* Hon. mem. Swedish Royal Acad. 1975; People's Artist of the RSFSR 1966, People's Artist of the USSR 1976, Hero of Socialist Labour 1991, Lenin Prize 1970 and other awards. *Address:* c/o Victor Hochhauser Ltd, 4 Oak Hill Way, London N.W.3, England. *Telephone:* (095) 299-58-71 (Moscow) (home).

**ROZSA, Pál;** Composer; b. 14 March 1946, Szombathely, Hungary; m. Éva Molnár, 28 Jan 1977, 2 d. *Education:* Chemical Engineering, Moscow State University; Private tuition, Composition, Sándor Szokolay and Zsolt Durkó. *Career:* Works performed in France, Italy, Germany, Sweden, Denmark, Poland, Austria, the United Kingdom, Canada, USA, South Africa, Hong Kong; Many works commissioned by renowned musicians; mem, Hungarian Composers Union, 1984–; Hungarian Music Society, 1990–. *Compositions:* Around 400 works including symphonic works, concertos, 5 operas, 7 string quartets, wind quintets, brass music, songs, oratorios and cantatas, church music, wind band, transcriptions of classical works. *Recordings:* 4 records; Many recordings for Hungarian Radio; 1 opera recorded by Hungarian Television. *Honours:* 15 works awarded 1st, 2nd or 3rd prizes at international or national composers competitions. *Address:* Zsókavár u.2 XI/50, Budapest XV, 1157, Hungary. *Telephone:* (36) 1418-4547. *E-mail:* erozsa@office.mta.hu.

**RUBENACKER, Jutta;** German violinist; *Professor of Violin, Hochschule für Musik und Theater, Hannover;* b. 25 May 1955, Karlsruhe, Germany; one s. *Education:* violin lessons and masterclasses. *Career:* mem., Bartholdy Quartet, Ensemble Neublang, Art Ensemble, Das Neue Ensemble, Rubernadzer Quartet, Duo Parlando; solo violist of the Sudwestdeubahe Kammer Orchester, Chamber Orchestra of Southwest Germany; concerts as soloist and chamber music, played mainly in Europe; masterclasses in Norway; many performances with Tatjana Prelevic, Xaver Thoma, David Wilde, Johannes Schollhorn, Stefan Schleiermacher, Tatjana Kumarova, Yougi Pagh-Pan, Sofia Gubaiduluia, Wolfgang Rihm; Prof. of Violin, Hochschule für Musik und Theater, Hannover 1993–. *Honours:* Hessischer Rundjunk-Preis 1974, Art and Promotion for music, Nieder, Sadisen 1998. *Address:* Helmstedter Str 1, 30519 Hannover, Germany.

**RUBENS, Sibylla;** Singer (Soprano); b. 1970, Germany. *Education:* Studied at Trossingen and Frankfurt Musikhochschule; Further study with Elise Cavelti in Basle. *Career:* Frequent Concerts with Helmuth Rilling and Bachakademie Stuttgart, including Tour of Japan, 1995 with Mozart's C Minor Mass; Bach's St John Passion under Rilling and Philippe Herreweghe, 1996; Deutsche Symphony Orchestra Berlin under Ashkenazy and Janowski, in Mendelssohn's Lobesgesang and Schumann's Scenes from Faust; Season 1997–98 with the Fauré Requiem and Poulenc's Stabat Mater at the Concertgebouw, Amsterdam, Ein Deutsches Requiem in Stuttgart and a tour of Messiah with the Windsbache Knabenchor; St John Passion under Ton Koopman, The Creation with Michael Schonwandt and tour with the group Tafelmusik; Other engagements in Italy, France, Czech Republic, Poland and Norway; Opera includes Mozart's Pamina and Beethoven's Marzelline. *Recordings include:* Schubert's Lazarus, arranged by Denisov (Hänssler); Mozart's Requiem (Harmonia Mundi). *Address:* Kunstler Sekretariat am Gasteig, Rosenheimerstrasse 52, 81699 Munich, Germany.

**RUBIN, Cristina;** singer (soprano); b. 1958, Milan, Italy. *Education:* Milan Conservatoire, opera school of La Scala. *Career:* debut at Bergamo in 1985 as Mimi; sang Anna in Puccini's Le Villi at Torre del Lago and Trieste; sang at Teatro Goldoni in Venice as Agata in Il Flamino by Pergolesi, Trieste in 1987 as Suzel in L'Amico Fritz, as Mimi at Zürich in 1986 and Mozart's Countess at Piacenza; concerts with Beethoven's Missa Solemnis, Schumann's Manfred and Mendelssohn's Lobesgesang Symphony.

**RUCKER, Mark;** Singer (Baritone); b. 1957, Chicago, USA. *Career:* Debut: Cincinnati, 1985, as Amonasro, in Aida; Philadelphia, 1986, as Verdi's Renato, New York City Opera, 1988, as Rigoletto; European debut at Nice, 1989, as Tonio in Pagliacci; Vienna Staatsoper, 1993, as Alfio in Cavalleria Rusticana; Verdi's Macbeth at New Orleans and Enrico in Lucia di Lammermoor for Portland Opera, 1994; Rigoletto for Milwaukee Opera, 1996; Season 2000 as Rigoletto at Miami and Amonasro in Amsterdam; Concerts include Messiah, Elijah and Donna nobis pacem by Vaughan Williams. *Recordings include:* Amonasro in Aida. *Honours:* Winner, Pavarotti Competition at Philadelphia, 1985. *Address:* Milwaukee Opera Company, 820 East Knapp St, Milwaukee, WI 53302, USA.

**RUDAKOVA, Larisa;** Singer (soprano); b. 1964, Russia. *Career:* Many performances in Russia and Eastern Europe in operas by Rossini (Il Barbiere di Siviglia), Donizetti (Lucia di Lammermoor), Charpentier (Louise) and Glinka (Ruslan and Lyudmila); Also sings Rossini's Bel raggio lusinghier (Semiramide); Contestant at the 1995 Cardiff Singer of the World Competition; Sang Antonida in Glinka's A Life for the Tsar, St Petersburg, 1998. *Current Management:* Askonas Holt Ltd, Lonsdale Chambers, 27 Chancery Lane, London, WC2A 1PF, England. *Telephone:* (20) 7400-1700. *Fax:* (20) 7400-1799. *E-mail:* info@askonasholt.co.uk. *Website:* www.askonasholt.co.uk.

**RUDEL, Julius;** Conductor; b. 6 March 1921, Vienna, Austria. *Education:* Vienna and Mannes School of Music in USA. *Career:* Rehearsal Pianist for New York City Opera; Conductor for Johann Strauss's The Gypsy Baron, NY, 1944, with overall command, 1957, and was responsible for many premieres of works by American and foreign composers, and for revivals of many neglected operas; Guest Conductor for La Scala Milan, Covent Garden, Teatro Colón in Buenos Aires, Vienna State Opera and the opera houses of Berlin, Munich, Paris and Hamburg; Conducted Rigoletto at the Metropolitan in 1989, Hamlet by Thomas at Chicago in 1990, and Der Rosenkavalier at Toronto in 1990; Season 1992 conducted La Bohème at Bonn, Don Carlo at Nice and Tosca at Buenos Aires; Conducted Faust at the Met, 1996; Die Zauberflöte for Los Angeles Opera, 1998. *Recordings include:* Julius Caesar by Handel; The Merry Widow by Lehar; Silverlake by Kurt Weill; Ginastera's Bomarzo; Works by Massenet, Donizetti, Offenbach, Verdi, Bellini, Boito and Charpentier; Many television recordings. *Honours:* Julius Rudel Award established in his honour for young conductors, 1969.

**RUDENKO, Bela Andreyevna;** Singer (soprano); b. 18 Aug. 1933, Bokovo-Antratsit, Ukraine, Russia. *Education:* Studied at the Odessa Conservatory with Olga Blagovidova. *Career:* Debut: Odessa in 1955 as Gilda in Rigoletto; Sang at Kiev from 1965 notably as Glinka's Ludmila, Rosina in Il Barbiere di Siviglia, Lakmé and Natasha in War and Peace; Bolshoi Theatre Moscow from 1972; Also successful in operas by Ukranian composers. *Recordings include:* Ruslan and Ludmila and A Life for The Tsar, by Glinka. *Honours:* State Prize of USSR. *Address:* c/o TG Shevchenko Theatre, Ul Vladimirskaya 50, Kiev, Ukraine.

**RUDERS, Poul;** Danish composer; b. 27 March 1949, Ringsted, Denmark; m. Annette Gerlach. *Education:* Royal Danish Music Acad. *Career:* performances with all major Danish symphony orchestras; performances by London Sinfonietta, Ensemble Intercontemporain, Speculum Musicae, New York Philharmonic, Philharmonia, Capricorn, Lontano; Psalmodies for Guitar and Ensemble, 1990, and frequent performances of works at several int. festivals; mem. Danish Composers' Guild, SPNM, England. *Compositions:* major orchestral pieces: Capriccio Pian e Forte 1978, Manhattan Abstraction 1982, Thus Saw St John 1984, The Drama Trilogy: Dramaphonia, Monodrama, Polydrama 1987–88, Himmelhoch-Jauchzend zum Tode betrübt, symphony 1989, Violin Concerto No. 2 1991, Gong for Orchestra 1992, Symphony No. 2 1997; chamber works: String Quartet No. 1 1971, No. 2 1979, Four Compositions 1980, Greeting Concertino 1982, 4 Dances in one movement 1983, Vox In Rama 1983, Concerto in Pieces (commissioned by BBC Symphony Orchestra) 1995, The Handmaid's Tale (opera commissioned by the Royal Theatre Copenhagen) 2000, Kafkas's Trial (opera with libretto by Paul Bentley, commissioned by The Royal Opera Co., Copenhagen) 2001–03, Listening Earth (commissioned by Berlin Philharmonic) 2002, Final Nightshade (commissioned by New York Philharmonic) 2003; numerous solo pieces for various instruments. *Recordings include:* Four Dances, with London Sinfonietta conducted by Oliver Knussen 1983–89, Corpus Cum Figuris, commissioned by Ensemble Intercontemporain 1984–90, Corpus Cum Figuris: Point PCD 5084, Violin Concerto No. 1 Unicorn-Kanchana, 9114, Psalmodies: Bridge 9037, Symphony: Chan 9179. *Honours:* Charles Heidsieck Prize, Royal Philharmonic Orchestra, London 1991. *Current Management:* c/o Chester Music, 14–15 Berners Street, London, W1T 3LJ, England. *E-mail:* poulmus.ruders@mail.tele.dk. *Website:* www.poulruders.net.

**RUDY, Mikhail;** Concert Pianist; b. 3 April 1953, Tashkent, USSR. *Education:* Moscow Conservatory with Jakov Flier. *Career:* After winning prizes at competitions in Leipzig and Paris he made his western debut in 1977, playing Beethoven's Triple Concerto in Paris with Rostropovich and Stern;

Guest appearances with the Berlin Philharmonic, Orchestre de Paris, Concertgebouw, Boston Symphony, Montreal Symphony Orchestra, London Philharmonic and Toronto Symphony; US debut 1981 with the Cleveland Orchestra conducted by Lorin Maazel; Festivals include Schleswig-Holstein, Berlin, Tanglewood, Lockenhaus and Vienna; Salzburg Easter Festival, 1987 with Karajan; Chamber music concerts with the Amadeus Quartet until 1987, Guarneri Quartet and Vienna Philharmonic Wind Ensemble; London debut with the London Symphony Orchestra under Michael Tilson Thomas, 1988; Promenade Concerts 1989, Prokofiev's 2nd Concerto; Subject of French television Documentary Le grand Echiquier, 1989; Debut with Dresden Staatskapelle, 1991; Season 1991–92 with concerts in Cleveland and Munich; Returned to Russia, 1990, concerts with the St Petersburg Philharmonic; Music Director, St Riquier Festival; Waldbühne Concert with Berlin Philharmonic and Mariss Jansons, 1994; Janáček, Stravinsky and Schubert concert at the Wigmore Hall, London, 1997. *Recordings include:* Brahms and Ravel recital (EMI); Concertos by Rachmaninov and Tchaikovsky with St Petersburg Philharmonic and Mariss Jansons; Shostakovich Piano Concerto No. 1 with Berlin Philharmonic; Stravinsky: integral of Petroushka ballet (Transcriptions: Stravinsky/Rudy); Wagner: Siegfried Idyll; 2 piano improvisations with jazz pianist Micha Alperin. *Honours:* Chevalier des Arts et des Lettres, Prizewinner, 1971 Bach Competition, Leipzig; First Prize, Marguérite Long Competition, Paris, 1975; Grand Prix du disque Liszt, Budapest; Grand Prix du Disque Acad. Charles Cros (Scribiane); Grand Prix, Acad. Française (Rachmaninov concerti with Mariss Jansons; Symanovski recital); Deutsche Schalplatte Kritik Preis (Shostokovich). *Current Management:* Harrison/Parrott Ltd, 12 Penzance Place, London, W11 4PA, England. *Telephone:* (20) 7229 9166. *Fax:* (20) 7221 5042. *Website:* www.harrisonparrott.com.

**RUDZINSKI, Zbigniew;** Composer; b. 23 Oct. 1935, Czechowice, Poland; m. Ewa Debska, 13 July 1965, 1 d. *Education:* Warsaw University, 1956; MA, Composition Diploma with distinction, State High School for Music, Warsaw, 1956–60. *Career:* Professor of Composition, 1973–, Head of Composition Department, 1980–81, Rector (director), 1981–84, Academy of Music, F Chopin, Warsaw; President, Warsaw District, Polish Composers' Union, 1983–85, Secretary General, 1985–. *Compositions include:* Orchestral: Sonata for 2 String Quartets, Piano and Kettle Drums, 1960, Contra Fidem, 1964, Moments Musicaux 1, 11, 111, 1965–68, Music By Night, 1970; Vocal/instrumental works: Four Folk Songs for soprano and piano, 1955; Sonata for clarinet and piano, 1958; Trio for 2 clarinets and bassoon, 1958; Epigrames for flute, choir and percussion, 1962; String Trio, 1964; Study for C for ensemble ad libitum, 1964; Impromptu for 2 pianos, 1968; Symphony for men's choir and orchestra, 1969; Requiem for the Victims of Wars for choir and orchestra, 1971; Tutti E Solo for soprano, flute, french horn and piano, 1973; Strings in the Earth for soprano and string orchestra, 1983; Three Romantic Portraits for 12 saxophones; Chamber: Quartet for 2 Pianos and Percussion, 1969, Sonata for Piano, 1975, Campanella for Percussion Ensemble, 1977, Tritones for Percussion Ensemble, 1979; Opera: The Mannequins, 1981, The Book Of Hours, songs for mezzo-soprano and piano trio, 1983, Das Sind Keine Träume, songs for mezzo-soprano and piano, 1986; Three Pictures at an Exhibition for flute, piano and vibraphone, 1996. *Address:* ul Poznanska 23m 26, 00-685 Warsaw, Poland.

**RUFFINI, Alessandra;** Singer (Soprano); b. 1961, Italy. *Education:* Studied at the Milan Conservatory. *Career:* Sang Arianna in Vivaldi's Giustino in 1985 and appeared as Gilda at Treviso and Rovigo in 1987; Sang at Vicenza in 1988 as Elena in Gluck's Paride e Helena, Palermo in 1991 as Mariana in Wagner's Das Liebesverbot, and at Rome Opera in 1992 as Rossini's Adina and Leila in Les Pêcheurs de Perles; Other roles include Amina in La Sonnambula (Cremona, 1988) and Adina in L'Elisir d'amore (Piacenza 1992); Sang Pauline in Donizetti's Les Martyrs, Nancy, 1996. *Recordings include:* Rosina in Morlacchi's Il Barbiere di Siviglia; La Locandiera by Salieri; La Cecchina by Piccinni. *Address:* Rome Opera, Teatro dell'Opera, Piazza B Gigli 8, 00184 Rome, Italy.

**RUFO, Bruno;** Singer (Tenor); b. 1941, Italy. *Career:* Debut: Spoleto in 1965 as Pinkerton; Many appearances at La Scala Milan, Rome, Naples and as Radames in 1981 at Verona Arena; Further engagements at Bologna, Parma, Hamburg, Munich, Vienna, the Deutsche Oper Berlin and Düsseldorf; Sang Manrico at Liège, and Samson in season 1986–87; Television appearances have included Verdi's Ernani. *Address:* c/o Opéra Royal de Wallonie, 1 Rue des Dominicains, 4000 Liège, Belgium.

**RUGGEBERG, Claudia;** Singer (Contralto); b. 1955, Hamburg, Germany. *Education:* Studied in Hamburg with Judith Beckmann. *Career:* Many appearances throughout Germany in concerts and recitals; Guest engagements at the Hamburg and Oldenburg Operas, Bregenz Festival, 1985–86 in Die Zauberflöte, and Gelsenkirchen and Stuttgart in 1987 in La Gioconda and Die Soldaten; Sang in Eugene Onegin at Zürich in 1991 and has appeared elsewhere including Barcelona, Bologna, Cologne and Krefeld; Has sung mainly in opera houses of Hamburg, Bonn, Cologne, Stuttgart, Aalto-Theater Essen; Ring Production (Erda), Dessau, Die Verurteilung des Lukullus, Handel, Giulio Cesare, 1992–97; Teatro Liceo Barcelona: Schoenberg Moses und Aron, Götterdämmerung, Walküre, Eugene Onegin; Teatro Communale Bologna: Walküre (Riccardo Chailly); Teatro alla Scala Milano, Elektra (Giuseppe Sinopoli), 1994; Asia-Concert tour with the Staatskapelle Dresden, Giuseppe Sinopoli: Elektra in Japan and Taiwan, 1995; Sang at Marseille, 1997 and Toulouse, 1999; Professor at the Essen Musikhochschule, 1990–.

*Recordings:* CDs: Braunfels: Die Verkündigung, 1994; Schoeck, Rohm, Shostakovich Lieder, 1997. *Address:* Wesselswerth 50, 45239 Essen, Germany.

**RUITUNEN, Esa;** Singer (Baritone); b. 1949, Finland. *Education:* Studied at the Sibelius Academy, Helsinki, 1974–80. *Career:* Vicar at the Temppelaukio Church at Helsinki, 1975–84; Appearances in Lieder recitals and concerts of sacred music throughout Scandinavia and Northern Europe and in the USA; Opera engagements at Helsinki and Savonlinna as Monterone, Escamillo, Pizarro, Enrico in Lucia di Lammermoor, Klingsor and Valentin; Appeared as guest at Essen in Merikanto's Juha and at Los Angeles in 1992 in the premiere of Sallinen's Kullervo; Sang Alberich in Das Rheingold at Helsinki, 1996; King Fisher in The Midsummer Marriage at Munich, 1998; Season 1999–2000 as Grigoris in The Greek Passion by Martinů, at Bregenz and Covent Garden; Enescu's Oedipe at the Deutsche Oper Berlin and the General in the premiere of Maria's Love by Kortekangas, at Savonlinna. *Address:* Finnish National Opera, Blvd 23–27, 00180 Helsinki, Finland.

**RUK-FOCIC, Bozena;** Singer (soprano); b. 31 Oct. 1937, Zagreb, Yugoslavia. *Education:* Studied with Zlatko Sir in Zagreb. *Career:* Debut: Basle in 1960 as Micaela in Carmen; Member of Croatian National Opera, Zagreb; Guest appearances in Bucharest, Athens, Roma, Palermo, Naples, Trieste, Genoa, Luxembourg, Netherlands, Graz, Bern, Belgrade, Vienna, Berlin, Stuttgart, Hamburg and at Covent Garden (as Eva in Die Meistersinger); La Scala as Sieglinde in Walküre in 1970 and in the Italian premiere of Dallapiccola's Ulisse; Further engagements in Kiev, Budapest, Houston, Pittsburgh, Seattle, Washington, Zürich, Geneva, Barcelona and Salzburg; Other roles include Jaroslavna in Prince Igor, Alceste, Madama Butterfly, Mozart's Countess, Verdi's Leonora and Aida, Wagner's Elsa, Elisabeth and Sieglinde, Strauss's Ariadne and Weber's Agathe, Desdemona in Otello, Tosca, Elisabetta in Don Carlos, Manon, Arabella, Marguerite in Faust, and Amelia in Simon Boccanegra; Many appearances as concert singer.

**RUMBOLD, Ian Francis,** BMus; British editor; *Senior Research Fellow, Department of Music, University of Nottingham*; b. 29 March, Grantham, England; m. Valerie Proctor. *Education:* King's School, Grantham, Lincolnshire, Univ. of Birmingham, Jesus Coll., Cambridge. *Career:* Research Fellow, Clare Hall, Cambridge 1981–83; Sir James Knott Research Fellow, Newcastle upon Tyne 1983–85; freelance editor and teacher 1985–86; Lecturer in Music, Univ. of Exeter 1986–87; Research Assoc. (New Berlioz Edition) Univ. of Manchester 1987–99, Royal Coll. of Music 1999–2003; Sr Research Fellow, Dept of Music, Univ. of Nottingham 2004–; mem. Royal Musical Asscn. *Publications:* Editions for New Berlioz Edition Vols 14, 15, and 22B; contrib. to The New Grove Dictionary of Music and Musicians, The New Oxford Companion to Music and many journals. *Address:* 33 Selly Wick Drive, Selly Park, Birmingham, B29 7JQ, England (home). *Telephone:* (121) 472-4994 (home). *Fax:* (121) 472-4994 (home). *E-mail:* ianrumbold@aol.com (home).

**RUNDGREN, Bengt;** Singer (Bass-Baritone); b. 21 April 1931, Karlskrona, Sweden. *Education:* Studied with Arne Sunnegaard and Ragnar Hulten in Stockholm. *Career:* Sang in operetta then made opera debut as the Commendatore, Stockholm in 1962; Member of the Royal Opera, Stockholm until 1969; Sang Osmin in Die Entführung at Drottningholm, 1965–67; Member of Deutsche Oper Berlin from 1969, often being heard as Leporello in Don Giovanni; Metropolitan Opera in 1974 as Hagen, repeating the role at Bayreuth in the 1976 centenary production of The Ring; Sang the Commendatore in Don Giovanni at Stockholm in 1988; Fafner in Siegfried at Helsinki, 1998; Also heard as concert singer. *Honours:* Swedish Court Singer, 1975. *Address:* c/o Finnish National Opera, PO Box 176, Helsingkatu 58, 00251 Helsinki, Finland.

**RUNGE, Peter-Christoph;** Singer (baritone); b. 12 April 1933, Lubeck, Germany. *Education:* Studied with Lilly Schmidtt de Giorgi in Hamburg. *Career:* Debut: Flensburg in 1958 as Guglielmo in Così fan tutte; Sang in Wuppertal, 1959–64, Deutsche Oper am Rhein, Düsseldorf, 1964–; Roles include Monteverdi: Orfeo; Mozart: Count, Figaro, Guglielmo, Papageno, Alfonso, Speaker, Rossini's Cenerentola, Dandini, Barber, Raimbaud, Le Comte Ory; Donizetti: Belcore, Malatesta; Strauss repertoire, Harlekin, Musiklehren and Olivier, Barbier; Puccini: Turandot, Marcello and Scaunard in La Bohème; Wagner: Beckmesser and Wolfram; Berg: Wozzeck; Glyndebourne Opera, 1966–73, 1982, 1983 as Papageno, Pelléas and Amida in the Leppard/Cavalli L'Ormindo, 1967–68; Edinburgh Festival in 1972 in the British premiere of Zimmermann's Die Soldaten as Stolzius, and Corpo in Cavallieri's Rappresentione; Guest appearances in Vienna Staatsoper, Brussels, Stockholm, Amsterdam, Warsaw, Bolshoi, Berlin, Hamburg and Zürich, Bogota, Verona, Paris, Nice, Buenos Aires, Berlin, Salzburg; Scottish Opera, 1970–74; World Premiere of Goehr's Behold the Sun, Düsseldorf in 1985 and BBC production; Udo Zimmermann's Schüsterfrau, Düsseldorf 1987; Wexford Festival in 1990 as Major Max von Zastrow in The Rising of The Moon by Maw; Dresden Festival, 1997–98 as Parmenione in Rossini's L'Occasione; Concert artist often heard in classical and contemporary repertoire; Oratorios and Missae include Bach, Handel, Mozart, Schubert, Bruckner, Brahms, Mendelssohn, War Requiem by Britten, Lucas Passion by Penderecki; Radio concerts and recordings with BBC London, Edinburgh, Paris, Berlin, Hamburg, Munich, Cologne, Milan, Rome, Madrid, Stockholm, Brussels and Netherlands; Teacher, Music High Schools in Düsseldorf and Aachen, also gives Masterclasses. *Recordings include:* Cavalli's L'Ormindo; Music by Monteverdi, Schütz and Bach; Handel's Apollo and Dafne; Auber's

Manon Lescaut. *Honours:* Kammersänger, 1990; Honorary Professorship, 1996. *Current Management:* Athole Still International Management, Forresters Hall, 25–27 Westow Street, London, SE19 3RY, England. *Telephone:* (20) 8771-5271. *Fax:* (20) 8768-6600. *Website:* www.atholestill.com.

**RUNKEL, Reinhild;** Singer (Mezzo-Soprano); b. 25 Dec. 1943, Volkach am Main, Germany. *Education:* Studied in Wuppertal. *Career:* Sang at the Nuremberg Opera, 1975–82; Guest engagements at Lisbon, Reggio Emilia, Paris and San Francisco, 1985, and Florence as Magdalene in Meistersinger in 1986; Salzburg Festival in 1987 in Moses and Aron by Schoenberg; Sang Fricka in Ring performances at Bologna, Stuttgart and Cologne, 1987–88; Appearances at the Zürich Opera from 1985 as Herodias, Fricka and Clytemnestra in a Ruth Berghaus production of Elektra in 1991; Stuttgart Staatsoper in 1992 as Begbick in Aufstieg und Fall der Stadt Mahagonny; Other roles include Erda, Waltraute, Brangaene, Lyon 1990, Jocasta in Oedipus Rex and the Nurse in Die Frau ohne Schatten; Fricka in Die Walküre for Netherlands Opera, 1998; Sang the Nurse in Die Frau ohne Schatten at La Scala and Munich, 1999; Clytemnestra in Elektra in Sydney and at the Savonlinna Festival, 2000; Frequent concert appearances. *Recordings include:* Fortune Teller in Arabella and Nurse in Die Frau ohne Schatten conducted by Solti; Beethoven's 9th. *Address:* c/o Zürich Opera, Falkenstrasse 1, 8008 Zürich, Switzerland.

**RUNNICLES, Donald;** British conductor; *Music Director, San Francisco Opera*; b. 16 Nov. 1954, Edinburgh, Scotland. *Education:* Edinburgh and Cambridge Univs, London Opera Centre. *Career:* Repetiteur, Mannheim Nat. Theatre from 1980, debut with Les Contes d'Hoffmann; Kapellmeister from 1984, conducting Fidelio, Le nozze di Figaro, Un Ballo in Maschera, Die Walküre and Parsifal; Principal Conductor, Hanover from 1987, leading Salome, Jenůfa, Tosca, Don Giovanni, Werther; regular engagements with the Hamburg Staatsoper, including Turandot, The Bartered Bride, Die Zauberflöte, Manon Lescaut, Carmen, Don Carlos, Zar und Zimmermann, Il Trovatore, Il Barbiere di Siviglia, L'Elisir d'amore, Lady Macbeth of Mtsensk; Gen. Music Dir, Freiburg from 1989, with Lady Macbeth, Billy Budd, Peter Grimes; assisted James Levine at Bayreuth, then conducted Lulu at the Metropolitan 1988, followed by Die fliegende Holländer 1990, and Die Zauberflöte; conducted The Ring at San Francisco 1990; Vienna Staatsoper from season 1990–91, with Il Barbiere di Siviglia, Don Giovanni, Madama Butterfly, La Traviata and Prince Igor; Glyndebourne debut 1991, with Don Giovanni; Music Dir, San Francisco Opera 1992–; season 1992–93 with Lady Macbeth of the Mtsensk District at Vienna Volksoper; The Fiery Angel, Guillaume Tell, Boris Godunov at San Francisco; Don Giovanni at Munich; Tannhäuser at Bayreuth; Der Ring des Nibelungen at Bayreuth; other repertory includes Idomeneo at Hanover; Der Freischütz; symphonic engagements in Darmstadt, Odensee, St Gallen, Copenhagen and with NDR Orchestra, Hamburg; season 1997–98 at San Francisco with Death in Venice, Le nozze di Figaro and Pelléas et Mélisande; Billy Budd and the Ring at the Vienna State Opera 2001; led new production of Katya Kabanova at San Francisco 2002; conducted Schoenberg's Gurrelieder at the London Proms 2002; Tristan und Isolde (over three concerts) for the BBC SO 2002–03; conducted world première of John Adams's opera Doctor Atomic 2005; Principal Guest Conductor, Atlanta Symphony Orchestra. *Recordings include:* Mozart Requiem 2005. *Address:* c/o San Francisco Opera, 301 Van Ness Avenue, San Francisco, CA 94102, USA. *Website:* www.sfopera.com.

**RUNSWICK, Daryl;** Composer, Musician and Singer; b. 12 Oct. 1946, Leicester, England. *Education:* MA, hons, Music, Corpus Christi College, Cambridge, 1964–67. *Career:* Musical Director, Footlights Club, 1966–67; Jazz Bass Player, especially with C Laine and J Dankworth, 1968–82; Concert Bass Player, especially with London Sinfonietta, 1970–82; Session Player, bass, bass guitar, keyboards, 1970–81; Arranger, Record Producer, especially King's Singers, 1971–; Composer of film and television music, 1976–; Tenor Singer in Electric Phoenix, 1983–; Musical Director, Green Light Music Theatre Company, 1990–; Professor of Composition and Media Studies, Trinity College of Music, London. *Compositions:* Scafra Preludes; 6 Episodes forming a Threnody; Moto interrotto/Ripresso; Mouth Symphony; Four by Five; I Am A Donut; Four Nocturnes; Main-Lineing; From Two Worlds; Cool>Warm>Hot. *Recordings:* With Electric Pheonix including: Berio, Cage, Nordheim, Wishart; With London Sinfonietta including: Songs for Dov, Agon, King Priam; With Nash Ensemble including: The Soldier's Tale. *Current Management:* Faber Music Ltd. *Address:* 34A Garthorne Road, London SE23 1EW, England.

**RUOFF, Axel D.;** Composer; b. 24 March 1957, Stuttgart, Germany. *Education:* State University for Music, Stuttgart and Academy for Music, Kassel, 1975–84; Diplomas in Piano and Music Theory, cum laude, 1979 and Diploma for Composers, 1984; National University for Fine Arts and Music, Tokyo, Japan, 1985–87. *Career:* Head of Department, Stuttgart Music School, 1981–88; Lecturer, State University for Music, Trossingen, 1985–87; Concurrently Guest Professor in Composition at Morioka College in 1988, selected for the Forum for Young Composers, Berlin; Fellowship from the Art Foundation of Baden, Württemberg; Fellowship from the Japanese Ministry of Culture for study at the National University for Fine Arts and Music in Tokyo; Professor at State University for Music, Stuttgart, 1992. *Compositions:* Prozession for Orchestra, 1983; Concerto for flute and orchestra, 1984; Correlations, cello solo, 1983; Jemand In Vorbeigehen for voice and piano, 1984; Via Dolorosa for organ, 1985; Fassaden for violin solo, 1985; String Quartet, 1986; Salomo-Variations for choir, 1986; Nacht Und Träume for orchestra, 1987–88; String Quartet No. 2, 1988; Piano Concerto, 1989. *Recordings:* Various records; Broadcasts for German, other European and Japanese stations. *Publications:* Publishing contracts with Edition Moeck, Con Brio in Berlin and Celle and Mieroprint in Münster. *Honours:* Valentino Bucchi, Rome, 1985, 1987; 1st Prize, ICONS, Torino, 1988; 2nd Prize, Ensemblia, Mönchengladbach, 1986; 1st Prize, Corciano, Perugia, 1991. *Address:* Möhringer Land Str 53, 7000 Stuttgart 80, Germany.

**RUOHONEN, Seppo;** Singer (Tenor); b. 25 April 1946, Turku, Finland. *Education:* Studied in Helsinki, with Luigi Ricci in Rome and with Anton Dermota in Vienna. *Career:* Debut: Helsinki in 1973 as Alvaro in La Forza del Destino; Appearances with Finnish National Opera as Verdi's Duke and Manrico, Tchaikovsky's Lensky and Hermann, and Don Ottavio; Savonlinna in 1977 in The Last Temptations by Kokonnen, with Sallinen's The Red Line, repeated at the Metropolitan, NY in 1983; San Diego Opera as Riccardo in Un Ballo in Maschera; Returned to Savonlinna in 1983 as Don Carlos and as Erik in Der fliegende Holländer; Has sung at Frankfurt from 1978 and made guest appearances in Berlin, Dresden, Leeds, Glasgow, Stuttgart and Wiesbaden as the Duke of Parma in Doktor Faust, Puccini's Cavaradossi, Luigi and Pinkerton, and Jenik in The Bartered Bride; Sang Florestan at the 1992 Savonlinna Festival; Inquisitor in Dallapiccola's Il Prigioniero for Tampere Opera, 1996. *Recordings include:* The Last Temptations.

**RUPP, Andrew;** Singer (baritone); b. 1970, England. *Education:* St John's College, Cambridge and with Linda Esther Gray. *Career:* Concerts with The Sixteen, The Cardinall's Musick and the Tallis Scholars; Repertoire includes Mozart and Fauré Requiems, Messiah, Bach's Christmas Oratorio, St Matthew Passion and B minor Mass; British premiere of Prokofiev's Eugene Onegin on South Bank; Glyndebourne Festival in Le Comte Ory, Dove's Flight, and as John in Birtwistle's The Last Supper; Somnus and Apollo in Semele by Eccles, Junius in The Rape of Lucretia for Opera de Caen and Purcell's Aeneas at Aix; European tour as the Ferryman in Britten's Curlew River; Mozart's Count for Kentish Opera and tour with the Gabrieli Consort 2001. *Current Management:* Athole Still International Management, Forresters Hall, 25–27 Westow Street, London, SE19 3RY, England. *Telephone:* (20) 8771-5271. *Fax:* (20) 8768-6600. *Website:* www.atholestill.com.

**RUSHTON, Edward,** MMus; British composer and pianist; b. 1972. *Education:* Chetham's School of Music with Renna Kellaway, Colin Touchin and Michael Ball, King's Coll., Cambridge with Robin Holloway and John York, RSAMD with James McMillan, attended summer schools with Sir Peter Maxwell Davies, Judith Weir, Magnus Lindberg, Colin Matthews, master-classes with Irwin Gage at the Zürich Conservatory. *Career:* composer-in-residence, Musikfesttage of the Orpheum Stiftung, Zürich 2002; freelance composer and pianist; works performed and commissioned by Endymion Ensemble, London Sinfonietta, Schubert Ensemble, Birmingham Contemporary Music Group, Faber Music, Camerata Zürich, Tonhalle Orchestra Zürich, Vokalensemble Cantapella, Orchestra of the Nat. Theatre Mannheim; performances as accompanist with Harry White (saxophone). *Compositions:* opera: Leinen aus Smyrna 2001, The Young Man with the Carnation 2002, Philoctetes, Birds. Bark. Bones. 2004, Harley 2005; chamber music: Rounds, L'An Mil, Combat in the Year Thousand. *Honours:* British Composer Award British Acad. of Composers and Songwriters 2005.

**RUSHTON, Julian Gordon,** BA, MusB, MA, DPhil; British academic and writer; *Professor Emeritus, School of Music, University of Leeds*; b. 22 May 1941, Cambridge, England; two s. *Education:* Trinity Coll., Cambridge, Magdalen Coll., Oxford. *Career:* Lecturer, Univ. of East Anglia 1968–74; Lecturer in Music and Fellow, King's Coll., Cambridge 1974–81; West Riding Prof. of Music, Univ. of Leeds 1982–2002, Prof. Emer. 2002–; Chair. Editorial Bd, Musica Britannica 1993–; mem. Royal Musical Asscn (Pres. 1994–99), American Musicological Soc. (Corresp. mem.). *Publications:* Berlioz: Huit Scènes de Faust, La Damnation de Faust, Cipriani Potter, Symphony in G minor (ed.), W. A. Mozart: Don Giovanni 1981, The Musical Language of Berlioz 1983, Classical Music: A Concise History 1986, W. A. Mozart: Idomeneo 1993, Berlioz: Roméo et Juliette 1994, Elgar: Enigma Variations 1999, The Music of Berlioz 2001, The Cambridge Companion to Elgar (ed. with Daniel Grimley) 2004, Mozart, an Extraordinary Life 2005, Mozart (The Master Musicians) 2006; contrib. to New Grove Dictionary of Music and Musicians, New Grove Dictionary of Opera, other books and professional journals. *Address:* School of Music, University of Leeds, Leeds, LS2 9JT (office); 362 Leymoor Road, Golcar, Huddersfield, HD7 4QF, England (home). *Telephone:* (113) 343-2579 (office); (1484) 649108 (home). *Fax:* (113) 343-2586 (office). *E-mail:* julianrushton@totalise.co.uk (home); j.g.rushton@leeds.ac.uk (office).

**RUSSELL, Ken;** British film director and stage producer; b. 3 July 1927, Southampton; s. of Henry Russell and Ethel Smith; m. 1st Shirley Kingdam (divorced 1978); four s. one d.; m. 2nd Vivian Jolly 1984; one s. one d.; m. 3rd Hetty Baines 1992 (divorced 1997); one s. *Education:* Nautical Coll., Pangbourne. *Career:* fmr actor and freelance magazine photographer. *Films:* French Dressing 1964, Billion Dollar Brain 1967, Women in Love 1969, The Music Lovers 1970, The Devils 1971, The Boyfriend 1971, Savage Messiah 1972, Mahler 1973, Tommy 1975, Lisztomania 1975, Valentino 1977, Altered States 1981, Gothic 1986, Aria (segment) 1987, Salome's Last Dance 1988, The Lair of the White Worm 1988, The Rainbow 1989, Whore 1990, Prisoners of Honour 1991, Lion's Mouth 2000, The Fall of the Louse of Usher 2002; acted in film The Russia House 1990. *Opera directed:* The Rake's Progress (Maggio

Musicale, Florence) 1982, Die Soldaten (Opéra de Lyon) 1983, Madama Butterfly (Spoleto) 1983, L'Italiana in Algeri (Geneva) 1984, La Bohème (Macerata Festival) 1984, Faust (Vienna) 1985, Mefistofele (Genoa) 1987, Princess Ida (London Coliseum) 1992, Salome (Bonn) 1993. *Television directed:* documentaries: Elgar, Bartok, Debussy, Henri Rousseau, Isadora Duncan, Delius, Richard Strauss, Clouds of Glory, The Mystery of Dr Martini, The Secret Life of Arnold Bax, Elgar: Fantasy of a Composer on a Bicycle 2002; series: Lady Chatterley's Lover. *Publications:* A British Picture: an Autobiography 1989, Altered States: The Autobiography of Ken Russell 1991, Fire Over England 1993, Mike and Gaby's Space Gospel 1999. *Honours:* Hon. DLitt (Univ. Coll., Salford) 1994; Prix Italia 1985. *Address:* 16 Salisbury Place, London, W1H 1FH, England.

**RUSSELL, Lynda;** Singer (Soprano); b. 1963, Birmingham, England. *Education:* Studied in London with Meriel St Clair and in Vienna with Eugene Ludwig. *Career:* Has sung with Glyndebourne Opera as the Queen of Night, Fortuna in Monteverdi's Ulisse and Marzelline in Fidelio; Opera engagements at Barcelona, Madrid, Nice, Venice, Vicenza, Rome, Bologna and Strasbourg; British appearances as Handel's Partenope and with Opera North and English National Opera; Trieste in 1990 as Donna Elvira; Concert showings at the festivals of Athens, Barcelona, Granada, San Sebastian, Cuence, Venice, Berne, Munich and Siena; Brahms Requiem under Jesus Lopez-Cobos and Beethoven's 9th with Walter Weller; Has sung Mozart's oratorios Davidde Penitente and Betulia Liberata in Italy; Further repertoire includes Wolf's Italienisches Liederbuch, Beethoven's Missa Solemnis under Weller, and Ah, Perfido, Mozart's Exultate and Coronation Mass; Mozart bicentenary concerts in London, Birmingham, Winchester and Lahti in Finland in 1991; Season 1996–97 with Bach's Jauchzet Gott in Vienna, Britten's Illuminations in Scotland, Mozart's Requiem with the Ulster Orchestra, and Dalila in Handel's Samson with The Sixteen; Sang Xanthe in Die Liebe der Danaë by Strauss at Garsington, 1999. *Recordings:* Handel Dixit Dominus with The Sixteen.

**RUSSELL, Malcolm Howard Alexander,** GRSM, ARAM, LRAM, FRCO; British musician; b. 17 Oct. 1945, Long Eaton, England; m. Judith Russell; three d. *Education:* Royal Acad. of Music, studied with Peter Hurford, Harald Vogel, Piet Kee and Ewald Kooiman. *Career:* educational work 1969–94; f. several choirs; Conductor Phoenix Singers 1976–96; 'The Bach Experience' Complete Organ Works of J. S. Bach 1991–94; Founder and Artistic Dir, East Anglian Acad. of Organ and Early Keyboard 1997; complete performances of Bach Clavieruburg III in England and Netherlands 1999–2000; cycles of Handel Concertos and Mendelssohn Sonatas; organ, harpsichord, clavichord recitals in UK, Italy, Netherlands and Catalonia; mem. British Inst. of Organ Studies, Incorporated Soc. of Musicians, British Clavichord Soc. *Recordings:* Bach from Framlingham 1997. *Publications:* contrib. to Organists' Review, Choir and Organ. *Address:* 14 Norfolk Crescent, Framlingham, Woodbridge, Suffolk, IP13 9EW, England (home). *Telephone:* (1728) 724456 (home). *E-mail:* russell.org.acad@macunlimited. net (home).

**RUSSO, William;** Composer; b. 25 June 1928, Chicago, Illinois, USA. *Education:* Studied with Lenni Tristano, 1943–46, John Becker, 1953–55 and Karel Jirak, 1955–57. *Career:* Trombonist and Chief Composer, Arranger with the Stan Kenton Orchestra, 1950–54; Taught at the Manhattan School of Music, 1958–61 and formed and conducted the Russo Orchestra, Columbia College Chicago, 1965–67 and Antioch College, 1971–72; Founded and directed the Center for New Music and Free Theatre at Columbia College, 1965–75; Returned to teaching at Columbia in 1979. *Compositions include:* Operas: John Hooten, BBC, 1963, The Island, BBC, 1963, Land of Milk and Honey, Chicago, 1967, Antigone, Chicago, 1967, A Cabaret Opera, New York, 1970, Aesop's Fables, Chicago, 1971, The Shepherds' Christmas, Chicago, 1979, Isabella's Fortune, New York, 1974, Pedrolino's Revenge, Chicago, 1974, A General Opera, Chicago, 1976, The Pay Off, Chicago, 1984, Talking To The Sun, Chicago, 1989; Ballets: The World Of Alcina, 1954, Les Deux Errants, Monte Carlo, 1956, The Golden Bird, Chicago, 1984; 2 Symphonies, 1957 and 1958; Music for Blues and Jazz Bands, Rock Cantatas and Sonata for Violin and Piano, 1986. *Publications include:* Composing Music: A New Approach, 1988. *Address:* c/o ASCAP, ASCAP Building, 1 Lincoln Plaza, New York, NY 10023, USA.

**RUT, Josef;** Violinist and Composer; b. 21 Nov. 1926, Kutná Hora, Czechoslovakia; m. Dr Milada Rutová, 14 Feb 1953 (died 2001), 1 s. *Education:* Studied with Professor Bedřich Voldan; State Conservatory of Music, Prague. *Career:* Debut: Prague in 1951; Violinist for Radio Prague Symphony Orchestra, 1953–83; Composer from 1983; mem, Society of Czech Composers. *Compositions:* 49 compositions based on own 12 note tonal theory. *Recordings:* Sonata for double bass and strings; String Quartets No. 1 and 2; Symphonies No. 2 and 3; Sonata for winds No. 1; Wind Quintet; Concerto for violin and orchestra; Duo for violin and violoncello; Concerto for horn and strings; Variations for orchestra; Sonate for piano; Concerto for trumpet and strings; Sonate for violin and piano; String Quartet No. 3 with tenor solo on the words of St Paul; Sonata for viola and piano; Duo for violins; Variations for violoncello and piano; Meditation over Kyrie eleison for violin, viola and violoncello. *Publications:* Studies for two violins; Small Dialogues for trumpet and trombone; Five Little Pieces for flute and piano; 12 Note Tonal Theory, 1969; Die Musik und ihre Perspektive vom Gesichtspunkt der Relativitätstheorie (International Review of the Aesthetics and Sociology of Music), 1980; Manual of Rhythm, with Jan Dostal, 1979 and 1984; Beitrag zur übersichtlicheren Notierung des Rhythmus, 1982; The Relativistic Theory of

Musical Motion, 1990; Search for Order as the Inspiration for Music Creation – Philosophy of Music, 2000. *Address:* Zborovská 40, 15000 Prague 5, Czech Republic.

**RUTHERFORD, James;** Singer (Bass); b. 1970, England. *Education:* Durham University; Royal College of Music, with Margaret Kingsley; National Opera Studio, London, 1998–99. *Career:* Appearances as Falstaff for British Youth Music Opera, Nick Shadow, Caronte in Orfeo for Kent Opera, and Rossini's Don Magnifico for Clonter Opera; Marziano in Alessandro Severo and Tullio in Arminio for the London Handel Society; Christus in St Matthew Passion and Handel's L'Allegro ed il Moderato, 2001; Concerts include Telemann's Don Quichotte with the Orchestra of the Age of Enlightenment, Verdi and Brahms Requiems, Haydn's Creation with the Britten Sinfonia and St Matthew Passion at St George's Church, Hannover Square; Messiah at Salisbury Cathedral, the Missa Solemnis at Exeter Cathedral and the B minor Mass at St John's Smith Square; Season 2000–01 with Mozart's Figaro for Opera North and Welsh National opera, The Dream of Gerontius with the Hallé Orchestra and L'Allegro ed il Moderato for the London Handel Festival; Season 2001–2002 as First Shepherd in Daphne and Kothner in Die Meistersinger, at Covent Garden. *Address:* c/o Royal Opera House (Contracts), Covent Garden, London, WC2.

**RUTMAN, Neil;** Pianist; b. 12 July 1953, California, USA. *Education:* BMus, San Jose State University, 1976 with Aiko Onishi; MMus, Piano Performance, Eastman School of Music, University of Rochester, 1977; Student of Cecile Genhart; DMA, Piano Performance, Peabody Institute of The Johns Hopkins University, 1983, under Ellen Mack; Private piano studies with Leon Fleisher, Frank Mannheimmer and Gaby Casadesus. *Career:* Debut: US debut at Carnegie Hall in 1985; London debut at Wigmore Hall in 1985; Washington DC debut at Phillips Gallery in 1985; Associate Professor of Piano at Goucher College, Baltimore, 1983–; Masterclasses on interpretation of French piano music of Fauré, Debussy, and Ravel, at Chateau de la Gesse, Toulouse, France, University of Colorado, Denver, 1986, and Wright State University, Dayton, OH, 1986; Recitalist at Chateau de la Gesse in 1985, at Cheltenham International Festival of Music in 1986 and soloist for Denver Symphony in 1986; US State Department recital tour of Yugoslavia and soloist for Metropolitan Orchestra at Carnegie Hall in 1986; Recitalist at Merkin Hall, NYC with 3 recitals of the music of Ravel, Debussy, Fauré and Poulence with American premiere each evening, 1987. *Recordings:* 3 Movements of Petrouchka by Stravinsky; 2 Mozart Piano Concerti, K482 and K414; Préludes Book 1 and 2 by Debussy. *Current Management:* Thea Dispeker, NYC, USA. *Address:* 20990 Valley Green Dr, Apt 700, Cupertino, CA 95014-1846, USA.

**RUTTER, Claire;** Singer (Soprano); b. 1972, South Shields, County Durham, England. *Education:* Studied at the Guildhall School of Music and the National Opera Studio. *Career:* Sang in Birtwistle's Yan Tan Tethera for Opera Factory (1986) and Donna Anna for British Youth Opera; Violetta for Welsh National Opera (1994) and Scottish Opera from 1995, as Mozart's Countess, Terinka in The Jacobin, and Violetta; Other roles include Tatiana, Mimi and Alice Ford; Further appearances at the Buxton and Chester Festivals, at the Wigmore Hall and in South America and South Africa; Sang Mozart's Elettra for Scottish Opera, 1996 and Violetta, 1998; Sang Mimi at Hong Kong, 1998; Sang Gilda for ENO and WNO, 1999; La Gioconda for Opera North and Donna Anna in London, 2000–01. *Address:* c/o Scottish Opera, 39 Elmbank Crescent, Glasgow, G2 4PT, Scotland.

**RUTTER, John Milford,** MA, DMus; British composer and conductor; *Director, The Cambridge Singers;* b. 24 Sept. 1945, London; m. JoAnne Redden 1980; two s. (one deceased) one step-d. *Education:* Highgate School and Clare Coll., Cambridge. *Career:* Dir of Music Clare Coll., Cambridge 1975–79; part-time Lecturer in Music Open Univ. 1975–87; founder and Dir The Cambridge Singers 1981–. *Compositions include:* The Falcon 1969, Gloria 1974, Bang! (opera for young people) 1975, The Piper of Hamelin (opera for young people) 1980, Requiem 1985, Magnificat 1990, I my best beloved's am (unaccompanied choral work for BBC Sounding the Millennium series) 1999, Mass of the Children 2003; numerous carols, anthems and songs; orchestral works and music for TV. *Recordings include:* original version of Fauré Requiem 1984. *Publications:* Opera Choruses (ed.) 1995, European Sacred Music (ed.) 1996, Christmas Motets (ed.) 1999. *Honours:* Hon. Fellow Westminster Choir Coll., Princeton, Hon. DMus (Lambeth) 1996. *Address:* Old Laceys, St John's Street, Duxford, Cambridge, CB2 4RA, England.

**RUUD, Ole Kristian;** Conductor; b. 2 Oct. 1958, Oslo, Norway; m. Karen Johnstad Ruud, 26 Mar 1988, 2 s. *Education:* Norwegian Academy of Music, 1979–83; Sibelius Academy, 1984–85. *Career:* Debut: Radio Concert, Oslo Philharmonic Orchestra, 1985; Chief Conductor, North Norwegian Chamber Orchestra, 1986–89; Chief Conductor, Trondheim Symphony Orchestra, 1987–95, Norrkoping Symphony Orchestra, 1996–99; Touring Concerts with Trondheim Symphony Orchestra, Germany, 1988, 1995, Bergen Philharmonic, Germany, 1991, Jeunesse Musicale Orchestra, Europe, 1993, Berlin, 1996, Stockholm Chamber Orchestra, Japan, 1995, 1999; Professor of Conducting at Oslo Academy, 1999–. *Recordings:* Norwegian Composers: Oslo Philharmonic, Trondheim Symphony, Stavanger Symphony Orchestra; International Composers: Swedish Radio Symphony Orchestra, Norrkoping Symphony Orchestra, Bergen Philharmonic, Trondheim Symphony. *Honours:* E Grieg Prize, 1992; Norwegian Newspaper Best Review Prize, 1993; Lindeman Prize, 1994; Johan Halvorsen Prize, 1996.

**RUZICKA, Peter;** Composer and Intendant; b. 3 July 1948, Düsseldorf, Germany. *Education:* Piano, Oboe and Composition, Hamburg Conservatory, 1963–68; PhD, 1977, Munich and Berlin. *Career:* Intendant, Berlin Radio Symphony Orchestra, 1979–87; Fellow, Bavarian Academy of Fine Arts, Munich, 1985; Free Academy of Arts, Hamburg, 1987. *Compositions:* Esta Noche, for the victims of the Viet Nam War, 1967; Antifone-Strofe for 25 strings and percussion, 1970; Elis, for mezzo, oboe and orchestra, 1970; Sonata for solo cello, 1970; 3 string quartets, 1970, 1970, 1992; Metastrophe for 87 instrumentalists, 1971; Sinfonia for 25 strings, 16 vocalists and percussions, 1971; Outside-Inside, Music Theatre, 1972; In Processo di Tempo for 26 instrumentalists and cello, 1972; Versuch, 7 Pieces for strings, 1974; Stress for 8 percussion groups, 1972; Einblendungen for orchestra, 1973–77; Feed Back for 4 orchestral groups, 1974; Torso for orchestra, 1974; Emanazione Variations for flute and 4 orchestral groups, 1975; Zeit for organ, 1975; Stille for cello, 1976; Abbruche for orchestra, 1977; Gestalt and Abbruch for voices, 1979; Impuls zum Weitersprechen for viola and orchestra, 1981; Satyagraha for orchestra, 1985;... der die Gesange zerschlug for baritone and ensemble, 1985; Metamorphosen uber ein Klangfeld von Joseph Haydn, for orchestra, 1990; Vier Gesänge nach Fragmenten von Nietzsche, for mezzo and piano, 1992; Klangschatten for string quartet, 1992; Tallis, for orchestra, 1993;... Inseln, randlos, for violin, chamber orchestra and chorus, 1994; Music Premiered at Gottingen, Stuttgart, Berlin, Hilversum, Hamburg, Munich, Vienna and Savonlinna. *Address:* Alphonsstrasse 17, 22043 Hamburg, Germany.

**RUŽICKÁ, Rudolf;** Czech composer and teacher; b. 25 April 1941, Brno; m. Bozena Ruzickova 1967; two s. *Education:* Brno Conservatory, Janáček Acad. of Performing Arts. *Career:* Prof. of Composition and Music Theory, Brno and Kromeriz Conservatories, Brno State Univ., Janáček Acad.; Pres., Soc. for Electro-acoustic Music in the Czech Republic; Chair. of the Jury Musica Nova Competition. *Compositions:* over 100 instrumental, chamber, vocal, electro-acoustic and computer compositions, including three cantatas, five symphonies, six concertos, ten suites. *Recordings:* some 60 compositions recorded for albums, radio and television. *Publications:* Use of Computers in Creating Works of Art; contrib. numerous articles on music theory of computer composition and automatic notation, to various publications. *Honours:* numerous honours, prizes and awards for electro-acoustic and computer music. *Address:* Serikova 32, 637 00 Brno, Czech Republic (office). *Telephone:* (5) 4122-0174 (office). *E-mail:* ruzicka@fi.muni.cz (office). *Website:* www.musica.cz/ruzicka (office).

**RŮŽIČKOVÁ, Zuzana;** Czech harpsichordist; b. 14 Jan. 1927; m. Viktor Kalabis 1952. *Education:* Pilsen School of Music and Acad. of Performing Arts, Prague. *Career:* interned in concentration camps including Auschwitz and Bergen-Belsen 1942–45; concert harpsichordist in Europe, Japan, Canada and the USA 1956–; music teacher Acad. of Performing Arts (AMU) 1951–, Acad. of Music and Dramatic Art, Bratislava 1978–82, Zürich Masterclass, Switzerland 1976–; Prof. of Music AMU 1990–. *Recordings include:* J. S. Bach, Purcell, Handel, Haydn, Scarlatti; more than 70 recordings. *Honours:* Hon. mem. Nat. Early Music Asscn, Oxford, UK 1988; winner Arbeitsgemeinschaft der öffentlich-rechtlichen Rundfunkanstalten der Bundesrepublik Deutschland (ARD) Competition, Munich (Germany) 1956, State Prize of Czechoslovakia 1970, Nat. Artist of Czechoslovakia 1989, Medal of Arts and Sciences, Hamburg, Germany 1992, Czech Critics' Medal 2003, Grand Prix du Disque Charles Cros; Gold and Platinum Discs, Supraphon. *Address:* Slezská 107, 130-00 Prague 3, Czech Republic. *Telephone:* (2) 67312104.

**RYABCHIKOV, Victor;** Pianist; b. 13 Feb. 1954, Tashkent, Uzbekistan; m. Golovina Irina, 31 Oct 1987, 1 d. *Education:* State Music Conservatory, Tashkent, 1972–79; Moscow Conservatory, 1977–79. *Career:* Concert as soloist and with orchestra in various cities across Russia from 1979 and in France, Switzerland, the United Kingdom, Sweden, Netherlands, Italy, South Africa and Germany from 1993; Numerous appearances on television and radio in Russia, Sweden and Switzerland; Founding Vice-President of Glinka Society, Moscow, 1997; Artistic Director, Glinka Festival, Moscow, 1997; Wigmore Hall debut, 2000. *Recordings:* CD, Russian Piano Music of XIX Century; Mikhail Glinka–Complete Piano Music in 3 Vols; Complete Piano Music by Borodin and Kalinnikov; Piano Music by Anton and Nikolai Rubinstein; Live recording, Chopin in Stockholm, 1999; Tchaikovsky – The Seasons and other piano pieces; Moments musicaux by Schubert and Rachmaninov. *Radio:* Writer/presenter, series of 14 broadcasts on Russian 19th century composers, Radio Orphei, 2002–03. *Honours:* Winner, 5th Republic Competition of Piano and Special Prize, Union of Composers, Russia, 1976; Pianist of the Year, APN, Moscow, 1992. *Current Management:* Tyndale-Biscoe Promotions, Stockholm. *Address:* Barvikha 21-7, Odinzovski R-N, Moscow 143083, Russia.

**RYABETS, Oleg;** Singer (Male Soprano); b. 28 June 1967, Kiev, Ukraine. *Education:* Kiev State Conservatory and Moscow State Academy of Music, 1988–94, with Professors K Radchenko and Z Dolukhanova. *Career:* Debut: Soprano part in Schnittke's Symphony No. 2 with Great Symphony Orchestra conducted by G Rozhdestvensky, Bolshoi Moscow State Conservatory Hall, 1990; Professional stage performer, 1977–; Soloist, State Boys Choir and State Chapel Choir of Kiev, performing in European countries, 1977–90; Sang with Vivaldi State Chamber Orchestra in 17–19th century music programme in Russian and Italian tours, 1990–93; Soprano role in Pergolesi's Stabat Mater, Moscow and Prague, 1992–93; Amour in Gluck's Orpheus, Hermitage Theatre, St Petersburg, 1993; Concerts and recitals in Moscow and St

Petersburg, including special recital dedicated to 1st and only official visit to Russia by Queen Elizabeth II, Tchaikovsky Great Concert Hall, Moscow, 17 Oct 1994; Performed in Petersburg's Seasons Music Festival and Ludwigsburg Festival conducted by W Gönnenwein, sang in recital at French Embassy, Vienna, and appeared as Count Myshkin in world premiere of V Kobekin's NFB at Sacro Art Festival, Bochum and Ludwigsburg, Germany, 1995; Lenin in world premiere of The Naked Revolution by D Soldier, New York, 1997; Aminta in Galuppi's Il Re Pastore, Italy, 1998. *Recordings:* Solo Soprano, Stabat Mater by G Pergolesi, 1993; Italian music of 17–18th centuries, Mr Soprano sings Bel Canto, 1996; King Solomon's Song, cantata composed for O Ryabets by V Kobekin. *Honours:* Audio tape with his voice preserved next to only recorded castrato singer Sgnr A Mareschi in British National Sound Archives, London, 1996–.

**RYAN, Barry;** Singer (Tenor); b. 1956, Australia. *Education:* Graduated with Honours, the NSW Conservatorium Opera School 1981. *Career:* Principal tenor with Cologne Opera 1988–92; Australian Opera debut 1993, as David in Die Meistersinger (returned 1998 as Laca in Jenůfa, under Charles Mackerras); Season 1996–97 with Royal Opera debut, in Peter Grimes, as Armand in Henze's Boulevard Solitude at Basle and Froh in Das Rheingold at La Scala; Erik in Der fliegende Holländer for Australian Opera and as return to Covent Garden, in Elektra and Katya Kabanova; Concerts included 1988 Australian Bicentennial at Drury Lane, London, the Mozart Requiem in Bergen, Beethoven's Ninth in Tokyo and Hindemith's Cardillac at the Amsterdam Concertgebouw (1997); Further appearances at the Opéra-Comique and the Komische Oper, Berlin; Sang Alfred in Die Fledermaus at Sydney, 2000. *Honours:* Awards at the Shell Aria, Metropolitan Opera Auditions and Marten Bequest for Singing. *Address:* c/o Australian Opera, PO Box 291, Strawberry Hills, NSW 2012, Australia.

**RYAN, Kwamé;** conductor; b. 1976, Canada. *Education:* Oakham School, England, Gonville and Caius Coll., Cambridge, studied with Peter Eötvös. *Career:* concert tours of Austria, France and Hungary with Peter Eötvös; Asst to Lothar Zagrosek at Stuttgart Opera 1998–99; Music Dir, Freiburg Opera 1999–2003, leading Tosca, Katya Kabanova, Der fliegende Holländer, Eugene Onegin, Fidelio and Nixon in China, Goebbels' Surrogate Cities, Fidelio and Maderna's Hyperion; season 2001–02 with Three Sisters by Eötvös at Opéra de Lyon, Nono's Prometeo in Lisbon and Brussels and Surrogate Cities by Heiner Goebbels at Freiburg; season 2002–03 with premiere of Percussion Concerto by Tüür, Grisey's Les Espaces Acoustiques at Lyon; season 2003–04 with Hartmann's Simplicius Simplissimus at Stuttgart State Opera; debut with Paris Nat. Opera with premiere of L'espace derniere by Matthias Pintscher 2004, UK debut at the Edinburgh Festival 2004; season 2004–05 featuring concerts with the Orchestra of Hamburg State Opera, Berliner Sinfonie, Deutsche Kammerphilharmonie Bremen, Scottish Chamber Orchestra, City of Birmingham Symphony Orchestra, Royal Scottish Nat. Orchestra and Baltimore Symphony Orchestra; guest appearances at many festivals, including Salzburg, Strasbourg Musica, Berlin Biennale, Budapest Spring Festival, Metapher in Stuttgart, Donaueschingen Musiktage, Wien Modern, Wittener Tage für Neue Musik, Rhine Music Festival in Cologne and the Festival d'Automne in Paris; he has worked with many orchestras and ensembles, including the Bavarian, Baden-Baden, Freiburg, Stuttgart and Saarland Radio Symphonies, the Hungarian State Orchestra, the Netherlands Radio Chamber Orchestra, the Luxembourg Philharmonic Orchestra and the Sudfunkchor Stuttgart. *Current Management:* Harrison/Parrott Ltd, 12 Penzance Place, London, W11 4PA, England. *Telephone:* (20) 7229-9166. *Fax:* (20) 7221-5042. *Website:* www.harrisonparrott.com.

**RYBARSKA, Lydia;** Singer (Soprano); b. 1958, Czechoslovakia. *Career:* Sang Rusalka at the National Theatre, Prague; Season 1988–89 as Luisa Miller at Philadelphia and Amelia in Un Ballo in Maschera at Zürich; Guest with the Slovak National Opera at Edinburgh, 1990, in Prince Igor (as Jaroslavna) and Suchoň's The Whirlpool; Bregenz Festival, 1993, as Abigaille in Nabucco; Bratislava, 1996, as Margherita in Mefistofele; Further appearances at the Paris Opéra Bastille (as Amelia) and Stuttgart; Concerts include Beethoven's Ninth in London and the Missa Solemnis in Vienna. *Address:* Slovak National Opera, Gorkeho 4, 81506 Bratislava, Slovakia.

**RYBNIKOV, Alexei;** Russian composer; b. 17 July 1946, Moscow. *Education:* Moscow Conservatory. *Career:* Dir, Russian State Symphony 1986–87; founder, Ribnikov Theatre Studio, Moscow 1990; performances of works throughout Russia, in USA, France, UK and Germany. *Compositions include:* Theatre Pieces: The Star and Death of Joachino Murieti, 1976; Juno and Avos, 1980; Liturgy for the Catechumens, 1991; A Night Song, ballet, 1997; 2 piano sonatas, 1962, 1966; 2 symphonies, 1969, 1974; Russian overture, 1967; The Jester, Capriccio for orchestra, 1968; Concerto for string quartet and orchestra, 1971; Piano Concerto, 1971; Bayan Concerto, 1972.

**RYDL, Kurt;** Singer (Bass); b. 8 Oct. 1947, Vienna, Austria. *Education:* Studied in Vienna and Moscow. *Career:* Debut: Stuttgart in 1973 as Daland in Der fliegende Holländer; Guest appearances in Venice, Barcelona and Lisbon; Sang at Bayreuth Festival in 1975; Vienna Staatsoper from 1976 as Rocco in Fidelio, Zaccaria in Nabucco, Procida in Vêpres Siciliennes, Mephistopheles in Faust, King Philip in Don Carlos, Kecal in The Bartered Bride, the Landgrave

in Tannhäuser and Marke in Tristan und Isolde; Salzburg Festival in 1985 in Il Ritorno d'Ulisse by Henze/Monteverdi; Tour of Japan with Vienna Staatsoper in 1986; Sang Baron Ochs in Turin and at Monte Carlo and Florence in 1987 and 1989; Salzburg Festival, 1987–89 as Mozart's Osmin, and La Scala Milan in 1990 as Rocco; Sang Pimen at Barcelona and Rocco at the 1990 Salzburg Festival; Season 1991–92 as Titurel at La Scala, Verdi's Zaccaria at the Vienna Volksoper, Ramfis in Aida at Tel-Aviv, Padre Guardiano at Florence and the Grand Inquisitor at the Verona Arena; Sang Hagen in Götterdämmerung at Covent Garden, 1995; returned 1997, in Pfitzner's Palestrina; Grand Inquisitor at Edinburgh, 1998; Season 2000–01 as Baron Ochs at the Deutsche Oper Berlin, Mozart's Osmin in Geneva, Dodon in The Golden Cockerel at Bregenz and Wagner's Pogner at Covent Garden; Morosus in Die schweigsame Frau at the Vienna Staatsoper and Wagner's Hagen (concert) in Sydney. *Recordings include:* Salome; Opera scenes by Schubert; Alceste; Manon Lescaut. *Address:* c/o Staatsoper, Opernring 2, 1010 Vienna, Austria.

**RYHANEN, Jaako;** Singer (Bass); b. 2 Dec. 1946, Tampere, Finland. *Education:* Studied in Helsinki. *Career:* Member of the Finnish National Opera at Helsinki from 1974; Appearances at the Savonlinna Festival and in Moscow and New York with the Helsinki Company; Further engagements in Madrid, Hamburg, Berlin, Munich, Zürich and Stuttgart; Paris Opéra in 1987, as Daland, and at Monte Carlo in 1988; Season 1991 as Daland at Munich, Titurel in Parsifal at Tampere and Mozart's Bartolo at Helsinki; Sang Daland at Santiago in 1992, and Sarastro at the Savonlinna Festival; Sang Fiesco in the original version of Simon Boccanegra at Covent Garden, 1997; Wagner's Daland at Lille, 1998; Season 2000–01 as Verdi's Banquo for Cologne Opera, Fiesco and Boris Godunov in Helsinki and Sarastro at Savonlinna; Boris for the Deutsche Oper am Rhein; Concerts with the Israel Philharmonic and throughout Scandinavia. *Address:* Finnish National Opera, Bulevardi 23–27, 00180 Helsinki 18, Finland.

**RYSANEK, Lotte;** Singer (Soprano); b. 18 March 1928, Vienna, Austria. *Education:* Vienna Conservatory with Richard Grossman. *Career:* Debut: Klagenfurt in 1950 as Massenet's Manon; Member of the Vienna Staatsoper as Marzelline in Fidelio, Marguerite in Faust, Pamina, Fiordiligi, Marenka in The Bartered Bride and Donna Elvira, and parts in operas by Wagner and Verdi; Guest appearances at the Vienna Volksoper in Graz, Berlin, Düsseldorf and Hamburg; Sang at Bayreuth in 1958; Well known in operetta and as a concert singer. *Recordings include:* Roles in operetta. *Address:* c/o Staatsoper, Opernring 2, 1010 Vienna, Austria.

**RYSSOV, Michail;** Singer (bass); b. 25 Aug. 1955, Crimea, Russia. *Career:* Principal Bass at the Opera in Minsk, 1983–87, in Don Giovanni, Don Carlos, Aida, La Forza del Destino, Macbeth, Nabucco, I Vespri Siciliani, Faust, Eugene Onegin, Boris Godunov, Mefistofele; Treviso, 1989, as the Commendatore in Don Giovanni; Has recently sung Ramfis at the Deutsche Oper Berlin and at the Verona Arena; Philip II at Deutsche Oper am Rhein, Düsseldorf; Prince Gremin and The Inquisitor in Don Carlos, at La Fenice, Venice; Sang Ramfis in Aida at the 1996 Verona Arena. *Honours:* Winner, Glinka Competition, 1984; International Verviers Competition, Belgium, 1987; International Ettore Bastianini Competition, Siena, 1988; International New Voice Competition in Pavia and the Toti dal Monte Competition in Treviso, 1989; Season 2000 as Verdi's Padre Guardiano at Verona and Procida at St Gallen; Kutzman in the premiere of Tatiana by Azio Corghi, at La Scala. *Current Management:* Athole Still International Management, Forresters Hall, 25–27 Westow Street, London, SE19 3RY, England. *Telephone:* (20) 8771-5271. *Fax:* (20) 8768-6600. *Website:* www.atholestill.com.

**RZEWSKI, Frederic (Anthony);** Composer and Pianist; b. 13 April 1938, Westfield, Massachusetts, USA; m. Nicole Abbeloss, 3 c. *Education:* BA, Harvard University, 1958, study with Thompson and Piston; MFA, Princeton University, 1960, study with Sessions and Babbitt; Italy, 1960–61 with Dallapiccola. *Career:* Pianist and teacher in Europe from 1962; Played in the premieres of Stockhausen's Klavierstuck X and Plus Minus; Co-founded electronic ensemble, Musica Electronica Viva, Rome, 1966; Returned to New York in 1971; Professor of Composition at the Royal Conservatory, Liège from 1977; Visiting Professor of Composition at Yale University in 1984. *Compositions:* For Violin, 1962; Composition for 2, 1964; Nature Morte for instruments and percussion, 1965; Zoologischer Garten, 1965; Spacecraft, 1967; Impersonation, audiodrama, 1967; Requiem, 1968; Symphony, 1968; Last Judgement for trombone, 1969; Falling Music for piano and tape, 1971; Coming Together for speaker and instruments, 1972; Piano Variations On The Song No Place To Go But Around, 1974; The People United Will Never Be Defeated, 36 variations for piano, 1975; 4 Piano Pieces, 1977; Satyrica for jazz band, 1983; Una Breve Storia D'Estate for 3 flutes and small orchestra; A Machine for 2 pianos, 1984; The Invincible Persian Army for low voice and prepared piano, 1984; The Persians for 4 voices, actors and ensemble, 1985; The Triumph of Death, oratorio, 1988; Roses, for 8 instruments, 1989; Piano Sonata, 1991; The Road, for piano, 1995–98; Scratch Symphony, 1997; Spiritus, for recorder and percussion, 1997. *Recordings:* As pianist, numerous items of contemporary music. *Address:* c/o ASCAP, ASCAP Building, 1 Lincoln Plaza, New York, NY 10023, USA.

# S

**SAARI, Jouko Erik Sakari;** Conductor and Musical Director; b. 23 Nov. 1944, Stockholm, Sweden; m. Raija Syvänen, 1 s., 1 d. *Education:* Sibelius Academy, 1962–68; Music Science, Helsinki University, 1965–67; Organist degree, 1966; Music Education degree, 1966; Conservatory degree in Trumpet, 1966; Conducting, Indiana University, USA, 1969–70; Music Director degree, 1966; Church Music Division degree, 1968; Conducting Diploma, 1968. *Career:* Musical Director, Helsinki Opera Society, 1971; Conductor, Tampere City Orchestra, 1973–74; Chorus Master, 1974–75, Conductor and Coach, 1976–78, National Opera Finland; Musical Director, Lahti Symphony Orchestra, 1978–84; Conductor, Gothenburg Opera House, Stora Teatern, 1984–85, Guest Conductor, 1985–88; Broadcast recordings with Finnish Radio Symphony Orchestra, 1971, 1973–75 and with Swedish Radio Symphony Orchestra, 1974, 1976–77; Concerts in USA, Canada, Germany, Hungary, Denmark, Sweden and Finland; Guest Conductor, Hämeenlinna Symphony Orchestra, 1989–93; Appearances on Swedish Radio and on Finnish Radio and Television; Freelance Conductor and Organist. *Compositions:* For Brass Band recorded with Töölö Brass Band; For voice, choir, organ and trumpets published by Sulasol, Finland. *Address:* Laaksokatu 5B23, 15140 Lahti, Finland.

**SAARIAHO, Kaija;** Finnish composer; b. 1952; m. Jean-Baptiste Barrière; one s. one d. *Career:* freelance composer of orchestral and instrumental music with live electronics and computers; music performed in most major festivals, including Salzburg Festival 1996; Graalthéatre for violin and orchestra, performed at the London Proms 1995. *Compositions include:* Verbledungen, 1984, Lichtbogen 1986, Du Cristal...à la fumée 1988–90, Graalthéatre 1994, Château de l'âme 1995, Oltra mar 1998, Miranda's Lament, for soprano and ensemble 1998, Neiges, for 8 cellos 1998, L'amour de loin (opera) 2000 (British premiere Barbican Hall, London 2002, Grawemeyer Award for Music 2003), Nymphea Reflection, for orchestra 2001, Orion, for orchestra 2002, Aile du Songe, for flute and ensemble 2001, Cinq Reflects, for soprano, baritone and orchestra 2001, Terrestre, for flute and ensemble 2002. *Recordings:* Maa, Verblendungen, Lichtbogen, Io, Stilleben. *Address:* c/o Chester Music, 8–9 Frith Street, London, W1V 5TZ, England.

**SAARINEN, Eeva-Liisa;** Singer (Mezzo-Soprano); b. 1951, Finland. *Education:* Studied at the Sibelius Academy, Helsinki, from 1972. *Career:* Sang throughout Northern Europe from 1981 in concerts and recitals; Stage debut at Helsinki in 1983 as Cherubino; Further roles with the Finnish National Opera have been Rosina, Cenerentola, the Composer in Ariadne auf Naxos, Marja in Merikanto's Juha, and Hansel; Has sung in the premieres of Sallinen's The King Goes Forth to France at Savonlinna in 1984 and Kullervo at Los Angeles in 1992; Fricka in Das Rheingold at Helsinki, 1996; Sang in the premiere of Luther by Kari Tikka, Helsinki 2000. *Recordings include:* Kullervo Symphony by Sibelius. *Address:* c/o Finnish National Opera, Blvd 23–27, 00180 Helsinki, Finland.

**SAARMAN, Risto;** Finnish singer (tenor); b. 25 Jan. 1956, Jyvaskyla. *Education:* Sibelius Acad., Helsinki. *Career:* Finnish National Opera from 1984, at first as M Triquet in Eugene Onegin; Beppe; Borsa in Rigoletto; Don Curzio; Later sang: Tamino, Don Ottavio, Ferrando, Belmonte, Almaviva, Lensky and Albert Herring; Savonlinna Festival and Opéra de Lyon, 1987, as Tamino and Belmonte; Aix-en-Provence, 1990, as Belmonte and Almaviva; Sang Jacquino at the 1992 Savonlinna Festival; Concert engagements in the St John and St Matthew Passions; Masses by Haydn, Handel, Mozart and Beethoven; L'Enfance du Christ by Berlioz and Mendelssohn's Second Symphony; Lieder repertoire includes: Dichterliebe; Die schöne Müllerin; Songs by Strauss.

**SABBATINI, Giuseppe;** Singer (Tenor); b. 11 May 1957, Rome, Italy. *Education:* Studied Double Bass at the Santa Cecilia Conservatory, Rome; Private study in Singing. *Career:* Debut: As Opera Singer, Edgardo in Lucia di Lammermoor at Spoleto, 1987; Played double bass in various Italian orchestras; Following opera debut, has sung in Faust, La Bohème, Werther, Massenet's Manon, Linda di Chamounix, La Traviata, Rigoletto, I Puritani, L'Elisir d'amore, Fra Diavolo, Les Pêcheurs de Perles, Eugene Onegin, Idomeneo, Maria Stuarda, Les Contes d'Hoffmann, La Favorita, Falstaff; Guillaume Tell; Dom Sébastien, by Donizetti; Roméo et Juliette; Performances at main theatres such as Teatro alla Scala, Milan, Vienna Staatsoper, Opéra-Bastille, Paris, Covent Garden, London, Chicago Lyric Opera, Suntory Hall, Tokyo, Carnegie Hall, New York City, Hamburg Staatsoper, San Francisco Opera; Gran Teatre del Liceu, Barcelona; Japan Opera Foundation Tokyo; Sang in Massenet's Thais at Nice, 1997; Engaged as Arnold in Guillaume Tell at the Vienna Staatsoper, 1998; Season 1998 as Gounod's Roméo at Turin and Donizetti's Roberto Devereux at Naples; Concert repertoire includes: Rossini's Stabat Mater, Rome, 1991, Bologna, 1992; La Damnation de Faust, Florence, 1995; La Damnation de Faust in London and New York both in 1996; Stabat Mater in Amsterdam, 1997; Sang Massenet's Werther at Parma and Des Grieux at La Scala, 1999; Season 2000–01 as Mozart's Mitridate at the Paris Châtelet, Lensky at the Vienna Staatsoper and Alfredo at Covent Garden; Beethoven's Ninth at the Ravenna Festival, Nemorinio for La Scala and Des Grieux at the New York Met (debut). *Recordings include:* La maga Circe; Gala Opera Concert–l'arte del belcanto; Le Maschere, by Mascagni; Canzone Sacre; Mozart Gala–Suntory Hall, Tokyo;

Simon Boccanegra; La Bohème; Don Giovanni; Messe Solennelle; Recital; Mitridate, re di Ponto. *Address:* c/o Prima International Artists Management, Palazzo Zambeccari, Piazza de'Calderini 2/2, 40124 Bologna, Italy.

**SABIN, Nigel;** Composer and Clarinettist; b. 25 Nov. 1959, England (Resident in Australia from 1974). *Education:* BMus hons, University of Adelaide; Manhattan School of Music, 1992, with David Del Tredici; Study with Richard Meale in Australia. *Career:* Musician-in-Residence, University of Queensland, 1988–95. *Compositions:* Job's Lament for clarinet, 1984; Inner-City Counter-Points, for clarinet, viola, cello and piano, 1989; Four Studies for flute, clarinet, violin and guitar, 1990; Points of Departure for violin, viola, piano and clarinet, 1991; Time and Motion Studies: Postcards From France for clarinet and viola, 1991; Voyages to Arcadia for small orchestra, 1992; Terra Australia for soprano and ensemble, 1992; Another Look At Autumn, for piano, 1993; Faint Qualm for piano, 1993; Love Songs for orchestra, 1993; Angel's Flight for small orchestra, 1994. *Honours:* ASME Young Composers Award, 1981, 1984. *Address:* c/o APRA, 1A Eden Street, Corws Nest, NSW 2065, Australia.

**SACCÀ, Roberto;** Singer (tenor); b. 12 Sept. 1961, Sendehorst, Westfalen, Germany. *Education:* Musikhochschule of Stuttgart and Karlsruhe. *Career:* sang in Germany from 1985 and in Israel, Switzerland, France and England; concert tour of Brazil, 1987 with appearances at Teatro Municipal Rio de Janeiro; Stadttheater Würzburg, 1987–88, Wiesbaden from 1988; sang at the Fermo Festival as Leandro in a 1990 revival of Paisiello's Le Due Contese; debut at La Scala, Milan with Henze's Das Verratene Meer, 1990; Brussels and Salzburg Festival in Ulisse by Dallapiccola, 1993, and Vienna, Musikvereinsaal, 1993; mem. of Zürich Opera, 1994–97; in 1994 sang Le Pêcheur in Le Rossignol at Salzburg Festival, and in Mozart's Der Schauspieldirektor under Harnoncourt; Season 1994–95 as Rinuccio in Puccini's Gianni Schicchi Bruxelles under Pappano, Vienna, title role of Orfeo, Alessandro in Mozart's Il Re Pastore under Harnoncourt, Don Ramiro in a new production of La Cenerentola, Don Ottavio in Don Giovanni and Almaviva in Il Barbiere di Siviglia; Fidelio under Solti in the Salzburg Festival; Sang in Handel's Alcina at the 1997 Vienna Festival; Season 1998 as Mozart's Ferrando at Glyndebourne and Lindoro in Paisiello's Nina at Zürich, with Cecilia Bartoli; Season 1999 in Zürich as Oberon under Gardiner, Don Ottavio and Ramiro in Cenerentola; Berlin with Leukippos in Daphne under Thielemann and Don Ottavio in Baltimore; sang Alfredo in Traviata in Cologne and Munich and Tamino in The Magic Flute under Runniclers at San Francisco, 2000, and Nemorino in L'Elisir d'amore there in 2001; sang Haydn's Orfeo at Covent Garden, 2001; Traviata and Magic Flute in Vienna; Berbiere in Paris; Sang Tamino in Seville, 2002, 2003; Rinuccio, Opéra Bastille, and Tokyo under Ozawa, Entfuhrung Munich, 2004; Inauguration concert of Le Fenice, Venice under Muti, 2004; Tokyo Bohéme under Ozawa; Entfuhrung Berlin; Traviata under Mehta in Munich; Rigoletto in Chile; Inauguration Performance La Fenice with La Traviata under Maazel in Venice. *Recordings:* Handel's Messiah; Capriccio with Vienna Philharmonic; Meistersinger von Nürnberg; Il Re Pastore; Don Giovanni and Cosí fan tutte under Harnoncourt and several solo CDs. *Contributions:* Openwelt; Orpheus; Opernglas, Merker. *Honours:* winner, Opera Prize in Geneva, Switzerland, 1989. *Current Management:* Mag Kurt-Walther Schober, Opernring 8-13, 1010 Vienna, Austria. *Website:* www.roberto-sacca.com.

**SACCO, P. Peter;** Composer and Singer (tenor); b. 25 Oct. 1928, Albion, New York, USA. *Education:* Pupil of Vivian Major and William Willett at Fredonia State University; Eastman School of Music, 1953–58 with Barlow, Rogers and Hanson; MM, 1954, DMus, 1958. *Career:* Studied composition with Wolfgang Niederste-Schee in Frankfurt, 1950–52; Clarinettist with 4th Division Infantry Band; Music Faculty of San Francisco State University, 1959–80; Visiting Professor at University of Hawaii, 1970–71; Concert Tenor. *Compositions:* Dramatic: Jesu, oratorio, 1956, Midsummer Night's Dream Night, oratorio, 1961, Mr Vinegar, chamber opera, 1967, Solomon, oratorio, 1976; Orchestral: Symphony No. 1, 1955, No. 2, The Symphony Of Thanksgiving, 1965–76, No. 3, The Convocation Symphony, 1968, Piano Concerto, 1964, Four Sketches on Emerson Essays, 1963, 2 Piano Sonatas, 1951, 1965, Violin Concerto, 1969–74, Moab Illuminations, for solo piano, 1972, 5 Songs for mezzo-soprano and strings; Chamber: Clarinet Quintet, 1956, String Quartet, 1966, Variations On Schubert's An Die Musik for piano four hands, 1981; 60 Solo songs, 25 choruses, four cantatas and 11 anthems.

**SACCOMANI, Lorenzo;** Singer (Baritone); b. 9 June 1938, Milan, Italy. *Education:* Studied in Milan with Vladimiro Badiali and Alfonso Siliotti. *Career:* Debut: Avignon in 1964 as Silvio in Pagliacci; Sang the Herald in Lohengrin at Venice then appeared in many Italian houses, notably La Scala, Milan, in operas by Puccini, Gounod, Massenet and Verdi; London in 1972 in a concert performance of Caterina Cornaro by Donizetti; US debut at Dallas in 1972 as Henry Ashton in Lucia di Lammermoor; Sang at Verona Arena in 1983, and Geneva in 1985 as Guy de Montfort in Les Vêpres Siciliennes; Further appearances in Frankfurt, New York, Chicago and Buenos Aires; Other roles include Escamillo, Zurga in Les Pêcheurs de Perles and Verdi's Nabucco, Germont, Ezio in Attila, Amonasro, Rigoletto, Luna and Francesco in I Masnadieri; Season 1998 as Gérard in Andrea Chénier at Monte Carlo. *Recordings include:* Caterina Cornaro; Pagliacci.

**SACHS, (Stewart) Harvey;** Canadian writer; b. 8 June 1946, Cleveland, OH, USA; m. 1st Barbara Gogolick 1967 (divorced); one s.; m. 2nd Maria Cristina Reinhart 2001; one d. *Education:* Cleveland Institute of Music, Oberlin College Conservatory, OH, Mannes College of Music, NY, Conductors' Workshop, University of Toronto. *Career:* Conducting, Peterborough Symphony Orchestra, Canada, 1972–75; Guest Conductor, Pomeriggi Musicali, Milan, Italy, 1977; Angelicum, Milan, 1977; Canadian Opera Touring Company, 1979; CBC Vancouver Chamber Orchestra, 1982, 1984; Orchestre Symphonique de Québec, 1984; Toronto Chamber Players, 1984, 1985; Full-time Writer, 1985–; numerous documentaries for radio. *Television:* Toscanini – The Maestro (documentary), for Bravo, PBS and other networks worldwide. *Publications:* Toscanini, biography, 1978; Virtuoso, 1982; Co-author Plácido Domingo's My First 40 Years, 1983; Music in Fascist Italy, 1987; Arturo Toscanini from 1915 to 1946: Art in the Shadow of Politics, exhibition catalogue, 1987; Reflections on Toscanini, 1991; Rubinstein: A Life, biography, 1995; Co-author Sir Georg Solti's Solti on Solti (Memoirs), 1997; Ed. and translator, The Letters of Arturo Toscanini, 2002; contrib. to The New Yorker, TLS, New York Times. *Honours:* Fellow, John Simon Guggenheim Foundation, 1981, Cullman Center for Scholars and Writers, The New York Public Library, 1999–2000. *Current Management:* Denise Shannon Agency, Suite 1603, 20 West 22nd Street, New York, NY 10012, USA. *Telephone:* (212) 414-2911. *Fax:* (212) 414-2930. *E-mail:* dshannon@deniseshannonagency.com.

**SACKMAN, Nicholas;** Composer; b. 12 April 1950, London, England. *Education:* Dulwich College, Nottingham University and Leeds University with Alexander Goehr. *Career:* Ensembles and Cadenzas performed in 1973 at the International Gaudaemus Week and the BBC Young Composers' Forum; A Pair of Wings for 3 Sopranos and Ensemble premiered at the 1974 ISCM Festival and Ellipsis for Piano and Ensemble premiered at Leeds Festival in 1976; Doubles for 2 Instrumental Groups and Flute Concerto commissioned by the BBC and String Quartet by the Barber Institute of Fine Arts, Birmingham; Alap for Orchestra premiered by the BBC Philharmonic Orchestra in 1983 and Hawthorn for Orchestra premiered at the 1993 London Proms; Taught in London and is now Senior Lecturer at the Music Department of Nottingham University. *Compositions include:* Simplicia, musical for schools, 1980; The World A Wonder Waking for mezzo-soprano and ensemble, 1981; The Empress of Shoreditch, musical for schools, 1981; Holism for viola and cello, 1982; Time-Piece for brass quintet, 1982–83; Piano sonata, 1983–84; Corronach for ensemble, 1985; Sonata for trombone and piano, 1986; Paraphrase for wind, 1987; Flute concerto, 1988–89; String Quartet No. 2, 1990–91; Hawthorn for orchestra, 1993, revised 1994; Scorpio for multi-percussion and piano, 1995; Caccia for piano and orchestra, 1998; Koi for four flutes, 1999; Meld for piano, brass and percussion, 1999; Sextet for wind, 2000; Way Back When, for orchestra, 2000; Ballo, for ensemble, 2002; Mosaic, for orchestra, 2002; Fling, for flute, cello and piano, 2002; Cross hands, for piano, 2002; Puppets, for four percussionists, 2003; Vivace, for small orchestra, 2004. *E-mail:* nicholas@sackman.co.uk. *Website:* www.sackman.co.uk.

**SADÉ, Gabriel;** Singer (Tenor); b. 1959, Romania. *Education:* Studied in Israel and at the Guildhall School, London. *Career:* New Israeli Opera at Tel-Aviv from 1986, as Nemorino, Alfredo, Rodolfo, Faust and Pedrillo; Seattle Opera, 1991, as Don Ottavio; Stuttgart Staatsoper from 1992, as Jim Mahonney, Rodolfo and the Duke of Mantua; Tel-Aviv, 1994–95, as Dmitri in Boris Godunov and in the premiere of Tal's Josef; Cologne Opera, 1995–96, as Lensky and Pinkerton; Other roles include Cavaradossi at Dresden, 1994, and Stuttgart, 1998, and Don José at Bologna and Modena; Season 2000–01 as Radames at Cincinnati and Alpha in the premiere of Alpha and Omega by Gil Shohat, in Tel-Aviv. *Recordings include:* Verdi's Requiem.

**SADIE, Julie Anne,** BA, BMus, MA, PhD; American/British cellist, viola da gamba player, lecturer and writer on baroque music; b. 26 Jan. 1948, Eugene, OR, USA; m. 1st Daniel Vertrees 1968; m. 2nd Stanley Sadie 1978; one s. one d.; m. 3rd David Goode 2005. *Education:* Univ. of Oregon, Cornell Univ., City Univ. *Career:* taught at the Eastman School of Music, Rochester, NY 1974–76, Queen's Coll., Taunton, Somerset 2002–05; freelance musician, lecturer and writer on Baroque music; Lecturer in Baroque Music, King's Coll., London 1982; Lecturer in Early Music, Royal Coll. of Music, London 1986–88; Ed., The Consort: European Journal of Early Music 1993–95; Administrator of The Handel House Trust Ltd 1994–98; mem. Royal Soc. of Musicians 1996–, Holst Birthplace Trust 1999–2003, Cossington Concert Trust 2001–; Ford Foundation Fellowship 1970–74. *Recordings:* as member of orchestra, with the Academy of Ancient Music in Mozart's Paris Symphony and with the English Bach Festival in Rameau's Castor et Pollux. *Publications:* The Bass Viol in French Baroque Chamber Music, 1980; Companion to Baroque Music (editor), 1991; The New Grove Dictionary of Women Composers (edited with Rhian Samuel), 1994; with Stanley Sadie, Calling on the Composer: a Guide to European Composer Houses and Museums 2005; contrib. to Gramophone; The Musical Times; Early Music; Chelys; Proceedings of the Royal Musical Association. *Honours:* Univ. of Oregon Distinguished Alumna Award 2005. *Address:* The Manor, Cossington, Bridgwater, Somerset TA7 8JR, England.

**SAÉDEN, Erik;** Singer (Baritone); b. 3 Sept. 1924, Vanersborg, Sweden; m. Elisabeth Murgard. *Education:* Studied at the Royal College of Music, Stockholm and at the Royal Opera School; Private studies with Arne Sunnegardh, Martin Ohman and W Freund. *Career:* Royal Opera Stockholm from 1952 as Mozart's Figaro and Count, Wagner's Sachs, Beckmesser, Pogner, Dutchman and Wolfram, Verdi's Iago, Renato, Macbeth, Germont, Ford and Nabucco; Berg's Wozzeck, Stravinsky's Nick Shadow, Tchaikovsky's Eugene Onegin, Busoni's Faust and the title role in Dallapiccola's Il Prigionierlo; created leading roles in Blomdahl's Aniara, Werle's Drommen om Thérèse, Berwald's Drottningen av Golconda, Dallapiccola's Ulisse (1968), Rosenberg's Hus med Dubbel Ingang and Ligeti's Le Grand Macabre, (1978); Guest Appearances at Bayreuth, Edinburgh, Covent Garden, Montreal; Also Savonlinna as Father Henrik in Singoalla; recorded the role in complete recording of Singoalla; mem, Stockholm Academy of Music. *Recordings include:* The Speaker in Bergman film version of Die Zauberflöte; Swedish Romances, Schubert's Winterreise. *Honours:* Swedish Court Singer; Order Litteris et Artibus. *Address:* Höglidsv 17 A, 182 46 Enebyberg, Sweden.

**SAFFER, Lisa;** American singer (soprano); b. 1964. *Career:* Philadelphia Opera 1987–88, as Flora in The Turn of the Screw, Susanna, and Poppea in Handel's Agrippina; Los Angeles Opera 1990, as Mozart's Re Pastore; Handel Festival at Göttingen 1992–93, as Poppea, in Ottone as Teofana, and Polinessa in Radamisto; ENO 1996, and Opéra Bastille, Paris 1994, as Marie in Zimmermann's Die Soldaten; season 1996 as Cavalli's Calisto for Glimmerglass Opera, USA, and Despina in Così fan tutte at Philadelphia; season 1998 as Handel's Partenope for Glimmerglass Opera; sang Xanthe in Die Liebe der Danaë by Strauss at Avery Fisher Hall, NY 2000; Almirena in Handel's Rinaldo for New York City Opera; Lulu in a new production of Berg's opera for ENO (Royal Philharmonic Soc. Award 2003) 2002. *Recordings include:* Handel's Agrippina, Judas Maccabaeus and Radamisto. *Current Management:* Janice Mayer & Associates LLC, 250 W 57th Street, Suite 2214, New York, NY 10107, USA. *Telephone:* (212) 541-5511. *Fax:* (212) 541-7303. *Website:* www.janicemayer.com.

**SAHL, Michael;** Composer; b. 2 Sept. 1934, Boston, Massachusetts, USA. *Education:* Studied with Israel Citkowitz, 1947–57; BA, Amherst College, 1955; MFA, Princeton University with Sessions, 1957; Berkshire Music Center and Florence in 1957 on a Fulbright Fellowship. *Career:* Buffalo/Lukas Foss Ensemble, 1965–66; Lincoln Center Repertory Company, 1966; Organist, Spencer Memorial Church; Pianist/arranger for Judy Collins, 1968–69; String Quartet, 1969; Music Director, WBAI-FM, 1972–73; Music theatre works, 1975; Tango Project with William Schimmel, 1981; Film work, 1963–. *Compositions include:* String Quartet, 1969; Doina, violin and jazz trio, 1979; Boxes, opera, 1980; Symphony 1983, big band with electric violin, 1983; Tango from Exiles Cafe, for piano solo, 1984; Dream Beach, opera, 1987; Jungles, for electric violin, electric guitar, piano, bass and drums, 1992; John Grace Ranter, opera, 1996; Trio, violin, cello and piano, 1997. *Recordings:* Tropes on the Salve Regina; A Mitzvah for the Dead; Symphony 1983; Doina; Prothalamium; Exiles Cafe Tango; New album, White Rabbit, 1997. *Publications:* Making Changes: A Practical Guide to Vernacular Harmony, 1977. *Honours:* Prix Italia, 1980 for Civilizations And Its Discontents; Nominated for Academy Award, 1990; Seagrams Award in Opera for Boxes; Nominated for Grammy, 1982. *Address:* c/o ASCAP, ASCAP Building, 1 Lincoln Plaza, New York, NY 10023, USA.

**SAINSBURY, Lionel;** British composer; b. 2 June 1958, Wilts. *Career:* Adjudicator, European Piano Teachers' Asscn Composers Competition, 2001; mem., British Acad. of Composers and Songwriters, Performing Right Soc., Mechanical Copyright Protection Soc. *Compositions:* Twelve Preludes for piano premiered by Jack Gibbons, St John's Smith Square, 1987, featured in composer's own performance on Classic FM, 1993; Cuban Dance No. 2 for violin and piano premiered by Tasmin Little and Piers Lane, Wigmore Hall, 1993; Two Nocturnes for strings premiered by William Boughton and the English String Orchestra, Malvern, 1994; Fiesta for two pianos performed by Jeremy Filsell and Francis Pott, Grocer's Hall, London, 1995; Violin Concerto first broadcast by Lorraine McAslan with the BBC Concert Orchestra conducted by Barry Wordsworth, BBC Radio 3, 1995; South American Suite for piano premiered by Jack Gibbons, Holywell Music Room, Oxford, 1996; Two Cuban Dances (originally for solo piano, arranged for piano four hands) premiered by Black/Katayama duo, Nuits Musicales de Beynac-en-Périgord, 1998; Soliloquy for solo violin premiered by Oliver Lewis, Dartington International Summer School, 1998; Incantation for piano premiered by the composer, St John's Coll., Oxford, 2000; Cuban Fantasy for piano broadcast in composer's own performance on BBC Radio 3, 2002; public premiere of Violin Concerto given by Lorraine McAslan with the Bournemouth Symphony Orchestra conducted by Adrian Lucas, Worcester Three Choirs Festival, 2002. *Recordings:* Cuban Dance No. 2 on 'Tchaikovskiana', Tasmin Little/John Lenehan, 2003; Two Nocturnes for strings on English String Miniatures Vol. 5, Royal Ballet Sinfonia/Gavin Sutherland, 2004. *Honours:* Mendelssohn Scholarship, 1980. *Address:* Boot Cottage, Brook End, Chadlington, Chipping Norton, Oxon., OX7 3NF, England. *Website:* www.lionelsainsbury.com.

**ST CLAIR, Carl;** American conductor; *General Music Director, Deutsches Nationaltheater und Staatskapelle Weimar.* *Education:* Texas Univ. *Career:* Conducting Fellow, Tanglewood Music Centre 1985; asst conductor, Boston Symphony Orchestra 1986–90; conductor and Music Dir, Arin Arbor Symphony Orchestra 1985–92, Cayuga Chamber Orchestra 1986–92, Pacific Symphony Orchestra 1996–2005; Gen. Music Dir, Deutsches Nationaltheater und Staatskapelle Weimar 2005–; guest conductor New York Philharmonic, Los Angeles Philharmonic, Philadelphia Orchestra, Austin Lyric Opera, and orchestras of Baltimore, Colorado, Houston, Minnesota, Indianapolis, Nashville, New Jersey, New Mexico, Phoenix, Pittsburgh, Saint Paul, San Antonio, San Jose, Seattle, Toronto, Montréal and Vancouver; has conducted European orchestras, including the radio orchestras of Stuttgart, Frankfurt, Saarbrücken, Hannover and Vienna, and the Frankfurt Opera Orchestra,

Bamberg Symphony, Stuttgart Philharmonic, Essen Philharmonic, Staatsphilharmonie; has appeared at festivals, including Schleswig-Holstein Festival, Pacific Music Festival, Japan, Cabrillo Festival, Grant Park Music Festival, Round Top Festival, Tanglewood Festival. *Recordings:* Corigliano, Concerto for Piano and Orchestra 1994, Elliot Goldenthal, Fire Water Paper (A Vietnam Oratorio) 1996, Takemitsu, From Me Flows What You Call Time 1998, Villa-Lobos, Symphonies No. 1 and 11 1999, Villa-Lobos, Symphonies No. 4 and 12 2001, Foss, Piano Concertos and Elegy for Anne Frank 2001, Music of Gabrieli 2002, Danielpour, An American Requiem 2002, Villa-Lobos, Symphonies No. 3 and 9 2002, Mozart, Sinfonia Concertante (with Karen Dreyfus, Glenn Dicterow) 2003, Villa-Lobos, Symphony No. 7 2004. *Honours:* NEA/Seaver Conductors Award 1990. *Address:* Deutsches Nationaltheater und Staatskapelle, Theaterplatz 2, Weimar 99423, Germany (office). *E-mail:* presse@nationaltheater-weimar.de (office). *Website:* www.nationaltheater-weimar.de (office).

**SAINT-CLAIR, Carol;** Singer (Soprano); b. 1951, Texas, USA. *Education:* Studied at Texas State University. *Career:* Sang at the Gelsenkirchen Opera, 1977–82, Klagenfurt, 1982–87 and Osnabruck Opera from 1987; Guest appearances throughout Germany and South America in such roles as Mimi, Marzelline in Fidelio, Euridice, Blanche in The Carmelites, Donna Anna and Tatiana in Eugene Onegin; Frequent concert appearances. *Address:* c/o Osnabruck Opera, St ädtische Buhnen, Osnabruck GmBH, Domhof 10–11, 4500 Osnabruck, Germany.

**ST HILL, Krister;** Singer (baritone); b. 1957, Sweden. *Career:* debut, sang Escamillo in 1982; Roles in Sweden have included Sancho Panza in Massenet's Don Quichotte, Belcore and Nick Shadow in The Rake's Progress at Malmö City Theatre, Lord Sidney in Rossini's Il Viaggio a Reims, Bohème, Ned Keene, Peter Grimes, Valentin, Faust and Wolfram in Tannhäuser; Sang at Garsington Opera, Oxford, as Ernesto in Haydn's Il Mondo della Luna, at Houston as Donny in the premiere of New Year by Tippett in 1989, Glyndebourne Opera in 1990 in the British premiere of New Year and lieder recitals in Scandinavia and abroad which included Wigmore Hall recitals with Elisabeth Söderström. *Recordings include:* three solo albums; Title role in Jonny Spielt Auf by Krenek; Hindemith's Requiem. *Current Management:* Nordic Artists Management, Sveavagen 76, 11359 Stockholm, Sweden.

**SAKAMOTO, Ryûichi,** MA; Japanese composer, musician and actor; b. 17 Jan. 1952, Tokyo; m. Akiko Yano 1979. *Education:* Shinjuku High School, Composition Dept, Tokyo Fine Arts Univ. *Career:* began composing at age of ten; mem. group Yellow Magic Orchestra 1978–83; worked with David Sylvian 1982–83; solo recording artist, composer 1982–; conductor, arranger, music for Olympic Games opening ceremony, Barcelona, Spain 1992. *Film appearances:* Merry Christmas Mr Lawrence 1982, The Last Emperor 1987, New Rose Hotel 1998. *Film soundtracks:* Daijôbu, mai furendo 1983, Merry Christmas Mr Lawrence 1982, Koneko monogatari 1986, The Last Emperor (with David Byrne and Cong Su, Acad. Award) 1987, Ôritsu uchûgun Oneamisu no tsubasa 1987, The Laser Man (title song) 1988, The Handmaid's Tale 1990, The Sheltering Sky 1990, Tacones lejanos 1991, Topâzu 1992, Wuthering Heights 1992, Wild Palms (TV series) 1993, Little Buddha 1993, Rabbit Ears: Peachboy 1993, Wild Side 1995, Snake Eyes 1998, Love is the Devil 1998, Gohatto 1999, Poppoya (theme) 1999, Alexei to izumi 2002, Derrida 2002, Femme Fatale 2002, Los Rubios 2003. *Recordings include:* albums: Thousand Knives 1978, B-2 Unit 1980, Hidariudeno (A Dream Of The Left Arm) 1981, Coda 1983, Ongaku Zukan (A Picture Book Of Music) 1984, Illustrated Musical Encyclopedia 1984, Esperanto 1985, Miraiha Yarô (A Futurist Chap) 1986, Media Bahn Live 1986, Oneamisno Tsubasa (The Wings Of Oneamis) 1986, Neo Geo 1987, Playing The Orchestra 1988, Tokyo Joe 1988, Sakamoto Plays Sakamoto 1989, Grupo Musicale 1989, Beauty 1989, Heartbeat 1991, Neo Geo (with Iggy Pop) 1992, Sweet Revenge 1994, Soundbites 1994, Hard To Get 1995, 1996 1996, Music For Yohji Yamamoto 1997, Smoochy 1997, Discord 1998, Love Is The Devil 1998, Raw Life 1999, Intimate 1999, Space 1999, BTTB 1999, Gohatto 1999, Complete Index of Gut 1999, Cinemage 2000, Casa 2002; singles: Bamboo Houses (with David Sylvian) 1982, Forbidden Colours (with David Sylvian) 1983, Field Work (with Thomas Dolby) 1986, Risky 1988, We Love You 1991, Moving On 1994, Prayer/Salvation 1998, Anger 1998. *Current Management:* David Rubinson Management, PO Box 411197, San Francisco, CA 94141, USA.

**SAKS, Gidon;** Singer (Bass baritone); b. 5 Jan. 1960, Rechovot, Israel. *Education:* Studied at Univ. of Capetown, Royal Northern College of Music with John Cameron, Univ. of Toronto with Patricia Kern; Int. Opera Studio, Zürich. *Career:* Debut: Stratford Festival Canada as The Mikado; Sang with Canadian Opera Company in Magic Flute, Belle Helene, Fanciulla del West, Poppea, Barbiere di Siviglia, Carmen, Merry Widow, Tales of Hoffmann, La Bohème, Anna Bolena, Fliegende Hollander, Luisa Miller, Beatrice et Benedict and Boris Godunov; Gelsenkirchen Opera in Hero und Leander, Punch and Judy, Der Freischütz, Poppea, Gianni Schicchi, Die Zauberflöte, Im Weissen Rossl, Die Blinden (world premiere), L'Italiana in Algeri, Barbiere di Siviglia, Der Rosenkavalier; Bielefeld Opera in Der Zauberflöte, Das Wunder der Heliane, Der Singende Teufel, La Juive, Verlorene Ehe von Katharina Blum (world premiere), Die Bakchantinnen, Street Scene, Ariadne auf Naxos; New Israeli Opera in La Bohème and Bartered Bride; Ariadne auf Naxos in Madrid; L'Incoronazione di Poppea in Brussels; Billby Budd, Don Giovannik Giulio Cesare and Magic Flute for Scottish Opera; Billy Budd and Don Carlo in Geneva; Billy Budd, Fanciulla del West, Rigoletto, Semele with Vlaamse Opera; Boris Godunov in Dublin and Das Liebesverbot in Wexford;

Fidelio and Freischutz at Berlin Staatsoper; Fidelio and Nozze di Figaro with Welsh Nat. Opera; Borish Godunov, Freischutz, Rake's Progress and Twilight of the Gods with English Nat. Opera; Harvey Milk in Houston, New York and San Francisco; Luisa Miller USA; Fidelio in Florence and Helsinki; Don Carlo in Palermo; Billy Budd, Salammbo and L'Espace Dernier at Bastille Paris; Nozze di Figaro in Cincinnati; Concerts include Berliner Festwochen with Fischer Dieskau and Ashkenazy in Franck's Beatitudes, Shostakovitch 13th Symphony in Liverpool, Execution of Styenka Razin in Florence with Bychkov and Verdi Requiem in Toronto; As Dir and Designer: Puny Little Life Show in Cape Town; Wozzeck, Cavalleria Rusticana, Happy End and Don Giovanni in Manchester; Paisiello Barbiere in Gattierres, Grande Macabre in Vienna; Cosí fan Tutte, Eugene Onegin, Don Giovanni and Carmen for Aberdeen Int. Youth Festival; teaches singing privately and in masterclasses. *Recordings:* Hercules; Billy Budd; Pilgrim's Progress; Silbersee; Ferne Klang; Der Kreidekries; Opera Gala; Harvey Milk. *Address:* c/o Harlequin Agency Ltd, 203 Fidlas Road, Llanishen, Cardiff CF14 5NA, Wales.

**SALA, Ofelia;** Singer (Soprano); b. 1970, Valencia, Spain. *Education:* Valencia Conservatoire; Courses with Victoria de los Angeles, Elly Ameling and Renata Scotto. *Career:* Appearances in opera and concert at Leipzig, Lyon, Munich (Prinzregententheater), Vienna, Barcelona and Prague; Repertoire includes Sophie in Der Rosenkavalier, Pamina, Gretel, Oscar, and Henze's Elizabeth Zimmer; Angel in Messiaen's St François d'Assise, at Leipzig 1998, in Outis by Berio at La Scala, Gilda (Bonn Opera) and Mozart's Servilia (Netherlands Opera, 2000); Engaged with the Deutsche Oper Berlin, from 2001; Concerts include the Requiems of Brahms and Mozart, Haydn's Creation, Vivaldi's Gloria and Mozart's C minor Mass. *Honours:* Prize Winner, Montserrat Caballé, Francisco Viñas and Vervier Competitions. *Address:* c/o Theateragentur Dr G. Hilbert, Maximilianstrasse 22, 80539 Munich, Germany.

**SALAFF, Peter;** Violinist; b. 1942, USA. *Career:* Member of the Cleveland Quartet, 1968–92, with regular tours of the USA, Canada, Europe, Japan, Russia, South America, Australia, New Zealand and the Middle East; Faculty, Eastman School Rochester and in residence at the Aspen Music Festival, co-founding the Center for Advanced Quartet Studies; Tour of Russia and 5 European countries in 1988; Season 1988–89 with appearances at the Metropolitan Museum and Alice Tully, New York; Concerts in Paris, London, Bonn, Prague, Lisbon and Brussels; Appearances at Salzburg, Edinburgh and Lucerne Festivals; Many complete Beethoven Cycles and annual appearances at Lincoln Center's Mostly Mozart Festival; In addition to standard works his repertory has included performances of works by Ives, John Harbison, Sergei Slonimsky, Samuel Adler, George Perle, Christopher Rouse and Toru Takemitsu. *Recordings:* Repertoire from Mozart to Ravel and collaborations with Alfred Brendel in Schubert's Trout Quintet, Pinchas Zukerman and Bernard Greenhouse with Brahms' Sextets, Emmanuel Ax, Yo-Yo Ma and Richard Stoltzman. *Address:* Eastman School of Music, 26 Gibbs Street, Rochester, NY 14604, USA.

**SALERNO-SONNENBERG, Nadja;** Violinist; b. 10 Jan. 1961, Rome, Italy. *Education:* Curtis Institute of Music (came to USA 1969); The Juilliard School. *Career:* Television, CBS 60 minutes; 60 minutes II; Sunday Morning; NBC 's National News; The Tonight Show; A and E's Artist of the Week; PBS' Live from Lincoln Center; Backstage/Lincoln Center; The Charlie Rose Show; City Arts; PBS/BBC Series the Mind; PBS Sesame Street; Subject of documentary: Speaking in Strings, 1999. *Recordings include:* Speaking in Strings; Humoresque; Night and Day; Bella Italia; It Aint Necessarily So; Vivaldi The Four Seasons; Nadja Salerno-Sonnenberg, Sergio and Odair Assad. *Honours:* Violin Competition, Walter W Naumburg International, 1981; Avery Fisher Career Grant, 1983; Ovation Award for Mendelssohn/Massenet/Saint Saëns, 1988; Avery Fisher Prize, 1999. *Current Management:* ICM Artists Ltd. *Address:* c/o M L Falcone, Public Relations, 155 West 68th Street, Suite 1114, New York, NY 10023, USA. *Telephone:* 212 580 4302.

**SALKELD, Robert,** ARCM; British teacher, examiner and editor; b. 16 April 1920, Newcastle upon Tyne; two s. one d. *Education:* Royal Grammar School, Newcastle upon Tyne, Newcastle Conservatoire of Music, Royal Coll. of Music. *Career:* Head of Music Dept, Collingwood School, Peckham 1957–60; tutor, Morley Coll. 1950–69; Prof., London Coll. of Music 1961–69, examiner 1961–82; extensive work at festivals, summer schools and courses 1949–72; mem. Royal Musical Asscn. *Publications:* Concert Pieces (four books) 1951, Play the Recorder Series (six books) 1966, Chester Recorder Series (12 books) 1970, Editions including Byrd, Weldon, Valentine, Arne, Hook etc.; contrib. to Music in Education 1954–76. *Honours:* Hon. FLCM 1977. *Address:* c/o HSBC, 58 High Street, Winchester, SO23 9BZ, England (office).

**SALLINEN, Aulis Heikki;** Finnish composer and professor of arts; *Chairman, TEOSTO (Finnish Composers' Copyright Society);* b. 9 April 1935, Salmi; s. of Armas Rudolf Sallinen and Anna Malanen; m. 1st Pirkko Holvisola 1955 (died 1997); four s.; m. 2nd Maisa Lokka 1999. *Education:* Sibelius Acad. *Career:* primary school teacher 1958–60; Man. Finnish Radio Orchestra 1960–69; Prof. of Arts Sibelius Acad. 1979–2000; Chair. TEOSTO (Finnish Composers' Copyright Society); mem. Swedish Royal Music Acad. 1979; mem. Finnish Composers' Asscn, Sec., Chair.; mem. Bd Finnish Nat. Opera. *Compositions include:* eight symphonies, violin concerto, cello concerto, flute concerto and other orchestral music, five string quartets and other chamber music; film score for The Iron Age 1983. *Operas include:* The Horseman 1975, The Red Line 1978, The King Goes Forth to France 1982, Kullervo 1988, The

Palace 1993, King Lear 1999. *Honours:* Hon. DPhil (Turku) 1991, (Helsinki) 1994; Nordic Council Music Prize 1978, Wihuri Int. Sibelius Prize 1983. *Address:* TEOSTO, Lauttasaarentie 1, 00200 Helsinki 20, Finland (office). *Telephone:* (9) 681011 (office). *Fax:* (9) 677134 (office). *E-mail:* teosto@teosto.fi (office). *Website:* www.teosto.fi/teosto/webpages.nsf (office).

**SALMENHAARA, Erkki;** Composer and Musicologist; b. 12 March 1941, Helsinki, Finland. *Education:* Studies, Sibelius Academy, Helsinki with Joonas Kokkonen and Vienna with Ligeti, 1963; PhD, University of Helsinki, 1970. *Career:* Faculty Member, University of Helsinki, 1963–; Chairman, Society of Finnish Composers, 1974–76. *Compositions:* 4 Symphonies, 1962, 1963, 1963, 1972; 2 Cello Sonatas, 1960–69, 1982; Elegy for 2 string quartets, 1963; Wind Quintet, 1964; Requiem Profanum, 1969; Quartet for flute, violin, viola and cello, 1971; Nel Mezzo Del Cammin Di Nostra Vita, for orchestra, 1972; The Woman of Portugal, Opera, 1972 (premiered Helsinki 1976); Suomi-Finland, Unsymphonic Poem, 1967; Canzonetta per Archi, 1972; Illuminations for orchestra, 1972; Horn Concerto, 1973; Sonatine for 2 violins, 1973; Canzona per piccola, orchestra, 1974; Poema for violin or viola and strings, 1976; Introduction and Chorale for organ and orchestra, 1978; String Quartet, 1978; Lamento per orchestra d'archi, 1979; Concerto for 2 violins and orchestra, 1980; Sonatine for flute and guitar, 1981; Violin Sonata, 1982; Sonatella for piano four hands, 1983; Adagietto for orchestra, 1982; Sinfonietta per archi, 1985; Introduction and Allegro for clarinet, cello and piano, 1985; Cello Concerto, 1987; Isle of Bliss for baritone, soprano and orchestra, 1990; Publications include; The History of Finnish Music, 1995. *Address:* c/o TEOSTO, Lauttasaarentie 1, 00200 Helsinki, Finland.

**SALMINEN, Matti;** Finnish singer (bass); b. 7 July 1945, Turku. *Education:* Sibelius Acad., Helsinki, and studied in Rome. *Career:* debut, Helsinki Opera as King Philip in Don Carlos 1969; sang in Cologne, Zürich and Berlin 1972–76 in the principal bass parts; La Scala, Milan 1973 as Fafner and at Savonlinna Festival 1975 as the Horseman, Sarastro, Philip, Don Carlos, Daland and Ramphis; sang at Bayreuth from 1978 as Daland, the Landgrave, Titurel, King Mark and in The Ring operas; Metropolitan Opera from 1981 as King Mark, Rocco, Osmin, Fasolt, Fafner, Hunding and Hagen; sang in Berlin 1985 and Munich 1987 as Fasolt, Hunding and Hagen; Prince Khovansky at San Francisco 1984, in Barcelona 1988, and Boris Godunov 1984 at Zürich and 1985 in Barcelona; sang in 1988 in the Ponnelle productions of L'Incoronazione di Poppea, Die Zauberflöte and Die Entführung and several principal bass parts in Vienna, Hamburg, Paris, Chicago and Tokyo; sang Hunding in Die Walküre at the Metropolitan 1990, also televised, Rocco in Fidelio at the Los Angeles Music Center, Daland at the 1990 Savonlinna Festival; season 1992–93 as Daland at the Metropolitan, Rocco at Zürich and Savonlinna, King Philip at the Deutsche Oper Berlin and Sarastro at the Savonlinna Festival; sang the Landgrave in Tannhäuser at Savonlinna 1996; sang Padre Guardiano in La Forza del Destino at Savonlinna 1998; season 2000–01 as Wagner's Hagen at the Deutsche Oper Berlin, Daland at Liège, King Mark for the Salzburg Festival, Gurnemanz for Washington Opera and Hunding in Zürich; title role in the premiere of Sallinen's Lear, at Helsinki; premiere of Rautavaara's Rasputin (title role) at Helsinki 2003. *Recordings:* St Matthew Passion, The Landgrave in Tannhäuser, The Ring, Sallinen's The Horseman, Daland, Mozart's Requiem, Osmin, Sarastro. *Honours:* Opera Actual magazine Award for best bass 2005. *Current Management:* Theateragentur Dr Germinal Hilbert, Maximilianstrasse 22, 80539 Munich, Germany. *E-mail:* agentur@hilbert.de. *Website:* www.hilbert.de.

**SALMON, Philip;** singer (tenor); b. 1960, England. *Education:* Royal College of Music. *Career:* debut recital at the City of London Festival followed by the St Matthew Passion with the Rotterdam Philharmonic, Beethoven's 9th with the Ulster Orchestra and Netherlands Philharmonic, and Mozart's Requiem with the Florida Philharmonic; Sang in Massenet's La Vièrge at St Etienne in 1991; Operatic repertoire includes Mozart's Tamino and Belmonte for Pavilion Opera and Debussy's Pelléas at Marseille and Strasbourg, 1990–91; Sang Belmonte in Die Entführung at the Buxton Festival in 1991 and Albert Herring at St Albans; Sang Tamino at the Gaiety Theatre, Dublin, 1996. *Honours:* Young Musicians Recordings Prize. *Current Management:* Robert Gilder & Co., Enterprise House, 59–65 Upper Ground, London, SE1 9PQ, England. *Telephone:* (20) 7928-9008. *Fax:* (20) 7928-9755. *E-mail:* rgilder@robert-gilder.com.

**SALOMAA, Petteri;** Singer (Baritone); b. 1961, Helsinki, Finland. *Education:* Studied at the Sibelius Academy and with Hans Hotter and Kim Borg. *Career:* Debut: Finnish National Opera, Helsinki 1983, as Mozart's Figaro; Appeared at the Ludwigsburg and Schwetzingen Festivals, 1984; Wexford Festival 1985, as the King in Ariodante; Drottningholm from 1986, as Leporello and Nardo in La Finta Giardiniera; Geneva Opera 1987, as Papageno and Amsterdam 1988, as Masetto, conducted by Nikolaus Harnoncourt; North American debut 1988, with Messiah in San Francisco, followed by Figaro with Michigan Opera; Season 1989–90 at Freiburg Opera as Faninal, Ned Keene, the Father in Hansel and Gretel and in Purcell's King Arthur; 1989–91 at Freiburg Opera as Billy Budd, Posa, Ned Keene and Belcore, 1991 at Frankfurt Opera as Papageno and Guglielmo, 1993 as Conte Robinson in Il matrimonio Segreto; Sang in Purcell's King Arthur at the Châtelet and Covent Garden, 1995; Other roles include Oreste in Iphigénie en Tauride, Posa, Billy Budd and Albert in Werther; Sang Silvio in Pagliacci with Tampere Opera, 1996; Sang in premiere of Bergman's The Singing Tree, Helsinki, 1995; Season 2000–01 in Legrenzi's La Divisione del Mondo, Swetzingen and Innsbruck Festivals; Captain in Death of Klinghoffer, by

John Adams, Helsinki, 2001. *Recordings include:* Beethoven's Ninth Symphony; La Finta Giardiniera; The Fiery Angel by Prokofiev, and Peer Gynt with the Berlin Philharmonic; Le nozze di Figaro; Mendelssohn Elijah. *Honours:* 1st Prize, National Singing Competition at Lappeenranta, 1981. *Address:* Festium Agency, Partiotic 34, 00370 Helsinki, Finland.

**SALOMAN, Ora (Frishberg);** American musicologist and professor of music; b. 14 Nov. 1938, Brooklyn, NY; m. Edward Barry Saloman, 1 July 1968. *Education:* PhD in Musicology, MA in Musicology, AB in Music, Columbia University, New York; Studied violin with Vladimir Graffman and Ivan Galamian, chamber music with Raphael Hillyer, Claus Adam and William Kroll. *Career:* Chairman, Department of Music, 1978–84, Professor of Music, Baruch College and The Graduate Center, City University of New York; Visiting Scholar in Residence, Queen's University, Ontario, Canada, 1999; mem. Editorial Advisory Board, American Music, 1995–97. *Publications:* Beethoven's Symphonies and J. S. Dwight: The Birth of American Music Criticism 1995, Essay in Music and Civilisation: Essays in Honor of Paul Henry Lang 1984, Essay in Music and the French Revolution 1992, Essay in Mainzer Studien zur Musikwissenschaft: Festschrift Walter Wiora 1997. *Contributions:* Acta Musicologica, Musical Quarterly 1974, 1992, 1996, Music and Man, American Music 1988, 1990, International Review of the Aesthetics and Sociology of Music 1989, The Journal of Musicology 1992, The New Grove Dictionary of Opera 1992, St James International Dictionary of Opera 1993, Journal of the Royal Musical Association 1994, American National Biography 1999, Reader's Guide to Music 1999, Revised New Grove Dictionary of Music and Musicians 2001, Dictionary of Literary Biography 2001, Die Musik in Geschichte und Gegenwart 2001, The Opera Quarterly 2003, Encyclopaedia of New England Culture 2005, Journal of Musicological Research 2005. *Honours:* National Endowment for the Humanities Fellowship 1989. *Address:* Baruch College, City University of New York, Department of Fine and Performing Arts, 1 Bernard Baruch Way, Box B7-235, New York, NY 10010, USA (office). *E-mail:* ora_saloman@baruch.cuny.edu.

**SALONEN, Esa-Pekka,** FRCM; Finnish conductor and composer; *Music Director, Los Angeles Philharmonic Orchestra;* b. 30 June 1958, Helsinki. *Education:* Sibelius Acad., Helsinki, studied composition with Rautavaara and conducting with Panula, studied in Italy. *Career:* Prin. Guest Conductor, Philharmonia Orchestra 1984–94, Oslo Philharmonic Orchestra 1985–; Music Dir and The Walt and Lilly Disney Chair, LA Philharmonic Orchestra 1992–; Prin. Conductor Swedish Radio Symphony Orchestra 1985–95; Artistic Adviser New Stockholm Chamber Orchestra 1986; Artistic Dir Helsinki Festival 1995–96. *Compositions:* orchestral: Concerto for alto saxophone and orchestra 1980–81, Giro 1982–97; chamber music: YTA I for alto flute 1985, YTA II for piano 1985, YTA III for cello 1986, FLOOF for soprano and chamber ensemble 1990, Mimo II 1992, LA Variations 1996, Gambit 1998, Five Images after Sappho 1999, Mania 2000, Foreign Bodies 2001. *Honours:* Royal Philharmonic Soc. Opera Award 1995, Litteris et Artibus Medal (Sweden) 1996, Royal Philharmonic Soc. Conductor Award 1997, Officier Ordre des Arts et des Lettres (France). *Address:* Los Angeles Philharmonic Orchestra, 151 S Grand Avenue, Los Angeles, CA 90012, USA. *Website:* www.laphil.org.

**SALTA, Anita;** Singer (Soprano); b. 1 Sept. 1937, New York, USA. *Education:* Studied in New York. *Career:* Debut: Jacksonville 1959, as Aida; Appearances at such German Opera House Centres as Stuttgart, Wuppertal, Nuremberg, Dortmund, Kassel, Essen and Hanover; Other roles have included Gluck's Alceste, Mozart's Countess, Donna Elvira and Fiordiligi, Marguerite, the Trovatore and Forza Leonoras, Traviata, Desdemona, Hélène and Elisabeth de Valois; Tatiana, Antonida in A Life for the Tsar, Marenka, Mimi, Butterfly, Santuzza, Elsa, Eva, Chrysothemis, the Marschallin and Katerina Izmailova; Many concert appearances. *Address:* c/o Theatre, Rolandstrasse 10, 4300 Essen, Germany.

**SALTER, Richard;** British singer (baritone); b. 12 Nov. 1943, Hindhead, Surrey, England. *Education:* Univ. of Cambridge, Royal Coll. of Music, London and Vienna Acad. of Music with Christain Moeller, Ilse Rapf and Anton Dermota. *Career:* sang with King's Singers and gave concert performances 1968; opera debut Darmstadt 1973; sang further in Frankfurt and at Glyndebourne; Kiel Opera 1979, as Don Giovanni; guest appearances in Berlin and Hanover; Hamburg Staatsoper 1979, as Lenz in the premiere of Wolfgang Rihm's Jakob Lenz; sang Beckmesser at the Paris Opéra 1988; Hamlet in Rihm's Die Hamletmaschine at Hamburg; season 1992–93 as the Master in Höller's Meister und Margarita at Cologne, and Cortez in the premiere of Rihm's Die Eroberung von Mexico at Hamburg; sang Coupeau in the premiere of Klebe's Gervaise Macquart, Düsseldorf 1996; Berg's Wozzeck at Montpellier 1998; season 2000–01 as Beckmesser at Nuremberg; Dr Schön in Lulu at Dusseldorf and Bielefeld; sang Milton in the premiere of Jörg Widmann's Gesicht im Spiegel, at Munich 2003; season 2004–05 sang Fra Melitone in La forza del destino at Nürnberg, sang in Ariadne auf Naxos, Don Pizzaro in Leonore, the title role in Gianni Schicchi, and Marcel in Il Tabarro all at Munich; sang The Magistrate in the premiere of Philip Glass's Waiting for the Barbarians, at the Erfurt Theatre, Germany 2005. *Address:* c/o Bayerische Staatsoper, Max-Joseph-Pl. 2, 8000 Munich 22, Germany.

**SALTER, Robert;** Violinist; b. 1960, England. *Education:* Wells Cathedral School and Guildhall School, London, with David Takeno. *Career:* Founder member of the Guildhall String Ensemble, with concerts in Europe, the Far East and North America; Solo engagements at the Barbican and Wigmore Halls, London and elsewhere in England and Europe; Leader of Glyndebourne

Touring Opera, 1992–; Guest Leader with the English Chamber Orchestra, London Pro Arte and orchestra of the Royal Opera (debut with Giulio Cesare at the Barbican, 1997). *Recordings:* many albums with the Guildhall String Ensemble. *Honours:* Prizes for solo and chamber music performance, GSMO.

**SALTER, Timothy,** MA, LRAM, ARCO, MTC, FRCM; British composer, conductor and pianist; *Professor of Composition, Royal College of Music;* b. 15 Dec. 1942, Mexborough, Yorks. *Education:* St John's Coll., Cambridge, Univ. of London. *Career:* Musical Dir The Ionian Singers; pianist (chamber music) on tours in the UK and internationally; conductor and pianist on recordings and broadcasts; Prof. of Composition, Royal Coll. of Music; f. Usk Recordings to promulgate new and neglected works 1995. *Compositions:* instrumental works, chamber music, songs, choral works and orchestral works. *Recordings include:* many choral and piano works, two string quartets and other chamber music, including Fantasy on a Theme by J. S. Bach for Piano, String Quartets Nos 1 and 2, Abstractions for oboe trio, Lacrimae rerum for cello, organ and chorus; English folk song arrangements; Katharsios for chorus, piano and percussion; Perspectives, set two, for piano, After the Sun for baritone, oboe/cor anglais and piano, Chimera for violin and piano. *Address:* 26 Caterham Road, London, SE13 5AR, England. *Telephone:* (20) 8318-2031 (office). *E-mail:* ts@timothysalter.com (office). *Website:* www.timothysalter.com.

**SALVADORI, Antonio;** Singer (Baritone); b. 1950, Venice, Italy. *Education:* Studied at the Conservatorio Benedetto Marcello, Venice. *Career:* Sang first in Il Barbiere di Siviglia and Pagliacci; La Scala 1977, in Luisa Miller, with Caballé and Pavarotti; Verona Arena fro m 1978, notably as Amonasro (1988); Marcello and Belcore at La Scala 1987–88, tour with the company to Japan 1988; Has sung Rossini's William Tell in Milan, Linz, Nice, Zürich and New York (concert performance at Carnegie Hall); Vienna Staatsoper 1988, as Ezio in Attila; Sang Simon Boccanegra at Cremona, 1990; Other appearances at Chicago, Venice (Gerard in Andrea Chénier), Turin and Hamburg (Don Carlo in Ernani); Sang Iago at Palermo, 1999. *Address:* c/o Opernhaus Zürich, Falkenstrasse 1, 8008 Zürich, Switzerland.

**SALVATORI, Roberto;** Singer (Baritone); b. 1970, Trinidad. *Education:* Studied, Guildhall School, London, England and the Britten/Pears School at Aldeburgh; Masterclasses with Sena Jurinac and Sherrill Milnes. *Career:* Roles with Pavilion Opera have included Mozart's Don Giovanni, Count and Guglielmo, Rossini's Figaro, Donizetti's Enrico in Lucia di Lammermoor, Dr Malatesta and Belcore; Germont and Scarpia with European Chamber Opera, Sid in Albert Herring at Aldeburgh and Berkely in Marschner's Vampyr for BBC television; Principal with English National Opera from 1995, with Ping, Escamillo and Marcello (La Bohème) in first season; Stolzius in the British company premiere of Zimmerman's Soldaten, 1996; Season 1998–99 as Marcello and Escamillo for ENO and in Massenet's Esclarmonde for Chelsea Opera Group; Sang Iago in Verdi's Otello at ENO and Jochanaan in Salome at the Spier Festival in South Africa. *Honours:* Scholarship from the Countess of Munster Trust. *Current Management:* Penelope Marland Artists' Management. *Address:* c/o ENO Press Office, English National Opera, St Martin's Lane, London WC2N 4ES, England.

**SALWAROWSKI, Jerzy (Hubert);** Conductor and Musical Director; b. 7 Sept. 1946, Kraków, Poland; m. Ewa Czarniecka, 19 Sept 1976, two s. *Education:* Kraków Music High School, Conducting and Composition, Graduated 1970; Warsaw Chopin Music Academy, docent symphony and opera conducting, 1997. *Career:* Assistant Conductor, Kraków Philharmonic Choir, 1970–71; Second Conductor, Opole Philharmonic Orchestra, 1972–78; Second Conductor, Katowice-Silesian Philharmonic, 1978–81; Substitute Art Director, Silesian Philharmonic, 1982–84; Substitute Art Director, Polish Radio National Symphony Orchestra, 1985–; Guest Conductor, Łódź Great Opera House, tours in Europe; Artistic Director, Pomeranian Philharmonic Orchestra, 1988–90; Artistic Director, Lublin State Philharmonic Orchestra, 1991–93; Artistic Director, Szczein Symphony Orchestra and Torunn Chamber Orchestra; Principal Guest Conductor, Szczecin Philharmonic Orchestra, Torun Chamber Orchestra; Artistic Dir, of festival, Torun: Music and Architecture; Tours in Europe (France, Portugal, Spain, Germany) with symphony and opera music; Prof., Paderewski Music Acad. Poznań, 1999–; Dir, Orchestra and Opera Conductorship Inst.;. *Compositions:* Transcriptions and theatre music. *Recordings:* All Gershwin's Pieces for piano and orchestra, with A Ratusinski; All Symphonic Poems by M Karlowicz; J Sibelius: En Saga and Violin Concerto, with V Brodski, for Musical Heritage Society, first digital in Poland; H Wieniawski, Violin Concerto, with V Brodski; Mozart CD, All Church Sonatas with Pomeranian Philharmonic Orchestra and Karol Golebiewski, 1988; Lessel, Grand Rondeau and Piano Concerto, with Silesian Philharmonic and Jerzy Sterczynski, 1992; Mendelssohn, Hebrides Overture, Violin Concerto and 4th Symphony (Italian) with Krzysztof Jakowicz, 1997; Permanent recording for Polish radio and television over 250 each year; Television concerts, television cycles, Musical Drawing Room. *Publications:* New Elaborations of Karlowicz Scores in PWM Edition. *Contributions:* Permanent Reviews. *Honours:* Gold Plate Award, for Gershwin Album, 1993. *Address:* ul. Wietnamska 63B, 40-765 Katowice, Poland.

**SALZMAN, Eric;** Composer and Writer on Music; b. 8 Sept. 1933, New York, USA. *Education:* BA, Columbia College, Columbia University, 1954; MFA, Princeton University, 1956; Teachers include Otto Luening, Ussachevsky, Jack Beeson, Roger Sessions and Milton Babbitt; Continued studies in Europe with Petrassi in Rome and Darmstadt. *Career:* Music critic for the New York Times, 1958–62, New York Herald Tribune, 1963–66; Teacher at Queen's

College, NY, 1966–68; Director, New Images of Sounds, series of concerts at Hunter College; In 1970 founded Quog Music Theater, to explore new ideas in the performing arts; Co-founder and Artistic Director of American Music Theater Festival with Marjorie Samoff, Philadelphia, 1983–. *Compositions include:* String Quartet, 1955; Flute Sonata, 1956; Inventions for orchestra, 1959; Verses and Cantos for 4 voices, instruments and electronics, 1967; Larynx Music, dance piece with tape, 1968; The Conjurer, multimedia spectacle, 1975; Civilization and its Discontents, opera buffa for radio, 1977; Noah, spectacle, 1978; The Passion of Simple Simon, for performance at the Electric Circus in Greenwich Village; Variations on a Sacred Harp Tune for harpsichord, 1982; Boxes, radio opera with Michael Sahl, 1983; Big Jim and the Small-Time Investors, music theatre, 1985; The Last Words of Dutch Schulz, music theatre, 1996; Body Language, mixed media, 1996; Adaptation of Gershwin's Strike up The Band, 1984. *Publications include:* 20th Century Music: An Introduction, 1967, new edition, 1987; Civilization and Its Discontents and Making Changes, a handbook of vernacular harmony, both with Michael Sahl; The New Music Theater, 1998. *Address:* American Music Theater Festival, 1 Franklin Plaza, Philadelphia, PA 19103, USA.

**SAMARITANI, Pier Luigi;** stage designer, costume designer and opera director; b. 29 Sept. 1942, Novare, Italy. *Education:* Accademia de Brera, Milan, Centre d'Art Dramatique, Paris. *Career:* debut as Director, Werther, Florence, 1978; Assisted Stage Designer, Lila de Nobili, Paris; Set Designer, Théâtre du Gymnase, Paris 1962, Teatro dell'Opera, Rome 1964; Dance Design for American Ballet Theatre, 1980; Stage Designer for many companies in USA and Europe; Exhibited Stage Designs Spoleto Festival, 1972; Ernani at the Met and Eugene Onegin for the Lyric Opera of Chicago/Werther in Vienna, Paris and Florence, Butterfly in Berlin (1987); Season 1992 with Andrea Chénier at Florence and Turin and Die Meistersinger at Spoleto. *Current Management:* Herbert H. Breslin Inc., 119 W 57th Street, New York, NY 10019, USA.

**SAMPSON, Carolyn;** Singer (soprano); b. 1974, England; m. *Education:* Univ. of Birmingham, 1995. *Career:* opera includes Amor in The Coronation of Poppea (ENO), Tanterabogus in The Fairy Queen (ENO in London and on tour to Barcelona), La Musica and Euridice in Orfeo (Barbican, London), Antonia in The Tales of Hoffmann at the St Endellion Festival, First Niece in Peter Grimes for Opéra National de Paris; concert engagements with City of London Sinfonia, Manchester Camarata, Le Chapelle Royale, ChorwerkRuhr, Il Giardino Armonico, Music of the Baroque Chicago, RIAS Kammerchor, Holland Sinfonia, Sonnerie, The King's Consort (including US tour, 2001), The Sixteen, Ex Cathedra, Halle Orchestra, Scottish Chamber Orchestra, Collegium Vocale, Gent, Washington Bach Consort, The Royal Concertgebouw Orchestra, Freiburg Baroque Orchestra, The English Concert, Orchestra of the Age of Enlightenment, Le Concert d'Astrée, The Gabrieli Consort, Orchestre des Champs Elysées; festival appearances include BBC Proms, Mostly Mozart (New York), Beaune, Leipzig, Saintes, Halle, Salzburg, Istanbul; recitals in the Proms Chamber Music series, The Wigmore Hall, BBC Wales, BBC Scotland, and the Hampstead and Highgate Festival, London. *Recordings include:* Kuhnau, Knüpfer, Vivaldi, Monteverdi, Zelenka, Lalande, Rameau, Bach, Orfeo, Buxtehude, Carmina Burana. *Current Management:* Caroline Phillips Management, The Old Brushworks, 56 Pickwick Road, Corsham, Wiltshire, SN13 9BX, England. *Telephone:* (1249) 716716. *Fax:* (1249) 716717. *E-mail:* cphillips@caroline-phillips.co.uk. *Website:* www.caroline-phillips.co.uk/sampson.

**SAMSING, Boris (Leon);** Violinist; b. 31 Dec. 1943, Copenhagen, Denmark; m., 1 s., 1 d. *Education:* Funen Academy of Music; Bern and Prague. *Career:* Debut: Funen Academy, 1963; Member, Sonderjylland Symphony Orchestra, 1964–69; Principal, Sjaelland Symphony Orchestra, 1969–75; Member, Kontra Quartet, 1973–; principal, Danish Radio Symphony Orchestra, 1975–; Representative ensemble af the Danish State, 1989–92; Teacher, Royal Danish Academy of music; Toured all over the world with Kontra Quartet; Workshops as a violinist with Kontra Quartet. *Recordings:* Carl Nielsen; Per Norgaard; Rued Langgaard; Vagn Holmboe; Niels W Gade; Poul Ruders; Hans Abrahamsen; Mozart; Schubert; Tchaikovsky; 33 recordings with the Kontra Quartet. *Honours:* Peder Moller Award; Nominations of the Nordic Council; The Gramophone Recording of the Year; Danish Musicians Union Award. *Address:* Vejlemosevej 10, 2840 Holte, Denmark.

**SAMSON, (Thomas) James,** BMus, MMus, PhD, LRAM; university teacher; b. 6 July 1946, Northern Ireland. *Education:* Queen's University, Belfast, University College, Cardiff. *Career:* Research Fellow in Humanities, University of Leicester, England, 1972–73; Lecturer in Music, 1973–86, Reader in Musicology, 1986–91, Professor of Musicology, 1991–94, University of Exeter; Badock Professor of Musicology, University of Bristol, 1994–2002; Professor of Music, Royal Holloway, University of London, 2002–; mem, Council Member, Royal Musical Association. *Publications:* Music in Transition, 1977; The Music of Szymanowski, 1980; The Music of Chopin, 1985; Chopin Studies, 1988; Man and Music, vol. 7, The Late Romantic Era, 1991; The Cambridge Companion to Chopin, 1992; Chopin: The Four Ballades, 1992; Chopin Studies 2 (with John Rink), 1994; Chopin, Master Musicians series, 1996; The Cambridge History of Music, 2002. *Contributions:* Rocznik Chopinowski, Journal of the American Musicological Society, Nineteenth-Century Music, Tempo, Journal of Musicology, Music Analysis, Music and Letters, Musical Times. *Honours:* Szymanowski Centennial Medal, 1982; Order of Merit, Polish Ministry of Culture, 1990; Fellow of the British Academy, 2000.

*Address:* Music Department, University of Bristol, Royal Fort House, Tyndall Avenue, Bristol BS8 1VJ, England.

**SAMUEL, Gerhard;** Conductor, Composer and Professor of Music; b. 20 April 1924, Germany. *Education:* BM, Eastman School of Music; MM, Yale University. *Career:* Conductor, Ballet Ballads on Broadway, 1947–48; Attached to Cultural Attache, American Embassy, Paris, 1948–49; Associate Conductor and Violinist, Minneapolis Symphony, 1949–59; Director and Conductor, Collegium Musicum, Minneapolis Civic Opera, 1949–59; Director and Conductor, San Francisco Composers Forum, 1959–71; Music Director Oakland Symphony Orchestra, 1959–71; Music Director/Conductor, San Francisco Ballet, 1960–70; Guest Conductor, San Francisco Opera; Conductor, Ojai Festival, 1971; Associate Conductor, Los Angeles Philharmonic Orchestra, 1970–73; Director and Conductor, Ojai Festival, 1971; Conductor of Orchestra and Opera and Director of Conducting Program, California Institute of the Arts, 1972–76; Director of Orchestral Activities, College-Conservatory of Music, University of Cincinnati, 1976–97; Conductor, Music Director, Cincinnati Chamber Orchestra, 1983–91; Guest Conductor, USA, South America, Mexico, Canada, the Philippines, England, Belgium, France, Germany, Norway, Sweden, Russia, China, Poland and Switzerland; Chief Guest Conductor, Oakland Ballet Company, 1983–86; Conducted the premiere of Harold Blumenfeld's Seasons in Hell, Cincinnati, 1996; Music Director, Cosmopolitan Orchestra, New York City, 1997–. *Compositions:* Over 70 including: Requiem for Survivors, orchestral, 1973; Looking at Orpheus Looking, orchestral, 1971; Out of Time, A Short Symphony, 1978; Chamber Concerto for flute in the Shape of a Summer, orchestral, 1981; Emperor and the Nightingale, small ensemble, 1980; Fanfare for a Pleasant Occasion, small ensemble, 1981; Thoughts For Sandy on His Birthday, small ensemble, 1983; Harlequin's Caprice, solo harpsichord, 1980; On the Beach at Night Alone, orchestral, 1980; The Naumburg Cadenza, solo violin, 1985; Nocturne on an Impossible Dream, small ensemble, 1986; Nicholas and Concepcion, orchestral, 1987; As Imperceptibly as Grief, orchestral, 1988; Christ! What are Patterns For?, small ensemble, 1988; Henry's Cadenza, solo violin, 1989; Apollo and Hyacinth, small ensemble, 1989; After a Dirge, small ensemble, 1993; His Cincinnati Philharmonia Orchestra participated in the 1989 Mahler Cyle, Châtelet Theatre, Paris, and Festival 98 in Lisbon; In Search of Words, orchestral, 1995. *Current Management:* Corbett Arts Management, San Francisco, California, USA. *Address:* c/o ASCAP, ASCAP Building, One Lincoln Plaza, New York, NY 10027, USA.

**SAMUELSON, Mikael;** Singer (Baritone); b. 9 March 1951, Stockholm, Sweden. *Education:* Studied with Birgit Stenberg and Erik Werba. *Career:* Has sung in Sweden from 1968 in opera, oratorio, music theatre and films; Royal Opera Stockholm as Rossini's Figaro, Drottningholm Theatre 1987 and 1989, as Mozart's Figaro and Papageno; Sang in Die Schöpfung 1988; Appearances with the Stockholm Music Drama Ensemble in Pagliacci, Mahagonny and Death in Venice; Television engagements in Drömmen om Thérèse by Werle and Kronbruden by Rangströ m; Has appeared as cabaret artist in Sweden and Finland. *Address:* c/o Drottningholms Slottsteater, PO Box 27050, 102 51 Stockholm, Sweden.

**SANCHEZ, Ana Maria;** Singer (Soprano); b. 1966, Elda, Alicante, Spain. *Education:* Studied at the Alicante Conservatory and in Madrid with Isabel Penagos and Miguel Zanetwi. *Career:* Sang in concerts and recitals in Spain, France and Germany; Stage debut as Abigaille in Nabucco at Palma (1994) followed by Donna Anna at Valencia and elsewhere; Mathilde in Guillaume Tell at Lisbon, Leonora in La Forza di destino at Barcelona and Chrysothemis in Elektra at Valencia; Sang the Trovatore Leonora at Zürich, season 1996–97, and has appeared further in Roberto Devereux and Tannhäuser in Bibao, Salud in La Vida Breve at Malaga and in Don Giovanni at Hamburg; Engaged to return to Valencia 1998, as Gutrune in Götterdämmerung; Concerts include the Verdi Requiem and song recitals. *Honours:* Prizewinner in competitions at Bilbao and Enna (Italy), 1992–93. *Address:* c/o Opernhaus Zürich, Falkenstrasse 1, 8008 Zürich, Switzerland.

**SAND, Annemarie;** Singer (Mezzo-Soprano); b. 26 Nov. 1958, Copenhagen, Denmark. *Education:* Studied at the Royal Academy of Music and the National Opera Studio. *Career:* Appeared with English National Opera from 1987 as the Page in Salome, Linetta in The Love of Three Oranges, and Dryad in Ariadne auf Naxos; Welsh National Opera, 1989 as the Composer in Ariadne, conducted by Charles Mackerras; Other roles include Mother Goose in The Rake's Progress, Nancy in Albert Herring, Charlotte, Octavian, Hansel and the Mother in Amahl and the Night Visitors; Many concert appearances including Mozart's Requiem at the Teatro San Carlo, Naples, and 12 concerts in Denmark, 1989; Season 1992 as Kate Pinkerton for ENO and in Oliver's Mario and the Magician at the Almeida Theatre; Season 1993 included BBC Proms debut in The Wreckers, Ethyl Smyth. *Honours:* Elena Gerhardt Lieder Prize; Minnie Hauk Prize; Clifton Prize for Best Recital. *Address:* c/o English National Opera, St Martin's Lane, London, WC2, England.

**SAND, Malmfrid;** singer (soprano); b. 1955, Oslo, Norway. *Education:* studied in Oslo and London. *Career:* debut, sang Pamina in Die Zauberflöte at Oslo; Appearances as Fiordiligi in Brussels, London and at the Bath Festival; Irene in Tamerlano for Orpheus Opera and Isaura in Jérusalem by Verdi for BBC Radio 3; Wexford Festival 1983, as the Queen in Marschner's Hans Heiling, returning as Donna Anna in Gazzaniga's Don Giovanni and in Busoni's Turandot; Recent engagements as Electra in Idomeneo for the English Bach Festival and Manon for Dorset Opera, 1991; Concert Repertoire

includes Vivaldi Gloria, Messiah, Dvořák's Requiem; Concerts and Recitals in Scandinavia, the USA and Europe, notably with the Stavanger Symphony, the Oslo NRK Symphony and the Harmonien Symphony Orchestra of Bergen; Sang Mrs Maurrant in Weill's Street Scene, Turin, 1995. *Current Management:* Robert Gilder & Co., Enterprise House, 59–65 Upper Ground, London, SE1 9PQ, England. *Telephone:* (20) 7928-9008. *Fax:* (20) 7928-9755. *E-mail:* rgilder@robert-gilder.com.

**SANDEL, Marina;** Singer (Mezzo-soprano); b. 1959, Stuttgart, Germany. *Education:* Studied in Frankfurt and Stuttgart, and with Brigitte Fassbaender. *Career:* Concert appearances in Europe and Israel from 1984; Essen Opera from 1989, with guest engagements in opera at Karlsruhe, Mannheim and Ludwigsburg; Roles have included Dorabella, Hansel, Laura in La Gioconda (Bremen, 1996) and Octavian in Der Rosenkavalier; Essen, 1996, in the premiere of Bibalo's Miss Julie and as Nicklausse in Les contes d'Hoffmann. *Address:* c/o Essen Opera, Rolandstrasse 10, 4300 Essen 1, Germany.

**SANDERLING, Kurt;** German conductor; b. 19 Sept. 1912, Arys; m. 1st Nina Bobath 1941; m. 2nd Barbara Wagner 1963; three s. *Career:* Conductor Moscow Radio Symphony Orchestra 1936–41, Leningrad Philharmonic 1941–60, Chief Conductor Dresden State Orchestra 1964–67; Guest appearances at Prague, Warsaw, Salzburg and Vienna Festivals; with Leipzig Gewandhaus Orchestra, New Philharmonia Orchestra 1972–; conducted LA Philharmonic 1991; Chief Prof. of Conducting, Leningrad Conservatory; retd 2002. *Honours:* many awards and prizes (USSR and GDR). *Address:* c/o Norman McCann International Artists Ltd, The Coach House, 56 Lawrie Park Gardens, London, SE26 6YJ (office); The Music Partnership Ltd, 41 Adlebert Terrace, London, SW8 7BH, England (office); Am Iderfenngraben 47, 13156 Berlin, Germany. *Telephone:* 9167558. *Fax:* 9167558.

**SANDERLING, Michael;** Concert Cellist; b. 1967, Berlin, Germany. *Education:* Studied at the Berlin Musikhochschule. *Career:* Principal of the Leipzig Gewandhaus Orchestra, 1987–92; Solo career from 1992, notably with the Boston Symphony Orchestra, Los Angeles Philharmonic Orchestra, Berlin and Bamberg Symphonies, Philharmonia, Royal Philharmonic Orchestra and Tonhalle Zürich; Chamber concerts with the Trio Ex Aequo at the Schleswig-Holstein, Lucerne and Salzburg Festivals. *Honours:* Prizewinner at the Maria-Canals Competition Barcelona, JS Bach Competition Leipzig and ARD Competition, Munich. *Address:* c/o World-wide Artists, 6 Petersfield Crescent, Coulsdon, Surrey CR5 2JQ, England.

**SANDERLING, Thomas;** Conductor; b. 2 Nov. 1942, Nowosibirsk, USSR. *Education:* School of the Leningrad Conservatory; German High School of Music, East Berlin. *Career:* Debut: Conducted Berlin Symphony Orchestra, 1962; Chief Conductor, Reichenbach, 1964; Music Director, Opera and Concerts, Halle, Democratic Republic of Germany, 1966; Permanent Guest Conductor, German State Opera, Berlin, 1978–; Moved to West Germany in 1983; Has conducted at most major centres in Germany and throughout Europe including Stockholm, Oslo, Helsinki, Milan, Rome, London, Salzburg and Amsterdam; Gave the German premiere of Shostakovich's Symphonies 13 and 14 with Berlin Radio Symphony Orchestra, 1969, and A Petterson's 8th Symphony in 1979; Outstanding success with productions of Magic Flute and Marriage of Figaro at Vienna State Opera, 1979; Has worked with Rotterdam Philharmonic, Bournemouth Symphony Orchestra, Philharmonia (London), Vienna Symphony Orchestra and in Nice, Vancouver, Rochester, New Zealand, Japan, Israel and Australia, with recent productions of Figaro (Nice) and Don Giovanni (Austria and Helsinki). *Recordings:* Shostakovich: Michelangelo cycle (recording premiere) and Symphonies 2 and 4; Handel: Alexander's Feast and Italian Cantatas; Wolfgang Strauss: Symphony No. 1; Udo Zimmermann: Ein Zeuge der liebe. *Honours:* Berlin Critics' Award, 1970. *Address:* The Music Partnership Ltd, 41 Adlebert Terrace, London, SW8 1BH.

**SANDERS, Ernest H.;** Musicologist; b. 4 Dec. 1918, Hamburg, Germany; m. Marion Hollander 1954, 1 s., 1 d. *Education:* MA, Music Historical Musicology, 1952, PhD, in the same, Columbia University, 1963. *Career:* Department of Music, Columbia University, Lecturer, 1954–58, Instructor, 1958–61 and 1962–63, Assistant Professor, 1963–65 and 1966–67, Associate Professor, 1967–72, Professor, 1972–86, Chairman, Department of Music, 1978–85. *Publications:* English Polyphony of the Thirteenth and Early 14th Centuries (Polyphonic Music of the Fourteenth Century Vol. XIV, 1979); Vols XVI and XVII, co-editor. *Contributions:* Numerous articles dealing with aspects of mediaeval polyphony in Journal of the American Musicological Society; The Musical Quarterly; Acta Musicologica; Archiv für Musikwissenschaft; Music and Letters; Musica Disciplina; The New Grove Dictionary; Various Festschriften; Most of these collected in French and English Polyphony of the 13th and 14th Centuries–The Notation of Notre-Dame Organa Tripla and Quadrupla, forthcoming; 3 articles on Beethoven's Opp 125 and 123. *Honours:* Fulbright Research Scholarship, 1965–66 (England); Guggenheim Fellowship (supplementary), 1965–66; ACLS Fellowship, 1969–70; Senior Research Fellowship, National Endowment for the Humanities, 1973–74. *Address:* 885 West End Avenue 8B, New York, NY 10025-3524, USA (home). *Telephone:* (212) 865-0527 (home). *E-mail:* sanders885@juno.com (home).

**SANDERS, Graham,** FLCM; singer (tenor); b. 1963, Chichester, England; m. *Education:* London Coll. of Music, and studied in USA with William McGraw at the Univ. of Cincinnati, James King and William Johns at Indiana Univ. *Career:* appearances at Bonn Opera as Roderigo in Otello (debut role), Laca in Jenůfa and Florestan in Fidelio; Bremen Opera 1994–2000, as Wagner's Erik and Walther, Bacchus in Ariadne auf Naxos and Canio in Pagliacci; further engagements as Siegmund in Die Walküre at Graz, Kiel and Darmstadt, Laca at Dresden and Polixenes in Ein Wintermärchen by Boesmans at Braunschweig; season 2001–02 as Otello at Budapest and Siegfried for Scottish Opera; engaged for Götterdämmerung at Edinburgh 2003. *Honours:* Lauritz Melchior Heldentenor Society scholarship 1990. *Current Management:* ICM, 4–6 Soho Square, London, W1D 3PZ, England. *E-mail:* classical@icmtalent.com. *Website:* www.cmtalent.com.

**SANDISON, Gordon;** Singer (Baritone); b. 1949, Aberdeen, Scotland. *Education:* Studied at the Royal Scottish Academy. *Career:* Has sung with Scottish Opera from 1973 as Papageno, the Figaros of Rossini and Mozart, Malatesta, Don Giovanni, Belcore, Don Alfonso, Falstaff, Marcello; Covent Garden debut, 1984, as Fléville in Andrea Chénier, followed by Mandarin, Morales, Starveling, Montano, Masetto and the Doctor and Shepherd in Pélleas et Mélisande; Further appearances with English National Opera, Théâtre du Châtelet Paris, Opera Northern Ireland and the Glyndebourne, Wexford and Edinburgh Festivals; Sang in Carmen at Earls Court, London and on Tour to Japan; Rossini's Bartolo for ENO, 1995; Sang Frank in Die Fledermaus for Opera Holland Park, 1998; Season 2000–01 as the Mayor in Jenůfa at Glyndebourne and Rossini's Bartolo for ENO. *Address:* c/o Phoenix Artists Management, 6 Windmill Street, London, W10 1HF, England.

**SANDMEIER, Rebekka,** BA, MA, PhD, LRSM; German musicologist; b. Berlin. *Education:* Trinity Coll., Dublin, Ireland. *Career:* Lecturer in Musicology, Trinity Coll., Dublin 1994–97, Conservatory of Music, Dublin 1996–97; violin teacher, Lüchow-Dannenberg 1997–98; Lecturer in Musicology, Univ. of Paderborn 1998, Münster Univ. 1999–; mem. Editorial Bd Die Musik in Geschichte und Gegenwart 2001–; mem. Gesellschaft für Musikforschung, ACMP. *Publications:* Text and Music in German Operas of the 1920s 1998, Denen Kennern... Winifried Schlepphorst zum 65. Geburtstag 2002, Die Sammlung Nordkirchen: Kammermusik 2004; contrib. to Die Musik in Geschichte und Gegenwart. *Honours:* Trinity Postgraduate Award 1992–95. *Address:* Musikwissenschaftl. Seminar, Schossplatz 6, 48149 Münster, Germany (office). *Telephone:* (251) 8324560 (office). *Fax:* (251) 8324450 (office). *E-mail:* sandmeier@uni-muenster.de (office). *Website:* www.uni -muenster.de/Musikwissenschaft (office).

**SANDON, Nicholas (John);** Musicologist; b. 16 Feb. 1948, Faversham, Kent, England; m. Edith Virginia Edwards, 1 July 1975, 1 step-s., 2 step-d. *Education:* Studied, 1967–71, BMus, 1970, University of Birmingham; PhD, University of Exeter, 1983. *Career:* Lecturer in Music, 1971–86, Head, Music Department, 1983–86, Professor of Music, 1993–, University of Exeter; Professor of Music, Head, Music Department, University College, Cork, Ireland, 1986–93; mem, Royal Musical Associatiiun; Plainsong and Medieval Society, Council Member; Henry Bradshaw Society. *Publications:* John Sheppard's Masses, 1976; Oxford Anthology of Medieval Music, 1977; The Use of Salisbury, 1986–99; Many other editions of English church music; General Editor of Antico Edition. *Contributions:* Early Music; Music and Letters; Musica Disciplina; Proceedings of the Royal Musical Association; Royal Musical Association Research Chronicle; Musical Times; Music Review; The Consort; BBC Radio 3; Journal of Theological Studies. *Honours:* University Scholar at Birmingham, 1967–70. *Address:* Department of Music, University of Exeter, Exeter EX4 4PD, England.

**SANDSTRÖM, Sven-David;** Composer; b. 30 Oct. 1942, Motala, Sweden; m. Gudrun Sandströ m. *Education:* Stockholm University, 1963–67; State College of Music, 1968–72 with Lidholm; Further study with Ligeti and Norgard. *Career:* Joined Faculty of State College of Music Stockholm, 1980. *Compositions:* Stage: Strong Like Death, Church opera, 1978; Hasta O Beloved Bride, chamber opera, 1978; Emperor Jones, music drama, 1980; Incidental Music for Strindberg's Dream Play, 1980; Ballet Den elfte gryningen, 1988; Music, ballet, 1995; The City, opera, 1998; Vocal: Pictures, 1969; Intrada, 1969; In the Meantime, 1970; Around a Line, 1971; Through and Through, 1972; Con tutta Forza, 1976; Clumination, 1977; Agitato, 1978; The Rest is Dross, 1980; Guitar Concerto, 1983; Invignings fanfar, 1988; Cello Concerto, 1989; Piano Concerto, 1990; Percussion Concerto, 1994; Concerto for recorder, harpsichord and strings, 1996; Soft Music for clarinet strings and percussion, 1996. Chamber: String Quartet, 1969; Mosaic for string trio, 1970; 6 Character Pieces, 1973; Metal, Metal for 4 percussionists, 1974; Utmost, premiered by Pierre Boulez, London 1975; Within for 8 trombones and percussion, 1979; Drums for timpani and 4 percussionists, 1980; Spring Music for percussion, 1997; Vocal: Inventions for 16 voices, 1969; Lamento, 1971; Birgitta-Music I, 1973; Expression, 1976; A Cradle Song/The Tiger, after Blake, 1978; Requiem, for the child victims of war and racism, 1979; Agnus Dei, 1980; Piano and organ music; Moses, Oratorio, 1997.

**SANDVE, Kjell Magnus;** Singer (Tenor); b. 1957, Karmoy, Norway. *Education:* Studied at the Oslo State Opera School, 1979–82. *Career:* Sang at the Nationaltheater Weimar, 1982–84 and Norwegian National Opera at Oslo from 1983, with guest appearances at Copenhagen, Opéra Bastille as Hylas in Les Troyens, the Staatsoper Berlin as Belmonte in 1989, and at Munich as Sifare in Mitridate in 1990; Other roles include Don Ottavio, Ferrando, Nemorino, Alfredo, Lensky and Nielsen's David; Sang Verdi's Macduff at Oslo, 2000. *Recordings include:* Songs by Grieg. *Address:* Norwegian National Opera, PO Box 8800 Youngstorget, 0028 Oslo, Norway.

**SANGER, David John,** FRAM, FRCO, ARCM; British organist; b. 17 April 1947, London; s. of Stanley C. Sanger and Ethel L. F. Sanger. *Education:*

Eltham Coll., London and Royal Acad. of Music. *Career:* studied organ in Paris with Marie-Claire Alain and later with Susi Jeans 1966–68; freelance soloist and teacher of organ 1969–; has performed throughout Europe and in USA and Canada; Prof. of Organ, RAM 1983–89, Visiting Prof. of Organ 1989–97; has recorded six organ symphonies of Louis Vierne and complete organ works of César Franck. *Publication:* Play the Organ (organ tutor for beginners) 1990. *Honours:* Hon. FASC; First Prize, Int. Organ Competition, St Albans 1969, Kiel 1972. *Address:* Old Wesleyan Chapel, Embleton, Cumbria, CA13 9YA, England. *Telephone:* (17687) 76628. *Fax:* (17687) 76628. *E-mail:* david .sanger@virgin.net (home). *Website:* www.davidsanger.co.uk (home).

**SANTI, Nello;** Conductor; b. 22 Sept. 1931, Adria, Rovigo, Italy. *Education:* Studied at the Liceo Musicale in Padua and with Coltro and Pedrollo. *Career:* Debut: Teatro Verdi, Padua, 1951, Rigoletto; Conductor of the Zürich Opera from 1958; Covent Garden debut, 1960, with La Traviata; Vienna Staatsoper and Salzburg Festival debuts, 1960; Metropolitan Opera, 1962, Un Ballo in Maschera; Regular appearances from 1976; La Scala, Milan, 1971; Paris Opéra, 1974; Guest engagements in Berlin, Munich, Florence, Geneva, Lisbon and Madrid, in the operas of Rossini, Bellini, Donizetti, Verdi, Puccini and Mascagni; Orchestral concerts with L'Orchestre National, Paris; RIAS, West Berlin, and the Munich Philharmonic; New Philharmonia Orchestra and the London Symphony; Returned to Covent Garden, 1982, La Fanciulla del West; Conducted Aida in a new production by Vittorio Rossi; Conducts regularly at the Metropolitan Opera House, New York, Arena di Verona and throughout Italy and Germany; Rigoletto at Verona, 1997 and Nabucco at Zürich, 1998; Season 2003/04 includes: Barbiere di Siviglio, Nabucco, Tosca and Rigoletto with the Opera House of Zurich, Donizetti's Don Pasquale in Montecarlo, new productions of Bellini's I Capuleti e Montecci at the Opera of Rome and Verdi's Nabucco at the Summer Festival of Caracalla in Rome and a new production of Puccini's La Bohème at the Teatro San Carlo di Napoli. Concert Engagements include a summer concert with the Philharmonic Orchestra of Montecarlo, symphonic concerts with the Oslo Philharmonic Orchestra and further concerts with the NHK Symphony Orchestra in Tokyo. *Recordings:* Pagliacci; L'Amore dei Tre Re; Complete Verdi tenor arias, with Carlo Bergonzi; Aria recitals with Placido Domingo; Videos of Otello, La Bohème, Nabucco, Rigoletto, Andrea Chénier, Falstaff and the Verdi Requiem. *Honours:* Medallion de la Cité de Zürich; Commendatore of the Republic of Italy. *Address:* Wildbachstrasse 77. CH-8008 Zürich Switzerland.

**SANTUNIONE, Orianna;** Singer (Soprano); b. 1 Sept. 1934, Sassolo, Modena, Italy. *Education:* Studied in Milan with Carmen Melis and Renato Pastorino. *Career:* After debut as Giordano's Fedora sang in Rome, Genoa, Bologna, Trieste, Naples, Parma and Palermo; Covent Garden, London 1965, as Amelia in Un Ballo in Maschera and Elisabeth de Valois; Further appearances in Nice, Rouen, Turin, Venice, Munich, Hamburg, Amsterdam, Dallas, Philadelphia and Cincinnati; Verona Arena, 1967–77; Other roles include Desdemona, Elsa, Medea, Santuzza, Nedda, both Leonoras of Verdi, Mathilde in Guillaume Tell, Francesca da Rimini, Tosca, Madama Butterfly and Aida. *Recordings include:* Madame Sans-Gêne by Giordano; Pimmalione by Donizetti; Otello and Lohengrin for Italian television. *Address:* c/o Arena di Verona, Piazza Bra 28, 37121 Verona, Italy.

**SAPAROVA-FISCHEROVA, Jitka;** Opera Singer (Soprano); b. 7 April 1964, Brno, Czechoslovakia; m. Miroslav Fischer, 19 Oct 1991, 1 d. *Education:* High School of Musical Art. *Career:* Debut: Mozart's Zauberflöte; Soloist of Chamber Orchestre, Baroque and Renaissance Music, Musica Aeterna, 1985–86; Soloist of Slovak National Theatres Opera from 1986; Operas include: Faust; Le nozze di Figaro; Rigoletto; Suor Angelica; Carmen; mem, Association of Slovak Theatres. *Recordings:* Rigoletto; La Sonnambula. *Honours:* 1st Prize, 1985 Competition of M Schneider Trnausee; Laureate of Singing Competition of Antonín Dvořák. *Address:* Dankovskeho 14, 811 03 Bratislava, Slovakia.

**SARADJIAN, Vagram;** Cellist; b. 15 July 1948, Yerevan, Armenia. *Career:* Debut: Yerevan, Armenia, 1956; US debut, Carnegie Hall, 1990; Winner of Russian National Competition aged 18; Won several major contests including Tchaikovsky International Competition, 1970; Geneva International Cello Competition, 1975; Recitals performed around the world in halls including: Gaveau in Paris; La Scala in Milan, Victoria Hall in Geneva, Musikverein in Vienna, Teatro Colón in Buenos Aires, Carnegie Hall in New York, Great Hall of the Moscow Conservatory, Leningrad Philharmonic Hall; International tours playing with conductors including Gergiev, Khachaturian, Kondrashin, Svetlanov, Rostropovich, Shostakovich, Temirkanov; Premiered works by composers including Alexander Tchaikovsky, Gia Kancheli, Karen Khachaturian; Appearances include: Valery Gergiev's Stars of the White Nights Festival in St Petersburg; Extensive tour of Argentina and Uruguay; Extensive European tour with Maxim Vengerov and Vag Papian; Engaged for performances in Chicago, Los Angeles, Philadelphia, tours in Russia, Switzerland, Poland and Germany; Taught at Connecticut College, New London, Connecticut and Oberlin Conservatory, Oberlin, Ohio; Faculty, Aaron Copland School of Music, Queens College, City University of New York and Pierchase Conservatory (SUNY); Professor of Violoncello, University of Houston, Texas. *Recordings:* Karen Khachaturian Cello Concerto (USSR Symphony Orchestra); Saint-Saëns, Concerto No. 1; Tchaikovsky Rococo Variations; Dvořák's Concerto in B Minor, op 104 (Moscow Philharmonic); Karen Khachaturian, Sonata for Cello and Piano; Eduard Mirzoian–Sonata for Cello and Piano. *Honours:* Fourth Prize, Tchaikovsky International Competition, Moscow, 1970; Gold Medals, Geneva Prize Winner, Switzerland,

1975; International Music Festivals in Sofia, 1976, Prague, 1980; First Prize, Aram Khachaturian International Music Awards, New York, 1990.

**SARASTE, Jukka-Pekka;** Finnish conductor; *Music Director, Oslo Philharmonic Orchestra*; b. 22 April 1956, Heinola; m. Marja-Lisa Ollila; three s. one d. *Education:* Sibelius Acad., Helsinki. *Career:* debut with Helsinki Philharmonic 1980; Prin. Conductor and Music Dir Finnish Radio Symphony Orchestra 1987–2001; Music Dir Toronto Symphony Orchestra 1994–2001; Prin. Guest Conductor BBC Symphony Orchestra 2002–05; Chief Conductor and Music Dir Oslo Philharmonic Orchestra 2006–; has been guest conductor with Boston Symphony Orchestra, Cleveland Orchestra, San Francisco Orchestra, Frankfurt Radio Orchestra, NY Philharmonic Orchestra, London Philharmonic Orchestra, Orchestre Philharmonique de Radio France, BBC Symphony Orchestra, Munich Philharmonic Orchestra; has toured Japan, Hong Kong, Taiwan, Germany, USA, Canary Islands Festival; Artistic Adviser Finnish Chamber Orchestra. *Recordings include:* complete Sibelius symphonies 1995 (with Finnish Radio Symphony Orchestra) Mussorgsky (with Toronto Symphony Orchestra) Nielsen Symphonies 4, 5 (with Finnish Radio Symphony Orchestra), Romeo and Juliet Suite (Prokofiev). *Current Management:* c/o Till Janczukowicz, Columbia Artists Management GmbH, 18 Albrechtstrasse, 10117 Berlin, Germany. *Telephone:* 172 2518526. *Address:* c/o Oslo Philharmonic Orchestra, Oslo Konserthus, Munkedamsveien 14, 0250 Oslo, Norway. *Website:* www.oslophil.com.

**SARBU, Eugene;** Violinist; b. 6 Sept. 1950, Pietrari, nr. Rimnicu Vilcea, Romania. *Education:* Following studies in Bucharest and Paris joined Curtis Institute, Philadelphia, for further study with Ivan Galamian; Later at Juilliard, New York, and with Nathan Milstein in Zürich. *Career:* Made first solo appearance aged 6; Won National Festival of Music Award in Bucharest, 1958; Regular solo recitals and concerts in England; Promenade Concert debut, 1982; Performances in USA, Europe, Australia and South America; Far East tour 1987–88, with the New Japan Philharmonic in Tokyo; Plays a Cremonese Violin by Tomasso Balestieri made in 1756. *Recordings:* Sibelius Concerto for EMI with the Hallé Orchestra, 1980; Vivaldi's Four Seasons and Mozart Concertos with European Master Orchestra, 1988. *Honours:* Winner, Paganini and Carl Flesch Competitions, 1978; George Enescu Medal, 1995. *Address:* c/o Hispania Clásica S.L., Los Madrazo 16 bajo, 28014 Madrid, Spain.

**SARDI, Ivan;** Singer (Bass); b. 7 July 1930, Budapest, Hungary. *Education:* Studied with Antonio Mekandri at the Martini Conservatory Bologna. *Career:* Debut: Brescia 1951, as Padre Guardiano in La Forza del Destino; Sang in Naples, Bologna, Genoa, Trieste and Catania, as Mozart's Masetto and Bartolo and in Operas by Verdi; Glyndebourne 1956, as Don Alfonso; Further appearances in Florence, Milan and Lisbon; Staatsoper Munich, 1956–61; Member of the Deutsche Oper Berlin from 1961; Concerts in Munich, Hamburg, Vienna and elsewhere in Europe; Sang Schigolch in Lulu at Dresden, 1992. *Recordings:* Don Giovanni, Le nozze di Figaro, Verdi Requiem, Der junge Lord by Henze; Sparafucile in Rigoletto; Guillaume Tell. *Address:* c/o Deutsche Oper Berlin, Richard Wagnerstrasse 10, 100 Berlin 1, Germany.

**SARDINERO, Vincenzo;** Singer (Baritone); b. 12 Jan. 1937, Barcelona, Spain. *Education:* Studied at the Liceo Conservatory in Barcelona. *Career:* Sang first in operettas and Spanish zarzuelas; Opera debut Barcelona 1964, as Escamillo; In 1967 sang Germont in La Traviata at Barcelona and in Lucia di Lammermoor at La Scala, Milan; New York City Opera 1970, as Tonio in Pagliacci; Covent Garden debut 1976, as Marcello in La Bohème; Further appearances Lisbon, Rome, Vienna, Madrid, Lyon, Paris, Munich, Hamburg, Basle, Budapest and the Aix-en-Provence Festival; Season 1991–92 as Marcello at Barcelona and Rigoletto at Palma; Other roles include Nottingham in Roberto Devereux, Valentin (Faust), Alphonse XI (La Favorite) and Verdi's Renato, Posa and Luna. *Recordings include:* L'Amico Fritz; L'Atlantida; Turandot; Manon Lescaut; Lucia di Lammermoor; Un Giorno di Regno; La Navarraise by Massenet; Edgar by Puccini; La Straniera by Bellini.

**SARFATY, Regina;** Singer (Mezzo-soprano); b. 1932, Rochester, New York, USA. *Education:* Studied at the Juilliard School, New York. *Career:* Sang with New Mexico Opera from 1948; Santa Fe Opera from 1957, notably in the 1968 US premiere of The Bassarids by Henze; New York City Opera from 1958, as Cenerentola, Maria Golovin in the opera by Menotti, Jocasta (Oedipus Rex) and Dorabella; Frankfurt Opera from 1963, as Carmen and Octavian; Sang Octavian at Glyndebourne, 1960, and returned in 1984, as Adelaide in Arabella; Sang Mme de Croissy in Dialogues des Carmélites at Baltimore, 1984; Member of the Zürich Opera, notably as the Countess Geschwitz in Lulu and in the premiere of Die Erretung Thebens by Kelterborn, 1963. *Recordings:* Excerpts from Die Walküre, conducted by Stokowski; The Rake's Progress, conducted by Stravinsky, and the Choral Symphony, conducted by Bernstein.

**SARGENT, (Donald) Anthony,** MA, FRSA; British arts administrator; *General Director, The Sage Gateshead*; b. 18 Dec. 1949, s. of Sir Donald Sargent, KBE, CB and Mary Raven; m. 1st Sara Gilford 1978 (divorced); m. 2nd Caroline Gant 1986; one d. *Education:* King's School, Canterbury, Oriel Coll., Oxford, Magdalen Coll., Oxford, Christ Church, Oxford. *Career:* numerous posts with BBC TV and radio 1974–86, including Man. Concert Planning 1982–86, Partnerships and Programme Development Man. BBC Music Live 1999–2000; Artistic Projects Dir South Bank Centre, London 1986–89; Head of Arts Birmingham City Council 1989–99; Gen. Dir The Sage Gateshead 2000–; Gen. Dir North Music Trust 2000–. *Honours:* Hon. Fellow Birmingham Conservatoire 1999. *Address:* The Sage Gateshead, POB 254, Gateshead, NE8 2YR, England (office). *E-mail:* anthony.sargent@ thesagegateshead.org (office). *Website:* www.thesagegateshead.org (office).

**SARGON, Simon A.;** composer and pianist; *Professor of Music, Southern Methodist University*; b. 6 April 1938, Bombay, India; m. Bonnie Glasgow 1961, 1 d. *Education:* BA, Brandeis University, 1959; MS, Juilliard School, 1962. *Career:* Debut: Carnegie Hall, with Jennie Tourel, 1963; Musical Staff, New York City Opera, 1960; Associate Conductor, Concert Opera, 1962–68; Pianist for concerts of Jennie Tourel, 1963–71; Faculty Member, Juilliard School, 1967–69; Chairman, Voice, Rubin Academy, Jerusalem, 1971–74; Faculty, Hebrew University, Jerusalem, 1973–74; Director of Music, Temple Emanu-El, 1974–2001; Faculty, SMU, 1983–. *Compositions:* Patterns in Blue, 1976; Elul: Midnight, 1980; Praise Ye the Lord, 1980; Sing His Praise, 1981; The Queen's Consort, 1982; Lord Make Me to Know My End, 1985; Voices of Change, commission, 1988; Symphony No. 1, Holocaust, premiered by Dallas Symphony, 1991; Jump Back; Before the Ark. *Recordings:* Music for French Horn and Piano; Huntsman, What Quarry; Deep Ellum Nights, Shema, A Clear Midnight, Flame of the Lord, Questings, Divertimento for Piano. *Publications:* Shemà; At Grandmother's Knee, 1995; Waves of the Sea, 1995; Sunflowers 1997, Scott's Rag 2002, Bitter for Sweet 2003, Let it be You 2003. *Honours:* First Prize, Nat. Art Song Competition 1992. *Address:* 3308 Dartmouth Avenue, Dallas, TX 75205, USA. *Telephone:* (214) 768-2241 (office); (214) 526-8084 (home). *E-mail:* ssargon@smu.edu (office); ssargon@aol .com (home). *Website:* simonsargon.com (home).

**SÁRI, József;** Composer; b. 23 June 1935, Lenti, Hungary; m. 2 d. *Education:* Ferenc Liszt Academy of Music, Budapest; Composition; Choral conducting. *Career:* Tutor, Music School, Budapest, 1962–71; Freelance Composer, Germany, 1971–84; Teacher of Music Theory, F Liszt Academy, 1984; Director of department, 1992; Adviser at Hungarian Radio, 1997; Composer's Portrait, broadcast by three major radio stations, Germany, 1992. *Compositions:* Fossils, 1974; String Quartet, 1975; Alienated Quotations for 2 pianos, 1982; Symbols, 1978; Attributes, 1990; Questions for Hillel, 1996; Concertino, 1992–95; Zenith, 1995; Parallel Lines which Cross before the Infinite, for flute and strings, 1997; Con Spirito for orchestra, 1998; Sonnenfinsternis, opera, 2000. *Recordings:* Time Mill; Farewell to Glenn Gould; Four Inventions; Fossils; Legend; His complete works for flute; works for dulcimer and brass instruments. *Honours:* Erkel Prize, 1991; Bartók Pásztory Prize, 1995; Artist of Merit, 1998. *Address:* 2011, Budakalasz, Szent Laszlo 41, Hungary. *Website:* www.bmc.hu/sari.

**SARICH, Paul;** Composer and Percussionist; b. 18 Sept. 1951, Wellington, New Zealand. *Education:* BSc, Victoria University of Wellington, 1971; Study with Leonard Salzedo and James Blades, 1981. *Career:* Percussionist, Various Australian Bands and Orchestras, 1973–93; Lecturer, Victoria College of the Arts, 1991–; New Notations, London, 1994–95. *Compositions:* Fantasia in G Minor for violin, 1981; Sonata for side drum and 3 percussion, 1981; Fantasia on a fragment of Martinů, for orchestra, 1982; Chaconne in B Flat for tuba, 1986; Concerto for bass trombone and orchestra, 1986; Antiphons for 2 percussions, 1986; Divertimento for viola, cello, double bass and percussion, 1986; Five in the Afternoon, trumpet, keyboards and percussion, 1986; Dance Suite for 3 tubas, 1987; Concerto da Camera, for percussion and strings, 1988; Music for tubes and sticks, 1988; Songs of Light and Shade for soprano and ensemble, 1989; Concerto Pieces for timpani and piano, 1990; Percussion Mass, 1991; The Illusionist for bass and piano, 1992; Fiesta, for soprano, timpani, 4 percussion and flamenco dancers, 1993; Essay for brass quintet and 8 tubas, 1993; Austranimalia for chorus, bass, percussion and piano, 1994; Invocation and dance for saxophone and clarinet trio, 1994; Three Neruda Love Songs for soprano and ensemble, 1994. *Address:* c/o APRA, 1A Eden Street, Crows Nest, NSW 2065, Australia.

**SARROCA, Suzanne;** Singer (Soprano); b. 21 April 1927, Carcassonne, France. *Education:* Studied at the Toulouse Conservatoire, 1946–48. *Career:* Debut: Carcassonne 1949, as Massenet's Charlotte; Sang Carmen in Brussels, 1951; Paris Opéra and Opéra-Comique from 1952, as Tosca, Rezia, Marina (Boris Godunov), Aida, Marguerite in La Damnation de Faust, Leonore and Octavian 1957, 1966; Also sang in Les Indes Galantes by Rameau; Guest appearances in Marseille, 1961 (Donna Anna), Rome 1965 (Elisabeth de Valois) and in Buenos Aires, Geneva, New York, London, Lisbon, Strasbourg and Toulouse; Salzburg Festival 1968, in Cavalieri's La Rappresentazione di Anima e di Corpo; Further engagements in Rio de Janeiro, Hamburg and Vienna; Modern repertoire included La Voix Humaine by Poulenc and Schoenberg's Erwartung; Director of the Centre d'art Lyrique at Strasbourg, 1983–85.

**SASAKI, Ken;** Concert Pianist; b. 14 Sept. 1943, Sendai, Miyagi, Japan. *Education:* Studied at University of Arts, Tokyo and at Warsaw Conservatoire; Attended Masterclasses of Vlado Perlemuter in Paris and Danuta Lewandowska in Warsaw. *Career:* Given many concerts in France, Poland, Netherlands, Switzerland, Austria, Germany, Japan; British debut 1972, at the Wigmore Hall; Coast to coast tour of the USA, 1979; Queen Elizabeth Hall, London, 1986 playing Bach's 1st Partita, Gaspard de la Nuit and Chopin's 2nd Sonata; Further appearances with the Warsaw Chamber Orchestra and the Berlin Octet; Other repertory includes Concertos by Bach (D minor) and Beethoven (C minor and G major); Mozart K449 and K466; Chopin No. 1 and Schumann; Ravel in G; Rachmaninov Nos 1 and 3; Mozart Sonatas K310, K311; Chopin Sonatas, Etudes Ballades, Nocturnes, Preludes and Polonaise; Schumann Fantasie Op 17, Fantasiestücke, Etudes Symphoniques and

Kreisleriana; Ravel Miroirs and Le Tombeau de Couperin; Debussy Images and Suite Bergamasque; Prokofiev 3rd and 7th Sonatas and Scriabin Etudes; Scarlatti Sonatas. *Recordings include:* Chopin Etudes. *Honours:* Stefanie Niekrasz Prize, 1984.

**SASS, Sylvia;** Singer (Soprano); b. 21 July 1951, Budapest, Hungary. *Education:* Studied at the Liszt Academy Budapest with Ferenc Revhegyi. *Career:* Debut: Budapest State Opera 1971, as Frasquita in Carmen; First major role as Gutrune, 1972; Sang Giselda in I Lombardi, 1973 and repeated the role at Covent Garden, 1976; Sofia 1972, Violetta (also at Aix-en-Provence 1976); Scottish Opera debut 1975, Desdemona; At the Budapest Opera 1977, sang in the premiere of Mózes by Zsolt Durkó; Metropolitan Opera 1977, Tosca; Guest engagements at the State Operas of Hamburg and Munich and at the Paris Opéra and La Scala Milan; Other roles include Norma, Penelope (Il Ritorno d'Ulisse), Tatiana, Elvira (Ernani), Alceste, Odabella (Attila), Medea, Santuzza, Elisabeth de Valois, Lady Macbeth, Donna Elvira and Donna Anna, Countess Almaviva, Mimi, Manon Lescaut, Turandot, Adriana Lecouvreur, Nedda (Pagliacci), Juliette and Marguerite by Gounod, and Salome (Budapest 1989); Has sung Bartók's Judith on BBC television and in Montpellier and Metz, 1989; Many concert performances in music by Strauss and Wagner; Modern repertoire includes Sogno di un Tramonto d'Autumno by Malipiero; Wigmore Hall debut 1979, in songs by Strauss and Liszt; Invited to return for András Schiff's Beethoven-Bartók series, Sept 1990; Season 1993, as Adriana Lecouvreur at Budapest. *Recordings include:* Don Giovanni, Arias by Puccini and Verdi, Liszt and Bartók songs (Decca); Verdi Stiffelio, Il Trittico, Duke Bluebeard's Castle by Bartók (Philips); Wagner Wesendonck Lieder, Vier Letzte Lieder by Strauss, Medea, Ernani, I Lombardi, Macbeth, Attila, Faust, Mózes by Durkó, Erkel's Hunyadi László (Hungaroton).

**SASSON, Deborah;** Singer (Soprano); b. 1955, Boston, Massachusetts, USA; m. Peter Hofmann, 1983, divorced 1990. *Education:* Studied at Oberlin College with Ellen Repp and Helen Hodam; New England Conservatory, Boston with Gladys Miller. *Career:* Debut: Hamburg Staatsoper 1979, as Maria in West Side Story; Sang at the Stadttheater Aachen, 1979–81; Guest appearances in Hamburg, Berlin, Venice and San Francisco; Has sung at the Bayreuth Festival from 1982; Other roles include Norina, Adina, Gilda, Rosina, Despina and Zerlina. *Recordings include:* Arias and Duets with Peter Hofmann; Mahler's 8th Symphony, from Tanglewood. *Address:* c/o PO Box Bayreuther Festspiele, 8580 Bayreuth 1, Germany.

**SATANOWSKI, Robert Zdzislaw;** Conductor and Music Director; b. 20 June 1918, Łódź, Poland; m.; two s. *Education:* Technical Univ., Warsaw 1935–39, Theory of Music and Conducting, Acad. of Music, Łódź, Poland 1951. *Career:* debut, Łódź State Philharmonic 1951; Conductor, Lubin State Philharmonic 1951–54; Artistic Dir, Principal Conductor, Bydgoszcz State Philharmonic 1954–58; Gen. Music Dir, Staedtische Oper Karl Marx Stadt/ former and later Chemitz 1960–62; Gen. and Artistic Dir, State Opera Poznan 1962–69; founder and Artistic Dir, Poznan Chamber Orchestra 1963–69; Gen. Music Dir, Staedtishe Buehnen Krefeld-Moenchengladbach 1969–76, State Opera House, Kraków 1975–77, State Opera House, Wroclaw 1977–82, Grand Theatre Warsaw/National Opera 1981–91; Conductor, Aachen Opera 1991–92; Guest Conductor, operatic works, Staatsoper Vienna, Dresden, Berlin, Bolshoi Moscow State Opera Bucharest, Operhaus Dresden, Oslo Opera House, Opera House Seattle, USA, National Opera House Genoa, Royal Opera Liège, Zagreb Opera House, Istanbul Festival; symphony concerts in Paris, London, Moscow, Berlin, Dresden, Leipzig, Bucharest, Genoa, Stockholm, Gothenburg, Leningrad, Tehran, Ankara, Madrid, Vienna, Düsseldorf and Warsaw. *Compositions:* symphony, chamber and vocal works composed – 1958. *Recordings:* with National Philharmonic, Warsaw, Warsaw Grand Theatre Orchestra, State Symphony Orchestra, Poznan, Poznan Chamber Orchestra, mainly Polish, classical and contemporary, symphony and operatic works; Halka, 1998. *Address:* Teatr Wielki, ul Moliera 3/5, 00-950 Warsaw, Poland.

**SATO, Shunske;** Violinist; b. 1984, Tokyo, Japan. *Education:* Juilliard School, New York, with Dorothy DeLay, from 1995. *Career:* Debut: Philadelphia Orchestra, 1994; Appearances with the St Petersburg Philharmonic under Yuri Temirkanov, National Symphony Orchestra, with Christopher Hogwood, Baltimore and Minnesota Orchestras, and elsewhere in USA; Season 2000–01 with the Mariinsky Orchestra under Gergiev, the Beethoven Concerto at the Bonn Festival, European tour with the St Petersburg Symphony Orchestra, Munich Radio Orchestra under Zdenek Macal, Swiss debut recital in Basle, and Italian concert with Riccardo Muti. *Address:* c/o Musicaglotz, 11, Rue Le Verrier, 75006 Paris, France.

**SATOH, Somei;** Composer; b. 19 Jan. 1949, Sendai, Japan. *Education:* Studied in Japan. *Career:* Freelance Composer in Advanced Idioms, including Non-Western Techniques and Instruments; Resident in New York, 1983–84. *Compositions include:* Hymn for the Sun for 2 pianos and tape delay, 1975; Cosmic Womb, 1975; Incarnation I and II, 1977–78; The Heavenly Spheres Are Illuminated by Light, for soprano, piano and percussion, 1979; Birds in Warped Time I and II, 1980; Lyra for 2 harps, percussion and strings, 1980; Sumeru I and II, 1982, 1985; A Journey Through Sacred Time, 1983; Naohi for piano, 1983; Hikari for trumpet and piano, 1986; Shirasagi for string quartet, 1987; Stabat Mater for soprano and chorus, 1987; A Gate into Infinity for violin, piano and percussion, 1988; Homa for soprano and string quartet, 1988; Towards the Night for strings, 1991; Kami No Miuri for mezzo and 7 instruments, 1991; Burning Meditation, for baritone, harp, tubar bells and

string quartet, 1993 (revised version, New York, 1995); Lanzarote for soprano saxophone and piano, 1993. *Address:* c/o JASRAC, 3-6-12 Uehara, Shibuya-ku, Tokyo 151, Japan.

**SAULESCO, Mircea (Petre);** Violinist; b. 14 Sept. 1926, Bucharest, Romania; m. (1) 3 c., (2) Gunilla Sandberg-Saulesco, 1 c. *Education:* Bucharest Conservatory; Diploma, Bucharest Musical Academy, 1944; Studied with various masters including Iosif Dailis, Garbis Avachian, Georges Enesco and Jacques Thibaud; Studied Piano and Composition with various masters. *Career:* Debut: Bucharest, 1941; Member, Bucharest Radio Symphony Orchestra, 1938–50; Founder, Saulesco String Quartet, 1945; Member 1950–58, Leader 1957–58, Bucharest State Philharmonic Orchestra Georges Enesco; Numerous chamber music and solo concerts in Eastern Europe until 1958; Member and one of the Leaders, Symphony Orchestra, Swedish Broadcasting Corporation, 1958–89; Founder, Swedish Saulesco Quartet, 1962; Co-Founder, Leygraf (piano) Quartet, 1965; Numerous television and radio appearances; Various foreign concert tours; mem, Mazer Society for Chamber Music. *Recordings include:* Alfven Violin Sonata; Mozart Piano Quartets No. 1 G minor and No. 2 E flat major; Atterberg String Quartet op 11; Verdi, String Quartet E minor. *Honours:* Swedish Record Prize, Grammis, 1970, 1972; Austrian Mozart Prize, 1974. *Address:* Pepparkaksgrand 26, 128 66 Sköndal, Sweden.

**SAUNDERS, Arlene;** Singer (Soprano) and Teacher; b. 5 Oct. 1935, Cleveland, Ohio, USA. *Education:* Baldwin-Wallace College and New York. *Career:* Debut: Operatic, as Rosalinde with National Opera Company, 1958; New York City Opera debut as Giorgetta in Il Tabarro, 1961; European debut as Mimi, Teatro Nuovo, Milan, 1961; Joined Hamburg State Opera, 1964; Also sang Pamina, Glyndebourne Festival, England, 1966 and Louise, San Francisco Opera 1967, Beatrix Cenci (world premiere) with the Washington DC Opera Society 1971, Eva, Metropolitan Opera 1976, Minnie, Royal Opera Covent Garden, London 1980; Farewell operatic appearances as the Marschallin, Teatro Colón, Buenos Aires, 1985; Other roles were Natasha (War and Peace), Nadia in The Ice Break (US premiere Boston, 1979), Mozart Donna Elvira and Fiordiligi, Wagner's Sieglinde, Elsa, Senta and Elisabeth, Tosca, Manon, Arabella and the Countess in Capriccio; Teacher, Rutgers University, New Jersey and Abraham Goodman School, New York, 1987–. *Honours:* Gold Medal, Vercelli Vocal Competition; Kammersängerin, Hamburg State Opera, 1967.

**SAUNDERS, Christopher;** Singer (Tenor); b. 1971, Queensland, Australia. *Education:* University of Queensland and the Guildhall School, London. *Career:* Appearances with Opera Queensland from 1993, including Ernesto in Don Pasquale and Aufidio in the local premiere of Mozart's Lucio Silla; Other roles include Jacquino for English Touring Opera, Tobias in Sweeney Todd for Opera North, Ferrando in Così fan tutte, and Jupiter in Handel's Semele; Concerts include Britten's Serenade at the Barbican Hall and Britten's St Nicolas. *Honours:* The Hammond Prize, Queensland. *Address:* Harlequin Agency Ltd, 203 Fidlas Road, Cardiff CF4 5NA, Wales.

**SAUNDERS, Jenny;** Singer (soprano); b. 1970, England. *Education:* Studied with Marjorie Thomas at the Royal Academy of Music and with Mary Thomas. *Career:* Concerts include Mozart's C Minor Mass in Canterbury Cathedral, Mendelssohn's Elijah in Scotland, the Christmas Oratorio in Oslo and the Brahms Requiem at the St Endellion Easter Festival; Further engagements with Messiah and Carmina Burana at the Albert Hall, Gounod's St Cecilia Mass and the Fauré Requiem at the Festival Hall and Mendelssohn's Midsummer Night's Dream with the Academy of St Martin in the Fields; Appearances with the Opera Company as Helen in Mefistofele and Mozart's Barabarina and Susanna; Season 1996–97 as Zerlina for Opera East, in Dido and Aeneas at Covent Garden and The Fairy Queen on tour to Spain and Greece; Despina for Country Opera and Nannetta for Palace Opera; 1997 concerts at St John's Smith Square (Exsultate Jubilate and St Matthew Passion) St Paul's Cathedral (Vivaldi's Gloria) and Wells Cathedral (Haydn's Creation); Papagena with Opera Factory; Season 1998 with the Sandman and Dew Fairy in Hansel and Gretel for Palace Opera. *Honours:* Winner, Soprano Section, 1992 Great Grimsby International Singers Competition. *Current Management:* Hazard Chase Ltd, Norman House, Cambridge Place, Cambridge, CB2 1NS, England. *Telephone:* (1223) 312400. *Fax:* (1223) 460827. *Website:* www.hazardchase.co.uk.

**SAUNDERS, Rebecca;** Composer; b. 19 Dec. 1967, London. *Education:* Studied with Wolfgang Rihm in Karlsruhe, 1991–94, and with Nigel Osborne in England, 1994–97. *Career:* Freelance composer in New York, Brussels, Berlin and elsewhere. *Compositions include:* Behind the Velvet Curtain for trumpet, piano, harp and cello, 1992; Into the Blue for clarinet, bassoon, percussion; piano, cello and double bass, 1996; Two pieces based on Molly Bloom's Monologue, from Ulysses, 1996; String Quartet, and double bass, 1998; Cinnabar, for ensemble, 1999; Duo for viola and percussion, 1999. *Honours:* Prize Winner, Berlin Academy at Art (1995) and Siemens Foundation (1996). *Address:* c/o Edition Peters, 10–12 Backes St, London N1 6DN, England.

**SAUTER, Lily;** Singer; b. 16 Nov. 1934, Zürich, Switzerland. *Education:* Studied in Milan and Zürich. *Career:* Sang at the Deutsche Oper am Rhein Düsseldorf, 1961–64; Zürich Opera, 1965–66; Stuttgart Staatsoper, 1964–83; Guest appearances at the State Operas of Hamburg and Munich, Berlin, Frankfurt, Barcelona, Venice, Milan, Genoa and Edinburgh; Roles have included Mozart's Susanna, Blondchen and Despina, Rosina, Martha, Norina,

Adina, Marzelline, Lortzing's Gretchen and Marie, Musetta, Nannetta, Sophie in Der Rosenkavalier, Aennchen, and Regina in Mathis der Maler; Television appearances in Germany and Switzerland. *Address:* c/o Staatsoper Stuttgart, Oberer Schlossgarten 6, 7000 Stuttgart, Germany.

**SAVAGE, Stephen (Leon);** Concert Pianist, Conductor and Teacher; b. 26 April 1942, Hertford, England; 2 s. *Education:* Vienna Akademie with Bruno Seidlhofer; Royal College of Music with Cyril Smith. *Career:* Debut: Wigmore Hall, London, 1966; Concerts, Radio, Television, Recordings in England, Canada, Australia, Japan; Concertos with Boult, A Davis, Zollman and others including 1st Australasian performance, Lutoslawski Concerto 1989; Director, Brisbane Tippett Festival 1990; Dedicatee of major works by Justin Connolly and Roger Smalley; Professor of Piano and Co-Director, 20th Century Ensemble, Royal College of Music, 1967–81, Artistic Director, Conductor, Griffith University Ensemble, Brisbane, Australia; Master Teacher to Australian National Academy of Music, Melbourne; Frequent Residencies include, Universities of Adelaide, Toronto, Hong Kong, Guildhall School of Music, Royal Academy of Music, Royal College of Music (Honorary Associate Professor); Noted for performances of classical repertoire and 20th Century Music including important first performances. *Recordings:* Roger Smalley, Accord for 2 Pianos with the Composer; Tippett, sonatas 1 and 3; Beethoven Sonatas Op 109, 110, 111. *Honours:* Dannreuther Prize, 1964; Hopkinson Medal, Worshipful Company of Musicians, Medal, 1965; Recommendation of Tippett Sonatas 1 and 3 by Gramophone, 1986. *Address:* c/o Queensland Conservatorium of Music, Griffith University, PO Box 28, Brisbane, Albert Street, 4002 Brisbane, Australia.

**SAVARY, Jérôme;** French theatre director and actor; *Director, Opéra Comique;* b. 27 June 1942, Buenos Aires, Argentina; s. of Jacques Savary and Claire Hovelaque; one s. two d. *Education:* Collège Cévenol, Haute-Loire, les Arts-Déco, Paris. *Career:* studied music Paris; moved to France 1947; became jazz musician New York 1961; returned to France; f. Compagnie Jérôme Savary 1965, subsequently called Grand Magic Circus, then Grand Magic Circus et ses animaux tristes 1968–; theatre dir 1969–; Dir Centre Dramatique Nat. du Languedoc-Roussillon, Béziers and Montpellier 1982–85; Dir Carrefour Européen, Théâtre-du 8e, Lyon 1985–; Dir Théâtre Nat. de Chaillot, Paris 1988–2000; Dir Opéra Comique, Paris 2000–(07); Dir about 80 plays and shows in Europe, Brazil, Argentina, Canada, USA, Israel; several TV films of plays and operas and three films for cinema. *Publications:* La Vie privée d'un magicien ordinaire 1985, Ma vie commence à 20h30 1991, Magic Circus 1966–96, 30 ans d'aventures et d'amour 1996, Havana Blues 2000. *Honours:* Chevalier, Ordre des Arts et des Lettres, Chevalier, Légion d'honneur, Grand Badge of Hon. (Austria), Prix Dominique for Cyrano de Bergerac, Molière Award for best musical 1987, Victoire de la Musique for Best Musical (for Cabaret) 1987, Best Dir for Cabaret Spain 1993. *Address:* Opéra Comique, 5 rue Favart, 75002 Paris, France. *Telephone:* 1-42-44-45-40 (office). *Fax:* 1-49-26-05-93 (office). *E-mail:* mtarot@free.fr (office). *Website:* www.opera-comique.com (office).

**SAVASKAN, Sinan (Carter);** Composer and Conductor; b. 11 Aug. 1954, England; m. Sarah Carter, 2 s., 2 d. *Education:* PhD, University of York; MMus, University of Surrey; BA Hons, University of London, Middlesex; Diploma Studies, Chiswick Music Centre. *Career:* Composer of orchestral, chamber and performing arts related music; Conductor and member of London based ensembles; Contemporary Arts Ensemble; Battersea Orchestra; Deputy Director of Music, Westminster School, London; Works featured at the 2002 International Rostrum of Composers, Paris; mem, British Academy of Composers and Songwriters; Association of Professional Composers; Executive Committee Member of British Academy of Composers and Songwriters PRS; MCPS. *Compositions:* String Quartet No. 3, Panic in Needle Park, commissioned and premiered by Balanescu String Quartet, 1990; Anthems for the Sun No. 2 for organ, played by Martin Ball, Westminster Abbey, 1994; Three Dances for chamber orchestra, BBC Philharmonic Forum Award Winner, 1997; Symphony No. 2, commissioned and premiered by BBC Symphony Orchestra, 1997; Symphony No. 3, commissioned and premiered by SEM Orchestra, New York, 1998. *Recordings:* Intercontinental Communication Disaster 1877; String Study No. 3. *Contributions:* Regular contributor to The Times Supplements. *Honours:* Dio Award (ACGB), 1985; BBC Symphony Orchestra Commission, 1997; Winner, Foundation for Contemporary Performance Arts, USA, 1998. *Current Management:* Sarah Moyse Artist Management. *Address:* 27 Dorchester Court, London SE24 9QX, England.

**SAVCHENKO, Arkadiy Markovich;** Belarusian opera singer (baritone); b. 6 April 1936, Vitebsk, Byelorussia; s. of Mark Iosifovich Savchenko and Marfa Stratonovna Savchenko; m. Glasova Serafima Semienovna 1977; two s. *Education:* Moscow Conservatoire. *Career:* soloist with Byelorussian (now Belarus) Bolshoi Theatre 1960–; Faculty mem., Prof., Vocal Dept, Belarus Acad. of Music 1987–. *Roles include:* Yevgeny in Tchaikovsky's Yevgeny Onegin, Kizgaylo in Smolsky's Ancient Legend, Telramund in Wagner's Lohengrin, Malatesta in Donizetti's Don Pasquale, Jermon in Verdi's Traviata, Valentin in Gounod's Faust, Rigoletto in Verdi's Rigoletto, Renato in Verdi's A Masked Ball, Tomsky, Eletsky in Tchaikovsky's Queen of Spades, Gryaznoy in Rimsky-Korsakov's The Tsar's Bride, Don Giovanni in Mozart's Don Giovanni, Amonasro in Verdi's Aida, Di Luna in Verdi's Trovatore, Rodrigo in Verdi's Don Carlos, Sharpless in Puccini's Madame Butterfly, Escamillo in Bizet's Carmen, Figaro in Rossini's The Barber of Seville, Prince Igor in Borodin's Prince Igor, Bolkonsky in Prokofiev's War and Peace, Alfio in

Mascagni's Cavalleria Rusticana etc., Iago in Verdi's Otello, Robert in Tchaikovsky's Iolanta, Mizgir in Rimsky-Korsakov's Snowmaiden, Tonyo in Leoncavallo's Pagliacci. *Honours:* People's Artist of USSR 1985. *Address:* Bolshoi Teatr, 1 Parizhskaya Kommuna Square, 220029 Minsk (Theatre); 8–358 Storozhovskaya Str., 220002 Minsk, Belarus (home). *Telephone:* (17) 219-22-01 (Theatre); (17) 239-15-51 (home). *Fax:* (17) 34-05-84.

**SAVIDGE, Peter;** Singer (baritone); b. 1952, Essex, England. *Education:* Cambrdge University. *Career:* Debut: English Music Theatre, 1976, as Papageno; Appearances with Opera North as Mozart's Count, Storch in Intermezzo, Don Giovanni, Valentin, Nardo in La finta giardiniera, Sharpless (Butterfly), Eugene Onegin; Welsh National Opera as Papageno, Marcello, Danilo, and Rossini's Figaro; Lescaut in Massenet's Manon, Ned Keene in Peter Grimes and the Baron in Massenet's Chérubin at Covent Garden, 1994; Seven baritone roles in Death in Venice at Nancy and Liège; Belcore (L'Elisir d'amore) at Opéra Comique, Paris; Ned Keene at Genoa, Strasbourg and Cologne; Season 1999–2000 world premiere of A Friend of the People by Horne at Scottish Opera; Count at Garsington; L'Anima del Filosofo by Haydn at Lausanne; Season 2000–01, title role in world premiere of Abélard et Heloïse for Strasbourg and Paris; 2003: Chnegos in Punch and Judy; Birtwistle in Porto; Gunther in Götterdämmerung for Scottish Opera and at Edinburgh Festival; Sang Szymanowski's Stabat Mater with Rotterdam Philharmonic, under Valerie Gergier, 2003. *Recordings include:* Britten's Albert Herring and Handel's Hercules; Mr Coyle in Channel 4's television film of Britten's Owen Wingrave, 2001; Bantock songs with David Owen Norris. *Current Management:* Musicmakers International Artists Representation, Tailor House, 63–65 High Street, Whitwell, Hertfordshire SG4 8AH, England. *Telephone:* (1438) 871708. *Fax:* (1438) 871777. *E-mail:* musicmakers@compuserve.com. *Website:* www.operauk.com. *Address:* 1, The Bank, Little Compton, Moreton-in-Marsh, Gloucestershire GL56 0RX, England.

**SAVOIE, Robert;** Singer (Baritone); b. 21 April 1927, Montreal, Canada. *Education:* Studied with Pauline Donalda in Montreal and with Antonio Narducci in Milan. *Career:* Debut: Teatro Nuovo Milan 1953, as Scarpia; Sang with many seasons for L'Opéra de Montréal and made guest appearances with the Paris Opéra and the Opéra du Rhin Strasbourg; Opera houses in Nice, Toulouse, Lyon, Marseille, Dallas, Washington, Pittsburgh and London; Other roles have been Mozart's Leporello, Don Giovanni, Count Figaro and Guglielmo; Escamillo; Verdi's Iago, Amonasro and Ford in Falstaff; Puccini's Gianni Schicchi and Sharpless; Golaud in Pelléas et Mélisande, Albert in Werther and Ramiro in L'Heure Espagnole; Artistic Director, City of Lachine, Quebec, Canada, now retired; The Lachine Music Festival; Vocal teacher at the Music Faculty, McGill University of Montreal; President, Founder, L'Orchestra Metropolitan of Montreal. *Recordings include:* Posa in the French version of Don Carlos. *Publications:* Memoires: Figaro-ci Figaro-la, 1998. *Honours:* Officer of the Order of Canada; Dr hc in Music, University of Moncton, Canada; Dr hc in Laws, Concordia Univ., Canada. *Address:* 2100 Du Calvados, St Bruno, Quebec J3V 3K2, Canada.

**SAVOVA, Galina;** singer (soprano); b. 1945, Sofia, Bulgaria. *Career:* sang first at the Sofia Opera before an international career at the opera houses of Rome, Naples, Karlsruhe and Bologna; Metropolitan Opera debut 1982, as Amelia in Un Ballo in Maschera; Other roles include Chrysothemis (Elektra), Puccini's Minnie, Turandot and Tosca, Amelia (Simon Boccanegra), Yaroslavna in Prince Igor and Leonore; In 1989 sang Aida at the Teatro São Carlos, Lisbon; Chicago Lyric Opera, 1992 as Turandot; Season 2000–01 as Frosja in Semyon Kotko by Prokofiev, with Kirov Opera at Covent Garden, and Mme Blanche in Prokofiev's The Gambler at the New York Met.

**SAVOVA, Olga B.;** Russian actress and singer (mezzo-soprano); b. 14 Nov. 1964, Leningrad; m. Yefimov Dmitri; two s. *Education:* Leningrad State Inst. of Music Theatre and Cinematography, Leningrad State Conservatory. *Career:* actress at Leningrad Tovstonogov Drama Theatre –1995; singer at Mariinsky Opera Theatre (Kirov Opera) 1995–; repertoire includes Verdi's Requiem, Emilia in Othello, Eboli in Don Carlos, Flora in La Traviata, Carmen, Amneris and Preziosilla, Olga in Eugene Onegin, Prokofiev's Semyon Kotko, Azucena in Il Trovatore, Marfa in Tsar's Bride, Bobilikha in Rimsky-Korsakov's The Snow Maiden, Blanche in The Gambler by Prokofiev, Lyubov in Mazeppa, Marina Mnishek in Boris Godunov, Hélène in War and Peace, Paulina in The Queen of Spades and Teresa in La Sonnambula; performances in France, Belgium, Holland, Italy, Japan, China and Israel. *Honours:* Voci Verdiani International Competition prizewinner, Italy 1992. *Address:* St Petersburg State Academic Mariinsky Opera Theatre, Teatralnaya pl.1, St Petersburg 130000, Russia (office).

**SAWALLISCH, Wolfgang;** German conductor; *Music Director, Philadelphia Orchestra;* b. 26 Aug. 1923, Munich; m. Mechthild Schmid. *Education:* Wittelsbacher Gymnasium, Munich. *Career:* studied under Profs. Ruoff, Haas and Sachsse; mil. service 1942–46, POW in Italy; conductor Augsburg 1947–53; Musical Dir Aachen 1953–58, Wiesbaden 1958–60, Cologne Opera 1960–63; Conductor Hamburg Philharmonic Orchestra 1960–73, Hon. mem. 1973–; Prin. Conductor Vienna Symphony Orchestra 1960–70, Hon. mem. and Hon. Conductor 1980; Prof. Staatliche Hochschule für Musik, Cologne 1960–63; Musical Dir Bayerische Staatsoper Munich 1971–92; Prin. Conductor Bayerisches Staatsorchester –92; Perm. Conductor Teatro alla Scala, Milan; conducted at many Festivals; recordings in Germany, USA and Britain; Hon. Conductor NHK Symphony Orchestra, Tokyo 1967; Artistic Dir Suisse Romande Orchestra, Geneva 1973–80; Dir Bayerische Staatsoper,

Munich 1982–92; Music Dir Philadelphia Orchestra 1993–. *Publications:* Im Interesse der Deutlichkeit – Mein Leben mit der Musik 1988, Kontrapunkte 1993. *Honours:* Dr hc (Curtis Inst., Philadelphia), (Princeton Univ.); Accademico Onorario Santa Cecilia; Österreichisches Ehrenkreuz für Kunst und Wissenschaft, Bayerischer Verdienstorden, Bruckner-Ring of Vienna Symphony Orchestra 1980, Grosses Bundesverdienstkreuz (mit Stern), Bayerische Maximiliansorden für Wissenschaft und Kunst 1984, Orden der aufgehenden Sonne am Halsband, Japan, Robert-Schumann-Preis 1994, Suntory Special Music Prize, Japan, Golden Baton Toscanini Teatro Scala, Milan; Chevalier Légion d'honneur, Commdr des Arts et des Lettres, Cavaliere di Gran Croce (Italy). *Address:* Hinterm Bichl 2, 83224 Grassau/Chiemsee, Germany; The Philadelphia Orchestra, 260 S Broad Street, 16th Floor, Philadelphia, PA 19102, USA (office). *Telephone:* (215) 893-1900 (office); (49) 86412315. *Fax:* (215) 893-1948 (office); (49) 86414501 (home). *E-mail:* graphil@gmx.de (home).

**SAWER, David;** Composer; b. 14 Sept. 1961, Stockport, England. *Education:* Univ. of York; DPhil studies with Richard Orton; further studies with Mauricio Kagel in Cologne. *Career:* music performed by the London Sinfonietta and Music Projects, London; commissions from MusICA 1986, the Kirklees Metropolitan Council, the 1988 Almeida Festival, King's Lynn Festival, BBC Singers, and BBC Symphony Orchestra; directed premiere productions of Kagel's Pas de Cinq and Kantrimiusik (Huddersfield Festival 1983, 1984) and as soloist in Kagel's Phonophonie at the 1987 Summerscope season on the South Bank; music for radio and theatre productions; Composer in association with the Bournemouth Orchestras, 1995–96; opera, From Morning to Midnight, premiered by ENO, 2001. *Compositions:* Music theatre: Etudes for 2–6 actors/musicians, 2 trumpets, percussion, 1984; Food of Love for actress and piano, 1988; The Panic, chamber opera, for 4 voices and 6 instruments, 1990–91; From Morning to Midnight, opera, 7 scenes, Sawer, from G. Kaiser: Von morgens bis mitternachts, 1998–2001; Orchestral: Byrnan Wood for large orchestra, 1992; The Memory of Water for 2 violins and strings, 1993; Trumpet Concerto, 1994; Tiroirs for chamber orchestra, 1996; The greatest happiness principle, 1997; Musica Ficta for chamber orchestra, 1998; Piano Concerto, 2002; Vocal: Rhetoric for soprano, viola, cello and double bass, 1989; Songs of Love and War for 24 voices, 2 harps and 2 percussion, 1990; Sounds: Three Kandinsky poems for chorus, 1996, 1999; Stramm Gedichte for chorus, 2001; Chamber: Solo Piano for piano, 1983; Cat's-Eye for chamber ensemble, 1986; Take Off for instrumental ensemble, 1987; Good Night for flute and piccolo, harp, violin, viola and cello, 1989; The Melancholy of Departure for piano, 1990; Hollywood Extra for chamber ensemble, 1996; Between for harp, 1998. *Recordings include:* Byrnan Wood; The Melancholy of Departure; Songs of Love and War. *Contributions:* New Grove Dictionary of Opera, entry on Kagel. *Honours:* DAAD Scholarship, 1984–85; Sony Radio Award, for Swansong, 1990; Fulbright-Chester-Schirmer Fellowship in Composition, 1992–93; Paul Hamlyn Foundation Award, 1993; Arts Foundations's Composer Fellowship, 1995; British Acad. of Composers and Songwriters Award, 2003. *Current Management:* Allied Artist Agency, 42 Montpelier Square, London, SW7 1JZ, England. *E-mail:* info@alliedartists.co.uk.

**SAWYER, Philip (John);** Lecturer, Organist and Continuo Player; b. 3 Feb. 1948, Birmingham, England; m. (1) Judith Susan Timbury, 9 Jan 1981, (2) Patricia Anne McAlister, 3 Feb 1996. *Education:* Royal College of Music, 1966–68; ARCM, 1966; ARCO, 1967; Peterhouse, Cambridge, 1968–71; BA, Honours, 1971; MA, 1975; Organ study in Amsterdam with Piet Kee, 1970; Study at the Nice Conservatoire with René Saorin, 1973–74; MMus, 1986. *Career:* Assistant Director of Music, Trent College, 1971–73; Lecturer, 1975–, Head of the School of Music, 1987–99, Napier University (formerly Napier College/Polytechnic); Organist, Choirmaster: St Cuthbert's Parish Church, Edinburgh, 1975–78; Nicolson Square Methodist Church, Edinburgh, 1978–83, Director of Music, St Andrew's and St George's Church, Edinburgh, 1983–86; Director of Music, St Mary's Collegiate Church, Haddington, 1999–; Organ recitals: Westminster Abbey, Notre Dame, Paris, Nice Cathedral, Monaco Cathedral, St Laurens, Alkmaar, St Bavo's RC Cathedral, Haarlem, Hillsborough Parish Church, N Ireland; Universities of: St Andrews, Edinburgh, Glasgow, Aberdeen; Cathedrals: Edinburgh, Glasgow, Dundee; Founder and Director, Edinburgh Organ Week; First performances of newly-commissioned organ works by Alan Ridout and others; 1st Performance of The Seven Sacraments of Poussin by John Mcleod in Edinburgh, Glasgow and London, 1992; Appearances as Continuo Player with: Scottish Chamber Orchestra, Scottish Baroque Ensemble; Conductor, Scottish Chamber Choir, 1994–97. *Recordings:* Solo Organ recitals for BBC Radio 3 and Radio Scotland; Harpsichord Continuo with Scottish Chamber Orchestra, conductor, Gibson, with music by Handel; BBC Radio Scotland recording of 1st performance of The Seven Sacraments of Poussin, Edinburgh, 1992. *Contributions:* Various to journals of British Institute of Organ Studies. *Address:* The Ian Tomlin School of Music, Napier University, Craighouse Road, Edinburgh EH10 5 LG, Scotland.

**SAXTON, Robert,** MA (Cantab.), DMus (Oxon.); British composer and university lecturer; *University Lecturer and Tutorial Fellow in Music, Worcester College, Oxford;* b. 8 Oct. 1953, London; s. of Ian Saxton and Jean Saxton (née Infield). *Education:* St Catharine's Coll., Cambridge, Worcester Coll., Oxford, studied privately with Elisabeth Lutyens and Luciano Berio, Univ. of Oxford. *Career:* Lecturer, Univ. of Bristol 1984–85; Fulbright Arts Award, Visiting Fellow Princeton Univ., USA 1985–86; Head of Composition, Guildhall School of

Music and Drama 1990–98; Head of Composition, RAM, London 1998–99; Univ. Lecturer and Tutorial Fellow, Worcester Coll., Oxford; mem. Bd South Bank Centre, London 1997–; mem. Royal Soc. of Musicians; Patron Soc. of English Speakers and Singers. *Compositions include:* orchestral: Ring of Eternity 1982, Concerto for Orchestra 1984, Viola Concerto 1986, In The Beginning 1987, Elijah's Violin 1988, Music to Celebrate the Resurrection of Christ 1988, Violin Concerto 1989, Cello Concerto 1992, Ring, Time for wind orchestra 1994; ensemble: Piccola Musica per Luigi Dallapiccola 1981, Processions and Dances 1981; vocal: Cantata No. 3 1981, Éloge for soprano and ensemble 1981, Chaconne for double chorus 1981, Caritas (opera) 1991, Paraphrase on Mozart's Idomeneo 1991; chamber: Chiaroscuro for percussion 1981, Piano Sonata 1981, Fantasiestuck for accordion 1982, The Sentinel of the Rainbow for sextet 1984, A Yardstick to the Stars 1994; choral: I Will Awake the Dawn 1987, At the Round Earth's Imagined Corners 1992, Psalm, a song of ascents 1992, O Sing unto the Lord a New Song 1993, Canticum Luminis for choir and orchestra 1994, Fanfare for the Golden Wedding Anniversary of Queen Elizabeth II, Songs, Dances and Ellipses 1997, Prayer Before Sleep 1997, Music for St Catharine 1998, Sonata on a Theme of William Walton for cello 1999, A Yardstick to the Stars 2000, The Dialogue of God and Zion for chorus 2000, Invocation, Dance and Meditation 2001, The Child of Light (carol), ...From a Distant Shore... 2001, Alternative Canticles 2002, Five Motets for nine voices 2003, Song without Words 2004. *Recordings:* Concerto for Orchestra, Sentinel of the Rainbow, Circles of Light, Ring of Eternity, Violin Concerto, In the Beginning, I Will Awake the Dawn, Paraphrase on Mozart's Idomeneo, Caritas, opera, At the Round Earth's Imagined Comers, Night Dance, Music to Celebrate the Resurrection of Christ, Chacony, Piano Sonata, A Yardstick to the Stars 2000, Eloge, Processions and Dances, Invocation, Dance and Meditation 2001, Songs, Dances and Ellipses 2001. *Publications:* The Process of Composition from Detection to Confection 1998; contrib. Where Do I Begin? (article in Musical Times) 1994, reviews in TLS. *Address:* Worcester College, Oxford, OX1 2HB, England (office).

**SAY, Fazil;** Turkish composer and pianist; b. 1970, Ankara. *Education:* Ankara State Conservatory, Robert Schumann Inst., Düsseldorf, Berlin Conservatory. *Career:* performances as soloist with orchestras, including New York Philharmonic, Israel Philharmonic, Baltimore Symphony, St Petersburg Philharmonic, Tokyo Symphony, BBC Philharmonic, Orchestre Nat. de France, Munich Philharmonic, Vienna Kammerorchester; has appeared worldwide at concert halls, including Concertgebouw Amsterdam, Berlin Philharmonie, Vienna Musikverein, Suntory Hall in Tokyo, Carnegie Hall, Avery Fisher Hall; has performed at festivals, including Lucerne Festival, Ruhr Piano Festival, Rheingau Music Festival, Verbier Festival, Montpellier Festival, Beethoven Festival Bonn, Salzburg Festival, Lincoln Center Festival, Harrod's Piano Series, World Piano Series in Tokyo; collaborations with musicians, including Yuri Bashmet, Shlomo Mintz, Maxim Vengerov, Akiko Suwanai, Abdullah Ibrahim, Bobby McFerrin; formed quartet with Kudsi Ergüner, performances at Montreux Jazz Festival, Istanbul Jazz Festival, Juan-les-Pins Festival; works commissioned by Turkish Ministry of Culture, Radio France and Kurt Masur, ETH Zürich, City of Vienna Mozart Year; artist-in-residence, Radio France 2003, Bremen Festival 2005. *Compositions include:* Four Dances for Nasreddin Hoca for piano 1990, Fantasiesücke for piano 1993, Chamber Symphony for string orchestra 1996, Sinfonia Concertante for piano and large orchestra 1994, 25 Songs for voice and piano 1994, Piano Concerto No. 2 'Silk Road' for piano and chamber orchestra 1994, Two Romantic Ballads for piano and strings 1995, Guitar Concerto 1996, Three Ballads for piano 1997, Black Earth for piano 1997, Violin Sonata 1997, Nazim oratorio for piano, vocalists, narrator, orchestra and chorus 2001, Piano Concerto No. 3 2001, Paganini Jazz for piano and orchestra 2003, Alla Turca (Jazz Fantasy after Mozart) for piano and orchestra 2003, Requiem for Metin Altiok oratorio for piano, chamber orchestra and chorus 2003, Ten Pieces for jazz quartet (with Kudsi Ergüner), Four Pieces for DJ and piano (with Mercan Dede) 2003. *Recordings include:* Mozart, Piano Sonatas 1998, Bach 1999, Gershwin, Rhapsody in Blue 2000, Stravinsky, Le Sacre du Printemps 2000, Tchaikovsky, Piano Concerto No. 1 2001, Liszt, Piano Sonata in B minor, Mozart, Piano Concertos Nos 12, 21 and 23 2004, Beethoven, Appassionata 2005; own compositions: Piano Concerto No. 2 'Silk Road' 1998, Nazim, Requiem for Metin Altiok, Black Earth 2004. *Honours:* winner Young Concert Artists Int. Auditions 1994. *Current Management:* Käch Artists & Promotion, Wolfgang Mohr, Graumannsweg 19, Hamburg 22087, Germany. *Telephone:* (40) 25336793 (office). *Fax:* (40) 25336796 (office). *E-mail:* WJMohr@t-online.de (office). *Website:* www.kaechartists.com (office); www.fazilsay.com.

**SAYER, Roger (Martin);** British organist; *Director of Music, Rochester Cathedral;* b. 1 May 1961, Portsmouth, Hants.; m. Nancy Sayer, 4 October 1986, one s., one d. *Education:* Royal College of Music, 1979–84; Organ Scholar, St Paul's Cathedral, London, 1980–84. *Career:* Organist and Dir of Music, Rochester Cathedral 1994–; Prof. of Organ, Trinity College of Music; Dir of Music, Rochester Choral Soc.; Organ concerts in many parts of the world; Examiner, Associated Board of the Royal Schools of Music; Adjudicator, National Federation of Music and Drama; mem, Honorary FNMSM; ARCM; FTCL; LRAM. *Recordings:* Great European Organs; Hallgrimskirja, Iceland; Rochester Cathedra, A Classic Selection, Magnificat and Nunc Dimitus; A Choral Portrait, Vaughan Williams; A Classic Selection 2. *Honours:* Third Prize, International Organ Competition, St Albans, 1989; Winner, Organ Prizes, Royal College of Music, 1989. *Address:* 107 Cecil Road, Rochester,

Kent, ME1 2HR, England. *Telephone:* (7720) 773163 (Mobile). *E-mail:* rms2001@bigfoot.com.

**SAYERS, Gavin;** singer (tenor); b. 7 Jan. 1962, England. *Education:* Guildhall School of Music with Johanna Peters and Maureen Morelle. *Career:* sang Arturo in a concert performance of Lucia di Lammermoor, British premiere of Nino Rota's La Notte di un nevrastenico at Morley College, 1990; Concert repertoire includes Puccini's Messa di Gloria; Hiawatha's Wedding Feast by Coleridge-Taylor; Haydn's Nelson Mass and Maria Theresa Mass; Messiah and Mozart Mass in C; Hymn of Praise by Mendelssohn (2nd Symphony); Elijah (Harrow Choral 1990); Britten's Serenade (East Surrey Orchestra 1991) performed in a variety of amateur operatic performances.

**SAYLOR, Bruce;** American composer; *Professor, Queens College*; b. 24 April 1946, Philadelphia, Pa. *Education:* studied at the Juilliard School of Music with Hugo Weisgall and Roger Sessions; Accad. di Santa Cecilia in Rome with Petrassi and Evangelisti, CUNY Graduate School with Weisgall and George Perle. *Career:* Instructor, Queens Coll. 1970–76, Prof. 1979–; Instructor, New York Univ. 1976–79; Composer-in-Residence, Chicago Lyric Opera 1992–94. *Compositions include:* Ballets Cycle; Inner World Out; Wildfire; Notturno for piano and orchestra; Woodwind Quartet; Symphony in Two Parts, Turns and Mordents for flute and orchestra; Duo for violin and viola; St Elmos Fire for flute and harp; Lyrics for soprano and violin; Love Play for mezzo and ensemble; Song from Water Street for mezzo; See You in the Morning, mezzo and ensemble; Orpheus Descending, opera in two acts; My Kinsman, Major Molineux, opera in one act; Songs from Water Street; See You in the Morning; A Scattering of Salts, concerto for piano and chorus 1997; Dreams for 2 choruses and orchestra 1998; Visions of Dante for piano 1999; The Scrimshaw Violin, opera in one act 2000; The Book in Your Hearts, for mezzo, baritone, chorus, orchestra 2000; Cantos from The Inferno, for clarinet and piano 2000; Proud Music of the Storm, for children's chorus and orchestra 2002; Dante's Violin 2001; Good News! for soprano, chorus and orchestra 2003; Swimming with Yevgeny, for mezzo and ensemble 2003; It had Wings, for mezzo and orchestra 1989; With Anthems Sweet for chorus and orchestra; Archangel, for orchestra. *Recordings:* Jessye Norman, In the Spirit 1997, Jessye Norman at Notre-Dame, and four song cycles performed by Constance Beavon. *Publications include:* The Writings of Henry Cowell. *Honours:* Gretchaninoff Prize 1965, Rogers and Hammerstein Scholarship 1968, Fulbright Fellowship 1969, NEA 1973, 1976, Mellon Foundation 1979–82, Guggenheim Fellowship 1982, Ingraham Merrill Award 1990, Charles E. Ives Scholarship and Music Award, American Acad. of Arts and Letters. *Address:* 318 W 85th Street, New York, NY 10024, USA. *Telephone:* (718) 997-3857 (office).

**SCALCHI, Gloria;** singer (mezzo-soprano); b. 23 July 1956, Trieste, Italy. *Education:* studied with Iris Adami Corradetti and with Joseph Metternich in Munich; seminars at the Rossini Acad., Pesaro. *Career:* sang Angelina in La Cenerentola at Catania, 1988; further appearances at the Rome Opera as Emma in Rossini's Zelmira, conducted by Philip Gossett, and as Andromaca in Rossini's Ermione; Concertgebouw Amsterdam as Maffio Orsini, in Lucrezia Borgia; Verona as Rosina and Angelina; Bologna as Sinaide in Mosè; Carnegie Hall, Ermione; San Francisco, Zelmira; Monte Carlo, Roberto Devereux; Paris, Rossini's Petite Messe Solennelle and Vivaldi's Juditha Triumphans; Musikverein Vienna, Cherubini's D Minor Requiem; Rossini Festival Pesaro, 1990, as Somira in Ricciardo e Zoraide; Season 1996 as Verdi's Preziosilla at the Met and Pippo in La Gazza Ladra at Palermo; season 1998 as Donizetti's Léonor at Rome and Rosina at Genoa; season 1999–2000 as Hassem in Donizetti's Alahor in Granata, at Palermo, Rossini's Isabella at the Deutsche Oper Berlin and Fenena in Nabucco at the Verona Arena. *Recordings include:* Semiramide, La Favorite, Maometto II, Lucrezia Borgia, Stabat Mater, Messa da Requiem, Juditha Triumphans. *Honours:* G.Verdi Prize for best emerging singer, Parma 1991, Best interpreter of the year, Mondov 1992, Ebe Stignani Prize, Lugo di Romagna 1996, Ester Mazzoleni Prize, Palermo 2000. *Current Management:* Hilbert Artists Management, Maximilianstrasse 22, Munich 80539, Germany. *Telephone:* (89) 290747-0. *Fax:* (89) 29074790. *E-mail:* agentur@hilbert.de. *Website:* www.hilbert.de.

**SCALTRITI, Roberto;** Singer (Baritone); b. 1969, Modena, Italy. *Education:* Graduate, The G B Martini Conservatory in Bologna; The School of Music of Fiesole; Studying with Ryland Davies;. *Career:* Debut: Philadelphia 1986, as Alcindoro in La Bohème; Appearances as Schaunard in Hamburg, as Masetto at Glyndebourne and the Festival Hall (1996, under Solti), Mozart's Count in Amsterdam and at the Opéra of Nice; Figaro with the Welsh National Opera, Publio in La Clemenza di Tito at the Théâtre des Champs-Elysées; Further roles in La Gazza Ladra (Nantes), Cimarosa's Maestro di Cappella (Florence) and Handel's Rinaldo (Beaune Festival); Season 1996–97 with Belcore at Lyon Opéra, Guglielmo and Don Giovanni in Amsterdam, Alidoro in La Cenerentola at Genoa; Don Giovanni produced by Peter Brook and conducted by Claudio Abbado in Aix en Provence; Monteverdi's Orfeo in Florence for the season 1998–99. *Recordings include:* Rigoletto with Riccardo Chailly; La Traviata with Zubin Mehta; Handel's Riccardo I with Christophe Rousset; Masetto in Don Giovanni, under Solti; Belcore in L'Elisir d'amore; Amadeus and Vienna–Arias with Christophe Rousset. *Honours:* Winner, 1985 Opera Company of Philadelphia Luciano Pavarotti International Voice Competition. *Address:* c/o IMG Artists, 54 Avenue Marceau, 75008 Paris, France.

**SCANDIUZZI, Roberto;** Singer (Bass); b. 14 July 1958, Treviso, Italy. *Career:* Debut: Sang Bartolo in Mozart's Figaro under Riccardo Muti at La Scala, 1982; Appearances in Opera at Paris, Munich, Hamburg, Amsterdam, Venice, Rome, US Debut in Verdi's Requiem, 1991; Sang Fiesco in a new production of Simon Boccanegra at Covent Garden, 1991; Other conductors have included Patanè, Giulini, Colin Davis; Festival engagements 1992 at Florence as Padre Guardiano in La Forza del Destino, Ramfis at Caracalla and Philip II and Zaccaria at Verona; Sang Zaccaria at Zürich, 1998; Season 2000–01 at the Munich Staatsoper as Verdi's Banquo, King Philip and Fiesco, Boito's Mefistofele in Vienna, Cherubini's Creon at Montpellier (concert) and Verdi's Attila at Frankfurt (concert); Verdi Requiem in Verona, Dresden and Florence; Other roles include Silva, Attila, Mefistofele and Don Giovani. *Recordings include:* Aida conducted by Mehta, I Puritani, Turandot and Simon Boccanegra. *Address:* c/o Theateragentur Dr G. Hilbert, Maximilianstrasse 22, D–80539 München, Germany.

**SCARABELLI, Adelina;** Singer (Soprano); b. 1950, Milan, Italy. *Education:* Studied in Brescia. *Career:* Sang at the Piccola Scala, Milan from 1977; La Scala Milan from 1981, debut as Barbarina in Le nozze di Figaro; Salzburg Festival, 1984–85, as Despina and the Italian Singer in Capriccio; Florence 1988, as Lauretta in Gianni Schicchi; Rome Opera 1989, as Aminta in Mozart's Il re Pastore and as Susanna; She sang Zerlina in Don Giovanni at Parma in 1989; Other roles include Mozart's Servilia (La clemenza di Tito) and Ismene (Mitridate), Verdi's Oscar and Nannetta, Puccini's Musetta and Liu, and Micaela in Carmen; Season 1996 as Rachelina in Paisiello's La Molinara at Bologna, and Olga in Fedora at La Scala; Anaide in Rota's Italian Straw Hat at Milan. *Address:* c/o Teatro Dell'Opera, Piazza Beniamino Gigli 8, 00184 Rome, Italy.

**SCAUNAS MARKOS, Simona;** Pianist; b. 12 Nov. 1965, Rimnicu Vilcea, Romania. *Education:* Baccalaureate Diploma, High School of Art, George Enescu, Bucharest, 1984; Conservator of Arts and Music, George Enescu, Iasi. *Career:* Recitals at Romanian Athene, Bucharest, 1989 and in other cities of Romania; Participant in Young Talents Piatra-Neamt; Museum of Republic, 1987–88; Concerts with: Bacau Symphony Orchestra, 1987 and Craiova Oltenia Philharmonic Orchestra, 1988; Radio appearances in musical programmes and with recitals, 1987 and 1988; Television, 1987; Participant in Young Talents Festival, 1984, 1986, 1987, 1988; Piano recitals and Chamber Music collaboration in German cities of Darmstadt, Erfurt, Freiburg, Gotha, Heiligenstadt, Nordhausen, Osnabrück, Sonderhausen, also in Poland and Italy; International Masterclasses for Pianists. *Recordings:* Radio appearances, 1989 and 1990. *Address:* Morgenröte Str 7, 99734 Nordhausen, Germany.

**SCEBBA, Miguel (Angel);** Pianist, Composer and Professor of Music; b. 6 Nov. 1948, San Martin, Buenos Aires, Argentina. *Education:* National Conservatory of Music, Buenos Aires, 1972; Postgraduate work at Tchaikovsky Conservatory, Kiev, 1974–76, Moscow, 1977–78. *Career:* Debut: Piano soloist with Orchestra of San Martin, Buenos Aires, Beethoven Concerto No. 3, 1966; Concerts in more than 15 countries in the world, among them: Two major tours in USSR, 1981, 1985; International festival, Settembre Musicale Triestino, 1983; Numerous appearances in Germany, 1986–90, on Radio RIAS-Berlin, Tübingen, Konstanz; Theater Colon, Buenos Aires, 1992; Artist-in-Residence, Miami University, Ohio, USA, 1994–97; Full Professor, National University of San Juan, Argentina; 2 tours in Europe, 2000. *Compositions:* Four symphonies, 1987, 1996, 1998, 1999, recorded by National University of San Juan; Organ Book, 1975; 10 string quartets; 5th Symphony, 2001. *Recordings:* Piano solo, Schumann, sonata op 22, Debussy, l'Isle Joyeuse, Ginastera sonata No. 1, Con Anima, São Paulo, Brazil, 1989; Argentina Musical, 1997; Liszt B minor sonata. *Address:* Dominguito 1572, 5400 San Juan, Argentina. *E-mail:* miguel.scebba@interredes.com.ar.

**SCHAAF, Johannes;** stage director; b. 7 April 1933, Bad Cannstatt, Germany; m. Stella Kleindienst. *Education:* studied medicine. *Career:* Worked at the Stuttgart Schauspielhaus, then directed plays in Ulm and Bremen; Further theatre work at Munich (Twelfth Night), Vienna and Salzburg (Beaumarchais, Buchner and Lessing); Director of award winning films from 1967 (with some acting) and television programmes featuring Sviatoslav Richter, Edith Mathis, Peter Schreier and Dietrich Fischer-Dieskau; Opera productions have included Les Contes d'Hoffmann (Vienna Volksoper), Idomeneo (Vienna Staatsoper), Eugene Onegin (Geneva and Bremen) and Capriccio and Die Entführung (Salzburg); Produced Le nozze di Figaro at Covent Garden 1987 and was invited to return for Così fan tutte and Idomeneo (1989), Don Giovanni 1992; Also engaged for Fidelio (1989) and Die Frau ohne Schatten (1992) at Geneva Opera, The Nose by Shostakovich at Frankfurt (1990) and Schreker's Der Ferne Klang at Brussels; Engaged to produce Boris Godunov to open the New Israel Opera House, 1994; Season 1995–96 with Simon Boccanegra at Stuttgart; Le nozze di Figaro at Confidencen, Stockholm, 1998; Directed Katya Kabanova for San Francisco Opera, 2002. *Publications:* contrib. to Geo, on subjects including Chinese Opera.

**SCHACHTSCHNEIDER, Herbert;** Singer (Tenor); b. 5 Feb. 1919, Allenstein, Germany. *Education:* Studied at the Musikhochschule Berlin. *Career:* Sang at the Stadttheater Flensburg from 1953; Further engagements at Mainz and Essen; Holland Festival 1958; Cologne Opera 1959–72; Sang at the Festival Hall, London 1963, in the British premiere (concert) of Schoenberg's Von Heute auf Morgen; Roles included Florestan, Walther, Tannhäuser, Lohengrin, Parsifal, Radames, Don Carlos, Cavaradossi and Don José; Guest appearances in Germany and elsewhere in Europe; Professor at the

Musikhochschule Saarbrücken from 1975. *Address:* Musikhochschule des Saarlandes, Bismarckstrasse 1, Saarbrücken, Germany.

**SCHADE, Michael;** Singer (Tenor); b. 23 Jan. 1965, Geneva, Switzerland. *Education:* Curtis Institute. *Career:* Early experience as Ernesto in Belgium and Rameau's Pygmalion with Opera Atelier in Toronto; Professional debut in 1990 as Jacquino with the Pacific Opera of British Columbia; Sang Tamino at Bologna, 1991; Appeared as Iago in Rossini's Otello at Pesaro; Vienna Staatsoper debut in 1991 as Almaviva; Season 1991–92 as Alfred in Fledermaus at Geneva, Almaviva with Edmonton and Canadian Operas, Ernesto with Vancouver Opera and Elvino in La Sonnambula at Macerata; Season 1992–93 as Jacquino in San Francisco and the Chevalier in Dialogues des Carmélites at Geneva; Sang Roderigo in Otello, 1993; Engaged by Vienna Staatsoper as Ferrando, Almaviva, Nemorino, Tamino and Nicolai's Fenton; Salzburg Festival in 1994 in a staged version of Mozart Arias; Cologne Opera as Telemaco in Monteverdi's Ulisse and Elvino at Trieste; Sang Tamino, 1995, Haydn's Creation, 1995 and Fidelio, 1995; Oedipus Rex at Toronto, 1997; Sang Tamino at Salzburg, 1997, and La Scala, 1998; Appeared in Merry Widow at Paris Opéra in 1998 and as Alfred in Fledermaus at the Metropolitan Opera in 1998–99; Concert repertoire includes Beethoven's Missa Solemnis, The Creation, The Seasons and Bach's St Matthew Passion, Mozart's Requiem, Carmina Burana, Schumann's Paradies und die Peri under John Eliot Gardiner and Elijah with the Cleveland Orchestra; Wagner's David at Chicago, 1999, Ottavio at Los Angeles, Vienna and Ravenna, 1999; Season 2000–01 at the Met as Rossini's Almaviva and Tamino, Henry in Die schweigsame Frau at the Vienna Staatsoper, Cherubini's Jason at Salzburg (concert) and Idomeneo at Dresden. *Recordings include:* Haydn's Maria Theresa Mass under Trevor Pinnock; The Creation and The Seasons; St Matthew Passion, Elijah, St Paul under Rilling; Die Zauberflöte under Gardiner; Mozart Requiem under Abbado. *Current Management:* IMG Artists. *Address:* c/o IMG Artists, Lovell House, 616 Chiswick High Road, London W4 5RX, England.

**SCHADLER, Elisabeth;** Pianist; b. 10 Nov. 1963, Feldbach, Styria, Austria. *Education:* Private lessons, 15 years, Hochschule für Musik, Graz; Masterclasses. *Career:* Concerts and recitals at Vienna Konzerthaus and Musikverein; Many European countries with Vienna Chamber Orchestra, Graz Symphony Orchestra; Notable partners; Festivals; Teacher, Kunstuniversität, Graz, 1987–; Member, EPTA, Austria; Professorship at the Conservatory Klagenfurt, 1999–. *Recordings:* Double concertos for violin, piano and orchestra, 1996. *Honours:* Second prize, International Competition Vercelli, 1985; Second prize, International Schubert Competition, Dortmund, 1987; Winner, International competition, Schubert and Music of the 20th Century, Graz, 1989; Third prize, Lied. *Address:* Friedrichgasse 29, 8010 Graz, Austria.

**SCHAEFER, Peter;** Composer and Musician (Sitar); b. 14 Sept. 1956, Sydney, New South Wales, Australia. *Education:* BA, 1977, BMus, hons, 1984, University of Sydney; DCA, University of Wollongong, 1998; Study with Peter Sculthorpe, Barry Conyngham Ustad Ali Akbar Khan, Ashok Roy. *Career:* Faculty Member, New South Wales Conservatory, 1984–90; University of Wollongong, 1990–92; Founding Member of Peter Schaefer Ensemble; Performer of Indian and electro-acoustic music. *Compositions:* Toward, for string quartet, 1980; See, for synthesizer and/or computer and digital delay, 1983; Petal... Silence, For 2 pianos and tape, 1983; Chien... Still, for orchestra, 1984; Spans, for ensemble and tape, 1989; Time Breathing, Dance Theatre, for ensemble and ape, 1990; Quartet Vibra, for string quartet and tape, 1991; Open/Secret, Music Theatre, for children, 1994; Expans Series (I–VII), for ensemble and tape, 1990–; Tao Streams, orchestra project, 1995–. *Honours:* 2 MBS-FM Radiophonic Tape Composition Prize, 1985. *Address:* c/o APRA, 1A Eden Street, NSW 2065, Australia.

**SCHAEFFER, Bogusław,** DPhil; Polish composer, music critic and playwright; b. 6 June 1929, Lwów (now Lviv, Ukraine); s. of Władysław Schaeffer and Julia Schaeffer; m. Mieczysława Hanuszewska 1953; one s. *Education:* State Higher School of Music (student of A. Malawski), Jagiellonian Univ., Kraków (student of Zdzisław Jachimecki). *Career:* wrote first dodecaphonic music for orchestra, Music for Strings: Nocturne 1953; Assoc. Prof. State Higher School of Music, Kraków 1963–, Extraordinary Prof. of Composition, Higher School of Music, Mozarteum, Salzburg 1986–89, Prof. 1989–; Chief Ed. Forum Musicum 1967–; leads Int. Summer Courses for New Composition in Salzburg and Schwaz (Austria) 1976–. *Main compositions:* Extrema, Tertium datur, Scultura, S'alto for saxophone, Collage and Form, Electronic Music, Visual Music, Heraclitiana, Jangwa, Missa Sinfonica, Piano Concerto, Maah, Sinfonia, Hommage à Guillaume for two cellos and piano 1995, Sinfonietta for 16 instruments 1996, Symphony in One Movement 1997, Enigma for Orchestra 1997, Four Psalms for choir and orchestra 1999, Musica Omogènea for 32 violins 1999, Si Gueris Miracula for soprano and orchestra 2000, Model XXI (wendepunkt) for piano 2000, De Profundis for soprano and chamber orchestra 2000, Monophonie VIII for 24 violins 2000, Ave Maria for soprano and orchestra 2000, opera Liebesblicke, Mini opera, also film and theatre music, Miserere, Organ Concerto, 8 string quartets, Orchestral and Electronic Changes, Concerto for Violin, Piano and Orchestra, Symphony/Concerto for 15 solo instrumentalists and orchestra, Heideggerriana, Winter Musik for horn and piano, Concerto for percussion, electronic media and orchestra. *Plays include:* Three Actors 1970, Darknesses 1980, Screenplay for Sins of Old Age 1985, The Actor 1990, Rehearsals 1990, Séance 1990, Tutam 1991, Rondo 1991, Together 1992, Toast 1991, Harvest

1993, Promotion 1993, Daybreak 1994, Multi 1994, Largo 1996, Stage Demon 1998, Alles 1998, Advertisement 1998, Farniente 1998, Chance 1999, Dwa Te (Two Te) 2000, Skala 2000; plays trans. into 16 languages. *Publications:* Nowa Muzyka. Problemy współczesnej techniki kompozytorskiej (New music. Problems of Contemporary Technique in Composing) 1958, Klasycy dodekafonii (Classics of Dodecaphonic Music) 1964, Leksykon kompozytorów XX wieku (Lexicon of 20th Century Composers) 1965, W kręgu nowej muzyki (In the Sphere of New Music) 1967, Mały informator muzyki XX wieku 1975, Introduction to Composition (in English) 1975, Historia muzyki (Story of Music) 1980, Kompozytorzy XX wieku (20th Century Composers) 1990, Trzy rozmowy (kompozytor, dramaturg, filozof) (Three Conversations: Composer, Playwright and Philosopher) 1992. *Honours:* Hon. mem. Int. Soc. for Contemporary Music 1998; Gold Cross of Merit 1969; Kt's Cross of Polonia Restituta Order 1972; numerous prizes include G. Fitelberg Prize 1959, 1960, 1964, A. Malawski Prize 1962, Minister of Culture and Arts Prize 1971, 1980, Union of Polish Composers Prize 1977, Alfred Jarzykowski Award 1999. *Address:* Osiedle Kolorowe 4, m.6, 31-938 Kraków, Poland; St. Julienstrasse, 5020 Salzburg, Austria. *Telephone:* (12) 6441960 (Poland). *E-mail:* bsch@ceti .pl (office). *Website:* www.usc.edu/dept/polish_music/composer/schaeffer .html#intro.

**SCHÄFER, Christine;** Singer (Soprano); b. 3 March 1965, Frankfurt, Germany. *Education:* Studied at the Berlin Musikhochschule and with Arleen Auger and Aribert Reimann. *Career:* Has sung widely in concert from 1988, notably with such ensembles as the Windsbacher Knaben Chor and the Berlin Philharmonic Choir; Sang Zerbinetta in Ariadne auf Naxos in Munich; Opera engagements at Brussels from 1991 as Papagena, Zerlina and Gilda; San Francisco debut as Sophie in 1993 and returned in 1994 as Zdenka; Pamina and Elisa in Il Re Pastore at Netherlands Opera; Pierrot Lunaire at the Châtelet and Berlin Staatsoper; Sang title role in Berg's Lulu at Salzburg (1995, 1999) and Glyndebourne (1996); Sang Constanze at the 1998 Salzburg Festival; Sang Gilda in Rigoletto at Covent Garden, 2001 (also televised); New York Met debut as Lulu, 2001. *Honours:* Prizewinner at the Mozart Competitions in Vienna and Rome in 1991. *Address:* c/o IMG Artists, Lovell House, 616 Chiswick High Road, London W4 5RX, England.

**SCHÄFER, Markus;** Singer (Tenor); b. 13 June 1961, Andernach am Rhein, Germany. *Education:* Studied in Koblenz, Karlsruhe. *Career:* Sang at the Zürich Opera from 1985; Hamburg, 1986; Deutsche Oper am Rhein, Düsseldorf, from 1987; Sang Fenton in Die Lustige Weiber von Windsor at Duisburg, 1991; Damon in Acis and Galatea at the Queen Elizabeth Hall; Other concerts include the Evangelist in Bach's Passions; Messiah, Elijah, St Paul, Die Schöpfung and Rossini's Stabat Mater; Opera roles include Paisiello's Almaviva, Pedrillo, Ramiro and Caramelo in Eine Nacht in Venedig; Mozart's Ferrando at the Berlin Staatsoper, 1997; Tamino at the Berlin Komische Oper, 1999. *Recordings include:* St Paul, Mendelssohn's Christus, Beethoven's Mass in C, Haydn's L'Infedeltà Delusa; Mozart's Mass K139. *Address:* c/o Deutsche Oper am Rhein, Heinrich Heine Allee 16, 4000 Düsseldorf, Germany.

**SCHAFER, Raymond (Murray);** Composer, Writer on Music and Educationist; b. 18 July 1933, Sarnia, Ontario, Canada. *Education:* Studied at the Toronto Conservatory with Guerrero (piano) and Weinzweg (composition). *Career:* Worked freelance for the BBC in Europe, 1956–61; Founded Ten Centuries Concerts 1961, Toronto; Artist-in-Residence, Memorial University, Newfoundland, 1963–65; Simon Fraser University British Columbia, 1965; Research into acoustic ecology from 1971. *Compositions:* Concerto for harpsichord and 8 instruments, 1954; Minnelieder for mezzo and wind quintet, 1956; Sonatina for flute and keyboard, 1958; In Memoriam: Iberto Guerrero for strings, 1959; Protest and Incarceration for mezzo and orchestra, 1960; Brebeuf for baritone and orchestra, 1961; Canzoni for Prisoners, orchestra, 1962; Untitled Composition for orchestra, 1963; Loving/Toi, music theatre, 1963–66; Requiems for the Party Girl, 1966; Threnody, 1966; Kaleidoscope for multi-track tape, 1967; Son of Heldenleben for orchestra and tape, 1968; From the Tibetan Book of the Dead for soprano, chorus and ensemble, 1968; Yeow and Pax for chorus, organ and tape, 1969; No Longer than Ten Minutes for orchestra, 1970; Sappho for mezzo and ensemble, 1970; String Quartet, 1970; Okeanos for 4-track tape, 1971; In Search of Zoroaster for male voice, chorus, percussion and organ, 1971; Music for the Morning for the World, 1970; Beyond the Great Gate of Light, 1972; Arcana for low voice and ensemble, 1972; East for chamber orchestra, 1972; Paria I–X music theatre, 1969–97; North White for orchestra, 1972; String Quartet No. 2, Waves, 1976; Adieu Robert Schumann for alto and orchestra, 1976; Hymn to the Night for soprano and orchestra, 1976; Cortège for orchestra, 1977; Apocolypsis, music theatre, 1980; RA, multimedia piece based on the Egyptian God, 1983; Flute Concerto, 1985; String Quartet No. 4, 1989; Tristan and Iseult, for vocal soloists, 1992; Accordion Concerto, 1993; String quartets Nos 5 and 6, 1989, 1993; The Falcon's Trumpet, 1995; Musique pour la parque Fontaine, for 4 bands, 1995; Viola Concerto, 1997; Seventeen Haiku, for chorus, 1997. *Publications include:* Edition of Ezra Pound's Opera Le testament de Francois Villon, 1960; British Composers in Interview, 1963; Ezra Pound and Music, 1977; The Thinking Ear, 1986. *Honours:* Canada Council Grants, 1961, 1963; Ford Foundation Award, 1968; Canadian Music Council Medal, 1972; Donner Foundation Grant, 1972; Guggenheim Fellowship, 1974.

**SCHAFF, Gabriel (Jacob Gideon Polin);** Violinist; b. 9 Nov. 1959, Philadelphia, Pennsylvania, USA; m. Nancy McDill, 18 Dec 1988, 1 d.

*Education:* BMus, 1981, Assistant teaching for Erick Friedman, 1979–81, Manhattan School of Music, New York City, 1981; Additional Studies, New School of Music and Temple University, Philadelphia; Studies with Norman Carol, Philadelphia Orchestra. *Career:* Extensive symphonic, opera, ballet and chamber music performances at Lincoln Center, Carnegie Hall and throughout Metropolitan New York City; Violin Soloist in Soviet-American Exchange Concerts organised by Claire Polin with performances in Philadelphia, New York, Moscow, Leningrad and Helsinki, 1979–88; Several commissions and premieres of works by US and Russian composers. *Recordings:* Recording on numerous labels; North/South Consonance. *Address:* c/o Manhattan School of Music, Violin Faculty, 120 Claremont Avenue, New York, NY 10027, USA.

**SCHAGIDULLIN, Albert;** Opera Singer (bass); b. 1 May 1966, Baschkizia; m., 1 s. *Education:* Moscow Conservatory, 1988–92. *Career:* Debut: Dublin, Enrico Grand Opera, 1991; Hamburg State Opera, 1993–97; Easter and Summer Festival, Salzburg, 1993, 1994; Visited Tokyo with Vienna State Opera, 1994; Salzburg, 1998; Opera di Roma, 1994; Bregenz Summer Festival, 1995–96; Messa di Gloria, Vienna Symphony, 1996; Oslo Philharmonic, 1996; Munich Staatsoper, 1997; Lyon Opéra, 1998. *Recordings:* Boris Godunov; Three Sisters by Peter Eötvös. *Publications:* F Times, 1991; Hamburger Abendblatt, 1992; Corriere della Sera, 1994; Salzburger Nachrichten, 1995. *Contributions:* Opera International, 1998; Opern Glas, 1998. *Honours:* Special prize for best young singer, Francisco Viñas Competition, Barcelona, 1990; 3rd prize, Maria Callas Competition, Athens, 1991; 2nd prize, Belvedere Competition, Vienna, 1991; 2nd prize, CIEM Competition, Geneva, 1991; 1st prize, Vervier Competition, 1991; Winner, Pavarotti Competition, Philadelphia. *Current Management:* Askonas Holt Ltd, Lonsdale Chambers, 27 Chancery Lane, London, WC2A 1PF, England. *Telephone:* (20) 7400-1700. *Fax:* (20) 7400-1799. *E-mail:* info@askonasholt.co.uk. *Website:* www.askonasholt.co.uk.

**SCHARFENBERGER, Tobias;** Singer (Baritone); b. 1 Sept. 1964, Grafelfing, Munich, Germany. *Education:* Studied in Hannover and Karlsruhe. *Career:* Sang at Stuttgart, 1991 in the premiere of Perseo e Andromeda by Sciarrone; Deutsche Oper am Rhein at Düsseldorf as Ottakar in Der Freischütz and in Krenek's Orpheus; German premiere of Schnittke's Life with an Idiot, Gelsenkirchen, 1991; Bielefeld Opera from 1995 as Papageno, Siegfried in Schumann's Genoveva and in the local premiere of Weir's Blond Eckbert, 1996; Season 1999–2000 as Nicomedes in Zemlinsky's König Kandaules at Cologne and as Kilian in Der Freischütz at the Komische Oper Berlin; Concert and oratorio appearances. *Address:* Bielefeld Opera, Bruhnenstrasse 3–5, 4800 Bielefeld, Germany.

**SCHARINGER, Anton;** Singer (Baritone); b. 5 March 1959, Austria. *Education:* Studied at Vienna Conservatory. *Career:* Sang with the Salzburg Landestheater, 1981–83; Vienna Volksoper from 1987; Sang Dr Falke in Fledermaus at Amsterdam, 1987; Mozart's Figaro at Ludwigsburg, 1989; Salzburg Festival, 1991; Guest appearances at Cologne, Zürich; Other roles include, Masetto and Guglielmo; Sang the Captain in Gurlitt's Wozzeck at Florence, 1998; Many concert engagements, notably in sacred works by Bach; Television appearances include Bass Solos in the St Matthew Passion, with the Neubeuern Choral Society and the Munich Bach Collegium. *Recordings include:* Die Zauberflöte with Les Arts Florissants, 1996; Masetto in Don Giovanni; Mozart's L'Oca del Cairo. *Address:* c/o Zürich Opera, Falkenstrasse 1, 8008 Zürich, Switzerland.

**SCHARLEY, Denise;** Singer (Mezzo-soprano); b. 1923, France. *Education:* Studied at the Paris Conservatoire. *Career:* Debut: Paris Opéra Comique 1942, as Geneviève in Pelléas et Mélisande; Appeared at the Opéra Comique until 1947, as Carmen, Dulcinée, Charlotte and Mignon; Sang at the Théâtre de la Monnaie, Brussels, 1947–48; Sang in Rome as Carmen; Paris Opéra from 1951, as Maddalena in Rigoletto, Dalila, Amneris, Wagner's Erda, Fricka and Mary; Puck in Oberon, Bellone in Les Indes Galantes and Madame de Croissy in the local premiere of Les Dialogues des Carmélites; Guest appearances in Geneva, Lyon and Barcelona; Marseilles 1961, as the Countess in The Queen of Spades. *Recordings include:* Werther and Carmen; Carmélites; L'Enfant et les Sortilèges. *Address:* c/o Théâtre National, 8 Rue Scribe, 75009 Paris, France.

**SCHÄRTEL, Elisabeth;** Singer (Contralto); b. 6 Oct. 1919, Weiden, Oberpfalz, Germany. *Education:* Studied with Helma Rodgier and Wilma Kaiser and with Anna Bahr-Mildenburg in Munich; Further study with Henny Wolff in Hamburg. *Career:* Sang first at Regensburg, then at Freiburg; Brunswick, 1951–57; Bayreuth Festival from 1954, as Mary in Der fliegende Holländer, Erda, Magdalene and Waltraute; Cologne Opera from 1960 (sang in the premiere of Zimmermann's Die Soldaten, 1965); Appearances in Florence, Lisbon and Vienna as Adelaide in Araballa, Magdalene and Brangaene; Deutsche Oper Berlin as Kundry, Brangaene and the Kostelnicka in Jenůfa; Concert Recitals, 1973. *Recordings:* Der fliegende Holländer; Der Zigeunerbaron.

**SCHASCHING, Rudolf;** Singer (Tenor); b. 12 April 1957, Engelhartszell, Austria. *Education:* Studied at the Vienna Musikhochschule, 1978–83. *Career:* Sang at the Saarbrucken Opera from 1983 as Tamino, Don Ottavio, Pinkerton, Cassio, Max, Oedipus Rex and Idomeneo; Sang Loge, Siegmund and Siegfried, 1987–90; Guest appearances at the Vienna Staatsoper as Aegisthus in 1992, Zürich and elsewhere; Concerts include Beethoven's Ninth,

Bruckner's Te Deum and Haydn's Seasons. *Address:* c/o Staatsoper Wien, Opernring 2, 1010 Vienna, Austria.

**SCHAUERTE-MAUBOUET, Helga (Elisabeth);** German organist; *Organ Teacher, Paris Conservatory;* b. 8 March 1957, Lennestadt; m. Philippe Maubouet, 22 July 1988; one d. *Education:* BA, (Abitur), St Franziskusschule, Olpe, 1976; State Examinations, Philosophy and Pedagogy, University of Cologne, 1982; Music and Artistic Maturity, 1982, Organ Playing, 1985, Musikhochschule, Cologne; Conservatory of Rueil-Malmaison, France, 1983. *Career:* debut: Public appearance as organist, aged 10; Chief Organist at local parish church, aged 13; Organist, German Lutheran Church, Paris 1982–; Organ Teacher, Conservatory Paris, 9th arrondissement and in Andresy 1993–; Recitals, lectures, master classes, Europe and USA, including Royal Academy of Music, London, University of Michigan, USA; Radio performances, Germany, France, and Denmark; Concerts include: Performance, integral of Jehan Alain's and Buxtehude's organ works, Paris, 1986; 1st Performance, Jean Langlais' organ works, Bach and Miniature II and Mort et Resurrection. *Recordings:* Integral of Jehan Alain's Organ Works; Poulenc Organ Concerto; Works of Langlais, Vierne, Dupré, Boëllmann, Dubois, J. S. Bach, Homilius, Walther, Kittel, Kellner, Buttstett, Armsdorff, Muthel and Max Reger; Complete Organ Works of Buxtehude. *Publications:* Jehan Alain: Das Orgelwerk, Eine monographische Studie, 1983; Jehan Alain: L'Homme et l'Oeuvre, 1985; Deutsche und französische Weihnachtslieder, 1997; Noël dans la tradition, Traditionelle Weihnacht, 1997; Boëllmann: Complete Organ Works, Vols I & II, 2002, 2003; Vol. III, 2004; Handbuch Orgelmusik, 2002, Marc-Antoine Charpentier: Te Deum (H. 146/148), Messe de Minuit 2004, Dubois: Complete Organ Works, Vol. I 2005. *Honours:* Cultural Prize of Olpe 1987. *Address:* 25 rue Blanche, 75009 Paris, France. *Website:* www.orguefrance.org/schauerte.htm.

**SCHAVERNOCH, Hans;** Stage Designer; b. 1955, Australia. *Education:* Studied at the Vienna Akademie. *Career:* Has designed productions of Erwartung, Iphigénie en Aulide, Elektra and La Clemenza di Tito in Vienna; Tannhäuser and Werther at Hamburg, Orfeo and Die Zauberflöte at the Komische Oper Berlin; Collaborations with Producer Harry Kupfer in Berlin, at Salzburg for the premiere of Penderecki's Die schwarze Maske and the 1988 Ring des Nibelungen at Bayreuth; Metropolitan Opera with Der fliegende Holländer, Erwartung and Bluebeard's Castle; Paris Opéra with Der Rosenkavalier, Il Trittico, and Katya Kabanova; Royal Opera Covent Garden designs include Ariadne auf Naxos; Followed by Così fan tutte, Idomeneo, Elektra and La Damnation de Faust; Other designs include Alceste at Versailles, Pelléas et Mélisande at Cologne, Liszt St Elisabeth in Vienna, Parsifal and the Ring at the Berlin Staatsoper and Khovanshchina in Hamburg; Rimsky's Legend of the Invisible City of Kitezh at the Bregenz Festival and Komische Oper, Berlin, 1995–96; Boris Godunov at the Vienna Volksoper. *Address:* c/o Deutsche Staatsoper, Unter der Linden, Berlin, Germany.

**SCHEIBNER, Andreas;** Singer (Baritone); b. 18 Jan. 1951, Dresden, Germany. *Education:* Studied in Dresden with Gunther Leib. *Career:* Debut: Gorlitz 1972, as Dr Caius in Die Lustige Weiber Von Windsor; Sang at Butzen, 1974, Stralsund 1976–79, Postdam 1979–83; Engaged at the Dresden Staatsoper from 1983; Roles have included Mozart's Don Giovanni, Guglielmo, Papageno, Belcore, Eugene Onegin, Count Luna, Silvio, Marcello, Lortzing's Zar and Kilian in Der Freischütz; Concert appearances in Austria, Netherlands, Poland and throughout Germany; Season 1999–2000 as the Count in Capriccio at Dresden, Barbier in Die schweigsame Frau for the Vienna Staatsoper, and Jochanaan in Salome at Zagreb; Hans Sachs in Madrid, 2001. *Recordings include:* Der Freischütz, conducted by C Davis; Bach Cantatas. *Address:* c/o Semper-Oper, 8012 Dresden, Germany.

**SCHEIDEGGER, Hans Peter;** Singer (Bass); b. 23 Feb. 1953, La Bottiere, Jura, Switzerland. *Education:* Studied at Berne University and in Essen with Jakob St ämpfli and Paul Lohmann. *Career:* Debut: Geneva Opera 1983, as Curio in Giulio Cesare, conducted by Charles Mackerras; Has appeared at Lucerne and elsewhere in Switzerland as Fiesco (Simon Boccanegra), Britten's Theseus and Collatinus, Bartók's Duke Bluebeard, Zuniga, Leporello, Walter (Luisa Miller), Trulove (The Rake's Progress) and Rocco; Has sung at Karlsruhe from 1986, as King Henry (Lohengrin), Gremin, the Commendatore, Sarastro, Pogner and the Doctor in Wozzeck; Other roles include Zoroastro in Handel's Orlando, Publio in La Clemenza di Tito, and Ferrando in Il Trovatore; Sang Rocco and King Marke at Basle, 1990; Concert repertoire includes Bach Cantatas, B minor Mass, St John Passion and Christmas Oratorio; Beethoven Missa Solemnis; Dvořák Requiem, Te Deum and Mass in D; Haydn Schöpfung, Jahreszeiten, Harmonie and Nicholas Masses; Salve Regina; Handel Messiah, Saul and Hercules; Mozart Requiem and other Masses; Schubert Mass in A flat and G; Graun Der Tod Jesu; Keiser Markus Passion; Telemann Matthew and Luke Passions; Conductors have included Armin Jordan, Horst Stein, Jeffrey Tate, Roderick Brydon, Kurt Sanderling, Charles Farncombe, Wolfgang Gönnenwein and David Lloyd-Jones; Sang Wotan and the Wanderer at Hannover, 1999; Season 2000–01 as Enkidu in the premiere of Gilgamesh by V.D Kirchner, Monteverdi's Seneca, Rangoni in Boris Godunov and Strauss's Orestes. [Change address to]: Staatstheater Hannover, Opernhaus, Opernplatz 1, 30159 Hannover, Germany. *Address:* Badisches Staatstheater, Baumeisterstrasse 11, 7500 Karlsruhe, Germany.

**SCHEJA, Steffan;** Concert Pianist; b. 1950, Sweden. *Education:* Studied at the Stockholm College of Music, Juilliard School, New York. *Career:* Debut:

Concert with Swedish Radio Symphony Orchestra, 1962; New York debut 1972, followed by concerts with the French Radio Symphony Orchestra, Philharmonia Hungarica, Munich Philharmonic, English Chamber Orchestra, NHK Symphony Tokyo and the major Scandinavian Orchestras; Solo Recitals and Lieder Accompanist to Håkan Hagegard, Barbara Bonney and Barbara Hendricks; Director of Chamber Music Festival at Gotland, Sweden, from 1986; Broadcasting engagements, tours of Europe, the USA and Asia; Recital programmes with Violinist Young Uck Kim. *Recordings include:* Albums as Concert Soloist and as Recitalist. *Address:* c/o Gottschalk Impresario A/S, Tollbugaten 3, N–0152 Oslo, Norway.

**SCHELLE, Michael;** Composer and Music Educator; b. 22 Jan. 1950, Philadelphia, Pennsylvania, USA; m. Joyce Tucciarone, 15 Jan 1972, 1 s., 1 d. *Education:* BA, Villanova University, 1972; BM, Butler University, 1974; MM, Hartt School of Music, University of Hartford, 1976; PhD, University of Minnesota, 1980; Private study with Aaron Copland, 1976–77. *Career:* Teaching Assistant, Hartt School of Music, University of Hartford, 1974–77; Instructor, Teaching Associate, University of Minnesota School of Music, 1977–79; Instructor, Carleton College, 19679; Instructor of Music 1979–81, Assistant Professor 1981–87, Associate Professor 1987–, Composer-in-Residence 1981–, Director, New Music Ensemble 1981–, Jordan College of Fine Arts, Butler University; Guest Composer, Lecturer, various universities and colleges, with orchestras and at festivals. *Compositions:* Stage: The Great Soap Opera, chamber opera, 1988; Orchestral: Lancaster Variations, 1976; Masque–A Story of Puppets, Poets, Kings and Clowns, 1977; El Medico, 1977; Pygmies for youth orchestra and tape, 1982; Pygmies II for youth orchestra and speaker, 1983; Golden Bells for orchestra and chorus, 1983; Completion of an unfinished score by N Dinerstein; Oboe Concerto, 1983; Swashbuckler!, 1984; Concerto for 2 pianos and orchestra, 1986; Kidspeace for orchestra and voices, 1987; (restless dreams before) The Big Night, 1989; Symphonic Band: King Ubu, 1980; Cliff Hanger March, 1984; Seven Steps from Hell, 1985; Chamber Music; Piano Pieces; Vocal Music includes: Swanwhite–Letters to Strindberg from Harriet Bosse, cycle for soprano and piano, 1980. *Honours:* Many composition awards and prizes, various commissions including Indianapolis Symphony Orchestra, Buffalo Philharmonic Orchestra, Kansas City Symphony. *Address:* 5939 N Rosslyn Ave, Indianapolis, IN 46220, USA.

**SCHELLEN, Nando;** Artistic Director, Stage Director; b. 11 Oct. 1934, The Hague, Netherlands; m. Deborah Raymond, 19 June 1991. *Career:* Director Nederlandse Operastichting, Amsterdam, 1969–87; Stage Director from 1982, with debut at Holland Festival with The Magic Flute, 1982, American continent debut, 1983 with Lohengrin at Toronto and Edmonton for the centennial of Richard Wagner's death; directed productions of Eugene Onegin in 1986, and The Merry Wives of Windsor 1987 in Germany, and Salto Mortale, 1989, and Our Town, 1990 in Netherlands; Nabucco 1999 Bulgaria/Netherlands; Background managerial, musical and theatrical; Produced 14 World premieres during his engagement at Netherlands Operastichting, also initiated major policy changes there including expansion of season from initially 90 to 165 performances; General Artistic Director of Sweelinck Conservatory of Music, Amsterdam, 1991–93; General Artistic Director of Indianapolis Opera, USA, 1993–96; Director of Opera Workshop at Oberlin Summer School at Casaimaggiore, 1998–; Director of Opera Theater at Northern Arizona University, Flagstaff, Arizona, USA, 2000–; Directed in USA: The Telephone, 1993, 2001; Rigoletto, 1994; Erwartung, 1994; Salomé, 1995; Ariadne auf Naxos, 1996; Così fan tutte, 1997, 1998, 2001; Samson et Dalila, 1998; Don Giovanni, 2000; Into the Woods, 2000; La Voix Humaine 2001; The Magic Flute, 2001; Little Night Music, 2002; Director of Opera Workshop at Oberlin Summer School at Casalmaggiore, 1998–. *Address:* 3841 Woodridge Way, Flagstaff, AZ 86004, USA.

**SCHELLENBERGER, Dagmar;** singer (soprano); b. 8 June 1958, Oschatz, Germany. *Education:* Musikhochschule, Dresden with Prof. Ilse Hahn. *Career:* from 1984 with Komische Oper, Berlin, singing: Donna Anna, in Dargomyzhsky's The Stone Guest; Eurydice, in Orfeo ed Eurydice; Rosalind (1995); guest artist in many German theatres including Dresden, as Aennchen in Freichütz and Laura in Weber's Die drei Pintos; in Leipzig as Hanna in The Merry Widow; Berlin Staatsoper as Agathe in Der Freischütz; Susanna in Le nozze di Figaro, at Hamburgische Staatsoper; US debut as Eurydice with Komische Oper Berlin and as Elena, in Donna del Lago, 1992; Opera of Bordeaux debut as Woglinde, in Das Rheingold; Italian debut with RAI Roma; in France: Beethoven 9th, Bordeaux, 1992; title role in L'incoronazione di Poppea, Opéra de Marseille, 1993; other engagements include: Countess in Le nozze di Figaro for Opera Northern Ireland; Anne in Marschner's Hans Heiling, Netherlands Opera; all four sopranos, Contes d'Hoffmann, Komische Oper Berlin; Donna Anna, in Don Giovanni, 1993; Adina, in L'Elisir d'amore; Norina in Don Pasquale; Webern Cantatas with Beethoven Academy, Antwerp and Brussels; Brahms, Ein Deutsches Requiem with Berlin Philharmonic; Messiah with Cleveland Orchestra; Donna Anna at Strasbourg Festival; sang Anna Maria Strada in the premiere of Farinelli by Matthus, Karlsruhe, 1998; season 2000–01 as Volkhova in Rimsky's Sadko at Venice and as Lehar's Hanna Glawari at the Leipzig Gewandhaus. *Recordings include:* Mozart's Bastien und Bastienne; Hasse's Mass with Capriccio; Handel's L'Allegro, il penseroso ed il moderato; Mozart's Kleinere Kirchenwerke; Solo Recital of Mozart Arias; Marenka in The Bartered Bride. *Honours:* winner Dvořák Int. Voice Competition 1982, Kammersängerin, Germany 1988. *Current Management:* Helen Sykes Artists' Management, 100 Felsham Road, Putney, London, SW15 1DQ, England. *Telephone:* (20) 8780-0060. *Fax:* (20) 8780-8772. *E-mail:* info@helensykesartists.com. *Website:* www.helensykesartists.co.uk.

**SCHELLENBERGER, Hansjörg;** German oboist; b. 1948, Munich. *Education:* Musikhochschule Munich, Tech. Univ. of Munich. *Career:* deputy solo oboist, Cologne Radio Symphony Orchestra 1971–75, solo oboist 1975–77; worked with Berlin Philharmonic Orchestra under Herbert von Karajan 1977, apptd solo oboist 1980; teacher, Hochschule der Künste, Berlin 1981–91; founder and Dir, Haydn Ensemble Berlin; mem., Wind Ensemble of Berlin Philharmonic, Ensemble Wien-Berlin; regular performances as duettist with Rolf Koen (piano), Wolfgang Schulz (flute), Margit-Anna Süss (harp); has performed with conductors, including Claudio Abbado, Carlo Maria Giulini, Riccardo Muti, James Levine; masterclasses at Accademia Chigiana, Siena, Scuola di Musica, Fiesole. *Recordings include:* Poulenc, Chamber Music 1989, Nielsen, Quintet for winds 1991, Mozart, Sinfonia Concertante K.197b 1992, Salon Music of the 19th Century 1992, Hansjörg Schellenberger and Margit-Anna Süss, Duo Recital 1992, Mozart, Posthorn Serenade 1993, Mozart, Divertimenti 1994, Mozart and Beethoven, Quintets (with Daniel Barenboim) 1994, Wilhelm Friedemann Bach, Six Duets 1994, Lachner, Nonet/Piano Quintet 1995, Martin/Ibert/Lutoslawski, Concertante 1998, Britten, Musik mit Oboe 1998, Bach, Sonaten 1998, Brahms/Mozart, Violin Concertos 2000. *Honours:* first prize Competition of German Conservatories 1971, second prize Int. ARD Competition, Munich 1972, Cultural Promotion Prize of Bavaria 1972. *Current Management:* Schellenberger Hansjörg Musikproduktion, Albulaweg 3, Berlin 12107, Germany. *Telephone:* (30) 7415740 (office).

**SCHEMTSCHUK, Ludmilla;** Singer (Mezzo-soprano); b. 14 Sept. 1946, Donetsk, Ukraine. *Education:* Studied at the Odessa Conservatory. *Career:* Sang at the Minsk Opera from 1970; Bolshoi Theatre Moscow from 1978, as Pauline (The Queen of Spades), Azucena, Amneris, Eboli, Dorabella, Ortrud, Fricka, Carmen and Charlotte (Werther); Has sung at the Vienna Staatsoper from 1985 as Laura in La Gioconda, Marina (Boris Godunov), Ulrica and Marfa in Khovanshchina; Guest appearances at the Verona Arena (Azucena 1985), Munich, Hamburg, Caracalla Festival, Rome and Stuttgart (Santuzza 1987); Countess in The Queen of Spades at Buenos Aires, 1995; Sang with Kirov Opera in Tchaikovsy's Mazeppa, as Lyubov, 1998; Season 2000 as Solokha in Tchaikovsky's Cherevichki, at Cagliari, and Ulrica at Barcelona; Concert tours of Finland, Bulgaria and Hungary. *Recordings include:* Video of La Gioconda with Domingo. *Address:* c/o Staatsoper, Opernring 2, 1010 Vienna, Austria.

**SCHENK, Otto;** Opera Producer; b. 12 June 1930, Vienna, Austria. *Education:* Studied acting with Max Reinhardt and production at the Unversity of Vienna. *Career:* Debut: First opera production Die Zauberflöte, Salzburg Landestheater, 1957; Don Pasquale at the Vienna Volksoper, 1961; Vienna Festival 1963, Dantons Tod and Lulu; Salzburg Festival 1963, Die Zauberflöte and Der Rosenkavalier; Jenůfa at the Vienna Staatsoper 1964; Chief Stage Director from 1965; Further productions include Macbeth and Der Freischütz; Opera productions in Frankfurt, Berlin, Munich (Der Rosenkavalier 1975) and Stuttgart; Metropolitan Opera from 1970; Tosca, Fidelio, Tannhäuser, Les Contes d'Hoffmann, Arabella and Der Ring des Nibelungen (1986–88); La Scala Milan 1974, Le nozze di Figaro; Covent Garden 1975, Un Ballo in Maschera; Savonlinna Festival 1991, The Bartered Bride; Elektra and Die Meistersinger at the Metropolitan, 1992–93. *Recordings include:* Video of Der Ring des Nibelungen, from the Metropolitan. *Address:* c/o Bayerische Staatsoper, Postfach 745, 8000 Munich 1, Germany.

**SCHERLER, Barbara;** Singer (Contralto); b. 10 Jan. 1938, Leipzig, Germany. *Education:* Studied at the Berlin Musikhochschule and with Margarete Barwinkel. *Career:* Sang at Frankfurt 1959–64; Cologne Opera 1964–68; Deutsche Oper Berlin from 1968, notably in the 1984 premiere of Gespenstersonate by Reimann; Guest appearances in London, Brussels, Lisbon, Mexico City, Zürich and Venice; Noted concert artist, particularly in works by Bach. *Recordings:* Bach Cantatas; Masses by Mozart; Penthesilea by Schoeck.

**SCHEUERELL, Douglas Andrew;** Musician and Teacher; b. 31 May 1948, Madison, Wisconsin, USA; m. Victoria Ann Scheuerell, 4 Aug 1992, 1 s. *Education:* Bachelor of Music with distinction, University of Wisconsin, Madison, 1971; Teaching certificate K-12, Wisconsin, California and Oregon; Ali Akbar College of Music, San Rafael, California; Ali Akbar Khan, Swapan Chaudhuri, 1981–98; Jnan Prakash Ghosh, 1985–86; Workshops with Samir Chatterjee. *Career:* Musician, Madison, 1966–74; Intern Choral Director, Sun Prairie High School, Wisconsin, 1970; Recording Artist, Stas WHA and WHA-TV, Madison, 1973–74; Musician, Composer, Missing Link Theatre Company, Berkeley, California, 1977–78; Faculty Member, East Bay Centre for the Performing Arts, Berkeley, 1977–78; Family Light Music School, Sausalito, California, 1978; Elizabeth Waters Dance Ensemble, Albuquerque, New Mexico, 1979–80; Accompanist, University of New Mexico School of Dance, Albuquerque, 1979–80; Tabla soloist and accompanist, North Indian classical music, 1988–; Tabla tutor, Eugene, Oregon, 1988–93; Faculty Member, University of Oregon School of Music, Eugene, 1993–; Residencies in California schools National Endowment for the Arts, 1977–78; Performance grantee, Lane Regional Arts Council, Eugene, 1989; Faculty Development grantee, University of Oregon, Eugene, 1996; Performances for Percussive Arts Society; Asia Society. *Recordings:* Badger A Go-Go; Vanish Into Blue. *Address:* 65 N Lawrence Street, Eugene, OR 97401, USA.

**SCHEVCHENKO, Larissa;** Singer (Soprano); b. 1952, Kiev, Russia. *Education:* Graduated St Petersburg Conservatoire, 1976. *Career:* Appearances with the Kirov Opera, St Petersburg, from 1976 as Aida, Olga in The Maid of Pskov by Rimsky-Korsakov, Lisa in The Queen of Spades and Maria in War and Peace; Other roles include Tatiana, Leonora (Il Trovatore), Mimi and Maria in Tchaikovsky's Mazeppa; Sang with the Kirov Opera in London, 1999–2000, as Katerina in Lady Macbeth of Mtsensk (Barbican Hall) and Maria in War and Peace (Covent Garden). *Honours:* Grand Prix in Holland, 1978 and Gold Medal in Belgium, 1979; Glinka All-Union Competition; Honoured Artist of the Republic and People's Artist of Russia. *Address:* c/o Mariinksy Theatre, 1 Theatre Square, St Petersburg, Russia.

**SCHEXNAYDER, Brian;** Singer (Baritone); b. 18 Sept. 1953, Port Arthur, Texas, USA. *Education:* Studied at the Juilliard School New York. *Career:* Sang in Operas by Verdi and Puccini while at Juilliard; Metropolitan Opera from 1980 as Ashton (Lucia di Lammermoor), Marcello (La Bohème), Guglielmo and Lescaut in Manon Lescaut; Paris Opéra 1982–83, as Marcello; Sang Marcello at the Metropolitan 1989, Valentin in Faust, 1990. *Address:* c/o Metropolitan Opera, Lincoln Center, New York, NY 10023, USA.

**SCHIAVI, Felice;** Singer (Baritone); b. 4 July 1931, Vimercate, Italy. *Education:* Studied with Riccardo Malipiero in Monza and with Carlo Tagliabue, Carlo Alfieri and Enrico Pessina in Milan. *Career:* Has sung widely in Italy from 1955, notably at Rome, Parma, Bologna, Trieste, Naples, Milan and Venice; Verona Arena, 1977; Vienna Staatsoper 1984, as Paolo in Simon Boccanegra; Further appearances in Nice, Marseille, Edinburgh, Prague, Barcelona, Moscow, Munich, Glasgow, Cardiff and Warsaw; Other roles include Amonasro, Renato, Luna, Iago, Posa, Don Carlos (La Forza del Destino), Simon Boccanegra, Scarpia, Gerard, Barnaba and Escamillo. *Address:* c/o Vienna Staatsoper, Opernring 2, 1010 Vienna, Austria.

**SCHIDLOWSKY, Leon;** Composer; b. 21 July 1931, Santiago, Chile. *Education:* Studies, National Conservatory, Santiago, 1940–47 and Germany, 1952–55. *Career:* Founded Performance Group, Agrupacion Tonus, for the Promotion of New Music; Teacher, Santaigo Music Institute, 1955–63; Professor, Composition, University of Chile, 1962–68; Emigrated to Israel, 1969; Faculty Member, Rubin Academy, Tel-Aviv. *Compositions:* Jeremias for 8 mixed voices and strings, 1966; String Quartet, 1967; Wind Quintet, 1968; Sextet, 1970; Bai Yar for strings, piano and percussion, 1970; Rabbi Akiba, Scenic Fantasy, 1972; Images for strings, 1976; Lux in Tenebris for orchestra, 1977; Adieu for mezzo and chamber orchestra, 1982; Missa in Nomine Bach for chorus and 8 instruments, 1984; Trilogy for orchestra, 1986; Ballade for violin and orchestra, 1986; Piano Quartet, 1988; String Quartet No. 2, 1988; Laudatio for orchestra, 1988; Kaleidoscope for orchestra, 1989; Trio In Memoriam Vruno Maderna, 1990; Sealed Room for 12 instruments, 1991; Silvestre Revueltas, Oratorio, 1994; Am Grab Kafkas for woman singer playing crotales, 1994; I Will Lay My Hand Upon My Mouth, for orchestra, 1994; Dybbuk, opera, 1994; Laudate, for chorus, 1995; Absalom, for orchestra, 1996; Before Breakfast, monodrama, 1997; Lamento for soprano, string quartet and percussion, 1998. *Address:* c/o Ministry of Education and Culture, Music Department, Hashalum Street 23, PO Box 131, Even Yehuda 40500, Israel.

**SCHIEFERSTEIN, Eva;** German pianist and harpsichordist; b. 17 March 1955, Büdesheim. *Education:* Sociology, Political Science, Ludwig Maximilians University, Munich; Studied at Richard Strauss Konservatorium, Munich, and Salzburg Mozarteum; Masterclasses with Elisabeth Leonskaja, Peter Feuchtwanger and others. *Career:* Debut: Municipal Hall, Friedberg, Germany, 1983; Specialised in contemporary music, lied accompaniment and chamber music; Chamber concerts, Meran, 1984, Berlin, 1986, Bayreuth, 1989, Reims, 1991, Dresden, 1992, Wartburgkonzerte, 1997, Salzburg, 2002, Prague 2003, elsewhere; Concertised at Festivals for Contemporary Music, Bacau, Romania, 1994, Bucharest, Romania, 1995, Belgrade, Yugoslavia, 1998; Recorded for Bavarian Broadcasting Station, Deutschland Radio, SWF Radio; mem, European Piano Teachers Association; GEDOK; Committee Member, Münchner Tonkünstlerverband. *Recordings:* as pianist/harpsichordist of Munich Flute Trio: Musik in Sanssouci, Oper im Salon, Masterpieces of Barocque Chamber Music, Noble Tafelmusik, Musik am Hofe August des Starken (Music at the Court of August the Strong), Friedrich der Grosse (Flute Music from Sanssouci), Münchener Flötentrio – Kompositionen für das Münchener Flötentrio; as soloist: Klaviernacht; Carl Maria von Weber: Tänzerische Klaviermusik. *Honours:* Special Prize as Lied Accompanist, Brahms Competition, Hamburg 1985. *Address:* Baldurstr. 31, 80637 Munich, Germany. *Telephone:* 089 1576614. *Fax:* 089 1576614.

**SCHIEMER, Gregory,** BMus, PhD; Australian composer, electronic instrument designer and academic; *Associate Professor of Music Technology;* b. 16 Jan. 1949, Dunedoo, NSW. *Education:* Univ. of Sydney, Control Data Inst., Macquarie Univ. *Career:* computer technician, Digital Equipment Australia 1976–81; Lecturer in Composition, New South Wales Conservatorium 1986–2002; Sr Lecturer in Music Technology, Faculty of Creative Arts, Univ. of Wollongong 2003, Assoc. Prof. 2004–; mem., Int. Computer Music Asscn; Sec. Australasian Computer Music Asscn. *Compositions include:* (most with purpose-built electronics) Laotian Wood for piccolo, flute, alto flute, soprano saxophone, tenor saxophone and harp, 1970–72; Brolga for computer generated tape, 1973; Iconophony for piano, 1973; Body Sonata for theremin controlled analogue electronics, 1974; A Rain Poem for theremin controlled digital synthesiser, 1975; Ground-Harp for theremin controlled analogue

electronics, 1977; Karamojan Wood for 2 marimbas, 1978; Mandala I and II for Tupperware Gamelan, 1981–82; Porcelain Dialogue for Tupperware Gamelan, 1982–83; Monophonic Variations for percussion and interactive MIDI system, 1986; Music for Shreelata for percussion, Tupperware Gamelan and computer generated tape, 1986; Polyphonic Variations for percussion and interactive MIDI system, 1988; Spectral Dance for MIDI Tool Box and Tupperware Gamelan, 1991; Talk-Back Piano for MIDI Tool Box and Disklavier, 1991; Voltage-Control Piano Studies for MIDI Tool Box and Disklavier, 1991; Token Objects for MIDI Tool Box and Tupperware Gamelan, 1993; Machine Dance for MIDI Tool Box and clarinet, 1994; Shantivanam for carnatic violin and MIDI Tool Box, 1995; Shantivanam II for veena and A4 MIDI Tool Box, 1996; Vedic Mass for 2 sopranos and 2 mezzo-sopranos, 19998; Transposed Hexanies for computer generated tape, 2000–01; Tempered Dekanies for computer generated tape, 2002; Tampatablatarangalila for tabla and MIDI Tool Box, 2002; A Dekany In Memorian for computer generated tape, 2003. *Honours:* various grants, Univ. of Sydney 1990–95, Australia Council Composer's Fellowship for musical instrument design at CSIRO Div. of Radiophysics 1994, Australian Research Council Collaborative Project for musical applications of 3D audio with Lake Technology 1997, Australian Research Council Discovery Project for mobile J2ME musical instrument devt 2003–05, Research Infrastructure Grant for 3D audio, Univ. of Wollongong 2003, Australian Research Council Linkage Project with Capital Authority and Olympic Carillon International 2005–07. *Address:* Faculty of Creative Arts, Building 25, University of Wollongong, 2522, Australia (office). *Telephone:* (2) 4221-3584 (office). *Fax:* (2) 4221-3301 (office). *E-mail:* schiemer@uow.edu.au (office).

**SCHIFF, András;** Hungarian pianist; b. 21 Dec. 1953, Budapest; s. of Odon Schiff and Klara Schiff (née Csengeri). *Education:* Franz Liszt Acad. of Music, Budapest with Pal Kadosa, Gyorgy Kurtag and Ferenc Rados, pvt lessons with George Malcolm, England. *Career:* recitals in London, New York, Paris, Vienna, Munich, Florence; concerts with New York Philharmonic, Chicago Symphony, Vienna Philharmonic, Concertgebouw, Orchestre de Paris, London Philharmonic, London Symphony, Philharmonia, Royal Philharmonic, Israel Philharmonic, Berlin Philharmonic, Cleveland, Philadelphia, Washington Nat. Symphony; played at Salzburg, Edinburgh, Aldeburgh, Feldkirch Schubertiade, Lucerne and Tanglewood Festivals; f. Musiktage Mondsee Festival 1989 (Artistic Dir 1989–98); f. own orchestra Cappella Andrea Barca 1999. *Recordings include:* Bach Goldberg Variations, Bach Partitas, Bach Piano Concertos, Mendelssohn Concertos 1 and 2, all the Schubert Sonatas, Schubert Trout Quintet, Schumann and Chopin 2, all the Mozart Concertos, Bach Two- and Three-part Inventions, Bach Well-Tempered Klavier, Beethoven Violin and Piano Sonatas with Sandor Vegh, Beethoven Piano Concertos, Bartok Piano Concertos, Tchaikovsky Piano Concerto, Bach English Suites (Grammy Award 1990), Bach French Suites, Lieder with Peter Schreier, Robert Holl and Cecilia Bartoli, etc., Beethoven Piano Sonatas Op. 2 Nos 1–3 and Op. 7 No. 4 2005. *Television:* The Wanderer – A Film About Schubert with Andras Schiff (BBC Omnibus, narrator), Chopin with Andras Schiff (BBC Omnibus, narrator). *Honours:* Prizewinner at 1974 Tchaikovsky Competition in Moscow and Leeds Piano Competition 1975, Liszt Prize 1977, Premio della Accad. Chigiana, Siena 1987, RPS/Charles Heidsieck Award for best concert series of 1988–89, Wiener Flotenuhr 1989, Bartok Prize 1991, Royal Philharmonic Soc.'s Instrumentalist of the Year 1994, Claudio Arrau Memorial Medal 1994, Kossuth Prize 1996, Sonning Prize, Copenhagen 1997, Palladio d'Oro della Città di Vicenza 2003, Musikfest Prize, Bremen 2003. *Current Management:* Terry Harrison Artists Management, The Orchard, Market Street, Charlbury, Oxon. OX7 3PJ, England. *Telephone:* (1608) 810330. *Fax:* (1608) 811331. *E-mail:* artists@terryharrison.force9.co.uk (office). *Website:* www.terryharrison.force9.co.uk (office).

**SCHIFF, Heinrich;** Austrian cellist and conductor; b. 18 Nov. 1951, Gruunden. *Education:* studied cello in Vienna with Tobias Kühne and André Navarra. *Career:* London and Vienna debuts 1973; subsequently undertook extensive concert tours in Europe, Japan and USA appearing with maj. orchestras; interpreter of contemporary music including work of Lutosławski, Henze, Krenek and Penderecki and has given first performances of many new works; Artistic Dir Northern Sinfonia 1990–91; prin. guest conductor, Deutsche Kammerphilharmonie 1990–92; Prin. Conductor, Musikkollegium, Winterthur and Copenhagen Philharmonic Orchestra 1995–; guest conductor of many int. orchestras. *Address:* Künstlersekretariat Astrid Schoerke, Mönckebergallee 41, 30453 Hannover, Germany. *Telephone:* (511) 401048. *Fax:* (511) 407435.

**SCHILDKNECHT, Gregor;** Swiss singer (baritone); b. 18 Oct. 1936, Biel. *Education:* Univ. of Music, Vienna with Adolf Vogel, studied in Nuremberg with Domgraf Fassbänder, in Düsseldorf with Carino. *Career:* sang at the Oldenburg Opera 1965–67, Coburg 1968–73, Detmold 1973–74, Krefeld 1974–77, and Bielefeld 1977–80; guest engagements from 1980 at the Berlin Staatsoper, Hamburg, Düsseldorf, Karlsruhe, Geneva, Amsterdam, Brussels and Prague; roles have included parts in operas by Mozart, Donizetti, Rossini; Verdi's Luna, Rigoletto, Germont, Macbeth, Posa, Amonasro and Carlo in La Forza del Destino; Wolfram, Scarpia, the villains in Hoffmann and Mandryka in Arabella; concert engagements in Germany, Netherlands, Switzerland and USA. *Address:* 2555 Brügg bei Biel, Switzerland.

**SCHILLER, Allan;** British concert pianist; b. 18 March 1943, Leeds, Yorks. *Education:* Associate, Royal College of Music, Performance and Diploma, 1959; Moscow Conservatoire. *Career:* Debut: Hallé Orchestra with John

Barbiroli, Leeds Town Hall, 1954; Edinburgh Festival, Scotland, 1954; Promenade Concert, London, 1957; Subject of Philpott File, television documentary; Toured in Canada, Europe, Russia; Professor, Guildhall School of Music; mem, Incorporated Society of Musicians; Bristol Savages. *Recordings:* Recital, 1958; Chopin and Mozart; Bridge and Elgar Quintets with Coull Quartet; Complete Chopin Waltzes. *Honours:* Harriet Cohen Medal 1966. *Address:* 14 Lilymead Avenue, Knowle, Bristol 4, Avon, England. *Telephone:* (117) 972-3423 (office). *E-mail:* allan.schiller@virgin.net (office). *Website:* allanschiller.com (home).

**SCHILLER, Christoph;** Concert Violist; b. 17 May 1951, Zürich, Switzerland; m. Louise Pelerin 1981, 1 s. *Education:* Realgymnasium Zürichberg; Matura, 1970; University of Zürich; North Carolina School of Arts, 1972–73; Accademia Chigiana, Siena, Italy; Nordwestdeutsche Musikakademie, Detmold, Germany. *Career:* Violist of New Zürich String Quartet, 1973–88 with tours in Europe, Israel, Scandinavia and North and South America; Viola soloist with orchestras throughout Europe; Professor at the Zürich and Basle Conservatories; Founder and Artistic Director of Ensemble Mobile, 1989–. *Recordings:* Charles Koechlin, Viola Sonata; Willy Burkhard, works for viola; Giacinto Scelsi, Solo and Chamber Music; String Quartets by Brahms, Mendelssohn, Debussy, Ravel, Dvořák, Grieg and Haydn; Chamber works by various Swiss composers. *Honours:* Soloist's Prize of Swiss Musicians Association, 1976. *Current Management:* Pro Musicis, Silvia Ackermann, Rütistrasse 38, 8032, Zürich, Switzerland. *Address:* Bombachstr 21, 8049 Zürich, Switzerland.

**SCHIML, Marga;** Singer (Mezzo-soprano); b. 29 Nov. 1945, Weiden, Germany; m. Horst Laubenthal. *Education:* Studied with Hanno Blaschke in Munich and with Hartmann-Dressler in Berlin. *Career:* Debut: Basle Opera 1967, in Tigrane by Hasse; Has sung in Vienna, Munich, Graz, Basle and Zürich; Appearances at the Orange and Salzburg Festivals; Bayreuth Festival 1981, 1986, as Magdalene in Die Meistersinger and in Parsifal and Der Ring des Nibelungen; Sang at Turin 1986, as Fricka in Das Rheingold; Maggio Musicale Florence 1989, Annina in Der Rosenkavalier. *Recordings:* Puck in Oberon, La Clemenza di Tito; Mozart Masses, Der Ring des Nibelungen; Choral Symphony; Masses by Weber. *Address:* c/o Festspielhaus, 8580 Bayreuth, Germany.

**SCHINDHELM, Michael;** German music administrator and novelist; *General Director, Stiftung Oper Berlin;* b. 1960, Eisenach. *Education:* Internationalen Universität Woronesh, Voronezh State Univ. *Career:* Dir Theater Nordhausen 1990–92, Gera City Theatres 1992–96, Basel Theatre 1996–2005; Gen. Dir Stiftung Oper Berlin (Berlin Opera Foundation) 2005–. *Television:* Lied von der Steppe (documentary, co-dir). *Publications:* novels: Roberts Reise 2001, Zauber des Westens 2001, Das Kamel auf der Startbahn 2004, Die Herausforderung 2005; trans.: Anton Chekhov, Onkel Wanja, Maxim Gorki, Nachtasyl; libretto: Lied von der Steppe. *Address:* Stiftung Oper Berlin, Unter den Linden 41, Berlin 10117, Germany (office). *Telephone:* (30) 20649530 (office). *Fax:* (30) 20649459 (office). *E-mail:* p.koneerding@oper -in-berlin.de (office). *Website:* www.oper-in-berlin.de (office).

**SCHIPIZKY, Frederick (Alexander);** Composer, Conductor, Bassist and Teacher; b. 20 Dec. 1952, Calgary, Alberta, Canada; m. Ruth Fagerburg (violinist), 4 Aug 1984. *Education:* BMus, Composition, University of British Columbia, 1974, study with Elliot Weisgarber and Jean Coulthard; Private study with Harry Freedman and Sophie Eckhardt-Gramatte Courtenay, 1974 and with Murray Adaskin at Victoria Conservatory, 1975–76; MMus in Composition and Double Bass at Juilliard School, NY, 1976–78, with Roger Sessions, David Diamond and David Walter; D.Mus in Music Composition, University of Toronto, 1994, with John Beckwith and John Hawkins. *Career:* Appearances on CBC radio and television with Vancouver Symphony Orchestra, and as Composer, Conductor and Bassist; Bassist for Vancouver Symphony Orchestra; Teacher of Theory and Composition at Vancouver Academy of Music; Faculty, Courtenay Youth Music Centre, 1986; Performed with Montreal Symphony Orchestra; Faculty, Douglas College since 1989; Performed with Esprit Orchestra and Arraymusic; mem, Associate Composer, Canadian Music Centre; Canadian League of Composers. *Compositions:* Symphonic Sketches, 1977; Fanfare for The Royal Visit, 1983; Divertimento for string orchestra, 1983; Symphony No. 1, 1985, commissioned by Vancouver Symphony Orchestra for Japan tour 1985; Symphony No. 2, 1988; From Under The Overture, 1990; Aurora Borealis, 1992; Concerto for contrabass and orchestra, 1994. *Address:* 5390 Larch Street, Vancouver, British Columbia, V6M 4C8, Canada.

**SCHIRMER, Astrid;** Singer (Soprano); b. 8 Nov. 1942, Berlin, Germany. *Education:* Studied at the Berlin Musikhochschule with Johanna Rakow and Elisabeth Grümmer. *Career:* Debut: Coburg, 1967, as Senta in Der fliegende Holländer; Has sung at the Hanover Opera and widely in Germany, notably in Cologne, Mannheim, Berlin, Stuttgart and Nuremberg; Guest appearances in Barcelona and Zürich; Other roles include Santuzza, Leonore, Brünnhilde, Aida, Amelia (Un Ballo in Maschera), Sieglinde, Ariadne, Arabella, Tosca, Turandot and Lady Billows in Albert Herring; Many concert appearances.

**SCHIRMER, Ulf;** Conductor; b. 1959, Germany. *Education:* Studied in Bremen and in Hamburg with Horst Stein and Christoph von Dohnányi. *Career:* Assistant to Lorin Maazel at the Vienna Staatsoper and from 1984 conducted Berio's Un Re in Ascolto, Erwartung, Lulu and Henze's Orpheus there; Music Consultant from 1993–95, leading Ariadne, Tannhäuser, Rosenkavalier, Fidelio, Katya Kabanova, Figaro, Parsifal and Cardillac, also

Raymonda (with Rudolf Nureyev); Antigone (Orff) at Salzburg Festival, 1989; Bregenz Festival from 1994, with Der fliegende Holländer, Nabucco, Fidelio and Martinů's Greek Passion; Music Director at Wiesbaden, 1988–91; Concerts with the Vienna Philharmonic from 1992; Engagements with the Berlin Philharmonic from 1993; Principal Conductor, Danish National Radio Symphony Orchestra, 1995–; From 1995/6 season, engagements with London, Israel and Rotterdam Philharmonics and Pittsburgh, St Louis and Gothenburg Symphony Orchestras; Nielsen's Maskarade and Berg's Lulu with the Danish Radio Symphony Orchestra; Schubert Bicentenary concert in Copenhagen, 1997; Tristan, 1997 and Ring, 2001, in Graz; Rosenkavalier and Lulu at the Bastille in Paris; Professor of Music Analysis, Academy of Music, Hamburg. *Recordings include:* Capriccio, with Te Kanawa (Decca), Lulu (Chandos); Maskarade (2 Grammy nominations). *Address:* c/o Artists Management Zürich, Rütisstrasse 52, 8044 Zürich-Gockhausen, Switzerland.

**SCHIRRER, René;** Singer (Bass-baritone); b. 1957, France. *Education:* Studied in Strasbourg, Basle and Salzburg. *Career:* Sang with the Groupe Vocal de France and with Lyon Opéra from 1983; Edinburgh Festival, 1985; in Pelléas et Mélisande and Chabrier's Etoile; Aix-en-Provence, 1987 in Lully's Psyché, Karlsruhe, 1990, as Rangoni in Boris Godunov and Montreal, 1993 in Les Troyens; Herald in Lohengrin at Lyons, 1995; Appearances with Opéra du Rhin, Strasbourg, including title role in Honegger's Les Aventures du Roi Pausole, 1998; Other roles include Peter Quince, Zaccaria in Nabucco and Rossini's Basilio; Sang Gounod's Frère Laurent at Strasbourg and Indra in Le Roi de Lahore by Massenet at St Etienne, 1999–2000. *Recordings:* Le Roi Arthus by Chausson, Iphigénie in Aulide, Handel's Tamerlano and Leclair's Scylla et Glaucus. *Address:* Opéra du Rhin, 19 Place Broglie, 67008 Strasbourg Cédex, France.

**SCHLAEPFER, Jean-Claude;** Swiss composer and teacher; b. 11 Jan. 1961, Geneva. *Education:* Conservatoire supérieur du Musique, Geneva, Academy of Music, Paris with Betsy Jolas, Diplomas in Musical Education and Musical Culture. *Career:* Composer; Professor, Department of Harmony and Analysis at the Conservatoire supérieur de Musique; Professor, Department of Musical Languages, University of Geneva. *Compositions include:* Esquisses en trois tableaux for violin and piano 1987, Instances I for piano or harpsichord 1987, Les Mots (3 melodies) for mezzo soprano and piano 1987–88, 3 Caprices, for violin in memory of N. Paganini, 1988, Impressions for 15 strings solo 1988; 5 Pieces for orchestra, in homage of Anton Webern, 1988, Dialogues, for solo violoncello 1989; Stabat Mater for soprano, mixed choir and orchestra 1990, 7 Preludes for two pianos 1991; Motets for soprano voice, viola da gamba and harp 1992; Trois reves (Three Dreams) on poems by Georg Trakl for narrator, soprano, alto, wind quintet, string quartet and piano 1992, Concerto Solitude for violin and chamber orchestra 1993; Instances II for solo horn (commissioned by Geneva International Music competition) 1993, Visibili et Invisibili, for men's and children's choir a capella, 1994, Exil for symphony orchestra (commissioned by Orchestre de la Suisse romande) 1994–95, Instances III for marimba alone 1994, Psaume for flute (C and G), oboe (and English horn), violoncello and organ 1994, Ascensus for trumpet and string orchestra 1995, L'impossible absence for symphony orchestra 1995, La Rose de Jérico for soprano voice and piano 1995, Chant de lune for flute, oboe, clarinet, percussion, violin, viola and violoncello 1996, Missa Brevis for soprano and string quartet 1996, He de Re for violoncello and piano 1996, Instances IV for violin solo 1997–98, Trio a Karin for violin, violoncello and piano 1999, Lamentations de Jeremie for string orchestra 2000. *Recordings:* Impressions; Stabat Mater and 7 Preludes for two pianos, Radio Suisse Romande, Jean-Claude Schlaepfer, Portrait (including Exil, Motets, Ascensus, Missa brevis, Chant de lune, Trio a Karin, Visibili et invisibili). *Honours:* Composition Award, Geneva Conservatory 1988. *Address:* c/o Editions Bim, PO Box 300, 1674, Vuarmarens, Switzerland. *Telephone:* (21) 909-1000. *Fax:* (21) 909-1009. *E-mail:* order@editions-bim.com. *Website:* www.editions-bim.com.

**SCHLEE, Thomas (Daniel);** Composer, Organist and Festival Director; b. 26 Oct. 1957, Vienna, Austria; m. Claire Aniotz, 24 May 1986, 1 s., 1 d. *Education:* Theresianische Akademie Wien, Hochschule für Musik, Vienna; Composition and Organ, Conservatoire National Supérieur de Musique, Paris, France; University of Vienna: Dr phil, Musicology, History of Arts, Theresianische Akademie Wien, University of Vienna. *Career:* Many organ concerts, Europe, USA and former USSR; Participant, various international festivals; Music Dramaturg, Salzburger Landestheater, 1986–89; Teacher, Wiener Musikhochschule and University Salzburg, 1988–90; Artistic Director of the Bruckner Hall Linz and International Bruckner Festival, 1990–98; Project director of La Cite Céleste by the Guardini Foundation, Berlin; President of the Foundation from 1998–2001; Nominated Music Director of the Brucknerhaus Linz, Upper Austria, 1990; Vice-Director, International Beethoven Festival, Bonn, 1999; Nominated Director of Carinthian Summer Festival, Austria, 2004; mem. governing body of the Guardini Foundation. *Compositions:* Organ, vocal, instrumental and orchestral music; Edited Bärenreiter, Leduc, Lemoine, Choudens, Combre, Schola Cantorum Doblinger, Universal Edition, Billaudot, Butz, Schola Cantorum;. *Recordings:* Radio and television recordings, various European countries including: Messiaen at La Trinité; E Reuchsel. *Publications:* La Cité céleste–Olivier Messiaen, 1998. *Contributions:* Books: Ecrivains Français et l'Opéra (Legende de Tristan, Tournemire), 1986; Studien zur Wertungsforschung 20 ('Cinq Rechants' by Messiaen), 1988; Meilensteine der Musik, 1991; Numerous music journals; Editor, Universal Organ series; Almanach zum Internationalen Beethovenfest Bonn 1999, 2000; Les Solitudes de Jean Françaix, 2001. *Honours:*

Chevalier des Arts et Lettres 1991; Joaquin Rodrigo Medal 1997, Landeskulturpreis für Musik Oberösterreich 1998, Kirchenmusikpreis der Staat Neuss 2002, Förderungspreis des Österr. Bundeskanzleramtes, 2003. *Address:* Hofmühlgasse 7a/7, 1060 Vienna, Austria.

**SCHLEMM, Anny;** Singer (Mezzo-soprano); b. 22 Feb. 1929, Neu-Isenburg, Frankfurt, Germany. *Education:* Studied with Erna Westenberger in Berlin. *Career:* Sang at the Berlin Staatsoper and the Berlin Komische Oper from 1949; Cologne Opera 1950–51; Has sung at Frankfurt Opera from 1951; Guest appearances in Hamburg, Munich and Berlin; Glyndebourne 1954, as Zerlina; Bayreuth Festival 1978–86, as Mary in Der fliegende Holländer; Netherlands Opera Amsterdam 1978, Herodias and Clytemnestra; Cologne 1981, as the Kostelnicka in Jenůfa; Covent Garden debut 1984, Madelon in a new production of Andrea Chénier; Other roles include Susanna, Desdemona, the Marschallin, Octavian and Marenka in The Bartered Bride; Sang Clytemnestra in Elektra at Stuttgart, 1989; Modern repertoire has included Miranda in Martin's The Tempest, Europera I and II by Cage (premiere at Frankfurt 1987), Mumie in Reimann's Gespenstersonate and Mother in Cerha's Baal (Vienna 1992); Sang the Countess in The Queen of Spades for Opera Flanders (1999) and Mamma Lucia in Cavalleria Rusticana at Frankfurt, 2001. *Recordings:* Madama Butterfly, Pagliacci; Hansel und Gretel; Der fliegende Holländer from Bayreuth; Video of Andrea Chénier. *Address:* 6078 Neeu-Isenburg, Graf-Folke-Bernasotte, Str 12, Germany.

**SCHLICK, Barbara;** Singer (Soprano); b. 21 July 1943, Würzburg, Germany. *Education:* Musikhochschule Würzburg; Paul Lohmann in Wiesbaden; Further study in Essen. *Career:* Engaged by Adolf Scherbaum for his Baroque Ensemble in 1966; Concert engagements in Munich, Hamburg, Rome, Geneva, Paris, Prague, Leningrad and New York; Russian tour 1971 and tour of the USA and Canada with the Chamber Orchestra of Paul Kuentz in 1972; Tour of Israel and USA 1975–76 with the Monteverdi Choir under Jürgen Jürgens; Festival appearances in Aix, Paris, Berlin, Kassel and Herrenhausen; Sang at the Göttingen Handel Festival 1980, York Early Music Festival 1988, CPE Bach's Die Letzten Leiden; Further appearances at the Haydn series on South Bank with the Orchestra of the Age of Enlightenment and in Mozart's Requiem with the Amsterdam Baroque Orchestra; Repertoire includes Carissimi's Jephte; Vivaldi's Gloria; Passions and Cantatas by Bach; Handel's Messiah, Acis and Galatea and Caecilia Ode; Haydn's Creation and Seven Last Words, Mozart's Requiem and Stravinsky's Cantata; Songs by Dowland, Purcell, Handel, Scarlatti and Haydn. *Recordings include:* Gagliano's La Dafne; Bach's St Matthew Passion; Jephtha by Reinthaler; Hasse's Piramo e Tisbe; Handel's Giulio Cesare and Rosalinda. *Address:* Greingstrasse 9, 8700 Würzburg, Germany.

**SCHMALFUSS, Peter;** Pianist and Professor of Piano; b. 13 Jan. 1937, Berlin, Germany; m. Sylvia Heckendorn, 7 Mar 1966. *Education:* Staatliche Hochschule für Musik, Saarbrücken with Walter Gieseking, Alexander Sellier, Adrian Aeschbacher; Studied with Wilhelm Kempff, Beethoven Seminary, Positano, Italy. *Career:* Appearances as soloist and with orchestras in over 40 countries since 1960; Premieres of contemporary works; Many concert tours to Asia and North Africa; Concerts and participation on many Music Festivals in 4 continents, China, 1989, South America, 1990, Canada and USA, 1992, Japan, 1993. *Recordings:* Works of R Schumann, Grieg, Chopin, Smetana, Szymanowski, Mozart, Beethoven, Debussy. *Publications:* Editor of educational literature for piano. *Honours:* Title, Honorary Professor of the State Institute of Education, Moscow, 1993.

**SCHMECKENBECHER, Jochen;** Singer (Baritone); b. 1967, Heidelberg, Germany. *Education:* Studied at Cologne with Kurt Moll. *Career:* Sang at Hagen Opera, 1990–93, as Mozart's Count and Dandini in Cenerentola; The Count in Lortzing's Wildschütz; Komische Oper Berlin from 1993 as Papegano, Silvio and Schaunard, and in Rimsky's The Tale of Tsar Saltan; Further engagements at Hamburg, Bonn, the Châtelet, Paris and Geneva Opera; Season 1997–98 with Papageno at Dallas Opera; Frequent concert appearances. *Address:* Komische Oper Berlin, Behrenstrasse 55–57, 10117 Berlin, Germany.

**SCHMID, Benjamin;** Violinist; b. 13 Sept. 1968, Vienna, Austria. *Education:* Music Universities, Salzburg, Vienna, Philadelphia; Diploma, Curtis Institute, Magister Artium, Salzburg. *Career:* Debut: Salzburg Festival, 1986; Over 500 concertos and recitals, St Petersburg Orchestra, Paris, London, Berlin, Vienna, in Europe, USA, Canada and Japan; Chamber music and violin solo recitals, radio and television appearances in Europe, USA and Canada; Professional Jazz Player; Repertory includes more than 50 concertos from Baroque to Contemporary music; The Three Great Cycles for violino-solo; Most of the important duo sonatas from 18th and Contemporary Music. *Recordings:* Concertos: All of Bach; 3 Mozart; Haydn C Major; Brahms D major; Violin concerto; Violin solo, Bach, 6 sonatas and partitas; Paganini; Ysaÿe, 6 sonatas, recitals; Brahms, Ravel, Kreisler solo recital. *Honours:* First prizes, Concours-Menuhin, Paris, 1985; Leopold Mozart, Augsburg, 1991; Carl-Flesch-International, 1992; Guest Professor, Hochschule Mozarteum, Salzburg, 1996–98. *Address:* Ziegelstadelstrasse 19A, 5026 Salzburg, Austria.

**SCHMID-LIENBACHER, Edith;** Singer (Soprano); b. 1959, St Andra, Kartnen, Germany. *Education:* Studied at Klagenfurt and Vienna. *Career:* Vienna Volksoper from 1985, as Janáček's Vixen, Leila in Les Pêcheurs de perles and Lauretta in Gianni Schicchi; Bregenz, Aix and Salzburg Festivals, 1985, 1989, 1993; as Papagena in Die Zauberflöte; Sang Mozart's Susanna at Cologne, 1996; Other roles include Fortuna in Handel's Giustino, Despina,

Adele in Die Fledermaus and Christel in Der Vogelhändler; Sang Mozart's Constanze at the Vienna Volksoper, 2001. *Recordings:* Die Zauberflöte. *Address:* c/o Wiener Volksoper, Wahringerstrasse 78, A–1090 Vienna, Austria.

**SCHMIDT, Andreas;** German singer (baritone); b. 30 June 1960, Düsseldorf; m. Eva Grundhoff 1989; one s. one d. *Education:* studied piano, organ, conducting in Düsseldorf, singing in Düsseldorf and Berlin. *Career:* youngest mem. Deutsche Oper Berlin 1983; debut Hamburg State Opera 1985, Munich State Opera 1985, Covent Garden London 1986, Vienna State Opera 1988, Geneva Opera 1989, Salzburg Festival 1989, Aix-en-Provence Festival 1991, Metropolitan New York 1991, Edin. Festival 1991, Paris Bastille 1992, Paris Garnier 1993, Glyndebourne Festival 1994, State Opera Berlin 1995, Amsterdam Opera 1995, Bayreuth Festival 1996; has sung with major orchestras, including Berlin, Geneva, Vienna, Munich, London, New York, Israel Philharmonic orchestras, Cincinnati, Cleveland Symphony orchestras, La Scala, Milan. *Honours:* first prize Deutscher Musikwettbewerb, several German and int. awards and prizes. *Current Management:* IMG Artists, Media House, 3 Burlington Lane, London, W4 2TH, England. *Address:* Fossredder 51, 22359 Hamburg, Germany.

**SCHMIDT, Anne-Sophie;** Singer (Soprano); b. 1968, France. *Education:* Strasbourg Conservatoire. *Career:* Debut: Aminta in Mozart's Il Re Pastore and Fiordiligi at Marseille, 1990; Appearances in Figaro and Boris Godunov at the Opéra Bastille, and as Italian Singer in Capriccio at the Salzburg Festival; Berlin Staatsoper in Honegger's Jeann d'Arc au Bûcher, in Haydn's I Pescatrici at Toulouse, as Donna Elvira at Nancy and Poulenc's Blanche de la Force at Toronto: also seen at Savonlinna and the London Proms; Season 1995 as Mélisande at Marseilles, followed by performances at the Paris Châtelet, Turin, Bucharest and Bologna; Further engagements in Werther, opposite Alfredo Kraus, at Seville, and concerts with leading European orchestras; Sang Susanna at Compiègne (1997) and Poulenc's La Voix Humaine, 2000. *Recordings include:* Arias from operas by Gounod and Massenet and Mélodies by Satie (Harmonia Mundi). *Address:* c/o Musicglotz, 11, rue le Verrier, 75006 Paris, France.

**SCHMIDT, Annerose;** Pianist and Professor; b. 5 Oct. 1936, Wittenberg, Germany. *Education:* Studied with Hugo Steurer, Hochschule für Musik, Leipzig, 1953–58. *Career:* Debut: Wittenberg, 1945; Numerous engagements as Soloist with major orchestras including: Gewandhaus Orchestra, Leipzig; Dresden State Orchestra; Royal Philharmonic Orchestra, London; New Philharmonic Orchestra, London; Cleveland Orchestra; Chicago Symphony Orchestra; Tonhalle Orchestra, Zürich; Danish Radio Symphony Orchestra, Copenhagen; Concertgebouw Orchestra, Amsterdam; Residentie Orchestra, The Hague; NHK (Japan Broadcasting Orchestra) Symphony Orchestra, Tokyo; Many festival appearances including Salzburg, Holland, Prague Spring, Berlin, Dresden, Warsaw Autumn; Professor, Hochschule für Musik Berlin, 1986–; Television appearances include Beethoven's 5th Piano Concerto; Rector, Hanns Eisler Hochschule für Musik, Berlin, 1990–. *Recordings:* Many as soloist with orchestra and as recitalist. *Honours:* Diploma, International Chopin Competition, Warsaw, 1954; 1st Prize, International Robert Schumann Competition, Zwickau, 1956; Artist's Prize, 1961; National Prize, 1965; Gold Bartók Medal, 1974. *Address:* Friedrich-Engels-Damm 131, Bad Saarow 75521, Germany.

**SCHMIDT, Carl (Brandon);** Professor of Music and Director of Graduate Studies; b. 20 Oct. 1941, Nashville, Tennessee, USA; m. Elizabeth Jane Kady, 25 June 1967, 2 s., 1 d. *Education:* AB, Stanford University, 1963; AM 1967, PhD 1973, Harvard University; Diploma, Fontainebleau School of Music, 1961; Conducting with Boulanger, Solfège-Dieudonné. *Career:* Debut: Conducting, Stanford, California 1963, London, 1971; Assistant Professor, Wabash College, 1970–73, Bryn Mawr College 1973–79; Professor, The University of the Arts, 1978–. *Publications:* Antonio Cesti: Il Pomo d'oro (Music for Acts III and V from Modena, Biblioteca Estense, Ms Mus E 120), Recent Researches in the Music of The Baroque Era, Vol. 42, 1982; A Catalogue raisonné of the Literary Sources for the Tragédies Lyriques of Jean-Baptiste Lully; General Editor, Jean-Baptiste Lully: The Collected Works; The Music of Francis Poulenc (1899–1963): A Catalogue; Jean-Baptiste Lully: Actes du colloque/Kongressbericht; The New Grove Dictionary of Opera, 1992; Journal of Musicology. *Address:* 250 South Broad Street, Philadelphia, PA 19120, USA.

**SCHMIDT, Emma;** Austrian pianist; b. 8 Feb. 1944, Vienna; m.; one s. *Education:* Master's degree, Hochschule für Musik, Graz, Austria; Masterclasses, Salzburg and Siena. *Career:* Teacher; College of Music, Graz and Hannover; Soloist in Austria, Portugal, South America, Germany and Italy; Recitals and chamber music in Vienna, Salzburg, London, Berlin, Hamburg, Düsseldorf, Hannover, Brussels, Warsaw, Belgrade, Segovia, Zagreb, Moscow, Rome, Milan, Turin and Florence; Several tours in Hong Kong and Korea; Radio productions across the world; Television concerts. *Recordings include:* La Ricordanza by Carl Czerny; George Gershwin's Rhapsody in Blue and 3 Preludes; Leoš Janáček, Piano Sonata and On the Overgrown Path I; Scott Joplin, Ragtimes; Alfred Schnittke, Concerto for Piano; Erwin Schulhoff's Concerto for piano; Franz Schubert, Winterreise; Smetana, Bohemian Dances; Alexandre Tansman, Sonatine Transatlantique; P. I. Tchaikovsky, Piano Trio; Alban Berg, Op. 1 Piano Sonata; Arnold Schönberg, 3 Klavierstücke Op. 11; J. S. Bach-Ferruccio Busoni, Chaconne; F. Schreker-I. Strasfogel, Kammersymphonie. *Honours:* Austrian Cross of Honour for Science and Arts 2002;

Bösendorfer Prize, Vienna, 1969; First prize, Vittorio Gui Chamber Music Competition, Florence, 1979. *Address:* Scheibengasse 14, 1190 Vienna, Austria. *E-mail:* emma.schmidt@utanet.at (office). *Website:* web.utanet.at/schm2337.

**SCHMIDT, Erika;** Singer (Soprano); b. 12 Jan. 1913, Quirnheim, Germany. *Education:* Studied in Frankfurt. *Career:* Sang at Frankfurt 1935–67 in operas by Mozart, Weber, Verdi, Strauss and Wagner; Guest appearances throughout Germany; Paris Opéra 1941; Holland Festival 1958, Von Heute auf Morgen by Schoenberg, conducted by Hans Rosbaud; Glyndebourne Festival 1965, as the Marschallin; Lieder recitals; Oratorio performances. *Address:* Staatliche Hochschule für Musik, Escherheimer Landstrasse 33, Postfach 2326, Frankfurt, Germany.

**SCHMIDT, Hansjürgen;** Composer; b. 26 Aug. 1935, Jena-Burgau, Germany; m. Annemarie Illig, 11 July 1959, 2 s. *Education:* Studied Philosophy at Friedrich-Schiller University, Jena; Musical Theory, Franz Liszt Hochschule Weimar, 1968; Diploma as Composer; MMus, Akademie der Künste Berlin, 1979. *Career:* Freelance composer in Jena from 1970; Lectureship in Theory of Music in Weimar, 1986–87; Lectureship at Volkshochschule in Erlangen since 1990; mem, Union of Composers, Thüringen. *Compositions:* Winterpastorale, 1976; Streichquartett II, 1979; Schwanengesang, 1983; Nachtstück and Toccata, 1987; Sinfonie III, 1989. *Recordings:* Nachtstück and Toccata, 1995; Chthulu Suite; Schütz-Fantasie, electronic music. *Honours:* Kunstpreis of the District of Gera, 1980. *Address:* Siedlung Sonnenblick 1, 07749 Jena, Germany.

**SCHMIDT, Manfred;** Singer (Tenor); b. 27 June 1928, Berlin, Germany. *Education:* Studied with Jean Nadolovitch and with Herbert Brauer in Berlin. *Career:* Concert Singer from 1956; Many Radio Concerts; From the Bielefeld Opera moved to Cologne 1965, singing Ernesto, Ottavio, Tamino, Almaviva and other lyric roles; Sang at the Festivals of Salzburg, Holland, Perugia, Flanders and Prague; Guest appearances in London, Paris and Milan. *Recordings include:* Opera excerpts. *Address:* c/o Musikhochschule Berlin, Ernst-Feuter-Platz 10, D–10587 Berlin, Germany.

**SCHMIDT, Ole;** Danish conductor and composer; b. 14 July 1928, Copenhagen; s. of Hugo Schmidt and Erna S. P. Schmidt; m. Lizzie Rode Schmidt 1960; two d. *Education:* Royal Danish Acad. of Music, Copenhagen. *Career:* conducting debut 1955; Conductor, Royal Theatre, Copenhagen 1959–65; Chief Conductor, Hamburg Symphony 1969–70; Conductor Danish Radio Concert Orchestra 1971–73; Chief Conductor and Artistic Dir Århus Symphony 1978–84; Perm. Guest Conductor, Royal Northern Coll. of Music, Manchester 1986–89; Chief Conductor and Artistic Dir The Toledo Symphony, Ohio 1989–. *Honours:* Carl Nielsen Legat 1975; Gramex Award 1975, H. C. Lumbye Award 1988. *Address:* Mariot, Gazax et Bacarrisse, 32230 Marciac, France; Puggaardsgade 17, 1573 Copenhagen V, Denmark (home).

**SCHMIDT, Peter-Jurgen;** Singer (Tenor); b. 25 Jan. 1941, Meiningen, Germany. *Education:* Studied in Weimar. *Career:* Debut: Weimar 1968, as Oberto in Alcina; Sang at Weimar until 1980, Staatsoper Berlin from 1981, notably in 1989 premiere of Graf Mirabeau by Siegfried Matthus; Guest appearances in concert and opera at London, Oslo, Linz, Salzburg, Graz and Germany, Japan and Korea; Schwetzinger Festival 1989, as Bacchus in Ariadne auf Naxos; Other roles include Don José, Hoffmann, Radames, Walther Von Stolzing, Lohengrin and Laca in Jenůfa; Season 1999–2000 at Chemnitz and the Brooklyn Academy of Music in the premiere production of Weill's The Eternal Road. *Recordings include:* Levins Muhle by Udo Zimmermann and Graf Mirabeau. *Address:* c/o Staatsoper Berlin, Unter Den Linden 7, 1086 Berlin, Germany.

**SCHMIDT, Werner Albert;** Composer and Educator; b. 29 July 1925, Bad Kissingen, Germany. *Education:* Studied Philosophy with Ernesto Grassi; Musicology and old German Language and Literature, University of Munich, graduated 1969; Conducting and Composition under Hans Rosbaud, Joseph Haas and Karl Höller, Academy of Music, Munich, 1946–50; Masterclass Diploma in Composition, 1950; Pedagogic State Examination, State Academy of Music, Munich, 1972; Further studies with Carl Orff, Karl A Hartmann (composition) and Kurt Eichhorn (conducting); PhD. *Career:* Freelance Composer in Munich (Musica Viva, Munich, 1954); Worked as Pianist with symphony and jazz orchestras; Music Teacher, Grammar School and Junior Music School in Wangen/Allgau; Head of City Orchestra; Teacher of Music Theory, 1975–91, Professor, 1980–92, State Academy of Music, Mannheim; mem, Several professional organizations; Deutsche Johan-Strauá Gesellschaft. *Compositions include:* Kassation, for strings, 1947; Partita, for piano, 1948; Sonata per il pianoforte, 1949; Sonate, Das Ballett, for violin and piano, 1950; Tollhausballade, for speaker and chamber orchestra, 1952, new edition without speaker, 1956; Tre Pezzi drammatici per archi, 1953–54; Symphony 'Aufstand der Massen' (Praeludium und Toccata) for large orchestra, 1953–55; Concerto grosso, for jazz combo and wind ensemble, 1955–56; Hieroglyphik, for large orchestra, 1956–57; Faszination, music for a filmic ballet, for 2 percussionists, 1957; Positiv-Negativ-Synthesis, for 4 instrumental respect vocal groups, 1958; Apokalypsis, for large orchestra, speaker and 6 vocalists, 1982–86. *Publications:* Theorie der Induktion, 1974. *Honours:* Achievement Awards, Bavarian Academy of Fine Arts, Munich; Composition Prize, Competition of German Composers' Association. *Address:* Herzogstr 20, 68723 Schwetzingen, Germany.

**SCHMIDT, Wolfgang;** German singer (tenor); b. 1955, Kassel. *Education:* Frankfurt Musikochschule. *Career:* sang first with the Pocket Oper Nuremburg, then at the Court Theatre Bayreuth 1982–84; Kiel 1984–86; Dortmund from 1986, notably as Otello and as Siegfried in Wagner's Opera; appearances at the Eutin Festival 1983–87, as Tamino, Max and Huon in Oberon; Bregenz Festival 1989, as Erik in Fliegende Holländer; Bayreuth 1992, as Tannhäuser; further engagements at Essen, Karlsruhe, Hanover, Stuttgart; sang First Armed Man in Die Zauberflöte at the 1991 Salzburg Festival; Tristan at the Opéra Bastille, Paris 1998; season 1999 as Siegfried at San Francisco, Loge, Siegmund and Siegfried in Hannover; Walther and Florestan for the Deutsche Oper am Rhein; Siegfried and Siegmund at the Berlin Staatsoper and Cologne 2000; sang Siegfried at the 2002 Bayreuth Festival; concert repertoire includes the Missa Solemnis with appearances in Mexico City, Parma, Prague. *Recordings include:* Die Zauberflöte, Weill's Lindberghflug. *Current Management:* K. E. Haase, Martiusstr. 3, 80802 Munich, Germany. *Telephone:* (89) 394190. *Fax:* (89) 342674. *E-mail:* ks@wolfgangschmidt.com. *Website:* www.wolfgangschmidt.com.

**SCHMIEGE, Marilyn;** Singer (Mezzo-soprano); b. 1955, Milwaukee, Wisconsin, USA. *Education:* Studied at Valparaiso University, BMus; MMus at Boston University; Further study at the Zürich Opera Studio. *Career:* Debut: Wuppertal as Dorabella, 1978; Theater am Gärtnerplatz, Munich as Cherubino, Rosina, Hänsel, Orlovsky, 1978–82; Teatro La Fenice, Venice, 1981; Aix-en Provence as Zaide in Il Turco in Italia, 1982; Munich Radio 1982 as Dido by Jan Novák conducted by Kubelik, 1982; Düsseldorf as Cherubino, 1983; La Scala title role in Orfeo by Rossi, 1983; Vienna Staatsoper debut as Rosina, later as Octavian, the Composer, 1985; Stuttgart as Charlotte in Werther, later as Lady Macbeth of Mtensk, Marguerite in Berlioz's Damnation de Faust, 1985; Aldeburgh Festival in Das Lied von der Erde, 1985; Hamburg Staatsoper as the Composer and Rosina, 1985, later as Venus in Tannhäuser; Dresden Staatsoper as the Composer, Octavian, 1986, later as Kundry; New York Philharmonic with Novák's Dido, 1986; Cologne as Lady Macbeth, 1988; Munich Staatsoper Octavian, 1988 later as Cherubino, Jeanne d'Arc, Silla in Palestrina, Dorabella, Venus, 1991; Carmen at Berlin Komische Oper, 1991; Judith in Berlin Schauspielhaus, 1993; Amsterdam as Marie in Wozzeck and at the Paris Châtelet as Waltraute in Götterdämmerung, 1994; Sang Marie in Wozzeck at Catania, 1996; Kundry in Parsifal for Nationale Reisopera, Netherlands, 1998; Season 1999–2000 as Countess Geschwitz in Lulu at Liège and Sieglinde for the Vienna Staatsoper. *Recordings include:* Vivaldi's Catone in Utica, Galuppi's La Caduta d'Adamo; Haydn Cantatas and Orfeo ed Euridice; Cherubino in Mozart's Figaro, directed by Colin Davis; Dido by Novák, directed by Kubelik; Schreker Die Gezeichneten; Mélodies of Gabriel Fauré, 1994.

**SCHNAPKA, Georg;** Singer (Bass); b. 27 May 1932, Schlesisch Ostrau, Czechoslovakia; m. Elisabeth Schwarzenberg. *Education:* Studied at the Bruckner Conservatory Linz with Andreas Sotzkov. *Career:* Debut: Heidelberg 1954, as Repela in Wolf's Der Corregidor; Sang 1964–85 at the Vienna Volksoper in the buffo repertory, also appeared with the Vienna Staatsoper; Guest appearances in Hamburg, Munich, Stuttgart, Saarbrucken, Düsseldorf, Wuppertal, Cologne and Frankfurt; Further engagements in Florence (Maggio Musicale), Venice, Amsterdam, Strasbourg, Lisbon, Bucharest and Zürich; American centres include New York City Opera, Baltimore and Washington DC; Main roles have included Philip II in Don Carlos, Daland, Fafner, Hunding, Sarastro, Pimen, Osmin, Leporello, Nicolai's Falstaff, Baron Ochs and Rossini's Bartolo; Many concert engagements. *Address:* Opernhaus, Kuhstrasse 12, 4600 Dortmund, Germany.

**SCHNAUT, Gabriele;** Singer (Mezzo-soprano, Soprano); b. 24 Feb. 1951, Mannheim, Germany. *Education:* Studied in Frankfurt with Elsa Cavelti, in Darmstadt with Aga Zah-Landzettel and in Berlin with Hannelore Kuhse. *Career:* Sang in Stuttgart from 1976; Darmstadt, 1978–80; Member of the Mannheim Opera from 1980; Bayreuth Festival from 1977, as Waltraute, Venus and Sieglinde, Chicago 1983, as Fricka in a concert performance of Die Walküre; Dortmund 1985, as Isolde; Has sung at Stuttgart, Frankfurt, Hamburg, Barcelona, Rome and Warsaw; Covent Garden debut 1989, as Sieglinde in a new production of Die Walküre conducted by Bernard Haitink; Sang in Düsseldorf and Hamburg 1989, as Lady Macbeth and Els in Schreker's Der Schatzgräber; Brünnhilde in Die Walküre at Cologne, 1990; Bayreuth 1987–89, as Ortrud in Lohengrin; Sang Isolde at San Francisco, 1991, Elektra at the Opéra Bastille, Paris, 1992; Sang the Walküre Brünnhilde at the 1997 Munich Festival, Isolde at Catania, 1996; Other roles include Octavian, Sextus (La Clemenza di Tito), Dorabella, Carmen, Brangaene, Kundry and Marie in Wozzeck; Season 1998 as Isolde at Cologne and 1999 as Elsa at Bayreuth; Sang Isolde at Covent Garden, 2000; Season 2001–02 as Isolde at Amsterdam, Turandot at the Vienna Staatsoper and Brünnhilde in new productions of Die Walküre and Siegfried at the Munich Staatsoper. *Recordings include:* St Matthew Passion by Bach; Sancta Susanna and Lieder by Hindemith. *Address:* c/o Theateragentur Dr G. Hilbert, Maximillian-Strasse 22, D–80539 München, Germany.

**SCHNEBEL, Dieter;** Composer; b. 14 March 1930, Lahr, Germany. *Education:* Studied at the Freiburg Hochschule für Musik, at Darmstadt and the University of Thubingen, 1952–56. *Career:* Active in the Lutheran Church, from 1976; Professor of Experimental Music and Musicology at the Berlin Hochschule für Musik; Work with the experimental theatre group Die Maulwerker, from 1978; Collaborations with Director Achim Freyer on Maulwerke and Cage-up. *Compositions include:* Music Theatre Maulwerke,

1968–74, Laut-Gesten-Laute, Zeichen-Sprache and St Jago (Music and pictures on Kleist 1989–91); Orchestral, Compositio 1956, revised 1964; Webern Variations 1972; Canones, 1975; In motu proprio, 1975; Diapason, 1977; Orchestra, 1977; Schubert-Phantasie, 1978; Wagner-Idyll, 1980; Thanatos-Eros, 1982; Sinfonie-Stucke, 1985; Beethoven-Sinfonie, 1985; Mahler Moment for strings, 1985; Raumklang X, 1988; Chamber, Reactions, 1961; Visable Music I, 1961; Nostalgie for Conductor, 1962; Espressivo, music drama for pianist, 1963; Concert sans orchestre for piano and audience, 1964; Ansclage-auschlage, 1966; Quintet, 1977; Pan for flute, 1978; Monotonien for piano and electronics, 1989; Vocal, Fur Stimmen (… missa est) for chorus, 1961; Glossolalie 61, 1961; Bach-Contrapuncti for chorus, 1976; Jowaegerli for 2 speakers, voices and chamber ensemble, 1983; Lieder ohne Worte, 1980–86; Missa Dahlemer Messe, 1984–87; Sinfonie X for orchestra, 1992; Majakowskis Tod, chamber opera, 1987; Totentantz, ballet-oratorio, 1989–94; Motetus II for two choruses, 1997; Ekstasis for soprano, chorus and orchestra, 1997; Museumstücke I/II for mobile voices and instruments; Produktionprozesse series, 1968–75; Graphic works including mo-no: Musik Zum Lesen, 1969. *Publications include:* Study of Stockhausen's early works: Mauricio Kagel, Cologne, 1970; Denkbare Musik: Schriften 1952–72, Cologne, 1972; Anschläge-Ausschläge, Essays, 1993. *Address:* Hektorstr. 15, 10711 Berlin, Germany.

**SCHNEEBERGER, Hansheins;** Violinist; b. 16 Oct. 1926, Berne, Switzerland. *Education:* Studied at the Berne Conservatory, with Carl Flesch in Lucerne and with Boris Kamensky. *Career:* Debut: 1946, in the Swiss premiere of Bartók's Second Violin Concerto; Teacher at the Biel Conservatory, 1948–58; Basle Musikakademie, 1961–91; Leader of String Quartet, 1952–59, and the North German Symphony Orchestra, Hamburg; Premieres of Martin's Violin Concerto and Bartók's First concerto (1952, 1958, with Paul Sacher); Further performances of music by Klaus Huber, Heinz Holliger and Elliott Carter. *Recordings include:* Schumann Sonatas and concerto; Bach Sonatas and Partitas for solo violin, Bartók Sonata for solo violin. *Address:* c/o Basle Musikakademie, Leonhardsstrasse 6, 4501 Basle, Switzerland.

**SCHNEIDER, David E.;** Musicologist and Clarinettist; b. 14 June 1963, Berkeley, California, USA; m. Klára Móricz 1994. *Education:* AB cum laude, Harvard University, 1985; MA, 1990, PhD, 1997, University of California at Berkeley; Private Clarinet studies with Donald Carrol, Leon Russianoff, Pasquale Cardillo, Greg Smith and Robert Marcellus; Chamber Music study with Nancy Garniez, Leon Kirchner and György Kurtag. *Career:* Member, Alaria Chamber Ensemble, New York City, 1986–88; Valentine Professor of Music, Amherst College, Amherst, Massachusetts, 1997–; mem, American Musicological Society. *Recordings:* Copland Clarinet Concerto, 1988. *Publications:* Bartók and Stravinsky, 1995; The Culmination Point as a Fulcrum Between Analysis and Interpretation, 1996; Expression in the Time of Objectivity: Nationality and Modernity in Five Concertos by Béla Bartók, PhD dissertation; A Context for Béla Bartók on the Eve of World War II, 1997. *Honours:* American Musicological Society 50 Fellowship, 1996. *Address:* Amherst College, Box 2258 Music, Amherst, MA 01002-5000, USA. *E-mail:* deschneider@amherst.edu.

**SCHNEIDER, Gary M.;** Conductor and Composer; b. 1950, USA. *Career:* Founder, Music Director and Principal Conductor of the Hoboken Chamber Orchestra; Debut in Europe at the International Zelt Musik Festival in Freiburg; New York debut with the American Composers Orchestra performing his Concerto for Jazz Clarinet and Orchestra; Has also conducted the Chamber Symphony of Princeton, and the New York Festival Orchestra; Artist-in-Residence at Denison University, Ohio and Composer-in-Residence at the Rockport (Massachusetts) Chamber Music Festival. *Compositions include:* Sonata for solo cello, 1976; String Quartet, 1977; Study for a Ballet, for piano, 1981; Piano Sonata, 1989; Nocturne for bassoon and strings, 1988; The Bremen Town Musicians, 1989; The Tell-Tale Heart and The Voice of Eternity for soloists and ensemble. *Publications:* compositions have been published by leading publishers. *Address:* c/o ASCAP, ASCAP Building, 1 Lincoln Plaza, New York, NY 10023, USA.

**SCHNEIDER, Gundula;** singer (mezzo-soprano); b. 1965, Dresden, Germany. *Education:* studied in Karlsrule and at Dresden Music Academy; masterclasses with Brigitte Fassbaender and Sena Jurinac. *Career:* appearances from 1997 with Dortmund Opera as Carmen, the Composer in Ariadne auf Naxos, Hansel, and Orlovsky in Die Fledermaus; guest engagements in Dresden, Strasbourg and the Komische Oper Berlin as Annio in La Clemenza di Tito; Cherubino at Dusseldorf and Bellini's Adalgisa at Kassel; festival engagements at the Dresdner Musikfestspiele and Rossini Festspiele Bad Wildbad; recitals at the Paris Opéra-Comique, Liederhalle Stuttgart and Carnegie Hall, New York. *Honours:* special prize 27th Antonin Dvorak International Singing Competition 1992, laureate Brahms Internationaler Wettbewerb, Hamburg 1994, Pro Musicis Int. Award 1995. *Current Management:* Pro Musicis, 140 W 79th Street, Suite 9F, New York, NY 10024, USA. *Telephone:* (212) 787-0993. *Fax:* (212) 362-0352. *Website:* www.promusicis.org.

**SCHNEIDER, Peter;** Conductor; b. 26 March 1939, Vienna, Austria. *Education:* Academy for Music and Dramatic Art, Vienna; conducting with Hans Swarowsky. *Career:* Sang with the Wiener Sängerknaben as a boy; Head of Studies at the Landestheater Salzburg from 1959 (conducting debut with Handel's Giulio Cesare); Principal Conductor in Heidleberg, 1961, Deutsche Oper am Rhein, Düsseldorf, from 1968; Performances of operas by Janáček, Berg, Wagner, Mozart, Verdi and Dallapiccola; Guest Conductor in Warsaw,

Florence and Edinburgh; Music Director in Bremen 1978–85, Mannheim 1985–87; Bayreuth Festival from 1981; Der fliegende Holländer, Der Ring des Nibelungen and Lohengrin; Conducted the Vienna Opera in Der Rosenkavalier on its 1986 tour of Japan, and the Vienna Philharmonic at the Salzburg Festival; Further appearances as a Conductor of opera in Vienna, Berlin, London, Bologna, Barcelona and Madrid; Concerts in San Francisco; Die Soldaten by Zimmermann at the Vienna Staatsoper, 1990; Conducted Tristan und Isolde in Japan 1990 and San Francisco, 1991; Music Director of the Bavarian State Opera, Munich, 1993; Led Walküre and Meistersinger at the 1997 Munich Festival; Lohengrin at Barcelona, 2000. *Current Management:* Ingpen & Williams Ltd, 7 St George's Court, 131 Putney Bridge Road, London, SW15 2PA, England.

**SCHNEIDER, Urs;** Swiss conductor and music director; b. 16 May 1939, St Gallen. *Education:* Zürich Conservatory, studied conducting with Rafael Kubelik, Igor Markevitch, Otto Klemperer. *Career:* debut with own orchestras at age 15; founder, Conductor, Artistic Dir, Ostschweizer Kammerorchester, Camerata Helvetica; guest conductor, USA; Music Dir, Camerata Stuttgart; Music Dir, Camerata Academica Salzburg; Chief Conductor, Music Dir, Haifa Symphony Orchestra; concerts, operas, radio and television; guest conductor, numerous major orchestras and opera houses worldwide; over 4000 performances in 70 countries; mem., Jury of the Concours des Jeunes Chefs d'Orchestre, Festival International de Besançon; Jury of Conductors' Competition, Silvestri, Bucharest and competitions in Israel, Taiwan and USA; Principal Conductor, Artistic Dir, Nat. Taiwan Philharmonic Orchestra; First Guest Conductor of Prague Chamber Soloists; mem. Swiss Musicians' Asscn, Schweiz Berufsdirigenten Verband. *Recordings:* 60 records. *Honours:* MFA Int. (New York) 1969; Cultural Prize, City of St Gallen. *Address:* Gattestrasse 1B, 9010 St Gallen, Switzerland. *Telephone:* (71) 2223980 (office). *Fax:* (71) 2223889 (office). *E-mail:* urs.schneider.conductor@freesurf.ch (office). *Website:* www.ursschneider.com (office).

**SCHNEIDER, Victoria,** BM, MM; opera and concert singer (soprano); b. 28 Oct. 1952, Reading, PA, USA; m. Riccardo Malipiero 1988 (deceased). *Education:* Eastman School of Music, Rochester, NY. *Career:* debut Staatsoper Stuttgart, Germany 1981; regular collaboration with Staatsoper Stuttgart and many concert appearances throughout Germany 1981–85, increased activity, Italy 1984–; appearances at Teatro alla Scala, Milan, Teatro Comunale di Bologna, Teatro dell'Opera di Roma, Teatro dell'Opera di Genova; many concerts with major Italian orchestras, Santa Cecilia, Rome, with Radio Orchestras (RAI) of Milan, Turin, Naples; Festival Wien Modern 1992; Paris debut at Théâtre du Châtelet 1993; Berg's Altenberg-Lieder and Der Wein with Staatsorchester Saarbrücken 1995; engagement with Frankfurt Opera 2000; concert repertoire ranges from baroque to contemporary, including Handel's Messiah, Beethoven's Mass in C Major and Missa Solemnis, Mozart's Mass in C Minor, Mahler's Kindertotenlieder, many Strauss Orchesterlieder, Wagner's Wesendoncklieder, Berg's Sieben Frühe Lieder, Shostakovich's Seven Lyrics of Alexander Blok, Dallapiccola's An Mathilde and Commiato; many world premieres with works by R. Malipiero, S. Sciarrino, Donatoni, Gentilucci, Guarnieri and others; numerous concerts, including Schoenberg's op 10 with Arditti String Quartet 1989, Elliott Carter with the Ensemble Contrechamps and the Nieuw Ensemble 1998, 1999, Shostakovich and Beethoven with the Ensemble Recherche 1999–2000, Bach with the Orchestra Sinfonica Abruzzese 2000, Verdi and Schoenberg with the Quartetto di Fiesole 2001. *Radio recordings include:* Vara Radio (Netherlands), Suddeutscher Rundfunk (Stuttgart), Bayerischer Rundfunk (Munich), Radio Bremen, RSI (Lugano), Italian National Radio RAI. *Address:* Via Stradella 1, 20129 Milan, Italy.

**SCHNEIDER-SIEMSSEN, Gunther;** stage designer and set designer; b. 7 June 1926, Augsburg, Germany; m. Eva Mazar 1969; four c. *Education:* Akademie für Kunst, Munich. *Career:* film designer, 1946–51; Head Designer, Landestheater, Salzburg, 1951–54; Head Designer, Marionetten Theater, Salzburg, 1951–; State Theater, Bremen, 1954–; Designed Der Ring des Nibelungen at Covent Garden, 1962–64; Guest Designer numerous opera houses; Professor, Stage Design, International Summer Academy Fine Arts, Salzburg, 1968–87; Designer, Salzburg Festival, 1965–89; Designer, Easter Festival, 1967–89; Notable productions include Boris Godunov, Tristan und Isolde, Die Frau ohne Schatten and Berio's Un Re in Ascolto; Designer Met Opera New York and cities in USA, including the Ring in New York (also televised and recorded 1990); Stage Director in South Africa, USA, Germany, Austria and Slovenia, 1982–; President, Society of the Stage of the Future; Rotary. *Publications:* contrib. to professional journals. *Honours:* Fellow, MIT, USA, 1980–85. *Address:* 4 Schlickgasse, Vienna, Austria.

**SCHNEIDERMAN, Helene;** singer (mezzo-soprano); b. 1955, Flemington, NJ, USA. *Education:* Westminster Choir Coll., Princeton, Univ. of Cincinnati Coll. *Career:* sang at Heidelberg Opera 1982–, Stuttgart 1984–, with guest appearances at Düsseldorf, Munich, Orlando and New York City Opera; season 1990 with the Rossini Festival at Pesaro and Smeaton in Anna Bolena at the Concertgebouw; other roles have included Monteverdi's Penelope Isabella, Carmen and Rosina at Stuttgart; Covent Garden season 1995–96, as Cherubino and Dorabella; appearances with conductors, including Bernard Haitink, Salzburg 1993, Bernstein, Arias and Barcarolles, Bonn, Solti, and Alberto Zedda, Pesaro; season 1998 with Cenerentola for New Israeli Opera. *Recordings include:* Copland's Eight Poems of Emily Dickinson. *Current Management:* Robert Gilder & Co., Enterprise House, 59–65 Upper Ground,

London, SE1 9PQ, England. *Telephone:* (20) 7928-9008. *Fax:* (20) 7928-9755. *E-mail:* rgilder@robert-gilder.com.

**SCHNITZLER, Michael;** Violinist; b. 1940, California. *Education:* Studied in Vienna Music Academy. *Career:* Member and soloist in the chamber orchestra Wiener Solisten, 1963–67; First concertmaster of Vienna Symphony, over 1000 concerts, touring USA, Japan and Europe; Appearances as soloist under Giulini, Abbado, Sawallisch and Jochum; Performances of Haydn and other composers in Vienna and elsewhere from 1968; Co-Founder, The Haydn Trio of Vienna 1968 and has performed in Brussels, Munich, Berlin, Zürich, London, Rome, Paris; New York debut 1979 and has made frequent North American appearances with concerts in 25 States; Professor of Violin at Vienna Music University, 1984–; Debut tour of Japan, 1984 with further travels to the Near East, Russia, Africa, Central and South America; Series at the Vienna Konzerthaus Society from 1976, with performances of more than 100 works; Summer Festivals at Vienna, Salzburg, Axi-en-Provence, Flanders and Montreux; Masterclasses at the Royal College and Royal Academy of London, Stockholm, Bloomington, Tokyo and the Salzburg Mozarteum; Leader of Vienna Johann Strauss Orchestra, 2000–; Master classes at the University of Indiana, Bloomington, Eastman School, Rochester, Mozarteum, Salzburg, RAM, RCM, London, Sweden, Holland and Japan; Juror at international competitions in Vienna, Salzburg and Osaka. *Recordings:* Complete Piano Trios of Beethoven and Schubert, Mendelssohn D Minor, Brahams B Major, Tchaikovsky A Minor, Schubert Trout Quintet; Albums of Works by Haydn, Schumann, Dvořák and Smetana. *Address:* Sternwartestrasse 58, A-1180 Wien Austria.

**SCHOLL, Andreas;** German singer (countertenor); b. 1967, Eltville. *Education:* Schola Cantorum Basiliensis, Basel, Switzerland. *Career:* mem. Kiedricher Chorbuben choir as child; soloist, Pueri Cantors Gathering, St Peter's Basilica, Rome 1981; debut int. recital at Théâtre de Grévin, Paris 1993; opera debut in Handel's Rodelinda, Glyndebourne Festival Opera, England 1998; performed at Belgian Royal Wedding Dec. 1999; teacher, Schola Cantorum Basiliensis, Basel 2000–; numerous int. tours and recitals, working with the world's leading Baroque conductors and ensembles, including London Proms 2005. *Recordings include:* Handel's Messiah, Solomon, Italian Cantatas and Opera Arias, Bach's Christmas Oratorio, St Matthew Passion, St John Passion, Solo Cantatas for Alto and B Minor Mass, Vivaldi's Stabat Mater (Gramophone Award) 1996, Nisi Dominus (Edison Award) 2001, Monteverdi's L'Orfeo and 1610 Vespers, works by Pergolesi and Caldara; Heroes (Echo Classic Award) 1999, Wayfaring Stranger 2001, Arcadia 2003, Arias for Senesino 2005. *Honours:* Conseil de l'Europe Award 1992, Fondation Claude Nicolas Ledoux Award 1992, Cannes Classical Award 1998, Artist of the Year, German Kultur Radio 1998, Belgian Musical Press Union Prize 1999. *Current Management:* HarrisonParrott Ltd, 12 Penzance Place, London, Wa1 4PA, England. *Website:* www.harrisonparrott.com.

**SCHOLLUM, Benno;** Singer (Baritone); b. 1953, Klagenfurt, Austria. *Education:* Studied at the Vienna Musikhochschule with Josef Greindl and with his father, Robert Schollum; Masterclasses in New York and Vienna with Sena Jurinac and others. *Career:* Has performed in Austria and elsewhere in operettas by Lehar, Johann Strauss, Milloecker and Offenbach; Operas by Mozart, Britten, Lortzing, Mascagni; Lieder by Loewe, Schubert, Wolf, Strauss, Grieg, Brahms and others; Oratorios include Schmidt's Das Buch mit Sieben Siegeln, the Brahms Requiem and Cantatas and Masses by Bach and Mozart; Festival appearances at Vienna, Antibes, Carinthian Summer and Gstaad; Guest Engagements in France, Yugoslavia, Italy, USA, South America, South Africa, Germany, Netherlands and Luxembourg; Berlin Philharmonic debut in Herbst by Antal Dorati; British debut, 1991 with the English Symphony Orchestra in Arias by Mozart; Stage roles include Papageno; Teacher at the Vienna Musikhochschule from 1983. *Recordings:* Schubert's Winterreise with Graham Johnson; Beethoven's Symphony No. 9 with Yehudi Menuhin. *Publications:* Sprecherziehung in der Praxis der Gesangsausbildung, 1993. *Honours:* MA, 1993. *Current Management:* Eleanor Hope, London. *Address:* 9 Southwood Hall, Wood Lane, London N6 5UF, England.

**SCHOLZ, Andreas;** Singer (Baritone); b. 14 Dec. 1964, Leipzig. *Education:* Felix Mendelssohn Musikhochschule, Leipzig, 1985–91. *Career:* Sang at Leipzig Opera from 1991, as Zuniga in Carmen, Schaunard, Guglielmo, Lortzing's Tsar Peter, Rossini's Figaro and Sander in Grétry's Zémire et Azore; Further appearances in Schoenberg's Moses and Aron and Hiller's Der Jagd; Dresden Opera as the Constable in Strauss's Friedenstag; Soloist with the Leipzig Gewandhaus Orchestra; Further concerts in Munich and Berlin. *Honours:* Prizewinner at Competitions in Karlovy Vary and Berlin, 1990. *Address:* Oper Leipzig, Opernhaus Augustusplatz 12, 7010 Leipzig, Germany.

**SCHOLZE, Rainer;** Singer (Bass); b. 13 May 1940, Sudetenland Germany. *Education:* Studied at the Cologne Musikhochschule. *Career:* Sang in the Chorus of the Lübeck Stadt Theatre, 1962–66; Discovered by Gerd Albrecht and sang small roles; Studied further and sang solo at Lübeck from 1966–70; Engaged at Brunswick, 1970–71; Kassel, 1971–81; Appeared at Kiel 1981–83 and made guest outings to Munich, Dresden, Hamburg; Has often appeared in operas by Mozart, Rossini, Lortzing and notably as Baron Ochs. *Recordings include:* Masetto in Don Giovanni; Reinmar in Tannhäuser; Larkens in Fanciulla del West.

**SCHOMBERG, Martin;** Singer (Tenor); b. 7 Nov. 1944, Hoxter, Westfalen, Germany. *Education:* Studied at the Hamburg Musikhochschule with Jakob

St ämpfli. *Career:* Debut: Mainz 1972, as Lenski in Eugene Onegin; Many appearances at the Opera houses of Cologne, Hamburg, Düsseldorf; Zürich Opera in lyric roles and in the 1974 premiere of Ein Wahrer Held by Klebe; Concert engagements at the Salzburg Festival and elsewhere; Roles have included Mozart's Belmonte, Ottavio and Tamino, Nencio in Haydn's L'Infedeltà Delusa, Florindo in Le Donne Curiose by Wolf-Ferrari, the Italian Tenor in Rosenkavalier and Alfred in Fledermaus. *Address:* Opernhaus Zürich, Falkenstrasse 1, 8008 Zürich, Switzerland.

**SCHONBACH, Dieter;** Composer; b. 18 Feb. 1931, Stolp, Pomerania, Germany. *Education:* Studied in Detmold and Freiburg with Gunter Bialas and Wolfgang Fortner. *Career:* Music Director of the Bochum Schauspielhaus, 1959–73; has also worked at theatres in Munster and Basle; lectured in India and S America for Goethe Inst. 1972–73. *Compositions include:* Die Geschichte von einem Feuer, mixed-media show with puppet, 1970; Bedrohung und Uberleben, multimedia opera, Cologne, 1971; Hysteria-Paradies Schwarz, mixed-media show after The Tempest, Wiesbaden, 1971; Hymnus II-Morgen nach dem Feuer, mixed-media show, Munich, 1972; Come S Francesco, Munster, 1979; Divina Comedia (Dante), multimedia show, Düsseldorf, 1985; Barocke Prunkoper, Come Signori... nach Lully, 1985–87, Versailles; Reineke Fuchs, musiktheater nach Goethe, Baden-Baden, 1988; Barocke Prunkoper, Il Pomo D'oro, nach Cesti, Vienna, 1989; Fläche und Raum zur Musik, after Wassily Kandinsky, 1996; Farben und Klange, in memory of Kandinsky for orchestra, 1958; Piano Concerto, 1958; Canticum Psalmi Resurrectionis, 1959; Kammermusik for 14 instruments, 1964; Hoquetus for 8 wind instruments, 1964; Revised form of Così fan tutte by Mozart for 6 instruments, 1992; Cover over piano concerto by Mozart (K491) for great orchestra, 1999, Nostradamus (multimedia opera) 2000, Entwicklung einer neuen Kompositionstechnik – direkte Umwandlung grafischbildnerischer Konzepte ins Musikalische 2003, 'Interstellares Konzert' 2004. *Honours:* Joint Winner, Stamitz Prize of Stuttgart, 1972. *Address:* GEMA, Postfach 80 07 67, 81607 Munich, Germany. *Website:* www.dieter-schonbach.de (office).

**SCHONBECK, Uwe;** Singer (Tenor); b. 1961, Essen, Germany. *Education:* Studied at the Essen Musikhochschule. *Career:* Appearances at Krefeld Opera from 1985; Frankfurt 1990 and at the Deutsche Oper am Rhein at Düsseldorf; Geneva 1991 as Mime in The Ring, also at Frankfurt, 1995; Vienna Staatsoper, 1993 as Herod in Salome; Salzburg, 1994 as Sellem in The Rake's Progress; Munich 1996 as Billy II in the premiere of Bose's Slaughterhouse Five; Other roles include Arnalta in Monteverdi's Poppea; Rameau's Platée and Nemorino; Modern repertory includes Troades by Reimann; Judith by Matthus; Macbeth by Bibalo. *Recordings:* Stephen Climax by Hans Zender. *Address:* c/o Bavarian State Opera, Max-Joseph-Platz, 80530 Munich, Germany.

**SCHÖNBERG, Stig Gustav;** Swedish composer and organist; b. 13 May 1933, Vastra Husby. *Education:* Stockholm Musikhogskolan, studied composition with Lars-Eric Larsson, Karl-Birger Blomdahl, organ with Flor Peeters in Belgium. *Career:* freelance composer with performances throughout Sweden; many concert tours and church performances throughout Scandinavia, Europe, USA and Japan as organist. *Compositions include:* Introduction and Allegro for strings 1959, Concerto for organ and strings 1962, Sinfonia Aperta 1965, three Concertinos for strings 1966, Madeleine and Conrad (ballet) 1967, Fantasia for strings 1967, numerous String Quartets 1961–84, Impromptu Visionario for orchestra 1972, Flute Sonata 1974, Concerto for two flutes and strings 1976, Symphony No. 2 1977, Pastoral for horn and organ 1979, Concerto for organ and orchestra 1982, Missa Coralis 1983, Missa da Pacem 1985, Concerto for organ and brass orchestra 1987, Sonata alla ricercata for organ and violin 1989, Bassoon Concerto 1992, Te Deum for choir and strings 1993, Gloria 1994, Symphony No. 3 1996, Variations on a Swedish Folktune for string orchestra 1999, Prince Hat Under the Earth (children's opera) 1999, Concerto for piano and orchestra 2001, Dance of the Crocodile for soprano and string quartet 2002, Concerto for violin and orchestra 2002, Messa Misura for two voices and organ or wind orchestra 2003, Missa for two voices and organ 2003, Capriccio elegante for two violins 2004, Sonata for violin and organ 2004, Symphony No. 4 2004; also choruses and songs. *Honours:* Royal Swedish Acad. of Music Award for Organ 2003. *Current Management:* c/o STIM, Sandhamnsgatan 79, PO Box 27327, 102 54 Stockholm, Sweden. *Telephone:* (411) 533730 (home). *E-mail:* sgschoenberg@home.se (home).

**SCHÖNE, Wolfgang;** Singer (Bass Baritone); b. 9 Feb. 1941, Bad Gandersheim, Germany. *Education:* Studied with Naan Pold in Hanover and Hamburg, Diploma in 1969. *Career:* Winner of awards from 1966 at Bordeaux, Berlin, Stuttgart and 's-Hertogenbosch; Concert tours and lieder recitals in Belgium, Netherlands, France, Denmark, USA, Mexico, Argentina and England; Appeared in film, The Chronicle of Anna Magdalena Bach; Opera career from 1970 at the State Operas of Stuttgart, Vienna and Hamburg, notably as Guglielmo, Wolfram and Count Eberbach in Der Wildschütz by Lortzing; Schwetzingen Festival 1983 as Tom, in the premiere of The English Cat by Henze; Komische Oper Berlin in 1984 as Golaud in Pelléas et Mélisande; Sang in the 1984 reopening of the Stuttgart Opera, as Don Giovanni; Season 1988–89 sang Gunther at Turin, Alidoro in Cenerentola at Salzburg and Barak at Cologne; Hamburg in 1990 as Wolfram; Sang Orestes and Pentheus in The Bassarids at Stuttgart in 1989; Sang Wolfram in Hamburg in 1990, the Count in Capriccio at 1990 Salzburg Festival, Dr Schön in Lulu at the Paris Châtelet, 1992; Amfortas in Parsifal at the Opéra Bastille,

Paris, 1997; Gunther in Götterdämmerung for Netherlands Opera, 1998; Season 2000–01 as the Wanderer in Siegfried at Stuttgart, Prus in The Makropulos Case at Hamburg, Amfortas in the Albert Hall, London, Strauss's Barak in Barcelona and Marschner's Hans Heiling for the Deutsche Oper, Berlin; Hans Sachs at Hamburg, 2002. *Recordings:* Bach Cantatas; St Matthew Passion by Schütz; Theresienmesse by Haydn; Bach B minor Mass; Doktor und Apotheker by Dittersdorf; Giulio Cesare by Handel; Lulu; Video of Der Freischütz.

**SCHØNWANDT, Michael;** Conductor; b. 10 Sept. 1953, Copenhagen, Denmark; m. Amalie Malling, 23 Mar 1991. *Education:* BMus, Musicology, Copenhagen University, 1975; Conducting and Composition, Royal Academy of Music, London, England, 1975–77. *Career:* Debut: Copenhagen, 1977; Concerts throughout Europe, Debut Royal Danish Opera, 1979; Guest Conductor, Covent Garden, London, Paris Opéra, Wiener Staatsoper, Bayreuth Festival; Principal Guest Conductor, Théâtre Royal de la Monnaie, Brussels, 1984–87; Principal Conductor, Collegium Musicum, Copenhagen, 1981–; Principal Guest Conductor, Nice Opera, 1987–91; Danish Radio Symphony Orchestra, 1989–2000; Principal Conductor, Berliner Sinfonie Orchestra, 1992–98; Permanent Conductor, Vienna State Opera, 1990; Conducts regularly in London (Philharmonia, BBC), Paris, (Orchestre Philharmonique), Vienna, Berlin; Music Director Royal Danish Opera and Orchestra, 2000–. *Recordings:* More than 50 CDs include: Mozart Piano Concertos and Violin Concertos; Beethoven Piano Concertos; Niels W Gade Complete Symphonies; Kuhlau's Lulu, Complete Opera; Schoenberg and Sibelius Pelléas and Mélisande, Berlioz Requiem; Richard Strauss: Salome, complete opera; Weyse: Complete Symphonies; Nielsen: Complete Symphonies. *Honours:* Numerous Musical Prizes, Denmark; Knighthood from HM Queen of Denmark, 1997; Carl Nielsen Prize, 1997. *Current Management:* Ingpen & Williams Ltd, 7 St George's Court, 131 Putney Bridge Road, London, SW15 2PA, England. *Address:* Svalevej 24, 2900, Hellerup, Denmark.

**SCHOPPER, Michael;** Singer (Bass-baritone); b. 1942, Passau, Germany. *Education:* Munich Musikhockschule. *Career:* Debut: Bach's Christmas Oratorio under Karl Richter, 1968; Many appearances in concerts and opera in the Baroque and classical repertory; In Europe and North and South America; Founded ensemble Musica Poetica, for performance of Renaissance and Baroque music, 1974; Sang Monteverdi's Seneca at Montpellier, 1989; and in Cavalli's Giasone at the Châtelet, Paris; Innsbruck Festival 1990–93 in Cesti's L'Orontea, as Sancho Panza in Conti's Don Chisciotte and Monteverdi's Seneca and Nettuno; Frankfurt, 1994 as Pfalzgrafen in Holzbauer's Gunther von Schwarzburg and Polyphemus in Handel's Acis and Galatea at Göttingen; Magdeburg, 1996 in the title role of Telemann's Der neumodische Liebhaber Damon. *Recordings:* Giulio Cesare and Bach cantatas; Bach Matthew Passion; Telemann's Pimpinone; Winterreise; Poppea and Stradella's San Giovanni Batista; Keiser's Masaniello Furioso; Gunther von Schwarzburg. *Address:* c/o Konzertbüro Andreas Braun, Sülzgürtl 86, D–50937 Köln, Germany.

**SCHOTT, Howard (Mansfield);** Musicologist and Harpsichordist; b. 17 June 1923, New York, NY, USA. *Education:* BA, 1943, JD, 1948, Yale University, DPhil (Oxon), 1978; Studied Applied Music at Mannes College, NY; Musicology with Barry Brook, Emanuel Winternitz, HC Robbins Landon, City University of New York, Leo Schrade, Yale, Joseph Kerman and John Caldwell at Oxford; Keyboard with Ralph Kirkpatrick at Yale and Hans Neumann at Mannes College; Composition with Richard Donovan and Luther Noss at Yale. *Career:* Lecturer at New England Conservatory, Boston, MA, 1988–; Lectures at Oxford, King's College London, Harvard, Yale (Sanford Fellowship, 1979), Cornell, Paris, and City University of New York; Consultant to Boston Early Music Festival, East Nakamichi Festival, also Victoria and Albert Museum and Metropolitan Museum of Art. *Publications:* Playing The Harpsichord, 1971, 3rd edition, 1979, Italian edition, 1982, German edition, 1983; Oeuvres Complètes De J J Froberger, 1980–; Editor, The Historical Harpsichord Series, 1984–; Catalogue of The Musical Instruments in The Victoria and Albert Museum, I: Keyboard Instruments, 1985. *Contributions:* Many articles in The New Grove Dictionary and New Harvard Dictionary of Music; Regularly to The Musical Times and to Early Music, including The Harpsichord Revival, and From Harpsichord to Pianoforte. *Address:* Brook House, Suite 402, 44 Washington Street, Brookline, MA 02146, USA.

**SCHRANZ, Karoly;** Violinist; b. 1950, Hungary. *Education:* Studied with András Mihaly at the Franz Liszt Academy in Budapest, with members of the Amadeus Quartet and Zoltán Szekely. *Career:* Founder Member of the Takacs Quartet, 1975; Many concert appearances in all major centres of Europe and USA; Tours of Australia, New Zealand, Japan, South America, England, Norway, Sweden, Greece, Belgium and Ireland; Resident at the London Barbican, 1988–91, with masterclasses at the Guildhall School of Music; Visits to Japan in 1989 and 1992; Bartók Cycle for the Bartók-Solti Festival at South Bank in 1990; Great Performers Series at Lincoln Center and Mostly Mozart Festival at Alice Tully Hall, NY; Appeared at Mozart Festivals at South Bank, Wigmore Hall and Barbican Centre in 1991; Bartók Cycle at the Théâtre des Champs Elysées in 1991, and Beethoven Cycles at the Zürich Tonhalle, in Dublin, at the Wigmore Hall and in Paris, 1991–92; Plays Amati instrument made for the French Royal Family and loaned by the Corcoran Gallery, Gallery of Art, Washington DC. *Recordings:* Schumann Quartets, Op 41; Mozart String Quintets, with Denes Koromzay; Bartók 6 Quartets; Schubert Trout Quintet, with Zoltán Kocsis; Haydn Op 76; Brahms Op 51, Nos 1 and 2;

Chausson Concerto, with Joshua Bell and Jean-Yves Thibaudet; Works by Schubert, Mozart, Dvořák and Bartók. *Honours:* Winner, International Quartet Competition, Evian, 1977; Winner, Portsmouth International Quartet Competition, 1979. *Address:* c/o Phelps, Takacs Quartet, 6 Malvern Road, London, E8 3LT, England.

**SCHREIBMAYER, Kurt;** Singer (Tenor); b. 1953, Klagenfurt, Germany. *Education:* Studied at the Graz Musikhochschule. *Career:* Sang at Graz, 1976–78, then at the Vienna Volksoper; Further appearances at the Theater am Gartnerplatz Munich, 1987–88, Deutsche Oper am Rhein Düsseldorf from 1987, Hamburg Staatsoper and the Zürich Opera; Théâtre Royal de la Monnaie, Brussels from 1987 as Števa in Jenůfa and Luka in From The House of the Dead in 1990; Bayreuth Festival engagements, 1986–90, as Froh, Walter von der Vogelweide and Parsifal; Returned to Vienna Volksoper in 1988 as Max in Der Freischütz; Has sung at Liège as Lohengrin, 1988–89; Other roles include Fra Diavalo, Babinsky in Shvanda the Bagpiper, Pedro in Tiefland, Gomez in Die drei Pintos, Wenzel in Zemlinsky's Kleider Machen Leute, and parts in operettas; Sang in Mona Lisa by Max von Schillings at the Vienna Volksoper, 1996 and Dimitri in Boris Godunov, 1998; Season 2000 as Shuisky in Boris Godunov and Zemlinsky's König Kandaules at the Vienna Volksoper, Siegmund in Graz. *Address:* c/o Théâtre Royal de la Monnaie, 4 Leopoldstrasse, 1000 Brussels, Belgium.

**SCHREIER, Peter;** German tenor and conductor; b. 29 July 1935, Meissen. *Education:* Dresden Hochschule für Musik. *Career:* sang with Dresden State Opera 1959–63; joined Berlin Staatsoper 1963; has appeared at Vienna State Opera, Salzburg Festival, La Scala, Milan, Sadler's Wells, London, Metropolitan Opera, New York and Teatro Colón, Buenos Aires; recital début London 1978; début as conductor 1969; has conducted recordings of several choral works by J.S. Bach, Mozart and Schubert; retd as opera singer 1999 but continues to conduct. *Address:* c/o Norman McCann Ltd., The Coach House, 56 Lawrie Park Gardens, London, SE26 6XY (office); c/o Askonas Holt, Lansdale Chambers, 27 Chancery Lane, London, WC2A 1PF, England (office); Calberlastr. 13, 01326 Dresden, Germany.

**SCHRÖDER, Jaap;** Violinist; b. 31 Dec. 1925, Amsterdam, Netherlands; m. Agnès Jeanne Françoise Lefèvre, 3 d. *Education:* Diploma, Amsterdam Conservatory; 1st Prize, Ecole Jacques Thibaud, Paris, 1948. *Career:* Debut: Holland 1949; Leader, Radio Chamber Orchestra, 1950–63; Founder, Chamber Music ensembles Quadro Amsterdam, and Concerto Amsterdam, 1962, Quartetto Esterhazy 1973–81; Smithson String Quartet, 1983; Professor of violin, Amsterdam Conservatory, Yale School of Music, Basel Schola cantozum; mem, Netherlands String Quartet, 1952–69. *Recordings:* Numerous recordings on major record labels. *Address:* Gerard Brandtstraat 18, Amsterdam, Netherlands.

**SCHRÖTER, Gisela;** Singer (Mezzo-soprano); b. 19 Aug. 1933, Sardenhnen, East Prussia, Germany. *Education:* Studied at the Berlin State Conservatory and with Rudolf Dittrich at the Studio of the Dresden Staatsoper. *Career:* Debut: Dresden 1957, as a page in Lohengrin; Sang at the Dresden Staatsoper until 1964 in the mezzo and dramatic soprano repertory, notably as the Dyer's Wife in Die Frau ohne Schatten; Bayreuth Festival 1959, as a Flowermaiden in Parsifal; Berlin Staatsoper from 1964, as Carmen, Octavian and the Composer in Ariadne; Guest appearances in Barcelona, Lausanne, Bratislava, Vienna, Hamburg, Prague, Budapest, USA and Soviet Union; Guested with the Staatsoper in North America as Sieglinde, Kundry, the Composer and Marie in Wozzeck; Sang Herodias, Salome, in Berlin 1987; Many Concert appearances. *Recordings:* Hansel and Gretel, Der Wildschütz; Wozzeck; Schumann's Genoveva. *Address:* c/o Deutsche Staatsoper, Unter den Linden 7, 1086 Berlin, Germany.

**SCHROTT, Thomas;** Italian violinist; b. 24 Nov. 1966, Milan. *Education:* Milan Conservatory, Parma Conservatory A. Boito, Mannes Coll. of Music, New York; studied violin with Aaron Rosand and Lewis Kaplan; masterclasses, Mozarteum, Salzburg, Centre Int. de Formation Musicale, Nice, Accad. Musicale Chigiana, Siena, Scuola di Musica di Fiesole. *Career:* played extensively in Italy for most concert socs including: Teatro all Scala di Milano, Pomeriggi Musicali di Milano, Ravello Festival, Sagra Musicale Umbra, Bologna, Teatro Comunale, Mantua, Teatro Bibiena, Piccolo Teatro di Milano, Accad. Musicale Pescarese, Accad. Filarmonica Romana (Teatro Olimpico), Turin, Lingotto (Auditorium G-Agnelli), Piccolo Teatro Regio, Genoa, Teatro Modena, Cantiere d'Arte Contemporanea di Monteputciano; many concerts in USA, Switzerland, Germany, Austria, France, Finland, Romania, South Africa, India, Bahrain, Mauritius, Turkey; soloist, various orchestras including: Moldava Symphony Orchestra, Orchestra della Sagra Musicale Umbra, Festival Strings Lucerne, Bombay Chamber Orchestra; mem. Festival Strings Lucerne 1995–; performs regularly at major European festivals including: Lucerne Festival, Musikverein in Vienna, Alte Oper Frankfurt, Köln Philhannonie, Rencontres Musicales d'Evian, Naantali Festival, Ossiach Festival, Festival G. Enescu, Bucarest, Engadiner Konzertwochen, Festival di Stresa, 21st Musicbiennale, Zagreb, Biennale di Venezia 2001, SKIP Festival, St Petersburg, DOM Cultural Centre, Moscow, Quirinale, Rome 2003; Principal Violin, Sentieri Selvaggi, Milan; performer (with Daniel Bosshard) complete cycle of J.S. Bach's sonatas for violin and harpsichord; Guest Concertmaster, Milano Classica, Orchestra da Camera della Lombardia. *Recordings:* F. Chopin – Complete Chamber Music; with Sentien Selvaggi: La Formula del Fiore, Musica Coelestis, Bad Blood, Child, La Buona Novella; other: Audible Noise, Milioni di Minuti. *Address:* via

Treviglio 17, 20128 Milano, Italy. *Telephone:* (2) 2592609. *E-mail:* thschrott@libero.it.

**SCHUBACK, Thomas;** Conductor and Pianist; b. 1943, Sweden. *Education:* Studied at the Stockholm College of Music. *Career:* Conductor, Royal Opera Stockholm from 1971; productions at the Drottningholm Theatre include L'Incoronazione di Poppea, L'Arbore di Diana by Martin y Soler, Mozart's Così fan tutte and Gluck's Paride ed Elena; Musical Director of Lyric Opera of Queensland from 1982; Guest Appearances with San Diego Opera and at Sydney and Copenhagen; Season 1992–93 included performances with the Drottningholm Theatre at the Barbican Centre, London; Concerts with major Swedish Orchestras and elsewhere in Scandinavia, USA and Australia; Lieder Accompanist to Gösta Winbergh, Barbara Bonney and others; Professor of Vocal Coaching, State Oper School, Stockholm. *Recordings include:* Electra by Haeffner. *Current Management:* Ulf Tornqvist Artists Management. *Address:* St Eriksgatan 100, 113 31 Stockholm, Sweden.

**SCHUBEL, Max;** American composer; *President, Opus One Recordings, Inc.*; b. 11 April 1932, New York. *Education:* Graduated, New York University, 1953; Further Composition Study with Frank Martin. *Career:* freelance composer; many performances throughout N America; Founder and Pres. Opus One Recordings, Inc. for the Recording of New and Unfamiliar Concert and Electronic Music 1966–. *Compositions:* Insected Surfaces, Concerto for clarinet and 4 instruments, 1965; Exotica, for cello and harpsichord, 1967; 3 String Quartets, 1968, 1980, 1981; Everybody's Favourite Rag, for piano, 1979; Divertimento for piano, trumpet and chamber orchestra, 1980; B Natural, for prepared piano, 1980; Guale for orchestra, 1984; Punch and Judie, for chamber orchestra, 1985; The Spoors of Time for viola and piano, 1986; Scherzo for orchestra, 1987; Septet, 1988; Super Scherzo, for chamber orchestra, 1989; String Quintet, 1989; Sygnet for orchestra, 1995; Cyrèniäde for voice and orchestra, 1997; Elation, for cello, voice and orchestra, 2000; April's Ascension into Blue Destiny, 2003; Aurora Angelica for orchestra, 2003; Rhapsody for English Horn, cello and orchestra, 2003; Toccatina for piano, 2003; Trio for violin, cello and piano, 2000, Cellophonica for cello and orchestra 2004. *Honours:* residencies at MacDowell Colony, Ossabaw Island, Wurlitzer Foundation, and Wolf Trap; grants from Nat. Endowment for the Arts, Ford Foundation, Martha Baird Rockefeller Foundation. *Address:* Box 604, Greenville, ME 04441, USA. *Telephone:* (207) 997-3581. *Fax:* (207) 997-3581.

**SCHUDEL, Regina;** Singer (Soprano); b. 1964, Zürich, Switzerland. *Education:* Berlin Hochschule and Opera Studio of the Vienna Staatsoper. *Career:* Debut: Vienna, 1988 as Quiteria in Die Hochzeit des Camacho by Mendelssohn; Berlin Kammeroper from 1988, as Leda in Europa und der Stier by Helge Jorus and in Henze's Elegy for Young Lovers; Sang Rosina in Paisiello's Il Barbiere di Siviglia; Guest appearances at Krefeld, the Bregenz Festival and throughout Germany and Switzerland; Many concert and recital engagements; Leipzig Opera from 1991. *Recordings:* Die Hochzeit des Comacho; Das Wunder der Heliane by Korngold; Wozzeck by Manfred Gurlitt. *Address:* c/o Leipzig Opera, Augustusplatz 12, 7010 Leipzig, Germany.

**SCHUDEL, Thomas;** Canadian composer; b. 8 Sept. 1937, Defiance, Ohio, USA. *Education:* BSc, 1959, MA, 1961, Ohio University; Composition Studies with Leslie Bassett and Ross Lee Finney, University of Michigan, DMA 1971. *Career:* Faculty Member, University of Regina, Canada, 1964–; Bassoonist, Regina Symphony Orchestra, 1964–70. *Compositions:* Set No. 2, for brass and wind quintets, 1963; Violin Sonata, 1966; String Quartet, 1967; 2 Symphonies, 1971, 1983; Variations, for orchestra, 1977; Winterpiece, for chamber orchestra and dancers, 1979; Triptych, for wind ensemble, 1979; A Dream Within a Dream, for chorus, 1985; A.C.T.S, for narrator and ensemble, 1986; Dialogues, for trombone and percussion, 1987; Concerto, for piccolo, strings and percussion, 1988; Concerto, for alto trombone and chamber orchestra, 1990; An Emily Dickinson Folio, for soprano and ensemble, 1991; Trigon, for 2 saxophones and percussion, 1992; A Tangled Web, for chamber orchestra, 1993; The Enchanted Cat, children's operetta, 1993; Pick Up The Earth, Gold and Rose, and Another Love Poem, all for chorus, 1994; Sinfonia Concertante, for saxophone quartet and band, 1994. *Honours:* 1st Prize, 1972 City of Trieste International Competition. *Address:* 149 Shannon Road, Regina, SK S4S 5H6, Canada.

**SCHULLER, Gunther Alexander;** American composer, conductor, music educator and record producer; b. 22 Nov. 1925, New York, NY; s. of Arthur E. Schuller and Elsie (Bernartz) Schuller; m. Marjorie Black 1948 (died 1992); two s. *Education:* St Thomas Choir School, New York, Manhattan School of Music. *Career:* Principal French horn, Cincinnati Symphony Orchestra 1943–45, Metropolitan Opera Orchestra 1945–59; teacher, Manhattan School of Music 1950–63, Yale Univ. 1964–67; Head Composition Dept, Tanglewood 1963–84; Music Dir First Int. Jazz Festival, Washington 1962; active as conductor since mid-1960s with maj. orchestras in Europe and USA; reconstructed and orchestrated Der Gelbe Klang by De Hartmann/Kandinsky; Pres. New England Conservatory of Music 1967–77; Pres. Nat. Music Council 1979–81; Artistic Co-Dir, then Artistic Dir Summer Activities, Boston Symphony Orchestra, Berkshire Music Center, Tanglewood 1969–84, Festival at Sandpoint 1985–98; founder and Pres. Margun Music Inc. 1975–2000, GM Records 1980; mem. American Acad. of Arts and Sciences, American Acad. of Arts and Letters. *Compositions include:* Horn Concerto No. 1 1945, Vertige d'Eros 1946, Concerto for cello and orchestra 1946, Jumpin' in the Future

1946, Quartet for Four Brasses 1947, Oboe Sonata 1947, Duo Concertante for cello and piano 1947, Symphonic Study (Meditation) 1948, Trio for Oboe, Horn, Viola 1948, Symphony for brass and percussion 1950, Fantasy for Unaccompanied Cello 1951, Recitative and Rondo for violin and piano 1953, Dramatic Overture 1951, Five Pieces for Five Horns 1952, Adagio for flute, string trio 1952, Music for Violin, Piano and Percussion 1957, Symbiosis for violin, piano, percussion 1957, String Quartet No. 1 1957, Contours 1958, Woodwind Quintet 1958, Spectra 1958, Concertino for jazz quartet and orchestra 1959, Seven Studies on Themes of Paul Klee 1959, Conversations 1960, Lines and Contrasts for 16 horns 1960, Abstraction for jazz ensemble 1960, Variants on a Theme of Thelonious Monk 1960, Music for Brass Quintet 1960, Contrasts for woodwind quintet and orchestra 1961, Variants (ballet with choreography by Balanchine) 1961, Double Quintet for woodwind and brass quintets 1961, Meditation for concert band 1961, Concerto for piano and orchestra 1962, Journey into Jazz 1962, Fantasy Quartet for four cellos 1963, Threnos for oboe and orchestra 1963, Composition in Three Parts 1963, Five Bagatelles for Orchestra 1964, Five Etudes for orchestra 1964, The Power Within Us 1964, Five Shakespearean Songs for baritone and orchestra 1964, String Quartet No. 2 1965, Symphony 1965, American Triptych (on paintings of Pollock, Davis and Calder) 1965, Sacred Cantata 1966, Gala Music concerto for orchestra 1966, The Visitation (opera) 1966, Movements for flute and strings, Six Renaissance Lyrics, Triplum I 1967, Study in Textures for concert band 1967, Diptych for brass quintet and orchestra 1967, Shapes and Designs 1968, Concerto for double bass and orchestra 1968, Consequents for orchestra 1969, Fisherman and his Wife (opera) 1970, Concerto da Camera No. 1 1971, Capriccio Stravagante 1972, Tre Invenzioni 1972, Three Nocturnes 1973, Five Moods for tuba quartet 1973, Four Soundscapes 1974, Triplum II 1975, Violin Concerto 1976, Concerto No. 2 for horn and orchestra 1976, Diptych for organ 1976, Concerto No. 2 for orchestra 1977, Concerto for contrabassoon and orchestra 1978, Deaï for three orchestras 1978, Sonata Serenata 1978, Octet 1979, Concerto for trumpet and orchestra 1979, Eine Kleine Posaunenmusik 1980, In Praise of Winds symphony for large wind orchestra 1981, Concerto No. 2 for piano and orchestra 1981, Symphony for organ 1981, Concerto Quaternio 1984, Concerto for alto saxophone 1983, Duologue for violin and piano 1983, On Light Wings piano quartet 1984, Piano Trio 1984, Concerto for viola and orchestra 1985, Concerto for bassoon and orchestra 1985, Farbenspiel Concerto No. 3 for orchestra 1985, String Quartet No. 3 1986, Chimeric Images 1988, Concerto for string quartet and orchestra 1988, Concerto for flute and orchestra 1988, Horn Sonata 1988, On Winged Flight: A Divertimento for Band 1989, Chamber Symphony 1989, Five Impromptus for English horn and string quartet 1989, Impromptus and Cadenzas for chamber sextet 1990, Song and Dance for violin and concert band 1990, Concerto for piano three hands 1990, Violin Concerto No. 2 1991, Brass Quintet No. 2 1993, Reminiscences and Reflections 1993, The Past is the Present for orchestra 1994, Sextet for left-hand piano and woodwind quintet 1994, Concerto for organ and orchestra 1994, Mondrian's Vision 1994, Lament for M 1994, Blue Dawn into White Heat concert band 1995, An Arc Ascending 1996, Ohio River Reflections 1998, A Bouquet for Collage 1988, Fantasia Impromptu for flute and harpsichord 2000, Quod Libet for violin, cello, oboe, horn and harp 2001, String Quartet No. 4 2002, Concerto da Camera No. 2 2002, String Trio 2003, Encounters for jazz orchestra and symphony orchestra 2003. *Publications:* Horn Technique 1962, Early Jazz: Its Roots and Musical Development, Vol. I 1968, Musings: The Musical Worlds of Gunther Schuller 1985, The Swing Era: The Development of Jazz 1930–45 1989, The Compleat Conductor 1997. *Honours:* Hon. DMus (Northeastern Univ.) 1967, (Colby Coll.) 1969, (Ill. Univ.) 1970, (Williams Coll.) 1975, (Rutgers Univ.) 1980, (Oberlin Coll.) 1989, (Fla State Univ.) 1991; Creative Arts Award, Brandeis Univ. 1960, Nat. Inst. Arts and Letters Award 1960, Guggenheim Grant 1962, 1963, ASCAP Deems Taylor Award 1970, Rogers and Hammerstein Award 1971, William Schuman Award, Columbia Univ. 1989, McArthur Foundation Fellowship 1991, McArthur'Genius' Award 1994; Gold Medal American Acad. of Arts and Letters 1996, Order of Merit, Germany 1997, Max Rudolf Award 1998, Pulitzer Prize in Music 1999. *Address:* 167 Dudley Road, Newton Center, MA 02459, USA. *Telephone:* (617) 332-6398. *Fax:* (617) 969-1079.

**SCHULTE, Eike (Wilm);** singer (baritone); b. Plettenberg, Germany. *Education:* Cologne Musikhochschule with Joseph Metternich, Salzburg Mozarteum. *Career:* mem., Deutsche Oper am Rhein Düsseldorf 1956–69, Bielefeld Opera 1969–73 and Hessisches Staatstheater Wiesbaden 1973–88; sang the Herald in Lohengrin at Bayreuth 1988 and toured Japan with the Bayreuth Festival Company 1989; Munich Staatsoper from 1989 as Faraone in Mosè by Rossini, the Father in Hansel and Gretel and Schtschelkalov in Boris Godunov; baritone role in staged performances of Carmina Burana 1990; sang Beckmesser in Die Meistersinger at the Paris Opéra and in Munich; guest engagements in Vienna, Hamburg, Cologne, Bonn, Trieste, Rome and Brussels, notably as Figaro and Rigoletto; sang Kurwenal in Japan in 1990 conducted by Peter Schneider, Mahler's 8th Symphony with the London Philharmonic under Klaus Tennstedt in 1991; season 1991–92 included: Lohengrin at Vienna State Opera, Zemlinsky, VARA Holland and Brahms Requiem with Hamburg Philharmonic; season 1993–94 included: Hansel and Gretel, Rosenkavalier and Meistersinger in Munich, Ariadne auf Naxos in Cologne and Rigoletto in Tel-Aviv; season 1994–95 included: Gunther in a new Ring production at Paris, Tannhäuser at Bayreuth Festival and debut with the Philadelphia Orchestra in Ariadne auf Naxos in Philadelphia and Carnegie Hall, New York; sang the Herald in Lohengrin at the Accademia di Santa Cecilia, Rome 1996 and at New York Met 1998; also in 1998–99 sang Meistersinger at the Deutsche Oper Berlin; Alidoro in Cenerentola in Dresden, Rosenkavalier at the Munich Opera Festival and Parsifal in Chile; season 1999–2000 debuts with Gunther at La Scala, Herald in Lohengrin at Florence Opera and Beckmesser at the Lyric Opera, Chicago; season 2002–03 with Meistersinger at the Royal Opera House in London and the Vienna State Opera, Die Zauberflöte and Der Rosenkavalier in Munich, Götterdämmerung at the Tenerife Festival, Fidelio in Milan and Monte Carlo, Lohengrin in Berlin and La Cenerentola in San Fransisco. *Recordings include:* Berlioz's L'enfance du Christ, Wagner's Lohengrin, Beethoven's 9th, Haydn's Creation and Wagner's Das Rheingold. *Current Management:* c/o Haydn Rawstron Ltd, 36 Station Road, London, SE20 7BQ, England. *Website:* www.haydn-rawstron.com; www.eike-wilm-schulte.de.

**SCHULTZ, Andrew;** Composer and University Professor; b. 18 Aug. 1960, Adelaide, South Australia. *Education:* Composition studies with Colin Brumby; BMus, Queensland University, 1982; Composition Studies with George Crumb, Conducting with Richard Wernick, University of Pennsylvania, USA, 1983; Composition with David Lumsdaine, MMus, Kings College, London, England, 1986; PhD, Queensland University, 1987. *Career:* Head of Composition and Music Studies, Guildhall School of Music and Drama and Visiting Professor, Faculty of Creative Arts, University of Wollongong, New South Wales; Compositions performed and broadcast widely, Australia, USA, Europe; Commissions, University of Melbourne, Perihelion, Seymour Group, Elision, Flederman, Queensland Philharmonic Orchestra, Hunter Orchestra, Sydney Symphony Orchestra, 4 MBS-FM, Duo Contemporain, Musica Nova; Discography includes: Garotte, 1981, on Tropic of Capricorn, Qld Symphony Orchestra, CD; Barren Grounds on Tapestry, CD; Ekstasis on Australian Vocal Music, 1992, CD; Chamber Music of Andrew Schultz, CD. *Compositions:* Spherics, flute, trombone, 1 percussion, piano, synthesizer, cello, 1985; Stick Dance, clarinet, marimba, piano, 1987; Sea-Change piano, 1987; Black River, opera, 1988; Barren Grounds, clarinet, viola, cello, piano, 1990; Ekstasis, 1990, 6 solo voices; Calling Music, 1991, chamber orchestra; The Devil's Music, 1992, large orchestra; Diver's Lament, large orchestra, 1995; Violin Concerto, 1996; In Tempore Stellae, Symphony No. 1, choir and orchestra, 1998; Going Into Shadows, 3-act opera, 2000. *Honours:* Composer Fellowship, Australia Council Music Board, 1982; Queensland University Medal, 1982; Fulbright Award, 1983; Commonwealth Postgraduate Research Award, 1983; Commonwealth Scholarship and Fellowship Plan Award, 1985; Albert H Maggs Composition Award, 1985; Hilda Margaret Watts Prize, Kings College London, 1986; Australian National Composers Opera Award, 1988; Composer Fellowship, Australia Council, 1990; APRA Classical Composition of the Year, 1994. *Address:* Professor of Composition, University of Wollongong, NSW 2522, Australia. *E-mail:* info@andrewschultz.net. *Website:* www.andrewschultz.net.

**SCHULZ, Gerhard;** Violinist; b. 23 Sept. 1951, Austria. *Education:* Studied in Vienna, Düsseldorf and USA. *Career:* 2nd violin of the Alban Berg Quartet from 1978; Many concert engagements, including complete cycles of the Beethoven Quartets in 15 European cities 1987–88, 1988–89 seasons; Bartók-Mozart cycle in London, Vienna, Paris, Frankfurt, Munich, Geneva and Turin, 1990–91; Annual concert series at the Vienna Konzerthaus and festival engagements world-wide; Associate Artist at the South Bank Centre, London; US appearances in Washington DC, San Francisco, NY, Carnegie Hall. *Recordings:* Complete quartets of Beethoven, Brahms, Berg, Webern and Bartók; Late quartets of Mozart, Schubert, Haydn and Dvořák; Ravel and Debussy quartets; Live recordings from Carnegie Hall, Mozart, Schumann; Konzerthaus in Vienna, Brahms, Opéra-Comique Paris, Brahms. *Honours:* Grand Prix du Disque; Deutsche Schallplatenpreis; Edison Prize; Japan Grand Prix; Gramophone Magazine Award. *Address:* Intermusica Artists' Management, 16 Duncan Terrace, London N1 8BZ, England.

**SCHULZ, Walther;** Cellist; b. 1940, Vienna, Austria. *Education:* Studied in Vienna. *Career:* Debut: New York 1979; Debut Tour of Japan 1984; Performances of Haydn and other composers in Vienna and elsewhere from 1968; Co-Founder of the Haydn Trio of Vienna, 1968 and has performed in Brussels, Munich, Berlin, Zürich, London, Paris and Rome; Frequent North American appearances with Concerts in 25 States; Further travels to the Near East, Russia, Africa, Central and South America; Series at the Vienna Konzerthaus Society from 1976 with Performances of more than 100 works; Summer Festivals at Vienna, Salzburg, Aix en Provence, Flanders and Montreux; Masterclasses at the Royal College and Royal Academy in London, Stockholm, Bloomington, Tokyo and the Salzburg Mozarteum. *Recordings:* Complete Piano Trios of Beethoven and Schubert, Mendelssohn D Minor, Brahms B major, Tchaikovsky A Minor, Schubert Trout Quintet; Albums of Works by Haydn, Schumann, Dvořák, Smetana. *Address:* c/o Gerhild Baron Artists, Dornbacher Strasse 4/111/2, A–1170 Wien, Austria.

**SCHUMAN, Patricia;** singer (soprano); b. 4 Feb. 1954, Los Angeles, USA. *Education:* Santa Cruz University, CA. *Career:* Sang minor roles with San Francisco Opera then appeared with the Houston Opera and in a touring company; Engagements at the NYC Opera, the Paris Opéra, Teatro La Fenice Venice and in Washington DC; Sang on tour with Peter Brook's version of Carmen; Théâtre de la Monnaie Brussels from 1983 as Dorabella, Zerlina, and as Angelina in La Cenerentola; St Louis 1986 and in US premiere of Il Viaggio a Reims by Rossini; Théâtre du Châtelet, Paris 1989, in the title role of L'Incoronazione di Poppea; Miami Opera and Long Beach Opera 1989, as Antonia in Les Contes d'Hoffmann and as Mozart's Countess; Seattle Opera 1990, as Blanche in Les Dialogues des Carmélites; Has also sung at the Vienna

Staatsoper and in the concert hall; Metropolitan Opera debut, Donna Elvira, 1990; The Voyage, by Glass, 1996; Covent Garden debut 1992, as Donna Elvira; Salzburg Festival 1997, in La Clemenza di Tito, also at Covent Garden, 2000; Sang Schumann's Genoveva in Leeds and London, 2000; Alice Ford in Falstaff at Cologne and Covent Garden, 2001. *Recordings:* Roggiero in Rossini's Tancredi; Messiah, Handel; Video of Monteverdi's Poppea, Schwetzingen 1993, title role. *Address:* c/o PG & PM, 7 Whitehorse Close, Royal Mile, Edinburgh, EH8 8BU, Scotland.

**SCHUNK, Robert;** Singer (Tenor); b. 5 Jan. 1948, Neu-Isenburg, Frankfurt, Germany. *Education:* Studied with Martin Grundler at the Frankfurt Musikhochschule. *Career:* Sang at Karlsruhe 1973–75; Bonn Opera 1975–77; Dortmund 1977–79; Bayreuth Festival from 1977, as Siegmund, Erik and Melot; Hamburg Staatsoper 1981, as the Emperor in Die Frau ohne Schatten; Bregenz Festival 1983, Max in Der Freischutz; Engagements in Munich, Vienna, Frankfurt, London, Cologne and Berlin; Tour of Japan with the Hamburg Staatsoper 1984; Sang Florestan at the Met and Naples, 1986–87; Siegmund in New York and Munich, 1987, 1989; Emperor in Die Frau ohne Schatten and Vladimir in Prince Igor at Munich, 1989; Sang Wagner's Erik at Naples, 1992; Florestan in Fidelio at Catania, 1998. *Recordings:* Erik in Der fliegende Holländer, from Bayreuth.

**SCHURMANN, Gerard;** Composer and Conductor; b. 19 Jan. 1924, Kertosono, Java; m. Carolyn Nott, 26 May 1973, 1 d. *Education:* Composition with Alan Rawsthrone; Piano with Kathleen Long; Conducting with Franco Ferrara. *Career:* Aircrew, 320 Squadron, RAF, 1941–45; Acting Netherlands Cultural Attaché, London, 1945–48; Resident Orchestral Conductor, Radio Hilversum, 1948–51; Freelance Composer/Conductor, 1950–; Guest Conductor, France, Italy, Spain, Switzerland, Czechoslovakia, Germany, Netherlands, Scandinavia, Ireland, USA; mem, Performing Right Society; American Society of Composers, Authors and Publishers; MCPS; APC; AMPAS; BAFTA; Composers' Guild of Great Britain; Phyllis Court Club. *Compositions include:* Orchestral: 6 Studies of Francis Bacon, 1969; Variants, 1970; Attack and Celebration, 1971; Piano Concerto, 1972–73; Violin Concerto, 1975–78; The Gardens of Exile, concerto, cello, orchestra, 1989–90; Man in the Sky, 1994; Concerto for orchestra, 1994–95; Man in the Sky, 1996; Chamber, instrumental: Serenade, 1971; Contrasts, 1973; Leotaurus, 1975; Wind Quintet, flute, oboe, clarinet, horn, bassoon, 1976; 2 Ballades for piano, 1, Hukvaldy, 2, Brno, 1981; Duo, violin, piano, 1984; Quartet for piano and strings (violin, viola, cello, piano), 1986; Ariel, oboe, 1987; Quartet No. 2 for piano and strings, 1997; String Quartet, 2003; Vocal, choral: Song cycle, Chuenchi, 1966; Summer is Coming, madrigal, SATB, unaccompanied, 1970; The Double Heart, cantata, SATB, unaccompanied, 1976; Piers Plowman, opera cantata, 2 acts, 1979–80; Nine Slovak folk songs, high voice, piano or orchestra, 1988; Six Songs of William Blake, 1997; Gaudiana, Symphonic Studies for orchestra, 1999–2002; Trio for clarinet, cello and piano, 2001. *Recordings:* 6 Studies of Francis Bacon; Variants; Chuench'i; The Double Heart; Claretta; Piers Plowman; The Gardens of Exile; Piano Concerto; Violin Concerto; Concerto for Orchesta; Duo for violin and piano; Attack and Celebration; The Film Music of Gerard Schurmann; The Gambler; Man in the Sky. *Contributions:* Introductory essay to 3 vols on Alan Rawsthorne, 1984; Essay about working on the music for the film Lawrence of Arabia, 1990. *Honours:* Numerous. *Current Management:* The Marion Rosenberg Office. *Address:* 3700 Multiview Drive, Hollywood Hills, Los Angeles, CA 90068, USA.

**SCHÜTZ, Siiri;** Pianist; b. 26 July 1974, Berlin, Germany. *Education:* Carl Phil E. Bach Gymnasium, Berlin, 1985–91; studied with Annerose Schmidt at the Hochschule für Musik, Berlin, 1991–96; Diploma at the Hochschule für Musik, Hanns Eisler, Berlin, 1996; studied with Leon Fleisher at the Peabody Conservatory, Baltimore, 1996–98; Musikhochschule, Cologne. *Career:* performed in place of Claudio Arrau in the Cologne Philharmonic and Murray Perahia in Düsseldorf, debut with the Berlin Philharmonic Orchestra, conducted by Claudio Abbado (this concert was recorded and used in the film, The First Year), 1991; further concerts include the Schleswig Holtstein Festival, the Schwetzinger Mozart Festival and the Ruhrfestspiele, with the Tonhalle Orchestra Zürich, the Bern Symphony Orchestra, and the Berlin Rundfunk Symphony Orchestra; played chamber music during the Berliner Festwochen, 1993, and in the Faust cycle of the Philharmonic Orchestra in Berlin, 1994. *Honours:* First Prize in the International Piano Competition, Aussig, 1989; Jütting Award, Stendhal, Germany, 1996; Jürgen Ponto Stiftung fellowship; Studienstiftung des Deutschen Volkes fellowship. *Current Management:* Konzert-Direktion Hans Adler, Auguste-Viktoria-Str. 64, 14199 Berlin. *Telephone:* (30) 825–6333. *Fax:* (30) 826–3520. *Website:* www.musikadler.de. *Address:* Üderseestr. 17, 10318 Berlin, Germany. *Telephone:* (30) 5038–1718. *E-mail:* atischuetz@aol.com. *Website:* www.siiri-schuetz.de.

**SCHWAGER, Myron August;** American professor of music; b. 16 March 1937, Pittsfield, Massachusetts; m. 1st Katharine Lake, Sept 1961; one s. one d.; m. 2nd Laurie Beth Lewis, June 1982; m. 3rd Susan Welch June 1999. *Education:* Massachusetts Inst. of Tech., 1955–56; BMus, Boston University, 1958; MMus, New England Conservatory of Music, 1961; MA, PhD, Harvard University, 1970. *Career:* Worcester Community School of the Performing Arts; Jesuit Artists Institute, Italy; Chair, Department of Music History, Hartt School of Music, University of Hartford, Connecticut 1974–92, Prof. Emer. 1993–; Former Principal Cellist, Springfield Symphony Orchestra; Appearances with Cambridge Society for Early Music, Boston Chamber Players, Consortium Musicale, Hawthorne Trio, Hartford Chamber Orchestra, and Karas String Quartet; Revived and reconstructed Francesco Cavalli's

La Virtu de'strali d'Amore, Venice, 1642 at Wadsworth Atheneum, Hartford, 31 July–1 Aug, 1987. *Contributions:* The Creative World of Beethoven, 1971; Current Musicology; Music and Letters; Early Music; Musical Quarterly, Studi musicali, American Music Teacher, The Beethoven Journal, Clavier. *Address:* 64 Avonwood Road, B16, Avon, CT 06001, USA.

**SCHWANBECK, Bodo;** Singer (Bass-Baritone); b. 20 July 1935, Scherwin, Germany. *Education:* Studied with Franz-Theo Reuter in Munich and with KH Jarius in Stuttgart. *Career:* Debut: Detmold 1959, as Varlaam in Boris Godunov; Has sung in Frankfurt, Hamburg, Munich, Manheim, Düsseldorf, and Lisbon and at the NYC Opera, Zürich Opera 1967, in the premiere of Madame Bovary by Sutermeister; French television as Mustafà in L'Italiana in Algeri; Théâtre de la Monnaie, Brussels, 1986; Sang at Madrid 1988, in Lulu; Brussels 1990, in From the House of the Dead; Covent Garden 1990, as Waldner in Arabella; Sang Antonio in Figaro with the Royal Opera on tour to Japan, 1992; Other roles include Baron Ochs, Osmin, Alfonso, Pizarro, Leporello, Mephistopheles, Nicolai's Falstaff, Don Pasquale, Dulcamara, Golaud, Don Magnifico and Wozzeck; Sang in Lulu at Palermo, 2001; Frequent concert appearances. *Address:* c/o Theatre Royal de le Monnaie, 4 Leopoldstrasse, 1000 Brussels, Belgium.

**SCHWANEWILMS, Anne;** German singer (soprano). *Education:* Cologne Musikhochschule with Hans Sotin. *Career:* mem., Cologne Opera Studio 1990–92, Cologne Opera 1993–95; freelance engagements 1995–; recent engagements haver included Die Walküre in Essen and Klagenfurt, Sieglinde/Walküre in Freiburg, Die Zauberflöte in Trieste (with Arnold Östman) and Salome with the Cologne Radio Symphony Orchestra; debut at the Bayreuth Festival in 1996 in roles of Gerhilde (Die Walküre) and Gutrune (Götterdämmerung) whilst covering the role of Kundry and has been reinvited to Bayreuth each year since; returned to Turin in 1998 to perform Gutrune and 3rd Norn in concert performances of Götterdämmerung; season 1999–2000 with Sieglinde at Bonn and Berlin, Senta at Lübeck, Adriano and Gutrune at Berlin; a new production of Götterdämmerung at Stuttgart and her first performance of Senta at the Hamburg State Opera 2000; recent concerts have included Zemlinsky's Der Zwerg with the Gürzenich Orchestra in Cologne, Mahler's Symphony No. 8 in Udine and a concert at the Kongresshalle in Lübeck (Weber/Schubert/Rubinstein) with Erich Wächter; further engagements with return visits to Bayreuth and concerts in Japan, Die Walküre (Gerhilde) in Hamburg, Hänsel und Gretel (Hexe) in Stuttgart, Wagner's Rienzi (Adriano) at the Komische Oper in Berlin, Die Walküre (Sieglinde) in Bonn, role of Judith in Barbe Bleue at the Brussels Opera and at the Schouwbund in Rotterdam, Beethoven's Symphony No. 9 in Leipzig for MDR and Wesendoncklieder (in the Mottl edition) in Freiburg; sang Beethoven's Leonore at the Châtelet 2002; Weber's Euryanthe at the London Proms 2002; engaged at Glyndebourne 2002–03, as Weber's Euryanthe and Mozart's Electra; Covent Garden debut as Chrysothemis in Elektra 2003; Ariadne in Ariadne auf Naxos, Covent Garden 2004. *Recordings:* Beethoven's Ninth (with Seiji Ozawa), Mahler's Eighth (with Riccardo Chailly), a Strauss recital (with the Hallé Orchestra), Mendelssohn's Lobgesang (with the Gewandhaus Orchester), Strauss Lieder recital for the BBC (with Roger Vignoles). *Honours:* Opernwelt magazine Singer of the Year 2002. *Current Management:* Haydn Rawstron Ltd, 36 Station Road, London, SE20 7BQ, England. *Website:* www.haydn-rawstron.com.

**SCHWANTER, Joseph,** BM, MM, DM; composer; b. 22 March 1943, Chicago, USA. *Education:* American Conservatory of Music, Chicago, Northwestern University. *Career:* Faculty mem., Eastman School of Music, Rochester 1970–, (Prof. of Composition 1980); composer-in-residence, St Louis Symphony 1982–85, Cabrillo Music Festival 1992. *Compositions:* Chronicon, for bassoon and piano, 1968; Consortium I and II, for flute and ensemble, 1970–71; Modus Caeliestis, for orchestra, 1973; Elixir, for flute and 5 players, 1975; And the Mountains Rising Nowhere, for orchestra, 1977; Canticle of the Evening Bells, for flute and 12 players, 1977; Wild Angels of the Open Hills, Song Cycle, for soprano and ensemble, 1977; Aftertones of Infinity, for orchestra, 1978; Sparrows, for soprano and chamber ensemble, 1979; Wind Willow, Whisper, for chamber ensemble, 1980; Dark Millennium, for orchestra, 1981; Through Interior Worlds, for ensemble, 1981; Distant Runes and Incantations, for piano and orchestra, 1984; Someday Memories, for orchestra, 1984; Witchnomad, Song Cycle, for soprano and orchestra, 1984; Dreamcaller, Song Cycle, for soprano, violin and chamber orchestra, 1984; A Sudden Rainbow, for orchestra, 1984; Toward Light, for orchestra, 1986; Piano Concerto, 1988; Freeflight, for orchestra, 1989; A Play of Shadows, Fantasy, for flute and orchestra, 1990; Velocities, for marimba, 1990; Percussion Concerto, 1991 (premiered 1995); Through Interior Worlds, Ballet, 1992 (concert version 1994); Symphony 'Evening Land' for soprano and orchestra, 1995; In Memories Embrace... for strings, 1996. *Honours:* Pulitzer Prize 1979.

**SCHWARTNER, Dieter;** Singer (Tenor); b. 6 Feb. 1938, Plauen, Germany. *Education:* Studied in Dresden. *Career:* Debut: Plauen in 1969 as the Baron in Der Wildschütz; Sang at Plauen until 1972, then at Dresden, 1972–78, and Dessau, 1978–79; Member of the Leipzig Opera from 1979 singing Ligeti's Le Grand Macabre and the Duke of Parma in Busoni's Doktor Faust in 1991; Guest appearances in Dresden and at the Berlin Staatsoper; Other roles have included Tamino, Faust, Max, Lionel in Martha, Florestan, Don José, Alvaro in La Forza del Destino and Walther von Stolzing; Many concert engagements. *Address:* c/o Stadtische Theatre, 7010 Leipzig, Germany.

**SCHWARTZ, Elliott Shelling,** AB, MA, EdD; American composer, writer and academic; *Professor of Music and Chair, Department of Music, Bowdoin College*; b. 19 Jan. 1936, Brooklyn, NY; m. Dorothy Rose Feldman 1960; one s. one d. *Education:* Columbia Univ. *Career:* Instructor, Univ. of Massachusetts 1960–64; Asst Prof. 1964–70, Assoc. Prof. 1970–75, Prof. of Music and Dept Chair 1975–, Bowdoin Coll., Brunswick, ME; Prof. of Composition, Ohio State Univ. 1985–86, 1988–91; visiting appointments, Trinity Coll. of Music, London (UK) 1967–, Univ. of California, San Diego 1978–79, Robinson Coll., Cambridge (UK) 1993–94, 1998–99; NEA grants 1978–83, American Composers' Alliance Rockefeller Foundation residencies, Bellagio, Italy 1980, 1989; mem. American Soc. of Univ. Composers, Coll. Music Soc. (past pres.). *Compositions:* Timepiece 1794 for chamber orchestra 1994, Rainbow for orchestra 1996, Alto Prisms for eight violas 1997, Mehitadel's Serenade for saxophone and orchestra 2001, Rainforest with Birds 2001, Voyager for orchestra 2002, Riverscape 2003. *Recordings:* Grand Concerto, Extended Piano, Mirrors, Texture for Chamber Orchestras, Concert Piece for Ten Players, Chamber Concerto, Cycles and Gongs, Extended Clarinet, Dream Music with Variations, Celebrations/Reflections for Orchestra, Memorial in Two Parts, Chiaroscuro, Elan, Aerie for six flutes, Equinox for orchestra, Voyager for orchestra, Timepiece 1794 for chamber orchestra. *Publications:* The Symphonies of Ralph Vaughan Williams 1964, Contemporary Composers on Contemporary Music (ed. with Barney Childs) 1967, Electronic Music: A Listener's Guide 1973, Music: Ways of Listening 1982, Music Since 1945: Issues, Materials and Literature (with Daniel Godfrey) 1993; contrib. to professional journals. *Honours:* Guaudeamus Prize (Netherlands) 1970, Maine State Award in the Arts and Humanities 1970. *Address:* PO Box 451, South Freeport, ME 04078, USA. *Telephone:* (207) 725-3320 (office); (207) 865-3722 (home). *Fax:* (207) 725-3748 (office); (207) 865-6652 (home). *E-mail:* eschwart@bowdoin.edu. *Website:* www.schwartzmusic.com.

**SCHWARTZ, Sergiu;** Israeli/American concert violinist, conductor and pedagogue; b. 1957, Romania. *Education:* studied with Dorothy DeLay, Juilliard School, New York, Yfrah Neaman, Guildhall School, London, Rami Shevelov, Rubin Academy, Tel-Aviv, Stefan Gheorghiu, Romania; additional studies with Sándor Végh, Felix Galimir, Leon Fleisher, Isaac Stern and Sergiu Celibidache. *Career:* New York debut at Carnegie Hall; London debut at Wigmore Hall in the Outstanding Israeli Artists series; North American debut at the Museum of Fine Arts, Montreal; soloist with over 200 leading orchestras in Europe, Israel and throughout the USA, including Dresden Staatskapelle, Jerusalem Symphony, London Symphony, Sarajevo, Dresden and Slovak Philharmonics, European Community Chamber Orchestra, National Orchestra of Mexico, Florida Philharmonic and Chicago's Grant Park Festival Orchestra and with numerous distinguished ensembles in the USA and world-wide; collaborations in performances with conductors, including Segiu Commissiona, James Judd, Peter Maag, Giuseppe Sinopoli and Bruno Weil; performances in major concert halls including Lincoln Center, Carnegie Recital Hall and 92nd Street Y (New York), Kennedy Center (Washington, DC), and Barbican Hall, Queen Elizabeth Hall and Wigmore Hall (London); frequent guest at int. music festivals, including Aspen, Newport, Bowdoin, Interlochen (USA), Israel, Switzerland, Finland, England, France, Romania and Bulgaria; conductor with European Community Chamber Orchestra, Concentus Hungaricus, Sarajevo Philharmonic, Israel Camerata Orchestra, Lynn Univ. Philharmonia and String Orchestra; broadcasts for major radio and TV stations, including the BBC, NPR and CNN; master classes conducted at music schools, colls and univs throughout the USA, including Interlochen Arts Acad., UCLA, Oberlin Conservatory, Eastman School, San Francisco Conservatory, Idyllwild Arts Acad., New York's La Guardia School for the Performing Arts, RAM (London), Reina Sofia Acad. of Music (Madrid) and Rubin Acad. of Music (Jerusalem); master courses in Romania, Bulgaria, Switzerland, Netherlands, Germany, Israel; judge in international violin competitions, including Tchaikovsky (Moscow), Pablo Sarasate (Spain), Henryk Szeryng (Mexico), Wieniawski (Poland), Novosibirsk (Russia), Int. Texaco-Sphinx (USA) and other competitions in France, Italy, Canada and the USA; teaching position, artist faculty, Conservatory of Music, Lynn Univ., Boca Raton, FL. *Recordings:* Works by Sibelius, Svendsen, Grieg, Spohr, Debussy, Schumann, R. Strauss, Bloch, Enescu, Smetana, Khachaturian, Millhaud, for Vox, Gega, Naxos, Arcobaleno, Romeo Records, Nonesuch, CBS and Discover/Koch International. *Honours:* America-Israel Cultural Foundation Award, Nat. Endowment for the Arts Solo Recitalist Fellowship, Nat. Foundation for the Advancement of the Arts; prizewinner, int. violin competitions in the USA, England, Switzerland and Chile. *Address:* C/o Joanne Rile Artists Management, 801 Old York Road, Noble Plaza, Suite 212, Jenkintown PA 19046 USA. *E-mail:* sergiuschwartz@aol.com. *Website:* members.aol.com/sergiuschwartz.

**SCHWARZ, Gerard;** American conductor; b. 19 Aug. 1947, Weehawken, NJ; m. Jody Greitzer 1984; two s. two d. *Education:* Professional Children's School, Juilliard School. *Career:* joined American Brass Quintet 1965; Music Dir Erick Hawkins Dance Co. 1966, Eliot Feld Dance Co. 1972; Co-Prin. Trumpet, New York Philharmonic 1973–74; Founding Music Dir Waterloo Festival 1975; Music Dir New York Chamber Symphony 1977–, LA Chamber Orchestra 1978–86; est. Music Today series, Merkin Concert Hall, New York 1981 (Music Dir 1988–89); Music Adviser Mostly Mozart Festival, Lincoln Center, New York 1982–84, Music Dir 1984–; Music Adviser Seattle Symphony 1983–84, Prin. Conductor 1984–85, Music Dir 1985–2001; Artistic Adviser Tokyu Bunkamura's Orchard Hall, Japan 1994–; Music Dir Royal Liverpool Philharmonic Orchestra 2001–06; Guest Conductor, Cosmopolitan

Symphony, Aspen Festival Chamber, Tokyo Philharmonic, Residentie, The Hague, St Louis Symphony, Kirov, St Petersburg, Royal Liverpool Philharmonic and Vancouver Symphony Orchestras, City of London Symphonia and London Mozart Players; has conducted many US orchestras and Hong Kong Philharmonic, Jerusalem Symphony, Israeli Chamber and English Chamber Orchestras, London Symphony, Helsinki Philharmonic and Monte Carlo Philharmonic Orchestras, Ensemble Contemporain, Paris and Nat. Orchestra of Spain; operatic conducting debut, Washington Opera 1982; has also conducted Seattle Opera 1986, San Francisco Opera 1991 and New Japan Philharmonic 1998; numerous recordings for Delos, Nonesuch, Angel and RCA labels; numerous TV appearances. *Honours:* Hon. DFA (Fairleigh Dickinson Univ., Seattle Univ.); Hon. DMus (Univ. of Puget Sound); named Conductor of the Year by Musical America Int. Directory of the Performing Arts 1994, Ditson Conductor's Award, Columbia Univ. 1989, two Record of the Year Awards, one Mumms Ovation Award. *Current Management:* Columbia Artists Management, 165 W 57th Street, New York, NY 10019, USA. *Telephone:* (212) 841-9500. *Fax:* (212) 841-9552. *E-mail:* info@cami.com.

**SCHWARZ, Hanna;** Singer (Mezzo-soprano); b. 15 Aug. 1943, Hamburg, Germany. *Education:* Studied in Hamburg, Hanover and Essen. *Career:* Debut: Hanover 1970, as Maddalena in Rigoletto; Eutin 1972, as Carmen; Member of the Hamburg Staatsoper from 1973; Guest appearances in Zürich (1975–), San Francisco (1977–), Vienna, Paris (Preziosilla 1977), Deutsche Oper Berlin (Cherubino 1978); Munich Staatsoper 1974, 1980, 1984; Bayreuth Festival 1976–85, as Fricka and Erda; sang in the first complete performance of Berg's Lulu, Paris Opéra 1979; Holland Festival 1985, as Brangaene in Tristan und Isolde; Paris 1987, as Cornelia in Giulio Cesare; Sang Fricka in Das Rheingold at Bonn and Cologne, 1990; Season 1992 as Orpheus and Fricka at Bonn; Sang Fricka at the New York Met, 1996–97; Mephistophila and Helen in the premiere of Schnittke's Historia von D Johann Fausten, Hamburg, 1995; Sang Brangaene at Cologne, 1998; Season 2000–01 as Fricka in the Ring and Berg's Countess Geschwitz at the Met; Waltraute at Cologne, the Nurse in Die Frau ohne Schatten at Dresden and Herodias for the Hamburg Staatsoper. *Recordings include:* Die Zauberflöte, The Queen of Spades, Lulu, Mahler's Rückert Lieder, Apollo et Hyacinthus by Mozart, Die Lustige Witwe; Les Contes d'Hoffmann, Humperdinck's Königskinder, Die Heimkehr aus der Fremde by Mendelssohn; Rhinedaughter in The Ring; Fricka in the Bayreuth Ring; Martha in Schubert's oratorio Lazarus; Mother in Hänsel und Gretel. *Address:* c/o Theateragentur Dr G. Hilbert, Maximillianstrasse 22, D–80539 München, Germany.

**SCHWARZENBERG, Elisabeth;** Singer (Soprano); b. 23 Sept. 1933, Vienna, Austria; m. Georg Schnapka. *Education:* Studied in Vienna. *Career:* Debut: Deutsche Oper am Rhein, Düsseldorf, 1956, as Eva in Die Meistersinger; Sang in Munich, Paris, Brussels, Nice, Turin, Dublin, Geneva and Zürich; Many appearances at the Vienna Volksoper; Düsseldorf 1957, in the premiere of Die Räuber by Klebe; Salzburg Festival 1961, in the premiere of Das Bergwerk zu Falun by Wagner-Régeny; Bayreuth 1962–72; Teatro San Carlo Lisbon 1967; Other roles included the Marschallin and Donna Elvira. *Address:* c/o Volksoper, Währingerstrasse 78, 1090 Vienna, Austria.

**SCHWARZKOPF, Dame Elisabeth** (see Legge-Schwarzkopf, Dame Elisabeth)

**SCHWEEN, Astrid;** Cellist; b. 1960, New York, USA. *Education:* Studied at the Juilliard School. *Career:* Soloist with The New York Philharmonic; Co-founder of the Lark String Quartet; Recent concert tours to: Australia; Taiwan; Hong Kong; China; Germany; Netherlands; US appearances at: The Lincoln Center, New York; Kennedy Center, Washington; Boston; Los Angeles; Philadelphia; St Louis; San Francisco; Repertoire includes: Quartets by Haydn, Mozart, Beethoven, Schubert, Dvořák, Brahms, Borodin, Bartók, Debussy and Shostakovich. *Honours:* Gold Medals at the 1990 Naumberg, 1991 Shostakovich Competitions; Prizewinner at the: 1990, Premio Paulio Borciani; 1990, Karl Klinger; 1991 London International String Quartet; 1991, Melbourne Chamber Music Competitions. *Address:* c/o Sonata (Lark Quartet), 11 Northpark Street, Glasgow G20 7AA, Scotland.

**SCHWEIGER, Stephanie (Kreszenz Berta);** Composer; b. 19 Dec. 1964, Regensburg, Germany. *Education:* Piano lessons and choir-singing from 1970; Studied Philosophy and Musicology in Regensburg, Munich and Berlin, 1986–91; Studied Composition at the Hochschule der Künste Berlin, with Gösta Neuwirth, Walter Zimmermann and Dieter Schnebel. *Career:* First compositions, 1980; Composer and Pianist in experimental ensemble, 1983–88; Appeared on radio at Westdeutscher Rundfunk, Sender Freies Berlin and other stations; Her works performed regularly, 1992–; Recent performances, 1998–, include at Darmstadt summer courses and at festivals in Rome, Paris, Berlin, Leipzig and elsewhere; Cooperated with Anna Clementi, Barre Bouman, ConGioco Ensemble, Accroche Note, Barbara Thun, Ariane Jessulat and others; mem, Freunde Guter Musik, Berlin, 1998. *Compositions:* 1au9tu9mn3 for 4 instruments and dancer, 1993; ekloge for mezzo-soprano, viola, guitar and percussion, 1996–97; frango phragmón for accordion, 1996–97; Skira for flute, violoncello, accordion, 1997; exilata for soprano and clarinet or bassoon, 1998: Film music: Nine pieces of music (One more time before I die), 1990; Die Vergessenen, 1997. *Recordings:* Sp19ri9ng one, 1991; Solo für Ebba, 1995. *Honours:* Commission from Berlin Senate, 1993; Commissions from G-Lock, Passau, 1994–98. *Address:* Barbarossastrasse 5, 10781 Berlin, Germany.

**SCHWEIKART, Dieter;** Singer (Bass); b. 9 Jan. 1942, Iserlohn, Germany. *Education:* Studied in Wuppertal with Becker-Brill and with Thomas Lo Monaco in Rome. *Career:* Sang in Saarbrucken from 1964; Appearances at Düsseldorf, Krefeld and Bonn; Hanover from 1976; Has sung in Dortmund, Hamburg, Frankfurt, Helsinki, Florence, Copenhagen and Cologne; Bayreuth Festival 1983–86, as Hans Foltz in Die Meistersinger and as Fafner in Der Ring des Nibelungen; Sang Daland in Der fliegende Holländer at Naples, 1992; Crespel in Les Contes d'Hoffmann at Cologne, 1998; Season 2000–01 at Cologne as Fafner and Sarastro. *Address:* c/o PO Box 100262, Bayreuther Festspiele, 8580 Bayreuth, Germany.

**SCHWEIZER, Alfred;** Composer; b. 4 Nov. 1941, Sevelen, Switzerland. *Education:* University of Berne; Berne Conservatory; Music Academy of Basle; Swiss Centre for Computer Music. *Career:* Professor, Winterthur Conservatory, 1970–71; Professor, 1971–2003, Acting Director, 1979–80, Biel Conservtory; Manager, Classic 2000, 1982–; mem, Schweizerischer Tonkünstlerverein; Schweizerischer Musikpädagogischer Verband. *Compositions:* 4 pieces for orchestra; 2 Concertinos for Violin and Strings; Metamusic for Percussion and Strings; Concerto for Piano and Orchestra; Concerto for Swiss folk instruments and small Orchestra; Canon for open Orchestra; The Year in Naïve Music; Christmas Music; Woodwind Quintet; Music for Piano Nos 1–7; Music for Guitars Nos 1–6; Music for Viola; Dorian Song for male voice, cello, piano; Phrygian Song for female voice, cello, piano; Lydian Song for female voice, violin, piano; Septet for flute, clarinet, piano, violin, viola, voice; Music for Brass Nos 1 and 2; Hip Hop for Wind Ensemble; Music for Christian, brass and two keyboards. *Recordings:* Orchestral Pieces Nos 1, 2, 3; Piano Concerto; Concertinos for Violin and Strings; Quartet ATON, open music; Alpine Sounds for four horns; Music for Piano Nos 1, 2, 3,4,5,6,7,8; Metamusic; Music for Guitars Nos 1, 2, 3, 4,5,6. *Honours:* Second Prize, International Composers Competition, Sanremo; Recognition Prize, Pro Arte Foundation, Berne; Recognition Prize, Canton Berne; Culture-Prize, City of Biel, 2001. *Address:* PO Box 17, CH-2513 Twann, Switzerland. *E-mail:* classic2000@bluewin.ch.

**SCHWEIZER, Daniel;** Conductor; b. 6 Nov. 1953, Herisau, Switzerland; m. Michiko Tsuda, 4 Oct 1980, 2 s. *Education:* Zürich Konservatorium 1972–76; Cello, Musikhochschule Essen, 1976–77; Conducting, Musikhochschule Freiburg, 1979–81. *Career:* Debut: With Zürich Symphony Orchestra, 23 Nov 1981; Concerts Founder, Zürich Symphony Orchestra, 1981; Concerts at festivals in Spain and Estoril, Portugal; Guest conductor, Germany, Czechoslovakia, Italy, France, Austria, Singapore, Korea, USA, Mexico, Estonia; mem, Schweizerischer Tonkünstlerverein. *Recordings:* Jecklin: Paul Muller, orchestral works; Motette: Marcel Dupré, Symphony G minor op 25, Dupré Concerto op 31 Demessieux op 9, Jongen Symphonie Concertante op 81, Classic 2000; Alfred Schweizer, orchestral works. *Contributions:* Neue Zürcher Zeitung. *Address:* Buecheneggstrasse 31, 8906, Bonstetten, Switzerland.

**SCHWEIZER, Verena;** Singer (Soprano); b. 9 May 1944, Solothurn, Switzerland. *Education:* Studied at the Zürich Conservatory, in Frankfurt, Basle with Elsa Cavelti, in Aachen and Freiburg and in Mannheim with Anna Reynolds. *Career:* Sang at Aargau 1971–72, Mainz 1973–75, Dortmund 1975–83; Sang at Freiburg from 1985 and guested at Stuttgart (1986 as Jenůfa, 1990 as Marenka in The Bartered Bride); Ludwigsburg 1984–89, as Fiodriligi and Mozart's Countess; Further appearances in Leeds (with the Dortmund Opera), Geneva, Cologne, Düsseldorf and Wiesbaden; Other roles include Susanna, Zerlina, Marcellina, Adina, Gilda, Micaela, Nannetta, Mimi, Sophie in Der Rosenkavalier, Anne Trulove and Desdemona; Concert engagements in Paris, Rome, Buenos Aires and Copenhagen; St Gallen 1983, in the premiere of P Huber's Te Deum. *Recordings include:* Christmas Oratorio by Saint-Saëns; Magnificat and other sacred music by Vivaldi (Erato); Così fan tutte (Harmonia Mundi); Hindemith's Cardillac (Wergo). *Address:* c/o Staatstheater Stuttgart, Oberer Schlossgarten 6, 7000 Stuttgart, Germany.

**SCHWENNIGER, Aurelia;** Singer (Mezzo-Soprano); b. 1938, Austria. *Career:* Sang at the Landestheater Linz, 1962–64, Augsburg, 1964–66, and at the Nationaltheater Mannheim, 1968–78; Roles have included Zenobia in Handel's Radamisto, Rosina, Fenena in Nabucco, Eboli, Amneris, Magdalene, the Composer in Ariadne auf Naxos, Silla in Palestrina, Janáček's Fox and Tchaikovsky's Maid of Orleans; Guest appearances at the Vienna Staatsoper, Rome and Cologne Operas and the Teatro San Carlos at Lisbon. *Address:* Mannheim National Theater, Nationaltheater Am Goetheplatz, 6800 Mannheim, Germany.

**SCHWETS, Stanislav;** Opera Singer (bass); b. 28 Jan. 1974, Ekaterinburg, Russia. *Education:* Studied under Professors P. Gluboky and V. Chachava, Moscow State Conservatory, 1992–97. *Career:* Debut: Banquo in Verdi's Macbeth, Dublin Opera, 1996; Filmed in Masterclass by Galina Vishnevskaya, Moscow, 1993; Frequent broadcasts on Russian television; Sang Rogozhin and David in world premieres of N. F. B. and Young David by V. Kobekin, at Sacro Art Festival, Germany, 1995, 1997; Sang in Te Deum by Handel and in Mass in B flat by Mozart, conducted by W Gönnenwein at Lüdwigsburger Festival, 1996; Sang Daland in Der fliegende Holländer for Metz Opera, France, 1997, and with Maryinsky company, conducted by Valery Gergiev in Toulouse and Madrid, Nov 1997; 1998 engagements with Basilio in Rossini's Il Barbiere di Siviglia and Leporello in Don Giovanni at Frankfurt Opera, Daland with Maryinsky Theatre conducted by Gergiev in Lisbon, and Pimen in Boris Godunov at Dublin. Has sung in concerts with V Chachava in

Moscow, St Petersburg and other Russian cities; Performed in Ekaterinburg in recital with Elena Obraztsova and Vazha Chachava. *Honours:* Grand Prix and Special Prize, Belvedere International Singers Competition, Vienna, 1994; Prizewinner, Rimsky-Korsakov International Singers Competition, St Petersburg, 1996. *Current Management:* Askonas Holt Ltd, Lonsdale Chambers, 27 Chancery Lane, London, WC2A 1PF, England. *Telephone:* (20) 7400-1700. *Fax:* (20) 7400-1799. *E-mail:* info@askonasholt.co.uk. *Website:* www.askonasholt.co.uk.

**SCIAMA, Pierre;** Singer (Countertenor); b. 1960, England. *Education:* Studied, Guildhall School with David Pollard and David Roblou, and at the GSM Early Music Course. *Career:* Sang Reason in Cavalieri's La Rappresentazione di Anima e di Corpo, Morley College, 1987; Purcell's Fairy Queen at the GSM conducted by William Christie; Sang in Rameau's Pygmalion at the Queen Elizabeth Hall and in Gluck's Alceste at Covent Garden and in Monte Carlo; Acis and Galatea with Midsummer Opera in Tours and St John's Smith Square, London, 1989; Appeared in Dido and Aeneas with the Early English Opera Society and as Apollo in Grabu's Albion and Albanus; Armindo in Handel's Partenope with Midsummer Opera.

**SCIARRINO, Salvatore;** Composer; b. 4 April 1947, Palermo, Italy. *Education:* Studied with Tulio Belfiore, 1964, and attended electronic music sessions at the Accademia di Santa Cecilia in Rome, 1969. *Career:* Artistic Director of Teatro Comunale in Bologna; Teacher in Milan, Florence and Citta del Castello; Milan Conservatory from 1974. *Compositions:* Instrumental pieces; Berceuse for orchestra 1967; Quartetto 1967; Da un divertimento 1970; Sonata du camera 1971; Arabesque for 2 organs 1971; Rondo for flute and orchestra 1972; Romanza for viola d'amore and orchestra 1973; Variazioni for cello and orchestra 1974; 2 Piano Trios, 1974, 1986; 2 Quintetes, 1976, 1977; Clair de Lune for piano and orchestra 1976; Kindertotenlied for soprano, tenor and chamber orchestra 1978; Flos Forum for chorus and orchestra 1981; Nox apud Orpheum for 2 organs and instruments 1982; String Trio 1983; 3 Piano Sonatas 1976, 1983, 1986; Violin Conceto, Allegoria nella notte 1985; Morte di Borromini for narrator and orchestra 1989; Florence, 1978; Lohengrin, 'azione invisible', Milan 1983; Perseo e Andromeda, Stuttgart 1991; Opera Luci Miei Traditrici, Schwetzingen, 1998; Infinito nero, theatre, 1998; Notturni for piano, 1999; Cantare con silenzio, for chorus, flute and percussion, 1999; Settimo quartetto, for string quartet, 1999. *Address:* c/o Staatstheater Stuttgart, Oberer Schlossgarten 6, 7000 Stuttgart, Germany.

**SCIBELLI, Carlo;** Singer (Tenor); b. 1970, New York. *Career:* Appearances throughout USA and Europe as Pinkerton, the Duke of Mantua, Faust, Rodolfo, Count Almaviva and Nemorino; Telemaco in Monteverdi's Ulisse; Lurciano in Ariodante; Fracasso in Mozart's Finta Semplice and Vladimir in Prince Igor; Season 1998-99, with Don Ottavio at Turin; Macduff at Cagliari and Alfredo at Covent Garden; Season 1999-2000, with Eduardo in Un giorno di regno for the Royal Opera, in Rosenkavalier at San Francisco and I Lombardi at Santiago. *Address:* c/o San Francisco Opera, Van Ness Avenue, War Memorial House, San Francisco CA 94102, USA.

**SCIMONE, Claudio;** Conductor and Musicologist; b. 23 Dec. 1934, Padua, Italy. *Career:* Studied with Franco Ferrara, Dmitri Mitropoulos and Carlo Zecchi., Founded the chamber ensemble I Solisti Veneti 1959; performances of 18th and 19th century Italian music, Mozart, Schoenberg and modern works (Donatoni, Bussotti, Malipiero and others); Tours of USA, Europe and Japan; wrote for La gazzetta del Veneto, 1952-57; Taught at Venice Conservatory, 1961-67; Chamber Music at Verona Conservatory, 1967-74; since then Director of Padua State Conservatory of Music; Permanent Conductor and Artistic Director of the chamber orchestra, Conducted Il Barbiere di Siviglia at Caracalla, 1992 and at the Verona Arena, 1996. *Recordings:* More than 200 recordings with I Solisti Veneti and other orchestras (London Philarmonia, Royal Philharmonic, English Chamber Orchestra, Bamberger Symphoniker, others), including L'Elisir d'amore (Ricciarelli, Carreras); Vivaldi flute concertos and Orlando Furioso; Concerti Grossi by Albinoni, Corelli and Geminiani; Marcello La Cetra; Italian flute and oboe concertos; Rossini string sonatas and Mozart's Salzburg Divertimenti; Operas by Rossini, including Zelmira, 1990. *Publications:* Editions of concertos by Tartini; Complete edition of Rossini; Segno, Significato, Interpretazione 1974; Numerous articles in music journals. *Honours:* Elizabeth Sprague Coolidge Memorial Medal 1969; Grammy record award (Los Angeles); several Grand Prix du Disque de l'Academie Charles Cros, Academie du Disque Lyrique and others. *Address:* Piazzale Pontecorvo 6, 35100 Padova, Italy.

**SCOGNA, Flavio Emilio;** Italian composer and conductor; b. 16 Aug. 1956, Savona; m. Fiorenza Iademarco 1993; two s. *Education:* N. Paganini Conservatory, Genoa, Univ. of Bologna, studied conducting with Franco Ferrara in Rome. *Career:* works performed in major int. venues, including Italian Radio (Rome, Naples), Centre Pompidou (Paris), Vienna Konzerthaus, and broadcast, RAI, BBC, Radio France, ORF, BRT; many commissions, Italian Radio, Vienna Konzerthaus, Pomeriggi Musicali of Milan; conductor, musical groups, nat. and int. orchestras such as RAI, Accademia Nazionale di St Cecilia, Israel Symphony Orchestra, Radio Broadcasting of Spain, Hungarian State Symphony Orchestra; appearances on Italian Radio, Teatro Massimo, Palermo, Teatro Opera Roma, Teatro Comunale, Firenze; teacher in several Italian conservatories such as S. Pietro a Maiella, Naples, and G. Rossini, Pesaro. *Compositions include:* Arioso per Guillermo 1984, Serenata for ensemble 1984, Anton (one-act opera) 1984, Incanto for string trio 1985, Come un'onda di luce for oboe, clarinet, violin, viola, cello 1985, Canto del

mare for flute, violin, cello 1985, Cadenza seconda for piano 1986, Sinfonia concertante for orchestra 1986-87, Frammento (after Mario Luz's poem) for soprano, piano 1987, La mar for marimba 1987, Concertino for 10 instruments 1987, Tre invenzioni for piano 1988, Risonanze for string quartet 1988, Fluxus for orchestra 1988, Verso for three winds and three strings 1988, Rifrazioni for soprano and orchestra 1989, Alternanze for piano and strings 1989, Musica reservata for strings and orchestra 1990, Salmo XII for mezzo-soprano, baritone, orchestra 1990, Relazioni for ensemble 1991, La memoria perduta (two-act opera) 1991-93, Diaphonia for viola, orchestra 1992, Trame for trumpet 1993, Aulos for oboe 1993, Concentus for orchestra 1994-95, Amadeus Mio Caro for chamber orchestra 1998. *Recordings:* as conductor: Planc, chamber ensemble; Serenata; Incanto; Anton; Alternanze and many others for leading recording companies. *Address:* Mrs. Philharmonica, Piazza del Colosseo 9, 00184 Rome (office); Via Gradoli 56, 00189 Rome, Italy (home). *Telephone:* (06) 77203017 (office); (06) 33266646 (home). *Fax:* (06) 70495523 (office); (06) 33266646 (home). *E-mail:* flavioscogna@libero.it (home).

**SCORSIN, Giuseppe;** Singer (Bass); b. 6 July 1961, Treviso, Italy. *Education:* Studied at Cremona University and the Verdi Conservatory, Milan. *Career:* Debut: Treviso 1990, as Bartolo in Le nozze di Figaro; Appearances at Monte Carlo in Gianni Schicchi, at Rovigo in La Bohème and La Scala in Franchetti's Cristoforo Colombo; Zürich Opera from 1992, in Semiramide, Butterfly, Lohengrin, The Rape of Lucretia, Macbeth, Salome, Otello, Roméo et Juliette and Die Zauberflöte; Lucerne Opera as Philip II in Don Carlo and at Lugano in Mendelssohn's Die Erste Walpurgisnacht; Further roles include Bellini's Oroveso, Rossini's Don Basilio and Ferrando in Il Trovatore, Pistola in Falstaff; Season 1996 in The Gambler at La Scala, as Orbazzano in Tancredi at Winterthur, and Don Basilio throughout Italy; Zürich Opera 1997-98: Sparafucile in Rigoletto; Il Prefetto in Linda di Chamounix (also at Bologna), Raimondo in Lucia di Lammermoor; Ashby in La fanciulla del West; Fabrizio in Wolf-Ferrari's Il Campiello at Bologna, 1998. *Honours:* Winner, 1990 Toti dal Monte Competition, Treviso. *Address:* Via Castellana 1/E, 31100 Treviso, Italy.

**SCOTT, John Gavin,** LVO, MA, MusB, FRCO; British organist and choir conductor; b. 18 June 1956, Wakefield. *Education:* Wakefield Cathedral School, St John's Coll., Cambridge. *Career:* asst, Southwark Cathedral 1979-85; asst sub-organist, St Paul's Cathedral 1979-85, sub-organist 1985-90, organist and Dir of Music 1990-2004; organist and Dir of Music, St Thomas, New York 2004–. *Compositions:* Arise, shine, your light has come, Easter Anthems, O mortal man, How can I keep from singing. *Recordings include:* solo organ albums and recordings with the choir of St Paul's Cathedral. *Publications:* Ash Wednesday to Easter for Choirs (compiler and ed., with Lionel Dakers), Epiphany to All Saints for Choirs (compiler and ed., with Malcolm Archer). *Honours:* Manchester Int. Organ Competition first prize 1978, Leipzig Int. J. S. Bach Competition winner 1984, American Guild of Organists Int. Performer of the Year 1998. *Address:* St Thomas Church, 1 W 53rd Street, New York, NY 10019-5496, USA (office). *Telephone:* (212) 757-7013 (office). *E-mail:* music@saintthomaschurch.org (office).

**SCOTTO, Renata;** Italian singer (soprano); b. 24 Feb. 1935, Savona; m. Lorenzo Anselmi. *Education:* Giuseppe Verdi Conservatory, Milan with Emilio Ghiriardini. *Career:* debut as Violetta, Teatro Nuovo, Milan 1953; joined La Scala opera co. from 1954; London debut at the Stoll Theatre 1957; US debut in Chicago 1960; Covent Garden debut 1962, as Madama Butterfly; roles at the Metropolitan Opera from 1965, directed Butterfly at the Metropolitan 1986 and sang there for the last time in 1987; numerous festival appearances; sang roles in Adriana Lecouvreur, Andrea Chénier, Anna Bolena, Cavalleria Rusticana, Der Rosenkavalier (Marschallin), Edgar, Falstaff, Gilda, I Capuleti e i Montecchi, I Lombardi, I Puritani, I Vespri Siciliani (Helena), L'Elisir d'amore, La Bohème, La Sonnambula (Amina), La Straniera, La Traviata, La Voix Humaine, Lucia di Lammermoor, Madama Butterfly, Manon Lescaut, Otello, Pagliacci, Pirata, Robert le Diable, The Medium, Tosca, Trittico, Turandot. *Publication:* More than a Diva (autobiog.) 1984. *Current Management:* Robert Lombardo Associates, 61 W 62nd Street, Suite 6F, New York, NY 10023, USA. *Telephone:* (212) 586-4453. *Fax:* (212) 581-5771. *E-mail:* lewis@rlombardo.com. *Website:* www.rlombardo.com.

**SCUDERI, Vincenzo;** Singer (Tenor); b. 1961, New York, USA. *Education:* Studied in New York and with Franco Corelli. *Career:* Long Island Opera, Pinkerton, Turiddu, Rodolfo; Appearances at Plovdiv and Zürich as Ishmaele in Nabucco and as Radames, 1987-89; Sang the Duke of Mantua on tour throughout France, 1989; Sang arias from Chénier and Fanciulla del West in Tribute Concert to Franco Corelli, Purchase, New York, 1991; Radames at the Baths of Caracalla, 1991. *Address:* Opera de Marseille, 2 Rue Moliére, 1321 Marseille Cédex 01, France.

**SCULTHORPE, Peter Joshua,** AO, OBE; Australian composer; b. 29 April 1929, Launceston, Tasmania; s. of Joshua Sculthorpe and Edna Moorhouse. *Education:* Launceston Grammar School, Univ. of Melbourne and Wadham Coll., Oxford. *Career:* Lecturer, Sr Lecturer in Music, Univ. of Sydney 1963-68; Visiting Fellow, Yale Univ. 1965-67; Reader in Music, Univ. of Sydney 1968-91; Prof. in Musical Composition and Sydney Moss Lecturer in Music 1992–; Visiting Prof. of Music, Univ. of Sussex 1971-72; commissions from bodies including Australian Broadcasting Comm., Birmingham Chamber Music Soc., Australian Elizabethan Theatre Trust, Australian Ballet, Musica Viva Australia, Australian Chamber Orchestra. *Compositions published include:* The Loneliness of Bunjil 1954, Sonatina 1954, Irkanda I

1955, II 1959, III 1960, IV 1961, Ulterior Motifs, a musical farce and music for various revues 1957–59, Sonata for Viola and Percussion 1960, Theme and Journey's End (from film They Found a Cave) 1962, The Fifth Continent 1963, String Quartet No. 6 1965, No. 7 1966, No. 8 1969, No. 9 1975, No. 10 1983, No. 11 1990, Sun Music I 1965, Sun Music for Voices and Percussion 1966, Sun Music III 1967, IV 1967, Morning Song for the Christ Child 1966, Red Landscape 1966, Tabuh Tabuhan 1968, Autumn Song 1968, Sea Chant 1968, Sun Music II 1969, Orchestral Suite (from film The Age of Consent) 1968, Sun Music Ballet 1968, Love 200 for pop group and orchestra 1970, The Stars Turn 1970, Music for Japan 1970, Dream 1970, Night Pieces 1971, Landscape 1971, How The Stars Were Made 1971, Ketjak 1972, Koto Music I 1973, II 1976, Rites of Passage 1973, The Song of Tailitnama 1974, Postcard from Nourlangie to Clapham Common 1993, From Saibai 1993, Memento Mori for orchestra 1993, From Ubirr for string quartet and didgeridoo 1994; various works for radio, TV, theatre and film. *Honours:* Hon. DLitt (Tasmania, Sussex); Hon. DMus (Melbourne); Australian Council Composers' Award 1975–77, Australian Film Inst. Award 1980, Ted Albert Award 1993, Sir Bernard Heinze Award 1994, ABC Classic FM Listeners' Choice Award 1998 and numerous other awards. *Address:* 91 Holdsworth Street, Woollahra, NSW 2025, Australia.

**SEAMAN, Christopher,** MA, ARCM; British conductor; b. 7 March 1942, Faversham; s. of Albert Edward Seaman and Ethel Margery (née Chambers) Seaman. *Education:* Canterbury Cathedral Choir School, The King's School, Canterbury, King's Coll., Cambridge. *Career:* Prin. Timpanist, London Philharmonic Orchestra 1964–68; Asst Conductor BBC Scottish Symphony Orchestra 1968–70, Chief Conductor 1971–77; Chief Conductor Northern Sinfonia Orchestra 1973–79; Prin. Conductor BBC Robert Mayer Concerts 1978–87; Conductor-in-Residence, Baltimore Symphony Orchestra 1987–98; Chief Guest Conductor Utrecht Symphony Orchestra 1979–83; Music Dir Naples Philharmonic Orchestra, Florida 1993–, Rochester Philharmonic Orchestra, NY 1998–; appears as guest conductor world-wide and has appeared in USA, Germany, France, Holland, Belgium, Italy, Spain, Australia and all parts of the UK. *Honours:* Hon. FGSM 1972. *Address:* 25 Westfield Drive, Glasgow, G52 2SG, Scotland.

**SEARS, Nicholas;** Singer (Tenor); b. 1965, Australia. *Education:* Trinity College, Cambridge; Guildhall School of Music, London. *Career:* Performed as a baritone singing major roles with the Welsh National Opera, Opera North, English National Opera, Scottish Opera and La Monnaie, Brussels; Concert appearances with the Songmakers' Almanac, the London Philharmonic Orchestra, the London Symphony Orchestra and the BBC Symphony and Philharmonic Orchestras; Having changed to tenor, made debut as the Chevalier in Poulenc's Dialogues des Carmélites at Aldeburgh and has since sung Achilles (King Priam) in Antwerp, Lysander (Midsummer Night's Dream), Essex and Spirit of the Mask (Gloriana), Telemachus (Ulisse) and Agenore (Re Pastore) for Opera North, Chevalier (Carmélites) Lucano (Poppea) for Welsh National Opera, Damon (Acis and Galatea) in Frankfurt, Grimoaldo (Rodelinda) for OTC in Ireland, High Priest (Idomeneo), Aufidio (Lucio Silla) and Da-ud (Die Aegyptische Helena) for Garsington, Sailor (Dido and Aeneas) at Covent Garden, and Shepherd (Orfeo) in Lugano; Further engagements for Opera North, Pluto (Orfeus in the Underworld), Grimaldo (Rodelinda) in New York, Gloriana in Barcelona, and Handel's Il Trionfo di Tempo e del Disinganno in Italy, Spain, Mexico, France and Belgium; Sang in Rodelinda at the 2000 Buxton Festival. *Recordings:* On this Bleak Hut by Philip Grange with the Gemini Ensemble; Lysander (Dream); Spirit of the Mask in Gloriana for the BBC. *Address:* 84 Algernon Road, Ladywell, London SE13 7AW, England.

**SEBASTIAN, Bruno;** Singer (Tenor); b. 1947, Udine, Italy. *Education:* Studied with Mario del Monaco. *Career:* Debut: Venice in 1969 in Donizetti's Belisario; Sang widely in Italy from 1970 notably as Arnold in Guillaume Tell at Florence, Wagner in Boito's Mefistofele at Caracalla and Radames at Verona; Sang Cavaradossi at Brussels in 1976, Otello at Basle, Manrico at Boston and the Metropolitan Opera, and Edgardo at Barcelona in 1987; Other roles include the Duke of Mantua, Macduff and Calaf (Helsinki, 1991); Sang Cavaradossi at the Prague State Opera, 2000. *Address:* Deutsche Oper Berlin, Bismarckstrasse 35, 1 Berlin 10, Germany.

**SEBESTA, Ronald;** Clarinettist; b. 22 July 1967, Senica, Czechoslovakia. *Education:* Diploma, Bratislava Conservatory, 1987; Studies, 1988–93, Diploma, 1993, Postgraduate study, Clarinet in the 20th century–virtuality and reality, 1995–, Academy of Music, Bratislava; 8 months study, Boulogne Conservatory, France, 1991–92. *Career:* Co-founder, VENI ensemble for contemporary music, with concerts in Bratislava (Evenings of New Music Festival), Prague, Berlin, Vienna, Perugia, Bucharest; Projects (workshops and concerts) with Younghi Pagh Paan, Siegfried Palm, Hans Deinzer, Louis Andriessen, James Tenney, Hugh Davies; Solo performance of Giacinto Scelsi's Kya, 1990; VENI ensemble recording for Die Hessische Rundfunk in Frankfurt, 1993; 1st Clarinettist, Slovak Radio Symphony Orchestra, Bratislava; Solo performance at Wien Modern Festival, 1994; Co-founder of Vapori del Cuore, improvising group, 1994; Solo performance of Mozart and Brahms Clarinet Quintets, 1995; 1st Clarinet, Cappela Istropolitana, chamber orchestra, Bratislava, 1995–; Co-founder, Opera Aperta ensemble, for classical and contemporary chamber music, 1997–; Solo performances of Mozart Clarinet Concerto, 1997–; mem, International Society for Contemporary Music, Slovak Section. *Recordings:* 2 CDs of VENI ensemble, 1990, 1992; Third CD, VENI ensemble, with music by Daniel Matej, 1995; CD of Opera Aperta ensemble, Postminimal set 2002; CD of Vapori del Cuore, Alpine Songs 2003. *Publications:* Clarinet quintet as a formation of chamber music and its place in the chamber music of classical-romantic tradition, diploma thesis, 1993. *Address:* Fandlyho 1, 81103 Bratislava, Slovakia. *E-mail:* info@operaaperta.com. *Website:* www.operaaperta.com.

**SEBESTYEN, Janos;** Hungarian organist, harpsichordist and academic; *Leading Professor of Harpsichord Faculty, Academy of Music, Budapest;* b. 2 March 1931, Budapest; s. of Dr Alexander Sebestyen and Rose Mannaberg. *Education:* Diploma, Ferenc Liszt Academy, Budapest. *Career:* recitals, radio and TV in Hungary; tours with organ and harpsichord recitals throughout Europe, USA, Japan and Philippines; radio recordings; Organ Four Hand Duo with Istvan Lantos; Founder and Leading Prof. of Harpsichord Faculty, Acad. of Music, Budapest 1970–; musical feature programme series, Radio Budapest; Pres. Jury, Int. Liszt Organ Competition, Budapest 1983, 1988 and 1993; mem. Jury, Organ Competition San Elpidio, Italy, 1998; mem. Jury, Int. Harpsichord Competition, Paris, 1976, Prague 1999, Pres. Budapest 2000. *Recordings:* more than 85 records, including Complete Organ Works of Liszt. *Publications:* Musical Conversations with Miklós Rózsa 1979, ... those Radio years 1925–1995, 1995. *Honours:* Cavaliere of the Italian Repub. 1984, Ufficiale 2003; Commdr, Order Infante Dom Henrique, Portugal 1996; Officer, Order of Isabelle la Católíca, Spain 1999; Cavalier, Order of the Southern Cross, Brazil 2000; Royal Order of the Nordic Star, Sweden 2000; Hungarian Order Officer's Cross 2000; Erkel Prize 1967, Liszt Prize 1974, Merited Artist 1982. *Address:* Fillér-u. 48, 1022 Budapest, Hungary (home). *Telephone:* (1) 3567675 (home). *Fax:* (1) 3567675 (home). *Website:* jsebestyen.org (home).

**SECUNDE, Nadine;** Singer (soprano); b. 21 Dec. 1953, Independence, Ohio, USA. *Education:* Oberlin Conservatory and Indiana University School of Music with Margaret Harshaw; further study in Germany on a Fulbright Scholarship. *Career:* Engaged first at the Hessisches Staatstheater Wiesbaden; Member of the Cologne Opera, where her roles have been Katya Kabanova, Elsa, Agathe, Elisabeth, Chrysothemis and Ariadne; Vienna Staatsoper debut as Sieglinde, Hamburg Staatsoper as Katya; Bayreuth Festival debut 1987, as Elsa in a Werner Herzog production of Lohengrin: returned 1988, as Sieglinde in the Harry Kupfer production of Der Ring des Nibelungen; Covent Garden and Chicago 1988, as Elsa and Elisabeth; returned to London 1990, as Chrysothemis; Sang Elisabeth at Munich, 1994, (also televised); Concert engagements include the Choral Symphony with the Los Angeles Philharmonic, conducted by Previn, and with the Orchestre de Paris under Barenboim; Penderecki's Dies Irae with the Warsaw Philharmonic; Sang Chrysothemis at Covent Garden (1997), and in the 1997 Munich premiere of Henze's Venus and Adonis; Netherlands Opera 1998 as Brünnhilde in Götterdämmerung; Sang Chrysothemis at Munich (2000) and Isolde at the Teatro Colón, Buenos Aires; Brünnhilde at Bilbao, 2002. *Current Management:* Ingpen & Williams Ltd, 7 St George's Court, 131 Putney Bridge Road, London, SW15 2PA, England.

**SEERS, Mary;** Singer (Soprano); b. 1958, England. *Education:* Studied at Girton College, Cambridge (choral exhibitioner) and in Rome and London. *Career:* Appearances with the Landini Consort, the Consort of Musique, The Scholars and the Hilliard Ensemble; Festival engagements at Aix-en-Provence, Schleswig-Holstein and Greenwich; Tour of the United Kingdom and Italy 1988 with Pärt's St John Passion; Concerts in Sydney and Tokyo 1989 with John Eliot Gardiner and the Monteverdi Choir; Concerts include Bach B minor Mass, Wrocław (Poland) with City of London Sinfonia; Other repertoire includes Mozart's C minor Mass, the Monteverdi Vespers (Bruges Festival), Messiah (St Martin in the Fields) and music by Finzi and Purcell; Further engagements at the Almeida, Cheltenham and Orkney Festivals and concerts with the Scottish Chamber Orchestra and the East of England Orchestra; US concerts in Chicago and New York, Pärt's St John Passion; Opera: with Music Theatre Wales, role of Madeleine in Philip Glass, The Fall of The House of Usher; Festivals: Warsaw Contemporary Music Festival (Pärt Passio), 1992; Television: Took part in BBC 2 documentary with English Chamber Orchestra and Corydon Singers; Monteverdi Vespers with The Sixteen. *Address:* c/o Music Theatre Wales, 5 Llandaff Road, Cardiff, CF11 9NF, Wales.

**SEGAL, Uri;** Israeli orchestral conductor; *Music Director, Louisville Orchestra;* b. 7 March 1944, Jerusalem; s. of Alexander and Nehama Segal; m. Ilana Finkelstein 1966; one s. three d. *Education:* Rubin Acad., Jerusalem and Guildhall School of Music, London. *Career:* debut with Seajillands Symphony Orchestra, Copenhagen 1969; Prin. Conductor Bournemouth Symphony Orchestra 1980–82, Philharmonia Hungarica 1981–85; Music Dir Israeli Chamber Orchestra, Chautauqua Festival, NY 1990–, Louisville Orchestra, Ky 1999–; Founder/Chief Conductor Century Orchestra, Osaka 1990–98, Laureate Conductor 1998–; fmr Prin. Guest Conductor Stuttgart Radio Symphony; orchestras conducted include Berlin Philharmonic, Stockholm Philharmonic, Concertgebouw, Orchestre de Paris, Vienna Symphony, Israel Philharmonic, London Symphony, London Symphony, London Philharmonic, Philharmonia, Orchestra de la Suisse Romande, Warsaw Philharmonic, Spanish Nat. Orchestra, Pittsburgh Symphony, Chicago Symphony, Detroit Symphony, Dalls Symphony, Houston Symphony, Montreal Symphony and Rochester Symphony; tours have included Austria, Switzerland, Spain, Italy, France, UK, Scandinavia and the Far East; operatic debut conducting The Flying Dutchman at Sante Fe Opera 1973; has since conducted opera in Italy, France, Germany, Japan, Israel and USA; recent guest appearances with Hamburg Symphony, Düsseldorf Symphony, Polish

Nat. Orchestra, Orchestre Nat. de Lille, Rochester Philharmonic, Detroit Symphony Orchestra. *Recordings:* Mahler Symphony No. 4 (with NZ Symphony Orchestra), music by Britten (Bournemouth Symphony), Stravinsky's Firebird Suite and Symphony in C with the Suisse Romande Orchestra), Mozart Piano Concertos with Radu Lupu and the English Chamber Orchestra, Schumann's Piano Concerto with Ashkenazy and the London Symphony, Beethoven Piano Concertos with Rudolf Firkusny and the Philharmonia. *Honours:* First Prize, Int. Mitropoulos Conducting Competition, New York 1969. *Current Management:* Michal Schmidt Artists Management, 59e 54th Street, Suite 83, New York, NY 10022, USA. *Website:* www .louisvilleorchestra.org (office).

**SEGERSTAM, Leif;** Conductor and Composer; b. 2 March 1944, Vasa, Finland. *Education:* Violin, Piano, Conducting, Composition, Sibelius Academy, Helsinki until 1963; Conducting diploma, Juilliard School of Music, New York, USA, 1964; Postgraduate diploma, 1965. *Career:* Debut: Violin soloist Helsinki, 1963; Conductor, Royal Opera Stockholm, 1968–72 and Musical Director, 1971–72; 1st Conductor, Deutsche Oper Berlin, 1972–73; General Manager Finnish National Opera, 1973–74; Chief Conductor ORF (Austrian Radio) Vienna 1975–82; Musical Director, Finnish Radio Symphony Orchestra, Helsinki, 1977–87: Principal Guest Conductor from 1987; General Music Director, Staatsphilharmonie Rhenland-Pfalz 1983–89; Honorary Conductor, 1989; Conductor of the Danish Radio Symphony Orchestra from 1988; Chief Conductor of the Helsinki Philharmonic Orchestra, 1995–; Led Tannhäuser at the 1997 Savonlinna Festival and began a new Ring cycle at Stockholm with Das Rheingold; Conducted Die Walküre and Siegfried at Helsinki, 1998; mem, Royal Academy of Music, Sweden. *Compositions include:* Divertimento for strings 1963; 6 Cello Concertos; 3 Piano Concertos; 57 Symphonies 1977–98 (nos. 20–25 to be given without conductor); 8 Violin Concertos; 6 Double Concertos; Many works for orchestra under title Composed orchestral works called Thought, the most famous being, Monumental Thoughts, Martti Tavela in memorium; Orchestral Diary Sheets, 5 Songs of Experience after Blake and Auden for soprano and orchestra 1971; 28 String Quartets; 3 Piano Trios; 4 String Trios; Episodes for various instrumental combinations. *Recordings:* Works by Mahler, Sibelius, Brahms, Scriabin, Petterson, Schnittke, Rott, Ruders, Koechlin, Schmitt, Roussel, Caplet, Roger-Ducasse and own compositions. *Honours:* Second Prize with Symphony IV, Sibelius, 1991; Record of the Year, Sibelius III symphony (Chandos), 1992. *Address:* c/o Jankko, Tölögatan 7 A5, 00100 Helsinki, Finland.

**SEIFERT, Gerd-Heinrich;** Horn player; b. 17 Oct. 1931, Hamburg, Germany; m. 29 June 1957, 3 s., 1 d. *Education:* Music High School, Hamburg, 1944–49; Studied horn with Albert Doscher. *Career:* Debut: Soloist, Horn Concerto (Strauss), 1948; Substitute, Hamburg Philharmonic Orchestra, 1947–49; Solo Horn, Düsseldorfer Symphoniker, 1949–64; Solo Horn, Bayreuth Festival, 1961; Solo Horn, Berlin Philharmonic Orchestra, 1964–; Performed with Düsseldorfer Waldhorn Quartett, also 13 Bläser Philharmonic Orchestra and Philharmonic Octet, Berlin; Teacher of Horn, Music High School, Berlin, 1970–. *Recordings:* With Berlin Philharmonic Orchestra/Octet (Hindemith); Octet, Nonet (Spohr); Serenade for 13 Wind instruments by Mozart, and other Chamber music; Concert Piece for 4 horns (Schumann). *Contributions:* Brass Bulletin. *Honours:* 1st Prize, ARD Competition, Munich, 1956; 125 Siegfried Calls at Bayreuth Festival since 1961; Grand Prix du Disque. *Address:* Xantenerstrasse 1, 1000 Berlin 15, Germany.

**SEIFERT, Ingrid;** Austrian violinist; b. 1952. *Education:* studied violin in Salzburg and Vienna. *Career:* played with the Concentus Musicus, Vienna and studied further in Netherlands; With Charles Medlam co-founded London Baroque, 1978; With London Baroque led the first performance of Scarlatti's Una Villa di Tuscolo and a revival of Gli Equivoci Sembiante, for the BBC; Season 1990–91 included: Dido and Aeneas at Paris Opéra; Music by Blow and Lully, Opéra Comique; Aci, Galatea e Polifemo in Spain, Netherlands and England; Cantatas by Handel and Rameau in Austria, Sweden and Germany, with Emma Kirkby; Other recent repertoire includes: Charpentier Messe de Minuit; 4 Violin music by Telemann, Vivaldi and Wassenaar; Bach Brandenburg Concertos; Monteverdi Tancredi and Clorinda; Salzburg Festival debut, 1991, with music by Mozart; Further festival engagements at Bath, Beaune, Versailles, Ansbach, Innsbruck and Utrecht. *Recordings:* Marais La Gamme; Theile Matthew Passion; Bach Trio Sonatas; Charpentier Theatre Music; Handel Aci, Galatea e Polifemo; Blow Venus and Adonis; Purcell Chamber Music, (Harmonia Mundi); Purcell Fantasias; Bach Violin Sonatas; Monteverdi Orfeo; Handel German Arias; A Vauxhall Gardens Entertainment; English Music of the 18th Century; François Couperin Apotheose de Lulli, Corelli Chamber Music; Complete Trios of Handel, Purcell; Chamber Music by Lawes; Pachelbel, Complete Chamber Music; Vivaldi Sonatas op. 1; Handel Latin Motets, with Emma Kirkby; Bach Trio sonatas; Couperin Apotheose de Lulli, Corelli etc; Rameau Pièces de Clavecin en concert. *Address:* Brick Kiln Cottage, Hollington, nr Newbury, Berks., RG20 9XX, England.

**SEIFFERT, Peter;** Singer (Tenor); b. 4 Jan. 1954, Düsseldorf, Germany; m. Lucia Popp, 1986, deceased 1993. *Education:* Studied at the Robert Schumann Musikhochschule Düsseldorf. *Career:* Sang first with the Deutsche Oper am Rhein Düsseldorf in Der Wildschütz and Fra Diavolo; Member of the Deutsche Oper Berlin from 1982, notably as Lensky, Jenik in The Bartered Bride, Huon (Oberon) and Faust; Bayerische Staatsoper Munich 1983, as Fenton in Die Lustigen Weiber von Windsor: has returned in Der Barber von Bagdad by Cornelius and as Narraboth and Lohengrin; Vienna Staatsoper and La Scala Milan debuts 1984; Covent Garden debut 1988, as Parsifal in a new

production of Wagner's opera conducted by Bernard Haitink; Season 1988/89 sang Faust at the Deutsche Oper Berlin and Lohengrin in Munich (repeated 1990); Sang at Salzburg 1992, as Narraboth; Concert engagements include Mozart's Requiem with Giulini in London, and the Choral Symphony with Muti in Philadelphia; Sang Walther von Stolzing in Die Meistersinger at the 1996 Bayreuth Festival; Season 1998 with Max in Der Freischütz at Rome; Season 2000–01 as Lohengrin at the Deutsche Oper Berlin, Walther in Munich in, Rienzi in Dresden and Erik for Zürich Opera; Parsifal at Bayreuth, 2002. *Recordings:* Elijah; Zar und Zimmerman; Matteo in Arabella, conducted by Jeffrey Tate; Die Fledermaus, conducted by Domingo; Gianni Schicchi (Patanè); Erik in Der fliegende Holländer, conducted by Pinchas Steinberg; The Choral Symphony (Muti) and Mozart's Mass in C Minor with Levine; Mendelssohn's Lobgesang and Beethoven's Symphony No. 9 with Sawallisch; Solo Records of Operetta; Solo Record of Opera; Freischitz; Fidelio; Liszt, Faust Symphony, conducted by Simon Rattle. *Honours:* Kammersänger of the Bavarian State Opera. *Address:* Bavarian Staatsoper, Maximilianstrasse, Munich, Germany.

**SEIFRIED, Reinhard;** Conductor; b. 25 July 1945, Freising, Germany; m. Fenna Kügel, 31 Oct 1991, 2 d. *Education:* Hochschule für Musik in Munich, trade examination and master class for conducting; Assistant Conductor with Rudolf Kempe, Rafael Kubelik, Karl Richter, Leonard Bernstein. *Career:* Debut: Conductor in Staatstheater am Gärtnerplatz, Munich, 1976; Conductor, Nürnberg, 1986; Chief Conductor, Remscheider Symphoniker, 1991; Music Director, and Chief Conductor of Oldenburgisches Staatsorchester, 1993–; Guest Conductor, Europe, Japan and USA. *Recordings:* Mendelssohn-Bartholdy, all symphonies with Irish National Symphony Orchestra, Dublin; Smetana, Ma Vlast, with Slovak State Philharmonic Košice. *Current Management:* FAME Management, Claudius Hirt, Lucerne. *Address:* Oldenburgisches Staatstheater, Theaterwall 18, 26122 Oldenburg, Germany.

**SEILER, Mayumi;** Violinist; b. 1963, Japan (German/Japanese parentage). *Education:* Studied in Japan and at the Salzburg Mozarteum, with Sándor Végh. *Career:* Concerts with the Australian Chamber Orchestra, Hong Kong Philharmonic, Royal Philharmonic, and the Academy of St Martin in the Fields at the 1994 London Proms. *Recordings include:* Concertos as director/soloist with the City of London Sinfonia (Virgin Classics). *Honours:* Christina Rechter Steiner Prize, Salzburg Mozarteum. *Address:* City of London Sinfonia, 11 Drum Street, London E1 12H, England.

**SEILTGEN, Annette;** Singer (Mezzo-Soprano); b. 26 June 1964, Wuppertal, Germany. *Education:* Leopold Mozart Conservatory in Augsburg and the Studio of the Bavarian State Opera. *Career:* Kassel Opera, 1990–92, as Rosina, Wellgunde in The Ring and Strauss's Composer; Theater am Gärtnerplatz, Munich, 1992–96; as Hansel, Cherubino, Rosina and Cornet in Matthus's Die Weise von Liebe und Tod; Guest appearances from 1989 at Mannheim, Heidelberg, Bielefeld, and Hannover notably as Octavian in Der Rosenkavalier; Deutsche Oper am Rhein at Düsseldorf from 1996, with Andronico in Handel's Tamerlano, 1998; Guest appearance in Madrid at the Theatro Real as Sextus in Mozart's La Clemenza di Tito, 1999; Season 1999–2000 as Dusseldorf as Olga in Three Sisters by Peter Eötvös, Ruggiero in Alcina and three roles in Lulu; Guest appearances in Nice and Santiago de Chile; Other roles include Don Ramiro in La finta giardineira by Mozart. *Address:* c/o Deutsche Oper am Rhein, Operhaus Düsseldorf, Heinrich-Heine-Alle 16a, 40213 Düsseldorf, Germany.

**SEIPP, Joachim;** German singer (bass baritone); b. 1956, Pohlheim; one d. *Education:* studied with Prof. Martin Gründler, Frankfurt Musikhochschule, Prof. Carla Castellani, Milan and with Milkana Nikolova, Vienna. *Career:* Sang at Kiel Opera, 1982–86; Karlsruhe 1985–86; Hanover 1986–91; Landestheater Innsbruck from 1991; Repertoire; Marquese di Posa, Rigoletto, Iago, Scarpia, Wotan in Ring, Four Villains in Les Contes d'Hoffmann, Carmina Burana by Carl Orff, Germont, Ford in Falstaff and Mozart's Count; Title role in Dallapiccola's Il Prigioniero; Guest appearances at the Ludwigsburg Festival as the Count, 1987 and 1989; Sang at Wiesbaden in Henze's Das verratene Meer, 1990; Der Kaiser von Atlantis by Victor Ullmann, La Monnaie, Brussels; Sang at Innsbruck as Iago (1999) and Albert in Werther, 2001; Der Fliegende Holländer in Domstufen Festival in Erfurt under the direction of Werner Herzog; Further roles include Kurwenal in Tristan and Isolde and Pizarro in Fidelio under Brigitte Fassbaender and Conte Luna in Il Trovatore and Amonasro in Aida; Concert repertory includes Schubert's Schwanengesang, Wolf's Italian Song Book and all great oratorios and major concert pieces. *Recordings:* Carmina Burana with Orchestra Tenerife under Victor Pablo 1996, Die Frau Ohne Schatten under Fassbaender 2004. *Honours:* First Prize, VdmK Gesangswettbewerb, Berlin. *Address:* c/o Landestheater Innsbruck, Rennweg 2, 6020 Innsbruck (office); Birchach 20, 6112 Wattenberg, Austria (home). *Telephone:* (5224) 52309 (home). *E-mail:* seipp .austria@web.de (home).

**SEIVEWRIGHT, (Robert) Peter,** BA, MA; concert pianist and lecturer; b. 11 July 1954, Skipton, England. *Education:* Worcester College, Oxford; FRCO Diploma, Royal Northern College of Music with Ryszard Bakst. *Career:* Tutor, University of Keele, 1979–83; Instructor in Music, University of Leicester, 1980–84; Lecturer in Music, Royal Scottish Academy of Music and Drama, 1984–; University Pianist, University of Strathclyde, 1990–93; Concerts throughout the United Kingdom, Ireland, Norway, Germany, Belgium, Denmark (eight recital tours), Latvia, Estonia, Viet Nam, Australia (five concert tours) and China, including Huddersfield Contemporary Music

Festival 1983, 1984, Tivoli Concert Hall and Århus Festival, Denmark, 1986, Munch-Museum, Oslo, 1986; Heilbronn International Piano Forum 1993, Germany International Masters of the Keyboard series, Bruges, Belgium, 1994, International All-Stars Piano Festival, Liepaja, Latvia, 1997, Concerto appearances with leading orchestras including Hallé Orchestra, Bradford Chamber Orchestra, Scottish Sinfonietta, Strathclyde Sinfonia, Paragon Ensemble, Liepaja Symphony Orchestra, recordings BBC Scotland, BBC Radio 3, Radio Denmark, 3MBs and ABC (Australia). *Recordings include:* Contemporary Scottish Piano Music; Complete Piano Music of Carl Nielsen, 2CDs, 1995; Piano Music by Victor Bendix, 1998; Complete Piano Sonatas of Baldassare Galuppi 1706–1785, 10 CDs; Variations and Fugue on a theme of Telemann and Variations and Fugue on a theme of Bach by Max Reger, 1999. *Current Management:* Tivoli Festival Agency, 20 H. C. Andersens Boulevard, Copenhagen V, Denmark. *Address:* The Old Joinery, Lintfieldbank, Coalburn, Lanarkshire ML11 0NJ, Scotland.

**SELBIG, Ute;** Singer (Soprano); b. 18 Aug. 1960, Dresden, Germany. *Education:* Dresden Musikhochschule until 1985. *Career:* Sang with Dresden Kreuzchor; Tours of Japan, 1988 and Canada, 1991; Member of Dresden Opera from 1985, as Zerlina, Nannetta, Aennchen in Der Freischütz, Musetta, Susanna, Sophie in Der Rosenkavalier, Pamina and Fiordiligi; Guest appearances throughout Europe and at Los Angeles and St Louis; Zdenka in Arabella at Geneva, 1994; Guardian of the Threshold in Die Frau ohne Schatten at Dresden, 1997; Season 2000–01 at Dresden as Donna Elvira, Pamina, Marzelline in Fidelio and Ilia in Idomeneo (concert). *Recordings:* Mozart Arias; Sacred Music by Mozart; Das Lied von der Glocke by Bruch. *Honours:* Prizewinner in competitions at Prague and Leipzig. *Address:* c/o Semper Oper Dresden, Theaterplatz 2, 01067 Dresden, Germany.

**SELBY, Kathryn Shauna,** BA, MM; concert pianist; b. 20 Sept. 1962, Sydney, Australia. *Education:* Sydney Conservatorium of Music, Bryn Mawr College, PA, Curtis Institute of Music, Juilliard School of Music. *Career:* debut, YMCA, 92nd Street, NY, 1981; Wigmore Hall in London in 1987; Appearances with Sydney Symphony Orchestra, Philadelphia Orchestra, Pittsburgh, St Louis and Cincinnati Symphony Orchestras, Calgary and Erie Philharmonic, Indianapolis Symphony Orchestra, Shreveport Symphony Orchestra, among others; As Chamber Musician at Spoleto Festival, Australia in 1986, Marlboro Music Festival, Caramoor Festival, Concerto Soloists of Philadelphia, Hartford Chamber Orchestra, Kennedy Center Washington; Founding Member of Selby, Pini, Pereira Trio, Australia with appearances and tours, Musica Viva in Australia, 1985, 1987; ABC Film, Mozart in Delphi with Australian Chamber Orchestra for ABC Australia; Recitals in New York, Washington DC, Seattle, Portland, Pittsburgh, Philadelphia, Sydney, London and Munich.

**SELBY, Philip;** British composer; b. 6 Feb. 1948, s. of George Selby and Sarah Selby (née Knott); m. Rosanna Burrai 1974; one s. *Education:* Manor Park Grammar School, Nuneaton, Royal Northern Coll. of Music. *Career:* composition studies with G. Petrassi, C. Camilleri and Karlheinz Stockhausen; appeared as guitar soloist, Birmingham Town Hall 1966, Royal Albert Hall, London 1970, All-India Radio and TV, Pakistani TV, Youth Palace, Tehran, Istanbul Univ.; début as composer with first performance of From the Fountain of Youth (for guitar and chamber orch.), Leamington 1975; mem. British Acad. of Composers and Songwriters, Inc. Soc. of Musicians, Performing Right Soc. *Compositions include:* Suite for guitar 1965–67, Two Meditations for Piano 1972–74, Symphonic Dance for orchestra 1973, Ten Little Studies for Guitar Solo 1973–76, Fantasia for guitar 1974, Rhapsody for piano and orchestra 1975, Three Scottish Songs for voice and violin 1975, A Nature Meditation for violin and small orchestra, Guitar Concerto 1976–77, Suite for String Quartet 1977–78, Sonatina for piano 1978, Spirit of the Earth for flute 1978, Branch Touches Branch, pastorale 1979, Isa Upanishad (cantata sacra for double chorus and orchestra) 1979–87, Sonata for timpani 1980, Greek Suite for Oboe Solo 1981, Siddhartha (dance symphony) 1981–84, Logos for trumpet 1982, Ring Out Ye Bells (carol) 1988, Symphony of Sacred Images (for soprano and bass soli, double chorus and orchestra) 1986–92, Anthem for Gibraltar (unison voices and organ) 1994, Beatus Vir (motet) 1995, String Quartet No. 1 (Non Potho Reposare, Amore Coro) 1996–97, Autoritratto Vittorio Alfieri (for soprano, violin and guitar) 1998, Sonata Atma Brahma for Piano 1998–99, Fear no more the Heat of the Sun, madrigal 2001, Agape for solo violin 2001–02, Agape II for solo viola 2002, Eight Poems of J. G. Brown, song cycle 2005. *Honours:* Chevalier Ordre Souverain et Militaire de la Milice du Saint Sépulcre 1988. *Address:* Hill Cottage, Via 1 Maggio 93, 00068 Rignano Flaminio, Rome, Italy. *Telephone:* (0761) 507945.

**SELEZNEV, Georgi;** singer (bass); b. 21 Oct. 1938, Tbilisi, Georgia. *Education:* studied at Toilisi and the Leningrad Conservatory. *Career:* bass soloist at the Maly Opera Leningrad 1972–78; appearances with the Bolshoi Opera Russia 1978–, on tour to Western Europe and USA; solo debut in the West as Konchak and Galitzky in Prince Igor at Trieste, 1985; returned as Dosifei, in Khovanshchina; title role in Salammbô by Mussorgsky for RAI in Rome; appeared in all international tours of Bolshoi Company in recent years; engagements such as: Verdi Requiem under Chailly, with Royal Concertgebouw Orchestra in Amsterdam; Oroveso, with Joan Sutherland as Norma, at Opera Pacific and with Michigan Opera; Boris at Wiesbaden Festival; Pimen at Opéra du Rhin, Strasbourg, repeated at Bordeaux, 1993; returned to Bordeaux as Timur, in production of Turandot, director Alain Lombard, 1994; Boris Godunov at St Petersburg, 1997. *Recordings include:* Salammbô, Oroveso in Norma. *Honours:* Lenin Prize.

**SELIG, Franz-Josef;** Singer (Bass); b. 11 July 1962, Germany. *Education:* Studied at the Cologne Musikhochschule with Claudio Nicolai. *Career:* Concert Tours of Italy, Germany, France, Switzerland, Netherlands and Turkey; Engaged at the Essen Opera from 1989, as the King in Aida, Herr Reich in Die Lustige Weiber von Windsor and Sarastro in Die Zauberflöte; Sang Mozart's Speaker at Frankfurt, 1991, and Fafner in Das Rheingold at Covent Garden; USA debut in Fidelio at San Francisco, 1995; St John Passion with Solti, 1997–98; Season 1998 with Mozart's Sarastro, and Samiel and Hermit in Der Freischütz at La Scala; Season 1999–2000 as Mozart's Commendatore at La Scala and the Vienna Staatsoper, Camillo in the premiere of Wintermärchen by Boesmans, at Brussels, and King Marke for the Deutsche Oper Berlin. *Recordings include:* Die Zauberflöte; Sacred Music by Mozart.

**SELLARS, Peter,** BA; American theatre and opera director; b. 27 Sept. 1957, Pittsburgh, PA. *Education:* Harvard Univ. *Career:* Dir Boston Shakespeare Co. 1983–84; Dir and Man. American Nat. Theater at J. F. Kennedy Center, Washington, DC 1984–; Artistic Adviser, Boston Opera Theatre 1990; Fellow MacArthur Foundation, Chicago 1983. *Productions include:* Ajax, Armida, Così fan tutte, The Death of Klinghoffer, Die Zauberflöte, Don Giovanni, The Electrification of the Soviet Union, Le Grand Macabre, Idomeneo, The Lighthouse, The Marriage of Figaro, Mathis der Maler, Merchant of Venice, The Mikado, El Niño, Nixon in China, Orlando, The Rake's Progress, Saul and Orlando, St Francois d'Assise, Tannhäuser, Theodora, Zangezi. *Address:* American National Theater, Kennedy Center, Washington, DC 20566, USA.

**SELLHEIM, Eckart;** Pianist, Fortepianist and Accompanist; b. 29 Oct. 1939, Danzig. *Education:* Hamburg Conservatory; Piano, Accompanying, Musikhochschule, Cologne; Concert Diploma, 1963; Musicology, Music History, History of Art, Theatre, Cologne University. *Career:* Lecturer, Rheinische Musikschule, Cologne, 1963–69; Professor, Piano, Musikhochschule, Cologne, 1969–83; Piano, Piano Chamber Music, University of Michigan, Ann Arbor, USA, 1983–89; Piano Accompanying, Director of Accompanying, Arizona State University, Tempe, 1989–; Concert tours: Germany, Austria, England, France, Spain, Italy, Poland, Netherlands, USA, Latin America, Middle East; Duo with Friedrich-Jürgen Sellheim, Cello, 1965–; Several 100 Radio recordings, Germany, Europe, USA. *Recordings include:* With Fr J Sellheim, Cello: Mendelssohn, 2 Cello Sonatas; 2 Variations Concertantes; Lied Ohne Worte, 1976; Brahms, 2 Cello Sonatas, 1977; Schumann, Fantasiestücke, Adagio und Allegro, Stücke im Volkston, 1978; Schubert, Arpeggione-Sonata, Chopin, Cello Sonata, Polonaise Brillante, Grand Duo Concertant, 1980; Ravel, Violin Sonata, 1985; Transcriptions of Chopin, Bach, Weber, Gluck, Schumann, Schubert, Rakoczi March, also Brahms Transcriptions by Max Reger and Theodor Kirchner, 1990. *Publications:* Editor, Spielbuch für Klavier. *Contributions:* Friedrich Gruetzmacher, 1966; Oskar von Pander, 1968; Instrumentale Ausbildung-Klavier, 1980; Die Klavierwerke W Fr Bachs, Concerto, 1984. *Address:* 2416 West Nopal Avenue, Mesa, AZ 85202, USA.

**SELLICK, Phyllis,** OBE, FRAM, FRCM; British concert pianist; b. 16 June 1911, Newbury Park, Essex; m. Cyril Smith 1937 (died 1974); one s. (deceased) one d. *Education:* Glenarm Coll., Ilford, Royal Acad. of Music and in Paris. *Career:* Prof., Royal Coll. of Music, London; Vice-Pres. Inc. Soc. of Musicians Centenary Year 1982–83; Malcolm Arnold, Bliss, Gordon Jacob, Tippett and Vaughan Williams have dedicated works to her; adjudicator of numerous important piano competitions, including BBC Young Musician of the Year and Leeds Int. Piano Competition; appeared as pianist on radio in film 49th Parallel 1941. *Radio:* talk on piano playing (BBC Radio 3) 2001, Castaway on Desert Island Discs (BBC Radio 4) 2002. *Address:* Beverley House, 29A Ranelagh Avenue, Barnes, London, SW13 0BN, England. *Telephone:* (20) 8876-5143.

**SELTZER, Dov;** Composer, Conductor, Orchestrator and Musician; b. 26 Jan. 1932, Iasi, Romania; m. Grazielle Fontana, 15 May 1968, 1 step-s. *Education:* Piano, Theory, privately, 1944–47; Piano, General Music, Haifa and Tel-Aviv Conservatory, 1949–50; Composition with Mordecai Setter, 1950–53, with Herbert Bruen, 1952–54; Diploma, Composition, Mannes College of Music, 1958; BS, Music, State University of New York, 1960. *Career:* Music Director, Composer, Israel Army Nachal Theatrical Group, 1950–53; Music Teacher, Afek School, Haifa; Arranger, Music Director, Oranim Zabar Folk Singers and Theodore Bikel for Elektra, Columbia Co, USA, 1956–58; Music Teacher, Mannes College of Music, New York, 1958–60; Freelance Composer, Conductor for theatre, musicals, films, records, Israel, USA, France, Italy, England, Germany, elsewhere; Conducted Israel Philharmonic and Jerusalem Symphony Orchestra, concert of his music, 1987; Music Director, Conductor, Three Penny Opera film version, 1988;. *Compositions include:* 15 musicals including: The Megillah, 1966; Kazablan, 1967; I Like Mike, 1968; To Live Another Summer, 1971; Comme la neige en été, 1974; Stempeniu, symphonic poem, 1985; This Scroll, cantata for Ben Gurion centenary, 1986; Music for Thieves In The Night, German television series, 1988; The Assisi Underground; Hassidic Rhapsody, violin solo, symphonic orchestra, 1989–90; The Gold of the Ashes, rhapsodic poem, 1991–92; Notre Dame de Paris, opera after novel by Victor Hugo, 1993–94; Lament to Yitzhak (requiem in memory of Yitzhak Rabin) world premiere, 1998, Mann Auditorium Tel-Aviv, Zubin Mehta conducting the Israel Philharmonic Orchestra. *Address:* 19 Netiv Hamazalot, Jaffa, Israel.

**SELWAY, Emma;** Singer (Mezzo-soprano); b. 1970, England. *Education:* Royal Academy, London; National Opera Studio. *Career:* Debut: Kate Pinkerton in Madama Butterfly for English National Opera, 1995; Sang Cefisa in Rossini's Ermione at Glyndebourne, 1995 (Musician in Manon Lescaut, 1999); Glyndebourne Tour 1996 and 1999, as Mozart's Dorabella and Sesto; Further engagements as Dorabella for Opera North, Idamante for Opera Northern Ireland and Cenerentola for Welsh National Opera; Sang Charlotte in Die Soldaten by Zimmermann, and Strauss's Octavian for English National Opera; Concerts include Debussy's Le Martyre de St Sebastian (Hallé Orchestra) and Mahler's 2nd symphony, with the Jersey Symphonic Orchestra; Anna in Weill's Seven Deadly Sins at Batignano. *Address:* c/o English National Opera. St Martin's Lane, London, WC2, England.

**SEMENCHUK, Ekaterina;** Singer (Mezzo-soprano); b. 1976, Minsk, Russia. *Education:* Minsk Music School; Byelorussian Music Academy; St Petersburg Conservatoire. *Career:* Young Singers' Academy of the Mariinsky Theatre, St Petersburg, from 1999; Roles have included the Nurse and Olga in Eugene Onegin, Marta in Iolanta, Puccini's Suzuki, Lyubasha in The Tsar's Bride by Rimsky-Korsakov and Pauline in The Queen of Spades; Sang Lehl in Rimsky's The Snow Maiden and Sonya in War and Peace with the Kirov Opera at Covent Garden, 2000. *Honours:* Diplomas for opera and recital singing, International Dvórak Competition, Prague, 1997; Winner, International Obraztsova competition, 1999. *Address:* c/o Kirov Opera, Mariinsky Theatre, 1 Theatre Square, St Petersburg, Russia.

**SEMKOW, Jerzy (Georg),** MA (Mus); Polish conductor; b. 12 Oct. 1928, Radomsko; s. of Aleksander Semkow and Waleria Sienczak Semkow. *Education:* Jagiellonian Univ., Kraków, State Higher School of Music (student of A. Malawski), Kraków and Leningrad Music Conservatoire. *Career:* Asst Conductor, Leningrad Philharmonic Orch. 1954–56; Conductor, Bolshoi Opera and Ballet Theatre, Moscow 1956–58; Artistic Dir and Prin. Conductor, Warsaw Nat. Opera 1960–62; Perm. Conductor, Danish Royal Opera, Copenhagen 1965–68; Prin. Conductor Italian Radio and TV (RAI) Orchestra, Rome 1969–73; Conductor Cleveland Symphony Orchestra 1970–71; Musical Dir and Prin. Conductor Saint Louis Symphony Orchestra 1975–; Artistic Dir and Prin. Conductor, Rochester Philharmonic Orchestra, New York 1986–; Guest Conductor Berlin Philharmonic, London Philharmonic, Nat. Orchestra of Madrid, Orchestre de la Suisse Romande, Orchestre Nat. de France and the orchestras of Paris, Strasbourg, Lyon, Bordeaux, Monte Carlo, Jerusalem, Stockholm, Frankfurt, St Petersburg, Toronto, New York, Cleveland, Chicago, Boston, Detroit, Washington, Cincinatti, Houston, Dallas, Pittsburgh, Rochester, Utah and Minneapolis; engagements at Covent Garden, La Scala, Milan, Staatsoper, Berlin, Staatsoper, Vienna, Teatro Real, Madrid, Paris Opera, Teatro del Opera, Rome, Maggio Musicale, Florence, La Fenice, Venice, Grand Theatre, Geneva, etc.; master classes at Yale Univ., Manhattan School of Music, New York. *Recordings include:* Boris Godunov (Musorgski) with Polish Nat. Radio Symphony Orchestra, Kniaź (Borodin) with Group from Opera of Sofia, Symphony No. 3 and Symphonic Concerto No. 4 (Szymanowski), Symphony Nos 2 and 3 (Scriabin) with Nat. Philharmonic Symphony Orchestra, Warsaw, Beethoven works with Saint Louis Orchestra, Mozart Symphonies (Disque d'Or). *Honours:* Commdr Cross, Order of Polonia Restituta, Ordre des Arts et des Lettres. *Current Management:* c/o ICM Artists, 40 West 57th Street, New York, NY 10019, USA. *Website:* www.icmtalent.com/musperf/profiles/60228.html.

**SEMMINGSEN, Tuva;** Norwegian singer (mezzo-soprano); b. 1975. *Education:* Royal Danish Opera, with Prof. Kirsten Buhl-Moller, Ingrid Bjoner and Anthony Rolfe Johnson. *Career:* professional debut in role of Cherubino (Figaro) at Theatre Royal, Copenhagen and Gran Teatro Fenice, Venice 2001; appeared as Angelina (La Cenerentola), Heksemutter Mortensen, Parsifal, Maskarade, Rosina (Il Barbiere di Siviglia) and Sesto (Giulio Cesare) Royal Danish Opera; Feodor (Boris Godunov) for Teatro Nacional de Sao Carlos; British operatic debut in La Gazzetta by Rossini, Garsington Opera; concerts: Mozart and Rossini arias with Gothenburg Symphony Orchestra under Mario Venzago, Schubert's Mass in E Flat with Danish Nat. Symphony and Choir under Andras Schiff, Mozart Requiem with Trondheim Symphony Orchestra, Juditha Triumphans with The King's Consort, Judas Maccabaeus with Danish Nat. Symphony Orchestra, Bach Cantatas with Danish Radio Symphony Orchestra and Haydn's Stabat Mater for Danish Radio Sinfonietta. *Recordings include:* Vivaldi's Sum in Medio and Gloria e Imeneo with The King's Consort (Hyperion). *Current Management:* HarrisonParrott Ltd, 12 Penzance Place, London, W11 4PA, England. *Telephone:* (20) 7229-9166. *Fax:* (20) 7221-5042. *Website:* www.harrisonparrott.com.

**SEMPERE, José;** Singer (Tenor); b. 9 Jan. 1955, Catalonia, Spain. *Education:* Barcelona Conservatory; La Scala Opera School, Milan. *Career:* Debut: Ford in Salieri's Falstaff, Parma, 1987; Appearances at Modena, Ferrara, Rome and Reggio Emilia; Season 1991–92 as the Duke of Mantua at Covent Garden, London, in Auber's Masaniello at Ravenna and Ernesto in Don Pasquale at Naples; Guest appearances at Oslo, 1989 as Rodolfo and at Bergamo, Donizetti's Poliuto, 1993; Madrid as Edgardo in Lucia di Lammermoor; Sang at St Etienne, 1993 and as Duke of Mantua at Verona, 1994; Arturo in I Puritani, Vienna Staatsoper and Lisbon, 1995–96; Sang Don Pedro in Persiani's Ines de Castro at Jesi, 1999. *Recordings:* Poliuto. *Address:* c/o Teatro San Carlos, Rua Serpa Pinto 9, 1200 Lisbon, Spain.

**SENATOR, Ronald,** BMus, PhD, FTCL; British composer; b. 17 April 1926, London; m. Miriam Brickman 1986. *Education:* Univ. of Oxford with Egon Wellesz, Univ. of London with Arnold Cooke, Trinity Coll. of Music. *Career:* Ed. Counterpoint 1947–50; Prof. of Composition, Guildhall School of Music 1981; fmr Sr Lecturer in Music, Univ. of London; Visiting Prof., Univs of Queensland and Melbourne, Australia, City Univ. of New York and MIT, USA, Toronto and McGill Univs, Canada, and Tel-Aviv Univ., Israel; Founding mem. Montserrat Composers' Asscn for Sacred Music; Founding Dir Nat. Asscn of Music Theatre; mem. Performing Rights Soc., American Soc. of Composers, Authors and Publishers, British Acad. of Composers and Songwriters, BMI. *Compositions:* Insect Play, Echoes, Pageant of London, Trotsky (musical), Kaddish for Terezin, Basket of Eggs, Streets of London, Francis and the Wolf, Mobiles, Spring Changes, My Animals, Sun's in the East, Poet to his Beloved, Holocaust Requiem 1990; incidental music for film and theatre, including Lightning (film), Siberia (play). *Publications:* General Grammar of Music 1975, Musicolor 1975, The Gaia of Music 1986, Requiem Letters (autobiog.) 1996. *Address:* 81 Hillcrest Avenue, Yonkers, NY 10705, USA. *E-mail:* ronaldsenator@hotmail.com (home). *Website:* www.ronaldsenator.com (home).

**SENDEROVAS, Anatolijus;** Composer; b. 21 Aug. 1945, Uljanovsk, Russia; 1 d. *Education:* Graduated from the Lithuanian Academy of Music (Vilnius), 1967; Postgraduate studies at the Rubin Israel Academy of Music (Tel-Aviv University), 1990; St Petersburg N. Rimski-Korsakoff Conservatory, 1967. *Career:* International Arts Manager, 2002; Berliner Morgeupost, 2002. *Compositions:* A Maiden and Death (ballet), staged at the Lithuanian Opera and Ballet Theatre, Vilnius, 1982; Symphony No. 2 (Music, St Petersburg), 1984; Mary Stewart (ballet), staged at the Vanemuine Theatre, Tartu, Estonia, 1988; Two Songs of Shulamith, for voice and piano, 1992; Der Tiefe Brunnen for voice and 5 instruments, 1993; Simeni Kahoteam al Libeha; Paratum cor Meum, Concerto for Cello, Mixed Choir, Piano (Clavinova) and Symphony Orchestra, 1995; Simeni Kahotam al Libeha (Set Me As A Seal on Your Heart) for soprano, bass, percussion solo and symphony orchestra, 1995; Shma Israel (Hear O Israel) for cantor, male choir and symphony orchestra, 1997; Cantus I, Cantus II for cello solo, 1997; Concerto in Do for Cello and Symphony Orchestra, 2002, Premiered Young Euro Classic, Berlin, 2002 by D. Geringas and the Lithuanian Symphony Orchestra, conducted by Robertas Servenikas. *Recordings:* Simeni Kahotam al libeha (Set me as a seal on your heart); Shma Israel; Concerto in Do. *Publications:* Berliner Zeitung, 1977; Ruch Muzyczny, 1978; Frankfurter Allegmeine Zeitung, 1982; Festival Zeitung, 1992; The Independent, 2003; International Arts Manager, 2002; Die Welt, 2002; Der Tagesspiegel, 2002. *Honours:* Laureate of the Lithuanian National Award, Euopeian Composers Prize, 2002; Lithuanian Grand Duke Gediminas Order Bearer; 2nd Prize Winner at the International Composers Competition in Prague, 1993; Certificate holder at the International W.Lutoslawski Contest, Kil, Sweden, 1994; Lithuanian National Award, 1997; European Composers Prize, Berlin, 2002 for Concerto in Do for Cello and Symphony Orchestra. *Address:* Lakstingalu 5, 15173 Nemencine, Vilnius raj, Lithuania. *Telephone:* +370 6 9999 576. *Fax:* +370 5 2370 995. *E-mail:* asenderovas@yahoo.com. *Website:* www.mie.lt/c_senderovas.htm.

**SÉNÉCHAL, Michel;** Singer (Tenor); b. 11 Feb. 1927, Tavery, France. *Education:* Studies, Paris Conservatoire. *Career:* Debut: Théâtre de la Monnaie, Brussels, 1950; Many Appearances at the Paris Opéra and Opéra Comique and elsewhere in France; Roles have included Ferrando, Don Ottavio, Tamino, Hylas in Les Troyens, Rossini's Almaviva and Comte Ory; Successful in Such Character Roles as Rameau's Platée (Aix 1956, Brussels Opéra Comique 1977), Erice in Cavalli's L'Ormindo (Glyndebourne), M. Triquet in Eugene Onegin, Valzacchi and Scaramuccio in Ariadne auf Naxos; Glyndebourne Debut, 1966, as Gonzalve in L'Heure Espagnole; Salzburg Festival 1972–88, notably as Mozart's Basilio; Metropolitan Opera debut 1982, as the Villains in Les Contes d'Hoffmann, returned 1997 and 2002, as Basilio; Season 1985 with the premieres of Landowski's Montségur at Toulouse and Boehmer's Docteur Faustus at the Paris Opéra; Director, Opera School at the Opéra, 1980–. *Honours:* Officier de l'Ordre National de la Légion d'Honneur; Officier de l'Ordre des Arts et des Lettres; Commandeur de l'Ordre du Mérite National. *Address:* c/o Metropolitan Opera, Lincoln Center, New York, NY 10023, USA.

**SENIA, Paul (Anthony);** Composer and Conductor; b. 26 Aug. 1925, Brooklyn, New York, USA; Divorced, 1 s., 3 d. *Education:* MM and MA, Composition, Theory, Juilliard School of Music, 1948; DMA, Composition, Los Angeles Conservatory, 1961; PhD, Music History, Toronto, 1971. *Career:* Debut: Saint-Saëns Piano Concerto, Carnegie Hall, 1939; Conductor, Los Angeles Conservatory Orchestra, 1960–62; Founder, Conductor, Simi Valley Symphony, 1964–67; Musical Director, Conductor: Los Angeles Civic Arts Symphony, 1964–; Los Angeles Pops Symphony, 1969–; American Theatre of the Opera, 1974–; New American Chamber Strings, 1980; British debut, Gershwin Concerto in F with Leeds Symphony; West Coast premieres, Eugene Zador's operas Christopher Columbus, 1976, Inspector General, 1978, Jehu, 1980; Guest Conductor, US Symphony orchestra: American Korean, Philadelphia, Rochester, Utah, Detroit and Miami Philharmonic, Bank of America Radio Orchestra and Boston Pops, European Symphony, Leeds, Chesterfield, Harrogate Chamber Orchestra (England), Brussels Symphony. *Compositions:* Work for piano, strings and vibraphone; Art Songs, 1945; 42 string quartets, 1948–60; Fisherman and the Mermaid, ballet, 1952, opera, 1954; Variety Suite for orchestra, 1953; Piano Suite (Belle South), 1953; 3 Piano Sonatinas,

1954; Brass Processional, 1956; Choral works, 1956–70; Divertimento, strings, 1961; Symphony No. 1, based on Psalm 23, with soloists and choruses, 1966; 3 Woodwind Quintets, 1968, 1991; 2 Cello Sonatas, 1973; 3 Violin Sonatas, 1969–1972; Crystals, ballet, 1993; Triple Concerto, violin, viola, cello, 1995. *Address:* c/o Sienna Enterprises, 5337 Northridge Drive, Palmdale, CA 93551, USA.

**SENN, Marta;** singer (mezzo-soprano); b. 1958, Switzerland. *Education:* legal training in Columbia; musical study in USA. *Career:* Rosina and in title role of Rossi's Orfeo, at several American Opera Houses and La Scala, 1984; Charlotte in Stuttgart, Paris, Hamburg and Nantes; Giulietta in Les Contes d'Hoffmann in Madrid; Isabella in Rome; Massenet's Dulcinée at the Liceo, Barcelona; US tour with Placido Domingo; Annius in La Clemenza di Tito and Rossini's Angelina at the Salzburg Festival, 1988; Season 1988–89, as Sara in Roberto Devereux at Naples and Meg in new production of Falstaff at Bologna; Fenena in Nabucco and Verdi's Preziosilla at Verona Arena; Carmen at Munich State Theatre; Carmen at Stuttgart State Theatre; Liceo, Barcelona, Olympics Arts Festival; Charlotte in Werther; Concerts and recording role of Salud, in La Vida Breve, Venezuela and Minnesota Orchestra, 1993; Debut role of Carmen, Paris Opéra, 1994; Charlotte, in Lisbon and Rome; Dorabella in Toulon and Fidalma in Il Matrimonio Segreto at Bologna; Season 1996 as Charlotte at Naples. *Recordings include:* Maddalena in Rigoletto, from La Scala, conducted by Riccardo Muti; Musetta, in La Bohème, at Venice; Lola in Cavalleria Rusticana; Salud in La Vida Breve, Mata conducting, 1993; El Amor Brujo, original version. *Honours:* winner Concours International de Paris 1982, first prize Baltimore Opera Nat. Auditions 1982. *Current Management:* Fedeli Opera International, via Montegrappa 3, 40121 Bologna, Italy. *Address:* c/o Dorian Recordings, 8 Brunswick Road, Troy, NY 12180-3795, USA. *Telephone:* (518) 274-5475. *E-mail:* info@dorian.com.

**SEOW, Yit Kin,** LRSM; British/Singaporean pianist; b. 28 March 1955, Singapore. *Education:* Yehudi Menuhin School and Royal Coll. of Music, England. *Career:* went to UK 1967; toured USA 1972; winner BBC Piano Competition 1974; toured Russia for BBC 1988. *Performances:* Promenade Concerts, Royal Albert Hall and Royal Festival Hall (with Philharmonia Orchestra), London 1975; appeared Beethovenfest, Bonn 1977, Hong Kong Arts Festival (with Berlin Radio Symphony Orchestra) 1977, Promenade Concerts (with Royal Philharmonic Orchestra) 1982, Poland 1984, Hong Kong Asian Arts Festival 1984, with St Petersburg Philharmonic 1998. *Recordings:* Satie, Schubert 1989. *Honours:* Rubinstein Prize 1977, Gold Disc of Yellow River Concerto 1984. *Address:* 8 North Terrace, London, SW3 2BA, England. *Telephone:* (20) 7584-5393. *Fax:* (20) 7584-5393. *E-mail:* yitkinseow@yahoo.com.

**SEQUI, Sandro;** Stage Director; b. 10 Nov. 1933, Rome, Italy. *Education:* Studied Literature and Philosophy at Rome University. *Career:* Directed La Sonnambula at the Teatro La Fenice Venice, 1961; Staging of I Puritani seen at Florence, 1971, Metropolitan 1976, Rome 1990; Guillaume Tell at Florence 1972, Les Contes d'Hoffmann at Dallas 1975; Staged the premiere production of Mannino's Il Principe Felice at La Scala, 1987; Rigoletto at the Chicago Lyric Opera, 1991; Fille du Régiment, Metropolitan, 1995–. *Address:* Lungotevere Sanzio 1, 00153 Rome, Italy.

**ŞERBAN, Andrei;** Romanian stage director; b. 21 June 1943, Bucharest; s. of Gheorghe Şerban and Elpis Şerban; m.; two c. *Education:* Bucharest Theatrical and Cinematographic Art Inst. *Career:* int. scholarships: Ford 1970, Guggenheim 1976, Rockefeller 1980; associated with Robert Brustein's American Repertory Theatre Company for more than twenty years since 1970; worked also with LaMama Theatre, Public Theater, Lincoln Center, Circle in the Square, Yale Repertory Theatre, Guthrie Theatre, ACT, New York City, Seattle and Los Angeles Operas; in Europe: at Paris, Geneva, Vienna, and Bologna Opera Houses, Welsh Nat. Opera, Covent Garden, Théâtre de la Ville, Helsinki Lilla Teatern, Comédie Française, among others; worked with Shiki Co. of Tokyo, Japan; has delivered numerous lectures; Gen. Man. Nat. Theatre of Romania 1990–93; Dir Oscar Hammerstein Center for the Performing Arts, Columbia University, New York 1992–. *Productions include:* (in Romania) Ubu Roi 1966, Julius Caesar 1968, Jonah 1969, An Ancient Trilogy (Medea, The Trojan Women, Elektra) 1990; (in USA) Medea (Euripides) 1970, The Cherry Orchard 1972, Fragments of a Trilogy (Medea, Elektra, The Trojan Women) 1974, As You Like It 1976, Uncle Vanya 1979, The Umbrellas of Cherbourg 1980, The Seagull 1981, Three Sisters 1983, The Miser 1988, Twelfth Night 1989, Sweet Table at the Richelieu 1989, Hamlet 2000, The King Stag 2001. *Opera productions include:* Eugene Onegin 1980, Turandot 1984, Norma 1985, Fidelio (Covent Garden) 1986; Paris Opera: L'Ange de feu 1991, Lucia Di Lammermoor 1995, The Puritans 1997, L'Italienne a Alger 1998, Les Indes Galanates 1999. *Honours:* Prize for the Best Performance, World Students' Theatre Festival, Zagreb 1965, Obie Awards, Tony Award, George Abbott Award, Soc. of Stage Dirs and Choreographers, prizes at Avignon, Belgrade and Shiraz Festivals. *Address:* Teatrul Naţional, Bd N. Bălcescu 2, Bucharest, Romania. *Telephone:* 614-56-92.

**SERBO, Rico;** Singer (Tenor); b. 9 May 1940, Stockton, California, USA. *Education:* Studied in San Francisco. *Career:* Debut: San Francisco 1965 as Ramiro in Cenerentola; Sang in Opera at Seattle, Santa Fe and San Francisco, Europe from 1970, notably with Netherlands Opera and at Koblenz, Essen and the Theater am Gärtnerplatz Munich; Further engagements at San Diego, New York City Opera, Houston, Toronto and Vancouver; Sang at New Orleans, as Arvino in the US premiere of I Lombardi; Deutsche Oper and

Theater des Westens Berlin, and at Belfast; Other roles have included Mozart's Ferrando and Tamino, Almaviva, Ernesto, Fenton, Alfredo, Tom Rakewell, Rodolfo, Boito's Faust, Lord Barrat in Der Junge Lord and Tony in Elegy for Young Lovers. *Recordings include:* Donizetti's L'Assedio di Calais.

**SERDIUK, Nadezhda;** Singer (Mezzo-Soprano); b. 1975, Moscow, Russia. *Education:* Tchaikovsky Conservatoire, Moscow. *Career:* Young Singers' Academy at the Mariinsky Theatre, St Petersburg, from 1999; Masterclasses with Christa Ludwig, Marilyn Horne and Renata Scotto at the Metropolitan Opera Young Singers' Programme; Roles with Kirov Opera have included Gluck's Orfeo, Olga in Eugene Onegin, Nadezhda in Vera Sheloga by Rimsky-Korsakov and Lyubava in Sadko; Sang Beautiful Spring in Rimsky's Snow Maiden with the Kirov at Amsterdam and London (Covent Garden), 1999–2000; Other roles include Lyubasha in Rimsky's The Tsar's Bride. *Honours:* Prizewinner, International Glinka and Rimsky-Korsakov Vocal Competitions, 1998; Participant in the 1999 Cardiff Singer of the World Competition. *Address:* c/o Kirov Opera, Mariinsky Theatre, 1 Theatre Square, St Petersburg, Russia.

**SEREBRIER, José,** MA; American conductor and composer; b. 3 Dec. 1938, Montevideo, Uruguay; s. of David Serebrier and Frida Serebrier (née Wasser); m. Carole Farley 1969; one d. *Education:* Univ. of Minn., Curtis Inst. of Music, Phila. *Career:* started conducting at age of 12; went to USA 1956; studied composition with Aaron Copland and Vittorio Giannini, Curtis Inst., Phila 1956–58 and conducting with Antal Dorati and Pierre Monteux; guest conductor in USA, S America, Australia and Europe; Assoc. Conductor American Symphony Orchestra, with Leopold Stokowski 1962–68; conducted alongside Leopold Stokowski world première of Charles Ives' Fourth Symphony, Carnegie Hall, New York 1964; conducted first performance in Poland of Charles Ives' Fourth Symphony 1971 and premieres of over 100 works; Composer-in-Residence with Cleveland Orchestra 1968–70; Music Dir Cleveland Philharmonic Orchestra 1968–71; Artistic Dir Int. Festival of Americas, Miami 1984–, Miami Festival 1985– (also Founder). *Compositions:* Solo Violin Sonata 1954, Quartet for Saxophones 1955, Pequeña música (wind quintet) 1955, Symphony No. 1 1956, Momento psicológico (string orchestra) 1957, Solo Piano Sonata 1957, Suite canina (wind trio) 1957, Symphony for Percussion 1960, The Star Wagon (chamber orchestra) 1967, Nueve (double bass and orchestra) 1970, Colores mágicos (variations for harp and chamber orchestra) 1971, At Dusk, in Shadows (solo flute), Andante Cantabile (strings), Night Cry (brass), Dorothy and Carmine (flute and strings), George and Muriel (contrabass), Winter (violin concerto) 1995, Winterreise (for orchestra) 1999; composed music for several films; all compositions published and recorded; over 175 recordings to date. *Television includes:* int. TV broadcast of Grammys' Ceremony, LA 2002, conducting suite from Bernstein's West Side Story. *Publications:* orchestration of 14 songs by Edvard Grieg 2000, orchestration of Gershwin's works 2002; more than 100 works published by Peer Music, Kalmus, Peters Editions. *Honours:* Nat. Endownment for Arts Comm. Award 1969, Ditson Award for Promotion of New Music, Columbia Univ. 1980, Deutsche Schallplatten Critics' Award 1991, UK Music Retailers' Asscn Award for Best Symphony Recording (Mendelssohn symphonies) 1991, Diapason d'Or Recording Award, France, Best Audiophile Recording (Scheherazade), Soundstage 2000, BMI Award, Koussevitzky Foundation Award, Latin Grammy for Best Classical Album of 2004. *Address:* 20 Queensgate Gardens, London, SW7 5LZ, England. *Fax:* (212) 662-8073 (office). *E-mail:* caspil23@aol.com (office). *Website:* www.naxos.com (office).

**SEREMBE, Gilberto;** Conductor and Professor of Orchestral Conducting; b. 17 Dec. 1955, Milan, Italy; m. Elisabetta Brusa, 3 May 1997. *Career:* Professor of Composition, Brescia Conservatorio, 1979–81; Assistant, Teatro alla Scala, Milan, 1980; Professor of Orchestral Rehearsing: Mantova Conservatorio, 1982–83, Conservatorio G Verdi, Milan, 1984–86, Brescia Conservatorio, 1986–88, Genoa Conservatorio, 1989–97; Professor of Orchestral Conducting, International Superior courses, Accademia Musicale Pescarese, 1988–; Professor/Conductor, Orchestra of the Conservatorio di Brescia, 1997–; Guest Conductor: Pomeriggi Musicali Orchestra, Milan, 1976–77, 1980–83, 1987, 1990, 1992, 1994, AIDEM Orchestra, Firenze, 1979, Angelicum Chamber Orchestra, Milan, 1980–83, San Remo Symphony Orchestra, 1980–87, Teatro Massimo Symphony Orchestra, Palermo, 1986–88, Orchestra Regionale della Toscana, Florence, 1986–88, 1995, Stradivari Orchestra, Milan, 1991–92, and Hungarian tour, 1991, Teatro Regio Symphony Orchestra, Turin, 1991, Toscanini Symphony Orchestra, Parma, 1993, Brescia Symphony Orchestra, 1996, 1998, 1999, Orchestra Sinfonica Triveneta, 1997–98, Filarmonia Veneta of Teatro Comunale, Treviso, 1997; Orchestra Stabile di Bergamo, 1998; Orchestra Sinfonia di Pescana, 1999, 2001, 2003; Abroad: Gothenburg Symphonic Orchestra, Sweden, 1989, BRT Radio Television Symphony Orchestra, Brussels, 1991, Turku Philharmonic, Finland, 1991, Tirana Radio and Television Symphony Orchestra, Albania, 1994–95, Summer Stage in Conducting, Valencia, Spain, 1999. *Current Management:* Via Zanella 43/1, 20133 Milan, Italy.

**SERENI, Mario;** Singer (Baritone); b. 25 March 1928, Perugia, Italy. *Education:* Studied at the Accademia di Santa Cecilia in Rome and at the Accademia Chigiana, Siena. *Career:* Debut: Florence 1953, in Lualdi's Il Diavolo nel Campanile; Sang in The Stone Guest by Dargomyzhsky, Florence, 1954; Palermo 1955, as Wolfram in Tannhäuser; Metropolitan Opera from 1957: almost 400 performances in 26 roles, including Gerard, Sharpless, Germont, Amonasro, Belcore and Marcello; Vienna 1965, Verona Arena 1965–74; Further engagements in London, Chicago, Dallas, Houston, London,

Milan and Buenos Aires. *Recordings:* Madama Butterfly; Andrea Chénier; La Bohème; Cavalleria Rusticana; Elisir d'amore; Aida; La Traviata; Ernani; Turandot; Lucia di Lammermoor. *Address:* c/o Arena di Verona, Piazza Bra 28, 37121 Verona, Italy.

**SERKIN, Peter Adolf;** American concert pianist; b. 24 July 1947, New York; s. of Rudolf Serkin and Irene Busch. *Education:* Curtis Inst. of Music. *Career:* debut, New York 1959. *Performances:* concert appearances in recital and with orchestras world-wide including Philadelphia, Cleveland, New York, Chicago, Berlin, London, Zürich, Paris and Japan; has premiered works composed for him by Knussen, Takemitsu, Lieberson, Berio; has given benefit performances to aid hunger and war victims. *Honours:* Dr hc (New England Conservatory) 2001; Premio Accademia Musicale Chigian Siena 1983. *Current Management:* Cramer Marder Artists, 127 W 96th Street, #13B, New York, NY 10025, USA. *Telephone:* (212) 864-1005. *Fax:* (212) 864-1066. *E-mail:* ccumella@aol.com.

**SERMILÄ, Jarmo Kalevi,** MA; Finnish composer and musician (trumpet, flugelhorn); b. 16 Aug. 1939, Hämeenlinna; m. Ritva Vuorinen 1962. *Education:* Helsinki Univ., Sibelius Acad. *Career:* worked for Finnish broadcasting co. (YLE), Artistic Dir YLE Experimental Studio 1973–79; Pres. Finnish Section, Int. Soc. for Contemporary Music 1975–79; Composer-in-Residence, Hämeenlinna 1977–82; freelance composer 1982–; Artistic Dir Time of Music Contemporary Music Festival, Viitasaari 1987–99; state grant for composition 1990; mem. Soc. of Finnish Composers, Vice-Pres. 1981–2005. *Compositions include:* A Circle of the Moon, Allegrìa, At Bizarre Exits, La Place Revisitée, Labor, Manifesto, Merlin's Mascarade (ballet), Mimesis 2, Movimenti, On the Road, Pentagram, Quattro Rilievi, Random Infinities, Technogourmet, Train of Thoughts, Wolf Bride (ballet). *Recordings:* Quattro Rilievi, At Bizarre Exits, Random Infinities, Movimenti, Technogourmet, Citymusic. *Honours:* Hon. Prof. 2005; hon. mem. Finnish Composers' Soc. 2005; Hon. Reward, Sibelius Fund of the Finnish Composers' Soc. 2006; Janacek Medal 1978, Hämeenlinna City Music Prize 1981, Smetana Medal 1984, Häme Prov. Art Soc. Award 1988, State Grant for Composition 1990–2003. *Address:* Niittykatu 7 A 7, 13100 Hämeenlinna, Finland. *Website:* www.sermila.net.

**SEROV, Edward;** Symphony Orchestra Conductor; b. 9 Sept. 1937, Moscow, Russia; Guenrietta Serova, 29 June 1961, 2 s. *Education:* Gnessin Institute, Moscow, 1954–59; Tchaikovsky Conservatoire, Kiev, 1958–61; Rimsky-Korsakov Conservatoire, Leningrad, 1961–64. *Career:* Debut: Kiev Opera, 1960; Conductor, Leningrad Philharmonic Orchestra, 1961–68, 1985–90; Founder, Chief Conductor, Uljanovsk Philharmonic, 1968–77; Chief Conductor, Leningrad Chamber Orchestra, 1974–85; Founder, Chief Conductor, Volgograd Philharmonic Orchestra, 1987–; Professor, Leningrad (now St Petersburg) Conservatoire, 1987–; Chief Conductor, Odense Symphony Orchestra, Denmark, 1991–96; Chief Conductor Saratov Philharmonic Orchestra, 1995–; Foreign Tours: Japan, USA, France, Germany, Austria, Spain, Sweden, Norway, Finland, Denmark, Czechoslovakia, Hungary, Yugoslavia, others. *Recordings include:* works of Webern, Tishchenko, Arensky, Mozart, Rubenstein, Tchaikovsky, Prokofiev, Sviridov, Purcell, Tartini, Bartók, Slonimski, Hindemith, Mendelssohn, Bach, Nielsen, Rossini, Ginastera, Shostakovich, Rodrigo, Elgar, Suk, Schumann, Spohr and Schubert. *Contributions:* The Exploit of Service to Music; The Soviet Music Magazine, 1980; About Conductor's Art, The Soviet Music, 1980; The original Symphonic Narration, The Music Life magazine, 1984; Meditation about G Sviridov to book on Sviridov; Others. *Honours:* People's Artist of Russia Honorary Title, President of Russia, 1990; Order of Honour, President of Russia, 1998. *Address:* Warschawskaja str 124 kw 95, St Petersburg 196 240, Russia.

**SERRA, Enric;** Singer (Baritone); b. 24 July 1940, Barcelona, Spain. *Education:* Studied in Barcelona. *Career:* Debut: Teatro del Liceo Barcelona, 1966, as Morales in Carmen; Has sung in Spain (Madrid, Valencia, Bilbao and Barcelona) from 1969, notably as Falstaff, Scarpia, Escamillo, Enrico, Belcore and Alcandro in Pacini's Saffo, 1987; Guest engagements in Zürich, Cologne, Nice, Tours, Naples, Venice, Bogota and Caracas, as Don Pasquale, Rossini's Figaro, Alfonso (La Favorita) and Don Carlos in La Forza del Destino; At Schwetzingen as Italiana in Algeri and Lescaut in Manon Lescaut and at Barcelona, 1990;; Don Magnifico in La Cenerentola at Hamburg, 1998; Sang Belfiore in Haydn's Il mondo della luna at Maastricht, 1999; Other roles include Mozart's Leporello and Alfonso, Escamillo, Valentin in Faust, Scarpia, and Verdi's Count Luna; Concert repertoire includes Falla's L'Atlantida (Madrid 1977); Rossini's Barbiere at München's Bayerische Staatsoper, 1989, and also at the New York Metropolitan Opera, 1997–99; Further roles include: Massenet's Mandy, Marcello, Albert, Michonet and Grand Prêtre from Saint-Saëns' Samson et Dalila; Concerts in Madrid's Teatro Real, Barcelona's Palau Musica, Paris' Salle Pleyel and ORTF, London's Royal Festival Hall, Rome's RAI, Tokyo's Suntory Hall and Granada's Music Festival. *Recordings include:* Madama Butterfly, with Caballé; Tosca with Aragall; Italiana in Algeri. *Address:* Gran Teatro del Liceo, Sant Pau I bis, 08001 Barcelona, Spain.

**SERRA, Luciana;** Singer (soprano); b. 4 Nov. 1946, Genoa, Italy. *Education:* Genoa Conservatoire and with Michele Casato. *Career:* debut, Budapest Opera 1966, in Cimarosa's Il Convito; mem. of Tehran Opera 1969–76; sang Gilda in Rigoletto at Genoa 1974; Bologna 1979, in La Sonnambula; Covent Garden 1980, as Olympia in Les Contes d' Hoffmann; Rossini's Aureliano in Palmira at Genoa 1980; Hamburg 1982 and La Scala Milan 1983, as Lucia; US debut at Charleston as Violetta; Chicago Lyric Opera 1983 as Lakmé; Parma

1986 as Lucia; Rossini Opera Festival Pesaro 1987 in L'Occasione fa il Iadro (Rossini); Vienna 1988 as the Queen of Night; Maggio Musicale Florence 1989, as Elvira in I Puritani; sang Gilda at Turin 1989, Hanna Glawari at Trieste 1990; Santiago 1990, as Donizetti's Marie; Schwetzingen Festival 1990, in Fra Diavolo at La Scala and Pamira in Le Siège de Corinthe at Genoa; sang Olympia at Genoa 1996; other roles include Rosina, Fiorilla; Ophelia, Philine; Bellini's Giulietta; Norina; Adina; Linda di Chamounix and Marie in La Fille du Régiment; Season 1998 with Gounod's Juliette at Palermo and Puccini's Lauretta at Torre del Lago; Rossini's Rosina at Santiago, 2000; concert appearances in pre-classical works and music by Vivaldi, Mozart, Rossini and Rimsky-Korsakov. *Recordings:* Zerline in Fra Diavolo (Cetra); Torquato Tasso by Donizetti; Die Zauberflöte; Les Contes d'Hoffmann; Don Pasquale; Barbiere di Siviglia, Gianni di Parigi; Fille du Régiment; La Scala di Seta and L'Occasione fa il Ladro. *Current Management:* Allied Artists Agency, 42 Montpelier Square, London, SW7 1JZ, England.

**SERRAIOCCO, Danielo;** Singer (Bass); b. 1960, San Giovanni Teatino, Italy. *Education:* Accademia di Santa Cecilia, Rome. *Career:* Debut: Spoleto, 1987 as Raimondo in Lucia di Lammermoor; Sang at Spoleto in Così fan tutte, Don Carlos, Mahagonny and L'Italiana in Algeri; Savonna, 1988 in a revival of Rossini's Ciro in Babilonia; Season 1990 as Wurm in Luisa Miller at Rome, in La rosa bianca e la rose rossa by Simone Mayr and in Britten's The Rape of Lucretia at Naples; Santa Domingo, 1992, as Columbus in the premiere of 1492 by A Braga; Concerts include Bach and Mozart at Florence; Puccini's Messa di Gloria and Mozart's Requiem in London; Schubert's Mass in G, Rome. *Recordings:* Angelotti in Tosca; La Fanciulla del West. *Address:* Teatro San Carlo, Via S Carlo, 80132 Naples, Italy.

**SERVADEI, Annette,** BMus, FTCL, LTCL(T), LRSM(P), UDLM, UTLM; British pianist; b. 16 Oct. 1945, Durban, Natal, S Africa; m. 1972 (divorced 1981); one s. one d. *Education:* studied with concert pianist mother, further studies in Milan, Detmold, Salzburg, London with Ilonka Deckers, Klaus Schilde, Carlo Zecchi, Wilhelm Kempff. *Career:* first radio broadcast aged 10; concert debut with Durban Symphony Orchestra aged 12; debut, Wigmore Hall, London 1972; recitals and concertos in UK, Western Europe, USA, Africa; frequent radio and television broadcasts; Sr Piano Tutor, UOFS Bloemfontein 1974, Wits Univ., Johannesburg 1977–81; festival adjudicator, lecture recitals, masterclasses; played world premiere, Tavener's Palintropos, London 1980; resumed career after heart surgery 1988; championed music of Sibelius and Dohnanyi; career further interrupted by stroke 1997–2003, resumed public performances, specialising in Mozart 2003–; mem. Inc. Soc. of Musicians. *Recordings:* Britten and Khachaturian Piano Concertos with London Philharmonic Orchestra, 1987; Mendelssohn, Schumann and Brahms piano pieces; Sibelius complete piano music (five CDs), 1994–96; Dohnányi Piano, Vols 1 and 2. *Honours:* UK Sibelius Soc. Artist of the Year 1993. *Address:* 3 Bournemouth Drive, Herne Bay, Kent, CT6 8HH, England (home). *E-mail:* annetteservadei@tiscali.co.uk.

**SERVILE, Roberto;** Singer (Baritone); b. 1959, Genoa, Italy. *Education:* Studied with Paride Venturi. *Career:* Sang Don Carlos in Ernani at Modena and Marcello with Bohème at Treviso, 1984; Marcello with Pavarotti at Philadelphia, 1986; Rome Opera, 1989 in a revival of Rossini's Zelmira and 1994 as Enrico in Lucia di Lammermoor; Genoa, 1990 as Luna in Il Trovatore, Macerata, 1992 as Germont; Further appearances at Naples, from 1993, Santiago, 1994 and Hamburg, 1995; Season 1996 as Osaka in Mascagni's Iris at Rome and Azo in Donizetti's Parisina at Wexford; Season 1997–98 as Enrico at La Scala; High Priest in Samson and Delilah, Eugene Onegin at Turin and Nottingham in Roberto Devereux at Naples; Other roles include Verdi's Posa, Macbeth and Ford, Oreste in Iphigénie en Tauride, Escamillo, Belcore and Zurga in Les Pêcheurs de Perles; Season 2000–01 as Count Luna at Parma, Puccini's Lescaut at Catania and Belfiore in Verdi's Un giorno di regno at Bologna. *Recordings:* Il Trovatore; Il Barbiere di Siviglia. *Address:* c/o Turin Opera, Piazza Castello 215, 10124 Turin, Italy.

**SESTAK, Zdenek;** Composer; b. 10 Dec. 1925, Citoliby, Czechoslovakia; m. Marie Zatecka, 2 Sept 1950, 1 s., 1 d. *Education:* Gymnasium, Louny, 1936–44; Conservatorium de la Musique, Prague, 1945–50; PhD, Charles University, Faculty of Philosophy, 1945–50. *Career:* Professor of Music, 1952–57; Freelance Composer, 1957–; Dramaturge, Centre for Symphonic Music, Radio Czechoslovakia, Prague, 1968–70; mem, Association of Music Artists Tchèques. *Compositions include:* Symphonie II, 1970, III, 1971, IV, 1979, V Chronos, 1978 and VI L'Inquietude Eternelle du Coeur, 1979; Cycle des Cantates Spirituels sur les Textes de psaume, 1972–92; Concert for string orchestra, 1974; String Quintet, Concentus musicus, 1975; Sonata Symphonica, 1976; Sonata da Camera, 1978; Concerto for violin: Sursum corda, 1981; Concerto for viola: Meditations de Socrates, 1982; Memoria, La Fresque Symphonique de Variation, 1983; Fatum, Vocale-Symphonique Fragment d'Aprilès Sophocles, 1983; Concerto for violin: Jean le Violiniste, 1985; Queen Dagmar, oratorium, 1989; Les Cycles des Chants sur Vers de Villon, Michelangelo Buonarotti, Hora, Macha, Jelen, Sefl, King Salamon, Le Testament Ancien (Book of Ecclesiasticas); Evocations Paschales for trumpet and organ, 1992; Sonata for trumpet and organ, Dies Laetitiae, 1993; String Quartet VI, Variations de Mácha, 1993; String Quartet Vll, Soliloquia, 1994; Herakleitos (Movimenti musicali per novem stromenti a fiato), 1998; String Quartet IX, Sisyfos, 1999; String Quintet No. 2, Conscientia temporis, 2000; String Sextet, Laus Vitae, 2001. *Publications:* La Musique de Maîtres de Citoliby de 18 Siècle, 1968, 1985. *Address:* Pracska 2594-87, 106 00 Prague 10, Czech Republic.

**SETZER, Philip;** American violinist; b. Cleveland, OH. *Education:* The Juilliard School, New York, studied with Josef Gingold, Rafael Druian, Oscar Shumsky. *Career:* has performed with symphony orchestras, including Aspen Chamber, Memphis, New Mexico, Puerto Rico, Nat., Omaha, Anchorage, and the Cleveland Orchestra; festival appearances include Marlboro Music Festival; performed world premiere of Paul Epstein's Matinee Concerto 1989; founder mem. and co-leader Emerson String Quartet 1976–, performing at Alice Tully Hall, Lincoln Center and Carnegie Hall, New York, Wigmore Hall, South Bank Centre and Barbican Centre, London, Aspen Music Festival, Stony Brook Int. Chamber Music Festival; commissions and premieres with Emerson String Quartet include compositions by Mario Davidovsky 1979, Ronald Caltabiano 1981, Maurice Wright 1983, George Tsontakis 1984, Gunther Schuller 1986, John Harbison 1987, Richard Danielpour 1988, Richard Wernick 1991, Wolfgang Rihm 1993, Paul Epstein 1994, Ned Rorem 1995, Edgar Meyer 1995, Ellen Taaffe Zwillich 1998, Andre Prévin 2003, Joan Tower 2003, Nicholas Maw 2006; faculty mem. Isaac Stern Chamber Music Workshops, Carnegie Hall and Jerusalem Music Center; has given master-classes at RAM, Curtis Inst., San Francisco Conservatory, Cleveland Inst. of Music, The Mannes School; artist-in-residence and Visiting Prof. of Violin and Chamber Music, State Univ. of New York at Stony Brook. *Recordings:* with Emerson String Quartet: Schubert, Der Tod und das Mädchen/Beethoven, Quartetto Serioso 1990, Bartók, Complete String Quartets (Grammy Awards for Best Classical Recording, Best Chamber Performance) 1990, Prokofiev, String Quartets Nos 1 and 2 1992, Schubert, String Quintet in C 1992, Ives/Barber, String Quartets (Grammy Award for Best Chamber Performance) 1993, Dvořák, Piano Quartet/Piano Quintet 1994, Dvořák, American Quartet/Tchaikovsky, Quartet No. 1/Borodin, Quartet No. 2 1995, Mozart, String Quartets KV 387 and 421 1995, Debussy/Ravel, String Quartets 1995, Webern, Works for String Quartet/String Trio Op. 20 1995, Schumann, Piano Quintet Op. 44/ Piano Quartet Op. 47 1996, Beethoven, The String Quartets (Grammy Award for Best Chamber Performance) 1997, Beethoven, Key to the Quartets 1997, Meyer, String Quintet/Rorem String Quartet No. 4 1998, Curt Cacioppo, Monsterslayer 1998, Mozart, Flute Quartets 1999, Schubert, String Quintet/Late Quartets 1999, Mozart/Brahms, Clarinet Quintets 1999, Shostakovich, The String Quartets (Grammy Awards for Best Classical Recording, Best Chamber Performance) 2000, The Emerson Encores 2002, Bach, The Art of Fugue 2003, Haydn, The Seven Last Words 2004, Harbison/Wernick/Schuller, American Contemporaries 2005, Mendelssohn, The Complete String Quartets 2005. *Honours:* Dr hc (Middlebury Coll., Vermont) 1995; Hartford Univ. Medal for Distinguished Service 1994, Avery Fisher Prize 2004. *Current Management:* c/o Matthew Zelle, IMG Artists, 152 W 57th Street, Fifth Floor, New York, NY 10019, USA. *Telephone:* (212) 994-3500 (office). *Fax:* (212) 994-3550 (office). *E-mail:* mzelle@imgartists.com (office). *Website:* www.imgartists.com (office).

**SEXTON, Timothy A. P.,** BMus, DipEd; Australian composer, conductor and singer (bass-baritone); b. 10 Aug. 1960, McLaren Vale, S Australia; m. Suzanne Walker 1984; one s. one d. *Education:* Elder Conservatorium of Music, Univ. of Adelaide, studied composition with Richard Meale and Bozidar Kos, conducting with Shalom Ronly-Riklis, Gianluigi Gelmetti and David Porcelijn. *Career:* debut, conducted Tasmanian Symphony Orchestra 1994; debut as bass soloist, world premiere of Propriocepts Symphony 1997; conducted Australian premiere of Flamma Flamma 1998, Don Pasquale, Riders to the Sea, Mavra, SOSA 1998, The Mikado, SOSA, Mahogonny Songspiel, Treemonisha 1999, The Turn of the Screw, SOSA 2001, Akhnaten, Sweeney Todd, SOSA 2002, Einstein on the Beach 2004; mem., Music Arrangers' Guild of Australia. *Compositions:* Newcastle Coal Cantata, Escape of the Chrysalids (opera), Whispering Winds (choral song cycle), The Hole in the Sky (cantata). *Recordings:* Australia, Be Proud; Fanfare; A Universal Christmas. *Publications:* contrib. to Sounds Australian; Sing Out; many opera programmes throughout Australia. *Honours:* Henry Krips Memorial Conducting Scholarships 1994, 1997, Centenary of Fed. Medal for Services to Music. *Address:* PO Box 332, Birdwood, S Australia 5234, Australia. *E-mail:* tapsexton@bigpond.com (home).

**SFIRIS, Konstantin;** Singer (Bass); b. 1958, Waltessinikon, Arcadia, Greece. *Education:* Athens National Conservatory; Cologne Musikhochschule. *Career:* Sang at the Vienna Staatsoper 1981–87; Graz Opera from 1986, notably in the premieres of Der Rattenfänger by Cerha and Rashomon by Makayo Kuba; Guest appearances in opera and concert at Bregenz, Barcelona, San Francisco and Geneva; Sang Sparafucile in Rigoletto at Liège, 1989; Other roles include Philip II and the Grand Inquisitor in Don Carlos, Zaccaria in Nabucco, Procida (I Vespri Siciliani), Hunding in Die Walküre and Pimen in Boris Godunov; Wide concert repertory. *Honours:* Winner, Treviso International Competition, 1981. *Address:* c/o Vereinigte Buhnen, Kaiser Josef Platz 10, A-8010 Graz, Austria.

**SGOURDA, Antigone;** Singer (Soprano); b. 6 June 1938, Saloniki, Greece. *Education:* Athens Conservatory; Vienna Music Academy. *Career:* Sang at Bonn Opera 1960–62; Essen 1962–66; Glyndebourne Festival 1962–63, as Fiordiligi, and First Lady in Die Zauberflöte; Festival appearances at Schwetzingen, Holland and Athens (1971–73); Zürich Opera 1968–82, notably in operas by Mozart, including Lucio Silla; Frankfurt Opera 1968–82; Guest engagements at Dusseldorf, Vienna, Stuttgart and Munich (Israel tour, 1974); Sang Donna Anna in Don Giovanni at Edinburgh 1973 and Philadelphia 1977; Other roles have included Tatiana, Verdi's Amelia (Ballo in Maschera), Alice Ford, Violetta, and Aida; Katya Kabanova, Elizabeth I in Donizetti's Roberto

Devereux, Arabella and Ariadne. *Recordings include:* Don Giovanni (HMV); Beatrice di Tenda by Bellini (Fonit). *Address:* c/o Opernhaus Zürich, Falkenstrasse 1, CH-8008 Zürich, Switzerland.

**SHABALTINA, Svitlana;** Pianist and Harpsichordist; b. 3 Feb. 1948, Kiev, Ukraine. *Education:* Kiev Music School; Gnessin Academy of Music, Moscow; Postgraduate course at Gnessin Academy of Music. *Career:* Debut: Kiev International Festival of the Contemporary Music, 1982; Early Music Festival, Kraków, 1990; Kiev International Festival, Ukraine and the World of Baroque, Bach's Concertos for 2 harpsichords with Elizabieta Stefanska and the Kiev Chamber Orchestra, Kiev Organ Hall, 1994; Recital of Slav Composers music, Germany, 1994; Played music of Russian and Ukraine composers for piano and flute, Tolouse, France, 1996; Baroque music for harpsichord and flute, Teatro Regio di Torino, Italy, 1998; Recital harpsichord music, Kiev Philharmonic Hall, 1998; Professor of piano and harpsichord, Ukraine. *Recordings:* Ukraine early and contemporary music for Kiev radio and television, 1972–98; Music for harpsichord on CD, 1997; Beethoven sonata op 111, Schumann Kreisleriana op.16, Luboš Fiser Sonata 4 for piano on CD, 1998. *Honours:* Special diplomas as a best accompanist, Ukraine Cello competition, Kcharkow, 1984; International Cello competition, Kyshynev, 1985. *Address:* St Prytysko-Mykilska 2 Apt 26, Kiev 254070, Ukraine.

**SHADE, Ellen;** Singer (Soprano); b. 17 Feb. 1948, New York, USA. *Education:* Studied at the Juilliard Opera Center and with Cornelius Reid; Further study at the Sanata Fe Opera, 1969. *Career:* Debut: Frankfurt 1972, as Liu in Turandot; Sang Micaela at Pittsburgh 1972 (US debut); Further engagements in Cincinnati, Milwaukee, Dallas and New Orleans; Chicago 1976, as Emma in Khovanshchina, returning as Eve in the premiere of Penderecki's Paradise Lost, 1978; Metropolitan Opera debut, as Eva in Die Meistersinger; New York City Opera, 1981, Donna Elvira; Sang in Paradise Lost at La Scala in 1979 and has made further European appearances at Hamburg, Brussels, Vienna (Florinda in Schubert's Fierrabras, conducted by Abbado), and Geneva (Katya Kabanova, 1988); Returned to the Metropolitan as Sieglinde in Die Walküre, conducted by James Levine; Season 1992 as the Empress in Die Frau ohne Schatten, at Amsterdam and Salzburg; Other roles include Verdi's Alice Ford, Wagner's Elsa and Freia, Climene in Cavalli's Egisto and Agathe in Der Freischütz; As a concert singer has appeared with the New York Philharmonic, the Chicago Symphony and the Orchestras of Boston, Cleveland, Los Angeles, Minnesota, St Louis, Pittsburgh and the National Symphony and in Europe with the Radio Orchestras of Frankfurt, Berlin, Stuttgart, Baden-Baden, Rome and Turin; Invited to teach French Art Song with the Ravinia Festival in Chicago; Revival of Die Frau ohne Schatten in Amsterdam; Aida with the Metropolitan Opera; Sang Arabella at Covent Garden, 1996. *Recordings include:* Hans Pfitzner Cantata Von Deutscher Seele with the Frankfurt Radio Orchestra conducted by Horst Stein; Television recordings include Strauss's Empress and Saffi in Der Zigeunerbaron. *Address:* c/o IMG Artists, Lovell House, 616 Chiswick High Road, London W4 5RX, England.

**SHADE, Nancy Elizabeth;** American opera and concert singer (soprano); b. 31 May 1949, Rockford, IL. *Education:* De Pauw University, Indiana University; studied voice with Vera Scammon. *Career:* debut at Kentucky Opera Theatre, 1968, as Leonora in Il Trovatore; Lulu, Frankfurt Opera; Countess in Figaro, Hamburg State Opera; Manon Lescaut, Munich State Opera; Marguerite in Faust, San Francisco Opera; Madama Butterfly, New York City Opera; Marie in Die Soldaten, Lyons; Santa Fe 1984, in the US premiere of Henze's We Come to the River; Stuttgart 1988, as Marie in Die Soldaten (repeated Vienna 1990); Sang Schoenberg's Erwartung at the Prague State Opera, 2000. *Honours:* First prize, National Metropolitan Auditions, 1968. *Current Management:* Thea Dispeker, 59 E 54th Street, New York, NY 10022, USA.

**SHAGUCH, Marina;** Singer (Soprano); b. 1964, Krasnodar, Russia. *Education:* Studied at the Arts School in Maikop and at St Petersburg State Conservatoire. *Career:* Sang at the Kirov Opera Theatre in season 1991–92, notably in Mussorgsky's Sorochinsky Fair and Il Trovatore; Concert debuts at Grand Hall of the Moscow Conservatoire; Glinka Capella in St Petersburg; Further appearances throughout Russia, USA, Germany, Wales; Concert repertoire has included works by Handel, Mozart, Rimsky, Schumann, Schubert, Wolf, Dvořák and Brahms; Performed in The Legend of the Invisible City of Kitezh with Kirov Opera at the Barbican, 1995. *Honours:* Winner, Mussorgsky All Russia and Glinka National Singing Competitions; Second Prize, Tchaikovsky International Competition. *Address:* c/o Sonata, 11 Northpark Street, Glasgow G20 7AA, Scotland.

**SHAHAM, Gil;** Concert Violinist; b. 19 Feb. 1971, Champaign-Urbana, Illinois, USA. *Education:* Studied at the Rubin Academy in Jerusalem, in Aspen and at Juilliard with Dorothy DeLay. *Career:* Debut: Concert with the Jerusalem Symphony Conducted by Alexander Schneider; Appeared with the Israel Philharmonic under Zubin Mehta, 1982; Engagements with the New York Philharmonic; Season, 1987–88 with the London Symphony Orchestra at the Barbican, Bavarian Radio Orchestra in Munich, the RAI Turin and Recitals at La Scala and in Munich; Debut with the Philadelphia Orchestra and Tour of South America, 1988; Season, 1988–89 with the Berlin Philharmonic, Orchestre de Paris, Frankfurt Symphony and the Philharmonia under Sinopoli; Bruch and Sibelius Concertos with the London Symphony Orchestra, 1989; Recital Debut at the Wigmore Hall, London, 1990; Season 1995–96 with the Israel Philharmonic, the London Symphony Orchestra,

CBSO, Vienna Symphony Orchestra and the Philharmonia Orchestra; Recitals throughout Europe and the Far East. *Recordings include:* Bartók Concerto No. 2 (Boulez/Chicago Symphony Orchestra); Messiaen's Quartet for the End of Time. *Honours:* First Prize, 1982 Claremont Competition, Israel. *Current Management:* Harrison/Parrott Ltd, 12 Penzance Place, London, W11 4PA, England. *Telephone:* (20) 7229 9166. *Fax:* (20) 7221 5042. *Website:* www .harrisonparrott.com.

**SHAMEYEVA, Natalia;** Russian harpist; b. 30 Dec. 1939, Moscow; m.; one s. *Education:* Moscow Middle Special Music School; Musical Pedagogical Institute; Postgraduate courses, Moscow Conservatory. *Career:* Soloist, Moscow Concert Organisation, 1962–70; Solo Harpist, 1970–85; Principal Harpist, 1985–2003, Bolshoi Theatre Orchestra; Teacher, Moscow Conservatory, 1967–70; Teacher, Musical Pedogical Institute, 1977–79; teacher, Russian Acad. of Music 1985, Asst Prof. 1996, Prof. 2004–; Performances on radio stations; Masterclasses, USA, Holland, Switzerland, United Kingdom, Japan and Italy; Performances on major stages in Moscow; World premieres of Schnittke's Concerto for oboe, harp and orchestra; Baltin's Bylina for harp and orchestra; Ulyanich's Dreamings for harp, flute, saxophone and viola; First performances in Russia of Quintets by Villa-Lobos, V. d'Indy; A. Roussel, A. Caplet, Quartet by Haydn; mem. Russian Harp Soc., World Harp Congress. *Recordings include:* solo and chamber compositions for harp. *Publications:* The History of Development of Harp Music in Russia, Moscow, 1994; The Development of Harp Music in Russia, Bloomington, 1997; V Dulova, Creative portrait, Moscow, 1975; In Dulova's book, The Art of Harp Playing. *Honours:* Master of Art Criticism, 1992; Honoured Artist of Russia, 1993; 2nd prize, Laureat of the all Union Competition, 1963; 3rd prize, International Harp Contest, Israel, 1965; 1st prize, USA, 1969; International Woman of the Year, for Services to Music, IBC, Cambridge. *Address:* Liapidevskogo 14-68, Moscow 125581, Russia. *Telephone:* (95) 456-9196. *Fax:* (95) 504-4500.

**SHAMIR, Michal;** Singer (Soprano); b. 1960, Tel-Aviv, Israel. *Education:* Studied at the Rubin Academy of Music, Tel-Aviv, and in London. *Career:* Operatic debut at Gluck's Euridice; Followed by Cherubino and Elvira in L'Italiana in Algeri; European debut at Hamburg as Susanna, followed by Pamina, Gretel and Frasquita; Geneva Opera 1987, as Larissa in the premiere of La Forêt by Liebermann; Appearances with Frankfurt Oper as Susanna, Despina, Gilda, Marzellina and Jenny in Mahagonny; Has returned to Tel-Aviv for Violetta, Nedda and Marguerite; Basle Opera in Zemlinsky's Der Zwerg; Member of the Deutsche Oper Berlin; Concert repertoire includes Lutoslawski's Chantefleurs et Chantefables, performed with the composer in San Francisco and Helsinki; British debut as Violetta in La Traviata with Opera North, 1994; First Tatiana in Eugene Onegin at Lausanne, Switzerland, 1994; Violetta in Tel-Aviv, 1998; Sang Jenůfa at Essen and Omega in the premiere of Alpha and Omega, by Gil Shohat for New Israeli Opera, 2001. *Address:* c/o Valmalète, Bureau de Concerts, 7 rue Hoche, F–92300 Levallois Perret, France.

**SHANAHAN, Ian (Leslie);** Composer; b. 13 June 1962, Sydney, New South Wales, Australia. *Education:* BMus, University of Sydney, 1986; Study with Eric Gross and Peter Sculthorpe. *Career:* Faculty Member, Department of Music, University of Sydney, 1994–; New South Wales Conservatory, 1989–94; Commissions from Roger Woodward, 1993 and others. *Compositions:* Echoes/Fantasies for bass clarinet and percussion, 1984; Arcturus Timespace for amplified mandolin and percussion, 1987; Solar Dust for mandolin, 1988; Cycles of Vega for clarinet and 2 percussions, 1988–90; Lines of Light for amplified recorders and percussion, 1991–93; Ritual Canons for 4 tubas, 1982–93; Dimensions Paradisim for alto flute, 1993; Arc of Light, for piano, 1993; Gate of Remembrance, for amplified piano, 1993. *Honours:* Adolf Spivakovsky Prize, 1991. *Address:* c/o APRA, 1A Eden Street, Crows Nest, NSW 2065, Australia.

**SHANE, Rita Frances,** BA; American singer (soprano) and professor of voice; *Professor of Voice, Eastman School of Music, University of Rochester;* b. 1940, New York, NY; m. Daniel F. Tritter; one s. *Education:* Barnard Coll., studied with Beverly Peck Johnson, Santa Fe Opera apprentice programme, Hunter Coll. opera workshop. *Career:* appearances with Metropolitan Opera, Chicago Lyric, San Francisco, New York City Opera, most American companies, La Scala, Vienna Staatsoper, Bavarian State Opera, Turin, Strasbourg, Scottish, other opera houses in Europe, S America, orchestras of Philadelphia, Cleveland, Cincinnati, Santa Cecilia and Vienna in Europe, Israel Philharmonic; festival appearances include Salzburg, Vienna, Munich, Glyndebourne, Perugia, Aspen, Mostly Mozart (Canada); roles at Met Opera New York include the Queen of Night, Lucia, Berthe in Le Prophète, Pamira in The Siege of Corinth, Verdi's Gilda, Oscar and Violetta; recitals; sang title role in the premiere of Argento's Miss Havisham's Fire, New York City Opera 1979; American premieres of Henze's Elegy for Young Lovers (Hilda Mack), New York, Schat's Houdini (Cecilia) at Aspen and Reimann's Lear (Regan), San Francisco; Prof. of Voice, Eastman School of Music, Rochester, NY, Aspen School of Music and Festival, Colorado, Hamamatsu, Japan, Juilliard School, New York; pvt. studio, New York City. *Recordings:* Highlights from Handel's Athalia; Highlights from Handel's Rinaldo; Complete works of Schoenberg, vol. 2; R Strauss, Brentano Songs, Op 68 with orchestra (Louisville Premiere); Various private recordings including, Les Huguenots, Die Zauberflöte; Professor of Voice, Eastman School of Music, Rochester, New York. *Address:* c/o Daniel F. Tritter, 330 W 42nd Street, New York, NY 10036, USA. *Telephone:* (212) 947-2233 (office); (212) 787-6982 (home). *Fax:* (212) 244-2159

(office). *E-mail:* dtritter@speakeasy.net (office); rtritter@speakeasy.net (home).

**SHANKAR, Anoushka;** Indian sitar player and conductor; b. 9 June 1981, London; d. of Sukanya and Ravi Shankar. *Education:* San Dieguito Acad., San Diego, Calif., USA. *Career:* professional debut in New Delhi 1995 at age of 13; signed to Angel/EMI Classics 1997; regular performances since then at major concert halls in India, Europe, USA and Asia, including tours with Ravi Shankar ensemble; first solo tour in 2000; fundraising concerts for the Tibet Foundation Peace Garden 2000, Ramakrishna Centre, Kolkata 2000, Siri Fort Auditorium, New Delhi (conducting debut) 2001, World Economic Forum, New York 2002, Rainforest Foundation Benefit Concert, Carnegie Hall 2002, Elizabeth Glazer Pediatric AIDS Foundation Concert 2002, A Concert for Peace and Reconciliation, Lincoln Center's Avery Fisher Hall, New York 2003, Adopt a Minefield, Germany 2005. *Recordings include:* Anoushka 1998, Anourag 2000, Live at Carnegie Hall 2002; contributions to albums by Ravi Shankar, Sting, Jazmin and to Concert for George. *Film:* Dance Like a Man (actress) 2003. *Publication:* Bapi, The Love of My Life (pictorial biog. of Ravi Shankar) 2002. *Honours:* House of Commons Shield 1998, Nat. Council on Youth Leadership Award 1998, San Dieguito Acad. Award Winner 1999, Woman of the Year (India) 2003. *Current Management:* Sulivan Sweetland, 28 Albion Street, London, W2 2AX, England. *Telephone:* (20) 7262-0333. *Fax:* (20) 7402-5851. *E-mail:* info@sulivansweetland.co.uk. *Website:* www .sulivansweetland.co.uk; www.anoushkashankar.com.

**SHANKAR, Ravi;** Indian sitar player and composer; b. 7 April 1920, Varansi; m. Sukanya Rajan 1989; two d. (Anoushka Shankar and Norah Jones) one s. (deceased). *Education:* studied under Ustad Allauddin Khan of Maihar. *Career:* fmr Dir of Music All-India Radio and founder of the Nat. Orchestra; founder and Dir, Kinnara Schools of Music, Mumbai 1962, Los Angeles 1967; Visiting Lecturer Univ. of Calif. 1965; concert tours in Europe, USA and the East, major festivals include Edinburgh, Woodstock, Monterey; appeared in film, Raga 1974; elected to Rajya Sabha (Upper House) 1986; Fellow Sangeet Natak Akademi 1977. *Compositions include:* Concerto No. 1 for Sitar and Orchestra 1971, No. 2 1981, Ghanashyam (opera-ballet, premiered by City of Birmingham Touring Opera) 1989, Kalyan 2001, Mood Circle 2002. *Soundtracks:* for film: Pather Panchali, The Flute and the Arrow, Nava Rasa Ranga, Charly, Gandhi, Chappaqua; for television: Alice In Wonderland. *Recordings include:* Concertos 1 and 2 for Sitar and Orchestra, Raga Jageshwari 1981, Homage to Mahatma Ghandhi 1981, West Meets East (with Yehudi Menuhin and others), In London (live) 1999, In New York 2000, Full Circle: Carnegie Hall 2000, In San Francisco 2001, Collected 2001. *Publications:* My Music, My Life (autobiog.) 1968, Rag Anurag (Bengali), Ravi: The Autobiography of Ravi Shankar (with others) 1995, From India 1997, Mantram: Chant of India 1997, Raga Jogeshwari 1998. *Honours:* numerous hon. degrees; Silver Bear of Berlin 1966; Award of Indian Nat. Acad. for Music, Dance and Drama 1962; Award of Padma Bhushan 1967, Padma Vibhushan 1981, Deshikottam 1981, Int. Music Council UNESCO Award 1975, Ramon Magsaysay Award 1992, Praemium Imperiale 1997, Polar Music Prize 1998, Bharat Ratna (Jewel of India) Award 1999; Grammy Award 2000; Hon. KBE 2001; ISPA Distinguished Artists Award 2003. *Current Management:* Sulivan Sweetland, 28 Albion Street, London, W2 2AX, England. *Telephone:* (20) 7262-0333. *Fax:* (20) 7402-5851. *E-mail:* info@sulivansweetland.co.uk. *Website:* www.sulivansweetland.co.uk.

**SHANKS, Donald;** Singer (Bass-Baritone); b. 5 July 1940, Brisbane, Australia. *Career:* Sang first in operettas by Gilbert and Sullivan, then toured Australia with the Williamson-Sutherland Opera Company; From 1964 has sung with the Australian Opera, Sydney in over 70 roles including Boris in Boris Godunov, Don Pasquale, Phillip in Don Carlos, Baron Ochs in Rosenkavalier, Osmin, Zaccaria, Nabucco, Raimondo in Lucia di Lammermoor, Prince Gremin in Eugene Onegin, Gurnemanz, Parsifal; Sang at Covent Garden in 1974 and Paris Opéra in 1976; Various roles with Queensland Lyric Opera and Victoria State Opera; Season 1996 as Rocco in Fidelio, Zaccaria in Nabucco, Daland in Der fliegende Holländer, Sarastro in The Magic Flute in Sydney for the Australian Opera; Parson/Badger in The Cunning Little Vixen, 1997. *Honours:* O.B.E., 1976; AO, 1987. *Address:* c/o The Australian Opera, PO Box 291, Strawberry Hills, Sydney 2012, Australia.

**SHAO, En;** Conductor; b. 1954, Tianjin, China. *Education:* Piano studies from age 4, violin from 5; Peking Centre Music Conservatory and Royal Northern College of Music. *Career:* Deputy Principal Conductor of the Chinese Broadcasting Symphony Orchestra and Principal Guest Conductor of the Central Philharmonic Orchestra of Ogina and the National Youth Orchestra; Engagements in Europe from 1988; Associate Conductor of the BBC Philharmonic Orchestra, 1990; Principal Conductor and Artistic Adviser of the Ulster Orchestra, 1993; Guest Appearances with the Bournemouth Symphony, Northern Sinfonia, Royal Liverpool Philharmonic and other BBC orchestras; London debut 1992 with the London Symphony Orchestra; European engagements with the Oslo Philharmonic, the Berlin Symphony and the Czech Philharmonic; Prague Autumn Festival, 1993; Concerts with the ABC Orchestras in Australia and the Hong Kong Philharmonic; North American showings with the Toronto Symphony and the Colorado and Vancouver Symphonies; Royal Philharmonic Orchestra debut, 1994; Helsinki Philharmonic. *Honours:* Lord Rhodes Scholarship; First Edward Van Beinum Scholarship; Winner, Sixth Hungarian Television Conductors Competition. *Current Management:* IMG Artists, Lovell House, 616 Chiswick High Road, London W4 5RX, England.

**SHAPERO, Harold (Samuel);** Pianist, Teacher and Composer; b. 29 April 1920, Lynn, Massachusetts, USA. *Education:* Studied piano with Eleanor Kerr; Composition with Nicolas Slonimsky, Malkin Conservatory, Boston 1936–37; with Ernst Krenek, 1937, with Walter Piston, Harvard University, 1938–41; With Paul Hindemith, Berkshire Music Center, Tanglewood, summers 1940, 1941; Nadia Boulanger, Longy School of Music, 1942–43. *Career:* Pianist; Teacher 1952–, Founder-director, electronic music studio, Brandeis University. *Compositions:* Orchestral: 9-minuted Overture, 1940; Serenade, 1945; Symphony for classical orchestra, 1947; Sinfonia: The Travelers Overture, 1948; Concerto, 1950; Credo, 1955; Lyric Dances, 1955; On Green Mountain for jazz ensemble, 1957; for orchestra, 1981; Partita for piano and small orchestra, 1960; Trumpet Concerto, 1995; Chamber: String Trio, 1938; 3 Pieces for flute, clarinet and bassoon, 1939; Trumpet Sonata, 1940, String Quartet, 1941; Violin Sonata, 1942; 3 Improvisations for piano and synthesizer, 1968; 3 Studies for piano and synthesizer, 1969; 4 Pieces for piano and synthesizer, 1969; 4 Pieces for piano and synthesizer, 1970; Six for Five, woodwind quintet, 1994; Piano: Sonata for 4-hands, 1941; 3 sonatas, all 1944; Variations, 1947; Sonata, 1948; American Variations, 1950; Vocal: 4 Baritone Songs, 1942; 2 Psalms for chorus, 1952; Hebrew Cantata for soprano, alto, tenor, baritone, chorus and 5 instruments, 1954; 2 Hebrew Songs for tenor and piano, 1970, also for tenor, piano and string orchestra, 1980. *Recordings:* Several compositions recorded. *Honours:* American Prix de Rome, 1941; Naumburg Fellowship, 1942; Guggenheim Fellowships, 1947, 1948; Fulbright Fellowship, 1948. *Address:* c/o Music Department, Brandeis University, MA 02254, USA.

**SHAPIRO, Joel;** Concert Pianist and Teacher; b. 28 Nov. 1934, Cleveland, Ohio, USA. *Education:* AB, Columbia College, New York City; Private study with Beryl Rubinstein and Frank Sheridan; Brussels Royal Conservatory with Stefan Askenase; Premier Prix avec Distinction, 1959. *Career:* debut, New York City, 1963; As a Soloist with Royal Philharmonic Orchestra, 1968; Extensive annual concert tours including piano recitals, concertos and chamber music in the world's leading music centres; Numerous radio and television broadcasts; Professor of Piano, University of Illinois, 1970–93; Professor of Piano and Prorektor, Staatliche Hochschule für Musik, Leipzig, 1994–; Artistic Director International Summer Music Academy, Leipzig, 1999–. *Honours:* Winner, Young Concert Artists International Auditions, New York City, 1961; 1st Prize, Darche Competition, Brussels, 1962; Harriet Cohen International Bach Award, London, 1963; Awards from The International Institute, 1964 and Rockefeller Foundation, 1965. *Address:* Hochschule für Musik, Grassistrasse 8, 04107 Leipzig, Germany.

**SHAPIRRA, Elyakum;** Conductor; b. 1926, Tel-Aviv, Israel. *Education:* Studied with Bernstein and Koussevitzky at Tanglewood and the Juilliard School. *Career:* Assistant with the San Francisco Symphony Orchestra; Conducted the New York Philharmonic on tours to Canada and Japan, 1960–61; Associate Conductor of the Boston Symphony Orchestra 1962–67; Guest conductor with leading orchestras in England (1968) and the USA; Chief Conductor of the Malmö Symphony Orchestra, Sweden, 1969–74; Chief Conductor of the South Australian Symphony Orchestra at Adelaide, 1975; Has conducted opera in Scandinavia. *Recordings include:* Bruckner's F minor Symphony and G minor Overture with the London Symphony Orchestra.

**SHARAF, Hisham;** Iraqi musician (clarinet); *Artistic Director, Baghdad Symphony Orchestra. Education:* Baghdad School of Folk Music and Ballet;*Address:* Iraqi National Symphony Orchestra, Baghdad Convention Center, Green Zone, Baghdad, Iraq.

**SHARNINA, Ljubov;** Singer (Soprano); b. 1962, Moscow, Russia. *Education:* Studied at the Gnessin Institute, Moscow. *Career:* Sang at the Nemirovitsch-Danschenko Theatre Moscow from 1986, notably as Tatiana, Lisa, Iolanta, Nedda, Lisa in La Battaglia di Legnano, Zemfira in Rachmaninov's Aleko and Imogene in Bellini's Pirata; Guest engagements as Aida at Birmingham and Manchester, Desdemona at Aachen in 1990, the Trovatore Leonora at Leipzig in 1991, and Maria in Tchaikovsky's Mazeppa at Amsterdam in 1991; Many concert appearances in Cologne, Vienna, St Petersburg and North America. *Address:* Bolshoi Theatre, 103009 Moscow, Russia.

**SHARP, Norma;** Opera Singer (Soprano); b. 1945, Shawnee, Oklahoma, USA; m. Jens Niggemeyer, 1 s. *Education:* Kansas University, USA; Hochschule für Musik, Hamburg, Cologne. *Career:* 1970–77 Permanent Member of the opera houses of Regensburg, Augsburg, Karlsruhe as Lyric Soprano; Since 1978 freelance Opera Singer, regular guest at Berlin, Hamburg, Munich, Frankfurt, Cologne, Düsseldorf, Vienna; Further Guest Appearances at Dresden, Hannover, Stuttgart, Amsterdam, Antwerp, Ghent, Zürich, Basel, Bern, Geneva, Milan, Rome, Naples, Madrid, London, Glasgow, Prague, Budapest; Festivals: Bayreuth 1977–81, Glyndebourne, Vienna; Concerts throughout Europe with conductors including Pierre Boulez, Carlo Maria Giulini, Marek Janowski, Neville Marriner, Wolfgang Sawallisch, Giuseppe Sinopoli, Horst Stein; Professor of Voice, Hochschule für Musik, Hanns Eisler, Berlin, 1992–. *Recordings:* Tales of Hoffmann; Peer Gynt; Ring of the Nibelung; Tannhäuser. *Current Management:* Marguerite Kollo, Berlin. *Address:* Seestr 119, 13353 Berlin, Germany.

**SHAULIS, Jane;** Singer (Mezzo-soprano); b. 1950, New Jersey, USA. *Education:* Studies, Philadelphia Academy and Curtis Institute. *Career:* Appearances with New York City Opera, 1977–90; Metropolitan Opera, 1990–, Notably in the premieres of The Ghosts of Versailles by Corigliano and The Voyage by Glass; Further New York appearances in Idomeneo, Elektra,

Die Zauberflöte, The Ring, I Lombardi, Arabella and Peter Grimes; Season 1996–97 as Mozart's Marcellina, Mdme. Larina in Eugene Onegin and Marthe in Faust; Glyndebourne, 1990–, as Nan in New Year by Tippett and Ragonde in Le Comte Ory, 1997; Other Roles include Amneris at Buffalo, Azucena and Herodias for Kentucky Opera and the Countess in Andrea Chénier at Chicago; Fricka, Erda and Waltraute in The Ring at Artpark. *Address:* c/o New York Metropolitan Opera, Lincoln Center, New York, NY 10023, USA.

**SHAVE, Jacqueline;** Violinist; b. 1960, England. *Career:* Co-Founded the Brindisi String Quartet at Aldeburgh, 1984; Wigmore Hall Debut 1984, with Peter Pears; Concerts in a wide repertory throughout the United Kingdom and in France, Germany, Spain, Italy and Switzerland; Festival Engagements at Aldeburgh, Arundel, Bath, Brighton, Huddersfield, Norwich and Warwick; First London Performance of Colin Matthews 2nd Quartet, 1990; Quartet by Mark Anthony Turnage, 1992; Many BBC Recitals and Resident Artist with the University of Ulster. *Recordings include:* Quartets by Britten, Bridge and Imogen Holst; Works by Pierné and Lekeu. *Honours:* Prize Winner at the Third Banff International String Quartet Competition. *Address:* c/o Owen/White Management, 14 Nightingale Lane, London N8 7QU, England.

**SHAVERZASHVILI, George;** composer and pianist; b. 4 Aug. 1950, Tbilisi, Georgia; m.; one d. *Education:* State Conservatory, Tbilisi. *Career:* debut, piano 1970, composer 1980, Tbilisi; Concerts at Tbilisi, Moscow, St Petersburg, Tallinn, Budapest, Bratislava; Professor, State Conservatory, Tbilisi; mem, Georgian Composers Union, 1986. *Compositions:* Quintet for piano and string quartet; 3 Sonatas for piano; 2 Concerts for piano and orchestra, 1984, 1991; 2 Concertos for violin, 1990, 1995; Sonata for violin; Trio for piano, flute and clarinet, 1997; Alegg for string orchestra, 1998; 2 piano fantasies, 1998, 1999; Mass for chorus and orchestra, 1999; Maestoso for piano, 2000; Clouds for symphony orchestra, 2003. *Address:* Mosashvili Street 8, Ap 6, 380062 Tbilisi, Georgia.

**SHAW, Kenneth;** Singer (Bass-baritone); b. 1955, Georgia, USA. *Career:* Debut: New Orleans, 1980, as Morales in Carmen; Appearances at New Orleans and Kentucky Operas as Mozart's Count, Germont and Escamillo, 1989; Scarpia and Nilakantha in Lakmé; season 1986–87 as Sharpless in Butterfly at New York City Opera; Mefistofele at Three Cities Opera; Concert of Jenůfa at Carnegie Hall, 1988; Saratoga Festival, New York as Marcello; Other roles include Jochanaan in Salome; Sarastro, Kentucky Opera, 1998. *Recordings:* Jenůfa. *Address:* c/o Kentucky Opera, 101 South 8th Street, Louisville KY 40202, USA.

**SHAW, Teresa;** Singer (Mezzo-soprano); b. 1965, England. *Education:* Studied at the Royal Academy of Music. *Career:* Concert appearances in Debussy's Le Martyre de Saint Sebastien with the London Philharmonic under Kurt Masur; Vivaldi's Gloria with Richard Hickox; Handel's Dixit Dominus and Haydn's Nelson Mass conducted by David Willcocks; The Dream of Gerontius at the York and Ripon Festival, 1991; The Apostles and the Glagolitic Mass at Canterbury; Operatic roles include Octavian, Third Lady in Die Zauberflöte, Dorabella (Opera Factory) and Female Chorus in Goehr's Triptych; Season 1991 included Purcell Room, Conway Hall and Wigmore Hall recitals; Premiere production of The Death of Klinghoffer by John Adams in Lyon and Vienna; Season 1992 in title role of Oliver's Beauty and the Beast, at Portsmouth; Season 1996 as the Composer in Ariadne auf Naxos for Castleward Opera. *Recordings include:* Sorceress in Dido and Aeneas and Brahms Liebesliederwalzer, conducted by John Eliot Gardiner. *Honours:* Winner, Great Grimsby International Singing Competition, 1989.

**SHCHEDRIN, Rodion Konstantinovich;** Russian composer; b. 16 Dec. 1932, Moscow; s. of Konstantin Mikhailovich Shchedrin and Konkordia Ivanovna Shchedrin; m. Maya Plisetskaya 1958. *Education:* Moscow Conservatoire. *Career:* Chair. RSFSR (now Russian) Union of Composers 1973–90; USSR People's Deputy 1989–91; mem. Acad. of Fine Arts, Berlin, Bavarian Acad. of Fine Arts. *Compositions include:* operas: Not Only Love 1961, Dead Souls (operatic scenes in three acts) 1976, Lolita (after V. Nabokov) 1994; ballets: Humpbacked Horse 1960, Carmen Suite 1967, Anna Karenina 1972, The Seagull 1980, Lady with a Lapdog 1985; for orchestra: three symphonies 1958, 1965, 2000, 5 concertos for orchestra 1963, 1968, 1988, 1989, 1998; Self-Portrait 1984, Stykhira 1988, Old Russian Circus Music 1989; 6 concertos for piano and orchestra 1954, 1966, 1973, 1992, 1999, 2003, Concerto for cello and orchestra 1994, Concerto for trumpet and orchestra 1995, Two Tangos by Albéniz for orchestra 1996, Concerto dolce for viola and string orchestra 1997; other: Poetoria 1974, Musical Offering for organ and nine soloists 1983, The Sealed Angel (Russian Liturgy) 1988, Nina and the Twelve Months (musical) 1988, Piano Terzetto 1996, Concerto Cantabile (for violin and strings) 1997, Preludium for 9th Symphony by Beethoven 1999, Lolita-serenade 2001, Parabola concertante (for cello and strings) 2001, Dialogue with Shostakovich 2001, The Enchanted Wanderer (concert opera) 2002, Tanja-Katya 2002, My Age, My Wild Beast 2003; works for chamber orchestra, piano, violin, organ and cello and song cycles, music for theatre and cinema. *Honours:* Hon. mem. American Liszt Soc., Rachmaninov Soc., Int. Music Council, Hon. Prof., Moscow Conservatoire; Lenin Prize, USSR and Russian State Prizes, Russian Union of Composers Prize, Shostakovich Prize, Beethoven Soc. Prize. *Address:* Theresienstrasse 23, 80333 Munich, Germany (home); 25/9, Tverskaya St, apt. 31, 103050 Moscow, Russia (home). *Telephone:* (89) 285834 (Munich); (095) 299-72-39 (Moscow). *Fax:* (89) 282057 (Munich). *E-mail:* rshchedrin@yahoo.com (office). *Website:* www .shchedrin.de (office).

**SHEBANOVA, Tatiana;** Pianist; b. 12 Jan. 1953, Moscow, USSR; m. 18 Sept 1986, 1 s. *Education:* Undergraduate and Postgraduate Studies, Main Music School, Moscow Conservatory. *Career:* Represented Moscow Conservatory, various International competitions and meetings; Live concert performances include appearances in Czechoslovakia, Belgium, France, Germany, Switzerland, Italy, Netherlands, Greece, Portugal, Austria and many tours: Japan, Philippines, Yugoslavia, Poland, Spain; Repertoire includes about 30 recitals, about 30 piano concertos; 1st interpretation of Bach's 12 choral preludes in Feinberg's transcription, Moscow Conservatory; Teaching, Warsaw and Bygdoszoz Academies of Music, Poland. *Recordings:* Works by Tchaikovsky, Chopin (many), Szymanowski, Rachmaninov, Bach, Debussy, Brahms.

**SHEERIN, Mairead;** Singer (Soprano); b. 1972, England. *Education:* Birmingham Conservatoire; Royal College of Music, with Margaret Kingsley. *Career:* Concert engagements in Haydn's Paukenmesse and Harmoniemesse, Elijah, Mozart's Requiem and Coronation Mass, Messiah, the Fauré Requiem and Monteverdi's Vespers; European tour with the St Matthew Passion, as soloist with the English Concert under Trevor Pinnock, 2001; London Handel Festival, 2001, as Clelia in Muzio Scevola; Other roles include Serpetto in La Finta Giardiniera, Ravel's Enfant, Purcell's Sorceress and Yum-Yum in The Mikado. *Honours:* D'Oyly Carte Scholar, at the London Royal Schools Opera. *Address:* c/o Royal College of Music (vocal faculty) Prince Consort Road, London SW7, England.

**SHEFFIELD, Philip;** Singer (tenor); b. 1960, Kenya. *Education:* Studied at Cambridge University, Guildhall School and Royal College of Music; Further Study with Philip Langridge and Malcolm King. *Career:* Season 1989–90 in L'Incoronazione di Popea at Brussels, Hans Jürgen von Bose's 63: Dream Palace at Munich and Capriccio at Glyndebourne; Cavalli's Egisto for the Berlin Kammeroper, Scaramuccio at Antwerp and the Count in Die Tote Stadt in Netherlands; Other Repertoire Encludes Mozart's Ferrando and Tamino, and Agenore in Il Re Pastore; Lensky, Tamino, and Belmonte for Lucerne Opera; Recent Concert performances include Britten's Nocturne with the Berlin Symphony Orchestra in the Philharmonie, and again in Montepulciano, Haydn's L'isola disabitata in the Vienna Konzerthaus with Heinz Holliger, Alexander Goehr's Eve Dreams in Paradise with the BBC Philharmonic, Henze's Kammermusik 1958 in Amsterdam, Schreker's Der Schatzgraeber for the Dutch Radio Philharmonic Orchestra in the Amsterdam Concertgebouw, Stravinsky's Renard with the Ensemble Modern in Frankfurt, Berlin and Vienna, Bach's St John Passion (Evangelist) with the North Netherlands Orchestra, Berio's Sinfonia in Leningrad and Messiah in Antwerp with the Royal Flanders Philharmonic; Also many appearances throughout the United Kingdom including Monteverdi's Orfeo at the Proms, Poppea in the QEH and Bach's B Minor Mass in Canterbury, all with Roger Norrington; Recent operatic performances include Ferrando in Così fan tutte; Shere Khan and Harry in Baa Baa Black Sheep; Chevalier in Der Ferne Klang; Belmonte in Die Entführung; Tamino in Die Zauberflöte; Lensky in Eugene Onegin; Sang Theseus in Goehr's Arianna at Cambridge, 1996; Janáček's Schoolmaster (Vixen) at Birmingham, 1998. *Recordings include:* Berio's Sinfonia with Pierre Boulez; Baa Baa Black Sheep for BBC and Radio with CD to follow; Tippett's Midsummer Marriage for Thames television and 63 Dream Palace for Bayerischer Rundfunk. *Current Management:* Musicmakers International Artists Representation, Tailor House, 63–65 High Street, Whitwell, Hertfordshire SG4 8AH, England. *Telephone:* (1438) 871708. *Fax:* (1438) 871777. *E-mail:* musicmakers@compuserve.com. *Website:* www.operauk.com.

**SHEFSIEK, David,** MMus; opera house director; *Managing Director, Vancouver Opera. Education:* Univ. of British Columbia, Carnegie Mellon Univ. *Career:* fmr singer with Des Moines Opera, Sarasota Opera, Ohio Light Opera; previous admin. positions include Dir of External Affairs Pittsburgh Opera; fmr Dir of Resource Development Vancouver Opera, currently Man. Dir; fmr teaching positions at Univ. of British Columbia, Carnegie Mellon Univ. *Address:* Vancouver Opera Offices, 835 Cambie Street, Vancouver, BC V6B 2P4, Canada (office). *E-mail:* dshefsiek@vancouveropera.ca (office). *Website:* www.vancouveropera.ca (office).

**SHELLEY, Howard Gordon;** British concert pianist and conductor; b. 9 March 1950, London; s. of Frederick Gordon Shelley and Anne Taylor; m. Hilary MacNamara 1975; one s. one step-s. *Career:* professional début Wigmore Hall, London 1971; soloist with all London and provincial British orchestras; regular tours to USA and Canada, Australia, Hong Kong and Europe; three piano concertos written for him (Cowie, Chapple, Dickinson); conducting début with London Symphony Orchestra 1985; Assoc. Conductor, London Mozart Players 1990–92, Prin. Guest Conductor 1992–98; Music Dir, Prin. Conductor Uppsala Chamber Orchestra, Sweden 2001–03; opera conducting debut 2002; current engagements as conductor or soloist or combined role of conductor/soloist. *Repertoire:* from Mozart through Liszt to Gershwin; first pianist to perform in concert complete solo piano works of Rachmaninov 1983. *Recordings include:* the complete solo piano music of Rachmaninov (nine vols) and complete Rachmaninov song-cycle (three vols), Chopin Preludes, Sonatas, Scherzi, Impromptus, Schumann Carnival, Kinderszenen, Hummel solo piano works, complete piano concertos of Rachmininov, piano concertos of British composers Alwyn, Carwithen, Dickinson, Ferguson, Rubbra, Tippett and Vaughan Williams, piano concertos and rhapsodies for piano and orchestra of Gershwin, piano concertos of Balakirev, Korngold (Left Hand), Liapounov, Hindemith's Four Temperaments, Szymanowski's Symphony No. 4 and Messiaen's Turangalila;

conducting from the keyboard Shelley has recorded the Mendelssohn piano concertos (three vols) and Mozart piano concertos Nos 9, 12, 13, 14, 17, 19, 20–24, 27 (six vols), Hummel piano concertos (three vols), Cramer piano concertos (one vol.), Moscheles piano concertos (three vols); conducting the Royal Philharmonic Orchestra he has recorded Mozart symphonies 35 and 38 and Schubert symphonies 3 and 5 and with Tasmanian Symphony Orchestra Reinecke symphonies 2 and 3. *Television:* Documentary on Ravel with Tasmanian Symphony Orchestra (Australian Broadcasting Co.) featured Shelley as presenter, conductor and pianist (Gold Medal for Best Arts Biog., 40th New York Festival Awards); documentary on Rachmaninov by Hessische Rundfunk (Channel 4). *Honours:* Hon. FRCM 1993; Dannreuther Concerto Prize 1971. *Current Management:* Caroline Baird Artists, Pinkhill House, Eynsham, Oxon., OX29 4DA. *Telephone:* (1865) 882771 (office). *Fax:* (1865) 882771 (office). *Website:* www.carolinebairdartists.co.uk (office). *Address:* 38 Cholmeley Park, London, N6 5ER, England.

**SHELTON, Lucy,** BA, MusM; American concert singer (soprano). *Education:* Pomona Coll. (CA) and New England Conservatory of Music. *Career:* Asst Prof. of Voice Eastman School of Music, Univ. of Rochester, NY 1979; Visiting Prof. Cleveland Inst. of Music, OH 1986; appearances at Chamber Music NW, Bethlehem, Bach, Casals, Tanglewood and Aspen Music Festivals, with all major US orchestras, at BBC Promenade Concerts (London); numerous recitals and guest appearances; best known for 20th century repertoire (including premières of Carter, Knussen, Ruders, Grisey, Albert, Schwantner, Smirnov, etc); recordings with Nonesuch Records, Vox, Vanguard, Bridge, Smithsonian Inst., Deutsche Grammophon; teacher New England Conservatory, Tanglewood Music Center; Walter W. Naumburg Prize (jtly) 1977, (solo) 1980. *Address:* New England Conservatory of Music, 290 Huntington Ave, Boston, MA 02115, USA. *Website:* www.newenglandconservatory.edu.

**SHENG, Bright;** composer; b. 6 Dec. 1955, Shanghai, China. *Education:* Shanghai Conservatory, 1976–; Queens College, City University of New York and Columbia University, 1982–, with Chou-Wen Chung, Mario Davidovsky, George Perle and Hugo Weisgall. *Career:* freelance composer with many performances throughout the USA; Commissions from Peter Serkin and Gerard Schwarz; Opera, The Song of Majnun, with libretto by Andrew Porter, written for the Chicago Lyric Opera, 1992 (former Composer-in-Residence); Resident, Seattle Symphony Orchestra, 1992–94. *Compositions:* Three Pieces, for orchestra, 1982; Trio, for flute, harp and cello, 1982; Five Pieces, for oboe and cello, 1983; 2 String Quartets, 1984; Suite for piano, 1984; Four Poems From the Tang Dynasty, for mezzo and piano, 1984; Adagio, for chamber orchestra, 1987; Three Poems From the Sung Dynasty, for soprano and chamber orchestra, 1987; H'un (Lacerations): In Memoriam, 1966–76, for orchestra, 1987; Three Pieces for viola and piano, 1987; My Song, for piano, 1988; Three Chinese Love Songs, for soprano, viola and piano, 1988; Three Chinhai Folk Songs, for chorus, 1989; Four Movements, for piano trio, 1990; The Song of Majnun, Opera, 1992; Prelude, for orchestra, 1994; The Silver River (musical, libretto by David Henry Hwang) 1997, Madame Mao (opera) 2003.

**SHEPPARD, Craig;** Concert Pianist; b. 26 Nov. 1947, Philadelphia, USA. *Education:* Studied at the Curtis Institute of Music and the Juilliard School of Music. *Career:* Senior Artist-in-Residence, University of Washington, Seattle; Teacher, Yehudi Menuhin School, Surrey, 1978–88; Teacher, University of Lancaster, 1979–81; Teacher, Guildhall School of Music and Drama, 1981–86; Concert Experience as Soloist in most American and all the major British, German and Italian Orchestras; Conductors have included Georg Solti, James Levine, Leonard Slatkin, Michael Tilson Thomas, Pritchard, Neeme Järvi and Charles Mackerras; Television appearances on PBS America and BBC England. *Recordings:* Liszt; Rachmaninov; Rossini; Jolivet. *Honours:* Arthur Rubinstein Prize; Silver Medal, Leeds International Pianoforte Competition; Dealey Award; Young Musicians Foundation of Los Angeles 1st Prize. *Address:* c/o School of Music, University of Washington, Seattle, WA 98195-3450, USA.

**SHEPPARD, Honor,** FRMCM; British singer (soprano); b. 1931, Leeds, Yorks.; d. of George Sheppard and Winifred Sheppard (née Tonkin); m. Robert Elliott; one s. one d. *Education:* Leeds Girls' High School, Royal Manchester Coll. of Music. *Career:* recitalist and oratorio singer; appearances at major British and European festivals; First Soprano with the Deller Consort, specialising in 17th and 18th century music; extensive tours of N and S America, Canada and Europe 1961–; numerous broadcasts; Tutor in Vocal Studies, Royal Northern Coll. of Music 1987–. *Recordings include:* Belinda in Dido and Aeneas, conducted by Alfred Deller; The Fairy Queen, The Indian Queen and King Arthur; Handel's Acis and Galatea. *Honours:* Curtis Gold Medal, Royal Manchester Coll. of Music. *Address:* The Firs, 27 The Firs, Bowdon, Cheshire WA14 2TF, England (home).

**SHEPPARD, Kerrie;** Singer (Soprano); b. 1970, Mansfield, England. *Education:* Studied at the Guildhall School and the National Opera Studio. *Career:* Appearances as Mimi in La Bohème at the Mananan Festival; Premiere production of Birtwistle's The Second Mrs Kong at Glyndebourne; Other roles include Micaela, Donna Elvira, Fiordiligi in Così fan tutte; Concerts include engagements with the Bangkok Symphony, Exultate Jubilate by Mozart at Chichester, Beethoven's Mass in C at the Fishguard Festival, Carmina Burana; Concerts with the Liverpool Philharmonic and Bournemouth Symphony Orchestras. *Honours:* Decca prize, 1995 Kathleen

Ferrier Competition. *Address:* Harlequin Agency Ltd, 203 Fidlas Road, Cardiff CF4 5NA, Wales.

**SHEPPARD SKAERVED, Peter;** violinist; *Research Fellow, Royal Academy of Music;* b. 1966, England. *Education:* Royal Acad. with Ralph Holmes, Sidney Griller and Erich Gruenberg, and studied in Boston with Louis Krasner. *Career:* dedicatee of over 200 works for solo violin, including Henze, Matthews and Rochberg; regular appearances in over 30 countries; recordings on Naxos, Metier, Chandos; duo partnership with pianist Aaron Shorr; leader of the Kreutzer Quartet; Principal Lecturer at the Royal Acad. of Music from 1993, currently Research Fellow; Visiting Prof. Blair School of Music, Carl Nielsen Conservatory. *Address:* c/o Royal Academy of Music Strings Faculty, Marylebone Road, London, NW1 5HT, England (office). *Telephone:* (20) 7480-5145 (home). *E-mail:* sheppardskaerved@aol.com (home).

**SHERE, Charles;** Composer and Writer on Music; b. 20 Aug. 1935, Berkeley, California, USA; m. Lindsay Remolif Shere. *Education:* Graduated, University of California at Berkeley, 1960 and studied music at the San Francisco Conservatory. *Career:* Music Director at California radio stations, 1964–73; Instructor at Mills College, Oakland, 1973–84 and Critic for the Oakland Tribune, 1972–88. *Compositions include:* Fratture for 7 instruments, 1962; Small Concerto for piano and orchestra, 1964; Ces desirs du vent des Greogoriens for tape, 1967; Nightmusic for diminished orchestra, 1967; Handler of Gravity for organ and optional chimes, 1971; Music for Orchestra (Symphony), 1976; Tongues for poet, chamber orchestra and tape, 1978; String QuartetNo. 1, 1980; The Bride Stripped Bare by Her Bachelors, Even, opera, 1981 and 1984; Certain Phenomena of Sound for soprano and violin, 1983; Concerto for Violin with Harp, Percussion and Small Orchestra, 1985; Requiem with oboe, 1985; Ladies Voice, chamber opera, 1987; Symphony in 3 Movements, 1988; I Like it to be a Play for tenor baritone, bass and string quartet, 1989; Sonata: Bachelor Machine for piano, 1989; What Happened, chamber opera after Gertrude Stein (trilogy with Ladies Voices and I Like it to be a Play); Three more Stein songs for soprano, violin, piano and bass clarinet, 1997; Trio for violin, piano and percussion, 1997;. *Contributions:* EAR (monthly new-music magazinee), which he co-founded and published. *Address:* c/o ASCAP, ASCAP Building, 1 Lincoln Plaza, New York, NY 10023, USA.

**SHERLOCK, Elizabeth;** British double bassist and viola da gamba player; b. 27 April 1946, Hillingdon, Middlesex. *Education:* Royal Coll. of Music. *Career:* debut, Purcell Room with the Helicon Ensemble, viola da gamba 1972; Oviedo, playing Dittersdorf Sinfonia Concertante, double bass 1994; mem. of Collegium Sagittarii and Helicon Ensemble 1967–72; principal cellist of St Cecilia Orchestra, Norwich, Celtic Sinfonia, South Wales, Ryedale Festival Orchestra; changed to bass in 1989; mem. of Asturias Symphony Orchestra, Spain 1991–; founder mem. of ensemble, La Ghironda, specialising in early music. *Publications:* contrib. to British and int. Bass Forum magazine. *Honours:* Lesley Alexander Prize for Violoncello 1965–66. *Address:* Calle Jorge Tuya 4-1c, La Corredoria, Oviedo 33011, Asturias, Spain.

**SHERMAN, Alexandra;** Singer (mezzo-soprano); b. 1970, St Petersburg, Russia. *Education:* Studied in Jerusalem and at Victorian College of the Arts, Melbourne; Royal College of Music, with Margaret Kingsley. *Career:* Concert engagements include Bach's Passions, Elijah, Messiah, Mozart's Requiem and Vivaldi's Gloria; Lieder eines fahrenden Gesellen in Melbourne and Sydney, Les Nuits d'été and Elgar's Sea Pictures; Season 1999 included Prokofiev's Alexander Nevsky with the Queensland Symphony Orchestra, Pergolesi's Stabat Mater, and Russian Songs at St John's Smith Square; Season 2000–01, with Messiah in Manchester, B minor Mass in York, Schubert's A flat Mass with the London Mozart Players and Mahler's 2nd Symphony in Melbourne; London Handel Festival 2001, as Guido in Flavio and Irene in Muzio Scevola; European tour with the Academy of Ancient Music in Bach's Magnificat, 2001. *Honours:* Queen's Trust for Young Australians Award; Joan Sutherland Award. *Current Management:* Musicmakers International Artists Representation, Tailor House, 63–65 High Street, Whitwell, Hertfordshire SG4 8AH, England. *Telephone:* (1438) 871708. *Fax:* (1438) 871777. *E-mail:* musicmakers@compuserve.com. *Website:* www.operauk.com. *Address:* c/o Royal College of Music (Vocal Faculty), Prince Consort Road, London SW7, England.

**SHERRATT, Brindley;** Singer (bass); b. 1965, England; m. 2 children. *Education:* Royal Academy of Music. *Career:* Debut: Welsh National Opera, as Leporello; Appearances as Wurm in Luisa Miller at Lausanne, Commendatore in Don Giovanni and Basilio in Barbiere for Garsington Opera and the King in Ariodante for Reisopera, Netherlands; Concerts include St Matthew Passion (London Proms, 2002), Les Noces by Stravinsky under Boulez in Paris, The Creation with Trevor Pinnock at the Lucerne Festival and Messiah with Robert King in the USA; Bach Cantatas and Haydn Masses with John Eliot Gardiner; Season 2001–02 with Plutone in Haydn's Orfeo and Publio in La Clemenza di Tito at Covent Garden; Season 2002–03 as Melisso in Alcina at the New York Met, Verdi's Ferrando and Gremin in Eugene Onegin for Welsh National Opera and Britten's Theseus at La Monnaie, Brussels; Concerts with Gardiner and Christophe Rousset; Sarasto for ENO, Commendatore and Claudio in Agrippina for Santa Fe Opera; Hobson in Peter Grimes in Saltzburg with the Berlin Philharmonic and Sir Simon Rattle. *Current Management:* Musicmakers International Artists Representation, Tailor House, 63–65 High Street, Whitwell, Hertfordshire SG4 8AH, England.

*Telephone:* (1438) 871708. *Fax:* (1438) 871777. *E-mail:* musicmakers@compuserve.com. *Website:* www.operauk.com.

**SHICOFF, Neil;** singer (tenor); b. 2 June 1949, New York, USA; m. Judith Haddon. *Education:* Juilliard School with Jennie Tourel. *Career:* debut, Kennedy Center Washington as Narraboth in Salome 1975; Metropolitan Opera 1976–, as Rinuccio in Gianni Schicchi, Verdi's Duke of Mantua, Tchaikovsky's Lensky, Massenet's Werther, Offenbach's Hoffmann and Massenet's Des Grieux; European career from 1976; Don Carlos in Amsterdam, Alfredo and Cilea's Maurizio at the Munich Opera; Macduff in a BBC version of Macbeth and the Duke of Mantua at Covent Garden 1988; At La Scala he has sung Lensky and at the Paris Opéra Don Carlos; Gounod's Roméo for French television; Chicago Lyric Opera debut 1979; San Francisco 1981; Sang Cavaradossi at Stuttgart, 1990; Debut at Barcelona as Hoffmann, 1990; Returned to Covent Garden, 1993, as Pinkerton; Don José at the Opéra Bastille, Paris, 1997; Eléazar in La Juive at the Vienna Staatsoper, 1999; Season 2000–01 at the Met as Hoffmann and Manrico, Don José at the Deutsche Oper Berlin, Donizeti's Edgardo for Zürich Opera and Britten's Captain Vere at the Vienna Staatsoper; Engaged as Eléazar at the Met, 2002–03. *Recordings:* Macduff and the Duke of Mantua for Philips; Foresto in Attila, conducted by Muti. *Current Management:* Theateragentur Dr Germinal Hilbert, Maximilianstrasse 22, 80539 Munich, Germany. *Telephone:* (89) 290 7470. *Fax:* (89) 290 74790. *E-mail:* agentur@hilbert.de. *Website:* www.hilbert.de; www.shicoff.com.

**SHIFRIN, Kenneth (Ken) Allen,** BA, PhD; lecturer, tenor trombonist, alto trombonist, tenor tubist and bass trumpeter and music publisher; b. 25 Aug. 1952, Washington, DC, USA. *Education:* Duke University, Durham, NC, Univ. of Oxford. *Career:* Debuts: US/British premiere of Leopold Mozart Konzert für Posaune, 1974, 1996; World premiere of D to A for Ken Shifrin and Digital Analogue by David Maves; Associate Principal Trombone, Israel Philharmonic, 1976–77; Co-Solo Trombone, Radio Sinfonie Stuttgart, 1977–78; Principal Trombone, Israel Radio Symphony, 1978–92; Principal Trombone, City of Birmingham Symphony Orchestra, 1982–94; Posaune Voce Trio, 1994–; Publisher, Director, Virgo Music, 1987–; Leopold Mozart, Concerto for Alto Trombone, British Premiere, 1996, Czech Premiere, 1997; Leopold Mozart, Agnus Dei, British Premiere, 1996; Wolfgang Amadeus Mozart, Jener Donnerworte Kraft, 1996; Elizabeth Raum, Three Jazz Moods, British and USA Premieres, 1997; Word, St Thomas Sonata, Premier, 1999; Guest artist, Dvořák International Music Festival; Malta International Arts Festival; Masterclasses presented including Prague, Vienna, Manchester, University of Illinois, Duke University and Washington, DC; British Academy Research Board Fellowship 1998–2004; Academy of Sciences of the Czech Republic Scholar Exchange Fellowship 1998–2004. *Honours:* James Ingham Halstead Scholar, Oxford University; Oxford University Press Music and Letters Award. *Address:* 47 Colebank Road, Hall Green, Birmingham, B28 8EZ, England.

**SHIH, Patricia;** Concert Violinist; b. 1971, Canada. *Education:* Studied in Vancouver and with Josef Gingold at Indiana University. *Career:* Season 1987 with recitals in Warsaw and at the Carnegie Hall, New York; Many appearances with leading orchestras in the USA and Europe; Prokofiev's 2nd Concerto with the Toronto Symphony Orchestra, 1994. *Honours:* Prize Winner at Seattle Young Artists Festival, 1985 and Wieniawski Competition, Warsaw, 1986. *Address:* c/o World-wide Artists, 6 Petersfield Crescent, Coulsdon, Surrey CR5 2JQ, England.

**SHILAKADZE, Shavleg;** Composer and Conductor; b. 21 Feb. 1940, Tbilisi, Georgia; m. Liana Shilakadze, 25 Jan 1964, 2 s., 1 d. *Education:* Z Paliashvili Special Music School; Viola and Composition at V Saradjishvili Conservatoire, Tbilisi; Conducting at Rimsky-Korsakov State Conservatoire, Leningrad. *Career:* Debut: Composition, Tbilisi, 1959; Conducting, Tbilisi, 1967; Founder, Ensemble Camerata Tbilisi; Concerts at Tbilisi, Moscow, Leningrad, Kiev, Minsk, Tallinn, Vilnius and elsewhere, 1978–85; Founder, Art Director, chamber orchestra Concertino Tbilisi, 1988–; Concerts at Tbilisi, Germany, 1990, 1991, 1993, 1995, 1996, 1997 Spain, Mar, Oct–Nov, 1993, Switzerland, 1996; 1997; London, Edinburgh, 1998; Professor, Tbilisi Conservatoire; mem. Union of Georgian Composers. *Compositions include:* Sonata for viola and piano; Epitaph, chamber symphony; From Ancient Georgian Poetry, cantata; Concerto for oboe and chamber orchestra; 2 symphonies; Pages of Love, cantata; Concerto for bassoon and chamber orchestra; Concerto giocoso for 3 trumpets and percussion. *Recordings:* R Gabitchvadze's Chamber Symphony No. 4, 1980; G Djaparidze's Chamber Symphony, 1983; Sh Shilakadze's Epitaph, 1983; Camerata Tbilisi, conductor Sh Shilakadze. *Publications:* Articles: About Tbilisi's musical life, 1982; The unity of creative forces, 1984. *Address:* 20 T Tabidze st, 380079 Tbilisi, Georgia.

**SHILLING, Eric,** ARCM; singer; b. 12 Oct. 1920, London, England; m. Erica Johns; two c. *Education:* Guildhall School of Music, Royal College of Music, studied with Walter Hyde and Frank Titterton in London. *Career:* debut at Sadler's Wells as Marullo in Rigoletto 1945; in operas by Smetana, Wagner, Mozart, Donizetti, Rossini and Janáček; television apearances in Die Fledermaus, Orpheus in the Underworld, The Visitation, Trial by Jury and A Tale of Two Cities; sang in the British stage premiere of Prokofiev's War and Peace, London Coliseum 1972; further appearances in operas by Wagner, Mozart, Donizetti, Rossini, Puccini, Strauss, Prokofiev, Penderecki and Reimann; premieres, Story of Vasco by Crosse and Clarissa by Holloway; Somarone in a new production of Beatrice and Benedict; mem. ISM, Council

Equity. *Recordings:* has recorded for major record labels. *Honours:* Royal College of Music Opera Prize, Worshipful Company of Musicians Sir Charles Santley Memorial Prize 1991. *Address:* 49 Belgrave Road, Wanstead, London, E11 3QP, England.

**SHILLITO, Helen Claire,** BMus; British horn player; b. 18 Oct. 1975, Newcastle-upon-Tyne, England. *Education:* Royal College of Music, London, with Julian Baker, Tim Brown and Susan Dent; Franz Liszt Acad., Budapest, with Adam Friedrich; CESMD, Saintes, France, with Claude Maury and Martin Murner (natural horn). *Career:* Co-founder of Aurora Ensemble (wind quintet), 1995, giving wind quintet performances at ORF studios, Vienna, Purcell Room (London), English Music and Cheltenham International Festivals, South Bank Rimsky-Korsakov Festival and International Akademie Prag-Wien-Budapest; Co-founded Ensemble Piros (wind and strings), 2002, Alla Caccia (horn, violin and piano trio), 2003; Joined Broadwood Ensemble (wind and piano), 2002; Launched outreach education scheme Sounds Exciting, 2000; Has played with The Acad. of St Martin-in-the-Fields, BBC Symphony Orchestra, Northern Sinfonia, City of London Sinfonia, Scottish Symphony Orchestra, Scottish Ballet, Welsh Nat. Opera and (on the natural horn) with Europa Galante and Orchestre Champs-Elysées; mem. (with Aurora Ensemble) Live Music Now!. *Television:* The Aurora Ensemble, Channel 4 Wales, 2002. *Radio:* with Aurora Ensemble: BBC Radio 3 Young Artists' Forum Broadcasts, 1999. *Honours:* Prague-Vienna-Budapest Internationale Sommerakademie scholarship winner (with Aurora Ensemble), 1997 and 1997; Winner, Outstanding Musicians Series (with Aurora Ensemble) at St Martin-in-the-Fields, 1998 and 1999; Prizewinner, European Music d'Ensemble Competition, Paris, 2001; Winners, Manchester Mid-day Concert Series, 2003; Winners, Park Lane Group Series, 2004. *Address:* 40 Westgate Road, Faversham, Kent ME13 8HF, England (office); 47 Salisbury Gardens, Jesmond, Newcastle-upon-Tyne NE2 1HP, England. *Telephone:* (7885) 540950 (office); (7195) 532432 (home). *E-mail:* auroraensemble@ hotmail.com (office); helenshillito@ukonline.co.uk (home). *Website:* www .auroraensemble.com (office).

**SHIMELL, William;** British opera singer; b. 23 Sept. 1952, Ilford, Essex; s. of W. Shimell and F. E. Shimell; m. Olga Slavka 1996. *Education:* Westminster Abbey Choir School, St Edward's School, Oxford, Guildhall School of Music and Drama, Nat. Opera Studio, London. *Career:* best known for interpretations of Don Giovanni, Count Almaviva (Marriage of Figaro) and Don Alfonso (Così fan Tutte), which he has sung in opera houses world-wide including La Scala, Milan, Metropolitan Opera House, New York, Paris Opéra, Rome Opera, Vienna Staatsoper, Covent Garden; Assoc. Guildhall School of Music and Drama; numerous recordings. *Address:* c/o IMG Artists, Lovell, 616 Chiswick High Road, London, W4 5RX, England. *Telephone:* (20) 8233-5800. *Fax:* (20) 8742-8758.

**SHIMIZU, Takashi;** Violinist; b. 13 Jan. 1953, Yokosuka, Japan; m. Harue Shimizu, 18 Aug 1973, 1 s. *Education:* Yokosuka High School; University of Southern California, USA; Guildhall School of Music, London, England. *Career:* Debut: Tokyo; Performed with the Royal Philharmonic Orchestra, BBC Philharmonic Orchestra, London Mozart Players, City of Birmingham Symphony Orchestra, The Hague Philharmonic; Many television appearances in France, Belgium, Spain, USSR and Japan. *Recordings:* For international record labels. *Honours:* Bronze Medal, Queen Elizabeth Competition; 2nd Prize and Beethoven Sonata Prize, Carl Flesch Competition; 1st Prize, Granada International Competition. *Current Management:* John Wright. *Address:* 18 Alyth Garden, London NW11, England.

**SHIN, Youngok;** Singer (soprano); b. 1961, Republic of Korea. *Education:* Juilliard School, New York. *Career:* Debut: Spoleto Festival, USA, 1989 as Mozart's Susanna; Metropolitan Opera, New York, from 1990 as Gilda in Rigoletto and roles in Rossini's Semiramide and Bellini's Bianca e Fernando at Catania, 1991; Oscar in Ballo in Maschera at Paris Opéra Bastille, 1993; Gilda at Covent Garden, 1994; Season 1995–96, as Lucia di Lammermoor at Toronto and Elvira in I Puritani at Turin; Other roles include Leila in Les Pêcheurs de Perles. *Recordings:* Bianca e Fernando; Semiramide; Ave Maria. *Address:* c/o Metropolitan Opera, Lincoln Center, New York NY 10023, USA.

**SHINALL, Vern;** Singer (baritone); b. 22 June 1936, St Louis, USA. *Education:* Indiana University, Bloomington, with Charles Kullman. *Career:* Debut: Kansas City Opera, as Scarpia in Tosca, 1964; Appearances in opera houses in Philadelphia, Boston, Houston, New Orleans and St Paul; Main career at New York City Opera; Roles have included Escamillo, Pizarro in Fidelio, Rigoletto, Amonasro, Count Luna, Mephistopheles in Faust and Barnaba in La Gioconda; Wagner's Dutchman, Telramund and Wotan, Don Giovanni and the baritone roles in Les Contes d'Hoffmann; Modern repertory includes John Proctor in The Crucible by Robert Ward and Olin Blitch in Susannah by Carlisle Floyd; Many concert engagements. *Address:* c/o New York City Opera, NY Theater, Lincoln Center, New York, NY 10023, USA.

**SHINOZAKI, Yasuo;** Conductor; b. 19 Feb. 1968, Kyoto, Japan; m. 12 April 1998. *Education:* Toho-Gakuen Music University, 1986–90; Toho-Gakuen Music Graduate School, 1990–92; Toho-Gakuen Conducting Course, 1992–94; Vienna National Music University, Austria, 1995–98. *Career:* Debut: With Bolzano and Trento Orchestra, in Trento, Italy, 1993; Opera debut, Tokyo, 1993; Conducted Bolzano and Trento Orchestra, 1993, Szeged Symphony Orchestra, 1996, Tokyo City Philharmonic Orchestra, 1998, Shinsei (Japan) Symphony Orchestra, 1999. *Honours:* Winner, 2nd Prize, 3rd Antonio Pedrotti International Conducting Competition (1st Prize not awarded), 1993.

*Address:* c/o Shinsei Symphony Orchestra, Maruishi Building, 3–16–4 Nishi Ikebukuro, Toshima-Ku, Tokyo 171, Japan.

**SHIRAI, Mitsuko;** Singer (Contralto); b. 1952, Japan. *Education:* Studied in Stuttgart. *Career:* Appearances in Europe, Israel, Japan and USA; Recitals with piano accompanist Hartmut Holl and concerts with the Berlin Philharmonic, New Japan Philharmonic, Atlanta Symphony, Nouvel Orchestre Philharmonique de Paris and the Vienna Symphony; Conductors include Chailly, Inbal, Ahronovitch, Ferencic and Sawallisch; Repertoire includes Mahler Symphony No. 8, Berlioz Les Nuits d'Été, Berg 7 Early Songs, Hindemith Das Marienleben, Complete vocal works of Webern, Schubert Winterreise and Lieder by Brahms, Wolf and Schumann; Concert performances of Mozart's Lucio Silla, Wagner's Das Liebesverbot and Ariane et Barbe-Bleue; Opened Suntory Hall Tokyo with Alexander Nevsky by Prokofiev; Stage debut Frankfurt 1987, as Despina in Così fan tutte; Masterclasses with Hartmut Holl at the Savonlinna Festival, Schleswig-Holstein Festival, Aldeburgh Festival, in Switzerland and USA and at Isaac Stern's Music Centre in Jerusalem. *Recordings:* Mozart, Schumann and Brahms Lieder (Capriccio); Bach, Mozart and Spohr Lieder; Sacred music by Mozart (Philips); Frauenliebe und-leben by Schumann; Lieder by Mendelssohn and Schumann. *Honours:* Winner of Competitions in Vienna, 's-Hertogenbosch, Athens and Munich; Winner, Robert Schumann Prize, Zwickau, 1982.

**SHIRASAKA-TERATINI, Chieko;** Singer (Mezzo-soprano); b. 1956, Tokyo, Japan. *Education:* Studied in Tokyo, and Hamburg Musikhochschule, 1977-80. *Career:* Many opera appearances from 1981, notably at Bremerhaven and Bonn; Guest engagements at Hamburg, Innsbruck, Bremen and Montpellier; Roles have included Octavian, Hansel, Siebel in Faust, Mozart's Annio, Suzuki in Madama Butterfly, Verdi's Eboli, Preziosilla and Fenena (Nabucico); Ottavia in L'Incoronazione di Poppea, and Rossini's Rosina and Isabella; Many concert and rectial appearances, notably in USA, Japan, Poland and Netherlands. *Honours:* Prizewinner, 1980 's-Hertogenbosch Competition. *Address:* c/o Bonn Opera, Am Boeselagerhof 1, Pf 2440, D-53111 Bonn, Germany.

**SHIRLEY, George;** American tenor and academic; *Joseph Edgar Maddy Distinguished University Professor of Music, University of Michigan;* b. 18 April 1934, Indianapolis, Ind.; s. of Irving E. Shirley and Daisy Shirley (née Bell); m. Gladys Lee Ishop 1956; one s. one d. *Education:* Wayne State Univ. *Career:* debuts with Metropolitan Opera, New York Opera, Festival of Two Worlds (Spoleto, Italy), Santa Fé Opera 1961, Teatro Colón, Buenos Aires 1965, La Scala, Milan 1965, Glyndebourne Festival 1966, Royal Opera, Covent Garden, Scottish Opera 1967, Vienna Festival 1972, San Francisco Opera 1977, Chicago Lyric Opera 1977, Théâtre Municipal d'Angers 1979, Edin. Festival 1979, Nat. Opera Ebony, Philadelphia 1980, Spoleto Festival, Charleston, SC 1980, Tulsa Opera, Okla 1980, Ottawa Festival 1981, Deutsche Oper 1983, Guelph Spring Festival 1983, Bregenz Festival, Austria 1998; Prof. of Voice, Univ. of Md 1980–87; Prof. of Music, Univ. of Mich. 1987–, Joseph Edgar Maddy Distinguished Univ. Prof. of Music 1992–. *Honours:* Hon. HDH (Wilberforce Univ.); Hon. LLD (Montclair State Coll.); Hon. DFA (Lake Forest Coll.); Hon. DHumLitt (Northern Iowa) 1997; Nat. Arts Club Award 1960, Concorso di Musica e Danza (Italy) 1960; Distinguished Scholar-Teacher Award, Univ. of Md 1985–86. *Address:* c/o Ann Summers International, Box 188, Station A, Toronto M5W 1B2, Canada; University of Michigan School of Music, Ann Arbor, MI 48109, USA. *Telephone:* (416) 362-1422 (Canada); (734) 665-7821 (Mich.). *Fax:* (734) 763-5097 (office). *E-mail:* gis@ umich.edu (office); geotenor@netscape.net (home). *Website:* www.music.umich .edu (office).

**SHIRLEY-QUIRK, John,** CBE, BSc; British/American concert and opera singer and teacher; *Member of Voice Faculty, Peabody Conservatory, Johns Hopkins University;* b. 28 Aug. 1931, Liverpool; s. of Joseph Stanley and Amelia Shirley-Quirk; m. 1st Dr Patricia Hastie 1952 (died 1981); one s. one d.; m. 2nd Sara Watkins 1981 (died 1997); one s. two d. (one d. died 2001). *Education:* Holt School, Liverpool and Liverpool Univ. *Career:* Flying Officer, RAF (Educ. Br.) 1952–55; Asst Lecturer, Acton Tech. Coll. 1956–60; Vicar Choral, St Paul's Cathedral 1960–61; professional singer 1961–; mem. Voice Faculty, Peabody Conservatory, Johns Hopkins Univ., Baltimore, Md, USA 1992–; mem. Voice Dept, Coll. of Fine Arts, Carnegie-Mellon Univ., Pittsburgh, Pa 1994–98; many recordings and first performances, notably works of Benjamin Britten and Michael Tippett. *Music:* first performances of Benjamin Britten's last five operas 1964–73; The Ice Break (Michael Tippett) 1977. *TV appearances include:* Carmen, The Marriage of Figaro, Billy Budd, Messiah, Owen Wingrave, Death in Venice. *Films:* Death in Venice (dir Tony Palmer) 1981. *Honours:* Hon. RAM 1972; Hon. DMus (Liverpool) 1976; Hon. DUniv (Brunel) 1981. *Address:* 6062 Red Clover Lane, Clarksville, MD 21029, USA. *Telephone:* (410) 531-1315 (home). *Fax:* (410) 531-3335 (home). *E-mail:* jssq@peabody.jhu.edu (home). *Website:* www.peabody.jhu.edu (office).

**SHKOLNIKOVA, Nelli;** Violinist; b. 8 July 1928, Zolotonosha, Ukraine; m. (1) Boris Sokolov, deceased, (2) Alexander Gul, 14 Dec 1989. *Education:* Music studies, BMus, MMus, Moscow Conservatory, 1949–57; Honours degree in Violin. *Career:* Concert tours in USSR, Austria, Australia, Bulgaria, Czechoslovakia, France, Finland, Hungary, East Germany, Canada, USA, Norway, New Zealand, Japan, 1953–; Appeared with conductors such as Kondrashin, Rozhdestvensky, Munch, Cluytens, Sanderling, Masur, Ormandy; Professor of Violin at Indiana University School of Music, USA;

mem, American String Teachers' Association. *Recordings:* Tchaikovsky–Concerto in D op 35; Mozart–Concerto No. 4 in D K218; Mendelssohn–Concerto in E Minor; Beethoven–Sonata No. 2 in A major op 12 No. 2, Sonata No. 8 in G major op 30 No. 3; Copland–Sonata in G major; Handel–Sonata No. 1 in A major, Sonata No. 3; Pieces by Paganini, Prokofiev and others. *Contributions:* Reviews in Le Figaro, New York Post, Berliner Morgenpost, Arbeiderbladet, Pravda, others. *Honours:* Grand Prix at Marguerite Long-Jacques Thibaud Competition, Paris, France, 1953; Honoured Artist of Russian Republic, 1978. *Address:* 2814 St Remy Circle, Bloomington, IN 47401, USA.

**SHKOSA, Enkelejda;** Singer (Mezzo-soprano); b. 29 Sept. 1969, Tirana, Albania. *Education:* Studied at the State Conservatory, the Academy of Fine Arts, Tirana; Giuseppe Verdi Conservatory, Milan. *Career:* Many appearances at La Scala, Milan, Naples, Turin, Barbican Centre London (under Colin Davis), Strasbourg Cathedral (Pergolesi Stabat Mater) and the Rossini Festival, Pesaro; Season 1997–98 with Maddalena at the Opéra Bastille, Paris, Stockholm, Amsterdam, Bologna, Monte Carlo and Brussels. *Honours:* Winner, Leyla Gencer Competition, Istanbul, 1995. *Address:* c/o Pentagramma, Via Bicetti De' Buttinoni 1, 20156 Milan, Italy.

**SHMITOV, Alexei;** Concert Organist and Pianist; b. 1957, Moscow, Russia. *Education:* Studied at the Moscow Conservatoire, with Roisman and Nikolayeva. *Career:* Many concerts in Russia as organist and pianist; Piano concertos by Bach in Vilnius, Lithuania, and the Sonatas for violin and harpsichord and violin with Viktor Pikaisen; Organ recitals in: Lithuania; Estonia; Latvia; Bach Festival in West Berlin; Recitals with the tenor Alexei Martynov in music by Bach, Handel, Scheidt, Schütz, Mendelssohn, Schumann and Verdi; Recitals at the Prokofiev Centenary Festival in Scotland, 1991; Organ Repertoire includes works by Bach, Widor, Taneyev, Liszt and Shostakovich. *Honours:* 2nd Prize, Organ Competition in Dom Zu Speyer, Germany. *Address:* c/o Sonata, 11 Northpark Street, Glasgow G20 7AA, Scotland.

**SHOKOV, Vladimir;** Cellist; b. 1950, Crimea, Russia. *Career:* Co-founder, Rachmaninov Quartet, 1974, under auspices of the Sochi State Philharmonic Society, Crimea; Many concerts in Russia, and from season, 1975–76, tours to: Switzerland; Austria; Bulgaria; Norway; Germany; Participation in the 1976 Shostakovich Chamber Music Festival at Vilnius, and in festivals in Moscow and St Petersburg; Repertoire has included works by: Haydn, Mozart, Beethoven, Bartók, Brahms, Schnittke, Shostakovich, Tchaikovsky and Meyerovich. *Honours:* Prizewinner at the first All Union Borodin String Quartet Competition. *Address:* c/o Sonata, 11 Northpark Street, Glasgow G20 7AA, Scotland.

**SHORE, Andrew,** BA; British concert and opera singer (baritone); b. 30 Sept. 1952, Oldham, England; m. Fiona Macdonald 1976; three d. *Education:* University of Bristol, Royal Northern College of Music, London Opera Centre. *Career:* as stage manager and singer, Opera For All, 1977–79; debut as Antonio in Marriage of Figaro, Kent Opera, 1981; English National Opera debut, 1988, as Don Alfonso in Così fan tutte; Covent Garden debut, 1992, as Trombonok in Rossini's Il viaggio a Reims; Paris Opéra debut, 1995, as Sacristan in Tosca; US debut, 1996, as Dulcamara in L'Elisir d'amore, at San Diego; Principal roles with all British opera companies and in Paris, Lyon, Hamburg, Barcelona, Amsterdam, Copenhagen, Brussels, Vancouver, Ottawa, Tel-Aviv; Particularly known for Falstaff, Don Pasquale, Dulcamara, Don Alfonso, Papageno, Bartolo, Gianni Schicchi, and in the serious repertoire for Wozzeck, King Priam and Šiškov in Janáček's House of the Dead; Gianni Schicchi for ENO, 1998; Season 2000–01 as Janáček's Kolenaty at Hamburg, Mozart's Bartolo at Glyndebourne and Tippett's King Priam for ENO; Engaged as Hans Sachs for Opéra de Nantes, 2003. *Recordings:* Bartolo in Barber of Seville; Sacristan in Tosca; Benoit and Alcindoro in La Bohème; Dulcamara in L'Elisir d'amore; Title role in Don Pasquale; Video recording of Kolenaty in Janáček's Makropulos Case. *Current Management:* Ingpen & Williams Ltd, 7 St George's Court, 131 Putney Bridge Road, London, SW15 2PA, England.

**SHORE, Clare;** Composer; b. 18 Dec. 1954, Winston-Salem, North Carolina, USA. *Education:* BA cum laude with honours, Music, Wake Forest University, 1976; MMus, University of Colorado, 1977; DMA, Juilliard School of Music, 1984; Studied with Annette LeSiege, Wake Forest University, Charles Eakin and Cecil Effinger, University of Colorado, David Diamond, Vincent Persichetti and Roger Sessions, Juilliard School. *Career:* Teaching: Fordham University, Manhattan School of Music, University of Virginia, and George Mason University, 1981–; Numerous commissions; Works performed in Carnegie Recital Hall, Alice Tully Hall, Lincoln Center, Merkin Concert Hall, Spoleto Festival, Charleston, The Barns of Wolf Trap, National Gallery of Art, throughout USA and abroad. *Compositions:* All works published by leading music publishers. *Recordings include:* July Remembrances, CD; Nightwatch; Oatlands Sketches. *Honours:* Contemporary Records Society Grant, 1988. *Current Management:* E C Schirmer Music Company Inc. *Address:* 12329 Cliveden Street, Herndon, VA 22070, USA.

**SHORE, Howard;** Canadian film score composer; b. 18 Oct. 1946, Toronto, ON. *Education:* Berklee Coll. of Music, Boston, USA. *Career:* f. band Lighthouse; Musical Dir Saturday Night Live TV comedy show 1970s; began composing film music 1978; has collaborated on films by David Cronenberg, Peter Jackson; composed title music for Late Night with Conan O'Brien TV show 1993; mem. ASCAP. *Film scores include:* I Miss You, Hugs and Kisses 1978, The Brood 1979, Scanners 1980, Videodrome 1983, Nothing Lasts Forever 1984, After Hours 1985, Fire with Fire 1986, The Fly 1986, Heaven 1987, Nadine 1987, Dead Ringers 1988, Big 1988, Signs of Life 1989, She-Devil 1989, The Local Stigmatic 1989, An Innocent Man 1989, Made in Milan 1990, The Lemon Sisters 1990, Naked Lunch 1991, The Silence of the Lambs 1991, A Kiss Before Dying 1991, Prelude to a Kiss 1992, Single White Female 1992, Philadelphia 1993, Mrs Doubtfire 1993, Guilty As Sin 1993, Sliver 1993, M. Butterfly 1993, Nobody's Fool 1994, The Client 1994, Ed Wood (Los Angeles Film Critics' Asscn Award) 1994, Se7en 1995, Moonlight and Valentino 1995, White Man's Burden 1995, Before and After 1996, The Truth About Cats and Dogs 1996, Striptease 1996, Looking For Richard 1996, Crash 1996, That Thing You Do! 1996, The Game 1997, Cop Land 1997, Gloria 1999, Existenz 1999, Dogma 1999, Analyze This 1999, The Yards 2000, High Fidelity 2000, Esther Kahn 2000, The Cell 2000, Camera 2000, The Score 2001, The Lord of the Rings: The Fellowship of the Ring (Acad. Award for Best Original Score 2002, Grammy Award for Best Soundtrack) 2001, Spider 2002, Panic Room 2002, The Lord of the Rings: The Two Towers 2002, Gangs of New York 2002, The Lord of the Rings: The Return of the King (Golden Globe Award for Best Original Score 2004, Acad. Award for Best Song, for 'Into the West' 2004) 2003, The Aviator (Golden Globe Award for Best Original Score 2005) 2004. *Honours:* ASCAP Lifetime Achievement Award 2004. *Current Management:* Gorfaine/Schwartz Agency Inc, 13245 Riverside Drive, Suite 450, Sherman Oaks, CA 91423, USA. *Website:* www.gsamusic.com.

**SHOSTAKOVICH, Maksim Dmitriyevich;** American conductor; b. 10 May 1938, Leningrad, USSR (now St Petersburg, Russia); s. of the late Dmitriy Shostakovich; m. 1st; one s.; m. 2nd Marina Tisie 1989; one s. one d. *Education:* Cen. Music School, Moscow Conservatory. *Career:* studied conducting under Rabinovich, Gauk, Rozhdestvensky (q.v.); Asst Conductor, Moscow Symphony Orchestra; Conductor, State Academic Symphony Orchestra; piano debut age 19 in father's Second Piano Concerto; Prin. Conductor and Artistic Dir USSR Radio and TV Symphony Orchestra); requested and granted political asylum in USA while on tour with USSR Radio and TV Symphony Orchestra, Nuremberg April 1981; conducted Nat. Symphony Orchestra, Capitol steps, Washington, DC, USA May 1981; Prin. Guest Conductor Hong Kong Philharmonic 1982–; Music Dir New Orleans Symphony Orchestra 1986–91. *Performances:* Touring Western Europe with USSR Radio and TV Symphony Orchestra, Japan, USA 1971–81; has conducted all maj. N American orchestras and many in Europe, Asia, S America; conducted premiere of father's 15th Symphony and recorded virtually all father's symphonies in USSR; has performed with leading soloists, incl. Emil Gilels, Oistrakh, Rostropovich. *Honours:* Hon. Music Dir Louisiana Philharmonic Orchestra 1993–94. *Address:* c/o Columbia Artists Management, Inc., 165 West 57th Street, New York, NY 10019 (office); PO Box 273, Jordanville, NY 13361, USA.

**SHRAPNEL, Hugh (Michael);** Composer; b. 18 Feb. 1947, Birmingham, England. *Education:* Eltham College, 1960–65; Royal Academy of Music, 1966–69; Goldsmiths' College, London, 1984–88; BMus. *Career:* Scratch Orchestra, 1969–72; Promenade Theatre Orchestra, 1970–72; People's Liberation Music, 1975–79; Co-Founder of Redlands Consort, 1992 specialising in new music; Compositions widely performed in London, provinces and abroad including: Wigmore Hall, 1968; Purcell Room, 1970; San Diego, 1974; Conway Hall, 1986 and 1993; University of Redlands, Texas, 1986 and 1989; Leighton House, 1989, 1990, 1991; Slaughterhouse Gallery, 1991; Appointed Composer-in-Residence at Music Works, London; mem, British Academy of Composers and Songwriters; Performing Right Society. *Compositions:* Oakley St, 1971; Variations for viola, 1984; Unity, 1991; Cat Preludes, 1994; South of the River, 1993–95; West Pier, 1997; Many works for piano and educational music. *Honours:* Lady Holland prize for composition, 1969. *Current Management:* STR Music Marketing & Management. *Address:* 27A Shooters Hill Road, Blackheath, London SE3 7AS, England.

**SHTODA, Daniil;** Russian singer (tenor); b. 1977, St Petersburg. *Education:* Glinka Capella, St Petersburg Conservatoire. *Career:* debut, sang Fyodor in Boris Godunov at the Marrinksy Theatre while a child; Young Artists' Acad. of the Mariinksy Theatre from 1998; repertoire includes Lensky in Eugene Onegin, Elvino in La Sonnambula, The Indian Guest in Sadko by Rimsky-Korsakov, and Tsar Berendai in The Snow Maiden (concert) with the Kirov Opera at Covent Garden 2000; Wigmore Hall recital 2002; London Proms 2002. *Honours:* winner Mario Lanza Vocal Competition, third Rimsky-Korsakov and 11th Tchaikovsky Competitions. *Current Management:* Askonas Holt Ltd, Lonsdale Chambers, 27 Chancery Lane, London, WC2A 1PF, England. *Telephone:* (20) 7400-1700. *Fax:* (20) 7400-1799. *E-mail:* info@askonasholt.co.uk. *Website:* www.askonasholt.co.uk.

**SHULMAN, Andrew;** Cellist and Conductor; b. 1960, London, England. *Education:* Studies at the RAM and the RCM (Joan Dickson and William Pleeth). *Career:* Principal cellist of the Philharmonia (5 years) followed by solo and conducting career; repertoire includes concertos by Dvořák, Elgar, Beethoven (Triple), Vivaldi and Haydn; Strauss's Don Quixote and Bloch's Schelomo; Founder member of the Britten Quartet, debut concert at the Wigmore Hall, 1987; Quartet in Residence at the Dartington Summer School, 1987, with quartets by Schnittke; Season 1988–89 in the Genius of Prokofiev series at Blackheath and BBC Lunchtime Series at St John's Smith Square; South Bank appearances with the Schoenberg/Handel Quartet Concerto conducted by Neville Marriner, concerts with the Hermann Prey Schubertiade and collaborations with the Alban Berg Quartet in the Beethoven Plus series;

Tour of South America 1988, followed by Scandinavian debut; Season 1989–90 with debut tours of Netherlands, Germany, Spain, Austria, Finland; Tours from 1990 to the Far East, Malta, Sweden, Norway: Schoenberg/Handel Concerto with the Gothenburg Symphony; Festival appearances at Brighton, the City of London, Greenwich, Canterbury, Harrogate, Chester, Spitalfields and Aldeburgh; Collaborations with John Ogdon, Imogen Cooper, Thea King and Lynn Harrell; Formerly resident quartet at Liverpool University; Teaching role at Lake District Summer Music 1989; Universities of Bristol, Hong Kong 1990; Conductor of various orchestras including RCM String Ensemble, Proteus Orchestra, Norfolk Youth Orchestra, Leicester Symphony Orchestra, Britten-Pears Orchestra, Ambache Chamber Orchestra, Salomon Orchestra. *Recordings:* Beethoven Op 130 and Schnittke Quartet No. 3; Vaughan Williams On Wenlock Edge and Ravel Quartet; Britten, Prokofiev, Tippett, Elgar and Walton Quartets; Vivaldi Concertos; Solo Disc, Delius and Dyson. *Honours:* Piatigorsky Artist Award in Boston, USA, 1989–90. *Address:* c/o The Ambache, 9 Beversbrook Rd, London, N19 4QG, England.

**SHUTOVA, Marina;** singer (mezzo-soprano); b. 1961, Moscow, Russia. *Education:* Tchaikovsky Conservatory, Moscow, and studied with Judith Beckmann in Hamburg. *Career:* sang with the Bolshoi Opera at Moscow from 1981; La Scala Milan debut 1989, as Clara in Prokofiev's Duenna (repeated at Edinburgh and Glasgow with the Bolshoi in 1990); Metropolitan Opera debut 1991, as Olga in Eugene Onegin; season 1992/93 as Amneris at Düsseldorf, Azucena at Liège and concerts in Hamburg; season 1995/6 as Sonia in War and Peace in Vienna, Dalila at Toulon and Maddalena in Rigoletto at Orange; other roles include Solocha in Rimsky's Christmas Eve (Edinburgh 1992).

**SHUTTLEWORTH, Anna Lee,** ARCM, BA; British cellist; *cello teacher, University of Leeds*; b. 2 May 1927, Bournemouth; d. of Henry Lee Hadwen Shuttleworth and Inez E. D. Lee Shuttleworth; m. David Sellen. *Education:* St Christopher's School, Hampstead, Talbot Heath School, Bournemouth, Royal Coll. of Music, Boise scholarship to study with Pablo Casals and Enrico Mainardi. *Career:* cellist in Vivien Hind Quartet 1947; played with Philomusica, Jacques, Boyd Neel and BBC Concert Orchestras; broadcasts as soloist; recitals in London with Bernard Roberts in Purcell Room; Prof., Royal Coll. of Music 1967–96; examiner, Associated Board of the Royal Schools of Music 1969–96; cello teacher, Univ. of Leeds 1996–, also Univ. of Christchurch, Canterbury; cellist in Georgian Quartet and Leonardo Piano Trio with David Roth, Maureen Smith and Ian Brown; cello and piano recitals with John Thwaites 2003; mem. European String Teachers Asscn, Incorporated Soc. of Musicians, Musicians' Union. *Recordings:* cello continuo on recordings by Alfred Deller. *Publications:* Playing the Cello 1971; contrib. to ESTA and NEEMF Magazines 2001–03. *Honours:* Leslie Alexander Prize, Royal Coll. of Music. *Address:* 1 Buckingham Road, Leeds, LS6 1BP, England (home). *Telephone:* (113) 2758509 (home); (1227) 261975 (home). *E-mail:* selshut@btinternet.com (home).

**SICHKIN, Emilian (Boris);** Composer; b. 14 Aug. 1954, Kiev, Ukraine. *Education:* Moscow Conservatory of Music; Gorky Conservatory of Music; Gnesins College of Music; Private lessons with Professor Berlin; Audio Institute of America; School for the Media Arts; Diplomas in Recording Engineering, Synthesizers and Computers. *Career:* Debut: Carnegie Hall, 1991; Performances include Winds of Freedom at Carnegie Hall, 1991; Concerto for Astronauts, 1988, 1989; Piano Recital, Carnegie Hall, 1988; Television appearance, All My Children, ABC television; Broadcast appearances on WQXR, Voice of America, WNBC, WBAI, Heart of Space; mem, ASCAP; American Composers Forum. *Compositions:* Concerto for Astronauts; Winds of Freedom, symphonic suite; Ballet, The Demon; Romeo and Juliet, symphonic tragedy; Little Mermaid, symphonic overture. *Recordings:* Concerto for Astronauts; Romeo and Juliet. *Address:* 35-20 21 St, Suite 6C, L.I.C., NY 11106, USA.

**ŠICHO, Robert;** singer (tenor); b. 1967, Prague, Czechoslovakia. *Education:* State Conservatory, Prague, Music Acad., Prague, studied with Jana Jonasová. *Career:* soloist of the State Opera, Prague; appearances in many major theatres in the Czech Republic; frequent guest, Austria, Belgium, Norway, Netherlands, Germany, Greece, Switzerland, Japan; operatic roles include Ferrando in Così fan tutte, Tamino in Die Zauberflöte, Almaviva in Il Barbiere di Siviglia, Alfredo in La Traviata, Lensky in Eugene Onegin, Leandro in Busoni's Arlecchino, Prince in Rusalka, Hoffmann in Les contes d'Hoffmann, Turiddu in Cavalleria rusticana and Don José in Carmen; operetta roles include Rosillon in Die Lustige Witwe, title role in Paganini and Octavio in Giuditta (Lehar), Caramello in Eine Nacht in Venedig, Bárinkay in Der Zigeunerbaron (J. Strauss) and Paris in Offenbach's La Belle Hélène; extensive concert repertoire includes Mozart's Requiem, Verdi's Requiem, Orff's Carmina Burana, Beethoven's Ninth, Rossini's Messe Solennelle and Stabat Mater and Telemann's Die Tageszeiten. *Recordings include:* Caramello in Strauss's Ein Nacht in Venedig 1990, Telemann's Die Tageszeiten, for Czech radio and television 1995, Carmina Burana for radio and television 1998, Charpentier's Te Deum, for radio and television 1999. *Address:* Otavska 1677, PSD-25101 Ricany, Czech Republic.

**SICILIANI, Alessandro;** Conductor and Composer; b. 5 June 1952, Florence, Italy. *Education:* Studied piano, conducting and composition at the Milan Conservatoire and the Accademia Chigiana in Siena (conducting with Franco Ferrara). *Career:* Many appearances at leading opera centres in Italy, notably Rome, Naples, Palermo and Florence; Further engagements at Marseilles, Barcelona, Nice, Liège, New Orleans and Philadelphia; Metropo-

litan Opera debut 1988, with Pagliacci and Cavalleria Rusticana; Symphonic engagements throughout the USA, Far East and Europe; From 1988 principal guest conductor of the Teatro Colón, Buenos Aires, and of the Teatro Municipal, São Paulo; From 1992 Music Director of the Columbus, Ohio, Symphony Orchestra. *Compositions include:* Cantata; L'Amour peintre (ballet); Giona, oratorio. *Address:* Columbus Symphony Orchestra, 55 East State Street, Columbus, OH 45210, USA.

**SIDLIN, Murray,** MM; American conductor; b. 6 May 1940, Baltimore, Md. *Education:* Academia Chigiana, Siena, Cornell Univ. *Career:* Asst Conductor, Baltimore Symphony Orchestra 1971–73; Dir of Maryland Ballet Co. 1971–73; Prin. Conductor Baltimore Chamber Players 1971–73; Resident Conductor Nat. Symphony Orchestra under Dorati 1973–77, Wolf Trap American Univ. Music Acad. 1974; Host and Conductor Children's TV series Music is… 1977; Music Dir Tulsa Philharmonic Orchestra 1978–80; Music Dir Hew Haven Symphony 1977–88, Long Beach Symphony 1980–88, Resident Conductor Aspen Music Festival 1978–93; Resident Conductor Oregon Symphony Orchestra 1994–; Guest Conductor with numerous orchestras in N America, also performances in Europe and at the Festival Casals in Puerto Rico; Carnegie Hall debut 1975; winner of Baltimore Symphony Orchestra Young Conductor's Competition 1962. *Address:* c/o Oregon Symphony Orchestra, 711 South West Adler, Suite 200, Portland, OR 97205; Shaw Concerts Inc., 3436 Springhill Road, Lafayette, CA 94549, USA.

**SIDOROVA, Svetlana;** Singer (Mezzo-Soprano); b. 1970, St Petersburg, Russia. *Education:* St Petersburg Conservatoire and in Italy with Alberto Zedda and Carlo Bergonzi; Further study with Christa Ludwig. *Career:* Appearances from 1992 in Vienna, Paris, Berlin and Bologna (Janacek's Makropulos Case, 1994); Italiana in Algeri at the Pesaro Festival and Jocasta in Oedipus Rex at St Petersburg; Verdi's Amneris at Cologne, Kundry in Parsifal for the Kirov Opera and Eboli in Don Carlos at Essen; Sang in Pacini's L'Ultimo giorni di Pompeii at the Martina Franca Festival and Falla's Atlantida at Granada; Concerts include the Brahms Alto Rhapsody, Bach's Magnificat, Rossini's Stabat Mater (at Pesaro), Beethoven's Ninth and Alexander Nevsky by Prokofiev (Bologna); Other opera roles include Carmen, Ulrica, Maddalena and Olga in Eugene Onegin (Deutsche Oper, Berlin). *Honours:* Prizewinner at Competitions in Athens, Sienna, Brussels, Tokyo and Barcelona. *Address:* c/o Theateragentur Dr G. Hilbert, Maximilianstrasse 22, 80539 Munich, Germany.

**SIEBER, Gudrun;** Singer (Soprano); b. 1953, Germany. *Education:* Studied at the Düsseldorf Opera Studio. *Career:* Member of the Deutsche Oper am Rhein Düsseldorf 1974–83; Deutsche Oper Berlin from 1977, notably in the 1984 premiere of Reimann's Gespenstersonate; Sang at the Bayerische Staatsoper Munich, 1978–84, in operas by Gluck, Mozart and Lortzing; Schwetzingen Festival 1980 and 1982, Salzburg Festival, 1981, 1984 and 1986 as Papagena in Die Zauberflöte; Also sang Papagena at the Théâtre des Champs-Elysées, Paris, 1987; Sang in a double bill of Il Maestro di Capella (Cimarosa) and La Serva Padrona at the Deutsche Oper foyer, 1990; Other roles include Marie in Zar und Zimmermann; Amour in Hippolyte et Aricie and Kristen in Miss Julie by Bibalo; Sang Papagena and Marie in Lortzing's Zar und Zimmermann at the Deutsche Oper Berlin, 1999; Shepherd in Tannhäuser 2001; Many concert appearances. *Recordings include:* Schumann's Manfred (Schwann). *Address:* c/o Deutsche Oper Berlin, Richard Wagnerstrasse 10, 1000 Berlin, Germany.

**SIEBERT, Isolde;** German singer (soprano); b. 1960, Hunfield, Hesse. *Education:* studied in Fribourg. *Career:* mem. of the Basle Opera 1982–85; sang at Darmstadt 1985–87, debut as Zerbinetta; Hanover Opera from 1987, as Blondchen, Susanna, Gretel, Tytania in A Midsummer Night's Dream, and Papagena; Bregenz Festival and Liège 1986, 1988, as the Queen of Night in Die Zauberflöte; sang in the 300th anniversary performance of Steffani's Enrico Leone, Hanover 1989; many concerts and recital appearances; sang La Reine de la nuit in Die Zauberflote, Beaune 2004, Europa in Europa riconosciuta, La Scala, Milan 2004. *Recordings include:* Dvořák's Biblical Songs Op99 2002, Von Winter's Clarinet Concerto and Aria 2004. *Address:* c/o Orfeo, Chandos House, Commerce Way, Colchester, Essex CO2 8HQ, England.

**SIEDEN, Cyndia;** Singer (Soprano); b. 10 Sept. 1954, Glendale, California, USA. *Education:* Studied at Olympia, Washington, and with Elisabeth Schwarzkopf. *Career:* Sang Cunegonde in Candide for New York City Opera, 1989; Sang Sifare in Mozart's Mitridate at the 1989 Wexford Festival, the Queen of Night in Toulon, Adele in Fledermaus for Scottish Opera and Offenbach's Olympia at Seattle; Salzburg Festival debut as Amor in Orfeo ed Euridice, conducted by John Eliot Gardiner; Appearances with the Bayerische Staatsoper Munich as Rosina, Helena in the premiere of Reimann's Troades, 1986, Zerbinetta and Fiakermilli in Arabella; Further engagements at Nice as Blondchen and Aminta in Die schweigsame Frau at Palermo; Sang Xenia in a concert performance of Boris Godunov conducted by Abbado, 1984, Verdi's Oscar for Washington Opera, Donizetti's Marie with Florida Opera West, Nannetta at Omaha and Fido in the US Professional premiere of Britten's Paul Bunyan, at St Louis; Season 1990/91 as Blondchen at the Théâtre du Châtelet, Paris, and on tour to Amsterdam, London, Lisbon and Stuttgart; Recent appearances as the Queen of Night at the Opéra Bastille, Paris, and Lucia di Lammermoor at Seattle; Zerbinetta for English National Opera and at the Vienna Staatsoper, season 1992/93 with Sophie in Der Rosenkavalier at the Châtelet; Sang in Mozart's Mitridate at Salzburg, 1997; Handel's

Rodelinda at Halle, 1996; Sang Gilda in Rigoletto for Flanders Opera, 1999; Season 2000–01 as the Queen of Night for ENO and Gilda for Vlaamse Opera, Antwerp; Sang Morgana in Alcina at Göttingen, 2002; Concert repertoire includes Mozart's C minor Mass (Cleveland Orchestra), Carmina Burana, Bach's St John Passion at the Concertgebouw under Frans Brüggen, and Candide at the Barbican Centre, London. *Recordings include:* Guardian of the Threshold in Die Frau ohne Schatten, conducted by Sawallisch (EMI); Orfeo ed Euridice (Philips); Die Entführung aus dem Serail. *Address:* c/o Opera voor Vlaanderen, Schouwburgstrasse 3, B–900 Ghent, Belgium.

**SIEGEL, Jeffrey;** Concert Pianist; b. 18 Nov. 1942, Chicago, Illinois, USA; m. Laura Mizel, 20 May 1973, 1 s., 1 d. *Education:* DMA, Juilliard School of Music, 1971; Studies with Rudolph Ganz, Rosina Lhevinne, Franz Reizenstein, Ilona Kabos. *Career:* Debut: Soloist, Chicago Symphony, 1958; Soloist with Orchestras of New York, Philadelphia, Boston, Cleveland, Los Angeles, London Symphony, London Philharmonic, Royal Philharmonic, Philharmonia, BBC Orchestras; NHK Orchestra of Japan; Nacionale Orchestra of Buenos Aires, Teatro Colón; Berlin Philharmonic; Recitals in Carnegie Hall, Festival Hall, Concertgebouw, Brussels, Berlin, Munich, Zürich, Tokyo, Tel-Aviv, Oslo, Stockholm; Television appearances; Frequent radio appearances. *Compositions:* Cadenza for Mozart C Minor Concerto. *Recordings:* Dutilleux Sonata and Hindemith Third Sonata; Gershwin Complete Works for Piano and Orchestra with St Louis Symphony, 1974; Solo works of Rachmaninov. *Honours:* Silver Medal, Queen Elizabeth Competition, Brussles, 1968; Honorary Doctorate, National College of Education, Evanston, Illinois, 1976. *Current Management:* ICM Artists Management. *Address:* c/o Kansai Opera Group, 3–3–9 Bingo-Cho, Chyno-Ku, Osaka, Japan.

**SIEGEL, Laurence (Gordon);** Conductor; b. 23 July 1931, New York, NY, USA; m. 15 Oct 1959, 1 d. *Education:* BA, City College of New York, 1953; MM, New England Conservatory, Boston, 1955; Studied under Boris Goldovsky and Leonard Bernstein, Berkshire Music Center, Tanglewood, 1953, 1955. *Career:* Conductor, NBC Symphony, Carnegie Hall concerts including tribute to Fritz Kreisler; Appeared with Honolulu Orchestra, Shreveport Festival Orchestra, Alexandria Symphony, Jacksonville Symphony and Opera Company, Connecticut Grand Opera Company; Director, Miami International Music Competition, Theater of Performing Arts, Miami Beach, 7 seasons; World-wide conducting includes Orquesta Sinfonica de El Salvador, Orquesta Sinfonica de Las Palmas, Spain, Manila Metro Philharmonic Orchestra and Opera Association, Teatro Sperimentale di Spoleto Orchestra, Belgrade Symphony, Filharmonica de Stat Oradea-Romania; Regularly conducts RAI Milan Orchestra; Music Director, Conductor, Puccini Festival Orchestra, Italy, 1984, Pan American Sinfonica, 1991–, also Festival of the Continents, Key West, Florida; Music Director, North Miami Beach Orchestra; Guest Conductor, Kensington Symphony (California), São Paulo Symphony, Brazil, Orquesta Sinfonica Ciudad Asuncion, Paraguay (1994); Chief Conductor, Sakai City, Osaka Opera, Japan; Numerous operas include Così fan tutte, Faust, Butterfly, Tosca, La Bohème, La Traviata, Otello, Rigoletto, Die Fledermaus, Ernani, Il Trovatore, Suor Angelica, Hansel and Gretel, Samson and Delilah, La Périchole, Elisir d'amore, Carmen (1991, 1992), Merry Widow (1992–). *Recordings:* Tchaikovsky Album with New Philharmonia Orchestra, London; Others with London Symphony, London Philharmonic and Royal Philharmonic Orchestras and London Festival Orchestra. *Honours:* Numerous citations and medals of honour; D.Mus, 1993. *Current Management:* Pan American Sociedad de Artisias. *Address:* 5225 La Gorce Drive, Miami Beach, FL 33140, USA.

**SIEGEL, Wayne;** Composer; b. 14 Feb. 1953, Los Angeles, USA; m. 22 Mar 1980, 1 s., 1 d. *Education:* BA, Music Composition, University of California, Santa Barbara, 1975; Diplomeksamen, Composition, Royal Danish Academy of Music, Århus. *Career:* Active as Composer and Performer, Europe and USA, including many radio and television broadcasts and numerous commissions; Major performances include: Danish Radio Festival, Copenhagen, 1980; Nordic Music Days, Helsinki, 1980; German Radio, 1981; New Music America, Chicago, 1982; Warsaw Autumn, 1984; Nordic Music Days, 1984; Rostrum, Stockholm, 1988; Wigmore Recital Hall, 1997; Sydney Opera House, 1998, 1999; Cunningham Dance Studio, New York, 1999; mem, Administrative Director, West Jutland Symphony and Chamber Ensemble, 1984–86; Director, Danish Institute of Electro-acoustic Music, 1986–. *Compositions:* String Quartet, 1975–79; East LA for 4 Marimbas or 2 guitars, 1975; Narcissus ad fontem, 1976; Mosaic, 1978; Autumn Resonance, 1979; Domino Figures, 1979; Music for 21 Clarinets, 1980; Watercolor, Acrylic, Watercolor, 1981; Polyphonic Music, 1983; 42nd Street Rondo, 1984; Devil's Golf Course, 1985; Last Request, 1986; Cobra, 1988; Tracking, 1991; Livstegn (opera) 1994; Jackdaw, 1995; Movement Study, 1996; Savannah, 1997. *Recordings:* String Quartet and Watercolor, Acrylic, Watercolor; Autumn Resonance and Domino Figures; East LA Phase; 42nd Street Rondo. *Contributions:* Danish Music Periodical, Nutida Musik, Contemporary Music Review. *Honours:* Danish Art Council 3-Year Grant for Composition, 1978–81. *Address:* DIEM, The Concert Hall Århus, DK 8000 Århus, Denmark.

**SIEGELE, Ulrich,** DPhil; German musicologist; b. 1 Nov. 1930, Stuttgart. *Education:* Tübingen Univ. *Career:* Lecturer in Musicology, Tübingen Univ. 1965–71, Prof. of Musicology 1971–95. *Publications:* Die Musiksammlung der Stadt Heilbronn, 1967; Kompositionsweise und Bearbeitungstechnik in der Instrumentalmusik Johann Sebastian Bachs, 1975; Bachs theologischer Formbegriff und das Duett F-Dur, 1978; Zwei Kommentare zum Marteau sans maître von Pierre Boulez, 1979; Beethoven/Formale Strategien der

späten Quartette, 1990; Die Orgeln des Musikwissenschaftlichen Instituts im Pfleghof zu Tuebingen, 1992; articles in periodicals, collections by several authors, and musical encyclopaedias including Bach, Das Wohltemperierte Klavier I; Ulrich Siegele zum 70. Geburtstag (biog.) 2002. *Address:* Am Hasenborn 2A, 61389 Schmitten, Germany (home). *Telephone:* 60843456 (home).

**SIEPI, Cesare;** Italian singer (bass-baritone); b. 10 June 1923, Milan. *Education:* Milan Conservatory. *Career:* debut as Sparafucile in Rigoletto at Schio 1941; La Fenice Venice 1946 as Silva in Ernani; La Scala Milan 1946–58, notably as Donizetti's Raimondo, Verdi's Grand Inquisitor, Wagner's Pogner and as Mefistofele and Simon Mago in the 1948 Boito celebrations conducted by Toscanini; New York Metropolitan 1950–74, principally as Mozart's Don Giovanni and Figaro; also sang Philip II in Don Carlos, Gounod's Mephistopheles, Verdi's Padre Guardiano, Ramfis, Silva, Zaccaria and Fiesco; first Wagner role in German was Gurnemanz 1970; sang Don Giovanni at Salzburg 1950s (also filmed) and on his Covent Garden debut 1962; appeared as Roger in Verdi's Jérusalem at Parma 1985. *Recordings:* Mefistofele, L'Amore dei tre Re, Le nozze di Figaro, La Gioconda, Rigoletto, La Forza del Destino, La Bohème, Il Barbiere di Siviglia, Lucia di Lammermoor, Faust, Boris Godunov, La Juive, Don Carlos, La Favorita, Ernani, Norma, five complete recordings of Don Giovanni, including Salzburg film 2002. *Address:* c/o Metropolitan Opera, Lincoln Center, NY 10023, New York.

**SIERRA, Roberto;** Composer and Music Educator; b. 9 Oct. 1953, Vega Baja, Puerto Rico. *Education:* Puerto Rico Conservatory of Music; Graduated, University of Puerto Rico, 1976; Royal College of Music, London; University of London, 1976–78; Institute of Sonology, Utrecht, 1978; Studied with Gyorgy Ligeti, Hamburg Hochschule für Musik, 1979–82. *Career:* Assistant Director, 1983–85, Director, 1985–86, Cultural Activities Department, University of Puerto Rico; Dean of Studies, 1986–87, Chancellor, 1987–, Puerto Rico Conservatory of Music. *Compositions:* Salsa on the C String for cello and piano, 1983; Salsa for wind quintet, 1983; Cantos Populares for chorus, 1983; Cinco bocetos for clarinet, 1984; El Mensajero de Plata, chamber opera, 1984; Concerto Nocturnal for harpsichord, flute, clarinet, oboe, violin and cello, 1985; Jubilo for orchestra, 1985; Memorias Tropicales for string quartet, 1985; Dona Rosita for mezzo-soprano and wind quintet, 1985; El sueno de Antonia for clarinet and percussion, 1985; Invocaciones for voice and percussion, 1986; Cuatro ensayos orquestales for orchestra, 1986; Glosa a la sombra.for mezzo-soprano, viola, clarinet and piano, 1987; Essays for wind quintet, 1987; Mano a mano for 2 percussionists, 1987; El Contemplado, ballet, 1987; Glosas for piano and orchestra, 1987; Introduccion y Descarga for piano, brass quintet and percussion, 1988; Dascarga for chamber ensemble or orchestra, 1988; Entre terceras for 2 synthesizers and computer, 1988; Tributo for harp, flute, clarinet and string quartet, 1988; Bayoán, oratorio, 1991–3; Trio Tropical, for violin, cello and piano, 1991; Evocaciones, for violin and orchestra, 1994; Lux Aeterna, for chorus, 1996; Alegriá for orchestra, 1996; Cuentos, for chamber orchestra, 1997; Concerto for percussion and orchestra, 1998; Piano Pieces; Harpsichord pieces. *Recordings:* Number of works recorded. *Honours:* Several commissions; Many works performed in USA and Europe. *Address:* c/o Conservatorio de Musica de Puerto Rico, Apartado 41227, Minillas Station, Santurce, Puerto Rico 00940, USA.

**SIFFERT (TRAVASSOS), Henrik;** Dramatic Tenor, Opera Singer and Singing Teacher; b. 20 Sept. 1959, Porto Alegre, Brazil. *Education:* Psychology and Sociology, University Gama Filho, Rio de Janeiro; Conservatory H. Villa-Lobos, Rio de Janeiro; Musikhochschule, Cologne, Germany; Musikhochschule, Karlsruhe, Germany; Studied with Dieter Jacob in Cologne, Aldo Baldin in Karlsruhe, Floriana Cavalli in Milan, James King in Munich and Rina del Monaco in Pesaro. *Career:* Debut: As Baritone: Teatro Municipal Rio de Janeiro, 1978; As Dramatic Tenor: Youth Festival Bayreuth, as Max in Der Freischütz by Weber; Baritone, German television; Tonio in Pagliacci, ZDF, 1984; Schicchi in Gianni Schicchi, Puccini, Sudwestfunk television; International Festival, Wiesbaden, Gonzales in Guarany, Carlos Gomes, Teatro Municipal do Rio de Janeiro, and others; Recorded leider, operas, Zarzuelas and oratorios for German radio; Dramatic tenor, 1988; Lord Cecil, Bonynge, del Monaco, Liceo de Barcelona, 1990; Otello, Parsifal, Ismaele, and others; Recitals with orchestra and piano; Teacher, Department of Voice, Conservatory of Colmar, France; Creator, Artistic Director, European Academy of Singing, Guebwiller, Alsace, France. *Current Management:* Walter Beloch, Milan, Italy. *Address:* 1 rue des Tourneurs, 68000 Colmar, France.

**SIGHELE, Mietta;** Singer (Soprano); b. 1944, Rovereto, Italy; m. Veriano Luchetti. *Education:* Studied in Milan and Rome. *Career:* Debut: Sang Butterfly at Spoleto; Appearances at opera houses throughout Italy and in Vienna, Barcelona, Buenos Aires, Montreal, Chicago, Dallas and New Orleans; Verona Arena from 1979, as Micaela in Carmen; Ravenna Festival, 1986 and Torre del Lago, 1989 as Butterfly; Metropolitan Opera, 1989 as Micaela; Season 1991 as Liu in Turandot, at Verona and Prioress in The Carmelites at Rome; Engagements in operas by Mozart, Janáček, Wagner and Tchaikovsky. *Recordings:* Priestess in Aida; Meyerbeer's L'Africaine, Florence, 1971.

**SIGMUNDSSON, Kristinn;** Singer (Bass-Baritone); b. 1 May 1951, Reykjavík, Iceland. *Education:* Studied at Academy of Music in Vienna and in Washington DC. *Career:* Member of Wiesbaden Opera from 1989 as Don Giovanni, the Speaker in Die Zauberflöte and Eugene Onegin; Royal Court

Theatre Drottningholm, 1989–90 as Agamemnon and Thoas in Gluck's Iphigénie operas; Season 1990–91 includes: Geisterbote in Die Frau ohne Schatten at the Concertgebouw, Beethoven's 9th with the Essen Philharmonie and St John Passion in the Hague; Recital at the Stratford-upon-Avon Scandinavian Festival; Malcolm in La Donna del Lago for Vara Radio, Netherlands, 1992; Concert appearances with the Dutch Radio Orchestra, the Rotterdam Philharmonic and the NDR Symphony Orchestra, Hamburg; Season 1991–92 included: Don Giovanni at Stuttgart Opera, Mozart's Requiem at Drottningholm and Barber of Seville at Geneva; Season 1993–94 included: Alidoro and Speaker in Geneva, Mathis der Maler in Barcelona and Lady Macbeth of Mtsensk at the Maggio Musicale in Florence; Sang in a new production of The Bartered Bride at the Grand Théâtre in Geneva, 1994; Sang Mephistofeles in La Damnation de Faust at the Opéra National in Paris; Colline in 1996; Sang Klingsor in Parsifal at the Opéra Bastille, Paris, 1997; Season 1997–98 as Rossini's Mustafà at Dresden, the Hermit in Der Freischütz for the Royal Opera at the Barbican and Grand Inquisitor in Don Carlos at the Opéra Bastille, Paris; Season 2000 as Banquo at Cologne, Cherubini's Creon at Salzburg (concert) and Rossini's Mustafà for the Vienna Staatsoper; Season 2001–02 engagements included Barbiere at the Paris Bastille, Don Giovanni in Munich and Berlin, Lucia di Lammermoor in Munich, Die Walküre and Parsifal in Cologne and Eugene Ongin in Hamburg, Nabucco at the Arena di Nimes; Season 2002–03 with Der Rosenkavalier and a revival of Walküre in Cologne, Meistersinger at Covent Garden, Gounod's Faust, Parisfal, Der fliegende Holländer, Meistersinger and La Juive at the Opéra National de Paris, La Damnation de Faust in San Francisco, Don Giovanni in Munich, Don Carlos in Dallas, Der Rosenkavalier in Dresden and Die Walküre in Naples. *Recordings include:* Commendatore in Don Giovanni, conducted by Arnold Östman. *Honours:* Prizewinner, Belvedere Singing Competition in Vienna, 1983; Winner, Philadelphia Opera Competition, 1983. *Address:* c/o Haydn Rawstron Ltd, 36 Station Road, London SE20 7BQ, England.

**SIGURBJORNSSON, Thorkell;** Composer; b. 16 July 1938, Reykjavík, Iceland. *Education:* Reykjavík College of Music; Continuing Studies in USA. *Career:* Creative Associate, State University of New York, USA, 1973; Research Musician, Centre for Music Experiment, University of California, San Diego, 1975; Head of Theory and Composition, Reykjavík College of Music, Iceland, 1968–74; Bukolla, 1974; Wiblo, 1976; Cadensa and Dance; Seascape; Albumblatt, 1975; The Bull Man, ballet music; Caprice, 1986; Chamber Music: Differing Opinions; Intrada, 1971; For Renee, 1973; A Short Passion Story; Hasselby Icelandic Folk Songs, 1976; Ballade, 1960; Happy Music, 1971; Kissum, 1970; Copenhagen Quartet; For Better or Worse, 1975; Solstice, 1976; Auf Meinen Lieben Gott, 1981; Three Faces of Pantomine, 1982; Choir Music: Ode, 1975; Five Laudi, 1973; Beginning, 1978; Hosanna Son of David; Palm Sunday, 1978; The Artificial Flower; Seven Christmas Songs; David 121, 1984; Evening Prayers, 1983; Children's Music: Seven Songs from Apaspil; Apaspil, opera, 1966; Velferd; Four Icelandic Folk Songs; Three Songs; Gigjuleikur; The Ugly Duckling, 1981; The Last Flower, 1983; Electronic Music: La Jolla Good Friday I, 1975; La Jolla Good Friday II, 1975; fipur, 1971; Race Track, 1975; Trifonia for orchestra, 1990; Missa Brevis, 1993; Visit, string quartet, 1993; Life, Dreams and Reality, for orchestra, 1993; Runes, for horn and orchestra, 1994; The Girl in the Lighthouse, children's opera, 1997; Symphony, 1998; Wheel of Fortune, chamber opera, 1998; President, Icelandic League of Composers. *Address:* c/o STEF, Laufasvegi 40, 101 Reykjavík, Iceland.

**SIKI, Bela;** Pianist; b. 21 Feb. 1923, Budapest, Hungary; m. Yolande Oltramare, 18 Sept 1952, 1 s., 1 d. *Education:* University of Budapest; Academy Franz Liszt, Budapest; Conservatoire de Genève, Switzerland. *Career:* Numerous concert tours world-wide; Appearances with major orchestras around the world; Extensive concert tours and master classes in Japan, Australia, USA and Canada, 1988. *Recordings:* Has made numerous recordings including music by Bach, Ravel, Liszt (B minor sonata), Beethoven (late sonatas) and Bartók. *Publications:* Piano Literature, 1981. *Honours:* Liszt Competition, Budapest, 1942, 1943; Concours International d'Executions Musicales, Geneva, 1948. *Address:* School of Music, University of Washington, Seattle, WA 98195, USA.

**SIKORA, Elizabeth;** Singer (Soprano); b. 1950, Edinburgh, Scotland. *Education:* Studied at the Royal Scottish Academy and at Elsa Mayer Lismanns Opera Workshop. *Career:* Appearances with the Royal Opera Covent Garden in London and on Tour to Los Angeles, La Scala Milan, Japan, Korea and Greece; Solo Roles in Die Meistersinger, Butterfly, Die Frau ohne Schatten, Manon Lescaut, Parsifal, Rigoletto and Simon Boccanegra; Sang in the British premieres of Henze's Pollicino and Menotti's The Boy Who Grew Too Fast; Appearances as Carmen in Oundle and Germany with Royal Opera Education; Annina in La Traviata at the Albert Hall. *Address:* c/o Scottish Opera, 39 Elmbank Crescent, Glasgow, G2 4PT, Scotland.

**SILJA, Anja;** German singer (soprano) and producer; b. 17 April 1940, Berlin; m. Christoph von Dohnanyi; one s. two d. *Education:* studied with Egon van Rijn. *Career:* began concert career aged ten at Berlin Titania Palace; stage debut Brunswick 1956, as Rosina; mem., Stuttgart and Frankfurt operas 1958–59; sang the Queen of Night at Aix 1959; sang at Bayreuth Festival 1960–67, as Senta, Elsa, Eva, Elisabeth and Venus; London debut at Sadler's Wells Theatre as Leonore/Fidelio 1963; Covent Garden debut as Leonore 1969, returned as Cassandre in Les Troyens, Senta, Marie in Wozzeck, Kostelnicka in Jenůfa; Metropolitan Opera debut 1972, returned as Salome, Marie and

Kostelnicka; Vienna Staatsoper 1959–, in roles including Queen of Night, Salome, Elektra, Lulu; Paris Opéra 1964–, as Salome and Brünnhilde; Glyndebourne Opera debut as Kostelnicka 1989; sang the Nurse in Die Frau ohne Schatten at San Francisco 1989; debut as opera producer at Brussels with Lohengrin 1990; sang Emilia Marty at Glyndebourne 1995; season 1997 in The Makropulos Case at Glyndebourne and as Herodias at Covent Garden; Geschwitz in Lulu at Düsseldorf 2000; Clytemnestra at Madrid, Geschwitz and Herodias at Amsterdam, The Makropulos Case at Aix and The Bassarids in Amsterdam, Pierrot Lunaire by Schoenberg at Aix 2003; season 2004 as Madame de Croissy in Milan and Mère Marie in Hamburg and Paris (both in Dialogues des Carmelites), Emilia Marty in Berlin, Clytemnestra (Elektra) in Oviedo, Gräfin Geschwitz (Lulu) in Munich; season 2005 as Kostelnicka in Lyon and Barcelona, Emilia Marty in Lyon and Berlin, and Gräfin Geschwitz in Munich. *Recordings include:* Der fliegende Holländer, Tannhäuser, Lohengrin and Parsifal from Bayreuth, Lulu, Wozzeck, Jenufa, Pierrot Lunaire. *Honours:* Kammersängerin; Bundesverdienstkreuz 1988; Janacek Medal. *Current Management:* Artists Management Zürich, Rütistrasse 52, 8044 Zürich-Gockhausen, Switzerland. *Telephone:* (1) 8218957. *Fax:* (1) 8210127. *E-mail:* schuetz@artistsman.com. *Website:* www.artistsman.com.

**SILLA, Frederick;** Singer (Tenor) and Composer; b. 1948, Vienna, Australia. *Education:* Studied at the Vienna Musikhochschule with Friedrich Cerha and Anton Dermota. *Career:* Sang first at the Stadttheater Krefeld, then appeared at Opera Houses in Ulm, Kiel, Munster and Gelsenkirchen; Opera, Jagdszenen aus Niederbayern, premiered at Karlsruhe 1979; Member of the Staatstheater am Gärtnerplatz Munich from 1985; Roles have included Mozart's Ottavio, Tamino, Ferrando and Belmonte, Nemorino and Hoffmann; Modern Repertoire includes parts in The Lighthouse by Maxwell Davies, Jakob Lenz by Wolfgang Rihm and Die Veruteilung des Lukullus by Dessau; Guest Engagements in Pisa, Venice and Madrid, Concert appearances in Germany and elsewhere. *Address:* c/o Staatstheater am Gärtnerplatz, Gärtnerplatz 3, 8000 Munich, Germany.

**SILLS, Beverly;** American singer (soprano) and opera administrator; b. (Belle Silverman), 25 May 1929, Brooklyn, New York; d. of the late Morris Silverman and of Sonia Bahn; m. Peter Bulkeley Greenough 1956; one s. one d. three step-c. *Education:* studied with Estelle Liebling. *Career:* debut as Frasquita in Carmen, Philadelphia Civic Opera 1946; appeared at most of the maj. opera houses of Europe and Latin America, numerous recitals with leading orchestras throughout USA; retd from singing 1980; Gen. Dir New York City Opera 1979–88, Pres. of Bd 1989–90; Man. Dir Metropolitan Opera, New York 1991–94, Chair. 2002–05; Chair. Lincoln Center 1994–2002; Dir Warner Communications Inc., New York 1982–, American Express, Macy's. *Opera roles include:* Helen of Troy in Mefistofele (San Francisco Opera) 1953, Rosalinda in Die Fledermaus (New York City Opera) 1955, Charpentier's Louise, Mozart's Donna Anna, Gounod's Marguerite, the three heroines in Les Contes d'Hoffmann, Massenet's Manon, Bellini's Elvira (all New York City Opera) 1955–79, Cleopatra in Handel's Giulio Cesare, Mozart's Queen of the Night in The Magic Flute (Vienna State Opera) 1967, Pamira in L'Assedio di Corinto (La Scala, Milan) 1969, title role in Lucia di Lammermoor (Covent Garden) 1970, Pamira in L'Assedio di Corinto 1975, Massenet's Thais, and Donizetti's Norina and Violetta in La Traviata (all at Metropolitan Opera), Queen Elizabeth I in Roberto Devereux, Marie in Daughter of the Regiment, Rosina in Barber of Seville, the title roles in Anna Bolena and Maria Stuarda, Norma, and Lucrezia Borgia, final role in Menotti's La Loca 1979. *Television:* host, Live from Lincoln Center (series) 1998. *Publications:* Bubbles: A Self-Portrait 1976, Beverly (autobiog.) 1987. *Honours:* Kennedy Center Honor Award, Heinz Award 1995; Presidential Medal of Freedom, Chevalier, Ordre des Arts et des Lettres. *Current Management:* Vincent and Farrell Associates, 157 West Street, Suite 502, New York, NY 10019, USA.

**SILVA, Stella;** Singer (Mezzo-soprano); b. 6 Jan. 1948, Buenos Aires, Argentina. *Education:* Studied in Buenos Aires and at Vercelli, Italy. *Career:* Debut: Bordeaux 1969, as Preziosilla in La Forza del Destino; Many appearances in Opera Houses at Parma, Lyon, Nice, Strasbourg, Hamburg, Vienna, Berlin, Barcelona and Buenos Aires; Verona Arena, 1973–74, as Amneris; Other roles have included Carmen, Ulrica, Eboli, Azucena, Adalgisa, Charlotte, Dalila and Ortrud; Laura in La Gioconda, Leonora, Gluck's Orpheus and Holofernes in Vivaldi's Juditha Triumphans; Frequent Concert Appearances.

**SILVA-MARIN, Guillermo (Osvaldo);** Singer (Tenor) and Artistic Director; b. 11 April 1944, Ponce, Puerto Rico. *Education:* BA, University of Puerto Rico; Diploma, Opera, University of Toronto. *Career:* Artistic Director, Metropolitan Music Theatre, Scarborough, 1976–79; Founder and Artistic Director, Toronto Operetta Theatre, 1985; Founder, Summer Opera Lyric Theatre, 1986; General Manager, Opera in Concert, 1994; Staged over 21 operas and operettas including Donizetti's Elixir of Love, Rossini's Barber of Seville, Lehar's Land of Smiles, Offenbach's La Vie Parisienne and Strauss's Gypsy Baron with the Toronto Operetta Theatre, Summer Opera Lyric Theatre, Opera de San Juan and Sault Ste Marie Opera; 16 performances as tenor with the Canadian Opera Company, including Richard Strauss's Ariadne auf Naxos and Leoncavallo's Pagliacci; Appearances with Opera Lyra, Cincinnati Opera Association, New York City Opera, Metropolitan Opera, Mexico State Symphony, Toronto Symphony, Edmonton Symphony, Puerto Rico Symphony, Carnegie Hall, Canadian Broadcasting Corporation, CFMX-FM include Stravinsky's Oedipus Rex, Strauss's Die Fledermaus, Zeller's The Bird Seller and Puccini's La Bohème. *Current Management:* VKD International Artists, 9 Vernham Avenue, Willowdale, Ontario M2L 2B1, Canada.

**SILVASTI, Jorma;** Singer (Tenor); b. 9 March 1959, Leppavirta, Finland. *Education:* Studied at Savonlinna from 1975, Sibelius Academy Helsinki, 1978–81, Frankfurt, 1981–83. *Career:* Appearances with the Finnish National Opera at Helsinki from 1980; Frankfurt 1981–82, Krefeld, 1982–85; Karlsruhe, 1985–88; Savonlinna Festival from 1983 as Jenik (Bartered Bride), the Steersman in Fliegende Holländer and Tamino; Premiere of Veitsi by Paavo Heikinen, 1989; Sang Ottavio at the Vienna Volksoper, 1988, Henry Morosus in Schweigsame Frau at Dresden, 1989; Further engagements at Essen, Karlsruhe and Bremen; Created Kimmo in Sallinen's Kullervo with the Company of Finnish National Opera at the Dorothy Chandler Pavilion, Los Angeles, 1992; Other roles include Ferrando, Fenton, Gluck's Pylades, Almaviva, Steva in Jenůfa, Lensky, Belmonte (Vienna State Opera, 1993) Nemorino, Alfredo; Noted Concert and Oratorio Performer; Gregor in premiere of Sansibar by E Meyer at Schwetzingen with Bavarian State Opera Munich, 1994; Faust at the Dorothy Chandler Pavilion, Los Angeles; Further engagements: Stuttgart, Düsseldorf, Frankfurt, Hannover, Hamburg, Munich, Vienna State Opera; Sang Petruccio in The Palace, by Sallinen, at the 1996 Savonlinna Festival; Sang Parsifal at Brussels, 1998; Season 2000–01 as Berg's Alwa at the Vienna Staatsoper, Manolios in Martinů's The Greek Passion at Covent Garden and Edmund in the premiere of Sallinen's Lear, for Finnish National Opera; Laca in Jenůfa at Covent Garden, 2001; Dvořák's Stabat mater at the London Proms, 2002. *Address:* Finnish National Opera, Bulevardi 23–27, 00180 Helsinki, Finland.

**SILVER, Sheila,** BA, PhD; American composer; b. 3 Oct. 1946, Seattle, WA. *Education:* Univ. of Washington, Seattle, Inst. for European Studies, Paris, Univ. of California at Berkeley, Stuttgart Hochschule für Musik with Ligeti, Brandeis Univ. with Arthur Berger and Harold Shapero, Tanglewood, and further study at Paris and London. *Career:* freelance composer, with performances throughout the USA; has worked with film, including scores Alligator Eyes and Dead Funny; teacher of composition, then Prof. of Music at SUNY, Stony Brook from 1979. *Compositions include:* String quartet 1977, Galixidi for orchestra 1977, Dynamis for horn 1979, Canto for baritone and chamber ensemble 1979, Chariessa for soprano and orchestra (after Sappho) 1980, Two Elizabethan Songs for chorus 1982, Ek Ong Kar for chorus 1983, Dance Converging for viola, horn, piano and percussion 1987, The Thief of Love (opera) 1987, Window Waltz for bass clarinet, horn, strings, harpsichord, piano and percussion 1988, Song of Sarah for string orchestra 1988, Cello Sonata 1988, Oh, Thou Beautiful One for piano 1989, Dance of Wild Angels for chamber orchestra 1990, Six Préludes for piano 1991, Three Preludes for orchestra 1992, To the Spirit Unconquered trio for violin, cello and piano 1992, Transcending (three songs for Michael Dash, in memoriam) 1995, From Darkness Emerging harp and string quartet 1995, Piano Concerto 1996, Four Etudes and a Fantasy string quartet No. 2 1997, Winter Tapestry for chamber ensemble 1998, Subway Sunset for oboe and piano 1999, As the Earth Turns for oboe, bassoon, tape and video 1999, Chant for bass and piano 2000–04, Fantasy on an Imaginary Folk Song for flute and harp/string orchestra 2001, Lullaby for bassoon and piano 2001, Moon Prayer for two violins, two viola, two celli 2002, Midnight Prayer for orchestra 2003. *Recordings include:* To the Spirit Unconquered, Fantasy Quasi Theme and Variation, Piano Concerto and Six Preludes for Piano, Shirat Sarah, The Thief of Love, Who the Hell is Bobby Roos? (film score). *Address:* PO Box 292, Spencertown, NY 12165, USA. *Telephone:* (518) 392-3843 (office). *E-mail:* sheilasilver@hummingbirdfilms .com (office). *Website:* www.hummingbirdfilms.com (office).

**SILVERMAN, Faye-Ellen,** BA, MA, DMA; American composer, pianist, writer and educator; *Member of Faculty, Eugene Lang Faculty;* b. 2 Oct. 1947, New York, NY, USA. *Education:* Mannes College of Music, Barnard College, Harvard University, Columbia University. *Career:* Teaching Assistant, Columbia University, 1972–74; Adjunct Assistant Professor, City University of New York, 1972–77; Assistant Professor, Goucher College, 1977–81; Graduate Facility, Department of Music History and Literature, Peabody Institute, Johns Hopkins University, 1977–85; Faculty, Center for Compositional Studies, Aspen Music Festival, 1986; College and Extension Faculty at Mannes College of Music since 1991, the Eugene Lang Faculty since Autumn 2000; Works performed live and/or on radio and television in many countries. *Compositions include:* Kalends for brass quintet, 1981, Oboe-sthenics (chosen to represent USA at Int. Rostrum of Composers/UNESCO 1982) 1981; Winds and Sines for orchestra (Indiana State Univ Orchestral Composition Contest 1982) 1981; Restless Winds for woodwind quintet, 1986; Adhesions for orchestra, 1987; A Free Pen, a cantata for narrator, soloists, chorus and chamber ensemble, 1990; Journey Towards Oblivion for soprano, tenor and chamber ensemble, 1991; Azure Skies for violin, cello and harp, 1993; Connections for clarinet, cello and marimba, 1994; Just For Fun for chamber orchestra, 1994; At The Colour Cafe, for brass choir, 1997; Dialogue Continued horn, trombone, tuba, 2000, Wilde's World for tenor, viola and guitar 2000; Reconstructed Music, Piano Trio, 2002; Over 65 published compositions with Seesaw Music Corporation. *Recordings:* Oboe-sthenics by James Astryniec; Zigzags by Velvet Brown; Passing Fancies, Restless Winds and Speaking Alone by Aspen Music Festival Contemporary Ensemble under Stephen Mosko. *Publications:* 20th Century Section of the Schirmer History of Music. *Honours:* Winner, Parents' League Competition (aged 13) 1961, Gov.'s Citation 1982, 30 Sept. 1982 named 'Fay-Ellen Silverman Day' in Baltimore, Md by Mayor Donald Schaeffer, Virginia Liebeler Biennial Grant for Mature Women, Nat. League of American Pen Women 2002. *Address:* 330 West 28th Street 7G, New York, NY 10001, USA (home). *Telephone:* (212) 627-5162 (home). *E-mail:* FayeNote@post.harvard.edu (home). *Website:* www.cmc.net/ member/faye_silverman (home).

**SILVERMAN, Stanley (Joel);** American composer; b. 5 July 1938, New York, NY. *Education:* Boston Univ., Mills Coll., Columbia Univ., Berkshire Music Centre. *Career:* writer of incidental music for plays; composer of operas, chamber music and film music; two comms from Chamber Music Soc. of Lincoln Center; his music has been performed at int. festivals including Autumn Festivals of Paris and Madrid, European Cultural Centre of Delphi, Greece, Stratford Festival of Canada, Royal Exchange Theatre, Manchester, UK, RSC, Stratford-upon-Avon and London, UK, Shakespeare's Globe Theatre, London, UK; Advisor/Consultant, Rockefeller Foundation 1980; Advisor, Nat. Opera Inst., Washington, DC 1982; mem. Bd American Music Center, New York 1981–84, Theatre Communications Group 1986, Bd Dirs Lincoln Center Inst. 1986. *Compositions include:* operas and musical plays: Hotel For Criminals 1964, Elephant Steps, Tanglewood 1968, Dr Selavy's Magic Theatre, Stockbridge 1972, Hotel for Criminals, Stockbridge 1974, The American Imagination 1978, Up From Paradise (with Arthur Miller) 1980, Madame Adare, New York Opera 1981, The Columbine String Quartet Tonight, Stockbridge 1981, Up from Paradise, New York 1983, The Golem 1984, Africanus Instructus, New York 1986, A Good Life, Washington 1986, Black Sea Follies, Stockbridge 1986, Love and Science 1990, In Celebration 1990, Eridos 1999, Shakespeare and Our Planet 2001, Reveille (Trio No. 2) 2003; film scores: Nanook of the North 1975, Simon, 1979, Eyewitness 1981, I'm Dancing As Fast As I Can 1982, The Merchant of Venice 1989, Timon of Athens 1991, Measure for Measure 1992, The Molières Comedies 1994, Twelfth Night 1994; theatre music: Bent 1979, Othello 1982, The Little Foxes 1982, Private Lives 1983, The Bluebird of Happiness 1987, Caucasian Chalk Circle 1987, St Joan 1993, Timon of Athens 1993, The Government Inspector 1994, Uncle Vanya 1995, The Capeman (musical by Paul SImon) 1998, Ah, Wilderness!, Lincoln Center Theater; TV music: Behind the Scenes with David Hockney. *Honours:* Obie Award 1968, Drama Desk Award 1973, Naumburg Foundation Comm. Award 1977, Koussevitzky Foundation Comm. Award 1974, Grammy Award (as arranger) 1997, Guggenheim Fellowships, Grants from Nat. Endowment for the Arts, Rockefeller Foundation, Ford Foundation. *Address:* c/o Broadcast Music, Inc., 320 West 57th Street, New York, NY 10019 (office); 2600 Netherland Avenue, Apt 2904, Riverdale, NY 10463, USA (home). *Telephone:* (212) 586-2000 (office); (718) 549-7978 (home). *Fax:* (718) 549-7978 (home); (212) 245-8986 (office). *E-mail:* JBanks@BMI.com (office); BenRenaMus@aol.com (home).

**SILVERSTEIN, Joseph;** Violinist and Conductor; b. 21 March 1932, Detroit, Michigan, USA. *Education:* Studied with Reynolds and Zimbalist, Curtis Institute of Music, Philadelphia, 1945–50; with Gingold and Mischakoff. *Career:* Houston Symphony Orchestra; Denver Symphony Orchestra; Philadelphia Orchestra; Member, 1955–62, Concertmaster, 1962–83, Assistant Conductor, 1971–83, Boston Symphony Orchestra; Faculty Member, Berkshire Music Center, Tanglewood; Boston University; Interim Music Director, Toledo (Ohio) Symphony Orchestra, 1979–80; Principal Guest Conductor, Baltimore Symphony Orchestra, 1981–83; Music Director, Utah Symphony Orchestra, Salt Lake City, 1983–; Chautauqua (NY) Symphony Orchestra, 1987–; Guest conductor with various orchestras. *Recordings:* As violinist and conductor. *Honours:* Winner, Queen Elisabeth of Belgium competition, 1959; Naumburg Foundation Award, 1960. *Address:* c/o Utah Symphony Orchestra, 123 West South Temple, Salt Lake City, UT 84101, USA.

**SILVESTRELLI, Andrea;** Singer (bass); b. 1966, Ancona, Italy. *Education:* Rossini Conservatory, Pesaro. *Career:* Debut: Rodolfo in La Sonnambula at Spoleto, 1989; Sang Fiesco in Simon Boccanegra (1989), Banquo in Macbeth at Jesi and the Commendatore at Bologna and Rome; Season 1992-93 as Colline at Naples, the Monk in Don Carlos at La Scala and Baldassare in La Favorita at Philadelphia; Macerata Festival as Monterone in Rigoletto, Sarastro in Die Zauberflöte; Commendatore in Don Giovanni for the Holland and Ludwigsburg Festivals, Scottish Opera and in Toulouse (1995-96); Florence 1996 in Il Prigioniero by Dallapiccola and Capello in Bellini's I Capuleti at the Opéra Bastille; Season 1999-200 as Verdi's Lodovico at Munich, Oroveso in Norma at Geneva and Sparafucile (Rigoletto) at the Chicago Lyric Opera; Concerts in Italy and elsewhere. *Recordings include:* Don Giovanni; Don Carlos; Mahler's 8th Symphony. *Address:* c/o Teatro Comunale di Firenze, Via Solferino H. 15, 50123 Florence, Italy.

**SILVESTRINI, Roberta;** Conservatory Professor and Composer; b. 3 Jan. 1964, Milan, Italy; m. Lorenzo Brunelli, 21 July 1996. *Education:* G Rossini Conservatory, Pesaro; G B Martini Conservatory, Bologna; Composition with Franco Donatoni at Chigiana and S Cecilia Academies; Film Music with Ennio Morricone, 1991. *Career:* Debut: Institut Français, Naples, 9 Oct 1987; Collaborated with international solists, theatrical companies, national and foreign ensembles; Works performed at major venues and festivals including La Fenice Venice, Carnegie Hall New York, Harvard University, Gaudeamus Amsterdam, Academies S Cecilia and Chigiana; Broadcasts, RAI radio and television, Bayerische Rundfunk, others; Director, San Giovanni Choir; Professor, Fermo State Conservatory of Music; mem, Artistic Director, Association for Ancient and Contemporary Music. *Compositions include:* La toile d'araignée for flute quartet, 1989; Charmant for double bass, 1990; Agité, double bass, 1991; Crescendo intenso, violin, viola, cello, vibraphone, marimba, 1992; Energique, piano, 1993; Nuances éclatantes for saxophone quartet, 1993; Animé, viola, 1993; Pour Toi, guitar, 1994; Epaisseurs No. 2, 4 flutes, 2 pianos, 1995; Sursauts, 2 percussionists, 1995; L'Acquata, narrator, piano, 1998; Spruzzi d'onde for string quartet, 1998; Monsiue Oz Nerol le Fou, bass clarinet, 1999. *Recordings:* Animé; Effet unique; Spruzzi d'onde; La toile d'araignée; Toccata, antique organ; L'Acrobata, harp, ad lib narrator. *Publications:* Various. *Honours:* Finalist, Premio 900 Musicale Europeo, 1987; SIAE Scholarship, 1991. *Address:* Via della Marina 16, 60010 Montignano di Senigallia (AN), Italy.

**SILVESTROV, Valentin Vasilyevich;** Ukrainian composer; b. 30 Sept. 1937, Kiev. *Education:* Kiev State Conservatory (pupil of B. Lyatoshinsky). *Career:* author of compositions performed in USSR and many countries of Europe and in USA. *Compositions include:* 5 symphonies for large symphony orchestra 1963–82, Symphony for baritone with orchestra Echo Momentum on verses of A. Pushkin 1987, string quartets 1978, 1988, Dedication – symphony for violin and orchestra 1991, Mertamusica for piano and orchestra 1992, numerous chamber ensembles, piano pieces, vocal cycles, choruses. *Honours:* S. Koussevitsky Prize (USA) 1967, Prize of Gaudeamus Soc. (Netherlands) 1970. *Address:* Entuziastov str. 35/1, Apt. 49, 252147 Kiev, Ukraine (home). *Telephone:* (44) 517-04-47 (home).

**SIMA, Gabriele;** Singer (Mezzo-soprano); b. 1955, Salzburg, Austria. *Education:* Studied at the Salzburg Mozarteum and the Vienna Musikhochschule. *Career:* Sang in the Baroque repertoire with the Viennese ensemble Spectaculum and studied with Nikolaus Harnoncourt from 1979; Opera Studio of the Vienna Opera, 1979–82; Has sung at the Vienna Staatsoper from 1982, Tebaldo in Don Carlos, 1989; Salzburg Festival from 1980, notably as Johanna in the premiere of Cerha's Baal, 1981 and in the 1984 premiere of Berio's Un Re in Ascolto; Guest appearances at the Hamburg Staatsoper and at Zürich, Berlin from 1988; Opera and Concert tour of Japan, 1989; Other roles include Rosina, Cherubino, Octavian, Siebel, Annio (Titus), Idamante in Idomeneo, Feodor (Boris), Dorabella (Così), Zerlina; Season 2000–01 as Giunone in Legrenzi's La divisone del mondo, at Innsbruck and Schwetzingen; Handel's Agrippina at Graz and Carlotta in Die schweigsame Frau for the Opéra Bastille. *Recordings:* Handel's Jephtha (Telefunken); Tannhäuser, as Shepherd (Schwann); Barbiere di Siviglia, as Berta (Abbado). *Address:* Staatsoper, Opernring 2, 1010 Vienna, Austria.

**SIMCOCK, Iain Hamilton,** FRCO; British organist; b. 13 March 1965, Hemel Hempstead, England. *Education:* Solihull School, Christ Church Coll., Oxford, St Georges Chapel, Windsor Castle. *Career:* recitals for major venues all over the United Kingdom and Europe; Sub-organist of Westminster Abbey and Assistant Master of Music, Westminster Cathedral; Frequent broadcaster for BBC Radio 3; Recitals at Nôtre Dame de Paris, Strasbourg Cathedral, Proms Royal Albert Hall; Frequent tours of Scandinavia, Germany and France; mem, Royal College of Organists. *Recordings:* Christus; Vièrne Symphonies. *Publications:* contrib. articles on Music of Louis Vièrne for the Musical Times. *Honours:* Second Grand Prix, Chartes International Organ Competition. *Address:* 12 Vincent Square Mansions, Walcott Street, London SW1P 2NT, England.

**SIMIC, Goran;** singer (bass); b. 14 Oct. 1953, Belgrade, Yugoslavia. *Education:* Music High School of Belgrade and Sarajevo. *Career:* sang in opera at Sarajevo 1978–84; mem., Vienna Staatsoper from 1984, notably as Wurm (Luisa Miller), Timur, Sparafucile, the Commendatore, Colline, Pimen, Titurel and Rossini's Basilio; guest appearances in Russia, Japan, Yugoslavia and the USA; Salzburg Festival from 1986, notably as Horn in Un Ballo in Maschera, conducted by Karajan and by Solti 1990; other roles include Padre Guardiano, Ramphis, The Grand Inquisitor, Ferrando, Kecal in The Bartered Bride, Raimondo in Lucia di Lammermoor and Konchak in Prince Igor; season 2000–01 in Vienna as Mozart's Bartolo, Gremin in Eugene Onegin and Timur in Turandot. *Recordings include:* Un Ballo in Maschera, Khovanshchina conducted by Abbado, Anselmus in Schreker's Irrelohe 1995. *Honours:* prizewinner in competitions at Busseto 1981, Moscow 1982, Philadelphia 1985. *Address:* c/o Staatsoper, Opernring 2, 1010 Vienna, Austria.

**SIMIONATO, Giulietta;** Italian singer (mezzo-soprano); b. 12 May 1912, Forli. *Education:* Rovigo with Ettore Locatello and Padua with Guido Palumbo. *Career:* debut as Lola in Cavalleria Rusticana, Montagana 1928; sang in premiere of Pizzetti's Orséolo 1933; La Scala, Milan 1936–66, notably as Thomas' Mignon, Massenet's Charlotte, Rossini's Isabella, Rosina and Cenerentola, Donizetti's Giovanna Seymour and as Valentine in Meyerbeer's Les Huguenots; sang in premiere of Falla's L'Atlantida 1962; British debut 1947, as Mozart's Cherubino at Edinburgh; Royal Opera House Covent Garden 1953, as Bellini's Adalgisa and Verdi's Amneris and Azucena, opposite Callas; US debut San Francisco 1953; Chicago 1954–61; Metropolitan Opera debut 1959, as Azucena; last appearance as Servilia in La Clemenza di Tito, Piccola Scala 1966. *Recordings:* Il Matrimonio Segreto, Cavalleria Rusticana, La Cenerentola, Il Barbiere di Siviglia, L'Italiana in Algeri, Il Trovatore, La Favorita, Rigoletto, La Gioconda, Falstaff, Aïda, Un Ballo in Maschera, Carmen, Gluck's Orpheus, Meyerbeer's Valentine and in partnership with Maria Callas.

**SIMON, Abbey;** Concert Pianist; b. 8 Jan. 1922, New York, NY, USA; m. Dina Levinson Simon, 28 July 1942, 1 s. *Education:* Graduate, Curtis Institute of Music, Philadelphia, Pennsylvania. *Career:* Debut: Town Hall, New York, as winner of Walter W Naumberg Award, 1940; Concert tours in recital and with orchestra on six continents, 1940–; Professor of Piano, Juilliard School of Music, New York City; Cullen Chair for Distinguished Professor, University of

Houston, Texas. *Recordings:* Complete Chopin repertoire for solo piano and orchestra; Complete Ravel repertoire for solo piano and orchestra; All Rachmaninov's works for piano and orchestra plus transcriptions; Beethoven and Mozart Woodwind quintets Mendelssohn Variations and Songs Without Words; Many other recordings include the Piano Virtuoso and works by Schumann, Brahms and Liszt. *Honours:* First Prize, Walter W Naumburg Piano Competition; Best Recital of the Year, Federation of Music Clubs, New York; National Orchestral Award; Elizabeth Sprague Coolidge Medal, London; Harriet Cohen Foundation, London. *Current Management:* Gurtman & Murtha Associates Inc, New York City. *Address:* 45 Chemin Moise Deboule, 1209 Geneva, Switzerland.

**SIMON, Geoffrey;** Conductor; b. 3 July 1946, Adelaide, South Australia, Australia. *Education:* Studied at Melbourne University, the Juilliard School and Indiana University. *Career:* Guest appearances with leading orchestras, 1974–; Music Director, Australian Sinfonia, London; Music Director, Albany Symphony Orchestra, New York, 1987–89; Music Director, Cala Records, London, 1991–; Artistic Adviser, 1993–94, Music Director, 1994–, Sacramento Symphony, California; Regular concerts with The London Philharmonic, London Symphony and English Chamber Orchestras; Other engagements with the Munich, Israel and New Japan Philharmonic Orchestras, the American, City of Birmingham, Sapporo and Tokyo Metropolitan Symphonies, the Orchestras of the Australian Broadcasting Corporation and the Australian Opera; Conducted the Royal Philharmonic Orchestra in the premiere of Paul Patterson's 1st Symphony at the Cheltenham Festival; mem, Vice-President, Stokowski Society, 1993–. *Recordings:* Music by French composers of the 1920s and rare music by Respighi and Tchaikovsky; Patterson's Mass of the Sea; The Warriors and other works by Percy Grainger; Music by Debussy, Ravel, Respighi, Brahms, Borodin, Mussorgsky, Saint-Saëns and Barry Conyngham; The London Cello Sound–the 40 cellos of the London Philharmonic, Royal Philharmonic Orchestra, BBC Symphony Orchestra and the Philharmonia Orchestra, similarly, the London Violin Sound, the London Viola Sound and the London Trombone Sound. *Honours:* Prize Winner, John Player International Conductor's Award, 1974; Prix de la Ville de Paris, Académie du Disque Français, 1985; Gramophone Award for Respighi recordings. *Address:* c/o Cala Records Ltd, 17 Shakespeare Gardens, London N2 9LJ, England.

**SIMON, Laszlo;** Pianist and Professor; b. 16 July 1948, Miskolc, Hungary; m. Sabine Simon, 1978, 2 d. *Education:* Musica; education in Stockholm, Hannover, New York. Teachers: Hans Leygraf, Ilona Kabos, Claudio Arrau. *Career:* Debut: 1966; Appearances in Hamburg, Rome, Stockholm, Helsinki, Oslo, Berlin, Tokyo, Seoul, London, Porto, Professor, Karlsruhe State Academy, 1977–; Professor, Hochschule der Kunste, Berlin, 1981–; Stockholm 1988–; Masterclasses at Murashino Academy in Tokyo, 1988–. *Recordings:* Liszt; Clementi; Kodály; Schubert; de Frumerie; Velte. *Honours:* III Prize Busoni Competition, I Prize Casagrande Competition. *Current Management:* Konsertbolaget, Stockholm. *Address:* Hochschule der Kunste Berlin, Fasanenstr 1, 1000 Berlin, Germany.

**SIMONEAU, Léopold,** OC; Canadian singer (tenor); b. 3 May 1918, St Plavien, QC; m. Pierrette Alarie 1946; two d. *Education:* studied in Montréal with Salvator Issaurel and in New York with Paul Althouse. *Career:* debut, Montreal, Varietées Lyriques in 1941 as Hadji in Lakmé; sang in Montréal as Wilhelm Meister, Tamino and Ferrando, and Central City Colorado, Philadelphia and New Orleans; sang in Paris at Opéra-Comique in 1949 in Mireille by Gounod, Aix-en-Provence in 1950 in Iphigénie en Tauride; Glyndebourne Festival 1951–54 as Don Ottavio and Idamante; Paris in 1953 as Tom Rakewell in the French premiere of The Rake's Progress; La Scala debut in 1953, and Vienna Staatsoper in 1954; visited London's Festival Hall with the Vienna Company 1954; Salzburg Festival 1956–59 as Don Ottavio and Tamino; Chicago Lyric Opera 1959 as Alfredo; taught in Montréal after retirement from stage; apptd deputy head of the music division, Ministry of Cultural Affairs; co-founder and Dir, Opéra de Québec 1971; moved to California, USA 1972, teaching voice at San Francisco Conservatory of Music; moved to Victoria, BC 1978 with the Festival Concert Soc. summer music programme; established Canada Opera Piccola 1978–88. *Recordings:* Die Zauberflöte, Die Entführung, Così fan tutte, Don Giovanni, Orphée et Eurydice, Idomeneo, Iphigénie en Tauride, Berlioz's Requiem. *Publications:* L'art du Bel Canto 1995. *Honours:* Officier, Ordre des Arts et des Lettres 1990.

**SIMONELLA, Liborio;** Singer (Tenor); b. 10 Jan. 1933, Cordoba, Argentina. *Education:* Studied in Buenos Aires with Mario Melani and Angel Celega. *Career:* Debut: Teatro Colón, Buenos Aires, as Roberto in Le Villi by Puccini, 1967; Sang Jason in the premiere of Medea by Guidi-Drei, 1973; Teatro Colón, Rio de Janeiro and Santiago as Verdi's Alfredo and Duke of Mantua, Don José, Andrea Chenier, Hoffmann, Rodolfo and Cavaradossi; Season 1984 as Saint-Saëns's Samson at Santiago and Pierre in War and Peace at the Teatro Colón; Other roles have included Canio in Pagliacci and Aegisthus in Elektra; Many concert engagements. *Address:* Teatro Colón, Cerrito 618, 1010 Buenos Aires, Argentina.

**SIMONETTI, Riccardo;** Singer (Baritone); b. 10 Jan. 1970, Leigh, Lancashire, England. *Education:* Royal Northern College of Music, with Robert Alderson. *Career:* Sang Rodimarte in Scarlatti's Il Trionfo d'Onore at Liège, Trento, Caen and Brussels; English National Opera from 1996, notably as Bill in Mahagonny (debut role) and Papageno; Ping in Turandot at Nice, Albert in Werther for English Touring Opera, Britten's Demetrius for the Broomhill

Trust and Belcore for Clonter Farm Opera; Season 1997 with Mozart's Count for English Touring Opera and a principal contract with ENO; Season 1998 with ENO in The Tales of Hoffmann and the premiere of Dr Ox's Experiment by Gavin Bryars; Concerts include the St Matthew Passion with the Liverpool Philharmonic Orchestra, Messiah under David Willcocks and concerts with the Liverpool Philharmonic Choir. *Honours:* Winner, Anne Ziegler/Esso Award, 1993. *Address:* c/o IMG Artists, Lovell House, 616 Chiswick High Road, London W4 5RX, England.

**SIMONOV, Yuri (Ivanovich);** Conductor; b. 4 March 1941, Saratov, USSR. *Education:* Studied at the Leningrad Conservatory with Kramarov (viola) and Rabinovich (conducting). *Career:* Debut 1953, conducting school orchestra; Led several opera productions while a student; Principal Conductor of the Kislovodsk Philharmonic 1968–69; Assistant Conductor of the Leningrad Philharmonic 1968–69; Principal Conductor of the Bolshoi Theatre, Moscow, from 1970: Toured with Prince Igor to the Metropolitan Opera 1975; Premieres include Shchedrin's ballet Anna Karenina, 1972; Teacher at the Moscow Conservatory from 1975; Frequent Guest Conductor with British orchestras; Performances include: Das Rheingold, at Bolshoi Theatre, 1979; Eugen Onegin by Tchaikovsky, 1982 and La Traviata, 1986, Covent Garden; Mahler Festival in Paris with London Philharmonic Orchestra, 1989; The Queen of Spades, Bastille Opéra, Paris, 1993; Concert tours of Japan with NHK Orchestra, 1993–95; Der Ring des Nibelungen, Budapest Opera House, 1995–98; Shostakovich Symphony No. 4, with BNO, 1996. *Recordings include:* Glinka, Ruslan and Lyudmila, opera with the Bolshoi; Anna Karenina, ballet with the Bolshoi; Wagner, excerpts and overtures; Mahler, Symphony No. 1, with RPO; Tchaikovsky, Romeo and Juliet and 1812 Overture; Prokofiev, Romeo and Juliet and Lieutenant Kijé. *Honours:* Winner, Accademia di Santa Cecilia Competition, Rome, 1968; Artist of Merit of the USSR 1983. *Address:* Allied Artists Agency, 42 Montpelier Square, London SW7 1JZ, England.

**SIMPSON, Dudley (George);** Composer, Conductor and Pianist; b. 4 Oct. 1922, Melbourne, Victoria, Australia; m. Jill Yvonne Bathurst, 8 Oct 1960, 1 s., 2 d. *Education:* Studied piano with Vera Porter, Victor Stephenson, Melbourne University; Orchestration with Elford Mack, Melbourne, Dr Gordon Jacob, England; Composition with John Ingram, Australia. *Career:* Debut: 1st and 2nd M D Borovansky Ballet, Royal Ballet, Covent Garden; Guest Conductor, Royal Ballet, Covent Garden, 1960–62; Principal Conductor at British and European major festivals including: Monte Carlo, Nice, Athens and Middle East, 1961–63; 2 World tours with Dame Margot Fonteyn and Rudolph Nureyev, 1962–64; Conducted Tokyo Philharmonic Orchestra, Ballet Festival, 1985; Conducted premiere of own work Class, Ballet at Covent Garden, 1986. *Compositions:* The Winter Play, ballet, Sadler's Wells Royal Ballet; Here We Come, ballet, transcription for Orchestra, Canadian National Ballet; Ballet, Class, Royal Ballet School; Marguerite and Armand for Fonteyn and Nureyev, transcription for Orchestra; The Pastoral Symphony; Numerous television themes and incidental music including Shakespeare Canon for BBC; A Trilogy of Psalms for Choir. *Honours:* Diploma of Music (Hons). *Address:* 6 Tristania Grove, Menai, New South Wales, 2234, Australia.

**SIMPSON, Marietta;** Singer (Mezzo-soprano); b. 1954, Philadelphia, USA. *Education:* Temple University and in New York State. *Career:* Sang in concert with the Atlanta Symphony Orchestra and in Dallas, Los Angeles, Cincinnati and Detroit; Virginia Opera, 1985 as Pat in the premiere of Harriet, a Woman Called Moses by Thea Musgrave; Glyndebourne Festival, 1986–87; As Maria in Porgy and Bess, also at Covent Garden in 1992; Sang Alto Rhapsody by Brahms at Carnegie Hall, 1988; Virgil Thomson's Four Saints in Three Acts at Houston, Edinburgh and San Diego, 1996. *Recordings:* Porgy and Bess; Mendelssohn's Elijah. *Address:* c/o Houston Opera, 510 Preston Avenue, Houston TX 77002, USA.

**SIMS, Ezra;** Composer; b. 16 Jan. 1928, Birmingham, Alabama, USA. *Education:* BA, Birmingham Southern College, 1947; BMus, Yale University School of Music, 1952; US Army Language School, 1953; MA, Mills College, 1956. *Career:* Music Director, New England Dinosaur Dance Theatre, 1968–74; Member, Theory Faculty, New England Conservatory, 1976–78; President, Dinosaur Annex Music Ensemble, 1977–81; Composer; Lecturer at Mozarteum, 1992–93. *Compositions include:* Twenty Years After, 1978; All Done From Memory, 1980; Ruminations, 1980; Phenomena, 1981; Sextet, 1981; Solo After Sextet, 1981; Quartet, 1982; Pictures for an Institution, 1983; String Quartet No. 4, 1984; Night Unto Night, 1984; The Conversions, 1985; Solo in Four Movements, 1987; Quintet, 1987; Flight, 1989; Night Piece, 1989; Concert Piece, 1990; Duo, 1992; Invocation, 1992; Stanzas, 1995; Duo, 1996; Kumo Salute, 1999; String Quartet No. 5, 2001; If I told Him, 1996; Musing and Reminiscence, 2003. *Recordings include:* Sextet; String Quartet No. 2, 1962; Elegie–nach Rilke; Third Quartet; Quintet; Night Piece; Flight; Solo in Four Movements; Concert Piece; Come Away. *Publications:* Selected works, Frogpeak Music 1998; as I was saying…, Corpus Microtonole, 1987. *Contributions include:* Apologia pro Musica Sua, Jaarboch, 1992; Stichting Huyghens-Fokker; Reflections on This and That, in Perspectives of New Music, vol. 29 No. 1; Yet Another 72-Noter, in Computer Music Journal, vol. 12 No. 4. *Address:* Rosalie Calabrese Management. *E-mail:* rcmgt@yahoo.com. *Address:* 229 Hurley Street #2, Cambridge, MA 02141, USA. *E-mail:* ezrsims@aol.com.

**SIMSON, Julie,** BMusEd, MMus; American singer (mezzo-soprano) and academic; b. 13 Feb. 1956, Milwaukee, WI. *Education:* Western Michigan University, University of Illinois. *Career:* New York recital debut, Weill

Recital Hall, Carnegie Hall 1989; radio appearance, The Listening Room, New York Times Radio 1989; Lyric Opera Cleveland debut as Minerva in The Return of Ulysses 1991; Opera Colorado debut as Emilia in Otello 1991; other opera appearances with Santa Fe Opera, Dallas Civic Opera, Opera Colorado, Houston Opera Association; appeared as soloist with Milwaukee, Des Moines, Missoula, Denver, Cheyenne symphonies; George Crumb Festival featuring Ancient Voices of Children, Prague, Czech Republic; solo recital at Prague Spring Festival 1994; sang Suzuki in Madama Butterfly at Colorado Opera Festival 1999; La Dama in Macbeth for Opera Colorado 1999; soloist in Mahler's 2nd Symphony with the Omaha Symphony Orchestra 1999; Assoc. Prof. of Voice, University of Colorado. *Recordings:* Horatio Parker's Hora Norissima; Mahler's 8th Symphony. *Honours:* Mozart Prize, International Belvedere Competition, Vienna, 1985; Winner, East and West Artists International Competition for Carnegie Hall Debut; National 2nd Place Winner, NATS Artist Award. *Address:* University of Colorado-Boulder, College of Music, Campus Box 301, Boulder, CO 80309-0301, USA.

**SINGER, Malcolm (John);** British composer and conductor; *Director of Music, The Yehudi Menuhin School;* b. 13 July 1953, London; m. Sara Catherine Nathan, 15 July 1984. *Education:* Magdalene College, Cambridge; Studied with Nadia Boulanger, Paris and Gyorgy Ligeti, Hamburg. *Career:* Teacher, Yehudi Menuhin School; Department of PCS, Guildhall School of Music and Drama; Teacher of Composition, Guildhall School of Music and Drama and The Yehudi Menuhin School; Director of Music, The Yehudi Menuhin School 1998–; mem, APC; British Academy of Composers and Songwriters. *Compositions:* Time Must Have a Stop for orchestra and piano solo, 1976; The Icarus Toccata for piano duet, 1979; A Singer's Complaint, 1979; Making Music for narrator and orchestra, 1983; Nonet for strings, 1984; Sonata for piano, 1986; Yetziah, Music for Dance, 1987; Piano Quartet, 1989; York, a cantata, 1990; Kaddish for a cappella choir, 1991; Honk, for Ugly Culture, 1992; A Hopeful Place, for Yehudi Menuhin's 80th Birthday, 1996; Dragons, 1998. *Publications:* Articles of self by R Rollin in Musical Quarterly and K Potter in Musical Times. *Contributions:* Composer. *Address:* 29 Goldsmith Avenue, London, W3 6HR, England. *Telephone:* (1932) 584402 (office). *E-mail:* malcolmsinger@yehudimenuhinschool.co.uk (office).

**SINGLETON, Alvin;** American composer; b. 28 Dec. 1940, Brooklyn, NY. *Education:* New York Univ., Columbia Univ., Juilliard School of Music, Berkshire Music Center, Tanglewood, MA, Yale Univ., Accad. Naz. di Santa Cecilia, Ferienkurse für Neue Musik, Darmstadt, Germany and Instituto Musicale, Vicenza, Italy. *Career:* mem. Woodwind Quintet, Berkshire Music Festvial 1969; freelance composer, Graz, Austria 1973; composer-in-residence, Atlanta Symphony Orchestra 1985–88, Spelman Coll. 1988–91; Master Artist, Atlantic Center for the Arts 1992; composer-in-residence, Calif. State Univ., Los Angeles 1996; UNISYS composer-in-residence, Detroit Symphony Orchestra. *Compositions include:* Epitaph (choral) 1966, String Quartet No. 1 1967, Woodwind Quintet 1968–69, Cinque for piano 1969, Argoru I for piano 1970, Argoru II for cello 1970, A Seasoning 1971, Argoru III for flute 1971, Be Natural for strings 1974, Kwitana for chamber orchestra 1974, Messa (choral) 1975, Dream Sequence (opera) 1976, Extension of a Dream (ballet) 1977, Le Tombeau du Petit Prince for harpsichord 1978, Argoru IV for viola 1978, Such a Nice Lady 1979, Again for chamber orchestra 1979, Et nunc 1980, Necessity is a Mother (drama) 1981, A Yellow Rose Petal for orchestra 1982, Inside-Out for piano four hands 1983–84, La flora 1983, Argoru Va for clarinet 1984, Argoru Vb for flute 1984, Apple for woodwind 1984, Akwaaba 1985, Changing Faces for piano 1986, Shadows for orchestra 1987, After Fallen Crumbs for orchestra 1987, Fallen Crumbs (choral) 1987, Alleluia (choral) 1987, Gospel (choral) 1988, Argoru VI for percussion 1988, Bernsteinlied 1988, Eine Idee ist ein Stück Stoff (An Idea is a Piece of Cloth, for chamber orchestra) 1988, Secret Desire to be Black for strings 1988, Between Sisters 1990, Search 1990, The World is Here with Me (choral) 1990, Sinfonia Diaspora 1991, Even Tomorrow for orchestra 1991, Durch Alles for orchestra 1992, 56 Blows for orchestra 1993, Intezar for strings 1993, Cara mia Gwen for orchestra 1993, Fifty Times Around the Sun (for chamber ensemble) 1994, Argoru VII for percussion 1994, Somehow We Can for strings 1994, Sing to the Sun (choral) 1995, Blues Konzert 1995, Umoja: Each One of us Counts for orchestra 1996, Ein kleines Volkslied 1997, In Our Own House (for chamber ensemble) 1998, Praisemaker 1998, Mookestueck for electric viola 1999, Jasper Drag (for chamber ensemble) 2000. *Recordings including:* albums: Shadows 1992, Extension of a Dream 2002, Somehow We Can 2002. *Honours:* New York Univ. Marion Bauer Memorial Award 1967, Yale Univ. Rena Greenwald Memorial Prize 1969–70, Yale Univ. Woods Chandler Memorial Prize 1970–71, Kranischsteiner Musikpreis, Darmstadt 1974, Austrian Radio Musik-protokoll Kompositionpreis, Graz 1979, 1981, NEA grants 1980, 1990, MacDowell Colony fellowships 1987, 1989, 1991, 1994, 1995, 1997, City of Atlanta Mayor's Fellowship in the Arts 1989, ASCAP Standard Award 1997–98. *Address:* c/o European American Music Distributors LLC, 35 E 21st Street, New York, NY 10010, USA (office). *E-mail:* info@eamdllc.com (office). *Website:* www.eamdc.com.

**SINIMBERGHI, Gino;** Singer (Tenor); b. 26 Aug. 1913, Rome, Italy. *Education:* Studied at the Academia di Sant Cecilia, Rome. *Career:* Sang at the Berlin Staatsoper, 1937–44; Italy, 1944–68, notably as Ismaele in Nabucco; Sang in the Italian premiere of Hindemith's Long Christmas Dinner and appeared in Milan, Venice and at the Caracalla Festival; Frankfurt 1960 in Monteverdi's Orfeo, RAI Italian Radio 1970, in Rossini's La Donna del Lago.

*Recordings include:* Massenet's Thérèse; La Donna Del Lago, Donizetti Requiem; Nabucco.

**SINYAVSKAYA, Tamara Ilyinichna;** Russian opera singer (mezzo-soprano); b. 6 July 1943, Moscow; m. Muslim Magovaev 1974. *Education:* Moscow Music Coll. and State Theatre Art Inst. *Career:* soloist with Bolshoi Theatre 1964–; studied at La Scala, Milan 1973–74. *Opera roles include:* Olga in Tchaikovsky's Eugene Onegin, Carmen, Blanche and Frosya in Prokofiev's Gambler and Semyon Kotko, Vanya in Glinka's A Life for the Tsar, Ratmir in Glinka's Ruslan and Lyudmila, Lyubasha in Rimsky-Korsakov's The Tsar's Bride, Varvara in Not Love Alone. *Honours:* First Prize Int. Singing Competition, Sofia 1968, Grand Prix Int. Singing Competition, Belgium 1969, First Prize at Int. Tchaikovsky Competition, Moscow 1970; People's Artist of RSFSR 1976, People's Artist of USSR 1982. *Address:* c/o Bolshoi Theatre, Teatralnaya Pl. 1, Moscow, Russia.

**SIPPOLA, Una;** Singer (Mezzo-soprano); b. 1959, Janakkala, Finland. *Education:* Sibelius Academy, Helsinki. *Career:* Debut: Helsinki, 1985 as Amneris in Aida; Savonlinna Festival from 1986; Freiburg Opera from 1989, notably as Jane Seymour in Anna Bolena, 1991–92; Season 1992 at Hagen as Lizzie Borden in Jack Beeson's opera; Deutsche Oper am Rhein from 1993, as Eboli in Don Carlos, Venus in Tannhäuser; Laura in La Gioconda and Brangaene and Kundry; Bayreuth Festival, 1995 as Venus; Dresden Staatsoper, 1996 and 1998 as Brangaene and Amneris; Deutsche Oper Berlin from 2000, as Ortrud and other dramatic repertory; Many concert appearances. *Recordings:* Rossini's Petite Messe. *Address:* Dresden State Opera, Theaterplatz 2, 01067 Dresden, Germany.

**SIRKIA, Raimo;** Finnish singer (tenor); *Artistic Director, Savonlinna Opera Festival;* b. 7 Feb. 1951, Helsinki; s. of Raimo A. Sirkia and Lidia Sirkia; m. Cynthia Makris; one s. one d. *Education:* studied at the Sibelius Academy in Helsinki, 1977–80 and in Rome and London. *Career:* has sung at the Savonlinna Festival from 1982, and Kiel Opera from 1983 as Tamino, Lionel in Martha, Pollione and Cavaradossi; sang dramatic roles at Dortmund Opera from 1985 as Riccardo, Manrico, Otello, Alvaro, Walther, Parsifal, Don José, Bacchus, Huon in Oberon, Narraboth and Vladimir in Prince Igor; guest appearances at the Deutsche Oper am Rhein and member since 1991, Dresden, Stuttgart, Braunschweig, Karlsruhe, Basle, Stockholm, Copenhagen, Bordeaux and the Deutsche Oper Berlin (as Manrico in 1989); Hanover, Essen, Hamburg (Calaf in 1992); mem. Finnish Nat. Opera at Helsinki from 1989 singing Edgardo and Alfredo there and at Tallinn in 1990; sang at Savonlinna in 1990 as Radames and as Erik in Der fliegende Holländer; sang Idomeneo at the Finlandia Hall, Helsinki in 1991; has appeared as a guest soloist at many important opera houses throughout Europe; role of Canio at the Royal Opera House in Stockholm followed by new production of Pagliacci in Tampere, Finland, 1996; debut as Tannhäuser in the Savonlinna Opera Festival's new production in 1996 and as Siegmund in the same year; Siegfried in new production of Wagner's Ring at the Finnish National Opera in 1997; sang Siegmund at Helsinki 1998, Lohengrin, Athens 1999, Bayreuth 2000, Turin 2001, Macduff, Deutsche Oper, Berlin 2000, Tristan, Darmstadt 2000, Manrico and Otello, Finnish Nat. Opera 2000, Tristan, Venice 2002, Calaf, Savonlinna 2003, 2004; Singapore 2003; Artistic Dir Savonlinna Opera Festival 2002–; frequent concert appearances. *Recordings:* Jää mun lähellein 1984, Der fliegender Holländer (video) 1989, Opera Arias 1992, Amado mio 1994, Symphony No. 8 Mahler 1994, Juha 1995, Lemmen Virtaa 1996, Valkea Joulu – White Christmas 1996, Pohjalaisia (opera) 1997, Die Loreley (opera) 2003, Mare and Her Son 2005. *Honours:* Pro Finlandia Award 2003. *Address:* PO Box 176, SF 00251 Helsinki, Finland. *Website:* www.raimosirkia.com (home).

**SISA, Hans;** Singer (Bass); b. 1947, Linz, Austria; m. Sophia Larson. *Education:* Salzburg Mozarteum. *Career:* Appearances at the Theater am Gärtnerplatz, Munich, Bregenz Festival, Essen, Kiel and Lucca; Roles have included Verdi's Padre Guardiano, Fiesco, Ferrando and Sparafucile; Rossini's Basilio, Donizetti's Raimondo, Mozart's Count and King Henry in Lohengrin; Sang Nicolai's Falstaff at Basle, 1989, and Sarastro at Graz, 1995; Season 1999–2000 included Salome at Graz, Beethoven's 9th Symphony at Aachen, Freischütz at Savonlinna and the Landgraf in Tannhäuser at Baltimore, USA; Further engagements in Rheingold and Götterdämmerung at Graz, 2001; Other roles include Bellini's Oroveso, Berkley in Der Vampyr by Marschner and the Hermit in Der Freischütz; Many concert appearances, including Mahler's Das Klagende Lied, for Italian Radio. *Address:* c/o Graz Opera Vereinigte Buhnen, Kaiser Josef Platz 10, 8010 Graz, Austria.

**SISMAN, Elaine (Rochelle);** Musicologist; b. 20 Jan. 1952, New York City, USA; m. Martin Fridson, 14 June 1981, 1 s., 1 d. *Education:* AB, Cornell University, 1972; MFA, 1974, PhD, 1978, Princeton University. *Career:* Instructor, 1976–79, Assistant Professor, 1979–81, University of Michigan; National Endowment for The Humanities Fellowship, 1981–82; Assistant Professor, 1982–90, Associate Professor, 1990–94; Professor, Columbia University, New York, 1995–. *Publications:* Haydn and The Classical Variation, 1993; Mozart's Jupiter Symphony, 1993; Haydn and His World, 1997. *Contributions:* Haydn Studies, 1981; Small and Expanded Forms: Koch's Model and Haydn's Music, in Musical Quarterly, 1982; Haydn Kongress, Vienna, 1982, 1986; The Orchestra: Origins and Transformations, 1986; The New Harvard Dictionary of Music, 1986; Haydn's Theater Symphonies, Journal of the American Musicological Society, 1990; Brahms and the Variation Canon, 19th Century Music, 1990; Pathos and the

Pathétique, Beethoven Forum, 1994; Genre, Gesture and Meaning in Mozart's Prague Symphony, 1997; After the Heroic Style, Beethoven Forum, 1997. *Address:* Columbia University, Department of Music, 611 Dodge Hall, New York, NY 10027, USA.

**SITKOVETSKY, Dmitry;** American violinist; b. 27 Sept. 1954, Baku, USSR (now Azerbaijan); s. of Julian Sitkovetsky and Bella Davidovich; m. Susan Roberts. *Education:* Moscow Conservatory, The Juilliard School of Music. *Career:* debut with Berlin Philharmonic 1980; appearances with Vienna Symphony Orchestra, Orchestre de Paris and the Amsterdam, Rotterdam, Munich and Royal Philharmonic Orchestras in Europe and the Chicago, Cincinnati, Detroit, Montreal and Toronto Symphony Orchestras in North America, Carnegie Hall debut 1988; Artistic Dir Kuhmo Festival, Finland 1983–. *Honours:* First Prize Fritz Kreisler Competition, Vienna 1979, Avery Fisher Career Grant 1983.

**SITSKY, Larry;** Australian composer, pianist, musicologist, teacher and broadcaster; *Adjunct Professor, Monash University;* b. 10 Sept. 1934, Tientsin, China; m. 8 Feb. 1961; one s. one d. *Education:* Graduated, 1956, Postgraduate Studies, 1956–58, New South Wales State Conservatorium, Sydney, Australia; Studied with Egon Petri, San Francisco Conservatory of Music, USA, 1959–61; Higher Doctorate in Fine Arts, Australian National University, 1997. *Career:* First recital aged 11; Lived Australia, 1951–; Many recitals including contemporary Australian music, USA, 1959–61; Numerous commissions; Piano Teacher, Queensland State Conservatorium of Music, Guest Lecturer, Queensland University, 1961–65; Head, Keyboard Studies, 1966–78, Department Head, Composition, Electronic Music, 1978–81, Department Head, Composition, Musicology, 1981–, Canberra School of Music, ACT; External Examiner, Composition, Piano Performance, Australian Universities and Colleges of Advanced Education; Artistic Director, Bi-Centennial Recording Project; Director, Australian Contemporary Music Ensemble; Composer-in-Residence, University of Cincinnati, USA, 1989–90; Director, Conference Music and Musicians in Australian Culture 1930–1960, Sept 1993; Promotion to Reader, 1993; Granted Personal Chair, ANU 1994, Distinguished Visiting Fellow 2005; Adjunct Prof., Monash Univ. 2004–. *Compositions include:* Lenz (opera) 1982, De Profundis (opera) 1982, Fiery Tales (opera) 1982, De Profundis (opera) 1982, The Jade Flute 1982, Three Scenes from Aboriginal Life 1988, The Secret Doctrine: 7 Epigrams for percussion duo 1995, Opera, The Golem 1994, Signor Locatelli Visits Russia, for violin ensemble 1995, Beowulf Sonata for double bass and piano 1997, Sonatinetto for oboe and piano 1997, Bone of My Bones, 5 love lyrics for voice and piano, Enochian, Trio No. 7 for 2 cellos and piano 1999, Five Violin Concertos (1971–98), Symphony in Four Movements 2000, Symphony No. 2 for piano and orchestra 2004, String Quartets Nos 4 and 5 2004, The Way of the Seeker for piano 2004; concertos for various instruments; keyboard music. *Recordings:* numerous for major record labels; The Golem, 3 CD set; Piano concerto; Chamber instrumental music. *Publications include:* Music of the 20th Century Avante Garde; Australian Piano Music of the 20th Century; The repressed Russian Avant-Garde 1900–1929, book; Busoni and the Piano, book; Editor, Complete piano music of Roy Agnew; Anton Rubinstein, book, 1998, Australian Piano Music of the 20th Century. *Address:* 29 Threlfall Street, Chifley, ACT 2606, Australia (home). *Telephone:* (2) 6125-5765 (office); (2) 6281-1008 (home). *E-mail:* Larry.Sitsky@anu.edu.au (office).

**SITU, Gang;** Composer; b. 6 Dec. 1954, Shanghai, China. *Education:* Shanghai Teachers' University, 1978; Master of music in Composition, 1988; Music and Arts Institute of San Francisco. *Career:* Instructor in Music Theory, Music Department, Shanghai Teachers' University, 1979–85; Music Director, Chinese Cultural Productions, 1990–; Composer-in-Residence, Alexander String Quartet, 1998–2000; BMI, American Composers Forum; National Association of Composers; The Society of Composers Inc. *Compositions:* Symphonic Suite, 1988; Circle Series for Dance, 1992–94; Double Concerto for Violin and Erhu, 1994; Common Ground, 1994; Songs From the Land, San Francisco Suite, 1997; String Quartet No. 1, 1998; Rondo–String Quartet No. 2, 2000; Strings Calligraphy, 2000; String Symphony, 2000. *Recordings:* Sunlight, 1994; Dynaities, 1996; Concerto for Violin, Erhu and Strings, 1998; Songs from the Land, 1998. *Honours:* Commissioning awards, Ross McKee Foundation, 1994; SF California Art Commission, 1996; Composers Fellowship, Californian Arts Council, 1995; Compoer-in-Residence, Meet the Composer, 1998. *Address:* 1286 Pacific Avenue, San Francisco, CA 94109, USA.

**SIUKOLA, Heikki;** Singer (Tenor); b. 20 March 1943, Finland. *Education:* Studied at the Sibelius Academy, Helsinki; Sang in Opera at Tempere and Helsinki; Engaged at Wuppertal 1972–79, Krefeld 1980–83; Season 1989 as Erik at Oslo, Siegmund in Naples and Tristan at Basle and Nancy; Sang Tristan at Lyon 1990; Tannhäuser at Montpellier 1991; Other roles include, Andrea Chénier, Alfredo, Cavaradossi, Don Carlos, Pinkerton, Dick Johnson, and Hoffmann; Florestan in Fidelio, Lohengrin, Parsifal and Bacchus; Sang Samson for Palm Beach Opera, 1998; Sang Tristan at Strasbourg and Buenos Aires, 2000; Siegmund at the Vienna Staatsoper. *Address:* c/o Opéra et Concert, 1 rue Volney, F–75002 Paris, France.

**SIXTA, Jozef;** Composer; b. 12 May 1940, Jicin, Czechoslovakia. *Education:* Bratislava Conservatory, 1955–60, High School of Music, Bratislava, 1960–64; Postgraduate studies in Paris, 1971. *Career:* Lecturer at University of Music and Drama, Bratislava; mem, Slovak Music Union. *Compositions:* Symphony No. 1, 1964; String Quartet No. 1, 1965; Asynchronie, 1968; Noneto, 1970;

Flutes Quartet 1972; Solo for piano, 1973; Recitativo for violin solo, 1974; Octeto, 1977; Piano Sonata, 1985. *Recordings:* Variations for 13 instruments, 1967; Asynchronie, 1968; Noneto, 1970; Punctum Contra Punctum, 1971; Flutes Quartet, 1972; Solo for piano, 1973; Octeto, 1977; Piano Sonata, 1985; String Quartet No.2, 1985; Music for four Players, 1988; Symphony No.2, 1991; Trio for 3 clarinets, 1992; Musica, for ensemble, 1994. *Honours:* Prague Spring Festival Composition Competition, 1966; Radio Tribune UNESCO, Paris, 1970; Haydn Festival Competition, Austria, 1987; Jan Leveslav Bella Prize, 1987 and 1990. *Address:* Riazanska 68, 83102 Bratislava, Slovakia.

**SJÖBERG, Gitta-Maria;** Singer (Soprano); b. 1957, Sweden. *Education:* Århus Conservatory and Opera Studio. *Career:* Debut: Sang Mimi in La Bohème at Århus, 1987; Appearances with Jutland Opera, Århus and Royal Opera Stockholm as Desdemona, Madama Butterfly and Donna Elvira; Season 1989-90 as Micaela in Carmen at Stockholm and Amelia in Simon Boccanegra at Malmö; Guest appearances at Umea as Amelia in Un Ballo in Maschera; Royal Opera Stockholm 1996, as Butterfly; Season 1999-2000 as Mimi and Butterfly at Bonn Opera, Emilia Marty in The Makropulos Case at Dusseldorf. *Address:* c/o Svenska Konsertbyram AB, Jungfrugatan 45, S–11444, Stockholm, Sweden.

**SJÖBERG, Johan-Magnus (Göran);** Organist, Cantor and Composer; b. 7 June 1953, Östra Grevie, Sweden; m. Cajsa Finnströ m, 4 June 1983, 1 s., 1 d. *Education:* Organist-Cantor, 1972; Music Pedagogue, 1975; Choir Pedagogue, College of Music, Malmö, 1981. *Career:* Music Director, Sankt Hans Church, Lund, 1974–; Performed at Poznán Spring Festival, 1989, Warsaw Autumn Festival, 1992, Festival for Contemporary Church Music, Sweden, 1993; mem, Swedish Composers' Society. *Compositions:* Face It for wind quintet and tape; Via Dolorosa for flute and tape; Windows for chamber orchestra and tape; String Quartet 1 (Reverse); Around for flute and choir; Choral works. *Recordings:* Composer of: Windows, Basic Music; Ave Maria Stella and Ave Maria; Five; Reverse, 1995. *Honours:* Culture Award, Lund, 1988. *Address:* Flygelvägen 307, 224 72 Lund, Sweden.

**SJÖHOLM, Monica;** Singer (Soprano); b. 1945, Sweden. *Education:* Studied at the Stockholm Music High School. *Career:* Sang at Vastenda and with the Ensemble Sangens Makt, from 1972; Norrlandsoperan, Umea, from its foundation 1974, notably in L'Italiana in Algeri, as Donna Elvira, Rosina and Amelia (Un Ballo in Maschera); Other roles have included Alice Ford, Begbick in Weill's Mahagonny, Ragnhild in Den bergtagna by Ivan Hallströ m, Flora in The Medium, and in Fortunato by Ian MacQueen, 1993; Frequent concert appearances throughout Scandinavia. *Address:* c/o Norrlandsoperan, PO Box 260, S-901 08 Umea, Sweden.

**SJÖSTEDT, Sten;** Singer (Tenor); b. 1945, Malmö, Sweden. *Education:* Studied in Malmö, and at the Salzburg Mozarteum, 1966-69. *Career:* Debut: Trier Opera 1969, as Rodolfo in La Bohème; Malmö Opera 1969-74, notably in a revival of Dal Male il bene, by Abbatini; Stora Theatre, Gothenburg, from 1974; Guest appearances at San Diego (Ferrando, 1971), Oslo (as Massenet's des Grieux) and Arhus (as Hoffmann); Other roles have included Tamino, Manrico, Riccardo (Un Ballo in Maschera), Lensky and Faust; Modern repertory has included the title role in The Voyage of Edgar Allan Poe, by Dominick Argento. *Recordings include:* Tintomara, by Werle (Philips). *Address:* c/o (Stora Theatre), Göteborgs Opera, Christina Nilssons Gatan, S-A11 04 Göteborg, Sweden.

**SKALICKI, Wolfram;** Stage Designer; b. 1938, Vienna, Austria; m. Amrei Skalicki. *Education:* Studied in Austria. *Career:* Stage designs for San Francisco Opera from 1962, The Rake's Progress, The Ring (1967–72), Aida, Lady Macbeth of Mtsensk, L'Africaine, Andrea Chénier and Salome; Collaborations with costume designer Amrei Skalicki at the Vienna Burgtheater, Volksoper and Staatsoper; Productions in Lyon, Munich, Toronto, Buenos Aires, Hamburg, Miami, Athens and Geneva; Operas have included Lulu, Boris Godunov, Tristan und Isolde, Death in Venice, Hérodiade and Giovanna d'Arco; Andrea Chénier at the Metropolitan, Boris at Pittsburgh, Falstaff for Canadian Opera, Ariadne at Los Angeles; The Queen of Spades in Santiago and Elektra for Seattle Opera; Exhibitions at Bayreuth, Vienna, Zürich, New York and San Francisco; Professor at the University for Music and the Performing Arts, Graz. *Address:* c/o San Francisco Opera, War Memorial House, Van Ness Avenue, San Francisco, CA 94102, USA.

**SKARECKY, Jana (Milena);** Composer and Teacher; b. 11 Nov. 1957, Prague, Czechoslovakia; 2 d. *Education:* BMus, Honours Composition, Wilfrid Laurier University, Ontario, Canada, 1980; ARCT, Piano Performance, Royal Conservatory of Music, Toronto, 1984; MMus, Composition, University of Sydney, Australia, 1987. *Career:* Composer; Teacher, piano and theory, Canada, USA, Australia, 1977–; Faculty, Piano Theory, Royal Conservatory of Music, Toronto, Canada; Faculty, Halton Waldorf School, Canada; Compositions performed in North America, Europe, Australia and Japan; mem, Canadian League of Composers; Association of Canadian Women Composers; Canadian Music Centre. *Compositions include:* Sea Window, brass quintet, 1983; 3 Movements on Bach Themes, trumpet and strings/trumpet and organ, 1984; Oresteia, solo double bass, 1986; Rose of Sharon, solo harp, 1985; Night Songs, 4 percussionists, 1986; The Sign of the Four, solo tenor recorder, 1986; Aquamarine, orchestra, 1986; Dayspring, mezzo-soprano, piano, 1987; Lullabies, voice, 1988; Flame of Roses, flute, cello, piano, 1989; The Living Wind, mezzo, flute, cello, harp, 1990; Consort Royal recorder quartet, 1990; Sonata for viola and piano, 1992; La Corona, 3 motets, 1993; Sinfonia Lauretta, string orchestra, 1994; Into the Centre of Our Heart, chamber

ensemble, 1994; The Eye of the Phoenix for cello, 1995; Water, Fire, Air and Earth for piano, 1996; Streams for large orchestra, 1997; The Foundation Stone for piano, 1999; Green and Gold for soprano and piano, 2001; Song of Life, SATB choir, 2001; Planet Earth for soprano and piano, 2002; Numerous choral works. *Recordings:* Flame of Roses, on Spinners of Starlight CD produced by the Ardeleana Trio. *Publications include:* On Her Wings, 1993, solo organ; Love Is Come Again, SATB choir, 1995. *Address:* 2318 Bonner Road, Mississauga, Ontario L5J 2C6, Canada.

**SKARENG, Per;** Swedish classical guitarist; b. 28 June 1959, Gavle; m.; two d. *Career:* debut playing Concierto de Aranjuez, 1985; Swedish Radio Symphony; Stockholm Royal Philharmonic Orchestra, 1991; Norrkoping Symphony Orchestra, 1992; Estonia Symphony Orchestra, 1993; Gavleborgs Symphony Orchestra, 1993; Concierto para una Fiesta, 1984; Wigmore Hall, London, 1993; Toured Argentina, Cuba, Estonia and Switzerland; Concerts in Tallinn, Finland, with Pietersaari Symphony Orchestra; Macedonian Philharmonic Orchestra, Skopje; 8 recital programmes; Teacher, Music College, Vaasa, Finland; Senior Master, Royal College of Music, Stockholm; Guest lecturer, Music College in Stockholm, Oslo and Copenhagen; Artistic Director, International Guitar Festival, Galve. *Recordings:* El Colibri; Dag Wiren Little Serenade; CD with flautist Tobias Carron, 1995; CD with Tobias Carron with South American and Spanish music, 1998. *Address:* c/o Svenska Konteryybyran AB, Kerstin Hammarstrom, Executive Director, Jungfrugatan 45, 114 44 Stockholm, Sweden.

**SKELTON, Stuart;** Singer (Tenor); b. 1968, Australia; Studied in Australia, Cincinnati and San Francisco. *Career:* Debut: Alfredo for Rockdale Opera Company, Australia; Appearances with San Francisco Opera from 1996–, in Hamlet, Lohengrin, Carmen, Hoffman, Salome and Aida; Australian Opera debut 1993, in Die Meistersinger; Basilio and Don Curzio in Figaro for Western Opera Theater tour, 1995; Title role in Argento's The Aspern Papers for San Francisco Opera Center '96 Showcase production; Concerts include opera highlights with Louisville Symphony Orchestra and the Verdi Requiem with the Lubbock, Texas, Symphony Orchestra. *Honours:* Winner, Marianne Mathy Award and McDonald Aria Award, Australia. *Address:* c/o San Francisco Opera, War Memorial House, Van Ness Avenue, San Francisco, CA 94102, USA.

**SKEMPTON, Howard;** composer, accordionist and music publisher; b. 31 Oct. 1947, Chester. *Education:* studied with Cornelius Cardew 1960s. *Career:* freelance composer; Visiting Lecturer in Composition, Univ. of Adelaide, S Australia 1991; Concerto for oboe and accordion premiered and toured by Camerata Roman of Sweden 1997; Visiting Prof. in Music, De Montfort Univ. 2000–02, Hon. Prof. in Music 2003–; mem. British Acad. of Composers and Songwriters. *Compositions include:* Lento for orchestra 1990, Concerto for hurdy gurdy and percussion 1994, Gemini Dances for flute, clarinet, violin, cello, percussion and piano 1994, Shiftwork for percussion quartet 1994, Chamber Concerto 1995, We Who With Songs for chorus and organ 1995, Winter Sunrise (string trio) 1996, Delicate (ballet) 1996, The Flight of Song for chorus 1996, Two Poems of Edward Thomas for choir 1996, Into My Heart an Air that Kills for soprano, piano, 2 violins, viola and cello 1996, Concerto for oboe and accordion 1997, Clarinet Quintet 1997, Hot Noon in Malabar for soprano and piano trio 1997, Ballade for saxophone quartet and strings 1997, Concertante for violin and strings 1998, Prelude for orchestra 1999, The Voice of the Spirits for choir 1999, He Wishes for the Cloths of Heaven for choir 1999, Murallennium for choir and wind band 2000, The Bridge of Fire for choir 2001, Catch for string quartet 2001, Sarabande for string orchestra 2002, Rise up, my love, for choir 2002, Emerson Songs for soprano and baritone 2003, That Music Always Round Me for choir and orchestra 2003, Magnificat and Nunc Dimittis (The Edinburgh Service) for treble voices and organ 2003, Eternity's Sunrise for flute, clarinet, harp and string quartet 2003, Tendrils for string quartet 2004; numerous piano pieces, including Images 1989. *Honours:* British Composer Award British Acad. of Composers and Songwriters 2005. *Address:* c/o Repertoire Promotion Department, Oxford University Press, 70 Baker Street, London, W1U 7DN, England. *E-mail:* repertoire.promotion.uk@oup.com.

**SKETRIS, Paul;** singer (bass); b. 2 June 1960, Sarnia, Canada. *Education:* Univ. of Toronto, and Freiburg. *Career:* sang at Frankfurt Opera 1991–93, Magdeburg 1993–, as Sarastro, Gremin, King Phillip, Hunding, Rocco, Daland, Mephisto, Mozart's Bartolo and Alfonso, Fafner and Henry, in Lohengrin; premiere of Goldschmidt's Beatrice Cenci 1994; guest at Toronto, Vancouver, Hamilton and Japan (tour, Aida 2003) opera houses and Aldeburgh Festival; concerts include Beethoven's Ninth, Shostakovich's 14th Symphony, Bach's B minor Mass and Christmas Oratorio, Messiah, Mozart Requiem and Verdi Requiem; Canadian music features in his recital programmes; singing teacher, Univ. of Magdeburg 1997–. *Recordings:* Winterreise 2000, Christmas Music (Stille Nacht) 2003. *Address:* c/o Magdeburg Theatre, Universitätsplatz 13, Pf 1240, 39104 Magdeburg, Germany. *Website:* www.paulsketris.de.

**SKINNER, John York,** BMus, LRAM, ARAM; British singer (countertenor); b. 5 March 1949, York, England; m. 1st Juanesse Adele Reeve 1970 (divorced); m. 2nd Janet Lesley Budden 1976; two d. *Education:* York Minster Song School, Colchester Inst., RAM, London. *Career:* debut, Kassel Opera, West Germany; broadcasts on BBC, WDR, NDR, ORTF and Italian radio; opera appearances at Royal Opera House Covent Garden, La Scala Milan, Scottish Opera, Festival Ottawa and English Music Theatre. *Recordings:* works of John

Dowland with Consort of Musicke; Handel's Partenope; other Mediaeval, Renaissance and Baroque music. *Honours:* hon. mem. Royal Coll. of Music 1982. *Address:* Principal, Bermuda School of Music, PO Box HM 3149, Hamilton HMNX, Bermuda.

**SKOGLUND, Annika;** Singer (Mezzo-Soprano); b. 5 Nov. 1960, Vanersborg, Alvsborg, Sweden. *Education:* Studied at Royal Academy of Music, Gothenburg and London. *Career:* Sang Cherubino at Drottningholm 1988, followed by Suzuki at the Royal Opera in Stockholm; Returned to Drottningholm as Ramiro in La Finta Giardiniera and made Italian debut at Venice as Isolier in Le Comte Ory; Further engagements as Cherubino at Oslo, Suzuki in Stockholm and the Countess in Maw's The Rising of the Moon at the 1990 Wexford Festival; Concert repertoire includes the Lieder eines Fahrenden Gesellen with Oregon Symphony; Songs of the Auvergne and Kindertotenlider and Das Lied von der Erde. *Recordings include:* Video of La Finta Giardiniera. *Current Management:* Nordic Artist AB. *Address:* Sveavagen 76, 113 59 Stockholm, Sweden.

**SKOLOVSKY, Zadel;** Concert Pianist; b. 17 July 1926, Vancouver, Canada; m. Alice Glass, 29 July 1947, divorced 1953. *Education:* Piano, Conducting, Violin, various teachers including last (and youngest) student, Leopold Godowsky; Graduate Diploma, Curtis Institute of Music, Philadelphia, USA. *Career:* Debut: Solo Recital as Winner, Naumburg Award, New York Town Hall; Orchestral with New York Philharmonic, Carnegie Hall; Solo appearances, most great orchestras world-wide including New York Philharmonic, Philadelphia, Chicago, San Francisco, Toronto, London Philharmonic, Royal Philharmonic, BBC Symphony, French National Orchestra, Lamoureux, Israel Philharmonic, under conductors including Monteux, Munch, Bernstein, Maazel, Leinsdorf, Kubelik, Kletzki; Appearances, Mexico, South America, many world capitals; Allied Arts Piano Series, Chicago; Aaron Richmond Celebrity Series, Boston; Eaton Series, Toronto; Stage and television; Teaching, Professor of Music, 1975–87, Professor Emeritus, 1987–, Indiana University. *Recordings:* Various performances on major record labels. *Current Management:* Self. *Address:* 240 East 79th Street, Apt 10-A, New York, NY 10021, USA.

**SKOVHUS, Bo;** Danish opera singer; b. 22 May 1962, Ikast; s. of Freddy Jorgensen and Birthe Skovhus; one d. *Education:* Music Acad., Århus, Royal Music Acad. and Opera School, Copenhagen, and in New York. *Career:* début in Don Giovanni, Vienna Volksoper 1988, début as Silvio, Pagliacci Vienna Staatsoper 1991; regular guest singer with all maj. orchestras and opera cos including Metropolitan, New York, San Francisco, Houston, Munich State Opera, Hamburg State Opera, Berlin, Cologne, Covent Garden, Dresden, etc.; many recitals in Europe, USA and Japan; numerous lieder recitals with Helmut Deutsch, Stefan Vladar, Yefim Bronfman, Lief Ove Andsnes,Christoph Eschenbach and Daniel Barenboim; repertoire includes Don Giovanni, Almaviva (La Nozze de Figaro), Guglielmo (Così fan Tutte), Wolfram (Tannhauser), Olivier (Capriccio), Barber (Schweigsame Frau), Wozzeck, Hamlet, Billy Budd, Eugene Onegin, Yeletsky (Pique Dame), Danilo (Lustige Witwe), Eisenstein (Die Fledermaus). *Recordings include:* Don Giovanni (twice), Le Nozze di Figaro, The Merry Widow, Britten's War Requiem, Carmina Burana, Fidelio, Das Lied von der Erde, Wozzeck, Mirror of Perfection (Blackford), I Pagliacci, Der Waffenschmied (Lortzing), Maskarade (Nielsen), Venus (Schoek), Die Schöne Müllerin, Schwanengesang (Schubert), Dichterliebe (Schumann), Liederkreis Op. 24 (Schumann), Eichendorff Lieder (Wolf), Faust (Spohr), Oberon (Weber), Die Orchesterlieder (Strauss), Lyrische Sinfonie (Zemlinsky) (twice), Lieder (Zemlinski) and recording of arias by Britten, Gounod, Korngold, Verdi, Wagner, Thomas, Massenet and Tschaikowsky. *Honours:* Kammersänger (Austria) 1997. *Current Management:* Balmer & Dixon Management AG, Kreuzstrasse 82, 8032 Zürich, Switzerland. *Telephone:* (43) 244-8644. *Fax:* (43) 244-8649. *Website:* www.badix.ch.

**SKRAM, Knut;** Singer (Baritone); b. 18 Dec. 1937, Saebo, Norway. *Education:* Montana University and voice with George Buckbee; European studies with Paul Lohmann in Wiesbaden, Luigi Ricci in Rome and Kristian Riis in Copenhagen. *Career:* Oslo Opera from 1964 with debut as Amonasro in Aida; In 1967 won first prize in Munich Radio International Competition; Sang at Glyndebourne Festival, 1969–76, as Mozart's Guglielmo, Papageno and Figaro; Così fan tutte for French television in 1977; Sang at Aix-en-Provence, 1977–, in operas by Mozart and at Spoleto Festival in Italy from 1978; Concert appearances in Europe and America with regular broadcasts on television and radio in Scandinavia; Sang at Lyon in 1984 as Tchaikovsky's Eugene Onegin; Sang Jochanaan in Salome with the Berlin Staatsoper on tour to Japan in 1987, Amfortas, Amonasro and Kurwenal in Berlin, 1988–89 and appeared as Pizarro in Tel-Aviv and Buenos Aires in 1988; Bolshoi Opera debut in 1988 as Scarpia; Season 1989–90 sang in The Makropulos Case at the Deutsche Oper Berlin, Amfortas at the Spoleto Festival, Charleston, and Don Giovanni at Trieste; Sang Hans Sachs at Nice in 1992; Sang the Wanderer in Mike Ashman's production of Siegfried, Oslo, 1996; Season 1999–2000 as Scarpia at the Opéra-Comique, Paris, Creon in Oedipus Rex at Brussels. *Recordings include:* Video from Glyndebourne Festival of Le nozze di Figaro in 1973; Many recitals of Norwegian Songs.

**SKRIPKA, Sergei (Ivanovich);** Ukrainian conductor; b. 5 Oct. 1949, Kharkov; m. Skripka Evgenija 11 Oct. 1975; two d. *Education:* Graduated as Chorusmaster, Kharkov Institute of Arts, 1972; Graduated in Conducting Opera and Symphony Orchestras from Moscow State Conservatoire (studied under Professor Leo Ginzburg), 1977; Master's Degree, 1979. *Career:* Debut: Zhukovsky Symphony Orchestra, 1975; First performance in the USSR of R Keiser's St Markus Passion with the Moscow Chamber Orchestra, 1982; Tour with the Zhukowsky Symphony Orchestra, 1991; Britten's War Requiem in Berlin, 1991; Mozart's Requiem and Beethoven's 9th Symphony, with the Russian State Symphony Orchestra of Cinematography, Frankfurt am Main, 1992; mem, Professional Society of Cinematography, 1988. *Recordings:* Minin and Pozharsky (oratorio Liberation of Moscow by Degtyarev) 1990, Cello Concertos by Glièr and Mosolov with S Sudzilovsky (cello), 1996; Russian Overture and Symphonies Nos 2 and 4 by Shebalin. *Honours:* Honourable Person in Russian Arts, 1993; Artistic Leader and Main Conductor of the Russian State Symphony Orchestra of Cinematography; Professor of the Russian Academy of Music (Gnessin's Institute), 1997; People's Artist of the Russian Federation, 1998. *Address:* ul Isakovskogo 12-1-208, 123181 Moscow, Russia. *E-mail:* sergeiskripka@pochta.ru (home).

**SKRIVAN, Zvonimir;** Conductor; b. 12 Aug. 1938, Prague, Czechoslovakia; m. 1964, 1 d. *Education:* Academy of Music Arts in Prague. *Career:* Debut: Il Barbiere di Siviglia, Olomouc, 1967; Albert Herring; Jakobin; Dalibor, Devil and Kate; Bartered Bride, Jenůfa; Aida; Rigoletto; La Traviata; Un Ballo in Maschera; Lucia di Lammermoor; Faust; La Gioconda; Idomeneo; Così fan tutte; Le nozze di Figaro; Fidelio; Other operas and ballets in the Moravian Theatre in Olomouc, 1967–97; also National Theatre, Prague; Collaboration with Moravian Philharmonia Orchestra, Olomouc, Simon Boccanegra, Suor Angelica, Gianni Schicchi and Orfeo ed Euridice; mem, Association of Music Artists; Society of Music Theatre. *Recordings:* The Bell by Donizetti, Czech television, and operas, arias and duets for Czech radio. *Honours:* The Prize of Oldrich Stibor, 1976, 1983; Prize of Prague Opera Festival for Lucia di Lammermoor, 1995, Idomeneo, 1997. *Address:* Dobnerova Str N 20, 77900 Olomouc, Czech Republic.

**SKROWACZEWSKI, Stanisław;** Polish conductor and composer; b. 3 Oct. 1923, Lwów (now in Ukraine); s. of Paweł Skrowaczewski and Zofia Skrowaczewska (née Karszniewicz); m. Krystyna Jarosz 1956; two s. one d. *Education:* Lwów Conservatoire and State Higher School of Music, Kraków. *Career:* Conductor, Wrocław Philharmonic Orchestra 1946–47; further composition studies with Nadia Boulanger and P. Klecki, Paris 1947–49; Artistic Dir and First Conductor, Silesian Philharmonic Orchestra, Katowice 1949–54; First Conductor, Kraków Philharmonic Orchestra 1955–56; Dir Nat. Philharmonic Orchestra, Warsaw 1957–59; Musical Dir Minnesota Orchestra 1960–79; tours in Europe, N and S America, Israel, Japan, Australia; Prin. Conductor and Musical Adviser, Hallé Orchestra 1984–91; Musical Adviser St Paul Chamber Orchestra 1986–88, Milwaukee Symphony 1992–94. *Compositions include:* Symphony for String Orchestra, three other symphonies, Muzyka Nocą (Music by Night, suite of nocturnes), four string quartets, two overtures, Cantique des Cantiques (voice and orch.), Prelude, Fugue, Post-Ludium (orch.), English Horn Concerto 1969, Ricercari Notturni (orchestral), Clarinet Concerto, Violin Concerto 1985, Fanfare for Orchestra 1987, Sextet 1988, String Trio 1990, Triple Concerto 1992, Chamber Concerto 1993, Passacaglia Immaginaria 1995, Musica a quattro 1998, Concerto for Orchestra 1999, Trio for piano, clarinet and bassoon, six piano sonatas; also music for opera, ballet, film and theatre; recordings for Mercury, Philips, Angel, RCA Victor, IMP, Erato, Arte Nova, Vox, Albany. *Honours:* Commdr Cross of Polonia Restituta Order; Hon. DHL (Hamline Univ., St Paul, Minnesota) 1961; Hon. DMus (Macalester Coll., St Paul, Minn.) 1977; Dr hc (Univ. of Minnesota) 1979; Second Prize for 'Overture 1947', Szymanowski Competition, Warsaw 1947; Second Prize, Int. Competition for String Quartet, Liège, Belgium 1953; State Prize (3rd Class) 1956, First Prize, Int. Conductor's Competition, Rome 1956, Conductor's Award of Columbia Univ., New York 1973, Third Prize, Kennedy Center Friedheim Award Competition (for Ricercari Notturni) 1978; 5 ASCAP Awards for imaginative programming with Minneapolis Symphony 1961–79, Gold Medal, Bruckner-Mahler Soc. 1999, McKnight Distinguished Artist Award 2004. *Address:* PO Box 700, Wayzata, MN 55391, USA. *Fax:* (763) 473-7384.

**SKRZYPCZAK, Bettina,** DMus; Polish composer, musicologist and music journalist; b. 25 Jan. 1962. *Education:* Poznań Acad. of Music, Basle Musikakademie Studio for Electronic Music. *Career:* Lecturer in Music History, Theory and Aesthetics of Music, Univ. of Lucerne, Switzerland 1995–, Prof. 2002–; Lecturer, Internationale Ferienkurse für Neue Musik, Darmstadt, Germany 2004. *Compositions include:* Sonata for two pianos 1985, What is Black, What is White 1987, Lob der Erde 1991, String Quartet 1993, 'SN 1993 J' 1995, Oboe Concerto 1996, Piano Concerto 1998, Mouvement 1999, Miroirs 2000, Vier Figuren 2001, String Quartet No. 4 2003, Lettres 2004. *Recordings include:* Portrait Bettina Skrzypczak with String Quartet No. 3 (DVD), Portrait Bettina Skrzypczak (including Scène, Miroirs, Toccata sospesa, 'SN 1993 J', Fantasie, Piano Concerto). *Honours:* awards at Zagreb Music Biennale competition for young composers 1988, Tadeusz Baird competition, Warsaw 1990, Mannheim Int. Competition for Women Composers 1994, Basle Förderpreis 1996, Riehen Kulturpreis 2004. *E-mail:* info@bettina-skrzypczak.com. *Website:* www.bettina-skrzypczak.com.

**SKWORTSOW, Alexander;** Violinist; b. 24 May 1944, Novosibirsk, Russia; m. 2 s., 1 d. *Education:* School for Musically Gifted Children, Novosibirsk; Masterclass, Leningrad Conservatory. *Career:* Debut: Novosibirsk Symphony Orchestra; Concertmaster: Leningrad Concert Orchestra; Primarius String Quartet, St Petersburg; First Concertmaster: Lubecker Symphony; Vancouver Symphony; Various orchestras throughout Western Europe; Soloist in

Canada, USA, Germany and Western Europe. *Compositions:* Various cadenzas for violin concertos. *Recordings:* Yuri Boutsko trio, Holocaust commemorative CD, award winning; Musica with works by Liszt, Enescu and Paganini. *Contributions:* Das Orchester; Lubecker Nachrichten. *Honours:* Twice obtained first prize in National Music competition for USSR. *Current Management:* Starling Artist Management. *Address:* Augustinushof 130, 1216 LH Hilversum, Netherlands.

**SLABBERT, Wicus;** Singer (Baritone); b. 1941, Kroonstad, South Africa. *Education:* Studied at the University of Pretoria, BA, Fine Arts; With Josef Metternich in Germany. *Career:* Sang in German repertory at Düsseldorf from 1968 and Italian from 1973; Appearances at Essen, 1974–79 as Germont, Don Carlo, Rigoletto, Don Giovanni, Count Almaviva in Figaro, Scarpia, Jochanaan, Mandryka and Beckmesser; Staatsoper Kassel from 1979 notably as Macbeth, Iago, the Villains in Hoffmann and Dr Schön; Guest engagements at the Bregenz Festival from 1988 in Les Contes d'Hoffmann and Der fliegende Holländer, at Düsseldorf, Stuttgart, Theater am Gärtnerplatz Munich and Pretoria; Member of the Vienna Staatsoper since 1991 with performances as Boris in Lady Macbeth of Mtsensk and as Nabucco in 1992; Festival engagements at Edinburgh, Florence, Stockholm and Warsaw; Sang at Teatro Colón Buenos Aires in 1992 as Wagner's Dutchman, Alberich in the Ring and Tosca; Vienna Volksoper 1996, in Mona Lisa by Max von Schillings; Shostakovich's Boris in Bonn, 1998; Season 2000 as Falstaff, Nick Shadow and Gyges in Zemlinsky's Der König Kandaules, at the Veinna Volskoper; Dutchman at Dusseldorf. *Recordings include:* Bohni in Zemlinsky's Kleider Machen Leute. *Address:* c/o Staatsoper, 1010 Vienna, Austria.

**SLADE, Julian Penkivil,** BA; British writer and composer; b. 28 May 1930, London. *Education:* Trinity Coll., Cambridge amd Bristol Old Vic Theatre School. *Career:* joined Bristol Old Vic Co. as Musical Dir 1952; wrote and composed Christmas in King Street (with Dorothy Reynolds, James Cairncross), Bristol 1952; composed music for Sheridan's The Duenna, Bristol 1953; transferred to Westminster Theatre, London 1954; wrote and composed The Merry Gentleman (with Dorothy Reynolds), Bristol 1953; composed incidental music for The Merchant of Venice 1953; wrote musical version of The Comedy of Errors for television 1954, and for Arts Theatre, London 1956; wrote Salad Days (with Dorothy Reynolds), Bristol, and Vaudeville, London 1954, Duke of York's 1976; Free As Air, Savoy, London 1957; Hooray for Daisy!, Bristol 1959, Lyric, Hammersmith 1960; Follow That Girl, Vaudeville, London 1960; Wildest Dreams 1960; Vanity Fair (with Alan Pryce-Jones, Robin Miller), Queens Theatre, London 1962; Nutmeg and Ginger, Cheltenham 1963; Sixty Thousand Nights (with George Rowell), Bristol 1966; The Pursuit of Love, Bristol 1967; composed music for songs in As You Like It, Bristol 1970, A Midsummer Night's Dream and Much Ado About Nothing, Regents Park 1970; adapted A. A. Milne's Winnie the Pooh, Phoenix Theatre 1970, 1975; music and lyrics, Trelawny, Bristol, then London West End 1972; Out of Bounds 1973; wrote Now We Are Sixty (with Gyles Brandreth), Arts Theatre, Cambridge 1986–; revival of Nutmeg and Ginger, New Orange Tree Theatre, Richmond 1991; revival of The Comedy of Errors, Gray's Inn Hall 1994; revival of Salad Days, Vaudeville, London 1996; revival of Follow that Girl, Theatre Museum, Covent Garden, 70th birthday concert, Theatre Museum 2000; revival of Vanity Fair, Theatre Museum 2001. *Honours:* BASCA Gold Badge of Merit 1987. *Address:* 86 Beaufort Street, London, SW3 6BU, England.

**SLAMA, František;** Czech cellist and viola da gamba player; b. 19 Nov. 1923, Herálec; three s. two d. *Education:* Conservatory of Prague, Chamber of Instrumental Music with Václav Talich, Academy of Music and Dramatic Arts of Prague. *Career:* debut playing Schumann's Concerto A Minor (with Czech Philharmonic Orchestra), Rudolfinum Hall, Prague, 1952; Cellist in Talich's Czech Chamber Orchestra, 1946–48; Member, Czech Philharmonic Orchestra, 1951–; Soloist and Continuo Player of two of the first European ensembles of Ancient music, Pro Arte Antiqua and Ars Rediviva, 1951–; Ars Rediviva had 45 years' subscription concerts cycle of Baroque music at Rudolfinum Hall, Prague (6 concerts annually; Repertoire of over 300 compositions of Czech and European Masters), festivals in Czechoslovakia, Germany, Spain, Italy, Austria, Sweden; Radio and television broadcasts and recordings with J. P. Rampal, M. André, O. Peter, A. Adorján. *Recordings:* Purcell's Phantasy Upon One Note, 1959; Musical Offering, 1969, radio, 1985; Brandenburg Concertos, 1965; J D Zelenka, Lamentationes, 1970; J. S. Bach's Concerto G Minor for Viola da gamba, 1981; C. P. E. Bach's Sonatas, 1994; Series on viola da gamba and Jordi Savall, for Czech Radio Prague, 1995. *Address:* Na Sumave 1, 150 00 Prague 5, Czech Republic.

**SLATFORD, Rodney (Gerald Yorke);** Musician (Double Bass) and Publisher; b. 18 July 1944, Cuffley, Hertfordshire, England. *Education:* Royal College of Music with Adrian Beers. *Career:* Principal Bass with Midland Sinfonia, the Academy of St Martin-in-the-Fields and English Chamber Orchestra until 1981; Edited and published 100 works for his own Yorke Edition, devoted to double bass literature; Founder member of Nash Ensemble and guest appearances with leading string quartets; Tours to Australia, New Zealand and The Far East; 1st Double Bass recital at Sydney Opera House; Lectures in USA; Professor in Residence at Kusatsu International Summer Academy in Japan, 1984; Teaching at the Toho Academy in Tokyo and at the Conservatoire in Peking; Professor at Royal College of Music, 1974–84; From 1984, Head of School of Strings at Royal Northern College of Music, Manchester; Fellow RNCM, 1987; Established teaching method for double bass, 1978; Founder of the Yorke Trust to promote the training of young

bassists; Director and Founder, RNCM Junior Strings project, 1991; Chairman, European String Teachers Association, 1992; Regular Presenter of Radio 3, 1993. *Recordings include:* Rossini's Duetto in solo record with Academy of St Martin-in-the-Fields. *Publications:* The Bottom Line, 1985. *Contributions:* Woman's Hour; A Word in Edgeways; One Pair of Ears; Mainly for Pleasure, Radio 3; The Strad Magazine; New Grove Dictionary of Music and Musicians, 1980. *Address:* 31 Thornhill Square, London N1 1BQ, England.

**SLATINARU, Maria;** Singer (Soprano); b. 25 May 1938, Jassy, Romania. *Education:* Studied at the Bucharest Conservatory with Arta Florescu and Aurel Alexandrescu. *Career:* Debut: Bucharest in 1969 as Elisabeth de Valois; Appearances as guest at Mannheim, Stuttgart, Zürich, Wiesbaden and Düsseldorf; Sang at Basle and Florence in 1983 as Giorgetta in Il Tabarro, Strasbourg in 1984 as Elisabeth in Tannhäuser and has sung Tosca in San Francisco, Dallas in 1988 and elsewhere; Other roles include Verdi's Abigaille and Amelia in Simon Boccanegra, Leonore in Fidelio, Wagner's Sieglinde, Senta and Elsa, Santuzza and Puccini's Turandot, Minnie and Manon Lescaut.

**SLATKIN, Leonard Edward;** American conductor and pianist; *Music Director, National Symphony Orchestra;* b. 1 Sept. 1944, Los Angeles, CA; s. of Felix Slatkin and Eleanor Aller; m. Linda Hohenfeld 1986; one s. *Education:* Indiana Univ., Los Angeles City Coll., Juilliard School; studied violin, piano, viola, composition, conducting. *Career:* debut Carnegie Hall 1966; founder, Music Dir and Conductor St Louis Symphony Youth Orchestra 1979–80, 1980–81; Asst Conductor Youth Symphony of New York, Carnegie Hall 1966, Juilliard Opera, Theater and Dance Dept 1967, St Louis Symphony Orchestra 1968–71, Assoc. Conductor 1971–74, Music Dir and Conductor 1979–96; Prin. Guest Conductor Minn. Orchestra 1974–, Summer Artistic Dir 1979–80; Music Dir New Orleans Philharmonic Symphony Orchestra 1977–78; Music Dir Nat. Symphony Orchestra, Washington, DC 1996–(2008); Prin. Conductor BBC Symphony Orchestra 2000–04; Prin. Guest Conductor Royal Philharmonic Orchestra 2005–; guest conductor with orchestras worldwide, including most major US orchestras, Montréal, Toronto, Vienna, Vienna State Opera, London Symphony, London Philharmonia, English Chamber, Concertgebouw, Royal Danish, Stockholm, Scottish Nat., NHK Tokyo, Israel, Berlin, Stuttgart Opera; festivals include Tanglewood, Blossom, Mann Music Center, Mostly Mozart and Saratoga. *Honours:* five hon. degrees; two Grammy Awards. *Current Management:* Askonas Holt Ltd, Lonsdale Chambers, 27 Chancery Lane, London, WC2A 1PF, England. *Telephone:* (20) 7400-1700. *Fax:* (20) 7400-1799. *E-mail:* info@askonasholt.co.uk. *Website:* www.askonasholt.co.uk. *Address:* c/o National Symphony Orchestra, The John F. Kennedy Center for the Performing Arts, 2700 F Street NW, Washington, DC 20566, USA. *Website:* www.kennedy-center.org/nso.

**SLAVICKY, Milan;** Czech composer, producer, writer on music and lecturer; b. 7 May 1947, Prague; m. Eva Hachova 1972; two s. *Education:* Charles Univ., Prague, Janáček Acad. of Music Arts, Brno. *Career:* Sr Music Producer of Classics, Supraphon 1973–81; Producer of Electro-acoustic Music, Radio Prague 1981–82; freelance composer and producer 1982–90; Asst Prof., Film Faculty, Acad. of Music Arts, Prague 1990–94, Asst Prof. of Composition 1994–97, Assoc. Prof. 1997–2001, Prof. 2002–; Asst Prof. of Musicology, Charles Univ. 1990–97, Assoc. Prof. 1997–2001, Prof. 2002–; lectures given throughout Europe and many papers presented at congresses; compositions performed widely at leading festivals and broadcast world-wide. *Compositions:* orchestral: Hommage à Saint-Exupéry, Terre des hommes, Porta coeli, Two chapters from the Revelation, Ich dien, Synergy' Concerto: Way of the Heart for violin, wind and percussion, Requiem; chamber: Musica lirica, Musica notturna, Brightening I–IV, Dialogues with the Silence string quartet; organ music and compositions for solo instruments; vocal: Stay with Us, Sweet Loving for soprano and ensemble, Media Vita for soprano and viola, Veni Sancte Spiritus for soprano and ensemble, Electro-acoustic: In Praise of Harpsichord, Variations on a Laser Ray, Brightening V or Prague Autumn, Adventus. *Recordings:* over 550 albums as producer for many labels. *Publications:* Interviews from the House of the Artists, Gideon Klein: A Fragment of Life and Work. *Honours:* Carl-Maria-von Weber Prize, Dresden 1976, 1979, Second Prize Competition from Czech Ministry of Culture 1980, Prize of Brasilia 1985, Czech Music Critics' Award 1992. *Address:* Lukesova 39, 142 00 Prague 4, Czech Republic. *Fax:* (2) 44471870 (home). *E-mail:* milan.slavicky@iol.cz (office). *Website:* www.musica.cz/slavicky (office).

**SLAVKOVA, Maria;** Singer (Soprano); b. 1958, Tarnova, Bulgaria. *Career:* Sang at the National Opera, Sofia, from 1987; Mainz Opera from 1984 and Mannheim from 1990, as La Gioconda, Tosca, Senta, Leonore in Fidelio, Aida, Butterfly, Odabella in Attila and Margherita in Mefistofele; Guest appearances at Munich as Smetana's Marenka and Tokyo (Santuzza); Gelsenkirchen, 1995, as Leonore (also at Leipzig, 1996), Brunswick, 1994, as Elisabeth in Tannhäuser; Wagner's Sieglinde at Hamburg and Abigaille in Nabucco at Vienna; Venus and Elisabeth in Tannhäuser at Limoges and Toulon. *Address:* c/o Mannheim Opera, Mozartstr 9, 68161 Mannheim, Germany.

**SLAWSON, A. Wayne;** Composer and Professor of Music; b. 29 Dec. 1932, Detroit, Michigan, USA. *Education:* BA in Mathematics, 1955, MA in Music Composition, 1959, University of Michigan; PhD in Psychology, Harvard University, 1965. *Career:* Assistant Professor of Theory of Music, Yale School of Music, Connecticut, 1967–72; Associate Professor, 1972–84, Chair, Department of Music, 1972–78, Professor of Music, 1984–86, University of

Pittsburgh, Pennsylvania; Professor of Music, 1986–, Chair Department of Music, 1996–, University of California, Davis. *Compositions:* Electronic music works: Wishful Thinking About Winter, 1966, Variations for 2 violins, 1977, Colors, 1981, Greetings, 1985, Quatrains Miniature, 1986, If These Two Tolled, computer music, 1990, Interpolations of Dance for string quartet, 1992, Grave Trunks for computer music and video tape, with Harvey Himelfarb, 1992, Warm Shades, an octet for singers and woodwinds, 1993, Match for orchestra, 1994; Dual II for computer synthesised, speech derived sound and sound poet, 1997; Autumn rounds for computer synthesised, speech derived sound, 1999. *Publications:* Sound Color, 1985; Rap soft for computer-synthesized speech-derived sound, 2000. *Contributions:* Book Reviewer for Journal of Music Theory, 1986. *Honours:* Fellow, American Council of Learned Societies, 1978–79; Outstanding Publication Award, Society for Music Theory. *Address:* c/o Music Department, University of California, Davis, CA 95616, USA.

**SLEPKOVSKA, Denisa;** Singer (Mezzo-soprano); b. 1965, Košice, Czecho-slovakia. *Education:* Košice Conservatory. *Career:* Appearances with Slovak National Opera at Bratislava, with guest appearances in Greece, Austria, Germany, Edinburgh, Spain and Jerusalem; Concerts at Munich, Passau and Baden-Baden, 1992–95; Repertory includes Puccini's Suzuki, Mozart's Apollo and Cherubino, Verdi's Maddalena and Fenena; Nicklausse in Les Contes d'Hoffmann, Rossini's Rosina and Vlasta in Šárka by Fibich, Recordings include: Respighi's Bella dormente and Lucrezia. *Address:* Music International, 13 Ardilaun Street, London N5 2QR, England.

**SLIMACEK, Jan;** Czech composer; b. 31 July 1939, Kelc; m. Marie Chvatikova 1964; two d. *Education:* Prague Conservatory. *Career:* debut, Symfonietta for Strings, Tape Recording Czech Radio; Music Director, Radio Plzeň, 1967–; Sonatina for strings, Northern Music Festival, Ontario, 1988, Vassa, 1992; Divertimento for flute and piano, Inter Music Festival, Brno, 1983, Graz Wien, 1993; Quattro Intermezzi per Orchestra Gera, 1983, Musical Festival Rostow Don, 1988; Concertino for accordion, electravox and orchestra gera, 1976, Nuremberg 1982, Bern, 1983; Dramatic Picture Szczecin, Weimar, 1979; Piano Quartet, Warsaw, 1977; Three Etudes for piano, Bristol, 1981; Professor of Music, Gymnasium Plzeň, 1993–; mem, Association of Musicians and Musicologists. *Compositions include:* Piano Quartet; Sonatina for strings; Three Etudes for piano; Dramatic Picture; Songs for children's choir and piano; Variations for strings and harpsichord. *Recordings include:* Quattro Intermezzi per orchestra; The Victory Overture for orchestra; Musica per orchestra; Three Miniatures for chamber orchestra; Music per ottoni. *Address:* Mohylová 109, Plzeň 312 06, Czech Republic.

**SLONIMSKY, Sergey Michailovich,** PhD; Russian composer, teacher and pianist; *Professor, St Petersburg Conservatoire;* b. 12 Aug. 1932, Leningrad (now St Petersburg); s. of Michail Slonimsky and Ida Slonimskaya (née Kaplan); m. Raisa Slonimskaya (née Zankisova) 1973; one s. one d. *Education:* Leningrad Conservatoire. *Career:* Teaching Faculty, Music Theory and Composition, Leningrad (now St Petersburg) Conservatoire 1958–, Prof. 1976–; mem. Bd CIS Composers' Union (also mem. St Petersburg Br.). *Works include:* 13 symphonies 1958–2004, orchestral and vocal works, chamber works, opera, ballet, songs and choral pieces, including Carnival Overture 1957, Concerto Buffa, chamber orchestra 1966, Antiphones (string quartet) 1969, Virinea opera 1969, Icarus (ballet in three acts) 1973, Master and Margarita (chamber opera in three acts) 1970–85, Merry Songs for piccolo, flute and tuba 1971, Sonata for violoncello and piano 1986, Mary Stuart (opera performed at 1986 Edinburgh Festival, USSR and abroad), Hamlet (opera) 1990–94, Cerch: dell'Inferno secondo Dante 1992, 24 Preludes and Fugues for piano 1994, Ivan the Terrible 1994 (opera premiered at Samara 1998), 24 Preludes and Fugues for piano 1995, King Lear (opera after Shakespeare) 2001, The Magic Nut (ballet) 2005. *Recordings:* Requiem 2003, Magic Nut (ballet, libretto by Mihail Shemiakin) 2005. *Publications:* musicological study of Prokofiev's symphonies 1964, Burlesques, Elegies, Dithyrambs 2000, Free Dissonance 2005. *Honours:* Cavalier of Commdr's Cross of Poland; RSFSR Glinka State Prize 1983, RSFSR People's Artist 1987, State Prize of Russia 2002. *Address:* St Petersburg Conservatoire of Music, Teatralnaya ploshchad, St Petersburg (office); Canal Griboedova 9-97, 191186 St Petersburg, Russia (home). *Telephone:* (812) 571-85-85 (home). *Fax:* (812) 571-58-11 (office). *E-mail:* sloh@rambler.ru (home).

**SLORACH, Marie;** Singer (Soprano); b. 8 May 1951, Glasgow, Scotland. *Education:* Royal Scottish Academy of Music and Drama. *Career:* Member of the Scottish Opera, 1974–81 with roles including Marzelline in Fidelio, Marenka in The Bartered Bride, Zerlina in Don Giovanni, Eva in Die Meistersinger, Tatiana in Eugene Onegin, Fiordiligi in Così fan tutte and Jenifer in The Midsummer Marriage; Sang at Wexford Festival in Wolf-Ferrari's I Gioelli della Madonna and Smetana's The Kiss; Sang with English National Opera as Lisa in The Queen of Spades and Donna Elvira in Don Giovanni, Glyndebourne Touring Opera as Mozart's Donna Anna and Electra and Amelia in Simon Boccanegra; Opera North in Carmen, Die Meistersinger, Katya Kabanova and Così fan tutte, Dorset Opera as Gabriella di Vergy and Giovanna d'Arco and Australian Opera in Sydney as Amelia; Sang Ellen Orford in a new production of Peter Grimes for Opera North in 1989; Concert engagements with the Hallé, Liverpool Philharmonic and Scottish National Orchestras, London Mozart Players and London Sinfonietta. *Address:* c/o Music International, 13 Ardilaun Road, Highbury, London, N5 2QR, England.

**SLOVAK, Ladislav;** Conductor; b. 10 Sept. 1919, Bratislava, Czecholsovakia. *Education:* Studied at the Bratislava Conservatory, then the Academy of Music with Vaclav Talich, 1949–53, and Leningrad with Yevgeni Mravinsky, 1954–55. *Career:* Music Producer of the Czech Broadcasting Company at Bratislava, 1946–61; Conducted the Symphony Orchestra of Radio Bratislava, 1955–61 and Slovak Philharmonic Orchestra, 1961–81; Tours of Germany, the United Kingdom and France; Tours with the Czech Philharmonic Orchestra to China, India, Japan, New Zealand and Russia in 1959 and the USA in 1967; Chief Conductor of the Prague Symphony Orchestra, 1972–75 and of the South Australia Symphony Orchestra at Adelaide in 1966 and 1972–73; Conducted the premieres of works by Alexander Moyzes, Eugen Suchon, Dezider Kardos and other Slovak composers; Conductor and Professor of the Academy of Music Bratislava. *Recordings include:* Tchaikovsky Symphonies with the Czech and Slovak Philharmonics; Shostakovich Symphonies Nos 2 and 9; Bartók Music for Strings, Percussion and Celesta; Prokofiev 5th Symphony; Music by Kubik, Ryba, Suchon, Cikker and Kardos; Shostakovich Complete Symphonies with the Symphony Orchestra of Radio Bratislava. *Address:* Banicka 3, 81104 Bratislava, Slovakia.

**SLUYS, Jozef;** Belgian organist; *organist, Cathedral of SS Michael and Gudule, Brussels;* b. 22 Oct. 1936, Gaasbeek; two s. one d. *Education:* Lemmens Inst., Malines, Royal Conservatoire of Music, Brussels. *Career:* Prof. of Organ, Lemmens Inst., Louvain –1987; Dir Acad. of Music, Schaerbeek, Brussels 1968–95; organist, Cathedral of SS Michael and Gudule, Brussels 1971–; Artistic Dir Cathedral Concert series and Brussels Int. Organ Week; Founder-Dir Historical Concerts, Church of Our Blessed Lady, Lombeek; recitalist; performed on radio and television, Belgium and abroad; appearances in many European countries; toured fmr Soviet Union 1987, USA, Zaïre, NZ, S Africa; represented Belgium at first World Organ Festival, Cambridge, UK; Cultural Amb. of Flanders 1996–97. *Recordings:* On the Walcker organ in Riga, works of F. Mendelssohn 1987; Organ works of Belgian composers A. De Boeck, E. Tinel, J. N. Lemmens, J. Jongen, Flor Peeters; Chamber music of Marcel Dupré; J. S. Bach works on organs of Gottfried Silbermann; Romantic Music of Belgian Composers, works for organ (Van Bever, Brussels) viola, violin, piano and cello 1999. *Honours:* Commdr, Ordre des Arts et Lettres 1990; Fuga Trophy 2000. *Address:* Domstraat 8, 1602 Vlezenbeek, Belgium (home). *Telephone:* (2) 219-26-61 (office); (2) 532-50-80 (home). *Fax:* (2) 219-26-61 (office); (2) 532-50-80 (home). *E-mail:* semorgweek@yucom.be (office); jozef@sluys.org (home). *Website:* www.jozef.sluys.org (home).

**SMALLEY, Denis Arthur,** BMus, DipMus, DPhil; New Zealand composer; *Professor of Music, City University, London;* b. 16 May 1946, Nelson. *Education:* Univ. of Canterbury, Victoria Univ. of Wellington, Diplôme de Musique Electro-Acoustique et de Recherche Musicale, Paris Conservatoire, Univ. of York, England. *Career:* Head of Music, Wellington Coll. 1969–71; Northern Music Critic, The Guardian 1972–75; Composition Fellow 1975–76, Sr Lecturer in Music, Univ. of East Anglia, Norwich 1976–94; Prof. of Music, City Univ., London 1994–. *Compositions:* Gradual 1974, Pentes 1974, Ouroboros 1975, Pneuma 1976, Darkness After Time's Colours 1976, Chanson de Geste 1978, The Pulses of Time 1979, Word Within 1981, Vortex 1982, Tides 1984, Clarinet Threads 1985, O Vos Omnes 1986, Wind Chimes 1987, Piano Nets 1990, Valley Flow 1992, Névé 1994, Empty Vessels 1997, Base Metals 2000, Ringing Down the Sun 2002, Resounding 2004. *Recordings:* Gradual, Pentes, Chanson de Geste, The Pulses of Time, Pneuma, Vortex, Tides, Clarinet Threads, Wind Chimes, Piano Nets, Valley Flow, Névé, Base Metals, Empty Vessels, Tides, Pentes. *Publications:* Spectro-Morphology and Structuring Processes, The Language of Electro-Acoustic Music 1986, The Listening Imagination: Listening in the Electro-acoustic Era 1992; contrib. Does Acousmatic Music Exist?, in Musiques et Recherches 1991, Spatial Experience in Electro-acoustic Music, in Musiques et Recherches 1991, Defining Transformations, in Interface 1993, Defining Timbre, Refining Timbre, in Contemporary Music Review 1994, Spectromorphology: Explaining sound shapes, in Organised Sound 1997, Établissement de cadres relationels pour l'analyse de la musique postschafférienne in Ouïr, Écouter, Comprendre Après Schaeffer 1999. *Honours:* Fylkingen Prize 1975, 1st Prize, Bourges Electro-acoustic Awards 1983, Special Prize, International Confederation of Electro-acoustic Music 1983, Prix Ars Electronica 1988. *Address:* Music Department, City University, Northampton Square, London, EC1V 0HB, England (office). *Telephone:* (20) 7040-8270 (office). *Website:* www.city.ac.uk/music (office).

**SMALLEY, Roger;** Composer and Pianist; b. 26 July 1943, Swinton, Manchester, England. *Education:* Studied at the Royal College of Music with Fricker and White; Later study with Walter Goehr at Morley College and with Stockhausen in Cologne. *Career:* Composer-in-Residence at King's College Cambridge, 1967; Co-founded and directed a four-man group, Intermodulation, 1970, disbanded in 1976; Has specialised as pianist in the music of Stockhausen; Appointed to University of Western Australia in 1976 as teacher, composer and performer. *Compositions include:* Piano Pieces I–V, 1962–65; Septet for tenor, soprano and ensemble, 1963; Variations for strings, 1964; Gloria Tibi Trinitas l for orchestras, 1965; Missa Brevis, 1967; Missa Paraodia l for piano, 1967; The Song Of The Highest Tower for solo voices, chorus and orchestra, 1968; Transformation l for piano and ring modulator, 1969; Pulses for 5 x 4 players, 1969; Melody Study ll for 4–12 players, 1970; Beat Music for 4 electronic instruments and orchestra; Zeitenbenen for ensemble and four-track tape, 1973; Accord for 2 pianos, 1974–75; 6 Modular

Pieces for 4 flutes, 1977; William Derrincourt, entertainment for baritone, male chorus and ensemble, 1977; String Quartet, 1979; Konzertstuck for violin and orchestra, 1980; Symphony, 1980–81; Movement for flute and piano, 1980; The Narrow Road to the Deep North, music theatre, 1983; Piano Concerto, 1985; Strung Out for 13 solo strings, 1988; Ceremony 1 for percussion quartet, 1987; Piano Trio, 1991; Poles Apart, for ensemble, 1992; The Southland for double chorus and Antipodean ensemble 1986; rev. 1993; Chimera for orchestra, 1994; Figures in a Landscape, for ensemble, 1994; Music for an Imaginary Ballet, for percussion, 1994; Close to the Edge, for orchestra, 1995. *Publications include:* Essays on Stockhausen, Debussy, Messiaen and Peter Maxwell Davies for Musical Times and Tempo. *Address:* c/o Music Department, University of Western Australia, Perth, Western Australia, Australia.

**SMALLWOOD, Robert;** Composer; b. 22 July 1958, Melbourne, Australia. *Education:* BMus, University of Melbourne, 1980; Accademia Chigiana, Siena, 1985; Study with Barry Conyngham and Nigel Butterley. *Career:* Freelance Composer; Musician-in-Residence, Orange City, 1987–90. *Compositions include:* Trio Sonatina for 2 clarinets and piano, 1976; Discovery for orchestra, 1979; Sunshine Disaster for choir and band, 1981; Reminiscences for clarinet and percussion 1982; Kyrie, 1984; Elements for speaker, children's chorus and band, 1985; Wake up my Soul for children's and adult choirs, and orchestra, 1987; Living Land, for chorus, children's choir and ensemble, 1988; Three Little Poems for speaker, for flute, clarinet and cello, 1980; Psalm 150 for soprano, chorus, strings, piano and organ, 1991; Three Greek Dances, for flute/piccolo, clarinet and string quartet, 1993. *Honours:* Twin Cities Church Musicians Competition, 1992. *Address:* c/o APRA, 1A Eden Street, Crows Nest, NSW 2065, Australia.

**SMEDING, Marten;** Singer (Tenor); b. 1960, Netherlands. *Career:* Appearances at Théâtre de la Monnaie, Brussels, in Salome, Khovanshchina, Parsifal and Otello, season 1999–2000; Holland Festival, 1996, in Enescu's Oedipe; Netherlands Opera from 1992, in Samson et Dalila, Parsifal and The Carmelites; Strauss's Bacchus at Frankfurt and Gounod's Faust in Romania; Concerts include Evangelist in the Bach Passions, Lieder by Schubert and Schumann, and Janáček's Diary of One who Disappeared; Pompeo in Benvenuto Cellini with the Rotterdam Philharmonic Orchestra at the Festival Hall, London, 1999. *Honours:* Semi-finalist at 's-Hertogenbosch Singers' Competition, Netherlands.

**SMEETS, Roger;** Singer (Baritone); b. 1959, Maastricht, Netherlands. *Education:* Studied at the Maastricht Conservatory. *Career:* Has sung with Netherlands Opera from 1984, including the 1985 premiere of Wintercruise by Henkemans; Komische Oper Berlin as Don Giovanni, Eugene Onegin and Wagner's Dutchman; Opera Zuid in Kerkrade, Netherlands, from 1990, notably as Mozart's Figaro; Major roles in recent years with Netherlands Opera; Steuermann in Tristan at Amsterdam, 2001. *Address:* Netherlands Opera, Waterloodein 22, 1011 PG Amsterdam, Netherlands.

**SMELLIE, Michael;** Australian music company executive; *Chief Operating Officer, Sony BMG Music Entertainment. Education:* Sydney Univ. of Technology. *Career:* fmr Finance Dir, Man. Dir PolyGram Australia 1981–93; Man. Dir BMG Australia 1993; Sr Vice-Pres. BMG Entertainment Asia-Pacific 1994–2001; COO BMG Entertainment 2001–04; COO Sony BMG Music Entertainment 2004–. *Address:* Sony BMG Music Entertainment, 550 Madison Avenue, New York, NY 10036, USA (office). *Website:* www.sonybmg.com (office).

**SMETANIN, Michael;** Australian composer; *Chair of Composition, Sydney Conservatorium, University of Sydney;* b. 1 Oct. 1958, Sydney. *Education:* BM, Composition, New South Wales State Conservatorium of Music, 1981; Australian Broadcasting Corporation's orchestral summer schools, 1981 and 1982; Composition study with Louis Andriessen at Royal Conservatorium, The Hague. *Career:* Composer in Residence, Musica Viva, 1988; jury mem. Int. Gaudeamus Music Week 1999; Chair of Composition Sydney Conservatorium Univ. of Sydney 2002–. *Compositions:* Ensemble: Per Canonem, 1982, revised 1984, Lichtpunt, 1983, The Speed Of Sound, 1983, Ladder Of Escape, 1984, Track, 1985, Vault, 1986, Bellvue ll, 1987, Fylgir, 1989, Spray, 1990, Strange Attractions, 1991; Orchestral: After The First Circle, 1982, Black Snow, 1987, Zyerkala, Blitz, 1989, Women and Birds in Front of the Moon, 1991; Vocal: 3 Songs, 1981, The Skinless Kiss Of Angels, for mezzo, baritone and ensemble, 1992; Tube-makers, 1995; Adjacent Rooms, 1992; Children's music: Music for Children and Dancers, 1988; Instrumental and keyboard: Afstand, 1983, Sting, 1987, Stroke, 1988. *Recordings:* Works on CD; Ladder Of Escape; Spray; Sting, Skinless Kiss of Angels. *Honours:* Paul Lowin Orchestral Award 1999. *Address:* c/o Australian Music Centre, PO Box N690, Grosvenor Street, Sydney 2000, Australia. *Telephone:* (2) 9634-1612 (home). *E-mail:* msmetanin@conmusic.usyd.edu.au (office).

**SMIETANA, Krzysztof,** FGSM; Musician and Violinist; b. 11 Oct. 1956, Kraków, Poland. *Education:* Secondary High School of Music; Kraków Acad. of Music; ASS postgraduate course, Guildhall School of Music and Drama, London. *Career:* debut, 1974; appearances with major orchestras such as London Symphony Orchestra, Philharmonia, BBC Symphony Orchestra; performed at 1997 Proms Festival; numerous broadcasts for BBC Radio 3 and Polish National Radio; very active in chamber music; leader with orchestras such as Chamber Orchestra of Europe, London Symphonietta and London Symphony Orchestra; violinist in London Mozart Trio; Prof. of Violin at Guildhall School of Music and Drama. *Recordings:* Brahms – Sonatas for

Violin and Piano, with Caroline Palmer; Panufnik – Violin Concerto, with London Musici; Fauré Violin Sonatas, with John Blakely, piano; Stravinsky – Violin Concerto, with Philharmonia, conducted by Robert Craft. *Honours:* Prizes at competitions: Thibaud, Paris; Kreisler, Vienna; Flesch, London; Brahms, Hamburg; Lipizer, Gorizia.

**SMIRNOV, Dmitri Nikolayevich;** Russian composer; b. 2 Nov. 1948, Minsk; m. Elena Firsova 1972; two c. *Education:* studied with Nikolai Sidelnikov, Edison Denisov, Yuri Kholopov at Moscow Conservatoire, 1967–72; studied with Philip Herschkowitz (privately). *Career:* Ed., Sovetsky Kompozitor publishing house, 1973–80; freelance composer, 1980–; operas Tiriel and The Lamentations of Thel (after William Blake)(chamber) performed in Freiburg and Almeida Theatre, London; Symphony No. 1 The Seasons in Tanglewood, 1989; oratorio A Song of Liberty premiered in Leeds, 1993; Prof., Composer-in-Residence, Keele Univ., 1993–98; Oratorio Song of Songs premiered in Geneva, 1998; Visiting Fellow at Goldsmiths College of Music, London, 2002–. *Compositions include:* Five piano sonatas, 1967, 1980, 1992, 2000, 2001; three violin sonatas, 1969, 1979, 1997; two piano concerti, 1971, 1978; six string quartets, 1973, 1985, 1993 (two), 1994, 1998; two piano trio, 1977, 1992; three symphonies, 1980, 1982, 1995; three violin concerti, 1990, 1995, 1996; two cello concerti, 1992, 2001; Songs of Destiny, voice, organ, 1980; Six Poems by William Blake, voice, Organ; Dirge Canons, ensemble; Serenade, ensemble, 1981; Farewll Song, viola, harp; Fantasia, saxophone quartet; The Night Rhymes, voice, orchestra, 1982; Two Ricercares for strings, 1993; Tiriel, 1985; Partita, solo violin, 1985; Thel, 1986; Mozart Variations, orchestra; The Visions of Coleridge, voice, ensemble, 1987; The Songs of Love and Madness, voice, ensemble, 1988–92; Angels of William Blake, piano, 1988; Blake's Pictures, visionary ballet, ensemble, 1988–92; From Evening to Morning, mixed chorus, 1990; Trinity Music, clarinet, violin, piano, 1990; A Song of Liberty, 1991; Three Blake's Songs, voice, ensemble, 1991; Job's Studies, solo clarinet, 1991; Wonderful Stories, voice, ensemble, 1991; The Angels of Albion, piano, 1991; Diptich, organ, 1992; Orcades, solo flute, 1992; Piano Quintet, 1992; Ariel's Songs, voice, ensemble; Magic Lamb, voice, ensemble; The Bride in Her Grave, an opera, 1995; Between Scylla and Charybdis, for strings; Song of Songs for soprano, tenor, chorus and orchestra, 1997; MMass; Opus 111 for clarinet, cello and piano; Twilight for voice and ensemble, 1998; Three Quarks for Muster Msrk, percussion; Portrait for wind ensemble; Shadows in Light for viola and harp, 1999; Well Tempered Piano, 2000 (completed); Saga fopr solo cello; Innocence of Experience for tape, 2001; Metaplasms I and II for Piano; The Stony Path for voice, cello and piano, 2002; Triple Concerto No.2 fopr violin, harp and double-bass with orchestra; Dream Journey for voice, flute and piano, 2003. *Articles:* On Webern, Boulez, Ligeti, Ferneyhow, Birtwhistle, Shostakovich, Denisov, Schnittke, Gubaidulina etc. *Publications:* The Book on Philip Herschkowitz: A Geometer of Sound Crystals (in English), Verlag Ernst Kuhn, Berlin, 2003. *Honours:* First Prize for Solo for Harp, Maastricht 1976. *Current Management:* Boosey & Hawkes, 1st Floor, Aldwych House, 71–91 Aldwych, London, WC2B 4HN, England. *Website:* www.boosey.com/smirnov. *E-mail:* dmitrismirnov@ntlworld.com (home).

**SMIRNOV, Oleg;** Cellist; b. 1950, Moscow, Russia. *Education:* Studied at the Moscow Conservatoire with Professor Kosolapova. *Career:* Co-founder, Amisted Quartet, 1973 (now Tchaikovsky Quartet); Many concerts in Russia with a repertoire including works by: Haydn, Mozart, Beethoven, Schubert, Brahms, Tchaikovsky, Borodin, Prokofiev, Shostakovich, Bartók, Barber, Bucchi, Golovin, Tikhomirov; Recent concert tours to: Mexico, Italy and Germany. *Recordings include:* Recitals for the US Russian Company Arts and Electronics. *Honours:* Prizewinner at the Béla Bart ók Festival and the Bucchi Competition. *Address:* c/o Sonata (Tchaikovsky Quartet), 11 Northpark Street, Glasgow G20 7AA, Scotland.

**SMIT, Henk;** Singer (Bass-baritone); b. 1937, Netherlands. *Education:* Toronto and Amsterdam Conservatories. *Career:* Sang at Netherlands Opera from 1963 as Puccini's Lescaut, Pistol in Falstaff, Rossini's Bartolo and Don Magnifico, Verdi's Ramphis, Zaccaria and Simon Boccanegra; Pizarro, the Dutchman, Speaker in Die Zauberflöte and the Man in Schoenberg's Die glückliche Hand; Premiere of Otto Ketting's Ithaka, 1986; Tel-Aviv, 1984, as Tiresias in Oedipus Rex, Paris Opéra, 1985, as Varlaam in Boris Godunov, Amsterdam, 1986, in Zemlinsky's Der Kreidekreis; Sang Falstaff at Enschede, 1990, and Wagner's Klingsor at Montpellier, 1995; Concerts throughout Europe and the USA; Season 1998 as Dikoy in Katya Kabanova at Salzburg and Alberich in Siegfried and Götterdämmerung at Amsterdam. *Address:* c/o Netherlands Opera, Waterlooplein 22, 1011 Amsterdam, Netherlands.

**SMITH, Carol;** Singer (Soprano); b. 1960, Huddersfield, England. *Education:* Guildhall School and National Opera Studio. *Career:* Appearances at Glyndebourne in Albert Herring and L'Enfant et les Sortilèges; Melissa in Handel's Amadigi for Dublin Opera Theatre at Prague, Paris and Warsaw; Handel's Solomon at the Prague Spring Festival and Tamerlano at Melbourne and Lisbon; Recitals include Carnegie Hall and the Aldeburgh Festival; Concerts with the Philharmonia, London Mozart Players, Hallé Orchestra and Berlin Symphony Orchestra; Mozart's C minor Mass at Tenerife and Henze's Der Prinz von Homburg (as Natalie) for the BBC; Season 1999 with Haydn's Seasons for City of London Sinfonia and Beethoven's 9th for Northern Sinfonia. *Recordings include:* Rossini's Ricciardo e Zoraide. *Honours:* Concert Artists Guild Award, New York.

**SMITH, Catriona;** Singer (Soprano); b. 1963, Scotland. *Education:* Studied at the Royal Scottish Academy and the University of Toronto, Opera Division. *Career:* Sang Britten's Lucretia and Miss Wordsworth at the Banff Summer Arts Festival in 1988, Cathleen in Riders to the Sea by Vaughan Williams at Toronto and Pamina for British Youth Opera; Wigmore Hall recital debut in 1988; Sang at Kent Opera as Juno in The Return of Ulysses; Festival engagements include Aldeburgh in Goehr's Triptych and English Bach Festival in Idomeneo; Sang Clorinda in La Cenerentola at Covent Garden in 1991 and engaged at the Stuttgart Staatsoper, 1991–95; Other roles include Mozart's Countess, Rossini's Berta, Dido, Frasquita, Susanna and Barbarina in Le nozze di Figaro; Roles in Stuttgart include Pamina, Gilda, Nayad, Sophie in Der Rosenkavalier, Erénoira (world premiere) and Zerlina; Madeline in Debussy's Fall of the House of Usher, 1996; Morgana in Alcina at Stuttgart, 1998; Season 2000–01 as Offenbach's Olympia, at Stuttgart, and Norina in Donizett's I Pazzi per progetto. *Honours:* Winner, Maggie Teyte Competition, 1987. *Address:* c/o Stuttgart Staatsoper, Oberer Schlossgarten 6, 7000 Stuttgart, Germany.

**SMITH, Craig;** Singer (Baritone); b. 1960, England. *Education:* Studied at the Royal Northern College of Music, with Nicholas Powell. *Career:* Roles at the RNCM included Sharpless, Pandolfe in Cendrillon, Zurga in Les Pêcheurs de Perles and Lionel in The Maid of Orleans by Tchaikovsky; Cecil in Jonathan Miller's production of Maria Stuarda at Buxton and Smirnov in Walton's The Bear, at Los Angeles; Zürich Opera from 1995, as Morales in Carmen, Paris in Roméo et Juliette and the Wig Maker in Ariadne auf Naxos; Other roles include Nabucco (Bad Hersfeld, 1996) and Sharpless, with the Royal Liverpool Philharmonic; Concert repertory includes CPE Bach's Magnificat, Rossini's Petite Messe Solennelle at Winchester Cathedral, L'Enfance du Christ at the Queen Elizabeth Hall, London, Carmina Burana at the Royal Concert Hall, Glasgow, and in Terra Pax by Frank Martin, at Schaffhausen and Ravensburg. *Honours:* Peter Moores Foundation and Robert Stanley Ford Scholarships. *Address:* Portland Wallis Artists' Management, 50 Great Portland Street, London W1N 5AH, England.

**SMITH, Daniel W.,** BM, MA; bassoon player; b. 11 Sept. 1939, New York, NY, USA; m. Judith Smith 1961; one s. one d. *Education:* Manhattan School of Music, Columbia University, Mannes College of Music. *Career:* debut at Carnegie Recital Hall, New York; European debut, Wigmore Hall, London; Soloist on recordings and in concert with English Chamber Orchestra, I Solisti di Zagreb, Royal Philharmonic Orchestra, Orchestra da Camera di Santa Cecilia, New York Virtuosi Chamber Symphony, Santa Cruz Symphony, Rome Festival Orchestra, Florida Chamber Symphony, New York String Ensemble, AIH Roma Orchestra; Recitals: BBC Concert Hall, London; Carnegie Recital Hall, New York; Wigmore Hall, London; Merkin Concert Hall, New York; Bruno Walter Auditorium, New York; Diligentia Hall, The Hague; Atelier, Belgium; Distinguished Artists Series, Long Island, New York; B'nai Brith Festival, Purcell Room, London; Premiered Contrabassoon Concerto of Gunther Schuller with Santa Cruz Symphony. *Recordings:* Vols 1–6 (37 concerti), Antonio Vivaldi with English Chamber Orchestra and I Solisti di Zagreb; 3 Bassoon Concertos with English Chamber Orchestra; Bassoon Bon-Bons with Royal Philharmonic Orchestra; English Music for Bassoon and Piano with pianist Roger Vignoles; Vols 1 and 2, 18th Century Bassoon concerti with Ravina Chamber Ensemble; Vivaldi Concerti with Ravina Chamber Ensemble; Music for Bassoon and String Quartet with Coull String Quartet; 5 Bassoon Concertos with English Chamber Orchestra.

**SMITH, Hale,** BM, MM; American composer and pianist; b. 29 June 1925, Cleveland, OH. *Education:* Central High School, Cleveland Inst. of Music. *Career:* began composing aged eight 1933; began playing in night clubs 1939; pianist in jazz ensemble conducted by Ernie Freeman and horn in ensemble led by Evelyn Freeman 1939–42; served in US Army and played piano and string bass in bands 1943–45; conductor and composer, Karamu House, Cleveland 1949–55; principal arranger for Forestorn 'Chico' Hamilton 1958–62; composed for film, TV and radio; worked as arranger and collaborator with Eric Dolphy, Dizzy Gillespie, Ahmad Jamal, Melba Liston, Oliver Nelson, Randy Weston and others from 1958; music consultant, C. F. Peters Corpn 1961–; Music Ed., Edward B. Marks Music Corpn 1961–63; Ed. and Gen. Music Adviser, Frank Music Corpn 1963–64; consultant on copyright infringement 1963–; composer-in-residence Symphony of the New World 1966–67; Ed., Sam Fox Music Publishers 1968–70; teacher at C. W. Post Coll., Long Island Univ., Brookville, NY 1968–69; teacher, Univ. of Conn., Storrs 1970–84; retired to give full attention to composing and arranging 1984–; first Pres. and Chair. of Bd, Arts Council of Freeport, NY from 1965; mem. Nat. Advisory Bd, Center for Black Music Research, Chicago 1983–; mem., New York State Council for the Arts 1993–97. *Compositions include:* Four Mosaics for piano 1948, Three Songs 1949, Two Kids 1950, Beyond the Rim of Day 1950, Yerma (incidental music) 1951, The Valley Wind 1951–55, Lysistrata (incidental music) 1952, Orchestral Set 1952, Blood Wedding (incidental music) 1953, Duo for violin and piano 1953, In Memoriam: Beryl Rubinstein 1953, Sonata for cello and piano 1955, Five Songs for soprano and violin 1956, Epicedial Variations for violin 1956, Two Love Songs of John Donne 1958, Three Brevities for solo flute 1961, Contours for Orchestra 1961, By Yearning and By Beautiful 1964, Somersault: A Twelve Tone Adventure for band 1964, Take A Chance: An Aleatoric Episode for band 1964, Trinal Dance 1965, Faces of Jazz for piano 1965, Bold New Approach (incidental music) 1966, Evocation for piano 1966, Music for harp and orchestra 1967, Expansions 1967, Nuances of Hale Smith (incidental music) 1968, Exchanges

1970, Anticipations, Introspections and Reflections for piano 1971, Comes Tomorrow: Jazz Cantata 1972, Concert Music for piano and orchestra 1972, Come Back, My Youth 1972, Introduction, Cadenzas, and Interludes for eight players 1974, I'm Coming Home 1974, Ritual and Incantations 1974, Variations for six players 1975, For One Called Billy for piano 1975, Toussaint L'Ouverte: 1803 1976, Innerflexions 1977, Solemn Music 1979, Symphonic Spirituals 1980, Meditations in Passage 1980–81, Joplin's Dirty Rags (for musical theatre) 1983, Variation a Due 1984, Three Patterson Lyrics 1985, March and Fanfare for an Elegant Lady 1986, Mirrors: Rondo-Variations for Two Pianos 1988, Dialogues and Commentaries for seven players 1991, I'm Going To Sing 1991, Tra La La Lamia 1991, Variations on a Quasi Classical Tune for string orchestra of young players 1992, Riverain 1993, Ask Your Mama for jazz ensemble 1994, Recitative and Aria for English horn solo 1995, A Ternion of Seasons 1996, Breaking Bread with Egbert for piano 1997, Music for Martyrs 1997. *Publications:* contrib. to numerous journals. *Honours:* BMI Student Composer's Award 1952, Black Music Caucus of the Music Educators Nat. Conf. Outstanding Achievement Award 1982, 1989, American Acad. and Inst. of Arts and Letters Composers' Award 1988, Keys to the City of New Orleans 1991. *Address:* 225 Pine Street, Freeport, NY 11520, USA.

**SMITH, Jennifer;** singer (soprano) and academic; *Professor of French Mélodie, Royal College of Music, London;* b. 13 July 1945, Lisbon, Portugal; one s. one d. *Education:* Lisbon Conservatory and French Lycé, Lisbon, studied with Winifred Radford in London, Pierre Bernac in London and Paris, Hans Keller in London. *Career:* debut, sang Jeptha, Carissimi, Lisbon 1966; sang in Europe before moving to England 1971; operatic roles have included Countess Almaviva for WNO, Scottish and Kent Operas; Gluck's Orfeo at the Wexford Festival; Rameau's Les Boréades and Hippolyte et Aricie at Aix-en-Provence; L'Incoronazione di Poppea conducted by Leonhardt; Aminta in Il Re Pastore, Lisbon; Cybelle in Lully's Atys at the Opéra-Comique Paris and in New York; Electra in Mozart's Idomeneo, Lisbon 1995; Praskovia Ossipovna in Shostakovich's The Nose, Lausanne; Foresta's Wife and Screech Owl in Janáček's The Cunning Little Vixan, ROH debut 2002; concert repertoire includes works by Bach, Handel, Poulenc, Purcell, Britten and Berlioz (Les Nuits d'Eté); appearances with the English Chamber Orchestra, London Bach Orchestra, the English Concert, Steinitz Bach Players and the Orchestra of the Age of Enlightenment; conductors include Rattle, Willcocks, Leppard, Pinnock, Gardiner, Boulez, Mackerras and Kempe; tour of Europe with the B Minor Mass, conducted by Frans Brueggen; song recitals in Portugal, France, Germany, Switzerland, Belgium and England; television appearances include Scarlatti's Salve Regina with George Malcolm, Handel's Judas Maccabaeus conducted by Norrington and Purcell's Come, Ye Sons of Art Away and Tony Palmer's film of Purcell; sang the Queen of Night (Mozart Experience, London) conducted by Norrington, QEH 1989; Rameau at Versailles (Flore and Nais) with the English Bach Festival 1989; season 1992 as Music in Monteverdi's Orfeo at ENO, Iphigénie en Tauride with the English Bach Festival at Covent Garden and in Conti's Don Chisciotte at Innsbruck; sang the Queen of Night with Hamilton Opera 1996; title role in the first performance since 1744 of Artaserse by Terradellas, Barcelona 1998; sang The Cunning Little Vixen, Covent Garden 2002, La Nozze di Figaro, Aix-en-Provence, France, also in Japan and in Baden-Baden, Germany 2002, Shostakovitch's Le Nez, Lausanne, Switzerland 2002, Nantes and Augers, France 2002; Prof. of French Mélodie, Royal Coll. of Music, London 1998–. *Recordings:* Bach Mass in B Minor, Magnificat/Corboz, Cantata 208; Carissimi Jephté; Falla Retablo de Maese Pedro and Psyche/Rattle; Gabrieli Sacrae Symphoniae; Handel Hercules and L'Allegro/Gardiner, Il Trionfo del Tempo, Silete Venti/Pinnock; Messiah, Amadigi; Haydn Mariazeller Mass and Little Organ Mass/Guest; Lully Dies Irae, Miserere and Te Deum/Paillard; Rameau's Nais/McGegan, Castor et Pollux/Farncombe and Les Boréades/Gardiner; Purcell King Arthur, Indian Queen and Fairy Queen/Gardiner, Come Ye Sons of Art/Pinnock; Vivaldi Gloria and Kyrie/Corboz, Beatus Vir and Dixit Dominus/Cleobury; Schubert Lieder; Platée (Rameau), Titon et l'Aurore (Mondonville) Alycone (Marais) Il Trionfo del Tempo (Handel), La Resurrezione (Handel), all with Marc Minkowski; Xerxes (Handel) with McGegan; Orphée aux enfers (Offenbach), with Minkowski; French Cantatas; Saudade, amor e morte, with Manuel Morais; Ottone (Handel) with Robert King; King Alfred (Arne); Chants de L'âme (Greif) with the composer at the piano; Le Nez (Shostakovitch) 2004, Fauré Complete Mélodies 2004–05. *E-mail:* je.ma.smith@ care4free.net (home).

**SMITH, Lawrence (Leighton);** Conductor and Pianist; b. 8 April 1936, Portland, Oregon, USA; m. (1) 2 s., (2) Kathleen Dale, 4 June 1976, 1 d., 1 step-s., 1 step-d. *Education:* BM, Music, Mannes College of Music, New York, 1959; Studied piano with Ariel Rubstein, Portland and Leonard Shure, New York. *Career:* Teacher at Mannes College of Music, 1959–62, University of Texas, 1962–63, Boston University, 1963–64, Curtis Institute of Music, 1968–69 and California Institute of The Arts, 1970–72; Professional debut as pianist in 1962; Assistant to Erich Leinsdorf, Berkshire Music Center, Tanglewood, Massachusetts, 1962–64; Assistant Conductor with Metropolitan Opera, New York, 1964–67; Music Director with Westchester Symphony Orchestra, New York, 1967–69; Principal Guest Conductor with Phoenix Symphony Orchestra, Arizona, 1971–73; Music Director with Austin Symphony Orchestra, Texas, 1972–73 and Oregon Symphony Orchestra, Portland, 1973–80; Artistic Adviser, Principal Guest Conductor, North Carolina Symphony Orchestra, Raleigh, 1980–81; Music Director, San Antonio Symphony Orchestra, 1980–85 and Louisville Orchestra, 1983–, and at Music Academy of the West, Santa Barbara, California, 1985–; Guest Conductor with various orchestras in the USA and abroad; mem, American Federation of Musicians. *Recordings:* Various. *Honours:* 1st Prize, Dimitri Mitropoulos International Conducting Competition, New York, 1964. *Address:* c/o Louisville Orchestra, 609 West Main Street, Louisville, KY 40202, USA.

**SMITH, Malcolm;** Singer (Bass); b. 22 June 1933, Rockville Center, New York; M. Margaret Younger. *Education:* Oberlin Conservatory and Indiana University, Bloomington. *Career:* Debut: Inquisitor in Prokofiev's The Fiery Angel, New York City Opera, 1965; Sang at the City Opera until 1970, New York Metropolitan from 1975; Guest appearances at Chicago, Seattle, Houston, Miami and San Francisco; Deutsche Oper am Rhein, Dusseldorf, from 1972, with further engagements in Milan, Vienna and throughout Germany; Season 1985-86 as Ramphis in Aida at Cincinnati and Fafner in Das Rheingold at Turin; Paris Théâtre du Châtelet, as Mephisto in Schumann's Faust and Salzburg Festival 1986 in the premiere of Die schwarze Maske by Penderecki; Dusseldorf 1991, as Drago in Schumann's Genoveva; Season 2000-2001 as Debussy's Arkel at Cincinnati, the Grand Inquisitor (Don Carlos) and Mussorgsky's Pimen at Dusseldorf; Further roles in operas by Beethoven, Rossini, Mussorgsky and Wagner (King Marke at Trieste, 1969). *Recordings include:* Tristan und Isolde, Das Rheingold, War and Peace, Oedipus Rex, Mahler's 8th Symphony. *Address:* c/o Deutsche Oper am Rhein, Heinrich Heine Allee 16a, D-40213 Dusseldorf, Germany.

**SMITH, Maureen (Felicity);** British violinist; b. Leeds, Yorks.; m. Geoffrey Rivlin 27 Aug. 1974; two d. *Education:* Royal Manchester College of Music; Indiana University, USA. *Career:* Debut: Royal Festival Hall in 1961; Soloist with most leading British orchestras; Debut at London Promenade Concerts in 1965; Regular broadcasts for BBC Radio 3 and numerous television appearances; Appearances at major festivals including Aldeburgh and Leeds, Brighton, Cheltenham, English Bach and Three Choirs; Professor of Violin, Royal College of Music, 1997, appointed Deputy Head of Strings, 2002; mem, European String Teachers Association. *Recordings:* Mendelssohn Violin Concerto; Milhaud Duos; Brahms and Mahler Piano Quartets; Mozart and Haydn violin and viola duos. *Honours:* Hon. ARAM 1996; BBC Violin Competition 1965, Gulbenkian Foundation Fellowship 1966, Leverhulme Fellowship 1966. *Address:* Royal College of Music, Prince Consort Road, London, SW7 2BS (office); 8 Heath Close, London, NW11 7DX, England (home). *Telephone:* (20) 7591-4863 (office); (20) 8458-4827 (home). *E-mail:* mfsmith@rcm.ac.uk (office); maureensmithriv@btinternet.com (home).

**SMITH, Philip;** American trumpeter; b. Long Island, NY; m.; two c. *Education:* Juilliard School. *Career:* mem., Chicago Symphony 1975; co-prin. trumpet, New York Philharmonic 1978, prin. trumpet 1988–; worked with conductors, including Zubin Mehta, Kurt Masur, Erich Leinsdorf, Leonard Bernstein, Neeme Järvi, Bramwell Tovey; notable performances with New York Philharmonic include world premieres of Joseph Turrin's Trumpet Concerto, Lowell Liebermann's Concerto, Siegfried Matthus's Double Concerto for Trumpet, Trombone, and Orchestra, and the US premiere of Jacques Hetu's Trumpet Concerto; performed Turrin's Chronicles (world premiere) with Univ. of New Mexico Wind Ensemble; appeared as guest soloist with Edmonton Symphony, Newfoundland Symphony, Columbus Symphony, Pensacola Symphony, Hartford Symphony, and Beaumont Symphony, also with US President's Own Marine Band, La Philharmonie des Vents des Québec, Hanover Wind Symphony, Ridgewood Concert Band, many major univ. wind ensembles, US Army Brass Band, Goteborg Brass (Sweden), Black Dyke Mills and Ridged Containers Bands (UK), Hannaford Street Silver Band and Intrada Brass (Canada), numerous US and Salvation Army brass bands; has contributed to festivals, including Caramoor Int. Music Festival, Grand Teton Music Festival, Swiss Brass Week, Bremen Trumpet Days, Oslo Trumpet Week, Harmony Ridge Festival, Scotia Festival of Music, numerous Int. Trumpet Guild conferences; guest teacher The Juilliard School; mem. Resounding Praise ensemble. *Recordings:* Orchestral Excerpts for Trumpet 1995, Philip Smith 1997, Fandango 2000, My Song of Songs 2002. *Address:* New York Philharmonic, Avery Fisher Hall, 10 Lincoln Center Plaza, New York, NY 10023-6990, USA (office). *Website:* www.newyorkphilharmonic.org (office).

**SMITH, Richard Langham,** BA, FRSA; British musicologist; *Arnold Kettle Distinguished Scholar, Open University*; b. 10 Sept. 1947, London; one d. *Education:* Univ. of York, further study with Edward Lockspeiser and at Amsterdam Conservatory. *Career:* harpsichordist and musicologist, specialising in French music; Lecturer, Univ. of Lancaster –1979, City Univ., London –1995, Univ. of Exeter 1995–2005; Visiting Prof. of Music, Gresham Coll. 2003–04; Arnold Kettle Distinguished Scholar, Open Univ. 2005–; Visiting Lecturer, Univ. of Cambridge 2005–. *Compositions:* reconstruction of Debussy's unpublished opera, Rodrigue et Chimène premiered at Opéra de Lyon 1993. *Publications:* Debussy on Music (trans. and ed.) 1977, Debussy, Pelléas et Mélisande, Cambridge Opera Handbook (with R. Nichols) 1989, Debussy Studies 1997, Debussy: Rodrigue et Chimène, Durand (ed.) 2003; contrib. numerous articles and reviews on Debussy in journals, including Music and Letters, Times Literary Supplement, 19th Century Music, Cahiers Debussy, Musical Times, The Listener, Early Music, The Strad, Frequent Broadcaster, BBC Radio 2, 3 and 4, and France Musique. *Honours:* Chevalier, Ordre des Arts et des Lettres. *Address:* Faculty of Arts, Open University, Milton Keynes MK7 6AA (office); Higher Summerlands, 4 Longlands, Dawlish, Devon EX7 9NE, England (home). *Telephone:* (1908) 653176 (office); (1626) 864105 (home). *E-mail:* r.langhamsmith@open.ac.uk (office).

**SMITH, Robert Dean;** Singer (Tenor); b. 1965, Kansas, USA. *Education:* Pittsburgh State University and Juilliard, New York. *Career:* Lyric-baritone roles in German opera houses early in career; Tenor repertoire has included Wagner's Walther, Parsifal and Lohengrin, Verdi's Don Carlo and Manrico, Enzo in La Gioconda and Beethoven's Florestan; Don José, Pinkerton, Cavaradossi, Des Grieux in Manon Lescaut, Offenbach's Hoffmann and Kardinal Albrecht in Mathis der Maler by Hindemith; Bayreuth Festival 1997–2002, as Walther von Stolzing and Siegmund in Die Walküre; Further engagements in Vienna, Paris, Barcelona, Tokyo and Berlin; Season 2000–01 with Die Meistersinger at the Royal Opera, Beethoven's Missa Solemnis at Carnegie Hall and Walther at San Francisco; Engaged as Siegmund in Tokyo and as Bacchus in Ariadne auf Naxos, 2002; Other concerts include the Verdi Requiem, The Dream of Gerontius and Rossini's Petite Messe. *Address:* c/o Theateragentur Dr G. Hilbert, Maximilianstrasse 22, 80539 Munich, Germany.

**SMITH, Roger;** Cellist; b. 1945, England. *Career:* Principal Cello with the Academy of St Martin in the Fields and member of the Academy of St Martin's Octet; Teacher at the Menuhin School; Co-Founder and Cellist of the re-constituted London String Quartet giving performances throughout the United Kingdom of English works and the recognised repertory. *Address:* c/o Academy of St Martin in the Fields Chamber Ensemble, Station House, Staverton, Totnes, Devon, TQ9 6 AG.

**SMITH, Trefor (Leslie);** Pianist; b. 4 July 1948, Aberdeen, Scotland. *Education:* MA Honours, Music, Aberdeen University, 1970; BMus, Liverpool University, 1971; Associate (Performance), Royal Manchester College of Music, 1973; Concert Examination, State College of Music, Hamburg; Further studies with Wilhelm Kempff, Vlado Perlemuter, Paul Badura-Skoda and Hans Leygraf. *Career:* Numerous appearances in Germany, the United Kingdom, France, Italy, Spain, Norway, Ireland, Austria, USA, India, Turkey, Poland and Russia; Various radio recordings; Staff and Professor of Piano, Musikhochschule, Hamburg. *Recordings:* 2 records of Piano Music by Theodore Kirchner (1823–1903); 2 CDs of Brahms Piano Sonatas and Beethoven Piano Sonatas; Radio recordings for North German Radio, RTE Dublin and NRK Oslo. *Address:* c/o Barbara Dennerlein, Newtone Management & BEBAB Records, Andreas-Wagner-Str. 39 A, 85640 Putzbrunn (Solalinden), Germany.

**SMITH, Wilma;** Violinist; b. 1960, New Zealand. *Education:* Studied at the New England Conservatory. *Career:* Leader of the Boston based Lydia Quartet; Co-founded the New Zealand String Quartet under the auspices of the Music Federation of New Zealand; Debut concert in Wellington in 1988; Concerts at the Tanglewood School in the USA, The Banff International Competition in Canada and performances with the Lindsay Quartet at the 1990 International Festival of The Arts; Soloist with the New Zealand Symphony Orchestra and Artist-in-Residence at Victoria University; Tour to Australia in 1990 for Music Viva Australia; Tours of New Zealand in 1992 and concerts in New York in 1993. *Recordings include:* Various.

**SMITH-LOMBARDINI, Maryelizabeth Anne;** Opera Singer and Artistic Director; b. 1 Sept. 1957, Norfolk, Virginia, USA; m. Danilo Lombardini, 30 Oct 1987. *Education:* BMus, 1979, MMus, 1980, University of Michigan, Ann Arbor; G Verdi Conservatory, Milan, Italy, 1980–83; La Scala Opera Studio, 1982–84, Diploma; Apprentice, Vienna State Opera, Austria, 1984–86. *Career:* Debut: Azio Corghi's Gargantua, Teatro Regio, Turin, 1984; Specialist in 20th century music; Vienna State Opera and Genoa Opera debuts, 1985; La Scala, 1991, in leading role in Henze's Das Verratene Meer, returning 1992 as Andromeda in Sciarrino's Perseo e Andromeda, 1993 for Donatoni's Il Velo Dissolto, 1996 for Berio's Outis; Catania and Venice debuts, 1997; Concert activity includes regular appearances at La Fenice, Venice; Artistic Director, Laboratorio Lirico, Sicilian Chamber Music Society, 1994–96; Professor, A Scontrino State Music Conservatory, Trapani, 1995–96; Artistic Director, Operalaboratorio, City of Palermo Foundation Teatro Massimo-Ars Nova, 1997–; Directo, Palermo-Detroit Cultural Exchange for Opera (Young Artists), 1998–. *Recordings:* La Griselda, Vivaldi; Stabat Mater, Boccherini. *Current Management:* Agentia Lirica Internazionale, Milan. *Address:* Via del Celso 95, 90134 Palermo, Italy.

**SMITH-MAXER, Carolyn;** Singer (Soprano); b. 1945, Oklahoma City, USA. *Education:* Studied in Chicago. *Career:* Debut: Basle Opera 1967, as Gilda in Rigoletto; Sang as Komische Oper Berlin from 1969, notably as Gershwin's Bess; Staatsoper Berlin 1974, in the premiere of Kunad's Sabellicus; Dresden Staatsoper 1976, as Mozart's Constanze; Appeared at the Frankfurt Opera until 1984 and sang at Bremen 1989-90; Frequent opera and concert engagements in Chicago; Repertory has included soubrette and coloratura roles, in addition to Negro spirituals. *Address:* c/o Bremen Theater, pf. 101046, D-2800 Bremen, Germany.

**SMITHERS, Don (Le Roy);** Music Historian; b. 17 Feb. 1933, New York, USA; m. (2) 1 Sept 1967, 1 d.; 1 s. and 1 d. from previous marriage. *Education:* BS, Music, Physics and Philosophy, Hofstra University, 1957; Seminars in Musicology, New York University, 1957–58; Studied Renaissance and Reformation History, Columbia University, New York, 1958; PhD, History of Music, University of Oxford, England. *Career:* Associate Professor, Department of Fine Arts and School of Music, Syracuse University, 1966–75; Lectures and papers on Baroque ornament, Festival Books, the history of music and musical instruments and the history of musical performance for various groups, colleges and universities; Solo concert performances on Baroque trumpet, cornetto, and various Renaissance wind instruments; Co-founder, First Musical Director and sometime conductor of Oxford Pro Musica, Oxford, 1965–. *Recordings:* About 50 solo and ensemble recordings with various European and American groups including New York Pro Musica, The Leonhardt Consort, Concentus Musicus Wien and Early Music Consort of London. *Publications include:* The Music and History of the Baroque Trumpet Before 1721, 1973; A Catalogue of Telemann's Music with Brass, 1995. *Contributions:* Many articles to professional journals and book chapters. *Honours:* Research Fellow and study with Professor Arthur Mendel, Princeton University, 1978; The Japan Foundation Grantee; ASECS/Folger Institute Fellowship, 1984. *Address:* 55 Van Houten Fields, West Nyack, NY 10994, USA.

**SMITKOVA, Jana;** Singer (Soprano); b. 26 Dec. 1942, Prague, Czechoslovakia. *Education:* Studied at the Prague Conservatory and Music Academy. *Career:* Debut: Liberec, 1967, as Nancy in Martha by Flotow; Sang with the Brno Opera, 1968–70, Ceske Budejovice, 1970–73; Member of the Komische Oper Berlin from 1973, debut as Katya Kabanova; Frequent guest appearances in Dresden, notably as Agathe in Der Freischütz at the 1985 reopening of the Semper Opera House; Has also sung at the National Theatre, Prague, and in other East European centres; Sang Ludmila in Harry Kupfer's production of The Bartered Bride at Covent Garden, 1989, on visit with the company of the Komische Opera; Other roles include Pamina, Puccini's Butterfly and the leading role in Die Kluge by Orff. *Recordings include:* Opera sets for two recording companies; Der Freischütz and Beethoven's Ninth. *Honours:* Prize of the Prague Spring Festival, 1963. *Address:* Leipzigerstr 41 06/08, 10117 Berlin, Germany.

**SMITS, Stefanie;** Opera Singer (Soprano); b. 13 Sept. 1966, Speyer, Rhein. *Education:* German Abitur in French and German, 1986; Studied at Hochschule für Musik, Karlsruhe, with Diploma in Music Pedagogy; Diplomas for opera and for lied and oratorio, Hochschule für Darstellende Kunst und Musik, Frankfurt/Main. *Career:* Debut: Telemann Festival, Magdeburg, as Nigella in Der neumodische Liebhaber Damon, 1996; Donna Anna in Don Giovanni in Berlin, 1997; Debut with Norske Opera Oslo as Tosca in Kristiansand, 1998; Dame in George Taboris's production of Magic Flute in Berlin, 1998; Guest performance as Suor Angelica at Frankfurt, 1999; Engaged with Landestheater Coburg to sing Mimi in La Bohème, Arabella, Rosalinde in Fledermaus and Manon by Massenet. *Recordings:* Der neumodische Liebhaber Damon with La Stagione Frankfurt with DLF Köln. *Honours:* Scholarship, Stiftung Frederique Brion, Basel, 1991; Silver Medal, Maria Callas Competition, Athens, 1997. *Current Management:* Karin Müller Kunstconsulting PR, Kulturmanagement GmmbH, 10117 Berlin, Germany.

**SMOLKA, Jaroslav;** Musicologist and Composer; b. 8 April 1933, Prague, Czechoslovakia; m. Jara Popelová, 8 Sept 1956, 1 s., 1 d. *Education:* Musicology, Charles University, Prague, 1951–56; Composition, Academy of Performing Arts, Prague. *Career:* Recordings Director of LP Supraphon, 1956–62, and then Panton, 1969–72; Assistant, 1962, Docent (Assistant Professor), 1968, Professor of History and Theory of Music, 1991; Leader of Development for Theory and History of Music Academy of Performing Arts, Prague; mem, Atelier 9O, The Society of Czech Composers and Musicologists. *Compositions:* The Play About Teeth, chamber comic opera, 1977–78; The Cock is Sitting Over the Cloud, cycle of female choruses, 1964; Choral Overture, for orchestra, 1982; The Dialog of Forms, symphony for large orchestra, 1989; String Quartet No. 2, 1963–65; Sonata for Pianoforte No. 2 Kontrasty, 1978–79; The Mist of Depression, for viola solo, 1982; Just Don't Be Afraid, concerto for cello and large orchestra. *Publications:* Ladislav Vycpálek: His Evolution as a Composer, 1960; Ceska hudba našeho stoleti, 1961; Ceská kantáta a oratorium, 1970; The Fugue in the Czech Music, 1987; Smetanova vokální tvorba (The Vocal Music of Bedrich Smetana), 1980; Smetanova symfonická tvorba (The Symphonic Music of Bedrich Smetana), 1984; Dejiny hudby (History of Music, Leader of Authors team), 2001. *Address:* Nad Bertramkou 4, 15000 Prague 5, Czech Republic.

**SMOLYANINOVA, Soya;** singer (soprano); b. 1960, Russia. *Education:* Gnessin Inst., Moscow. *Career:* appearances at the Bolshoi Opera from 1986, as Tatiana, Lisa in The Queen of Spades, Emma (Khovanshchina), Yaroslavna (Prince Igor), the Trovatore Leonora, Tosca and Desdemona; guest appearances at Leipzig, Dresden and the Deutsche Oper Berlin, as Amelia, Tosca and Tatiana; soloist with the Gewandhaus Orchestra, Leipzig, and other leading orchestras; Semper Oper Dresden from 1995, as Abigaille in Nabucco, Madama Butterfly and the Forza Leonora; season 1996 as Leonora and Tosca at Antwerp; engaged as Turandot 1998.

**SMYTHE, Russell;** Singer (baritone); b. 19 Dec. 1949, Dublin, Ireland. *Education:* Studied at Guildhall School of Music and London Opera Centre. *Career:* English Music Theatre Company from 1976 as: Tom Jones, Dandini and Ballad Singer in Stephen Oliver's Tom Jones, Rossini's Cenerentola and Britten's Paul Bunyan; Welsh National Opera from 1977 as Billy Budd, Onegin, Papageno, Count Almaviva and Rossini's Figaro; Covent Garden from 1983 as Malatesta in Don Pasquale, Falke in Der Fledermaus and Guglielmo; has sung with English National Opera: Pelléas, Papageno, Figaro, Tarquin in The Rape of Lucretia, Prince Andrei in War and Peace; Hamburg Staastoper from 1980 as Guglielmo, Figaro, Papageno and in Ariadne and Pelléas; Vienna from 1982 as The Count in Der Wildschütz, Harlequin and Falke; Paris Opéra from 1985 as Harlequin and Apollon in Alceste by Gluck; Brother in Dr Faust; North American debut 1986 as Papageno at Vancouver; Sang in Oberon at

Lyon and in La Finta Giardiniera, Amsterdam, Berlin and Brussels; Buxton Festival 1988 as Donizetti's Torquato Tasso; Sang Rossini's Figaro for Opera North, 1989; Don Giovanni, Dublin, 1990; Frankfurt: Finta, 1990; Basel Opera as Orestes in Iphigénie en Tauride, Germont in Traviata and Belcore in L'Elisir d'amore, 1991; Catania: Papageno; Madrid: Ned Keene, in Peter Grimes; ENO: Albert, in Werther; Season 1992 included Ping in Turandot, Antwerp, Eugene Onegin, Tel-Aviv; Season 1993–94 Onegin, Scottish Opera; Orfeo, Monteverdi, Nancy; Season 1994–95 included Henri de Valois in Le Roi Malgré Lui for Opera North; Balstrode in Peter Grimes, Scottish Opera, The Forester, Cunning Little Vixen, Opera Zuid: (Maastricht) Sharpless in Madama Butterfly for Welsh National Opera; Season 1995–96 included Peter, Hansel and Gretel for Scottish Opera; Shishkov in House of the Dead for Opéra du Rhin, Strasbourg; Season 1996–97 as Apollo in Orfeo for Netherlands Opera and Ned Keen in Peter Grimes at La Monnaie; Season 1998–99 at De Vlaamse Opera as Ping in Turandot, Aeneas in Dido and Aeneas, and Arbace in Idomeneo. Concert engagements include Berlioz's L'Enfance du Christ with the Hallé Orchestra and Messiah at Valencia; Recently sang in Orfeo for English Bach Festival and Shishkov in From the House of the Dead, BBC Symphony Orchestra. *Recordings:* Nardo, Brussels Opera; Thésée in Hippolyte et Aricie, Rameau, Archiv; Extensive recording for Radio 3; Video Disc of Menotti's The Telephone. *Current Management:* Athole Still International Management, Forresters Hall, 25–27 Westow Street, London, SE19 3RY, England. *Telephone:* (20) 8771-5271. *Fax:* (20) 8768-6600. *Website:* www .atholestill.com.

**SNIPP, Peter;** singer (baritone); b. 1964, London, England. *Education:* Guildhall School. *Career:* appearances as Masetto with Opera North and in the title role of the premiere of Judith Weir's The Vanishing Bridegroom for Scottish Opera; Eugene Onegin for Kentish Opera and in Zaide and Les Boréades for City of Birmingham Touring Opera; Principal with English National Opera from 1994, singing Malatesta, Harlequin (Ariadne), Guglielmo and Patroclus in King Priam; Concerts include the War Requiem in Finland, Carmina Burana under Jane Glover and the Steersman in Tristan with the London Philharmonic Orchestra; Sang in Henze's Prince of Homburg for ENO, 1996, as Papageno, 1998 and as Figaro in Le Nozze in 1999. *Recordings include:* Il Barbiere di Siviglia, with ENO. *Current Management:* Robert Gilder & Co., Enterprise House, 59–65 Upper Ground, London, SE1 9PQ, England. *Telephone:* (20) 7928-9008. *Fax:* (20) 7928-9755. *E-mail:* rgilder@robert-gilder.com.

**SNOWMAN, (Michael) Nicholas,** MA; British music administrator; *General Director, Opera National du Rhin;* b. 18 March 1944, London; s. of the late Kenneth Snowman and Sallie Snowman (née Moghilevkine); m. Margo Michelle Rouard 1983; one s. *Education:* Hall School and Highgate School, London, Magdalene Coll., Cambridge. *Career:* Asst to Head of Music Staff, Glyndebourne Festival 1967–69; co-founder and Gen. Man. London Sinfonietta 1968–72; Admin. Music Theatre Ensemble 1968–71; Artistic Dir Institut de Recherche et de Coordination Acoustique/Musique (IRCAM), Centre d'Art et de la Culture Georges Pompidou 1972–86; co-founder and Artistic Adviser Ensemble InterContemporain 1975–92, mem. Bd 1992–, Vice-Chair. 1998–; mem. Music Cttee Venice Biennale 1979–86; Artistic Dir Projects in 1980, 1981, 1983, Festival d'Automne de Paris; Programme Consultant Cité de la Musique, La Villette, Paris 1991–92; Gen. Dir (Arts) South Bank Centre, London 1986–92, Chief Exec. 1992–98; Gen. Dir Glyndebourne Opera 1998–2000, Opera Nat. du Rhin 2002–; Chair. Wartski; mem. British Section, Franco-British Council 1995–; Trustee New Berlioz Edn 1996–; Gov. Royal Acad. of Music 1998–. *Publications:* The Best of Granta (co-ed.) 1967, The Contemporary Composers (series ed.) 1982–; papers and articles on music, cultural policy and France. *Honours:* Chevalier, Ordre nat. du Mérite, Officier, Ordre des Arts et des Lettres, Polish Order of Cultural Merit. *Address:* c/o Wartski, 14 Grafton Street, London, W1X 4DE, England; 9 rue de Bain Finkwiller, 67000 Stasbourg, France (home). *Telephone:* (3) 88-75-48-64 (office); (6) 64-77-81-30 (home). *Fax:* (3) 88-25-52-59 (office). *E-mail:* wartski@wartski.com; nsnowman@onr.fr. *Website:* www.wartski.com; www .onr.fr.

**SNYDER, Barry;** Concert Pianist and Teacher; b. 6 March 1944, Allentown, Pennsylvania, USA. *Education:* BM, Master's Degree, Performance and Literature, Artist Diploma in Piano, Eastman School of Music, University of Rochester. *Career:* Debut: Soloist with Allentown Symphony Orchestra; Has performed throughout the USA, Canada, Europe, Poland, South America and Asia; Appearances with orchestras of Montreal, Atlanta, Houston, Baltimore, National, Detroit and Kraków in Poland, with such conductors as Sixten Ehrling, David Zinman, Charles Dutoit, Robert Shaw, Leopold Stokowski; Chamber music with Jan DeGaetani, Dong-Suk Kang, Zvi Zeitlin, Ani Kavafian, Bonita Boyd, Cleveland Quartet, Composers' Quartet, Eastman Brass Quintet, New York Brass Quintet; Founding Member of Eastman Trio with tours to Europe and South America; Professor of Piano, Eastman School of Music, 1970–; Has given masterclasses with solo recitals. *Recordings:* 38 CDs including Dohnányi, solo recording; Dohnányi chamber works with Cleveland Quartet; Complete cello music of Fauré with Steven Doone, cellist; Stephen Jaffe's Two Piano Sonata with Anton Nel. *Address:* 166 Orchard Drive, Rochester, New York, NY 14618-2344, USA.

**SOBEHARTOVA, Jitka;** Singer (Soprano); b. 1950, Czechoslovakia. *Education:* Studied in Prague. *Career:* Sang in operetta at the Karlin Music Theatre, Prague; Opera roles at Usti nad Labern 1977-84, including Marenka in The Bartered Bride, Susanna, and Marguerite in Faust; National Theatre,

Prague, from 1984, notably as Zerlina in Don Giovanni, Musetta (La Bohème), Aennchen (Der Freischütz) and roles in operas by Dvořák and Smetana; Many concert appearances in Eastern Europe. *Recordings include:* The Cunning Peasant by Dvořák (Supraphon). *Address:* National Theatre, PO Box 865, 112 30 Prague 1, Czech Republic.

**SOBOLEVA, Galina;** Cellist; b. 1960, Moscow, Russia. *Education:* Studied at Moscow Conservatoire with Valentin Berlinsky. *Career:* Member of the Prokofiev Quartet (founded at Moscow Festival of World Youth and the International Quartet Competition, Budapest); Many concerts in former Soviet Union and on tour to Czechoslovakia, Germany, Austria, USA, Canada, Spain, Japan and Italy; Repertoire includes works by Haydn, Mozart, Beethoven, Schubert, Debussy, Ravel, Tchaikovsky, Bartók and Shostakovich. *Address:* c/o Sonata (Prokofiev Quartet), 11 Northgate Street, Glasgow G20 7AA, Scotland.

**SOCCI, Gianni;** Singer (Bass); b. 19 March 1939, Rome, Italy. *Education:* Studied at the Accademia di Santa Cecilia in Rome and with Franco Cavara. *Career:* Debut: Piccolo Teatro Comico Rome in 1965 as Achmed in Paisiello's Il Re Teodoro in Venezia; Sang in the buffo repertory at opera houses in Milan, Rome, Naples, Florence, Turin, Venice, Genoa and Trieste; Guest appearances in Brussels, Copenhagen, Toulouse, Strasbourg, Paris, Cologne, Frankfurt, Philadelphia, Montreal, Quebec, Monte Carlo and Barcelona; Many performances in operas by Mozart, Cimarosa, Rossini and Donizetti; Sang at Teatro Lirico Milan in 1975 in the premiere of Al Gran Sole Carico d'Amore by Luigi Nono; Concert engagements in Italy and elsewhere.

**SÖDERSTRÖM, Elisabeth Anna;** Swedish singer (soprano); b. 7 May 1927, Stockholm; m. Sverker Olow 1950; three s. *Career:* studied singing under Andrejewa de Skilonz and Opera School, Stockholm; engaged at Royal Opera, Stockholm 1950–; appearances at Salzburg 1955, Glyndebourne 1957, 1959, 1961, 1963, 1964, 1979, Metropolitan Opera, New York 1959, 1960, 1962, 1963, 1983, 1984, 1986, 1987, 1999; frequent concert and TV appearances in Europe and USA; toured USSR 1966; Artistic Dir Drottningholm Court Theatre 1993–97. *Recordings include:* complete Rachmaninov songs with Vladimir Ashkenazy, Janáček's operas Katya Kabanova, Jenufa and the Makropoulos Case conducted by Sir Charles Mackerras. *Roles include:* Fiordiligi (Così fan tutte), Countess and Susanna (Figaro), Countess (Capriccio), Christine (Intermezzo); sang three leading roles in Der Rosenkavalier 1959. *Publications:* I Min Tonart 1978, Sjung ut Elisabeth 1986. *Honours:* Hon. mem. RAM, Hon. Prof. 1996; Singer of the Court (Sweden) 1959; Hon. CBE; Stelle della Solidarietà dell'Italia; Commdr of the Order of Vasa 1973, Commdr des Arts et Lettres 1986; Prize for Best Acting, Royal Swedish Acad. 1965, 'Litteris et Artibus' Award 1969, Ingmar Bergman Award 1988. *Address:* Drottningholms Slottsteater, Box 15417, 10465 Stockholm (office); Hersbyvägen 19, 18142 Lidingo, Sweden. *Telephone:* (8) 765-22-89 (home). *Fax:* (8) 566-931-01.

**SOFFEL, Doris;** Singer (Mezzo-Soprano); b. 12 May 1948, Hechingen, Germany. *Education:* Early studies as violinist, then voice with Marianne Schech in Munich, 1968–73. *Career:* Bayreuth Youth Festival in 1972, in Das Liebesverbot; Stuttgart State Opera, 1973–76; Sang Waltraute at Bayreuth and began career as a concert artist; Noted in Bach and other Baroque music; Sang at Bregenz Festival in 1977 as Puck in Oberon; Sang Monteverdi's Poppea in Toronto in 1983 and took part in the Hamburg premiere of JC Bach's Amadis de Gaule; Sang at Covent Garden in 1983 as Sextus in La Clemenza di Tito and Orlovsky in Die Fledermaus; Fricka (Solti/Hall), Bayreuth Festival, 1983; Mahler 3rd (Tennstedt), New York Carnegie Hall, 1983; Sang in the world premiere of Reimann's Troades in Munich, 1986; Sang Octavian in a production of Der Rosenkavalier at the renovated Brussels Opera House, and Angelina in La Cenerentola at the Berlin Staatsoper in 1987; L'Italiana in Algeri/Isabella, Schwetzingen, Zürich, Cologne, 1987; Television appearances include Das Lied von der Erde in 1988; Sang in the premiere of Penderecki's Ubu Rex at Munich in 1991; Season 1992 as Cassandra in Reimann's Troades at Frankfurt and Elizabeth in Donizetti's Maria Stuarda at Amsterdam; Verdi's Preziosilla at Munich in 1994; Bartók's Bluebeard's Castle (Judith), Deutsche Oper Berlin (Kout/Friedrich), 1994; Werther (Charlotte) at Parma with Alfredo Kraus and Damnation of Faust at Munich, 1995; Returned to London 1997 for Mahler/Brahms recital at St John's Smith Square; Season 2000–01 as Kundry at the Deutsche Oper Berlin; Frick and Waltraute for Cologne Opera, Countess Geschwitz in Palermo and Schoeck's Penthesilea for the Maggio Musicale, Florence; Ortrud in Lohengrin at Bologna, 2002. *Recordings include:* Bach Cantatas and Magnificat; Flotow's Martha; Lortzing's Der Wildschütz; Haydn's St Cecilia Mass; Das Liebesverbot; Schumann's Requiem; Zemlinsky's Eine Florentinische Tragödie; Troades; Parsifal; Mahler No. 2; Beethoven's Missa Solemnis; Wolf's Der Corregidor; Mahler 3; Mahler 8; Kindertotenlieder; Lieder eines fahrenden Gesellen; Mahler's Rückertlieder; Virtuoso Arias, Anna Bolena. *Current Management:* Ingpen & Williams Ltd, 7 St George's Court, 131 Putney Bridge Road, London, SW15 2PA, England.

**SOGNY, Michel;** Artistic Director, Manager, Composer and Author; b. 21 Nov. 1947, Pau, France. *Education:* Doctor of Philosophy, Paris; Masters Degree in Psychology and Literature; Ecole Normale de Musique de Paris. *Career:* Debut: Piano recital of own compositions, Paris, 1990; Book on Liszt, 1975; New Piano method, 1978; Producer, International recitals of gifted pupils; Founder, Paris Piano School, 1974; Numerous radio and television programmes; Television film on Liszt, 1982; Educational methods adopted by

ILO, Geneva, 1985; Creation of Michel Sogny Foundation for young and talented under-privileged children, 2000; mem, Treasurer of French Association Franz Liszt, Paris, 1972. *Compositions:* Numerous concert pieces for piano; Numerous didactic compositions for piano. *Recordings:* Michel Sogny Live at Espace Cardin, 1990; Prolegomenes to a Musical Eidetic; Michel Sogny Live at Villa Schindler. *Publications:* Admiration Créatrice Chez Liszt, 1975; La Methode eu Questions, 1984; Le Methode eu Action, 1987. *Contributions:* Tribune de Genève, 1993; Record critique in classical review Harmony, Paris, 1980. *Honours:* Peace Medal of UN, New York, 1986; Honorary diploma from UNESCO for his work, 1995. *Address:* Villa Schindler, Obermarkstr 45, 6410 Teifs, Austria.

**SOHAL, Naresh;** Composer; b. 18 Sept. 1939, Harsipind, Punjab, India. *Education:* University of Punjab; London College of Music; Leeds University. *Career:* Asht Prahar performed by London Philharmonic Orchestra under Norman del Mar at the Royal Festival Hall in 1970; BBC have commissioned four major works including The Wanderer, first performed during the 1982 Promenade Concerts, under Andrew Davis; From Gitanjali commissioned by Philharmonic Society of New York, first performed by New York Philharmonic Orchestra under Zubin Mehta in 1985; Represented the West in 2 East-West encounters in the Netherlands and Bombay in 1983; Television credits include music score for Sir William in Search of Xanadu for Scottish television and three episodes of Granada television's series, End of Empire, 1985; Member of BBC 's Central Music Advisory Committee and the equivalent committee in Scotland; mem, Society for the Promotion of New Music. *Compositions include:* Orchestral: Indra-Dhanush, 1973, Dhyan 1, 1974, Tandava Nritya, 1984; Chamber and instrumental: Shades I, 1974, Shades II, 1975, Shades III, 1978, Chakra, 1979, Shades IV, 1983, Brass Quintet No. 2, 1983; Vocal and choral: Inscape, 1979, The Wanderer, 1981, From Gitanjali, 1985; Maya, music theatre, 1997; Satyagraha for orchestra, 1997. *Contributions:* Tempo Magazine. *Address:* c/o British Music Information Centre, 11 Stratford Place, London, W1, England.

**SOHN, Sung-rai;** South Korean violinist and conductor; b. 23 Sept. 1950, Seoul; m. Patricia Esposito Gilleran 1980; one s. three step-d. *Education:* BM, Peabody Conservatory of Music (full scholarship student of Berl Senofsky), Baltimore, Maryland, USA; MFA, Sarah Lawrence College (scholarship student of Dorothy DeLay); Quartet Seminar, Juilliard School of Music. *Career:* Debut as a winner of Artists International Competition and Jack Kahn Music Award, Carnegie Recital Hall, New York City, 1980; Founder, Music Director/Conductor, Philharmonic Lawrencia Chamber Orchestra; Founder, 1st Violinist, Laurentian String Quartet; Appeared: Korean National television (KBS Radio); WNYC, New York, in Rising Star, Live, and the Bosendorfer Concert Series; The Listening Room, WQXR, New York; NPR, USA; MaineTelevision Network; Kansas Television Network; Sendai Television Network, Japan; Toured Canada, USA, Europe, Africa, Asia. *Recordings:* Barber String Quartet Op 11; Rochberg String Quartet No. 3; C P E Bach Concerto in A major; Ginastera Piano Quintet. *Publications:* Careers in Music, 1980. *Address:* 69 Mile Road, Suffern, NY 10901, USA.

**SOJAT, Tiziana;** Singer (Soprano); b. 28 April 1955, Rome, Italy. *Education:* Studied with her mother, Alda Noni, and Elisabeth Schwarzkopf. *Career:* Debut: Dublin in 1984 as Elsa in Lohengrin; Sang Mimi at Ljubljana in 1984; Concert performances of Dido and Aeneas and Gianni Schicchi at Lausanne in 1985; Sang with the company of San Carlo, Naples, in Pergolesi's Stabat Mater at New York; Croatian National Opera at Zagreb in 1988 as Sieglinde in Die Walküre; Marseilles in 1989 as Elena in Mefistofele; Engaged at Karlsruhe Opera from 1989, notably as Butterfly and Arabella; Concert performances at Turin, Dubrovnik, Rome and Milan; Freelance career, giving several concertts and Liederabende in Tokyo, one of which for the Richard Strauss Society of Japan, 1995–. *Recordings include:* Lieder by Wolf, Schumann, Liszt and Mahler; CD War Songs by Franz Lehar and Kurt Weill, 1996. *Address:* Badisches Staatstheater, Baumeisterstrasse 11, 7500 Karlsruhe, Germany.

**SOJER, Hans;** Singer (Tenor); b. 20 March 1943, Innsbruck, Austria. *Education:* Studied with Franziska Lohmann. *Career:* Debut: Innsbruck in 1967 as David in Meistersinger; Sang at Innsbruck until 1971, Bonn, 1971–73, Wiesbaden, 1973–81, and Hanover, 1981–; Roles in operas by Rossini, Donizetti, Mozart, Wagner and Strauss, at Graz, Cologne, Mannheim, Düsseldorf, Frankfurt, Berlin, Lisbon and Karlsruhe; Sang at Bregenz and Schwetzingen Festivals; Sang the Steersman and Narraboth at Barcelona in 1988, Ernesto at Kiel and Count Riccardo in Wolf-Ferrari's Quattro Rusteghi at Hanover in 1991; Concert repertoire includes Beethoven's 9th and cantatas and Passions by Bach. *Recordings include:* Brighella in Ariadne auf Naxos. *Address:* c/o Niedersachsische Staatstheater, Opernplatz 1, 3000 Hanover, Germany.

**SOKHIEV, Tugan;** Russian conductor; *Principal Guest Conductor, Orchestre National du Capitole de Toulouse;* b. 1977, Vladikavkaz. *Education:* St Petersburg State Rimsy-Korsakov Conservatoire. *Career:* Guest Conductor, State Philharmonic Orchestra of Northern Ossetia; Prin. Conductor, State Symphony Orchestra of Russia; has also conducted Iceland Opera, Welsh Nat. Opera, Danish Radio Sinfonietta, Strasbourg PO, Orchestre della Toscana, Bavarian Staatsoper, Swedish Radio SO, Nuremberg Opera; conducts regularly at Mariinsky Theatre, St Petersburg; Prin. Guest Conductor, Orchestre Nat. du Capitole de Toulouse, France 2005–. *Honours:* prize-winner Prokoviev Int. Conducting Competition 1999. *Current Management:* c/o Rona

Eastwood, Askonas Holt Ltd, Lonsdale Chambers, 27 Chancery Lane, London, WC2A 1PF, England. *Telephone:* (20) 7400-1700 (office). *Fax:* (20) 7400-1799 (office). *E-mail:* info@askonasholt.co.uk (office). *Website:* www.askonasholt.co.uk (office). *Address:* Orchestre National du Capitole de Toulouse, BP 41408, 31014 Toulouse Cedex 6, France. *Website:* www.onct.mairie-toulouse.fr.

**SOKOLOV, Grigory Lipmanovich;** Russian pianist; b. 18 April 1950, Leningrad (now St Petersburg). *Education:* Leningrad Conservatory (pupil of Moisey Halfin). *Career:* numerous guest appearances in London, Paris, Vienna, Berlin, Madrid, Salzburg, Munich, Rome and New York; has worked with leading conductors including Myung-Whun Chung, Neeme Järvi, Herbert Blomstedt, Valery Gergiev, Sakari Oramo, Trevor Pinnock, Andrew Litton, Vassilly Sinajskij, Jukka-Pekka Saraste, Alexander Lazarev, John Storgards, Moshe Atzmon, Walter Weller and Evgeny Svetlanov; has performed with orchestras including New York Philharmonic, Montreal Symphony, Münchner Philharmoniker, Leipzig Gewandhaus, Philhannonia, Amsterdam Concertgebouw and Detroit Symphony; Prof., Leningrad (St Petersburg) Conservatory 1975–. *Recordings:* several live recordings including works by Bach, Beethoven, Brahms, Chopin, Rachmaninoff, Prokofiev, Schubert, Schumann, Scriabin and Tchaikovsky; DVD of 2002 Paris recital directed by Bruno Monsaingeon. *Honours:* Second Prize, All-Union Competition of Musicians 1965, First Prize, Int. Tchaikovsky Competition 1966, People's Artist of Russia 1988. *Current Management:* c/o Artists Management Co., Piazza R. Simoni 1, 37122 Verona, Italy. *Telephone:* (45) 8014980 (office). *E-mail:* office@amcmusic.com (office). *Website:* www.amcmusic.com (office).

**SOKOLOV, Ivan Glebovitch;** Russian composer, pianist and educator; b. 29 Aug. 1960. *Education:* Gnesin Musical College, composition with Nik Sidelnikov, piano with Lev Maumov. *Career:* Assistant Probationer under Nik Sidelnikov, 1984–86, Moscow Conservatoire; Concerts, as soloist and with others in Moscow, Leningrad, Sverdlovsk, Kharkov, Briansk, Tashkent, Alma-Ata, Lvov and Tallinn among others, 1985–; Repertoire includes Stockhausen, Cage, Crumb, Scriabin, Shostakovich, Prokofiev, Debussy and Brahms; Festival appearances include Moscow Autumn, 1987–90, Alternative, 1988–90, Festival of Music in Russia and Germany, 1990, and Schleswig-Holstein Music Festival, Hamburg, 1991; Solo concert, playing Chopin in 1991; Teacher of Composition at Musical College, 1986–; Leader of classes in Instrumentation and Musical Score Reading at Moscow Conservatoire, 1988–. *Compositions include:* 10 Pieces for flute and piano, 1983; The Night, cantata, 1983; Rus Pevutchaya, cantata, 1985; Blazhenstvo I Beznadezhnos, vocal cycle, 1986; Volokos for piano, 1988; Sonata for flute and piano, 1988; 13 Pieces for piano, 1988; Eshtche, 7 pieces for piano, 1989; Knigy Na Stole for piano, 1989; Zvezda for soprano and piano, 1990; O, flute solo, 1990; Korably V More for 2 pianos, 1990; Igra Bez Natchala I Konza for percussion, 1991; Mysli O Rachmaninove for piano, 1991; Summer for narrator, actress and strings, 1994; Opera-Cryptophonics, 1995; KA-24 Non-Presludes, for piano and percussion ensemble, 1995; Secret Letters for violin, viola, piano and synthesizer, 1995; I. Sokolov, for fortepiano, 1997. *Address:* uliza Staryi Gaiy, dom 1, korpus 1, Kvartira 116, 111539 Moscow, Russia.

**SOKOLOV, Vladimir;** Clarinettist; b. 21 Feb. 1936, Uckshor, Republic of Komi, Russia; m. Irina Sokolova. *Education:* City of Siktivkar Music School, Republic of Komi, 1950–54; Orchestra Faculty, Moscow Conservatory, 1954–59;. *Career:* Debut: With Moscow Conservatory Symphony Orchestra at the Grand Hall, Moscow Conservatory, 1955; Clarinettist, Radio and Television Symphony Orchestra, 1960–63; Clarinettist, USSR State Symphony Orchestra, 1963–92; Clarinettist, Russian National Symphony Orchestra, 1992–94; Teacher, 1973–, Professor, 1992–, Moscow Conservatory; Teacher, Central Music School, 1977–; Professor, Korean National Institute of Arts, Seoul, 1994–. *Recordings:* Concertos by Mozart, Krommer and Weber; Sonatas by Brahms, Glinka, Grechaninov, Artemov, Saint-Saëns, Poulenc; Works by French composers; Duets, Trios, Quartets, Quintets by Mozart, Beethoven, Brahms, Glinka, Khachaturian, Power. *Address:* Presnensky Val h 40, Apt 41, 123557 Moscow, Russia.

**SOLARE, Juan María;** Argentine/Italian composer and pianist; *Teacher and Conductor, University of Bremen;* b. 11 Aug. 1966, Buenos Aires; s. of Juan Solare and Beatriz Entenza. *Education:* Conservatorio Nacional, Buenos Aires; Postgraduate studies, Musikhochschulen, Cologne and Stuttgart. *Career:* Prof., Conservatorio, Tandil, 1986–93; Teacher and Conductor, Univ. of Bremen, Germany 2002–; Piano Teacher, Musikschule of Bremen 2002–; piano recitals (tango music and contemporary music); composition comms from Centropara la Difusion de la Musica Contemporanea, Madrid 2002, 2004, Kunststiftung NRW, Düsseldorf 2003, Landesmusikrat Bremen, Germany 2004; compositions performed at Ferienkurse, Darmstadt 1992, 1994, 1998; columnist, Clasica 1990–, Doce Notas 1996–; interviews with diverse musicians including Kagel, Nono, Iachenmann, Stockhausen, Juan Carlos Zorzi, Rihm, Nuria Schönberg-Nono, Luis de Pablo, Pedro Sáenz. *Compositions:* more than 250 works including Veinticinco de Agosto (chamber opera) 1983, Neverness (string quartet), Passacaglia uber Heidelberg (trio), Pope for voice, An Angel of Ice and Fire for orchestra, Subte (radio piece), El es (piano trio), Palmas for 8 percussionists, Faq (piano four hands), Anamnesis (septet), Sufi Motetten for choir, piano music (about 30 pieces); music for Internet animations (art movies) and short films. *Publications:* Musica y Ajedrez, Planteo de un metodo 1998, El encuentro de Mahler y Freud 1996, Una ventana a El Sur 2001, Dónde estás, hermano?: die ewige Utopie 2001, Mis Maestros de Composición 2001, Gequälte Satire 2002, La música de Al Capone 2003, Doce aspectos del Doce 2003, Interkultur in der Elektroakus-

tischen Musik Iberoamerikas 2004, Cage, ajedrecista 2005. *Honours:* First Composition Prize, Promociones Musicales de la Argentina 1990, Third Prize, Walter Witte Viola Foundation, Frankfurt 2001, prize winner, Brewer Komponistenwettbewerb, Bremen, Germany 2004, Second Prize (as pianist of ensemble Die Kugel) 6th Internationaler Wettbewerb für junge Kultur, Düsseldorf 2000; scholarships from Fundacion Antorchas, Argentina 1986, 1988, Internationales Musikinstitut, Darmstadt 1992, 1994, German Academic Exchange Service 1993–94, Instituto de la Juventud, Spain 1996, Ministerio de Educación y Cultura, Spain 1996, Heinrich-Strobel Foundation, Baden-Baden 1998–99, Kilnstlerhauser Worpswede, Germany 2001–02. *Address:* Adam-Stegerwaldstr. 15, 51063, Cologne, Germany (office). *Telephone:* (221) 881474 (office). *Fax:* (221) 881474 (office). *E-mail:* solare@surfeu.de (office). *Website:* www.tango.uni-bremen.de (office); www.ciweb.com.ar/solare (home).

**SOLBIATI, Alessandro;** Composer; b. 5 Sept. 1956, Busto Arsizio, Italy; m. Emuanuela Piemonti, 2 Feb 1985, 1 s., 1 d. *Education:* 2 Years, Faculty of Classics, University of Milan; Diploma in Piano and in Composition, Conservatory G. Verdi, Milan. *Career:* Debut: Biennale, Venice, 1981; Numerous commissions from Teatro alla Scala, RAI, French Ministry of Culture, Radio France, Mozarteum, South Bank of London, Gulbenkian Foundation, Lisbon, University of Paris; Performances at numerous festivals including Lille, Avignon, Strasbourg, Radio France Presences, 1992, 1994, 1997, Huddersfield, England, Wien Modern, Holland Festival, Zagreb, Musicale of Florence, Sydney, Maastricht, Moscow. *Compositions:* Trio d'archi, 1981; Sonata, 1986; Nel deserts, 1986; Canto per Ania, for cello and instruments, 1992; Quartetto con lied, for string quartet and child's voice, 1992; Inno, radiophonic production, 1997; Sinfonia, for orchestra, 1998; Sonata, for piano, 1998. *Recordings:* Solbiata: Chamber Recordings, 1999; Nel Deserto, oratorio and ensemble; Quartetto con Lied, Quartetto Borciani; Trio, Trio Matisse; Tre pezzi, for guitar, Filomena Moretti; Tre pezzi, for guitar, Halasa; Inno. *Publications:* Progettualita Pormale nell'Ultimo Moderna, in Studies in Bruno Maderna, 1989. *Contributions:* Journals and periodicals. *Honours:* First Prize, International Composition Award, Turin, 1980; First Prize, International Composition Award, RAI-Paganini, Rome, 1983; Targa d'Argento, Prize Saint Vincent, 1983. *Address:* Viale Argonne 39, 20133 Milano, Italy.

**SOLDH, Anita;** Swedish singer (soprano); b. 26 Sept. 1949, Stockholm. *Education:* Stockholm Univ., Stockholm and Vienna Music Acads, studied with Erik Saéden, and with Luigi Ricci in Rome. *Career:* sang with Norrlands Opera 1975–77, notably as Britten's Lucretia and Mozart's Countess, Royal Opera Stockholm from 1977 with debut as Eva in Die Meistersinger, returning as Senta, Elizabeth, Arabella, Octavian, Chrysothemis, Mozart's Countess, Elvira, Vitelia and Pamina, Tchaikovsky's Tatiana and Maid of Orleans; concert tours of the USA, Brussels and Europe 1984, as Cherubino; Bayreuth Festival 1983–84 as Freia in Das Rheingold; sang Elsa in Lohengrin at Stockholm 1989 and First Lady in Die Zauberflöte at the Drottningholm Court Theatre, and the Queen in Vogler's Gustaf Adolf en Ebba Brahe 1990; season 1991–92 as Agave in the premiere of Backanterna by Daniel Börtz, production by Ingmar Bergman, and at Drottningholm in Haeffner's Electra and as Gluck's Eurydice; concert repertoire includes Schoenberg's Erwartung, Berg's Frühe Lieder and Haydn's Schöpfung. *Recording:* Idomeneo from Drottningholm (as Elettra, video). *Current Management:* Svenska Konsertbyrån AB, Jungfrugatan 45, 114 44 Stockholm, Sweden. *Telephone:* (8) 665 80 88. *Fax:* (8) 665 80 66. *E-mail:* info@svenskakonsertbyran.se. *Website:* www.svenskakonsertbyran.se.

**SOLÉN, Christer;** singer (tenor); b. 1939, Gustavs, Finland. *Education:* Royal Music Academy, Stockholm, and with Luigi Ricci in Rome. *Career:* Sang at Herrenhausen 1969-70, as Sextus in Handel's Giulio Cesare; Norrlandsoperan at Umea from 1974, as Rossini's Lindoro, Don Ottavio, Male Chorus in The Rape of Lucretia; Folksoperan Stockholm from 1981, as Pinkerton, Radames and Tamino; Stora Theatre Gothenburg in The Lighthouse by Peter Maxwell Davies (1984) and title role in The Voyage of Edgar Allan Poe, by Argento; Other roles have included Hoffmann, Fatty in Weill's Mahagonny, Oedipus Rex, and Eufemio in Gli Equivoci, by Storace; Many concert appearances throughout Europe.

**SOLLBERGER, Harvey;** Composer, Conductor and Flautist; b. 11 May 1938, Cedar Rapids, Iowa, USA. *Education:* BA 1960, University of Iowa; Composition with Jack Beeson and Otto Luening at Columbia University, New York (MA 1964). *Career:* Co-founded the Group for Contemporary Music, New York 1962; Regular tours as flautist and conductor; Faculty Member, Columbia University 1966–82; Manhattan School of Music, 1972–83; Indiana University School of Music 1983–92; Professor of Music at the University of California, San Diego, from 1992; Music Director, La Jolla Symphony Orchestra, 1998–. *Compositions include:* Chamber Variations for 12 players, 1964; Music for Sophocles's Antigone, electronic, 1966; Musica Transalpina, 2 motets for soprano, baritone and 9 players, 1970; Folio, 11 pieces for bassoon, 1976; Sunflowers, for flute and vibraphone, 1976; Music for Prepared Dancers, 1978; Interrupted Night for 5 instruments, 1983; Double Triptych for flute and percussion, 1984; Persian Golf, for strings, 1987; Aurelian Echoes for flute and alto flute, 1989; Passages, for soloists, chorus and orchestra, 1990; The Advancing Moment for flute, clarinet, violin, cello, piano and percussion, 1993; CIAO, Arcosanti for 8 instruments, 1994; In Terra Aliena for 5 soloists and orchestra, 1995; Grandis Templum Machinae for soprano, mezzo, baritone, chorus and 21 Instruments, 1996; To the Spirit Unappeased and Peregrine, for flute and clarinet, 1998; New Millennium Memo for solo flute, 2000. *Honours:* Guggenheim Fellowships, 1969, 1973. *Address:* Department of Music 0326, University of California, San Diego, La Jolla, CA 92093, USA. *E-mail:* hsollberger@ucsd.edu.

**SOLODCHIN, Galina;** Violinist; b. 29 April 1944, Tientsin, China. *Education:* Studied at the New South Wales Conservatorium. *Career:* Freelance musican, including member of Delmé Quartet from 1967; Many performances in the United Kingdom and Europe in the classical and modern repertory; Concerts at the Salzburg Festival and the Brahms Saal of the Musikverein Vienna; Season 1990 included Haydn's Seven Last Words in Italy and elsewhere, three Brahms programmes at St John's Smith Square with Iain Burnside on piano; Concerts at St David's Hall in Cardiff with Quartets by Tchaikovsky and Robert Simpson including premiere of his 13th Quartet; Appearances in Bremen, Hamburg and Trieste followed by festival engagements in 1991; Other repertory includes works by Paul Patterson, Daniel Jones, Wilfred Josephs, Iain Hamilton and Bernard Stevens. *Recordings include:* Haydn's Seven Last Words; Vaughan Williams's On Wenlock Edge; Gurney's Ludlow and Tame; Simpson Quartets 1–9 and String Trio; Daniel Jones 3 Quartets and Bridge No. 2; Bliss's No. 1 and 2; Josef Holbrooke Piano Quartet and Clarinet Quintet; Brahms Clarinet Quintet; Dvořák F major Quartet; Verdi Quartet; Strauss A major Op 2; Hummel No. 1, 2 and 3; Bernard Stevens Theme and Variations and Quartet No. 2 and Lyric Suite for String Trio; Beethoven Op 74 and Op 95; Favourite Encores. *Address:* c/o 33 Whittingstall Road, Fulham, London SW6, England.

**SOLOMON, Maynard Elliott,** BA; American music historian and writer; b. 5 Jan. 1930, New York, NY; m. Eva Georgiana Tevan 1951; two s. one d. *Education:* Brooklyn Coll., CUNY, Columbia Univ. *Career:* co-founder, co-owner, Vanguard Recording Soc. Inc 1950–86; teacher, CUNY 1979–81; Visiting Prof., SUNY at Stony Brook 1988–89, Columbia Univ. 1989–90, Harvard Univ. 1991–92, Yale Univ. 1994–95; Scholarly Adviser, Beethoven Archive, Bonn 1995–; Graduate Faculty, Juilliard School 1998–; Assoc. Ed., American Imago 1976; mem. PEN. *Publications:* Marxism and Art 1973, Beethoven 1977, 1998, Myth, Creativity and Psychoanalysis 1978, Beethoven Essays 1988, Mozart: A Life 1995, Some Romantic Images in Beethoven 1998, Late Beethoven: Music, Thought, Imagination 2003; contrib. articles to Beethoven Jahrbuch: Music and Letters, Musical Quarterly: 19th Century Music, Journal of the American Musicological Society. *Honours:* ASCAP–Deems Taylor Awards 1978, 1989, 1995, Kinkeldey Award American Musicological Soc. 1989, hon. mem. 1999, 2000. *Address:* 1 W 72nd Street, Apt 56, New York, NY 10023, USA.

**SOLOMON, Yonty,** BMus, FRCM; British/South African concert pianist; b. 6 May 1938, Cape Town; s. of David and Chaze Riva Solomon. *Education:* Univ. of Cape Town. *Career:* studied with Dame Myra Hess in London, Guido Agosti in Rome, Charles Rosen (q.v.) in USA; Concert début in Wigmore Hall, London 1963; recitals and concertos in UK, Italy, Netherlands, USA, Canada, Romania, South Africa; gave first performances of works dedicated to him by Richard Rodney Bennett (q.v.), Wilfred Mellers, Merilaainen, Wilfred Josephs; given solo performing rights by composer Kaikhosru Sorabji 1976–77 for all his works; panel of judges of Royal Overseas League Commonwealth Music Competition 1974–; many TV and radio engagements; many recitals devoted to Charles Ives, J. S. Bach (The Well-Tempered Klavier and Klavierübung), Janáček, Boulez, Granados, Albéniz and much rarely performed piano music; first performance of unpublished scores by K. S. Sorabji 1978; Prof. of Piano, Royal Coll. of Music, London 1978–; Visiting Artist-in-Residence, Nottingham Univ. 1980–; Master classes in piano and chamber music at Int. Musicians Seminar (Cornwall) 1982; Leverhulme (Royal Coll. of Music) Project 1999; Scholarships from Univ. of Cape Town. *Publications:* Schumann Symposium 1973, Bach's "48", Analysis and Historical Survey 1972. *Honours:* Hon. mem. Royal Philharmonic Soc.; Hon. Royal Coll. of Music (London) 1982; Harriet Cohen Beethoven Medal 1962, Commonwealth Award. *Address:* 56 Canonbury Park North, London, N1 2JT, England. *Telephone:* (20) 7226-8123. *Fax:* (20) 7226-8123. *E-mail:* yonty .solomon@btinternet.com (home).

**SOLTESZ, Stefan;** Hungarian conductor; b. 6 Jan. 1949, Nyiregyhaza. *Education:* Vienna Hochschule für Musik with Dieter Weber, Hans Swarowsky, Reinhold Schmidt and Friedrich Cerha. *Career:* Conductor at the Theater an der Wien, Vienna, 1971–73; Coach and Conductor at Vienna Staatsoper, 1973–83; Salzburg Festivals, 1978, 1979, 1983 being assistant to Karl Böhm, Christoph von Dohnányi and Karajan; Guest Conductor of the Graz Opera, 1979–81; Permanent Conductor of the Hamburg Staatsoper, 1983–85 and Deutsche Oper Berlin 1985–97; General Music Director of the State Theatre at Brunswick, 1988–93; Music Director of the Flanders Opera, Antwerp/Ghent, 1992–97 Guest Conductor with the Opéra Royale de Wallonie at Liège, Bavarian State Opera in Munich, Bonn Opera, Leipzig Opera, Vlaamse Opera Antwerp, Stuttgart State Theater, Nederlandse Oper at Amsterdam, Festival de Radio France et Montpelleier, Aix-en-Provence, Paris Opéra, Vienna State Opera, Frankfurt Opera, Semper Opera, Dresden, Teatro Bellini, Catania, Hamburg Opera, Teatro Colón, Buenos Aires, Washington Opera, Kennedy Center and ROH, London, San Francisco Opera, Zürich Opera; Toured Japan with the German State Opera Unter den Linden, 1990; Concerts in Bologna, Hamburg, Mexico City, Naples, Paris, Salzburg, Turin, Vienna, Munich, Essen, Berlin, Karlsruhe, Hannover, Dresden, Genoa, Basel and Zagreb among others; Since 1997 Artistic Director of the Aalto Musiktheater in Essen and Music Director of the City of Essen, Germany.

*Recordings include:* Swan Lake Excerpts with Vienna Symphony; La Bohème with Lucia Popp and Francisco Araiza; Opera Arias with Lucia Popp; Opera Arias with Grace Bumbry; Don Giovanni, by Giuseppe Gazzaniga, with Munich Radio Orchestra; The Chalk Circle by Alexander Zemlinsky; Orchestral Songs by Hugo Wolf with Dietrich Fischer-Dieskau. *Honours:* Cultural Prize, Foundation of Savings Banks of the Rhineland (Germany) 2004. *Address:* Aalto Musiktheater Essen, Opernplatz 10, 45128 Essen, Germany (office). *Telephone:* (201) 8122291 (office). *Fax:* (201) 8122280 (office).

**SOLUM, John Henry,** BA; American concert flautist, writer and educator; b. 11 May 1935, New Richmond, WI; m. Millicent Hunt 1960; two s. *Education:* Princeton Univ., studied with William Kincaid in Philadelphia. *Career:* solo debut 1953; soloist, Philadelphia Orchestra 1957; New York debut recital 1959; soloist chamber music player worldwide; guest appearances with orchestras in over 50 cities, many radio broadcasts, festival appearances in Europe, N America; teacher, Vassar Coll. 1969–71, 1977–, Indiana Univ. 1973, Oberlin Conservatory 1976; Co-Dir Bath Summer School of Baroque Music, England 1979–89, Connecticut Early Music Festival 1982–99. *Compositions:* Cadenzas, Mozart's Flute Concertos. *Recordings:* Ibert, Jolivet, Honegger Flute Concertos 1975, Two Malcolm Arnold Flute Concertos 1977, Romantic Music for Flute and Orchestra 1978, Mozart Flute Concertos 1980, Telemann Duets 1981, Bach Flute Sonatas 1988, Vivaldi Bullfinch Concerto 1992, Bach, Handel, Telemann Trio Sonatas 1992, Sonatas by Telemann, Handel, Vinci, Scarlatti, J. C. Bach, C. P. E. Bach, Mozart 1994, Works by Kupferman, Laderman, Beeson, Luening, Kraft and Nowak 1994, Handel Trio Sonata in C Minor 1995, Hummel's chamber arrangements of Mozart symphonies 35 and 36 1997, Shadow by David MacBride 1995, Works by J. S. Bach, C. P. E. Bach, W. F. Bach and J. C. Bach 2001, Trio Sonatas by de la Barre, Hotteterre, Couperin, Leclair 2003, Music composed for Lord Abingdon by Haydn, Abel, Gretry, J. C. Bach 2003, Six Concertos for Two Flutes by Telemann 2004. *Publication:* The Early Flute 1992. *Honours:* winner Philadelphia Orchestra Youth Contest 1957. *Address:* 10 Bobwhite Drive, Westport, CT 06880, USA. *E-mail:* jhsolum@optonline.net.

**SOLYOM, Janos Paul;** Hungarian/Swedish concert pianist and conductor; b. 26 Oct. 1938, Budapest; s. of Dr I. Solyom and M. Weill; m. Camilla Lundberg 1987. *Education:* Franz Liszt Acad. of Music, Budapest. *Career:* pvt. studies with Ilona Kabos in London and with Nadia Boulanger in Paris; int. concert career 1958–; mem. Royal Swedish Acad. of Music. *Honours:* Royal Swedish Medal for Outstanding Artistic Merit 'Litteris et Artibus'. *Address:* Norr Mälarstrand 54, VII 112 20 Stockholm, Sweden. *Telephone:* (8) 652-42-72. *Fax:* (8) 652-42-72. *E-mail:* pianos@solyom.com (home). *Website:* www .solyom.com (home).

**SOLYOM-NAGY, Sandor;** Singer (Baritone); b. 21 Dec. 1941, Siklos, Hungary. *Education:* Ferenc Liszt Academy of Music, Budapest, 1960. *Career:* Budapest State Opera, 1964–; Numerous guest performances in Berlin, Brussels, Bratislava, Prague, Cologne, Barcelona, Moscow, Leningrad, Genoa, Rome, The Hague, Rotterdam, Paris, Rio de Janeiro, São Paulo, Sofia, Varna and Vienna; Frequent guest appearances with Bavarian State Opera at Munich in Germany and Vienna State Opera in Austria and Japan; Regular guest artist at Bayreuth Festival from 1981 including Grail Knight in Parsifal in 1992; Sang Palatine Gara in Erkel's Hunyadi László at Budapest in 1989; Sang Amonasro at Budapest, 2000. *Recordings:* Numerous records including Liszt's Christus Oratorio, The Legend of Elisabeth, Via Crucis, Goldmark's The Queen of Sheba, Agamemnon in Gluck's Iphigénie en Aulide, the title role in Kodály's Háry János and in Strauss's Guntram and Respighi's La Fiamma. *Honours:* Liszt Prize, 1972; Merited Artist of Hungary, 1977; Hector Berlioz Prize, French Record Academy; Grand Prix, French Record Academy; Charles Cros Prize; Golden Orpheus Prize, French Record Academy; Excellent Artist of Hungary, 1987; Kossuth Prize, 1998. *Address:* c/o Budapest State Opera, Budapest, Hungary.

**SOMACH, Beverly;** Violinist; b. 17 Jan. 1935, New York, NY, USA; m. S George Silverstein, 20 August 1959, 2 s., 2 d. *Education:* BS, Columbia University, 1956; Certificate of Completion of Studies with Jascha Heifetz, University of California, Los Angeles, 1959. *Career:* Recitals, Town Hall, Carnegie Hall, Lincoln Center, Alice Tully Hall, New York City; Recitals in London (Wigmore Hall, Purcell Room), Edinburgh, Glasgow, Stockholm, Copenhagen, Zürich, Paris, Tokyo, Hong Kong, Montreal; Soloist with Orchestra: New York Philharmonic, Chicago Symphony, Los Angeles Symphony, American Symphony, Orchestra Luxembourg. *Recordings:* For Newport Classic, Heritage Society, Radio Free Europe, Voice of America. *Contributions:* New York Times; Musical America. *Current Management:* Seymour F. Malkin Management.

**SOMARY, Johannes (Felix);** Musician; b. 7 April 1935, Zürich, Switzerland; m. Anne Van Zandt, 20 July 1963, 2 s., 1 d. *Education:* BA, Yale University, 1957; MMus, Yale School of Music, 1959. *Career:* Debut: As Conductor with Washington Square Music Festival, New York, 1960; Founder, Music Director and Conductor of Amor Artis, New York City, 1962–; Chairman, Arts and Music Department, Horace Mann School, New York City, 1971–2002; Conductor for Fairfield County Chorale, 1975–, Great Neck Choral Society, 1982–94, Taghkanic Chorale, 1992–99; Artist-in-Residence at St Jean Baptiste Church, 1985–; Music Dir, St Patrick's Cathedral, 2001–03; Appeared as Guest Conductor at Madeira Bach Festival, 1985, Dubrovnik Music Festival, 1986, Sion Music Festival, Switzerland, 1990, with Polish radio and television Orchestra, 1990, and with Royal Philharmonic, London,

New Orleans Philharmonic, others; Composition commissions include This Is Life, oratorio for Jefferson Music Festival, 1994, The Ultimate Quest, for Great Neck Choral Society, Liturgy in E-flat, for Blessed Sacrament Fathers' Centennial Celebration, and Te Deum, for Benedictinus, premiered in Rome, 2000; Violin Concerto, premiered in St Petersburg, Russia, 2004; mem, American Choral Directors' Association; Chorus America; American Symphony Orchestra League. Recordings include: Handel's Messiah, Theodora, Jephtha, Semele, Bach's Mass in B Minor, and St Matthew Passion as Conductor with the English Chamber Orchestra; Additional recordings of works by Haydn, Tchaikovsky, Schütz, Mozart, Prokofiev, Kurt Weill; Mozart's Requiem (Amor Artis Chorus and Orchestra), 1996; Haydn's Creation, 1998; Vivaldi's Four Seasons; Handel's Acis and Galatea; Saint-Saëns's Requiem. Current Management: MPL, c/o Michael Leavitt, 170 West 74th Street, New York, NY 10023, USA. Address: 620 West 254th Street, Bronx, New York, NY 10471, USA.

**SOMFAI, László,** DipMus, DMus; Hungarian musicologist; Professor Emeritus, Ferenc Liszt Academy of Music; b. 15 Aug. 1934, Jászladány; m. Dorrit Révész-Somfai; one s. one d. Education: Ferenc Liszt Acad. of Music, Budapest, Hungarian Acad. of Sciences, Budapest. Career: Music Librarian at National Széchényi Library, Budapest until 1962; Head of Budapest Bartók Archives, Institute for Musicology, Hungarian Academy of Sciences, 1972–2004; Professor of Musicology, Ferenc Liszt Academy of Music, 1980–2004, Prof. Emer. 2005–; mem, Zentralinstitut der Mozartforschung, Salzburg; Joseph Haydn Institut, Cologne; Corresponding Member, Hungarian Academy of Sciences; mem, American Musicological Society, British Academy, Academia Europaea; Last President, International Musicological Society. Publications: Haydn als Opernkapellmeister (co-author) 1960, Joseph Haydn: Sein Leben in Zeitgenössischen Bildern 1966, Anton Webern 1968, The Keyboard Sonatas of Joseph Haydn 1979, 18 Bartók Studies 1981, Béla Bartók: Composition, Concepts and Autograph Sources 1996; studies on Haydn, Liszt, Stravinsky, Webern and Bartók; critical editions in Mozart Neue Ausgabe, Gluck Neue Ausgabe, Musica Rinata; Ed., Documenta Bartókiana. Address: Falk Miksa u 12, V4, 1055 Budapest, Hungary.

**SON, Dang Thai;** Pianist; b. 1950, Hanoi, Viet Nam. Education: Diploma, 1976; Moscow Tchaikovsky Conservatory, 1983. Career: Appearances at Several Major Festivals, including, Berlin, Geneva, Ravinia, Miami, Paris, Brescia, Bergamo, Cannes, Prague Spring, Dubrovnik, Bratislava, Russian Winter, December Nights, Chopin Festival of Nohant, Ruhr Piano Festival; Tour of North America, 1989; Played with World-Famous Orchestras including, Leningrad Philharmonic, Montreal Symphony, BBC Philharmonic, Dresden Philharmonic, Staatskapelle Berlin, Oslo Philharmonic, Warsaw National Philharmonic, Prague Symphony, NHK Symphony, Helsinki Philharmonic, Sydney Symphony, Hungarian Symphony, Moscow Philharmonic; Appearances with the Virtuosi of Moscow, the Polish, Moscow and Zürich Chamber Orchestras and with Sinfonia Varsovia; Honorary Professor, Kunitachi Music College, Tokyo. Honours: Gold Medal, 10th International Chopin Piano Competition, Warsaw, 1980. Address: c/o Latitude 45, Arts Promotion Inc, 109 St Joseph Blvd West, Montreal, QC H2T 2P7, Canada.

**SONDEREGGER, Peter;** Swiss composer and musician; b. 2 Oct. 1960, St Gallen. Education: Konservatorium Basel with Jacques Wildberger, Musikhochschule Karlsruhe, Germany with Wolfgang Rihm. Career: performer of 16th- and 17th-century music. Compositions: Delirien I–III, chamber ensembles and live electronics, 1981–83; Piano Concerto No. 1, 1985; Tombeau per tre Clarinetti, 1985; Eclairs Errants, piano and orchestra, 1986–87; Webern-Variations to Symphony Op 21, for orchestra, 1987; Zeit, Verjüngendes Licht, clarinet, viola and guitar, 1987–88; 73 Pezzi Degli Scrovegni, piano, 1989–90; Missa Incontri, piano trio, 1990–91; Auslöschung, for panflute and double-string quartet, 1991; Conductus II, violin and organ, 1993–94; Various other compositions for chamber ensembles, piano solo, guitar Solo; Quaenam sit divina caligo, for female voices and violins, 1994; La Mallorquina, for violin and piano, 1995; Conductus IV for 2 saxophones. Recordings: Tombeau per tre Clarinetti; Zeit, Verjüngendes Licht. Honours: scholarships to Heinrich Strobel-Stiftung des Südwestfunks 1986, Schweizerischer Tonkünstlerverein 1987. Address: Unterdorf 10, 4203 Grellingen, Switzerland.

**SONDHEIM, Stephen Joshua,** BA; American composer and lyricist; b. 22 March 1930, New York, NY; s. of Herbert Sondheim and Janet Fox. Education: George School, Newtown, PA, Williams Coll., Williamstown, MA, private instruction. Career: Pres. Dramatists' Guild 1973–81, Council mem. 1981–; Visiting Prof. of Drama and Musical Theatre, Univ. of Oxford Jan.–June 1990; mem. American Acad. and Inst. of Arts and Letters 1983–. Compositions: television: Topper (co-author) 1953, Evening Primrose (music and lyrics) 1967; lyrics: West Side Story 1957, Gypsy 1959, Do I Hear a Waltz? 1965, Candide 1973; music and lyrics: A Funny Thing Happened on the Way to the Forum 1962, Anyone Can Whistle 1964, Evening Primrose 1966, Company 1970, Follies 1971, A Little Night Music 1973, The Frogs 1974, Pacific Overtures 1976, Sweeney Todd 1978, Merrily We Roll Along 1981, Sunday in the Park with George 1984, Into the Woods (Drama Critics' Circle Award 1988) 1986, Follies 1987, Assassins 1991, Passion 1994, Wise Guys 2001; anthologies: Side by Side by Sondheim 1976, Marry Me a Little 1980, You're Gonna Love Tomorrow 1983, Putting It Together 1993; screenplays: (with Anthony Perkins) The Last of Sheila 1973, Birdcage 1996, Getting Away Murder 1996; film scores: Stavisky 1974, Reds 1981, Dick Tracy 1989; incidental music: The Girls of Summer 1956, Invitation to a March 1961,

Twigs 1971. Honours: Antoinette Perry Awards for Company 1971, Follies 1972, A Little Night Music 1973, Sweeney Todd 1979; Drama Critics' Awards 1971, 1972, 1973, 1976, 1979; Evening Standard Drama Award 1996; Grammy Awards 1984, 1986; Nat. Medal of Arts 1997, Praemium Imperial 2000. Current Management: c/o John Breglio, 1285 Avenue of the Americas, New York, NY 10019, USA.

**SONEK, Frantisek;** Pianist and Conductor; b. 12 April 1933, Opava, Czechoslovakia; m. Lubomíra Záskodná, 1 Aug 1959, 2 d. Education: Piano and conducting at Conservatory in Ostrava; Conducting at Janáček Academy of Music Arts in Brno (JAMU). Career: Debut: Ballet, Fairy-tale about John by Oskar Nedbal in Theatre Ostrava (as conductor), Czech Republic; Teacher at Conservatories of Ostrava and Brno, 1965–69; Then Janáček Academy of Music Arts (JAMU) in Brno mainly as Pianist-Choral Répétiteur, 1969–; Also Pianist-Choral Répétiteur in Opera House of Opava, 1960–64: Conductor-Assistant, Janáček Opera in Brno (music of Smetana, Dvořák, Janáček, Bizet, Moniuszko, Rimsky-Korsakov, Tchaikovsky); mem, Chief and Conductor of Amateur Symphony Orchestra of Railwaymen in Brno, 1978–. Recordings: Janáček's operas Jenůfa and Excursions of Mr Brouček. Contributions: JAMU: About Janáček's Glagolitic Mass and its Problems, 1972. Address: Milénova 12, Brno 38, Czech Republic 63800.

**SONNTAG, Ulrike;** German singer (soprano); b. 1959, Esslingen. Education: Studied with Eva Sava and Dietrich Fischer-Dieskau; Hartmann-Dressler. Career: Debut: Sang Oriane in Amadis de Gaul by J C Bach as guest with the Hamburg Staatsoper, 1983; Sang at the Stadttheater Heidelberg, 1984–86; Nationaltheater Mannheim, 1986–88; Has appeared in concerts all over Europe, festivals of Salzburg, Vienna, Berlin, Frankfurt, Schwetzingen and in the USA (Los Angeles), China, Brazil, Japan; Member of the Stuttgart Opera from 1988, as Euridice, Susanna, Donna Elvira, Marcellina, Pamina, Marie, Ännchen, Micaela, Nedda, Frau Fluth, Gretel, Sophie in Der Rosenkavalier and Helena (A Midsummer Night's Dream); Sang Aennchen in Der Freischütz at the 1988 Ludwigsburg Festival; Member of Vienna State Opera for 1991–94, repertoire including Susanna, Pamina, Micaela, Zdenka, Musetta; Pamina, 1992; Freischütz production, Trieste, 1994; Wildschütz production, Cologne, 1994; Lieder tour, Moscow and St Petersburg, 1994; Guest appearances: Deutsche Oper, Berlin; Frankfurt, Belinda, Marcellina, Musetta; Monte Carlo, Ännchen, 1990; Cairo, Rosina in Haydn's La Vera Costanza, 1990; Trieste, Ännchen, 1994, Euridice, 1995; Tel-Aviv Opera with Der Freischütz, 1996; Appeared in Don Giovanni at Berlin in 1997; Season 1998 in Cagliari with Wagner's Die Feen and with Carmen at St Margarethen in Austria. Recordings include: Bach Cantatas; Bach: B minor Mass with Rilling; Mignon lieder, Schubert, Schumann, Wolf; Milhaud, songs and chamber music; Hindemith: Das Unaufhörliche; Bach; Video of Der Freischütz, DVD of Die Zauberflöte, CD: Herbsttag (Rilke Songs). Address: Steigstrasse 21, 71394 Kernen, Germany. E-mail: UlrikeSonntag@z.zgs.de (home).

**SOOTER, Edward;** Singer (Tenor); b. 8 Dec. 1934, Salina, Kansas, USA. Education: Studied at the Friends University in Wichita with Elsa Haury, Kansas University with Joseph Wilkins and the Hamburg Musikhochschule with Helmut Melchert. Career: Debut: Bremerhaven, 1966, as Florestan; Sang in Kiel, Karlsruhe, Wiesbaden, Munich, Frankfurt and Cologne; Metropolitan Opera from 1979, as Florestan, Tannhäuser, Otello, Aeneas in Les Troyens, Walther, Tristan and Lohengrin; Sang Siegmund in Ring cycles at Seattle; New Orleans Opera, 1992, as Florestan; Other roles include Parsifal, Don José, Canio, Aegisthus, Manrico, Ernani, Samson, and Babinsky in Schvanda the Bagpiper; Sang Siegmund at Flagstaff, 1996. Address: c/o Thea Dispeker Artists' Management, 59 E 54th, New York, NY 10021, USA.

**SOPRONI, Jozsef;** Composer; b. 4 Oct. 1930, Sopron, Hungary. Education: Studied at the Budapest Academy of Music, 1949–56. Career: Faculty Member at Bela Bartók School, Budapest, from 1957; Professor, Budapest Academy of Music, from 1977 (on faculty from 1962); Rector at Budapest Academy 1988–94. Compositions include: Concerto for Strings 1953; 10 String quartets, 1958–94; Carmina polinaesiana cantata for women's chorus and ensemble, 1963; Ovidi metamorphoses, for soprano, chorus and orchestra, 1965; 2 Cello concertos, 1967, 1984; 6 Symphonies, No. 1 1975, No. 2 The Seasons 1977, No. 3 Sinfonia da Requiem, for soloists, chorus and orchestra, 1980, No. 4 1994, No. 5 1995, No. 6, 1995; Horn sonata, 1976; Six Bagatelles for wind quintet, 1977; Late Summer Caprices for string trio and piano, 1978; 2 violin sonatas, 1979, 1980; Violin Concerto, 1983; Comments on a Theme by Handel, for orchestra, 1985; Antigone, opera, 1987; Three Pieces for orchestra, 1988; Magnificat for soloists, chorus and orchestra, 1989; Missa Scarbantiensis, 1991; Missa Choralis, 1992; Missa super B-A-C-H, 1992; Litaniae Omnium Sanctorum, 1993; Pslam XXIX for chorus, organ, trumpet and trombone, 1993; Missa Gurcensis for chorus and ensemble, 1994; Te Deum, for soloists, chorus and orchestra; Livre d'orgue, 9 pieces, 1994; 12 Piano sonatas, 1996–98; Piano concerto, 1997; Chamber Concerto No. 2, for 12 instruments, 1998; Das Marienleben, for soprano and piano, 1998. Piano Music, songs and choruses. Address: II Pajzs-u 22/b, 1025, Budapest, Hungary.

**SORDELLO, Enzo;** Singer (Baritone); b. 20 April 1927, Pievebovigliano, Macerata, Italy. Education: Studied at the Torino Conservatory and Scuola di Perfezio namento per Giovani Artisti del Teatro Alla Scala of Milan. Career: Debut: Teatro Toselli in Cueno as Enrico in Lucia di Lammermoor, 1952; La Scala, 1954–75, as Cinna in La Vestale opposite Callas; Later appeared in Milan as Belcore, Albert in Werther, Gerard in Andrea Chénier in 1955 and as

Tonio; Sang at Metropolitan Opera in 1956 as Marcello, Malatesta, Enrico and Ashtou, Vienna Staatsoper in 1959, Stoll Theatre in London in 1960 and Glyndebourne Festival, 1961–62, as Belcore; Frequent broadcasts on RAI. *Recordings include:* La Fanciulla del West; La Vestale, Pagliacci; Madama Butterfly; Lucia di Lammermoor. *Publications:* Enzo Sordello, Autobiografia-Veritá di vu Baritono (Il "Fattaçcio" Çallas-Sordello-Metropolitan of New York). *Address:* Villa America, 12018 Roccavione, Cueno, Italy.

**SORENSON VON GERTTEN, Iwa (Cecilia);** Singer (Soprano); b. 5 Sept. 1946, Gothenburg, Sweden; m. Gustf von Gertten, 5 July 1980, 2 s. *Education:* Music Conservatory, Gothenburg, 1966–74; Staatliche Hochschule für Musik, Cologne, 1970–71; Trained as Singer, Singing Teacher and Organist, School of Theatre and Opera, Gothenburg, 1974–75, 1976–77. *Career:* Debut: Malmö, Sweden, as Norina in Donizetti's Don Pasquale, 1978; Opera soloist at Malmö Stadsteater, 1978–79 and Royal Opera of Stockholm, 1979–; Major roles include Rosina in The Barber of Seville, Musetta in La Bohème, Sophie in Der Rosenkavalier, Zdenka in Arabella, Fiordiligi in Così fan tutte, Susanna in The Marriage of Figaro, Blonde in The Abduction from the Seraglio, Aminta in Il Re Pastore, Violetta in La Traviata, Marguerite in Faust, and Olympia in Tales of Hoffmann; Roles in operettas include Adele in Die Fledermaus, Laura in Der Bettelstudent by Millöcker, Josephine in HMS Pinafore, and Fiametta in Boccaccio by von Suppé; Concert repertoire includes Handel's Messiah and Judas Maccabaeus, Haydn's Creation, Mendelssohn's Elijah, and Mozart's Requiem and Mass in C minor; Recitals with piano of German Lieder, French Art Songs, Swedish repertoire and contemporary music. *Recordings:* Mostly 19th and 20th Century Swedish Music. *Honours:* 3 Gramophone Prizes, 1983, 1984, 1985. *Address:* Hogbergsgatan 26B, 11620 Stockholm, Sweden.

**SORG-ROSE, Margarete;** German composer and publisher; b. 11 April 1960, Remscheid; d. of Margarete Sorg. *Education:* piano and conducting studies in Mainz, composition in Cologne with Hans Werner Henze and Krzysztof Meyer, Univs of Mainz and Tübingen. *Career:* Bachchor (choir) coach, Mainz 1985–87; Production Asst Zweites Deutsches Fernsehen (ZDF), Mainz 1987; freelance composer 1992–; works performed at nat. and int. concerts and festivals, including Festival Cantiere Int. d'Arte Montepulciano (Italy) 1990; compositions include pieces for orchestra, choir, Lieder and chamber music. *Honours:* Johann-Wenzel-Stamitz-Förderpreis for Composition 1993, Kompositionsauftrag des Landes Rheinland-Pfalz 1994, Kompositionsaufträge der Villa-Musica-Stiftung 1995, 1997, Auftragskomposition der Mozart-Gesellschaft Kurpfalz e.V. 1996, Art-Gedok-Nadel 1996 and other prizes. *Address:* Henkellstr. 3, 65187 Wiesbaden, Germany. *Fax:* (611) 691216. *E-mail:* margaretesorg-rose@t-online.de.

**SOROKINA, Elena;** Pianist and Music Historian; b. 6 April 1940, Moscow, USSR; m. Alexander Bakhchiev, 28 Nov 1962, 1 d. *Education:* Graduated, Central School of Music, 1958; MA, Performance, MA, History of Music, 1963, PhD, 1965, Moscow State Conservatory. *Career:* Debut: Duet concert (with husband), Mozart, Schubert, Central Arts House, Moscow; Professor, 1965–, Chief, Chair of Russian Music History, 1992–, Moscow State Conservatory; Regular duet performances, Beethoven, Mozart, Weber, Schumann, Schubert, Brahms, Glinka, Borodin, Rachmaninov, other Russian composers, music genres, history of Moscow Conservatory, 1969–; Series of television programmes, chamber music concerts, 1970s; Tours lecturing on Russian music, France, Austria, Latin America; International/national festivals of music, Moscow, Leningrad (with husband); Mozart International Festival, Tokyo (1991); English tour (Cambridge, London), Soviet and British modern piano duets; Concerts with husband, Israel, Italy, Germany, USA, 1992–93; 8 programmes, all Schubert piano duets, with husband; Piano duo festivals, Novosibirsk and Ekaterinburg, 1993–95; Works dedicated to her and husband by Boyarsky, Lubovksy, Fried, Manukyan and Moore. *Recordings include:* Piano duets with husband: Rachmaninov; Russian Salon Piano Music; Mozart; Schubert; Music of France; Weber, Schumann, Mendelssohn; V Persichetti; Bartók, Lutoslawski; Enescu; Albums: Music of Old Vienna; J. S. Bach, his family and pupils; Music for 6 and 8 hands (with G Rozhdestvensky, V Postnikova). *Publications:* Piano Duet (history of genre), 1988. *Address:* 4-32 Koshkin Str, Moscow 115409, Russia.

**SOTIN, Hans;** German singer (bass); b. 10 Sept. 1939, Dortmund; m. Regina Elsner 1964; three c. *Education:* Dortmund Musikhochschule. *Career:* with Opera House, Essen 1962–64; State Opera, Hamburg 1964–, State Opera, Vienna 1970–; perm. mem. Bayreuth Festival 1971–; guest appearances worldwide; pvt. singing teacher. *Recordings include:* Tannhäuser, Aida, Fidelio, Salome, Così fan tutte, Die Walküre, Parisfal, Paukenmesse. *Honours:* Forderpreis des Landes, Friedrich Oberdörfer Preis, Kammersänger. *Address:* c/o Askonas Holt Ltd, Lonsdale Chambers, 27 Chancery Lane, London, WC2A 1PF, England; 2106 Bendestorf, Schulheide 10, Germany. *Telephone:* (4183) 6614.

**SOUDANT, Hubert;** Dutch conductor; b. 16 March 1946, Maastricht. *Education:* studied at Maastricht Conservatory, with Franco Ferrara in Italy and at Netherlands Radio Course in Hilversum. *Career:* Asst Conductor with Hilversum Radio Orchestra 1967–70; has conducted Orchestra of Radio France and Nouvel Orchestre Philharmonique, with which he gave the French premiere of Mahler's 10th Symphony at Strasbourg in 1979; conducted premieres of Rene Koering's opera Elseneur and Nana Symphonie by Marius Constant 1980; Conductor Symphony Orchestra of Utrecht 1982; Musical Dir with Orchestra Sinfonica dell'Emilia Romagna Arturo Toscanini, Parma 1988; Guest Conductor in England, Germany, Belgium, Italy, Scandinavia, South

Africa and Japan; conducted Ernani in Parma 1990, Berlioz's Faust in Turin 1992. *Recordings:* Tchaikovsky 4th and 6th Symphonies and Romeo and Juliet with London Philharmonic, Liszt Piano Concertos with London Philharmonic Orchestra. *Honours:* Winner, Int. Competition for Young Conductors at Besançon 1971, Second Prize, Herbert von Karajan Int. Conducting Competition 1973, First Prize, Guido Cantelli Int. Conducting Competition, Milan 1975. *Current Management:* Baron & Weingartner KEG, International Artists Management, Bösendorferstrasse 4/12, 1010 Vienna, Austria. *Telephone:* (1) 489-61-54. *Fax:* (1) 489-61-54-44. *E-mail:* schwemle@baronartists.com. *Website:* www.baronartists.com.

**SOUKUPOVA, Vera;** Singer (Contralto); b. 12 April 1932, Prague, Czechoslovakia. *Education:* Studied in Prague with L Kaderabek and A Mustanova-Linkova. *Career:* Has sung in concert from 1955; Stage debut in 1957 at Pilsen; Member of the Prague National Opera from 1960; Tour of Russia in 1961 and sang Dalila in Bordeaux; Guest appearances in Vienna, France and Switzerland; Sang at State Operas of Hamburg and Berlin, 1969–71; Prague National Opera in 1983 as Radmila in Smetana's Libuše. *Recordings:* Erda in The Ring; Dvořák's Stabat Mater; Lieder by Mahler; Choral Symphony; Libuše; The Brandenburgers in Bohemia; The Bride of Messina by Fibich; Oedipus Rex; Janáček's Glagolitic Mass. *Address:* c/o National Theatre, PO Box 865, 112 30 Prague 1, Czech Republic.

**SOUNOVA, Daniela;** Singer (Soprano); b. 17 May 1943, Prague, Czech Republic. *Education:* Studied in Prague. *Career:* Debut: Sang at the National Theatre Prague, from 1973, notably in the 1974 premiere of Coriolanus by Jan Cikker and lyric roles in operas by Mozart, Smetana, Bizet, Puccini and Prokofiev; Guest appearances at Bologna and the Edinburgh Festival; Sang Donna Elvira in the bi-centenary performances of Don Giovanni, in Prague, 1987; Savonlinna Festival 1991, in Dvořák's Rusalka; Many concert and recital engagements. *Recordings include:* Rusalka, The Jacobin by Dvořák, The Bride of Messina by Fibich, and Don Giovanni (Supraphon); Mahler's 8th Symphony (Ariola –Eurodisc). *Address:* c/o National Theatre, PO Box 865, 11230 Prague 1, Czech Republic.

**SOUSTROT, Marc;** Conductor; b. 15 April 1949, Lyon, France. *Education:* Studied trombone at the Lyon Conservatoire, 1962–69, and conducting with Manuel Rosenthal at the Paris Conservatoire, 1969–76. *Career:* Assistant to André Previn with the London Symphony Orchestra, 1974–76; Deputy Conductor, 1976, then Musical Director of the Orchestre Philharmonique of the Loire; Artistic Director of the Nantes Opera, 1986–90; Conducted the premieres of Claude Baliff's Fantasio Grandioso in 1977, 1st Piano Concerto by Maurice Ohana in 1981, and Concerto for Orchestra by Alain Louvier, 1987; Conducted Tristan and Isolde at Nantes, 1989, Manon Lescaut, 1990, Les Contes d'Hoffmann at Geneva in 1990, and Carmen at the Bregenz Festival, Austria; Conducted Rheingold at Bonn, 1997. *Recordings:* Trumpet Concertos with Maurice André; Music by Franceschini, Scarlatti, Vivaldi, Tartini and Telemann with the Monte Carlo National Opera Orchestra. *Honours:* Winner, Rupert Foundation Competition for Young Conductors, London, 1974; International Competition at Besançon, 1975. *Address:* Orchestra of Bonn, Germany.

**SOUTHAM, Ann;** Composer; b. 4 Feb. 1937, Winnipeg, Manitoba, Canada. *Education:* Composition at the Royal Conservatory of Music, Toronto; electronic music at the University of Toronto. *Career:* Associated with the Toronto Dance Theatre and other modern dance companies, and Arraymusic and other concert music ensembles and soloists. *Compositions:* Throughways: Improvising Music, for ensemble, 1988; In a Measure of Time for two pianos, 1988; Song of the Varied Thrush, for string quartet, 1991; The Music so Far for clarinet and piano, 1992; Webster's Spin, for strings, 1993; Remembering Schubert, for piano, 19993; Full circles, for trumpet, violin, vibraphone and piano, 1996; Electro Acoustic: Emerging Ground, 1983; Tuning, and Re-Tuning, for Viola and tape 1982, 1985; Music for Slow Dancing, 1985; Fluke Sound, 1989; Figures for solo piano and string orchestra, 2002. *Address:* c/o SOCAN, 41 Valleybrook Drive, Don Mills, Ontario, M3B 2S6, Canada.

**SOUTHGATE, Sir William David,** Kt; Conductor and Composer; b. 4 Aug. 1941, Waipukarau, New Zealand. *Education:* Otago University and the Guildhall School of Music. *Career:* Freelance Composer in London and guest musical director of the Royal Shakespeare Company; Conductor and Arranger for the Phoenix Opera Company; Musical Director of the Wellington Youth Orchestra from 1977; Musical Director of the Christchurch Symphony Orchestra from 1984; Has conducted operas by Rossini, Verdi and Johann Strauss for the Wellington and Canterbury Opera Companies; Prsenter of music programmes on New Zealand radio and television; Toured Finland as Conductor, 1986, Sweden and Finland, 1989; Debut in Honolulu Symphony, 1989; Tour of New Zealand with the Royal New Zealand Ballet Company, 1989; Premieres of children's opera Faery Tale and Cello Concerto in New Zealand, 1990; Also engaged for the Dunedin Sinfonia, New Zealand, 1991; St Matthews Chamber Orchestra, New Zealand, 1991; SWF Sinfonia Orchestra, Spohr Competition, Baden-Baden, 1991; Christchurch Symphony Orchestra, New Zealand, 1991; New Zealand Symphony Orchestra, 1992. *Recordings include:* Second Symphony. *Honours:* Guildhall School conducting prize; 2nd prize, Besançon Conducting Competition.

**SOVERAL, Isabel;** Composer; b. 25 Dec. 1961, Oporto, Portugal. *Education:* Lisbon Conservatory, 1984-88, with Joly Braga Santos; NY State University at Stony Brook, from 1988. *Career:* Lecturer at the University of Aveiro. *Compositions:* Contornos, I, for two clarinets (1987), II, for oboe and bassoon

(1987), III, for four clarinets (1990); Pensando, enredano sombras, for low voice and orchestra, 1991; Quadramorphosis (1993); Anamorphoses I, for clarinet and tape (1993), II, marimba, vibraphone and tape (1994), III, violin and tape (1995), IV, cello and tape (1997), V, for string quartet (1997); Le Navigateur du soleil incandescent, for baritone, chorus, orchestra and tape, 1998; Un Soir, for baritone and ensemble, 1998. *Address:* c/o SPA, Av. Duque de Loulé 31, 1098 Lisbon Codez, Portugal.

**SOVIERO, Diana;** Singer (Soprano); b. 1952, USA. *Career:* Sang first at St Paul in 1974 appearing as Lauretta in Gianni Schicchi and as Massenet's Manon; Joined the New York City Opera in 1976 and sang further at Miami, San Francisco and Chicago; Metropolitan Opera debut in 1986 as Juliet in Roméo et Juliette; European engagements at Paris, Rome, Florence, Milan, Vienna and Hamburg; Geneva in 1988 as Gretchen in Doktor Faust by Busoni, Philadelphia and San Diego in 1988 as Margherita in Mefistofele and Marguerite in Faust; Sang Juliet and Manon at Montreal in 1989; Covent Garden debut in 1989 as Nedda; Season 1992 as Tosca with Opera Pacific at Costa Mesa, Puccini's Trittico heroines at Dallas, Manon Lescaut at Miami and Adriana Lecouvreur at Sydney; Other roles include Puccini's Butterfly and Mimi, Leila in Les Pêcheurs de Perles and Norina in Don Pasquale; Sang Maddalena in Andrea Chénier at Seattle, 1996 and Monte Carlo 1998; Tosca for Palm Beach Opera, 1998. *Address:* c/o Seattle Opera Association, PO Box 9248, Seattle, WA 98109, USA.

**SOYER, David;** American cellist; b. 24 Feb. 1924, Philadelphia, Pa. *Education:* studied with Emanuel Feuermann and Pablo Casals. *Career:* Played with Bach Aria Group, Guilet Quartet, New Music Quartet and Marlboro Trio; Performed in chamber music with Rudolf Serkin at Marlboro Festival and prompted by Alexander Schneider to co-found the Guarneri String Quartet in 1964; Many tours of American and Europe notably with appearances at the Spoleto Festival in 1965, to Paris with Arthur Rubinstein and London in 1970 in the complete quartets of Beethoven; Noted for performances of the Viennese Classics and works by Walton, Bartók and Stravinsky; Season 1987–88 included tour of Japan, concerts at St John's Smith Square, and Queen Elizabeth Hall in London; Faculty at Curtis Institute, Philadelphia and the University of Maryland. *Recordings include:* Mozart's Quartets dedicated to Haydn; Complete Quartets of Beethoven; With Arthur Rubinstein, Piano Quintets of Schumann, Dvořák and Brahms; Piano Quartets by Fauré and Brahms. *Honours:* hon. doctorates at University of South Florida and State University of New York; Edison Award for Beethoven Recordings, 1971; Many Grammy Awards for recordings. *Address:* 6 West 77th Street, New York, NY 10024, USA.

**SOYER, Roger;** Singer (Bass); b. 1 Sept. 1939, Thiais, France. *Education:* Studied at the Paris Conservatoire with Georges Daum and Georges Jouatte. *Career:* Sang at the Paris Opéra from 1963; Sang at La Scala Milan in 1963 as Tirésias in Les Mamelles de Tirésias by Poulenc, Aix-en-Provence Festival from 1965 as Pluto in Monteverdi's Orfeo, Don Giovanni, Don Basilio and Arkel, Paris in 1965 in Rameau's Hippolyte et Aricie, Wexford Festival in 1968 in La Jolie Fille de Perth by Bizet and US debut at Miami in 1973 as Frère Laurent in Roméo et Juliette by Gounod; Sang at Paris Opéra from 1972 in the premiere of Sud by Stanton Coe, and as Don Giovanni, Procida in Les Vêpres Siciliennes, Ferrando in Il Trovatore, Colline and Mephistopheles, Metropolitan Opera in 1972 and Edinburgh Festival in 1973 as Don Giovanni in a new production of Mozart's opera under Daniel Barenboim; Guest appearances in Cologne, Brussels, Geneva, Chicago, Lisbon, Prague, San Antonio and Salzburg; Sang Rodolfo in La Sonnambula at Geneva in 1982, Sulpice in La Fille du Régiment at Dallas in 1983 and sang in L'Heure Espagnole at Turin in 1992. *Recordings:* Les Troyens and Benvenuto Cellini conducted by Colin Davis; Les Pêcheurs de Perles; L'Enfance du Christ; Mozart's Requiem; Lakmé; Werther; Maria Stuarda by Donizetti; Pelléas et Mélisande; Dardanus by Rameau; David et Jonathas by Charpentier. *Address:* c/o Grand Théâtre de Genève, 11 Boulevard du Théâtre, 1211 Geneva 11, Switzerland.

**SPACAGNA, Maria;** American singer (soprano); b. 1951, Rhode Island. *Education:* New England Conservatory. *Career:* sang with Dallas Opera from 1977, New York City Opera, 1978, St Louis Opera, 1982, and Detroit, 1986; Sang Puccini's Liu at Toronto in 1983 and appeared at Santa Fe, New Orleans and Trieste in 1987; Debut at La Scala Milan in 1988 as Butterfly; Sang at Spoleto Festival in 1988 as Ismene in Traetta's Antigone, sang Mimi for New Orleans Opera in 1989, Liu and Butterfly at Costa Mesa California and Greater Miami Opera in 1990; Appearances at Memphis, the Cologne Opera and elsewhere as Violetta, Susanna, Zerlina, Norina, Gilda, Marguerite, Rusalka, Micaela, Lauretta and Mascagni's Lodoletta; Sang Madama Butterfly at Santa Fe, 1996 and at Montreal 1997; active concert career.

**SPAGNOLI, Pietro;** Singer (Bass-baritone); b. 1958, Rome, Italy. *Career:* Member of Sistine Chapel Choir, and sang in concert; Stage debut Martina Franca, 1987, as Gaffredo in Bellini's Il Pirata, and returned as Achillas in Giulio Cesare and Mangetto in La buona figliuola by Piccinni; La Scala from 1991; Season 1991–92 as Leporello at Prague and Publio in La Clemenza di Tito at the Salzburg Festival; Rome Opera, 1995, as Don Alfonso and Paris Palais Garnier, 1996, as Alidoro in La Cenerentola; Other roles include Rossini's Bartolo and Dandini, Belcore in L'Elisir d'amore and Talbot in Giovanna d'Arco; Sang Mozart's Figaro at Turin, 1998; Sang Rossini's Dandini at Monte Carlo, Taddeo for New Israeli Opera, and Don Alfonso at Aix, 2000. *Recordings include:* L'Elisir d'amore; Rossini's Tancredi. *Address:* c/o Turin Opera, Piazza Castello 215, 10124 Turin, Italy.

**SPAHLINGER, Mathias;** Composer; b. 15 Oct. 1944, Frankfurt, Germany. *Education:* Studied composition and music education with Erhard Karkoschka and Konrad Lechner. *Career:* Lecturer at the Hochschule der Kunst, Berlin, 1978-81; Professor of Karlsruhe Hochschule für Musik, 1983-90; Professor of Composition at Freiberg, 1990-. *Compositions:* Morendi, for orchestra, 1974; éphémène, for percussion and piano, 1977; Extension, for violin and piano; String Quartet, 1982; Inter-mezzo, for piano and orchestra, 1986; Passage/Paysage, for orchestra, 1990; Und als wir, for 54 strings, 1993; Gegen unendlich, for ensemble, 1995; Akt, eine Treppe Herabsteigend, for trombone, bass, clarinet and orchestra, 1998. *Honours:* Boswil Foundation Prizes. *Address:* c/o GEMA, Rosenheimer Str. 11, 81677 Munic, Germany.

**SPANO, Robert;** American conductor and pianist; *Music Director, Atlanta Symphony Orchestra*; b. 1970, Conneaut, OH. *Education:* Oberlin Conservatory, Curtis Inst. with Max Rudolf. *Career:* Music Dir and the Robert Reid Topping Chair, Atlanta Symphony Orchestra 1997–(2009); Music Dir, Brooklyn PO; Dir of Festival of Contemporary Music, Tanglewood 2003–04; appearances with symphonies of Boston, Houston, San Francisco and Chicago; opera engagements at Santa Fe (US premiere of Saariaho's L'amour de loin 2002), New York (Saariaho's Château de l'âme) and Houston (Eugene Onegin); season 2002–03 with the Cleveland and St Louis Symphonies, L'Amour de loin with the BBC SO and the City of Birmingham SO; further modern repertory includes El Niño by Adams, Del Tredici's Child Alice and Billy Budd (Seattle Opera); chamber musician (piano) with mems of American orchestras. *Recordings include:* Rimsky-Korsakov: Scheherazade and Vaughan Williams: A Sea Symphony, Del Tredici: Paul Revere's Ride and Theofanidis: The Here and Now. *Honours:* Dr hc (Bowling Green State Univ., Curtis Inst. of Music) 2004. *Address:* Atlanta Symphony Orchestra, 1293 Peachtree Street, Suite 300, Atlanta, GA 30309-3552, USA. *Website:* www .atlantasymphony.org.

**SPARNAAY, Harry (Willem);** Bass Clarinettist; b. 14 April 1944, Amsterdam, Netherlands; m. Roswitha Sparnaay-Mol. *Education:* Amsterdam Conservatory. *Career:* Debut: Amsterdam in 1969; Performances with many leading orchestras including the BBC Symphony, Rotterdam Philharmonic, ORTF, Concertgebouw and Radio Chamber Orchestra Hilversum; Soloist at festivals of Warsaw, Zagreb, Graz, Madrid, Poitiers, Witten, Como, Paris, Naples and the ISCM World Music Days at Boston, Athens and Bonn; Concerts in Europe and America; Professor of Bass Clarinet and Contemporary Music at Sweelinck Conservatory, Amsterdam-Rotterdam Conservatory and Royal Conservatory, The Hague; Composers who have written for him include Donatoni, Ferneyhough, Bussotti, Isang Yun and Barry Anderson (premiere of ARC), 1987; Appeared at Hudderfield Festival in 1987 with Time And Motion Studies by Ferneyhough; Tour of the United Kingdom in 1989 on the Contemporary Music Network, playing Echange by Xenakis. *Recordings:* Bass Clarinet Identity; Harry Sparnaay/Lucien Goethals; Composers' Voice; Music by Thon Tbuynel; Music by Earle Brown; Bass Clarinet Idenitity 2; The Garden of Delight. *Honours:* First Prize, Bass Clarinet Soloist, International Gaudeamus Competition, 1972. *Address:* Z Buiten Sparne 120, 2012 AD Haarlem, Netherlands.

**SPASOV, Bozhidar;** Composer and Musicologist; b. 13 Aug. 1949, Sofia, Bulgaria. *Education:* Moscow Conservatory, 1970-76, with Edison Denisov. *Career:* Lecturer at Sofia Academy of Music, from 1976; Folkwang Hochschule, Essen, 1990 -; Music performed at Festivals in Dresden, Essen, Darmstadt and Rome. *Compositions:* The Bewitched, chamber opera, 1975; Sinfonie, 1978; Konzertmusik for wind, percussion and two pianos, 1982; Dialog I for two ensembles, 1983; Glagolitic Concerto, for mezzo, harpsichord and 13 strings, 1984; The Beginning, for mezzo and ensemble, 1987; De Profundis, for ensemble, 1988; Violin Concerto, 1988; Prabel 12 for chamber ensemble 1992; Oboe Concerto, 1995; Sandglass for trombone, keyboard and electonics, 1996; The Flight of the Butterfly, for mezzo, flute and harpsichord, 1997. *Address:* c/o MUSICATOR, 63 Tsar Assen Str, 1463 Sofia, Bulgaria.

**SPEECH, Bernadette;** Composer; b. 1 Jan. 1948, Syracuse, USA. *Education:* Columbia University, NY, and in Siena with Franco Donatoni, 1976; State University of NY, Buffalo, with Morton Feldman. *Career:* Administrator of the Composers Forum, 1988-94 and The Kitchen, 1995-. *Compositions:* Shattered Glass, for percussion, 1986; Telepathy Suite, for speaker and ensemble, 1998; Inside Out, for piano, 1987; Les ordes pour quatre, string quartet, 1988; Resoundings, piano four hands, 1990; It Came to me in a Dream, for baritone and ensemble, 1990; Trio des trois, I–III, 1991–92; Angels in the Snow, for piano, 1993; Woman without Adornment, for speaker and ensemble, 1995; Parallel Windows–Unframed, for piano and orchestra, 1995. *Address:* c/o ASCAP, ASCAP Building, One Lincoln Plaza, New York, NY, 10023, USA.

**SPEISER, Elisabeth;** Swiss singer (soprano); b. 15 Oct. 1940, Zürich; m. Hans Jecklin; two c. *Education:* Acad. of Music, Winterthur. *Career:* debut in Zürich; concerts in all European countries and North and South America; Guest at many festivals; Many concerts with Karl Richter; Opera debut as Pamina in Die Zauberflöte, Ludwigsburger Schloss Festspiele, 1972–73; Glyndebourne Festival, 1973; Mélisande, St Gallen, 1974; Euridice, Ludwigsburger Schloss Festspiele, 1975; Many Lieder recitals with Irwin Gage; Television and radio appearances in Germany, Italy, Switzerland; Glyndebourne Festival as Euridice, 1982; mem, Swiss Tonkunstlerverband. *Recordings include:* Secular Cantatas and Geistliche Lieder by JS Bach; Caecilien Mass by Haydn; Carissimi Cantatas; Berg/Schoenberg Lieder; Gluck's Orfeo ed Euridice; Schubert, Lieder, 1984 and 1989; Brahms, Lieder, 1985; Haydn's

Arianna a Naxos and English songs, CD, 1987. *Address:* Au Village, 1742 Autigny, Switzerland.

**SPELINA, Karel;** Czech violist; *Professor (Viola and Chamber Music), Prague Conservatory;* b. 2 Nov. 1936; m. Marie Husickova 7 June 1958; two d. *Education:* Tech. Coll., Conservatory of Music, Plzeň. *Career:* debut with Plzeň Radio Quartet 1963; Principal Viola, Plzeň Radio Orchestra 1962–70, Czech Philharmonic Orchestra 1970–2002; mem. Ars Rediviva Ensemble 1970–, Martinů Piano Quartet 1979–2002; Prof., Prague Conservatory 1994–; has played concertos and orchestral works by Berlioz, J. Reicha, A. Vranitzky, J. V. Stamitz, J. K. Vanhal, J. S. Bach, Martinů, and other composers; sonatas and chamber music by Bach and sons, Telemann, Handel, Mendelssohn, Hindemith, Brahms, Shostakovich, Martinů, Honegger, Milhaud, and others; mem. AHUV, Prague; teacher, Sándor Végh Int. Chamber Music Acad., AMEROPA Int. Chamber Music Acad. *Recordings:* Sonatas of C. P. E. Bach and W. F. Bach, Sonatas of A. Honegger and D. Milhaud, Sonatas of Hindemith, Concertos of Josef Reicha, Complete Sonatas of J. K. Vanhal, first World Recording 1997. *Honours:* City of Plzeň Prize 1968. *Address:* Sturova 32/1153, 14200 Prague 4, Czech Republic. *Telephone:* kspelina@volny.cz (home).

**SPEMANN, Alexander;** Singer (Tenor) and Composer; b. 1 June 1967, Wiesbaden, Germany. *Education:* Studied with Gertie Charlent at the Peter Cornelius Conservatory, Mainz and with Martin Grundler at the Frankfurt Musikhochschule. *Career:* Debut: Tenor solo in Beethoven's Ninth, Milan, 1989; Stage debut as First Armed Man in Die Zauberflöte at Wiesbaden; Many concert and opera appearances at Essen, Vienna, Stuttgart, Cologne, Frankfurt, Munich and Hamburg; Engaged with Bonn Opera from 1993–97, singing Kronthal in Lortzing's Wildschütz, and making debut in a Wagner role as Erik in Der fliegende Holländer; Freelance Film and Theatre music composer, including music for the Hessiche Staatstheater, Wiesbaden; Engaged with Darmstadt since 1997 as young heroic tenor, singing Son-Chong in Land des Lächelns, Don José in Carmen and many other roles; Sang Berg's Alwa at Mainz, 1999; Season 2000–01 as Florestan in the 1805 version of Fidelio, Don José and Herod in Salome. *Recordings include:* Count Rudolf in Weber's Silvana (Marco Polo); Jenik in The Bartered Bride, with the orchestra of North German Radio. *Honours:* Winner, Robert Stolz Competition, Hamburg 1996. *Address:* c/o NWB Apollon & Hermes, PR-Arts-Media Services Production, Im Floegerhof 12, 53819 Neunkirchen/Cologne, Germany.

**SPENCE, Patricia;** Singer (Mezzo-soprano); b. 12 Jan. 1961, Salem, Oregon, USA. *Education:* Studied in San Francisco. *Career:* Debut: San Francisco Opera as Anna in L'Africaine; Has performed the Princess in Suor Angelica, Mother Goose in The Rake's Progress and Meg Page in Falstaff at San Francisco; New York City debut, 1988, as Rosina; Opera Colorado, 1989 as Mistress Quickly; European debut as Edwige in Guillaume Tell at Verona followed by Mozart's Requiem at St Petersburg, Malcolm in La Donna del Lago at La Scala, 1992, and Cenerentola with Phoenix Opera, Arizona; Further engagements as Farnace in Mitridate at St Louis, Tsaura in Tancredi at La Scala, Lola at the Arena di Verona, Cenerentola at Covent Garden, (United Kingdom debut, 1993), and Ramiro in La Finta Giardinera for Welsh National Opera; recitals at Göttingen and Hesse Handel Festivals, further Handel performances with Nicholas McGegan and appearances with San Francisco, Detroit, St Louis and Sacramento Symphonies, and Fresno and Mexico City Philharmonics; Sang Handel's Poro at the Halle Festival, 1998. *Recordings include:* Flora in La Traviata; Handel's La Resurrezione, Messiah and Ottone, conducted by McGegan. *Honours:* Il Cenacolo Award in the 1987 Merola Opera Programme, San Francisco Opera Centre. *Current Management:* Neil Funkhauser. *Address:* c/o San Francisco Opera, War Memorial Opera House, San Francisco, CA 94102, USA.

**SPENCE, Toby;** Singer (Tenor); b. 1968, England. *Education:* Choral scholar at New College, Oxford; Opera School of the Guildhall School. *Career:* Debut: Barbican Hall with the Gothenburg Symphony Orchestra in The Tempest by Sibelius; Concerts with RIAS Berlin in Handel's Theodora, at the Wigmore Hall in Schubertiade series and at the Brighton Festival in the Missa Solemnis; Further concerts include the St Matthew Passion, with Frans Brueggen, Die Schöpfung by Haydn and On Wenlock Edge, by Vaughan Williams (Cheltenham Festival); Other orchestras include the Bournemouth Symphony Orchestra, Royal Philharmonic and Cleveland Orchestra; Season 1995–96 included Welsh National Opera debut, as Idamante in Idomeneo, Pane in La Calisto under René Jacobs at Brussels, and in Verdi's Alzira at Covent Garden; Season 1996–97 at the Salzburg Festival in Mitridate, as Tamino at Brussels and with the Israel Philharmonic and San Francisco Symphony Orchestras; Sang in Roméo et Juliette by Berlioz at the London Festival Hall, 1999; Jacquino in Fidelio at the Paris Châtelet, 2002. *Recordings include:* Albums with DGG, Decca, BMG and EMI; St Matthew Passion (Philips Classics). *Address:* 408 The Royle Building, 23–41 Wenlock Road, London, N1 7SH.

**SPERSKI, Krzysztof;** Violoncellist and Teacher; b. 11 June 1942, Kraków, Poland; m. Janina Duda, 24 June 1967, divorced 1986, 1 s. *Education:* MA (cello class of Professor R Suchecki), Academy of Music, Gdansk, 1969; Doctorate (Adjunct qualification), Academy of Music, Poznan, 1978; Habilitation (Docent qualification), Academy of Music, Łódź, 1985. *Career:* Debut: Debut recital by Association of Polish Artist Musicians, Gdansk, 1964; Soloist of symphony concerts, recitals, chamber concerts in Poland and foreign concert tours, Finland, the United Kingdom, Sweden, Germany, Romania,

Bulgaria, Iceland, Czechoslovakia, Austria, Greece, Italy, Denmark, Lithuania, Peru, Switzerland, Netherlands, Belgium, Russia, Chile; Professor of Cello, Academy of Music, Gdansk; Guest Professor, Music Masterclasses, Mynä m äki, Finland, 1976, International Music Seminar, Kozani, Greece, 1990–99, Masterclasses Santiago, Chile, 1998–2000, Lima, Peru, 2000; mem, Association of Polish Artist Musicians. *Recordings:* Radio and television recordings; CD, Slavic Music, 1994; Music Treasures of Gdansk, 1997. *Publications:* About faults of position, left and right hand of young cellists, 1979; Characteristics of Musical Utterance, 1981; Remarks of Performing Violoncello Baroque Music in the Light of Traditions and Contemporary Requirements, 1988; Polish Violoncello Pedagogic Literature, 1988. *Honours:* Award for Polish Culture, 1979; Distinction of Merit, Town of Gdansk, 1981; Gold Cross of Merit, 1985. *Address:* ul Goralska 55/A/9, 80-292 Gdańsk, Poland.

**SPICER, Paul,** FRSA; British choral conductor, composer and record producer; b. 1952. *Education:* New Coll., Oxford, Royal Coll. of Music, London. *Career:* taught music at Uppingham School and Ellesmere Coll. 1974–84; Producer, BBC Radio 3 1984–86; Sr Producer, BBC Midlands Region 1986–2001; founder and Dir, Finzi Singers 1987–; Artistic Dir, Lichfield Int. Arts Festival 1990–2001; Dir, Abbotsholme Arts Soc. 1990–2001; Conductor, Birmingham Bach Choir 1992–, Royal Coll. of Music Chamber Choir 1995–, Whitehall Choir, London 2000–; Prof. of Choral Conducting, Royal Coll. of Music. *Compositions include:* The Darling of the World for choir and orchestra 1986, Piano Sonata 1988, A Song for Birds (song cycle) 1990, Prelude in homage to Maurice Duruflé for organ 1990, Kiwi Fireworks for organ 1994, Dies Natalis for choir 1995, Man, Wretched Man for choir and organ 1997, Easter Oratorio 2000, The Deciduous Cross for choir and orchestra 2003. *Recordings include:* God's Great New Day: Music from Easter Oratorio, five albums with Finzi Singers, three albums with Birmingham Bach Choir, including J. S. Bach: The Seven Motets. *Publications:* Herbert Howells 1998. *Honours:* Hon. Research Fellow Univ. of Birmingham 2000, Hon. Fellowship Birmingham Conservatoire 2001; Walford Davies Organ Prize Royal Coll. of Music. *Current Management:* c/o Val Withams, Choral Connections, 28 Wright's Lane, Prestwood, Great Missenden, HP 16 OLH, England. *E-mail:* paul@paulspicer.com. *Website:* www.paulspicer.com.

**SPICKA, Daniel (Hilarius);** Music Festival Art Director, Early Music Instrument Maker and Collector; b. 5 Feb. 1939, Prague, Czechoslovakia; m. The Hon Victoria W Reilly, 13 Jan 1973, 2 d. *Education:* Architecture, Czech Technical University, Prague, 1956–62; Evening course in Conducting, Prague Conservatoire, 1960–63; Private studies of Piano, Viol, Classical Guitar. *Career:* Debut: With Vejvanovsky Consort, Prague, 1959; With Camerata RSX, 1977; Valtice Baroque Festival, 1989; Founder, Camerata RSX, 1st authentic Renaissance Consort in Bohemia; Co-Founder of Valtice Baroque Opera Festival, South Moravia, Czech Republic; Performances on Czech and Austrian television, BBC and Czech Radio; Dramaturg of Valtice Baroque Opera Festival, 1989–; Noted for introducing authentic Early Music performances to Czech music scene, by bringing books, magazines, recordings and plans of instruments from the West to former Czechoslovakia; mem, Czech Music Society, Early Music Branch. *Recordings:* Gagliano–La Dafne, 1992; Monteverdi–Balli, 1994. *Contributions:* Various Czech music magazines, 1982–; Articles on Valtice Festival in The Independent, 1990, Die Presse, 1990, 1992, The Times, 1992. *Current Management:* Avant Promotion. *Address:* U Mrázovky 7, 15000 Prague 5, Czech Republic.

**SPIERS, Colin James,** BA; Australian composer and pianist; b. 24 July 1957, Brisbane, Qld. *Education:* Queensland Conservatorium. *Career:* Faculty mem., Univ. of Queensland 1980–90, Newcastle Conservatorium 1990–; founding mem., Perihelion Ensemble; solo pianist, recital accompanist and composition teacher. *Compositions include:* Fantasy on Theme of Keith Jarrett for piano 1987, Divertimento for strings 1987, Tales from Nowhere for piano 1988, Sonata for solo viola 1988, Day of Death and Dreams for tenor and piano 1989, UWJ for viola and piano 1991, Flecks for piano 1991, Cadenzas and Interludes for string orchestra 1991, Deranged Confessions, Desperate Acts, Divine Symmetry, Delicate Games piano sonatas 1990–98, ZYJ for trumpet and piano 1993, Music, Like the Dark Husk of Earth, Abiding for string orchestra 1994, NSJ for clarinet, bassett-horn and piano 1995, Mutations for piano 1996, five Bagatelles for piano 1996–97, Sonata for cello and piano 1999, The Last Thoughts of Prokofiev for piano 2003, Blue into Blue for orchestra 2004, Collide for orchestra 2004. *Honours:* Queensland Conservatorium Medal of Excellence 1979, Jean Bogan Composition Prize 1995. *Address:* 16 Kimian Avenue, Waratah West, NSW 2298, Australia (home). *Telephone:* (02) 49218925 (office). *E-mail:* Colin.Spiers@newcastle.edu.au (office).

**SPIEWAK, Tomasz,** BEd; Australian (b. Polish) pianist and composer; b. 12 Sept. 1936, Kraków; s. of Antoni Spiewak and Janina Mermon; one s. one d. *Education:* State Primary and Secondary Music School, Kraków, Jagiellonian Univ., Kraków and Univ. of Melbourne, Australia. *Career:* full-time teacher, Box Hill Coll. of Music, Melbourne, Australia 1982–2001; two years in Polish army ensemble, Desant as pianist, composer and arranger; five years in Polish comedy theatre, Wagabunda as musical dir, pianist, composer, arranger and bandleader; two years in Polish radio and TV orchestra as pianist, composer and arranger; pianist, organist and arranger in a quartet, toured through Scandinavia 1971–74; currently part-time teacher of aural training, Defence Force School of Music, Melbourne. *Compositions include:* Quartet for Saxophones in four movements 1988, 11 studies for marimba 1988–94, three marimba duets 1988–94, six preludes for vibraphone 1988–95, Sonatina for B flat saxophone and piano 1990, Duo Sonata for tenor and baritone saxophones 1990, Trio for alto and baritone saxophones and piano 1991, Sonata for trombone and piano 1992, Roller Coaster for violoncello 1996, pieces for bassoon and piano 1996, Floral Suite for alto saxophone and piano 2000, Scherzetto for baritone saxophone and piano 2000, Walking Dance for baritone saxophone and piano 2000, Second Quartet for saxophones, featuring baritone saxophone 2000, Kaleidoscope for alto saxophone and piano 2002, Blue Ride for alto saxophone and piano 2002, Palindrome for saxophone quartet 2003, Quartet for Saxophones No. 3 (from Rag to Funk) 2003, six pieces for saxophone solo 2004, six pieces for clarinet solo 2004, Sonata for tenor saxophone and pianoforte 2005. *Publications:* Aural Training for Musicians and Music Students Vols I–IV 1991–96, The Performing Ear (with Jenni Hillman) 2001, Vocalises for Modern Singers Vols I–III 2002, Essential Instrumental Ensemble Kit: Exercises in sight reading and aural training 2005. *E-mail:* tspiewak@bigpond.net.au.

**SPIEWOK, Stephen;** Singer (Tenor); b. 1 Dec. 1947, Berlin, Germany. *Education:* Musikhochschule, Weimar, and with Johannes Kemter in Dresden. *Career:* Debut: Weimar 1971, as Nicolai's Fenton; Dresden Staatsoper 1971-80, notably in the 1979 premiere of Vincent, by Kunad; Leipzig Opera and Berlin Staatsoper 1980-90, including the 1984 premiere if Kunad's Amphitryon; Ludwigsburg Festival 1989, as Ephrain in the premiere of Judith, by S. Matthus; Sang Arbace in Idomeneo at the Komische Oper, Berlin, and Morosus at Wiesbaden (Die schweigsame Frau, by Strauss); Guest appearances throughout Europe and in Japan as Tamino, the Duke of Mantua, Števa in Jenůfa, and Andres in Wozzeck; Many concert engagements. *Address:* c/o Komische Oper, Behrenstrasse 55-S7, D-10117 Berlin, Germany.

**SPILLER, Andres;** Argentine oboist and conductor; b. 24 Dec. 1946, Buenos Aires; m. Marcela Magin; two s. one d. *Education:* Conservatorio Nacional; Private studies, Hochschule für Musik, Cologne, Germany; Summer courses with Heinz Holliger, Bruno Maderna, Franco Ferrara, Michael Gielen, Volker Wangenheim. *Career:* Assistant Conductor, National Symphony Orchestra and Oboe Soloist; Oboe Soloist, Camerata Bariloche and Soloist of Bach Academy, Buenos Aires; Conductor, La Plata Chamber Orchestra; Performed with Koeckert Quartet in Munich; Other European appearances include Madrid, Rome and Radio Zürich; Toured America and Europe with Camerata Bariloche; Professor of Oboe and Chamber Music. *Recordings:* Death of an Angel; Tango. *Honours:* DAAD Fellowship for study in Germany; Sociedad Hebraica Prize; 2nd Prize, Promacions Musicales; Premio Konex, 1989, 1999. *Address:* Medrano 47, 5øA, 1178 Buenos Aires, Argentina. *Telephone:* (11) 49811470 (home). *Fax:* (11) 49811470 (home). *E-mail:* spillermagin@abacomet.com.ar (home).

**SPINK, Ian;** Emeritus Professor; b. 29 March 1932, London, England; m. 7 c. *Education:* BMus, London, 1952; MA, Birmingham, 1958. *Career:* Lecturer, Senior Lecturer, University of Sydney, New South Wales, 1962–68; Senior Lecturer, Reader, Professor, London University (RHUL), 1969–97; Emeritus Professor, 1997–, Dean of Faculty of Arts, 1973–75 and 1983–85; Dean of Faculty of Music, University of London, 1974–78; Member of Senate, 1975–81. *Publications include:* The English Lute-Songs, Vol. 17, 1961, 2nd edition, 1974, Vol. 18, 1963, Vol. 19, 1966; An Historical Approach to Musical Form, 1967; Editor, English Songs 1625–1660, Musica Britannica, Vol. 33, 1971; English Song, Dowland to Purcell, 1974, revised edition, 1986; Editor, Arne, The Judgement of Paris, Musica Britannica, Vol. 42, 1979; Purcell, A Song for the Duke of Gloucester's Birthday, 1695, Purcell Society Edition, Vol. 4, 1990; The Seventeenth Century, Blackwell History of Music in Britain, Vol. 3, 1992; Purcell, Timon of Athens, Vol. 2, 1994; Restoration Cathedral Music, 1660–1714, 1995; Purcell, Dramatic Music Part II vol. 20, 1998; Henry Lawes, Cavalier Songwriter, 2000; Purcell, Catches, Vol. 22a, 2000; Purcell, Duets, Dialgoues and Trios, Vol. 22B, 2001. *Address:* Royal Holloway, University of London, Egham, Surrey TW20 0EX, England.

**SPINNLER, Burkard;** Pianist; b. 17 July 1954, Goldbach, Germany; m. Claudine Orloff, 1 Oct 1983, 2 s., 1 d. *Education:* Staatsexamen, Musikhochschule Würzburg, with J von Karolyi, 1978; Diplome Superieur, Brussels Royal Conservatory, with J Cl Vanden Eynden, 1982; Ecole de Maitrise Pianistique, 1981–84; Private studies with Eduardo del Pueyo in Brussels. *Career:* Debut: With University Orchestra at Würzburg in 1978; Recording for Bavarian Radio in 1979, for Belgian Radio RTB, 1984; Appearances as soloist and in chamber music in Germany, Belgium and France; Special J Godowsky commemorative programme, 1989; Regular concerts on 2 pianos with Claudine Orloff, including Musique en Sorbonne, Paris, 1991; Live radio engagement, Hommage à Milhaud, RTB Brussels in 1992 and 1999; Private research of Liszt unpublished works and 136 unedited letters of Francis Poulenc; Teaches at Brussels Conservatory, 1985–; Further live recordings for Belgian and French radio in 1995 and 1998. *Publications:* Zur Angemessenheit Traditionelles Formbegriffe in der Analyse Mahlerscher Symphonik, in Form und Idée in G Mahlers Instrumentalmusik, 1980. *Current Management:* F E de Wasseige Music Management. *Address:* 109 Avenue E Van Becelaere, 1170 Brussels, Belgium.

**ŠPITKOVA, Jela;** Slovakian violinist; *Professor of Violin, Banska Bystrica Music Academy;* b. 1947. *Education:* Bratislava Conservatory and in Vienna with Riccardo Odnoposoff, Prague Coll. of Music, Tchaikovsky Conservatory Moscow with David and Igor Oistrakh. *Career:* has performed with leading Czech Orchestras and in 40 other countries, including South and North America and Africa; recitals in Paris, Rome, Moscow, Berlin, Prague, Amsterdam and Vienna; television and radio recordings in Spain, Norway, Denmark, Austria, France, Finland and Russia; Leader of the Mozarteum Orchestra 1980; soloist with Slovak Philharmonic in Bratislava; repertoire includes concertos by Tchaikovsky, Brahms, Beethoven, Sibelius, Mendelssohn, Mozart, Bach and Haydn, Lalo Symphonie Espagnole, Sonatas by Brahms, Beethoven, Franck, Schumann, Prokofiev, Mozart, Handel, Debussy and Dvořák; Concertmaster, Mozarteum Orchestra in Salzburg 1980–94; Teacher of Violin, Vienna Music Acad. 1985–; Prof. of Violin, Banska Bystrica Music Acad., Slovakia; Docent, Prague Music Acad. 2002; Prof., Bratislava Music Acad. 2004–. *Recordings:* CDs and recordings for Slovak Radio: Mendelssohn Violin Concerto in E Minor; Bruch Violin Concerto; Chausson, Poème; Tchaikovsky Serenade Melancholique; Brahms Sonata Nos 1, 2 and 3; Ravel's Tzigane; Sibelius Violin Concerto; Suchon Sonatine op 11; Haydn Violin Concerto in C Major; Dittersdorf Violin Concerto in G Minor, Sibelius Violin Concerto in D Minor, Tchaikovsky Violin COncerto in D Major, Beethoven Violin COncerto in D Major, Suk Fantasy in G Minor, Lalo Symphonie Espagnole, Hummel Concerto for Violin, Piano and Orchestra, Schuman Sonatas Nos 1 and 2, Debussy Sonata, Enescu Sonato No. 2. *Honours:* 3rd Prize, National Youth Festival, Sofia, 1968; 3 Prizes in international violin competition, Tibor Varga, Switzerland, 1969; 3rd Prize, international competition, Emily Anderson, Royal Philharmonic Society, London, 1969. *Address:* Belopotockeho 2, 81105 Bratislava, Slovakia (home). *Telephone:* (2) 52492535 (home). *E-mail:* jela.spitkova@post.sk (home).

**SPIVAKOV, Vladimir Teodorovich;** Russian violinist and conductor; b. 12 Sept. 1944, Ufa, Bashkiria; m. Satinik Saakyants; three d. *Education:* Moscow State Conservatory, postgraduate with Yury Yankelevich. *Career:* studied violin since age of six with B. Kroger in Leningrad; prize winner in several int. competitions including Tchaikovsky, Moscow; Founder and Conductor Chamber Orchestra Virtuosi of Moscow 1979–; Founder and Artistic Dir Music Festival in Colmar, France 1989–; Artistic Dir and Chief Conductor Russian Nat. Symphony Orchestra 1999–2003; founder, Artistic Dir and Chief Conductor Nat. Philharmonic Orchestra of Russia 2003–; Guest Conductor of several orchestras including Chicago Symphony Orchestra, LA Philharmonic, London Symphony Orchestra, English and Scottish Chamber Orchestras; f. Int. Charity Foundation 1994. *Recordings:* more than 20 CDs on Capriccio, RCA Victor Red Seal and BMG Classics including works by Brahms, Berg, Chausson, Franck, Prokoviev, Ravel, Tchaikovsky, Richard Strauss, Schubert, Sibelius, Shostakovich. *Honours:* Les Insignes de Chevalier de la Légion d'Honneur 1994 USSR State Prize 1989, USSR People's Artist 1990, Triumph Prize, Nat. Cultural Heritage Award, Russia's Artist of the Year 2002, First Prize Montreal Competition, Marguerite Long St Jacques Thibaud Competition, Paris, Nicolo Paganini Int. Violin Competition, Genoa, Int. Tchaikovsky Competition, Moscow. *Address:* c/o Columbia Artists Management, 165 West 57th Street, New York, NY 10019, USA (office); Vspolny per. 17, Apt 14, Moscow, Russia. *Telephone:* (095) 290-23-24 (Moscow); 1-45-25-50-85 (Paris). *Fax:* 1-45-25-04-60 (Paris).

**SPOORENBERG, Erna;** Singer (Soprano); b. 11 April 1926, Yogyakarta, Java. *Education:* Studied in the Netherlands with Julius Rontgen and Aaltje Noordewier-Reddingius. *Career:* Debut: Hilversum concert in 1947 with Mozart's Motet Exsultate Jubilate; Opera debut at the Vienna Staatsoper in 1949; Sang in Vienna, Hamburg in 1962, Düsseldorf and Amsterdam in operas by Mozart and as Debussy's Mélisande, and at Bordeaux in 1964 in La Dame Blanche by Boildieu; Concert tours of Germany, South Africa, Russia, Austria and Scandinavia; US debut at Lincoln Center in New York in 1967; Recital partnership with the pianist, Geza Frid. *Recordings:* Pelléas et Mélisande conducted by Ansermet; Die Schöpfung; Mahler's 8th Symphony; Bach Cantatas; Masses by Haydn.

**SPOTORNO, Marianangela;** Singer (Soprano); b. 1970, Rome. *Education:* First studied cello, then singing with Magda Laszlo and Elio Battaglia. *Career:* Debut: Elisabetta in Cimarosa's Il Matrimonio Segreto, for the Walton Trust at Ischia and in Scotland, 1992; Sang in Offenbach's Barbe-bleue at Bologna and Messina, Mozart's Fiordiligi and Susanna at Cagliari; Sang the title role in Manon Lescaut at the Glyndebourne Festival, 1997, and engaged 1997–98 as Antonia in L'Elisir d'amore; Concerts include: Beethoven's Christus am Olberge, at Treviso, and opera concert with Domingo in Finland; Sang the voice of the soprano Guiditta Pasta for Italian television film of the life of Giulio Ricordi. *Address:* c/o Teatro Massimo Bellini, Via Perrotta 12, 95131 Catania, Italy.

**SPRATLAN, Lewis;** Composer; b. 5 Sept. 1940, Miami, Florida, USA. *Education:* Composition studies with Yehudi Wyner, Gunther Schuller and Mel Powell at Yale University (BA, 1962, MM, 1965); George Rochberg and Roger Sessions at Tanglewood, 1966. Career Faculty Member, Pennsylvania State University, 1967–70; Amherst College from 1970 (Chairman of Music Department, 1977–94, Professor from 1980). *Compositions include:* Missa Brevis, 1965; Cantate Domine for men's chorus, winds and tape, 1968; Serenade for 6 instruments, 1970; Moonsong for chorus and ensemble, 1970; Two Pieces for orchestra, 1971; Woodwind quintet, 1971; Fantasy for piano and chamber ensemble, 1973; Ben Jonson for soprano, violin and cello, 1974; Life is a Dream, opera, 1977; Coils for ensemble, 1980; String Quartet, 1982; When Crows Gather for 3 clarinets, violin, cello, and piano, 1986; Hung Monophonies for oboe and 11 instruments, 1990; Night Music for violin, clarinet and percussion, 1991; In Memorian for soloists, chorus and orchestra,

1993; A Barred Owl baritone and 5 instruments, 1994; Concertino for violin, cello and cello and double baritone and 5 instruments, 1994; Concertino for violin, cello and double bass, 1995; Psalm 42, for soprano, baritone and ensemble, 1996. *Address:* c/o ASCAP, ASCAP Building, 1 Lincoln Plaza, New York, NY 10023, USA.

**SPRATT, Geoffrey (Kenneth);** British musician; *Director, Cork School of Music;* b. 16 Sept. 1950, London; m. 1st Frances Vivien Squire; two s.; m. 2nd Elizabeth Searls. *Education:* BA, Honours with Distinction in Practical Work, 1973; PhD, University of Bristol, 1980. *Career:* Professional freelance flute and viola player with Cyprus Broadcasting Company Orchestras, 1969–70, and various British Orchestras, 1970–76; Part-time Tutor, Open University, 1973–76 and University of Bristol, 1974–76; Lecturer in Music, University College, Cork, Ireland, 1976–92; Founder-Conductor, UCC Choir and Orchestra, 1976–92; Conductor, UCC Choral Society, 1978–86, Madrigal '75 Chamber Choir; Director, Cork School of Music, 1992–; Founder-Conductor, Irish Youth Choir and the Fleischmann Choir of the Cork School of Music; Conductor, Canticum Novum Chamber Choir; Guest Conductor: National Symphony Orchestra of Ireland, RTÉ Concert Orchestra, RTÉ Chorus, RTÉ Chamber Choir, Irish Chamber Orchestra, Orchestra St Cecil, Galway Baroque Singers; Chairman, Association of Irish Choirs and Cork Orchestral Society; Council, Music Teachers' Association of Ireland, 1977–. *Recordings:* Choral music of Séamas de Barra sung by the Irish Youth Choir and Madrigal '75; Sacred Choral Music of Angel Climent sung by the Irish Youth Choir. *Publications:* Catalogue des oeuvres de Arthur Honegger, Geneva and Paris, 1986; Co-author with M Delannoy, Honegger, Geneva and Paris, 1986; The Music of Arthur Honegger, Cork, 1987. *Honours:* Napier Miles Prize, Bristol University, 1972. *Address:* Cork School of Music, Union Quay, Cork, Ireland (office). *Telephone:* (21) 4270076 (office). *Fax:* (21) 4276595 (office). *E-mail:* gspratt@cit.ie (office).

**SQUIRES, Shelagh;** Singer (Mezzo-soprano); b. 17 Aug. 1936, England. *Education:* Guildhall School, London. *Career:* Debut: Glyndebourne 1968, in Die Zauberflöte; Sang Cherubino for Phoenix Opera, 1969; Sadler's Wells/ English National Opera from 1972, as Mozart's Marcellina, Tisbe in Cenerentola, Filippevna in Eugene Onegin, Emilia in Othello, and Mamma Lucia in Cavalleria Rusticana; Appearances in the first local stage performances of War and Peace; Penderecki's The Devils of Loudun, Janáček's Osud (1984), Christmas Eve by Rimsky-Korsakov, and the premiere of Robin Holloway's Clarissa (1990); Other roles in The Ring of the Nibelung, as Rosette in Manon, Jezibaba in Rusalka and Mrs Sedley in Peter Grimes. *Recordings include:* Othello, The Ring (EMI); Video of Gloriana. *Address:* c/o Engish National Opera, St Martin's Lane, London, WC2, England.

**SRABRAWA, Daniel;** Violinist; b. 1948, Kraków, Poland. *Education:* Studied with Z Slezer in Kraków. *Career:* Leader of Kraków Radio Symphony Orchestra, 1979; Joined Berlin Philharmonic Orchestra in 1983 and became leader in 1983; Co-founder of the Philharmonic Quartet Berlin giving concerts throughout Europe, USA and Japan; British debut in 1987 playing Haydn, Szymanowski and Beethoven at Wigmore Hall; Played at Bath Festival in 1987 with Mozart, Schumann and Beethoven Op 127; Other repertoire includes quartets by Bartók, Mendelssohn, Nicolai, Ravel and Schubert, and quintets by Brahms, Weber, Reger and Schumann. *Address:* c/o Vogtr Artists, Philharmonia Quartet, 1714 Stockton St, Suite 300, San Francisco, CA 94133–2930, USA.

**SRAMEK, Alfred;** Singer (Bass); b. 5 April 1951, Nichtelbach, Vienna, Austria. *Education:* Studied with Ludwig Weber and Hilde Zadek. *Career:* Has sung with the Vienna Staatsoper from 1975 in Palestrina and as Don Pasquale, Dulcamara, Beckmesser, Masetto, Leporello and Figaro; Sang at Salzburg Festival from 1976, and Bregenz Festival in 1982; Season 2000–01 at the Vienna State Opera in Lulu, Figaro (as Bartolo), Wozzeck and Billy Budd; Dulcamara in L'elisir d'amore; Many concert appearances. *Recordings:* Lohengrin; Wozzeck; Don Giovanni; Ariadne auf Naxos; Die Lustigen Weiber von Windsor; Karl V by Krenek; Video of Wozzeck, as First Workman, conducted by Abbado. *Address:* c/o Staatsoper, Opernring 2, 1010 Vienna, Austria.

**STAAHLEN, Torhild;** Norwegian singer (mezzo-soprano); b. 25 Sept. 1947, Skien; m. Neil Dodd 1975. *Education:* Music Conservatory, Oslo, Nat. Opera School. *Career:* debut, Oslo, as Suzuki in Madama Butterfly 1971; has sung 65 roles from the mezzo-alto repertoire, including the title role in Carmen, Octavian in Der Rosenkavalier, Azucena in Il Trovatore, Ulrica in Un Ballo in Maschera, Amneris in Aida, Erda in Das Rheingold, Waltraute in Götter-dämmerung, La Principezza in Suor Angelica, Olga in Eugene Onegin, Prince Orlovsky in Die Fledermaus, and Valencienne in The Merry Widow; character roles include Heriodas in Salome, Marcellina in The Marriage of Figaro, La Vecchia Madelon in Andrea Chenier, and The Secretary in Jeppe by Geir Tveitt; frequent radio and television broadcasts; sings many oratorios, including the Bach Passions and Handel's Messiah; concert repertoire includes Brahms' Alto Rhapsody, Wagner's Wesendonck Lieder, Beethoven's Ninth Symphony, Mahler's Second and Fourth Symphonies, Elgar's Sea Pictures, Heise's Bergljot, Handel's Samson, and Pergolesi's Stabat Mater; guested in Sweden, Denmark, Finland, Germany, England, Scotland and the USA; has sung under conductors, including Heinrich Hollreiser, Paavo Berglund, Maurice Handford, Heinz Fricke, Antonio Pappano, Michael Schönwandt, Silvio Varviso, Erich Wächter and Berislav Klobuchar; inaugurated Torhild Staahlen Prize for Singers, Musicians and Composers 1991;

mem. Norsk Musikerforbund, Norsk Operasangerforbund. *Recording:* Expression 1991. *Honours:* Fund for Performing Artists State Artist's Stipendium, Friends of Music in Telemark Prize of Honour 1981, City of Oslo Cultural Stipendium, Vel Medal. *Address:* Breidablikkveien 24, 1167 Oslo, Norway.

**STAAR, René;** Composer and Violinist; b. 30 May 1951, Graz, Austria. *Education:* Sibelius Academy, Helsinki, 1968-69; Vienna Hochschule für Msuik, 1963-79, with Hans Swarowsky and Roman Haubenstock –Ramati, Violin with Nathan Milstein in Zürich. *Career:* Co-founder, Ensemble Wiener College 1986; Member of Vienna PO, from 1988; Director of Graz-Petersburg Ensemble, 1993; Founder, Ensemble Wien-Paris, 1996. *Compositions:* Structures I-VI, for various ensembles, 1981-82; Just an Accident, Requiem, 1986; Das wachsende Schloss, for violin and orchestra, 1986; Bagatellen auf den Namen György Ligeti, for piano, 1989-96, Metamorphosen eines labyrinths for violin and strings, 1991; Versunkene Träume, for string quartet, 1993; Metropolitan Midnight Music, 1993; Heine Fragments, for soprano, baritone and ensemble, 1997; Monumentum pro Thomas Alva Edison, for violin, guitar and double bass, 1998. *Address:* c/o AKM, Baumanstrasse 10, 1031 Wien, Postfach 259, Austria.

**STABELL, Carsten;** Singer (Bass); b. 5 Sept. 1960, Trondheim, Norway. *Education:* Studied at the Norwegian Opera School, Oslo. *Career:* Debut: Oslo in 1984 as the King in Aida; Sang at Stuttgart Opera from 1986 as Osmin, Sarastro, the Commendatore, Pietro in Simon Boccanegra and the Hermit in Der Freischütz; Sang Rustomji in Philip Glass's Satyagraha in 1990; Concert repertoire includes Bach's Magnificat and St John Passion, Messiah, Judas Maccabaeus, Acis and Galatea, Die Schöpfung, the Requiems of Mozart and Verdi and Liszt's Christus; Engaged as the Commendatore at Opera Geneva and Sarastro at the Opéra de Paris Bastille in 1991, and in Perseo e Andromeda by Sciarrino at La Scala Milan in 1992; Season 1998 with Oroveso in Norma at Philadelphia and Fafner in Siegfried for Netherlands Opera; Sang Fasolt at Edinburgh, Daland in Ghent, King Marke for Houston Opera and Banquo at the Vienna Staatsoper, 2000–01. *Address:* c/o Staatstheater Stuttgart, Oberer Schlossgarten 6, 7000 Stuttgart 1, Germany.

**STABLER, Gerhard;** Composer; b. 20 July 1949, Wilhelmsdorf, Germany. *Education:* Studied at Detmold Music Academy, 1968–70 and with Nicolaus Huber (composition) and Gerd Zacher (organ) at the Essen Hochschule, 1970–76; Further courses with Stockhausen, Kagel and Ligeti, at Cologne and Darmstadt. *Career:* Stanford University computer music centre, 1983, 1986; Faculty Member, Essen Hochschule 1989–94; Concert, lecture tours and guest professorships in Europe, Asia and North and South America from 1985. *Compositions include:* Drüber, for 8 screamers, cello and tape, 1972; Das Sichere ist nicht sicher, spiral rondo for 8 instruments and tape, 1982; Schatten Wilder Schmerzen, for orchestra, 1985; Warnung mit Liebeslied for harp, accordion and percussion, 1986; . . . strike the ear. . . for string quartet, 1988; October for flute, violin and double bass, 1988; Den Müllfahren von San Francisco, for 17 instruments, 1990; Ungaretti Lieder for mezzo or baritone and percussion, 1990; Sünde, Fall, Beil, opera after Catherine Howard by Dumas, 1992; Traum 1/9/92, for soprano saxophone, cello, piano and ensemble, 1992; CassandraComplex, music theatre, 1994; (Apparat), for chorus, clarinet, accordion, double bass and percussion, 1994; Karas.Krähen, for tape, 1994; Winter, Blumen, for countertenor, or solo string instruments, 1995; Internet, various works for solo instruments or chamber music ensembles, 1995–98; Spuren, for saxophone quartet, 1995; Dali, for piano solo, 1996; Poetic Arcs, for ensemble, 1996; Cassandra, music for dance, 1996; Burning Minds, for 12 voices, 1997; Bridges, for mezzo and accordion, 1997; Ausnahme.Zustand for orchestra, 1998; Time for Tomorrow, theatre music, for voice percussion and tape, 1998; Metal Seasons for violin solo, brass ensemble, percussion and airplanes, 1999. *Honours:* Cornelius Cardew Memorial Prize, London, 1982; Fellowship in composition, Heinrich-Strobel-Stiftung, 1985–86; Niederdachsen Scholarship, 1987–88; Japan Foundation Scholarship, 1994. GEMA, Rosenheimer Str 11, 81667 Munich, Germany.

**STACY, Thomas;** American oboist and English hornist; b. 15 Aug. 1938, Little Rock, AR. *Education:* Eastman School of Music, Univ. of Rochester, NY. *Career:* solo English horn, New Orleans Symphony Orchestra 1960–61, San Antonio Symphony Orchestra 1961–62, Minneapolis Symphony Orchestra 1962–72, New York Philharmonic Orchestra 1972–; guest engagements with leading orchestras throughout USA; commisioned and premiered works by Stanislav Skrowaczewski, Gunther Schuller, Ned Rorem and Vincent Persichetti; teacher, Juilliard School, NY 1973–, Mannes Coll. of Music 1998–; has given masterclasses at the Royal Acad., London and throughout Asia; Dir, Stacy English Horn Seminar. *Recordings include:* Three Concerti, New York Legends. *Address:* New York Philharmonic Orchestra, Avery Fisher Hall, 10 Lincoln Center Plaza, New York, NY 10023-6990, USA. *Website:* www.newyorkphilharmonic.org.

**STADELMANN, Christian;** Violinist; b. 1958, Berlin, Germany. *Education:* Studied with Charlotte Hampe and Thomas Brandis in Berlin. *Career:* Former Member of the Junge Deutsche Philharmonie and Co-founder of its Chamber Orchestra; Member of the Berlin Philharmonic 1985, leader of the 2nd violins, 1987; Second Violinist of the Philharmonia Quartet, Berlin, 1986; Many concerts with the Quartet in all European major cities and regular tours to the USA, Japan and South America. *Recordings include:* Quartets by Reger, Beethoven, Shostakovich, Szymanowski, Janáček for leading recording companies. *Address:* c/o Berlin Philharmonisches Orchester, Herbert von Karajan Strasse 1, 10785 Berlin, Germany.

**STADLER, Irmgard;** Singer (Soprano); b. 28 March 1937, Michaelbeuern, Salzburg, Austria. *Education:* Studied at Salzburg Mozarteum and Vienna Academy of Music. *Career:* Debut: Stuttgart 1962, as Micaela; Salzburg Festival 1961–62, in Idomeneo, Mozart's Requiem 1962–63; Glyndebourne Festival 1967–72 as Sicle in L'Ormindo, Donna Elvira, Juno in La Calisto and the Composer (Ariadne auf Naxos); Member of Stuttgart Opera since 1963; Guest appearances in Vienna, Munich, Berlin, Lisbon, Venice and Rome; Most important roles: Elvira, Cherubino, Fiordiligi, Elektra (Idomeneo), Octavian and Marschallin, Eva, Gutrune, Alice, Agathe, Marenka (Bartered Bride), Rusalka, Jenůfa, Katya Kabanova, Lisa (Queen of Spades), Tatiana, Marina and Marie in Wozzeck; Concert appearances in sacred music by Bach, Mozart, Bruckner and Lieder Recitals; Sang Theresa in the premiere of Giuseppe & Sylvia by Adriana Hölszky, Stuttgart, 2000. *Address:* c/o Staatstheater Stuttgart, Oberer Schlossgarten 6, D-70173 Stuttgart, Germany.

**STADLMAIR, Hans;** Conductor; b. 3 May 1929, Neuhofen, Austria. *Education:* Studied at the Vienna Academy of Music, 1946–52 with Clemens Krauss and Alfred Uhl and in Stuttgart, 1952–56 with Johann Nepomuk David. *Career:* Conducted the Stuttgart Chorus and became conductor of Munich Chamber Orchestra, 1956; Tours of Europe, North and South America, Asia, Africa, Canada and India; Has conducted own realisation of the Adagio from Mahler's 10th Symphony. *Compositions:* Concerto Profano for Violin, Cello and Orchestra; Concerto Capriccioso for two Flutes and Orchestra (composed for A Nicolet and J Pierre Rampal); Adagietto for Strings, Ecce Homo, 5 Novelletten for Strings; Sinfonia: 'Da Pacem Domine' für Alphorn, Röhrenglocken and Strings, 1988; Lacrimae Metamorphosen for Strings; Essay for clarinet and strings. *Recordings:* W A Mozart, Piano Concertos Nr 8 KV246, Lützow and Nr 9 KV271, Jeunehomme; F Danzi: Phantasie on La ci darem la mano from Don Giovanni, K Stamitz; Concerto for Clarinet Nr 3 B flat (E Brunner–Clarinet); Haydn's Seven Last Words; Scarlatti Il Giardino di Amore; Mozart Bassoon Concerto, Clarinet Concerto and Violin Concerto K219; Vivaldi Four Seasons; Koch-Schwann: Hans Stadlmair. *Contributions:* Riemann Musiklexikon. *Honours:* Medaille: München Leuchtet, 1989; Bundesverdienstkreuz am Bande, 1989; Musikpreis der Stadt München, 1994. *Address:* Dachauerstr 175, 80636 München, Germany.

**STADLMAIR, Vincent;** Cellist; b. 1959, Vienna, Austria. *Education:* Vienna Acad. of Music. *Career:* mem. of the Franz Schubert Quartet, Vienna from 1983; many concert engagements in Europe, USA, and Australia including appearances at the Amsterdam Concertgebouw, the Vienna Musikverein and Konzerthaus, the Salle Gaveau Paris and the Sydney Opera House; visits to Zürich, Geneva, Basle, Berlin, Hamburg, Rome, Rotterdam, Madrid and Copenhagen; festival engagements include Salzburg, Wiener Festwochen, Prague, Spring Schubertiade at Hohenems, the Schubert Festival at Washington DC and the Belfast and Istanbul Festivals; tours of Australasia, Russia and USA; frequent concert tours of the UK; featured in the Quartet Concerto by Spohr with the Liverpool Philharmonic in Liverpool at the Festival Hall; many appearances at the Wigmore Hall and Cheltenham Festival; teacher at the Vienna Conservatory and Graz Musikhochschule; masterclasses at the Royal Northern Coll. of Music, Lake District Summer Music. *Recordings include:* Schubert's Quartet in G, D887; Complete Quartets of Dittersdorf; Mozart's String Quartet in D, K575, and String Quartet in B flat, K589.

**STAEHELIN, Martin;** Musicologist; b. 25 Sept. 1937, Basel, Switzerland; m. Elisabeth Schenker. *Education:* Diploma, Teacher Querflöte, 1962, School Music Diploma, 1963, Music Academy, Basel; PhD, University of Basel, 1967. *Career:* Teacher of Latin, Greek and Music, Basel, 1963; Musicology Teacher, University of Zürich, 1971–76; Head of Beethoven Archives, Bonn, Germany, 1976–84; Teacher, 1976–77, Professor, 1977–83, University of Bonn; Professor, University of Göttingen, 1983–; Honorary Director of J. S. Bach Institut, Göttingen, 1992; mem. Akad. der Wissenschaften, Göttingen, 1987, Academia Europaea, London, 1995; Emeritus Univ., Göttingen, 2002. *Publications:* Editor, H Isaac, Messen, 1970, 1973; Der Grüne Codex der Viadrina, 1971; Die Messen Heinrich Isaacs, 3 vols, 1977. *Contributions:* Archiv für Musikwissenschaft; Die Musikforschung; Fontes Artis Musicae; Schweizer Beiträge zur Musikwissenschaft; Tijdschrift van de Vereniging voor Nederlandse Muziekgeschiedenis; Schweizerisches Archiv für Volkskunde. *Address:* Musicology Seminar of Georg August University, Kurze Geismarstrasse 1, 37073 Göttingen, Germany.

**STAFFORD, Ashley George,** BA, MA; British singer (countertenor); b. 3 March 1954, Holland, near Oxted, Surrey, England; m. Shauni Lee McGregor 1977; two s. *Education:* Westminster Abbey Choir School, Trinity School Croydon, Christchurch Oxford with Simon Preston, studied with Douglas Guest, Hervey Alan, Paul Esswood, Helga Mott, Jessica Cash. *Career:* debut, Purcell Room, 1975; sang in opera at Aix-en-Provence, Lyon, Oxford and London and in concert at major festivals throughout Europe, in Sydney and Melbourne, 1989, Japan, 1987 and 1989, Taiwan in 1989, USA and Canada including Bath, Edinburgh, Three Choirs, Berlin, Rome, Venice, Madrid, Barcelona, Lisbon, New York, Boston and Ottawa, 1980–86; Sang in Judith Weir's A Night at the Chinese Opera for Kent Opera; Many appearances on radio and on television including Messiah in France; Visiting Professor of Voice at Royal College of Music, London in 1989; mem, Incorporated Society of Musicians; Equity; Committee, Royal Society of Musicians. *Recordings include:* Purcell's Ode to St Cecilia, King Arthur, From the Nativity of Time (Songs sacred and secular); Handel's Israel in Egypt, Dettingen Te Deum; Valls's Mass Scala Aretina; Motets by Bach, Power, Dunstable and Josquin; Haydn's Nelson Mass; Scarlatti's Stabat Mater; Schütz's Muzikalisches Exequien; Handel's Alexander's Feast. *Honours:* Young Musician, Greater London Arts Association. *Address:* Fenton House, Banbury Road, Chipping Norton, Oxon OX7 5AW, England.

**STAHL, David,** BA, MA, MM; American symphony and opera conductor; b. 4 Nov. 1949, New York, NY; m. Karen Doss Stahl 1989; one s. two d. *Education:* Queens College, CUNY. *Career:* debut at Carnegie Hall, New York, 8 Dec 1973; Assistant Conductor, New York Philharmonic, 1976, and Cincinnati Symphony Orchestra, 1976–79; Music Director, St Louis Philharmonic, 1976–81; Broadway and international tour of West Side Story, 1980–82; Charleston (South Carolina) Symphony Orchestra, 1996–; Guest Conductor, Pittsburgh, Atlanta, Dallas, Indianapolis, St Louis, Buffalo, Baltimore, Long Beach, Edmonton, New World, San Jose, Winnipeg, and Louisville Symphonies; New York City Opera, Spoleto Festival, Lake George Opera, Dayton, Detroit, Hawaii and Tulsa opera companies; Overseas: RAI orchestra, Rome, Teatro Massimo, Palermo, Teatro Comunale, Genoa, Festival of two worlds, Spoleto, Orchestre Colonne, Paris, Orchestra del Sodre, Montevideo and Seoul (South Korea) Philharmonic, Toronto Symphony Orchestra, Montreal Opera, Washington Opera; Stadtheater National Mannheim, Darmstadt, Bernstein Festival in the Concertgebouw, Amsterdam; Principal Guest Conductor, Bavarian Staatsbtheater am Gaertnerplatz; Guest Conductor: NDR Symphony, Hamburg; Bamberg Symphony; Staatskapelle Dresden; L'Orchestre National de Lyon; Helsinki Philharmonic; Düsseldorf Symphony; Berlin Symphony Orchestra; Munich Philharmonic, Radio Symphony Orchestra of Stuttgart, Radio Philharmonie, Hannover; Chief Conductor Bavarian Staatstheater am Gaertnerplatz, 1999–. *Recordings:* Proto concertos for double bass; Portraits in Blue and Grey with Charleston Symphony; Poulenc Double Piano Concerto. *Honours:* ASCAP Award for Adventuresome Programming; Order of the Palmetto (highest award in South Carolina). *Current Management:* Colbert Artists Management Inc., 111 W 57th Street, New York, NY 10019, USA. *Address:* 14 George Street, Charleston, SC 29401, USA.

**STAHLAMMER, Semmy;** Musician and Violinist; b. 5 March 1954, Eskilstuna, Sweden. *Education:* Soloist Diploma, Royal Music College, Stockholm, 1972; Juilliard School of Music, USA, 1972–74; BMus, Curtis Institute of Music, 1975–79; Studied with Jaime Laredo, Ivan Galamian, Felx Galimir, Isidore Cohen, Szymon Goldberg, Paul Makanowitsky, Josef Silverstein, Josef Gingold, Nathan Milstein, Isaac Stern and Henryk Szeryng. *Career:* Debut: With Stockholm Philharmonic Orchestra, 1964; First Concertmaster of Stockholm Royal Opera, 1979–83; Artistic Director, Chamber Music in The Mirror Hall, 1982–; Artistic Director, Chamber Music in The Parks, 1986–; Teacher at Stockholm Royal Music College, 1987–. *Recordings:* Collections of Swedish 20th century music; Alfred Schnittke's Labyrinths; JS Bach's Sonatas and Partitas for Solo Violin. *Honours:* Winner of JS Bach International Violin Competition, Washington DC, 1985. *Address:* Norr Málarstrand 24, 112 20 Stockholm, Sweden.

**STAHMER, Klaus Hinrich,** PhD; composer; b. 25 June 1941, Szczecin, Stettin, Poland. *Education:* Hamburg Musikhochschule, Kiel Univ. *Career:* Lecturer, Würzburg Hochschule für Musik 1969–79, Prof. 1979–2004; Dir Tage der Neuen Musik 1972–2000; Dir Würzburg New Music Studio 1989–2000. *Compositions:* Quasi un requiem for speaker and string quartet 1974, Espace de la solitude (ballet) 1977, Soundscape (sound sculptures) 1985, Momentaufnahmen for speaker and ensemble 1986–89, Musik der Stille for piano 1994–98, Noa, Noa for ensemble 1996, Sacred Site for piano 1996, Embith-kâ for string quartet 1998. *Honours:* Würzburg Arts Prize 1995, Händel Prize 1999. *Address:* c/o GEMA, Rozenheimerstr 11, 8166 Munich, Germany (office). *Website:* www.khstahmer.de.

**STAICU, Paul;** Conductor, Professor and Horn Player; b. 7 June 1937, Bucharest, Romania; m. Irina Botez, 6 July 1963, 1 s. *Education:* Graduate Diploma in Horn, Prague Academy of Music, 1961; Graduate Diploma at Vienna Academy of Music, with conductor Hans Swarowsky. *Career:* Debut: As Horn Soloist, 1954 and as Conductor, 1963, Bucharest Radio and Philharmonic Orchestra; Horn Soloist, 1954–79; Solo Horn with Bucharest Philharmonic, 1961–69; Chief Conductor of Chamber Orchestra, 1966; Professor of Chamber Music, 1966–; Camerata, 1978; H von Karajan Foundation, Medal with Camerata, orchestra, 1974; Professor of Horn, 1969–89, Chief Conductor of Symphony Orchestra, Bucharest Music Academy, 1975–78; Chief Conductor, Symphony and Chamber Orchestra, Constanta Romania, 1978–79; Professor, Conservatoire of Music, Montbeliard, France, 1990; Director, School of Music, Exincourt, France, 1990; Chief Conductor, Ensemble Orchestral Montbeliard, France, 1992; Television and radio performances in Romania and abroad; Summer classes at Bayreuth, Gourdon, Europe, USA and Canada tours; Membership, Munich and Prague International Music Competitions. *Recordings:* No. 3, Beethoven Horn Sonata; Mozart and Beethoven Quintets; Mozart's Horn Concertos as Soloist and Conductor; Haydn Concertos as Conductor; Haydn Symphonies 100–103 as Conductor; Radio: Beethoven Symphony No. 4, Schoenberg Verklärte Nacht and Shostakovich's Symphony No. 14. *Publications:* Studiu introductiv si exercitii zilnice pentru corn (Introductory studies and daily exercises for horn).

**STAIER, Andreas;** Harpsichordist and Pianist; b. 13 Sept. 1955, Göttingen, Germany. *Education:* Baccalaureate in Göttingen; Studies in Piano, Harpsichord, Chamber Music in Hanover and Amsterdam. *Career:* Harpsichordist in Musica Antiqua, Köln, 1983–86; Professor, Schola Cantorum, Basle, Switzerland, 1987–96; Concerts in USA, Europe and Australia. *Recordings:* Haydn Piano Sonatas; J. S. Bach Harpsichord Works; CPE Bach Harpsichord Works; Chamber Music; Lieder; D Scarlatti; L Dussek; Schubert and Schumann, Piano solo works, concertos and lieder; Mozart Piano Sonatas. *Current Management:* Claudia Nitsche, Jean Michel Forest,. *Address:* Franzstr 19, 50931 Cologne, Germany.

**STALDER, Hans Rudolf;** Clarinettist and Musician; b. 9 July 1930, Zürich, Switzerland; m. Ursula Burkhard, 11 April 1957. *Education:* Konservatorium, Zürich; Bayerische Staatskonservatorium, Würzburg, Germany; Private studies with Louis Cahuzac, Paris. *Career:* International Soloist on clarinet, Bassethorn and Chalumeau, also with Chamber Music groups including: Stalder Quintet, Zürich Chamber Ensemble, Zürich Clarinet Trio; Teacher at Musik Akademie, Basle and Schola Cantorum Basiliensis; mem, Schweizerischer Tonkunstlerverein. *Recordings include:* First recording of Mozart Clarinet Concerto in original version with Bassetclarinet, 1968; Bassethorn Concerto from A Rolla; Das Chalumeau ein Portrait. *Address:* Wengi 2, 8126 Zumikon, Switzerland.

**STALLMAN, Robert;** Flautist; b. 12 June 1946, Boston, Massachusetts, USA; m. Hannah Woods, 26 Sept 1981. *Education:* BMus, 1968, MMus, 1971, New England Conservatory of Music; Paris Conservatoire, France, 1968–69. *Career:* Major solo appearances include Library of Congress (Washington), Carnegie Hall, Weill Hall, Alice Tully Hall, Avery Fisher Hall (New York), Symphony Hall (Boston), Salle Pleyel (Paris), Suntory Hall (Tokyo), Wigmore Hall (London); Radio and television appearances, nationwide USA, Canada, France and Spain; Guest Artist appearances include American Symphony, Mostly Mozart Festival, Netherlands and Suk Chamber Orchestras, Lincoln Center Chamber Music Society, Chamber Orchestra of Philadelphia, Speculum Musicae, Muir, Mendelssohn, Martinů and Orion String Quartets; Festivals, Brazil, Canada, Czech Republic; Finland, France, Netherlands, Japan, USA; Founder, Artistic Director, Cambridge Chamber Players and Marblehead Music Festival, 1976–96; Composers for whom he has premiered works include Elliott Carter, Richard Danielpour, Stephen Dodgson, Robert Helps, John Harbison, Karel Husa, William McKinley, Alexander St. Lawrence; Teaching: Aaron Copland School of Music, Queen's College, New York, 1980–; Académie Internationale d'Eté, Nice, France, 1985; Boston Conservatory, 1986–90; New England Conservatory, 1978–82; Masterclasses, USA, Canada, Mexico, England, France, Germany; Japan; Editor of flute repertoire, International Music Co, New York, 1984–; also, G Schirmer, New York, 1996–. *Recordings:* Blavet Sonatas; Incantations (20th century solo flute works); Gypsy Flute; Handel Sonatas; Leclair Sonatas; Bach Sonatas; The American Flute; Schubert Sonatas; The Nightingale in Love (French Baroque music); Telemann Concerti; Vivaldi Concerti; Dodgson Concerto with the Northern Sinfonia; McKinley Concerto with the Prism Orchestra. *Publications:* 40 include Flute Workout, 1995; The Flutist's Détaché Book, 1997. *Address:* 1530 Locust Street, #11A, Philadelphia, PA 19102, USA. *Website:* flute@robertstallman.com.

**STAMENOVA, Galina;** Violinist; b. 5 Oct. 1958, Sofia, Bulgaria. *Education:* Musical studies from age 5 with her mother; Studies with Dorothy DeLay, Juilliard School of Music, New York. *Career:* Debut: With André Previn and London Symphony Orchestra at Royal Festival Hall; American debut with Dallas Symphony in 1984; Performances with most leading British orchestras, Antwerp Philharmonic and orchestras in Bulgaria; Radio and television appearances in Bulgaria, Netherlands, the United Kingdom and Belgium; Accomplished recitalist having appeared at Harrogate and Aspen Music Festivals, live on BBC and Radio VARA in Netherlands and several other European countries. *Recordings:* Saint-Saëns No. 3, Chausson-Poème, Sofia Radio Orchestra with Vassil Stefanov conducting. *Honours:* Several first prizes for young violinists. *Address:* 33 Greinstraat, 2060 Antwerp, Belgium.

**STAMM, Harald;** Singer (Bass); b. 29 April 1938, Frankfurt am Main, Germany. *Education:* Studied with Franz Fehringer. *Career:* Debut: Gelsenkirchen, 1968; Sang at Cologne and Frankfurt, Hamburg Staatsoper, 1975, in the premiere of Der Gestiefelte Kater by Bialas; Many appearances in German opera houses and in Budapest Venice, Rome and Nice; Metropolitan Opera from 1979; Salzburg Festival 1985, in the Henze version of Monteverdi's Ulisse; Bregenz Festival 1986, as Sarastro in Die Zauberflöte; Other roles include: Mozart's Commendatore, Beethoven's Rocco, Verdi's Grand Inquisitor and Zaccaria, Wagner's Daland, Marke, Fasolt and Hunding and Massenet's Don Quixote; Covent Garden debut in 1987 as Raimondo in Lucia di Lammermoor; Sang the King in Schreker's Der Schatzgräber at Hamburg, 1989; King Henry in Lohengrin at Brussels and Lisbon, 1990; Season 1992 as Gurnemanz at Eseen; King Henry in Lohengrin at Hamburg, 1998; Hamburg State Opera 1999–2000, as Arkel in Pelléas and Wagner's Landgrave. Also heard in recital and concert. *Recordings:* Lieder by Liszt and Franz; Vier Ernste Gesänge by Brahms; Dittersdorf's Doktor und Apotheker; Schumann's Manfred; Massimila Doni by Schoeck. *Honours:* Nominated Kammersänger by Hamburg Opera, 1989; Professor at Hochschule der Künste Berlin, 1993. *Address:* c/o R & B GmbH, Plankengasse 7, A–1010 Vienna, Austria.

**STÄMPFLI, Jakob;** Singer (Bass); b. 26 Oct. 1934, Berne, Switzerland. *Education:* Studied at the Berne Conservatory and in Frankfurt with Paul Lohmann. *Career:* Gave concerts in Germany while still a student; Sang with the Chorus of St Thomas's Leipzig, conducted by Gunter Ramin; Many performances of sacred music by Bach in Europe, USA and Japan; Sang also with the Schola Cantorum Basiliensis; Lieder recitals with music by Brahms, Schubert and Schumann; Professor at the Saarbrücken Musikhochschule from 1960 then at the Hamburg Musikhochschule. *Recordings:* Cantatas by Buxtehude; Bach Cantatas; Monteverdi's Orfeo; Christmas Oratorio; St Matthew Passion and Magnificat by Bach; Plutone in L'Orfeo conducted by Michel Corboz. *Address:* c/o Hochschule für Musik, Harvestehuderweg 12, 2000 Hamburg 13, Germany.

**STANDAGE, Simon;** Violinist; b. 8 Nov. 1941, High Wycombe, Buckinghamshire, England; m. Jennifer Ward, 15 Aug 1964, 3 s. *Education:* Studied at Cambridge; Violin studies with Ivan Galamian in New York, 1967–69. *Career:* Associate member of the London Symphony Orchestra and deputy leader of the English Chamber Orchestra; Appointed Leader of the English Concert in 1973; Leader of the Richard Hickox Orchestra and the City of London Sinfonia; Founded the Salomon Quartet in 1981 giving performances of 18th century repertoire on original instruments; Teacher of Baroque violin at the Royal Academy of Music from 1983; Founded Collegium Musicum 90 in 1990; Associate Director of Academy of Ancient Music, 1991–95; Professor of Baroque Violin, Dresdner Akademie für Alte Musik, 1993–. *Recordings:* Vivaldi op 8 (including Four Seasons), op 3 (L'Estro Armonico), op 4 (La Stravaganza), op 9 (La Cetra), J. S. Bach Violin Concertos, Leclair complete concertos, Mozart and Haydn complete violin concertos, Mozart mature string quartets and quintets, Haydn quartets opp 17, 20, 33, 42, 50, 54/55, 64, 71/74, 77 and 103. *Address:* 106 Hervey Road, London SE3 8BX, England.

**STANDFORD, Patric;** Composer; b. 5 Feb. 1939, Barnsley, Yorkshire, England; m. Sarah Blyth Hilton. 2 s., 1 d. *Education:* GGSM, London, 1963; FGSM, London, 1973; MMus, London, 1979; Studied with Rubbra, Mendelssohn Scholarship 1964, Malipiero in Italy; Lutoslawski in Poland; Stanley Glasser at London University. *Career:* Professor of Composition, Guildhall School of Music, London, 1969–80; Head of Music Leeds University at Bretton Hall, 1980–93. *Compositions include:* 6 symphonies, 1971–2004; Taikyoku for 2 pianos and percussion, 1976; A Christmas Carol Symphony, 1978; Variations for orchestra, 1979; Cello Concerto; Violin Concerto; Christus Requiem, oratorio; 2 string quartets; Choral and instrumental works; Villon, opera; Ballet scores: Celestial Fire and Reflexions; Film and video music; Clarinet Quintet; The Prayer of St Francis for chorus and orchestra, 1996; Concertino for harpsichord and orchestra, 1998; The Emperor's Orchestra, for narrator and orchestra, 2001. *Recordings:* The Prayer of St Francis (Hungariton); A Christmas Carol Symphony (Naxos); Ballet Suite Celestial Fire (ASV). *Contributions:* (features, concert and CD reviews) Yorkshire Post, Choir and Organ, Music and Vision (internet). *Honours:* City of Geneva Ernst Ansermet Award, 1987; Budapest International Composers' Award, 1997; Belgian International ClarinetFest Prize, 1999. *Address:* c/o RTS Music, 17 Bradford Road, Wakefield, West Yorkshire WF1 2RF, England. *E-mail:* standford@rtsmusic.demon.co.uk. *Website:* www.impulse-music.co.uk/standford.htm.

**STANHOPE, David;** Composer, Conductor and Horn Player; b. 19 Dec. 1952, Sutton Coldfield, England (Resident in Australia from 1958). *Education:* Studied in Melbourne. *Career:* 2nd Horn Australian Symphony Orchestra 1970; Conductor Australian Opera 1986–, conducted Berg's Lulu 1994, The Turn of the Screw 2005. *Compositions include:* Quintet No. 3 for brass quintet 1983, The Australian Fanfare for 9 trumpets in 3 choirs 1983, Four Concert Studies for 4 trombones 1985, Felix Randall, for high voice and piano 1986, Concerto for Band 1988, Droylsden Wakes for wind or brass band 1990, Folksongs for Band 1990–91, Endpiece for orchestra 1991, Three Poems for soprano and string orchestra, String Songs, Three Folksongs for brass quintet. *Honours:* Prize Winner International Horn Society Composition Contest 1979. *Address:* c/o APRA, 1A Eden Street, Crows Nest, NSW 2065, Australia.

**STANHOPE, Paul Thomas;** Composer; b. 25 Nov. 1969, Wollongong, NSW, Australia. *Education:* BA (Hons), University of Sydney, 1992; MA (Hons), University of Wollongong, 1994; Study with Peter Sculthorpe, 1995–96. *Career:* Faculty Member, University of Wollongong, 1994–95; University of Sydney, 1995–. *Compositions include:* Liquid Marimba for tape, 1991; Morning Star for string quartet, 1992; Missa Brevis for chorus, 1992; The Taste of Midnight for flute, piano and clarinet, 1993; Morning Star II and III for ensemble, 1993; Kandeyala for orchestra, 1994; Satz for mandolin quartet, 1994; Rin, for tape, 1994; Snap, for clarinet, 1994; Geography Songs for chorus, 1994–95; No More than Movement... or Stillness, for tape, 1995; Kraftwerk Overture, for string orchestra, 1995; Rain Dance for violin, 2 violas and cello, 1995; Stars Sounding for orchestra, 1996. *Honours:* Australian Voices Festival Young Composers Award, 1995. *Address:* c/o APRA, 1A Eden Street, Crows Nest, NSW 2065, Australia.

**STANKOV, Angel (Mirchov);** Concert Violinist, Conductor and Violin Duo Chamber Player (with Josif Radionov); b. 28 April 1948, Sofia, Bulgaria; m. Meglena Stankova, 1 d. *Education:* State High School; Bulgarian State Music Academy, Sofia; Specialised in London with Professor Parikian of the Royal Academy of Music. *Career:* Debut: Pleven Philharmonic Orchestra, Beethoven Concerto, 1970; Regular appearances with Sofia Phiharmonic Orchestra and foreign orchestras; Appearances on Bulgarian radio and television; Concert Master, Sofia Philharmonic, 1981–2000; Live recital, Hague Radio, 1991; North France and Soviet television appearances, 1991; Foreign tours to almost all European countries and Cuba; International Music Festivals, Llandaff, the United Kingdom, 1975, Brno, Czechoslovakia, 1989, Warsaw, Bydgoscz and Crete, Greece, 1983; Professor of Violin and Chamber Music, Sofia State Music Academy; Performer as soloist and as member of violin duo with Josif Radionov; First Violin of the Sofia Quartet, 2002; Teaching one term at the North Carolina School of the Arts, 2003; Recitals in the USA, 2003. *Recordings:* Bulgarian radio and television; BBC London; BBC Oxford; Hague Radio; Prague Radio; Some concertos specially dedicated to the Violin Duo by outstanding Bulgarian and foreign composers, also individual pieces; Conducted all Beethoven Symphonies Cycle, 1999–2000. *Honours:* First Prize and Gold Medal, First International Chamber Music Festival, Osaka, 1993; Nominated Artist of the Year, Bulgaria, 1997. *Address:* 58 William Gladstone Street, 1000 Sofia, Bulgaria.

**STANKOVYCH, Yevhen Fedorovych;** Composer; b. 19 Sept. 1942, Svaliava, Ukraine. *Education:* Kiev Conservatory, 1963-70. *Career:* Works performed throughout Russia and in USA and Asia; Composer-in-residence at Berne, 1996. *Compositions:* Prometheus, ballet, 1985; Five Symphonies, 1973, 1975, 1976, 1977, 1980; String Quartet, 1973; Dictum, for ensemble, 1987; Black Elegy, for chorus and orchestra, 1991; Kaddish-Requiem, for tenor, bass, chorus and orchestra, 1991; Music for Heavenly Musicians, woodwind quintet, 1993; Requiem for Those Who Died of Famine, 1993; Sonata, for clarinet, 1996; Elegy, string quartet, 19997; Ave Maria, for orchestra, 1997; May Night, and The Night before Christmas, ballets after Gogol. *Address:* c/o RAO, 6a B. Bronnaya, Moscow 103670, Russia.

**STANTCHEV, Ognian Nikolov;** Violist and Professor; b. 1937, Sofia, Bulgaria. *Education:* Graduated, State Academy of Music, Sofia, 1960; Specialization, Chamber Music with Joseph Calvet, Paris Conservatory, 1967; Specialization, Tchaikovsky Conservatory, Moscow, Russia, 1976. *Career:* Lecturer, 1962–81, Assistant Professor, 1981–88, Professor, 1988–, State Academy of Music, Sofia; First Viola, Sofia Philharmonic Orchestra, 1962–66; Violist, Orpheus Quartet, 1966–72; Violist, Tilev Quartet, Bulgarian National Radio, 1972–78; First Viola, Sofia Philharmonic Orchestra, 1979–88; Violist, Sofia Quartet, Bulgarian National Radio, 1988–93; Numerous concerts and many broadcasts of chamber music, especially string quartets; Numerous concert tours in Czech Republic, Hungary, Germany, Austria, Poland, France, Italy, England, USA and Greece; Holds Masterclasses, Summer Academy Prague-Vienna-Budapest, 1997–; Jury Member, viola competition in Vienna, 1998; mem, Union of Musicians, Bulgaria. *Recordings:* Shostakovich Sonata for viola and piano; Debussy string quartet op 10; Prokofiev string quartet op 50; Four quartets for flute and strings, Mozart; Mozart quartet K 458; Haydn op 76 No. 2; Borodin string quartet No. 1; Sofia String quartet; For Bulgarian Radio: Britten, Lachrimae op 48; Hindemith, Meditation. Prizewinner, international competitions in Helsinki for stringed instruments, 1962; Second Prize, Stringed Quartet Competition, Kolmar, France, 1978. *Address:* Drujba 2, bl 206, en 3, ap 57, Sofia 1582, Bulgaria.

**STANZELEIT, Susanne;** Violinist; b. 1968, Germany. *Education:* Studies with Leonid Kogan and at Folkwang Hochschule in Essen (diploma 1989) and with Yfrah Neaman at the Guildhall School of Music; Masterclasses with Nathan Milstein, Sándor Végh and György Kurtag at Prussia Cove. *Career:* Recitals throughout Germany, Italy, Hungary, Netherlands, Canada, USA and England; Concerto appearances with leading orchestras, leader of Werethina Quartet (Haydn, Mendelssohn and Bartók at Purcell Room, 1993) and Prometheus and Ondine Ensembles; Purcell Room Recital, 1993 with Julian Jacobson, playing Strauss, Schubert's C Major Fantasy and Beethoven, Op 96; Broadcasts with BBC Radio 3, teaching and performing with the Paxos Festival in Greece, Dartington Summer School (1993) and International Bartók Festival in Hungary. *Recordings:* Bartók's music for violin and piano, Delius sonatas for violin and piano, Stanford, Bantock, Dunhill. *Address:* c/o Encord Concerts, Caversham Grange, The Warren, Mapledurham, Berks RG4 7TQ, England.

**STAPP, Olivia;** Singer (Mezzo-Soprano); b. 30 May 1940, New York, USA. *Education:* Studied with Oren Brown in New York and Ettore Campogalliani and Rodolfo Ricci in Italy. *Career:* Debut: Spoleto Festival in 1960 in L'Amico Fritz; Sang in Vienna, Berlin, Wuppertal, Turin and Basle; Sang at Indiana University at Bloomington in the 1971 premiere of Eaton's Heracles; Sang at New York City Opera from 1972 notably as Carmen and Norma, Metropolitan Opera from 1982 as Lady Macbeth and Tosca, Paris Opéra in 1982, La Scala Milan, 1983–84 as Turandot and Electra in Idomeneo, and Geneva in 1985 as Elena in Les Vêpres Siciliennes; Other roles include Verdi's Ulrica and Mistress Quickly, Santuzza, Dorabella, Isabella, Rosina, Idalma in Il Matrimonio Segreto and Jocasta in Oedipus Rex; Sang Lady Macbeth at Geneva and Venice in 1986, Elektra and Abigaille at Frankfurt and Zürich, 1988–89, at Paris in 1989 in La Noche Triste by Prodomidès, and sang Shostakovich's Katherina at Hamburg in 1990. *Recordings include:* Cyrano de Bergerac by Alfano.

**STAREK, Jiri;** conductor; b. 25 March 1928, Mocovice, Czechoslovakia; m. Eva Itis 1964; one s. *Education:* State Conservatory of Music, Acad. of Music Arts, Prague. *Career:* Conductor and Chief Conductor, Czech Radio, Prague 1953–68; Chief Conductor and Music Dir, Chamber Orchestra Collegium Musicum Pragense 1963–68; guest conductor for many int. symphony orchestras; Artistic Leader, Sinfonietta RIAS, Berlin 1976–80; Chief Conductor, Trondheim Symphony Orchestra, Norway 1981–84; Prof. and Head of Conductors Class, Music Acad., Frankfurt am Main 1975–97, Dean Artistic

Dept 1980–90; Principal Guest Conductor, ABC West Australia Symphony Orchestra 1988–90; Gen. Music Dir, Pfalztheater Kaiserslautern, Germany 1989–92; after 22 years in exile, returned to Prague, conducting Czech Philharmonic Orchestra, State Philharmonic Orchestra, Brno, Janáček Philharmonic Orchestra, Ostrava, Prague Symphony Orchestra, Radio Symphony Orchestra Prague 1990–; Chief Conductor, State Opera Prague 1996–; appearances at many leading int. music festivals, including Salzburg, Prague, Berlin, Schleswig-Holstein; mem. Czech Soc. of Arts and Sciences, Dvořák Soc. (London), Schubert Soc. (Prague). *Recordings:* with Prague Symphony Orchestra FOK, Radio Symphony Orchestra Prague, Sinfonietta-RIAS, Berlin, Radio Symphony Orchestra Stuttgart, Frankfurt, Munich, Berlin, for BBC (London and Glasgow). *Honours:* Hon. Chief Conductor, Karlsbad Symphony Orchestra; OIRT Award (for Z. Sestak: Vocal Symphony) 1964, Czech Radio Awards (for operas, W. Egk's Columbus, Shostakovich's The Nose, Dallapiccola's The Prisoner) 1966–67, Czech Music Council Award 1997, The Artist's Life Foundation Award 2003. *Address:* Brunnenweg 18, 61352 Bad Homburg vdh, Germany (home). *Telephone:* (61) 72450593 (home). *E-mail:* prof-j-starek@lycos.de (home).

**STARKER, Janos;** American cellist and academic; *Distinguished Professor of Cello, School of Music, Indiana University;* b. 5 July 1924, Budapest, Hungary; s. of Margit Starker and Sandor Starker; m. 1st Eva Uranyi 1944 (divorced); one d.; m. 2nd Rae Busch 1960; three d. *Education:* Franz Liszt Acad. of Music, Budapest. *Career:* Solo Cellist, Budapest Opera House and Philharmonic Orchestra 1945–46; Solo Cellist, Dallas Symphony Orchestra 1948–49, Metropolitan Opera Orchestra 1949–53, Chicago Symphony Orchestra 1953–58; Resident Cellist, Indiana Univ. 1958–, Prof. of Music 1961, now Distinguished Prof. of Cello; inventor of Starker bridge for orchestral string instruments; worldwide concert tours. *Publications:* Method 1964, Bach Suites 1971, Concerto Cadenzas, Schubert-Starker Sonatina, Bottermund-Starker Variations, Beethoven Sonatas, Beethoven Variations, Dvořák Concerto; numerous magazine articles, essays and record cover notes. *Honours:* Hon. mem. American Fed. of Musicians, Royal Acad. of London 1981, Indiana Acad. of Arts and Sciences, American Acad. of Arts and Sciences; Chevalier Ordre des Arts et Lettres 1997; Hon. DMus (Chicago Conservatory) 1961, (Cornell Coll.) 1978, (East West Univ.) 1982, (Williams Coll.) 1983, (Lawrence Univ.) 1990; Grand Prix du Disque 1948, George Washington Award 1972, Sanford Fellowship Award, Yale 1974, Herzl Award 1978, Ed Press Award 1983, Kodály Commemorative Medallion, New York 1983, Arturo Toscanini Award 1986, Indiana Univ. Tracy Sonneborn Award 1986, Indiana Gov.'s Award 1995, Medal of Paris 1995, Grammy Award 1998, Indiana Univ. Pres.'s Medal for Excellence 1999, Pres. of Hungary's Gold Medal 1999. *Current Management:* Colbert Artists, 111 West 57th Street, New York, NY 10019, USA. *Address:* c/o Department of Music, Office MA155, Indiana University, Bloomington, IN 47405-2200, USA. *E-mail:* starker@indiana.edu. *Website:* www.music.indiana.edu.

**STAROBIN, David Nathan,** BM; American classical guitarist; b. 27 Sept. 1951, New York, NY; m. Rebecca Patience Askew 1975; one s. one d. *Education:* Peabody Conservatory, studied with Manuel Gayol, Abert Valdes Blain and Aaren Shearer. *Career:* debut at Carnegie Recital Hall, New York, 1978; European at Wigmore Hall, London, 1979; Played the premiere performances of over 200 new compositions written for him including solo works, concerti and chamber music; Composers who have written for him include Elliott Carter, Charles Wuorinen, Barbara Kolb, David Del Tredici, Tod Machover, Milton Babbitt, Roger Reynolds, Robert Saxton, Mel Powell, Elisabeth Lutyens, Lukas Foss, Poul Ruders, George Crumb and Mario Davidovsky; Member of Speculum Misicae. *Recordings:* New Music with Guitar, vols 1, 2, 3 and 4; A Song From The East, music from Russia and Hungary; Twentieth Century Music for Voice and Guitar; Newdance. *Publications:* Editor: Looking for Claudio, 1978, Three Lullabies, 1980, Changes, 1984, Acrostic Song, 1983. *Honours:* AFIM Award Best Solo Classical Album, Newdance, 1999. *Current Management:* Bridge Records Inc, GPO Box 1864, New York, NY 10116, USA.

**STARYK, Steven S.;** violinist, concertmaster and academic; b. 28 April 1932, Toronto, Canada; m. 1963; one d. *Education:* Royal Conservatory of Music, Toronto, private studies in New York. *Career:* debut in Toronto; Concert Master, Royal Philharmonic, London, Concertgebouw Amsterdam, Chicago Symphony and Toronto Symphony; Prof. of Violin, Amsterdam Conservatory, Oberlin Conservatory, Northwestern Univ., Univ. of Victoria and Acad. of Music, Vancouver; Visiting Prof., Univ. of Ottawa, Univ. of Western Ontario; Prof., Royal Conservatory of Music, Toronto; Prof., Faculty of Music, Univ. of Toronto; Prof. and Head String Division, Univ. of Washington, Seattle, USA 1987–98, Prof. Emeritus 1999–; organizer of Quartet Canada; extensive concert tours, radio and television broadcasts in N America, Europe and the Far East. *Recordings:* 190 compositions on 45 albums. *Publications:* Fiddling with Life (biog., co-author) 2000. *Honours:* Hon. DLitt (York Univ., Toronto) 1980; Canada Council Arts Awards 1967, 1975, Shevchenko Medal 1974, Queen Elizabeth Centennial Award 1978, Univ. of Washington, Seattle Distinguished Teaching Award 1995. *Address:* 12068 E Bella Vista Cr, Scottsdale, AZ 85259, USA.

**STAUFFER, George (Boyer);** Musicologist and Organist; b. 18 Feb. 1947, Hershey, Pennsylvania, USA; m. Marie Caruso, 26 May 1985, one s. *Education:* BA, Dartmouth College, 1969; PhD, Columbia University, 1978; Organ study with John Weaver and Vernon de Tar. *Career:* Director of Chapel Music and Organist, Columbia University, 1977–99; Adjunct Assistant

Professor of Music, Yeshiva University, 1978–79; Assistant, Associate and Professor of Music, Hunter College and Graduate Center, City University of New York, 1979–2000; President, American Bach Society, 1996–2000; Dean, Mason Gross School of the Arts, Rutgers University, 2000–. *Publications:* Author, Organ Preludes of J. S. Bach, 1980 and J. S. Bach: Mass in B minor, 1997; Co-editor, J. S. Bach as Organist, 1986; Editor, The Forkel–Hoffmeister and Kuhnel Correspondence, 1990, and Bach Perspectives 2, 1996; Co-author, Organ Technique: Modern and Early, 2002; General Editor, Yale Music Masterworks series. *Contributions:* Early Music; Musical Quarterly; Bach-Jahrbuch. *Address:* 30 Euclid Avenue, Hastings-on-Hudson, NY 10706, USA.

**STEANE, John Barry;** British music journalist and writer; b. 12 April 1928, Coventry, England. *Education:* Univ. of Cambridge. *Career:* teacher of English, Merchant Taylors' School, Northwood 1952–88; reviewer, Gramophone 1973–, Musical Times 1988–, Opera Now 1989–. *Publications:* Marlowe: A Critical Study 1964, Dekker: The Shoemaker's Holiday (ed.) 1965, Tennyson 1966, Jonson: The Alchemist (ed.) 1967, Marlowe: The Complete Plays 1969, Nashe: The Unfortunate Traveller and Other Works 1972, The Grand Tradition: Seventy Years of Singing on Record 1973, Opera on Record (co-author, three vols) 1979–85, Song on Record (co-author, two vols) 1986–88, Choral Music on Record 1991, Voices: Singers and Critics 1992, Elisabeth Schwarzkopf: A Career on Record (with Alan Sanders) 1995, Singers of the Century (three vols) 1996, 1998, 2000, The Gramophone and the Voice 1999; contrib. to The New Grove Dictionary of Music and Musicians 1980, 2001, The New Grove Dictionary of Opera 1992. *Address:* 32 Woodland Avenue, Coventry, CV5 6DB, England (home). *Telephone:* (2426) 674842 (home).

**STEBLIANKO, Alexei;** Tenor; b. 1950, Russia. *Education:* Studied at the Leningrad Conservatory. *Career:* Has sung at the Kirov Theatre Leningrad as Lensky (debut), Radames, Manrico, Don José, Des Grieux, Andrei in Mazeppa, Herman in The Queen of Spades, Andrei Khovansky, Dmitri in Boris Godunov, Cavaradossi, Lohengrin, Canio and Pierre Bezukhov in War and Peace; Tours of Europe with the Kirov Company, including Covent Garden debut as Hermann in 1987; Sang at La Scala in 1982 as Aeneas in Les Troyens, and Covent Garden, 1989–90 as Jason in Médée, Vladimir in Prince Igor, both being new productions, and Manrico; Season 1992 as Otello at Reggio Emilia; Television appearances include Prince Igor, also on video; Sang Herman in The Queen of Spades at Bonn, 1996; Season 2000 as Pierre in War and Peace, as guest with the Mariinsky Company at Covent Garden; Mussorgsky's Boris Godunov at the London Proms, 2002. *Address:* Allied Artists, 42 Montpelier Square, London, SW7 1JZ, England.

**STEDRON, Milos;** Composer; b. 9 Feb. 1942, Brno, Czechoslovakia. *Education:* Musicology and music theory at Brno Academy, 1965–70. *Career:* Researched Janáček's music and worked in administration at the Moravian Museum in Brno, 1963–72; Teacher of theory at University of Brno from 1972. *Compositions include:* Operas: The Apparatus, after Kafka, 1967, Culinary Cares, Brno, 1979, The Chameleon, Or Josef Fouche, Brno, 1984; Ballets: Justina, 1969, Ballet Macabre, 1986; Annals of the Predecessors of the Avant-garde, chamber orchestra, 1997; Orchestra: Concerto for Double Bass and Strings, 1971, Diagram for Piano and Jazz Orchestra, 1971, Music for Ballet, 1972, Wheel, symphony, 1972, Cello Concerto, 1975, Sette Villanelle for Cello and Strings, 1981, Musica Concertante for Bassoon and Strings, 1986, Lammento for Viola and Orchestra, 1987; Chamber: Musica Ficta for Wind Quintet, 1968, String Quartet, 1970, Trium Vocum for Flute, Cello and Drums, 1984, Danze, Canti e Lamenti for String Quartet, 1986;Qudra, for ensemble, 1992; Trio for violin, cello and piano, 1993; String Quartet, 1994; Dances of King Lear, for cello, early music instruments and percussion, 1996; Vocal: Mourning Ceremony, cantata, 1969, Vocal symphony for Soprano, Baritone and Orchestra, 1969, Attendite, Populi, cantata for Chorus and Drums, 1982, Dolorosa Gioia Ommaggio á Gesualdo, Madrigal Cantata, 1978, Death Of Dobrovsky, cantata-oratorio, 1988; Missa Sine ritu, for mezzo and cello, 1996; Solo instrumental music and piano pieces. *Address:* c/o OSA, Cs armady 20, 160-56 Prague 6, Bubenec, Czech Republic.

**STEELE-PERKINS, Crispian;** trumpeter; b. 18 Dec. 1944, Exeter, England; m. Jane Elisabeth Mary 1995. *Education:* Guildhall School of Music. *Career:* many appearances in the Baroque repertoire at the Barbican and Royal Festival Halls with the City of London Sinfonia and the English Chamber Orchestra; Sadler's Wells Opera 1966–73; Royal Philharmonic 1976–80; played Haydn's Trumpet Concerto at the 1982 Edinburgh Festival; performances on the Natural Trumpet with The King's Consort, The English Baroque Soloists, The Taverner Players and The Parley of Instruments; Prof. of Trumpet, Guildhall School of Music 1980; workshops and masterclasses as preludes to concert presentations; season 1989–90 in Boston, Tokyo, Lisbon, Stuttgart and Gstaad; British festival engagements at Edinburgh, the Proms, City of London, Cambridge, Chester, Dartington, Leeds and Glasgow; US tour in 1988 and tour of Japan in 1990; The King's Consort 1985–; full-time trumpet soloist 1990–; Bach's Magnificat with The Sixteen at QEH, London 2000; mem. Royal Soc. of Musicians. *Recordings include:* 13 solo albums, Mr Purcell's Trumpeter (with the City of London Sinfonia under Richard Hickox), Messiah (featuring English trumpet of Handel's time), Shore's Trumpet, Let the Trumpet Sound, Six Trumpet Concertos, some 80 film tracks. *Publications:* contrib. articles to Historic Brass Journal. *Honours:* Historic Brass Soc. Christopher Monk Award 2004. *Address:* c/o Hyperion Records Ltd, PO Box 25, London, SE9 1AX, England.

**STEFANESCU, Ana Camelia;** Singer (Soprano); b. 8 June 1974, Bucharest, Romania. *Education:* Dinu Lipatti High School of Music, Bucharest; University of Music, Bucharest studying with Professor Andreiana Rosca. *Career:* Romanian National Opera, as Lucia di Lammermoor, Rosina, the Queen of Night in Die Zauberflöte, Zerbinetta, and Zerlina; Season 1997–98 as the Queen of Night at the Teatro Comunale, Florence, and at the Vienna State Opera; Deutsche Staatsoper, Berlin; Concerts and recitals in Romania, Poland, France, Netherlands, Luxembourg, the United Kingdom, Belgium and Switzerland; Season 1998–99 new productions in Berlin Deutsche Staatsoper with René Jacobs including Narsea in Solimano by Adolf Hasse; Concerts with José van Dam, José Carreras, performances at Teatro Real in Madrid and with the National Orchestra of Spain, several International Festivals; Roles include: Adina from L'elisir d'amore, Adele from Strauss' Die Fledermaus, the Fire, the Princess and the Lark from Ravel's l'Enfant et sortileges, Sophie from Massenet's Werther and Gilda from Verdi's Rigoletto. *Recordings:* Many recordings for Romanian radio and television, and WDR in Cologne. *Honours:* Prize Winner, Verviers International Competition and the Queen Elisabeth International Music Competition, Belgium; The Romanian Critics Award, 1997; Finalist of the Placido Domingo Competition, 1998. *Address:* c/o IMG Artists, Lovell House, 616 Chiswick High Road, London W4 5RX, England.

**STEFANESCU-BARNEA, Georgeta;** Romanian pianist and academic; *Professor, Ciprian Porumbescu Conservatory;* b. 25 April 1934, Satu-Mare; m. Jean Barnea 1958; two s. *Education:* Lyceum, Cluj, G. H. Dima Academy of Music, Cluj, Ciprian Porumbescu Conservatory, Bucharest, additional studies in Weimar, Germany, Switzerland, France. *Career:* piano teacher, Music Lyceum 1957–60; Univ. Lecturer, Ciprian Porumbescu Conservatory, Bucharest 1960–91, Univ. Reader 1991–, Prof. 1995–; numerous concerts and piano recitals in Romania, Germany, Switzerland, Czechoslovakia, England; appearances on Romanian radio and television, Radio Weimar, Suisse Romande Radio, Geneva. *Publications include:* Mihai Burada–Homage Album (three vols) 1993, Martian Negrea–Piano Pieces 1994, Romanian Sonatines for Piano (ed., two vols) 1994, many other pedagogical albums by H. Herz, Schubert, Grieg, Chopin, Haydn, Mozart and Beethoven, Romanian Pieces for Piano of the XIXth Century (ed., two vols) 1975, Romanian Sonatines for Piano (ed.) 1985, Lieds of Romanian Contemporary Creation (ed., two vols) 1987, Little Pieces for Piano Four Hands (ed., three vols) 1989, Album of Little Romanican Pieces for Piano 1997. *Address:* Str Compozitorilor Nr 32, Bl F8, Apt 24 Sect Vl, 77353 Bucharest 66, Romania; c/o Conservatorul Ciprian Porumbescu, Strada Stribei Vodá 33, 70732 Bucharest, Romania (office).

**STEFANOVIC, Ivana;** Composer; b. 14 Sept. 1948, Belgrade, Yugoslavia. *Education:* Belgrade Academy of Music, and with Gilbert Amy in Paris. *Career:* Radio Belgrade from 1976, founder of Sound Workshop (1985) and head of Music Production, 1990. *Compositions:* Hommage à François Villon, for voices and early instruments, 1978; Fragment of a Possible Order, for two pianos and ensemble, 1979; Interpretation of a Dream for flute, two speakers and tape, 1984; Lingua/Phonia/Patria, 1989; Psalm, for mezzo and choir, 1990; Isadora, ballet, 1992; Tree of life, for strings, 1997. *Address:* c/o SOKOJ, PO Box 213, Mišarska 12–14, 1100 Belgrade, Serbia and Montenegro.

**STEFANOWICZ, Artur;** Polish singer (countertenor); b. 1968, Szczecin. *Education:* Chopin Acad. of Music with Jerzy Artysz, studied with Paul Esswood and Jadwiga Rappe. *Career:* appearances from 1990 with the Warsaw Chamber Opera in Mozart's Ascanio in Alba, Apollo et Hyacinthus and Mitridate; Since 1991, appearances with orchestras and ensembles such as Orchestra Teatro La Fenice, Sinfonia Varsovia, Warsaw National Philharmonic, DSO Berlin, Capella Savaria, Musica Aeterna, Comnattimento Consort Amsterdam, Il Fondamento, Collegium Instrumentale Brugense, Les Arts Florissants, Netherlands Wind Ensemble, Orchestra of the Age of Enlightenment, Akademie für Alte Musik; Engagements include Warsaw and Budapest Chamber Opera, Opéra Comique Paris, Opéra Marseille, Théâtre des Champs Elysées, Théâtre du Châtelet, Opéra du Rhin, Florida Grand Opera, Miami, New York City Opera, Concertgebouw and De Nederlandse Opers Amsterdam, De Doelen Rotterdam, De Vlaamse Opera, Deutsche Staatsoper Berlin etc.; Festival engagements at Halla, Warsaw and Bratislava and concerts with the Vienna Philharmonic, Clemencic Consort and Ensemble Mosaique; Sang Ottone in Monteverdi's Poppea for Netherlands Opera in 1995; Various Mozart roles, including Farnace in Mitridate Re di Ponto, 1995; Recital at the Lincoln Center, New York with the Polish Chamber Orchestra, 1996 and the roles of Ottone at the Massachusetts Music Festival and Orlofsky in Austria, also in 1996; Repertoire includes Mozart's Ascanio, Farnace, Apollo, Handel's Arsamenes from Xerxes, Tolomeo from Julio Cesare, Polinesso from Ariodante, Unulfo from Rodelinda, Tamerlano, Didymus from Theodore, Orlando, Orfeo and Monteverdi's Ottone from L'Incoronazione di Poppea. *Recordings include:* Mozart operatic arias for the Polskie Nagrania company, with the Warsaw Symphony Orchestra and Karol Teutsch; Stabat Mater by Pergolesi, and by Vivaldi; Recital for Polish Radio with the Hedos Ensemble, 1994; Orlofsky in Die Fledermaus for BMG/Arte Nova Classics; Vespro della Beata Vergine by Monteverdi for Erato; Christmas Cantatas by Bach and Stölzel for Forlane; The Roes' Room by Josef Skrzek and Lech Majewski for Polygram, Cantatas by Handel and Vivaldi for Koch. *Honours:* Venanzio Rauzzini Prize for the best counter-tenor at the Mozart Singing Competition in Vienna. *Address:* Helen Sykes Artists Management, 100 Felsham Road, Putney, London SW15 1DQ, England.

**STEFANSSON, Finnur (Torfi)**, MA; Composer; b. 20 March 1947, Iceland; m. 1st, two s., one d., 2nd, two d., 3rd Steinunn Johannesdottir, 18 Aug. 2002. *Education:* University of Iceland, 1972; University of Manchester, 1974; Reykjavík College of Music, 1985; University of California, 1989. *Career:* Government and Law, Iceland; Member of Parliament, 1978; Ombudsman, Ministry of Justice, 1980; Lecturer, Reykjavík College of Music, 1991–94; Music Critic, 1991–94; Composer, 1994–; mem, Icelandic Society of Composers. *Compositions:* Works for Full Orchestra: Piece I, 1986; Piece II, 1988; Piece III, 1992; Piece IV, 1995; Piece V, 1997; Piece VI, 2001; Piece VII, 2003; Opera: The Shinbone and the Shell, 1992; Oratoria: The Seventh Word of Christ, 2003; Concertos: Concerto for violin and orchestra, 1996; for clarinet, bassoon and orchestra, 1991; Concerto Grosso, 1992; Chamber Music: String quartets, 1989, 1994, 1998; Wind quintets, 1993, 1996; Violin and piano, 1985, 1998; Flute and piano, 2001; Clarinet and piano, 1993; Piano Solo, 1987, 1995, 1997; Choral: My mother said, 1999; Cradle song, 1996; Christmas night, 2001; Solo songs to Icelandic and English texts. *Recordings:* Waves in the field, 2000. *Current Management:* Iceland Music Information Center. *Address:* Vesturfold 44, 112 Reykjavik, Iceland. *E-mail:* fts@li.is.

**STEFFEK, Hanny;** Singer (Soprano); b. 12 Dec. 1927, Biala, Poland. *Education:* Studied at the Vienna Music Academy and the Salzburg Mozarteum. *Career:* Sang in concert from 1949 with opera debut in 1951; Sang at the Graz Opera from 1953 then the Frankfurt Opera, and at the Munich Staatsoper, 1957–72; Salzburg Festival, 1950–55 as Papagena, Ilia and Blondchen, Covent Garden in 1959 as Sophie in Der Rosenkavalier, Aix-en-Provence in 1960 and Teatro Fenice Venice in 1962; Sang at the Vienna Staatsoper, 1964–73; Sang Christine in the British premiere of Intermezzo by Strauss at Edinburgh in 1965. *Recordings include:* Despina in Così fan tutte; Das Buch mit Sieben Siegeln by Franz Schmidt. *Address:* c/o Bayerische Staatsoper, Postfach 745, 8000 Munich 1, Germany.

**STEFFENS, Walter;** Professor and Composer; b. 31 Oct. 1934, Aachen, Germany. *Education:* Basic music education with Toni and Max Spindler; Conducting with Rolf Agap; Music theory and composition with Klussmann, Maler and Philipp Jarnach at Musikhochschule Hamburg; Musicology, phonetics, theology, arts and general history at University of Hamburg. *Career:* Dozent (lecturer) in Composition and Music Theory at Hamburg Conservatorium, 1962–69; Professor of Composition and Music Theory, masterclasses, Hochschule für Musik, Detmold, 1969–. *Compositions:* Operas: Eli, librettos by composer, after Mystery of The Sorrow of Israel by Nelly Sachs, Dortmund, 1967; Under Milk Wood, English and German versions, librettos by composer, after Dylan Thomas, Hamburg State Opera, 1973, 1977 Staatstheater Kassel opening; Grabbes Leben, libretto by Peter Schütze, Landestheater Detmold, 1986, Hamburg State Opera; Der Philosoph, librettos by Schütze, Landestheater Detmold, 1990; Die Judenbuche, libretto by Schütze, after Annette von Droste-Hülshoff, Dortmund, 1993, Gelsenkirchen during the New Music Theatre Days; Bildvertonugen, over 50 individual musical settings after paintings by Bosch, Marc Chagall, Klee, Picasso, Soto and others, Kassel, 1977 and 1992; Chamber music, Lieder, Concertos, Symphonies, ballet music and oratorio. *Address:* Rosenstr 15, 32756 Detmold, Germany.

**STEFIUK, Maria;** Singer (Soprano); b. 1967, Kiev, Ukraine. *Education:* Studied at the Kiev State Conservatoire. *Career:* Debut: Kiev Opera in 1982 as Violetta; Many appearances in Kiev, Moscow and St Petersburg as Lucia, Zerlina, Marguerite de Valois, Mimi, Leila in Les Pêcheurs de Perles and Marfa in The Tsar's Bride; Guest engagements in Dresden, Madrid, Wiesbaden, London, Paris, Washington, Tokyo and Sydney, including many concert appearances; Sang at La Scala Milan in Sorochintsy Fair by Mussorgsky. *Address:* c/o Sonata Ltd, 11 North Park Street, Glasgow G20 7AA, Scotland.

**STEGER, Ingrid;** Singer (Soprano and Mezzo-Soprano); b. 27 Feb. 1927, Roding, Germany. *Education:* Studied in Munich at the Musikhochschule. *Career:* Debut: As Azucena in Passau, 1951; Sang in opera at Augsburg, 1952–54, Kassel, 1954–59, Trier, 1958–60 and Oberhausen from 1960; Further engagements at Berlin Staatsoper, 1965–68, Parma and Venice, 1965 and 1968, Salzburg Easter Festival, 1967, Graz, 1974–75 and Karlsruhe, 1975–77; Sang Elektra at San Francisco in 1973 and appeared further at the state operas of Vienna, Hamburg and Stuttgart; Sang until 1986 in such roles as Rodelinda, Leonore, Senta, Elsa, Ortrud, Elisabeth, Isolde, Kundry, the Composer in Ariadne, Lady Macbeth, Amneris, Amelia in Un Ballo in Maschera, Santuzza, Turandot, Judith in Bluebeard's Castle and Schoeck's Penthesilea. *Recordings include:* Die Walküre conducted by Karajan. *Address:* c/o Stuttgart Staatsoper, Oberer Schlossgarten 6, 7000 Stuttgart, Germany.

**STEIGER, Anna;** Singer (Soprano); b. 13 Feb. 1960, Los Angeles, California, USA. *Education:* Guildhall School of Music, London; Further study with Vera Rozsa and Irmgard Seefried. *Career:* Associated with Glyndebourne Opera from 1983 singing Micaela on tour in 1985, Poppea at the 1986 Festival and in the 1987 premiere production of Osborne's The Electrification of the Soviet Union; Sang at Lausanne Opera in 1985 in La Cenerentola, Opera North in 1986 as Musetta, Covent Garden Opera from 1987 in Parsifal and Jenůfa, English National Opera in The Makropulos Case, and Geneva Opera as Concepcion in L'Heure Espagnole; Sang Despina in Così fan tutte for Netherlands Opera in 1990, and Eurydice in Milhaud's Les Malheurs d'Orphée at the Queen Elizabeth Hall in 1990; Season 1991–92 as Despina

at Stuttgart, a Hooded Figure in the premiere of Osborne's Terrible Mouth at the Almeida Theatre, and Zerlina for Netherlands Opera; Sang in Verdi's Un Giorno di Regno for Dorset Opera, 1994; Sang the Marquise in La Fille du régiment at St Gallen, 2000; Concert engagements include BBC recitals, Clarissa's Mad Scene by Holloway with the London Symphony, Les Illuminations with Bournemouth Sinfonietta and Fauré's Requiem with Scottish National Orchestra. *Recordings:* Poème de L'Amour et de La Mer by Chausson, with the BBC Scottish Symphony Orchestra. *Honours:* Peter Pears Award, 1982; Richard Tauber Award, 1984; John Christie Award, 1985. *Address:* c/o Stadtheater St Gallen, Museumstrasse 24, CH –9000 St Gallen, Switzerland.

**STEIGER, Rand;** Composer and Conductor; b. 18 June 1957, New York, USA. *Education:* New York High School of Music and Art, 1972–75; Percussion and Composition at the Manhattan School of Music (BMus 1980); California Institute of the Arts, with Brown, Subotnick and Powell (MFA 1982); Yale University with Elliott Carter, Betsy Jolas and Jakob Druckman; Further study at IRCAM, electronic music studios, Paris. *Career:* Faculty, University of Costa Rica, 1984–85, California Institute of the Arts, 1982–87 and University of California at San Diego, from 1987; Conductor and Director of contemporary music performances with SONOR at San Diego and with the Los Angeles Philharmonic New Music Group; From 1981 member new-music ensemble E.A.R., based at California Institute of the Arts. *Compositions include:* Brave New World for voices and electronics, 1980; Dialogues II for marimba and orchestra, 1980; Quintessence for 6 instruments, 1981; Currents Caprice, electronic, 1982; Kennedy Sketches for marimba and vibraphone, 1982; In Nested Symmetry for 15 instruments and electronics, 1982; Tributaries for chamber orchestra, 1986; Tributaries for Nancarrow, for six computer-controlled pianos, 1987; ZLoops for clarinet, piano and percussion, 1989; Mozart Tributary for clarinet quintet, 1991; The Burgess Shale for orchestra, 1994; Resonant Vertices, for ensemble, 1996; Frames, for ensemble, 1998; Diaspora for cello and percussion, 1999; Lemma I and II, for percussion and electronics 1997, 1999. *Honours:* First Composer Fellow of the Los Angeles Philharmonic, 1987–88. *Address:* c/o ASCAP, ASCAP Building, 1 Lincoln Plaza, New York, NY 10023, USA.

**STEIN, Caroline;** Singer (Soprano); b. 1963, Germany. *Education:* Musikhochschule, Cologne. *Career:* Debut: Würzburg Municipal Theatre; Sang with Wiesbaden State Opera from 1989, as Adele, Zerlina and The Queen of Night, Hannover Opera 1991-99, as Adina, Norina, Olympia, Sophie in Der Rosenkavalier, Zerbinetta, Susanna, and Venus in Ligeti's Le Grand Macabre; Further engagements at the Komische and Deutsche Operas, Berlin, and at Leipzig, Lisbon, Dresden and Munich; Blonde in Die Entführung at Quebec and Covent Garden (2000); Flower Maiden in Parsifal at Bayreuth, and roles in Henze's König Hirsch at Hannover and Rihm's Die Eroberung von Mexico at Frankfurt; London Proms Concerts, 2000-2001. *Address:* Semper Oper, Dresden, Theaterplatz 2, D-01067 Dresden, Germany.

**STEIN, Horst;** German conductor; b. 2 May 1928, Elberfeld. *Education:* Cologne Musikhochschule. *Career:* conducted first at Wuppertal, then at the Hamburg Staatsoper 1951–, and Berlin Staatsoper 1955–61; Opera Dir in Mannheim 1963–70; conducted the S American premiere of Schoenberg's Gurrelieder at Buenos Aires 1964; Bayreuth Festival from 1969 with Parsifal and Der Ring des Nibelungen; Principal Conductor, Vienna Staatsoper 1970–72; Music Dir, Hamburg Staatsoper 1972–79; Dir, Hamburg Philharmonic 1973–76; has conducted Tristan und Isolde in Buenos Aires, Der fliegende Holländer in Sofia and Parsifal at the Paris Opéra; Conductor, Orchestre de la Suisse Romande 1980–85; Dir, Bamberg Symphony from 1985, Basle Symphony from 1987; conducted Fidelio at the 1990 Salzburg Festival; Parsifal at the Opéra Bastille, Paris 1997; often heard in the symphonies of Bruckner. *Address:* c/o Bamberger Symphoniker, Mußstraße 1, 96047 Bamberg, Germany (office). *Website:* www.bamberger-symphoniker.de (office).

**STEIN, Peter;** Stage Director; b. 1 Oct. 1937, Berlin, Germany. *Career:* Worked with Munich Kammerspiele from 1964 directing Saved by Edward Bond in 1967; Directed plays by Brecht in Munich, Goethe and Schiller in Bremen; Co-founded the Berlin Schaubuhne Company in 1970 and was Artistic Director until 1985; Debut as opera director with Das Rheingold in Paris, 1976; For Welsh National Opera has directed Otello in 1986, Falstaff in 1988, Pelléas et Mélisande in 1992 and Peter Grimes in 1999; Director of Drama at Salzburg Festival, 1992–97; Staged Schoenberg's Moses und Aron at Salzburg, 1996; Engaged for Simon Boccanegra, 2000. *Recordings include:* Videos of Welsh National Opera productions, as director for television.

**STEINAUER, Mathias;** Composer; b. 20 April 1959, Basel, Switzerland; m. Elena Gianini, 3 June 1991. *Education:* Teaching Diploma, Piano, with P Efler, Teaching Diploma, Composition Theory, with R Moser, R Stuter, J Wildberger, Musik-Akademie, Basel, 1978–86; Private Study with G Kurtág, Budapest. *Career:* Various concerts of own music, radio productions, film music, 1982–; Founder, Komponisten Forum, 1982; Teacher of Music theory, and composition at the Hochschule für Musik and Theater Winterthur, Zürich, 1986. *Compositions include:* Music for xylophone, marimba and 2 musical boxes, 1984; Musik in fünf Teilen for 3 cellists and 2 percussionists, 1985; Andante for percussion trio, 1985; Vier Klangbilder for baritone, large orchestra, female choir, 18 recorders, words by H Erni, 1986; Visions for 12 wind instruments, 2 percussionists, piano, 1987; Drei Skizzen for string quartet, 1987; Duat, 14 signs for chamber orchestra. 1988;... wir Risse im

Schatten..., concerto for flute and orchestra, 1988–89; Blutenlese for 2 choirs, soprano, children's voice, ensemble, words by 12 authors, 1990–91; Undici Duettini for violin and viola, 1991; Speculum Sibyllinum, 1992; Omaggio ad Italo Calvino for clarinet, horn, violin and piano, 1993; Il rallentamento della sarabanda for piano, percussion and orchestra, 1993–95; Die gehaubte Braut, a little wedding music for mezzo-soprano and organ, 1994; Jahreszeiten for percussion trio, 1994; Alta fedeltà for 2 violins and tape, 1996; Rumori cardiacl for flute, clarinet, violin, cello and piano, 1996; Nacht, pipe dreams for chamber orchestra; Koren Fantasie, 1997. *Recordings:* For various radio stations in Switzerland. *Address:* c/o Konservatorium Winterhur, Tossertobelstrasse 1, CH 8400 Winterhur, Switzerland.

**STEINBACH, Heribert;** Singer (Tenor); b. 17 May 1937, Duisberg, Germany. *Education:* Studied in Düsseldorf, and in Cologne with Clemens Glettenberg. *Career:* Sang at the Cologne Opera, 1964–66, and Staatstheater Karlsruhe, 1966–68; Member of the Deutsche Oper am Rhein Düsseldorf, 1968–76, and Munich Staatsoper, 1977–80; Sang at Bayreuth Festival, 1971–76 as Froh and Melot; Guest engagements at the Paris Opéra in 1976 and 1978, and Lisbon and Barcelona in 1978; Sang Loge in Das Rheingold at the 1979 Maggio Musicale Florence and again at the Teatro Colón Buenos Aires in 1982; Sang Tristan at Lausanne in 1983, Walther von Stolzing at the Metropolitan in 1985 followed by Siegfried at Kassel; Sang at Teatro Regio Turin, 1987–88 as Siegmund in Die Walküre; At the first season of the new Musiektheater Rotterdam in 1988 sang Siegfried in Der Ring des Nibelungen; Sang Herod in Salome in 1989 at Lyric Opera of Queensland. *Recordings:* Pfitzner's Palestrina; Tristan und Isolde conducted by Bernstein; Die Soldaten by Zimmermann. *Address:* c/o Hochschule für Musik Rheinland, Vocal Faculty, Robert-Schumann-Institut, Fischerstrasse 110, D–40416 Dusseldorf, Germany.

**STEINBERG, Pinchas;** Conductor; b. 12 Feb. 1945, New York, USA. *Education:* Studied in New York and at Tanglewood; Composition studies with Boris Blacher in Berlin. *Career:* Took part in the 1964 Tanglewood Festival and became Professor and Assistant at the University of Indiana; Associate Conductor at the Lyric Opera Chicago from 1967, making his debut with Don Giovanni; Conducted leading orchestras in Europe from 1972; Conducted at the Frankfurt Opera from 1979 and has led performances in Stuttgart, Hamburg and Berlin and at Covent Garden, Paris Opéra and the San Francisco Opera; Musical Director at Bremen, 1985–89, Chief Conductor at the Verona Arena in 1989 and Conductor of the Austrian Radio Symphony Orchestra notably in Janáček's Everlasting Gospel and Dvořák's Te Deum in 1990; Appeared at Bregenz Festival in 1990 with Catalani's La Wally and conducted Rossini's Tancredi at the 1992 Salzburg Festival; L'amore dei tre re at the 1994 Montpellier Festival; Further opera includes Rienzi for Radio France, Rigoletto at Orange, Nabucco at the Opéra Bastille, Tosca at Houston and Trovatore in Geneva; Un Ballo in Maschera at Monte Carlo, 1998; Die Walküre at Toulouse, 1999. *Honours:* Winner, Florence International Conductors' Competition, 1972. *Address:* c/o Poilvé, 16 avenue Franklin D. Roosevelt, F–75008 Paris, France.

**STEINBERGER, Birgit;** Singer (soprano); b. 1967, Berghausen, Salzach, Austria. *Education:* Studied with Wilma Lipp in Salzburg, Charlotte Lehmann in Hannover and with Kurt Widmer. *Career:* Debut: Heidelberg 1991, as Serpetta in La Serva padrona by Pergolesi; Sang at Basle Oper 1992-1994, then at Vienna Volks and State Operas, as Susanna, Marzelline in Fidelio, Papagena, Marie in Lortzing's Zar and Zimmermann, Nicolai's Anne, and Musetta in La Bohème; Operetta roles include Franziska in Wiener Blut, Rosalinde in Die Fledermaus and Lehar's Valencienne. *Honours:* Prizewinner. Hugo Wolf Competition, Stuttgart, 1990. *Address:* c/o Volksoper, Währingerstrasse 78, A-1090 Vienna, Austria.

**STEINECKER, Anton;** Slovak composer; b. 9 Dec. 1971, Bratislava. *Education:* Bratislava Conservatory, Kroměříž Conservatory, Czech Republic, Acad. of Music and Drama, Bratislava with Jozef Sixta and Dušan Martincek, Acad. of Music and Drama, Prague with Svatopluk Havelka and Juraj Filas, Jerusalem Rubin Acad. of Music and Dance with Mark Kopytman, Acad. of Music and Drama, Bratislava with Dušan Martincek and Vladimír Bokes, Hochschule für Musik Saar, Germany with Theo Brandmüller, also studied with Tadeáš Salva. *Career:* debut, Ground for oboe and viola, Mirbach Concert Hall, Bratislava 1993; works performed at festivals in Slovakia, Czech Repub., Germany, Russia, Israel, France, Austria, Poland and USA; Lecturer, Acad. of Arts, Banská Bystrica, Slovakia 2001–02; masterclasses Bohemia Festival, Czech Repub. with Dušan Martinček 1996, Eighth Int. Summer Programme in Composition, CASMI, Czech Repub. with Ladislav Kubík 2001, Ostrava New Music Days and Festival, Czech Repub. with Jean-Yves Bosseur, Alvin Lucier, Petr Kotik, Christian Wolff and Tristain Murail 2001, 2003, Int. Music Acad. Masters de Pontelevoy, France with Mark Kopytman 2002, New Music Darmstadt, Germany with Brian Ferheyhough and Chaya Czerhovin 2003, Days for Interpretation and Performance Praxis, Hochschule für Musik Saar, Germany with Theo Brandmüller and Toshio Hosokawa 2003, 2004; mem. Slovakian Composers' League. *Compositions:* Piano Trio 1994, Jaj, Bože môj! for a capella SATB choir (third prize Year of Slovak Music Composition Competition 1995) 1993–94, Ground for oboe and viola 1993, Invention for violin, viola or cello 1994–95, Preludium e Quasi una passacaglia for string orchestra 1994, Impressions for piano 1995–96, Moments musicaux for string trio 1996, Notturno for horn 1996, String Quartet No. 1 1996–98, Variants for clarinet 1998, String Trio 1998–99, Memories for percussion 1998–99, Wind Quintet 2000, String Quartet No. 2 Choral Variations 2000, Es umfingen mich

die Wogen des Todes Cantata for baritone, SATB choir and chamber orchestra 2000, Chamber Opera in Four Scenes (libretto by Daniila Charms) 2001, String Quartet No. 3 Preludium – Fragmente 2001–02, Preludium for violoncello, violin or viola 2001–02, Notturni for cimbalom 2001–04, Impressions for clarinet 2002, Quasi una sonata for cimbalom 2003–05, Quintet for cimbalom and string quartet 2003. *Recordings include:* with Slovak Radio: Ground for oboe and viola 1994, Notturno for horn 1997, String Trio 2001, Wind Quintet 2001, Preludium e Quasi una passacaglia for string orchestra 2002, Notturni for cimbalom 2004; with Saarlandischem Rundfunk Saarbrücken: Impressions for clarinet 2003, Notturni for cimbalom 2004; other: Kohelet for baritone and piano trio 2000, Miserere mei Domine for a capella, SAATB choir 2002, Preludium for violincello 2002. *Publication:* contrib. to Slovak Music 1998. *Honours:* most-played composition prize Slovak Protection League of Authors 2004. *Address:* Tolsteho 2, 81106 Bratislava, Slovakia (home). *E-mail:* anton_steinecker@hotmail.com (home).

**STEINER, Elisabeth;** Singer (Mezzo-Soprano); b. 17 March 1935, Berlin, Germany. *Education:* Studied in Berlin with Frida Leider. *Career:* Sang at the St ädtischen Oper Berlin from 1961 with debut in Blacher's Rosamunde Floris; Sang at Salzburg Festival in 1962 as Artemis in Gluck's Iphigenia in Aulis; Discovered by Rolf Liebermann and engaged for the Staatsoper Hamburg; Sang in many premieres there including Von Einem's Der Zerrissene in 1964, Penderecki's The Devils of Loudun in 1969, Kelemen's Der Belagerungszustand in 1970 and Stefen's Under Milk Wood in 1973; Appeared often at Bayreuth and in guest engagements at the Maggio Musicale Florence, Metropolitan Opera, New York and La Scala Milan; Sang at Vienna Staatsoper in 1980 in the premiere of Jesu Hochzeit by Gottfried von Einem; Sang the Countess in Lortzing's Wildschütz, Hamburg, 1994. *Recordings:* Roles in Tiefland, Die Fledermaus, The Devils of Loudun, Rienzi and Eine Nacht in Venedig. *Address:* c/o Staatsoper, Opernring 2, 1010 Vienna, Austria.

**STEINER, Frederick,** BM, PhD; American composer, conductor and musicologist; b. 24 Feb. 1923, New York, NY; m. Shirley Laura Steiner; two d. *Education:* Inst. of Musical Art, New York, Oberlin Conservatory of Music, Ohio, Univ. of Southern California. *Career:* composer, conductor, radio in New York; Music Dir, radio programmes This is Your FBI, To Los Angeles 1947, many other radio programmes; worked for Columbia Broadcasting System 1950; Lecturer in History and Art of Film Music, Univ. of Southern California 1984–89, Coll. of Santa Fe 1990–93; mem. Acad. of Motion Picture Arts and Sciences, American Musicological Soc., AFofM, ASCAP, Soc. of Composers and Lyricists, Film Music Soc. (bd of advisers). *Television music compositions include:* Andy Griffith, Danny Thomas, Gunsmoke, Have Gun Will Travel, Hogan's Heroes, Rocky and Bullwinkle Show, Movie of the Week, Fractured Fairy Tales, Rawhide, Star Trek, Twilight Zone, Hawaii Five-O, Dynasty, Amazing Stories, Tinytoons, Perry Mason theme, Dudley Doright theme. *Film music compositions include:* Della, First To Fight, Hercules, The Man From Del Rio, Run For The Sun, St Valentine's Day Massacre, Time Limit, Shipwreck, The Color Purple. *Other compositions:* Navy Log March, Five Pieces for String Trio, Tower Music for brass and percussion, Pezzo Italiano for cello and piano, Act Without Words for percussion ensemble, Indian music for viola and piano; transcriptions. *Recordings:* King Kong (conductor, score by Max Steiner), Great American Film Scores, Music from the Television Series Star Trek. *Publications:* foreword, in Music on Demand (R. R. Faulkner) 1983, Music for Star Trek, in Wonderful Inventions (Iris Newsom) 1985, Fred Steiner on Film Music, in Film Score (Tony Thomas) 1991, Interlude, in Hollywood Holyland (Ken Darby) 1992, Arthur Honegger's Les Ombres: Fragment of a Lost Score, in The Rosaleen Moldenhauer Memorial: Music History from Primary Sources (eds Jon Newsom and Alfred Mann) 2000; contrib. to Journal of the Arnold Schoenberg Institute, Film Music Notebook, Quarterly Journal of the Library of Congress, New Grove Dictionary of American Music, Dictionary of American Biography, New Grove Dictionary of Music and Musicians, album sleeve notes. *Honours:* City of Los Angeles Special Recognition Certificate, Film Music Soc. Award of Merit. *Address:* 1086 Mansion Ridge Road, Santa Fe, NM 87501, USA.

**STEINER, Paul;** Singer; b. 19 Aug. 1948, Horgen, nr. Zürich, Switzerland. *Education:* studied with Elsa Cavelti in Basle, and Adalbert Kraus in Stuttgart. *Career:* many appearances in opera houses in Switzerland, notably at Paolino in Il Matrimonio Segreto, Milford in Rossini's Cambiale di matrimonio, Marquis in Zar und Zimmermann by Lortzing; concert engagements throughout Germany and Switzerland in repertory from Baroque to contemporary music; many premiere performances, including Une songe d'une nuit d'été, by R. Gerber, Biel 1984. *Recordings include:* Cantatas by Mozart and Schubert; Markus Passion, attributed to Bach (Collegium Musicum); Lieder by Othmar Schoeck. *Address:* c/o Stadttheater Biel, Burggasse 19, 2502 Biel, Switzerland.

**STEINHARDT, Arnold;** Violinist; b. 1 April 1937, Los Angeles, California, USA. *Education:* Studied at the Curtis Institute, Philadelphia, with Ivan Galamian. *Career:* Debut: With Los Angeles Philharmonic, 1951; Assistant Concertmaster, Cleveland Orchestra under George Szell; Performed in chamber music with Rudolf Serkin at the Marlboro Festival and prompted by Alexander Schneider to co-found the Guarneri String Quartet, 1964; Many tours of America and Europe, notably in appearances at the Spoleto Festival in 1965, to Paris with Arthur Rubinstein and London in 1970, in the complete quartets of Beethoven; Noted for performances of Viennese classics, works by Walton, Bartók and Stravinsky; Season 1987–88 included opening concert in New Concert Hall at Shufmotomo Festival, Japan and British appearances at

St John's Smith Square and Queen Elizabeth Hall; Faculty Member of Curtis Institute at University of Maryland. *Recordings include:* Mozart's Quartets dedicated to Haydn; Complete Quartets of Beethoven; With Arthur Rubinstein, Piano Quintets of Schumann, Dvořák and Brahms; Piano Quartets by Fauré and Brahms. *Honours:* Edison Award for Beethoven recordings, 1971.

**STEINSKY, Ulrike;** Singer (Soprano); b. 21 Sept. 1960, Vienna, Austria. *Education:* Studied with Margaret Zimmermann, Hilde Zadek and Waldemar Kmentt in Vienna. *Career:* Many performances as Constanze in Die Entführung while a student; Debut at the Vienna Staatsoper in 1983 as the Queen of Night; Has also sung in Die Zauberflöte with the Cologne Opera in Tel-Aviv, Covent Garden in Los Angeles in 1984 and at the 1985 Bregenz Festival; Appeared with the Bayerische Staatsoper Munich, 1984–90 and at Zürich from 1985 as Zerline in Fra Diavolo in season 1989–90; Further guest engagements at Cologne, Dortmund, Barcelona as Fiakermilli in Arabella in 1989 and at Hamburg in 1990; Season 1992 as Fiakermilli at La Scala; Other roles include Adele in Die Fledermaus, Musetta, Zerlina, Pamina, Despina, Aennchen and Papagena; Has also sung in operettas by Oscar Straus, Lehar and Millöcker; Concert performances of Così fan tutte, Don Giovanni and Mozart's La Finta Giardiniera; Sang Pamina at the Loreley Fstival, 2000. *Recordings:* Die Fledermaus. *Address:* c/o Wiener Staatsoper, 1010 Vienna, Austria.

**STEJSKAL, Margot;** Singer (Soprano); b. 9 Feb. 1947, Engelsdorf, Leipzig, Germany. *Education:* Studied in Weimar and at Leipzig Musikhochschule with Hannelore Kuhse. *Career:* Debut: Cottbus, as Musetta in 1975; Sang in opera at Cottbus until 1977, Staatsoper Dresden, 1977–80, and Chemnitz, 1980–84; Sang Sophie in Der Rosenkavalier at the opening of Semper Oper Dresden, 1985; Guest appearances at Berlin Staatsoper and elsewhere in Germany; Other roles have included Blondchen, Susanna, Nannetta and Adele in Die Fledermaus; Many concert appearances. *Recordings include:* Der Rosenkavalier. *Address:* c/o Semper Oper Dresden, 8012 Dresden, Germany.

**STELLA, Antonietta;** Singer (Soprano); b. 15 March 1929, Perugia, Italy. *Education:* Studied at the Accademia di Santa Cecilia, Rome. *Career:* Debut: Leonora in Il Trovatore, Spoleto, 1950; Rome debut, 1951, as Leonora in La Forza del Destino; Germany from 1951, in Stuttgart, Wiesbaden and Munich; Sang as guest all over Italy; Verona Arena and La Scala debuts, 1953; At the New York Metropolitan (debut 1956) she sang Aida, Butterfly, Tosca, Elisabeth de Valois (Don Carlos), Violetta and Amelia (Un Ballo in Maschera); At Naples in 1974 sang in the premiere of Maria Stuarda by de Bellis. *Recordings:* Roles in Verdi's Simon Boccanegra, Un Ballo in Maschera, Don Carlos, Il Trovatore, Aida and Il Battaglia di Legnano; Donizetti's Linda di Chamounix; Puccini's La Bohème and Tosca; Giordano's Andrea Chénier.

**STEMME, Nina;** Swedish singer (soprano); b. 1966, Stockholm. *Education:* studied in Stockholm. *Career:* Stockholm Royal Opera as Cherubino 1994; Stora Theatre Gothenburg as Donna Elvira and Butterfly; Bayreuth Festival as Freia in Das Rheingold 1994–95; Cologne Opera from 1995, as Pamina, Butterfly, Mozart's Countess, and Mimi 1998; sang Katerina in Martinů's Greek Passion at Bregenz 1999; Elsa at Basle and Tosca for Cologne Opera; season 2000–01 as Senta at Antwerp, Marguerite for the Savonlinna Festival, Manon Lescaut for ENO and Tatiana in Brussels, Senta at the New York Met; sang Elisabeth in Tannhäuser at the Deutsche Oper, Berlin 2003; sang Isolde in Tristan und Isolde at Beyreuth, Elisabeth in Tannhauser at Geneva, and Amelia in Un Ballo in maschera at the Royal Opera House, London 2005; many concert appearances. *Honours:* winner Placido Domingo Competition 1993, finalist Cardiff Singer of the World Competition 1993. *Current Management:* Artists Management Zürich, Rütistrasse 52, 8044 Zürich-Gockhausen, Switzerland. *Telephone:* (44) 821 89 57. *Fax:* (44) 821 01 27. *E-mail:* schuetz@artistsman.com. *Website:* www.artistsman.com.

**STENE, Randi;** Singer (mezzo-soprano); b. 1967, Norway. *Education:* Studied at the Norwegian State Academy of Music, Oslo, and the Opera Academy, Copenhagen. *Career:* Salzburg Festival from 1992, in Salome and Dallapiccola's Ulisse; Premiere of Reigen by Boesmans at Brussels, 1993; Season 1993–94 as Octavian at the Théâtre du Châtelet, Paris, and Dorabella at the Royal Opera, Copenhagen; Season 1995–96 with Cherubino at Covent Garden, Olga in Eugene Onegin at the Opèra Bastille, Paris, and Carmen in Brussels; Returned to London 1997, as Silla in a new production of Palestrina by Pfitzner; Hansel at the Théâtre du Châtelet, Paris, 1997; Concert repertory includes Szymanowski's Stabat Mater (London Proms, 1996), Dvořák's Requiem (Edinburgh Festival, 1996), Missa Brevis by Bach (Salzburg), the Christmas Oratorio, Zemlinsky's Maeterlinck Lieder and Falla's Three Cornered Hat (with the Berlin Symphony Orchestra); Schubert's A-flat Mass with the Oslo Philharmonic Orchestra and Sibelius's Kullervo Symphony with the Stockholm Philharmonic Orchestra. *Recordings include:* Vivaldi Cantatas; Opera Arias, with Kathleen Battle; Salome, under Christoph von Dohnányi; Kullervo Symphony. *Honours:* Finalist, 1991 Cardiff Singer of the World Competition. *Current Management:* Askonas Holt Ltd, Lonsdale Chambers, 27 Chancery Lane, London, WC2A 1PF, England. *Telephone:* (20) 7400-1700. *Fax:* (20) 7400-1799. *E-mail:* info@askonasholt.co.uk. *Website:* www.askonasholt.co.uk.

**STENZ, Markus;** Conductor; b. 28 Feb. 1965, Bad Neuenahr, Germany. *Education:* Studied at the Cologne Musikhochschule in Salzburg, with Gary Bertini and Noam Sheriff. *Career:* With Ozawa and Bernstein at Tanglewood, 1988; Association with Hans Werner Henze includes Elegy for Young Lovers at Venice, 1988, and The English Cat in Berlin, 1989; Premieres of Das

Verratene Meer (Berlin, 1990) and Venus und Adonis (Munich, 1997); Musical Director of the Montepulciano Festival, 1989–92; Conducted Figaro at Los Angeles 1994 and Hamburg, 1996; English National Opera debut 1995, Don Giovanni; Principal Conductor of the London Sinfonietta from 1994, leading it at the 1994 Proms in Music by Kurtag, Ives and Xenakis; Season 1993–94 with the Berlin Symphony Orchestra, Scottish Chamber Orchestra and BBC Symphony Orchestra; Season 1994–95 included debuts with the Hallé Orchestra, Royal Stockholm Philharmonic, and Philharmonic of Rotterdam, Helsinki and Hamburg; Debut appearances with the Sydney and Melbourne Symphony Orchestras in season 1995–96 and Prom concert with Weill's Der Silbersee; Other operas include Henze's Bassarids in Hamburg (1994), Hans Zender's Stephen Climax in Brussels and Weill's Mahagonny in Stuttgart; Season 1997–98 included debuts with the Minnesota Orchestra and the Chicago Symphony Orchestra; Chief Conductor and Artistic Director, Melbourne Symphony Orchestra, 1998–. *Current Management:* Ingpen & Williams Ltd, 7 St George's Court, 131 Putney Bridge Road, London, SW15 2PA, England.

**STEPANOV, Oleg;** Pianist; b. 2 May 1956, Riga, Latvia; m. Natasha Vlassenko 1981, 1 d. *Education:* Undergraduate, Postgraduate, Moscow Tchaikovsky Conservatory. *Career:* Appeared as duo with Cellist Daniel Shafran; Appeared solo and as Chamber Music Player in Germany, Italy, Hungary, Sweden, Poland, Cuba, Bulgaria, Russia, Hong Kong and Australia; Lecturer in Piano, Queensland Conservatorium, Griffith University, Brisbane, Australia; Founder, Artistic Director, The Lev Vlasenko Piano Competition, Brisbane. *Honours:* First Prize, Grand Prize, Vittorio Gui Chamber Music Competition, Citta di Firenze, Italy, 1988. *Address:* 26 Ninth Ave, St Lucia, Brisbane, Qld 4067, Australia.

**STEPHAN, Erwin;** Singer (Tenor); b. 23 June 1949, Worms, Germany. *Education:* Studied in Frankfurt, Osnabruck and Karlsruhe; Further study with James King. *Career:* Debut: Flensburg, 1978; Sang in opera at Luneburg, Coburg and Giessen; Saarbrucken, 1984–86 in debut as Florestan and sang Tannhäuser from 1985, notably at Dortmund, Bremen, Geneva and the 1986 Orange Festival; Freiburg in 1987 as Otello, Huon in Oberon at Catania and Max in Der Freischütz at Cologne; US debut in 1989 as Walther von Stolzing at Seattle; Other roles have included Don José and Ismaele in Nabucco; Opera performances at Semper Oper Dresden and concert showings in France, Austria, Switzerland, Japan and South America. *Address:* c/o Semper Oper Dresden, 8012 Dresden, Germany.

**STÉPHANY, Anna,** MMus; singer (mezzo-soprano). *Education:* King's Coll., London, GSMD. *Career:* operatic roles include Smeraldina in The Little Green Swallow, Concepçion in L'Heure Espagnole, title role in Mignon, Marcellina in The Marriage of Figaro (all GSMD), Juno in Semele, Dorabella in Così fan tutte (both British Youth Opera); sang with Glyndebourne Festival Chorus 2002, 2003; has performed with The Bach Choir, Holst Singers, The Philharmonia Chorus; oratorio performances include Mendelssohn's Elijah with Richard Hickox, Barbican 2000, Stravinsky's Mass, Southwark Cathedral, Handel's Messiah with Sir David Willcocks, Royal Albert Hall 2003, Elgar's Dream of Gerontius with Michael George and Adrian Thompson, Exeter Cathedral 2004, Mendelssohn's Angel, St Peters Church, Kensington 2004, Mozart's Requiem, Guildford Cathedral 2005, Handel's Dixit Dominus with Highgate Choral Soc. 2005; recitals with pianist Jonathan Beatty include Die schöne Magelone, Hampstead Parish Church 2004, Brahms, Wolf and Hahn, St Mary on the Strand Church 2004; mem. Nat. Opera Studio, London 2005–. *Recordings:* Tomás Luis de Victoria, Motets 2003, Tenebrae, Gaudete 2004, Tenebrae, Rachmaninoff Vespers 2005. *Honours:* Clonter Opera Prize 2005, Joaninha Trust Award 2005, Kathleen Ferrier Award 2005, GSMD Gold Medal 2005. *Address:* c/o National Opera Studio, The Clore Building, 2 Chapel Yard, Wandsworth High Street, London, SW18 4HZ, England (office). *E-mail:* info@nationaloperastudio.org.uk (office). *Website:* www.nationaloperastudio.org.uk (office).

**STEPHEN, Pamela (Helen);** Singer (Mezzo-soprano); b. 1965, England; m. Richard Hickox. *Career:* Debut: Cathleen in The Rising of the Moon, Wexford, 1990; Appearances with Opera North as the Composer in the Mozart/Griffiths Jewel Box, Cherubino, Donna Clara in Gerhard's Duenna and Cynthia in Benedict Mason's Playing Away (Munich and London); Prince in Massenet's Cenrillon for WNO, Dafne in Peri's Euridice at Batignano and Juno in Semele for the City of London Festival; Season 1999–2000 with Sonya in War and Peace at Spoleto, Verdi's Maddalena for Los Angeles Opera, and Nero in Agrippina by Handel; Concerts including Haydn's Nelson Mass at the London Proms, Britten's Phaedra with the Los Angeles CO and Dream of Gerontius for the Scottish National Orchestra; Elgar's Sea Pictures at Lisbon.

**STEPHENSON, Donald James,** ARCM; British singer (tenor); b. 15 Feb. 1947, Leeds, England; m. (divorced); one s. one d. *Education:* Royal Manchester Coll. of Music, Nat. Opera Studio, ITEC. *Career:* ENO 1972–75; English Opera Group 1975; English Music Theatre 1976–78; freelance opera singer 1978–; festival appearances in the UK and Europe; film Death in Venice (Benjamin Britten, English Music Theatre); regular television and radio broadcasts; principal tenor, WNO; roles include Radames in Aida, Don José in Carmen, title role in Parsifal, Siegmund in Die Walküre, Max in Der Freischütz; Glyndebourne and Aldeburgh Festivals; numerous British premieres; world premieres include No. 11 Bus (Peter Maxwell Davies, London, Rome and New York) 1985; other appearances include Freiburg Opera in roles, including Alwa in Lulu 1986, Erik in Fliegende Holländer

1988; Scottish Opera as Florestan in Fidelio 1984, Red Whiskers in Billy Budd 1987; Opera North as Mark, Midsummer Marriage, Tippett 1985, Wiesbaden 1986; Florestan, Fidelio at Regensburg and Kaiserslautern Operas 1987–88, Hoffmann in Tales of Hoffmann, Stockholm 1990, First Jew in Salome, ENO 1991, Bob Boles in Peter Grimes 1992; Missa Solemnis, RAH 1992; sang Filaura in Cesti's Il Pomo d'Oro at Batignano 1998; mem. Equity, Int. Therapy Education Council. *Honours:* Arts Council Scholarship to study with Otakar Kraus 1974. *Address:* 55 Milner Street, York, YO24 4NJ, England.

**STEPHENSON, Michael;** Saxophonist; b. 16 Nov. 1963, Charlotte, North Carolina, USA; m. Cheryl Ann Swanson, 6 August 1988. *Education:* BMus, North Carolina School of Arts; MMus, Ithaca College. *Career:* Debut: New Century Saxophone Quartet, Carnegie Hall, New York City, 1993; White House; Ambassador Auditorium; Boston Symphony Hall; Concertgebouw, Amsterdam; Kennedy Centre. *Recordings:* With New Century Saxophone Quartet: Drastic Measures; Main Street, USA; Home Grown; New Century Christmas; Standard Repertoire. *Current Management:* Robert Besen, Besen Artists. *Address:* 102 Prince Road, Greenville, NC 27858, USA.

**STEPHINGER, Christoph;** Singer (Bass); b. 4 June 1954, Herrshing, Germany. *Education:* Studied at Munich Hochschule and the Opera Studio of Bayerische Staatsoper; Further study with Kurt Moll. *Career:* Sang at Bielefeld Staadttheater, 1982–86, Staatstheater Hannover from 1986; Guest appearances at Düsseldorf, Dortmund, Karlsruhe, Hamburg, Berlin, Nice and Spleto; Roles have included Wagner's Guernemanz, King Henry, Pogner and Daland, Mozart's Commendatore, Osmin, Sarastro and Alfonso, Kecal in The Bartered Bride and Jim in Maschinist Hopkins by Max Brand (at Bielefeld); Concert repertoire includes Herod in L'Enfance du Christ by Berlioz, with the Gächinger Kantorei under Helmuth Rilling in 1989; Sang Fasolt and Hunding in new productions of Das Rheingold and Die Walküre at Hannover in 1992; Season 1999–2000 as Leporello at the Theater am Gärtnerplatz, Munich, and Lothario in Mignon. *Address:* c/o Niedersachsische Staatstheater, Opernplatz 1, 30159 Hannover, Germany.

**STEPTOE, Roger Guy,** BA, ARAM; British composer, pianist and teacher; *Professor of Harmony, Analysis, Ecole Nationale de Musique, de Danse et l'Art Dramatique;* b. 25 Jan. 1953, Winchester, Hampshire, England. *Education:* Univ. of Reading and Royal Acad. of Music. *Career:* debut as composer at Purcell Room 1977, as pianist at Wigmore Hall 1982; first Vaughan Williams Composer-in-Residence, Charterhouse 1976–79; Prof. of Composition, Royal Acad. of Music 1980–91; US debut as composer and pianist at Federal Hall, NY 1991; Administrator of Contemporary Music Projects, Royal Acad. of Music 1989–91, for Int. Composer Festivals 1991–93; Prof. of Harmony, Analysis, Ecole Nationale de Musique, de Danse et l'Art Dramatique, Brive-la-Gaillarde, France 2001–; French debut as pianist and composer, Salle Cortot, Paris 2003; mem. Incorporated Soc. of Musicians. *Compositions include:* opera: King of Macedon (libretto by Ursula Vaughan Williams) 1979; orchestral: Dance Music for Symphonic Brass 1976, Two Miniatures for strings 1977, Oboe Concerto 1982, Tuba Concerto 1983, Clarinet Concerto 1989, Cello Concerto 1991, Cheers 1993, Impressions Correziennes 1999, This Side of Winter 2002; choral: Two Madrigals 1976, In Winter's Cold Embraces Dye (cantata for soprano, tenor, chorus and chamber orchestra) 1985, Life's Unquiet Dream (cantata for baritone, chorus and chamber orchestra) 1992; chamber: String Quartet No. 1 1976, No. 2 1985, No. 3 2002, No. 4 2003, Clarinet Quintet 1981, Four Sonnets for brass quintet 1984, Oboe Quartet 1989, Piano Quartet 2001; vocal: Aspects for high voice and piano 1978, Chinese Lyrics for soprano and piano 1982, Chinese Lyrics for mezzo or counter-tenor and piano 1983, The Bond of the Sea for bass-baritone and piano 1983, Five Rondos for soprano, baritone and piano 1989, Sonnets to Delia for baritone and piano 1993; instrumental: Three Preludes for piano 1976, Piano Sonata No. 1 1980, No. 2 1988, No. 3 2003, Prelude for guitar 1981, Equinox for piano 1981, Violin Sonata No. 1 1983, No. 2 1986, In the White and the Walk of the Morning (five poems for two guitars) 1989, Prelude La Dame de Labenche 2001, Prelude for viola and piano 2002, Clarinet Sonata 2003. *Address:* c/o Stainer & Bell Ltd, Victoria House, 23 Gruneison Road, London, N3 1DZ, England (office); 7 rue Jean Gentet, 19140 Uzerche, France (home). *E-mail:* post@stainer.co.uk (office); roger.steptoe@nordnet.fr (home).

**STERN, David;** Conductor; b. 1965, USA. *Career:* Music Director of the Philharmonisches Orchester, Westphalen, 1995: Principal Guest Conductor, 1998–; Music Director of the European Academy of Music, Aix-en-Provence, 1997–2000; Led the Philharmonia Orchestra, London, at the Albert Hall in a Yehudi Menuhin Memorial Concert; collaborations with the Peking Festival and several orchestras in China; Principal Guest Conductor of Opéra de Rouen, 2001–; Season 2000–01 with the Gurzenich Orchestra and the Royal Flanders Orchestra; Regular appearances with period instrument orchestra Concerto Köln, including tours of Europe and USA, 2002–2003. *Address:* c/o IMG Artists, Lovell House, 616 Chiswick High Road, London, W4 5RX.

**STERNBERG, Jonathan,** AB; American conductor; *Musical Director, Bach Festival of Philadelphia;* b. 27 July 1919, New York; m. Ursula Hertz 1957; one s. one d. *Education:* Washington Square Coll., New York Univ., Harvard Summer School, Juilliard School of Music, Manhattan School of Music, studied with Leon Barzin and Pierre Monteux. *Career:* initial engagements, Nat. Youth Administration Symphony Orchestra 1940–42; Shanghai Municipal Symphony 1945–46; professional debut Vienna Symphony Orchestra 1947; guest conductor with major orchestras and opera cos worldwide 1950–; Conductor, Halifax Symphony Orchestra, Nova Scotia 1957–58; Musical Dir,

Royal Flemish Opera 1962–66, Harkness Ballet 1966–68, Atlanta Opera and Ballet 1968–69; Visiting Prof. of Conducting, Eastman School of Music (Univ. of Rochester) 1969–71; Prof., Temple Univ. Coll. of Music 1971–89, Prof. Emeritus 1989–; Lecturer, Chestnut Hill Coll., Philadelphia 1989–92; Faculty, Int. Conductors' Workshop and Masterclasses, Zlin, Marienbad, Karlsbad (Czech Republic), Kharkov (Ukraine), Philadelphia, New York – 2005; conducted premiere performances in Europe, S Africa, China and USA of music by Bloch, Ives, Rorem, Blackwood, Persichetti, Prokofiev, Messiaen, Lajtha, von Einem, Diamond, Skrowaczewski, Hindemith; Ed.-at-Large Podium Notes (Conductors' Guild newsletter) 1982–; Musical Dir, Philadelphia Bach Festival 2003–; mem. Int. Arts Medicine Asscn (vice-pres. 1981–85), Bartok Soc. of America (vice-pres. 1972–78), Conductors' Guild (vice-pres. 1991–96, hon. life mem. 2003). *Recordings include:* several Haydn symphonies, Nelson Mass, Mozart Posthorn Serenade, several Bach cantatas, Rossini Stabat Mater, Prokoviev Piano Concerto No. 5 (Brendel), Mozart Piano Concerti (Badura-Skoda), Schubert Symphonies Nos 2, 4, 5, Bassett Variations for Orchestra, Ives Set of Pieces, Telemann Pimpinone. *Publications:* contrib. scores and parts to Journal of the Conductors' Guild 1983–2000. *Honours:* Citation Award for Outstanding Service to American Music 1972, Temple Univ. Faculty Research Award 1983, Distinguished Alumnus Award Third Street Music School Settlement 1988, Maestro Soc. Conducting Teacher of the Year 2001. *Address:* 5 West Chestnut Hill Avenue, Philadelphia, PA 19118, USA. *E-mail:* maestro@temple.edu.

**STERNDALE-BENNETT, Barry Monkhouse,** BA, FIAM, FRSA; British singer (baritone) and music administrator; b. 9 March 1939, London, England. *Education:* Univ. of Chicago, London Coll. of Music. *Career:* mem. Philharmonia Chorus 1962–96; appearances as soloist at festivals and on TV and radio in UK, Europe and Canada; Visiting Fellow Univ. of Reading 1996–2005; consultant to TCL 2000–05; Chair. Music Preserved Council 2004–; trustee and Dir Pro Corda, The Nat. School for Young Chamber Music Players 2004–, Bewley Music Trust 2004–; custodian of Sir William Sterndale-Bennett Library; mem. Royal Philharmonic Soc., British Music Soc., Int. Mendelssohn Foundation. *Publications:* contrib. several articles to Journal of the British Music Soc. *Address:* White Windows, Longparish, Hants. SP11 6PB, England (home). *E-mail:* b.sbennett@andover.co.uk (home).

**STERNKLAR, Avraham;** Pianist, Composer and Educator; b. 21 Oct. 1930, Trieste, Italy; m. Evelyn Katz, 10 July 1953, one s. *Education:* Piano with L Kestenberg and composition with P Ben Haim, Israel; Juilliard School of Music, New York, USA, 1949–54; Piano with J Friskin and E Steuermann; Composition with V Giannini; Graduate work, chamber music. *Career:* Debut: Tel-Aviv, Israel; Recitals, broadcasts and performances with Israel Philharmonic, Jerusalem Symphony; Music Correspondent, Israel Broadcasting Service, 1949–52; Film; Siena Pianoforte, numerous concerts throughout USA, Canada and Europe as soloist, chamber music and as soloist with orchestras; Guest performer at Festivals; Lecturer at seminars and workshops; Specialist in Contemporary Music; Premiered many works several of which are now recorded; Faculty Member, Chamber Music Workshop, sponsored by Training Orchestra, Long Island and New York University; Appeared in concerts with Mischa Elman, Ruggiero Ricci, Oscar Shumsky, Zvi Zeitlin, Tossy Spivakovsky, Jascha Horenstein, the Hofstra String Quartet and the Bayview Chamber Players; Associate Professor of Piano Performance at Aaron Copland School of Music, Queens College, 1992. *Compositions:* For Piano: Sonatinas, Sonata, Trapezium, Etudes, A Promise Fulfilled, a set of 10 piano pieces based on the paintings of Tea Sternklar, The General Schwarzkopf March, works for one piano four hands and for two pianos; Violin and Piano sonata, Cello and Piano sonata, Clarinet and Piano sonata; Introduction and Dance for Flute and Piano, songs, chamber music, choral works, recorder works, 12 duets for 2 violins, educational music; Etudes for Piano; Sonatina for Flute, Oboe and Bassoon; Silhouttes for solo Harp. *Honours:* Recipient of 17 Meet the Composer Awards; 3 Best of the Year Awards from the Piano Quarterly Magazine. *Current Management:* E Florence. *Address:* 14 Jerold Street, Plainview, NY 11803, USA. *E-mail:* composers@sprynet.com. *Website:* www.clearstarinternational.com/asbio .html.

**STEUERMAN, Jean Louis;** Concert Pianist; b. 16 March 1949, Rio de Janeiro, Brazil; m. Monica Laport, 14 Aug 1981, 2 s. *Career:* Debut: Rio de Janeiro, 1963; Appearances world-wide with major orchestras with British debut in 1976; Recent engagements with Royal Philharmonic under Menuhin, Britten's Concerto at Athens Festival, with London Symphony Orchestra under Abbado and Liverpool Philharmonic and Gewandhaus Orchestra under Masur; Played Bach's D minor Concerto at the 1985 Promenade Concerts in London; Tour of Japan in 1989 with Stuttgart Chamber Orchestra, Schumann's Concerto with the Hallé Orchestra; Season 1989–90 season included recital at Salle Gaveau in Paris, Mendelssohn's G minor Concerto with Florida Philharmonic Orchestra and Tippett's Concerto with Helsinki Philharmonic; Further tours of Switzerland, with EC Youth Orchestra under James Judd, Italy and Japan, with the Gustav Mahler Youth Orchestra of Vienna, Czechoslovakia and Ireland; Recitals in San Francisco and Scotland; Chamber music concerts with leading instrumentalists notably at the Menuhin Festival in Gstaad and Kuhmo Chamber Music Festival. *Recordings include:* Bach Partitas; Italian Concerto; French Overtures; Chromatic Fantasia and Fugue; Capriccio; Preludes and Fugues; Concerti; Scriabin Sonatas 3, 4 and 5. *Honours:* 2nd Prize, Leipzig Bach Competition, 1972.

*Address:* c/o London Artists, 10 Guild Street, Stratford-upon-Avon, Warwickshire, CV 37 6RE, England.

**STEVENS, Risë;** Singer (Mezzo-Soprano); b. 1 June 1913, New York, USA. *Education:* Juilliard School with Anna Schoen-Rene; Study in Europe with Marie Gutheil-Schoder and Herbert Graf. *Career:* Sang at Prague Opera in 1936 as Mignon in Thomas's opera, as Strauss's Octavian in 1938 at the Vienna Staatsoper and at the Teatro Colón, Buenos Aires, at Glyndebourne Festival in 1939 as Dorabella and Cherubino, and at Metropolitan Opera, 1938–61 as Mignon, Carmen, Dalila, Orfeo, Ponchielli's Laura and Mussorgsky's Marina, 337 performances in New York and on tour; Sang in Chicago and San Francisco in 1940, Paris Opéra in 1949 as Octavian, and Glyndebourne in 1955 as Cherubino; Retired from stage in 1965 and became Director of the Metropolitan National Company until 1967, and President of the Mannes College of Music, 1975–78; Adviser to the Metropolitan's Young Artists Development Programme. *Recordings:* Carmen; Le nozze di Figaro; Orpheus and Euridice; Die Fledermaus. *Address:* c/o Metropolitan Opera, Lincoln Center, New York, NY 10023, USA.

**STEVENSON, Robert (Murrell);** Professor of Music; b. 3 July 1916, Melrose, New Mexico, USA. *Education:* AB, University of Texas, 1936; Piano at Juilliard School of Music, New York; Composition and musicology at Yale University; Private lessons in composition with Stravinsky, 1939, piano with Artur Schnabel, 1940; PhD, Eastman School of Music, Rochester, NY, 1942; Theology degrees, Harvard and Princeton; BLitt, Musicology, Oxford University, United Kingdom, 1954. *Career:* Instructor at University of Texas, 1941–43, 1946; US Army Chaplain, 1942–46; Recitals as concert pianist in USA and the United Kingdom, 1942–47; Lecturer of Church Music at Westminster Choir College, NJ, 1946–49; Music Faculty, 1949–, Professor of Music, 1961–, Faculty Research Lecturer, 1981–, University of California, Los Angeles; Visiting Professor to various universities. *Compositions include:* Orchestral, works performed by Philadelphia Orchestra, conducted by Leopold Stokowski; Pieces for piano, clarinet and piano, organ, mixed chorus. *Publications:* Prolific writings especially on Latin American, Spanish and Portuguese music, Italian Renaissance, and Baroque including Music In Mexico, Historical Survey, 1952, Patterns of Protestant Church Music, 1953, Cathedral Music in Colonial Peru, 1959, Spanish Cathedral Music in The Golden Age, 1961, Renaissance and Baroque Musical Sources in the Americas, 1970, Guide to Caribbean Music History, 1975, Antologia da Música Portuguesa 1490–1680, 1984; Francisco Barbieri, 1986. *Contributions:* Over 400 articles in New Grove Dictionary, 1980; Numerous contributions to prestigious journals and books. *Honours:* Research and teaching awards and fellowships; Honorary Degrees. *Address:* Department of Music, University of California, 405 Hilgard Avenue, Los Angeles, CA 90024, USA.

**STEVENSON, Ronald;** Composer, Pianist and Writer on Music; b. 6 March 1928, Blackburn, Lancashire, England; m. Marjorie Spedding, 18 Aug 1952, 1 s., 2 d. *Education:* Royal Manchester College of Music, 1945–48; Accademia di Santa Cecilia, Rome, 1955. *Career:* Debut: Albert Hall Proms in 1972 with own 2nd Piano Concerto; Senior Lecturer in Composition at University of Cape Town, 1963–65; 12 Busoni programmes on Radio 3, 1973; Busoni documentary on BBC television, 1974; mem, Royal Society of Musicians, United Kingdom; Composers' Guild; Savile Club; Scottish Arts Club. *Compositions include:* Prelude, Fugue and Fantasy on Busoni's Faust for Piano, 1949–59; Harpsichord Sonata, 1968; Peter Grimes Fantasy for Piano, 1970; 9 Haiku for Soprano, Tenor and Piano, 1971; Violin Concerto, The Gypsy, 1979 commissioned by Menuhin; St Mary's May Songs, song cycle, poems by Chaucer, Tennyson, Rossetti, Joyce for Soprano and String Orchestra premiered in Edinburgh, 1988; Cello Concerto, commissioned by RSNO, 1995; A Carlyle Suite, for piano, 1995; Many settings for voice and piano and for chorus of Scottish folk songs; Transcriptions of works by Purcell, Bach, Chopin, Berlioz, Delius, Britten, Berg and Grainger. *Recordings:* Stevenson plays Stevenson piano works; Passacaglia on DSCH; Grainger's Salute to Scotland; Cathedrals in Sound; Taken into the Mountains; Piano Concertos 1 and 2; Piano Music from Scotland; The Essence of Busoni; Twentieth Century Operatic Fantasias; Busoni for Two Pianos; In memoriam John Ogdon; Essentially Scottish; In memoriam Benjamin Britten; Eurocantica; Twentieth Century Scottish Choral Music. *Publications:* Numerous publications for piano; Western Music: A Brief Introduction, 1971; Editor, Bernhard Ziehn: Canonical Studies, 1976; Editor, Time Remembered, a symposium for the 80th birthday of Alan Bush, 1981; The Paderewski Paradox, 1992; Biography: Ronald Stevenson, a musical biography by Malcolm MacDonald, 1989. *Contributions:* Various publications and many learned journals. *Honours:* Harriet Cohen International Music Award for 1966 Busoni Centenary radio broadcasts; Fellow, RNCM. 1966; Honorary Fellow, RIAS, 1992; DUniv, Stirling, 1996; HonD.Mus, Aberdeen, 1998; LLD, Dundee, 1998. *Address:* Townfoot House, Main Street, West Linton, Peeblesshire EH46 7EE, Scotland.

**STEWART, Donald George,** MusB; American musician (clarinet), composer and music industry executive; *President, Trillenium Music Company;* b. 8 Jan. 1935, Sterling, IL; m. Susan Ann Trainer 1963 (divorced 1979); one d. *Education:* Indiana Univ., Manhattan School of Music, School of Jazz, studied with Ray Harris, Bernhard Heiden, Gunther Schuller, clarinet with Russianoff, Cioffi and Moyse. *Career:* second clarinet, Birmingham Symphony Orchestra, Alabama 1954–56, Florida Symphony, Orlando 1963; played with numerous jazz ensembles, including Ornette Coleman, David Baker, Sammy Davis 1957–65; freelance copyist 1958–88; woodwind in various

orchestras, New York 1967–72; founder, Boehm Quintette, New York 1968–88, debut at Carnegie Recital Hall 1972; over 1,000 chamber music concerts, festival appearances, with Boehm Quintette and other groups; music asst, New York State Council on Arts 1970–74; panellist, Vermont Council on the Arts 1976–78; founder 1978, bd mem., treasurer 1982, Chamber Music America; founder, pres., Trillenium Music Co. 1986–; pres. 1987–89, bd mem. 1985–95, Opera North, Norwich, VT; bd mem., Vermont Symphony Orchestra 1989–93; mem. ASCAP, American Federation of Musicians, American Soc. of Music Copyists (bd of dirs 1970–87, treasurer 1984–87), American Music Centre, Music Publishers' Asscn, Retail Print Music Dealers' Asscn. *Compositions:* Seven Little Etudes for orchestral woodwind section, A Book of Sliding Things for eight trombones, tuba and bass, Gesualdo Stanzas for large ensemble, 200-bar Passacaglia, two string quartets, Sonata No. 1 for horn and piano, No. 2 for wind quintet, String Quartet Nos 1 and 2, Saxophone Quartet, Brass Quintet, Duet for Flute and Bass Clarinet, Violin Sonata, Never Leave Me Blue for SSAATTBB, piano and string bass, Piccolo Concerto 1973, August Lions, for youth orchestra 1978, Song of Arion 1985, First Blue Symphony, for large orchestra 1988, Book of Sliding Things 1989, Green Mountain Christmas Card, opera 1993, Never Seek To Tell Thy Love, for voice and ensemble 1998, Duo for violin and cello 1999, Sinfonia for Strings and Percussion 2000, A Quartet of Flutes 2003; transcriber, composer, arranger. *Recordings include:* three records with Boehm Quintette, Marlboro Recordings, Music of Arthur Berger. *Publications:* over 100 titles in print. *Address:* Trillenium Music Company, POB 51059, Sarasota, FL 34232-0329 (office); 1515 Fivethorne Lakes Drive, Sarasota, FL 34240, USA (home). *Telephone:* (941) 377-7375 (office). *Fax:* (941) 377-9043 (office). *E-mail:* don@trillmusic .com (office). *Website:* www.trillmusic.com.

**STEWART, Jeffrey;** singer (tenor); b. 1970, England. *Education:* Guildhall School and National Opera Studio. *Career:* appearances with Opera North in The Thieving Magpie and The Magic Flute (Tamino); Nadir in The Pearl Fishers for ETO and Narraboth in Salome for ENO; Edgardo for European Chamber Opera and Ernesto at Düsseldorf; Other roles include Don José at Dartington, Števa in Jenůfa, Maurizio in Adriana Lecouvreur, 1999, the Duke of Mantua and Mozart's Ferrando; Season 1999–2000 as Count Ivrea in Un giorno di regno, and Italian Singer in Der Rosenkavalier, for the Royal Opera; Concerts include Bach's B minor Mass, The Dream of Gerontius and Mozart's Requiem. *Current Management:* Robert Gilder & Co., Enterprise House, 59–65 Upper Ground, London, SE1 9PQ, England. *Telephone:* (20) 7928-9008. *Fax:* (20) 7928-9755. *E-mail:* rgilder@robert-gilder.com.

**STEWART, Murray,** MA, FRCO, ARCM, LRAM; British conductor; *Artistic Director, London Pro Arte Orchestra;* b. 1954, London, England. *Education:* Trinity Hall, Cambridge, studied with Daniel Roth in Paris, with Harold Gray, Meredith Davies and Charles Mackerras. *Career:* as organist recorded the complete works of Franck and works by Vierne; Artistic Dir and Principal Conductor, London Pro Arte Orchestra and London Pro Arte Baroque Orchestra, conducted premieres by Ropartz, Langlais, Sallinen, Kokkonen, Szymanowski, Howells, Patterson, Chapple, Hellawell, Burgon, Blake, Hakim, Walker and Leighton; guest conducting engagements with the Philharmonia Orchestra, Bournemouth Symphony Orchestra, Bournemouth Sinfonietta, Ulster Orchestra, City of London Sinfonia, East of England Orchestra, and with the Prague Radio Symphony Orchestra, Musici de Praga and the Aarhus Symphony Orchestra; studio recordings for the BBC with the BBC Concert Orchestra; Conductor, East London Chorus; former conductor, Collegium Musicum of London, Bristol Choral Soc. and Finchley Children's Music Group. *Recordings include:* works by Jean Langlais, Mozart's Requiem, complete orchestral works of Maurice Duruflé (with the BBC Concert Orchestra), Rodriguez de Ledesma's Requiem Mass (world premiere recording). *Address:* 17b St Augustine's Avenue, South Croydon, Surrey CR2 6JN, England (office). *Telephone:* (20) 8688-2901 (office). *Fax:* (20) 8688-2901 (office). *E-mail:* m.stewart@londonproarte.co.uk (office). *Website:* www .londonproarte.co.uk.

**STEWART, Thomas,** MusB; American opera singer; b. 29 Aug. 1928, San Saba, Tex.; s. of Thomas James Stewart and Gladys Naomi (Reavis) Stewart; m. Evelyn Lear (q.v.) 1955; one s. one d. *Education:* Baylor Univ., Juilliard School of Music, Hochschule für Musik, Berlin. *Career:* joined Berlin Opera 1958; first performance at Bayreuth Festival 1960; has performed at Metropolitan Opera, New York, Royal Opera House, Covent Garden, London, La Scala, Milan, Vienna State Opera, Grand Opera, Paris, Bavarian State Opera, San Francisco Opera, Chicago Opera, Hamburg Opera; appears with all maj. orchestras of the world; gives recitals internationally with Evelyn Lear; Fellow, American Univ. 1967; Artistic Adviser Vocal Arts Soc. 1995. *Major roles include:* Hans Sachs (The Mastersingers of Nuremberg), Falstaff, Wotan (The Ring cycle), The Flying Dutchman, Scarpia (Tosca), Iago (Otello), Golaud (Pelléas et Mélisande), Amfortas (Parsifal). *Honours:* Hon. mem. Advisory Bd George London Foundation for Singers, NY 1994; numerous honours, awards and prizes including Richard Wagner Medal 1963, Berlin Kammersänger 1963; Grammy Awards 1969, 1971. *Address:* Thomlyn Artists Inc., 3413 Olandwood Court, Ste. 203, Olney, MD 20832, USA.

**STICH-RANDALL, Teresa;** Soprano; b. 24 Dec. 1927, West Hartford, Connecticut, USA. *Education:* Hartford School of Music; Columbia University, New York. *Career:* While at college in New York created Gertrude Stein in Thomson's The Mother Of Us All in 1947 and the title role in Luening's Evangeline in 1948; Season 1949–50 sang Priestess in Aida and Nannetta in Falstaff conducted by Toscanini; European debut at Florence in

1951 as the Mermaid in Oberon; Sang at Salzburg Festival in 1952 in concert with arias by Mozart, at Vienna Staatsoper, 1952–, Aix-en-Provence Festival, 1953–71 as Mozart's Pamina, Constanze, Countess, Donna Anna and Fiordiligi; Chicago Lyric Opera debut in 1955 as Gilda; Sang at Metropolitan Opera, 1961–65 as Fiordiligi and Donna Anna; Concert performances of works by Bach and Handel, retired in 1971. *Recordings:* Così fan tutte; A Life for The Tsar; Falstaff; Aida; Hercules; Orpheus and Euridice; Rodelinda; Le nozze di Figaro; Don Giovanni; Beethoven's 9th Symphony; Brahms Requiem; Mozart's Coronation Mass. *Honours:* Austrian Kammersängerin, first American to be so honoured, 1962.

**STILES, Frank,** BSc, BMus, LGSM, AGSM; British composer, conductor and violist; b. 2 April 1924, Chiswick, London, England; m. 1st Estelle Lewis 1969; m. 2nd Elizabeth Horwood 1988. *Education:* Imperial Coll., Durham Univ., Paris Conservatoire. *Career:* Principal Conductor, Priory Concertante of London; composer-in-residence, Protoangel Visions, Normanby by Spital, Lincolnshire 2003–; mem. Composers' Guild of Great Britain, Incorporated Soc. of Musicians, Royal Soc. of Musicians, Asscn for British Music (chair.), British Acad. of Composers and Songwriters. *Compositions:* Dramatic Cantata, Masada, Song Cycle Mans' Four Seasons, Triple Concerto, Mirage for solo piano, Concoid organ work, In Memoriam choral work, five symphonies, seven concertos, other orchestral works, works for string orchestra, five string quartets, trios, duos and solo works, various other chamber, choral and vocal works, Four Miniatures for solo clarinet, Fantasia for 12 violas, The Great Lakes symphonic suite, Sonata No. 3 for viola and piano 2005. *Recordings:* Guitar Sonata, String Quartet No. 3, Keyboard Sonata, Concerto For Five, First Piano Concerto, Equinox for Solo Piano, Sonata for Solo Violin No. 2 2000, Sonata for Violin and Piano No. 2 2000, String Quartet No. 6 2001. *Publications:* contrib. to Composer, Musician. *Honours:* City of London Prize for Composition 1955. *Address:* 43 Beech Road, Branston, Lincoln LN4 1PP, England.

**STILLER, Andrew (Philip);** Composer; b. 6 Dec. 1946, Washington, District of Columbia, USA; Ernestine Steiner, 25 May 1975. *Education:* BA, Zoology, University of Wisconsin, 1968; MA, 1972, PhD, 1976, Composition, State University of New York. *Career:* Center of Creative and Performing Arts, 1971–73; Decapod Wind Quintet, 1975; Age of Reason Ensemble, 1981; Buffalo New Music Ensemble, 1984–85; Network for New Music, 1986–89; Solo shows, Buffalo, 1979, 1972, 1973, 1976; Works also heard at 2nd and 3rd North American New Music Festivals, 1984, 1985; Consultant, New Grove Dictionary of Opera, 1990; Founder and Director, Kallisti Music Press, 1991–; mem, American Society of Composers, Authors and Publishers. *Compositions:* Orchestral: Periodic Table of Elements; Foster Song; Magnification: Procrustean Concerto, 1994; Chamber music: Numerous works including Sonata, Chamber Symphony; Also various pieces, keyboard and vocal. *Recordings:* A Descent into the Maelstrom; The Mouse Singer; A Periodic Table of the Elements; The Water is Wide, Daisy Bell; Sonata a3 pulsatoribus. *Publications:* Handbook of Instrumentation, 1985; Buffalo Philharmonic Orchestra, 1985. *Contributions:* Opus; Philadelphia Inquirer; Buffalo News; Revised New Grove Dictionary of Music and Musicians; New Grove Dictionary of Opera; Musical Quarterly; Musical America. *Address:* 810 South Saint Bernard Street, Philadelphia, PA 19143, USA.

**STILWELL, Richard Dale,** MusB; American baritone; b. 6 May 1942, St Louis; s. of Otho John Clifton and Tressie (née Parrish) Stilwell; m. 1st Elizabeth Louise Jencks 1967 (divorced); m. 2nd Kerry M. McCarthy 1983. *Education:* Anderson Coll., Univ. of Indiana. *Career:* with Metropolitan Opera Co., New York 1970–; appearances in major roles Washington Opera Soc., Marseilles Opera Co., Santa Fe Opera, San Francisco Opera Co., Paris Opera Co., La Scala, Covent Garden, Hamburg State Opera, Glyndebourne Opera Festival, Van. Opera Co., Chicago Opera Co., Tanglewood Festival, Israel Philharmonic, Boston Symphony, LA Philharmonic, etc.; soloist with Nat. Symphony, Washington, Chicago Symphony, American Symphony, Carnegie Hall, Boston Symphony, LA Philharmonic, etc.; mem. American Guild Musical Artists. *Honours:* Nat. Soc. of Arts and Letters Award 1963, Fisher Foundation award Metropolitan Opera Auditions 1965. *Address:* c/o Columbia Artists Management, Arbib Division, 165 W 57th Street, New York, NY 10019, USA.

**STOCKER, Markus;** Violoncellist; b. 2 April 1945, Basel, Switzerland; m. Mei-Lee Ong, 21 Mar 1975, 2 d. *Education:* University of Basel; Teachers and soloist diplomas under August Wenzinger, Academy of Music, Basel. *Career:* Debut: At London, Paris, Vienna, Berlin, New York, Tokyo, Beijing; Concerts throughout Europe, USA, Far East, Israel and Russia; Performed at Lucerne, Salzburg and Menuhin Festivals, Marlboro and Lockenhaus; Appearances with Rudolf Serkin, Martha Argerich, Sándor Végh, Gidon Kremer; Professor at Winterhur and Zürich Conservatories; Piano Trio with violinist Wanda Wilkomirska and pianist Werner Genuit, 1985; European premiere, Cello Concerto by Oscar Morawetz, Memorial of Martin Luther King, Zürich, 1995; Professor of Cello, Queensland Conservatorium, Brisbane, 1995–; mem, Association of Swiss Musicians; Indooroopilly LC. *Recordings:* Live recording of Bach Suites; Mendelssohn, Complete Works for Cello and Piano; Swiss composers: Martin and Honegger; Rachmaninov and Shostakovich with Victor Yampolsky, 1994. *Honours:* 1st Prize, Bloomington, IN, USA, 1972; Grand Prix, Maurice Marechal International Cello Competition, Paris, 1972; Soloists Prize, Association of Swiss Musicians, 1973. *Address:* 11 Tarcoola Street, St Lucia, Brisbane, Qld 4067, Australia.

**STOCKHAUSEN, Karlheinz;** German composer; b. 22 Aug. 1928, Mödrath bei Cologne; s. of Simon Stockhausen and Gertrud Stupp; m. 1st Doris Andreae 1951; one s. three d.; m. 2nd Mary Bauermeister 1967; one s. one d. *Education:* Cologne Nat. Music Conservatory, Univs. of Cologne and Bonn. *Career:* worked with Olivier Messiaen and with the "Musique Concrète" Group in Paris 1952–53; with Westdeutscher Rundfunk Electronic Music Studio, Cologne 1953–, Artistic Dir 1963–77; first composition of purely electronic music (Studie 1 for sinewaves) 1953; co-ed. Die Reihe (Universal Edn) 1954–59; lecturer at the Int. Summer School for New Music, Darmstadt 1955–74; concert tours throughout the world since 1958; Founder and Artistic Dir Cologne Courses for New Music 1963–68; f. ensemble for live electronic music 1964–; Int. World Fair Expo 70, Osaka; Prof. of Composition Staatliche Hochschule für Musik, Cologne 1971–77; Stockhausen annual courses for composers and interpreters of music, Kürten 1998–; mem. Royal Swedish Acad., Akad. der Künste, Berlin, American Acad. and Inst. of Arts and Letters and others; Assoc. mem. Acad. royale des sciences, des lettres et des beaux arts (Belgium) 2004. *Compositions:* 296 works including Chöre für Doris 1950, Drei Lieder (alto voice and chamber orchestra) 1950, Choral (chorus) 1950, Sonatine (violin and piano) 1951, Kreuzspiel (oboe, clarinet, piano, 3 percussion) 1951, Formel (orchestra) 1951, Etude (musique concrète) 1952, Schlagtrio 1952, Spiel (orchestra) 1952, Punkte (orchestra) 1952 (new version 1962), Klavierstücke I–IV 1952–53, Kontra-Punkte (ten instruments) 1952–53, Elektronische Studien 1953–54, Klavierstücke V–X 1954–61, Zeitmasze (five woodwind) 1955–56, Gruppen (three orchestras) 1955–57, Klavierstück XI 1956, Gesang der Jünglinge (electronic) 1955–56, Zyklus (percussionist) 1959, Refrain (three players) 1959, Carré (four orchestras and four choruses) 1959–60, Kontakte (piano, percussion and/or electronic sounds) 1959–60, Originale (musical theatre) 1961, Momente (soprano, four choral groups and 13 instrumentalists) 1962–64, Plus Minus 1963, Mikrophonie 1 (tam-tam, two microphones, two filters and potentiometers) 1964, Mixtur (orchestra, four sine-generators and ring-modulators) 1964, Mikrophonie II (choir, Hammond organ and four ring-modulators) 1965, Stop (orchestra) 1965, Telemusik (electronic music) 1966, Solo (melodic instrument and feedback) 1966, Adieu (wind quintet) 1966, Hymnen (electronic and concrete music with or without soloists) 1966–67, Prozession (tam-tam, viola, electronium, piano, filters and potentiometers) 1967, Ensemble (process planning) 1967, Kurzwellen (six players) 1968, Stimmung (six vocalists) 1968, Aus den sieben Tagen (fifteen compositions of intuitive music) 1968, Musik für ein Haus (process planning) 1968, Spiral (soloist with short-wave receiver) 1968, Dr. K-Sextett 1969, Fresco (four orchestral groups) 1969, Hymnen Dritte Region (electronic music with orchestra) 1969, Stop (ensemble) 1969–73, Pole (two players/singers) 1970, Expo (three players/singers) 1970, Mantra (two pianists) 1970, Sternklang (park music for 5 groups instrumentalists/singers), Trans (orchestra) 1971, Für kommende Zeiten (17 texts of intuitive music) 1968–70, Alphabet for Liège (13 musical pictures for soloists and duos) 1972, 'Am Himmel wandre ich' (12 American Indian songs) 1972, Ylem (19 or more players) 1972, 'Atmen gibt das Leben' (choir with orchestra or tape) 1974, Inori (Adorations for soloists and orchestra) 1973–74, Herbstmusik (4 players) 1974, Musik im Bauch (six percussionists and music boxes) 1975, Tierkreis (12 melodies of the star-signs) 1975, Harlekin (clarinet) 1975, The Little Harlequin (clarinet) 1975, Sirius (electronic music and trumpet, bass-clarinet, soprano and bass) 1975–77, Amour (5 pieces for clarinet or flute) 1976, Jubiläum (for orchestra) 1977, In Freundschaft 1977, Licht, die sieben Tage der Woche (for solo voices/instruments, dancers, choir, orchestra, ballet, electronic and concrete music) 1977–2000, an operatic cycle that includes Donnerstag aus Licht 1981, Samstag aus Licht 1984, Montag aus Licht 1988, Dienstag aus Licht 1991, Freitag aus Licht 1996, Mittwoch aus Licht 1998 and other scenes for a combination of forces, Sonntag aus Licht Lichter – Wasser (for soprano, tenor and orchestra with synthesizer) 1999, Litanei 97 (for chorus) 1997, Engel-Prozessionen for choir a capella 2002, Düfte-Zeiten for seven vocalists, boy's voice and synthesizer 2003, Hoch-Zeiten for choir and orchestra 2003. *Recordings:* over 130 records; from 1991 a complete album of all his works was being released. *Publications:* Texte zur Musik (10 vols) 1952–62, 1963–70, 1970–77, 1977–84, 1984–91, Stockhausen on Music – Lectures and Interviews 1989, Towards a Cosmic Music 1990, Stockhausen beiden international Ferienkurse in Darmstadt 1951–96. *Honours:* Hon. PhD (Freie Univ. Berlin) 1966; Hon. DPhil (Queen's Univ., Belfast) 2004; Hon. mem. Royal Acad. of Music, London; Hon. Patron Sonic Arts Network, UK; many prizes including Preis der deutschen Schallplattenkritik 1964, Grand Prix du Disque 1968, Diapason d'Or 1983, UNESCO Picasso Medal 1992, Polar Music Prize 2001, German Music Publrs Society Award for score Michaelion 2002, for score Stop and Start 2004; Bundesverdienstkreuz (1st Class), Commdr, Ordre des Arts et des Lettres (France) 1985. *Address:* Kettenberg 15, 51515 Kürten (office); Stockhausen-Verlag, 51515 Kürten, Germany. *Telephone:* (2268) 1813 (office). *Fax:* (2268) 1813 (office). *E-mail:* stockhausen-verlag@stockhausen.org (office). *Website:* www .stockhausen.org (office).

**STOCKHAUSEN, Markus;** Trumpeter and Composer; b. 2 May 1957, Cologne, Germany. *Education:* Cologne Hochschule für Musik. *Career:* Debut: K-H Stockhausen's Sirius, Washington DC, 1976; Participation in the premieres of Aries (1977) and the Licht cycle of operas; Donnerstag (Michaels Reise um die Erde, 1981), Samstag (oberlip-pentanz, 1984) and Dienstag (Invasion and Pietà, 1991); Jazz collaborations including the group Possible Worlds, 1995–; Duo partners include the pianist Majella Stockhausen (b Cologne, 1961); Film and theatre music composition with brother, Simon

Stockhausen (b Bensberg, 1967); Lecturer at Cologne Hochschule für musik, from 1996. *Recordings include:* Michaels Reise um die Erde (DGG); New Colours of Piccolo Trumpet (1993); Clow and Jubilee (1996). *Address:* Hochschule für musik, Dagobertstrasse 38, 50668 Cologne, Germany.

**STOCKIGT, Janice Beverley,** BMus, MMus, PhD; Australian musicologist; b. 14 July 1938, Melbourne, Vic. *Education:* Univ. of Melbourne. *Career:* mem. American Musicological Soc., Australian Musicological Soc., Int. Musicological Soc. *Publications:* Die 'Annuae Literae' der Leipziger Jesuiten 1719–1740: Ein Bach-Dokument 1992, Zpráve o návsteve císare Karla VI. s choti v Klementinu v roce 1723 1992, Einflüsse auf Zelenkas Kompositionsstil am Beispiel seiner Vesperpsalm-Vertönungen von etwa 1725 bis 1730 1993, Jan Dismas Zelenka's Setting of Psalm 150: Chvalte Boha Silného 1995, The Life and Afterlife of Jan Dismas Zelenka 1996, Hinweise auf die Originalauffüh-rungen von Zelenkas Vesperpsalmen (Indications of the Original Perfor-mances of Zelenka's Vespers Psalms) 1997, Die Übertragung Prager Vesperquellen nach Dresden durch Zelenka: Ein Beispiel anhand einer Gruppe anonymer Vertonungen (The Transmission of Prague Vespers Sources to Dresden by Zelenka: An Example of a Group of Anonymous Settings) 1997, Music as a Proselytizing Force of the Jesuits in Saxony 1998, The Prague Sources of Zelenka's Vespers Psalm Collection 1998, Szenen in Zelenka's Vespers Psalm Settings 1998, Jan Dismas Zelenka (1679–1745): A Bohemian Musician at the Court of Dresden 2000; contrib. to The Oxford Companion to Australia, The New Grove Dictionary of Music and Musicians. *Honours:* Univ. of Melbourne Chancellor's Prize 1994, Harbison-Higinbotham Research Scholarship 1994, Univ. of Melbourne Woodward Medal 2001, British Acad. Derek Allen Prize 2001. *Address:* c/o Faculty of Music, University of Melbourne, Parkville, Vic. 3052, Australia.

**STØDLE, Tori;** Pianist; b. 1 July 1942, Oslo, Norway; m. Hakon Stodle 1975; one s. one d. *Education:* studied with Robert Riefling in Oslo, Jurgen Uhde in Stuttgart, and Adele Marcus in New York. *Career:* debut, Oslo in 1970 and New York in 1990; recitals in Norway, UK, Germany, Russia, Italy, Netherlands, Denmark and USA; several television and radio programmes for Norwegian broadcasting; guest artist at major music festivals, including Chamber Music Festival at Tromso, Bergen Festival and North Norwegian Festival; piano soloist for world premieres of Ketil Vea's Piano Concertos Nos 1 and 3; Music from the Top of the World, recital of music by 19th- and 20th-century Norwegian composers, sponsored by various Norwegian organiza-tions, Weill Recital Hall, Carnegie Hall, New York 1990; The Dream of a Sound, television portrait 1991; promotes new music; works dedicated to her by several Norwegian composers; Assoc. Prof. of Piano, North Norwegian Music Conservatory, Tromso; mem. of two Norwegian music asscns, European Piano Teachers' Asscn. *Recordings:* Music From The North, Music From The Top Of The World, Berg, Bibalo and Brahms 1996, Landscapes in Music (works by Norwegian composer David Monrad Johansen) 2000. *Honours:* Northern Lights Prize 1991. *Address:* Fogd Dreyersgt 21, 9008 Tromso, Norway.

**STOIANOV, Konstantin;** Violinist; b. 1950, Russia. *Education:* Studied at the Antwerp Conservatory from age 9 and in Berlin and Würzburg. *Career:* Numerous solo appearances with leading orchestras; Radio broadcasts in Belgium, France and Italy; Leader of the Royal Philharmonic Orchestra of Flanders: Co-Leader of the London Philharmonic, 1990; Professor at the International Menuhin Academy at Gstaad.

**STOICA, Adrian-Oliviu;** Pianist; b. 27 Oct. 1955, Cluj-Napoca, Romania; m. Marcela-Iustina Stoica, 1 Sept 1979. *Education:* Musical studies, Piano with Georg Sava and Harald Enghiurliu, Chamber Music with Ferdinand Weiss, 1974–78, graduated, 1978, George Dima Academy of Music, Cluj; Master-classes, 1 year; MA degree equivalent; Masterclasses, Weimar, Germany, 1975, 1977, with Rudolf Kehrer. *Career:* Debut: Played Mozart's Concerto in C major, K 415, with Oradea Symphony Orchestra, 1972; Permanent Piano Soloist, Sibiu State Philharmonic Orchestra, 1989–91; Recitals; Guest Soloist, concerts with all philharmonic orchestras in Romania; Tours abroad: Washington DC, Midland-Odessa (Texas), New York, 1979, Boston, Massa-chusetts, 1993, 1994, New Jersey, 1994, Galesburg and Monmouth, Illinois, 1996, USA; Thuringia, 1979, Hannover-Langenhagen, 1994, 1996, Germany; Czech Republic, 1984; Poland, 1985; Russia and Baltic Republics, 1986, 1989; Valencia, Spain, 1992, 1994; Lecturer, University of Music, Bucharest. *Recordings:* Paul Richter: Op 58, Concerto in C minor for piano and orchestra, and op 121, Variations for piano and orchestra. *Honours:* Full Scholarship to George Dima Academy of Music; Fellowship, Romanian Ministry of Culture. *Address:* Bd Magheru No. 9, ap 133, 70161 Bucharest, Romania.

**STOJADINOVIC-MILIC, Milana;** Composer; b. 13 July 1962, Belgrade, Yugoslavia; m.; two s. *Education:* Composition, Belgrade Faculty of Music, 1987; postgraduate studies, 1994. *Career:* debut, String Quartet Melodia, Radio Belgrade Programme for Classical Music, 1985; Prof. of Harmony and Analysis, High School for Music, Belgrade; Asst, Dept of Music Theory, Faculty of Music, Belgrade; live performances at festivals in Yugoslavia, Slovenia, Croatia, Germany, Italy, Bulgaria, Greece, UK; mem., Asscn of Composers of Serbia. *Compositions:* Melody for string quartet, 1985; Dream, for flute and piano, 1986; Mimicry for symphony orchestra, 1987; Aurora Borealis for symphony orchestra, 1989; Duo Symbolico for piano and symphony orchestra, 1994; Kaleidoscope for wind quintet, 2001; Tango Sentimental for violin, double bass, accordion and piano (in memory of Astor Piazzola), 2002; Haven't You Forgotten Something? for flute and bassoon,

2002; Tears, a cycle of songs for unusual trio: voice (soprano), alt-flute and piano, first live performance, Belgrade, 2003. *Recordings:* Albums: Aurora Borealis, 1989; Duo Simbolico, 1995; Contemporary Music from the Balkans, 1999; Kaleidoscope, on The International Review of Composers, 2002; Tango Sentimental, on New Tango After Piazzola, 2002. *Honours:* three annual Asscn of Composers of Serbia awards, 1985, 1986, 1988; two International Festival of Composers awards, 1992, 1994; Belgrade October Prize, 1987; Vasilije Mokraniac Prize, 1989; Josip Slavenski Prize, 1987. *Address:* Palmoticeva 5/15, 11000 Belgrade, Serbia and Montenegro. *Telephone:* (11) 3232765.

**STOJANOVIC, Milka;** Singer (soprano); b. 13 Jan. 1937, Belgrade, Yugoslavia. *Education:* Studied at La Scala Opera School and with Zinka Milanov. *Career:* Sang with Belgrade National Opera from 1960, notably at Edinburgh Festival in 1962 and at Oslo and Lausanne in 1968 and 1971; Further appearances at Graz, 1962, Metropolitan Opera, 1967–68, Vienna, Bari, Munich, Cologne and Barcelona, 1970–71; Opera and concert engage-ments in Denmark, England, Hungary, Hamburg, Frankfurt, Dresden, Berlin, Zürich, Oslo, Copenhagen, Helsinki, Rome, Venice, Bologna, Palermo, Syracuse, Valencia, Athens, Ankara, Cairo, Caracas, Russia, Sofia, Budapest, Bucharest, and Czechoslovakia; Also festival appearances at Prague Spring and Salzburg; Roles have included Verdi's Aida, Desdemona and Amelia in Un Ballo in Maschera, Leonore, Mimi, Liu, Mozart's Countess, La Gioconda, Marenka, Santuzza and Tatiana; Roles in Verdi's Simon Boccanegra, Traviata and Vespri Siciliani, Madama Butterfly, Fidelio, Lohengrin, Tchaikovsky's Queen of Spades, Borodin's Prince Igor. *Address:* c/o Narodno Pozoriste, Francuska 3, 11000 Belgrade, Serbia and Montenegro.

**STOJANOVIC-KUTLACA, Svetlana;** Harpsichordist; b. 2 May 1957, Skopje, Macedonia; m. Djuro Kutlaca, 23 Feb 1980, 1 d. *Education:* Completed Secondary Music School, 1975; BA, Piano, 1981, BA, Harpsichord, 1991, MA, Harpsichord, 1993, Faculty of Music Art, Belgrade; Masterclasses with Huguette Dreyfus, France, 1989, 1990, Colin Tilney, England, 1996; Curso de perfeccionamiento with Genoveva Galvez, Madrid, 1989–90; Specialisation with Paul Simmonds, Brighton, England, 1996, 1997. *Career:* Debut: Harpsichord recital, Real Conservatorio Superior da Musica, Madrid, April 1990; Performed J. S. Bach's D minor Concerto, 5th Brandenburg Concerto, and Rameau's Pièces de clavecin en concerts, Belgrade, 1991; Cycle of 4 concerts and lectures on Improvisation, Folklore, Description, Polyphony, Belgrade, 1992; Over 50 harpsichord recitals, Yugoslavia, 1992–97; Harpsi-chord recitals, Aranjuez and Alcala de Henares, Spain, 1993, Brighton and Lewes, England, 1996; Repertoire includes works by Frescobaldi, Couperin, Rameau, Scarlatti, Soler, J. S. Bach, Balbastre; Teaches harpsichord, Josip Slavenski High School, Belgrade. *Recordings:* Vivaldi's Four Seasons, CD, 1993; Balbastre's Premier Livre de Clavecin, tape, 1994; For Radio Belgrade: Cycle of 4 concerts and lectures, Improvisation, Folklore, Description, Polyphony, 1992, Bach Goldberg Variations, 1995, Frescobaldi, Picchi, Froberger, F Couperin, D Scarlatti, M Kuzmanovic, 1997. *Publications:* The elements of Spanish folklore music in Domenico Scarlatti's harpsichord sonatas, MA thesis. *Address:* Branicevska 11, 11000 Belgrade, Serbia and Montenegro.

**STOKER, Richard,** FRAM, ARAM, ARCM; British composer, conductor, writer, poet and painter and actor; b. 8 Nov. 1938, Castleford, Yorkshire, England; s. of the late Capt. Bower Morrell Stoker and of Winifred Harling; m. Gillian Patricia Stoker 1986. *Education:* Breadalbane House School, Castleford, Huddersfield Univ. with Harold Truscott, Coll. of Art, Royal Acad. of Music and Drama, composition with Sir Lennox Berkeley, conducting with Maurice Miles, private study with Nadia Boulanger, Paris. *Career:* performance debut with BBC Home Service 1953, Nat. and Int. Eisteddfods, Wales 1955–58; conducting debut 1956; asst librarian, London Symphony Orchestra 1962–63; Prof. of Composition RAM 1963–87 (tutor 1970–80); composition teacher St Paul's School 1972–74, Magdalene Coll., Cambridge 1974–76; Ed. The Composer magazine 1969–80; apptd Magistrate, Inner London Commission 1995–2003, Crown Court 1998–2003; Adjudicator, Royal Philharmonic Soc. Composer's Award, Cyprus Orchestral Composer's Award for the Ministry of Culture 2001–, BBC Composers' Awards; mem. Composers' Guild 1962– (mem. exec 1969–80); founder mem. RAM Guild Cttee 1994– (hon. treas. 1995–); founder mem. European-Atlantic Group 1993–; mem. Byron Soc. 1993–2000, Magistrates' Asscn 1995–2003, English and Int. PEN 1996–2005; mem. and treas. Steering Cttee Lewisham Arts Festival 1990, 1992; founder-mem. Atlantic Council 1993, RSL, Creative Rights Alliance 2001–; concert appearances as pianist including Queen Elizabeth Hall, Purcell Rooms, Leighton House, RAM, Pizza on the Park, Barnet Festival. *Art:* exhbns, various works in pvt. collections including Trinity Coll. of Music. *Composi-tions include:* four symphonies 1961, 1976, 1981, 1991; 12 nocturnes; two jazz preludes; overtures: Antic Hay, Feast of Fools, Heroic Overture; three string quartets, three violin sonatas, Partita for Violin and Harp or Piano, Sonatina for Guitar, two piano sonatas, three piano trios, A York Suite for piano, Piano Variations, Piano Concerto, Partita for Clarinet and Piano, Wind Quintet; organ works: Partita, Little Organ Book, Three Improvisations, Symphony; Monologue, Passacagalia, Serenade, Petite Suite, Nocturnal, Festival Suite; choral works and song cycles: Benedictus, Ecce Homo, Proverb, Psalms, Make Me a Willow Cabin, Canticle of the Rose, O Be Joyful, A Landscape of Truth; piano works: Zodiac Variations, Regency Suite, A Poet's Notebook; vocal works: Music That Brings Sweet Sleep, Aspects of Flight, Four Yeats Songs, Four Shakespeare Songs, Johnson Preserv'd (three-act opera), Thérèse

Raquin (in preparation), Chinese Canticle, Birthday of the Infanta; music for film and stage includes Troilus and Cressida, Portrait of a Town, Garden Party, My Friend – My Enemy. *Recordings:* appearances on numerous CDs and records. *Films:* appearances include Red Mercury Rising, Woken, Daddy's Girl, Portrait of a Town, Lear and Goncril, The Shrink, Bedtime Story, The Usual, The End of the Line. *Radio:* interviews and discussions on BBC Radio Three, Four, World Service, New York Times Radio, Radio New York, Wall Street Radio, Radio Algonquin. *Publications:* Portrait of a Town 1970, Words Without Music 1974, Strolling Players 1978, Open Window – Open Door (autobiog.) 1985, Tanglewood (novel) 1990, Between the Lines 1991, Diva (novel) 1992, Collected Short Stories 1993, Sir Thomas Armstrong – A Celebration 1998, Turn Back the Clock 1998, A Passage of Time 1999; contrib. to anthologies, including Triumph, Forward, Outposts, Spotlight, Strolling Players, American Poetry Soc. publications, reviews and articles for periodicals, including Records and Recording, Books and Bookmen, Guardian, Performance, The Magistrate, poems in numerous anthologies and internet publications; contrib. to Oxford Dictionary of Nat. Biography 2004 (adviser 2003–). *Honours:* BBC Music Award 1952, Eric Coates Award 1962, Dove Prize 1962, Nat. Library of Poetry (USA) Editors' Choice Award 1995, 1996, 1997, American Biographical Soc. Man of the Year 1997, 1998. *Address:* Ricordi & Co. (London) Ltd, 210 New King's Road, London, SW6 4NZ, England (office). *Telephone:* (20) 7371-7501 (office); (20) 8852-9608 (home); (7906) 843812 (mobile). *Fax:* (20) 7371-7270. *E-mail:* richardstoker@serendipity.p9.org.uk. *Website:* serendipity.p9.org.uk/richardstoker.htm.

**STOKES, Harvey J.,** BM, MM, PhD; American composer and academic; b. 14 Sept. 1957, Norfolk, VA; m.; one s. two d. *Education:* East Carolina Univ., Univ. of Georgia, Michigan State Univ. *Compositions:* four string quartets, Dominion Fragments, Ethnic Impressions, Concerto No. 2 for oboe and strings, two piano sonatas, Values and Proposals no. 6, Music for 12 trumpets, In Memoriam SCA, Sonata for violin and piano, Sonata for cello and piano, Sonata for viola and piano, four symphonies, Quintet No. 3 for winds, Three Psalm Fragments, The Triumphant Men for wind ensemble 2003, Sonata for horn and piano. *Recordings:* String Quartet No. 1, String Quartet No. 2, String Quartet No. 3 (with The Oxford String Quartet). *Publications:* A Selected Annonated Bibliography on Italian Serial Composers 1989, Compositional Language in the Oratorio the Second Act 1992. *Honours:* first prize New England Conservatory New Works Competition 1983, first prize Lancaster Summer Arts Festival Orchestral Composition Contest 1983. *Address:* 1412 Hastings Drive, Hampton, VA, USA 23663 (office). *Telephone:* (757) 727 5410 (office); (757) 850 6456 (home). *E-mail:* harvey.stokes@hamptonu.edu (office); hstok1412@aol.com (home).

**STOLL, David Michael,** MA, ARAM, FRSA; British composer; b. 29 Dec. 1948, London, England. *Education:* Worcester Coll., Oxford, Royal Acad. of Music, London. *Career:* Music Dir, Greenwich Young People's Theatre 1971–75; subsequently freelance; Dir, British Acad. of Composers & Songwriters (fmr chair.), British Music Rights; education work includes leading the Dept for Education and Skills-commissioned project, 'Building Music'; commissioned by UK Govt to write a book on the teaching of music composition in primary schools; consultant on music and creativity in schools; mem. Incorporated Soc. of Musicians. *Compositions:* concert music: Piano Quartet 1987, Sonata for two pianos 1990, Piano Sonata 1991, String Trio 1992, Fanfares and Reflections (sextet) 1992, String Quartet No. 1 1994, Monument 1995, The Bowl of Nous (cantata) 1996, False Relations (opera) 1997, Motet in Memoriam 1998, Midwinter Spring (symphonic poem) 1998, String Quartet No. 2 1999, Cello Concerto 2000, Octave Variations (tuba quartet) 2001, The Path to the River (octet) 2001, Cello Sonata 2001, Fools by Heavenly Compulsion (String Quartet No. 3) 2002, Sonnet for string orchestra 2002, Pot-Pourri for orchestra 2002, Theatre Dreams for brass quintet 2003, A Colchester Suite for pipes 2003; media music: commissions include several signature tunes and much media and library (production) music; for theatre: several scores, including Teller of Tales (musical, co-composer), As You Like It (RSC production) 2003. *Recordings:* Chamber Music 1993, The Shakespeare Suite 2000, String Quartets 2001, The Fair Singer 2002, Fools by Heavenly Compulsion 2004. *Publications:* contrib. several articles on music, philosophy and related subjects. *Honours:* Hadow Open Scholarship in Composition to Worcester Coll., Oxford 1967. *E-mail:* info@davidstoll.co.uk. *Website:* www.impulse-music.co.uk/stoll.htm; www.creative-confidence.com.

**STOLL, Klaus;** Double Bass Player; b. 24 May 1943, Rheydt, Germany. *Education:* Cologne Musikhochschule. *Career:* Member of Niederrheinische Sinfoniker, 1959-65; Berlin Philharmonic from 1965, Principal Bass 1992-; Professor at Salzburg Mozarteum, 1990-; Premieres include Skalkottas Concerto and concertos for cello and double bass by Harald Genzmer and Helmut Eder; Many duo recitals with cellist Jörg Baumann, as Philharmonisches Duo Berlin, 1981-94; Further engagements with András Schiff, Heinz Holliger, Ruggiero Ricci and Viktoria Mullova; Plays Maggini Bass of 1610. *Publications include:* Repertoire Philharmonisches Duo Berlin (ed.) *Address:* c/o Berlin Philharmonic Orchestra, Herbert Von Karajan Str, D-10785 Berlin, Germany.

**STOLLERY, Pete,** BMus, PGCE, MA, PhD, FRSA; British composer and academic; *Senior Music Lecturer and Programme Director, University of Aberdeen;* b. 24 July 1960, Halifax, England; m. Catherine Sutcliffe 1988; two s. one d. *Education:* Univ. of Birmingham. *Career:* Ed., Journal of Electroacoustic Music, Res Musica; Sr Music Lecturer and Programme Dir, Univ. of Aberdeen; frequent radio broadcasts around the world; Chair. Sonic Arts

Network 1996–2000. *Compositions:* Shortstuff 1993, Shioum 1994, Altered Images 1995, Onset/Offset 1996, Peel 1997, ABZ/A 1998, Thickness 2000, Vox Magna 2003, Banchory Ears 2004, Serendipities and Synchronicities 2004. *Honours:* Musica Nova 1994, CIMESP 1997, Pierre Schaeffer Award 1998, Musica Nova 2003. *Address:* University of Aberdeen, Hilton Campus, Hilton Place Aberdeen, AB24 4FA (office); 3 Whitehills Cottages, Monymusk, Inverurie, Aberdeenshire AB51 7SS, Scotland (home). *Telephone:* (1467) 651425 (home); (1224) 274601 (office). *Fax:* (1224) 274877 (office). *E-mail:* p.stollery@abdn.ac.uk (office). *Website:* www.petestollery.com.

**STOLTZMAN, Richard (Leslie);** Clarinettist; b. 12 July 1942, Omaha, Nebraska, USA; m. Lucy Chapman. *Education:* BA, Ohio State University, 1964; MM, Yale University, 1967; Teachers included Donald McGinnis, Kalmen Opperman and Keith Wilson. *Career:* Debut: Metropolitan Museum, New York; Taught at the California Institute of the Arts, Valencia, 1970–75; Program Director, 1971–74, and Board Member of Western Region of Young Audiences; Co-founder with Peter Serkin, Ida Kavafian and Fred Sherry of chamber group, Tashi, 1973; Mozart concert debut at Carnegie Hall, 1976; Performed with Amadeus Quartet at the Aldeburgh Festival, 1978, and New York Philharmonic with James Levine, 1979; Performances with the Cleveland, Emerson, Guarneri, Tokyo and Vermeer Quartets; Concert programmes with transcriptions and commissioned pieces; Debut at the Promenade Concerts in London with Mozart's Concerto, 1989; Premiere of Rautavaara Concerto with BBC and Leonard Slatkin, 2003. *Compositions:* Edition of Schubert's Arpeggione Sonata, Sonatinas in A minor, D385 and D384; Saint-Säens's Romanza for Clarinet and Harp. *Recordings include:* World premiere Toru Takemitsu's Fantasma/Cantos with BBC Wales; Brahms and Weber Quintets with Tokyo Quartet; Mozart, Beethoven and Brahms Trios with Yo-Yo Ma and Emmanuel Ax; Schubert and Schumann with Richard Goode; Laser Disc, Vienna Konzerthaus, 1791, 1891, 1991–Mozart, Brahms, Takemitsu, with Rafael Frubeck de Burgos; Finzi Concerto and Bagatelles with Guildhall Concerti for Richard Stoltzman by Einar Englund, Lukas Foss, William T McKinley with Berlin Radio Orchestra under Lukas Foss; Steve Reich, New York Counterpoint. *Honours:* Avery Fisher Prize, 1977 and 1986; Yale University Order of Merit; Grammy Award, 1983, 1996; Emmy Award for Copland Concerto Video. *Address:* c/o Frank Salomon Associates, 201 West 54th Street 4C, New York, USA.

**STONE, Carl (Joseph);** Composer and Radio Producer; b. 10 Feb. 1953, Los Angeles, CA. *Education:* California Institute of the Arts, with Morton Subotnick. *Career:* Independent Composers Association, from 1974; Director of KPFA Radio; Performances and lectures throughout Japan, 1989. *Compositions:* (Electro-Acoustic) Thoughts in Stone, 1980; Ho ban, with piano, 1984; Wave Heat, 1984; Samanluang, 1986; Shing Kee, 1986; Jang toh, 1988; Chao nue, 1990; Noor mahal, 1991; Kamiya bar, 1992; Acid Karaoke, 1994; Electric Flowers, with pipa, 1994; Mae ploy, with string quartet, 1994; The Wagon Wheel, with pipa, 1995; Sampling Neurosis 1996; Wei fun, 1996. *Honours:* Asian cultural Council Grant, 1989. *Address:* c/o ASCAP, ASCAP Building, One Lincoln Plaza, New York, NY 10023, USA.

**STONE, Elisabeth;** Cellist; b. 1975, England. *Education:* Royal College of Music, with Simon Rowland-Jones and Chillingirian Quartet. *Career:* Co-founded Tavec String Quartet at RCM, 1999; Frequent performances at music society venues throughout Britain; London engagements at Queen Elizabeth Hall, St Martin in the Fields and Serpentine Gallery (BBC Proms); National Gallery, 2001, performing Schubert's Octet as member of Piros Ensemble (founded 2000); Workshops and other educational projects, notably in the North East of Britain. *Honours:* Prizewinner Music d'ensemble competition, Paris, 2001; Rio Tinto Ensemble Prize; Helen Just String Quartet Prize. *Address:* c/o Royal College of Music, Prince Consort Road, London, SW7 2 BS, England.

**STONE, Karen;** British opera house director and fmr singer; *General Director, Dallas Opera;* b. Yorkshire. *Education:* RAM, Conservatorio di Musica Santa Cecilia, Rome. *Career:* fmr opera singer, gave numerous performances; prod. and dir at venues, including Glyndebourne Festival, Brighton Festival, ROH, Maggio Musicale Fiorentino, Teatro Lirico di Parma, Opéra de Monte Carlo, Teatro Communale di Bologna, Bavarian State Opera, Houston Grand Opera, Los Angeles Opera, Auckland Opera Co., Teatro Colón-Bogotá, Savonlinna Opera Festival; fmr Asst Dir Freiburg Opera; fmr Staff Producer and Dir ENO; Deputy Dir Cologne Opera, then Dir 1995–2000; Gen. Man. Theatres of Graz, Austria 2000–03; Gen. Dir Dallas Opera 2003–. *Address:* Dallas Opera, Campbell Center I, 8350 N Central Expressway, Suite 210, Dallas, TX 75206, USA (office). *E-mail:* karen@dallasopera.org. *Website:* www.dallasopera.org (office).

**STONE, William;** Singer (Baritone); b. 1944, Goldsboro, North Carolina, USA. *Education:* Studied at Duke University and University of Illinois. *Career:* Sang at first in concert and oratorios; Opera debut as Germont in La Traviata in 1975 at Youngstown, Ohio; European debut in 1977 at Spoleto Festival in Napoli Milionaria by Nino Rota, and New York City Opera debut in 1981; Sang at Lyric Opera Chicago in 1978 as Adam in the premiere of Penderecki's Paradise Lost and again at La Scala in 1979; Maggio Musicale Florence in 1979 as Wozzeck, as Orestes in 1981, at Opéra Comique in Paris in 1984 as Purcell's Aeneas, Aix-en-Provence in 1987 as Ford in Falstaff; Further guest engagements at Trieste, Rome, Naples and Brussels as Germont, Paolo and Simone in Simon Boccanegra; Many appearances at the New York City Opera including Mozart's Count in 1990 and sang at Santa Fe in 1980 in the

US premiere of Schoenberg's Von Heute auf Morgen; Sang at Wexford Festival in 1989 as the Templar in Marschner's Der Templer und die Jüdin; Other roles include Rossini's Figaro, Enrico, Malatesta, Verdi's Ezio and Posa, Zurga, Albert in Werther, Golaud, Alfio and Eugene Onegin; Sang the title role in the US stage premiere of Busoni's Doktor Faust, New York City Opera, 1992; Sang Wozzeck at the 1994 Spoleto Festival; Sharpless in Butterfly at Chicago, 1998; Concert repertoire includes the St Matthew Passion, Messiah, Missa Solemnis, Beethoven's 9th and Ein Deutsches Requiem. *Recordings:* Mussorgsky's Salammbô; Hindemith's Requiem; Walton's Belshazzar's Feast; Robert Ward's Arias and Songs; Bach B minor Mass; Mahler's Symphony No. 8; Schubert's Mass in G; Bach's Magnificat; Mozart's C minor Mass; Video of Messiah with Robert Shaw. *Address:* c/o Columbia Artists Management Inc, Arbib-Treuhaft Dn, 165 West 57th Street, New York, NY 10019, USA.

**STOROJEV, Nikita;** Singer (bass); b. 9 Nov. 1950, Harbin, China. *Education:* Studied at Tchaikovsky Conservatoire, Moscow. *Career:* Bolshoi Theatre, Moscow, from 1978, as Pimen, Prince Igor, Gremin, Basilio and fafner; Appearances from 1983 at Vienna, Paris, Rome, Florence, Berlin, London, New York, San Francisco and Toronto; Repertoire has included Verdi's Zaccaria, Ramphis and Grand Inquisitor, Sarastro, Mephistopheles, Boris Godunov and Ivan Khovansky; Sang in Prokofiev's War and Peace at San Francisco, Rimsky's Mozart and Salieri at the Komische Oper in Berlin and Montreal, 1992; Rimsky's Ivan the Terrible at the Rome Opera, 1993, followed by Verdi Requiem at the Festival Deauville and Tchaikovsky's Iolanta at Dresden Festival; Song Recitals with David Ashkenazy and concert features with the Songs and Dances of Death at Festival Hall, 1991, and Gorecki's Beatus Vir at New York. *Recordings include:* Shostakovich 13th and 14th Symphonies; War and Peace; Gorecki's Beatus Vir and Songs of the Forest by Shostakovich; Mozart and Salieri. *Honours:* Diapason d'Or and Choc de la Musique. *Current Management:* Athole Still International Management, Forresters Hall, 25–27 Westow Street, London, SE19 3RY, England. *Telephone:* (20) 8771-5271. *Fax:* (20) 8768-6600. *Website:* www.atholestill.com.

**STOTT, Kathryn Linda,** ARCM; British pianist; b. 10 Dec. 1958, Nelson, Lancs.; d. of Desmond Stott and Elsie Cheetham; m. 1st Michael Ardron 1979 (divorced 1983); m. 2nd John Elliot 1983 (divorced 1997); one d. *Education:* Yehudi Menuhin School (under Marcel Ciampi, Vlado Perlemuter, Louis Kentner) and Royal Coll. of Music, London (under Kendall Taylor). *Career:* fifth prizewinner, Leeds Int. Piano Competition 1978; debut Purcell Room, London 1978; has since performed extensively in recitals and concertos both in UK and in Europe, Far East, Australia, Canada and USA; ten appearances at Henry Wood Promenade concerts; Dir Fauré and the French Connection Festival, Manchester 1995, Piano 2000, Manchester 2000, Piano 2003, Manchester 2003. *Recordings:* 20 recordings, including premieres of concertos by George Lloyd and Michael Nyman. *Honours:* Martin Scholarship 1976, Churchill Scholarship 1979, Croydon Symphony Award, Chappell Medal, Royal Amateur Orchestral Soc. Silver Medal 1979; Chevalier, Ordre des Arts et Lettres 1996. *Address:* c/o Jane Ward, 11 The Cresson, 43 Bidston Road, Oxton, Merseyside CH43 6UJ, England (office). *Telephone:* (151) 513-2716. *Fax:* (151) 513-2716. *E-mail:* ward.music@ntlworld.com (office). *Website:* www.kathrynstott.com (office).

**STOUT, Alan Burrage,** MA; Composer; b. 26 Nov. 1932, Baltimore, MD, USA. *Education:* John Hopkins Univ., Peabody Conservatory, Univs of Copenhagen and Washington, Seattle, with Vagn Holmboe, Wallingford Riegger and Henry Cowell. *Career:* Music Department at Northwestern University, 1962–; George Lieder, Second Symphony, Fourth Symphony and Passion premiered by the Chicago SO. *Compositions:* 10 String Quartets, 1953–62; 4 Symphonies, 1959–1970; George Lieder for baritone and orchestra, 1962; Cello Sonata 1965; Solo for soprano and orchestra, 1968; Nocturnes for mezzo, speaker and ensemble, 1970; Pulsar for brass and timpani, 1972; Passion, for orchestra, 1975; Five Visages de Laforgue for soprano and orchestra, 1997; Pilva for orchestra and organ, 1983; Tryptich for female voices, chorus and orchestra, 1983; Waves of Light and sound, for chamber orchestra, 1993; Brass Quintet, 1997; Stele, for organ, 1997. *Address:* c/o ASCAP, ASCAP Building, One Lincoln Plaza, New York, NY 10023, USA.

**STOYANOV, Boyko (Stoykov);** Composer, Conductor, Pianist and Music Teacher; b. 4 May 1953, Sliven, Bulgaria; m. Rikako Akatsu, deceased, 2 d. *Education:* Bulgarian State Academy of Music, Sofia, 1974–75; Frederick Chopin Academy of Music, Warsaw, Poland, 1975–82; Toho Gakuen School of Music, Tokyo, Japan, 1981–82. *Career:* Conductor, Varna Philharmonic Orchestra, 1983–; Iwaki Symphony Orchestra, Japan, 1984–; Private music school, Iwaki Musica, 1984; Tokyo debut with Tokyo Symphony Orchestra, 1986; Conducted with Tenerife Symphony Orchestra, 1991–; Kaguyahime, opera for children, premiered in Vienna, 1993; Broadcasts on Bulgaria Radio Varna, Japan Fukushima Central Television, TV V and NHK, Radio RFC, Poland Radio, Austria Television; mem, Piano Teachers National Association, Japan; Japan Computer Music Association. *Honours:* 1st Prize, Folk Song Section, Bulgarian National Folk Music Competition, 1959; Varna Prize for Popular Song, 1965; 2nd Prize for Conducting and Arrangement, Bulgarian National Folk Music Competition, 1972; Distinction, Wroclaw Arrangement Competition, 1979; International Composers Competition, 1985; International Electro-acoustic Music Competition, 1990. *Address:* 35 Baba, Nishiki-machi, Iwaki City, Fukushima 974-8232, Japan.

**STOYANOVA, Krassimira;** Singer (Soprano); b. 1969, Bulgaria. *Education:* University of Plovdiv, Bulgaria. *Career:* Debut: Violetta in La Traviata at

Opava, 1994; Appearances at the National Theatre, Sofia, from 1995 as Gilda, Susanna, Cecilia in Il Guarany and Delia in Fosca, both by Gomes, Rachel in La Juive; Mozart's Vitellia and Ilia (Idomoneo); Vienna Staatsoper from 1998 as Micaela, and in other roles; Further engagements as Mozart's Countess at Helsinki, Rachel in Tel-Aviv and Nedda in Pagliacci in Buenos Aires; Season 2001–2002 as Donna Anna at Covent Garden, Carmen (Micaela) with the Bavarian Staatsoper and Valentine in Les Huguenots at Carnegie Hall, New York; Concerts include Beethoven's Ninth Symphony, conducted by Philippe Herreweghe in Europe and Japan, and under Riccardo Muti at the Ravenna Festival. *Address:* c/o Theateragentur Dr G. Hilbert, Maximilianstrasse 22, 80539 Munich, Germany.

**STRAHAN, Derek William,** BA; Australian composer, actor, singer and writer; *Director, Revolve Pty Ltd;* b. 28 May 1935, Penang, Malaysia; m. (divorced); one s. one d. *Education:* Campbell Coll., Belfast, Northern Ireland, Univ. of Cambridge. *Career:* Dir, Revolve Pty Ltd; mem. Australian Music Centre, APRA, Music Arrangers' Guild of Australia, Australian Writers' Guild, Media Entertainment and Arts Alliance. *Radio:* presenter Words and Music (Eastside Radio FM) 1984–. *Film and TV appearances:* Number 96 1974, Fantasy 1991, Inspector Shanahan Mysteries (episode, Cult of Diana) 1992. *Film and TV writing:* The Unisexers (TV series) 1975, Chopper Squad (TV series) 1978, Leonora (screenplay, also dir) 1984, Fantasy (screenplay, also dir) 1991. *Compositions for film:* 30 documentaries, including Shell's Australia 1969–73, Aliens Among Us 1974, Garden Jungle 1974, Artisans of Australia 1985; films, including Leonora 1984, Fantasy 1991. *Compositions include:* String Quartet No. 1: The Key 1980, Clarinet Quintet No. 1 in D: The Princess 1980, The Quay for orchestra 1986, Rose of the Bay song cycle for mezzo-soprano, clarinet and piano 1987, String Trio No. 1 in F 1987, Piano Trio in F 1987, Sydney 200 for orchestra 1988, China Spring for cello and piano 1989, Escorts Trio 1989, Atlantis for flute and piano 1990, Solo Cello Suite No. 1 1991, Solo Cello Suite No. 2 1992, Atlantis Variations for piano 1992, Voodoo Fire for clarinet, percussion and keyboards 1994, Eden in Atlantis for soprano, flute and piano 1994, Clarinet Concerto No. 1 2001, Eden in Atlantis (opera libretto) 2002, Calypso in Exile for soprano and wind quintet 2003. *Publications:* contrib. numerous articles to music publs and websites. *Address:* POB 128, Petersham, NSW 2049, Australia (office). *Telephone:* (2) 95583645 (office). *Fax:* (2) 95583645 (office). *E-mail:* dstrahan@revolve.com .au. *Website:* www.revolve.com.au.

**STRAKA, Peter;** Tenor; b. 22 Feb. 1950, Zlin, Czechoslovakia. *Education:* Düsseldorf Conservatory; Cologne Music High School; Artistic development, International Opera Studio, Zürich. *Career:* Member, Zürich Opera; Guest at many opera houses and in concert; Appearances include New York Metropolitan debut as Boris and Kudryasch in Katya Kabanova under Charles Mackerras, 1991, returning as Boris, 1999; Season 1991–92 as Alwa in Lulu at the Châtelet, Paris, Titus in La Clemenza di Tito in Nice; Florestan at Zürich Opera, 1992, also Berlin State Opera, Covent Garden, Nice, Paris; Returned to the Châtelet as Lenski in Eugene Onegin; Lurcano in Monteverdi's Poppea, Salzburg Festival, 1993; Opened Season 1993 as Erik in Der fliegende Holländer at Bastille Opéra, Paris, then Loge in Rheingold at the Châtelet, Boris at Zürich; Mazal and Petrik in Janáček's Excursions of Mr Brouček and Narraboth in Salome under Mackerras at Bavarian State Opera, Munich, 1995; Erik at Munich State Opera and Zürich, Boris at the Bastille, Alwa in Copenhagen programme, Oedipus in Oedipus Rex at Zürich, 1996; Prince in Rusalka at Zürich Opera, Laca in Jenůfa at Amsterdam Opera for Holland Festival's 50th Anniversary, Mahoney in Mahagonny at the Bastille, 1997; Laca in Zürich, Siegmund in Walküre at Caracas Opera, 1998; Season 2000–01 at Zürich Opera as Elemer in Arabella, Narraboth, and Berg's Alwa; Boris in Katya Kabanova at the Munich Staatsoper; Concerts with London Philharmonia, Munich Philharmonic under Celibidache, Bavarian Radio Orchestra under Colin Davis, Concentus Musicus Wien under Harnoncourt, other leading orchestras and conductors; Concert repertoire includes Mahler's 8th Symphony, Janáček's Glagolitic Mass and Our Father, Beethoven Ninth, Zivny in Janáček's Osud, Bruckner's Te Deum, Puccini's Messa di Gloria, Stravinsky's Oedipus, Bach B minor Mass, Richard Strauss Lieder. *Recordings:* Several operatic and concert performances. *Address:* Ränkestrasse 34, 8700 Küsnacht, Switzerland.

**STRANGE, (John) Allen,** MA; composer; b. 26 June 1943, Calexico, CA, USA. *Education:* California State University, Fullerton, University of California at San Diego with Harry Partch, Pauline Oliveros and Kenneth Gaburro. *Career:* co-founder, electronic music performances groups Biome (1967–72) and Electronic Weasel Ensemble, 1974; President of International Computer Music Association, 1993–98. *Compositions:* Soundbeams, for ensemble and electronics, 1977; Second Book of Angels, for string quartet and tape, 1979; Santa Fe, string quartet, 1980; Velocity Studies, for violin and tape, 1983; Sleeping Beauty, 1989; Ursa Major, tape, 1989; Antigone, theatre music, 1989; Cygnus, kinetic sculpture, 1992; Phoenix and the Harlequin, tape, 1995; Physical States, theatre, 1996; Chimera, for orchestra and tape, 1997; The Phoenix Set, tape, 1999; Goddess, for violin and electronics, 1999. Address c/o ASCAP, ASCAP Building, One Lincoln Plaza, New York, NY 10023, USA.

**STRANZ, Ulrich;** Composer; b. 10 May 1946, Neumarkt St Veit, Bavaria, Germany. *Education:* Munich Musikhochschule, with Günter Bialas, 1968–72. *Career:* Performances of music throughout German-speaking Europe. *Compositions:* Déjà vu, for oboe d'amore and chamber orchestra, 1973; Tachys, for solo strings and orchestra, 1974; Klangbild, for orchestra,

1976; Musik für Klavier und Orchester no. 1, 1978–82, no, 2 1992; Four String quartets, 1976, 1981, 1993, 1999; Auguri, for viola and small orchestra, 1981; Janus, for violin, piano and 13 wind instruments, 1986; Piano Trio, 1986; Symphony no. 1 1990; Aus dem Zusammenhang. for eesemble, 1997; Der Sinn des Lebens for soprano, flute, violin and viola, 1998; Music for Two Violoncelli and Orchestra, 1999. *Address:* c/o GEMA, Rozenheimer Str. 11, 81667 Munich, Germany.

**STRASHKO, Yevgeny;** Singer (Tenor); b. 1967, Crimea, Russia. *Education:* Graduated St Petersburg Conservatoire, 1998; Musikhochschule Graz and Salzburg. *Career:* Appearances with the Kirov Opera, St Petersburg, from 1995 as Tamino, Alfredo, Steersman in Der fliegende Holländer and Young Gypsy in Rachmaninov's Aleko; Further roles include Tchaikovsky's Lensky and Herman, Dimitri in Boris Godunov, Kuragin in War and Peace and Prokofiev's Semyon Kotko; Sang in Rimsky-Korsakov's Snow Maiden (Concert) with the Kirov Opera at Covent Garden, 2000; Also appears as Genarro in Prokofiev's Maddalena and gives recitals of Russian German and Italian songs. *Honours:* Prizewinner at competitions in Russia, Germany and Sweden. *Address:* c/o Kirov Opera, Mariinsky Theatre, 1 Theatre Square, St Petersburg, Russia.

**STRATAS, Teresa Anastasia Strataki,** OC; Canadian opera singer; b. 26 May 1938, Toronto, Ont.; d. of Emmanuel Stratas and Argero Stratakis; m. Tony Harrison. *Education:* Univ. of Toronto. *Career:* began singing career in nightclubs in Toronto; début at Toronto Opera Festival 1958; won audition to Metropolitan Opera, New York 1959; performances there include Berg's Lulu, Jenny in Brecht and Weill's Mahagonny, Suor Angelica, Lauretta and Giorgetta in Il Trittico; major roles in opera houses worldwide include Paris (Lulu 1979), Brussels (Lulu 1988), Boston (Mimi 1989), Chicago (Mélisande 1992); appeared as Violetta in Zeffirelli's film of La Traviata 1983; appeared in Broadway musical Rags 1986; cr. role of Marie Antoinette in Ghosts of Versailles, premièred Metropolitan Opera, NY 1992; Il Tabarro and Pagliacci at the Met 1994. *Honours:* LLD hc (McMaster Univ.) 1986, (Toronto) 1994, (Rochester) 1998, (Juillard School of Music), (Royal Conservatory of Music); Canadian Music Council Performer of the Year 1979, Drama Desk Award for Leading Actress in a Musical on Broadway 1986–87, Gemini Award for Best Supporting Actress (for Under the Piano) 1997, three Grammy Awards, Opera Canada Award for Creative Artist 2003. *Current Management:* Vincent & Farrell Associates, 157 W 57th Street, Suite 502, New York, NY 10019, USA. *Address:* The Ansonia, 2109 Broadway, New York, NY 10023, USA (office).

**STRATE, Petra-Ines;** Singer (Soprano); b. 7 Sept. 1945, Jessen an der Alster, Germany. *Education:* Magdeburg Musikhochschule, and with Gunther Leib, Dresden. *Career:* Debut: Magdeburg 1971, as Pamina in Die Zauberflöte; Sang at Magdeburg until 1973; Halle Opera from 1973, Leipzig Opera from 1984; Guest appearances throughout Germany as Mozart's Countess, Donna Anna and Fiordiligi, Agathe in Der Freischütz, and Liu in Turandot; Many appearances in operas by Handel at the Halle Festival; Often heard in oratorios by Bach, Haydn and Handel. *Address:* c/o Oper Leipzig, Augustusplatz 12, D-7010 Leipzig, Germany.

**STRAUCH, Jacek;** Singer (Baritone); b. 1953, London, England. *Education:* Studied at the Royal College of Music and National Opera Studio in London. *Career:* Debut: Kent Opera in 1978 as Rigoletto; Sang in opera at Würzburg, 1980–82, and Saarbrucken, 1982–85; Guest appearances in Modena and Pretoria, South Africa in 1985; Berne Opera in 1987 as Wozzeck, English National Opera in 1988 as Alfio and as Jaroslav Prus in The Makropulos Case; Season 1988–90 as Amfortas, Iago and the Hoffmann Villains at Brunswick, Kurwenal at Saarbrücken and Gunther in Götterdämmerung; Other roles include Mozart's Count; Broadcast engagements in Germany, England and Norway; Sang Pacheco in the premiere of Macmillan's Ines de Castro, Edinburgh, 1996; Season 2000–01 as Wotan in The Ring at Graz, followed by Nicolai's Falstaff, Verdi's Renato at Barcelona and Tomsky in The Queen of Spades for the Munich Staatsoper. *Honours:* Winner, Kathleen Ferrier Competition, 1978; Prizewinner, Belvedere International at Vienna, 1984. *Address:* c/o Grant Rogers Management, 8 Wren Crescent, Hertfordshire WD23 1AN, England.

**STRAUSSOVA, Eva;** Singer (Soprano); b. 7 June 1934, Cheb, Czechoslovakia. *Education:* Studied with Elisa Stunzner and with Rudolf Dittrich at the Dresden Opera Studio, 1956–59. *Career:* Debut: Landestheater Dessau in 1959 as Helmwige in Die Walküre; Sang at Dessau until 1963, notably as Eva in Die Meistersinger, then joined the Staatsoper Berlin in major roles including Wagner's Elisabeth and Gutrune, Amelia in Un Ballo in Maschera, Donna Anna, Turandot, Elektra, Fiordiligi, Leonore and Katerina Izmailova; Guest engagements in Zürich, Berne, West Germany, Russia and Austria; Sang Isolde at Aachen Opera. *Recordings:* Various albums.

**STREATFIELD, Simon;** Violist and Conductor; b. 3 May 1929, Windsor, Berkshire, England; m. Elizabeth Winship, 2 d. *Education:* Eton College; Royal College of Music, London. *Career:* Principal Viola, Sadler's Wells Opera, 1953–55, London Symphony Orchestra, 1956–65 and Vancouver Symphony Orchestra, Canada, 1965; Assistant Conductor, 1967, Associate Conductor, 1972–77, Music Director and Conductor of the Vancouver Bach Choir, 1969–81; Season 1970–71 included concerts with the City of Birmingham Symphony, the Royal Choral Society, the BBC and with the Vancouver Bach Choir in Netherlands; Visiting Professor at Faculty of Music, University of West Ontario, 1977–81; Conductor, Regina Symphony Orchestra, Canada, 1981–84; Conductor, Manitoba Chamber Orchestra, 1982–; Conductor,

Quebec Symphony Orchestra, 1984–; Has also conducted the National Arts Centre Orchestra in Ottawa, the Danish Radio Symphony, the Oslo Philharmonic and the Belgian Radio Symphony. *Recordings include:* Telemann Viola Concerto; Berlioz Harold en Italie.

**STREET, Tison;** Composer and Violinist; b. 20 May 1943, Boston, MA, USA. *Education:* Harvard University, with David Del Tredici and Leon Kirchner (MA 1971). *Career:* Lecturer at Berkeley, 1971–72, Harvard University, 1979-83, and Boston University, 1995-; Co-leader of the Boston Ballet Orchestra, 1992-97. *Compositions:* String Quartet, 1972; String Quintet, 1974; Adagio for oboe and strings 1977; Montsalvat for orchestra, 1980; Divertimento for piano, 1983; Six Fantasies on a Hymm Tune for string quartet, 1984; Violin Concerto 1986; Fantasia, for six cellos, 1988; Bright Sambas, for orchestra, 1993; Symphony no. 2, 1993; Ave maris stella, for chorus, 1994; The Jewel Tree, ballet, 1998. *Honours:* Prix de Rome, 1973; Guggenheim Fellowship 1981; Commissions from the New York PO and Boston Ballet. *Address:* c/o ASCAP, ASCAP Building, One Lincoln Plaza, New York, NY 10023, USA.

**STREHLE, Wilfried;** German violist; b. 1947, Stuttgart. *Education:* studied at Stuttgart and Detmold Hochschulen. *Career:* violist with Sudfunk-Sinfonie-Orchester at Stuttgart; soloist with Chamber Orchestra Tibor Varga until 1971, then principal violist with Berlin Philharmonic Orchestra; co-founder, Brandis String Quartet 1976, with chamber concerts in Paris, Munich, Hamburg, Milan, Tokyo and London, and appearances with Wiener Singverein and Berlin Philharmonic; festival engagements at Edinburgh, Tours, Bergen, Salzburg, Lucerne, Florence and Vienna; co-premiered the third Quartets of Gottfried von Einem and Giselher Klebe in 1981 and 1983, and the Clarinet Quintet of Helmut Eder 1984. *Recordings include:* albums in the standard repertory from 1978, Quartets by Beethoven, Schulhoff, Weill and Hindemith, and the Schubert String Quintet. *Honours:* European Chamber Music Award 1997. *Address:* c/o Berlin Philharmonie, Herbert-von-Karajan-Strasse 1, 10785 Berlin, Germany.

**STREIT, Kurt;** Singer (Tenor); b. 14 Oct. 1959, Itazuke, Japan. *Education:* Studied at the University of New Mexico with Marilyn Tyler. *Career:* Member of apprentice programmes at San Francisco and Santa Fe, also at the Texas Opera Theater; Appearances with the Milwaukee Skylight Comic Opera and in Dallas; European career with the Hamburg Staatsoper singing in operas by Mozart, Donizetti and Rossini; Guest appearances at Schwetzingen in 1987, Aix-en-Provence in 1989, Salzburg in 1989 and at Glyndebourne as Tamino in the 1990 production of Die Zauberflöte by Peter Sellars; Has also sung at opera houses in Vienna, Munich, Brussels, Leipzig, Düsseldorf and San Francisco (1990); Covent Garden debut in 1992 as Ferrando; Concert engagements with the London Symphony, Orchestre National de France, St Petersburg Philharmonic, Hamburg Staatsorchester and the English Chamber Orchestra; Promenade Concerts in London in a 1990 concert performance of Die Zauberflöte; Sang Orfeo in Haydn's Orfeo ed Euridice at South Bank, London, 1997; Belmonte at Covent Garden, 1996; Grimoaldo in Rodelinda at Glyndebourne, 1998; Season 2000–01 as Mozart's Tito for the New York City Opera, Almaviva in Seattle, Rossini's Ramiro in Los Angeles and Cassio in Otello at Covent Garden. *Recordings include:* Gluck's Echo et Narcisse; Ferrando in Così fan tutte (also at Glyndebourne in 1990), with Daniel Barenboim and the Berlin Philharmonic; Die Entführung aus dem Serail. *Address:* c/o IMG Artists, Lovell House, 616 Chiswick High Road, London W4 5RX, England.

**STRINDBERG, Henrik;** Composer; b. 28 March 1954, Kalmar, Sweden. *Education:* Stockholm Royal College of Music, with Gunnar Bucht, Brian Ferneyhough and Sven-David Sandström, 1985–87; Computer music programs at IRCAM, Paris, 1987–89. *Compositions:* In Yellow and Red, suite for orchestra, 1979; String Quartet, 1982; Hustle and Bustle, for ensemble, 1984; Scenario, for wind band, 1984; Petite chronique berlinoise, two pianos, 1984; Bambu, electro-acoustic, 1984; Midsommar, for soprano and ensemble, 1986; The First Lay about Gudrun, for mezzo and guitar, 1987; Within Trees, for orchestra, 1988; Etymology, for piano, string quartet, soprano, saxophone and double bass, 1990; Two Pianos, 1992; Nattlig Madonna, for chamber orchestra, 1994; Clarinet Concerto, 1998. *Address:* c/o STIM. Sandhamnsgatan 79, PO Box 29327, S–102 54 Stockholm, Sweden. *Telephone:* 0046 8783 8800. *Fax:* 0046 8662 6275.

**STROE, Aurel;** Composer; b. 5 May 1932, Bucharest, Romania. *Education:* Bucharest Conservatory, 1951–56; Darmstadt summer courses, 1966–69, with Ligeti, Stockhausen and Maurico Kagel. *Career:* Reader in Composition at Bucharest Conservatory, 1962–; Professor at Mannheim Hochschule für musik, 1986–93; Commissions from Royan Festival, French Ministry of Culture and Kassel Opera. *Compositions:* Le Paix, opera after Aristophanes 1973; String quartet, 1973; Clarinet Concerto, 1976; Le Jardin des Structures for trombone and tape, 1976; Les Choephores music theatre, 1977; Missa Puerorum, 1983; Piano sonata no. 2, 1983, no. 3 1993; Agememnon, music theatre, 1983; Eumenides, opera after Sophocles, 1985; Accords et continues, for orchestra, 1988; Capricci e Ragas for violin and chamber orchestra, 1990; L'Enfant et le Diable, opera, 1990; Mozart Sound Introspection, string trio, 1994; Préludes lyriques, for orchestra, 1999. *Address:* c/o UCMR, Calea Victoriei 141, Sector 1 Bucharest, Romania. *Telephone:* 40212127966. *Fax:* 40212107211. *E-mail:* umcr@itcnet.ro.

**STROHM, Reinhard,** PhD, FBA; musicologist; *Heather Professor of Music, University of Oxford;* b. 4 Aug. 1942, Munich, Germany. *Education:* Univ. of Munich and Technical Univ., Berlin with Carl Dahlhaus. *Career:* Lecturer

1975–83, Prof. 1990–96, King's Coll. London; Prof., Yale Univ. 1983–90; Heather Prof. of Music, Univ. of Oxford 1996–; corresponding mem. American Musicological Soc., Göttinger Akad. der Wissenschaften. *Publications:* Hasse, Scarlatti, Rolli 1975, Wagner Collected Edition (co-ed.) 1970–82, Zu Vivaldis Opern schaffen 1975, Italienische Opernarien des Frühen Settecento, 1720–1730 1976, Die Italienische Oper im 18 Jahrhundert 1979, Music in Late Medieval Bruges 1985, Essays on Handel and Italian Opera (contrib.) 1985, Music in Late Medieval Europe 1987, The Rise of European Music, 1380–1500 1993, On the Dignity and the Effects of Music: Two Fifteenth-Century Treatises (with J. D. Cullington) 1996, Dramma per musica: Italian Opera Seria in the Eighteenth Century 1997, Song Composition in the 14th and 15th Centuries: Old and New Questions 1997, The Eighteenth Century Diaspora of Italian Music and Musicians 2001, Music as Concept and Practice in the Late Middle Ages (The New Oxford History of Music, Vol. III, with B. Blackburn) 2001; contrib. to learned books and journals. *Honours:* Royal Musical Asscn Dent Medal 1977. *Address:* c/o Faculty of Music, University of Oxford, St Aldate's, Oxford, OX1 1DB, England. *E-mail:* reinhard.strohm@music.ox.ac.uk.

**STROPPA, Marco;** Composer; b. 8 Dec. 1959, Verona, Italy. *Education:* Verona, Milan and Venice Conservatories; Michigan Institute of Technology 1984–86, computer music. *Career:* Composer and researcher at IRCAM, electronic music studios, Paris, from 1982; Professor of Composition, Stuttgart Musikhochschule, from 1997. *Compositions:* Traiettoria, with piano, 1984; Etude pour Pulsazioni, for 18 instruments, 1985–89; Spirali, with string quartet, 1988; Träumen vom Fliegen, ballet, 1990; Leggere il decamerone, 1990; Miniature estrose, piano, 1991–95; Danza per miniature estrose, ballet, 1995; Auras, 1996; Upon a Blade of Grass, for piano and orchestra, 1996. *Honours:* Kompositionspreis, Salzburg Easter Festival, 1996. *Address:* c/o SIAE (Sezione Musica), Viala della Letteratura 30, 00144 Rome (EUR), Italy.

**STROW-PICCOLO, Lynn;** singer (soprano); b. 17 June 1947, Waterburg, CT, USA. *Education:* Hartford Univ., studied with Carlo Alfieri in Parma. *Career:* debut at Siena Opera, 1975; Season 1976-77 as Leoncavallo's Zaza for RAI, and guest appearances in San Diego, and Turin; Further engagments at New Orleans, Santiago, Miami, Oslo and Marseille; Norma in Bellini's opera at Covent Garden, 1987; La Scala, Vienna Staatsoper and elsewhere in Europe as Maria Stuarda, both Leonoras of Verdi, Elisabeth in Don Carlos, Desdemona, Odabella and Amelia (Un Ballo in Maschera); Manon Lesaut, Mascagni's Isabeau, and Sieglinde in Die Walküre. *Honours:* winner Giuseppe Verdi Competition, Bussetto 1974.

**STRUCKMANN, Falk;** Singer (Baritone); b. 23 Jan. 1958, Heilbronn, Germany. *Education:* Studied at the Stuttgart Musikhochschule. *Career:* Debut: Kiel, 1985; Kiel Opera, 1985–89, Basle Opera, 1991; Vienna State Opera, 1990, as Scarpia and Escamillo; Berlin State Opera from 1992, as Amfortas, the Wanderer in Siegfried, the Dutchman, Pizarro and Jochanaan in Salome; Bayreuth Festival from 1993 as Kurwenal, Donner, Gunther and Amfortas; Kurwenal and Wotan at the Vienna State, US debut Chicago, 1995, as Orestes in Elektra (concert); New York Metropolitan debut, 1997, as Wozzeck; La Scala, 1997, as the Wanderer; Berlin Staatsoper, 1996 and 1998, as Telramund and Hans Sachs; Other roles include Barak in Busoni's Turandot, Rangoni in Boris Godunov and Bartók's Bluebeard; Sang Kurnwenal at Florence, Wozzeck at the Berlin Staatsoper and Strauss's Barak in Vienna, 1999; Season 2000–01 as Gunther for Cologne Opera, Pizarro at the Met, Hans Sachs in Madrid, Wagner's Dutchman and Wotan in Berlin. *Recordings include:* Tristan und Isolde, and Lohengrin conducted by Barenboim; Video of Parsifal, Berlin 1992; Bluebeard's Castle, under Eliahu Inbal. *Address:* c/o Music International, 13 Ardilaun Road, London N5 2QR, England.

**STRUMMER, Peter;** Canadian/American (b. Austrian) singer (bass-baritone); b. 8 Sept. 1948, Vienna, Austria; m. Linda Roark. *Education:* Cleveland Inst. of Music. *Career:* debut as Antonio in Le Nozze di Figaro with the Atlanta Symphony Orchestra 1972; Metropolitan Opera debut as Beckmesser 1985; debut with New York City Opera as the Sacristan in Tosca 1998–99; season 1999–2000 engagements included San Francisco Opera as Benoit/Alcindoro in La Bohème and as Borov in Giordani's Fedora for the Domingo Gala, New York City Opera as Don Prudenzio in Il Viaggio a Reims and as the Sacristan in Tosca, De Brétigny in Manon with Milwaukee's Florentine Opera Company, the Sacristan in Tosca with Manitoba Opera, Geronte in Manon Lescaut with Opera Pacific, and a concert performance as Alberich in Das Rheingold with L'Opéra de Montréal; season 2001–02 included appearances at San Francisco Opera as the Sacristan in Tosca and as Bogdanovic in The Merry Widow, New York City Opera as the Sacristan in Tosca and as Colonel Vandeveer in John Philip Sousa's The Glass Blowers, Opera Colorado as the Sacristan in Tosca, and Florentine Opera as Faninal in Der Rosenkavalier; season 2002–03 engagements included New York City Opera as Talpa in Il Tabarro and as Simone in Gianni Schicchi, Dr Bartolo in Il Barbiere di Siviglia with New York City Opera, Mustafa in L'italiana in Algeri with L'opéra de Montréal, Sulpice in La Fille du Régiment with Opera Ontario, and Benoit/Alcindoro in La Bohème with Utah Opera; season 2003–04 engagements include San Francisco Opera as Benoit/Alcindoro in La Bohème and as the Badger in The Cunning Little Vixen, New York City Opera in the title role of Don Pasquale and as Candy in Of Mice And Men, Florentine Opera and Opera Lyra Ottawa in the title role of Don Pasquale, and New Orleans Opera as Alberich in Das Rheingold; other roles include Baron Zeta in The Merry Widow, Beckmesser in Die Meistersinger von Nürnberg, Bottom in A

Midsummer Night's Dream, Dansker in Billy Budd, Dikoj in Katya Kabanova, Don Alfonso in Così fan Tutte, Don Magnifico in La Cenerentola, Dr Bartolo in Le Nozze di Figaro, Frank in Die Fledermaus, Kecal in The Bartered Bride, Leporello in Don Giovanni, Mamma Agatha and the Impresario in Viva la Mamma, Melitone in La Forza del Destino, Raimbaud and the Gouverneur in Le Comte Ory, Shishkov in From the House of the Dead, the Mayor in Jenůfa, the Music Master in Ariadne auf Naxos, the Parson in The Cunning Little Vixen, Varlaam in Boris Godunov; numerous radio and television broadcasts, including Melitone in La Forza del Destino and the Sacristan in Tosca (CBC) and the Music Master in Ariadne auf Naxos (PBS). *Recordings:* Devilshoof in The Bohemian Girl, with Central City Opera. *Current Management:* Pinnacle Arts Management/Uzan Division, 889 Ninth Avenue, Suite 1, New York, NY 10019, USA. *Telephone:* (212) 397-7926. *Fax:* (212) 397-7920. *E-mail:* Vuzan@pinnaclearts.com. *Website:* www.peterstrummer.com.

**STRYCZEK, Karl-Heinz;** Singer (Baritone); b. 5 May 1937, Nichelsdorf, Germany. *Education:* Leipzig Musikhochschule. *Career:* Debut: Dresden-Radebeul, 1964, as Germont; Dresden Staatsoper from 1966, Berlin Staatsoper, 1970; Premiere of Levins Muhle by U Zimmermann at Dresden, 1973; Guest appearances at Paris Opéra, Helsinki, Wiesbaden and Barcelona (Telramund in Lohengrin, 1992); Dresden, 1992 and 1994, in Hoffmann and as Oger in Reimann's Melusine; Other roles include Pizarro, Wozzeck, Scarpia, Mozart's Count, Amonasro, Iago and Carlos in La Forza del Destino; Dresden Staatsoper 2000–01 as the Speaker in Die Zauberflöte, and in the premiere of Celan, by Peter Ruzicka; Many concert and oratorio engagements. *Recordings include:* Donner in Das Rheingold; Die Kluge and Carmina Burana. *Address:* Dresden Semper Oper, Theaterplatz 2, 01067 Dresden, Germany.

**STUART, Debra;** Singer (Mezzo-Soprano); b. 1969, Scotland. *Education:* Studied at the Royal Scottish Academy and the Guildhall School of Music. *Career:* Opera appearances at Covent Garden, English National Opera and with the English Touring Opera; Roles include Mozart's Annius and Dorabella, Rosina, Meg Page and Britten's Hermia; Concerts with Frans Brüggen and the Songmakers' Almanac; Sang in A Midsummer Night's Dream at Aldeburgh in 1995 and festival engagements at Aix-en-Provence and Bordeaux; Further repertoire includes Les Nuits d'Été (BBC); Sang Luca in the premiere of Woolrich's In the House of Crossed Desires, Cheltenham, 1996.

**STUBBS, Stephen;** chitarrone player, archlute player and ensemble director; b. 1951, Seattle, WA, USA. *Career:* Director of Tragicomedia, ensemble performing in the Renaissance and Baroque repertory; Concerts, the United Kingdom and leading European early music festivals; Gave Stefano Landi's La Morte d'Orfeo at the 1987 Flanders Festival; Francesca Caccini's La Liberazione di Ruggiero dall'Isola d'Alcina at the 1989 Swedish Baroque Festival, Malmö; Conducted Monteverdi's L'Incoronazione di Poppea for Norrlands Opera in Umeå, Sweden, 1993; Conducted Monetverdi's L'Orfeo at Netherlands Opera, Amsterdam, 1995. *Compositions:* Pegasus and the Griffin, one-hour chamber opera for three singers and chamber ensemble, libretto by Peter Bockström, performed Malmö, 1994. *Recordings:* Solo lute recordings, David Kellner's XVI. Auserlesene Lauten-Stücke; J. S. Bach and S L Weiss Lute Suites; With Tragicomedia, Proensa (Troubadour songs); My Mind to Me a Kingdom (Elizabethan ballads); A Musicall Dreame (duets from Robert Jones 1609 collection); Orpheus I Am (masque and theatre music by Robert Johnson and William Lawes); Sprezzatura (Italian instrumental music); Il Ballo dell'Ingrate (and other theatrical music by Monteverdi); The Notebook of Anna Magdalena Bach; Le Canterine Romane (music for 3 sopranos by Luigi Rossi); Concert programmes including all recorded repertoire and other 17th and 18th century music including Orpheus Britannicus (best of Purcell's secular music for up to 5 singers, violins and oboes); Purcell, Songs of Welcome and Farewell, Tragicomedia, 1995. *Publications:* contrib. L'Armnonia Sonora: continuo orchestration in Monteverdi's L'Orfeo, to Early Music, 1994. *Current Management:* Robert White Artist Management, 182 Moselle Avenue, London, N22 6EX, England.

**STUCKY, Steven,** BM, MFA, DMA; American composer and conductor; b. 7 Nov. 1949, Hutchinson, KS. *Education:* Baylor Univ., Cornell Univ. with Karel Husa, studied conducting with Daniel Sternberg. *Career:* faculty mem. Cornell Univ. from 1980, Chair Music Dept 1992–97; composer-in-residence Los Angeles Philharmonic Orchestra, later consulting composer for new music 1988–; Ernest Bloch Visiting Prof. of Music Univ. of Calif. at Berkeley 2003; Guggenheim Foundation Fellowship 1986; Bogliasco Fellowship 1997; American Acad. of Arts and Letters Goddard Lieberson Fellowship 2002. *Compositions include:* Two Holy Sonnets of Donne for mezzo, oboe and piano 1982, Sappho Fragments for mezzo and ensemble 1982, Voyages for voice and wind orchestra 1984, Double Concerto for violin, oboe and chamber orchestra 1985, Concerto for Orchestra 1987, Threnos for wind ensemble 1988, Son et Lumière for orchestra 1988, Angelus for orchestra 1989, Serenade for wind quintet 1989, Impromptus for orchestra 1991, Four Poems of A. R. Ammons for baritone and ensemble 1992, Funeral Music for Queen Mary (arrangement of Purcell) 1992, Ancora for orchestra 1994, Fanfares and Arias for wind ensemble 1994, Concerto for two flutes and orchestra 1994, Pinturas de Tamayo for orchestra 1995, Cradle songs 1997, Concerto Mediterraneo 1998, Ad Parnassum 1998, American Muse 1999, Nell'ombra, nella luce 2000, Partita-Pastorale 2000, Etudes (concerto for recorder and chamber orchestra) 2000, Skylarks 2001, Noctuelles (orchestration of Ravel) 2001, Concerto for percussion and wind orchestra 2001, Whispers 2002, Colburn Variations 2002,

Spirit Voices for percussion and orchestra 2002–03, Second Concerto for orchestra (Pulitzer Prize for Music 2005) 2003, Jeu de timbres 2003, Sonate en forme de préludes 2003–04, Piano Quartet 2004–05. *Publications include:* Lutoslawski and his Music 1981. *Address:* De Witt Building, PO Box 21, 215 N Cayuga Street, Ithaca, NY 14850, USA.

**STUDEBAKER, Thomas;** Singer (Tenor); b. 1970, Illinois, USA. *Career:* Debut: St Louis Opera, 1995; Appearances throughout USA, including engagements with the Metropolitan (Ruiz in Il Trovatore); Sang Narraboth in Salome at Santa Fe, 1998; Season 1999–2000 with appearances at Montreal and Seattle. *Honours:* Finalist in 1999 Singer of the World Competition, Cardiff. *Address:* c/o Metropolitan Opera, Lincoln Center, New York, NY 10023, USA.

**STUDER, Cheryl;** American soprano opera singer; b. 24 Oct. 1955, Midland, Mich.; m. 2nd Ewald Schwarz; two d. (one by previous m.). *Education:* Interlochen Arts Acad., Oberlin Coll. Cleveland, Ohio and Univ. of Tennessee. *Career:* studied singing with Gwendolyn Pike, at Berkshire Music Centre, at Tanglewood with Phyllis Curtin and at Hochschule für Musik, Vienna with Hans Hotter; engaged for concert series with Boston Symphony Orchestra by Seiji Ozawa (q.v.) 1979; opera debut as the First Lady in The Magic Flute, Munich 1980–82; with Darmstadt State Theatre, Germany 1982–84, Deutsche Oper, Berlin 1984–86; US debut as Micaela in Carmen, Lyric Opera of Chicago 1984; debut at Bayreuth 1985, Royal Opera House, Covent Garden 1987, Metropolitan Opera, New York 1988; sings wide variety of roles, especially Wagner, Verdi, Mozart and Strauss. *Honours:* Int. Music Award 1993, Vocalist of the Year (USA) 1994. *Address:* c/o Deutsche Oper Berlin, Richard Wagnerstrasse 10, 1000 Berlin, Germany (office); c/o International Performing Artists Inc., 125 Crowfield Drive, Knoxville, TN 37922, USA.

**STUDER, Ulrich;** Singer (Baritone); b. 27 Aug. 1945, Bern, Switzerland. *Education:* Studied at Bern Conservatory and Musikhochschule Munich. *Career:* Many appearances at Opera Houses in Italy, Netherlands (The Hague), Austria (Innsbruck), Australia and Czechoslavakia; Concert and Broadcast engagements in Switzerland, Germany and France, notably in Bach's Sacred Music and contemporary works by Burkhard, Milhaud and Huber; Recitals featuring German Lieder and French Chansons; Opera performances at Bern, 1979–83, and at Basle, Lausanne and Munich; Roles have included Morales in Carmen, Belcore, Malatesta, Valentin, Creonte in Haydn's Orfeo, Masetto, Suppé's Boccaccio and Monteverdi's Orfeo; Season 2000–01 at Halle as Don Alfosno, Escamillo, and Elmiro in Rossini's Otello (concert). *Recordings include:* Cantatas by Bach and Charpentier; Messe des Morts by Gilles; Cantatas by Vivaldi; Elviro in Handel's Serse; Lully's Armide; Erode in Stradella's San Giovanni Battista. *Address:* c/o Opern- and Konzertsänger, Mittelstrasse 14–15, 06108 Halle/Saale, Germany.

**STUDNICKA, Vladimir;** Composer and Music Director; b. 24 Aug. 1935, Czechoslovakia; 2 d. *Education:* Completed Composition studies, 1957, and Classical Guitar Performance, 1966, Conservatory of Music. *Career:* Debut: Suite for Orchestra performed by Janáček Philharmonic Orchestra in 1957; Teacher at Music School, 1961–75; Music Director, Radio Ostrava, 1975–; Works as a Conductor; Established and conducted the Beskydska Muzika Harmonic Folk Orchestra. *Compositions:* All kinds especially concert pieces for orchestra, adaptations of folk songs of the Janáček region, and chamber and symphony works including: Suite for Orchestra, 1957; The May Dance, recorded, Prague Radio, 1973; The Beskydy Nocturno, Radio Ostrava, 1984; The Ondra's Dance, Radio Ostrava, 1985; Salut JV Stich-Punto for 12 Horns, Radio Ostrava, 1986. *Recordings include:* Radio recordings of many smaller pieces. *Publications:* The Round, 1985; The Song Of The Rising Sun by Wilhelm Halter, 1990; Slazsky Dance Musikvarlag Rundal, 1993. *Address:* ul Prof Jana Soupala 1607, 70800 Ostrava-Poruba, Czech Republic.

**STUMPF, Peter (Daniel);** Cellist; b. 16 Jan. 1963, Syracuse, New York, USA. *Education:* BM, Curtis Institute of Music, 1985; Artist Diploma, New England Conservatory, 1990; Teachers: David Wells, Orlando Cole, Lawrence Lesser. *Career:* Debut: Boston Symphony Orchestra, Symphony Hall, Boston, 1979; Participant at Marlboro Music Festival, 1985–; Tours with Music From Marlboro; Member, Philadelphia Chamber Music Society Players, 1994–; Piano Trio with Mitsuko Uchida and Mark Steinberg, 1995–; Solo recitals at the Jordan Hall, Boston, 1989–90, Phillips Collection, Washington DC, 1991, 1994, 1996, Corcoran Gallery, Washington DC, 1997; Solo appearances at: Aspen Festival, Colorado, 1984; Boston Philharmonic, 1989; Virginia Symphony, 1992; National Repertory Orchestra, 1992; Philadelphia Orchestra Chamber Music Series, 1990–; Chamber Music with Wolfgang Sawallisch in Carnegie Hall and Concertgebouw; Teaching Chamber Music at the Curtis Institute of Music, 1994–. *Honours:* Second Prize, Evian International String Quartet Competition, 1983; First Prize, Aspen Concerto Competition for Cello, 1984; First Prize, Washington International Competition, 1991; Serving on Board of Trustees for Yellow Barn Festival, Putney, Vermont, USA, 1995–. *Address:* 400 South Sydenham Street, Philadelphia, PA 19146, USA.

**STUMPHIUS, Annegeer;** Singer (Soprano); b. 1963, Netherlands. *Career:* Glyndebourne Touring Opera, 1987, as Fiordiligi; Munich Festival, 1988, as Europa in Strauss's Die Liebe der Danaë; Sang Britten's Helena at Glyndebourne, 1989; First Lady in Die Zauberflöte, 1991; Season 1991 as Vitellia in La Clemenza di Tito at Enschede and Zürich, Ilia in Idomeneo at Amsterdam; Season 1993–94 as Ellen Orford at Munich and Vitellia at Dresden; Munich, 1996, as Echo in Ariadne and Naxos; Jenůfa at Hildesheim, 2001; Further engagements as Donna Anna at Dresden, Jenůfa at Hilde-

sheim, Mozart's Countess at Salzburg and Donna Elvira at Munich; Wellgunde and Helmwige in Munich Ring, under Zubin Mehta. *Recordings include:* Bach B minor Mass; Haydn's Seasons, under Helmuth Rilling; Mendelssohn Lobgesang; Bach St John Passion; Gluck Pilgrims to Mecca. *Current Management:* Agentur Haase, Munich. *Address:* c/o Bavarian State Opera, Max-Joseph-Platz, 80539 Munich, Germany.

**STUPPNER, Hubert;** Composer; b. 18 Jan. 1944, Trodena, nr. Bolzano, Italy. *Education:* Bolzano Conservatory and University of Padua (Doctorate, 1965); Darmstadt 1970–74, with Ligeti, Xenakis and Stockhausen. *Career:* Founded International Festival of Contemporary Music at Bolzano, 1975; Director of Bolzano Conservatory, from 1981. *Compositions:* Historia Naturalis, for soprano, mezzo, six voices, two flutes and two percussion, 1976; Totentanz, chamber opera, 1978; Die Stimme der Sylphiden for orchestra, 1979; Quasi una Sinfonia, 1981; Chamber concerto, 1981–84; String quartet no. 1, 1984, no. 2 1987, no. 3 1990; Symphony no.1, 1985; Piano Concerto, 1984; Chamber Symphony, 1986; Symphony no. 2 1986; Café Eros, theatre, 1986; Salomes Tanz for soprano and orchestra, 1988; Bergkristall, for violin and piano, 1989; Hiob, oratorio, 1991; Folk Songs for soprano and ensemble, 1994; Corrida, for orchestra, 1996. *Address:* c/o SIAE (Sezione Musica), Viale della Letteratura n.30, 00144 Rome, Italy.

**STUR, Svetozar;** Conductor and Composer; b. 21 Feb. 1951, Bratislava, Czechoslovakia; m. Nadezda Sturova, 12 November 1977. *Education:* Graduate, conservatoire in Bratislava, 1972; Graduate, Academy of Music and Performing Arts, Bratislava, 1977. *Career:* Debut: Taras Bulba by Janáček with the Slovak Philharmonic Orchestra, Bratislava, 1977; Artistic Head of Orchestra, Slovak Folklorist Ensemble, Lucnica, 1972–77; Assistant Conductor, Slovak Philharmonic Orchestra, Bratislava, 1977–79; First Conductor, Cairo Conservatoire Orchestra, 1979–80; Conductor, Symphony Orchestra of Czech Radio, Bratislava, 1980–81; Recording Own Compositions for Films and Television with Fisyo Orchestra, Prague, 1980–; Assistant Conductor, Slovak National Theatre, Bratislava, 1980–87; Conductor, Slovak State Folk Ensemble, Bratislava, 1988–90; Freelance Composer, for films, television and theatre, 1991–. *Address:* Grosslingova 28, 811 09 Bratislava, Slovakia.

**STURROCK, Kathron;** Pianist; b. 17 July 1948, Bournemouth, England. *Education:* Studied at the Royal College of Music and with Alfred Brendel in Vienna; Further study with Mstislav Rostropovich in Moscow. *Career:* Concert and television appearances throughout Europe and in North America, India and Australia; Regular performances for the BBC and concerts in the major London halls; Director, the chamber music ensemble, The Fibonacci Sequence; Has taught at Morley College, the Royal College of Music, Royal Academy of Music and the Birmingham School of Music; Artist in Residence at the Brisbane Conservatoire, 1987; British Council tour of Oman in 1989; BBC recitals include Schubert's Wanderer Fantasy, Beethoven Op 109, and Rawsthorne Ballade; Prom debut in 1994 in Rawsthorne 2 Piano Concerto with Piers Lane. *Recordings include:* Bliss Viola Sonata with Emanuel Vardi; Beethoven Spring Sonata; Brahms Violin and Viola Sonatas; Cello Sonatas by Beethoven, Schnittke, Shostakovich and Kabalevsky; Songs by Rebecca Clarke with Patricia Wright; Chamber Works of Alan Rawsthorne; Songs by Sir Arthur Bliss. *Honours:* Sofia International Opera Competition, as accompanist; Martin Musical Scholarship Fund and The Countess of Munster Award, RCM. *Address:* 81 Lacy Road, London SW15 1NR, England.

**STUTZMANN, Natalie;** Singer (Contralto); b. 6 May 1965, Suresnes, France. *Education:* Nancy Conservatory; Studied singing with her mother, Christiane Stutzmann, with Hans Hotter and at the Paris Opéra School. *Career:* Sang in recitals and concerts at London Wigmore Hall, Paris Théâtre Champs-Elysées, New York Carnegie Hall; La Scala, Milan; Amsterdam Concertgebouw; Berlin Philharmonie, Vienna Musikverein, Tokyo Suntory Hall; Sang Mozart's Ombra Felice at the Salzburg Festival, 1994; Gluck's Orpheus at Lyon, 1998; Giulio Cesare by Handel at Bordeaux, 1999. *Recordings include:* Schumann complete lieder, Fauré, Debussy, Ravel, Chausson, mélodies, Handel and Mozart Arias, Bach Cantatas and Passions, and Brahms Alto Rhapsody; Handel Amadigi. *Address:* c/o Opéra et Concert, 1 Rue Volney, F–75002 Paris, France.

**SUART, Richard Martin,** ARAM, FRAM; British singer (baritone); b. 5 Sept. 1951, Blackpool, England; m. Susan Cook 1981; two s. one d. *Education:* sang in choir of St John's Coll.; Royal Acad. of Music. *Career:* roles in contemporary opera include The Black Minister in Le Grand Macabre, Der Gatte in Reigen at Amsterdam, Dad/Café Manager in Greek for ENO, Old Musician in Broken Strings (Param Vir) for Netherlands Opera, Chaplinoperas (Mason) throughout Europe with Ensemble Modern, Eight Songs for a Mad King in London, Paris, Helsinki, Milan and Strasbourg, Stan Stock in Playing Away (Mason) also French Ambassador in Of Thee I Sing (Gershwin) for Opera North; other roles include Frank in Die Fledermaus, Benoit and Alcindoro in La Bohème for ENO, Don Inigo Gomez in L'Heure Espagnole for Grange Park Opera; Savoy Opera performances include the patter roles in Gilbert and Sullivan, particularly Ko-Ko (The Mikado), in London, Venice, New York; presents one-man show, As a Matter of Patter. *Recordings include:* most of the Savoy operas, Candide, A Midsummer Night's Dream, The Geisha, The Rose of Persia, The Fairy Queen and Ligeti's Le Grand Macabre. *Current Management:* Musichall, Vicarage Way, Ringmer, BN8 5LA, England. *Address:* Yardley Bank, 29 Yardley Park Road, Tonbridge, Kent TN9 1NB, England. *E-mail:* info@richardsuart.co.uk. *Website:* www.richardsuart.co.uk.

**SUBEN, Joel Eric,** BMus, MFA, PhD; American conductor, composer and academic; b. 16 May 1946, New York, NY; m. 1st Judith Ann Gundersheimer 1979 (divorced 1985); m. 2nd Linda Rodgers 1993. *Education:* Eastman School of Music, Brandeis University, Hochschule Mozarteum, Salzburg, studied conducting with Jacques-Louis Monod. *Career:* Music Director and Permanent Conductor of Peninsula Symphony of VA, 1982–87; Guest Conductor includes: Silesian Philharmonic Orchestra, Poland, 1986 and 1994, New Jersey Composers Orchestra, 1987–, Polish Radio National Symphony Orchestra, 1993, Janáček Philharmonic Orchestra, 1994 and 1996, Slovak Radio Symphony Orchestra, Bratislava, 1995 and North Bohemian Philharmonic Orchestra, Czech Republic, 1996; Director of Orchestras, College of William and Mary, VA, 1983–92; Artistic Director, Brooklyn Heights Music Festival, 1986; Guest Lecturer, NY Philharmonic Pre-Concert Lecture Series, 1989–; Music Director, Composers Chorus, 1992–; Music Adviser, Wellesley Philharmonic, MA, 1993–. *Compositions include:* Gesualdo Triptych, for String Orchestra, 1984; Symphony in Old Style for Orchestra, 1987; Concerto Classico for Flute and Small Orchestra, 1991; Breve Sogno for Large Orchestra, 1993. *Publications:* Debussy and Octatonic Pitch Structure, University Microfilms, 1980. *Current Management:* Linda Rodgers Associates, 628 Bloomfield Street, Hoboken, NJ 07030, USA.

**SUBLETT, Virginia;** Singer (Soprano); b. 29 July 1952, Kansas City, Kansas, USA. *Education:* BMus, Louisiana State University, Baton Rouge, 1974; Master of Arts in Music, University of California at San Diego, 1994; Doctorate of Musical Arts, UCSD, 1997; Private vocal study with Carol Webber, Isabel Penagos, and Michael Jackson Parker. *Career:* Sang the Queen of Night in The Magic Flute (Mozart), New York City Opera and San Diego Opera; La Princess and La Rossignol in L'Enfant et les Sortilèges (Ravel), New York City Opera; Nannetta in Falstaff (Verdi), Tytania in A Midsummer Night's Dream (Britten), and Oberto in Alcina (Handel), Los Angeles Opera; Ismene in Mitridate (Mozart) and Servilia in La Clemenza di Tito (Mozart), L'Opéra de Nice; Numerous appearances as soprano soloist with Los Angeles Philharmonic Orchestra, San Diego Symphony Orchestra, Illinois Symphony Orchestra, New Jersey Symphony Orchestra, and Los Angeles Baroque Orchestra; Founder and Co-conductor of Cappella Gloriana vocal ensemble, 1996; Member of Adjunct Faculties at University of California at San Diego and University of San Diego, 1992; Director of Choral Scholars and University-Community Choir at UCSD, 1997–99; mem, American Guild of Musical Artists, National Association of Teachers of Singing; American Choral Directors' Association. *Current Management:* Classical Performing Artists Management. *Address:* c/o CPAM, 3760 29th Street, San Diego, CA 92104, USA.

**SUBOTNICK, Morton Leon,** MA; American composer; b. 14 April 1933, Los Angeles; s. of Jack Jacob Subotnick and Rose Luckerman; m. 1st Linn Pottle 1953 (divorced 1971); one s. one d.; m. 2nd Doreen Nelson 1976 (divorced 1977); m. 3rd Joan La Barbara 1979; one s. *Education:* Univ. of Denver, Mills Coll. *Career:* Co-Founder, San Francisco Tape Music Center 1961–65; fmr Music Dir, Ann Halprin's Dance Co. and San Francisco Actors' Workshop, fmr Music Dir of Lincoln Center Repertory Theatre; Dir of electronic music at original Electric Circus, St Mark's Place, New York 1967–68; Artist-in-Residence, New York Univ. School of the Arts 1966–69; Co-Dir Center for Experiments in Art, Information and Tech., Calif. Inst. of Arts, Valencia 1969–, also Co-Chair. Composition Dept; Visiting Prof. in Composition, Univ. of Md 1968, Univ. of Pittsburgh 1969, Yale Univ. 1982, 1983; has toured extensively as a lecturer and composer/performer; Composer-in-Residence DAAD, West Berlin 1981, MIT 1986. *Compositions include:* Silver Apples of the Moon, The Wild Bull, Trembling, The Double Life of Amphibians, The Key to Songs, Return: The Triumph of Reason (electronic composition in honour of the return of Halley's Comet) 1986, In Two Worlds 1987–88, And The Butterflies Begin to Sing 1988, A Desert Flowers 1989, All my Hummingbirds have Alibis, Jacob's Room (opera) 1993, Making Music 1996, Intimate Immensity 1997, Echoes from the Silent Call of Girona 1998. *Honours:* Brandeis Award for Music 1983 and numerous other grants and awards. *Address:* 121 Coronado Lane, Santa Fe, NM 87507, USA.

**SUBRTOVA, Milada;** Opera Singer (Dramatic Soprano); b. 24 May 1924, Lhota, Kralovice, Czechoslovakia; m. Jan Hus Tichy. *Education:* Business School, Prague; Private studies with tenor Zdenek Knittl, Prague. *Career:* Debut: As Giulietta in Offenbach's Les Contes d'Hoffmann, Theatre 5 May, Prague; Opera and concerts, Czechoslovakia including National Theatre Prague and Czech Philharmonic, Prague, Italy, Poland, Romania, Bulgaria, England, Yugoslavia, Switzerland, Spain, Iceland, Germany, Netherlands, Austria; Recitals, songs and opera arias of romantic composers, Radio Prague; Roles included: 3 female roles (Hoffmann); Norma, Dona Anna (Don Giovanni), Constanze (Entführung), Fiordiligi (Così fan tutte), Pamina (Die Zauberflöte), Gilda (Rigoletto), Violetta (La Traviata), Elisabeth (Don Carlo), Abigaille (Nabucco), Mimi (La Bohème), Butterfly, Tosca, Turandot, Santuzza (Cavalleria), Charpentier's Louise, Marguerite (Faust), Micaela (Carmen), Woman (Poulenc's La Voix Humaine), Ännchen and Agathe (Der Freischütz), Elsa (Lohengrin), Sieglinde (Die Walküre), Tatyana (Eugene Onegin), Marenka (Bartered Bride), title roles in Libuše, Rusalka, Jenůfa, many others; Concerts include Beethoven's 9th; Bach, B minor mass; Martinů, Gilgamesh; Honneger, Jeanne d'Arc; Janáček, Glagolitic Mass; Schoenberg, Gurreleider; Mahler's 4th; Dvořák, Stabat Mater; Berlioz, Damnation of Faust. *Recordings:* Portrait recital; Complete operas: At Well, Blodek, conductor Frantisek Skvor, 1959; Rusalka, conductor Zdenek Chalabala,

1960; The Devil's Wall, conductor Zdenek Chalabala, 1961; Libuše, conductor Jaroslav Krombholc. *Honours:* 1st Prize, International Vocal Competition, Prague Spring Festival, 1954. *Address:* Belohorska 70, 16900 Prague 6, Czech Republic.

**SUDBIN, Yevgeny;** Russian pianist; b. 1980, St Petersburg. *Education:* St Petersburg Conservatory with Lyubov Pevsner, Hochschule Hanns Eisler, Berlin, Purcell School of Music, London with Christopher Elton, RAM. *Career:* has performed concerts and recitals throughout Europe and N America, including Rudolfinum, Prague, Philharmonie, Cologne, Gewandhaus, Leipzig, Schauspielhaus, Berlin, Nat. Concert Hall, Dublin, Salle de l'UNESCO, Paris, Serate Musicali, Milan, British Embassy, Paris, Tonhalle, Zurich, Konzertreihe, Wolfsberg, Nuits Romantiques Festival, France, Sommets Musicaux and the Verbier Festival, Switzerland; chamber music concerts with the Chilingirian String Quartet and violinists Ilya Gringolts and Julia Fischer. *Recordings:* London Octave, Better Baroque, Scarlatti, Piano Sonatas 2005, Sudbin plays Rachmaninov 2005. *Honours:* first prize Steinway Piano Competition, Berlin 1992, 1993, 1995, winner Concertino Praga Int. Piano Competition 1994, second prize Vendome Prize 2000, prize winner Dublin Int. Piano Competition 2000, Alfred Brendel Prize, Philharmonia Orchestra Musical Prize, winner Jaques Samuels Piano Competition 2003, Orpheum Public Award for the best interpretation of a Mozart Concerto. *Current Management:* Grant Rogers Musical Artists' Management, 8 Wren Crescent, Bushey Heath, Hertfordshire WD23 1AN, England. *Telephone:* (20) 8950-2220 (office). *Fax:* (20) 8950-3570 (office). *E-mail:* info@ngrartists.com (office). *Website:* www.ngrartists.com (office). *Address:* c/o BIS Records AB, Stationsvägen 20, Åkersberga 184 50, Sweden (office).

**SUHONEN, Antti;** Singer (Bass-Baritone); b. 5 Nov. 1956, Nurmes, Finland. *Education:* Studied at Sibelius Academy and at the National Opera Studio, Helsinki and at the International Opera Studio, Zürich; Masterclasses with Charles Farncombe, Herbert Brauer and Victoria de Los Angeles. *Career:* Made debut at Zürich, 1986, engaged at Karlsruhe, 1987–91, and at Helsinki from 1991–; Made guest appearances at Dresden, Wiesbaden, Hanover and Mannheim and also at Munich State Opera, Berlin State Oera, Essen and Royal Opera in Copenhagen; Karlsruhe, 1989, in shared premiere of Graf Mirabeau by Siegfried Matthus; Appearances at Helsinki and elsewhere as Mozart's Leporello, Masetto, Figaro and Alfonso, Sparafucile, Dulcamara, Basilio, Varlaam and Rangoni in Boris Godunov, Melitone in La Forza del Destino, Méphistopélès in Gounod's Faust; Sang Klaus in premiere of Linkola's Elina, Helsinki, 1992 and Fruitseller in Bergman's The Singing Tree in Helsinki, 1995; With Berlin State Opera, Wagner's Ring, Kupfer and Barenboim, 1996; Savonlinna Festival, 1992, as Don Fernando in Fidelio; Bluebeard in Bartók's Bluebeard's Castle, 1994; Season 1999 with the Israel Philharmonic Orchestra under Zubin Mehta in Ariadne auf Naxos, Chicago Symphony orchestra under Pierre Boulez in Schoenberg's Moses und Aron and the Finnish National Opera in Wagner's Ring; Season 1999–2000 as Wagner's Gunther in Helsinki and the Forester in The Cunning Little Vixen, for the Deutsche Oper Berlin; Guest appearances at Deutsche Oper, Berlin, 2000–; Alongside his opera career he frequently appears as soloist in numerous concerts. *Recordings:* Rautavaara: Thomas, 1986, Sampo, 1995; Mozart: Die Zauberflöte, 1988; Pacius: Kung Karls Jagd, 1991; Sang Ossip in The Palace, by Sallinen, at the 1996 Savonlinna Festival. *Address:* c/o Finnish National Opera, Helsinginkatu 58, SF 00260 Helsinki 18, Finland.

**SUITNER, Otmar;** Austrian conductor; b. 16 May 1922, Innsbruck; s. of Karl Suitner and Maria Rizzi; m. Marita Wilckens 1948. *Education:* Pädagogium Innsbrück, Mozarteum Salzburg. *Career:* Music Dir in Remscheid 1952–57; Gen. Dir of Pfalzorchester in Ludwigshafen 1957–60; Gen. Dir of State Opera Dresden 1960–64; Gen. Dir German State Opera Berlin 1964–89; Hon. Conductor Nippon Hoso Kyokai Orchestra, Tokyo 1973–88; Guest Conductor San Francisco, Tokyo, Vienna, Bayreuth Festival, etc.; many recordings; led course for conductors, Int. Summer Acad. Univ. Mozarteum, Salzburg 1975, 1976; Prof. 1968; Prof. in Conducting, Hochschule für Musik, Vienna 1977–. *Honours:* Commendatore, Gregorian Order 1973; Austrian Ehrenkreuz for Science and Art 1982. *Address:* Platanenstr. 13, 13156 Berlin, Germany; Widerhoferplatz 4/48, 1090 Vienna, Austria.

**SUK, Josef;** Czech violinist (retd); b. 8 Aug. 1929, Prague; s. of Josef Suk and Marie Suková; grandson of Josef Suk; great-grandson of Antonin Dvořák; m. Marie Bláhová 1951. *Education:* Prague Conservatory and studied with Jaroslav Kocian. *Career:* First Violinist, Prague String Quartet 1950; f. Suk Trio 1952; soloist with Czech Philharmonic Orchestra 1961–; Prof., Vienna Conservatoire 1979–86; has given concerts as a soloist or with trio throughout the world; announced retirement from professional career 2001; Pres. Prague Spring Foundation, Antonin Dvořák Foundation; numerous recordings. *Honours:* Hon. mem. Int. Antonín Dvořák Soc. 1999; Chevalier, Légion d'honneur 2002; Dr hc (Acad. of Music, Prague) 2003; Grand Prix du Disque 1960, 1966, 1968, 1974, 1978, Czechoslovak State Prize 1964, Edison Prize 1972, Wiener Flötenuhr 1974, Honoured Artist 1970, National Artist 1977, Golden Disc of Nippon Columbia 1978, Plaque of 100th Anniversary of Béla Bartók's Birth 1981, Czech State Prize 1999, Platinum Record Supraphon 1999, Medal of Merit 1999, Prize, Masaryk Acad. of Peforming Arts 2001. *Address:* Karlovo náměstí 5, 12000 Prague 2, Czech Republic. *Telephone:* (2) 24919765. *Fax:* (2) 24919765.

**SUKIS, Lilian;** Singer (Soprano); b. 29 June 1939, Kaunas, Lithuania. *Education:* Toronto University. *Career:* Debut: Toronto 1964, as Lady Billows in Britten's Albert Herring; Metropolitan Opera from 1965, notably as Pamina in Die Zauberflöte; Bayerishe Staatsoper, Munich, and elsewhere in Germany from 1969, as Violetta, Mozart's Countess and Fiordiligi, Micaela in Carmen, Liu in Turandot, and Verdi's Luisa Miller; Sang Strauss's Daphne at Munich, and in the 1972 premiere of Sim Tjong by Isang Yun. *Recordings include:* Ascanio in Alba, by Mozart (Philips); Die Lustige Weiber von Windsor (Decca); Mozart's La finta giardiniera (DGG). *Address:* c/o Bayerische Staatsoper, Max-Josephs-Platz, D-8-539 Munich, Germany.

**SULEIMANOV, Stanislav;** Russian singer (bass); b. 1945, Baku. *Education:* Baku Conservatory. *Career:* sang at the Bolshoi Theatre Moscow from 1977; since 1989 also the creator of the first Contract Musical Theatre 'Forum'; repertoire includes: Boris and Varlaam in Boris Godunov, Rimsky's Salieri, Scarpia in Tosca, Malatesta in Rachmaninov's Francesca da Rimini, Boris in Lady Macbeth, Pontius Pilate in Master and Margarita by S. Slonimsky; guest appearances throughout Russia, USA, Japan, Netherlands, Belgium, Luxembourg, Italy, Spain, Greece and Germany; concerts and Lieder recitals. *Address:* Halturinskaja str 4-1-58, 107392 Moscow, Russia.

**SULLIVAN, Ghillian;** Singer (Soprano); b. 1954, Adelaide, South Australia. *Education:* Studied with Audrey Langford, in London. *Career:* Debut: Opera 80 in 1980, as Mozart's Countess; Season 1981–82 as Britten's Tytania for GTO and Donizetti's Adina for Opera North; Fiordiligi at Sydney, 1983; Leeds, 1983–84, in the premiere of Rebecca by W Josephs, and the English premiere of Krenek's Jonny spielt auf; Wiesbaden and Aachen, 1985–86, as Constanze; Cologne, 1987 as Musetta; Victoria State Opera debut, 1986, as Donna Elvira; English National Opera from 1989, including tour of Russia; Principal Guest Artist at Opera Australia from 1985 to the present day; Many major roles including Traviata, Lucia, Gilda, Donna Anna and Rosalinde; Guest appearances at all State companies and with Sydney Symphony Orchestra; Sang Bizet's Leila and Rosalinde in Die Fledermaus at Sydney, 2000; Concert and oratorio engagements. *Recordings:* First solo CD, Vocal Gems. *Address:* c/o Jenifer Eddy Artists Management, Suite 11, The Clivedon, 596 St Kilda Road, VIC 3004, Australia.

**SULZEN, Donald,** MMus; pianist and accompanist; b. 17 Feb. 1955, Kansas City, KS, USA. *Education:* Ecole Normale de Musique de Paris, Univ. of North Texas. *Career:* performed at major festivals throughout the world; regular appearances with well-known singers, such as Julie Kaufmann, Michiè Nakamaru, Anna Caterina Antonacci, Daphne Evangelatos, Doris Soffel, Marilyn Schmiege, Ofelia Sala, James Taylor, Laura Aikin and Thomas Cooley; pianist Munich Piano Trio 2001–; television and radio performances for Bayerischer Rundfunk Munich, WDR Cologne, Radio France Paris, RAI 1 Rome, Nippon TV Tokyo, RAI 3 Naples; teacher, Richard Strauss Conservatory and Hochschule für Musik, Munich. *Recordings include:* Gabriel Fauré Melodies with Marilyn Schmiege (Le Monde de la Musique Prix du Choc 1994), Johannes Brahms Lieder und Duette with Julie Kaufmann and Marilyn Schmiege, George Enescu Cello Sonatas with Gerhard Zank, Franz Liszt Songs–Schmiege, Hans Pfitzner Lieder with Julie Kaufmann, Songs of John Duke with James Taylor and works of Alberto Ginastera, including solo piano pieces, Songs and Cycles of Ned Rorem with Laura Aikin, Songs and Trios of Joseph Haydn with Julie Kaufmann and the Munich Piano Trio, Songs and Trios of Joseph Haydn with James Taylor and the Munich Piano Trio. *Address:* Baaderstr. 19, 80469 Munich, Germany.

**SUMEGI, Daniel;** Singer (bass); b. 1965, Australia. *Education:* studied in Australia, Venice, San Francisco, Vienna, New York. *Career:* appearances with San Francisco Opera from 1991 in La Traviata, Andrea Chénier, A Midsummer Night's Dream, Der Rosenkavalier, Capriccio, Il Trovatore, Fiery Angel, Die Meistersinger, Pique Dame, Tannhäuser, King Priam, Salome and Aida; La Bohème at the Golden Gate Theatre 1996; world premiere in Asdrubila, Barcelona Olympic Games, 1992; Season 1994–95 with Hermit in Freischutz at Trieste, Sarastro at Victoria State Opera; Season 1995–96 with Ramfis and Rossini's Basilio for Australia Opera, Gounod's Mefisto and Verdi's Banquo for Holland's Reiseopera, Britten's Theseus at Turin, Gremin for Victorian State Opera; Seneca in Monteverdi's Poppea for Glimmerglass Opera at Brooklyn Acad., Ratcliffe in Billy Budd at the Opéra Bastille and Alonso in Il Guarany for Washington Opera; Season 1996–97 Ramphis and the Commendatore for Victoria State Opera, Basilio for Opera Australia, Commendatore in Oviedo, and Sarastro in Die Zauberflöte for Bonn Opera; Season 1997–98 Colline and Saint Saens Old Hebrew for Opera Australia, Banquo at Houston, Peter Grimes and Boris Godunov at Metropolitan Opera, Sant Saens High Priest at Palm Beach, Billy Budd at Opera Bastille, Lady Macbeth of Mtsensk at Opera Nantes; Season 1998–99 with Faust at Opera Australia, Wagner's Hagen at State Opera of South Australia, The Crucible and Boris for Washington, Pizzaro at Utah, Mefisto in Minneapolis and Fafner in Sydney; Season 1999–2000 with I Lombardi in Santiago de Chile, Ramphis and the Commendatore in Houston, I Puritani's Georgio, Tosca's Scarpia and Otello's Lodovico in Washington and Baron Ochs for WNO; Season 2000–01 as Fiesco for Opera Australia and Mahler's 8th for Olympic Games, Scarpa in Adelaide, Mozart's Speaker in San Diego, Verdi's Grand Inquisitor in DC and Richard Tucker Gala at Covent Garden; Season 2001–02 as Wagner's Klingsor in Adelaide, Hoffmann Villains and Kurwenal for Opera Australia, Opera de Montreal Gala Concert, Don Carlo at the Met, Wagner's Pogner in Antwerp and Daland in San Diego; Washington Opera Japan Tour of Tosca, Otello and Sly; Season 2002–03 as Scarpia at WNP, Medea's Creonte in Montpellier, Puccini's Timur in Dallas, Daland in Minneapolis, Escamillo for Opera Australia, Elijah for Sydney Phiharmonia and Stiffelio's Jorg for Minneapolis,

Daland at Austin Lyric and Escamillo at WNO; Season 2003–04: Messiah in Minnesota, Dutchman in Sydney and Austin. *Honours:* Winner: 1987 Melbourne Sun Aria, 1987; Sydney McDonald's Aria, 1994; Met Opera National Council Auditions, 1994; Sullivan Foundation Grant, 1994; Finalist of 1992 Pavarotti and 1995 Placido Domingo Operalia Competition. *Current Management:* Vincent & Farrell Associates, 165 East 83 No. 5E, New York, NY 10028, USA; Ingpen & Williams Ltd, 7 St George's Court, 131 Putney Bridge Road, London, SW15 2PA, England.

**SUMMERLY, Jeremy,** BA, MMus; Conductor and Musicologist; b. 28 Feb. 1961, Stoke-on-Trent, England. *Education:* Lichfield Cathedral School, Winchester Coll., Univ. of Oxford, London Univ. *Career:* Studio Man., BBC Radio 1982–89; Lecturer in Academic Studies, Royal Acad. of Music 1989–95; Head of Academic Studies, Royal Acad. of Music 1996–; Conductor, Oxford Camerata 1983; Conductor, Schola Cantorum of Oxford 1990–96; freelance writer and presenter for BBC Radio, including Record Review and CD Review (BBC Radio 3) 1990–, The English Cadence (BBC Radio 3) 1995, Choir Works (BBC Radio 3) 1996–98, Front Row (BBC Radio 4) 2002–; organist, Christ Church, Chelsea 1999–2002; debut as conductor at BBC Promenade Concerts, July 1999; mem. Royal Musical Asscn, American Musicological Soc. *Recordings:* Schütz: Christmas Story 1995, J. S. Bach: Magnificat 1995, Fauré Requiem 1994, Handel: Coronation Anthems 2002. *Publications:* Gaudete: Medieval Songs and Carols 1999, Passetime with Good Company: Medieval Songs 2002, Fair Oriana: Elizabethan Madrigals 2002; contrib. to Early Music, The Musical Times, Choir and Organ, Leading Notes, Classic CD. *Honours:* European Cultural Prize (Basel) 1995, Hon. ARAM 1997, Hon. FASC 2002. *Current Management:* Sigma Management, Suite 729, 78 Marylebone High Street, London, W1V 5AP, England. *Telephone:* (20) 7381-4692 (office). *Fax:* (20) 7460-0742 (office). *E-mail:* sigma@camerata.demon.co .uk (office). *Website:* www.camerata.demon.co.uk (office).

**SUMMERS, Hilary;** Contralto; b. 1965, Newport, Gwent, Wales. *Education:* Reading University, Royal Academy of Music and the National Opera Studio. *Career:* Concert appearances at Festival Hall, Barbican Centre, Purcell Room and St John's Smith Square; Sang in The Dream of Gerontius with Liverpool Philharmonic and Henze's Novae de Infinito Laudes with London Sinfonietta; Other modern repertory includes Schoenberg's Pierrot Lunaire and works by Berio, Stravinsky, Webern, Berg, Rihm and Jonathan Harvey; Opera debut as a Valkyrie in Die Walküre for Scottish Opera in 1992; Has also sung in Die Königskinder for English National Opera and appeared as Britten's Lucretia, Ursule in Béatrice et Bénèdict, Cornelia in Giulo Cesare, Mercèdès in Carmen, Gaea in Daphne, Martha in Mefistofele and Anna in Les Troyens; Sang Medoro in Handel's Orlando at the Brooklyn Academy of Music, 1996; Season 1998 as Trasimede in Handel's Admeto at Beaune and Montpellier and in Australia; Sang Stellea in the premiere of Carter's What Next?, Berlin Staatsoper 1999; Schwetzingen and Innsbruck 2000, in Legrenzi's La divisione del mondo; Created the role of Irma in Peter Eotvos' opera Le Balcon at the Aix Festival, 2002. *Recordings include:* Messiah with the King's College Choir. *Honours:* The Worshipful Company of Musicians Silver Medal; Shinn Fellowship, Royal Academy of Music; Recital Diploma, Royal Academy of Music. *Current Management:* Ingpen & Williams Ltd, 7 St George's Court, 131 Putney Bridge Road, London, SW15 2PA, England.

**SUMMERS, Jonathan;** Singer (Baritone); b. 2 Oct. 1946, Melbourne, Australia. *Education:* Studied with Bettine McCaughan in Melbourne and with Otakar Kraus in London. *Career:* Debut: Kent Opera in 1975 as Rigoletto; Royal Opera House Covent Garden company member, 1976–86; roles include: High Priest in Samson et Dalila, Figaro, Papageno, Balstrode, Marcello, Demetrius, Silvio, Sharpless, Paolo, Ford, Nabucco and Iago; Other British appearances include: English National Opera as Rodrigo, Renato, Macbeth, Boccanegra, Onegin, Kurwenal; Scottish Opera as Count Almaviva and Don Giovanni; Opera North as the High Priest, Onegin and Amonasro in Aida; Glyndebourne as Ford in Falstaff. Welsh National Opera, Germont Pére and Kurwenal; European engagements at Hamburg, Munich, Florence, Las Scala, Avignon, Paris Opéra and Geneva; American and Australian engagements include: Metropolitan Opera in 1988, debut Australian Opera in 1981, Sydney Opera in Le nozze di Figaro; Season 1994 at Australian Opera, Sydney as Germont and appearances in Chicago, London, Toulouse and Lausanne; Season 1995 included Michele, Il Tabarro in Trittico with the Australian Oper, Sydney, Don Carlo and Kurwenal for ENO and Nabucco with WNO; Season 1996 included Nabucco in Melbourne, Germont, La Traviata, for Scottish Opera and Figaro in The Marriage of Figaro with ENO; Season 1997 as Amonasro with Opera North; Iago with Royal Opera House and Scarpia in Tosca at Spear Festival, South Africa; Season 1998 included Traviata with the New Israeli Opera and WNO, Balstrode in Peter Grimes with the Royal Opera at Savonlinna and Amfortas in Parsifal with ENO; Season 1999 included Kurwenal in Tristan and Isolde with WNO, the title role in Wozzeck with Opera Australia and Balstrode in Peter Grimes with ENO; Season 2000–01 with Opera North, as Barnaba in La Gioconda, and Simon Boccanegra; Season 2001 included Amfortas in Parsifal with State Opera of South Australia; Pere Germont in La Traviata with Israeli Opera; Season 2002 included Prus in Vec Makropulos with Houston Grand Opera, Scarpia in Tosca with Buhnen der Stadt, Cologne, Alfio and Tonio in Cavalleria Rusticana and Pagliacci with Opera Australia, Scarpia in Tosca with Opera Australia. *Recordings include:* Peter Grimes; Samson et Dalila; The Bohemian Girl; Sea Symphony; Carmina Burana; Videos of Samson et Dalila, Il Trovatore and Nabucco. *Address:* c/o

Patricia Greenan, 19b Belsize Park, London NW3 4DU, England. *E-mail:* patricia@greenanartists.fsnet.co.uk.

**SUMMERS, Patrick;** American conductor; *Music Director, Houston Grand Opera*; b. 1960, San Francisco. *Education:* Indiana Univ. School of Music. *Career:* conducted season preview concerts with the San Francisco Opera from 1989; Opera Center Showcase productions include Handel's Ariodante, Reimann's Ghost Sonata and Shield's Rosina; projects for the Merola Opera Program include Bohème, Butterfly, Pasquale and Falstaff; Lucia di Lammermoor for the Western Opera Theater; Music Dir, San Francisco Opera Center, leading Carmen and Bohème on tour to Japan 1991, 1993 and La Fille du Régiment for the Opera Guild 1994; performances with the San Francisco Opera include Tosca, the US premiere of Rossini's Ermione and the local premiere of his Otello; La Traviata and Così fan tutte; associated with the Shanghai Conservatory of Music in productions of Rigoletto and Don Pasquale; Asian premiere of Tosca at the Shanghai Opera House; Italian debut in season 1993–94 with Manon Lescaut for Rome Opera, Canadian debut with Lucia di Lammermoor at Calgary; Australian debut with Cenerentola at Sydney and Melbourne 1994; L'Incoronazione di Poppea for Dallas Opera 1995, Tosca at Lisbon; Music Dir, Houston Grand Opera 1998–; Nabucco at Opera Australia 2005. *Honours:* named Outstanding San Franciscan by the San Francisco Chamber of Commerce 1991. *Current Management:* Askonas Holt Ltd, Lonsdale Chambers, 27 Chancery Lane, London, WC2A 1PF, England. *Telephone:* (20) 7400-1700. *Fax:* (20) 7400-1799. *E-mail:* info@askonasholt.co.uk. *Website:* www.askonasholt.co.uk. *Address:* c/o Houston Grand Opera, 510 Preston Street, Houston, TX 77002, USA. *Website:* www.houstongrandopera.org.

**SUNDIN, Nils-Göran;** Music Director, Composer and Author; b. 18 May 1951, Växjö, Sweden. *Education:* Diploma, Choirmaster and Organist, Lund, 1968; Master's Degree, Musical Theory, Pedagogy of Musical Theory, Stockholm State School of Music; PhilCand, Musicology, History of Literature and Fine Arts, Stockholm University; PhD, Philosophy of Music, USA, 1988; MedCand, Lund University. *Career:* Lecturer in Music Theory and Interpretation at Stockholm State College of Music and Edsberg College of Music, Sollentuna, 1975–85; Lecturer in Music History at Stockholm University, 1976; Music Critic, Svenska Dagbladet, 1977–81; Executive Music Chief, Kronoberg Music Foundation, Växjö, 1987–; mem, STIM; Sveriges Författaförbund; New York Academy of Sciences; International Musicological Society. *Compositions:* Numerous for piano, chamber music, voice, choir and orchestra including: Symphony For Peace for Orchestra and Choir with poems by Dag Hammarskjöld, commissioned for The Great Peace Journey, Invitazione, Emmanuel Swedenborg In Memoriam, 1988, Concerto St George for Piano and Orchestra, 1990; Violin Concerto, 1994. *Publications:* Books include: Musical Interpretation in Performance, 1983, Bilder Ur Musikens Historia, 1984, Musical Interpretation Research, 1984, MIR vols I–II, 1984, Aesthetic Criteria of Musical Interpretation in Contemporary Performance, 1994. *Contributions:* About 300 articles and reviews in numerous publications including Nutida Musik, Bonniers Musiklexikon, Sohlmans Musiklexikon. *Address:* c/o STIM, Sandhamnsgatan 79, PO Box 27327, S–10254 Stockholm, Sweden.

**SUNDINE, Stephanie;** Singer (Soprano); b. 1954, Illinois, USA. *Education:* Studied in Illinois and New York. *Career:* Sang with the New York City Opera, 1981–84 as Ariadne, Santuzza and Margherita in Boito's Mefistofele; Sang the title roles in the US premieres of Prokofiev's Maddalena at St Louis in 1982 and Judith by Siegfried Matthus at Santa Fe in 1990; Best known as Strauss's Salome at Covent Garden (debut) in 1988, Metropolitan Opera (debut) in 1990 and Welsh National Opera in 1991; Sang Isolde at Nantes in 1989 and Fusako in the premiere production of Henze's Das Verratene Meer at the Deutsche Oper Berlin in 1990; Other roles include Janáček's Emilia Marty, Tosca, La Gioconda and Elsa; Sang the Foreign Princess in Rusalka at San Francisco, 1995. *Address:* c/o San Francisco Opera, War Memorial House, Van Ness Avenue, San Francisco, CA, USA.

**SUNDMAN, Ulf Johan,** DipMus; Swedish organist and music director; b. 27 Feb. 1929, Stockholm; m. Anna-Greta Persson 1954; one d. *Education:* Hogre Organistexamen, Hogre Kantorsexamen, Musiklararexamen, Royal Acad. of Music, Stockholm, Int. Acad. for Organ, Haarlem, Netherlands. *Career:* organist, Skelleftea St Olovs Church 1954–81, Gavle Heliga Trefaldighets Church 1981–94; organ concerts in Sweden, Finland, Norway, Germany, Austria, Netherlands, Switzerland, France, Italy, Spain, Czechoslovakia, Poland, USSR 1974, 1976, 1979, Denmark and Belgium; organ music festivals, Gottingen, West Germany 1972, 1987, Vilnius, USSR 1974, Madrid 1982, Naples, Toulon 1983, Ratzeburg 1985, Verona and Asola 1986, Buren 1987, Gottingen 1987, Zug 1988, Biella 1988; concerts on Radio Sweden and Radio Netherlands. *Recordings:* Soviet (Melodia) Sweden (Proprius), (Opus 3). *Honours:* Royal Acad. of Music P. A. Berg Medal, Stockholm, Culture Prize of the Town of Skelleftea 1972, Province of Vasterbotten 1973, Gavle 1994. *Address:* N Köpmangatan 22A, 803 21 Gavle, Sweden.

**SUNNEGARDH, Thomas;** Singer (Tenor); b. 11 July 1949, Stockholm, Sweden. *Education:* Studied at The Royal School of Music in Stockholm. *Career:* Sang at Vadstena Academy, 1978–79; Appeared in Die Fledermaus and Der Vogelhändler with National Touring Company; Royal Opera Stockholm from 1982 as Albert Herring, Walther von der Vogelweide, Taverner, Ferrando, Fra Diavolo, Tamino and Steuermann in Der fliegende Holländer; Has sung Lohengrin in Stockholm, Moscow with Bolshoi,

Wiesbaden and Stuttgart conducted by Silvio Varviso, 1990; Macduff at the Bergen Festival, 1988; Other roles include Florestan, Erik and Parsifal in Denmark and Antwerp, and parts in Iphigénie en Aulide and Genoveva at Deutsche Oper am Rhein, and Die Meistersinger at Nice, 1992; Season 1991–92 sang Lohengrin at Barcelona, Parsifal at Århus, Die Meistersinger at Nice Opera, Der fliegende Holländer at Royal Opera Covent Garden, Das Lied von der Erde with London Philharmonic Orchestra); Season 1992–93 with Meistersinger at Brussels, Deutsche Oper Berlin, Munich, Tokyo, Stuttgart, Dutchman/Erik in Munich, Parsifal in Essen and Deutsche Oper Düsseldorf, Lohengrin in Frankfurt, Berlin, Tokyo and Toulouse; Season 1993–94 in Lohengrin in Frankfurt, Der fliegende Holländer in Munich, and Walter in Stuttgart; Season 1994–95 with Walter von Stolzing in Stuttgart, Fidelio and Lohengrin in Düsseldorf and Toulouse; Sang Paul in Korngold's Die tote Stadt at Stockholm, 1996; Engaged for Lohengrin in Seville and concert performances of Wozzeck with the Swedish Radio Symphony Orchestra and Rheingold at the Canary Islands Festival; Season 2001–02 with Capriccio in Stockholm, Tannhäuser in Gothenburg; Berg's Alwa and Rhiengold/Loge in San Francisco, a Wagner Gala Concert in San Diego, concert performances of Fidelio in Lübeck, performances of Beethoven IX at the Gewandhaus in Leipzig, concerts for RAI Torino (Bach's Magnificat and Chapentier's Te deum) and a new production of Gefors' Clara at the Royal Opera Stockholm; Season 2002–03 with The Bells by Rachmaninov at Malmö and Tristan in Gothenburg, and further performances of Tannhäuser at the Royal Opera Stockholm. *Recordings:* Role of Froh with Cleveland Orchestra under Christoph von Dohnányi, 1993. *Address:* Artistsekretariat ulf Törnquist, Sankt Eriksgatan 100, 2 tr., S-113 31 Stockholm Sweden.

**SUNSHINE, Adrian;** Conductor and Teacher; b. 1940 New York City, USA; m. Sheila Genden, 1 s., 1 d. *Education:* San Francisco State University; University of California, Berkeley; Private instrumental studies with Gabriel Sunshine (father), Janet Hale, Georg Gruenberg, Herman Reinberg; Conducting teachers: Pierre Monteux, Leonard Bernstein, Paul Klecki. *Career:* Performances: Philharmonia (London); BBC Orchestras; BBC Opera; São Carlos Opera (Lisbon); Bournemouth, Berlin, Leningrad, Cleveland, Geneva, Paris, Vienna, Philharmonia Hungarica, Athens, Budapest, Bucharest, Cluj, Lausanne, Lugano, Amsterdam, Denmark, Sweden, Poland, Miami, San Francisco, Buenos Aires, Rio de Janeiro, São Paulo, Caracas, Mexico City, Israel, Ankara, Madrid, Barcelona, Bilbao, Luxembourg, Bangkok, Kuala Lumpur, Tai Pei; Festivals include: Blossom, Athens, São Paulo, Montreux-Vevey, Ascona, London, Cheltenham, Gulbenkian, Reims, Lille, Seville, Romania, Chamonix, San Sebastian, Sion, Cadiz; Previously Founder-Conductor, San Francisco Chamber Orchestra; music director, Gulbenkian Orchestra, Lisbon; Principal Guest Conductor, Romania; Director Crete International Festival; Music director, London Chamber Players; Co-conductor, Camerata Budapest; Permanent Guest conductor, Bucharest Philharmonic Orchestra; Previously Visiting Professor, Bowling Green State University, Ohio; Guest Lecturer, University of London Institute of Education; Director, Orchestra-in-Residence Music Programme, Middlesex University, London; Visiting Lecturer, Smith College, Massachusetts; Visiting Professor, Romanian Academy of Music; mem, Conductors' Guild. *Recordings:* Works by Schoenberg, Shostakovich, Perera, Wheelock and Ives. *Publications:* Various articles on music. *Current Management:* Armonia, Santander, Spain; Bureau de Concerts Camile Kiesgen, 252 Faubourg St Honore, 75008 Paris, France. *Address:* PO Box 84, London NW11 8 AL, England.

**SURJAN, Giorgio;** Singer (bass); b. 21 Oct. 1954, Rijeca, Yugoslavia. *Education:* Studied in Ljubljana and at the Opera School of La Scala. *Career:* Sang in Yugoslavia from 1977; La Scala, 1980, in a concert version of Mussorgsky's Salammbô; Pesaro Festival, 1984 and 1987, in Il Viaggio a Reims and Ermione; Aix Festival, 1988, as Publio in La Clemenza di Tito and Astarotte in Rossini's Armida; Season 1991–92 as Rossini's Alidoro at Covent Garden, Gluck's Thoas at La Scala and Frère Laurent in Gounod's Roméo et Juliette at Martina Franca; Season 1995–96 as Polidoro in Rossini's Zelmira at Pesaro, Fiesco in Simon Boccanegra at Turin, and the Villains in Hoffmann at Genoa; Season 1998 as Balthasar in La Favorita at Rome, Governor in Le Comte Ory at Florence, Banquo at Genoa and Escamillo at Macerata; Season 2000–01 as Monteverdi's Seneca in Florence, Rossini's Mosè in Verona, Rodolfo in La Sonnambula at Palermo, Alfonso (Luzrezia Borgia) in Bologna and Walter in Luisa Miller for Opéra Lausanne. *Recordings include:* La Forza del Destino; Anna Bolena; Salammbô. *Address:* c/o Teatro Comunale di Firenze, Via Solferino 15, 50123 Florence, Italy.

**SUSA, Conrad;** Composer; b. 26 April 1935, Springfield, Pennsylvania, USA. *Education:* BFA, Carnegie Institute of Technology at Pittsburgh, 1957; Juilliard School, New York, with William Bergsma and Vincent Persichetti. *Career:* Composer in Residence at the Old Globe Theatre, San Diego, 1959–60; Music Director of APA-Phoenix Repertory Company in New York, 1961–68, and the American Shakespeare Festival in Stratford, CT, 1969–71; Dramaturg of the Eugene O'Neill Center in Connecticut, 1986–. *Compositions include:* Operas: Transformations, Minneapolis, 1973, Black River: A Wisconsin Idyll, St Paul, 1975, The Love Of Don Perlimplin, Purchase, NY, 1984; The Dangerous Liaisons, 1994, rev. 1997; The Wise Women, church opera, 1994; A Sonnet Voyage, symphony, 2003; Choral: Dawn Greeting, 1976, The Chanticleer's Carol, 1982, Earth Song, 1988; A Midnight Clear, 1992; Piano pieces. *Address:* c/o ASCAP, ASCAP Building, One Lincoln Center, New York, NY 10023, USA.

**SUSHANSKAYA, Rimma;** Concert Violinist; b. 1950, Leningrad, Russia. *Education:* Studied at Leningrad and Moscow Conservatoires with David Oistrakh; PhD. *Career:* Emigrated to America in 1977 and has given many concerts there, in South America, throughout Russia and in Europe; Orchestras include Czech, Moscow, and St Petersburg Philharmonic Orchestras and Prague Radio Symphony Orchestra; Orchestral and recital tours of Russia, Finland and Czechoslovakia; London recital debut in 1987 at the Wigmore Hall, followed by Tchaikovsky's Concerto with the Royal Liverpool Philharmonic Orchestra and the City of Birmingham Symphony Orchestra; Based in the United Kingdom, residing in London, Stratford and New York. *Honours:* First Prize, Prague International Competition; Ysaye Medal. *Address:* Manhattan, 5 Lock Close, Kingfisher Court, Stratford-upon-Avon, Warwickshire, CV 37 6TY, England.

**SUSS, Reiner;** Singer (Bass); b. 2 Feb. 1930, Chemnitz, Germany. *Education:* Member of the Thomas Choir, Leipzig, 1939–48; Hochschule für Musik Leipzig, 1948–53. *Career:* Sang with Radio Leipzig, 1953–56 and the opera company at Bernburgan Der Saale, 1956–57 with debut in Tiefland by d'Albert; Sang at Theater der Stadt Halle, 1957–59 notably as Ochs in Der Rosenkavalier and member of the Staatsoper Berlin from 1959 as Leporello, Beckmesser, Nicolai's Falstaff, Kecal in The Bartered Bride, Varlaam and Baculus in Der Wildschütz; Dr Bartolo in Barbiere, Kovalyov in The Nose by Shostakovich, Don Pasquale, and Osmin in Entführung; Guest engagements at the Vienna Staatsoper and in Budapest, Helsinki, Lyon, Lausanne, Florence, Moscow, Prague, Warsaw and Tokyo. *Recordings include:* Tannhäuser conducted by Franz Konwitschny; Tosca; Der Wildschütz; La Serva Padrona; Mozart's Zaide; Die Kluge and Der Mond by Orff; Don Pasquale. *Address:* c/o Deutsche Staatsoper, Unter den Linden 7, 1086 Berlin, Germany.

**SUSTIKOVA, Vera;** Musicologist; b. 9 Jan. 1956, Uh Hradiste, Czechoslovakia; m. Sustik Jaroslav, 15 July 1982, 1 d. *Education:* Philosophical Faculty, Charles University in Prague, PhD, 1982; Conservatory in Brno (Guitar); Guitar-Masterclasses with Professor Cotsiolis (Greece); Musicology at the PF of Charles University in Prague. *Career:* Debut: Muzeum of Czech Music in Prague; 100 let spolecen pusobeni smetanova dila, Prague, 1984; Bedrich Smetana, 1824–1884, Prague, 1994; Opera and song without Singing Musical Melodram, Stanford, California, 1996; Fibich-Melodrama-Art nouveau, Prague 2000; Author of major exhibitions: History of Czech Musical Culture, 1986; Smetana-Dvořák, Litomyšl, 1988; B Smetana's Memorial in Benatky n j, 1991; Bedrich Smetana, Legend of My Country, Montreal, Ottawa, Toronto, 1994; Zdeněk Fibich 1850–1900, Prague 2000/2001; Dramaturgist and director of Concert tour with melodramas of Zdeněk Fibich, Los Angeles, San Francisco, Stanford, Portland, Vancouver, Montreal, Toronto, New York, 1996; Founder and dramaturgist of International Workshops of Melodrama, from 1997; International Festival of Cncert Melodrama, Prague from 1998; International Zdeněk Fibich Competition in the interpretation of melodrama, in Prague, from 1999. *Publications include:* Bedrich Smetana–Legend of My Country, 1994; Zdenek Fibich–Master of Scenic Melodrama, 1996; Zdeněk Fibich 1850–1900, 2000; Zdeněk Fibich Concert Melodramas Christmas Eve and Water Sprite (Noten Edition), 2003. *Address:* Pstrossova 35, Prague 1, 11008, Czech Republic.

**SUTER, Jeremy Langton,** MA, FRCO, ARCM; British organist; b. 3 March 1951, London, England; m. Susan; two d. *Education:* Royal Coll. of Music, Magdalen Coll., Oxford. *Career:* organist and Choirmaster, All Saints, Northampton 1975–81; Asst Organist, Chichester Cathedral 1981–91; Master of Music, Carlisle Cathedral 1991–; mem. Royal Coll. of Organists, Incorporated Soc. of Musicians. *Address:* 6 The Abbey, Carlisle, CA3 8TZ, England (home). *Telephone:* (1228) 526646 (home). *Fax:* (1228) 547049 (office). *E-mail:* jeremy.suter@virgin.net (home).

**SUTER, Louis-Marc,** PhD; Swiss musicologist and academic; b. 2 Feb. 1928, Fribourg; m. Monique Suter 1955; four s. *Education:* Univ. of Fribourg and Berne Conservatory of Geneva. *Career:* debut 1955; Int. Academic Orchestra, Salzburg; Lausanne Chamber Orchestra; Suisse Romande Orchestra; fmr Prof. of Musicology, Univ. of Berne, now Prof. Emeritus; mem. Int. Soc. for Musicology, Société Suisse de Musicologie, Asscn Suisse des Musiciens. *Publications:* Four concert works of Serbian composers 1989, Norbert Moret, compositeur 1993, Le langage musical de l'Europe occidentale 2005; contrib. Claude Debussy: 'Pour les accords', Etude No. 12 pour piano (in Revue Musicale de Suisse Romande) 1983, Ronsard: 'Les Amours' de 1552 mises en musique (in Actes du Colloque de Neuchâtel) 1985, Pelléas et Mélisande in Performance (in Debussy in Performance) 1999, Les graduels en la 1999. *Address:* route du Pré de l'Ile 1, 1752 Villars-sur-Glâne, Switzerland (office). *Telephone:* (264) 025 845 (home). *Fax:* (264) 015 845 (home).

**SUTHERLAND, Dame Joan,** OM, AC, DBE, FRCM; Australian singer (soprano, retd); b. 7 Nov. 1926, Sydney, NSW; d. of William McDonald Sutherland and Muriel Beatrice Sutherland (née Alston); m. Richard Bonynge (q.v.) 1954; one s. *Education:* St Catherine's School, Waverley, Sydney. *Career:* debut as Dido in Purcell's Dido and Aeneas, Sydney 1947; Royal Opera Co., Covent Garden, London 1952–88, with first role as First Lady in The Magic Flute 1952; performed worldwide at Vienna State Opera, La Scala, Milan, Teatro Fenice, Venice, Paris Opera, San Francisco Opera, Chicago Lyric, The Metropolitan, New York, Australian Opera, Sydney, Hamburg, Canadian Opera, Buenos Aires, and at Glyndebourne, Edinburgh, Leeds and Florence festivals; repertoire included Amelia (A Masked Ball), Aida, Eva (The Mastersingers), Gilda (Rigoletto), Desdemona (Othello), Agathe (Der

Freischütz), Olympia, Giulietta, Antonia, Stella (Les Contes d'Hoffmann), Jenifer (The Midsummer Marriage), lead role in Lucia di Lammermoor, Norma, and roles in I Puritani, Dialogues of the Carmelites, Euridice, La Traviata, Adriana Lecouvreur, Lucrezia Borgia, Semiramide, Don Giovanni, Faust, Die Zauberflöte, Dido and Aeneas, The Merry Widow, Les Huguenots; last operatic role as Marguerite de Valois in Les Huguenots for Australian Opera 1990, retd from performing 1991. *Publications:* The Joan Sutherland Album (autobiog., with Richard Bonynge) 1986, A Prima Donna's Progress: the Autobiography of Joan Sutherland 1997. *Honours:* hon. life mem. Australia Opera Co. 1974; Commdr, Ordre des Arts et des Lettres 1989; Hon. DMus (Sydney) 1984; recipient of Kennedy Center Honors 2004, depicted on two Australian postage stamps 2004. *Current Management:* Ingpen & Williams Ltd, 7 St George's Court, 131 Putney Bridge Road, London, SW15 2PA, England.

**SUTHERLAND, Rosalind;** British singer (soprano); b. 8 May 1963, Glasgow, Scotland. *Education:* qualified as a nurse, London Coll. of Music and Royal Northern Coll. of Music. *Career:* appearances include Madama Butterfly (WNO, San Francisco Opera, Opera North), Nedda in Pagliacci (Minneapolis Opera, WNO, New Israeli Opera), Liu in Turandot (WNO, Mannheim Opera), Mimi in La Bohème (San Francisco Opera, ENO, WNO, New Israeli Opera), Jenůfa (WNO), Micaela in Carmen (WNO), Governess in Turn of the Screw (Minneapolis Opera), Musetta in La Bohème (Toronto Opera Co.). *Honours:* Peter Moores Scholarship, winner Anne Ziegler Prize for a Singer Showing Outstanding Promise. *Current Management:* IMG Artists, Lovell House, 616 Chiswick High Road, London, W4 5RX, England.

**SUTTER, Ursula;** Singer (Mezzo-Soprano); b. 26 March 1938, Berne, Switzerland. *Education:* Studied in Berne and Stuttgart. *Career:* Sang at Biel-Solothurn, 1961–63, Trier, 1963–64, Essen, 1964–66 and engaged at Stuttgart Staatsoper, 1966–85, notably in the premiere of Orff's Prometheus in 1968; Guest appearances at State Operas of Vienna, Munich and Hamburg, Cologne, Nuremberg and Düsseldorf; Further engagements at Bucharest, Lisbon, Monte Carlo, Essen and Schwetzingen Festival (premiere of Henze's The English Cat in 1983); Roles have included Dorabella, Cherubino, Rosina, Isabella, Maddalena, Preziosilla, Magdalene in Meistersinger, the Composer in Ariadne and Britten's Lucretia. *Address:* c/o Stuttgart Staatsoper, Oberer Schlossgarten 6, 7000 Stuttgart, Germany.

**SUWANAI, Akiko;** Concert Violinist; b. 1959, Tokyo, Japan. *Education:* Studied at the Toho Gakuen School of Music College, with Dorothy DeLay at Juilliard and Cho-Liang and Cho-Liang at Columbia University, New York. *Career:* Many concert engagements since becoming the youngest ever winner of the Tchaikovsky Competition, Moscow; Conductor have included Bychkov, Rostropovich, Rozhdestvensky, Ozawa, Marriner, Conlon, Previn, Svetlanaov and Temirkanov; Boston Symphony debut 1996, and performances with the Orchestre de Paris, Cincinnati, Pittsburgh and Seattle Symphonies and Academy of St Martin in the Fields; Ravinia and Evian Festivals, recital at the Amsterdam Concertgebouw and concert with the Toho Gakuen Orchestra at Carnegie Hall; Further engagements with the State Symphony of Russia, Russian National Orchestra and Budapest Symphony; Tours of Japan and South America. *Recordings include:* Concertos No. 1 by Bruch and Scottish Fantasia, with Neville Marriner (Phillips Classics, 1997); The Winners Gala at the Tchaikovsky Competition at Moscow; Prizewinner at the 35th International Paganini Violin Competition, the fourth International Japan Competition and the Queen Elizabeth International Competition, Belgium. *Current Management:* Ingpen & Williams Ltd, 7 St George's Court, 131 Putney Bridge Road, London, SW15 2PA, England.

**SUZUKI, Hidetaro;** Violinist and Conductor; b. 1 June 1937, Tokyo, Japan; m. Zeyda Ruga, 16 May 1962, 2 s., 1 d. *Education:* Toho School of Music, Tokyo, 1953–56; Curtis Institute of Music, Philadelphia, Pennsylvania, USA, 1956–63; Studied with Efrem Zimbalist. *Career:* Debut: Tokyo, 1951; Concertmaster, Quebec Symphony, Canada, 1963–78; Professor, Conservatory of Province of Quebec, 1963–79; Professor, Laval University, 1970–79; Concertmaster, Indianapolis Symphony, Indiana, USA, 1978–; Concert appearances as soloist, recitalist, conductor, the United Kingdom, Western Europe, Soviet Union, Central America, USA, Canada, Japan, South East Asia; Director of Chamber Music Series Suzuki and Friends, 1980. *Recordings:* Beethoven Sonatas; Hidetaro Suzuki Encore Album; Franck, Ravel Sonatas; Beethoven Piano Trios, Marlboro Festival; 3 CDs of violin/piano repertoires with pianist Zeyda Ruga Suzuki. *Honours:* Laureat, Tchaikovsky International Competition, 1962; Laureat, Queen Elizabeth International Competition, 1963, 1967; Laureat, Montreal International Competition, 1966; Served as Jury Member, Montreal International Competition, 1979; International Violin Competition, 1982, 1986, 1990, 1994. *Address:* 430 West 93rd Street, Indianapolis, IN 46260, USA.

**SVANIDZE, Natela;** Composer; b. 4 Sept. 1926, Akhaltsikhe, Georgia; m. Peter Tomadze, 15 June 1952, 1 d. *Education:* Studies at Tbilisi State University, French Literature; Graduated from the Tbilisi State Conservatoire, 1951. *Career:* Debut: Symphonic poem, Samgori, conducted by Odyssey Dymitriady, Tbilisi, 1951; Performances: Improvisation, violin, piano, 1956; Fairytale, piano, Tbilisi, 1960; Kvarkvare, symphonic poem, conducted by Lile Kilaze, Radio Tbilisi, 1963; Burlesque, symphonic poem, conducted by Lile Kiladze, Tbilisi, 1966; Symphony No. 1, conducted G Rozdestvensky, Radio Moscow, Paris, Belgrade, 1969; Pirosmani, oratorio, conducted by Lile Kiladze, Tbilisi, 1972, by Kataeff, Moscow, 1974 and by Provatoroff, Samara,

1976; Professor of the Georgian State Institute of Theatre and Cinema, Tbilisi; mem. Board member, The Georgian Composers' Union. *Compositions:* Symphony No. 1, for strings, piano and percussion instruments, 1967; Lamentatia Georgica, oratorio for speaker, female sextet, two choruses, instruments and tape, 1974; Symphony No. 2, for big orchestra, 1983; Gaul-Gavkhe, cantata, mixed choruses, big orchestra, 1995; Monodrama for voice, piano, cassa a pedal, piatto and tape, 1999. *Honours:* Honoured Art Worker of the Georgian SSR, 1981; Professor, 1991. *Current Management:* Professor of the Institute of Theatre and Cinema, Tbilisi. *Address:* Griboedoff Str 4, Apt 7, 380 008, Tbilisi, Georgia.

**SVARC-GRENDA, Ivana;** Pianist; b. 17 Feb. 1970, Yugoslavia. *Education:* Music Academy in Zagreb; Peabody Conservatory of Music, Baltimore; Hochschule der Kunste, Berlin; Mozarteum, Salzburg. *Career:* Winner of the Kosciuszko Chopin Competition, New York; Winner Croatian National Artists Competition; Solo appearances at Carnegie Recital Hall; Lincoln Center Library, New York; Kennedy Center, Washington DC; Philharmonie Berlin; Alte Oper Frankfurt; Chamber Music appearances, Salle Cortot, Paris; Philharmonie Berlin; Schauspielhaus Berlin; Glinka Hall, St Petersburg; Orchestra appearances with Zagreb Philharmonic, Solisti di Zagreb and Croatian Chamber Orchestra; Berlin Symphony Orchestra; Gives master courses at International Summer school, Hvar, Croatia. *Recordings:* Cello-piano duo with Monika Leskovar. *Honours:* Milka Trnina prize for the best Croatian Musician, 1996; Porin award for the best Croatian recording, 1996. *Address:* Kastlenstr 26A, 81827 Munchen, Germany.

**SVECENY, Jaroslav;** Concert Violinist; b. 8 Dec. 1960, Hradec Kralove, Czechoslovakia; m. Monika Svecena. *Education:* Studied at the Prague Conservatoire and the Prague Academy of Arts with Vaclav Snitil; Masterclasses with Nathan Milstein at Zürich and Gidon Kremer at Kuhmo. *Career:* Concert appearances in Germany, Spain, France, Italy, the United Kingdom, Finland, Denmark, USA, Russia, Poland, Hungary and Romania; Participated in several festivals in Berlin, Constance, Helsinki, Bilbao, Madrid, Granada, Havana, Prague, Leipzig and Palermo; Repertoire includes Concertos by Dvořák, Beethoven, Brahms, Mozart, Bach, Vivaldi, Haydn, Reicha and Martinů, Reicha Complete Works for Violin and Piano, Benda 24 Capriccios (only artist with this repertoire), and sonatas by Brahms, Beethoven, Dvořák, Benda, Handel and Ysaÿe. *Recordings include:* Reicha 4 Sonatas, Grand Duo Concertante and Rondo; Sonatas by Benda, Stamitz, Corelli, Handel and Tartini; Vivaldi Four Seasons. *Honours:* Winner, Pablo de Sarasate International Violin Competition. *Address:* c/o Czech Arts & Concert Agency, Korunni 60, CZ–12000 Praha-Vinohrady, Czech Republic.

**SVEINSSON, Atli Heimir;** Composer, Conductor and Administrator; b. 21 Sept. 1938, Reykjavík, Iceland. *Education:* Studied at the Reykjavic College of Music and with Petzold and BA Zommermann at the Cologne Hochschule für Musik; Composition studies with Pousseur and Stockhausen at Darmstadt and Cologne. *Career:* Freelance composer and conductor throughout Iceland and Scandinavia; Chairman, Society of Icelandic Composers, 1972–83. *Compositions include:* Tautophony, for orchestra, 1967; Flower Shower, for orchestra, 1973; Flute Concerto, 1975; Septet, 1976; Twenty-One Sounding Minutes for flute, 1980; Bassoon Concerto, Trobar Clus, 1980; The Silken Drum, opera, 1982; Trombone Concerto, Jubilus, 1984; Recitation, for piano and orchestra, 1984; Bicentennial, for string quartet, 1984; Trio, for violin, cello and piano, 1985; The Night on our Shoulders, for soprano, alto, women's chorus and orchestra, 1986; Dreamboat, concerto for violin, harpsichord and orchestra, 1987; Vikivaki, television opera, 1990; Opplaring, for soprano and wind instruments, 1991; Dernier Amour, chamber opera, 1992; Rock-erauschen, Bruit des Robes for chamber orchestra, 1993; Poem to the Virgin Mary, for chorus, 1995; The Isle of Moonlight, 1995, performed Peking, 1997; Signs of Fire, for piano and wind, 1995; Discords, for cello, strings and piano, 1997; Independent People, incidental music, 1999; The Conversion of Iceland, opera, 2000. *Honours:* Nordic Council Prize, 1976. *Address:* c/o STEF, Laufasvegi 40, 101 Reykjavík, Iceland.

**SVENDEN, Birgitta;** Singer (Mezzo-Soprano); b. 20 March 1952, Porjus, Sweden. *Education:* Studied at the Stockholm Opera School. *Career:* Has sung at the Royal Opera in Stockholm as Cherubino, Olga and Erda; Sang a Rhinemaiden in The Ring under Solti at Bayreuth in 1983, at Nice Opéra from 1985 in Carmen and as Meg Page and Anna in Les Troyens; Created Queen Christina in Hans Gefors' opera in 1988; Sang at Metropolitan Opera from 1988 as Erda in Das Rheingold and Siegfried and Maddalena in Rigoletto, Seattle Opera in 1989 as Magdalena in Die Meistersinger, Ravinia Festival Chicago in Mahler's 3rd Symphony under James levine, and at La Scala, Munich and San Francisco in 1990 as Magdalena, Erda and First Norn; Covent Garden debut in 1990 in a new production of Siegfried under Bernard Haitink; Sang at Théâtre du Châtelet, Paris, as Margret in a production of Wozzeck by Patrice Chéreau under Daniel Barenboim; Engaged for BBC Philharmonic in Verdi's Requiem in 1991, Gürzenich Orchestra in Mahler's 3rd in 1992, and Los Angeles Philharmonic in Mahler's 3rd; Sang in Eugene Onegin and Die Meistersinger at Metropolitan Opera in 1993; Season 1993 with Mahler's 3rd at Boston and Carnegie Hall under Ozawa, Mahler's 3rd and 8th at Rome and Rotterdam under Conlon, Missa Solemnis at Paris under Solti, and Octavian in Der Rosenkavalier at Paris Châtelet; Season 1994 with new Ring productions at Bayreuth, Covent Garden and Cologne; Season 1996–97 as Wagner's Magdalena at Bayreuth, Erda at the Met; Season 2000–01 as Erda in Das Rheingold at the Met and Brigitta in Die tote Stadt at Strasbourg; mem. Royal Swedish Academy of Music. *Recordings:* Das

Rheingold; Mahler; Elgar; Siegfried; Zemlinsky. *Honours:* Royal Court Singer (Hovsångerska) 1995 by King of Sweden. *Address:* Artistsekretariat Ulf Törnqvist, Sankt Eriksgatan 100, 2tr, 113 31, Stockholm, Sweden.

**SVENSSON, Peter;** Singer (Tenor); b. 1963, Vienna, Austria. *Career:* Sang in the 1988 Vienna Festival under Claudio Abbado; Season 1991–92 at the Prague State Opera, as Wagner's Rienzi and Zemlensky's Der Zwerg and Eine Florentinische Tragödie; Lucerne, 1993, as Strauss's Bacchus (also at Cologne); Sang Tannhäuser at Prague, 1994, and Claudio in Das Liebesverbot by Wagner at Wexford; Season 1995–96 as Hermann in The Queen of Spades at Mainz, Tannhäuser at Meiningen and in the premiere of The Marx Sisters at Bielefeld; Guest appearances as Siegmund at the Châtelet, Paris, and as Max in Der Freischütz, Florestan and Strauss's Herod; Sang Oedipus Rex at Naples, 2001. *Address:* c/o Buhnen der Stadt Bielefeld, Bruhnenstrasse 3–9, Pf 220, 4800 Bielefeld, Germany.

**SVETE, Tomaz;** Composer and Conductor; b. 29 Jan. 1956, Ljubljana, Slovenia. *Education:* Graduated in Composition, 1980 and Conducting, 1981, Academy of Music, Ljubljana; Studied with Professor F Cerha, Hochschule für Musik und Darstellende Kunst, Vienna, Diploma with Distinction, 1986; Studies in conducting with Otmar Suitner, Diploma 1988 and electro-acoustic music with Dieter Kaufmann, Vienna; Magister Artis of the Hochschule für Musik und Darstellende Kunst, Vienna, 1989. *Career:* Debut: 1st composition performance, Ljubljana, 1978; Works performed in: Ljubljana, Skopje, Opatija, Zagreb-Music Biennial, Vienna, Salzburg, Prague, Brno-Moravian Autumn, Amsterdam, Rotterdam, Middleburgh, Torino, Trieste, Klagenfurt, Spittal-Drau, Tirana, Leipzig, Melk, St Pölten- Niederösterreich International; Conductor of Slovene Philharmonic and Pro Arte Orchestras, of Singkreis Währing, Vienna and Brno Radio Symphony Orchestra; Professor of Composition, Karl Prayner Conservatory, Vienna; Concert of own works in Brahmssaal, Musikverein, Vienna; Freelance Composer in Vienna; Docent in composition at Pedagogical Faculty, Maribor, Slovenia; Guest Professor for Composition, University of Hartford, Connecticut, 1999–2000. *Compositions include:* Requiem, 1991; The Rape from Laudach Sea, opera, 1993; Isomerisms for Chamber Ensemble; Rappresentazione Sacra for Double Bass Solo and Flute Quartet, Ljubljana, 1994; Sonata Solaris for Violoncello and Piano, Salzburg, 1994; Sacrum Delirium, cantata for Soloists, Chorus, Ensembles and Orchestra (Italian Prize); 1994; Hommage à Slavko Osterc for Piano, Ljubljana, 1995; Evocazione, soprano and chamber ensemble, 1995; Poet and Rebellion, opera, 1996; Concert de la Nuit, double bass, violin, harp and orchestra, 1997; Kriton, opera after Plato, 2000. *Recordings:* Jugoton, 1986 and Kriton. *Address:* Prusnikova 2, SL-2000 Maribor, Slovenia.

**SVETLEV, Michail;** Singer (Tenor); b. 6 March 1943, Sofia, Bulgaria. *Education:* Studied at the Sofia Conservatoire. *Career:* Debut: Passau in 1971 as Manrico; Appearances in Munich, Hamburg, Berlin and Vienna, and La Scala Milan in 1979; US debut as Riccardo in Un Ballo in Maschera at Washington DC in 1980; Further US appearances at Houston in 1980, San Francisco in 1980 and 1983, and Philadelphia in 1982; Sang Dmitri in Boris Godunov at Covent Garden in 1983 and has appeared elsewhere as Verdi's Radames and Gabriele Adorno, Andrea Chénier and Cavaradossi; Season 1985–86 as Hermann in The Queen of Spades at Marseilles and Lykov in Rimsky's The Tsar's Bride at Monte Carlo; Other roles include the Duke of Mantua, Don Carlos, Bacchus, Lensky, Edgardo and the Prince in Rusalka. *Address:* c/o Opéra de Monte Carlo, Place du Casino, Monte Carlo.

**SVOBODA, Tomas;** Composer, Pianist, Conductor and Professor of Music; b. 6 Dec. 1939, Paris, France; m. Jana Demartini, 9 Oct 1965, 1 s., 1 d. *Education:* Degree in Percussion, 1956, Composition, 1958, Conducting, 1962, Conservatory of Music, Prague, Czechoslovakia; Degree in Composition, University of Southern California, USA, 1969. *Career:* Debut: FOK Prague Symphony Orchestra, Symphony No. 1, Op 20, 1957. *Compositions:* Symphonies 1–6; Overture of the Season, Op 89; Festive Overture, Op 103; Nocturne for orchestra, Op 100; Serenade for orchestra, Op 115; Sinfonietta (à la Renaissance), Op 60; Reflections for orchestra, Op 53; Concerto for piano and orchestra, Op 71; Concerto for violin and orchestra, Op 77; Ex Libris, Op 113; Child's Dream for children's choir and orchestra, Op 66; Concerto for chamber orchestra, Op 125; Journey, cantata for mezzo-soprano, baritone, choir and orchestra, Op 127; Dance Suite for orchestra, Op 128; Concerto No. 2 for piano and orchestra, Op 134; Concerto for marimba and orchestra, Op 148; Meditation for oboe and strings, Op 143, 1993; Rememberance, Chorale for trumpet and orchestra, Op 152a, 1997; 121 chamber pieces include Children's Treasure Box for piano, 1977–78; Woodwind Quintet Op 111, 1983–97; Duo Concerto for trumpet and organ; 53 keyboard compositions. *Recordings:* Symphony No. 4 (Apocalyptic), Op 69; Ex Libris, Op 113, for orchestra; CD recording (Mirecourt Trio), Passacaglia and Fugue for piano trio, Op 87; Concerto for chamber orchestra, Op 125; Trio for flute, oboe and bassoon Op 97; Concerto for Marimba and Orchestra, Op.148; Concerto No.1&2 for Piano and Orchestra; Overture of the Season for ORchestra; Symphony No.1 (Of Nature) for Orchestra; Autumn for Piano. *Publications:* Chaconne for Strings, Op.166a; Oriental Echoes, for String Orchestra, Op.140; Prelude and Fugue for String Orchestra, Op.172; Swing Dance, for Orchestra, Op.135a; Aria for Soprano and four instruments, Op.153; Autumn, for Koto, Op.110; Brass Quintet, Op.112; Celebration of Life, Cantata on Aztec Poetry, op.80; Chorales from 15th Century for English Horn and Strings, op.52f; Chorale in E flat for Piano Quintet (homage to Aaron Copland) Op.118; Concealed Shapes for two Pianos, Xylophone and Marimba, Op.163; Concertino for Oboe, Brass Choir and Timpani, Op.46; Czernogorsk Fugue for Choir, Op.14; Duo for Xylophone and Marimba, Op.141; Farewell Matinee for Brass Quintet, Op.160; Five Studies for Two Timpanists, Op.160; Forest Rhythms for Flute, Viola and Xylophone, Op.150; Intrata for Brass Quintet, Op.127a; March of the Puppets for Guitar, Xylophone and four Temple Blocks, Op.95; Morning Prayer, for four Percussion, Op.101; Nocturne for Organ four hands, Op.155; Nocturne for Piano, Op.84; Offertories for Organ Vol. I, Op.52a; Partita in D for Viola da Gamba and Harpsichord, Op.161; Quartet, for four French Horns, Op.145; Sonata for Guitar, Op.99; Sonata for Violin and Piano, Op.73; Storm Session, for Electric Guitar and Bass Guitar, Op.126; String Quartet No.2, Op.102; Suite for Piano and 5 Percussionists, Op. 83; Veritas Veritatum, for Men's Choir, Op.129a; Wedding March, for Organ, Op.94. *Honours:* ASCAP Foundation/ Meet the Composer Award, 1985; Oregon Governor's Arts Award, 1992; American Record Guide, 2001 Critics Choice Award for Piano Trios CD. *Current Management:* Thomas C Stangland, Portland, USA. *Address:* c/o Thomas Stangland Co, PO Box 19263, Portland, OR 97280, USA. *E-mail:* info@TomasSvoboda.com. *Website:* www.TomasSvoboda.com.

**SVORC, Antonin;** Singer (Bass-Baritone); b. 12 Feb. 1934, Jaromer, Czechoslovakia. *Education:* Studied with Jan Berlik in Prague. *Career:* Debut: State Theatre of Liberec as Pizarro in Fidelio, 1955; Member of the National Theatre, Prague, from 1958; Visited Edinburgh with the company in 1964 in the British premiere of From the House of the Dead by Janáček; Guest appearances at the Berlin Staatsoper and in Vienna, Paris, Dresden, Cologne, Düsseldorf, Kassel, Zürich, Trieste, Venice and Barcelona; Sang in Prague in 1974 in the premiere of Cikker's Coriolanus and as Chrudos in Libuše at the 1983 reopening of the National Opera; Sang as guest at the Paris Opéra in 1988 in From the House of the Dead. *Recordings:* Operas by Smetana including Dalibor and Libuše. *Honours:* National Artists of Czechoslovakia, 1985. *Address:* c/o National Theatre, PO Box 865, 112 30 Prague 1, Czech Republic.

**SWAFFORD, Jan (Johnson),** BA, MMA, DMA; American writer and composer; b. 10 Sept. 1946, Chattanooga, TN; m. Julie Pisano 1973 (divorced 1979). *Education:* Harvard Univ., Yale School of Music, Tanglewood. *Career:* Asst Prof., Boston Univ. School for the Arts 1977–78; Visiting Asst Prof. Hampshire Coll., Amherst 1979–81; Amherst Coll. 1980–81; freelance composer and writer 1981–; Lecturer in English, Tufts Univ.; Massachusetts Artists' Foundation grant 1983; Harvard-Mellon Fellowship 1988; NEA Composers Fellow 1991; mem. American Music Center, Minnesota Composers' Forum, Composers' Forum. *Compositions:* Passage 1975, Peal 1976, Landscape with Traveller 1981, Shore Lines 1982, Labyrinths 1983, Music Like Steel Like Fire 1983, In Time of Fear 1984, Midsummer Variations 1985, Chamber Sinfonietta 1988, They Who Hunger 1989, Requiem in Winter 1991, Iphigenia Choruses 1993. *Publications:* The Vintage Guide to Classical Music 1992, The New Guide to Classical Music 1993, Charles Ives: A Life with Music 1996, Johannes Brahms: A Biography 1997; contrib. articles and reviews to Symphony, New England Monthly, Musical America, Yankee. *Honours:* prizewinner New England Composers' Competition 1984, L. L. Winship-PEN New England Award 1997. *Address:* c/o English Department, Tufts University, 210 East Hall, Medford, MA 02155, USA. *E-mail:* jswaffor_AT_tufts .edu.

**SWANSTON, Roderick Brian;** Professor of Music Theory; b. 28 Aug. 1948, Gosport, England. *Education:* Music Scholar, Stowe School, 1961–66; Royal College of Music, 1966–69; Organ Scholar at Pembroke College, Cambridge, 1969–71; MA; BMus; Graduate, Royal Schools of Music; Fellow, Royal College of Organists; Licentiate of Royal Academy; Associate of Royal College of Music. *Career:* Organist at Christ Church, Lancaster Gate, 1972–77, and St James, Sussex Gardens, 1977–80; Conductor of Christ Church Choral Society, 1972–80; Part-Time Tutor at University of London, Department of Extra Mural Studies, 1972–; Academic Adviser in Music to Birkbeck College, University of London, Centre for Extra Mural Studies, 1987–; Visiting Lecturer for many organizations including English National Opera, Royal Opera House, Covent Garden, BBC, Oxford University and Goldsmiths' College. *Compositions:* A Time There Was for Tenor, Choir and Strings; Let Us Gather Hand In Hand for Choir and Brass à 5, recorded by BBC. *Recordings:* Organ recital from Framlingham Parish Church. *Publications:* Concise History of Music. *Address:* Royal College of Music, Prince Consort Road, London SW7, England.

**SWAYNE, Giles;** Composer; b. 30 June 1946, Hitchin, Hertfordshire, England. *Education:* Ampleforth, Trinity Coll. Cambridge; RAM, London; studies with Nicholas Maw, Harrison Birtwistle, Oliver Messiaen; conducting course at Siena 1968. *Career:* early work performed by SPNM and at Aldeburgh and Bromsgrove Festivals; Orlando's Music and Pentecost Music performed by several major orchestras; opera repetiteur at Wexford Festival 1972–73 and Glyndebourne 1973–74; teaching staff at Bryanston School 1974–76; first major int. success with composition Cry for 28 voices for BBC premiered London 1980, later 1988, Proms 1983, 1994, also Amsterdam Concertgebouw 1982, Vienna Modern Festival and Stuttgart 1997; companion piece Havoc premiered Proms 1999; visited West Africa in 1980 to study the music of the Jola people of Senegal and The Gambia; lived in Ghana 1990–96; teaches composition Cambridge Univ.; mem. PRS, APC, MCPS. *Compositions include:* Six Songs of Love & Lust, La Rivière 1966, The Kiss 1967, Sonata for String Quartet 1968, Three Shakespeare Songs (SATB choir) 1969, Chamber Music for Strings, Four Lyrical Pieces for Cello and Piano 1970, The Good Morrow (mezzo and piano), Paraphrase (organ), String Quartet No. 1 1971, Trio (flute, oboe and piano), Canto for Guitar 1972, Canto for Piano, Canto for

Violin 1973, Orlando's Music for Orchestra, Synthesis (2 pianos) 1974, Scrapbook (piano), Canto for clarinet, Duo (violin and piano), Charades (school orchestra) 1975, Suite for guitar, Pentecost-Music for Orchestra, Alleluia! (SA choir, harp, percussion) 1976, String Quartet no. 2 1977, A World Within, ballet with tape 1978, Phoenix Variations (piano), Cry for 28 amplified voices 1979, The Three Rs (primary school orchestra), Freewheeling (violin, viola, bass) 1980, Count-Down (SATB choir), Canto for Cello 1981, Rhythm Studies 1 & 2 (school percussion), Magnificat (SATB choir) 1982, Riff-Raff (organ), A Song for Haddi (ensemble) 1983, Le Nozze di Cherubino (opera), Symphony for Small Orchestra, Naaotwa Lalà (for orchestra) 1984, Missa Tiburtina for SATB choir 1985, Into the Light (ensemble), Solo for Guitar 1986, godsong (mezzo & ensemble), Nunc Dimittis (SATB choir and organ), O Magnum Mysterium (treble voices and organ) 1986, Tonos for ensemble 1987, Veni Creator I & 2 (SATB choir and organ), Songlines for Flute and Guitar, The Coming of Saskia Hawkins (organ) 1987, Harmonies of Hell (large ensemble), The Song of Leviathan (large orchestra) 1988, No Quiet Place (SA choir and ensemble), No Man's Land for solo bass voice, SATB choir, ensemble 1990, Circle of Silence for 6 male voices 1991, Zebra Music (piano), The Song of the Tortoise (narrator, SATB, small orchestra) 1992, The Owl & the Pussycat I (narrator, ensemble), String Quartet no. 3 1993, Fiddlesticks (violin & bass), Goodnight, Sweet Ladies (soprano & piano), Squeezy (accordion) 1994, All about Henry (string orchestra), The Tiger (SATB choir), Communion Service in D (congregation and organ), A Convocation of Worms (countertenor & organ) 1995, Two romantic songs (SATB choir), Ophelia drowning (flute & SATB choir), The Silent Land (cello & 40-part choir) 1996, Tombeau (piano), Beatus vir (SATB choir & organ), Mr Leary's Mechanical Maggot (string orchestra), Chinese Whispers (organ & orchestra), Miss Brevissima (SATB choir), Petite Messe Solitaire (SATB choir & unison voices), Echo (violin & piano) 1997, Winter Solstice Carol (flute & SATB choir), Groundwork (theorbo) Merlis Lied (voice & piano) 1998, The Flight of the Swan (flute & SATB choir), Havoc (24 voices, countertenor, ensemble & small orchestra) 1999, Perturbèd Spirit (countertenor & organ), Canto for flute, The Akond of Swat (2 narrators & ensemble) 2000, Mancanza (solo guitar & orchestra), The Murder of Gonzago (wind quintet) 2001, Epitaph and Refrain (ensemble) 2002, The Owl & the Pussycat II (treble voices & piano), Midwinter (SATB choir), Sangre viva (trumpet & piano) 2003, Stabat mater (SATB choir and soloists), Stations of the Cross Book I (organ), Mr Bach's Bottle-Bank (organ) 2004. *Address:* Gonzaga Music, 43 Victor Road, London, NW10 5XB, England. *E-mail:* giles@havocry.ndo.co.uk.

**SWEENEY, William;** Composer; b. 5 Jan. 1950, Glasgow, Scotland. *Education:* Royal Scottish Academy 1967–70; Royal Academy of Music, London, 1970–73, with Harrison Birtwistle and Alan Hacker. *Career:* Lecturer on Composition at the University of Glasgow. *Compositions:* Three Poems from Sangschaw for soprano, three clarinets and piano, 1977; Maqam for orchestra, 1984; Sunset Song, for orchestra, 1986; The Heights of Macchu Picchu, for soprano, harp and percussion, 1988; The New Road, for tenor saxophone and orchestra, 1989; El Pueblo, for baritone and ensemble, 1989; Concerto Grosso, for nine clarinets, strings and timpani, 1990; St, Blane's Hill, for orchestra 1991; A Set for the Kingdom, for strings, 1991; Two Lyrics, for two sopranos and chorus, 1992; A Drunk Man Looks at the Thistle, for speaker baritone and ensemble, 1992; The Woods of Rassay for soprano, baritone and orchestra, 1993; Seeking Wise Salmon, for soprano, clarinet, trombone and two synthesizers, 1994; October Landscapes, for orchestra, 1994; The Lost Mountain, for wind band, 1996; All that Came in the Coracle, for mezzo and ensemble, 1999. *Address:* c/o PRS Ltd, 29–33 Berners St, London, W1T 3 AB, England. *Telephone:* (20) 7580 5544. *Fax:* (20) 7306 4455.

**SWEET, Sharon;** Singer (Soprano); b. 16 Aug. 1951, New York, USA. *Education:* Studied with Margaret Harshaw at the Curtis Institute, Philadelphia and with Marinka Gurewich in New York. *Career:* Sang in private recitals at Philadelphia then appeared in the title role in concert performance of Aida at Munich, 1985; Dortmund Opera, 1986–88, debut as Elisabeth in Tannhäuser; Deutsche Oper Berlin from 1987, notably as guest in Zürich and Japan as Elisabeth and in the Ring; Paris Opera and Hamburg, 1987 as Elisabeth de Valois; Season 1987–88 as Desdemona in Brunswick, Dvořák's Stabat Mater at the Salzburg Festival, Gurrelieder in Munich under Zubin Mehta and Wagner's Elisabeth at the Vienna Staatsoper; Norma in a concert performance of Bellini's opera at Brussels, 1988; US debut as Aida at San Francisco in 1989; Season 1992 as Aida in Dallas and the Trovatore Leonora at Orange; Sang in the house premiere of Verdi's Stiffelio at the Metropolitan Season, 1993–94 returned 1997, as Aida; Aida at Covent Garden, 1995, returned as Turandot, 1997; Norma at Rome, 1999; Sang Turandot at the Dresden Staatsoper, 2001. *Recordings include:* Verdi's Requiem. *Address:* c/o IMG Paris, 54 Ave Marceau, F–75008 Paris, France.

**SWENSEN, Joseph Anton;** American conductor and composer; *Principal Conductor, Scottish Chamber Orchestra;* b. 4 Aug. 1960, New York City; m. 2nd Kristina Algot-Sörensen; three s. (one from previous marriage). *Education:* Juilliard School. *Career:* Prin. Guest Conductor Stockholm Chamber Orchestra 1994–97, Lahti Symphony Orchestra 1995–2000; Prin. Conductor Scottish Chamber Orchestra (SCO) 1996–; Prin. Guest Conductor BBC Nat. Orchestra of Wales 2000–; toured Japan with SCO 1995, USA 1999; debut at Edinburgh Int. Festival with SCO 1998; cycle of Beethoven performances to mark 25th anniversary of SCO 1999; conducted new production of The Marriage of Figaro at the Royal Danish Opera 1999; regular appearances with Royal Stockholm Philharmonic and Swedish Radio Symphony Orchestras;

guest conductor with Los Angeles Philharmonic, Toronto Symphony, Dallas Symphony, London Philharmonic, City of Birmingham Symphony, Oslo Philharmonic, Finnish Radio Symphony, Gothenburg Symphony and Ulster Orchestras, Lausanne Chamber Orchestra; own orchestral works have been performed by various orchestras. *Current Management:* Van Walsum Management Ltd, 4 Addison Bridge Place, London, W14 8XP, England. *Telephone:* (20) 7371-4343. *Fax:* (20) 7371-4344. *Website:* www.vanwalsum.co.uk.

**SWENSEN, Robert;** Singer (Tenor); b. 1961, USA. *Career:* Sang at the New Jersey Festival, 1987 and 1988, as Rossini's Count and Britten's Lysander; Season 1990 with Tybalt in I Capuleti e i Montecchi at Geneva and Nadir in Les Pêcheurs des Perles at the Paris Opéra-Comique; Carnegie Hall, New York, 1992, as George Brown in La Dame Blanche by Boieldieu: Matsumato Festival, 1993, as Oedipus Rex and Amenofi in Nabucco at Venice; Season 1995–96 in Mozart's Mitridate at Turin and Gianetto in La Gazza Ladra at Palermo; Concerts include Mozart's Requiem at Cologne. *Recordings include:* Bach's St John Passion; Haydn's Orfeo ed Euridice; Bach's Christmas Oratorio; Oedipus Rex, also on video. *Address:* c/o Teatro Regio de Torino, Piazza Castello 215, 10124 Turin, Italy.

**SWENSON, Ruth Ann;** American opera singer (coloratura soprano). *Career:* Debut San Francisco (CA) 1983, Royal Opera House, Covent Garden (London) 1996; has sung in Berlin, Geneva (Switzerland), Paris, etc. *Operas include:* Orlando, Rigoletto, Elisir d'amore, Lucia di Lammermoor, Puritani, Semele. *Recordings include:* Coloratura Arias from the Golden Age 1996, Roméo et Juliette (with Placido Domingo) 1996.

**SWERTS, Piet;** Belgian composer and conductor; b. 14 Nov. 1960, Tongeren. *Education:* Lemmensinstituut, Leuven and masterclasses with Witold Lutoslawski. *Career:* Prof. of Composition, Piano and Analysis, Lemmensinstituut, Leuven 1982–. *Compositions:* String Quartet No. 1 1982, Paysages Métaphysiques for orchestra 1982, Piano Concerto No. 1 1984, String Quartet No. 2 1985, Yoshiwara for soprano and 14 instruments 1986, Symphony No. 1 1990, Piano Concerto No. 2 1986, Ajas (opera) 1986, Marcuspassie for soloists, choirs and orchestra (St Mark Passion) 1988, Rotations for piano and orchestra 1988, Magma for concerto for violin, cello and strings 1989, String Quartet No. 3 1991, Piano Concerto No. 3 1991, Rapsodia for bassoon and string quartet 1991, Missa semplice 1993, Zodiac for violin and orchestra 1993, String Quartet No. 4 1993, Les Liaisons dangereuses (opera) 1994, Cello Concerto 1996, Symphony No. 2 Morgenrot 1997, The Titanic Saga for wind orchestra 1998, Minerva for orchestra 2002, Nursery Songs for soprano and orchestra 2003, Concertino for alto saxophone and concert band 2004. *Recordings include:* Piet Swerts speelt Piet Swerts: Muziek voor piano 1985–1995, Marcuspassie, Symphony No. 2, The Titanic Saga. *Honours:* Baron Flor Peeters Prize 1983, Prijs Lemmens Tinel for piano and composition 1985, BAP Prize 1985, SABAM Prize 1986, Camille Huysmans Composition Prize 1986, Prize for Composition of the Province of Limburg 1986, First Prize, Concours Musical Int. Reine Elisabeth de Belgique 1993. *Address:* Grauwe Steenberg 1, 3060 Bertem, Belgium (home). *Telephone:* (1) 648-00-52 (home). *Fax:* (1) 648-00-52 (home). *E-mail:* piet.swerts@scarlet.be (home). *Website:* www.pietswerts.be (home).

**SWIERCZEWSKI, Michel;** Conductor; b. 1960, France. *Education:* Studied with Jean-Claude Hartemann in Paris and Charles Mackerras at the Vienna Hochschule. *Career:* Made debut in 1976 and was then assistant conductor to Pierre Boulez and Peter Eötvös at the Ensemble Intercontemporain, 1983–85 and for Claudio Abbado at La Scala, including the premiere of Nono's Prometeo, 1985–86; Paris Opéra in 1986 with Georges Prêtre; Has conducted such contemporary music ensembles as Itineraire, Musique Oblique, Antidogma and New Music Ensemble, giving many premieres; Guest engagements in France, Germany, Italy, Spain, Portugal and Australia; Conducted Die Fledermaus at Lyon, 1996. *Recordings:* La Conférence des Oiseaux by Michael Levinas; Works by Roussel with the Gulbenkian Foundation Orchestra; Complete Symphonies of Méhul. *Honours:* Finalist, 1984 Tanglewood International Conducting Competition; Prize, Villa Medicis Hors Les Murs. *Current Management:* Agence Thelen, 15 avenue Montaigne, 75008 Paris, France.

**SWINGLE, Ward (Lamar);** Choral Conductor, Composer, Arranger and Clinician; b. 21 Sept. 1927, Mobile, Alabama, USA; m. Françoise Demorest, 23 Sept 1952, 3 d. *Education:* BM, MM, Piano Major, Cincinnati Conservatory of Music, 1947–51; Masterclasses with Walter Gieseking at Saarbrücken, Germany, 1951–53. *Career:* Solo piano recitals and accompanist, 1953–55; Conductor of Ballets de Paris, France, 1955–59; Founded Swingle Singers, a world-wide touring concert group, 1963; Numerous radio and television appearances with Swingle Singers in most major capitals and about 2000 concerts around the world, 1963–91. *Compositions:* Over 100 arrangements and compositions for the Swingle Singers. *Recordings:* About 30 with the Swingle Singers including Bach's Greatest Hits, Going Baroque, and Luciano Berio's Sinfonia. *Honours:* 5 Grammy Awards, 1964, 1965, 1966, 1970; Grand Prix du Disque, 1964; Edison Award, 1970. *Current Management:* Piers Schmidt, 45a Chalcot Road, London, NW1 8LS, England. *Address:* c/o ASCAP, ASCAP Building, One Lincoln Plaza, NY 10023, USA.

**SWINNEN, Peter;** Belgian composer; b. 31 Jan. 1965, Lier. *Education:* Royal Conservatory, Brussels, Muziekkapel Konigin Elisabeth, Waterloo, masterclasses with Michael Finnissy and Brian Ferneyhough. *Career:* taught cello at music schools 1990–97; teacher of analysis, Royal Conservatory, Brussels

1992–, of music technology 2002–, of composition 2004–; software development for aural training at Leuven Univ. 1997–2004, for musical analysis at Brussels Univ. 2004–; freelance work for BRTN-television; frequent performances of live electronics with various ensembles. *Compositions include:* Diorama 1989, FugaEneas 1990, Escurial 1991, The Petrifying Blue (chamber opera) 1992, Hombre alado 1995, The Black Lark's Ballad (symphonic poem, tribute to Frank Zappa) 1995, Een pimpelpaarse wiebelfiets 1996, La Vieille dame et la fille nomade 1998, Toaminà'k 1998, Sinfonia I 1998, Ciaccona 2000, Annotazione 2000, Pas-de-deux 2001, Maitre Tsa (mini opera for children) 2003. *Compositions for films:* Andres 1992, Het Verhoor 1998, The Voice of the Violin 1998. *Recordings include:* Ciaccona, The Black Lark's Ballad, Quar'l. *Honours:* Prijs CERA – Jeugd en Muziek Vlaanderen 1991, Prov. of Antwerp Prijs voor Muziekcompositie 1992, Prix de Musique Contemporaine, Québec 1997, winner Queen Elisabeth Int. Music Competition Nat. Composition Contest, Belgium 1997, 2001. *Address:* Frans Gasthuislaan 33/4, 1081 Brussels, Belgium. *Telephone:* (2) 425-24-18. *E-mail:* info@peterswinnen.be. *Website:* www.peterswinnen.be.

**SYDEMAN, William;** American composer; b. 8 May 1928, New York. *Education:* Mannes Coll. with Roy Travis, Hartt Coll., studied with Goffredo Petrassi and Roger Sessions. *Career:* Lecturer, Mannes Coll. 1959–70, Rudolf Steiner Coll., CA from 1980; commissions from Boston SO and Chamber Music Soc. of the Lincoln Center. *Compositions:* over 600 chamber, orchestral and choral works, including Three Concertos da Camera for violin and orchestra 1959, 1960, 1965, Piano Sonata 1961, Homage to L'Histoire du Soldât 1962, Three Studies for orchestra 1959, 1963, 1965, Music for viola, winds and percussion 1996, Concerto for piano four hands and orchestra 1967, Full Circle for three solo voices and ensemble 1971, 18 Duos for two violins 1976, Duo for violin and cello 1979, A Winter's Tale (incidental music) 1982, Sonata for violin and piano 1987, Duo for cello and double bass 1992, Duo for oboe and piano 1996, Jonathan's Trombone 1996, The Odyssey (opera). *Honours:* Boston Symphony Merit Award, Koussevitzky Foundation, Nat. Inst. of Arts and Letters. *Address:* c/o ASCAP, ASCAP Building, One Lincoln Plaza, New York, NY 10023 (office); 20834 New Bowie Boulevard, Nevada City, CA 95959, USA (home). *E-mail:* jaysyde@earthlink.net (home).

**SYLVAN, Sanford;** Singer (Baritone); b. 1952, USA. *Career:* Debut: Concert with New York Philharmonic Orchestra, under Pierre Boulez, 1977; Sang at the Marlboro Festival from 1982 and collaborated with Peter Sellars as Handel's Orlando, as Mozart's Don Alfonso, 1986, and Mozart's Figaro, 1987; Premieres of Nixon in China by John Adams at Houston, 1987, and The Death of Klinghoffer at Brussels, 1991; Albert Hall, London, 1990, as Xun in Tippett's The Ice Break; Glyndebourne, 1994, as Leporello; Houston, New York and Edinburgh, 1996, as St Agnatius in Virgil Thomson's Three Saints in Four Acts; Klinghoffer at Barbican Hall, London, 2002; London Proms, 2002. *Recordings include:* Nixon in China and The Death of Klinghoffer. *Address:* c/o Houston Opera Association, 510 Preston Avenue, Houston, TX 77002, USA.

**SYLVESTER, Michael;** Singer (Tenor); b. 21 Aug. 1951, Noblesville, Indiana, USA. *Education:* Studied with Margaret Harshaw at Bloomington. *Career:* Sang Radames and Pinkerton at Stuttgart, 1987, at Cincinnati Opera from 1987 as Pinkerton and Sam in Floyd's Susannah, New York City Opera debut in 1987 as Rodolfo in La Bohème and further engagements at La Scala and Santiago as Pinkerton in 1990, Paris Opéra as Pollione in Norma, Hamburg Staatsoper as Rodolfo and Don José, and Vienna Staatsoper as Cavaradossi; Covent Garden debut in 1990 as Samson, followed by Gabriel Adorno in a new production of Simon Boccanegra in 1991; Sang at Bregenz Festival in 1990 as Hagenbach in La Wally, and at Metropolitan Opera in debut, 1991, as Rodolfo in Luisa Miller followed by Don Carlos in 1992; Appearances as Radames at Deutsche Oper Berlin, Chicago, Orange Festival and Seattle in 1992; Further engagements at Bonn as Bacchus in 1990, San Francisco as Calaf, Venice as Don Carlos and Geneva as Foresto in Attila; Sang Radames at the Met, 1996–97; Season 2000–01 as Eleazar in La Juive for New Israeli Opera, Giasone in Cherubini's Médée at Montpellier, Calaf at the Met, Gabriele Adorno for Australian Opera and Puccini's Dick Johnson in Toronto. *Recordings include:* Title role in Oberon; Don Carlos conducted by James Levine; Video of Simon Boccanegra from Covent Garden with Solti conducting. *Address:* c/o Metropolitan Opera, Lincoln Center, New York, NY 10023, USA.

**SYNKOVA, Milada;** Czech pianist, harpsichordist and opera repetiteur; b. 16 May 1933, Bratislava, Czechoslovakia. *Education:* Conservatoire of Music, Brno; University of Bratislava, 1951–63. *Career:* debut, Slovak Nat. Theatre, Bratislava 1963; concerts worldwide; harpsichordist, pianist and Asst to Prof. Viktor Málek (Conductor), Chamber Orchestra Camerata Slovaca 1969–; singer, pianist and Asst to Prof. Ladislav Holásek (Conductor), Bratislava City Choir 1973–; performed in chamber orchestras in Edinburgh, Jerusalem, Budapest and Seoul; co-operates regularly (with Prof. Milau Sládek) with The Mime Theatre ARENA, Bratislava; taught professional training courses in piano, singing and Czech music at Sungshin Women's Univ., Seoul, Republic of Korea 2000; opera teacher, SUNCHON Summer Music Camp, Republic of Korea 2004, 2005; worked with Milan Sládek Pantonimentheater, Cologne, Germany 2005; currently Tutor, Acad. of Music Arts, and Opera Repetiteur, Opera of the Slovak Nat. Theatre. *Recordings:* for Czechoslovak radio, television. *Address:* 13 Joann Court, Monmouth Junction, NJ 08852, USA.

**SZEGEDI, Anikó;** Hungarian pianist; b. 22 March 1938, Budapest; m. J. Szavai 1966; one d. *Education:* F. Liszt Acad. of Music, Budapest. *Career:* debut with Chopin Piano Concerto, Budapest Acad. of Music 1961; concerts in Budapest, Vienna Brahms Saal, Leningrad, Kiev, Dresden, London, Berlin, and Paris Salle Gaveau. *Recordings:* Beethoven Eroica Variations, Haydn Sonatas, Beethoven Piano Concerto and Triple Concerto (with D. Koracs and M. Pereuy), Schumann Carnaval, Kreisleriana. *Honours:* third prize Int. Schumann Piano Concerts, Zwickau 1963, F. Liszt Prize, Budapest 1973. *Address:* Szt Istvan krt 16, 1137 Budapest, Hungary; 93 boulevard de Port-Royal, Paris 75013, France. *E-mail:* szentistvan16@netquick.hu.

**SZEGHY, Iris,** ArtD; Slovak composer; b. 5 March 1956, Presov, Czechoslovakia; m. Pedro Zimmermann. *Education:* Kosice Conservatory, Acad. of Music, Bratislava. *Career:* resident composer, Akad. Schloss Solitude, Stuttgart 1992–93; visiting composer, Univ. of California, San Diego 1994; composer-in-residence, Hamburg State Opera 1995, Kunstlerhauser Worpswede 1999; several portrait concerts, Hamburg, San Diego, Stuttgart, Bremen; participation in many festivals of music; composer-in-residence, Künstlerhaus Boswil, Switzerland 2001, Künstler Wohnung Stein am Rhun, Switzerland 2002. *Compositions:* Concerto for violoncello and orchestra 1989, Homewards for symphony orchestra 1997, De Profundis for voice and two melodic instruments 1990, Midsummer Night's Mystery for two percussionists 1992, Musica folclorica for clarinet, percussion and piano 1996, Tableaux d'un parc for chamber ensemble 2000, Vielleicht, dass uns etwas aufginge for soprano and string orchestra 2003, Ahrufung des Grossen Bären for soprano, flute and piano 2003; broadcasts on Slovak, German and Swiss radio stations. *Recordings include:* Portrait, Hastedt Verlag Bremen 2001. *Honours:* several composition scholarships and prizes. *Address:* Nürenbergstrasse 17, 8037 Zürich, Switzerland (home). *Telephone:* (1) 3632966. *Fax:* (56) 6663032 (home). *E-mail:* szeghy@bluewin.ch (home).

**SZEMZO, Tibor;** Composer and Performer; b. 7 Feb. 1955, Budapest, Hungary. *Education:* Budapest Academy. *Career:* Composes diverse groups; Performs with quartet, Group 180; Solo performances; Ensemble, The Gordian Knot, 1998; Written 12 records; Written works for films; Performed: Contemporary Music Week, Budapest, 1981–; Autumn Festival, Paris, 1982; Steyerischer Herbst, Austria; New Music America, Houston, 1986; Donaufest, St Polten, 1988; Dokumenta, Kassel; Wiener Festwochen, 1988; Ars Electronica, Linz, 1988 and 1989; Urban Aboriginal Festival, Berlin, 1992; NIPAF, Nagano, 1993; Music Now from Hungaary, Yoahama, 1994; Warsaw Autumn Festival, Poland, 1995; Unsung Music, 1996; Izumiwaka '96, Tokyo; Zona Europa de Est, 1996; Romania Literatur Im Marz, Vienna and other countries. *Recordings:* Water Wonder, 1983; Snapshot From the Island, 1987; Private Exits, 1989; Meteo/The Dreams of Eckermann, 1990; Sub-Carpathia, 1981; Ain't Nothing But a Little Bit of Music for Moving Pictures, 1992;; The Conscience/Narrative Chamber Pieces, 1993; Duo, 1984; The Last Hungarian PVC, 1994; The Sex Appeal of Death/Airy Wedding, 1994; Tractatus, 1995; Symultan, 1997; Relative Things, 1998. *Address:* 2093 Budajeny, Kossuth Str 43, Hungary.

**SZETO, Caroline,** BMus, MMus, PhD; Australian composer; b. 15 Sept. 1956. *Education:* Univ. of Sydney, studied with Peter Sculthorpe. *Career:* worked at Univ. of Sydney 1990–91; commissions from ABC 1991, Sydney Metropolitan Opera 1993, Song Co. 1994, 1997, Sydney Mandolins 1995, 1997, Bernadette Balkus and Michael Kieran Harvey 1999, ENERGEX Brisbane Festival 2000, Nat. Festival of Women's Music 2001. *Compositions include:* Three Pieces for guitar 1984, Catalogue for string quartet 1985, C.C. 33 for concert band 1985, Sheng for orchestra 1986, Images of Li Po for ensemble 1987, Missa Brevis 1987, Energy for orchestra 1990, Study No. 1 and 2 for tuba 1990, Moon on Night's Water for piano 1990, Lament of the Boobook for computer-based instruments 1991, Yunny's Treat for piano 1991, ABC Fanfare for orchestra 1992, In a Garden for computer-based instruments 1992, A Game for violin 1992, The Third Station of the Cross for clarinet, double bass and percussion 1993, The Sweet Apple for six vocal soloists 1994, Energy II for orchestra 1994, Mandolin Dance 1995, Prelude for mandolin ensemble 1997, Monkeys Cry for six vocal soloists and two percussionists 1997, Cycles for guitar 1997, Mandolin Concerto 1998–99, Buffo for bassoon and piano 1998, Toccata for two pianos 1999, Cello Dance for cello and piano 1999, Impulse for oboe, clarinet, French horn and bassoon 2000, Dawn Day Dusk for koto and guitar 2001. *Recordings:* Yunny's Treat 1993, Mandolin Dance 1996, Energy for Orchestra 1997, ABC Fanfare for Orchestra 1997, Moon on Night's Water 1998, Prelude 1999, Cello Dance 2004. *Honours:* Ignaz Friedman Memorial Prize 1985, Donald Peart Memorial Prize 1986, two first prizes City of Sydney Eisteddfod 1991, Australia Council for the Arts Composer Fellowship 1994. *Address:* PO Box 163, Mosman, NSW 2088, Australia (office). *E-mail:* mail@carolineszeto.com (office). *Website:* www.carolineszeto.com (office).

**SZEVERENYI, Ilona;** Music Professor and Dulcimer Player; b. 12 Aug. 1946, Gyula, Hungary; m. Ferenc Gerencser, 25 Mar 1967. *Education:* Studied with Ferenc Gerencser, Liszt Ferenc Academy of Music, Budapest, graduating 1968. *Career:* Regular concerts as Soloist and with her chamber orchestras, Hungary and throughout Europe, 1968–; Founder, dulcimer duo, 1972; Numerous recitals, France, Germany, Italy; Premieres of more than 70 works including 3 concertos by contemporary composers; With her students founded Pantaleon, ensemble for 4 dulcimers, 1996; Teaching, Béla Bartók Music Secondary School, 1986–, Liszt Ferenc Academy of Music, 1989–; Developed curriculum for low, medium and advanced levels of dulcimer instruction. *Compositions:* Several published compositions for dulcimer. *Recordings*

*include:* Pieces for 2 dulcimers, 1980; Contemporary works for dulcimer solo, 1986; CD with selection from J. S. Bach's pieces arranged for dulcimer solo, 1995; Lachrymae, a CD featuring the music of J. Dowland, S.L. Weiss and J.S.Bach's solo works, Hungarton, 2003; Participant in records of 10 composers. *Publications:* Co-author, Cimbalon Tutor, 1982; Publications in field of music education. *Contributions:* Parlando music journal. *Address:* Krecsanyi utca 12, 1025 Budapest, Hungary.

**SZIGETI, István;** Hungarian composer; b. 16 Oct. 1952, Budapest; Orsolya Srankó; two d. *Education:* Béla Bartók Conservatory, Budapest with Miklós Kocsár and Sándor Szokolay, Ferenc Liszt Acad. of Music with Zoltán Pongrácz. *Career:* worked for Hungarian Radio 1975–; Musical Ed. 1982–; Artistic Dir, electro-acoustic music studio, Hungarian Radio HEAR Studio 1994–; Head of Young Composers' Group, Budapest 1986–89; Pres., Hungarian Composers' Union; Pres., László Lajtha Soc. *Compositions include:* Souvenir de K 1981, Elka 1984. *Honours:* special prize Int. GMEB Electro-acoustic Music Centre Composers' Competition, Bourges 1981, 1984, Kodály Scholarship 1984, Lajtha Prize 1999, Erkel Prize 2000. *Address:* HEAR Studio, Hungarian Radio PLC, u. Brody S. 5-7, 1800 Budapest, Hungary (office). *E-mail:* hear@radio.hu (office).

**SZILAGYI, Karoly;** Singer (Baritone); b. 1949, Oradea Mare, Romania. *Education:* Studied at the Cluj Conservatory. *Career:* Sang Morales and Rigoletto at the Cluj Opera, then engaged at the Gelsenkirchen Opera 1980–85, Essen 1985–89; Guest appearances at the Vienna Staatsoper, Zürich Opera and St Gallen and throughout Germany, Hungary and Austria; Liège 1990, as Rigoletto; Also sings in operas by Donizetti and Puccini; Sang Coppelius in Les Contes d'Hoffmann at Essen, 1996; Sang Verdi's Miller at Essen, 2001. *Address:* c/o Essen Opera, Theater Essen, Rolandstrasse 10, W-4300 Essen 1, Germany.

**SZIRMAY, Marta;** Singer (Mezzo-Soprano); b. 1939, Kaposvar, Hungary. *Education:* Studied at the Budapest Conservatory. *Career:* Member of the Hungarian State Opera from 1964 singing the mezzo repertory in operas by Wagner and Verdi, and Cologne Opera from 1976; Covent Garden debut in 1977 as Clytemnestra in Elektra with later London appearances as Erda in Das Rheingold and Mistress Quickly in Falstaff; Further appearances in Hamburg, Berlin, Vienna, Barcelona, Venice and Naples; Sang at Salzburg Festival in 1985 as Ericles in Il Ritorno d'Ulisse by Monteverdi, arranged by Henze; Other roles include Gaea in Daphne, Gluck's Orpheus and Brangaene in Tristan and Isolde; Season 1992 in Corghi's Blimunda at Turin. *Address:* c/o Teatro Region di Turino, Piazza Castello 215, 10124 Turin, Italy.

**SZMYTKA, Elzbieta;** Singer (Soprano); b. 1956, Prochowice, Poland. *Education:* Studied in Kraków, 1975–82 with Helena Lazarska. *Career:* Sang at the Kraków Opera from 1978 then at Bytom and Wroclaw; Toured to West Germany and Luxembourg as Blondchen in Die Entführung; Sang widely in Western Europe from 1983 notably at Ghent, Antwerp and Brussels as Despina, Blondchen and Serpina, and as Nannetta, 1987–88; Sang at Aix-en-Provence Festival, 1987–88 as Nannetta and as Servilia in La Clemenza di Tito, Holland Festival in 1987 as Serpina in La Finta Giardiniera, at the Vienna Staatsoper in 1988 as Papagena, and in Amsterdam and Antwerp in 1989 as Gilda and Zerbinetta; Sang at Glyndebourne Festival in 1991 as Ilia in Idomeneo and Servilia in La Clemenza di Tito, Salzburg Summer Festival in 1992 as Alyeya in From the House of the Dead and Mozartwoche in 1993 as Cinna in Lucio Silla; Sang Vitellia in Gluck's La Clemenza di Tito at the Théâtre des Champs-Elysées, Paris, 1996; Other roles include Susanna, Norina and Aennchen in Der Freischütz; Engaged for Mozart's Lucio Silla and Entführung at the 1997 Salzburg Festival; Season 1999–2000 as Mozart's Elettra at Lyon, Mélisande in Toronto and Donna Anna for the Berlin Staatsoper. *Recordings include:* La Finta Giardiniera; Despina in Così fan tutte; Mozart Arias; Die Entführung; Il Matrimonio Segreto; Music by Szymanowski conducted by Simon Rattle. *Address:* c/o PG & PM, 7 Whitehorse Close, Royal Mile, Edinburgh, EH8 8BU, England.

**SZOKOLAY, Sándor;** Hungarian composer; b. 30 March 1931, Kunágota; s. of Bálint Szokolay and Erzsébet Holecska; m. 1st Sári Szesztay 1952; m. 2nd Maja Weltler 1970; four s. one d. *Education:* Békéstardos Music High School, Budapest Music Acad. *Career:* music teacher Budapest Conservatory 1952–55; Musical Adviser and Ed. Hungarian Radio 1955–59; composition teacher Budapest Music Acad. 1959–66; musical adviser Hungarian TV 1966–; Chair. Hungarian Kodály Soc. *Works include:* Blood Wedding (opera) 1963, Hamlet (opera) 1968, Az iszonyat balladája (The Ballad of Horror), Tetemrehivás (Ordeal of the Bier), Samson (opera) 1973, Csalóka Péter (children's opera, text by Sándor Weöres) 1985, Ecce Homo (passion-opera) 1987, Dublin Concerto for violin 1991; Oratorios: A tüz márciusa (March Fire), Istár pokoljárása (Ishtar's Descent to Hell), Hungarian Psalm; has also written cantatas, songs, chamber music and choral works. *Honours:* has won prizes in Warsaw, Moscow, Vienna, Merited Artist Distinction 1976, Honoured Artist Distinction 1986, Bartók-Pásztory Prize 1987. *Address:* c/o Martin Perdoux, 5014 Chaparral Way, San Diego, CA 92115, USA.

**SZŐLLŐSY, András,** DPh; Hungarian composer, music historian and academic; *Professor of History and Theory of Music, Liszt Ferenc Academy of Music;* b. 27 Feb. 1921, Szászváros, Transylvania; s. of János Szőllősy and Julia Tóth; m. Éva Keményfy 1944. *Education:* Univ. of Budapest; studied composition at Budapest Acad. of Music with Zoltán Kodály and Iános Viski and with Goffredo Petrassi at Accad. Santa Cecilia, Rome, Italy. *Career:* Prof. of History and Theory of Music, Liszt Ferenc Acad. of Music Budapest 1950–.

*Compositions include:* Oly korban éltem (Improvisation of Fear) (ballet) 1963; orchestral works: five Concertos, Musica per Orchestra 1972, Trasfigurazioni 1972, Musica Concertante 1973, Preludio, Adagio e Fuga 1973, Sonorità 1974, Musiche per Ottoni 1975, Concerto for Harpsichord and Strings 1979, Pro Somno Igoris Stravinsky Quieto 1979, Fabula Phaedri for vocal ensemble 1982 (composed for the King's Singers), In Pharisaeos (for choir) 1982, Tristia (for strings) 1983, Planctus Mariae (for female choir) 1983, Suoni di tromba 1984, Miserere (composed for the King's Singers) 1985, Fragments 1985, Quartetto di Tromboni 1986, Canto d'autunno (for orchestra) 1986, Due Paesaggi (for piano) 1987, String Quartet 1988, Elegy (for dixtuor) 1992, Passacaglia Achatio Máthé in memoriam (for string quartet and cello) 1997, Addio (for 10 strings) 2002; songs; incidental music for plays and films. *Publications:* Kodály művészete 1943, Honegger 1960, 1980; Ed. writings of Kodály and Bartók. *Honours:* Commdr, Ordre des Arts et Lettres 1987; top qualifier, UNESCO Prize, Tribune Int. des Compositeurs, Paris 1970, Erkel Prize 1971, Merited Artist title 1974, Outstanding Artist 1982, Kossuth Prize 1985, Bartók-Pásztory Prize 1986, 1998. *Address:* Somlói ut 12, 1118 Budapest, Hungary. *Telephone:* (1) 466-0035. *Website:* www.musicacademy .hu (office).

**SZŐNYI, Erzsébet;** Hungarian musician; b. 25 April 1924, d. of Jenő Szőnyi and Erzsébet Piszanoff; m. Dr. Lajos Gémes 1948; two s. *Education:* Music Acad., Budapest and Paris Conservatoire. *Career:* teacher of music at a Budapest grammar school 1945–48, Music Acad., Budapest 1948–; leading Prof. of Music Acad. 1960–81; Vice-Pres. Int. Soc. for Music Educ. 1970–74; Co-Chair. Hungarian Kodály Soc. 1978–, Bárdos Soc. 1988–, Forum of Hungarian Musicians 1995–; Hon. Pres. Hungarian Choir Asscn 1990–; Gen. adviser on methodology, Int. Kodály Soc. 1979–; mem. Chopin Soc. of Warsaw, Liszt Soc. of Hungary; mem. Bd Hungarian Composers' Soc. 1999–. *Compositions include:* Concerto for Organ and Orchestra; symphonic works: Musica Festiva, Divertimento 1 and 2, Prelude and Fugue, Three Ideas in Four Movements; operas: Tragedy of Firenze, A Gay Lament, Break in Transmission, Elfrida (madrigal opera) 1987–, several children's operas; chamber music, oratorios, vocal compositions, etc. *Publications:* Methods of Musical Reading and Writing, Kodály's Principles in Practice, Travels in Five Continents, Twentieth-Century Musical Methods. *Honours:* Erkel Prize 1959, Hungarian Repub. Medal 1993 Apácai Csere János Prize 1994, Bartók-Pásztory Prize 1995, 2004, Prize for Artistic Excellence 2000, Zoltán Kodály Prize 2001, Hungarian Heritage Prize 2004, Hungarian Choir Asscn Medal 2004. *Address:* Ormódi-utca 13, 1124 Budapest XII, Hungary. *Telephone:* (1) 356-7329.

**SZÖRENYI, Suzana;** Pianist and Lecturer; b. 23 Oct. 1929, Bucharest, Romania; m. Corneliu Radulescu, 26 Sept 1968 (divorced). *Education:* Diploma, C Porumbescu Bucharest National University of Music1954; Piano Studies with Dusi Mura and Music Forms with Tudor Ciortea. *Career:* Debut: Recital, Romanian Atheneum, Bucharest, 1946; Professor by the Music Academy, Bucharest; Soloist, Symphony Concertos, Piano Solo Recitals, Piano Duets, Lieder, Chamber Music, Tours abroad; Recordings for Romanian Broadcasting, from Romanian and Universal repertoire; Premieres of recorded and stage performances of Romanian music by George Enescu, Constantin Silvestri, Hilda Jerea, Dan Constantinescu, and others; Premieres of works by Beethoven, Brahms, Schumann and Mendelssohn in Romania; Television films with famous pages of the pianistic literature; Participation in George Enescu International Festival, Bucharest–11th Edition, September 1988; Tour abroad: Germany and Switzerland, with Cornelia Binonzetti (violin), 1991; Also to Austria, 1996; Participation in the Gala, first EPTA Congress in Romania, Constanto, 1992; Interpretation of Nietzsche's works; Lieder, violin, piano and four hands works; Participation as accompanist at several international contests with singers and instrumentalists in France, Switzerland, Poland, Hungary, Russia, Czech Republic and Romania; Participation as soloist with the G. Enescue Philharmonie Orchestra in the opening concert of the International Piano Competition and Festival, Dinu Lipattis, in Bucharest, 1995. *Recordings:* Lieder by Brahms with Marta Kessler; Romanian Lieder with Emilia Petrecu; Romanian Dances for two Pianos by Dinu Lipatti with Hilda Jerea; Beethoven's complete works for piano–four hands; Symphony Concertante for Two Pianos and String Orchestra by Dinu Lipatti, and George Enescu's works for piano–four hands with Corneliu Radulescu; Original four-hands works by Brahms, Schumann, Mendelssohn-Bartholdy and Max Reger (with Corneliu Radulescu). *Contributions:* Musica Revue; Elore, Newspapers. *Honours:* A life dedicate to music award from the M.Jora society of Music Critics, 2000. *Current Management:* Academia de Muzica Bucuresti, Str Stirbei Voda 33, Romania. *Address:* Colentina 37-VI/26, 72.245 Bucharest 10, Romania.

**SZOSTTEK-RADKOVA, Krystina;** Singer (Mezzo-Soprano); b. 14 March 1933, Katowice, Poland. *Education:* Studied at the Katowice Conservatory with Faryaszevska and Lenczevska. *Career:* Debut: Katowice in 1960 as Azucena in Il Trovatore; National Opera Warsaw from 1962 as Eboli, Amneris, Ortrud, Kundry and other roles in the dramatic mezzo repertory; Guest engagements in Vienna, Hamburg, Berlin, Prague, Sofia, Belgrade, Moscow and Leningrad; Sang at Paris Opéra in 1981 as Ulrica in Un Ballo in Maschera, Grand Théâtre, Geneva, in 1983 as Herodias in Salome and appeared at the Théâtre de la Monnaie, Brussels, and the Opéra de Lyon in operas by Verdi and Wagner; Sang Fricka in The Ring at Warsaw in 1988; Concert tours of France and South America. *Recordings:* Many opera albums and works by Penderecki and Tadeusz Baird. *Address:* Teatr Wiekli, Plac Teatrainy, 00-076 Warsaw, Poland.

**SZUCS, Marta;** Singer (Soprano); b. 1964, Hungary. *Education:* Studied violin at first, then singing in Budapest. *Career:* Sang in concert in Hungary and abroad, 1976–78; Guest appearances at Hamburg Staatsoper and Frankfurt from 1979; Member of the Hungarian National Opera from 1981 with debut as Gilda; Further engagements at Vienna Staatsoper, La Traviata's Violetta, 1985–87; Scottish Opera as Gilda in 1984 and Anna in Anna Bolena in 1989, Liège, 1986–87 as Lucia di Lammermoor, and Monte Carlo in 1988 in Cimarosa's Il Pittore Parigino; Sang Anaide in Moïse et Pharaon by Rossini at Budapest in 1992. *Address:* c/o Hungarian State Opera House, Nepoztarsasag utja 22, 1061 Budapest, Hungary.

**SZYMAŃSKI, Paweł;** Composer; b. 28 March 1954, Warsaw, Poland. *Education:* Warsaw Acad. of Music with Tadeusz Baird; Vienna with Roman Haubenstock-Ramati. *Compositions:* String quartet 1975, Partitas I–IV for orchestra 1977–86, Gloria, for female chorus and orchestra 1979, 10 Pieces, for sting trio 1979, La folia, tape 1979, Appendix, for ensemble 1983, Lux Aeterna, for chorus and ensemble 1984, Trope, for piano 1986, Through the Looking Glass I and II for chamber orchestra 1987, 1994, III for harpsichord and string quartet 1995, A Study of Shade, for chamber orchestra 1989, Quasi una Sinfonietta 1990, Miserere, for male voices and ensemble 1993, Piano Concerto 1994, Sonata for piano 1995, Recalling a Serenade, for clarinet and string quartet 1996, Muzyska filmowa 1996. *Address:* c/o ZAiKS, 2 Hipoteczna Street, 00 092 Warsaw, Poland. *Telephone:* (4822) 828 17 05. *Fax:* (4822) 828 13 47. *E-mail:* sekretariat@zaiks.org.pl. *Website:* www.zaiks.org.pl.

# T

**TABACHNIK, Michel;** Swiss/French conductor and composer; b. 10 Nov. 1942, Geneva; m. Sabine Tabachnik 1981; two s. one d. *Education:* studied piano, conducting, writing and composition. *Career:* Asst to Markevitch and Boulez; debut with BBC, London; Nat. Orchestra, Paris; Berlin Philharmonic; has conducted all major orchestras, including NHK Tokyo, Orchestre de Paris, Israel Philharmonic, Berlin Philharmonic, London Philharmonic, St Cecilia, Rome, Suisse Romande, Geneva, Concertgebouw, Amsterdam. *Compositions:* Cosmogonie for orchestra, Haisha for choir and orchestra, Le Pacte des onze for choir and orchestra, L'Arch for soprano and orchestra, Concerto for piano, Quatuor, Les Perseides for orchestra. *Recordings:* Schumann, Grieg, Lalo, Saint-Saëns, Xenakis. *Address:* 1985 Villaz-La Sage, Switzerland (office). *Fax:* (27) 2841409 (office). *E-mail:* office@tabachnik.org (office). *Website:* www .tabachnik.org.

**TABAKOV, Emil;** Conductor and Composer; b. 1947, Bulgaria. *Education:* Bulgarian State Conservatory, degree in conducting, composition and double bass. *Career:* Founded and conducted the Bulgarian State Conservatoire Chamber Orchestra of Sofia, 1977; Director of the Sofia Soloists Chamber Orchestra, 1979–, touring Bulgaria, Europe, Asia, Latin America, Australia and the USA; Principal Conductor of the Sofia Philharmonic Orchestra, 1985 with tours of the USA, Japan, Hong Kong, South America and the United Kingdom; Guest Conductor in Denmark, Sweden, Germany, Poland, Brazil, Romania, Greece and France; Conducted The Queen of Spades at Turin, 1998. *Compositions:* Concerto for Double Bass and Orchestra; Turnovgrad Velki; 1393 Cantata; Concerto for Percussion; Three Symphonies. *Recordings:* Mozart, The Complete Church Sonatas; Works by JS Bach, Handel, Haydn, Mendelssohn, Shostakovich, Britten and Schoenberg (with the Sofia Soloists); Complete Symphonies of Mahler, Rachmaninov and Bruckner (with the Sofia Philharmonic Orchestra). *Honours:* Prizewinner, Nikolai Malko International Competition for Young Conductors, Copenhagen, 1977. *Address:* c/o Teatro Regio di Torino, Piazzo Castello 215, 10134 Turin, Italy.

**TACHEZI, Herbert;** Organist, Harpsichordist and Composer; b. 12 Feb. 1930, Wiener Neustadt, Austria. *Education:* Vienna Music Academy. *Career:* Teacher at Vienna Secondary Schools, 1952–67; Vienna Academy 1958, Professor from 1972; Performances with the Vienna Soloists and Solisti di Zagreb, from 1960; Keyboard soloist with the Concentus Musicus, 1964–; Organist of the Vienna Hofmusikkapelle, 1974; Concert tours throughout Europe and in the USA. *Compositions:* Sacred vocal music, keyboard works, chamber and orchestral music. *Recordings include:* Handel Organ Concertos; Organ works by J. S. and C. P. E Bach. *Honours:* Theodor Körner Prize, Vienna, 1965. *Address:* c/o AKM, Baumanstrasse 10, 1031 Wien, Postfach 259, Austria. *Telephone:* 00431 717 140. *Fax:* 00431 717 14107.

**TACUCHIAN, Ricardo,** BMus, DMA; Brazilian composer and conductor; *Professor, University of Rio de Janeiro;* b. 18 Nov. 1939, Rio de Janeiro; m. Maria de Fátima G. Tacuchian; two s. *Education:* Universidade do Brasil, Universidade Federal do Rio de Janeiro, Univ. of Southern California, USA. *Career:* Prof., UFRJ –1995; Prof., UNIRIO 1995–, Pro-Rector 1999–2000; Visiting Prof., State Univ. of New York at Albany 1998, Universidade Nova de Lisboa 2002–03; Conductor, UNIRIO Chamber Orchestra 2002–04; life mem. Brazilian Music Acad. 1981. *Compositions include:* symphonic pieces, cantatas, chamber music, instrumental soli and tape music. *Recordings:* fifty albums. *Publications:* O Requiem Mozartiano de José Maurício (in Revista Brasileira de Música 19) 1991, Estrutura e Estilo na Obra de Béla Bartók (in Revista Brasileira de Música, v. 21, 1–17) 1994–95, Música pós-moderna no final do século (in Pesquisa e Música No. 2, 25–40) 1995, Fundamentos Teóricos do Sistema-T, Debates: Cadernos do Programa de Pós-graduação (in Música 1, 45–68) 1997; contrib. more than 60 papers to Brazilian music journals. *Honours:* Univ. of Southern Calif. Academic Achievement Award 1990, Hon. Conductor, Santa Maria Symphony Orchestra 1996, grants and scholarships from Fulbright Comm., Rockefeller Foundation, Other Minds, Appolon Stiftung, Capes and CNPQ (both in Brazil); ALMB Brasilia Carlos Gomes Laurel Prize Medal 1996. *Address:* Rua Carlos Góis 327, ap. 702, 22440-040 Rio de Janeiro, RJ, Brazil (home). *Fax:* (21) 25113350 (home). *E-mail:* rtacuchi@cybernet.com.br.

**TADDEI, Giuseppe;** Singer (Baritone); b. 26 June 1916, Genoa, Italy. *Education:* Studied in Rome. *Career:* Debut: Rome in 1936 as The Herald in Lohengrin; Sang in Rome until 1942 as Alberich and Germont and in Dallapiccola's Volo di Notte; Sang at Vienna Staatsoper, 1946–48 as Amonasro, Rigoletto and the Figaros of Mozart and Rossini, Cambridge Theatre in London, 1947, as Scarpia and Rigoletto, Salzburg Festival in 1948 as Mozart's Figaro, and La Scala, 1948–61 as Malatesta, the villains in Les Contes d'Hoffmann and Pizarro; Sang Wagner's Dutchman, Gunther and Wolfram elsewhere in Italy, and Mozart's Papageno and Leporello; US debut at San Francisco in 1957 as Macbeth; Sang at Chicago in 1959 as Barnaba, Teatro Masimo Palermo in 1959 in Beatrice di Tenda by Bellini and Covent Garden, 1960–67, as Macbeth, Rigoletto, Iago and Scarpia; Sang at Bregenz Festival, 1968–71, as Falstaff, Dulcamara and Suplice in La Fille du Régiment, Vienna Staatsoper in 1980 in Il Tabarro, Metropolitan Opera debut in 1985 as Falstaff, Vienna Staatsoper in 1986 as Scarpia, to celebrate 70th birthday, and sang Gianni Schicchi at Torre del Lago in 1987; Appeared at Stuttgart Staatsoper in 1990 as Falstaff. *Recordings:* La Bohème; Ernani;

Un Ballo in Maschera; Guillaume Tell; Rigoletto; Falstaff; Don Giovanni; Il Maestro di Capella; Andrea Chénier; Le nozze di Figaro; Così fan tutte; L'Elisir d'amore; Mosè in Egitto; Linda di Chamounix; Falstaff; Tosca; Macbeth. *Address:* c/o Staatstheater Stuttgart, Oberer Schlossgarten 6, 7000 Stuttgart 1, Germany.

**TADDEI, Ottavio;** Singer (tenor); b. 15 July 1926, Tuscany, Italy. *Education:* Studied in Siena. *Career:* Debut: Sienna, as Rodolfo in La Bohème, 1953; Sang the Duke of Mantua and Edgardo at Rome, 1954; Appearances at Milan, Florence, Modena and San Jose in Costa Rica; Teatro San Carlo, Naples, 1959, as Mateo in Conchita by Zandonai; Sang at Teatro Comunale in Florence from 1960, and made tours of the Netherlands, Turkey and England; Many broadcasts for Italian radio, RAI including The Queen of Spades in 1963; Sang in Hamburg, Nuremberg and Frankfurt from 1966 notably as Pinkerton; Sang in Monteverdi's Poppea at Rome, 1966. *Address:* Teatro Comunale di Firenze, Via Solferino 15, 50123 Florence, Italy.

**TADEO, Giorgio;** Singer (Bass); b. 2 Oct. 1929, Verona, Italy. *Education:* Studied in Parma with Ettore Campogalliani and at the Opera School of La Scala, Milan. *Career:* Debut: Palermo in 1953 as Mephistopheles in Faust; Sang at Turin, Rome, Florence and Trieste as well as La Scala; Sang at Verona Arena in 1955 and 1973–74; Covent Garden debut in 1974 as Don Pasquale; Further engagements at Buenos Aires, Mexico City, Dallas, Chicago, Paris and Salzburg. *Recordings include:* Tosca; Andrea Chénier conducted by Chailly; Leonore by Paer; Antonio in Le nozze di Figaro; Manon Lescaut.

**TAGLIASACCI, Monica;** Singer (Mezzo-soprano); b. 1959, Turin, Italy. *Education:* Studied in Venice. *Career:* Sang in Rossini's Tancredi at Turin and at La Scala in Rossini's Il Viaggio a Reims, I Lombardi and Die Frau ohne Schatten; Suzuki in Butterfly at Ravenna, Verona and Zürich; Guest appearances at the Vienna Staatsoper in L'Italiana in Algeri, at Philadelphia as Dorabella and at Florence as Pantalis in Boito's Mefistofele; Bayerische Staatsoper at Munich, 1991–91; Sang Teresa in La Sonnambula at Rome, 1996. *Address:* c/o Bavarian State Opera, Max Joseph Platz, Pf 100148, 8000 Munich 1, Germany.

**TAGLIAVINI, Franco;** Singer (Tenor); b. 29 Oct. 1934, Novellara, Reggio Emilia, Italy. *Education:* Studied at Liceo Musicale Vercelli and with Zita Fumagalli-Riva. *Career:* Debut: Teatro Nuovo Milan in 1961 as Canio in Pagliacci; Bologna in 1962 as Pinkerton; Sang Edgardo in Lucia di Lammermoor at Tunisia, and at Rome Opera as Dmitri in Boris Godunov, Cavaradossi and Lensky; US debut in 1964 as Ismaele in Nabucco and Calaf in Turandot at San Francisco; Sang Alfredo for Dallas Opera in 1965; La Scala debut in 1965 in Mosè by Rossini; Sang at Royal Opera House, Covent Garden, 1967–76 as Pollione, Cavaradossi, the Duke of Mantua and Macduff, and Chicago Lyric Opera, 1969–73 as Turiddu, Calaf, Pinkerton, Alfredo and Riccardo in Un Ballo in Maschera, I Due Foscari and Maria Stuarda; Appearances at the Metropolitan Opera, NY in Norma, Un Ballo in Maschera, Tosca, Vespri Siciliani and Macbeth; Guest appearances in Munich, Paris, Berlin, Vienna, Parma, Geneva, Zürich, Verona and Brussels; Other roles include Enzo in La Gioconda, Don Carlos, Don José, Des Grieux in Manon Lescaut, Paolo in Francesca da Rimini and Maurizio in Adriana Lecouvreur; Sang Rodolfo in Luisa Miller at Brussels in 1982; Retired in 1989. *Recordings include:* Te Deum by Berlioz; Madame Sans-Gêne by Giordano; Olympie by Spontini; Adriana Lecouvreur and Francesca da Rimini for Italian television.

**TAGLIAVINI, Luigi Ferdinando,** PhD; Italian organist, harpsichordist and musicologist; b. 7 Oct. 1929, Bologna. *Education:* Conservatoires of Bologna and Paris with Marcel Dupré (organ) and Riccardo Nielsen (composition), Univ. of Padua. *Career:* teacher of organ 1952–54, librarian 1953–60, Martini Conservatory, Bologna; Organ Prof., Monteverdi Conservatory, Bolzano 1954–64; founder and co-editor, L'Organo 1960; many concert appearances in Europe and N America, playing the harpsichord and organ; Visiting Prof., Cornell Univ. 1963, SUNY, Buffalo 1969; Dir, Inst. of Musicology at Fribourg Univ. 1965, Prof. 1971–; Ed., Monumenti di Musica Italiana. *Recordings include:* two-organ works (with Marie-Claire Alain). *Publications:* contrib. to Neue Mozart-Ausgabe, 3 vols: Ascanio in Alba, Betulia Liberata, Mitridate Re di Ponto; Articles in L'Organo, Musik in Gesicht und Gegenwart, Ricordi, La Musica, Larousse de la Musique. *Address:* c/o Department of Musicology, University of Fribourg, Miséricorde, Bureau 2020, Av. de l'Europe 20, 1700 Fribourg, Switzerland.

**TAHOURDIN, Peter,** LTCL, MMus; Composer; b. 1928, England. *Education:* Studied composition with Richard Arnell, Trinity College of Music, London, graduated in 1952; Postgraduate studies at Toronto University, Canada, 1966–67. *Career:* Visiting Composer at University of Adelaide, 1965; Staff, Faculty of Music, University of Melbourne, 1973–88; Chairman, Composers Guild of Australia, 1978–79; mem, Australian Performing Right Association; Fellowship of Australian Composers. *Compositions:* Orchestral: Sinfonietta No. 1, 1952, No. 2, 1959, Diversions for orchestra, 1958–59, Symphony No. 1, 1960, No. 2, 1968–69, No. 3, 1979, No. 4, 1987, Fanfares And Variations, A Festival Overture, 1983; Symphony No. 5, 1994; Cello and orchestra: Sinfonia Concertante, 1966; Ensemble: Three Pieces for wind quintet, 1959, Quartet for oboe and strings, 1963, Celebration, 1979, Quartet for strings, 1982, Raga Music 3–Elision, 1988, Trio for clarinet, piano and cello, 2003; Instrumental:

Sonata for clarinet and piano, 1962, Dialogue No. 1, 1971, No. 2, 1976, No. 3, 1978, No. 4, 1984, Raga Music 4 for Two, 1990, Music for solo viola, 2001, Music for solo bassoon, 2002; Piano: Capriccio, 1963; Exposé, 1995; Vocal: Raga Music 1, The Starlight Night, 1985; Choral: Seven Gnomic Verses, 1968, King Oswald's Victory, 1970; Music Theatre: Ern Malley–A Dramatic Testament, 1975–76; Stage: Inside Information, 1 act opera, 1955, Illyria, 1 act ballet, 1965; Heloise and Abelard, chamber opera in two acts, 1991; The Tempest, opera in three acts after Shakespeare, 2000; Works for tape and education works. *Recordings:* CD, Exposé: The Chamber Music of Peter Tahourdin, 1998. *Address:* c/o Australian Music Centre, PO Box N690, Grosvenor Place, New South Wales 1220, Australia.

**TAÏRA, Yoshihisa;** Composer; b. 3 March 1937, Tokyo, Japan. *Education:* studied in Tokyo and with Messiaen at the Paris Conservatoire. *Career:* Lecturer at Ecole Normale de Musique, Paris; music performed by the Ensemble Intercontemporain, in Tokyo and Tanglewood and throughout Europe. *Compositions:* Hierophonie II for 15 instruments, 1970, III for four flutes 1971; Stratus, for flute and harpsichord and 22 strings, 1971; Trans-Appearance for 29 instruments, 1977; Delta for chamber orchestra, 1981; Pénombres I-IV, for various instruments, 1981–91; Tourbillon for six percussions, 1984; Polydère, for orchestra, 1987; Monodrame I for percussion (1984), II for bassoon (1986), III for guitar (1988); Hexaphonie, for string sextet, 1992; Pentamorphe, wind quintet, 1993; Filigrane for flute and piano, 1994; Réminiscence flute concerto, 1998. *Honours:* Lily Boulanger Prize, 1971; Prix Florent Schmitt, 1985; Officier, Ordre des Arts et des Lettres.

**TAKACS, Klara;** Singer (Mezzo-Soprano); b. 24 April 1945, Hungary. *Education:* Studied at the Ferenc Liszt Academy Budapest. *Career:* Has sung at the Hungarian State Opera from 1973 notably as Orpheus, Adalgisa, Goldmark's Königin von Saba, Cenerentola and Cherubino; Guest appearances at Europe's leading opera houses and concert halls; Sang with the Vienna Staatsoper on a tour to Japan in 1986, Teatro Colón Buenos Aires in 1987 as Charlotte and as Eudossia in La Fiamma by Respighi and sang Mozart's Marcellina at the 1992 Salzburg Festival. *Recordings:* Médée by Cherubini with Sylvia Sass; Die Königin von Saba; Boito's Nerone; Hunyádi Lászlo by Erkel; Haydn's Apothecary; Mozart's Requiem; Liszt's Legend of Saint Elizabeth; Missa Solemnis by Beethoven; Mahler Lieder eines Fahrenden Gesellen; Kodály's Háry János; Sacred Music by Haydn. *Honours:* Prizewinner, Erkel International Singing Competition, Budapest, 1975; Liszt Prize Laureate; Grand Prix de L'Academie du Disque, Paris, 3 times. *Address:* c/o Hungarian State Opera, Nepoztarsasag utja 22, 1061 Budapest, Hungary.

**TAKACS, Tamara;** Singer (Mezzo-Soprano); b. 1950, Hungary. *Education:* Studied with Joszef Reti at the Ferenc Liszt Academy in Budapest until 1978. *Career:* Has sung at Hungarian State Opera House from 1978 as Vivaldi's Griselda, Orpheus, Mozart's 2nd Lady and Dorabella, Verdi's Azucena, Maddalena, Ulrica, Emilia, Mrs Quickly and Eboli, Wagner's Waltraute and Magdalena, Charlotte and Carmen; Sang Orzse in Kodály's Háry János in 1988; Appeared as Judit in Duke Bluebeard's Castle at Covent Garden in 1989 on a visit with the Hungarian State Opera; Season 1992 as Public Opinion in Orphée aux Enfers, at Budapest; Concert repertoire includes Purcell's Ode for St Cecilia's Day, Vivaldi's Stabat Mater, Gloria, Juditha Triumphans and Nisi Dominus, Donizetti and Verdi Requiems, Messiah and Rossini's Stabat Mater. *Recordings:* Numerous albums. *Address:* Hungarian State Opera, Nepoztarsasag utja 22, 1061 Budapest, Hungary.

**TAKÁCS-NAGY, Gábor;** Hungarian violinist; b. 17 April 1956, Budapest; s. of László Takács-Nagy and Matild Pataki; m. Lesley (née Townson) de Senger 1991; two d. *Education:* Béla Bartók Conservatory and Franz Liszt Music Acad. of Budapest. *Career:* f. Takács String Quartet 1976, Takács Piano Trio 1996; concert tours from 1980 every year throughout Europe, every other year in Australia, USA, Japan, South America; Leader, Festival Orchestra of Budapest 1993–99; Prof. Conservatoire de Musique, Geneva 1997–, Acad. of Music, Sion 1998–, Conductor, Swiss and Hungarian Orchestras 2002–. *Honours:* first prize Evian competition 1977, Menuhin competition (Portsmouth) 1981, Scholarship award, Banff School of Fine Arts, Liszt Prize 1983. *Address:* Case postale 186, 1245 Collonge-Bellerive, Switzerland. *Telephone:* (22) 752-55-68. *Fax:* (22) 752-55-68. *E-mail:* ldstn@hotmail.com (home).

**TAKAHASHI, Takako;** Japanese pianist; b. Sapporo. *Education:* Toho Gakuen School of Music, Tokyo and Polish Nat. Frederic Chopin Music Acad., studied with Nobuyoshi Kato, Jan Ekier, Koji Shimoda. *Career:* currently based in Poland; has performed at festivals, including Yokohama Int. Piano Concert, Marianske Lazne Int. Chopin Festival, Duszniki Int. Chopin Festival, Nohant Int. Chopin Festival, Rimini Int. Music Festival. *Recordings:* Russian Piano Masterpieces 1994, Voyage de Chopin Vols 1–6. *Honours:* second prize and best contemporary music performance Porto City Int. Music Competition 1989, first prize Radziwill Int. Piano Competition, Antonin, Poland, fifth prize Int. Frederic Chopin Piano Competition, Warsaw 1990, Chopin Soc. Prize for best recital 1996. *Address:* c/o Exton Records, 6-5-8 Akasaka, Minato-ku, Tokyo 107-0052, Japan (office). *E-mail:* takako@japoland.pl (office). *Website:* www.takako-takahashi.com.

**TAKEZAWA, Kyoko;** Concert Violinist; b. 1977, Japan. *Education:* studied with Dorothy DeLay, Juilliard School. *Career:* concerts with Philadelphia Orchestra and Charles Dutoit, New York Philharmonic, BBC Symphony Orchestra under Andrew Davis, Leipzig Gewandhaus orchestra; and London Symphony Orchestra with Tilson Thomas. Many appearances with leading orchestras in Europe, North America and Japan; Mainly Mozart Festival,

New York, 1999; Co-director of Suntory Festival Soloists of Suntory Hall, Tokyo, including collaborations with Isaac Stern (violin), Yo-Yo Ma (cello), Wolfgang Sawallisch (piano) and Josef Suk (violin); Royal Concertgebouw Orchestra, Amsterdam, with the Elgar Violin Concerto, conducted by Leonard Slatkin, 2001; Szymanowski's Violin concerto No.1 at the London Proms, 2002; Chamber music performances in Europe and North America; Juror Indianapolis Violin Compeition 2002. *Recordings include:* Elgar Concerto, with Bavaria Radio Symphony Orchestra under Colin Davis; Bartok's Second Violin Concerto with London Symphony Orchestra under Michael Tilson Thomas; both Mendelssohn Concertos, with Bamberg Symphony Orchestra under Klaus Peter Flor (RCA Victor Red Seal); Barber's Violin Concerto with the Saint Louis Symphony Orchestra under Leonard Slatkin. *Honours:* Gold Medal Second Quadrennial Int. Violin Competition 1986, Winner Indianapolis Violin Competition, Idemitsu Award for Outstanding Musicianship. *Address:* c/o IMG Artists, Lovell House, 616 Chiswick High Rd, London W4 5RX, England.

**TAKOVA, Davina;** Singer (soprano); b. 1968, Sofia, Bulgaria. *Career:* appearances with Sofia Opera from 1992, with guest appearances at La Scala, as the Queen of Night and Lucrezia Borgia, and the Royal Opera as Rimsky's Queen of Shemakha and Violetta 2001; Gilda at Geneva, Rome, Frankfurt and Detroit; Lucia di Lammermoor at Bergamo, Florence, Amsterdam Concertgebouw and Tel-Aviv; Teatro Real, Madrid, in revival of 1660 opera by Juan Hidalgo, Celos aun del aire matan; Violetta in Berlin, Munich, Hamburg and Verona (Arena); season 2001–02 as Pamyre in Rossini's Le Siège de Corinthe at Lyon, Bellini's Elvira at Trieste and Violetta at Geneva. *Honours:* Winner, Francisco Vinas Computation 1993, Toti del Monte Competition 1994.

**TAL, Josef;** Israeli composer; b. 18 Sept. 1910, Pinne, now Poland; m. 1940, one s. *Education:* Hochschule für Musik, Berlin. *Career:* Dir, Jerusalem Acad. of Music, Israel 1948–52, Centre for Electronic Music 1961; Head of Musicology Dept, Incumbent Arthur Rubinstein Cathedra, Hebrew Univ., Jerusalem 1965; mem. Berlin Acad. of Arts, 1975; hon. mem. American Acad. and Inst. of Arts and Letters. *Compositions include:* Eight Operas: Saul At Ein Dor, 1957, Ammon And Tamar, 1961, Ashmedai, 1971, Massada 967, 1973, Die Versuchung, 1976, Der Turm, 1987, Der Garten, 1988, Josef, 1993; 6 Symphonies, 6 Piano Concertos and 5 Concertos for different instruments: Requiem: The Death Of Moses; Chamber Music Works, Vocal Music, Cantatas; Psychodrama Die Hand. *Recordings:* Else, hommage; three Essays for Piano. *Publications:* Autobiography, 1984; Ars Nova in the third Millennium, 2000. *Honours:* three Engel Prizes, Tel-Aviv Municipality; Unesco Fellowship, 1957; Israel State Prize, 1971; Art Prize of the City of Berlin, 1975; Wolf Prize, 1982; Verdienstkreuz 1 Klasse, BDR, 1984; Commandeur de l'Ordre des Artes et des Lettres, France, 1985. *Address:* 3 Guatemala Street, Jerusalem 96704, Israel.

**TALARICO, Rita;** Singer (Soprano); b. 30 May 1941, Rome, Italy. *Education:* Studied in Rome with Gabriella Besanzoni and at the Accademia di Santa Cecilia with Maria Teresa Pediconi. *Career:* Debut: As Eleonora in Il Furioso all'Isola di San Domingo by Donizetti, at the 1967 Spoleto Festival; Has sung at leading Italian opera houses and in Lyon, Rouen, Montreal, New York and Philadelphia; Other roles include Elvira in I Puritani, Amina in La Sonnambula, Leila in Les Pêcheurs de Perles, Mimi, Violetta, Medora in Il Corsaro, Elsa, Agathe, Donna Anna, Susanna, Countess Almaviva, Marguerite, Carolina in Il Matrimonio Segreto and Margherita in Mefistofele; Sang at La Scala in 1985 in Orfeo by Luigi Rossi. *Recordings include:* Il Furioso all'Isolo di San Domingo.

**TALBOT, Michael Owen,** BA, BMus, PhD, ARCM, FBA; writer; *Emeritus Professor of Music, University of Liverpool;* b. 4 Jan. 1943, Luton, Bedfordshire, England; m. Shirley Mashiane 1970; one s. one d. *Education:* Royal Coll. of Music, London, Clare Coll., Cambridge. *Career:* Lecturer 1968–79, Sr Lecturer 1979–83, Reader 1983–86, James and Constance Alsop Prof. of Music 1986–2003, Emeritus Prof. of Music 2003–, Univ. of Liverpool; mem. Royal Musical Asscn, Società Italiana di Musicologia; corresponding Fellow, Ateneo Veneto. *Publications:* Vivaldi 1978, Albinoni: Leben und Werk 1980, Antonio Vivaldi: A Guide to Research 1988, Tomaso Albinoni: The Venetian Composer and his World 1990, Benedetto Vinaccesi: A Musician in Brescia and Venice in the Age of Corelli 1994, The Sacred Vocal Music of Antonio Vivaldi 1995, Venetian Music in the Age of Vivaldi 1999, The Musical Work: Reality or Invention (ed.) 2000, The Finale in Western Instrumental Music 2001, The Business of Music (ed.) 2002, The Chamber Cantatas of Antonio Vivaldi 2006; contrib. to professional journals, including Early Music, Music and Letters, Music Review, Musical Times, Journal of the Royal Musical Association, Soundings, The Consort, Note d'Archivio, Händel Jahrbuch, Informazioni e Studi Vivaldiani, Studi Vivaldiani, Journal of Eighteenth Century Music, Recercare. *Honours:* Cavaliere del Ordine al Merito, Italy 1980, Oldman Prize 1990, Serena Medal 1999. *Address:* c/o School of Music, The University of Liverpool, Liverpool, L69 7WW, England. *Fax:* (151) 794 3141 (office). *E-mail:* mtalbot@liv.ac.uk (office).

**TALI, Anu;** Estonian conductor; *Artistic Director, Nordic Symphony Orchestra;* b. 18 June 1972. *Education:* Tallinn Music High School, Estonian Acad. of Music, Sibelius Acad., Finland, St Petersburg Conservatory, Russia with Ilya Mussin and Leonid Kortshmar. *Career:* conducting debut with the Estonian Nat. Symphony Orchestra; guest conductor with Lahti SO, Oulu SO, Tampere PO and Jyväskylä Chamber Orchestra in Finland, Tonkünstler SO and I Frauen Kammerorchester in Austria, Norrlands Opera and Gävle SO in Sweden, Liepaja SO, Latvia, Bratislava Soloists, Slovakia, Vanemuine Opera, Estonia, Moscow SO, Tokyo PO, Japan Philharmonic, Frankfurt Radio SO, Strasbourg Philharmonic, Tyrol SO, New Jersey SO; co-f., Artistic Dir and Conductor Nordic Symphony Orchestra (fmrly Estonian-Finnish Symphony Orchestra) 1997–, with themed seasons, Musical Capitals of the World 1998–99, Life and Death 1999–2000, Symphony 2000–01, Musica Grande 2001–02, Passion or Passion 2002–03, A la Russe 2003–04. *Recordings:* with Nordic SO: Swan Flight 2001, Action Passion Illusion 2005. *Current Management:* Stafford Law, Candleway, Broad Street, Sutton Valence, Kent ME17 3AT, England. *Website:* www.stafford-law.com. *Address:* Nordic Symphony Orchestra, c/o Estonia Concert Hall, Estonia Avenue 4, Tallinn 10148, Estonia (office).

**TALICH, Jan;** Violist; b. 30 Oct. 1945, Pilzen, Czechoslovakia. *Education:* Studied at the Prague Conservatory. *Career:* Co-founded the Talich Quartet in 1961; After success in competitions at Komeriz and Belgrade gained title of Laureate by the Association of International Music Festivals in Bayreuth; Moved from leader of Talich Quartet to Violist in 1972; Appearances in Europe and North America, Egypt, Iraq, Indonesia and Japan; Annual visits to France from 1976 including the complete Beethoven quartets; Engagements with festivals and music clubs in the United Kingdom; Played at Wigmore Hall in London in 1991 with the quartets of Smetana, Beethoven's Op 74, Brahms A minor and Mozart D minor, and at Bath and Bournemouth Festivals in 1991; Played at Queen Elizabeth Hall in 1991, and Janáček's 2nd Quartet for BBC 2's The Late Show. *Recordings:* Various albums. *Address:* c/o Clarion–Seven Muses, 64 Whitehall Park, London N19 3 TN, England.

**TALLEY-SCHMIDT, Eugene;** Singer (Tenor) and Professor of Voice and Chairman of Voice Department, Houston Baptist University; b. 10 Feb. 1932, Rome, Georgia, USA; m. Jeanette Lombard Pecorello, 22 Nov 1960, 2 s. *Education:* San Diego State College; Indiana University; Opera Arts, Atlanta, GA; Teatro dell'Opera, Rome, Italy; Diploma, Teatro Lirico, Spoleto, Italy; Voice study with Ethel Wilkerson, Rome, GA, John Walsh and Raoul Couyas, San Diego, CA. *Career:* Debut: USA debut as Jenik in The Bartered Bride at San Diego, CA; European debut as Fritz in L'Amico Fritz at Spoleto, Italy; Leading Tenor with Deutsche Oper am Rhein, Düsseldorf, Staatsoper Hamburg, Wuppertal and Munster Operas; Sang over 50 leading tenor roles at opera houses in USA and Europe; Television and radio performances in Europe and America; Performed at international festivals and appeared with Atlanta, Birmingham, Mobile, Miami, Palm Beach, Indianapolis, Rome, and San Diego Symphony Orchestras. *Recordings:* Robert Schumann, Complete Duets for tenor and soprano. *Address:* 3506 Oyster Cove Drive, Missouri City, TX 77459, USA.

**TALMI, Yoav;** Iraeli conductor and composer; *Artistic Director and Conductor, Orchestre Symphonique de Québec, Canada;* b. 28 April 1943, Kibbutz Merhavia; m. Er'ella Talmi, 2 Sept 1964, 1 s., 1 d. *Education:* Diploma, Rubin Academy of Music, Tel-Aviv, 1961–65; Postgraduate Diploma, Juilliard School of Music, New York, 1965–68; Summer study courses with Walter Suskind, Aspen, 1966; Bruno Maderna, Salzburg, 1967; Jean Fournet, Hilversum, 1968; Eric Leinsdorf, Tanglewood, 1969. *Career:* Co-Conductor, Israel Chamber Orchestra, Tel-Aviv, 1970–72; Artistic Director and Conductor, Gelders Symphony Orchestra, Arnhem, 1974–80; Principal Guest Conductor, Munich Philharmonic Orchestra, 1979–80; Music Director and Principal Conductor, Israel Chamber Orchestra, 1984–88; Music Director, New Israeli Opera, 1985–89; Music Director, San Diego Symphony, USA, 1989–96; Artistic Director and Conductor Orchestre Symphonique de Québec, Canada 1999–; Chief Conductor Hamburg Symphony 2000–04; Guest Conducting with the Berlin and Munich Philharmonics, London Symphony and Philharmonia, London and Royal Philharmonics, Amsterdam's Concertgebouw, Israel and New Japan Philharmonics, NHK Symphony, Vienna Symphony, St Petersburg and Oslo Philharmonics, Tonhalle Orchestra, Zürich, Detroit, Pittsburgh, Houston, Dallas and St Louis Symphonies; Los Angeles and New York Chamber Symphonies. *Compositions:* Elegy for strings, timpani and accordion; Dreams for choir a capella; Music for flute and strings; Overture on Mexican Themes, (recorded by Louisville Orchestra); 3 monologues for flute solo, (published); Inauguration Fanfare for brass ensemble. *Recordings:* Bruckner: Symphony No. 9, Oslo Philharmonic; Tchaikovsky Symphony No.1, Quebec Symphony Orchestra; Glière Symphony No.3, San Diego; Rachmaninov's Isle of the Dead; Brahms; Sextet-4 Serious Songs, San Diego Symphony; Tchaikovsky and Schoenberg with the Israel Chamber Orchestra; Bloch, Barber, Puccini and Grieg with the Israel Chamber Orchestra; Berlioz: Overtures; Symphonie Fantastique, Romeo and Juliet, San Diego Symphony; Harold in Italy with San Diego Symphony; Works for Flute and Piano with Erella Talmi. *Honours:* Dr hc (Laval, Québec) 2000)Koussevitzky Memorial Conducting Prize, Tanglewood, USA, 1969; Rupert Foundation Conductors' Competition, London, 1973; Boskovitch Prize for Composition, Israel, 1965; Ahad Ha'am Award LA Centre for Jewish Culture and the American-Israel Cultural Foundation, 1997. *Current Management:* Michal Schmidt Management, 59 East 54th Street, Suite 83, New York, NY 10022, USA. *Telephone:* (212) 421-8500. *Fax:* (212) 421-8583. *Address:* PO Box 1384, Kfar Saba 44113, Israel (home). *E-mail:* talmi@netvision.net.il.

**TALVI, Ilkka Ilari;** violinist and concertmaster; b. 22 Oct. 1948, Kuusankoski, Finland; m. Marjorie Kransberg 1984; three d. *Education:* Sibelius Academy, Helsinki with Arno Granroth, Univ. of Southern California, USA

with Jascha Heifetz, Curtis Institute of Music with Ivan Galamian, with Riccardo Odnoposoff in Vienna and Gabriel Bouillon in Paris. *Career:* debut with orchestra aged 10; recital debut aged 15, Helsinki; Performances as soloist and recitalist in Europe and USA; Lecturer at Sibelius Academy, Finland, 1969–75 and at Pori School of Music, 1970–76; Concertmaster with Malmö Symphony, Sweden, 1976–77; Working in motion picture business at Los Angeles, USA, 1977–85; Principal with Los Angeles Chamber Orchestra, 1979–85; Guest Concertmaster, 1983–85, Concertmaster, 1985–, Seattle Opera; Concertmaster, Waterloo Festival, New Jersey, 1988–. *Recordings* include: Klami Violin Concerto, Albert Im Concordiam. *Honours:* numerous honours and prizes in Finland. *Address:* 3456 10th Avenue W, Seattle, WA 98119, USA.

**TAMAR, Iano;** Singer (Soprano); b. 15 Oct. 1963, Kashbergi, Georgia. *Education:* Studied at the Tbilisi Conservatory. *Career:* Sang at the Tbilisi Opera from 1989; Best known in the title role of Rossini's Semiramide, which she has sung at the Pesaro Festival, under Alberto Zedda and at the Zürich Opera (1992); Has also sung the Rossini Stabat Mater at Dresden, Natasha in War and Peace, Mozart's Countess and Amelia (Ballo in Maschera); Sang Ottavia in Pacini's L'Ultimo giorno di Pompei, Martina Franca Festival, 1996; Lady Macbeth at Naples, 1998 and Fiordiligi at Miami; Sang Fausta in Massenet's Roma at Martina Franca, 1999; Season 2000–01 as Amelia (Ballo in Maschera) at Bregenz, Lady Macbeth for the Deutsche Oper Berlin, Donna Anna at La Coruña and Elvira in Ernani at the Vienna Staatsoper. *Address:* c/o Zürich Opernhaus, Falkenstrasse 1, 8008 Zürich, Switzerland.

**TAMAYO, Arturo;** Conductor; b. 3 Aug. 1946, Madrid, Spain. *Education:* Studied at the Royal Conservatoire Madrid, harmony with A Barrera, and composition with Francisco Cales and Gerardo Gombau. *Career:* Gave concerts in Spain from 1967; Studied further with Pierre Boulez at Basle and at the Musikhochschule Fribourg-in-Brisgau; Studied conducting with Franc Travis, 1971–76, and composition with Wolfgang Fortner and Klaus Huber; Assisted Huber at Fribourg from 1974 and directed concerts of contemporary music; Frequent appearances at the Deutsche Oper Berlin from 1982 notably with the 1983 premiere of Wolfgang Rihm's ballet, Tutuguri; Conducted the premiere of Kelterborn's Ophelia at the 1984 Schwetzingen Festival, and Maurice Ohana's La Celestine at the Paris Opéra in 1988; Théâtre des Champs Elysées in Paris, 1990 with the local premiere of La Noche Triste by Jean Prodomidès; Graz 1996, Busoni's Doktor Faust. *Address:* c/o Théâtre des Champs Elysées, 15 Avenue Montaigne, 75012 Paris, France.

**TAMBERG, Eino;** Estonian composer; *Head of the Composition Department, Estonian Academy of Music;* b. 27 May 1930, Tallinn. *Education:* Tallinn Conservatory with Eugen Kapp. *Career:* recording engineer, Estonian Radio 1953–59, later Music Supervisor; Artistic Consultant, Estonian Composers' Union 1960–69; Teacher, Estonian Conservatory 1967–78; Head of Composition Dept, Estonian Acad. of Music 1978–87, 1989–, Prof. 1983–; mem. Estonian Composers' Union, Estonian Theatre Union. *Compositions include:* opera: The Iron House 1965, Cyrano de Bergerac 1974, The Flight 1983, Soaring 1983, The Beings 1992, We'd Like to Become Human 2001 (all premiered in Tallinn); ballet: Ballet-Symphony (Schwerin) 1959, The Boy and the Butterfly (Tallinn) 1963, Joanna Tentata (Tallinn) 1971, Through the Looking Glass 2001; oratorio: Moonlight Oratorio 1962, Amores 1981; symphonic work: Concerto Grosso 1956, Symphonic Dances 1957, Toccata 1967, two Concerti for trumpet and orchestra 1972, 1997, four Symphonies 1978, 1986, 1989, 1998, Concerto for violin and orchestra 1981, Concerto for mezzo-soprano and orchestra 1986, Alto Saxophone Concerto 1987, Concerto in D Fixe for clarinet 1996, Second Trumpet Concerto 1997, Concerto for bassoon and orchestra 2000, Concerto for cello and orchestra 2001, Concerto for flute and orchestra 2003; chamber music: Five Romances on poems of Sandor Petöfi 1955, String Quartet 1958, two Quintets for woodwind 1975, 1984, Three Simple Songs on poems of Viivi Luik 1986, Waiting for flute, clarinet, percussion, violin and cello 1991, Music for Five for brass quintet 1992, A Play for Five in Four Acts for saxophone quartet and percussion 1994, Desiderium concordiae for flute, clarinet, percussion, piano and cello 1997, Piano Quartet for flute, clarinet, cello and piano 2000; vocal: Fanfares of Victory (cantata) 1975, songs and piano pieces. *Honours:* World Youth and Student Festival Gold Medal, Moscow 1957, Prize of the Soviet Estonia 1967, 1987, People's Artist of the Estonian SSR 1975, Annual Estonian Music Award 1979, 1984, Estonian Culture Award 1999, Annual Award of the CEE 2002;elected Resident Composer ENSO 1997–98; 4th Class Order, Nat. Coat of Arms 1997. *Address:* 10145 Tallinn, Lauteri 7-23, Estonia (home). *Telephone:* 6455342 (home). *E-mail:* emic@emic.ee (home).

**TAMBOSI, Olivier;** Opera Director; b. 7 July 1963, Paris, France. *Education:* Vienna Music Academy. *Career:* Formed Neue Oper Wien, 1988 and was Artistic Director until 1993; Productions included Medea, Die Zauberflöte, Macbeth, Pimpinone by Telemann, Don Pasquale and Lulu; Artistic Director at Klagenfurt Opera, 1993–96 with Manon Lescaut, Death in Venice, Così fan tutte, Cav and Pag, Les Contes d'Hoffmann and Rigoletto; Productions from 1996 include Der Rosenkavalier and Lulu at Mannheim; Macbeth at Strasbourg and Bohème and Jenůfa at Hamburg; Season 1999–2000 with Pelléas et Mélisande at Linz, Falstaff for the Lyric Opera of Chicago; Tristan at Berne; Katya Kabanova in Hamburg; Mozart's Die Entführung in Klagenfurt; Season 2000–01 with Jenůfa at Covent Garden and Saariaho's L'Amour de Loin at Berne; Engaged for Lulu at Klagenfurt (2002), Un Ballo in Maschera at Chicago (2003), Jenůfa, Met Opera, New York, (2003); Luisa Miller at Covent Garden (2003) and Falstaff at Salzburg

(2004). *Address:* c/o IMG Artists, Lovell House, 616 Chiswick High Road, London W4 5RX, England.

**TAMULENAS, Eva;** Singer (Mezzo-soprano); b. 1943, Narva, Estonia. *Education:* Studied in Milwaukee and Vienna. *Career:* Sang at first with the Royal Opera Copenhagen and from 1977 at Gelsenkirchen; Roles have included Hansel, Rosina, Orlofsky, Olga, Maddalena and the title role in Miss Julie by Antonio Bibalo; Einem's Der Besuch der alten Dame (1991); Sang Third Lady in Die Zauberflöte at Gelsenkirchen, 2000; Many concert engagements. *Address:* Gelsenkirchen Opera, Musiktheater im Revier, Kennedyplatz, Pf 101857, W-4650 Gelsenkirchen, Germany.

**TAMULIONIS, Jonas;** Composer; b. 10 Jan. 1949, Alytus, Lithuania; Divorced, 2 s. *Education:* Graduated from the Faculty of Music of the Vilnius Pedagogical Institute, 1970; Composition with Professor Eduardos Balsys at the Lithuanian State Conservatoire, 1976. *Compositions include:* For string quartet: Two Quartets, 1973, 1982; Diary, 1978; For string orchestras: Concertino, 1974; Toccata Diavolesca, 1988; Pastoral Suite, 1990; Three symphonies, 1976, 1978, 1986; For wind orchestra: Festive Overture, 1978; Spanish Rhapsody, 1981; Sonatas: for two guitars, 1978, two pianos, 1979, two birbynes (Lithuanian folk wind instrument), 1988; For chamber orchestra: Epitaph, 1981; Cantatas: I Sing of Lithuania, 1981; Children's Earth (verse by J Marcinkevicius), 1988; To My Motherland (verse by J Mikstas), 1989; Sinfonia Rustica, 1989; Oratorio: Six Dedications To The Town (text by various Lithunanian poets), 1985; Reminiscence for two violins and two accordions, 1989; Recollection for glass instruments, 1992; Trio for flute, viola, guitar and piano, 1993; Vocal music includes: Seven Love Elegies for soprano and chamber ensemble, 1982; Summer Psalms for soprano and piano (verse by J Marcinkevicius), 1985; Three Prayers for baritone and piano, (verse by B Brazdzionis), 1989; For Choir: Single Words, 1980; The Tears of Ablinga, 1984; Tres retratos con sombra (verse by F García Lorca), 1992; Los juegos, 1997; For accordion: Sonatina, 1978; Metamorphoses, 1984; Polyphonic Pieces, 1990; Ten Etudes, 1995; For guitar: Eleven preludes, 1982; Suite of Intervals, 1987. *Recordings:* CD: On The Coast, 1990; Numerations, Patterers, 1992; Ex Anima, 1994; Home Psalames, 1995; The Sea, 1996. *Honours:* 2nd Prize, Symphony No. 1, Moscow, Russia, 1967; 1st prize, Canciones de la Tierra, Spain, 1995; 1st Prize, Oda al Atlántico, Spain, 1997; 1st Prize, Los juegos, Spain, 1997. *Address:* Tauro 8-11, 2001 Vilnius, Lithuania.

**TAN, Dun,** MA; Chinese composer; b. 18 Aug. 1957, Si Mao, Hunan Province; s. of Tan Xiang Qiu and Fang Qun Ying; m. Jane Huang 1994; one s. *Education:* Cen. Conservatory of Music, Beijing and Columbia Univ., USA. *Career:* violist, Beijing Opera Orchestra 1976–77; Vice-Pres. Cen. Conservatory of Music 1978–; works performed by major orchestras in China and at festivals world-wide; four recordings of his major orchestral works, oriental instrumental music, chamber music and electronic music issued by China Nat. Recording Co.; works also include 14 film scores for US and Chinese films, six modern ballet scores, music for several stage plays; orchestral piece commissioned by Inst. for Devt of Intercultural Relations Through the Arts, USA for Beijing Int. Music Festival 1988; Artistic Dir Fire Crossing Water Festival Barbican Centre, London 2000. *Film scores:* Aktion K 1994, Nanjing 1937 1995, Fallen 1997, In the Name of the Emperor 1998, Wo hu cang long (Crouching Tiger Hidden Dragon) (Grammy Award 2001, Acad. Award 2001, British Acad. Film Award 2001, Classical BRIT Contemporary Music Award 2001) 2000, Ying xiong (Hero) 2002. *Compositions:* orchestral works: Li Sao (symphony) 1979, Five Pieces in Human Accent for piano 1980, Feng Ya Song for string quartet 1982, Fu for two sopranos, bass and ensemble 1982, Piano Concerto 1983, Symphony in two movements 1985, On Taoism for orchestra 1985, Traces for piano 1989, Eight Colours for string quartet 1989, Silk Road for soprano and percussion 1989, Orchestral Theatre I: Xun 1990, Soundshape 1990, Silent Earth 1991, Jo-Ha-Kyu 1992, Death and Fire: Dialogue with Paul Klee 1992, Orchestral Theatre II: Re 1992, CAGE for piano 1993, Circle for four trios, conductor and audience 1993, The Pink 1993, Autumn Winds for instruments and conductor ad lib 1993, Memorial Nineteen for voice, piano and double paper 1993, Orchestral Theatre III: Red 1993, Yi concerto for cello 1994, Heaven, Earth, Mankind symphony for the 'Bian Zhong' bronze bells (composed in celebration of the Hong Kong handover) 1997, 2000 Today: A World Symphony for the Millennium: A Musical Odyssey for the Ages 1999, Water Passion after St Matthew 2000, The Map concerto for cello, video and orchestra 2003; opera: Out of Beijing 1987, Nine Songs 1989, Marco Polo 1994, Peony Pavilion 1998, Tea 2002. *Honours:* second place Weber Int. Chamber Music Composition Competition, Dresden 1983, Suntory Prize 1992, Grawemeyer Award 1998, Musical America Composer of the Year 2003. *Address:* 367 W 19th Street, Suite A, New York, NY 10011, USA (office). *Telephone:* (212) 627-0410 (office). *Fax:* (917) 606-0247 (office). *E-mail:* tan_dun@hotmail.com (office). *Website:* www.tandun.com (office).

**TAN, Lihua;** Conductor; b. 22 Oct. 1955, Jiangsu, China; m. Lumin Qiao, October 1980, 1 d. *Education:* Graduated, Shanghai Conservatory of Music. *Career:* debut, conducting Bruch's Violin Concerto and Dvořák Symphony No. 9, Wuhan Orchestra, Wuhan, China; Conductor, Chinese Ballet, 1990–96; Conductor, China Central Philharmonic Symphony Orchestra, 1993–; Music Director, Principal Conductor, Beijing Symphony Orchestra; Chinese premieres include: Pines of Rome, Dvořák Symphony No. 7, Prokofiev Symphony No. 5; Guest conducting appearances include: New York Youth Symphony, Seattle Federal Way Symphony, Russian National Symphony; Venues include New York City's Avery Fisher Hall, Lincoln Center; Moscow's Tchaikovsky Conservatory of Music. *Recordings:* Beethoven Symphony No. 5; Brahms

Symphony No. 4, with Beijing Symphony Orchestra; Dvořák Symphony Nos 8 and 9; Haydn Symphony No. 94; Mendelssohn, Saint-Saëns and Tchaikovsky Violin Concertos, China Central Philharmonic Symphony Orchestra. *Publications:* Article, Conducting Technique and Instrumental Performance, 1988. *Current Management:* Bary Plews, Australia. *Address:* Beijing Symphony Orchestra, No. A-1 Eight Poplar, Shuang Jing, Chao-Yang District, Beijing 100022, People's Republic of China.

**TAN, Melvyn;** British concert pianist and early music specialist; b. 13 Oct. 1956, Singapore; s. of Tan Keng Hian and Wong Sou Yuen. *Education:* Anglo-Chinese School, Yehudi Menuhin School, Royal Coll. of Music. *Career:* performs on historical keyboard instruments, which he has introduced to audiences around the world; has now extended repertory to include modern piano; performs regularly in music festivals in USA, Japan, Far East, Australia and throughout Europe. *Recordings include:* Debussy Préludes 2005. *Current Management:* Valerie Barber Management, Suite 305, Mappin House, 4 Winsley Street, London, W1N 7AR, England. *Telephone:* (20) 7436-1115. *Fax:* (20) 7436-5090.

**TANAKA, Karen,** BA; Japanese composer; b. 7 April 1961, Tokyo. *Education:* Tōhō Gakuen School of Music, Tokyo, studied with Berio in Florence, IRCAM composition technology course. *Career:* Visiting Assoc. Prof., Univ. of California at Santa Barbara. *Compositions include:* Anamorphose (piano concerto) 1986, Crystalline I, II and III 1988, 1995–96, 2000, Hommage en cristal 1991, Initium 1993, Metallic Crystal 1994–95, Echo Canyon 1995, Metal Strings 1996, The Song of Songs 1997, Frozen Horizon 1998, Guardian Angel 2000. *Honours:* Gaudeamus Prize 1987. *Current Management:* G. Schirmer Promotion Department, 257 Park Avenue S, 20th Floor, New York, NY 10010, USA. *Website:* www.schirmer.com (office).

**TANG, Muhai;** Conductor; b. 10 July 1949, Shanghai, China. *Education:* Music Conservatory at Shanghai; Music Hochschule, Munich, Germany; Masterclass Diploma. *Career:* Conducted the Berlin Philharmonic, London Philharmonic, Orchestre de Paris, San Francisco Symphony, Montreal Symphony, Santa Cecilia Orchestra, Rome, Tonhalle Orchestra Zürich, Helsinki Philharmonic, Hallé Orchestra, Scottish National Symphony Orchestra, National Symphony Orchestra of Spain, Mozarteum Orchestra Salzburg, Polish Chamber Orchestra, Oper Orchestra Hamburg, Frankfurt, Munich, Bonn, Monte Carlo, Radio Symphony Orchestra Munich, Berlin, Hamburg, and Cologne; Chief Conductor of Peking Central Philharmonic and Gulbenkian Orchestra of Lisbon; Classic Aid Television Gala Concert, UN Geneva, 1986. *Current Management:* Askonas Holt Ltd, Lonsdale Chambers, 27 Chancery Lane, London, WC2A 1PF, England. *Telephone:* (20) 7400-1700. *Fax:* (20) 7400-1799. *E-mail:* info@askonasholt.co.uk. *Website:* www.askonasholt.co.uk. *Address:* c/o Keils, Treibjagdweg 31, 1 Berlin 37, Germany.

**TANGGAARD, Svend Erik;** Composer and Writer; b. 25 Jan. 1942, Copenhagen, Denmark; m. Margit Bendtsen, 29 Feb 1980, 2 d. *Education:* Piano and Composition studies with Helge Bonnen, Copenhagen, 1962–67; Studies in Munich, 1968–70. *Career:* Debut: Royal Academy of Fine Arts, 1962; Performances of own works by Danish Radio Symphony Orchestra, Aalborg Symphony Orchestra, Southern Jutland Symphony Orchestra, Odense Symphony Orchestra and Moritz Fromberg Quartet; Several transmissions on Danish Radio, NDR and Swedish Radio; Performances at the Art Association, Gronningen and other art galleries. *Compositions:* 5 Symphonies; Concerto for orchestra; 12 String Quartets; 3 Fuga String Quartets op 150; Piano, Violin (2), Viola, Cello, Oboe, Flute, Trumpet and Clarinet Concertos; Overtures Nos 1 and 2, for chamber orchestra; Concertos Nos 1, 2 and 3, for 14 wind instruments, 2 double basses and percussion, and Concerto, for violin, viola and orchestra; Vox Humana, for orchestra, soprano, bass and tape recorder; The Bells, for orchestra and reader; Songs, 3 Wind Quintets; 3 Solo Cello Suites; 2 Solo Violin Sonatas, Piano Sonata, Day and Night; 3 Italian Prayers, for mezzo-soprano and viola; 3 Cantatas, for tenor and wind quintet; 25 Selected Songs From Omar Khayyam's Rubaiyat, for basso and 3 instruments; Songs for small ensembles; Memoria Futuris, Nos II and III, for string orchestra, 1997, Nos IV and V, for wind quintet, 1998; Opus 200, String Quartet No. 16, 1999. *Address:* Nikolaj Plads 7, 4, 1067 Copenhagen K, Denmark.

**TANGUY, Eric;** French composer; b. 27 Jan. 1968, Caen. *Education:* Caen Conservatoire, Darmstadt Ferienkurse, Conservatoire Nat. Supérieur de Musique, Paris. *Career:* composer-in-residence, Champagne-Ardenne 1995, Lille 1996, Orchestre de Bretagne 2001–03. *Compositions include:* Avènement de la ligne 1988, Alloys 1988, Océan N.Y. Fantaisie 1989, Azur B 1990, Azur C 1990, Towards 1991, Wadi 1992, Solo 1993, Concerto pour violon 1990, Towards 1991, Concerto pour flûte et 16 instruments 1992, Célébration de Marie-Madeleine 1995, Le Jardin des délices 1996, Éclipse 1999, Concerto for cello and orchestra No. 2 2000, Chronos (opera) 2002, Ouverture 2002. *Honours:* Darmstadt Stipendienpreis 1988, Villa Medici extra-mural prize 1989, Paris Conservatoire first prize for composition 1991, Darmstadt Kranichstein Musikpreis 1992, Institut de France André Caplet Prize 1995, SACEM Hervé Dugardin Prize 1997. *Address:* c/o Patricia Alia, Editions Salabert, 5 rue du Helder, 75002 Paris, France (office).

**TANGUY, Jean-Michel;** Flautist; b. 15 Nov. 1944, France. *Education:* French Baccalaureate, Lycee Français, Berlin; Jean-Pierre Rampal, Nice, Paris; Aurèle Nicolet, Berlin; Freiburg, Breisgau Staatliche Hochschule für Musik. *Career:* Debut: Orchestra der Beethovenhalle, Bonn, Germany;

Performances with Bonn Orchestra, Rotterdam Philharmonic, Orchestre National de Belgique, Brussels; Chargé de Cours Conservatoire Royal de Bruxelles; Professor of Flute, Hochschule für Musik, Heidelberg-Mannheim, 1992–; mem, Jury Member, International Flute Competition, Jean-Pierre Rampal, 1994, 1998; Guest Member, National Flute Convention, Chicago, 1986, Atlanta, 1999. *Recordings:* Telemann Flute Concertos; Heidelberger Chamber Orchestra, JS Bach Trios, CPE Bach–Sonatas; JS Bach–Flute Sonatas; Sommermusik with Belgian Windquintett. *Honours:* Prize, International Music Competition, Geneva, 1973; Scholarship, DAAD; Masterclasses: Belgium, France, Italy, Germany, Austria, Korea. *Address:* 17 rue Guimard, 1040 Brussels, Belgium.

**TANYEL, Seta;** Concert Pianist; b. 1950, Istanbul. *Education:* Studied at Vienna Hochschule for Musik with Dieter Weber and with Louis Kentner in London. *Career:* Orchestral and recital debuts in New York, Philadelphia, Detroit and London in 1978; Extensive touring in Europe, the Middle East, Russia and the USA performing with such orchestras as the Vienna Symphony, Israel Philharmonic, Stuttgart Philharmonic, the Philharmonia and London Symphony Orchestra; Taught at Yehudi Menuhin School in London from 1986–1989; A pianist with an international reputation in both standard and lesser-known Romantic piano repertoire, recent performing projects include the long overdue revival in the piano music of Xaver Scharwenka. *Recordings include:* Shostakovich, Khachaturian, Poulenc and Bax 2-piano works (Chandos); Brahms and Beethoven solo recital; Grieg and Schumann Piano Concertos with London Symphony Orchestra/Fruhbeck de Burgos; Brahms Piano Concerto No. 1 with the Philharmonia/Vaclav Neumann; Scharwenka Piano Concerto No. 1 and Chopin Piano Concerto No. 1 with the Philharmonia/Rizzi; Chopin, Sharwenka and Moszkowski solo recitals; Scharwenka chamber works with piano (Complete) (Collins Classics). *Honours:* Prizewinner at International Beethoven Competition in Vienna in 1973, at first Arthur Rubinstein Piano Master Competition in Israel in 1974 and at Queen Elisabeth of Belgium Competition in 1975. *Address:* c/o Philharmonia Orchestra (Artist Contracts), 1st Floor, 125 High Holborn, London, WC1V 6QA, England.

**TAPPY, Eric;** Singer (Tenor); b. 19 May 1931, Lausanne, Switzerland. *Education:* Studied with Fernando Carpi in Geneva, Ernst Reichert in Salzburg and Eva Liebenberg in Hilversum. *Career:* Debut: Strasbourg in 1959 as the Evangelist in Bach's St Matthew Passion; Concert performances of Milhaud's Les Malheurs d'Orphée and Martin's Le Mystère de la Nativité and Monsieur de Pourceaugnac; Sang in the premiere of Klaus Huber's Soliloquia in 1962; Stage debut at Opéra-Comique Paris in 1964 as Rameau's Zoroastre; Sang at Herrenhausen in 1966 as Monteverdi's Orfeo, Geneva Opera in 1966 in the premiere of Milhaud's La Mère Coupable, and Hanover in 1967 in L'Incoronazione di Poppea; Covent Garden debut in 1974 in the title role of La Clemenza di Tito; US debut in 1974 as Don Ottavio at San Francisco returning in Poppea and as Idomeneo, 1977–78; Sang at Rome Opera in 1980 as Titus; Appearances in Chicago, Drottningholm, Aix-en-Provence, Salzburg as Tamino, Amsterdam, Lyon, Brussels and Lisbon; Other roles include Schoenberg's Aron, Pelléas, Lysander in A Midsummer Night's Dream, Don Ramiro, Lensky and Stravinsky's Oedipus; Concert repertoire includes music by Handel, Haydn, Campra, Carissimi, Vivaldi, Bach, Berlioz and Schütz; Retired in 1982. *Recordings include:* Monteverdi's Orfeo and Poppea; Zoroastre; Pelléas et Mélisande; Die Jahreszeiten by Haydn; Die Zauberflöte; La Clemenza di Tito.

**TARASCHENKO, Vitalij;** Singer (Tenor); b. 1953, Kyrgyzstan, USSR. *Career:* Sang in opera at Moscow and Warsaw; Florence, 1990, as Prince Vsevolod in Rimsky's Kitezh; Dimitri in Boris Godunov at Bologna; Bregenz Festival, 1993, as Andrei in Mazeppa and Ismaele in Nabucco; Season 1993–94 as Calaf at Hamburg and Amsterdam, Turiddu at the Vienna Staatsoper and Hermann in The Queen of Spades at the Paris Opéra Bastille; Venice and Zürich, 1995, as Andrei and Lensky in Eugene Onegin; Member of the Bolshoi Opera, Moscow, from 1992; Other roles include Vladimir in Prince Igor, Gabriele Adorno in Simon Boccanegra, and Cavoradossi; Season 1997–98 as Prince Guidon in Rimsky's Tsar Saltan, at Florence, and Paolo in Rachmaninov's Francesca da Rimini, at St Petersburg; Sang Dimitri in Boris Godunov with the Bolshoi Company in London, 1999; Season 1999–2000 as Ugo in Mascagni's Parisina, at Montpellier, and Tchaikovsky's Herman for WNO. *Address:* c/o Bolshoi Opera, Bolshoi Theatre, 103009 Moscow, Russia.

**TARASSOVA, Marianna;** Singer (Mezzo-Soprano); b. 1962, St Petersburg, Russia. *Education:* St Petersburg Conservatoire; Masterclasses at Aldeburgh, 1992. *Career:* Appearances with the Kirov Opera from 1993, as Carmen, Amneris, Cherubino, Olga in Eugene Onegin, Purcell's Dido, Konchakovna in Prince Igor and Blanche in The Gambler by Prokofiev; Other roles include Lyubava in Sadko and Young Boy in The Invisible City of Kitezh, both by Rimsky-Korsakov, Polina in The Queen of Spades, Marfa (Khovanshchina) and Clara in Prokofiev's Betrothal in a Monastery; Concert repertory includes Mahler Symphony no. 3, the Verdi Requiem and songs by Shostakovich for mezzo and orchestra; Recitals and concerts in the USA, and world-wide tours with the Kirov Opera, including summer season at the Royal Opera, Covent Garden, 2000. *Address:* c/o Kirov Opera, Mariinsky Theatre, 1 Theatre Square, St Petersburg, Russia.

**TARBUK, Mladen;** Composer, Conductor and Producer; b. 19 July 1962, Sarajevo; m. Jasna Cizmek, 29 Jan 1994, 2 s. *Education:* Diploma, Conducting, Music Academy, Zagreb, 1987; Diploma, Conducting, Hochschule für Musik und darstellende Kunst, Graz, 1988; Postgraduate Study, Conducting, Hochschule für Musik und darstellende Kunst, Vienna, 1991–92; Diploma, Composition, Music Academy, Zagreb, 1994. *Career:* Das Rheingold, Elektra and many other operas and ballets, Croatian National Opera, Zagreb, 1990–91; Premiere, Udo Zimmermann's White Rose, Slovenian National Theatre, Maribor, 1991; World Premiere, Schwertsik's Café Museum, Deutschlandsberg, 1993; Concert of composers from Alpe-Adria region, Moscow Autumn festival, 1996; Concert of Croatian music composers, Symphonic Orchestra of Croatian Radio and Television, broadcast by European Broadcasting Union, 1998; World Premiere, Villardi's Judas, Brussels, 1999; World Premiere, Medida del tiempo, conducted by Friedrich Cerha, 1991; Performance of Zildjian Concerto, World Music Days, Manchester, 1998; Chief Conductor, Symphonic Wind Orchestra, Croatian Military Forces, 1992–99; Principal Conductor, Symphonic Orchestra of Croatian Radio and Television, 1999; Lecturer, 1989, Senior Lecturer, 1997, Assistant Professor of Music Theory, 1997, Zagreb Music Academy. *Compositions include:* A tre for string trio, 1990; Discusiones amorosas, for choir, 1993; Zildjian Concerto, for percussion and orchestra, 1995. *Recordings:* Zildjian Concerto, Sticks&Strings&Winds, recorded by Honey & Rock; Croatian Masses. *Address:* Katicev Prilaz 7, 10010 Zagreb, Croatia.

**TARLING, Judith,** ARAM; British violinist and violist; b. 1947, England. *Career:* Leader of the Parley of Instruments; frequent tours of the UK and abroad, including the British Early Music Network; performances in Spain, France, Germany, Sweden, Netherlands, Poland, Czechoslovakia, USA and Colombia; US debut in New York 1988; many concerts with first modern performances of early music in new edns by Peter Holman; numerous broadcasts on BBC Radio 3 and elsewhere; English Eighteenth-Century Music, such as Dr Arne at Vauxhall Gardens, William Boyce's Solomon, and John Stanley Six Concertos in seven parts, Op 2, these works performed with Crispian Steele-Perkins on trumpet and Emma Kirkby as soprano, among others; principal viola, Brandenburg Consort, with recordings including Bach Brandenburg Concertos and Suites; Handel arias, flute concertos by Quantz and C. P. E. Bach; principal viola, Hanover Band 1981–2002, with numerous recordings including complete symphonies of Beethoven, Schubert and Haydn; repertoire includes Renaissance Violin Consort Music, such as Music by Michael Praetorius, Peter Philips, music for Charles I by Orlando Gibbons and Thomas Lupo, Baroque Consort Music by Monteverdi and Matthew Locke anthems, motets and ceremonial music, Purcell Ayres for Theatre, Georg Muffat's Armonico Tributo sonatas of 1682, Heinrich Biber's Sonate tam Aris, Quam Aulis Servientes of 1676, Vivaldi sonatas and concertos for lute and mandolin, concertos for recorders, and J. S. Bach's Hunt Cantata, No. 208, Italian and German sacred music with Robin Blaze. *Publications:* Baroque String Playing for ingenious learners 2000, The Weapons of Rhetoric: A Guide for Musicians and Audiences 2004. *Address:* 3 North Street, Punnetts Town, Heathfield, East Sussex, England. *E-mail:* judytarling@btinternet.com.

**TARR, Edward Hankins,** DPhil; trumpeter and musicologist; b. 15 June 1936, Norwich, CT, USA. *Education:* Univ. of Hamburg, studied trumpet with Roger Voisin in Boston, Adolph Herseth in Chicago, musicology with Leo Schrade in Basle. *Career:* founder, Edward Tarr Brass Ensemble 1969, giving many performances of Renaissance, Baroque and contemporary music in Europe and the USA; early repertoire includes the trumpet works of Torelli; modern repertoire includes works by Kagel, Stockhausen and Krol; has collaborated on the reconstruction of early instruments with the German firm, Meinl and Lauber and the Swiss firm, Adolf Egger and Son; trumpet teacher, Rheinische Musikschule Cologne 1968–70; cornett and natural trumpet teacher, Schola Cantorum Basiliensis 1972–2001; trumpet teacher, Basle Conservatory 1974–2001; Baroque trumpet teacher, Musikhochschule Karlsruhe from 2001, Prof. 2003–; Baroque trumpet teacher, Musikhochschule Lucerne 2002–; brass ensemble teacher, Musikhochschule Frankfurt am Main 2003–; Dir of the Trumpet Museum, Bad Säckingen, Germany 1985–2003. *Publications include:* Die Trompete 1977; contrib. over 70 articles to The New Grove 1980 and 2000 edns; contrib. to performing edns of Baroque, Classical and Romantic Music. *Honours:* Hon. DrMus (Oberlin Coll.) 2003. *Address:* c/o Trumpet Museum, PO Box 1143, 79702 Bad Säckingen, Germany.

**TARRÉS, Enriqueta;** Singer (Soprano); b. 18 March 1934, Barcelona, Spain. *Education:* Studied at the Barcelona Conservatory with Concepcion Callao de Sanchez Parra. *Career:* Debut: Valencia in 1956 as the Trovatore Leonora; Sang in Spain notably at the Teatro Liceo, Barcelona, Basle and Wuppertal Opera, 1960–64; Glyndebourne in 1962 and 1964 as Ariadne and Elettra in Idomeneo, and Hamburg Staatsoper from 1964, visiting Sadler's Wells in 1966 as the Empress in the first British performance of Die Frau ohne Schatten by Strauss; Engaged with Düsseldorf, Cologne and Stuttgart Operas; Sang at Metropolitan Opera in 1973 as Mimi, Lausanne in 1983 as the Marschallin, Verona in 1984 as Carmen, and sang the Mother in Luis de Pablo's El Viajero Indiscreto at the Teatro de la Zarzuela at Madrid in 1990; Frequent concert appearances. *Recordings:* Falla's Atlantida; Orff's Trionfi; Les Huguenots; Idomeneo. *Address:* c/o Arena di Verona, Piazza Brà 28, 37121 Verona, Italy.

**TARUSKIN, Richard Filler,** PhD; American musicologist, critic and writer; *Professor, University of California at Berkeley;* b. 2 April 1945, New York, NY. *Education:* Columbia Univ. *Career:* Asst Prof. 1975–81, Assoc. Prof. of Music 1981–87, Columbia Univ.; Visiting Prof., Univ. of Pennsylvania 1985; Assoc. Prof. 1986–89, Prof. 1989–, Univ. of California at Berkeley; Hanes-Willis Visiting Prof., Univ. of North Carolina at Chapel Hill 1987; music critic for Opus, New York Times; Fulbright-Hays Traveling Fellowship 1971–72;

Guggenheim Fellowship 1987; mem. American Musicological Soc. *Publications include:* Opera and Drama in Russia 1981, Busnoi: The Latin-Texted Works (ed., two vols) 1990, Musorgsky: Eight Essays and an Epilogue 1993, Stravinsky and the Russian Traditions: A Biography of the Works Through Mavra (two vols) 1995, Text and Act: Essays on Music and Performance 1995; contrib. articles on Russian composers and operas in New Grove Dictionary of Opera (four vols) 1992; many articles and reviews in professional journals and general periodicals. *Honours:* Dent Medal, England 1987, ASCAP Deems Taylor Award 1989. *Address:* c/o Department of Music, University of California at Berkeley, Berkeley, CA 94720, USA.

**TARVER, Kenneth;** Singer (Tenor); b. 1965, Detroit, USA. *Education:* Oberlin College Conservatory and Yale University School of Music. *Career:* Stuttgart Staatsoper 1994–97, as Tamino, Ferrando, Almaviva and Lindoro; Tamino in Don Giovanni at Aix-en-Provence, Milan, Stockholm and Tokyo, 1998; Season 2000–01 at Covent Garden, London, as Fenton in Falstaff and Roderigo in Otello by Rossini; Further appearances at the Deutsche Oper and State Opera, Berlin, and the New York City Opera; Concerts include Bach's St Matthew Passion, conducted by Chailly and Berlioz series in London, conducted by Colin Davis, 2000; Roméo et Juliette, Béatrice et Bénédict and Les Troyens; London Proms, 2002. *Recordings:* DVD of Falstaff, Covent Garden, 2000. *Honours:* Winner, Metropolitan Opera National Competition. *Address:* c/o Deutsche Oper Berlin, 10 Richard Wagnerstrasse, 100 Berlin, Germany.

**TASKOVA, Slavka;** Singer (Soprano); b. 16 Nov. 1940, Sofia, Bulgaria. *Education:* Studied at the Accademia di Santa Cecilia with Gina Cigne and in Milan with Lina Pagliughi. *Career:* Debut: Milan in 1966 as Rosina in Il Barbiere di Siviglia; Has sung in Venice, Bologna, Berlin, Munich, Paris, Vienna, Sofia, Warsaw and Zagreb; Sang at Schwetzingen Festival in 1971 in the premiere of Reimann's Melusine, Teatro Lirico Milan in 1975 in the premiere of Nono's Al Gran Sole Carico d'Amore, and Genoa in 1983 as Violetta. *Recordings include:* Anacréon by Cherubini. *Address:* c/o Teatro Carlo Felice, 16100 Genoa, Italy.

**TATE, Jeffrey Philip,** CBE, MA, MB, BChir; British conductor; *Musical Director, Teatro di San Carlo, Naples;* b. 28 April 1943, Salisbury, Wilts.; s. of Cyril H. Tate and Ivy Ellen Naylor (née Evans). *Education:* Farnham Grammar School, Christ's Coll. Cambridge and St Thomas's Hosp. London. *Career:* trained as medical doctor 1961–67; joined London Opera Centre 1969; joined staff of Royal Opera House, Covent Garden 1970; made recordings as harpsichordist 1973–77; Asst to Pierre Boulez (q.v.) for The Ring, Bayreuth 1976–81; Asst to Sir John Pritchard, Cologne Opera 1977; conducted Gothenburg Opera, Sweden 1978–80; Metropolitan Opera début 1979; Covent Garden debut 1982; Chief Guest Conductor, Geneva Opera 1983–95; Prin. Conductor, English Chamber Orchestra 1985–, Royal Opera House, Covent Garden 1986–91; Prin. Guest Conductor, Royal Opera House, Covent Garden 1991–94; Orchestre Nat. de France 1989–98; Chief Conductor and Artistic Dir Rotterdam Philharmonic Orchestra 1991–94; Chief Conductor Minnesota Orchestra Summer Festival 1997–; Prin. Guest Conductor Teatro La Fenice 1999; Musical Dir Teatro di San Carlo, Naples 2005–; appears with maj. orchestras in Europe and America; numerous recordings with English Chamber orchestra; Pres. Asscn for Spina Bifida and Hydrocephalus 1989–, Music Space Trust 1991–; other charitable positions. *Honours:* Hon. DMus (Leicester) 1993; Hon. Fellow Christ's Coll. Cambridge, St Thomas's and Guy's Hosp. Medical School; Grand Prix du Disque (for complete recording of opera Lulu) 1995, Premio della Critica Musicale 'Franco Abbiati' Spettacolo prize (for Königskinder, with Paul Curran) 2003; Officier, Ordre des Arts et des Lettres 1995, Chevalier, Légion d'honneur 1999. *Address:* Fondazione Teatro di San Carlo, Via San Carlo 98/F, 80132 Naples, Italy. *Website:* www .teatrosancarlo.it.

**TATTERMUSCHOVA, Helena;** Singer (Soprano); b. 28 Jan. 1933, Prague, Czechoslovakia. *Education:* Studied at the Prague Conservatory with Vlasta Linhartova. *Career:* Debut: Ostrava in 1955 as Musetta; National Theatre Prague from 1959; Visited Edinburgh with the company in 1964 and 1970 in the British premieres of Janáček's From The House Of The Dead and The Excursions of Mr Brouček; Guest appearances at opera houses in Barcelona, Brussels, Amsterdam, Warsaw, Naples, Venice and Sofia; Repertoire included works by Janáček, Smetana, Mozart, Puccini and Strauss; Also sang in concert. *Recordings:* Orfeo ed Euridice; Trionfi by Orff; The Makropulos Case; From the House of the Dead; Glagolitic Mass; The Cunning Little Vixen. *Address:* Detska 13, 100 00 Prague 10, Czech Republic.

**TATUM, Nancy;** Singer (Soprano); b. 25 Aug. 1934, Memphis, Tennessee, USA; m. Wiley Tatum. *Education:* Studied with Zelma Lee Thomas in Memphis and with Samuel Margolis and Wiley Tatum in New York. *Career:* Debut: Saarbrucken in 1962 as Santuzza; Has sung in Paris, Geneva, Lyon, Minneapolis, Vancouver and Sofia; Member of the Deutsche Oper am Rhein, Düsseldorf, from 1964, and Metropolitan Opera from 1973; Further appearances in Budapest, Bucharest, Zagreb, Brussels and Amsterdam; Repertoire includes major roles in operas by Wagner and Verdi.

**TAUB, Robert David;** Concert Pianist; b. 25 Dec. 1955, New York, NY, USA; m. Tracy Elizabeth Milner 1983. *Education:* AB, Princeton Univ., 1977; MMus, 1978, DMA, 1981, Juilliard School. *Career:* concert pianist performing throughout the USA, Europe, Asia and Latin America with orchestras including the MET Opera Orchestra, Boston Symphony Orchestra, LA Philharmonic, BBC Philharmonic, Philadelphia Orchestra; Concerto and

solo repertoire covering the Baroque to contemporary music; numerous works composed for him by Milton Babbitt, Mel Powell, Jonathan Dawe, David Bessell, Ludger Brummer and others; performances broadcast live on nat. radio including BBC, RTE, NPR. *Recordings:* Beethoven, Complete Piano Sonatas; Scriabin, Complete Piano Sonatas; Milton Babbitt, Piano Works, Three Compositions; Schumann, Davidsbündlertänze and two Lizst transcriptions; Mel Powell, Duplicates: Concerto for 2 Pianos, 1990; Persichetti, Piano Concerto; Sessions, Piano Concerto; Bartók, Sonata; Shifrin, Responses; Kirchner, Sonata. *Television:* featured in US nat. TV special The Big Idea. *Publications:* Playing the Beethoven Piano Sonatas (book); contributions to many music journals. *Current Management:* California Artists Management, 41 Sutter Street, Suite 420, San Francisco, CA 94104-4903, USA. *Telephone:* (415) 362-2787. *E-mail:* don@calartists.com. *Website:* www.calartists.com.

**TAUTU, Cornelia;** Composer; b. 10 March 1938, Odorhei, Romania; m. Valentin Curocichin, 6 Aug 1976, 1 d. *Education:* Ciprian Porumbescu Conservatory, Bucharest; Postgraduate studies at Long Island University, NY, USA, 1971–72. *Compositions:* Film Music: Tragic Holiday, Stage Music for: Prometheus (Aeschylus), La Locandiera (Goldoni), Medees (Seneca), Cherry Orchard (Chekhov); Symphonic: Counterpoint for String Orchestra, Segments for String Orchestra, Inventions for Piano and Orchestra, Dice, symphonic sketch, Palingenesia–Poem For 1907 for Orchestra; Engravings for Orchestra, Sinfonietta, Symphony No. 1, 1907, 1987, Concerto for Piano and Orchestra, 1989; Chamber: Concerto for 12 Instruments, Inventions for Piano, Collage for String Quartet, Carol Echoes, quintet for Flute, Oboe, Clarinet, Bassoon and Horn, Homage For Peace for String Quintet, Sonata, Trio for Flute, Piano and Harp, 8 progressive pieces for piano, 1988, Three Lieder, rhymes, by M Eminescu; Choral: Triptych 1991; Dixatuor, for ensemble and percussion, 1993; Inventions No.2 for piano and orchestra, 1996; Palingenesia, septet, 1996. *Address:* c/o UCMR-ADA, Cala Victoriei 141, 71102 Bucharest, Romania.

**TAVENER, Alan;** Conductor, Organist and Manager; b. 22 April 1957, Weston-Super-Mare, Avon, England; m. Rebecca Jane Gibson, 30 Aug 1980. *Education:* Organ Scholar, Brasenose College, Oxford, 1976–79; ARCO/ARCM 1978, graduated with BA Honours, Music, 1979; Subsequently gained MA degree. *Career:* Director of Music, University of Strathclyde, 1980–; Founder Director, Cappella Nova, 1982–; Conducted several world premieres of new choral works, including John Tavener's Resurrection, Glasgow, 1990; and James MacMillan's Seven Last Words, Glasgow, 1994. *Recordings:* Robert Carver, the Complete Sacred Choral Music, 3 CDs, 1990; Scottish Medieval Plainchant, Columba, most Holy of Saints, 1992; Twentieth Century Scottish Choral Music, 1992; Sacred Music for Mary Queen of Scots, 1993; Sacred Music of Robert Johnson, 1996; Scottish Medieval Plainchant, The Ceremonies of St Kentigern, 1997; Now Let Us Sing: A Scottish Christmas, 1998. *Address:* Director of Music, University of Strathclyde, Livingstone Tower, Richmond Street, Glasgow G1 1XH, Scotland.

**TAVENER, Sir John,** Kt; British composer; b. 28 Jan. 1944, London; s. of Kenneth Tavener and Muriel Tavener; m. 1st Victoria Marangopoulou 1974 (divorced 1980); m. 2nd Maryanna Schaefer 1991; two d. *Education:* Highgate School and RAM. *Career:* Organist St John's Church, London 1960; Prof. of Composition, Trinity Coll. of Music, London 1968–; youngest composer ever performed at Promenade Concert, London 1969, at Royal Opera House, Covent Garden (Thérèse) 1979; works performed in UK, USA, fmr USSR, Greece, Poland, Australia, Germany, Scandinavia, S America and elsewhere; converted to Russian Orthodox Church 1974; works recorded on numerous labels. *Compositions include:* The Whale, Celtic Requiem, Últimos Ritos, Palintropos, Antigone, Thérèse, Akhmatova-Rekviem, Liturgy of St John Chrysostom, 16 Haiku of Seferis, Sappho – Lyrical Fragments, Great Canon of St Andrew of Crete, Prayer for the World, Kyklike Kinesis, Ikon of Light, A Gentle Spirit, All-Night Vigil Service of the Orthodox Church (commissioned by Orthodox and Anglican Churches, for Christ Church Cathedral, Oxford 1985), Two Hymns to the Mother of God, Trisâgion, Mandelion; Eis Thanaton (a ritual), Ikon of St Cuthbert, God is with Us, Acclamation for Patriarch Demetrios, Akathist of Thanksgiving, Meditation on the Light, Panikhida, Ikon of Saint Seraphim, The Protecting Veil, Resurrection, Magnificat and Nunc Dimittis, The Hidden Treasure, Eonia, Mary of Egypt, The Repentant Thief, We Shall See Him as He Is, The Last Sleep of the Virgin, The Annunciation, Hymns of Paradise, Akhmatova Songs, The Child Lived, The Apocalypse, Let's Begin Again, Wake Up and Die, The Toll Houses, Agraphon, Vlepondas, The Last Discourse, Diodia, Song for Athene (performed at funeral of Diana, Princess of Wales), Nipson Fall and Resurrection, Total Eclipse, A New Beginning, Eternity's Sunrise, The Bridegroom, Lamentations and Praises, Life Eternal, Song of the Cosmos, The Veil of the Temple 2003. *Publication:* The Music of Silence – A Composer's Testament. *Honours:* Hon. FRAM, Hon. Fellow Royal School of Church Music, Hon. Fellow Trinity Coll. of Music, London; Hon. DMus (New Delhi) 1990, (City of London Univ.) 1996; Prince Rainier Int. Prize 1965, First Prize Sacred Music Int. Composition Contest 1972, Gramophone Award (for The Protecting Veil) 1992. *Address:* c/o Chester Music, 8–9 Frith Street, London, W1D 3JB, England.

**TAYLOR, Ann;** Singer (Mezzo-soprano); b. 1966 Wrexham, North Wales. *Education:* Royal Northern College of Music, Guildhall School and the National Opera Studio. *Career:* Appearances with Opera North as Ramiro in La Finta Giardiniera, Feodor in Boris Godunov (also at the London Proms), Cherubino, and Donna Clara in the British premiere of Gerhard's The Duenna; Dorabella, Ramiro, Phoebe in Yeomen of the Guard and Handel's

Ariodante for Welsh National Opera; Kristina in The Makropulos Case and Oreste in La Belle Hélène for Scottish Opera, Rosina and Mozart's Annius for Glyndebourne Touring Opera; Premiere of Berkeley's Baa Baa Black Sheep at the 1993 Cheltenham Festival; Schumann's Manfred at Monnaie, Brussels, and Cherubino for the Bavarian State Opera; Concerts include Chabrier's La Sulamite at the Queen Elizabeth Hall, Schumann's Scenes from Faust at the 1994 Edinburgh Festival, Les Nuits d'Eté, and Nancy in Albert Herring under Steuart Bedford; Season 1997 with Hänsel for Opera Zuid, and Glyndebourne Festival debut, as Kate in Owen Wingrave; Sang the Stewardess in the premiere of Jonathan Dove's Flight for GTO at Glyndebourne, and also GFO (television) 1998 and Rosina in the Barber of Seville for Opera North; Pippo in The Thieving Magpie and Varvara in Katya Kabanova with Opera North, 1999, and Sarah in Tobias and the Angel for Almeida Opera; Concert, Les Noces, Stravinsky Ensemble Modern, Barbican. *Recordings include:* The Duenna; Baa Baa Black Sheep; Albert Herring; Flight by Jonathan Dove; Messiah, with Hallé Orchestra. *Current Management:* Ingpen & Williams Ltd, 7 St George's Court, 131 Putney Bridge Road, London, SW15 2PA, England.

**TAYLOR, Daniel;** Canadian singer (countertenor); b. 1969. *Education:* McGill Univ., Univ. of Montréal. *Career:* concerts with Tafelmusik, Netherlands Radio Chamber Orchestra, Dallas Symphony Orchestra, Portland Baroque, Winnipeg and Quebec Symphonies, Kammerchor Stuttgart and American Bach Soloists; Repertoire includes Messiah (at Göttingen), St Matthew Passion (Berkeley), King Arthur (with Les Violons du Roi), and Rodelinda; Sang Bertarido in Rodelinda at Broomhill and Halle, 1996; Tolomeo in Giulio Cesare at Rome, 1998; Handel's Israel in Egypt at the London Proms, 2002. *Recordings include:* Jommelli, La Didone Abandonata, and Zelenka Missa Omnium Sanctorum.

**TAYLOR, Hilary;** Singer (Soprano); b. 1970, Melbourne, Australia. *Education:* Melbourne Conservatorium and Victorian College of Arts; National Opera Studio, London. *Career:* Appearances with Victorian State Opera, Australian Opera, Glyndebourne and Salzburg Festivals, and Raymond Gubbay productions; Concerts with Tasmanian and Melbourne Symphonies and BBI Classic Café recitals from the Floral Hall, Covent Garden; Royal Opera engagements in Der Rosenkavalier, The Greek Passion by Martinů, Turandot and Die Entführung. *Honours:* Opera foundation Australia Shell Covent Garden Scholarship, 1996. *Address:* Royal Opera House (chorus), Covent Garden, London, WC2, England.

**TAYLOR, James;** singer (tenor); b. 1966, Dallas, TX, USA. *Education:* Texas Christian University, Munich Hochschule with Adalbert Kraus. *Career:* debut as Tony in West Side Story, with the Fort Worth Symphony Orchestra 1990; opera appearances in Stuttgart (Monteverdi's Ulisse and Fliegende Holländer) and the Grand Priest in Idomeneo at Brussels; Concerts include: Bach's St Matthew Passion in Munich, and the St John Passion with the Vienna Philharmonic; Beethoven's Missa Solemnis, Mendelssohn's Elijah and Bach Cantatas, conducted by Philippe Herreweghe; season 1997 with Mozart's Requiem at Zürich and Bach's B Minor Mass with the Cleveland Orchestra under Christoph von Dohnányi. *Recordings include:* Orff's Catulli Carmina, Bach's Magnificat and Mass in A (with Helmuth Rilling), Missa solemnis and Mendelssohn's St Paul (Herreweghe). *Address:* Kunstler Sekretariat, Rosenheimerstrasse 52, 81669 Munich, Germany.

**TAYLOR, Paul Wegman;** Conductor; b. 30 Sept. 1954, Cleveland, Ohio, USA. *Education:* Private violin lessons aged 6–16 years old, with grandfather Willem Wegman; School orchestras; Youth orchestras; Family recitals; Studied horn from 15 years old; Studied at Juilliard with John Chambers and John Cerminaro; New York Freelance including solo horn, Greenwich Symphony Orchestra, extra New York Philharmonic, Metropolitan Opera and numerous other engagements including chamber music, 1975–83; Conducting studies, David Gilbert, Maurice Peress, Walter Hugler, 1986–, San Francisco State University; Juilliard School; Queens College, City University of New York. *Career:* Kammerphilharmonie Budweis CR Wiener Oper Theater, 1992–94; Conductor of Choirs and Amateur Orchestras in Zürich, 1993–2000; Guest Conductor, Tonhalle Orchestra, 1994; Founder, Conductor, Mauritius Ensemble, Switzerland, 1995–; Thuner Stadtsorchester, Switzerland, 1998; Artistic Director, Jakobstads Orchestra, Finland, 2000; Teacher of Horn, Uster, Switzerland; mem, Conductors Guild; International Horn Society. *Recordings:* Hornist with the New York Philharmonic: Ein Heldenleber, Strauss; Ring Excerpts, Wagner. *Honours:* Winner, Conducting Competition, Biel, Bienne Summer Academy, 1994; Guest engagement: Kammerphilharmonie, Budweis, CR, 1995. *Current Management:* Sirkka Varonen Artists. *Address:* Vasterbyvagen 222, 68560 Eegmo, Finland.

**TAZZINI, Rinaldo;** Producer, Director and Artistic Director; b. 15 Feb. 1942, New York City, USA; m. Helen Neswald, 15 Sept 1965, 1 s., 2 d. *Education:* High School of Music and Art, New York City; BA, Music, Hunter College; Mannes School of Music with Paul Berl and Carl Bamberger; Conservatorio di Cherubini with Cecilia Castelana-Zotti, Florence, Italy; Accademia di Chigiana with Gino Bechi; Accademia di Santa Cecilia with Tito Gobbi. *Career:* Sang at New York City Opera, 1971–72, Teatro dell'Opera, Rome, Italy, 1972–74, Teatro Massimo Bellini at Catania in 1974, and Teatro Lonigo in 1974; Artistic Director and Director of Productions at Brooklyn Opera Society, USA, 1977–; Madama Butterfly at Japanese Garden in New York City, being the first opera for television shot on location in USA, 1980; Producer, Director of the George Gershwin Festival Tour in 1982; Creator, Director, Hot Rags Musical at Lincoln Center in 1983. *Address:* c/o Bernard

Lewis, Director of Communications, The Brooklyn Opera Society, Borough Hall, Brooklyn, NY 11201, USA.

**TCHISTJAKOVA, Trina;** Singer (mezzo-soprano); b. 1965, Moscow, Russia. *Education:* Graduated from the Gnesin Russian Academy of Music, Moscow, 1989. *Career:* Soloist with the Theatre Studio of the Gnesin Academy, from 1988; Principal with the Moscow Municipal Theatre, from 1990 (tour of Italy 1991, as Ratmir in Glinka's Ruslan and Lyudmila); Season 1994–95 Marina in Boris Godunov at Liège, the Verdi Requiem at Lincoln Center, New York, and Ruslan and Lyudmila at Carnegie Hall; Marfa in Khovanshchina at the Bolshoi, 1995; Season 1996–97 as Marina at Turin and Salzburg; Eugene Onegin and The Queen of Spades at Trieste; Kirov Opera St Petersburg as Cherubino, Marguerite in La Damnation de Faust, Amneris and Eboli; Concert repertory includes Skriabin's 1st Symphony (in Sweden and Germany), Beethoven's Ninth and Prokofiev's Alexander Nevsky (with the Philharmonia Orchestra). *Recordings include:* Verdi Arias; Azucena in Il Trovatore. *Honours:* Winner, Viñas Singing Competition, Barcelona, 1993. *Current Management:* Askonas Holt Ltd, Lonsdale Chambers, 27 Chancery Lane, London, WC2A 1PF, England. *Telephone:* (20) 7400-1700. *Fax:* (20) 7400-1799. *E-mail:* info@askonasholt.co.uk. *Website:* www.askonasholt.co.uk.

**TEAR, Robert,** CBE, MA, FRSA, RCM, RAM; British opera and concert singer; b. 8 March 1939, Barry, Wales; s. of Thomas Arthur Tear and Edith Tear; m. Hilary Thomas 1961; two d. *Education:* Barry Grammar School, King's Coll., Cambridge. *Career:* embarked on solo career as tenor after singing as member of King's Coll. Choir 1957–60 and St Paul's Cathedral Choir; joined English Opera Group 1964; worked with leading conductors (including Karajan, Giulini, Bernstein, Solti) and appeared in numerous operas by Benjamin Britten 1964–68; has appeared at Royal Opera House, Covent Garden on regular basis since his debut in The Knot Garden 1970; US conducting debut in Minneapolis 1985; debut with ENO in The Turn of the Screw 1988–89; debut as Aschenbach in Death in Venice with Glyndeboume Touring Co. 1989–90, later filmed by BBC TV; has subsequently worked with BBC Nat. Orchestra of Wales, London Mozart Players, Northern Sinfonia, English Chamber Orchestra, Philharmonia Orchestra, Royal Liverpool Philharmonic, Royal Scottish National Orchestra, Toulouse Chamber Orchestra, Tapiola Sinfonietta and Scottish Chamber Orchestra; recent opera performances have included Opera Nat. de Paris Bastille (Marriage of Figaro), Los Angeles Opera (Tales of Hoffmann), Royal Opera House (Falstaff), Welsh Nat. Opera (Eugene Onegin) and Bayerische Staatsoper (Saul); appearances in all major festivals; close asscn with Sir Michael Tippett 1970–97; first Prof. of Int. Singing, Royal Acad. of Music, London 1985–. *Recordings:* more than 250 records for every major record label, including premier recording of Tippett's opera King Priam 1981. *Publications:* Victorian Songs and Duets, Tear Hear (autobiog.) 1990, Singer Beware 1995, 10 Christmas Carols. *Honours:* Hon. Fellow, King's Coll. Cambridge 1989, Welsh Coll. of Music and Drama 1994; Hon. DMus (Royal Scottish Acad. of Music and Drama). *Current Management:* Askonas Holt Ltd, Lonsdale Chambers, 27 Chancery Lane, London, WC2A 1PF, England. *Telephone:* (20) 7400-1700. *Fax:* (20) 7400-1799. *E-mail:* melanie.moult@askonasholt.co.uk. *Website:* www.askonasholt.co.uk.

**TEARE, Christine;** singer (soprano); b. 1959, Isle of Man. *Education:* Royal Academy of Music with Marjorie Thomas, studied with Rudolf Piernay. *Career:* debut with Welsh National Opera, Cardiff, as Donna Anna, 1983; Covent Garden, 1983, as Helmwige, Ortlinde and Third Norn in The Ring; Season 1985–6 as a Flower Maiden in Parsifal for English National Opera, and Donna Anna for Opera North; Welsh National Opera 1985–89 as Mozart's Countess, Amelia (Ballo in Maschera), Third Norn in Götterdämmerung, Berta (Barbiere di Siviglia) and the Empress in Die Frau ohne Schatten; Broadcasts with the BBC. *Recordings include:* Osud by Janáček, and Parsifal (ENO and WNO; EMI).

**TEDE, Margery;** Singer (Mezzo-Soprano); b. 1940, USA. *Education:* Studied at San Francisco State College, Madrid Conservatory and the Hochschule für Musik in Berlin. *Career:* Sang with the San Francisco Opera as Fricka, Amneris, Azucena, Judith in Bluebeard's Castle, Jocasta and Herodias in Salome; Sang Countess Carolina in the local premiere of Henze's Elegy for Young Lovers, conducted by Christopher Keene; Lake Tahoe Summer Music Festival as Susan B Anthony in Virgil Thomson's The Mother of Us All; Concert appearances with the San Francisco Symphony under Seiji Ozawa and in Mozart's Coronation Mass in New York; Sang in opera, concerts and recitals in Europe, Central America, Alaska and the South Pacific; Sang the world premiere of Roger Nixon's Three Transcendental Songs in New York and songs by Charles Ives in Hamburg; Now retired as singer and active as teacher. *Honours:* International Scholarship from the Federation of Music Clubs. *Address:* Steorra Enterprises, 243 West End Avenue, Suite 907, New York, NY 10023, USA.

**TEITELBAUM, Richard (Lowe);** Composer, Performer and Teacher; b. 19 May 1939, New York City, USA. *Education:* BA, Haverford College, 1960; MMus, Yale University School of Music, 1964; Mannes School, 1960–61; Accademia di Santa Cecilia, Rome, 1964–65; Composition with Luigi Nono in Venice, 1965–66; Wesleyan University World Music Program, 1970–71. *Career:* Founding Member, Musica Electronica Viva, Rome, 1966; Instructor at California Institute of the Arts, 1971–72; Founder and Director, Electronic Music Studio, Art Institute of Chicago, 1972–73; Co-Director and Visiting Professor, York University, Toronto, 1973–76; Soloist at Berlin Philharmonic Hall, Concertgebouw, Centre Pompidou, and WDR Cologne among others,

1984–86; Visiting Professor, Vassar College, Full Professor, Bard College, 1988–89; mem, American Music Center; Composers Forum; College Music Society; International Computer Music Society. *Compositions include:* Intersections for Piano, 1964; In Tune for Live Electronics, 1966; Digital Piano Music, 1983; Concerto Grosso for Robotic Pianos, Winds, Trombone and Synthesizers; Iro Wa Nioedo for 20 Buddhist Monks; Golem, interactive opera, 1989–94; Dal Niente, for midi piano, sampler and computer, 1997. *Recordings include:* Hi Uchi Ishi, 1977; Time Zones, 1977; Concerto Grosso, 1987; Golem, Cyberband, Live at Merkin Hall. *Honours:* Fulbright Scholarships, Italy, 1964–66, Japan, 1976–77; Meet the Composer/NEA Grant, Mary Flager Cary Trust, 1976, 1979, 1988. *Address:* 250 Cold Brook Road, Bearsville, NY 12409, USA.

**TELLEFSEN, Arve;** Violinist; b. 13 Dec. 1936, Trondheim, Norway. *Education:* Studied with Arne Stoltenberg, Henry Holst and Ivan Galamian, New York, 1960. *Career:* Numerous recitals and concerts in Europe; Professor of The Academy of Music in Oslo from 1985; Tour of Norway in 1985 with the RPO under Ashkenazy; Oslo Philharmonai concerts in 1987 with Mariss Jansons, Neeme Järvi and Esa-Pekka Salonen; British engagements with David Zinman, Jerzy Maksymiuk, Marek Janowski, Okko Kamu, Vernon Handley and Kurt Sanderling; Festival concerts at Schleswig-Holstein, Lockenhaus and Montreux; Founded Oslo Chamber Music Festival in 1989; Season 1997 premiered the Concerto by Nordheim, with the Oslo Philharmonic Orchestra. *Recordings include:* concertos by Nielsen, Shostakovich, Berwald, Aulin, Valen, Sinding, Svendsen and Sibelius; Beethoven and Grieg Sonatas; Bruch and Beethoven concertos with the London Philharmonic Orchestra; Shostakovich 1 and Sibelius with the Royal Philharmonic. *Honours:* First Prize, Princess Astrid's Competition for Young Norwegian Artists, 1956; Harriet Cohen International Award, 1962; Awarded the prize of Bergen Festival, 1964; Grieg Prize, 1973.

**TEMESI, Maria,** (Maria Toth); Singer (soprano); b. 1957, Szeged, Hungary. *Education:* Studied at Franz Liszt Academy; At Szeged, Piano; Singing Teacher, Opera Singer diplomas, Budapest; Masterclasses at Weimar Music Academy and Mozarteum, Salzburg. *Career:* Debut: Budapest State Opera as Elsa, in Wagner's Lohengrin, under G Patanè, 1982; Appearances: Staatsoper Hamburg, Oper der Stadt Köln, Semperoper Dresden, Staatsoper Berlin, Komische Oper Berlin, Opernhaus Zürich, Teatro Farnese Parma, Teatro de la Zarzuela Madrid, Opéra de Nice, Théâtre du Capitole Toulouse, Opera Company of Philadelphia, Smetana Theatre Prague, Herodes Atticus Ampthitheatre Athens, Opernhaus Graz, Montevideo Teatro Solis, Uruguay; Main Roles: Vitellia in La Clemenza di Tito, Adriana Lecouvrer, Tatiana, Lisa in The Queen of Spades, Amelia in Ballo in Maschera, Leonora in Trovatore, Elisabeth de Valois, Elena in Vespri Siciliani, Desdemona, Alice in Falstaff, Elsa in Lohengrin, Eva in Meistersinger, Elisabeth in Tannhäuser, Estrella in Schubert's Alfonso und Estrella, Sieglinde in Die Walküre, Mimi in La Bohème and Manon in Manon Lescaut; Brünnhilde in Götterdämmerung at Budapest, 1998; Concert performance of Guntram by Strauss, Manhattan Cable television, NY; Götterdämmerung (Gutrune); Mahler's 2nd Symphony under Dorati; Handel's Messiah under Gönnenwein; La Clemenza di Tito conducted by John Pritchard, Cologne; Liederabenden, Budapest Music Academy; Lisbon Fundacao Calouste Gulbenkian; Cairo Academy of Arts; Beethoven: Missa Solemnis (Milano, RAI); Verdi: Requiem; Dvořák, Requiem; Britten: War Requiem (Zagreb); Rossini: Stabat Mater; Pergolesi: Stabat Mater. *Recordings:* Liszt, Missa Choralis; Mahler, 8th Symphony. *Honours:* Prizewinner in competitions in Athens, 1979, Toulouse, 1980; 1st Prize, Rio de Janeiro, 1981; Winner, Pavarotti Competition, Philadelphia, 1985; Szekely Mihaly Plaquette, Budapest, 1995. *Address:* Templom u 22, 1028 Budapest, Hungary.

**TEMIRKANOV, Yuriy Khatuyevich;** Russian conductor; *Music Director, Baltimore Symphony Orchestra*; b. 10 Dec. 1938, Nalchik; s. of Khatu Sagidovich Temirkanov and Polina Petrovna Temirkanova; m. Irina Guseva (deceased); one s. *Education:* Leningrad Conservatoire. *Career:* first violinist with Leningrad Philharmonic Orchestra 1961–66; Conductor for Maly Theatre and Opera Studio, Leningrad 1965–68; Chief Conductor, Leningrad Philharmonic Orchestra 1968–76, Kirov Opera and Ballet Co. 1976–88; Prof. Leningrad Conservatoire 1979–88; Artistic Dir State Philharmonia 1988–; Prin. Guest Conductor Royal Philharmonic Orchestra and Philadelphia Orchestra; Chief Conductor, London Philharmonic Orchestra 1992–97; Prin. Guest Conductor, Danish Radio Orchestra 1997–; Music Dir Baltimore Symphony Orchestra 1999–07; guest conductor in a number of countries, including Scandinavia (Sweden 1968), USA and the UK (Royal Philharmonic Orchestra 1981–). *Opera productions include:* Porgy and Bess (at Maly), Peter the Great (at Kirov), Shchedrin's Dead Souls (at Bolshoi and Kirov), Tchaikovsky's Queen of Spades and Eugene Onegin (Kirov) 1979. *Honours:* USSR People's Artist 1981, Glinka Prize, USSR State Prize 1976, 1985. *Address:* Baltimore Symphony Orchestra, Meyerhoff Symphony Hall, 1212 Cathedral Street, Baltimore, MD 21201-5545, USA. *Website:* www .baltimoresymphony.org.

**TEMPERLEY, Nicholas;** American musicologist; b. 7 Aug. 1932, Beaconsfield, England; m. Mary Dorothea Sleator, 17 Sept 1960, 1 s., 2 d. *Education:* ARCM, Royal College of Music, 1952; BA, BMus, MA, PhD, King's College, Cambridge University, 1952–59. *Career:* Assistant Lecturer, Music, Cambridge University and Fellow, Clare College, Cambridge, 1961–66; Assistant Professor, Musicology, Yale University, USA, 1966–67; Associate Professor 1967–72, Professor 1972–96, Professor Emeritus, 1996–, Chairman Musicol-

ogy Division 1972–75, 1992–96, University of Illinois. *Publications include:* Books: Raymond and Agnes, Edward J Loder, performed Cambridge, 1966; Symphonie Fantastique, Berlioz, New Berlioz Edition, 1972; English Songs 1800–60, Musica Britannica Vol. 43, 1979; London Pianoforte School 1766–1860, 20 vols, Garland, 1984–87; Haydn's Creation, with authentic English text, 1987; Music of English Parish Church, 2 vols, 1979; Athlone History of Music in Britain, vol. 5, Romantic Age, 1981; Haydn: The Creation, 1991; Co-Editor, The Hymn Tune Index, 4 vols, 1998; Bound for America: Three British Composers, 2003. *Contributions:* numerous musical journals; New Grove Dictionary. *Address:* 805 West Indiana Street, Urbana, IL 61801, USA.

**TENENBOM, Steven;** Violist; b. 1965, USA. *Education:* Curtis Institute of Music with Michael Tree and Karen Tuttle. *Career:* soloist with the Brandenburg Ensemble and Rochester Philharmonic Orchestra, guest artist with the Guarneri Quartet, Beaux Arts Trio and Chamber Music Society of Lincoln Center; festival engagements at Chamber Music Northwest, Aspen, music from Angel Fire and Bravo Colorado; violist with the Orion String Quartet, including concerts throughout North America and in Europe; Brahms and Schubert evening in season 1996–97 at Lincoln Center, and opening night Gala in honour of Marilyn Horne; faculty mem. at Mannes Coll. of Music and Hartt School of Music, New York. *Current Management:* Ingpen & Williams Ltd, 7 St George's Court, 131 Putney Bridge Road, London, SW15 2PA, England.

**TENNFJORD, Oddbjorn;** Singer (bass); b. 1941, Oslo, Norway. *Education:* Studied at the Bergen and Oslo Conservatories, in Essen with Clemens Kaiser-Breme, in Rome with Luigi Ricci and in London with Roy Henderson. *Career:* Has sung with the Norske Opera Oslo from 1971 as Osmin, Don Pasquale, Basilio, Falstaff, Pogner, Boris Godunov, Sarastro, Wotan, King Marke, Gremin and Fiesco; Concert and opera engagements for Norwegian radio and television, in Germany, Italy, Poland, Sweden, Denmark, Israel, Yugoslavia, France and USA; Appearances with Scottish Opera as The Commendatore, Daland, Sarastro and Fafner; Bologna in 1988 and Ravenna Festival in 1989 as the Grand Inquisitor in Don Carlos; Sang with Scottish Opera as Fafner in Das Rheingold and the Commendatore and as Daland at Oslo in 1989; Numerous guest appearances world-wide include: Baron Ochs and Daland in Montpellier, Daland in Cologne, Tokyo, Barcelona and Las Palmas, Baron Ochs in Osaka, The Grand Inquisitor in Bologna and Ravenna, Sarastro, Fafner, The Commendatore and Frank (Die Fledermaus) with the Scottish Opera; Since 1994 freelance: Gurrelieder with Mariss Jansons and the Oslo Philharmonic Orchestra, King Marke in Brussels with Antonio Pappano, Duke Bluebeard with Neeme Järvi and Gothenburg Symphony Orchestra, Vespri Siciliani, Rheingold and Die Walküre at Den Norske Opera; Season 1996–97 included Baron Ochs at Deutsche Oper, Berlin, Boris Godunov at Kungliga Operan, Stockholm, Marke and Commendatore in Brussels and Der Friedenstag and Don Giovanni at Sächsische Staatsoper, Dresden; Season 1998–99, Sang Wagner's Klingsor at Brussels, Baron Ochs at Royal Opera, Stockholm, Daland at Hamburg Staatsoper and The National Opera, Oslo. *Address:* Olaf Bulls Vei 32, 0765 Oslo, Norway.

**TENSTAM, Ulrica;** Singer (Mezzo-soprano); b. 1963, Sweden. *Education:* Gothenburg 1983–87, Opera Studio Stockholm, 1987–89. *Career:* Debut: Oslo 1987, as Ramiro in Mozart's La finta giardiniera; Drottningholm Festival from 1989, as Klytemnestra in Gluck's Iphigenie en Aulide, and other roles; Stockholm Folkoperan as Rossini's Rosina; Royal Opera Stockholm from 1992, as Rosina, Nicklausse in Les Contes d'Hoffmann and Dalila; Ystad Opera 1993, as the Mother in Szokolay's Blood Wedding; Hermia in A Midsummer Night's Dream; Other roles include Gluck's Orpheus (Stockholm, 1991); Frequent concerts throughout Scandinavia. *Address:* Kungliga Teater, PO Box 16094, S–103 22 Stockholm, Sweden.

**TENZI, Fausto;** Singer (Tenor); b. 1 April 1939, Lugano, Switzerland. *Education:* Studied in Milan. *Career:* Sang at La Scala Milan, Théâtre des Champs Elysées, Paris, Teatro Comunale, Bologna and in Florence, Lucerne, Aachen and Perugia; Engaged at Buxton Festival, England and made concert appearances in Rome, Paris, Berlin, Moscow, Leningrad and North America; Other roles include Don José, Edgardo, Manrico, Don Carlos, Pinkerton, Rodolfo, Turiddu and Ivan Khovansky in Khovanshchina. *Recordings include:* The Queen of Spades; Scriabin's 1st Symphony.

**TERAMOTO, Mariko,** BA, MA, PhD; Japanese musicologist; *Professor, Musashino College of Music*; b. 6 June 1948, Tokyo. *Education:* Musashino Coll. of Music, Tokyo, Nat. Univ. of Fine Arts and Music, Tokyo, Univ. of Frankfurt am Main. *Career:* Lecturer, Nat. Univ. of Fine Arts and Music 1985–89, 1996–97; Asst Prof. 1984–87, Prof. 1988–97, Meisei Univ.; Lecturer 1984–97, Asst Prof. 1998–2001, Prof. 2002–, Musashino Coll. of Music; mem. Int., American and Japanese Musicological Soc., Gesellschaft für Musikforschung, Internationale CMV Weber-Gesellschaft, Internationale Heinrich Schütz Gesellschaft. *Publications:* Die Psalmmotettendrucke des Johannes Petrejus in Nürnberg 1983, Katalog der Musikdrucke des Johannes Petrejus in Nürnberg 1993, Shihen-no-Ongaku (Music of the Psalms) 2004; contrib. to Journal of the Japanese Musicological Soc., musicological reference books. *Address:* 2-10-16 Shimo-ochiai, Shinjuku-ku, Tokyo 161-0033, Japan (office).

**TERENTYEVA, Nina Nikolayevna;** Russian singer (mezzo-soprano); b. 9 Jan. 1946, Kusa, Chelyabinsk Region; d. of Nikolai Fedorovich and Tatyana Vladimirovna Terentyev; one d. *Education:* Leningrad State Conservatory (class of Olga Mshanskaya). *Career:* soloist Kirov (now Mariinsky) Theatre

1971–77, Bolshoi 1979; leading solo mezzo-soprano. *Russian repertoire includes:* Marta (Khovanshchina), Lubasha (Tsar's Bride), Lubava (Sadko), Marina Mnishek (Boris Godunov), also Amneris (Aida), Azucena (Il Trovatore), Delila (Samson and Delila), Eboli (Don Carlos), Santuzza (Cavalleria Rusticana) and others; participated in productions of maj. theatres of the world including Covent Garden (Amneris, 1995), Metropolitan-Opera (Eboli, 1993), La Scala (oratorio Ivan Grozny with R. Muti, 1994), also in Deutsche Oper and Staatsoper Berlin, Munich, Hamburg, Bordeaux, Los Angeles opera houses; participated in int. festivals; concert repertoire comprises Russian classics. *Honours:* People's Artist of Russia. *Address:* Bolshoi Theatre, Teatralnaya pl. 1, 103009 Moscow, Russia (office). *Telephone:* (095) 971-67-61 (home).

**TEREY-SMITH, Mary,** BMus, MA, PhD; British musicologist, conductor and vocal coach; *Professor Emerita, Western Washington University;* b. 4 Dec. 1933, Budapest, Hungary; m. C. A. C. Smith (deceased). *Education:* Liszt Acad. of Music, Univ. of Vermont, USA, Eastman School of Music, Univ. of Rochester. *Career:* debut as conductor, Tatabanya Symphony Orchestra, Budapest 1951; vocal coach, then asst conductor, Hungarian State Opera 1950–56; resident conductor, Tatabanya Symphony Orchestra 1951–56; vocal coach, Toronto Royal Conservatory Opera School, Canada 1957–58; Asst Prof. 1967–72, Assoc. Prof. 1972–85, Prof. of Music History and Literature 1985–2001, Prof. Emer. 2001–, Western Washington Univ.; Dir, Western Washington Univ. Opera Workshop 1967–75, Dir of the Collegium Musicum Ensemble 1969–2001 (five biannual European summer tours with the Collegium Musicum 1990–2000, performing in Hungary, Italy, Austria, Switzerland, Liechtenstein, Slovakia and Romania); musical adviser and frequent conductor of Capella Savaria 1999–, with tours in Baroque music; research project on the church music of Gregor J. Werner. *Recordings:* Four Orchestral Suites from Operas by J. P. Rameau conductor, with the Capella Savaria Baroque Orchestra) 1996, Syrens, Enchanters and Fairies—18th-Century Overtures from the London Stage (dir, with the Capella Savaria Baroque Orchestra), Thomas Arne—The Complete Solo Cantatas, G. J. Werner: Masses and Offertories composed for the Esterházy Family. *Publications:* French Baroque Partbooks in the Uppsala University Library 1979, Joseph Kämpfer, a Contrabass Virtuosos from Pozsony (Bratislava) 1983, French Baroque Orchestral Dances (ed.) 1986, Prosperina Rapita: An Unknown Opera Fragment 1990, International Dictionary of Opera: Rameau: Les Boréades (essay) 1993; contrib. Orchestral Practice in the Paris Opéra 1690–1764 (in Studia Musicologica xxxi) 1989, The Spread of the French Influence in Europe (in Studia Musicologica xxxi) 1989, Passio Jesu Christi by F. F. Fasch (in The Fasch Yearbook) 1997, articles in Revised New Grove Dictionary of Music 2000, articles, studies and reviews to books and periodicals, including Music and Letters, Notes. *Honours:* Canada Council grant 1966–67, ACLS grant 1975–76, Harvard Fellowship 1976. *Address:* Department of Music, Western Washington University, 516 High Street, Bellingham, WA 98225-9107, USA (office). *Telephone:* (360) 650-3130 (office). *Fax:* (360) 650-7538 (office). *E-mail:* tereysm@cc.wwv.edu (office).

**TERFEL, Bryn,** CBE; British singer (bass baritone); b. (Bryn Terfel Jones), 9 Nov. 1965, Pantglas, Snowdonia, Wales; s. of Hefin Jones and Nesta Jones; m. Lesley Halliday 1987; three s. *Education:* Ysgol Dyffryn Nantlle, Penygroes, Gwynedd and Guildhall School of Music and Drama. *Career:* debut, WNO as Guglielmo 1990; sang Mozart's Figaro at Santa Fe Opera and ENO 1991; Royal Nat. Opera, Covent Garden debut as Masetto in Don Giovanni 1992, repeated on tour to Japan; sang at Salzburg Festival as the Spirit Messenger in Die Frau ohne Schatten, and as Jochanaan in Salome 1992, returning as Leporello in Patrice Chéreau's production of Don Giovanni 1994; further appearances at Vienna Staatsoper as Mozart's Figaro 1993, at Chicago as Donner in Das Rheingold, debuts at New York Metropolitan Opera 1994, Sydney Opera House 1999, and frequent guest soloist with Berlin Philharmonic Orchestra; sang in the Brahms Requiem under Colin Davis and at Salzburg Easter Festival under Abbado (Herbert von Karajan In Memoriam) 1993; sang Nick Shadow in The Rake's Progress for WNO 1996, Figaro at La Scala 1997, Scarpia for Netherlands Opera 1998, Falstaff at the reopening of the Royal Opera House, Covent Garden 1999; 4 male roles in Les Contes d'Hoffmann, and Don Giovanni, both at Metropolitan Opera, New York, and Nick Shadow in The Rake's Progress for San Francisco Opera 1999–2000; London Proms 2002; baritone roles in Les Contes d'Hoffmann at the Opéra Bastille, Sweeney Todd in Chicago, and Falstaff and Don Giovanni at Covent Garden 2002–03; Mephistopheles in Faust, Wotan in Das Rheingold and Die Walküre at Covent Garden 2004; many concert appearances in Europe, USA, Canada, Japan and Australia; Pres. Nat. Youth Choir of Wales, Festival of Wales; Vice-Pres. Llangollen Int. Eisteddfod; Founder, Faenol Festival 2000–. *Recordings include:* Salome, Le nozze di Figaro, An Die Musik, Wagner Arias, Britten's Gloriana, Beethoven's Ninth Symphony, Brahms' Requiem, Schwanengesang, Cecilia and Bryn, If Ever I Would Leave You, Handel Arias, Vagabond (Caecillia Prize 1995, Gramophone People's Award 1996) 1995, Opera Arias (Grammy Award for best classical vocal performance) 1996, Something Wonderful (Britannia Record Club Members' Award) 1997, Don Giovanni 1997, Bryn (Classical BRIT Award for Best Album 2004) 2003, Simple Gifts 2005. *Honours:* Hon. Fellow, Univ. of Wales, Aberystwyth, Welsh Coll. of Music and Drama, Univ. of Wales, Bangor; Hon. DMus (Glamorgan) 1997; White Robe, Gorsedd; recipient, Kathleen Ferrier Scholarship 1988; Gold Medal Award 1989; Lieder Prize, Cardiff Singer of the World Competition 1989; Young Singer of the Year, Gramophone magazine 1992; British Critics' Circle Award 1992; Newcomer of Year, Int. Classic Music

Awards 1993, Classical BRIT Award for Male Artist of the Year 2004, 2005. *Current Management:* Harlequin Agency, 203 Fidlas Road, Cardiff, CF14 5NA, Wales. *Telephone:* (29) 2075-0821. *Fax:* (29) 2075-5971.

**TERRACINI, Lyndon;** Singer (Baritone); b. 1950, Australia. *Education:* Studied in Australia. *Career:* Debut: With Australian Opera at Sydney Opera House as Sid in Albert Herring, 1976; Sang in London in 1983 as Ivan in Brian Howard's Inner Voices; Sang Daniello in the local premiere of Krenek's Jonny Spielt Auf in 1984; US debut in 1984 at the Cabrillo Music festival in Australian Folksongs; German debut in the title role in Hans Zender's Stephen Climax at Frankfurt; Italian debut as Sancio Panza in the world premiere of Henze-Paisiello Don Quischotte at the Montepulciano Festival; Has sung with Opera Factory Zürich as Agamemnon and Orestes in the Iphigenias by Gluck; Sang Der Alte in Reimann's Ghost Sonata and Landsknecht in Hartmann's Simplicius Simplicissimus; Appearances in Ullmann's posthumous The Emperor of Atlantis and as Marcello in La Bohème and Byron in the premiere of Richard Meale's La Mer de Glace at Sydney, 1991; Sang Don Giovanni in Adelaide in 1991 and appearances with Opera Factory London as Figaro on stage and on film for Channel 4 television; Sang the title role in the premiere of Casanova Confined, by Andrew Ford, Barossa Festival, Australia, 1996. Concert repertoire includes Syringa by Elliott Carter, with Collegium Musicum, Zürich, and El Cimarrón by Hans Werner Henze. *Address:* Performing Arts, 6 Windmill Street, London W1 1HF, England.

**TERRANOVA, Vittorio;** Singer (Tenor); b. 18 June 1945, Licata, Sicily. *Education:* Studied in Milan. *Career:* Debut: Mantua 1970, as Arturo in I Puritani; Many appearances at opera houses throughout Italy, and at the Spoleto and Florence (Maggio Musical) festivals; Rosini's Almaviva at Amsterdam, 1971; Guest engagements at the Vienna Staatsoper, Bregenz festival, Teatro Colón Buenos Aires, New York City Opera and Chicago Lyric Opera; Other roles have included Verdi's Fenton, Alfredo and the Duke of Mantua, Nadir in Les Pêcheurs de Perles, Don Ottavio, Ferrando, Faust, and Lyonel in Martha; Further roles in operas by Donizetti (Alamiro in Belisario, Buenos Aires), Cimarosa and Paisiello; Many concert engagements. *Address:* c/o New York City Opera, Lincoln Center, New York, NY 10023, USA.

**TERVO, Markku;** Singer (Bass); b. 1955, Helsinki, Finland. *Education:* Sibelius Academy, Helsinki; Further study with Hendrik Rootering. *Career:* Sang with Finnish National Opera, 1977–79, Karlsruhe Opera 1981–86, Krefeld 1986–89 and Freiburg, 1989–94; Returned to Karlsruhe, 1994; Roles have included Mozart's Osmin, and Sarastro, Rossini's Basilio, Verdi's Ferrando, Sparafucile and King Philip (Don Carlos); Wagner's Daland and Hagen, and Claggart in Billy Budd; Guest engagements throughout Germany, and in Luxembourg; Concerts throughout Europe, notably with Bach's Christmas Oratorio, St John Passion and Magnificat, L'Enfance du Christ by Berlioz, the Verdi Requiem and Shostakovich 13th Symphony (Babi-yar). *Recordings include:* Götterdämmerung (Bella Musica). *Address:* c/o Staatstheater Karlsrhe, Baumesterstrasse 11Pf 1449, D–7550 Karlsruhe, Germany.

**TERZAKIS, Dimitri,** DipMus; Greek composer; *Emeritus Professor, Felix Mendelssohn Musikhochschule;* b. 12 March 1938, Athens; s. of Angelos and Louisa Terzakis; m. Magdalena; one d. *Education:* Hellenic Conservatory, Athens, Cologne Musikhochschule with Zimmermann. *Career:* co-founder, Greek Soc. for Contemporary Music 1966; Lecturer, Robert Schumann Inst., Düsseldorf 1974; teacher and Prof. of Composition, Düsseldorf Hochschule 1987–93, Berne Hochschule 1990–94, Felix Mendelssohn Musikhochschule, Leipzig 1994– (currently Prof. Emer.). *Compositions include:* Ikona for strings 1963, Oboe Concerto 1968, Okeaniden for chorus and orchestra 1968, Ichochronos (electronic) 1968, Torquemada (opera) 1976, Circus Universal (chamber opera) 1976, four string quartets 1969, 1976, 1982, 1990, Tropi for orchestra 1976, Passionen (oratorio) 1979, Erotikon for soprano and three instruments 1979, Lachesis for orchestra 1984, Hermes (opera) 1984, Brass Quintet 1984, Six Monologues for soprano and orchestra 1985, Violin Concerto 1986, Das sechste Siegel for chorus and ensemble 1987, Per aspera ad Astra for orchestra 1990, Ikaros-Daidolos for soprano quartet and brass orchestra 1990, Der Holle Nachklang II for soprano and organ 1993, Daphnis and Chloe for soprano and viola 1994, Lieder ohne Worte for soprano 1994, Alto saxophone concerto 1995, Pensier for piano 2002, Mythem (Rapsodia) 2002. *Address:* Pölitzstr 26, 04155, Leipzig, Germany (home). *Telephone:* 3419614431 (home). *E-mail:* dimitriterzakis@gmx.de (home).

**TERZAKIS, Zachos;** Singer (Tenor); b. 1945, Athens, Greece. *Education:* Degree in Geology, University of Athens; Studied voice at Apollonion Odeon, Athens, 1969. *Career:* Engaged at National Lyric Theatre of Athens, roles included Alfredo in La Traviata, Pinkerton in Madama Butterfly and Elvino in Sonnambula; Sang in Athens Festival; Greek radio and television appearances; German debut as Turiddu in Cavalleria rusticana, Kiel, 1978; Engaged in Bielefeld, roles included Cassio in Otello, Singer in Rosenkavalier and Tamino in Magic Flute, 1979–82; Member, Nuremberg-Opera, roles included Rodolfo in Bohème, Almaviva in Barbiere di Siviglia and Adorno in Simon Boccanegra, 1982–87; Since 1987, freelance opera singer, appearances in many European venues including Opernhaus Zürich, Staatsoper Berlin, Volksoper Wien and National Opera Athens; sang Hoffman at Bregenz Festival, 1987; Other festival appearances include Luzerner Festwochen and Casals Festival in Puerto Rico; Debut as Titus in Staatsoper Vienna, and Jason in Medea by Mikis Theodorakis in Bilbao, 1991; Teatro dell Opera,

Rome, as Rudolf von Habsburg in Mayerling, 1993; Numerous concert recitals including Tivoli Copenhagen, Concert House Stockholm and Palais des Beaux Arts, Brussels; Staging Director, Medea, at Meiningen, 1995, and German translator; Numerous radio broadcasts. *Recordings:* Greek opera, Mother's Ring by Kalomiris, tenor solo, 1985; Penderecki's Polish Requiem, 1992; Missa Solemnis; Lehar's Operetta Highlights; Die lustige Witwe; Markopoulos's Orpheus Liturgy. *Honours:* Gold Medal of Excellence, Apollonion Odeon, Athens, 1976; First Prize, Maria Callas Scholarship Competition, 1976; Grammy Award nomination, 1992. *Address:* Bergstrasse 15, 91086 Falkendorf, Germany.

**TERZIAN, Alicia;** Composer, Conductor, Lecturer and Musicologist; b. 1 July 1934, Cordoba, Argentina; Divorced, 1 d. *Education:* Philosophical Studies, National University of Argentina; Research in Musicology, Latin American music; Private study in Conducting with Mariano Drago. *Career:* Debut: Premiere of String Quartet, Wagneriana Association, Buenos Aires, 1955; Organizer, Argentine Music Council of UNESCO, and also Jeunesses Musicales; Over 2000 lectures on 20th Century music history world-wide; Organizer, Foundation Encuentros Internacionales de Musica Contemporanea, 1968; Founder, Grupo Encuentros, to promote Latin American music; Performances for television and radio and over 400 concerts world-wide; As composer, works performed world-wide by leading soloists, orchestras and chamber ensembles. *Compositions include:* Stage: Hacia la luz, ballet, 1965; Bestiela, theatre music, 1981; El enano, theatre music, 1964; Orchestral works: Three Pieces for strings, orchestra of guitar quartet, 1954; Concertio para violin, 1955; Atmosferas, symphonic band, 1969; Carmen Criaturalis, solo horn, string orchestra and percussion, 1971; Off the Edge, baritone, string orchestra and percussion, 1992; Chamber Music: Y cuya luy es como la profunda oscuridad, group and tape, 1982; Les yeux fertiles, mezzo and group with percussion, 1997; Au dela des rêves, for piano, clarinet and violin, 2001; Instrumental: Libro de canciones de Federico Garcia Lorca for voice and piano, 1954; Atmosferas, duo piano, 1969; Yagua yu yuca, solo percussion, 1992; Canto a Vahan for piano and tape, 1996; Offer to Bach, for organ, 2000; Le viol des anges for 4 to 6 percussionists, 2000/01; Multimedia: Sinfonia Visual en dos movimientos, tape and slides, 1972; Canto a mí misma, string orchestra, tamtam and electronic sound transformation and loudspeakers in concert hall, 1986; Buenos Aires me vas a matar, 1990; Frémissement, organ and tape, 2000. *Recordings:* Violin Concerto, Voces and Canto a mi misma, 1997; Toccata for Piano; Juegos para Diana. *Honours:* Hon. mem., Int. Music Council, 2003; First Prize of Municipality of Buenos Aires, 1964; Francisco Solano Award, 1968; Outstanding Young Musicians Prize, Argentina, 1970; Nat. Fund for the Arts Prize, 1970; First Nat. Prize for Music, 1982; Gomidas Int. Prize, 1983; Médaille des Palmes Académiques, France, 1992; St Sahuk and St Mesrop Medals, Pope Vasken I of Armenian Church, 1992; Alberto de Castilla Medal of Columbia, 1994; Mozart Medal, Int. Music Council, 1995. *Address:* Santa Fe 3269-4B, Buenos Aires 1425, Argentina. *E-mail:* aterzian@aliciaterzian.com.ar. *Website:* www.aliciaterzian.com.ar.

**TERZIAN, Anita;** Singer (Mezzo-Soprano); b. 12 Oct. 1947, Strasbourg, France. *Education:* Studied at the Juilliard School, New York with Jennie Tourel. *Career:* Debut: Brussels in 1973 as Rosina; Has appeared at many operatic centres in Europe and the USA: Opéra du Rhin, Strasbourg, Brussels, Liège and San Francisco Opera; Best known in such coloratura mezzo repertoire as Rossini's Isabella and Sinaide in Mosè, Elisetta in Il Matrimonio Segreto and Sesto in La Clemenza di Tito; Other roles include Carmen, Charlotte, Olga, Orlofsky and Konchakovna in Prince Igor; Many concert appearances. *Recordings include:* Title role in Handel's Serse. *Address:* c/o Opéra du Rhin, 19 Place Broglie, 67008 Strasbourg Cédex, France.

**TETZLAFF, Christian;** Violinist; b. 29 April 1966, Hamburg, Germany. *Education:* Studied at the Lubeck Conservatory with Uwe-Martin Haiberg and in Cincinnati with Walter Levine. *Career:* Debut at the Berlin Festival and with the Cleveland Orchestra followed by regular appearances with the Berlin and Vienna Philharmonic, London Symphony Orchestra, City of Birmingham Symphony Orchestra, Orchestra Philharmonie de Paris, Gewandhausorchestra Leipzig, Munich Philharmonic, NHK Orchestra Tokyo, the New York Philharmonic, Boston and Chicago Symphonies and Academy of St Martin in the Fields; Season 1996–97 with the Houston Symphony Orchestra under Eschenbach and the Boston Symphony Orchestra under Franz Welser-Möst; Brahms Double Concerto and Shostakovich No. 1 with the Bavarian Radio Symphony Orchestra; Bach Sonatas and Partitas in Brussels and Paris 1997; Vienna Philharmonic concert at the 1997 Salzburg Festival; Chamber music series at the Vienna Konzerthaus: has collaborated with Leif Ove Andses, Yo-Yo Ma, Sabine Meyer and Heinrich Schiff; Beethoven's Concerto at the 1999 London Prom concerts; Berg's concerto at the London Proms, 2002; Has worked with many distinguished conductors including Boulez, Dohnanyi, Eschenbach, Gatti, Harding, Herreweghe, Paavo Jarvi, Levine, Nagano, Salonen, Saraste, Slatkin, Tilson Thomas and Vanska. *Recordings include:* Bach Sonatas and Partitas; Mozart Violin Concertos, with the Deutsche Kammerphilharmonie; Complete works for Violin and Orchestra by Sibelius. *Honours:* Recordings of the Bach Sonatas and Partitas and Sibelius's complete works for violin and orchestra were both awarded the Diapason d'Or. *Current Management:* Harrison/Parrott Ltd, 12 Penzance Place, London, W11 4PA, England. *Telephone:* (0)20 7313 3511. *E-mail:* matt.fretton@harrisonparrott.co.uk. *Website:* www.harrisonparrott.com.

**TEZIER, Ludovic;** Singer (Baritone); b. 1968, Marseilles, France. *Education:* Studied in Paris and Switzerland. *Career:* Engagements with Lyon, Marseilles, Tours and Bordeaux Opéras; Opéra-Comique, Paris, as Don Giovanni, Marcello, Escamillo, Harlequin (Ariadne auf Naxos), Sharpless, and Britten's Demetrius; Season 1996–97 in Handel's Radamisto and as Frédéric in Lakmé at Marseilles, Guglielmo at Bordeaux; Mozart Count, Marcello and Belcore at Lyon; Season 1997–98 as Malatesta, and Mercutio in Roméo et Juliette, at Bordeaux, with Escamillo, Don Giovanni and Talbot in Donizetti's Maria Stuarda at the Opéra-Comique; Glyndebourne 1997–98, as Comte Ory in a new production of Rossini's opera. *Address:* c/o Opera de Bordeaux, Grand Théâtre Municipal, Place de la Comédie, 33074 Bordeaux, France.

**THALLAUG, Edith;** Singer (Mezzo-Soprano); b. 16 June 1929, Oslo, Norway. *Education:* Studied with Giurgia Leppee and Joel Berglund in Stockholm. *Career:* Debut: Stage debut as actress in 1952; Song recital in Oslo in 1959; Stage debut as Dorabella at Gothenburg in 1960; Sang at Royal Opera Stockholm from 1964 notably as Carmen, Cherubino, Rosina, Bradamante in Alcina, Maddalena in Rigoletto, Eboli, Azucena, Amneris, Venus, Fricka, Waltraute, Octavian and The Composer in Ariadne, Judith in Bluebeard and Miss Julie; Frequent appearances at the Drottningholm Court Theatre from 1964; Sang at Glyndebourne Festival in 1971 as Dorabella, Basle in 1976 in Schoenberg's Gurrelieder and on Swedish television as Carmen; Guest engagements in Oslo, Copenhagen, Moscow, USA, Japan, Korea, Germany, La Scala Milan, Italy, Paris, Prague and Vienna. *Recordings include:* CD: Songs by De Falla, Montsalvatge, Ravel and many other recordings of Scandinavian Songs; Opera Arias, Songs by Grieg, and duets with Gösta Winbergh. *Honours:* Critic Prizes for La Cenerentola, Oslo, 1972; Court Singer, 1976; Grieg Prize, 1978; Drottningholm Court Theater, Gold Medal, 1979; Litteris et Artibus, 1982. *Address:* c/o Kongliga Teatern, PO Box 16094, 10322 Stockholm, Sweden.

**THANE, Amanda;** Singer (Soprano); b. 1960, Australia. *Education:* New South Wales Conservatorium of Music, Sydney. *Career:* Roles with the Australian opera since 1983 include Fiordiligi, Violetta, Marzelline, Constanze, Mimi, Norina, Pamina, Mozart's Countess, Micaela, Lauretta, Antonia, Leila, Nedda, Liu, Valentine (in Joan Sutherland's farewell performance of Les Huguenots), Governess, Maria Stuarda, Eva, Euridice and Gilda; Additional roles sung with other Australian companies include: Madama Butterfly, Rosalinde, Alice Ford, Marenka and Suor Angelica; Royal Opera House Covent Garden debut season 1991–92 as Valentine in new production of Les Huguenots and Antonia in Les Contes d'Hoffmann; Other roles at Royal Opera include Mimi, Lina in Verdi's Stiffelio and Amelia (Boccanegra); European debut 1993, as Lina in Stiffelio with Opera Forum, the Netherlands; Donna Elvira in Don Giovanni for Grand-Théâtre de Bordeaux; Many concert appearances throughout Australia, United Kingdom, Europe, USA, Japan and Korea; Teacher of Voice in London. *Honours:* Prizewinner, Metropolitan Opera Auditions, New York; Winner, ABC Instrumental and Vocal Competition; Queen Elizabeth II Silver Jubilee Award for Young Australians; Australian Music Foundation Award, London, Churchill Fellowship, 1990 (Australia). *Address:* c/o 70 Chandos Avenue, London W5 4ER, England.

**THAW, David;** Singer (Tenor); b. 19 June 1928, New York, USA; m. Claire Watson, deceased 1986. *Education:* Studied at Columbia University, with Giovanni Martinelli in New York and Giuseppe Pais in Milan. *Career:* Debut: Vichy in 1950 as Vincent in Mireille; Sang at the Theater am Gärtnerplatz Munich from 1955, with debut as the Duke of Mantua, Frankfurt am Main Opera from 1958 with debut as Lenski in Eugene Onegin and a visit to London with the company in 1963 in Fidelio, Salome and Die Entführung, Bayreuth Festival in 1961 as Froh in Das Rheingold and member of the Bayerische Staatsoper Munich from 1963; Guest appearances in Berlin at Deutsche Oper and Staatsoper, Hanover and elsewhere; Sang at Salzburg Festival, 1964–68, and Munich in 1986 in the premiere of Belshazzar by VD Kirchner; Many appearances in musicals notably as Professor Higgins in My Fair Lady. *Address:* c/o Bayerische Staatsoper, Postfach 745, 8000 Munich 1, Germany.

**THEBOM, Blanche;** Singer (Mezzo-Soprano); b. 19 Sept. 1918, Monessen, Pennsylvania, USA. *Education:* Studied with Margharete Matzenauer and Edyth Walker in New York. *Career:* Debut: Sang in concert from 1941; Stage debut in 1944 at Philadelphia with the Metropolitan Opera as Brangaene; Sang in New York until 1966 as Marina, Eboli, Baba the Turk, Herodias, Orlofsky and in Wagner roles as Venus and Fricka; Sang at Chicago in 1946 as Brangaene, San Francisco Opera, 1947–59 with debut as Amneris, Glyndebourne in 1950 as Dorabella, Covent Garden in 1957 as Dido in the first British professional performance of Les Troyens and a tour of Russia in 1958; Directed the Atlanta Opera Company, 1967–68; Professor at the University of Arkansas. *Recordings:* Tristan und Isolde, conducted by Furtwängler; The Rake's Progress.

**THEISEN, Kristin;** Singer (Soprano); b. 13 Jan. 1955, Oslo, Norway. *Education:* Studied German, Oslo University, 1 year; Vocal Pedagogic studies, Music Conservatorium, Oslo for 4 years; Norwegian State Opera School, 3 years; Studied in Vienna, Salzburg and Bayreuth; Teachers: Erna Skaug, Ingrid Bjoner, Kim Borg, Anna Reynolds and Jean Cox. *Career:* Debut: Recital, Oslo, 1979; As opera singer, Leoncavallo's Nedda, Gelsenkirchen, 1982; Has appeared in Hamburg, Frankfurt, Nuremberg, Catania, Strasbourg, Eutin, Basel and Lubeck; Television, radio and film in Norway, Austria and Poland; Important opera roles: Agathe in Freischütz, Rezia in Oberon, Susanna in Figaro, Giulietta in Hoffmann, Ellen Orford in Peter Grimes, Euridice in Orpheus and Euridice, Sieglinde in Walküre, Senta in Holländer;

mem, Leader of The Norwegian Opera Singer Society. *Recordings:* Zigeuner-lieder with Audin Kayser, piano; Irmgard in Franz Schreker's opera Flammen, conducted by Frank Strobl. *Current Management:* Kollo, Berlin and Heissler-Remy, Düsseldorf. *Address:* Sarbuvollveien 8A, 1322 Hovik, Norway.

**THEODOLOZ, Annelise;** Singer (Soprano); b. 1954, Switzerland. *Education:* Violin pupil of Carl Flesch and Tibor Varga at early age; Award-winning graduate, Lausanne Conservatory and Guildhall School of Music and Drama, London. *Career:* Debut: As Dorabella in Così fan tutte and Dalila in Samson et Dalila, National Hungarian Opera under conductor János Kovács; Has performed as Soloist in major concert halls and on radio, with Orchestre de la Suisse Romande, Israel Chamber Orchestra, Bach Solisten Amsterdam, Orchestre National de Lyon and many others all over Europe, in Middle East, Japan and Canada; Works with conductors such as Michel Corboz, Jesus Lopez-Cobos, Zoltán Nágy, Helmuth Rilling; French debut as Bradamante in Handel's Alcina, 1998; Further roles include Berlioz's Béatrice et Bénédict in Nancy and Tours under M Ossonce; Debut as soprano lirico spinto with Leonora's aria from Verdi's La Forza del Destino at Geneva, 2000. *Current Management:* Catherine Schoendorff Félix. *Address:* c/o Catherine Schoendorff Félix, Avenue du Tribunal-Fédéral 25, 1005 Lausanne, Switzerland.

**THEURING, Günther;** Conductor and University Professor; b. 28 Nov. 1930, Paris, France. *Education:* choirboy, Vienna; univ. studies in law and musicology; studied orchestral conducting with Hans Swarowsky and choir conducting with Ferdinand Grossmann, at Univ. of Music. *Career:* Regens Chori at St Rochus Church, Vienna, 1950; Conductor, Vienna Acad. Chorus, 1954; founder, Conductor, Vienna Jeunesse-Chorus, 1959; Conductor, Contraste Ensemble for Contemporary Music, 1971; concerts with Munich, Leipzig and Berlin Radio Choirs, Rias Chamber Choir, Berlin, Danish Radio Choir, Copenhagen, ORF Choir, Vienna, others; Conductor, orchestras including Vienna Symphony Orchestra, ORF Symphony Orchestra, Tonkünstler Orchester Wien, Mozarteum Orchestra, Salzburg, Orchestra Scala, Milan, Jerusalem Symphony Orchestra; Gewandhausorchester, Leipzig, Danish Radio Orchestra, Copenhagen, Leipzig Radio Orchestra, Prague Symphony, Slovakian Philharmonic, Bratislava, and Vienna Chamber Orchestra; Artistic Dir, Vienna master courses, 1971–; Prof. Ordinarius, Univ. of Music, Vienna, 1973–; Music Dir, Alpbach European Forum, –1982; Artistic Dir, First World Symposium for Choral Music, held in Vienna 1987. *Recordings include:* concert extracts. *Honours:* First prize, Choir Competition, Arezzo, 1956; Gold Badge of Service, Republic of Austria, 1970; Cross of Honour for Science and Arts, Republic of Austria, 1984; Ferdinand Grossmann Prize, 1999. *Address:* Landstrasser Hauptstrasse 67, Vienna 1030, Austria. *E-mail:* guenther.theuring@aon.at.

**T'HEZAN, Helia;** Singer (Soprano); b. 23 Aug. 1934, Rieumes, France. *Education:* Studied at the Toulouse Conservatoire and the Musikhochschule, Berlin. *Career:* Debut: Bordeaux in 1958 in Armide by Lully; Sang at the Paris Opéra and the Opéra-Comique from 1959, Covent Garden in 1965 in the title role of Gluck's Iphigénie en Tauride, Glyndebourne in 1966 as Charlotte in Werther, and Monte Carlo in 1973 in the premiere of La Reine Morte by Rossellini; Has sung at Lyon, Marseille, Geneva, Rome, Trieste, Turin, Lisbon and Philadelphia; Sang at the Paris Opéra in 1988 as Juno in Orphée aux Enfers. *Recordings include:* Manon by Massenet. *Address:* Théâtre National, 8 Rue Scribe, 75009 Paris, France.

**THIBAUD, Pierre;** Trumpeter; b. 22 June 1929, Proissans, France. *Education:* Studied violin and trumpet at the Bordeaux Conservatoire; Premier Prix for cornet playing at the Paris Conservatoire. *Career:* Principal Trumpet with the Orchestre de Paris Opéra, Ensemble Ars Nova, Domaine Musicale, Musique Vivante, Musique Plus and the Chamber Orchestra Fernand Oubradous; Further experience with the Concerts Lamoureux, Concerts Colonne and Musique de la Garde Republicaine; Founded the Brass Quintet Ars Nova and collaborations with the Société des Concerts du Conservatoire and IRCAM (electronic music studios), Paris; Concert appearances with leading European orchestras in the standard classics; Also plays music by Marius Constant, Xenakis, Messiaen, Varèse, Berio and Enesco; Professor of Trumpet at the Paris Conservatoire, 1975. *Recordings:* Brandenburg Concerto No. 2; Concertos by Haydn, Hummel and Telemann. *Address:* Conservatoire National Superieur de Musique de Paris, 209 Avenue Jean-Jaures, 75019, Paris, France.

**THIBAUDET, Jean-Yves;** French pianist; b. 7 Sept. 1961, Lyon. *Education:* Paris Conservatoire, Lyon Conservatory of Music. *Career:* now based in LA and Paris; appears with maj. orchestras in USA and Europe including Royal Concertgebouw, London Philharmonic, Royal Philharmonic, Orchestre Nat. de France etc.; regular visitor to major US and European music festivals; in recital has collaborated with mezzo-sopranos Brigitte Fassbaender and Cecilia Bartoli, Renee Fleming and cellist Truls Mørk; debut, BBC Promenade Concerts 1992, continuing to 2001; records exclusively for Decca (over 20 recordings). *Films:* Portrait of a Lady 1997, Bride of the Wind 2001. *Television:* Piano Grand! (PBS/Smithsonian Special) 2000. *Honours:* Chevalier, Ordre des Arts et Lettres 2001; Prix du Conservatoire, Paris Conservatory 1976, winner, Young Concert Artists Auditions 1981, Echo Award 1990, 1998, Schallplattenpreis 1992, Gramophone Award 1998, Edison Prize 1998, Choc de la Musique 1999, 2003, Diapason d'Or for his recordings of works by Debussy 2000, Premio Pegasus 2002, Echo Classical Music Awards 2002. *Current Management:* Mastroianni Associates, 161 West 61st Street, Suite 17E, New York, NY 10023; c/o M. L. Falcone Public Relations, 155 West 68th Street, Suite 1114, New York, NY 10023, USA. *Telephone:* (212) 580-4302. *Fax:* (212) 787-9638.

**THIEDE, Helga;** Singer (Soprano); b. 6 Feb. 1940, Berlin, Germany. *Education:* Berlin Musikhochschule. *Career:* Debut: Schwerin 1967, as Marina in Wolf-Ferrari's Quattro Rusteghi; Sang at Schwerin until 1971, Dessau 1972–84 and Dresden Staatsoper from 1984; Roles have included Leonore in Fidelio (1989), Chrysothemis in Elektra (also at Berlin Staatsoper and Kiel), Ariadne, the Marschallin, Wagner's Eva and Elisabeth, Eglantine in Euryanthe, the Mother in Dallapiccola's Il Prigioniero, and the Kostelnička in Jenůfa (1996); Many concert engagements throughout Germany. *Address:* c/o Semper Opera, Theaterplatz 2, D–01607 Dresden, Germany.

**THIELEMANN, Christian;** German conductor; *Music Director, Munich Philharmonic Orchestra;* b. 1 April 1959, Berlin. *Education:* Berlin Hochschule für Musik, Karajan Foundation Orchestra Acad., Berlin. *Career:* musical coach in Berlin, with Karajan from 1979, at Berlin, Salzburg and Munich; asst to Daniel Barenboim at Paris, Berlin and Bayreuth; Principal Conductor, Deutsche Oper am Rhein Düsseldorf 1985; Music Dir, Nuremberg Opera 1988–92; American debut season 1991–92, with Elektra at the San Francisco Opera; Der Rosenkavalier at the New York Met 1993, Arabella 1994; regular concerts with the New York Philharmonic Orchestra and Philadelphia and Minnesota Orchestras; British debut with Jenůfa at Covent Garden 1988, returning for Elektra 1994 and the British premiere of Pfitzner's Palestrina 1997; further opera includes Capriccio in Florence, The Makropulos Case in Bologna, Don Giovanni in Berlin and Lohengrin on tour to Japan with the Deutsche Oper Berlin; season 1996 with Otello in Bologna (Principal Guest Conductor), Tristan and Meistersinger with the Deutsche Opera; further concerts with the Chicago Symphony Orchestra, Philharmonia Orchestra and the Munich Philharmonic Orchestra; Strauss's Aegyptische Helena for the Royal Opera at the Festival Hall 1998; returned to Covent Garden with Palestrina 2001; Music Dir, Deutsche Oper Berlin 1997–2004, Guest Dir 2004–; Music Dir Munich Philharmonic Orchestra 2004–. *Recordings include:* Wagner and Strauss, with René Kollo; Beethoven Cantatas, orchestral music by Wagner, Strauss and Pfitzner, Schumann 2nd Symphony and Beethoven Nos 5 and 7; Video of Arabella, from the Met, with Kiri Te Kanawa. *Current Management:* Columbia Artists (Conductors Division), 165 West 57th Street, New York, NY 10019, USA.

**THIEME, Helga;** Singer (Soprano); b. 27 Feb. 1937, Oberlengsfeld, Germany. *Education:* Studied in Frankfurt. *Career:* Sang in opera at Basle, 1962–65; Bielefeld, 1965–67, Wiesbaden, 1967–68, Hamburg, 1968–83, notably in the premieres of The Devils of Loudun by Penderecki in 1969 and Josef Tal's Ashmedai in 1971, Bremen, 1974–76, St Gallen from 1980 and Zürich, 1984–85; Guest engagements at Berne, Deutsche Oper Berlin, state operas of Munich and Stuttgart, Düsseldorf, Vienna Volksoper, Barcelona and Cologne; Roles have included Susanna, Zerlina, Despina and the Queen of Night, Norina and Adina, Lortzing's Gretchen and Marie, Gilda, Aennchen, Marenka, Sophie in Der Rosenkavalier, Isotta in Die schweigsame Frau and Ida in Henze's Junge Lord. *Recordings include:* The Devils of Loudun. *Address:* c/o Staatl. Hochschule für Musik, 30175 Hannover, Germany.

**THIEME, Ulrich;** Professor of Recorder and Musicologist; b. 5 Aug. 1950, Hamm, Germany. *Education:* State Diploma, Music Teaching, 1973; Concert Diploma, Recorder, 1974; PhD, Musicology. *Career:* Television appearances with broadcasts for several German stations, 1969–; Recorder Teacher at Academy of Music in Cologne, 1973–78 and Academy of Music at Hannover, 1978–; Concert tours throughout Europe, Eastern Asia and South America and 50 concerts with recorder and lute-guitar duo in Germany; mem, Vice-President, ERTA, European Recorder Teachers Association, German Section. *Recordings:* Jürg Baur's Tre Studi per Quattro; Bach's Brandenburg Concertos; Baroque Recorder Music by various composers including Delalande, Bonocini and Mancini. *Publications:* Studien zum Jugendwerk A Schoenbergs, 1979; Affektenlehre im Barocken Musikdenken, 1984. *Contributions:* Editor of Baroque Recorder Music (Castello, Monteclair); TIBIA. *Honours:* 1st Prize, German Young Musicians Competition, 1967. *Address:* c/o Staatliche Hochschule für Musik, D-3 Hannover, Germany.

**THIOLLIER, François-Joël;** concert pianist; b. 12 Nov. 1943, Paris, France; m. Beatrice Fitch 1978; one s. *Education:* studied in Paris with Robert Casadesus, Juilliard Preparatory College. *Career:* many concerts in over 30 countries including appearances with the Orchestre de Paris, Nouvel Orchestre Philharmonique, Moscow and Leningrad Philharmonic Orchestras, the Hague Residentie Orkest, Tokyo and Berlin Philharmonics and RAI in Italy; Concert halls include Amsterdam Concertgebouw, Théâtre des Champs Elysées, Teatro Real of Madrid, Accademia di Santa Cecilia, Rome, and Victoria Hall Geneva; Played the Busoni Concerto in Berlin. *Recordings:* Complete works of Rachmaninov and Gershwin; Beethoven Sonatas Op 27 No. 2, Op 13 and Op 57; Liszt Sonata and Complete Songs for Tenor and Piano; Brahms Sonata Op 5; Paganini Variations; Mozart Sonata K330 and Quintet K452. *Honours:* Prizewinner at International Piano Competitions: Viotti, Casella, Busoni, Pozzoli, Montreal, Tchaikovsky Moscow, Marguérite Long, Paris, Queen Elisabeth, Brussels. *Current Management:* Patricia Garrasi, Via Manzoni, 20121 Milan, Italy.

**THOMAS, Augusta (Read);** Composer; b. 24 April 1964, Glen Cove, New York, USA. *Education:* Studied at Northwestern University (1983–87) and with Jacob Druckman at Yale University (MM 1988); Postgraduate studies at the Royal Academy of Music, London 1988–89. *Career:* Freelance composer;

Faculty member, Eastman School of Music, Rochester, New York, 1993–2001; Prof. of Music, Northwestern University, Chicago, IL; Mead Composer-in-Residence, Chicago Symphony Orchestra, 1997–(2006); mem., Bd of Dirs, American Music Center, 2000–. *Compositions include:* Vigil for cello and chamber orchestra, 1992; Ligeia, chamber opera, 1994 (Int. Orpheus Prize); Words of the Sea, for orchestra, 1996; Orbital Beacons, for orchestra, 1997; Ritual Incantations, cello concerto, 1999; Ceremonial, for orchestra, 1999; Daylight Divine, 2001; Prayer Bells, for orchestra, 2001; In My Sky at Twilight, 2002; Silver Chants the Litanies, homage to Luciano Berio, for solo horn and ensemble; Tangle, for orchestra; Galaxy Dances, ballet for orchestra; Gathering Paradise, for solo soprano and orchestra; Grace Notes, for orchestra. *Honours:* International Orpheus Prize for Opera, Spoleto Italy, 1994; Charles Ives Fellowship, 1994; Rockefeller Foundation Grant, 1997; New York State Artist Fellowship, 1998; Koussevitzky Award, 1999; Siemens Award, 2000; American Academy Award, 2001. *Address:* c/o PO Box 769, Lee, MA 01238, USA. *Website:* www.augustareadthomas.com.

**THOMAS, Caryl,** MA, ARCM; British harpist; b. 23 Oct. 1958, Aberystwyth, Dyfed, Wales; m. Huw Williams 1985. *Education:* Welsh Coll. of Music and Drama, New York Univ., USA. *Career:* debut, Carnegie Hall, NY 1981; freelance harpist, concentrating on solo and concert work with great emphasis on BBC Radio 3 and Channel 4 television broadcasting; appearances include London debut at Wigmore Hall, concerto soloist with BBC Nat. Orchestra of Wales 1982, and Mozarteum Orchestra at Salzburg, Austria 1984. *Recordings:* Mozart Concerto for flute and harp (with London Philharmonic Orchestra, flautist Jonathan Snowden and conducted by Andrew Litton) 1987, French Impressions (with Prometheus Ensemble). *Address:* Hendre'r Wenallt, St Athan Road, Cowbridge, South Glamorgan CF71 7LT, Wales.

**THOMAS, David;** British singer (bass); b. 26 Feb. 1943, Orpington; m. Veronica Joan Dean 1982; three d. *Education:* St Paul's Cathedral Choir School, London, King's School, Canterbury, Choral Scholar, King's Coll., Cambridge. *Career:* began singing as boy chorister in St Paul's Cathedral Choir, London; repertoire ranges from Baroque and Classical, and includes works by Walton, Tippet, Britten, Stravinsky, Schoenberg and Schnittke; tours to Europe, USA and Japan; appearances at int festivals, including Tanglewood, Salzburg, Edingburgh, Luzerne, Stuttgart, Aldeburgh and BBC Promenade Concerts; has appeared with many of the major symphony orchestras and ensembles in UK, including City of Birmingham Symphony, London Philharmonic, Royal Philharmonic, Philharmonia, Hallé, Royal Liverpool Philharmonic, Chamber Orchestra of Europe, London Classical Players, Scottish Chamber Orchestra, Manchester Camerata, Northern Sinfonia, Taverner Consort, Acad. of Ancient Music and London Baroque, and has worked regularly with conductors including Simon Rattle, John Eliot Gardiner, Nicholas McGegan and Christopher Hogwood; notable engagements in UK include TV recording of Beethoven's 9th Symphony with London Classical Players conducted by Roger Norrington, Handel's Orlando at BBC Proms conducted by Christopher Hogwood and Die Schöpfung' with Chamber Orchestra of Europe and Frans Bruggen; regular concerts with soprano Emma Kirkby and lutenist Anthony Rooley; sang Sarasto in Covent Garden Festival's production of Die Zauberflöte and the Commendatore in Don Giovanni and General Spork in Cornet Cristoph Rilke's Song of Love and Death for Glyndebourne Touring Opera; other engagements have included performances of the Christmas Oratorio in Leipzig and Berlin, a series of Messiahs in Italy and concerts with the Orchestre de la Swiss Romande, Fundaçao de Sao Carlos in Lisbon, Wiener Akademie, with Kammerchor Stuttgart in concerts in Göttingen, and Handel's Serse and Resurrezione in Brighton and Göttingen; engagements in USA have included Messiah with Los Angeles Philharmonic in the Hollywood Bowl, Haydn's Creation with Boston Symphony Orchestra and Simon Rattle, Messiah at Lincoln Center with Acad. of Ancient Music, Schubert's Winterreise at Cornell University and Handel's Judas Maccabaeus, Susanna and Theodora with Philharmonia Baroque and Nicholas McGegan; teaches at Trinity Coll. of Music, London. *Recordings include:* more than 100 records, including Handel's Serse (Hanover Band/Nicholas McGegan), Handel's Susanna, Apollo and Daphne and Judas Maccabaeus (Philharmonia Baroque/Nicholas McGegan), Handel's Semele, Purcell's Fairy Queen and Bach's Magnificat (Monteverdi Choir/English Baroque Soloists/John Eliot Gardiner), Handel's Acis, Galatea e Polifemo (London Baroque/Charles Medlam), Handel's Messiah and Israel in Egypt, Bach's B Minor Mass and St John Passion (Taverner Consort & Players/Andrew Parrot), Coffee Cantata with Emma Kirkby, Mozart's Requiem (Hanover Band/Roy Goodman), Stravinsky's Pulcinella (City of London Sinfonia/Richard Hickox) and Die Schöpfung (City of Birmingham Orchestra/Simon Rattle); solo record Aria for Montagnana. *Current Management:* Allied Artists, 42 Montpelier Square, London, SW7 1JZ. *Telephone:* (20) 7589-6243. *Fax:* (20) 7581-5269. *Website:* www.alliedartists.co.uk. *Address:* 74 Hyde Vale, Greenwich, London, SE10 8HP, England. *E-mail:* davidthomas@london.com.

**THOMAS, Gwion;** Singer (Baritone); b. 1954, Wales. *Education:* Studied at the Royal Northern College of Music. *Career:* Appearances with Welsh National Opera, Royal Opera Garden Venture, Kent Opera and the Aldeburgh Festival (in the title role in the premiere of Lefanu's Wildman, 1995); Other roles include Orestes, Mozart's Don Giovanni, Count and Papageno, and Britten's Tarquinius, Billy Budd and Ned Keene; Television appearances in Weir's Night at the Chinese Opera and Scipio's Dream; Concerts with the BBC Symphony Orchestra, London Philharmonic Orchestra.

**THOMAS, Matthew (Elton);** Singer (Baritone); b. 1963, Canada. *Career:* Performances as Kuligin in Katya Kabanova for the Canadian Opera Company, and Marcello in La Bohème at Vancouver; Mozart's Count, Guglielmo and Don Giovanni at the Banff Centre of the Performing Arts; Ourrais in Gounod's Mireille and Le Conte in Massenet's Grisélidis for Opera in Concert, Toronto; British performances include Rigoletto for Clonter Opera Farm and English Touring Opera (1996); Rossini's Figaro for ETO, Belcore (L'Elisir d'amore) for Mid Wales Opera and Valentin in Faust for Dublin Grand Opera Society; Further appearances as Hercules/The Herald in Gluck's Alceste for Scottish Opera and Don Giovanni for Opera on a Shoestring, Glasgow; Concert repertoire includes Carmina Burana, Messiah, Elijah, and the Requiems of Brahms, Fauré and Duruflé. *Address:* c/o English Touring Opera, 250a Kennington Lane, London, SE11 5RD, England.

**THOMAS, Michael Tilson** (see Tilson Thomas, Michael)

**THOMAS, Nova;** Singer (Soprano); b. 1960, North Carolina, USA. *Education:* Studied at the University of Bloomington with Eileen Farrell. *Career:* Debut: Mimi in La Bohème at North Carolina; Appearances at opera houses in Cologne, Hamburg, Belfast (Opera Northern Ireland), St Louis, Seattle, San Diego, Detroit and New York City Opera; Season 1991–92 in Cologne and Paris as Giulia in La Scala di Seta; Roles have included Violetta, the Four Heroines in Les Contes d'Hoffmann, the Trovatore Leonora and Anna Bolena; Further engagements as Mozart's Constanze for Cologne Opera, Norma with Seattle Opera and Hoffmann under Richard Bonynge; Sang Adalgisa in Norma at Philadelphia, 1998. *Recordings include:* Title role in The Bohemian Girl, under Bonynge. *Honours:* Winner, Metropolitan Opera National Council Auditions, 1984. *Address:* c/o Opera Co of Philadelphia, 510 Walnut Street, Suite 1600, Philadelphia, PA 19106, USA.

**THOMAS, Peter;** Violinist; b. 1944, South Wales. *Education:* Studied in England, winning the Menuhin Prize at Bath Festival, 1958. *Career:* Second Violinist of the Allegri Quartet, 1963–68; Co-Founder of Orion Piano Trio, becoming resident ensemble at Southampton University; Leader of BBC National Orchestra of Wales, 1972, then Philharmonia; Leader of City of Birmingham Symphony Orchestra and Artistic Director of Birmingham Ensemble; String Adviser to Gustav Mahler Youth Orchestra, Vienna; Purcell Room, London, recital 1993, with works by Schubert, Berio (Sequenza VIII), Schoenberg and Busoni (2nd Sonata). *Honours:* With Orion Piano Trio: BBC Prize for British and Commonwealth Ensembles. *Address:* Camerata Artists, 4 Margaret Road, Birmingham B17 0 EU, England.

**THOMAS, Steven Murray,** BA, DipMus; Canadian stage producer and television producer; b. 26 June 1946, Peterborough, ON; m. Irene Wronski 1985. *Education:* University of Western Ontario, Royal Conservatory of Toronto. *Career:* debut with New Jersey State Opera in 1976; Producer, Artistic Director, Actor, Dramatic Theatre, 1964–72; Producer and Stage Director for Opera (freelance), 1972–78; Production Manager, Opera Festival at National Arts Centre, Ottawa, 1978–79; Artistic Director for Opera Hamilton, 1979–86; Producer, television opera, CHCH-TV, Hamilton, 1979–86; Operas produced for television include La Bohème, La Traviata, Madama Butterfly, The Barber of Seville, Rigoletto, Aida, Manon Lescaut, The Marriage of Figaro, Hansel and Gretel and Carmen. *Honours:* CANPRO Awards for Excellence in the Performing Arts, Canadian Television National Competition, for La Bohème, 1980, La Traviata, 1981, The Barber of Seville, 1983, and Aida, 1985; Canadian Music Council Award for television, La Traviata, 1983. *Address:* 226 Westmount Avenue, Toronto, ON M6E 3M8, Canada.

**THOMASCHKE, Thomas Michael;** German concert and opera singer (bass); b. 2 Aug. 1943, Pirna; m. 1964; one s. one d. *Education:* Dresden Hochschule für Musik. *Career:* debut in Freiberg, Germany, in Tosca, 1963; Sang in Leipzig, Dresden, and at the Komische Oper Berlin in the 1960s; La Scala, Bavarian State Opera, Glyndebourne, Covent Garden, Paris, Lisbon, Buenos Aires, Vienna, Edinburgh, Cape Town, Rome, Florence and Amsterdam; Has sung Figaro, Don Giovanni, Rocco (Fidelio), Sarastro (Magic Flute), Gurnemanz (Parsifal); Sang Ramphis in Aida at Cape Town, 2000; Artistic Director of Festival Mitte Europa. *Recordings include:* Bach and Handel, conducted by Nikolaus Harnoncourt; Weber, Freischütz, Philips, Colin Davis; Beethoven 9th Symphony, Yehudi Menuhin. *Publications:* contrib. to Opernwelt. *Honours:* Schumanpreis, 1966; Tschaikowskypreis, 1970; 1st Prize, Preis Hertogenbosch, 1971. *Address:* Fliederweg 108, 50859 Cologne, Germany.

**THOME, Diane;** Composer, Pianist, University Professor and Lecturer; b. 25 Jan. 1942, Pearl River, New York, USA. *Education:* Studied piano with Dorothy Taubman, New York, composition with Robert Strassburg, Darius Milhaud at Aspen, Colorado, Roy Harris at Inter-American University, PR; PhD in Music, Princeton University, 1973; Alexander Boscovich (Israel); Milton Babbitt, Princeton. *Career:* Taught music at Princeton University, New Jersey, 1973–74; Taught theory and 20th century music at SUNY, Binghampton, 1974–77; Professor of Theory and Composition at University of Washington School of Music, Seattle; mem, SCI Inc; BMI; CMS. *Compositions include:* Chamber: 3 Pieces, 1958, 3 Movements, 1958, Sonatine, 1960, Suite, 1961, Quartet, 1961, Constellations, 1966; Electronic music: Le Berceau De Miel, 1968, Spectrophonie, 1969, Polyvalence, 1972, January Variations, 1973, Los Nombres, 1974, Alexander Boscovich Remembered, 1975, Anais, 1976, Sunflower Space, 1978, Winter Infinities, 1980, To Search The Spacious World, 1986, The Ruins Of The Heart for Soprano, Orchestra and Tape, 1991,

Angels for Virtual Reality Artwork, 1992, The Palaces Of Memory for Large Chamber Ensemble or Chamber Orchestra and Tape, 1993; Masks of Eternity, 1994; Unseen Buds, for chorus and tape, 1995; Unfold, Entwine, 1998; Like a Seated Swan, for viola and tape, 2000; Multimedia works: In My Garden, 1956, Caprice, 1957, Night Passage, 1973; Anais; Bright Air/Brilliant Fire; Levadi (Alone); Unfold Entwine; Unseen Buds; Orchestral: 3 Movements, 1962, S'Embarquement, 1971, The Golden Messengers, 1984, Lucent Flowers, 1988; Piano works: Sonatine, 1959, Pianismus; Sacred works: Three Psalms, 1979; Vocal: Ash On An Old Man's Sleeve, 1962, Spring And Fall: To A Young Child, 1962, Cantata, 1964, Songs On Chinese Verses, 1964, The Yew Tree, 1979, 3 Sonnets By Sri Aurobindo: Settings for Soprano and Orchestra, 1984; Lucent Flowers; Celestial Canopy, 1999. *Recordings include:* Palaces of Memory, electro-acoustic music; The Ruins of the Heart; Three Psalms; Pianismus; The Yew Tree; The Palaces of Memory, 1995; Bright Air/Brilliant Fire, 2000. *Address:* University of Washington School of Music, Box 353450, Seattle, WA 98195, USA.

**THOMPSON, Adrian;** Singer (tenor); b. 1954, London, England. *Education:* Guildhall School of Music and Drama, London. *Career:* opera engagements with the Glyndebourne Festival, Scottish Opera, Handel Opera Society and at the Buxton, Aldeburgh, Wexford, Lausanne and Göttingen Festivals; roles include Ariodante, Snout and Flute in A Midsummer Night's Dream, Albert Herring, Podesta, Pedrillo in Die Entführung, Le nozze di Figaro, Così fan tutte, Bardolph in Falstaff, Conti's Don Quixote in Sierra Morena, the Simpleton in Boris Godunov and Nurse in L'Incoronazione di Poppea; sang Alfred in Die Fledermaus at Belfast, 1990, the title role in Haydn's Orlando Paladino at Garsington Manor, Oxford, and Britten's Flute at Sadler's Wells, 1990 (Snout at Glyndebourne, 1989); concert performances throughout Europe and the UK in works by Purcell, Bach, Handel, Berlioz, Schoenberg and Tippett; Britten repertoire includes Les Illuminations, The Serenade, Nocturne, Canticles and Song Cycles; appearances with leading British orchestras, the Netherlands Chamber Orchestra, Nash Ensemble and Stockholm Bach Choir; frequent Promenade Concerts and recitals at the Aldeburgh, Bath, Lichfield and Buxton festivals; has sung Schubert's Die schöne Müllerin at the Wigmore Hall and songs by Schubert and Schoenberg at South Bank; recitals in Israel, Canada, Germany, France and Switzerland; recitals in USA, Salome in Netherlands, Handel's Tamerlano at Karlsruhe and Irus in Monteverdi's Ulisse at the Coliseum, London, 1992–93; sang Grimoaldo in Rodelinda with Broomhill Opera, 1996; Schoolmaster in Janáček's Vixen at Spoleto, 1998; Albert Gregor in The Makropulos Case at Cologne, 2000. *Recordings include:* Gurney's Ludlow and Teme; Beggar's Opera. *Current Management:* Caroline Phillips Management, The Old Brushworks, Pickwick Road, Corsham, Wiltshire, SN13 9BX, England. *Telephone:* (1249) 716716. *Fax:* (1249) 716717. *E-mail:* cphillips@caroline-phillips.co.uk. *Website:* www.caroline-phillips.co.uk/thompson.

**THOMPSON, Donald (Prosser);** University Professor, Conductor and Writer; b. 28 Feb. 1928, Columbus, Ohio, USA; m. Ana Christina Figueroa Laugier, 23 Jan 1972, 2 s., 1 d. *Education:* AB, University of Missouri, 1952; MA, University of Missouri, 1954; Akademie für Musik, Vienna, Austria; Eastman School of Music; PhD, University of Iowa, 1970. *Career:* Retired as Professor and Chair, Department of Music, University of Puerto Rico, 1956–85; Conductor, opera, music theatre, television, San Juan, Puerto Rico, 1956–; Music Critic San Juan Star, 1957–60, 1975–94; Consultant in Arts Management, 1985–. *Contributions:* Manual para monografias musicales, 1980; The New Grove Dictionary of Music, 1980; The New Grove Dictionary of American Music, 1986; Music Research in Puerto Rico, 1982; The Puerto Rico Symphony Orchestra, 1985; The New Grove Dictionary of Opera, 1992; El joven Tavarez; nuevos documentos y nuevas perspectivas, 1993; Diccionario de musica espanola e hispanoamericana, 1994. *Contributions:* Revista musical chilena, 1984; African Music, 1975–76; Inter American Music review, 1989; Revista musical de Venezuela, 1989; Bibliografia musicologica latinoamericana, 1992, 1993; Latin American Music Review, 1983, 1985, 1990, 1993. *Address:* Calle Acadia N-64, Rio Piedras, Puerto Rico.

**THOMPSON, Lesleigh (Karen);** Composer and Pianist; b. 8 Nov. 1966, Bulawayo, Rhodesia (now Zimbabwe), Australian resident since 1977. *Education:* BMus 1991, MMus 1994, The University of Melbourne. *Career:* Lecturer in Music Techniques at the University of Melbourne, 1993–96; Studied with Brenton Broadstock, 1989–93; Stephen Ingham, 1994–97; Examiner, Australian Music Examinations Board, 1997–. *Compositions include:* Toccata for piano, 1989; Captive, for ensemble, 1991; Enost, for string quartet, 1992; Sonata for Piano: Mad Men, Mad Times, 1992; Sphygmus for piano, 1992; Exuviae for piano, 1993; Facade for guitar, 1994; Clandestine, for orchestra, 1994; Sweet Talk, for guitar and cello, 1995; Roulette, for piano, 1996. *Honours:* New Audience Award for Composition, 1990; Albert H Maggs Award, 1993. *Address:* c/o APRA, 1A Eden Street, Crows Nest, NSW 2065, Australia.

**THOMPSON, Margaret;** Singer (Mezzo-soprano); b. 26 Aug. 1962, Glenlovee, New York. *Education:* New England Conservatory, Boston and University of Delaware; Salzburg Mozarteum with Grace Bumbry. *Career:* Sang Carmen, and Orlofsky in Die Fledermaus, in USA; Koblenz and Pforzheim opera houses, from 1991, and Bielefeld Opera from 1995; Roles have included Rosina, Cherubino, Strauss's Composer, Eboli, Charlotte in Werther, Queen of the Spirits in Marschner's Hans Heiling, Britten's Oberon, Suzuki, and Margaretha in Schumann's Genoveva (Bielefeld 1995); Mahler's Rückert Lieder at Salzburg, 1996; Other concert repertory in works by Bach,

Handel, Haydn, Mozart and Penderecki; Sang in German, premiere of Blond Eckbert, by Judith Weir, at Bielefeld. *Honours:* Winner Sylvia Geszty Competition; Luxembourg, 1995. *Address:* c/o Bühnen der Stadt Bielefeld, Brunhenstrasse 3–9, Pf. 220, 4800 Bielefeld, Germany.

**THOMPSON, Martin;** Singer (Tenor); b. 1956, USA. *Career:* Many appearances at leading European and American opera houses; Roles have included Werther, Hoffmann, Gounod's Roméo, Edgardo, Pinkerton, Peter Grimes, Don José, Lensky, Rodolfo, and Orombello in Bellini's Beatrice di Tenda; Concerts include Beethoven's Ninth Symphony at San Francisco, Cherubini's Mass in D Minor (Stuttgart) and Britten's War Requiem; Season 1997–98 with Covent Garden and Metropolitan Opera debuts (as the Duke of Mantua, and Pinkerton), Hoffmann in Philadelphia and Pinkerton at Santa Fe; Other repertory includes Tom Rakewell (Philadelphia, 1997), the title role in Mozart's Mitridate (Wexford Festival, 1988), Nadir in Les pêcheurs de Perles and the title role in Argento's Voyage of Edgar Allan Poe (Dallas Opera); Santa Fé Opera 1999–2000, as Don José, Pinkerton and the Duke of Mantua; Puccini's Des Grieux for ENO 2000, Foresto in Attila at Chicago and Rodolfo in Luisa Miller for the Deutsche Oper Berlin. *Address:* c/o Metropolitan Opera, Lincoln Center, New York, NY 10023, USA.

**THOMPSON, Michael,** FRAM; British horn player; *Professor of Horn, Royal Academy of Music;* b. 4 Jan. 1954, London. *Education:* RAM, London with Ifor James. *Career:* Principal Horn, BBC Scottish Symphony Orchestra 1972–75, Philharmonia Orchestra, London 1975–85, London Sinfonietta; Prof. of Horn (Aubrey Brain Chair), Royal Acad. of Music 1984–; concert repertory includes concertos of Haydn and Mozart, Sea Eagle by Maxwell Davies, and Des Canyons aux Etoiles, by Messiaen; premieres of works by Benedict Mason, Simon Bainbridge and Anthony Powers. *Recordings include:* Standard Concertos and the Quintets of Franz Danzi and Antoine Reicha. *Address:* Royal Academy of Music, Marylebone Road, London, NW1 5HT, England. *Website:* www.ram.ac.uk.

**THOMPSON, (Robert) Ian,** MA, ARCM, ARCO; British singer (tenor), harpsichordist, conductor and artistic director; b. 5 April 1943, Bradford, Yorks., England; m. Judith Welch 1970. *Education:* Queens' Coll., Cambridge, Royal Coll. of Music, London; singing with Campogalliani, Italy. *Career:* BBC Chorus 1966–67; Vicar Choral, St Paul's Cathedral, London 1967–77; opera and concert singer with Kent Opera and Opera North; debut, Royal Opera House, Covent Garden 1993; since debut at Rossini Festival, Pesaro 1991; has appeared regularly at leading European theatres, including La Scala, Milan, San Carlo Naples, Regio, Turin, Bastille and Châtelet, Paris, Strasbourg, Bordeaux and Lyon; broadcasts in most European countries; Visiting Lecturer, Royal Scottish Acad. of Music and Drama, Glasgow 1996–; Artistic Dir Lonsdale Music; 60e Parallèle with Philippe Mancury; Ariadne auf Naxos, with Giuseppe Sinopoli; mem. Incorporated Soc. of Musicians, Royal Coll. of Organists, The Alpine Club, Amaryllis Consort. *Recordings:* with Pro Cantione Antiqua, Early Music Consort, Società Cameristica di Lugano and Capella Clementina; Dr Wittkop in 60 Parallèle, Scaramuccio in Ariadne auf Naxos. *Address:* Hill Top, Tearnside, Kirkby Lonsdale, Cumbria, LA6 2PU, England (home).

**THOMPSON, Terence James,** ABSM (TTD); British composer and teacher (retd), clarinettist and saxophonist; b. 19 Jan. 1928, Staffordshire, England. *Education:* Birmingham School of Music. *Career:* music master, West Bromwich Technical High School 1950–59; clarinet tutor, Birmingham School of Music 1954–55; Head of Music, March End School; mem. Performing Right Soc., British Acad. of Composers and Songwriters, Musicians' Union, Central Composers' Alliance, Birmingham Conservatoire Asscn (Alumnus), Mechanical Copyright Protection Soc., Light Music Soc., NUT. *Compositions:* Boogie and Blues, Suite Chalumeau Swing, Suite City Scenes, Back to Bach, two syncopated dances. *Recordings:* London Saxophone Quartet in digital, Two Light Pieces 1999, A Cumbrian Voluntary 2000. *Publications:* Romance in Sepia 1985, Something Blue 1983, Song and Dance 1994, A Cumbrian Voluntary 2000. *Address:* 58 Willenhall Road, Bilston, West Midlands WV14 6NW, England. *Telephone:* (1902) 495646 (home).

**THOMSON, Brian Edward,** AM; Australian film, theatre and opera designer; b. 5 Jan. 1946, Sydney; s. of Austin Thomas Thomson and Adoree Gertrude Thomson. *Education:* Applecross Sr High School, Perth Tech. Coll., Univ. of New South Wales. *Career:* Supervising Designer, closing ceremony of Olympic Games, Sydney 2000; Production Designer, Centennial of Fed. Ceremony 2001; Designer, opening and closing ceremonies, Rugby World Cup 2003. *Musicals:* Hair, Jesus Christ Superstar (London and Australia), The Rocky Horror Show (original London production and worldwide), Chicago, The Stripper, Company, Chess, The King and I (Broadway production 1996, London Palladium), How to Succeed in Business Without Really Trying, South Pacific, Hello, Dolly!, Merrily We Roll Along, Grease, Happy Days. *Theatre:* Housewife Superstar!!! (London and New York); The Threepenny Opera (opening season, Drama Theatre, Sydney Opera House); Big Toys (the Old Tote); A Cheery Soul, Chinchilla, Macbeth, The Doll Trilogy, The Ham Funeral, A Midsummer Night's Dream, The Crucible, The Homecoming, Uncle Vanya, Death and the Maiden, Coriolanus, Falsettos, King Lear, Arcadia, Medea, Mongrels, Third World Blues, After the Ball, White Devil (also at Brooklyn Acad. of Music), Up for Grabs (all for Sydney Theatre Co.); Arturo Ui, Rock-Ola (Nimrod); Lulu, Shepherd on the Rocks Crow (State Theatre Co. of S Australia); Ghosts, The Tempest, The Master Builder, Buzz, Frogs, Aftershocks, Radiance, Up the Road, Burnt Piano, The Laramie Project

(Company B Belvoir); Angels in America (Melbourne Theatre Co.); Soulmates, One Day of the Year (Sydney Theatre Co.), My Zinc Bed, Buried Child (Company B Belvoir), Dame Edna Back With A Vengeance, Broadway 2004, Three Furies, Sydney Festival 2005. *Film and television:* Barlow and Chambers, Shadow of the Cobra (both mini-series); Shirly Thompson vs. the Aliens, The Rocky Horror Picture Show, Starstruck, Rebel, Night of Shadows (also dir), Ground Zero, Turtle Beach, Frauds. *Dance:* Synergy, Fornicon (Sydney Dance Co.), Tivol (Sydney Dance Co. and Australian Ballet). *Opera:* Death in Venice, The Makropulos Affair (Adelaide Festival); Turandot, Aida, Summer of the Seventeenth Doll (Vic. State Opera); Voss, Death in Venice, Tristan und Isolde, Katya Kabanova, The Eighth Wonder (The Australian Opera); Billy Budd (Welsh Nat. Opera, Opera Australia, Canadian Nat. Opera), Sweeney Todd (Lyric Opera of Chicago). *Honours:* Australian Film Inst. Award for production design, Rebel 1985, Ground Zero 1987, Sydney Theatre Critics' Award for Best Designer 1989, 1992, 1993, 1994, Mo Award 1994, 1995, Tony Award for The King and I 1996. *Address:* 5 Little Dowling Street, Paddington, NSW 2021, Australia. *Telephone:* (2) 9331-1584 (office); (4) 1164-3323 (home). *E-mail:* bt@brianthomson.biz (office). *Website:* www.brianthomson.biz (office).

**THOMSON, Heather;** Opera Singer (Soprano); b. 7 Dec. 1940, Vancouver, Canada; m. Perry Price. *Education:* Studied at the Toronto Conservatory with Herman Geiger-Torel and Irene Jessner. *Career:* Debut: Toronto in 1962 in Hansel and Gretel; Debut with Sadler's Wells as Micaela followed by Mimi, Marguerite in Faust and Anne Trulove in The Rake's Progress; Canadian Opera Company roles include Manon, Rosalinda in Die Fledermaus, Donna Anna and Donna Elvira in Don Giovanni, Ellen in Peter Grimes, Marguerite in Faust, Mother in Hansel and Gretel, Mimi in La Bohème, Tatyana in Eugene Onegin, Lady Billows in Albert Hessing, and world premieres of Heloise and Abelard by Wilson, and Mario and The Magician by Sommers and the title role in Beatrice Cenci, by Goldschmidt in Magdeburg, Germany; Has sung with Welsh National Opera as well as throughout the British Islies, Holland, Czech Republic, Germany, Chile, Monterideo, Poland, Norway, China, the Phillipines and in USA; Roles with New York City Opera include Violetta, Nedda, Donna Anna and Donna Elvira, Marguerite, Rosalinda, and Agathe in Der Freischütz; 1993–94 season as Lady Macbeth in Chemnitz in Germany, Violetta in La Traviata in Toledo, Ohio, Hanna in The Merry Widow at Victoria BC and concerts in Germany and Canada; Sang Rosalinda in Die Fledermaus in Regina, Sash in 2002; Teacher at the School of Music, University of British Columbia in Vancouver and at the New England Vocal Studios, which she established with her husband Perry Price in 1997 in Danbury, CT, USA. *Recordings:* Sang Manon for CBC television; Lady Billows in Albert Herring for CBC and BBC radio; Mother in Hansel and Gretel for CBC-Radio. *Address:* c/o Canadian Opera Company, 227 Front Street East, Toronto, M5A 1E8, Canada.

**THOMSON, Neil;** Conductor; b. 1966, London, England. *Education:* Studied at the Royal Academy of Music with George Hurst and at the Royal College with Norman del Mar and Christopher Adey. *Career:* Director, Manson Ensemble at RAM giving many performances during the Messiaen Festival in 1987 and the Henze Festival in 1988; Conducted major orchestral and instrumental works of Paul Patterson at venues around the United Kingdom; Founded the contemporary music group, Terre Nova in 1986, with its debut at St John's Smith Square; Concerts at the Purcell Room, South Bank and the Huddersfield Contemporary Music Festival; Worked with such soloists as Christopher Bunting in Dvořák's Cello Concerto and the Brahms Double Concerto with Emanuel Hurwitz, And Suddenly It's Evening by Elisabeth Lutyens with Philip Langridge, and Philip Gammon with Saint-Saëns's 2nd Concerto; Concerts with the Royal Tunbridge Wells Symphony Orchestra; Music Director, Sadler's Wells Youth Ballet Workshop; Concerts with the Bombay Chamber Orchestra in India. *Honours:* Bursary for Conductors, National Association of Youth Orchestras.

**THORBURN, Melissa Rachel,** BMus, MMus; American opera and concert singer (mezzo-soprano); b. 9 July 1956, Monmouth, IL; m. Timothy Richard Sobolewski 1985; one s. *Education:* Louisiana State University, New England Conservatory, studied with Yvonne Lefèbure in Paris. *Career:* Handel's Messiah with Philadelphia Orchestra, 1987–91, annually; Sang in Berlioz's L'Enfance du Christ with Seattle Symphony, WA, in 1987, Gounod's Faust as Siebel with Deutsche Oper Berlin in 1988, Pergolesi's Stabat Mater with the Puerto Rico Symphony in 1988, Mozart's Le nozze di Figaro as Cherubino with Sarasota Opera, FL, in 1988; Mozart's Requiem with Los Angeles Philharmonic in 1991, and Handel's Messiah with National Symphony in 1992; Mozart's Requiem and Schubert's Mass in E flat with Indianapolis Symphony conducted by Richard Hickox, 1994; Bach's Mass in B Minor with Winter Park Bach Festival, Florida, 1994; Bach's Christmas Oratorio and Cantata No.78 with Baldwin-Wallace Bach Festival, Ohio, 1995; Mendelssohn's Lobgesang with Vancouver Symphony and recitals at the Bermuda Festival, 1996; Mendelssohn's A Midsummer Night's Dream with Philadelphia Orchestra conducted by Charles Dutoit, 1997, and with St Louis Symphony, 1998. *Recordings:* Vaughan Williams's Serenade to Music with the New York Virtuosi Chamber Symphony; Sousa's Désirée. *Current Management:* Thea Dispeker Inc. Artists Representative, 59 E 54th Street, New York, NY 10022, USA. *Address:* c/o Music Department, SUNY, 222 Baird Hall, Buffalo, NY 14260, USA.

**THORN, Benjamin,** BA, PhD; Australian composer, editor and recorder player; b. 31 Jan. 1961, Canberra. *Education:* Univ. of Sydney, studied with Larry Sitsky and Donald Hollier. *Career:* Univ. of Sydney 1986; Nat. Printing Industry Training Council 1991; performances as recorder player with the Renaissance Players and other groups. *Compositions include:* Visioni di Cavoli for ensemble, 1985; Pipistrelli Gialli for bass recorder and live electronics, 1985; Chasing for 3 recorders, 1985; Croutons Il for clarinet, 1985; Magnificat for chorus, 1985; The Voice of the Crocodile for bass clarinet, 1988; The Pobble for chorus, 1988; Chick Peas for two mandolins, 1990; Two Diagonals and a Squiggle for recorder and percussion, 1991; Missa Sine Verbum, 1991; Croutons III for baroque flute, 1992; Croutons IV for harpiscord, 1992; Songs for my father's wedding, bass recorder, 1995. *Publications:* Editor, two vols of recorder music, Recorders at Large, Works of Sitsky, Strozzi and Castello. *Honours:* jt winner Fellowship of Australian Composers Competition 1991. *Address:* c/o APRA, 1A Eden Street, Crows Nest, NSW 2065, Australia.

**THORN, Penelope;** British singer (soprano); b. 19 Sept. 1957, Kent, England. *Education:* Guildhall School of Music and studied with Tito Gobbi in Italy. *Career:* sang with Karlsruhe Opera from 1980 as Adriana Lecouvreur, Alice Ford, Amelia in Ballo in Maschera, Princess in Rusalka, Giorgetta in Il Tabarro, Freia, Giulietta and Armida in Handel's Rinaldo, also at Barcelona; sang at Düsseldorf and Mannheim, then appeared at Hannover from 1985 as Tosca, Abigaille and Jenůfa; Freia and Gutrune in Der Ring des Nibelungen for Deutsche Oper am Rhein; guest appearances at Giessen in Menotti's Mara Golovin 1986 and at Bielefeld as the Forza Leonora and Asteria in Boito's Nerone; Zürich as Freia and Gutrune and at Nice as Minnie in La Fanciulla del West; has sung Senta at Freiburg, Lyon and Mannheim, Strauss's Empress at Karlsruhe and Bremen and Third Norn in Götterdämmerung at Munich Staatsoper and in Berlin, under Christian Thielemann; appearances at Saarbrücken as Aida, Salome, Leonore, Butterfly and Elsa; engaged as Salome at Stuttgart 1996; sang Third Norn in Götterdämmerung at Deutsche Oper Berlin 2000. *Honours:* Winner, Voci Verdiane, Bussetto 1985. *Current Management:* Konzertdirektion Fritz Dietrich GmbH, Sigmund-Freud-Strasse 1, 60435 Frankfurt am Main, Germany. *Telephone:* (69) 544504. *Fax:* (69) 5484107. *E-mail:* info@konzertdirektion-dietrich.de. *Website:* www.konzertdirektion-dietrich.de.

**THORNER-MENGEDOTH, Jane;** Singer (Soprano); b. 1955, Seattle, USA. *Education:* Studied at Seattle, Munich, Milan, and Geneva. *Career:* Sang in concert at Vienna, with Schreker's Das Spielwerk und die Prinzessin and Pfitzner's Von deutscher Seele; Geneva Opera, 1984, as Alceste; Season 1985 as Salome at Seattle, Leonore at Lucerne, Tippett's Andromache at Nancy and Schreker's Princess at Wuppertal; Sang Abigaille in Nabucco at the Bregenz Festival, 1993–94; Other roles include Cherubini's Medea, and Wagner's Senta, Sieglinde and Gutrune; Festival engagements at Lucerne, Basle and Lausanne; Concerts with the Berlin Philharmonic Orchestra, Metropolitan Orchestra Tokyo and Orchestra of the Santa Cecilia, Rome. *Address:* c/o Bregenz Festival Theatre, Postfach 311, 6901 Bregenz, Austria.

**THORNTON-HOLMES, Christopher;** Singer (baritone); b. 1959, England. *Education:* Royal Northern College of Music. *Career:* Glyndebourne Tour and Festival from 1985, as Morales in Carmen, Jankel in Arabella, Paolo in Simon Boccanegra, Narumov in The Queen of Spades and Zaretsky in Eugene Onegin (1994); Engagements with Scottish Opera Go Round as Puccini's Sharpless, and Don Giovanni, Amonasro for New Sussex Opera and Verdi's Renato and Rigoletto, Mozart's Count and Eugene Onegin; Further engagements at the Royal Opera, Covent Garden, and La Scala Milan. *Recordings:* Emilia di Liverpool by Donizetti (Opera Rava).

**THORPE, Marion;** Pianist, Writer, Musical Administrator and Teacher; b. (Marion Stein), 1926, Vienna, Austria; m. 1st The Earl of Harewood; 2nd Rt Hon. Jeremy Thorpe, three s., one step-s. *Education:* Private study with Franz Osborn. *Career:* Lectures, talks and interviews; Programme notes; mem., Aldeburgh Productions; Co-Founder, Leeds International Pianoforte Competition; Trustee, Britten-Pears Foundation; Friends of Covent Garden. *Publications:* Editor: Form and Performance by Erwin Stein, 1962; Classical Songs for Children, 1964; Series of 19 vols of Piano Lessons and Pieces, The Waterman/Harewood Series, 1967–. *Address:* 2 Orme Square, London W2 4RS, England.

**THORSEN, Marianne;** Concert Violinist; b. 1972, Trondheim, Norway. *Education:* Studied in Norway, at the Suzuki Institute, London, the Purcell School, and the Royal Academy in London with György Pauk. *Career:* Solo performances in Berlin, with the Slovak Chamber Orchestra, Philharmonia, BBC Symphony Orchestra and orchestras throughout Norway; Recitals at the Bergen International Festival; Member of the Leopold String Trio. *Recordings:* Svendsen's Romance with the Stavanger Symphony Orchestra; Albums with the Trondheim Soloists. *Address:* c/o BLH Artists Management, Strindvegen 38, N–7502 Trondheim, Norway. *E-mail:* blh@c2i.net.

**THURLOW, Sarah;** Clarinettist; b. 29 May 1974, Bromley, Kent, England. *Education:* BMus, MMus, PGDipRCM, DipRCM, ARCM, with Robert Hill, Stephen Trier and Michael Harris, Royal College of Music; Study with Hans Deinzer, Scuola Internazionale di Perfezionamento Musicale, Bobbio, Italy; Private study with Andrew Marriner and Nicholas Bucknall. *Career:* Debut: St John's Smith Square, 1996; Philharmonia/David Parry Recital Debut, accompanied by Nigel Clayton, Purcell Room, 1999; Solo recitals: Kirckman concerts, Park Lane Group broadcast; Fresh Young Musicians, Purcell Room; Numerous appearances for music clubs and societies; Concertos: including touring with European Union Chamber Orchestra; Orchestral: Freelance with London Symphony Orchestra, Academy of St Martin in the Fields, Sinfonia 21, London Chamber Orchestra, Age of Enlightenment, BBC Philharmonic, Manchester Camerata, Viva; Chamber: Founded Contemporary Consort in 1998; Performances at Cheltenham, Brighton, Kings Lynn and York Late Music Festivals. *Address:* 64A South Eden Park Road, Beckenham, BR3 3BG, England.

**THURMER, Harvey;** Violinist; b. 1950, Vienna, Austria. *Education:* Vienna Acad. of Music. *Career:* mem. of the Franz Schubert Quartet, 1983–90; many concert engagements in Europe, USA, and Australia including showings in the Amsterdam Concertgebouw, the Vienna Musikverein and Konzerthaus, the Salle Gaveau Paris and the Sydney Opera House; visits to Zürich, Geneva, Basle, Berlin, Hamburg, Rome, Rotterdam, Madrid and Copenhagen; festival engagements include Salzburg, Wiener Festwochen, Prague Spring Schubertiade at Hohenems, the Schubert Festival at Washington DC and Belfast and Istanbul Festivals; tours of Russia, Australasia and USA, and frequent concert tours of the UK; featured in the Quartet Concerto by Spohr with the Liverpool Philharmonic at the Liverpool Festival Hall; Wigmore Hall series includes Master Concerts, Russian Series, Summer Nights, and Coffee Concerts; performance of Alun Hoddinott's Quartet at the 1989 Cheltenham Festival featured on BBC Welsh television; teacher at the Vienna Conservatory and Graz Musikhochschule; masterclasses at the Royal Northern Coll. of Music and at the Lake District Summer Music. *Recordings include:* Schubert's Quartet in G, D877; Complete Quartets of Dittersdorf.

**THWAITES, Penelope (Mary);** Pianist and Composer; b. 18 April 1944, Chester, England; m. Edward Jackson, 5 Dec 1981, one s., one d. *Education:* BMus, 1st class Hons, Melbourne University, Australia, 1965; Postgraduate study: Piano with Albert Ferber, Composition with William Reed. *Career:* Debut: Wigmore Hall, London, 1974; Regular concerts and broadcasts in London; Tours on 5 continents; Concertos with leading orchestras, Australia, the United Kingdom, America; Lectures, lecture recitals, radio, television and video appearances; Artistic Director, First London International Grainger weekend, 1998; Founder and Chairman, Performing Australian Music Competition, London, 2001. *Compositions include:* Ride! Ride!, 1976; Dancing Pieces, 1989; A Lambeth Garland, 1990; Instrumental and organ works. *Recordings:* Australian Piano Music, 1981; Percy Grainger: complete original music for 4 hands, with John Lavender, Vol. 1, 1989, Vol. II, 1991, Vol. III, 1993; Percy Grainger: Chosen Gems for Piano, solo, 1992; Her own songs recorded, 1985, 1991; Ten recordings in Chandos Grainger Edition; Musical, Ride, Ride, 1999. *Contributions:* The Singer, 1996; BBC Music Magazine, 1997. *Honours:* Order of Australia (AM) 2001; International Grainger Society Medallion 1991. *Current Management:* Siva Oke Music Management. *Address:* 23 Lyndale Avenue, Child's Hill, London NW2 2QB, England.

**THYM, Jürgen;** Musicologist; b. 2 July 1943, Bremervörde, Germany; m. Peggy Dettwiler, 6 June 1992. *Education:* Diploma in School Music, Hochschule für Musik, Berlin, 1967; PhD, Musicology, Case Western Reserve University, 1974; Studies in theory and composition with Reinhard Schwarz Schilling, counterpoint with Ernst Pepping, 12-tone technique with Josef Rufer and musicology with Reinhold Brinkmann, Rudolph Stephen and Jon G Suess. *Career:* Visiting Instructor at Oberlin College, USA, 1973; Instructor, Assistant Professor, Associate Professor, Professor, 1973–, Chair of Musicology, 1982–, Eastman School of Music, Rochester, NY. *Publications:* The Solo Song Settings of Eichendorff's Poems by Schumann and Wolf, 1974; Translations of Kirnberger's The Art of Strict Musical Composition, 1982, and Schenker's Counterpoint, 1987; 100 Years of Eichendorff Songs, 1983; Schoenberg Collected Works Edition, vol. XIV, 1988, vol. XIII, 1993. *Contributions:* Articles in Journal of Music Theory, Notes, American Choral Review, Comparative Literature, Journal of Musicological Research, Fontes Artis Musicae, Musica Realtà and Aurora, Eichendorff year book, among others; Essays on Mendelssohn and Schumann.

**TIBBELS, Nicole;** Singer (Soprano); b. 1960, England. *Education:* Sheffield University and the Guildhall School, London. *Career:* Sang with the Swingle Singers and has made many concert appearances in music by Berio; Other repertory includes Dies by Wolfgang Rihm, Mason's Concerto for Viola Section, Nenia by Birtwistle, and songs by Stravinsky; Opera engagements as the Queen of Night with Richard Hickox, and the European Chamber Opera, Alice Ford and Rossini's Clorinda for Pimlico Opera, Serpina in La Serva Padrona for Broomhill Opera and Mozart's Constanze for Perth Festival Opera; Royal Opera Covent Garden debut 1997, as La Comtesse in Massenet's Chérubin; 1997–98 appearances as La Folie in Platée by Rameau and Fido in Paul Bunyan; Premieres of works by Maxwell Davies, Bainbridge, Berio, Michael Finnissy, Jonathan Lloyd and Nigel Osborne. *Recordings include:* Berio's Sinfonia, and works by Bryars, Smalley, Cage and Stockhausen. *Address:* c/o Allied Artists, 42 Montpelier Square, London, SW7 1JZ, England.

**TICHY, Georg;** Singer (Baritone); b. 9 June 1944, Vienna, Austria. *Education:* Studied with Hilde Zadek in Vienna. *Career:* Debut: Vienna Staatsoper in 1973 in Tristan und Isolde; Sang in Vienna in operas by Verdi, Rossini, Mozart, Puccini, Britten and Wagner; Sang at Maggio Musicale Florence in 1984 as Rigoletto and at Bregenz Festival in 1986 as Papageno; Sang in Schubert's Fierrabras and Wagner's Lohengrin at Vienna in 1990; Sang Ned Keene in the house premiere of Peter Grimes, Vienna Staatsoper, 1996; Season 2000–01 at Covent Garden as Faninal in Der Rosenkavalier, Don Carlo in Ernani and Verdi's Renato for the Vienna Staatsoper; Frequent concert appearances. *Recordings:* Ariadne auf Naxos; Parsifal; Alfonso und

Estrella by Schubert. *Address:* c/o Vienna Staatsoper, Opernring 1, Vienna, Austria.

**TIEBOUT, Torsten;** Violist; b. 21 Sept. 1963, Kassel, Germany. *Education:* Music studies in Hamburg, Hannover, Trossingnen and Helsinki with Prof Stanley Weiner, Hatto Beyerle, Emile Cantor, Hermann Voss and Teemu Kupiainen; Masterclasses with Csaba Erdlyi, Kim Kashkashian, Bruno Giuranna, Tabea Zimmermann, Rainer Moog and Wolfram Christ. *Career:* Debut: As Soloist, with Helsinki University Orchestra in first performance in Finland of revised version of Bartók's Viola Concerto, conductor John Storgårds, 13 April 1996; Member of Finnish Radio Symphony Orchestra, 1991–95; Principal of Tampere Philharmonic Orchestra, 1995–96; Principal Violist of Helsinki Philharmonic Orchestra, 1996–. *Recordings:* Numerous radio recordings as chamber musician with Cable Quartet, especially contemporary music. *Address:* Paciuksenkatu 4 A 24, 00290 Helsinki, Finland.

**TIEPPO, Giorgio;** Singer (Tenor); b. 1953, Varese, Italy. *Education:* Studied at the Giuseppe Verdi Conservatory, Milan, and with Pier Miranda Ferraro. *Career:* Sang in concert from 1977 and made opera debut at Pavia 1983, as Don Ruiz in Donizetti's Maria Padilla; Appeared as Don Ruiz in Parma and Ravenna and sang further in La Bohème and Lucia di Lammermoor at Bergamo; Pinkerton in Butterfly at Genoa, Bologna, Turin and New Orleans; Vienna, Mannheim and Dublin debuts as Cavaradossi; Verona Arena in Nabucco, Il Trovatore, Un Ballo in Maschera, Norma and Aida; Appearances at the Zürich Opera as Rodolfo (season 1996–97), Cavaradossi, and Luigi in Il Tabarro; Further engagements in New York, Dallas, Berlin, Rome and Helsinki. *Honours:* Winner, Voci Nuove Verdiane Competition, Bergamo; Voci Verdiane in Busseto. *Address:* c/o Opernhaus Zürich, Falkenstrasse 1, 8008 Zürich, Switzerland.

**TIERNEY, Vivian;** Singer (soprano); b. 26 Nov. 1957, London, England. *Career:* Sang as Principal Soprano with D'Oyly Carte Opera Company; Freelance, 1982–, at first with Sadler's Wells Opera Company in Kalman's The Gypsy Princess and Lehar's The Count of Luxembourg; Edwige in Offenbach's Robinson Crusoe for Kent Opera; Hanna Glawari in Die Lustige Witwe for Opera North; English National Opera from 1987 as Frasquita, Euridice in Orpheus in the Underworld and Regan in the British premiere of Reimann's Lear, 1989; Sang title role in world premiere of Robin Holloway's Clarissa, 1990; Has sung with Freiburg Opera as Lady Macbeth of Mtsensk, Ellen Orford and Giulietta (Les Contes d'Hoffmann); Has appeared in Handel's Alceste at Versailles; Mimi in La Bohème at Montpellier Festival; Euridice in Milhaud's Les Malheurs d'Orphée at Frankfurt; Donna Anna for Flanders Opera; Sang in Sullivan's cantata The Golden Legend for Colorado Springs Orchestra; Appearance with Opera 80 as Donna Anna; Marie in Wozzeck (Almeida Festival, 1988); Other roles include the Marschallin in Der Rosenkavalier, Jenny (in Mahagonny), Rosalinde in Die Fledermaus, and Malinka in The Excursions of Mr Brouček; Mimi in La Bohème for English National Opera, 1992; Gypsy Princess (Los Angeles); Sang Ellen Orford in a new production of Peter Grimes at Glyndebourne, 1992; Renata in The Fiery Angel in Freiburg, 1993; Berg's Marie for Opera North, 1993; Sang Gutrune in Götterdämmerung at Covent Garden, 1996; Season 1998 with Jitka in Smetana's Dalibor for Scottish Opera; Season 2000 as Korngold's Marietta at Cologne, Ellen Orford at Glyndebourne and Mrs Foran in the premiere of The Silver Tassie, by Turnage, for ENO. *Current Management:* Athole Still International Management, Forresters Hall, 25–27 Westow Street, London, SE19 3RY, England. *Telephone:* (20) 8771-5271. *Fax:* (20) 8768-6600. *Website:* www.atholestill.com.

**TIKKA, Kari (Juhani);** Conductor and Composer; b. 13 April 1946, Siilinjärvi, Finland; m. Eeva Relander, 18 May 1979, 3 s., 1 d. *Education:* Oboe Diploma, Conducting Diploma, Sibelius Academy, Helsinki; Private study with Arvid Jansons and Luigi Ricci. *Career:* Debut: Helsinki, 1968; Conductor: Tampere Theatre, 1969–70; Finnish National Opera, Helsinki, 1970–72, 1979–; Finnish Radio Symphony Orchestra, 1972–76; Royal Swedish Opera, Stockholm, 1975–77; Symphony Orchestra Vivo, Helsinki, 1986–97; Guest Conductor, Scandinavia, Western and Eastern Europe, Israel and USA. *Compositions:* Frieda, opera; Luther, opera; Two Aphorisms; Due Pezzi; Many songs; Cantatas; The Prodigal Son, oratorio; Concerto for Cello; Music for choir; Chamber music. *Recordings:* Vivo-Tikka; Triplet; Jumala on rakkaus; Armolaulu: Armolaulu, VIVO Finlandia. *Address:* Mannerheimintie 38 A 4, 00100 Helsinki, Finland. *E-mail:* kari.tikka@kolumbus.fi.

**TILLEY, David;** Singer (Baritone); b. 1960, England. *Education:* Studied with Mark Wildman and David Mason. *Career:* Appearances in Das Liebesverbot by Wagner at Wexford and Howard Goodall's Silas Marner for CBTO; Lesbo in Handel's Agrippina at Cambridge, Frost King in Purcell's King Arthur at Croydon and Adonis in Blow's Venus and Adonis; Other roles include Leporello and parts in Purcell's Fairy Queen (English Bach Festival, 2001) and Jonathan Dove's Tobias and the Angel for the Almeida Festival; Further roles in Rigoletto and Die Zauberflöte. *Address:* c/o English Bach Festival, 15 South Eaton Place, London, SW1W 9ER, England.

**TILLI, Johann;** Singer (Bass); b. 11 Nov. 1967, Kerimäki, Finland. *Education:* Studied at the Sibelius Academy, Helsinki. *Career:* Appearances at the Savonlinna Festival, Finland, as Sarastro, the King in Aida, Banquo and Landgraf and other roles; National Opera, Helsinki, as Lodovico and High Priest Baal (Nabucco); Commendatore and Rossini's Basilio at Oslo, with further engagements at Amsterdam, Brussels, Tel-Aviv and Hannover;

Member of the Hamburg Opera from 1990; First Bass with Düsseldorf Oper, 1996–97; Has worked with many conductors including Abbado, Cillario, de Burgos, Fricke, Harnoncourt, Steinberg, Sawallisch and Wallberg; Three Bass Concert with Matti Salminen, Jaakko Ryhänen and conductor Leif Segerstam in Helsinki, 1995; Wotan in Die Walküre at Helsinki, 1998; Season 2000–01 as Fasolt at Bayreuth, Gremin for Cologne Opera and Colonna in Wagner's Rienzi at Dresden (concert). *Recordings include:* Gazzaniga's Don Giovanni (Sony Classics); Mahler's 8th Symphony; Schumann Genoveva; Dessau: Haggaddah; Highlights from Savonlinna; Lady Macbeth of the Mtsensk District (DGG). *Address:* c/o Hamburg Staatsoper, Grosse Theaterstrasse 34, Pf 302448, 20354 Hamburg, Germany.

**TILLIKAINEN, Sauli;** Singer (Baritone); b. 7 Dec. 1952, Finland. *Education:* Studied at the Sibelius Academy Helsinki and in Vienna with Anton Dermota and Hans Hotter. *Career:* Debut: Sang in concert from 1981; Sang with the Finnish National Opera from 1984 and as guest at the Moscow Bolshoi, Stockholm, Dresden and Copenhagen; Roles have included Guglielmo, Don Giovanni, Escamillo, Mozart's Count, Germont, Eugene Onegin, Ruprecht in The Fiery Angel and the title roles in Lionardo by Werle and Thomas by Rautavaara; Kennedy Center, Washington, in Ein Deutsches Requiem and the Kullervo Symphony by Sibelius; Sang Valmonte in Sallinen's The Palace, Savonlinna Festival, 1996; Season 2000–01 as Helsinki as Edgar in the premiere of Sallinen's Lear, and Germont in Traviata; Lieder recitals in music by Schubert and Schumann. *Address:* Finnish National Opera, Bulevardi 23–27, 00180 Helsinki 18, Finland.

**TILLING, Camilla;** Singer (soprano); b. 1972, Sweden. *Education:* Gothenburg University; Royal College of Music, with Margaret Kingsley. *Career:* Debut: Camiletta and Mergelina, in intermezzi by Jommelli, Vadstena Summer Opera; Appearances in Gothenburg as Offenbach's Olympia, Sophie in Der Rosenkavalier, and Rossini's Rosina (2000–01); Mozart's Blonde and Susanna in London and Aix; Corinna in Il Viaggio a Reims for New York City Opera, Purcell's Belinda in Geneva and Nannetta in Falstaff at the New York Met (2001); Concerts include Handel's Saul in Brussels, and engagements with the London Mozart Players, King's Consort and Corydon Singers; Glyndebourne Festival debut 2000, as First Niece in Peter Grimes.

**TILNEY, Colin;** Harpsichordist; b. 31 Oct. 1933, London, England. *Education:* Studied harpsichord with Mary Potts at Cambridge and with Gustav Leonhardt in Amsterdam. *Career:* Soloist and ensemble player in the United Kingdom and Europe from the early 1960s; US debut in 1971; Repertoire has included music by Renaissance and Baroque composers; Has performed on various clavichords, harpsichords, virginals and early pianos, employing both historical instruments and modern copies. *Recordings include:* Parthenia, a collection of pieces by Byrd, Bull and Gibbons published in 1611; Complete Keyboard Works of Matthew Locke and the Suites of Purcell and Handel; CD of Bach's Toccatas, 1990. *Publications include:* Edition of the harpsichord music of Antoine Forqueray. *Address:* c/o Conifer Records, Horton Road, West Drayton, Middlesex UB7 8JL, England.

**TILSON THOMAS, Michael;** American conductor, pianist and composer; *Music Director, San Francisco Symphony Orchestra;* b. 21 Dec. 1944, Los Angeles, CA; s. of Theodor Thomas and Roberta Thomas. *Education:* Univ. of S Calif. *Career:* conductor, Young Musicians' Foundation Orchestra, Los Angeles 1963–67; conductor and pianist, Monday Evening Concerts 1963–68; musical Asst Bayreuth 1966–67; Asst Conductor, Boston Symphony Orchestra 1969, Assoc. Conductor 1970–71, Prin. Guest Conductor 1972–74; New York debut 1969; London debut with London Symphony Orchestra (LSO) 1970; Dir Young People's Concerts, New York Philharmonic 1971–77; Music Dir Buffalo Philharmonic 1971–79; Prin. Guest Conductor, Los Angeles Philharmonic 1981–85; Music Dir Great Woods Inst. 1985, Music Dir Great Woods Festival 1987–88; Prin. Conductor, LSO 1988–95, Prin. Guest Conductor 1995–; founder and Artistic Dir, New World Symphony 1988–; Music Dir San Francisco Symphony Orchestra 1995–; Artistic Dir Pacific Music Festival; guest conductor with orchestras and opera houses in USA and Europe. *Compositions include:* Poems of Emily Dickinson, premiered by Renée Fleming and San Francisco Symphony Orchestra. *Recordings include:* Mahler Symphonies 1, 3 and 6 (with San Francisco Symphony Orchestra), four-hand version of Stravinsky's Rite of Spring (with Ralph Grierson), Charles Ives' 2nd Symphony (with Concertgebouw Orchestra), complete works of Carl Ruggles (with Buffalo Philharmonic), various musicals by Weill and Gershwin, works of Bach, Beethoven, Prokofiev, Reich and Cage. *Honours:* Tanglewood Koussevitzky Prize 1968, Ditson Award for contrib. to American music 1994, Musical America Conductor of the Year 1994, American Music Center Award 2001, two Gramophone Awards, five Grammy Awards including Best Classical Album 2004, Classic FM Gramophone Award for Artist of the Year 2005. *Current Management:* Van Walsum Management Ltd, 4 Addison Bridge Place, London, W14 8XP, England. *Telephone:* (20) 7371-4343. *Fax:* (20) 7371-4344. *E-mail:* chouse@vanwalsum.co.uk (office). *Website:* www.vanwalsum.co.uk. *Address:* c/o San Francisco Symphony, Davies Symphony Hall, 201 Van Ness Avenue, San Francisco, CA 94102, USA. *Website:* www.sfsymphony.org.

**TIMARU, Valentin;** Composer; b. 16 Oct. 1940, Sibiu, Romania; m. Maria Chisbora, 20 May 1976, 1 s., 1 d. *Education:* Licence in Musical Pedagogy, 1964, Licence in Musical Composition, 1972, George Dima Conservatory, Cluj; Doctor of Musicology, 1982. *Career:* Debut: As Author of Musical Portrait, 30 Jan 1970; Music Teacher, Buftea, Bucharest, 1964–68; Music Inspector for Cultural Department of Cluj District, 1968–70; University Assistant in

Musical Theory, 1970; University Lecturer in Musical Forms, 1977; University Professor of Musical Forms, 1990. *Compositions:* 2 String Quartets, 1968, 1992; 4 Cantatas for Choir and Orchestra, 1971, 1976, 1980, 1992; Symphony No. 1, 1972, No. 2, 1988, No. 3, 1988, No. 4, 1990, No. 5, 1999; Violin Concerto, 1976; Double Concerto for Double Bass and Percussion, 1980; 3 Oratorios, 1981, 1984, 1999; Lorelei, opera, 1989; Liturgy for Mixed Choir (Liturgy of Ioan Chrysostomos), 1994; The Ciuleandra Ballet (after the novel of Liviu Rebreanu), 1998; Lieder, works for choirs, miscellaneous chamber music. *Publications:* Musical Form Theory, vol. I, 1990, vol. II, 1994, vol. III, 1998; Enescian Symphonism (Analysis of Enescu's Symphonies), 1992; The Art of Musical Ensemble (Orchestral and Vocal), 1998; Our Holy Music, 2001; Dictionary of Notions and Terminology, 2003; Musical Analysis between Genre Conscience and Form Conscience, 2003. *Honours:* Romanian Composers' Union Prize, 1986, 1992, 1995, 2003; Romanian Acad. Prize, 1995. *Address:* Gheorghe Dima Music Academy, 25 I.C. Bratianu Street, PO Box 195, 400750 Cluj-Napoca, Romania. *E-mail:* v_timaru@yahoo.com.

**TINNEY, Hugh;** pianist; b. 28 Nov. 1958, Dublin, Ireland. *Education:* Trinity College, Dublin, 1976–79; Private piano studies with Mabel Swainson, Louis Kentner, Bryce Morrison and Maria Curcio; LRSM Diploma, 1974. *Career:* debut, Purcell Room, London in 1983; Performed concertos and recitals in 30 countries in 4 continents; Radio broadcasts in 12 countries and 2 recitals for Irish television, RTE; Concerto appearances on Irish, Italian and Spanish television; Recitals at Queen Elizabeth Hall in London, Musikverein, Vienna, Kennedy Center, Washington; Appearances at festivals include Newport, Rhode Island, Granada, and Prague Spring Festival; Performances with Gulbenkian, Lisbon, Spanish National, Spanish Radio, and Brazil Symphony Orchestras; Proms debut in 1989 with BBC National Orchestra of Wales; Other performances with British orchestras such as London Philharmonic, Philharmonia, Royal Philharmonic, Royal Liverpool Philharmonic, City of Birmingham and Royal Scottish Orchestras. *Recordings:* Liszt Recital–Dante Sonata, Benediction de Dieu dans La Solitude; Harmonies Poétiques et Réligieuses, Liszt, 1993. *Current Management:* Tennant Artists, Unit 2, 39 Tadema Road, London, SW10 0PZ, England. *Telephone:* (20) 7376-3758. *Fax:* (20) 7351-0679. *E-mail:* info@tennantartists.demon.co.uk. *Address:* 258b Camden Road, London NW1 9AB, England.

**TINSLEY, Pauline;** Singer (Soprano); b. 27 March 1928, Wigan, England. *Education:* Northern School of Music, Manchester, LRAM 1949; Opera School, London; Further study with Eva Turner and Eduardo Asquez. *Career:* Professional engagements in the United Kingdom from 1961 include London debut as Desdemona, Rossini's Otello; leading roles in Verdi's I Masnadieri, Ernani, Il Corsaro and Bellini's Il Pirata; Welsh National Opera from 1962 as Susanna, Elsa, Lady Macbeth, Sinaide (Rossini's Moses), Abigaille, Aida, Tosca, Turandot, Kostelnicka (Jenůfa), Elektra and Dyer's Wife (Frau Ohne Schatten) 1981; Sadler's Wells/English National Opera from 1963 as Gilda, Elvira (Ernani), Fiordiligi, Queen of Night, Countess, Donna Elvira, Beethoven's Leonore and Fidelio, Leonora (Force of Destiny), Elizabeth (Mary Stuart), 1973, Mother/Witch (Hansel and Gretel), 1987, Kabanicha (Katya Kabanova), 1989; Covent Garden from 1965 as Overseer (Elektra), Amelia (Ballo in Maschera), 1971, Helmwige and 3rd Norn (The Ring), Santuzza, 1976, Mère Marie (Carmélites), 1983, Lady Billows (Albert Herring), 1989; Various roles with Scottish Opera including Kostelnicka and Opera North (Fata Morgana in Love for 3 Oranges) and with Handel Opera Society; From 1966, performed abroad in Germany, Netherlands, Italy, USA, Canada, Switzerland, Czechoslovakia, Spain and Belgium; Concerts, recitals, broadcasts and television operas; Wexford Festival as Lady Jowler in The Rising of the Moon, 1990; Sang Lady Billows at Garsington, 1996; Sang Grandmother Burya in Jenůfa, for Opera North, 1995 and 2002, and for Netherlands Opera 1997 and 2001. *Recordings include:* Electra in Idomeneo (Philips). *Address:* c/o Music International, 13 Ardilaun road, Highbury, London N5 2QR, England.

**TIPO, Maria;** Pianist; b. 23 Dec. 1931, Naples, Italy. *Education:* Studied with her mother, Ersilla Cavallo. *Career:* Debut: Public piano performance aged four; Many solo engagements from 1949 throughout Europe, USA, Central and South America, Africa, Russia, Japan and the Middle East, including many performances in the USA after discovery by Arthur Rubinstein in 1952; Teacher at the Bolzano, Florence and Geneva Conservatories; Performances of works by Clementi, Scarlatti and other Italian composers, Beethoven, Mozart, Schumann, Ravel, Debussy, Chopin, Brahms; Has performed with the Berlin Philharmonic, Vienna Philharmonic, Boston Symphony, London Philharmonic, Concertgebouw Orchestra in Amsterdam, Czech Philharmonic, Orchestre de Paris, Salzburg Mozarteum, La Scala in Milan, S Cecilia in Rome and many others; Chamber music performances with the Amadeus Quartet, Salvatore Accardo and Uto Ughi; Judge at many international competitions; President, Centro Studi Musicali F Busoni. *Recordings include:* Piano Sonatas by Clementi; Bach's Goldberg Variations; Eighteen Scarlatti Sonatas. *Honours:* Many awards include: Prizewinner at the 1949 Geneva and 1952 Queen Elisabeth of the Belgians Competitions; First Music Critics Prize, 1985; Gargano Award; Ernest Hemingway Award; Personality of the Year Award. *Address:* c/o Accademia Santa Cecilia, Via Vittoria 6, 00187 Rome, Italy.

**TIPTON, Thomas;** Singer (Baritone); b. 18 Nov. 1926, Wyandotte, Michigan, USA. *Education:* Studied at Michigan State College with Herbert Swanson and at Ann Arbor with Chase Baromeo. *Career:* Debut: New York City Opera in 1954 as Bob in The Old Maid and The Thief by Menotti; Sang two seasons in New York, then visited Europe; Sang at Mannheim Opera, 1960–63,

Stuttgart, 1964–66, and Bayerische Staatsoper Munich from 1966; Guest appearances in Vienna, Berlin and Hamburg; Sang at Salzburg Festival, 1964–65, Bayreuth Festival in 1967 as Wotan and the Herald in Lohengrin, and at Covent Garden, 1972–74 as Rigoletto; Other roles included Nabucco and Macbeth; Concert appearances in North and South America. *Publications:* Thomas Tipton ein Leben in Bildern, Munich, 1987. *Address:* c/o Bayerische Staatsoper, Postfach 745, 8000 Munich 1, Germany.

**TIRIMO, Martino,** FRAM, Dip RAM; British concert pianist and conductor; *Professor, Trinity College of Music;* b. 19 Dec. 1942, Larnaca, Cyprus; s. of Dimitri Tirimo and Marina Tirimo; m. Mione J. Teakle 1973; one s. one d. *Education:* Bedales School, England (Cyprus Govt Scholarship), Royal Acad. of Music, London, Vienna State Acad. *Career:* first public recital, Cyprus 1949; conducted seven performances of La Traviata with singers and musicians from La Scala, Milan, at Cyprus Opera Festival 1955; prizewinner Int. Beethoven Competition, Vienna 1965; London début Wigmore Hall 1965; jt winner Munich Int. Piano Competition 1971; winner Geneva Int. Piano Competition 1972; gave first public performance of complete Schubert sonatas (including unfinished ones with own completions), London 1975; first public performance of Beethoven piano concertos cycle directed from keyboard in two consecutive evenings, Dresden 1985, London 1986; first performance Tippett piano concerto in several European countries 1986–87; concerto performances with major orchestras worldwide as well as recitals, radio and TV appearances Europe, USA, Canada, SA and Far East 1965–; four series of performances of complete Beethoven piano sonatas 2000, two series devoted to the maj. piano works of Robert and Clara Schumann 2001; six-concert series devoted to the major piano works of Chopin 2002; began Mozart piano concertos series, directing from keyboard 2001–; f. Rosemunde Trio with violinist Ben Sayevich and cellist Daniel Veis 2002; performed with Vienna Philharmonic during Olympics, Athens Festival 2004, Olympic Games torch bearer 2004; composed film score The Odyssey 1998; Prof. and Visiting Artist Trinity Coll. of Music, currently Prof. 2003–; Visiting Prof., Royal Scottish Acad. of Music and Drama; Liszt Scholarship, Boise Foundation Scholarship, Gulbenkian Foundation Fellowship 1967–69; mem. jury in various int. piano competitions 1995–. *Recordings include:* Brahms piano concertos, Chopin concertos, Tippett piano concerto, Rachmaninov concertos, complete Debussy piano works, complete Schubert piano sonatas, complete Janacek piano works, complete Mendelssohn works for piano and cello, Tchaikovsky and Shostakovich piano Trios (Rosamunde Trio), several other recordings with mixed repertoire. *Television:* live performance of Tippett piano concerto from Coventry Cathedral for BBC TV in celebration of composer's 90th birthday and the 50th birthday of the UN. *Publications include:* urtext edn of complete Schubert piano sonatas in 3 vols 1997–99. *Honours:* Gold Medal, Associated Bd of Royal Schools of Music 1959, Macfarren Medal, Royal Acad. of Music 1964, Silver Disc 1988 and Gold Disc 1994 for recording of Rachmaninov 2nd Concerto and Paganini Rhapsody and other prizes and awards. *Address:* 1 Romeyn Road, London, SW16 2NU, England. *Telephone:* (20) 8677-4847. *Fax:* (20) 8677-6070. *E-mail:* martino@tirimo.fslife.co.uk. *Website:* www.tcm.ac.uk (office).

**TISCHENKO, Leonid;** Singer (Bass); b. 1969, Kiev, Ukraine, Russia. *Education:* Studied at the Moscow and Kiev Conservatories. *Career:* Has sung with the National Opera of the Ukraine at Kiev as Pimen (Boris Godunov), Verdi's King Phillip and Gremin in Eugene Onegin; Concerts at Strasbourg 1999, in the Mozart Requiem, and at the Concertgebouw Amsterdam in Rossini's Stabat Mater; further engagements with the Verdi Requiem and other works in Germany, Italy, the USA, Austria, France and Hungary; has also conducted the Ukraine State Symphony Orchestra. *Address:* National Opera of the Ukraine, Kiev, Ukraine.

**TISHCHENKO, Boris Ivanovich;** Russian composer; b. 23 March 1939, Leningrad; s. of Ivan I. Tishchenko and Zinaida A. Tishchenko; m. Irina A. Donskaya 1977; three s. *Education:* Leningrad Conservatory, with post-grad. course under Shostakovich. *Career:* Prof. at St Petersburg Conservatory. *Compositions include:* vocal works and ballets: Lenin Lives (cantata) 1959, The Twelve (ballet) 1963, Requiem (words by A. Akhmatova) 1966, Fly-bee (ballet) 1968, A Cockroach (operetta) 1968, The Stolen Sun (opera) 1968, Yaroslavna (The Eclipse, ballet) 1974, Beatriche (ballet) 2005; symphonies: French Symphony 1958, Sinfonia Robusta 1970, Violin Symphony (2nd Violin Concerto) 1981, The Siege Chronicle 1984, Pushkin's Symphony 1998, 7 symphonies 1961–94; other works: 10 piano sonatas 1957–97, violin and cello solo sonatas, Sonata for family of flutes and organ 1999, Rondo, Capriccio and Fantasy for violin and piano, also concertos for violin, piano, cello, flute and harp 1962–77, Concerto alla marcia for 16 soloists 1989, The Dog's Heart – Novels for chamber ensemble based on M. Bulgakov 1988, Concerto for clarinet and piano trio 1990, Piano Quintet 1985, String quartets 1957–84, Twelve Inventions and Twelve Portraits for Organ 1964, 1994, orchestral and instrumental suites and pieces, vocal cycles and ensembles, choral works, music for drama productions and films; edns and instrumentations of some works by Monteverdi, Grieg, Mahler, Prokofiev and Shostakovich. *Honours:* Russian Order of Merit for the Homeland, Fourth Class 2002; 1st Prize, Int. Contest of Young Composers, Prague 1966, RSFSR State Prize (Glinka) 1978, People's Artist of RSFSR 1987, Prize of Mayor of St Petersburg 1995, Pushkin Gold Medal 2000, Union of Composers of Russia Prize 2002, Prize of Honour of Russian Author's Society 2003. *Address:* Rimsky-Korsakoff Avenue 79, Apt 10, 190121 St Petersburg, Russia (home). *Telephone:* (812) 114-75-16 (home). *E-mail:* boristishchenko@rambler.ru (home).

**TISNE, Antoine;** Composer; b. 29 Nov. 1932, Lourdes, France. *Education:* Studied at the Paris Conservatoire with Riviere and Darius Milhaud, among others. *Career:* Inspector of Music for the French Ministry of Culture, 1967–92; Inspector for the municipal conservatories of Paris, from 1992; Professor of compositions and orchestration at the Paris Conservatoire. *Compositions include:* 4 piano concertos, 1959, 1961, 1962, 1992; 4 string quartets, 1956, 1979, 1979, 1989; Cantique de Printemps, 1960; Wind Quintet, 1961; Violin Sonata, 1963; Cosmogonies for 3 orchestras, 1967; Violin Concerto, 1969; Ondes Flamboyantes, for strings, 1973; Impacts for ondes martenots and 2 string orchestras, 1973; Isle de Temps for ondes martenot sextet, 1980; La Ramasseuse de sarments, music theatre, 1982; Instant, ballet, 1985; L'Heure des Hommes, oratorio, 1985; Reliefs irradiants de New York, for orchestra, 1979; Le Chant des Yeux, oratorio, 1986; Les Voiles de la nuit, 1991; De la Nuit et L'Aurore, for oboe and strings, 1991; La Voix de l'Ombre, for flute and string trio, 1991; Dans la lumière d'Orcival, for chorus, 1992; Invocation, for baritone and orchestra, 1993; Pour l'amour d'Alban, opera. *Honours:* Grand Prix Musical of the City of Paris, 1979. *Address:* c/o SACEM, 225 Avenue Charles de Gaulle, 92521 Neuilly sur Seine Cédex, France.

**TITOV, Alexander;** Conductor; b. 1950, St Petersburg, Russia. *Education:* Graduated St Petersburg Conservatoire, 1981. *Career:* Assistant conductor to Gennadi Rozhdestvensky and Mstislav Rostropovich; Conductor at the Kirov Opera and Ballet, St Petersburg from 1991; Repertoire has included La Traviata, Prokofiev's The Gambler and Love for Three Oranges, Stravinsky's Rossignol, Katerina Izmailova and Ruslan and Lyudmila; Ballets include Chopiniana, The Sleeping Beauty, The Firebird and Schéhérazade; Conducted the Kirov Ballet in summer season at Covent Garden, 2000; Professor at the St Petersburg Conservatoire. *Honours:* Winner, International Minon Competition, Tokyo, 1988. *Address:* c/o Kirov Opera, Mariinsky Theatre, St Petersburg, Russia.

**TITTERINGTON, David Michael;** Concert Organist; b. 10 Jan. 1958, Oldham, England. *Education:* BA, 1980, Organ Scholar, 1977–81, Pembroke Coll., Oxford; studied under Marie-Claire Alain, Conservatoire National de Rueil-Malmaison, Paris, 1982–85;. *Career:* debut, Royal Festival Hall, 1986; recitals in cathedrals and halls throughout the UK; concert tours of Germany, Scandinavia, France, USA, Far East, New Zealand and Australia; appearances at major international festivals at Hong Kong, Harrogate, Istanbul, Adelaide, Sydney and Brighton; concert hall appearances include Wigmore Hall, Royal Festival Hall, Munich, Acad. for Performing Arts, Hong Kong; television appearances on BBC 2 and Anglia television; Prof. of Organ, Royal Academy of Music, London, 1990–; Concertos with Berlin Symphony, BBC Symphony Orchestra, City of London Sinfonia and English Sinfonia; Recitals, Concertos and Masterclasses world-wide at major venues and festivals including BBC Proms, Hong Kong, Sydney, New Zealand, Tokyo; Head of Organ Studies, Royal Acad. of Music, 1996–. *Recordings:* Messiaen; La Nativité du Seigneur; Eben; Job; Eberlin; Toccatas; over 30 recordings for BBC and networks world-wide. *Publications:* edited works of Petr Eben; Organ Works (ed.). *Current Management:* Denny Lyster Artists' Management, PO Box 155, Stanmore, Middlesex HA7 3WF, England. *Telephone:* (20) 8954-5521. *Fax:* (20) 8954-9168. *E-mail:* artists@dennylyster.co.uk. *Website:* www.dennylyster.co.uk.

**TITUS, Alan;** Singer (baritone); b. 28 Oct. 1945, New York, NY, USA. *Education:* Studied with Askel Schiotz at the Colorado School of Music and with Hans Heinz at Juilliard. *Career:* Debut: Washington DC in 1969 in La Bohème; Sang the Celebrant in the premiere of Bernstein's Mass at Washington DC, 1971; Sang at New York City Opera in 1972 in Summer and Smoke; American debut at Amsterdam in 1973 in Debussy's Pelléas; Sang at Metropolitan Opera in 1976 as Harlekin in Ariadne auf Naxos, Glyndebourne in 1979 as Guglielmo, Deutsche Oper am Rhein Düsseldorf in 1984 as Don Giovanni, and Santa Fe in 1985 in Strauss's Intermezzo; Engagements at Aix-en-Provence, Hamburg and Frankfurt; Sang at Maggio Musicale Florence in 1987 as Olivier in Capriccio; Sang Dandini at San Francisco in 1987, at Munich as Valentin and sang in Mathis der Maler in 1989, Bologna 1990 as Storch in the Italian premiere of Intermezzo; Sang Kovalyov in The Nose by Shostakovich at Frankfurt in 1990; Season 1992–93 in Arabella at La Scala, the title role in Donizetti's Il Duca d'Alba at Spoleto, and Hans Sachs at Frankfurt; Sang the title role in Hindemith's Mathis der Maler at Covent Garden, 1995; Sang Pizarro in Fidelio at Rome, 1996; Altair in Strauss's Aegyptische Helena at the Festival Hall, 1998; Season 2000–01 as Kurwenal at Covent Garden and Strauss's Barak for the Dresden Staatsoper; Sang Wotan in The Ring at Bayreuth, 2001. *Recordings include:* Haydn's La Feldeltà Premiata; La Bohème; L'Elsir d'Amore; Don Giovanni; La Wally; Le nozze di Figaro; Falstaff; Paradies und die Peri; Genovea; Carmen. *Current Management:* L. S. Artists, Lydia Störle, Orlando Strasse 8, 8000 Munich 2, Germany.

**TITUS, Graham;** Singer (Baritone); b. 15 Dec. 1949, Newark, Nottinghamshire, England. *Education:* MA, Clare College, Cambridge University (Organ Scholar); FRCO; Cologne Musikhochschule. *Career:* Debut: Purcell Room, London in 1974; Appearances with New Opera Company, Handel Opera and English National Opera; Radio recitals from 1974 and appearances on Dutch radio and television; Concert tour of South America; Recital and oratorio work throughout the United Kingdom including the Aldeburgh Festival in 1975 and the Glyndebourne Festival in 1979 as Guglielmo. *Honours:* Winner of Young Musicians Competition, 1974 and 's-Hertogenbosch Competition, 1977.

*Address:* c/o English National Opera, St Martin's Lane, London WC2N 4ES, England.

**TJEKNAVORIAN, Loris-Zare;** American/Armenian composer and conductor; b. 13 Oct. 1937, s. of Haikaz and Adriné Tjeknavorian; m. 1st Linda Pierce 1964 (divorced 1979); one s.; m. 2nd Julia Cory Harley-Green 1986. *Education:* Vienna Acad. of Music, Salzburg Mozarteum. *Career:* studied with the late Carl Orff 1963–64; worked in USA until 1970; fmr Teaching Fellow, Univ. of Michigan; fmr Composer-in-Residence, Concordia Coll., Minnesota; Composer-in-Residence, Ministry of Culture and Fine Arts; Prin. Conductor, Tehran Opera 1972–79; artist with RCA 1976–; Composer-in-Residence American-Armenian Int. Coll., La Verne Univ., Calif. 1979–; Prin. Conductor and Artistic Dir Armenian Philharmonic Orchestra, Yerevan, Armenia 1989–; principally associated with London Symphony Orchestra with whom he has recorded; Chair. Bd of Trustees, Inst. of Armenian Music, London 1976–80; Order of Homayoun; several int. tours as a conductor. *Works include:* Requiem for the Massacred 1975, Simorgh (ballet music), Lake Van Suite, Erebouni for 12 strings 1978, a piano concerto, several operas, several chamber works, Credo Symphony Life of Christ (after medieval Armenian chants) 1976, Liturgical Mass, Violin Concerto, oratorios Lucifer's Fall and Book of Revelation, Mass in Memoriam 1985, Othello (ballet), ballet suites for orchestra, five symphonies. *Current Management:* Thea Dispeker Artist Representative, 59 E 54th Street, New York, NY 10022, USA. *Telephone:* (212) 421-7676. *Address:* c/o State Philharmonia, Mashtotsi Prospekt 46, Yerevan, Armenia (office); 347 W 57th Street, Apt 37C, New York, NY 10019, USA (home).

**TOCZYSKA, Stefania;** Polish singer (mezzo-soprano); b. 19 Feb. 1943, Gdansk. *Education:* Gdansk Conservatory with Barbara Iglikovska. *Career:* debut, Danzig as Carmen 1973; sang in Poland as Azucena, Leonora in La Favorita and Dalila; Western debut in 1977 as Amneris at Basle Opera; sang at Vienna Staatsoper 1977 as Ulrica in Un Ballo in Maschera, returning as Carmen and as Verdi's Azucena, Eboli and Preziosilla; sang at Munich and Hamburg 1979 as Eboli in Don Carlos, San Francisco Opera as Laura in La Gioconda, Amneris and in Roberto Devereux, Royal Opera Covent Garden 1983–84 as Azucena and Amneris, Bregenz Festival and Chicago Lyric Opera 1986 as Giovanna Seymour in Anna Bolena, Houston Opera 1987 as Adalgisa and Amneris, and Barcelona 1987 and Hamburg 1990 as Venus in Tannhäuser; sang Laura in La Gioconda at the Metropolitan Opera 1989, at Washington and Houston 1990 as Amneris and Dalila, and appeared in Aida at the Caracalla Festival at Rome 1990; season 1992 as Azucena at Munich, Massenet's Dulcinée at Toulouse, Donizetti's Maria Stuarda at Barcelona and Carmen at the Munich Festival; sang Amneris at the Met 1997; season 2000–01 as Amneris at Maastricht, and in Moniuszko's The Haunted Castle at Warsaw.

**TODD, Will,** BA, MMus; British composer; b. 14 Jan. 1970, Durham, England; s. of Derek and Iris Todd; m. Bethany Halliday; one s. one d. *Education:* Bristol Univ. with Raymond Warren and Adrian Beaumont. *Compositions:* Isambard Kingdom Brunel (opera, premiered at Colston Hall, Bristol) 1993, Midwinter for chorus 1994, St Cuthbert (oratorio, premiered at Durham Cathedral) 1996, The Burning Road (commissioned for Crouch End Festival Chorus) 1996, The Screams of Kitty (musical, with librettist David Simpatico, performed at Boston Conservatory) 2001, The Blackened Man (opera, with librettist Ben Dunwell, Linbury Studio Theatre Covent Garden) (prizewinner Int. Giuseppe Verdi Competition) 2002, Mass in Blue (commissioned by Herts. Chorus) 2003. *Recordings:* The Burning Road, Saint Cuthbert (Northumbrian Anthology), Mass in Blue. *Address:* 39 Grover House, Vauxhall Street, London, SE11 5LJ (office); 1 Blue Coat Court, Claypath, Durham, DH1 1TX, England (home). *Telephone:* (20) 7793-7013 (office); (191) 384-3766 (home). *E-mail:* will@willtodd.com. *Website:* www.willtodd.com.

**TODISCO, Nunzio;** Singer (Tenor); b. 1942, Italy. *Career:* Has sung in Italy and at Orange, Lisbon, Rome and Zürich from 1970; US debut at San Francisco in 1978 as Pollione in Norma; Sang Loris in Fedora at the Metropolitan Opera and in Naples, 1989; Sang at Verona Arena in 1989 as Ismaele in Nabucco; Other roles include Verdi's Carlo in I Masnadieri, Foresto in Attila, Arrigo in La Battaglia di Legnano, Manrico, Ernani and Radames, Puccini's Dick Johnson, Luigi and Cavaradossi and Licinius in La Vestale by Spontini; Sang Ismaele at Verona in 1992. *Address:* c/o Arena di Verona, Piazza Brà 28, 37121 Verona, Italy.

**TODOROV, Nedyalcho (Georgiev);** Violinist and Professor; b. 27 Oct. 1940, Plovdiv, Bulgaria; m. Veneta Assenova Todorova, 26 Nov 1967, 1 s., 1 d. *Education:* MA, State Academy of Music, Sofia, 1964; Gnessini State Music Pedagogy Institute, Moscow, 1973–74. *Career:* Violin Teacher, Secondary School of Music, Plovdiv, 1964–67; Violin Professor, Deputy Rector, 1974–79, Rector, 1979–83, Academy of Music and Dance Art, Plovdiv; Director, 1970–72, Concertmaster, 1976–79, Plovdiv Philharmony; 1st Violinist, Plovdiv String Quartet, 1978–; Director, Educational Department, Ministry of Culture, Sofia, 1983–91; Recitals, soloist with orchestra, chamber music concerts; Repertoire includes concertos of Bach, Mozart, Beethoven, Mendelssohn, Bruch, Hindemith, Shostakovich, V Stoyanov, Ivan Spassov, sonatas, pieces, duos, trios, quartets. *Recordings:* Luigi Boccherini: String Quartet Op 33 No. 6, A major; Quintet for oboe, violins, viola and violoncello Op 45 No. 1, G major, Quintet Op 45 No. 2, F major, Quintet Op 45 No. 3, D major with Plovdiv String Quartet and Boryu Pamoukchiev, oboe, 1988; 4 concertos for violin, oboe and orchestra: Telemann, C minor, Fasch, D minor,

Vivaldi, B flat major, Bach, D minor, soloists: self, violin, Pamoukchiev, oboe, with Jambol Chamber Orchestra, conductor N Sultanov, 1988. *Publications:* 1st performances, recordings, editions (pieces for violin and piano, duos for 2 violins and chamber ensembles by modern Bulgarian composers), 6 vols, 1977–88; Recordings, editions (collections of classical concertos for oboe and violin), 1990; Bulgarian Violin Literature (editor), catalogue, 1992; Avramov Catalogue, 1999. *Address:* Complex Hippodrome, Block 139, Entr A, Apt 33, 1612 Sofia, Bulgaria. *E-mail:* todorov@inet.bg.

**TODOROVIC, Nicholas;** Singer (Bass-Baritone); b. 1965, Christchurch, New Zealand. *Education:* University of Canterbury and Queen's Conservatorium of Music. *Career:* Appearances with Mercury Opera, Auckland, as Hermann in The Queen of Spades and Morales in Carmen; Don Giovanni with the Lyric Opera of Queensland and Papageno with Victoria State Opera; British debut as the villains in Les Contes d'Hoffmann, for Stowe Opera; Season 1996–97 as Masetto for Victoria State Opera and Johnny Dowd in the premiere of Summer of the Seventeenth Doll by Richard Mills, at the Melbourne International Arts Festival; Masetto in Don Giovanni for Auckland Opera (with Kiri Te Kanawa) and Schaunard in La Bohème at Melbourne; Resident in the United Kingdom. *Address:* c/o Victoria State Opera, 77 Southbank Blvd, Melbourne, VIC3205, Australia.

**TODOROVICH, Zoran;** Singer (Tenor); b. 1962, Bulgaria. *Education:* Belgrade Conservatoire and in Zagreb with Zinka Milanov. *Career:* National Theatre, Belgrade, from 1985 as Rossini's Almaviva, Shuisky in Boris Godunov and Donizetti's Tonio; State Opera Hanover 1994–99; Pinkerton at the Vienna and Berlin State Operas, 1997–98, Faust at the Deutsche Oper, Berlin; Season 1999–2000 as Leopold in La Juive (Vienna), US debut as Rodolfo at San Francisco, Lensky for Nice Opera and Alfredo in La Traviata at Zürich; Season 2000–01 as Lensky in Tokyo, Rodolfo at Hamburg and the Berlioz Faust in Zürich; Further engagements in Roberto Devereux by Donizetti in Munich, Edgardo and the Duke of Mantua for Hamburg Opera and Alfredo at Frankfurt; Concerts include the Verdi Requiem (Munich), Gounod's Mors et Vita and Rossini's Stabat Mater. Other opera roles include Mozart's Titus (at Madrid). *Recordings include:* Mors et Vita. *Address:* c/o Theateragentur Dr G. Hilbert, Maximilianstrasse 22, 80539 Munich, Germany.

**TOFFOLUTTI, Ezio;** Stage Designer; b. 1941, Venice, Italy. *Education:* Studied set design and art at the Accademia delle Belle Arti, Venice. *Career:* Designer at the Volksbuhne, Berlin, 1971–79; Collaboration with such opera producers as Harry Kupfer, Johannes Schaaf and Jerome Savary (Rossini's Le Comte Ory at the 1997 Glyndebourne Festival, also televised); Engagements also include Rigoletto in Berlin, Die Meistersinger at La Scala, and Idomeneo at the Salzburg Festival; Grand Theatre, Geneva, with Così fan tutte and at the Palais Garnier, Paris; Season 1997–98 with Il Matrimonio Segreto in Vienna and Die Entführung aus dem Serail at Trieste. *Address:* c/o Grand Théâtre de Genève, 11 Boulevard de Théâtre, 1211 Geneva 11, Switzerland.

**TOIVANEN, Heikki;** Singer (Bass); b. 1947, Mikkeli, Finland; m. Ingrid Haubold. *Education:* Studied at the Sibelius Academy, Helsinki, and in Germany. *Career:* Sang at the Finnish National Opera, 1973–74, Wuppertal, 1974–76, and Karlsruhe, 1977–84; Bayreuth Festival, 1977–78, as Fasolt and Titurel; Guest appearances throughout Europe and in South America; Many concert engagements. *Address:* Staatstheater Karlsruhe, Baumeisterstrasse 11, Pf 1449, W-7500 Karlsruhe, Germany.

**TOKODY, Ilona;** Hungarian soprano; b. Szeged; d. of András Tokody and Ilona Nagy. *Education:* Liszt Ferenc Music Acad., Budapest. *Career:* won Kodály singing competition 1972, Erkel competition of Inter-konzert Agency 1973, Ostend competition operatic category 1976; joined State Opera, Budapest 1976; regular guest performer Staatsoper Wien and Deutsche Oper West-Berlin; appearances in opera houses and concert halls worldwide, including Metropolitan Opera House, Royal Opera House Covent Garden, Vienna State Opera, San Francisco Opera, Teatro Colón, Buenos Aires, Liceo, Barcelona, Bavarian State Opera, San Carlo, Naples, Rome Opera, Bolshoi, Carnegie Hall, New York, Musikverein, Vienna, Royal Opera, Copenhagen. *Operatic roles include:* leading roles in La Forza del Destino, Don Carlos, Suor Angelica, Madama Butterfly, Il Trovatore, Aida, La Juive, La Bohème, Manon Lescaut; Nedda (I Pagliacci), Micaela (Carmen), Alice (Falstaff), Giselda (I Lombardi), Desdemona (Otello). *Recordings include:* Suor Angelica, Nerone, La Fiamma, Brahms Requiem, Il Tabarro, Guntram, Iris, Ilona Tokody – Portrait Of The Artist 1995, Beethoven – Symphony No. 9 2000. *Address:* c/o Hungarian State Opera, Andrássy ut 22, 1062 Budapest, Hungary. *Telephone:* (1) 312-550.

**TOLE, Vasil S.;** Albanian composer and musicologist; b. 22 Nov. 1963, Përmet. *Education:* Tirana Conservatory, Folkwang Hochschule, Essen, Athens Univ. *Career:* Music Dir, Naïm Frashëri Palace of Culture 1988–91; Artistic Dir, Elrena Gjika Ensemble 1988–91; Lecturer, Tirana Conservatory 1991–; founder, New Albanian Music Asscn 1993; founder, Ton de Leeuw Int. Competition for New Music, Tirana 1997; Dir, Theatre of Opera and Ballet, Tirana 1997–99; Dir, State Ensemble of Folk Songs and Dances 1997–99. *Compositions include:* Suite 1986, Symphonic Poem 1987, Kontrast 1989, Concerto for Orchestra 1990, Epitaf dhe britmë 1992–93, Pheromones 1993, Genotype 1996, Trias 1996, RIP 1997, Dikotomi 2000, Eumenides (opera) 2004. *Recordings:* Trias 1997, Epitaf dhe britmë 1996. *Publications:* Music and Literature 1997, SAZET 1998, Albanian folk polyphony 1999, Etnostructure and Etnosemantic 2000, Encyclopedia of Albanian Folk Music 2001,

The Albanian National Anthem 2003, The Albanian Intangible Heritage 2004, Cluster, Musicology and Composition 2004. *Honours:* Asscn of Albanian Composers Prix des Jeunesses Musicales 1990, Ministry of Culture MUZA Prize 2001. *Address:* Rr 'Sitki Çiço', Pallatet 9 kate, Shkalla 2, Ap. 4, Tirana, Albania. *Telephone:* 4 374127. *Fax:* 4 222857. *E-mail:* tole@vasiltole.com. *Website:* www.vasiltole.com.

**TOLIVER, Edmund;** Singer (Bass); b. 1947, Greenport, USA. *Education:* Michigan University (MM) and in Vienna. *Career:* Vienna Staatsoper as Pistol in Falstaff, Nightwatchman in Die Meistersinger and Hector in Les Troyens; Coburg Opera, 1985–87; Graz Opera, 1987–92, Dortmund from 1992; Sang Fasolt, Fafner, Hunding and Hagen in Ring cycles at Graz and Salzburg Landestheaters, 1988–89; Detroit, 1985, as the King in Aida, Linz, 1988, as Boito's Mefistofele; Paris Châtelet, 1994, as Hunding and Fafner, and 1996 in The Rake's Progress; Sang King Marke in Tristan at Enschede, 1999; Further appearances in Berlin, Munich, Zürich and New York; Frequent concert engagements. *Recordings include:* Bonze in Madama Butterfly. *Address:* c/o Châtelet Théâtre Musical, 2 Rue Edouard Colonne, 75001 Paris, France.

**TOMASI, Loretta;** opera company director; *Chief Executive, ENO. Career:* fmr chartered accountant with Coopers & Lybrand, Perth, Melbourne and London eight years, then with Tyndall Holdings PLC, London three years; Finance Dir, Stoll Moss Theatres nine years, later Man. Dir, Really Useful Theatres 2000–; Exec. Dir and Finance Dir, ENO 2003–05, Chief Exec. 2005–. *Address:* English National Opera, London Coliseum, St Martin's Lane, Trafalgar Square, London, WC2, England (office). *Website:* www.eno.org.

**TOMASSON, Tomas;** Singer (bass); b. 1968, Iceland. *Education:* Studied at the Reykjavík College of Music and the Royal College of Music Opera School, London. *Career:* Sang at first with Icelandic Opera, as Sparafucile (Rigoletto), Mozart's Sarastro and Lodovico in Otello; Further engagements as Arasse in Handel's Siroe at the RCM, the Commendatore at Valencia, Masetto at Covent Garden (1996) and in Copenhagen, Colline in La Bohème at the Royal Albert Hall (1997) and Pimen in Boris Godunov at Turin; Further Handel roles include Cadmus and Somnus in Semele at the Berlin Staatsoper, and Christian in Rinaldo at Geneva; Concerts include Haydn's Nelson Mass, Mozart's Coronation Mass and Requiem, Tippett's A Child of our Time with the Icelandic Symphony Orchestra, Bach's St Matthew Passion at the United Kingdom Handel Festival and Verdi's Requiem at the Mayfield Festival. *Current Management:* Athole Still International Management, Forresters Hall, 25–27 Westow Street, London, SE19 3RY, England. *Telephone:* (20) 8771-5271. *Fax:* (20) 8768-6600. *Website:* www.atholestill.com.

**TOMASZEWSKI, Rolf;** Singer (Bass); b. 18 March 1940, Deutzen, Leipzig, Germany. *Education:* Studied in Dresden with Johannes Kemter. *Career:* Debut: Wittenberg in 1959 as Baculus in Lortzing's Der Wildschütz; Teacher until 1971 then sang in opera at Dresden-Radebeul, 1971–75; Performances at the Dresden Staatsoper and elsewhere in Germany from 1975 as Sarastro, Osmin, the Commendatore, Don Alfonso, Kaspar in Der Freischütz, the Landgrave in Tannhäuser, King Henry in Lohengrin and buffo roles; Many concert appearances. *Address:* c/o Semper-Oper, Dresden 01067, Germany.

**TOMITA, Yo,** BMus, MMus, PhD; Japanese academic; *Reader, Queen's University, Belfast;* b. 17 Dec. 1961, Fukushima, Japan. *Education:* Musashino Academia Musicale, Tokyo and Univ. of Leeds, UK. *Career:* Postdoctoral Research Fellow, Queen's Univ., Belfast 1995–2000, Lecturer 2000–01, Reader 2001–; mem. Royal Musical Asscn, Neue Bach-Gesellschaft, American Bach Soc., Soc. for Musicology in Ireland, Japan Musicological Soc. *Publications:* J. S. Bach's Das Wohltemperierte Clavier II 1993, edns of Fugal Composition: A Guide to the Study of Bach's 48 by Joseph Groocock 2003, Bach studies from Dublin (with Anne Leahy) 2004; contrib. to Oxford Composer Companions: J.S. Bach 1999, Cambridge Mozart Encyclopedia 2006, many journals. *Honours:* Martha Goldsworthy Arnold Fellowship, Riemenschneider Bach Inst., Berea, OH, USA 2002. *Address:* School of Music and Sonic Arts, Queen's University, Belfast, BT7 1NN, Northern Ireland (office). *Telephone:* (28) 90975206 (office). *Fax:* (28) 90975053 (office). *E-mail:* y.tomita@qub.ac.uk (office). *Website:* www.music.qub.ac.uk/tomita (office).

**TOMLINSON, Ernest,** FRCO; Composer; b. Sept. 1924, Rawtenstall, England; m.; four c. *Education:* composition, organ, piano and clarinet, Royal Manchester Coll. of Music, Manchester Univ., 1941; MusB, Composition; ARMCM, Organ, 1947. *Career:* mem., Rossendale Male Voice Choir; arranger, group of music publishers, 1947; Organist, Church in Mayfair; Dir, Church choir; Musical Dir, Chingford Amateur Dramatic and Operatic Society, 1951–53; broadcast with his own orchestras and singers, 1995–; conducted his own compositions, Royal Festival Hall, Royal Albert Hall, London, Tchaikovsky Hall, Moscow; founder, Northern Concert Orchestra; Rossendale Male Voice Choir, 1976–81; co-founder, Rossendale Festival Choir; founder, Ribble Vale Choir, Longridge, 1989; Conductor, Slovak Radio Symphony Orchestra, Bratislava; Conductor, RTE Concert Orchestra, Dublin; New Zealand Symphony Orchestra, Wellington; mem., Composers' Guild of Great Britain (exec. cttee, Chair., 1964), Performing Right Society (Composer-Dir, 1965–94), Light Music Society (Chair.). *Compositions:* Overtures; Suites; Rhapsodies; two symphonies for combined jazz and symphony orchestras; three concertos; one-act opera, Head of the Family; background music for use in films, television; brass band and wind band and organ music; Fantasia on Auld Lang Syne; Fantasia on North-Country Tunes, commissioned by the Hallé Orchestra, 1977. *Recordings:* conducted on five albums, British Light Music, 1991–. *Honours:* Ivor Novello Award, 1974; Special Composers' Guild Award.

*Address:* Lancaster Farm, Chipping Lane, Longridge, Preston, Lancashire PR3 2NB, England.

**TOMLINSON, Sir John Rowland,** CBE; British singer (bass); b. 22 Sept. 1946, Accrington, Lancs.; s. of Rowland Tomlinson and Ellen Greenwood; m. Moya Joel 1969; one s. two d. *Education:* Accrington Grammar School, Manchester Univ. and Royal Manchester Coll. of Music. *Career:* debut at Glyndebourne Festival 1972, ENO 1974, Royal Opera House, Covent Garden 1976; since then has appeared in many operas throughout Europe and N America, including Parsifal, Tristan und Isolde and Lohengrin; has sung role of Wotan/Wanderer in The Ring Cycle, Bayreuth Festival 1988–98; other significant roles include Boris in Boris Godunov, ENO (Manchester) 1982, Don Basilio in Il Barbiere di Siviglia, Covent Garden 1985, Moses, ENO 1980, Fiesco in Simon Boccanegra, ENO 1988, Mephistopheles in Damnation of Faust, Santiago, Chile 1990, Attila, Opera North 1990, Filippo II in Don Carlos, Opera North 1992, König Marke in Tristan and Isolde, Bayreuth Festival 1993, Mephistopheles in Damnation of Faust, La Fenice, Venice 1993, Claggart in Billy Budd, Covent Garden 1994, Hans Sachs in Die Meistersinger, Berlin Staatsoper 1995, Kingfisher in Midsummer Marriage, Covent Garden 1996, Bluebeard in Bluebeard's Castle, Berlin Philharmonic 1996, Four Villains in Tales of Hoffmann, ENO 1998, Moses in Moses and Aaron, New York Metropolitan Opera 1999, Golaud in Pelléas et Mélisande, Glyndebourne 1999, Mephistopheles in Damnation of Faust, Munich Staatsoper 2000, Hagen in Götterdämmerung, Bayreuth 2000, Baron Ochs in Rosenkavalier, Staatsoper Dresden 2000, Borromeo in Palestrina, Covent Garden 2001, Gurnemanz in Parsifal, New York Metropolitan 2001; numerous broadcasts, recordings, opera videos and concert performances. *Honours:* Hon. FRNCM; Hon. DMus (Sussex) 1997, (Manchester) 1998; Singer of the Year, Royal Philharmonic Soc. 1991, 1998, Evening Standard Opera Award 1998. *Current Management:* Music International, 13 Ardilaun Road, Highbury, London, N5 2QR, England. *Telephone:* (20) 7359-5183.

**TOMMASI, Carlo;** Stage Designer; b. 1950, Italy. *Education:* Brera Academy. *Career:* Designs for Rigoletto at Munich, in production by Roman Polanski, Carmen in Tokyo, Otello at Bregenz and Tannhäuser in Frankfurt; Premiere production of Berio's La Vera Storia (La Scala, 1982), La Cenerentola in Brussels (1983) and L'Incoronazione di Poppea at Nancy; Further designs at La Monnaie for The Cunning Little Vixen, Der Rosenkavalier, Der fliegende Holländer and Der Freischütz; Collaborations with Nicholas Joël at Théâtre du Capitole, Toulouse, for Falstaff (1991) and Roméo et Juliette (1993 also at the Royal Opera, Covent Garden); Further work includes Leonore at Genoa and Les Contes d'Hoffmann at Toulouse. *Address:* c/o Théâtre du Capitole, Place du Capitole, 31000 Toulouse, France.

**TOMOWA-SINTOW, Anna;** Austrian singer (soprano); b. 22 Sept. 1943, Stara Zagora, Bulgaria; m. Albert Sintow 1963; one d. *Education:* Nat. Conservatory of Sofia with Zlatew Tscherkin. *Career:* debut Leipzig Opera 1967; joined Deutsche Staatsoper, Berlin 1969; guest engagements at most leading European and US opera houses, including La Scala, Milan, Vienna, Covent Garden, London, Paris, Bavarian State Opera and Bolshoi, Moscow; debut N America at Metropolitan Opera, New York 1978; has toured Japan with La Scala di Milano and Berlin Philharmonic under von Karajan; regular guest at Salzburg Festival since 1973; has sung in several TV productions; recording and film of Verdi Requiem with von Karajan. *Recordings include:* Lohengrin, Le Nozze di Figaro, Don Giovanni, Die Zauberflöte, Mozart Coronation Mass, Mozart Requiem, Brahms German Requiem, Strauss Four Last Songs and Capriccio monologue, Beethoven Missa Solemnis, Ariadne auf Naxos (in preparation), Madame Butterfly, La Traviata, Tosca, Eugene Onegin, recitals of Verdi arias and of Italian and German arias. *Major roles include:* Arabella, Ariadne, Madelaine (in Capriccio), Countess Almaviva, Elsa (in Lohengrin), Elisabeth (in Tannhäuser), Aida, Tosca, Madame Butterfly, Traviata, Manon Lescaut, Maddalena (in Andrea Chenier), Leonora (in La Forza del Destino), Marschallin (Rosenkavalier), Yaroslavna, etc. *Honours:* winner Kammersängerin Prize. *Current Management:* Cæcilia Lyric Department, Rennweg 15, 8001 Zurich, Switzerland. *Telephone:* (1) 221 33 88. *Fax:* (1) 211 71 82. *E-mail:* caecilia@caecilia-lyric.ch. *Website:* www.caecilia .ch.

**TOMTER, Lars Anders;** Violist; b. 30 Nov. 1959; 1 d. *Education:* Piano, 5 years, Violin, 8 years, Violin and Viola, Conservatory, 13 years, Max Rostal Bern Conservatory, 3 years, Sándor Végh, Mozarteum, Salzburg, 2 years. *Career:* Solo Performances, USA, Germany, Vienna, Scandinavia, Madrid, Budapest, Frankfurt, Cologne, Paris, London; Soloist with such orchestras as Academy of St Martin-in-the-Fields, City of Birmingham and Frankfurt Radio Symphony Orchestras, Philharmonic Orchestra of Frankfurt, Hungarian National Philharmonic Orchestra, Los Angeles Chamber Orchestra, Oslo and Bergen Philharmonics, Danish Radio Symphony Orchestra, Stockholm New Chamber Orchestra, Gavleborg, Norwegian Radio, Trondheim and Stavanger Symphony Orchestras; Proms debut with RPO, 1998; Artistic Director, Risar Chamber Music Festival; Walton's concerto at the London Proms, 2002. *Recordings:* Walton Concertos; Franck and Vieuxtemps Sonatas; Mozart's Sinfonia Concertante with Norwegian Chamber Orchestra and Iona Brown; Schumann and Brahms Sonatas with Pianist Leif Ove Andsnes. *Honours:* Numerous awards and prizes. *Address:* c/o Martin Muller, Vintrup 4, 59320 Ennigerloh Ostenfelde, Germany.

**TONE, Yasunao;** American composer and multimedia artist; b. 31 March 1935, Tokyo, Japan. *Education:* Japanese National University, Chiba, Tokyo

University of the Arts. *Career:* founded performance group Ongaku at Tokyo, 1960; Wrote tape pieces Geography, and Music performed by Merle Cunningham Dance Company; Settled in New York 1972, participating in avant garde and computer music festivals in North America and Europe, FLUXUS festivals 1979–87 and Venice Biennale (1990). *Compositions include:* Intermedia Art Festival, 1969; Multi Performance, 1972; Voice and Phenomenon, 1976; The Wall and the Books, 1982; Word of Mouth, 1988. *Publications include:* Can Art be Thought, 1970. *Honours:* New York Foundation for the Arts Fellowship, 1987.

**TOOLEY, Sir John,** Kt, MA; British arts administrator and arts consultant; b. 1 June 1924, Rochester, Kent; s. of the late H. R. Tooley; m. 1st Judith Craig Morris 1951 (divorced 1965); three d.; m. 2nd Patricia J. N. Bagshawe 1968 (divorced 1990); one s.; m. 3rd Jennifer Anne Shannon 1995 (divorced 2003). *Education:* Repton School and Magdalene Coll., Cambridge. *Career:* Sec. Guildhall School of Music and Drama 1952–55; Asst to Gen. Admin., Royal Opera House, Covent Garden 1955–60, Asst Gen. Admin. 1960–70, Gen. Admin. 1970–80, Gen. Dir 1980–88; Chair. Almeida Theatre 1990–97, Fabric Advisory Cttee Salisbury Cathedral 1992–2005, Salisbury Cathedral Girl Choristers Trust 1995–2006, Nureyev Foundation 1995–; Pres. Salisbury Festival 1988–2005; Chair. Monument Insurance Brokers Ltd 1997–2002; consultant, Int. Man. Group 1988–97, Ballet Opera House, Toronto 1989–90, Istanbul Foundation for Culture and Arts 1993–, Antelope Films 1993–; Dir London Philharmonic Orchestra 1998–, Britten Estate 1989–96, South Bank Bd 1991–97, Compton Verney Opera Project 1991–97, Welsh Nat. Opera 1992–2000, David Gyngell Holdings Ltd 1996–97; Gov. Royal Ballet 1994–97; adviser, Borusan Philharmonic Orchestra, Istanbul 2005–; Trustee Britten Pears Foundation 1988–99, Walton Trust 1988–2000, Wigmore Hall 1989–2001, Almeida Theatre 1990–2002, Performing Arts Labs 1992–97, Cardiff Bay Opera House 1995–96, Sidney Nolan Trust 1995–, Mozartfest, Bath 2001–. *Publication:* In House 1999. *Honours:* Hon. FRAM; Hon. GSM; Hon. mem. Royal Northern Coll. of Music; Hon. ISM; Hon. Fellow, Magdalen Coll. Cambridge 2005; Commendatore of Italian Repub. 1976; Hon. DUniv (Univ. of Central England) 1996; Queen Elizabeth II Coronation Award 2005. *Address:* 18 Grange Court, Cambridge, CB3 9BD, England (home). *Telephone:* (1223) 358737 (office); (1223) 351995 (home). *Fax:* (1223) 358737 (office). *E-mail:* tooley@btinternet.com (home).

**TOOVEY, Andrew;** Composer; b. 21 Feb. 1962, London, England. *Education:* Studied at the Universities of Surrey and Sussex with Jonathan Harvey and at Dartington with Morton Feldman. *Career:* Music has been performed by Alan Hacker, Michael Finnissy, the Mistry Quartet and the Endimion Ensemble; Director of Ixion, founded in 1987, giving performances of works by Cage, Feldman, Ferneyhough, Finnissy, James Dillon and Xenakis; Composer in Residence at the Banff Centre, Canada, 1997. *Compositions:* Chamber and ensemble: Winter Solstice, 1984, String Quartet, 1985, Cantec for Viola and Piano, 1986, Ate, 1986, Shining for Violin and Cello, 1987, Shining Forth, 1987, Shimmer Bright for String Trio, 1988, White Fire, 1988, Snow Flowers, 1988, Black Light, 1989, An Die Musik, 1989, Adam, 1989; Solo instruments: Veiled Wave 1 and 2, for Flute and Clarinet, 1985, Artaud for Piano, 1986, Fragments After Artaud, 1988, Lament, Strathspey, reel for Violin, 1988, Out Jumps Jack Death and Down There By The Sea for Piano, 1989, UBU, opera in 2 acts (five scenes), 1990–92, The Juniper Tree, opera in one act (4 scenes), 1993; The Moon Falls through the Autumn, for piano, 1995; Out!, for two pianos and orchestra, 1995; Red Icon, for large symphony orchestra, 1996; Oboe Concerto, 1997; In the Shallow Grave, opera, 1999. *Recordings include:* Artaud; Out Jumps Jack Death; Red Icon and The Juniper Tree, 1998. *Honours:* Tippett Prize for Untitled String Quartet; Terra Nova Prize for Ate; Bernard Shore Composition Award for Cantec; Young Concert Artists Trust Associate Composer, 1993–. *Current Management:* Ycat. *Address:* 57B Station Road, Willesden, London NW10 4UX, England.

**TÖPPER, Hertha;** singer (mezzo-soprano); b. 19 April 1924, Graz, Austria. *Education:* Graz Conservatory. *Career:* debut, Graz 1945 as Ulrica in Un Ballo in Maschera; sang in Graz 1945–52, at Munich Staatsoper from 1952 notably in the 1957 premiere of Hindemith's Die Harmonie der Welt, at Bayreuth Festival from 1951 as Brangaene and Fricka, and visited Covent Garden with the Munich Co. 1953 as Clairon in Capriccio; sang at San Francisco 1960 and Metropolitan Opera 1962 as Octavian in Der Rosenkavalier, and at Munich 1972 in the premiere of Isang Yun's Sim Tjong; other roles include Verdi's Eboli and Amneris, Mozart's Dorabella, Magdalena in Die Meistersinger and Nancy in Martha; sang Branhaene with Bayreuth Co. in Osaka; retired from stage 1981; often heard in sacred music by Bach; Prof., Munich Musikhochschule from 1971. *Recordings:* Die Meistersinger; Bluebeard's Castle; Oedipus Rex; Schoenberg's Gurrelieder; Bach's B minor Mass; Octavian in Der Rosenkavalier from London's Covent Garden. *Honours:* Bayer Kammersängerin 1955, Deutsches Bundes Veraienstkreuz 1 Klasse 1985, Bayer Maximiliansorden für Wissenschaft und Kunst 1995. *Address:* Knöbelstrasse 2, 80538 München, Germany.

**TORADZE, Alexander;** Pianist; b. 1955, Tbilisi, Georgia. *Education:* Graduated the Tchaikovsky Conservatory Moscow 1978. *Career:* Resident in the USA from 1983, giving concerts in every major centre and appearing with such conductors as Ashkenazy, Dutoit, Eschenbach, Masur, Mehta, Ozawa and Rattle; European engagements with the Kirov Orchestra (under Valery Gergiev) Rotterdam Philharmonic Orchestra, London Symphony and Philharmonic, CBSO and Philharmonia Orchestra; Season 1997 with the Los Angeles Philharmonic Orchestra under Esa-Pekka Salonen, Toronto Symph-

ony Orchestra under Jukka-Pekka Saraste, the Orchestra National de France and the Rotterdam Philharmonic Orchestra under Gergiev; Festival appearances at the London Proms, Hollywood Bowl, St Petersburg White Nights, Saratoga and Schleswig-Holstein; From 1991, Martin Endowed Professor in Piano at Indiana University South Bend; Prokofiev's concerto No. 3 in C major at the London Proms, 2002. *Recordings include:* Prokofiev's 7th Sonata, Ravel's Miroirs, Three Movements from Petrushka, Pictures at an Exhibition, Gaspard de la Nuit (EMI/Angel); Prokofiev Concertos, with the Kirov Orchestra and Gergiev (Philips Classics). *Current Management:* Askonas Holt Ltd, Lonsdale Chambers, 27 Chancery Lane, London, WC2A 1PF, England. *Telephone:* (20) 7400-1700. *Fax:* (20) 7400-1799. *E-mail:* info@askonasholt.co.uk. *Website:* www.askonasholt.co.uk.

**TORCHINSKY, Yuri;** Violinist; b. 1949, Kharkiv, Ukraine (United Kingdom resident from 1991); 1 s. *Education:* Tchaikovsky Conservatory Moscow, 1975–80; Postgraduate Conservatory Assistant, 1980–83. *Career:* Debut: Brahms Violin Concerto with the Kharkov Philharmonic Orchestra conducted by Vakhtang Gordania; Leader of the Bolshoi Theatre in Moscow with numerous performances, concerts and tours, as soloist and orchestra leader, world-wide including the Metropolitan Opera in New York and at many opera theatres and concert halls in USA, Italy, Austria, France, Netherlands, Germany, Japan and elsewhere; Radio appearances with recitals in Moscow and on television in Yugoslavia; Several appearances at the Albert Hall in London, television and radio recordings of Promenade Concerts performance, at the Barbican Hall, Royal Festival Hall, New Symphony Hall and Town Hall in Birmingham; Many concerts and radio and CD recordings as guest leader of London Symphony Orchestra as well as tours to France, Switzerland, Austria, Portugal and Italy; Solo appearances at Royal Opera House, 1995; Guest Leader with such orchestras as BBC National Orchestra of Wales, Philharmonia, Royal Philharmonic, and BBC Manchester; Leader of the Royal Ballet Symphonia Orchestra of the Birmingham Royal Ballet. *Address:* 14 Ellery Road, Upper Norwood, London SE19 3QG, England.

**TORKE, Michael;** American composer and pianist; b. 22 Sept. 1961, Milwaukee, WI. *Education:* Eastman School of Music, Rochester. *Career:* commissions from New York City Ballet and The Huddersfield Festival; European performances with the Danish Radio Symphony Orchestra, the Ensemble Intercontemporain, London Sinfonietta and Lontano; as pianist has recorded on several labels. *Compositions:* Laetus for piano solo 1982, Ceremony of Innocence for flute, clarinet, violin, cello and piano 1983, Ecstatic Orange for ensemble 1984, Vanada for keyboards, brass and percussion 1984, The Yellow Pages 1984, Bright Blue Music for ensemble 1985, Verdant Music for ensemble 1986, The Directions (one-act opera based on The Yellow Pages) 1986, Adjustable Wrench for ensemble 1987, Black and White for wind instruments, percussion and synthesizer 1988, Copper for brass quintet and orchestra 1988, Ash for orchestra or chamber orchestra 1989, Slate (ballet for Concertante Group and orchestra) 1989, Rust for piano and wind instruments 1989, Run for orchestra 1992, Four Proverbs for voice and ensemble 1993, King of Hearts (chamber opera) 1994, Book of Proverbs for soprano, baritone, chorus and orchestra 1996, Overnight Mail and Change of Address for ensemble 1997, Brick Symphony 1997, Pentecost for soprano, organ and strings 1997, Strawberry Fields (chamber opera) 1999, The House of Mirth (opera for the New York City Opera) 2004. *Honours:* Prix de Rome, Koussevitzky Foundation Award. *Address:* c/o Composers & Repertoire Department, Boosey & Hawkes Inc., 35 E 21st Street, New York, NY 10010-6212, USA. *Website:* www.boosey.com/torke.

**TÖRNQUIST, Pirkko;** Singer (Soprano); b. 1955, Finland. *Education:* Helsinki Conservatory and Sibelius Academy; With Vera Rozsa in London, Nicolai Gedda in Stockholm and with Anitta Välkki. *Career:* Many appearances as opera and concert singer throughout Finland and Europe; Finnish National Opera at Helsinki from 1990, as Amelia in Ballo in Maschera, Tosca, Tatiana in Eugene Onegin, Mozart's Countess and Elsa in Lohengrin; Maija in Pohjan's Daughter, by Merikanto; Savonlinna Festival, 1990–91, as Aida; Sang Sieglinde in Die Walküre at Helsinki, 1998. *Honours:* Prize Winner, 1993 Competition, Vienna Belvedere. *Address:* c/o Finnish National Opera, PO Box 176, Helsingkatu 58, 00251 Helsinki, Finland.

**TORRES, Victor;** Singer (Baritone); b. 1965, Buenos Aires, Argentina. *Education:* Studied in Buenos Aires and with Gerard Souzay. *Career:* Debut: Bilbao, 1991, as Germont; Sang in South Africa as Verdi's Posa and Luna; Teatro Colón, Buenos Aires, from 1993, as Masetto in Don Giovanni and Paolo Orsini in Rienzi; Season 1993–94 at the Châtelet, Paris, and Lyon as Germont; Further appearances as Donizetti's Enrico at the Paris Opéra and as Purcell's Aeneas and Bartók's Bluebeard at San Francisco; Season 1997–98 as Don Alfonso in Così fan tutte at the Berlin Staatsoper and Germont at Opéra de Nancy; Many concert engagements, notably in Bach's St John Passion, Messiah, Haydn's Creation and Schumann's Scenes from Faust; Sang Yeletzky in The Queen of Spades at Florence, 1999. *Recordings include:* Monteverdi Vespers.

**TORRES-SANTOS, Raymond;** Composer, Arranger, Keyboardist, Conductor and Music Educator and Music Critic; b. 19 June 1958, Puerto Rico. *Education:* BA, Puerto Rico University and Conservatory of Music, 1980; MA 1982, PhD 1986, University of California, Los Angeles; Ferienkurse für Neue Musik, 1982; CCRMA, Stanford University, 1985; Centro di Sonologia Computazionale, Padua University, Italy, 1988. *Career:* Arranger, Music Director, for best American singers and entertainers; Composer of film music, studio musician in Hollywood; Professor, California State University, San Bernardino, 1986–91; Chairman of Music Department, University of Puerto Rico, 1991–93; Chancellor, Puerto Rico Conservatory of Music, 1994–98; Visiting Professor, CUNY, 2000–01. *Compositions include:* Sinfonietta Concertante for Orchestra, 1980; Summertime, Clarinet Consort, 1982; Exploraciones for String Orchestra, 1982; Areytos: a Symphonic Picture, 1985; Enchanted Island, Piano and Tape, 1986; Monchin del Alma: Ballet, 1988; El Pais de los Cuatro Pisos: A Symphonic Overture, 1988; Viaggio Senza Destinazione for Tape, 1988; Danza for Orchestra, 1991; La Cancion de las Antillas: A Symphonic Poem, 1992; Fantasia Caribena, for Orchestra, 1992; Salsa y tres Sones, for piano or harp solo; Requiem for Mezzo-Soprano, Baritone, Mixed Chorus, Children's Choir and Orchestra, 1995; Odalisque, ballet, 1997; Concertino for clarinet, French horn, piano, percussion and strings, 1998; Trio for clarinet, cello and piano, 1998; Overture for Orchestra, 1998; Conversation with Silence, for soprano and ensemble, 1999; Millennium Symphony for orchestra, 2000; Jersey Polyphony for chorus, 2000; Juris Oratorio, for chorus, 2000; Performed and/or commissioned by the Casals Festival, Vienna Philharmonic, New Jersey Chamber Music Society, Continuum, Bronx Arts Ensemble, Quintet of the Americas, Paquito de Rivera, Inter-American University, Youth Symphony of the Americas, San Juan Ballet and Pops Orchestra; American Composers Orchestra; Boston Pops; Symphony Orchestra from Puerto Rico, Queens, London, Virginia, Pacific, Northwestern University and University of California at Los Angeles. *Recordings:* 25 as Arranger and/or Conductor. *Address:* PO Box 361743, San Juan, Puerto Rico 00936-1743, USA.

**TORTELIER, Yan Pascal;** French conductor and violinist; b. 19 April 1947, Paris; s. of the late Paul Tortelier and of Maud Tortelier; m. Sylvie Brunet-Moret 1970; two s. *Education:* Paris Conservatoire and Berks. Music Centre. *Career:* debut as concert violinist, Royal Albert Hall 1962; has since toured extensively world-wide; Konzertmeister, Assoc. Conductor of Orchestre du Capitole de Toulouse 1974–82; Prin. Conductor and Artistic Dir, Ulster Orchestra 1989–92; Prin. Conductor BBC Philharmonic 1992–2002. *Publication:* première orchestration of Ravel's Piano Trio (world première concert 1992). *Honours:* Hon. DLitt (Ulster) 1992; Dr hc (Lancaster) 1999. *Address:* c/o IMG Artists Europe, 616 Chiswick High Road, London, W4 2RX, England.

**TORZEWSKI, Marek;** singer (tenor); b. 1960, Poland. *Education:* Poznan Academy of Music. *Career:* debut, Łódź Opera 1984 as Edgardo in Lucia di Lammermoor; Sang in Idomeneo at the Théâtre de la Monnaie Brussels, 1984; Appearances in La Finta Giardiniera at Vienna, Salzburg, Amsterdam, Berlin and New York, 1985; Further engagements at Brussels and in Hamburg, Montpellier, Philadelphia and Lausanne; Season 1989–90 in L'Incoronazione di Poppea in Paris, Rosenkavalier, Così fan tutte and Fierrabras by Schubert in Brussels, Don Ottavio at Toulouse and Glyndebourne Festival debut as Fenton in Falstaff; Season 1991–92 as Tamino at Lausanne, Alfredo for Scottish Opera and the Mozart Requiem under Muti at La Scala, Milan; Debut with the Berlin Philharmonic 1992, singing in Nono's Il Canto Sospeso, under Abbado; Opera National de Lisbon, Eugene Onegin–Lensky, Staatsoper Leipzig, Così fan tutte–Ferrando, 1993; Théâtre Municipal de Lausanne, Iphigénie en Tauride–Pylade, 1994. *Recordings include:* Il Canto Sospeso (Deutsche Grammophon). *Current Management:* Robert Gilder & Co., Enterprise House, 59–65 Upper Ground, London, SE1 9PQ, England. *Telephone:* (20) 7928-9008. *Fax:* (20) 7928-9755. *E-mail:* rgilder@robert-gilder.com.

**TOTENBERG, Roman;** Violinist and Conductor; b. 1 Jan. 1911, Łódź, Poland; m. 30 July 1941, 3 d. *Education:* Baccalaureate, Warsaw; Chopin School, Warsaw; Chopin School of Music Diploma, Warsaw, Gold Medal, 1929; Hochschule für Musik with Carl Flesch, Berlin, Mendelssohn Prize, 1932; Paris Institut Instrumentale with Georges Enesco, 1933. *Career:* Soloist with most major orchestras, Europe, USA, South America; Formerly Director Chamber Music radio station WQXR New York and Director of Longy School, Cambridge, Massachusetts; Professor of Music, Boston University, 1962–; Summers: Kneisel Hall Blue Hill, Maine, 1975–; Formerly Music Academy of the West, Salzburg Mozarteum, Berkshire Music Centre and Aspen Festival; Co-Chairman, String Department, Boston University. *Recordings:* Brahms and Lipinski Concertos, Titanic, 1990; Beethoven and Szymanowski Concertos, VGR, 1992; Bloch Concerto, Vanguard, 1992; All Bach Sonatas and Partitas, Schumann Sonatas, German Baroque Concerti, Musical Heritage. *Publications:* Cadenzas to Mozart concerti, co-author, 1998. *Address:* 329 Waverley Avenue, Newton, MA 02458, USA.

**TOVEY, Bramwell,** FRAM; British conductor and composer; *Music Director, Vancouver Symphony Orchestra;* b. 1955, England. *Career:* many concerts in a broad repertoire throughout Europe and Canada, including numerous premieres; Artistic Dir, Winnipeg Symphony Orchestra 1989–2001, establishing the Winnipeg New Music Festival; Music Dir, Vancouver Symphony Orchestra 2000–; Chief Conductor and Music Dir, Orchestre Philharmonique du Luxembourg 2002–; debut, Concertgebouw, Amsterdam 2004; guest conductor with orchestras, including NYPO, Toronto Symphony, National Arts Centre Orchestra, Trondheim Symphony in Norway, New York Philharmonic, Royal Scottish Nat. Orchestra, London Philharmonic. *Compositions include:* Cello Concerto 2001, Requiem for a Charred Skull (Juno Award for Best Classical Composition 2003), Eighteen (film score) 2005. *Honours:* Dr hc (Manitoba), (Winnipeg); Joan Chalmers Nat. Award for Artistic Direction 1999; Member of the Order of Manitoba 2000. *Address:* c/o

Vancouver Symphony Orchestra, Orpheum Theatre, 601 Smithe Street, Vancouver, BC V6B 5G1, Canada. *Website:* www.vancouversymphony.ca.

**TOWER, Joan Peabody,** MA; American composer; b. 6 Sept. 1938, New Rochelle, NY. *Education:* Bennington Coll. (VT) and Columbia Univ. (NY). *Career:* Pianist Da Capo Chamber Players 1969–84; apptd Assoc. Prof. Bard Coll., New York 1972; Composer-in-Residence St Louis Symphony 1985–87; comms from Contemporary Music Soc., Jerome Foundation, Massachusetts State Arts Council, Schubert Club, Richard Stolzman, St Louis Symphony, Elmar Oliveira, NY Philharmonic, Chicago Symphony, Fromm Foundation, Nat. Endowment for the Arts; Guggenheim Fellow 1976; Nat. Endowment for the Arts Fellow 1974, 1975, 1980, 1984; New York State Council for Arts Award 1980; American Acad. and Inst. of Arts and Letters Award in Music 1983. *Compositions include:* Amazon, Amazon II, Sequoia, Silver Ladders (Grawemeyer Award, Univ. of Louisville 1990) 1985, Breakfast Rhythms, Black Topaz, Wings, Fantasy, Cello Concerto, Piano Concerto, Clarinet Concerto. *Address:* Bard College, Annandale-On-Hudson, NY 12504, USA.

**TOWSE, David,** ARCM, LRAM; British violinist; b. 1956, Bridlington, England. *Education:* Royal Coll. of Music with Leonard Hirsch, Peter Element and Herbert Howells. *Career:* leader of the East Riding County Youth Orchestra and British Youth Symphony Orchestra 1972; leader of the London Youth String Ensemble while at the Royal Coll. of Music; joined Royal Philharmonic Orchestra 1978, Assoc. Leader 1982, (performances of piano quintets and quartets with the Forellen Ensemble (mems of the RPO) at music clubs and festivals throughout the UK, left RPO 1998; freelance in and around London, guest leading, directing and coaching ensembles, teaching and performing as a soloist, also chamber music both for concerts and private functions. *Address:* 47 Abbotswood Road, London, SW16 1AJ, England.

**TOZZI, Giorgio;** singer (bass); b. 8 Jan. 1923, Chicago, Illinois, USA. *Education:* Studied with Rosa Raisa, Giacomo Rimini and John Daggert Howell. *Career:* Debut: Tarquinius in The Rape of Lucretia, on Broadway, 1948; Studied further in Italy and sang Rodolfo in La Sonnambula at the Teatro Nuovo Milan, 1950; La Scala 1953, in La Wally by Catalani; Metropolitan Opera from 1955, as Alvise (La Gioconda), Sparafucile, Pimen, Boris Godonov, Mozart's Figaro, Daland, Pogner, Sachs, Rocco and Philip II; Created the Doctor in Barber's Vanessa (1958); San Francisco from 1955, as Ramfis, Calkas in Troilus and Cressida and Archibaldo (L'Amore dei tre Re); Salzburg Festival 1958, 1961 in Vanessa and as Fiesco in Simon Boccanegra; Hollywood Bowl 1956, in the US premiere of David by Milhaud; La Scala 1962, in a revival of Les Huguenots; Appearances in Florence, Palermo, Hamburg, Frankfurt, Lisbon and Munich as Sarastro, Padre Guardiano, Don Giovanni, Gurnemanz, Arkel and Gremin; Boston Opera 1977, in the US premiere of Ruslan and Lyudmila by Glinka; Active in films, television and musical comedy. *Recordings:* Rigoletto, Guillaume Tell; Der fliegende Holländer; Vanessa; La Forza del Destino; Aida; La Bohème; Le nozze di Figaro; Luisa Miller; Il Trovatore, La Fanciulla del West, Rigoletto.

**TRACEY, Edmund;** Translator, Administrator and Librettist; b. 14 Nov. 1927, Preston, England. *Career:* Music Critic for The Observer 1958–65; Sadler's Wells (later English National Opera) Director from 1965, as dramaturg and repertory planner; Translated for ENO such texts as Les contes d'Hoffmann 1970, Aida, 1978 and Manon, 1979; La Finta Giardiniera by Mozart for English Music Theatre at Sadler's Wells, 1976; Librettist for Malcolm Williamson's Lucky-Peter's Journey (after Strindberg), Sadler's Wells 1969. *Address:* English National Opera, St Martin's Lane, London WC2N 4ES, England.

**TRACK, Gerhard;** Conductor and Composer; b. 17 Sept. 1934, Vienna, Austria; m. Micaela Maihart, 3 Aug 1958, 2 s. *Education:* Music Theory, Conducting and Piano, Academy of Music and Performing Arts, Vienna, Austria; Teacher Training College, Vienna, Austria, 1953; Member, Vienna Boys Choir, 1942–48. *Career:* Debut: Conductor, Vienna Boys Choir, 1953; Conductor, Vienna Boys Choir, 1953–58; Music Director, St John's Symphony Orchestra, Associate Professor, Music, St John's University, Men's Chorus, Minnesota, USA, 1958–69; Music Director, Metropolitan Youth Symphony Orchestra, Minneapolis, Minnesota, USA, 1965–69; Music Director, Pueblo Symphony Orchestra, Chorale and Youth Symphony; Founder, annual Mozart Festival, Pueblo, Colorado, USA; Thatcher Professor of Music, University of Southern Colorado, Pueblo, Colorado, 1969–86; Music Director and Conductor, Choral Society of Young Vienna (Jung-Wien), 1986–96; Orchester Pro Musica International and Vienna Serenade Orchestra, Vienna, 1986–; Teacher: Conservatory of the City Vienna and Hochschule (University) for Music and Performing Arts. Vienna, 1987–89; Director, Conservatory of the City of Vienna, 1989–99; President, Austrian Composers Society, 1988–92; Music Director, Vienna Male Choral Society, 1990–2003; International Guest Conductor, Europe, USA, Asia and Australia; President and Founder, PMI Music Publication, California. *Compositions:* Over 600 compositions, orchestral works, choral compositions and arrangements, 1 opera, chamber music, songs, 3 children's operas, 11 Masses, published in Europe and USA. *Recordings:* Many for major recording companies. *Contributions:* Sacred Music; Oesterreichische Musikzeitschrift. *Honours:* Golden Honorary Cross for Merits, Republic of Austria,Golden Honorary Cross of Vienna and Honarary Cross for Science and Art, 1st Class Austria. *Current Management:* PMI, 10730 Riverside Drive, North Hollywood, CA 91602, USA. *Address:* Praterstrasse 76/8, 1020 Vienna, Austria.

**TRAMA, Ugo;** Singer (bass); b. 4 Aug. 1932, Naples, Italy. *Education:* Studied with Emilia Gubitosi in Naples, at the Accademia Chigiana in Siena and at the Accademia di Santa Cecilia Rome. *Career:* Debut: Spoleto Festival 1951, as Banquo in Macbeth; Sang in Cairo and the Italian provinces; Holland Festival 1960, as Fiesco in Simon Bocanegra; Wexford festival 1961, as Silva in Ernani; Dallas Opera 1961; San Francisco Opera 1965; Appearances at the Maggio Musicale Florence, Teatro Liceo Barcelona and Strasbourg; Glyndebourne 1964–79, as Asdrubale in La Pietra del Paragone, Giove and Pane (Calisto), Atinoo and Tempo (Il Ritorno d'Ulisse), Bartolo (Le nozze di Figaro), Pistol (Falstaff) and Farfallo (Die schweigsame Frau). *Recordings include:* Ramphis in Aida; La Cenerentola (Deutsche Grammophon); Il Ritorno d'Ulisse (CBS).

**TRAN, Quang Hai;** Ethnomusicologist, Educator, Musician and Composer; b. 13 May 1944, Viet Nam; m. Bach-Yen Quach, 17 June 1978, one d. *Education:* National Conservatory of Music, Saigon, 1961; Sorbonne, Paris, 1963; Institut d'Ethnologie, 1964; Diploma, Centre d'Etudes de Musique Orientale, Institut de Musicologie, Paris, 1969; State Diploma, Professor of Traditional Music, 1989. *Career:* Ethnomusicologist, Musée National des Arts et Traditions Populaires, 1968–87, Musée de l'Homme, Paris, 1968–; Professor, Centre d' Etudes de Musique Orientale, 1970–75; Lecturer, Universities of Paris X and Nanterre, 1987; Over 2000 concerts in 45 countries, 1966–; Played at many international music festivals and in films including Le chant des Harmoniques (co-author, principal actor, composer), 1989. *Compositions include:* 300 pop songs; Ve Nguon, electro-acoustic, 1975; Shaman, 1982; Nui Ngu Sông Huong, monochord, 1983; Voyage chamanique, voice, 1986; Solo Thai, zither, 1989; Tambours 89, percussion, tape, 1989; Vinh Ha Long, 1993; Hôn Viêtnam, 1993; For Jew's harp: Nostalgie au Pays Mông, 1997; Vietnam Mon Pays, 1997; Tuva Tuva (with overtone singing), 1997; Ambiance des Hauts Plateaux du Vietnam, 1997. *Recordings:* Numerous records on Vietnamese music including: Landscape of the Highlands, 1997; Jew's Harps of the World, 1997; Vietnam Music of the Mountains, 1997; Over 150 television programmes throughout the world; Over 250 radio programmes, the latest with BBC Radio 3 on World Routes in December 2003 and January 2004. *Publications:* Am Nhac Viet Nam, 1989; Musique du Monde (with Michel Asselineau and Eugène Bérel), 1993, in English, 1994; Tuyen tap 50 cakhuc (Book of 50 Songs) with Vo My Ngoc, 1999. *Contributions:* Numerous to New Grove Dictionary of Music and Musicians, Encyclopedia Universalis, others. *Honours:* Grand Prix of the Academy of the Charles Cros, Paris, 1983; Gold Medal of the Academy of Asia, 1986; Grand Prize of the International Scientific Film, Parnu, Estonia, 1990; Prize of Best Ethnomusicological Film, Parnu, Estonia, 1990; Prize of Best Film on Scientific Research, International Film Festival, Palaiseau, France, 1990; Grand Prize of the 2nd International Scientific Film Festival, Montreal, Canada, 1991; Special Prize of Overtone Singing, Kyzyl, Tuva, 1995; Medal of Cristal, 1996; Grand Prize of the Academy Charles Cros, 1997; Medal of Honour of the City of Limeil Brevannes, France, 1998; Special Prize of Jew's Harp Performer, Je's Harp International Festival, Molln, Austria, 1998; Knight of the Legion of Honour, 2002. *Address:* 12 rue Gutenberg, 94450 Limeil Brevannes, France. *E-mail:* tranquanghai@hotmail.com. *Website:* www.tranquanghai.org; www.tranquanghai.net; www.ethnomus.org; tranquanghai.phapviet.com.

**TRANTER, John;** singer (bass); b. 1946, Chesterfield, Derbyshire, England. *Education:* London Opera Centre, singing with John Dethick in Sheffield. *Career:* debut, Hobson in Peter Grimes, Châtelet Opera in Paris; Opera for All; Kent Opera as the Commendatore in Don Giovanni and Seneca in L'Incoronazione di Poppea; ENO from 1976 as Sarastro, Colline, Monterone in Rigoletto, Verdi's Grand Inquisitor Opera North as Zaccaria in Nabucco, Rossini's Don Basilio, Daland in Der fliegende Holländer, Gremin in Eugene Onegin, Pogner in Die Meistersinger and Trulove in The Rake's Progress; WNO as Wagner's Fasolt and Hagen, and Grigoris in The Greek Passion; other engagements in Nancy, Nîmes, Wellington and Lausanne; other roles include Oroveso (Norma), Ramphis (Aida), Nourabad (Les pêcheurs de Perles), Henry VIII (Anna Bolena) and Tiresias (Oedipus Rex); Fafner at Covent Garden and Pope Leone in Attila at Covent Garden 1990; Banquo in Metz, France, and engagements in Marseille; debut in Pittsburgh as Varlaam (Boris) 1991; season 1992 as Melchtal in Guillaume Tell at Covent Garden and Monterone for Opera North; has sung in concert at the Royal Albert Hall, Royal Festival Hall, Canterbury Cathedral, York Minister and Leeds Town Hall; also sang with the Scottish Opera as Gremin, King in Aida and in Billy Budd, Pearl Fishers; sang Fafner in Siegfried and the King in Aida at Santiago 1996–98; Hobson in Peter Grimes at La Scala 2000. *Current Management:* Music International, 13 Ardilaun Road, Highbury, London, N5 2QR, England.

**TRAUBOTH, Andrea;** German singer (soprano); b. 2 April 1959, Seefeld, Munich, Germany. *Education:* studied in Munich. *Career:* sang with the Dortmund Opera 1983–86, Munich Staatsoper from 1986 and Cologne Opera from 1988; Dresden 1986–87, notably as Musetta and Donna Anna; sang Pamina at Essen 1990, and Elsa at Kiel 1992; further appearances at the Komische Oper, Berlin, La Scala, Milan and in Madrid, as Agathe, Senta, Rusalka and Micaela; concerts in Netherlands, Greece, France and England; season 1999–2000 at Cologne as Agathe and First Lady in Die Zauberflöte. *Address:* c/o Hochschule für Musik Köln, Theaterstraße 2–4, 52062 Aachen, Postfach 1265, 52013 Aachen, Germany.

**TRAVIS, Roy (Elihu);** Composer; b. 24 June 1922, New York, NY, USA; m. 3c. *Education:* Studied with Otto Luening at Columbia University; MA 1951; Schenkerian studies privately with Felix Salzer, 1947–50; Studied with Bernard Wagenaar at Juilliard; MS, 1950; and with Darius Milhaud, Conservatoire National, Paris, on a Fulbright grant, 1951–52. *Career:* Teacher at Columbia University, 1952–53, Mannes College of Music 1952–57 and the University of California at Los Angeles, 1957–91, Professor 1968–91. *Compositions include:* Symphonic Allegro 1951; First Piano Sonata, 1954; Songs from Shakespeare's Tempest, 1954; String Quartet 1958; African Sonata, 1966; Duo Concertante for violin and piano 1967; The Passion of Oedipus, opera, Los Angeles 1968; Collage for orchestra 1968; Piano Concerto 1969; Barma, Septet, 1968; Switched-On Ashanti for flute, piccolo and tape (including African instruments and synthesized sounds), 1973; Songs and Epilogues for bass and orchestra, 1975; The Black Bacchants, opera, 1982; Dover Beach for bass and piano, 1983; Concerto for violin, tabla and orchestra, 1988; Various piano pieces and songs. *Publications include:* Five Preludes for piano; Songs and Epilogues for bass and piano; African Sonata; Duo Concertante; Piano Concerto Collage; Toward a New Concept of Tonality, 1959; Tonal Coherence in the First Movement of Bartók's Fourth String Quartet, 1970; The Recurrent Figure in the Britten/Piper Opera Death in Venice, 1987; Traditional Ashanti Dances as a Compositional Resource: Tachema-chema and Sikyi, 1995. *Address:* 16680 Charmel Lane, Pacific Palisades, CA 90272, USA.

**TREACHER, Graham;** Conductor, Composer and Lecturer; b. 1932, England. *Career:* Conducted the London New Music Singers 1958–63, with the first performances of works by Davies and Bennett, British premieres of works by Penderecki and Schoenberg; Tours of Europe, Henry Wood Promenade Concerts; Conductor at Morley College, London, Holst Choir and Opera Group; Director of the Thaxted Festival, Essex until 1963; Assistant Chorus Master Royal Opera House, Covent Garden 1962–64 for the British premiere of Schoenberg's Moses und Aron; Associate conductor of the BBC Scottish Symphony Orchestra and Chorus, 1964–67; Director of the Purcell School, London, 1968–70; Director of Music at the University of Warwick, 1969–70; Lecturer in Style, Interpretation and Conducting, University of York, 1972–85; Founder of the Amati Ensemble, baroque quartet, playing harpsichord and chamber organ, 1978–85; Director and conductor, Northern Music Theatre 1980–84, with first performances of works by Vic Hoyland, Philip Grange and British premieres of Kagel and Henze; Artistic Director of the John Loosemore Early Music Centre, Devon, 1988–92. *Compositions include:* Music for children, vocal and instrumental music including music for Strings, Percussion and Celestine, for the 1990 Orkney Summer Festival; Choral music with settings of Chaucer and Christmas music. *Publications include:* Editions of Gesualdo (Cantiones Sacrae 1603) and Pallavicino's three act Carnival opera Messalina, for performance at the Vadstena International Opera Festival, Sweden; Dixit Dominus by Pallavicino. *Address:* Warren Cottages, Hippenscombe, Nr Marlborough, Wilts SNB 3NN, England.

**TREE, Michael;** Concert Violinist and Violist; b. 19 Feb. 1934, Newark, New Jersey, USA; m. Johanna Kreck, 1 s., 1 d. *Education:* Diploma, Curtis Institute of Music, 1955. *Career:* Debut: Carnegie Hall, 1954; Soloist with major American orchestras; Solo and chamber music appearances at major festivals, including Israel, Athens, Spoleto, Casals, Marlboro; Founding member, Guarneri String Quartet; Faculty member, Curtis Institute of Music University of Maryland, Rutgers University, Manhattan School of Music; Repeated appearances on the Today Show and first Telecast of Chamber Music Live from Lincoln Center; mem, President of the First American String Quartet Congress at University of Maryland and Smithsonian Institute, 1989. *Recordings:* Over 60 chamber music works on Columbia, Nonesuch, Philips and RCA labels; Complete Beethoven quartets, 10 works for piano and strings, with Artur Rubinstein; Collaborations with Emanuel Ax, Jaimie Laredo, Leonard Rose, Alexander Schneider, Rudolf Serkin and Pinchas Zuckerman. *Honours:* New York City Seal of Recognition, 1982; Honorary degress, Doctor of Fine Arts, University of South Florida, State University of New York at Binghampton. *Current Management:* Herbert Barrett Management.

**TREFAS, György;** Hungarian singer (bass); b. 6 Oct. 1931, Budapest; m. Szabó Katalin 1972. *Education:* studied with Werner Alajos, Makai Mihály, Lendvay Andor, Hetényi Kálmán. *Career:* debut in Csokonai Theatre, Debrecen, Hungary; bass characters of operas: Verdi's King Philip, Don Carlos, Attila and De Silva in Ernani; Rocco, Fidelio; Duke Bluebeard, Bartók: Duke Bluebeard's Castle – radio recording, Dresden, Antwerp, Zaccaria, Nabucco, Sofia; Magdeburg, Mephisto, Faust; Ibert; Angelica; King Nero television film; Sarastro, Zauberflöte; Osmin, Entführung; Family portrait film, Hungarian television. *Address:* Bethlen-U 42-44, 4026 Debrecen, Hungary.

**TREKEL, Roman;** Singer (Baritone); b. 1962, Pirna, Saxony, Germany. *Education:* Studied at the Berlin Musikhochschule 1980–86 and with Siegfried Lorenz and Hans Hotter. *Career:* Sang with the Berlin Staatsoper from 1986, notably in Erwin and Elmire by Reichardt 1987 and Ullmann's Emperor of Atlantis 1989; Many roles in operas by Mozart in Berlin and elsewhere; Season 1992 as Ulysses in Erendira by Violet Dinescu and as Tarquinius in The Rape of Lucretia with the Berlin Kammeroper; Concerts and Lieder recitals in Germany, Belgium, Austria, Czechoslovakia, Sweden and England; Berlin Staatsoper 1999–2001, as Leonhard in Die Brautwahl by Busoni, Ottokar in Der Freischütz and Don Alfonso. *Recordings include:* Title role in Telemann's Orpheus. *Honours:* Prizewinner, Dvořák Competition, 1985; Karlovy Vary, 1987; DDR Competition Germany; 1989 International Lieder Competition Walter Gruner in London. *Address:* Stuttgart Staatsoper, Oberer Schlossgarten 6, 7000 Stuttgart 1, Germany.

**TREKEL-BURCKHARDT, Ute;** Singer (Mezzo-soprano); b. 3 Nov. 1939, Pirna, Saxony, Germany. *Education:* Studied in Berlin with Rita Meinl-Weise. *Career:* Debut: Komische Oper Berlin 1963, as the Page in Salome; Sang at the Komische Oper until 1978, then joined the Staatsoper Berlin; Guest appearances in Vienna, Cologne, Brussels, Madrid and Dresden; Cologne 1984, as Renata in The Fiery Angel by Prokofiev; Nancy 1985, as The Woman in Schoenberg's Erwartung; Created Queen Marguerite in Sutermeister's Le roi Bérenger at Munich in 1985; Other roles include the Countess Geschwitz in Lulu, Mozart's Sextus and Cherubino, Verdi's Eboli, Amneris and Ulrica, Strauss's Nurse (Die Frau ohne Schatten), Composer and Octavian, and Wagner's Fricka, Kundry and Ortrud (Wiesbaden 1988); Sang Venus in Tannhäuser as guest with the Berlin Staatsoper at Las Palmas in 1986; Sang Clytemnestra in Elektra at the Komische Oper Berlin, 2000; Many concert appearances. *Address:* Deutsche Staatsoper, Unter den Linden 7, 1086 Berlin, Germany.

**TRELEAVEN, John;** British singer (tenor); b. 10 June 1950, Cornwall, England. *Education:* studied in London and Naples. *Career:* with Welsh Nat. Opera has sung Tamino, Alfredo (La Traviata), Pinkerton, Nadir (Les Pêcheurs de Perles) and Mark in The Midsummer Marriage); at ENO his roles have included Don José, Cavaradossi, Faust (Berlioz), Erik in Der fliegende Holländer, the Prince in Rusalka, Hoffmann, Don Carlos and Wozzeck in a new production of Berg's Opera 1990; Royal Opera, Covent Garden, debut as Tamino, followed by Froh in Das Rheingold and Peter Grimes 1989; appearances with Scottish Opera have included Florestan, Jenik (The Bartered Bride), Werther and Radames; Opera North as Dick Johnson (La Fanciulla del West), Cavaradossi, Radames and Peter Grimes; Further engagements in The Damnation of Faust at the Adelaide Festival, Pylades (Iphigénie en Tauride) at the Paris Opéra, Verdi's Attila at the Concertgebouw, Amsterdam and Prince Golitisin (Khovanshchina) at the San Francisco Opera 1990; concert performances include a 1981 debut at Royal Festival Hall in Puccini's Messa di Gloria and Rossini's Stabat Mater; Verdi Requiem under Nello Santi at the 1984 Festival de la Mediterranée; Dream of Gerontius with Scottish Nat. Orchestra 1989; concert performance of Bernstein's Candide at Barbican, London 1989; Season 2000 sang Lohengrin at Barcelona 2000, at Karlsruhe, as Apollo in Daphne, Siegmund and Tristan, Siegfried at Mannheim and Chemnitz; sang Weill's Jim Mahonney at Genoa and Tristan in Amsterdam 2001; Tristan for BBC Symphony Orchestra at Barbican, London 2002–03; Season 2003–04 sang Lohengrin at Hamburgische Staatsoper, Siegfried at Lyric Opera, Chicago, Die Walküre with Bamberger Symphoniker, Götterdämmerung in Tokyo, Siegfried and Götterdämmerung at Gran Teatre del Liceu, Barcelona, Tristan at Opéra de Rouen; Season 2004–05 sang Tristan (konzertant) at Lucerne Festival, Siegfried and Götterdämmerung in Helsinki, Liederabend in Wiesbaden, Gurrelieder in Melbourne, Siegfried at Staatsoper, Vienna, Tristan in Mannheim Gala, Die Walküre for Semperoper Dresden, Meistersinger in Hamburg, Das Lied von der Erde in New Orleans, Gurrelieder in Los Angeles, Siegfried and Götterdämmerung for Lyric Opera, Chicago, Meistersinger and Lohengrin in Hamburg, Tristan in Frankfurt and Brisbane at Queensland Music Festival. *Recordings include:* solo parts: Le Prophète, Meyerbeer, conducted by Henry Lewis; L'Assedio di Calais, Donizetti; Il Trovatore, Colin Davis, with José Carreras; Il Tabarro, Maazel with Placido Domingo; Rachmaninov Vespers, Candide, Leonard Bernstein; Videos of Rusalka for English National Opera; Richard Dauntless in Ruddigore; Candide; John Treleaven as Siegfried in Siegfried and Götterdämmerung at the Gran Teatre del Liceu Barcelona on DVD 2006. *Current Management:* Theateragentur Dr Germinal Hilbert, Herr Rudolf Meindl, Maximilianstrasse 22, 80539 Munich, Germany. *Telephone:* (89) 290-747-0. *Fax:* (89) 290-747-90. *E-mail:* meindl@hilbert.de. *E-mail:* mennicken.beate@t-online.de. *Website:* www.johntreleaven.com.

**TRELIŃSKI, Mariusz;** Polish opera, film and theatre director; *Artistic Director, Polish National Opera. Education:* State School of Film, Television and Theatre, Łódź. *Career:* began career working for Television Theatre; Artistic Dir Karol Irzykowski Studio 1990–92; dir of plays, including Lautréamont-Dreams (Studio Theatre), Macbeth (Powszechny Theatre); opera directing debut with Madama Butterfly, Polish Nat. Opera, Warsaw 1999 (with subsequent productions in Washington 2001, Mariinsky Theatre, St Petersburg 2005); other operas directed in Warsaw include Szymanowski's King Roger (Karol Szymanowski Award 2001) 2000, Otello 2001, Eugene Onegin 2002, Don Giovanni 2002 (also for Los Angeles Opera 2003), The Queen of Spades 2004 (also for Staatsoper, Berlin 2003); has also directed Giordano's Andrea Chénier for Washington Nat. Opera 2004, Teatr Wileki, Poznań 2004, Polish Nat. Opera 2005; Artistic Dir Opera Narodowa (Polish Nat. Opera), Teatr Wielki, Warsaw 2005–. *Films as director:* Zad Wielkiego Wieloryba (Stern of the Giant Whale, TV) 1987, Pożegnanie jesieni (The Farewell to Autumn) 1990, Łagodna (The Gentle One) 1995, Egoiści (Egoist) 2000. *Honours:* Andrzej Munk Award 1990, Minister of Culture Award for Best Debut 1990. *Address:* Opera Narodowa, Teatr Wielki, Plac Teatralny 1, PO Box 59, Warsaw 00-950, Poland (office). *Telephone:* (22) 692-05-01 (office). *Fax:* (22) 826-04-22 (office). *E-mail:* office@teatrwielki.pl (office). *Website:* www.teatrwielki.pl (office).

**TRETYAKOV, Viktor Viktorovich;** Russian violinist; b. 17 Oct. 1946, Krasnoyarsk; m. Natalia Likhopoi; one d. *Education:* Moscow Conservatory (pupil of Yury Yankelevich). *Career:* First Prizes, All-Union Competition of Violinists 1965, Int. Tchaikovsky Competition 1966; concert career since mid-1960s, soloist of Moscow Philharmonic 1969; tours Europe, America, Japan;

participant in numerous European music festivals; Artistic Dir and Conductor Moscow (now Russian) Chamber Orchestra 1983–90; Prof., Head of Chair of Violin, Moscow Conservatory 1983–90; Prof., Hochschule für Musik, Cologne 1996–. *Honours:* State Prize of Russia 1981, USSR People's Artist 1987, "Triumph" Prize (Russia) 2003. *Address:* Berliner Konzertagentur Monika Ott, Dramburger, Str. 46, 12683 Berlin (office); Burgblick 9b, 53177 Bonn, Germany (home). *Fax:* (228) 9329641 (home).

**TREW, Graham Donald,** MVO, MMus, AGSM, PGCE, FRSA; British singer (baritone), teacher and adjudicator; b. 18 July 1948, Epping, England. *Education:* Guildhall School of Music and Drama, Univ. of London, Bretton Hall. *Career:* performed, English Opera Group, Nottingham Music Theatre, Cockpit Opera Workshop (20 productions and title role in video of Marriage of Figaro); recitals, Wigmore Hall, Purcell Room, QEH, Barbican, Royal Nat. Theatre; oratorio and concerts throughout England, Europe, USA, Caribbean and South Africa; English song recitals for BBC Radio 3, Friday Night is Music Night, Songs from the Shows, Melodies for You, for BBC Radio 2; Gentleman of Her Majesty's Chapel Royal, St James's Palace 1975–2002; Prof., RAM 2002–; Assoc. Prof., Trinity Coll. of Music; teaches privately and at Tonbridge School; Guest Lecturer, Royal Acad. of Music lieder class and Birmingham Conservatoire; Adjudicator throughout England, including British Fed. of Music Festivals; mem. Equity, Royal Soc. of Musicians. *Recordings:* English song recordings with Roger Vignoles, recordings with John Alley, Marcello-Cantatas, Rodolphe, Florence, The Holy Boy with Simon Weale, James Bowman and Richard Lewis. *Honours:* Gold Medal Guildhall School of Music and Drama 1973, Gramophone Magazine Award for Vocal Record of the Year (for A Shropshire Lad) 1980, Queen's Silver Jubilee Medal 1977, Queen's Golden Jubilee Medal 2002. *Address:* Melin-y-Grogue, Llanfair Waterdine, Knighton, Powys, LD7 1TU, Wales (home). *Telephone:* (1547) 510327 (home). *Fax:* (1547) 510327 (home). *E-mail:* graham.trew@virgin.net (home).

**TRIFONOVA, Olga;** Singer (soprano); b. 1969, St Petersburg, Russia. *Education:* St Petersburg Conservatoire. *Career:* Appearances at the Mariinksy Theatre, St Petersburg, from 1994 as Mozart's Queen of Night and Barbarina, Rosina, Lucia di Lammermoor, Xenia in Boris Godunov, Frasquita in Carmen and Louisa in Prokofiev's Betrothal in a Monastery; Salzburg debut 1998, as Flowermaiden in Parsifal, New York Met 1999, in The Queen of Spades; Sang the title role in The Snow Maiden by Rimsky-Korsakov (Concert) with the Kirov Opera at Covent Garden, 2000; Other roles include Stravinsky's Nightingale, Amina in La Sonnambula, Gilda, Glinka's Lyudmila and Chloë/Prilepa in The Queen of Spades. *Recordings include:* Le Rossignol (London Philharmonic under Robert Craft). *Address:* c/o Kirov Opera, Mariinsky Theatre, 1 Theatre Square, St Petersburg, Russia.

**TRIMARCHI, Domenico;** Italian singer (bass-baritone); b. 21 Dec. 1940, Naples, Italy. *Education:* studied at Naples Conservatory, Accad. di Belle Arti and with Gino Campese. *Career:* debut at Teatro La Fenice Venice as Belcore in L'Elisir d'amore 1964; has sung widely in Italy (Verona Arena 1975–78), Edinburgh, London, Stuttgart, Frankfurt, Chicago and Dubrovnik; Teatro Regio Parma as Falstff in the operas by Salieri and Verdi 1987; repertoire also includes Leporello, Alfonso, Papageno, Arbace and Count Almaviva (Mozart), Varlaam (Mussorgsky), Germont, Paolo and Fra Melitone (Verdi), Dulcamara, Belcore, Don Pasquale, Malatesta, Enrico and Alfonso (Donizetti), Dallapic-cola's Job, Marcello, Sharpless and Gianni Schicchi (Puccini); sang Donizetti's Mamma Agata at Luga di Romagna 1988, Marchese in Linda di Chamounix at Trieste 1989, Leporello at Parma; sang in Wolf-Ferrari's Quattro Rusteghi at Geneva 1992. *Recordings:* Haydn's La Vera Costanza, L'Incontro Improvviso and Il Mondo della Luna, Il Barbiere di Siviglia, Vivaldi's Tito Manlio, Tosca (Philips), Elisa e Claudio by Mercadante, La Straniera by Bellini, La Cenerentola (CBS), Pimpinone by Albinoni. *Honours:* Winner, Venice Int. Competition 1970. *Address:* Studiomusica s.r.l., Via Farini 53, 41100 Modena, Italy. *Telephone:* (059) 245486. *E-mail:* gabriele.monici@studiomusica.net. *Website:* www.studiomusica.net.

**TRITT, William;** Concert Pianist; b. 1950, Canada. *Education:* Studied at the Ecole Vincent d'Indy in Montreal with Lucille Brassard and Yvonne Hubert; Further study with Yvonne Lefébure in Paris and György Sebok at Indiana University. *Career:* First solo appearance aged 15 with the Little Orchestra Society at Avery Fisher Hall, New York; Further engagements with the Montreal Symphony and the CBS Orchestra in Quebec; Boston Pops Orchestra and the Chicago Symphony at the Ravinia Festival; Cincinnati and Houston Symphony Orchestras; Nationwide appearances in Canada, including Toronto, Edmonton, Winnipeg and Halifax; London recital debut 1981, Wigmore Hall. *Recordings include:* Bach D minor Concerto; Beethoven C major Concerto and Schumann A minor; Liszt Totentanz. *Honours:* Winner of all major competitions in Canada, 1966–71.

**TROITSKAYA, Natalia Leonidovna;** Russian singer (soprano); b. 18 May 1956, Moscow. *Education:* Gnesins Music Inst. *Career:* left USSR 1980, winner of int. competitions in Toulouse, Vercelli, Barcelona; debut as opera singer in Theatro Liseo, Barcelona with José Carreras 1981; performs as guest singer La Scala, Covent Garden, Deutsche Oper Berlin, Wiener Staatsoper, Colón Buenos Aires, Rome Opera; participated in numerous music festivals including Arena di Verona; debut in Moscow as Adrienna Lecouvrer with La Scala 1989; f. fund for promotion of young singers, Moscow 1994–97. *Opera roles include:* Lisa (Queen of Spades), Violetta (La Traviata), Aida, Maddalena (Andre Chenier), Leonora (Il Trovatore), Elisabeth (Don Carlos), Desdemona

(Othello), Amelia (Un Ballo in Maschera), Mavra (Mavra), Yaroslavna (Prince Igor). *Honours:* Gold Rose Prize of Critics (Germany).

**TROJAHN, Manfred;** Composer; b. 22 Oct. 1949, Cremlingen, Brunswick, Germany. *Education:* Studied at the Niedersächsische Musikschule, Brunswick, 1966–70; Composition at the Hamburg Hochschule, 1970–77. *Career:* Freelance composer including Residency at the Villa Massimo in Rome, 1979–80; Teacher of composition at the Robert Schumann Hochschule, Düsseldorf, 1991. *Compositions include:* Opera Enrico (1991); 4 symphonies, 1973, 1978, 1985, 1992; 3 string quartets, 1976, 1980, 1983; Fünfsee-Bilder für messosopran und orchester, 1979–83; Flute Concerto, 1983; Requiem, 1985;... une campagne noire de soleil, 7 ballet scenes for chamber ensemble, 1983–93; Sonatas for violin and cello, 1983; Variations for orchestra, 1987; Cinq Epigraphes for orchestra, 1987; Fragmente für Antigone, 6 pieces for string quartet, 1988; Transir for orchestra, 1988; Aubade for 2 sopranos, 1990; Ave Maria for chorus, 1991; Grodek for baritone and 8 instruments, 1991; Quattro Pezzi for orchestra, 1992; Divertissement for oboe and chamber orchestra, 1993; Cornisches Nachtlied for orchestra, 1994; Was ihr Wollt (As You Like It), opera, 1997–98. Liebeslieder, for soprano and orchestra, 1997; Palinsesto, for soprano and string quartet, 1997; Violin Concerto, 1999; La Clemenza di Tito by Mozart with newly composed recitatives by Trojahn, premièred Netherlands Opera, Amsterdam, 2002; Limonen aus Sizilien: Drei italienische Geschichten (opera), premièred Cologne City Theatre, 2003; Occhi mie for tenor, 2002; Three Songs by John Keats for Mezzo-soprano and six instruments, 2002; Rhapsodie for Clarinet and Orchestra, 2001/02. *Address:* 44 rue Dauphine, 75006 Paris, France.

**TROPP, Vladimir;** Pianist; b. 9 Nov. 1939, Moscow, Russia; m. Tatiana Zelikman 1961; one s. *Education:* Gnessin Children's Music School; Gnessin Specialized Music School; Gnessin Institute. *Career:* concert tours in Russia, Netherlands, USA, Italy, Japan, Finland, Germany, Ireland, Costa Rica, Republic of Korea, Czechoslovakia, Cuba; masterclasses and concerts in American univs, conservatories of Holland and Ireland, London Royal Acad. of Music, Italy, France, Japan; numerous chamber music festivals; performances on radio and television in Russia, Netherlands, Germany, USA, Finland, Costa Rica; performances with major orchestras; Prof. of Piano, Dept of Russian, Gnessin Acad. of Music, Chief of Piano Dept. *Recordings include:* works by Chopin, Brahms, Tchaikovsky, Rachmaninov, Scriabin, Medtner. *Contributions:* articles in magazines and newspapers in Russia. *Address:* Dmitry Ulianov Str 4, Block 2, Apt 251, Moscow 117333, Russia.

**TROST, Rainer;** Singer (Tenor); b. 1966, Stuttgart, Germany. *Education:* Munich Hochschule, with Adalbert Kraus. *Career:* Member of the Hanover Staatstheater, 1991–95; Sang Ferrando in Così fan tutte at the Hamburg Opera 1992 and toured in Mozart's opera with the Monteverdi Choir and Orchestra; Sang Ferrando at Munich 1993, Don Ottavio at Dresden and Vienna, Tamino in Geneva and Berlin (1994) and Eginhard in Schubert's Fierrabras at Florence (1995); Further engagements at the Cologne Opera, Opéra National de Paris, as Belmonte in Vienna and Hamburg and as Ferrando at Covent Garden, Glyndebourne, 1994 (debut role), returning 1997; Season 1998–99 sang Orsino in the premiere of Manfred Trojahn's Was ihr Wollt, Munich, Entführung, Don Giovanni and Zauberflöte in Vienna, Don Giovanni in Hamburg and concerts of Tristan und Isolde with the Berlin Philharmonic under Abbado; Season 1999–2000 included Zauberflöte and Fidelio in Munich, Così fan tutte at Salzburg Festival with Abbado, Katya Kabanova for Netherlands Opera and concerts for Gesellschaft der Musikfreunde in Vienna; Season 2001 as Fenton and Ferrando in Munich, Belmonte at Hannover and Des Grieux in Henze's Boulevard Solitude at Covent Garden; Further engagements include Don Giovanni, Zauberflöte, Così fan tutte, Fidelio and Falstaff in Munich, Zauberflöte at Vienna State Opera and Così fan tutte in Salzburg, with concert engagements of Fidelio in Munich and Katja Kabanowa in Brussels and Barcelona; Concerts include Mozart's Mass in C Minor, with the Monteverdi Choir and Orchestra; Die Schöpfung, with the Hamburg Philharmonic Orchestra and the Cologne Radio Symphony Orchestra; Bach's Christmas Oratorio (NDR SO) and the St Matthew Passion, with the Concertgebouw Orchestra. *Recordings include:* CD and video of Così fan tutte (DGG). *Address:* c/o Haydn Rawstron Ltd, 36 Station Road, London SE20 7BQ, England.

**TROTTER, Thomas Andrew,** MA, ARCM; British organist; b. 4 April 1957, Birkenhead, England. *Education:* Royal Coll. of Music, London, Univ. of Cambridge, Conservatoire Rueil-Malmaison, France. *Career:* debut, Royal Festival Hall 1980; regular broadcasts on BBC Radio 2 and 3; performances at festivals throughout Europe; Proms debut 1986; concert tours of USA, Australia and Japan; organist for St Margaret's Church, Westminster, London 1982–; City of Birmingham 1983–; Messiaen recitals, Edinburgh Festival 1994. *Recordings:* The Grand Organ of Birmingham Town Hall, Liszt Organ Works and Reubke Sonata, Jehan Alain Organ Works, Charles-Marie Widor Organ Works, Antonio Soler Concertos for Two Organs, Olivier Messiaen Organ Works, The Ride of the Valkyries: Organ Transcriptions, Liszt Organ Works vol. 2, Mozart Organ Works. *Honours:* Organ Scholar St George's Chapel, Windsor and King's Coll., Cambridge (John Stewart of Rannock Scholarship in Sacred Music 1979; RCM Walford Davies Prize 1976, first prize and Bach Prize St Alban's Int. Organ Competition 1979, Prix de Virtuosité 1981. *Address:* c/o Town Hall, Birmingham, B3 3DQ, England.

**TROUP, Malcolm;** Concert Pianist, Professor Emeritus of Music, City University and Former Director of Music, Guildhall School of Music and

Drama; b. 22 Feb. 1930, Toronto, Canada; m. (1) Carmen Lamarca Subercaseaux, 1 d., (2) Wendela Lumley. *Education:* DPhilMus. University of York; Associate, Royal Conservatory of Music (ARCT), Toronto; FGSM; LLD, Memorial University of Newfoundland; Hon D.Mus, City University. *Career:* Debut: With CBC Symphony Orchestra, Toronto, aged 17; Recitals and Concertos with leading orchestras in Europe, North and South America; Premieres, important modern works; Frequent broadcaster with the BBC; External Examiner, Universities of York, Keele, London; Member of International Juries: Chopin Competition of Australia, CBC National Talent Competition, Young Musician of the Year; 1st Dvořák International Piano Competition, 1997; Rome 1997 and 2002 International Piano Competition and 1st Claudio Arrau International Piano Competition, Chillan, Chile, 2003; Vice President, World Piano Competition, London; President of Jury, 1st EPTA International Piano Competition, Zagreb, 1999, Reykjavík, 2000; Founder and Vice-President Asociación Latinoamericana de Profesores de Piano (ALAPP/Chile); Director, London International String Quartet Competition; President, Oxford International Piano Festival, 1999–; Governor of Music Therapy Charity; Chairman of European Piano Teachers Association; Chairman of Beethoven Piano Society of Europe; Trustee of Jewish Music Trust; Freeman of the City of London, 1971; Liveryman of Worshipful Company of Musicians, 1973; Court Member, 1991, Master 1999. *Recordings:* Major record labels. *Publications:* Editor, The Piano Journal. *Contributions:* The Messiaen Companion, London: Faber and Faber, 1995; The Science and Psychology of Music Performance, New York: OUP, 2002. *Honours:* Medal Winner in the Harriet Cohen International Awards, 1965; Liszt Medal of the American Liszt Society, 1998. *Address:* 86 Lexham Gardens, London W8 5JB, England.

**TROWELL, Brian (Lewis);** Professor of Music; b. 21 Feb. 1931, Wokingham, Berkshire, England; m. Rhianon James, 1958, 2 d. *Education:* Christ's Hospital; MA 1959, PhD 1960, Gonville and Caius College, Cambridge. *Career:* Assistant Lecturer later Lecturer in Music, Birmingham University, 1957–62; Freelance Scholar, Conductor, Opera Producer, Lecturer and Editor, 1962–67; Head of BBC Radio Opera, 1967–70; Regents' Professor, University of California, Berkeley, USA, 1970; Reader in Music, 1970 then Professor of Music, 1973, KCL; Visiting Gresham Professor of Music, City University, 1971–74; King Edward Professor of Music, University of London, King's College, 1974–88; Chairman of Editorial Committee, Musica Britannica, 1983–93; President, Royal Musical Association; Chairman, Handel Institute Trust and Council, 1987–98; Heather Professor of Music, University of Oxford, 1988–96; Professor Emeritus, 1996–. *Publications:* The Early Renaissance, Pelican History of Music, vol. II, 1963; Four Motets by John Plummer, 1968; Joint Editor, John Dunstable: Complete Works, Editor, M F Bukofzer, 2nd revised edition, 1970; Editor, Invitation to Medieval Music, vol. 3, 1976, vol. 4, 1978; Opera translations. *Contributions:* Dictionaries of music and articles in books and learned journals including: Libretto II, The New Grove Dictionary of Opera, London, 1992, Acis, Galatea and Polyphemus: a serenata a tre voci?, Music and Theatre: Essays in Honour of Winton Dean, 1987, Elgar's Use of Literature in Edward Elgar Music and Literature, 1993. *Address:* Faculty of Music, Oxford University, St Aldate's, Oxford OX1 1 DB, England.

**TRPČESKI, Simon;** pianist; b. 1979, Skopje, Macedonia. *Education:* University of St Cyril and St Methodius, Skopje and with Boris Romanov. *Career:* concert appearances in Romania, Bulgaria, Italy, France, Portugal and Republic of Korea; played Prokofiev's Third Concerto at the World Piano Competition, London 2000; played at Jacobins Festival, Toulouse 2000; further concerts in Russia, Yugoslavia, Czech Republic, Turkey, Canada, Switzerland, Norway, UK, Australia and USA; repertoire centres on Russian music and Chopin; season 2001–02 at Wigmore Hall, London debut, Saint-Saëns Concerto No. 2 with the Bournemouth Symphony Orchestra and concerts in Australia and Malaysia; Royal Festival debut with the Philharmonia Orchestra; recent engagements include collaborations with Sydney and Melbourne Symphony Orchestras, the Tonhalle Orchestra, the Bergen Philharmonic, Seattle Symphony, Royal Liverpool Philharmonic, Scottish Chamber Orchestra, Stockholm Philharmonic Orchestra and the Hallé Orchestra. *Honours:* winner Yamaha Music Foundation of Europe, Skopje 1998, second prize World Piano Competition, London 2000, Royal Philharmonic Soc. Young Artist Award 2003, Gramophone Award 2003. *Current Management:* IMG Artists, Lovell House, 616 Chiswick High Road, London, W4 5RX, England. *E-mail:* Cdyer@imgworld.com.

**TRUAX, Barry;** Composer; b. 10 May 1947, Chatham, Ontario, Canada. *Education:* Studied physics and mathematics at Queen's University Kingston, BS, 1969; MM, Electronic music at the University of British Columbia, 1971, and at the Institute of Sonology, University of Utrecht, 1971–73. *Career:* Collaboration with Murray Schafer at World Soundscape Project in Vancouver; Director of Sonic Research Studio, and Professor in Communication Department, Simon Fraser University, 1976–, and School for the Contemporary Arts. *Compositions include:* Four Sonic Landscapes, 1971–79; Gilgamesh, for voices, chorus, ensemble and tape, 1974; Nautilus for percussion and tape, 1976; East Wind for amplified recorder and tape, 1981; Nightwatch for marimba and tape, 1982; Etude for cello and tape, 1983; Divan, and Wings of Nike, for computer images and tape, 1985–87; Tongues of Angels for English horn and oboe d'amore, 1988; Dominion for chamber ensemble and tape, 1991; Song of Songs, for oboe d'amore, tape and computer images, 1993; Bamboo, Silk and Stone, for Asian instruments and tape, 1994; Inside, for bass oboe and tape, 1995; Wings of Fire, for cello and tape, 1996; Androgyne, Mon Amour, for double bass and tape, 1997; Powers of Two, for singers, dancers, video and tape, 1995–99; Twin Souls, Islands. *Recordings:* Digital Soundscapes, Pacific Rim, Song of Songs, Inside. *Publications include:* Handbook for Acoustic Ecology (1978) CD-ROM, 1999, and Acoustic Communication (1984), 2001. *Honours:* Magisterium, International Electro-acoustic Competition, Bourges, 1991. *Address:* c/o School of Communication, Simon Fraser University, Burnaby, BC V5A 1S6, Canada. *Website:* www.sfu.ca\~truax.

**TRUBASHNIK, Simon;** Oboist; b. 16 Sept. 1939, Odessa; Divorced, 1 d. *Education:* Central Music School for Gifted Children, Moscow Conservatoire; Diploma, 1953, Graduate Diploma, Moscow Conservatoire, 1958. *Career:* Debut: Solo, Youth Festival, Berlin, 1955; Principal Oboe, Moscow Philharmonic Orchestra, 1955–72; Principal Oboe, Moscow Chamber Orchestra, 1958–72; Associate Principal Oboe, Israel Philharmonic Orchestra, 1972–75; Principal Oboe, Belgium National Opera, 1976–85; Principal Oboe, Halifax Symphony, Canada, 1986–87; Professor, Royal Conservatory of Music, Toronto, 1987–; Solo with Moscow Philharmonic and Moscow Chamber Orchestras (World Tours); Radio Luxembourg Orchestra of Belgium; Mozart Chamber Orchestra, Brussels; Opera Orchestra of Ghent; Toronto Chamber Players; Kingston Philharmonic; McGill Chamber Orchestra; mem, American Federation of Musicians. *Recordings:* Bach Concerto (with David Oistrakh) and Concertos by Mozart and Strauss with Moscow Philharmonic Orchestra; Italian Baroque Concerts with Luxembourg Radio Orchestra; 100 Orchestral Records with Moscow Philharmonic Orchestra. *Honours:* Gold Medal, Moscow Conservatoire, 1958. *Current Management:* Sol Hurock Management. *Address:* 100 Upper Madison #610, North York, Ontario M2N 6M4, Canada.

**TRUEFITT, Alison;** Singer (Soprano); b. 1958, England. *Education:* Studied at London University and the Royal Academy of Music. *Career:* Debut: Sang at the Purcell Room, London, 1979; Has appeared in recital with the Songmakers' Almanac and with the BBC in songs by Britten, Bartók, Fauré, Holst, Milhaud, Poulenc, and Tippett; With orchestra or ensemble in works by Gerald Finzi, Stephen Dodgson and Frank Martin; Promenade Concerts debut in La Forza del Destino; Sang Gluck's Iphigenia with Opera Factory, 1985, and created Kathe in John Metcalf's The Crossing (tours of the USA, the United Kingdom and Canada); Sang in the British stage premiere of Schubert's Fierrabras, Oxford University 1986; English National Opera 1988, as Manassah in Salome; Sang Donizetti's Rita, Madame Herz in Mozart's Impresario and Musetta with London Chamber Opera 1988; Appearances with London Chamber Opera 1988; Appearances as the Queen of Night with Birmingham Touring Opera, 1988–89; Other repertory includes Leila in Les pêcheurs de Perles, the Governess in The Turn of the Screw, Britten's Phaedra and Major Stone in Weill's Happy End; Translated Orfeo for Opera North, 1990, and has provided several sets of surtitles for Covent Garden. *Address:* c/o Royal Opera House, Covent Garden, London WC2E 9 DD, England.

**TRUSSEL, Jacques;** Singer (Tenor); b. 7 April 1943, San Francisco, California, USA. *Education:* Studied at Ball State University, Muncie, Indiana and in New York. *Career:* Sang at first in concert then made opera debut at the Oberlin Festival 1970, as Pinkerton; Has appeared in Boston, Dallas, Houston, Santa Fe, New Orleans, Chicago (from 1976), Pittsburgh (1979), Washington (1981) and San Francisco (Loge in Das Rheingold 1990); Sang Don José at Cincinnati 1988 and has appeared as Rodolfo, Cavaradossi, Berg's Alwa, Araquil in La Navarraise by Massenet, Števa in Jenůfa, Max (Der Freischütz) and Nero in L'Incoronazione di Poppea (Geneva 1989); Sang at Houston in the title role of Hugh the Drover by Vaughan Williams (US premiere 1973) and in the 1974 word premiere of The Seagull by Pasatieri; European debut Spoleto Festival 1976, as Hermann in The Queen of Spades; Sang Alwa at Florence 1985 and at Chicago 1987; Covent Garden and Nancy 1989, as Peter Grimes and as Sergei in the French premiere of Lady Macbeth of Mtsensk by Shostakovich; Appeared with Greater Miami Opera 1990, as Pollione in Norma; London appearances 1991, as Don José; Season 1991/92 as Alexey in the US premiere of The Gambler, at Chicago; Sergei at the Opéra Bastille, Monteverdi's Nero in Florence, Don José in Birmingham and Roderick in The Fall of the House of Usher by Philip Glass at the Maggio Musicale; Sang Golitsin in Khovanschina at Brussels, 1996; Herod in Salome at Vancouver, 1998 and at Cincinnati, 2000. *Address:* c/o Vancouver Opera, Suite 500, 845 Cambie Street, Vancouver British Columbia V6B 4Z9, Canada.

**TRYON, Valerie Ann,** FRAM; Canadian (b. British) pianist and academic; b. 5 Sept. 1934, Portsmouth; d. of Kenneth Montague Tryon and Winifred Tryon (née Lunan). *Education:* Royal Acad. of Music, London. *Career:* performances in the UK include Cheltenham Festival, Royal Festival Hall, Royal Albert Hall, Royal Opera House, Covent Garden, Aldeburgh Festival; has performed throughout Canada and the USA, including Library of Congress, Washington, DC; currently pianist in Rembrandt Trio; Artist-in-Residence McMaster Univ., Hamilton, Ont. 1978–86, Assoc. Prof. 1986–. *Recordings include:* Liszt's Sonata for Violin and Piano, Rachmaninov and Hoddinott, Valerie Tryon plays Richard Baker's most requested pieces, These You Have Loved, Valerie Tryon Piano, The Joy of Piano, Debussy Songs (Juno Winner with Claudette Leblanc) 1994. *Honours:* Hon. DLitt (McMaster Univ.); Dove Prize 1955, Harriet Cohen Int. Music Award 1967, Franz Liszt Medal of Honour, Hungarian Ministry of Culture 1986. *Address:* McMaster University, Department of Music, Hamilton, Ontario, L8S 4L8 (office); 609 Tuscarora Drive, Ancaster, Ontario, L9G 3N9, Canada (home). *Telephone:* (416) 525-9140 (office); (416) 648-5883 (home). *Fax:* (416) 527-0100 (office).

**TRYTHALL, (Harry) Gilbert,** BA, MMus, DMA; composer and teacher; b. 28 Oct. 1930, Knoxville, TN, USA; m.; two d. *Education:* University of Tennessee, Northwestern University, Cornell University; studied with David Van Vactor, Wallingford Riegger, Robert Palmer and Donald Grout. *Career:* Assistant Professor of Music, Knox College, Galesburg, Illinois, 1960–64; Professor of Music Theory and Composition, 1964–75; Chairman, School of Music, George Peabody College for Teachers, Nashville, Tennessee, 1975–; Professor of Music, 1975–, Dean, Creative Arts Center, 1975–81, Virginia University, Morgantown, West Virginia; Guest Lecturer at various universities and colleges. *Compositions:* Operas: The Music Lesson, 1960; The Terminal Opera, 1982, revised 1987; The Pastimes of Lord Caitanya, chamber opera, 1992; Orchestral: A solemn Chant for strings, 1955; Symphony No. 1, 1958, revised 1963; Harp Concerto, 1963; Dionysia, 1964; Chroma I, 1970; Cindy the Synthe (Minnie the Moog) for synthesizer and strings, 1975; Chamber: Flute Sonata, 1964; A Vacuum Soprano for brass quintet and tape, 1966; Entropy for brass, harp, celesta, piano and tape, 1967; Echospace for brass and tape, 1973; Choral music; Piano pieces; Organ music; Electronic scores; Mixed media pieces; Film music. *Publications:* Principles and Practice of Electronic Music, 1974; Eighteenth Century Counterpoint, 1993; Sixteenth Century Counterpoint, 1994. *Address:* 41 W Main, Morgantown, WV 26505, USA.

**TSCHAIKOV, Basil Nichols,** FRNCM, FRSA; British clarinettist; b. 30 May 1925, London, England; m. 1st; two d.; m. 2nd Dorothy Gallon 1966. *Education:* Royal Coll. of Music. *Career:* London Philharmonic Orchestra 1943–47; Royal Philharmonic Orchestra 1947–55; Philharmonia Orchestra 1958–79; Visiting Lecturer, Middlesex Polytechnic 1959–79; Prof., Royal Coll. of Music 1964–84; Dir Nat. Centre for Orchestral Studies, Goldsmiths' Coll., London 1979–89; Artistic and Exec. Nat. Orchestra for Europe 1989–90; Ed.-in-Chief Musical Performance, Harwood Academic Publrs 1993–2001; mem. Musicians' Union, Music Preserved (fmrly Music Performance Research Centre) (Chair. 1987–2003, Pres. Emer. 2003–). *Compositions:* First Tunes and Studies, Play the Clarinet. *Recordings:* with various chamber ensembles. *Publications:* Play the Clarinet Teachers; Handbook, How to Be a Musician. *Honours:* Hon. mem. Royal Coll. of Music 1966. *Address:* Hillside Cottage, Hillbrow, Liss, Hants., GU33 7PS, England (home). *E-mail:* bnickt@homecall.co.uk (home).

**TSCHAMMER, Hans;** Singer (Bass); b. 1945, Schlesien, Germany. *Education:* Würzburg Musikhochschule and Salzburg Mozarteum. *Career:* Sang at the Deutsche Oper am Rhein from 1975, notably as Pogner, Hagen, Daland, the Landgrave in Tannhäuser and Gurnemanz; Guest appearances at Hamburg, Zürich and San Francisco (Hunding, 1983); Bayreuth Festival, 1985–86; Further appearances at the New York Metropolitan, 1983, Bregenz Festival as Daland, 1990, and Covent Garden as Rocco, 1991; Other roles include the Commendatore in Don Giovanni and Prince Gremin (Toulouse, 1990 and 1993); Season 1994–95 as Sarastro at Turin and Gurnemann at Montpellier; Season 1998 as King Marke for Flanders Opera and at Monte Carlo; Sang Rocco in Fidelio at Rome, Daland in Dresden and Pogner for the Deutsche Oper Berlin, 2000; Concerts include Mozart's C minor Mass. *Address:* c/o Opéra et Concert, Rue Volney, 75002 Paris, France.

**TSCHERGOV, Michail;** Bulgarian singer (tenor, baritone); b. 1 Oct. 1928, Novo Selo. *Education:* studied in Sofia. *Career:* sang with the Vraza Opera, 1952–53 (debut as Nemorino), at Rostock, 1966–68, as Max, Alvaro and Dimitri; Sang widely in Eastern Europe as Otello, Canio, Des Grieux and Pedro in Tiefland; Other roles have included Calaf, Don José, Florestan, Tannhäuser, Siegmund and Rodolfo; Sang Otello at Frankfurt, 1988, and from 1990 such baritone roles as Verdi's Rigoletto and Renato. *Address:* c/o Bulgarian National Opera, Boul Dondoukov 58, 1000 Sofia, Bulgaria.

**TSONEVA, Plamena,** MA, MAS; Bulgarian musicologist and arts manager; *Production Manager, Varna Summer International Music Festival;* b. 19 Nov. 1954, Baltchik. *Education:* Dobri Hristov High School of Music, Varna, Pancho Vladigerov Music Acad., Sofia, Acad. for Music and Dance, Plovdiv, Int. Centre for Culture and Management, Salzburg and Linz Univ., Austria. *Career:* Dept of Culture, Dobrich Municipality 1978–85; Bulgarian Nat. Inst. of Culture, Branch Dobrich 1985–88; musicologist and Production Man., Varna Summer Int. Music Festival and Int. Summer Music Acad. 1988–; recent projects include Balkan Musicians in the Varna Summer Festival 2002, Varna Summer Int. Music Acad., with assistance from the British Council, Folkwang Hochschule, Essen, Germany 2002; meeting point of Young Talents supported by the EC Culture 2000 Program; participation in, as representative of the Varna Festival, projects initiated by the European Festivals Asscn 1998–2003. *Publications:* catalogues and brochures for Varna Summer Int. Music Festival, texts and articles about the festival image, programmes and performers 1989–2004, Varna Summer Int. Festival and Creative Urban Policy summary, 'The Balkan City – Stage for the End of the XX Century' in conference book for Yugoslav Performing Arts Centre, Belgrade 2000, script for a documentary 'Choir Singing in Dobrich' (Bulgarian Nat. TV/Branch Varna) 2002, contrib. to Das Musiktheater in Exil und Diktatur und seine Rezeption – Salzburg 2003 with paper, Bulgarian Opera during the period 1944–89, Journeys of Expression II, in cultural festivals/events and tourism Vienna 2003, Centre for Tourism and Cultural Change Sheffield Hallam Univ., in asscn with IFEA Europe, The City and the Festival, 'A mast or a-muse' Rotterdam 2001, Boekman Foundation, Topic Arts and Culture in Education – Policy and Practice in Europe, Analysis of the Situation in Bulgaria. *Address:* Varna Summer International Music Festival, Varna Municipality, 43 Osmi Primorski Polk Blvd., 9000 Varna, Bulgaria (office).

*Telephone:* (359) 52659123 (office). *Fax:* (359) 52659236 (office). *E-mail:* plconeva@varna.bg (office). *Website:* www.varnasummerfest.org.

**TSONTAKIS, George;** American composer; b. 24 Oct. 1951, New York. *Education:* Juilliard School, Karlheinz Stockhausen, Rome, studied with Roger Sessions. *Career:* freelance composer; faculty mem., Aspen Music School, Colorado 1976–, founding dir Aspen Contemporary Ensemble 1991–98; Asst in Electronic Music, Juilliard 1978; Asst Prof., Brooklyn Coll. Conservatory 1986–87. *Compositions include:* Scenes from the Apocalypse for soloists, chorus and orchestra 1978, The Epistle of James, Chapter I for narrator, chorus and orchestra 1980, Erotkritos oratorio for chorus and orchestra 1982, Five Signs and a Fantasy for orchestra 1985, Fantasia Habanera for orchestra 1986, four string quartets 1980, 1984, 1986, 1989, Bird-wind Quintet 1983, Brass Quintet 1983, Brass Quintet 1984, Saviours for soprano, chorus and orchestra 1985, The Past, The Passion for 15 players 1987, Galway Kinnell Songs for mezzo, piano and string quartet, The Sowers of the Seed for orchestra 1989, Heartsounds quintet for piano and strings 1990, Stabat Mater for soprano, chorus and orchestra 1990, four symphonic quartets 1992–96, Gemini for horn, violin, cello and piano 1996, Dust for horn, violin and piano 1998, Violin Concerto 1998, Violin Concerto No. 2 (Grawemeyer Award for Music Composition 2005) 2003. *Address:* c/o Aspen Music School, 2 Music School Road, Aspen, CO 81611, USA.

**TSOUPAKI, Calliope;** Composer and Pianist; b. 27 May 1963, Piraeus, Greece. *Education:* Studied at the Hellinicon Conservatory, Athens and at Nikos Skalkottas Conservatory (1985); With Louis Andriessen at the Hague Royal Conservatory; Summer courses at Darmstadt with Iannis Xenakis, Olivier Messiaen and Pierre Boulez (1985–88). *Career:* Freelance composer and pianist; Gaudeamus International Music Week at Amsterdam, 1991 and 1993; Composer in residence at the 1993 Budapest Young Artists Foundation; Featured composer at 1995 San Francisco Other Minds Festival. *Compositions include:* Eclipse for orchestra, 1986; Earinon for 8 horns and percussion, 1986; Revealing Moment for alto flute, 1987; Moments I and II for piano, 1988; For Always for female voice, tape and lights, 1989; Your Thouht for voice, tape and lighting, 1989; Silver Moments for 2 pianos and 2 percussion players, 1989; Mania for amplified violin, 1989; Visions of the Night, for amplified chamber ensemble, 1989; Sappho's Tears for violin, tenor recorder, and female voice, 1990; When I was 27, for amplified viola and double bass, 1990; Song for Four, for string quartet, 1991; Echoing Purple for violin and ensemble, 1992; Eros and Psyche, for wind octet and double bass, 1992; Orphic Fields for flute, 2 harps and 2 pianos, 1993; Phantom for tuba, 1994; Her Voice for harp, 1994; Ethra for flute, string trip and harp, 1995; Epigramma for chorus and orchestra, 1995; Lineos for chorus and ensemble, 1995; Hippolutos, music theatre after Euripides, 1996; Medea, stage, 1996; Interface, for ensemble, 1996; Siren, for narrator and chamber orchestra, 1997; No Name I, for oboe and violin, 1997; E guerre morte, after Tasso, for chorus and ensemble, 1997.

**TSUTSUMI, Tsuyoshi;** Japanese concert cellist and professor of music; *Professor of Music, Indiana University; President, Toho Gakuen School of Music, Tokyo;* b. 28 July 1942, Tokyo; m. Harue Saji 14 May 1978; one s. one d. *Education:* Toho Gakuen High School of Music, Tokyo, Indiana Univ., USA. *Career:* debut: Tokyo, Japan 1955; soloist (Iwaki), European Tour, NHK Symphony Orchestra of Tokyo 1960; soloist (Ozawa), Chicago Symphony, Ravinia Festival, Ravinia Park, Chicago, Illinois, USA 1967; soloist (Ozawa), American and European Tour, New Japan Philharmonic 1974; soloist (Akiyama), American Symphony, New York City 1978; soloist (Ceccato), Czech Philharmonic, Prague, Czechoslovakia 1984; Prof. of Music, School of Music, Univ. of Illinois, Urbana, USA; Prof. of Music, School of Music, Indiana Univ., Bloomington, USA 1988–; Pres. Toho Gakuen School of Music, Tokyo 2004–. *Recordings:* Bach, Unaccompanied Suites, complete; Beethoven, Sonatas and Variations (Turini, piano); Dvořák Concerto, Czech Philharmonic (Košler, conductor); Haydn, Concertos, English Chamber Orchestra; Yashiro Concerto, Tokyo Symphony Orchestra, conducted by Ohtomo. *Publications:* An Illinois Diary (The Cello and I), 1991, My Life with Cello 2003. *Honours:* First Prize, Int. Casals Competition, Budapest, Hungary 1963, Prize, Nat. Acad. of Arts (Japan) 1993. *Address:* School of Music, Indiana University, Bloomington, IN 47405 (office); 2715 Bluff Court, Bloomington, IN 47401, USA (home). *Telephone:* (812) 855-1552 (office); (812) 339-4629 (home). *Fax:* (812) 856-5006 (office); (812) 332-9523 (home).

**TSYDYPOVA, Valentina;** Singer (soprano); b. 1955, Buritia, Russia. *Education:* Graduated the Novosibirsk Conservatory 1984. *Career:* Sang at the Ulan-Ude Opera Theatre 1984–89; Novosibirsk Opera Theatre 1989–92; Kirov Opera St Petersburg from 1992, notably on tour to Italy, Israel, Spain, the Met Opera in New York, France, Finland and Germany; Guest appearances as Butterfly at the Opéra Bastille, Paris (1993) and in Hamburg and Berlin, Tosca at the Savonlinna Festival and Gorislava in Ruslan and Lyudmila at San Francisco; Other roles include Tchaikovsky's Tatiana, Maria (Mazeppa) and Lisa, Elisabeth de Valois, Desdemona, Aida, Santuzza and Yaroslavna; Concerts include Wigmore Hall recital (1995) and the Verdi Requiem at the Bastille Opéra. *Recordings include:* Rimsky's Sadko and Glinka's Ruslan and Lyudmila, with the Kirov Opera (Philips). *Honours:* People's Artist of the Buriatian Republic. *Current Management:* Askonas Holt Ltd, Lonsdale Chambers, 27 Chancery Lane, London, WC2A 1PF, England. *Telephone:* (20) 7400-1700. *Fax:* (20) 7400-1799. *E-mail:* info@askonasholt.co .uk. *Website:* www.askonasholt.co.uk.

**TSYPIN, George;** Set Designer; b. 1954, Russia. *Education:* Studied architecture in Moscow and set design in New York. *Career:* Collaborations with producer Peter Sellars include premiere of Osborne's The Electrification of the Soviet Union (1987) and Handel's Theodora (1996) at Glyndebourne; Premiere production of The Death of Klinghoffer by John Adams seen at Brussels, San Francisco, Lyon and New York, 1991; Messiaen's St Francois d'Assise (1992) and Le Grand Macabre by Ligeti (1997) at the Salzburg Festival; First staging by British company of Hindemith's Mathis der Maler, Covent Garden 1995; Further engagements with Salome and Katerina Izmailova at the Kirov, St Petersburg; The Gambler at La Scala, Die Zauberflöte in Florence and Orfeo and Euridice in Zürich; Oedipus Rex in Japan, Rigoletto for Canadian Opera with further work on Tannhäuser, Don Giovanni and Pelléas et Mélisande; Engaged for The Ring at Netherlands Opera (concluding with Götterdämmerung, 1999).

**TUCAPSKY, Antonin,** PhDr; Czech/British composer and academic (retd); b. 27 March 1928, Opatovice, Czechoslovakia; m. Beryl Musgrave 1972; one s. one d. *Education:* Teachers' Training Coll., Masaryk Univ., Brno, Janáček Acad. of Music, Brno. *Career:* debut: Ostrava; conductor of various choirs 1954–65, Children's Radio Choir, Ostrava 1960–62; Chief Conductor Moravian Teachers' Choir 1964–73; appearances on Czech Radio, Supraphon Records, BBC Radio and TV, Belgian Radio; fmr Prof. of Composition, Trinity Coll., London. *Compositions include:* In Honorem Vitae, Lauds, 5 Lenten Motets (choral cycles), The Time of Christmas, The Sacrifice (cantatas), Four Dialogues for clarinet and piano, Pocket Music for wind quintet, Adieu, Moravian Polka for orchestra, Missa Serena (oratorio), Stabat Mater (oratorio), The Undertaker (opera), Triptychon for symphony orchestra 1991, Concertino for piano and string orchestra 1992 Concerto for violin and orchestra 1993, String Quartet No. 2 1993, Viola Concerto 1996, Piano Trio No. 2 'Eclogues' 1996, Oboe Quintet 1997, Clarinet Concerto 1999, Te Deum 1999, Kohelet 2000, Three Psalms (cantatas) 2001, Rondo Capriccioso for bassoon and piano 2002, Concerto Semplice for cimbalom and orchestra 2003, Preludes for piano 2004, Missin Sol for SATB choir and organ 2005. *Recordings:* Choral Music, Comoedia, Cantata, Veni Sancte Spiritus, BBC Recordings; Viola Concerto; Stabat Mater, Mary Magdalene (Somm Records). *Publications:* Sightreading and Sightsinging, 1969; Janáček's Male Choruses and Their Interpretation, 1971. *Honours:* Janáček Gold Medal 2004. *Address:* 50 Birchen Grove, Kingsbury, London, NW9 8SA, England (home). *Telephone:* (20) 8200-5200 (home).

**TUCCI, Gabriella;** Singer (Soprano); b. 4 Aug. 1929, Rome, Italy. *Education:* Studied at the Accademia di Santa Cecilia with Leonardi Filoni. *Career:* Debut: Teatro Giglio Lucca 1951, as Violetta; Spoleto Festival 1952, as Leonora in La Forza del Destino; Florence 1953, as Cherubini's Médée; Tour of Australia 1955; La Scala Milan from 1959, as Mimi and in the Italian premiere of A Midsummer Night's Dream; Verona Arena 1959–69; US debut San Francisco 1959, as Madeleine in Andrea Chénier; Metropolitan Opera, 1960–73 as Butterfly, Aida, Euridice, Leonora in Trovatore and La Forza del Destino, Violetta and Marguerite; Covent Garden 1960, as Tosca; Appearances at Buenos Aires, Sydney, Oslo, Johannesburg, Dallas, New Orleans and Philadelphia; Other roles include Desdemona, Anaide in Mosé by Rossini, Luisa Miller, Micaela and Elvira in I Puritani; Teacher at Indiana University from 1983. *Recordings:* Pagliacci; Il Trovatore; Requiems by Bellini and Donizetti. *Address:* Music Faculty, Indiana University, Bloomington, IN 47405, USA.

**TUCEK, Rene;** Singer (baritone); b. 8 Jan. 1936, Plzeň, Czechoslovakia. *Education:* Studied in Plzeň with M. Gartnerova and in Vienna with F. Schuch-Tovini. *Career:* Debut: Brno 1960, as Count Luna in Il Trovatore; Sang first in Brno, Plzeň and Ceske Budejovice; Prague National Theatre from 1971, in the standard repertory and in operas Prokofiev, Martinů, Gershwin and Myslivicek; Guest appearances in Spain, Austria, Bulgaria, Luxembourg and Cuba; Has sung in concert and in song recitals; Teacher at the Prague Conservatory from 1973. *Recordings:* The Jacobin by Dvořák and operas by Smetana. *Address:* c/o National Theatre, PO Box 865, 112 30 Prague 1, Czech Republic.

**TUCKER, Mark;** British singer (tenor); b. 10 Aug. 1958, England. *Education:* Univ. of Cambridge and Guildhall School of Music and Drama, London. *Career:* active as concert and opera singer with particular interest in Italian repertoire, has performed and recorded alongside many of its leading exponents, including Gardiner, Harnoncourt and Jacobs; career highlights include a performance at Queen Elizabeth Hall in the title-role of Monteverdi's L'Orfeo; appearances at Salzburg Festival in Monteverdi Vespers of 1610 under Harnoncourt, and again under John Eliot Gardiner at Basilica San Marco, Venice; world premiere of Shchedrin's Vek Moy with Ashkenazy (piano) and Koelner Philharmonic; recent operatic engagements include L'Orfeo with Pinchgut Opera in Sydney, Hyllos (Hercules) in Potsdam, Platee in Lisbon, Eurimaco (Il ritorno d'Ulisse in patria) with Boston Baroque, Danceny in world premiere of Swerts' Les liaisons dangereuses for Flanders Opera, Gomatz (Zaide) at La Monnaie and for Opera du Rhin, Lysander (A Midsummer Night's Dream) in Turin, The Novice (Billy Budd) for Royal Opera, Covent Garden and Marzio (Mitridate) under Christophe Rousset at Theatre du Chatelet, Paris; concerts have included Elgar's Dream of Gerontius with Orchestra dell'Accademia Nazionale di Santa Cecilia under Ashkenazy, Andromeda Liberata with Venice Baroque Orchestra under Marcon, Beethoven's Mass in C for La Fenice under Gardiner; appearances with London Symphony Orchestra in L'enfant et les sortileges under Previn,

Handel's Messiah with New York Philharmonic conducted by Hickox. *Recordings include:* A Midsummer Night's Dream, L'incoronazione di Poppea, Bach B Minor Mass, Fennimore and Gerda by Delius 1997, Percy Grainger Songs, Vivaldi's Andromeda Liberata. *Current Management:* Harrison/Parrott Ltd, 12 Penzance Place, London, W11 4PA, England. *Telephone:* (20) 7229-9166. *Fax:* (20) 7221-5042. *E-mail:* info@harrisonparrott.com. *Website:* www.harrisonparrott.com.

**TUCKWELL, Barry Emmanuel,** AC, OBE, FRCM, FRSA; Australian horn player and conductor; b. 5 March 1931, Melbourne, Australia; s. of Charles Tuckwell and Elizabeth Hill; m. 1st Sally E. Newton 1958; one s. one d.; m. 2nd Hilary J. Warburton 1971; one s.; m. 3rd Susan T. Levitan 1992. *Education:* Sydney Conservatorium. *Career:* French horn player with Melbourne Symphony Orchestra 1947, Sydney Symphony Orchestra 1947–50, Hallé Orchestra 1951–53, Scottish Nat. Orchestra 1954–55, Bournemouth Symphony Orchestra, London Symphony Orchestra 1955–68; Horn Prof., RAM 1963–74; f. Tuckwell Wind Quintet 1968; int. soloist and recording artist; Conductor of Tasmanian Symphony Orchestra 1980–83; Music Dir and Conductor Md Symphony Orchestra 1982–98; Pres. Int. Horn Soc. 1969–76, 1993–95; Guest Conductor Northern Sinfonia 1993–; mem. Bd of Dirs, London Symphony Orchestra 1957–68, Chair. 1961–68; mem. Chamber Music Soc. of Lincoln Center 1974–81; Fellow Royal Coll. of Music, Royal Soc. of Arts. *Publications:* Playing the Horn, 50 1st Exercises 1978, The Horn (Yehudi Menuhin Music Guides) 1981, entire horn repertoire of G. Schirmer Inc. (Ed). *Honours:* hon. degrees from RAM, Guildhall School of Music and Drama, Sydney Univ.; Harriet Cohen Int. Award for Solo Instruments 1968, George Peabody Medal for outstanding contribs to music in America. *Address:* Gallo & Giordano, 76 West 86th Street, New York, NY 10024 (office); 13140 Fountain Head Road, Hagerstown, MD 21742, USA.

**TULACEK, Thomas;** Violinist; b. 26 April 1955, Prague. *Education:* Studied at the Prague Conservatory, the Prague Academy of Musical Arts and the Guildhall School of Music. *Career:* First Violin Section, BBC Scottish Symphony Orchestra, 1985–89; Leader, New Chamber Orchestra, Oxford, 1990–; Associate Professor, Trinity College of Music, London, 1991; Recital work has taken him to countries such as Italy, Switzerland, France, Israel and the Czech Republic and has recorded for Czech Radio and Radio Vatican; Since 1990 has been performing regularly with the English pianist Steven Wray and they have formed a piano trio with Jaroslav Ondracek; Concerto performances have included works by Prokofiev, Bruch, Haydn, Mozart and most recently Nielsen, with the Teplice Symphony Orchestra, in the Czech Republic. *Address:* 1 Brookes Court, Longley Road, London SW17 9LF, England.

**TUMA, Jaroslav;** Czech organist; b. 1956. *Education:* Prague Academy of Arts with Milan Sleehta and Zuzana Ruzicková, summer school at Haarlem, Netherlands with Hans Haselböck, studied improvisation and Bach interpretation with Piet Kee. *Career:* Laureate of organ competitions in Prague, Linz, Leipzig, Nuremberg and Haarlem; Festival appearances by Nuremberg, Linz, Prague and Mechelen; Engagements in Europe, Japan and the USA; Concerts with Czech Philharmonic Orchestra, Three years cycle of complete organ works by J. S. Bach in Prague; Repertoire includes works by Bach, Franck, Liszt, Reger, Hoffhaimer, Sweelinck, Isaac and Husa; Accompanies major soloists on the harpsichord. *Recordings:* L. and H. Hassler, Muffat; Handel; Series organs of Bohema I–IV, Czech compositions for harpsichord. *Current Management:* Bohemia-Concert, PO Box 5, 100 05 Prague, Czech Republic. *Address:* c/o Prague Academy of Arts, Dominumilc, Alsovo náb e i 12, 110100 Prague 1, Czech Republic.

**TUMAGIAN, Eduard;** Singer (Baritone); b. 1944, Bucharest, Romania. *Career:* Sang at Bucharest from 1968 as Papageno, Alfonso, Mozart's Count, and Wolfram in Tannhäuser; Opéra du Rhin Strasbourg from 1974, as Germont, Iago, Enrico in Lucia di Lammermoor, Scarpia, Marcello, Belcore, Escamillo and Eugene Onegin; Guest appearances at Lyon, Stuttgart, Karlsruhe and Orange; Sang Rigoletto at Basle 1981 and appeared further with Welsh and English National operas, Frankfurt (Renato 1983), Nice (I Puritani and Vespri Sicilaini (Montfort), I Due Foscari and Riccardo III by Flavio Testi; Paris Opéra 1985, as Germont; US debut 1986 at Pittsburgh as Don Carlo in La Forza del Destino; Carnegie Hall New York in concert performances of Béatrice et Bénédict and Nabucco; Recent appearances at the Deutsche Oper Berlin, Staatsoper Hamburg, Vienna Staatsoper (Scarpia in season 1988–89), Toulouse (La Franciulla del West) and Oviedo Festival (Simon Boccanegra and La Favorita); Season 1991 as Nabucco at Trieste and Buenos Aires, Rigoletto at Philadelphia; Sang Vaudémont in Iolanta and Verdi's Germont at Orange and Baltimore, 1999; Concert repertoire includes music by Bach, Handel, Beethoven, Mussorgsky, Britten and Shostakovich (14th Symphony at the 1984 Salzburg Festival). *Recordings include:* Miller in video of Luisa Miller from Opéra de Lyon; Napoleon in War and Peace; Turandot.

**TUMANYAN, Barseg;** Singer (bass baritone); b. 1958, Jerevan, Armenia. *Education:* Studied at the Komitas Conservatoire and at La Scala, Milan; Further study with Evgeny Nesterenko at the Moscow Conservatoire, 1985. *Career:* Sang with the Spenderian Opera (Armenia) from 1980; Performances of Basilio at the Teatro San Carlo Naples 1988; Appeared in Gala Concert for Armenia at Covent Garden 1989, and invited back to sing in La Bohème, Les Contes d'Hoffmann and Carmen; US debut with Boston Opera as Ramfis in Aida, 1989; Appearances in USA, 1989 with the Armenian State Opera; Sang Colline in La Bohème at Covent Garden and Monte Carlo, 1990; King Philip in

Don Carlos at Los Angeles; Wigmore Hall recital, June 1990; Sang Moser in I. Masnadieri with the Royal Opera, 1998; Sang Ramphis in Aida at Dublin, and Gounod's Mephisto at Lyon, 2000. *Honours:* Prizewinner, Bussetto Competition, 1983; 2nd Prize, Tchaikovsky Competition, Moscow 1986; Joint First Prize, Rio de Janeiro Competition, 1987. *Current Management:* Askonas Holt Ltd, Lonsdale Chambers, 27 Chancery Lane, London, WC2A 1PF, England. *Telephone:* (20) 7400-1700. *Fax:* (20) 7400-1799. *E-mail:* info@askonasholt.co .uk. *Website:* www.askonasholt.co.uk.

**TUNLEY, David Evatt,** AM, DLitt, MMus, FAHA; Australian musicologist and academic; *Emeritus Professor and Honorary Senior Research Fellow, Department of Music, University of Western Australia*; b. 3 May 1930, Sydney; s. of Leslie Tunley and Marjorie Tunley; m. Paula Patricia Laurantus 1959; one s. two d. *Education:* The Scots Coll., Sydney, State Conservatorium of Music, Sydney. *Career:* music master, Fort Street Boys' High School, Sydney 1952–57; joined staff of Dept of Music, Univ. of Western Australia 1958, Personal Chair. of Music 1980–, now Emer., Head Dept of Music 1985–90, Hon. Sr Research Fellow in Music 1994–; studied under Nadia Boulanger with French Govt Scholarship 1964–65; Scholar-in-residence, Rockefeller Foundation, Bellagio, Italy 1987; Fowler Hamilton Visiting Research Fellow, Christ Church, Oxford 1993; Visiting Scholar, Wolfson Coll. Oxford 1996; Founder/Conductor Univ. Collegium Musicum, 1976–83; Founder/Chair. York Winter Music Festival, 1982–; Founder/Dir The Terrace Proms, Perth; Nat. Pres. Musicological Soc. of Australia 1980–81; Chair. Music Bd, Australia Council 1984–85. *Compositions include:* Concerto for Clarinet and Strings 1966 (revised 2000), A Wedding Masque 1970, Immortal Fire 1999. *Publications:* The 18th-Century French Cantata 1974, Couperin 1982, Harmony in Action 1984, The French Cantata in Facsimile, 17 Vols 1990, Romantic French Song in Facsimile (6 Vols) 1994, The Bel Canto Violin: the life and times of Alfredo Campoli 1906–1991 1999, Salons, Singers and Songs: A Background to Romantic French Song 1830–70 2002, François Couperin and The Perfection of Music 2004; contribs to the New Grove Dictionary of Music and Musicians, The New Oxford History of Music. *Honours:* Hon. DMus (Western Australia); Chevalier Ordre des Palmes Académiques. *Address:* Department of Music, University of Western Australia, Nedlands 6009, Western Australia (office); 100 Dalkeith Road, Nedlands 6009, Western Australia, Australia (home). *Telephone:* (8) 9386-1934 (home). *E-mail:* dtunley@cyllene.uwa.edu.au (office). *Website:* www.music.uwa.edu.au/welcome_to_uwa_music (office).

**TUNNELL, Jonathon;** Cellist; b. 1955, England. *Career:* Debut: Wigmore Hall, 1984, with Peter Pears; Member of the Tunnell Trio; Co-founded the Brindisi String Quartet at Aldeburgh 1984; Concerts in a wide repertory throughout the United Kingdom and in France, Germany, Spain, Italy and Switzerland; Festival engagements at Aldeburgh (residency 1990), Arundel, Bath, Brighton, Huddersfield, Norwich and Warwick; First London performance of Colin Matthews's 2nd Quartet, 1990, premiere of David Matthews's 6th Quartet 1991; Quartet by Mark Anthony Turnage 1992; Many BBC recitals and resident artist with the University of Ulster. *Recordings include:* Quartets by Britten, Bridge and Imogen Holst; Works by Pierné and Lekeu. *Honours:* Prizewinner, Third Banff International String Quartet Competition in Canada, 1989, with Brindisi Quartet. *Address:* c/o Owen-White Management, 14 Nightingale Lane, London N8 7QU, England.

**TUOMELA, Tapio Juhani,** DipMus, MMus; Finnish composer and conductor; *Artistic Director, Time of Music Festival*; b. 11 Oct. 1958, Kuusamo; m. Helena Tuovinen 1985; three d. *Education:* Sibelius Acad., Helsinki, Eastman School of Music, Rochester, NY, USA. *Career:* debut concert of own compositions, Helsinki Festival 1991; performances of own works at UNM Festivals (Young Scandinavian Composers) 1985–89, Scandinavian Music Days 1990, 1994, 1996, Time of Music Festival, Viitasaari 1993, 1997, Tampere Biennale 1994, 1996; performances in the USA, Germany, Russia, Hungary, Netherlands, all Scandinavian countries; profile concerts in Antwerp 2000, Paris 2003; also active as a conductor, including numerous first performances in Scandinavia; Artistic Dir, Time of Music Festival 2000–. *Compositions include:* L'échelle de l'évasion for chamber orchestra 1989, Symphony 1991, The Ear's Tale chamber opera (Finnish Nat. Opera commission) 1993, Jokk for orchestra 1995, Mirage for ensemble 1997, Mothers and Daughters (opera from the Kalevala) 1999, Lemminkäinen, Nordan, Lappic, Vuohenki Luohti, two Quintets, The Escape Ladder. *Recordings:* Symmetry quintet, L'échelle de l'évasion, conductor of world premiere recording of ballet music Maa, by K. Saariaho and some late pieces for string orchestra by Sibelius 1995. *Honours:* first prize City of Lahti Children's Choir Competition 1997. *Address:* Temppelikatu 14 A 12, 00100 Helsinki, Finland (home). *Telephone:* (9) 490-586 (home). *Fax:* (9) 4541-1630 (home). *E-mail:* ttuomela@siba.fi (home). *Website:* www.webusers.siba.fi/~ttuomela.

**TURBAN, Ingolf;** Violinist; b. 17 March 1964, Munich, Germany; m. Barbara Meier, 28 July 1994, 2 s. *Education:* Studied at the Munich Musikhochschule with Gerhart Hetzel and at Aspen, Colorado with Dorothy DeLay and Jens Ellerman. *Career:* Debut: Munich, 1986, with the Munich Philharmonic; National Symphony Orchestra, Washington DC, USA, 1991; Leader of the Munich Philharmonic, 1985–88; Solo career since 1988 in Europe, USA, Canada and Israel; Professor, Stuttgart Musikhochschule, 1995–. *Compositions:* Cadenzas to numerous violin concertos; a Niccolò, for 5 violins, 1998. *Recordings:* Numerous including: World premieres, Paganini Caprices with piano accompaniment by Schumann; Hartmann Solo Sonatas and Suites; Ernst Pieces; Respighi with English Chamber Orchestra; Marek with the Philharmonia, London. *Current Management:* Art Productions, Marbach-strasse 19A 81369 Munich, Germany. *Address:* Nordstrasse 4, 82131 Stockdorf, Munich, Germany.

**TURBET, Richard Beaumont,** BA, MLitt; British librarian; *Special Collections Cataloguer and Music Librarian, University of Aberdeen;* b. 5 Feb. 1948, Ilford, Essex, England; m.; two s. *Education:* Bancroft's School, Woodford, Essex, Univ. Coll., London, Leeds Polytechnic, Univ. of Aberdeen. *Career:* trainee asst librarian, Univ. of Dundee 1969–70; grad. teaching asst, Univ. of Calgary, Canada 1971–72; Asst Librarian, Nat. Cen. Library 1972–74; Librarian, Prison Service Coll., Wakefield 1974–77; Asst Librarian, Univ. of Aberdeen 1977–90, Sub-Librarian 1990–2003, Special Collections Cataloguer and Music Librarian 2003–; Layclerk, Wakefield Cathedral 1976–77, Aberdeen Cathedral 1977–92; mem. Royal Musical Asscn, Int. Asscn of Music Libraries, British Music Soc., Viola da Gamba Soc., Elgar Soc., Armstrong Gibbs Soc., Nat. Early Music Asscn, Friends of Cathedral Music. *Publications:* William Byrd: A Guide to Research 1987, Tudor Music: A Research and Information Guide 1994, William Byrd: Lincoln's Greatest Composer 1993, Byrd Studies (ed with Alan Brown) 1992, Music Librarianship in the United Kingdom (ed) 2003, Annual Byrd Newsletter (ed) 1995–2004 2005; contrib. to Sundry sorts of Music Books (Festschrift for O. W. Neighbour 1993), Aspects of British Song 1992, Branches of Literature and Music 2000, New Grove Dictionary of Music and Musicians (second edn), Oxford Dictionary of National Biography, British Catalogue of Music Periodicals, and more than 100 articles in journals. *Honours:* C. B. Oldman Prize 1994. *Address:* The Library, University of Aberdeen, Meston Walk, Old Aberdeen, AB24 3UE (office); 140 Newburgh Road, Bridge of Don, Aberdeen, AB22 8QY, Scotland (home). *Telephone:* (1224) 274266 (office); (1224) 704601 (home). *Fax:* (1224) 273956 (office). *E-mail:* r.turbet@abdn.ac.uk (office).

**TURCHI, Guido;** Composer; b. 10 Nov. 1916, Rome, Italy. *Education:* Studied at the Rome Conservatory and with Pizzetti at the Accademia di Santa Cecilia. *Career:* Taught at the Rome Conservatory, Director, Parma and Florence Conservatories 1967–72; Artistic Director, Accademia Filarmonica Romana 1963–66, and Teatro Comunale Bologna, 1968–70; Artistic Director, Accademia di Santa Cecilia from 1972–75; Accademia Musicale Chigiana do Siena, 1978–88. *Compositions include:* Opera II buon soldato Svejk, La Scala Milan 1962; Trio for flute, clarinet and viola 1945; Invettiva for small chorus and 2 pianos 1946; Concerto for string orchestra 1948; Piccolo concerto notturno 1950; 3 Metamorfosi for orchestra 1970; Dedalo, ballet, Florence 1972; Dedica for flute 1972; Adagio for orchestra, 1983; Parabola for orchestra, 1993; Exil, for singers and chamber orchestra, 1996; Te Lucis Ante-Terminum, for chorus and string orchestra, 1988; 6 Bagatelles, for chamber orchestra, 1999; Fantasia, for string quintet, 1999; Choruses, songs and incidental music. *Recordings:* Exil, 1995; Fantasia, 1990; 6 Bagatelles, 1999. *Address:* Cannaregio 233, 30121 Venice, Italy.

**TURCO, Enrico;** Italian singer (bass); b. 1962, Genoa. *Education:* Accademia di Santa Cecilia, Rome. *Career:* sang at first in concert and made stage debut in 1987, as King Philip in Don Carlos; Macerata Festival, 1991, as Leporello, and Frankfurt Alte Oper in a concert of Franchetti's Cristoforo Colombo; Guest appearances at La Scala, Turin, Parma and the Scottish Opera; Sang Capello in Bellini's Capuleti at Reggio Emilia, 1998. *Address:* c/o Teatro Regio, Via Garibaldi 16, 43100 Parma, Italy.

**TURETZKY, Bertram (Jay);** Double Bass Player and Composer; b. 14 Feb. 1933, Norwich, Connecticut, USA. *Education:* Studied at the Hartt School of Music (graduated 1955), at New York University (musicology with Curt Sachs) and with David Walter; Further study at the University of Hartford, MM 1965. *Career:* Played double bass in various orchestras and ensembles; Solo debut at Judson Hall, New York, Oct 1064, with works by Donald Erb and Barney Childs; Novel performing techniques have been exploited by such composers as Donald Martino, Richard Felciano, Paul Chihara, Kenneth Gaburro, George Perle and Ben Johnston. *Compositions:* Collages I–IV 1976–81; Reflections on Ives and Whittier for double bass and tape 1979–81; In memoriam Charles Mingus 1979; Baku for tape 1980. *Publications include:* The Contemporary Contrabass 1974; Editions of double bass studies for the American String Teachers Association; Editor of series published by the University of California Press on contemporary performance techniques. *Address:* ASCAP, ASCAP Building, 1 Lincoln Plaza, New York, NY 10023, USA.

**TURKOVIC, Milan;** Austrian Bassoonist; b. 14 Sept. 1939, Zagreb, Yugoslavia. *Education:* Studied in Vienna. *Career:* Performed with the Philharmonia Hungarica, then soloist with the Bamber Symphony and member of the Bamberg Wind Quintet; Soloist with the Vienna Symphony from 1967, with freelance concert performances from 1984; Further concerts at the Salzburg Mozarteum and with Concentus Musicus at Vienna, under Harnoncourt; Created Helmut Eder's concerto in 1968 and with Helmut and Wolfgang Schulz formed the Vienna Trio. *Address:* c/o Salzburg Mozarteum Orchestra, Erzbischof-Gebhardstrasse 10, 5020 Salzburg, Austria.

**TURNAGE, Mark-Anthony;** British composer; *Composer-in-Residence, Chicago Symphony Orchestra;* b. 10 June 1960, Corringham, Essex; s. of Roy Turnage and Patricia Knowles; m. 1st Susan Shaw 1989 (divorced 1990); m. 2nd Helen Reed 1992; two s. *Education:* Hassenbrook Comprehensive School, Palmers Sixth Form, Grays, Royal Coll. of Music with Oliver Knussen and John Lambert and Tanglewood, USA with Hans Werner Henze and Gunther Schuller. *Career:* first opera, Greek, premiered at first Munich Biennale 1988; Composer in Asscn with City of Birmingham Symphony

Orchestra, composing three major works 1989–93; Composer in Asscn with ENO 1995–99; Assoc. Composer in Asscn with BBC Symphony Orchestra 2000–03; Momentum, BBC 3 composer weekend dedicated to his music, Barbican Hall, London 2003; composer-in-residence London Philharmonic Orchestra 2005–, Chicago Symphony Orchestra 2006–(08). *Compositions include:* Night Dances for orchestra 1980, Lament for a Hanging Man for soprano and ensemble 1983, Sarabande for soprano saxophone and piano 1985, On All Fours for chamber ensemble 1985, Release for eight players 1987, Greek opera in two acts 1987, Three Screaming Popes for orchestra 1988, Greek Suite for mezzo soprano, baritone and ensemble 1989, Kai for solo cello and ensemble 1989, Some Days 1989, Momentum for orchestra 1990, Killing Time television scena 1991, Drowned Out 1992, Your Rockaby saxophone concerto 1992, Blood on the Floor for large ensemble 1994, Dispelling the Fears 1994, Twice Through the Heart for mezzo and 16 players 1997, Country of the Blind 1997, Four-Horned Fandango 1997, The Silver Tassie opera in four acts 1997, Silent Cities for orchestra 1998, About Time for two orchestras 1999, Evening Songs for orchestra 2000, Another Set To for trombone and orchestra 2000, Fractured Lines for two percussionists and orchestra 2000, Scorched for jazz trio and orchestra (with John Scofield) 2000, On Opened Ground concerto for viola and orchestra 2000, Bass Inventions for double bass and ensemble 2001, The Torn Fields for orchestra 2001, Dark Crossing 2001, A Quick Blast 2001, The Game is Over for orchestra 2002, Riffs and Refrains 2005. *Honours:* Guinness Prize for Composition 1982, Benjamin Britten Young Composers' Prize 1983, BMW Music Theatre Prize 1988, Laurence Olivier Award 2001. *Current Management:* Van Walsum Management Ltd, 4 Addison Bridge Place, London, W14 8XP, England. *Telephone:* (20) 7371-4343. *Fax:* (20) 7371-4344. *E-mail:* vwm@vanwalsum.co.uk (office). *Website:* www .vanwalsum.co.uk (office).

**TURNER, Bruno;** Choral Director; b. 7 Feb. 1931, London. *Education:* studied Gregorian chant and Renaissance choral music. *Career:* many performances of Medieval and Renaissance music, notably as Dir of Pro Cantione Antiqua; liturgical reconstruction of the Missa Tecum Principium by Robert Fayrfax, 1962; Iberian, English and Franco-Flemish choral music of the 15th and 16th centuries. *Recordings include:* albums of early choral music on various labels. *Publications include:* Mapa Mundi Editions. *Address:* Apdo 172, Garrucha 04630, Almeria, Spain. *E-mail:* bruno.t@freedom255.com.

**TURNER, Charles (Lloyd);** Musicologist, Bibliographer and Performer; b. 10 July 1948, Houston, Texas, USA. *Education:* BMus, 1970; MMus, 1976; MSLS, 1979, University of Texas; D.Mus, Indiana University, 1986. *Career:* Founding Director, La Primavera, Early Music Ensemble; Concert tours of Texas, California, Southwest USA; Tour of Mexico sponsored by US State Department; Musicologist, Director of Hartt Early Music Ensemble, Hartt School, University of Hartford. *Recordings:* Popular Elizabethan Music; The Greater Passion Play from Carmina Burana. *Publications:* Bibliographer, Medieval Music, 1986; The Isorhythmic Motet in Continental Europe, Proportion and Form, 1986; Articles in Journal of the Lute Society of America, Lute Society Quarterly, Journal of the American Musicological Society, Journal of the International Trumpet Guild, Early Music, Notes and Music Analysis; Reviews in Notes; Associate Editor,Notes 2001–03;. *Address:* Hartt School, University of Hartford, 200 Bloomfield Avenue, West Hartford, CT 06117, USA.

**TURNER, Claramae;** Singer (Contralto); b. 28 Oct. 1920, Dinuba, California, USA. *Education:* Studied with Nino Comel, Armando Angini and Giacomo Spadoni at San Francisco and with Dick Marzollo in New York. *Career:* Debut: San Francisco 1942, in Les Contes d'Hoffmann; Sang at the Metropolitan Opera 1946–50, notably as Amneris; Sang in the premieres of Menotti's The Medium (1946), The Tender Land by Copland (1954) and Bomarzo by Ginastera (1967); Teatro Liceo Barcelona 1957–58; Chicago Lyric Opera 1956, as Azucena; Sang Diego 1967, in the US premiere of Der junge Lord by Henze; Appearances in Buenos Aires, Mexico City, Venice, Monte Carlo, Boston, Dallas, Houston, Baltimore, Philadelphia and Pittsburgh. *Recordings:* Un Ballo in Maschera, conducted by Toscanini; Bomarzo.

**TURNER, Jane;** Singer (Mezzo Soprano); b. 1960, County Durham, England. *Education:* Guildhall School of Music; Opera Studio, London. *Career:* West German debut as Wellgunde and Siegrune in The Ring at Bayreuth, 1984, as a Flower Maiden and Flosshilde; British Opera debut 1985 as Carmen with the Glyndebourne Tour; Flora in Peter Hall's production of Traviata at the Festival, 1987; Covent Garden debut 1987, as Ann Who Strips in the Hytner production of The King Goes Forth to France; returned as a Flower Maiden in Parsifal and as Flosshilde in Das Rheingold; English National Opera as Maddalena in Rigoletto and as Lola in Cavalleria Rusticana; Sang Siebel in Faust at Dublin, 1995. *Address:* c/o English National Opera, St Martin's Lane, London, WC2, England.

**TURNER, Margarita;** Singer (Soprano); b. 11 March 1943, Perth, Australia. *Education:* Studied in London and West Germany. *Career:* Debut: Krefeld 1969, as Micaela; Appearances in opera at Cologne, Saarbrucken, Wiesbaden and Wuppertal; 15 year career at the Essen Opera as Fiordiligi, Pamina, Marguerite, Martha, Marenka, Violetta, Marzelline (Fidelio), Mélisande, Eva, Concepcion and Nedda; Sophie in Der Rosenkavalier, Mimi, Liu, Rosalinde and Luise in Der Junge Lord by Henze; Frequent concert engagements; Teacher at the Essen Musikhochschule; Season 2000–01 at Essen, in Elektra, Faust and Jenůfa. *Address:* c/o Theater, Rolandstrasse 10, 4300 Essen, Germany.

**TURNER, Paul;** Composer; b. 16 April 1948, Morwell, Victoria, Australia. *Education:* BMus, 1977, Mus, 1980, University of Melbourne; Study with Barry Conyngham. *Career:* Composer-in-the-Community, Hamilton, Victoria, 1981; Faculty Member, University of Adelaide, 1987–92. *Compositions include:* Panels II for violin, clarinet and piano, 1974; Grand Pocket Sonata in B Minor for piano, 1986; Herbivores for piano, 1987; Sonata, for tape, 1994; A Spangled Pandemonium Escapes from the Zoo, for ensemble; Chronic Interludes I–III for saxophone and piano; Geraniums or Nasturtiums for saxophone and piano; Instrumental Rationality, for various combinations; Icarus Flying, for guitar or tape; Machines I–III for harp and tape; Phrygian Misery for saxophone and piano. *Address:* c/o APRA, 1A Eden Street, Crows Nest, NSW 2065, Australia.

**TURNER, Robert Comrie,** CM, BMus, MMus, DMus; Canadian composer; b. 6 June 1920, Montréal; m.; two s. one d. *Education:* McGill Univ., Royal Coll., George Peabody Coll. *Career:* Music Prod., Canadian Broadcasting Corp, Vancouver 1952–68; Lecturer in Music, UBC 1955–57; Asst Prof., Music Acadia Univ., Wolfville 1968–69; Prof. of Composition, Univ. of Manitoba, Winnipeg 1969–85, Prof. Emeritus 1985–; composer-in-residence, MacDowell Colony, Peterborough, NH 1987; Fellow Canada Council 1966–67; mem. Music Publishers of Canada, Canadian League of Composers, Canadian Music Centre. *Compositions:* two operas, three symphonies, four concertos, A Group of Seven for viola, reciter and orchestra, Johann's Gift to Christmas for narrator and orchestra, The Third Day (Easter cantata for soloists, chorus and orchestra), The River of Time for chorus and orchestra, Shades of Autumn for orchestra, Opening Night (theatre overture) 1960, String Quartet No. 2 1963, Six Voluntaries for organ 1963, Little Suite for harp 1971, Prophetic Song 1971, Four Fragments for brass quintet 1972, A Merry-Mournful Mood 1972, Nocturne for orchestra 1972, Eidolons 1977, Chamber Concerto for bassoon and 17 instruments 1977, Manitoba Memoir for strings 1989, Two Choral Pieces 1990, Vestiges for piano 1990, The Phoenix and the Turtle, Time for Three, Four Last Songs, House of Shadows 1994, Festival Dance 1997, Diverti-memento for chamber orchestra 1997. *Recordings:* RCI Anthology of Canadian Music, Sonata for violin and piano, Five Canadian Folksongs, Vestiges for piano, Robert Turner Portrait, Ovation IV. *Honours:* Commemorative Medal for 125th Anniversary of Confed. of Canada 1993, Queen's Golden Jubilee Award 2003. *Address:* One Evergreen Place #2602, Winnipeg, MB, R3L 0E9, Canada. *Telephone:* (204) 478-1440.

**TURNOVSKY, Martin;** Czech conductor; b. 29 Sept. 1928, Prague, Czechoslovakia. *Education:* Music Acad., Prague; studied Conducting with Dedecek and Ančerl, Prague Acad. of Music; pvt. studies in conducting with Szell 1956. *Career:* Conductor Czech Army Symphony Orchestra 1955–60, State Philharmonic Orchestra, Brno 1960–63; Music Dir Plzeň Radio Orchestra 1963–66, Dresden State Opera and State Orchestra 1966–68; Guest Conductor with numerous well-known orchestras including Radio Orchestra, Berlin, Cleveland Orchestra, New York Philharmonic Orchestra, Detroit Symphony Orchestra, Toronto Symphony, Stockholm Philharmonic Orchestra, BBC Northern Orchestra, Manchester 1968, Norwegian Opera, Oslo 1975–80, Bonn Opera 1979–83, Prague Symphony Orchestra 1992; opera engagements with Deutsche Oper Berlin, Welsh Nat. Opera (British opera debut, Eugene Onegin 1988), Staatsoper Stuttgart, Royal Opera Stockholm and Savonlinna Festival, Finland; Season 1992–93 conducted Otello and Un Ballo in Maschera at Prague State Opera; American opera debut with Jenůfa at Cincinnati 1998; Dvořák's Rusalka with Seattle Opera 1998. *Recordings:* numerous recordings for Supraphon, including 4th Symphony of Bohuslav Martinů (Grand Prix du Disque 1968). *Honours:* Österreichisches Ehrenkreuz für Wissenschaft und Kunst 1. Klasse; First Prize, Int. Competition for Conductors, Besancon, France 1958. *Current Management:* Baron & Weingartner KEG, International Artists Management, Bösendorferstrasse 4/12, 1010 Vienna, Austria. *Telephone:* (1) 489-61-54. *Fax:* (1) 489-61-54-44. *E-mail:* schwemle@baronartists.com. *Website:* www.baronartists.com.

**TUROK, Paul (Harris);** Composer; b. 3 Dec. 1929, New York City, USA; m. Susan Kay Frucht, 24 Mar 1967. *Education:* BA, Queens College, 1950; MA, University of California, Berkeley, 1951; Special studies at Juilliard School of Music, 1951–53; MS, Baruch College, 1986. *Career:* Music Director, Experimental television, US Army, Augusta, GA, 1954; Music Director, KPFA, Berkeley, 1955–56; Lecturer, City College of New York, 1960–63; Visiting Professor, Williams College, 1964. *Compositions:* Operas: Richard III, A Secular Masque, Scene Domestic; Orchestral: American Variations, Chartres West, Ultima Thule, Great Scott!, Joplin Overture, Sousa Overture, Danza Viva, Concertos for Violin, English Horn, Trombone, Cello, Oboe, Symphony; Chamber Music: 4 String Quartets, English Horn Quintet, Sonatas for Flute, Bassoon, Horn, Trumpet, Viola, Cello, Harp, Harpsichord; Numerous other works; Organ: Toccata; Piano: Passacaglia, Transcendental Etudes; Brass: Elegy, Quintet; Vocal: Lanier Songs, Evocations, To Music, Three Popular Songs. *Address:* c/o G Schirmer Incorporated, 24 East 22nd Street, New York, NY 10010, USA.

**TURPIN, Kathryn;** Singer (Mezzo-soprano); b. 1968, England. *Education:* History of Art, New Hall, Cambridge; Opera School, Royal College of Music; Samling Foundation; Welsh Arts Council Scholar. *Career:* Lady de Hautdesert in Birtwistle's Gawain at the Royal Opera House; Margaretha in Schumann's Genoveva at Garsington; Bizet's Djamileh at Cap Ferrat; Lucretia in The Rape of Lucretia for Music Theatre Wales; Carmen at the Festival de la Vezère; Cherubino at Neuchâtel; Ulisse in Deidamia, London Handel Society; Madame Popova in The Bear at Cambridge; Conductors worked for include

Simon Rattle, Neville Marriner, David Willcocks, Elgar Howarth, Matthew Best and Martyn Brabbins; Orchestras include CBSO, Orchestra of the Age of Enlightenment, London Sinfonietta, Bournemouth Sinfonietta, London Mozart Players, Hanover Band, Orchestre National de Lille, Orchestre de Besançon, National Youth Orchestra of Wales, Academy of St Martin in the Fields. *Recordings:* In The Beginning, Copland, with the Choir of St John's College, Cambridge; Duruflé Requiem; Broadcasts for BBC Radio 3 and Classic FM. *Address:* 109 Sugden Road, London SW11 5 ED, England.

**TURSKA, Joanna (Lucja);** Flautist; b. 16 Oct. 1958, Warsaw, Poland; m. Roman Siczek, 28 June 1986, 1 d. *Education:* MMus, Flute Performance, Warsaw Academy of Music; Postgraduate Studies; Royal Conservatory, The Hague, Netherlands; Conservatories in Creteil and Paris, France; Teachers include E Gajewska, F Vester, A Marion (flute), S T Preston, P Sechet (baroque flute). *Career:* Appearances at recitals, chamber music concerts and as soloist with orchestras in Europe and America including: Germany, France, Italy, Switzerland, Austria, Netherlands, Belgium, Luxembourg, Poland, Cuba, USA; Performances at such festivals as Paris, Youth Music Festival (Bayreuth, Germany), Warsaw Autumn, New Music Festival and Early Music Festival (Chicago, USA). *Recordings:* Solo, chamber music and orchestral performances recorded by Polish radio and television, Belgian radio, French radio, and US radio, television Classical and ethnic channels; Album for winners of Premio Ancona competitions. *Address:* 1426 Portsmouth, Westchester, IL 60153, USA.

**TUSA, Andrew;** singer (tenor); b. 1966, England. *Education:* New College, Oxford, Pears-Britten School. *Career:* sang in the Play of Daniel at the Queen Elizabeth Hall 1989, followed by Asterion in Rameau's Nais for the English Bach Festival; Concert engagements include Messiah with the Leicester Bach Choir, St John Passion in Krefeld, soloist with Gothic Voices in Milan and Second Shepherd in Monteverdi's Orfeo at the 1990 Salzburg Festival; Appearances with the Gabrieli and Taverner Consorts, Christmas Oratorio under Andrew Parrott in Oslo, Masses by Mozart in Barbican Hall, 1991, St Matthew Passion with Birmingham Bach Society and Messiah with the Stavanger Symphony in Norway. *Recordings include:* Mozart's Salzburg Masses with the Winchester College Choir and Monteverdi Madrigals with I Fagiolini. *Current Management:* Robert Gilder & Co., Enterprise House, 59–65 Upper Ground, London, SE1 9PQ, England. *Telephone:* (20) 7928-9008. *Fax:* (20) 7928-9755. *E-mail:* rgilder@robert-gilder.com.

**TUSA, Sir John,** Kt, MA; British broadcaster and administrator; *Managing Director, Barbican Centre;* b. 2 March 1936, Zlín, Czechoslovakia (now Czech Repub.); s. of Jan Tusa and Lydie Sklenarova; m. Ann Hilary Dowson 1960; two s. *Education:* Gresham's School, Holt, Trinity Coll., Cambridge. *Career:* joined BBC as general trainee 1960; Producer, Talks and Features, BBC World Service 1964–66; Ed., Forum World Features 1966–67; Presenter, The World Tonight, Radio 4 1970–78, 24 Hours, BBC World Service 1972–78, Newsweek, BBC2 1978–79, Newsnight, BBC2 1979–86, Timewatch, BBC2 1982–84, One O'Clock News BBC 1993–95; Chair. London News Radio 1993–94; Pres. Wolfson Coll., Cambridge Feb.–Oct. 1993; Man. Dir BBC World Service 1986–92; Man. Dir Barbican Centre 1995–; Chair. Advisory Cttee, Govt Art Collection 1993, BBC Marshall Plan of the Mind Trust 1992–99; mem. Bd ENO 1994–2005; Freeman City of London 1997; Trustee Nat. Portrait Gallery 1988–2000, Design Museum 1998–2000, British Museum 2000–; Chair. Wigmore Hall Trust 1999–; Visiting Prof., Dept of Arts Policy and Man., City Univ. *Publications:* The Nuremberg Trial 1983 (with Ann Tusa), The Berlin Blockade (with Ann Tusa) 1988, Conversations with the World 1990, A World in Your Ear 1992, Art Matters 1999, On Creativity 2003. *Honours:* Hon. mem. RAM 1999, Guildhall School of Music and Drama 1999; Order of the White Rose (Finland) 1998; Dr hc (Heriot-Watt) 1993; Hon. LLD (London) 1993; Hon. DLitt (City Univ.) 1997; Royal TV Soc. (RTS) TV Journalist of the Year 1984, BAFTA Richard Dimbleby Award 1984, Broadcasting Press Guild Award 1991, RTS Presenter of the Year 1995, Broadcasting Press Guild Radio Programme of the Year (for 20/20 – A View of the Century) 1995. *Address:* Barbican Centre, Silk Street, London, EC2Y 8DS, England (office). *Telephone:* (20) 7382-7001 (office). *Fax:* (20) 7382-7245 (office); (20) 7704-2451. *Website:* www.barbican.org.uk.

**TUTINO, Marco;** Composer; b. 30 May 1954, Milan, Italy. *Education:* Studied at the Giuseppe Verdi Conservatory, Milan. *Career:* Works performed at the 1976 Gaudeamus Festival in Amsterdam; Operas produced in Genoa, Alessandria, Livorno and Modena. *Compositions:* A synthesis between 19th century procedures and more modern methods. *Compositions include:* Operas Pinnochio, Genoa 1985; Cirano, commedia lirica, Alessandria 1987; La lupa, Livorno 1990; Le vite immaginarie, chamber opera, Modena 1990. *Address:* c/o Sezione Musica, Viale della Letteratura n.30, 00144 Roma (EUR), Italy.

**TUVÅS, Linda;** Singer (Soprano); b. 1972, Stockholm, Sweden. *Education:* Studied at Stockholm University, the Birkagarden School of Music and the Guildhall School, London. *Career:* Engagements as Mozart's Donna Anna and Fatima in Grétry's Zémire et Azor at Drottningholm and the Théâtre Champs-Elysées, Paris; Kate Pinkerton, Jano in Jenůfa and Micaela (Carmen) for Gothenburg Opera; Further roles as Musetta for Welsh National Opera, Tatiana for British Youth Opera and the title role in Il Segretto di Susanna for Newbury Opera; Also sings Massenet's Grisélidis, Arminda in La Finta Giardiniera by Mozart, and Offenbach's Giulietta; Sang Barbarina in Le nozze di Figaro at the 1997 Glyndebourne Festival; Season 1998 as Amor in Poppea for WNO, Varvara (Katya Kabanova) for the Glyndebourne Opera. *Address:*

c/o Neil Dalrymple, Music International, 13 Ardilaun Road, London N5 2QR, England.

**TWARDOWSKI, Romuald,** (Adam Lass), DipMus; Polish composer; *Professor, Warsaw Academy of Music*; b. 17 June 1930, Wilno; m. Alice Stradczuk 1981; one s. *Education:* Wilno Conservatory, Higher School of Music, Warsaw, studied with Nadia Boulanger in Paris. *Career:* Prof., Warsaw Acad. of Music. *Compositions include:* opera: Cyrano de Bergerac 1963, Tragedy 1969, Lord Jim 1976, Maria Stuart 1979, Story of St Catherine 1985; works for orchestra, choirs, theatre, cinema: Old Polish Concerto for strings 1988, Little Concerto for vocal orchestra 1988, Michelangelo Sonnets for baritone and piano 1988, Lithuanian Variations for winds/quartet 1988, Niggunim for violin and orchestra 1991. *Recordings include:* Gershwin Variations for symphony orchestra (Polish Radio, Kraków) 1980, Spanish Fantasy for cello and orchestra (Polish Radio, Warsaw), Alleluia for mixed choir 1990, Espressioni for violin and piano 1990, Niggunim, chassidim tunes for violin and piano or orchestra, numerous recordings of own compositions. *Publication:* It Has Been, It Has Not Passed (biog.) 2000. *Honours:* Grand Prix, Monaco 1965, 1973, first prize Prague Spring Competition 1966, Order of Polonia Restituta. *Address:* ul Miaczynska 54 m 61, 02-637 Warsaw, Poland (home). *Telephone:* (22) 8483862 (home).

**TYL, Noel;** Singer (Baritone); b. 31 Dec. 1936, West Chester, Pennsylvania, USA. *Career:* Studied with Gibner King in New York. *Address:* New York City Opera, Lincoln Center, New York, NY 10023, USA.

**TYLER, James;** Lutenist and Viol Player; b. 3 Aug. 1940, Hartford, CT, USA. *Education:* Hartt College of Music. *Career:* Debut: New York Pro Musica, 1962; Appearances with early music ensembles in USA and Europe, including Studio der Frühen Musik, Munich; Early Music Consort, London, and Musica Reservata from 1969; Co-founded the Consort of Musicke and was co-director until 1972; Julian Bream Consort, 1974–; Founded London Early Music Group 1976, with performances of Renaissance Music, Director of Early Music Program at UCLA, from 1986. *Publications include:* The Early Guitar, 1980; A Brief Tutor for the Baroque Guitar, 1984; Edition, Gasparo Xanetti's II scolaro, 1984; Mixed ensembles, in A Performer's Guide to Renaissance Music, 1994. *Address:* c/o Early Music Program, University of California LA, 5151 State University Drive, Los Angeles, CA 90032, USA.

**TYLER, Marilyn;** Singer (soprano); b. 6 Dec. 1928, New York, NY, USA. *Education:* studied with Friedrich Schorr in New York and with Toti dal Monte in Venice. *Career:* sang first in operetta; Basle Opera 1948; Netherlands Opera 1955, as Violetta; sang title role in Die Entführung; Bayreuth; Bayreuth 1961, Brünnhilde in Die Walküre; appearances in Italy, Germany, North America and Israel. *Recordings include:* Die Zauberflöte, Die Entführung, Serse by Handel, Stravinsky's Pulcinella.

**TYNAN, Kathleen;** Soprano; b. 1960, Ireland. *Education:* Royal Irish Academy of Music, Dublin; Guildhall School of Music and Drama, London. *Career:* Selected by RTE, representative Ireland, Cardiff Singer of the World Competition, 1987; Sang for Opera Theatre Company, Expo '98, Lisbon; Cork Opera House; Performed songs with pianist Dearbhla Collins and Irish Piano Trio in recitals, Theatre Royal, Wexford, Belfast Waterfront Hall, RHA Gallery, Dublin, Boyle Arts Festival, St James's, Picadilly; New work for voice and electronics by Fergus Johnston, 2000; Opera Ireland; Wexford Festival Opera; RTE television production Riders to the Sea; Opera South, Cork; Olympia Theatre, Dublin; Opera Theatre Company, Dublin; Queen Elizabeth Hall, London; Toured France; Bermuda Festival for MidSummer Opera; Sang Marzelline for new adaptation in English, Zulu and Afrikaans, Broomhill Opera/Opera Africa, with Northern Sinfonia; Toured the United Kingdom extensively; Extensive concert and song recital; London Festival orchestra; St John's Smith Square; Liverpool Cathedral Festival; National Symphony Orchestra, Ireland; Concerts with RTE Concert Orchestra; Presented recitals for music network, Ireland; Broadcasts for BBC Radio Ulster. *Recordings:* Debut CD, Romancing Rebellion. *Address:* 63 Dominic Street, Shandon, Ireland.

**TYNES, Margaret;** Singer (Soprano); b. 11 Sept. 1929, Saluda, Virginia, USA. *Education:* Studied with Emil Cooper in New York and with Tullio Serafin in Italy. *Career:* Debut: New York City Opera 1952, as Fata Morgana in The Love for Three Oranges; Montreal 1959, as Lady Macbeth; Has sung in Spoleto (as Salome), Vienna, Budapest, Toronto, Milan, Prague, Naples and Bologna; Metropolitan Opera debut 1973, as Jenůfa; Other roles have included Norma, Aida, Desdemona, Dido and Marie in Wozzeck; Many concert appearances.

**TYREN, Arne;** Singer (Bass-Baritone); b. 27 Feb. 1928, Stockholm, Sweden. *Education:* Studied with Ragnar Hulten at the Stockholm Opera School. *Career:* Debut: Royal Opera Stockholm 1955, as Bartolo in Le Nozze di Figaro; Has sung in Scandinavia as Leporello, Baron Ochs, the Grand Inquisitor, Sarastro and Wozzeck; Drottningholm Festival from 1955, as Bartolo in Paisiello's Il Barbiere di Siviglia, Don Alfonso, Il Maestro di Capella, Buonafede in Haydn's Il Mondo della luna and Seneca in L'Incoronazione di Poppea; Sang at Stockholm in the premieres of Blomdahl's Aniara (1959) and Herr von Hancken (1965) and Tintomara by Werle (1973); Edinburgh Festival 1959, Wozzeck; Further engagements in Hamburg, Cologne, Turin, Lisbon and Tel-Aviv; Director of the Stockholm Opera School from 1977. *Recordings include:* Aniara (Columbia). *Honours:* Swedish Court Singer 1978. *Address:* Opera School, Kungliga Teatern, PO Box 16094, 10322, Stockholm, Sweden.

**TYRRELL, John,** BMus; musicologist; *Professor, Cardiff University*; b. 17 Aug. 1942, Salisbury, Southern Rhodesia. *Education:* Univ. of Cape Town, Univ. of Oxford. *Career:* fmr Assoc. Ed., Musical Times; editorial staff mem., New Grove Dictionary of Music –1976; Lecturer, Nottingham Univ. 1976, Reader in Opera Studies 1989; Exec. Ed., The New Grove Dictionary of Music and Musicians second edn 1996–2001; Professorial Research Fellow, Cardiff Univ. 2000, Prof. in the School of Music, Cardiff Univ. 2003–. *Publications include:* Leoš Janáček: Kát'a Kabanová 1982, Czech Opera 1988, Janáček's Operas: A Documentary Account 1992, Intimate Letters: Leoš Janáček to Kamila Stösslová (ed. and trans.) 1994, Leoš Janáček: Jenůfa (co-ed.) 1996, Janáček's Works: A Catalogue of the Music and Writings of Leoš Janáček (co-author) 1997, My Life with Janáček: The Memoirs of Zdenka Janáčková (ed. and trans.) 1998. *Honours:* Dr hc (Masaryk Univ. of Brno) 2002. *Address:* School of Music, University of Cardiff, 31 Corbett Road, Cardiff, CF10 3EB, Wales. *Website:* www.cardiff.ac.uk/music/people/JT.html; www.czechmusic.co.uk.

**TYRRELL, Lisa (Jane);** Soprano; b. 7 June 1967, Salford. *Education:* Chetham's School of Music, Manchester: Entered as a singer aged 11 years, 2nd study, piano; Drama, Guildhall School of Music, London; Banff Centre, School of Fine Arts, Canada. *Career:* Debut: Pamina in Die Zauberflöte, English Touring Opera, 1990; Zerlina in Don Giovanni with the English Touring Opera; Lace Seller in Death in Venice at Glyndebourne Festival Opera; Semire in Les Boreádes, Birmingham Touring Opera; Judith in European Story, Garden Venture (Covent Garden); Naiad in Ariadne auf Naxos, Garsington Opera; Euridice in Orfeo, Scottish Opera-go-Round; Debut at the Welsh National Opera in The Doctor of Myddfai; as the Child, a new opera written by Peter Maxwell Davies; Debut at the Royal Opera, Covent Garden as Barbarina in The Marriage of Figaro; *Concerts include:* St John Passion in Salzburg, Handel's Messiah in St John's Smith Square; Concerts with Fretwork at St John's; Monteverdi Vespers; Ariadne auf Naxos at Endellion Festival, with Richard Hickox; Vivaldi's Gloria at St Paul's Cathedral and Brazil; Brahms' Requiem; The Fairy Queen, ENO Bayliss Programme; New commission by Peter Maxwell Davies, with Scottish Chamber Orchestra, 1997; Janáček's Vixen with City of Birmingham Touring Opera, 1998. *Honours:* Associate (with distinction) of G S M D, 1989; Wyburd Trust Award (for advanced lieder study), 1990; Wingate Scholar, 1996; Channel 4 at G S M D; Also BBC Film with Peter Skellern, Where Do We Go From Here, following students of Chetham's. *Address:* c/o Music International, 13 Ardilaun Road, London, N5 2QR, England.

**TZINCOCA, Remus;** Conductor and Composer; b. 1920, Iassy, Romania; m. Anisia Campos. *Education:* Iassy Conservatory of Music, Conservatoire National Superieur de Musique de Paris; disciple and musical assistant of George Enescu. *Career:* debut, led Colonne Orchestra with George Enescu as soloist, Paris; Conducted major orchestras in Europe and North America including: London Philharmonic, Zürich Tonhalle, Lamoureux, Pasdeloup and Colonne in Paris, Radiotelevision Francaise, New York Philharmonic, Cleveland Orchestra, CBC Orchestra, Bucharest Philharmonic; Radio Television and Bucharest Opera; Founder, Musical Director, Newport Music Festival, Rhode Island, USA; Founder, Musical Director, New York Orchestra da Camera, with concerts at Metropolitan Museum, Carnegie Hall and Town Hall; Discovered with Anisia Campos, original version, in Romanian, of Bartók's Cantata Profana, in New York Bartók Archives and gave premiere in Bucharest with the Philharmonic Orchestra, 1984. *Compositions:* oratorios, symphonies, lieder and a Byzantine Mass. *Address:* 632 Avenue Herve-Beaudry, Laval, QC H7E 2X6, Canada.

# U

**UCHIDA, Mitsuko;** Japanese pianist; *Artist-in-Residence, Cleveland Orchestra*; b. 20 Dec. 1948, Tokyo; d. of Fujio Uchida and Yasuko Uchida. *Education:* Vienna Acad. of Music with Prof. R. Hauser. *Career:* debut Vienna 1963; recitals and concerto performances with all major London orchestras, Chicago Symphony, Boston Symphony, Cleveland Orchestra, Berlin Philharmonic, Vienna Philharmonic, New York Philharmonic, Los Angeles Philharmonic and others; played and directed the cycle of 21 Mozart piano concertos with the English Chamber Orchestra, London 1985–86; gave US premiere of piano concerto Antiphonies by Harrison Birtwistle 1996; Perspectives recital series at Carnegie Hall 2003; Co-Dir Marlboro Music Festival; Artist-in-Residence, Cleveland Orchestra 2002–. *Recordings include:* Mozart Complete Piano Sonatas and 21 Piano Concertos (English Chamber Orchestra and Jeffrey Tate), Chopin Piano Sonatas, Debussy 12 Etudes, Schubert Piano Sonatas, Beethoven Piano Concertos, Schoenberg Piano Concerto. *Honours:* Hon. CBE 2001; First Prize Beethoven Competition Vienna 1969, Second Prize Chopin Competition Warsaw 1970, Second Prize Leeds Competition 1975, Gramophone Award (Mozart Piano Sonatas) 1989, Gramophone Award (Schoenberg Piano Concerto) 2001, Royal Philharmonic Soc.'s Instrumentalist Award 2004. *Current Management:* Van Walsum Management Ltd, 4 Addison Bridge Place, London, W14 8XP, England. *Telephone:* (20) 7371-4343. *Fax:* (20) 7371-4344. *Website:* www.vanwalsum.co.uk.

**UDAGAWA, Hideko;** Japanese violinist; b. 1960. *Education:* Tokyo Univ. of Arts,Juilliard School of Music, New York, studied with Nathan Milstein in London. *Career:* orchestral debut with London Symphony Orchestra under Sir Charles Mackerras, playing Bruch's G minor concerto, Barbican Hall, London; television appearances and radio broadcasts, concerts in USA and Europe; recitals at Queen Elizabeth Hall, Lincoln Center; concerto performances with London Symphony Orchestra, the Philharmonia, the Royal, London and Liverpool Philharmonics, the City of Birmingham Symphony, the English Chamber and the Polish Chamber Orchestras, Berlin Symphony and the Bucharest Philharmonic Orchestra. *Recordings:* virtuoso violin pieces, Heifetz Transcriptions, Brahms and Bruch Concertos with Charles Mackerras and London Symphony, Aram Khachaturian Sonata and Dances 2005. *Current Management:* c/o Deborah Meyer, Grant Rogers Musical Artists' Management, 8 Wren Crescent, Bushey Heath, Hertfordshire WD23 1AN, England. *Telephone:* (20) 8950-2220. *Fax:* (20) 8950-3570. *E-mail:* dmeyer@ngrartists .com. *Website:* www.NGRArtists.com; www.hidekoudagawa.com.

**UDALOVA, Irina;** Singer (Soprano); b. 1957, Nikolaevsk na, Amur, Russia. *Education:* Studied at the Kishinev Conservatory. *Career:* Sang in opera at Aschchabad, Turkmenistan, notably as Tatiana, Iolanta, Amelia (Ballo in Maschera) and Nedda; Bolshoi Opera, Moscow, from 1985, as Militrissa in The Tale of Tsar Sultan, and Tchaikovsky's Lisa and Maid of Orleans; Guest with the Bolshoi at Glasgow 1990 and elsewhere as Voyslada in Rimsky's Mlada. *Recordings include:* Judith by Serov (Melodya). *Address:* c/o Bolshoi Theatre, 103009 Moscow, Russia.

**UEHARA, Ayako;** Japanese pianist; b. 1980, Takamatsu. *Education:* Yamaha Music School, Yamaha masterclass, studied with Fumiko Eguchi, Shinji Urakabe, Vera Gornostaeva. *Career:* concert debut with Nat. Symphony Orchestra, Tokyo 1994; concert performances with orchestras, including Japan PO, Moscow SO, Moscow Radio SO, Russian Nat. SO, Washington Nat. SO, Prague SO, Bamberg SO, LSO, Dresden Philharmonic, Toscanini Philharmonic; toured Australia with Sydney SO and Paavo Jarvi, Japan with Berlin Radio Orchestra and Marek Janowski; recitals at Wigmore Hall, London, Fondo per l'Ambiente Italiano, Ruhrgebiet Piano Festival, Int. Chopin Festival, Poland, Dubrovnik Festival, Croatia, Tokyo Opera City Recital Hall. *Recording:* Tchaikovsky Grand Sonata 2003. *Honours:* first prize Int. Competition for Young Pianists, Ettlingen, Germany, second prize Sydney Int. Piano Competition 2000, second prize Hamamatsu Int. Piano Competition 2000, first prize Int. Tchaikovsky Competition, Moscow 2002. *Current Management:* c/o Wray Armstrong, IMG Artists, Lovell House, 616 Chiswick High Road, London, W4 5RX, England. *Telephone:* (20) 7957-5000 (office). *Fax:* (20) 7957-5801 (office). *E-mail:* warmstrong@imgartists.com (office). *Website:* www.imgartists.com (office).

**UGORSKI, Anatol;** Pianist; b. 28 Sept. 1942, Leningrad, Russia. *Education:* Studied at the Leningrad Conservatoire. *Career:* From 1962 has given many concerts and recitals, including works by Boulez, Messiaen, Berg and Schoenberg; Teacher at the Leningrad Conservatoire from 1982, Resident in Germany, 1990.

**UHLIK, Tomislav;** Composer and Conductor; b. 24 Oct. 1956, Zagreb, Croatia; m. Lidija; one s. one d. *Education:* Theory of Music, 1981, Conducting, 1989, Zagreb Music Acad. *Career:* Music Dir, Lado Folklore Ensemble, 1983–85; Conductor, Komedija Theatre, Zagreb, 1992–; regular guest conductor of the symphonic wind orchestra of the Croatian army; mem., Croatian Composers' Asscn. *Compositions:* Six Episodes for Wind Quintet, 1986; The Body of Our Lord (liturgical cantata for folk choir and tambouras), 1990; Divertimento for Strings, 1991; Melancholy Variations for Harp Solo, 1991; Don Quixote and Dulcinea, for cello and double bass; Concerto for Horn and Wind Orchestra, 1997. *Honours:* First Prize for the Nocturne, for mixed choir a cappella, Matetic Days Festival in Ronjgi, 1988; Croatian Ministry of

Culture Award, for Hymne for Soprano and Orchestra. *Address:* 10010 Zagreb, Varicakova 4, Croatia.

**UHRMACHER, Hildegard;** singer (soprano); b. 15 Dec. 1939, Mönchen Gladbach, Germany. *Education:* Studied in Waldniel and Düsseldorf. *Career:* debut, Deutsche Oper am Rhein, 1964, as Vespina in Haydn's L'Infedeltà delusa; Sang at Kassel Opera, 1967–73, Hamburg from 1974, Munich, 1970–78; Further appearances at Vienna, Amsterdam, Florence and Cardiff; Staatsoper Stuttgart, 1981–89; Roles have included Salome, The Queen of Night, Constanze, Zerbinetta, Gilda, Traviata, Musetta and Flotow's Martha; Düsseldorf, 1995, as Hanna Glawari and Mannheim, 1996 in Amandas Traum by Harold Weiss; Modern repertoire also includes Zimmermann's Die Soldaten (Hanover, 1989) and works by Dessau and Britten.

**ULBRICH, Andrea (Edina);** Hungarian singer (mezzo-soprano); b. Budapest; d. of József Ulbrich and Eva Mészdros; one s. *Education:* Budapest Music Academy. *Career:* has sung with the Hungarian National Opera at Budapest from 1988, notably as Nicklausse in Les Contes d'Hoffmann, Sextus in Clemenza di Tito, Mercédès in Carmen and as Flotow's Nancy; Frankfurt, 1991, in a concert of Franchetti's Cristoforo Colombo; Guest at Ludwigshafen, 1992, as Cherubino; Dorabella (Così fan tutte), Olga (Onegin), Judith (Bluebeard's Castle), Octavian (Der Rosenkavalier), Rosina (Barber of Seville), Dryad (Ariadne auf Naxos), Priestess (Aida), Mirinda in Cavalli's Ormindo, Angelina (La Cenerentola), Lolette (La Rondine-Puccini) and others; Guest at Deutsche Oper Berlin, Oper Frankfurt, Brüssel, Klagenfurt, Wiener Konzerthaus, appearing as Amneris in Verdi's Aida, Eboli in Verdi's Don Carlos, Cuniza in Verdi's Oberto and Melibea in Rossini's Il Viaggio a Leims, La Principessa in Puccini's Suor Angelica, Sara in Donizetti's Robert Devereux; has sung with the Deutsche Operam Rhein from 1996. *Recordings include:* La Canterina, Haydn; Donizetti and Rossini songs and duets; Opera Gala, Berlin; Die Hochzeit des Camacho, Mendelssohn; Serenata, Scarlatti; opera film Così fan tutte (Mozart). *Honours:* Prizewinner at the Dvořák Competition, Prague and Paris competition; Belvedere Competition, Vienna; Mandi Prize Fondation from Hungarian State Opera, 1989; Grand Prix, Brussels Bel Canto competition, 1990; Béla Bartók-Pasztory Ditta Prix, 1992; Mihaly Szekely Prize, 1994. *Address:* c/o Hungarian National Opera, Népöztársaság utja 22, 1061 Budapest, Hungary. *Telephone:* (1) 3848658 (home). *Fax:* (1) 3848658 (home).

**ULEHLA, Ludmila;** Composer and Pianist; b. 20 May 1923, Flushing, NY. *Education:* Manhattan School of Music, with Vittorio Giannini. *Career:* Professor of Manhattan School from 1947; Chairperson of Composition Department, 1970–89. *Compositions include:* Piano Concerto, 1947; Violin Concerto, 1948; Two Piano Sonatas, 1951, 1956; String Quartet, 1953; Music for Minstrels, 1969; Michelangelo: A Tone Portrait, 1970; Five Around for ensemble, 1972; In Memoriam, piano trio, 1972; Fountains, Castles and Gardens, for soprano, clarinet and keyboard, 1977; The Great God Pan for chorus and flute, 1979; Temple at Abydos for trombone, harp, woodwind and strings, 1981; Inspirations from Nature, for piano, 1985; Symphony in Search of Sources, 1990; Bassoon Sonata, 1992; Sybil of the Revolution, chamber opera, 1993; Mississippi for flute, trombone, guitar and percussion, 1995; Visions, for ensemble, 1997; Undersea Fantasy, for orchestra, 1999; Vivo, for orchestra, 1999. *Honours:* Awards and Grants from ASCAP. *Address:* c/o ASCAP, ASCAP Building, One Lincoln Plaza, New York, NY 10023, USA. *Telephone:* 001 212 621 6000. *Fax:* 001 212 724 9064.

**ULFUNG, Ragnar;** Singer (Tenor); b. 28 Feb. 1927, Oslo, Norway; Opera Producer. *Education:* Studied at the Oslo Conservatory and in Milan. *Career:* Debut: Sang in concert from 1949; first stage role in Menotti's The Consul, Oslo, 1952; Member of Royal Opera Stockholm from 1958; Sang Renato in Un Ballo in Maschera at Covent Garden 1960; Sang Don Carlos at Covent Garden for two seasons, 1963–64; Returned in the premiere of Maxwell Davies's Taverner, 1972 and as Mime in the Götz Friedrich production of the Ring, 1974–6; Metropolitan Opera debut 1972, as Mime; Later sang Strauss's Herod, Wagner's Loge, Berg's Captain and Weill's Fatty in New York; Other appearances include Strauss's Liebe der Danaë and Penderecki's Die schwarze Maske in Santa Fe, as Kent in Reimann's Lear in San Francisco and Tom Rakewell in The Rake's Progress; Concert performances of Messiaen's St Francois d'Assise in London and Lyon; Sang Herod in Salome at San Francisco 1986; Paris Opéra and Geneva 1988, as Shuisky (Boris Godunov) and in The Fiery Angel; Alfred in Die Fledermaus as Oslo, 1988; Festival Hall London 1989, Aegisthus in Elektra; Herod at Los Angeles; Valzacchi in Der Rosenkavalier at Santa Fe 1989; Sang Goro in Butterfly at Lyon, 1990; Season 1992 as the Witch in Hansel and Gretel at Los Angeles, Fatty in Mahagonny at Geneva and Valzacchi in Rosenkavalier at the Santa Fe Festival; Debut as stage director Santa Fe 1973, with La Bohème; Other stagings include Lulu for Santa Fe, Otello in Stockholm and Der Ring des Nibelungen in Seattle; Sang Hauk in The Makropulos Case, Chicago, 1995; Bill Poster in US premiere of A Dream Play by Lindberg, Santa Fe, 1998; Sang Aegisthus in Elektra at Santa Fe, 2000. *Recordings include:* Monostatos in Ingmar Bergman's version of Die Zauberflöte. *Address:* c/o Santa Fe Opera, PO Box 2408, Santa Fe, NM 87504, USA.

**ULIVIERI, Nicola;** Singer (Baritone); b. 1972, Italy. *Education:* Graduated Claudio Monteverdi Conservatory, 1992. *Career:* Debut: Wolf-Ferrari's I Quattro Rusteghi, 1993; Appearances from 1995 as Conte Robinson in Il matrimonio Segreto and Don Giovanni; Rotta's La notte di un nevrastenico at Cosenza and Spoleto; Guido in Mercadante's Elena da Feltre at the 1997 Wexford Festival; Season 1998 as Publio in La Clemenza di Tito at Ferrara and Don Giovanni at Cologne and on tour in Europe. *Recordings include:* Dottor Mangiacarta in Spontini's Li puntigli delle donne; Guido in Elena da Feltre. *Honours:* Winner, 1995 Belli Competition at Spoleto and Riccardo Zandonai Competition at Rovereto. *Address:* c/o AMP Productions, Conso di Porta Ticinese 89, 1–20123 Milan, Italy.

**ULLMANN, Elisabeth;** Austrian organist; *Professor, Mozarteum, Salzburg;* b. 20 April 1952, Zwettl; m. Prof. Bigenzahn 1981; one s. *Education:* music studies in Vienna, London and Salzburg. *Career:* debut: First Prize, Bach Competition, Leipzig 1976; has given numerous recitals and performed on radio and TV; Artistic Dir 20th Anniversary Int. Stift Zwettl Organ Festival, Austria; Prof., Mozarteum, Salzburg 1988–. *Recordings:* Muffat, Apparatus Complete (Diapason Award); Hindemith Organ Sonatas; Mozart, Complete Church Sonatas; Haydn, Great Organ Mass; Wagenseil, Concerti per organo; Gottlieb Muffat, Selected keyboard music. *Contributions:* Fono Forum. *Honours:* First Prize, Bruckner Competition 1978. *Address:* Bennoplace 8/28, 1080 Vienna, Austria. *E-mail:* elisabeth.bigenzahn-ullmann@moz.ac.at (office). *Website:* elisabeth-ullmann.at.

**ULLMANN, Jakob;** German composer, organist and philosopher; b. 12 July 1958, Freiberg. *Education:* studied in Naumburg 1975–78, School of Sacred Music, Dresden 1979–82; influenced by Schoenberg and John Cage; doctoral cand. 2003. *Compositions include:* Komposition for string quartet, 1985; Symmetries on Aleph Zero, 1–3, for ensemble, 1987; Ensemblekomposition, theatre music, 1986–; Alakata, for ensemble, 1989; Due Frammenti, for orchestra, 1990; Komposition I–III for orchestra, 1991, 1993, 1994; Meeting John Cage under the Tropic of the late Eighties, graphic score, 1990; Disappearing Musics, 1990; Pianissimo, for viola and electronics, 1990; Echoing A Distant Sound, for ensemble, 1991–93; A Catalogue of Sounds for 13 solo strings, 1996; voice, books and Fire I 1991–2004, voice, books and Fire II (1–5), graphic score 1991–2005, Solo (flute), Solo (trombone), Solo (organ) 1992–93, composition for string quarter 2 1997–99, kol 1 for ensemble 2000, kol 2 for ensemble 2001. *Address:* c/o GEMA, Rosenheimstr. 11, 8166 Munich, Germany (office). *Telephone:* (89) 4800300 (office); (30) 2858767 (home). *Fax:* (89) 48003495 (office); (30) 2858767 (home). *E-mail:* tloen_uqbar@gmx.de (home).

**ULLMANN, Marcus;** Singer (Tenor); b. 1970, Olbernhau, Germany. *Education:* Dresden Kreuzchor and Musikhochschule; Lieder classes with Dietrich Fischer-Dieskau. *Career:* Concerts and opera with Helmuth Rilling (Bach B minor Mass), Sylvain Cambreling, Leopold Hager and Peter Schreier; Orchestras include Bamberg SO, Staatskapelle Berlin and Dresden, Gewandhaus Orchestra, Munich PO and Salzburg Mozarteum; Sang in Schoenberg's Moses und Aron, under Kent Nagano, at the Vienna Konzerthaus, 2001; Festival appearances at Milan, Savonlinna, Philadelphia, Madrid, Utrecht and Salzburg. *Address:* c/o Wiener Konzerthaus, A–1010 Vienna, Austria.

**UNDERWOOD, John;** Violist; b. 11 Oct. 1932, Luton, Bedfordshire, England. *Education:* Studied with Frederick Riddle at the Royal College of Music. *Career:* Co-principal viola of the RPO under Beecham, 1962–62; Cofounder of the Delmé Quartet 1962; Many performances in the United Kingdom and Europe in the classical and modern repertory; Concerts at the Salzburg Festival and the Brahms Saal of the Musikverein Vienna; Season 1990 included Haydn's Seven Last Words in Italy and elsewhere, three Brahms programmes at St John's Smith Square with Iain Burnside, piano; Concerts at St David's Hall Cardiff with quartets by Tchaikovsky and Robert Simpson (premiere of 13th quartet); Appearances in Bremen, Hamburg and Trieste, followed by festival engagements, 1991; Other repertory includes works by Paul Patterson, Daniel Jones, Wilfred Josephs, Iain Hamilton and Bernard Stevens. *Recordings include:* Haydn Seven Last Words; Vaughan Williams On Wenlock Edge and Gurney's Ludlow and Teme; Simpson quartets 1–9 and String Trio (Hyperion); Daniel Jones 3 quartets and Bridge No. 2 (Chandos); Bliss Nos 1 and 2; Josef Holbrooke Piano Quartet and Clarinet Quintet (Blenheim); Brahms Clarinet Quintet and Dvořák F major (Pickwick); Verdi Quartet and Strauss A major Op 2 (Hyperion). *Address:* c/o J Williams, 33 Whittingstall Road, Fulham, London SW6, England.

**UNG, Chinary;** American composer; b. 24 Nov. 1942, Prey Lovea, Cambodia. *Education:* studied clarinet at the Manhattan School of Music; studied composition with Chou Wen-Chung at Columbia Univ. DMA, 1974. *Career:* Regents Prof. at Arizona State Univ., Tempe, 1987–95; Prof. of Music at Univ. of California at San Diego, 1995–. *Compositions include:* Tall Wind for soprano and ensemble, after e. e. cummings, 1969; Anicca for chamber orchestra, 1970; Mohori for mezzo and ensemble, 1974; Khse Buon for cello, 1979; Child Song I–VII for various instrumental ensembles, 1979–89; Inner Voices for chamber orchestra (Grawemeyer Award 1989), 1986; Grand Spiral 'Desert Flowers Bloom' for orchestra, 1993; Water Rings for chamber orchestra, 1993; Antiphonal Spirals for orchestra, 1995; '...Still Life after Death' for high voice and ensemble, 1995. *Honours:* Kennedy Center Friedheim Award, 1991; Koussevitszky Foundation Commission, 1992. *Address:* c/o ASCAP, ASCAP Building, 1 Lincoln Plaza, New York, NY 10023, USA.

**UNGER, Gerhard;** Singer (Tenor); b. 26 Nov. 1916, Bad Salzungen, Thuringia, Germany. *Education:* Studied at Eisenach and the Berlin Musikhochschule. *Career:* Sang lyric roles at Weimar from 1947, Tamino, Pinkerton and Alfredo; Bayreuth Festival 1951–52 as David in Die Meistersinger; Guest appearances at the Dresden Opera as Tamino and Pinkerton; Engaged at the Berlin Staatsoper from 1952, Stuttgart from 1982; Member of the Hamburg Staatsoper 1962–73, appearing also in Vienna, Milan, Paris, Metropolitan New York and London (Alwa in Lulu at Sadler's Wells, 1966); Salzburg Festival 1961–64, as Pedrillo in Die Entführung and Brighella in Ariadne auf Naxos; Character roles later in career (Captain in Wozzeck, Mime and Shuratov in From the House of the Dead) in Europe and North and South America (Mime at Dallas 1984); Bregenz Festival 1980 as Pedrillo, Stuttgart 1987 as Mime (last major role). *Recordings include:* Der Waffenschmied, Steuermann in Fliegende Holländer, Die Meistersinger, Alwa in Lulu; Die Entführung, Die Meistersinger; Fidelio, Königskinder by Humperdinck, Die Zauberflöte, Carmina Burana, Elektra, Ariadne auf Naxos, Der Rosenkavalier, Tannhäuser (EMI); La Finta Giardiniera. *Address:* c/o Stuttgart Staatsoper, Oberer Schlossgarten 6, 7000 Stuttgart, Germany.

**UNGVARY, Tamas;** Swedish/Hungarian composer, conductor, double bass player and teacher; b. 12 Nov. 1936, Kalocsa; one d. *Education:* Budapest, Mozarteum, Salzburg, Austria, Béla Bartók Conservatory, Budapest. *Career:* Solo Double Bass, Camerata Academica, Salzburg 1967–69; Composer at four ISCM Festivals; has broadcast on all major European radio stations; lecturer on computer music; Artistic Man. EMS, Stockholm, Sweden and Dir of Kinetoauditory Communication Research, Royal Inst. of Tech., Stockholm; Leader, EA-Music Courses, Vienna Univ. of Music and Performing Art 1992–. *Compositions include:* Seul, Traum des Einsamen, Akonel No. 2 for Flute and Tape, Interaction No. 2 for Organ and Tape, Ite missa est, Dis-Tanz for Ensemble and Tape, Istenem Uram! for Tape, Sentograffito, live computer music 1993, Grattis for Tape 1994, Recollection No. 1 1996. *Publications:* articles and book chapter on design of musical cyberinstruments published in scientific journals. *Honours:* Hon. Prof. (Austrian Govt) 1996–. *Address:* Hagalundsgatan 31, 16966 Solna, Sweden (home). *Telephone:* (8) 828991 (home). *Fax:* (8) 828991 (home). *E-mail:* ungvary@mdw.ac.at (home).

**UNRUH, Stan;** Singer (Tenor); b. 20 Nov. 1938, Beaver, Oklahoma, USA. *Education:* Studied at the Juilliard School, New York. *Career:* Debut: Geneva 1970, as Melot in Tristan; Appearances at Paris, Orange, Rouen, Bordeaux (Lohengrin 1979 and Aeneas 1980) and Toulouse; Member of the Krefeld Opera 1977–85, notably in Der Ring des Nibelungen; New York City Opera, 1976, as Erik in Der fliegende Holländer, Strasbourg 1977, as Parsifal; Further guest appearances at Barcelona, 1978, Brunswick and Innsbruck 1983, Buenos Aires, 1985 (Siegfried in Götterdämmerung) and Freiburg 1986, in the premiere of Hunger und Durst by Violeta Dinescu; Sang at the Staatstheater Kassel, 1989–90; Other roles include Wagner's Tristan, Siegmund, Loge and Walther von Stolzing, Florestan, Shuratov in From the House of the Dead, Max, Don José, Samson, Stravinsky's Oedipus and Bacchus. *Address:* Staatstheater, Friedrichplatz 15, 3500 Kassel, Germany.

**UNWIN, Nicholas,** ARCM, LGSM, DipRCM; British concert pianist; b. 1962, Cambridge, England. *Education:* studied at Royal Coll. of Music and with Philip Fowke. *Career:* played Bartók, Lambert and McCabe at the Purcell Room, London 1986; Bartók's 2nd Concerto at St John's Smith Square (also on BBC Radio 3); Wigmore Hall recital 1987; BBC recital 1989, followed by Univ. of Birmingham and Leeds Town Hall; Artist-in-Residence, King's Lynn Festival 1989, with Nights in the Gardens of Spain and Ravel's G major Concerto; BBC documentary on Michael Tippett 1990, playing the Second Sonata; specialised in Spanish music, culminating in Images of Iberia at Blackheath Concert Halls; performed Tippett in Madrid and Radio France, also at Barbican's Tippett Festival 1994; first work written for him by Luis De Pablo 1997. *Recordings:* Tippett Sonata 4, with Robert Saxton and Colin Matthews 1995, Tippett Sonatas 1–3 1995, Joaquin Nin: Piano Works 1998, Albeniz: Iberia 1999, Jean-Michel Damase: Piano Works 2003. *Honours:* Chappell Gold Medal and Cyril Smith Recital Prize, Royal Coll. of Music, Winner, Lambeth Music Award, Hastings Concerto Festival and Brant Piano Competition, Schott Award 1990. *E-mail:* nicholas@nicholasunwin.com (home). *Address:* Old Mill House, Langham, Colchester, CO4 5NU, England (home). *Website:* www.nicholasunwin.com (home).

**UPSHAW, Dawn,** MA; American singer (soprano); *Charles Franklin Kellogg and Grace E. Ramsey Kellogg Professor of the Arts and Humanities, Bard College Conservatory of Music;* b. 17 July 1960, Nashville, TN; m. Michael Nott 1986; one d. *Education:* Illinois Wesleyan Univ. and Manhattan School of Music, Metropolitan Opera School. *Career:* sang in the US premiere of Hindemith's Sancta Susanna 1983; joined young artists devt program at the Metropolitan Opera, New York after winning int. auditions sponsored by Young Concert Artists 1984; sang at the Met, appearing as Countess Ceprano, Echo (Ariadne), Adina, Despina, Susanna, Sophie (Werther), the Woodbird and Zerlina 1985–; has performed with major orchestras, opera cos and chamber groups in the USA and Europe, including the Netherlands Opera Co., Vienna opera, Hamburg (Germany) opera, Berlin Philharmonic, Los Angeles Philharmonic, Rotterdam Philharmonic (Netherlands) and Chicago Symphony Orchestras; festival appearances include Salzburg Festival as Barbarina 1987, as L'Ange in St Francois at Salzburg 1992, 1998, Clemene in Saariaho's L'Amour de loin 2000, Aix-en-Provence as Despina and Pamina 1988–89, Anne Trulove 1992, sang Pamina at the London Proms 1990, Judith Weir's Natural History 1999, sang Theodora at Glyndebourne 1996;

appearances include at the Barbican and at Covent Garden, London, at the Paris Châtelet; other roles include Marzelline (Fidelio), Constance in Les Dialogues des Carmélites, Mozart's Cherubino, Daisy in Harbison's The Great Gatsby, Janáček's Vixen; Charles Franklin Kellogg and Grace E. Ramsey Kellogg Prof. of the Arts and Humanities, Bard Coll. Conservatory of Music 2005–. *Operas include:* Rigoletto, Simon Boccanegra, Khovanshchina, Carmen, La Clemenza di Tito, Dialogues of the Carmelites, The Magic Flute 1985, Death in the Family 1986, Alice in Wonderland, The Marriage of Figaro (also on TV), L'elisir d'amore 1988, Così fan Tutte 1988, Idomeneo 1988–89, Werther 1988–89, Don Giovanni 1989–90. *Recordings include:* Ariadne auf Naxos, songs by Rachmaninov, Hugo Wolf, Richard Strauss, Charles Ives and Kurt Weill, songs and pieces by Samuel Barber, John Harbison, Stravinsky and Gian-Carlo Menotti (Grammy Award for Best Classical Vocal Soloist 1990), Bach's Magnificat and Vivaldi's Gloria 1989, Lucio Silla, L'elisir d'amore. *Honours:* jt first prize Naumburg Competition 1985. *Current Management:* IMG Artists, Lovell House, 616 Chiswick High Road, London, W4 5RX, England.

**URBAIN, Mady;** Singer (Mezzo-soprano); b. 27 April 1946, Montegnée, Belgium. *Education:* Studied at the Liège Conservatoire and in Vienna and Salzburg. *Career:* Sang at the Liège Opera from 1967, and made many guest appearances elsewhere in Belgium and throughout France; Roles have included Amneris, Preziosilla, Mistress Quickly, Carmen, Marcellina, Charlotte, Puccini's Princess (Suor Angelica) and Suzuki, Strauss's Adelaide and Mère Marie in The Carmélites; Concerts include Messiah, Bach's B Minor Mass, the Verdi Requiem and Beethoven's Ninth; Professor at the Grètry Academy, Liège, from 1970. *Address:* c/o Opéra de Wallonie, 1 Rue des Dominicains, 4000 Liège, Belgium.

**URBANNER, Erich;** Composer and Conductor; b. 26 March 1936, Innsbruck, Austria. *Education:* Vienna Music Academy, with Hans Swarowsky; Darmstadt courses, with Bruno Maderna and Karl-Heinz Stockhausen. *Career:* Professor at Vienna Music Academy, 1969–; Director of Institut für Electroakustik und Experimentelle Musik, 1986–89. *Compositions include:* String quartets nos 2 and 3, 1957, 1972; Piano Concerto, 1958; Flute Concertino, 1959; Der Gluckreich, comic opera, 1963; Oboe Concerto, 1966; Violin Concerto, 1971; Concerto "Wolfgang Amadeus," 1972; Sinfonietta 79, 1979; Cello Concerto, 1981; Requiem 1983; Ninive, oder Das Leben geht weiter, opera, 1987; Concerto for saxophone quartet and orchestra, 1989; Quasi una fantasia, for 15 instruments, 1993; Zyklus, for organ, 1993; Begegnung for 12 instruments, 1996; Formen in Wandel, piano, 1996. *Address:* c/o AKM, Baumannstr 10. 1031 Wien, Postfach 259, Austria. *Telephone:* 00431 717 140. *Fax:* 00431 717 14107/262/195.

**URBANOVÁ, Eva;** Czech singer (soprano); b. 20 April 1961, Slaný. *Education:* Acad. of Musical Arts. *Career:* opera début at Plzeň Josef Kajetan Tyl Theatre 1987; soloist, Plzeň Opera 1988–90; Chief of Opera Singer section, Conservatory Plzeň 1989; soloist, Nat. Theatre Prague 1990–, Metropolitan Opera, New York 1996–; charity concert tours with Karel Gott, Czech Repub. 1998; concert tours and opera performances in Canada, France, Italy, USA (Dvořák operas), Hong Kong (Janáček operas) and Germany (Verdi opera); charity concerts after floods in Czech Repub. 2002–. *Recordings:* Duets (with Karel Gott) 1998, Czech Opera Airs 1998, Czech Christmas Carols 2000. *Honours:* Classic Prize for propagation of Czech music in the world 1999. *Address:* Národní divadlo, National Theatre, Ostrovní 1, 110 00 Prague 1, Czech Republic (office). *Telephone:* (2) 24910312 (office). *Fax:* (2) 24911524 (office).

**URIA-MONZON, Beatrice;** Singer (Mezzo-soprano); b. 28 Dec. 1963, Agen, France. *Education:* Studied in Marseille and the Opera School of the Paris Opéra. *Career:* Debut: Nancy, 1989, as Cherubino; Lyon and Aix, 1989, as Smeraldine in The Love for Three Oranges by Prokofiev; Sang Mignon at Avignon, 1990, Charlotte in Werther, 1991; Berlioz's Béatrice at Toulouse and Marguerite in La Damnation de Faust at Bregenz, 1992; Carmen at the Opéra Bastille, 1993, at Buenos Aires and Verona; New productions of Carmen at St Etienne, and Toulouse (1997); Season 2000–01 as Carmen at Houston and the Vienna Staatsoper, Offenbach's Giulietta for the Festival d'Orange and Massenet's Hérodiade at St Etienne. *Recordings include:* Beethoven's Ninth; The Love for Three Oranges; Carmen. *Address:* c/o Théâtre du Capitole, Place du Capitole, 31000 Toulouse, France.

**URMANA, Violeta;** Lithuanian singer (mezzo-soprano); b. 1959. *Education:* Vilnius and Munich High Schools for Music. *Career:* sang at the Munich Opera from 1992; State Opera of Stuttgart 1994; Lucerne Opera as Princess Eboli, and Bayreuth as Waltraute 1994; Opéra Bastille and Ravenna Festival 1995, as Fenena in Nabucco; Season 1996 at La Scala as Wagner's Fricka and La Haine in Gluck's Armide; Azucena at the Deutsche Oper Essen; further roles include Santuzza, Preziosilla and Eboli in Don Carlos (Vienna Staatsoper); concerts include Das Lied von der Erde in Bologna and Bach's B minor Mass at Wuppertal 1996; season 1998 as Kundry at the Deutsche Oper Berlin, Eboli with the Royal Opera at Edinburgh, Bartók's Judith at Aix; Act II of Parsifal with Placido Domingo at St Petersburg; season 2000–01 as Azucena at La Scala, Adalgisa in Seville, Santuzza at Florence, Amneris in Geneva, Waltraute for the Bayreuth Festival and Kundry at the Met (debut role); sang Kundry at Covent Garden 2002; Les Troyens in Florence and Iphigénie en Aulide in Milan 2002; Ariadne auf Naxos, Metropolitan Opera, New York 2005. *Honours:* Premio della Critica Musicale 'Franco Abbiati' 2003. *Current Management:* Caecilia Lyric Department, Rennweg 15, 8001 Zürich, Switzer-

land. *Telephone:* (1) 221 33 88. *Fax:* (1) 211 71 82. *E-mail:* caecilia@caecilia-lyric.ch. *Website:* www.caecilia.ch.

**URRILA, Irma;** Singer (Soprano); b. 29 Jan. 1943, Helsinki, Finland. *Education:* Studied in Helsinki, Milan and Essen. *Career:* Debut: Helsinki 1964, as Mimi in La Bohème; Sang with the Finnish National Opera, notably as Pamina, and in the 1975 premiere of The Last Temptations by Jonas Kokkonen; Premiere of Antonio Bilbalo's Macbeth, Oslo, 1990; Sang throughout Scandinavia in concert and opera; Many broadcast appearances; Pamina in the film version of Die Zauberflöte, directed by Ingmar Bergman. *Recordings include:* Die Zauberflöte; The Last Temptations (DGG). *Honours:* Prize-winner in Competitions at Lonigo (1965) and Parma (1996). *Address:* c/o Finnish National Opera, PO Box 176, Helsingkatu 58, 002 51 Helsinki, Finland.

**URROWS, David Francis,** AB, MMus, DMA; American composer and music historian; b. 25 Oct. 1957, Honolulu, HI. *Education:* Brandeis Univ., Univ. of Edinburgh, UK, Boston Univ. *Career:* compositions performed, commissioned and broadcast in USA, Asia and Europe; lecturer at several US univs; organist and choral conductor. *Compositions:* String Quartet 1978, Piano Sonata 1979, A Midsummer Night's Dream (opera) 1980, Quintet for winds 1981, Three Vailima Episodes for soprano and string orchestra 1984, A New England Almanack for baritone and piano 1985, Sonata for oboe and harp 1985, Partita: Nun Komm, der Heiden Heiland for organ 1985, Sonata San Angelo for two violas 1986, Ricordanza dell Umbria for piano 1987, Lycidas (oratorio) 1987, Winterreise for soprano and chamber orchestra 1988, Sonata for violin and piano 1991, Epiphany Cantata 1993, Nova Gaudia 1997, Exaltabo te 2005. *Publications include:* Sea Ballads and Songs in Whalsay, Shetland 1983, The Choral Music of Christopher le Fleming 1986, Randall Thompson: A Bio-Bibliography 1991, Otto Dresel: Collected Vocal Music (ed.) 2002. *Address:* Department of Music and Fine Arts, Hong Kong Baptist University, Kowloon Tong, Hong Kong (office). *Telephone:* 3411-7596 (office). *Fax:* 3411-7870 (office). *E-mail:* urrows@hkbu.edu.hk (office).

**URSULEASA, Mihaela;** Romanian concert pianist; b. 1978, Brasov. *Education:* Brasov Music School with Stela Dragulin, Vienna Musikhochschule with Heinz Medjimorec. *Career:* Salzburg Festival debut with the Mozarteum Orchestra 1998; tour of Germany with the Acad. of St Martin in the Fields under Sir Neville Mariner 2000; London debut at South Bank Centre, Harrods Int. Piano Series 2002; European tour with the Gothenburg Symphony Orchestra under Neeme Järvi 2003; debut with RAI Torino, Hallé Orchestra, Bournemouth Symphony Orchestra 2003, Wigmore Hall debut 2004. *Honours:* winner Clara Haskil Int. Piano Competition 1995. *Address:* c/o Schmid UK, 4 Addison Bridge Place, London W14 8XP, England. *Website:* www.ursuleasa.com.

**URTEAGA, Irma;** Argentine composer and pianist; b. 7 March 1929, San Nicolás, Buenos Aires. *Education:* Nat. Conservatory and Instituto del Teatro Colón, Buenos Aires. *Career:* Prof., Instituto del Teatro Colón 1964–84 (Coach 1974–1978, Prof., Summer Courses 1985–93), Nat. Conservatory 1974–88; Coach, Opera from Ecuador 1986, 1987, 1988. *Compositions:* Piano Sonata 1968, String Quartet 1969, Ambitos, for orchestra 1970, Existenciales, for voice and piano 1974, Designios, for flute, clarinet, viola, and piano 1976, Expectacion for soprano and mixed choir 1977, Turbulencias, for violin and piano 1979, Suenos de Yerma, for mezzo and ensemble 1986, La maldolida, chamber opera 1987, El mundo del ser, for mezzo and orchestra 1990, Luz de mundos, for choir 1990, Los alumbramientos, for children choir or female choir string orchestra 1992, Escalénicas for piano 1992, Cánticos para sõnar, for voice and piano 1993, Marimba Concerto 1994, Tiempo de memorias for clarinet, violin and piano 1996, Variaciones sobre un tema de Beatriz Sosnik, for piano 1997, Aquellos villancicos, for choir 1999, Todavia Buenos Aires, for saxophone quartet 2000, Ayer del Buen Ayre, for piano 2001 (two-piano version 2004), Tangoforte, for violin, French horn and piano 2003 (violin, cello and piano version 2004), Mar verde, verde... for baritone, soprano and percussion 2004. *Address:* Rio Bamba 944, 6-C, 1116 Buenos Aires, Argentina. *Telephone:* (11) 48130435 (home). *Fax:* (11) 48130435 (home). *E-mail:* irmaurteaga@uolsinectis.com.ar (home). *Website:* www.musicaclasicaargentina.com (home).

**USHAKOVA, Natalia;** Singer (Soprano); b. 1969, Tashkent, Russia. *Education:* Graduated Munich Conservatoire, 1999. *Career:* Appearances with the Kirov Opera, St Petersburg, from 1998, as Maria in Mazeppa, Lyuba in Prokofiev's Semyon Kotko, Tatiana (Eugene Onegin) and Mozart's Countess and Donna Elvira; Sang with the Kirov Opera in Summer season at Covent Garden, 2000. *Honours:* Prizewinner, Wroclaw International (1993), 1st Pechkovsky, St Petersburg (1994) and Volkswagen (1997) Competitions. *Address:* c/o Kirov Opera, Mariinsky Theatre, 1 Theatre Square, St Petersburg, Russia.

**USPENSKY, Vladislav Aleksandrovich;** Russian composer and academic; *Professor of Composition, Leningrad State Conservatory;* b. 7 Sept. 1937, Omsk; s. of Alexander Grigoryevich Kolodkin and Vera Pavlovna Uspenskaya; m. Irina Yevgenyevna Taimanova 1963. *Education:* Leningrad State Conservatory. *Career:* postgrad. studies under Dmitri Shostakovich; teacher of music theory Leningrad State Conservatory 1965–67, Dean of Musicology 1967–72, Prof. of Composition 1982–; Guest Composer-in-Residence Seoul Univ., Korea 1995, Lima Univ., Peru 1997, Boston Univ. USA; Chair. Music Council of Cultural Cttee, St Petersburg Govt 1996–; Vice-Pres. Union of Composers of St Petersburg 1972–; Gen. Dir Int. Musical Children's Festival

1995–. *Compositions:* Phantasmagoria, Vepres, Requiem, Liturgie, Temperaments, Toccata, Sonata-Phantasia, States, Sonata for the Violin and Piano, Anna Karenina (musical), Trombone Concertino 1963, Double Piano Concerto 1965, Music for Strings and Percussion 1967, The War Against Salamanders (opera) 1967, To the Memory of a Hero (ballet) 1969, Intervention (opera) 1970, A Road to the Day (ballet) 1974, Symphonic Frescoes 1977, For You to the Sea (ballet) 1978, Nocturne for low voice and orchestra 1980, Expectation 1982, With You and Without You (oratorio) 1984, Cranes Flying (ballet) 1984, Towards the Light (symphony) 1985, Dedication (symphony) 1988, The Mushroom's Alarm (ballet) 1990, All Night Vigil 1990, The Departure of the Soul (funeral service) 1992, A Dithyramb of Love for two pianos and orchestra 1995, Trombone Concerto 1995, Concerto for low voice and orchestra 1997, Casanova in Russia (musical) 1998, Temptation of Jeanna (musical) 1999; music for plays, including Revizor, over 100 songs, music for films, theatre and TV productions. *Publication:* D. Shostakovich in My Life. *Honours:* People's Artist of Russia, D. Shostakovich Prize 1997, Order of Merit of Homeland 1998, Order of Catherine the Great 2002; music festival in his honour, St Petersburg autumn 2002. *Address:* Composers' Union, B. Morskaia 45, St Petersburg (office); Admiralteysky canal 5 Apt. 26, St Petersburg, Russia (home). *Telephone:* (812) 117-35-48 (office); (812) 117-74-35 (home). *Fax:* (812) 117-35-48 (office).

**USTVOLSKAYA, Galina Ivanovna;** Russian composer; b. 17 June 1919, Petrograd (now St Petersburg). *Education:* Leningrad Conservatory (pupil of Shostakovich). *Career:* teacher, then Prof. of Composition N. Rimsky-Korsakov School of Music in St Petersburg 1947–. *Compositions:* author of maj. orchestral compositions rarely performed in USSR up to late 1980s due to ban on contemporary sacred music, including five symphonies: 1 1955, 2 (Genuine Eternal Beauty) 1979, 3 (Jesus, Messiah, Rescue Us) 1983, 4 (Pray) 1987, 5 (Amen) 1989/90; also numerous compositions for different instruments and piano pieces, including Dona nobis pacem, for piccolo, tuba and piano 1970/71, Dies irae, for eight double basses, percussion and piano 1972/73, Benedictus qui Venit, for four flutes, four bassoons and piano 1974/75. *Address:* Prospect Gagarina 27, Apt. 72, 196135 St Petersburg, Russia (home). *Telephone:* (812) 373-15-12 (home).

# V

**VACCHI, Fabio;** Italian composer; b. 19 Feb. 1949, Bologna. *Education:* Bologna Conservatory, Tanglewood, USA. *Career:* has written for Berlin Philharmonic Orchestra, Teatro alia Scala, Opera Nat. de Lyon, Radio France, Opera Comique and Theatre du Chatelet, Paris, Nat. Symphony Orchestra, Washington, DC, Pittsburgh Orchestra, Wien Modem; compositions have been conducted and commissioned by Claudio Abbado, Ricardo Muti, Zubin Mehta, Kyung Hwa Chung, Daniel Harding, Sir Neville Marriner, Luciano Berio. *Compositions:* II Viaggio 1989, Luoghi immaginari 1987–92, La station thermale 1993, Dai Calanchi di Sabbiuno (by Claudio Abbado) (1997), Les Oiseaux de passage 1998, Quartette No. 3 (by Tokyo Quartett, Lully Award, USA 2002), Tre Veglie (Salzburger Festspiele 2000), film soundtrack II Mestiere delle armi, Dir Ermanno Olmi (David Donatello Prize 2002), Diario dello sdegno (by Riccardo Muti and Terra Comune, opening of the new Rome Auditorium 2002), II Letto della storia (Abbiati Prize) 2003; film soundtrack Gabrielle, Dir Patrice Chereau 2005. *Honours:* Koussevitsky Prize for Composition, Tanglewood, 1974. *Address:* c/o BMG RICORDI, Via Berchet 2, 20121 Milan, Italy. *Telephone:* (2) 88812257. *Fax:* (2) 88812323.

**VACEK, Milos;** Composer; b. 20 June 1928, Horni Roven, Pardubice, Czechoslovakia. *Education:* Studied at the Prague Conservatory, 1942–47; Academy of Musical Arts, 1947–51. *Career:* Freelance composer from 1954. *Compositions include:* Operas Jan Zelivsky, composed 1956–58, performed Olomouc 1984; Brother Zak, Ostrava, 1982; Romance of the Bugle, Ceske Budejovice 1987; Mikes the Tomcat, Brno 1986; Ballets: The Comedian's Fairytale, 1958, Wind in the Hair, 1961, The Mistress of the Seven Robbers 1966, Meteor, 1966; Lucky Sevens, 1966; Musicals: The Night is my Day (on Bessie Smith) 1962; The Emperor's New Clothes, 1962; Madame Sans Gene, 1968; Wind from Alabama, 1970; Orchestral: Sinfonietta, 1951; Spring Suite for wind instruments and strings, 1963; Serenade for Strings, 1965; May Symphony, 1974; Poem of Fallen Heroes for alto and orchestra, 1974; Olympic Flame, symphonic poem, 1975; A Solitary Seaman, symphonic picture, 1978; World's Conscience, in memory of Lidice, 1981; Trombone Concerto, 1986; Symphony No.2, 1986; Chamber and piano music. *Address:* Spojovaci 401, 252 45 Zvole u, Prague, Czech Republic.

**VĂDUVA, Leontina;** French singer (soprano); b. 1 Dec. 1960, Rosiile, Romania; d. of Maria Ciobanu; m. Gheorghe Codre. *Education:* Bucharest Conservatoire. *Career:* gained political asylum in France; debut in Massenet's Manon, Toulouse 1987; appeared as Ninetta in La Gazza Ladra at the Théâtre des Champs Elysées, Paris 1988; Covent Garden debut as Manon 1988; appeared at Covent Garden as Gilda in Rigoletto 1989; sang Drusilla at Théâtre du Châtelet, Paris, and at the Grand Théatre, Geneva; other roles included appearances in Les Pêcheurs de Perles and L'Elisir d'amore at Toulouse, Manon at Montpellier, Bordeaux, Avignon, Paris (Opéra Comique) and Vienna, Rigoletto at Bonn, Donizetti's Il Campanello di Notte at Monte Carlo, Les Contes d'Hoffmann in Paris (Théâtre du Châtelet) and London (Covent Garden), Ismene in Mitridate by Mozart at the Châtelet, Micaela in Carmen at Covent Garden (returned 1996 as Mimi); sang Juliet in Romeo and Juliet at Covent Garden, Adina at Barcelona, Marguerite and Mimi at Los Angeles, Poulenc's Blanche at La Scala, Offenbach's Antonia for Festival d'Orange and Adina at Savonlinna 2000; season 2003–04 as Euridice at Barcelona, as Marguérite in Turin, Alice Ford for Bordeaux Opéra and Mimi on tour of Japan for Catania Opera. *Recordings:* Mitridate, Le nozze di Figaro 1993. *Honours:* Chevalier, Ordre des Arts et des Lettres 1998, Grand Officer Order of Merit (Romania); winner Concours de Chant, Toulouse 1986, winner 's-Hertogenbosch Competition, Netherlands 1987, Olivier Award for Outstanding Achievement in Opera 1988, Medal of the City of Toulouse. *Current Management:* Stafford Law, Candleway, Broad Street, Sutton Valence, Kent ME17 3AT, England. *Website:* www.stafford-law.com. *E-mail:* leontina@leontinavaduva.com. *Website:* www.leontinavaduva.com.

**VAGGIONE, Horacio;** Composer; b. 21 Jan. 1943, Cordoba, Argentina. *Education:* Composition, Arts School, National University of Cordoba. *Career:* Co-Founder, Experimental Music Centre, University of Cordoba, 1964–69; Alea Electronic Music Group, Madrid, Spain, 1969–74; Computer Music Project, University of Madrid, 1970–73; Guest Composer, IRCAM/Centre Georges Pompidou, 1981–85 Groupe de Musique Experimentale de Bourges, France, 1983; Technische Universität, West Berlin, 1987–88; Director, Electro-acoustic Music Studio, University of Paris VIII, 1985–. *Compositions:* 48 including symphonic, chamber and electronic music; Myr-S, for cello and electronics, 1996; Frauyage for violin, cello and tape, 1997; Nodal for tape; Performances of works at Festivals of Warsaw, Stockholm, Berlin, Kassel, Frankfurt, Amsterdam, Helsinki, Oslo, Paris, Venice, La Rochelle, Bourges, Geneva, Lausanne, Milan, Turin, Rome, Madrid, Athens and at UNESCO's Rostrum of Composers, World Music Days, Los Angeles Olympic Arts Festival, ICMC (Rochester, Illinois, The Hague, Venice, Paris, Cologne), British Arts of London, Berlin Kulturstadt Europas 88, Darmstadt Ferienkurse für Neue Musik. *Recordings:* ADDA, Paris; Le Chant du Monde, Paris; WERGO, Germany. *Address:* Editions Salabert, 22 Rue Chauchat, 75009 Paris, France.

**VAJDA, Janos;** Hungarian composer; b. 8 Oct. 1949, Miskole. *Education:* Franz Liszt Acad., Budapest 1968–75, Amsterdam Conservatory. *Career:* Prof., Budapest Acad. 1981–. *Compositions:* De Angelis, wind quintet, 1978; Stabat Mater, 1978; Barabbas, opera, 1978; Farewell, for orchestra, 1980;

Sinfonia Retrograde, 1980; Mario and the Magician, opera, 1980–85; The Moment of Truth, ballet, 1981; Don Juan, ballet, 1981; Via Crucis, for chorus, 1983; The Circus is Coming, ballet, 1984; Duo, for violin and cello, 1989–91, Missa in A 1990, Magnificat 1991; Double Concerto, violin and cello, 1993; Leonce and Lena, opera, 1990–95; Violin Concerto, 1995; Two String Quartets, 1995, 1997; Piano Sonata, 1996; O Magnum Mysterium, for chorus, 1999, Titanic 2000, Missa in H 2000, Missa in D 2001, Trio for violin, cello and piano 2001, String Quarter No. 3 2001, Sinfonietta 2001, Így volt, Így se (oratorio) 2002. *Honours:* Erkel Prize 1981, Bartók-Pasztory Prize 1990, Kossuth Prize 2003. *Current Management:* c/o ARTISJUS, Mészáros u. 15–17, PO Box 593, 1539 Budapest 114, Hungary. *Telephone:* (1) 212-1553. *Fax:* (1) 212-1544. *Address:* Pomázi str. 9, 2000 Szenteudre, Hungary (home). *Telephone:* (626) 316222 (home). *E-mail:* vajdanet@axelero.hu (home). *Website:* kincsestar .radio.hu/ktz (office).

**VAJNAR, Frantisek;** Conductor; b. 15 Sept. 1930, Strasice u Rokycan, Czechoslovakia. *Education:* Studied violin and conducting at the Prague Conservatoire. *Career:* Played in the orchestra of the Prague National Theatre; 1950–53, conducted the ensemble of Czech Army, 1953–55; Conducted at the State Theatre of Karlina 1955–60, Ostrava 1960–62; Director of the Nejedly Theatre Usti nad Labem 1962–73, with operas by Smetana (complete), Dvořák, Janáček, Wagner, Verdi, Puccini, Strauss, Prokofiev, Henze and Hartmann; Conductor at the National Theatre Prague 1973–79, Artistic Director from 1985; Chief Conductor of the Czech Radio Symphony Orchestra 1979–85, Guest Conductor of the Czech Philharmonic; Director of the Collegium Musicum Pragense and guest conductor in Australia, Brazil, Germany, France, Greece, Italy, Japan, Poland, Scandinavia, Russia and Switzerland; Festival appearances at Salzburg, Vienna, Prague; Conducted Prokofiev's Betrothal in a Monastery at the 1979 Wexford Festival; Teacher at Prague Academy of Arts. *Recordings include:* Smetana The Kiss; Shostakovich 10th and 15th Symphonies (Czech Philharmonic); Beethoven Overtures; Brixi Organ Concertos; Mozart arranged Wendt Le nozze di Figaro; Dvořák's The Cunning Peasant. *Address:* c/o National Theatre, PO Box 865, 11230 Prague 1, Czech Republic.

**VAKARELIS, Janis;** Concert Pianist; b. 1950, Greece. *Education:* Studied at the Vienna Music Academy with Nikita Magaloff and Bruno Leonardo Gelber. *Career:* Engagements from 1979 with the Gewandhaus Orchestra, Mozarteum Orchestra of Salzburg, Zürich Chamber, Monte Carlo Philharmonic, Berlin Symphony, Stuttgart Philharmonic, Staatskapelle Dresden and BBC Symphony; Conductors have included Rattle, Weller, Masur, Kurt Sanderling, Ashkenazy, Litton and Rowicki; Recitals at the Concertgebouw in Amsterdam and the Teatro Real Madrid; Festival appearances at Spoleto and Athens, BBC Prom Concerts 1986. *Recordings include:* Prokofiev's 3rd Concerto and works by Brahms and Liszt; Labels include RCA, ASV and RPO. *Honours:* Winner, 1979 Queen Sofia Competition, Madrid; Pan-Hellenic Piano Competition and the Prix d'Academie d'Athenes. *Address:* c/o Primusic, Herrengasse 6–8/2/22, A–1010 Vienna, Austria.

**VALADE, Pierre-André;** French conductor; b. 14 Oct. 1959, Brive; m. 2004. *Education:* As a flautist: Michel Debost's Private Class, Paris, 1979–81; Occasional lessons from Marcel Moyse, Maxence Larrieu and Alain Marion. *Career:* Flautist 1979–95; Numerous stage including ensemble, chamber music and soloist appearances in repertoire from Mozart 1982–95; Soloist: numerous world premieres including Eolia by Philippe Hurel, Paris, Radio-France, 1983; Jupiter by Philipe Manoury on Flute-4x, IRCAM, Paris, 1987; ... explosante-fixe... by Pierre Boulez, for Flute, Computer and Ensemble, Paris, 1991; Concerts with Ensembles: Ensemble Musique Oblique, 1983–93; Ensemble InterContemporain, 1985–90, including London Proms, 1985, US Tour with Pierre Boulez, 1986; ... explosante-fixe... in New York, Carnegie Hall, with P. Boulez, 1993; Director, Collection Pierre-André Valade, Edition Henry Lemoine, Paris, 1985–95; Career as a Conductor: Co-Founder and Musical Director of Court-circuit Ensemble, Paris, 1991–; Guest Conductor: West Australian Symphony Orchestra, 1995, 1996,1998; Melbourne Symphony Orchestra, 1998; London Sinfonietta, 1999, 2000; Ensemble InterContemporain, 2000–(05); Ensemble Modern, 2001–04; Philharmonia Orchestra, 2003–04, BBC Symphony Orchestra, 2001–04; Tonhalle Orchester, Zürich, 2003–04; Orchestre Symphonique de Montréal, 2003, 2005; Major Festivals: Festival of Perth, Australia (1996, 1998); Ultima Festival, Oslo Norway, 1998–2004; Festival de Strasbourg, 1995–2003; Festival of Bath, UK, 1999; Aldeburgh, UK, 2002; Festival Présence de Radio-France, Paris, 1998, 1999, 2005; Festival Agora, Ircam, Paris, 1998–2002; London Proms, 2002, 2004; Lucerne Festival, 2002, 2004; Salzburg Easter Festival, 2002, Montréal Nouvelles Musiques Festival 2003–05; mem, International Contemporary Music Society. *Recordings:* A Schoenberg: Pierrot Lunaire, Harmonia Mundi, 1992; A Jolivet: The Complete Works for Flute, 1993, H. Birtwistle: Theseus Game. *Publications:* La Flute dans le Repertoire du XXe Siècle pour Ensemble Instrumental, 1987; Flute et Creations, 1991. *Honours:* Chevalier dans l'Ordre des Arts et des Lettres, 2001; Grand Prix de la Nouvelle Académie du Disque Français. *Current Management:* Allied Artists, 42 Montpelier Square, London SW7 1JZ, England. *Telephone:* (20) 7589-6243. *E-mail:* andrew@alliedartists.co.uk. *E-mail:* www.pavalade.com.

**VALCARCEL, Edgar;** Pianist and Composer; b. 4 Dec. 1932, Puno, Peru; m. Carmen Pollard, 1 Jan 1958, 2 s., 2 d. *Education:* Catholic University, Lima, Peru; National Conservatory of Music, Lima; Instituto Torcuato de Tella, Buenos Aires, Argentina; Columbia Princeton University, New York, USA. *Career:* As Pianist: Soloist, National Symphony Orchestras of Lima, Rio de Janeiro and La Habana; As Composer: Commissions, V Inter-American Festival, Washington DC, 1971, Rochester Festival, 1972, Maracaibo Festival, Venezuela, 1977; Works premiered at Panamerican Union Peer International Corporation, 1968, Tonos, Darmstadt, 1977, Veracruz University, Mexico, 1983; Head of Music Department, Newton College, Lima. *Compositions:* Dichotomy III, for 12 instruments, 1968; Montaje 59, for chamber ensemble, 1977; Chegan IV, for choir, 1977; Karabotasat Cutintapata, for orchestra, 1977; 4 Children's Songs, 1983. *Recordings:* American Contemporary Music, EDS-030-Stereo; Edul, Organization of American States; Antologia Music Peruana Siglo XX, Vol. III, Edubanco. *Honours:* Professor honoris causa, Puno University, Peru; National Award for Composition Award, Caracas, Venezuela, 1981. *Address:* Avenida Angamos (Oeste) 862-C, Miraflores, Lima 18, Peru.

**VALDES, Maximiano;** Conductor; b. 17 June 1949, Santiago, Chile. *Education:* Studied in Santiago, at the Santa Cecilia Rome and with Franco Ferrara. *Career:* Assistant conductor at La Fenice, Venice, 1976–80; Principal guest with the Spanish National Orchestra from 1984 and music director of the Buffalo Philharmonic, USA, from 1989; Guest appearances in England, Scandinavia and France (Paris Opéra). *Honours:* Prizewinner at the 1978 Rupert Foundation Competition, London, and the 1980 Nikolai Malko Competition, Copenhagen. *Address:* c/o Cramer/Marder Artists, 3436 Springhill Road, Lafayette, CA 94549, USA.

**VÁLEK, Vladimír;** Czech conductor; b. 2 Sept. 1935, Nový Jičín; m. 1st Jana Adamová; m. 2nd Hana Patočková 1986; two s. one d. *Education:* Acad. of Musical Arts, Bratislava, Acad. of Performing Arts, Prague. *Career:* conductor with several Czech orchestras 1962–75; Conductor FOK Prague Symphony Orchestra 1975–87; Chief Conductor Prague Radio Symphony Orchestra 1985–; Conductor Czech Philharmonic 1996–; Prin. Guest Conductor Orchestra Osaka Symphoniker 2003–; Guest Conductor with many orchestras world-wide including The Big Radio Orchestra Leipzig, Tonkuenstler and ORF (Vienna), Israeli and Japan Philharmonics. *Performances:* concert tours include Japan, France, Spain, USA and Singapore; has appeared as guest conductor with numerous symphony orchestras in many countries. *Recordings:* more than 100 classical music recordings and more than 1,000 recordings for radio. *Honours:* Music Critics' Award, MIDEM Classic Cannes (for recording of piano concertos by Ervin Schulhoff) 1996. *Address:* Český rozhlas, Vinohradská 12, 120 00 Prague 2 (office); Nad údolím 24, 140 00 Prague 4, Czech Republic (home). *Telephone:* (2) 2155-1400 (office); (2) 4177-1463 (home). *Fax:* (2) 2155-1413 (office). *E-mail:* socr@cro.cz (office). *Website:* www.cro.cz/socr (office).

**VALENTE, Benita;** American singer (lyric soprano); b. 19 Oct. 1934, Delano, CA; d. of Lorenzo Giuseppe and the late Severina Antonia (née Masonati) Valente; m. Anthony Checchia 1959; one s. *Education:* Delano High School, Music Acad. of the West, Santa Barbara, CA, Curtis Inst. of Music, Philadelphia, PA and Metropolitan Opera Studio, New York. *Career:* concert debut in New York 1960; singer with Freiburg Opera, then Nuremberg Opera, Germany 1966; US opera debut in The Magic Flute at the Metropolitan Opera, New York 1973; has performed with major nat. and int. orchestras; nat. and int. opera performances and concert recitals include New York Town Hall 1966, Mostly Mozart Festival, New York 1967, Rome 1968, Aspen Music Festival, Zurich, Switzerland, Columbus Opera 1999, Strasbourg, France, Frankfurt, Germany, Netherlands etc.; teacher Aspen Music Festival; winner Metropolitan Opera, New York auditions 1960. *Operas include:* The Magic Flute, Turn of the Screw, Falstaff, Orfeo, Vanqui. *Recordings include:* Schubert and Brahms songs on Marlboro Festival album 1960, David del Tredici's Night Conjure-Verse 1966. *Address:* c/o Anthony Checchia, 135 S 18th Street, Philadelphia, PA 19103, USA.

**VALERA, Roberto;** Composer; b. 21 Dec. 1938, Havana, Cuba. *Education:* Havana Conservatory; Warsaw School of Music, 1965–67. *Career:* Professor of Composition, Instituto Superior de Arte, Havana, 1976–. *Compositions include:* Toccata, for piano, 1965; Conjuro for soprano and orchestra, 1967; Devenir for orchestra, 1969; Iré a Santiago, for mixed chorus, 1969; Tres Impertinencias, for 12 instruments, 1971; Quisiera for mixed chorus, 1971; Es rojo, for baritone, flute and piano, 1979; Violin Concerto, 1982; Concierto por la paz, for saxophone and orchestra, 1985; Ajiaco, tape, 1989; Nadie oye, female chorus, 1990; Palmas tape, 1991; Tierra de sol, cielo y tierra, for ensemble, 1992; Periodo espacial, tape, 1993; Yugo y estrella, for soprano, baritone, chorus and orchestra, 1995; Hic et Nunc, tape, 1996; Concierto de Cojimer, for guitar and orchestra, 1998. *Address:* c/o ACDAM, Calle 6 no. 313 entre 13y15, Vedado La Habana CP –10400, Cuba.

**VALERA CHAMIZO, Roberto,** MM; Cuban composer and teacher; *Professor of Composition and Contemporary Techniques, Instituto Superior de Arte;* b. 21 Dec. 1938, Havana. *Education:* Havana Municipal Conservatory, Havana Pedagogical School, Havana Univ., Warsaw Conservatory, Poland. *Career:* teacher at elementary and high schools, Havana 1957–64; began composing 1961; Musical Adviser, Cuban Inst. of Cinematographic Arts and Industry 1961–64, 1967–68; taught harmony, counterpoint, composition and contemporary techniques, Alejandro García Caturla School of Music 1967–76, Asst

Dir 1967–68; taught classes in harmony, counterpoint, composition and contemporary technique, Nat. School of the Arts 1967–76, Asst Dir 1972, Dir 1973–76; Prof. of Composition and Contemporary Techniques, Music Faculty, Instituto Superior de Arte, Havana 1976–, Asst Dean 1976–79, 1987–90; mem. Asscn of Musicians (pres. 1989–92). *Compositions for film:* Revolución en el mar 1961, Minerva traduce el mar 1964, Pueblo de estrellas bajas 1964, Era Nickel Co. 1964, Escena de los mueles 1967, Páginas del diario de José Marti 1967, El mar 1967, La salación 1967, Sigma 33 1967, Tránsito 1967, Angola victoria de la esperanza 1967, Che, hoy y siempre 1967, El cero 1967. *Compositions:* Mi niña 1960, Soy como un niño distraido 1960, Es por ti 1960–63, Las cebollas mágicas 1961, Estudio ritmico (ballet) 1962, Siete piezas para piano 1962, Ensayo (ballet) 1963, Chachachá 1963, Música para cuerdas 1964, Toccata 1965, Cuarteto de cuerdas 1966, Cinco mínimas 1966, Conjuro 1967, Culturosamente 1968, Iré a Santiago 1969, Devenir 1969, Claustros de mármol 1970, Tres impertinencias 1971, Quisiera (or Guaguancaglia, quasi una passacaglia) 1971, Retrato de Camilo 1972, Qué yo pueda tocar 1973, Así cantaba que yo la ví 1975, Extraplan 1975, Compañero Presidente 1975, Dos líneas 1976, Diálogos para uno solo 1978, Vocalizo 1978, Es rojo 1979, Capitán Camilo 1979, La pequeñas balada de Plovdiv 1980, Solo de guitarra 1980, Tiempo para un tiempo 1980, Movimiento concertante 1980, Tiempo para un tiempo 1980, Responde tú 1980, Concierto para violín y orquesta 1982, Rondo cubana 1984, Concierto por la paz 1985, Cuba, tu cielo y tu bandera 1985, Cubana 1986, Lágrimas barrocas 1988, Madrigal 1988, Ajiaco 1989, La barbacoa 1989, Si a mí me hubieran dicho 1989, Yo soy el que te canta 1989, La vida empieza a correr 1989, Nadie oye 1990, Palmas 1991, Tierra de sol, cielo y tierra 1992, Aquí en Varadero 1992, Período espacial 1993, Yugo y estrella 1995, Hic et Nunc 1996, Concierto de Cojímar 1998. *Honours:* Premio Alcaldia 1960, Highest Nat. Cultural Award 1982, winner Cuban Nat. Compositional Contest, Ministry of Cultural Affairs 1985; Order Alejo Carpentier 1988. *Address:* c/o Ana Margarita Cabrera, Instituto Superior de Arte, Calle 120, No. 1110 entre 9na y 13, Cubanacan Playa, Havana, 12100, Cuba (office).

**VALJAKKA, Taru Aura Helena;** Finnish singer (mezzo-soprano); b. 16 Sept. 1938, Helsinki; d. of Oiva and Aili (née Kivirinta) Kumpunen; m. Risto Valjakka 1960; one s. one d. *Education:* Sibelius Acad., Helsinki, Mozarteum Salzburg, Austria and Santiago de Compostela, Spain. *Career:* Guest Prof., Estonian Music Acad. 1966–; singer with Finnish Nat. Opera 1969–89; Guest Singer, Int. Soc. for Contemporary Music 1968–90; Singing Prof., Tallinn Music Acad. 1995–; performances include Bolshoi Theatre (Moscow, USSR, now Russian Fed.) 1982, 1984, Metropolitan, New York, USA 1984, Teatro Colón, Buenos Aires 1987, and appearances in Europe, N and S America, Canada, fmr USSR, Japan and People's Repub. of China. *Recordings:* Reittersman (also film), Red Line, Lady Macbeth of Mtsensk, Peer Gynt, The Damask Drum (also film). *Honours:* Second Prize, Rio de Janeiro singing competition 1966, Sibelius Prize 1978, Pro Finlandia Medal 1989. *Address:* Bulevardi 19A 2, 00120 Helsinki, Finland. *Telephone:* (0) 6932995.

**VÄLKKI, Anita;** Singer (Soprano); b. 25 Oct. 1926, Saakmaki, Finland. *Education:* Studied with Tynne Haase, Jorma Huttunen and Lea Piltti in Helsinki. *Career:* Performed first as an actress and sang in operettas at theatre in Kokkola; Sang at the Helsinki National Opera from 1955; Royal Opera Stockholm from 1960, as Aida, Santuzza and Brünnhilde; Covent Garden 1961–64, as Brünnhilde; Metropolitan Opera 1962–66, Senta, Turandot, Venus, Brünnhilde, Kundry; Bayreuth Festival 1963–64; Guest appearances in Mexico City, Palermo and Philadelphia; Savonlinna Festival Finland 1983, as Mary in Der fliegende Holländer; sang at Helsinki 1986, in Juha by Merikanto. *Recordings include:* Third Norn in Götterdämmerung, conducted by Solti (Decca); The Horseman by Sallinen. *Address:* c/o Finnish National Opera, Bulevardi 23–27, SF 00180 Helsinki 18, Finland.

**VALLE, José (Nilo);** Conductor, Composer and Teacher; b. 20 Feb. 1946, Santa Catarina State, Brazil. *Education:* Paraná Music College (Music License and Fine Arts Degrees); National School of Music, Federal University of Rio de Janeiro (Graduate degrees in Composition and Conducting; MMusic and DMA in Orchestral Conducting, University of Washington School of Music, USA. *Career:* Debut: Federal University of Rio de Janeiro Symphony Orchestra, 1983; Teacher, Music Theory, Parana Music College; Assistant Conductor, Federal University of Rio de Janeiro, 1981–83; Conductor of the Florianópolis Choral Association, 1985–86; Assistant Conductor at the University of Washington, 1989–91; Conductor and Founder, Proconart Ensemble for Contemporary Music, University of Washington, 1989–91; Conductor, Founder, Camerata Simfonica, Seattle, Washington, 1989–91; Founder, and since 1993 Music Director and Conductor, Santa Catarina Symphony Orchestra, Florianópolis, Santa Catarina State, Brazil; President Director of the Santa Catarina Cultural Association. *Address:* CP 1004, 88010-970 Florianopólis, Santa Catarina State, Brazil.

**VALLER, Rachel;** Australian pianist; b. 14 Sept. 1929, Sydney; m. Walter Travers 28 Feb. 1965. *Education:* BA, 1952; DipEd, 1960; LTCL, 1947; Conservatorium of Music, University of Sydney; Pupil of Ignaz Friedman. *Career:* Debut: Sydney, 1940; Soloist, Associate Artist Chamber Ensembles, ABC radio and television; Appearances with Sydney, Melbourne and Queensland Symphony Orchestras; Toured with cellist André Navarra, with Violinists Wanda Wilkomirska, Stoika Milanova, Zvi Zeitlin, Erick Friedman, Erich Gruenberg, Thomas Zehetmair and bassoonist George Zukerman. *Recordings:* Lesser known piano works of Beethoven issued to mark Beethoven bicentenary, 1970; Schubert's Sonatinas with violinist Susanne Lautenbacher to commemorate 150th anniversary of his death,

Germany, 1978. *Honours:* Harriet Cohen Commonwealth Medal, 1956; O A M Medal of the Order of Australia, 1995. *Address:* 22 Allen's Parade, Bondi Junction, NSW 2022, Australia. *E-mail:* waltrav@bigpond.com.

**VAN ALLAN, Richard,** CBE; British opera singer; b. 28 May 1935, Clipstone, Notts.; s. of Joseph Arthur Jones and Irene Hannah Jones; m. 1st Elizabeth Mary Peabody 1963 (divorced 1974); m. 2nd Rosemary Pickering 1976 (divorced 1987); two s. one d. *Education:* Brunt's Grammar School, Mansfield, Worcester Teaching Training Coll., Birmingham School of Music; studied singing under David Franklin and Jani Strasser. *Career:* with Sadler's Wells Opera (now ENO) 1968, as Prin. Bass, Royal Opera House, Covent Garden 1971–, with Paris Opera 1975, with Boston Opera, Mass. and San Diego Opera, Calif. 1976; Dir Nat. Opera Studio, London 1986–2001; mem. Bd Dirs ENO 1995–98; Fellow, Birmingham Schools of Music 1991. *Performances:* first appearance with Glyndebourne Festival Opera 1964; with Welsh Nat. Opera 1967, debut Colón Theatre, Buenos Aires 1978, Le Monnaie, Brussels 1982, Miami 1985, Seattle 1987, Metropolitan, New York 1991, Madrid 1991, Barcelona 1992, Vic. State Opera, Melbourne 1995, Saito Kinen and Florence Festivals 2002, Die Zauberflöte (Royal Opera House) 2003. *Television:* world premiere of Flight. *Honours:* Hon. mem. RAM 1987; Hon. Fellow, Birmingham Conservatoire; John Christie Award, Glyndebourne 1967, Grammy Award (The Nat. Acad. of Performing Arts and Sciences) for Don Alfonso (Così fan tutte), Sir Charles Santley Memorial Prize, Worshipful Co. of Musicians 1995. *Address:* 18 Octavia Street, London, SW11 3DN, England. *Telephone:* (20) 7228-8462. *Fax:* (20) 7228-4367. *E-mail:* rvanallan@aol.com (home).

**VAN ALTENA, Marius;** Dutch singer (countertenor); b. 10 Oct. 1938, Amsterdam; m. Marianne Syses; two s. *Education:* Conservatory of Music, Amsterdam. *Career:* debut, Germany, 1970; Concerts throughout Europe and the US with early music groups; Further tours to Japan and Australia; Holland Festival, 1974, in Eumelio by Agazzari and in Seelewig by Staden; Returned 1980, for Gluck's L'Isle de Merlin; Performed with Vienna-based group Spectaculum, 1980–84, in stage works by Fux, Leopold I and Conti; Later turned to conducting. *Recordings include:* Leopold I's Il figliuol prodigo; Madrigals by Monteverdi (RCA); Bach Concertos with Harnoncourt and Gustav Leonhardt, 1985; Hodges Ensemble with Paul V Nevel, 1990–97; Camerata Trajectina, 1988–97. *Address:* Bloemberg 8, 7924 PW Veeningen, Netherlands.

**VAN APPLEDORN, Mary Jeanne,** BM, MM, PhD; American composer and academic; *Paul Whitfield Horn Professor of Music Theory and Composition, Texas Technical University;* b. 2 Oct. 1927, Holland, MI; d. of John and Elizabeth Rinck. *Education:* Eastman School of Music, University of Rochester, New York. *Career:* solo piano debut, Weill Recital Hall, New York City, 1956; solo performer, Concerto Brevis for piano, American University, Washington DC, 1960; piano accompaniment, Concerto for trumpet and piano, with Robert Birch, trumpet for International Trumpet Guild, Albuquerque, New Mexico, 1985; Paul Whitfield Horn Professor of Music Theory and Composition, School of Music, Texas Tech University, Lubbock 1950–; ASCAP, Standard Panel Awards, 1980–2004. *Compositions:* Rhapsody, for violin and orchestra, 1996; Incantations for Oboe and Piano, 1998; Galilean Galaxies for flute, bassoon and piano, 1998; Five Psalms for tenor, trumpet and piano, 1998; Gestures for clarinet quartet, 1999; Meliora for symphony orchestra, 1999 and Meliora for symphonic band 2002; Commission from San Francisco Women's Symphony for Year 2000 Millennium performances; Symphony for Percussion Orchestra, 2000; Fanfare for trumpets, drums and cymbals, 2001; A Symphony of Celebration for Youth Orchestra 2002; Passages III for Clarinet, Cello and Piano 2003; Sonata for Guitar 2003. *Publications:* Cycles of Moons and Tides 1995; Trio Italiano, 1996. *Address:* 1629 16th Street, Apt 216, Lubbock, TX 79401, USA (home).

**VAN ASPEREN, Bob;** Harpsichordist; b. 8 Oct. 1947, Amsterdam, Netherlands. *Education:* Studied at the Amsterdam Conservatoire, with Gustav Leonhardt. *Career:* From 1971 many concerts as soloist and in concert; Appearances with La Petite Bande and Quadro Hotteterre; Founded the ensemble Melante 81, for the tercentenary of Telemann; Teacher at the Hague Conservatoire, 1973–88, Berlin Hochschule from 1987. *Address:* Berlin Hochschule für Musik, Ernst Reuter Platz 10, 1000 Berlin 10, Germany.

**VAN AST, Jochen;** singer (baritone); b. 1970, Amsterdam, Netherlands. *Education:* studied in Jerusalem; Guildhall School. *Career:* appearances with The Opera Company, Kent Opera; British Youth Opera and in Hong Kong; Roles have included Mozart's Count and Guglielmo, Dandini in Cenerentola, Clonter Opera; Purcell's Aeneas and Marullo in Rigoletto, Stowe Opera; Purcell's Fairy Queen at Athens and Granada; Le Bourgeois Gentilhomme, Covent Garden; Fledermaus on tour to the USA, 1999; Gershwin's Of Thee I Sing, debut with Opera North, 1998; Concerts include Bach's Passions and Magnificat; Messiah; Judas Maccabaeus; Haydn's Creation and Seasons; Mozart's Requiem. *Address:* Music International, 13 Ardilaun Road, London N5 2QR, England.

**VAN BARTHOLD, Kenneth;** Indonesian pianist and teacher; b. 10 Dec. 1927, Surabaya, Java; m. 1st Prudence van Barthold; m. 2nd Sarianne van Barthold; m. 3rd Gillian van Barthold; two s. two d. *Education:* Bryanston School, Paris Nat. Conservatoire of Music (class of Yves Nat). *Career:* debut, Bournemouth Municipal Orchestra 1944; Wigmore Hall 1956; frequent recitals in London Piano Series, Queen Elizabeth Hall and throughout UK; concerts in Canada, France, Israel and Ireland, including broadcasts; concerto

appearances with many orchestras, including London Symphony Orchestra, English Chamber Orchestra, London Classical Players and Polyphonia under Sir Adrian Boult, Raymond Leppard, Sir Roger Norrington and Bryan Fairfax; Dir of Studies, Victoria Coll. of Music 1953–1959; Prof. of Piano, Trinity Coll. of Music 1959–65; Head of Music, City Literary Inst. 1960–1983; Univ. of Edinburgh annual master-classes during Int. Festival 1968–; Sr Piano Tutor, Inner London Educ. Authority 1983–90; Lecturer on 19th- and 20th-century Opera, Wimbledon Coll. of Art 1983–94; master-classes in Israel, Canada and throughout UK; int. juror in France and Canada; has written and presented 21 hour-long documentaries on TV, including first ever full-length studio documentary (BBC) 1964; further frequent appearances interviewing, linking, profiling and performing on both BBC and ITV. *Recordings:* Decca/Argo: Mozart Recital, Sonatas K284 and K332, Chopin Recital, Ballade No. 4, Mazurkas, Etudes etc., Schumann Recital; Decca: Couronne Compilation; Darmo: Liszt Sonata, 4 Chopin Ballades, Hommage à Pierre Max Dubois. *Publications:* The Story of the Piano (co-author) 1976; reviewer for BBC Music Magazine, various articles. *Honours:* Critics Award (TV) 1972. *Address:* Arvensis, Stour Lane, Stour Row, Shaftesbury, Dorset, SP7 0QJ, England (home). *E-mail:* kvanbarthold@aol.com (home).

**VAN BLERK, Gerardus J. M.;** Concert Pianist; b. 14 May 1924, Tilburg, Netherlands; m. A. Van den Brekel. *Education:* Studied Piano with Professor W. Andriessen, Amsterdam Conservatory; Piano-Soloist (Prix d'excellence); Studied with Yves Nat, Paris, France 1950–52. *Career:* Solo concerts with Concertgebouw Orchestra, Residentie Orchestra, The Hague, Rotterdam Philharmonic Orchestra with Haitink, Jochum, Fournet; Recitals, Chamber Music, Accompaniments (instrumental and singers); Professor of Piano, Royal Conservatory, The Hague. *Recordings:* Hindemith, Kammermusik Number 2, Klavierkonzert, op 36 Number 1; Chopin, Grand duo Concertant, Polonaise brillante op 3, Sonata in G minor op 65 with Anner Bylsma (violoncellist); Max Reger; Sonata for Cello and Piano, Caprice and Romance with Anner Bylsma; Brahms Lieder with Jard Van Nes (Alto); French violin sonatas; works of M Ravel. *Address:* Prinsengracht 1095, 1017 Amsterdam, Netherlands.

**VAN BOER, Bertil Herman, Jr;** Musicologist and Conductor; b. 2 Oct. 1952, Florida, USA; m. Margaret Fast 1977. *Education:* PhD, Uppsala University, Sweden, 1983. *Career:* Musical Director, Opera Kansas, 1989–; Assistant/Associate/Full Professor, Wichita State University, 1987–; Assistant Professor of Music, Brigham Young University, UT, 1983–87; Instructor, Shasta College, 1981–83. *Publications:* Dramatic Cohesion in the Works of Joseph Martin Kraus, 1989; Joseph Martin Kraus: Systemtisch-thematiches Werkverzeichnis, 1988; Joseph Martin Kraus Der Tod Jesu, 1987; The Symphony: Richter, Sweden I and II, 1983–86; Gustav III and the Swedish Stage, 1993. *Contributions:* Articles in Fontes, Svensk tidskrift for Musikforskning, Journal of Musicology, Journal of Musicological Research. *Address:* 316 S Belmont, Wichita, KS 67218, USA.

**VAN BUREN, John (Hidden);** Composer; b. 21 Sept. 1952, Portland, Oregon, USA; m. Margret Ulrike Schaal, 9 June 1988. *Education:* Reed College, Portland, 1970–72; Oregon State University, 1972–74; Composition with Milko Kelemen, Piano with Edgar Trauer, Electronic Music with Erhard Karkoschka, 1973–79, Diploma, Composition, 1979, Staatliche Hochschule für Musik, Stuttgart, Germany. *Career:* His works broadcast on various German radio stations, 1974–; Other performances of his works include ZDF national television, 1979. St ädtisch Bühne Mainz Ballet, 1981, American Composers' Orchestra, in Carnegie Hall, 1987, Deutsche Sinfonie Orchester, Berlin, 1994; Organiser, new music concerts, Stuttgart, notably as Artistic Director and Manager, Musica Nova Society; Has taught music at Ludwigsburg University, John-Cranko Ballet School of Stuttgart State Opera, City School of Music, Stuttgart; Dozent, Hochschule für Music Nürnberg-Augsburg, Augsburg; Taught International Masterclass in Verulà, Spain. *Compositions include:* Streichquartett, 1981; Fünf Gesänge nach Catull, 1984–85; Les Nuages de Magritte for violin, cello, piano, 1989 Mementos, Symphony No. 1, 1989–90; Aufbruch for orchestra, 1992. *Recordings:* Mementos, 1994; String Quartet Nr 2, 1996; Night Scenes for orchestra, 1996; Flute Concerto, 1998; Luxe, Calme et Volupté for violoncello and Piano, 1998; All major works recorded by Süddeutscher, Westdeutscher, Hessischer Südwest and Sender Freies Berlin radio stations. *Address:* Daimlerstrasse 29, 70372 Stuttgart, Germany.

**VAN DAM, José;** Luxembourg singer (bass); b. 25 Aug. 1940, Brussels, Belgium; m. *Education:* Acad. de Musique, Brussels, Conservatoire Royal, Brussels. *Career:* debut in Paris in Carmen (Escamillo) 1961, with Grand Théâtre, Geneva 1965–67, Deutsche Oper, Berlin 1967–, Salzburg Festival, opera and concerts 1966–, Festival d'Aix en Provence 1966–, title role in St-François d'Assise (Messiaen) Paris 1983–84, Wozzeck at Royal Opera House, Covent Garden 1983–84, debut in Meistersinger (Hans Sachs), Brussels 1985. *Honours:* Grand Prix de l' Acad. Française du Disque 1979, Orphée d'Or, Académie Lyrique Française 1980, Prix Européen des Critiques 1985. *Current Management:* Ariën Arts & Music Management BVBA, De Boeystraat 6, 2018 Antwerp, Belgium.

**VAN DE SANT, Cecile;** Dutch singer (mezzo-soprano); b. 1970. *Education:* Sweelinck Conservatory, and in New York; Studies with Regine Crespin, Charlotte Margiono and Robert Holl. *Career:* appearances at the Göttingen Festival in cantatas by Handel and Vivaldi, and as Tauride in Handel's Arianna in Creta; Sang Gualtiero in Bononcini's Griselda at Utrecht and Handel's Tamerlano in Amsterdam; Other roles include Amastre in Xerxes, Monteverdi's Nerone, Jezibaba in Rusalka, Gluck's Orfeo, and Cherubino;

Concerts include Mahler's Lieder eines fahrenden Gesellen and Knaben Wunderhorn, Elijah, Les Nuits d'été, the Alto Rhapsody and sacred music by Bach; Haydn's Seven Last Words at the Concertgebouw. Amsterdam; Season 2000–2001 with Cenerentola at Kaiserslautern, Unulfo in Rodelinda at Göttingen and Messenger in Monteverdi's Orfeo at Munich; Olga in Eugene Onegin for Opera North, and Rosina for Opera Holland Park, London. *Current Management:* Athole Still International Management, Forresters Hall, 25–27 Westow Street, London, SE19 3RY, England. *Telephone:* (20) 8771-5271. *Fax:* (20) 8768-6600. *Website:* www.atholestill.com.

**VAN DE VATE, Nancy (Hayes);** American composer and record producer; *President and Artistic Director, Vienna Modern Masters*; b. 30 Dec. 1930, Plainfield, NJ; m. 1st Dwight Van de Vate, Jr 9 June 1952; one s. two d.; m. 2nd Clyde Arnold Smith 23 June 1979 (died 1999). *Education:* Eastman School of Music, University of Rochester, 1948–49; AB, Wellesley College, 1952; MM, University of Mississippi, 1958; D.Mus, Florida State University, 1968; Postdoctoral study, Electronic Music, Dartmouth and University of New Hampshire, 1972. *Career:* Opera premieres: In the Shadow of the Glen, Cambridge, Mass, USA, 1999; All Quiet on the Western Front (Acts II & III), NY City Opera, 2003; Im Westen nichts Neues, Osnabrück, Germany, 2003; Orchestral premieres: Distant Worlds, Concerto for Percussion and Orchestra, Concertpiece for Cello and Small Orchestra all premiered by Polish Radio Symphony Orchestra of Kraków, Szymon Kawalla conductor, 1987–89; Premieres, Musica Viva Festival, Munich, Aspekte, Salzburg, Poznan Spring Festival, Poland; Chernobyl, for orchestra, Vienna 1994; Dark Nebulae, Vienna Musikverein, 2000; President and Artistic Director Vienna Modern Masters 2000–. *Compositions:* Cocaine Lil, 5 singers, percussion; Teufelstanz, percussion ensemble; A Night in the Royal Ontario Museum, soprano, tape; Pura Besakih for large orchestra; Nine Preludes for Piano; Twelve Pieces for Piano; Trio for Violin, Violoncello and Piano; Many choral, vocal, brass and solo string works; Viola Concerto; Four Sombre Songs, for mezzo and orchestra; *Premieres:* Katyn, 1989, Polish Radio Symphony Orchestra and Chorus, S Kawalla, Conductor; Concerto for Violin and Orchestra, 1992, Vienna Konzerthaus, Vienna Musiksommer; Operas: Nemo: Jenseits von Vulkania; In the Shadow of the Glen; All Quiet on the Western Front; Where the Cross is Made. *Recordings:* Operas Nemo: Jenseits von Vulkania, All Quiet on the Western Front, and In the Shadow of the Glen. Orchestral works, Polish Radio Symphony Orchestra of Kraków; Many solo and chamber works also commercially recorded; Violin Concerto No. 2, 1996; Suite from Nemo for Orchestra, 1996. *Publication:* Journeys Through the Life and Music of Nancy Van de Vate 2005. *Honours:* Faculty Citation for Distinguished Achievement in Composition, Florida State Univ. 1999, Wellesley Coll. Alumnae Achievement Award 2001. *Address:* Khleslplatz 6, #2309, 1120 Vienna, Austria. *Telephone:* (1) 545-1778. *Fax:* (1) 545-1778. *E-mail:* nvandevate@yahoo.com. *Website:* www.xs4all.nl/~gdv/vmm.

**VAN DELDEN, Alex (Lex);** actor and singer (tenor); b. 21 June 1947, Amsterdam, Netherlands; s. of Lex van Delden and Jetty van Dijk. *Education:* Drama School, Amsterdam, studied singing with Jan Keizer, Marianne Blok and Andrew Field. *Career:* debut 1967; Opera: Gianni Schicchi (G Puccini); Turandot (F Busoni); Die Fledermaus (Johann Strauss); Il Ritorno d'Ulisse (Claudio Monteverdi); Ariadne auf Naxos (Richard Strauss); and others; also extensive stage, film and TV work. *Compositions include:* Active as composer for theatre: Romeo and Juliet (W Shakespeare); Dance of Death (A Strindberg); The Spanish Brabantine (Bredero). *E-mail:* lexvandelden@onetel.net.uk.

**VAN DEN HOEK, Martijn;** Concert Pianist; b. 1955, Rotterdam, Netherlands. *Education:* Studied at the Rotterdam Conservatory, in Moscow with Valeri Kastelskii, in Budapest with Pal Kadosa and in Weimar with Ludwig Hofmann; New York with Joseff Raieff and Eugene Liszt; Further study in Vienna with Paul Angerer. *Career:* Has performed as soloist with the Amsterdam Concertgebouw Orchestra, the Wiener String Quartet and the National Hungarian Post Orchestra; Performances in Belgium, France, Germany, Austria, Portugal, USA, Japan and Hong Kong; Recital with the BBC, London; Repertoire includes concertos by Bach, Bartók, Beethoven, Chopin, Haydn, Hummel, Mozart and Schumann; Sonatas by Beethoven, Berg, Brahms, Chopin, Haydn, Mozart, Scarlatti, Schubert, Impromptus and Moments Musicaux, Schoenberg's Op 23; Schumann's Kreisleriana and Faschingsschwank aus Wien; Liszt Consolations, Sonata, Spanish Rhapsody, Valses oubliées and Opera transcriptions. *Honours:* Prix d'Excellence and Goethe Prize, 1978; Public Prize of the City of Amsterdam, 1981; First Prize, International Liszt Competition in Utrecht, 1986.

**VAN DER KAMP, Harry;** Dutch singer (bass); b. 1947, Kampen. *Education:* studied with Alfred Deller, Pierre Bernac, Max von Egmond and Herman Woltman. *Career:* appearances in solo recitals and in oratorios; Conductors include Nikolaus Harnoncourt, Gustav Leonhardt and Ton Koopman; Leading parts in operas by Monteverdi, Handel, Mozart, Pergolesi and Rossini in Milan, Venice and elsewhere in Europe; Engagements at the Berlin, Carinthian, Flanders, Spoleto and Holland Festivals; Founder and Director of the Dutch vocal ensemble Gesualdo Consort Amsterdam; Member and Artistic Adviser of Netherlands Chamber Choir; Guest Teacher at the Early Music Academy in Bremen and Antwerp; Sang in the Towards Bach concert series on London's South Bank, Aug 1989; Sang in Cesti's L'Orontea at the 1990 Innsbruck Festival of Ancient Music; Season 1999–2000 as Valeso in Handel's Theodora at Göttingen, and in the premiere of Rêves d'un Marco Polo by Claude Vivier, at Amsterdam. *Recordings include:* Le Testament de François Villon, by Ezra Pound. *Honours:* Edison Prize, for Ezra Pound Recording. *Address:* c/o De Netherlandse Opera, Waterlooplein 22, 1011 PG Amsterdam, Netherlands.

**VAN DER LINDE, Clint;** Singer (Countertenor); b. 1976, South Africa. *Education:* Boy soprano in Drakenberg Boys' Choir School, S. Africa, 1988; University of Pretoria, 1996; Eton College; Choral College of Music, with Ashley Stafford; Bach studies with Peter Schreier. *Career:* Appearances with the Orchestra of the Age of Enlightenment in Bach's B minor Mass; Title roles in Lotario, Ottone and Flavio for the London Handel Festival (1999, 2000, 2001); St Matthew Passion at St George's Hanover Square, 2001. *Honours:* Queen Elizabeth, the Queen Mother Scholarship, RCM; Kathleen Ferrier Bursary for Young Singers. *Address:* c/o Royal College of Music, Prince Consort Road, London, SW7, England.

**VAN DER MEER, Ruud;** Dutch singer (baritone) (retd); b. 23 June 1936, The Hague; m. Annetje Schonk 1979; one s. two d. *Education:* Royal Conservatory, The Hague, Mozarteum, Salzburg, studied with Pierre Bernac in Paris. *Career:* debut, Concertgebouw, Amsterdam 1967; concerts, recitals and oratorio in USA, Western and Eastern Europe; regular BBC radio recitals, Dutch and German radio stations; Man. Special Projects and Int. Relations, Princess Christina Concours, Netherlands 1991–. *Recordings include:* Bach Cantatas with Harnoncourt, Vienna, Bach St Matthew Passion with Royal Concertgebouw Orchestra, Duparc, Schumann and Brahms Lieder, Bach's St John Passion (Grand Prix du Disque) 1970. *Honours:* Kt, Order of Orange Nassau 1990, Order of the Dutch Lion 2001. *Address:* L. V. Leeuwesteyn 71, 2271 HJ Voorburg, Netherlands. *Telephone:* (70) 3870130 (office). *Fax:* (70) 3860433 (office). *E-mail:* meerruud@planet.nl (office).

**VAN DER PUTTEN, Thea;** Dutch singer (soprano); b. 1950, Eindhoven. *Education:* Hague Conservatory. *Career:* sang in the 1980 Holland Festival and with Netherlands Opera in La Cenerentola, Hansel and Gretel, Die Zauberflöte and La Vie Parisienne; Nedda in Pagliacci, 1985; Komische Oper Berlin, 1988, as Donna Elvira, and in the 1986 premiere of Ketting's Ithaka, at the opening of the Amsterdam Muziektheater; Many concert engagements; Teaches singing at the Royal Conservatory, The Hague. *Recordings include:* Die Zauberflöte. *Address:* Netherlands Opera, Waterlooplein 22, 1001 PS Amsterdam, Netherlands.

**VAN DER ROOST, Jan (Frans Joseph);** Composer; b. 1 March 1956, Duffel, Belgium; m. Bernadette Johnson, 16 May 1980, 2 s., 2 d. *Education:* Lemmens Institute, Leuven; Royal Academy of Music, Antwerp and Ghent; Graduated in Music Theory, Harmony, Counterpoint, Fugue, Musical History, Trombone, Choral Conducting and Composition; Professor at the Lemmensinstituut in Leuven; Guest Professor, Shobi Institute of Education, Tokyo; Nagoya Univ. of Arts. *Compositions:* Divertimento, for piano, 1982; Canzona Gothica, for trombone and piano, 1982; Melopee e Danza, for 2 guitars, 1982; Per Archi, for string orchestra, 1983; 3 Bagatels, for flute and piano, 1984; Rikudim, for band, orchestra or string orchestra, 1985; Van Maan en Aarde (Of the Moon and the Earth), for mixed choir, 1985; Mozaieken (Mosaics), for orchestra, 1986; Concerto Grosso, for cornet, trombone and brass band, 1986; Jaargang (Turning of the Year), for choir and piano, 1986–87; Puszta, for band, 1987; Excalibur, for brass band, 1987; Elckerlyc (Everyman), Oratorio for soloists, choir and orchestra, 1987; Obsessions, for brass instrument and piano, 1987–88; Arghulesques, for clarinet quartet, 1988; Spartacus, for band, 1988; Symphony, for orchestra, 1988–89; Chemical Suite, for trombone quartet, 1990; Amazonia, for band, 1990; Met Annie in Toverland, for children's choir and ensemble, 1990; Olympica for band, 1992; Stonehenge for brass band, 1992; A Year has Four Lives, for female choir and guitar, 1993; Exodus, Oratorio, for soloists, choir, organ and brass band, 1994; Concierto de Homenaje for guitar and orchestra, 1995; Rhapsody for horn, winds and percussion, 1995; Poème Montagnard for band, 1996; canTUBAllada for solo tuba, 1997; Contrasto Grosso for recorder quartet and string quartet, 1997; Et in Terra Pax for band, 1998; Credentium for band, 1998; Canti d'Amore for baritone and chamber orchestra, 1999; Concerto Doppio for 2 clarinets and string orchestra, 1999; Sinfonia Hungarica for band, 2000; Albion for brass band, 2001; Concerto per Tromba for trumpet, cembalo and string orchestra, 2001; I Continenti for recorder quartet, 2002; Partita for guitar quartet, 2002; Sirius for orchestra, 2002; Sinfonietta for band, 2003; Contemplations for choir and organ, 2003. *Recordings include:* Per Archi, Canti D'Amore, Contrasto Grosso and Concerto Doppio (EMI Classics). *Address:* Albrecht Rodenbachlaan 13, 2550 Kontich, Belgium.

**VAN DER SCHAAF, Jerrold;** singer (tenor); b. 1952, Battle Creek, MI, USA. *Education:* University of Michigan. *Career:* sang at the Aachen Opera, 1977–80, at Essen, 1980–83, and at Stuttgart Staatsoper, 1987–93 notably as Checchi in Henze's König Hirsch, Janáček's Števa, Tamino, Wagner's Steuermann and Don Ottavio; Guest at Frankfurt in 1983 as Hylas in Les Troyens and elsewhere in Germany in Jommelli's Fetonte; Sang at Vienna Staatsoper from 1989 notably as Tamino. *Recordings include:* Die Entführung; Die Soldaten. *Address:* c/o Staatsoper Wien, Opernring 2, 1010 Vienna, Austria.

**VAN DONGEN, Maria;** Dutch singer (soprano); b. 23 March 1928. *Career:* sang Mozart's Countess and Pamina at Amsterdam; Member of the Zürich Opera, 1959–65, debut as the Forza Leonora; Guest appearances at Frankfurt, London, (Countess at the Albert Hall), Bologna, Parma (Elisabeth, 1963), and Pisa (Elsa); Amsterdam 1963–67, as Donna Elvira; Munich from 1964, Vienna from 1967 as Ariadne, Fiordiligi, Senta and Desdemona; Munich Opera 1967, as Strauss's Danae, and as Irene in Rienzi; Further engagements at Barcelona and Hamburg (as Leonora in Fidelio), Graz, the Deutsche Oper Berlin, Piccola Scala Milan and the Salzburg Festival (First Lady in Die Zauberflöte, 1963–64); Sang Leonore at the Landestheater Salzburg, 1971; Frequent concert engagements. *Address:* c/o Vienna State Opera, Opernring 2, 1010 Vienna, Austria.

**VAN EETVELT, Francois;** Belgian singer (bass-baritone); b. 23 May 1946, Bornem. *Education:* Brussels and Antwerp Conservatories and in Italy and Germany. *Career:* sang Amfortas in Parsifal at Antwerp in 1976 and has sung there and in Brussels, Prague, Leipzig, Bratislava, Dresden and Helsinki as Don Giovanni, Wagner's Donner, Gunther, Wolfran and Kurwenal; Sang Apollo in Monteverdi's Orfeo, Jochanaan and Tarquinius in The Rape of Lucretia; Sang in the premiere of Das Schloss by André Laporte at Brussels in 1986; Festival engagements at Flanders and Aldeburgh; Television appearances include Monteverdi's Orfeo. *Honours:* Winner, Belcanto Competition, Ostend in 1978. *Address:* Theatre Royal de la Monnaie, 4 Leopoldstrasse, 1000 Brussels, Belgium.

**VAN EGMOND, Max;** singer (baritone); b. 1 Feb. 1936, Semarang, Indonesia. *Education:* studied in Netherlands with Tine van Willigen-de Lorme. *Career:* after winning prizes in Netherlands, Brussels and Munich made many appearances as concert singer, notably in Baroque music, Netherlands, England, Brazil, Germany, Austria, Italy, Poland, Belgium, USA and Canada; Engagements at most leading music festivals and centres; Radio and television broadcasts; Teacher of singing at the Amsterdam Musieklyceum from 1973. *Recordings:* St Matthew and St John Passions by Bach; Bach Cantatas conducted by Gustav Leonhardt and Nikolaus Harnoncourt; Der Tag des Gerichts by Telemann; Reger's Requiem; Il Ritorno d'Ulisse, Orfeo and Il Combattimento by Monteverdi; St Luke Passion by Schütz; Schubert's Schwanengesang; Lully's Alceste. *Honours:* Winner, 's-Hertogenbosch Competition, 1959; Edison Awards for Gramophone Recordings, 1969, 1971. *Address:* Willemsprakweg 150-1, Amsterdam 1007, Netherlands.

**VAN GEMERT, Theo;** singer (baritone); b. 20 Oct. 1940, Kerkrade, Netherlands. *Education:* Maastricht Conservatory. *Career:* fmr professional footballer, including Dutch national team, before career as a singer; sang at Aachen, 1970–71 as Germont and Jochanaan, and at Wuppertal from 1973 as Wotan and Gunther in The Ring, Creonte in Médée, Rigoletto, Iago, Nabucco, Count Luna, Simon Boccanegra, Telramund, Amfortas and Orestes; Guest appearances in Germany, France, Netherlands and Barcelona; Sang Hindemith's Cardillac at Wuppertal, 1991 and the Grand Inquisitor in Don Carlos, 1996; Season 2000–01 at Eutin and Hagen, in Der Freischütz and Der Kuhhandel by Weill. *Address:* c/o Städtische Buhnen, Spinnstrasse 4, 5600 Wuppertal, Germany.

**VAN GINKEL, Peter;** singer (bass-baritone); b. 10 March 1933, Eindhoven, Netherlands. *Education:* Quebec Conservatory, studied with Kurt Herbert Adler in San Francisco. *Career:* debut, Woodstock, New York, as Colonel Ibbetson in Peter Ibbetson by Deems Taylor; Has appeared at most Canadian opera houses and in Chicago in the premiere of Penderecki's Paradise Lost in 1978; German engagements at Cologne, Dortmund, Stuttgart, Mannheim, Düsseldorf and Nuremberg; Roles have included Mozart's Figaro and Alfonso, Verdi's Iago and Rigoletto, Caspar, Wagner's Dutchman, Wotan and Alberich, Escamillo, Wozzeck and Jochanaan; Engaged at Basle Opera, 1979–80; Many concert appearances. *Recordings include:* Lieder by Beethoven and Wolf. *Address:* c/o Stadtische Buhnen, Richard Wagner-Platz 2-10, 8500 Nuremberg, Germany.

**VAN GOETHEM, Patrick;** Belgian singer (countertenor); b. 1968. *Education:* private studies. *Career:* Flemish Schola Cantorum Cantate Domingo; member of various ensembles; Appearances with Laudantes Consort; Permanent soloists' ensemble; Performed with Ricercar Consort, Les Rumeurs Souterraines and Akademia; Appearances at festivals all over Europe; Passau Mozart Festival; Festival van Vlaanderen, Bruges; Ensemble Vocal Regional de Champagne-Ardenne; Dresden State Theatre; Bach weekends of the European Music Festival; Musica Antiqua Köln; Concentus Musicus Wien; Freiburger Barokorchestra and Hasse; Dresden Chamber Choir; Baroque Orchestra; Sang alto solos in Rotterdam; Sang with Orquesta Ciudad de Malaga; Netherlands Bach Society; Netherlands Handel Society; Concerto Köln; Baroque cantatas; Bach cantatas in Leipzig, as part of the Bach 250 celebrations. *Recordings:* 3 Bach cantatas; Monteverdi 1610 Vespers; Zelenka Te Deum; Heinichen Mass Opus 9; Scheidt Magnificat. *Address:* Kloosterstraat 114, 9420 Erpe-Mere, Belgium.

**VAN HOVE, Luc;** Composer; b. 3 Feb. 1957, Wilrijk, Belgium. *Education:* Antwerp Conservatory, with Wiilem Kersters. *Career:* Lecturer at Antwerp Conservatory and Lemmens Institute, Leuven, from, 1984. *Compositions:* Wood-Wind Quintet, 1982; Trois poèmes (Verlaine) for soprano, chorus and chamber orchestra, 1984; Two symphonies, 1989, 1997; Septet, 1989; Cello Sonata, 1991; Aria, for cello, 1992; Triptych, oboe concerto, 1993; String Quartet, 1994; Piano Concerto, 1995; Nonet, 1995; Strings, 1997. *Address:* c/o SABAM, Rue d'Arlon 75–77, B–1040 Brussels, Belgium. *Telephone:* (2) 2868211. *Fax:* (2) 2311800.

**VAN IMMERSEEL, Jos;** Harpsichordist and Conductor; b. 2 April 1928, Monaco. *Education:* Studied at the Antwerp Conservatoire, notably with Flor Peeters and Kenneth Gilbert. *Career:* Professor at the Anvers Conservatoire

from 1972 and Artistic Director at the Sweelinck Conservatoire Amsterdam, 1981–85; Founded the Baroque Orchestra Anima Eterna, 1985 and Professor of Piano at the Paris Conservatoire from 1992; Many recitals and concerts throughout France; Conductor of the ensemble Anime Eterna and let it in Handel's Serse for Flanders Opera, 1996. *Address:* Conservatoire National, 14 Rue de Madrid, 75008 Paris, France.

**VAN KAMPEN, Bernhardt Anthony;** British viol player, violone player, double bassist and artist; b. 4 March 1943, Bushey, Herts.; s. of Hans Bernhardt Albert van Kampen and Dorothy Frances van Kampen (née Smithers); m. Julia Henriette Margarete Bockhacker 1991; one d. *Education:* Hornsey Coll. of Art, Guildhall School of Music and Drama, studied with Josef Rač z, and with Prof. František Pošta, Solo Bassist of the Czech Philharmonic Orchestra, viola da gamba with Alison Crum and Mark Caudle. *Career:* Art Ed. Aldus Books 1964–66; Founder-mem. New BBC Orchestra (later Acad. of the BBC) 1966; Prin. Bass, New BBC Orchestra 1967–68; freelance in London with London Symphony Orchestra, Royal Philharmonic Orchestra and others; BBC Symphony Orchestra 1972–78; freelance musician and artist, composer, arranger and conductor, viols, violone and baroque and classical double-bass with various early music groups; teacher, pianist and harpsichordist; Founder and Dir Harmonie Universelle. *Exhibitions:* London, North Cornwall (St Endellion), Goch, Nivelles, Friedersdorf, Waldbröl, Berlin, Reichshof-Hespert, Gummersbach, Bonn, etc. *Recordings:* with BBC Symphony Orchestra, Acad. of Ancient Music, London Classical Players, City of London Sinfonia, Hanover Band, London Sinfonietta and many others. *Address:* Harmonie Universelle, Heinrich-Krapoth-Strasse 4, 51647 Gummersbach/Hülsenbusch, Germany (office). *Telephone:* (2261) 28067 (office). *Fax:* (2261) 28067 (office).

**VAN KESTEREN, John;** Dutch singer (tenor); b. 4 May 1921, The Hague. *Education:* studied in The Hague with Lothar Wallerstein and with Nadia Boulanger in Paris; Further study with Vera Schwarz in Salzburg. *Career:* debut, Scheveningen 1947, as the Italian Singer in Der Rosenkavalier; Sang operetta in Netherlands, on Dutch Radio and in Utrecht; Sang at the Komische Oper Berlin from 1951, Städtische Oper Berlin from 1953; Salzburg Festival from 1957, as Basilio in Le nozze di Figaro and in concert; Guest appearances in Vienna (from 1954), Düsseldorf, Munich, Stuttgart, Frankfurt, Ghent, Milan, the Drottningholm Festival (Stockholm), New York City Opera, Boston, Cincinnati, Dallas and Buenos Aires; Many concert appearances. *Recordings:* Belmonte in Die Entführung; Le Postillon de Lonjumeau by Adam; Pfitzner's Palestrina, Ariadne auf Naxos, Die Kluge by Orff; Leonore by Paer; Carmina Burana.

**VAN KEULEN, Isabelle;** violinist and violist; b. 16 Dec. 1966, Mijdrecht, Netherlands. *Education:* Sweelinck Conservatoire, Amsterdam, Salzburg Mozarteum with Sándor Végh, masterclasses with Max Rostal and Vladimir Spivakov. *Career:* debut as violist 1992; has appeared from 1983 with Berlin Philharmonic, Vienna, Detroit, Minnesota and BBC National Orchestra of Wales, NHK of Tokyo and the Concertgebouw; Conductors have included Baumgartner, Chailly, Colin Davis, Dutoit, Ehrling, Leitner, Leppard, Marriner, Neumann, de Waart and Zinman; Appearances at the Salzburg Festival and tours with the Bamberg Symphony and Gidon Kremer's Lockenhaus Soloists; BBC Proms debut 1990, in Mozart with the Rotterdam Philharmonic; Strauss's Concerto with the BBC Philharmonic and the Dutilleux Concerto with the Concertgebouw; Other repertoire includes concertos by Bach, Haydn, Henkemans, Schnittke, Spohr and Stravinsky, in addition to the standard items; Messiaen's Quartet for the End of Time at the 1999 London Prom concerts; as violist has collaborated with the Hagen, Orlando and Borodin Quartets. *Recordings include:* Saint-Saëns and Vieuxtemps Concertos, London Symphony; Schubert's Octet; Shostakovich Sonatas for Violin and Viola (Fidelio). *Honours:* Silver Medal, International Yehudi Menuhin Violin Competition, 1983; Winner, Eurovision Young Musician of the Year Competition, 1984. *Current Management:* Georgina Ivor Associates, 66 Alderbrook Road, London SW12 8AB, England.

**VAN KOOTEN, Katie;** American singer (soprano). *Education:* Biola Univ., CA with Jeanne Robinson, and GSMD with Rudolf Piernay, masterclasses with Sir Colin Davis, Graham Johnson, Martin Katz, Eugene Asti, Ian Burnside, Robin Bowman, Earl Patriarco. *Career:* professional debut as Magda in La Rondine at ROH, Covent Garden 2004; roles include Pamina in Die Zauberflöte, Aminta in Il Re Pastore, Kate Pinkerton in Madama Butterfly, Eurydice in Orphée, Arbate in Mitridate; concert appearances include Mozart's Requiem with LPO and Vladimir Jurowsky, Kensington and Chelsea Music Soc. Recital at Leighton House; mem. Jette Parker Young Artists Programme, ROH. *Current Management:* c/o Peter Wiggins, IMG Artists, 44 rue Blanche, Paris 75009, France. *Telephone:* 1-44-31-00-10 (office). *Fax:* 1-44-31-44-40 (office). *E-mail:* artistsparis@imgartists.com (office). *Website:* www.imgartists.com (office).

**VAN MECHELEN, Werner;** Belgian singer (bass-baritone); b. 1961, Turnhout. *Education:* studied under Roland Bufkens, Vocalist's Diploma, Lemmens Institute, Leuven; Masterclasses with Dietrich Fischer-Dieskau, Elisabeth Schwarzkopf, Robert Holl, Mitsuko Shirai, Hartmut Höll, Malcolm King. *Career:* Performances of Passions, Oratorios and orchestral Lieder in Cologne, Geneva, Brussels, Amsterdam, Paris, Barcelona and Tel-Aviv; Has worked with conductors Stefan Soltesz, Sigiswald Kuijken, Ton Koopman, Antonio Pappano, S Varviso, others; Has sung Mozart's Count and Figaro, Guglielmo, Don Giovanni, Leporello, Papageno, also Schaunard in La Bohème, Dandini in La Cenerentola, Belcore in L'Elisir d'amore, Wolfram in

Tannhäuser, Animal Trainer and Athlete in Lulu; Guest appearances in Zürich, Liège, Antwerp, Wiesbaden, Braunschweig, Bielefeld, Coburg, Limoges, elsewhere; Sang under direction of Kuijken in Caldara's opera I Disingannati at Innsbruck Baroque Festival, 1993, and with same ensemble performed Don Giovanni, 1995, Pergolesi's Livietta e Tracollo, 1996, Le nozze di Figaro, 1998; Repertoire includes all great lieder-cycles; Often sings to piano accompaniment of Jozef De Beenhouwer, Eric Schneider and others; Conducts Kemp Oratorio Society concerts; Engaged to sing in Wozzeck for La Bastille, Rigoletto for open-air festival in Belgium, Marcello in Liège and Kothner in Meistersinger at Antwerp. *Recordings:* For Belgian and foreign radio and television; Discs with Baroque music; Richard Strauss Lieder. *Address:* Goedeluchtstraat 12, 8420 Wenduine, Belgium. *E-mail:* arioso@skynet.be.

**VAN NES, Jard;** Dutch singer (mezzo-soprano); b. 15 June 1948. *Career:* debut in Mahler's 2 Symphony under Bernard Haitink at Concertgebouw, 1983; Appearances in Bach's St Matthew Passion under Nikolaus Harnoncourt and in Mahler's 8th Symphony; Tour of North America with Minnesota Orchestra and Edo de Waart, 1987–88; Further concerts in Paris, London, Oslo, Montreal and Ludwigsburg; Stage debut with Netherlands Opera 1983, as Bertarido in Rodelinda; Double bill of Hindemith's Sancta Susanna and Mörder, Hoffnung der Frauen 1984; Season 1986–87 with parts in Il Ritorno d'Ulisse, Die Meistersinger (Magdalena) and Tristan und Isolde as Brangaene; Sang in Ligeti's Le Grand Macabre at the Paris Châtelet and the Salzburg Festival, 1997; Sang Mrs Sedley in Peter Grimes at Glyndebourne, 2000. *Recordings:* Mozart Requiem, Brahms Alto Rhapsody, Mahler 2nd Symphony and Zemlinsky Lieder; Messiah; Beethoven's Ninth; Handel's Theodora and Das Lied von der Erde. *Address:* c/o Netherlands Opera, Waterlooplein 22, 1011PG, Amsterdam, Netherlands.

**VAN REE, Jean;** singer (tenor); b. 7 March 1943, Kerkrade, Netherlands. *Education:* studied with Else Bischof-Bornes in Aachen and Franziska Martienssen-Lohmann in Düsseldorf. *Career:* debut, Mainz, 1963, in Zar und Zimmermann; Sang in Basle, Augsburg and Cologne; Guest appearances in Amsterdam, Hamburg, Hanover, Salzburg and Frankfurt; Augsburg, 1971, in the premiere of Rafael Kubelik's opera on the life of Titian, Cornelia Faroli; Teatro Regio Turin, 1983, in Lulu; Antwerp and Ghent, 1984, as Matteo in Arabella; Other roles include Don Ottavio, Hoffmann, Count Almaviva, Alfredo, and Mephistopheles in Doktor Faust by Busoni; Metropolitan Opera, 1978, as Bicias in Massenet's Thaïs; Sang Berg's Alwa at Barcelona and Vienna, 1987; Sang the Captain in Wozzeck at Enschede, Netherlands, 1993. *Recordings include:* Les Brigandes, by Offenbach. *Address:* c/o Staatsoper, Opernring 2, 1010 Vienna, Austria.

**VAN SANTE, Sophia Maris Christina;** Dutch singer (mezzo-soprano); b. 11 Aug. 1925, Zaandam. *Education:* Amsterdam Muzieklyceum with van der Sluys and Ruth Horna; Further studies with Marietta Amstad in Italy. *Career:* many appearances from 1960 with the Amsterdam Opera as the Woman in Schoenberg's Erwartung, Marie in Wozzeck and Judith in Duke Bluebeard's Castle; also sang in the Dutch premieres of Henze's Der Junge Lord and Dallapiccola's Il Prigioniero. *Recordings include:* Der Rosenkavalier.

**VAN STEEN, Jac;** Dutch conductor; *Music Director, Deutsches Nationaltheater Weimar;* b. 1956, Eindhoven. *Education:* Brabants Conservatory. *Career:* conducted Univ. of Leiden Student Orchestra and Nat. Youth Orchestra; participant in BBC European Conductors' Seminar, London 1986; Music Dir Nijmegen Bach Choir 1986–90, Amsterdam Nat. Ballet – 1994; Permanent Guest Conductor Bochum Symphony, Germany 1992–94; Chief Conductor Nuremberg Symphony 1997–2002; fmr Music Dir, Neues Berliner Kammerorchester; Music Dir Deutsches Nationaltheater Weimar 2002–; Chief Conductor Staatskapelle Weimar 2002–, Musikkollegium Winterhur 2002–; Prin. Guest Conductor, BBC Nat. Orchestra of Wales 2005–; appearances as guest conductor in Holland, Germany and the UK include Rotterdam Philharmonic, Netherlands Philharmonic, Residentie Orkest Den Haag, Hamburg Symphonic Orchestra, Saarbrücken Orchestra, Mannheim Nat. Theatre Orchestra, BBC SO, BBC Philharmonic, Hallé Orchestra, London Sinfonietta; world premieres include Jonathan Harvey's Concerto for Percussion and Orchestra, with BBC SO, London, Christian Jost's Lux Aeterna, with Residentie Orkest Den Haag 2003; Prof., Royal Conservatory of Music, The Hague and Fontys Music Acad., Tilburg. *Recordings:* David Bedford, Symphony No. 1 1998, Elgar/Lutoslawski, Cello Concertos 2001, Themes and Variations 2001, David Matthews, In the Dark Time 2001, Thea Musgrave, Memento Vitae 2003, Purcell/Handel/Mozart, Arias 2003, Love from a Stranger (film scores) 2004, Bruch, Das Lied von der Glocke 2005. *Address:* Deutsches Nationaltheater, 2 Theaterplatz, Weimar, Thuringia 99423, Germany. *Website:* www.nationaltheater-weimar.de.

**VAN TASSEL, Charles;** singer (baritone); b. 28 Aug. 1937, New York, USA. *Education:* studied in New York and with Luigi Ricci, Rome. *Career:* debut, Contemporary Chamber Players, Chicago, in Weisgall's Purgatory, 1967; Sang at Bremerhaven Opera 1968–71, Kassel 1971–75, Wiesbaden and Hamburg Staatsoper; Appearances with Netherlands Opera from 1975, notably as Guglielmo, Enrico in Lucia di Lammermoor, Verdi's Ford, and Nabucco, and Yeletsky in The Queen of Spades; Holland Festival 1983, as the man in Mörder, Hoffnung der Frauen, by Hindemith; Further engagments as Escamillo, Mozart's Count, Marcello, Verdi's Posa, Jochanaan in Salome, and Demetrius in A Midsummer Night's Dream; Sang Mussorgsky in the premiere of Symposion by Peter Schat, Amsterdam, 1994; Teacher at the Sweelinck

Conservatory; Frequent concert appearances. *Recordings include:* Die Zauberflöte (Erato); Schreker's Die Gezeichneten (Marco Polo); Messiaen's St François d'Assise (KRO). *Address:* c/o Netherlands Opera, Waterlooplein 22, 1011 PG Amsterdam, Netherlands.

**VAN VLIJMEN, Jan;** Dutch composer and administrator; b. 11 Oct. 1935, Rotterdam. *Education:* studied composition with Kees van Baaren. *Career:* Director of the Amersfoort Music School, 1961–65; Lecturer in Theory at Utrecht Conservatory, 1965–67; Deputy Director of the Royal Conservatory, The Hague, 1967, Director, 1971; General Manager of Netherlands Opera, 1985–88; Director of the Holland Festival, 1991–97. *Compositions include:* Strijkkwartet No. 1, 1956 and No. 2, 1958 both for String Quartet; Gruppi for Orchestra, 1962, revised 1980; Sonata for Piano and Large Ensemble, 1966; Quintetto a fiati No. 2 for Wind Quintet, 1972; Axel, opera with Reinbert de Leeuw, 1977; Faithful for Viola, 1984; Nonet for Ensemble, 1985; Solo II for Clarinet, 1986; R Escher–Summer Rites at Noon for 2 Orchestras, 1987; Such a Day of Sweetness for Soprano and Orchestra, 1988; Un Malheureux Vêtu de Noir, opera, 1990; Concerto for Piano and Orchestra, 1991; Tombeau (Solo III), for Violoncello, 1991; Inferno (Dante), cantate for Choir and Large Ensemble, 1993; A Schoenberg–6 Kleine Klavierstücke, Op 19 arrangement for Orchestra (published), 1993; After Schoenberg Op 19: Solo IV, against that time, for flute and contralto, 1994–95; Quintetto for strings, 1995–96; Monumentum for large orchestra and mezzo-soprano, 1998; Sei pezzi for violin and piano, 1998; Choeurs for chamber choir and several instruments, 1999; Gestures I and II for violin and piano, 1999; Arrangements of Schoenberg and Zemlinsky. *Recordings:* Un malheureux de Noir; Sonata, Omaggio a Gesualdo and Inferno; Concerto. *Honours:* Officier des Arts et des Lettres, France; Officier in de orde van de Nederlandse Leeuw, Netherlands; State Prizes; Prizes from the City of Amsterdam. *Address:* Eerste Breeuwerstraat 24, 1013 MK Amsterdam, Netherlands.

**VAN VROOMAN, Richard;** singer (tenor); b. 29 July 1936, Kansas City, MO, USA. *Education:* Kansas City Conservatorium, Salzburg Mozarteum with Max Lorenz. *Career:* debut, Bregenz Festival 1962, as Lorenzo in Fra Diavalo; Many appearances in West Germany, Austria and Switzerland, notably at the Zürich Opera 1964–78; Guest engagements at Salzburg 1964–65, Aix-en-Provence, with the Deutsche Oper am Rhein and the Paris Opéra and in Lisbon, Geneva, Frankfurt, Hamburg, Rome, Bordeaux and Marseille; Glyndebourne Festival 1968, as Belmonte in Die Entführung; Best known in operas by Mozart, Rossini and Donizetti and in the Baroque repertoire; Many concert appearances. *Recordings:* Wozzeck (CBS); Mozart Davidde Penitente and Handel Acis and Galatea (Schwann); Doktor und Apotheker by Dittersdorf; Cimarosa Requiem (Philips); Haydn Salve Regina (EMI). *Address:* c/o Opernhaus Zürich, Falkenstrasse 1, 8008 Zürich, Switzerland.

**VANAUD, Marcel;** Singer (Baritone); b. 1952, Brussels, Belgium. *Education:* Studied at the Brussels Conservatoire and at Liège. *Career:* Sang at the Liège Opera 1975–83, notably as Papageno, Escamillo, Alfonso in La Favorita, Renato and Ourrais in Mireille; Guest appearances at Pittsburgh and New Orleans 1984; New York City Opera 1985 as Zurga in Les Pêcheurs de Perles; Théâtre de la Monnaie Brussels as Raimund in Comte Ory and Mozart's Figaro; Season 1987–88 as Lescaut at Montreal, Posa in Don Carlos at Tulsa, Figaro at Santa Fe and Raimbaud at Toulouse; La Scala Milan 1989 in the premiere of Doktor Faustus by Manzoni; Returned to Liège 1992 as Mephistopheles in La Damnation de Faust and sang Germont at Los Angeles; Festival de Radio France at Montpellier 1992, as Sacchini's Oedipus and in Chateau des Carpathes by Philippe Hersant; Season 2000–01 as Count Luna at Montpellier, Amonasro in Geneva, and the Dutchman at Liège. *Recordings include:* Les contes d'Hoffmann and Franck's Les Béatitudes; Karnac in Le Roi d'Ys.

**VANDERSTEENE, Zeger;** Singer (Tenor); b. 5 June 1940, Ghent, Belgium. *Career:* Sang at first in concert and appeared in opera from 1980; Théâtre de la Monnaie at Brussels, 1981–84, as Evandre in Alceste and Steuermann in Fliegende Holländer; Théâtre du Châtelet, Paris, 1983, in Rameau's Les Indes Galantes; Bologna, 1987, in Gluck's La Danza; Sang Aegisthus in Elektra at Antwerp, 1990; Song recitals in works by Schubert, Schumann and Fauré. *Recordings include:* Castor et Pollux by Rameau (Telefunken); Armide by Lully (Erato). *Address:* Antwerp Opera, Ommeganchshtrasse 59, 2018 Antwerp, Belgium.

**VANDERVELDE, Janika;** American composer; b. 1955, Ripon, WI. *Education:* Univ. of Wisconsin; Univ. of Minnesota, with Dominick Argento (PhD 1985). *Career:* comms from Minnesota Orchestra, St Paul Chamber Orchestra and Dale Warland Singers; Faculty, Minnesota Center for Arts Educ. 1990–; Composer-in-Residence, Minnesota Chorale 1999–2002. *Compositions:* Genesis I, for oboe and piano 1983, II, piano and trio 1983, III, flute, viola and harp 1984, IV, for violin, clarinet and piano 1987, V, four guitars 1987, VI, string trio 1988, VII, for saxophone, piano and percussion 1989; Clockwork Concerto, for viola and orchestra, 1987; Hildegard, video opera, 1989; O viridissima virga, for chorus and percussion, 1992; Polyhymnia for chorus and orchestra, 1992; Seven Sevens, opera, 1993; Echoes across the Stara Planina, for female chorus and orchestra, 1995; The Dreamweaver, for speaker and orchestra, 1996; Cafés of Melbourne, for accordion and orchestra, 1997; Beijing Cai Hong, for chorus and pipa, 1997; Wataridori, for chorus and oboe, 1997; Pacific Transit for pipa and orchestra, 1998; Cosmos for speaker and orchestra, 1999; Tutti for Earth and Heaven for chorus and organ, 1999; Cançao de Embalar for chorus, 2000; Dance Ablaze! for chorus and percussion, 2001; Adventures of the Black Dot for speaker, 4 instruments and chorus, 2001; O factura dei for chorus, percussion and electric bass, 2002; Birds of Oz for chorus 2003, Monapacataca (String Quartet No. 1) 2004, Villancico for chorus and percussion 2004, Candoncilla del primer deseo for chorus and percussion 2004, Mar for chorus 2005. *Recordings:* published by Albany, Cinnabar, Innova, Nat. Public Radio, and others. *Publications:* music published by Boosey & Hawkes, Earthsongs, and Hothouse Press. *Honours:* Lili Boulanger Award 1994, American Composers Forum/Jerome Foundation Commissioning Awards 1980, 1985, 1990, 1992, 1995, Bush Foundation Fellowships 1986, 1995, McKnight Foundation Fellowships 1984, 1994, 2003, Meet The Composer New Residencies Award 1999, Minnesota State Arts Board Fellowships 1985, 2003. *Address:* c/o Hothouse Press, 1631 Highland Parkway, Saint Paul, MN 55116, USA. *Telephone:* (651) 690-3000. *Fax:* (651) 690-4559. *E-mail:* janikav@visi.com (office). *Website:* www.janikavandervelde .com.

**VANDOR, Ivan;** Composer; b. 13 Oct. 1932, Pecs, Hungary. *Education:* Diploma in Composition, S Cecilia; MA Ethnomusicology, UCLA, 1970. *Career:* Member, Musica Elettronica Viva, 1966–68; Member, Nuova Consonanza Improvis Group, 1967–68; Research in Tibetan Buddhist Music, 1970–71; Director, International Institute for comparative Music Studies, Berlin, 1977–83; Founder, Director, Scuola Interculturale di Musica, 1979–; Professor, Composition, Conservatory of Music, Bologna, 1979–; Professor of Music, Conservatory of Music S Cecilia. *Compositions:* Quartetto Per Archi, 1962; Moti, 1963; Serenata, 1964; Dance Music, 1969; Esercizi, 1966; Winds, 1970; Cronache, 1981; Cronache II, 1989; Concerto for Violoncello and orchestra, 1991; Fantasie for piano and orchestra, 1992; Offrande II, 1993; some short pieces for Harpsichord. *Publications:* La Musique du Bouddhisme Tibetain, 1976; Die Musik des Tibetischen Buddhismus, 1978; Editor, The World of Music, 1975–85. *Address:* Viale Parioli 73, 00197 Rome, Italy.

**VANEEV, Vladimir;** Singer (Bass); b. 1961, Russial. *Education:* Graduated Gorky Conservatoire, 1986. *Career:* Sang with the Mussorgsky Opera, St Petersburg, 1986–97; Kirov Opera from 1997, as Verdi's Philip II and Grand Inquisitor Boris and Pimen in Boris Godunov and Prince Gremin in Eugene Onegin; Further appearances as Dosifei in Khovanshchina, Ruslan, Wagner's Wotan and Dutchman and Boris in Katerina Izmailova; Sang Ivan Khovansky in Khovanshchina with the Kirov at Covent Garden, 2000; Other roles include Prince Galitsky and Khan Konchak in Prince Igor, Monterone (Rigoletto), Remeniuk in Prokofiev's Semyon Kotko and Kochubei in Mazeppa; Sang Klingsor in Parsifal, with the Kirov at the Royal Albert Hall, 1999. *Honours:* Honoured Artist of Russia; Prize Winner Voce Verdiani, All-Russian Chaliapin and Russian State Competitions. *Address:* c/o Kirov Opera, Mariinksy Theatre, 1 Theatre Square, St Petersburg, Russia.

**VANELLI, Adriana;** Singer (Soprano); b. 1957, Detroit, USA. *Education:* Cleveland Institute of Music. *Career:* Sang at New York Grand Opera as Butterfly, Mimi and Aida, Liu in Turandot and Nedda in Pagliacci for Stamford State Opera, Mozart's Countess in Nevada and Tosca for New Jersey Opera; Violetta for Connecticut Grand Opera 1985 and Desdemona at Providence, 1986; European debut as Liu, at Hamburg; Tatiana in Eugene Onegin for Netherlands Opera, Manon Lescaut at Wiesbaden (1985) and Tosca at Nice (1986); Deutsche Oper Berlin 1986-89; Sang Annina in Menotti's The Saint of Bleecker Street, 1989; Concert engagements in Europe and North America. *Address:* c/o Deutsche Oper, Richard Wagner Strasse 10, D-10585 Berlin, Germany.

**VANESS, Carol;** Singer (Soprano); b. 27 July 1952, San Diego, California, USA. *Education:* Studied in California with David Scott and in 1976 won the San Francisco Opera Auditions. *Career:* San Francisco 1977, as Vitellia in La Clemenza di Tito; New York City Opera from 1979, as Alcina, Antonia in Les Contes d'Hoffmann, Vitellia, Flotow's Frau Fluth, Mimi, and Leila in Les pêcheurs de Perles, Rigoletto (Gilda), Traviata (Violetta); Donna Anna, Glyndebourne Opera from 1982, as Donna Anna, Electra in Idomeneo, Fiordiligi and Amelia Boccanegra (1986); Covent Garden debut 1982, as Mimi: returned for Vitellia and Dalila in Handel's Samson; Countess Almaviva, 1989; Rosalinda in Der Fledermaus; Metropolitan Opera from 1984, as Armida in Rinaldo, Fiordiligi, Electra and the Countess in Figaro, Manon; Australian Opera 1985, Amelia in Un Ballo in Maschera; Seattle Opera 1986, as Massenet's Manon; Desdemona, 1986; Violetta, 1988; Leonora in Trovatore, 1989; Concert appearances in the Choral Symphony in Paris, the Verdi Requiem in Philadelphia and at the Lincoln Center New York with Pavarotti; Sang in Beethoven Missa solemnis at the Barbican Hall, London, 1989; Royal Opera, Vitellia in La Clemenza di Tito 1989; Trovatore 1990 at the Metropolitan Opera and Faust (Marguerite); Don Giovanni (Anna) at Covent Garden, 1992; Season 1992/93 as Iphigénie en Tauride at La Scala, Mathilde in Guillaume Tell at San Francisco and Olympia at the Met; Sang Desdemona at the Metropolitan, 1994; Norma at Seattle, 1994, (Amelia, Ballo in Maschera, 1995); Fiordiligi at the Met, 1997; Elisabeth de Valois at the Opéra Bastille, 1998; Season 2000–01 as Donna Elvira for San Francisco Opera, the Trovatore Leonora in Washington and Mathilde in Guillaume Tell for the Vienna Staatsoper; Sang Tosca at Covent Garden, 2002. *Recordings include:* Donna Anna in the Glyndebourne production of Don Giovanni conducted by Bernard Haitink; Masses by Haydn; Glyndebourne, Haitink, Così fan tutte; Beethoven's Ninth with Dohnányi and Cleveland Orchestra; Missa Solemnis with Tate and the ECO; Don Giovanni (Elvira), conducted by Muti, EMI;

Tosca, Philips; Rossini, Stabat Mater, Philips (Bychkov). *Address:* c/o Herbert H Breslin, 119 West 57th Street, NY 10019, USA.

**VÄNSKÄ, Osmo;** Finnish conductor; *Music Director, Minnesota Orchestra*; b. 28 Feb. 1953, Sääminki. *Education:* Sibelius Acad., Helsinki with Jorma Panula. *Career:* co-principal clarinet, Helsinki PO 1977–82; Principal Guest Conductor, Lahti SO 1985, Music Dir 1988–; Music Dir, Iceland SO 1993–96, Tapiola Sinfonietta 1990–92; Chief Conductor BBC Scottish SO –2002; Music Dir, Minnesota Orchestra 2003–(11); guest conductor with Chicago SO, Cleveland Orchestra, Boston SO, San Francisco SO, Detroit, Houston and Saint Louis Symphonies, Munich PO, Leipzig Gewandhaus Orchestra, Oslo PO, Concertgebouw Orchestra, BBC SO, Czech PO, Orchestre Nat. de France; symphonic cycles of Beethoven, Sibelius and Nielsen with BBC Scottish SO; Tapiola by Sibelius and Nielsen's 4th at the London Proms 2002. *Recordings include:* Sibelius Edition (with Lahti SO), albums of Kalevi Aho, Sofia Gubaidulina, Kokkonen and Rautavaara, Nielsen Symphonies. *Honours:* Royal Philharmonic Soc. Award 2002, Musical America Conductor of the Year 2005. *Current Management:* Harrison/Parrott Ltd, 12 Penzance Place, London, W11 4PA, England. *Telephone:* (20) 7229 9166. *Fax:* (20) 7221 5042. *Website:* www.harrisonparrott.com. *Address:* c/o Minnesota Orchestra, Orchestra Hall, 1111 Nicollet Mall, Minneapolis, MN 55403, USA. *Website:* www.minnesotaorchestra.org.

**VARADY, Julia;** German/Romanian singer (soprano); b. 1 Sept. 1941, Oradea, Romania; m. Dietrich Fischer-Dieskau 1977. *Education:* studied in Cluj with Emilia Popp and in Bucharest with Arta Florescu. *Career:* debut, Cluj as Fiordiligi 1962; guest appearances at the Budapest and Bucharest Operas; moved to Frankfurt 1972; sang Violetta at Cologne 1972; Munich from 1973, as Vitellia in La Clemenza di Tito, Lady Macbeth, Butterfly, Giorgetta (Il Tabarro), Elektra in Idomeneo, Santuzza, Liu, Leonora (La Forza del Destino), Elisabeth de Valois and Cordelia in the premiere of Lear by Reimann 1978; Scottish Opera 1974, as Gluck's Alceste; Metropolitan Opera 1978, Donna Elvira; tours of Japan, Israel and the USA; appearances at the Berlin, Edinburgh, Munich and Salzburg Festivals and at the Promenade Concerts London; La Scala Milan 1984, in Idomeneo; other roles include Countess Almaviva, Judith (Bluebeard's Castle), Tatiana, Desdemona and Rosalinde; sang Wagner's Senta at Munich 1990, Covent Garden 1992; Vitellia in La Clemenza di Tito at the Queen Elizabeth Hall 1990; appeared as Abigaille in Nabucco at the 1990 Munich Festival; season 1992–93 as the Trovatore Leonora at Munich, in concert performances with the Glyndebourne Company of Fidelio and Elisabeth de Valois at the Deutsche Oper Berlin; returned to Berlin 1997, as Senta; Aida at the 1997 Munich Festival; concert repertoire includes arias by Mozart and Beethoven, Vier Letzte Lieder by Strauss, Britten's War Requiem, the Verdi Requiem, the Faust oratorios of Schumann and Berlioz; Requiem by Reimann (premiere 1982); soloist in the Verdi Requiem at Berlin 2000; recital in Madrid 2003; Prof. 1999–. *Recordings include:* Lucio Silla by Mozart, Die Fledermaus, Il Matrimonio Segreto, Lear, Idomeneo, La Clemenza di Tito, Duke Bluebeard's Castle, Gli Amori di Teolinda by Meyerbeer, Cavalleria Rusticana, Les Contes d'Hoffmann, Arabella, Don Giovanni, Handel's Saul, Mozart's Le Nozze di Figaro, works Verdi and Richard Strauss, Wagner's Wesendonk Lieder. *Honours:* Maximillian's Orden, Bayerische Herdnistorden.

**VARCOE, Stephen;** Singer (baritone); b. 19 May 1949, Lostwithiel, Cornwall, England; m. Melinda Davies 1972; three s. (one deceased) two d. *Education:* Cathedral Choir School and King's School, Canterbury; MA, King's College, Cambridge; Guildhall School of Music, London. *Career:* concerts in most major British and European festivals; specialist in Lieder, French Mélodies and English song; many appearances on British, French and German radio stations; sang Sarastro in Die Zauberflöte at the Mozart Experience, London, 1989; Haydn's L'Infedeltà Delusa at Antwerp in 1990; created Zossima in the premiere of Tavener's Mary of Egypt, Aldeburgh, 1992; Peri's Eurydice in Drottningholm, 1997; sang Bartley in Riders to the Sea, Vaughan Williams Festival, London, 1997. *Recordings:* over 130 albums including: Purcell's Indian Queen, Fairy Queen, King Arthur and The Tempest; Handel's Partenope, L'Allegro, Triumph of Time and Truth, Alessandro and Israel in Egypt; Bach's B Minor Mass, Masses, Cantatas and Matthew and John Passions; Fauré's Requiem; Finzi's Songs of Thomas Hardy; Rameau's Motets, French Mélodies; Britten's Cantata Misericordium and Tavener's Mary of Egypt; Schubert's Lieder. *Publication:* Sing English Song, 2000. *Contribution:* Cambridge Companion to Singing, 2000. *Honours:* Gulbenkian Foundation Fellowship, 1977. *Current Management:* Caroline Phillips Management, The Old Brushworks, Pickwick Road, Corsham, Wiltshire, SN13 9BX, England. *Telephone:* (1249) 716716. *Fax:* (1249) 716717. *E-mail:* cphillips@caroline-phillips.co.uk. *Website:* www.caroline -phillips.co.uk/varcoe.

**VARGA, Balint (Andras);** Music Publisher and Music Interviewer; b. 3 Nov. 1941, Budapest, Hungary; m. Katalin Zsoldos, 14 Jan 1977, 2 d. *Education:* Teacher's degree, English and Russian, University of Budapest, 1960–65; Hungarian Journalists' School, 1966–67; Studied piano privately for 13 years. *Career:* Regular radio programmes in Budapest, 1965–; Some foreign radio programmes; Occasional programmes on Hungarian Television; Head of Promotion, Editio Musica Budapest, 1971–; Deputy Director of the Hungarian Cultural Institute, Berlin, 1991–. *Publications:* Conversations with Lutoslawski, 1974; Conversations with Iannis Xenakis, 1980; Conversations with Luciano Berio, 1981; 4 other anthologies of musical interviews published in Hungarian 1972, 1974, 1979, 1986; Translated Aaron Copland's The New

Music into Hungarian 1973, also two books published in English and one published in German. *Contributions:* Regular articles in Muzsika. *Address:* 1020 Berlin, Fischerinsel, 10301, Germany.

**VARGA, Gilbert;** Conductor; b. 17 Jan. 1952, London, England; m. 2 children. *Education:* Studied with Franco Ferrara, Sergiu Celibidache and Charles Bruck. *Career:* Principal Conductor, Hofer Symphoniker, 1980–85; Chief Conductor of the Philharmonia Hungarica, 1985–90; Principal Guest Conductor, Stuttgart Chamber Orchestra, 1992– 1996; Principal Guest Conductor, Malmö Symfoniorkester, 1997–99; Music Director Orquestre Sinfonica de Euskadi, 1998–; Guest engagements include Orchestre de Paris, Rotterdam Philharmonic, Hallé Orchestra, City of Birmingham Symphony, BBC Philharmonic, Bavarian Radio, Gürzenich Orchestra Cologne, Toronto Symphony, Indianapolis Symphony, Sydney Symphony Orchestra; Yomiuri Nippon Symphony, Tokyo; Scottish Chamber ORchestra; Orchestre de la Suisse Romande; Göteborg Symphony Orchestra; Cologne Radio; Minnesota Orchestra; Santa Caecilia Roma; Saint Louis Symphony; RAI Torino. *Recordings include:* Symphony No. 6 of Anton Rubinstein and solo cello concertos with BBC Philharmonic and Rolland; Ravel recording with Orquestre Sinfonica de Euskadi and recordings with Munich Chamber Orchestra and Bamberg Symphony. *Address:* c/o Intermusica Artists Management Ltd, 16 Duncan Terrace, London N1 8BZ, England.

**VARGAS, Milagro;** Singer (Mezzo-soprano); b. 1958, USA. *Education:* Studied at Oberlin College and the Eastman School of Music with Jan DeGaetani. *Career:* Member of the Stuttgart Staatsoper 1983–88, notably in the premiere of Akhnaten by Philip Glass (1984) and as Cherubino, Nancy in Albert Herring, Orlofsky, and Lybia in Jommelli's Fetonte; Komische Oper Berlin as Cherubino, Heidelberg Festival as Ramiro in La Finta Giardiniera; Sang Charlotte in Zimmermann's Die Soldaten at Strasbourg and Stuttgart, 1988; Sang Ravel's Shéhérazade at the Cabrillo Festival 1986 and has appeared elsewhere in concert at the Aspen and Marlboro Festivals, with the Philadelphia Orchestra and the Rochester Philharmonic; Season 2000–01 as Nemorino at Houston, Lensky in Florence, Donizetti's Roberto Devereux for the Vienna Staatsoper and Don Carlos for Washington Opera; Duke of Mantua at Covent Garden, 2002. *Recordings include:* Akhnaten; Die Soldaten. *Address:* c/o Staatsoper Stuttgart, Oberer Schlossgarten 6, 7000 Stuttgart 1, Germany.

**VARGAS, Ramon;** Singer (Tenor); b. 1959, Mexico City, Mexico. *Career:* Has sung in opera a Mexico City as Fenton in Falstaff, Nemorino, Don Ottavio and Count Almaviva; Sang Gelsomino in Il Viaggio a Reims at the Vienna Staatsoper, 1987; Pesaro and Salzburg Festivals, 1987, Mexico City 1988 as Tamino: Further appearances at Lucerne 1989, Zürich 1990 as Lorenzo in Fra Diavalo and Enschede Holland, as Fenton; Season 1991–92 as Leicester in Rossini's Elisabetta at Naples, Almaviva at Rome, Rodrigo in a concert performance of La Donna del Lago at Amsterdam and Paolina in Il Matriomonio Segreto at Martina Franca; Sang Rossini's Almaviva at the Verona Arena, 1996; Alfredo Germont at the Opéra Bastille, 1998–99; Rodolfo in La Bohème at Covent Garden, 1999 and at the New York Met, 2002; London Proms, 2002. *Recordings include:* Rossini's Il Turco in Italia; Massenet's Werther. *Address:* c/o Opernhaus Zürich, Falkenstrasse 1, 8008 Zürich, Switzerland.

**VARGYAS, Lajos (Karoly);** Musical Folklorist and Ethnographer; b. 1 Feb. 1914, Budapest, Hungary; m. 17 Dec 1949. *Education:* Pupil of Kodály in Musical Folklore, Budapest University; Church Music at Budapest Music Academy, 1936–37; Doctor of Ethnography, Linguistics and Hungarian Literature, 1941; Academic D.Mus, 1963. *Career:* Assistant Professor at Budapest University, 1952–54; Director of Folk Music Research Group, Hungarian Academy, 1970–73; President, Committee for Scientific Classification in Musicology and Ethnography, Hungarian Academy; Music Committee, Hungarian Academy. *Recordings:* Mongolian Folk Music, UNESCO, 1971. *Publications include:* Aj falu zenei élete (The Musical Life of the Village Aj), 1941; Compiler, Kodály: A Magyar népzene; A peldatart szerkesztette Vargyas Lajos (The Hungarian Folk Music: Collection of Tune Examples by L Vargyas), 1952; A magyar vers ritmusa (The Rhythm of the Hungarian Verse), 1952; Author and Editor, Studia Memoriae Belae Bartók Sacra, 1956, 1957 and 1959; Aj falu zenei anyaga (The Tune Material of The Village Aj), 1960, 1961 and 1963; Magyar vers–Magyar Nyelv (Hungarian Verse–Hungarian Language), 1966; Researches into The Mediaeval History of Folk Ballad, 1967; Zoltan Kodály: Folk Music of Hungary, 2nd revised and enlarged edition, 1971; Balladaskonyv (Books of Ballads with their tunes), 1979; Hungarian Ballads and The European Ballad Tradition, in Hungarian, 1976, English 1983; A magyarság népzenéje (Folkmusic of the Hungarians), 1981, 1993; Keleti hagyomany–nyugati kultura, Tanulmanyok (Eastern Traditions–Western Culture, Essays), 1984; Magyar Néprajz V Népköltészet (Hungarian Ethnography Folkpoetry), 1988; Kodály hatrahagyott foljegyzesei l (Kodály's Records Left Behind), editor, 1989, 1993; Corpus Musicae Popularis Hungaricae VIII/A-B, editor, 1993; Keritésen kivül (Emlékek életemböl) (Memoirs), 1993; Magyar népballadák (Hungarian Folkballads), 1994. *Honours:* Erkel Prize, 1980; Széchényi Prize, 1991. *Address:* 1022 Budapest, Szemlohegy Str 4/B, Hungary.

**VARNAY, Astrid;** American opera singer (soprano) (retd); b. 25 April 1918, Stockholm, Sweden; d. of Alexander Varnay and Mária Jávor; m. Hermann Weigert 19 May 1944. *Education:* studied privately with her mother and with Paul Althouse; studied repertoire with Herman Weigert in New York. *Career:*

debut: Metropolitan Opera 1941, as Sieglinde; sSang at the Metropolitan until 1956, as Brünnhilde, Isolde, Senta, Eva, Elsa, Elisabeth, Kundry, Venus, Ortrud, the Marschallin, Amelia Boccanegra, Santuzza, Elektra and Salome; sang Telea in the premiere of Menotti's The Island God 1942; also sang in concert with New York Philharmonic at Carnegie Hall and in Lewisohn Stadium; song recitals accompanied by Hermann Weigert; Chicago Lyric Opera debut 1944, Sieglinde; San Francisco Opera debut 1946–61, notably as Gioconda and Leonore; Mexico City 1948, as Aida, Leonora (Il trovatore), Desdemona and Gioconda; Covent Garden debut 1948, as Brünnhilde in Siegfried; returned to London 1951, 1958–59 and 1968 (the Kostelnička in Jenůfa); Bayreuth Festival 1951–67, as Brünnhilde, Isolde, Ortrud, Kundry and Senta; Paris Opéra and La Scala Milan, as Isolde, 1956, 1957; Stuttgart 1959, as Jocasta in the premiere of Ödipus der Tyrann by Orff; character roles from 1962: Clytemnestra, Herodias and the title role in Einem's Der Besuch der Alten Dame; Salzburg Festival 1964–65, as Elektra; Prof., Düsseldorf Musikhochschule 1970–; taught vocal interpretation at Opera Studio of Bavarian State Radio; returned to the Metropolitan 1975, as the Kostelnička, then sang Herodias, Clytemnestra and Begbick in Mahagonny. *Recordings:* Der fliegende Holländer, Lohengrin (Decca); Ödipus der Tyrann (Deutsche Grammophon); Cavalleria Rusticana (HMV); pvt. recordings from Bayreuth and the Metropolitan; Der Ring des Nibelungen conducted by Clemens Krauss, Bayreuth 1953 and conducted by Joseph Keilberth 1955 (Testament); Gotterdammerung, Bayreuth 1951 (Testament, released 1999); Elektra (Orfeo); Salome 1953 (Orfeo), Schonberg's 2nd Quartet, conducted by Dimitri Mitropoulos; sang in recordings released 1964–65 by Decca: Andrea Chénier and The Rake's Progress, both conducted by Riccardo Chailly; Opera Scenes and Orchestral Songs (Deutsche Grammophon, released in 2004). *Publications include:* 55 Years in Five Acts (co-author with Donald Arthur, first published in German trans. as Hab' mir's gelobt 1998) 2000. *Honours:* Maximilansorden, Bavaria 1980, Kammersängerin; Wilhelm-Pitz Medal, Bayreuth, 1988. *Address:* c/o Bayerische Staatsoper, Max-Joseph-Platz 2, 80539 Munich, Germany.

**VARONA, Luciano;** Argentine stage designer and costume designer; b. 14 Aug. 1930, Mendoza. *Education:* Escuela Superior de Bellas Artes, Buenos Aires. *Career:* debut at Teatro Colón, Buenos Aires 1959, Prokofiev's The Love for Three Oranges; Collaborated with Tito Capobianco at the New York City 1966–73, with Giulio Cesare, The Golden Cockerel, Manon, Lucia di Lammermoor and Donzetti's Tudor trilogy; Handel's Ariodante for the opening of the Kennedy Center at Washington, DC, 1971; San Francisco and Vancouver Opera 1972–73, with Norma and Lucrezia Borgia; further association with Capobianco at the Deutsche Oper Berlin and the Netherlands Opera 1971–74, Attila, Aida, Rodelinda and La Traviata; Returned to the Teatro Colón 1981–88, with designs for Romeo et Juliette, Die Zauberflöte, Carmen and Die Entführung. *Address:* c/o Teatro Colón, Cerrito 618, 1010 Buenos Aires, Argentina.

**VARPIO, Marja-Leena;** Singer (Soprano); b. 1956, Helsinki, Finland. *Education:* Munich Musikhochschule and Salzburg Mozarteum. *Career:* Vienna Kammeroper 1985-87, as Paisiello's Rosina, Susanna, and Blondchen in Die Entführung; Vienna Volksoper 1987-90, as Mozart's Despina and Papagena; Festival appearances as Schwetzingen, Vienna and Savonlinna (Telemann's Pimpinone, 1990); Premiere of Adriana Hölszky's Bremer Freiheit, Munich 1998; Season 1993-94 as Axiniain in Katerina Izmailova at Stuttgart and Musetta for Finnish National Opera; Other roles include Mozart's Countess, and Lucia in Hindemith's The Long Christmas Dinner; Frequent engagements in operetta; Concerts include Mozart's Requiem, Beethoven's Ninth, Masses by Haydn, and Carmina Burana. *Address:* c/o Finnish National Opera, PO Box 176, Helsingkatu 58, 002 51 Helsinki, Finland.

**VARVISO, Silvio;** Conductor; b. 26 Feb. 1924, Zürich, Switzerland. *Education:* Studied at the Zürich Conservatory and in Vienna with Clemens Krauss. *Career:* Debut: St Gallen 1944, Die Zauberflöte; Assistant, then Principal Conductor of Basle Opera, 1950–62; Conducted opera in Berlin and Paris, 1958; San Francisco Opera from 1959 (US premiere of A Midsummer Night's Dream, 1961); Metropolitan Opera from 1961, Lucia di Lammermoor, Die Walküre, Die Fledermaus, Die Meistersinger, and Italian repertory; Glyndebourne and Covent Garden 1962, Le nozze di Figaro and Der Rosenkavalier; Principal Conductor of the Royal Opera, Stockholm 1965–71; Bayreuth Festival 1969–74; Die Meistersinger, Der fliegende Holländer and Lohengrin; Conducted new production of La Bohème at Covent Garden, 1974; Musical Director at Stuttgart 1972–80; has led performances of Rossini, Donizetti, Bellini, Strauss, Mozart and Wagner; Musical Director of the Paris Opéra 1980–85; Conducted Lohengrin at Stuttgart 1990, Manon Lescaut at Barcelona; Season 1992/93 with Tosca at Antwerp and Die Frau ohne Schatten in Florence; Conducted La Fanciulla del West at Ghent, 1996; Turandot at Antwerp, 1998. *Address:* c/o Staatstheater Stuttgart, Oberer Schlossgarten 6, 7000 Stuttgart 1, Germany.

**VÁSÁRY, Tamás;** Hungarian concert pianist and conductor; *Chief Musical Director and Principal Conductor, Budapest Symphony Orchestra (Symphony Orchestra of the Hungarian Radio and Television);* b. 11 Aug. 1933, Debrecen; s. of Jozsef Vasary and Elizabeth (née Baltazár) Vasary; m. Henriette Tunyogi 2000. *Education:* Ferenc Liszt Acad. of Music, Budapest under Lajos Hernádi, József Gát and Zoltán Kodály. *Career:* first solo performance aged eight; studied with Ernst von Dohnányi at Ferenc Liszt Acad. of Music –1954; remained at Ferenc Liszt Acad. as Asst Prof. to Zoltán Kodály; recitals in

Leningrad (now St Petersburg), Moscow and Warsaw; settled in Switzerland 1958; London debut 1961, New York 1962; debut as conductor in Menton Festival of Music 1971; has since appeared in Europe, S Africa, S America, USA, Canada, India, Thailand, Hong Kong, Australia, Japan and Mexico; Jt Music Dir Northern Sinfonia, Newcastle, UK 1979–82; Musical Dir Bournemouth Sinfonietta 1988–96; Chief Musical Dir and Prin. Conductor Budapest Symphony Orchestra (Symphony Orchestra of the Hungarian Radio and Television) 1993–; Guest Conductor London Philharmonic, Royal Philharmonic, Philharmonia, New York Philharmonic, Dallas and Houston Symphonies, Detroit Symphony; performances at Salzburg, Edin. and Merano Music Festivals; records for Deutsche Grammophon. *Principal recordings:* three records of works of Liszt; eight of works of Chopin and various recordings of works of Rachmaninoff, Dohnányi, Debussy and Mozart; all symphonies and overtures of Beethoven, Schubert and Schumann 1997–98; further records for Hungaroton. *Honours:* Liszt Prizes: Queen Elizabeth (Belgium), Marguerite Longue (Paris); Chopin Prizes: Int. Competition, Warsaw, Int. Competition, Brazil; Bach and Paderewski Medals (London), Kossuth Prize, Presidential Gold Medal 1998, Hungarian Heritage Prize. *Address:* Magyar Rádió Zenekari Iroda, Bródy Sándor u. 5-1, 1800 Budapest, Hungary (office). *Telephone:* (1) 328-8326 (office). *Fax:* (1) 328-8910 (office).

**VASILYEVA, Alla;** Concert Cellist; b. 1933, Moscow, Russia. *Education:* Studied at the Central Music School and at the Moscow State Conservatoire, with Rostropovich. *Career:* Joined the Moscow Chamber Orchestra under Rudolf Barshai 1958 and remains as principal cellist; many tours with the Moscow Chamber Orchestra and as solo recitalist, notably in modern Russian works; Plays her own arrangements of works by Respighi and Vivaldi. *Recordings:* Works by Bach, Geminiani, Vivaldi, Moshei Wainberg, Boris Tchaikovsky, Khrennikov and Shostakovich. *Address:* c/o Sonata, 11 Northpark Street, Glasgow G20 7AA, Scotland.

**VASKS, Peteris;** Composer; b. 16 April 1946, Aizpute, Latvia. *Education:* Studied double bass at Lithuanian Conservatory, Vilnius, 1964–70; Composition at Latvian Conservatory, Riga, until 1978. *Career:* Double bassist in orchestras throughout Latvia and Lithuania, 1963–74; Lecturer at Riga Music School, 1989–. *Compositions:* Music for Fleeting Birds, wind quintet, 1977; Three string quartets, 1997, 1984, 1995; In Memoriam for two pianos, 1997; Cantabile for strings, 1979; Book for Cello, 1979; In Memory of a Friend, wind quintet, 1982, Message for orchestra, 1982; Piano Trio, 1985; Double Bass Sonata, 1986; Latvija, chamber cantata, 1987; English Horn Concerto, 1989; Symphony, Voices, for strings, 1991; Litene, for 12 voices, 1992; Cello Concerto, 1994; Violin Concerto, 1997; Dona nobis pacem, for chorus and seven instruments, 1997; Symphony No. 2, 1998. *Address:* c/o AKKA/LAA, 12 Kr, Barona Str, Riga PDP, LV-1426, Latvia.

**VASSAR, Frédéric;** Singer (Baritone); b. 1948, France. *Education:* Studied at the Opera Studio of the Théâtre de la Monnaie, Brussels. *Career:* Sang first as bass in Opera at Brussels from 1973 (Alberich), then at Ghent (Wotan, Hoffmann, Boccanegra) and for French Radio; Sang Mephistopheles in Faust at Marseilles, 1977, followed by visits to Strasbourg, Avignon, Dublin and Orange; Engagements at Liège, 1985–86 as (Escamillo, Ourrais in Mireille), Angers, Metz (Golaud), Don Giovanni and the Villains in Hoffmann; Season 1989–90, as Mephistopheles at Avignon, Lescaut at Nantes, Telramund at Limoges and Scarpia for Opera Northern Ireland in Belfast. *Honours:* Winner, 1976 Voix d'or Enrico Caruso and Henri Duparc, France; Winner, Toti dal Monte.

**VASSILEV, Vasko;** Bulgarian/British violinist and concertmaster; *Concertmaster, Royal Opera House, London*; b. 1970, Sofia, Bulgaria. *Education:* studied in Moscow. *Career:* after early competition success, joined Orchestra of Royal Opera House, 1991, as youngest ever leader and Concertmaster; solo career in Europe, North America and the Far East; European tour with the Royal Opera Orchestra 1998, with Mendelssohn and Tchaikovsky Concertos; Artistic Director of the Soloists of the Royal Opera House Orchestra 1998; Laureate of the String Ensemble. *Recordings include:* Solo and chamber music including Brahms Sonatas and Concerto by John Adams (Harmonia Mundi; Trittico Classics and Erato); Tartini Devil's Trill Sonata and The Original Four Seasons, with the Royal Opera String Ensemble and Vanessa Mae. *Honours:* prizewinner at Jacques Thibaud, Carl Flesch and Paganini Competitions. *Address:* Royal Opera House (Contracts), Covent Garden, London, WC2E 9DD, England (office). *Telephone:* (20) 7930-0330 (office). *Fax:* (20) 7930-0440 (office). *E-mail:* inbox@trittico.org (office). *Website:* www .vaskovassilev.com (office).

**VASSILIEV, Alexander;** German singer (bass); b. 20 March 1971, St Petersburg, Russia. *Education:* Tchaikovsky Conservatory, Moscow, 1989–93, with Evgeny Nesterenko; Masterclasses with Ernst Haefliger in Moscow, Hanna Ludwig at Salzburg and Astrid Varnay at Munich. *Career:* appearances at the Bavarian State Opera, Munich 1994–95, Freiburg Opera 1995–97, Cologne Opera 1997–2000; roles have included Bottom in Britten's Midsummer Night's Dream, Alidoro in Rossini's Cenerentola, Don Basilio in Rossini's Il Barbiere di Seviglia, Figaro in Mozart's Le Nozze di Figaro, Leporello in Mozart's Don Giovanni, Colline in Puccini's La Bohème, Mephistopheles in Gounod's Faust, and many others; appearances at operas of Paris, Bologna, Geneva, Amsterdam and St Petersburg; concerts and recitals at Cologne Philharmony, Concertgebouw, Amsterdam, Palao de la Musica Catalana, Barcelona, as well as in Strasbourg, Freiburg, Stuttgart, Paris, Davos, Città di Castello and Duisburg. *Recordings:* CD recordings with

Radio France/Naïve and Westdeutscher Rundfunk/CPO. *Current Management:* c/o Haydn Rawstron Ltd, 36 Station Road, London, SE20 7BQ, England. *Telephone:* www.haydn-rawstron.com.

**VASSILIEVA, Elena;** Singer (Soprano); b. 1956, France. *Education:* Studied at the Paris Conservatoire. *Career:* Won various awards in the early 1980s and sang in Henze's Boulevard Solitude at Paris, 1984; Has sung in operas by Puccini, Massenet, Verdi, Strauss and Mozart and notably as Tatiana in Eugene Onegin; Saffi in Der Zigeunerbaron at Liège; Many concert appearances, including modern repertory and songs by Russian composers. *Address:* Opéra de Wallonie, 1 Rue des Dominicains, 4000 Liège, Belgium.

**VATER, Wolfgang;** Singer (Bass-baritone); b. 1949, Bremerhaven, Germany. *Education:* Hanover Musikhochschule, 1969–75. *Career:* Sang at Bielefeld from 1975, notably as Leporello; Bremen Opera from 1986; Gelsenkirchen, 1987, as Faber in Tippett's The Knot Garden; Season 1991 at Bielefeld in the premiere of Katharina Blum by Tilo Medek; Kothner in Die Meistersinger at Wiesbaden and Wiedehopf in Die Vögel by Braunfels; Other roles include Mephistopheles in Faust, Don Alfonso in Così fan tutte and Gessler in Guillaume Tell; Many concert and oratorio appearances. *Recordings include:* Werther; Strauss's Daphne. *Address:* c/o Buhnen der Stadt Bielefeld, Bruhnenstrasse 3–9, Pf 220, 4800 Bielefeld, Germany.

**VAUGHAN, Denis (Edward);** Orchestral Conductor and Organist; b. 6 June 1926, Melbourne, Australia. *Education:* BMus, University of Melbourne, 1947; Royal College of Music, London, England, 1947–50. *Career:* Debut: As Conductor, Royal Festival Hall, London, 1953; Annual harpsichord concerts, Royal Festival Hall, 1948–58; Concert to honour Toscanini, with Bernstein, Klemperer, Celibidache and Maazel, Parma, 1959; Adviser to UNESCO and Berne Union on musical aspects of copyright matters, 1962–67; Music Director, Australian Elizabethan Theatre Trust, 1966; Orchestral concerts, operas in Europe, Australia, USA, Canada, 1970–2002; Munich State Opera House, 1972–80; Musical Director, State Opera of South Australia, 1981–84; Operas conducted include Così fan tutte, Faust, Fidelio, Falstaff, Boris Godunov, The Rake's Progress, Giulio Cesare; Concert in Vienna to celebrate the Austrian Millennium, 1996. *Recordings include:* 23 with Orchestra of Naples, including complete Schubert symphonies, 12 Haydn, 11 Mozart, Re Pastore etc, RCA Victor/BMG. *Publications:* Le Discrepanze Nei Manoscritti Verdiani, La Scala, 1959; Preface on organ articulation and phrasing, Stanley Voluntaries, 1959; Puccini's Orchestration, Royal Musical Association, 1961; The Evaluation of Errors and Omissions in Dvořák's Manuscripts, Prague, 1999. *Current Management:* Hazard Chase Ltd, Norman House, Cambridge Place, Cambridge, CB2 1NS, England. *Telephone:* (1223) 312400. *Fax:* (1223) 460827. *Website:* www.hazardchase.co.uk. *Address:* 41 Floral Street, London WC2E 9DG, England. *Telephone:* (20) 7836-7399. *Fax:* (20) 7836-2289. *E-mail:* denisvaughan2001@yahoo.co.uk.

**VAUGHAN, Elizabeth;** Singer (Soprano); b. 12 March 1937, Llanfyllin, Montgomeryshire, Wales. *Education:* Royal Academy of Music; FRAM. *Career:* Debut: Welsh National Opera, 1960, as Abigaille in Nabucco; Covent Garden from 1961, as Mimi, Liu (Turandot), Teresa (Benvenuto Cellini), Gayle (The Ice Break, world premiere), Andromache and Hecuba (King Priam), Mozart's Elvira and Electra, Madama Butterfly, and Verdi's Amelia (Boccanegra), Abigaille, Alice (Falstaff), Leonore (Trovatore), Gilda and Violetta; Opera North as Tosca, Lady Macbeth and Abigaille; Welsh National Opera as Tosca, Leonora (La Forza del Destino) and Maddalena in Andrea Chénier; English National Opera as Aida, Penelope Rich (Gloriana) and Beethoven's Leonore; Metropolitan Opera debut, 1972, as Donna Elvira; Guest engagements in Vienna, Berlin, Paris, Hamburg, Munich and Prague; Appearances in Australia, Canada, South America, Japan; Toured USA with English National Opera, 1984; Now Mezzo with major companies, roles of Herodias, Kabanicha (Katya Kabanova), and the Witch in Hansel and Gretel; Sang the Overseer in Elektra at Covent Garden, 1997; La Frugola in Il Tabarro for ENO, 1998; Season 1999 Princess in Suor Angelica and Old Prioress in Carmélites; Sang Herodias in Salome for Scottish Opera, 2000. *Honours:* Honorary D.Mus, University of Wales. *Current Management:* IMG Artists Europe, London, England. *Address:* c/o IMG Artists Europe, Lovell House, 616 Chiswick High Road, London W4 5RX, England.

**VAUGHAN WILLIAMS, (Joan) Ursula Penton,** FRCM; writer; b. 15 March 1911, Valletta, Malta; m. 1st Michael Forrester Wood 1933 (died 1942); m. 2nd Ralph Vaughan Williams 1953 (died 1958). *Career:* writer of songs, song cycles, libretti for cantatas and opera libretti; cttees: RVW Ltd., Ralph Vaughan Williams Trust. *Publications:* No Other Choice 1941, Fall of Leaf 1944, Need for Speech 1948, Silence and Music 1959, Ralph Vaughan Williams (biog.) 1964, Aspects 1984, Paradise Remembered (autobiog.) 2002, Complete Poems 2003; seven vols of poems, three novels, two books of photographs of Ralph Vaughan Williams; libretti for operas and cantatas by various composers. *Honours:* Hon. FRAM, Hon. RNCM. *Address:* 66 Gloucester Crescent, London, NW1 7EG, England.

**VAVILOV, Gennadi (Alekseevich);** Composer and Professor; b. 7 May 1932, Russia; m. Natalia Romanenko, 17 Mar 1971, 1 s. *Education:* Musical High School, 1958; Theory on Music and Composing, Leningrad Conservatory, 1966; Moscow Conservatory, 1973–83; Petrozavodsk University, 1978. *Career:* Debut: Performing of Cantata for Choir and Symphony Orchestra, Moscow, 1959; Composer, 1958; Teacher of Theory of Music and Composition, 1958; Professor of Theory of Music, Instruments and Scores of Symphony Orchestra, 1989; Lecturer of Music, 1982; Music Accompaniment, 1982. *Compositions* include: Symphony No. 1, Voroneh, 1982; Philadelphia, USA, 1992; Symphony No. 4, Finland, 1990; Sochi, Russia, 1996; Symphony No. 3, Moscow, 1973; Sonata No. 2 for piano, Paris, France, 1996; Piano music: Allegro Barbaro, Dreams... Bushnell, USA, 1998; Original musical themes, traditions of Russian classical music, intonations characteristic for Karelian and Finnish Folk Tunes. *Recordings:* 3 records, Symphonietta for full symphony orchestra, Sonata for piano, Karellia tunes for symphony orchestra; Songs About Karelia, 1985; More than 13 works recorded to Gold Fund of Radio Russia. *Contributions:* Typical Features of Opera Orchestra by Mussorgsky, 1984; Some Problems in the Usage of Folk in Composing, 1985; Polifonia forms in the Symphony Music, 1985. *Honours:* 2nd place in the competitions of Young Composers, Moscow, 1958; Television Competition of the USSR, Moscow, 1959. *Address:* Lenin Street 13-3, 185000 Petrozavodsk, Russia.

**VAVRINECZ, Béla;** Composer, Conductor and Ethnomusicologue-historian; b. 18 Nov. 1925, Budapest, Hungary; m. Amalia Endrey, 1950, 1 s., 6 d. *Education:* Diploma in Composition, 1950, Diploma in Conducting, 1952, Budapest Academy of Music. *Career:* Debut: Budapest Academy of Music, 1949; First Conductor, Philharmonic Orchestra, Györ, 1957–58; Chief Conductor, Ministry of Home Affairs Symphony Orchestra, Budapest, 1961–73; Artistic Director, Dance Ensemble Budapest, 1974–83; Artistic Director, Ensemble Duna Budapest, 1983–85; Works frequently performed on radio and television. *Compositions:* 2 operas; 2 ballets; 112 musical pieces for dance theatre; 12 incidental works; 4 oratoria; Gisela, 1991; Chronicle of Somogy, 1999; 6 cantatas; 18 works for choir and orchestra; 20 works for symphony orchestra, including Symphonie, 1955; 6 works for chamber orchestra; 7 concerts; 45 chamber music works; Solo pieces; 33 choral works; 1 Mass; Songs; Arrangements; Music for wind bands. *Recordings:* Numerous. *Publications:* Kodály Memorial Book, 1953. *Address:* Cinkotai utca 39, 1141 Budapest, Hungary.

**VEALE, John,** MA; British composer; b. 15 June 1922, Shortlands, Kent, England; m. Diana Taylor 1944 (divorced 1971); one s. two d. (one deceased). *Education:* Repton School and Univ. of Oxford, studied with Thomas Armstrong, Egon Wellesz, Roger Sessions, Roy Harris. *Career:* Commonwealth Fellowship, USA 1949–51; Research Fellowship, Corpus Christi Coll., Oxford 1952–54; film correspondent, Oxford Mail 1964–80; copy ed., Oxford Univ. Press 1968–87; mem. Performing Right Soc. Ltd, British Acad. of Composers and Songwriters, Royal Philharmonic Soc. *Compositions:* Symphonies 1, 2 and 3 1947, 1965, 1996, Clarinet Concerto, Violin Concerto, Panorama for orchestra, Metropolis concert overture for orchestra, Elegy for flute, harp and strings, String Quartet, Kubla Khan for baritone solo, mixed chorus and orchestra, Song of Radha for soprano and orchestra, Demos Variations for orchestra, Apocalypse for chorus and orchestra, Triune for oboe/cor anglais and orchestra, Encounter for two guitars, Three Sydney Streetscenes for chorus and instrumental ensemble 1994, Triptych for recorder and string quartet. *Recordings:* Clarinet Concerto, Three Sydney Streetscenes, Violin Concerto. *Publications:* contrib. articles and reviews to various publications. *Address:* 7 Nourse Close, Woodeaton, Oxford, OX3 9TJ, England. *Telephone:* (1865) 558156.

**VEASEY, Josephine,** CBE; British singer (mezzo-soprano) (retd) and vocal consultant; b. 10 July 1930, London; m. Ande Anderson 1951 (divorced 1969); one s. one d. *Career:* mem. chorus Covent Garden Opera Company 1948–50, returned as soloist 1955; prin. mezzo-soprano, Royal Opera House, Covent Garden; has sung every major mezzo-soprano role in repertory; many foreign engagements have included Salzburg Festival, La Scala, Milan, Metropolitan Opera House, New York and Paris Opera; Prof., RAM 1982–83; vocal consultant, ENO 1985–94. *Recordings:* has made recordings with Karajan, Solti, Bernstein and Colin Davis. *Honours:* Hon. RAM. *Address:* 5 Meadow View, Whitchurch, Hants., RG28 7BL, England (home). *Telephone:* (1256) 896813 (home).

**VECCIA, Angelo;** Singer (Baritone); b. 1963, Rome, Italy. *Education:* Studied at the Santa Cecilia Academy, Rome, and the Juilliard School, New York. *Career:* Debut: Sang Mozart's Figaro at Juilliard; Gave concerts at the Lincoln Center, New York, and elsewhere in America, and appeared in Tosca with Placido Domingo; Appearances throughout Italy as Rossini's Figaro, Belcore, Marcello (at Verona, Venice and Florence) and Silvio; Further roles in Gluck's Iphigénie en Tauride at La Scala, Rimsky's Golden Cockerel at Rome and Schoenberg's Moses und Aron in Florence; Zürich Opera as Sharpless (Madama Butterfly), Gianni Schicchi and Marcello; Season 1997 in Bohème and Turandot at Tel-Aviv, Il Barbiere di Siviglia at Zürich and Lucia di Lammermoor at La Scala; Sang as guest in Aida at Berlin and in the 1996 Christmas Concert under Riccardo Chailly at the Amsterdam Concertgebouw. *Address:* c/o Opernhaus Zürich, Falkenstrasse 1, 8008 Zürich, Switzerland.

**VEDERNIKOV, Alexander Aleksandrovich;** Russian conductor; b. 11 Jan. 1964, Moscow; s. of Aleksander F. Vedernikov and Natalya Guryeva; m. Olga Aleksandrovna Vedernikova. *Education:* Moscow P. I. Tchaikovsky State Conservatory. *Career:* Asst, then Conductor Prin. Symphony Orchestra of Russian TV and Radio 1989–95; Founder and Chief Conductor Russian Philharmonic Orchestra 1995–98, 2000–; Musical Dir and Chief Conductor Bolshoi Theatre of Russia 2001–; conducted opera and ballet productions in European theatres including Covent Garden, London, La Scala, Milan and symphony orchestras in Russia. *Address:* Bolshoi Theatre, Teatralnaya pl. 1, Moscow (office); Pyryeva str. 4, korp. 1, apt. 24, 119285 Moscow, Russia (home). *Telephone:* (095) 292-18-48 (office); (095) 147-52-17 (home).

**VEDERNIKOV, Alexander Filoppovich;** Russian singer (bass); b. 23 Dec. 1927, Mokino, nr Kirov. *Education:* studied in Moscow with Alpert-Khasina. *Career:* debut, Bolshoi Theatre Moscow 1957, as Ivan Susanin in Glinka's A Life for the Tsar; Appearances in Moscow, Leningrad, Tbilisi and Kiev as Boris and Varlaam in Boris Godunov, Dosifey (Khovanshchina) and Konchak in Prince Igor; Engagements with the company of the Bolshoi at Paris, New York and Milan as Philip II and the Grand Inquisitor in Don Carlos and Massimilione in Verdi's I Masnadieri; Toured West Germany with the Bolshoi 1987; Other roles include Daland in Der fliegende Holländer, Prince Gremin (Eugene Onegin), Kutuzov in War and Peace and Mephistopheles (Faust). *Recordings include:* The Stone Guest by Dargomyzhsky; Rimsky-Korsakov's The Snow Maiden, Pimen in a video of Boris Godunov from the Bolshoi (National Video Corporation). *Address:* c/o Bolshoi Theatre, Pr Marxa 8/2, 103009 Moscow, Russia.

**VEERHOFF, Carlos Heinrich;** German/Argentine composer; b. 3 June 1926, Buenos Aires, Argentina. *Education:* Berlin Hochschule für Musik with Hermann Grabner and Boris Blacher, in Cologne with Walter Braunfels, and in Switzerland with Hermann Scharchen. *Career:* freelance composer in Munich 1952–, Stuttgart, Argentina and Paris. *Compositions:* Pavane royal, ballet, 1950; Sinfonische Invention for Orchestra, 1951; Sinfonia panta-rhei, 1954; Sinfonischer Satz for Orchestra, 1954; Targusis, Opera 1955–57; Symphony, 1956, Symphonie Spirales 1958; El porquerizo del rey, ballet, 1958; Mirages for orchestra, 1961; Die goldene Maske, opera 1962–63, rev. 2002; Tanz des lebens, puppet opera, 1962; Five Bagatellen for Brass Orchestra, 1965; Akroasis for orchestra, 1965; Gesänge auf dem Wege for Baritone and Orchestra, 1966; Textur, for orchestra, 1970; Symphony no. 2, 1972; Es gibt doch Zebrastreifen, opera, 1972; Two Violin Concertos, 1976, 1992; Dualis, ballet 1975; Nonett, 1976; Gesänge aus Samsâra, 1976, rev. 1984; Piano Concerto No. 1, 1979; Dorefamie for Orchestra, 1980; Pater noster for chorus and orchestra, 1985; Concerto for cello, double bass and orchestra, 1988; Piano Concerto No. 2, 1989 rev. 1998; Concerto for percussion solo and orchestra, 1994; Desiderata, for chorus, solo voices and orchestra (Symphony No. 6), 1996; Burleske, for chorus, 1982, rev, 1998, Mana (opera) 1999–2006, Piano Concerto No. 3 2004–05. *Current Management:* c/o GEMA, Rosenheimerstr. 11, 81667 Munich, Germany. *Telephone:* (89) 4800300. *Fax:* (89) 48003495. *Address:* Gabriele Münter Platz 3, 82418 Murnau, Germany (home).

**VEIRA, Jonathan;** Singer (Bass Baritone); b. 1960, England. *Education:* Studied at Trinity College of Music, London; The National Opera Studio. *Career:* Debut: Soloist, Wexford, 1986; At Glyndebourne appeared as Lemokh in the premiere of The Electrification of the Soviet Union; Die Entführung and Capriccio; Other engagements include a tour with Opera 80; Antonio, in Le nozze di Figaro at the Prom concerts and Tippett's New Year for the Glyndebourne Tour; Broadcasts of Mahagonny and Rossini's Tancredi for the BBC; Television appearances in La Traviata, The Electrification of the Soviet Union and Death in Venice; Engagements with Opera Factory, London; As a concert artist has performed at many major London venues; Has broadcast Leoncavallo's La Bohème and Königskinder for RTE Dublin; Television appearances include The Marriage of Figaro, La Traviata and Death in Venice; In 1993 he sang his first Papageno in a new production of The Magic Flute conducted by Jane Glover at the Covent Garden Festival; Sang Bartolo (Barber of Seville) for Opera Northern Ireland and at Garsington Festival in 1994; Other performances include a premiere of a new opera by Stuart Copeland in the Barbados Festival, Bottom (A Midsummer Night's Dream), for Covent Garden Festival and Scarpia in a concert performance of Tosca for the opening of the 1994 Bournemouth International Festival; In 1995 he sang Dulcamara (L'Elisir d'amore) for Opera Northern Ireland, Dr Bartolo (The Marriage of Figaro), Melitone (La Forza del Destino) and Calchas (La Belle Hélène) for Scottish Opera; Engagements in 1996 included Leporello (Don Giovanni) for Auckland Opera with Kiri Te Kanawa, Melitone with the Royal Danish Opera, Dr Bartolo for Opéra de Nice; Banker (Lulu) and roles for Glyndebourne Festival Opera; 1997 with Bartolo for Welsh National Opera; Sharpless (Madama Butterfly), Dr Bartolo (Le Nozze di Figaro) for Opera Ireland; Dr Kolonaty (The Makropulos Case) for Glyndebourne at the Proms, Royal Albert Hall; Engagements in 1998 included Baron Zeta, The Merry Widow, for Royal Opera; Dr Bartolo, The Marriage of Figaro, Zürich Opera; Vaarlam, Boris Gedonov, Welsh National Opera; Tonio, Pagliacci, Opera Ireland; Jake, Porgy and Bess, BBC Proms; Engagements in 1999–2000 included Talum Hadjo in Delius's Godunov, The Magic Fountain at Scottish Opera; Title role in Falstaff, Royal Danish Opera, Copenhagen, Mustafà, The Italian Girl in Algiers, Garsington Festival; Kecal, The Bartered Bride, Glyndebourne Festival and tour; Season 2000–01 as Leporello with GTO, Bunoafede in Haydn's Il mondo della luna at Garsington and Janáček's Kolenaty at the Academy of Music, New York. *Recordings:* Two solo albums; Featured soloist on recording of operatic excerpts for Opera Rara; Elgar's The Spanish Lady, CD. *Honours:* Winner, Peter Pears Singing Competition; Anna Instone Memorial Award. *Address:* 4 Lincoln Road, Guildford, Surrey GU2 6JT, England.

**VEJZOVIC, Dunja;** Singer (soprano); b. 20 Oct. 1943, Zagreb, Yugoslavia. *Education:* Studied in Zagreb, Stuttgart, Weimar and Salzburg. *Career:* Sang first at Zagreb, then in Frankfurt, Düsseldorf, Vienna, Hamburg and Stuttgart; Bayreuth Festival 1978–80, as Kundry in Parsifal: also sang the role at the Salzburg Easter Festival; Metropolitan Opera 1978–79, as Venus in Tannhäuser; Paris Opéra 1982, Ortrud; Teatro Liceo Barcelona 1983 in the title role of Hérodiade by Massenet; La Scala Milan 1984, as Venus; Théâtre de la Monnaie, Brussels 1984, Senta in Der fliegende Holländer; Also sings Chimène in Le Cid by Massenet; sang Ortrud at the Vienna Staatsoper, 1990; Season 1992 as Kundry in Robert Wilson's production of Parsifal at Houston. *Recordings:* Parsifal, conducted by Karajan (Deutsche Grammophon); Christus by Liszt; Lohengrin and Der fliegende Holländer (EMI). *Address:* c/o Allied Artists Agency, 42 Montpelier Square, London SW7 1JZ, England.

**VELAZCO, Jorge;** Conductor and Music Director; b. 12 Jan. 1942, Mexico City, Mexico. *Education:* General Law degree, National University of Mexico; Student of Conrado Tovar (Piano), Antonio Gomezanda (Piano, Music Theory), Rodolfo Halffter (Composition, Music Analysis), Lukas Foss, Franco Ferrara at Accademia Musicale Chigiana, Siena, Herbert von Karajan (Conducting). *Career:* Assistant Chairman, Mexico Federal Government's Music Department, 1972–73; Professor, National Conservatory, Mexico City, 1973–84; Chairman, Music Department, 1973–74, Vice-President for Cultural Affairs, 1974–76, Researcher in Music, 1974–, National University of Mexico; Visiting Professor, Wyoming and Michigan State Universities, Phoenix College, University of Houston, University of Oviedo (Spain), 1975–94; Associate Conductor, 1977–81, Music Director, 1985–89, UNAM Philharmonic; Assistant to Herbert von Karajan at Salzburg Easter Festival, 1977; Founder, Music Director, Minería Symphony Orchestra, 1978–84; Principal Guest Conductor, Florence Chamber Orchestra, Italy, 1990–; Director, International Studies, Texas Music Festival, Houston, 1992–; Artistic Director and Conductor, Mineria Symphony Orchestra, 1995–; Guest Conductor, National Orchestra of Spain, Interamerican Music Festival Orchestra, several major US and European orchestras; mem, Sociedad Española de Musicología; Royal Musical Association, London; International Musicological Society. Cedros 18, San Miguel Ajusco, Tlalpan DF, Mexico 14700. *Recordings:* Several with Berlin Radio Symphony Orchestra, Florence Chamber Orchestra, Berlin Symphony and Sinfonietta RIAS. *Publications:* Edgard Varèse, Perfil de un Revolucionario, 1975; De Música y Músicos, 1981; Dos Músicos Eslavos, 1981; El Pianismo Mexicano del Siglo XIX, 1983–84; Federico II, El Rey Músico, 1986; La Versión Original de 'Janitzio' de Silvestre Revueltas, 1986; La Música por Dentro, 1988; Antonio Gomezanda y el Nacionalismo Romántico Mexicano, 1991. *Honours:* Guggenheim Fellow, 1987; Wortham Chair in Performing Arts, University of Houston, 1991, 1994.

**VELIS, Andrea;** Singer (Tenor); b. 7 June 1932, New Kensington, Pennsylvania, USA. *Education:* Studied with Louise Taylor in Pittsburgh, at the Royal College of Music, London, and at the Accademia di Santa Cecilia, Rome. *Career:* Debut: Pittsburgh 1954, as Goro in Madama Butterfly; Appearances in Chicago, Cincinnati, Philadelphia and San Francisco; Metropolitan Opera from 1961 in 1,600 performances of 50 operas, including La Fanciulla del West, Death in Venice, Hansel and Gretel, Eugene Onegin, The Ring (Mime), Les Contes d'Hoffmann, Otello, Der Rosenkavalier, Tosca and Boris Godunov; Sang Mardian in the premiere of Barber's Antony and Cleopatra, 1966. *Recordings include:* Tosca (HMV). *Address:* c/o Metropolitan Opera, Lincoln Center, New York, NY 10023, USA.

**VELLA, Joseph;** Composer and Conductor; b. 9 Jan. 1942, Gozo, Malta. *Education:* Accademia Musicale, Siena, with Franco Donatoni and Franco Ferrara; University of Durham, until 1970. *Career:* Guest appearances as conductor in Europe, USA, Asia; Musical Dir, Astra Opera House, Gozo, 1970–; Associate Professor, Univ. of Malta, 1994–. *Compositions:* Over 150 works including Trio for violin, horn and piano, 1968; Sinfonia De profundis, 1969; Clarinet Quintet, 1973; The Seasons, Madrigal cycle, 1980; String Quartet, 1981; Piano concerto 1984; Sinfonietta, for strings, 1984; A Canticle Cantata, 1985; Sinfonia No. 2, 1989; Blood on the Verna, oratorio, 1989; Brass Quintet, 1992; Love Textures, for baritone and orchestra, 1993; Violin Concerto, 1993; Cello Concerto, 1995; Flute Concerto, 1996; Concerto Barocco for bassoon and orchestra, 1998; Concerto for 2 pianos solo, 2000; Sinfonietta for 13 woodwind players, 2001; Symphony No. 3 (The Apocalypse Verses), 2003. *Address:* c/o Music Dept, University of Malta, Sliema, Malta. *E-mail:* joseph.vella@um.edu.mt.

**VELLA, Richard;** Composer and Professor of Music; b. 1 Dec. 1954, Melbourne, Victoria, Australia. *Education:* BA 1978, MA 1981, La Trobe University. *Career:* General Editor, Music Currency Press, 1989–; Professor, La Trobe University, 1996–97; Advisory Professor, 1998–99; Artistic Director, Calculated Risks Opera Productions, 1990–. *Compositions include:* Tales of Love, opera, 1990; A Piano Reminisces, 1991; Remember, Unending Love, for chorus, 1992; The Last Supper, opera, 1993; Concerto for Trombone, 1995; Commissions from Astra Choir, One Extra Dance Company, The Elizabethan Theatre Trust, and others. *Publications:* Musical Environments, 2000. *Honours:* Commonwealth Postgraduate Research Award, 1979. *Address:* c/o Red House Editions, PO Box 2123, Footscray, Vic 3011, Australia.

**VENGEROV, Maxim;** Russian violinist and violist; *Professor of Violin, Saarbrücken University;* b. 20 Aug. 1974, Novosibirsk, Western Siberia, USSR; s. of Alexander Vengerov and Larissa Vengerov. *Career:* studied with Galina Tourchaninova and Zakhar Bron; first recital aged five; debut Moscow, playing Schubert's Rondo Brillant 1985; US debut with New York Philharmonic 1990; performs concerts and recitals with all maj. int. orchestras including Concertgebouw, Russian State Symphony, Berlin Philharmonic, London Philharmonic, St Petersburg Philharmonic, Chicago Symphony, Los Angeles Philharmonic, Mozarteum, Vienna Philharmonic, Hallé and English Chamber Orchestras; worked with Abbado, Mehta, Simonov, Barenboim,

Menuhin; solo recital programme of Bach, Ysaÿe, Shchedrin and Paganini 2002–03; Prof. of Violin, Musikhochschule des Saarlandes, Saarbrücken Univ.; apptd UNICEF Envoy for Music 1997. *Recordings include:* Sonatas by Beethoven and Brahms and Paganini 1st Concerto 1992, Sonatas by Mozart, Beethoven and Mendelssohn 1992, Virtuoso Violin Pieces, Bruch and Mendelssohn Violin Concertos, Britten Violin Concerto and Walton Viola Concerto (Classical BRIT Critics' Award 2004, Grammy Award 2004) 2002. *Honours:* 1st Prize Jr Wieniawski Competition Poland 1984, Winner Carl Flesch Int. Violin Competition 1990, Gramophone Young Artist of the Year 1994, Ritmo Artist of the Year 1994, Gramophone Record of the Year 1996, Edison Award 1997, Gramophone Artist of the Year 2002. *Current Management:* c/o Nicola-Fee Bahl, NFBM Ltd, 28 Smalley Close, London, N16 7LE, England. *Telephone:* (20) 7254-9606. *Fax:* (870) 0941600. *E-mail:* Nicola-Fee@ nfbm.com. *Website:* www.nfbm.com.

**VENN, Edward John,** BA, MA, PhD, LRSM; Lecturer; b. 31 Oct. 1974, Watford, England. *Education:* Univ. of Birmingham. *Career:* Lecturer, Dept of Music, Lancaster Univ. 2001–; cttee mem., Soc. for Music Analysis 2004–. *Publications:* 'Idealism and Ideology in Tippett's writings', in Michael Tippett: Music and Literature (ed. Suzanne Robinson), The Music of Hugh Wood. *Address:* Department of Music, Lancaster University, Lancaster, LA1 4YW, England (office). *Telephone:* (1524) 593105 (office). *E-mail:* e.venn@lancaster.ac.uk (office). *Website:* www.lanc.ac.uk/staff/venn (office).

**VENTRE, Carlo;** Singer (Tenor); b. 23 Feb. 1969, Montevideo, Uruguay. *Education:* Studied in Uruguay and in Italy (from 1991). *Career:* Appearances at La Scala Milan under Riccardo Muti as the Duke of Mantua, and Ismaele in Nabucco; Further engagements at Rome, Ravenna, Trieste, Athens, Tokyo and Cologne; Wexford Festival 1995, in Pacini's Saffo; Season 1996–97 included British debut, as Rodolfo with Welsh National Opera, and American debut as the Duke of Mantua for Opera Pacific; Engaged as the Duke by Michigan Opera, as Pinkerton in Trieste and Edoardo di Sanval in Un Giorno do Regno by Verdi at Parma. *Recordings include:* Pacini's Saffo. *Honours:* Gino Becchi Prize at the 1990 Francisco Vinas Competition; Winner, 1995 Luciano Pavarotti Competition, Philadelphia. *Address:* c/o IMG Artists, Lovell House, 616 Chiswick High Road, London W4 5RX, England.

**VENTRIGLIA, Franco;** Opera Singer (Bass); b. 20 Oct. 1927, Fairfield, Connecticut, USA; m. 1945. *Education:* American Theatre Wing, Toti Dal Monte International School of Bel Canto in Rome and Venice. *Career:* Debut: Teatro Massimo Palermo, Italy, Meistersinger, Tullio Serafin, Conductor; Appearances in various operas, Academia Di S Cecilia, Rome; La Scala, Vienna Staatsoper, Berlin Staatsoper; San Carlo; Regio di Parma; Regio di Torino; Comunale di Firenze; King's Theatre, Edinburgh; Chicago Lyric; Dallas Opera; Wexford Festival; La Fenice Venezia; Arena di Verona; Teatro de L'Opera Roma; Milwaukee; Concertgebouw, Amsterdam; Dutch Radio; Roles have included Rossini's Basilio, Raimondo, Elmiro (Otello by Rossini), Walter and Wurm in Luisa Miller, Loredano (I due Foscari), the Grand Inquistor, Alvise, Colline and Sparafucile (Rigoletto); mem, AGMA. *Recordings:* La Traviata, RCA; Manon Lescaut, EMI; Angelium, Vedette Records. *Contributions:* Opera News.

**VENTRIS, Christopher;** Singer (Tenor); b. 5 May 1960, London, England. *Education:* Studied at the Royal Academy of Music. *Career:* Joined Glyndebourne Festival Chorus, 1987; Touring opera debut, 1988 as Vanya in Katya Kabanova; Later appearances as Tom Rakewell with Glyndebourne Festival Opera and The Porter in Death in Venice, Jacquino in Fidelio, and Števa in Jenůfa with GTO; Opera work with Opera North, ENO and Royal Opera; Performed in: Magic Flute, 1993 in Geneva, King Priam and Eugene Onegin, 1994 at Antwerp and Flying Dutchman, 1992 and Salome, 1995 at Leipzig; Concert work throughout Europe includes: Beethoven 9th Symphony, Mendelssohn's Second Symphony, (Lobgesang) and Elijah, and Tippett's Child of Our Time; Further engagements include: Steuermann at Amsterdam in 1995, Midsummer Marriage with Royal Opera, Title role in Parsifal at Antwerp; Debut at La Scala as Max in Der Freischütz, 1998; Engaged as Parsifal at San Francisco, 2000, and Siegmund in Die Walküre at Cologne, 2001. *Recordings:* Caritas, Saxton; Blonde Eckbert, Weir. *Honours:* Esso GTFO Singers Award, 1988–89; John Christie Award, Glyndebourne; Associate of Royal Academy of Music, 1993. *Address:* c/o IMG Artists Europe, Lovell House, 616 Chiswick High Road, London W4 5RX, England.

**VENUTI, Maria;** Singer (Soprano); b. 1953, New York, USA. *Education:* Eastman School, Rochester, and Detmold Musikhochschules with Helmut Kretzschmar and Gunter Weissenborn. *Career:* Sang at the Vienna Staatsoper from 1976, Lyric Opera Chicago from 1978; Appearances throughout Europe in operas by Mozart, Amor in Orfeo ed Euridice, Oscar (Un ballo in Maschera), Sophie in Der Rosenkavalier and Bizet's Micaela; Engagements at Augsburg, Kassel (Mozart's Ilia, 1984), Salzburg and Brussels; Concert repertoire has included Schubert's Lazarus, Utrecht Te Deum by Handel, and the Mozart Requiem. *Recordings include:* Inez, in Il Trovatore, under Karajan (EMI). *Address:* Augsburg Opera, Kasernstrasse 4-6, Of 111949, D-86044, Augsburg, Germany.

**VENZAGO, Mario;** conductor; *Music Director, Indianapolis Symphony Orchestra;* b. 1 July 1948, Zürich, Switzerland. *Education:* Univ. of Zürich, Zürich and Vienna Conservatories, notably with Hans Swarowsky. *Career:* Prin. Conductor, Collegium Musicum at Winterthur 1977; Conductor, Lucerne Opera House, then Prin. Conductor for broadcast recordings, Orchestre de la Suisse Romande, Geneva –1986; American debut at the

Hollywood Bowl with the Los Angeles Philharmonic Inst. Orchestra 1988; Music Dir, Heidelberg Opera 1986–89, Deutsche Kammer-philharmonie, Frankfurt/Bremen 1989–92, Graz Opera House, Austria 1990–95, Basel Symphony Orchestra 1997–2003, Basque Euskadi Nat. Orchestra, Spain 1998–2001; Artistic Dir, Baltimore Symphony Orchestra's Summer MusicFest 2000–03; Principal Guest Conductor, Malmö Symphony Orchestra 2001–03; Prin. Conductor, Gothenburg Symphony Orchestra 2004–; Music Dir, Indianapolis Symphony Orchestra 2002–06. *Recordings:* works by Schumann, Janáček and others. *Current Management:* Bulmer and Dixon Ltd, Granitweg 2, 8002 Zürich, Switzerland. *Address:* c/o Indianapolis Symphony Orchestra, 32 E Washington Street, Suite 600, Indianapolis, IN 46204-2919, USA.

**VERA-RIVERA, Santiago Oscar;** Professor and Composer; b. 2 Nov. 1950, Santiago, Chile; m. Maria Angelica Bustamante, 25 May 1974, 2 s., 1 d. *Education:* University of Chile; Doctorate in Musicology, University of Oviedo, Spain, 1991. *Career:* Professor, University of Chile, 1974–81, University of Tarapaca, 1984; Acad Pedag Santiago, 1981–85; University Metropolitana, 1986; Escuela Moderna de Musica, 1976–87; Intem/OAS, 1984. *Compositions:* Choral, piano, electronic, percussion, guitar and orchestral pieces include: Apocaliptika II, 1988; Silogistika I for flute and guitar, 1989; Silogistika II for voice, clarinet, violin, violoncello and piano, 1989; Silogistika III for voice and orchestra. *Recordings include:* Tres Temporarias, 1987; Cirrus, 1987; Tres acuareskas, 1989; Chiloé, Tierra de Agua, 1989; CD: Musica Para el Fin de Siglo. *Publications:* Harmony for two voices, 1990; Contributor to Dictionary of Music, Hispano Americano and Espanola, 1989–92; Informúsica, Spain, 1992; Voices for Hispano-Americano and Española, Dictionary of Music of Ten Chilean Composers; Complete Catalogue of Chilean and Latin American Classical Music. *Address:* San Juan 4967, Santiago, Chile.

**VERBITSKY, Leonid;** Composer, Conductor and Arranger; b. 9 Dec. 1930, Kharkov, USSR. *Education:* Musical Secondary School, Kiev, Russia, 1938–49; Conservatoire (Evening Department), Kiev, Russia, 1949–53. *Career:* Singing Teacher, Secondary School, Kiev, Russia, 1953–55; Member of Orchestra and Arranger, Republican State Variety Orchestra, 1955–66; Conductor, Kiev State Russian Dramatic Theatre, 1966–71; Conductor and Arranger, Ukrainian Masters of Arts Concert Team, Kiev State Opera and Ballet Theatre, 1971–74; Leader of the Orchestra, Music Ensembles Union, Kiev, 1974–79; Moved to USA and settled in New York City, 1979–; Numerous tours of Russia conducting variety orchestras; Many performances on television and radio. *Compositions:* Over 400 compositions include: Music for 9 cartoons; 3 theatrical plays; Several television and radio plays; More than 300 songs and romances including: The Girl is Going; Blue Roses; The Cranes; The Black Eyes' Charm; It is Good When It is Good. *Recordings:* 20 compositions recorded. *Publications:* More than 200 compositions published by different publishing houses. *Address:* 200 Corbin Place, #6F, Brooklyn, NY 11235, USA.

**VERBITSKY, Vladimir,** PhD; Russian conductor; *Music Director and Chief Conductor, Voronezh State Symphony Orchestra;* b. 24 Oct. 1943, Leningrad; m. Ninel; one s. one d. *Education:* studied piano, choral, operatic and symphony conducting, Leningrad Conservatoire, graduated in piano 1966. *Career:* various orchestral appointments, including Music Dir and Chief Conductor Voronezh State Philharmonic 1972–; Guest Conductor, State Orchestra of the USSR, Moscow 1976–89; Chief Conductor, Slovak Philharmonic Orchestra, Bratislava, Czechoslovakia 1982–84; Music Dir State Orchestra of Victoria, Melbourne, Australia 1987–88; Guest Conductor, West Australian Symphony Orchestra 1987–91, Prin. Guest Conductor 1992–97, Conductor Laureate 1997–; publs and recordings of classical music with major orchestras world-wide. *Honours:* Herbert von Karajan Int. Young Conductors' Competition diploma, Berlin 1973, Laureate Villa Lobos Int. Young Conductors' Competition, Rio de Janeiro 1975, Laureate Hungarian Radio and Television Int. Conductors' Competition, Budapest 1976, People's Artist of Russian Fed. 1993; Order of Honour USSR Govt 1980, Order for Services to the Fatherland 2004. *Current Management:* c/o Dr Boehm, Künstleragentnstur Dr Raab & Dr Boehm, Plankengasse 7, 1010 Vienna, Austria. *Telephone:* (1) 5120501. *Fax:* (1) 5127743. *E-mail:* drboehm@jbartists .at. *Website:* www.rbartists.at. *Current Management:* c/o Manager Robert Slotover, Allied Artists, 42 Montpelier Square, London, SW71JZ, England. *Telephone:* (20) 7589-6243. *Fax:* (20) 7581-5269. *E-mail:* robert@alliedartists .co.uk. *Website:* www.alliedartists.co.uk. *Current Management:* c/o Kenneth Wentworth, Jonathan Wentworth Associates Ltd, 10 Fiske Place, Suite 530, Mt Vernon, NY 10550-3205, USA. *Telephone:* (914) 667-0707. *Fax:* (914) 667-0784. *E-mail:* kenneth@jwentworth.com. *Website:* www.jwentworth com. *Address:* West Australian Symphony Orchestra, PO Box Y3041, East St George's Terrace, Perth, WA 6832, Australia (office). *Telephone:* (8) 93260051 (office). *Fax:* (8) 93260080 (office). *E-mail:* venningk@waso.com.au (office). vnverbitsky@aol.com. *Website:* www.waso.com.au (office).

**VERBRUGGEN, Marion;** Recorder Player and Teacher; b. 2 Aug. 1950, Amsterdam, Netherlands. *Education:* Study with Kees Otten, Amsterdam Conservatory, 1966; With Frans Brüggen, Muziek Lyceum, Amsterdam, and Royal Conservatory, The Hague, 1967; B Diploma, 1971; Solo degree cum laude, 1973. *Career:* Performances with various ensembles and solo concerts; Netherlands, USA, Canada, Japan, most European countries; Regular guest, Gustav Leonhardt, Amsterdam Baroque Orchestra, Musica Antiqua, Cologne, Tafelmusik Toronto, many others; Plays at Holland Festival of Early Music; Television appearances, Netherlands, Norway, Belgium, Italy, Federal Republic of Germany, USA; Teacher: Royal Conservatory, The Hague; Utrecht

Conservatory; Guest Teacher, Malmö Conservatory, Sweden; Masterclasses and workshops, Stanford University, Toronto, Montreal, New York, Philadelphia, Malmö, Trondheim, Copenhagen, Jerusalem. *Recordings:* For EMI, Philips/Seon, Titanic, Hungaroton, ASV London, L'Oiseau Lyre, Monumenta Belgicae Musicae; Archiv, Harmonia Mundi. *Address:* Vondelstraat 99, 1054 GM Amsterdam, Netherlands.

**VERBY, Theo;** Composer; b. 5 July 1959, Delft, Netherlands. *Education:* Royal Conservatory, The Hague, 1978–85. *Career:* Lecturer in Composition; Amsterdam Sweelinck Conservatory, 1997–; Commissions from London Sinfonietta, Residentie-Orkest and Royal Concertgebouw Orchestra. *Compositions:* Caprice Symphonique, 1976; Triplum for wind instruments, 1982; Random Symphonies. electronic, 1985; Contrary motion, for orchestra, 1986; Inversie, for ensemble, 1987; Expulsie, for ensemble, 1990; De Peryton, for seven wind instruments, 1990; Triade for orchestra, 1991, rev, 1994; Whitman, for soprano and orchestra, 1992; Notturno, for oboe, two horns and strings, 1995; Conciso, for ensemble, 1996; Alliage for orchestra, 1996; Six Rilke Lieder for baritone and small orchestra, 1998. *Honours:* Amsterdam Art fund Award, 1987. *Address:* c/o BUMA, PO Box 725, 1180 AS Amstelveen, Netherlands. *Telephone:* 0031 20540 7911. *Fax:* 0031 20540 7496.

**VERCO, Wendy;** Singer (Mezzo-soprano); b. 1945, Melbourne, Australia. *Education:* Studied at Sydney Conservatory and in London at Opera Studio. *Career:* Debut: Opera 80, 1982, as Orlofsky in Die Fledermaus; Appearances with Opera 80 as Dorabella and with Welsh National Opera as Maddalena in Rigoletto and Meg Page in Falstaff; Glyndebourne Festival from 1981, in Poppea, Idomeneo and Arabella; Opera North, 1985, as Irene in Tamerlano, Covent Garden, 1986, as Rossweise in Die Walküre; Welsh National Opera on tour to Japan, 1990; Sang Clytemnestra in Gluck's Iphigénie operas at the Théâtre des Champs Elysées, Paris, 1991; Concerts with the City of Birmingham Symphony Orchestra and the London Mozart Players. *Recordings:* Videos of Poppea, Arabella and Idomeneo from Glyndebourne.

**VERCOE, Elizabeth (Walton);** American composer; b. 23 April 1941, Washington DC; one s. one d. *Education:* BA in Music, Wellesley College, 1962; MMus in Composition, University of Michigan, 1963; Doctor of Musical Arts in Composition, Boston University, 1978. *Career:* Instructor of Musical Theory, Westminster Choir College, 1969–71; Assistant Professor of Music, Framlingham State College, Massachusetts, 1973–74; Composer, Cité Internationale des Arts, Paris, France, 1983–85 and Charles Ives Center for American Music, 1984, 1992; Co-Director of Women's Music Festival, Boston, 1985, MacDowell Colony, 1992, and St Petersburg, Russia, Spring Music Festival, 1993; Director, Society of Composers Festivals, 1995–96; Lecturer Regis College, Weston Massachusetts, 1997–; Residency, Civitella Ranieri Center, Italy, 1998; Acuff Chair of Excellence, Austin Peay State Univ., TN, 2003. *Compositions include:* Fantasy for piano; Duo for violin and cello; Sonario for cello; Three Studies for piano; Irreveries from Sappho for SSA and piano or soprano and piano; Herstory II for soprano, piano and percussion; Herstory III; Persona for piano; Rhapsody for violin and orchestra; Despite our Differences No. 1 for piano trio, No. 2 for piano and orchestra, 1988; Plucked String Editions: A la Fin tout seul for mandolin and optional piano; A Dangerous Man for baritone and piano, 1990; Changes for chamber orchestra, 1991; Four Humors for clarinet and piano, 1993; Herstory IV for soprano and mandolin or marimba, 1997; Umbrian Suite for piano 4-hands, 1999; Kleemation for flute and piano, 2003; To Music for solo flute, 2003, Four Humors for clarinet and piano. *Recordings:* Herstory III, on Owl; Herstory II; 13 Japanese Lyrics for soprano, piano and percussion; Fantasy for Piano; Irreveries from Sappho for voice and piano; Fantasia for flute and percussion, Four Humors for clarinet and piano. *Publications:* various works published; contribs: The Lady Vanishes?, in Perspectives of New Music 1982, A Composer's View, in the Journal of Early Music America 1990. *Honours:* Meet the Composer Grants 1981, 1987, 1994, 1999, Massachusetts Artist Fellowship 1985, Project Grant, Artists' Foundation 1983. *Address:* 74 Judy Farm Road, Carlisle, MA 01741, USA. *E-mail:* elizverco@yahoo.com (office). *Website:* www.pennynation.com/hyptonic/evercoe (office).

**VERGARA, Victoria;** Singer (Mezzo-soprano); b. 1948, Santiago, Chile. *Education:* Studied in Santiago and in New York with Nicola Moscona, and Anton Guadagno, and at the Juilliard School with Daniel Ferro and Rose Bampton. *Career:* Sang minor roles in the USA, before New York City Opera debut, 1977; Sang at Detroit from 1977, Santiago 1978; Houston Grand Opera from 1980; Has sung Carmen at San Francisco, Cincinnati, Zürich, Lisbon, Vancouver, Philadelphia, Seattle, New Orleans and Berlin; Chicago Lyric Opera 1982, Vienna Staatsoper 1984, as Amneris; Washington Opera 1987, as the Duchess of Alba in the premiere of Menotti's Goya, opposite Placido Domingo; Metropolitan Opera debut 1988, as Carmen; Teatro Liceo Barcelona 1989, in the premiere of Cristobal Colon by Leonardo Balada, with Caballé and Carreras; Season 1990 sang Herodias (Salome) at Santiago and at the Zarzuela Theatre Madrid in El viajero indiscreto, as Dona; Other roles include Donna Elvira, Cherubino, Federica in Luisa Miller, Maddalena, Rosina, Dalila, Nicklausse, Charlotte and Massenet's Dulcinée. *Recordings include:* Maddalena in Rigoletto. *Address:* c/o IM Röhrich 55, 6702 Bad Dürkheim 2, Germany.

**VERMEERSCH, Jef;** Singer (Baritone); b. 7 Feb. 1928, Bruges, Belgium. *Education:* Studied in Bruges, Ghent and Antwerp, 1960, as Wotan in Das Rheingold; Sang at Gelsenkirchen from 1966; Member, Deutsche Oper Berlin from 1973; Guest appearances in Germany and Brussels, Amsterdam, Lyon,

Venice, Lisbon, Prague, Geneva, San Francisco, Barcelona and Stockholm; Salzburg Easter Festival 1973, as Kurwenal in Tristan and Isolde, conducted by Karajan; Bayreuth Festival 1981–83, Kothner in Die Meistersinger; Other roles included Hans Sachs, Amfortas, the Dutchman, Boris Godunov, Golaud, Pizarro, Kaspar, the title role in Giulio Cesare by Handel, Leporello, Jochanaan, Kepler in Hindemith's Die Harmonie der Welt, Falstaff, Amonasro and St Just in Von Einem's Dantons Tod; Sang Kothner at Bayreuth 1988; Kurwenal at Wuppertal 1989;*Address:* Wuppertal Bühnen, Spinnstrasse 4, 5600 Wuppertal.

**VERMILLION, Iris;** Soprano; b. 1960, Bielefeld, Germany. *Education:* Studied flute at first then voice with Mechthild Bohme and Judith Beckmann. *Career:* Debut: Brunswick in 1986 as Zulma in L'Italiana in Algeri and as Barbara in Eine Nacht in Venedig; Sang Dorabella and Octavian in Brunswick; Deutsche Oper Berlin from 1988 as a Rhinemaiden, Hansel and Cherubino; Darmstadt in 1988 as Judith in Duke Bluebeard's Castle; Sang Dorabella with Netherlands Opera in Amsterdam in 1990; Salzburg Festival in 1990 as Clairon in Capriccio; Other roles include Werther, Charlotte and Mozart's Sextus; Also sings in the St Matthew Passion and Mozart's Davidde Penitente; Sang Bianca in Zemlinsky's Florentinische Tragödie at Florence, 1995; Season 2000 as Strauss's Composer at La Scala, Waltraute for the Vienna Staatsoper, premiere of Rihm's St Luke Passion at Stuttgart and Adriano in Wagner's Rienzi at Dresden (concert). *Recordings include:* Second Lady in Die Zauberflöte under Neville Marriner. *Honours:* Prize Winner at Cardiff Singer of World Competition. *Address:* c/o Deutsche Oper Berlin, Richard Wagnerstrasse 10, 1000 Berlin, Germany.

**VERNEROVA-NOVAKOVA, Ludmila;** Singer (Soprano); b. 6 Dec. 1962, Prague, Czechoslovakia; m. Pravomil Novák, 1 d. *Education:* Academy of Musical Arts, Prague. *Career:* Debut: National Theatre, Prague, 1987; Bach Academy at Stuttgart, Germany, three times: Handel, Messiah; Bach Mass in B Minor; Mozart Festival at Citta del Castello, Italy, 1991; Mozart's Missa C Major; Sommerfestspiele at Stuttgart, 1993; Festival at Marbella, Spain, 1994: Beethoven's Missa Solemnis; Festival Prague Spring, 1995: Mozart's Concert Arias; Festival in Ludwigsburg, Germany, 1995: Mozart's Requiem; Music Festival Bratislava, Slovakia, 1997: Mozart's Missa C Minor; Festival Prague Autumn, 1997; Other repertory includes: Myslivecek's Isaac; Purcell's Dido and Aeneas (Dido, Belinda); Britten's Beggar's Opera; Mozart's Nozze di Figaro (Countess), Don Giovanni (Donna Anna); Bizet's Carmen (Micaela); Sang under conductors V Neumann, H Rilling, G Delogu, W Gönnenwein, F Bernius, G Albrecht, Ch Dohnányi and others in most European countries; Her repertoire also includes Handel's Samson, Judas Maccabaeus, Rodelinda, Alcina, Jephtha, several cantatas; Beethoven's 9th Symphony and Songs; Bach's St John Passion, St Mark Passion, Mass in B minor, Magnificat, numerous cantatas; Haydn's Die Schöpfung, Stabat Mater, Vier Jahreszeiten and Masses; Schubert's Stabat Mater, Masses, Salve Regina, Erstes Offertorium (Op 45); Brahms' Ein Deutsches Requiem, Songs; Dvořák's Stabat Mater, Mass in D, Songs; also music by Mendelssohn, Schumann, Rameau, Pergolesi, Carissimi, Vivaldi, Zelenka, Buxtehude and others. *Recordings:* 42 CDs include: Dvořák's Stabat Mater; Haydn's Nelson Mass, Stabat Mater; Schubert's Mass No. 3 BFlat; Pergolesi's Stabat Mater; J. S. Bach's St John Passion; Mozart's Coronation Mass, Vesperae Solemnes. *Address:* Kafkova 8, Prague 6-Dejvice, CZ 160 00.

**VERNET, Isabelle;** Singer (Soprano); b. 1966, Paris, France. *Education:* Studied with Regine Crespin in Paris. *Career:* Sang in Der Rosenkavalier at Paris, 1989; Season 1991 as Fauré's Pénélope at Nancy and in La Vie Parisienne at Geneva; Opéra de Lyon, 1993–95, as Offenbach's Giulietta and Donna Elvira; Frankfurt, 1994, as Gluck's Iphigénie en Tauride; Season 1996 as Alceste at Scottish Opera and Nice, Phèdre in Hippolyte et Aricie at the Palais Garnier, Paris; Season 1998 as Vitellia in La Clemenza di Tito for Welsh National Opera; Engaged as Iphigénie at Bordeaux, 2000; Sang the Trovatore Leonora at Montpellier and Mozart's Elettra in Toronto, 2000. *Recordings include:* Oedipe by Enescu; Le Domino Noir by Auber. *Address:* c/o OIA, 16 ave Franklin Roosevelt, 75008 Paris, France.

**VERNHES, Alain;** Singer (Baritone); b. 1944, France. *Career:* Sang at the Opéra de Lyon, 1969–72, and made many appearances throughout France; Opéra d'Avignon, 1982–85, with such singers as Caballé, Aragall and Bruson; Orange Festival, 1987, as Vitellius in Massenet's Herodiade, and Opéra du Rhin, Strasbourg, as Zuniga in Carmen; Avignon, 1992, as Ourrais in Gounod's Mireille; Has also sung Puccini's Marcello and Scarpia in concert performances; Sang Melitone in La Forza del Destino at Orange, 1996; Marquis in The Carmélites at Amsterdam, 1998; Season 2000–01 as Massenet's Des Grieux at Monte Carlo, in Chausson's Le Roi Arthus at Edinburgh and Ramon in Gounod's Mireille for Opéra de Nice; Massenet's Sancho Panza for Washington Opera and Lotharo in Mignon at Toulouse. *Address:* Opéra d'Avignon, Rue Racine, 84000 Avignon, France.

**VERNON, Richard;** Singer (Bass); b. 1950, Memphis, Tennessee, USA. *Education:* Studied at Memphis State University. *Career:* Debut: Memphis 1972, as Pimen in Boris Godunov; Has sung with Houston Opera Studio from 1977, in operas by Verdi; Appearances with Washington Opera and Pittsburgh Opera; Metropolitan Opera from 1981, in L'Enfant et les Sortilèges, and as Titurel (Parsifal) and the Commendatore (Don Giovanni); Sang Foltz in a new production of Die Meistersinger at the Metropolitan, 1993. *Address:* c/o Metropolitan Opera, Lincoln Center, New York, NY 10023, USA.

**VERONELLI, Ernesto;** Singer (Tenor); b. 1948, Milan, Italy. *Education:* Studied at the Giuseppe Verdi Conservatory, Milan. *Career:* Has sung in operas by Verdi, Puccini, Massenet and Giordano at Paris, Zürich, Berlin, Barcelona, Vienna and Verona; Debut with the Royal Opera Covent Garden at Manchester as Cavaradossi, 1983, later singing Chevalier Roland in Esclarmonde, opposite Joan Sutherland; Season 1985–86 sang Canio at the Metropolitan, Cavaradossi in Pretoria and Pinkerton at the Cologne Opera; Calaf in Detroit and Radames at Toronto; Other roles have been Verdi's Macduff, Carlo (Giovanna d'Arco), Don Carlos and Manrico.

**VERRETT, Shirley;** American singer (soprano); b. 31 May 1931, New Orleans; d. of Leon Verrett and Elvira Verrett; m. Louis Lomonaco 1963; one d. *Education:* Juilliard School of Music, New York. *Career:* Prof. of Voice, School of Music, Univ. of Mich. 1996–; operatic début as mezzo-soprano taking title role of Carmen, Spoleto Festival 1962; same role for début at Bolshoi Opera, Moscow 1963, New York City Opera 1966, Florence 1968, Metropolitan Opera, New York 1968; sang at Covent Garden, London in roles of Ulrica (Un Ballo in Maschera) 1966, Amneris (Aida) 1967, Eboli (Don Carlos) 1968, Azucena (Il Trovatore) 1970; début at San Carlo, Naples as Elisabetta (Maria Stuarda) 1969, at La Scala, Milan as Delilah (Samson et Dalila) 1970, at Vienna Staatsoper as Eboli 1970, at Teatro Liceo, Barcelona as Eboli 1971, at Paris Opera as Azucena 1972; other mezzo-soprano roles in Orfeo (Gluck), as Dido (Les Troyens), Judith (Bluebeard's Castle), Neocle (Siege of Corinth), Adalgisa (Norma, first performance at Metropolitan, New York 1976); made début as soprano in title role of La Favorita, Dallas Civic Opera 1971; début at San Francisco Opera in title role of L'Africaine 1972; first artist to sing roles of both Dido and Cassandra in one single full-length production of Les Troyens, Metropolitan 1973; other soprano roles: Lady Macbeth, La Scala 1975 and with La Scala at Kennedy Center, Washington, DC 1976, also with Opera Co. of Boston 1976; title role of Norma, Metropolitan Opera 1976 (in the same season took mezzo-soprano role of Adalgisa, being the first singer since Grisi to sing both roles); New Prioress in Dialogues of the Carmelites, Metropolitan 1977; now sings only soprano roles; Amellia, La Scala 1978, title role in Favorita, Metropolitan 1978; in Tosca at Metropolitan, New York 1978; début appearance at Opera Bastille, Paris 1990; appeared in film Maggio Musicale 1990, as Nettie Fowler in Broadway production of Carousel 1994–95; frequent appearances with US and European opera houses, with US symphony orchestras; has appeared as soloist on Milan's RAI; was subject of BBC TV feature Profiles in Music 1971, of documentary Black Diva 1985. *Honours:* Dr hc (Holy Cross Coll., Worcester, Mass., Northeastern Univ.); Commdr des Arts et des Lettres 1984. *Address:* Herbert Breslin Inc., 6124 Liebig Avenue, Bronx, NY 10471 (office); School of Music, University of Michigan, 1100 Baits Drive, Ann Arbor, MI 48109, USA.

**VERROT, Pascal;** French conductor; b. 9 Jan. 1959, Lyon, France. *Education:* studied at the Sorbonne and Conservatoire, Paris. *Career:* Asst to Seiji Ozawa at Boston Symphony from 1985, giving concerts at Symphony Hall Boston and Tanglewood; further concerts with Boston Chamber Players; guest engagements in Japan, throughout N America and France; Music Dir Quebec Symphony Orchestra 1991–2005. *Honours:* Prizewinner, Tokyo Int. Competition 1985. *Address:* 154 avenue Maréchal Foch, 69110 Ste-Foy Les Lyon, France.

**VERROUST, Denis;** French flautist and musicologist; b. 21 Feb. 1958, Vincennes, France; m. Marguerite Sopinski 1986. *Education:* Baccalaureate A 1975, DEUG, Econs 1979, Grad. Saint-Maur CNR, DE, flute teacher 1988. *Career:* flute teacher; Prof. of Flute in Palaiseau, France 1979–; appearances, St Malo Festival, Brittany, 1980–90; several tours in France, Germany, Netherlands as soloist with Cologne Chamber Orchestra; solo and chamber music concerts in France and abroad; Dir of Collection for Billaudot Edn, Paris 2004–; Chief Ed. French Flute Asscn 1990–2000, Pres. 1991–2004; Founder and Pres. Jean-Pierre Rampal Asscn 2005–; Co-founder and Artistic Dir Au temps de Mozart Music Festival, Palaiseau 2003–; Recording Producer for Traversières label and for recordings of the Jean-Pierre Rampal Asscn; researcher and leading authority on the late classical and romantic flute repertoire. *Radio:* programmes for Radio-France and Radio Classique, Paris. *Recordings:* A. Stamitz, Sinfonia concertante in D for 2 flutes (with C. Arimany, Wrocław Chamber Orchestra, Dir J.L. Moraleda) 1996. *Publications:* five titles proposed and ed for Billaudot Edn, Paris 1980 and 1982; J.S. Bach: Sinfonia from Cantata BWV 209; four characteristic XIXth century pieces by W. Popp, F. Doppler and A. Fürstenberg; two titles edited for Stravaganza Edn, Paris: Mozart, Haydn, Rossini (Overtures for two flutes) and A. Hugot (Trios for two flutes and bass) 1987; Jean-Pierre Rampal, A Half-Century of Recordings (ed. La Flute Traversière, S. Faulisi) 1991; Concertos for two flutes by C.L. Dieter and I. Pleyel 2004, 2005 respectively; numerous contribs to professional journals. *Address:* 16 avenue Aubert, 94300 Vincennes, France. *Telephone:* 1-4-65-64-41. *E-mail:* denis.verroust@wanadoo.fr.

**VERSCHRAEGEN, Herman (Elie Bertha);** Organist, Director of Music and Organ Master; b. 4 April 1936, Ghent, Belgium; m. Genevieve Van Hove, 2 July 1963, 1 s., 1 d. *Education:* Several First Prizes and Higher Diploma in Organ, Royal Conservatory of Music, Ghent, 1960; Virtuosity Prize, Organ, 1965. *Career:* Debut: Ghent, 1957; Organist, St Josef Church, Antwerp, 1962; Master of Music Theory and History, Music Academy of Wilrijk, 1963–73; Organ Master, Music Academy of Aalst, 1965–73 and Music Academy of Geel, 1966–73; Director, Music Academy of Wilrijk-Antwerp, 1974–; Organ Master, Royal Conservatory of Music, Brussels, 1976–; Over 700 organ concerts and recitals in Austria, Belgium, Czechoslovakia, Denmark, Germany, France, Netherlands, Israel, Italy, Japan, Poland, South Africa, Sweden, Switzerland, England, USA, Philippines; Several seminars about C Franck and the Flemish Organ School and also masterclass in Japan; Member of Jury of International Organ Contests, Nuremberg 1970, Lokeren 1972; Recitals for International Broadcasting Corporations Belgium, Denmarks Radio, Suddeutscher Rundfunk, Hessischer Rundfunk, Bayerischer Rundfunk, Sender Freies Berlin, Sudwestfunk, NDR, Czechoslovakia, Sweden, Radio Geneva, Bern, Zürich, Suisse Romande, USA, South Africa. *Compositions:* Fantasy for Organ. *Recordings:* Handel, Bach, Couperin, Van den Gheyn (Polydor). *Address:* 5 Schansweg, 2610 Wilrijk-Antwerpen, Belgium.

**VEZNIK, Vaclav;** Stage Director; b. 1 Aug. 1930, Brno, Moravia, Czechoslovakia; m. Helena Rozsypalova, 28 Sept 1957, 1 s., 1 d. *Education:* The Masaryk State University (Philosophy), 1949–50; The Janáček Academy of Music, 1950–54; Operatic Production, Stage Director; Private study of violin and singing. *Career:* Debut: Donizetti's Don Pasquale, State Theater Brno, 1955; Stage Director, State Theater, Brno, 1954; Guest Directors at all theatres in Czech Republic and Slovakia, 1955–97; Guest directions in Norway, Germany, Switzerland, Italy, Spain, Belgium, Austria, Yugoslavia, 1968–95: 173 operatic productions include: Janáček's Fate (world premiere), 1958; Martinů's The Marriage (Czech premiere), 1960; Fischer's Rome, Julia and the Darkness (world premiere), 1962; Martinů's The Voice of the Forest (World Stage Production), 1964; Martinů's Alexander bis (Czech premiere), 1964; Von Einem's Dantons Tod (Czech premiere), 1966; Gershwin's Porgy and Bess (Czech premiere), 1968; Szokolay's The Blood Wedding (Czech premiere), 1971; Television productions: Prokofiev's Duenna, Prague, 1972; Janáček's Jenůfa, Brno, 1972; Rimsky-Korsakov's The Golden Cockerel, Prague, 1973; Janáček's The Excursions of Mr Brouček, Brno, 1978; Janáček's The Cunning Little Vixen, Brno, 1979; Verdi's Simon Boccanegra, Brno, 1984; Verdi's Nabucco, Brno, 1989; Professor at The Janáček Musik Academy, Brno, 1990–. *Contributions:* Many articles about opera productions in Program (journal of the Janáček Opera, Brno). *Honours:* Bedrich Smetana Medal, 1974, Leoš Janáček Medal, 1978–79, Czech Ministry of Culture. *Address:* Brenkova 3, Brno 613 00, Czech Republic.

**VIALA, Jean-Luc;** Singer (Tenor); b. 5 Sept. 1957, Paris, France. *Education:* Studied in Paris with Michel Sénéchal. *Career:* Debut: Paris Opéra-Comique 1983 in Pomme d'Apis by Offenbach; Sang at the Opéra-Comique in César Franck's Stradella and has made many appearances at provincial French opera houses; Glydebourne Festival 1986, as the Italian Singer in Capriccio, Dublin 1987, Aix-en-Provence Festival 1989, as the Prince in the Love of Three Oranges; Recent engagements at the Opéra de Lyon including Rodolfo 1990; Sang in Sacchini's Oedipe à Colone for the Festival de Radio France at Montpellier, 1992; Other roles include Paolino in Il Matrimonio Segreto, Giannetto (La Gazza Ladra), Fenton, George Brown in La Dame Blanche and Iopas in Les Troyens; Sang Belfiore in Il Viaggio a Reims at Liège, 2000. *Recordings include:* Guercoeur by Magnard and Les Brigands by Offenbach; Narraboth in the French version of Salome, Osmin in Gluck's La Rencontre Imprévue and Bénédict in Béatrice et Bénédict, all with the Lyon Opéra; The Love for Three Oranges; Engaged as George Brown in La Dame Blanche at St Etienne, 1996–97; Rossini's Otello at the Theater an der Wien, Vienna, 1998. *Address:* c/o Opéra de Lyon, 9 Quai Jean Moulin, 69001 Lyon, France.

**VICAR, Jan,** PhDr, CSc; Czech musicologist and composer; *Professor of Theory and History of Music, Academy of Music and Performing Arts;* b. 5 May 1949, Olomouc, Czechoslovakia; m. 1st Anna Betkova 1979; two s.; m. 2nd Eva Slavickova 2001; one s. one d. *Education:* Conservatory in Ostrava, Palacky Univ., Olomouc, Acad. of Music and Performing Arts, Prague 1981. *Career:* Lecturer, Dept of Music, Palacky Univ. 1973–85, Prof. and Head, Dept of Musicology 1990–98, 2000–03; Sr Lecturer, Acad. of Music and Performing Arts, Prague 1985–, Prof. of Theory and History of Music 1998–; Ed.-in-Chief Hudebni Rozhledy 1986–89; Prof. of Composition, Birmingham-Southern Coll., Ala, USA 2005; mem. Czechoslovak Soc. of Arts and Sciences. *Compositions:* String Quartet 1978, Nones 1979, Music For Strings and Timpani 1980, The Cry 1981, Japanese Year (prizes 1980) 1979, Night Prayer 1996, Instructions of Surruppak 1996, Choruses and Songs For Children 1997, Three Marches for Dr Kabyl for brass band 1999, Vivat universitas! 2000, Preludes/Phantasms 2000, Musica profunda 2003, Toward the Mountain 2004. *Publications:* Akordeon a Jeho Hudebni Uplatneni (The Accordion and Its Music Use) 1981, Vaclav Trojan 1989, Hudebni Kritika A Popularizace Hudby (Musical Criticism and Popularization of Music) 1997, Music Aesthetics (with Roman Dykast) 1998, Imprints: Essays on Czech Music and Aesthetics 2005. *Honours:* Mickly's Dissies 1995, Fulbright Scholar-in-Residence 1998–99. *Address:* Malostranske Namesti 13, 118 00 Prague 1, Mala Strana, Czech Republic. *E-mail:* janvicar@seznam.cz (office).

**VICK, Graham;** British opera producer; b. 30 Dec. 1953, Liverpool, England. *Career:* productions for ENO include Ariadne auf Naxos, The Rape of Lucretia, Madama Butterfly, Eugene Onegin, Timon of Athens by Stephen Oliver (world premiere 1991), and The Marriage of Figaro; for Opera North, Così fan tutte, Die Zauberflöte and Katya Kabanova; for Glyndebourne Festival, Queen of Spades, Lulu, Eugene Onegin and Manon Lescaut; Artistic Dir Birmingham Opera Co.; European engagements in Brussels, Bonn, Venice, Netherlands, Berlin, Paris, Italy and St Petersburg; Covent Garden debut in 1989 with British premiere of Un Re in Ascolto by Berio, returning for Mozart's Mitridate 1991 and Die Meistersinger 1993, The Midsummer Marriage at Royal Opera House 1996; Parsifal for Opéra Bastille, Paris

1997; Season 1998–99 with Don Carlos at Opéra Bastille, Così fan tutte at Glyndebourne, Ernani in Vienna and Moses and Aron at the Met in New York; Il Trovatore at the Met 2001. *Television includes:* Il Segreto di Susanna for Scottish TV, The Rape of Lucretia for Channel Four, a live BBC TV broadcast of War and Peace from St Petersburg, and The Queen of Spades from Glyndebourne. *Honours:* Hon. Prof. of Music, Univ. of Birmingham; Chevalier, Ordre des Arts et Lettres; Premi Abbiati Award as Best Dir for Mahagonny at the Teatro Communale in Florence and a Soc. of West End Theatres (SWET) Olivier Award for Mitridate at the Royal Opera, Covent Garden. *Current Management:* Ingpen & Williams Ltd, 7 St George's Court, 131 Putney Bridge Road, London, SW15 2PA, England.

**VICKERS, Jon,** CC, RAM; Canadian singer (tenor); b. 29 Oct. 1926, Prince Albert, Saskatchewan; s. of William Vickers and Myrle Mossip; m. 1st Henrietta Outerbridge 1953 (died 1991); three s. two d.; m. 2nd Judith Stewart 1993. *Career:* began career as concert and opera singer in Canada; joined Royal Opera House, Covent Garden (London) 1957; sang at Bayreuth Festival, Vienna State Opera, San Francisco, Chicago Lyric Opera, Metropolitan Opera, La Scala, Milan, Paris Opera, Boston, Buenos Aires, Athens, Ottawa, Houston, Dallas, Hamburg, Berlin, Munich, Athens Festival, Salzburg Festival, Festival of Orange, Tanglewood Festival, Rio de Janeiro. *Films include:* Carmen, Pagliacci, Norma, Otello. *Recordings:* Messiah, Otello, Aida, Die Walküre, Samson and Delilah, Fidelio, Italian Arias, Verdi Requiem, Peter Grimes, Das Lied von der Erde, Les Troyens, Tristan und Isolde; Enoch Arden (poem by Alfred Lord Tennyson, piano played by Mark Ammelain). *Honours:* Hon. LLD (Sask.); Hon. CLD (Bishop's Univ.); Hon. MusD (Brandon, Univ. of Western Ont.); Hon. LLD (Guelph); Hon. Civ. LD (Laval); Hon. DMus (Univ. of Ill.); Critics Award, London 1978, Grammy Award 1979. *Address:* PO Box 290 WKBX, Warwick, WK 03, Bermuda.

**VIDAL, Elizabeth;** Singer (Soprano); b. 1961, Nice, France. *Education:* Studied in Paris with Elisabeth Grümmer and Eric Tappy. *Career:* Sang at Opéra de Lyon from 1985, as Nannetta, Mozart's Blondchen, Charpentier's Glauce (Médée) and Paisiello's Rosina; Aix-en-Provence, 1987, in Lully's Psyché, Spoleto, 1989, as Offenbach's Olympia; Season 1991 as Auber's Manon Lescaut at the Paris Opéra Comique and Strauss's Sophie at Montpellier; Queen of Night at Avignon and Olympia at Covent Garden; Sang Oscar in Un Ballo in Maschera at Santiago, 1996; Sophie in Massenet's Werther at Venice, 1998; Concerts include Mozart's Requiem and Haydn's Creation. *Recordings include:* Scylla et Glaucus by Leclair.

**VIDOVSZKY, László;** Hungarian composer; *Professor, Franz Liszt Academy;* b. 25 Feb. 1944, Békéscsaba. *Education:* Franz Liszt Acad., Budapest, 1962–67; further study with Messiaen in Paris, 1970–71. *Career:* Co-f. Budapest New Music Studio, 1970; Lecturer, Pécs Univ., 1984–93; Prof., Pécs Univ. 1993–, Franz Liszt Acad., Budapest 1999–. *Compositions:* Music for Györ, for orchestra, 1971; Double for two prepared pianos, 1968–72; Autokoncert, 1972; Circus, electronic, 1975; Schroeder's Death for Piano, 1975; Encounter, Melodrama, 1980; Narcissus and Echo, opera, 1981; Motetta, for chorus and horn, 1981; Une Semaine de beauté, synthesizer, 1983–89; Romantic Readings for Ensemble or Orchestra, 1985; Twelve Duos for Violin and Viola, 1989; Danses Allemandes for String Quartet, 1989;; Etudes for MIDI-piano, 1989–93; Lear, ballet, 1988; German Dances, for orchestra, 1990; Soft Errors, for ensemble 1990; Black Quartet, percussion, 1993–97, Cinema, for ensemble and tape, 1993; Nine Little Greeting Chorales to Kurtág, for piano, 1996; Ady: the Black Piano, for orchestra, 1997; Flute Sonata, 1997; Silly Old Muzak, Electronic, 1997; Zwölf Streichquartette, for String Quartet, 2000; Sonata for Violin and Radio, 2001;. *Current Management:* c/o ARTISJUS, Mészáros u. 15–17, PO Box 593, 1539 Budapest 114, Hungary. *E-mail:* vid@art.pte.hu. *Address:* Mogyorós köz 7, 7635 Pécs, Hungary (home).

**VIER, Michael;** Singer (Bass-baritone); b. 27 Aug. 1963, Hamburg, Germany. *Education:* Studied in Hamburg and Paris. *Career:* Sang Mozart's Count at Pforzheim, then at Bielefeld from 1986, as Nelusko in L'Africaine, as Spohr's Faust and in Gerhard's Duenna; Bernstein's Songfest, with the composer, in London and Moscow; Season 1993–94 as the Herald in Lohengrin at Kiel and Papageno at Zürich; Cologne Opera from 1995, as Papageno, Sharpless and Elviro in Handel's Xerxes; Melot in Tristan und Isolde, 1998; Season 1999–2000 at Cologne in Der König Kandaules by Zemlinsky, Die Vogel by Braunfels, and as Guglielmo and Marcello. *Recordings include:* Spohr's Faust and Lortzing's Ali Pascha von Janina. *Address:* Oper der Stadt Köln, Offenbachplatz Pf 180241, 50505 Cologne, Germany.

**VIGAY, Denis,** FRAM; British cellist; b. 14 May 1926, Brixton, London; m. Greta Vigay 24 July 1952; one s. two d. *Education:* Royal Acad. of Music, London. *Career:* debut: BBC 1941; Principal Cello, Royal Liverpool Philharmonic Orchestra, BBC Symphony Orchestra; Soloist, BBC Promenade Concerts, Royal Albert Hall; Soloist, Principal Cello, Academy of St Martin-in-the-Fields. *Recordings:* Complete Chamber Works of Handel, Schubert Octet, Beethoven Septet, Mendelssohn Octet, Complete Boccherini Guitar Quintets, Mozart Clarinet Quintet, Mozart Oboe Quartet, Mozart Horn Quintet, Fantasia on a Theme of Corelli by Michael Tippett. *Address:* 12 Chesterfield Road, Finchley, London, N3 1PR, England (home).

**VIGNOLES, Roger (Hutton);** Pianoforte Accompanist and Conductor; b. 12 July 1945, England; m. (1) Teresa Ann Elizabeth Henderson 1972, diss 1982, (2) Jessica Virginia Ford, 1982. *Education:* Canterbury Cathedral Choir School; Sedbergh School; BA, BMus, Magdalene College, Cambridge; Royal

College of Music, London (ARCM). *Career:* Accompanist of national and international reputation, regularly appearing with the most distinguished international singers and instrumentalists, in London and provinces and at major music festivals including Aldeburgh, Cheltenham, Edinburgh, Brighton, Bath, Salzburg, Prague, etc; Broadcasting for BBC Radio 3 and television; International tours include USA, Canada, Australia, New Zealand, Hong Kong, Scandinavia; Recitals at Opera Houses of Cologne, 1982; Brussels, 1983; Frankfurt, 1984; Lincoln Center, New York, 1985; San Francisco, 1986; Tokyo, 1985 and 1987; Repetiteur, Royal Opera House, Covent Garden, 1969–71; English Opera Group, 1968–74; Australian Opera Company, 1976; Professor of Accompaniment, Royal College of Music, 1974–81; Conducted Handel's Agrippina at the 1992 Buxton Festival; Accompanist to Inger Dam-Jensen in Strauss, Poulenc and Nielsen at the V & A, London, 1999; London Proms Chamber Music, 2002. *Recordings include:* English song, various, with Graham Trew, Baritone; Lieder by Schumann and Brahms/Dvořák; Cabaret Songs by Britten, Gershwin and Dankworth with Sarah Walker, Mezzo; Premiere recording of The Voice of Love (Nicholas Maw); Franck and Grieg cello sonatas with Robert Cohen, Cello; The Sea, songs and duets with Sarah Walker and Thomas Allen, Baritone; Parry Violin Sonatas with Erich Gruenberg, Violin. *Honours:* Honorary RAM, 1984. *Address:* 1 Ascham Street, Kentish Town, London NW5 2PB, England.

**VIGNON, Lucille;** Singer (Mezzo-soprano); b. 1963, Paris, France. *Education:* Studied in Paris and Venice and with Isabel Garcisanz. *Career:* Debut: Treviso, 1988, as Tisbe in Cenerentola; Appearances throughout France and Italy as Cenerentola, Rosina, and Pippo in La Gazza Ladra; Sara in Donizetti's Roberto Devereux at Montpellier and Bologna; Season 1991 as Fenena at Caracalla and Anne Boleyn in Henry VIII by Saint-Saëns at Compiègne; Other roles include Maddalena in Rigoletto, Nicklausse in Les Contes d'Hoffmann and Léonor in La Favorite, at Nantes; Oreste in La Belle Hélène at Montpellier and at Zürich, 1994–95; Concerts include works by Berio, and the Verdi Requiem. *Address:* c/o Opernhaus Zürich, Falkenstrasse 1, 8008 Zürich, Switzerland.

**VIHAVAINEN, Ilkka;** Singer (Bass-baritone); b. 18 Oct. 1960, Finland. *Education:* Studied at the Sibelius Academy, 1984–87, and in Berlin and Zürich. *Career:* Sang with the Zürich Opera as Lord Walton in I Puritani, Belcore, Garibaldo in Rodelinda and Nick Shadow in The Rake's Progress; Royal Opera Stockholm, 1988, as the Commendatore in Don Giovanni, and the Savonlinna Festival in Sallinen's The King goes forth to France; Concert appearances in Bach, Mozart's Requiem and Haydn's Creation. *Address:* Finnish National Opera, Bulevardi 23–27, 00180 Helsinki 18, Finland.

**VIHAVAINEN, Satu;** Singer (Soprano); b. 1958, Finland. *Education:* Graduated Sibelius Academy, Helsinki, 1982. *Career:* Sang in concert from 1981, Finnish National Opera from 1982; Roles have included Micaela, Nedda, Donna Elvira, Susanna, Mimi and Marguerite; Savonlinna Festival from 1981, as First Lady and Pamina in Zauberflöte, Priestess in Aida and Marzelline in Fidelio; Guested at Los Angeles, 1992, in premiere of Sallinen's Kullervo; Sang Freia in Das Rheingold at Helsinki, 1996; Sang Wagner's Gutrune at Helsinki, 1999; Many concert engagements. *Address:* Finnish National Opera, Bulevardi 23–27, 00180 Helsinki 18, Finland.

**VILÉGIER, Jean Marie;** Stage Director; b. 1940, France. *Education:* Ecole Normale Supérieure Paris. *Career:* Lecturer at the Theatre Studies department, University of Nancy; Director of Théâtre National de Strasbourg, 1990–93; Founder and Director of L'Illustré Théâtre; Opera productions have included La Cenerentola (1983), Lully's Atys (1986), La fée Urgèle by Duni and Favart (1991), Charpentier's Médée (1993) and Rameau's Hippolyte et Aricie, 1996; Tours of Atys, Médée and Hippolyte to the Brooklyn Academy, New York; Further collaborations, with William Christie include Handel's Rodelinda at Glyndebourne, 1998. *Recordings include:* Rodelinda (video).

**VILJAKAINEN, Raili;** Singer (Soprano); b. 1954, Helsinki, Finland. *Education:* Studied at the Sibelius Academy, 1973–78; Further study with Luigi Ricci in Rome. *Career:* Has sung in Stuttgart from 1978 as Aennchen in Der Freischütz, Sophie, Pamina, Ilia, Micaela, Mimi, Liu, Eva, Freia in Das Rheingold and Countess in Figaro; Guest appearances at the Savonlinna Festival, Salzburg and the Saratoga Springs Festival; Concert appearances in works by Bach, Mozart, Beethoven, Handel and Mahler; Has sung at Carnegie Hall, New York and in Finland, throughout Germany, Austria, USA, Australia, France and Spain; Sang Pamina at the Savonlinna Festival, 1981–90, Tatiana in Eugene Onegin and Desdemona in Otello at Helsinki; Contemporary music in Paris, Biennale Helsinki, Opera in Bonn, and in Sciarrino's Lohengrin; Sang Ellen Orford in Helsinki and Berlin, 1999. *Recordings:* Aennchen in Der Freischütz. *Honours:* 1st Prize, Timo Callio Competition at Savonlinna Festival, 1976; 1st Prize, 's-Hertogenbosch Competition, Netherlands, 1977. *Address:* c/o Finnish National Opera, Helsinginkatu 58, 00260 Helsinki, Finland.

**VILLA, Edoardo;** Singer (Tenor); b. 19 Oct. 1953, Los Angeles, USA. *Education:* Studied at the University of Southern California and with Martial Singher, Horst Gunter and Margaret Harshaw. *Career:* Many appearances in opera throughout the USA and abroad; Paris Opéra 1986, as Don Carlos, Houston 1988, as Don José; Sang at the Munich Staatsoper, 1988, and has appeared widely in Canada; Sang Jacopo Foscari in I Due Foscari with the Opera Orchestra of New York, 1992; Other roles include Corrado in Il Corsaro, Ruggero in La Rondine, Hoffmann, the Italian Singer in Rosenkavalier and

Albert Herring; Season 1999–2000 as Enzo in La Gioconda for Miami Opera and Radames at Heidenheim. *Recordings include:* Le Roi d'Ys by Lalo.

**VILLAROEL, Veronica;** Singer (Soprano); b. 1962, Chile. *Education:* Studied in Chile and the USA. *Career:* Debut: Santiago, 1988, as Marguerite in Faust; Sang Antonia at the 1989 Spoleto Festival, Fiordiligi at Barcelona, 1990 (returned for Violetta 1992); Season 1991 as Nedda at Miami, Traviata at Milwaukee and Mimi at Opéra de Lyon; Los Angeles and Théâtre du Châtelet, Paris, as Violetta; Sang Nedda in Pagliacci at Los Angeles; Season 2000 as Desdemona for Washington Opera, Nedda and Boito's Margherita at the Met, Hélène in Verdi's Jérusalem at Genoa and the Trovatore Leonora for the Teatro Colón, Buenos Aires; London Proms, 2002; Many concert engagements. *Address:* 256 West 85th Street #2C, New York, NY 10024, USA.

**VILLARS, John;** Singer (Tenor); b. 1965, Panama City, Florida, USA. *Education:* Juilliard Opera School, New York. *Career:* Sang Midir in Boughton's The Immortal Hour at Juilliard, 1994; Season 1997-98 as the Drum Major in Wozzeck at Salzburg and Bacchus in Ariadne auf Naxos at Florence; Season 1998-99 as Calaf for Canadian Opera, Apollo in Strauss's Daphne at the Deutsche Oper Berlin and the Drum Major in Gurlitt's Wozzeck, Enée in Les Troyens at Salzburg, 2000; Other roles include Strauss's Emperor, Werther, Stravinsky's Oedipus Rex, Cavaradossi and Don José; Concerts include Mahler's 8th Symphony, at the London Proms, 2002. *Recordings include:* Video of Ariadne auf Naxos, Dresden 1999. *Honours:* Winner, National Competition for Young Opera Singers, New York, 1994. *Address:* c/o Staatsoper Dresden, Theaterplatz 2, D-01067 Dresden, Germany.

**VILLAZÓN, Rolando;** Mexican singer (tenor); b. 1972, Mexico City. *Education:* Espacios Acad., Nat. Conservatory of Music, studied with Arturo Nieto, Enrique Jaso, Gabriel Mijares, San Francisco Opera Merola Program, Pittsburgh Opera Young Artists Program, masterclasses with Joan Sutherland. *Career:* European debut as Des Grieux in Manon, Genoa 1999; has performed at Hamburg State Opera, Lyon Opera, Rome Opera, Bregenz Festival, Bellas Artes Mexican Opera, Antibes Festival, Munich State Opera, Berlin Deutsche Oper and Staatsoper, Glyndebourne Festival, Paris Bastille Opera, Oviedo, Trieste, Brussels La Monnaie, Los Angeles Opera, Pittsburgh Opera, Macerata Festival, Orange Festival and New York City Opera; operatic roles include Tebaldo in I Capuleti e i Montecchi, Don José in Carmen, Nemorino in L'Elisir d'Amore, Rodolfo in La Bohème, Edgardo di Ravenswood in Lucia di Lammermoor, Roberto Conte di Leicester in Maria Stuarda, Roméo in Roméo et Juliette, Manon in Des Grieux, The Duke in Rigoletto, Macduff in Macbeth, Alfredo Germont in La Traviata, title roles in Les Contes d'Hoffmann, Don Carlo and Faust. *Recordings:* Gounod, Romeo y Julieta 2002, Wagner, Der Fliegende Holländer 2002, Italian Opera Arias 2004, Gounod and Massenet Arias 2005. *Honours:* Victoires de la Musique 2003; Zarzuela Prize, second prize Placido Domingo's Operalia 1999. *Current Management:* Zemsky/Green Artists Management, 104 W 73rd Street, New York, NY 10023, USA; c/o Dominique Riber, Opéra et Concert, 7 rue de Clichy, Paris 75009, France (office). *Website:* www.rolandovillazon.com.

**VILMA, Michele;** Singer (Mezzo-soprano); b. 23 Feb. 1932, Rouen, France. *Education:* Studied at the Rouen Conservatoire. *Career:* Debut: Sang Léonor in La Favorite at Verviers; Appearances at the Rouen Opera, notably as Dalila, and elsewhere in France as Charlotte, Carmen, Herodiade, Azucena and Dulcinée in Don Quichotte by Massenet; Paris Opéra from 1970 as Eboli, Fricka and the Kostelnicka in Jenůfa; Marseille Opéra as Laura in La Gioconda, Fricka at Bayreuth and Brangaene at the Metropolitan; Sang Clytemnestra in Elektra at the Opéra de Toulouse. *Address:* c/o Opéra de Paris, Théâtre National, 8 Rue Scribe, 75009 Paris, France.

**VINCO, Ivo;** Singer (Bass); b. 8 Nov. 1927, Verona, Italy; m. Fiorenza Cossotto. *Education:* Studied at the Liceo Musicale Verona and at La Scala Opera School with Ettore Campogalliani. *Career:* Debut: Verona 1954, as Ramfis in Aida; Appearances at La Scala and in Rome, Naples, Bologna, Venice, Turin and Florence; Sang at the Verona Arena almost every year from 1954; Further appearances in Vienna, Hamburg, Berlin, Buenos Aires, Paris, Lisbon, Barcelona, Monte Carlo, Moscow, Chicago, Miami and Seattle; Metropolitan Opera debut 1969; Roles include Raimondo (Lucia di Lammermoor), Alvise (La Gioconda), the Grand Inquisitor, Oroveso (Norma), Sparafucile (Rigoletto), Ferrando (Il Trovatore) and Bartolo (Le nozze di Figaro); Sang Alvise in La Gioconda at Barcelona, 1988; Ramphis at Palma, 1992. *Recordings include:* Lucia di Lammermoor, Il Trovatore, Rigoletto, Don Carlos; La Gioconda, Le nozze di Figaro, Iris by Massenet; Norma. *Address:* c/o Arena di Verona, Piazza Bra 28, 37121 Verona, Italy.

**VINE, Carl;** Australian composer, pianist and conductor; b. 8 Oct. 1954, Perth. *Education:* studied with Stephen Dornan and John Exton at the Univ. of Western Australia. *Career:* co-founder of contemporary music ensemble Flederman, 1979; appearances as conductor and pianist in the UK, Europe and the USA; resident composer with the Sydney Dance Co, 1979, London Contemporary Dance Theatre, 1979, Australian Chamber Orchestra, 1987 and Univ. of Western Australia, 1989; Lecturer in Electronic Music at the Queensland Conservatorium, 1980–82; Artistic Dir of Musica Viva Australia since 2001. *Compositions include:* Cafe Concertino, 1984; Canzona, 1985; Love Song for trombone and tape, 1986; Six Symphonies (no. 6 Choral Symphony), 1986–96; Defying Gravity for 4 percussion, 1987; Percussion Concerto, 1987; Piano Sonata, 1990; The Tempest, ballet, 1991; String Quartet No. 3, 1993; Esperance for chamber orchestra, 1994; Five Bagatelles for piano, 1994; Inner World for cello and tape, 1994; Gaijin for koto, strings and electronics, 1994;

Oboe Concerto, 1996; Flag Handover Music (for Atlanta Olympic Games), 1996; Metropolis, for Melbourne Symphony Orchestra, 1997; Piano Concerto, for Sydney Symphony Orchestra, 1997; Piano Sonata No. 2, 1998; Pipe Dreams (flute concerto), 2002; V (an orchestral fanfare), 2002. *Honours:* John Bishop Memorial 1990. *Address:* c/o Faber Music Ltd, 3 Queen Square, London, WC1N 3AU, England. *E-mail:* carlvine@iinet.net.au (office). *Website:* www.carlvine.com (office).

**VINE, David Charles,** BMus, ARCM; British conductor, harpsichordist, composer, pianist and teacher; b. 1943, London. *Education:* Royal College of Music, London, 1961–65; Studied piano with Cornelius Fischer, Bernard Roberts, Eric Harrison, piano accompaniment with Joan Trimble, harpsichord with Millicent Silver, baroque ensemble playing with Hubert Dawkes, conducting with Adrian Boult; Univ. of Canterbury, New Zealand. *Career:* Tutored in Baroque Music, Guildhall School of Music and City Literary Institute; Founder of London Telemann Ensemble; Settled in New Zealand in 1974; Conductor of New Zealand National Youth Orchestra, Wellington Polytechnic Orchestra, Dunedin Sinfonia and Schola Cantorum, Amici Chamber Orchestra, Christchurch Symphony Orchestra, Orpheus Choir, Phoenix Choir of Wellington, and Cantoris; Musical Director of Gisborne Choral Society, Christchurch Operatic Society, Jubilate Singers, Perkel Opera, Academy Chamber Orchestra and Ensemble Divertimento; Orchestral keyboard: New Zealand Symphony Orchestra; Recitalist, presenter and announcer with Radio NZ 's Concert FM; Musical Director, Phoenix Choir and Academy Opera, conducting 7 New Zealand premieres of Handel, Mozart and Puccini operas; Has lectured at universities of Canterbury, Auckland, Waikato, and is at Massey University of Wellington. *Recording:* Serenata. *Publications:* Handel: Suite in C minor, reconstruction for two keyboards 1992, A Caldara, 16 Sonatas for cello and continuo, Doblinger, Vienna 1996–. *Honours:* 1st Prize, three times, Northampton Eisteddfod Piano Section, acknowledged as one of New Zealand's finest harpsichordists, piano accompanists and conductors. *Address:* PO Box 12675, Thorndon, Wellington, New Zealand. *Telephone:* (4) 9774260. *E-mail:* david.vine@paradise.net.nz.

**VINIKOUR, Jory;** American harpsichordist; b. 12 May 1963, Chicago, Ill. *Education:* Peabody Conservatory, 1981–83; BA, 1986, MA, 1988, Mannes College of Music, 1986; Doctoral studies, Rutgers University, 1988–90; Artist Diploma, Conservatoire Nationale Supèrieure de Musique de Paris, 1990–93. *Career:* recitals at festivals in Deauville, Paris, Monaco, Prague, London, Latin America, USA; soloist with Rotterdam Philharmonic, Orchestre Philharmonique de Radio France, Flanders Opera Orchestra, Orchestre de Chambre de Grenoble, Moscow Chamber Orchestra; major contemporary music concerts in France, Germany and Netherlands; major performances of contemporary works including Amsterdam Festival of Contemporary Harpsichord Music, Festival Presence, Radio France; numerous performances of Michael Nyman's harpsichord concerto. *Recordings:* J.S. Bach: Toccatas for Harpsichord 1998, Soloist, Goldberg Variations 2001, Music for a While (with Anne Sofie von Otter) 2001, soundtrack, Jefferson in Paris, continuist, Les Musiciens du Louvre, Les Arts Florissants. *Honours:* Fulbright Award 1990, Medaille d'Or and Prix d'Excellence, Conservatoire Nationale de Musique de Rueil-Malmaison 1991, Prix de Virtuosité, Conservatoire Nationale de Musique de Rueil-Malmaison 1992, Nadia et Lily Boulanger Foundation 1994, First Prize, Int. Harpsichord Competition of Warsaw 1993, First Prize, Int. Harpsichord Competition, Prague 1994. *Address:* 39 rue Manin, 75019 Paris, France. *Telephone:* 1-42-02-63-85; (6) 18-65-84-77 (Mobile). *Fax:* 1-42-02-53-42. *E-mail:* jvinikour@mac.com. *Website:* www.joryvinikour.org; ical .mac.com/jvinikour/professional; homepage.mac.com/jvinikour.

**VINK, Elena;** Singer (Soprano); b. 1962, Netherlands. *Education:* Studied at the Hague Conservatory. *Career:* Broadcast performances with conductors Jean Fournet, Kenneth Montgomery and Hans Vonk; Netherlands Opera as Lucia di Lammermoor, Constanze, Gilda, Poppea and Oscar; Mozart's Queen of Night at Lausanne, Brussels, the Berlin Staatsoper and the Opéra Bastille, Paris (1994); Sang in Mozart's Sogno di Scipione at Aix, 1991; Bath Festival, 1992, as Musetta; Amsterdam from 1994, as Aminta in Il Re Pastore, in The Nose by Shostakovich and as the Dove in Heppener's A Soul of Wood, 1998. *Recordings include:* Donna Anna in Don Giovanni.

**VINTON, John;** Writer on Music; b. 24 Jan. 1937, Cleveland, Ohio, USA. *Education:* Ohio State University, 1954–58; New York University, 1958–63; University of Southern California, 1965–66. *Career:* Editorial and Research Assistant, Bela Bartók Archives, New York, 1962–65; General Manager, Dance Theatre Workshop, New York, 1971–73; Assistant Music Critic, Washington Star-News, 1966–67; Left music field and specialized in story telling in literature of Adirondack mountains. *Publications:* Dictionary of Contemporary Music, 1974; Published in England as Dictionary of 20th Century Music; Essays after a Dictionary, 1977; A Treasury of Great Adirondack Stories, 1991. *Contributions:* Music Quarterly; Music Review; Music and Letters; Journal of the American Musicological Society; Arte Musical; Studia Musicologica; Sohlmans Musiklexikon; Notes. *Honours:* Research on Béla Bartók won bronze medal from Hungarian Academy of Sciences, 1981. *Address:* 167 Hicks Street, Brooklyn, NY 11201, USA.

**VINZING, Ute;** Singer (Soprano); b. 9 Sept. 1936, Wuppertal, Germany. *Education:* Studied with Martha Mödl. *Career:* Sang at Lubeck 1967–70, notably as Marenka in The Bartered Bride and Senta in Der fliegende Holländer; Wuppertal Opera 1971–76, sang Brünnhilde in Der Ring des Nibelungen; Has sung in Hamburg, Munich, Vienna, Buenos Aires, Geneva,

and Seattle (as Brünnhilde); Paris Opéra 1977, 1985, as Brünnhilde and Isolde; Teatro Liceo 1983; Metropolitan Opera from 1984, debut as Elektra; Other roles include Ortrud, Kundry, Leonore and the Dyer's Wife in Die Frau ohne Schatten; Teatro Colón, Buenos Aires 1987, as Elektra; Sang Isolde at Florence 1988; Elektra at Marseilles 1989; Sang Ortrud at Buenos Aires 1991. *Recordings include:* Elektra; Die Frau ohne Schatten, conducted by Sawallisch.

**VIR, Param;** Composer; b. 6 Feb, 1952, Delhi, India. (British national). *Education:* Delhi University; Dartington Summer School, 1983–84, with Peter Maxwell Davies; Guildhall School, London, with Oliver Knussen. *Career:* Composition Fellow at Tanglewood, 1986; Broken Strings and Snatched by the Gods commissioned by Hans Werner Henze for the Munich Biennale, 1992; Ion premiered at Aldeburgh, 2000. *Compositions:* The Demons of Bara Tooti, music theatre, 1980; Besura Desh, theatre, 1982; Fall Out, musical, 1984; Contra-pulse, for ensemble, 1985; Pragati, concertante, 1986; Antiphons and Elegies, for chamber orchestra, 1986; Before Krishna, for strings, 1987; Krishna, children's opera, 1988; Brahma, Vishnu Sita, for six solo voices, 1988; Snatched by the Gods, chamber opera, 1900; Broken Strings chamber opera, 1992; Horse Tooth White Rock, for orchestra, 1994; The Comfort of Angels, for two pianos, 1995; Tender Light for viola da gamba, 1996; Ultimate Words: Infinite Song, for baritone, six percussion and piano, 1997; Ion, opera after Euripides, 2000. *Honours:* Tippett Composition Award, Britten Prize, 1987. *Address:* c/o PRS Ltd, 29–33 Berners St, London, W1T 3 AB, England. *Telephone:* (20) 7580-5544. *Fax:* (20) 7306-4455.

**VIRAGH, Endre;** Professor of Organ and Orchestra Conductor; b. 23 March 1928, Vasvár, Hungary; m. Margit Piláth, 21 Sept 1958. *Education:* Graduated in Organ playing, Liszt Ferenc Academy of Music, Budapest, 1955; Studied with J Reinberger, Prague, 1958–59, with M Dupré, Paris, 1960, and with Germani, Rome and Siena, 1965, 1967, 1968. *Career:* Debut: Bartók Conservatoire, Miskolc, 1955; Principal Parish Church, Budapest, 1961; Regularly appears as soloist at concert on Hungarian radio and television; Organ recitals in Brune and Siena; Permanent interpreter at prestigious organ concerts; Extensive repertoire includes all organ works of J. S. Bach, Liszt, and César Franck, sonatas of Mendelssohn and Hindemith, organ works by modern composers such as Dupré, Messiaen, Janáček and Kodály, and organ concertos including Vivaldi's 2nd; mem, Saint Cecilia OMCE; Ferenc Liszt Society; Zoltán Kodály Society; Lajos Bardos Society. *Recordings:* Video: Assisi, Italy, 1982; Castelgandolfo, Italy, 1991; Professor of Organ at Miskolc from 1955, and at Belá Bartók Conservatoire, Budapest, from 1969. *Honours:* Diploma of Honour, Siena, 1967; Pro-Arte Prize, 1980; Eminent Pedagogue of Organ, 1991; Rectorate Honourable Mention, 1992. *Address:* Róbert-Károly krt 12 a, 1138 Budapest, Hungary.

**VIRKHAUS, Taavo;** Symphony Orchestra Conductor; b. 29 June 1934, Tartu, Estonia; m. Nancy Ellen Herman 1969. *Education:* BM, University of Miami, Florida, 1951–55; MM 1957, DMA 1967, Eastman School of Music, Rochester, New York; Pierre Monteux Masterclass 1960 and 1961; Fulbright Grant to Cologne, Germany, 1963–64. *Career:* Debut: Conducting the Miami Ballet Guild Orchestra, 1956; Director of Music, University of Rochester, 1966–77; Music Director and Conductor, Duluth-Superior Symphony Orchestra, Duluth, Minnesota, 1977–94; Huntsville AL Symphony Orchestra, 1990–2003, Conductor Emeritus, 2003–; Guest Conductor with Rochester Philharmonic; Baltimore Symphony; Estonian SSR State Symphony; Minnesota Orchestra; Music Director and Conductor of Huntsville, Alabama, Symphony Orchestra, 1990–. *Compositions:* 5 Symphonies, 2 Violin Concerti. *Honours:* Howard Hanson Prize, 1966. *Current Management:* Joanne Rile Artists Management, Philadelphia, Pennsylvania, USA. *Address:* 111 Lake Shore Drive, Madison, AL 35758, USA.

**VIRSALADZE, Eliso Konstantinovna;** Georgian pianist; b. 14 Sept. 1942, Tbilisi. *Career:* studied under grandmother, Prof. Anastasia Virsaladze; then at Tbilisi Conservatory; won first prize at All-Union Competition of Performing Musicians, Moscow 1961; Bronze Medal at Tchaikovsky Competition 1962, Prize at Schumann Competition; teacher Moscow Conservatory 1962, Prof.; played as a soloist all over the world and on tour in Europe and USA with Leningrad Philharmonic; soloist with USSR Symphony Orchestra in UK 1983–84, Germany 1984–85; f. Tkvarcheli Music Festival and Summer School; many other tours as soloist in Europe and Japan; master classes in Munich 1996. *Honours:* USSR People's Artist 1989, Georgian State Prize 1983. *Address:* Moscow Conservatory, Bolshaya Nikitskaya str. 13, Moscow, Russia. *Telephone:* (095) 268-69-12 (home).

**VISCONTI, Piero;** Singer (Tenor); b. 1947, Valenze, Piedmont, Italy. *Education:* Studied in Rome. *Career:* Debut: Naples, 1975, as Rodolfo in La Bohème; Sang at Miami, 1979, Rome Opera from 1978 (debut as Ernani); Vienna Staatsoper 1980, as Edgardo, the Duke of Mantua at the 1981 Verona Arena, Barcelona and Mannheim from 1982; US appearances at Houston and Philadelphia, Verdi Requiem in London, 1985, and Sydney Opera, 1986; Other roles include Almaviva, Arturo in La Straniera, Pollione in Norma, Nemorino, Foresto, Gabriele Adorno, Pinkerton, Calaf, Enzo and Andrea Chénier. *Address:* Opéra de Montpellier, 11 Boulevard Victor Hugo, 3400 Montpellier, France.

**VISHNEVSKAYA, Galina Pavlovna;** Russian singer (soprano); b. 25 Oct. 1926, Leningrad (now St Petersburg); m. Mstislav Rostropovich (q.v.); two d. *Career:* studied with Vera Garina 1942–52; Leningrad Musical Theatres 1944–52; leading soloist, Bolshoi Theatre 1952–74; left Soviet Union 1974;

stripped of citizenship 1978 (citizenship restored 1990); retd from operatic stage as Tatiana (Eugene Onegin) Paris 1982; numerous parts in operas, notably Leonora in Fidelio and Tatiana in Eugene Onegin (also in the film), Aida (Aida), Kupava (Snow Maiden), Liza (Queen of Spades), Cio-Cio-San (Madame Butterfly), Margaret (Faust), Natasha (War and Peace), Cherubino (Marriage of Figaro), Marfa (Tsar's Bride), Violetta (Traviata), Liu (Turandot), Katerina (Lady Macbeth of Mtsensk); acted in A. Chekhov Moscow Arts Theatre 1993–94; f. opera School in Moscow 1999. *Publication:* Galina (autobiog.) 1985. *Address:* Gazetny per. 13, Apt. 79, 103009 Moscow, Russia. *Telephone:* (095) 229-04-96 (Moscow); 1-42-27-85-06 (Paris).

**VISSE, Dominique;** French singer (countertenor); b. 30 Aug. 1955, Lisieux; m. Agnès Mellon. *Education:* chorister at Notre Dame in Paris, Versailles Conservatory, studied with Alfred Deller, René Jacobs and Nigel Rogers. *Career:* opera debut at Tourcoing 1982, in Monteverdi's Poppea; sang Flora in the first modern performances of Vivaldi's L'Incoronazione di Dario at Grasse 1984; Charpentier's Actéon at Edinburgh 1985, Nirenus in Nicholas Hytner's production of Giulio Cesare at the Paris Opéra 1987, Delfa in Cavilli's Giasone 1988 Innsbruck Early Music Festival; created Geronimo in the premiere of Le Rouge et Noir by Claude Prey, Aix 1989; sang Annio in Gluck's La Clemenza di Tito at Lausanne 1991; sang the Nurse in Monteverdi's Poppea at Buenos Aires 1996; season 1998–99 with La Calisto at the Berlin Staatsoper, the Salzburg Festival, the Barcelona Opera and the New York Lincoln Center; at La Scala Milan in Luciano Berio's opera, Outis; instrumentalist in medieval and Renaissance music; founder, Ensemble Clement Janequin; sang with Les Arts Florissants under William Christie; sang Narciso in Handel's Agrippina at Brussels 2000, Nirenus at the Paris Palais Garnier 2002. *Recordings include:* L'Incoronazione di Dario by Vivaldi, Charpentier's Acteon, Les Arts Florissants and David et Jonathan, Cavalli's Xerxes and Giasone, Octavia's Nurse in L'Incoronazione di Poppea, Rameau's Anacréon and Hasse's Cleofide. *Current Management:* c/o Ian Malkin, Satirino, 59 rue Orfila, 75020 Paris, France. *Telephone:* 1 43 15 06 04. *Fax:* 1 53 01 33 46. *E-mail:* ianmalkin@satirino.fr. *Website:* www.satirino.fr; www.dominique-visse.com.

**VISSER, Lieuwe;** Singer (Bass); b. 23 Aug. 1940, Diemen, Netherlands. *Education:* Studied with Jo van de Meent in Amsterdam and at the Accademia di Santa Cecilia, Rome with Giorgio Favaretto. *Career:* Debut: Netherlands Opera Amsterdam, as Don Basilio in Il Barbiere di Siviglia; Has sung with Netherlands Opera in the 1974 premiere of The Picture of Dorian Gray by Kox and as Masetto, 1984; Glyndebourne Festival 1981, in A Midsummer Night's Dream; Centre France Lyrique Paris 1983, in the stage premiere of Frankenstein by Gruber. *Recordings include:* Lucrezia Borgia by Donizetti.

**VITALI, Marisa;** Singer (Soprano); b. 1964, South Africa. *Education:* Studied in Cape Town and New York. *Career:* Sang at Bonn Opera from 1989, as Rosina, Strauss's Composer, Wellgunde and Donna Elvira; Guest appearances elsewhere in Germany as Traviata, Liu in Turandot, Suor Angelica, Micaela, Mélisande and Offenbach's Antonia; Fiora in Montemezzi's L'Amore dei tre Ré at Hanover, 1993, and Despina at Catania; Season 1995–96 as Nedda in Pagliacci at Verona, Maria in Guglielmo Ratcliff by Mascagni at Livorno, and Donna Elvira at the Deutsche Oper Berlin. *Honours:* Winner, Francisco Viñas Competition, Barcelona, 1989. *Address:* c/o Deutsche Oper Berlin, Richard Wagner Str 10, 10585 Berlin, Germany.

**VITMAN, Yelena;** Singer (Mezzo-Soprano); b. 1969, Russia. *Education:* St Petersburg Conservatoire. *Career:* Appearances at the Mariinsky Theatre, Kirov Opera, from 1996; Roles have included Lyubava in Sadko and Lyubasha in The Tsar's Bride, both by Rimsky-Korsakov; Olga in Eugene Onegin, Puccini's Suzuki, Konchakovna in Prince Igor and Siebel in Faust; Sang with the Kirov Opera in summer season at Covent Garden, 2000; Other roles include Clarice in The Love for Three Oranges, and Maria Bolkonskaya in War and Peace. *Honours:* Prizewinner at Wroclaw (1992) and St Petersburg (1994) Vocal Competitions. *Address:* c/o Kirov Opera, Mariinsky Theatre, 1 Theatre Square, St Petersburg, Russia.

**VLAD, Marina (Marta);** Romanian composer; b. 8 March 1949, Bucharest; m. Ulpiu Vlad 15 Sept. 1973; one s. *Education:* Music High School, Bucharest, 1960–65; High School, T L Caragiale, 1965–67; Graduate in Composition, The C Porumbescu Academy of Music, 1973. *Career:* University Assistant at the C Porumbescu Academy of Music, 1973–91; Prof., Nat. Univ. of Music, Bucharest 1991–2002; mem. Union of Composers of Romania. *Compositions:* Recorded at the Romanian Radio: Sonata for Violin and Piano, 1978; Rondo for Piano, 1978; Symphony Movement, 1979; Images for String Orchestra, 1980; Sonata for Piano, 1981; String Quartet No. 1, 1981; String Quartet No. 2, 1982; Legend and In Search of The Game for Piano, 1983; String Trio No. 1, Inscriptions for Peace, 1984; String Trio No. 2, Dream of Peace, 1985; String Trio No. 3, 1986; This Country's Land, cantata for Solo Voice, Choir and Orchestra, a verse by Jon Brad, 1987; Light Rays, trio for Flute, Oboe and Clarinet, 1988; Thoughts for the Future, quartet for Flute, Violin, Viola and Cello, 1989; In Search of The Game No. 2 for Piano, 1994; Still Life I for oboe solo, 1996; Still Life II for clarinet solo, 1997; Still Life III for piano solo, 1997; Still Life IV for violin solo, 1998; Still Life V for viola solo, 1999; Still Life VI for cello 2000, Still Life VII for flute solo 2000, Still Life VIII for bassoon solo 2002, Two contrastive pieces for orchestra 2004. *Recordings:* String Quartet No. 2 and Sonata for Piano, 1984. *Publications:* Sonata for Violin and Piano, 1982; Rondo for Piano, 1983; String Trio No. 1, Inscriptions for Peace, 1986; Dream of Peace, String Trio No. 2, 1988; Light Rays, trio for Flute Oboe and Clarinet, 1989. *Honours:* Prize granted by the Conservatory of Music, C Porumbescu for

The Cantata Resonance 1972. *Address:* Str. Andrei Popovici 18, Bl 8A, Sc c et IV, Apt 39, 011724 Bucharest, Romania.

**VLAD, Roman;** Italian composer and writer on music; b. 29 Dec. 1919, Cernauti (now Ucraina). *Education:* Cernauti Conservatory and in Rome with Casella. *Career:* active as a pianist and lecturer from 1939; Artistic Director of the Accademia Filarmonica in Rome, 1955–58 and 1966–69; President, Accademia Filarmonica, Rome; Artistic Director of the Maggio Musicale Fiorentino, 1964 and of the Teatro Comunale, Florence, 1968–72; Taught at Dartington Summer School, 1954–55; Co-Editor of the Enciclopedia dello Spettacolo, 1958–62 and the Nuova Rivista Musicale Italiana, 1967–; President of the Italian section of the ISCM, 1960–83; Professor of Composition at the Perugia Conservatory, 1968; Supervisor of the Turin Radio Symphony Orchestra, 1973–80; Artistic Adviser of the Turin Settembre Musica Festival from 1985; President of Society of Italian Authors and Publishers (SIAE) 1987–94, Governmental Commissioner 1992–94; President of CISAC, 1982–84, 1992–96; Artistic Director, Teatro alla Scala, Milan, 1994–96. *Compositions:* Ballets: La Strada sul caffè, 1943; La Dama delle Camelie, 1945; Fantasia, 1948; Masques Ostendias, 1959; Die Wiederkehr, 1962; Il Gabbiano, 1968; Il Sogno, 1973; Operas: Storia di una Mamma, 1951; Il Dottore di Vetro, 1960; La Fantarca, 1967; Orchestral: Sinfonietta, 1941; Suite, 1941; Sinfonia all'antica, 1948; Variazioni Concertanti su una Serie di 12 Note dal Don Giovanni di Mozart for Piano and Orchestra, 1955; Musica per Archi, 1957; Musica Concertata for Harp and Orchestra, 1958; Ode Super Chrysae Phorminx for Guitar and Orchestra 1964; Divertimento Sinfonico, 1967; Vocal: 3 Cantatas, 1940–53; Lettura di Michelangelo for Chorus, 1964; Immer Wieder for Soprano and 8 Instruments, 1965; Piccolo Divertimento Corale, 1968; Lettura di Lorenzo Magnifico for Chorus, 1974; La Vespa di Toti for Boys' Voices and Instruments, 1976; Chamber: Divertimento for 11 Instruments, 1948; String Quartet, 1957, Serenata for 12 Instruments, 1959; Il Magico Flauto di Severino for Flute and Piano, 1971; Cinque elegie su testi biblici, 1990; Melodia variata, 1990; Stagioni giaponesi, 24 Haiku, 1993–94; Piano Music; Music for more than 100 films. *Publications include:* Collected Essays, 1955; Luigi Dallapiccola, 1957; Storia della Dodecafonia, 1958; Stravinsky, 1958, revised 1973 and 1979; Essays on Busoni, Schoenberg and Stravinsky; Introduzione alle cultura musicale, 1988; Capire la musica 1989. *Address:* Via XXIV Maggio N 51, 00187 Rome, Italy. *Telephone:* (06) 6797686 (office).

**VLAD, Ulpiu;** Romanian composer; *Professor, National University of Music*; b. 27 Jan. 1945, Zarnesti; m. Marina Marta Vlad 15 Sept. 1973; one s. *Education:* Music High School, Bucharest, 1958–64; Academy of Music C Porumbescu, Bucharest, 1964–71; Seminar in Composition, Conservatory of Music, Santa Cecilia, Rome. *Career:* debut: Septet for Winds and Piano, 1970, Conservatory of Music C Porumbescu; Researcher in Romanian Folk Music, Academy of Music, Bucharest, 1972–77; Researcher in Romanian Folk Music, Institut de Cercetari Etnologice si Dailectologice, Bucharest, 1977–80; Editor, 1980–84, Manager, 1984–92, Romanian Musical Publishing Company; Music Department Director, Romanian Ministry of Culture, 1992–93; Prof., Nat. Univ. of Music (fmrly Acad. of Music), Bucharest 1990–; Romanian TV and radio appearances; mem., Union of Composers and Musicologists, 1973. *Compositions include:* Sonata for oboe and piano (harpsichord), 1969; This is Earth, cantata foro mixed choir and orchestra, verse by Eugen Frunz, 1970; As Hardly from Depths, symphonie concertante for violoncello, pianoforte and orchestra, 1971, revised 1981; First Symphony Roads in The Light, 1979; Lights in The Sunset, symphonic work, 1991; The Secret of Dreams, quintet for Winds No. 2, 1992; The Time of Mirrors, for chamber orchestra, 1974; Mosaic, chamber-vocal-symphonic cycle, with unlimited possibilities of combinations between the different instruments of the orchestra and a vocal quartet, 1974–78; Flowers for peace, string quartet, 1982; Voices of peace, quintet for winds and tape, 1986; String trio, 1987; Sun-lit Landscape, string trio no. 2, 1987; On this Sunny Land, string trio no. 3, 1988; String Trio, 1990; The Joy of the Passage, string trio no. 4, 1991; The Joy of Dreams I, quintet for flute, violin, viola, cello and percussion, 1990; From the Joy of Dreams, Concerto for string orchestra, 1991; The Game of Dreams I, Concerto for chamber orchestra, 1992; The Time of Dreams, quartet for flute, clarinet, piano and percussion, 1993; Suddenly Dreams, concerto for Chamber Orchestra, 1994; The Legend of Dreams, septet for flute, oboe, clarinet, piano, bassoon, percussion, violin and cello, 1994; The Light of Dreams, symphonic work, 1995; Beyond Dreams, music for wind, string and keyboard, 1996; The Secret of Dreams III, septet for flute, oboe, clarinet, bassoon, horn, percussion and piano, 1996; Resonances in the future, solo pieces for flute, oboe, clarinet, bassoon, horn, percussion, violin, viola, cello, piano, harp, 1997–2001; Interlocking Dreams, for 3 flutes, oboe, clarinet, bassoon, horn, violin, viola and accordion, 1997; Interlocking Dreams II, 3 pieces for wind quintet, string quartet, trumpet, percussion, piano and harp, 1998; Resonances on White Background, quartet for saxophones, trombone, percussion and piano, 1998; Interlocking Dreams III, 3 pieces for wind quintet, string trio, saxophone, trumpet, percussion, piano, soprano and improvising ensemble, 1999; Resonances on a Mauve Background for oboe, clarinet, bassoon, violin, cello, percussion 2000, Resonances on a Light Blue Background for flute and cello 2000, Resonances on a Green Background for flute, harp and cello 2001, Resonances on Pale Background – Concerto for harp and string orchestra 2002, The Poetry of Dreams, 3 pieces for chamber ensemble and tape (dedicated to victims of the Holocaust) 2003, Resonances on a Light Blue Background II for flute, trumpet and cello 2004, Through the Light of Resonances – Piece for Cello and Chamber Orchestra 2004. *Recordings:*

Mosaic, 2 versions, 1980; Dreams 1; The Joy of Achievement – Wedding Songs; Beyond Dreams III, 1998; Suddenly Dreams, 2000, Beyond Dreams V 2004. *Publications include:* Mosaic, 1982; 1st Symphony, Roads in The Light, 1985; 2nd Symphony, From our Hearts, 1988; Inscriptions in Hearts, 1989; Dreams ll, 1992; The Spring, String Trio No. 1, 1994, The Legend of Dreams 1999. *Honours:* Officer, Order of Cultural Merit 2004; Oboe Prize, Festival of Young Performers of Romania 1964; Special Prize of Univ. of Music, Bucharest 1971; Medal for Distinction in Culture (2nd Class) 1983; George Enescu Prize of the Acad. of Romania 1985; First Prize, Union of Composers and Musicologists, Nat. Festival of Song, Romania 1987; Prize, Union of Romanian Composers and Musicologists 1991, 1995, 2000, 2003. *Address:* Str. Andrei Popovici 18, Bl 8A, Sc c et IV, Apt 39, 011724 Bucharest, Romania. *Telephone:* (21) 2306712. *E-mail:* romanvlad@dnt.ro. *Website:* composers21.com/compdocs/vladu.htm.

**VLATKOVIC, Radovan;** Horn Player; b. 1962, Zagreb, Croatia. *Education:* Zagreb Academy of Music and the Northwest German Music Academy at Detmold. *Career:* Principal of the Berlin Radio Symphony Orchestra, 1982–90; Solo engagements from 1979, notably at Salzburg 1984, the Vienna Konzerthaus, the Barbican, the Théâtre de la Ville in Paris, Pushkin Museum Moscow, Metropolitan Museum New York, Orchestra Hall Chicago and Suntory Hall, Tokyo; Soloist with leading orchestras and chamber music performer with Gidon Kremer, Heinz Holliger, András Schiff and Aurèle Nicolet; Professor of Horn, Stuttgart Hochschule für Musik, 1992–. *Recordings include:* Mozart's Four Concertos and R Strauss Concertos with the English Chamber Orchestra conducted by Jeffrey Tate. *Honours:* Prizes at the Wind Instruments Competition in Ancona, 1979; Horn Competition in Liège, 1981; 1st Prize, International ARD Competition in Munich, 1983; German Music Critics' Prize three times for recordings of solo (Mozart) and chamber music (Gubaidulina, Hindemith) Repertoire. *Current Management:* Ingpen & Williams Ltd, 7 St George's Court, 131 Putney Bridge Road, London, SW15 2PA, England.

**VODICKA, Leo (Marian);** Singer (Tenor); b. 1950, Brno, Czechoslovakia. *Education:* Studied at the Janáček Academy of Arts with Josef Valek. *Career:* Has sung in most Czech opera houses, notably the Janáček Opera Brno and the Prague National Theatre; Guest engagements in Bologna, Rome, Milan, Geneva, Zürich, Berne, Graz, Salzburg, Cologne, Paris, Nice, Tokyo, Osaka and in Bulgaria, Hungary, the former Soviet Union and East Germany; Major roles have included Verdi's Rigoletto, Don Carlos, Manrico and Otello; Puccini's Cavaradossi, Des Grieux, Pinkerton and Rodolfo; Janáček's Laca and Boris, the Prince in Rusalka and Smetana's Jenik and Dalibor; Don José and Stravinsky's Oedipus; Concert repertoire includes Verdi Requiem; Dvořák Stabat Mater and Requiem; Janáček Amarus, Glagolitic Mass, Diary of One Who Disappeared and Everlasting Gospel; Martinů's Field Mass and Bartók's Cantata Profana; Staatsoper Vienna for role of Prince in Rusalka by Dvořák, 1990; Vienna, L Janáček-Glagolitic Mass and Osud (Fate), 1990; Solo tour in Japan/Tokyo, Koriyama, Kumamoto, Matsuyama with airs from Carmen, Andrea Chénier, La Forza del Destino, Otello, Tosca, Traviata, conducted by Shigeo Genda, 1992; Season 2000 as Don José, Max in Der Freischütz and Cavaradossi, at the Prague State Opera. *Recordings:* Smetana The Kiss, The Secret and Libuše; Dvořák The Cunning Peasant; Foerster Eva; Janáček Amarus conducted by Charles Mackerras (Supraphon); Antonin Dvořák–Dimitrij, title role, conducted by Gerd Albrecht, Supraphon, 1989; London BBC, Diary of One Who Disappeared, with Radoslav Kvapil-piano, 1993. *Current Management:* Pragokoncert, Maltézské nam 1, Prague 1, Czech Republic. *Address:* Zlichovska 6, Prague, Czech Republic.

**VOGEL, Siegfried;** Singer (Bass); b. 6 March 1937, Chemnitz, Germany. *Education:* Studied in Dresden with H Winkler and J Kemter. *Career:* Debut: Dresden Staatsoper 1959, as Zizell in Si j'etais roi by Adam; Sang Mozart roles in Dresden; Sarastro, Osmin and the Commendatore; Berlin Staatsoper from 1965 as Leporello, Alfonso, Hunding, Basilio, Count Almaviva, Escamillo, Kecal and Ochs; Guest appearances in Moscow, Paris, Lausanne (Hans Sachs and Baron Ochs 1983), Brussels and Vienna; Further engagements at La Scala and in Venice, Stockholm, Helsinki, Amsterdam and Cairo; Bayreuth Festival 1985–86, as Biterolf in Tannhäuser; Sang Kaspar, Rocco and the King Henry in Lohengrin, 1986 at the Berlin Staatsoper; Metropolitan debut 1986, as Hunding, sang Morosus in Die schweigsame Frau at Palermo, 1988; Bayreuth 1989, as Fasolt, Biterolf and Titurel; Toronto Opera 1990, as the Doctor in Wozzeck; Sang the Athlete in Lulu at the Semper Oper Dresden, 1992; Concert repertoire includes sacred music by Bach and Handel; Sang Rocco in Fidelio at the 1996 Edinburgh Festival; Sang Saul in the premiere of Weill's The Eternal Road, Chemnitz 1999; Fafner in The Ring at the Berlin Staatsoper, 2001. *Recordings:* Der Freischütz; Ariadne auf Naxos, Die Meistersinger, Zar und Zimmermann, Genoveva, Rienzi; St Matthew Passion; Karl V by Krenek. *Address:* c/o Berlin Staatsoper, Unter den Linden 7, 1086 Berlin, Germany.

**VOGEL, Volker;** Singer (Tenor); b. 13 Oct. 1950, Karlsruhe, Germany. *Education:* Studied at the Hanover Musikhochschule. *Career:* Sang at the Dortmund Opera, then at Freiburg, 1984–85, and the Vienna Volksoper, 1984–90; Zürich Opera from 1991; Guest appearances in Barcelona, Berlin, Bregenz and Verona; Vienna, 1990, in the premiere of Einem's Tuliphant; Salzburg and London, 1992, in Weill's Sieben Todsünden; Other roles include Mozart's Pedrillo and Beethoven's Jacquino; Season 1999–2000 as Herod in Salome and Shuisky in Boris Godunov, at Dublin; Wagner's Melot and Mime for Zürich Opera. *Recordings include:* Zemlinsky's Kleider machen Leute;

Monostatos in Die Zauberflöte. *Address:* Opernhaus Zürich, Falkenerstrasse 1, 8008 Zürich, Switzerland.

**VOGLER, Jan;** Cellist; b. 18 Feb. 1964, Berlin, Germany. *Education:* Hanns Eisler Hochschule für Musik, Berlin; Basle Music Academy, Switzerland, Teachers Josef Schwab, Heinrich Schiff. *Career:* Concert Master, cello, Staatskapelle Dresden, 1985–; Concerts as soloist, orchestras including Berlin Radio Orchestra 1986, 1987, 1989, Staatskapelle Dresden, Berlin Chamber Orchestra, Dresden Chamber Orchestra, Virtuosi Saxoniae; US debut, Chicago 1987; Marlboro Festival, USA 1988, 1989; numerous radio broadcasts, live recordings; recitals, many countries. *Current Management:* Kunstleragentur, Krausenstrasse 9/10, 1080 Berlin. *Address:* Bahnhofstrasse 47, 1123 Berlin, Germany.

**VOGT, Lars;** concert pianist; b. 8 Sept. 1970, Düren, Germany; m. Tatiana Komarova. *Education:* Hanover Conservatoire with Prof. Kämmerling. *Career:* numerous concerto and recital performances throughout Europe, Asia and North America; London debut, Royal Albert Hall 1990; work with numerous British orchestras, including Philharmonia, London Symphony, Royal Scottish Nat. and all BBC Orchestras; Berlin concerto debut with Deutsches Symphonie-Orchester under Leonard Slatkin; performed with LA Philharmonic, including Hollywood Bowl under Simon Rattle; played 16-concert tour of Australia 1997; Far East tour, including performances with NHK Symphony, Tokyo 1998; season 1998–99 included engagements with Salzburg Mozarteum Orchestra, Leipzig Gewandhaus, City of Birmingham Symphony; played Mostly Mozart Festival, New York; debut with Atlanta and Montreal Symphony Orchestras; recitals in London, Salzburg, Berlin, Rome, Amsterdam and Bilbao; played Brahms with Skampa Quartet, Wigmore Hall, London; Beethoven concerto cycle with Gurzenich Orchestra under James Conlon; founder, chamber music festival in Heimbach, Germany 1998; season 1999–2000 included engagements with the Komische Oper Berlin, Dresden Philharmonic, BBC Nat. Orchestra of Wales; Lutoslawski's Piano Concerto in Zürich, Dresden, Stuttgart, Bremen and Vienna; recitals in London, Los Angeles and Montreaux and chamber concerts in London, Vienna, Salzburg, Lucerne and Frankfurt; premiere of a new concerto by Tatiana Komarova 2001; Schumann's concerto in A minor at the London Proms 2002. *Recordings:* Schumann Concerto, Grieg Concerto with City of Birmingham Symphony and Simon Rattle, first two Beethoven concertos with Simon Rattle, 19th and 20th century Russian works, Haydn sonatas and Schumann's Kreisleriana and Bunte Blätter, Beethoven Sonatas op 10 No. 1 and Op 111, Prokofiev and Shostakovich cello sonatas with Truls Mork, Hindemith piano concerto No. 1 with Berlin Philharmonic and Claudio Abbado. *Honours:* Diapason d'Or for Prokofiev and Shostakovich cello sonatas. *Current Management:* Askonas Holt Ltd, Lonsdale Chambers, 27 Chancery Lane, London, WC2A 1PF, England. *Telephone:* (20) 7400-1700. *Fax:* (20) 7400-1799. *E-mail:* info@askonasholt.co.uk. *Website:* www.askonasholt.co.uk.

**VOICULESCU, Dan;** Composer, Musicologist and Professor of Counterpoint and Composition; b. 20 July 1940, Saschiz-Sighisoara, Romania. *Education:* diplomas in composition and piano, Acad. of Music Gh. Dima, Cluj, 1958–64; classes with V. Mortari, Venice, Italy, 1968, K. Stockhausen, Cologne, Germany, 1971–72; DMus, 1983. *Career:* Prof. of Counterpoint and Composition, Acad. of Music, Cluj, 1963–2000, National Univ. of Music, Bucharest, 2000–; Ed., Lucrari de Muzicologie (Musicological Works), Cluj, 1979–91; mem., Union of Romanian Composers. *Compositions:* Sinfonia Ostinato, 1963; Visions Cosmiques, 1968; Music for strings, 1971; Pieces for orchestra, 1973; Suite from Codex Caioni for strings, 1996; Inflorescences, for strings, 2001; Fables, Dialogues, Sonata, Croquis, Sonantes, Spirals, 3 Toccatas for piano solo, 6 Sonatas for flute solo, Sonata for clarinet solo; Sketches and Sonata for oboe solo; Fiorituri for violin and piano; Dilemmas, for seven; Concertant Diptych, for Baroque ensemble; Cantata for baritone, choir and orchestra, 1977; Homage to Blaga for mixed choir; Mass for children's choir; Four vols choral music for children; Book Without End, 3 vols of piano pieces for children; 50 Lieder for voice and piano; The Bald Chanteuse, chamber comic opera, 1993. *Publications:* Polyphony of Baroque in the Works of J. S. Bach, 1975; Polyphony of the 20th Century, 1983; Bachian Fugue, 1986. *Honours:* Union of Romanian Composers Prizes, 1972–1978, 1995; G. Enescu Prize from the Romanian Acad., 1984. *Address:* Str. Carol Davila 67, 050452 Bucharest, Romania.

**VOIGT, Deborah;** Singer (soprano); b. 4 Aug. 1960, Chicago, USA. *Education:* San Francisco Opera's Merola Program. *Career:* debut, Shostakovich's 14th Symphony, San Francisco Chamber Symphony; European engagements include Schubert's Fierrabras at Brussels, Electra in Idomeneo for Finnish National Opera, 1991, and Elvira in Ernani for Chelsea Opera Group, 1990; Other opera performances in concert include Das Rheingold with the Minnesota Orchestra, Weber's Agathe in New York, Die Walküre, La Wally and Il Piccolo Marat for Dutch Radio; Season 1990–91, with Amelia, Ballo in Maschera, at San Francisco and Strauss's Ariadne with the Boston Lyric Opera; Metropolitan Opera debut 1991, as Amelia; Season 1992–93 included Leonora in Il Trovatore with the Metropolitan Opera and as Amelia in Un ballo in maschera with the Lyric Opera of Chicago; Highlights of the 1993–94 season included her debut with the Berlin Philharmonic in Zemlinsky's Lyrische Symphonie, performances of the Verdi Requiem and her debut with the Philadelphia Orchestra in a series of highly acclaimed Wagner concerts in Philadelphia and Carnegie Hall; Made her first concert appearance with Luciano Pavarotti in Lincoln Center's Pavarotti Plus! gala, 1994; European engagements in 1995–96 included Senta in Wagner's Der fliegende Holländer with the Vienna Staatsoper and a gala concert in Tel-Aviv under Daniel Oren, and as Amelia, Covent Garden (debut), 1995; Amelia at the Metropolitan, 1997; Season 1998 with Sieglinde on Act I of Die Walküre at St Petersburg and Strauss's Aegyptische Helena for the Royal Opera, London, in concert; season 2002 as Danae in Die Liebe der Danae at the Salzburg Festival, Ariadne in Ariadne auf Naxos at San Francisco Opera, in Elektra at the New York Met, and in Tosca at Vienna State Opera. *Recordings include:* Strauss's Ariadne auf Naxos; La Forza del Destino; Strauss's Die Frau ohne Schatten. *Honours:* Prizewinner, Metropolitan Opera Auditions and the Pavarotti International Competition at Philadelphia; Winner, 1989 Bussetto Verdi Competition and 1990 Tchaikovsky International at Moscow; Opera Debut of the Year, New York Times, 1991; Title role in Strauss's Die Liebe der Danaë, Salzburg Festival 2002. *Current Management:* Prima International Artists Management, Piazza de' Calderini 2/2, 40124 Bologna, Italy. *Telephone:* (051) 264056. *Fax:* (051) 230766. *E-mail:* prima@primartists.com. *Website:* www.primartists.com. *Address:* IMG Artists, Lovell House, 616 Chiswick High Road, London, W4 5RX, England. *Telephone:* (20) 8233-5800. *Fax:* (20) 8233-5801. *E-mail:* artistseurope@imgworld.com. *Website:* www.imgartists.com; www.deborahvoigt.com.

**VOKETAITIS, Arnold;** Singer (Bass); b. 11 May 1931, New Haven, Connecticut, USA. *Education:* Studied in New York. *Career:* Debut: New York City Opera 1958, as Vanuzzi in Die schweigsame Frau; Sang in New York as Britten's Theseus, Creon in Oedipus Rex and the Father in the local premiere of Douglas Moore's Carrie Nation, 1968; Guest engagements at Houston, Miami, Pittsburgh, Mexico City, San Antonio, Montreal and Vancouver; Chicago 1968–73 in Le Rossignol, Madama Butterfly, Carmen, I Due Foscari, Werther and Billy Budd; Other roles have included Don Magnifico (Metropolitan Opera National Touring Company), Don Pasquale, Dulcamara, Basilio and John Hale in The Crucible by Robert Ward, Milwaukee 1976. *Recordings:* Le Cid by Massenet.

**VOLANS, Kevin;** Irish composer; b. 26 July 1949, Pietermaritzburg, South Africa. *Education:* Univs of Witwatersrand and Aberdeen, Hochschüle für musik, Cologne with Karl-Heinz Stockhausen, Mauricio Kagel and Alois Kontarsky. *Career:* Lecturer in Composition, Univ. of Natal 1981–85; composer-in-residence, Queen's Univ., Belfast 1986–89, Princeton Univ. 1992. *Compositions include:* White Man Sleeps, for two harpsichords, bass viol and percussion, 1982 (arranged as String Quartet no. 1, 1986); Walking Song, for ensemble, 1984; She Who Sleeps with a Small Blanket, for percussion, 1985; Kneeling Dance, for two pianos, 1985 (version, for six pianos, 1992); Into the Darkness, for ensemble, 1987; Hunting, Gathering, string quartet no. 2, 1987; The Songlines, string quartet no. 3, 1988, rev, 1993; Chevron, dance, 1990; The Ramanujan Notebooks, string quartet no. 4, 1990; The Man with Footsoles of Wind, chamber opera, 1993; Plane-song, film music, 1993; Concerto, for piano and wind, 1995; Blue, Yellow, dance, 1995; Dancers on a Plane, string quartet, 1995; Slow, for piano and wind, 1996; Asanga, for percussion, 1997; Violin Concerto, 1997; Double Violin Concerto, 1999; Piano Trio, 2001; Concerto for Double Orchestra, 2002; Strip Weave for orchestra, 2002; Trumpet and String Quartet 1 & 2, 2002; String Quartet No. 7 (Similarity 1), 2002; Confessions of Zeno, 2002. *Current Management:* Van Walsum Management Ltd, 4 Addison Bridge Place, London, W14 8XP, England. *Telephone:* (20) 7371-4343. *Fax:* (20) 7371-4344. *Website:* www.vanwalsum.co.uk.

**VOLKERT, Gudrun;** Singer (Soprano); b. 1942, Brno, Czeckoslovakia. *Education:* Studied at the Linz Conservatory. *Career:* Sang dramatic roles at Klagenfurt 1966–67, Kiel 1967–74, Bielefield 1974–83; Guest appearances at Brunswick 1983–88, Kassel from 1984, Hamburg 1986 and Turin 1987; Performances as Brünnhilde in Der Ring des Nibelungen at Rotterdam, 1988, Warsaw 1988–89, and Seattle 1991; Sang Cherubini's Médée at Wuppertal 1988, followed by Isolde 1989; Metropolitan Opera 1990, as Brünnhilde; Scottish Opera 1991, as Leonore in a new production of Fidelio; Other roles include Senta, Ortrud, Salome, the Marschallin, Gioconda, Tosca, Turandot and the Countess in Die Soldaten. *Address:* c/o Seattle Opera Association, PO Box 9248, WA 98109, USA.

**VOLKONSKY, Andrey Mikhaylovich;** Composer and Harpsichordist; b. 14 Feb. 1933, Geneva, Switzerland. *Education:* Studied with Nadia Boulanger and Dinu Lipatti in Paris; Moscow Conservatory, 1950–53. *Career:* Associated with Rudolf Barschai and Chamber Orchestra of Moscow; Performances of his music by Pierre Boulez in London and Berlin (1967) after ban by Soviet authorities; Emigrated to France 1973 and worked for Belaieff Foundation, in aid of needy musicians. *Compositions:* String trio, 1951; Concerto for Orchestra, 1953; Piano Quintet, 1955; Two string quartets, 1955, 1958; Serenade for an Insect, for chamber orchestra, 1958; Les plaintes de Shchaza for soprano and ensemble, 1961; Itinerant Concerto, for low voice and ensemble, 1963–67; Les mailles du temps for three instrumental groups, 1969; Immobile, for piano and orchestra, 1978; Was noch lebt, for mezzo and string trio, 1985; Psalm 148, 1989; Crossroads for synthesizer and ensemble, 1992. Publications include: The Foundation of Temperament, Moscow, 1998. *Address:* c/o SACEM, 225 avenue Charles de Gaulle, 92521 Neuilly Sur Seine Cédex, France.

**VOLKOV, Solomon;** American musicologist; b. 17 April 1944, Ura-Tyube, Tajikistan. *Education:* Leningrad Conservatory. *Career:* Artistic Dir, Leningrad Experimental Studio of Chamber Opera 1965–70; staging of Fleischmann's Rothschild's Violin, completed by Shostakovich; research at Russian

Inst., Columbia Univ. 1976. *Publications:* Young Composers of Leningrad 1971, Remembrance of the 'Leningrad Spring' 1974, Testimony: The Memoirs of Dmitri Shostakovich (ed.) 1979, Scissors and Music: Music Censorship in the Soviet Union 1983, Balanchine's Tchaikovsky 1985, Yevgeny Mravinsky, Leningrad's Master Builder 1988, From Russia to the West: the Musical Memoirs of Nathan Milstein (with N. Milstein) 1990, St Petersburg: A Cultural History 1995, Conversations with Joseph Brodsky 1998, Shostakovich and Stalin 2004; contrib. articles in journals and newspapers 1959–. *Address:* c/o Alfred A. Knopf, 1745 Broadway, New York, NY 10019, USA.

**VOLKOVA, Svetlana;** Singer (Soprano); b. 1950, Russia. *Career:* Many appearances throughout Russia in concerts and opera; Kirov Opera, St Petersburg, from 1990, as Pauline in The Gambler by Prokofiev, Sonya in War and Peace, the Hostess in The Fiery Angel and Fata Morgana in The Love for Three Oranges; Sang with the Kirov Opera in summer season at Covent Garden, 2000; Other roles include Tisbe in Cenerentola, Susanna (Khovanshchina), Herodias in Salome, Mozart's Marcellina, Fricka in Das Rheingold, Larina (Eugene Onegin) and Skomoroshina in Sadko by Rimsky-Korsakov. *Address:* c/o Kirov Opera, Mariinksy Theatre, 1 Theatre Square, St Petersburg, Russia.

**VOLLE, Michael;** Singer (Baritone); b. 1959, Germany. *Education:* Studied in Stuttgart and Trossingen with Joseph Metternich and Rudolf Piernay. *Career:* Sang first at Mannheim, then three seasons at Bonn as Mozart's Guglielmo, Count, Don Giovanni and Papageno, Marcello in La Bohème and Rossini's Figaro; Further engagements at Hanover, Wiesbaden, Dresden, Düsseldorf, Leipzig and Paris; Season 1997–98 with Covent Garden and La Scala debuts, as the Herald in Lohengrin and the Speaker in Die Zauberflöte; Other roles include Silvio, Don Fernando (Fidelio) and Ottokar in Der Freischütz; Don Giovanni at the 1998 Schwetzingen Festival; Season 2000–01 as Billy Budd, Eugene Onegin and Mozart's Count at Cologne, Don Giovanni at the Berlin Staatsoper and Ford in Falstaff at Brussels; Bach's St Mathew Passion at the London Proms, 2002; Many concert appearances. *Recordings include:* Britten's War Requiem; Schubert's Mass in A-flat and Bach's Christmas Oratorio. *Honours:* Winner of numerous competitions. *Address:* c/o Oper der Stadt Bonn, Am Boeselagerhof 1 Pf 2440, 5300 Bonn, Germany.

**VOLODOS, Arcadi;** concert pianist; b. 24 Sept. 1972, St Petersburg, Russia. *Education:* St Petersburg and Moscow Conservatories, Paris Conservatoire with Jacques Rouvier, Madrid Conservatory with Dmitri Bashkirov. *Career:* frequent recital and concerto engagements in Russia and Europe; Carnegie Hall, New York debut 1998; Salzburg Festival debut 2002; repertoire includes Bach, Mozart, Schumann and Russian Masters. *Recordings include:* Mozart's Rondo alla Turca, transcriptions of songs by Rachmaninov, Scriabin Sonata No. 10 and Schumann Bunte Blätter, Schubert Sonatas D157 and D894. *Current Management:* Columbia Artists Management International, Albrechtstrasse 18, Berlin 10117, Germany. *Telephone:* (30) 20 64 8078. *Fax:* (30) 20 45 3480.

**VOLPE, Joseph;** American music administrator; b. 2 July 1940, Brooklyn, NY; m. Jean Anderson. *Career:* joined the Metropolitan Opera as apprentice carpenter, New York 1964, apptd Master Carpenter 1966, Tech. Dir 1978–81, Asst Man. 1981–90, Gen. Man. 1990–2006; guest lecturer Columbia Univ., New York Univ. Stern School of Business, Wharton School of Business. *Address:* The Metropolitan Opera, Lincoln Center, New York, NY 10023, USA (office). *Website:* www.metoperafamily.org/metopera/ (office).

**VOLZ, Manfred;** Singer (Bass-baritone); b. 1949, Darmstadt, Germany. *Career:* Sang in concert from 1972; Stage debut as Mozart's Figaro at Trier, 1980; Further engagements as Melitone in La Forza del Destino and Papageno; Engaged at Aachen 1981–83, Kassel from 1985, as Alberich, Ford, Amonasro, Mozart's Count, and Faninal; Bad Gandersheim 1986, as the King in Der Kluge by Orff; Sang Alberich in Ring cycles at Rotterdam 1988 and Dortmund 1991; Season 2000–01 at Kassel as Banquo, Faninal in Der Rosenkavalier, Berg's Dr Schön and Rangoni in Boris Godunov; Concert repertoire includes Verdi's Requiem. *Address:* c/o Opernhaus, Kuhstrasse 12, 4600 Dortmund, Germany.

**VON ALPENHEIM, Ilse;** pianist; b. 11 Feb. 1927, Innsbruck, Austria; m. Antal Dorati 1969 (died 1988). *Education:* Salzburg Mozarteum with Franz Ledwinka and Winfried Wolf. *Career:* soloist with major European and US orchestras; many engagements as recitalist and chamber music player. *Recordings:* complete Haydn piano music, Schubert complete chamber music with piano.

**VON BINZER, Kim;** Denmark singer (tenor); b. 2 March 1952. *Career:* sang with the Choir of Danish Radio in Copenhagen; Soloist with Jutland Opera, Århus, 1979–87; Roles include Tamino in Zauberflöte, Ramiro in La Cenerentola, Alfred in Fledermaus, Piquillo in Offenbach's La Périchole, Goro in Madama Butterfly; Aix-en-Provence Festival, 1985, in Monteverdi's Orfeo; Royal Opera Copenhagen from 1987 as Count Almaviva in Il Barbiere, Tamino in Zauberflöte, Ferrando in Così fan tutte, Don Ottavio in Don Giovanni and Cassio in Otello; Opera productions for Danish Radio and Television; Frequent concert engagements; Stage Director, Royal Opera Copenhagen, 1994–; Head, Opera Academy, 1999–. *Recordings:* Fynsk Foraar by Nielsen; Kuhlau's Lulu. *Address:* c/o The Royal Opera, PO Box 2185, 1017 Copenhagen, Denmark.

**VON BOSE, Hans-Jurgen;** German composer; b. 24 Dec. 1953, Munich. *Education:* Hoch Conservatory, Frankfurt am Main, 1969–72; Pupil in composition of Hans Ulrich Engelmann; In piano of Klaus Billing, Hochschule für Musik Frankfurt am Main, 1972–75; Opera 63; Dream Palace performed at Munich, 1990; Slaughterhouse Five premiered at the 1996 Munich Festival. *Compositions:* Stage; Blutbund, chamber opera, 1974; Das Diplom, chamber opera, 1975; Die Nacht aus Blei, kinetic action, 1980–81; Die Leiden des jungen Werthers, lyrical scenes, 1986; 63: Dream Place, 1990; Slaughterhouse Five, 1995; *Orchestra:* Morphogenesis, 1975; Symphony No. 1, 1976; Musik für ein Haus voll Zeit, 1977; Songs for Tenor and Chamber Orchestra, 1977; Travesties in a Sad Landscape for Chamber Orchestra, 1978; Symphonic Fragment for Tenor, Baritone, Bass, Chorus; Orchestra, 1980; Variations for 15 strings, 1980; Idyllen, 1983; Sappho-Gesänge for Mezzo-Soprano and Chamber Orchestra, 1982–83; Labyrinth I, 1987; Oboe Concerto, 1986–87; 5 Children's Rhymes for Alto and 5 Instrumentalists, 1974; Threnos-Hommage à Bernd Alois Zimmermann for Viola and Cello, 1975; Solo Violin Sonata, 1977; Variations for Cello, 1978–79; Vom Wege abkommen for viola, 1982; Guarda el Canto for Soprano and String Quartet, 1982; Studie I for Violin and Piano, 1986; Lorca-Gesänge for Baritone and 10 instruments, 1986; Wind Sextet, 1986. *Address:* c/o GEMA, Herzog-Wilhelm Strasse 38, 8000 Munich 2, Germany.

**VON DER WETH, Alexandra;** Singer (Soprano); b. 1972, Coburg, Germany. *Education:* Studied in Munich. *Career:* Debut: Leipzig 1993, in Grétry's Zémire et Azor; Appearances with the Deutsche Oper am Rhein, Düsseldorf, from 1996 as Mozart's Pamina and Sandrina, Manon, Lucia di Lammermoor and Alcina; Season 1999–2000 as Micaela at Cologne, Fiordiligi at the Glyndebourne Festival and Musetta for the Vienna Staatsoper; Lulu and Violetta at Düsseldorf; Season 2000–01 with Lucia at Santa Fe, Musetta at the New York Met and Violetta in Chicago; Covent Garden debut 2001, as Manon Lescaut in Henze's Boulevard Solitude; Engaged as Strauss's Daphne at Covent Garden (Concert), 2002. *Recordings include:* Concert arias by Mozart and Beethoven; Lieder by Clara Schumann. *Address:* c/o Deutsche Oper am Rhein, Heinrich Heine Allee 16a, 40213 Düsseldorf, Germany.

**VON DOHNÁNYI, Christoph;** German conductor; *Principal Conductor, Philharmonia Orchestra;* b. 8 Sept. 1929, Berlin; s. of Hans von Dohnányi and Christine (née Bonhoeffer) von Dohnányi; brother of Klaus von Dohnányi; m. 1st Renate Zillessen; one s. one d.; m. 2nd Anja Silja (q.v.) 1979; one s. two d. *Education:* Munich Musikhochschule. *Career:* abandoned legal training to study music 1948; studied in USA under grandfather, Ernst von Dohnányi 1951; répétiteur and conductor under Georg Solti, Frankfurt Oper 1952–56; Gen. Music Dir Lübeck 1957–63, Kassel 1963–66; London debut with London Philharmonic Orchestra 1965; Chief Conductor of Cologne Radio Symphony Orchestra 1964–69; Gen. Music Dir and Opera Dir, Frankfurt 1968–77; Chief Conductor and Intendant, Hamburg State Opera 1977–84; Music Dir (desig.) Cleveland Orchestra 1982–84, Music Dir 1984–; Prin. Guest Conductor Philharmonia Orchestra 1994, Prin. Conductor 1997–; numerous guest appearances; numerous recordings of symphonies with Cleveland Orchestra and opera recordings. *Honours:* Dr hc (Kent State Univ., Case Western Univ., Oberlin Coll., Eastman School of Music, Cleveland Inst. of Music); Commdr, Ordre des Arts et des Lettres; Commdr's Cross, Order of Merit (Germany); Commdr's Cross (Austria); recipient Richard Strauss Prize, Bartok Prize, Goethe Medal, Frankfurt, Arts and Science Prize, City of Hamburg, Abraham Lincoln Award. *Current Management:* Harrison/Parrott Ltd, 12 Penzance Place, London, W11 4PA, England. *Telephone:* (20) 7229-9166. *Fax:* (20) 7221-5042. *Website:* www.harrisonparrott.com.

**VON DOHNÁNYI, Oliver;** Czech conductor; b. 2 March 1955, Trencin; m. Natalia Melnik 1996; one d. *Education:* Konzervatorium in Bratislava (violin, conducting and composition), Academy of Music Prague, Hochschule für Musik, Vienna (both conducting). *Career:* Conductor of the Radio Symphony Orchestra, Bratislava, 1979–86; Principal Conductor of the Slovak National Opera House in Bratislava, conducted new productions of Borodin's Prince Igor, Puccini's Tosca, Rossini's Il Barbiere di Siviglia, Smetana's The Bartered Bride, Verdi's Rigoletto, Gounod's Faust; Conductor, Slovak Philharmonic Orchestra; Istropolitana Chamber Orchestra; Music Director of the National Theatre in Prague, 1993–96; Conducted Smetana's Libuše, Gounod's Romeo and Juliet, Puccini's La Bohème, Verdi's Rigoletto, Prokofiev's Cinderella, and two Mozart operas; Don Giovanni and The Marriage of Figaro, which toured Japan, 1995, 1997; Regular guest conductor Czech National Symphony Orchestra, Prague, Yomiuri Nippon Symphony Orchestra in Tokyo, Hungarian State Philharmonic, Portugal State Symphony Orchestra, Northern Philharmonic in Leeds, Kosice State Philharmonic, Brno State Philharmonic and Slovak Sinfonietta, Zilina; Also conducts at the Danish Royal Opera House, Copenhagen, National Theatre, Brno, Teatro San Carlo, Naples, the Royal Liverpool Philharmonic, English National Opera, English Chamber Orchestra, London Mozart Players, Northern Philharmonic in Leeds, BBC Belfast and Irish National Symphony Orchestra; Conducted Verdi's Falstaff and a new production of Boito's Mephistopheles for English National Opera, 1999. *Recordings:* Smetana's Libuše and My Country (with National Theatre of Prague); Famous Russian Masterpieces; Bach's St John Passion; Works by F Mendelssohn-Bartholdy. *Address:* Renoirova 2A, 152 00 Prague 5, Czech Republic. *E-mail:* o.v.dohnanyi@volny.cz.

**VON GYLDENFELDT, Graciela;** singer (soprano); b. 22 June 1958, Buenos Aires, Argentina. *Education:* studied in Buenos Aires. *Career:* debut as Norina in Don Pasquale at Buenos Aires in 1979; Sang at Bern Opera from 1980, debut as Gilda, then as Zerlina, Martha, Pamina, Echo in Ariadne auf Naxos and Corilla in Donizetti's Convenzione Teatrali; Sang at Vienna Staatsoper,

1982–86, Salzburg Festival, 1984–86, as Frasquita and Tebaldo in productions of Carmen and Don Carlos conducted by Karajan; Sang at Enschede Netherlands from 1988 as Suor Angelica, Mimi and Donna Elvira; Member of Kiel Opera as Chrysothemis, Katya Kabanova and Ellen Orford, 1989–94; Sang the Princess in Zemlinsky's Es War Einmal in 1991, Marietta in Die Tote Stadt; Cincinnati, 1991 as Carmen; Appearances at Teatro Comunale, Florence, as Elena in Mefistofele and concert engagements in Beethoven's 9th and Janáček's Glagolitic Mass, Salud in La Vida Breve of Manuel de Falla at Dallas Opera, 1993; Teatro Colón, Buenos Aires debut as Donna Elvira in Don Giovanni; Appearances throughout Germany as Amelia in Simon Boccanegra and Madama Butterfly; Sang Amelia at Freiburg, 1995; Sang Elena in Mefistofele at Buenos Aires, 1999. *Recordings:* Mefistofele as Elena, with Samuel Ramey, 1990. *Address:* Muhliusstrasse 70, 24103, Kiel, Germany.

**VON HALEM, Victor;** German singer (bass); b. 26 March 1940, Berlin. *Education:* Musikhochschule Munich with Else Domberger. *Career:* has sung at the Deutsche Oper Berlin, 1966–; Guest appearances in Hamburg, Munich, Stuttgart, Cologne, Rome, Geneva, Montreal, Athens and London; Roles include: Wagner's Daland, Pogner, King Henry, Fafner, Fasolt and Hans Sachs, Verdi's Padre Guardiano, The Grand Inquisitor, Mozart's Sarastro and Osmin, Puccini's Colline; Mephistopheles at Strasbourg, St Bris in Les Huguenots at Berlin and at the Spoleto Festival in Parsifal as Gurnemanz; Sang King Heinrich in Lohengrin at Nice, and in Meistersinger as Hans Sachs at Spoleto, Charleston; La Scala debut 1994, Walküre, Hunding; Dallas Opera debut 1994 in Der fliegende Holländer; San Francisco 1994, Tannhäuser, Landgraf; Season 1995–96 as the Commendatore at San Francisco and Ramphis at Verona; Many concert appearances. *Address:* c/o Deutsche Oper Berlin, Richard Wagnerstrasse 10, 10585 Berlin, Germany.

**VON JORDIS, Eelco;** Austrian opera and concert singer (bass); b. 11 May 1943, Graz, Austria. *Education:* studied in Graz, Zürich and Milan. *Career:* debut, Graz 1967, as the Monk in Don Carlos; sang at Regensburg Opera 1969–72, Saarbrucken and Kassel 1972–79; Bielefeld Opera from 1979, notably as Mephisto in Faust by Spohr 1993; further engagements throughout Germany and in Milan, Brussels and Zagreb; other roles include Mozart's Alfonso, Don Giovanni and Sarastro, Verdi's King Philip and Ramphis, Scarpia in Tosca, Boris Godunov, Prince Igor, Daland and Wagner's Landgrave; guest appearances in Russia and North America; Dresden Semperoper, 1999–2001, Gianni Schichi, Music Master in Ariadne; Opera Leipzig 1998, Gustav in Abraum, Herchet; Opera Hamburg 1984–1991, Ferrando in Trovatore, Grandinquisitore in Don Carlo; Munich Nat. Opera 1984–1988, Monterone in Rigoletto; Felsensteinoper in Dessau 1997–2002, Die Kluge (Orff), Don Alfonso in Così fan tutte, Reich in Lustige Weiber; Prof of Solo Singing; performances for Deutschland Radio, Cologne, including Karl Löwe's Hiob. Oratorium. *Recordings:* Ludwig Spohr, Faust, Mephistofeles, CPO; Catott-Romanzia Mario Ruffini, E. Pentirario-Editoria Ellectronica; Charles Gounod, Margarethe. *Publication:* Gedichte 2003. *Honours:* Second Prize, Schubertwettbewerb, Vienna 1967, Third Prize, Staatlicher Preis (Udssr) Paliaschwilli Tiflis Georgien 1976. *Address:* Bremerstrasse 28, 33613 Bielefeld, Germany (office); Via Santa Lucia 8, 09045 Quartu SE, Italy (home). *Telephone:* (521) 130730 (office); (070) 3355661843 (home). *Fax:* (521) 130730 (office).

**VON KANNEN, Günter;** singer (bass-baritone); b. 22 March 1940, Rheydt, Germany. *Education:* studied with Paul Lohmann and Franziska Martienssen. *Career:* sang first at the Pfalztheater Kaiserslautern; subsequently member of the troupe in Bonn and Karlsruhe, and from 1979–90 Principal Bass at the Zürich Opera; since 1992, at the Staatsoper in Berlin; Guest appearances in Cologne, Hamburg, Deutsche Oper Berlin, Washington DC, Vienna, Brussels, Dresden, Amsterdam, Paris Châtelet, with NHK Symphony Tokyo (Pizarro under Ferdinand Leitner), Israel Philharmonic (Doktor in Wozzeck under Daniel Barenboim), Chicago Symphony Orchestra (Klingsor in Parsifal); Sang at the Festivals of Santa Fe, Salzburg, Drottningholm, Schwetzingen, Aix-en-Provance, Lucerne; From 1988–92, Alberich in the Bayreuth Festival's Ring cycle, conducted by Daniel Barenboim and produced by Harry Kupfer; Sang also Klingsor at Bayreuth, (conductor James Levine); Alberich at both Berlin Opera Houses and at Hamburg State Opera; Alberich in the Bayreuth Millennium Cycle 2000, conductor Giuseppe Sinopoli, producer Jürgen Flimm; Other important roles are Hans Sachs (Meistersinger); Ochs Von Lerchenau (Rosenkavalier), La Roche (Capriccio); Cardillac; Sang Alberich in Harry Kupfer's production of The Ring at the Berlin Staatsoper, 1996; Sang Morosus in Die schweigsame Frau by Strauss, Dresden, 1998; Season 2000–01 as the Doctor in Wozzeck at La Scala and Falstaff in Dresden, Alberich at Bayreuth and the Berlin Staatsoper. *Recordings include:* Lebendig Begraben by Schoeck (Atlantis); Bartolo in Nozze di Figaro (Barenboim); Klingsor in Parsifal (Barenboim/Berlin Philharmonic); Osmin in Entführung aus dem Serail; Tiresias in Oedipus Rex by Stravinsky (Neeme Järvi); Manasse in Brautwahl by Busoni (Barenboim); Commendatore in Gazzaniga's Don Giovanni; Alberich in the Bayreuth Ring (Barenboim); Doktor in Wozzeck and Pizarro in Fidelio (Colin Davis); Capriccio/La Roche, conductor Georges Prêtre. *Current Management:* Balmer & Dixon Management AG, Kreuzstrasse 82, 8032 Zürich, Switzerland. *Telephone:* (43) 244-8644. *Fax:* (43) 244-8649. *Website:* www.badix.ch.

**VON MAGNUS, Elisabeth;** Singer (Mezzo-soprano); b. Vienna, Austria. *Education:* Drama School, Salzburg; Vocal studies with Hertha Töpper, Munich, and S Schouten, Netherlands. *Career:* Own programme on Austrian

Radio; Soloist in nearly all European countries, Japan and the USA; Venues include the Alte Oper, Frankfurt, the Barbican Centre, London, the Vienna Musikverein, the Concertgebouw, Amsterdam, the Berlin Philharmonic and the Cologne Philharmonic; Has sung with conductors such as Abbado, Harnoncourt, Weill, Hans Vouk; N. Marnines; Adam Fischer, Herreweghe, and Ton Koopman; US debut in 1991 with St Matthew Passion with the Los Angeles Philharmonic under Peter Schreier; Salzburg Festival debut in Mozart's C Minor Mass, Monteverdi's L'Incoronazione di Poppea and Vespers of 1610, 1993; Has appeared in many and varied roles at several leading opera houses and music festivals with recitals of songs ranging from Haydn to Berg and Weill; Has featured on numerous radio and television broadcasts including Mozart's Le nozze di Figaro from Zürich Opera House; Sang Piramus in Hasse's Piramo e Tisbe, Wiener Schauspielhaus, 2001. *Recordings include:* Zigeunerbaron; Stabat mater; Bach's Christmas Oratorio and Magnificat; Shostakovich, Sieben Romanzen with Stononi Trio; Arianna and Canzonettes by Haydn (Challenge Records). *Address:* Künstleragentur Dr Raab and Dr Böhm, Plankeng 7, 1010 Vienna, Austria.

**VON OSTEN, Sigune;** German singer (soprano); b. 8 March 1950, Dresden. *Education:* studied in Hamburg and Karlsruhe and with Elisabeth Grümmer and Eugen Rabine. *Career:* debut singing John Cage's Aria at Hanover 1973; Noted interpreter of 20th century repertoire at the Dresden and Salzburg Festivals, the Bonn and Vienna Festivals at Venice, Berlin, Donaueschingen, Madrid, Strasbourg, St Petersburg, Moscow and Tokyo; Concert tours, radio and television recordings of Europe, the USA, Japan and South America and opera engagements at Stuttgart, Wiesbaden, Paris, Venice and Lisbon; Repertoire includes Berg's Marie and Lulu and the Woman in Schoenberg's Erwartung; Shostakovich, Lady Macbeth; Sang Fusako in Henze's Des verratene Meer at Wiesbaden, 1991 and the Mother in Turnage's Greek, Wuppertal 1992; Worked with composers such as Halffter, Penderecki, Denisov, Messiaen, Cage, Scelsi and Nono; Sang in Orff's De temporum fine comoedia at Munich, 2000. *Recordings:* Penderecki Luke Passion; Messiaen, Harawi; Noche pasiva by Halffter and Dittrich's Engführung; Songs by Ives, Satie, Cage. *Address:* c/o Hessisches Staatstheater, Postfach 3247, 8200 Wiesbaden, Germany.

**VON OTTER, Anne-Sofie;** Swedish singer (mezzo-soprano); b. 9 May 1955, Stockholm. *Education:* Conservatorium, Stockholm, studied interpretation with Erik Werba (Vienna) and Geoffrey Parsons (London), vocal studies with Vera Rozsa. *Career:* mem. Basel Opera, Switzerland 1982–85; début France at Opéra de Marseille (Nozze di Figaro—Cherubino) and Aix-en-Provence Festival (La Finta Giardiniera) 1984, Rome, Accad. di Santa Cecilia 1984, Geneva (Così fan tutte—Dorabella) 1985, Berlin (Così fan tutte) 1985, USA in Chicago (Mozart's C minor Mass) and Philadelphia (Bach's B minor Mass) 1985, London at Royal Opera, Covent Garden (Le Nozze di Figaro) 1985, Lyon (La Finta Giardiniera) 1986, La Scala, Milan (Alceste) 1987, Munich (Le Nozze di Figaro) 1987, Stockholm (Der Rosenkavalier) 1988, The Metropolitan Opera, New York (Le Nozze di Figaro) 1988, The Royal Albert Hall, London (Faust) 1989, Handel's Ariodante 1997; Glyndebourne (Carmen) 2002, Théâtre des Champs Elysées (Handel's Serse) 2003; repertoire extends from baroque music, German lieder through opera to 20th century music; recorded For the Stars with Elvis Costello 2001; has given recitals in New York, Paris, Brussels, Geneva, Stockholm, Vienna and London. *Honours:* Hon. DSc (Bath) 1992. *Current Management:* IMG Artists, Lovell House, 616 Chiswick High Road, London, W4 5RX, England. *Telephone:* (20) 8233-5800. *Fax:* (20) 8233-5801. *E-mail:* info@imgartists.com. *Website:* www.imgartists.com.

**VON SCHWEINITZ, Wolfgang;** German composer; b. 7 Feb. 1953, Hamburg. *Education:* American Univ., Washington, DC, Hamburg Hochschule für Musik with György Ligeti. *Career:* Center for Computer Research in Music and Acoustics, Stanford Univ., Calif., USA 1975–76; Resident Composer, German Acad., Rome, Italy 1978–79; Opera 'azione musicale' Patmos Premiered at Munich 1990; Guest Prof. in Composition, Weimar 1994–96. *Compositions:* 2 Symphonies 1973, 1974, Mozart Variations, for orchestra 1976, String Quartet 1977, Die Brücke, for tenor, baritone and chamber orchestra 1978, Piano Concerto 1979, Papiersterne Song Cycle, for mezzo and piano 1981, Englische Serenade, for 6 wind instruments 1984, Mass, for soloists, chorus and orchestra 1984, Music for 4 saxophones 1984, Patmos, azione musicale 1990, Morgenlied, for flute 1990, . . . wir aber singen, Symphonic Cycle in 3 Parts, for cello and orchestra 1992, 1995, 1996, Franz and Morton for piano trio 1993–94, O-Ton Automne, Linguistikherbst, song on a poem by Oskar Pastior for soprano and piano 1996, Helmholtz-Funk for 8 computer-controlled sine generators and 2 ringmodulated pianos with natural tuning 1997, Klang auf Schön Berg La Monte Young for string trio and live-electronic ring modulation 1999, JUZ (ein Jodelschrei) for amplified tenor trombone and CD or hard disk recorder 1999, Naturgesang mit Fröschen und Rotbauchunken (live electronic sound performance) 2000, des Himmel Höhe glänzet, song in just intonation for soprano and 2 violins 2002, Die Kantate oder, Gottes Augenstern bist du 2003, Radio Play by and with Friederike Mayröcker, Plainsound – Litanei for cello solo 2004, Plainsound Symphony, for clarinet, ensemble and orchestra 2004–05. *Publications:* Kursbuch 122 'Die Zukunft der Moderne' 1995, Alef Bet/Kometendeutsch, Psalm 119 in Sinn-Silben- und akzentgetreur Übersetzung des Althebräischen Wortlauts (a radically literal German trans. of Psalm 119) 1999; several articles in music journals and magazines including Neue Zeitschrift für Musik, Neue Musik, Positionen, MusikTexte. *Honours:* Schneider-Schott Prize for Young Composers 1986, Plöner-Hindemith Preis 1988. *Address:* Eisenbahnstrasse 12,

10997 Berlin, Germany (home). *E-mail:* schweinitz@plainsound.org (home). *Website:* plainsound.org (home).

**VON STADE, Frederica;** American mezzo-soprano; b. 1 June 1945, Somerville, NJ; m. 1st Peter Elkus 1973 (divorced); two d.; m. 2nd Michael G. Gorman 1991. *Education:* Mannes Coll. of Music, New York. *Career:* opera début with Metropolitan Opera, New York (in Le Nozze di Figaro) 1970; has also sung Paris Opera, San Francisco Opera, Lyric Opera of Chicago, LA Music Center Opera, Salzburg Festival, Covent Garden, London, Spoleto Festival, Boston Opera Co., Santa Fe Opera, Houston Grand Opera, La Scala, Milan; recital and concert artist. *Music:* over 60 recordings include Frederica von Stade Sings Mozart and Rossini Opera Arias, French Opera Arias, Songs of the Cat with Garrison Keillor. *Honours:* Dr hc (Yale Univ.), (Boston Univ.), (Georgetown Univ. School of Medicine), (Mannes School of Music); two Grand Prix du Disc awards, Deutsche Schallplattenpreis, Premio della Critica Discografica and many other awards and prizes; Officier Ordre des Arts et des Lettres. *Current Management:* Columbia Artists Management Inc., Jeffrey D. Vanderveen, 165 W 57th Street, New York, NY 10019, USA.

**VONDRÁCEK, Lukás;** Czech concert pianist; b. 1986, Ostrava. *Education:* Acad. of Music, Latowice, Vienna Musikhochschule and Ostrava Univ. *Career:* debut: first public recital aged four; performed in various piano festivals in USA, including Gilmore Festival, Ravinia Rising Stars Series and New York Int. Piano series; UK recital performances include appearances at Buxton, Ryedale, Music at Oxford and Harrogate Festivals; recital debut in Paris La Cite, Brussels Palais des Beaux Arts and Madrid Auditorio Nacional; has performed with Czech Philharmonic, St Petersburg Philharmonic, Hong Kong Philharmonic, Lake Forest Symphony, Cape Town Philharmonic, Flemish Radio Orchestra, Orquesta Filarmonica de Galicia, Iceland and Dallas Symphony Orchestras and has toured with NHK Symphony in Japan; projects in 2004–05 included debuts with Helsinki Philharmonic, BBC BBC Orchestra, Deutsches Symphonie-Orchester, Berlin and Cincinnati Symphony Orchestra. *Recordings:* CD debut: Prodigy – Lukas Vondracek, repertoire including Mendelssohn, Liszt, Janacek and Dohnanyi. *Current Management:* HarrisonParrott Ltd, 12 Penzance Place, London, W11 4PA, England. *Telephone:* (20) 7229 9166. *Fax:* (20) 7221 5042.

**VOROPAEV, Dmitri;** Russian singer (tenor); b. 1980, Baku. *Education:* M. I. Glinka Choral Coll., St Petersburg Conservatory. *Career:* joined Mariinsky Young Singers' Acad., Moscow 2000; Mariinsky Theatre debut as Don Ottavio in Don Giovanni 2002; roles include Chevalier Belfiore in Il Viaggio a Reims, Mariinsky Theatre and in Paris 2005, Maese Pedro in El Retablo de Maese Pedro, Vienna 2004, Un laquais in La Guerre et la Paix, Opera Bastille 2005, L'innocent in Boris Godunov, La Monnaie, Brussels, Kennedy Center's Opera House, Washington; appeared in Ten Tenors concert, RFH 2004. *Current Management:* c/o Mark Hildrew, Askonas Holt Ltd, Lonsdale Chambers, 27 Chancery Lane, London, WC2A 1PF, England. *Telephone:* (20) 7400-1700 (office). *Fax:* (20) 7400-1799 (office). *E-mail:* info@askonasholt.co.uk (office). *Website:* www.askonasholt.co.uk (office).

**VOSCHEZANG, Hans;** Dutch singer (baritone); b. 1970, Netherlands. *Education:* Utrecht School of Arts, Guildhall School of Music and Drama, London, UK. *Career:* appearances in Netherlands and London as Masetto in Don Giovanni, Purcell's Aeneas, Nick Shadow, Silvio (Pagliacci), Argante in Rinaldo, Ctésippe in Faure's Pénélope, Gianni Schicchi, and Esteban Montejo in Henze's El Cimarrón; concerts in Wuppertal, with the Brabants Orchestra, Orchestre Symphonique de la Monnaie under Marc Soustrot, Acad. of Ancient Music with Paul Goodwin, Hanover Band, London Philharmonic Orchestra, Netherlands Radio Philharmonic Orchestra; recent engagements include Conte Almaviva with European Camerata in Amsterdam and Brussels, Robert in Les Vêpres Siciliennes for The Saturday Matinee in the Concertgebouw and Junius in The Rape of Lucretia in UK its Hungarian premiere; debut at the Liceu, Barcelona in Saint-Saens Henry VIII 2002, Glyndebourne Festival in new production of Carmen 2002. *Recording:* Carmen, Glyndebourne Festival (BBC/OpusArte DVD) 2002. *Honours:* Prizewinner, Hertogenbosch Int. Singing Competition, Netherlands 2000. *Website:* www.hansvoschezang.com.

**VOSS, Ealynn (Elverta Lynn);** Opera Singer (Soprano); b. 10 March 1949, Pittsburgh, Pennsylvania, USA. *Education:* BS, Vocal Performance major, Oberlin Conservatory of Music, 1971. *Career:* Operatic appearances at various US venues, and in Canada, Australia, Spain, Japan, Netherlands and Denmark; Frequent appearances in Turandot title role include Arizona Opera (1988), Opera Carolina, 1990, Miami Opera, 1990, the Australian Opera (1991, 1994) New York City Opera (1991, 1992), Arena di Verona in Japan (1991) Baltimore Opera, 1992, San Francisco, 1993, Michigan Opera, 1994, Houston Grand Opera, 1994 and Copenhagen Opera, Denmark (1996); Sang the Foreign Princess in Rusalka at the Spoleto Festival, USA, 1988, and again at Seattle Opera, 1990; Ariadne (Ariadne auf Naxos) at Victoria State Opera, Australia, 1988, and Los Angeles Music Center Opera, 1992, where she also sang Chrysothemis in Elektra, 1991, 1994, Amelia (Un Ballo in Maschera), 1991, 1994, and Senta (Der fliegende Holländer), 1995; Manitoba Opera, Canada, 1989, as Lady Macbeth, returning as Amelia (1992); Other appearances include Elvira (Ernani) at the Oviedo Festival, Spain, 1991, Tove in Gurre-Lieder at the Concertgebouw Amsterdam, 1995, and Brünn-hilde in Götterdämmerung at the Aspen Festival; Concerts include Beethoven's 9th with Santa Barbara Symphony and Verdi's Requiem with Pasadena Symphony; Debut with the Rome Opera singing Turandot in 1996. *Record-*

*ings:* Video, Turandot with Australian Opera, 1991. *Current Management:* Columbia Artists Management Inc. *Address:* 508 South First Avenue, Elizabeth, PA 15037-1320, USA.

**VOSS, Friedrich;** German composer; b. 12 Dec. 1930, Halberstadt; m. Erna Lewann 10 Dec. 1965; one s. *Education:* Abitur, Gymnasium Halberstadt, 1949; Studied composition and piano, Hochschule für Musik, West Berlin, 1949–54. *Career:* Performances with: Berlin Philharmonic Orchestra, under Karajan; Radio Symphony Orchestra, Berlin, under Maazel; Japan Philharmonic Orchestra, under James Loughran; in Germany, Western Europe, USA, Australia, Asia, South Africa, Latin America; Television performances in Madrid, Johannesburg, Adelaide (Australia). *Compositions include:* more than 75 works: 5 symphonies; 2 violin concertos; 1 cello concerto; 1 cello concertino; 5 string quartets; 1 saxophone quartet; concertino for organ, strings and timpani; 2 works for choir; Hamlet overture; Dithyrambus for Orchestra; Metamorphosis for Orchestra; ballet, Die Nachtigall und die Rose; opera, Leonce und Lena; Cantata of Psalms for soloists, choir and orchestra; Missa MM (Versöhnungsmesse) for soloists, chorus and orchestra (Composers' Prize, Catholic and evangelical churches in Baden-Württemberg, 2001). *Recordings:* About 100 broadcasting recordings in Germany and Western Europe; CD: CTH 2069, THOROFON (4 works). *Honours:* 1st Place, Composers' Competition, Munich Chamber Orchestra, 1955; Stuttgart Music Prize, 1960; Berlin Art Prize (Young Generation), 1961; Düsseldorf Robert Schumann Prize, 1962; Villa Massimo Award, 1964, 1977; Johann Wenzel Stamitz Prize, Mannheim, 1985. *Address:* Hoppenstedts Weg 5, 29308 Winsen /Aller, Germany. *Telephone:* (5143) 911752 (office).

**VOSS, Hermann;** Violist; b. 9 July 1934, Brunen, Germany. *Education:* Studied in Düsseldorf with Maier and in Freiburg with Végh. *Career:* Former Member of Karl Munchinger's Stuttgart Chamber Orchestra in Heibronn; Co-Founded the Melos Quartet of Stuttgart, 1965; First concert tours sponsored by the Deutsches Musikleben Foundation and represented West Germany at the Jeunesse Musicales in Paris, 1966; International concert tours from 1967; Bicentenary concerts in the Beethoven House at Bonn, 1970, and soon toured the USSR, Eastern Europe, Africa, North and South America, the Far East and Australia; British concerts and festival appearances from 1974; Cycle of Beethoven quartets at Edinburgh Festival, 1987; Wigmore Hall, St John's Smith Square and Bath Festival, 1990; Associations with Rostropovich in the Schubert Quintet and the Cleveland Quartet in works by Spohr and Mendelssohn; Teacher at the Stuttgart Musikhochschule. *Recordings:* Complete quartets of Beethoven, Schubert, Mozart and Brahms; Quintets by Boccherini with Narcisco Ypes and by Mozart with Franz Beyer. *Honours:* (with members of the Melos Quartet) Grand Prix de Disque and Prix Caecilia from the Academie du Disque in Brussels.

**VOSTRIAKOV, Alexander;** Singer (Tenor); b. 1948, Kurgan Region, Russia. *Education:* Studied in Kursk and at the Kharkov Institute of the Arts. *Career:* Member of the Kharkov Opera from 1973, then Dnepropetrovsk Opera Theatre until 1983; Principal of the Kiev National Opera from 1983, notably as Lohengrin and Ismaele in Nabucco; Tour of the United Kingdom in 1996 with the Perm State Opera as Lensky in Eugene Onegin. *Address:* c/o Sonata Ltd, 11 North Park Street, Glasgow G20 7AA, Scotland.

**VOYTIK, Viktor Antonovich;** Composer; b. 3 Oct. 1947, Grodno, Belarus. *Education:* Conservatories of Belarus and Moscow. *Career:* Lecturer at Conservatory of Belarus from 1980. *Compositions:* Two Symphonies. 1972, 1974; How the Gnat went Wooing, Cantata, 1972; Remembering Khatin, oratorio, 1973; Suite in the Olden Style for orchestra, 1973; Cossack songs, cantata, 1974; Paraphrases, Suite for orchestra, 1975; Day of the Homeland,

oratorio, 1977; Sonata for two cimbaloms, 1979; String Quartet, 1979; Clarinet Concerto, 1984; Cimbalom Concerto, 1988; Suite, for male voices, 1990; Patriotic Chant for chorus and orchestra, 1991; The Last Autumn of the Poet for soprano, baritone and ensemble, 1992; Spring Song, opera, 1995; Journey to the Alphabet Castle, 1996. *Address:* c/o RAO, 6a B. Bronnya, Moscow 103670, Russia. *Telephone:* 007095 203 3777/200. *Fax:* 00 7095 200 1263.

**VRIEND, Jan;** Composer, Conductor and Pianist; b. 10 Nov. 1938, Benningbroek, Netherlands. *Education:* Conservatory of Amsterdam, 1960–67; Paris, GRM/ORTF and Schola Cantorum, 1967–68; Institute of Sonology, Utrecht, 1965–66; Self taught in mathematics. *Career:* Founder and first conductor of ASKO-Amsterdam, 1964; Conductor of choirs orchestras and ensembles, 1961–70; Conductor of Stroud Symphony Orchestra, 1989–94; Lectured on many topics concerning composition, the use of mathematics in composition and philosophy of music. *Compositions include:* Paroesie for 10 Instruments, 1963–67; Huantan for organ and 4 groups of wind instruments, 1968; Ensembles for mixed choir, 1971; Elements of Logic for wind orchestra, 1972; Heterostase for piano, flute and bass clarinet, 1980; Gravity's Dance for piano, 1983; Jets d'Orgue, I, II and III, 1984–90; Hallelujah I for large orchestra, 1986–97; Hallelujah II for 26 instruments, 1987; 3 Songs for Soprano and Orchestra, 1991; Symbiosis for 9 instruments, 1992; Khepera for altoflute and altoclarinet, 1997; Du-Dich-Dir for mixed choir, 1998; Piano Quintet, 1999; Choirbook part 1 for male choir, 1999; In Paradisum for large ensemble, 2000; Grosse Fuge for 6 percussion and organ, 2001. *Publications:* Essays on the music of Xenakis and Varèse and on musical life in Netherlands, published in Netherlands and France. *Honours:* Schnittger Organ Prize for Herfst, 1966; Prize for Composition, Amsterdam Conservatory, 1967; International Gaudeamus Prize, 1970. *Address:* 22 Pooles Lane, Selsley, Stroud GL5 5JT, England.

**VRONSKY, Petr;** Conductor; b. 4 March 1946, Prague, Czechoslovakia; 1 d. *Education:* Violin, Conservatoire Plzeň, 1967; Conducting, Academy of Music Arts, Prague, 1972. *Career:* debut, Prague, 1971; Opera, Plzeň, 1971; Opera, Usti Nad Labem, Aussig, 1974; State Philharmonic Orchestra, Brno, 1979–91; Senior Lecturer, Prague, 1990; Kammeroper Wien, 1991; Dance Theatre, Haag, 1995; Guest Conductor, Czech Philharmonic Orchestra, Prague, Symphony Orchestra, Prague, National Theatre, Prague, State Opera, Prague, Metropolitan Orchestra, Tokyo, Radio Symphony Orchestra, Munchen, Philharmonic Orchestra, Dortmund; mem, Association of Music Scientists and Musicians, Prague. *Honours:* Conducting Competition Prizes, Olomouc, 1970, Besancon, 1971, Berlin, 1973. *Address:* Majerskeho 2049, PO Box 124, 14900 Prague 4, Czech Republic.

**VUORI, Harri;** Composer; b. 10 Jan. 1957, Lahti, Finland. *Education:* Sibelius Academy, 1978–89, with Eino Rautavaara. *Career:* Department of Musicology, Helsinki University, 1993–; Composer-in-residence, Hyvinkää Orchestra, 1997. *Compositions:* Piano Sonata, 1976; In Natural State, for ensemble, 1978; String Quartet, 1979; The Seasons, in Natura Naturally, for four female voices and ensemble, 1982; Like a Bird's footprints in the Sky, chamber opera, 1983; Mystical metamorphoses nocturnae, for two sopranos and ensemble, 1985; Kri, for orchestra, 1988; Songs of Dreaming and Death, for soprano and cello, 1990; Interrupted Movements, for chamber orchestra, 1991; Above and Below, for wind and percussion, 1991; Violin Sonata, 1996; The Mandelbrot Echoes, for orchestra, 1996; Sky Line, electro-acoustic, 1997; Invitation to a Nocturnal Dance, for two viols and harpsichord, 1997; Awakenings, for chorus, 1997. *Address:* c/o TEOSTO, Lauttasaarentie 1, SF–00200 Helsinki, Finland. *Telephone:* 00358 0681 011. *Fax:* 00358 9677 134.

**WAAGE, Lars;** Singer (Bass-baritone); b. 1948, Århus, Denmark. *Education:* Studied at the Århus Conservatory. *Career:* Sang with the Lubeck Opera, 1975–80, as King Henry in Lohengrin and Wagner's Gurnemanz; Jyske Opera at Århus from 1980, notably as Wotan and Gunther in The Ring; Guest appearances as Sharpless, Iago, Pizarro, Mephistopheles and Kurwenal; Concert singer in France, Germany and Italy. *Address:* Århus Opera, Thomas Jensens Allee, 8000 Århus, Denmark.

**WÄCHTER, Erich;** Conductor; b. 3 July 1945, Bielefeld, Germany. *Education:* Hochschule für Musik, Berlin. *Career:* Repetiteur at Kaiserslautern, 1969–71, Kapellmeister der Opera, 1971–74; Kapellmeister at the Saarbrucken State Opera, 1974–77; Musical Director of the Saarbrucken City Choir; Musical Assistant, Bayreuth, 1975 (and conducted Der fliegende Holländer and Die Zauberflöte at Tbilisi); Conductor at the Baden State Opera in Karlsruhe, 1977–85; Guest Conductor, Wiesbaden (with Der Rosenkavalier, Carmen and La Forza del Destino); Lecturer in Music at State Music Academy, Karlsruhe, 1980; Kapellmeister at Darmstadt, 1985–87 and National Theatre at Mannheim, 1987–90; General Music Director, Lübeck Opera, 1987–; Also engaged by the Stuttgart Opera, Vienna Volksoper, Oslo, Munich State Opera, Hamburg, Leipzig, Dresden, Stockholm and Antwerp, and Zürich Opera; Leiter des Hochschulorchesters und Leiter der Dirigierabteilung Musikhochschule Lübeck, 1993.

**WADDINGTON, Henry;** Singer (Bass); b. 1968, Kent, England. *Education:* Royal Northern College of Music, with Barbara Robotham. *Career:* Debut: As Bottom in A Midsummer Night's Dream, at the RNCM; Glyndebourne Touring Opera from 1992, in The Rake's Progress, and in the premiere of Birtwistle's The Second Mrs Kong (1994); Appearances in Le Comte Ory and Tchaikovsky's The Enchantress for New Sussex Opera, as Colline for GTO, Farlaf in Ruslan and Lyudmila for Dorset Opera, as Falstaff for Opera North and Fiorello in Il Barbiere di Siviglia for Royal Opera House; Count Lamoral in Arabella and Mozart's Antonio at the Glyndebourne Festival, 1996–97; Season 1998 with Major Domo in Capriccio at Glyndebourne, Verdi's Ribbing for WNO, Don Magnifico in Cenerentola for English Touring Opera, Count Horn in Ballo in Maschera for WNO and Oroe in Semiramide for Chelsea Opera Group; 1999, Banquo in Macbeth for ETO; Concerts include: Mozart's Requiem with the English CO at the Barbican Hall, Sir John in Love for British Youth Opera, the Verdi Requiem, and The Rake's Progress with the BBC Symphony Orchestra at the Festival Hall (1997). *Current Management:* Ingpen & Williams Ltd, 7 St George's Court, 131 Putney Bridge Road, London, SW15 2PA, England.

**WADE, Simon;** Composer; b. 28 Aug. 1958, Devonport, Tasmania, Australia. *Education:* BA (Mus), Tasmanian Conservatory, 1979; Master of Creative Arts, Film and Communications Diplomas, 1995. *Career:* Tasmanian Conservatory, 1980; University of Sydney, 1988; Rare Birds Productions Co, 1993; Commissions from Tasmanian Opera Co, New England String Quartet, and others. *Compositions include:* Saxophone Quartet, 1984; Extracts for saxophone and piano, 1984; Songs from Shakespeare, for chorus and orchestra, 1984; Introduction to the String Quartet, 1985; The Other Meaning, song cycle for tenor and piano, 1985; Sequences for clarinet and piano, 1985; The Watching Clock, chamber opera, 1992; The Herald Angel, for alto trombone and piano, 1993; Computer-generated music for film and theatre, 1993–. *Address:* c/o APRA, 1A Eden Street, Crows Nest, NSW 2065, Australia.

**WADSWORTH, Matthew;** British lutenist. *Education:* Chetham School of Music, RAM, Royal Conservatory, The Hague. *Career:* founder mem., Ricordo Ensemble 1997–; Wigmore Hall solo debut 2003; US concert tour 2005; continuo player and chamber musician with leading early music ensembles; lute song recitals with Faye Newton; workshops with Live Music Now! for visually impaired children; guest tutor, Royal Northern Coll. of Music. *Recordings:* Away Delights (lute solos and songs from Shakespeare's England), 14 Silver Strings (music by Kapsberger and Piccinini). *Honours:* London Student of the Year Award for development of Braille lute tablature 1997. *Current Management:* Chameleon Arts Management, 32 St Michael's Road, Sandhurst, GU47 8HE, England. *Telephone:* (20) 8521-4959. *E-mail:* concerts@matthewwadsworth.com. *Website:* www.matthewwadsworth.com.

**WADSWORTH, Stephen;** Stage Director, Translator and Librettist; b. 3 April 1953, Mount Kisco, New York, USA. *Career:* Artistic Director and Stage Director of the Skylight Opera in Milwaukee; Productions of Monteverdi's three principal operas, from 1982; Wrote libretto for Bernstein's A Quiet Place 1983 and has directed productions of it at La Scala, Milan and in Vienna; For Seattle Opera has directed Jenůfa, Fliegende Holländer, and Gluck's Orphée; Handel's Xerxes at Milwaukee 1985 and Partenope at Omaha, 1988; Fidelio and La Clemenza di Tito for Scottish Opera, 1991; Die Entführung at San Francisco 1990, other productions include Le nozze di Figaro and Alcina (St Louis) and Simon Boccanegra (Netherlands Opera); Head of the Opera Program at the Manhattan School of Music, 1991; Translations of Monteverdi's Orfeo and Handel's Xerxes, Alcina and Partenope; Covent Garden debut 1992, Handel's Alcina; Staging of Xerxes seen at Santa Fe, Los Angeles and Boston (1996). *Honours:* Chevalier, Ordre des Arts et des Lettres. *Address:* c/o Boston Lyric Opera, 114 State Street, Boston, MA 02109, USA.

**WAGEMANS, Peter-Jan;** Composer; b. 7 Sept. 1952, The Hague, Netherlands. *Education:* Studied at the Hague Conservatory, and with Klaus Huber in Freiburg. *Career:* Lecturer at Hague Conservatory, 1978–84; Rotterdam Conservatory, 1982–; Promoter of modern music concerts at Rotterdam, from 1990. *Compositions include:* Symphony, 1972; Wind Quintet, 1973; Musiek, I–IV, 1974, 1977, 1985, 1988; Cantata, 1979; Octet, 1980; Trio, for clarinet, violin and piano, 1985; Klang, for orchestra 1986; Wie, for alto, two clarinets and two horns, 1987; Walk on Water, for trumpet and ensemble, 1988; Rosebud, for orchestra and female chorus, 1988; Requiem for strings and percussion, 1992; Panthalassa, for wind, 1994; Wind Quintet no. 2, 1994; Concerto for two pianos, 1994, rev, 1997; Nachtvlucht for soprano and orchestra, 1997; String Quartet, 1998. *Honours:* Matthijs Vermeulen Prize, 1990. *Address:* c/o BUMA, PO Box 725, 1180 AS Amstelveen, Netherlands. *Telephone:* 0031 20540 7911. *Fax:* 0031 20540 7496.

**WAGENAAR, Diderik;** Composer; b. 10 May 1946, Utrecht, Netherlands. *Education:* Royal Conservatory, The Hague. *Career:* Lecturer at Royal Conservatory. 1969–. *Compositions include:* Canzonas, for 15 brass instruments, double bass and two pianos, 1976, Tam Tam, for ensemble 1978; Canapé, for clarinet, violin, cello and piano 1980, Metrum, for four saxophones and orchestra, 1984; Limiet, for string quartet, 1985; Triforium, for wind ensemble and percussion, 1988; Tessituur, for orchestra, 1990; Solenne, for six percussion, 1992; Cat Music, for two violins, 1994; Trios Poèmes en prose, for soprano and orchestra, 1995; Rookery Hill, for ensemble, 1998; Galilei, for chamber orchestra, 1999; Arrangement of Berg's Altenberglieder for medium voice and ensemble, 1985. *Honours:* Matthijs Vermeulen Prize, 1996. *Address:* c/o BUMA, PO Box 725, 1180 As Amstelvven, Netherlands.

**WAGENFUHRER, Roland;** Singer (Tenor); b. 1964, Hof/Saale, Germany. *Education:* Studied at the Nuremberg Conservatory, from 1982. *Career:* Member of the Bavarian State Opera Studio 1987–89, as Ferrando and as Chlestakov in Der Revisor; Landestheater Coburg 1989–95, as Jenik in The Bartered Bride, Lensky, Don José and Wagner's Erik; Dresden Semper Oper from 1995, as Max, Laca (Jenůfa), Desportes in Zimmermann's Soldaten and Dionysos in The Bassarids by Henze; Guest appearances as Florestan at the Bregenz Festival (1995–96), Tamino in Cologne, Walther von Stolzing in Lubeck and Erik at the Vienna Staatsoper; Season 1997–98 as Florestan at the Komische Oper Berlin and Hoffmann at Cologne; Engagements for 1998 in The Bartered Bride in Munich, Fliegender Holländer at the Bayreuth Festival and New York Met, and Freischütz/Max in Vienna; Lohengrin at Bayreuth, 1999; Further engagements include Elijah in Zürich, Beethoven's 9th in Brussels and Duisburg, Bruch's Moses-Oratorium in Berlin and Munich, and Berlioz's Faust Studies in Paris; Season 2000–01 as Florestan at Munich and Dresden, Lohengrin for the Bayreuth Festival and Wagner's Erik at the Met. *Address:* c/o Theateragentur Dr G. Hilbert, Maximillianstr 22, D–80539 Munich, Germany.

**WAGNER, James;** Singer (Tenor); b. 1949, New Orleans, Louisiana, USA. *Education:* Studied at Rochester University and in Vienna. *Career:* Sang at the Frankfurt Opera, 1975–76, Kassel, 1976–80, New York City Opera, 1981–82, Vienna Volksoper, 1983–84; Theater am Gärtnerplatz, Munich, 1985–88, and elsewhere, as Almaviva, Xerxes, Belmonte, Giasone in Cherubini's Médée, Florestan, Edgardo, and Dionysos in Henze's Bassarids; Guest appearances in Berne, Bologne (1987), Venice (1990) and Greece; Season 2000–01 in the Verdi Requiem in Vienna and as Rossini's Otello (concert) at Halle. *Recordings include:* Amadis de Gaule by J C Bach (Hanssler). *Address:* Theater am Gärtnerplatz, Gärtnerplatz 3, W-8000 Munich 5, Germany.

**WAGNER, Wolfgang;** German opera director; b. 30 Aug. 1919, Bayreuth; s. of Siegfried Wagner and Winifred Wagner (née Williams); grandson of Richard Wagner; m. 1st Ellen Drexel 1943; one s. one d.; m. 2nd Gudrun Mack (née Armann) 1976; one d. *Career:* mil. service 1938–40; stage man. at Bayreuth Festival 1940; Asst with Preussische Staatsoper, Berlin 1940–44; returned to Bayreuth after war, worked with brother (the late Wieland Wagner) as dir annual Wagner operatic festival 1951–66, on his own 1967–; directed more than 400 performances 1953–; numerous guest appearances and int. tours; mem. Bayerische Akad. der Schönen Künste 1986. *Productions include:* Andreasnacht (Berlin 1944), The Rhinegold (Naples 1952), The Valkyrie (Naples 1952, 1953, Barcelona 1955, Venice 1957, Palermo 1962, Osaka 1967), Lohengrin (Bayreuth 1953, 1967, Taormina 1991, Tokyo 1997), Siegfried (Naples 1953, Brussels 1954, Venice 1957, Bologna 1957), The Flying Dutchman (Bayreuth 1955, Dresden 1988), Tristan and Isolde (Barcelona 1955, Bayreuth 1957, Venice 1958, Palermo 1960, Osaka 1967, Milan 1978), Parsifal (Barcelona 1955, Bayreuth 1975, 1989), Don Giovanni (Brunswick 1955), The Mastersingers of Nuremberg (Rome 1956, Bayreuth 1968, 1981, 1996, Dresden 1985), The Nibelung's Ring (Venice 1957, Bayreuth 1960, 1970), Götterdämmerung (Venice 1957), Tannhäuser (Bayreuth 1985). *Publication:* Acts (autobiog.). *Honours:* Ehrensenator Graz 1987, Munich 1988, Tübingen 1988; Bayerischer Maximiliansorden 1984; Dr hc (Univ. of Bayreuth) 1994. *Address:* c/o Bayreuther Festspiele, PO Box 100262, 95402 Bayreuth, Germany. *Telephone:* 92178780.

**WAHLGREN, Per-Arne;** Singer (Baritone); b. 1953, Sweden. *Education:* Studied at the opera school of the Royal Opera Stockholm. *Career:* Debut: Norrland Opera 1978, as Don Giovanni; Sang at the Stora Teater Gothenburg from 1979 as Germont and Belcore; Guest appearances at the Theater an der Wien, Vienna 1980, in the premiere of Jesu Hochzeit by Gottfried von Einem; Royal Opera Stockholm from 1981, as Mozart's Count and Guglielmo, Marcello, Sharpless and Wolfram; Humbert Humbert in the premiere of Rodion Shchedrin's Lolita under the direction of M Rostropovich, 1994; Further engagements at Nice in Tannhäuser and The Queen of Spades, at Lausanne in Dido and Aeneas and in Madrid in Mendelssohn's Elijah; Stockholm 1986 in the premiere of Christina by Hans Gefors; Drottningholm Court Theatre 1991, as Orestes in a revival of Electra by J C F Haeffner; Sang Frank in Korngold's Die tote Stadt, Stockholm, 1995. Concert repertory includes Bach's Passions, Christmas Oratorio and Cantatas, the Brahms Requiem, Messiah, Utrecht Te Deum by Handel, the Fauré Requiem, Lieder eines fahrenden Gesellen and Carmina Burana. *Recordings include:* Dido and Aeneas. *Address:* Kungliga Teatern PO Box 16094, 10322 Stockholm, Sweden.

**WAHLUND, Sten;** Singer (Bass); b. 1943, Stockholm, Sweden. *Education:* Stockholm Music High School, 1964–70, with Erik Saéden. *Career:* Debut: Royal Opera Stockholm, 1969, as Sarastro; Appearances in Stockholm and at the Drottningholm Baroque Theatre, as the Commendatore, Rossini's Basilio, the Grand Inquisitor in Don Carlos, and Don Pasquale; Premieres of Christina by Hans Gefors, 1986, and Doktor Glas by Arne Mellnäs, 1994; Season 1995–96 at Stockholm as Gurnemanz in Parsifal and Pimen in Boris Godunov; Other roles include Mephistopheles in Faust, Fafner, and King Henry in Lohengrin; Sang King Marke in Tristan at Karlstad, 2000; Frequent concert engagements in Scandinavia and elsewhere. *Address:* Royal Opera, Stockholm, PO Box 16094, 10322 Stockholm, Sweden.

**WAKASUGI, Hiroshi,** BMus; Japanese conductor; *Permanent Conductor, NHK Symphony Orchestra;* b. 31 May 1935, Tokyo. *Education:* Tokyo Nat. Univ. of Fine Arts and Music, studied conducting with Hideo Sati and Nobori Kaneko. *Career:* conducted the Kyoto Symphony Orchestra from 1975; regular concerts with the Berlin Philharmonic, Vienna Symphony, Munich Philharmonic, Toronto Symphony, Montréal Symphony, Pittsburgh Symphony, NHK Symphony, Bavarian Radio Symphony and the Frankfurt Museum Soc.; Chief Conductor, Cologne Radio Symphony 1977–83; US debut 1981, with the Boston Symphony Orchestra; Music Dir, Deutsche Oper am Rhein Düsseldorf 1981–86; Prin. Guest Conductor, Dresden State Opera and the Dresden Staatskapelle 1982–91; Chief Conductor, Tokyo Metropolitan Orchestra; Chief Conductor and Artistic Dir, Tonhalle Orchestra Zürich 1987–91; Music Dir, Tokyo Metropolitan Symphony Orchestra 1986–95, Prin. Conductor 1987–95; Permanent Conductor, NHK Symphony Orchestra 1995–; has conducted first Japanese performances of Schoenberg's Gurrelieder and Pelléas und Mélisande, Wagner's Parsifal, Der fliegende Holländer, Rheingold and Siegfried, Strauss's Capriccio and Ariadne auf Naxos, and many contemporary works; Lohengrin at Tokyo 1998; currently Artistic Dir Centre for the Performing Arts, Shiga, and of Tokyo Chamber Opera; Prof. Emeritus, Tokyo Nat. Univ. of Fine Arts and Music; Artistic Consultant (Opera), New Nat. Theatre, Tokyo 2005–(07, Artistic Dir (Opera) 2007–10); mem. Japan Art Acad. *Honours:* Suntory Prize 1987. *Address:* c/o New National Theatre Tokyo, 1-1-1 Hon-machi, Shibuya-ku, Tokyo 151, Japan. *Website:* www.nhkso .or.jp; www.nntt.jac.go.jp.

**WAKEFIELD, John,** FRAM; British academic and singer (tenor); b. 21 June 1936, Yorkshire, England; m. Rilla Welborn; two s. one d. *Education:* Royal Acad. of Music. *Career:* debut, WNO 1960; Macduff, Glyndebourne 1964; Rinuccio at Royal Opera House 1965; other roles include Fenton, Tamino, Paris, Don Ottavio, Ferrando, Belmonte, Idamante, Rodolfo, Orfeo, Cavalli's Ormindo, Essex in Britten's Gloriana and Saul; mem. Equity, NATFHE. *Recordings:* La Traviata, Ormindo, The Mikado, Messiah. *Honours:* Kathleen Ferrier Scholarship 1958, 's-hertogenbosch Tenor Prize 1959, Hon. FTCL. *Address:* 12 Avenue Gardens, Teddington, Middlesex TW11 0BH, England.

**WALACINSKI, Adam;** Composer; b. 18 Sept. 1928, Kraków, Poland. *Education:* Studied at the Kraków Conservatory, 1947–52; Private studies in composition with Stefan Kisielewski. *Career:* Violinist in the Kraków Radio Orchestra, 1948–56; Teacher at the Kraków Conservatory, 1972–92, Professor, 1993–96, Prorector; Music Critic, Dziennik Polski, 1962–; Collaborates with PWM Music Cyclopedia as Area Editor of 20th Century composers; Member of the Grupa Krakowska, for promotion of the New Music; Chairman, Kraków section, Polish Composers Union, 1971–87. *Compositions include:* Alfa for orchestra, 1958; String Quartet, 1959; Intrada for 7 players, 1962; Canto Tricolore for flute, violin and vibraphone, 1962; Horizons for chamber orchestra, 1962; A Lyric Before Falling Asleep for soprano, flute and 2 pianos, 1963; Concerto de Camera for violin and strings, 1964; Fogli volanti for string trio, 1985; Canzona for cello, piano and tape, 1966; Epigrams for chamber ensemble, 1967; Refrains and Reflections for orchestra, 1969; Notturno 70 for 24 strings, 3 flutes and percussion, 1970; Torso for orchestra, 1971; Divertimento interrotto for 13 players, 1974; Mirophonies for soprano and ensemble, 1974; Ballada for flute and piano, 1986; Little Autumn Music for flute and string trio, 1986; Drama e Burla for orchestra, 1988; Pastorale, for flute, oboe, violin, 1992; La vida es sueno, reminiscences from Calderon, for flute, guitar and viola, 1998; Aria for orchestra, 1998; Spirale of Time for 15 players, 2000; Music for theatre, cinema and television. *Honours:* State Award, 1966; Prize of the City of Kraków, 1976. *Address:* ul Arciszewskiego 4, 30-138 Kraków, Poland.

**WALDHANS, Jiri;** Conductor; b. 17 April 1923, Brno, Czechoslovakia. *Education:* Studied at the Brno Conservatory until 1948 and with Igor Markevitch in Salzburg. *Career:* Repetiteur and Chorus Master at the Ostrava Opera, 1949–51; Conducted the Brno State Philharmonic, 1951–54, Ostrava Symphony Orchestra 1955–62; Returned to the Brno State 1962–80; Janáček Academy at Brno from 1980; Guest Conductor in Czechoslovakia and elsewhere in Europe. *Recordings include:* Dvořák Cello Concerto with the Czech Philharmonic (Supraphon); 15 Pages after Dürer's Apocalypse by Luboš Fišer; Janáček's Lachian Dances, Jealousy (Jenůfa) Overture, The Fiddler's Child and The Ballad of Blanik Hill; Suites from Martinů's Ballets Istar and Spalicek; Cello Concertos by Milhaud, Beethoven's Piano Arrangement of his Violin Concerto and early Concerto in E flat 1784, with Felicia Blumenthal. *Address:* Slezske divadlo, Marketing Manager, Ales Waldhans, Horni Namesti 13, 749 69 Opava, Czech Republic.

**WALENDOWSKI, Dario;** Singer (Tenor); b. 1 Aug. 1955, Łódź, Poland. *Career:* Debut: Łódź, 1980, as Alfredo in La Traviata; National Opera Warsaw from 1982, as Donizetti's Edgardo, Nadir in Les Pêcheurs de Perles, Tamino, Captain, Tebaldo (Capuleti ed i Montecchi) and Shuisky in Boris Godunov; Engagements in Austria from 1985 and Germany, 1989; Oberhausen and Giessen Operas as Count Almaviva, the Duke of Mantua, Rodolfo, Jontek (Halka), Edgardo, Des Grieux, Macduff, Romeo, Jenik (Bartered Bride), Don José, Hoffmann and Pinkerton; Staatstheater Schwerin from 1993, as Cavaradossi, Pedro (Tiefland), Sly, Radames, Faust, Nemorino, and Manrico; Guest appearances at the Bolshoi (Moscow), Mannheim, Berlin, Madrid, Hamburg, Barcelona and Paris; Form 1996 guest appearances at Lübeck and Rostock as Alva (Lulu), Don Alvaro (La Forza del Destino); Modern repertory includes Jedidia in Penderecki's The Black Mask; Der schöne Herr Herrmann ( Hindemith's Neues vom Tage), Sandy (The Lighthouse), Pierrot/Soldât. *Address:* c/o Mecklenburgisches Staatstheater, Alte Garten, 2751 Schwerin, Germany.

**WALKER, David;** Stage Designer; b. 18 July 1934, Calcutta, India. *Education:* Studied at the Central School of Arts and Crafts, London, 1952–56. *Career:* Designs for Joan Littlewood's Theatre from 1955; Opera designs for Werther and La Bohème at Glyndebourne, 1966–67; Royal Opera House designs (some in collaboration with producer John Copley), 1965–82; Suor Angelica, Così fan tutte, Don Giovanni and Semele; Costumes for Carmen at the Metropolitan, 1972; Manon Lescaut at Palermo and Lucia di Lammermoor at La Fenice, Venice; Production designs for La Traviata and Der Rosenkavalier at English National Opera, 1973, 1975; Sets and costumes for Donizetti's Roberto Devereux at the Teatro dell'Opera Rome, 1988 and at Naples, 1998; Collaborated with John Conklin on designs for Der Rosenkavalier at Santa Fe, 1989; ENO designs for La Traviata seen at Philadelphia, 1992. *Address:* c/o English National Opera, St Martin's Lane, London WC2N 4ES, England.

**WALKER, Diana;** Singer (Soprano); b. 1958, Salt Lake City, Utah, USA. *Career:* Has sung at the New York City Opera, 1983–, as Leila (Les Pêcheurs de Perles), Gilda, Adele, Micaela, Barbara (Argento's Casanova) and Ninetta (The Love of Three Oranges); Seattle Opera in the title roles of The Ballad of Baby Doe and Lucia di Lammermoor; Utah Opera as the Queen of Night; European debut as Blondchen in Die Entführung with Nice Opera; Modern repertory includes Laetitia in The Old Maid and the Thief with St Louis Opera, Abigail in The Crucible by Robert Ward and Ariel in Lee Hoiby's The Tempest (Kansas City); Performances of the ballet Alice, after Del Tredici's In Memory of a Summer Day, in Toronto, Chicago, Washington DC, Florida, California, New York (Metropolitan Opera) and London; Sang Lakmé for Chicago Opera Theatre, 1990; Premieres of Victoria Bond's Travels in Virginia, 1995; Concert repertory includes, Messiah, Handel's Joshua and Rinaldo (at Kennedy Center) and Mahler's 4th Symphony; Further roles include Donizetti's Norina, Adina and Marie; Gluck's Iphigénie; Mozart's Mme Silberklang, Blondchen and Susanna; Strauss's Sophie and Zerbinetta; Verdi's Nannetta and Ophelia in Hamlet by Thomas; Guest artist with Miami Chamber Symphony, Brooklyn Symphony, New York, Utah Symphony, Kansas City Philharmonic, Roanoke, Virginia Symphony, Aspen Symphony. *Current Management:* c/o Anthony George Management, 250 W 77th Street, No. 304, New York City, NY 10024, USA.

**WALKER, George Theophilus, Jr,** BMus, DMA; American composer, pianist and educator; *Professor Emeritus of Music, Rutgers University;* b. 27 June 1922, Washington, DC; two s. *Education:* Oberlin Coll., Curtis Inst. of Music, Univ. of Rochester. *Career:* first professional concert, Shiloh Baptist Church, Washington, DC 1939; organist Oberlin Theological Seminary 1939–41; debut as pianist at Town Hall, New York 1945; numerous recitals world-wide; teacher, Dillard Univ., New Orleans 1953–54, Dalcroze School of Music, New York 1960–61, New School for Social Research, New York 1960–61, Smith Coll., Northampton, MA 1961–68, Peabody Inst. Conservatory at Johns Hopkins Univ., Baltimore 1975–78; Visiting Prof. of piano and piano literature, Univ. of Colorado at Boulder 1968–69; Distinguished Prof. of Music, Univ. of Delaware, Newark 1975–76; teacher of piano, theory, music history and composition, Rutgers Univ., Newark, NJ 1969–92, Chair of Music Dept 1975–77, Prof. Emeritus 1992–; John Hay Whitney Fellowship 1958; Bok Foundation grant for European concerts 1963; Bennington Composers Conference Fellowships 1967, 1968; Guggenheim Fellowships 1969, 1988; MacDowell Colony Fellowships 1966–69; Yaddo Fellowship 1969; Rutgers Univ. Research Council grant 1969; Rockefeller Fellowships 1971, 1974; NEA grants 1971, 1975, 1978, 1984. *Compositions include:* Lyric for Strings 1947,

18 songs for voice and piano 1941–94, arrangements of spirituals for voice and piano 1947–62, five piano sonatas, two string quartets, two sonatas for violin and piano, concertos for cello, trombone, violin and piano, Concerto for piano and orchestra, Concerto for trombone and orchestra, Cantata for soprano, tenor boys' choir and chamber orchestra, Mass for chorus and orchestra, Address for orchestra, three Sinfonias for orchestra, Serenata for chamber orchestra, Sonata for cello and piano, Music for Brass, Poem for soprano and chamber ensemble, Variations for orchestra, Antifonys for chamber orchestra, Orpheus for chamber orchestra 1994, Lilacs for soprano or tenor and orchestra (Pulitzer Prize 1996) 1995, Pageant and Proclamation for orchestra 1997, Tangents for chamber orchestra 1999, Wind Set for woodwind quintet 1999, Modus for two guitars, winds and strings 1999. *Recordings include:* George Walker in Recital 1994, George Walker A Portrait 1994, George Walker (Chamber Works) 1995, George Walker plays Bach, Schumann, Chopin and Poulenc 1997, The Music of George Walker 1997, George Walker: Works for Chamber Orchestra. *Publications:* Make Room for Black Classical Music (in New York Times) 1992, The Lot of the Black Composer 1992, Recordings of Solo Piano Works: George Walker in Recital, George Walker Plays Bach, Schumann, Chopin and Poulenc, Lilacs: The Music of George Walker 2000, George Walker: American Virtuoso 2001, George Walker in Concert 2002, George Walker: Composer-Pianist 2005. *Honours:* Univ. of Rochester Distinguished Scholar medal 1996, Dr hc (Lafayette Coll., Easton) 1982, (Oberlin Coll.) 1983, (Curtis Inst.) 1997, (Montclair State Univ.) 1997, (Bloomfield Coll.) 1997; Religious Arts Festival Award 1961, Carnegie Mellon Inst. Harvey Gaul Prize 1963, Koussevitzky Award 1988, Pulitzer Prize 1996, American Acad. of Arts and Letters Award 1999, American Classical Music Hall of Fame 2000. *Address:* 323 Grove Street, Montclair, NJ 07042, USA.

**WALKER, Helen;** Singer (Soprano); b. 1952, Tunbridge Wells, England. *Education:* Guildhall School, London, with Noelle Barker. *Career:* Sang Verdi's Giovanna d'Arco, 1977; Glyndebourne Festival as Fiordiligi, Monteverdi's Poppea 1984, and Helena in A Midsummer Night's Dream; Glyndebourne Touring Opera as Pamina, Ann Trulove in The Rake's Progress, and Ninetta in The Love of Three Oranges; Opera North as Pamina, and Fenena in Nabucco; Helena at Aldeburgh and Covent Garden; Handel roles include Polissena in Radamisto (Handel Opera Society) and Teseo, for the English Bach Festival at Sadler's Wells Theatre; Foreign engagements in Hong Kong and Nancy (with Glyndebourne Touring Opera), Montpellier and La Fenice, Venice (as Anne Trulove); Sang a Maid in Elektra at Covent Garden, 1990; Freia, Sieglinde and Gutrune in the City of Birmingham Touring Opera version of the Ring; Premiered Leaving by Turnage, Symphony Hall and Radio 3, 1992. *Recordings:* Dido and Aeneas (1st Witch), Philips. *Honours:* Winner, Susan Longfield Competition, 1977; Ricordi Prize for Opera; Mozart Memorial Prize, 1978; South East Arts Young Musicians Platform; Glyndebourne Touring Award; Christie Award, Glyndebourne.

**WALKER, John (Edward);** Singer (Tenor); b. 19 Aug. 1933, Bushnell, Indiana. *Education:* Studied at the Universities of Denver, Urbana and Bloomington. *Career:* Debut: Berne 1963, as Tamino; Appearances in Europe at Zürich, Cologne, Frankfurt, Stuttgart and Brussels; US engagements at San Francisco, Dallas, Santa Fe, Chicago, Seattle, San Diego, Omaha and Portland; Other roles have included Mozart's Belmonte, Don Ottavio and Ferrando, Nadir, Almaviva, Alfredo, Fenton, Ernesto, Nemorino, Werther, Lensky and Britten's Lysander; Has also sung Jenik in The Bartered Bride, Nureddin in the Barber of Baghdad, Albert Herring, and David in Die Meistersinger; Many concert and oratorio engagements. *Address:* c/o Staatsoper Stuttgart, Oberer Schlossgarten 6, 7000 Stuttgart 1, Germany.

**WALKER, Malcolm;** Singer (Baritone); b. 1958, USA. *Career:* Sang Pelléas at the Opéra du Rhin, Strasbourg, and Monteverdi's Orfeo at Milan; Glyndebourne, 1985, as Morales in Carmen and 1987–88 in L'Enfant et les Sortilèges; Don Giovanni on tour to Hong Kong; Lille Opéra in The Rake's progress and Geneva Opera in Manon; Pelléas at the Vienna Staatsoper, La Scala, Florence, Seattle (1993) and Venice (1995); Other roles include Varbel in Cherubini's Lodoiska, at Montpellier, Fürst in Guillaume Tell at Théâtre des Champs Elysées, and Massenet's Lescaut at Opéra-Comique (1999). *Recordings include:* Gluck's Les Pèlerins de la Mecque; Chabrier's Le Roi malgré Lui. *Address:* c/o Seattle Opera Association, PO Box 9248, Seattle, WA 98109, USA.

**WALKER, Nina;** Pianist, Opera Coach and Chorus Master; b. 30 May 1926, Hyde, Cheshire, England; m. Francis Barnes, 2 s., 1 d. *Education:* Pianoforte, Composition, Royal Manchester College of Music, 1945–50; Studied with Alfred Cortot 1953, Lausanne, Bridget Wild, 1965. *Career:* Accompanist and Solo Pianist, Arts Council Recitals, Germany, Italy, Sweden, Greece; Solo Pianist, Marquis de Cuevas Ballet, Paris, 1957; Accompanist, Caballé, La Scala, Milan, Spain, Japan, Germany, Royal Opera House, 1975–90; Masterclasses, Pavarotti, etc.; Chorus Master, Royal Choral Society 1970–75, Huddersfield Choral Society 1980–83; Music Staff, Royal Opera House, 1974–83; Chorus Master 1981–83; Founder, Director, Nimbus Records, 1973. *Recordings:* Nimbus Records, Schubert Song Cycles, Shura Gehrman; Argentinian Songs, Raul Gimenez; Rossini, Soirées Musicales, June Anderson; Complete Schubert Piano Duets, Adrian Farmer; Fauré and Duparc Songs, Shura Gehrman; Mussorgsky (Songs and Dances of Death) Songs I Love, Jenny Drivala, Soprano (Somm Records). *Honours:* Open Scholarship, RMCM, 1946; LRAM, 1948; ARMCM, 1948; Hilary Haworth Memorial Prize, 1949; Edward Hecht Prize, 1949; FRMCM, 1970. *Address:* 12 Ainsdale Road, Ealing, London W5 1JX, England.

**WALKER, Penelope;** singer (mezzo-soprano); b. 12 Oct. 1956, Manchester, England; m. Phillip Joll, two c. *Education:* GSMD, 1974–78 (AGSM and advanced studies); National Opera Studio, 1979–80. *Career:* debut, Royal Albert Hall, 1976; Prom Debut, Grimgerde in Die Walküre with Gwyneth Jones and the National Youth Orchestra, 1989; Canada with Regina Symphony Orchestra, 1993, singing Wesendonck Lieder, and Chausson's Poème de l'amour et de la mer; Royal Opera House, Covent Garden, Die Walküre, 1994; BBC television and radio, including Elgar documentary with Simon Rattle and CBSO, Operatic debut in Paris, 1982 with Opéra-Comique; London debut at Camden Festival, Maria Tudor (Pacini) Opera Rara; ENO, Siegrune (Die Walküre), Kate Pinkerton (Madama Butterfly) and Madame Sosostris (Midsummer Marriage); Opera North, Madame Sosostris; Welsh National Opera, Fricka (Das Rheingold and Die Walküre), Anna in The Trojans, Madame Larina in Eugene Onegin, Tornrak-Main Protagonist in Metcalf Opera; Geneviève, Pelléas; Zürich Opera, 1991, 3rd Lady; Hedwig (William Tell); Mozart Requiem; Grimgerde (Die Walküre), Chatelêt Ring, 1994; Debut at La Scala, 1994; Rossweisse, Covent Garden, 1994; Sang Handel's Riccardo Primo at the 1996 Göttingen Festival. *Recordings:* London Opera, Hippolyta (Midsummer Night's Dream), Virgin, Hickox; Schwertleite (Die Walküre) C. Dohnányi, Cleveland Symphony, Decca; Flosshilde and Fricka, Das Rheingold, Operavox Animated Opera, television; Geneviève, (Pelléas et Mélisande) WNO Video, Peter Stein production, Pierre Boulez; New Israeli Opera, Mamma Lucia (Cavalleria Rusticana). *Current Management:* Robert Gilder & Co., Enterprise House, 59–65 Upper Ground, London, SE1 9PQ, England. *Telephone:* (20) 7928-9008. *Fax:* (20) 7928-9755. *E-mail:* rgilder@robert-gilder.com.

**WALKER, Robert (Ernest);** Composer; b. 18 March 1946, Northampton, England. *Education:* Chorister at St Matthew's Church, Northampton; Choral Scholar, Organ Scholar, at Jesus College, Cambridge. *Career:* Organist and Schoolmaster in Lincolnshire; Freelance Composer from 1975; Featured Composer at 1982 Greenwich Festival; Living composer, Eastern Orchestral Board 1990–91; Works performed by Royal Philharmonic Orchestra at Chichester and Exeter Festivals; Regular broadcasts on BBC Radio 3. *Compositions:* Orchestral, Pavan for violin and strings 1975, At Bignor Hill 1979, Chamber Symphony No. 1 1981, Variations on a Theme of Elgar 1982, Charms and Exultations of Trumpets 1985, Symphony No. 1 1987; Vocal, The Sun on the Celandines 1973, Psalm 150 1974, Requiem 1976, The Norwich Service 1977, Canticle of the Rose 1980, The Sun Used to Shine for tenor, harp and strings 1983, Magnificat and Nunc Dimittis in D 1985, Missa Brevis 1985, Singer by the Yellow River for soprano, flute and harp 1985, Five Summer Madrigals 1985, Jubilate 1987, English Parody Mass for choir and organ 1988; Instrumental, String Quartet No. 1 1982, Five Capriccios 1 and 2 1982–85, Piano Quintet 1984, Passacaglia for 2 pianos, Serenade for flute, harp, violin and cello, Journey into Light, A Choral Symphony 1992 and Music for BBC1, BBC2 and Channel 4; Melelivida, after Catullus, for chorus, percussion, piano and strings, 1997. *Address:* c/o PO Box 46, UBVD 80571, Bali, Indonesia.

**WALKER, Sandra;** Singer (Mezzo-soprano); b. 1 Oct. 1948, Richmond, Virginia, USA. *Education:* Studied at the University of North Carolina and the Manhattan School of Music, New York. *Career:* Debut: San Francisco 1972, as Flosshilde in Das Rheingold; Sang in opera at Philadelphia, Chicago and the New York City Opera; European engagements at Gelsenkirchen, 1985 and Wiesbaden, 1987; Sang the Nurse in Ariane et Barbe-bleue at Amsterdam, 1989; San Francisco Opera 1989 and 1992, as Bradamante in Vivaldi's Orlando Furioso and Hedwige in Guillaume Tell; Lyric Opera Chicago 1990–91, as Olga in Eugene Onegin and Marta in Mefistofele; Other roles include Carmen, Suzuki, Lola, the Marquise in La Fille du Régiment and Frugola in Il Tabarro; Hostess in Boris Godunov at the New York Met, 1998. *Address:* c/o San Francisco Opera, War Memorial Opera House, San Francisco, CA 94102, USA.

**WALKER, Sarah Elizabeth Royle,** CBE, FRCM, FGSM, LRAM; British singer (mezzo-soprano); b. Cheltenham; d. of Elizabeth Brownrigg and Alan Royle Walker; m. Graham Allum 1972. *Education:* Pate's Grammar School for Girls, Cheltenham and Royal Coll. of Music (RCM). *Career:* studied violin and cello and then voice (with Ruth Packer and Cuthbert Smith) at RCM; Martin Musical Trust Scholarship to begin vocal studies with Vera Rozsa 1967; operatic débuts: Kent Opera, Ottavia in Coronation of Poppea 1969, Glyndebourne Festival, Diana/Giove in La Calisto 1970, Scottish Opera, Didon in Les Troyens 1971, ENO, Wellgunde in The Ring 1971; prin. singer with ENO 1972–76; début Royal Opera House, Covent Garden as Charlotte in Werther 1979; début Metropolitan Opera, New York, as Micha in Handel's Samson 1986; has sung opera in Chicago, San Francisco, Göttingen, Geneva, Vienna and Brussels; concert repertoire includes, in addition to standard works, contemporary and avant-garde works by Berio, Boulez, Cage, Ligeti, Xenakis and others; sang Rule Britannia at last night of 1985 and 1989 BBC Promenade Concerts, London; recital début, Wigmore Hall, London 1979; recital tours Australia, N America, Europe; numerous recordings including Handel's Hercules and Julius Caesar and Stravinsky's Rake's Progress; video recordings of Gloriana (title role), Julius Caesar (Cornelia) and King Priam (Andromache); Prince Consort Prof. of Singing RCM 1993–; vocal performance consultant Guildhall School of Music and Drama 1999–; Pres. Cheltenham Bach Choir 1986–; Liveryman Worshipful Co. of Musicians. *Address:* c/o Askonas Holt Ltd, Lonsdale Chambers, 27 Chancery Lane, London, WC2A 1PF, England. *E-mail:* megamezzo@sarahwalker.com (home). *Website:* www .sarahwalker.com (home).

**WALKER, Thomas;** Music Historian; b. 5 Nov. 1936, Malden, Massachusetts, USA; m. Barbara Bland, 30 Jan 1965, 1 d. *Education:* AB, Harvard University, 1961; Fulbright Scholarship, Copenhagen, 1961–62; Graduate Study, University of California, Berkeley. *Career:* Assistant Professor, State University of New York, Buffalo, 1968–73; Lecturer, University of London King's College, 1973–80; Professor Ordinario di Storia della Musica, Universita della Calabria, 1980–81; Universita di Ferrara, 1981–; mem, Consiglio Direttivo, Societa Italiana di Musicologia; Responsible for Rivista Italiana di Musicologia. *Publications:* Edited to date (with Giovanni Morelli and Reinhard Strohm), 8 vols of Drammaturgia Musicale Veneta, Milan, Ricordi, 1983–. *Contributions:* Musica Disciplina, Journal of the A.M.S Musica/Realta, Rivista Italiana di Musicologia; Concert Criticism for The Times and other London newspapers, 1973–77.

**WALKER, Timothy Alexander,** AM, BA, DipEd, AMusA, DipFinMgt; Australian arts administrator; *Chief Executive and Artistic Director, London Philharmonic Orchestra;* b. 23 Nov. 1954, Hobart, Tasmania; s. of Keith James Walker and Elaine Walker (née Edwards). *Education:* Univ. of Tasmania at Hobart, Univ. of New England at Armidale. *Career:* Concert Man., Canberra School of Music 1981–87; Marketing and Development Man., Australian Chamber Orchestra 1987–89, Gen. Man. 1989–99; Chief Exec. World Orchestras 1999–2003; Chief Exec. and Artistic Dir London Philharmonic Orchestra 2003– (also Dir and Trustee); Dir Asscn of British Orchestras; Trustee Henry Wood Hall; mem. Int. Soc. for Performing Arts, Royal Philharmonic Soc. *Honours:* Sidney Myer Performing Arts Awards 1999, Australian Inst. of Arts Man. Nugget Award 2000. *Address:* London Philharmonic Orchestra, Level 4, 89 Albert Embankment, London, SE1 7TP, England (office). *Telephone:* (20) 7840-4218 (office). *Fax:* (20) 7840-4201 (office). *E-mail:* timothy.walker@lpo.org.uk (office). *Website:* www.lpo.org.uk (office).

**WALKER, William;** Singer (Baritone); b. 29 Oct. 1931, Waco, Texas, USA. *Education:* Studied at the Texas Christian University in San Antonio. *Career:* Debut: Fort Worth Opera 1955, as Schaunard in La Bohème; Appearances at Opera Houses in New Orleans, Santa Fe, Milwaukee, San Antonio, Vancouver, Washington and Fort Worth; Metropolitan Opera New York from 1962, as Mozart's Guglielmo and Papageno, Malatesta, Verdi's Germont, Ford, Amonasro and Rigoletto, Valentin, Rossini's Figaro, Marcello, Alfio, Tonio, Escamillo. Noted Concert Artist. *Address:* c/o Metropolitan Opera, Lincoln Center, New York, NY 10023, USA.

**WALLACE, Ian Bryce,** OBE, MA; British singer, actor and broadcaster; b. 10 July 1919, London; s. of the late Sir John Wallace and Mary Temple; m. Patricia Gordon Black 1948; one s. one d. *Education:* Charterhouse and Trinity Hall, Cambridge. *Career:* debut, Schaunard in Puccini's La Bohème, London 1946; appeared at Glyndebourne 1948–61 with roles, including Masetto in Don Giovanni, Bartolo in Le nozze di Figaro and Il Barbiere di Siviglia, Don Magnifico in La Cenerentola and Matteo in Arlecchino; continued to appear in opera in Britain and briefly in Italy until 1970s, appearances including Berlin Festwoche 1954, Teatro Reale, Rome 1955, Scottish Opera 1966–75; later appeared on concert platforms and also in plays, reviews, musicals and pantomimes, as well as in many television and radio shows, notably My Music (BBC) 1966–93; Pres. Inc. Soc. of Musicians 1979–80, Council for Music in Hospitals 1987–99. *Film appearances include* Plenty, Tom Thumb. *Radio:* panellist, 'My Music' (BBC). *Television appearances include:* The Mikado, Singing for Your Supper (opera series, Scottish TV), Porterhouse Blue. *Recordings:* Ian Wallace—My Music, Mikado, Iolanthe, Your Hundred Favourite Hymns, Glyndebourne recordings of Le nozze di Figaro, La Cenerentola, Il Barbiere di Siviglia, Le Comte Ory. *Publications:* I Promise Me You'll Sing Mud (autobiog., vol. I) 1975, Nothing Quite Like It (autobiog., vol. II) 1982, Reflections on Scotland 1988. *Honours:* Hon. MusD (St Andrews Univ.) 1991; Hon. mem. RAM, Royal Coll. of Music. *Current Management:* PFD, Drury House, 34–43 Russell Street, London, WC2B 5HA, England. *Telephone:* (20) 7344-1000. *Fax:* (20) 7836-9539. *E-mail:* postmaster@pfd.co.uk. *Website:* www.pfd.co.uk.

**WALLACE, Stephen;** British singer (countertenor); b. 1970, England. *Education:* Royal Northern Coll. of Music. *Career:* Appearances as Athamas in Handel's Semele for English National Opera and the Staatsoper Berlin; Gluck's Orpheus for English Touring Opera, Orlofsky in Die Fledermaus for Dublin Lyric Opera and Anfinomus in Monteverdi's Ulysses for Opera North; Athamas, and Hasse's Solimano at the Innsbruck Early Music Festival; Madam Bubble in The Pilgrim's Progress by Vaughan Williams at Manchester and Bach's Magnificat for Israel Camerata; Season 2001 with James the Less in Birtwistle's The Last Supper, at Glyndebourne, Monteverdi's Orfeo in Brussels, Gassmann's L'Opera Seria in Paris and Death in Venice for Opera Zuid; Concerts with Les Arts Florissants and Akadamie für Alte Musik Berlin. *Current Management:* Musichall, Vicarage Way, Ringmer, BN8 5LA, England. *Telephone:* (1273) 814240. *Fax:* (1273) 813637. *E-mail:* info@musichall.uk.com. *Website:* www.musichall.uk.com.

**WALLACE, William,** BMus, PhD; Canadian/American composer and educator (retd); b. 25 Nov. 1933, Salt Lake City, UT; m. Harriette Kippley 1957; two s. *Education:* Univ. of Utah, Univ. of Oxford. *Career:* educator, Rutgers and McMaster Univs; commissioned concerti 1995, 1996, 1998, 1999; mem. Canadian League of Composers, Canadian Music Centre, Soc. of Composers, Authors and Music Publrs of Canada. *Compositions:* Concerto Variations for orchestra, Concerto for piano and orchestra, Concerto for clarinet, violin and orchestra, Concerto for clarinet, violin, piano and orchestra, Concerto for piano and orchestra, several chamber works. *Recordings:* Dances and Variations (with London Symphony), Luminations, Epilogue (with Warsaw Chamber Orchestra), Concerto for clarinet, violin, piano and orchestra (with Janáček Symphony Orchestra), Concerto for clarinet, violin and orchestra (with Martinu Symphony Orchestra), Concerto for piano and orchestra (with Slovak Radio Symphony Orchestra). *Publications:* Concerto Variations 1990, Symphonic Variations 1990, Dance Suite: Introduction and Passacaglia 1990. *Address:* PO Box 203, Wilson, WY 83014-0203, USA (home). *Telephone:* (307) 733-3570 (home). *E-mail:* wwallcomp@aol.com (home).

**WALLAT, Hans;** Conductor; b. 18 Oct. 1929, Berlin, Germany. *Education:* Studies at the Conservatory of Scherwin. *Career:* Debut: Metropolitan Opera, 1971; Conductor at Stendal 1950–51; Meiningen 1951–52; Schwerin Opera, 1953–56; Conductor at Leipzig Opera, 1958–61; Stuttgart, 1961–64; Deutsche Oper Berlin, 1964–65; Music Director at Bremen, 1965–70; Mannheim, 1970–80; Regular appearances at the Vienna Staatsoper from 1968; Bayreuth from 1970; Music Director at Dortmund, 1979–85; Deutsche Oper am Rhein, Düsseldorf, from 1986; Conducted new production of Macbeth, 1988; Led the Company in Schreker's Die Gezeichneten at the 1989 Vienna Festival: Many engagements at the Hamburg Staatsoper. *Address:* c/o Deutsche Oper am Rhein, Heinrich-Heine Allee 16, 4000 Düsseldorf, Germany.

**WALLEN, Errollyn,** BMus, MMus; British composer and musician (keyboard); b. 10 April 1958, Belize City, Belize. *Education:* Dance Theatre of Harlem, New York, USA, Goldsmiths' Coll., London, King's Coll., London and The Performing Arts Lab, London. *Career:* joined alternative cabaret band, Pulse as composer, singer and keyboardist 1983–85; freelance keyboard player 1985; opened Wallen Parr recording studio and music-production co., London 1986; composer for corporate video, film and TV 1986–; mem. and composer, Nanquidno 1987; composer-in-residence, Newcastle Electric Music 3 Festival 1988; founder mem., Ensemble X 1990; part-time lecturer, Nottingham Trent Univ. 1991; guest performer and lecturer, Ga State Univ., Atlanta 1991; external examiner, Brighton Univ. 1996; leader of composition workshops in various schools, and in asscn with London Sinfonietta and Hayward Gallery 1997; founder mem. Women in Music 1987–; mem. Performing Rights Soc., British Asscn of Songwriters, Composers and Authors. *Compositions:* It's a Quarter to Nine 1968, Song Cycle 1976, Deaths and Entrances 1979, Concert 1980, Three Piano Pieces 1980, Three Elizabethan Songs 1980, Violin 1981, We Four Kings 1981, Quartet for wind instruments and cello 1982, Trio for two flutes and vibraphone 1982, Lines 1982, Music for small orchestra 1983, Still Lives 1983, Variations for string quartet 1983, Pulse Songs 1983–85, Psalm 150 1986, Second String Quartet 1988, Big Business 1988, Take 1988, Mythologies 1988, Memorias de un corazón en un pueblo pequeño 1988, It All Depends on You 1989, Jelly Dub Mix 1990, The Girl in My Alphabet 1990, Favourite Things 1990, In Our Lifetime 1990, The Singing Ringing Tree 1991, Dark Heart 1991, Until You Do 1991, Having Gathered his Cohorts 1991, I Hate Waiting 1991, Mondrian 1992, Heart 1992, E.D.R. 1993, Four Figures with Harlequin (opera) 1993, 1-2-3-4 (ballet) 1993, Waiting (ballet) 1993, Concerto for percussion and orchestra 1993–94, My Lazy Goodheart 1994, Are You Worried about the Rising Cost of Funerals?: Five Simple Songs 1994, Gastarbeiter 1994, Teeth 1994, Dogness 1994, Phonecalls from Besieged Cities 1994, Chorale 1995, Jig 1995, Look! No Hands! (opera) 1995, The Constant Nymph (for radio) 1996, Prelude 1996, Hunger 1996, Music for Alien Tribes 1996, Earth Stood Hard as Iron 1996, The Devil and the Doctor 1997, One Week Short of a Valentine 1997, Shit in her Eyes 1997, Chrome 1997, Never Ending 1997, Horseplay (ballet) 1997, Oil 1997–98. *Recordings:* The Girl In My Alphabet 1990, Meet Me At Harold Moore's 1998, Errollyn 2004, Spirit Symphony – Speed-Dating for Two Orchestras (BBC Radio 3 Listeners Award British Composer Awards British Acad. of Composers and Songwriters 2005). *Honours:* Arts Council Bursary 1987, Holst Award 1991, Peter Whittingham Award 1995. *Address:* c/o Volker Schirp, Peters Edition, 10–12 Baches Street, London, N1 6DN, England (office). *E-mail:* errollyn@errollynwallen.com (office). *Website:* www.errollynwallen.com.

**WALLÉN, Martti;** Opera Singer (Bass); b. 20 Nov. 1948, Helsinki, Finland. *Education:* Sibelius Academy, Helsinki. *Career:* Debut: Helsinki; Finnish National Opera, 1973–75; Principal Bass, Royal Opera, Stockholm, 1975–; Roles include Colline (Bohème), Ferrando, Philip II (Don Carlos), Sparafucile (Rigoletto), Spirit Messenger (Die Frau ohne Schatten), Dikoy (Katya Kabanova), Baron Ochs, Marke, Landgraf, Daland, Orestes, Pimen, Falstaff; Roles in Finnish modern operas such as The Last Temptations (Paavo), The Horseman (Judge); Sang Fasolt in Das Rheingold at Helsinki, 1996. *Address:* c/o Finnish National Opera, Bulevardi 23–27, 00180 Helsinki 18, Finland.

**WALLER, Adalbert;** Singer (baritone); b. 1932, Danzig, Germany. *Education:* Studied in Frankfurt. *Career:* Opera appearances at Bielefeld, 1958–59; Passau, 1962–65; Aachen, 1968–74, as Rigoletto, Scarpia, Alfio; Sang Telramund in Lohengrin, 1976–77; Sang Wozzeck in the Brazilian premiere of Berg's opera, São Paulo, Cologne, 1981, as the Dutchman; Member of Frankfurt Opera Company, from 1981; Brunswick, 1985 as Reimann's Lear and Antwerp 1982, as Dr Schön in Lulu; Further engagements as Alberich in Der Ring des Nibelungen at Buenos Aires, 1982; Kurwenal at Bologna, 1984; Season 2000–01 in Reimann's Gespenstersonate, at Berlin, and Schigolch in Lulu at the Vienna Staatsoper; Other centres as Hans Sachs, Wotan, Falstaff, Count Luna.

**WALLEZ, Jean-Pierre;** French violinist and conductor; *Professor of Violin, Geneva Conservatory;* b. 18 March 1939, Conservatoire de Lille, Conservatoire

Nat. Supérieure de Musique, Paris, France. *Education:* Lille and Paris Conservatories. *Career:* Founder and Leader Ensemble Instrumental de France 1968–83; Leader Orchestre de Paris 1975–77; Founder and Dir Ensemble Orchestral de Paris 1978–87; first Guest Conductor Sonderjyllands Symfoniorkester, Denmark; Musical Dir Orchestre Royal de Chambre de Wallonie, Örebro Orchestra, Sweden; Prin. Guest Conductor Orchestra Ensemble Kanazawa, Japan 1994–2000, Orchestre Pasdeloup, Paris 1996–2002; Artistic Dir Albi Music Festival 1974–91; premiered works by Landowski, Bondon, Martinů, Jolivet, Florentz, Finzi, Sciortino, Loussier, Hersant, Capdenat, Bon; Prof. of Violin, Geneva Conservatory 1987–. *Honours:* Commandeur, Ordre nat. du Mérite, Chevalier, Légion d'Honneur, Officier, Ordre des Arts et Lettres. *Current Management:* Agence Artistique Monique Cazeneuve, 5–7 avenue Mac-Mahon, 75017 Paris, France. *Telephone:* 1-43-80-15-86. *Fax:* 1-46-22-58-76. *E-mail:* mcazeneuve@free.fr. *Website:* www.monique-cazeneuve.com. *Address:* 15 route de Florissant, 1206 Geneva, Switzerland (home). *E-mail:* jwallez@dplanet.ch (home).

**WALLFISCH, Elizabeth,** FRAM; Australian violinist; *Professor of Baroque Violin, Royal Conservatoire, The Hague;* b. 28 Jan. 1952, Melbourne; m. Raphael Wallfisch. *Career:* began performing on 'modern' violin; early professional engagements included concerto performances with orchestras in Australia and the UK, including the London Mozart Players and the Royal Liverpool Philharmonic Orchestra; concerts, recordings and broadcasts, both as concerto soloist (often directing from the violin), and as a recitalist with the Locatelli Trio (later renamed Convivium), which she founded in 1989 with Paul Nicholson and Richard Tunnicliffe; regularly leads the Orchestra of the Age of Enlightenment and the Raglan Baroque Players and, occasionally, the London Classical Players under Roger Norrington; has performed works from the later periods, including Spohr's Concerto No. 8 for the BBC with the Ulster Orchestra under Roy Goodman; the Brahms Double Concerto with Raphael Wallfisch; the Viotti Concerto No. 22 with the Hanover Band; the Brahms Violin Concerto with the Orchestra of the Age of Enlightenment under Charles Mackerras; regular visits to her native Australia where, in 1992, she was welcomed as Artist-in-Residence at Melbourne Univ., returned in 1993 with the Locatelli Trio for four week tour and in 1995 and 1996 toured and performed as soloist; featured soloist and leader of orchestra at the annual Carmel and Boulder Bach Festivals, USA; Locatelli Trio made USA debut at the Frick Collection 1994; visited Utrecht, Irsee and Amsterdam Locatelli Festivals 1995; has directed the Britten-Pears Orchestra, Hanover Band, Les Musiciens du Louvre, Nordwestdeutsche Philharmonie, Camerata of Athens, Israel Chamber Orchestra, American Bach Soloists, Brandywine Baroque, Australian Chamber Orchestra, Queensland Philharmonic, Melbourne Chamber Orchestra, the Acad. of Melbourne, Brandenburg Orchestra of Australia; recent enagements include debut with MDR Orchestra Leipzig performing Myslivecek Concerto and directing from the violin; Handel Concertos with the Orchestra of the Age of Enlightenment; Vivaldi's L'Estro Armonico with Les Musiciens du Louvre; Concertos with Netherlands Bach Soc., Staatstheater Wiesbaden and Tafelmusik, Toronto. *Recordings:* Complete Violin Concerti by Bach (including those reconstructed from Bach's Harpsichord Concertos in D minor and G minor), Haydn, including the Sinfonia Concertante, recently recorded a series of early Italian Violin Sonatas with the Locatelli Trio, Locatelli, Tartini and Corelli with Albinoni and Veracini, Trio have also recorded Handel Sonatas Op 1, Locatelli Violin Concertos Op 3, 'L'Arte del Violino' performed by Elizabeth Wallfisch with Raglan Baroque Players under Nicholas Kraemer, Locatelli Concerti Grossi (also with Raglan Baroque Players), Locatelli Opus 8 Sonatas with The Locatelli Trio, solo recording of Bach Solo Sonatas and Partitas. *Publications:* The Art of Playing 'Chin-Off' for the Brave and the Curious 2003. *Current Management:* Clarion/Seven Muses, 47 Whitehall Park, London, N19 3TW, England. *Telephone:* (20) 7272-4413. *E-mail:* admin@c7m.co.uk.

**WALLFISCH, Lory;** Pianist, Harpsichordist and Professor of Music; b. 21 April 1922, Ploesti, Romania; m. Ernst Wallfisch, 12 Nov 1944, deceased 1979, 1 s. *Education:* Royal Academy of Music, Bucharest; Studied with Florica Muzicescu and M Jora. *Career:* Debut: Duo with Ernst Wallfisch, Bucharest, 1943; Taught: Bucharest; Switzerland; Cleveland, USA; Detroit; Smith College, Northampton, Massachusetts, 1964–; Professor of Music; Visiting Professor, International Menuhin Music Academy, Switzerland; Masterclasses and lectures, USA and abroad; Lecture-performances on Enescu, Lipatti, other Romanian composers; Formerly Pianist-Harpsichordist, Wallfisch Duo with violist husband; Concerts, television appearances, radio recordings, USA, Canada, Europe, North Africa, Israel; Occasional appearances as soloist and in chamber music; Participated in music festivals, Western Europe and the United Kingdom; In recent years has played in premieres of Lipatti's works in Switzerland, Italy, Germany and Moscow; Member of Jury, International Piano Festival and Competition, University of Maryland, 1986. *Recordings:* For various labels; Several CDs as pianist of the Wallfisch-Duo (with late husband) reissued; All-ENESCU: solo, piano sonata and cello sonata with cellist Julius Berger. *Address:* 7 Jay Court, Avon CT 06001, USA.

**WALLFISCH, Raphael;** British cellist; b. 15 June 1953, London, England; s. of Peter Wallfisch. *Education:* Royal Acad with Derek Simpson, studied with Amarylis Fleming, Amadeo Baldavino in Rome, Gregory Piatigorsky in California. *Career:* since winning the 1977 Gaspar Cassado Int. Cello Competition in Florence, appeared widely in Europe, Australia, USA with Indianapolis Symphony Orchestra 1988; chamber music formerly with Heifetz

in California; with Amadeus Quartet, recitals with his father; Solti on television; piano trio concerts with Ronald Thomas and Anthony Goldstone; performances with most major British orchestras, including Prokofiev's Sinfonia Concertante at the Festival Hall, Promenade Concerts, London 1989, James Macmillan's Concerto at the 1999 Proms. *Recordings:* Tchaikovsky's Rococo Variations, Strauss's Don Quixote and Romanze, Britten's Cello Symphony, Prokofiev's Sinfonia Concertante, Concertos by Shostakovich, Barber, Kabalevsky, Khachaturian, Finzi, Bax, Moeran, Bliss, Dvořák and Brahms, Delius Violin and cello concerto (with Tasmin Little), Cello Concerto. *Address:* Clarion-Seven Muses, 64 Whitehall Park, London N19 3TN, England.

**WALLIS, Delia;** singer (mezzo-soprano); b. 1944, Chelmsford, Essex, England. *Education:* Guildhall School of Music, London. *Career:* debut at Wexford Festival, 1968, as Annius in La Clemenza di Tito; Welsh National Opera from 1968, as Hansel and Cherubino, Covent Garden, from 1970; Glyndebourne, 1971–72, 1976, as Cathleen in Maw's The Rising of the Moon; Composer in Ariadne auf Naxos and Cherubino; Has sung at the Hamburg Staatsoper, from 1973. *Recordings:* Manon Lescaut, EMI.

**WALLSTRÖM, Tord;** Singer (Baritone); b. 1952, Sweden. *Education:* Stockholm Music Academy. *Career:* Engagements at the Royal Opera, Stockholm, the Drottningholm Theatre, and at Gothenburg; Appearances in Soliman II by J M Kraus and as Masetto in Don Giovanni; Essen Opera and Stockholm from 1985, as Telramund in Lohengrin, Don Giovanni, Cecil in Roberto Devereux, Tonio in Pagliacci and Klingsor in Parsifal (1995); Guest appearances in Scandinavia and Germany as Handel's Giulio Cesare and Arsamenes (Xerxes), Mandryka in Arabella and Fra Melitone in La Forza del Destino; Frequent concert engagements. *Recordings include:* Soliman II by Kraus, and Don Giovanni.

**WALMSLEY-CLARK, Penelope;** Singer (Soprano); b. 19 Feb. 1949, London, England. *Career:* Sang the Queen of Night in Die Zauberflöte at Covent Garden; Returned for British premiere of Berio's Un Re in Ascolto, 1989; Glyndebourne Festival in The Electrification of the Soviet Union by Nigel Osborne; Has sung the Queen of Night for Geneva Opera, and English National Opera, 1989; Ligeti's Le Grand Macabre in Vienna; Concert engagements include the Brahms Requiem at the City of London Festival; Carmina Burana with the London Symphony Orchestra; Elijah in Liverpool with Marek Janowski; Shostakovich Symphony No. 14, with City of London Sinfonia; Title roles in Maria Stuarda and Norma, Leonora in La Forza del Destino and Il Trovatore, all with Scottish Opera; Concert performances of the operas Moses und Aron at the Festival Hall and Elegy for Young Lovers at La Fenice, Venice; Further appearances in Vienna, Berlin, Salzburg, Frankfurt, Czechoslovakia and Russia; Conductors include Birtwistle, Boulez, Colin Davis, Charles Groves, Haitink, Norrington and Leppard; Sang as Guinevere in the world premiere of Birtwistle's Gawain at Covent Garden, 1991; Donna Anna for English National Opera, 1995; Hecuba in King Priam for Flanders Opera, 1996. *Recordings:* A Mind of Winter by George Benjamin with London Sinfonietta; Song Offerings by Jonathan Harvey, with London Sinfonietta; Gawain, complete opera, under Elgar Howarth; Le Grand Macabre, by Ligeti. *Address:* c/o Allied Artists, 42 Montpelier Square, London SW7 1JZ, England.

**WALSH, Louise;** Singer (Soprano); b. 16 March 1966, Dublin, Ireland. *Education:* Trinity College, and College of Music, Dublin; Royal Northern College of Music, and National Opera Studio, London. *Career:* Opera engagements as Susanna, and La Fée in Cendrillon, for RNCM; Britten's Tytania for the Broomhill Trust, Janáček's Vixen for Opera Northern Ireland and in Handel's Tamerlano for the Covent Garden Festival; Stuttgart Opera (contract 1995–97) in Hansel and Gretel, as Serpina in La Serva Padrona, Servilia in La Clemenza di Tito, Pauline in La Vie Parisienne for Stuttgart Opera, Xenia in Boris Godunov and Musetta in La Bohème; Ilia in Idomeneo for Opera Northern Ireland, 1997; Adele in Die Fledermaus, for Opera Ireland, 1998, and Carl Rosa opera company, 1999; Rosina in Sarlatan by P. Hass, for Wexford Festival Opera, 1998; Anne Trulove in The Rake's Progress for Opera Theatre, 1999; Concerts include Bach's St John Passion and Mass in B Minor, Elijah, Carmina Burana, Messiah and Mozart's Mass in C Minor; Engaged as a Flowermaiden at Brussels, 1998 (production of Parsifal). *Honours:* Prizewinner, 1994 Vienna Belvedere International Singing Competition; Elizabeth Harwood Memorial Scholarship, Curtis Gold Medal for Singing and Ricordi Prize for Opera, at the RNCM. *Current Management:* Neil Dalrymple at Music International. *Address:* 89 Ridgemount Gardens, London WC1E 7AY, England.

**WALTER, Bertrand;** Violinist; b. 17 March 1962, Metz, France. *Education:* Studied at the Metz and Paris Conservatories. *Career:* After study with Franco Gulli at the University of Indiana (1985–86) became co-leader of the Orchestre Philharmonique de France; With violist Laurent Verney and cellist Dominique de Williencourt founded the string trio BWV and has given many recital concerts throughout France. *Honours:* Prizes at the Paris Conservatoire and the 1980 Paganini International Competition. *Address:* Orchestre Philharmonique de France, 116 Avenue de Pres Kennedy, 75786 Paris, Cédex 16, France.

**WALTER, Horst;** Musicologist; b. 5 March 1931, Hannover, Germany; m. Liesel Roth, 1959, 2 s. *Education:* Musicology, German Philology, Philosophy, University of Cologne; DPh. *Career:* Scientific Co-operator, Joseph Haydn Institute, Cologne, 1962–92; Director of the Institute, 1992–96. *Publications include:* Music History of Lüneburg, from end 16th Century to Early 18th

Century, Tutzing, 1967; Editor, Complete Haydn Edition Symphonies i/4, i/17. 1964, 1966; Baryton trios xiv/5, 1968; La Vera Costanza xxv/8, 1976; Keyboard Concertos xv/2, 1983; Accompanied Keyboard Divertimenti and Concertini xvi, 1987; Wind-band Divertimenti and Scherzandi viii/2, 1991; String Quartets op.76, op.77 and op.103, xii/6, 2003; G van Swieten's Manuscript Notebooks of The Creation and The Seasons; Haydn Studies i/4, 1967; Haydn's Pianos, Haydn Studies, ii/4, 1970; The Biographical Relationship Between Haydn and Beethoven, Report of Bonn Conference, 1970, 1973; An Unknown Schütz Autograph in Wolfenbüttel, Festschrift K G Fellerer, 1973; The Posthorn Signal in the Works of Haydn and Other 18th Century Composers, Haydn Studies iv/1, 1976; Haydn's Pupils at the Esterhazy Court, Festschrift H Hüschen, 1980; Haydn Bibliography, 1973–83, Haydn Studies v/4, 1985; Haydn Bibliography 1984–90, Haydn Studies vi/3, 1992; Hanky-panky Around Haydn, Haydn Studies, vi/4, 1994; String Quartets Dedicated to Haydn, Tradition and Reception, Report of the Gesellschaft für Musikforschung Köln 1982, 1985; On Haydn's "Characteristic" Symphonies, Internationales Musikwissen- schaftliches Symposium Eisenstadt 1995, Eisenstadt 2000. Contributions: Music Past and Present, MGG; New Grove Dictionary; Proceedings International Haydn Conference, Washington DC, USA 1975, 1981; International Haydn Congress, Vienna 1982, 1986. Address: Herkenfelder Weg 146, 51467 Bergisch Gladbach, Germany.

**WALTER, Rudolf,** DPhil; professor of musicology; b. 24 Jan. 1918, Gross Wierau, Silesia; m. Marianne Marx 1946; one s. three d. Education: Univs of Breslau, Strasbourg and Mainz, Coll. of Stuttgart, Univ. of Mainz. Career: founder and conductor of Kissinger Kantorei and Cappella Palatina Heidelberg; radio broadcasts in Germany, Austria, Switzerland, Czechoslovakia and France; Prof. of Musicology, Univ. of Mainz. Recordings: 12 organ albums; choral album of Monteverdi's Mass for four voices. Publications include: M. Brosig 1988, J. C. F. Fischer 1990, Musikgeschichte der Zisterzienserabtei Grüssau von 1700 bis zur Aufhebung 1810 mit Musikinventar 1996, Organ works of J. A. Silbermann, Organ works of J. Ph Seuffert, The Organ works of O. Messiaen, Max Reger's Sacred Music, Silesian Musicology, Sueddeutsche Orgelmeister des Barock (ed., 21 vols), Orgelwerke von Schlick, Tunder, Sweelinck, Reichardt, Merulo, Fasolo, Trabaci, Gottlieb Muffat, Organum in missa cantata (three vols), Sacred vocal works of German, English, French, Spanish and Italian Masters, J. C. F. Fischer, Psalmi vespertini, J. C. Fischer, Litaniae Lauretanae, and T. Fritsch, Novum et insigne opus musicum (120 motets in two vols), F. X. A. Murschhauser, Vespertinus... cultus in Denkmäler der Tonkunst in Bayern, J. J. Fux (8 Offertoria and 10 Offertoria in two vols, in Gesamtausgabe der Werke), Musikinventare der Breslauer Kathedrale von 1761 u. 1825 1988, Musikinventare der Kreuzheren in Neisse von 1825 1997, Musikinventare der Jesuiten u. Pfarrkirche Glatz 1997, Musik zur Verehrung der hl Hedwig aus Schlesien 1995, Die Rezeption der Kirchenmusik Carl Ditters von Dittersdorfs in Schlesien 1997, Das Reimoffizium der hl Hedwig 1997, Joseph Ignaz Schnabels Figuralmusik zur Vesper (in Festschrift J. J. Menzel) 1998, Ein schlesisches Reise-Diarium zum Zisterzienser-Generalkapitel 1771 1999, Zur Kirchenmusikpflege an Hl. Geist, Heidelberg, 17–20 Jh, in Jahrbuch zur Geschichte von Heidelberg, Band 8–10 2003–05; contrib. articles on southern German organ music, Austrian musicology, to books, including New Grove 2001, and to journals. Address: Lessing Strasse 3, 69214 HD-Eppelheim, Germany. Telephone: (6221) 764743 (home).

**WALTHER, Ute;** Singer (Mezzo-soprano); b. 23 June 1945, Jena, Germany. Education: Musikhochschule, Berlin. Career: Debut: Schwerin, 1968, as Octavian in Der Rosenkavalier; Sang at Rostock, 1974–80, Dresden Staatsoper from 1980 and Deutsche Oper Berlin, 1986; Tours of Japan with the Vienna Staatsoper and Deutsche Oper companies, as Fricka and Waltraute in The Ring; Guest appearances at Warsaw, Cologne (Brangaene in Tristan, 1990), the Moscow Bolshoi, Edinburgh Festival and Madrid; Season 1995–96 at Berlin as Brangaene, Dorabella, Cherubino, Carmen, Eboli in Don Carlos, Amneris, and the Hostess in Boris Godunov; Sang the Witch in Hansel and Gretel, season 1997–98; Season 2000 at the Deutsche Oper as Brangaene, Wagner's Mary, Nicolai's Frau Fluth and Meg Page in Falstaff; Many concert appearances, notably in music by Bach. Address: c/o Deutsche Oper Berlin, Richard Wagner Str 10, 10585 Berlin, Germany.

**WALZ, Melanie;** Singer (Soprano); b. 1965, Stuttgart, Germany. Career: Many appearances in concert and opera throughout Europe, notably in contemporary music; Sang in Einstein on the Beach and The Fall of the House of Usher by Philip Glass, at Stuttgart; Hamburg, Staatsoper 1997, in the premiere of Helmut Lachenmann's Mädchen mit den Schwefelhölzern; Engagements at the Vienna Konzerthaus in Luigi Nono's La fabbrica illuminata and Intolleranza, Noti by Heinz Holliger, and Schoenberg's Moses und Aron (2001); Basle Theatre from 1998, as Mozart's Blondchen and Sophie in Der Rosenkavalier. Address: Hamburgische Staatsoper, Grosse Theatesstrasse 34, D-20354 Hamburg, Germany.

**WANAMI, Takoyoshi;** Concert Violinist; b. 1945, Tokyo, Japan; m. Mineko Tsuchiya. Education: Studied with Kichinouska Tsuji, Saburo Sumi and Toshiya Eto. Career: Debut: Played the Glazunov Concerto with the Japan Philharmonic, 1963; Performed with orchestras including the Leipzig Gewandhaus, City of Birmingham Symphony, Bournemouth Symphony, BBC Philharmonic, BBC National Orchestra of Wales, London Mozart Players, Zürich Chamber, Festival Strings Lucerne, Vienna Chamber, Slovak Chamber and Boston Pops; Conductors include R Barshai, G Bertini, R Fruhbeck de Burgos, K Masur, T Otaka and S Ozawa; Collaborated with

pianists including S Lorenzi, B Canino, E Lush, G Pratley and H Barth; Duo partnership with the pianist Mineko Tsuchiya since 1980; Festivals: Lucerne International Music Festival 1980 and 1988; Festival Estivalde in Paris, 1981; Schaffhausen Bach Festival, 1982; Seon Bach Festival, 1984; Japan Week in Cairo, 1986; Meiningen Summer Festival, 1991; Tours: USA, 1973, 1981, 1989; Soviet Union, 1983, 1989, 1991; Egypt and Morocco, 1986; Gave numerous recitals at Queen Elizabeth Hall, Purcell Room and Wigmore Hall in London including a Solo Recital of 20th Century Violin Music in 1987; In Tokyo, directing Izumigoh Festival Orchestra, 1991; Annual recital entitled, Christmas Bach Series, 1991–; Two performances with Academy of St Martin in the Fields under Neville Marriner in Japan, 1994; Performed Brahms' Concerto in Budapest, 1994; Recital with Mineko Tsuchiya at St John's Smith Square in London, 1995; Fiftieth Birthday Concert in Tokyo in April 1995; Recital at St Johns, London, 1997. Recordings include: Tchaikovsky, Bruch and Mendelssohn Concertos with the Philharmonia; Bach Concertos with the London Mozart Players; Brahms and Schumann Concertos with London Philharmonic; Bach Solo Sonatas and Partitas (Complete) Ysaÿe Six Solo Sonatas; Brahms Violin Sonatas with Mineko Tsuchiya. Publications: Autobiography, The Gift of Music, 1994. Honours: Suntory Music Award, 1995; Prize Winner at the 1965 Long-Thibaud Competition and the Carl Flesch International, London 1970; Ysaÿe Medal, 1970; Mobil Music Award, 1993. Address: 61 Woodhill Crescent, Kenton, Harrow HA3 0LU, England.

**WANG, Jian;** Chinese cellist; b. 1969, Shanghai. Education: Shanghai Conservatoire, Yale School of Music. Career: debut, Brahms Double Concerto with Maxim Vengerov and the Mahler Youth Orchestra under Claudio Abbado 1995; appeared with Royal Concertgebouw Orchestra and Riccardo Chailly in Amsterdam and on tour in China 1996; has performed with many of the world's leading orchestras, including Philadelphia, Cleveland, Minnesota and Chicago Symphony Orchestras, NHK Symphony, Hong Kong Philharmonic, Zurich Tonhalle, Stockholm Philharmonic, Santa Cecilia, Halle, Mahler Chamber and the Orchestre National de France; played with many conductors, including Dutoit, Krivine, Sawallisch, Bergland, Eschenbach, Chung, Hickox, Neeme Jarvi, Ashkenazy, Wigglesworth and Harding. Recordings include: Brahms Double Concerto (with Berlin Philharmonic Orchestra, Claudio Abbado and Gil Shaham), Haydn Concerti (with the Gulbenkian Orchestra under Muhai Tang), Messaien's Quartet for the End of Time (with Myung-Whun Chung, Gil Shaham and Paul Meyer), Brahms, Mozart and Schumann chamber music (with Pires and Dumay), Baroque album (with the Camerata Salzburg). Current Management: Askonas Holt Ltd, Lonsdale Chambers, 27 Chancery Lane, London, WC2A 1PF, England. Telephone: (20) 7400-1700. Fax: (20) 7400-1799. E-mail: info@askonasholt.co.uk. Website: www.askonasholt.co.uk.

**WANG, Jin;** Chinese conductor; Director of Music, Komische Oper Berlin; b. 1960, Beijing. Education: Vienna Acad. of Music, studied with Karl Österreicher, Leopold Hager, Zubin Mehta, Leonard Bernstein. Career: has conducted orchestras, including Göteborg Symphony, Oslo Philharmonic, Helsinki Philharmonic, Finnish Nat. Radio Symphony, Berlin Radio-Symphony, Royal Liverpool Philharmonic, Toscanini Symphony, Yomiuri Nippon Symphony, Tokyo, Seoul Philharmonic, Singapore Symphony, Taiwan Nat. Symphony; fmr Chief Conductor Moravian Philharmonic Orchestra, Prin. Guest Conductor Janácek Philharmonie, Prin. Guest Conductor Romanian Radio Symphony; Conductor and Dir of Music, Komische Oper Berlin 2003–, performances there include Carmen, Don Giovanni, Der Freischütz, La Bohème, Rigoletto, The Rider with the Wind in his Hair, Albert Herring; Guest Prof. of Conducting, Swedish Royal Acad. of Music, Göteborg Music Acad. Compositions include: Tibet Impressions, Suites 1–3. Honours: prizewinner Prague Spring Conducting Competition 1991, Nicolai Malko Competition, Arturo Toscanini Competition. Address: Komische Oper Berlin, Stiftung Oper in Berlin, Behrenstraße 55–57, Berlin 10117, Germany (office). E-mail: info@komische-oper-berlin.de (office). Website: www.komische-oper-berlin.de (office).

**WANGEMANN, Hendrikje;** Singer (Soprano); b. 1961, Kropstädt, Germany. Education: Leipzig Musikhochschule. Career: Debut: Armida in Handel's Rinaldo at Halle; Sang at Halle, 1887–91, as Asteria in Handel's Tamerlano, Gilda, Susanna, Marzelline in Fidelio, Nannetta in Falstaff and Micaela in Carmen; Leipzig Opera from 1991, as Musetta, Zerlina (1994) and Amanda in Ligeti's Le Grand Macabre; Guest appearances in Austria, Switzerland, Hungary and Germany; Other roles include Mozart's Pamina and Servilia, Baroness in Lortzing's Der Wildschütz and Jenny in Weill's Mahagonny; Season 1996 in Greek by Marc Anthony Turnage, at Leipzig. Recordings include: Deutsche Sinfonia by Hanns Eisler.

**WANGENHEIM, Volker;** German conductor, composer and academic; b. 1 July 1928, Berlin; m. Brigitte Antweiler; one d. Education: Musikhochschule, Berlin. Career: founder, Principal Dir, Berlin Mozart Orchestra 1950–59; Conductor, Dir of Studies, Mecklenburg State Opera, Schwerin 1951–52; Conductor, Orchestra Berlin Musikfreunde 1952–55, Berlin Academic Orchestra 1954–57; first concert with Berlin Philharmonic Orchestra 1954; guest conductor, Germany and worldwide 1953–; Music Dir, City of Bonn; Principal Conductor, Orchestra of Beethovenhalle and Philharmonic Choir, Bonn; Artistic Dir, Bonn Beethoven Festivals 1957–78; Gen. Music Dir, Bonn 1963–78; Prof., Musikhochschule, Cologne 1972–99; int. conducting class; Dean, Artistic Dept I 1991–93; mem. of the Bd, German Music Council 1980–88; jury mem., int. music competitions, Besançon 1991, Copenhagen 1995, Geneva 1996; co-founder, Principal Conductor, Artistic Dir, German

Nat. Youth Orchestra 1969–84; co-founder, German Nat. Student Orchestra. *Recordings:* classical, Baroque, chamber orchestra, symphonic and choral. *Compositions:* Sonatina for orchestra, Sinfonietta Concertante, Concerto for strings, Sinfonia Notturna, Sinfonie 1966, Klangspiel I and II, Hymnus Choralis for String Quintet, Choral works a cappella, Mass: Stabat Mater, Pater Noster, Nicodemus Iesum nocte visitat, Cantus de cognitione, Canticum sponsae, Hymnus Mariae, Parvulus natus est nobis, Domine, probasti me, Non moriar, sed vivam, Quid est homo, Deus caritas est, Dei iudiciorum altitudo, Antiphonae Marianae, Cantus de luce, Cantica de pace, Altenkirchener Hymnar, Te Deum, Pange Lingua, Veni Creator, Veni Sancte Spiritus, O Lux beata Trinitas, Lucis Creator optime, Nolite thesaurizare, Lucerna corporis tui, Lex charitatis, Emitte Lucem tuam, Pacem relinquo vobis, Verba de confessionibus Augustini, Rerum, Deus, tenax vigor, Vox clara ecce intonat, Christe, redemptor omnium, A solis ortus cardine, Qui habitat in adiutorio Altissimi, Cor mundum crea in me, Exsultate, iusti, in Domino, Amoris sensus erige, Lux aeterna, Lumen potens, Telluris ingens conditor, Verbum Ruth, Caeli enarrant, Dei providentia, Misericordiae Domini, Dignus est Agnus, Rex sum ego, Seclebit Dominus Rex, Quaerite Dominum, Redemisti nos Domine, Cogitationes Cordis eius, Psalms 1, 13, 23, 57, 62, 67, 70, 84, 86, 90, 93, 103, 114, 121, 123, 130, 131, 133, German and European folk songs. *Honours:* City of Berlin Arts Prize 1954, German Cross of Merit 1972, Order of Merit for Polish Culture 1978. *Address:* Gerhart-Hauptmann-Strasse 12, 57610 Altenkirchen, Germany.

**WARD, David W. B.;** Musician, Pianist, Conductor, Teacher and Lecturer; b. 28 Dec. 1942, Sheffield, Yorkshire, England; m. Elizabeth Gladstone 1963, 1 s., 1 d. *Education:* Music Scholar at Bryanston School, Dorset, 1956–61; Music Exhibitioner, Caius College, Cambridge, 1962–63; Royal College of Music, London, 1963–67; Studied with Nadia Boulanger, Paris, 1968–69. *Career:* Debut: Purcell Room, London, 1972; Many concerts as soloist in the United Kingdom, Netherlands, France, Germany, America and Australia; Conductor of La Spiritata Chamber Orchestra and others; Professor at Royal College of Music, 1969–; Well-known for interpretation of Mozart; Now playing harpsichord and more especially the fortepiano; Teacher of fortepiano, Birmingham Conservatoire; Examiner, Associated Board of Royal Schools of Music; Much recital work in the United Kingdom and Netherlands. *Recordings:* Mozart Piano Music, 3 records; Tapes of Duets with Susan Rennie and Solo Works; Aslo radio recordings with BBC, RTE and ORTF; Mozart piano and violin sonatas with Yossi Zivoni; Haydn Trios and Piano Solos with Badinage, on fortepiano and original instruments; Duets and solos by J. C. and C. P. E. Bach, Haydn and first recording of a new piece by David Stoll for two fortepianos with Marejka Smit-Sibinga, Amsterdam; Mozart Keyboard Music on fortepiano; David Stoll Chamber Music, including a Piano Sonata and a Two Piano Sonata with Noel Skinner. *Address:* 4 Patten Road, London SW18 3RH, England.

**WARD, Joseph;** Singer (Tenor) and Vocal Consultant; b. 22 May 1942, Preston, Lancashire, England. *Education:* Studied at the Royal Manchester College of Music; FRMCM; FRNCM. *Career:* Debut: Royal Opera House, Covent Garden, 1962; Many appearances in opera in the USA, London, Germany, Portugal, France and Austria; Formerly Head of vocal studies at the Royal Northern College of Music; Formerly Principal Tenor, Royal Opera House, Covent Garden; Consultant in Opera and Vocal Studies at the Hong Kong Academy for performing arts; Director of Opera, Freelance; Course Director, European Opera Centre, Manchester from 1998 (Tosca and Mozart's Lucio Silla); Many BBC broadcasts. *Recordings:* Norma, Beatrice di Tenda, Montezuma, Wuthering Heights, Pilgrim's Progress and Albert Herring; Numerous others for major labels. *Honours:* O.B.E., 1991. *Address:* c/o Royal Northern College of Music, 124 Oxford Road, Manchester, M13 9RD, England.

**WARD, Nicholas;** Violinist; b. 1954, England. *Education:* Royal Northern Coll. of Music and in Brussels. *Career:* joined the Royal Philharmonic in 1977 and is co-leader of the City of London Sinfonia and Dir of the Northern Chamber Orchestra, Manchester; mem. of the Instrumental Quintet of London, with repertoire including works by Jongen, Mozart, Debussy and Villa-Lobos; mem. of the Melos and Radcliffe Ensembles. *Current Management:* Upbeat Classical Management, PO Box 479, Uxbridge, UB8 2ZH, England. *Telephone:* (1895) 259441. *Fax:* (1895) 259341. *E-mail:* info@ upbeatclassical.co.uk. *Website:* www.upbeatclassical.co.uk.

**WARD JONES, Peter Arthur,** MA, FRCO; Music Librarian, Musicologist, Organist and Harpsichordist; b. 30 March 1944, Chester, England; m. Shirley Bailey 1978 (died 2001); one s. one d. *Education:* Balliol Coll., Oxford. *Career:* part-time Prof., Royal Coll. of Music 1967–69; music librarian, Bodlian Library, Oxford 1969–; harpsichordist, City of Oxford Orchestra 1968–99; conductor, Oxford Harmonic Soc. 1971–2000; mem. of editorial bd, Leipzig Mendelssohn edition 1993; mem. Royal Coll. of Organists, Royal Musical Asscn, Mendelssohn-Gesellschaft. *Publications:* Catalogue of the Mendelssohn Papers in the Bodlian Library Oxford Vol. 3 1989, Revision of P. Radcliffe's Mendelssohn 1990, The Mendelssohns on Honeymoon 1997, Mendelssohn: an Exhibition 1997; contrib. to Music and Letters, Brio, Mendelssohn-Studien, RMA Research Chronicle, New Grove Dictionary of Music and Musicians 1980, 2000, Die Musik in Geschichte und Gegenwart (second edn), Festschrift Rudolf Elvers, The Encyclopaedia of Oxford. *Honours:* F. J. Read prize (FRCO) 1962. *Address:* 25 Harbord Road, Oxford, OX2 8LH, England.

**WARD-STEINMAN, David,** BMus, MM, DMA; American composer; *Distinguished Professor of Music Emeritus, San Diego State University*; b. 6 Nov. 1936, Alexandria, LA; m. 1st Susan Diana Lucas 1956 (divorced 1993); one s. one d.; m. 2nd Patrice Dawn Madura 2001. *Education:* Florida State Univ., Univ. of Illinois, Princeton Univ., Nat. Music Camp, Interlochen, Aspen Music School, Berkshire Music Center, Tanglewood, studied in Paris, France, and Australia. *Career:* Prof. of Music, San Diego State Univ. 1961–2004, Distinguished Prof. of Music Emer. 2004–; Composer-in-Residence, Brevard Music Centre, NC; Univ. Research Lecturer, San Diego State Univ. 1986–87; Faculty, California State Summer School for the Arts, Loyola Marymount Univ., Los Angeles 1988; Adjunct Prof. of Music Ind. Univ. 2004–; numerous commissions; major orchestral performances of his work include those by Chicago Symphony, Japan Philharmonic, New Orleans Philharmonic, San Diego Symphony, Orchestra USA, Belgrade Radio Orchestra, Yugoslavia, and the Seattle Symphony; additional performances by Joffrey Ballet, San Diego Ballet Co., California Ballet Co. *Compositions:* major works for orchestra, ballet, band, chamber groups, vocal ensembles. *Recordings:* Concerto No. 2 for chamber orchestra, Fragments from Sappho, Duo for cello and piano, Brancusi's Brass Beds, Child's Play, Three Songs for clarinet and piano, Sonata for piano, The Tracker, Scorpio, Western Orpheus Concert Suite, Sonata for Piano Fortified (Moiré), Cello Concerto, Chroma Concerto, Cinnabar Concerto, Prisms and Reflections, Borobudur, Night Winds, Sonata for Piano Fortified. *Address:* 1159 Winners Circle, Bloomington, IN 47401, USA (home). *Telephone:* (812) 824-3505. *E-mail:* dwardste@mail.sdsu.edu (office); dwardste@indiana.edu.

**WARFIELD, Sandra;** Singer (Mezzo-Soprano); b. 6 Aug. 1929, Kansas City, Missouri, USA; m. James McCracken, died 1988. *Education:* Studied at the Kansas City Conservatory with Harold von Duze; Further study with Irran Petina, Elsa Seyfart and Joyce McClean. *Career:* Debut: Metropolitan Opera, 1953, in Le nozze di Figaro; Sang in New York until 1957, as Marcellina, Madelon in Andrea Chénier, La Cieca and Ulrica, then moved to Europe; Sang at the Zürich Opera from 1959, notably in the premiere of The Greek Passion by Martinů and as Fides, Azucena, Dalila, Amneris and Léonor in La Favorita; San Francisco Opera, 1963, Dalila; Appearances in Berlin, Vienna, Perugia and elsewhere in Europe as Carmen and Fricka; Metropolitan Opera, 1972; Samson et Dalila, with James McCracken. *Recordings:* Les Contes d'Hoffmann; Le nozze di Figaro.

**WARING, Kate;** Composer; b. 22 April 1953, Alexandria, Louisiana, USA; m. 22 May 1981, 1 s., 1 d. *Education:* BMus, Flute Performance, 1975, MMus, Composition, 1977, Louisiana State University; Doctorate Science Humaine, Sorbonne, Paris, France, 1984. *Career:* Solo Flute Recitals in Italy, France, Germany, USA; Original Compositions performed in USA, Italy, France, Switzerland and Germany; Radio Performances of Compositions on Swiss, German and USA Radio; Founder of annual American Music Week in Germany concert series; Appearances on American PBS and Worldnet Television. *Compositions:* Over 60 Works; Variations, Flute and Harpsichord, 1984; Assemblages, Soprano, Flute, Trombone, Percussion and Piano, 1977; 3 Act Ballet, Acteon, for large Orchestra, 1983; Chamber Opera, Rapunzel, 1988; Remember the Earth Whose Skin You Are, an Oratorio, 1994. *Address:* Zum Kleinen Oelberg 41, 53639 Königswinter, Germany.

**WARNER, Deborah;** British theatre and opera director; *Director, Fitzroy Productions*; b. 12 May 1959, Oxford; d. of Ruth Warner and Roger Warner. *Education:* Sidcot School, Avon, St Clare's, Oxford, Cen. School of Speech and Drama, London. *Career:* Founder and Artistic Dir Kick Theatre Co 1980–86; Resident Dir RSC 1987–89; Assoc. Dir Royal Nat. Theatre 1989–98; Assoc. Dir Abbey Theatre, Dublin 2000; has also staged productions at ENO (Bach's St John Passion and Janacek's Diary of One Who Vanished), Glyndebourne Festival Opera (Don Giovanni 1994, Fidelio 2001), Royal Opera House(Turn of the Screw), Opera North (Wozzeck), London Proms (concert of Honegger's Jeanne d'Arc au Bûcher), and has staged productions for Fitzroy Productions, Odeon Theatre, Chaillot and Bobigny Theatre, Paris, Salzburg Festival (Coriolan), LIFT and Perth Int. Arts Festival, Lincoln Center Festival, New York, Bavarian State Opera (The Rape of Lucretia) 2004; Dir Fitzroy Productions. *Productions* include: Titus Andronicus (RSC), King John (RSC), Electra (RSC), Hedda Gabler (Abbey Theatre, Dublin/West End), The Good Person of Sichuan (Royal Nat. Theatre), King Lear (Royal Nat. Theatre), Richard II (Royal Nat. Theatre), The Powerbook (Royal Nat. Theatre), The Waste Land (Fitzroy Productions), Medea (Abbey Theatre/West End/Broadway), The St Pancras Project (LIFT), The Tower Project (LIFT)The Angel Project (Perth Int. Arts Festival and Lincoln Center Festival). *Films:* The Waste Land 1996, The Last September 1999. *Television* includes: Richard II (BBC), Hedda Gabler (BBC), Don Giovanni (Channel 4). *Honours:* Officier, Ordre des Arts et Lettres 2000; Evening Standard Award 1988, 1998, 2002, Laurence Olivier Award 1989, 1992, New York Drama Desk Award 1997, South Bank Arts Award 1998, OBIE Award 2003. *Current Management:* c/o Leah Schmidt, The Agency, 24 Pottery Lane, London, W11 4LZ; c/o Askonas Holt, Lonsdale Chambers, 27 Chancery Lane, London, WC2A 1PF, England. *Telephone:* (20) 7727-1346 (The Agency, theatre); (20) 7400-1700 (Askonas Holt, opera).

**WARNER, Keith;** British stage director; b. 6 Dec. 1956, England. *Education:* Univ. of Bristol, studied in London and at Bayreuth. *Career:* early work in fringe theatre; staff producer, ENO 1981–, Assoc. Dir 1984–89, staging Rossini's Moïse, Dargomizhsky's Stone Guest, Pacific Overtures, Werther; Co-producer (with David Pountney) A Midsummer Marriage, The Flying

Dutchman and The Queen of Spades; Assoc. Dir Scottish Opera, with Carmen, Tosca, Werther, Die Zauberflöte and Iolanthe; Handel's Flavio at Florence and Batignano; further productions of Trovatore at Dortmund, Norma in Bielefeld and Un Ballo in Maschera with the Canadian Opera Co.; Madama Butterfly and Casken's Golem at Omaha, The Queen of Spades in Madrid, Tannhäuser for the Brighton Festival, My Fair Lady for Houston; production of Janáček's The Makropulos Case in Oslo 1992; Dir and Designer Der fliegende Holländer in Minneapolis, transferring to Omaha and Portland, Weill's Lost in the Stars for the Brighton Festival; Head of Productions, Omaha Fall Opera and the Omaha festival from 1992 (Eugene Onegin and Weisgall's Gardens of Adonis 1992); Dir Tosca for ENO 1994, Pagliacci and Cavalleria Rusticana at Berlin Staatsoper, From the House of the Dead for Opéra du Rhin and Carmen at Turin 1996, Carmen for Minnesota Opera and La Finta Giardinera for Opera Zuid 1997, The Turn of the Screw at La Monnaie, Brussels 1998, Der fliegende Holländer for Opera Pacific, Il Trittico for Spoleto Festival, USA and Lohengrin for Bayreuth Festival 1999; Season 2000 with Der fliegende Holländer for de Vlaamse Opera, The Cunning Little Vixen for Portland Opera, Manon Lescaut for ENO, Lohengrin for Bayreuth Festival and God's Liar for La Monnaie, Brussels (for which he also wrote the Libretto), Wagner's Ring at Covent Garden 2005. *Address:* c/o Royal Opera House, Bow Street, Covent Garden, London, WC2E 9DD, England. *Telephone:* (20) 7240-1200) (office). *E-mail:* info@roh.org.uk. *Website:* www.royaloperahouse.org.

**WARRACK, John,** MA, DLitt, ARCM; British musicologist; b. 9 Feb. 1928, London; m. Lucy Beckett 1970; four s. *Education:* Winchester Coll., Royal Coll. of Music. *Career:* freelance oboist 1951–54; Asst Music Critic, Daily Telegraph 1954–61; Chief Music Critic, Sunday Telegraph 1961–72; Dir, Leeds Musical Festival 1977–83; Univ. Lecturer in Music and Fellow, St Hugh's Coll., Oxford 1984–93; Editorial Bd, Cambridge Opera Journal, New Berlioz Edn, Neue Weber Gesamtausgabe; mem. Royal Musical Asscn. *Publications:* Concise Oxford Dictionary of Opera 1964, Carl Maria von Weber 1968, Tchaikovsky Symphonies and Concertos 1969, Tchaikovsky 1973, Tchaikovsky Ballet Music 1979, Carl Maria von Weber: Writings on Music (ed.) 1981, Oxford Dictionary of Opera 1992 (concise version 1996), Richard Wagner: Die Meistersinger von Nürnberg 1994, German Opera 2001; contrib. to Musical Times, Music and Letters, Opera, Gramophone, International Record Review, opera translations, articles in the New Grove Dictionary of Music and Musicians 1980. *Honours:* Royal Coll. of Music Colles Prize 1951. *Address:* Beck House, Rievaulx, Helmsley, York YO62 5LB, England. *E-mail:* warrack@aelred.demon.co.uk.

**WARREN, Raymond Henry Charles;** British composer and academic; b. 7 Nov. 1928, Weston-super-Mare, England; m. Roberta Smith 1953; three s. one d. *Education:* Corpus Christi Coll., Cambridge with Robin Orr, studied with Michael Tippett and Lennox Berkeley. *Career:* teacher, Queen's Univ. of Belfast 1955–66, Prof. of Composition 1966–72; Prof. of Music, Bristol Univ. 1972–94; mem. ISM, BACS. *Compositions:* incidental music for 11 plays by W. B. Yeats: The Lady of Ephesus (chamber opera) 1959, Finn and the Black Hag (children's opera) 1959, Graduation Ode (three-act opera) 1963; church operas: Let my People Go 1972, St Patrick 1979, In the Beginning 1982; The Passion (oratorio) 1962, Violin Concerto 1966, Three Symphonies 1965, 1969, 1996, Three String Quartets 1965, 1975, 1977, Oratorio Continuing Cities 1989, Violin Sonata 1993; song cycles: The Pity of Love (Yeats) 1965, Songs of Old Age (Yeats) 1968, In My Childhood (MacNeice) 1998, Two Wind Quintets 2003, Ballet shoes (ballet) 2001. *Publication:* Opera Workshop 1995. *Address:* 4 Contemporis Court, Merchants Road, Bristol, BS8 4HB, England.

**WARREN-GREEN, Christopher;** Violinist and Educator; b. 30 July 1955, Cheltenham, England. *Education:* Royal Academy of Music. *Career:* Debut: Solo, Berlin; London, 1984; Leader, BBC National Orchestra of Wales, 1977; Philharmonia Orchestra, 1980; Academy of St Martin-in-the-Fields, 1985; Music Director, London Chamber Orchestra, 1987; Tours a soloist, 1983–; Television Presenter, BBC Music and Arts; Professor, Royal Academy of Music, 1985–. *Recordings:* Mozart Violin concerti; Vivaldi Four Seasons; 4 records Haydn Concerti, Philharmonia; Mendelssohn Concerto; Tchaikovsky; Exclusive to Virgin Classics, 1987–; Berlin Chamber Akademie. *Honours:* Honorary ARAM, 1983.

**WASCHINSKI, Jörg;** Singer (Countertenor); b. 1966, Berlin, Germany. *Education:* Trained in Church Music, then at the Berlin Music College, Masterclasses with Barbara Schlick and Peter Schreier. *Career:* Many appearances in Germany and elsewhere in Europe in the Baroque music repertory; Operas by Jommelli at Stuttgart. *Recordings include:* Title role in Jommelli's Il Vologeso. *Honours:* Second Prize, International J H Schmetzer Competition for Baroque Music, Melk, 1996; Prize of the German State Association at the State Singing Competition, Berlin. *Address:* c/o Orfeo International Music GmbH, 8000 Munich, Germany.

**WASSERTHAL, Elfriede;** Singer, (Soprano); b. 12 March 1911, Lubeck, Germany. *Career:* Debut: Stettin 1935, as Marzelline in Fidelio; Sang in Essen and Düsseldorf, then at the Deutsche Oper Berlin, Charlottenburg, debut as Fiordiligi; Sang at Düsseldorf, 1941, in the premiere of Die Hexe von Passau by Gerster; Hamburg Staatsoper 1947–64, notably as Tosca, Desdemona, Jenůfa and Magda Sorel in The Consul; Visited Edinburgh Festival with the Hamburg Company 1952, for the British stage premiere of Mathis der Maler by Hindemith; Staatsoper Berlin 1951, as Selika in L'Africaine; Sang at Covent Garden as Eva, Sieglinde, Donna Elvira, Elsa and Marie in Wozzeck; Copenhagen, 1960; Frequent concert appearances.

**WASSILJEV, Nikolai;** Singer (Tenor); b. 1957, Leningrad, Russia. *Education:* Studied in Leningrad. *Career:* Has sung with the Bolshoi Opera from 1982, with guest appearances at La Scala Milan and the Metropolitan Opera, New York; Roles have included Alfredo, Cavaradossi, Turiddu, Lensky, Prince Gvidon in Rimsky's Tale of Tsar Saltan, Vladimir in Prince Igor and Dimitri in Boris Godunov; Sang in Mlada at New York, 1991. *Honours:* Prizewinner at the 1984 Glinka Competition and the 1986 Voci Verdiane at Busseto. *Address:* c/o Bolshoi Opera, 103009 Moscow, Russia.

**WASSON, Jeffrey;** Musicologist; b. 24 Aug. 1948, Illinois, USA. *Education:* BMus, 1970, MMus, 1973, PhD, Music History and Literature, 1987, Northwestern University; Boston College, 1989; Brandeis University, 1995; Boston University, 2000. *Career:* Instructor, 1980–85, Visiting Associate, 1990, 1993, Northwestern University; Professor of Music, Director of Music, Barat College, Lake Forest, Illinois, 1985–2001; Barat College of De Paul University, 2001–; Director of Music, St Mary of the Angels Church, Chicago, 1992–97; Lecturer at Universities of Yale, Michigan, Minnesota, Brandeis, Boston, De Paul, Michigan State, Loyola of Chicago and Nebraska. *Recordings:* Jacket Annotations. *Publications include:* Editor, A Compendium of American Musicology: Essays in Honour of John F Ohl; Self Study Modules of History of Music in the Middle Ages and Renaissance; First Mode Gradual Salvum fac Servum: Modal Practice Reflected in a Chant that Begins on B-Flat. *Contributions:* The Hymnal, 1982; Companion and Reader's Guide to Music History and Theory; Encyclopaedia of the Romantic Era. *Address:* 1500 Oak Avenue, Evanston, IL 60201, USA.

**WATERHOUSE, William;** Bassoonist and Author; b. 18 Feb. 1931, London, England. *Education:* Studied at the Royal College of Music with Archie Camden, Gordon Jacob. *Career:* Played first with the Philharmonia Orchestra, 1951–53; Royal Opera House Orchestra, 1953–55; First bassoon, Italian-Swiss Radio Orchestra in Lugano, 1955–58; First bassoon, London Symphony Orchestra, 1958–64; BBC Symphony, 1964–82; Member of the Melos Ensemble from 1959, including tours of Europe and USA; Many solo appearances; Tutor in Bassoon, 1966–96, Fellow, 1991–, Royal Northern College of Music; Curator, RNCM Collection of Historic Musical Instruments, 1996–; Honorary Archivist of the Galpin Society, 1983; Visiting Faculty at Indiana University, 1972, Melbourne, 1983, Sarasota, 1985, Haus Marteau, Lichtenberg, 1986–98; Banff 1987, Victoria, 1988; Tanglewood, 1999; Competition Juror at Munich, 1965, 1975, 1984, 1990, Prague, 1986, Eindhoven, 1988, Markneukirchen, 1990, Victoria, British Columbia, 1993, Potsdam, 1996 and 1998; Member of Arts Council of Great Britain Music Advisory Panel, 1983–85; Joint President of the British Double Reed Society, 2002; Honorary member of the International Double Reed Society, 2003; Honorary member of the I D R S, Deutschland, 2001; Dedicatee of works by Gordon Jacob, Jean Françaix, Elliott Schwartz and other composers. *Recordings:* Numerous with Melos Ensemble and various orchestras; First recording of Anton Liste Sonata, 1999. *Publications:* Numerous editions of wind music; Translations; Articles for New Grove Dictionary; Bibliography of Bassoon Music, 1962; Joint Editor of Universal Bassoon Edition; The New Langwill Index: a Dictionary of Musical Wind-Instrument Makers and Inventors, 1993; Yehudi Menuhin Music Guides: The Bassoon, 2003. *Address:* 86 Cromwell Avenue, London N6 5 HQ, England.

**WATERMAN, David Allen Woodrow,** MA, PhD; British cellist; b. 24 March 1950, Leeds, England. *Education:* Trinity Coll., Cambridge, studied with Martin Lovett, William Pleeth, Jane Cowan and Sándor Végh. *Career:* cellist, Endellion Quartet (founded 1979); resident at Cambridge Univ. 1992–, Royal Northern Coll. of Music 2001–; has coached cello and quartet at Int. Musicians' Seminar, Prussia Cove (Cornwall, UK) 1991–; Co-Dir Rathbone-Dickson Course at Westonbirt (Glos., UK); has also taught at Menuhin School, RAM, Guildhall School of Music and Drama and MIT, Boston, USA; appearances at Kennedy Center, Washington, DC, Ambassadors Auditorium, Los Angeles, many times at London, Bath Festival, Concertgebouw, Amsterdam, Lucerne and Gstaad Festivals, Switzerland, Spoleto and Fiesole Festivals, South Bank Festival, City of London Festival, Aldeburgh Festival; tours of USA, Australia, New Zealand and most major European centres and radio stations, South Africa, South America and Western Europe, with Endellion Quartet. *Recordings:* award-winning recordings of Quartetto Intimo, John Foulds; complete Britten Chamber Music, Haydn, Mozart, Dvořák, Smetana, Bartók, Martinů, Walton, Schubert, Beethoven and Frank Bridge, Thomas Ades' Arcadia. *Publications:* contrib. to European String Teachers' Association Magazine, American Record Guide, chapter in Cambridge Companion to the String Quartet. *Honours:* (with Endellion Quartet) Royal Philharmonic Soc. Award for Best Chamber Ensemble 1996. *Current Management:* Hazard Chase Ltd, 25 City Road, Cambridge, CB1 1DP, England. *Telephone:* (1223) 312400. *Fax:* (1223) 460827. *Website:* www .hazardchase.co.uk. *Address:* 27 Lancaster Grove, London, NW3 4EX, England.

**WATERMAN, Dame Fanny,** DBE, DMus, FRCM; British pianist and piano teacher; *Chairwoman, Leeds International Pianoforte Competition*; b. 22 March 1920, Leeds, England; d. of Myer and Mary (née Behrmann) Waterman; m. Geoffrey de Keyser 1944; two s. *Education:* Allerton High School (Leeds) and Royal Coll. of Music (London) with Tobias Matthay and Cyril Smith. *Career:* co-founder (with Marion Harewood) Leeds Int. Pianoforte Competition 1961, Chair. 1963–, Chair. of Jury 1981–; Vice-Pres. European Piano Teachers Asscn 1975–; Trustee Edward Boyle Memorial Trust 1981–; Gov Harrogate Festival 1983; mem. Int. Juries, Vienna 1977, 1993, Terni

(Italy) 1978, Munich 1979, 1986 and Leipzig (Germany) 1980, 1984, Calgary (Canada) 1982, Salt Lake City (USA) 1982, 1984, Viña del Mar (Chile) 1982, 1987, 1992, Maryland (USA) 1983, Cologne (Germany) 1983, 1986, Pretoria (S Africa) 1984, 1992, Santander (Spain) 1984, Rubinstein 1986, 1989, Moscow 1986, Vladigerov (Bulgaria) 1986, Lisbon 1987, 1991, CBC Toronto (Canada) 1989. *Television:* Piano Progress (series on ITV, Channel 4). *Publications:* Piano Tutors (series, with Marion Harewood) 1967–, Fanny Waterman on Piano Playing and Performing 1983, Young Violinists Repertoire (series, with Paul de Keyser) 1984, Music Lovers' Diary 1984–86, Merry Christmas Carols 1986, Christmas Carol Time 1986, Nursery Rhyme Time 1987, Piano for Pleasure (books 1–2) 1988, Me and My Piano: Repertoire and Duets (books 1–2) 1988, Animal Magic 1989, Piano Competition: the story of Leeds (jtly) 1990. *Honours:* Hon. MA (Leeds) 1966, Hon. MusDoc (Leeds) 1992, Hon. DUniv (York) 1995. *Address:* c/o Leeds International Pianoforte Competition, Piano Competition Office, University of Leeds, Leeds, LS2 9JT, England. *Website:* www.leedspiano.com.

**WATERMAN, Ruth (Anna);** Violinist; b. 14 Feb. 1947, Harrogate, Yorkshire, England. *Education:* Juilliard School, New York; Royal Manchester College of Music,. *Career:* Recitals and concerts throughout Europe and USA, radio and television, lecture-recitals, lecturing, coaching; Concerts include Bath Festival with Yehudi Menuhin as Conductor, 1966; Televised Prom, 1966; New York recital debut, International Artists series, Carnegie Hall Corporation, 1974; Concertos with London Symphony, BBC Symphony, BBC Scottish, English Chamber, Orpheus Chamber Orchestra and others; Festivals include Aldeburgh, Montreux; BBC Radio 3, complete Bach Sonatas, 1992; Lecture-recitals at Wigmore Hall, South Bank, Great Performers at Lincoln Center, New York, 2000, Avery Fisher Hall, New York, 1997; Recital at Hermitage Museum, St Petersburg, 2001; Radio interviews and talks for BBC, WNYC New York, Bayerischer Rundfunk, 1996; Professor, Queens College, City University of New York, 1975–92; Faculty Member, New York University, Royal Academy of Music; Masterclasses and lectures: Oxford University, 1994, Juilliard School, 2000, Royal Northern College of Music, New England Conservatory, Menuhin School; St Petersburg Conservatoire; mem, ISM; Fellow, George Bell Institute. *Recordings:* Bach Brandenburg Concertos, 1985; Bach Sonatas with Keyboard, 1997. *Publications:* Articles on interpretation and reviews for The Strad, BBC Music Magazine. *Honours:* Critic's Choice, Gramophone, 1997. *E-mail:* j.craxton@ruthwaterman.com.

**WATERS, Rosalind;** Singer (Soprano); b. 1965, Somerset. *Education:* Welsh College of Music and Drama, Cardiff and Royal College of Music. *Career:* Appearances with Musicians of the Globe, under Philip Pickett, the Gabrieli Consort, Corydon Singers and the Monteverdi Choir (tours of Europe); Handel's Saul in France, Mozart's Requiem in Madrid and Gubaidulina's The Canticle of the Sun in London, with Mstislav Rostropovich; Further engagements at the Purcell Room and Elizabeth Hall, London, and at the Strasbourg Festival; Elizabethan Lute Songs in Tel-Aviv; Tour of Spain, France and Turkey with Florilegium. *Recordings:* Albums with the New London Consort and the Philharmonia Orchestra (Suor Angelica). *Address:* c/o New London Consort, 8/9 Rust Square, London SE5 7 LG, England.

**WATERS, Susannah;** Singer (Soprano); b. 1965, England. *Education:* Studied at Guildhall School of Music and Drama, graduated 1989. *Career:* Debut: Sang Belinda, in Dido and Aeneas at Symphony Place, NY, 1986; The Princess in L'Enfant et les Sortilèges at 1989 Aldeburgh Festival and Louise in German production of Henze's The English Cat; Season 1990–91: Nannetta in Falstaff, Scottish Opera, Papagena at Glyndebourne, Philine in Thomas' Mignon at the Vienna Volksoper and Cherubino for Opera Factory, London, Many recital and oratorio appearances; Season 1991–92: Despina in Così fan tutte, Zerlina in Don Giovanni for Opera Factory, London; Martha, Sarasota Opera, USA; 1st Niece, in Peter Grimes for Glyndebourne Festival Opera; Dorlinda, in Orlando for Musica nel Chiostro, Italy; Season 1992–93: Gilda in Rigoletto for Opera Northern Ireland, Pamina in The Magic Flute, Scottish Opera, Susanna, in The Marriage of Figaro for Opera Factory, Cunegonde in Candide at Musica nel Chiostro; Season 1993–94: Fairy Godmother, in Cendrillon and Dalinda, in Ariodante, Welsh National Opera, Blonde, in Abduction from the Seraglio, for Sante Fe Opera; Season 1994–95: Atlanta in Xerxes, LA Music Center Opera, Cupidon and Nereid, in King Arthur at Théâtre du Châtelet, Paris and Covent Garden; Despina, Welsh National Opera; Belinda for Royal Opera of Stockholm at Drottningholm; Elizabeth, in Elegy for Young Lovers at Lausanne and on South Bank, London, 1997; Sang Salome in Stradella's San Giovanni Battista, Batignano, 1996; New York City Opera and Los Angeles 1997, as Atlanta in Serse and Countess in Fedora. *Recordings:* As Evato in King Arthur, with William Christie and Les Arts Florissants. *Current Management:* IMG Artists Europe, Tom Graham. *Address:* c/o 4 Tremadoc Road, London SW4 7NE, England.

**WATERS, Willie Anthony;** Conductor; b. 1952, Miami, Florida, USA. *Education:* Studied at the University of Miami. *Career:* Assistant Conductor of the Memphis Opera, 1973–75; Music Assistant to Kurt Herbert Adler at San Francisco Opera, 1975–79; Music Director of the San Antonio Festival, 1983–84; Artistic Director of the Greater Miami Opera for whom he has conducted La Gioconda, L'Italiana in Algeri, Madama Butterfly, Ernani, 1984–85, Of Mice and Men by Floyd, Rigoletto, Cav and Pag, 1985–86, Salome, La Traviata, Hamlet, Aida, 1986–87, Bellini's Bianca e Falliero, Tosca, Otello, 1987–88, Le nozze di Figaro, Die Walküre, La Forza del Destino, 1988–89, I Vespri Siciliani, Idomeneo, Elektra, 1989–90, Così fan tutte and Falstaff, 1990–91; Has also worked with the Detroit Symphony Orchestra, Fort Worth

Opera, Miami City Ballet, Florida Symphony Orchestra, Cincinnati, Chautaqua and Connecticut Opera Companies, Australian Opera Sydney, Cologne Opera, Sudwestfunk Orchestra and Essen Philharmonic, debuts 1990–91; Season 1991–93 conducting Aida with Connecticut Opera, Greater Miami Opera, SWF Sinfonieorchester, Baden-Baden, Florida Philharmonic Orchestra, and Macbeth with Charlotte Opera; Led an all-black Bohème at Cape Town, 1997–98.

**WATKIN, David Evan;** British cellist; b. 8 May 1965, Crowthorne. *Education:* studied with Sharon McKinley, Wells Cathedral School with Margaret Moncrieff and Amaryllis Fleming, St Catherine's Coll., Cambridge with William Pleeth. *Career:* St John's Smith Square debut recital 1989; Lincoln Centre, New York debut 1999; principal cello, Orchestre Révolutionaire et Romantique, English Baroque Soloists, Orchestra of the Age of the Enlightenment, Acad. of Ancient Music, Philharmonia Orchestra 2002–; revived the realization of figured bass on the cello; mem., Eroica Quartet 1999–. *Recordings include:* Corelli Op. 5 Violin Sonatas (realized figured bass, with Trio Veracini), Farewell to Hirta (music by Francis Pott), Vivaldi Cello Sonatas, Beethoven Cello Sonatas. *Publications:* article on the Beethoven Cello Sonatas, in Performing Beethoven. *Current Management:* c/o Eroica Quartet, Early Music Agency, 22 Michael Road, London, E11 3DY, England. *E-mail:* louise@earlymusicagency.com (office).

**WATKINS, Glenn;** Musicologist; b. 30 May 1927, McPherson, Kansas, USA. *Education:* BA 1948, MMus 1949, University of Michigan; PhD, University of Rochester, 1953; Diploma, American Conservatory, Fontainebleau, 1956. *Publications:* Gesualdo, Complete Works, co-editor, 1959–66; Gesualdo: The Man and His Music, 1973, 2nd edition, 1991; S D'India, Complete Works, co-editor, 1980–; Soundings Music in 20th Century, 1988; Pyramids at the Louvre, 1994; Proof Through the Night: Music and the Great War, 2003. *Honours:* Fulbright, England, 1953–54; National Book Award Nominee, 1974; Senior Fellow, National Endowment for the Humanities, 1976–77. *Address:* 1336 Glendaloch Circle, Ann Arbor, MI 48104, USA.

**WATKINS, Michael Blake;** British composer; b. 4 May 1948, Ilford, Essex; m. Tessa Marion Fryer 1975; two d. *Education:* studied guitar and lute with Michael Jessett, composition with Elisabeth Lutyens and Richard Rodney Bennett. *Career:* Fellow in Television Composition, LWT 1981–83. *Compositions:* orchestral works: Clouds and Eclipses for guitar and strings 1973, Aubade for brass band 1973, Horn Concerto 1974, Violin Concerto 1977, Etalage for symphony orchestra 1979, Trumpet Concerto 1988, Cello Concerto 1992, Viola Concerto 1998; chamber works: Solus for guitar solo 1975, The Wings of Night for solo violin 1975, All That We Read in Their Smiles for tenor, horn and piano 1977, The Spirit of the Universe for soprano and ensemble 1978, The Spirit of the Earth for guitar solo 1978, String Quartet 1979, The Magic Shadow Show for cello and ensemble 1980, Sinfonietta for 12 instruments 1982, Clarinet Quintet 1984, Somnial for guitar solo 1988, La Mort de l'aigle for solo trumpet 1993, Piano Quintet 1995, The River of Time for guitar trio 1996, Viola Concerto 1998. *Recordings:* Trumpet Concerto (with Håkan Hardenberger and the BBC Philharmonic Orchestra conducted by Elgar Howarth), La Mort de l'aigle (with trumpet played by Håkan Hardenberger), The River of Time (with Zagreb Guitar Trio). *Honours:* Menuhin Prize 1975, Carl Flesch Composition Prize 1976, Guinness Prize 1978. *Current Management:* Novello Publishing Ltd, 8–9 Frith Street, London, W1D 3JB, England. *Telephone:* (20) 7434-0066. *Fax:* (20) 7287-6329. *Website:* www.chesternovello.com.

**WATKINS, Sara (Van Horn);** Oboist and Conductor; b. 12 Oct. 1945, Chicago, Illinois, USA; m. John Shirley Quirk, 29 Dec 1981, 1 s., 2 d. *Education:* BMus, Oberlin Conservatory of Music, 1967; Studied with Ray Still, Marc Lifschey, Marcel Moyse; Fellowship student at Tanglewood Music Festival, 1967. *Career:* Principal Oboist, American National Opera Company, 1967; Honolulu Symphony Orchestra, 1969–73; National Symphony Orchestra, 1973–81; Professor of Oboe, University of Hawaii, 1969–73; Catholic University, 1973–81; Oberlin Conservatory, 1984; In residence, Scottish Academy of Music, 1985; Oboe Soloist, Conductor, 1981–; Oboe Soloist at Aldeburgh, Sofia, Spoleto Festivals, Vienna, The Hague, Moscow, Leningrad, London, São Paulo, New York and other major US cities; Recent conducting appearances in Glasgow, Cambridge, London Queen Elizabeth Hall, Britten-Pears School, Snape Maltings, Paris, New York Glimmerglass Opera; mem, Musicians' Union of Chicago and London; Conductors' Guild, USA. *Recordings:* CDs: Britten Chamber Music with John Shirley-Quirk, Osian Ellis, Philip Ledger; Handel Cantatas, Arias and Sonatas with Yvonne Kenny, John Shirley-Quirk, Martin Isepp. *Current Management:* Columbia Artists Management. *Address:* 51 Wellesley Road, Twickenham, Middlesex TW2 5RX, England.

**WATKINSON, Andrew;** Musician; b. 1955, England. *Career:* founder member and leader of the Endellion String Quartet from 1979; many concerts in Amsterdam, Frankfurt, Paris, Munich, Rome and Salzburg; appeared at South Bank Haydn Festival in 1990, the Wigmore Hall Beethoven Series and the Quartet Plus Series in 1994; Quartet-in-Residence at the Univ. of Cambridge from 1992 and Residency at MIT, USA 1995. *Recordings include:* works by Haydn, Bartók, Barber, Dvořák, Smetana and Walton. *Current Management:* Hazard Chase, Norman House, Cambridge Place, Cambridge CB2 1NS, England. *Telephone:* (1223) 312400. *Fax:* (1223) 460827. *Website:* www.hazardchase.co.uk.

**WATKINSON, Carolyn;** Singer (Mezzo-soprano); b. 19 March 1949, Preston, Lancashire, England. *Education:* Royal Manchester College of Music; Muzieklyceum, The Hague, Netherlands. *Career:* Early specialisation in Baroque music, and sang with Syntagama Musicum, Grande Ecurie de la Chambre du Roi, with Jean-Claude Malgoire and Gächinger Kantorei, under Helmuth Rilling; Sang Phèdre in Hippolyte et Aricie at Covent Garden and Versailles, 1978, English Bach Festival; Nero in L'Incoronazione di Poppea with Netherlands Opera, 1979; Guest in Stuttgart as Rossini's Rosina and at Ludwigsburg as Mozart's Cherubino, 1980; 1981 as Handel's Ariodante at La Scala, Milan; 1982 Edinburgh Festival, Ariodante; Glyndebourne Festival debut, 1984, as Cherubino, returned as Cenerentola; Aix-en-Provence debut, 1985, as the Messenger in Monteverdi's Orfeo; Concerts include Mahler's 3rd and 8th Symphonies, conducted by Haitink, Das Lied von der Erde, and appearances with the Royal Liverpool Philharmonic, BBC Symphony, Scottish Chamber and National Orchestras and the Philharmonia; Sang with Boston Symphony at Tanglewood, 1985; Engagements in Paris, Vienna, San Francisco, Washington DC, Madrid, Barcelona; Toured Australia, 1987, and appeared at Sydney Opera; Sang in Gloucester Cathedral performance of St John Passion, shown by BBC television on Good Friday, 1989; Sang Nero in L'Incoronazione di Poppea at Montpellier, 1989; Purcell's Dido conducted by John Eliot Gardiner at Salerno Cathedral, 1990; Nero at the 1990 Innsbruck Festival. *Recordings:* Handel Messiah (Hogwood), Rinaldo and Xerxes; Solomon (Gardiner); Mozart Requiem; Bach B Minor Mass (Schreier) and St Matthew Passion; Solo album recorded live at her debut, Wigmore Hall recital, London. *Address:* c/o Opéra et Concert, 1 Rue Volney, F–75002 Paris, France.

**WATSON, Janice;** Singer (Soprano); b. 1964, England. *Education:* Studied at the Guildhall School, further study with Johanna Peters. *Career:* Concert repertory has included the Four Last Songs of Strauss, Stravinsky's Pulcinella, Les Nuits d'Eté by Berlioz, Mahler's 4th Symphony and Berio's Sinfonia (Barbican Hall, London); Has sung the Brahms Requiem with Dulwich Choral Society, Haydn's Nelson Mass and Seasons at the Usher Hall, Edinburgh; Bach's Magnificat, Christmas Oratorio and St Mark Passion on South Bank, Britten's Les Illuminations at Salisbury Cathedral; Elgar's The Spirit of England with the Hallé Orchestra; Messiah in St Alban's Cathedral and Beethoven's Missa Solemnis with the Chichester Singers; Hummel's E flat Mass and Schubert's Stabat Mater at the Queen Elizabeth Hall; Mendelssohn's Elijah with the Bristol Bach Choir; Further repertory includes Handel's Saul, Mendelssohn's Hymn of Praise (2nd Symphony), Vaughan Williams's Pastoral Symphony and Beethoven's Mass in C (Barcelona Palace of Music); Recitals with the Songmakers' Almanac and in the crush bar at Covent Garden; Opera engagements at Glyndebourne, in Monteverdi's L'Incoronazione di Poppea at the City of London Festival and Musetta in La Bohème at Covent Garden (1990); With Welsh National Opera has sung Musetta, Fiordiligi, Micaela, Adèle in Le Comte Ory, Pamina and Rosalinde (Die Fledermaus); US and Canadian debuts in Messiah, conducted by Trevor Pinnock, 1990; Eugene Onegin for Welsh National Opera and recently Lucia di Lammermoor, Daphne for San Francisco Opera and at Santa Fe (1996), Les Illuminations by Benjamin Britten at the Proms, Messiah at the Barbican with Richard Hickox; Engaged as Pamina at the Berlin Staatsoper and Arabella at San Francisco, 1998; Beethoven's Choral Symphony with the London Symphony Orchestra at the 1999 London Proms; Season 1999–2000 as Mozart's Elettra at Santa Fe, Micaela for Chicago Lyric Opera, Governess in The Turn of the Screw for ENO and Ellen Orford at Amsterdam; Mendelssohn's Elijah at the London Proms, 2002. *Address:* Elm Cottage, Portsmouth Road, Milford, Godalming, Surrey, GU8 5DU.

**WATSON, Lillian;** Singer (Soprano); b. 4 Dec. 1947, London, England. *Education:* Studied at the Guildhall School of Music and the London Opera Centre. *Career:* Sang first at the Wexford Festival, then with the Welsh National Opera; Glyndebourne from 1976, as Susanna, Despina, Sophie, Tytania in A Midsummer Night's Dream and Blondchen (1988); Covent Garden debut, 1971, as Barbarina in Le nozze di Figaro; Appearances in die Entführung, Der Rosenkavalier and Arabella; Guest engagements with English National Opera and Scottish Opera and in Munich, Paris, Rouen, Marseilles and Bordeaux; Salzburg Festival, 1982, as Marzelline in Fidelio; Vienna Staatsoper in Le nozze di Figaro; Sang Strauss's Sophie at the Théâtre des Champs-Elysées, 1989; Norina in Don Pasquale at Amsterdam; Title role in The Cunning Little Vixen at Covent Garden, 1990; Sadler's Wells Theatre, 1990, as Britten's Tytania; Television engagements in Don Pasquale and Orpheus in the Underworld. Sang Fairy Godmother in Massenet's Cendrillon for Welsh National Opera, 1993 and at Ghent, 1998; Bella in The Midsummer Marriage at Covent Garden, 1996; Despina, 1997; Sang Britten's Tytania at Rome 1999 and Naples 2001. *Recordings:* Carmen; Le nozze di Figaro; Monteverdi Madrigals and Handel's Israel in Egypt; Die Entführung aus dem Serail; The Cunning Little Vixen; Così fan tutte; Britten's A Midsummer Night's Dream. *Address:* c/o IMG Artists, Lovell House, 616 Chiswick High Road, London W4 5RX, England.

**WATSON, Linda;** Singer (Soprano and Mezzo-soprano); b. 1959, San Francisco, USA. *Education:* New England Conservatory, Boston; Vienna, with Erik Werba and Waldemar Kmentt; Berlin, with Hannelore Kuhse. *Career:* Sang in Vienna from 1986; Aachen Opera 1992-1995, as Jezibaba in Rusalka, Santuzza, and Offenbach's, Giulietta; Essen and Leipzig 1995-97, as Wagner's Venus and Brangaene, Azucena Marina in Boris Godunov and Sieglinde in Die Walküre; Guest appearances in Prague (the Marschallin,

1996), Vienna Staatsoper (Venus, 1997) and Hamburg; Deutsche Oper am Rhein as Sieglinde, Kundry and Isolde, from 1997; Bayreuth Festival 1998, as Kundry in Parsifal; Further engagements in London, Moscow, Tokyo, Boston and Amsterdam (Venus 1998); Season 1998-99 as Leonore in Fidelio at Dusseldorf, Brünnhilde in Siegfried at Bonn and Isolde for the Maggio Musicale, Florence Elisabeth in Tannhäuser at Toulouse; Complete Ring cycles, as Brünnhilde, at Barcelona, Vienna and Amsterdam, from 2003. *Address:* c/o IMG Artists, Lovell House, 616 Chiswick High Road, London, W4 5RX, England.

**WATT, Alan;** Singer (Baritone); b. 1947, Aberdeen, Scotland. *Education:* Scottish Academy of Music, Glasgow. *Career:* Debut: Scottish Opera, Glasgow, 1970; Sang as Háry János by Kodály at the 1971 Buxton Festival; Glyndebourne Festival and Touring Opera from 1973, as Marcello, Guglielmo and Figaro; Appearances in The Cunning Little Vixen, Strauss's Intermezzo and The Visit of the Old Lady by Einem; Covent Garden, 1976, in the premiere of Henze's We Come to the River; Wexford Festival, 1978, as Ernesto in Haydn's Il mondo della luna; Sang Guglielmo at Venice, 1983, and Strasbourg, 1989, Figaro at Vienna, 1986, and for Welsh National Opera, 1987; Papageno at Tel-Aviv, 1991; Festival Hall, London, 1998, as Pish-Tush in The Mikado; Many concert and oratorio engagements. *Address:* c/o D'Oyly Carte Opera Co, Valley Park, Cromer Gardens, Wolverhampton WV 6 0UA, England.

**WATTS, André;** Pianist; b. 20 June 1946, Nuremberg, Germany. *Education:* Studied with Genia Robiner, Doris Bawden and Clement Petrillo, Philadelphia Musical Academy; Artist's Diploma, Peabody Conservatory of Music, Baltimore, 1972, and with Leon Fleisher. *Career:* Debut: Soloist, Haydn's Concerto in D Major, Philadelphia Orchestra Children's Concert, 1955; Soloist, Franck's Symphonic Variations, Philadelphia Orchestra, 1960; Soloist, Liszt's Concerto No. 1, with Bernstein and New York Philharmonic Orchestra, 1963; European debut, London Symphony Orchestra, 1966; New York recital debut, 1966; World tour, 1967; First pianist to play a recital on live network television in USA, New York, 1976; Celebrated 25th anniversary of debut as soloist with New York Philharmonic Orchestra, Liszt Concerto No. 1, the Beethoven Concerto No. 2 and Rachmaninov Concerto No. 2, telecast nationwide, 1988; Rachmaninov's concerto No. 2 in C minor at the London Proms, 2002. *Recordings:* Various. *Honours:* Honorary Doctorates from Yale University, 1973, Albright College, 1975; Film documentary of his career; Avery Fisher Prize, 1988. *Address:* c/o Columbia Artists' Management Inc., 165 West 57th Street, New York, NY 10019, USA.

**WATTS, Andrew;** Singer (Countertenor); b. 1967, Middlesex, England. *Education:* Royal Academy of Music. *Career:* Appearances at the Almeida and Montepulciano Festivals in works by Smirnov, McQueen and Henze; Opera roles include Tolomeo in Giulio Cesare, Lidio in Cavalli's L'Egisto, Handel's Sosarme, Scarlatti's Tigrane and Britten's Oberon, Arsamenes in Xerxes, and Monteverdi's Orfeo (1999–2000) for English National Opera; Double bill of Dido and Aeneas and Venus and Adonis for De Vlaamse Opera; Season 1998–99 as Gluck's Orpheus at Sydney and for ENO, and in Cesti's Il Pomo d'Oro at Batignano; Season 2000 in Birtwistle's Gawain at Covent Garden and premiere of Guarnieri's Passione Secondo Matteo at La Scala; Concerts include Bach's Passions and Magnificat, Chapentier's Te Deum (at Lourdes), Purcell's Indian Queen in France, Messiah at Oxford, Handel's Jephtha on tour to Italy and Judas Maccabaeus in France. *Address:* Music International, 13 Ardilaun Road, London N5 2QR, England.

**WATTS, Helen Josephine,** CBE; British contralto (retd); b. 7 Dec. 1927, Milford Haven, Wales; d. of Thomas Watts and Winifred Morgan; m. Michael Mitchell 1980. *Education:* St Mary and St Anne's School, Abbot Bromley. *Career:* singer in Glyndebourne and BBC choruses; toured Russia with English Opera Group 1964; concert tours in USA 1967–85 (retd); has appeared with all major European and American orchestras; numerous recordings; has sung at the Salzburg Festival, Covent Garden and the Hong Kong Festival; major appearances include: The Ring at Covent Garden; Mozart Opera at Salzburg Festival; four Promenade concerts 1974. *Recordings include:* Handel Arias, Orfeo, Bach's B Minor Mass, Beethoven's Mass in C Minor, The Dream of Gerontius, The Apostles, Götterdämmerung. *Honours:* Hon. FRAM. *Address:* c/o Askonas Holt Ltd, Lonsdale Chambers, 27 Chancery Lane, London, WC2A 1PF, England (office).

**WAYENBERG, Daniel (Ernest Joseph Carel);** Pianist and Composer; b. 11 Oct. 1929, Paris, France. *Education:* Studied with his mother and with Marguérite Long. *Career:* Played in private houses, 1939–46; Public debut, Paris, 1949; Opening recital of the Chopin Centenary Festival, Florence, 1949; Besançon Festival, 1951; US debut, Carnegie Hall, 1953, conducted by Mitropoulos; Numerous concerto appearances throughout the world (tours of USA and Indonesia, 1955); Repertoire centres on 19th century classics but also plays Haydn and Stockhausen; Teacher at Conservatory of Rotterdam. *Compositions:* Ballet Solstice, 1955; Sonata for violin and piano; Concerto for 5 wind instruments and orchestra; Capella, symphony; Concerto for 3 pianos and orchestra, 1975. *Recordings:* Numerous concertos including Brahms, Tchaikovsky, Beethoven, Gershwin and Rachmaninov. *Current Management:* Concert Director, Samama 8C, Netherlands. *Address:* 17 rue Thibault, 94520 Mandres-Les Roses, France.

**WEAVER, James (Merle);** Harpsichordist, Pianist and Fortepianist; b. 25 Sept. 1937, Champaign, Illinois, USA. *Education:* BA, 1961, MM, 1963, University of Illinois, Urbana-Champaign; Studied with Gustav Leonhardt, Sweelinck Conservatory, Amsterdam, 1957–59. *Career:* Many appearances as keyboard artist; Curator of historic instruments at the Smithsonian Institution, Washington DC, USA, 1967; Co-founder of Smithsonian Chamber Players, 1976; Teacher, Cornell University and American University; Various masterclasses in 18th century performance practice. *Recordings include:* Smithsonian Collection. *Address:* c/o Smithsonian Chamber Players, Smithsonian Institution, Washington DC 20560, USA.

**WEAVING, John (Weymouth);** Singer (Tenor); b. 23 Feb. 1936, Melbourne, Australia. *Education:* Studied with Browning Mummery in Melbourne, Audrey Langford in London and Ken Neate in Munich. *Career:* Debut: Sadler's Wells in 1960 as Eisenstein in Die Fledermaus; Has sung in operas by Wagner with the English National Opera; Engagements at opera houses in Kiel, Essen, Hanover, Lyon, Wiesbaden and Munich; Other roles included Florestan, Huon in Oberon, Alvaro in La Forza del Destino, Otello, Don José, Bacchus, Herman in The Queen of Spades, and Sali in A Village Romeo and Juliet; Many concert appearances. *Address:* c/o English National Opera, St Martin's Lane, London WC2N 4ES, England.

**WEBB, Jonathan;** Conductor; b. 1963, England. *Education:* University of Manchester. *Career:* Appearances with New Israel Opera with Jenůfa, Così fan tutte, Midsummer Night's Dream, Faust, Carmen, Don Pasquale, Butterfly, Der Freischütz, Hoffmann, Samson et Dalila, Cavalleria Rusticana, Pagliacci, Traviata, L'Elisir d'amore, Cenerentola and Lucia di Lammermoor; Head of Music, Opera Ireland; Resident Conductor New Israeli Opera; Festival appearances in Turin and Rome; Don Pasquale, Der Zigeunerbaron and Die Zauberflöte at the Vienna Volksoper; Peter Grimes in Genoa and Balfe's The Rose of Castile at Wexford; Figaro, The Rape of Lucretia, Falstaff and L'Histoire du Soldât in Ireland; Co-production between Kirov Opera and New Israel Opera of Lady Macbeth of Mtsensk; Season 1999–2000 with L'Italiana in Algeri, Tosca, La Juive, Macbeth and Eugene Onegin in Tel-Aviv; Mahagonny for the Deutsche Oper Berlin, La Traviata in Cologne and Turandot for the Caesarea Festival; Season 2000–01 with Tancredi in Venice and Carmen at the Deutsche Oper, Berlin. *Address:* Music International, 13 Ardilaun Road, London N5 2QR, England.

**WEBB, Peter;** Composer and Conductor; b. 29 Feb. 1948, Melbourne, Victoria, Australia. *Education:* BA, University of Melbourne, and Teaching Certificate, 1970. *Career:* Oboe and Cor Anglais in the Adelaide Symphony Orchestra, 1975–95; Conductor and Teacher; Commissions from ABC, Adelaide Harmony Choir, Unley Chamber Orchestra, and others. *Compositions include:* Songs of the Wind, song cycle for soprano and orchestra, 1978; Quintet for Brass, 1980; Sonata for Clarinet and Piano, 1981; Songs of the Shadows, song cycle for mezzo soprano and orchestra, 1985; The Christmas Kangaroo for narrator and orchestra, 1986; Sextet for pairs of horns, clarinets and bassoons, 1987; Sonata for bassoon and piano, 1987; Five Blake Songs for chorus and orchestra, 1988; Trio for clarinet, bassoon and piano, 1989; Sinfonietta for orchestra, 1990; Trio for 2 oboes and piano, 1992; Trio for flute, oboe and piano, 1992; Sonata for Cor Anglais and piano, 1995; Sonata for cello and piano, 1998; Retrospection for 8 cellos, 1999; Sonata for flute and piano, 2001. *Address:* c/o APRA, 1A Eden Street, Crows Nest, NSW 2065, Australia. *E-mail:* pjwebb@senet.com.au.

**WEBBER, Oliver;** Violinist; b. 1969, Essex, England. *Education:* Wells Cathedral; Cambridge; The Hague, Netherlands. *Career:* Appearances from 1995 with the Charivari Agréable Sinfonie, Gabrieli Consort and Florilegium; Violin and Viola with the Revolutionary String Quartet, Red Priest and the Consort of Musicke; Soloist with Florilegium, the Avison Baroque Ensemble, La Serenissima and London Musical Arts; Exponent of early and Baroque music performance practice, including ornamentation and the use of gut strings; European tour with the London Handel Festival, 2001. *Address:* c/o Florilegium, 21 Village Road, Finchley, London N3 1TL, England.

**WEBER, Margit;** Pianist; b. 24 Feb. 1924, Ebnat-Kappel, St Gallen, Switzerland. *Education:* Studied organ with Heinrich Funk in Zürich and piano with Max Egger and Walter Lang at the Zürich Conservatory. *Career:* Frequent concert tours of the USA and Europe; Festival appearances at Lucerne, Munich, Venice, Berlin and Vienna; Has given the premieres of Martinů's Fantasia Concertant, 1958, Stravinsky's Movements in 1960, and Tcherepnin's Bagatelles and 5th Piano Concerto; Has performed Moeschinger's Piano Concerto in 1962, Schibler's Ballade for Piano and Strings in 1963, Fortner's Epigrams for Piano in 1964, Vogel's Horformen for Piano and Strings in 1972; Concert classes at the Zürich Musikhochschule from 1971. *Recordings include:* Mozart Concerto K414 under Baumgartner; Nights in the Gardens of Spain; Franck Symphonic Variations; Weber's Konzertstück; Stravinsky's Movements with the Berlin Radio Symphony Orchestra under Fricsay. *Honours:* Hans Georg Nägeli Medal of Zürich, 1971.

**WEBER, Peter;** Singer (Baritone); b. 1955, Vienna, Austria. *Education:* Diploma, Hochschule für Musik, Vienna. *Career:* Engaged by the Studio of the Vienna Staatsoper, 1976; Member of ensemble of the Vienna Staatsoper, 1978; Engaged at the Nuremberg Opera in 1980 and Hanover Staatsoper in 1982; Regular appearances at the Salzburg Festival and the Vienna Festwochen from 1977; Appeared at Glyndebourne Festival 1985–89 as Mandryka in Arabella and Olivier in Capriccio; Debut at the Teatro Colón in Buenos Aires in 1986 as Mozart's Count; Debuts at the Teatro Liceo Barcelona and the Teatro dell'Opera Rome in 1988; Guest engagements in Hamburg, Düsseldorf, Geneva, Paris and Milan; Sang Mandryka at Covent Garden in 1990; USA debut as Amonasro at Dallas Opera in 1991; Contracted to Vienna State Opera in 1992; Other roles include Silvio, Sharpless, Malatesta, Falke and the

Secretary in Der Junge Lord by Henze, Don Giovanni, Don Alfonso, Telramund, Pizarro, Amfortas, Eisenstein, Onegin; Debuts as Wagner's Gunther and Strauss's Barak at Hanover in 1993; Concerts and recitals in Europe and the USA; Radio and television appearances; Engaged as the Count in Capriccio, Vienna 1996–97; Season 2000–01 as Wozzeck at La Scala, the Speaker in Die Zauberflöte, Kurwenal and the Chosen One in Schoenberg's Die Jakobsleiter, at the Vienna Staatsoper; Hindemith's Mathis at Hannover. *Recordings:* Ariadne auf Naxos; Un Ballo in Maschera; Die Frau ohne Schatten; Die Zauberflöte; Schoeck Penthesilea; Schubert Alfonso und Estrella; Haydn's Die Feuerbrunst. *Honours:* Prizewinner, Hugo Wolf Competition in Salzburg in 1976; Interpretation Prize from the Mozartgemeinde Vienna in 1976; International Schubert-Wolf Competition, Vienna in 1978. *Address:* c/o Vienna State Opera, Ringstrasse, Vienna, Austria.

**WEBSTER, Gillian;** British singer (soprano); b. 2 May 1964, Scotland; m. Brian Kay. *Education:* studied at Royal Northern College of Music and Nat. Opera Studio. *Career:* began her career with Royal Opera, Covent Garden in roles of Pamina and First Lady in Die Zauberflöte, La Contessa in Le nozze di Figaro, Ilia in Idomeneo, Servilia in La clemenza di Tito, First and Second Nieces in Peter Grimes, Micaela in Carmen, Mimi, Euridice, Marzelline in Fidelio, Woglinde and Wellgunde in Der Ring des Nibelungen, Le Coq d'Or, Kátya Kabanova, Rigoletto, Médée, Elektra and Prince Igor 1988; appearances with the English Bach festival, Scottish Opera, Glyndebourne Festival and ENO; roles have included Micaela, Pamina and Leila in Les Pêcheurs de Perles, Agilea Handel's Teseo and Ilia in Idomeneo; sang Klim (debut) in The Making of the Representative from Planet 8 by Philip Glass for ENO; sang Micaela with Welsh Nat. Opera 1990; TV appearances include Gluck's Euridice at Covent Garden; sang Mozart's Countess with Royal Opera at Shaftesbury Theatre 1998; int. opera appearances have included Pamina in Stuttgart, Euridice at the Komische Oper Berlin, La Contessa for Vlaamse Opera, Servilia for L'Opéra de Nancy, Micaela in Tours, Mimi in Las Palmas, Comtesse de la Roche in Die Soldaten and Elsa in Lohengrin in Nantes, Elsa in Dijon, First Lady in Bordeaux, Geneva, Aix-en-Provence, Chorégies d'Orange, Amsterdam, and at Bastille and Ginevra with Les Musiciens du Louvre; noted exponent of Baroque music and later vocal works of Mahler, Strauss, Mozart and Beethoven; has performed with conductors including Bernard Haitink, Jeffrey Tate, John Eliot Gardiner, Sir Georg Solti, Marc Minkowski, Paul McCreesh, Sir Yehudi Menuhin and Sir Colin Davis; concert engagements have included Mahler Symphony No. 4 with New York Philharmonic, Four Last Songs with L'Orchestre de l'Opéra de Nancy, Beethoven Missa Solemnis with Madrid Nat. Orchestra, Pallas Athene in Gluck's Paride ed Elena and Galatea with Les Musiciens du Louvre; recent engagements have included First Lady in Die Zauberflöte for Royal Opera, Galatea in Acis and Galatea with Les Musiciens du Louvre under Marc Minkowski, Messiah with City of Birmingham Symphony Orchestra and with Gabrieli Consort, Haydn and Mozart Masses with Birmingham Festival Choral Soc., Mendelssohn Second Symphony at Three Choirs Festival and performances with L'Orchestre de l'Opéra de Nancy; chamber music recitals with Alice Ader Ensemble, Arpeggione quartet, Talich quartet and Wanderer Trio in works by Shostakovich, Chausson, Schubert and Schoenberg. *Recordings:* role of Juno in Offenbach's Orpheus in the Underworld with Chorus and Orchestra of the D'Oyly Carte Opera Co. under John Owen Edwards 1994, Beethoven Choral Symphony, Second Niece in Peter Grimes, Pallas in Athene Paride ed Elena, Covent Garden DVDs of Orfeo and Die Zauberflöte. *Honours:* John Noble Award, Scottish Opera 1986. *Current Management:* Helen Sykes Artists' Management, 100 Felsham Road, Putney, London, SW15 1DQ, England. *Telephone:* (20) 8780-0060. *Fax:* (20) 8780-8772. *E-mail:* info@helensykesartists.com. *Website:* www.helensykesartists.com.

**WEDD, Peter;** Singer (Tenor); b. 1970, England. *Education:* Graduated Guildhall School, 1996, and National Opera Studio, 1998. *Career:* Season 1998–99 in Die Lustige Witwe and Paul Bunyan for the Royal Opera, Pavel Haas's Sarlatan and Zandonai's I Cavalieri di Ekebù at Wexford; Don José for Welsh National Opera, Britten's Lysander at Singapore, Tamino for European Chamber Opera and Federico in L'Arlesiana for Opera Holland Park; Covent Garden season 1999–2000 in Gawain, Der Rosenkavalier, The Greek Passion, Die Meistersinger and La Battaglia di Legnano; Concerts include Mozart's Requiem, Haydn's Mass in Time of War, Messiah, the Glagolitic Mass, St John Passion and The Dream of Gerontius; Britten's Serenade at Neuchâtel. *Address:* Music International, 13 Ardilaun Road, London N5 2QR, England.

**WEGMAN, Rob Cornelis,** MPhil, PhD; Dutch musicologist; b. 26 Jan. 1961, Emmen; m. Helene van Rossum; one s. one d. *Education:* Univ. of Amsterdam. *Career:* Asst Lecturer, Univ. of Amsterdam 1983–85; Researcher, Univ. of Amsterdam 1987–91; Weston Jr Research Fellow, Univ. of Oxford 1991–93, British Acad. Post-Doctoral Research Fellow 1993–95, concentrating on 15th-century polyphony; Asst Prof., Princeton Univ. 1995–2000, Assoc. Prof. 2000–. *Publications include:* edn of Choirbook of the Burgundian Court Chapel 1989, Born for the Muses: The Life and Masses of Jacob Obrecht 1994, 'Who was Josquin?' (chapter in The Josquin Companion) 2001, 'Historical Musicology: Is it Still Possible?' (chapter in A Critical Introduction to the Cultural Study of Music), The Crisis of Music in Early Modern Europe 1470–1530. *Honours:* Westrup Prize 1990, Music and Letters Award 1992, American Musicological Soc. Alfred Einstein Award 1996, Royal Musical Asscn Edward J. Dent Medal 1998. *Address:* Department of Music, Woolworth Center of Musical Studies, Princeton University, Princeton, NJ 08544, USA (office). *Telephone:* (609) 258-

4248 (office). *Fax:* (609) 258-6793 (office). *E-mail:* rwegman@phoenix
.princeton.edu (office). *Website:* www.princeton.edu (office).

**WEGNER, John;** Singer (Bass-baritone); b. 1950, Germany. *Education:*
Victorian College of the Arts, Australia. *Career:* Australian Opera, 1981–92,
as Britten's Theseus, Collatinus and Swallow, Mozart's Commendatore and
Leporello, Escamillo, Baron Ochs, Banquo and Boris Godunov; Falstaff for
Queensland Opera; 1992–95 with Karlsruhe Opera as Orestes, Wotan,
Cardillac (Hindemith), Prince Igor and Iago; Wagner's Dutchman at Berne
and Leipzig, Scarpia at Sydney and Copenhagen; Wotan and the Wanderer in
The Ring, at Adelaide, 1999; Bayreuth debut, 1997, as Donner in Das
Rheingold; Season 1999–2000 as Escamillo and Scarpia for Opera Australia,
Wotan at Toulouse and Alberich in Götterdämmerung at Stuttgart; Season
2000–01 as the Dutchman, Boris and Wotan at Düsseldorf, Scarpia in
Brussels, Kurwenal for Opera North in Leeds and on tour to Germany;
Jochanaan in Salome at the Berlin Staatsoper and Telramund at Sydney.
*Recordings:* Wotan/Wanderer in The Ring, from Stuttgart (Bella Music).
*Honours:* Mo Award as Operatic Performer of the Year 1998–89 from the
Australian Entertainment Industry. *Address:* Music International, 13
Ardilaun Road, London N5 2QR, England.

**WEHOFSCHITZ, Kurt;** Singer (Tenor); b. 3 May 1923, Vienna, Austria.
*Education:* Studied at the Vienna Music Academy. *Career:* Debut: Linz in
1948 as Wilhelm Meister; Sang at Kiel, 1953–54, Munich, 1956–59 notably as
Ulrich Greiner-Mars in the premiere of Hindemith's Harmonie der Welt in
1957; Sang at Düsseldorf, 1959–64, Frankfurt, 1964–66 notably in The Photo
of the Colonel by Humphrey Searle, Düsseldorf in 1960 as Creon in the
German premiere of Oedipe Re by Enescu; Guest appearances at Zürich,
Lisbon, Rio de Janeiro and the Vienna Staatsoper; Sang at the Vienna
Volksoper until 1980; Other roles have included Mozart's Belmont and Basilio,
Leandro in Haydn's Mondo della Luna, Strauss's Leukippos and Flamand,
Alfredo, Germont, Don Carlos, Riccardo and Tom Rakewell. *Recordings
include:* Carmen.

**WEIDENAAR, Reynold (Henry);** Composer and Video Artist; b. 25 Sept.
1945, East Grand Rapids, Michigan, USA. *Education:* BMus, Composition,
Cleveland Institute of Music, 1973; MA, 1980, PhD, 1989, Composition, New
York University; Studied composition with Donald Erb and Brian Fennelly.
*Compositions include:* Between The Motion And The Act Falls The Shadow,
1981; Love Of Line, Of Light And Shadow: The Brooklyn Bridge, 1982; Night
Flame Ritual, 1983; The Stillness, 1985; The Thundering Scream Of The
Seraphim's Delight, 1987; Long River, 1993; Long into the Night, Heavenly
Music Flowed Out Of the Street, 1995; Swing Bridge, 1997. *Recordings:* The
Tinsel Chicken Coop, 1978, 1982; Twilight Flight, 1986; Harmony, 1986;
Imprint: Footfalls To Return, 1986; Night Flame Ritual, 1986. Bass Bars,
videotape, 1988; Long River, for piano and tape, 1993; Magic Music from the
Telharmonium, 1997; Swing Bridge, clarinet and tape, 1997. *Publications:*
Magic Music From The Telharmonium, 1995. *Contributions:* New Music
America: A Moveable Fest, in The Independent, 1984; Down Memory Lane:
Forerunners of Music and The Moving Image and So You Want to Compose for
The Moving Image, in Ear Magazine, 1985; Live Music and Moving Images:
Composing and Producing The Concert Video, in Perspectives of New Music,
1986; The Alternators of the Telharmonium, 1986, in Proceedings of the
International Computer Music Conference, 1991. *Address:* William Paterson
University, Department of Communication, Wayne, NJ 07470, USA.

**WEIDINGER, Christine,** BA; American singer (soprano); b. 31 March 1946,
Springville, NY; m. Kenneth Smith 1976. *Education:* Grand Canyon Coll.,
Phoenix, studied singing with Marlene Delavan in Phoenix, Adrian de Peyer
in Wuppertal, Dean Verhines in Los Angeles. *Career:* debut as Musetta in La
Bohème at the Metropolitan 1972; sang at Metropolitan Opera 1972–76,
Stuttgart and Bielefeld Operas, Germany 1979–; roles include Malvina in
Heinrich Marschner's Der Vampyr, Anina in Bellini's La Sonnambula, Berthe
in Meyerbeer's Le Prophète, Elizabeth I in Donizetti's Roberto Devereux, Inez
in L'Africaine, Lucia and Juliet in I Capuleti e i Montecchi, Pamira in Rossini's
Siege of Corinth, Eupaforice in Heinrich Graun's Spanish Conquest,
Constanze in Abduction from the Seraglio, Electra in Idomeneo, Leonora in
Trovatore, Adèle in Le Comte Ory, Vitellia in La Clemenza di Tito, Tancredi,
Violetta, Gilda, Donna Anna, Mimi, Liu, and the title roles in Thea Musgrave's
Mary, Queen of Scots, Donizetti's Lucia di Lammermoor, Bellini's Norma,
Bellini's Beatrice di Tenda. *Recordings:* Handel's Rinaldo with Marilyn
Horne, L'Africaine with Caballé and Domingo, Die Freunde von Salamanka
by Schubert, Médée with Caballé and Lima, Mitridate by Mozart. *Honours:*
Nat. first prize Metropolitan Opera Auditions 1972. *Current Management:*
Robert Lombardo Associates, 61 W 62nd Street, Suite 6F, New York, NY
10023, USA.

**WEIGLE, Jorg-Peter;** Conductor; b. 1953, Greifswald, Germany. *Education:*
Studied at the Thomasschule, Leipzig, 1963–71; Hochschule für Musik, East
Berlin from 1973. *Career:* First kapellmeister at the State Symphony
Orchestra of Neubrandenburg, 1978–80; Conductor of the Leipzig Radio
Chorus, 1980; Chief Conductor of the Dresden Philharmonic Orchestra;
Repertoire has included Bach's Christmas Oratorio, St John Passion and B
Minor Mass, symphonies by Beethoven, Haydn, Mozart, Shostakovich and
Schubert, and Janáček's Sinfonietta; Visited Wales and the West Country
with the Dresden Philharmonic in 1989, with works by Beethoven, Brahms,
Weber and Tchaikovsky, Hamburg and Spain in 1989 and Czechoslovakia in
1990; Season 1990–91 included Mahler's Das klagende Lied, Haydn's

Symphony No. 92, Mozart's Requiem and Concertante K364, Sibelius's
Symphonies 2, 3 and 7, Brahms' 2nd Symphony and D Minor Concerto,
Berg's Violin Concerto; Concert performance of Meyerbeer's Il Crociato in
Egitto, to celebrate the bicentenary of the composer's birth. *Recordings:*
Albeniz' Iberia Suite; Falla's Three Cornered Hat; Mozart's Horn Concertos,
Arias and Duets; Ravel's Rhapsodie Espagnole; Reger's Böcklin Tone Pictures
and Mozart Variations. *Address:* Dresden Philharmonic Orchestra, Kultur-
palast am Altmarkt, 8012 Dresden, Germany.

**WEIKERT, Ralf;** Austrian conductor; b. 10 Nov. 1940, St Florian, Linz.
*Education:* Bruckner Conservatory, Linz, State Acad., Vienna with Hans
Swarowsky. *Career:* coach, conductor, Landestheater Salzburg 1963; concerts
in Austria, Scandinavia from 1965; conductor, Bonn Opera 1966, Music Dir
1968; Salzburg Festival (concert) 1971; guest conductor, Royal Opera
Copenhagen 1972, with works by Mozart, Verdi, Stravinsky; Hamburg
Staatsoper from 1975, with Don Quichotte, works by Mozart, Puccini and
Donizetti; Vienna Staatsoper debut 1974, Il Trovatore; Zürich Opera 1976–80,
with Le nozze di Figaro, Arabella, Fidelio, La Cenerentola and Il Barbiere di
Siviglia; Deutsche Oper Berlin 1978–80, Figaro and Don Pasquale; US debut
1980, with the City Opera's Giulio Cesare in New York and Los Angeles;
Teatro La Fenice, Venice 1981, with Tancredi by Rossini; further engage-
ments in Barcelona, Munich, Vienna 1968–88, Rosenkavalier, Carmen, Die
Entführung and L'Elisir d'amore; Metropolitan Opera 1987–90, Elisir,
Barbiere and Bohème; Finnish Nat. Opera 2001–2004, with La Fanciulla
del West, Die Entführung aus dem Serail, Arabella, Der Ring des Nibelungen,
Arena di Verona 1987, La Traviata; concert engagements with leading
orchestras in Berlin, Vienna, Scandinavia, Paris, Japan, Hungary, West
Germany, the UK (English Chamber Orchestra, WNO, Acad. of St Martin in
the Fields); festival appearances at Salzburg (Mozart Matinées, Serenades
and Cenerentola), Aix-en-Provence, Orange, Bregenz and Lucerne; conducted
Offenbach's Barbe Bleue at Stuttgart 1996, Fidelio at Catania 1998; Verdi's I
Vespri Siciliani at Palermo 2004. *Recordings:* Rossini Tancredi (Schoeck
Lebendig Begraben), James Morris Recital, Love Duets Araiza-Lind, Barbiere
di Siviglia (Metropolitan Opera, video), Alexander von Zemlinsky: Kleider
Machen Leute (opera), Eugen d'Albert: Die tote Stadt (opera), Rossini's
Barbiere di Siviglia, L'Italiana in Algeri (DVD). *Honours:* Mozart Prize 1966,
Dr Karl Böhm Prize 1975. *Address:* Neubruchstrasse 5, 8127 Zürich,
Switzerland. *Telephone:* 1-980-3473. *Fax:* 1-980-3473. *E-mail:* ralf.weikert@
bluewin.ch.

**WEIKL, Bernd;** Austrian singer (baritone); b. 29 July 1942, Vienna.
*Education:* Mainz Conservatoire and Hochschule für Musik, Hanover. *Career:*
mem. Hamburg State Opera 1973–, Deutsche Oper Berlin 1974–; Guest
Artist, Bayreuth Festivals 1973–75; Covent Garden debut in 1975 as Rossini's
Figaro; Metropolitan Opera debut in 1977 as Wolfram; guest engagements at
La Scala Milan, Bavarian State Opera, Salzburg Festival; performed Iago at
Stuttgart 1990, Boccanegra at Hamburg 1991, Dutchman at Bayreuth 1990,
Sachs at the Metropolitan 1993, Jochanaan at San Francisco 1997, Kurwenal
in Tristan und Isolde at Munich 1998. *Current Management:* Askonas Holt
Ltd, Lonsdale Chambers, 27 Chancery Lane, London, WC2A 1PF, England.

**WEIL, Bruno;** Conductor; b. 24 Nov. 1949, Hahnstatten, Germany.
*Education:* Studied with Franco Ferrara in Italy and with Hans Swarowsky
in Vienna. *Career:* Conducted at the opera houses of Wiesbaden and
Brunswick; Debut with the Berlin Radio Symphony Orchestra in 1977;
Concerts with the Berlin Philharmonic from 1979; Music Director of Augsburg
Opera, 1979–89; Debut at the Deutsche Oper Berlin in 1980 with Weill's Die
Sieben Todsünden; Salzburg Festival from 1982 including Don Giovanni at
the 1988 Festival; Conducted Fidelio for Radio France in Paris, 1984, and led
the Yomiuri Nippon Symphony Orchestra in Japan; In 1985 conducted Aida at
the Vienna Staatsoper and Ariadne auf Naxos at Bordeaux, and in 1986 Le
nozze di Figaro at Trieste; Initiated series of Mozart operas in joint production
with the Vienna Volksoper and Austrian television, 1987; Conducted Die
Entführung aus dem Serail in Bonn and Die Zauberflöte in Karlsruhe, 1987;
US debut in 1988 in a Schubertiade in New York; Concerts in Netherlands
with the Residentie Orchestra and Rotterdam Philharmonic; Concerts with
the Los Angeles Philharmonic and the BBC Scottish Symphony from season
1988–90; Tour of Germany with the English Chamber Orchestra; Season
1990–91 with the Orchestre National de France and the Montreal Symphony;
Conducted Brahms with the Orchestra of the Age of Enlightenment, London,
1997. *Recordings:* Various albums with the Deutsche Philharmonie. *Honours:*
Second Prize, Herbert von Karajan Conductors' Competition in 1979. *Current
Management:* Ingpen & Williams Ltd, 7 St George's Court, 131 Putney Bridge
Road, London, SW15 2PA, England.

**WEIL, Tibor V.;** Singer (baritone), Pianist, Cellist, Impresario and
Economist; b. 16 May 1942, Hungary. *Education:* Economist, Mackenzie
University, São Paulo, Brazil; MA, New York University, USA; Pianist and
cellist, Budapest Music High School, Salvador Music High School, Pro Arte
Music High School. *Career:* Debut: Piano and Cello in 1960; Concerts,
television appearances in São Paulo, Rio de Janeiro, and Salvador, 1958–;
Regular chamber music performances; Frequent concerts as lieder and light
opera singer, sacred music and requiems, 1989–; mem, Pro Arte, São Paulo;
Managing Adviser, Centro de Musica Brasileira. *Honours:* Viscua Konserva-
toire Scholarship, 1956; Pro Arte Scholarship, 1959. *Address:* TAW Promotions SP, Rua Angatuba 80, Bairro, Pacaembu, CEP 01247 São Paulo SP,
Brazil.

**WEILERSTEIN, Donald;** Violinist; b. 14 March 1940, Washington DC, USA. *Education:* BS; MS, Juilliard School of Music, 1966. *Career:* Debut: New York, 1963; Founding First Violinist, Cleveland Quartet, 1969–89; Professor of Violin and Chamber Music; Cleveland Institute of Music, 1967–71, 1989–, SUNY at Buffalo, 1971–76, Eastman School of Music, NY, 1976–89; mem, American String Teachers' Association. *Recordings:* Complete Brahms Quartets; Complete Beethoven Quartets; Schubert 2 cello Quintet; Schubert Trout Quintet; Mendelssohn and Schubert Octets; Complete Violin and Piano and Solo Violin Works of Ernest Bloch; Sonatas of Dohnányi and Janáček; The Complete Sonatas of Robert Schumann with pianist Ulvian Hornik Weilerstein, 1995; The Complete Sonatas and Partitas of J. S. Bach, 2000. *Publications:* Chapter on Violin Technique in Medical Problems of Instrumental Musicians, 2000. *Honours:* NEA Grant; Grammy nominations for recorded works; Prizewinner, Munich Competition for violin and piano duo. *Current Management:* Jane Deckoff. *Address:* 2645 Fairmount Blvd, Cleveland Heights, OH 44106, USA.

**WEIN, Erika;** Singer (Mezzo-Soprano); b. 2 Sept. 1928, Vienna, Austria. *Education:* Studied at the Vienna Music Academy with Erik Werba. *Career:* Sang at the Vienna Volksoper, 1952–53, Bremen, 1953–59, and Düsseldorf, 1959–64; Engagements at the Zürich Opera, 1964–80, notably in the premieres of Sutermeister's Madame Bovary in 1967, and Kelterborn's Ein Engel Kommt nach Babylon, 1977; Guest appearances in Berlin, the State Operas of Munich, Hamburg, Stuttgart, Frankfurt and Cologne, at the Holland Festival, Florence, Lyon, Buenos Aires, Paris, San Francisco and Turin; Roles included: Carmen, Azucena, Amneris, Eboli, Ulrica, Ortud, Fricka, Brangane, Venus, Orpheus, Marina in Boris Godunov, Clytemnestra and Berg's Marie; Concert showings in works by Bach, Beethoven and Brahms; Lieder recitals and concerts in Germany, Switzerland, Spain and Austria. *Recordings include:* Highlights from Rigoletto and Nabucco. *Address:* c/o Opernhaus Zürich, Falkenstrasse 1, 8008 Zürich, Switzerland.

**WEINGARTNER, Elisabeth;** Singer (Mezzo-Soprano); b. 23 Jan. 1938, Sissach, Switzerland. *Education:* Studied in Basle and with Res Fischer in Stuttgart. *Career:* Sang at the Basle Opera, 1973–81 and made guest appearances at Nantes, Paris, Trier and Cannes; Roles have included Dorabella in Così fan tutte by Mozart, Carmen by Bizet, Isabella in L'Italiana in Algeri, Idamantes in Idomeneo, Geneviève in Pelléas, Annina, and the Hostess in Boris Godunov; Sang at Strasbourg in 1984 in the premiere of H H Ulysse by Prodromidès; Concert and lieder engagements in France and Switzerland and at Liège, Stuttgart and Vienna; Sang in Verdi's Requiem in Paris with Orchestra Lamoureux and Dvořák's Requiem at San Sebastian in Spain. *Recordings include:* H H Ulysse. *Address:* Opéra du Rhin, 19 Place Brogile, 67008 Strasbourg Cédex, France.

**WEINSCHENK, Hans-Jorg;** Singer (Tenor); b. 14 Nov. 1955, Stuttgart, Germany. *Career:* Sang in Opera at Heidelberg, 1974–76, and Wuppertal, 1976–80; Member of the Zürich Opera, 1981–85, and Theater am Gärtnerplatz Munich from 1984; Guest appearances at Lausanne in 1985, and the Grand Opera Paris in 1986; Sang in the premiere of Der Meister und Margarita by Kunad, Karlsruhe, 1986; Roles have included such buffo and character repertory as Pedrillo, the Witch in Hansel and Gretel, Monostatos, David in Die Meistersinger and the Steuermann in Fliegende Holländer; Frequent concert engagements; Sang in The Cunning Little Vixen at Karlsruhe, 1996 and in Hindemith/Milhaud/Weill/Toch programme, 1998; Season 2000–01 as Flaminio in A. Scarlatti's Il trionfo dell'onore, at Halle, Victorin in Die tote Stadt, Mozart's Basilio and Finn in Ruslan and Lyudmila, at Karlsruhe. *Address:* c/o Badische Staatstheater Karlsruhe, Baumersterstrasse, 11, Pf 1449, W-7500 Karlsruhe, Germany.

**WEIR, Dame Gillian Constance,** DBE, FRCM; British/New Zealand concert organist and harpsichordist; b. 17 Jan. 1941, Martinborough, New Zealand; d. of Cecil Alexander Weir and Clarice Mildred Foy Weir (née Bignell); m. 1st Clive Rowland Webster 1967 (divorced 1971); m. 2nd Lawrence Irving Phelps 1972 (died 1999). *Education:* Wanganui Girls' Coll., NZ and Royal Coll. of Music, London, pvt. studies with Marie-Claire Alain, Anton Heiller, Nadia Boulanger. *Career:* winner St Albans Int. Organ Festival Competition 1964; debuts Royal Festival Hall and Royal Albert Hall, London 1965; worldwide career since 1965 as organist and latterly as harpsichordist; has appeared with all leading British orchestras and with many abroad, under leading conductors; many radio and TV appearances; adjudicator in int. competitions and artist-in-residence at major univs including Yale; frequent adjudicator at int. competitions; gives lectures and master classes in many countries; organ consultant, Birmingham Symphony Hall; Visiting Prof. of Organ, Royal Acad. of Music, London 1997–98; Prince Consort Prof. of Organ, Royal Coll. of Music, London 1999–; many premières including first British performance of Messiaen's Méditations of 1972; many works written for her including concertos by William Mathias and Peter Racine Fricker; many recordings including 7-CD set complete organ works of Olivier Messiaen 1995 and complete works of César Franck 1997; presenter and performer 6-part BBC TV series 1989; various TV documentaries for NZTV; subject of South Bank Show, ITV 2000; Concerto soloist First Night of the Proms 1967 and Last Night of the Proms 1999, many other Proms appearances; Pres. Inc. Asscn of Organists (first woman Pres.) 1981–83, Inc. Soc. of Musicians 1992–93, Soloists' Ensemble 1998–; mem. Exec. Council, Royal Coll. of Organists (first woman mem.) 1981–85, Council (first woman mem.) 1977–, Pres. (first woman Pres.) 1994–96; mem. Council Royal Philharmonic Soc. 1996–2001; mem. Royal Soc. of Musicians of GB 1996–; Trustee Eric Thompson Charitable Trust

1993–. *Publications:* contrib. to The Messiaen Companion 1995; articles in professional journals. *Honours:* Hon. FRCO 1975; Hon. Fellow Royal Canadian Coll. of Organists 1983; Hon. mem. RAM 1989; Hon. DMus (Victoria Univ. of Wellington, NZ) 1983, (Hull) 1999, (Exeter) 2001, (Leicester) 2003, (Aberdeen) 2004; Hon. DLitt (Huddersfield) 1997; Hon. DUniv (Univ. of Cen. England) 2001; Int. Performer of Year Award, American Guild of Organists 1981; Turnovsky Prize for Outstanding Achievement in the Arts 1985; Silver Medal, Albert Schweitzer Asscn (Sweden) 1998, Evening Standard Award for Outstanding Solo Performance in 1998, Lifetime Achievement Award, NZ Soc. 2005. *Current Management:* c/o Karen McFarlane Artists Inc., 2385 Fenwood Road, Cleveland, OH 44118-3803, USA. *Telephone:* (216) 397-3345. *Fax:* (216) 397-7716. *E-mail:* john@concertorganists.com. *Website:* www.dennylyster.free -online.co.uk; www.gillianweir.com.

**WEIR, Judith,** CBE, MA; British composer; b. 11 May 1954, Cambridge. *Education:* North London Collegiate School, King's Coll. Cambridge. *Career:* composer-in-residence, Southern Arts Asscn 1976–79; Fellow in Composition Univ. of Glasgow 1979–82, Creative Arts Fellowship, Trinity Coll. Cambridge 1983–85, composer-in-residence Royal Scottish Acad. of Music and Drama 1988–91; Fairbairn Composer in Asscn with City of Birmingham Symphony Orchestra 1995–98; Artistic Dir Spitalfields Festival 1995–2000; Visiting Prof. in Opera Studies, Univ. of Oxford 1999–2000; Visiting Prof., Princeton Univ., USA 2001; mem. Bd of Govs Royal Opera House 2003–. *Compositions include:* King Harald's Saga 1979, Consolations of Scholarship 1985, A Night At The Chinese Opera 1987, Missa Del Cid 1988, Heaven Ablaze In His Breast 1989, The Vanishing Bridegroom 1990, Music Untangled 1991–92, Heroic Strokes of the Bow 1992, Blond Eckbert 1993, Musicians Wrestle Everywhere 1994, Moon and Star 1995, Forest 1995, Storm 1997, We Are Shadows (South Bank Show Award 2001) 2000, The Voice of Desire (British Composer Award for vocal work) 2004. *Honours:* Dr hc (Aberdeen) 1995; Critics' Circle Award for most outstanding contrib. to British Musical Life 1994. *Address:* c/o Chester Music, 8–9 Frith Street, London, W1D 3JB, England. *Telephone:* (20) 7434-0066. *Fax:* (20) 7287-6329.

**WEIR, Scot;** Singer (Tenor); b. 1954, New Mexico, USA. *Education:* Studied at Colorado University and in Graz. *Career:* Sang at the Gelsenkirchen Opera, 1981–85, notably as Don Ottavio, Lenski and Xerxes; Wiesbaden Opera, 1985–89, as Almaviva, Medoro in Haydn's Orlando Paladino, Belfiore in La finta giardiniera, and Veit in Lortzing's Undine; Sang Hylas in Les Troyens at Brussels (1992) and has appeared as guest in Canada, Israel, Japan and the USA; Sang Monteverdi's Ulisse at Vienna, 1998. *Recordings include:* Franck's Les Béatitudes; Mozart C minor Mass. *Address:* Théâtre Royale de la Monnaie, 4 Leopoldstrasse, 1000 Brussels, Belgium.

**WEISBERG, Arthur;** Bassoonist, Conductor and Teacher; b. 4 April 1931, New York City, USA. *Education:* Studied bassoon with Simon Kovar, conducting with Jean Morel, Juilliard School of Music, New York. *Career:* Bassoonist with Houston Symphony Orchestra, Baltimore Symphony Orchestra, and Cleveland Orchestra; Member of New York Woodwind Quintet, 1956–70; Founder-Director of Contemporary Chamber Ensemble, NY, 1969–; Chief Conductor, Iceland Symphony Orchestra, Reykjavík, 1987–88; Guest Conductor with various orchestras including New York Philharmonic, 1983, 1984; Teacher, Juilliard School of Music, 1960–68, State University of New York, Stony Brook, 1971–89, Yale University, 1975–89. *Publications:* The Art of Wind Playing, 1973. *Address:* 12008 South 35th Ct, Phoenix, AZ 85044, USA.

**WEISBROD, Annette;** Pianist; b. 9 Dec. 1937, Blackburn, Lancashire, England; m. Charles Kirmess, 21 Jan. 1967. *Education:* Teaching Diploma, Chamber Music Diploma, Zürich Conservatory; Soloist and Concert Diploma, Basle Conservatoire. *Career:* Debut: Wigmore Hall in London, 1960; Concert appearances world-wide; Radio and television appearances in Switzerland, Germany, England, France, the former Yugoslavia and China; Professor at Berne Conservatoire; mem, Swiss Tonkünstler Verein; Swiss Musikpädagogischer Verein; International Piano Teachers Association; Soroptimist International, Zürich; Business and Professional Women, Zürich. *Recordings:* Over 50 albums including: Haydn Trios with the Swiss Festival Trio; Complete Works for Piano and Cello by Beethoven; Several piano concertos and many piano works. *Address:* Heuelstr 33, 8032 Zürich, Switzerland.

**WEISE, Klaus;** Conductor; b. 30 Jan. 1936, Kolpin, Poland. *Education:* Studied at Berlin, Dresden and Leipzig. *Career:* Conducted first at Wuppertal, then principal conductor of the Essen Opera; Musical director at Fribourg Opera, 1978–81, Kiel, 1981–85, and Dortmund, 1985–90; Director of the Nice Opera and Philharmonic Orchestra, from 1990. *Address:* Théâtre de l'Opéra de Nice, 4 and 6 Rue St François de Paule, 06300 Nice, France.

**WEISEL-CAPSOUTO, Robin;** Singer (Soprano); b. 1952, USA. *Education:* Studied at Oberlin College, University of Illinois, with Jennie Tourel in Jerusalem and with Heather Harper in London. *Career:* Debut: Sang Vivaldi's Gloria with the Jerusalem Symphony Orchestra in 1974; Sang in Mahler's 4th with Israel Philharmonic, 1976; Opera engagements in USA and Israel as Gluck's Amor, Lucy in The Beggar's Opera, and in La Voix Humaine, Le Roi David, Bacchus and Ariadne by Thomas Arne and Rameau's Les Fêtes d'Hébé; Sang Zerlina with New England Opera Company in 1984, and The Governess in The Turn of The Screw for New Israeli Opera in 1992; Concert repertoire includes Bach's B minor Mass, Carissimi's Jephté, Solomon and other oratorios by Handel.

**WEISS, Ferdinand,** DipMus, MA; Austrian composer and educator; b. 6 June 1933, Vienna; m. Ingeborg Scheibenreiter 1967; two s. *Education:* Viennese Acad. of Music. *Career:* debut as composer, Eisenstadt 1957; freelance composer, private teacher of music theory, conductor and orchestra musician 1960–; Music Master, Vienna Conservatory and Baden Pedagogische Academie; Man., Concert Chamber Ensemble, Lower Austria Composer's Soc.; Pres., Inoek; performances, concerts and radio broadcasts worldwide. *Compositions include:* three symphonies, concertos for flute, oboe, clarinet, trumpet and trombone, chamber music, Lieder; Quattrofonia for saxophone quartet, 5 Scènes pour quatuor de guitares, a sa fin for orchestra 1994, Avec un Souffle du Tristesse for flute and string orchestra 1997, Quartetto Egiziano 2002, Quartet for flute, violin, violoncello, piano 2004. *Honours:* Award of Vienna 1960, Award of the Austrian State 1972, Award of Lower Austria 1970, 1984. *Address:* Christalnigg-Gasse 11, 2500 Baden, Austria (office). *Telephone:* (2252) 22632 (office). *Fax:* (2252) 22632 (office).

**WEISS, Howard A.,** BM, MM; American violinist, conductor, concertmaster and educator; b. 1935, Chicago, IL. *Education:* Chicago Musical College, Roosevelt University. *Career:* founder, Music Director, Conductor, Rochester Philharmonic Youth Orchestra, 1970–89, with 12 tours including England, Scotland, 1984, Germany, Austria, Switzerland, 1986, Dominican Republic, 1987, Alaska, 1988; Jamaica, 1989, also on Voice of America; Advisory Board, Young Audiences of Rochester, 1975–; Rochester Chamber Orchestra, 1981–; Professor, Violin: Eastman School of Music, Rochester, 1981–, Nazareth College, Rochester, 1983–85; Concertmaster: Chicago Chamber Orchestra, 1962–70, San Francisco Ballet Orchestra, 1962, Virginia Symphony, 1964, Rochester Philharmonic, 1967–87 (Concertmaster Emeritus, 1987–), Eastern Music Festival, Greensboro, North Carolina, 1976–80, Grand Teton Music Festival Seminar, Jackson Hole, Wyoming, 1983–86, Rochester Oratorio Society, 1987–, Bear Lake Music Festival, Utah, 1992–93; Music Director, Conductor String Orchestra, Siena Festival, Italy, 1998–; 1st Violinist, Cleveland Orchestra, 1965–67; Violin Soloist, over 45 concerti with Cleveland Orchestra, Rochester and New Orleans Philharmonics, Chicago Grant Park Symphony, Cincinnati, Chicago and Rochester Chamber Orchestras, Siena Festival, Italy; Violin soloist with conductors James Levine, David Zinman, Alexander Schneider, Walter Hendl and Gerard Schwarz; Soloist in the US premiere of the Carl Nielsen Violin Concerto, 1967; Soloist in the Rochester, New York premieres of the violin concertos of Berg, Nielsen and Vaughan Williams; Soloist, complete concerti for violin and orchestra of J. S. Bach (5), Rochester Bach Festival, of Haydn (3), Rochester Chamber Orchestra; Violinist of Brockport Piano Trio, 1971–74; Leader, Hartwell String Quartet, 1975–78; Participant, Casals Festival, Puerto Rico, 1975–80; Chamber music with Misha Dichter, Leonard Rose, Lynn Harrell, Yo-Yo Ma; Elly Ameling, Jaime Laredo, Walter Trampler, Lillian Fuchs, James Buswell, Gary Karr, Alan Civil, Lukas Foss. *Recordings:* Amram Elegy for Violin and Orchestra, David Zinman, Rochester Philharmonic; Music Director, Conductor, Rochester Philharmonic Youth Orchestra. *Honours:* Outstanding Graduate of 1966, Roosevelt University, 1973; Monroe County (New York) Medallion, 1986. *Address:* 228 Castlebar Road, Rochester, NY 14610, USA.

**WEISSENBERG, Alexis;** Bulgarian pianist; b. 26 July 1929, Sofia. *Career:* studied piano and composition with Pancho Vladigerov aged three, also with Olga Samaroff at Juilliard School, New York 1946; debut aged 14; numerous appearances in Europe, South America, USA, Japan; American debut with New York Philharmonic; soloist with Berlin, Vienna, Japan, Czechoslovak Philharmonics, Philadelphia, Cleveland, Minnesota, Royal Danish and Salzburg Festival orchestras, Boston, Chicago, Pittsburgh Symphony orchestras, Orchestre de Paris and others; recording artist with RCA, Angel. *Recordings include:* works by Bach, Bartók, Beethoven, Brahms, Chopin, Debussy, Franck, Haydn, Liszt, Mozart, Mussorgsky, Prokofiev, Rachmaninov, Ravel, Saint-Saens, Scarlatti, Schumann, Stravinsky. *Honours:* First Prize, Philadelphia Youth competition 1946, First Prize, Int. Leventritt Competition 1947. *Current Management:* c/o Michal Schmidt, Thea Dispeker Inc., 59 East 54th Street, New York, NY 10022, USA. *E-mail:* info@ alexisweissenberg.com (office). *Website:* www.alexisweissenberg.com (office).

**WEITHAAS, Antje;** German concert violinist; b. 1966. *Education:* Hanns Eisler Hochschule, Berlin. *Career:* frequent concerts with the Deutsches Symphony Orchestra and Vladimir Ashkenazy, Leipzig Gewandhaus Orchestra, Suisse Romande and Acad. of St Martin in the Fields; Los Angeles Philharmonic Orchestra, Boston Symphony Orchestra and Minneapolis Orchestra; Philharmonia, BBC Symphony Orchestra, Dresdner Staatskapelle and Scottish Chamber Orchestra; season 1995–96 with recitals at the Bath Festival and Wigmore Hall, London, San Francisco Symphony Orchestra Debut Series and in Toronto; season 1996–97 with the Orchestre de Paris, Zürich Tonhalle, Gothenburg Symphony Orchestra, BBC Symphony Orchestra, and tour of Germany with the Bournemouth Symphony Orchestra; season 1998–99 with Scottish Chamber Orchestra, English Northern Philharmonic and BBC Symphony Orchestra; other engagements with the Royal Liverpool Philharmonic Orchestra and the Hallé Orchestra; with the Trio Ex Aequo, resident at the Vancouver Festival; season 1999–2000 with the Royal Liverpool Philharmonic, Brabant and Residentie Orchestras, Orchestra de Palermo and the Malaysian Philharmonic; season 2001–02 with the Tokyo Metropolitan, Copenhagen Philharmonic, Ulster, Capetown Philharmonic and Swedish Chamber Orchestras; season 2002–03 with the Gothenburg Symphony, BBC Philharmonic, Scottish Chamber and Lisbon Gulbenkian Orchestras; season 2003–04 with the Orchestre de Chambre de Lausanne,

BBC Nat. Orchestra of Wales; season 2004–05 with the Bournemouth Symphony Orchestra, Gothenburg Symphony; regularly performs chamber music with the Ex Aequo Trio, Vancouver Festival resident 1998–99; festivals include Kuhmo, Bath, Vancouver, Heimbach, Mondsee, Risör and Delft; plays Peter Greiner violin 2001. *Honours:* winner of Wieniawski, Kreisler and Joseph Joachim Competitions. *Current Management:* Markus Bröhl Artists and Concerts, Sülzburgstrasse 112, 50937 Cologne, Germany. *Telephone:* (221) 282-5185 (office). *Fax:* (221) 282-5899 (office). *E-mail:* markusbroehl@ artistsandconcerts.de (office). *Website:* www.artistsandconcerts.de.

**WELBORN, Tracey;** Singer (Tenor); b. 1967, Stoneville, North Carolina, USA. *Education:* Curtis Institute of Music, Philadelphia. *Career:* School teacher until 1989; Opera engagements with Lausanne Opera, Boston Lyric Opera, Spoleto USA, Opera Co of Philadelphia and Portland Opera; Season 1993–94 with Rossini's Lindoro for Utah Opera, Ernesto and Tamino for Canadian Opera and Gluck's Pylade at Strasbourg; Season 1994–95 with Paris in La Belle Hélène for Scottish Opera, Ferrando at Pittsburgh and Jupiter in Semele at Spoleto, Italy; Concerts include Candide with the San Francisco Symphony Orchestra, Messiah with the Baltimore Symphony Orchestra, Honegger's King David, and Mozart's Requiem; Phoenix Symphony Orchestra in Bach's St Matthew Passion; Season 1997 with Mozart's Belmonte at Edmonton, Don Ottavio at Costa Mesa and in Prokoviev's The Duenna at Geneva; title role in Rossini's Le Comte Ory, at Glyndebourne; Season 1998 with Bernstein's Candide at Turin and in Prokofiev's Duenna at Geneva. *Recordings include:* Paolo in Il Matrimonio Segreto. *Honours:* Winner, Washington International Competition and Mario Lanza Competition. *Address:* c/o Allied Artists, 42 Montpelier Square, London SW7 1JZ, England.

**WELCHER, Dan;** Composer and Conductor; b. 2 March 1948, Rochester, New York, USA. *Education:* BMus, 1969, Eastman School at Rochester (composition with Samuel Adler); MM, 1972, Manhattan School of Music and postgraduate studies in electronic music at the Aspen Music School, 1972. *Career:* Bassoonist with the Rochester Philharmonic Orchestra, 1968–69, and US Military Band at West Point, 1969–72; Louisville Orchestra, 1972–78; Assistant Conductor with the Austin, Texas Symphony Orchestra (1980–90); Faculty of University of Texas 1978, Full Professor from 1989; Faculty of Aspen Music Festival, 1976–93. *Compositions include:* Flute Concerto, 1974; 2 Wind Quintets, 1972, 1977; Concerto da Camera for bassoon and chamber orchestra, 1975; Trio for violin, cello and piano, 1976; The Visions of Merlin for orchestra, 1980; Partita for horn, violin and piano, 1980; Vox Femina for soprano and ensemble, 1984; Quintet for clarinet and strings, 1984; Prairie Light for orchestra, 1985; Arches: An Impression for concert band, 1985; Evening Scenes: Three Poems of James Agee, 1985; Della's Gift, opera, 1986; The Yellowstone Fires for wind ensemble, 1988; Clarinet Concerto, 1989; Bridges, 5 pieces for strings, 1989; 2 string quartets, 1987, 1992; 2 symphonies, 1992, 1994; Violin Concerto, 1993; Piano Concerto, Shiva's Drum, 1994; Zion for wind ensemble, 1994; Bright Wings, for orchestra, 1996; Brass Quintet, 1983; Oratorio, JFK: The Voice of Peace, 1999; Oboe Concerto Venti di Mare, 1999; Orchestral works: Beyond Sight, 1999; Zion, 2000; Wind Ensemble Works: Symphony #3 (Shaker Life), 1998; Perpetual Song, 2000; Songs without Words, 2001; Minstrels of the Kells, 2002; Glacier, 2003. *Honours:* Residencies, MacDowell Colony, 1989, and Bellagio, 1997; Composer-in-Residence with the Honolulu Symphony Orchestra, 1990–93; Guggenheim Fellowship, 1997; 3 National Endowment for the Arts awards;Artistic Advisory Board, Lotte Lehmann Foundation, 01–. *Address:* c/o ASCAP, ASCAP Building, One Lincoln Plaza, New York, NY 10023, USA.

**WELKER, Hartmut;** German opera singer (bass-baritone); b. 27 Oct. 1941, Velbert, Rhineland; m. Edeltraut 1982; one s. one d. *Education:* studied for tech. career, took up singing 1972. *Career:* debut, Opera, Aachen 1974; British debut, Edinburgh Festival with London Symphony Orchestra/Abbado 1983; Aachen Opera 1974–80; since then has had three-year contract with Karlsruhe Opera; sang at La Scala (Lohengrin with Abbado), Geneva, Paris (Khovanshchina); sang Don Pizarro (Fidelio), Madrid and at Maggio Musicale, Florence, Italy and for Scottish Opera 1984; appeared in Hamburg, Munich and Stuttgart, Boris Godunov in North America with Chicago Symphony Orchestra/Abbado, Vienna State Opera, Berlin and Hamburg in productions of Fidelio, Flying Dutchman, Salome, Lohengrin; Covent Garden debut in Fidelio 1986; sang also with Philharmonia Orchestra/Muti, also at Turin, Vienna, Madrid, Bologna, Naples, Tokyo, Chicago; Season 1988 included appearances in San Francisco, Berlin, Geneva, with further visits to La Scala, Covent Garden and Salzburg; sang in London as Pizarro and Kaspar 1986–89, Theater an der Wien and Turin in Schubert's Fierrabras and as Wozzeck 1989, Telramund in Lohengrin at Vienna Staatsoper and Deutsche Oper Berlin 1990; other roles include Kurwenal, Klingsor, Macbeth, Carlos in La Forza del Destino, Amonasro, Barnaba and Scarpia; sang Pizarro in Fidelio at the Metropolitan, New York 1991, Wozzeck at Catania 1996, Pizarro in Beethoven's Leonore at Théâtre de Champs Elysées, Paris 1998; Season 1997–98, Semperoper, Dresden as Kurwenal, Holländer, Pizarro; further roles as Amfortas in Parsifal, and Wotan and Alberich in Wagner's Ring, Bayreuth 2000–; Season 2000 as Alberich at Cologne and Scarpia at Essen, Kurwenal, Amonasro and Wotan for Karlsruhe Opera, Kurwenal in Tristan und Isolde at Bayreuth Festival 2006. *Recordings include:* Zemlinksy's Der Traumgörge as Kaspar/Hans, Notre Dame by F. Schmidt as Archidiakonus, Fierrabras, Brutamonte 1992, Fidelio (Pizarro), Lohengrin (Telramund), Das Wunder der Heliane, Korngold 1992, Arcesius in Die toten Augen, d'Albert 1997. *Honours:*

Kammersänger. *Address:* Frühlingstrasse 10, 76327 Pfintzal/Wöschbach, Germany (home). *Telephone:* (7240) 942548. *Fax:* (7240) 942549. *E-mail:* edeltraut.welker@web.de.

**WELLEJUS, Henning;** Composer; b. 23 Aug. 1919, Roskilde, Denmark; m. Inge Osterby, 2 c. *Education:* Studied with composer Svend Erik Tarp and conductor Giovanni Di Bella; University of Copenhagen. *Career:* Debut: Copenhagen; mem, Danish Composers Society. *Compositions include:* 3 Symphonies; 4 Concerts for violin and orchestra, oboe and orchestra, cello and orchestra, and piano and orchestra; Symphonic Fantasies: The History of the Year, Nina; Our Childhood's Friends and from Hans Christian Anderson's picturebook, 2 suites from ballet, The Swan; Wind Quintet; Flute Serenade Just for Fun, for flute, violin, viola and cello; 2 String Quartets; Several Songs; Trio for clarinet, viola and piano; The Dream, ballet; Passacaglia for orchestra; A Freedom Overture; Copenhagen Rhapsody; A Danish Summer Pastorale; Grates Nune Omnes Reddamus Domini, for soprano, chorus and orchestra; A Danish Requiem for soprano, baritone and orchestra; A Trio for Piano, Violin and Oboe; 3 Symphonic Fantasies, Dionysia, A Summer Morning in Hornboek and the Distant Morningsong of the Stars; a Trio for Violin, Viola and Cello; Operas; The Changed Bridegroom and Barbara; Several songs and numerous other works. *Recordings:* CD of music of his concert for violin and orchestra; CD of orchestra music; CD of Wind Quintet. *Honours:* Lange-Müller Stipendich, 1956; Aksel Agerbys Mindelegat, 1957; Det Anckerske Legat, 1958; Aügüst and Theodore Kassels Familie-og, Künstnerlegat, 1987; Cross, Order of Knighthood, Denmark. *Address:* Godthaabsvej 99, 2000 Frederiksberg, Denmark.

**WELLER, Dieter;** Singer (Bass Baritone); b. 25 May 1937, Essen, Germany; m. Dorte Fischer. *Education:* Studied with Erwin Rottgen in Essen; Further study in Cologne. *Career:* Debut at Bremerhaven, 1963–66 as Padre Guardiano in La Forza del Destino; Member of the Frankfurt Opera from 1966; Appeared in San Francisco in 1974 as Wurm in Luisa Miller; Further appearances in Berlin, Düsseldorf, Hamburg, Brussels and Edinburgh; Sang at Teatro Regio Turin in 1983 in Berg's Lulu, at Metropolitan Opera in 1985 as the Music Master in Ariadne auf Naxos; Season 2000 as Joe in Mahagonny at Hamburg and Reimann's Lear for the Dresden Staatsoper; Many appearances in operas by Rossini, Lortzing, Weber, Smetana, Wagner and Wolf-Ferrari; Frequent concert engagements. *Recordings:* Der Freischütz and Martha; Der Zwerg by Zemlinsky.

**WELLER, Walter;** Austrian conductor; b. 30 Nov. 1939, s. of Walter and Anna Weller; m. Elisabeth Samohyl, 1966; one s. *Education:* Realgymnasium, Vienna, Akademie für Musik, Vienna. *Career:* f. Weller Quartet 1958–69; mem. Vienna Philharmonic 1958–60, First Leader 1960–69; Conductor, Vienna State Opera 1969–75; Guest Conductor with all main European, American and Japan Broadcasting Corpn orchestras 1973–; Chief Conductor, Tonkünstler Orchestra, Vienna 1974–77; Principal Conductor and Artistic Adviser, Royal Liverpool Philharmonic Orchestra 1977–80, Guest Conductor Laureate 1980; Prin. Conductor, Royal Philharmonic Orchestra 1980–85, Chief Guest Conductor 1985–; Chief Guest Conductor, Nat. Orchestra of Spain 1987–; Prin. Conductor, Music Dir Royal Scottish Nat. Orchestra 1992–97, now Conductor Emer.; Chief Conductor and Artistic Adviser, Opera Basel and Allgemeine Musikgesellschaft Basel 1994–95. *Honours:* Medal of Arts and Sciences (Austria) 1968, Grand Prix du Disque, Charles Cross for Duke's Symphony in C, Great Silver Cross of Honour (Austria) 1998. *Address:* c/o Harrison-Parrott Ltd, 12 Penzance Place, London, W11 4PA, England. *Telephone:* (20) 7229-9166 (office). *E-mail:* info@harrisonparrott.co.uk (office). *Website:* www.harrisonparrott.co.uk (office); www.music.at/walter-weller (home).

**WELLINGTON, Christopher Ramsay,** MA, ARCM; British violist and viola d'amore player; b. 5 Feb. 1930, London, England; m. 1st Joanna Donat 1954; one s. one d.; m. 2nd Eileen Darlow 1988. *Education:* Univ. of Oxford, Royal Coll. of Music. *Career:* Sadler's Wells Opera Orchestra 1954–58; Philharmonia Orchestra 1958–65; principal viola, London Bach Orchestra, Philomusica of London, Tilford Bach Orchestra; principal viola of Southern Pro Musica; viola player of Zorian String Quartet, Amici String Quartet, Nemet Piano Quartet, Music Group of London, Rasumovsky String Quartet; frequent soloist at QEH; Prof. of Viola, Univ. Coll., Chichester; warden solo performers section Incorporated Soc. of Musicians 1986–87; Prof. Royal Coll. of Music 1972–96; Prof. Trinity Coll. of Music 1996–2001. *Recordings:* Elegiac Meditation by Robin Milford, works by Haydn, Rubbra, Charles Ives, Shostakovich with Amici Quartet, works by Elgar, Vaughan Williams, Frank Bridge, Schubert with Music Group of London, works by Jadin, Vachon, Boughton, Holbrooke, Padre Soler with Rasumovksy String Quartet. *Publications:* Concerto for viola and orchestra by William Walton (Vol. 12, ed.) 2002. *Address:* 7 Fraser Gardens, Emsworth, Hants PO10 8PY, England (home). *Telephone:* (1243) 378300 (home). *Fax:* (1243) 378300 (home). *Website:* www.rasumovsky.com.

**WELLS, Jeffrey;** Singer (Bass-baritone); b. 1957, USA. *Career:* Sang Donizetti's Raimondo at New Orleans in 1985; Season 1986–87 as Assur in Semiramide and Ferrando in Il Trovatore at Washington; Sang Stravinsky's Nick Shadow at Glyndebourne, 1989, and Rossini's Basilio at Toronto; Metropolitan Opera from 1990, in Semiramide, Billy Budd, Carmen (as Zuniga), and A Midsummer Night's Dream, 1996; Guest appearances at Washington as Enrico in Anna Bolena, 1993, at Bonn as Escamillo, 1994, Detroit as Don Giovanni, 1995, and San Francisco, 1996–98, as Glinka's Ruslan, and Escamillo; Sang the Rheingold Wotan at San Francisco, 1999;

Britten's Claggart in Seattle and Toronto, 2001. *Recordings include:* Il Trovatore. *Address:* San Francisco Opera, War Memorial House, Van Ness Avenue, San Francisco, CA 94102, USA.

**WELSBY, Norman;** Singer (Baritone); b. 7 Feb. 1939, Warrington, Cheshire, England. *Education:* Studied at the Royal College of Music in Manchester and with Gwilym Jones and Otakar Kraus in London. *Career:* Debut: Sadler's Wells Opera, London in 1968 as Masetto; Many appearances at Covent Garden and with English National Opera in the standard repertoire and in modern works; Sang Gunther in The Ring, under Reginald Goodall, 1973–74; Sang in the premiere (concert) of The Magic Fountain by Delius, BBC, 1977; Sang Pentheus in the British premiere of The Bassarids for ENO in 1974 and The General in the premiere of We Come to The River, at Covent Garden in 1976; Many concert appearances. *Recordings include:* The Ring of the Nibelung conducted by Reginald Goodall; The Magic Fountain. *Address:* c/o English National Opera, London Coliseum, St Martin's Lane, London WC2N 4ES, England.

**WELSER-MÖST, Franz;** Austrian/Liechtenstein conductor; *Music Director, Zürich Opera;* b. 16 Aug. 1960, Linz; m. *Education:* Musikgymnasium, Linz and Staatliche Musikhochschule, Munich. *Career:* Chief Conductor, Jeunesse Orchestra, Linz 1982–85, Norrköping Symphony Orchestra 1985, Musikkollegium Winterthur, Switzerland 1986; Music Dir London Philharmonic Orchestra 1990–96; Music Dir Zürich Opera 1995–2002, Principal Conductor 2002–05; Music Dir 2005–(11); Music Dir Cleveland Orchestra 2002–(12); has also appeared at Vienna Staatsoper, Deutsche Oper Berlin, Glyndebourne Festival; regularly works with Berlin Philharmonic and orchestras of Philadelphia, Los Angeles, New York and Boston. *Recordings include:* Mendelssohn Symphonies Nos 3 and 4, Schumann Symphonies Nos 2 and 3, Bruckner Symphony No. 7, Strauss Waltzes, Carl Orff's Carmina Burana, Stravinsky's Oedipus Rex, Bartok's Miraculous Mandarin, Kodaly's Peacock Variations, Kancheli's Symphony No. 3, Pärt's Symphony No. 3, Fratres, Schmidt's Symphony No. 4 (Gramophone Award 1996) (all with LPO), World Premiere Recording of Johann Straus Jr's Simplicius with Zurich Opera Orchestra. *Honours:* Outstanding Achievement Award from Western Law Centre, LA, for work for people with disabilities, Musical America's Conductor of the Year 2003. *Current Management:* IMG Artists, Lovell House, 616 Chiswick High Road, London, W4 5RX, England. *Telephone:* (20) 8233-5911 (office); (20) 8233-5801 (office). *E-mail:* cdennes@imgworld.com (office). *Address:* c/o Opernhaus Zürich, Falkenstrasse 1, 8008 Zürich, Switzerland. *E-mail:* info@opernhaus.ch. *Website:* www.opernhaus.ch.

**WELSH, Moray Meston,** BA, LRAM, ARCM, GradDip; British cellist; *Principal Cellist, London Symphony Orchestra;* b. 1 March 1947, Haddington, Scotland; s. of D. A. Welsh and C. Welsh (née Meston); pnr Jonathan Papp. *Education:* York Univ. and Moscow Conservatoire. *Career:* debut, Wigmore Hall 1972; cello solo appearances in UK, USA, USSR, Europe and Scandinavia; appeared with major UK orchestras, including London Symphony Orchestra, Royal Philharmonic Orchestra, BBC Symphony; festivals at Bath, Edinburgh, Aldeburgh, Bergen and Helsinki; appeared as soloist internationally under Colin Davis, Previn, De Burgos, Haitink; chamber music performances with Previn, Bashmet, Midori, Galway and Chung; Prin. Cellist London Symphony Orchestra 1992–. *Recordings include:* concertos by Boccherini, Vivaldi, Alexander Goehr, Hoddinott, Hugh Wood (Sunday Times record of the year); recorded with James Galway, Kyung-Wha Chung, Allegri Quartet, Alberni Quartet; cello and orchestra music by Herbert Howells with LSO; Rachmaninov Complete Works for Cello and Piano. *Radio:* frequent broadcasts on BBC Radio 3. *Honours:* British Council Scholarship 1969, Gulbenkian Fellowship 1970. *Address:* 32 Dartmouth Road, London, NW2 4EX, England (home). *Telephone:* (20) 8933-3032 (home). *Fax:* (20) 8933-3032 (home).

**WEN, De-Qing;** Composer; b. 10 July 1958, Jian Yang, Fujian, China. *Education:* Art Department, Fujian Normal University, 1978–82; China Conservatory of Music, Beijing, 1988–90; Conservatoire de Musique de Genève, Switzerland, 1992–96; Conservatoire National Supérieur de Musique de Lyon, France, 1993–94. *Career:* debut as composer, Ningxia Ensemble, China, 1984; Concert Portrait performed by Ningxia Ensemble, Xining, 1986; Music for Fan Jun's film My Childhood in Ruijing, 1990; Concert Portrait performed by Ensemble Contrechamps and Ensemble CIP, Geneva, 1995; Concert Portrait performed by Quatuor du Temps, La Chaux-de-Fonds, 1998; Concert Portrait tour in China, 1999. *Compositions:* Ji I and Ji II for piano, 1992–93; Complainte for 1 speaker of Beijing Opera and 3 percussionists, 1994; Le souffle for 6 instruments, 1994; String Quartet No. 1, 1995; Spring, River, Flowers, Moon, Night for 12 women's voices, 1995; Traces II for 9 instruments, 1996; Divination for 6 instrumentalists, 1997; Petit Chou variation for erhu and string quartet, 1997; String Quartet No. 2, 1997; Ballade, for pipa and string quartet, 1998; Kung-fu, for percussion solo, 1998; Quatre Poésies for chamber orchestra, 1999. *Recordings:* De-qing Wen, Ensemble Contrechamps and CIP, Quatuor du Temps, recorded for Radio Suisse Romande, Espace 2, 1996. *Publications:* Musical Works, China, 1997, Switzerland, 1998. *Address:* 36 Avenue de la Roseraie, 1205 Geneva, Switzerland.

**WENKEL, Ortrun;** German singer (mezzo-soprano, alto); b. 25 Oct. 1942, Buttstadt, Thuringia; m. Peter Rothe 1966. *Education:* Franz Liszt Hochschule Weimar, Hochschule für Musik, Frankfurt, Lohmann masterclass and operatic studies with Cavelti. *Career:* debut concert, as student, in

London, 1964; Opera in Heidelberg, 1971; Performed at opera houses throughout Europe including Milan Scala, Covent Garden, Bayerische Staatsoper, Hamburg, with appearances at the Salzburg Festival, Munich Opera Festival and festivals of Schwetzingen, Edinburgh, Berlin and Vienna, notably as Penelope in the Zürich production of the Monteverdi Cycle; Has given numerous lieder recitals and made guest appearances with symphony orchestras in New York, London, Berlin, Vienna, Paris, Bayreuth, Amsterdam, Buenos Aires and Rio de Janeiro among others; Alto part of Erda in Wagner's Rheingold and Siegfried; Debuts in new mezzo soprano roles as Adriano in Wagner's Rienzi, Staatsoper Prague, Fricka in Wagner's Rheingold and Walküre, Herodias in Salome and Klytämnestra in Elektra by Richard Strauss, Spring Festival, Budapest, 1999; Magda Schneider in Kühr/Turrini's Tod und Teufel, world premiere, Graz, Steirischer Herbst, 1999; Beroe in Henze's The Bassarids at New York and Moscow; Bernarda in Relmann's Bernarda Albas Haús, Swiss premiere, Bern, 2002; Numerous concert engagements. *Recordings include:* Boulez Bayreuth Centenary Ring, The Ring with Dresdner Staatskapelle; Mahler's 3rd Symphony and 8th Symphony; Mozart's Requiem; The Magic Flute; Schoenberg's Jacob's Ladder; Dvořák's Stabat Mater; Handel's Xerxes; Solo recitals of Italian Baroque music; St Matthew Passion by Bach and several of his cantatas; Zemlinsky Lieder, Schreker and Shostakovich Lieder; Henze's The Bassarids; Wagner's Ring with Badische Staatskapelle, 1995. *Honours:* Grammy Award for Wagner's Ring des Nibelungen, principal soloist, 1982; Deutscher Schallplattenpreis for Mozart's Requiem, 1983. *Address:* Eichendorffstrasse 25, 69493 Hirschberg-Leutershausen, Germany.

**WENKOFF, Spas;** Singer (Tenor); b. 23 Sept. 1928, Tirnovo, Bulgaria. *Education:* Studied with J Jossifov in Sofia, Madame Saffiriva in Russe and Johannes Kemter in Dresden. *Career:* Debut: Tirnovo 1954, in Keto and Kote by Dolidse; Sang in Russe, Bulgaria, 1962–65, East Germany from 1965, Dobben, Madgeburg, Halle and the Staatsoper Berlin; Sang Tristan at Dresden Staatsoper in 1975, and Tristan and Tannhäuser at Bayreuth Festival, 1976–83; Has sung roles in operas by Verdi and Puccini as well as leading parts in operas by Wagner; Sang Tannhäuser at Vienna Staatsoper in 1982; Further appearances at the Deutsche Oper Berlin in 1984, Munich and Cologne; Sang Tannhäuser at Berne in 1987.

**WENNBERG, Siv (Anna Margareta);** Dramatic Soprano; b. 18 Sept. 1944, Timrå, Sweden. *Education:* Ingesunds Musikskola, Sweden; Musikaliska Akademien Stockholm; Qualified Pianist, Organist and Music Director. *Career:* Debut: Royal Opera House, Stockholm in 1972; Opera performances from 1972 throughout Europe; Extensive concert appearances with roles including Brünnhilde in Siegfried and Die Walküre, Empress in Die Frau ohne Schatten (television), Amelia in Ballo in Maschera (television), Alice in Falstaff, Puccini's Tosca, Leonora in Fidelio, Mozart's Donna Elvira, Daisy Doody in Aniara, Euridice in Orpheus in the Underworld and Beatrice in von Suppé's Boccaccio; Television and radio appearances in Sweden, throughout Europe and the USA; Permanent member of the Royal Opera Stockholm; Sang Verdi title role, Aida and Lady Macbeth; Wagner: Senta, Elisabeth, Elsa and Sieglinde; Strauss: Elektra, Salome, Ariadne. *Recordings:* Scandinavian Songs with Geoffrey Parsons; Wagner's Rienzi, Irene, with Dresden Staatskapelle; Royal Opera Stockholm Gala excerpt from Aida, 1995; Schubert and Strauss songs with Jan Eyron, 1997. *Honours:* First prizes at Jussi Björling Competition and Scandinavian Singing Contest, 1971; Swedish Opera Prize for Wagner's Isolde, 1988; Appointed Court Singer by King Carl Gustaf XVI of Sweden, 1994. *Current Management:* Svenska Konsertbyrån, Jungfrugatan 45, 11444, Stockholm, Sweden. *Address:* Odengatan 32, 11351 Stockholm, Sweden.

**WERDER, Felix;** Australian composer; b. 24 Feb. 1922, Berlin, Germany. *Career:* settled in Australia, 1941; Adult Education Class Music Lecturer, 1956–; music critic, The Age, Melbourne, 1960–77; Founder and Dir, Australia Felix Ensemble, presenting new Australian works by young composers. *Compositions include:* Kisses for a Quid, opera, 1960; En Passant, ballet, 1964; The General, opera, 1966; Agamemnon, opera, 1967; The Affair, opera, 1969; The Vicious Square, opera, 1971; The Conversation, opera, 1973; Banker, music theatre, 1973; La Belle Dame sans Merci, ballet, 1973; Quantum, ballet, 1973; Cranach's Hunt, horn concerto, 1974; Six Symphonies, 1948–79; Sans souci, flute concerto, 1974; Synorgy for synthesizer, winds and organ, 1974; The Tempest, electronic music for V100, 1974; Index for chamber ensemble, 1976; Bellyful, music theatre, 1976; The Director, music theatre, 1980; Board Music, for piano, 1983; The Medea, opera, 1985; Opening for contrabass and flute, 1987; Concerto for Orchestra, 1987; Concert Music for bass clarinet and orchestra, 1987; Renunciation for viola and orchestra, 1987; Business Day, music theatre, 1988; Two Fantasias for string trio, 1988; Saxophone Quintet, 1988; Belzaser, choral cantata, 1988; Off Beat for cello and piano, 1990; Four Violin Sonatas, 1958–88; Los Dramas, for soprano and chamber ensemble, 1990; The Wenzel Connection, clarinet concerto, 1990; Music for a While, for chamber orchestra, 1991; Taffelmusik, for clarinet, cello and piano, 1991; Piano Quartet, 1991; Symphony No. 7 (Pique Dame), 1992; Sisiphus, for solo cello and string orchestra, 1993; Hawthorn Konzert, for solo violin, percussion and string orchestra, 1994; Gryphiusad, for voice and orchestra, 1995; Catullus and John Donne, Songs, 1996; San Souci, sinfonia concertante, 1997; Uber die Maniere for full orchestra, 1998; Klav**4, for 4-handed piano. *Recordings:* No. 3, Laocoon; Tower Concerto; Concerto for Violin; String Quartets 4, 6, 9; Requiem, for soprano and ensemble; Aspect, collection of

works. *Publications:* More than Music, 1991; Music and More, 1994. *Address:* c/o Locked Bag 3665, St Leonards, NSW 2065, Australia.

**WERRES, Elisabeth;** Singer (soprano); b. 1954, Bonn, Germany; m. Anthony Bramall (conductor). *Education:* Cologne Conservatory under D. Jacob. *Career:* Debut age 22, Cologne Opera in small roles for one season; Resident soprano, Staatstheater Karlsruhe, 1978–80: roles included Rosina, Marguerite in Gounod's Faust, Adele, Eurydice, Frau Fluth; Resident soprano, Dortmund Opera, 1980–82: roles included Nedda, Susanna, Musetta, Gilda, Aminta, Adina; Resident soprano, Staatsoper Hannover, 1989–1997: roles included Tatjana, Rosalinde, Musetta, Freia, Merry Widow, Marschallin, Mazenka, Helmwige; Guest engagements in over 30 theatres in Europe including Staatsoper Hamburg, Staatsoper Munich, Deutsche Oper Berlin, Cologne Opera, Komische Oper Berlin, Essen, Leipzig, Zürich, Mannheim, Strasbourg, Wiesbaden, Weimar, Dortmund, Karlsruhe, Amsterdam, Vienna Volksoper: roles included Rosalinde, Marie in Wozzeck, Turandot by Busoni, The Merry Widow, Milada in Dalibor, Chrysothemis in Elektra, Arabella, Countess in Figaro, Elena in I Vespri Siciliani and especially Feldmarschallin in Der Rosenkavalier; Concerts in Barcelona, Chicago, Tokyo, Hamburg, Essen, Stuttgart, Karlsruhe, Strasbourg, Luxembourg, Vienna, Munich, Cologne, Zürich, Luzern, Berlin: Beethoven's 9th, Strauss' 4 Last Songs, Weill's Seven Deadly Sins, Wozzeck Fragments, opera and operetta galas; Prof. of voice, Univ. of the Arts, Berlin, 2003–. *Recordings:* Laura in Hindemith's opera Neues Vom Tage, conductor Jan Latham-Koenig; Offenbachiade: Gala for opening of Cologne Philharmonic, conductor Pinchas Steinberg. *Honours:* Special Award, Mozart Competition Würzburg, 1977. *Address:* Wehrastr. 11, 76199 Karlsruhe, Germany.

**WERTHEN, Rudolf;** Violinist and Conductor; b. 16 July 1946, Malines, Belgium. *Education:* Studied at the Ghent and Brussels Conservatories, with André Gertler. *Career:* Soloist with the NDR Symphony Orchestra at Hamburg and professor at the Robert Schumann Institute, Detmold; Flanders Chamber Orchestra from 1977 and musical director of Flanders Opera at Antwerp, from 1992; Has rediscovered and premiered the 7th Concerto of Vieuxtemps and the Russian Concerto of Lalo. *Honours:* Prizewinner of competitions at Vienna, Amsterdam and Brussels. *Address:* Robert Schumann Institute and Hochschule für Musik, Allee 22, 4930 Detmold, Germany.

**WEST, Ewan Donald,** BA, MA, MBA, DPhil; British writer on music; b. 9 Aug. 1960, Cheltenham, Gloucestershire, England. *Education:* Exeter Coll., Oxford, Cranfield School of Management. *Career:* Lecturer on History of Music, Worcester Coll., Oxford 1986–94; Jr Research Fellow, Mansfield Coll., Oxford 1988–92; Dir of Studies in Music, Somerville Coll., Oxford 1989–94; mem. American Musicological Soc., Royal Musical Asscn. *Publications:* The Hamlyn Dictionary of Music 1982, The Oxford Dictionary of Opera (with John Warrack) 1992, The Concise Oxford Dictionary of Opera (third edn, with John Warrack) 1996; contrib. to Music and Letters, Austrian Studies. *Honours:* Univ. of Oxford James Ingham Halstead Scholar 1985–87. *Address:* 14 Moorhouse Road, London, W2 5DJ, England (office). *Telephone:* (20) 7221-6001 (home). *E-mail:* wean_west@hotmail.com (home).

**WEST, John;** American singer (bass); b. 25 Oct. 1938, Cleveland, OH. *Education:* Curtis Institute with Martial Singher, in New York with Beverley Johnson. *Career:* debut in San Francisco in 1963 as Sarastro; Many appearances at US opera centres including Houston, Philadelphia, Seattle, Santa Fe, Portland, San Francisco, Washington and Fort Worth; Guest engagements at Vancouver, Mexico City, Hanover and Spoleto; Other roles have included Don Alfonso, Oroveso in Norma, Basilio, Mephistopheles of Gounod and Berlioz, Boris Godunov, Ramphis, Arkel, Ochs, La Roche in Capriccio, Hunding and Tiresias; Frequent concert engagements. *Address:* c/o San Francisco Opera, War Memorial Opera House, San Francisco, CA 94102, USA.

**WEST, John Frederic;** singer (tenor); b. 4 March 1952, Dayton, OH, USA. *Education:* Manhattan School of Music and American Opera Center at Juilliard, New York. *Career:* sang Tamino and Stravinsky's Tom Rakewell at Glens Falls, 1975; Scottish Opera, 1980, as Gabriele Adorno; Season 1982–83 as Manrico and Calaf at the New York City Opera; Waldemar in Schoenberg's Gurrelieder at the Edinburgh Festival; Toronto, 1986, as Apollo in Strauss's Daphne, Bacchus in Ariadne auf Naxos at Washington and the Metropolitan Opera, 1993; Wagner's Tristan at the reopening of the Prinzregententheater, Munich, 1996; Season 1997–98 as Tannhäuser at the Metropolitan and Tristan at the Nationaltheater, Munich; Tristan at Covent Garden, 2001; Engaged as Siegfried in The Ring at the Deutsche Oper, Berlin, 2003. *Recordings include:* DVD of Tristan, from Munich. *Current Management:* Robert Gilder & Co., Enterprise House, 59–65 Upper Ground, London, SE1 9PQ, England. *Telephone:* (20) 7928-9008. *Fax:* (20) 7928-9755. *E-mail:* rgilder@robert-gilder.com.

**WEST, Kevin;** Singer (Tenor); b. 1960, England. *Education:* Studied at the Guildhall School with Walter Gruner. *Career:* Sang first with the D'Oyly Carte Opera Company; Appearances with Opera 80 as Sellem in The Rake's Progress and Don Ottavio, and Britten's Peter Quint for Music Theatre Wales; Engagements with Opera Restor'd in English Baroque Music and throughout the United Kingdom; Sang Monteverdi's Orfeo at the Prom Concerts in London; English National Opera debut, 1989 as David in The Mastersingers; Has also sung with English National Contemporary Opera Studio, Opera Factory as Trimalchio in Maderna's Satyricon in 1990 and the Montepulciano Festival in Henze's The English Cat in 1990; Appeared with Opera Northern

Ireland in 1991 as Mozart's Don Basilio (repeated for Opera North, 1996); Sang in Bernstein's Candide at Turin, 1997; Concert repertoire includes Bach's St John Passion and Easter Oratorio, works by Handel, Mozart and Schubert and Tippett's A Child Of Our Time at South Bank in London.

**WEST, Stephen;** Singer (bass-baritone); b. 1950, New York, USA. *Education:* Curtis Inst., Philadelphia, and with Jerome Hines in New Jersey. *Career:* debut, Bonze in Butterfly at Philadelphia 1973; sang with the Metropolitan Opera, Chicago, Washington, Seattle and many others; New York City Opera from 1995, as Boito's Mefistofele and Verdi's Attila; Deutsche Staatsoper, Berlin as Weber's Kaspar and Paris Bastille as Berg's Dr Schön; concert appearances with the Philadelphia Orchestra at Carnegie Hall, and with the Denver and Montreal Symphony Orchestras; season 1997–98 as Adams in the premiere of Amistad by Anthony Davis at Chicago, and Kolenaty in The Makropulos Case by Janáček at the New York Metropolitan; further engagements as King Henry in Lohengrin at Bayreuth, Dr Schön at the Met, Gounod's Mephistopheles at Baltimore and Massenet's Comte des Grieux for Dallas Opera; season 2000–01 as Mars in Henze's Venus and Adonis, at Santa Fe and Acrobat in Lulu at the Met. *Honours:* prizewinner at Met Audition and Tchaikovsky Competition. *Current Management:* Herbert Barrett Management, 266 W 37th Street, 20th Floor, New York, NY 10018, USA. *Telephone:* (212) 245-3530. *Fax:* (212) 397-5860. *Website:* www .herbertbarrett.com.

**WESTENRA, Hayley Dee;** New Zealand singer; b. 10 April 1987, Christchurch. *Career:* performer in classical, pop and traditional Maori choral styles; fmr Amb. to Save The Children, Hong Kong; Amb. for UNICEF. *Television appearances:* American Dreams (NBC-TV) 2003, Great Performances (PBS-TV) 2004. *Recordings:* albums Hayley Westenra 2001, Pure 2003, My Gift To You 2004, Odyssey 2005. *Current Management:* c/o Giselle Allier, Bedlam Management Ltd, PO Box 34449, London, W6 0XU, England. *E-mail:* hayleyw@bedlammanagement.com. *Website:* www.hayleywestenra .com.

**WESTERGAARD, Peter;** Composer and Professor of Music; b. 28 May 1931, Champaign, Illinois, USA. *Education:* AB, Magna cum Laude, Harvard College, 1953; MFA, Princeton University, 1956; Studied Composition with Walter Piston, Darius Milhaud, Roger Sessions, and Wolfgang Fortner. *Career:* Assistant Professor 1963–66, Columbia College; Visiting Lecturer with rank of Associate Professor, Princeton University, 1966–67; Associate Professor, Amherst College, 1967–68; Princeton University, 1968–71; Professor, Princeton University, 1971–; Chairman, Department of Music, Princeton University, 1974–78, 1983–86; Director, Princeton University Orchestra, 1968–73; Board of Directors: American Music Centre, 1969–72; International Society for Contemporary Music, 1970–74; Director, Princeton University Opera Theatre, 1970–; Visiting Professor, University of British Columbia, 1987; Lecturer, International Music Seminar, University of Bahia, Brazil, 1992; Interdepartmental Committee for the Program in Musical Performance, Princeton University, 1992–93; William Shubael Conant Professor of Music, Princeton University, 1995–; Acting Chair, Department of Music, 1995. *Compositions include:* 5 Movements for Small Orchestra, 1959; Cantata II, 1959, III, 1966; Quartet for Violin, Vibraphone, Clarinet and Violoncello, 1961; Variations for 6 Players, 1967; Mr and Mrs Discobbolos, 1967; Divertimento on Discobbolic Fragments, 1967; Noises, Sounds and Sweet Airs, 1968; Tuckets and Sennets, 1969; Cantata I, 1956; Two Rhymes, for soprano and violin, 1979, 1997; Ariel Music, 1987; Ode, 1989; The Tempest, Opera in Three Acts after William Shakespeare, 1990; Ringing Changes, 1996; All 4s, 1996; anyone lived in a pretty how town, 1996; Byzantium for baritone and percussion quartet on poems by Yeats, 1997; Chicken Little, an opera for children, 1997; Cantata VI, To The Dark Lady, 1998; Chaconne, 1999; Epithalamium, 2000; Singing Translations of The Magic Flute, Don Giovanni, Der Freischütz, Fidelio (original version of 1805), Così fan tutte, The Marriage of Figaro, Cinderella and The Coronation of Poppea. *Address:* 40 Pine Street, Princeton, NJ 08542, USA.

**WESTERN, Hilary;** Singer (Soprano); b. 1948, Cardiff, Wales. *Education:* Studied at the Royal Academy of Music and the London Opera Centre. *Career:* Sang at the Wexford and Glyndebourne Festivals and in Angers as Mimi and Toulouse as Frasquita; Appearances as Fiordiligi in Grenoble, Anchorage and Britain; Sang Mimi, Papagena and Diana for Opera North; Ariadne, Louise, Micaela, Christine in Blake's Toussaint, Musetta and Diana; Sang at Almeida Festival in 1990 in the world premiere of Europeras III and IV by John Cage; Performances of Birtwistle's Punch and Judy, The Beggar's Opera and Orfeo with Opera Factory; Schoenberg's Pierrot Lunaire for Ballet Rambert; Has sung in the musicals, chess and A Little Night Music, in the West End and at the Chichester Festival in Born Again. *Honours:* Arts Council Award, to study with Martin Isepp in New York.

**WESTLAKE, Nigel;** Composer and Clarinettist; b. 6 Sept. 1958, Perth, Western Australia. *Education:* Clarinet with Don Westlake, 1970–78; Bass Clarinet with Harry Sparnay, 1983; Composition self taught. *Career:* Freelance clarinettist from 1975; Principal of Australia Ensemble, 1987–92, with tours throughout Australia and abroad; Tour of Australia and England 1992, with John Williams' group, Attaca; Film and television music. *Compositions include:* Onomatopoeia for bass clarinet and digital delay, 1984; Omphalo Centric Lecture, for 4 percussion, 1984; Entomology, for chamber ensemble and tape, 1988; Refractions at Summercloud Bay, for bass clarinet, flute and string trio, 1989; Malachite Glass, for bass clarinet and percussion quartet,

1990; Antarctica Suite, for guitar and orchestra (from the film score), 1992; Tall Tales But True, for 2 guitars and ensemble, 1992; Songs from the Forest, for guitar duo, 1994; High Tension Wires, for string quartet, 1994; Invocations, concerto for bass clarinet and orchestra, 1995; Babe: orchestral excerpts from the film, 1996; Piano Sonata, 1997. *Honours:* Gold Medal, New York radio festival, 1987; APRA Award, Babe, Best Film Score, 1996. *Address:* c/o APRA, PO Box 576, Crows Nest, NSW 2065, Australia.

**WETHERELL, Eric (David);** Composer and Conductor; b. 30 Dec. 1925, Tynemouth, Northumberland, England; m. (1) Jean Bettany, 4 July 1949, 1 s., 1 d., (2) Elizabeth Major, 16 Jan 1976, 2 d. *Education:* BA, BMus, The Queen's College, Oxford, 1945–47; Royal College of Music, 1948–49. *Career:* Horn Player, 1949–59; Repetiteur, Royal Opera House, Covent Garden, 1960–63; Assistant Music Director, Welsh National Opera, 1963–69; Music Director, HTV, 1969–76; Chief Conductor, BBC Northern Ireland Orchestra, 1976–81; Senior Music Producer, BBC Bristol, 1981–85. *Compositions:* Choral, Solo Songs, Orchestral including Airs and Graces and Welsh Dresser for Orchestra, Bristol Quay for String Orchestra, Your Gift to Man for Chorus; Music for television plays and films. *Publications:* Life of Gordon Jacob, 1995; Arnold Cooke, 1996; Patrick Hadley, 1997; Albert Sammons, 1998. *Address:* c/o British Music Information Centre, 11 Stratford Place, London, W1, England.

**WETHERILL, Linda;** Flautist; b. 1950, USA. *Career:* Recital and concerto Soloist in major cities of Europe, Canada, USA; Principal Flautist with the orchestras of Hessischer Rundfunk Frankfurt and of Pierre Boulez's IRCAM at Pompidou Centre, Paris, France; Repertoire includes Baroque, Classic, Romantic and Impressionist works; Performed and premiered the flute music of Luciano Berio, Pierre Boulez, Elliott Carter, Olivier Messiaen, Goffredo Petrassi and Karl-Heinz Stockhausen; Taught master classes in English, French, German, Spanish and American Conservatories. *Recordings:* Numerous for DTR and Deutsche Grammophon. *Honours:* Won New York Young Artists debut, 1979; First American and first flautist to be featured artist, 35 year running World Peace Festival, Llangollen, Wales, 1982; Selected by West German Broadcasting Association for a 10 country European Concerto debut, 1975.

**WEWEL, Gunter;** Singer (Bass); b. 29 Nov. 1934, Arnsberg, Sauerland, Germany. *Education:* Studied with Johannes Kobeck in Vienna, Rudolf Watzke in Dortmund, Emmi Muller in Krefeld. *Career:* Member of the Dortmund Opera from 1963; Guest appearances in Düsseldorf, Cologne, Karlsruhe, Hanover, Budapest, Paris, Zürich, Salzburg, Munich; Radio and Television engagements in Germany, France; Roles include Wagner's Daland, Titurel, Fafner, King Mark, Landgrave and King Heinrich; Philip II in Don Carlos, Gremin in Eugene Onegin and Beethoven's Rocco; Mozart's Sarastro, Osmin and Commendatore; Nicolai's Falstaff and Rossini's Bartolo. *Recordings include:* Die Zauberflöte conducted by Sawallisch; Schumann's Paradies und die Peri under Henryk Czyz; Suppé's Boccaccio with Willi Boskovsky; Die Königskinder, Mendelssohn's Die Beiden Pädagogen, Les Contes d'Hoffmann and Millöcker's Gasparone, conducted by Heinz Wallberg; La Vie Parisienne, with Willy Mattes.

**WHEATLEY, Patrick;** Singer (Baritone); b. 1950, Hinckley, Leicestershire, England. *Education:* Studied at London Opera Centre, 1973. *Career:* Appeared with English National Opera, 1974–80, as Germont, Amonasro, Marcello, Sharpless, Donner, Gunther, De Bretigny (Manon), Albert (Werther), Schelkalov (Boris Godunov) and the King in Dalibor; Guest appearances as Escamillo, Kothner, Hans Sachs and Talbot and Cecil in Maria Stuarda; Other roles include Renato (Northern Ireland Opera Trust); Ezio in Attila (University College Opera); Falstaff and Papageno (City of Birmingham Touring Opera); Zurga in Les Pêcheurs de Perles (Scottish Opera); Jochanaan, and Yeletsky in The Queen of Spades (Chelsea Opera Group); Nabucco (Opera West); Mercutio in Roméo et Juliette (Las Palmas); Don Pasquale (Neath Opera); Rigoletto (Welsh National Opera); Sang Wotan and the Wanderer in a version of Wagner's Ring for the City of Birmingham Touring Opera, 1990–91; Concert engagements in Italy, Belgium and Spain and at the Promenade Concerts, London. *Address:* Music International, 13 Ardilaun Road, London N5 2QR, England.

**WHEELER, Antony,** BMus, MPhil; composer, clarinettist and saxophonist; b. 9 Aug. 1958, Dunedin, New Zealand. *Education:* Queensland Conservatory, Shanghai Conservatory, Hong Kong University, studied with Ann Boyd. *Career:* clarinettist with Queensland Symphony Orchestra and Philharmonic Orchestra 1980–82; ABC Sinfonia 1983–85, Sydney Symphony Orchestra 1983–85; Freelance Teacher and Performer, 1987–95; Lane Cove Public School, 1992–99; Trinity Grammar School, 1996–99; Australian Institute of Music, 1992–99; Active in wide range of performance styles, including traditional Chinese music, contemporary, improvisation, using clarinet, saxophone, qin, ruan; mem. APRA; Musicians' Union of Australia; Australian Music Centre. *Compositions include:* many for Chinese instruments; Piano Variations, 1982; Incidental Music for Ubu the King, for ensemble, 1983; Sarabande and Fugue, brass quintet, 1984; Winter, 1986; Bodhisattva of the Silk Road, 1986; Cold Moon Shines South of the River, 1987; Approach to Peace, for Chinese orchestra, 1988; Snake, 1988; Wind Quintet in Five Movements, 1988; Love Songs of the Grasslands for chorus and string orchestra, 1989; Rising, for Chinese orchestra, 1990; Hearing Thunder on the Fishing Boat, for Chinese percussion ensemble, 1990; Back to the Bush for clarinet, saxophone and piano, 1990; Birthday Variations, wind quintet, 1991;

Now Close the Windows, for tenor and piano, 1991; Jin Beng Bong, for Chinese ensemble, 1998. *Address:* c/o APRA, 6–12 Atchison Street, St Leonards, NSW 2065, Australia.

**WHELAN, Paul;** Singer (Baritone); b. 29 Sept. 1966, Christchurch, New Zealand. *Education:* Studied at the Wellington Conservatoire and the Royal Northern College of Music. *Career:* Concerts and Recitals in New Zealand, the USA and Europe; Nielsen's 3rd Symphony under Simon Rattle, Messiah in Russia with Yehudi Menuhin and in London with the London Mozart Players; Vaughan Williams's Five Mystical Songs and Sea Symphony, Messiah at the Albert Hall under Charles Farncombe; Opera engagements include roles in Death in Venice for Glyndebourne Opera, Schaunard in La Bohème at Stuttgart, Masetto in Bordeaux, 1993, Britten's Demetrius for Australian Opera and on tour in France and Guglielmo for Dublin Grand Opera; Welsh National and Scottish Opera debuts 1994, as Timur in Turandot and Mozart's Figaro; Messiah with Hallé Orchestra, conductor Roger Vignoles; Verdi, Requiem, Budapest Symphony Orchestra, conductor Paolo Olmi; Recitals at Blackheath and Wigmore Halls, London; Sang Demetrius at the Edinburgh Festival, 1994 and Schaunard for Netherlands Opera; Covent Garden debut 1996, as Schaunard; Don Giovanni for Opera Australia, 1997; Season 1998–99 included Guglielmo and the baritone roles in Death in Venice; Marcello at the Bastille; Apollo in Gluck's Alceste at Netherlands Opera; Gil in Il Segreto di Susanna; Tarquinius in The Rape of Lucretia; The Count in Figaro with Scottish Opera; Escamillo in Carmen with Welsh National Opera; Season 2000–01 as Christus in Bach's St John Passion for ENO, Mephisto in The Damnation of Faust, with the BBC Philharmonic, and the Villains in Hoffmann, in New Zealand; Concert engagements with RIAS Berlin Chamber Choir for Messiah. *Honours:* Brigitte Fassbaender Award for Lieder. *Address:* c/o IMG Artists, Lovell House, 616 Chiswick High Road, London W4 5RX, England.

**WHETTAM, Graham (Dudley);** Composer; b. 7 Sept. 1927, Swindon, Wiltshire, England; m. (1) Rosemary B. Atkinson, 20 Nov 1948, (2) Janet Rosemary Lawrence, 31 Mar 1959, 4 s., 1 d. *Education:* Self-taught Composer. *Career:* Debut: Concert: C.B.S.O., Birmingham, 1950; Radio: BBC 3rd Programme, 1951; Works in concert and broadcast in the United Kingdom and abroad; Has withdrawn recognition of works written mostly prior to 1959. *Compositions include:* Orchestra: Clarinet Concertos No. 1, 1959, No. 2, 1982; Introduction and Scherzo Impetuoso, 1960; Sinfonia Contra Timore, 1962; Cello Concerto, 1962; Sinfonia Intrepida, 1976; Sinfonia Drammatica, 1978; Hymnos for Strings, 1978; Symphonic Prelude, 1985; Ballade for Violin and Orchestra, 1988; Choral: The Wounded Surgeon Plies the Steel, 1960; Magnificat and Nunc Dimittis, 1962; Do Not Go Gentle Into That Good Night, 1965; Consecration, 1982; A Mass for Canterbury, 1986; Chamber Music: 3 String Quartets, 1967, 1978, 1980; Sextet for Wind and Piano, 1970; Quintetto Concertato, Wind Quintet, 1979; Percussion Partita for Six Players, 1985; Quartet for Four Horns, 1986; Piano, Prelude, Scherzo and Elegy, 1964, revised 1986; Prelude and Scherzo Impetuoso, 1967; Night Music, 1969; Solo Violin Sonatas No. 1, 1957, revised 1987, No. 2, 1972; Solo Violin Sonata No. 3, 1989; Suite for Timpani, 1982; Solo Cello Sonata, 1990; Andromeda for Percussion Quartet, 1990; Concerto Ardente for Horn and Strings, 1992; Les Roseaux au Vent for Two Oboes, Cor Anglais and Strings, 1993; Romanza for Solo Violin (also arr. for Solo Viola and Solo Cello), 1993; Les Roseaux au Vent, for 2 oboes, bassoon and strings, 1993; Concert for Brass Quintet, 1993; Three Shakespearian Elegies, 1994; Evocations, for orchestra, 1995; Concerto drammatico for cello and orchestra, 1998; Promethean Symphony, 1999. *Recordings:* Quartet for Four Horns, 1989. *Contributions:* Listener; Times Educational Supplement; Guardian. *Address:* Meriden Music, The Studio Barn, Silverwood House, Woolaston, Nr Lydney, Gloucestershire GL15 6PJ, England.

**WHITBOURN, James,** MA; British composer and conductor; b. 17 Aug. 1963. *Education:* Magdalen Coll., Oxford. *Career:* began career making programmes for the BBC; commissions include compositions for the funeral of HM The Queen Mother, for the Westminster Abbey service in memory of victims of 11 Sept. 2001 terrorist attack; collaborated with poets, Michael Symmons Roberts and Andrew Motion; numerous collaborations with Choir of Clare Coll., Cambridge; Conductor and Dir of vocal ensemble, The Choir; has conducted BBC Philharmonic in performances of his own works. *Compositions:* for chorus and orchestra: Son of God Mass 2000, The Mystery of Love 2001, A Prayer of Desmond Tutu 2004, Missa Carolae 2004, Annelies 2004; for soloist(s) and orchestra: Pika 2000, The Wounds 2001, Whirlwind 2002; for a capella chorus: Magnificat and Nunc Dimittis, Eternal Rest, Give us the Wings of Faith 2002; for film and TV: Miracle of Tears 1998, Cherub Song 1999, Burmese Journey 2000, Living Voices 2001, Son of God 2001, Bridge over Tay 2002, Bible Mysteries (aka Ancient Evidence) 2004, Four Wedding Songs 2004, D-Day 60 2004. *Recording:* A Finer Truth 2001. *Honours:* Royal Television Soc. Craft Award, Sony Gold Award. *Current Management:* c/o Chester Music Ltd and Novello Publishing Ltd, 8–9 Frith Street, London, W1D 3JB, England.

**WHITE, (Edwin) Chappell,** BA, BMus, MFA, PhD; educator and musicologist; b. 16 Sept. 1920, Georgia, USA; m. Barbara Tyler 1959; one s. two d. *Education:* Emory University, Westminster Choir College, Princeton University. *Career:* Instructor, Agnes Scott College, 1950–52; Instructor and Associate Professor, Emory University, 1952–74; Professor, Kansas State University, 1974–91 now retired; Violist with Atlanta Symphony, 1950–57; Music Critic, Atlanta Journal, 1959–72; Visiting Professor, University of

Georgia, 1970–71, Indiana University, 1972–73; Brown Foundation Fellow, University of the South, 1993; mem, College Music Society, President, 1979–80; American Musicological Society; Visiting Professor, University of the South, 1993–2002. *Publications:* G B Viotti: A Thematic Catalogue of His Works, 1985; Intro to Life and Works of R Wagner, 1969; Editor, 4 Concertos by G B Viotti, 1976, and 3 Concertos by J Myslivecek, 1994; From Vivaldi to Viotti: A History of The Classical Violin Concerto, 1992. *Contributions:* 15 articles in New Grove Dictionary, 1980; Journal of American Musicological Society; Fontes Artis Musiche; Musical Quarterly. *Honours:* Research Grant, NEH, 1982–83. *Address:* 150 Bobtown Circle, Sewanee, TN 37375, USA.

**WHITE, Frances,** BMus, MA; composer; b. 30 Aug. 1960, Philadelphia, USA. *Education:* University of Maryland, Princeton University. *Career:* technical asst to John Cage 1985–87, collaborating on works for computer-generated tape; freelance composer. *Compositions include:* Ogni pensiero vola, for tape, 1985; Chiaroscura, for percussion and tape, 1986; Design for an Invisible City for tape, 1987; Valdrada, 1988; Still Life with Piano, for piano and tape, 1989; Resonant Landscape, interactive computer-music, 1990; Trees for 2 violins, viola and tape, 1992; Nocturne, 1992; Walks Through Resonant Landscapes 1–5 for tape, 1992; Winter Aconites (commission from ASCAP in memory of John Cage) for clarinet and ensemble, 1993. *Honours:* First Prize, programme music category, 18th Bourges International Electro-Acoustic Music Competition, 1990; ASCAP Awards, 1990, 1993, 1994.

**WHITE, Harry;** University Professor of Music; b. 4 July 1958, Dublin, Republic of Ireland; m. Eithne Graham 1980; two s. *Education:* Univ. Coll. Dublin; Univ. of Toronto; Trinity Coll., Dublin. *Career:* part-time Lecturer, St Patrick's Coll., Maynooth, 1984–85; Asst Lecturer in Music, 1985–88, Coll. Lecturer, 1988–93, Prof. of Music, 1993–, Univ. Coll. Dublin; Visiting Prof. of Music, Univ. of Western Ontario, 1996; Visiting Prof. of Musicology, Ludwig-Maximilians-Universität, Munich, 1999; General Ed., Irish Musical Studies (Dublin), 1990–; Foreign Corresponding Ed., Current Musicology (New York), 1996–; mem., Irish RILM Cttee (Chair. 1992–), Editorial Board of the International Review of the Aesthetics and Sociology of Music (Zagreb, 2001–), Society for Musicology in Ireland (founding mem., 2003–). *Publications:* Johann Joseph Fux, Il Trionfo della Fede (ed.), 1988; Musicology in Ireland (co-ed.), 1990; Johann Joseph Fux and the Music of the Austro-Italian Baroque (ed.), 1992; Music and the Church (co-ed.), 1993; Music and Irish Cultural History (co-ed.), 1995; The Maynooth International Musicological Conference: Selected Proceedings (co-ed.), 1996; The Keeper's Recital: Music and Cultural History in Ireland 1770–1970, 1998; Musical Constructions of Nationalism (co-ed.), 2001. *Contributions:* Acta Musicologica, Bach, Fontes Artis Musicae, International Review of the Aesthetics and Sociology of Music, Irish University Review, Eighteenth Century Ireland, Irish Review, Journal of American Studies, Kirchenmusikalisches Jahrbuch, Canadian Journal of Irish Studies, Modern Drama, Journal of Musicology, Studies in Music from the University of Western Ontario, College Music Symposium, Atti del Antiquae Musicae Italicae Studiosi, Music and Letters, The New Grove Dictionary of Music and Musicians (revised edn, 2001). *Address:* Department of Music, University College Dublin, Belfield, Dublin 4, Ireland.

**WHITE, Ian David;** Violist; b. 16 Sept. 1941, London; m. Annelise White, 16 Feb 1987, 4 c. *Education:* Royal College of Music, 1956–60; Viola making with Dr Arthur Councell, 1957–62; Decoration in Baroque music with Dr Carl Dolmetsch, 1967–72. *Career:* Debut: With Royal Philharmonic Orchestra, 1960; First appearance in Wigmore Hall, 1966, Purcell Room, 1967, Smith Square, 1969; Music for A Man for All Seasons; Chamber music on BBC television; Performances with English Chamber Orchestra, with Benjamin Britten; Hold the Front Page; Lectures at Royal College of Music and Guildford University; mem, Viola d'Amore Society of Great Britain; American Viola d'Amore Society; Principal Viola, BBC London Studio Strings, March 1970– March 1987; Principal Viola L'estro Armonico, 64 Haydn Symphonies CBS Masterworks 1976–90; Leader of the Misbourne Orchestra 1982–94. *Compositions:* Arrangements of Trio in E flat for Viola, Cello and Bass, by Michael Haydn, Concertos for Viola d'Amore by Vivaldi, Böhm, Carl Stamitz and W F Rust, Pfeiffer Trio, Quantz Trios. *Recordings:* Brandenberg Concertos with English Chamber Orchestra and Benjamin Britten; Nisi Dominus by A Vivaldi; Christmas Story, Heinrich Schütz; St John Passion, J. S. Bach, at King's College, Cambridge–Instruments with Sympathetic Strings. *Publications:* Arrangements: Lute and Viola d'Amore Concerto, Vivaldi, 1978; Divertimento for Viola d'Amore, by Karl Stamitz; La Chasse by Hraczek; Trios by Pfeiffer and Graupner. *Contributions:* Profile in the Strad, 1968; Articles in Bucks Examiner. *Honours:* Alfred Gibson Viola Prize and Percy Carter Buck Prize, Royal College of Music, 1958–60. *Current Management:* Viola d'Amore Society. *Address:* 4 Constable Road, Felixstowe, Suffolk IP11 7 HH, England.

**WHITE, Jeremy;** Singer (bass-baritone); b. 1953, Liverpool, England. *Education:* Studied at Queen's College and Christ Church, Oxford; Singing Studies with David Johnston, Elisabeth Fleming. *Career:* Many performances with early music ensembles in the United Kingdom and Europe; Acis and Galatea for Swiss Television, debut at the Amsterdam Concertgebouw in Bach cantatas under Ton Koopman; Performances in Vienna, Budapest and Turku (Finland); Bach's St John Passion in England and Spain with The Sixteen; CPE Bach's Oratorio Auferstehung und Himmelfahrt Jesu, in Munich; Bach's Magnificat and Christmas Oratorio in Oxford and London with King's College Choir and English Chamber Orchestra; Handel/Mozart Messiah in Paris and Lucerne; Bach's Passions in English Cathedrals; Modern concert repertoire includes Abraham and Isaac by Stravinsky, and music by Berio and Taverner; Has sung in The Lighthouse by Maxwell Davies, Walton's The Bear (title role), Pfitzner's Palestrina (Cardinal Morone), Les Troyens and Der Rosenkavalier (the Notary, Aix-en-Provence Festival); Roles in operas by Mozart and Rossini; Recent engagements 1993: Tour of Verdi's Requiem, including Paris and the Flanders Festival; Series of performances of Arvo Pärt's Passio in Jerusalem, Seville and throughout Poland and Finland, Berio in Helsinki conducted by the composer and Beethoven's Ninth Symphony for Swiss Radio; Sang Don Prudenzio in Rossini's Il Viaggio a Reims, Covent Garden, 1992; Sang Webern's Second Cantata with Pierre Boulez in a broadcast from Birmingham Symphony Hall; Season 1993–94: Contemporary Music Network tour as Peter in Jonathan Harvey's Passion and Resurrection, followed by a return to the Royal Opera to sing Benoit in La Bohème; Visit to Brazil with the Scottish Chamber Orchestra; Return to Swiss Radio in Lugano; Concert appearances with The Sixteen and The Taverner Players in Beethoven and Schütz in Germany, Norway and Switzerland, and Handel's La Resurrezione in Paris and Bourges; Concerts in London and the provinces; Sang in Pfitzner's Palestrina at Covent Garden, 1997; Season 1998 with Talbot in Verdi's Giovanna d'Arco in London and Leeds; Sang Colonna in Wagner's Rienzi for Chelsea Opera Group, 1999; Season 2000–01 as Rossini's Selim for ENO and Mesner in Tosca at Covent Garden. Recordings include: John Tavener's Great Canon of St Andrews; Monteverdi's Vespers, with The Sixteen; Handel Israel in Egypt conducted by Andrew Parrott. Current Management: Musicmakers International Artists Representation, Tailor House, 63–65 High Street, Whitwell, Hertfordshire SG4 8AH, England. Telephone: (1438) 871708. Fax: (1438) 871777. E-mail: musicmakers@compuserve.com. Website: www.operauk.com. Address: c/o Royal Opera, Contracts, Covent Garden, London WC2, England.

**WHITE, John,** ARAM, ARCM, FRAM; British viola player, teacher, author and editor; b. 28 May 1938, Leeds, Yorks.; m. Carol Susan Shaw 1964; one s. one d. Education: Royal Acad. of Music, Huddersfield Tech. Coll. Music Dept. Career: mem. Alberni String Quartet 1960–67, Stadler Trio 1967–76; Prof. of Viola in the Jr Dept, Royal Acad. of Music 1967–76, Prof. of Viola 1975–2002, Head of Instrumental Studies 1984–1991, Pres. of RAM Club 2001–02; Sr Lecturer, Hockerill Coll. of Educ. 1970–78; Tutor, Royal Northern Coll. of Music 1974; Viola Tutor, European Union Youth Orchestra 1984–1992; gave master-classes at Beijing Conservatory, China 1997, in Greece, Holland, Sweden and Ireland; jury mem. Lionel Tertis Int. Viola Competition 1994 (also Exec. Cttee mem. Workshop 1978–), Int. William Primrose Viola Competition 1999, Allessandro Rolla Int Viola Competition, Maastricht, Netherlands 2006; mem. Royal Soc. of Musicians. Recordings: Haydn String Quartets, Rawsthorne String Quartets. Publications as editor: Three Miniature String Quartets by Richard Stoker 1968, Sonatina for Viola and Piano by Alan Bush 1980, Ballade for Viola and Piano, Minna Keal, Scales and Arpeggios for viola players by Watson Forbes 1993, A Book of Daily Exercises by Watson Forbes 1994, Sonata Impromptu Violin and Viola by William Alwyn 1994, Pastoral Fantasia Viola and Strings (piano) by William Alwyn 1994, Nocturne for Viola and Cello by Gordon Jacob 1995, Sussex Lullaby 1995, Intrada 1996, Autumn Sketches 1998, Rhapsody by Alan Richardson, Introduction and Andante Op. 5 for six violas by B.J. Dale 1996, Phantasy for viola and piano 1997, Rhapsody for viola and piano 1998, Viola Concerto by York Bowen 1998, Three Pieces for Oboe, Viola and Piano by Alan Richardson 1999, Trio Sonata for Bass Clarinet, Viola and Piano by Alan Richardson 2000, English Dance for Viola and Piano by Dale/Bowen 2003, Slavonic Dance for Viola and Piano op. 46, No. 4 by Dvorák/Harding 2003, The Arrival of the Queen of Sheba for six-part Viola Ensemble by Handel (Dennison) 2002, Concert Piece for Viola and Orchestra, and Viola and Piano by Gordon Jacob 2003, Romance in D flat for Viola and Piano by York Bowen 2004, Sonata op. 129 for Viola and Piano by C. V. Stanford 2004, Two Albums – Viola Music Associated with Lionel Tertis 2006, Fantasia for Viola and Organ by York Bowen 2006, Concerto Allegro for Viola and Piano by York Bowen 2006, Romance in A for Viola and Piano by York Bowen 2006, Poem for Viola, Harp (Piano) and Organ by York Bowen 2006. Publications: An Anthology of British Viola Players 1997, Lionel Tertis – The First Great Virtuoso of the Viola 2006. Honours: Asscn of the Inst. of Educ., Univ. of London; Int. Viola Congress Special Services Award, Sweden 2000. Address: 36 Seeleys, Harlow, Essex, CM17 0AD, England (home).

**WHITE, John;** Composer; b. 5 April 1936, Berlin, Germany. Education: Studied with Elisabeth Lutyens at the Royal College of Music, 1954–57. Career: Music Director of the Western Theatre Ballet, 1959–60; Teacher of Composition at the Royal College of Music, 1961–66; Tuba Player with the London Gabrieli Brass Ensemble, 1971–72. Compositions include: 136 Piano Sonatas, 1957–96; 26 Symphonies 1965–90; 35 Ballets 1957–93; Music for Films and Television; Operas Stanley and the Monkey King, London 1975, and the Trial; Orpheus: Eurydice, London 1976; Music Theatre Man-Machine Interface. Address: c/o PRS Ltd, Member Registration, 29–33 Berners Street, London W1P 4AA, England.

**WHITE, John David;** Composer and Cellist; b. 28 Nov. 1931, Rochester, Minnesota, USA; m. Marjorie Manuel 1952, 2 s., 1 d. Education: BA, University of Minnesota 1953; MA 1954; PhD 1960; Eastman School of Music, University of Rochester, 1960. Career: University of Wisconsin, Kent State University, Music Department, Chair, Whitman College, 1978–80; Dean, School of Music, Ithaca College 1973–75; Professor and Head of Composition and Theory, University of Florida 1980–; Active Cellist in recital and chamber music; Soloist with Atlanta, Rochester, Madison and Akron Orchestras;

Composer of 50 works, performances by Cleveland, Atlanta, Rochester, Madison and Akron Orchestras; Music published by G. Schirmer, Galaxy, Carl Fischer, Lawson-Gould; Author of Five Books; Taught at University of Michigan. Compositions: Symphony No. 2, 1960; Symphony No. 3; Legend of Sleepy Hollow, 1962; 3 Choruses from Goethe's Faust; 3 Madrigals for Chorus and Orchestra; Numerous choral works, 1960–87; Variations for Clarinet and Piano; Zodiac, Chorus and Piano; Music for Oriana, 1979 (for Violin, Cello and Piano); Pied Beauty, Chorus and Piano; Eiseleic Madrigals; Sonata for Cello and Piano, 1982; Music for Violin and Piano, 1983; Concerto for Flute and Wind Ensemble, 1984; Symphony for Wind Band, 1985; Dialogues for Trombone and Piano, 1984; Symphony for A Saint, 1987; Songs of the Shulamite, 1988; Mirrors for Piano and Orchestra, 1990. Recordings: Variations for Clarinet and Piano, Advent 5005. Publications: Understanding and Enjoying Music, 1968; Music in Western Culture, 1972; Guidelines for College Teaching of Music Theory, 1981; The Analysis of Music, 2nd Edition, 1984. Contributions: Journal of Music Theory; Journal for Musicological Research; Music and Man. Address: 5715 NW 62nd Court, Gainesville, FL 32606, USA.

**WHITE, Wendy;** Singer (Mezzo-soprano); b. 1959, USA. Career: Sang Valencienne in The Merry Widow at Washington, 1984, Carmen at Cincinnati, 1985; New York City Opera, 1986, as Charlotte in Werther (also at Nice, 1990); Chicago Lyric Opera from 1987, as Siebel in Faust, Charmian in Barber's Antony and Cleopatra, and Suzuki in Butterfly (1998); Metropolitan Opera from 1990, in La Traviata, Rusalka, Les Troyens (as Anna), Otello and Andrea Chénier (1996); Magdalena in Die Meistersinger, 1998; Sang Cherubino in Corigliano's The Ghosts of Versailles, Metropolitan and Chicago, 1995; Sang Mascagni's Lola, Annina in Der Rosenkavalier and Fenena (Nabucco) at the Met, 1999–2001. Recordings include: Parsifal, and Bernstein's A Quiet Place. Address: c/o Metropolitan Opera, Lincoln Center, New York, NY 10025, USA.

**WHITE, Sir Willard Wentworth,** Kt, CBE, BA; Jamaican/British opera singer (bass); b. 10 Oct. 1946, Ewarton, St Catherine, Jamaica; s. of Egbert White and Gertrude White; m. Gillian Jackson 1972; three s. one d. Education: Excelsior School, Kingston and Juilliard School of Music, NY. Career: debut with New York City Opera as Colline in La Bohème 1974–75; European debut as Osmin with Welsh Nat. Opera 1976; has performed in most int. opera houses, including Royal Opera House, Covent Garden, England, La Scala, Italy, Glyndebourne, England, Scotland; roles include: Porgy, Orestes, Banquo, King Henry (Lohengrin), Pizarro, Wotan, Mephistopheles, Boris Godunov, Golau, Leporello, Prince Kovansky, Napoleon; extensive concert appearances; appeared as Othello, RSC, Stratford-upon-Avon; Falstaff at Aix Festival 2001, Klingsor in Parsifal, Covent Garden 2001, Bartok's Bluebeard 2002, Messiaen's St Francis, San Francisco 2002, Wotan in the Ring, Aix and Salzburg 2005. Recordings include: Porgy and Bess, Mozart Requiem, Orfeo, Die Aegyptische Helena, Acis and Galatea. Honours: Prime Minister of Jamaica's Medal of Appreciation 1987. Current Management: IMG Artists Europe, 616 Chiswick High Road, London, W4 5RX, England.

**WHITEHEAD, Gillian;** Composer; b. 23 April 1941, Whangarei, New Zealand. Education: University of Auckland; BMus, University of Wellington; MMus, University of Sydney, New South Wales; Studied with Peter Maxwell Davies in Adelaide, then in the United Kingdom. Career: Lived in the United Kingdom and Europe, 1967–81; Appointed 1st Composer-in-Residence, Northern Arts, Newcastle upon Tyne, England, 1978; Lecturer in Composition, Sydney Conservatorium of Music, New South Wales, Australia, 1981; Various commissions funded by Music Board of Australia Council, Arts Council of Great Britain, New Zealand Arts Council. Compositions: Published and/or Recorded: Missa Brevis, 1963; Qui Natus Est, Carol, 1966; Fantasia on Three Notes, Piano Solo, 1966; Whakatau-Ki, Chamber Music with Voice, 1970; La Cadenza Sia Corta, Piano Solo, 1974; Tristan and Iseult, for 4 Singers, Mimes and Puppets, Instrumental Ensemble, 1975; Voices of Tane, Piano Solo, 1976; At Night the Garden Was Full of Flowers, for 4 Recorders, 1977; The Tinker's Curse, Children's Opera, 1979; Requiem, for Male Soprano and Organ (Dance Score), 1981; The King of the Other Cowboy, chamber opera, 1984; The Pirate Moon, chamber opera, 1986; Resurgences, for orchestra, 1989; Angels Born at the Speed of Light, 1990, for string quartet; Moments, for chorus, 1993; The Art of Pizza, chamber opera, 1995. Honours: Recipient of numerous grants including New Zealand Queen Elizabeth II Arts Council and Vaughan Williams Trust. Current Management: Helen Lewis. Address: c/o Helen Lewis, 10 John Street, Woollahra, New South Wales 2025, Australia.

**WHITEHOUSE, Frank, Jr;** Emeritus Professor; b. 20 Nov. 1924, Ann Arbor, Michigan, USA; m. Helen Alice Schimkat, 1 s., 3 d. Education: AB, University of Michigan, College of Literature, Science and the Arts, 1953; MD, University of Michigan Medical School, 1953. Career: Active duty, World War II, 1942–46, Pilot B-29; Internship, Blodgett Memorial Hospital, Michigan, 1953–54; Faculty Member, University of Michigan Dept of Microbiology and Immunology, 1954–95; Visiting Scientist, Queen Victoria Hospital, East Grinstead, England, 1971; Senior Fulbright Lecturer, Bahrain University, 1979; Retired, 1995; Composer of religious and secular music; mem. ASM. Compositions: Religious music: Hymn for the Human Family; Memorial Day Anthem; Scottish Advent Carol; Meditation for Mary; Master Builder; Easter Anthem; All Children at Play; The Gift of the Church is Love; Introit; Amen; The Genius of Jesus; Secular music: The Lioness March; Big Time Flo' from Kokomo; Here's To You Maize and Blue; Dr Chase Patent Medicine Show.

*Recordings:* Here's To You Maize and Blue on the University of Michigan Marching Band CD, The Spirit of Michigan. *Publications:* Numerous publications, subjects include microbiology and immunology; Civil War Surgeon's Diary, in progress. *Honours:* Hopwood Literary Award, University of Michigan, 1947; Departmental and Medical School Award for distinguished contributions to medical and undergraduate education, 1995; Air Medal USAAF, 1995. *Address:* 3411 Woodland Road, Ann Arbor, MI 48104-4257, USA.

**WHITFIELD, John (Peter);** Conductor, Musical Director and Bassoonist; b. 21 March 1957, Darlington, County Durham, England. *Education:* Chetham's School of Music, 1973–75; Keble College, Oxford, 1975–78; National Youth Orchestra, 1973–77; European Community Youth Orchestra, 1978; International Youth Orchestra; Bassoon Studies with Charles Cracknell, Martin Gatt and Mordechai Rechtmann, Tel-Aviv. *Career:* Debut: South Bank Conducting Debut, 27 March 1983; Israel Chamber Orchestra; City of London Sinfonia; English Baroque Orchestra; London Sinfonietta; London Symphony Orchestra, also tours; London Symphony Orchestra Israel Chamber Orchestra; Founder and Musical Director of Endymion Ensemble; Many concerts in London and the United Kingdom festivals as bassoonist, conductor, with soloists; commissioned and conducted premieres of works by David Bedford, Dominic Muldowney, Nigel Osborne, Michael Nyman, Giles Swayne, Anthony Payne; Assistant Conductor for Spitalfields Festival Production and EMI recording of Armide (Gluck) with Felicity Palmer in title role; Assistant to Richard Hickox; Stage Debut as Conductor of Birtwistle's Down by the Greenwood Side at the Bath Festival, also broadcast by Radio 3. *Recordings:* Stravinsky record including Symphonies of Wind and Dumbarton Oaks and Britten Record with Gomez and Palmer on EMI. *Current Management:* Music & Musicians Artists Management, London. *Address:* 45 Chalcot Road, London NW1 8lS, England.

**WHITICKER, Michael;** Composer; b. 1954, Gundagai, New South Wales, Australia. *Education:* Degree, Composition, New South Wales Conservatorium of Music, 1982; Studied with Richard Troop; Postgraduate Composition Studies, West Germany with Isang Yun and Witold Szalonek. *Compositions:* Orchestral Works: Ad Marginem, 1986; Tartengk, 1985; Tya, 1984; Works for the Stage: The Bamboo Flute, 1982; Gesualdo, 1987; Ensemble Works: Hunufcu, 1979; Korokon, 1983; Quidong, 1983; Kwa, 1986; Winamin, 1986; Orpheus and Persephone, 1987; Plangge, 1987; Venus Asleep, 1987; Min-amé, 1988; Ad Parnassum, 1989; Redror, 1989; Solo Instrumental Works: Vibitqi, 1980; Tulku, 1982; If Buifs, 1981; Kiah, 1986; The Hands, The Dream, 1987; In Prison Air, 1988; On Slanting Ground, 1988; Vocal Works: A Voice Alone, 1982; Night Swimming, 1984; Sheaf Tosser, 1984; As Water Bears Salt, 1989; Works for Students: Boinko the Billio, 1979; Homage to Alban Berg, 1980; Liexliu, 1980; Introduction for Concert Band, 1985; Karobaan, 1985; Taldree, 1985; The Bankstown Pageant, 1985; The Hollow Crown, 1985; The Serpent Beguiles, 12985; Three Episodes, 1985; Works for Tape Alone: Cement Mounted Inlays, 1981; Model Sequence II, 1981; Slid PC, 1982; Ballets: Factor X, 1980; Passion, 1989; Film Scores: Atlantis, 1981; Conferenceville, 1982; The Bus Trip, 1982; Man, The Skin Cancer of the Earth, 1991 for Three Voices, Sax, Percussion and Tape; Jellingroo, 1990 for Didjeridoo, Flute and Cello; Encircled by Lillies, 1991, for Soprano, Tenor and Piano. *Address:* c/o Australian Music Centre, PO Box 49, Broadway 2007, Australia.

**WHITTALL, Arnold,** MA, PhD; British musicologist; b. 11 Nov. 1935, Shrewsbury, Shropshire. *Education:* Emmanuel Coll., Cambridge. *Career:* Lecturer, Univ. of Nottingham 1964–69; Sr Lecturer, Univ. Coll., Cardiff 1969–75; Reader, King's Coll., London 1976–81; Prof. of Musical Theory and Analysis 1981–96; Visiting Prof., Yale Univ. 1985. *Publications include:* Post-Twelve Note Analysis 1968, Stravinsky and Music Drama 1969, Schoenberg Chamber Music 1972, Music Since the First World War 1977, The Music of Britten and Tippett 1982, Romantic Music 1987, Wagner's Later Stage Works 1990, The Emancipation of Dissonance: Schoenberg and Stravinsky 1993, Musical Composition in the Twentieth Century 1999, Exploring Twentieth Century Music 2003.

**WHITTLESEY, Christine;** Singer (soprano); b. 12 Jan. 1950, New York City, USA. *Education:* Studied in Boston. *Career:* Sang with opera companies in Boston, Washington and Santa Fe; Concerts with the New York Pro Musica Antique and other Chamber Ensembles; Resident in Europe from 1981: Concert engagements with the Sudwestfunk and Austrian Radio, conducted by Boulez and Michael Gielen; Tours of Russia and South America with Ensemble Modern; Ensemble Intercontemporain in Paris and Ensemble Kontrapunkte in Vienna; Debut with the BBC Symphony 1988, in Pli selon Pli under Boulez; Sang in Dallapiccola's Ulisse with the BBC Symphony Orchestra under Andrew Davis and appeared at the Henze Festival at the Barbican Centre, London, 1991, with the BBC Philharmonic and the Scottish Chamber Orchestra; Further concerts in Berlin, Salzburg, Strasbourg and Warsaw: Season 1992–93 with Debussy's Damoiselle Elue in the Netherlands and Russian songs in Paris; Performs at all major music festivals. *Recordings include:* Homage to T. S. Eliot by Gubaidulina; Schoenberg: String Quartet No. 2; Harrison Birtwistle: Three Celan Settings; Benedict Mason: Self-Referential Songs and Realistic Virelais; Mahler Symphony No. 4; Dieter Schnebel: Dahlemer Messe. *Current Management:* Ingpen & Williams Ltd, 7 St George's Court, 131 Putney Bridge Road, London, SW15 2PA, England.

**WHITWORTH-JONES, Anthony,** CA; British arts administrator; *General Director, Garsington Opera;* b. 1 Sept. 1945, Bucks.; s. of Henry Whitworth-Jones and Patience Martin; m. Camilla Barlow 1974; one d. *Education:* Wellington Coll. *Career:* Admin. Dir London Sinfonietta 1972–81; Admin. Glyndebourne Touring Opera 1981–89, Opera Man. Glyndebourne Festival Opera 1981–89, Gen. Dir Glyndebourne 1989–98; Chair. Michael Tippett Musical Foundation 1998–; Gen. Dir The Dallas Opera 2000–02; Artistic Dir Casa de Musica, Oporto, Portugal 2004–05; Gen. Dir Garsington Opera 2005–; mem. Bd Spitalfields Festival 2003–. *Address:* 81 St Augustine's Road, London, NW1 9RR, England (home). *Fax:* (20) 7482-7017 (home).

**WIBAUT, Frank;** Concert Pianist; b. 10 Nov. 1945, London, England; m. Kay Alexander. *Education:* Studied at the Royal College of Music; ARCM. *Career:* Debut: Wigmore Hall, London, 1969; Concert performances in Netherlands, Belgium, Denmark, Germany, Ireland, Spain and Malta; Frequent broadcaster on radio and television; Member, The Camirilla Ensemble; mem, Musicians Union; Incorporated Society of Musicians. *Recordings:* The Romantic Chopin; Favourite Piano Classics; Elgar's From the Bavarian Highlands (in original form); Piano Quintets by Elgar, Suk and others. *Honours:* Senior Foundation Scholarship, Leverhulme Scholarship and Countess of Munster Award, Royal College of Music; 1st Prize, Chopin Competition, London; Chappell Gold Medal; BBC Piano Competition, 1968. *Address:* Highfield Lodge, 68 Harborne Road, Edgbaston, Birmingham B15 3 HE, England.

**WICH, Gunther;** Conductor; b. 23 May 1928, Bamberg, Germany. *Education:* Studied in Freiburg, 1948–52. *Career:* Conducted at the Freiburg Town Theatre, 1952–59; Opera Director at Graz, 1959–61; General Music Director at Hanover, 1961–65; Conducted the first production of Schoenburg's three one-act operas as a triple bill, 1963; General Music Director, Deutsche Oper am Rhein, Düsseldorf/Duisburg, 1965–87; Took the Company to Edinburgh, 1972, for the British premiere of Zimmermann's Die Soldaten; Covent Garden debut 1968, Die Zauberflöte; Professor of Conducting, Musikhochschule, Würzburg, 1982–94; Guest Conductor with major orchestras in Europe, Japan and the USA; Has led the Capella Colonsiensis on tours to North and South America. *Recordings include:* Handel's Concerti Grossi Op 3 and Alexander's Feast; Haydn's Symphonies Nos 82 and 85; Serenades by Dvořák, Mozart and Tchaikovsky; Early Mozart Piano Concertos with Martin Galling; Pfitzner's Violin Concerto with Susanne Lautenbacher, 21. *Address:* c/o Spitalrain 10, 97234 Reichenberg, Germany.

**WICKS, Camilla;** Concert Violinist and Professor of Violin; b. 1925, USA; m. 5 c. *Education:* Fellowship to Juilliard School aged 10. *Career:* Debut: New York Town Hall aged 13; Solo appearances with the Hollywood Bowl Orchestra, the Los Angeles and New York Philharmonic Orchestras and the Chicago Symphony; Many concerts with European Orchestras from age 18; Played the Sibelius Concerto before the composer in Helsinki and has also featured the Bloch Concerto in addition to the standard repertory; Frequent engagements in Norway and elsewhere in Scandinavia; Teaching appointments 1960s–; notably faculties of North Texas State University, California State College at Fullerton, San Francisco Conservatory of Music, Banff Centre for the Performing Arts, University of Washington and University of Southern California; Professor and Head of the String Department, Royal Academy of Music, Oslo; Professor of Violin, University of Michigan School of Music, 1984; Shepherd School of Music at Rice University, Houston, Texas, 1988–; Continuing performances in recital and as orchestral soloist and in Chamber Music Concerts. *Recordings:* Several albums, including the Sibelius Concerto. *Address:* Shepherd School of Music, Rice University, Houston, Texas, USA.

**WIDDICOMBE, Gillian,** ARAM; British music critic and journalist; b. 11 June 1943, Aldham, Suffolk, England; m. Sir Jeremy Isaacs 1988. *Education:* Royal Acad. of Music, Gloucester Cathedral. *Career:* music division, BBC 1966; Glyndebourne Festival Opera 1969; critic and journalist on various publications, including Financial Times 1970–76, The Observer 1977–93; subtitles for television opera productions; Opera Consultant, Channel Four 1983–88; Arts Ed., The Observer 1988–93; Features Writer, The Independent 1993–95; Dir, Jeremy Isaacs Productions 1995–; Production Exec., Cold War 1998; Assoc. Prod., Millennium 1999; Prod., Artsworld TV Programmes, including Star Recitals with Paco Peña, Amanda Roocroft and Simon Preston 2000–; Poulenc, A Human Voice (for BBC 2). *Honours:* Prix Italia 1982, BP Award for Arts Journalism 1986. *Address:* 80 New Concordia Wharf, Mill Street, Bermondsey, London, SE1 2BB, England.

**WIDMANN, Jörg;** Composer and Clarinettist; b. 19 June 1973, Munich, Germany. *Education:* Studied clarinet with Professor Gerd Starke at the Hochschule für Musik and with Charles Neidich at the Juilliard School, New York; Studied composition with Hans Werner Henze, Wilfried Hiller and Wolfgang Rihm. *Career:* Debut: As soloist in Mozart's Clarinet Concerto with members of Munich Philharmonic on a tour of Japan (aged 12); Soloist with orchestras including: Münchener Rundfunkorchester, Sinfonia Varsovia, Capella Istropolitana. *Compositions include:* Absences, 1990; La Verrière Lilas, 1991; Jardin du Luxembourg, 1992; Carillon, 1992–93; Kreisleriana, 1993; 180 Beats per minute, 1993; Tränen der Musen, 1993; Stimmbruch, 1994; Nickel List, 1994; Badinerie, 1994; Wunder Verwirklichen, 1995; Knastgesänge, 1995; Trauergesang und Frühlingsmusik, 1995–96; Three Rilke Fragments, 1996; Beitrage, Lea and Rachel, Lilith, 1996; Fleurs du Mal, 1996–97; Fünf Bruchstücke, 1997; Mullewapp, 1997; Sieben Abesänge Auf Eine Tote Linde, 1997; Insel der Sirenen, premiere, with Isabelle Faust on violin in Warsaw, Autumn 1997; Kleine Morgenstern-Szene for Soprano, Cymbalon und Schlagzeug, 1997; Werk für Klarinette, Streichquartett und

Klavier, 1997; Sieben Miniaturen; Pas de deux, Ritual, für zwei Flöten und Orchester, 1997. *Recordings:* As composer and clarinettist, Honours: Kulturförderpreis of city of Munich, 1996; 1st Prize, Wettwerb deutscher Musikhochschulen, Berlin, 1996; 1st Prize, Carl Maria Von Weber Competition, Munich, 1996; Bavarian State Prize for Young Artists, 1997. *Address:* Barerst 3, 80333 München, Germany.

**WIDMER, Oliver;** Singer (Baritone); b. 1965, Zürich, Switzerland. *Education:* Studied at the Basle Music Academy with Kurt Widmer; Masterclasses with Fischer-Dieskau in Berlin, 1986 and 1989. *Career:* Concert appearances at the Salzburg Festival, Festival de Musique de Strasbourg, the Vienna Musikverein, the San Francisco Symphony Hall and the Leipzig Gewandhaus; Recitals at the Schubertiade in Hohenems, the Wigmore Hall, London, the Residenz in Munich, Alte Oper Frankfurt, Fêtes Musicales de Touraine, Louvre de Paris, the Vienna Konzerthaus and the 1992 Aldeburgh Festival; Zürich Opera from 1991 as Mozart's Papageno and Guglielmo, Olivier in Capriccio and Harlequin in Ariadne auf Naxos; Salzburg Festival 1993, conducted by Harnoncourt; Season 2000–01 as Guglielmo for Zürich Opera, Rocco in Pa ër's Leonora at Wintherthur and Christus in the St Matthew Passion at La Scala. *Recordings:* Die Zauberflöte and Schreker's Die Gezeichneten. *Honours:* Prizewinner at ARD Competition Munich, Hugo Wolf International Competitions Stuttgart and the Othmar Schoeck Competition in Lucerne. *Address:* c/o R & B Kunstleragentur, Plankengasse 7, A–1010 Vienna, Austria.

**WIEDSTRUCK, Yvonne;** Singer (soprano); b. 1960, Potsdam, Germany. *Education:* Studied in Germany. *Career:* Sang first at Altenburg, in Rusalka, Hänsel und Gretel, La Bohème and Faust; Komische Oper Berlin as Despina, Zerlina, Euridice, Susanna, Micaela, the Daughter in Hindemith's Cardillac and Stella in Goldschmidt's Der Gewaltige Hahnrei; Schwetzingen Festival, 1992, in the premiere of Desdemona und ihre Schwestern, by Siegfried Matthus; Appearances as Octavian in Der Rosenkavalier at the Deutsche Oper Berlin and Covent Garden (1995); La Scala debut 1996, in Das Rheingold under Riccardo Muti, and debut as Beethoven's Leonore at Essen Opera, 1997; Engaged as the Composer in Ariadne auf Naxos, Bayerische Staatsoper Munich, 1998; Resident artist at the Deutsche Oper Berlin from 1996; Concert repertory includes Bach's St Matthew Passion (under Kurt Masur), Schubert's E-flat Mass, Pergolesi's Stabat Mater and Les Illuminations by Britten; Pfitzner's choral fanatasia Das Dunkle Reich under Rolf Reuter; Season 2000–01 at the Deutsche Oper as Rossini's Zulma, Octavian and Gertrude in Hans Heiling; Waltraute at Bayreuth (2002) and Brangaene at Glyndebourne, 2003. *Recordings include:* Songs by Shostakovich.

**WIEGOLD, Peter (John);** Composer, Conductor and Teacher; b. 29 Aug. 1949, Ilford, Essex, England. *Education:* BMus, MMus, University College of Wales, Aberystwyth; PhD, University of Durham. *Career:* Director of Gemini, regular tours of the United Kingdom including many broadcasts; Many residencies involving local participation in shared concerts; Artistic Director, Performance and Communication Skills Project, Guildhall School of Music; Has directed many workshops in music and music theatre including those with London Sinfonietta, Royal Opera House, English National Opera, Scottish Chamber Orchestra and City of London Sinfonia; Junge Deutsche Philharmonie in Greece, Canada, Spain and Sweden; London Symphony Orchestra; mem, Past Member, Council and Executive Committee of SPNM. *Compositions include:* Gemini; Sing Lullaby; The Flowers Appear on the Earth; Preludes I–V; The Dancing Day; Songs from Grimm; Half-hour opera commissioned by the Royal Opera House, performed 1989; the Seventh Wave for cello and tape, 1997; Earth Receive/an Honoured Guest, for cor anglais and string trio, 1998; Kalachakrá, for 18 players, 2000; Farewells Take Place in Silence, Octet, 2001. *Honours:* Several Arts Council awards. *Address:* 82 Lordship Park, London N16 5UA, England.

**WIENER, Otto;** Singer (Baritone); b. 13 Feb. 1913, Vienna, Austria. *Education:* Studied in Vienna with Kuper and Hans Duhan. *Career:* Sang in Concert from 1939; Stage debut Graz 1953, as Simon Boccanegra; Sang at the Salzburg Festival from 1952; in Pfitzner's Palestrina 1955 and in the stage premiere of La Mystère de la Nativité by Martin, 1960; Deutsche Oper am Rhein Düsseldorf, 1956–59; Bayreuth Festival from 1957, as Hans Sachs, Gunther and the Dutchman; Member of the Vienna Staatsoper from 1957, Munich Staatsoper, 1960–70; Guest appearances in Paris, London, Rome and Brussels, often in operas by Wagner; Glyndebourne Festival 1964, as La Roche in Capriccio; Retired from stage 1976 and led an Opera School at the Vienna Staatsoper. *Recordings include:* Missa Solemnis, conducted by Klemperer; Faninal in Der Rosenkavalier; Lohengrin; St Matthew Passion. *Address:* c/o Staatsoper, Opernring 2, 1010 Vienna, Austria.

**WIENS, Edith,** OC; Canadian singer (soprano); b. 1950. *Career:* concert engagements with orchestras in Berlin, London, Israel, Munich, New York (Philharmonic), and with Cleveland, Philadelphia, San Francisco, Montréal and London Symphony Orchestras; broadcasts on Bavarian Radio, Dresden Staatskapelle, Leipzig Gewandhaus Orchestra; conductors include Barenboim, Georg Solti, Colin Davis, Haitink, Kurt Masur, Marriner, Sawallisch and Tennstedt; Salzburg debut 1984, with the Boston Symphony under Ozawa, with whom she has also sung Mozart's Ilia in Japan; other operatic roles include Donna Anna (at Glyndebourne under Haitink, in Paris and at Amsterdam under Harnoncourt) and Mozart's Countess (Buenos Aires); St Matthew Passion in Paris and Salzburg under Masur, with whom she also appeared in Mendelssohn's Elijah in New York; L'Enfant et les Sortilèges at

Carnegie Hall; Mahler's 4th Symphony in Munich; recitals in Paris, Vienna, Florence, Buenos Aires, New York and Montréal; Concertgebouw, Amsterdam, and the Pushkin Museum, Moscow; jury mem. of int. competitions; Rotarian 2001; Prof. of Voice, Hochschule für Musik, Augsburg, and Hochschule für Musik und Theater München 2000. *Recordings include:* Schubert, Schumann, Strauss and Zemlinsky Lieder, the title role in Schumann's Das Paradies und die Peri (Grammy Award 1990, Maurice Fleuret (Paris) Prize 1991), Flowermaiden in Parsifal, conducted by Barenboim, Mahler's 8th Symphony, conducted by Tennstedt, Haydn's Creation conducted by Neville Marriner, Brahms Lieder, Zemlinsky's Lyrical Symphony with the Swiss Romande Orchestra. *Honours:* Hon. DMus (Oberlin Coll., USA) 1997. *Address:* Georg-Schuster-Str. 10, 82152 Krailling, Germany. *Website:* www.edithwiens.com.

**WIESE, Henrik;** Flautist; b. 22 July 1971, Vienna, Austria. *Education:* Studied with Ingrid Koch, Roswitha Staege and Paul Meisen at Musikhochschule Hamburg and Musikhochschule Munich. *Career:* Engaged as 1st Principal Flautist, Bavarian State Opera, Munich, 1995–; Solo concerts with various orchestras including Berlin Radio Symphony Orchestra, Orchestra of the Beethovenhalle in Bonn, Polish Chamber Philharmonic, others; Solo concerts with Berlin Radio Symphony Orchestra, Hanover Radio-Philharmonie of NDR, Lower Saxonian State Orchestra. *Recordings:* Chamber music works including Mozart, Flute Quartets and Overtures arranged for flute and string quartet, with Artemis; Bach Flute Sonatas with Anikó Soltész. *Publications:* Several editions at Henle Edition. Contributions to Mozart-Jahrbuch, 1997. *Honours:* Prizewinner at national compositions, such as German Music Competition, 1995;, Elise Meyer Competition, 1996; Prizewinner at international competitions such as Kobe International FLute Competition 1997, Markneukirchen and Munich International Music Competition 2000. *Address:* Franziskanerstrasse 2, 81669 Munich, Germany. *Website:* www.henrikwiese.de.

**WIGGLESWORTH, Mark;** British music director and conductor; b. 19 July 1964, Ardingly, Sussex, England. *Career:* Assoc. Conductor, BBC Symphony Orchestra 1991–93; Music Dir, Opera Factory 1991–94; Music Dir, Premiere Ensemble 1989–; Music Dir, BBC Nat. Orchestra of Wales 1996–2000; Principal Guest Conductor, Swedish Radio Orchestra 1988–2001; worked in the UK with BBC Symphony, BBC Scottish Symphony, London Philharmonic, London Symphony, Bournemouth Symphony, English and Scottish Chamber Orchestras, Royal Scottish Nat. Orchestra, European Community Youth Orchestra; conducted Premiere Ensemble and BBC Nat. Orchestra of Wales in Centenary Season of BBC Proms; guest conductor in Europe, including Berlin Philharmonie and Deutsches-Symphonie Orchester Berlin; conductor with BBC Nat. Orchestra of Wales, Mahler Festival at the Concertgebouw, Amsterdam 1995, Royal Concertgebouw Orchestra, Rotterdam Philharmonic, Residentie Orchester, Radio Philharmonie and Netherlands Wind Ensemble, Netherlands, Welsh Nat. Opera, ENO, Santa Cecilia of Rome, Israel Philharmonic; European engagements include Oslo Philharmonic, Swedish Radio Orchestra, tour with Deutsche Kammerphilharmonie, Mozarteum Orchestra at Salzburg Festival; also engagements with Chicago, Cleveland, Philadelphia, Minnesota and Los Angeles Philharmonic Orchestras, St Louis, Toronto and San Francisco Symphony Orchestras, and at the Hollywood Bowl; debut with Sydney Symphony Orchestra, New York Philharmonic and at Glyndebourne with Peter Grimes 2000; Covent Garden debut with Die Meistersinger 2002. *Honours:* first prize Int. Kondrashin Competition, Netherlands 1989. *Current Management:* Askonas Holt Ltd, Lonsdale Chambers, 27 Chancery Lane, London, WC2A 1PF, England. *Telephone:* (20) 7400-1700. *Fax:* (20) 7400-1799. *E-mail:* info@askonasholt.co.uk. *Website:* www.askonasholt.co.uk.

**WILBRAHAM, John;** Trumpet Player; b. 15 April 1944, Bournemouth, England; m. Susan Drake. *Education:* Royal Academy of Music, London; LRAM; ARCM. *Career:* New Philharmonia Orchestra, 1966–68; Royal Philharmonic Orchestra, 1968–72; BBC Symphony Orchestra from 1972; Many appearances as soloist in the trumpet concerto repertory; mem, Savage Club; ISM. *Recordings include:* Concertos by Haydn, Hummel, Mozart, Telemann and Torelli. *Honours:* Silver Medal, Worshipful Company of Musicians, 1965. *Address:* 14b Elizabeth Mews, London NW3, England.

**WILBY, Philip;** Composer; b. 18 July 1949, Pontefract. *Education:* Leeds Grammar School, with Herbert Howells and at Keble College, Oxford. *Career:* Violinist with the Covent Garden Orchestra and City of Birmingham Symphony Orchestra; Senior Lecturer at Leeds University from 1972. *Compositions:* Orchestral Sunstudy; The Wings of Morning, 1988; Vocal: Et Surrexit Christus for 3 Sopranos and Ensemble, 1979; Ten Songs of Paul Verlaine for Baritone and Piano, 1983; The Temptations of Christ for Soprano and Ensemble, 1983; Winter Portrait in Grey and Gold for Voice and Ensemble, 1977–85; Cantiones Sacrae: In Darkness Shine, 1987; Magnificat and Nunc Dimittis, 1988; Easter Wings for Soprano and Ensemble, 1989; A Passion of our Times, 1997; Chamber: Little Symphony for Brass, 1985; The Night and All The Stars, Horn Quintet, 1985; Sonata Sacra: In Darkness Shine for Clarinet, Viola and Piano, 1986; And I Move Around The Cross for Double Wind Quintet, 1985; Two Concert Studies for Violin and Piano, 1986; Capricorn Suite for 4 Trombones, 1987; Parables for Cello and Piano, 1988; Classic Images, Partita for Brass Quintet, 1988; Concert music for Winds, 1988; Green Man Dancing, Wind Quintet, 1988; Breakdance for Recorder and Tape, 1988; Wind Band: Firestar, 1983; Symphonia Sacra: In Darkness Shine, 1986; Catcher of Shadows, 1988; Laudibus in sanctis, 1994; Keyboard: Roses for the Queen of Heaven, 1982; Two Preludes on English Tunes, 1987; Lifescape-Mountains, 1987;. . . Aunque es de Noche, 1989; Mozart Reconstructions include Concerto for Violin and Piano K315f and Concerto for Violin, Viola, Cello and Orchestra K320e, for the Philips Mozart Edition; Commissions include Symphony for the BBC Philharmonic. *Address:* c/o Chester Music, 8/9 Frith Street, London W1V 5TZ, England.

**WILD, Earl;** American pianist and composer; b. 26 Nov. 1915, Pittsburgh, Pa; s. of Royland Wild and Lillian G. Wild. *Education:* Carnegie Tech. Coll., Pittsburgh. *Career:* studied with Selmar Jansen, Egon Petri, Helene Barrere, Volya Cossack and Paul Doguereau; first American soloist to perform with NBC Orchestra conducted by Toscanini 1942, has performed with symphony orchestras and given recitals in many countries; staff pianist, composer, conductor ABC TV, New York 1945–68; has appeared with Sir Malcolm Sargent, Jascha Horenstein, Sir Georg Solti, Arthur Fiedler; played first TV piano recital 1939; has played for seven US presidents, including inauguration of Pres. J. F. Kennedy; Carnegie Hall, New York 2005; teacher, Juilliard School of Music 1977–, Manhattan School of Music 1981–83; numerous recordings for RCA, EMI, Columbia, Nonesuch, Readers Digest and Vanguard Records. *Compositions include:* Piano Concerto, The Turquoise Horse (choral work) and ballet music, oratorios, solo piano music, choral work and popular songs.

**WILDE, David (Clark);** Pianist, Composer, Conductor and Professor of Piano; b. 25 Feb. 1935, Manchester, England; m. (1) Jeanne Lukey, 23 May 1956, 1 s., 1 d., (2) Jane Heller, 14 June 1984. *Education:* Privately, Solomon/Reizenstein, 1945–47; Royal Manchester College of Music, Piano (Elinson), Composing (Hall), Conducting (Cohen), 1948–53; Nadia Boulanger, privately and American Conservatoire, Fontainebleau; Caird Foundation Scholar, 1963–64. *Career:* Concerts, USA, Canada, Australia, New Zealand, India, Brazil, France, Belgium, Netherlands, Spain, Germany, Hungary, Russia; International recording and concert artist for BBC, 1961–; Henry Wood Proms from 1961; Soloist, Royal concert in HM the Queen's presence, Royal Festival Hall, and at BBC television inaugural concert, Manchester (Hallé Orchestra, Barbirolli), 1962; Edinburgh, Cheltenham, Three Choirs, Perth (Australia) festivals; Tours, all leading British orchestras; Conductor, Worthing Symphony, season 1967–68; Writer, narrator, pianist, BBC television Liszt and Bartók documentary programmes, 1972–73; Guest Conductor, Royal Philharmonic, 1975; Liszt in Weimar, film, Granada television, 1986; Soloist, Tippett's Concerto, BBC Philharmonic, conducted Tippett (Manchester), Edward Downes (London Proms), 1988. *Compositions:* Love, song for baritone and cello, 1981; Jens, Heidi und die Schneekönigin, 1984; Vocalise, mezzo soprano, guitar; Die Jahreszeiten, song cycle, 1986; Mandala, solo viola, 1986; Piano trio, 1987–88; String quartet, 1991; The Cellist of Sarajevo, solo cello, 1992; Suite, Cry Bosnia-Herzogovina, violin, piano, 1993. *Recordings include:* Schumann Fantasie; Liszt Sonata; Complete Beethoven Sonatas with Gruenberg, violin. *Publications:* Transcriptions for piano, chapter in Franz Liszt, The Man and His Music, 1970; Liszt's Consolations, complete (editor), 1978. *Address:* c/o J Audrey Ellison International Artists' Management, 135 Stevenage Road, Fulham, London SW6 6PB, England.

**WILDE, Mark;** Singer (tenor); b. 1960, Dundee, Scotland. *Education:* Read Music, University of East Anglia; Choral Scholar, Norwich Cathedral Choir; Foundation Scholar, Royal College of Music; Thomas Allen Scholar, RCM. *Career:* Lay Clerk, Queen's Free Chapel of St George, Windsor Castle; Performs regularly throughout the United Kingdom and abroad in oratorio and recital; Bach's St Matthew Passion, Helsinki; Britten's War Requiem, Westminster Cathedral, Norwich Cathedral; Berlioz Te Deum, Orleans Cathedral; Mozart's Requiem, Israel; Monteverdi Vespers, Norway; Handel's Arminio, RCM; Maxwell Davies' The Lighthouse and Vivaldi's Ottone in Villa and Giustino for BBC Radio 3; Ferrando, Royal Academy of Music and Pimlico Opera Tour; Many recitals and oratorio appearances, including appearances with Osmo Vanska, Liège Philharmonic Orchestra, Southend Festival Choir, The Aldeburgh Music Club, Birmingham Festival Choral Society; Solo recitals in London and Aberdeen; Title role in Albert Herring, Perth Festival, 1998; Buxton Festival and appearances in recital and oratorio, 1999. *Recordings:* Requiem with the National Youth Choir of Great Britain and music by Wren Baroque Ensemble. *Current Management:* Hazard Chase, Norman House, Cambridge Place, Cambridge CB2 1NS, England. *Telephone:* (1223) 312400. *Fax:* (1223) 460827. *Website:* www.hazardchase.co.uk. *Address:* St Michael's Cottage, Church Lane, Bray SL6 2AF, England.

**WILDING, Simon,** BMus; British singer (bass); b. b. 10 May 1970, Leigh, Lancashire, England. *Education:* Royal Northern College of Music with Robert Alderson, and with Patrick Mcguigan. *Career:* at Royal Northern College of Music, sang Quince and Snug in separate productions of Britten's Midsummer Night's Dream; Geronimo in Il Matrimonio Segreto; and Walter Raleigh in Donizetti's Roberto Devereux; Luka in Walton's The Bear at Manchester and the UK/LA Festival at Los Angeles; Sang Count Ceprano in Rigoletto for English National Opera; and Foltz in Die Meistersinger (ROH debut), ein Brabantische Edle in Lohengrin, and the Cappadocian in Salome at Covent Garden; Also covered and performed roles including Theseus in A Midsummer Night's Dream; The Drunken Poet in The Fairy Queen; The Speaker in The Magic Flute; Kotwitz in The Prince of Homburg; General in Die Soldaten; 5th Jew in Salome; Other roles include Jove in La Calisto and roles in Il Pomo d'Oro for the Batignano Festival; Sang Fasolt in Das Rheingold and Hagen in Götterdämmerung for the Mastersingers and Wagner Soc. *Recordings include:* Cappadocian in Salome (ROH);

Lt Ratcliffe in Billy Budd (Hallé); Dick Deadeye in HMS Pinafore (D'Oyle Carte). *Honours:* Wagner Bursary Award for most promising singer of Wagner, 1991. *Current Management:* Robert Gilder & Co., Enterprise House, 59–65 Upper Ground, London, SE1 9PQ, England. *Telephone:* (20) 7928-9008. *Fax:* (20) 7928-9755. *E-mail:* rgilder@robert-gilder.com. *E-mail:* simon@wilding608.freeserve.co.uk.

**WILDING-WHITE, Raymond,** MM, DMA; composer and teacher; b. 9 Oct. 1922, Caterham, Surrey, England. *Education:* Juilliard School, New England Conservatory, Tanglewood with Copland and Dallapiccola, Boston University with Gardner Read. *Career:* teacher at Case Institute of Technology, Cleveland, 1961–67 and De Paul University, Chicago (1967–88); Founder and Director of the Loop ensemble, 1969–89, for the performance of contemporary music; Many music education broadcasts on WFMT-FM, Chicago, including series Our American Music, 1976, and a memorial tribute to John Cage 1992. *Compositions include:* Piano Concerto, 1949; The Tub, chamber opera, 1952; The Selfish Giant, television fable, 1952; Even Now for baritone and orchestra, 1954; Paraphernalia for chorus and five instruments, 1959; The Lonesome Valley, ballet, 1960; Yerma, opera, 1962; Concertante for viola, violin, horns and strings, 1963; Bandmusic, 1966; Encounters, ballet, 1967; 6 string quartets, 1948–88; Violin Concerto, 1978; Beth, musical, 1989 (renamed Trio 1994); Gifts, liturgical drama, 1993; Symphony of Symphonies, 1995.

**WILKE, Elisabeth;** Singer (Mezzo-Soprano); b. 19 May 1952, Dresden, Germany. *Education:* Studied at the Musikhochschule Dresden. *Career:* Debut: Dresden 1974, as Hansel; Appearances with the Dresden Staatsoper-Semper Oper in Germany and on tour as Dorabella, Amastris in Handel's Serse, Olga (Eugene Onegin) and Tisbe in Cenerentola, 1992; Sang Veronika in the premiere of Der Goldene Topf by E Mayer, 1989; Zulma in L'Italiana in Algeri at Dresden, 1997; Soloist in the St Matthew Passion at Magdeburg, 2000. *Recordings include:* Symphoniae Sacrae by Schütz (Capriccio); Saint-Saëns Christmas Oratorio; Missa Brevis by C P E Bach; J. S. Bach's St Matthew Passion. *Address:* c/o Semper Oper, 8012 Dresden, Germany.

**WILKENS, Anne;** Singer (Mezzo-Soprano); b. 1 July 1947, Romford, England. *Education:* Guildhall School of Music; London Opera Centre; Further Study with Eva Turner. *Career:* Sang in Verdi's Ernani at the Festival Hall, 1972; The Nose by Shostakovich for the New Opera Company, 1973; Sang with English Opera Group in operas by Britten, in Aldeburgh, Venice and Brussels; Sang in world premieres of Death in Venice, 1973, and Musgrave's The Voice of Ariadne, 1974; Member of the Royal Opera Company, Covent Garden, 1974–78, as Olga in Eugene Onegin, Maddalena in Rigoletto, and in the world premiere of Henze's We Come to the River, 1976; Appearances with Handel Opera Society; Handel roles include Julius Caesar, Dejanaira (Hercules) and Ezio; Welsh National Opera 1979, as Brangaene in Tristan und Isolde; Guest appearances in Frankfurt (Azucena), Marseille and Stuttgart (Brangaene); Bayreuth 1983, in the Solti/Hall production of The Ring; Karlsruhe from 1983, as Eboli in Don Carlos and as Wagner's Venus, Fricka, Ortrud and Waltraute; Sang in the premiere of Der Meister und Margarita by Kunaud, Karlsruhe, 1986; Sang Neris in Cherubini's Médée for Opera North, 1996; Mme Larina in Eugene Onegin for ENO, 1997; Season 2000–01 as Wagner's Mary at Covent Garden and in Dublin; Concert engagements with the London Symphony Orchestra, Hallé Orchestra, Bournemouth Symphony and in Netherlands, Spain, Brussels and Stockholm. *Recordings include:* Tristan und Isolde, conducted by Reginald Goodall. *Address:* c/o English National Opera, St Martin's Lane, London, EC 2, England.

**WILKINS, Caroline;** Composer; b. 31 July 1953, Somerset, England. *Education:* BMus, Royal College of Music, London, 1975; Cologne Music Academy, with Mauricio Kagel, 1987–88. *Career:* Composer and performer with new music projects in Australia, 1984–86; Freelance composer in Germany, 1989–; Commissions from Ensemble Köln (1991), the Hilliard Ensemble (1994) and others; Festival Participation at Darmstadt, Rheinland, Zürich and Witten, 1990–94. *Compositions include:* Piece for Accordion and Phonograph, 1988; Piece for Accordion with Screens, 1988; Arias for Phonograph and Singers, 1988; Piece for 17 Tones, for 2 pianos, 1990; Piece for Player Piano and Piano, 1990; Loquela, for 1 to 8 female voices, 1991; Automatophone, for ensemble, 1991; The Bird Organ is Made of Wood for Percussion, 1991; Camera Aeolia for organ, 1992; Auroram Lucifer for chorus, 1993; For These My Friends and Yours for 4 male voices, 1994; With Circle and Axis, for string quartet, 1998. *Honours:* First Prize, Frauenmusik-Forum, Berne, 1992. *Address:* c/o Ms F. Zimmermann, Edition Modern, Tre Media Musikverlage, Karlsruhe, Germany. *Website:* www.tremediamusicedition.de.

**WILKINS, Margaret (Lucy),** BMus, LRAM, AMusD; British composer and music educator (retd); b. 13 Nov. 1939, Kingston upon Thames; m. Nigel E. Wilkins 11 Asst Prof. Aug. 1962 (divorced 1977); two d. *Education:* Trinity Coll. of Music, London, Univ. of Nottingham. *Career:* debut: BBC; works performed world-wide, South Bank and Wigmore Hall, London, and elsewhere in UK, Canada, Germany, Italy, Switzerland, Bulgaria, Austria, Netherlands, America, Spain, Romania and Poland; comms: BBC Scottish Symphony Orchestra, Univ. of St Andrews, New Music Group of Scotland, William Byrd Singers, John Turner, Julie Wilson, Goldberg Ensemble, Kirklees Cultural Services, Philip Mead; festivals: Durham, Edinburgh, Huddersfield, Nottingham, Donne in Musica, Llangollen Eisteddfod, ISCM, World Music Days, Poland and Slovenia, Middelburg, Netherlands, New Music, Bucharest; music teacher, Mansfield Grammar School, Nottingham 1961–62; pvt. teacher of piano and theory, St Andrews, Scotland 1964–1976; Founder-mem. and performer, Scottish Early Music Consort 1970–76; Sr Lecturer, Huddersfield Polytechnic/Univ. of Huddersfield 1976–99, Subject Leader in Composition 1984–92, MA in Music Composition Course Leader 1990–2003, Module Area Leader in Composition 1997–2003, Prin. Lecturer in Music 1999–2003, CALMA Fellowship 2000; Artistic Dir Polyphonia 1989–95; Maude Clarke Visiting Prof., Queen's Univ., Belfast 1995; External Assessor for BA in Performing Arts, Anglia Polytechnic Univ. 1997–2001; External Examiner for PhD, Univ. of Edinburgh 2000, Univ. of Leeds 2002; Doctoral Comm., Univ. of Music, Bucharest, Romania 2001. Compositions include: Struwwelpeter 1973, Hymn to Creation 1973, Etude 1974, Circus 1975, Ave Maria 1975, Music of the Spheres 1975, Gitanjali 1981, Aspects of Night 1981, Epistola da San Marco 1987, Réve, Réveil, Révélations, Réverbérations 1988, Revelations of the Seven Angels 1988, Symphony 1989, Kanal 1990, Musica Angelorum 1991, Stringsing 1992, L'Attente 1994, Study in Black and White No. 3 1996, Folk Works 1996, Fearful Apathy 1997, Ring Out, Wild Bells 1998, Rituelle 1999, Trompettes de Mort 2003. Recordings: Deus ex Machina (Keith Jarvis, solo organ), Organ Mixtures 1988, Struwwelpeter for soprano, 3 clarinets, percussion, piano 1997, Study in Black & White Nos 1 and 2 for solo piano, Ananda Sukarlan (solo piano), The Pentatonic Connection 1994, Musica Angelorum, Struwwelpeter, Burnt Sienna, 366″ for solo trombone, Symphony (Alison Wells, Barrie Webb, Firebird Ensemble, Sofia Soloists, Orchestra Simfonica Timisoara), Free Spirit 2003, Revelations of the Seven Angels (Orchestra e Coro Simfonica Timisoara, conductor Barrie Webb) 2004. Publications: Pirouette for solo oboe, and Pas de Quatre for 4 oboes, in Modern Wind Music, Vol. 2 (ed. John Turner) 1985, Aries for descant recorder, in Pieces for Solo Recorder, Vol. 1 (ed. John Turner) 1986, Circuit for bassoon & piano, in Modem Wind Music, Vol. 4 (ed. John Turner) 1986, 366″ for solo trombone 1988, Struwwelpeter for soprano, 3 clarinets, percussion, piano, in Music File (ed. Micheal Burnett, Stanley Thornes) 1997, Study in Black & White N0.3 for solo piano, in British Contemporary Music Anthology 1996–97 1997, Study in Black & White Nos 1, 2 and 3 for solo piano 1998. Honours: Scottish Arts Council Bursary for Composers 1970, Winner, The New Cantata Orchestra of London's Competition for Young British Composers (Concerto Grosso) 1970, Winner, Cappiani Prize for Women Composers (The Silver Casket) 1971, First Prize, Halifax (Canada) Int. Competition for Teaching Music (Instrumental Interludes) 1973, Hinrichsen Foundation Award for Composers (UK) 1979, Arts Council of GB Bursary for Composers 1981–82, First Prize, Miriam Gideon Int. Prize for Composers (Struwwelpeter) 2000, LTSN Palatine Devt Award (UK) 2002. Address: 4 Church Street, Golcar, Huddersfield, HD7 4AH, West Yorks., England (home). Telephone: (1484) 652762 (home). E-mail: margaretlucywilkins@btinternet.com (home). Website: composers21.com/compdocs/wilkinsm.htm.

**WILKINSON, Katie;** Violist; b. 1960, England. Career: Debut: Wigmore Hall 1984, with Peter Pears; Co-Founded the Brindisi String Quartet at Aldeburgh, 1984; Concerts in a wide repertory throughout the United Kingdom and in France, Germany, Spain, Italy and Switzerland; Festival engagements at Aldeburgh (residency 1990), Arundel, Bath, Brighton, Huddersfield, Norwich and Warwick; First London Performance of Colin Matthews's 2nd Quartet 1990, premiere of David Matthews's 6th Quartet, 1991; Quartet by Mark Anthony Turnage, 1992; Many BBC recitals and Resident Artist with the University of Ulster. Recordings include: Quartets by Britten, Bridge and Imogen Holst; Works by Pierné and Lekeu. Honours: (with Brindisi Quartet) Prizewinner at the Third Banff International String Quartet Competition in Canada, 1989. Address: c/o Owen-White Management, 14 Nightingale Lane, London N8 7QU, England.

**WIŁKOMIRSKA, Wanda,** MMus; Polish violinist; b. 11 Jan. 1929, Warsaw; d. of Alfred Wiłkomirski and Dorota Temkin; divorced since 1976; two s. Education: Higher State of Music, Łódź, Franz Liszt Acad. of Music, Budapest and pvt. studies with Henryk Szeryng, Paris. Career: public debut playing a Mozart Sonata aged seven; first appearance with orchestra aged 15, in Kraków; numerous recordings; concerts in 50 countries with most of the major orchestras throughout the world; toured as soloist with, amongst others, Nat. Philharmonic, Warsaw and Minnesota Symphony; has given world premiere performances of numerous contemporary works including works by Baird and Penderecki; has toured with her sister and brother as the Wilkomirska Trio and has performed with Martha Argerich, Gidon Kremer, Daniel Barenboim, Misha Maisky and others; defected whilst on tour of FRG March 1982; Prof., Hochschule für Musik, Heidelberg-Mannheim 1983–98; Guest Prof., Sydney Conservatorium of Music, Australia 1999–; has worked with Australian Nat. Acad. of Music, Melbourne 2001–; master classes in Melbourne and Sydney; mem. Jury Hannover Int. Violin Competition 1997, 2000, Kendall Nat. Violin Competition (Australia). Honours: Officer's Cross of Polonia Restituta Order 1953, Commdr's Cross with Star 2001, Order of Banner of Labour 2nd Class 1959, (1st Class) 1964; Polish State Prize 1952, 1964; several foreign prizes, including Second Prize, Leipzig 1950, Bach Competition Award of Democratic German Radio, Culture and Arts Prize (1st Class) 1975, Orpheus Prize, Polish Musicians' Asscn 1979. Address: Sydney Conservatorium of Music, Building C41, The University of Sydney, Sydney NSW 2006, Australia (office). Telephone: (2) 93511222 (office). Fax: (2) 93511287 (office). E-mail: info@greenway.usyd.edu.au (office). Website: www.music.usyd.edu.au (office).

**WILKOMIRSKI, Jozef,** MA; Polish conductor, composer, broadcaster, lecturer and journalist and writer; Chief Manager and Artistic Director,

Sudettic Philharmonic, Walbrzych; b. 15 May 1926, Kalisz; m. Margaret Zasinska 1980; one d. Education: State High School of Music, Warsaw and Warsaw Univ. Career: debut, Warsaw Philharmonic 1950; Asst Conductor, Kraków Philharmonic 1950–51; Conductor, Poznan Philharmonic 1954–57; Dir and Chief Conductor, State Philharmonic M. Karlowicz in Szczecin 1957–71; founder, Chief Man. and Artistic Dir, Sudettic Philharmonic, Walbrzych 1978–, later renamed the Sudettic Philharmonia; guest conductor in numerous countries in Europe, Asia and America; composer from 1968; numerous radio and television programme appearances, including over 300 lectures. Compositions: two sinfoniettas, Symphonic Poems, Symphonic Suite (Royal Castle in Warsaw), sonatas for violin, cello and double bass, Harp Concerto, Concerto for violin and cello, trio, songs. Publications: contrib. over 400 articles and pieces of journalism. Honours: Gold Medal of Pomeranian Gryphon 1960, Musical Prize of the City of Szczecin 1961, Medal for Merit in Culture 1967, Prize for Public Cultivation of Music 1970, Prize of the City of Walbrzych 1979, Prize of Lower Silesia Press 1982, Prize of the Province of Walbrzych 1983, Medal of National Education 1984, Cultural Award of the City of Walbrzych 1999, Key of Success Prize 2003, Prize of the Province of Lower Silesia 2003; Cross of Warsaw Insurrection 1985, Order of the Banner of Labour (First Class) 1986, Cross of the Home Army 1995, Medal of the Veteran of the War for Independence 1995, Commander's Cross with the Star of the Order Polonia Restituta 1998. Address: Sudettic Philharmonia, ul Slowackiego 4, 58-300 Walbrzych, Poland. Telephone: 74 842-28-73. Fax: 74 842-28-73. E-mail: filharmonia@pako.pl. Website: www.filharmonia.pako.pl.

**WILL, Jacob;** Singer (Bass); b. 8 June 1957, Hartsville, South Carolina, USA. Education: Studied at the Cincinnati Conservatory and at San Francisco Opera Studio. Career: Sang Masetto at San Francisco, followed by appearances with Long Beach and Anchorage Operas, as Basilio in Il Barbiere di Siviglia; Carmel Beach Festival as Mozart's Figaro; Appearances throughout the USA as Don Giovanni, Frank in Die Fledermaus, and Dulcamara; Sang in Europe from 1986, Zürich Opera from 1988 as Basilio and Melcthal in Guillaume Tell; St Gallen as Sparafucile and Raimondo in Lucia di Lammermoor, Barnaba in Andrea Chénier, 1989; Vancouver 1990, as Oroveso, Bregenz Festival 1992, as Zuniga in Carmen; Concert engagements include Rossini's Petite Messe Solennelle, Lincoln Center, 1989; Sang the Speaker in Die Zauberflöte at Zürich and Giachino in Pa ër's Leonora at Winterthur, 2000. Recordings include: Zemlinsky's Kleider Machen Leute. Address: c/o Opernhaus Zürich, Falkenstrasse 1, 8008 Zürich, Switzerland.

**WILLCOCK, Christopher John;** Composer; b. 8 Feb. 1947, Sydney, New South Wales, Australia. Education: BMus (Hons), University of Sydney, 1974; Theological Doctorates at Paris, 1987. Career: Trinity Mass for Cantor, chorus, congregation and organ, 1977; Psalms for Feasts and Seasons, 1977; Convict and the Lady, for chorus and chamber ensemble, 1978; Lines from Little Gidding for chorus and organ, 1978; Friday 3.30 for chorus and string orchestra, 1986; Easter Moon for chorus and brass instruments, 1988; Two Pastorals for voice and harpsichord, 1990; Duo for Oboe and Harpsichord, 1992; Plaint Over Dili for oboe and harpsichord, 1992; The Frilled Lizard for viola and harp, 1993; Here be Dragons, for harpsichord, 1994. Honours: Dr Percy Jones Award for Outstanding Services to Liturgical Music, 1993. Address: c/o APRA, 1A East Street, Crows Nest, NSW 2065, Australia.

**WILLCOCKS, Sir David (Valentine),** Kt, CBE, MC, MusB, MA, FRCO, FRCM; British musician; b. 30 Dec. 1919, Newquay, Cornwall; s. of T. H. Willcocks; m. Rachel Blyth 1947; two s. (one deceased) two d. Education: Clifton Coll. and King's Coll., Cambridge. Career: served with 5th Bn, Duke of Cornwall's Light Infantry (rank of Capt.) 1940–45; Fellow, King's Coll., Cambridge 1947–51, Fellow and Dir of Music 1957–73, Lecturer in Music, Cambridge Univ. and Cambridge Univ. Organist 1957–74; Conductor Cambridge Univ. Music Soc. 1958–73; Organist Salisbury Cathedral 1947–50, Worcester Cathedral 1950–57; Conductor, Worcester Three Choirs Festival and City of Birmingham Choir 1950–57; Musical Dir Bach Choir, London 1960–98; Pres. Royal Coll. of Organists 1966–68 (Vice-Pres. 1968–), Incorporated Soc. of Musicians 1978–79, Nat. Fed. of Music Socs 1980–90 (Vice-Pres. 1990–), Asscn of British Choral Dirs 1993–; Dir Royal Coll. of Music, London 1974–84 (Vice-Pres. 1984–); conductor in many recordings with the Choir of King's Coll. Cambridge, The Bach Choir (Conductor Laureate 1998–) and the Royal Coll. of Music Chamber Choir; Fellow Royal School of Church Music 1977, Royal Scottish Acad. of Music and Drama 1982. Honours: Freeman, City of London 1981; Hon. RAM 1965, Guildhall School of Music and Drama 1980; Hon. FRNCM, FRSAMD; Hon. Fellow Royal Canadian Coll. of Organists 1967, Trinity Coll. of Music 1976, King's Coll., Cambridge 1979; Hon. mem. Royal Philharmonic Soc. 1999; Hon. DMus (Exeter) 1976, (Leicester) 1977, (Westminster Choir Coll., Princeton) 1980, (Bristol) 1981, (St Olaf Coll., Minn.) 1991, (Royal Coll. of Music) 1998, (Univ. of Victoria, BC) 1999; Hon. DLitt (Sussex) 1982, (Memorial Univ. of Newfoundland) 2003; Hon. DSL (Trinity Univ., Toronto) 1985; Hon. DFA (Luther Coll., Ia) 1998; Hon. LLD (Toronto) 2001; Hon. MA (Bradford) 1973; Harvard Glee Club Medal 1992, Distinguished Musician Silver Medal, Inc. Soc. of Musicians 1999, Distinguished Visitor Silver Medal, Univ. of Toronto 1999, Silver Medal Worshipful Co. of Musicians 1999. Address: 13 Grange Road, Cambridge, CB3 9AS, England. Telephone: (1223) 359559. Fax: (1223) 355947. E-mail: david_willcocks@dvwcambs.freeserve.co.uk.

**WILLEN, Niklas Olov;** Swedish conductor; b. 30 March 1961, Stockholm; m. Anna Schulze 1997; three s. one d. Education: Royal Coll. of Music, Stockholm. Career: debut with Gavleborg Symphony Orchestra 1988; conductor, Royal

Opera, Stockholm, Gothenburg Opera; Principal Conductor, The Sundsvall Chamber Orchestra 1993–97; Principal Guest Conductor, Royal Stockholm Philharmonic Orchestra 1993–96; guest appearances in Norway, Finland, Denmark, Germany, England, Scotland, Ireland, USA; mem. Swedish Soc. of Musical Artists. *Compositions:* Lux Aeterna for Choir 1983, Bassoon Concerto 1988, Wind Quintet 1993. *Recordings include:* symphonies by Hugo Alfrein with Royal Scottish Nat. Orchestra. *Honours:* second prize Nordic Competition 1990. *Current Management:* Patrick Garvey Management, Cedar House, 10 Rutland Street, Filey, North Yorkshire YO14 9JB, England. *Website:* www .patrickgarvey.com.

**WILLI, Herbert;** Composer; b. 7 Jan. 1956. *Education:* Abitur; MPhil, University of Innsbruck; Diploma in Composition and MA, Mozarteum, Salzburg; Studies with Helmut Eder and Boguslav Schaeffer. *Compositions:* Opera Schlafes Bruder (libretto by Robert Schneider); Orchestral works: Der Froschmäusekrieg–for sprechgesang, 3 orchestral groups and tape, 1989; Räume für Orchester, 1991; Konzert für Orchester, 1991–92; Flötenkonzert, 1993; Chamber music: Stück für Flöte solo, 1985, 1986; Streichquartett, 1986; Trio für Violine, Horn und Klavier, 1992; Concerto for Orchestra, 1992; Flute Concerto, 1993; Begegnung, for orchestra, 1999; Performances of his works: New York (Carnegie Hall), London (Royal Albert Hall), Vienna (Konzerthaus/ Musikverein), Salzburg Festival (Grosses Festspielhaus), Berlin Philharmonic Hall, performed by international orchestras Vienna Philharmonic, Berlin Philharmonic, Cleveland Orchestra, conducted by Claudio Abbado and Christoph von Dohnányi. *Honours:* Prize of the Republic of Austria, 1986; Rome Prize, 1987, 1988; Rolf Liebermann Scholarship, 1990; Ernst-von-Siemens Prize, 1991; Composer in Residence, Salzburg Festival, 1992. *Current Management:* Schott Musik International.

**WILLIAM, Louis Hagen;** Singer (Bass-Baritone); b. 1950, New Orleans, USA. *Education:* Studied at University of Los Angeles Opera Workshop and at Paris Conservatoire. *Career:* With Lyon Opéra sang Sarastro, Daland and the Landgrave in Tannhäuser, Paris Opéra Company in Turandot and L'Heure Espagnole; Other roles include Mephistopheles, Nilakanta in Lakmé, Rossini's Bartolo and the villains in Les Contes d'Hoffmann; Has sung in various versions of Porgy and Bess with the Royal Liverpool Philharmonic, the Scottish Chamber Orchestra under Carl Davis, the Ulster Orchestra under Yan Pascal Tortelier, and the Hallé and Royal Philharmonic Orchestras; Has also sung in Handel's Judas Maccabaeus and on French Radio and Television. *Recordings include:* Negro Spitituals (Quantum) and Mozart Concert Arias. *Honours:* First Prizes for Opera and Concert Singing at the Paris Conservatoire.

**WILLIAMS, Adrian;** Composer and Pianist; b. 30 April 1956, Watford, Hertfordshire, England. *Education:* Royal College of Music, London. *Career:* Composer-in-Residence, Charterhouse, 1980–82; Founder Director, Presteigne International Festival, 1983–92. *Compositions:* Sonata for Solo Cello, 1977; String Quartet No. 2, 1981; Tess, Orchestral Poem, 1982; Cantata: September Sky, 1985; Mass, 1986; Chaconne for Guitar, 1986; Images of a Mind, Cello and Piano, 1986; Cantata: Not Yet Born, 1986; Leaves from the Lost Book, 1987; Dies Irae, 1988; Music for the Film Gernika, 1987; Cantata: The Ways of Going, 1990; String Quartet No. 3, 1991; The King of Britain's Daughter, 1993. *Honours:* Menuhin Prize, 1978; Guinness Prize, 1986. *Address:* c/o BMI, 79 Harley House, Marylebone Road, London, NW1, England.

**WILLIAMS, Bradley;** Singer (tenor); b. 1965, Texas, USA. *Education:* University of Texas and Cincinnati Conservatory of Music. *Career:* Debut: As Ernesto in Don Pasquale with the Metropolitan Opera Guild, 1991; Performances include Korngold's Die Tote Stadt with New York City Opera and Zimmermann's Die Soldaten; Opera Orchestra of New York as Georges in Boieldieu's La Dame Blanche; Don Ramiro in La Cenerentola and Giannetto in La Gazza Ladra at Gran Teatro del Liceu in Barcelona; 1992 included Italian debut as Salvini in world premiere of Bellini's Adelson e Salvini at Teatro Massimo Bellini; Beppe in Pagliacci for New York City Opera; Canadian debut as Ernesto in Don Pasquale in Edmonton; Arturo in I Puritani in Malaga; Carmina Burana at Teatro Regio Torino under Hubert Soudant; Alphonse in Hérold's Zampa at the Wexford Festival; 1995, created role of Scott for Houston Grand Opera's world premiere of Wallace and Korie's Harvey Milk; Count Almaviva in Il Barbiere di Siviglia; Performances of Handel's Judas Maccabaeus and Messiah with Collegiate Chorale for Carnegie Hall debut; Australian debut as Tonio in Fille du Régiment with Opera Australia, 1997; Connecticut Opera debut as Ernesto; Ernesto for Opéra de Québec and Ferrando in Così fan tutte for Dayton Opera; Lindoro in l'Italiana in Algeri for Garsington Opera Festival, Oxford; Season 1998–99 included Duke in Rigoletto in Anchorage, Alaska, debut at Strasbourg's Opéra du Rhin as Tonio in Fille du Régiment and Edgardo in Lucia di Lammermoor in Anchorage. *Recordings:* Salvini in Adelson e Salvi; Harvey Milk with San Francisco Opera. *Current Management:* Athole Still International Management, Forresters Hall, 25–27 Westow Street, London, SE19 3RY, England. *Telephone:* (20) 8771-5271. *Fax:* (20) 8768-6600. *Website:* www.atholestill.com.

**WILLIAMS, Camilla;** American singer; *Professor of Voice, Indiana University;* b. 8 Oct. 1922, Danville, VA; m. Charles T. Beavers 1950. *Education:* Virginia State Coll., studied with Marion Szekely-Freschl. *Career:* sang role of Madama Butterfly as first black singer, New York City Centre 1946; sang Aida, New York City Centre 1948; New York performance of Mozart's Idomeneo, Little Orchestra Soc. 1950; tour of Alaska 1950; European tour (London) 1954; performance of Menotti's Saint of Bleecker Street 1955; American Festival, Belgium 1955; African tour for US State Dept (14 countries) 1958–59; tour of Israel 1959; guest of Pres. Eisenhower, Concert for Crown Prince of Japan 1960; tour of Formosa, Australia, New Zealand, Korea, Japan, Philippines, Laos, South Viet Nam 1962; New York performance of Handel's Orlando 1971; tour of Poland 1974; appearances with orchestras, including the Royal Philharmonic, Vienna Symphony, Zürich, Tonhalle, Berlin Philharmonic, New York Philharmonic, Chicago Symphony, Philadelphia Orchestra, BBC Orchestras, Stuttgart Orchestra, Geneva, Belgium; Prof. of Voice, Brooklyn Coll. 1970–73, Bronx Coll. 1970–, Queens Coll. 1974–, Indiana Univ., Bloomington 1977–. *Address:* School of Music-Studio MU104B, Indiana University, Bloomington, IN 47405, USA.

**WILLIAMS, Daniel Lewis;** Singer (bass); b. 1960, USA. *Education:* University of Utah, Salt Lake City; Musikhochschule, Munich and with Kurt Böhme and Kurt Moll. *Career:* Many appearances at opera houses throughout Germany and Italy, with roles including Ramphis in Aida, Gremin, Sarastro, Hunding, Rocco and Daland; Baron Ochs in Der Rosenkavalier at Frankfurt, Palermo, Munich and Genoa; Season 2000–2001 as King Marke at Genoa, Fafner and Hagen in The Ring at Marseille, Claggart in Billy Budd at Venice, Sarastro in Weimar and Daland for Opera di Trieste; Concerts include the Verdi Requiem in Nuremberg, Schoenberg's Gurrelieder, Shostakovich Symphony no. 14, Stravinsky's Threni and Beethoven's Mass in C (both in Venice). *Current Management:* Athole Still International Management, Forresters Hall, 25–27 Westow Street, London, SE19 3RY, England. *Telephone:* (20) 8771-5271. *Fax:* (20) 8768-6600. *Website:* www.atholestill.com.

**WILLIAMS, Edgar Warren;** Professor, Composer and Conductor; b. 12 June 1949, Orlando, Florida, USA; m. Christine Anderson, 19 June 1971, 1 s., 1 d. *Education:* BA, Duke University, 1971; MA, Columbia University, 1973; MFA 1977; PhD 1982, Princeton University. *Career:* Teaching Assistant, Columbia University, 1972–73; Assistant in Instruction, Princeton University, 1977–78; Visiting Lecturer in Music, University of California, Davis, 1978–79; Assistant Professor, The College of William and Mary, Williamsburg, Virginia, 1979–82; Associate Professor, 1982; Guest Conductor with orchestras including Bennington Composers Conference Ensemble, 1969–70 and Columbia Composers Ensemble, 1973; Conductor, William and Mary Orchestra, 1979–82. *Compositions:* Numerous published including: Three Songs, 1977; Across a Bridge of Dreams, 1979–80; Amoretti, 1980; Some Music for Merry Wives, 1982; Landscapes With Figure, 1983; Now Showing, for wind and percussion, 1993; Pentimenti, for chamber orchestra, 1993; String Quartet II, 1996; String Quartet III, 1997; Nosferata: A Symphony of Horror, for large orchestra, 1998; Lone, for solo saxophone, 1998. *Publications:* Harmony and Voice Leading, with Taylor and Miller, 1993; Introduction to Music, 1993. *Contributions:* In Theory Only; 19th Century Music. *Address:* Department of Music, College of William and Mary, Williamsburg, VA 23185, USA.

**WILLIAMS, Harriet,** DipDrama; British singer (mezzo-soprano); b. 1969, London; d. of Gordon Williams and Claerwen Williams; m.; one c. *Education:* Arts Educational School, Guildhall School with Johanna Peters, studies with Hazel Wood. *Career:* WNO from 1993 in operas by Mozart, Strauss, Berlioz, Verdi and Janáček; Purcell's Dido at Bath, Suzuki in Butterfly at the Mananan Festival and Cenerentola for Clonter Opera; other roles include Mozart's Cherubino and Dorabella; concerts include the Mozart and Verdi Requiems, St Matthew Passion, Haydn's Nelson and St Theresa Masses and Mahler's Rückert Lieder; season 1998–99 with Poppea for WNO and The Dream of Gerontius with the Liverpool Philharmonic; season 2003 Carmen for English Pocket Opera; Storge in Handel's Jephtha with Konzertcher Darmstadt with performances in Baberihausen, Frankfurt, Amorbach and Darmstadt; season 2004 Cherubino for WNO, Old Sister 1 in Babette's Feast for Royal Opera in Linbury Studio, Nenila in The Enchantress for Grange Park Opera; season 2005 Marcellina for Opera 2005 in Cork, Hannah Kennedy, Maria Stuarda, Grange Park Opera. *Honours:* Countess of Muster Scholarship 1991, Sir James Laird Travelling Scholarship 1991, Ian Fleming Award 1991, Sybil Tutton Award 1992. *Current Management:* Helen Sykes Artists Management, 100 Felshan Road, Putney, London, England. *E-mail:* harrietejwilliams@yahoo.com.

**WILLIAMS, Helen;** Singer (Soprano); b. 1959, Merseyside. *Education:* Royal Northern College of Music. *Career:* Appearances with Glyndebourne Festival and Tour in 1980s, including Sashka in Osborne's The Electrification of the Soviet Union, and Emme in Albert Herring on tour to Italy; Engagements from 1994 include Handel's Rodelinda in Dublin and in Jephtha with The Sixteen in Rome and London; Dalinda in Ariodante and Amor in Gluck's Orfeo, for English National Opera; Britten's Helena for Opera North and Flaminia in Hayden's Mondo della luna for Netherlands Opera; Sang Naiad in Ariadne auf Naxos and Mozart's First Lady for Scottish Opera; Concerts include The Poisoned Kiss by Vaughan Williams (London and Birmingham), Messiah at the Albert Hall and Handel's Israel in Egypt at St John's Smith Square (2000); Season 2000–2001 with Polinesso in Handel's Radamisto for Opera North and Rodelinda at Aldeburgh and New York. *Recordings include:* Gianetta in L'Elisir d'amore and Frasquita in Carmen (Chandos). *Address:* c/o Opera North, 26 New Briggate, Leeds, Yorkshire, LS1 6NU, England.

**WILLIAMS, Howard;** Conductor; b. 25 April 1947, Hemel Hempstead, Hertfordshire, England; m. Juliet Solomon 1977, 1 s, 1 d. *Education:* King's

School, Canterbury; BA, New College, Oxford; BMus, Liverpool University; Advanced conducting course, Guildhall School of Music and Drama. *Career:* Conducted over 40 opera productions with English National Opera and elsewhere, including Punch and Judy and The Knot Garden for Channel 4 television; Other modern repertory includes the premieres of Holloway's Liederkreis and Concertino No. 1, Hamilton's Anna Karenina, and Cowie's Choral Symphony and Concerto for Orchestra; Many productions with Royal Ballet at Covent Garden and abroad; Regular Guest Conductor with BBC Symphony Orchestra, BBC National Orchestra of Wales; Regular appearances with Royal Philharmonic, Scottish National, Bournemouth Symphony, Northern Sinfonia, English Chamber, London Sinfonietta and Royal Liverpool Philharmonic; Regular visitor overseas to orchestras in France, Belgium, Netherlands, Sweden and Hungary; Principal Conductor, Pècs Symphony Orchestra, Hungary, 1989–, being first British conductor to hold appointment in Hungary; Led Chelsea Opera group in Massenet's Esclarmonde, 1998; Season 2000–01 as Chief Conductor of Oxford Orchestra da Camera, concerts with Prague and Portuguese Symphony Orchestras and Bavarian Radio Symphony Orchestra. *Compositions:* Shadowdance, 1991. *Recordings include:* three vols of music by Frank Bridge, including his opera The Christmas Rose; Bizet's Ivan The Terrible. *Current Management:* Connaught Artists Management Ltd, 2 Molasses Row, Plantation Wharf, London, SW11 3UX, England. *Telephone:* (20) 7738 0017. *Fax:* (20) 7738 0909. *E-mail:* classicalmusic@connaughtartists.com. *Website:* www.connaughtartists.com.

**WILLIAMS, Huw;** Organist; b. 2 June 1971, Swansea, Wales. *Education:* Organ Scholar, Christ's College, Cambridge; 2 years Postgraduate at RAM; Organ Scholar, St Paul's Cathedral, London; Organ lessons, Netherlands. *Career:* Assistant Organist, Hereford Cathedral; Three Choirs Festival; Sub-Organist, St Paul's Cathedral; BBC broadcasts with both Cathedral Choirs; mem, ISM. *Recordings:* 10 recordings with Cathedral Choirs, Hereford and St Paul's. *Honours:* Fellow of Royal College of Organists; Limpus Prize, 1991; Music degree, Cambridge, 1992; Countess of Munster Music Scholar, 1993–95; Ian Fleming Musical Trust Scholar, 1994–95; Associate of the Royal Academy of Music, 2001. *Address:* 4A Amen Court, London EC 4M 7BU, England.

**WILLIAMS, Janet;** American singer (soprano); b. 1965, Detroit. *Career:* debut, San Francisco Opera 1989, as Despina in Così fan tutte; roles at San Francisco included Adele in Die Fledermaus, Nannetta, Musetta, and Elvira in L'Italiana in Algeri; guest at Los Angeles as Mozart's Blondchen and at Wexford as Rezia in Gluck's La Rencontre imprévue 1991; season 1992–93 as Zerlina in Lyon and Rosina at Washington; Berlin Staatsoper from 1992, as Pamina, Graun's Cleopatra, and Oresia in Telemann's Orfeo; Deutsche Oper Berlin 1996, as Handel's Semele; Verdi's Oscar at the Paris Opéra Bastille and Elisa in Mozart's Il Re Pastore at Nice 1994; Adele in Die Fledermaus at the New York Met 1996; season 1997–98 in Opera Gala at San Francisco, and as Manon in Henze's Boulevard Solitude at Frankfurt; sang Poppea in Handel's Agrippina at Graz 2000; concerts include Tippett's A Child of Our Time at Berlin and Mozart's Requiem at New York. *Recordings include:* Messiah and Graun's Cesare e Cleopatra. *E-mail:* info@janetwilliams.de. *Website:* www.janetwilliams.de.

**WILLIAMS, Jeremy Huw;** British singer (baritone); b. 1965, England. *Education:* St John's Coll., Cambridge, Nat. Opera Studio, studied with April Cantelo. *Career:* debut, Guglielmo in Così fan tutte with WNO; appearances with L'Opéra de Nantes as Papageno, Olivier in Capriccio and title role in Karetnikov's Till Eulenspiegel; Escamillo, Germont, and Marcello in La Bohème for WNO; further engagements for Music Theatre Wales, Opera Ireland and the City of Birmingham SO; Buxton Festival, Holland Park Opera and Ulm, Germany; sang M. Gaye in the Lully/Molière Bourgeois Gentilhomme, for the English Bach Festival at the Linbury Theatre, Covent Garden 2001. *Honours:* Welsh Music Guild Sir Geraint Evans Award 2005. *Current Management:* Robert Gilder & Company, Enterprise House, 59–65 Upper Ground, London, SE1 9PQ, England. *Telephone:* (20) 7928-9008. *Fax:* (20) 7928-9755. *E-mail:* rgilder@robert-gilder.com. *Address:* Ty Gwyn, 111 Heol Isaf, Radyr, Cardiff, CF15 8DW, Wales. *Telephone:* (29) 2084 3753. *Fax:* (29) 2041 8965. *E-mail:* jhw@jeremyhuwwilliams.com. *Website:* www.jeremyhuwwilliams.com.

**WILLIAMS, John,** AO, OBE; classical guitarist; b. 24 April 1941, Melbourne, Australia; s. of Len Williams and Melaan Ket; m. 1st Linda Susan Kendall 1964 (divorced); one d.; m. 2nd Sue Cook 1981 (divorced); one s.; m. 3rd Kathleen Panama 2000. *Education:* Friern Barnet Grammar School and Royal Coll. of Music, London. *Career:* studied guitar with father, Segovia and at Accad. Chigiana, Siena; has toured widely and appears frequently on TV and radio; numerous transcriptions and gramophone recordings as solo guitarist and with leading orchestras; f. The Height Below (ensemble) with Brian Gascoigne 1974, John Williams and Friends (ensemble) and founder-mem. groups Sky 1979–84 and John Williams' Attacca 1991–; current ensembles include John Williams and Richard Harvey's World Tour and WEB with John Etheridge and Patrick Bebey, as well as solo recitals worldwide; Artistic Dir South Bank Summer Music Festival 1984–85, Melbourne Arts Festival 1987. *Films:* composed and played music for film Emma's War. *Recordings:* include Takemitsu Played by John Williams (music by Toru Takemitsu, with the London Sinfonietta) 1991, several of Rodrigo's Conciertos de Aranjuez, Vivaldi Concertos 1991, The Seville Concert/The Film Profile of John Williams (also on laserdisc and VHS) 1993, From Australia (featuring music by Peter Sculthorpe and Nigel Westlake) 1994, The Great

Paraguayan 1995, concerti by Richard Harvey and Steve Gray 1996, John Williams Plays the Movies 1997, The Black Decameron (music by Leo Brouwer) 1997, The Guitarist 1998, Schubert and Giuliani 1999, The Magic Box 2002, El Diablo Suelto 2003, The Ultimate Guitar Collection 2004. *Honours:* Hon. FRCM, FRAM, FRNCM; Dr hc (Melbourne). *Current Management:* c/o Askonas Holt Ltd, 27 Chancery Lane, London, WC2A 1PF, England. *Telephone:* (20) 7400-1700. *Fax:* (20) 7400-1799. *Website:* www.johnwilliamsguitar.com.

**WILLIAMS, John Towner;** American composer; b. 8 Feb. 1932, Flushing, NY. *Education:* Juilliard School, UCLA. *Career:* pianist Columbia Pictures; jazz pianist working with Henry Mancini on television scores; conductor Boston Pops Orchestra 1980–98. *Film scores:* The Secret Ways 1961, Diamond Head 1962, None But the Brave 1965, How to Steal a Million 1966, Valley of the Dolls 1967, The Cowboys 1972, The Poseidon Adventure 1972, Tom Sawyer 1973, Earthquake 1974, The Towering Inferno 1974, Jaws (Acad. Award) 1975, The Eiger Sanction 1975, Family Plot 1976, Midway 1976, The Missouri Breaks 1976, Raggedy Ann and Andy 1977, Black Sunday 1977, Star Wars (Acad. Award) 1977, Close Encounters of the Third Kind 1977, The Fury 1978, Jaws II 1976, Superman 1978, Dracula 1979, The Empire Strikes Back 1980, Raiders of the Lost Ark 1981, E.T.: The Extra Terrestrial (Acad. Award) 1982, Return of the Jedi 1983, Indiana Jones and the Temple of Doom 1984, The River 1985, Space Camp 1986, The Witches of Eastwick 1987, Empire of the Sun (BAFTA Award for Best Score) 1988, 1941 1989, Always 1989, Born on the Fourth of July 1989, Indiana Jones and the Last Crusade 1989, Stanley and Iris 1990, Presumed Innocent 1990, Home Alone 1990, Hook 1991, JFK 1993, Far and Away 1993, Home Alone 2: Lost in New York 1993, Jurassic Park 1993, Schindler's List (Acad. Award) 1993, Sabrina 1995, The Reivers 1995, Nixon 1995, Sleepers 1996, Rosewood 1996, Land of the Giants 1997, Seven Years in Tibet 1997, The Lost World: Jurassic Park 1997, Amistad 1997, Lost in Space 1997, Time Tunnel 1997, Saving Private Ryan 1998, Star Wars: Episode I – The Phantom Menace 1999, Angela's Ashes 1999, Harry Potter and the Sorcerer's Stone 2001, Star Wars: Episode II – Attack of the Clones 2001, Minority Report 2002, Harry Potter and the Chamber of Secrets 2002, Catch Me if You Can 2002, Harry Potter and the Prisoner of Azkaban 2004, The Terminal 2004, Star Wars: Episode III – Revenge of the Sith 2005, War of the Worlds 2005, Harry Potter and the Goblet of Fire 2005, Memoirs of a Geisha (Golden Globe for Best Original Score in a Motion Picture 2006) 2005, Munich 2005. *Recordings:* John Williams Plays The Movies 1996, Music From The Star Wars Saga 1999, Jane Eyre 1999, Themes From Academy Award Winners, Over The Rainbow: Songs From The Movies 1992, John Williams Conducting The Boston Pops 1996, The Hollywood Sound 1997, From Sousa To Spielberg, Best Of John Williams 1998, Treesong 2001, Call Of The Champions (official theme of 2002 Winter Olympics, Salt Lake City) 2001, John Williams Trumpet Concerto 2002, American Journey 2002; recordings of film scores. *Honours:* numerous hon. degrees; two Emmy Awards, three Golden Globes, 16 Grammy Awards, recipient of Kennedy Center Honors 2004, Classical BRIT Award for Soundtrack Composer of the Year 2005. *Current Management:* Michael Gorfaine, Gorfaine & Schwartz, 13245 Riverside Drive, Suite 450, Sherman Oaks, CA 91423, USA. *Website:* www.johnwilliams.org.

**WILLIAMS, Julius (Penson);** Composer and Conductor; b. 22 June 1954, Bronx, New York, USA; m. Lenora B Williams, 7 Aug 1977, 1 s., 1 d. *Education:* Music major, Andrew Jackson High School, 1972; BS, Herbert H Lehman College, City University of New York, 1977; MM, Hartt School of Music, 1980; Aspen Music School, 1984; Professional Fellow, Aspen, 1985. *Career:* Debut: Premiere of A Norman Overture, New York Philharmonic and Zubin Mehta, 1985; Music Director, CPTV, 1984–85; Arts Award Guest Conductor, Connecticut Opera, 1983; Dallas Symphony, 1986; Savannah Symphony, 1987; Assistant Conductor, Aspen Music Festival, 1985; Conductor, Composer-in-Residence, Nutmeg Ballet, Connecticut, 1986–88; Guest Conductor, New Haven Symphony, May 1987; Guest Conductor, Amor Artist Chamber Orchestra, 1987; Artistic Director, New York State Summer School of the Arts (Choral Studies), 1988–; Principal Guest, School of Orchestral Studies; Associate Professor, University of Vermont; Artist-in-Residence, Saratoga Arts Festival, Aug 1988; National television, CBS Sunday Morning with Charles Kuralf, 11 Sept 1988. *Compositions:* A Norman Overture; Toccatina for Strings; Incommendation of Music; The Spring; Rise Up Shepherd and Follow; Vermont's Escape; Alison's Dream; The Fall, Summers Good Ecelin. *Contributions:* American Choral Directors' Journal Choral Review, 1982. *Current Management:* Euphonia Artist Management, PO Box 809, Cambridge, MA 02238, USA. *Address:* Henderson, 7th Ave, Apt 4K, New York, NY 10026-2231, USA.

**WILLIAMS, Laverne;** Singer (Tenor); b. 1935, San Francisco, California, USA. *Education:* Master's Degree, University of California; Alfred Hertz Memorial Scholarship and Rockefeller Foundation Scholarship for studies in Europe. *Career:* Concerts and Opera appearances ranging from Baroque to Contemporary; L'Incoronazione di Poppea, Salome, Idomeneo and Porgy and Bess, Switzerland; Appeared with Jessye Norman in Great Day in the Morning, Paris; Porgy and Bess, Glagolitic Mass and Jenůfa under Simon Rattle, United Kingdom; Appearances with most major orchestras in London and the United Kingdom including London Symphony, Royal Philharmonic and the Royal Liverpool Philharmonic Orchestra; Directed and sung in an experimental evening of spirituals, Almeida Theatre; Performed Virgil Thomson's Four Saints in Three Acts, Almeida Theatre; European Opera appearances include Zürich, Lyon and Brussels operas; Television and Radio appearances include: Gershwin's Blue Monday in Switzerland; Hermann Prey Show for German television; Here Comes the Classics and excerpts from Carmen Jones, BBC television; Club Mix, Channel 4; Leading role, European premiere of Carmen Jones; Weber's Oberon, Edinburgh Festival, Tanglewood and Frankfurt, 1986. *Recordings:* Great Day in the Morning, with Jessye Norman. *Honours:* Competition successes in 'S-Hertogenbosch, Rio de Janeiro and Barcelona.

**WILLIAMS, Louise;** British violist; b. 23 Sept. 1955, England. *Education:* Royal Acad. of Music, Juilliard School of Music, New York. *Career:* co-founder and second violinist, Endellion Quartet 1979–83; violist, Chilingirian Quartet 1987–92; mem., Raphael Ensemble 1996–2003; quintet pnr, Lindsay Quartet 1995–; founder-mem., Merel Quartet 2002–; freelance chamber musician and soloist. *Recordings:* Complete Quartets of Bartók and Dvořák, Bartók Piano Quintet, Dvorak Quintets, Mozart Flute Quartets, Beethoven Serenade, Haydn Quartets, Prokofiev Quartets, Mendelssohn Viola Quintets, Bridge Sextet, Quintet and Viola Duo, Bridge Music for Viola and Piano. *Address:* 10a Paultons Street, London, SW3 5DP, England (office). *Telephone:* (7767) 685058 (office). *E-mail:* louisevla@ukonline.co.uk. *Website:* www.merelquartet .com.

**WILLIAMS, Peter Fredric,** BA, MusB, MA, PhD, LittD; British musicologist, academic, writer, organist and harpsichordist; b. 14 May 1937, Wolverhampton, Staffordshire, England; m. Rosemary Seymour 1982; three s. one d. *Education:* Birmingham Inst., St John's Coll., Cambridge. *Career:* Lecturer 1962–72, Reader 1972–82, Prof. 1982–85, Dean 1984, Univ. of Edinburgh; Dir, Russell Coll. of Harpsichords, Edinburgh 1969; Founder-Ed., The Organ Yearbook 1969–; Arts and Sciences Distinguished Prof. 1985–95, Dir, Graduate Center for Performance Practice Studies 1990–96, Duke Univ., Durham, NC, USA; John Bird Prof., Univ. of Wales, Cardiff 1996–2002; mem. British Inst. of Organ Studies (chair.). *Publications:* The European Organ 1450–1850 1966, Figured Bass Accompaniment (two vols) 1970, Venta/Peeters the Organ of the Netherlands (trans.) 1971, Bach Organ Music 1972, A New History of the Organ From the Greeks to the Present Day 1980, The Organ Music of J. S. Bach (three vols) 1980–84, Bach, Handel and Scarlatti: Tercentenary Essays (ed.) 1985, Playing the Works of Bach 1986, The Organ 1988, Playing the Organ Music of Bach 1988, Mozart: Perspectives in Performance (ed. with L. Todd) 1991, The Organ in Western Culture 750–1250 1992, The King of Instruments: How Do Churches Come to Have Organs? 1993, The Chromatic Fourth During Four Centuries of Music 1995, Cambridge Studies in Performance Practice (series ed., four vols) 1995, Music to Hear, or Fears for Higher Music Study 2001, Bach: The Goldberg Variations 2001, The Life of Bach 2005; several vols of keyboard music by Bach and Handel; contrib. to scholarly books and journals. *Honours:* Hon. Fellow, Royal Scottish Acad. of Art, Research Fellow, Cornell Univ., New York, Curt Sachs Award, American Musical Instrument Soc. 1996. *Address:* c/o Department of Music, Corbett Road, University of Wales, Cardiff, CF10 3EB, Wales.

**WILLIAMS, Sioned;** Harpist; b. 1 July 1953, Mancot, Clwyd, North Wales; m. Kim A L Sargeant, 6 August 1977. *Education:* Welsh College of Music and Drama, 1971–74; Recital Diploma, Royal Academy of Music. *Career:* Debut: Purcell Room, Park Lane Group Young Artists/20th Century Music, 1977; Carnegie Hall, New York, USA (Concert Artists Guild Award), 1980; Appearances world-wide with London Symphony Orchestra, Philharmonia, London Philharmonic Orchestra, RPO, BBC Symphony Orchestra, BBC Philharmonic, CBSO, Royal Ballet, London Sinfonietta, Royal Opera House, ENO, WNO, SNO; Solo and Concerto performances, premiering over 80 works; Chamber Music with Uroboros, Gemini, Spectrum, Endymion, Divertimenti, Koenig, Grosvenor, Circle; Theatre, radio, television and festival appearances; Professor of Harp, Royal College of Music Junior Department, 1976–85; Royal Academy of Music, 1983–84; London College of Music, 1985–86; Trinity College of Music, 1986–; Adjudicator at major Welsh Eisteddfods, 1981–. *Compositions:* Cyfres i'r Delyn, 1973 (special prize, 17th International Harp Week); Serenata e Danza, 1983. *Recordings:* Harp Music, John Thomas; Harp Music, John Parry; Spun Gold for Flute and Harp; Ceremony of Carols, Britten; Nielsen with James Galway. *Publications:* Editor, John Parry: Four Sonatas, 1982; Four Sonatas, 1982; J. S. Bach: Suite BMV1006a, 1986. *Honours:* Numerous Prizes, Awards and Scholarships including Bursary, Arts Council Advanced Training Scheme, 1982. *Address:* 181 Gloucester Road, Cheltenham, Gloucester GL51 8NQ, England.

**WILLIAMS, Wayne;** Singer (Tenor); b. 1960, Cleveland, Ohio, USA. *Education:* Studied at the Cleveland Music Settlement and with Gerard Souzay in Geneva. *Career:* Concert appearances with the Suisse Romande, Chamber Orchestra of Lausanne, Berne Symphony, Tonhalle Zürich, YMSO (London), Orchestra Haydn (Italy) and the Shanghai Symphony (China); Conductors have included Armin Jordan, Peter Maag, Horst Stein, Lopez-Cobos, James Blair, Paul Angerer and Herbert Handt; Recitals throughout the USA and Europe with Dalton Baldwin; Appearances in Paris in Dvořák's Requiem and Stabat Mater, Switzerland in The Creation and St Matthew Passion; Opera repertoire includes Schubert's Fierrabras, L'Elisir d'amore, La Traviata and A Midsummer Night's Dream. *Recordings include:* Poulenc Gloria; Great Day in the Morning, with Jessye Norman; Dvořák Stabat Mater.

**WILLIAMS-KING, Anne;** singer (soprano); b. 1960, Wrexham, Wales. *Education:* Royal Northern College of Music, National Opera Studio, London. *Career:* sang with the Welsh National Opera as Lenio in The Greek Passion by

Martinů, Mimi, Gilda, Fiordiligi, Marzelline in Fidelio and Micaela; Covent Garden debut in 1988 as Freia in Das Rheingold; Appearances with Opera North as Mimi and in Rebecca by Josephs and A Village Romeo and Juliet by Delius; Scottish Opera as Freia and Violetta, invited to return as Jenůfa, Madama Butterfly and Mimi; Foreign engagements include Anne Trulove in The Rake's Progress at Berne; Frequent concert appearances with leading British orchestras and on television; Sang Butterfly with Scottish Opera at Edinburgh, 1990; Suor Angelica for ENO, 1998; Season 1999–2000 as Lisa in The Queen of Spades, at Antwerp, and Janáček's Emilia Marty at Osnabrück.

**WILLIS, Helen;** Singer (Mezzo-Soprano); b. 25 July 1959, Newport, Gwent, Wales; m. Robert Venn, 17 Dec 1983. *Education:* Diploma, Royal Academy of Music, 1977–83. *Career:* Debut: Wigmore Hall, London, 1983; Member of Glyndebourne Festival Chorus, 1983–85; Solo Operatic debut with Welsh National Opera as Siegrune in Die Walküre in 1984; Concerts and recitals throughout the United Kingdom and abroad; Broadcasts include Sea Pictures and Wesendonck Lieder with BBC National Orchestra of Wales. *Honours:* Triennial Young Welsh Singer of the Year, 1982.

**WILLIS, Nuala;** Singer (mezzo-soprano); b. 1950, England. *Career:* Worked as Designer and Costumier and as Actress in England in North America; Sang with Opera Studio in Brussels and small roles with the Glyndebourne Tour; Aldeburgh Festival in Eugene Onegin and A Midsummer Night's Dream; Guest appearances at Nancy, Metz, Marseilles (Herodias in Salome), Geneva (Larina in Eugene Onegin), Marseilles (Jezibab in Rusalka) and Zürich (The Hostess in Boris Godunov); At Covent Garden appeared in A Midsummer Night's Dream, Eugene Onegin and Faust as Martha; In Ireland has sung Widow Bebick (Mahagonny) at Wexford and Clytemnestra in Elektra conducted by Janos Fürst, in Dublin; Season 1989–90 included Herodias in the Swedish Folkopera's Salome at the Edinburgh Festival; Ulrica in Un Ballo in Maschera for Canadian Opera in Toronto; Royal National Theatre in Sondheim's Sunday in the Park with George; Engagements with the D'Oyly Carte Opera; Sang the Elephant in Paran Vir's Broken Strings at the Almeida Theatre, 1996; Older Woman in the premiere of Dove's Flight, Glyndebourne, 1998; Season 1999–2000 as Stravinsky's Mother Goose at Lausanne and Glyndebourne and premiere of Ion by Param Vir, at Aldeburgh. *Current Management:* Athole Still International Management, Forresters Hall, 25–27 Westow Street, London, SE19 3RY, England. *Telephone:* (20) 8771-5271. *Fax:* (20) 8768-6600. *Website:* www.atholestill.com.

**WILLS, Arthur,** OBE, BMus, DMus, ADCM, FRSCM, FRCO; British composer and cathedral organist; b. 19 Sept. 1926, Coventry, England; m. Mary Elizabeth Titterton 1953; one s. one d. *Education:* St John's School, Coventry, St Nicholas Coll., Canterbury. *Career:* organist, Ely Cathedral 1958–90; Prof., Royal Acad. of Music 1964–92; organ recitals in Europe, USA, Australia and New Zealand. *Compositions:* Organ Concerto 1970, An English Requiem 1971, Guitar Sonata 1974, Three Poems of E. E. Cummings for tenor, oboe and piano 1974, Love's Torment (Four Elizabethan Love Songs) for alto and piano 1975, The Fenlands (Symphonic Suite for brass band and organ) 1981, Overture: A Muse of Fire for brass band 1983, Concerto Lirico for guitar quartet 1987, When the Spirit Comes (Four Poems of Emily Brontë for mezzo-soprano and piano) 1985, Piano Sonata '1984', The Dark Lady (Eight Sonnets of Shakespeare for baritone and piano) 1986, Sacrae Symphonia: Veni Creator Spiritus 1987, Choral Concerto: The Gods of Music 1992, Eternity's Sunrise, Three Poems by William Blake 1992, A Toccata of Galuppi's, Scena for countertenor and string quartet 1993, Missa Sancti Stephani 2001, Missa Incarnationis 2002, Crossing the Bar 2004. *Recordings include:* Missa Sancti Stephani, Missa Incarnationis, Music for Organ and Brass, The Praises of the Trinity, Full Stops, Music of Six Centuries, Wondrous Machine!: Organ Music of Arthur Wills. *Publications:* Organ (Menuhin Music Guide Series) 1984; contrib. to Musical Times. *Honours:* Hon. RAM 1974. *Address:* Paradise House, 26 New Barns Road, Ely, Cambridgeshire CB7 4PN, England (home). *Telephone:* (1353) 662084 (home). *Fax:* (1353) 662084 (home). *E-mail:* artwill@ argonet.co.uk (home). *Website:* www.impulse-music.co.uk/arthurwills.htm (home).

**WILSON, Catherine;** Singer (soprano); b. 1936, Glasgow, Scotland. *Education:* Royal Manchester Coll. of Music with Elsie Thurston; further study with Ruth Packer in London and Maria Carpi in Geneva. *Career:* debut, Sadler's Wells, London in 1960 as Angelina in La Cenerentola; Glyndebourne in 1960 in Die Zauberflöte; Sadler's Wells in 1965 in the premiere of Bennett's The Mines of Sulphur; Scottish Opera in the 1977 Edinburgh Festival, title role in Thea Musgrave's Mary Queen of Scots; Scottish Opera in 1974 in the premiere of Hamilton's The Catiline Conspiracy; guest appearances in Aldeburgh, Cologne, Geneva, Boston, Houston, Louisville and ENO in London, and Santa Fe; often heard in operas by Mozart, Rossini, Puccini, Strauss and Britten and as a concert singer; teacher at Royal Northern Coll. of Music, 1980–91; performance coach, William Walton Trust, 1990–95. *Recordings include:* Albert Herring by Britten, The Merry Widow, Dido and Aeneas. *Honours:* Fellow, Royal Manchester Coll. of Music. *Address:* 18 St Mary's Grove, London, N1, England.

**WILSON, Charles Mills,** MusBac, MusDoc; Canadian composer (retd); b. 8 May 1931, Toronto; m. Elizabeth Wilson; two s. one d. *Education:* Toronto Conservatory with Godfrey Ridout, Toronto Univ., Berkshire Music Center with Lukas Foss and Carlos Chavez. *Career:* Head of the Music Dept, Guelph Collegiate Inst. 1962–70; composer-in-residence, Canadian Opera Co. from 1972, and Univ. of Guelph in Ontario; chorus master, Canadian Opera Co.;

Assoc. Composer, Canadian Music Centre; Choral Conductor, Bach-Elgar Choir of Hamilton, ON 1992–; mem. Canadian League of Composers. *Compositions include:* four string quartets 1950, 1968, 1975, 1983, The Strolling Clerk from Paradise (chamber opera) 1952, Symphony in A 1954, Sonata de Chiesa for oboe and strings 1960, String Trio 1963, The Angels of the Earth (oratorio) 1966, En Guise for baritone and strings 1968, Concert 5x4x3 for string quintet, woodwind quartet and brass trio 1970, Johnny Fibber (operetta) 1970, Phrases from Orpheus (multimedia opera) 1971, Dona Nobis Pacem for choir and brass sextet 1972, The Summoning of Everyman (church opera) 1973, Heloise and Abelard (opera in three acts) 1973, The Selfish Giant (children's opera) 1973, Sinfonia for double orchestra 1973, Image Out of Season for chorus and brass quintet 1973, Christo Paremus Canticum for chorus and orchestra 1973, Symphonic Perspectives: Kingsmere for orchestra 1974, Missa Brevis for chorus and organ 1975, Psycho Red (opera in two acts) 1980, Kamouraska (opera in three acts) 1979, Revelations to John: A Festival Cantata for three choirs and organ, Symphony No. 1 1998, Seasons of Life song cycle for contralto and piano 1998, Cantata for Palm Sunday for choir, soli, strings and piano 1998, Images for contralto and flute 1999, Cantata for Tenebrae 1999, The Cave song cycle for contralto and piano 2000, Dream Telescope song cycle for contralto and chamber orchestra 2001, She, to Him song cycle for contralto, oboe and piano 2002, Cantata for the Resurrection for choir, soli and strings and harpsichord or piano 2004. *Address:* 610 Wildwood Crescent, Gabriola, BC V0R 1X4, Canada (home). *Telephone:* (250) 247-0136 (home). *E-mail:* ce-wilson@shaw.ca (home).

**WILSON, Christopher;** lutenist and vihuela player; b. 1951, England. *Education:* Royal College of Music with Diana Poulton. *Career:* specialised in the performance of Renaissance music throughout the United Kingdom; concert tours of Europe, Scandinavia, USA, the Baltic States, Russia and the Far East; as well as working with his own group Kithara, interest in the lute song repertoire has led him to work with such song recitalists as countertenor Michael Chance and the tenor Rufus Müller; performs with Fretwork, Gothic Voices, the Consort of Musicke and the English Baroque Soloists; Concerts 1993–94 included tours to Sweden, Hong Kong and Japan, Poland and Taiwan. *Recordings:* appeared on over 50 recordings and on solo recordings.

**WILSON, Christopher R.,** BA, MA, DPhil; British academic; *Senior Lecturer in Music and Head of Department, University of Reading*; b. 1 Oct. 1952, Hull, England; m. Christine; three c. *Education:* Univ. of Oxford. *Career:* temporary Lecturer, Univ. of St Andrews 1978; Lecturer, Univ. of Reading 1979; Sr Lecturer and Head of Music Dept, Univ. of Reading 2001–; mem. Royal Musical Asscn (council 1989–92, 2001–03), Finzi Trust Friends. *Publications:* Campion, A Critical Study 1989, Campion and Coprario Treatises 2003; contrib. to A Shakespeare Music Catalogue 1991, Grove Opera 1992, New Oxford Companion to Music 2002, Music and Letters 1979–, Early Music 1981–. *Honours:* Louise Dyer Award 1978, Leverhulme Trust research project grant 2001–04. *Address:* Department of Music, University of Reading, 35 Upper Redlands Road, Reading, RG1 5JE, England (office). *Telephone:* (118) 3788415 (office). *Fax:* (118) 3788412 (office). *E-mail:* c.r.wilson@rdg.ac.uk (office). *Website:* www.rdg.ac.uk/music (office).

**WILSON, Elisa,** AMusA; Australian singer (soprano); b. 22 Oct. 1965, Perth, Western Australia; d. of Cyril William Wilson and Gloria Elwyn Stitfold; m., three s. *Education:* WA Conservatorium, Perth; Univ. of Western Australia. *Career:* debut: Despina in Cosí fan Tutte, WA Opera, and Adele in Die Fledermaus; Other engagements throughout Australia for Western Australia Opera Company include Nanetta in Falstaff, the Sandman and Dew Fairy in Hansel & Gretel, Micaela in Carmen, Pamina in The Magic Flute, Gilda in Rigoletto, Susanna in The Marriage of Figaro, Norina in Don Pasquale, Adina in The Elixir of Love, Musetta in La Bohème, Leila in The Pearl Fishers, Alice Ford in Falstaff and world premieres, Nanette in The Eureka Stockade and Heloise in HEloise and Abelard. Also performed Greta in Brian Howard's Metamorphosis and Mrs Green in Harrison Birtwistle's Down by the Greenwood Side for other companies in WA; Donna Elvira in Don Giovanni and The Girl in The Emperor of Atlantis for Victoria State Opera; Echo in Ariadne auf Naxos, Spoleto Festival, Melbourne; debut with Opera Australia as Helena in A Midsummer Night's Dream at Edinburgh Festival, 1994 and in Sydney; Handel's Alcina in Sydney and Melbourne; Rosalilnda in Die Fledermaus and Musetta in La Bohème at Sydney Opera House; Concert appearances as soloist with Australian Symphony Orchestra and other Australian orchestras, with Vienna Male Voice Choir and Opera Australia; live broadcasts of operas Rita and Susanna's Secret for ABC. *Recording:* Bruckner's Mass in D Minor (soprano soloist). *Leisure interests:* martial arts, genealogy. *Honours:* Creative Development Fellowship ArtsWA, 1994; Armstrong-Martin Opera Award, 1992; Dame Mabel Brookes Award, 1992; ABC Prize, 1992. *Current Management:* Patrick Togher Artists Management, Suite 25, 450 Elizabeth Street, Surry Hills, NSW 2010, Australia. *Telephone:* (2) 9319-6255 (office). *Fax:* (2) 9319-7611 (office). *E-mail:* pjtogher@ozemail .com.au (office). *Website:* www.patricktogher.com.

**WILSON, Fredric (Woodbridge);** Musicologist; b. 8 Sept. 1947, Point Pleasant, New Jersey, USA. *Education:* BA, Music, Lehigh University, Bethlehem, Pennsylvania, 1969; MA, Musicology, New York University, 1977. *Career:* Director, The Wall Choirs, New Jersey, 1969–81; Editor, Allaire Music Publications, 1980–; Curator, The Pierpont Morgan Library, New York City, 1981; Professor of Museum Studies, Graduate School of Arts and Science, New York University, 1994–; Musical and Textual Consultant to opera companies. *Compositions:* More than 50 musical editions published,

including motets by Gallus, Charpentier, mass by Lotti. *Publications:* Introduction to the Gilbert and Sullivan Operas, 1989; Index to the Opus Musicum of Jacob Handl, 1992; General Editor, The W S Gilbert Edition, 1986–; Complete Savoy Opera Libretti, Folio Society, 1994. *Contributions:* New Grove Dictionary of Opera; Many papers and articles to various publications; Organised conferences in English Opera, New York, 1985, Gilbert and Sullivan, New York, 1989, Purchase College, 1994; Organised exhibitions at Pierpont Morgan Library, 1985, 1989, Kentucky Center for the Arts, 1987, 1988, Purchase College, 1994. *Address:* Pierpoint Morgan Library, 29E 36th Street, New York, NY 10016, USA.

**WILSON, Gordon;** Singer (Tenor); b. 1968, Scotland. *Education:* Studied at the Royal Scottish Academy. *Career:* Appearances at Covent Garden, Glyndebourne, Scottish Opera, Opera North and the Buxton Festival; Sang Philidor's Tom Jones at Drottningholm and in Massenet's Chérubin at Covent Garden; Roles have included Nathaniel in Hoffmann, Alfredo, the Duke of Mantua, Riccardo in Oberto, Jenik in The Bartered Bride and Walton's Troilus; Concerts with the Ulster Orchestra, Northern Sinfonia and Manchester Camerata.

**WILSON, Ian,** BMus, DPhil; Northern Irish composer; b. 26 Dec. 1964, Belfast. *Education:* Univ. of Ulster. *Career:* AHRB Research Fellow in Creative and Performing Arts, Univ. of Ulster 2000–03; featured composer at Presteigne Festival 2005. *Compositions include:* Prime 1987, Running, Thinking, Finding 1989, BIG 1991, Drive 1992, Winter's Edge (String Quartet No. 1) 1992, Rise 1993, The Capsizing Man and other stories 1994, Rich Harbour 1994–95, I Sleep at Waking 1995, The Seven Last Words (Piano Trio No. 2) 1995, Six Days at Jericho 1995, For Eileen, after rain 1995, Catalan Tales (Piano Trio No. 3) 1996, Towards the Far Country 1996, From the Book of Longing 1996, A Haunted Heart 1996, Lim 1998, Spilliaert's Beach 1999, In Blue Sea or Sky 2000, Verschwindend 2001, Winter Finding 2005. *Recordings:* Winter's Edge, Spilliaert's Beach, In Blue Sea or Sky, The Seven Last Words, Catalan Tales and Six Days at Jericho, Winter's Edge, The Capsizing Man and other stories and Towards the Far Country, String Quartets 1–3, From the Book of Longing, Drive, Spilliaert's Beach, BIG, For Eileen, after rain, Verschwindend, Lim and A Haunted Heart. *Honours:* Ultima Festival, Oslo composition prize 1991, Macaulay Fellowship 1992, elected to Aosdána 1998. *E-mail:* mail@ianwilson.org.uk. *Website:* www.ianwilson.org.uk.

**WILSON, James;** British/Irish composer; b. 27 Sept. 1922, London, England. *Education:* Trinity Coll. of Music, London. *Career:* resident in Ireland from 1948; freelance composer of music for stage and other works. *Compositions:* three symphonies, The Hunting of the Snark (children's opera) 1965, Twelfth Night (three-act opera) 1969, Letters to Theo (one-act opera) 1984, Grinning at the Devil (two-act opera) 1989, The King of the Golden River 1990, A Passionate Man (two-act opera) 1995, Virata (four-scene opera), numerous concerti, including those for viola, violin, wind quintet, clarinet, harpsichord, chamber music, choral works and numerous song cycles. *Address:* 10a Wyvern, Killiney Hill, Co Dublin, Ireland (home). *Telephone:* (1) 285-0786 (home). *E-mail:* jwilson@iol.ie (home).

**WILSON, Olly Woodrow, Jr;** American composer, musician and academic; *Professor of Music Emeritus, University of California at Berkeley*; b. 7 Sept. 1937, St Louis, MO. *Education:* Washington Univ., St Louis, Univ. of Ill. at Urbana-Champaign, Univ. of Iowa, Iowa City, Univ. of Ill. Studio for Experimental Music, studied African music in Ghana. *Career:* played jazz piano with local groups in St Louis; played double bass in several orchestras; UNISYS composer-in-residence, Detroit Symphony; Instructor and Asst Prof., Fla-A&M Univ. 1960–62, Assoc. Prof. 1964–65; Asst Prof., Oberlin Conservatory, OH 1965–70; visiting artist, American Acad., Rome, Italy 1977–78; taught at Univ. of Calif., Berkeley 1970–86, Asst Chancellor Int. Affairs 1986–90, Assoc. Dean Grad. Div. 1986–90, Prof. 1992–93, Dept Chair 1993–97, Jerry and Evelyn Hemmings Chambers Prof. of Music from 1995, Prof. of Music Emeritus; mem. advisory cttee to Nat. Black Music Center 1967–70; consultant on music, African-American Historical and Cultural Soc., San Francisco 1975–80; Bd Dirs, Cazadero Music Camp, Berkeley 1975–80; Nat. Advisory Bd, Meet the Composer 1980–; Bd Dirs, Contemporary Music Players 1988–; Bd Govs., San Francisco Symphony 1991–; Bd Dirs, Koussevitzky Foundation 1992–; Bd Dirs, Oakland E Bay Symphony 1993–; elected to American Acad. of Arts and Letters 1995; mem. ASCAP. *Compositions:* Trio for flute, cello and piano 1957–58, Prelude and Line Study 1959, String Quartet 1960, Structure for orchestra 1960, Two Dutch Songs 1960, Wry Fragments 1961, Gloria 1961, Violin Sonata 1961, Soliloquy 1962, Dance Suite 1962, And Death Shall Have No Dominion 1963, Sextet 1963, Dance Music No. 1 1963, Three Movements for orchestra 1964, Chanson Innocent 1964, Dance Music No. 2 1965, Piece for Four 1966, Biography 1966, Cetus 1967, In Memoriam Martin Luther King Jr 1968, Piano Piece 1969, Voices 1970, The Eighteen Hands of Jerome Harris (ballet) 1971, Black Mass (incidental music) 1971, Black Martyrs 1972, Akwan 1972, Spirit Song 1973, Echoes 1974, Sometimes 1976, Trio for piano, violin and cello 1977, Reflections 1979, Expansions 1979, Trilogy for orchestra 1979–80, Lumina 1981, Sinfonia 1983–84, No More 1985, Houston Fanfare 1986, Expansions II 1987, Moe Fragmenti 1987, A City Called Heaven 1988, Viola Concerto 1990, Of Visions and Truth 1990–91, I Shall Not Be Moved 1991–92, Expansions III 1993, Soweto's Children 1994–95, Shango Memory 1995, Fanfare for the Millennium for brass quintet and electronic sound 1996, Hold On 1997–98. *Publications:* contrib. numerous articles to Black Perspective in Music, Black Music Research Journal, American Organist, New Perspectives on Jazz and others. *Honours:* Dartmouth Arts Council Prize for electronic compositions 1968, Guggenheim Fellowship 1971–72, 1977–78, American Acad. of Arts and Letters and Nat. Inst. of Arts and Letters Achievement in Music Composition Award 1974, Washington Univ. Distinguished Alumni Award 1991, Missouri Historical Soc. Award 1991, Lincoln Center Chamber Music Soc. Elise Stoeger Prize 1992, Jerry and Evelyn Hemmings Distinguished Chair in Music 1995. *Address:* Department of Music, University of California at Berkeley, 104 Morrison Hall, Room 1200, Berkeley, CA 94720-1200, USA (office). *E-mail:* ollywil@socrates.berkeley.edu (office).

**WILSON, Paul,** MA, ARCM; British singer (tenor, baritone); *Director of Drama, Whitgift School, Croydon*; b. 1952, Gloucester, England. *Education:* Jesus Coll., Oxford and Royal Coll. of Music. *Career:* appearances with ENO, WNO and Scottish Opera, Kent Opera, Glyndebourne Festival, Chelsea Opera and Opera North; engagements abroad with the Opera Factory Zürich, Pocket Opera Nürnberg and Nairobi Opera; roles include Tom Rakewell, Andrea Chénier, Bacchus, Mark in The Wreckers, and Don José; Royal Opera Covent Garden in Handel's Samson, Ariadne auf Naxos, King Priam and Der Rosenkavalier; WNO debut in 1987 as Florestan, and ENO debut in 1988 as Monostatos; sang in the world premieres of Golem by John Casken and Cage's Europeras III and IV (Almeida Festival 1989–90) and Oliver's Timon of Athens (ENO 1991); Opera North from 1990 in Gianni Schicchi and L'Heure Espagnole; sang Siegmund and Siegfried in Birmingham Touring Opera's truncated Ring performances in the UK 1990–91; concert repertory includes The Dream of Gerontius, the Glagolitic Mass, Verdi's Requiem and Beethoven's 9th Symphony, conducted by Roger Norrington; performance of Stravinsky's Les Noces with the Nat. Youth Orchestra of Spain; Aldeburgh Festival in 1990 in Goehr's Triptych; Garsington Manor Opera in Ariadne auf Naxos 1993; Kong in Harrison Birtwistle's The Second Mrs Kong, Glyndebourne 1995; now sings as a baritone; retired from full-time performing 1996; Dir of Drama, Whitgift School, Croydon 1998–. *Recordings:* Golem, John Gasken 1991, Caritas, Robert Saxton 1992, Four Seafarers' Songs, Alan Bush 1999. *Honours:* First Wagner Soc. Bayreuth Bursary 1983, Arts Council Bursary. *Address:* 76 Avondale Road, South Croydon, CR2 6JA, England (office). *Telephone:* (20) 8681-2938 (office). *E-mail:* paul@wilson4586.freeserve.co.uk (office).

**WILSON, Richard E.;** Composer, Pianist and Professor of Music; b. 15 May 1941, Cleveland, Ohio, USA; m. Adene Stevenson Green 1971, 1 s., 1 d. *Education:* AB, Harvard University, 1963; MA, Rutgers University, 1966; Cello studies with Ernst Silberstein, piano with Leonard Shure, composition with Robert Moevs. *Career:* Works performed in New York, London, Tokyo, San Francisco, Los Angeles, Bogota, Stockholm, The Hague, Vienna, Aspen, Boston, Chicago; Assistant Professor, 1966, Associate Professor, 1970, Professor, 1976–, Mellon Chair in Music, 1988–, Vassar College, Poughkeepsie, New York; Composer in Residence, American Symphony, 1992–; Commissions from The Library of Congress; Naumburg, Koussevitzky and Fromm Foundations; Chamber Music America; The Chicago Chamber Musicians. *Compositions include:* String Quartets 1–4; Symphonies 1–2; Opera: Aethelred the Unready; Concertos for violin, bassoon, piano and Triple Concerto for horn, bass clarinet and marimba; Eclogue, Fixations, Intercalations for solo piano; The Ballad of Longwood Glen for tenor and harp. *Recordings include:* Bassoon Concerto; Piano Concerto; Symphony No. 1; Aethelred the Unready; complete choral works; String Quartets 3 & 4; Affirmations for chamber ensemble; Transfigured Goat for 2 singers and instruments. *Publications include:* entire catalogue. *Honours:* Stoeger Prize for Chamber Music Composition, 1994. *Address:* 27 Vassar Lake Drive, Poughkeepsie, NY 12603, USA. *E-mail:* riwilson@vassar.edu.

**WILSON, Robert M.;** American theatre and opera director and artist; b. 4 Oct. 1941, Waco, Tex.; s. of D. M. Wilson and Velma Loree Wilson (née Hamilton). *Education:* Univ. of Tex., Pratt Inst. *Career:* began creating innovative theatre in New York in the 1960s; worked mainly in Europe in the 1980s and 1990s, directing original works as well as traditional opera and theatre; Guggenheim Fellow 1971, 1980; Trustee Nat. Inst. of Music Theatre; mem. Dramatists Guild, Soc. des Auteurs et Compositeurs Dramatiques, Soc. of Stage Dirs. and Choreographers, PEN American Center, American Acad. of Arts and Letters; hon. Dir American Repertory Theatre; has given lectures and workshops at numerous insts. *One-man exhibitions of drawings and sculpture:* Iolas Gallery, NY, Palazzi Gallery, Milan, Galerie Fred Lanzenberg, Brussels, Musée Galliera, Paris 1972, 1974, Contemporary Art Center, Cincinatti 1980, Galerie der Stadt, Stuttgart, Galerie Herald Behm, Hamburg 1988, Anne Marie Verna Galerie, Zurich 1989, Museum of Fine Arts, Boston 1991, Centre Georges Pompidou, Paris 1991, Galerie Fred Jahn, Munich 1991, IVAM, Valencia 1992, Museum Boymans-Van Beuningen Rotterdam 1993, Galeria Luis Serpa, Lisbon 1995, Thaddeus Ropac Gallery Salzburg and Paris 1996, Clink Street Vaults, London 1996, Art Cologne, Cologne 1996, Villa Stuck Museum, Munich 1997, Palazzina dei Giardini, Modena 1998–99, Harvard Grad. School of Design Cambridge Mass. 1999 Rotunda della Besana, Milan 2000, Oberammergau Passion Theater 2000, Guggenheim Museum, New York and Bilbao 2000–01, Kunstindustrimuseet, Copenhagen 2001. *Dance created and choreographed:* Snow on the Mesa (for Martha Graham Dance Co.) 1995. *Stage appearances include:* Deafman Glance 1970, The Life and Times of Joseph Stalin (Dir) 1974, A Letter for Queen Victoria 1974, Einstein on the Beach 1976, 1984, Death, Destruction and Detroit 1979, The Golden Windows 1982, 1985, The Civil Wars 1983–85, Hamletmachine 1986, Doktor Faustus 1989, The Black Rider 1990, King Lear 1990, The Magic Flute

1991, Alice 1993, Der Mond in Gras 1994, The Death of Molière 1994, Hamlet: A Monologue 1995, Prometeo 1997, Saints and Singing 1997, Monsters of Grace 1998, Dream Play 1998, Scourge of Hyacinths 1999, The Days Before 1999, Hot Waters 2000, Relative Light 2000. *Plays directed and designed include:* Deafman Glance 1970, Einstein on the Beach 1976, Death, Destruction and Detroit 1979, The Golden Windows 1982, the CIVIL warS 1983–85, Hamletmachine 1986, Doktor Faustus 1989, The Black Rider 1990, The Magic Flute 1991, Doktor Faustus Lights the Lights 1992, Alice 1992, Madame Butterfly 1993, Hanjo 1994, Hamlet: A Monologue 1995, Time Rocker 1996, Lady from the Sea 1998, Das Rheingold 2000, POEtry 2000, Woyzeck 2001. *Films include:* Overture for a Deafman, Monsters of Grace 1998. *Videos include:* The Spaceman 1976, 1984, Video 50 1978, Stations 1982, La Femme à la Cafétière 1989, Mr. Bojangles' Memory 1991, La Mort de Molière 1994. *Publications include:* The King of Spain 1970, Einstein on the Beach: An Opera in Four Acts (with Philip Glass q.v.) 1976, A Letter for Queen Victoria 1977, Death, Destruction and Detroit 1979, the CIVIL warS 1985, Mr. Bojangles' Memory 1991, RW Notebook 1999. *Honours:* Dr. hc Calif. Coll. of Arts and Letters, Pratt Inst. New York City; numerous awards and decorations including the Maharam Award for Best Set Design 1975, Lumen Award 1977, First Prize San Sebastian Film and Video Festival 1984, Picasso Award 1986, Inst. Skowhegan Medal for drawing 1987, Grand Prix Biennale, Barcelona Festival of Cinema Art 1989, Germna Theatre Critics Award 1990, Brandeis Univ. Poses Creative Arts Award 1991, Venice Biennale Golden Lion Award for Sculpture 1993, Dorothy and Lillian Gish Prize 1996, Tadeusz Kantor Prize 1997, Harvard Excellence in Design Award 1998, Pushkin Prize 1999; Most Outstanding Theater Designer of the Seventies, U.S. Inst. of Theater Tech. 1977. *Address:* RW Work Ltd, 155 Wooster Street, Suite 4F, New York, NY 10012, USA. *Telephone:* (212) 253-7484. *Fax:* (212) 253-7485 (office). *Website:* www.robertwilson.com (office).

**WILSON, Timothy;** singer (countertenor); b. 18 July 1961, England. *Education:* Royal Academy of Music. *Career:* operatic engagements include Handel's Orlando and Britten's Death in Venice for Scottish Opera, Dido and Aeneas in Frankfurt, Gluck's Orfeo in Kassel, L'Incoronazione di Poppea in Gelsenkirchen, The Fairy Queen in Florence, A Midsummer Night's Dream in Kentucky, the modern premiere of Cesti's Il Pomo d'Oro in Vienna, and the world premieres of Maxwell Davies's Resurrection in Darmstadt, and Luis de Pablo's El Viajero Indiscreto in Madrid; Season 1990–91 with Vivaldi in Prague, Messiah in Valencia, Bach in the Philippines and the title role in Handel's Xerxes at Innsbruck; Covent Garden debut in 1992 as Oberon in A Midsummer Night's Dream; Sang in Agrippina at Buxton Festival, Alcina at the Halle Festival and Giulio Cesare at Ludwigshafen, 1992–93; Further concert appearances with Mackerras, Hickox, Pinnock, Herreweghe, Leonhardt, Norrington and Parrott; Venues include Netherlands, France, Germany, Austria, Spain, Italy and the United Kingdom including the Promenade Concerts. *Recordings include:* Alcina, Purcell's Come Ye Sons of Art Away and Handel's Israel in Egypt.

**WILSON-JOHNSON, David Robert,** BA, FRAM; British baritone; b. 16 Nov. 1950, Northampton; s. of Harry K. Johnson and Sylvia C. Wilson. *Education:* Wellingborough School, Northants., British Inst. of Florence, St Catharine's Coll., Cambridge and Royal Acad. of Music. *Career:* debut at Royal Opera House, Covent Garden in We Come to the River 1976; has since appeared in Billy Budd, L'Enfant et les Sortilèges, Le Rossignol, Les Noces, Boris Godunov, Die Zauberflöte, Turandot, Werther, Madame Butterfly; Wigmore Hall recital début 1977; BBC Promenade Concert debut 1981; appeared at Edin. Festival 1976, Glyndebourne Festival 1980 and at festivals in Bath, Bergen, Berlin, Geneva, Graz, Netherlands, Hong Kong, Jerusalem, Orange, Paris and Vienna; Paris Opéra debut in Die Meistersinger 1989; played St Francis of Assisi (title role) in Olivier Messiaen's 80th birthday celebrations 1988; American debut in Paulus (title role) 1990; ENO debut (in Billy Budd) 1991, Netherlands Opera debut in Birtwistle's Punch and Judy 1993; Founder Dir Ferrandou Summer Singing School 1985–; Gulbenkian Fellowship 1978–81. *Films include:* A Midsummer Marriage 1988. *Recordings include:* Schubert's Winterreise, Mozart Masses from King's College, Cambridge, Haydn's Nelson Mass, Schoenberg's Ode to Napoleon, King Priam, Punch and Judy, La Traviata, Lucrezia Borgia and Michael Berkeley's Or Shall We Die?, Belshazzar's Feast, L'Enfance du Christ, The Kingdom (Elgar), The Ice Break (Tippett), Odes (Purcell), Caractacus (Elgar), Black Pentecost (Maxwell Davies), Mass in B Minor (Bach) Peter Grimes, Damnation of Faust. *Honours:* Nat. Fed. of Music Soc. Award 1977, Evening Standard Award for Opera 1989. *Address:* Prinsengracht 455, 1016 HN Amsterdam, Netherlands (home); 28 Englefield Road, London, N1 4ET, England. *Telephone:* (20) 7254-0941 (London); 5-65-10-94-11 (France); (20) 7728104 (home). *E-mail:* ferrandou@aol.com (office); jumbowj@aol.com (home). *Website:* www.gmn.com (office).

**WIMBERGER, Peter;** Singer (Bass-Baritone); b. 14 May 1940, Vienna, Austria. *Education:* Studied at the Vienna Music Academy with Paul Schöffler and Adolf Vogel. *Career:* Debut: Dortmund 1963, as Pietro in Simon Boccanegra; Appearances in the opera houses of Frankfurt, Karlsruhe, Kassel, Düsseldorf, Munich, Warsaw and Copenhagen; Barcelona 1985, as the Wanderer in Siegfried; Festivals of Bregenz and Florence; Repertoire includes principal roles in operas by Mussorgsky, Mozart, Wagner, Rossini, Verdi and Strauss; Sang at Palermo and Naples, 1988, as Amfortas; Rangoni at the Vienna Staatsoper, 1988; Kuno in Der Freischütz, 1996; mem, Vienna Staatsoper from 1968. *Recordings:* Haydn's Harmoniemesse; Spirit Messenger in Die Frau ohne Schatten by Strauss. *Address:* c/o Landestheater, Promenade 39, A 4010 Linz, Austria.

**WINBECK, Heinz;** Composer and Teacher; b. 11 Feb. 1946, Piflas, Landshut, Germany. *Education:* Studied piano and conducting at the Munich Richard Strauss Conservatory, 1964–67; Composition with Harald Genzmer and Gunter Bialas at the Munich Hochschule, 1963–73. *Career:* Conductor and Composer at Ingolstadt and Wunsiedel, 1974–78; Teacher at the Munich Hochschule 1980–88, Professor of Composition at the Würzburg Hochschule, from 1988; Composer in Residence at the Cabrillo, California, Music Festival, 1985. *Compositions include:* In Memorian Paul Celan, for soprano, flute, piano and percussion, 1970; Sie Tanzt for baritone and ensemble, 1971; Sonosillent, for cello and strings, 1971; Musik for wind quintet, 1971; Espaces, for 4 percussionists, piano and flute, 1972; Nocturne I for chamber ensemble, 1972; Lenau-Fantasien for cello and chamber orchestra, 1979; 3 String Quartets, 1979, 1980, 1984; Chansons a Temps, for women's voices and 13 instruments, 1979; 4 Symphonies, 1983, 1987, 1988, 1993; Blick in den Strom, for String Quintet, 1993. *Honours:* Music Prize of the Akademie der Schonen Kunste, Berlin, 1985. *Address:* c/o GEMA, Rosenheimer Str 11, 81667 Munchen, Germany.

**WINDMULLER, Yaron;** Singer (Baritone); b. 1956, Israel. *Education:* Studied in Tel-Aviv, Munich with Ernst Haefliger and in Vicenza with Malcolm King; Further study at the Opera Studio of the Bayerische Staatsoper. *Career:* Debut: City of London Festival in 1982, in Gluck's Armide; Sang as soloist with the Israel Philharmonic, and as member of Theater am Gärtnerplatz, Munich, from 1986, as Purcell's Aeneas, Mozart's Count, Guglielmo, Don Giovanni and Papageno, Wolfram, Marcello, Hans Jürgen von Bose's Werther and Kaspar in Der Zaubergeige by Werner Egk; Sang Trinity Moses in Weill's Mahagonny at Frankfurt in 1990; Sang Paolo in Simon Boccanegra at Wellington, 2000; Many concert appearances and Lieder recitals. *Address:* c/o Staatstheater am Gärtnerplatz, Gartnerplatz 3, 8000 Munich 1, Germany.

**WINKLER, Hermann;** Singer (Tenor); b. 3 March 1924, Duisburg, Germany. *Education:* Studied at the Hanover Conservatory. *Career:* Sang at the Bayreuth Festival from 1957, notably as the Steersman in Der fliegende Holländer in 1965 and Parsifal, 1976–77; Member of the Zürich Opera from 1970; Frankfurt Opera, 1970 as Lohengrin and Florestan; Munich in 1972 as Mozart's Don Ottavio and Idomeneo; Salzburg Festival and Deutsche Oper Berlin, 1976, 1981 in Idomeneo; USA debut in 1980 as Don Ottavio; Sang Florestan in USA and Japan in 1981; Covent Garden debut in 1984 as the Captain in Wozzeck; Zürich Opera in 1985 as the Emperor in Die Frau ohne Schatten; Guest appearances in Vienna and Hamburg; Sang Herod in Salome at La Scala, 1987, and Loge at Bologna; Season 1987–88 at the Teatro Real Madrid in Wozzeck and Lulu; Marseilles and Barcelona in 1989 as Aegisthus in Elektra; Sang in Peter Grimes at Zürich in 1989; Many appearances in the concert hall, often in Das Lied von der Erde by Mahler. *Recordings:* Arabella; Mahler's 8th Symphony; Idomeneo; Drum Major in Wozzeck.

**WINKLER, Peter,** BA, MFA; American composer, pianist and musicologist; *Professor of Music, State University of New York at Stony Brook;* b. 26 Jan. 1943, Los Angeles, CA; s. of David P. Winkler and Elizabeth Babcock Winkler. *Education:* Univ. of California at Berkeley with Andrew Imbrie and Seymour Schifrin, Princeton Univ. with Milton Babbitt and Earl Kim. *Career:* music faculty, State Univ. of New York, Stony Brook from 1971, Prof. of Music 1999–; Ed., Journal of Popular Music Studies 1992–95. *Compositions include:* String Quartet, 1967; Humoresque for piano, 1970; Symphony, 1978; Clarinet Bouquet: Four Concert Rags, 1976–80; Recitativo e Terzetto for woodwind trio, 1980; Professionally Speaking (satirical review, with Frederic Block and Ernst Muller), 1986; Yaa Amponsah: Fantasy on a Ghanaian Popular Song for violin and piano, 1988; No Condition is Permanent, for Pierrot ensemble, 1989; Solitaire, for solo clarinet, 1989; Waterborne, for violin and tape, 1991; Saboreando el Gusto Cubano, for violin, piano and percussion, 1994; Tingle-Tangle: A Wedekind Cabaret, collaboration with Eric Bentley, William Bolcom and Arnold Black, 1994; Nine Waltzes for piano trio, 1997; Serenade for String Orchestra, 1998; Out! The Musical (book and lyrics: Winston Clark) for male chorus, piano, bass and drums, 1997–98; Returning to the Root, for horn and piano, 2000; Requiem Aeternam, for chorus, 2001; Partita for Baroque Ensemble, 2001; A Midsummer Overture for orchestra, 2002; Gili's Music for bassoon and cello, 2003; Gathering Reel for chamber orchestra, 2004. *Honours:* MacDowell Colony Fellowship 1971. *Address:* c/o Department of Music, Stony Brook University, Stony Brook, NY 11733-5475 (office); 15 Bayview Avenue, East Setauket, New York, NY 11733, USA (home). *Telephone:* (631) 751-7672 (home). *E-mail:* peter.winkler@sunysb.edu (office). *Website:* naples.cc.sunysb.edu/cas/music.nsf/pages/winkler.

**WINKLER, Wolfgang;** Musicologist; b. 12 June 1945, Graz, Austria; m. Elisabeth; one d. *Education:* Universität Graz. *Career:* Brucknerkonservatorium Linz, Bibliothek und musikwissenschaftliches Referat 1978; Referent für U. Musik im ORF Landesstudio 1979; Head of Music, ORF 1985; Artistic Dir and CEO, LIVA 1998. *Publications:* contrib. to Musik in Österreich (Gottfried Kraus Verlag), Musicolociga austriaca 11, Umkunst (Publikation der Hochschule für künstlerisches und industrielle Gestaltung, Linz), 20 Jahre Bruckenhaus, Gedanken zu Balduin Sulzer (Musikarchiv der Österreichisch Nationalbibliothek), Musikgeschichte Österreichs, Neue Musik und Medien, echt falsch Will die Welt betrogen werden? (Kremayr und Scheriau). *Address:* Untere Donaulände 7, Linz, 4020, Austria (office). *Telephone:* (732) 7612 2025

(office). *Fax:* (732) 7612 2030 (office). *E-mail:* w.winkler@liva.co.at (office). *Website:* www.wolfgang-winkler.at (office).

**WINSCHERMANN, Helmut;** Oboist and Conductor; b. 22 March 1920, Munich, Germany. *Education:* Studied in Essen and Paris. *Career:* Principal with the Frankfurt Radio Symphony Orchestra, 1945–51; Co-founded Collegium Instrumental Detmold, 1954, and became professor at the Detmold Academy, 1956; Appearances with the Capella Coloniensis and Stuttgart Chamber Orchestra; Founded the Deutsche Bachsolisten, giving many performances throughout Europe and elsewhere; Premiered La tomba di Igor Stravinsky by Giselher Klebe, 1979. *Address:* Detmold Hochschule für Musik, Allee 22, 4930 Detmold, Germany.

**WINSLADE, Glenn;** Singer (Tenor); b. 1958, Australia. *Education:* Studied at the New South Wales Conservatorium and at Vienna Conservatory. *Career:* Has sung with English National Opera as Ferrando, Victoria State Opera as Belmonte, Walter von der Vogelweide and Don Ottavio, Scottish Opera as Mozart's Titus and Australian Opera as Oronte in Alcina; Covent Garden debut in 1990 as Vogelgesang in Die Meistersinger; Further appearances with Glyndebourne Festival and Touring Opera, New Sadler's Wells Opera in Merry Widow, Freiburg Opera, Semper Oper Dresden as Belmonte, Stuttgart Opera and the Netherlands Opera in Idomeneo; Other roles include Tamino, The Prince in The Love of Three Oranges, Stroh (Intermezzo), Elemer in Arabella, Amenophis in Mosè, Ernesto and Nemorino, Fracasso in La Finta Semplice, Lindoro and Alfredo, Jacquino in Fidelio, Steuermann in Der fliegende Holländer and Jason in Cherubini's Médée; Mozart's Titus for Welsh National Opera; Engaged as Wagner's Rienzi at the Vienna Staatsoper, 1998; Strauss's Emperor at Covent Garden, 2001; Sang in Mahler's 8th at Vienna, 2002; Concert engagements with the Musica Antiqua Vienna, Duke University, NC, RAI Milan and The BBC. *Recordings include:* Messiah with the Scottish Chamber Orchestra; Merry Widow. *Honours:* Winner, Australian Opera Auditions, Esso/Glyndebourne Touring and John Christie Glyndebourne Awards. *Address:* c/o Musiespana, c/José Marañon, 10-40 Izqda, E–28010 Madrid, Spain.

**WINSTIN, Robert;** Composer, Conductor and Pianist; b. 6 June 1959, Chicago, Illinois. *Education:* Advanced Studies, Chicago Musical College; Roosevelt University; University of Colorado. *Career:* Debut: Pianist, Carnegie Hall, 1986; First American composer to have work and perform in mainland China, 1995; Shanghai and Beijing, piano concerto No. 2; Music Director and Principal Conductor, Metropolis Youth Symphony; Music Director and Principal Conductor, Derriere Guard Festival Orchestra; Musical Director and Principal Conductor, Millennium Symphony; Executive Director, Foundation for Music; mem, ASCAP; NARAS; Derriere Guard Society. *Compositions:* Dedo, opera; Scherto Burlesque; Symphony No. 2; Symphony No. 5; Piano concerto No. 2; Cello Concerto, Millennium Symphony. *Recordings:* Piano Art; Simple Songs; Piano concerto No. 2; Favourites; Dedo. *Publications:* Scherzo Burlesque, 1988; Symphony No. 2, 1989; Piano Art, 1995; Symphony No. 5, 1996; Etudes, 1993; Cello Concerto, 1997; Piano concerto, 1994. *Contributions:* Music editor, Nit and Wit magazine, 1985–88; Radio producer and writer, Nuovo Voce, 1990–. *Honours:* Joseph Jefferson Citations Wing Recommendation for Oedipus Requiem, 1989; Concours Caveat Prim Palm D'Or, 1992; Barrettson Prize in American Music, Piano concerto No. 1, 1998. *Current Management:* ERM. *Address:* c/o ERM 3712 N Broadway #264, Chicago, IL 60613, USA.

**WINTER, Louise;** Singer (mezzo-soprano); b. 29 Nov. 1959, Preston, Lancashire, England; m. Gerald Finley. *Education:* Studied at Chetham's School of Music and at the Royal Northern College of Music with Frederick Cox. *Career:* With Glyndebourne Touring Opera (from 1982) has sung Tisbe in La Cenerentola, Dorabella in Così fan tutte and Mercédès in Carmen; Sang Zerlina on Glyndebourne's tour to Hong Kong, Nancy in Albert Herring at the 1986 summer festival and in the Ravel double bill in 1987–88; Covent Garden debut in 1988 as a Flowermaiden in Parsifal; Has sung Janáček's Varvara and Ravel's Concepcion for Opera North; Netherlands Opera as Rosina in Il Barbiere di Siviglia and Second Lady in Die Zauberflöte; Glyndebourne Festival, 1988–90, in Katya Kabanova, Il Barbiere di Siviglia and the Ravel double bill; Appearances with the Canadian Opera Company in Eugene Onegin and as Dorabella in Così fan tutte in 1991; Concert engagements with the König Ensemble and in the Choral Symphony conducted by Simon Rattle; Season 1997 with Carmen and the Berlioz Marguerite for English National Opera and Jocasta in Oedipus Rex at the Festival Hall; Season 1998 with Eduige in Rodelinda at Gyndebourne and Marina in Boris Gounov for New Sussex Opera, Berlioz's Damnation of Faust in Sydney and Mahler's Des Knaben Wunderhorn in Kuala Lumpur with Malaysian Philharmonic Orchestra; Britten's Phaedre at the 1999 London Proms; Sang Carmen for ENO, 2001; London Proms, 2002. *Recordings:* Songs of Frank Bridge, 1997; Lucia di Lammermoor with Hanover Band, conducted by Charles Mackerras. *Current Management:* Askonas Holt Ltd, Lonsdale Chambers, 27 Chancery Lane, London, WC2A 1PF, England. *Telephone:* (20) 7400-1700. *Fax:* (20) 7400-1799. *E-mail:* info@askonasholt.co.uk. *Website:* www.askonasholt.co.uk.

**WINTER, Nils Tomas;** Composer; b. 1 March 1954, Arboga, Sweden. *Education:* University studies in archaeology, law, Spanish and Portuguese; Studied composition with Werner Wolf Glaser, 1980–94, Daniel Börtz, 1981, and Miklós Maros, 1995. *Career:* Debut: Swedish National Radio programme, Monologue No. 10 for Bassoon and Monologue No. 2 for Guitar, 1982; FST 1998–; Society of Swedish Composers. *Compositions:* Sargasso for saxophone quartet, 1995–96; Istros for string quartet, 1996–97; Symphony No. 1 1998–99; Piano trio, 2000. *Honours:* Three scholarships, 1997–2001. *Address:* Tunadalsgatan 34 D, 731 40 Köping, Sweden.

**WINTER, Quade;** Composer and Singer (Tenor); b. 1950, Oregon, USA. *Career:* Debut: Sang Max in Der Freischütz at San Francisco; Has sung the Duke of Mantua for Eugene Opera, Canio at Anchorage, Don Ottavio at the Carmel Bach Festival and Ishmael in Nabucco for San Francisco Opera; Appeared in US premiere of The Excursions of Mr Brouček, with the Berkeley Symphony; Concerts have included Beethoven's Ninth with the Stockton Symphony and the Verdi Requiem at the San Francisco Festival of Masses, conducted by Robert Shaw; European debut as Hermann in The Queen of Spades with Graz Opera in 1982; La Scala Milan in 1982 as Cherubini's Anacréon; Roles with the Stadtheater Würzburg have included Don Carlos, Lensky, Herod, Rodolfo and Canio; Has sung Parsifal at Graz and Herod in Heidelberg and Seattle; Scottish Opera debut as Mark in The Midsummer Marriage, in 1989; Music for Gilbert and Sullivan's Thespis performed by Ohio Light Opera, 1996. *Address:* Music International, 13 Ardilaun Road, London N5 2QR, England.

**WINTER, Sidonie;** British singer (soprano); b. 1965, England. *Education:* Univ. of East Anglia, Royal Acad. of Music and Nat. Opera Studio. *Career:* frequent concerts throughout the UK, including Wigmore Hall, St John's Smith Square and South Bank; Proms debut as Lady Angela in Patience; other concerts include Messiah and Handel's Dixit Dominus, the Mass in D Minor by Haydn, Beethoven's Mass in C and Elgar's Apostles; opera debut as Leila in Iolanthe for D'Oyly Carte Opera; other roles include Siebel in Faust, Elena (Aroldo), Sofia (Lombardi) and Priestess (Aida, Covent Garden 1996); Fiordiligi at Ischia for the Walton Trust, Geisha in Mascagni's Iris for Chelsea Opera Group, Mozart's Countess and Donna Elvira at Aldeburgh; Lady Billows in Rheinsberg Sieglinde for Wagner Soc. *Address:* 12 Pond Road, Stratford, London, E15 3BE, England.

**WIRKKALA, Merja;** Singer (Soprano); b. 7 Oct. 1954, Kaustinen, Finland. *Education:* Studied at the Sibelius Academy, Helsinki. *Career:* Sang with the Helsinki Opera from 1976, notably as Nannetta, Zerlina, Despina, Susanna, Kaisa in Merikanto's Juha, and Siebel; Sang Marzelline in Fidelio at the Vienna Staatsoper (1980), Zerlina at Covent Garden, 1981, and the title role in the premiere of Elina by Liukolas at Helsinki, 1992; Guest in Juha at the Edinburgh Festival, 1987. *Address:* Finnish National Opera, Bulevardi 23–27, 00180 Helsinki 18, Finland.

**WIRTZ, Dorothea;** Singer (Soprano); b. 13 March 1953, Tuttlingen, Germany. *Education:* Studied in Berlin with Hugo Diez and in Munich with Hanno Blaschke. *Career:* Sang at the Munich Staatsoper, 1979–80, Kassel, 1980–84; Member of the Zürich Opera from 1984; Guest appearances in Düsseldorf, Venice, Naples, Lisbon, Bologna, Berlin, Cologne, Wiesbaden, Florence and Strasbourg; Roles include Olympia in Les Contes d'Hoffmann, Blondchen, the Queen of Night, Zerlina, Despina, Ilia in Idomeneo, Rosina, Sophie in Der Rosenkavalier, Zerbinetta, Norina, Adina, Marzelline and the Woodbird in Siegfried; Sang Blondchen at Buenos Aires in 1987; Professor at the Freiburg Musikhochschule, from 2000; Concert Repertoire includes works by Handel, Mozart, Bach and Schumann including Paradies und die Peri. *Recordings include:* Strauss's Daphne. *Address:* c/o Operhaus Zürich, Falkerstrasse 1, 8008 Zürich, Switzerland.

**WISE, Patricia;** Singer (Soprano); b. 31 July 1944, Wichita, Kansas, USA. *Education:* Studied at Kansas University, Santa Fe, and in New York with Margaret Harshaw. *Career:* Debut: Susanna in The Marriage of Figaro, Kansas City in 1966; Appearances at the Houston Opera, New York City Opera, New Orleans, Philadelphia, Chicago, San Francisco, Washington, Miami, Baltimore, San Antonio and Pittsburgh; Carnegie Hall, New York in 1971 in Handel's Ariodante, Covent Garden, London in 1971 as Rosina in Rossini's Barber of Seville with New York City Opera; Glyndebourne in 1972 as Zerbinetta in Ariadne auf Naxos; Vienna Staatsoper in 1983 as Pamina, Nannetta and Sophie; Sang at the 1984 Salzburg Festival in the premiere of Un Re in Ascolto by Berio; 1st appearance in Geneva in 1985 as Lulu; Repertoire includes roles in operas by Donizetti, Gounod, Gluck, and Verdi's Gilda; Sang with the Vienna Staatsoper, 1976–91, in 300 performances, many of which were Strauss or Mozart operas; Since 1985 has appeared in five other productions of Berg's 3 act Lulu, from Berlin to Paris; Sang Lulu at Madrid in 1987, Sophie in Der Rosenkavalier at Budapest, 1989, Gilda in Rigoletto at Madrid, 1989, Fiordiligi in Mozart's Così fan tutte, and Violetta in Verdi's Traviata, 1990; Guest appearances in European opera houses including La Scala, Munich, Berlin, Hamburg, Barcelona, Geneva, Glyndebourne and at Salzburg Festival. *Honours:* Kammersängerin, Vienna Staatsoper, 1996. *Address:* c/o Vienna Staatsoper (Artist Contracts), Opernring 2, 1010 Vienna, Austria.

**WISEMAN, Debra (Debbie),** MBE, GGSM; British composer and conductor; b. 10 May 1963, London; d. of Paul and Barbara Wiseman; m. Tony Wharmby 1987. *Education:* Trinity Coll. of Music, Kingsway Princeton/Morley Coll., Guildhall School of Music and Drama, London. *Career:* composer and conductor of music for film and TV productions 1989–; Visiting Prof. of Film Composition, Royal Coll. of Music 1995–; mem. Performing Right Soc., BAFTA, Musicians' Union, British Acad. of Composers and Songwriters. *Compositions include:* Inside Looking Out 1989, Squares and Roundabouts 1989, Echoes of Istria 1989, The Guilty, Lighthouse, Female Perversions, The Dying of the Light, Shrinks (Silents to Satellite Award for Best Original TV

Theme Music 1991), The Good Guys (Television and Radio Industries Club Award for TV Theme Music of the Year 1993), Tom and Viv 1994, The Project, Judge John Deed, P. O. W., Wilde Stories, The Upper Hand, The Churchills, Serious and Organised, The Second Russian Revolution, Little Napoleons, Children's Hospital, Death of Yugoslavia, Haunted 1995, Wilde 1997, The Fairy Tale of the Nightingale and the Rose 1999, The Fairy Tale of the Selfish Giant 1999, It Might be You, A Week in Politics, People's Century, What Did You Do In The War, Auntie?, The Cuban Missile Crisis, Vet's School, The Missing Postman, Tom's Midnight Garden, Absolute Truth, My Uncle Silas 2001, Othello 2001, Warriors (Royal TV Soc. Award) 2000, Oscar Wilde Fairy Stories 2002, Freeze Frame 2004, He Knew He Was Right 2004, The Truth About Love 2004, Arsène Lupin 2004. *Current Management:* c/o Roz Colls, Music Matters International, Crest House, 102–104 Church Road, Teddington, Middx TW11 8PY, England. *Telephone:* (20) 8979-4580. *Fax:* (20) 8979-4590. *E-mail:* dwiseman10@aol.com. *Website:* www.debbiewiseman.co.uk.

**WISHART, Trevor;** Composer; b. 11 Oct. 1946, Leeds, England; m. Jacqueline Joan Everett, 2 d. *Education:* BA Music, Oxford University; MA, Analysis of Contemporary Music, Nottingham University; DPhil, Composition, York University. *Career:* Foreign tours: Scandinavia, Australia, Japan, USA, Netherlands, Spain, Germany, IRCAM commission, Vox-5, 1986; Vox cycle performed at London Proms, 1988; Sound Designer, Jorvik Viking Centre Museum, York; Special Professor of Music, University of Nottingham, 1990–92; Visiting Fellow, Bretton Hall College of the University of Leeds, 1994; Research Fellow, University of Birmingham; Chair, Sonic Arts Network, 1990–92; Founder, Composers Desktop Project. *Compositions:* Red Bird; Anticredos; The Vox Cycle; Pastorale–Walden 2; Beach Singularity; Tongues of Fire, 1994; Fabulous Paris, 1997. Two Women, for DAAD, Berlin, 1998: American Triptych, for French Ministry of Culture, 1999. *Recordings:* Vox; Vox 5; Red Bird; Anticredos; October Music; Audible Design, 1994. *Publications:* Sounds Fun, educational music games, 1974 also in Japanese; On Sonic Art, 1985; Audible Design, 1994; Sun, Creativity and Environment; Sun-2, A Creative Philosophy; Whose Music, A Sociology of Musical Language. *Contributions:* Contact; Musics; Ear Magazine, New York; Interface, Utrecht; Computer Music Journal, USA; Musica Realta, Milan. *Honours:* Prizewinner: Bourges International Electro-Accoustic Music Festival, 1978, Gaudeamus International Festival, Netherlands, 1979, Linz Ars Electronica, 1985, 1995.

**WISLOCKI, Leszek;** Polish composer and pianist; *Professor, Academy of Music, Wrocław;* b. 15 Dec. 1931, Chorzow; m. Renata Krumpholz 1968; two s. *Education:* Acad. of Music, Wrocław. *Career:* concerts as pianist and composer for Polish radio and television. *Compositions:* Andante and Presto for xylophone and piano, Two Miniatures for violin and cello, Sonata for oboe and cello, Ostinato and Toccatina for piano solo, Polonaise for piano solo, Suita Lubuska for wind orchestra, Songs for choir a cappella (male and female), four symphonies, Rhapsody for the great symphonic orchestra 1996, three concerti for instruments (piano, oboe, bassoon) and orchestra, VIth Piano Trio 1997, Dilectissimo Papae Ioanni Paulo Secundo ad honorem maximum for ten brass instruments and four kettle drums (for 46th Int. Eucharistic Congress, Wrocław) 1997, Cantata The Shepherd Goes for choir and symphonic orchestra (for 46th Int. Eucharistic Congress, Wrocław) 1997, XIth String Quartet 2002, Two Sonnets for baritone and piano (text by John Gracen-Brown) 2002, Concerto for orchestra 2003. *Recordings:* for Radio-Wrocław, Andante and Presto for xylophone and piano. *Address:* ul Komandorska 48-8, 53-343 Wrocław, Poland (home). *Telephone:* (71) 367-61-38 (home).

**WISPELWEY, Pieter;** Dutch cellist; b. 1965. *Career:* appearances with the Rotterdam Philharmonic, under Kent Nagano, L'Orchestre des Champs Elysées (Philippe Herreweghe), BBC SO, Netherlands Radio SO (Frans Brüggen), and the Camerata Academica Salzburg (Roger Norrington); further engagements in Argentina, Japan, S Africa and Australia; Bach-Marathon concerts with the six solo suites throughout Europe 2000, including the Wigmore Hall; tours with Nat. Orchestra of Lille and Baseler Kammerorchester 2001; with piano pnr, Dejan Lazic, performed complete Beethoven cello sonatas, Edinburgh Festival 2001; repertoire also includes works by Kagel, Carter and Schnittke. *Recordings include:* Suites by Bach, Britten and Reger, Sonatas by Schubert, Brahms and Beethoven, Concertos by Haydn, Vivaldi, Elgar, Dvořák and Schumann. *Honours:* Netherlands Music Prize, Diapason d'Or. *Address:* c/o Ariën Arts, de Boeystraat 6, 2018 Antwerp, Belgium.

**WIT, Antoni;** Polish conductor and professor of music; *Managing and Artistic Director, Warsaw Philharmonic;* b. 7 Feb. 1944, Kraków; m. Zofia Ćwikiewicz. *Education:* State Higher School of Music, Kraków. *Career:* Asst Conductor Warsaw Philharmonic, 1967–70, Man. and Artistic Dir 2002–; conductor, Poznań Nat. Philharmonic 1970–72; Artistic Dir Pomeranian Philharmonic, Bydgoszcz 1974–77; Dir and Artistic Chief Polish Radio Symphony Orchestra and Choir 1977–83; Dir Polish Nat. Radio Symphony Orchestra, Katowice 1983–2000; Artistic Dir Orquesta Filarmonica de Gran Canaria, Las Palmas 1987–91; Prof., Fryderyk Chopin Acad. of Music, Warsaw 1997–; Dir and Artistic Chief Warsaw Philharmonic 2002–; has conducted The London Philharmonic, BBC Symphony Orchestra, Berliner Philharmoniker, Royal Philharmonic Orchestra, Orchestre National de Belgique, Tokyo Symphony Orchestra, Montreal Symphony Orchestra, Orquesta Nacional de España, Staatskapelle, Dresden, Accad. di Santa Cecilia, Rome, Tonhalle-Orchester. *Compositions:* soundtracks: Kronika wypadków miłosnych (The Chronicle of Love Affairs) 1986, Korczak 1990, Pan Tadeusz (Last Foray in Lithuania) 1999. *Recordings include:* more than 90 albums including symphonies by

Tchaikovsky, Górecki, Schumann, Penderecki, Lutosławski (all), Olivier Messiaen (Turangalila Symphony) (Cannes Classical Award—Midem Classique 2002), etc. *Honours:* numerous prizes include Second Prize, Herbert von Karajan Conducting Competition, Berlin 1971, Orfeusz (Critics' Award) 1984, 1996, Diapason d'Or, Grand Prix de Disque de la Nouvelle Académie du Disque 1992, Diamond Baton Award, Bd Dirs Polish Public Radio 1998. *Address:* Warsaw Philharmonic, The National Orchestra and Choir of Poland, ul. Jasna 5, 00-950 Warsaw, Poland (office). *Telephone:* (22) 5517102 (office). *Fax:* (22) 5517200 (office). *E-mail:* antwit@medianet.pl (office); sekretariat@filharmonia.pl (home). *Website:* www.filharmonia.pl (office).

**WITT, Kerstin;** Singer (Mezzo-soprano); b. 1960, Altentreptow, Brandenburg, Germany. *Education:* Hanns Eisler Conservatory, Berlin, 1977–85. *Career:* Appearances at the Dresden Staatsoper from 1988, as Donna Elvira, Strauss's Clairon (Capriccio), Octavian and Composer (Ariadne), Medea in Handel's Teseo, Leonore in Fidelio and Offenbach's Nicklauss; Modern repertory includes the Mother in Janáček's Osud, Countess Geschwitz in Lulu and Bartók's Judith; Guest appearances at Montpellier, Venice and elsewhere; Wagner roles include Brangaene in Tristan, and Magdalena in Die Meistersinger; Concerts include the Wesendoncklieder and Kindertotenlieder and Dvořák's Gypsy Songs; Sang Brangaene at Enschede (1999) and Herodias in Salome for the Dresden Staatsoper, 2001. *Recordings include:* Herodias in Salome.

**WITZENMANN, Wolfgang,** DipMus, DPhil; composer; b. 26 Nov. 1937, Munich, Germany; m. Renata Di Salvo 1977; one s. one d. *Education:* Musikhochschule Stuttgart, Universitaet Tübingen. *Career:* as composer: Gaudeamus-Festival, Netherlands 1967, 1968, 1970, 1971, Internationale Ferienkurse für Neue Musik, Darmstadt, Germany 1969, Autunno Musicale, Como, Italy 1975, Festival Internazionale Nuova Consonanza, Rome 1985, Festival Internazionale Terenzio Gargiulo, Naples 1986; founded Wolfgang Witzenmann Musikverlag 2003. *Compositions:* Choirs, Oden I–V for voice and piano, six cycles of Lieder, Operas Nivasio, Mary and Sappho, Oratorio Christus and Gilgamesh, Orchestra Eigenklänge Natur Deutschland-Lieder, Sinfonia 1 and 2 for orchestra, Violin Concerto, Antiphonales Konzert for trumpet and orchestra, piano and organ music, chamber music, and music for early instruments; arrangements from original works by Macque, Gesualdo, Bellini. *Recordings:* Monographic 1989. *Publications:* Domenico Mazzocchi (1592–1665), Dokumente und Interpretationen 1970. *Contributions:* Analecta Musicologica, Acta Musicologica, Die Musikforschung, Recercare, Rivista Italiana di Musicologica, Studi Musicali. *Honours:* Festschrift: 'Vanitatis fuga, aeternitatis amor' Wolfgang Witzenmann (zum 65), Geburstag 2005. *Address:* Via Mario Fascetti 67, 00136 Rome, Italy (home). *Telephone:* (06) 35498447 (home). *E-mail:* wo_witzenmann@msn.com (home). *Website:* www.literadur.de.

**WIXELL, Ingvar;** Baritone; b. 7 May 1931, Lulea, Sweden. *Education:* Studied in Stockholm with Dagmar Gustavson. *Career:* Debut: Sang at Gavle in 1952; Stockholm in 1955 as Papageno; Member of the Royal Opera Stockholm from 1956; Appeared with the company in Alcina at Covent Garden in 1960; Glyndebourne Festival in 1962 as Guglielmo in Così fan tutte; US debut at Chicago Lyric Opera in 1967 as Belcore in L'Elisir d'amore; Salzburg Festival 1966–69, as Count Almaviva and Pizarro; Hamburg Staatsoper in 1970 as Rigoletto and Scarpia; Covent Garden, 1972–77 as Simon Boccanegra, Scarpia, Belcore and Mandryka in Arabella; Metropolitan Opera from 1973 as Rigoletto, Germont, Amonasro, Marcello and Renato in Un Ballo in Maschera; Other roles include Don Carlo in La Forza del Destino, Count Luna, Posa and Pentheus in The Bassarids by Henze; Sang Amonasro at Houston in 1987; Covent Garden, 1987–90 as Rigoletto and Belcore; Stuttgart Staatsoper, 1990 as Scarpia; Sang in Tosca at Earl's Court in London, 1991; Sang Falstaff at Copenhagen, 1997; Scarpia at Malmö, 2000. *Recordings:* Le nozze di Figaro, Don Giovanni, Zaide, La Bohème, Un Ballo in Maschera, Tosca, Un Giorno di Regno, Il Trovatore, L'Elisir d'amore; Video of Tosca. *Address:* c/o Opéra et Concert, 1 Rue Volney, F–75002 Paris, France.

**WLASCHIHA, Ekkerhard;** Singer (Baritone); b. 28 May 1938, Pirna, Germany. *Education:* Studied at the Franz Liszt Musikhochschule in Leipzig and with Helene Jung. *Career:* Debut: Gera in 1961 as Don Fernando in Fidelio; Sang in Dresden and Weimar, 1964–70; Leipzig Opera from 1970 as Scarpia, Pizarro, Alfio, Tonio, Dr Coppelius, and Jochanaan in Salome; Sang in the premieres of Greek Wedding by Hannell in 1969 and The Shadow by Fritz Geissler in 1975; Lausanne Opera and Staatsoper Berlin in 1983 as Kurwenal and Telramund; Sang Kaspar in Der Freischütz at the reopening of the Semper Opera House in Dresden, 1985; Bayreuth Festival in 1986 as Kurwenal; Appeared on Russian television in Fidelio by Beethoven; Sang Telramund at the Berlin Staatsoper in 1990, and Alberich in a new production of Siegfried at Covent Garden in 1990; Returned to London 1997, as Bishop Ercole in Pfitzner's Palestrina and 1998 as Alberich at the Albert Hall; Season 2000–01 as Alberich and Klingsor at the Met, Pizarro in Dresden and Biterolf in Tannhäuser for the Munich Staatsoper. *Address:* c/o Allied Artists Agency, 42 Montpelier Square, London SW7 1JZ, England.

**WOHLER, Rudiger;** Singer (Tenor); b. 4 May 1943, Hamburg, Germany. *Education:* Studied at the Hamburg Musikhochschule. *Career:* Sang at Darmstadt, 1968–71; Sang at Zürich 1971–74 as Mozart's Belmonte, Ferrando, Tamino and Don Ottavio; Sang at Stuttgart from 1974 and has made guest appearances in Hamburg, Munich, Vienna and Frankfurt; Schwetzingen Festival in 1975 as Belmonte; Deutsche Oper Berlin from 1977; Sang Tamino at the 1981 Salzburg Festival; La Scala Milan in 1983 as Ferrando in Così fan tutte; Sang in Cavalli's L'Ormindo at the Hamburg Staatsoper 1984 and toured with the company to Japan; Stuttgart in 1984 as Don Ottavio in the newly restored opera house; Other roles include Fenton in Die Lustigen Weiber von Windsor, Lionel in Martha, Nemorino, Lensky and Almaviva in Il Barbiere di Siviglia; Many concert engagements and lieder recitals; Sang Idomeneo with the English Bach Festival at Covent Garden in 1990. *Recordings:* Jacquino in Fidelio; Cantatas by Bach, Fux and Scarlatti; Die Schöpfung by Haydn. *Address:* c/o Hamburgische Staatsoper, Grosse Theaterstrasse 34, 2000 Hamburg 36, Germany.

**WOHLHAUSER, René Claude;** Swiss composer; b. 24 March 1954, Zürich; two s. two d. *Education:* Basel Conservatory, Staatliche Musikhochschule, Freiburg with Klaus Huber, studied with Kazimierz Serocki, Mauricio Kagel, Herbert Brün, Heinz Holliger, Brian Ferneyhough. *Career:* works played by Arditti String Quartet, Basel, Biel and Luzern Symphony Orchestras, also at Schweizer Tonkünstlerfeste and Int. Darmstädter Ferienkurse für Neue Musik, Notre Dame de Paris, Toronto, Newcastle, Baku, Klangforum Wien and Schauspielhaus Berlin; portraits and works on radio programmes; lectures on musical and philosophical aspects of his works at Darmstadt, Winterthur and Basel; founder, Komponistenforum Basel and co-founder of Adesso, contemporary music of independently published composers. *Compositions include:* Duometrie for flute and bass clarinet 1985–86, Adagio assai for string quartet 1982–88, In statu mutandi for orchestra 1991–93, Vocis Imago for flute, clarinet, percussion, piano, violin and cello 1993–95, Gantenbein (opera) 2002–04. *Recordings:* Wer den Gesang nicht kennt, Drei Stücke für Klavier, Portrait. *Address:* Schillerstrasse 5, 4053 Basel, Switzerland.

**WOLF, Gerd;** Singer (Bass); b. 18 April 1940, Floha, Saxony, Germany. *Education:* Studied at the Berlin Musikhochschule. *Career:* Debut: Dresden Radesbeul in 1970 as the Hermit in Der Freischütz; Sang at Dresden and elsewhere in East Germany until 1982, Berlin Staatsoper from then as Mozart's Osmin, Leporello and Bartolo, Nicolai's Falstaff, Bett in Zar und Zimmerman, Geronimo in Il Matrimonio Segreto and the Doctor in Wozzeck; Guest appearances in Leipzig, Karlsruhe and with the Berlin Staatsoper company at Naples, Messina, Prague, Bratislava, Japan and Netherlands; Season 2000–01 in Berlin as Mozart's Bartolo and Kuno in Der Freischütz. *Recordings include:* Pfitzner's Palestrina; Graf Mirabeau by Siegfried Matthus; Ariadne auf Naxos. *Address:* Deutsche Staatsoper Berlin, Unter den Linden 7, 1086 Berlin, Germany.

**WOLF, Markus,** DipMus; violinist and violist; b. 28 May 1962, Vienna, Austria; two s. *Education:* Wiener Musikhochschule with Edith Bertschinger and Guenter Pichler, studied with Max Rostal in Klagenfurt and Bern, masterclasses with Nathan Milstein and Oscar Shumsky. *Career:* debut, Wiener Musikverein 1976, Wigmore Hall, London 1987, Suntory Hall, Tokyo 1990, Carnegie Hall (Weill Hall), New York 1996; violist, string trio with brothers Reinhold and Peter Wolf 1973–; appearances with the Alban Berg Quartet 1986; violinist, asst of Guenter Pichler, Wiener Musikhochschule 1983–89; Principal Concertmaster, Wiener Symphoniker 1987–88, Bavarian State Opera in Munich 1989–; guest leader, London Symphony Orchestra 1997–2002; founder, Beethoven Trio Wien 1981; mem. and teacher, Junge Muenchner Philharmonie 1999–2002; teacher, Richard Strauss Conservatory, Munich 2000–. *Recordings:* Mozart with Alban Berg Quartet, Tchaikovsky, Beethoven, Mendelssohn, Mozart, Schubert, Dvořák, Smetana, Suk, Mahler, Schoenberg and Korngold with Beethoven Trio Wien, Webern with Jérôme Granjon, Wagner with Wolfgang Sawallisch, Schoenberg with Zubin Mehta, Mendelssohn with Munich Youth Orchestra. *Address:* Bayerisches Staatsorchester München, Max Joseph Platz 2, 80539 Munich, Germany.

**WOLF, R. Peter;** Musicologist and Harpsichordist; b. 5 Dec. 1942, Washington DC, USA. *Education:* AB, Harvard University, 1965; MPhil, 1969; PhD, 1977, Yale University; Studied harpsichord with Gustav Leonhardt at Amsterdam Conservatorium, 1965–66 and with Ralph Kirkpatrick at Yale School of Music, 1966–70. *Career:* Debut: Carnegie Recital Hall, NY, 1975; Numerous concerts as harpsichord soloist and continuo player; Musician-in-Residence, NC State University, Raleigh; 2 television shows, NC Educational Network, 1972; Instructor in Music, SUNY, Stony Brook, 1972–78; Assistant Professor of Music, University of Utah, 1978–80, and at Rutgers University, 1980–85; Editor, Brouda Brothers Ltd, 1985–89; Director of Development, Hoboken Chamber Orchestra, 1989–; Member of Bowers-Wolf Duo, Salt Lake Chamber Ensemble, Apollo's Banquet, and New York Baroque. *Recordings:* Telemann's Instrumental Chamber Music with Concertmasters Ensemble; Private recording of works by Rameau, J. S. Bach, C. P. E. Bach; Violin Sonatas by Biber, 1681, with Sonya Monosoff and Judith Davidoff. *Publications include:* Joint Editor, ms Bauyn, New York; Editor, Rameau, Les Paladins, New York and Paris; Editor, facsimile edition of Rameau, Les Paladins, 1986. *Contributions:* The Scriblerian; Actes; Colloque International Rameau, Dijon, 1983; The Musical Quarterly; Journal of The American Musical Instrument Society; Recherches; Early Music; Journal of The American Musicological Society. *Address:* 37A Phelps Avenue, New Brunswick, NJ 08901, USA.

**WOLF, Reinhold (Michael);** Violinist; b. 23 May 1956, Vienna, Austria. *Education:* Piano lessons at age 6; 1st Violin instruction at Wiener Musikakademie at age 8, later chamber music lessons with Alban Berg Quartet; Kuenstlerische Diplompruefung mit Auszeichnung, 1976; Violin studies with G Poulet in Paris and Max Rostal in Cologne; Chamber music with Amadeus Quartet; Konzert-Examen mit Auszeichnung Cologne, 1981. *Career:* Established the Wolf Trio with brothers Markus on Viola and Peter on Violoncello; Concertmaster, World Youth Orchestra with L Bernstein at Tanglewood, USA at age 18; Concertmaster, Orchestra of the Deutsche Oper Berlin, 1982–; Soloist with various European orchestras; Appeared as Double Concerto partner of H Szeryng with Vienna Symphony Orchestra; Established ensemble, Contraste in Berlin, 1989. *Honours:* Special Prize, Jeunesse Musicales Austria for the Wolf Trio, 1973; 1st Prize as Soloist, Jugend Musiziert Competition, Austria, 1975. *Address:* c/o Deutsche Oper Berlin, Orchesterdirektion, Richard Wagnerstrasse 10, 10585 Berlin, Germany.

**WOLF, Sally;** Singer (Soprano); b. 1957, USA. *Career:* Santa Fe Opera from 1982, as the Queen of Night, in the premiere of Eaton's The Tempest (1985) and in Sallinen's The King goes forth to France; Has sung the Queen of Night throughout North America, at Covent Garden (1986) and with Opera North at Leeds (1987); Seattle Opera, 1992, as Lucia di Lammermoor, Netherlands Opera, 1990, as Constanze, and San Francisco, 1991, as Giunia in Mozart's Lucio Silla; Other roles include Eternita in La Calisto (at Santa Fe), Gilda, Violetta and Oscar; Sang Donna Anna at the 1996 Munich Festival and Mozart's Queen of Night at Los Angeles, 1998; Season 1999–2000 as Donna Elvira in Los Angeles, Amalia in Verdi's Masnadieri at Carnegie Hall and Mme Cortese in Il Viaggio a Reims at the New York City Opera. *Address:* Santa Fe Opera, PO Box 2408, Santa Fe, NM 87504, USA.

**WOLFF, Beverly;** Singer (Mezzo-Soprano); b. 6 Nov. 1928, Atlanta, Georgia, USA. *Education:* Studied with Sidney Dietch and Vera McIntyre at The Academy of Vocal Arts in Philadelphia. *Career:* Debut: Sang Dinah in a television production of Bernstein's Trouble In Tahiti, 1952; Has sung with the New York City Opera from 1958, with debut as Dinah; Appeared on NBC television in the premiere of Menotti's Labyrinth, 1963; Stage engagements in Mexico City, Cincinnati, Boston, Houston, Washington and San Francisco as Carmen, Adalgisa, Cherubino, Kabanicha in Katya Kabanova, Radamisto, Dalila and Sesto in Handel's Giulio Cesare; Concert appearances as Dalila and Sesto; Sang in the Premieres of Douglas Moore's Carrie Nation in 1966 and Menotti's The Most Important Man in 1971; Concert appearances with leading American orchestras. *Recordings:* Roberto Devereux by Donizetti; Rossini's La Pietra del Paragone; Giulio Cesare. *Honours:* Winner, Youth Auditions, Philadelphia, 1952.

**WOLFF, Christian;** Composer; b. 8 March 1934, Nice, France. *Education:* Influenced by John Cage, Morton Feldman and Earle Brown after moving to the USA; Studied classics at Harvard, PhD in 1963. *Career:* Taught at Harvard University, 1962–76; Teacher of Classics and Music at Dartmouth College from 1976; Strauss Professor of Music, Professor of Classics, Dartmouth College, New Hampshire, USA. *Compositions include:* Nine for Ensemble, 1951; Suite for Prepared Piano, 1954; Duo for Pianists 1 and ll, 1957–58; Music For Merce Cunningham, 1959; Duo for Violin and Piano, 1961; Summer for String Quartet, 1961; In Between Pieces for 3 players, 1963; Septet, 1964; Quartet for 4 Horns, 1966; Elec Spring I–III, 1966–67; Toss for 8 or more players, 1968; Snowdrop for Harpsichord, 1970; Burdocks for 1 or more Orchestras or 5 or more Players, 1971; Accompaniments, 1972; Lines for String Quartet, 1972; Changing The System, 1973; Exercises 1–24, 1973–84; Wobbly Music for Mixed Chorus and Instruments, 1976; Bread And Roses for Piano and for Violin, 1976; Dark As A Dungeon for Clarinet, 1977, for Trombone and Double Bass, 1977; The Death Of Mother Jones for Violin, 1977; Stardust Pieces for Cello and Piano, 1979; Isn't This A Time for Saxophone, 1981; Eisler Ensemble Pieces, 1983; Piano Song–I Am A Dangerous Woman, 1983; Peace March 1–3, 1983–84; I Like To Think Of Harriet Tubman for Female Voice, Treble and Alto, 1984; Piano Trio, 1985; Bowery Preludes, 1986; Long Peace March, for chamber ensemble, 1987; From Leaning Forward, songs, 1988; Rosas, for piano and percussion, 1990; Ruth, for piano and trombone, 1991; Merce, for percussion ensemble, 1993; Two Pianists, 1994; Memory, octet, 1994; Percussionist Songs, 1995; Percussionist Dances, 1997; John, David, for orchestra, 1998; Pebbles for violin and piano, 1999; Cello Suite Variation, 2000. *Recordings:* For Ruth Crawford; Stones; Bread and Roses; I Like to Think of Harriet Tubman. *Publications:* Cues: Writing and Conversations, book, 1998. *Honours:* John Cage Award for Music, 1996; Fromm Foundation Commissioning Grant, 1998. *Address:* 104 South Main Street, Hanover, NH 03755, USA.

**WOLFF, Hugh;** American conductor; b. 21 Oct. 1953, Paris; m. Judith Kogan; three s. *Education:* Harvard Univ. *Career:* Musical Dir New Jersey Symphony 1985–92; Prin. Conductor Saint Paul Chamber Orchestra 1988–92, Musical Dir 1992–2000; Prin. Conductor Frankfurt Radio Symphony Orchestra 1997–; regularly guest-conducts the major orchestras in N America and Europe. *Current Management:* Van Walsum Management Ltd, 4 Addison Bridge Place, London, W14 8XP, England. *Telephone:* (20) 7371-4343. *Fax:* (20) 7371-4344. *Website:* www.vanwalsum.co.uk.

**WOLFF, Jean-Claude;** Composer; b. Oct. 1946, Paris, France. *Education:* Studied Composition, Analysis, History of Music, at L'Ecole Normale de Musique de Paris, then at Conservatoire National Supérieur de Musique de Paris with Henri Dutilleux, Jean-Pierre Guezec, Michel Philippot, Ivo Malec; Electro-acoustic classes with Jean-Etienne Marie, Centre International de Recherches Musicales; Spent 3 summers following Composition courses with Franco Donatoni, Accademia Chigiana, Siena, Italy; Laureate, Académie de France, Rome (Villa Medici), 1978–80. *Compositions include:* About 40 works performed at various festivals and concerts of contemporary music in France

(Radio-France, International Musical Weeks in Orleans, Angers Music Festival, Contemporary Music Meetings at Metz) and abroad in Italy, Switzerland, Denmark, Spain, Netherlands; For several years has concentrated mainly on chamber music; Working on four pieces for piano solo or with violin or violoncello; Symphony for voices and large orchestra. *Honours:* 1st Prize, Vienna Modern Masters, 1991. *Address:* 39 rue Bouret, 75019 Paris, France. *E-mail:* jeanclaude.wolff@free.fr.

**WOLFF, Marguerite,** OBE; British concert pianist; b. 1930, London, England; m. Derrick Moss (deceased); two d. *Education:* Royal Acad. of Music with Thomas Khatt, Trinity Coll. of Music with Gertrude Agulkyi, studied with pianist, Louis Kentner. *Career:* soloist, London Symphony Orchestra, Royal Philharmonic Orchestra, Philharmonia, Bournemouth and Birmingham Orchestras; radio and television broadcasts with major orchestras; toured worldwide, including 12 tours of Far East (Nepal, India, Malaysia, Indonesia, Singapore, Hong Kong), nine tours of Africa, 14 tours of South America, four tours of Canada, numerous performances in Europe and the USA; Vice-Pres. Chopin Soc. *Recordings:* Bliss Piano Sonata, Liszt Society Recording, Wright Society Liszt recording. *Honours:* Hon. FTCL; American Liszt Soc. Award 2000, UK Award for Music Naples 2001. *Address:* Flat T, 82 Portland Place, London, W1B 1NS, England (home). *Telephone:* (20) 7436-5501 (home). *Fax:* (20) 7436-5502 (home). *E-mail:* margueritewolff@amserve .com (home).

**WOLLENBERG, Susan L. F.,** BA, MA, DPhil; British teacher; *Reader in Music, Oxford University;* b. 28 April 1949, Lancashire, England; m. L. Wollenberg; one s. one d. *Education:* Withington Girls' School, Manchester, Royal Northern Coll. of Music, Lady Margaret Hall, Oxford. *Career:* Clara Sophie Deneke Music Scholar, Lady Margaret Hall 1966–69; Halstead Postgraduate Scholar, Faculty of Music, Oxford 1969–72; Univ. Lecturer in Music, Faculty of Music, Oxford 1972–2002, Reader in Music 2002–; Fellow and Tutor in Music, Lady Margaret Hall 1972–; Lecturer in Music, Brasenose Coll., Oxford 1987–; mem. Royal Musical Asscn, Oxford Architectural and Historical Soc. *Compositions include:* The Survivor (song cycle). *Publications:* Music at Oxford in the 18th and 19th Centuries, Concert Life in 18th-Century Britain (ed. with S. McVeigh); contrib. to New Grove Dictionary of Music and Musicians, Oxford Dictionary of National Biography, various musical journals. *Address:* 131 Eynsham Road, Botley, Oxford, OX2 9BY, England (home). *Telephone:* (1865) 276125 (office). *Fax:* (1865) 276128 (office). *E-mail:* office@music.ox.ac.uk (office).

**WOLOVSKY, Leonardo;** Singer (Bass-Baritone); b. 1922, York, Pennsylvania, USA. *Education:* Studied at Oberlin College, Ohio. *Career:* Sang at first in concert then appeared with Maria Callas in Norma at Catania, 1952; Engaged at Wiesbaden Opera, 1953–57, Nuremberg, 1957–73; Guest appearances at Frankfurt, 1959–73, Bayerische Staatsoper Munich, 1961–69, Hanover, 1961–73, Hamburg, 1956–60; Sang also at Graz, Essen, Amsterdam, Zürich, Paris, Barcelona and Athens; Bielefeld 1988, as Simon Mago in Nerone by Boito; Other roles have included Enrico (Lucia di Lammermoor); Oroveso, King Philip, Nabucco, the Dutchman, Hans Sachs, the Wanderer in Siegfried and Boris Godunov; Concert repertoire included Beethoven's Ninth, the Verdi Requiem and Bach's Christmas Oratorio. *Address:* St ädtische Buhnen, Brunnenstrasse 3, 48000 Berlin 1, Germany.

**WOLPE, Michael,** MA; Israeli composer; b. 4 March 1960, Tel-Aviv. *Education:* Rubin Acad., Jerusalem, Univ. of Cambridge. *Career:* founder regional music school, Sdeh Boker kibbutz; teacher, High School of Sciences and the Arts 1991–; Rumin Acad., Jerusalem 1996–; Head of Music Dept, Israeli Arts and Sciences Acad. 1999–; founder and Artistic Dir, Sounds in the Desert festival. *Compositions include:* Capella Kolot 1988, Stabat Mater 1994, Concerto for flutes and orchestra 1995, Trio 1996, Songs of Memory 1998, Hatarat Nedarim 2002, Songs of the Land (cycle of symphonic poems), Kaprisma Nos 1–9 for the Jerusalem Ensemble Kaprisma. *Recordings:* Kaprisma No. 8. *Address:* c/o Israeli Arts and Sciences Academy, Massuah Road, Jerusalem 96408, Israel (office).

**WOLVERTON, Joseph;** Singer (tenor); b. 1970, Chicago, USA. *Education:* Juilliard School, New York; American Conservatory of Music, Chicago. *Career:* Appearances with Minnesota Opera as Alfredo, Leicester in Maria Stuarda and Mozart's Ferrando for Chautauqua Opera, and Bellini's Pollione with Toledo Opera; Faust and Hoffmann for Michigan Opera, Edgardo and Riccardo (Ballo in Maschera) at Knoxville, the Duke of Mantua at Seattle, and Pinkerton for New York City Opera; European engagements as Nemorino at Hamburg, Werther in Malaga and Pinkerton for Dublin Opera; Concerts include Beethoven's Ninth and Missa Solemnis, Berlioz Requiem, Mahler's Eighth and the Verdi Requiem; Season 2001–2002 as Cavaradossi at Brussels, Nemorino at Montreal and the Duke for Tulsa Opera; Other roles include Macduff, Rinuccio in Gianni Schicchi, Turiddu, and Mascagni's Silvano. *Current Management:* Athole Still International Management, Forresters Hall, 25–27 Westow Street, London, SE19 3RY, England. *Telephone:* (20) 8771-5271. *Fax:* (20) 8768-6600. *Website:* www.atholestill.com.

**WONG, Randall Kevin,** BMus, MMus, DMusA; American singer (male soprano, countertenor); b. 10 April 1955, Oakland, CA. *Education:* Stanford Univ., San Francisco State Univ. *Career:* opera debut, Bernabei's Ascanio, Teatro Olimpico, Vicenza, Italy; San Francisco Opera; NY City Opera; Houston Grand Opera in Harvey Milk; Houston Grand Opera in Monk's Atlas; JC Bach's Endimione at the Carmel Bach Festival and Jommelli's Demofoonte at the Schwetzingen Festival; mem, AGMA; NARAS. *Recordings:* Hasse's

Cleofide; Meredith Monk's Atlas; Wallace and Korie's Harvey Milk; Wallace and Korie's Kabbalah; Solo soprano cantatas of Vivaldi; Classical music composed by computer. *Publications:* Barbara Strozzi entry in Women Composers: Music Through The Ages vol. 2, GK Hall & Co, 1996. *Honours:* NY Dance and Performance Award, 1997; Recipient of the California Arts Council Touring Grant, 1986–. *Current Management:* c/o Donald Osborne, California Artists Management, 564 Market Street, Suite 420, San Francisco, CA 94104, USA. *Telephone:* (415) 362-2787. *Fax:* (415) 362-2838. *E-mail:* don@ calartists.com.

**WOOD, Hugh;** Composer; b. 27 June 1932, Parbold, Lancashire, England. *Education:* Studied at Oxford University and in London with W S Lloyd Webber; Further study with Anthony Milner, Iain Hamilton and Matyas Seiber. *Career:* Professor of Harmony at the Royal Academy of Music, 1962–65; Teacher at Morley College, 1958–67; Research Fellow in Composition, Glasgow University, 1966–70; Lecturer in Music, Liverpool University, 1971–73 and at Cambridge University from 1976; Talks on BBC Radio 3; Piano Concerto premiered at the 1991 Promenade Concerts. *Compositions:* Songs For Springtime for Chorus and Piano, 1954; Suite for Piano, 1956; String Quartet, 1957; Variations for Viola and Piano, 1958; Laurie Lee Songs, 1959; Songs To Poems By Christopher Logue, 1961; Trio for Flute, Viola and Piano, 1961; String Quartet No. 1, 1962; Scenes From Comus for Soprano, Tenor and Chorus, 1965; 3 Choruses, 1966; Songs To Poems By D H Lawrence, 1966; Capriccio for Organ, 1967; Quintet for Clarinet, Horn and Piano Trio, 1967; The Horses, song cycle, 1967; The Rider Victory, song cycle, 1968; Cello Concerto, 1969; String Quartet No. 2, 1970; Chamber Concerto, 1971; Violin Concerto, 1972; 2 Choruses, 1973; Songs To Poems By Robert Graves, 1973; Songs To Poems By Pablo Neruda for High Voice and Chamber Orchestra, 1973; String Quartet No. 4, 1978; Symphony, 1979–82; Piano Trio, 1984; Comus Quadrilles, 1988; Horn Trio, 1987–89; Cantata for Chorus and Orchestra, 1989; Marina for High Voice and Ensemble, 1989; Piano Concerto, 1990; Funeral Music (brass quintet), 1992; String Quartet No. 3, 1993; Poem, for violin and piano, 1993; The Kingdom of God, anthem, 1994; Variations for orchestra, 1997; Clarinet Trio, 1997; Greek Songs, 1998; Serenade and Elegy for string quartet and orchestra, 1999; String Quartet No. 5, 2001. *Address:* c/o Churchill College, Cambridge CB 3 ODS, England.

**WOOD, James (Peter);** Composer, Conductor and Percussionist; b. 27 May 1953, Barton-on-Sea, Hampshire, England; m. Penny Irish, 25 June 1977, 1 s., 1 d. *Education:* Radley College, 1966–71; ARCO, 1969; FRCO, 1971; Sidney Sussex College, Cambridge, 1972–75; BA, Music, 1975; Studied with Nadia Boulanger in Paris, 1971–72; RAM, 1975–76. *Career:* Conductor, Schola Cantorum of Oxford, 1977–81; Founder and Conductor of New London Chamber Choir, 1981; Professor of Percussion, Internationale Ferienkurse, Darmstadt, 1982–; Regular radio and television appearances; Artistic Adviser to Percussion Foundation and Percussion 88 and 90 Festivals; Founder and Director, Centre for Microtonal Music, 1990–; Director of Barbican's Annual Weekend of Microtonal Music. *Compositions include:* Phaedrus; Oreion, BBC Symphony Orchestra commission, premiered at 1989 Promenade Concerts; Stoicheia, Darmstadt commission; Ho Shang Yao; T'ien Chung Yao; Choroi Kaithaliai; Spirit Festival With Lamentations; Village Burial With Fire; Incantamenta; The Parliament of Angels, for 18 instruments, 1995; Children at a Funeral, for prepared piano, 1996; The Parliament of Angels, 1996; Séance, 1996; Mountain Language, 1998; Jodo, 1999; Journey of the Magic, 2000. *Recordings include:* Stoicheia; Music for Percussion and Voices; Stravinsky's Les Noces and other choral works; Bergman's Choral Works; 15th Century Flemish Choral Works, 2 records. *Contributions:* A New System for Quarter-Tone Percussion, in Musical Times and Percussive Notes. *Honours:* Lili Boulanger Prize, 1975; Lili Boulanger Memorial Award, 1980; Holst Foundation Award, 1995. *Current Management:* Colin Boyle. *Address:* Bancroft, Rectory Lane, Fringford, Bicester, Oxfordshire OX6 9DX, England.

**WOOD, Jeffrey (Neal);** Composer and University Professor; b. 3 Oct. 1954, Allentown, Pennsylvania, USA; 1 s. *Education:* BMus, Oberlin College Conservatory of Music, 1976; MMus, 1978, MA, 1980, PhD, 1982, State University of New York, Stony Brook. *Career:* Visiting Lecturer, University of New Mexico, Albuquerque, New Mexico Institute of Mining and Technology, 1983–84, Austin Peay State University, Clarksville, TN, 1984–. *Compositions:* Duo for Cello and Piano, 1982 (recorded); In Memoriam Magistri for Brass Quintet, 1982; Sonata for Cello and Piano, 1984; String Quartet No. 2, 1985; MCMXIV for Tenor and Piano, 1985; Now The Most High Is Born, 1985; Trio-Sonata for Cello, Piano and Percussion, 1986; The Dream Of The Rood for Tenor Solo, Chorus and Organ, 1986; Swifts for Violin and Cello, 1986; First Essay for Orchestra, 1986; Music for Concert Band, 1987; Comedies for Woodwind Quintet, 1988; Quartet for Flute, Violin, Cello and Piano, 1988; Lay Your Sleeping Head My Love for Soprano, Tenor and Piano, 1987; Kreigeslieder for Mezzo-Soprano and Piano, 1988; Time Let Me Hail And Climb for Chorus, Brass Quintet and Piano, 1990; The Killing for Tenor and Piano, 1989; Four Deadly Serious Songs for Baritone and Piano, 1990; Ballads For The Goodly Fere for Voice and Piano, 1991; Dances for 2 Pianos, 1992; Preludes for Piano Solo, 1992; Ghosts for Clarinet, Viola and Piano, 1993. *Recordings:* Comedies, by Quintet of the Americas, 1991. *Contributions:* In Theory Only, vol. 7, 1983. *Current Management:* Broadcast Music Inc. *Address:* Department of Music, Austin Peay State University, Clarksville, TN 37044, USA.

**WOODLAND, Rae,** FRSA; British singer (soprano) and teacher of singing; *President, Aldeburgh Music Club;* b. 1930, Nottingham, England; d. of Arthur Woodland; m. Denis Stanley 1950. *Education:* Opera School, London and private studies with Roy Henderson, Joan Cross and Vittorio Gui. *Career:* debut, Sadler's Wells Theatre, as Queen of the Night in Mozart's Magic Flute; notable appearances include Covent Garden debut in Sonnambula 1965, sang Diana in the Olympians at the Royal Festival Hall, soloist in the first performance of Angels of the Mind at Lancaster Univ., sang Handel's Messiah at Church of the Nativity, Bethlehem, sang in the productions of The Unknown Island for the Royal Festival Ballet and La Fête Étrange for the Royal Ballet, sang in Der Rosenkavalier at Glyndebourne before announcing her retirement from public performances; numerous broadcasts with the BBC; roles include Venus in Tannhäuser, Naiade in Ariadne auf Naxos, Fiordiligi in Così fan Tutte, Odabella in Attila, Electra in Idomeneo, Giselda in I Lombardi, Mimi in La Bohème, Donna Anna and Donna Elvira in Don Giovanni, Constanze in Entführung, Luisa in Luisa Miller, Marguerite in Mefistofele, Mistress Ford in Falstaff, Helmwige in Walküre, Flower Maiden in Parsifal, Female Chorus in Rape of Lucretia, Lady Billows in Albert Herring, Miss Jessel in Turn of the Screw, Eugenie in Nicholas Maw's Rising of the Moon, Frau III in Von Einem's Visit of the Old Lady, Guinone in The Return of Ulysses, Dama in Macbeth, roles in Il Trovatore, Aida; performances with opera companies including Scottish Opera, WNO, ENO, Glyndebourne Festival Opera, Sadler's Wells, Royal Opera Covent Garden, and several companies world-wide; numerous appearances at festivals, including Glyndebourne, Aix-en-Provence, Amsterdam, Edinburgh, Aldeburgh, Rome, Wiesbaden, Antwerp, Geneva, Lyon, Bergen, Brussels, Three Choirs Festival; Prof. of Singing, Royal Acad. of Music, London; vocal consultant, Britten Pears School, Snape; guest lecturer in Edinburgh, the Univs of Aberdeen, East Anglia and Nottingham; international adjudicator and examiner, Royal Acad. of Music, Guildhall School of Music, Royal Northern Coll. of Music, Royal Welsh School of Music, Trinity Coll. and the Royal Scottish Acad. of Music; adviser to Arts Council of Great Britain, Eastern Arts; Patron of Erin Arts; mem. Music Panel of the English Speaking Union, Aldeburgh Music Club (Pres.), Royal Acad. of Music Guild, Asscn of Teachers of Singing, Incorporated Soc. of Musicians, Equity, Asscn of English Singers and Speakers, WOY, WI. *Recordings include:* Messiah (John Tobin-Handel Soc.), Arthur Bliss's Birthday, Midsummer Night's Dream (Haitink), Montezuma (by Gunn, Bonynge), Idomeneo (Davis), Mahler No. 2 (Stokowski), Glyndebourne Macbeth and Ritorno d'Ulisse, The Queen of Night (BBC Proms), Glyndebourne Angels of the Mind, Sir Arthur Bliss, Shostakovich's Symphony No. 14, op 135 (Rudolf Schwarz and Northern Sinfonia), Rameau's Hippolyte et Aricie (Anthony Lewis), Ivor Novello Glamorous Night, ROUT – Sir Arthur Bliss' 80th Birthday, Attila-Verdi-Matheson The Dancing Years (Novello), 150 live broadcasts for BBC. *Honours:* Hon. RAM 1986; Opera School Classics Prize and Award 1959. *Address:* Brackendale, Priory Lane, Snape, Saxmundham, Suffolk IP17 1SD, England (home). *Telephone:* (1728) 688610 (home). *E-mail:* raewoodlandsnape@aol.com (home). *Website:* www.impulse-music.co .uk/woodland.htm.

**WOODROW, Alan;** Canadian singer (tenor); b. 1952, Toronto. *Education:* Royal Conservatory, Toronto and London Opera Centre. *Career:* sang with ENO from 1976 as Pedrillo, Don Ottavio, Froh (Das Rheingold), Lindoro, Vasek, Monostatos, Canio, Hermann, Don José, Edmund in Reimann's Lear and Walther von Stolzing; season 1992–93 as the Prince in The Love of Three Oranges, the Captain in Wozzeck, Herod in Salome and Siegmund in Die Walküre; has also sung Sergei in Lady Macbeth of Mtsensk at La Scala and the Bastille, Paris; season 1998 as Tannhäuser at Naples and Huon in Oberon at the Barbican Hall, London; concert engagements in Canada with the Mozart and Verdi Requiems, The Choral Symphony and Mahler's Eighth, A Mass of Life by Delius, Kodály's Psalmus Hungaricus; season 1999–2000 as Don José for ENO, Siegfried in The Ring at the Tyrol Festival, and Strauss's Emperor for the Munich Staatsoper; Bacchus in Naples, Peter Grimes at Aldeburgh and in Henze's Venus and Adonis, at Toronto; season 2004–05 as Siegfried in Gotterdammerung at Liège and Seattle, as Bacchus in Ariadne auf Naxos at Trieste, as Herodes in Salome at Palermo, and in the title role in Guntram at Catania; sang role of Siegfried in The Ring at Amazonas Opera Festival, Brazil 2005. *Recordings include:* Siegfried and Götterdämmerung (from the Tyrol Festival). *Current Management:* Athole Still International Management, Forresters Hall, 25–27 Westow Street, London, SE19 3RY, England. *Telephone:* (20) 8771-5271. *Fax:* (20) 8768-6600. *Website:* www .atholestill.com.

**WOODS, Elaine;** Singer (Soprano); b. 1958, Lancashire, England. *Education:* Studied at Oxford University and at the Royal Manchester College of Music with Elsie Thurston; Further study with Marjorie Thomas. *Career:* Debut: With Kent Opera as Violetta in 1979 at the Edinburgh Festival; Sang in Handel's Tolomeo at the Batigniano Festival in Italy, 1980; German debut in 1981 as Mimi in Mannheim; Bremen Opera from 1982 as Fiordigili, Tatiana, Eva, Liu and the Countess in Capriccio; In 1983 sang in JC Bach's Lucio Silla in Frankfurt and Acis and Galatea at Karlsruhe; Appeared as Pamina at the 1986 Bregenz Festival and sang Belinda in a new production of Dido and Aeneas at Frankfurt; With Welsh National Opera has sung Donna Elvira, Fiordigili and Mozart's Countess; Concert repertoire includes the Verdi and Mozart Requiems, Haydn's Creation and Seasons, Messiah and Beethoven's Missa Solemnis and Ninth Symphony. *Honours:* Prizewinner at the 1978 's-Hertogenbosch Competition. *Current Management:* Ingpen & Williams Ltd, 7 St George's Court, 131 Putney Bridge Road, London, SW15 2PA, England.

**WOODS, Thomas;** Australian conductor; b. 1959, Tanzania. *Education:* Western Australian Conservatorium, Perth and with Vladimir Ponkin at the Gnessin Institute, Moscow. *Career:* Asst Conductor with West Australian Opera Company for productions of Don Pasquale and Madama Butterfly, 1982–93; Asst Chorus Master and Conductor at the Australian Opera, 1994–, leading Il Barbiere di Siviglia, A Midsummer Night's Dream, La Traviata and The Gondoliers; with La Fille du Régiment in Sydney, Il Barbiere in Sydney and La Traviata in Perth, 1997. *Honours:* Cultural Exchange Scholarship, 1989.

**WOODWARD, Donna,** AA, BMus; American singer and voice teacher; b. 2 June 1946, Baltimore, MD; m. Juergen Stadtmueller 1983. *Education:* Virginia Intermont Coll., Coll. Conservatory of Music, Univ. of Cincinnati, Univ. of Hamburg, Germany. *Career:* coloratura and lyric soubrette, Stadtheater Lucerne 1970, Staatstheater Darmstadt 1971–73, Stadttheater, Heidelberg 1973–75, Nationaltheater, Mannheim 1975–86; frequent guest in (National theater) Munich, Cologne, Karlsruhe and Stuttgart; freelance from 1986; appearances in Germany, Switzerland, France and Belgium; teacher of voice, Voice Dept Univ. of Mainz 1991–2001, Hochschule für Musik, Heidelberg/Mannheim 1992–97, private studio in Frankfurt, Germany 1999–; mem. Delta Omicron, NATS. *Recordings:* Rosalia in Karl von Dittersdorf's Doktor und Apotheker. *Honours:* Giorno Memorial Prize 1969, Corbett Foundation stipend for study in Europe 1969. *Address:* Auf der Weide 4A, 65550 Limburg, Germany; 1694 Wayah Drive, Charleston, SC, USA. *E-mail:* woodstadt@aol.com.

**WOODWARD, Roger Robert,** OBE, AC; Australian pianist, conductor and composer; b. 20 Dec. 1942, Sydney; s. of Francis W. Woodward and Gladys A. Woodward; one s. one d. *Education:* Conservatorium of Music, Sydney and PWSH, Warsaw. *Career:* debut at Royal Festival Hall, London 1970; subsequently appeared with the five London orchestras; has performed throughout Eastern and Western Europe, Japan and the USA; has appeared at int. festivals and with the major orchestras throughout world; extensive repertoire and is noted for interpretation of Chopin, Beethoven, Bach and Twentieth Century Music; Artistic Dir Nat. Chamber Orchestra for Contemporary Music in Australia 'Alpha Centaure' 1989 and festivals in London; performs each season at leading int. festivals works by contemporary composers; Nat. Treas. 1998; Fellow Chopin Inst., Warsaw 1976; Kt (Breffini) 1985. *Address:* LH Productions, 2/37 Hendy Avenue, Coogee, NSW 2034, Australia. *E-mail:* woodward@metz.une.edu.au.

**WOOF, Barbara;** Composer; b. 2 Sept. 1958, Sydney, New South Wales, Australia. *Education:* BMus (Hons), University of Sydney, 1981; Royal Conservatory, The Hague; Study with Peter Sculthorpe and Jan van Vlijman. *Career:* Faculty Member, Utrecht School of Arts, the Netherlands, 1988–; Resident Composer with the Sydney Symphony Orchestra, 1992. *Compositions include:* Maldoror, for violin, 1983; Caoine, for alto saxophone, 1985; Hymns and Melodies, for saxophone quartet, 1989; Soundings, for gamelan, 1990; Banshee's Dance, for orchestra, 1992; Night Crossing, for orchestra, 1993; Táragató-Ray, for chamber ensemble, 1998; Alchimien du verbe, for voice and chamber orchestra, 1999; Naxos revisited, for soprano and 4 channel tape, 2003; Traumland, for sporano and chamber orchestra, 2003. *Recordings:* Soundings, for Gamelan. *Honours:* Winner, Martin Codex Composition Competition, Spain, 1985. *Address:* c/o DONEMUS, Paulus Potterstraat 16, 1016-CZ Amsterdam, Netherlands.

**WOOLFENDEN, Guy (Anthony);** Composer and Conductor; b. 12 July 1937, Ipswich, England; m. Jane Aldrick, 29 Sept 1962, 3 s. *Education:* Westminster Abbey Choir School; Whitgift School; Christ's College, Cambridge; MA (Cantab); LGSM; FBSM; Honorary LCM. *Career:* Head of Music, Royal Shakespeare Company, Stratford-upon-Avon and London, composed more than 150 scores for this company, 1963–98; Also composed scores for Burgtheater, Vienna; Comédie Française, Paris; Teatro di Stabile, Genoa and National Theatre, Norway; Also for films, radio, television; Conducted concerts with most British Symphony Orchestras; Conducted concerts and ballet in Canada, Germany, Japan, USA, Hong Kong, and France; Conducted opera for BBC radio, television and 3 productions with Scottish Opera; Conductor of Birmingham Conservatoire Wind Orchestra; Arranged and composed music for four full-length ballets by choreographer André Prokovsky: Anna Karenina, The Three Musketeers, La Traviata and The Queen of Spades, all now in the repertory of the world's major companies; Conducted Russian premiere of Anna Karenina with Kirov Ballet in St Petersburg, 1993; Artistic Director, Cambridge Festival, 1986–91. *Compositions:* composed 3 musicals: Comedy of Errors for RSC; A Children's Opera, The Last Wild Wood Sector 88 with Adrian Mitchell; Works for the Concert Hall include: Concertos, Chamber Music and Several works for Symphonic Band; Bassoon Concerto, 1999. *Recordings:* Music for Royal Shakespeare Company; Music for The Winter's Tale; Songs of Ariel; Gallimaufry featuring the wind music of Guy Woolfenden; Sweet Swan of Avon; Video: The Comedy of Errors, Antony and Cleopatra, Macbeth. *Address:* Malvern House, Sibford Ferris, Banbury, Oxon OX15 5RG, England.

**WOOLLAM, Kenneth Geoffrey;** British singer (tenor); b. 16 Jan. 1937, Chester, England; m. Phoebe Elizabeth Scrivenor; four d. *Education:* Chester Cathedral Choir School, Royal Coll. of Music. *Career:* debut, Sadler's Wells, London 1972; appearances with Royal Opera Copenhagen, Saul and David, David; Florestan in Frankfurt; ENO roles include Rienzi, Radames, Aida; sang with Scottish Opera, Royal Opera, Ghent, Opera du Nord, Warsaw Philharmonic Orchestra in various roles, including Walther in Die Meistersinger, Siegfried in The Ring, Laca in Jenůfa; sang Husband in world premiere of John Tavener's Gentle Spirit at Bath; three film appearances as Canio, Alfredo and Hoffmann; concerts and oratorios with leading socs; sang in the premieres of Hamilton's Royal Hunt of The Sun and Blake's Toussaint L'Ouverture 1977; Covent Garden debut 1988, as Aegisthus; Prof. of Singing, Royal Coll. of Music; vocal consultant to David Puttnam's film, Meeting Venus 1990; appointed vocal consultant to DeVlaamse Opera in Antwerp and Ghent, Belgium 1995; Pierre (War and Peace, Prokofiev); Tristan; mem. Incorporated Soc. of Musicians, Savage Club, Glass Circle. *Recordings:* Delius's Margot-La-Rouge, Berlioz's La Mort d'Orphée (conductor Jean Fournet) 1987, Songfest by Bernstein (TV), Elgar's Gerontius (BBC, conducted by Vernon Handley) 1987, Gurre-Lieder (televised Bergen Int. Festival), Herod in Salome (Edinburgh Festival) 1989. *Honours:* hon. mem. Royal Coll. of Music 1992. *Address:* 33 Marlborough Crescent, Bedford Park, Chiswick, London, W4 1HE, England.

**WOOLLETT, Elizabeth;** Singer (soprano); b. 13 March 1959, Hillingdon, Middlesex, England. *Education:* Studied at Royal Academy of Music from 1977. *Career:* Sang Magda in La Rondine and Irene in Donizetti's Belisario at the RAM; Opera North from 1984, as the Owl in The Cunning Little Vixen, Papagena, Kate Pinkerton, Mermaid in Oberon at Le Fenice, Venice, Anna in Intermezzo and Second Maid in the British premiere of Strauss's Daphne; Scottish Opera debut 1989, as Mozart's Susanna; Buxton festival, 1990, as Amenaide in Tancredi; Debut, Royal Opera House, Covent Garden, 1991, as Clorinda in La Cenerentola; Other roles include Adina (L'Elisir d'amore), Cherubino, Micaela, Bella (The Midsummer Marriage) and Despina; Isabella in L'Assedio di Calais by Donizetti for the Wexford Festival, 1991; Sang Weber's Agathe for Chelsea Opera Group, South Bank, 1997; Season 1998 as Musetta for ENO and Violetta for Castleward Opera; Has also sung for the BBC Radio 3 and has recorded works by Gilbert and Sullivan for TER records. *Honours:* Alec Redshaw Memorial Award. Grimsby, 1986. *Current Management:* Musicmakers International Artists Representation, Tailor House, 63–65 High Street, Whitwell, Hertfordshire SG4 8AH, England. *Telephone:* (1438) 871708. *Fax:* (1438) 871777. *E-mail:* musicmakers@compuserve.com. *Website:* www.operauk.com.

**WOOLLEY, Robert;** Harpsichordist and Organist; b. 8 Jan. 1954, London, England. *Education:* Royal College of Music 1970–75 with Ruth Dyson. *Career:* Harpsichordist, Organist, Member of the Purcell Quartet, debut concert at St John's Smith Square, London in 1984; Professor, The Royal College of Music; Extensive tours and broadcasts in France, Belgium, Netherlands, Germany, Austria, Switzerland, Italy and Spain; British appearances include four Purcell concerts at the Wigmore Hall, 1987, later broadcast on Radio 3; Tours of USA and Japan, 1991–92; Repertoire includes music on the La Folia theme by Vivaldi, Corelli, CPE Bach, Marais, Scarlatti, Vitali and Geminiani, instrumental songs by Purcell, music by Matthew Locke, John Blow and fantasias and airs by William Lawes, 17th century virtuoso Italian music by Marini, Buonamente, Gabrieli, Fontana, Stradella and Lonati, J. S. Bach and his forerunners Biber, Scheidt, Schenk, Reinken and Buxtehude; Many Concerts with other ensembles and as soloist. *Recordings include:* Complete Keyboard works of Henry Purcell; Solo recordings of Bach, Scarlatti, Frescobaldi, Couperin and Gibbons. *Address:* 11 Sterry Drive, Thames Ditton, Surrey KT 7 0YN, England.

**WOOLRICH, John;** Composer; b. 3 Jan. 1954, Cirencester, England. *Education:* English at Manchester University; Composition with Edward Cowie at Lancaster University. *Career:* Northern Arts Fellow in Composition at Durham University, 1982–85; Composer-in-Residence, National Centre for Orchestral Studies, 1985–86; Animateur of various educational and music-theatre projects; Visiting Lecturer and Composer-in-Residence, Goldsmiths College, London, 1987–88; Artistic Director, Composers Ensemble, 1989–; Tutor at Guildhall School of Music, 1990–91; Composition Teacher, Dartington Summer School, 1991–93; Professor, Stage Internacional de Musica de Cambra, 1992; Visiting Lecturer, Reading University, 1993; Lecturer, Royal Holloway University of London, 1994–98; Visiting Fellow, Clare Hall, Cambridge, 1999–2001. *Compositions include:* Four Songs After Hoffmann for Soprano and Clarinet, 1981; Spalanzani's Daughter for Instrumental Ensemble, 1983; Black Riddle for Soprano and Chamber Orchestra, 1984; The Barber's Timepiece for Orchestra, 1986; Dartington Doubles for Chamber Ensemble, 1988; Night Machines for Instrumental Ensemble, 1988; The Turkish Mouse for Soprano and Ensemble, 1988; Barcarolle for 6 Players, 1989; Lending Wings, 1989; The Ghost In The Machine, 1990; Berceuse, 1990; Quicksteps, 1990; The Death Of King Renaud, 1991; The Theatre Represents A Garden: Night, 1991; It Is Midnight, Dr Schweitzer, 1992; A Farewell, 1992; String Quartet, 1995; In the House of Crossed Desires, opera, 1996; Oboe concerto, 1996; String Trio, 1996; Cello Concerto, 1998; Little Walserings, for chorus, 1999; Accord, for mixed orchestra, 1999; Wind Sextet, 1999; A Shadowed Lesson, for piano and strings, 1999; Bitter Fruit for 16 players, 2000; Fanfarronda, for chamber orchestra, 2002; Watermark, for violin and bass clarinet, 2002; Good Morning-Midnight, five songs, for soprano and piano, 2002; Arcangelo Homage to Corelli, 2003. *Recordings:* Lending Wings; Ulysses Awakes; The Ghost In The Machine. *Honours:* Honorary Fellow, Trinity College, London, 1996. *Address:* c/o Faber Music Ltd, 3 Queen Square, London WC1N 3AU, England.

**WORDSWORTH, Barry;** Conductor; b. 20 Feb. 1948, Surrey, England. *Education:* Studied at the Royal College of Music, London; Conducting with Adrian Boult in London and harpsichord with Gustav Leonhardt in

Amsterdam. *Career:* Debut: Soloist in Frank Martin's Harpsichord Concerto at the Royal Opera House, for Kenneth Macmillan's ballet, Las Hermanas; Freelance conductor with the Royal Ballet, the Australian Ballet and the National Ballet of Canada (including performances at the Metropolitan, New York); Music Director of the BBC Concert Orchestra and the Brighton Philharmonic in 1989; Music Director of the Royal Ballet and the Birmingham Royal Ballet in 1991; Debut with the Royal Opera at Covent Garden with Carmen in 1991; Conducted the BBC Concert Orchestra at the 1991 Promenade Concerts; Piano Concerto by Bliss, Malcolm Arnold's Guitar Concerto, Vaughan Williams's 8th Symphony, and Act 3 of Sleeping Beauty; Conducted Last Night of The Proms, with the BBC Symphony Orchestra in 1993; Conducted New Queen's Hall Orchestra at the 1995 Proms; Raymond Gubay's Carmen at the Albert Hall, 1997; Poulenc's Les Biches and Roussel's 3rd Symphony at the 1999 London Proms; Conducted the BBC Concert Orchestra at the London Proms, 2002. *Recordings include:* Series of British music with the BBC Concert Orchestra, 1990–91. *Address:* ICM Artists, Oxford House, 76 Oxford Street, London W1R 1RB, England.

**WORKMAN, Charles;** Singer (Tenor); b. 1965, Arkansas, USA; m. Alexandra Harwood. *Education:* Studied at the Juilliard School, New York. *Career:* Appearances in operas by Mozart and Rossini at the New York Met, English National Opera, Geneva, Nice, Amsterdam and the Spoleto Festival; Further roles as Henn Smith in Bizet's Jolie Fille de Perth, Jupiter in Semele and Fenton in Falstaff; Season 1998 in Semele for Flanders Opera, as Giocondo in La Pietra del paragone at Garsington and Iago in Rossini's Otello at Pesaro; Season 1999–2000 as Alamar in Donizetti's Alahor in Granata, Ferrando at Ferrara and Monteverdi's Orfeo for the Munich Staatsoper; Don Ottavio at Salzburg, Cherubini's Anacréon in Venice and Belfiore in Il Viaggio a Reims, at La Coruña. *Recordings include:* Renaud in Gluck's Armide. *Address:* c/o Music International, 13 Ardilaun Road, London N5 2QR, England.

**WORTON-STEWARD, Andrew;** Composer, Organist and Lecturer; b. 20 Feb. 1948, Kent, England. *Education:* BA, DMus, Cincinnati Conservatory, USA, 1976; Diploma of Education; LLCM. *Career:* performances of own music world-wide including New York, Long Island, Milan, London, Manchester, Sydney, Australia; Music Adviser for Somerset Univ., England; recital tour on organ, Texas Gulf, USA, 1985, New York, 1986; concert of choral works, New York, 1986; BBC radio broadcast, 1987; concerts, Paris, 1987, Purcell Room, 1987; Organist at Holy Trinity, New York, 1987–88; commissions for Chichester Cathedral, 1987, Hove Festival, 1987, Hanover, 1988; Choral masterclass, Tallahassee, FL, USA, 1988; Organ recitals, St Thomas, and St James, New York, 1988; TVS documentary, Requiem, in the series Music Makers, 1989; course tutor and Lecturer, Open Univ.; ARCO. *Compositions (recorded):* Chamber Music, 1978; Soli 3, 1980; Via Crucis, 1983; My Eyes For Beauty Pine; Oecumuse. *Publications:* piano music published. *Address:* c/o White Lodge, 105 Pembroke Crescent, Hove, Sussex, England.

**WOSNITZA, Cornelia;** Singer (Soprano); b. 28 Nov. 1960, Dresden, Germany. *Education:* Studied at the Dresden Musikhochschule. *Career:* Sang Yniold in Pelléas and the Shepherd Boy in Tannhäuser at Dresden, 1979; Has appeared throughout Germany and in Russia, Amsterdam and elsewhere as Aennchen, Gretel, Blondchen, Norina, Susanna, Zerlina, Papagena and Musetta; Concert appearances in works by Bach, Handel, Mozart, Schumann, Strauss and Orff (Carmina Burana). *Honours:* Prizewinner at the 1981 Robert Schumann Competition at Zwickau and the 1985 Mozart Competition at Salzburg. *Address:* Dresden Staatsoper, Theaterplatz 2, 8010 Dresden, Germany.

**WOTTRICH, Endrik;** Singer (Tenor); b. 1964, Celle, Germany. *Education:* Studied both violin and voice in Würzburg with Ingeborg Hallstein, and in New York at the Juilliard School. *Career:* Debut: Wiesbaden, 1992, as Cassio in Otello; Berlin Staatsoper from 1993, as Tamino in Die Zauberflöte, Alfredo in La Traviata, Sänger in Rosenkavalier and Capriccio and Gernando in Haydn's L'isola disabitatà; Vienna Staatsoper, 1994, as Wagner's Steuermann and Théâtre du Châtelet, Paris, as Andres (Wozzeck) and in Fidelio, 1995–97; Bayreuth since 1996, as David in Die Meistersinger; Concerts include Verdi Requiem with Zubin Metha in Berlin; Das Lied von der Erde by Mahler, Matthäus Passion by Bach, Faustszenen by Schumann with Abbado and Harnoncourt; Season 1999–2000 as David at Bayreuth, Jacquino in Fidelio at La Scala and Don Carlos for Bonn Opera; Steuermann in Der fliegende Holländer at Chicago and Konrad in Hans Heiling for the Deutsche Oper, Berlin, 2001. *Recordings:* Many recordings including Braunfels's Die Vögel, Der Freischütz with Berlin Philharmonic (both Grammy nominated), Korngold, Ring des Polykrates, Kalman's Herzogin von Chicago as well as Beethoven's 9th Symphony. *Address:* Berlin Staatsoper, Unter den Linden 7, 1060 Berlin, Germany.

**WOYKE, Andreas;** Pianist; b. 28 April 1966, Siegen, Germany; m. Beate, 1 s., 1 d. *Education:* Jugendmusikschule Siegen, with Pál Molnar, Aldo Antognazzi, Julio Largacha, Siegfried Fiedler; Musikhochschule Cologne with Pavel Gililov; Musikhochschule Vienna, with Rudolf Kehrer. *Career:* Concerts in Germany at Philharmonie Cologne, Gasteig Munich, Tonhalle Düsseldorf; Concerts in Austria at Konzerthaus Vienna, Musikverein Vienna, Schloá Eggenberg Graz; Concerts throughout Europe and in USA, Canada, South Africa, Russia and Chile; Radio appearances in Germany, Austria, USA, Canada, South Africa; Television appearances in Germany, Switzerland and South Africa; mem, Studienstiftung des Deutschen Volkes, 1988–92. *Record-*

*ings:* Bach Concertos for 2, 3 and 4 pianos; Bremen Competition: Ginastera, Danzas Argentinas. *Honours:* First Prize, Bremen Piano Competition, 1987; First Prize, International Brahms Competition, Hamburg, Germany, 1992; Second Prize, UNISA-Transnet International Piano Competition, Pretoria, South Africa, 1996; First Prize, Knezkova-Hussey International Piano Competition, Bathurst, Canada, 1996. *Address:* Farmi 85, 8511 Greisdorf, Austria.

**WRAY, Steven (Donald);** Pianist; b. 10 June 1959, Bolton, Lancashire, England. *Education:* BA, Honours, Queen's College, Oxford, 1976–79; Private studies with Dorothea Law and Ruth Nye; International Summer Musical Academy at Salzburg, masterclasses with Hans Graf and Carmen Graf-Adnet, 1985–86; Further studies at Hochschule für Musik und Darstellende Kunst, Vienna. *Career:* Live Music Now! solo artist, 1985; Solo recital, Park Lane Group, Young Artists and Twentieth Century Music series, Purcell Room in London, 1988; Formation of duo with Czech violinist Tomas Tulacek in 1990; Concert and festival appearances, solo and duo recitals, and ensemble and concerto engagements in Austria, Czechoslovakia, Slovenia, the United Kingdom, Israel and Portugal. *Current Management:* Chameleon Arts Management. *Address:* 1 Brookes Court, Longley Road, London SW17 9LF, England.

**WRIGHT, Brian (James);** Conductor; b. 4 Aug. 1946, Tonbridge, Kent, England. *Education:* Gulbenkian Scholar, Guildhall School of Music; Guildhall School of Music; Studied with George Hurst and Jascha Horenstein; Munich Music Academy, Germany. *Career:* Debut: Royal Festival Hall, London, 1972 (Messiah); Professional singer (Tenor) with English Opera Group; Recitals Wigmore Hall 1971, Purcell Room 1972; Associate Conductor Goldsmith's Choral Union 1972; Musical Director 1973; Conductor Highgate Choral Society 1972; Assistant Conductor London Symphony Orchestra 1974–75; Conductor BBC Symphony Orchestra 1976–84; Berlioz Requiem 1982; Liszt's Christus, 1985–; guest Conductor with British orchestras: London Symphony (Mendelssohn 3, Sibelius 2); Philharmonia (Beethoven 6); Hallé (Brahms 2); Bournemouth Symphony (A Child of our Time, Verdi Requiem); Scottish National (Dvořák Requiem); Royal Liverpool Philharmonic (Hugh Wood Symphony); World and British premieres of works by Robert Simpson, Wilfred Josephs, Penderecki and Lutoslawski; First complete performance of Furtwängler's 3rd Symphony; Season 1988–89 conducted Tippett's Mask of Time on South Bank and Stravinsky's Pulcinella for BBC television; Season 1990 with the Bach B Minor Mass at the Barbican, the Verdi Requiem at the Festival Hall, and concerts with the RPO, BBC Symphony Orchestra and BBC National Orchestra of Wales; mem, ISM. *Honours:* Silver Medal, Cantelli Competition, Milan 1975. *Current Management:* Worldwide Artists. *Address:* c/o World-wide Artists, 6 Petersfield Crescent, Coulsdon, Surrey CR5 2JQ, England.

**WRIGHT, Peter,** MA; British organist and conductor; *President, Royal College of Organists;* b. Herts. *Education:* RCM with Richard Popplewell and Angus Morrison, Emmanuel Coll., Cambridge with Dame Gillian Weir, studied with Flor Peeters in Belgium. *Career:* mem. Royal Coll. of Organists from 1970, council mem. 1990–, Hon. Sec. 1997–2002, Chief Examiner 1997–2005, Vice-Pres. 2003–05, Pres. 2005–; apptd sub-organist Guildford Cathedral 1977; Prin. Conductor Guildford Chamber Choir 1984–1994, Surrey Festival Choir 1987–2001; organist and Dir of Music, Southwark Cathedral 1989–; numerous int. concerts and tours with Southwark Cathedral Choir, including performances at St Alban's Int. Organ Festival 2001, BBC Proms 2002. *Recording:* Augustin Barié, Organ Works. *Honours:* Hon. FGCM. *Address:* Royal College of Organists, Millennium Point, Curzon Street, Birmingham, B4 7XG, England (office). *E-mail:* admin@rco.org.uk (office). *Website:* www.rco.org.uk (office).

**WRIGHT, Peter Anthony,** BA, BMus, MA, PhD; musicologist; b. 14 April 1953, Vienna, Austria; m. Joanne Frew; two d. *Education:* Pembroke Coll., Oxford, Nottingham Univ. *Career:* freelance teacher and writer 1975–77, 1981–85; Lecturer, Exeter Univ. 1987–88; Lecturer, Nottingham Univ. 1988, Reader in Music 2000–; specialist in 15th-century music, especially source study; mem. Royal Musical Asscn (council 2001–04, cttee for Early English Church Music 2002–), American Musicological Soc., Plainsong and Mediaeval Music Soc., Royal Musical Asscn. *Publications:* The Related Parts of Trent, Museo Provinciale d'Arte, MSS 87 (1374) and 92 (1379) 1989, I codici musicali trentini 2 (ed.) 1996; contrib. to Early Music, Early Music History, Leading Notes, Music and Letters, Music and Musicians, Plainsong and Medieval Music, Revised New Grove Dictionary of Music and Musicians, Die Musik in Geschichte und Gegenwart. *Honours:* The Westrup Prize 1995. *Address:* Department of Music, University of Nottingham, University Park, Nottingham, NG7 2RD, England (office). *Telephone:* (115) 9514760 (office). *Fax:* (115) 9514756 (office). *E-mail:* p.a.wright@nottingham.ac.uk (office).

**WRIGHT, Rosemarie;** Concert Pianist; b. 12 Dec. 1931, Chorley, Lancashire, England; m. Michel Brandt, 28 Oct 1961, 2 s. *Education:* Royal Academy of Music, London; Staatsakademie, Vienna; Masterclasses with Edwin Fischer, Pablo Casals and Wilhelm Kempff. *Career:* Debut: Grosser Musikvereinssaal, Vienna, 1960; Concerts throughout Europe, USA, Far East, Australasia; Broadcasts world-wide; Concertos with London Philharmonic, Philharmonia, English Chamber Orchestra, London Mozart Players, BBC Orchestras, Vienna Symphony Orchestra, and Danish and French Radio; Professor of Piano: Royal Northern College of Music, Manchester, 1973–78, Royal Academy of Music, London, 1978–97; Pianist-in-Residence, Southampton University, 1972–80; mem, British Federation of Festivals for Music, Dance and Speech, Adjudicator. *Recordings:* Piano Music by Edward Macdowell; Vols 1, 2 and 3, and Double CD of Haydn Sonatas on 1799 Broadwood Fortepiano. *Honours:* Chappell Silver Medal, 1953; Tobias Matthay Fellowship, 1954; Haydn Prize, Vienna, 1959; Bösendorfer Prize, 1960. *Address:* 84 Filsham Road, Hastings, East Sussex TN 38 0PG, England.

**WRIGHT, William George C.;** British pianist; b. 14 Dec. 1936, Airdrie, Scotland; m. Janette Montgomery Rose 1961; two s. one d. *Education:* Royal Scottish Acad. of Music and Drama. *Career:* Liszt scholar; gives lectures and recitals in Belgium, Canada, Hungary and the USA; numerous radio and television appearances; mem. Liszt Soc., London, American Liszt Soc. *Recordings:* BBC Scotland world premiere recording of Liszt's Piano Piece in A flat S189 1987, first modern performance (BBC recording) of Liszt/de Swert Consolations I and IV and 'Enchâînement' de F. Liszt D11 for cello and piano (with Mark Bailey) 1991, first modern performance (BBC recording) of Liszt's Die Vätergruft, 1886 version for baritone and piano (with Christopher Underwood) 1998, first modern performance of Hérold/Herz/Liszt Cavatine de Zampa 2004. *Publications:* More Light on Young Liszt: Liszt 2000 2000, Liszt's Chamber Compositions and Transcriptions: The Liszt Companion 2002; contrib. to New Letters of Liszt, Journal of the American Liszt Society (vols 31 and 33), Letters from the Royal Library, Copenhagen: Liszt Saeculum Nr. 54 1995, New List Letters (The Hungarian Quarterly, vol. 44, no. 170) summer 2003, Hérold/Herz/Liszt Cavatine de Zampa 2004. *Address:* 24 Ayr Road, Giffnock, Glasgow, G46 6RY, Scotland. *E-mail:* williamgcwright@hotmail.com.

**WROBLEWSKI, Patryk;** Singer (Baritone); b. 4 Dec. 1956, Mishawaka, Indiana, USA. *Career:* Debut: Sang Malatesta at the 1980 Blossom Festival; Recent appearances as Fernando in La Gazza Ladra at Philadelphia, Silvio, Valentin and Monteverdi's Orfeo at Dallas; Lyric Opera of Chicago as Germont and Marcello and in Satyagraha by Glass; Opera Grand Rapids as Don Giovanni; Season 1991–92 with debut at New York City Opera as Zurga in Les pêcheurs de perles and as Silvio; Puccini's Lescaut with Greater Miami Opera and Silvio at the Munich Staatsoper (European stage debut); Season 1992–93 as Zurga in Holland, Taddeo in L'Italiana in Algeri at Dublin, and Marcello and Rossini's Figaro for the New Israel Opera; Concert appearances with the Chicago Symphony under Leppard and the Grant Park Concerts under Leonard Slatkin; Santa Fe Opera in Henze's Young Lord; Weill, The Protagonist; Dublin Grand Opera, Marcello in La Bohème; Manitoba Opera, Zurga, Carmen. *Honours:* Grand Prize, 1984 Rosa Ponselle International Competition; Winner, Luciano Pavarotti Competition, 1985. *Address:* c/o Opera Ireland, John Player House, 276–288 South Circular Road, Dublin 8, Ireland.

**WU, Mary Mei-Loc;** Pianist; b. 22 Dec. 1964, Hong Kong; m. James Wong, 4 July 1992. *Education:* Yehudi Menuhin School, 1976–83; Performer's Diploma of Royal College of Music, London, 1983–87; Banff Center of Fine Arts, Winter School Diploma, Canada, 1987–88; Master of Music, 1988–89, Doctorate of Musical Arts, 1989–92, State University of New York at Stony Brook, USA. *Career:* Debut: Queen Elizabeth Hall, London, 1979; Beethoven Sonata with Yehudi Menuhin in Germany, 1985; Bach Double Concerto with Vlado Perlemuter, London South Bank, 1986; Solo Recital, Wigmore Hall, London, 1994; Artist-in-Residence, Chinese University, Hong Kong, 1997. *Recordings:* Fantasias; Chinese Contemporary Piano Music; Piano Classico. *Address:* 135 Stevenage Road, Fulham, London SW6 6PB, England.

**WU, Zuqiang;** Chinese musician and composer; *Vice-Chairman, China Federation of Literary and Art Circles;* b. 24 July 1927, Beijing; s. of Jing-zhou Wu and Qin-qi (née Zhou) Wu; m. Li-qin Zheng 1953; one s. one d. *Career:* Vice-Pres. Cen. Conservatory of Music 1978–82, Pres. 1982–88, now Prof., Hon. Pres.; Vice-Pres. Chinese Musicians' Asscn 1985–; Vice-Exec. Chair. China Fed. of Literary and Art Circles 1988–92, Vice-Chair. 1992–; Adviser to China Nat. Symphony Orchestra 1996; Alt. mem. 12th CCP Cen. Cttee 1982–87; Perm. mem. Nat. Cttee 7th, 8th and 9th CPPCC 1988–2003. *Address:* Central Conservatory of Music, 43 Baojiajie West District, Beijing 100031, People's Republic of China (office). *Telephone:* (10) 66414887 (office). *Fax:* (10) 66417211 (office).

**WULKOPF, Cornelia;** Singer (Contralto); b. 1952, Braunschweig, Germany. *Education:* Detmold Music Academy, with Gunther Weissenborn. *Career:* Debut: Sang Sieglinde and Flosshilde at the 1977 Bayreuth Festival, in The Ring conducted by Pierre Boulez; Sang at the Bavarian State Opera from 1977, notably as Erda and Waltraute in The Ring, 1978; Lieder and Oratorio concerts from 1981, at Munich and elsewhere; Schmidt's Das Buch mit Sieben Siegeln, Salzburg, 1981; Cornelia in Giulio Cesare at the 1993 Schwetzingen Festival; Brangaene in Tristan at Hamburg, 1996; Sang Erda in Das Rheingold for Cologne Opera, and Amelfa in The Golden Cockerel at Bregenz, 2000; Wagner's Mary at Trieste 2001; Further concerts include Schubert's Lazarus, Vier Ernste Gesänge by Brahms and the Verdi Requiem. *Recordings include:* Mozart's Apollo et Hyacinthus. *Address:* c/o Hamburg Staatsoper, Grosse Theaterstrasse 34, 20354 Hamburg, Germany.

**WULSTAN, David,** BSc, BA, MA, FRSM; British academic; *Research Professor, University of Wales, Aberystwyth;* b. 18 Jan. 1937, Birmingham, England; m. Susan Nelson Graham 1967; one s. *Education:* Coll. of Technology, Birmingham, Magdalen Coll., Oxford. *Career:* founder and Dir, The Clerkes of Oxenford 1961–; numerous appearances on BBC television and Radio 3, Thames television, NWDR, BRT, Cheltenham, York, Bologna, Holland and Flanders Festivals, Proms and various films; Visiting Prof., Univ. of California, Berkeley 1977; Prof. of Music, Univ. Coll., Cork 1980; Prof. of Music, Univ. of Wales, Aberystwyth 1983–90, Research Prof. 1991–; Consulting Ed., Spanish Academic Press; mem. of council, Plainsong and Mediaeval Music Soc. *Compositions:* various Christmas carols, hymns, chants and film music. *Recordings:* Tallis, Sheppard, Gibbons: Church Music, Play of Daniel, Robert White. *Publications include:* Early English Church Music, vol. 3 1964, vol. 27 1979, Anthology of Carols 1968, Anthology of English Church Music 1971, Play of Daniel 1976, Coverdale Chant Book 1978, Sheppard: Complete Works 1979–, Tudor Music 1984, The Emperor's Old Clothes 2001, The Poetic and Musical Legacy of Heloise and Abelard 2003, Music from the Paraclete 2004, The Canterbury Dictionary of Hymnology 2005, Early Music and Three Haworth Hymns 2005; contrib. to Journal of Theological Studies, Journal of the American Oriental Society, Music and Letters, Galpin Society Journal, Musical Times (Iraq), English Historical Review, Plainsong and Medieval Music, Cantigueiros, Al-Masāq. *Address:* Ty Isaf, Llanilar, Aberystwyth, SY23 4NP, Wales.

**WUORINEN, Charles;** Composer; b. 9 June 1938, New York City, USA. *Education:* Attended Columbia University, BA 1961, MA 1963. *Career:* Founded the Group for Contemporary Music 1962; Teacher at Columbia University 1964–71; Professor of Music, Rutgers University, 1984–; Visiting Professor, New York University, 1990; Visiting Professor, State University of New York at Buffalo, 1989–94; San Francisco Symphony (and New Music Adviser to Music Director Herbert Blomstedt), 1985–89; American Academy in Rome, 1990. *Compositions include:* Stage: The Politics of Harmony 1968 and The W of Babylon; Opera: Haroun and the Sea of Stories, 2001; Orchestral: Music for orchestra 1956; Orchestral and Electronic Exchanges 1965; 3 Piano Concertos 1966, 1975, 1984; Contrafactum 1969; Grand Bamboula 1971; Concerto for amplified violin and orchestra 1972; A Reliquary for Igor Stravinsky, 1975; Tashi, 4 soloists and orchestra, 1976; Two-Part Symphony, 1978; The Magic Art: An Instrumental Masque, after Purcell, 1978; Short Suite, 1981; Crossfire, 1984; Bamboula Squared, 1984; Movers and Shakers, 1984; Rhapsody for violin and orchestra, 1984; The Golden Dance, 1986; Five, concerto for amplified cello and orchestra, 1987 Microsymphony, 1991–92; The Mission of Virgil, 1993; Concerto for Saxophone Quartet and Orchestra, 1993; The River of Light, 1995–96; The Great Procession, 1995; Symphony Seven, 1997; Chamber Music includes 3 String Quartets, 1971, 1979, 1987; String Trio, 1968; On Alligators, for 8 players, 1972; Speculum Speculi, 1972; Hyperion, 1975; Fortune, 1975; Fast Fantasy for cello and piano, 1977; Archaeopteryx, 1978; New York Notes, 1981; Sonata for violin and piano, 1988; String Sextet, 1989; Piano Quartet, 1994; Sonata for guitar and piano 1995; Horn Trio, 1981 and 1985; (Wuorinen) Cello variations III, 1997; Brass Quintet, 1999; An Orbicle of Jasp for cello and piano, 1999; String Quartet No. 4, 2000; Cyclops for chamber orchestra; Vocal Music includes: Genesis for chorus and orchestra, The Celestial Sphere, oratorio, 1980; Mass for soprano, chorus, violin 3 trombones and organ; Piano and Organ music; Many keyboard works including 3 Sonatas; A Winter's Tale (2 versions), soprano and chamber and w/piano, 1991, 1992; Fenton songs, for soprano and piano trio, 1997; Electronic: Time's Encomium, 1970. *Publications:* Charles Wuorinen, a Bio-Bibliography by Richard Burbank. *Honours:* Joseph Bearns Prize 1958, and Letters Award 1967; Guggenheim Fellowship, 1968–72; Pulitzer Prize for Time's Encomium, 1970; Rockefeller Foundation Fellowship, 1979, 1981, 1982; American Academy of Arts and Letters, 1985; MacArthur Foundation Fellowship, 1986–91. *Current Management:* c/o Howard Stokar Management. *Address:* c/o Howard Stokar Management, 870 West End Avenue, New York, NY 10025, USA.

**WÜTHRICH, Hans;** Composer; b. 3 Aug. 1937, Aeschi, Switzerland; m. Beatrice Mathez, 6 May 1977, 1 d. *Education:* Piano and Violin studies at Conservatory of Music, Berne, 1957–62; Studies of composition with Klaus Huber, Academy of Music, 1968–74; Doctor's Degree, University of Zürich, 1973. *Career:* Lecturer of Linguistics, Zürich University, 1971–85, and Teacher, Winterthur Conservatory, 1985–; Performances of compositions in Donaueschingen, 1978, 1985, at ISCM World Music Festival, Bonn in 1977 and at Athens in 1979. *Compositions:* Kommunikationsspiele, 1973; Das Glashaus, 1974–75; Netz-Werke I, II, 1983–85; Annaeherungen an Gegenwart, 1986–87; Procuste Deux Etoiles, 1980–81; Supplement: Netz-Werk III, 1987–89; Chopin Im TGV Basel-Paris, 1989; Wörter Bilder Dinge, 1990–91; Leve, 1992; Ah! Vous voila!, 1994; Happy Hour, 1995–97. *Recordings:* Procuste Deux Etoiles, 1980–81; Annäherungen an Gegenwart, 1986–87; Chopin im TGV Basel-Paris, 1989; Wörter Bilder Dinge, 1990–91. *Address:* Kirchgasse 4, 4144 Arlesheim, Switzerland.

**WYN-DAVIES, Catrin;** British singer (soprano); b. 1969, England. *Education:* Guildhall School of Music. *Career:* roles with Welsh National Opera (1994–96) have included Mozart's Ilia, Zerlina and Susanna, and Anne Trulove in The Rake's Progress; Season 1996–97 with Gilda for WNO, First Flower Maiden in Parsifal at the Paris Châtelet and Handel's Acis and Galatea with the English Concert; Concerts have included Soprano Solo in Schoenberg's Moses und Aron with the Philharmonia (1996), Handel's Orlando, Elijah with David Willcocks and Bach's Christmas Oratorio with René Jacobs on tour to Europe; Wigmore Hall debut recital 1994; Further opera roles include Kristine in The Makropulos Case and Monteverdi's Poppea (for WNO), 1998; Leader of the Flower Maidens in Parsifal at the Festival Hall, 1998; Engaged for the Beggar's Opera at Strasbourg; Sang Ginevra in Ariodante for ENO, London, 2002; Engaged as Jenůfa for WNO, 2003.

*Recordings include:* Sacred music by Vivaldi with the King's Consort; Weill's Der Silbersee under Marcus Stenz; Beethoven Folk Songs, with Malcolm Martineau. *Honours:* Kathleen Ferrier Decca Award 1994. *Current Management:* IMG Artists, Lovell House, 616 Chiswick High Road, London, W4 5RX, England. *Telephone:* (20) 8233-5800. *Fax:* (20) 8233-5801. *E-mail:* info@imgartists.com. *Website:* www.imgartists.com.

**WYN-ROGERS, Catherine;** Singer (contralto); b. 1958, England. *Education:* Studied at the Royal College of Music with Meriel St Clair and later with Ellis Keeler and Diane Forlano. *Career:* Regular concerts with the Bach Choir under David Willcocks in London and abroad; Frequent appearances with the United Kingdom's major orchestras; Tours with English Concert and Trevor Pinnock including Messiah in Germany and Vivaldi's Gloria in Rome for TV/ Deutsche Grammophon recording; Appearances at the Proms with the Sixteen, the National Youth Orchestra and the English Concert Opera including Il Ritorno d'Ulisse for English National Opera and Stuttgart, Maddalena in Rigoletto in Nantes, La Gioconda for Opera North, Die Zauberflöte for the ROH and Salzburg Festival; Sang First Norn in Götterdämmerung at Covent Garden, 1995; Sang in Palestrina and Pfitzner recital at Covent Garden, 1997; Mary Magdalene in The Kingdom by Elgar at the 1999 London Prom Concerts; Bach's Magnificat with the Sixteen, 2000; Season 2000–01 in the St John Passion and as La Cieca in La Gioconda for ENO, Adelaide in Arabella at Munich and Hero in Béatrice et Bénédict for WNO; Dvořák's Stabat mater at the London Proms, 2002. *Recordings:* Vaughan Williams's Serenade To Music and Magnificat with Matthew Best; Teixera Te Deum and Bach's Christmas Oratorio with the Sixteen; Elgar's Dream of Gerontius with Vernon Handley and the Royal Liverpool Philharmonic. *Honours:* College Song Recital Prize; Dame Clara Butt Award; Grantee, Countess of Munster Trust, RCM. *Current Management:* Askonas Holt Ltd, Lonsdale Chambers, 27 Chancery Lane, London, WC2A 1PF, England. *Telephone:* (20) 7400-1700. *Fax:* (20) 7400-1799. *E-mail:* info@askonasholt.co.uk. *Website:* www.askonasholt.co.uk. *Address:* 67 Whiteley Road, Upper Norwood, London, SE19 1JU, England.

**WYNER, Susan (Davenny);** Singer (Soprano); b. 17 Oct. 1945, New Haven, Connecticut, USA. *Education:* Graduated from Cornell University, 1965; Vocal studies with Herta Glaz, 1969–75. *Career:* Debut: Carnegie Hall recital in 1972; Alice Tully Hall recital in 1973; Orchestral debut with the Boston Symphony in 1974; Engagements with all leading orchestras in USA and Canada and with Israel Philharmonic and London Symphony; Repertoire includes Baroque and contemporary works; Operatic debut as Monteverdi's Poppea, New York City Opera, 1977; Metropolitan Opera in 1982 as Woglinde in Das Rheingold; Has sung in the premieres of Del Tredici's Adventures Underground in 1975 and Carter's A Mirror On Which To Dwell in 1965, and in the premieres of Memorial Music and Fragments from Antiquity by Yehudi Wyner; Also sings works by Rochberg (Quartet No. 2) and Reimann (Inane).

**WYNER, Yehudi,** BMus, MA, MMus; American composer, pianist and conductor; *Professor of Composition, Brandeis University;* b. 1 June 1929, Calgary, Alberta, Canada; m. 1st Nancy Joan Braverman 1951 (divorced 1967); two s. one d.; m. 2nd Susan Davenny Wyner 1967. *Education:* Juilliard School, Yale Univ. with Paul Hindemith, Harvard Univ. with Walter Piston. *Career:* American Acad. in Rome 1953–56; performed and recorded contemporary music in New York; directed the Turnau Opera; Prof., Yale School of Music from 1963, Chair. of Composition 1969–73; Music Dir, New Haven Opera Soc.; keyboard player with the Bach Aria Group; Berkshire Music Center 1975; Prof. of Music, State Univ. of New York, Purchase 1978, Dean of Music 1978–82; Visiting Prof., Brandeis Univ. 1988, Cornell Univ. 1989, Harvard Univ. 1991–93, 1996–98, 2003–04; Prof. of Composition, Brandeis Univ. 1990–; mem. American Composers' Alliance, American Music Center, American Acad. of Arts and Letters. *Compositions include:* Piano Sonata 1954, Three Informal Pieces for violin and piano 1961, Torah Service 1966, Cadenza

for clarinet and harpsichord 1969, Canto Cantabile for soprano and band 1972, Memorial Music for soprano and three flutes 1971–73, Intermedio for soprano and strings 1974, Fragments from Antiquity for soprano and orchestra 1978–81, Romances for piano quartet 1980, On This Most Voluptuous Night for soprano and seven instruments 1982, Wind Quintet 1984, String Quartet 1985, Toward the Center for piano 1988, Il Cane Minore for two clarinets and bassoon 1992, Concerto for cello and orchestra 1994, Lyric Harmony for orchestra 1995, Epilogue for orchestra 1996, A Mad Tea Party for soprano, two baritones and ensemble 1996, Horn Trio 1997, The Second Madrigal for soprano, string quartet, wind quintet and percussion 1999, Tuscan Triptych for string orchestra 2002, Commedia for clarinet and piano 2002, Piano Concerto 2004. *Honours:* Rome Prize fellow 1953–56, Univ. of Calif. Alfred E. Hertz fellow 1953–54, Guggenheim fellow 1960, 1977, Inst. of Arts and Letters grant 1961, NEA grantee 1976, Rockefeller Foundation fellow, Bellagio 1998, Lincoln Center Elise Stoeger Prize 1998. *Address:* c/o Associated Music Publishers, 257 Park Avenue S, New York, NY 10023 (office); 49 Brooks Street, Medford, MA 02155, USA (home). *Telephone:* (781) 736-3310 (office); (781) 396-3385 (home). *Fax:* (781) 736-3320 (office); (781) 396-5562 (home). *Website:* www.schirmer.com/composers/wyner/.

**WYSOCKI, Zdzislaw,** MA; Austrian (b. Polish) composer; b. 18 July 1944, Poznań, Poland; m.; one s. one d. *Education:* Music School, Poznań, Music High School Poznań, Univ. of Music, Poznań, Univ. of Music, Vienna, Austria. *Career:* debut, Poznań 1963; performances in Austria, Poland, Germany, France, the UK, Italy, Denmark, Portugal, Hungary, Ukraine, Slovakia, fmr Yugoslavia, Soviet Union, USA, Canada, Brazil, Japan; festivals in Germany, Brazil, Slovakia, Austria, Hungary, Italy, Portugal, Poland; world premieres include Double Concerto with Berkeley Symphony Orchestra under Kent Nagano 2002, Concerto Doppio with Ensemble Wiener Collage/René Staar, Salzburg Festival 2003; radio broadcasts in Poland, Austria, Germany, Japan, USA, France, Denmark, and television appearances in Poland. *Compositions include:* Missa in honorem Ioannis Pauli secundi op 30, Fantasia op 33, Quasi concerto grosso op 36, Quartetto op 46 1990, Movimento Saxophonquartet op 47 1991, Quasi Divertimento op 49 1993, Trio op 51, De finibus temporum op 52 1994, Etudes for chamber ensemble op 54, 56, 60 1996–2001, Gespräch mit einem guten Menschen (opera) 1992, Musica de la passione for strings 1999, Double Concerto op 63 2002, In Memoriam op 66 2002, Concerto Doppio op 67 2003. *Recordings:* Austrian contemporary music, works of Z. Wysocki op 46, 49, 51, 52, Ensemble Wiener Collage, Klang debuts Ensemble Graz, St Petersburg, Etudes op 54/7,9, guitar recital performed by Leo Witoszynskyj, Due Caratteri op 29, Violoncellomusik des 20 Jahrhunderts performances by Adalbert Skocic, Walter Delahunt, Fantasia op 33. *Honours:* L'Ordre du Merite en Faveur de la Culture Polonaise 1984; Theodor Körner Prize 1977, City of Vienna Recognition Prize 1977, Adolf Schärf Fund Z Prize for Artistic Merit 1984, first prize Int. Competition for Choir Composition, Vienna 1988. *Address:* Pfarrgasse 34-44/16/7, 1230 Vienna, Austria (home). *Telephone:* (1) 6153024 (home). *Fax:* (1) 6153024 (home).

**WYZNER, Franz;** Singer (Bass); b. 1932, Vienna, Austria. *Education:* Studied in Vienna. *Career:* Sang at the Landestheater in Salzburg, 1958–59, Gelsenkirchen, 1959–64, Wuppertal, 1964–85, notably in the German premiere of Crime and Punishment by Petrovic, 1971, and the first performance of The Gamblers by Shostakovich in the arrangement by K Meyer, 1986; Guest appearances at the Schwetzingen Festival, 1970, Vienna Volksoper in the Austrian premiere of The Burning Fiery Furnace by Britten in 1977, Salzburg Festival in Dantons Tod, 1983, Buenos Aires as Alberich in 1983, and Cologne in 1985; Other roles have included Mozart's Leporello, Figaro, Papageno and Alfonso, Kaspar in Der Freischütz, Don Magnifico, Mephistopheles, the Doctor in Wozzeck, and Kecal in The Bartered Bride. *Recordings include:* Dantons Tod, Orfeo. *Address:* Theater am Gärtnerplatz, Gärtnerplatz 3, 8000 Munich 1, Germany.

# X

**XIA, Liping;** Composer and Music Educator; b. Feb. 1935, China; m. 1963, 3 s. *Education:* Music Institute of China, graduated 1958. *Career:* Music Editor, radio station of Hainan, China; Leader, music group at radio station, Guangdong, China for 21 years; Music Professor, Hainan Normal Institute and Guangdong University of Foreign Studies for 20 years. *Compositions:* Song of Spring Ploughing, 1965; Song of Rubber Forest, 1981; Joy Over a Bumper Harvest, 1989; Having Classes, 1993; Dance Music in Praise of Youth, 1993. *Recordings:* The Pass to South Guangdong, 3rd part of the music programme series Along Today's Long March, 1986. *Publications:* Appreciation of Chinese Classical Music, 1993; Appreciation and Analysis of Ancient Chinese Melodies, 1993; A Music Course for College Students, 1999. *Contributions:* Chief Editor, University Music Education, Guangdong. *Address:* 388-5 Dong-Hua Doag Road Rm# 703, Guangzhou, People's Republic of China.

**XIONG, Jihua;** Chinese professor of conducting and composition; b. 24 Feb. 1932, Beijing; m. Cai Rengi 1953; two d. *Education:* Chengdu Arts School, studied conducting with Russian and German teachers. *Career:* debut conducting Shanghai Symphony Orchestra, 1958; debuted several new works including Recollection of the past on the Grassland (Gao Weijie, Tang Qingshi) and Symphonic Suite (Zou Lu) and Symphonic Poem, Chant of the River (Li Zhongyong); Conducted various master works including Bruch, Violin Concerto No. 1 in G minor; Chopin, Piano Concerto No. 1 in E Minor; Rachmaninov, Piano Concerto No. 2 in C minor, Beethoven, Symphony No. 3 (Eroica) and Symphony No. 5 (Fate); Dvořák, Symphony No. 9 New World; Tchaikovsky Symphony Pathétique; Rimsky-Korsakoff, Symphony Suite Scheherezade; Conducted orchestras for numerous films and plays; Conducted 200 dance theatres; Conducted several broadcast symphony concerts; Invited participant, 20th Century Classical Music Works Chinese Composers; Conducted all the major Chinese orchestras. *Compositions:* Wan Xi Sha, symphony, 1962; Die Lian Hua, orchestra piece, 1964; A Stormy October, film music, 1979; Mystic Giant Buddha, film music, 1981; The Soul of Hua Xia, television series of plays, 1984; Welcoming the New Year, solo works for pipa; Morning Song, solo for violin; Pour Out One's Heart, piano solo. *Recordings:* Recollections of the Past on Grassland. *Publications:* Article, How to Read the Orchestra Score. *Address:* c/o Sichuan Conservatory of Music, 6 Xinsheng Road, Chengdu, Sichuan 610021, China.

873

**YAHR, Carol;** Singer (Mezzo-soprano); b. 1959, USA. *Career:* Sang at the Cologne Opera, 1987, as Venus in Tannhäuser, Théâtre des Champs-Elysées, 1988, as Fricka in The Ring; Nice Opéra, 1988–89, as Geneviéve in Pelléas and Dido in Les Troyens; Seattle, 1989, as Wagner's Eva, Leonore at Innsbruck, 1990, and with Glyndebourne Tour; Scottish Opera and Innsbruck, 1991, as Sieglinde and Elisabeth; Sang the Walküre Brünnhilde at Wiesbaden, 1993; Sang Brünnhilde in The Ring for Norwegian Opera, 1996; Sang Isolde for Hawaiian Opera, 2000. *Address:* c/o Der Norske Opera, PO Box 8800, Youngstorget, N0028 Oslo, Norway.

**YAKAR, Rachel;** Singer (Soprano); b. 3 March 1938, Lyon, France. *Education:* Studied at the Paris Conservatoire and with Germaine Lubin. *Career:* Sang with Deutsche Oper am Rhein, Düsseldorf from 1964 in roles including Antonia in Les Contes d'Hoffmann; Sang at Aix-en-Provence in 1966 in Ariadne auf Naxos, Strasbourg Opera in 1967 in a new production of Der Junge Lord by Henze, Amsterdam, 1968–69 as Cleopatra in Giulio Cesare and as Marguerite, at Düsseldorf in 1969, and Paris Opéra in 1970 as Gilda and Micaela; Baroque repertoire from 1971 includes Deidamia by Handel; Munich Festival in 1974 as Donna Elvira, Bayreuth Festival in 1976 as Freia and Gerhilde in Patrice Chéreau's centenary production of Der Ring des Nibelungen, Glyndebourne Festival, 1977, 1980 as Donna Elvira and the Marschallin, Strasbourg and Düsseldorf in 1978 as Mélisande; Sang Cycle of operas by Monteverdi at Zürich in 1978; Geneva Opera in 1981 as Janáček's Jenůfa; Guest appearances in San Francisco, East Berlin, Edinburgh, Lausanne, Monte Carlo and Santiago; Other roles include Mozart's Ilia and Fiordigili; Sang Madame Lidoine in Dialogues des Carmélites at Lyon, 1990; Climène in Lully's Phaëton at Lyon, 1993. *Recordings include:* Rameau's Les Indes Galantes, and Pygmalion; Idomeneo; Monteverdi's Orfeo; Dido and Aeneas; Bach B minor Mass; Lully's Armide; Schütz's Christmas Story and Magnificat; Fux's and Scarlatti's Baroque Cantatas; Die Zauberflöte, from the Salzburg Festival conducted by James Levine.

**YAMASHITA, Kazuhito;** Japanese guitarist; b. 25 March 1961, Nagasaki; s. of Toru Yamashita. *Education:* Nagasaki Guitar Acad., studied with Kojiro Kobune, J. Thomas, Narciso Yepes, Andres Segovia, Toru Takemitsu. *Career:* debut recitals in Tokyo 1978, Paris 1979; concert at the Toronto Guitar Festival with his guitar transcription of Mussorgsky's Pictures at an Exhibition 1984; transcribed and performed Stravinsky's Firebird Suite, Dvořák's 'New World' Symphony for solo guitar, and Beethoven's Violin Concerto for guitar and orchestra; duo tour of USA with James Galway 1987; mem., Nagasaki Guitar Ensemble; 'The World of Kazuhito Yamashita' recital series, Casals Theatre, Tokyo 1989, 1994, 1999. *Compositions include:* Imaginary Forest for solo guitar 1982. *Recordings:* transcriptions of Mussorgsky's Pictures at an Exhibition, Stravinsky's Firebird Suite, Dvořák's 'New World' Symphony, J. S. Bach's Sonatas, Partitas and Suites for unaccompanied flute, violin, cello and lute, the complete works of Fernando Sor, Giuliani and Ponce. *Honours:* winner All-Japan Guitar Competition 1976, Ramirez competition, Spain 1977, Alessandria competition, Italy 1977, Concours International de Guitare, Paris 1977. *Address:* c/o Allegro Music Tokyo Inc, Meisen Bldg 502, 7-17-20 Roppongi, Minato-ku, Tokyo 106-0032, Japan (office).

**YANAGIDA, Takayoshi;** Composer; b. 27 March 1948, Sapporo, Hokkaido, Japan; m. Keiko Tsuhako 1973; one s. one d. *Education:* Musashino Music Coll., and Graduate School; Musik Hochschule, München. *Career:* debut, Iino Hall, Tokyo, 1969; Prof. of Music, Bunkyo Univ.; Composer for the Music of NHK Educational Program; mem., ISME, JSCM, JFC. *Compositions:* Mixed Chorus Suite, Kitano-kawa, MCS Pony of Stars; Seen in the Twilight, for flute, violin and piano; Beside a Stream, for piano. *Recordings:* Concert Tableau for wind orchestra; Johi-haku-un. *Publications:* Orchestra Project '93; Libretto on a Dreamy Vision for flute and orchestra (recorded and sent on the air by NHK), 1993; Selections from a Literary Calendar for clarinet and orchestra, 1998. *Honours:* First Prize in the 38th Japan Music Competition, Composition Division, 1969. *Address:* 7-23-13, Higashi-urawa, Midori-ku, Saitama-shi 336-0926, Japan.

**YANAGITA, Masako;** Violinist; b. 30 March 1944, Tokyo, Japan; m. Abba Bogin. *Education:* Artist Diploma, Mannes College of Music, New York City, USA; Studied with Eijin Tanaka, Louis Graeler, William Kroll. *Career:* Debut: Tokyo, 1966; Concert appearances throughout USA, Europe, Near and Far East; Soloist, orchestras in Japan, the United Kingdom, Germany, Philippines, USA; 1st Violinist, toured with Vieuxtemps String Quartet; Faculty Member, Mannes College of Music. *Recordings include:* Complete Schubert violin and piano repertoire (with Abba Bogin, pianist). *Honours:* Silverstein Prize, Berkshire Music Center, Massachusetts, 1966; Carl Flesch Competition, London, England, 1968; Paganini Competition, Genoa, Italy, 1968; Munich International Competition, 1969. *Current Management:* Raymond Weiss Artists Management, New York City, USA. *Address:* 838 West End Avenue, New York, NY 10025, USA.

**YANG, Guang;** Singer (mezzo-soprano); b. 1970, Peking, China. *Education:* Central Conservatory, Peking. *Career:* Concerts at Carnegie Hall, New York, Bournemouth, London, Newcastle and Stockholm; Verdi Requiem at the Wales National Eisteddfod; Philharmonic Orchestra at Symphony Hall, Birmingham, 1999; Opera roles include Rossini's Rosina (Welsh National Opera, 1999) and Mozart's Dorabella; Celebrity recital at the 1999 International Eisteddfod. *Honours:* Winner, 1997 Cardiff Singer of the World Competition. *Current Management:* Harlequin Agency Ltd, 203 Fidlas Road, Cardiff CF4 5NA, Wales.

**YANG, Liqing;** Composer; b. 30 April 1942, Sichuan, China; Divorced; one d. *Education:* BA, Shenyang Conservatory, 1970; MA in Composition, Shanghai Conservatory, 1980; Diplomas of composition and piano, Musikhochschule, Hannover, Germany, 1983. *Career:* Debut: Violin concerto, White Hair Girls, Shenyang Conservatory of Music, 1970; 24th Tage der Neuen Musik Hannover, poems from Tang Dynasty, Germany, 1982; Musique en Scene, France, 1997; Glocke Musikhall, Bremen, Germany, 1998; 17th Asian Art Festival, Hong Kong, 1997. *Compositions:* Grievances at Wujiang, 1986; Festive Overture, 1987; Prelude, Interlude and Postlude, 1991; Elegy, 1991, 1998. *Recordings:* Grievances at Wujiang, 1986; Taiwan, Linfair, 1995; Yang Liqing's Orchestral Works; Elegy. *Publications:* The Composition Techniques of Olivier Messiaen, 1989; Style Evolution in Orchestration, 1986–87; On Postmodernism in Contemporary Western Music, 1994; Contemporary Instrumentation Techniques, 2001. *Contributions:* Interview with Composer Yang Liqing, Chinese Music Yearbook, 1993. *Address:* 1855 Tianshan Road, Apt. 1710#, Shanghai 200051, Shanghai, People's Republic of China.

**YANG, Simon;** Singer (Bass); b. 1960, Seoul, South Korea. *Education:* Cologne Musikhochschule, with Kurt Moll. *Career:* Debut: Düsseldorf, 1992, as Giorgio in I Puritani; Sang at Karlsruhe Opera, 1993–95, then with the Hamburg Staatsoper; Roles have included Mozart's Sarastro and Commendatore, King Philip in Don Carlos and Padre Guardiano in La Forza del Destino; Fasolt and Fafner in The Ring at Karlsruhe; Concerts include Beethoven's Ninth, the Verdi Requiem and Schumann's Paradies und der Peri; Sang Osmin in Die Entführung at Vienna Schönbrunn, 1998; Season 2000–01 at Hamburg as Mozart's Bartolo, Varlaam in Boris Godunov and in Donizetti's Roberto Devereux (concert). *Recordings include:* Wagner's Ring. *Honours:* Winner, Vienna Belvedere Competition. *Address:* c/o Hamburg Staatsoper, Grosse Theaterstrasse 34, 20354 Hamburg, Germany.

**YANG, Sungsic;** Concert Violinist; b. 1966, Korea. *Education:* Studied at the Paris Conservatoire and with Yfrah Neaman at the Guildhall School of Music, 1987. *Career:* Debut: Recital in Seoul in 1977; Solo appearances throughout Europe including tour with the Seoul Philharmonic; Tchaikovsky and Mendelssohn Concertos with the Moscow Philharmonic at Seoul for the Olympic Festival in 1988; Paris concerto debut with Orchestre National de France, conducted by Lorin Maazel, 1988; BBC radio recording, 1988; Appearances with National Symphony Orchestra, RTE, Dublin, and Gävleborgs Symfoniorkester, Sweden, 1991; Plays a Joseph Guarneri del Gesu of 1720; Repertoire also includes concertos by Bach, Brahms, Bruch, Beethoven, Mozart, Prokofiev, Saint-Saëns, Sibelius and Wieniawski; Solo works by Bach, sonatas by Brahms, Beethoven, Debussy, Fauré, Franck, Tartini and Ysaÿe, and Stravinsky's Suite Italienne. *Honours:* Prizewinner in Paganini Competition, Genoa, Long-Thibaud Paris, and Indianapolis, USA; 1st Prize, Carl Flesch Competition, London, 1988.

**YANG, Tianjie;** Composer; b. 5 Sept. 1952, Changsha City, Hunan Province, China; m. Shuyun He, 9 June 1979, 1 d. *Education:* Graduate, Composing Department, Shanghai Conservatory of Music; Studies at Beijing Broadcast College. *Career:* debut, The Legend of Mountains, orchestral music played at Beijing Music Hall, 1979; Started professional composing, 1972; Created more than 1,000 pieces of music, many of which have been performed in the USA, Russia, Austria, Poland, Hong Kong and elsewhere; mem, Chinese Musicians' Institute, 1990–; Manager of China International Famous Association, 1999. *Compositions:* Orchestral Music: The Carnival of the Miaos; Spring of the Yao Shan; Symphony: Linhai Cuts Firewood; Erhu Concerto: Yearning; Dance Drama: Border Town; Opera: The Remote Days. *Recordings:* Music for the television serial, Nuo Yao. *Recordings:* Border Town, 1990; The Carnival of the Miaos, 1993; Spring of Yao Shan, 1994; Children Sing Ancient Poetries, 1994. *Publications:* On Opera Music's Reforming, 1991; Chinese Theatre: A Talk on the Music Creation of Dance Drama, Border Town, 1996. *Honours:* Title of National First Degree Composer; Wenhua Award (the most prestigious art award in China), 1996; World Cultural Celebrities' Achievement Award, 1998. *Address:* The Song and Dance Theatre of Hunan, 9 Ren Min Road, Changsha City, Hunan Province 410011, People's Republic of China.

**YANG, Youqing;** Conductor and Pianist; b. 10 Dec. 1952, Shanghai, China. *Education:* BA in Conducting, Shanghai Conservatory of Music, 1984; MA, 1997, DMA in Orchestral Conducting, 2000, School of Music, Michigan State University, USA; Studied with Distinguished Professor Leon Gregorian. *Career:* Debut: Brahms Symphony No. 4, Mozart Piano Concerto No. 20 and Berlioz Overture to Benvenuto Cellini, with Guangzhou Symphony Orchestra, 1984; Conductor, Symphony Orchestra of China National Opera Theatre, 1984–, appearances including World Premiere of opera Savage Land at 1st China Arts Festival in Beijing, 1987; Has appeared since 1986 as Guest Conductor for Shanghai Philharmonic Orchestra, Shangdong Symphony Orchestra, Central Philharmonic Orchestra of China, China Broadcasting

Symphony Orchestra, China Film Philharmonic Orchestra and at Zhou Xiaoyan Opera Centre, Shanghai; In 1995, Music Director of Chinese Musicians' Delegation Concert Tour in Europe, and Guest Conductor of Das Saarlandisches Staatsorchester Saarbrucken, with concerts at Kunst und Ausstellungshalle der Bundesrepublik Deutschland and Saarlandisches Staatstheater, Germany, at the Classic Open-Air in Solothurn, Switzerland, and the Municipal Theatre, Luxembourg; mem, Chinese Musicians' Association. *Contributions:* Looking for Perfect Combination of Mind and Music, interview in Contemporary China magazine, 1991. *Honours:* Merit Fellowship and Scholarship, Shanghai Conservatory of Music, 1982, 1983, 1984. *Address:* c/o Shanghai Symphony Orchestra, 105 Hunan Lu, Shanghai 200031, People's Republic of China.

**YANNAY, Yehuda;** Composer; b. 26 May 1937, Timisoara, Romania. *Education:* Graduated Rubin Academy of Music, Tel-Aviv, 1964; MFA, Brandeis University, USA, 1966 (study with Berger, Shapero and Krenek); DMA University of Illinois at Urbana, 1974. *Career:* Resident in Israel from 1951; Teacher of theory and composition at University of Wisconsin, Milwaukee, 1970–; Music from Almost Yesterday concert series, 1971–. *Compositions include:* Spheres for soprano and 10 instruments, 1963; Two Fragments for violin and piano, 1966; Wraphap, theatre music, 1969; Coloring Book from the Harpist, 1969; Concert for Audience and orchestra, 1971; The Hidden Melody for cello and horn, 1977; Concertino for violin and chamber orchestra, 1980; Celan Ensembles: Augentanz and Galgenlied for tenor and instruments, 1986–; In Madness There is Order for voice, projections and synthesizers, 1988–92; The Oranur Experiment, music video, Part 1, Journey to Orgonon for actor, projections and synthesizer, 1991; Five Pieces for Three Players for soprano saxophone, clarinet and marimba, 1994; Exit Music at Century's End, for orchestra, 1995; Geometry of Aloneness, for low voice, glass harmonica and slide projections, 1996; Marrakesh Bop, for flute and guitar, 1999. *Address:* c/o ASCAP, 1 Lincoln Plaza, New York, NY 10023, USA.

**YANOV-YANOVSKY, Dmitri Feliksovich;** Uzbekistan composer; b. 24 April 1963, Tashkent. *Education:* Tashkent State Conservatory. *Career:* founder and Artistic Dir, Int. Festival of Contemporary Music ILKHOM-XX, Tashkent. *Compositions include:* Bagatelles 1982, Piano Concerto 1983, Anno Domini 1985, Chang-Music I–V 1990–94, Lacrymosa 1991, Awakening 1993, Ritual 1994, Conjunctions 1995, Takyr 1995, Come and Go (for theatre) 1995, Hommage à Gustav Mahler 1996, The Little Match-Girl (ballet) 1996–97, Lux aeterna 1997, Music of Dreams 1999, Eh Joe (chamber opera) 2001, Twilight Music 2002, scores for over 40 films. *Recordings:* Chang-Music V (with Kronos Quartet), Lacrymosa, Dawn upshaw (with Kronos Quartet), Music of Dreams (with Elisabeth Chojnacka), Opus 111. *Honours:* second prize Int. Competition de Musique Sacrée, Fribourg 1991, ALEA III Int. Prize, Boston 1992, Cannes Int. Film Festival Special Award of Nantes 1992. *Address:* C-1 47-ap. 42, 700000 Tashkent, Uzbekistan. *Telephone:* 711 361382. *Fax:* 712 560296. *E-mail:* yanovsky@mail.tps.uz.

**YARBOROUGH, William;** Symphony Conductor; b. 3 Jan. 1926, Wilmington, North Carolina, USA; m. Ruth M Feldt, 29 Jan 1955. *Education:* BM, Chicago Musical College and University of Chicago; MM, Indiana University; Studied with Nadia Boulanger, Vittorio Rieti and Serge Koussevitsky; Studied at Peabody Conservatory and Berkshire Music Center. *Career:* Debut: As Conductor, aged 19, American Symphony in Paris; As Concert Violinist, aged 8; Music Director and Conductor, American Symphony Orchestra, Paris, France, Richmond Philharmonic Orchestra, Richmond, Virginia; CBS Radio broadcasts; Music Director, Conductor, Michigan Bach-Mozart Festival; Performances with Touring American Opera Company and American Chamber Orchestra at present; Music Director, Conductor, American Chamber Orchestra, Washington DC since 1980; Director, Wolf Trap American University Program for the Performing Arts, Washington, DC; Guest Conductor of many of the major symphonies in Europe and USA including Royal Philharmonic, Vienna Symphony, St Cecilia Orchestra in Rome, Boston Symphony and Philadelphia Orchestra; Numerous radio and television appearances; Speaker, Chicago Adult Education Council; Music Adviser, Old Dominion Symphony Council. *Contributions:* Journal of the American Musicological Society. *Address:* American Chamber Orchestra Society, 4201 Cathedral Avenue NW, Suite 706-E, Washington, DC 20016, USA.

**YARON, Gilah;** Singer (Soprano); b. 1941, Tel-Aviv, Israel. *Education:* Studied in Tel-Aviv with Tuerk Bernstein and with Gunter Reich, George London and Elisabeth Schwarzkopf. *Career:* Sang with the Israel Philharmonic and other orchestras from 1970; Israel Festival in 1972 in Bach's Magnificat; Sang in Switzerland and other European centres from 1975 including concert at Berlin Festival with works by Hindemith and Webern; Guest appearances in Austria, Belgium, Netherlands, Italy, Denmark and England; Sang Psaumes Hebraiques by Markevitch and Poèmes pour Mi by Messiaen; Other repertoire includes Penderecki's St Luke Passion, Mahler's 2nd Symphony and Mendelssohn's music for A Midsummer Night's Dream; Singing Teacher at The Rubin Academy of Music and Dance, Jerusalem, 1982–. *Address:* c/o PO Box 2179, Bat Yam 59121, Israel.

**YASSA, Ramzi;** Pianist; b. 15 March 1948, Cairo, Egypt; m. Brigitte Chevrot, 7 June 1978, 1 s., 1 d. *Education:* Lycee of Heliopolis; Diploma, Cairo Conservatory, 1968; Tchaikovsky Conservatory, Moscow, 1969–74; FTCL, 1972; Licence de Concert, Ecole Normale, Paris, 1977. *Career:* Appearances at The Barbican in London with Royal Philharmonic Orchestra, conductor

Charles Groves, Kennedy Center, Mann Auditorium with IPO, conductor Zubin Mehta, Musikverein, Palau, Barcelona, Théâtre des Champs Elysées and South Bank, London; Television Mondovision with Zubin Mehta in 1987; Inaugural concert, Cairo Opera House, 1988; BBC recordings and live broadcasts; Adjudicator for international piano competitions; Appearances with Yehudi Menuhin as conductor; Director of the Cairo Opera House, 1998–; Special Adviser for Music to the Egyptian Minister of Culture, 1999–. *Recordings:* Tchaikovsky's The Seasons, Ades, France; Prokofiev's Cinderella, 2nd Sonata, Belgium; Chopin's Ballades and Opus 22, Belgium; Beethoven Appassionata/Waldstein/Lieder von Goethe; Beethoven 5 Piano Concertos and Choral Fantasy Op 80. *Address:* 14 Rue Sainte Cecile, 75009 Paris, France.

**YASUNAGA, Toru;** Violinist; b. 14 Nov. 1951, Fukuoka, Japan. *Education:* Studied at the Toho Music Academy, Tokyo, and with Michael Schwalbe in Berlin. *Career:* Many appearances in Europe and the Far East as recitalist and in concert; Joined Berlin Philharmonic Orchestra, 1977, and became leader. *Honours:* Winner, Leu Cadia prize at the All Japan Music Competition, 1971. *Address:* c/o Berlin Philharmonic Orchestra, Philharmonie, Matthaikirchestrasse 1, W-10785 Berlin, Germany.

**YAUGER, Margaret;** Singer (Mezzo-Soprano); b. 1947, Birmingham, Alabama, USA; m. Malcolm Smith, 4 Oct 1975. *Education:* BM, Converse College; MM, New England Conservatory of Music; Special studies at American Opera Centre, Juilliard School of Music, New York City, and Goldovsky Opera Studio. *Career:* Debut: American National Opera Company, Sarah Caldwell, Conductor; Performances with New York City Opera, 1973–75, Lake George Opera Festival, 1972–74, Central City Opera Festival, 1973–76, Boris Goldovsky Opera Tour, 1973–74, Mexico City Opera, Teatro Regio Turin, Italy; Sang at Knoxville with Tennessee Opera, Birmingham Alabama Civic Opera, Fort Worth, Texas Opera; Deutsche Oper am Rhein, Düsseldorf, Germany, 1977–86; Sang at Krefeld, Hanover, Karlsruhe, Freiburg, Wiesbaden and Gelsenkirchen Opera Houses and with Solingen, Duisburg, Münchengladbach-Krefeld, and Trier Symphonies; Appearances on East Berlin Radio and with Dresden Philharmonic; Sang Fricka in Das Rheingold, Washington National Symphony, Margret in Wozzeck, with Boston Symphony Orchestra, 3rd Magd, Elektra with London Symphony Orchestra; Heidelberg Schloss, Festspiele, 1992; Sang in Verdi Requiem, Delaware Symphony Orchestra, 1993; Mahler Symphony No. 2, Roanoke Symphony, 1994; Choral Arts Society of Washington tour of France, 1996; Youngstown Symphony, 1996; Cincinnati Opera, 1996; Portland Maine Symphony, Cesky Krumlov Summer Festival, Czech Republic; Voice Teacher, University of Southern Maine, 1999–; mem, AGMA. *Recordings:* Beethoven Symphony No. 9, alto part, with Mexico City Symphony; Live recording of Rigoletto, New York City Opera. *Honours:* Miss Alabama Competition Scholarship; 3 Scholarships, William Mathis Sullivan Foundation. *Current Management:* Thea Dispecker, Artists' Representative, 59 East 54th Street, New York, NY 10022, USA. *Address:* 12 Locksley Road, Cape Elizabeth, ME 04107, USA.

**YE, Shaolan,** (Ye Qiang); Chinese opera singer, actor and playwright; b. Sept. 1943, Beijing; s. of Ye Shenglan. *Education:* China Acad. of Traditional Operas, Cen. Acad. of Drama. *Career:* actor, dir, playwright; Art Dir Zhanyou Peking Opera Troupe, PLA Beijing Mil. Command; mem. Exec. Council of Chinese Dramatists Asscn. *Peking operas include:* Lu Bu and Diao Chan, Luo Cheng, Story of the Willow Tree. *Honours:* won 1st Nat. Theatre Plum Blossom Award 1984; Fulbright Int. Scholar. *Address:* c/o Zhanyou Peking Opera Troupe, People's Liberation Army, Beijing Command, Beijing, People's Republic of China (office).

**YEEND, Frances;** Singer (Soprano); b. 28 Jan. 1918, Vancouver, Washington, USA. *Education:* Studied at Washington State University. *Career:* From 1943 sang in musicals and on the radio; Concert tour of USA in 1944; Sang Ellen Orford in the US premiere of Peter Grimes, at Tanglewood in 1946; World tour in 1947 with Mario Lanza and George London, as Bel Canto Trio; New York City Opera, 1948–65, as Violetta, Eva in Die Meistersinger, Micaela, Mozart's Countess and Marguerite; Metropolitan Opera, 1961–64, as Chrysothemis in Elektra and Gutrune in Götterdämmerung; European engagements in Barcelona, Edinburgh in 1951, London in Mimi in 1953, Munich, Verona in Turandot in 1958, and Vienna. *Recordings include:* Micaela in Carmen; Ein Deutsches Requiem by Brahms.

**YEN, Wen-hsiung,** BA, MA; American musician (piano, erhu), composer and conductor; *Music Director and Conductor, Chinese Music Orchestra of Southern California;* b. 26 June 1934, Tainan, Taiwan; m. Yuan Yuan 1961; three s. *Education:* Nat. Taiwan Normal Univ., Chinese Culture Univ., Univ. of California at Los Angeles, World Univ., studied piano with Qing-Yan Zhou, Fu-Mei Lee, composition with Paul Chihara Hsu, Chang-Houei and Mike Mitacek. *Career:* instructor, Taiwan Provincial Taichung Teacher Coll. 1961–62; Prof., Chinese Culture Univ. 1964–69; founder, Music Dir and Conductor, Chinese Music Orchestra of Southern California 1974–; founder, Chinese Culture School, Los Angeles 1976–; Lecturer, West Los Angeles Coll. 1978–82; Faculty, Dept of Music, Univ. of Maryland 1982–83; instructor, Los Angeles City Coll., California State Univ., Los Angeles 1984–, California State Univ., Northridge and Santa Monica City Coll. 1986–; founder and Pres., Chinese Musicians' Asscn of Southern California 1990–; conducted the orchestra for the Dragon Boat Festival at the Chinese Cultural Center in Los Angeles' Chinatown 1993 and for the opening ceremony of the annual Chinese Writers' Asscn of Southern California Conference 1993; mem. Soc. for

Ethnomusicology, Int. Council for Traditional Music, Soc. for Asian Music; Fellow UCLA. *Compositions:* Drinking Alone in the Moonlight (words L. Bai), Song of 911, Pure Even Tune (words L. Bai), Roc Flies Ten Thousand Miles, Mother Earth – Four Seasons, The Phoenix Hair Pin (words Lu You). *Recording:* East-West Music Concert (DVD) 2004. *Publications:* Taiwan Folk Songs Vol. I 1967, Vol. II 1969, A Dictionary of Chinese Music (co-author) 1967, A Collection of Wen-hsiung Yen's Songs Vol. I 1968, Vol. II 1987, Vol. III 2002, Chinese Musical Culture and Folk Songs 1989, A Study of Si Xiang Qi (article) 1989, Silk and Bamboo Expresses Emotion of Meaning 2000, Wen-hsiung's Composition Vol. 3 2000. *Honours:* Confucius Commemorative Day Ceremony Outstanding Teacher Award, Los Angeles 1984, UCLA Assocs of Ethnic Artists Award, Fed. of Overseas Chinese Asscns Award 2000, 2002. *Address:* c/o Chinese Cultural School of Los Angeles, 615 Las Tunas Drive, Suite B, Arcadia, CA 91007, USA.

**YERNA, Alexise;** Singer (Mezzo-soprano); b. 1959, Belgium. *Education:* Studied at the Brussels Conservatoire with Jules Bastin. *Career:* Sang in operas by Handel, Chabrier and Puccini at the Brussels opera studio; Opéra Wallonie at Liège from 1982, as Orlofsky and in operettas by Offenbach; Has appeared throughout Belgium and France at Lola, Pepa in Goyescas, Fenena (Nabucco) and the Priestess in Aida; Many concert engagements. *Address:* c/o Opéra de Wallonie, 1 Rue des Dominicains, 4000 Liège, Belgium.

**YEROFEEVA, Yelena;** Cellist; b. 1960, Moscow, Russia. *Education:* Studied at the Moscow Conservatoire with Alexei Shislov. *Career:* Co-founded the Glazunov Quartet 1985; Many concerts in the former Soviet Union and recent appearances in Greece, Poland, Belgium, Germany and Italy; Works by Beethoven and Schumann at the Beethoven Haus in Bonn; Further engagements in Canada and Netherlands; Teacher at the Moscow State Conservatoire and Resident at the Tchaikovsky Conservatoire; Repertoire includes works by Borodin, Shostakovich and Tchaikovsky, in addition to the standard works. *Recordings include:* The six quartets of Glazunov. *Honours:* (with the Glazunov Quartet) Prizewinner of the Borodin Quartet and Shostakovich Chamber Music Competitions. *Address:* c/o Sonata (Glazunov Quartet), 11 Northpark Street, Glasgow G20 7AA, Scotland.

**YIM, Jay Alan,** BA, MMus; Composer; b. 24 April 1958, St Louis, MO, USA. *Education:* University of California, Royal College of Music, London, England; studied at Dartmouth, England and Tanglewood. *Career:* Lecturer, Director of Electronic Music Studio, University of California, Santa Barbara, 1978–80; Composer-in-Residence, Cummington School of the Arts, 1984; Major festival performances at Huddersfield, 1982, International Computer Music Conference, 1985, Tanglewood in 1986 and 1987, and Gaudeamus in 1987. *Compositions:* Orchestral: Askesis, 1980–81, Eastern Windows, 1981, Karénas, 1986; Chamber: Palimpsest, 1979, Piak, 1981, Autumn Rhythm, 1984–85, Moments Of Rising Mist, 1986, Mille Graces, 1986, Geometry And Delirium, 1987; Solo instrument: Timescreen for Pianoforte No. 1, 1984, No. 2, 1983, Furiosamente for Piccolo, 1985, Más Furiosamente for Flute, 1985; Electronic: Kinkakuji, 1984, Shiosai, 1984. *Address:* c/o ASCAP, ASCAP Building, 1 Lincoln Plaza, New York, NY 10023, USA.

**YING, Shi Zhen;** Piano Professor; b. 29 Nov. 1937, China; m. Pan Yi Ming 1960, 2 s. *Education:* Bachelor Degree, 1960, Masters Degree, 1962, Central Conservatory of Music, Beijing. *Career:* Debut: Seven years of age; Piano teacher, Department of Central Conservatory of Music, Beijing, 1962–91; Performed numerous piano recitals and concerts in China and around the world; Recitals, The Tchaikovsky Conservatory of Moscow and other cities in Russia; Lecturer, many Chinese Conservatories including Hong Kong University, 1984; Music Adviser, Singapore Yamaha Music Academy, Singapore, 1991–; Examiner, Guildhall School of Music and Drama, England. *Compositions:* Many piano examination pieces. *Publications:* The Methods of Piano Teaching and Performance, 1990; Over 10 articles in magazines in China; Text books. *Honours:* 1st prize, Conservatory Piano Competition, 1961. *Address:* Blk 38, 14-2406 Upper Boon, Kent Road, 5380038, Singapore.

**YOES, Janice;** Singer (Soprano); b. 1947, USA. *Career:* Debut: New York City Opera in 1973 as Santuzza; Sang at the Augsburg Opera, 1975–77, Saarbrucken, 1976–77, and Karlsruhe, 1977–78; Engaged at Nuremberg, 1978–84, with guest appearances at Graz, 1980–83; Sang Strauss's Elektra at the Vienna Staatsoper, Marseilles, Madrid, the Deutsche Oper Berlin, Seattle and Santiago in 1984; Bregenz Festival in 1977 as Reiza in Oberon; Appearances as Brünnhilde in Der Ring de Nibelungen at Naples, Lisbon and Seattle, 1982–86; Further engagements at Basle, Trieste, Brunswick and Pretoria, 1987–88; Other roles have included Isolde, Salome and Lady Macbeth. *Address:* Opera of the Performing Arts Council, Transvaal PO Box 566, Pretoria 0001 Transvaal, South Africa.

**YORDANOV, Luben;** Violinist; b. 6 Dec. 1926, Sofia, Bulgaria. *Education:* Studied at the Paris Conservatoire, with Pierre Pasquier. *Career:* Has performed throughout Europe as concert soloist from 1951; Leader of the orchestra of the Monte Carlo Opera, 1958–67; Orchestre de Paris, 1967–91; Premiered the Concerto by André Jolivet, 1973, and became professor of chamber music at the Paris Conservatoire, 1987. *Address:* Conservatoire National Superieur de Musique et de Danse de Paris, 209 Avenue Jean-Jaures, Paris 75019, France.

**YORK, Deborah;** Singer (soprano); b. 9 Nov. 1964, Sheffield, Yorkshire, England. *Education:* Manchester University and the Guildhall School of Music, with Laura Sarti; Further study with Janice Chapman. *Career:* Opera engagements with Glyndebourne Touring Opera as Servilia in La Clemenza di Tito, Mirror in Birtwistle's The Second Mrs Kong; Emilia in Handel's Flavio for Dublin Touring Opera; Mozart's Barbarina at Covent Garden and Fortuna in Monteverdi's Poppea for Netherlands Opera (1995–96); Concerts include Pergolesi's Stabat Mater under Marc Minkowski, Purcell's Tempest with Ivor Bolton, Handel's Israel in Egypt with the Brandenburg Consort and Dixit Dominus with the Hallé Orchestra; Purcell's King Arthur with the King's Singers in Italy and with the English Concert at the 1995 London Proms; Further concerts with the Collegium Vocale, Ghent, under Phillipe Herreweghe; Other broadcasts include music by Purcell with the King's Consort for the BBC, and with the Gabrieli Players in France; Music for the Mona Lisa on Radio 3; Season 1997–98 with Gianetta in L'Elisir d'amore at Covent Garden, Semele at Berlin, Anne Trulove in concert with the London Symphony Orchestra and Handel's Jephtha at the 1997 London Proms; Acis and Galatea in Spain and the St John Passion at Montpellier; Sang Alceste in Handel's Admeto at Beaune, 1998; Season 2000–01 with Almirena in Handel's Rinaldo at Munich and Anne Trulove at Teatro Colón, Buenos Aires. *Current Management:* IMG Artists, Lovell House, 616 Chiswick High Road, London, W4 5RX, England. *Telephone:* (20) 8233-5800. *Fax:* (20) 8233-5801. *E-mail:* artistseurope@imgworld.com. *Website:* www.imgartists.com.

**YORK, John;** Pianist; b. 20 March 1949, Eastbourne, England; m. Fiona Osborne, 5 Sept 1981, 1 s., 1 d. *Education:* AGSM Diploma, Guildhall School of Music and Drama, London, 1971; Studied in Paris with Jacques Février, 1971–72; Vienna Hochschule with Dieter Weber, 1972–74. *Career:* Debut: Wigmore Hall, 1974; Recitals and concerts in the United Kingdom, Ireland, France, throughout Europe, USA, Canada, Brazil, Bermuda, Singapore, Malaysia; Australia; Partner to Raphael Wallfisch, cello; Member of York 2 Piano Duo; Classic FM, BBC radio, and CBC television and radio. *Recordings:* Many albums on several labels including: 3 albums of York Trio; Eminence and Black Box with Raphael Wallfisch. *Publications:* Selector and assistant in new issue of Mikrokosmos (Bartók); Fingers and Thumbs, 1993; 20th Century Collections, 1998. *Contributions:* Reviewer for Piano Magazine, The Strad. *Honours:* Debussy Prize, Paris, 1973. *Current Management:* Clarion/Seven Muses, London, England. *Address:* 38 Caterham Road, Lewisham, London SE13 5 AR, England. *Telephone:* (20) 8318-1824. *E-mail:* john@yorkpiano.freeserve.co.uk.

**YORK, Richard,** BEd; British musician and music historian; b. 15 May 1953, Northampton, England; m. Elizabeth York; two d. *Education:* Culham Coll., Abingdon and Northampton Coll. *Career:* freelance education workshop leader in schools and museums; music historian and interpreter at museums and heritage sites, including Victoria & Albert museum, London, Greenwich Foundation, English Heritage and Nat. Trust properties, and Elgar's birthplace museum; plays a large collection of instruments from medieval clarsach to Victorian concertina and hammer dulcimer; mem. Incorporated Soc. of Musicians, Int. Museum Theatre Alliance Europe, Asscn for Historical Interpretation. *Address:* 1 Exmoor Close, Northampton, NN3 3AU, England (home). *Telephone:* (1604) 639581 (home). *E-mail:* richard@richard-york.co.uk (office). *Website:* www.richard-york.co.uk (office).

**YOSHINO, Naoko;** Harpist; b. 1967, London, England. *Education:* Studied with Susan McDonald of Indiana University from 1974. *Career:* Soloist with leading orchestras from 1977, notably the Israel Philharmonic under Mehta in 1985, the Philadelphia Orchestra under Frühbeck de Burgos in 1987, and in Japan with Seiji Ozawa and Wolfgang Sawallisch; New York recital debut at Merkin Hall in 1987 and chamber concert with members of the Berlin Philharmonic; Soloist with the Berlin Philharmonic under Ozawa in 1988; Classic Aid concerts with Lorin Maazel in Paris, 1988, and Yehudi Menuhin at Gstaad Festival in 1988; London debut with James Galway in Mozart's Concerto K299 in 1990; London recital debuts in 1990; English Chamber Orchestra at the Barbican under Menuhin in 1990; Played at the World Harp Festival at Cardiff in 1991. *Recordings:* Album with the English Chamber Orchestra under Menuhin; 5 Other albums recorded: 3 as soloist, 1 with flute and 1 concerto album. *Honours:* Second Prize, First International Harp Contest, Santa Cecilia Academy in Rome, 1981; 1st Prize, 9th International Harp Contest in Israel, 1985. *Current Management:* Kajimoto Concert Management Ltd. *Address:* Kajimoto Concert Management Ltd, Kahoku Building 8-6-25 Ginza, Chuo-Ku, Tokyo, Japan.

**YOST, Ricardo;** Singer (Bass-baritone); b. 1943, Chile. *Education:* Studied in Santiago. *Career:* Sang at the Teatro Colón Buenos Aires from 1973, notably as Guglielmo, Rigoletto, Amonasro, Iago, Renato, Malatesta, Escamillo and Napoleon in Prokofiev's War and Peace; Has appeared throughout South America and in bass roles such as Mephistopheles and Rossini's Basilio; Sang Amonasro at Buenos Aires, 1996; Sang in Francesca da Rimini at Buenos Aires, 2000. *Address:* Teatro Colón, Cerrito 618, 1010 Buenos Aires, Argentina.

**YOUN, Kwangchul;** Singer (Bass); b. 1970, Korea. *Education:* Chong-Ju University; Sofia Music School and Berlin Hochschule der Künste, with Herbert Brauer. *Career:* Sang in concert at Seoul from 1998; South Korean State Opera 1988-90; Engaged at the Deutsche Oper Berlin from 1993; Bayreuth Festival debut 1996, in Die Meistersinger; Sang the Priest in Schoenberg's Moses und Aron, Vienna Konzerthaus 2001; Season 2001–02 with concerts in Berlin and Lyon, Mozart's Bartolo at Barcelona and High Priest in Idomeneo at the Salzburg Festival. *Address:* c/o Deutche Oper Berlin, Richard Wagnerstrasse 10, D-10568 Berlin, Germany.

**YOUNG, Douglas;** Composer, Pianist, Conductor, Writer and Broadcaster; b. 18 June 1947, London, England; m. Susan Anne Devlin, 22 Nov 1980, 1 d. *Education:* Trinity College of Music, Junior Exhibitioner, 1957–66; ATCL, Piano Performance, 1963; BMus, London Royal College of Music, 1969. *Career:* Debut: As Pianist, Royal Festival Hall, London, 1970; Works with Ronald Hynd, choreographer for Royal Ballet and München Staatsoper Ballet, 1970–; Fellow, Commoner in The Creative Arts, Trinity College, Cambridge, 1973–75; Composer-in-Residence, Leicester Education Authority, 1975–77; Founded internationally renowned ensemble, Dreamtiger, 1975; Trustee, LAMA; SPNM; BMIC. *Compositions include:* Works in all genres including several inspired by Apollinaire, Lewis Carroll, Joyce, Virginia Woolf and Borges; Series of Concerti, Night Journeys Under The Sea; Ludwig–Fragments Eines Rätsels, ballet in 2 acts, 1986; Mr. Klee Visits the Botanical Gardens, for string quartet, 1993; Herr Schoenberg Plays Ping-Pong, for piano, 1992–99; The Excursions of M. Jannequin, for piano, 1997–; The Eternal Waterfall, for cello and piano, 1998; The Lost Puzzle of Gondwana, stage, 1999. *Recordings include:* Virages–Region One for Cello and Large Orchestra; Trajet, Inter Lignes, 1980; The Hunting Of The Snark, 1982; Third Night Journey Under The Sea, 1980–82; Rain, Steam And Speed, 1982; Dreamlandscapes, Portrait Of Apollinaire, 1983; Dreamlandscapes Book ll, 1986. *Contributions:* Tempo; Music Teacher; Composer. *Honours:* Cobbett Prize for Chamber Music, 1968; Karl Rankl Prize for Orchestral Composition, Musica Nova, 1970–71. *Address:* c/o BMI, 79 Harley House, Marylebone Road, London, NW1, England.

**YOUNG, Josephine;** Cellist; b. 1960, Auckland, New Zealand. *Education:* Studied at the New England Conservatory, and in London with Christopher Bunting. *Career:* Debut: Concert in Wellington, 1988; Chamber musician and soloist in New Zealand; Co-founder of the New Zealand String Quartet in 1987 under the auspices of the Music Federation of New Zealand; Concerts at the Tanglewood School in USA, the Banff International Competition in Canada and performances with the Lindsay Quartet at the 1990 International Festival of the Arts, Wellington; Soloist with the New Zealand Symphony Orchestra and artist-in-residence at Victoria University, Wellington; Tour to Australia in 1990 for Musica Viva Australia; Tours of New Zealand in 1992 and concerts in New York, 1993. *Recordings:* Various albums.

**YOUNG, Julianne;** Singer (Mezzo-soprano); b. 1973, Cape Town, South Africa. *Education:* Royal College of Music, with Lillian Watson. *Career:* Concert engagements include Mozart's Requiem at King's College Chapel, Bach's Passions at St John's Smith Square (St John Passion with Peter Schreier, 2000) and Rossini's Petite Messe in Glasgow; Opera roles include Adalberto in Ottone and Vitige in Flavio, for the London Handel Festival, 2000–2001; Baba the Turk in The Rake's Progress; Further concerts include Linbury Theatre, Covent Garden, recital (2000), master class with Barbara Bonney, concert tour of Japan with the BBC Concert Orchestra and engagement with the Cape Town Symphony Orchestra, 2000. *Honours:* Winner, Lady Maud Warrender and Cuthbert Smith Prizes, RCM; John McCormack Golden Voice Competition, Ireland. *Address:* Royal College of Music, Prince Consort Road, London SW7, England.

**YOUNG, La Monte Thornton;** Composer and Performer; b. 14 Oct. 1935, Bern, Idaho, USA; m. Marian Zazeela, 1963. *Education:* Studied at Los Angeles City College, 1953–56, Los Angeles State College, 1956–57 and UCLA with Robert Stevenson; Further study with Andrew Imbrie at the Stockhausen masterclasses at Darmstadt and electronic music at the New School for Social Research, NY. *Career:* Performed and taught Kirana style of North Indian classical vocal music, with Pran Nath; Collaborations with Marian Zazeela; Associations with the Fluxus and Minimalist movements of artistic endeavour; Returned to California in 1959 and became Music Director of the Ann Halprin Dance Company, 1959–60; With Marian Zazeela made tours of USA and Europe with the Theatre of Eternal Music, 1969–75; Director of the Kirana Center for Indian Classical Music, 1971; Dream House maintained by the Dia Art Foundation's programme at Harrison Street, NY, 1979–85. *Compositions include:* Various pieces for electronic and mixed-media forces, 1959–67; Trio for Strings, 1958; Studies I–III, 1959; Arabic Numeral, 1960; Death Chant for Male Voices and Carillon, 1961; The Well-Tuned Piano, ongoing series of pieces for Prepared Piano; Orchestral Dreams, 1985; The Subsequent Dreams of China, 1993; The Empty Base, Sound environments, 1991–. *Publications include:* An Anthology, 1963, revised, 1970; Selected Writings, 1969. *Honours:* Woodrow Wilson Fellowship, 1959; Guggenheim Fellowship, 1966; Creative Arts Public Service Grants; Commission from the Dia Art Foundation, 1975–85. *Address:* c/o ASCAP, ASCAP Building, 1 Lincoln Plaza, New York, NY 10023, USA.

**YOUNG, Richard;** Violist; b. 1945, USA. *Education:* Studied at Indiana University and Catholic University; Teachers included Josef Gingold, Aaron Rosand and William Primrose. *Career:* Performed at Queen Elisabeth of Belgium Competition aged 13; Member of Faculty at Oberlin Conservatory of Music, 1972–84; Performances with the Rogeri Trio and the Hungarian Quartet in the USA, Europe, South America, Africa and Australia; Member of the Vermeer Quartet from 1985; Performances at all major US centres and in Europe, Israel and Australia; Festival engagements at Tanglewood, Aspen, Spoleto, Edinburgh, Mostly Mozart in New York, Aldeburgh, South Bank, Santa Fe, Chamber Music West and the Casals Festival; Resident quartet for Chamber Music Chicago; Annual masterclasses at the Royal Northern College of Music, Manchester; Member of the Resident Artists Faculty of Northern Illinois University; Producer of the Vermeer Quartet's Grammy-nominated

CD of Haydn's the Seven Last words of Christ; Mozart K421 and Beethoven op 95 with the Vermeer Quartet at the 2001 Bath Festival. *Recordings include:* Quartets by Beethoven, Dvořák, Verdi and Schubert; Brahms Clarinet Quintet with Karl Leister. *Address:* Allied Artists, 42 Montpelier Square, London SW7 1JZ, England.

**YOUNG, Simone,** AM; Australian conductor; *Music Director and General Manager, Staatsoper Hamburg;* b. 2 March 1961; m. Greg Condon; two d. *Education:* Sydney Conservatorium of Music. *Career:* Conductor Vienna Staatsoper, Bastille (Paris), Berlin Staatsoper, Cologne Opera, Royal Opera House (London), Metropolitan Opera (New York), Houston Grand Opera, Los Angeles Opera, New York Philharmonic Orchestra, Oslo Philharmonic Orchestra, Munich Philharmonic Orchestra, Maggio Musicale (Florence), ORF Radio Orchestra Vienna, NDR Hanover, NHK Symphony Orchestra (Japan), Hamburg Philharmonic Orchestra Sydney, Melbourne and West Australian Symphony Orchestras; Chief Conductor Bergen Philharmonic Orchestra 1999–2002; Music Dir Opera Australia 2001–05; Music Dir and Gen. Man. Staatsoper Hamburg 2005–. *Repertoire includes:* operas: Rigoletto, Tosca, La Traviata, Oberto, Der fliegende Holländer, Der Rosenkavalier, Macbeth, Elektra, La Bohème, Cavalleria Rusticana, Pagliacci, Tales of Hoffmann, Il Trovatore, Lohengrin, Eugène Onegin, Salomé, Fidelio, Peter Grimes, Wozzeck, La Juive, Der Ring des Nibelungen, Die Meistersinger von Nürnberg, Die Fledermaus, Die Frau ohne Schatten, Faust, Ariadne auf Naxos, Simon Boccanegra, Tannhäuser, Falstaff, Don Carlos, Andrea Chenier, Tristan und Isolde, The Marriage of Figaro, Don Giovanni, Lulu, Otello; extensive symphonic repertoire including works of Mahler, Strauss, Wagner, Brahms, Beethoven, Bruckner and Bartók. *Honours:* Chevalier, Ordre des Arts et des Lettres; Hon. DMus (Monash Univ.) 1998, (Univ. of New South Wales) 2001; Young Australian of the Year 1987. *Current Management:* Arts Management, Level 2, 420 Elizabeth Street, Surry Hills, Sydney, NSW 2010, Australia. *Telephone:* (2) 93102466 (office). *Fax:* (2) 93105334 (office). *E-mail:* enquiries@artsmanagement.com.au (office). *Address:* c/o Hamburgische Staatsoper, Große Theaterstraße 34, 20354 Hamburg, Germany. *Website:* www.hamburgische-staatsoper.de.

**YOUNG, Thomas;** Singer (Tenor); b. 1962, USA. *Career:* Debut: Sang the Inspector in the premiere of Under the Double Moon, by Anthony Davis, St Louis, 1989; New York City Opera from 1990, as Schoenberg's Aron, Molqi in The Death of Klinghoffer by John Adams (also in Brussels and San Francisco) and in Zimmermann's Die Soldaten; Season 1992 as Frère Elie in Messiaen's St François d'Assise, at Salzburg, and in Birtwistle's Punch and Judy at Amsterdam; Florence Maggio Musicale 1994, as Aron; Chicago Lyric Opera, 1997, as the Trickster God in the premiere of Amistad, by Anthony Davis; Concerts include Mendelssohn's Elijah, and modern repertory. *Recordings include:* The Death of Klinghoffer. *Address:* c/o Chicago Lyric Opera, 20 North Wacker Drive, Chicago, IL 60606, USA.

**YTTREHUS, Rolv;** Composer; b. 12 March 1926, Duluth, USA. *Education:* BS in music at University of Minnesota, 1950; MM with Ross Lee Finney, at University of Michigan, 1955; Further study with Brustad in Oslo, Boulanger in Paris, Sessions at Princeton (1957–60) and Petrassi in Rome, 1960–61. *Career:* Teacher at the University of Wisconsin, Oshkosh, 1969–77; State University of New Jersey, Rutgers, from 1977. *Compositions include:* Six Haiku for flute, cello and harp, 1959; Music for Winds, Percussion and Viola, 1961; Expression for orchestra, 1962; Sextet for 6 instruments, 1969; Music for winds, percussion, cello and voices, 1969; Angstwagen for soprano and percussion, 1971; Quintet, for flute, violin, clarinet, cello and piano, 1973; Gradus ad Parnassum, for soprano and chamber orchestra, after Nietzsche and Fux, 1979; Explorations for piano, 1985; Cello Sonata, 1988; Raritan Variation for piano, 1989; Symphony, 1995. *Address:* c/o ASCAP, 1 Lincoln Plaza, New York, NY 10023, USA.

**YU, Chun Yee;** Pianist; b. 12 July 1936, Shanghai, China; m. (1) Isabella Miao, Dec 1963, 2 s., (2) Jung Chang, June 1982. *Education:* Royal College of Music, England under Kendall Taylor; Agostic, Italy; Tagliaferro, France. *Career:* Examiner to the Associated Board of Royal School of Music; Professor of Piano, Royal College of Music; Represented Singapore at the First Asian Music Festival in Hong Kong; First appeared at the Royal Festival Hall in 1963 as soloist with London Philharmonic Orchestra; Has played extensively in the Far East and throughout the United Kingdom; Recently toured Taiwan and China. *Honours:* Recordi Prize for Conducting; Prizewinner, International Piano Competition; Scholarship to study in Siena under Agosti. *Address:* c/o Royal College of Music, London, SW7, England.

**YU, Julian Jing-Jun,** DipMus, MMus; Australian (b. Chinese) composer; *Teacher of Composition, University of Melbourne;* b. 2 Sept. 1957, Beijing, China; m. Marion Hazel Gray 1984. *Education:* Central Conservatory of Music, Beijing, Tokyo Coll. of Music, Queensland Conservatorium of Music, La Trobe Univ., Melbourne. *Career:* Teacher of Harmony, Cen. Conservatory of Music, Beijing 1977–85; emigrated to Australia 1985; Tanglewood Fellow 1988; Victorian Ministry for the Arts Music Advisory Panel 1991–93, 1995–96; Teacher of Composition, Univ. of Melbourne 1992–, Victorian Coll. of the Arts 1993–; work commissioned by ABC, Ensemble Intercontemporain, IRCAM, Chamber Made Opera, Australia Ensemble, Synergy Percussion, The City of Munich and the BBC Proms; jury mem. BMW Music Theatre Prize at Munich Biennale 1992, for ACL Young Composer's Competition 2003; works performed at Huddersfield Contemporary Music Festival 1990, ISCM World Music Days, Zürich 1991, New Mexico 1993, Luxembourg 2000, Lausanne

2004. *Compositions:* music for film, tv and stage productions –1986; Impromptu for piano 1987, Wu-Yu for orchestra 1987, Scintillation I, II and III 1987, Great Ornamented Fuga Canonica for orchestra 1988, Medium Ornamented Fuga Canonica for woodwind quintet 1988, Reclaimed Prefu I for two pianos 1989, The White Snake (music theatre) 1989, First Australian Suite for chamber orchestra 1990, Reclaimed Prefu II for SATB choir and two pianos 1990, In the Sunshine of Bach for a capella choir 1990, Hsiang-Wen (Filigree Clouds) for orchestra 1991, Philopentatonia for chamber orchestra 1994, Three Symphonic Poems 1994, Sinfonia Passacaglissima 1995, Marimba Concerto 1996, Lyrical Concerto for flute and orchestra 1996, Fresh Ghosts (opera) 1997, Concerto for zheng and orchestra 1999, Not a Stream but an Ocean for orchestra 1999, The Future of Water for choir and orchestra 2001, Pictures at an Exhibition modern chamber rendition 2001, The Possessed (opera) 2002, Clarinet Concerto on Chinese Themes 2002, Willow and Wattle for erhu and orchestra 2002, Chaconnissima for four percussionists and piano 2004. *Recordings:* Classical Allusion: Selected Works by Julian Yu, Dovetailing, Impromtu, In the Sunshine of Bach, Pictures at an Exhibition: Modern Version, Scintillation II, Scintillation III, Six Pieces for Young Pianists, Ten Chinese Folk and Art Songs, The Future of Water, Trio for Violin, Cello and Piano, Wu-Yu, Yellow Beanleaves. *Honours:* prize winner Int. New Music Composers' Competition 1987, 1988, 1989, 1990, Albert H. Maggs Composition Award 1988, Koussevitzky Tanglewood Composition Prize 1988, Paul Lowin Orchestral Prize 1991, 1994, Vienna Modern Masters Composition Award 1992, Adolf Spivakovsky Composition Prize 1993, Australia Council Composer Fellowship 1995. *Address:* c/o Australian Music Centre, PO Box N690, Grosvenor Place, NSW 1220, Australia (office). *Telephone:* (2) 92474677 (office). *Fax:* (2) 92412873 (office). *E-mail:* info@amcoz.com.au (office). *Website:* www.amcoz.com.au (office).

**YU, Long;** Conductor; b. 1965, China. *Career:* Many appearances with leading orchestras in Europe and the Far East; Artistic Director of the Peking International Festival, 1998–; Founder of the China Philharmonic Orchestra, 2000; Engagements with soloists including Frank-Peter Zimmermann (violin), Tiziana Fabbricini (soprano) and Nelson Freire (piano) in Australia, France, Germany and Hungary; Further concerts in Hong Kong, Poland, Singapore, Slovakia, Switzerland and China. *Recordings include:* Albums with the China Philharmonic (Deutsche Grammophon). *Current Management:* IMG Artists, Lovell House, 616 Chiswick High Road, London W4 5RX, England.

**YUASA, Takuo,** BMus; Japanese conductor; b. Osaka. *Education:* Univ. of Cincinnati, USA, in France with Igor Markevich, Hochschule, Vienna with Hans Swarowsky, in Siena with Franco Ferrara. *Career:* fmr Asst to Lovro von Matacic in Monte Carlo, Milan and Vienna; fmrly Principal Conductor Gumma Symphony Orchestra, Japan, Principal Guest Conductor BBC Scottish Symphony Orchestra; currently Principal Guest Conductor Ulster Orchestra, Northern Ireland –(2005); regularly performs throughout Europe and the Far East; has played with orchestras, including the Adelaide Symphony, BBC Scottish Symphony Orchestra, Berliner Symphoniker, Bournemouth Symphony Orchestra, Brabants Orkest, Gelders Orkest, Hallé Orchestra, Hong Kong Philharmonic, London Philharmonic, Luxembourg Philharmonic, Nat. Symphony Orchestra of Ireland, New Zealand Symphony Orchestra, North Netherlands Orchestra, Norwegian Radio Orchestra, Oslo Philharmonic, Polish Radio Nat. Symphony Orchestra, Queensland Orchestra, Royal Liverpool Philharmonic Orchestra, Royal Scottish Nat. Orchestra, Sonderjyllands Symphony Orchestra, Sydney Symphony Orchestra, Trondheim Symphony, Ulster Orchestra, Warsaw Nat. Philharmonic. *Honours:* Fitelberg Int. Conducting Competition special award, Katowice, Poland. *Current Management:* Patrick Garvey Management, 10 Rutland Street, Filey, North Yorkshire YO14 9JB, England. *Telephone:* (1723) 516613. *Fax:* (1723) 514678. *E-mail:* patrick@patrickgarvey.com. *Website:* www.patrickgarvey.com.

**YUEN, Nancy;** Singer (Soprano); b. 1965, Hong Kong. *Education:* Royal Academy of Music, London; Scholarship to study Lieder, Germany. *Career:* Extensive concert repertoire; 11 operatic roles; Worked with: Welsh National Opera; English National Opera; Mid-Wales Opera; Los Angeles Music Centre Opera; West Australian Opera; New Zealand International Festival of the Arts; Singapore Lyric Opera; Barbados Festival, 1995; Further engagements with ENO, Hong Kong Arts Festival, Singapore Lyric Opera and Kentish Opera; Extensive tour of Middle East and Far East; Regularly performs at Royal Festival Hall, Queen Elizabeth Hall and the Purcell Room; Recent engagements with: Opera Northern Ireland; Concerts in France and around the United Kingdom; Touring production in the Middle East and Far East; Festival of the Asian Performing Arts, Singapore; Singapore Lyric Theatre; Royal Albert Hall; Performances in Manchester and Sheffield; Lyric Opera productions, National concert Hall, Dublin; Toured France with London City Opera; Sang for Opera Queensland; Royal Albert Hall; Lyric Opera, NCH. *Recordings:* Recorded for BBC radio, Television Hong Kong, Radio FM, New Zealand. *Address:* 16 Maygrove Road, London NW6 2EB, England.

**YURISICH, Gregory;** Singer (Baritone); b. 13 Oct. 1951, Mount Lawley, Western Australia, Australia. *Education:* Studied in Perth. *Career:* Debut: Paolo in Simon Boccanegra for Australian Opera at Sydney, 1978; Roles in Australia have included Mozart's Masetto and Don Alfonso, Verdi's Germont and Melitone, Alberich in The Ring, Varlaam in Boris Godunov, Beethoven's Pizarro and Wagner's Dutchman; European debut, Frankfurt, 1989, as Bottom in A Midsummer Night's Dream; Covent Garden debut, 1990, as William Tell, returning as Dr Bartolo, the villains in Les Contes d'Hoffmann, Don Profondo in a new production of Il Viaggio a Reims, 1992; Pizarro in Fidelio and Scarpia in Tosca; For English National Opera has sung in two world premieres: Alcibiades in Timon of Athens by Stephen Oliver, 1991, and Cadmus in Bakxai by John Buller, 1992; Sang Stankar in a new production of Verdi's Stiffelio at Covent Garden, 1993; Other roles include Escamillo, Leporello (Glyndebourne 1991), King Henry in Anna Bolena, and Verdi's Iago, Simon Boccanegra, Rigoletto and Nabucco; Further engagements include: San Francisco and Geneva (Germont Père in La Traviata); Covent Garden (title role in Nabucco); Australia (title role in Falstaff); Vienna (Balstrode in Peter Grimes and title role in Rigoletto); Munich (title role in Nabucco); Sang in opening gala concert of Belfast Concert Hall, 1997; Tonio in Pagliacci at Washington; Sang the High Priest in Samson et Dalila at Los Angeles, 1999. *Recordings:* Leporello with Roger Norrington. *Address:* c/o English National Opera, St Martin's Lane, London, WC2, England.

# Z

**ZABARA, Maksim;** Bassoonist; b. 12 April 1957, Minsk, Belarus. *Education:* Belorus Lyceum of Music, 1982–91; Kiev Special Music School Lisenko, 1991–94; National Academy of Music, Ukraine, 1994–97. *Career:* Many recital and concert appearances in Belarus, Ukraine, Germany, Netherlands and Canada. Repertory includes CP Bach Sonatas, Concertos by Devienne, Françaix, Hummel, Mozart, Vivaldi and Weber; Sonatas by Glinka, Saint-Saëns and Schubert (arrangement of Arpeggione Sonata); Beethoven's Trio op 11 (arranged), Kreutzer's Trio op 43 and the Trio Pathétique by Glinka. *Honours:* Second Prize, Belarus Youth Woodwind Competition, 1991; Diploma of the International Woodwind Competition, Minsk, 1994. *Address:* c/o NWB Apollon & Hermes, PR-Arts-Media Services Production, Im Flögerhof 12, 53819 Neunkirchen-Cologne, Germany.

**ZABILIASTA, Lydia;** Singer (Soprano); b. 1959, Oleno-Koshorivka, Kirovohrad, Ukraine. *Education:* Studied in Kirovgrad and at the Kiev State Conservatoire; Further study with Giulietta Simionato at La Scala. *Career:* Principal at the National Opera in Kiev from 1982, with such roles as Elsa, Tatiana, Nedda, Xenia in Boris Godunov and Mimi; Tours to North and South America, Japan, Australia and the United Kingdom (with Perm Opera, 1996), adding roles of Abigaille in Nabucco and Madama Butterfly. *Honours:* Gold Medal, Tchaikovsky Singing Competition, Moscow, 1982. *Address:* c/o Sonata Ltd, 11 North Park Street, Glasgow G20 7AA, Scotland.

**ZACCARIA, Nicola;** Singer (Bass); b. 9 March 1923, Athens, Greece. *Education:* Studied at the Royal Conservatory, Athens. *Career:* Debut: Athens in 1949 as Raimondo in Lucia di Lammermoor; Has sung at many Italian centres; La Scala debut in 1953 as Sparafucile in Rigoletto; Sang in Milan in the standard bass repertory until1974, and created the Third Knight in the premiere of Pizzetti's Assassino nella Cattedrale, 1958; Vienna Staatsoper from 1956; Salzburg Festival from 1957 as the Minister in Fidelio, the Monk in Don Carlos, the Commendatore in Don Giovanni and Ferrando in Il Trovatore; Covent Garden in 1957 and 1959, as Oroveso in Norma, and Creon in Médée, both with Maria Callas; Further appearances in Brussels, Cologne, Geneva, Moscow, Rio di Janeiro, Mexico City, Berlin, Monte Carlo, Edinburgh, Aix and Orange; Dallas in 1976 as King Marke in Tristan and Isolde; Sang Colline in La Bohème at Macerata in 1982; Other roles included Verdi's Zaccaria in Nabucco and Silva in Ernani, Rodolfo in La Sonnambula and Sarastro in Die Zauberflöte. *Recordings include:* Norma; Aida; Un Ballo in Maschera; Il Trovatore; La Sonnambula; Rigoletto; Turandot; Barbiere di Siviglia; La Bohème; Falstaff; L'Italiana in Algeri; La Navarraise; Orlando Furioso; Mignon by Thomas; Beethoven's Missa Solemnis.

**ZACHARIAS, Christian;** pianist; b. 27 April 1950, Tamshedpur, India. *Education:* studied with Irene Slavin in Karlsruhe, Germany, with Vlado Perlemuter in Paris, France. *Career:* US debut with the Boston Symphony; appeared in the USA with the Boston Symphony, Cleveland Orchestra and New York Philharmonic, in Canada with the Montreal Symphony; regular appearances in the UK, including the Edinburgh Festival 1985 with the Polish Chamber Orchestra and Jerzy Maksymiuk; engagements at major European festivals include Salzburg and the piano festival at La Roque d'Antheron; chamber concerts with the violinist Ulf Hoelscher, the cellist Heinrich Schiff and the Alban Berg Quartet; British concerts include appearances with the London Symphony Orchestra, BBC Nat. Orchestra of Wales and Royal Liverpool Philharmonic. *Recordings:* Schubert, Scarlatti and Mozart Sonatas, Concertos by Beethoven with the Dresden Staatskapelle. *Honours:* won prizes in Geneva and in the Van Cliburn Competition 1969, won the European Broadcasting Union Ravel Prize 1975. *Current Management:* Kunstlersek A. Schoerke, Grazer Strasse 30, 30519 Hannover, Germany.

**ZACHARIASSEN, Mathias;** Singer (Tenor); b. 1968, Stockholm, Sweden. *Education:* Stockholm College of Opera, with Nicolai Gedda. *Career:* Debut: Eurimedes in Telemann's Orfeo, at the Staatsoper Berlin and Innsbruck Festival of Early Music, 1994; Opera engagements as the Singer in Der Rosenkavalier at Stockholm and Oslo, Mozart's Ferrando and Idamante at Brussels, Lenski and Elemer in Arabella at the 1996 Glyndebourne Festival; Season 1996–97 with Ferrando and Tamino at Graz, Don Ottavio in Oslo; Season 1998 with Jacquino in Leonore and Fidelio, Théâtre des Champs Elysées, Paris; Concerts have included Mozart's C Minor Mass in Oslo and Gothenburg, the Requiem with the Danish Radio Symphony Orchestra and Schubert's A-flat Mass; Verdi Requiem at Norrkoping; Further concerts in Helsinki, Trondheim, Bad Kissingen and Amsterdam. *Address:* c/o Svenska Konsertbyran AB, Jungfrugatan 45, S–114 44 Stockholm, Sweden.

**ZACHER, Gerd;** Concert Organist; b. 6 July 1929, Meppen, Germany. *Education:* Studied at Detmold with Gunter Bialas and in Hamburg. *Career:* Worked at the German Church, Santiago, before position as organist at the Lutheran Church, Hamburg Wellingsbutel, 1957–70; Director of the Church Music Institute at the Essen Hochschule and interpreter of many modern works; Has premiered music by John Cage (Variations, 1963), Mauricio Kagel (Phantasie, 1967), Ligeti (Two Studies, 1967) and Isang Yun (Fragment, 1975); Also a noted performer of works by Bach, Frescobaldi, Liszt and Cabezon.

**ZAGORZANKA, Barbara;** Singer (Soprano); b. 31 July 1938, Kazimierzow, Poland. *Career:* Sang at the Bydgoszcz Opera, 1960–67 as Butterfly, Gilda,

Tosca and Tatiana, Poznan from 1967 as Halka, Micaela, Elisabeth de Valois, Marguerite, Odabella in Attila, Mozart's Countess and Fiordiligi, and Lucia, and Warsaw Opera from 1967 as Aida, Liu, Leonore, Norma, Abigaille, Sieglinde and Roxana in Szymanowski's King Roger; Has sung Halka on tour to the USA and Roxana in Vienna in 1989; Concert of Penderecki's Utrenja at Frankfurt in 1992; Further guest appearances in Paris including Lisa in The Queen of Spades, and Wiesbaden. *Address:* Polish National Opera, Grand Theatre, Plac Teatrainy 1, 00-950 Warsaw, Poland.

**ZAGROSEK, Lothar;** Conductor and Composer; b. 13 Nov. 1942, Waging, Germany. *Education:* Studied in Vienna with Hans Swarowsky and with Karajan and Bruno Maderna. *Career:* Appointments at opera houses in Salzburg, Kiel and Darmstadt, 1967–73; Frequent appearances with the London Sinfonietta from 1978, conducting music by Weill, Ligeti, Messiaen and Stravinsky; Engagements in USA, notably San Diego and Seattle, from 1984; Guest Conductor for BBC Symphony Orchestra; Musical Director, Paris Opéra, 1986–88; Glyndebourne debut in 1987 with Così fan tutte; Conducted the premiere of Krenek's oratorio, Symeon Stylites, at the 1988 Salzburg Festival; Conducted the Paris Opéra Orchestra in York Höller's Der Meister und Margarita in 1989, the last new production at the Paris Opéra, Palais Garnier, before the opening of the Opéra de la Bastille; Conducted the BBC Symphony Orchestra at the 1989 Promenade Concerts in music by Markevitch, Mozart, Mendelssohn, Kodály and Brahms' Ein Deutsches Requiem; Conducted Peter Sellars production of Die Zauberflöte at Glyndebourne in 1990; Promenade Concerts in 1991; Season 1997–98 with King Roger, Die Entführung and Tosca at Stuttgart; Double bill of Bluebeard's Castle and Erwartung at Covent Garden, 2002. *Recordings include:* Jonny spielt auf (Krenek), Goldschmidt's Der gewaltige Hahnrei and Die Vögel by Braunfels, Gruber's Cello Concerto, Schnittke's Piano Concerto, Haydn's 47th Symphony, Brahms No. 1 and Mendelssohn's Violin Concerto; Appointed Music Director at the Stuttgart State Opera, 1996; Chief Conductor of the Städtische Theater, Leipzig; Led the premiere of Das Mädchen by Lachenmann, Hamburg, 1997. *Address:* Staatsoper Stuttgart, Oberer Schossgarten 6, Stuttgart, Germany.

**ZAHORTSEV, Volodymr Mykolayovych;** Composer; b. 27 Oct. 1944, Kiev, Ukraine. *Education:* Tchaikovsky Conservatory, Kiev. *Career:* Joined avant-garde group of post-Stalinist composers in Kiev; mem, The Composers Union of the Ukraine. *Compositions include:* Priskaski, song cycle, 1963; Violin Sonata, 1964; String Quartet, 1964; Sizes for 5 Instruments, 1965; Graduations for Chamber Group, 1966; Games for Chamber Orchestra, 1968; Symphony No. 1, 1968; Music for 4 Strings, 1968; Sonata for Strings, Piano and Percussion, 1969; Rhythms for Piano, 1970; Symphony No. 2 for Soprano, Tenor and Orchestra, 1978; Oboe Sonata, 1978; Music for 4 Strings, No. 2, 1978; A Day In Pereyaslavl for Soloists, Chorus and Orchestra, 1979; In The Children's Room, cantata, 1979; Chamber Concertos 1–4, 1981; Maty (Mother), Lvov, opera, 1985; Chamber Concerto No. 5, 1997; Epitaph No. 1, No. 2, No. 3, 1998; Sonata for piano No. 3, 1999. *Honours:* Zyatoshinsky Prize, 1997. *Address:* c/o Music Information of the Composers Union of the Ukraine, Ul Sofiuska 16/16, 252001 Kiev 1, Ukraine.

**ZAIDEL, Nahum;** Musician and Conductor; b. 20 Sept. 1933, Russia; m. 30 Aug 1976. *Education:* Graduated as Orchestra Soloist, Chamber Music Performer, and Teacher, P I Tchaikovsky State Conservatoire, Moscow, 1957; Studied conducting with Igor Markevitch and Genady Rozhdestvensky, 1963–66. *Career:* Solo Flautist, Moscow Chamber Orchestra under Rudolf Barschai, 1957–58, Moscow Radio Symphony Orchestra under Rozhdestvensky, 1959–72, and Jerusalem Symphony Orchestra, Israel, 1972–; Professor, Rubin Music Academy, Jerusalem, 1972–; Masterclasses for flute and appearances as guest conductor. *Recordings:* Works by Handel, Bach, Beethoven, Gluck, Hindemith, Prokofiev, Doppler, Vivaldi, Stamitz, Cimarosa, Salieri, Chaminade, Bloch, Dvořák, Stravinsky and Kurt Weill, for record and radio. *Honours:* 1st Prize for Flute, International Competition in Moscow, 1957. *Address:* Haviv Avshalom 4-7, Jerusalem 93802, Israel.

**ZAJICK, Dolora;** Singer (Mezzo-Soprano); b. 24 March 1952, Salem, Oregon, USA. *Education:* Studied at the University of Nevada with Ted Puffer and at the Manhattan School of Music with Helen Vanni and Lou Galtiero; Further study with Donald Hall. *Career:* Debut: San Francisco Opera in 1986 as Azucena; Metropolitan Opera debut in 1988 as Azucena; Season 1988–89 with further debuts at Lyric Opera of Chicago, Vienna Staatsoper, Rome's Caracalla Festival and the Verona Arena; Sang Rossini's Stabat Mater at the Cincinnati May Festival and Mahler's 8th Symphony at Washington DC under Rostropovich, Verdi's Requiem at Carnegie Hall and in Paris and London, Mahler's 2nd Symphony in Paris under Lorin Maazel; Season 1989–90 as Amneris and Azucena at the Metropolitan, Tchaikovsky's Maid of Orleans at Carnegie Hall, Il Trovatore in Toulouse and Florence, Aida in Reno, the Verona Arena and at the Caracalla Festival, as Marfa in Khovanshchina at San Francisco Opera, 1990, Eboli in Don Carlo at the Metropolitan, La Scala and in Reno, 1990; Sang Principessa in Adriana Lecouvreur at San Carlo, Naples, 1992, and Jezibaba in Rusalka at the Metropolitan in 1993; Other opera houses include Barcelona, Houston, Florence, Orange Festival, and Covent Garden with debut in 1994; Sang Amneris at the Verona Arena, 1996; Sang in Cav and Pag double bill, Met

1997; Paris Opéra Bastille debut 1998 as Eboli; Season 2000–01 as Azucena at the Met; Etoli at the Munich and Vienna State Opera and Verdi Requiem in Munich. *Recordings include:* La Forza del Destino and Verdi Requiem under Muti; Aida; Il Trovatore, 1991; Don Carlo, under Levine; Alexander Nevsky, under Rostropovich. *Honours:* Bronze Medal, Tchaikovsky International Competition, Moscow, 1982. *Address:* Edgar Vincent-Patrick Farrell Associates, 157 West 57th Street, Suite 502, New York, NY 10019, USA.

**ŻAK, Jerzy**, MA, ARCM; Polish musician and musicologist; *Senior Lecturer*, *Academy of Music, Kraków*; b. 31 March 1954, Łódź. *Education:* Higher School of Music, Łódź, Conservatorio Superior de Musica, Alicante, Early Music Centre, London. *Career:* chamber musician and basso continuo player on lute, theorbo and guitar; chamber concerts, recitals and participation or directing opera performances in Poland, several European countries and in Canada; several broadcasts on Polish radio, and television appearances 1980–; Asst, Acad. of Music, Łódź 1983–94; Sr Lecturer, Acad. of Music, Kraków 1993–; taught at int. summer courses in Wilanów, Poland (Early Music) 1993–94, and in Szczawno Zdrój, Poland (guitar) 1992–99; Artistic Dir, Days of Guitar Music, Int. Festival, Łódź 1984, 1986; Consultant, Akademie Weiss-Inst. for Lute Studies, Parc de Schoppenwihr, France 1992–; founder and Dir of the Kleine Cammer-Musik ensemble 1993–; researcher, chamber music with plucked instruments; specialist in historical plucked instruments, lute and guitar. *Recordings include:* A. Scarlatti, San Casimiro, Re di Polonia, oratorio (Direction), A. Cesti, Secular Chamber Sonatas (Continuo and direction), Silvius Leopold Weiss, Lute Music from Grüssau manuscript. *Publications:* contrib. articles to musicological journals. *Address:* Pustola 32A m 6, 01-107 Warsaw, Poland (home). *E-mail:* jurekzak@gazeta.pl (home).

**ZAKAI, Mira;** Singer (Contralto); b. 1942, Jerusalem. *Education:* Studied in Tel-Aviv with Jennie Tourel. *Career:* Debut: Vienna in 1976 with Mahler's Rückert Lieder; Further concerts with the Philharmonia Orchestra, Berlin Philharmonic (Mahler No. 2 under Abbado), in New York (Bach B minor Mass), and throughout Germany (Das Lied von der Erde and Mahler No. 3, 1987); Sang with Israel National Opera from 1990 in The Medium and Hansel and Gretel; Sang at Bonn in 1992 in Beethoven's Ninth; Opera includes Gluck's Orpheus with Scottish Opera, and Anne in Les Troyens with Opéra de Lyon; Has also sing with the following conductors: Guillini, Leinsdorf, Kubelik, Mehta, the premiere of Berio's orchestrations for Mhler Songs under Berio, Andrew Davis, Bertini, Menuhin in a concert for Pope John Paul in Castel Gandolfo, Rome, Zedda, Rizzi, Groves etc.; Collaborations with pianists including: Mikael Eliasen, Graham Johnson, Cristian Ivaldi, Andras Schiff and others; Professor at the Tel Aviv Rubin Academy of Music, part of the Tel Aviv University, teaching voice and heading the Lied and Oratorio Department. *Recordings include:* Mahler 2nd Symphony with the Chicago Symphony Orchestra and George Solti. *Honours:* Grammy Award for recording of Mahler's 2nd Symphony with the Chicago Symphony Orchestra and Sir George Solti; Special Prize for contribution to Israeli Music given by the ministry of education; BA Hebrew Literature and Theatre Arts from Tel Aviv University; BMus and MMus in singing from Tel Aviv University. *Address:* 6 Patai St. Givatayim 53203 Israel. *E-mail:* mzakai@post.tau.ac.il.

**ZALEWSKI, Wlodzimerz;** Singer (Bass-Baritone); b. 1949, Poland. *Career:* Sang at the Łódź Opera, 1975–82 and Gelsenkirchen from 1982; Bregenz Festival in 1978 as the Dutchman, and Philadelphia in 1988 as Don Alfonso in Così fan tutte; Professor at the Łódź Music Academy from 1981; Sang in the 1989 premiere of Michael Kohlhaas by Karl Kogler at the Landestheater, Linz; Appearances at Łódź and elsewhere as Boris Godunov; Other roles have included Hindemith's Cardillac, Kaspar in Der Freischütz, Basilio, Mustafâ, Wotan and Scarpia; Frequent concert appearances.

**ZAMBELLI, Marco;** Conductor; b. 1965, Genoa, Italy. *Education:* organ and composition, Geneva Conservatoire. *Career:* Chorus Master at the Grasse Boys Choir, 1988–89, Opéra de Lyon 1989–92 (including the premiere of Debussy's Rodrigue et Chimène); other repertory includes all major operas of Mozart, L'Elisir d'amore, La Bohème, Butterfly, Poppea, Orfeo and Il Trovatore; asst with such conductors as John Eliot Gardiner (Manon Lescaut at Glyndebourne and other repertory with Monteverdi/EBS), Luciano Berio and Woldemar Nelsson; Season 1996–97 with Pergolesi/Cimarosa double bill at Messina, La Cenerentola at Ascoli and Don Giovanni for Opera Zuid; Haydn's Creation in Cogliou, 1996; Madama Butterfly, 1996, and Don Pasquale and Rigoletto, 1997, at the Tenerife Opera Festival; Luisa Miller and Madama Butterfly for Opera North and Manon Lescaut at the 1997 Glyndebourne Festival; Così fan tutte.

**ZAMBELLO, Francesca,** BA; American opera producer and musical director; b. 24 Aug. 1956, New York. *Education:* American School of Paris, Colgate Univ. *Career:* Asst Dir Lyric Opera of Chicago 1981–82, San Francisco Opera 1983–84; Artistic Dir Skylight Music Theatre 1984–; guest producer San Francisco Opera, Teatro La Fenice, Savonlinna Festival, Houston Grand Opera, Nat. Opera of Iceland, Seattle Opera, San Diego Opera, Opera Theatre of St Louis, Rome Opera, Théâtre Municipal de Lausanne, Teatro Regio, Greater Miami Opera, Pesaro Festival, Parma and Wexford Festival. *Works directed include:* La Traviata (San Francisco Opera) 1983, La Voix Humaine (San Francisco Opera) 1986, Faust (San Francisco Opera) 1986, La Bohème (San Francisco Opera) 1988, Lucia di Lammermoor (New York Metropolitan Opera) 1992, Arianna (Royal Opera House, Covent Garden) 1994–95, Billy Budd (Royal Opera House, Covent Garden, Opéra Bastille) 1995–96, Khovanshchina (ENO) 1995–96, Tannhäuser (Copenhagen) 1995–96, Modern Painters (Santa Fe Opera) 1995–96, Prince Igor (San Francisco Opera) 1996, Lady in the Dark (Nat. Theatre, London) 1997, Iphigènie en Tauride (Glimmerglass Festival) 1997, Salammbô (Opéra Bastille) 1998, Tristan (Seattle) 1998, Napoleon (Shaftesbury Theatre, London) 2000, The Bartered Bride (Royal Opera House, Covent Garden) 2001, Don Giovanni (Royal Opera House, Covent Garden) 2002, Guillaume Tell (Opéra Bastille) 2003. *Honours:* several Olivier Awards, Nat. Opera Inst. grant. *Current Management:* Columbia Artists, 165 W 57th Street, New York, NY 10019, USA.

**ZAMBORSKY, Stanislav;** Pianist; b. 12 April 1946, Kosice; m. Zlata Olachova, 8 July 1972, 2 d. *Education:* Konservatorium Kosice; Academy of Music and Dramatic Arts, Bratislava; Franz Liszt Academy, Budapest; Doctor Degree, Academy of Arts, Bratislava. *Career:* Debut: Bratislava Music Festival; Many Concerts with Orchestra and Recitals in Netherlands, France, Bulgaria, Poland, Soviet Union, Germany, Italy, Sweden, Spain, Belgium, Kuwait, Cuba, Korea, Jerusalem. *Recordings:* Mozart, Haydn Concertos; Schumann, Sonata G minor; Liszt, Liebersträume, Au bord d'une source, Death of Isolde; Hummel Works for 4 hands piano; Sixta Piano Sonata; Bokes Piano concerto; Parik Dropping Foliage Songs, Hrusovsky Sonata No. 2; Mozart Piano Sonatas; Grieg Piano Concerto. *Honours:* 2nd Prize, Prague, 1968; 4th Prize, Utrecht, 1969; Frico Kafenda Prize, Excellent Interpretation, Slovak Music, Bratislava, 1995; Complete Musical Critic Prix, Bratislava, 1996. *Address:* Bieloruska 52, 821 06 Bratislava, Slovakia.

**ZAMIR;** singer (high tenor); b. 1953, USA. *Education:* Univ. of Massachusetts at Amherst, Univ. of Maine at Portland-Gorham, Chicago and San Francisco Conservatories of Music. *Career:* has appeared since 1985 in major cities of Israel, USA, Iceland, Germany, England and Cyprus in wide range of concert and operatic music; Conductors include Marc Minkowski, Christopher Hogwood, Nicholas McGegan, and Richard Westenberg; Has performed as Male Soprano, Countertenor and Baritone as well as Tenor, specializing as high tenor, Tenore di Grazia; Has sung in Die Fledermaus in 1977, Cendrillon in 1986, A Midsummer Night's Dream in 1987, La Bohème in 1988, Lucia di Lammermoor, Mefistofele, Attila, Platée and Cavalleria Rusticana in 1988, La Clemenza di Tito and Alcina in 1990, and Riccardo Primo with the English Bach Festival at Covent Garden in 1991.

**ZAMPARINO, Cesare;** singer (tenor); b. 1969, Italy. *Career:* sang Alfredo in Traviata at Rieti (1992) followed by the Duke of Mantua at Buenos Aires; Teatro San Carlo Naples from 1993, as Alfredo and as Alfred in Fledermaus; other repertory includes Rodolfo, Nemorino, Elvino (La Sonnambula), Edgardo, Ernesto and Cavaradossi.

**ZAMPIERI, Maria;** Singer (Soprano); b. 24 May 1941, Padua, Italy. *Education:* Studied at the Padua Conservatory. *Career:* Debut: Pavia in 1972; La Scala Milan from 1977 as Amalia in I Masnadieri, Leonora in Il Trovatore and Elisabeth de Valois; Trieste as Elvira in Ernani; Lisbon as Amelia Boccanegra; Vienna Staatsoper from 1979 in Il Giuramento, Attila and Macbeth; Deutsche Oper Berlin and Verona Arena as Aida; Covent Garden debut in 1984 as Tosca; Other engagements in Munich, Buenos Aires, San Francisco, Bregenz, Bonn and Frankfurt; Sang Francesca da Rimini at Karlsruhe in 1986; Season 1987–88 as Norma at Nîmes and Lady Macbeth at Spoleto; Stuttgart Staatsoper in 1990 as Tosca, Bregenz Festival in 1990 in the title role of La Wally; Debut as Salome at Vienna, 1991; Sang Suor Angelica at Zürich, 1996; Verdi's Elena and Lady Macbeth at the Vienna Staatsoper, 1999. *Recordings include:* Il Giuramento; Attila; Belisario by Donizetti; Macbeth. *Address:* Allied Artists, 42 Montpelier Square, London SW7 1JZ, England.

**ZAMUSZKO, Slawomir;** Polish composer, viola player and teacher of music theory; b. 30 Dec. 1973, Łódź. *Education:* H. Wieniawski State Music Lyceum, Łódź, G. & K. Bacewicz Univ. of Music, Łódź, F. Chopin Acad. of Music, Warsaw with Prof. Marian Borkowski, Computer Eng Dept Tech. Univ. of Łódź. *Career:* debut as composer, Stage Music for David Mercer's Flint with flute, horn, trombone, strings and synthesizer, 'Pole' Theatre Studio, Łódź 1993; viola player with Strings of Łódź Chamber Orchestra 1990–93, Polish Camerata Orchestra 1993–94; first and solo violist, Young Austrian Philharmony 1996–99; contrib. to Justus Frantz's Philharmony of Nations 1998; numerous concerts performing own work in Poland, Germany, Netherlands, USA, 47th Festival of Contemporary Music, Warsaw 2004, 11th Laboratory of Contemporary Music, Warsaw 1994; candidate mem. Polish Composers' Union; man. mem. The Culture Coalition Soc., Łódź. *Compositions include:* instrumental and vocal instrumental: Suite for viola solo 1995, Controversies an instrumental theatre for two flutes 1996, Portal 1 for horn and piano 1996, Concerto for clarinet and string orchestra 1998, An die unsterbliche Geliebte (cantata, after Beethoven) for baritone and orchestra 1998, Portal 2 for viola, cello and orchestra 1999, Preludes for piano 1999–2000, Requiem (text by Anna Akhmatova) for alto and string quartet 2000, Re-percussions for two trumpets and two percussion groups 2001, Preludes for organ 2001, Psalm XV for lyric soprano and chamber orchestra 2001–02, Portal 3 for chamber orchestra with concerting viola 2002, The Mask (after S. Lem) monodrama for female speaking voice and chamber orchestra 2004, Six Persons for cello and piano 2004; vocal: A Heart Grows Up song for four-voiced male choir a capella (text by Jan Kochanski) 1999, Lingvariations on theme of John Cage for speaking voice 2001; electronic: Babel FM for tape 1997, Play-tin for tape 1997, Ampliviola 1 for tape 2001–02, Ampliviola 2 for tape 2003; music for the spectacles of 'Pole' Theatre Studio in Łódź and motion pictures realized by students of Film/Television Directing and Cinematography Depts of L. Schiller State Film, Television and Theatre School in Łódź.

*Recordings:* Portal 1 for horn and piano 2000, Preludes for organ 2003. *Publications:* contrib. to Muzyka 21 2000–02, Koneser 2001–02, Musical Education in School 2002–03, Dobre Radio Broadcasting Corpn 2003–04. *Honours:* Ministry of Culture and Arts scholarship 1997–98, first prize Int. Composers' Competition, Cottbus, Germany 2000, 2003. *Address:* Gdanska 32, 90-716 Łódź (office); Piotrkowska 204/210 m 106, 90-369 Łódź, Poland (home). *E-mail:* zamek@mnc.pl. *Website:* www.mnc.pl/~zamek/zamek .htm#utwory.

**ZANABONI, Giuseppe,** DipMus; Italian organist, conductor and composer; b. 25 Nov. 1926, Pontelagoscuro; m. Clelia Losi 1951; one s. one d. (deceased). *Career:* debut 1945; major solo organ concerts world-wide; masterclasses in Europe and America; chamber and symphonic orchestra conductor, Italy; Dir of State Music Conservatorium, Piacenza 1968–93; Artistic Dir, V. L. Ciampi instrumental group for diffusion of ancient music; founder and Dir, Group V. Legrenzio Ciampi chamber music ensemble, Piacenza. *Compositions include:* Lyric Opera: Alcesti, 1949; Myrica, 1949; La Regina delle Nevi, 1952; Casello 83, 1956; De Placentiae Synodo, 1995–96; Cantatas: Apoteosi di S Giovanni B de la Salle, 1950; Cantata a Roma; I Bambini di Terezin, 1991; Chamber Music: Quartetto in Do for strings, 1949; Improvviso Drammatico, 1953; Meditazione for strings and organ, 1968; Luna Park, 1968; Quatuor for strings, 1988; Con Pincchio nel Regno della Fantasia, 1990; Menhir studio, 1992; Immagini e Suoni, 1993; Fantasia in Epidiapente, 1993; Tiphyscolon, impressioni sinfoniche su Cristoro Colombo, 1992; Choral Music: Missa Laudate Pueri Dominum, 1941; Requiem Aeternam, 1943; Missa Domine Non Sum Dignus, 1944; Esaltazione del Volto di S Corrado, 1994; La Fravezzosa, carme madricalis, 1984; For Organ: Toccata, 1966; Profilo di un Organo, 2nd suite, 1988; Musiche Nuove per un Organo Antico, 1985. *Recordings:* 10 albums of organ music in series, Antichi Organi Italiani, and instrumental music. *Publications:* Ciampi, 30 anni di musica a Piacenza, 1987. *Address:* Via Giulio Alberoni 33, 29100 Piacenza, Italy.

**ZANASI, Mario;** Singer (Baritone); b. 8 Jan. 1927, Bologna, Italy. *Education:* Studied at the Conservatorio Martini, Bologna; La Scala Opera School. *Career:* Debut: Cesena in 1954 in Lohengrin; Sang widely in Italy and at opera houses in Portugal, France, Belgium and Germany; Metropolitan Opera from 1958 as Sharpless in Butterfly, Escamillo, Marcello in La Bohème, Amonasro and Enrico in Lucia di Lammermoor; Sang at Covent Garden in 1958 and Verona Arena, 1957–72; Further appearances in Paris, Vienna, Chicago, Dallas, Miami, San Francisco and Munich. *Recordings:* Giulietta e Romeo by Zandonai; Madame Sans-Gêne by Giordano; Madama Butterfly; Maria di Rohan by Donizetti.

**ZANAZZO, Alfredo;** Singer (Bass); b. 14 Oct. 1946, Imperia, Italy. *Education:* Studied with Tancredi Pasero. *Career:* Debut: Verona Arena in 1981 as the King in Aida; Verona Arena, 1982–89, as Ramphis and Timur; Sang Wagner's Dutchman at Treviso in 1981, La Scala Milan in 1982 as Narbal in Les Troyens, and the King of Scotland in Ariodante; Season 1986–87 as Colline in La Bohème at the Paris Opéra, Padre Guardiano at Rome, Zaccaria and Masetto at Turin and Ramphis at the Metropolitan; Appearances at Luxor and the Vienna Staatsoper as Ramphis, Macerata Festival as Raimondo in Lucia di Lammermoor; Zürich Opera in 1988 as Banquo and Walter Furst in Guillaume Tell; Further engagements at the Geneva Opera as Pluto in Monteverdi's Orfeo, at Frankfurt as Raimondo, in Toronto as Procida in Les Vêpres Siciliennes and at Las Palmas as Alvise in La Gioconda; Teatro Margherita Genoa in 1991 as Roucher in La Gioconda; Sang Pagano in I Lombardi at Piacenza, 1995. *Address:* c/o Opernhaus Zürich, Falkenstrasse 1, 8008 Zürich, Switzerland.

**ZANCANARO, Giorgio;** singer (baritone); b. 9 May 1939, Verona, Italy. *Career:* debut at Teatro Nuovo Milan in I Puritani; Sang widely in Italy from 1971; International career from 1977, notably in London, Frankfurt, Rome, Hamburg, Paris and Zürich; Milan La Scala debut in 1981 as Ford in Falstaff; Metropolitan Opera debut in 1982 as Renato in Un Ballo in Maschera; Macerata Festival in 1983 as Posa in Don Carlos; Florence, 1984–85 as Germont and Posa; Covent Garden in 1985 as Gerard in Andrea Chénier; Other roles include Verdi's Rigoletto, Luna and Ezio in Attila, Escamillo, Tonio in Pagliacci and Albert in Werther; Hamburg and La Scala in 1988 as Count Luna and Guillaume Tell; Sang Ezio in Attila at Covent Garden in 1990, and in Donizetti's Parisina d'Este in Florence in 1990; Sang Michele in Il Tabarro at Zürich, 1996 and Nabucco there in 1998; Season 1999–2000 as Verdi's Renato in Venice and the High Priest in Samson et Dalila for Zürich Opera. *Recordings include:* Il Trovatore, conducted by Giulini; Andrea Chenier (G. Patane); La Traviata (Kleiber); La Forza del Destino, Rigoletto, Guillaume Tell, Attila, I Vespri Siciliani and Tosca all with Muti. *Current Management:* Stafford Law, Candleway, Broad Street, Sutton Valence, Kent ME17 3AT, England. *Website:* www.stafford-law.com.

**ZANDER, Benjamin;** Conductor; b. 1943, England. *Education:* studied with Benjamin Britten and Imogen Holst at Aldeburgh, at Florence with cellist Gaspar Cassado, at the Academica Chigiana in Siena, the State Conservatory Cologne and London Univ.; graduate work at Harvard and in New York. *Career:* faculty mem., New England Conservatory 1968–85, conducting the Youth Philharmonic Orchestra and the Conservatory's Symphony Orchestra; ten international tours with the Youth Philharmonic Orchestra, including South America, 1995; Artistic Dir, New England Conservatory at Walnut Hill School, 1986–; guest conductor with American orchestras and in the Far East, Russia, Italy, Germany and Israel; founding Dir of the Boston Philharmonic,

leading it in many concerts; debut with the London Philharmonic Orchestra, 1995, with Mahler's Sixth, returning for the Ninth Symphony. *Recordings include:* Mahler's Sixth Symphony, Beethoven's Ninth and The Rite of Spring, with the Boston Philharmonic Orchestra. *Address:* c/o Boston Philharmonic Orchestra, 295 Huntingdon Avenue, Suite 210, Boston, MA 02115–4433, USA.

**ZANETTOVICH, Renato;** Italian violinist; b. 28 July 1921, Trieste; m. Bianca Negri 1947; three s. *Education:* violin diploma. *Career:* debut with the Trio Di Trieste 1933; concerts and records with Trio Di Trieste world-wide; violin teacher at Conservatories of Bolzano 1950–55, Trieste 1955–70, Venice 1970–86; now teaching at Accademía Musicale Chigiana in Siena, Scuola Superiore Internazinale di Musica da Camera del Trio di Trieste in Duino; mem. Rotary Club, Trieste. *Publications:* Revision of Etudes by Kayser Op 20, Mazas Op 36, Dont Op 37, Sitt Op 32, Scale and Arpeggio Exercises, five books. *Honours:* Accademico di S Cecilia, Grande Ufficiale dell'Ordine Al Merito della Repubblica Italiana. *Address:* Via Catraro 9, Trieste, Italy (home). *Telephone:* (040) 305159 (home). *Fax:* (040) 307212 (home).

**ZANNINI, Laura;** Singer (Mezzo-Soprano); b. 4 April 1937, Trieste, Italy. *Education:* Studied at the Conservatorio Benedetto Marcello in Venice, with Gilda dalla Rizza, and with Bruno Maderna. *Career:* Debut: Spoleto in 1955 as Isabella in L'Italiana in Algeri; Sang leading roles at La Scala Milan, Genoa, Palermo, Naples, Parma, Venice, Turin and Trieste; Sang at Verona Arena in 1957, 1967, 1979–80, 1986, and Piccola Scala in 1966 in the premiere of Flavio Testi's Albergi dei Poveri; Further appearances at the Maggio Musicale Fiorentino, the State Operas of Vienna and Munich, the Paris Opéra, Brussels, Bordeaux, Wiesbaden, Copenhagen, London, Edinburgh, Moscow and Budapest; Sang Alisa in Lucia di Lammermoor at Bari and Tisbe in La Cenerentola at Glyndebourne, 1983; Also sang in operas by Henze, Britten, Menotti, Poulenc, Stravinsky, Schoenberg and Zandonai; Sang Caterina in L'Amico Fritz at Livorno, 1996. *Recordings:* Tisbe in La Cenerentola; Flora in La Traviata with Callas; Mascagni's Isabeau.

**ZANOLLI, Silvana;** Singer (Soprano); b. 14 Oct. 1928, Fiume, Italy; m. Otello Borgonova. *Education:* Studied at the Milan Opera School and with Luciano Tomerilli and Tomaso Japelli. *Career:* Debut: La Scala Milan in 1951 in La Buona Figliuola, by Piccinni; Appearances in leading roles at Rome, Palermo, Bologna, Parma, Turin, Trieste, Naples and Venice; Festival engagements at Florence and Rome with guest showings at Buenos Aires, the State Operas of Vienna, Stuttgart and Munich, at Brussels, Cologne, Rio de Janeiro, Geneva, Barcelona, Lisbon and London Covent Garden; Verona Arena, 1957–58 and Glyndebourne, 1959–60 as Clorinda in La Cenerentola; Also sang in Mexico City, Monte Carlo and New York at Metropolitan Opera. *Recordings:* Amelia al Ballo by Menotti; Cimarosa's Il Matrimonio Segreto; Il Campiello by Wolf-Ferrari.

**ZANOTELLI, Hans;** Conductor; b. 1927, Wuppertal, Germany; m. Ingeborg Schlosser. *Education:* Student in Cologne. *Career:* Choirmaster, Solingen, 1945; Conductor, Wuppertal in 1950, Düsseldorf, 1951–54, Bonn, 1954–55, Hamburg State Opera, 1955–57; General Music Director, Darmstadt, 1957–63, Augsburg, 1963–72; Chief Conductor, Stuttgart Philharmonic Orchestra, 1971–; Guest Conductor, Dresden Staatskapelle, 1964–67, Bavarian State Opera, 1968–71, Wurttemberg State Opera; Tours of many European countries; Conducted Der Rosenkavalier at Dresden for 300th anniversary and Verdi's Requiem at Dresden for anniversary of destruction of city in World War II. *Recordings:* Many. *Address:* Stuttgarter Philharmoniker, Leonhardplatz 28, 7000 Stuttgart, Germany.

**ZAROU, Jeannette;** Singer (Soprano); b. 1942, Ramallah, Palestine. *Education:* Studied at The Royal Conservatory of Music in Toronto with Irene Jessner, Halina Wyszkowski and Herman Geiger-Torel. *Career:* Debut: Priestess in Aida with Canadian Opera at Toronto, 1964; Sang Liu in Turandot for Canadian Opera in 1965; Member of the Deutsche Oper am Rhein, Düsseldorf, from 1967; Guest appearances in Toronto, Deutsche Oper Berlin, Hamburg and Munich State Opera, Cologne, Frankfurt, Karlsruhe, Nuremberg, Bordeaux and Rouen; Other roles have included Mimi, Marguerite, Ilia in Idomeneo, Pamina, and Sophie in Rosenkavalier; Modern repertoire has included Miss Wordsworth in Albert Herring and Blanche in Dialogues des Carmélites; Many concert appearances. *Recordings include:* Requiem by Draeske.

**ZARTNER, Rose Marie;** Pianist; b. 14 Sept. 1939, Nuremberg, Germany; m. Wolfgang Schwabe, 1 s., 1 d. *Education:* Studied in Nuremberg with Ernst Gröschel, Frankfurt am Main with Brauka Musulin; Concert Examen, Cologne, with Bruno Seidlhofer. *Career:* Many solo concert engagements and tours, in Germany and abroad; Numerous appearances as lieder accompanist in chamber engagements; Performed at recitals at Beethoven and Reger festivals, Bonn, Palais Schaumburg, German Federal Chancellery, Minsk and Bucharest; Concerts with Berlin Philharmonie, in Vienna, Salzburg, Nuremberg, Mannheim; Schwetzingen Musik Festival and Haydn Festival in Burgenland; Concerts with numerous orchestras including Bamberg and Nuremberg Symphonies, Symphony Orchestra of Romania, Orchester of Beethovenhalle and Classical Philharmonie, Bonn; Extensive classic repertory including works of Haydn and Mozart, also modern and unknown works; Numerous radio performances at home and in Europe; Many works dedicated to her; As member of Bonn Ensemble, appearances at International Music Days in Bonn and at Royal Danish Opera, Copenhagen, and in Seoul; Docent, Music School, Bonn and private tuition. *Recordings:* Works of Schumann, Haydn, Schubert, Dittersdorf, Reger. *Honours:* Cultural

Prize, Sudetendeutsche Landsmannschaft, 1975; Grand Cultural Prize, 1997. *Address:* Im Ringelsacker 49, 53123 Bonn, Germany.

**ZARZO, José;** Spanish French horn player; *Principal Horn, Gran Canaria Philharmonic Orchestra;* b. 6 Aug. 1966, Mexico City, Mexico; m. Mari Carmen Lobeira 1992; one s. one d. *Education:* studied music from age seven, with father; Royal Conservatory of the Hague, Netherlands with Prof. Vicente Zarzo, masterclasses with Profs Radovan Vlatkovic and Dale Clevenger. *Career:* debut, Orlando Festival with Orlando String Quartet, Heinz Holliger 1983; appeared on Dutch TV with Punto's Horn Concerto No. 5; has performed with almost all Dutch symphony orchestras 1989–; Principal Horn, Gran Canaria Philharmonic Orchestra, performing solo and recording major symphony repertoire 1989–; tours of major cities in Austria, Switzerland, Germany; founding mem. chamber music group, Ensemble Isola, with principals from Gran Canaria Philharmonic Orchestra and pianist Juan Francisco Parra; guest artist, Int. Horn Soc. symposium, Valencia 2004; mem. Int. Horn Soc. *Recordings:* Virtuoso Bläsermusik, Gustav Mahler's Symphony No. 5, Gustav Mahler's Symphony No. 4 (with Gran Canaria Philharmonic Orchestra, Adrian Leaper conductor), Choros of Villa Lobos, Horn in Trios, Isola Romantica. *Address:* Avenue Santiago de Cuba 22, 35330 Teror, Spain (home). *Telephone:* (92) 8631246 (home).

**ZAWADZKA, Barbara;** Composer; b. 21 Sept. 1951, Warsaw, Poland. *Education:* MA, Academy of Music in Kraków; Studied composition with Krzysztof Penderecki; French Government Scholarship to CNSM to study composition, theory and analysis with Guy Riebel, 1983–85; Studied composition and electro-acoustic and computer music at IRCAM, Paris, 1989. *Career:* Debut: Sixth International Wettgewerb–GEDOK, Mannheim, Germany, 1976; Lecturer at Kraków Music Academy since 1980; Has participated at the major music festivals in Poland, France, Germany, Norway, Switzerland and Hong Kong, 1988–; ISCM World Music Days. *Compositions:* Greya for tape; Monodrama for violin; Esperanza for tape; '4+1' quintet for oboe, cor anglais, clarinet, bass clarinet and piano; Sources for tape, 80 projectors and percussion; Games for clarinet, saxophone, cello, percussion and tape; Stabat Mater for choir; Locus Solus for piano; Motif of Space for strings. *Recordings include:* cassette, 1990; CD, 2000. *Publications:* Ruch Muzyczny, 1988; Ars Electronica, 1988; Boswil, 1988. *Address:* Academy of Music, Tomasza 43, 31-027 Kraków, Poland. *E-mail:* zbzawadz@cyf-kr.edu.pl.

**ZAWADZKA-GOLOSZ, Anna;** Composer; b. 1 Dec. 1955, Kraków, Poland; m. Jerry Golosz, 6 July 1986. *Education:* Diploma in Theory of Music, Academy of Music, Kraków, 1981; Studies in composition at the Academy of Music, Kraków under Krystyna Moszumanska-Nazar; Diploma, Academy of Music, Kraków and at the Hochschule für Musik, Theater und Tanz in Essen under Wolfgang Hufschmidt. *Career:* Teacher of Theory of Music, 1981–; Assistant at Academy of Music in Kraków; Performances in Poland and abroad including Warsaw Autumn–International Festival of Contemporary Music, 1986; mem, Polish Section of ISCM. *Compositions:* A Duo for Double Bass and Tape, 1980; Esoterikos for Soprano and Oboe Quartet, 1984; Senza for Double Bass, 1984; Girare for Percussion and Tape, 1986; Obraz w Pieciu Ujeciach (The Picture In Five Aspects), 1987; Vitrail ll for Clarinet, Cello, Accordion and Vibraphone, 1988. *Address:* ul Basztowa 5-28, 31-134 Kraków, Poland.

**ZAZOFSKY, Peter;** Concert Violinist; b. 1955, Boston, USA. *Education:* Studied with Joseph Silverstein, Dorothy DeLay and Ivan Galamian and at the Curtis Institute of Music. *Career:* Frequent appearances from 1977 with such orchestras as the Berlin and Rotterdam Philharmonics, the Vienna Symphony and the Amsterdam Concertgebouw Orchestra; North American engagements at Atlanta, Baltimore, Boston, Minnesota, Montreal, Philadelphia, San Francisco, Toronto and Vancouver; Tour of the USA with the Danish Radio Orchestra and recitals at the Kennedy Center and New York's Carnegie Hall; Further concerts in Israel and throughout Europe with such conductors as Dutoit, Zinman, Ormandy, Tennstedt and Ozawa; 1978 recital tour of South America; Season 1995–96 with concertos by Bartók and Mendelssohn in Germany and Belgium; Also plays Nielsen and Bernstein (Serenade). *Honours:* Prizewinner at the 1977 Wieniawski Competition, 1978 Montreal International and 1980 Queen Elisabeth of the Belgians Competition, Brussels; Avery Fisher Career Grant, 1985. *Address:* c/o Künstler Sekretariat am Gasteig, Rosenheimerstr 52, 81669 Munich, Germany.

**ZAZZO, Lawrence;** American singer (countertenor); b. 1970, Philadelphia. *Education:* King's Coll., Cambridge, Royal Coll. of Music with David Lowe. *Career:* concerts include Bach Cantatas at the 1997 Lufthansa Festival, London, Vivaldi Nisi Dominus and Handel's Messiah with the Israel Camerata, season 1996–97; opera debut as Oberon in A Midsummer Night's Dream at the RAM, London 1996; title role in Handel's Arminio and Alessandro Severo for the London Handel Festival, Bacco in Goehr's Arianna at Cambridge 1996, Athamas in Semele at Santa Fe Opera; 1998 season included Unulfo in Rodelinda at the Karlsruhe Handel Festival and with the Glyndebourne Touring Opera, title role in Cavalli's Giasone at the Spoleto Festival in Charleston, SC. *Recordings include:* Purcell's Jubilate, Britten's Rejoice in the Lamb, Bernstein's Chichester Psalms and Pergolesi's Stabat Mater. *Address:* c/o Allan Beavis, Phoenix Artists Management, Fourth Floor, 6 Windmill Street, London, W1P 1HF, England. *Telephone:* (20) 7636-5021. *Fax:* (20) 7631-4631. *E-mail:* allan@phoenixartists.co.uk. *E-mail:* larry@lawrencezazzo.com. *Website:* www.lawrencezazzo.com.

**ZEANI, Virginia;** Singer (Soprano); b. 21 Oct. 1925, Solovastru, Romania; m. Nicola Rossi-Lemeni, 1957 (deceased 1991). *Education:* Studied in Bucharest with Lucia Angel and Lydia Lipkovska, and with Aureliano Pertile in Milan. *Career:* Debut: Bologna, 1948, as Violetta; London debut, Stoll Theatre, 1953, as Violetta; La Scala, 1956, as Cleopatra in Giulio Cesare; Sang Blanche in premiere of Dialogues des Carmélites, 1957; Vienna and Paris debuts, 1957; Verona Arena, 1956–63; Took part in revivals of Donizetti's Maria di Rohan (Naples 1965), Rossini's Otello (Rome 1968), Verdi's Alzira (Rome 1970); Further appearances at Covent Garden, 1959, Metropolitan, 1966, and Budapest, Bucharest, Mexico City, Rio de Janeiro, Zürich, Amsterdam, Belgrade, Moscow, Madrid; Other roles included Aida, Desdemona, Tosca, Manon and Manon Lescaut, Lucia di Lammermoor, Elvira (I Puritani), Magda Sorel in The Consul (Menotti); Further engagements, Barcelona, Lisbon, Leningrad, Houston, Philadelphia, Berlin and New Orleans, 1966; Sang at Barcelona, 1977–78, as Giordano's Fedora; Sang 67 roles, 648 times Traviata around the world; Professor of Voice, 1980–, Distinguished Professor, 1994–, Emeritus Professor, 1995–, Indiana University School of Music, USA; mem, Accademia Tiberina-Roma; Commendatore of Italian Republic; Soroptimist Club of Rome. *Recordings:* La Traviata; Rossini's Otello; Elisa e Claudio by Mercadante; Rossini's Zelmira; Alzira; La Serva Padrona. *Honours:* 34 awards including: Gold Medal, Egypt, 1951; Gold Medal, Barcelona, 1963; Maschera d'Argento, 1965–70; Arena d'Oro, 1966; Diapason d'Oro, 1968; Viotti D'Oro, 1999; Una Vita per la Lirica, San Remo, 1999. *Address:* 2701 Robins Bow, Bloomington, IN 47401, USA.

**ZEAVIN, Carol;** Violinist; b. 2 May 1948, San Bernardino, California, USA. *Education:* Studied in New York. *Career:* Co-Founder of Columbia String Quartet, 1977, initially called Schoenberg String Quartet; Many performances in the standard and modern repertory, including the premieres of Wuorinen's Archangel and Second Quartet, 1978, 1980, Roussaki's Ephemeris, 1979, and quartets by Morton Feldman, 1980, Wayne Peterson, 1984, and Larry Bell, 1985; In 1979 at Abraham Goodman House, New York, played in the premiere of Berg's Lyric Suite with recently discovered vocal finale. *Recordings include:* String Quartet No. 3 by Lukas Foss and Ned Rorem's Mourning Song.

**ZEBINGER, Franz;** Austrian composer, harpsichordist and organist; b. 29 April 1946, Styria; m.; two s. one d. *Education:* Musikhochschule Graz, Univ. of Graz. *Career:* harpsichord and organist with Gamerith Consort, Ljubljana Barocni Trio, Ramovs Consort, Concilium Musicum; many recordings for radio, TV; concerts as a soloist, organ and forte piano; mem. Steirischer Tonkünstlerbund; Pres., Komponisten und Interpreten Burgenlands 2000–. *Compositions:* Carmen Miserabile 1988, Drachenkampf 1995, Markuspassion 1996, Heller als die Sonn 1998, Dies Illa 1999, Bruder Sonne, Schwester Mond 2002, Geschichte von Adam und Eva 2003, Feuer von Himmel 2004. *Recordings:* Gamerith Consort 1989, Dedications for Sax 1993, Stay a Weill 1994, Haydn Keyboard Trios 1994, Spectaculars 1997, Barrè en Bloc 1999, Franz Zebinger compositions 2000, Haydn music for Forte Piano on original instruments 2002. *Publications:* Ikonographie zum Musikleben der Etrusker (dissertation) 1982. *Honours:* Kulturpreis Burgenland 2004. *Address:* 7423 Kroisegg Nr 25, Austria. *Telephone:* (664) 505-4805. *Fax:* (3353) 7616. *E-mail:* franz_zebinger@web.de.

**ZECCHILLO, Giuseppe;** Singer (Baritone); b. 18 Dec. 1929, São Paulo, Brazil. *Education:* Studied at the Conservatorio Giuseppe Verdi at Milan and with Aureloano Pertile and Carlo Tagliabue. *Career:* Debut: Teatro Nuovo Milan in 1953 as Germont in La Traviata; Leading roles at La Scala, Rome, Bologna, Naples, Palermo, Parma, Turin, Trieste and Venice; Festival engagements at Caracalla, Verona, 1972–85, as Sharpless in Butterfly in 1983 and Florence, Maggio Musicale; Further appearances at the New York City Opera and in San Francisco and Monte Carlo; Distinguished in contemporary as well as standard repertory. *Recordings include:* Nina by Paisiello.

**ZECHBERGER, Gunther;** Composer and Conductor; b. 24 April 1951, Zams, Tyrol, Austria. *Education:* Studied at the Innsbruck Conservatory, 1968–74 and at University of Innsbruck with Witold Rowicki and Boguslaw Schaeffer. *Career:* Founder and Conductor of the Tyroler Ensemble für Neue Musik, 1984. *Compositions include:* Trio for Clarinet, Horn and Bassoon, 1973; Trio for Violins, 1975; Das Neue Preislied for Women's Chorus and Speaker, 1975; Schlus Stuck for Mixed Chorus and Orchestra, 1979; Mass for Mixed Chorus and Orchestra, 1979; Trombone Quartet, 1980; Stabat Mater for Mixed Chorus, 1981; Im Nebel for Mezzo and Orchestra, 1982; Study for 12 Strings, 1983; Hendekegon for 26 Instruments, 1984; Tieferschuttert for Mezzo, Trombone and Guitar, 1984; String Quartet, 1985; Chorus for 5 Musicians, 1985; Stabat Mater ll for Mezzo and Ensemble, 1985–88; Kammermusik for Conductor and 5 Musicians, 1986; Dear Mr J, 1987; Interview for Tape, 1987; Guitar Concerto, 1988; Duet for Guitars, 1988. *Address:* c/o AKM, III Baumanstrasse 8-10, Postfach 334-338, 1031 Vienna, Austria.

**ZECHLIN, Ruth;** Composer, Harpsichordist and Organist; b. 22 June 1926, Grosshartmannsdorf, Germany. *Education:* Studied composition with Johann Nepomuk David, organ with Karl Straube and Gunther Ramin, 1943–49. *Career:* Lecturer in Music from 1950 and Professor of Composition from 1969 at the Berlin Musikhochschule; Member of the Akademie der Künste Berlin 1970; mem, Akademie der Künste Berlin; Freie Akademi der Künste Mannheim. *Compositions include:* Reineke Fuchs, opera for actors, 1967; Ballet, La Vita, 1983; Opera Die Salamandrin und Die Bildsäule, 1989; Opera

Die Reise, 1991; Orchestral: 2 Violin Concertos, 1963, 1990, 3 Symphonies, 1965, 1966, 1971, 19 Great Mixed Chamber Music, 1966–93, 2 Chamber Symphonies, 1967, 1973, Piano Concerto, 1974; 4 Organ Concertos, 1974, 1975, 1980, 1984; 2 Harpsichord Concertos, 1975, 1986, Briefe, 1978, Situationen, 1980, Musik für Orchester, 1980, Metamorphosen, 1982, Musik Zu Bach, 1983, Kristallisation, 1987, Stufen, 1993; Varianten zu Goethes Märchen for chamber orchestra, 1998; Triptychon 2000 for orchestra, 1999; Triptychon zu Angelus Suesius for soprano, flute, strings, 1999; Chamber: 7 String Quartets, 1959–95, Reflexionen for 14 Strings, 1979, Konstellationen for 10 Winds, 1985, Akzente Und Flächen for 5 Percussions, 1993, Circulations for 8 Percussions, 1994; 5 Studien and 1 collage for chamber ensemble, 1996; Musikalische Antworten auf J. S. Bach for flute and organ, 1999; Vocal: Lidice Kantante, 1958, Canzoni alla Notte for Baritone and Orchestra, 1974, Der Sieg Von Guernica for 4 Voices, 1975, Das Hohelied for Tenor and Orchestra, 1979, Das A Und Das O for Mezzo Solo, 1990; Geistliche Kreise for 24 voice choir, 1995; Sonnengesang des Franz von Assisi for 8 voice choir, 1996; Stabat Mater for tenor and organ, 1999; Dies Irae for alto and organ, 1999; Scheyerer Messe for 4 voice choir, 1999; Piano, harpsichord and organ music. *Honours:* Gothepreis Berlin, 1962; Kunstpreis, 1965; Hanns-Eisler-Preis, 1968; Nationalpreis der DDR, 1975, 1982; Heidelberger Künstlerinnenpreis, 1996; Verdienstkreuz 1st class; BRD. *Address:* Adolf-Rebl-Str 1, 85276 Pfaffenhofen a. d. J1M, Germany.

**ZEDNIK, Heinz;** Tenor; b. 21 Feb. 1940, Vienna, Austria. *Education:* Studied with Marga Wissmann and at the Vienna Conservatory. *Career:* Debut: Graz in 1964 in La Forza del Destino; Vienna Staatsoper from 1964, notably in the 1976 premiere of Von Einem's Kabale und Liebe; Guest appearances in Nice, Moscow, Montreal and Baden; Bayreuth Festival from 1970 as David, the Steersman, Mime and Loge; Salzburg Festival in 1984 in the premiere of Berio's Un Re in Ascolto; Other roles include Mozart's Pedrillo and Monostatos, Beethoven's Jacquino and Peter the Great in Zar und Zimmermann; Salzburg Festival in 1986 in the premiere of Penderecki's Die schwarze Maske; Pedrillo, 1987–89; Mime at New York Metropolitan, 1989–90, also televised; Sang Baron Laur in Weill's Silbersee at the 1996 London Proms; Season 2000 at the Vienna Staatsoper as Bob Boles in Peter Grimes, the Villians in Les Contes d' Hoffmann, the Captain in Wozzeck, and Monk in Schoenberg's Die Jakobsleiter. *Recordings:* Parsifal; Lustige Weiber Von Windsor; Le nozze di Figaro; Wozzeck; Salome; Wiener Blut; Die Zauberflöte; Das Rheingold and Siegfried from Bayreuth. *Address:* c/o Allied Artists, 42 Montpelier Square, London, SW7 1JZ, England.

**ZEFFIRELLI, G. Franco Corsi;** Italian theatre, opera and film producer and designer; b. 12 Feb. 1923, Florence. *Education:* Liceo Artistico, Florence and School of Architecture, Florence. *Career:* designer Univ. Productions, Florence; actor Morelli Stoppa Co.; collaborated with Salvador Dali on sets for As You Like It 1948; designed sets for A Streetcar Named Desire, Troilus and Cressida, Three Sisters; producer and designer of numerous operas at La Scala, Milan 1952– and worldwide; Senator Forza Italia 1994–2002, cultural collaborator, Italian Ministry of Culture and Arts. *Exhibition:* Zeffirelli - The Art of Spectacle (Tokyo, Athens, Florence, Milan). *Operas include:* Lucia di Lammermoor, Cavalleria Rusticana, Pagliacci (Covent Garden) 1959, 1973, Falstaff (Covent Garden) 1961, L'elisir d'amore (Glyndebourne) 1961, Don Giovanni, Alcina (Covent Garden) 1962, Tosca, Rigoletto (Covent Garden) 1964, 1966, 1973, (Metropolitan, New York) 1985, Don Giovanni (Staatsoper-Wien) 1972, (Metropolitan, New York) 1990, Otello (Metropolitan, New York) 1972, Antony and Cleopatra (Metropolitan, New York) 1973, Otello (La Scala) 1976, La Bohème (Metropolitan, New York) 1981, Turandot (La Scala) 1983, 1985, (Metropolitan, New York) 1987, Don Carlos 1992, Carmen 1996, Aida (New Theatre, Tokyo) 1997, (Busseto) 2000, La Traviata (Metropolitan, New York) 1998, Tosca (Rome) 2000, Il Trovatore (arena di Verona) 2001, Aida (arena di Verona) 2002, La Bohème (La Scala) 2003, (Rome) 2003, Carmen (arena di Verona) 2003, I Pagliacci (Covent Garden, London) 2003, (Tel Aviv, Israel) 2005, Madame Butterfly (Arena Di Verona) 2004. *Theatre:* Romeo and Juliet (Old Vic, London) 1960, Othello (Stratford) 1961, Amleto (Nat. Theatre, London) 1964, After the Fall (Rome) 1964, Who's Afraid of Virginia Woolf (Paris) 1964, (Milan) 1965, La Lupa (Rome) 1965, Much Ado About Nothing (Nat. Theatre, London) 1966, Black Comedy (Rome) 1967, A Delicate Balance (Rome) 1967, Saturday, Sunday, Monday (Nat. Theatre, London) 1973, Filumena (Lyric, London) 1977, Six Characters in Search of an Author (London) 1992, Absolutely Perhaps! (London) 2003. *Films:* The Taming of the Shrew 1966, Florence, Days of Destruction 1966, Romeo and Juliet 1967, Brother Sun and Sister Moon 1973, Jesus of Nazareth 1977, The Champ 1979, Endless Love 1981, La Traviata 1983, Cavalleria Rusticana 1983, Otello 1986, The Young Toscanini 1987, Hamlet 1990, Sparrow 1994, Jane Eyre 1995, Tea with Mussolini 1998, Callas Forever 2002. *Ballet:* Swan Lake 1985; produced Beethoven's Missa Solemnis, San Pietro, Rome 1971. *Publication:* Zeffirelli by Zeffirelli (autobiog.) 1986. *Honours:* Hon. KBE 2005; Prix des Nations 1976 and numerous others. *Address:* Via Lucio Volumnio 45, 00178 Rome, Italy. *Fax:* (06) 7184213.

**ZEHETMAIR, Thomas;** Austrian violinist; *Music Director, Northern Sinfonia*; b. 23 Nov. 1961, Salzburg. *Education:* Salzburg Mozarteum, masterclasses with Max Rostal and Nathan Milstein. *Career:* concert appearances with the Boston, Chicago, Cleveland, Minnesota and San Francisco Orchestras, Philharmonia, English and Scottish Chamber, BBC Symphony, City of Birmingham, Rotterdam Philharmonic and Concertgebouw, Stockholm Philharmonic and Leipzig Gewandhaus; guest engagements at int. music festivals; chamber music with Gidon Kremer at Lockenhaus; London recital debut at Wigmore Hall 1993; concerto engagements with the BBC Philharmonic, Bournemouth Symphony, Northern Sinfonia and Scottish Chamber Orchestra 1993; Edinburgh Festival with Bach's works for solo violin 1995; Berlioz Harold in Italy, London Proms 1997; repertoire includes concertos by Szymanowski, Bach, Bartók, Henze, Berg and Prokofiev, in addition to the standard works; founder, Zehetmair Quartet; currently Music Dir, Northern Sinfonia. *Recordings:* Beethoven's Kreutzer and Spring Sonatas, Concertos by Brahms, Joseph and Michael Haydn, Mendelssohn, Mozart, Schumann and Sibelius, Berg's Chamber Concerto and Schoenberg's Violin Concerto under Heinz Hoffiger, Szymanowski, Concertos Nos 1 and 2 with Simon Rattle, Bartók Concertos Nos 1 and 2 with Ivan Fischer. *Address:* Northern Sinfonia, The Sage Gateshead, PO Box 254, Gateshead, NE8 2YR, England. *Website:* www.northernsinfonia.org.

**ZEHNDER, Kaspar;** Flautist and Conductor; b. 27 Aug. 1970, Bern, Switzerland. *Education:* Flute, with Heidi Indermühler, 1978–, Piano, with Agathe Rytz-Jaggi, 1981–, Theory and Conducting with Arthur Furer and Dr Ewald Körner, 1985, Berne Conservatory; Bachelor Type A, Ancient Languages, High College, Bern, Switzerland; Studies at Berne Music Academy, 1986–; Swiss School for Orchestra and Opera Conductors, 1991; Masterclasses with Ralf Weikert and Horst Stein, 1991–93; Private lessons and masterclasses, with Aurèle Nicolet, Basel and Siena, 1993–; Studies in Paris, free assistance with Charles Dutoit, Orchestre National de France, 1994; Member European Mozart Academy, 1995. *Career:* Soloist with Bern Symphony, 1988; Conductor, Basel Symphony, 1993; Conducting, Tchaikovsky Symphony Orchestra, Moscow, 1999–; Artistic Director Murten Classics Festival, 1999; Artistic director Swiss Chamber Opera, 2001–; Concerts throughout Europe with orchestras including: Capella Istropolitana, Bratislava, 2000; Prague Philharmonia, 2001; Bucharest Symphony Orchestra, 2001; Appeared at festivals including: Mecklenberg-Vorpommern, Germany and Le stelle del futuro, Venice, 1996; President, Swiss Brahms Society, 2000–; Swiss Musicians Society. *Recordings:* French Music for flute and piano; Sonatas for flute and piano by Franck, Martinů, Prokofiev. *Honours:* Swiss Youth Competition, 1984, 1986; Migros Foundation Scholarship, 1994; Honour Diploma, Accademia Chigiana, Siena, 1994, 1998. *Address:* Junkerngasse 13, 3011 Bern, Switzerland. *E-mail:* kaspar.zehnder@datecomm.ch.

**ZEITLIN, Zvi;** Concert Violinist and Professor of Violin; b. 21 Feb. 1923, Dubrovno, USSR; m. Marianne Langner, 1 s., 1 d. *Education:* Juilliard School of Music; Hebrew University, Jerusalem. *Career:* Debut: New York, 1951; Professor, Eastman School of Music, University of Rochester, New York; Head of Violin Department, Music Academy of the West, Santa Barbara, California; Concert tours world-wide; Appearances with leading world symphony orchestras; Broadcasts on radio and television; Editor, newly discovered Nardini Concerto, 1958; Working on six other Nardini concertos; mem, The Bohemians, New York; University of Rochester Faculty Club; New York State Teachers' Association; American Federation of Musicians. *Recordings:* Schoenberg Violin Concerto; Rochberg Variations; Schumann Sonatas; Schubert, Glinka and Tchaikovsky Trios with Eastman Trio, 1976–82. *Honours:* American Israel Society Award for furthering cultural relations between USA and Israel, 1957; Commissions of violin concertos by Gunther Schuller, Carlos Surinach and Paul Ben Haim; American Israel Cultural Foundation; 1st Kilbourn Professor, Eastman School of Music. *Current Management:* Thea Dispeker, New York City, USA. *Address:* 204 Warren Avenue, Rochester, NY 14618, USA.

**ZELJENKA, Ilja;** Composer; b. 21 Dec. 1932, Bratislava, Czechoslovakia; m. Maria Kimlickova, 13 April 1957, 1 d. *Education:* Gymnasium 1943–51; Compositions studies at Academy of Music and Drama, Bratislava, 1951–56. *Career:* Debut: 1956; Dramaturgist of the Slovak Philharmony, 1957–61; With Slovak Radio, 1961–68; Freelance Composer, 1968–90; Chairman of the Slovak Music Union, 1990–91; President of the International Festival of Contemporary Music, Melos-Ethos, 1991. *Compositions:* 5 Symphonies, 6 string quartets, 4 piano sonatas, 2 piano concertos, clarinet concerto, violin concerto, Dualogues for Violoncello and Chamber String Orchestra, Oswienczym Cantata, 2 piano quartets, Polymetric Music for 4 String Quintets, music for clarinet, piano and percussion, Metamorphoses XV for Chamber Ensemble and Reciter, Galgenlieder for Soprano, String Quartet, Clarinet, Flute and Piano, Mutations for Soprano, Bass, Wind Quintet and Percussion, Astecian Songs for Soprano, Piano and Percussion, and Plays for 13 Singers and Percussion. *Address:* 11A Zeljenka, Slavicie udolie 14, 81102 Bratislava, Slovakia.

**ZELTSER, Mark;** Concert Pianist; b. 3 April 1947, Kischiniev, Russia. *Education:* Graduated Moscow Conservatory, 1971. *Career:* Resident in USA from 1976; Played at the 1977 Salzburg Festival under Karajan and performed in Berlin with the Philharmonic in 1979; Debut with the New York Philharmonic, 1980; Further appearances with leading orchestras in Europe and America. *Address:* c/o Berlin Philharmonic Orchestra, Philharmonie, Matthaikirchstrasse 1, W-1000 Berlin, Germany.

**ZELTSER, Sandra;** Singer (Soprano); b. 1972, Paris, France. *Education:* Paris Conservatoire with Christiane Eda-Pierre, Guildhall School, London. *Career:* Covent Garden recital 1995, with appearances in Così fan tutte and Elektra 1997; Further engagements at Tatiana at the Paris Conservatoire, Linda di Chamounix at the Guildhall, Micaela for Mid Wales Opera and

Bizet's Leila for English Touring Opera; Arminda, La Finta Giardiniera for Opera Zuid in the Netherlands; Sang Melia in Mozart's Apollo et Hyacinthus, Britten Theatre, London, 1998; Micaela (Carmen) and Donna Elvira (Don Giovanni) for Opéra Comique in Paris; Spoleto Festival, 1999, Lauretta (Gianni Schicchi); Versailles, 1999, Il Viaggio a Reims (Rossini); Carmen (Micaela) Opéra de Nancy, 1999–2000; Engaged as Donna Elvira at Glyndebourne Festival, 2000. Concerts include Gounod's Requiem in France and recitals in Oxford and at the Wigmore Hall, London; Recital at the Opéra-Comique, 1999; Sang Natasha in new production of War and Peace for ENO, 2001; Anacreón by Cherubini. *Recordings:* Recital recording of songs, 2001. *Honours:* 1994 James Gulliver Prize; Bourse Lavoisier Scholarship; Prize Winner at the 1995 Maggie Teyte Competition. *Current Management:* Ingpen & Williams Ltd, 7 St George's Court, 131 Putney Bridge Road, London, SW15 2PA, England.

**ZEMTSOVSKY, Izaly (Iosifovich);** Ethnomusicologist; b. 22 Feb. 1936, St Petersburg, Russia; m. Alma Kunanbay, 29 Jan 1982. *Education:* MA, Philology, University of Leningrad, 1958; Diploma, Russian Folklore, Musicology and Composition, Leningrad Conservatoire, 1955–60, 1961; MA, PhD. *Career:* Debut: 1958; Senior Research Fellow, Head of Folklore Department, Leningrad State Institute of Theatre, Music and Cinema (now Russian Institute of History of the Arts, 1990–), 1960–95; Head, Department of Traditional Culture, Russian Pedagogic University, 1989–93; Vice-President, Jewish Musical Society of St Petersburg, 1992–96; Vice President, International Delphic Council, 1994–96; President, Delphic Movement in Russia, 1995–97; Fellow, Institute for Research in the Humanities, University of Wisconsin-Madison, 1995–; Visiting Professor in Slavic and E Bloch Professor in Music, University of California, Berkeley, 1997–99. *Publications include:* Russian Folk Song, 1964; The Russian Drawn-Out Song, 1967; Songs of Toropets: Songs of The Homeland of Moussorgsky, 1967; Song Hunters, 1967; The Poetry of Peasant Holidays, 1970; The Melodics of Calendar Songs, 1975; Folklore and The Composer, 1978; Tracing the Melody Vesnianka from P Tchaikovsky's Piano Concerto: The Historical Morphology of the Folk Songs, 1987; Russian Folk Music, in Grove's Dictionary of Music and Musicians, 1980; Boris Asaf'yev on Folk Music, 1987; Jewish Folk Songs: An Anthology, 1994; An Attempt at a Synthetic Paradigm, 1997. *Address:* 2550 Dana Street Apt 9B, Berkeley, CA 94704, USA.

**ZENATY, Ivan;** Concert Violinist; b. 1960, Czechoslovakia. *Education:* Studied at the Prague Conservatoire and the Academy of Arts, Weimar with André Gertler, Zürich with Nathan Milstein. *Career:* Solo appearances with all leading Czech orchestras in Austria, Bulgaria, England, Finland, Netherlands, Italy, Poland, Spain, Russia, Switzerland and Yugoslavia; Festival engagements in Prague, Dubrovnik, Moscow, Sofia, Berlin and Havana; Repertoire includes concertos by Bach, Haydn, Mozart, Vivaldi, Myslivicek, Sibelius, Dvořák, Vieuxtemps and Kalabis, Bach solo sonatas and Telemann solo fantasies, sonatas by Mozart, Beethoven, Vanhal, Schubert, Schumann, Brahms, Prokofiev, Dvořák, Janáček and Martinů. *Recordings:* Various albums. *Honours:* First Prize, Prague Spring Festival Competition, 1987. *Address:* c/o Prague Conservatory, na Rejdi ti 1, 110 00 Prague, Czech Republic.

**ZENDER, J(ohannes) W(olfgang) Hans;** German composer and conductor; b. 22 Nov. 1936, Wiesbaden; s. of Dr Franz Zender and Marianne (née Fromm) Zender; m. Gertrud-Maria Achenbach 1962. *Education:* Acad. of Music, Freiburg. *Career:* studied composition and piano; conductor, Freiburg im Breisgau 1959–63; Chief Conductor, Bonn City Theatre 1964–68; Gen. Dir of Music, Kiel 1969–72; Chief Conductor, Radio Symphony and Chamber Orchestras, Saarbrücken 1972–82; Gen. Dir of Music (Philharmonia and City Opera), Hamburg 1984–87; Chief Conductor Radio Chamber Orchestra, Netherlands Broadcasting Corpn; Prin. Guest Conductor Opéra Nat., Brussels 1987–90; Guest Conductor SWF Symphony Orchestra –1999; Prof. of Composition, Frankfurt Musikhochschule 1988; mem. Freie Akad. der Künste, Hamburg, Akad. der Künste, Berlin, Bayerische Akad. der Künste; numerous recordings. *Major works include:* Canto I–VIII 1965–96, Zeitströme 1974, Mujinokyo 1975, Litanei 1976, Lo-Shu I–VI 1977–89, Hölderlin Lesen (string quartet) 1979, Dialog mit Haydn 1982, Stephen Climax (opera) 1979–84, Don Quixote (opera) 1989–91, Schubert's Winterreise (for soloists, choir, large orchestra and live electronics) 1993–97. *Publication:* Happy New Ears (essays) 1991, Wir steigen niemals in den selben Fluss (essays) 1996. *Address:* c/o Astrid Schoeke, Moernckebergallee 41, 30453 Hannover; Am Rosenheck, 65812 Bad Soden, Germany. *Fax:* (6174) 930054.

**ZENTAI, Csilea;** Singer (Soprano); b. Hungary. *Education:* Studied at Budapest, and in Stuttgart. *Career:* Debut: Stuttgart Opera School, 1969, in Ibert's Angelique; Sang at Ulm Opera, 1969–1972, Bremen, 1973–79, Deutsche Oper am Rhein from 1979; Guest appearances at the State Operas of Stuttgart, Hamburg and Munich, Vienna Staatsoper as Mozart's Countess and Fiordigili, Luise (Junge Lord), Zürich as the Marschallin, Deutsche Oper Berlin as Elvira and Blumenmädchen 1, and Cologne Opera as Fiordigili, Agathe, Butterfly, Rosalinde, Countess and Marenka; Further engagements at Bordeaux, Brussels, Salzburg as Donna Anna in concert performance of Don Giovanni, and Moscow; Other roles have included Violetta, Composer, Jenůfa, Pamina, Rosalinde, Marguerite and Amaranta in La Fedeltà Premiata by Haydn, Konstanze, Susanna, Jlica, Donna, Elviva, Marzelline; Leonore (Fidelio and Troubadour), Tosca, Traviata, Lucia, Mimi, Nedde, Euydice, Antonia, Martha, Michaela; Concert appearances in Germany, Netherlands, Belgium, Italy, Spain, Mexico and Hungary; Title of Kammer-

sängerin of the Deutsche Oper am Rhein, 1990–; Professor, Folkwang Musikhochschule, 1991–. *Honours:* First Prize in s'Hertogeubosch (1968); Internqtional Vocal Competition; Silvermedallion in Toulouse (1968); First Prize in the "Francisco Viñas" Vocal Competition in Barcelona (1969). *Address:* c/o Deutsche Oper am Rhein, Heinrich Heine Allee 16, 40667 Dusseldorf, Germany.

**ZENZIPER, Arkadi;** Pianist; b. 10 April 1958, Leningrad, Russia; m. Tatjana Zenzipér, 10 Aug 1990, 3 s., 2 d. *Education:* Specialised Music School at Leningrad Conservatory, with T. Orlovsky; Final Examination with distinction, Leningrad Conservatory, 1981, after studying with N. Perlmann and G. Sokolov; Master's degree, 1984. *Career:* Debut: Television piano recital in Vilnius, Lithuania, 1982; Major concerts with orchestras: Berlin Symphonic Orchestra, 1990, Munich Klaviersommer, 1994, Ljubljana Festival, 1994; Stuttgart Chamber Orchestra, 2002; Krakauer Philharmonic Orchestra, 2001, 2002, 2004; Major chamber music concerts: Schleswig-Holstein Music Festival, 1989, 1990, Lucerne Festival, 1989, Concertgebouw, Amsterdam, 1990, 1991, Berlin Philharmonic Hall, 1992, and frequently at Berlin Konzerthaus; Radio performance of Prokofiev 4th and 5th Piano Concertos with Berlin Radio Orchestra, 1992; Television portrait and recording of Rachmaninov with Staatskapelle Dresden; La Chaise Dieu Music Festival with Orchestre Nat. de Lyon, 1998, 1999, 2000; Chamber music: Rheingau Festival, 1996; Dresdner Musikfestspiele, 1996; Tibor Varga Festival Sion, 1997; Beethovenhaus Bonn, 1997; Hitzacker-Festival, 1997; Prague Spring Festival, 2003; Rostica Music Festival London, 2003; Concerts with soloists of the Israeli Philharmonic Orchestra, 2003; Art Dir, Dreiklang Music Festival, 2001–; Regular Professor, Dresden Musikhochschule, 1993–. *Recordings:* Radio recordings of chamber music with RIAS-Berlin, Hessischer Rundfunk, South German Radio, Deutschland Radio; 9 CDs. *Current Management:* Pressando Musikagentur, Feuerbachstrasse 1, 04105 Leipzig, Germany. *Telephone:* (341) 4623088. *Fax:* (341) 4623089. *E-mail:* patrizia.meyn@t-online.de.

**ZERBINI, Antonio;** Singer (Bass); b. 1928, Italy. *Career:* Debut: Sang in La Forza del Destino at Spoleto in 1952; Sang at the Verona Arena, 1958–71 with debut as Ramphis in Aida; Further appearances at La Scala Milan, Moscow, Buenos Aires and the Paris Opéra; Théâtre de la Monnaie Brussels, 1960, 1962, 1969, and 1979 as the King in Aida, Mozart's Commendatore, Angelotti in Tosca, Timur in Turandot and Padre Guardiano in La Forza del Destino; Also sang in Nice and Monte Carlo in 1979; Verona Arena in 1981 as Sparafucile in Rigoletto; Sang Hieros in a revival of L'Assedio di Corinto by Rossini at Florence in 1982. *Recordings:* Tosca; Aida; Don Giovanni; L'Arlesiana; Donizetti's Maria Stuarda; I Lombardi; La Forza del Destino; Manon; Lucia di Lammermoor.

**ZETTERSTRÖM, Rune;** Swedish singer (bass); b. 1936, Vasteras. *Education:* Stora Teatern opera school, Gothenburg. *Career:* debut, Gothenburg 1966, as Mozart's Bartolo; guest engagements at Oslo 1970, Bergen 1972, 1975, Copenhagen 1976, London 1977; major roles include Seneca in L'Incoronazione di Poppea, Rossini's Basilio, Verdi's Renato, bass in Tintomara by Werle, Timur in Turandot, Puccini's Colline; sang the Lion in Werle's Animalen with the Stora Teatern at the Wiesbaden Festival 1981; further roles include Mozart's Figaro, Sarastro, Leporello, Osmin, Philip, in Don Carlos; guest engagements in Semperoper in Dresden 1988 with Osmin; sang Leporello at Stockholm 1996; Louis in the premiere production of Marie Antoinette by D. Börtz, Stockholm and Brighton 1998. *Recordings include:* Tintomara.

**ZHADKO, Victoria;** Conductor; b. 1967, Kiev, Ukraine. *Education:* Studied at the Kiev Conservatoire. *Career:* Deputy Conductor of the Kiev Radio Symphony Orchestra in 1993; Performances of Ukrainian music with the St Petersburg Philharmonic and guest engagements with the Rotterdam Philharmonic, Netherlands Radio, Helsinki, Wroclaw and Poznan Philharmonics; Repertoire includes the Viennese classics, Strauss, Tchaikovsky, Brahms, Liszt and Ravel; Teacher at the Kiev School of Arts and Odessa Conservatoire. *Address:* c/o Sonata Ltd, 11 North Park Street, Glasgow G20 7AA, Scotland.

**ZHANG, Jianyi;** American singer (tenor); b. 30 Aug. 1959, Shanghai, China. *Education:* Shanghai Conservatory of Music, Juilliard School. *Career:* debut as the Lover in Amelia al Ballo 1987; appeared as the Duke of Mantua in Rigoletto at Teatro Comunale di Firenze 1989; as Rodolfo in La Bohème at New York City Opera and Werther at Opera de Nice 1990–91; performed Nadir in the Pearl Fishers at Washington Opera and Opera Pacific 1991–92; Roldolfo at Opéra de Lyon and Opera Nice and Des Grieux in Manon at Opéra Comique Paris 1992–93; season 1993–94 as Don José in Carmen at the Nat. Opéra de Paris Bastille; Faust in Paris, Washington, Michigan Opera Theatre and Miami Grand Opera 1994–95; as Alfredo in La Traviata at Staatsoper Hamburg and Rodolfo at Stattsoper Stuttgart 1995–96; season 1996–97 as Faust at the Metropolitan Opera and The Duke of Mantua in Rigoletto at the Montréal Opera and as Nemorino in L'Elisir D'Amore at the New Israeli Opera; sang Rodolfo and Alfredo at New York City Opera and as Des Grieux at the Metropolitan Opera 1997–98; appearances as Rodolfo at Dallas Opera and Alfredo at Vancouver Opera and Tamino in The Magic Flute at Florentine Opera, Faust at Savonlinna Opera Festival at the Seattle Opera 1998–99; sang Meyerbeer's Robert for Deutsche Staatsoper, Berlin, Gerald in Lakmé at Montréal, Massenet's Des Grieux in Madrid and Cavaradossi at Hong Kong 1999–2001; Calos in Linda di Chamounix at Vienna State Opera, Faust at

Bavaria State Opera, Munich 2001–02; Leopold in La Juive at Vienna State Opera, Edgardo in Lucia di Lammermour at Metropolitan Opera and Palm Beach Opera, Nemorino in L'Elisir D'Amore at Frankfurt Opera 2002–03; Rodolfo in La Bohème at Metropolitan Opera, Ismaele in Nabucco at Metropolitan Opera, Cellini in Benvenuto Cellini at Metropolitan Opera 2003–04; Roméo in Roméo and Julliette at Beijing Int. Music Festival 2004–05. *Recordings:* Jianyi Zhang: Tenor (solo album), Great Opera Arias, Leopold in La Juive (DVD). *Honours:* first prize Belvedere Int. Opera Singer Competition, Vienna 1984, Grand Winner Luciano Pavarotti Int. Voice Competition, Philadelphia 1988, first prize EMF, New York 1989, first prize Opera Index of New York 1989, winner Metropolitan Opera Audition 1989. *Address:* c/o 62-54 97th Place Apt PH-1, Rego Park, NY 11374, USA.

**ZHANG, Xian;** Chinese conductor; *Associate Conductor, New York Philharmonic Orchestra;* b. Dandong. *Education:* Beijing Central Conservatory. *Career:* professional debut with Le Nozze di Figaro at Central Opera House, Beijing; conductor-in-residence China Opera House 1995–96; fmr conductor Jin Fan Symphony Orchestra; one year teaching at Beijing Central Conservatory; moved to USA 1998; Asst Prof. of Orchestra Conducting and Music Dir of the Concert Orchestra, Univ. of Cincinnati Conservatory of Music 2000–; Music Dir Lucca Festival Orchestra 2000; Assoc. Conductor New York Philharmonic Orchestra 2002–, collaborating with Lorin Maazel and conducting family and young people's concerts; has conducted Cincinnati Opera in La Traviata 2003, Don Giovanni 2004, La Bohème 2005; guest conductor with Cincinnati Symphony Orchestra, Colorado Symphony, Louisiana Philharmonic, Omaha Symphony, Charlotte Symphony, Orchestra of St Luke's, China Philharmonic, Auckland Philharmonia, LSO, Sinfonica Arturo Toscanini. *Honours:* winner Maazel/Vilar Int. Conductors' Competition 2002. *Address:* c/o New York Philharmonic, 10 Lincoln Center Plaza, New York, NY 10023-6990, USA (office). *Website:* www.newyorkphilharmonic.org (office).

**ZHAO, Pingguo;** Professor of Piano and Pianist; b. 1934, China; m. Ling Yuan 1956, 1 s., 1 d. *Education:* Graduated, Piano, Central Conservatory of Music, 1951; Studied at Central Conservatory of St Petersburg with Aram Taturan and Tachiana Kravchenko. *Career:* Joined Piano Faculty, Central Conservatory of Music, 1951; Took part in International Tchaikovsky Piano Competition, 1962; Professor of Piano; Performance tour of Japan with promising pupil, 1996; Numerous piano concert performances; Repertoire includes Beethoven Sonatas; Chopin pieces; Mozart Concertos; Tchaikovsky Concertos; Numerous lectures in cities world-wide including Russia, Ukraine, Los Angeles, Japan; Judge, several piano competitions; Grader, National Examinational Piano Playing. *Address:* Central Conservatory of Music, 43 Bao Jia Street, Beijing, People's Republic of China.

**ZHAO, Xiaosheng;** Composer, Pianist, Musicologist and Music Professor; b. 27 July 1945, Shanghai, China. *Education:* BA, Piano, 1967, MA, Composition, 1981, Shanghai Conservatory of Music. *Career:* Visiting Scholar, Visiting Professor, UMC, USA, 1981–84; Over 100 piano recitals in 20 main cities of China, in USA and Hong Kong; Created Taiji Composition, 1987, Tone-sets Motion Theory, 1991; Guest Host, Radio Shanghai, Oriental Radio Shanghai, STV and OTV, Shanghai; Editor-in-Chief, Shanghai Piano Guild, 1994, 1995; Vice Editor-in-Chief, Piano Artistry magazine. *Compositions include:* Six Concert Etudes for piano, 1976; 2 String Quartets, 1980, 1981; The Goddess of Hope, Piano Concerto, 1985; Four Movements of Jian, 1986; Taiji, piano solo, 1987; Three Movements of Yin-Yang for 16 players, 1987; Bi Xiao Pai Yun for flute, 1988; Double Concerto for Gaohu and Erhu and Chinese Orchestra, 1988; LuYao, pipa solo, 1989; Ting Qin for Erhu and Piano, 1989; Huan Feng, sheng solo, 1989; Hui Liu, quartet, 1989; Three Symphonic Suites, 1990; The Song of Earth, Sound of Man, Sacrifice to Heaven, ballet, 1990; Liao Yin, piano concerto, 1991; The Sun of Wilderness, ballet, 1991; Shi Lou for Chinese Chamber Orchestra, 1994; Pieces for piano solo: Stephen Hawking's View of Cosmos; Filter; Eight Scenes of West Lake; Qin Yun; Xiao Xue; A-Bing Sui Xiang (Capriccio from Blind Abing); Blake and White; Drum and Bell; 62343314; Echoes from Empty Valley; Ancient Sound of Mt Yu, 1999; More than 30 improvisations. *Recordings:* Music from His Heart–Zhao Plays His 14 Own Piano Pieces, 2CD album, 1999; How to Play The 'Music Note Book for Anna Magdalena Bach', 2VCD album, 1999. *Address:* Composition Department, Shanghai Conservatory of Music, 20 Fenyang Lu, Shanghai 200031, People's Republic of China.

**ZHIDKOVA, Elena;** Singer (Mezzo-soprano); b. 1972, Russia. *Education:* St Petersburg Conservatory and Opera Studio of Hamburg State Opera. *Career:* Mascagni's Lola and Maddalena in Rigoletto at Hamburg; Deutsche Oper Berlin as Olga in Eugene Onegin, Hansel, and Siebel in Faust; Guest appearances in Japan, at Théâtre du Châtelet, Paris, New York Lincoln Center and Barbican Hall, London; Season 2000–01 as Fides in Le Prophète at Kiel, Schwertleite in Die Walküre at Bayreuth and in The Ring at the Deutsche Oper; Concerts include Mahler's 8th Symphony in Rome, under Myung-Whun Chung. *Honours:* Prize Winner, Dvořák Competition, Prague. *Address:* c/o Theateragentur Dr G. Hilbert, Maximilianstrasse 22, 80539 Munich, Germany.

**ZHIKALOV, Yuri;** Singer (Tenor); b. 1948, Russia. *Education:* Graduated St Petersburg Conservatoire, 1972. *Career:* Many engagements in concerts and opera throughout Russia; Kirov Opera, St Petersburg, from 1977 as Lensky in Eugene Onegin, Mozart's Monostatos, Andrei in Mazeppa and Khovanshchina, and Finn in Ruslan and Lyudmila; Sang with the Kirov in summer

season at Covent Garden, 2000; Other roles include Prince Guidon in The Tale of Tsar Saltan by Rimsky-Korsakov, Norman in Lucia di Lammermoor, Mikhail and Nikita in Rimsky's The Maid of Pskov and Platon in War and Peace. *Address:* c/o Kirov Opera, Mariinsky Theatre, 1 Theatre Square, St Petersburg, Russia.

**ZHISLIN, Grigory Yefimovich;** Russian violinist and violist; b. 14 May 1945, Leningrad (now St Petersburg); s. of Sarra and Yefim Zhislin; m. Valentina Murashova 1980; one s. *Education:* Moscow State Conservatory (pupil of Yuny Yankelevich). *Career:* winner Int. Competitions of Paganini in Genoa 1967 and Queen Elizabeth in Brussels 1976; concerts in USSR and abroad 1966–; participated in maj. music festivals including Maggio Musicale Fiorentino, Warsaw Autumn, Prague Spring, Kuhmi Chamber Music, Berliner Biennale, Pablo Casals in Puerto Rico, Paganini in Genoa and others; teacher Kharkov Inst. of Arts 1971–73, Moscow Gnessin Pedagogical Inst. 1973–, Prof. 1978–90; Royal Coll. of Music London 1990–; Hochschule für Musik Würzburg 1993–; Visiting Prof. Oslo, Krakow, Warsaw Conservatories; masterclasses USA, Italy, France, Finland, Sweden. *Address:* 25 Whitehall Gardens, London, W3 9RD, England (home). *Telephone:* (20) 8993-8223. *Fax:* (20) 8993-8295.

**ZHIVOPISTEV, Vladimir;** Singer (Baritone); b. 1960, Dobrush, Byelorussia. *Education:* Odessa State Conservatoire. *Career:* Appearances at the Maly Opera Theatre, St Petersburg; Kirov Opera, Mariinsky Theatre, from 1996; Roles have included Giorgio Germont, Yeletsky in The Queen of Spades, Eugene Onegin, Rossini's Figaro and Goro in Madama Butterfly; Sang in War and Peace, Khovanshchina and Semyon Kotko (British premiere) with the Kirov at Covent Garden, 2000; Other roles include Robert in Tchaikovsky's Iolanta, the Indian Guest in Rimsky's Sadko, Spoletta in Tosca and Bayan in Ruslan and Lyudmila. *Honours:* Prize Winner, Lysenko International Vocal Competition. *Address:* c/o Kirov Opera, Mariinksy Theatre, 1 Theatre Square, St Petersburg, Russia.

**ZHU, Ai-La;** Singer (soprano); b. 1957, Nanking, China. *Education:* studied in Peking and Berlin and at the Hartt School of Music. *Career:* sang first with the Peking Central Opera notably as Butterfly, Violetta and Mimi; sang Micaela with Texas Opera, Mimi and Marguerite with Virginia Opera and Xola in the premiere of Under The Double Moon by A. Davis, with the St Louis Opera; appeared at Pepsicosummerfare as Zerlina in the Peter Sellars production of Don Giovanni; season 1990–92 as Violetta at Boston, Gilda at Philadelphia and Leila with Minnesota Opera; sang at Glyndebourne Festival 1990–91 as Pamina; also features in Lieder recitals.

**ZHU, Jian-Er;** Composer and Professor of Composition; b. 18 Oct. 1922, Tianjin, China; m. Qun Shu 1949, 2 s., 1 d. *Education:* Graduated, Moscow State Conservatory, 1960; Studied with Professor Sergey Balasanian. *Career:* Composer, Art Troupe, New 4th Army, 1945–49; Conductor, Brass Band, 1946–49; Composer, Shanghai and Peking Film Studios, 1949–63; Shanghai Opera House, 1963–75; Shanghai Symphony Orchestra, 1975–; Professor of Composition, Shanghai Conservatory of Music. *Compositions: Main Works:* Orchestral: Festival Overture, 1958; In Memorian, for Strings, 1978; Symphonic Fantasia, 1980; Sketches in Mountains of Guizhou, 1982; The Butterfly Fountain for Er-hu and Orchestra, 1983; A Wonder of Naxi, 1984; Symphonies No. 1, 1986; No. 2, 1987; No. 3 Tibet, 1988; No. 4, 1990; No. 5, 1991; No. 6, 1994; No. 7, 1994; No. 8, 1994; No. 9, 1999; No. 10, 1998; Sinfonietta, 1994; Concerto for Sona and Orchestra, 1989; Hundred Year Vicissitudes, 1996; Choral: Salute 1946, 1945; Gada-meilin, 1958; Symphony-Cantata Heroic Poems, 1960; A Cappella Cycle The Green, Green Water Village, 1981; Piano: Preludes, 1955; Theme and Var, 1956; Ballade, 1958; Five Yunnan Folk Songs, 1962; Quintet, 1992; Folk Instrumental Ensemble Day of Liberation, 1953; Song of the Spring, for Oboe and Piano, 1956; Numerous Songs. *Address:* 105 Hu Nan Road, Shanghai Symphony Orchestra, Shanghai 200031, People's Republic of China.

**ZHU, Kunqiang;** Musician (French horn); b. 10 April 1963, Bengbu, Anhui Province, People's Republic of Chinab. *Education:* Music Department, Army Art Academy of China. *Career:* Principal French Horn, Symphony Orchestra of the Chinese Army, 1983; Toured Russia, Hungary, Poland, Romania and Germany, 1988; Performed at the Hong Kong Arts Festival with the China Youth Symphony Orchestra, 1991; Macao Music Festival with the China Chamber Music Orchestra, 1995; Principal French Horn with the China National Symphony Orchestra, 1996–; Has toured China, and abroad, including Hong Kong Arts Festival, 1997, 1998 and 2000, Germany, the United Kingdom and Austria, 1998, Japan and the Osaka International Music Festival, 1999, Mexico, 2000, and Hong Kong and Macao, 2001; Co-founded and performs with the Wuxing Brass Quintet; mem, International Horn Society; Chinese Musician's Association. *Recordings include:* numerous works for television and film with the China Radio Symphony Orchestra and the China Film Orchestra; Chinese Folk Song Collection with the Wuxing Brass Quintet; Many Chinese and Western symphonic works with the China National Symphony Orchestra. *Honours:* First Prize at the Second Chinese Horn Competition, 1991. *Address:* c/o The China National Symphony Orchestra, 11-1 Hepingjie, Chaoyang District, Beijing 100013, People's Republic of China.

**ZHU, Xiao Mei;** French (b. Chinese) concert pianist; *Professor of Piano, Conservatoire National Supérieur de Paris;* b. Shanghai. *Education:* Nat. Music School for Gifted Children. *Career:* made first radio and TV appearances in Peking at age of six; sent to labour camp in Inner Mongolia at age of ten following Cultural Revolution 1970–76; continued playing piano in secret; left China for USA following visit of Isaac Stern in 1979; won several prizes in USA and began concert career; moved to Paris 1985, French citizenship 2000; Prof. of Piano, Conservatoire Nat. Supérieur de Paris; divides her time between teaching and worldwide concert schedule; regular guest performer at Théâtre de la Ville, Paris 1994–. *Recordings include:* major piano works of Bach, Scarlatti, Mozart, Schubert and Schumann. *Address:* 4 rue de Nevers, 75006 Paris, France. *Telephone:* 1-46-33-61-31. *Fax:* 1-46-33-61-31.

**ZHUKOV, Sergei;** composer; b. 30 Aug. 1951, Zhitomir, Ukraine; m. Natalia Zhukova 1982; two d. *Education:* Music Coll., Zhitomir, Moscow State Conservatory. *Career:* debut chamber music concert, Maliy Hall, Moscow Conservatory 1973; participated, All-Union and int. concerts, festivals, symposia, including Moscow Autumn Musical Festival 1981–2004, Warsaw Autumn 1988, Int. Musical Festival, Leningrad 1989, Charles Ives Festival, USA 1990, Week Van de Hedendaagse Musiek, Belgium 1991; teacher, Dept of Theory and Composition, Moscow State Conservatory 1991; mem. Union of Composers of Russia, Union of Theatre Workers of Russia. *Television and radio broadcasts:* Symphony (All-Union Radio) 1987, Moments, Running in Successions (oratorio, All-Union Television) 1987, Partita for violin solo (Donderdag, Dutch Radio) 1990, Landscape for clarinet solo (BRT-3, Belgium Radio), Solaris (ballet, Ukrainian television) 1991. *Compositions:* Black Keys for voice and ensemble 1973, Spivanochcki chamber cantata to traditional words 1975, On the Shore (soundtrack to verses by A. Tarkovsky) 1976, Echo (three poems by A. Pushkin) for soprano and piano trio 1979, Monologues (verses by M. Tsvetayeva) for soprano, string orchestra and percussion 1980, Sonata-Capriccio for solo cello 1980, Partita for violin solo 1983, Refracted Sounds wind quintet 1984, Symphony 1985, Moments, Running in Successions (verses by I. Bunin) for narrator, soloists, women and children's chorus, and symphony orchestra 1987, Sonata-Bussanda for piano 1988, Landscape for solo clarinet 1988, Solaris (ballet) 1990, Concerto for orchestra and solo percussions 1990, Image and Transfiguration for organ 1991, Concerto-Partes for string orchestra 1992, Lot of Nemesida choreographic composition for clarinetist, dancer, magnetic tape 1992, Farewell's Songs (verses by J. H. Leopold) for soprano, flute, cello and piano 1992, De Tuinman en de Dood (verses by P. N. van Eyck) for contralto and cello 1993, Concerto-Mystery for piano, violin, violoncello and orchestra 1994, Concerto Sacra for piano, violin, cello and orchestra 1997, Insomnia (ballet after Pushkin) 1999, In Search of the Missing Score for clarinet, harpsichord and soundtrack 2000, Book of Transformations for prepared piano 2000, Sempre Sonare for two pianos and percussion 2001, Fatum (ballet based on M. Lermontov's poem, Demon) 2001, Silentium concerto for piano and orchestra 2001, Hommage Holland for three organs 2002, Gethsemanian Night concerto for electric cello, mixed chorus, horns, percussion and prepared piano 2003, Angel's Day concerto for violin and orchestra 2004. *Recordings:* Spivanochcki 1982, Sonata-Capriccio 1983, Concerto Mystery 1998, Concerto Grosso 1998, Image and Transfiguration 2000. *Publications:* contrib. articles, including Some Aspects of Creation of Musical Compositions 1980, series of articles for The Musical Encyclopedia 1991. *Address:* Studencheskaja Str 44-28, Apt 128, 121165 Moscow, Russia. *Telephone:* (095) 249-5515. *Fax:* (095) 249-5515. *E-mail:* sergzhukov@umail.ru.

**ZIEGLER, Delores;** Singer (Mezzo-Soprano); b. 4 Sept. 1951, Atlanta, Georgia, USA. *Education:* Studied at the University of Tennessee. *Career:* Sang at first in concert then made stage debut as Flora in Traviata at Knoxville, Tennessee, 1978; Sang Maddalena in Rigoletto at St Louis in 1979; Bonn Opera from 1981 as Emilia in Otello, Dorabella and Octavian; Member of the Cologne Opera from 1982, notably as Cherubino, Orlofsky and Octavian; La Scala Milan, 1984–87 in Bellini's Romeo; Guest engagements in Munich, Oslo, San Diego, Toronto, Hamburg and at the Glyndebourne Fesival as Dorabella in 1984; Maggio Musicale Florence in 1989 as Idamantes; Salzburg Festival in 1988 as Mozart's Sextus; Metropolitan Opera, 1989–91 as Siebel and Octavian; Sang in Der Rosenkavalier with the Canadian Opera Company at Toronto, 1990; Sang Dorabella at Washington DC, 1996; Sang Mozart's Marcellina at the Met (1999) and in Rameau's Hippolyte et Aricie at Saint Louis, 2001; Many concert engagements. *Recordings include:* Bach's B minor Mass; Così fan tutte; Mozart's Mass in C; Second Lady in Die Zauberflöte; Le Roi d'Ys by Lalo. *Address:* c/o Cote Artists Management, 150 West 57th Street, Suite 803, New York, NY 10019, USA.

**ZIELINSKA, Lidia;** Composer; b. 30 Oct. 1953, Poznań, Poland; m. Zygmunt Zielinski, 3 Aug 1974, 1 d. *Education:* MA, State Higher School of Music, Poznan; Studied composition with Andrzej Koszewski. *Career:* Collaborated in Electronics Music Studio in Kraków, 1978–; Composers Workshops in Poland, Netherlands, France and Switzerland, 1979–87; Polish Radio Experimental Studio, 1980–81, 1986–, and Studio IPEM, Ghent, 1985; Polish Center of Art for Children and Youth, Artistic Group, Artificial Cult; Co-organised Multimedia Art Meetings, Obecnosc, Poznan; Festivals, Young Polish Music, Szczecin; Concerts and performances in Europe, Asia and USA; Assistant Professor, Academy of Music, Poznan, 1983–. *Compositions include:* Violin Concerto, 1979; Farewell Mr Toorop for Orchestra, 1981; Lullaby Gagaku for Double Bass, 1984; Sonnet On The Tatras for 4 Musicians, 1985; Music For Stanislaw Wyspianski for Tape, 1985; Glossa for Viola or Violin, 1986; Polish Dances for Tape after Father Baka, 1986; Pleonasmus for Oboe, Violin and String Orchestra, 1986; Kaleidoscope, Passacaglia for Percussion, Slides and Clapping Hands, for children, 1987; Concrete Music for Choir and Orchestra,

1987; The Same, 1988; Little Atrophic Symphony, 1988; Musica Humana or How Symphonies Are Born, radio piece, 1989; Jacquard Loom for 15 Musicians, 1991; Fago for Bassoon, Double Bass and Accordion or Electronic Keyboard, 1992; Venture Unknown, ballet, 1995; The Plot Theory of Sound, installation, 1996; Expandata, for percussion and tape, 1997. *Recordings:* Numerous. *Address:* ul Poplinskich 7-9, 61-573 Poznań, Poland.

**ZIESAK, Ruth;** Singer (Soprano); b. 9 Feb. 1963, Hofheim, Taunus, Germany. *Education:* Studied with Christoph Pregardien, at the Frankfurt Musikhochschule with Elsa Cavelti, and at the Frankfurt Opera School. *Career:* Debut: Heidelberg in 1988 as Valencienne in Die Lustige Witwe; Sang at Heidelberg as Pamina, Gilda, Sesto in Giulio Cesare and Despina; Deutsche Oper am Rhein in 1989 as Marzelline; Tour of Tokyo, Osaka and Kyoto with the Ludwigsburg Festival Ensemble, singing in Messiah and Mozart's Requiem, 1989; Sang Susanna at the Opéra Bastille, Paris, and Pamina, 1991, and at the Salzburg Festival, 1993; Season 1993–94 as Sophie in Rosenkavalier at the Deutsche Oper Berlin, 1993; Sang Ighino in Pfitzner's Palestrina at Covent Garden, 1997; Aennchen in Der Freischütz at La Scala, 1998; Season 2000–01 as Marzelline in Fidelio at Munich, and Aennchen in Der Freischütz; Mozart's Countess at Glyndebourne, 2003. *Recordings include:* Servilia in La Clemenza di Tito, under Harnoncourt. *Address:* c/o IMG Artists, Lovell House, 616 Chiswick High Road, London W4 5RX, England.

**ZIESE, Christa-Maria;** Singer (Soprano); b. 13 July 1924, Aschersleben, Germany; m. Rainer Ludeke. *Education:* Studied with Gottlieb Zeithammer and Josef-Maria Hausschild in Leipzig. *Career:* Debut: Leipzig in 1947 as Gretel; Sang at the Leipzig St ädtische Theater, 1951–77 notably as Fidelio, Santuzza, Tosca, Salome, Aida, Carmen, Turandot, Senta, Isolde and Venus; Guest appearances in Weimar, 1951–54, Dresden, Komische Oper Berlin, Moscow Bolshoi, Düsseldorf, Hamburg, Nice, Zürich and Brno; Many concert appearances. *Recordings:* Many. *Honours:* Bach Competition Dresden and International Competition in Prague, 1949.

**ZIFFRIN, Marilyn,** BM, MA; American composer and writer; *Professor Emerita, New England College, Henniker;* b. 7 Aug. 1926, Moline, IL; d. of Harry E. and Betty S. Ziffrin. *Education:* Univ. of Wisconsin, Columbia Univ., Univ. of Chicago. *Career:* teacher, Chicago Public Schools 1952–56; Asst Prof. of Music Northeastern Ill. Univ. 1956–66; Assoc. Prof. of Music New England Coll., Henniker, NH 1957–83, Prof. Emer. 1983–; MacDowell Colony Fellowships 1961, 1963, 1971, 1977, 1980, 1989. *Compositions include:* solo: Theme and Variations for piano 1949, Suite for piano 1955, Toccata and Fugue for organ 1956, Three Songs for woman's voice 1957, Rhapsody for solo guitar 1958, Four Pieces for guitar 1973, Three Movements for guitar 1989, Themes and Variations for organ 1990, Three Songs of the Trobairitz 1991, Recurrences piano solo 1998, Moods piano solo 2003, Three Songs for D'Anna 2003; chamber music: The Little Prince for clarinet and bassoon 1953, Make a Joyful Noise quintet for recorder 1966, In the Beginning for percussion ensemble 1968, XIII for chamber ensemble 1969, String Quartet 1970, Haiku for soprano, viola and harpsichord 1971, Movements for clarinet and percussion 1972, Sonata for organ and cello 1973, Trio for xylophone, soprano and tuba 1974, Trio for violin, cello and piano 1975, Quintet for oboe and string quartet 1976, Concerto for viola and woodwind quintet 1978, SONO for cello and piano 1980, White Lies (film score) 1983, Yankee Hooray piano duet 1984, Duo for alto recorders 1985, Conversations for double bass and harpsichord 1986, Tributum for clarinet, viola and double bass 1992, Flute Fun for two flutes 1995, Fantasy for two pianos 1995, Lines and Spaces for brass quintet 1996, For Love of Cynthia for baritone and classical accordion, or violin, horn and piano 1997, Two Songs for soprano, viola and piano 1998, String Quartet No. 2 1999, Two Movements for woodwind quintet 2000, Abbot's Duo for alto sax and violin 2001, Sonatina for trumpet and piano 2001, Trio for flute, clarinet and piano 2004; choral: Jewish Prayer 1950, Death of Moses 1954, Prayer 1966, Drinking Song and Dance, from Captain Kidd 1971, Chorus from Alcestis 1990, Choruses from the Greeks 1992, New England Epitaphs 1994, Cantata for Freedom 2000, Almanack 1688 2002; orchestral: Strings 1966, Soundscape 2000, Soundscape II 2002. *Publications:* Carl Ruggles: Composer, Painter and Storyteller 1994; contrib. to The New Grove Dictionary of Music and Musicians 1980, The New Grove Dictionary of American Music 1986. *Honours:* Special Mention Delius Composition Competition 1971, first prize Delius Composition Competition 1972, ASCAP Awards 1981–2004, Music Fix Prize 1996, New Hampshire MTA Composer of the Year 1997, Virginia Center for the Creative Arts Residency 1987. *Address:* PO Box 179, Bradford, NH 03221, USA.

**ZIKMUNDOVÁ, Eva;** Opera Singer (Soprano); b. 4 May 1932, Kromeriz, Czechoslovakia; Divorced, 1 s. *Education:* State Conservatory, Brno; Music Academy, Prague. *Career:* Debut: Opera House, Ostrava; Member of Opera Company of National Theatre, Prague, 1958–92; Assistant Producer, State Opera, Prague, 1992–95; Guest appearances at State Opera, Berlin, Hannover, Mannheim, Germany, Venice, Genoa, Naples, Italy, Lausanne, Switzerland, Vienna, Austria, Edinburgh, Scotland, Amsterdam, Netherlands, Warsaw, Poland, Budapest, Hungary, Sofia, Bulgaria, and Brussels, Belgium; Recitals for Czech Radio and Television; Professor of Singing at State Conservatory, Teplice. *Recordings:* Dvořák's St Ludmila and Moravian duets; Janáček's The Cunning Little Vixen; Numerous recordings of arias and duets. *Publications:* Translations into Czech of: Martienssen-Lohmann, Der wissende Sänger and Das bewusste Singen, 1994; Rodolfo Celletti: Storia del belcanto, 1998. *Honours:* Supraphon Annual Award for Cunning Little Vixen,

1974; Merited Member of The National Theatre, Ministry of Culture. *Current Management:* Pragokoncert, Prague 1, Czech Republic. *Address:* Mánesova 23, Prague 2, Czech Republic.

**ZILBERSTEIN, Lilya;** Concert Pianist; b. 19 April 1965, Moscow, Russia; m. Alexander Gerzenzon, 27 Aug 1988, 2 s. *Education:* Moscow Gnessin Special Music School with Ada Traub, 1972–83; Gnessin Music Pedagogical Institute, with Alexander Satz, 1983–90. *Career:* St Louis Symphony, Chicago Symphony, Berlin Philharmonic, London Symphony, Royal Philharmonic, Dresden Staatskapelle, Moscow Philharmonic, Finnish Radio; Montreal Symphony Orchestra; Teatro La Scala, 1999. *Recordings:* 8 CD's, 6 Recitals include: Concertos Nos 2, 3 by Rachmaninov with the Berlin Philharmonic and Claudio Abbado; Concerto by Grieg with Gothenburg Symphony and Neeme Järvi. *Honours:* lst Prize, Busoni International Piano Competition, 1987; International Prize of Academia Musicals Chigiana in Siena, Italy. *Current Management:* Konzertdirektion Dr Goette, Hamburg. *Address:* c/o Konzertdirektion Dr Goette, Brahmsallee 6, 20144 Hamburg, Germany.

**ZILIO, Elena;** Italian singer (soprano); b. 1941, Bolzano; m. Stillo Burchiellaro. *Education:* Conservatorio Monteverdi, Bolzano, Accademia Chigiana, Siena and Accademia di Santa Cecilia, Rome. *Career:* debut at Spoleto in 1963 as Sofia in Rossini's Il Signor Bruschino. Career. Has sung at La Scala Milan, Rome, Genoa, Palermo, Naples, Turin, Trieste, Venice and Verona Arena in 1970, 1973, 1978; Festivals at Caraccalla and Florence; Sang Lisa in La Sonnambula at Geneva in 1982; Chicago Opera in 1983 as Suzuki in Madama Butterfly; Milan at La Scala and Piccola Scala in 1983 as Amore in Cherubini's Anacréon and Dardane in La Rencontre Imprévue by Gluck; Sang Smeaton in Anna Bolena at Bergamo in 1983, returning in 1988 as the Page in Donizetti's Gianni di Parigi; With the company of the San Carlo Naples sang Giustinio in Pergolesi's Flaminio at Versailles and Spoleto, USA, 1983 and Wiesbaden in 1985; Cologne Opera in 1984 as Pippo in La Gazza Ladra: Returned to La Scala in 1985 in a revival of Rossi's Orfeo; Further appearances in Brussels, at Paris Opéra, in Boston, San Antonio, Montreal, Bregenz and Dubrovnik; Sang Elena in La Gazza Ladra at Palermo, 1996; Marquise in La Fille du Régiment at Rome, 1998; Sang Mistress Quickly in Falstaff at Lyon and Frankfurt, 1999–2000. *Recordings:* La Buona Figliola by Piccinni; La Straniera by Bellini; Un Giorno di Regno by Verdi. *Current Management:* Atelier Musicale, Via Caselle 76, San Lazzaro di Savena 40068, Italy. *Telephone:* (051) 19 98 44 44. *Fax:* (051) 19 98 44 20. *E-mail:* info@ ateliermusicale.com. *Website:* www.ateliermusicale.com.

**ZIMANSKY, Robert;** Violinist; b. 20 April 1948, Iowa City, USA; m. Lucia Borsatti, 9 April 1979. *Education:* University of Iowa, 1960–66; Juilliard School of Music, 1966–71; Masterclasses with various teachers, 1970–74. *Career:* Debut: Orchestra Hall, Chicago with Civic Symphony Orchestra; Resident Europe, 1972–; Leader of Symphonie-Orchester Graunke, 1972–73; Suddeutsche Rundfunk, 1974, and Orchestre de la Suisse Romande, 1975–99; Professor of Advanced Classes, Geneva Conservatory, 1980–; Soloist with Wolfgang Sawallisch, Horst Stein, Charles Dutoit, Leif Segerstam, David Zinman, George Cleve and Herbert Blomstedt; mem, Board of Directors, Association des Musiciens Suisses. *Recordings:* X and P Scharwenka Violin Sonatas; Bach 5th Brandenberg; Albéric Magnard Sonata; Schumann 3 Sonatas (award); Reger, Sonatas op 72 and 84; Schubert, Octet and Janáček complete violin works. *Honours:* Grand Prix du Disque, Academie Charles Cros, 1986. *Current Management:* Wismer-Casetti, 30, CH Du Vieux-Vesenaz, 1222 Vesenaz. *Address:* 6 Tour de Champel, 1206 Geneva, Switzerland.

**ZIMERMAN, Krystian;** Polish pianist and conductor; *Lecturer, Academy of Music, Basel;* b. 5 Dec. 1956, Zabrze; m. Maria Drygajło; one s. one d. *Education:* State Higher Inst. of Music, Katowice, student of Prof. Andrzej Jasiński. *Career:* Lecturer, Acad. of Music, Basel, Switzerland 1996–; Founder and Conductor Polish Festival Orchestra 1999–; collaborated with conductors Abbado, Bernstein, von Karajan, Ozawa, Muti, Maazel, Previn, Boulez, Mehta, Haitink, Skrowaczewski, Rattle and others; has performed in numerous European countries and the USA. *Recordings:* CD recordings include: works for piano and chamber music by Schumann, Grieg (with H. von Karajan), Mozart (with K. Danczowska), Schubert, Brahms, Chopin (with Polish Festival Orchestra – Chopin Piano Concertos), Liszt, Debussy and others. *Honours:* numerous prizes in prin. pianist competitions in Poland and abroad including First Prize, Beethoven Competition, Hradec Kralové 1973, Grand Prix IX Chopin Int. Pianist Competition, Warsaw 1975, Chigiana's Acad. Award for Best Young Pianist of the Year, Siena 1985, Orfeusz (Critics' Award), Polish Artists of Music Asscn 1988, Grand Prix de Disque, French Acad. 1989, Int. Critics' Award 1989. *Address:* Kernmatterstrasse 8B, 4102 Binningen, Switzerland.

**ZIMMER, Hans Florian;** German film score composer; b. 12 Sept. 1957, Frankfurt am Main, Germany; m. Vicki Carolyn (separated); one d. *Education:* in England. *Career:* mem. The Buggles (produced hit song Video Killed the Radio Star); pioneered use of digital synthesizers with computer tech. and traditional performers; mem. BMI. *Film scores:* Moonlighting 1982, Histoire d'O: Chapitre 2 1984, Success is the Best Revenge 1984, Insignificance 1985, Separate Vacations 1986, The Wind 1987, Terminal Exposure 1987, Rain Man 1988, Twister 1988, Taffin 1988, Spies Inc 1988, The Fruit Machine 1988, Burning Secret 1988, A World Apart (with Stanley Myers) 1988, Wiezien Rio 1989, Paperhouse 1989, Dark Obsession 1989, Black Rain 1989, Driving Miss Daisy 1989, Green Card 1990, Pacific Heights 1990, Nightmare at Noon 1990, Fools of Fortune 1990, Chicago Joe and the Showgirl

1990, Bird on a Wire 1990, Days of Thunder 1990, K2 (European version) 1991, Backdraft 1991, Regarding Henry 1991, Thelma & Louise 1991, Where Sleeping Dogs Lie 1992, The Power of One 1992, A League of Their Own 1992, Radio Flyer 1992, Toys 1992, Cool Runnings 1993, Calendar Girl 1993, Point of No Return 1993, True Romance 1993, Younger and Younger 1993, The House of the Spirits 1993, The Lion King (Acad. Award, Golden Globe) 1994, Africa: The Serengeti 1994, I'll Do Anything 1994, Renaissance Man 1994, Drop Zone 1994, Two Deaths 1995, Crimson Tide (Grammy Award) 1995, Nine Months 1995, Something to Talk About 1995, Beyond Rangoon 1995, Muppet Treasure Island 1996, Broken Arrow 1996, The Preacher's Wife 1996, The Whole Wide World, 1996, The Fan 1996, The Peacemaker 1997, As Good As It Gets 1997, The Last Days 1998, The Thin Red Line 1998, The Prince of Egypt 1998, Chill Factor 1999, Gladiator (Golden Globe) 2000, The Road to El Dorado 2000, Mission: Impossible II 2000, An Everlasting Piece 2000, Hannibal 2001, Pearl Harbor 2001, Riding in Cars with Boys 2001, Invincible 2001, Black Hawk Down 2001, Spirit 2002, The Ring 2002, Tears of the Sun 2003, Matchstick Men 2003, The Last Samurai 2003, Something's Gotta Give 2003, King Arthur 2004, Thunderbirds 2004, Shark Tale 2004, Lauras Stern 2004, Spanglish 2004, The Ring Two 2005, Madagascar 2005, Batman Begins 2005, The Weather Man 2005. *Television scores:* Wild Horses 1985, First Born 1989, Millennium 1992, Space Rangers 1993, The Critic (theme) 1994, High Incident (theme) 1996, Die Motorrad-Cops: Hart am Limit 1999, El Candidato 1999, Carnivàle (series) 2003, Threat Matrix (series title theme) 2003, The Contender (series) 2005. *Recordings:* Wings of Film 2001, numerous soundtrack recordings. *Current Management:* Gorfaine/Schwartz Agency Inc., 13245 Riverside Drive, Suite 450, Sherman Oaks, CA 91423, USA.

**ZIMMERMAN, Christopher;** Conductor; b. 1957, England. *Education:* Studied at Yale and the University of Michigan; Further study with Nadia Boulanger and at the Pierre Monteux School of Conducting, Maine. *Career:* Music Director of the Yale Bach Society, 1980; Conducted the Michigan University Symphony Orchestra in the USA and Europe; Worked with the Toronto Symphony, the Czech Philharmonic, 1983–85; London 1985, leading concerts with the Royal Philharmonic and the London Symphony Orchestras; Appearances with the Royal Liverpool Philharmonic and at the Concertgebouw in Amsterdam; Prague 1987, with the Prague Symphony Orchestra; Conducted the Seoul Philharmonic in Korea, 1989; Guest Music Director at Mexico City Opera; Music Director, City of London Chamber Orchestra, 1988–93; Most recent Guest Engagements: Edmonton Symphony Orchestra, 1993, Waterbury Symphony Orchestra, 1994; Further engagements in Finland and Venezuela; Music Director, Bangor Symphony Orchestra, Bangor Maine, and Music Director, Concert Orchestra, Cincinnati College Conservatory of Music, Cincinnati, Ohio, USA; mem, A S O L. *Current Management:* Kenneth Wentworth, Jonathan Wentworth & Associates Ltd. *Address:* Artist Management, Suite 503, 100 Stevens Avenue, Mount Vernon, New York 10550, USA.

**ZIMMERMAN, Franklin B.,** BLitt, PhD, FACLS; American musician, conductor and musicologist; b. 20 June 1923, Wanneta, KS; m. 1988; one s. five d. *Education:* Univ. of Southern California, Univ. of Oxford, studied French Horn with Aubrey Brain, conducting with Ernest Read, orchestration with Leon Kirchner and Ingolf Dahl. *Career:* created Music SoundScapes, a three-dimensional, animated and colour-coded graphic musical notation; debut, London 1957; founder and Dir, Pennsylvania Pro Musica playing over 5,200 concerts; mem. AMS, IMS. *Recordings:* Handel L'Allegro ed Il Penseroso 1981. *Publications:* Henry Purcell: Analytical Catalog 1963, Henry Purcell: Life and Times 1967, Henry Purcell: Thematic Index 1973, Words to Music 1965, Facsimile Editions: An Introduction to the Skill of Musick by John Playford (12th edn, corrected and amended by Henry Purcell, with index, introduction and glossary) 1972, Henry Purcell: a Guide to Research 1989, Henry Purcell (1659–1695): Analytical Essays on his Music 2001, Visible Music Sound-Scapes: A New Approach to Musical Notation and Understanding, Purcellian Melodies Indexed: A Thematic Index to the Complete Work of Henry Purcell; contrib. numerous articles and monographs. *Honours:* Arnold Bax Medal for Musicology 1958. *Address:* Visible Music SoundScapes Inc., Suite 1A, 225 S 42nd Street, Philadelphia, PA 19104, USA. *E-mail:* musica@dca.net. *Website:* www.visiblemusics.com/new.

**ZIMMERMAN, Willi;** Violinist; b. 1955, Switzerland. *Education:* Studied with the Alban Berg Quartet in Vienna. *Career:* Leader, Amati String Quartet, 1981–; Further study with members of the Amadeus and Bartók Quartets, and with Walter Levin; Many performances in Switzerland, USA and elsewhere in the classical repertoire, and in works by Szymanowski, Tailleferre, Cui, Steuermann, Vladimir Vogel, Kelterborn and Robert Suter; Recitals at Basle in 1986 and tours of the United Kingdom, 1990–91; Menuhin Festival at Gstaad in 1991; Recitals with Bruno Canino, Malcolm Frager, Bruno Giuranna, Karl Leister among others. *Honours:* With Amati Quartet: Grand Prix, Concours International at Evian, 1982, Art Prize of the Lions Club in 1985, and 1st Prize, Karl Klinger Competition in Munich, 1986. *Address:* c/o Dönch Amati Quartet, Eckenheimer Landstrasse 483, D–60435 Frankfurt, Germany.

**ZIMMERMANN, Frank Peter;** German violinist; b. 27 Feb. 1965, Duisburg; m. Young Joo Zimmermann; one s. *Education:* Folkwang Musikhochschule, Essen, Staatliche Hochschule der Künste, Berlin and with Herman Krebbers in Amsterdam. *Career:* made debut aged 10 playing Mozart's violin concerto in G major, K 216 in Duisburg; now performs with all maj. orchestras in world and has undertaken extensive tours in Europe, the USA, Japan and Australia;

also gives worldwide recitals, with pianists Alexander Lonquich –1994 and Enrico Pace 1998– and with Heinrich Schiff (q.v.) and Christian Zacharias; appeared with English Chamber Orchestra conducted by Sir Colin Davis at Buckingham Palace by special invitation of HRH The Prince of Wales 1991; soloist at Europa Concert given by Berlin Philharmonic under Bernard Haitink at Royal Albert Hall, London and televised live all over world 1993; recordings include concertos of Tchaikovsky, Brahms, Beethoven, Mozart, Prokofiev, Sibelius, Mendelssohn, Dvořák, Glazunov, Berg, Saint-Saëns, Weill and Stravinsky; in recital with Alexander Lonquich recorded all Mozart and Prokofiev sonatas and works by Ravel, Debussy, Janáček etc.; Brahms Double Concerto with Heinrich Schiff and London Philharmonic Orchestra 1997; Ligeti Violin Concerto with ASKO Ensemble and Reinbert de Leeuw 2001; many other recordings. *Honours:* Premio dell'Accademia Musicale Chigiana, Siena 1990, Rheinischer Kulturpreis 1994; numerous awards and prizes for recordings. *Address:* c/o Riaskoff Concert Management, Concertgebouwplein 15, 1071 LL Amsterdam, Netherlands. *Telephone:* (20) 6645353. *Fax:* (20) 6715106. *E-mail:* mail@riaskoff.nl (office).

**ZIMMERMANN, Margarita;** Singer (Mezzo-Soprano); b. Aug. 1942, Buenos Aires, Argentina. *Education:* Studied in Buenos Aires. *Career:* Debut: Teatro Colón Buenos Aires, as Orpheus in the opera by Gluck, 1977; European debut at the Landestheater in Salzburg, as Carmen and Ulrica in Un Ballo in Maschera; Covent Garden debut in 1980 as Cherubino; US appearances at Miami as Dalila in 1979 and San Francisco as Rosina in 1982; Further engagements at Naples, Bologna, Venice, Rome, Lyon, Geneva and Paris; Further roles include Mozart's Sextus, Idamante and Zerlina, Handel's Giulio Cesare and Agrippina, Juno in Cavalli's Ercole Amante and Wagner's Fricka; In 1988 sang at Piacenza and Madrid as Massenet's Charlotte and as Andromache in Rossini's Ermione; Appeared as Thérèse in the opera by Massenet at Opéra de Monte Carlo, 1989. *Recordings include:* The Singer in Manon Lescaut.

**ZIMMERMANN, Margrit;** Composer; b. 7 Aug. 1927, Bern, Switzerland. *Education:* Studied piano and theory with Jeanne Bovet and Walter Furrer in Bern, with Denise Bidal in Lausanne, and masterclasses with Alfred Cortot; Diploma in Pianoforte; Composition studies under Arthur Honegger, Ecole Normale de Musique de Paris; Study as conductor with Ewald Korner, Municipal Theatre of Bern; International masterclasses with Igor Markevitch, Monte Carlo, and Hans Swarowsky, Ossiach; Diploma in Composition, Giuseppe Verdi Conservatorium, Milan. *Career:* Music teacher, Bern; Composer. *Compositions:* Numerous including symphonic and scenic works, chamber music for a wide range of instruments, vocal and solo works for piano, strings, wind, percussion and guitar; Works include Panta Rhei, Op 39, 1987, Cloccachorda, Op 40, 1987, Die Gestundete Zeit, Op 52, 1987; Piano Time, Op 46, 1987; Quadriga, Op 51, 1987; Murooji, Op 57, for Guitar Solo; Trptychon, Op 58; Pianorama, Op 59; In Urbis Honorem, symphony for Orchestra and Choir; Jubilation, concert for Orchestra. *Recordings:* Cloccachordia; Piano Time; Quadriga; Pensieri; Orphische Taenze; Quartetto d'Archi. *Address:* Ostermundigenstrasse 22, 3006 Bern, Switzerland.

**ZIMMERMANN, Tabea;** German concert violist; *Professor of Viola, Hanns Eisler Hochschule für Musik;* b. 8 Oct. 1968, Lahr. *Education:* studied with Ulrich Koch and Sándor Végh. *Career:* Prof., Conservatoire in Frankfurt 1994–2002; Prof. of Viola, Hanns Eisler Hochschule für Musik, Berlin 2002–; frequent concerts with such soloists as Gidon Kremer, Heinz Holliger, Thomas Zehetmair, Steven Isserlis and Heinrich Schiff; appearances at Prades, Schleswig-Holstein, Lockenhaus, Marlboro and other chamber music festivals; regular recitals with pianist Hartmut Holl; concert engagements include Mozart's Sinfonia Concertante in Amsterdam, and at the Salzburg Festival; has also performed with the Bamberg Symphony under Christoph Eschenbach, at Frankfurt with Gary Bertini, Penderecki's Concerto with the composer conducting the Munich Philharmonic and concerts in Hamburg, Tokyo, Rome, Copenhagen, Helsinki and Israel; gave the world premieres of concertos by Mark Koptyman and Volker David Kirchner 1992; premiere of Ligeti's Viola Sonata at Cologne 1993; Alexander Goehr's Schlussgesang at the Aldeburgh Festival 1997, Berio's Concerto for clarinet and viola 1996, with Paul Meyer; recent engagements include the Mahler Chamber Orchestra; recitals in Italy, France and Belgium; Scottish Chamber Orchestra, Royal Concertgebouw, CBSO, Orchestre Nat. de Lyon; season 2002 with premieres of Recicanto by Heinz Holliger and Concerto by Sally Beamish; co-founder Arcanto Quartet with Antje Weithaas, Daniel Sepec and Jean-Guihen Queyras 2004–. *Recordings:* Mozart's Concertante K364, Bach Trio Sonatas, Gubaidulina Hommage, Chamber works by Bruch, Mozart and Schumann, The Concerto in Europe, Double Concertos and works by Penderecki, Berlioz's Harold in Italy with London Symphony Orchestra and Colin Davis. *Honours:* first prize competitions in Geneva and Budapest, Awarded Vatelot Viola, Paris, Frankfurter Musikpreis 1995, Accademia Musicale Chigiana, Sienna 1997. *Current Management:* Karsten Witt Musik Management GmbH, Leuschnerdamm 13, 10999 Berlin, Germany. *Telephone:* (30) 616921920. *Fax:* (30) 616921101. *E-mail:* info@karstenwitt.com. *Website:* www .karstenwitt.com.

**ZIMMERMANN, Udo;** German composer and conductor; b. 6 Oct. 1943, Dresden. *Education:* Dresden Musikhochschule with J. P. Thilman, masterclasses at the Akademie der Kunste, Berlin. *Career:* Composer and Prod., Dresden State Opera 1970; founder, Studio for New Music in Dresden 1974; Prof. of Composition, Dresden Hochschule für Musik 1978, Prof. of Experimental Music Theatre 1982; conducted the Bavarian Radio Symphony

Orchestra in the premiere of Hartmann's Sinfonia Tragica, Munich 1989; premiere of Bernhard Jesl's Opera Der König Stirbt at Bonn 1990; Intendant, Leipzig State Opera 1990–2001, Deutsche Oper 2001–02; Chair., Festspielhaus Hellerau, Dresden. *Compositions include:* Operas: Die Weisse Rose, 1967, Levins Muhle, 1973, Die Wundersame Schusterfrau, 1982; 5 songs for Baritone and Orchestra, 1964; Musik für Streicher, 1967; String Quartet, 1967; Sieh, Meine Augen for Chamber Orchestra, 1970; Mutazioni for Orchestra, 1972; Choreographien Nach Edgar Degas for 21 Instruments, 1974; Hymnus An Die Sonne, after Kleist, for Soprano, Flute and Harpsichord, 1976; Pax Questuosa for 5 Soloists, 3 Choirs and Orchestra, 1980. *Address:* c/o Festspielhaus Hellerau GmbH, Karl-Liebknecht-Strasse 56, 01109 Dresden, Germany.

**ZIMMERMANN, Walter;** Composer; b. 15 April 1949, Schwabach, Germany. *Education:* Studied piano, violin and oboe; Composition with Werner Heider and Otto Laske at Utrecht; Ethnological Centre Jaap Kunst in Amsterdam, 1970–73; Computer music in the USA, 1974. *Career:* Pianist in the Ars-Nova Ensemble of Nuremberg, 1968–70; Founded Beginner Studio at Cologne, 1977; Lecturer at Darmstadt, 1982, and Liège Conservatory from 1982; Professor of Composition, HDK Berlin. *Compositions include:* Lokale Musik, 15 works for various forces, 1977–81; Uber Die Dörfer, dramatic song for Soprano, Chorus and Orchestra, 1986; Fragmente der Liebe for Saxophone and String Quartet, 1987; Beginners Mind for piano, 1975; Wüstenwanderung for 1986; Festina lente for string quartet; Diastasis/Diastema for 2 orchestras without conductor, 1992; Distentio for string trio, 1990; Affeklenlehre for ensemble, 1995–. *Address:* c/o GEMA, Postfach 80 07 67, 81607 Munich, Germany.

**ZIMMERMANN, Wolfram;** Singer (Bass-Baritone); b. 17 April 1920, Stuttgart, Germany. *Education:* Studied with his father, at the Stuttgart and Vienna Academies and with Anna Bahr-Mildenburg. *Career:* Debut: Stuttgart in 1947 as Rossini's Basilio; Radio broadcasts in Germany and Austria; Sang Beckmesser in Die Meistersinger, under Furtwängler, at La Scala, 1952; Created title role in Titus Feuerfuchs by Heinrich Sutermeister for television in Austria, 1959; Vienna Staatsoper 1958–63, notably as Leporello, Mozart's Papageno and the Doctor in Wozzeck by Berg; Rome Opera in 1956, Graz in 1958, Barcelona, 1958–63, and Mexico City in 1966 as Beckmesser; Other roles include the title roles in Mozart's Figaro, Gounod's Mephistopheles and Donizetti's Don Pasquale; mem, Honorary Cavalier, Deutscherrn-Ritterbund Norimberga. *Recordings:* Zar and Zimmermann by Lortzing; Tannhäuser by Wagner. *Honours:* Diploma, International Song, Geneva, 1949; Bach Prize, Leipzig, 1950; Gold Medal, Accademia Italia, 1980. *Address:* Erbisleiten 6, 91227 Weissenbrunn, Gemeinde Leinburg, Germany.

**ZINKLER, Christiane;** Singer (Mezzo-Soprano); b. 23 Nov. 1947, Coburg, Germany. *Education:* Studied with Willi Domgraf-Fassbaender in Nuremberg and with Clemens Kaiser-Breme in Essen. *Career:* Debut: Deutsche Oper am Rhein, Düsseldorf, in 1968 as Messenger in Dallapiccola's Job; Member of the Dortmund Opera notably as Gluck's Orpheus, Erda and Fricka in Der Ring des Nibelungen, Ulrica, Hansel, Monteverdi's Poppea, Anina in Der Rosenkavalier, Cherubino and Dorabella; Guest appearances in Hamburg, Essen, Copenhagen, Wiesbaden and Florence; Many concert appearances. *Address:* c/o Opernhaus, Kuhlstrasse 12, 4600 Dortmund, Germany.

**ZINMAN, David Joel;** American conductor; *Music Director, Aspen Music Festival and School;* b. 9 July 1936, New York; s. of Samuel Zinman and Rachel Ilo (née Samuels) Zinman; m. 1st Leslie Heyman (deceased); one s. one d.; m. 2nd Mary Ingham 1974; one s. *Education:* Oberlin Conservatory, Ohio and Univ. of Minnesota. *Career:* studied conducting at Berkshire Music Center, Tanglewood and with Pierre Monteux; Asst to Monteux 1961–64; Music Dir Nederlands Kamerorkest 1964–77; Music Dir Rochester Philharmonic Orchestra, New York 1974–85; Baltimore Symphony Orchestra 1985–98; Prin. Guest Conductor Rotterdam Philharmonic Orchestra 1977–79; Chief Conductor 1979–82; Music Dir Tonhalle Orchestra, Zurich 1995; Music Dir (desig.) Aspen Music Festival and School 1997, Music Dir 1998–; numerous recordings. *Honours:* Grand Prix du Disque, Edison Award, Gramophone Best Selling Record (Górecki) 1993, Gramophone Award (Jungle Book) 1994, three Grammy Awards, Deutschen Schallplatten Prize, Peabody Medal 1996. *Address:* Aspen Music Festival and School, 2 Music School Road, Aspen, CO 81611, USA (office).

**ZINOVENKO, Yuri;** Singer (Bass); b. 1955, Simferopol, Ukraine. *Education:* Studied in Tashkent. *Career:* Sang first at the Kirov Opera, St Petersburg; Croatian National Opera, Zagreb, 1981–87; Further engagements at the Frankfurt Opera and the Staatstheater, Darmstadt; Guest appearances in Italy, Israel, Austria, Russia and the USA; Roles have included the Hermit in Der Freischütz, Water Sprite in Rusalka, Prince Gremin (Eugene Onegin), and Kochubey in Tchaikovsky's Mazeppa; Verdi roles include Zaccaria and Lodovico; Sang The Prophet in the first production this century of Zemlinsky's first opera, Sarema (Trier Opera, 1996); Concerts include Mozart's Requiem and Shostakovich's 13th Symphony, Babi-Yar. *Recordings include:* Sarema (Koch International). *Address:* c/o Theater der Stadt Trier, Am Augustinerhof, 5500 Trier, Germany.

**ZINSSTAG, Gérard;** composer; b. 9 May 1941, Geneva, Switzerland; m. 1984; one s. one d. *Education:* CNSM, Paris, Chigiana Acad., Siena, Musikhochschule, Zürich, studied with H. U. Lehmann, Helmut Lachenmann. *Career:* composer-in-residence, Berlin 1981 (DAAD); orchestral musician touring Europe, 1964–67; solo flute, Orchestra of Zürich, Tonhalle,

1967–75; participation in summer course, Darmstadt, 1976–78; seminar at University of California, Berkeley, 1979 and several in New York; founder of Festival of Zürich, Tage für neue Musik Zürich, 1986–; tour of Russia, Moscow and Baku, 1990; several conferences and lectures in Moscow, Taipeh, Paris (Sorbonne and IRCAM), Salzburg, Geneva, Zürich, Bamberg etc.; mem. Suisa, Composers' Forum, New York, ISCM. *Compositions:* Déliements; Wenn Zum Biespiel; Tatastenfelder; Suono Reale; Innanzi; Foris; Perforation; Altération; Trauma; Edition Modern Munich; Cut Sounds; Incalzando, 1981; Artifices, 1982–83; Sept Fragments, 1982–83; Stimuli, 1984; Tempi Inquieti, 1984–86; Eden Jeden, 1987; Artifices ll, 1988; Tempor, 1992; String Quartet no. 2, 1995; Tahir, 1995; Ergo, 1996; Hommage à Charles Racine, for mezzo and ensemble, 1997; Ubu Cocu, opéra bouffe, 2000; Passage, for orchestra, 2002; String Quartet no. 3. *Recordings:* Foris, Innanzi, etc; Tempor; Diffractions. *Publications:* Pro Musica, 1988; Revue Musicale Suisse, 1979–80. *Address:* Seefeldstr. 191, 8008 Zürich, Switzerland; 4 place Victor Basch, 30400 Ville-lés-Avignon, France.

**ZITEK, Vaclav;** Singer (Baritone); b. 24 March 1932, Tisa, Czechoslovakia. *Education:* Studied in Prague with Adrian Levicky. *Career:* Debut: Prague Opera Studio in 1957 as Germont in La Traviata; Member of the National Theatre, Prague, in operas by Mozart, Verdi, Tchaikovsky, Smetana, Dvořák, Martinů, Puccini, Strauss and Prokofiev; Guest appearances at the Bolshoi Theatre Moscow, the Staatsoper and Komische Oper Berlin, National Opera in Bucharest and the Bordeaux Opera; Sang at Prague National Theatre in 1983 as Premysl in Smetana's Libuše; Frequent concert and oratorio engagements. *Recordings:* Operas by Smetana, Dvořák's Jacobin and Šarka by Fibich; Šiškov in From the House of the Dead, and Jenůfa with the Vienna Philharmonic conducted by Charles Mackerras; Don Giovanni, Don Carlos, Trovatore, Pelléas et Mélisande, Faust, Macbeth, The Queen of Spades, Pagliacci; Smetana/Dalibor, Libuše, The Kiss, The Secret, The Devil's Wall; The Makropulos Case; From the House of the Dead; Jenůfa; The Cunning Little Vixen; Don Giovanni; Luisa Miller. *Honours:* Laureate of the State Prize, 1981; National Artist of Czechoslovakia, 1985; Prize of the National Academy of Recording and Science, Šiškov, in Janáček's From the House of the Dead, with the Vienna Philharmonic conducted by Charles Mackerras, 1981. *Address:* Ke skalkam 2450, 106 00 Prague 10, Czech Republic.

**ZIVA, Vladimir P.;** Russian conductor; b. 7 March 1957, Arkhangelsk; m. Ziva Anna; two s. *Education:* Leningrad State Conservatory, Moscow State Conservatory. *Career:* asst to principal conductor Symphony Orchestra of Moscow Philharmonics 1984–87; teacher Moscow State conservatory 1988–89; Artistic Dir and chief conductor Nizhne-Novgorod Philharmonic Orchestra 1988–2000; principal conductor St Petersburg Mussorgsky Theatre of Opera and Ballet 1990–92; Artistic Dir and principal conductor Moscow Symphony orchestra 2000–; co-founder Krasnodar Opera Co. 2003–; repertoire comprises classical and modern music; opera stage productions, in collaboration with B. Pokrovsky, include The Turn of the Screw, Albert Herring by B. Britten, Snow Maiden by P. Tchaikovsky. *Honours:* Hon. Artist of Russia, Conductor of the Year 1996, 1997; State Prize of Russian Federation 1995. *Address:* Kazanskaya str. 8/10 apt. 42, St Petersburg 191186, Russia (home). *Telephone:* 812-117 2337 (home).

**ZIVONI, Yossi,** FRNCM; violinist; *Professor of Violin, Royal College of Music;* b. 1939, Tel-Aviv, Israel; m. Jeanne 1962; one d. *Education:* Israel Acad. of Music, Tel-Aviv, Conservatoire Royal de Musique de Bruxelles, Belgium. *Career:* debut, Amsterdam, Netherlands 1964; concert tours in Europe, Israel, Australia, Canada, Far East and South America; Principal Tutor, Royal Northern Coll. of Music, Manchester; Prof. of Violin, Royal Coll. of Music, London 1997–; Leader Gabrieli String Quartet 1995–2000; mem. Royal Soc. of Musicians of Great Britain. *Recordings:* Mozart Sonatas, Bach Sonatas and Partitas, Mendelssohn Sonatas, Bartók Sonata for solo violin and violin duos, Schumann Quartets, Mozart Early Quartets (with Gabrieli Quartet). *Honours:* Hon. Fellow Royal Northern Coll. of Music; Paganini Int. Competition 1960, Bavarian Radio Int. Competition, Munich 1961, Queen Elisabeth Int. Competition, Brussels, Belgium 1963. *Current Management:* Anglo-Swiss Management Ltd, Suite 6, 72 Fairhazel Gardens, London, NW6 3SR, England.

**ZLATKOVA, Sonia;** Singer (Soprano); b. 1963, Tolbuchin, Bulgaria. *Education:* Studied in Varna and Sofia. *Career:* Sang in concert in France in 1988 and made her stage debut at Ruse in 1989 as Despina; Sang at Bulgarian National Opera at Sofia from 1989 as Gilda, Lucia, the Queen of Night and Rosina; Guest appearances at Bregenz in 1991 as Frasquita, at St Gallen as Oscar and at Kaiserslautern as the Queen of Night; Sang Pamina at Schönbrunn, Vienna, 1996; Sang Zerlina and Nannetta for Graz Opera, 1999–2001. *Address:* Bulgarian National Opera, Boulevard Dondoukov 58, 1000 Sofia, Bulgaria.

**ZNAIDER, Nikolaj;** violinist; b. 1975, Denmark. *Education:* Royal Danish Acad., Juilliard School of Music, Vienna Conservatory with Boris Kuschnir. *Career:* appearances with the Cleveland, Leipzig Gewandhaus and St Petersburg Philharmonic Orchestras; season 1999–2000 with the Berlin Philharmonic Orchestra under Daniel Barenboim, London Symphony under Rostropovich at the Barbican and on tour to Japan and London Philharmonic with Kurt Masur at the Royal Festival Hall; Los Angeles Philharmonic, Czech, Oslo and Munich Philharmonics, BBC Symphony and Budapest Festival Orchestra; Yehudi Menuhin Memorial Concert at the Albert Hall; tour of Australia 2000; Nielsen's concerto at the London Proms 2002; recitals in New York, Paris, Amsterdam and Lucerne; frequent guest with the Chicago Symphony Orchestra, Cleveland Orchestra, Detroit Symphony, Nat. Symphony, New York Philharmonic Orchestra and the Philadelphia Orchestra; he has collaborated with Daniel Barenboim, Herbert Blomstedt, Myung Whun Chung, Sir Colin Davis, Charles Dutiut, Valery Gergiev, Mariss Jansons, Neeme Järvi, Lorin Maazel, Kurt Masur, Zubin Mehta, Mstislav Rostropovich, Leonard Slatkin and Yuri Temirkanov. *Recordings:* Bruch No. 1 and Nielsen Concertos with the London Philharmonic and Lawrence Foster. *Honours:* winner Queen Elisabeth Violin Competition, Brussels 1997, first prize Carl Nielson Int. Violin Competition 1992. *Current Management:* IMG Artists, Lovell House, 616 Chiswick High Road, London, W4 5RX, England. *E-mail:* tcarrig@imgworld.com.

**ZOBEL, Ingeborg;** Singer (Soprano); b. 31 July 1928, Gorlitz, Schlesien, Germany. *Education:* Studied at the Dresden State Music Academy with Eduard Plate. *Career:* Debut: As Amelia in Un Ballo in Maschera, Cottbus, 1952; Sang in Schwerin, 1955–57, Rostock, 1957–66, and Weimar, 1966–72; Dresden Staatsoper from 1972, notably as Wagner's Brünnhilde, Isolde and Ortrud, the Marschallin, Tosca, Santuzza, Lady Macbeth and Leonore in Fidelio; Guest appearances in Leningrad, Barcelona, Budapest, Wiesbaden, Prague, Belgrade and Sofia; Teacher at the Franz Liszt Musikhochschule in Weimar. *Recordings:* Various albums. *Address:* c/o Dresden Staatsoper, 8012 Dresden, Germany.

**ZOGHBY, Linda;** Singer (Soprano); b. 17 Aug. 1949, Mobile, Alabama, USA. *Education:* Studied at Florida State University and with Elena Nikolaii. *Career:* Sang at first in concert; Stage debut at Houston in 1974 as Donna Elvira in Don Giovanni; Dallas Opera in 1976 as Giulietta in I Capuleti e i Montecchi; Glyndebourne Festival from 1978 as Mimi and in Haydn's La Fedeltà Premiata; Metropolitan Opera in 1982 and 1986 as Mimi and as Ilia in Idomeneo; Other roles include Mozart's Fiordigili and Pamina. *Recordings:* Haydn's L'Isola Disabitata and L'Incontro Improvviso.

**ZOLLER, Karlheinz;** Flautist; b. 24 Aug. 1928, Hohr-Grenzhausen, Germany. *Education:* Studied at the Detmold and Frankfurt Musikhochschule. *Career:* Many performances as concert soloist and chamber musician from 1950; Soloist with the Berlin Philharmonic, 1960–69, and teacher at the Berlin Musikhochschule; Professor at Hamburg before returning to Berlin; Has premiered the Double Concerto by Ligeti (1972) and the flute concerto by Isang Yun (1977). *Address:* Berlin Philharmonic Orchestra, Philharmonie, Matthaikirchstrasse, W-1000 Berlin, Germany.

**ZOLLMAN, Ronald;** Conductor; b. 8 April 1950, Antwerp, Belgium; m. Dominique G. Mols. *Education:* Diploma in Conducting, Brussels Conservatoire; Diploma, Academy Chigiana. *Career:* Has conducted throughout Europe, North and South America, and in Australia; Head of Conducting Faculty at the Royal Brussels Conservatory of Music; Musical Director of the Philharmonic Orchestra of UNAM, Mexico. *Recordings:* Belgian Music for Ministry of Culture, Brussels; various recordings with the National Orchestra of Belgium, the World Orchestra, the London Sinfonietta; Basle Symphony Orchestra, Northern Sinfonia, Barcelona Orchestra and Northern Sinfonia. *Honours:* Premio Firenze for Conductors, 1972. *Current Management:* Konsertbolaget, Kungsgatan 32, 11132, Stockholm, Sweden. *Address:* Rue Général de Gaulle 36, 1310 La Hulpe, Belgium.

**ZOUHAR, Vit;** Composer and Musicologist; b. 13 March 1966, Brno, Czechoslovakia; m. Karla Zemanová, 28 June 1997. *Education:* Master, 1989, Postgraduate degree, 1993, Composition, Janáček University of Music and Dramatic Arts, Brno; Composition, University of Music and Dramatic Arts, Graz, Accademia Chigiana, Siena; Master, Musicology, Masaryk University, Brno, 1996; Doctorate 2001, Janáček University of Music and Dramatic Arts, Brno. *Career:* Teacher, Musical Theory, State Conservatory, Brno, 1989; Assistant, Palacky University, Olomouc, 1992–; Teacher, 1992–, Guest Composer, 1993, Institute of Electronic Music, Graz, Austria; Guest Composer, Werkstadt Graz, 1994; Co-Founder, Teacher, Computer Music Study Room, Ostrava University, 1996; Works performed by State Philharmonic Orchestra Brno, Moravian Symphony Orchestra, DAMA DAMA percussion ensemble, Sonata a Tre, also many concerts, festivals, radio, television, including: Hörgänge Wien; Experimental Music Festival, Prague; IST alles, ballet, Czech television, 1992; The Garden, Forfest Music Festival, 1995; Like Water Is, ballet, Janáček Theatre, Brno, National Theatre, Prague, 1996; Wide Crossing, ballet, Graz Opernhaus, 1997; Prague Spring; Europalia Brussel; EXPO; Vice-Dean of the Pedagogical Faculty Palacký University Olomuc, 2003. *Compositions include:* Le Vedute di Bruna for string quartet, 1985; Agastia for large orchestra, 1988; The Sun Gate for 4 percussionists and large orchestra, 1989; Es scheint mir aber immer für violin, clarinet and piano, 1992; Ist alles for 2 guitarists, 1992; Close Encounters of Those Wild at Heart for stereo-orchestra, 1993; Like Water Is for clarinet, bassoon and piano, 1994; Wide Crossing, 1994; Il Pendolo for chamber ensemble, 1998; Coronide, chamber opera, 2000; Petite sirène, for four percussionists 2001; Rings of Levels, for a recorder quartet, 2003; Torso, chamber opera together with Tomáš Hanzlík, 2003. *Address:* CZ-67907 Kotvrdovice 175, Czech Republic.

**ZOUHAR, Zdenek;** Composer and Musicologist; b. 8 Feb. 1927, Kotvrdovice, Czechoslovakia. *Education:* PhD, Brno University, 1967; Studied composition at Brno Janáček Academy, 1967. *Career:* Head of Music Section at Brno University Library, 1953–61; Editor for Czech Radio, 1961–70; Professor at Brno Janáček Academy, 1962–. *Compositions include:* Sonatina for piano, 1948; Spring Suite for 3 violins, 1949; Partita for organ, 1956; Midnight Mass,

1957; '151' Music for wind quintet I, 1958; Trio for flute, contralto and bass clarinet, 1961; Divertimento I for 4 winds and percussion, 1965; Music for strings, 1966; 2 String Quartets, 1966, 1983; Symphonic Triptych, 1967; Music for wind quintet II, 1982; Triple Concerto for clarinet, trumpet, trombone and orchestra, 1970; Chamber radio opera, Metamorphosis, 1971; Variations On A Theme By B Martinů for symphonic orchestra, 1979; Musica Giocosa Per Archi, 1981; Brass Quintet, 1985; Comic opera, A Great Love, 1986; Oratorio, The Flames Of Constance, 1988; Divertimento III for Brno Brass Band, 1993; Pavel Haas Symphony (1941) completed by Šdenek Zouhar, 1994. *Address:* Halasovo ná m 4, CZ 638 00 Brno-Lesná, Czech Republic.

**ZSCHAU, Marilyn;** Singer (Soprano); b. 9 Feb. 1944, Chicago, Ilinois, USA. *Education:* Juilliard School of Music, 1961–65; Further study with John Lester in Montana. *Career:* Toured with Metropolitan National Company, 1965–66; Debut at Vienna Volksoper as Marietta in Die Tote Stadt, 1967; Vienna Staatsoper in 1971 as the Composer in Ariadne auf Naxos; New York City Opera from 1978, as Puccini's Minnie and Butterfly, Odabella in Attila, and Maddalena in Andrea Chénier; Metropolitan Opera debut in 1985 as Musetta in La Bohème; La Scala debut in 1986 as the Dyer's Wife in Die Frau ohne Schatten; Appearances world-wide in operatic roles including Aida, Leonora, Desdemona, Butterfly, Brünnhilde in Die Walküre and Götterdämmerung, Salome, Elektra, Prokofiev's Renata in The Fiery Angel, Shostakovich's Katerina in Lady Macbeth of Mtsensk, Santuzza and Manon Lescaut; Sang Puccini's Minnie at Reggio Emilia and Chicago in 1990, and The Fiery Angel at the 1990 Holland Festival; Other roles include: Janáček's Vixen and Kostelnicka in Jenůfa, the Marschallin and Octavian in Der Rosenkavalier, Mozart's Fiordigili, Countess and Pamina, Lucille in Dantons Tod, and Tatiana in Eugene Onegin; Sang Elektra at Buenos Aires, 1996; Season 1998 as Kostelnicka in Jenůfa at Santiago; Sang Elektra with New Israeli Opera at Savonlinna, 2000. *Recordings include:* Video of Covent Garden performance of La Bohème. *Honours:* Martha Baird Rockefeller Foundation Scholarships, 1962, 1963. *Address:* c/o Janine Meyer and Associates, Suite 1C, 201 West 54th Street, New York, NY 10019, USA.

**ZSIGMONDY, Denes;** Violinist; b. 9 April 1922, Budapest, Hungary; m. Anneliese Nissen, pianist, Aug 1947, 2 d. *Education:* Baccalaureate, University of Budapest; Franz Liszt Academy, Budapest; Studied with Geza de Kresz, Leo Weiner, Imre Waldbauer and others. *Career:* Soloist with Vienna and Berlin Symphonies, Tokyo, Budapest and Munich Philharmonies, Radio Orchestras ABC Sydney, Melbourne and Munich, Stuttgart Chamber Orchestra, and Salzburg Camerata; Performed with BBC Radio London, NHK Tokyo, Radio Paris and others; World premieres of works by Bialas, Eder, Genzmer, Rozsa and others; Professor, University of Washington, Seattle, USA, 1971–; Occasional masterclasses including New England Conservatory; Established annual Holzenhausen Festival in Ammerland, Bavaria with concerts and violin courses, 1978–; Visiting Professor, Boston University, 1981–82; Courses at the Summer Academy, Salzburg-Mozarteum, Austria and in Germany, Italy, Hungary, Poland and others, 1986–. *Recordings include:* The Virtuoso Violin; The Romantic Violin; Zsigmondy Plays Bartók, vols 1 and 2; Sonatas by Beethoven, Brahms, Grieg, Franck, Debussy and all Mozart and Schubert violin-piano music. *Address:* Bonselweg 10, 8193 Ambach, Bavaria, Germany.

**ZUKERMAN, Eugenia;** American flautist; b. (Eugenia Rich), 25 Sept. 1944, Cambridge, MA; m. 1st Pinchas Zukerman (divorced); m. 2nd David Seltzer 1988. *Education:* Juilliard School, New York with with Julius Baker. *Career:* debut, New York Town Hall 1971; has played with most major orchestras in the USA and Canada; tour of USA with English Chamber Orchestra; European performances with the Royal Philharmonic, Israel Chamber Orchestra and the Hamburg Bach Solisten; participation in Festival of Two Worlds at Spoleto, London's South Bank Festival and the Edinburgh Festival; collaborations with Jean-Pierre Rampal at Carnegie Hall 1976, and James Galway; music commentator on CBS News 'Sunday Morning' programme. *Address:* c/o 10 Barley Mow Passage, London, W4 4PH, England.

**ZUKERMAN, Pinchas;** Israeli violinist, violist and conductor; b. 16 July 1948, Tel-Aviv; s. of Yehuda Zukerman and Miriam Zukerman; m. 1st Eugenia Rich 1968 (divorced); two d.; m. 2nd Tuesday Weld 1985 (divorced); m. 3rd Amanda Forsyth 2004. *Education:* Israel Conservatory, Acad. of Music, Tel-Aviv, Juilliard School of Music, New York with Ivan Galamian. *Career:* debut in New York with New York Philharmonic 1969, in UK at Brighton Festival 1969; concert and recital performances throughout USA and Europe; debut as conductor, London 1970; appearances as conductor with orchestras world-wide; has performed at Spoleto, Pablo Casals and Edinburgh Festivals; Dir S Bank Summer Music 1978–80; Musical Dir St Paul Chamber Orchestra 1980–87; Prin. Conductor Dallas Symphony Orch. 1993–95 (Prin. Guest Conductor Int. Summer Music Festival 1990–95); Music Dir Baltimore Symphony Orchestra Summer MusicFest 1997–99; Music Dir Nat. Arts Centre Orchestra, Canada 1998–. *Film soundtracks:* Prince of Tides, Critical Care. *Honours:* Hon. DMus (Brown Univ.) 1989; winner Leventritt Competition 1967, Isaac Stern Award for Artistic Excellence (Nat. Arts Awards) 2002, Grammy Award for Best Chamber Music Performance 1980, Grammy Award for Best Classical Performance, Instrumental Soloist without Orchestra 1981. *Current Management:* Kirshbaum Demler and Associates, 711 West End Avenue, New York, NY 10025, USA. *Telephone:* (212) 222-4843. *E-mail:* kirshdem@aol.com (office). *Website:* www.kirshdem.com (office).

**ZUKOFSKY, Paul;** Violinist and Conductor; b. 22 Oct. 1943, Brooklyn, New York, USA. *Education:* BM, 1964, MS, 1964, Juilliard School of Music. *Career:* Creative Associate, SUNY, Buffalo, 1964–65; Various positions as violinist, and violin teacher, 1965–75; President, Musical Observations Inc, 1975–; Principal Investigator, Project Director, Limits, 1976–82; Conductor with various orchestras, 1977–79; Programme Co-ordinator, American Portraits, concert series at John F Kennedy Center, 1980–; Conductor, Contemporary Chamber Ensemble at Juilliard School of Music, 1984–; Founder, Principal Conductor, Sinfoniuhljomsveit Aeskunnar, 1985–; Director of Chamber Music Activities, The Juilliard School, 1987–89; Artistic Director, Summer Garden Concert Series, Museum of Modern Art, NYC, 1987–. *Recordings include:* As conductor: Various Icelandic Orchestral Works, 1987, Sixteen Dances by Cage, 1984; As violinist: Penderecki's Capriccio for Violin and Orchestra, 1968, Babbitt and Milton Sextets, 1972, Glass's Strung Out, 1977, Cage's Cheap Imitation, 1981, Sonata for Solo Violin, 1983, For John Cage, Feldman, Morton, 1984. *Contributions:* Articles in professional journals including The Psychology of Music, with Sternberg and Knoll. *Honours:* Nominee for Grammy Awards, 1972; Pick of the Pack, Time Magazine, 1975; ASCAP Community Orchestra Award, 1979; ASCAP Citation, 1979; Guggenheim Fellowship, 1983–84; National Endowment for The Arts Fellowship, 1983; Knight's Cross, Icelandic Order of the Falcon. *Address:* c/o The Juilliard School of Music (Violin Faculty), Lincoln Plaza, New York, NY 10023, USA.

**ZUPKO, Ramon;** Composer; b. 14 Nov. 1932, Pittsburgh, Pennsylvania, USA. *Education:* Studied with Vincent Persichetti at Juilliard (BS 1956, MS 1957) and with Schiske at the Vienna Academy of Music, 1958–59; Electronic music at Columbia University, and with Koenig at the University of Utrecht. *Career:* Teacher of Theory and Director of Electronic Music at the Chicago Musical College of Roosevelt University, 1967–71; Professor of Composition and Director of Electronic Music at Western Michigan University, Kalamazoo, 1971–97; Gilmore Foundation Commission, 1990. *Compositions include:* Variations for orchestra, 1961; Violin Concerto, 1962; Translucents, for strings, 1967; Tangents, for 18 bass instruments, 1967; Radiants, for orchestra, 1971; Proud Music of the Storm, multimedia theatre, 1976; Wind Song, piano concerto, 1979; Life Dances, for orchestra, 1981; Where the Mountain Crosses, song cycle for mezzo and piano, 1982; Canti Terrae, for orchestra, 1982; 2 Symphonies, 1984, 1986; Series of twelve Chamber Pieces, Fluxus, for various instrumental combinations (1977–94); Vox Naturae, Concerto for Brass Quintet and Orchestra, 1992; Chaconne for piano, 1995; The Nightingale, Opera, 1998. *Honours:* NEA Grants, Koussevitzky Foundation Award and Guggenheim Fellowship (1981–82). *Address:* 1540 North 2nd Street, Kalamazoo, MI 49009, USA.

**ZUR, Menachem,** DipEd, BMus, MFA, DMusA; Israeli composer and teacher of theory and composition; b. 6 March 1942, Tel-Aviv. *Education:* College for Teachers of Music, Jerusalem, Rubin Academy of Music, Mannes College of Music, NY, USA, Sarah Lawrence College, Columbia University. *Career:* Musical Adviser to the Israel Museum, Jerusalem; Chairman of the Music Education Department of the Rubin Academy of Music, 1991; Chairperson, Israeli Composers' League, 1992–94, 2000–; Chair, Israeli Composers' League, 2000–. *Compositions include:* Fantasy for Piano; Sonata for Cello and Piano; Several works for Tape; Prisma for two pianos; Double Concerto for Bassoon, French Horn and Chamber Orchestra; Clarinet Quintet; Piano Concerto; Tuba Concerto; Violin Concerto, Concerto Grosso; Centres, string quartet; Pygmalion, chamber opera; Sonata for Violin and Piano; 3 Symphonies; Prelude for Band; The Golem for 11 Instruments and Baritone Solo; Horn Trio; 2 Sonatas for Cello and Piano; Fantasy for Brass Quintet; Circles of Time for Piano Solo; Pieces for Choir: Hallelujah, Kedushah, Shiluvium, A Tale of Two Sandals; concerto for piano 4 hands and orchestra, 1997; String Sextet, 1998; Prisma for piano duet, 1999. *Recordings include:* Chants and Horizons for Magnetic Tape; Sonata No. 1 for Cello and Piano; Clarinet Quintet, electroacoustic music. *Publications:* Keyboard Harmony (co-author) 1980; contrib. to Musical Quarterly. *Honours:* Acum Prize for Life Achievements, 2001; Prime Minister Prize for Composition, 2001. *Address:* Rubin Academy of Music, Givat-Ram, Jerusalem, Israel.

**ZVETANOV, Boiko;** Singer (Tenor); b. 14 June 1955, Sofia, Bulgaria. *Education:* Studied at the Sofia Conservatory. *Career:* Sang with the Bulgarian National Opera from 1982 as the Duke of Mantua, Foresto in Attila, Fernando in La Favorita, Pollione and Radames; Concerts in Russia, Czechoslovakia and France (Verdi's Requiem at Paris), and the Italian Singer in Der Rosenkavalier at the Vienna Staatsoper; Sang at St Gallen in 1991 as Riccardo in Un Ballo in Maschera, Opernhaus Zürich as Lensky, Alvaro in Forza del Destino, Arnold in Guillaume Tell and Rodolfo; 1992 included Capriccio, Wiener Staatsoper, La Forza del Destino in Zürich, Guillaume Tell, La Bohème and Il Pirata in Zürich; 1993 included Hérodiade in Zürich, Cavalleria rusticana in Wiesbaden and Capriccio in Dresden; La Forza del Destino in Karlsruhe in 1993–94; Season 1994–95 included Rosenkavalier and Ballo in Maschera with Deutsche Oper Berlin; Lucia di Lammermoor at Teatro Principal in Valencia with L Alberti, 1995; Rosenkavalier, Oper der Stadt Bonn, director Spiros Argiris, 1995; Season 1999–2000 as Arvino in I Lombardi for Zürich Opera and Manrico at the Prague State Opera; Don Carlos in Mainz, 2002. *Recordings:* CDs of arias and duets from Verdi's operas. *Address:* Opernhaus Zürich, Falkenstrasse 1, 8008 Zürich, Switzerland.

**ZWEDEN, Jaap;** Violinist and Conductor; b. 1960, Amsterdam, Netherlands. *Education:* Amsterdam Conservatory and with Dorothy DeLay at Juilliard, New York. *Career:* Leader of the Royal Concertgebouw Orchestra from 1979;

Solo performances under conductors Haitink, Giulini, Solti and Bernstein; Conductor from 1995 including tours with the Berlin Symphony Orchestra, the Salzburg Mozarteum, the Israel CO and the Japanese CO; Music Director of the Netherlands Symphony Orchestra from 1997; Buenos Aires Philharmonic Orchestra in Argentina and on tour to Europe; US debut with the St Louis Symphony Orchestra, 1997; Principal guest conductor of the Brabant Orchestra, 1997; Season 1999–2000 with Netherlands Symphony Orchestra on tour to USA and debut with the London Philharmonic; Principal Conductor of the Residentie Orchestra, The Hague, from 2000. *Honours:* First prize, 1977 Dutch National Violin Competition. *Address:* c/o IMG Artists, Lovell House, 616 Chiswick High Road, London W4 5RX, England.

**ZWIAUER, Florian;** Violinist; b. 1954, Vienna, Austria. *Education:* Studied at the Vienna Academy of Music. *Career:* Co-founded the Franz Schubert Quartet, 1974; Won the European Broadcasting Union's International String Quartet Competition in Stockholm, 1974; Appearances at Amsterdam Concertgebouw, Vienna Musikverein and Konzerthaus, the Salle Gaveau, Paris, and Sydney Opera House; Visits to Zürich, Geneva, Basle, Berlin, Hamburg, Rome, Rotterdam, Madrid, Copenhagen, Stockholm, Dublin, Manchester, Munich, Lisbon and many more; Festival engagements include Salzburg, Wiener Festwochen, Prague Spring, Bregenz Festival, Schubertiade at Hohenems, the Schubert Festival at Washington DC and the Belfast and Istanbul Festivals; Tours of Australasia, USSR and USA; British debut at the Queen Elizabeth Hall, 1979; Frequent appearances at Wigmore Hall and Cheltenham Festival; 1st Leader of Vienna Symphony Orchestra, 1989–; Teacher at the Vienna Conservatory and Graz Musikhochschule; Masterclasses at the Royal Northern College of Music and at the Lake District Summer Music. *Recordings include:* Schubert's Quartet in G, D887; Complete quartets of Dittersdorf; Haydn's 3 Last String Quartets; The 10 late Mozart String Quartets; Complete Tchaikovsky string chamber music; Complete string quartets of Franz Schmidt, Erich Wolfgang Korngold; Complete string quartets of Hans Pfitzner. *Honours:* As Soloist won 2nd Prize at the W A Mozart International Violin Competition in Salzburg, 1978. *Current Management:* Künstleragentur Dr Raab and Dr Böhm, Plankengasse 7, 1010 Vienna, Austria. *Address:* Alszeile 15/14, 1170 Vienna, Austria.

**ZWILICH, Ellen Taaffe,** DMus; American composer; b. 30 April 1939, Miami, FL; d. of Edward and Ruth (née Howard) Taaffe; m. Joseph Zwilich 1969 (died 1979). *Education:* Florida State Univ. and Juilliard School (New York). *Career:* violinist, American Symphony, New York 1965–73; Composer-in-Residence, Santa Fe Chamber Music Festival 1990, American Acad., Rome 1990; Carnegie Hall Composer's Chair. 1995–; Guggenheim Fellow 1981; elected mem. American Acad. of Arts and Letters 1992. *Compositions include:* Einsame Nacht 1971, Im Nebel 1972, Sonata in Three Movements 1973, String Quartet 1974, Clarino Quartet 1977, Chamber Symphony 1979, Passages 1981, String Trio 1982, Symphony No 1: Three Movements for Orchestra (Grammy nomination) 1982, Fantasy for Harpsichord 1983, Double Quartet for Strings 1984, Concerto Grosso 1985, Concerto for Piano and Orchestra 1986, Tanzspiel 1987, Symphony No 2 (Grammy nomination) 1985, Piano Trio 1987, Concerto for Trombone and Orchestra 1988, Symbolon 1988, Concerto for Bass Trombone, Strings, Timpani and Cymbals 1989, Concerto for Flute and Orchestra (Grammy nomination) 1989, Concerto for Oboe and Orchestra 1990, Quintet for Clarinet and Strings 1990, Concerto for Violin, Cello and Orchestra 1991, Concerto for Bassoon and Orchestra 1992, Symphony No 3 (Grammy nomination) 1992, Concerto for Horn and String Orchestra 1993, Fantasy for Orchestra 1993, American Concerto for Trumpet and Orchestra 1994, A Simple Magnificat 1994, Triple Concerto 1995, Jubilation 1995, Peanuts Gallery 1996, Violin Concerto 1997, String Quartet No 2 1998, Lament for Piano 1999, Upbeat! 1999, Symphony No 4 1999, Lament for Cello and Piano 2000, Millennium Fantasy for Piano and Orchestra 2000, Partita for Violin and String Orchestra 2000, Clarinet Concerto 2002, 'Rituals' for 5 Percussionists and Orchestra 2003. *Honours:* Lifetime Hon. mem. American Fed. of Musicians; Hon. DMus (Oberlin Coll.) 1987, (Manhattanville Coll.) 1990, (Marymount Manhattan Coll., Converse Coll.) 1994, (New School, Mannes Coll.) 1995; Elizabeth Sprague Coolidge Chamber Music Prize 1974, Gold Medal G. B. Viotti, Vercelli, Italy 1975, Ernst Von Dohnanyi Citation 1981, Pulitzer Prize 1983, Acad. Award, American Acad. of Arts and Letters 1984, Arturo Toscanini Music Critics Award 1987, Florida Artists Hall of Fame 1993, Musical America Composer of the Year 1999. *Address:* 600 West 246th Street, Riverdale, NY 10471, USA.

**ZYKAN, Otto M.;** Composer and Pianist; b. 29 April 1935, Vienna, Austria. *Education:* Vienna Academy of Music. *Career:* many concert appearances, performing contemporary works. *Compositions:* Opera, Auszahireim, 1986; Sonata for cello and piano, 1958; String Quartet, 1958; Piano Concerto, 1958; Kyryptomnemie for winds, percussion, piano, 1963; Schon der Reihe ballet, 1966; Kurze Anweisung for orchestra, 1969; Miles Smiles, chamber music theatre, 1974; Symphonie der heilen welt, scenic concerto, 1977; Trio for violin, 1977; Ausgesucht Freundliches, concerto for 2 soloists, chorus, orchestra, 1979; Kunst Kommt von Gonnon, opera, 1980; Cello concerto, 1982; 3 String Quartets, with speaker, 1984; Krüppelsprache, for 5 voices, 1984; Engels Engel, scenic concerto, 1988; Wahr ist, dass der Tigerfrisst, choral opera, 1994; Piano Trio, 1997; Wanderers Nachtlied, for chorus, string quartet and tape, 1997; String Quartet, 2002; Messe! fur 12 Selipten, Chor und Orchester, 2003; Cello Koncert, 2004; Violin Koncert, 2004. *Honours:* Winner, Darmstadt Competition for pianist, 1958. *Address:* c/o AKM, III Baumanstrasse 8–10, Postfach 334-338, 1031 Vienna, Austria.

**ŻYLIS-GARA, Teresa;** Polish singer (soprano); b. 23 Jan. 1935, Wilno (now Vilnius, Lithuania); m.; one c. *Education:* State Higher School of Music, Łódź. *Career:* soloist, Kraków Philharmonic 1954–58 and Kraków Opera 1958–59; foreign contracts in operas: Oberhausen 1961–63, Städtische Bühnen, Dortmund 1963–65, Deutsche Oper am Rhein, Düsseldorf 1965–70; debuts abroad at Glyndebourne Festival 1965, Paris Opera 1966, Salzburg Festival 1968, San Francisco Opera 1968, Metropolitan Opera, New York 1968, Royal Opera House, Covent Garden 1968, Vienna Opera 1970, Aix-en-Provence Festival 1972, Nat. Theatre, Prague 1974, Orange Festival 1975, Nat. Theatre, Budapest 1976, Great Theatre, Warsaw 1976, La Scala, Milan 1977, Bolshoi Theatre, Moscow 1978, Teatro Colón, Buenos Aires 1981; regular performances at Metropolitan Opera, New York, Berlin, Hamburg, Munich, La Scala, Milan, Staatsoper, Vienna; also song recitals; renowned for interpretation of works by Szymanowski; Prof. of Music Art and Pedagogue of Vocal Art, State Higher School of Music, Łódź 1999. *Recordings include:* Mozart's Don Giovanni, Chausson's Le Roi Arthus, Richard Strauss' Ariadne auf Naxos, Bach's St Matthew Passion, Dvořák's Requiem, Verdi's Messa da Requiem, Mahler's Das Klagende Lied, and songs by Chopin, Moniuszko and Lalo. *Honours:* Commdr's Cross Order of Polonia Restituta 2000; Winner, All-Polish Competition of Young Vocalists, Warsaw, Prime Minister's Prize (1st Class) 1979. *Address:* 16A Boulevard de Belgique, Principality of Monaco. *Telephone:* (93) 305339. *E-mail:* teresa_zylis-gara@monaco377.com (office).

**ZYSSET, Martin;** Singer (Tenor); b. 1965, Solothurn, Switzerland. *Education:* Studied at the Berne Conservatory and with Ernst Haefliger, Edith Mathis and Roland Hermann. *Career:* Debut: Selzach Summer Festival, 1992, as Pedrillo in Die Entführung; Appearances at the Zürich Opera, 1992–, as Scaramuccio in Ariadne auf Naxos, Monostatos in Die Zauberflöte, Count Hohenzollern (Henze's Der Prinz von Homburg), Cassio, Jacquino and Tamino; Vienna Festival, 1994, in the premiere of Ein Narrenparadies by Ofer Ben-Amots; Further engagements with the Radio della Svizzera Italiana, in Antwerp and in Luxembourg (concert performance of Fidelio, under Leopold Hager); Other roles include Don Ottavio, Goro in Butterfly and Spoletta in Tosca; Season 2000–01 at Zürich as Johann Strauss's Simplicius Simplicissimus (also televised) and in Tosca, The Queen of Spades, Lulu and Carmen. *Honours:* Prizewinner at the 1990 Pro Arte Lyrica Competition, Lausanne. *Address:* c/o Opernhaus Zürich, Falkenstrasse 1, 8008 Zürich, Switzerland.

# Directory

Directory

# APPENDIX A: ORCHESTRAS

## Argentina

**Orquesta Filarmónica de Buenos Aires:** Cerrito 618, 0101 Buenos Aires; tel. 54 1 383 5199; fax 54 1 383 6167.

**Orquesta Sinfónica Nacional:** Córdoba 1155, 1055 Buenos Aires; tel. 54 1 45 4252.

## Armenia

**Armenian Philharmonic Orchestra:** Aram Khachaturian Concert Hall, Mashtotz 46, 375002 Yerevan; tel. 3741 560645; fax 3741 564965; e-mail apo@arminco.com; website www.apo.am; Gen. Man. Nika Babayan.

**Armenian State Symphony Orchestra:** Mashtotz 46, 375019 Yerevan; tel. 37 885 256 4965; fax 37 885 258 1142; Music Dir Loris Tjeknavorian; Man. George Avedissian.

## Australia

**Adelaide Symphony Orchestra:** PO Box 2131, Adelaide, SA 5081; tel. 61 8 8343 4834; fax 61 8 8343 4808; e-mail aso@aso.com.au; website www.aso.com.au; Gen. Man. Robert Clarke.

**Australian Brandenburg Orchestra:** 159A New South Head Road, Edgecliff, NSW 2027; tel. 61 2 9363 2899; fax 61 2 9327 2593; e-mail mail@brandenburgorchestra.org.au; Music Dir Bruce Applebaum.

**Australian Opera and Ballet Orchestra:** PO Box 291, Strawberry Hills, NSW 2021; tel. 61 2 9699 3184; Music Dir Simone Young.

**Canberra Symphony Orchestra:** PO Box 1919, Second Floor, Hobart Place, Canberra, ACT 2601; tel. 61 6 247 9191; fax 61 6 247 9026; e-mail info@cso.org.au; website www.cso.org.au; CEO Ian McLean.

**Melbourne Symphony Orchestra:** PO Box 9994, Melbourne, Vic. 3001; tel. 61 3 9626 1111; fax 61 3 9626 1101; e-mail mso@mso.com.au; website www.mso.com.au; Conductor Laureate: Hiroyuki Iwaki; Chief Conductor Marcus Stenz; Gen. Man. Steven Porter.

**Queensland Orchestra:** GPO Box 9994, Brisbane, Qld 4001; tel. (7) 3377-5000; fax (7) 3377-5001; e-mail info@thequeenslandorchestra.com.au; website www.thequeenslandorchestra.com.au.

**State Orchestra of Victoria (Orchestra Victoria):** PO Box 836, S Melbourne, Vic. 3205; tel. 61 3 9694 3600; fax 61 3 9694 3611; e-mail dana.moran@orchestravictoria.com.au; website www.stateorchestra.com.au; Man. Dir Peter Garnick; Admin. Officer Dana Moran.

**Sydney Symphony:** GPO Box 4338, Sydney, NSW 2001; tel. 61 2 9334 4644; fax 61 2 9334 4646; e-mail info@sydneysymphony.com; website www.sydneysymphony.com; Chief Conductor and Artistic Dir Gianluigi Gelmetti; Man. Dir Libby Christie.

**Tasmanian Symphony Orchestra:** Australian Broadcasting Corporation, PO Box 9994, Hobart, TAS 7001; tel. 61 03 6235 3646; fax 61 03 6235 3651; e-mail tso@tso.com.au; website www.tso.com.au; Chief Conductor David Porcelijn; Gen. Man. Julie Warn.

**Victorian Concert Orchestra:** 1 Treasury Place, Third Floor, Melbourne, Vic. 3002; Music Dir Martin Rutherford.

**West Australian Symphony Orchestra:** PO Box 9994, 191 Adelaide Terrace, Perth, WA 6000; tel. 61 8 9326 0011; fax 61 8 9220 0099; website www.waso.com.au; Music Dir Vernon Handley; Gen. Man. Henk Smit.

## Austria

**Austro-Hungarian Haydn Orchestra:** Favoritenstrasse 139/20, 1100 Vienna; tel. and fax 43 69 9 1032 4797; website www.haydnphil.com; Dir Adam Fischer.

**Bruckner-Orchester:** Promenade 39, 4020 Linz; tel. 43 70 761 1194; fax 43 70 761 1315; e-mail office@bruckner-orchester.at; website www.bruckner-orchester.at; Chief Conductor Martin Sieghart; Man. C.-F. Steiner.

**Grazer Philharmonisches Orchester:** Kaiser-Josef-Platz 10, 8010 Graz; Man. Dr Gerhard Brunner.

**The Haydn Academy:** Wiener Str 14, 2100 Linz; tel. 43 2 2627 2662; e-mail anton.gabmayer@gmx.net; Music Dir Anton Gabmayer.

**Haydn Sinfonietta Wien:** 1130 Vienna, Bossi Gasse 76; tel. 43 1 877 5208; fax 43 1 877 5208-17; e-mail haydn.sinfonietta@utanet.at; Music Dir Manfred Huss.

**Mozarteum Orchester:** Erzbischof-Gebhyardstrasse 10, 5020 Salzburg; tel. 43 66 284 3571; fax 43 66 284 357123; e-mail info@mozarteum.orchester.at; website www.mozarteum.orchester.at; Music Dir Hubert Soudant; Exec. Dir Dr Peter Ramsauer.

**Niederösterreichisches Tonkünstler-Orchester:** Elisabethstrasse 22/9, 1010 Vienna; Chief Conductor Fabio Luisi; Gen. Man. Peter Roczek.

**Orchester Pro Musica International:** Praterstrasse 76/8, 1020 Vienna; tel. 43 1 216 7333; fax 43 1 216 7333; Music Dir Gerhard Track; Man. Joanna Lewis.

**Österreichisches Rundfunk Symphonie Orchester:** Argentinierstrasse 30, 1040 Vienna; tel. 01 50101/18241; fax 01 50101/18358; e-mail rso-wien@orf.at; website www.rso-wien.orf.at; Chief Conductor Pinchas Steinberg; Gen. Man. Dr Andrea Seebohm.

**Wiener Kammerorchester (Vienna Chamber Orchestra):** Schachnerstrasse 27, 1220 Vienna; tel. 43 1 203 6357; fax 43 1 204 3750; e-mail wiener@kammerorchester.com; website www.kammerorchester.com; Chief Conductor Philippe Entremont; Gen. Man. Christian Buchmann.

**Wiener Musica Antiqua Ensemble:** Minoritenplatz 2, Arkadentrakt, 1010 Vienna; Music Dir Bernhard Kiebel.

**Wiener Philharmoniker:** Bösendorferstrasse 12, 1010 Vienna; tel. 43 1 505 6525; e-mail philoffice@wienerphilharmoniker.at; www.wienerphilharmoniker.at; Man. Peter Pecha.

**Wiener Symphoniker:** Lehargasse II, 1060 Vienna; tel. 43 1 591 8916; e-mail office@wiener-symphoniker.at; website www.wiener-symphoniker.at; Chief Conductor Vladimir Fedoseyev; Man. Rainer Bischof.

## Azerbaijan

**Azerbaijan Symphony Orchestra:** Baku.

## Belarus

**State Academic Symphony Orchestra of Byelorussia:** Pr Skoriny 50, 220005 Minsk, Belarus; tel. 17 2 315547; fax 17 2 319050; e-mail presto@belarustoday.com; Orchestra Dir Iosif Turko.

## Belgium

**Belgian Chamber Orchestra:** Buizenbergstrasse 1, 9830, St-Martens-Latem; Conductor Rudolf Werthen; Man. Dries Sel.

**Collegium Instrumentale Brugense:** Vijversdreef 9b, 8310 Bruges; tel. 32 50 353717; fax 32 50 362717; Music Dir Patrick Peire; Admin. Dir Lieve Geerolf.

**Collegium Vocale Gent:** Drongenhof 42, 9000 Gent, Belgium; tel. 32 9 265 90 50; fax 32 9 265 90 51; e-mail org@collegiumvocale.com; website www.collegiumvocale.com; Man. Stephane Leys.

**Ensemble Musique Nouvelle:** Place de Vingt Août 16, 4000 Liège; Music Dir Patrick Davin; Man. Michel Schoonbrood.

**Filharmonisch Orkest van der BRT:** Magdalenazaal Duquesnoystr. 14, 1000 Brussels; Music Dir Frank Shipway; Man. André Laporte.

**Grand Orchestre d'Harmonie de la Ville de Charleroi:** rue Biavent A, 6208 Charleroi; tel. 00 32 71 36 38 73; fax 00 32 31 39 38 73; Dir Christian Delcoux.

**Het Nieuw Belgisch Kamerorkest:** Bondgenteniaan 114, 3000 Leuven; Music Dir Jan Caeyers; Man. Jan Roekens.

**Koninklijk Filharmonisch Orkest van Vlaanderen:** Britselei 80, 2000 Antwerp; tel. 32 3 231 3737; fax 32 2 231 9126; website www.kfovv.be; Music Dir Walter Van Den Eeckhout.

**La Petite Bande:** Vital Decosterstraat 72, 3000 Leuven; tel. 32 1 623 0830; fax 32 1 622 7610; e-mail info@lapetitebande.be; website www.lapetitebande.be; Music Dir Sigiswald Kuijken.

**Orchestre National de Belgique:** Galerie Ravenstein, 28 Boite 6, 1000 Brussels; tel. 32 2 552 0460; fax 32 2 552 0468; e-mail info@nob-onb.be; website www.onb.be; Music Dir Mikko Franck.

**Orchestre Philharmonique de Liège et de la Communauté Française:** Salle Philharmonique, Blvd Piercot 25, 4000 Liège; tel. 31 4 220 0000; fax 31 4 220 0001; website www.opl.be; Music Dir Pierre Bartholomée; Man. Paul-Emile Mottard.

**Orchestre Royal de Chambre de Wallonie et de la Communauté Française:** rue de Nimy 106, 7000 Mons; tel. 65 584 7044; fax 6 532 1158; Music Dir Georges Octors; Man. Robert Leleu.

**Orchestre Symphonique de la RTBF:** Place Eugène Flagey 18, 1050 Brussels.

**Orchestre Symphonique du Théâtre Royal de la Monnaie:** 4 rue Léopold, 1000 Brussels; tel. 32 2 229 1227; fax 32 2 229 1386; Man. Bernt Sandstad.

**Philharmonische Vereniging van Antwerpen:** De Boeystraat 6, 2018 Antwerp; tel. 3 218 6975; fax 3 230 3523; Man. Albrecht Klora.

## Bosnia and Herzegovina

**Sarajevo Philharmonic Orchestra:** Obala Kulina Bana 9, 71000 Sarajevo; tel. 666-519; fax 666-521; e-mail sarphore@bsh.net.ba.

**Sarajevo Radio and Television Symphony Orchestra:** Sarajevo Radio and Television, 71000 Sarajevo.

## Brazil

**Orquestra Filharmônica do Rio de Janeiro:** Rua das Marrecas 25, Sala 901, Centro, 20013-120 Rio de Janeiro; tel. 55 21 240 7354; fax 55 21 262 4269; e-mail orquestra@filarmonica-rio.com.br; website www.filarmonica-rio.com .br; Music Dir Florentino Dias; Man. Regina Helena Macedo.

**Orquestra Sinfônica Brasileira:** Avenida Rio Branco 135, Room 918, 20040 Rio de Janeiro; tel. 55 21 225 2 6330; fax 55 21 250 8 9592; website.www.osb.-com.br; Music Dir Isaac Karabtchevsky.

**Orquestra Sinfônica do Teatro Nacional de Brasilia:** Avenida N2, Anexo do Teatro Nacional de Brasilia, 70000 Brasilia; Conductor Silvio Barbato.

## Bulgaria

**Bulgarian Radio and Television Symphony Orchestra:** 4 Dragan Tsankov Blvd, Sofia; tel. and fax 359 2 661812; Music Dir Milen Natcher.

**Sofia Philharmonic Orchestra:** Benkovski str 1, 1000 Sofia; tel. 359 2 883197; fax 359 2 874072; website www.sofiaphilharmonie.bg; Music Dir Emil Tabakov; Admin. Vassil Kostov.

**Vidin Philharmonic Orchestra:** 4 Gradinska Street, 3700 Vidin; tel. 359 94 24675; e-mail sinfonia@vidin.net; Music Dir Nayden Todorov; Man. Miroslav Krastev.

**Vratza State Philharmonic Orchestra:** 1 Bolev Square, 3000 Vratza; tel. 359 922 3434/3261; fax 359 926 0053; e-mail vratzaphil@mbox.digsys.bg; Principal Conductor Valeri Vatchev; Man. Dir Dimitar Panov.

## Canada

**Calgary Philharmonic Orchestra:** 205 Eighth Avenue, Calgary, AB T2G 0K9; tel. 1 403 571 0270; fax 1 403 294 7424; e-mail info@cpo-live.com; website www.cpo-live.com; Music Dir Hans Graf.

**Edmonton Symphony Orchestra:** Winspear Centre, Winston Churchill Square NW, Edmonton, AB T5J 4X8; tel. 1 403 428 1108; fax 1 403 425 1067; website www.edmontonsymphony.com; Music Dir Gregorz Nowak; Man. Dir Robert McPhee.

**Hamilton Philharmonic Orchestra:** Effort Trust Building, 105 Main Street E, Suite 1515, Hamilton, ON L8N 1G6; tel. 1 905 526 1677; fax 1 905 526 0616; e-mail office@hamiltonphilharmonic.org; website www .hamiltonphilharmonic.org; Artistic Dir Michael Reason; Gen. Man. Jack Nelson.

**Kingston Symphony:** PO Box 1616, Kingston, ON K7L 5C8; tel. 1 613 546 9729; fax 1 613 546 8580; e-mil info@kingstonsymphony.on.ca; Music Dir Glen Fast; Gen. Man. Andrea Haughton.

**Kitchener-Waterloo Symphony Orchestra:** 101 Queens Street N, Kitch-ener, ON N2H 6P7; tel. 1 519 745 4711; fax 1 519 745 4474; e-mail mail@ kwsymphony.on.ca; website www.kwsymphony.on.ca; Music Dir Chosei Komatsu; Man. Dir Mark Jarnison.

**National Arts Centre Orchestra:** PO Box 1534, Station B, Ottawa, ON K1P 5W1; tel. (613) 947-7000; fax (613) 943-1400; website www.nac-cna.ca; Man. Dir Christopher Deacon.

**Orchestra London Canada:** 520 Wellington Street, London, ON N6A 3R1; tel. 1 519 679 8558; fax 1 519 679 8914; e-mail olc.info@orchestra.london.on.ca; website www.orchestralondon.ca; Music Dir Timothy Vernon; Exec. Dir Robert Gloor.

**Orchestre Symphonique de Montréal:** 260 de Maisonneuve Blvd W, Second Floor, Montréal, QC H2X 1Y9; tel. 1 514 842 9951; fax 1 514 842 0728; website www.osm.ca; Music Dir Charles Dutoit; Man. Dir Robert Spickler.

**Orchestre Symphonique de Québec:** 130 Grande Alleé W, Québec, QC G1R 2G7; tel. 1 418 643 5598; fax 1 418 646 9665; e-mail info@osq.org; website www.osq.org; Artistic Dir Yoav Talmi; Man. Louis Laplante.

**Regina Symphony Orchestra:** 200 Lakeshire Drive, Regina, SK S4P 3V7; tel. 1 306 586 9555; fax 1 306 586 2133; e-mail rso2@sk.sympatico.ca; website www.reginasymphonyorchestra.sk.ca; Music Dir Vladimir Conta; Exec. Dir Pat Middleton.

**Saskatoon Symphony Orchestra:** Suite 703, Delta Bessborough Hotel, 601 Spadina Crescent E, Saskatoon, SK S7K 3G8; tel. 306 665-6414; fax 306 652-3364; e-mail saskatoonsymphony@sasktel.net; website www .saskatoonsymphony.org; Artistic Dir Douglas Sanford; Gen. Man. Karen Conway.

**Thunder Bay Symphony Orchestra:** PO Box 2004, Thunder Bay, ON P7B 5E7; e-mail info@tbso.ca; website www.tbso.ca; Music Dir Geoffrey Moull; Gen. Man. Erik Perth.

**Toronto Symphony:** Suite 550, 212 King Street W, Toronto, ON M5H 1K5; tel. 1 416 593 7769; fax 1 416 977 2912; website www.tso.on.ca; Music Dir Designate Peter Oundjian; Man. Dir Max Tapper.

**Vancouver Symphony Orchestra:** 601 Smithe Street, Vancouver, BC V6B 5G1; tel. 1 604 684 9100; fax 1 604 684 9264; e-mail reachus@ vancouversymphony.ca; website www.vancouversymphony.ca; Music Dir Bramwell Tovey.

**Victoria Symphony Orchestra:** 846 Broughton Street, Victoria, BC V8W 1E4; tel. 1 250 385 9771; fax 1 250 385 7767; e-mail administration@ victoriasymphony.bc.ca; website www.victoriasymphony.bc.ca; Music Dir Tania Miller; Gen. Man. Michael Aze.

**Winnipeg Symphony Orchestra:** Centennial Concert Hall, 555 Main Street, Room 101, Winnipeg, MB R3B 1C3; tel. 1 204 949 3950; fax 1 204 956 4271; website www.wso.mb.ca; Musical Dir Andrey Boreyko; Exec. Dir Howard Jang.

## Chile

**Orquesta Filarmónica de Santiago:** San Antonio 149, PO Box 18, Santiago; tel. 56 2 639 9735/9736; fax 56 2 633 7214; e-mail andrespinto@ municipal.cl; Man. Andrés Pinto.

## People's Republic of China

**Central Philharmonic Orchestra:** Beijing.

**Shanghai Symphony Orchestra:** 105 Hunan Lu, Shanghai 200031; tel. and fax 86 21 6433 3752; Conductor Chen Xie-Yang; Gen. Man. Cao Yiji.

## Colombia

**Orquesta Filarmónica de Bogotá (Bogota Philharmonic Orchestra):** Calle 39A, No. 14-57, PO Box 16034, Bogotá; tel. 57 1 340 6643; fax 57 1 288 3162; e-mail info@filarmonicabogota.org.co; website www.filarmonicabogota .gov.co; Music Dir Francisco Rettig; Exec. Dir Maria Cristina Sánchez.

**Orquesta Sinfónica de Colombia:** Teatro Colón, Calle 10, No. 5-32, Bogotá; tel. 57 243 5316; fax 57 820 854; Music Dir Federico Garcia Vigil; Man. Blanca Cecilia Carreno.

## Costa Rica

**Orquesta Sinfónica Nacional:** PO Box 1035, San José 1000; Music Dir Irwin Hoffman; Gen. Man. Gloria Waissbluth.

## Croatia

**Croatian Radio and Television Symphony Orchestra:** Dezmanova 10, 41000 Zagreb.

**Zagreb Philharmonic Orchestra:** Trg Stjepana Radica 4 pp909, Zagreb; tel. 385 1 606 0103; fax 385 1 611 1577; e-mail zqfilhar@zqf.hr; website www .zqf.hr; Dir Berislav Sipus.

## Czech Republic

**Brno State Philharmonic Orchestra:** Komenského nám 8, 602 00 Brno; tel. and fax 420 5 4221 2300; e-mail info@sfb.cz; website www.sfb.cz; Conductor Aldo Ceccato.

**Hradec Králové State Symphony Orchestra:** Náb e í Eli ino 777, 500 03 Hradec Králové tel. 495 211375; fax 495 211952; e-mail fhk@fhk.cz; website www.fhk.cz; Chief Conductor Frantisek Vajnar; Man. Radomir Malý.

**Janácek Philharmonic Orchestra:** 28 rijna 124, 702 00 Ostrava 1; tel. 420 69 661 9914; fax 420 69 661 9997; e-mail office@jfo.cz; website www.jfo.cz; Chief Conductor Christian Arming; Man. Miroslav Snyrich.

**Karlovy Vary Symphony Orchestra:** Náb e í CSP 1, 360 01 Karlovy Vary; website www.kso.cz; Music Dir Douglas Bostock; Man. Peter Kuli.

**Kosice State Philharmonic Orchestra:** Dom Umenia, Moyesova 66, 041 23, Kosice; tel. 421 95 622 4514.

**Moravian Philharmonic Orchestra:** Horni nám sti 23, 772 00 Olomouc; tel. 420 585 206 520; fax 420 585 220 124; website www.mfo.cz; Dir Vladislav Kvapil.

**National Theatre of Moravia and Silesia in Ostrava:** Csl., Legil, 701 04, Ostrava; tel. 420 69 6125144; fax 420 69 6112881; Dir Ludek Golat; Man. Dr G. Coates-Gibson.

**Plzeňská filharmonie (Radio Symphony Orchestra Pilsen):** náměstí Míru 10, 301 00 Plzeň; tel. and fax 420 377423336; e-mail plzenska .filharmonie@softech.cz; Chief Conductor: Hynek Farkač; Dir: Jan Motlík.

**Prague Radio Symphony Orchestra:** Vinohradská 12, 12099 Prague 2; tel. 420 2 2155 1412; fax 420 2 2155 1413; e-mail socr@cro.cz; Chief Conductor Vladimir Válek; Man. Lubomir Herza.

**Prague Symphony Orchestra (FOK):** Obecni dum, nám Republiky 5, 110 21 Prague 1; tel. 420 2 2231 5981/200 2425; fax 420 2 2231 0784; e-mail pso@

fok.cz; website www.fok.cz; Principal Guest Conductor Libor Pesek; Man. Dir Petr Polivka.

**South Bohemian State Orchestra:** Ceská ul 1, 370 21 Ceske Budejovice; Chief Conductor Ondrej Kukal; Dir Milan Kraus.

**West Bohemian Symphony Orchestra:** Tída Odborá u 51, 353 21 Mariánské Lazn; tel. 420 165 2141; fax 420 68 5228 511; Music Dir Radomil Elika; Man. Nadjda Domanjová.

## Denmark

**Ålborg Symfoniorkester:** Kjellerupsgade 14, 9000 Ålborg; tel. 45 98 131955; fax 45 98 130378; e-mail info@aalborgsymfoniorkester.dk; website www .aalborgsymfoniorkester.dk; Gen. Man.: Palle Kjeldgaard; Principal Chief Conductors: Lan Shui, Ari Rasilainen.

**Århus Symfoniorkester:** Musikhuset Århus, Thomas Jensens Allé, 8000 Århus; tel. 45 89 404040; fax 45 89 409091; e-mail symf@aarhus.dk; website www.aarhussymfoni.dk; Chief Conductor Giancarlo Andretta.

**Danish National Symphony Orchestra:** Rosenørns Allé 22, 1999 Copenhagen; tel. 45 3520 3040; fax 45 3520 6121; website www.dr.dk/rso; Chief Conductor: Thomas Dausgaard; Man.: Per Erik Veng; Principal Guest Conductor: Yuri Temirkanov.

**Odense Symphony Orchestra:** Claus Bergs Gade 9, 5000 Odense C; tel. 45 66 12 00 57; fax 45 65 91 00 47; e-mail orchestra@odensesymfoni.dk; website www.odensesymfoni.dk; Gen. Man. Per Holst.

**Royal Danish Orchestra:** PO Box 2185, 1017 Copenhagen; tel. 45 33 096701; fax 45 33 696767; e-mail admin@kgl-teater.dk; Principal Conductor Paavo Berglund.

**Sjaellands Symphony Orchestra:** Bernstorffsgade 9, 1577 Copenhagen V; Man. Maria Sørensen.

**Søndersyllands Symfoniorkester (Danish Philharmonic Orchestra, South Jutland):** Skovvej 16, 6400, Sønderborg; tel. 45 74 426161; fax 45 74 426106; e-mail info@sdisymfoni.dk; website www.sonderjyllands -symfoniorkester.dk; Gen. Man. Henrik Wenzel Andreasen.

**Tivoli Symphony Orchestra:** Tivoli, Vesterbrogade 3, 1620 Copenhagen V.

**West Jutland Symphony Orchestra:** Islandsgade 50, 6700 Esbjerg; tel. 45 75 139339; fax 45 75 133242; Admin. Dir Leif Pedersen.

## Dominican Republic

**Orquesta Sinfónica Nacional:** Palacio de Bellas Artes, Santo Domingo; Music Dir Carlos Piantini; Man. Sofia de Sturla.

## Ecuador

**Orquesta Sinfónica Nacional:** Casilla 2844, Calle Venezuela 666, Quito; Music Dir Alvaro Manzano; Man. G. Sáenz.

## Egypt

**Cairo Symphony Orchestra:** Egyptian Opera House, Geziro, Cairo 11211; tel. 202 342 0601; fax 202 342 0599; e-mail csorchestra@yahoo.com; website www.cairo-symphony.com.eg; Music Dir Ahmed Elsaedi.

## Estonia

**Eesti Riikliku Sümfooniaorkestri—ERSO (Estonian National Symphony Orchestra):** Estonia PO Box 4, 10143 Tallinn; tel. 372 6147787; fax 372 6313133; e-mail erso@erso.ee; website www.erso.ee; Dir Andres Sitan.

## Finland

**Finnish Radio Symphony Orchestra:** PO Box 14, 00 024 Yleisradio, Helsinki; tel. 358 9 1480 4366; fax 358 9 1480 3551; e-mail tuula.sarotie@yle.fi; website www.yle.fi/rso; Conductor of Honour Jukka-Pekka Saraste; Chief Conductor Sikari Oramo; Gen. Man. Tuula Sarotie.

**Helsinki Philharmonic Orchestra:** Finlandia Hall, Karamzininkatu 4, 00100 Helsinki; tel. 358 9 4024 265; fax 358 9 406484; website www.hel.fi/filharmonia; Chief Conductor Leif Segerstam; Man. Helena Ahonen.

**Tampere Philharmonic Orchestra:** PL 16, 31 101 Tampere; tel. 358 3 243 4111; fax 358 3 243 4400; e-mail orchestra@tampere.fi; website www.tampere .fi; Artistic Dir Eri Klas; Gen. Man. Maritta Hirvonen.

**Turku Philharmonic Orchestra:** Sibeliuksenkatu 2 A, 20 110 Turku; tel. 358 21 2314 577; fax 358 21 250 0480; e-mail orchestra@turku.fi; website www3.turku.fi/orkesteri; Man. Kalevi Kuosa.

## France

**Association des Concerts Colonne:** 2 rue Edouard Colonne, 75001 Paris; Music Dir Antonello Allemandi; Gen. Man. Guy Arnaud.

**Association des Concerts Lamoureux:** 252 rue de Faubourg St-Honoré, 75008 Paris; tel. 33 1 45 63 44 34; fax 33 1 45 62 05 41; Man. Annie Foultier.

**Association des Concerts Pasdeloup:** 18 rue de Berne, 75008 Paris; Man. Roger Landy.

**Ensemble Ars Nova:** 16 rue des Fossés St Jacques, 75005 Paris; tel. 33 1 43 26 74 84; fax 33 1 46 3334 59; Music Dir Marius Constant.

**Ensemble Instrumental de Grenoble:** 1 rue du Vieux Temple, 38000 Grenoble; Dir Marc Tardue; Man. Jean-Peter Roeber.

**Ensemble Intercontemporain:** 223 avenue Jean Jaurès, 75019 Paris; tel. 33 1 44 84 44 50; fax 33 1 44 84 44 61; website www.ensembleinter.com; Music Dir David Robertson; Man. Claude Le Cleach.

**Ensemble Orchestral de Haute-Normandie:** 50 ave de la Porte des Champs, 76000 Rouen; Music Dir Jean-Pierre Berlingen; Admin. Jean-Michel Bernard.

**Ensemble Orchestral de Paris:** 37 rue Anatole-France, 92309 Levallois-Perret Cedex, 75008 Paris; e-mail contact@eop.com.fr; website www.ensemble -orchestral-paris.com; Conductor John Nelson; Man. Alain Guillon.

**Ensemble Orchestral Harmonia Nova:** 74 rue de Faubourg St Denis, 75010 Paris; Music Dir Didier Bouture; Man. Daniel Gutenberg.

**La Chapelle Royale/Orchestre des Champs Elysees:** 10 rue Coquilliere, 75001 Paris; tel. 33 1 40 26 58 00; fax 33 1 40 26 38 37; website www .lachapelleroyale.com; Music Dir Philippe Herreweghe.

**La Grande Ecurie et la Chambre du Roy:** 19 rue de Biercy Vanry, 77640 Jouarre; tel. 33 1 60 22 98 45; fax 33 1 60 22 03 13; Music Dir Jean-Claude Malgoire.

**Les Arts Florissants:** 2 rue de Saint-Petersburg, 75008 Paris; tel. 33 1 43 87 98 88; fax 33 1 43 87 37 31; e-mail contact@arts-florissants.com; website www .arts-florissants.com; Music Dir William Christie; Gen. Admin. Luc Bouniol Laffont.

**Musique en Sorbonne:** 2 rue Francis de Croisset, 75018 Paris; tel. 33 1 42 62 71 71; fax 33 1 42 51 69 11; website www.musique-en-sorbonne.org; Gen. Man. Jim Houdayer.

**Nouvel Orchestre Philharmonique:** Radio France, 116 avenue du Président Kennedy, 75786 Paris Cédex 16; tel. 33 1 42 30 36 30; fax 33 1 42 30 47 48; Music Dir Marek Janowski; Artistic Dir Yvon Kapp.

**Opera de Rouen:** 7 rue du Docteur Rambert, 76 000, Rouen; tel. 33 2 35 98 50 98; fax 33 2 35 15 33 49; website www.operaderouen.com; Musical Dir Oswald Sallaberger; Dir Laurent Langlois.

**Orchestra Symphonique de Tours:** Grand Théâtre, 34 rue de la Scellerie, 37000 Tours; tel. 33 247 60 20 00; fax 33 247 60 20 40; e-mail theatre@ville -tours.fr; Dir: Jean-Yves Ossonce; Admin.: Luc Cavalier.

**Orchestre d'Auvergne:** 2 rue Urbain II, 63000 Clermont-Ferrand; tel. 04 73 14 47 47; fax 04 73 14 47 46; e-mail orchestre.d.auvergne@wanadoo.fr; Admin. Alain Riviere.

**Orchestre de Bretagne:** 42A rue St-Melaine, BP 30823 Rennes, Céedex 3; tel. 33 2 99 275 285; fax 33 2 99 275 276; e-mail administration@orchestre-de -bretagne.com; website www.orchestre-de-bretagne.com; Dir Jean-Marc Bador; Man. Jean-François Jeandet.

**Orchestre de Caen:** 1 rue du Carel, 14050 Caen Cédex 4; tel. 33 2 31 30 46 88; fax 33 2 31 30 46 87; website www.caen.fr/OrchestredeCaen; Music Dir Jean-Marc Laureau; Man. Delphine Chevallier; Artistic Dir Stephane Bechy.

**Orchestre de Chambre de Versailles:** 3 rue Descartes, 92310 Sèvres; Music Dir M. B. Wahl.

**Orchestre de Chambre Jean-François Paillard:** 50 rue Laborde, 75008 Paris; Music Dir Jean-François Paillard; Admin. Richard Siegel.

**Orchestre de Chambre Jean-Louis Petit:** 34 rue Corot, 92410 Ville d'Avray; tel. 33 1 47 09 22 82; fax 33 1 47 50 53 90; Music Dir Jean-Louis Petit.

**Orchestre de Chambre National de Toulouse:** 4 rue Clémence Isaure, 31000 Toulouse; tel. 33 5 62 30 34 40; fax 33 5 62 30 34 41; e-mail ocnt.ocnt@ wanadoo.fr; website www.espritsnomades.com/onct.html; Dir Alain Moglia; Man. Jean-Pierre Paragon.

**Orchestre de Chambre Paul Kuentz:** 144 rue du Faubourg St Antoine, 75012 Paris; Music Dir Paul Kuentz.

**Orchestre de Paris:** 25 rue de Mogador, 75009 Paris; tel. 33 1 56 35 12 00; fax 33 1 42 89 24 49; website www.orchestredeparis.com; Music Dir Christoph Eschenbach; Gen. Dir Georges-François Hirsch.

**Orchestre des Concerts Lamoureux:** 53 rue des Orteaux, 75020 Paris; tel. 33 1 58 39 30 30; fax 33 1 58 39 30 31; e-mail orchestrelamoureux@wanadoo.fr; website www.orchestrelamoureux.com; Chief Principal Yutaka Sado; Pres. Lionel Evans.

**Orchestre des Pays de Savoie:** 6 rue Metropole, 73000 Chambéry; tel. 33 4 79 33 42 71; fax 33 4 79 33 43 00; e-mail orchestrepayssavoie@wanadoo.fr; website www.savoie-culture.com; Music Dir Graziella Contratto; Pres. Andre Fumex; Admin. Dir Odile Ollagnon.

**Orchestre Français des Jeunes:** Maison de Radio France, 116 avenue du Président Kennedy, 75220 Paris Cédex 16; tel. 33 1 56 40 49 45; fax 33 1 56 40 49 90; e-mail ofjeunes@aol.com; website www.ofj.asso.fr; Music Dir Emmanuel Krivine; Admin. Dir Pierre Barrois; Man. Aude le Cleh.

**Orchestre Jean-François Gonzales:** 32 rue du Maréchal Joffre, Residence 7, 78000 Versailles; tel. 33 01 39 51 66 05; Music Dir J.-F. Gonzales-Hamilton.

**Orchestre Lyrique de Région Avignon Provence:** 258 chemin des Rémouleurs, Zl de Courtine, PO Box 967, 84093 Avignon Cédex 9; website www.ars-dom.com/olrap; Music Dir François Bilger.

**Orchestre National Bordeaux-Aquitaine:** PO Box 95, 33025 Bordeaux; tel. 33 5 56 00 85 20; fax 33 5 56 81 93 66; e-mail courrier@opera-bordeaux .com; website www.opera-bordeaux.com/artistes/onba.htm; Admin. Daniel Dourneau-Gabory; Music Dir Hans Graf.

**Orchestre National d'Ile de France:** 19 rue des Ecoles, 94140 Alfortville; tel. 33 1 41 79 03 40; fax 33 1 41 79 03 50; e-mail courrier@orchestre-ile.com; website www.orchestre-ile.com; Music Dir Jacques Mercier; Gen. Dir Marc-Olivier Dupin.

**Orchestre National de France:** Radio France, 116 avenue du Président Kennedy, 75786 Paris Cédex 16; tel. 33 1 42 30 26 03; fax 33 1 42 30 43 33; Music Dir Charles Dutoit; Gen. Man. Patrice d'Ollone.

**Orchestre National de Lille:** 30 place Mendès-France, PO Box 119, 59027 Lille Cédex; tel. 33 03 20 128240; fax 33 03 20 782910; e-mail jbrochen@orlille .com; website www.orlille.com; Man. Jacqueline Brochen.

**Orchestre National de Lyon:** 82 rue de Bonnel, 69431 Lyon Cédex 3; tel. 33 4 78 95 95 00; fax 33 4 78 60 13 08; website www.orchestrelyon.com; Music Dir David Robertson; Dir-Gen. Anne Poursin.

**Orchestre National de Montpellier:** Le Corum, PO Box 9056 34041, Montpellier Cédex 1; tel. 33 4 67 61 67 21; fax 33 4 67 61 67 20; website www .orchestre-montpellier.com; Musical Dir Friedemann Layer; Admin. Sophie Cuvillier.

**Orchestre National du Capitole de Toulouse:** Halle aux Grains, place Dupuy, 31000 Toulouse; tel. 33 5 61 63 13 13; fax 33 5 62 27 49 49; website www.onct.mairie-toulouse.fr; Music Dir Michel Plasson; Man. George Schneider.

**Orchestre Philharmonique de Lorraine:** 25 avenue Robert Schuman, 57008 Metz; tel. 33 3 87 55 12 02; fax 33 3 87 65 69 36; website www .orchestrenatinoal-lorraine.fr; Artistic Dir Jacques Mercier; Gen. Admin. Pascal Schwan.

**Orchestre Philharmonique de Montpellier:** Le Corum, PO Box 9056, 34041 Montpellier Cédex 01; tel. 33 04 67 61 67 21; fax 33 04 67 61 66 82; Music Dir Friedemann Layer; Dir Gen. René Koering; Admin. Jany Macaby.

**Orchestre Philharmonique de Nice:** 4 rue St François de Paule, 06300 Nice; tel. 33 4 92 17 4 0 00; fax 33 4 93 80 34 83; Music Dir Marcello Parni; Man. Pierre Medecin.

**Orchestre Philharmonique de Radio France:** 116 avenue du Président Kennedy, 75220, Paris Cédex 16; tel. 1 42 30 36 30; fax 1 42 30 47 48; e-mail philhar@radiofrance.com; Musical Dir Myung-Whun Chung; Admin. Jean-François Jeandet; Artistic Delegate Eric Montalbetts.

**Orchestre Philharmonique de Strasbourg:** Palais de la Musique et des Congrès, avenue Schutzenberger, 67000 Strasbourg Cédex; tel. 33 03 88 15 09 00; fax 33 03 88 15 09 01; e-mail opstrasbourg@aol.com; website www .philharmonique-strasbourg.com; Music Dir Ian Latham Koenig; Dir-Gen. Patrick Minard.

**Orchestre Philharmonique des Pays de la Loire:** 26 avenue Montaigne, PO Box 15246, 49052 Angers Cédex 2; tel. 33 41 24 11 20; fax 33 41 87 80 52; website www.onpl.fr; Music Dir Hubert Soudent; Gen. Admin. Maryvonne Lavigne.

**Orchestre Régional de Cannes-Provence Alpes Côte d'Azur:** 104 avenue Francis Tonner, PO Box 46, 06150 Cannes La Bocca Cédex; tel. 33 4 93 48 61 10; fax 33 4 93 90 27 79; Dir Philippe Bender; Man. Catherine Morschel.

**Orchestre Régional Poitou-Charentes:** 3 place Prosper Mérimée, PO Box 422, 86000 Poitiers Cédex; tel. 33 5 49 55 91 10; fax 33 5 49 60 12 21; Dir Charles Frey.

**Orchestre Symphonique de la Garde Républicaine:** 12 blvd Henri IV, 75004 Paris; Music Dir Roger Boutry.

**Orchestre Symphonique de Rhin-Mulhouse:** 38 Passage du Théâtre, 68100 Mulhouse; Music Dir Luca Pfaff; Man. Jean-Luc Fischer.

**Orchestre Symphonique et Lyrique de Nancy et de Lorraine:** 1 rue Sainte Catherine, 54000 Nancy; tel. 33 83 85 33 20; fax 33 83 85 30 66; Music Dir Sebastian Lang-Lessing; Man. Astrid Chepfer.

**Société des Concerts du Conservatoire:** 1 rue de la Bibliothèque, 13000 Marseille.

# Germany

**Akademie Hamburger Solisten:** Seilerstrasse 41, 20355 Hamburg; Music Dir Joachim Kerwin.

**Bach Collegium München e V:** Elisabethstrasse 9, 8000 Munich; Music Dir Florian Sonnleitner.

**Badische Staatskapelle Karlsruhe:** Baumeisterstrasse 11, 7500 Karlsruhe; Gen. Music Dir Anthony Brawall.

**Bamberger Symphoniker:** Mussstrasse 1, 96047 Bamberg; tel. 49 951 964 7100; fax 49 951 964 7123; e-mail intendanz@bamberger-symphoniker.de; website www.bamberger-symphoniker.de; Chief Conductor Jonathon Nott; Principal Guest Conductor Ingo Metzmacher.

**Bayerisches Staatsorchester:** Max-Joseph-Platz 2, 80539 Munich; tel. 49 89 218501; fax 49 89 2185 1003; website www.staatsorchester.de; Musical Dir Zubin Mehta; Gen. Dir Peter Jonas.

**Berliner Barock-Orchester:** Arnold-Knoblauch-Ring, 64, Pf 173, 1000 Berlin; Music Dir Konrad Latte.

**Berliner Philharmonisches Orchester:** Philharmonie, Matthäikirch-strasse 1, 14057 Berlin; tel. 49 30 254 880; fax 49 30 261 4887; website www .berliner-philharmoniker.de; Man. Elmar Weingarten; Music Dir Sir Simon Rattle.

**Berliner Sinfonie-Orchester:** Gendarmenmarkt, 1086 Berlin; Music Dir Michael Schønwandt; Man. Frank Schneider.

**Berliner Symphoniker:** Christstrasse 30, 14059 Berlin; tel. 49 30 321 1017; fax 49 30 325 5326; e-mail kontakt@berlin-symphoniker.de; website www .berliner-symphoniker.de; Music Dir Alun Francis; Chief Conductor Lior Shambadal; Man. Jochen Thärichen.

**Bochumer Symphoniker:** Prinz-Regent-Strasse 50-60, 44795 Bochum; tel. 49 02 34 910 8622; fax 49 02 34 910 8616; website www.bochum.de/ symphoniker; Gen. Music Dir Steven Sloane.

**Brandenburger Symphoniker:** Brandenburger Theater, Grabenstrasse 14, 14776 Brandenburg/Havel; tel. 3381 511 131; fax 3381 511 160; e-mail info@brandenburgertheater.de; website www.brandenburgertheater.de; Music Dir Michael Helmrath.

**Brandenburgische Philharmonie:** Zimmerstrasse 10, 1570 Potsdam; Music Dir Stefan Sanderling.

**Brandenburgisches Kammerorchester e V, A Thiemig:** Schopenhauer-strasse 9, 7513 Cottbus; e-mail bko@bko-berlin.de; website www.bko-berlin.de; Music Dir Rainer Johannes Kimstedt.

**Bremen Filharmoniker:** Wüstestätte 11, 28195 Bremen; tel. (421) 361 41 78; fax (421) 361-41-94; e-mail info@bremerphilharmoniker.de; website www .bremerphilharmoniker.de; Gen. Music Dir Lawrence Renes.

**Collegium Aureum:** Nordstrasse 2, 7800 Freiburg; Music Dir Franzjosef Maier.

**Concerto Grosso Frankfurt e V:** Ludwigstrasse 66, 6050 Offenbach; Music Dir Irina Edelstein.

**Detmolder Kammerorchester e V:** Bruchstrasse 25, Pf 1404, 32756 Detmold; tel. 05231 31603; fax 05231 31606; e-mail info@detmolder -kammerorchester.de; website www.detmolder-kammerorchester.de; Music Dir Christoph Poppen.

**Deutsche Bachsolisten:** Goddardstrasse 28, 5300 Bonn; Music Dir Helmut Winschermann.

**Deutsche Kammerakademie:** Oberstrasse 17, Pf 101452, 41460 Neuss 1; tel. 02131 904116; fax 02131 904127; Music Dir Johannes Goritzki.

**Deutsche Kammerphilharmonie:** Schwedlerstrasse 2–4, 60320 Frankfurt am Main 1.

**Deutsches Kammerorchester Frankfurt am Main:** Hans-Bredow-Strasse 42B, 6200 Wiesbaden; tel. 0611 464 619; fax 0611 464 755; e-mail concmanag@aol.com; website www.deutscheskammerorchester-frankfurt .com; Conductor Rista Savic.

**Deutsches Kammerorchester:** Lietzenburger Strasse 51, 1000 Berlin; e-mail info@dko-berlin.de; website www.dko-berlin.de; Music Dir Fritz Weisse.

**Deutsches Symphonie Orchester Berlin:** Charlottenstrasse 56, 10117 Berlin; tel. 49 30 2029 8711; fax 49 30 2029 8729; website www.dso-berlin.de; Chief Conductor Kent Nagano; Orchestral Dir Dr Thomas Schmidt.

**Dresdner Kammerorchester:** c/o Sächsische Staatskapelle Dresden, Theaterplatz 2, 8010 Dresden.

**Dresdner Philharmonie:** Kulturpalast am Altmarkt, Pf 120424, 01005 Dresden; tel. 49 351 486 6202/6287; fax 49 351 486 6306/6286; website www .dresdnerphilharmonie.com; Gen. Music Dir Rafael Frühbeck de Burgos; Artist Man. Dr Olivier von Winterstein.

**Duisburger Sinfoniker:** Beckarstrasse 1, 4100 Duisburg 1; Gen. Music Dir Bruno Weil.

**Düsseldorfer Symphoniker:** Ehrenhof 1, 40479 Düsseldorf; tel. 49 211 899 3606; fax 49 211 892 9143; Music Dir John Fiore; Man. Thomas Stuhrk.

**Folkwang Kammerorchester Essen e V:** Hollestrasse 1g, 45127 Essen; tel. 49 201 230034; fax 49 201 200696; e-mail fko.essen@web.de; website www .folkwang-kammerorchester.de; Man. Dir Ralph Sistermanns; Music Dir Stefan Fraas.

**Freies Kammerorchester Berlin e V:** Antonstrasse 25, 1000 Berlin; Music Dir Christoph Hagel.

**Gewandhausorchester zu Leipzig:** Augustusplatz 8, 04109 Leipzig; tel. 49 341 1270; fax 49 341 12 70200; website www.gewandhaus.de; Principal Conductor Herbert Blomstedt.

**Göttinger Symphonie-Orchester:** Godehardstrasse 19–21, 3400 Göttingen; Music Dir Christian Simonis.

**Gürzenich-Orchester:** Bischofsgartenstrasse 1, 50667 Cologne 1; tel. 0221 22122437; fax 0221 22123800; Gen. Music Dir James Conlon.

**Hamburger Mozart-Orchester:** Helgolandstrasse 12, 2000 Wedel; Music Dir Robert Stehli.

**Hamburger Symphoniker:** Dammtorwall 46, 20355 Hamburg; tel. 49 40 344851; fax 49 40 353788; website www.hamburger-symphoniker.de; Music Dir Miguel Gómez Martínez.

**Händelfestspielorchester:** Universitätsring 24, 06108 Halle an der Saale; tel. 49 345 511 10300; fax 49 345 511 0303; Music Dir Roger Epple; Orchestral Man. Bruno Scharnberg.

**Hofer Symphoniker:** Klosterstrasse 9–11, 95028 Hof; tel. 0049 9281 7200; fax 0049 9281 7272; e-mail info@hofer-symphoniker.de; website www.hofer -symphoniker.de; Man. Wilfried Anton.

**Hohner-Akkordeonorchester 1927 Trossingen e V:** Neuenstrasse 29, 78647 Trossingen-Schura; tel. 490 7425 20212; fax 490 7425 20462; e-mail mkeller@hohner.de; Pres. Matthias Keller.

**Jenaer Philharmonie:** Volkshaus Carl-Zeiss-Platz 15, 07743 Jena; tel. 0049 3641 590010; fax 0049 3641 590026; e-mail philharmonie@jena.de; website www.jenaer-philharmonie.de; Man. Bruno Scharnberg.

**Kammerorchester Merck:** Stefan Reinhardt, Pf 4119, 6100 Darmstadt.

**Kammerorchester Musica Juventa Halle:** Hegelstrasse 9, 06109 Halle an der Saale; Music Dir Roger Epple.

**Kammerorchester Schloss Werneck e V:** Balthasar-Neumann-Platz 8, Pf 65, 97440 Werneck; tel. 490 9722 91610; fax 490 9722 91611; e-mail info@ tammerorchester.de; website www.kammerorchester.de; Music Dir Ulf Klausenitzer.

**Klassische Philharmonie Telekom Bonn:** Theaterstrasse 10, 5300 Bonn 1; Music Dir Heribert Beissel.

**Kölner Kammerorchester e V:** Schlosstrasse 2, 5040 Bruhl; Music Dir Helmut Müller-Bruhl.

**Kölner Rundfunk-Sinfonie-Orchester:** Appellhofplatz 1, 50600; Principal Conductor Semyon Bychkov; Dir of Music Programming: Hermann Lang.

**Kürpfalzisches Kammerorchester:** D 6, 2, 6800 Mannheim 1; Music Dir Jiri Malát.

**Landessinfonieorchester Thüringen-Gotha:** Reinhardsbrunner Strasse 23, 5800 Gotha; Music Dir Hermann Breuer.

**Landestheaterorchester Coburg:** Coburger Landestheater, Schlossplatz 6, 96450 Coburg; tel. (49) 9561 898900; website www.landestheater.coburg.de; Gen. Music Dir: Alois Seidlmeier.

**Magdeburgische Philharmonie:** Theater der Landeshauptstadt Magdeburg, Pf 1240, 39002 Magdeburg; tel. 03 91 540 6500; Gen. Music Dir Mathias Husmann.

**Mainzer Kammerorchester e V:** Friedrich Naumann Str 9, 55131 Mainz; tel. 06131 839 198; fax 06131 834 128; e-mail info@mainzer-kammerorchester .de; website www.mainzer-kammerorchester.de.

**MDR Sinfonieorchester:** Augustusplatz 9a, 04105 Leipzig; tel. 49 341 300 8705; fax 49 300 8701; e-mail mdr-lkangkoerper@mdr.de; website www.mdr .de/konzerte; Gen. Man. Mario Plath; Chief Conductor Fabio Luisi.

**Mecklenburgische Staatskapelle:** Alter Garten, 2750 Schwerin; e-mail info@mecklenburgische-staatskapelle.de; website www.mecklenburghische -staatskapelle.de; Musical Dir Matthias Foremny.

**Münchener Kammerorchester e V:** Wittelsbacherplatz 2, 80333 Munich; tel. 089-636-35972; fax 089-280-171; e-mail hans-joachim-litzkow@ muenchner.de; website www.muenchener-kammerorchester.de; Music Dir Christoph Poppen.

**Münchener Philharmoniker:** Gasteig Kulturzentrum, Kellerstrasse 4/III, 81667 Munich; tel. 49 89 4809 8509; fax 49 89 4809 8513; e-mail philharmoniker@ muenchen.de; website www.muencher-philharmonie.de; Gen. Music Dir James Levine; Man. Bernd Gellermann.

**Münchener Symphoniker e V:** Drachslstrasse 14, 81541 Munich; tel. 08944 11960; fax 08944 119615; e-mail info@muenchner-symphoniker.de; website www.muenchner-symphoniker.de; Music Dir Christoph Stepp.

**Musica Antiqua Köln:** Brüsseler Str. 94, 50672 Köln; tel. 221 9232030; fax 221 9232031.

**Nationaltheater-Orchester Mannheim:** Mozartstrasse 11, 68161 Mannheim; tel. 49 0621 26044; fax 49 0621 23182; Musical Dir Adam Fischer.

**NDR-Sinfonieorchester:** Norddeutscher Rundfunk Hamburg, Rothenbaumchaussee 132, 20149 Hamburg; tel. 49 40 4156 2401/3545; fax 49 40 4156 3758/7569; e-mail sinfonie@ndr.de; website www.ndr.de/sinfonie; Chief Conductor Herbert Blomstedt; Dir of Music Programming Bernhard Hansen.

**Neubrandenburger Philharmonie:** Pfaffenstrasse 22, 17033 Neubrandenburg; tel. 49 39 5569 9811; fax 49 39 5582 6179; e-mail philharmonie.NB@t -online.de; website www.philharmonie-online.de; Chief Conductor Stefan Malzew; Man. Horst Beitz.

**Niederrheinische Sinfoniker:** Theater Mönchengladbach, Odenkirchener Strasse 78, 41236 Mönchengladbach; tel. 2166-6151-128; fax 2166-6151-134; e-mail gmd@theater-kr-mg.de; website www.theater-krefeld -moenchengladbach.de; Gen. Music Dir Graham Jackson.

**Niedersächsisches Staatsorchester:** Opernplatz 1, 3000 Hannover 1; Gen. Music Dir Christof Prick.

**Norddeutsche Philharmonie Rostock:** Patriotischer Weg 33, 18057 Rostock; tel. 49 38 1381 4650; fax 49 38 1381 4659; Gen. Music Dir Wolf-Dieter Hauschild.

**Nordwestdeutsche Philharmonie:** Stiftbergstrasse 2, 32049 Herford; tel. 39 52 198380; fax 5221 983821; e-mail info@nwd-philharmonie.de; website www.nwd-philharmonie.de; Music Dir Michail Jurowski.

**Nürnberger Symphoniker:** Bayernstrasse 100, 90471 Nürnberg; tel. 39 91 1474 0140; fax 39 91 1474 0150; e-mail info@nuernbergersymphoniker.de; website www.nuernbergersymphoniker.de; Man. Lucius A. Hemmer.

**Oldenburgisches Staatsorchester:** Theaterwall 28, 26122 Oldenburg; tel. 0441/2225-111; fax 0441/2225-221; website www.oldenburg.staatstheater.de; Gen. Music Dir Alexander Rumpf.

**Opernhaus-und Museumsorchester Frankfurt am Main:** Untermainanlage 11, 60320 Frankfurt am Main; Gen. Music Dir Sylvain Cambreling.

**Orchester der Beethovenhall Bonn:** Verwaltung, Wachsbleiche 2, 53111 Bonn 1; tel. 0228 630031; fax 0228 630376; e-mail info@beethoven-orchester .de; website www.beethoven-orchester.de; Gen. Music Dir Roman Kofman.

**Orchester der Deutschen Oper Berlin:** Richard-Wagner-Strasse 10, 10585 Berlin; tel. 49 30 34381; fax 49 30 348 8232; e-mail info@ deutscheoperberlin.de; website www.deutscheoperberlin.de/orchester; Gen. Music Dir Christian Thielemann.

**Orchester der Elbe-Saale Bühnen:** Thomas-Müntzer-Strasse 14/15, 4600 Wittenberg; Music Dir Klaus Hofmann.

**Orchester der Hansestadt Lübeck (Philharmonisches Orchester der Hansestadt Lübeck):** Beckergrube 16, 23552 Lübeck; tel. 0451 70880; website www.theater.luebeck.de; Gen. Music Dir Roman Brogli-Sacher.

**Orchester der Komischen Oper Berlin:** Behrenstrasse 55–57, 10117 Berlin; tel. 49 30 202600; fax 49 30 2026 0405; e-mail info@komische-oper -berlin.de; website www.komische-oper-berlin.de; Gen. Music Dir Kirill Petrenko.

**Orchester der Landesbühnen Sachsen:** Meissner Strasse 152, 8122 Radebeul; Music Dir Joachim Widlak; Man. Christian Schmidt.

**Orchester der Musikalischen Komödie Leipzig:** Dreilindenstrasse 30, 7033 Leipzig; Music Dir Roland Seiffarth.

**Orchester der Staatsoperette:** Pirnaer Landstrasse 131, 01257 Dresden; tel. 0351 207990; e-mail info@staatsoperette-dresden.de; website www .staatsoperette-dresden.de; Music Dir Volker Munch.

**Orchester der Stadt Ulm:** Ulmer Theater, Herbert-von-Karajan-Platz 1, 89073 Ulm; tel. 0049/0731/161-4500; fax 0049/0731/161-1619; e-mail PhilharmonieUlm@aol.com; website www.theater.ulm.de; Gen. Music Dir Alicja Mounk; Public Relations Karin Mayer.

**Orchester des Friedrichstadtpalastes Berlin:** Friedrichstrasse 107, 10117 Berlin; tel. 49 30 2326 2264/2265; fax 49 30 282 4578; website www .friedrichstadtpalastes.de; Music Dir Detlef Klemm; Man. Julian Herrey.

**Orchester des Hessischen Staatstheater Wiesbaden:** Christian-Zais-Strasse, 65022 Wiesbaden; tel. 61 113 2255; fax 61 113 2236; Gen. Music Dir Oleg Caetani.

**Orchester des Landestheaters Dessau:** Fritz-Hesse-Platz 1, 4500 Dessau; Gen. Music Dir Daniel Lipton.

**Orchester des Landestheaters Detmold:** Landestheater Detmold, Theaterplatz, 37256 Detmold; tel. 5231 97460; fax 5231 974701; e-mail info@ landestheater-detmold.de; website www.landestheater-detmold.de.

**Orchester des Landestheaters Mecklenburg:** Friedrich-Ludwig-Jahn-Strasse, 2080 Neustrelitz; Music Dir Golo Berg.

**Orchester des Meininger Theaters:** Bernhardstrasse 5, 98617 Meiningen; tel. 03693 451222; fax 03693 451301; e-mail kasse@das-meininger-theater.de; website www.das-meininger-theater.de; Music Dir Wolfgang Hocke.

**Orchester des Pfalztheaters Kaiserslautern:** Fruchthallstrasse, 6750 Kaiserslautern; Gen. Music Dir Lior Shambadal.

**Orchester des Staatstheaters am Gärtnerplatz:** 80469 Munich; tel. 089 20241 1; fax 089 20241-237; website www.staatstheater-am-gaertmerplatz.de; Music Dir: David Stahl; Man.: Prof. Klaus Schultz.

**Orchester des Staatstheaters Darmstadt:** Auf dem Marienplatz, 6100 Darmstadt.

**Orchester des Staatstheaters Kassel:** Staatstheater Kassel, Friedrichsplatz 15, 3500 Kassel; Gen. Music Dir Georg Schmöhe.

**Orchester des Theaters der Altmark-Landestheater Sachsen-Anhalt Nord:** Karlstrasse 4–6, 3500 Stendal; Music Dir Frank Jaremko.

**Orchester des Theaters des Westens:** Kantstrasse 12, 1000 Berlin 12; Music Dir Peter Keuschnig.

**Orchester des Theaters Nordhausen:** Kathe-Kollwitz-Strasse 15, 5500 Nordhausen; Music Dir Kurt Schafer.

**Orchester des Theaters Zwickau:** Gewandhausstrasse 7, Pf 308, 9541 Zwickau; Music Dir Welisar Gentscheff.

**Orchester des Vogtland-Theaters Plauen:** Theaterplatz 1–3, 9900 Plauen; Music Dir Paul Theissen.

**Osnabrücker Symphonieorchester:** Städtische Bühnen Osnabrück, Domhof 10/11, 49086 Osnabrück; tel. 0049 541 3233355; fax 0049 541 3233751; e-mail musikbuero.theateros@t-online.de; Music Dir Lothar Koenigs.

**Philharmonia Hungarica:** Lord Menuhin-Haus, Hochstrasse 34, 45768 Marl; tel. 02365 13031; fax 02365 15877; e-mail philharmonia-hungarica@t-online.de; website www.philharmonia-hungarica.com; Gen. Music Dir Jun Märkl.

**Philharmonic Essen:** Aatlo Musiktheater, Opernplatz 10, 45128 Essen; website www.theater-essen.asp.de; Gen. Music Dir Stefan Soltesz.

**Philharmonisches Kammerorchester Hamburg e V:** Musikhalle, Karl-Muck-Platz, 20355 Hamburg; Music Dir Wilfried Laatz.

**Philharmonisches Kammerorchester München e V:** Connolly-Strasse 15, 8000 Munich; Music Dir Michael Helmrath.

**Philharmonisches Kammerorchester Wernigerode GmbH:** Bahnhofstrasse 16, 38855 Wernigerode; tel. (3943) 94-95-14; fax (3943) 94-95-29; website www.kammerorchester-wr.de; Music Dir Christian Fitzner.

**Philharmonisches Orchester Augsburg:** Kasernstrasse 4–6, 86152 Augsburg; tel. 49 821 324 4935; fax 49 821 324 4935; Gen. Music Dir Rudolf Piehlmayer; Man. Matthias Gress.

**Philharmonisches Orchester der Landeshauptstadt Kiel:** Rathausplatz 4, 24103 Kiel; tel. 49 431 901 2856; fax 49 431 901 6288; website www.theater-kiel.de; Gen. Music Dir Georg Fritzsch.

**Philharmonisches Orchester der Staatstheaters Cottbus:** Lausitzer-Strasse 33, 03046; website www.staatstheater-cottbus.de; Gen. Music Dir Reinard Petersen.

**Philharmonisches Orchester der Stadt Bielefeld:** Brunnenstrasse 3, 4800 Bielefeld 1; website www.bielefelder-philharmoniker.de; Gen. Music Dir Peter Kuhn.

**Philharmonisches Orchester der Stadt Dortmund:** Kuhstrasse 12, 4600 Dortmund 1; Gen. Music Dir Moshe Atzmon.

**Philharmonisches Orchester der Stadt Gelsenkirchen:** Musiktheater im Revier, 4650 Gelsenkirchen; Gen. Music Dir Neil Varon.

**Philharmonisches Orchester der Stadt Nürnberg:** Städtische Bühnen Nürnberg, Musiktheater, Richard-Wagner-Platz 2–10, Nürnberg; Gen. Music Dir Eberhard Kloke.

**Philharmonisches Orchester des Staatstheaters Mainz GmbH:** Gutenbergplatz 7, 6500 Mainz 1; Gen. Music Dir Peter Erckens.

**Philharmonisches Orchester Erfurt:** Placidus-Muth-Strasse 1, 99084 Erfurt; tel. 0361 22330; website www.theater-erfurt.de; Gen. Music Dir Walter E. Gugerbauer.

**Philharmonisches Orchester Frankfurt an der Oder:** Collegienstrasse 7, 1200 Frankfurt an der an Oder; Gen. Music Dir Nikos Athinäos.

**Philharmonisches Orchester Freiburg:** Bertoldstrasse 46, 79098 Freiburg; tel. 49 761 2012807; website www.theater.freiburg.de; Music Dir Kwamé Ryan.

**Philharmonisches Orchester Gera:** Bühnen der Stadt Gera, Küchengartenalle 2, 07548 Gera; tel. 365 82790; fax 365 827 9135; Music Dir Wolfgang Wappler.

**Philharmonisches Orchester Hagen:** Elberfelder Strasse 65, 58095 Hagen 1; website www.theater.hagen.de; Gen. Music Dir Gerhard Markson.

**Philharmonisches Orchester Heidelberg:** Friedrichstrasse 5, 69117 Heidelberg; e-mail info@heidelberger-philharmoniker.de; website www.heidelberger-philharmoniker.de; Gen. Music Dir Thomas Kalb.

**Philharmonisches Orchester Regensburg:** Bismarckplatz 7, 08468 Regensburg; Gen. Music Dir Hilary Griffiths.

**Philharmonisches Staatsorchester Halle:** Kleine Brauhausstrasse 26, 06108 Halle an der Saale; tel. 49 345 221 3001; fax 49 345 221 3010; e-mail philharmonie@halle.de; website www.staatsorchester-halle.de; Gen. Music Dir Hendrik Vestmann.

**Philharmonisches Staatsorchester Hamburg:** Grosse Theaterstrasse 34, 20354 Hamburg; e-mail info@philharmonisches-staatsorchester-hamburg.de; website www.philharmnisches-staatsorchester-hamburg.de; Gen. Music Dir Ingo Metzmacher; Man. Peter Ruzicka.

**Pro Arte Ensemble Mainz e V:** Werderstrasse 8, 6200 Wiesbaden; Music Dir Juan Levy.

**Radiokammerorchester Hamburg:** Zum Forellenbach 11, 22113 Oststeinbek; tel. 040 712 3701; fax 040 713 8525; Music Dir Karl Henke.

**Radio-Sinfonie-Orchester Frankfurt:** Bertramstrasse 8, 60320 Frankfurt; tel. 069 155 2071; fax 069 155 2720; e-mail rso-frankfurt@hr-online.de; website www.rso-frankfurt.de; Orchestra Man. Medi Gasteiner-Girth.

**Radio-Sinfonieorchester Stuttgart des SWR:** 70150 Stuttgart; tel. 49 711 929-2590; fax 49 711 929-4053; Chief Conductor Roger Norrington; Orchestra Man. Felix Fischer.

**Remscheider Symphoniker:** Stadt Remscheid, Kulturverwaltungsamt, Konrad-Adenauer-Strasse 31/33, 5630 Remscheid; Gen. Music Dir Reinhard Seifried.

**Reussisches Kammerorchester:** Bühnen der Stadt Gera, Küchengartenalle 2, 6500 Gera; Music Dir Herbert Voigt.

**Rheinisches Kammerorchester Köln:** Steinfelder Gasse 11, 5000 Cologne 1; Music Dir Jan Corazolla.

**Robert Schumann Philharmonie:** Pf 756, 09007 Chemnitz.

**Robert-Schumann-Philharmonie:** Chemnitz, Käthe-Kollwitz-Strasse 7, 09111 Chemnitz; website www.theater-chemnitz.de; Gen. Music Dir Niksa Bareza.

**Rundfunkorchester des Hessischen Rundfunks:** Bertramstrasse 8, 60320 Frankfurt am Main 1; Music Dir Peter Falk; Dir of Music Programming Leo Karl Gerhartz.

**Rundfunkorchester des Südwestfunks:** Fliegerstrasse 36, 6750 Kaiserslautern; Music Dir Klaus Arp; Dir of Music Programming Dr Reimund Hess.

**Rundfunkorchester Hannover:** Rudolf-von-Benningsen-Ufer 22, 3000 Hannover; Chief Conductor Bernhard Klee.

**Rundfunk-Sinfonieorchester Berlin:** Haus des Rundfunks, Masurenallee 8–14, 14057 Berlin; website www.rso-berlin.com; Chief Conductor Marek Janowski.

**Rundfunk-Sinforneorchester Saarbrücken:** Funkhaus Halberg, Pf 1050, 6600 Saarbrücken; Chief Conductor: Günther Henbig; Dir of Music Programming: Dr Sobine Tomek.

**Saarländisches Staatsorchester Saarbrücken:** Schillerplatz, 6600 Saarbrücken; Gen. Music Dir Jun Märkl.

**Sächsische Staatskapelle Dresden:** Theaterplatz 2, 8010 Dresden.

**Schleswig-Holsteinisches Sinfonieorchester:** Rathausstrasse 22, 24937 Flensburg; tel. 0461 141000; website www.sh-landestheater.de; Gen. Music Dir Gerard Oskamp.

**Sinfonieorchester des Theaters der Hansestadt Stralsund:** Olaf-Palme-Platz, 2300 Stralsund; Music Dir Daniel Kleiner.

**Sinfonieorchester Wuppertal:** Spinnstrasse 4, 5600 Wuppertal; e-mail info@sinfonieorchester-wuppertal.de; website www.sinfonieorchester-wuppertal.de; Gen. Music Dir George Hanson.

**Sinfonietta Köln:** Auf der Kuhle 11, 5250 Engelskirchen; Music Dir Cornelius Frowein.

**Städtisches Orchester Aachen:** Stadttheater, 5100 Aachen.

**Städtisches Orchester Bremerhaven:** Theodor-Heuss-Platz, Pf 12051, 2850 Bremerhaven; Gen. Music Dir Leo Plettner.

**Städtisches Orchester Trier:** Am Augustinerhof, 5500 Trier; Gen. Music Dir Reinhard Petersen.

**Städtisches Philharmonisches Orchester Würzburg:** Theaterstrasse 21, 8700 Würzburg; Gen. Music Dir Jonathan Seers.

**Staatliches Orchester Sächsen:** Chemnitzer Strasse 46, 9125 Grüna.

**Staatskapelle Berlin:** Unter den Linden 7, 10117, Berlin; tel. 49 30 2035 4555; fax 49 30 2035 4480; website www.staatsoper-berlin.de; Gen. Music Dir Daniel Barenboim.

**Staatskapelle Weimar:** Theaterplatz 2, 99423 Weimar; website www.nationaltheater-weimar.de; Gen. Music Dir Julia Miehe.

**Staatsorchester Braunschweig:** Orchestervarstand Am Theater, 38100 Braunschweig; website www.staatsorchesterbraunschweig.de; Gen. Music Dir Jonas Alber.

**Staatsorchester Rheinische Philharmonie:** Eltzerhostrasse 6a, 56068 Koblenz; tel. 0261 30 12272; fax 0261 3012 277; e-mail info@rheinische-philharmonie.de; website www.rheinische-philharmonie.de; Gen. Music Dir Shao-Chia Lü Man. Hans Richard Stracke.

**Staatsorchester Stuttgart:** Oberer Schlossgarten 6, 70173 Stuttgart; website www.staatstheater-stuttgart.de; Gen. Music Dir Gabriele Ferro.

**Staatsphilharmonie Rheinland-Pfalz:** Heinigstrasse 40, 67059 Ludwigshafen; tel. 621 5990999; fax 621 5990950; website www.staatsphilharmonie.de; Music Dir Ari Rasilainen; Man. Raimund Gress.

**Stuttgarter Kammerorchester e V (Stuttgart Chamber Orchestra):** Johann-Sebastian-Bach-Platz, 70178 Stuttgart; tel. 49 711 6192121; fax 49 711 6192122; e-mail info@stuttgarter-kammerorchester.de; website www.stuttgarter-kammerorchester.de; Music Dir: Dennis Russell Davies; Man. Dir: Timan Kuttenkeuler.

**Stuttgarter Philharmoniker:** Leonhardblatz 28, 70182 Stuttgart; tel. 0711 216 7843; e-mail philharmoniker@stuttgart.de; website www.stuttgart.de/philharmoniker; Gen. Music Dir Jörg-Peter Weigle.

**Südwestdeutsche Philharmonie Konstanz:** Spanierstrasse 3, 7750 Konstanz; Gen. Music Dir Petr Altrichter.

**Südwestdeutsches Kammerorchester Pforzheim (South-West German Chamber Orchestra, Pforzheim):** Westliche Karl-Friedrich-Strasse 257a, 75172 Pforzheim; tel. 49 7231 464644; fax 49 7231 464643; e-mail swdko-pforzheim@t-online.de; website www.swdko.de; Music Dir: Sebastian Tewinkel; Man.: Andreas Herrmann.

**Südwestfälische Philharmonie:** Im Langen Feld 2, Pf 1320, 5912 Hilchenbach; Music Dir Hiroshi Kodama; Man. Volker Mattern.

**SWF-Sinfonieorchester Baden-Baden:** Hans-Bredow-Strasse, 7570 Baden-Baden; Chief Conductor Michael Gielen; Man. Mathias Weigmann.

**Symphonieorchester der Stadt Münster:** Neubrückenstrasse 63, 4400 Münster; Gen. Music Dir Will Humburg.

**Symphonieorchester der Stadt Solingen:** Konrad-Adenauer-Strasse 71, 5650 Solingen; Gen. Music Dir Christian Süss.

**Symphonieorchester des Bayerischen Rundfunks:** Rundfunkplatz 1, 8000 Munich; Chief Conductor Zubin Mehta.

**Telemann-Kammerorchester Sachsen-Anhalt:** Institut für Auffuhrungspraxis Michaelstein, Pf 24, 3720 Blankenburg; Music Dir Eitelfriedrich Thom.

**Theaterorchester Senftenberg:** Rathenaustrasse 6/8, 7840 Senftenberg; Music Dir Michael Keschke.

**Thüringen Philharmonie Suhl:** Bahnhofstrasse 8–10, Pf 306, 6000 Suhl; Gen. Music Dir Olaf Koch.

**Thüringer Symphoniker Saalfeld/Rudolstadt:** Thüringer Landestheater Rudolstadt, Anger 1, 6820 Rudolstadt; Music Dir Oliver Weder.

**Thüringisches Kammerorchester Weimar:** Theaterplatz 2, 5300 Weimar; Conductors Max Pommer, Claus Gebauer.

**Virtuosi Saxoniae:** Welterstrasse 16, 8029 Dresden; Music Dir Ludwig Güttler.

**Vogtlandphilharmonie:** Weinholdstrasse 7, 9800 Reichenbach; Music Dir Stefan Fraas.

**Waiblinger Kammerorchester e V:** Friedemann Enssle, Lindauer Strasse 40, 7150 Backnang; Music Dir Gerd Budday.

**Westdeutsche Sinfonia:** Am Kreispark 32, Pf 310154, 5090 Leverkusen; Music Dir Dirk Joeres.

**Württembergische Philharmonie Reutlingen:** Wilhelmstrasse 69, 7410 Reutlingen; Gen. Music Dir Roberto Paternostro.

**Württembergisches Kammerorchester Heilbronn:** Pf 3830, 7100 Heilbronn; Music Dir Jörg Faerber.

## Greece

**Athens Radio Symphony Orchestra:** 432 Messioghion Street, 15310 Athens; tel. 30 1 639 2721; fax 30 1 639 6012; Chair. Mikis Theodorakis.

**Athens State Orchestra:** 17-19 Vas. Georgious B'Str, 10675 Athens; tel. 30 2 1072576013; fax 30 2 10 72 57 600; Artistic Dir Aris Garoufalis.

**Orchestra of Colours:** 18 Alexandrou Soutsou, 10671 Athens; tel. 30 1 362 8074; fax 30 1 362 1477; Artistic Dir George Kouroupos.

**Thessaloniki State Symphony Orchestra:** 21 Ippodromiou Street, 54630 Thessaloniki; tel. 30 31 589156; fax 30 31 604854; e-mail koth@otenet.gr; Dir Mikis Michaelides; Pres. Konstantinos A. Yakoumis.

**Tsakalof Symphony Orchestra and Opera:** Platia G. Stavrou 5, 45444 Ioannina; tel. 30 651 33300; fax 30 651 70714; Principal Conductor George Chlitsios; Gen. Dir Aspasia Zerva.

## Guatemala

**Orquesta Sinfónica Nacional:** 3a Avenida 4-61, Zona 1, Guatemala City.

## Honduras

**Orquesta Sinfónica Nacional:** PO Box 4087, Tegucigalpa; tel. 504 220 7206; website www.osnh.hn; Music Dir Ramiro Soriano-Arce; Exec. Dir Jim Andonie.

## Hong Kong

**Hong Kong Philharmonic Orchestra:** Level 8, Administration Building, Hong Kong Cultural Centre, 10 Salisbury Road, Kowloon; tel. 852 2721-2030; fax 852 2311-6229; website www.hkpo.com; Chief Conductor and Artistic Dir: Edo de Waart; CEO: Paul S. W. Leung.

## Hungary

**Budapest Chamber Orchestra Franz Liszt:** Kiskorona utca 7, 1036 Budapest; tel. 1 250 4938; fax 1 270 0846; Dir János Rolla.

**Budapest Concert Orchestra MAV:** Muzeum utca 11, 1088 Budapest; tel. 36 1 338 2664; fax 36 1 338 4085; e-mail bcorch.mav@matavnet.hu; website www.bmc.hu/mav; Music Dir Tamás Gál; Man. Dir Géza Kovécs.

**Budapest Festival Orchestra:** Vörösmarty tér 1, 1369 Budapest; Music Dirs Ivan Fischer, Zoltán Kocsis; Man. Ildikó Gedényi.

**Budapest Philharmonic Orchestra:** Hajos utca 8–10, 1061 Budapest; tel. 36 1 3319 478; fax 36 1 138 8910; website www.bpo.hu; Music Dir Rico Saccani.

**Budapest Symphony Orchestra of the Hungarian Radio:** Brody Sandor utca 5–7, 1800, Budapest; tel. 36 1 328 8326; fax 36 1 328 8910; e-mail kelenta@iroda.radio.hu; Chief Musical Dir Tamas Vasary; Man. Dir Apor Héthy.

**Debrecen Philharmonic Orchestra:** Simonffy utca 1/c, 4025 Debrecen; tel. and fax 36 52 412 395; Artistic Dir Imre Kollar.

**Hungarian National Philharmonic Orchestra:** Vörösmarty tér 1, 1364 Budapest; tel. 36 1 411 6600; fax 36 1 422 6699; website www.hunphilharmonic.org.hu; Music Dir Gilbert Varga.

**Hungarian Symphony Orchestra:** 10–12 Pava utca, 1094, Budapest; tel. 36 1 215 5770; fax 36 1 215 5462; e-mail btg@tza.hu; website www.orchestra.matav.hu; Music Dir Tamás Vásáry.

**Nord Hungarian Symphony Orchestra Miskolc:** Fábián utca 6a, 3525 Miskolc; tel. 36 46 323488; fax 36 46 351497; Music Dir László Kovács; Man. László Sir.

**Pécs Symphony Orchestra:** Kossuth Lajos utca 19, 7621 Pécs; Music Dir Nicolas Pasquet; Admin. Péter Szkladányi.

**Savaria Symphony Orchestra:** Thököly utca 14, 9700 Szombathely; tel. 36 94 314 472; fax 36 94 316 808; website www.savaria-symphony.hu; Music Dir Robert Houlihan; Man. Tibor Menyhárt.

**Szeged Symphony Orchestra:** Festö utca 6, 6721 Szeged; tel. 36 62 420 256; fax 36 62 426 102; e-mail orch@symph-szeged.hu; website www.symph-szeged.hu; Dir and Principal Conductor: Sandor Gyüdi.

## Iceland

**Iceland Symphony Orchestra:** Háskólabió v/Hagatorg, PO Box 7052, 127 Reykjavík; tel. 354 545 2500; fax 354 562 4475; e-mail sinfonia@sinfonia.is; website www.sinfonia.is; Music Dir Rico Saccani; Man. Runólfur Birgir Leifsson.

**Reykjavík Chamber Orchestra:** Hauhlid 14, 105 Reykjavík; Man. Rut Ingolfsdottir.

## India

**Kolkata Symphony Orchestra:** 6B Sunny Park, Kolkata 700019.

**Delhi Symphony Orchestra:** 2 Humayun Road, New Delhi 110003; tel. 4623431; fax 24361918.

## Ireland

**Irish Chamber Orchestra:** Foundation Building, University of Limerick, Castletroy, Limerick; tel. 353 61 202620; fax 353 61 202617; e-mail ico@ul.ie; website www.icorch.com; Chief Exec. John Kelly; Artistic Dir Nicholas McGegan.

**Radio Telefis Éireann (RTÉ) Concert Orchestra:** Radio Telefis Éireann, Donnybrook, Dublin 4; tel. 353 1 208 2779; fax 353 1 208 2511; e-mail Anthony .Long@rte.ie; website www.rte.ie/music; Gen. Man.: Anthony Long; Principal Conductor: Laurent Wagner.

**Radio Telefis Éireann (RTÉ) National Symphony Orchestra:** National Concert Hall, Earlsfort Terrace, Dublin 2; tel. 353 1 208 2530; fax 353 1 208 2160; e-mail westerm@rte.ie; Exec. Dir Martyn Westermann.

## Israel

**Israel Chamber Orchestra:** Amot Mishpat House, 8 Shaul Ha'melech Blvd, 64733 Tel-Aviv; tel. 972 3 696 1167; fax 972 3 691 0104; e-mail ico2000@ netvision.net.iz; Music Dir: Noam Sheriff; Gen. Dir: Arie Bar-Droma; Chair.: Avigdor Levin.

**Israel Kibbutz Orchestra:** 60990 Shefayim; tel. 972 9 9503715; fax 972 9 9523643; Music Dir Noam Yeny; Man. Aharon Kidron; formerly Kibbutz Chamber Orchestra.

**Israel Northern Symphony Haifa:** PO Box 6746, 1a Keller Street, 34483 Haifa; tel. 972 4 836 3131; fax 972 4 837 6355; Music Dir Ronald Zollman.

**Israel Philharmonic Orchestra:** PO Box 23500, 1 Huberman Street, 61231 Tel-Aviv; tel. 972 3 629 3345; fax 972 3 629 0097; Music Dir Zubin Mehta; Gen. Sec. Avi Shoshani.

**Israel Pro-Musica Orchestra:** PO Box 7191, 31071 Haifa; Music Dir Dalia Atlas.

**Israel Sinfonietta:** Derech Hameshachrerim 12, 84299 Beer Sheva; tel. 7 623 1616; fax 7 623 5412;Artistic Dir Uri Mayer; Man. Misha Grass.

**Jerusalem Symphony Orchestra:** PO Box 4640, 91040 Jerusalem; tel. 972 2 5660211; fax 972 2 5669117; Music Dir David Shallon; Man. Dir Zusia Rodan; Artistic Dir Gideon Paz.

**Netanya Orchestra:** PO Box 464, 42103 Netanya; Music Dir Samuel Lewis; Gen. Man. Yafe Duek.

**Ramat Gan Chamber Orchestra:** PO Box 138, 13 Hertzel Street, Ramat Gan; Music Dir Zeev Steinberg; Man. Sarah Lash-Yolowitz.

**Rishon Le-Zion Symphony Orchestra:** 5 Habanim Street, 75254 Rishon Le-Zion; tel. 972 3 948 4842; fax 972 3 948 4843; Music Dir Asher Fisch; Gen. Dir Menachem Shai; Asst Conductor Ilan Schul.

**Technion Symphony Orchestra:** Churchill Auditorium, 32000 Haifa; Music Dir Dalia Atlas.

**Young Israel Philharmonic:** PO Box 11292, 1 Huberman Street, 61112 Tel-Aviv; Music Dir Ze-ev Dorman; Admin. Dir Yaffa Sharett.

## Italy

**I Solisti Veneti:** Piazzale Pontecorvo 4A, 35121 Padua; tel. 49 666 128; fax 49 875 2598; Conductor Claudio Scimone; Man. Mirella Gualandi.

**Orchestra Alessandro Scarlatti di Napoli della Radiotelevisione Italiana:** Via Marconi 5, 80125 Naples; Artistic Dir Massimo Fargnoli.

**Orchestra da Camera di Padova e del Veneto:** Via Marsilio da Padova 19, 35139 Padua; website www.pvorchestra.org; Artistic Sec. Cecilia Montovani.

**Orchestra della Toscana:** Via Verdi 20, 50122 Florence; tel. 39 55 234 0710; fax 39 55 200 8035; e-mail info@orchestradellatoscana.it; website www .orchestradellatoscana.it;

**Artistic Dir Sergio Sablich; Principal Conductor Lu Jia.**

**Orchestra Filarmonica Marchigiana:** Vicolo Aranci 2, 60121 Ancona; tel. 39 071 206168; fax 39 071 206730; e-mail filarmonica.marche@libero.it; Artistic Dir Gustav Kuhn.

**Orchestra Sinfonica dell'Accademia Nazionale de Santa Cecilia:** Via Vittoria 6, 00187 Rome; Music Dir Daniele Gatti.

**Orchestra Sinfonica di Milano della Radiotelevisione Italiana:** Via Conservatorio 12, 21011 Milan; Artistic Dir Mario Messinis.

**Orchestra Sinfonica di San Remo:** Corso Cavallotti 51, 18038 San Remo; Artistic Dir Giovanni Guglielmo.

**Orchestra Sinfonica di Torino della Radiotelevisione Italiana (RAI):** Piazza Fratelli Rossaro 15, 10124 Turin; tel. 39 11 812 3424; fax 39 11 817 7410; Artistic Dir Daniele Spini; Orchestral Man. Maria Sciavolino; Principal Conductor Eliahu Inbal.

**Orchestra Sinfonica Haydn di Bolzano e Trento:** Via Gilm 1A, 39100 Bolzano; tel. 0471 975 031; fax 0471 327868; e-mail haydn@dnet.it; website www.haydn-orchestra.com; Artistic Dir Hubert Stuppner.

**Orchestra Sinfonica Nazionale della RAI:** Piazza Rossaro, 10124 Torino; tel. 39 011 4961; fax 39 011 817 7410; Artistic Dir Daniele Spini.

**Orchestra Sinfonica Siciliana:** Via G. La Farina 29, 90141 Palermo; tel. 39 91 300609; fax 39 91 300155; Artistic Dir Giuseppe Catalso; Conductor Gabriele Ferro.

**Orchestra Sinfonico dell'Emilia Romagna Arturo Toscanini:** Via G. Tartini 13, 43100 Parma; tel. 39 521 274417; fax 39 251 272134.

## Japan

**Hiroshima Symphony Orchestra:** 15-10 Hatchobori, Naka-ku, Hiroshima 730; tel. 81 82 222 8448; fax 818 2222 8447; Music Dir Kazuyoshi Akiyaima.

**Japan Philharmonic Orchestra:** 1-6-1 Umezato, Suginami-ku, Tokyo 166; tel. 81 3 5378 6311; fax 81 3 5378 6161; e-mail office@japanphil.or.jp; website www.jphil.or.jp; Music Dir Kenichiro Kobayashi; Man. Dir Shuhei Deguchi.

**Kanagawa Philharmonic Orchestra:** Hanami-dai 4-2, Hodogaya-ku, Yokohama 240; tel. 81 45 331 4001; fax 81 45 331 4022; website www .kanaphil.com; Music Dir Yuzo Toyama; Exec. Dir Yutaka Ueno.

**Kansai Philharmonic Orchestra:** 7F Harp Oak 26h, 1-2-4 Benten, Minato-ku, Osaka-shi, Osaka; tel. 06 557 1381; fax 06 557 1383; Conductor Uri Mayer.

**Kobe Philharmonic Orchestra:** 1-9-1 San-no-miya-cho, Chuo-ku, Kobe-shi 650; Conductor Chitaru Asahina.

**Kunaicho Gakuba (Imperial Court Orchestra):** Imperial Palace, Tokyo 100.

**Kyoto Symphony Orchestra:** 103 Izumoji Tatemoto-cho, Kita-ku, Kyoto 603-8134; tel. 81 75 222 0331; fax 81 75 222 0332; website www.city.kyoto.jp/ bunshi/symphony; Chief Conductor: Naoto Otomo; Chief Guest Conductor: Hiroyuki Iwaki; Artistic Man. Mitsuru Yoshida; f. 1956; performs some 90 concerts each year, including 15 subscription concerts with world-famous conductors and soloists, and a series of concerts for children.

**Kyushu Symphony Orchestra:** 1-11-50 NoNaKuma, Jonan-ku, Fukuoka-shi 814-01; tel. 092 822 8855; fax 092 822 8833; Music Dir Ishimaru Hiroshi; Chair. Kenzou Tanaka.

**Nagoya Philharmonic Orchestra:** Nagoya City Music Plaza 4f 1-4-10, Kanayama Naka-ku Nagoya 460-0022; tel. 81 52 322 2774; fax 81 52 322 3066; e-mail eigyou@nagoya-hil.or.jp; Conductor Iimori Tajjiro; Man. Susumu Nonoyama.

**New Japan Philharmonic Orchestra:** Sumia Triphony Hall, 1-2-3 Kinshi, Sumida-ku, Tokyo 130-0013; tel. 813 5610 3820; fax 813 3822 0729; Hon. Artistic Dir Seiji Ozawa; Man. Chiyoshige Matsubara.

**NHK (Japan Broadcasting Corporation) Symphony Orchestra:** 2-16-49 Takanawa, Minato-ku, Tokyo 108; tel. 81 3 5793 8111; fax 81 3 3443 0278; Music Dir Charles Dutoit; Exec. Dir Takeshi Hara.

**Orchestra Ensemble Kanazawa:** Hirosaka 1-7-1, Kanazawa 920; tel. 076 232 0171; fax 076 232 0172; e-mail office@oek.jp; website www.oek.jp; Music Dir Hiroyuki Iwaki; Man. Dir Masayuki Yamada.

**Osaka Philharmonic Orchestra:** 1-1-44 Kishinosato, Nishinari-ku, Osaka 557-0041; tel. 81 6 6656 7711; fax 81 6 6656 7714; Music Dir Takashi Asahina; Sec.-Gen. Shoji Onodera.

**Osaka Symphony Orchestra:** 4-3-9 203 Tezukayama naka, Sumiyoshi-ku, Osaka 558; Music Dir Thomas Sanderling; Gen. Man. Tetsuo Shikishima.

**Sapporo Symphony Orchestra:** c/o Kyoiku Bunka Kaikan, Nishi 13-chome, Kita 1-jo, Chuo-ku, Sapporo 060; tel. 011 251 4774; fax 011 251 4776; Conductor Kazuyoshi Akiyama; Pres. Hideji Kitagawa.

**Shinsei Nihon Symphony Orchestra:** Maruishi Building, 3-16-4 Nishi Ikebukuro, Toshima-ku, Tokyo 171; Music Dir Ryusuke Numjiri; Exec. Dir Saburo Kurematsu.

**Tokyo City Philharmonic Orchestra:** 1-19-1-2-3 Sumiyoshi Koutu-ku, Tokyo, 135-0002; tel. 813 5624 4001; fax 813 5624 4114; e-mail mail@cityphil .gr.jp; website www.cityphil.jp; Music Dir Naohiro Totsuka; Exec. Dir Tatatsugu Kuwahata.

**Tokyo Metropolitan Symphony Orchestra:** c/o Tokyo Bunkakaikan, 5-45 Ueno Park, Taito-ku, Tokyo 110-0007; tel. 81 3 3822 0727; fax 81 3 3822 0729; Chief Conductor Koizumi Kauhiro; Exec. Dir Hiroshi Kainuma.

**Tokyo Philharmonic Symphony Orchestra:** Eiritsu Building, 3-3 Kanda Kajicho, Chiyoda-ku, Tokyo 10; tel. 81 3 3256 9696; fax 81 3 3256 9698; Conductor Kazushi Ohno; Dir Shogo Matsuki.

**Tokyo Symphony Orchestra:** 2-23-5 Hyakunin-cho, Shinjuku-ku, Tokyo 169-0073; tel. 03 3369 1661; fax 03 3360 8249; e-mail tokyosymphony@ musicinfo.com; website www.tokyosymphony.com; Music Dir Kazuyoshi Akiyama; Gen. Man. Shigteto Kanayama.

**Yomiuri Nippon Symphony Orchestra:** 7F Daiichi Nurihiko Bldg, 2-9-2 Kyobashi Chuo-ku, Tokyo 104-0031; tel. 81 3 3562-1540; fax 81 3 3562-1544; e-mail yomikyo@k3.dion.ne.jp; website yomikyo.yomiuri.co.jp; Principal Conductor: Gerd Albrecht; Dir Gen.: Takao Ohuchi.

## Republic of Korea

**Busan Philharmonic Orchestra:** 848-4 Daeyon 4 Dong, Nam-gu, Pusan; tel. 82 51 625 8130; fax 82 51 625 8138; e-mail 61pwc@hanmail.net; Music Dir Sung Kwak; Gen. Man. Won-Chul Park.

**Korean Broadcasting System (KBS) Symphony Orchestra:** 18 Yoido-dong, Youngdungpo-gu, Seoul 150-790; website www.kbsso.kbs.co.kr; Chief Conductor Othmar Maga.

**Seoul Philharmonic Orchestra:** 81-3 Sejong-Ro, Chong Ro-Gu, Seoul 110-050; tel. 82 2 736 2721; fax 82 2 738 0948; website www.seoulphilharmonic .org; Music Dir Kyung-Soo Won.

## Latvia

**Latvian National Symphony Orchestra:** 6 Amatu St, 1664 Riga; tel. 371 722 9357; fax 371 722 4850; e-mail secretary@lnso.lv; website www.lmuza.lv; Music Dir Olan Eits; Gen. Man. Ilona Brege.

**Latvian Philharmonic Chamber Orchestra:** Iagrera Str, Riga, 1050; tel. 371 9223201; fax 371 2451038; Man. Dir Linda Liepzig.

**Latvian Radio and Television Symphony Orchestra:** c/o Latvian Radio and Television, Riga.

**Riga Chamber Orchestra:** Kalku St 11a, 226350 Riga.

**Liepaja Symphony Orchestra:** Graudu 50, 3401, Liepaja; tel. 371 342 5538; fax 371 348 1478; e-mail lsovija@mail.anet.lv; Artistic Dir Imants Resnis.

## Lithuania

**Lithuanian National Symphony Orchestra:** Ausroz Vartu 5, 2001 Vilnius; tel. 370 2 627 047; fax 370 2 622 859; e-mail info@filharmonija.lt; Artistic Dir and Chief Conductor Juozas Domarkas.

**Lithuanian State Symphony Orchestra:** Zygimantu 6, 2600 Vilnius; tel. 370 2 628127; fax 370 2 220966; e-mail lvso@lvso.lt; website www.lvso.lt/en; Music Dir Gintaras Rinkevicius; Gen. Dir Gintautas Kevisas.

## Luxembourg

**Orchestre Philharmonique du Luxembourg:** BP 2243, 1022 Luxem-bourg; tel. 352 22 99 01205; fax 352 22 99 98; e-mail info@opl.lu; website www .opl.lu; Chief Conductor: Bramwell Tovey; Man. Benedikt Fohr.

## Malaysia

**Malaysian Philharmonic Orchestra:** Level 2, Tower 2, Petronas Twin Towers, Kuala Lumpur; tel. 603 581 3208; fax 603 581 3216; Musical Dir Kees Bakels.

## Mexico

**National Symphony Orchestra of Mexico:** Regina 52, Centro, 06080 Mexico City, DF; tel. 52 5 709 8118; fax 52 5 709 3533; Musical Dir Enrique Arturo Diemecke; Gen. Man. Aleiandro Toledano.

**Orquesta de Cámera de Bellas Artes:** Extemplo de Santa Teresa La Antigua, Lic Verdad 8 y Moneda, Centro, 06060 Mexico City, DF; Music Dir Ildefonso Cedillo; Man. Maricarmen Guerrero Meneses.

**Orquesta Filarmónica de Jalisco:** Teatro Degollado, 44100 Guadalajara, Jalisco; tel. 33 3658 3812; fax 52 614 9366; website www.ofj.com.mx; Music Dir José Guadalupe Flores; Man. Silvia Susana Hernández Huerta.

**Orquesta Filarmónica de la Ciudad de México:** Periférico Sur 5141, Sala Ollin Yoliztli, 14030 Mexico City, DF; tel. 52 905 606 8933; fax 52 905 606 8401; Principal Conductor Luis Herrera de la Fuente.

**Orquesta Filarmónica de la Universidad Autónoma de México:** Avda Insurgentes Sur 3000, Sala Nezahualcóyotl, 04510 Mexico City, DF, Coyoacán; Music Dir Ronald Zollman; Gen. Man. Maricarmen Costero.

**Orquesta Sinfónica del Estado de México:** Plaza Fray Andrés de Castro, Edificio C, 1°, Toluca, Mex C.P. 5000; tel. 52 72 44 5219; fax 52 72 45 6216; Music Dir Enrique Bátiz; Gen. Man. Maria Dolores Castillo.

**State of Mexico Symphony Orchestra:** Avenida José Vicente Villada No. 406 1er Piso, Col. Centro, 50000 Toluca; tel. 52 7 214 5219; fax 52 7 215 6216; Musical Dir Enrique Batiz; Admin. Dir Alfredo Higuera Hernandez.

## Moldova

**Symphony Orchestra of the National Philharmonic of Moldova:** 78 Mitropolitul, Varlaam Str., 2012 Chisinau; tel. 373 244 5879; fax 373 223 3509; e-mail somnph@ch.moldpac.md; Chief Conductor Valentin Doni.

## Monaco

**Orchestre Philharmonique de Monte Carlo:** BP 139, Place du Casino, 98007 Monte Carlo; tel. 00 377 92 16 23 17; fax 00 377 92 15 08 71; e-mail info@ opmc.mc; website www.opmc.mc; Music Dir Marek Janowski; Dir René Croesi; Artistic Dir Chandler Cudlipp.

## Netherlands

**Amsterdam Baroque Orchestra:** Meerwag 23, 1405 BC Bussum; website www.tonkoopman.nl; Music Dir Ton Koopman; Gen. Man. Hans Meijer.

**Arnhem Philharmonic Orchestra:** Velperbuitensingel 12, PO Box 1180, 6801 BD Arnhem; tel. 31 26 442 2632; fax 31 26 443 9966; e-mail info@ hetgeldersorkest.nl; Principal Conductor Lawrence Renes.

**Brabants Philharmonisch Orkest:** J. Van Lieshoutstraat 5, 5611 EE Eindhoven; tel. 31 40 265 5699; fax 31 40 246 3459; e-mail info@ brabantsorkest.nl; Man. Dir Stan Paardehooper; Chief Conductor Marc Soustrot.

**Forum Filharmonisch:** PO Box 1321, 7500 BH Enschede; Gen. Man. J. M. Bal.

**Het Gelders Orkest:** Velperbuitensingel 12, 6828 CV Arnhem; tel. 31 26 442 2632; fax 31 26 443 9966; website www.hetgeldersorkest.nl; Principal Conductor Martin Sieghart; Gen. Admin. H. Hierck.

**Koninklijk Concertgebouworkest:** Jacob Obrechtstraat 51, 1071 KJ Amsterdam; tel. 31 20 20 679 2211; fax 31 20 676 3331; e-mail info@ concertgebouworkest.nl; website www.concertgebouworkest.nl; Chief Con-ductor Riccardo Chailly.

**Limburgs Symphonie Orkest:** Statenstraat 5, 6211 TB Maastricht; tel. 043 350 7000; fax 043 350 7025; e-mail info@lso.nl; website www.lso.nl; Chief Conductor Ed Spanjaard.

**Metropole Orkest:** PO Box 125, 1200 AC Hilversum; tel. 31 0 35 67 14 160; fax 31 0 35 67 14 171; website www.metropoleorchestra.com; Music Dir Dick Bakker; Man. Fred Dekker.

**Nederlands Philharmonisch Orkest:** Beurs van Berlage, Damrak 213, 1012 ZH Amsterdam; tel. 31 020 521 75 00; fax 31 20 622 9939; website www .orkest.nl; Music Dir Hartmut Haenchen; Man. Dr J. W. Loot.

**Noordhollands Philharmonisch Orkest:** Klokhuisplein 2A, 2011 HK Haarlem; tel. 31 235 319248; fax 31 235 32 8533; Music Dir Lucas Vis; Man. Casper Vogel.

**Noord-Nederlands Orkest:** Emmaplein 2, PO Box 818, 9700 AV Groningen; tel. 31 35 6714 140; fax 31 35 6714 171; website www.noordnederlandsorkest .nl; Man. A. L. E. Verberne.

**Radio Filharmonisch Orkest Holland:** Heuvellaan 33, PO Box 125, 1200 AC Hilversum; tel. 31 35 6714 130; fax 31 35 6714 171; e-mail rfo@mco.nl; website www.rfo.nl; Chief Conductor Edo de Waart; Man. Stefan Rosu.

**Radio Kamerorkest:** PO Box 125, 1200 JB Hilversum; tel. 31 35 6714150; fax 31 35 6714171; Conductor Frans Bruggen; Man. Ferdinand L. J. Vrijma.

**Radio Symphonie Orkest:** Heuvellaan 33, PO Box 125, 1200 AC Hilversum; tel. 31 0 35 671 41 40; fax 31 0 35 671 41 71; e-mail rso@mco.nl; website www.nl -rso.org; Chief Conductor Eri Klas; Gen. Man. Henk Smit.

**Residentie Orkest:** PO Box 11543, 2502 AM The Hague; tel. 31 070 88 00 200; fax 31 070 36 519 07; e-mail info@residentieorkest.nl; website www .residentieorkest.nl; Chief Conductor Jaap van Zweden; Man. H. Van den Akker.

**Rotterdams Philharmonisch Orkest:** PO Box 962, 3000 AZ Rotterdam; tel. 31 10 217 1760; fax 31 10 411 6215; e-mail art.dir@rpho.nl; Chief Conductor Valery Gergiev; Man. Paul Zeegers.

## New Zealand

**Auckland Philharmonia:** PO Box 56024, Dominion Road, Auckland, New Zealand; tel. 649 639 7073; fax 649 630 9687; e-mail ap@akl-phil.co.nz; website www.akl-phil.co.nz; Music Dir Miguel Harth Bedoya.

**Auckland Philharmonic Orchestra:** PO Box 56-024, Mount Eden, Auck-land; tel. 9 638 7073; fax 9 630 9687; Gen. Man. Lloyd Williams.

**Christchurch Symphony Orchestra:** St Elmos Court, 47 Hereford Street, Christchurch; tel. 64 3 379 3886; fax 64 3 379 3861; e-mail office@chsymph.co .nz; website www.csymph.co.nz; Music Dir: Marc Taddei.

**New Zealand Symphony Orchestra:** PO Box 6640, Wellington 6001; tel. 64 4 801 3890; fax 64 4 801 3891; e-mail info@nzso.co.nz; website www.nzso.co.nz; Musical Dir James Judd; Chief Exec. Mark Keyworth.

**Southern Sinfonia:** PO Box 5571, Dunedin; tel. 03 477 5623; fax 03 477 5628; e-mail sinfonia@earthlight.co.nz; Gen. Man. Philippa Harris.

**Wellington Sinfonia:** Level 2, Municipal Office Bldg, 101 Wakefield Street, Wellington; tel. 64 4 801 3882; fax 64 4 801 3888; website www .wellingtonsinfonia.co.nz; Gen. Man. Christine Pearce.

## Norway

**Bergen Filharmoniske Orkester:** Grieghallen, Lars Hilles Gate 3a, 5015 Bergen; tel. 47 5521 6228; fax 47 5531 8534; website www.harmonien.no; Principal Conductor: Andrew Litton; Gen. Man.: Lorentz Reitan; f. 1765, one of Norway's two national orchestras; puts on some 70–90 concerts each year, international and national tours.

**Norsk Kammerorkester (Norwegian Chamber Orchestra):** Pilestredet 7, 0180 Oslo; tel. 47 2242 0770; fax 47 38 022991; e-mail post@kso.no; Artistic Dir Iona Brown.

**Oslo Filharmoniske Orkester:** PO Box 1607 Vika, 0119 Oslo; tel. 47 2201 4900; fax 47 2201 4901; website www.oslophil.com; Chief Conductor Mariss Jansons; Man. Trond Okkelmo.

**Stavanger Symfoniorkester:** Sandvigå 27, Bjergsted, 4007 Stavanger; tel. 47 51508830; fax 47 51508839; e-mail post@sso.no; website www.sso.no; Admin. Dir Thorstein Granly; Man. Dir Erik Landmark.

**Trondheim Symfoniorkester:** PO Box 774, 7001 Trondheim; tel. 47 7353 9800; fax 47 7353 9801; e-mail post@tso.no; website www.tso.no; Artistic Dir Roar Leinan; Chief Conductor Daniel Harding.

## Panama

**Orquesta Sinfónica Nacional:** Apto 9190, Panama City 6; Conductor Eduardo Charpentier de Castro.

## Paraguay

**Orquesta Sinfónica de la Ciudad de Asunción:** México 145, Asunción; tel. 595 21 492416; e-mail sfa@pol.com.py; website www.sfa.org.py; Music Dir Luis Szarán.

**Philomúsica de Asunción:** Guillermo Arias 884 y Dr Paiva, Asunción; tel. and fax 595 21 424005; e-mail szaran@pol.com.py; website www.szaran.org.py; Contact Glenda Campos.

## Peru

**Orquesta Sinfónica Nacional:** Avda Javier Prado Este 2465, Lima 41; tel. and fax 225-8882; e-mail osnperu@telefonica.net.pe; Artistic Dir and Conductor: Armando Sánchez Málaga.

## Philippines

**Manila Symphony Orchestra:** Manila Metropolitan Theater, Liwasang Bonifacio, PO Box 664, Manila; Music Dir Alfredo Buenaventura.

**National Philharmonic Orchestra:** PO Box 2650, Makati, Metro, Manila; tel. 63 817 2601; fax 63 815 3483; Music Dir Redentor Romero.

**Philippine Philharmonic Orchestra:** Cultural Center of the Philippines, Roxas Blvd, Manila; tel. 63 2 832 1125; fax 63 2 832 3683; Music Dir Oscar Yatco; Exec. Dir Amelita Guevara.

## Poland

**Baltic State Philharmonic Orchestra:** Aleja Zwyci stwa 15, 80-219 Gdańsk.

**Białystok State Philharmonic Orchestra:** Podlesna 2, 15-227 Białystok; Music Dir Miroslaw Blaszczyk.

**Chopin Chamber Orchestra:** 25/54 ul Gabrieli Zapolskiej, 30-126 Kraków; tel. 12 637 0684; Music Dir and Man. Boguslaw Dawidów.

**Czestochowa Philharmonic Orchestra:** Wilsona 16, 42-202 Czestochowa; tel. 48 034 3244230; fax 48 034 34 37; e-mail filharmonia@filharmonia.com.pl; website www.filharmonia.com.pl; Man. Dir: Leszek F. Hadrian; Music Dir: Jerzy Swoboda.

**Filharmonia Poznańska im. Tadeusza Szeligosdkiego (Tadeusz Szeligowski Poznań Philharmonic Orchestra):** ul. Św. Marcin 81, 61-808 Poznań; tel. 61 852 47 08; fax 61 852 34 51; e-mail filharmonia@filharmonia.poznan.pl; website www.filharmonia.poznan.pl; Gen. and Artistic Dir: José Maria Florêncio.

**Jelenia Gora State Philharmonic Orchestra:** ul 22-go Lipca 60, 58-500 Jelenia Gora; Music Dir Tadeusz Wicherek; Dir Zuzanna Dziedzic.

**Kraków Philharmonic Orchestra Karol Szymanowski:** Zwierzyniecka 1, 31-103 Kraków; tel. and fax 48 12 422 4312; e-mail fk@filharmonia.krakow.pl; website www.filharmonia.krakow.pl; Music Dir and Chief Conductor: Tomasz Bugay; Man.: Anna Oberc.

**National Polish Radio Symphony Orchestra:** Plac Sejmu Slaskiego 2, 40-032 Katowice; tel. 48 32 2518903; fax 48 32 2571384; e-mail nospr@nospr.org.pl; website www.nospr.org.pl; Gen. and Programme Dir: Joanna Wnuk-Nazarowa.

**New Polish Radio Orchestra:** J. P. Woronicza 17, 00-950 Warsaw; Artistic Dir and Principal Conductor Tadeusz Strugala.

**Polish Chamber Orchestra:** Centrum Sztuki Studio, Palac Kultury i Nauki, 00901 Warsaw; tel. 48 22620 0138; e-mail imp@sinfoniavarsovia.com; Music Dir Franciszek Wybranczyk.

**Polska Filharmonic Baltycka:** ul Olowianka 1, 80-751 Gdańsk; tel. 48 58 30 52 040; fax 48 58 30 52 040.

**Pomeranian State Philharmonic Orchestra Ignacy Paderewski:** Libelta 16, 85-080 Bydgoszcz; tel. 52 21 09 20; fax 52 21 07 52.

**Rzeszów State Philharmonic Orchestra Artur Malawski:** Chopina 30, 35-055 Rzeszów; Music Dir Adam Natanek.

**Silesian State Philharmonic Orchestra:** Sokolska 2, 40-084 Katowice; tel. 48 32 597571; fax 48 32 589885; Music Dir Jerzy Swoboda.

**Sinfonia Varsovia:** Centrum Sztuki Studio, Palac Kultury i Nauki, 00901 Warsaw; e-mail imp@sinfoniavarsovia.com; Artistic Dir Krysztof Penderecki; Music Dir and Man. Franciszek Wybranczyk.

**Sudettic Philharmonic Orchestra:** Slowackiego 4, 58-3000 Walbrzych; tel. 842 41 80; fax 842 28 93; Artistic Dir and Chief Man. Jozef Wilkomirski.

**Szczecin State Philharmonic Orchestra Mieczyslaw Karlowicz:** Dzierzy skiego 1, 70-455 Szczecin; Music Dir Stefan Marczyk; Man. Jadwiga Igiel.

**Warsaw Chamber Orchestra:** ul Freta 28/8, 00-227 Warsaw; tel. 22 31 63 63; fax 22 48 76 66; Artistic Dir Marek Sewen.

**Warsaw Philharmonic Orchestra:** ul. Jasna 5, 00 950 Warsaw; tel. 48 22 5517101; fax 48 22 5517200; e-mail filharmonia@filharmonia.pl; website www.filharmonia.pl; Artistic and Gen. Dir: Antoni Wit; national orchestra of Poland.

**W. Lutoslawski Philharmonic in Wrocław:** ul. Pilsudskiego 19, 50-044 Wrocław; tel. 4871 342 20 01; fax 4871 342 89 80; e-mail biuro@filharmonia.wroclaw.pl; website www.filharmonia.wroclaw.pl; Gen. Dir: Lidia Geringer d'Oedenberg; Artistic Dir: Mariusz Smolij.

**Zielona Góra State Philharmonic Orchestra:** Plac Powsta ców Wielkopolskich 10, 65-075 Zielona Góra; Music Dir Czeslaw Grabowski.

## Portugal

**Orquestra Gulbenkian:** Fundação Calouste Gulbenkian, Serviço de Música, Avda de Berna 45a, 1067-001 Lisbon; tel. 351 21 782 3000; fax 351 21 782 3041; e-mail musica@gulbenkian.pt; Principal Conductor and Artistic Dir: Lawrence Foster.

**Orquestra Sinfónica do Porto:** Radiodifusao Portuguesa, Rua Candido Reis 74/10, 4000 Porto; Music Dir Gunther Arglebe.

**Orquestra Sinfónica Portuguesa:** Rua Serpa Pinto 9, 1200 Lisbon; tel. 351 1 343 1734; fax 351 1 343 1735; Chief Conductor and Artistic Dir Alvaro Cassuto.

## Romania

**Bucharest Chamber Orchestra:** Allée Ioanid 4, Bucharest 70259; Music Dir Ion Voicu; Man. Madeleine Cretu.

**Bucharest State Philharmonic Orchestra George Enescu:** Ateneul Roman, Franklin Str 1, Bucharest.

**Iasi Philharmonic:** Str Cuza Voda 29, 6600 Iasi; tel. 240 32 114601; fax 240 32 214160; e-mail filarmonicais@mail.dntis.ro; Artistic Dir Bujor Prelipcean.

**Rumanian Radio and Television Symphony Orchestra:** Str Nuferilor 62-64, 79756 Bucharest.

## Russia

**Bolshoi Symphony Orchestra:** Bolshoi Theater, Petrovka St 1, Moscow; tel. 7 095 292 6570; fax 7 095 292 9032; Music Dir and Conductor Mark Ermler.

**Ensemble XXI Moscow (Moscow International Chamber Orchestra):** Voznesensky Per 8/5, Moscow 103009; tel. and fax 7095 229 1221; e-mail info@ensemblexxi.org; website www.ensemblexxi.org; Artistic Dir and Conductor Lygia O'Riordan.

**Moscow Chamber Orchestra:** Ul Gorkogo 37, Moscow; tel. 7095 956 7677; e-mail info@moscowchamberorchestra.com; website www.moscowchamberorchestra.com; Musical Dir Constantine Orbelian.

**Moscow Philharmonic Orchestra:** Ul Gorkogo 37, Moscow; Chief Conductor Vassily Sinaisky.

**Russian National Symphony Orchestra:** Studio Moscow, Alexeya Tolstovo St 26-33, 103001 Moscow; tel. 7 095 290 6262; fax 7 095 292 6511; Conductor Mikhail Pletnev.

**Russian State Philharmonic Orchestra:** 18 Murmansky Proezd, App 77, 129075, Moscow; tel. 7095 233 8996; Chief Conductor Valery Poljansky.

**St Petersburg Chamber Orchestra:** ul Brodskogo 2, St Petersburg.

**St Petersburg Philharmonic Orchestra:** Mikhailovskaya St 2, 219011 St Petersburg; tel. 7 812 311 7331; fax 7 812 311 2126; Chief Conductor Yuri Temirkanov.

**State Radio and Television Symphony Orchestra:** 24 Malaya Nikitskaya, 12812 Moscow; tel. 095 290 05 01; fax 095 573 61 75; e-mail letter@rtvsymphony.ru; Chief Dir Anatoly Nemudrov.

**State Symphony Orchestra of Russia:** Arbat 35, 121835 Moscow; Chief Conductor Evgeny Svetlanov.

## Serbia and Montenegro

**Belgrade Philharmonic Orchestra:** Studentski Trg 11, 11000 Belgrade; tel. 38111187533; fax 38111187533; Gen. Man. Branka Cvejic-Mezei.

**Belgrade Radio and Television Symphony Orchestra:** Hilendarska 2, 11000 Belgrade.

## Singapore

**Singapore Symphony Orchestra Ltd:** 11 Empress Place, Second Floor, Victoria Memorial Hall, 179558 Singapore; tel. 65 6336 4417; fax 65 6336 6382; e-mail ssonet@singnet.com.sg; website www.sso.org.sg; Music Dir Lan Shui.

## Slovakia

**Capella Istropolitna:** Schillerove 23, 811 04 Bratislava; Music Dir Ewald Daniel; Man. Karol Kopernický.

**Musica Aeterna:** 816 01 Bratislava; Chief Conductor Peter Zajicek.

**Slovak Chamber Orchestra:** 816 01 Bratislava; Chief Conductor Bohdan Warchal.

**Slovak Philharmonic Orchestra:** 816 01 Bratislava; tel. 00 421 25443 3351; website www.filharm.sk; Chief Conductor Ondrej Lenárd; Man. Tatiana Schoeferová.

**Slovak State Philharmonic, Kosice:** Dom Umenia, Moyzesova 66, 04123 Kosice; tel. 421 55 622 7216; e-mail sfk@sfk.sk; Chief Conductor Tomás Koutnik; Exec. Dir Julius Klein.

**Symphony Orchestra of the Slovak Radio:** Mýtna 1, 812 90 Bratislava; tel. 421 7/57273475; fax 421 7/57273386; Chief Conductor Robert Stankovsky; Man. Dir Milos Jurkovic.

## Slovenia

**Slovenian Philharmonic Orchestra:** Kongresni trg 10, 61000 Ljubljana; tel. 386 01 24 10 800; fax 386 01 24 10 900; e-mail slo-filharmonija@filharmonija.si; website www.filharmonija.si; Artistic Dir Marko Letonja.

**Slovenian Radio and Television Symphony Orchestra:** Tavcarjeva 17, 61000 Ljubljana.

## South Africa

**Cape Town Philharmonic Orchestra:** PO Box 4040, Cape Town 8000; tel. 27 21 418 9809; fax 27 21 425 1009; e-mail capephil@artscape.co.za; Principal Conductor Bernhard Ejueller.

**Cape Town Symphony Orchestra:** City Hall, Darling Street, Cape Town 8001.

**Kwa Zulu-Natal Philharmonic Orchestra:** PO Box 5353, Durban 4000; tel. 27 31 369 9438; fax 27 31 369 9559; e-mail kznpomar@iafrica.com; website www.kznpo.co.za; Artistic Dir Bongani Tembe.

**The National Orchestra:** PO Box 566, Pretoria 0001; Principal Conductor Carlo Franci; Gen. Man. Stephen Wikner.

**New Arts Philharmonic Orchestra (NAPOP):** PO Box 566, Pretoria 0001; tel. 27 12 322 1665; fax 27 12 322 3913; Principal Conductor Gerard Korsten.

## Spain

**Joven Orquesta Nacional de España:** Príncipe de Vergara, 28002 Madrid; Principal Conductor Edmon Colomer; Man. Juan Wesolowski y Fernández-Heredia.

**Orquesta Ciudad de Barcelona:** Via Laietan a 41, pral, 08003 Barcelona; Music Dir Garcia Navarro; Man. Jaume Masferrer.

**Orquesta del Principado de Asturias:** Corrado del Obispo s/n, Edificio del Conservatorio de Música Eduardo Martínez Torner, 33003 Oviedo; Music Dir Maximiano Valdes.

**Orquesta Nacional de España:** Príncipe de Vergara 146, 28002 Madrid; Principal Conductor Aldo Ceccato; Man. Dir Tomas Marco.

**Orquesta Pablo Sarasate:** 6° Izquierda, 31002 Pamplona; tel. 34 948 229217; fax 34 948 211948; e-mail pablosarasate@retemail.es; website www.pablosarasate.com/orquesta.htm; Artistic Dir Jacques Bodmer; Man. José Maria Montes Navio; Admin. Ricardo Salcedo.

**Orquesta Sinfónica de Baleares:** Calle Vicente Juan Rossello 22-B, 07013 Palma; tel. 34 971 287 565; fax 34 971 287 758; e-mail informacio@simfonica-de-balears.com; Music Dir Luis Remartínez Gómez; Man. Carlos Rubic.

**Orquesta Sinfónica de Barcelona i Nacional de Catalunya (OBC):** Via Laietana 41, 08003 Barcelona; tel. 34 3 317 1096; fax 34 3 317 5439; website www.obc.es; Artistic Dir Lawrence Foster.

**Orquesta Sinfónica de Euskadi (Basque National Symphony Orchestra):** Paseo Miramon 214, 20 140 San Sebastian, Basque Country; tel. 34 943 01 32 32; fax 34 943 30 83 24; e-mail medios@orquestadeeuskadi.es; website www.orquestadeeuskadi.es; Gen. Dir: Germán Ormazábal Artolazábal; Music Dirs: Gilbert Varga, Cristian Mandeal.

**Orquesta Sinfónica de Málaga:** Calle Ramos Marin s/n, 29012 Málaga; Music Dir Octav Calleya.

**Orquesta Sinfónica de Radiotelevisión Española:** Sor Angela de la Cruz 2, 7°, 28020 Madrid; Chief Conductor Sergiu Comissiona.

**Orquesta Sinfónica de Sevilla:** Cerrajeri 10, 2° izquierda, 41004 Seville; Music Dir Vjekoslav Sutej; Gen. Man. Francisco José Senra Lazo.

**Orquesta Sinfónica de Tenerife:** Pim. Cabildo de Tenerife, Plaza de España 1, 38001 Santa Cruz de Tenerife; tel. 34 922 23 9801; fax 34 922 23 9617; e-mail info@sinfonicadetenerife.com; website www.sinfonicadetenerife.com; Music Dir Victor Pablo Pérez; Gen. Man. Enrique Rojas.

**Orquestra de Valencia:** Palau de la Música, Paseo de la Alameda 30, 46023; tel. 34 96 337 5020; fax 34 96 337 0988; Conductor Miguel Angel Gohez Martínez.

## Sri Lanka

**Tamil Service Orchestra:** c/o Sri Lanka Broadcasting Corporation, Torrington Square, Colombo 7; tel. 1 697 491 10; fax 1 695 488.

## Sweden

**Gävle Symfoniorkester:** PO Box 1071, Kungsbacksvagen 22, 80134, Gävle; tel. 46 26 1729 30; fax 46 26 17 2935; e-mail gavle.symfoniorkester@gavle.se; website www.gavle.se/symfoniorkester; Music Dir Hannu Koivula; Gen. Man. Haukur F. Hannesson.

**Göteborgs Symfoniker (Gothenburg Symphony Orchestra):** Götaplatsen, 412 56 Göteborg; tel. 46 31 726 5300; fax 46 31 726 5370; e-mail info@gso.se; website www.gso.se; Principal Conductor: Neeme Järvi; the national orchestra of Sweden.

**Helsingborgs Symfoniorkester:** Konserthuset, 25221 Helsingborg; tel. 46 10 42 70; fax 42 12 31 97; e-mail konserthuset@helsingborg.se; website www.hso.nu; Music Dir Hannu Lintu.

**Malmö Symfoniorkester:** 205 80 Malmö tel. 46 40 34 35 10; fax 46 40 611 7505; e-mail office@mso.se; website www.mso.se; Music Dir: Christoph König; Gen. Man.: Lennart Stenkvist.

**Norrköpings Symfoniorkester:** PO Box 2144, 600 02 Norrköping; tel. 46 11 1551 50; fax 46 11 1551 55; website www.symfoniorkester.nu; Music Dir: Lü Jia; Man. Dir: Hans Barksjö.

**Norrlands Symphony Orchestra:** PO Box 360, 90108, Umea; tel. 46 0 90154300; fax 46 0 90125845; Marketing Asst Felicia Wipp.

**Orebro Symphony Orchestra and Swedish Chamber Orchestra:** Konserthuset, Farriksgatan 2, 702 10 Orebro; Music Dir Goran Nilson; Man. Karl Friman.

**Royal Baltic Symphony Orchestra:** Kungliga Slottet, 111 30 Stockholm; tel. 46 8 102247; fax 46 8 215911; Music Dir Mats Liljefors; Programme Man. Mathias Walin.

**Stockholms Filharmoniska Orkester:** PO Box 7083, 103 87 Stockholm; tel. 46 8 7860200; fax 46 8 50667720; website www.konserthuset.se; Chief Conductor: Alan Gilbert; Exec. and Artistic Dir: Stefan Forsberg.

**Sveriges Radios Symfoniorkester:** Berwaldhallen, Strandvägen 69, 105 10 Stockholm; tel. 46 8 784 1801; fax 46 8 784 5150; e-mail orkestern@bwh.sr.se; Gen. Man. Michael Tyden; Principal Conductor Manfred Honeck.

**Uppsala Kammarorkester:** PO Box 1510, 751 45 Uppsala; Music Dir Kjell Söderqvist; Man. Nils-Olof Sondell.

**Västeras Musiksällskap:** Sangargatan 3, 722 20 Västeras; Man. Ulf Stenberg.

## Switzerland

**Basler Kammerorchester:** PO Box 4001, 4051 Basel.

**Berner Symphonieorchester:** Münzgraben 2, 3000 Bern 7; tel. 41 31 328 2424; fax 41 31 328 2425; e-mail info@bernorchester.ch; website www.bernorchester.ch/ index3.htm; Chief Conductor Dmitri Kitaenko; Man. Margrit Lenz.

**Camerata Bern:** Mayweg 4, 3007 Bern; tel. 031 371 86 88; fax 031 371 38 35; Conductor Thomas Füri; Gen. Sec. Rose Brügger.

**Camerata Zürich:** Bergstrasse 50-G, 8712 Stáfa; Conductor Räto Tschupp; Sec. Rosemarie Kleinert.

**Collegium Academicum de Genève:** PO Box 539, 1211 Geneva 4; Music Dir Thierry Fischer; Man. Janine Mariz.

**Collegium Musicum Zürich:** Konzertgesellschaft, Steinwiesstrasse 2, 8032 Zürich; Man. Barbara Oehninger.

**Festival Strings Lucerne:** Dreilindenstrasse 93, 6006 Lucerne; tel. 41 420 62 63; fax 41 420 62 73; e-mail info@festivalstringslucerne.org; website www

.festivalstringslucerne.org; Artistic Dir: Achim Fiedler; Man. Dir: Samuel Steinemann; concerts and tours throughout the world.

**Luzerner Sinfonieorchester:** Zentralstrasse 44, 6003 Lucerne; tel. 41 210 50 50; fax 41 210 26 93; e-mail info@sinfonieorchester.ch; website www.sinfonieorchester.ch.

**Orchester Musikkollegium Winterthur:** Rychenbergstrasse 94, 8400 Winterthur; tel. 41 52 268 1560; fax 41 52 268 1570; Music Dir Jac van Steen; Dir Karl Bossert.

**Orchestra della Radiotelevisione della Svizzera Italiana:** 6903 Lugano.

**Orchestre de Chambre de Lausanne:** Chemin du Devin 72, 1010 Lausanne; Music Dir Jesús López-Cobos; Chair. Jean-Jacques Rapin.

**Orchestre de la Suisse Romande:** Promenade du Pin 3, 1211 Geneva; tel. 41 22 807 0017; fax 41 22 807 0018; e-mail music@osr.ch; website www.osr.ch; Chief Conductor Armin Jordan; Artistic Dir Fabio Luisi; Gen. Man. Jean Cordey.

**Radio-Sinfonie-Orchester:** Münsterplatz 18, 4051 Basel; Chief Conductor Nello Santi.

**Sinfonieorchester Basel:** Barfüsserplatz 8, Stadtcasino Basel, 4051 Basel; tel. 41 61 205 0095; fax 41 61 205 0099; e-mail info@sinfonieorchesterbasel.ch; website www.sinfonieorchesterbasel.ch; Dir: Franziskus Theurillat.

**Sinfonieorchester der Allgemeinen Musikgesellschaft Luzern:** Moosstrasse 15, 6003 Lucerne; Music Dir Olaf Henzold; Man. Peter Keller.

**Sinfonieorchester St Gallen:** Museumstrasse 1, 9004 St Gallen; tel. 41 071 242 05 05; website www.sinfonieorchestersg.ch; Music Dir: Jin Kout; Man.: Florian Scheiber.

**Sinfonietta Wetzikon:** Lindenhofstr 12a, 8624 Grüt; tel. 41 1 972 1898; fax 41 1 972 1897; Artistic Dirs Werner Bärtsch, Matthias Ziegler; Sec. Pauline d'Hooghe.

**Symphonisches Orchester Zürich:** PO Box 1923, 8021 Zürich; Music Dir Daniel Schweizer; Man. Paul Trachsel.

**The Masterplayers:** Via Losanna 12, 6900 Lugano; Conductor Richard Schumacher; Man. Dr D. V. Zschinsky.

**Tonhalle Orchester Zürich:** Gotthardstrasse 5, 8002 Zürich; tel. 41 1 206 34 44; fax 41 1 206 34 73; e-mail pr-marketing@tonhalle.ch; Exec. Dir: Trygve Nordwall; Artistic Dir: David Zinman; Dir of Admin.: Jürg Keller; Artistic Admin.: Etienne Reymond.

**Züricher Kammerorchester:** Muhlebachstrasse 86, PO Box 1011, 8032 Zürich; tel. 41 1 388 3600; fax 41 1 388 3610; Music Dir Howard Griffiths; Gen. Man. Thomas Pfiffner.

## Taiwan

**Taipei City Symphony Orchestra:** 25 Pa Teh Road, Sec 3, Taipei 10560; tel. 886 2 752 3731; fax 886 2 751 8244; Music Dir Chen Chiu-sen.

**Taiwan Symphony Orchestra:** 292 Ming-Sheng Road, Wu Feng, T'aichung; Conductor Tze-shiou Liu; Man. Po-chou Chang.

## Thailand

**Bangkok Symphony Orchestra:** Tejapaibil Building, Fifth Floor, 16 Plubplachai Road, Bangkok 10100; tel. 662 22308715; fax 662 6215751; e-mail bso_bangkok@hotmail.com; Music Dir John Georgiadis; Gen. Man. Witaya Tumornsoontorn.

## Turkey

**Istanbul State Symphony Orchestra:** Atatürk Kültür Merkezi-80090 Taksim, Istanbul; tel. 90 212 243 1068; fax 90 212 251 0507; e-mail istsymph@hotmail.com; Conductor Erol Erdinc; Man. Ozer Sezgin; Dir Turkmen Goner; Programme Controller Orhan Topguoglu.

**Izmir State Symphony Orchestra:** Büro SSK Ishani C Blok 4, Kat Konak, 352260 Izmir; tel. 90 232 484 8343; fax 90 232 484 5172; Music Dir Iosif Conta; Dir Numan Pekdemir.

**Presidential Symphony Orchestra:** Talatpasa Bulvari 38A, 06330 Ankara; tel. 90 312 309 1343; fax 90 312 311 7548; Music Dir Gürer Aykol.

## Ukraine

**Crimea State Symphony Orchestra:** PO Box 53, 98600 Yalta; tel. 380 654 32 5070; Chief Conductor Aleksey Goulianitsky.

**Crimean State Philharmonic:** 13 Litkens Street, 334200 Yalta.

**Karhkiv Philharmonic Orchestra:** Rymarskaya Street 21, 61057 Kharkiv; tel. 380 572 470527; fax 380 572 631212; e-mail itl360@online.kharkov.ua; Music Dir Yuriy Yanko; Exec. Dir Nicolai A. Saltovsky.

**Kiev Chamber Orchestra:** Volodymyrskiy Uzviz 2, 252001 Kiev.

**National Symphony Orchestra of Ukraine:** Volodymyrskiy Uzviz 2, 252001 Kiev; tel. and fax 380 44 229 6842; Artistic Dir and Conductor Theodore Kuchar.

**Odesa Chamber Orchestra:** 15 R. Vul. I. Bunina, 65026 Odesa.

**Odesa Philharmonic Orchestra:** 15 R. Vul. I. Bunina, 65026 Odesa; tel. and fax 7 048 222 6349.

**Ukrainian State Symphony Orchestra:** Khrestchatyk 26, 01001 Kiev; tel. 380 44 235 5272; fax 380 44 229 3322; e-mail radio_na@c-mail.ru; Chief Conductor V. Blinov.

## United Kingdom

**Academy of Ancient Music:** 10 Brookside, Cambridge CB2 1JE; tel. 1223 301509; fax 1223 327377; e-mail aam@aam.co.uk; website www.aam.co.uk; Dir Christopher Hogwood; Assoc. Conductor Paul Goodwin; Gen. Man. Christopher Lawrence.

**Academy of London:** Studio 26, Building 56, Magnet Road, GEC East Lane Estate, Wembley, Middlesex HA9 7RG; tel. 20 8908 4348; fax 20 8908 4713; Conductor Richard Stamp; Gen. Man. Elaine Baines.

**Academy of St Martin-in-the-Fields:** Raine House, Raine Street, Wapping, London E1W 3RJ; tel. 20 7702 1377; fax 20 7481 0228; e-mail info@asmf.org; website www.academysmif.co.uk; Life Pres. Neville Marriner; Man. Gillian Brierley; Artistic Dir Kenneth Sillito.

**All Souls Orchestra:** All Souls Music Office, St Paul's Church, Robert Adam Street, London W1M 5AH; tel. 20 7487 3508; fax 20 7224 6087; Principal Conductor Noël Tredinnick.

**Ambache Chamber Orchestra:** 9 Beversbrook Road, London N19 4QG; tel. (20) 7263-4027; e-mail polmear.ambache@telinco.co.uk; website www.ambache.co.uk; Music Dir Diana Ambache; Gen. Man. Sue Sharpe; specialists in the music of Mozart and female composers of the last 250 years, performing collaboratively without a conductor.

**Amici Chamber Orchestra:** 55 Rosedale, Welwyn Garden City, Hertfordshire AL7 1DP; tel. and fax 1438 715740; Conductor Nigel Springthorpe.

**Barbican Chamber Orchestra:** 10 Acacia Road, London E17 8BW; Principal Conductor Gregory Rose; Man. Paul Thomas.

**Basildon Symphony Orchestra:** 101 Queens Park Avenue, Bournemouth BH8 9LJ; Conductor and Artistic Dir Richard Studt.

**BBC Concert Orchestra:** BBC Hippodrome, North End Road, London NW11 7RP; tel. 20 7765 4010; fax 20 7765 4929; e-mail concert.orch@bbc.co.uk; website www.bbc.co.uk/orchestras; Principal Conductor Barry Wordsworth; Gen. Man. Ian Maclay.

**BBC National Orchestra of Wales:** Broadcasting House, Llandaff, Cardiff CF5 2YQ, Wales; tel. 02920 322442; fax 02920 322575; e-mail now@bbc.co.uk; website www.bbc.co.uk/wales/now/index.htm; Principal Conductor Richard Hickox; Orchestra Man. Byron Jenkins.

**BBC Philharmonic Orchestra:** New Broadcasting House, Oxford Road, Manchester M60 1SJ; tel. 161 244 4001; fax 161 244 4211; e-mail philharmonic@bbc.co.uk; website www.bbc.co.uk/orchestras/philharmonic; Principal Conductor Gianandrea Noseda; Conductor Laureate:Yan Pascal Tortelier; Man. Peter Marchbank.

**BBC Scottish Symphony Orchestra:** Broadcasting House, Queen Margaret Drive, Glasgow G12 8DG; tel. (141) 338 2606; fax (141) 307 4312; e-mail bbcsso@bbc.co.uk; website www.bbc.co.uk/bbcsso; Chief Conductor: Ilan Volkov; Dir: Hugh Macdonald; Man.: Alan Davis; f. 1935; plays world-wide.

**BBC Symphony Orchestra:** Maida Vale Studios, Delaware Road, London W9 2LG; tel. 20 7765 2956; fax 20 7286 3251; e-mail bbcso@bbc.co.uk; website www.bbc.co.uk/orchestras/so/; Chief Conductor Leonard Slatkin; Gen. Man. Paul Hughes.

**Ben Uri Chamber Orchestra:** 5 Bradby House, Carlton Hill, London NW8 9XE; tel. 20 7624 1756; Conductor Sydney Fixman.

**Birmingham Contemporary Music Group:** CBSO Centre, Berkley Street, Birmingham, B1 2LF; tel. 121 616 2616; fax 121 616 2622; e-mail info@bcmg.org.uk; website www.bcmg.org.uk; Artistic Dir Stephen Newbould.

**Birmingham Sinfonietta:** 41 St Agnes Road, Birmingham B13 9PJ; tel. 121 449 0225; Music Dir Jeremy Ballard; Man. Susan Savage.

**Blackheath Haus:** 23 Lee Road, London, SE3 9RQ; tel. 20 8318 9758; fax 20 8852 5154; Artistic Dir Peter Conway.

**Bournemouth Sinfonietta:** 2 Seldown Lane, Poole, Dorset BH15 1UF; tel. 1202 670611; fax 1202 687235; Principal Conductor Alexander Polianichko.

**Bournemouth Symphony Orchestra:** 2 Seldown Lane, Poole, Dorset BH15 1UF; tel. 1202 670611; fax 1202 687235; e-mail contact@bsolive.com; website www.bsolive.com; Principal Conductor Marin Alsop; Conductor Laureate Andrew Litton; Man. Dir Michael Henson.

**Brandenburg Consort:** Crooked Cottage, Dunkerton, Bath, Avon BA2 8BG; tel. 1761 431535; fax 1761 431538; Musical Dir Roy Goodman; Man. Charlotte de Grey.

**Brighton Philharmonic Orchestra:** 50 Grand Parade, Brighton, East Sussex BN2 2QA; tel. 1273 622900; fax 1273 697887; website www.brightonphil.co.uk; Principal Conductor Barry Wordsworth; Gen. Man. Ivan Rockey.

**Bristol Philharmonic Orchestra:** 11 Windsor Court, Victoria Terrace, Bristol BS8 4LJ; tel. 117 929 7597; fax 117 925 1301; website www.3sixty.co.uk/bristolphil/; Artistic Dir Derek Bourgeois; Gen. Man. Kenneth H. Gibbs.

**Britten Sinfonia:** 13 Sturton Street, Cambridge CB1 2SN; tel. 1223 300795; fax 1223 302092; e-mail info@brittensinfonia.co.uk; website www.brittensinfonia.co.uk; Concerts Dir Nikola White; Chief Exec. David Butcher.

**BT Scottish Ensemble:** Centre for Contemporary Arts, 350 Sauchiehall Street, Glasgow, G2 3JD; tel. 141 332 4747; fax 141 332 3555; website www.scottishensemble.co.uk; Artistic Dir Clio Gould; Gen. Man. Heather Duncan.

**Cantelli Chamber Orchestra:** 13 Cotswold Mews, 12–16 Battersea High Street, London SW11 3JB; Conductor Philip Ellis; Man. Alexander Waugh.

**Chamber Orchestra of Europe:** 8 Southampton Place, London WC1A 2EA; tel. 20 7831 2326; fax 20 7831 8248; e-mail redbird@coeurope.org; Artistic Adviser Claudio Abbado; Gen. Man. June Megennis.

**Cheltenham Chamber Orchestra:** 5 Deans Quarry, Burleigh, Stroud, GL5 2PQ; tel. (1453) 882268; fax (1453) 887262; e-mail piccpeter@aol.com; Orchestral Man. Peter Tomlinson.

**City of Birmingham Symphony Orchestra:** CSBO Centre, Berkley Street, Birmingham B1 2LF; tel. 121 616 6500; fax 121 616 6518; e-mail information@cbso.co.uk; website www.cbso.co.uk; Principal Conductor Sakari Oramo; Chief Exec. Stephen Maddock; Gen. Man. Mike Buckley.

**City of London Sinfonia:** 11 Drum Street, London E1 1LH; tel. 20 7480 7743; fax 20 7488 2700; e-mail info@cls.co.uk; website www.cityoflondonsinfonia.co.uk; Music Dir Richard Hickox; Gen. Man. Stephen Carpenter.

**City of Oxford Orchestra:** Midsummer Cottage, Boars Hill, Oxford OX1 5DG; tel. and fax 1865 744457; e-mail info@cityofoxfordorchestra.co.uk; website www.cityofoxfordorchestra.co.uk; Artistic Dir Roger Payne; Man. Dir John King.

**Collegium Musicum 90 Ltd:** 71 Priory Road, Kew, Surrey TW9 3DH; tel. 20 8940 7086; fax 20 8332 0879; Man. Francesca McManus.

**East of England Orchestra:** Derby College at Wilmorton, Pentagon Centre, Beaufort Street, Derby, DE21 6AX; tel. 1332 207570; fax 1332 207569; Principal Conductor Nicholas Kok.

**English Bach Festival Orchestra and English Bach Festival Baroque Orchestra:** 15 South Eaton Place, London SW1W 9ER; tel. 20 7730 5925; fax 20 7730 1456; Dir Lina Lalandi.

**English Baroque Orchestra:** 57 Kingswood Road, London SW19 3ND; tel. 20 8542 1661; fax 20 8540 1103; Music Dir Leon Lovett; Man. Robert Porter.

**English Baroque Soloists:** 61 Wandsworth High Street, SW18 2PT; tel. 20 8871 4750; fax 20 8871 4751; Music Dir John Eliot Gardiner; Gen. Man. Michael B. MacLeod.

**English Camerata:** 14 Dunstarn Drive, Leeds, LS16 8EH; tel. and fax 113 267 5821; Musical Dir Elizabeth Altman; Admin. John Harris.

**English Chamber Orchestra:** 2 Coningsby Road, London W5 4HR; tel. 20 8840 6565; fax 20 8567 7198; e-mail mail@englishchamberorchestra.co.uk; website www.englishchamberorchestra.co.uk; Principal Conductor Ralf Gothóni; Dir Pauline Gilbertson.

**English Classical Players:** 25B Epsom Lane South, Tadworth, Surrey KT20 5TA; tel. 1737 813273; fax 1737 215676; e-mail ecp@classicconcerts.co.uk; Artistic Dir Jonathan Brett; Exec. Dir Lyn Mumford.

**The English Concert:** 8 St George's Terrace, London NW1 8XJ; tel. 20 7911 0905; fax 20 7911 0904; e-mail ec@englishconcert.co.uk; website www.englishconcert.co.uk; Artistic Dir Andrew Manze; Man. Felix Warnock.

**English Festival Orchestra:** 151 Mount View Road, London N4 4JT; tel. 20 8341 6408; fax 20 8802 0595; e-mail tford@aol.com; Gen. Man. Trevor Ford.

**English National Opera Orchestra:** London Coliseum, St Martin's Lane, London WC2N 4ES; tel. 20 7836 0111; fax 20 7845 9277; website www.eno.org; Orchestra Man. Richard Smith; Music Dir Paul Daniel.

**English Northern Philharmonia:** Opera North, Grand Theatre, Leeds LS1 6NU; tel. (113) 243-9999; fax (113) 244-0418; e-mail info@operanorth.co.uk; website www.operanorth.co.uk; Principal Conductor Steven Sloane; Gen. Dir Richard Mantle.

**English Sinfonia:** 1 Wedgwood Court, Stevenage, Hertfordshire SG1 4QR; tel. 1438 350990; fax 1438 350930; e-mail info@englishsinfonia.org.uk; website www.englishsinfonia.org.uk; Chief Exec. Lucy Potter; Principal Conductor Nicolae Moldoveanu.

**English Sinfonietta:** The Barn, Layston Park, Royston, Hertfordshire SG8 9DS; tel. 1763 2424847; fax 1763 248048; Principal Conductor Steuart Bedford; Gen. Man. Graham Pfaff.

**English String Orchestra:** Rockliffe House, Church Street, Malvern, Worcestershire WR14 2AZ; tel. (1684) 560696; fax (1684) 560656; e-mail info@eso.co.uk; website www.eso.co.uk; Artistic/Music Dir: William Boughton; Admin.: Kate Hodson.

**English Symphony Orchestra:** Rockliffe House, Church Street, Malvern, Worcestershire WR14 2AZ; tel. (1684) 560696; fax (1684) 560656; e-mail info@eso.co.uk; website www.eso.co.uk; Artistic/Music Dir: William Boughton; Admin.: Kate Hodson.

**Esterhazy Orchestra:** 278 Kew Road, Richmond, Surrey TW9 3EE; tel. 20 8948 6140.

**European Union Chamber Orchestra:** Hollick, Yarnscombe, Devon EX31 3LQ; tel. 1271 858249; fax 1271 858375; e-mail eucorch1@aol.com; website www.etd.gb.com; Dir Gen. Ambrose Miller.

**European Union Youth Orchestra:** 65 Sloane Street, London SW1X 9SH; tel. 20 7235 7671; fax 20 7235 7370; e-mail info@euyo.org.uk; website www.euyo.org.uk; Music Dir Vladimir Ashkenazy; Gen. Man. Huw Humphreys.

**Gabrieli Consort and Players:** 372 Old Street, London EC1V 9LT; tel. 20 7613 4404; fax 20 7613 4414; e-mail info@gabrieli.com; Gen. Man. Ole Backhoej.

**Guildford Philharmonic Orchestra:** Millmead House, Millmead, Guildford, Surrey GU2 5BB; tel. 1483 444666; fax 1483 444732; e-mail guildfordphil@guildford.gov.uk; website www.guildfordphilharmonic.co.uk; Principal Conductor En Shao.

**Guildhall String Ensemble:** 41 Belmont Lane, Stanmore, Middlesex, HA7 2PU; tel. 20 8954 1380; fax 20 8954 9212; Dir Robert Salter.

**Hallé Orchestra:** The Bridgewater Hall, Manchester M1 5HA; tel. 161 237 7000; fax 161 237 7029; e-mail info@halle.co.uk; website www.halle.co.uk; Music Dir Mark Elder; Chief Exec. David Richardson.

**Hanover Band:** The Old Market, Upper Market Street, Hove, East Sussex BN3 1AS; tel. 1273 206978; fax 1273 329636; website www.hanoverband.com; Artistic Dir Caroline Brown.

**Henry Wood Chamber Orchestra:** 64 Ashley Gardens, Ambrosden Avenue, London, SW1P 1QG; Music Dir John Landor; Admin. William Corke.

**The King's Consort:** 34 St Mary's Grove, London W4 3LN; tel. 20 8995 9994; fax 20 8995 2115; e-mail info@tkcworld.com; website www.tkcworld.com; Artistic Dir Robert King.

**Kreisler String Orchestra:** 57 Sunnyside Road, Chesham, Buckinghamshire HP5 2AR; tel. and fax 1494 792572; Man. Robert Woollard.

**Langham Chamber Orchestra:** 9 Weylea Avenue, Burpham, Guildford, Surrey GU4 7YN; tel. 1483 573705; Orchestra Man. Peter Holt.

**Little Symphony of London:** 14 Beaumont Road, Purley, Surrey CR8 2EG; tel. and fax 20 8668 5883; Artistic Dir Darrell Davison.

**Liverpool Sinfonietta:** 40 Caulfield Drive, Greasby, Wirral, Merseyside L49 1SW; Music Dir Anthony Ridley.

**London Bach Orchestra:** c/o Goldberg Ensemble, 1 Rowsley Avenue, West Didsbury, Manchester M20 2XD; tel. and fax 161 446 2170; Artistic Dir Nicholas Kraemer.

**London Camerata:** 21 Halstead Road, Mountsorrel, Leicestershire LE12 7HD; tel. 116 230 3674; Conductor Paul Hilliam.

**London Chamber Orchestra:** c/o The London Chamber Society Ltd, 6 Hambalt Road, London SW4 9EB; tel. 20 8772 9741; fax 20 8772 9742; e-mail info@lco.co.uk; website www.lco.co.uk; Music Dir Christopher Warren-Green; Gen. Man. Step Parikian.

**London Chamber Players:** PO Box 84, London NW11 8AL; tel. 20 8455 9200; fax 20 8455 6799; e-mail london-players@excite.com; Conductor Adrian Sunshine; Admin. Sheila Genden.

**London Chamber Symphony:** Toynbee Studios, 28 Commercial Street, London E1 6LS; tel. 20 7247 2950; fax 20 7247 2956; Conductor Odalaine de la Martinez; Co-Dir Sophie Langdon.

**London Chanticleer Orchestra:** Tickerage Castle, Pound Lane, Framfield, Uckfield, East Sussex TN22 5RT; tel. 1825 890348; Sec. H. J. Graty.

**London City Chamber Orchestra:** 3/5 Bridge Street, Hadleigh, Ipswich, Suffolk IP7 6BY; tel. 1473 822596; fax 1473 824175; e-mail thomas.mcintosh@minstrelmusic.demon.co.uk; Conductor Thomas McIntosh; Gen. Man. Miranda Reckitt.

**London Concert Orchestra:** 29–31 East Barnet Road, New Barnet, Hertfordshire EN4 8RN; tel. 20 8216 3000; fax 20 8216 3001; Admin. Raymond Gubbay.

**London Festival Orchestra:** 13 Theed Street, London SE1 8ST; tel. 20 7928 9250; fax 20 7928 9252; e-mail orchestra@lfo.co.uk; website www.lfo.co.uk; Music and Artistic Dir Ross Pople; Man. Anne Storrs.

**London Handel Orchestra:** 32 Wolverton Gardens, London W6 7DX; tel. 20 8563 0618; fax 20 8741 5233; Musical Dir Denys Darlow; Admin. Joya Logan.

**London Jupiter Orchestra:** 57 White Horse Road, London E1 0ND; tel. 20 7790 5883; fax 20 7265 9170; Conductor Gregory Rose.

**London Mozart Players:** Suite 306, Park House, Park Street, Croydon CR0 1YE; tel. (20) 8686-1996; fax (20) 8686-2187; e-mail info@lmp.co.uk; website www.lmp.co.uk; Man. Dir: Antony Lewis-Crosby; Music Dir: Andrew Parrott.

**London Philharmonic Orchestra:** 89 Albert Embankment, London, SE1 7TP; tel. 20 7840 4200; fax 20 7840 4201; e-mail admin@lpo.org.uk; website www.lpo.co.uk; Artistic Dir Serge Dorny; Principal Conductor Kurt Masur.

**London Pro Arte Baroque:** 17b St Augustine's Avenue, South Croydon, Surrey CR2 6JN; tel. (20) 8688-2901; fax (20) 8654-9137; e-mail office@ londonproarte.co.uk; website www.londonproarte.co.uk; Artistic Dir Murray Stewart; Orchestra Man. Richard Thomas.

**London Pro Arte Orchestra:** 17b St Augustine's Avenue, South Croydon, Surrey CR2 6JN; tel. (20) 8688-2901; fax (20) 8654-9137; e-mail office@ londonproarte.co.uk; website www.londonproarte.co.uk; Artistic Dir Murray Stewart; Orchestra Man. John Cobb.

**London Repertoire Orchestra and Chamber Orchestra:** 56 Alexandra Road, Croydon, Surrey CR0 6EU; Conductor Francis Griffin.

**London Sinfonietta:** Dominion House, 101 Southwark Street, London SE1 0JF; tel. (20) 7928-0828; fax (20) 7928-8557; e-mail info@londonsinfonietta .org.uk; website www.londonsinfonietta.org.uk; Conductor Laureate: Oliver Knussen; Artistic Dir: Gillian Moore; Man. Dir: Cathy Graham.

**London Soloists' Chamber Orchestra:** PO Box 100, East Horsley KT24 6WN; tel. 1483 282666; fax 1483 284777; e-mail info@londonsoloists.com; website www.londonsoloists.com; Conductor David Josefowitz; Man. Nick Bomford.

**London String Orchestra:** 37 St Davids Road, Clifton Campville, nr Tamworth, Staffordshire B79 0BA; tel. 1827 373586; Conductor James Maddocks.

**London Symphony Orchestra:** Barbican Centre, Silk Street, London EC2Y 8DS; tel. 20 7588 1116; fax 20 7374 0127; e-mail admin@lso.co.uk; website www.lso.co.uk; Principal Conductor Colin Davis; Man. Dir Clive Gillinson.

**Manchester Camerata:** Zion Arts Centre, Stretford Road, Manchester M15 5ZA; tel. 161 226 8696; fax 161 226 8600; Principal Conductor and Artistic Dir: Douglas Boyd; Principal Guest Conductor: Nicholas Kraemer.

**Manchester Mozart Orchestra:** 30 Derby Road, Fallowfield, Manchester M24 6UW; Man. John Whibley.

**Melos Ensemble:** 35 Doughty Street, London WC1N 2AA.

**Monteverdi Choir and Orchestra:** Fourth Floor, 11 Westferry Circus, Canary Wharf, London E14 4HE; tel. (20) 7537-4004; fax (20) 7517-9874; Gen. Man.: Per Hedberg.

**Musiciens du Roi:** 6 Aldersmead Road, Beckenham, Kent BR3 1NA; Dir Lionel Sawkins.

**National Chamber Orchestra:** Fir Tree Lodge, Jumps Road, Churt, nr Farnham, Surrey GU10 2JY; tel. 1252 792315; fax 1252 795120.

**National Philharmonic Orchestra:** 7 Lowlands, 218 Eton Avenue, Hampstead, London NW3 3EJ; tel. 20 7722 1078; fax 1689 852311; Dir Sidney Sax.

**National Symphony Orchestra:** Fir Tree Lodge, Jumps Road, Churt, nr Farnham, Surrey GU10 2JY; tel. 1252 792315; fax 1252 795120.

**National Symphony Orchestra of London:** 177 John Ruskin Street, London SE5 0PQ; tel. 20 7703 3148; fax 20 7701 9479; e-mail enquiries@nso.co .uk; website www.nso.co.uk; Principal Conductor Martin Yates; Man. Dir/ Joint Artistic Dir Anne Collis.

**New English Concert Orchestra:** 23 Hitchin Street, Biggleswade, Bedfordshire SG18 8AX; tel. 1767 316521; fax 1767 317221; e-mail neco@ lindsaymusic.co.uk; Music Dir Douglas Coombes; Admin. Rose Miles.

**New English Orchestra:** 4 Link Road, Edgbaston, Birmingham B16 0EP; website www.newenglishorchestra.org; Principal Conductor: Nigel Swinford; Company Sec.: Julie Fry.

**New London Orchestra:** 4 Lower Belgrave Street, London SW1W 0LJ; tel. 20 7823 5523; fax 20 7823 6373; e-mail admin@nlo.co.uk; website www.nlo.co .uk; Artistic Dir Ronald Corp; Gen. Man. Julian Knight.

**New Queen's Hall Orchestra:** Trees, Ockham Road, South East Horsley, Surrey KT24 6QE; tel. 1483 281300; fax 1483 281811; e-mail info@nqho.com; website www.nqho.com; Artistic Dir John Boyden; Gen. Admin. James Thomson.

**Northern Ballet Theatre Orchestra:** West Park Centre, Spen Lane, Leeds LS16 5BE; tel. 113 274 5355; fax 113 274 5381; website www.nbt.co.uk; Music Dir John Pryce-Jones.

**Northern Chamber Orchestra:** 799 Wilmslow Road, Didsbury, Manchester M20 2RR; tel. 161 247 2220; fax 161 247 6899; e-mail info@norch.co.uk; website www.ncorch.co.uk; Music Dir Nicholas Ward; Gen. Man. Jonathan Thackeray; presents concerts in north-west England, associated education programmes.

**Northern Sinfonia of England:** The Sinfonia Centre, 41 Jesmond Vale, Newcastle upon Tyne NE1 1PG; tel. 191 240 1812; fax 191 240 2668; e-mail nsinfonia@ndirect.co.uk; website www.nsinfonia.ision.co.uk; Music Dir Thomas Zehetmair; Chief Exec. John Summers.

**Orchestra da Camera:** 41 Mill End, Kenilworth, Warwickshire CV8 2HP; tel. (1926) 858187; e-mail enquiries@orchestradacamera.com; website www .orchestradacamera.com; Artistic Dir: Rosalind Page.

**Orchestra of Sadler's Wells Royal Ballet:** Sadler's Wells Theatre, Rosebery Avenue, London EC1R 4TN; Man. Wendy Hacker.

**Orchestra of St John's, Smith Square:** The White House, Eltham College, Grove Park Road, London SE9 4QF; tel. 20 8857 8579; fax 20 8857 9340; e-mail info@osj.org.uk; Principal Conductor John Lubbock; Chief Exec. Nicky Goulder.

**Orchestra of the Age of Enlightenment:** Third Floor, 33 Henrietta Street, Covent Garden, London WC2E 8NA; tel. 20 7836 6690; fax 20 7836 6692; e-mail info@oae.co.uk; website www.oae.co.uk; Chief Exec.: Marshall Marcus; Dir of Planning: Charlotte Wadham; Dir of Development and Marketing: Katy Shaw; Chair.: Greg Malgaard.

**Orchestra of the Royal Opera House:** Covent Garden, London WC2E 9DD; tel. 20 7304 4000; fax 20 7212 9460; e-mail webmaster@roh.org.uk; website www.royalopera.org; Music Dir Antonio Pappano.

**Orchestra of Welsh National Opera:** c/o Welsh National Opera Ltd, Wales Millennium Centre, Bay Chambers, West Bute Street, Cardiff, CF10 5GG; tel. (29) 2040 2000; fax (29) 2040 2001; e-mail info@wno.org.uk; website www.wno .org.uk, www.wmc.org.uk; Orchestra Dir Peter Harrap.

**Orchestre Revolutionnaire et Romantique:** 61 Wandsworth High Street, Tower Place, London SW18 2PT; tel. 20 8871 4750; fax 20 8871 4751; e-mail info@monteverdi.org.uk; Music Dir Sir John Eliot Gardiner; Gen. Man. Michael MacLeod.

**Per Musica Chamber Orchestra:** 50 Cranfield Court, Homer Street, London W1; Music Dir Julian Reynolds; Admin. Joan Cruickshank.

**Philharmonia Orchestra:** First Floor, 125 High Holborn, London WC1V 6QA; tel. 20 7242 5001; fax 20 7242 4840; e-mail info@philharmonia.co.uk; website www.philharmonia.co.uk; Principal Conductor Christoph von Dohnányi; Man. Dir David Whelton.

**Purcell Orchestra:** 86 Park Hill, Carshalton Beeches, Surrey SM5 3RZ; tel. and fax 20 8669 4358; Artistic Dir Robin Page.

**Raglan Baroque Players:** 140 Muswell Hill Road, London N10 3JD; tel. 20 8444 2507; fax 20 8444 1795; e-mail raglanadmin@compuserve.com; Music Dir Nicholas Kraemer.

**Regent Sinfonia of London:** 17 Parliament Hill, London NW3 2TA; tel. 20 7435 5965; fax 20 7435 9166; Artistic Dir George Vass.

**Rossini Chamber Orchestra:** 10A Radipole Road, Fulham, London SW6 5DL; tel. 20 7736 3821; fax 20 8449 1664; Music Dir and Conductor Alexander Bryett.

**Royal Liverpool Philharmonic Orchestra:** Philharmonic Hall, Hope Street, Liverpool L1 9BP; tel. 151 210 2895; fax 151 210 2902; e-mail info@ liverpoolphil.com; website www.liverpoolphil.com; Music Dir Gerard Schwarz.

**Royal Philharmonic Orchestra:** 16 Clerkenwell Green, London EC1R 0QT; tel. 20 7608 8800; fax 20 7608 8801; e-mail info@rpo.co.uk; website www .rpo.co.uk; Music Dir Daniele Gatti; Man. Dir John Manger.

**Royal Scottish National Orchestra:** 73 Claremont Street, Glasgow G3 8EP; tel. 141 225 3500; fax 141 225 3505; e-mail admin@rsno.org.uk; website www.rsno.org.uk; Principal Conductor Alexander Lazarev; Chief Exec. Paul Hughes; Marketing Man. Fiona Brownlee.

**Scottish Chamber Orchestra:** 4 Royal Terrace, Edinburgh EH7 5AB; tel. 131 557 6800; fax 131 557 6933; e-mail info@sco.org.uk; website www.sco.org .uk; Principal Conductor Joseph Swensen; Man. Dir Roy McEwan.

**Sinfonia 21:** 14 Prince's Gardens, London, SW7 1NA; tel. 20 7584 2759; fax 20 7581 0970; e-mail info@sinfonia21.co.uk; Chief Exec. Oliver Rivers; Gen. Man. Claire Wright.

**Sinfonia of London:** 27 Grove Road, Beaconsfield, Buckinghamshire HP9 1UR; tel. (1494) 677934; fax (1494) 670433; e-mail info@sinfonia-of-london .com; website www.sinfonia-of-london.com; Exec. Dir: Peter Willison.

**South Yorkshire Symphony Orchestra:** Springfield Close, Eckington, Sheffield S21 4GS; tel. 1246 431562; website www.syso.co.uk/orchestra.htm; Music Dir Paul Scott.

**St James's Baroque:** 120 Chewton Road, London E17 7DN; tel. (20) 8223-0772; fax (20) 8926-2979; e-mail petermccarthy@waitrose.com; Dir: Ivor Bolton; Man.: Peter McCarthy.

**Taverner Players:** Ibex House, 42–46 Minories, London EC3N 1DY; tel. 44 1717 481 2103; fax 44 171 481 2865; Conductor Andrew Parrott; Admin. Victoria Newbert.

**Ulster Orchestra:** Elmwood Hall at Queens, 89 University Road, Belfast BT7 1NF; tel. 44 028 9066 4535; fax 44 028 9066 2761; website www.ulster-orchestra.org.uk; Gen. Man. Roger Lloyd; Principal Conductor and Artistic Dir Thierry Fischer; Chief Exec. David Byers.

**Vivaldi Concertante:** 35 Laurel Avenue, Potters Bar, Hertfordshire EN6 2AB; tel. and fax 1707 643366; Conductor Joseph Pilbery.

**Welsh Chamber Orchestra:** 100 Ystrad Fawr, Bridgend, Mid-Glamorgan CF31 4HW; tel. and fax 1656 658891.

**Worthing Symphony Orchestra:** Connaught Theatre, Union Place, Worthing, Sussex, BNII ILG; tel. 1903 231799; fax 1903 215337; Chief Conductor John Gibbons.

**Yorkshire Philharmonic Orchestras:** Torridon House, 104 Bradford Road, Wrenthorpe, Wakefield, West Yorkshire WF1 2AH; tel. 1924 371496; Gen. Man. Brian Greensmith.

## United States of America

**Albany Symphony Orchestra:** 19 Clinton Avenue, Albany, NY 12207; tel. (518) 465-4755; fax (518) 465-3711; e-mail info@albanysymphony.com; website www.albanysymphony.com; Music Dir David Alan Miller.

**American Composers Orchestra:** 37 W 65th Street, Sixth Floor, New York, NY 10023; Music Dir Dennis Russell Davies; Exec. Dir Jesse Rosen.

**American Symphony Orchestra:** 850 Seventh Avenue, Suite 1106, New York, NY 10019; Music Dir Leon Botstein; Exec. Dir Eugene Carr.

**Anchorage Symphony Orchestra:** 400 D Street, Suite 230, Anchorage, AK 99501; tel. 274 8668; fax 272 7916; e-mail aso@corecom.net; website www.anchoragesymphony.org; Music Dir Randall Craig Fleischer; Exec. Dir Sherri Reddick.

**Ann Arbor Symphony Orchestra:** 527 E Liberty Suite 208B, Ann Arbor, MI 48104; tel. 1 734 994 4801; fax 1 734 994 3949; website www.a2so.com/main.html; Music Dir Samuel Wong; Exec. Dir Mary Blaske.

**Arkansas Symphony Orchestra:** PO Box 7328, 2417 N Tyler, Little Rock, AR 72217; tel. 1 501 666 1761; fax 1 501 666 3193; Music Dir David Itkin; Exec. Dir JoAnn Greene.

**Aspen Festival Orchestra and Chamber Symphony:** PO Box AA, Aspen, CO 81612; Gen. Man. Thomas Eirman.

**Atlanta Symphony Orchestra:** 1293 Peachtree Street NE, Suite 300, Atlanta, GA 30309; tel. 1 404 733 4900; fax 1 404 733 4901; e-mail aso-info@woodruffcenter.org; website www.atlantasymphony.org; Music Dir Robert Spano; Pres. Allison Vulgamore.

**Austin Symphony Orchestra:** Symphony Square, 1101 Red River, Austin, TX 78701; tel. 1 512 476 6064; fax 1 512 476 6242; e-mail contact@austinsymphony.org; website www.austinsymphony.org; Music Dir Peter Bay; Exec. Dir Kenneth K. Caswell.

**Baltimore Symphony Orchestra:** Joseph Meyerhoff Symphony Hall, 1212 Cathedral Street, Baltimore, MD 21201; tel. 1 410 783 8000; fax 1 410 783 8077; e-mail webmaster@baltimoresymphony.org; website www.baltimoresymphony.org; Music Dir Yuri Temirkanov; Exec. Dir John Gidwitz.

**Berkeley Symphony Orchestra:** 1942 University Avenue, Suite 207, Berkeley, CA 94704-1073; tel. 1 510 841 2800; fax 1 510 841 5422; e-mail mail@berkeleysymphony.org; website www.berkeleysymphony.org/index.htm; Music Dir Kent Nagano; Exec. Dir Kelly Johnson.

**Boise Philharmonic:** 516 S Ninth Street, Boise, ID 83702; tel. 1 208 344 7849; fax 1 888 300 7849; e-mail info@boisephilharmonic.org; website www.boisephilharmonic.org; Music Dir James Ogle; Gen. Man. Margie Stoy.

**Boston Symphony Orchestra:** Symphony Hall, 301 Massachusetts Avenue, Boston, MA 02115; tel. (617) 266-1492; fax (617) 638-9367; website www.bso.org; Music Dir: James Levine; Man. Dir: Mark Volpe.

**Brooklyn Philharmonic Symphony Orchestra:** 30 Lafayette Avenue, Brooklyn, NY 11217; Music Dir Robert Spano; Exec. Dir Joseph Horowitz.

**Buffalo Philharmonic Orchestra:** 71 Symphony Circle, Buffalo, NY 14201; tel. 1 716 885 0331; fax 1 716 885 9372; e-mail amanton@bpo.org; website www.bpo.org; Music Dir Joann Falletta; Exec. Dir John Bauser.

**Cedar Rapids Symphony Orchestra:** 205 Second Avenue SE, Cedar Rapids, IA 52401; e-mail webmaster@crsymphony.org; website www.crsymphony.org; Music Dir Christian Tiemeyer; Exec. Dir Kathy Hall.

**Charleston Symphony Orchestra:** 160 E Bay Street, Charleston, SC 29401; tel. (843) 723-7528; fax (843) 722-3463; e-mail info@charlestonsymphony.com; website www.charlestonsymphony.com; Music Dir David Stahl; Exec. Dir Sandra Ferencz.

**Chautauqua Symphony Orchestra:** Chautauqua, NY 14722; tel. 1 716 357 6200; fax 1 716 357 9014; e-mail cso@ciweb.org; website symphony.ciweb.org; Music Dir Uriel Segal; Gen. Man. Marty W. Merkley.

**Chicago Chamber Orchestra:** 332 S Michigan Avenue, Suite 1143, Chicago, IL 60604; tel. 1 312 922 5570; fax 1 312 922 9290; Music Dir Dieter Kober; Gen. Man. Magdalene Lornez.

**Chicago Symphony Orchestra:** Symphony Center, 220 S Michigan Avenue, Chicago, IL 60604; tel. 1 312 294 3000; fax 1 312 294 3329; website www.chicagosymphony.org; Music Dir Daniel Barenboim; Exec. Dir Henry Fogel.

**Cincinnati Symphony Orchestra:** 1241 Elm Street, Cincinnati, OH 45202-7531; tel. (513) 621-1919; fax (513) 744-3535; website www.cincinnatisymphony.org; Music Dir: Paavo Jarvi; Pres.: Steven I. Monder.

**Cleveland Orchestra:** Severance Hall, 11001 Euclid Avenue, Cleveland, OH 44106; tel. 1 216 231 7300; fax 1 216 231 0202; e-mail info@clevelandorchestra.com; website www.clevelandorch.com; Music Dir Franz Welser-Möst; Exec. Dir Thomas W. Morris.

**Colorado Springs Symphony Orchestra:** PO Box 1692, Colorado Springs, CO 80901; Music Dir Christopher Wilkins.

**Columbus Symphony Orchestra:** 55 E State Street, Columbus, OH 43215; tel. 1 614 228 9600; fax 1 614 224 7273; website www.csobravo.com; Music Dir Alessandro Siciliani; Music Dir Designate Franz Welser-Most; Exec. Dir Susan Franano.

**Colorado Symphony Orchestra:** Denver Place, North Tower, 999 18th Street, Suite 2055, Denver, CO 80202; tel. 1 303 292 5566; fax 1 303 293 2649; e-mail administration@coloradosymphony.org; website www.coloradosymphony.org; Music Dir Laureate Marin Alsop.

**Dallas Symphony Orchestra:** 2301 Flora Street, Suite 300, Dallas, TX 75201; tel. 1 214 692 0203; website www.dallassymphony.com; Music Dir Andrew Litton; Exec. Dir Eugene Bonelli.

**Dayton Philharmonic Orchestra:** 125 E First Street, Dayton, OH 45422; website www.daytonphilharmonic.com; Music Dir Isaiah Jackson; Exec. Dir Curtis Long.

**Delaware Symphony Orchestra:** PO Box 1870, Wilmington, DE 19899; e-mail info@desymphony.org; website www.desymphony.org; Music Dir Stephen Gunzenhauser; Exec. Dir Curtis Long.

**Detroit Symphony Orchestra:** 3633 Woodward Avenue, Detroit, MI 48201; tel. 1 313 576 5700; fax 1 313 576 5101; website www.detroitsymphony.com; Music Dir Neeme Järvi; Exec. Dir Mark Volpe.

**Eastern Philharmonic Orchestra:** PO Box 22026, Greensboro, NC 27420; Music Dir Sheldon Morgenstern.

**Eugene Symphony Orchestra:** 45 W Broadway, Suite 201, Eugene, OR 97401; tel. 1 541 687 9487; website www.eugenesymphony.org/directory.htm; Music Dir and Conductor Miguel Harth-Bedoya; Exec. Dir Stuart Weiser.

**Fairbanks Symphony Orchestra:** PO Box 82104, Fairbanks, AK 99708; tel. 1 907 474 5733; e-mail symphony@fairbankssymphony.org; website www.fairbankssymphony.org; Musical Dir Eduard Ziberkant; Exec. Dir Jane Aspnes.

**Florida Orchestra:** 101 S Hoover Blvd, Suite 100, Tampa, FL 33609; tel. 1 813 286 1170; fax 1 813 286 2316; e-mail admin@floridaorchestra.org; website www.floridaorchestra.org; Music Dir Stefan Sanderling; Exec. Dir Kathryn Holm.

**Florida Philharmonic Orchestra:** 3401 NW Ninth Avenue, Fort Lauderdale, FL 33309; tel. 1 954 938 6700; Music Dir James Judd; Exec. Dir John Graham.

**Florida Symphonic Pops:** 120 NE First Avenue, Boca Raton, FL 33432; Artistic Dir Derek Stannard; Exec. Vice-Pres. Carol Simmons.

**Florida West Coast Symphony Orchestra:** 709 N Tamiami Trail, Sarasota, FL 34236; tel. 1 941 953 4252; fax 1 941 953 3059; e-mail marketing@fwcs.com; website www.fwcs.org; Music Dir Leif Bjalanf; Exec. Dir Gretchen Serrie.

**Fort Worth Symphony Orchestra:** 330 E Fourth Street, Suite 200, Fort Worth, TX 76102; tel. 1 817 665 6500; fax 1 817 665 6600; e-mail admin@fwsymphony.org; website www.fwsymphony.org; Music Dir John Giordano; Exec. Dir Ann Koonsman.

**Fresno Philharmonic Orchestra:** 2610 W Shaw Avenue, Suite 103, Fresno, CA 93711; tel. (559) 261-0600; fax (559) 261-0700; e-mail info@fresnophil.org; website www.fresnophil.org; Exec. Dir David H. Gaylin; Music Dir Theodore Kuchar.

**Glendale Symphony Orchestra:** PO Box 4626, Glendale, CA 91203; tel. 1 818 500 8720; e-mail info@glendalesymphony.org; website www.glendalesymphony.org; Music Dir Norman Henry Mamey.

**Grand Rapids Symphony Orchestra:** 169 Louis Campari Promenade, Suite 1, Grand Rapids, MI 49503; tel. 1 616 454 9451; fax 1 616 454 7477; website www.grsymphony.org; Music Dir David Lockington; Exec. Dir Peter W. Smith.

**Grant Park Symphony Orchestra:** 425 E McFetridge Drive, Chicago, IL 60605; Principal Conductor Hugh Wolff.

**Greater Bridgeport Symphony Orchestra:** 446 University Avenue, Bridgeport, CT 06604; tel. 1 203 576 0263; fax 1 203 367 0064; website www.bridgeportsymphony.org; Music Dir Gustav Meier; Gen. Man. Jena Maric.

**Greater Trenton Symphony Orchestra:** 28 W State Street, Suite 201, Trenton, NJ 08608; tel. 1 609 394 1338; fax 1 609 394 1394; website www.trentonsymphony.org; Exec. Dir and Principal Conductor John Peter Holly.

**Handel and Haydn Society:** Horticultural Hall, 300 Massachusetts Avenue, Boston, MA 02115; tel. 1 617 262 1815; fax 1 617 266 4217; e-mail info@handelandhaydn.org; website www.handelandhaydn.org; Music Dir Grant Llewellyn; Conductor Laureate Christopher Hogwood; Exec. Dir Mary A. Deissler.

**Hartford Symphony Orchestra:** 228 Farmington Avenue, Hartford, CT 06105; tel. 1 860 246 8742; fax 1 860 249 5430; e-mail website www.hartfordsymphony.org; Music Dir Edward Cumming; Exec. Dir Charles H. Owens.

**Honolulu Symphony Orchestra:** 650 Iwilei Road, Suite 202, Honolulu, HI 96817; tel. 1 808 524 0815; fax 1 808 524 1507; website www.honolulusymphony.com; Music Dir Samuel Wong.

**Houston Symphony Orchestra:** 615 Louisiana Street, Houston, TX 77002; tel. 1 713 224 4240; fax 1 713 222 7024; website www.houstonsymphony.org; Music Dir Hans Graf; Exec. Dir David M. Wax.

**Hudson Valley Philharmonic Orchestra:** 35 Market Street, Poughkeepsie, NY 12601; tel. website www.bardavon.org/hvp.htm; Music Dir Randall Fleischer; Man. Dir Karen Deschere.

**Huntsville Symphony Orchestra:** PO Box 2400, Huntsville, AL 35804; website www.hso.org; Music Dir Carlos Prieto; Exec. Dir Samuel Woodward.

**Indianapolis Chamber Orchestra:** 4603 Clarendon Road, Suite 36, Indianapolis, IN 46208; Music Dir Kirk Trevor; Exec. Dir Chad Miller.

**Indianapolis Symphony Orchestra:** 32 E Washington Street, Suite 600, Indianapolis, IN 46204-2919; tel. (317) 262-1100; fax (317) 262-1159; website www.indianapolissymphony.org; Music Dir: Mario Venzago; Pres. and CEO: Richard R. Hoffert.

**Jacksonville Symphony Orchestra:** 300 Westwater Street, Suite 200, Jacksonville, FL 32202; tel. 1 904 354 5547; fax 1 904 354 9238; website www.jaxsymphony.org; Music Dir Fabio Mechetti; Conductor Laureate Roger Nierenberg; Exec. Dir David Pierson.

**Kalamazoo Symphony Orchestra:** 359 South Kalamazoo Mall, Suite 100, Kalamazoo, MI 49007; tel. 1 269 349 7759; fax 1 269 349 9229; website www.kalamazoosymphony.com; Music Dir Raymond Harvey; Exec. Dir Stacy Ridenour.

**Kansas City Symphony Orchestra:** 1020 Central, Suite 300, Kansas City, MO 64105; tel. 1 816 471 1100; fax 1 816 471 0976; website www.kcsymphony.org; Conductor Timothy Hankewich; Gen. Man. Susan Franano.

**Knoxville Symphony Orchestra:** 406 Union Avenue, Suite 100, Knoxville, TN 37902; tel. 1 865 523 1178; fax 1 865 546 3766; website www.knoxvillesymphony.org; Music Dir Lucas Richman; Exec. Dir Constance Harrison.

**Long Beach Symphony Orchestra:** 110 W Ocean Blvd, Suite 22, Long Beach, CA 90802; website www.lbso.org; Music Dir: Enrique Arturo Diemecke; Exec. Dir: Jack A. Fishman.

**Long Island Philharmonic Orchestra:** 1 Hungtington Quadrangle, Suite LL 09, Melville, NY 11747; Music Dir Enrique Arturo Diemecke; Exec. Dir Jack Fishman.

**Los Angeles Chamber Orchestra:** 707 Wiltshire Blvd, Suite 1850, Los Angeles, CA 90017; tel. 1 213 622 7001; fax 1 213 955 2071; e-mail laco@laco.org; website www.laco.org; Artistic Adviser Jeffrey Kahane; Exec. Dir Ruth L. Eliel.

**Los Angeles Philharmonic Orchestra:** 151 S Grand Avenue, Los Angeles, CA 90012; tel. 1 213 972 7300; fax 1 213 617 3065; website www.laphil.org; Music Dir Esa-Pekka Salonen.

**Louisiana Philharmonic Orchestra:** 305 Baronne Street, Suite 600, New Orleans, LA 70112; tel. (504) 523-6530; fax (504) 595-8468; website www.lpomusic.com; Music Dir Klauspeter Seilbel; Exec. Dir Sharon Litwin.

**Louisville Orchestra:** 300 W Main Street, Suite 100, Louisville, KY 40202; tel. 1 502 587 8681; fax 1 502 589 7870; e-mail info@louisvilleorchestra.org;

website www.louisvilleorchestra.org; Music Dir Uriel Segal; Exec. Dir Wayne S. Brown.

**Maryland Symphony Orchestra:** 13 S Potomac Street, Hagerstown, MD 21740; tel. 1 301 797 4000; fax 1 301 797 2314; website www.marylandsymphony.org; Music Dir Elizabeth Schulze; Man. Dir Cassandra H. Wantz.

**Memphis Symphony Orchestra:** 3100 Walnut Grove, Suite 501, Memphis, TN 38111; tel. 1 901 324 3627; fax 1 901 324 3698; website www.memphissymphony.org; Music Dir David Loebel; Exec. Dir Martha Maxwell.

**Michigan Chamber Orchestra:** 60 Farnsworth, Detroit, MI 48202; Principal Conductor Andrew Massey; Gen. Man. Virginia Catanese.

**Milwaukee Symphony Orchestra:** 330 E Kilbourn Avenue, Suite 900, Milwaukee, WI 53202; tel. 1 414 291 6010; fax 1 414 291 7610; website www.milwaukeesymphony.org; Music Dir Andreas Delfs; Exec. Dir Joan Squire.

**Minnesota Orchestra:** 1111 Nicollet Mall, Minneapolis, MN 55403; tel. 612 371 5600; fax 1 612 371 0388; e-mail info@mnorch.org; website www.minnesotaorchestra.org; Music Dir Osmo Vänskä; Pres. David J. Hyslop.

**Mississippi Symphony Orchestra:** 201 E Pascagoula Street, Jackson, MS 39201; tel. 1 601 960 1565; website www.msorchestra.com; Music Dir Crafton Beck; Exec. Dir Philip K. Messner.

**Music Academy of the West Summer Festival Orchestra:** 1070 Fairway Road, Santa Barbara, CA 93108; tel. (805) 969-4726; fax (805) 969-0686; website www.musicacademy.org; Pres. David L.Kuehn; Vice-Pres. and Dean W. Harold Laster.

**Music of the Baroque Orchestra:** 343 S Dearborn, Suite 1716, Chicago, IL 60604; Music Dir Thomas Wikman.

**Naples Philharmonic:** 5833 Pelican Bay Blvd, Naples, FL 33963; e-mail info@thephil.org; website www.thephil.org; Music Dir Christopher Seaman; Pres. and CEO Myra Janco Daniels.

**Nashville Symphony Orchestra:** 2000 Glen Echo Road, Suite 204, Nashville, TN 37215; tel. 1 615 783 1200; fax 1 615 255 5656; website www.nashvillesymphony.org; Music Dir Kenneth Schemerhorn; Exec. Dir Stephen R. Vann.

**National Gallery Orchestra:** Sixth Street and Constitution Avenue NW, Washington, DC 20565; Music Dir George Manos.

**National Repertory Orchestra:** PO Box 38, Keystone, CO 80435; e-mail nro@NROMusic.com; website www.nromusic.com; Conductor Carl Topilow.

**National Symphony Orchestra:** John F. Kennedy Center for the Performing Arts, 2700 F Street NW, Washington, DC 20566; tel. 1 202 416 8000; fax 1 202 416 8105; website www.kennedy-center.org/nso; Music Dir Leonard Slatkin; Gen. Man. Richard Hancock.

**New Hampshire Symphony Orchestra:** 1087 Elm Street, Manchester, NH 03101; tel. (603) 669-3559; fax (603) 623-1195; e-mail info@nhso.org; website www.nhso.org; Exec. Dir: Douglas A. Barry; Music Dir: Kenneth Kiesler; f. 1974; .

**New Haven Symphony Orchestra:** 70 Audubon Street, New Haven, CT 06510; tel. (203) 865-0831; fax (203) 789-8907; website www.newhavensymphony.org; Music Dir: Jung-Ho Pak; Exec. Dir: Michael MacLeod.

**New Jersey Symphony Orchestra:** 2 Central Avenue, Newark, NJ 07102; tel. 1 201 624 3713; fax 1 201 624 2115; e-mail information@njsymphony.org; website www.njsymphony.org; Music Dir Zdenek Macal; Exec. Dir Lawrence Tamburri.

**New Mexico Symphony Orchestra:** 4407 Menaul Blvd NE, Albuquerque, NM 87190; tel. 1 505 881 9590; website www.nmso.org; Music Dir Guillermo Figueroa; Exec. Dir Kevin Hagen.

**New World Symphony:** 541 Lincoln Road, Third Floor, Miami Beach, FL 33139; tel. 1 305 673 3330; fax 1 305 673 6749; e-mail email@nws.org; website www.nws.org; Artistic Dir Michael Tilson Thomas; Artistic Admin. John Duffy.

**New York Chamber Symphony:** 92nd Street Y, 1395 Lexington Avenue, New York, NY 10128; Music Dir Gerard Schwarz; Man. Tom Gaitens.

**New York Philharmonic Orchestra:** Avery Fisher Hall, 10 Lincoln Center Plaza, Lincoln Center for the Performing Arts, Broadway at 65th St, New York, NY 10023; tel. 1 212 875 5900; fax 1 212 875 5717; website www.newyorkphilharmonic.org; Music Dir Lorin Maazel; Man. Dir Deborah Borda.

**New York Virtuosi Chamber Symphony:** C. W. Post College, Greenvale, NY 11548; website www.newyorkvirtuosi.org; Music Dir Kenneth Klein; Exec. Dir Yolanda Padula.

**North Carolina Symphony Orchestra:** 2 E South Street, Raleigh, NC 27601; tel. 1 919 733 2750; fax 1 919 733 9920; website www.ncsymphony.org; Music Dir Gerhardt Zimmerman; Exec. Dir Banks C. Talley Jnr.

**Oakland East Bay Symphony Orchestra:** 1999 Harrison Street, Suite 2030, Oakland, CA 94612; Music Dir Michael Morgan.

**Oklahoma City Philharmonic Orchestra:** 428 W California, Suite 210, Oklahoma City, OK 73102; website www.okcphilharmonic.org; Music Dir Joel Levine; Gen. Man. Alan D. Valentine.

**Omaha Symphony Orchestra:** 1605 Howard Street, Suite 310, Omaha, NE 68102; tel. 1 402 342 3836; fax 1 402 342 3819; website www.omahasymphony.org; Music Dir Bruce Hangen; Exec. Dir Roland Valliere.

**Oregon Symphony Orchestra:** 711 SW Alder, Suite 200, Portland, OR 97205; tel. 1 503 228 4294; fax 1 503 228 4150; website www.orsymphony.org; Music Dir Carlos Kalmar; Pres. Don Roth.

**Orpheus Chamber Orchestra:** 490 Riverside Drive, New York, NY 10027; tel. (212) 896-1700; fax (212) 896-1717; e-mail orpheusnyc@orpheusnyc.org; website www.orpheusnyc.org; Man. Dir: Ronnie Bauch.

**Pacific Symphony Orchestra:** 3631 S Harbor Blvd, Suite 100, Santa Ana, CA 92704; tel. 1 714 755 5788; fax 1 714 755 5789; e-mail pso@pso.org; website www.pacificsymphony.org; Music Dir Carl St Clair; Exec. Dir John E. Forsyte.

**Pasadena Symphony Orchestra:** 2500 E Colorado Blvd, Suite 260, Pasadena, CA 91107; tel. 1 626 793 7172; fax 1 626 793 7180; website www.pasadenasymphony.org; Music Dir Jorge Mester; Exec. Dir Wayne Shilkret.

**Philadelphia Orchestra:** Academy of Music, 260 S Broad Street, Suite 1600, Philadelphia, PA 19102; tel. 1 215 893 1900; fax 1 215 893 7649; e-mail philadelphia_orchestra@ philadelphiaorchestra.org; website www.philorch.org; Music Dir Christoph Eschenbach; Pres. and COO Joseph H. Kluger.

**Philharmonia Baroque Orchestra:** 180 Redwood Street, Suite 200, San Francisco, CA 94102; tel. 1 415 252 1288; fax 1 415 252 1488; e-mail info@philharmonia.org; website www.philharmonia.org; Music Dir Nicholas McGegan; Exec. Dir George Gelles.

**Philharmonia Virtuosi:** PO Box 645, North Salem, NY 10560-0645; e-mail bkapp@pvmusic.org; website pvmusic.org; Exec. Dir Barbara Kapp.

**Phoenix Symphony Orchestra:** 455 N Third Street, Suite 390, Phoenix, AZ 85004; tel. 1 602 495 1117; fax 1 602 253 1772; e-mail info@phoenixsymphony.org; website www.phoenixsymphony.org; Principal Guest Conductor Hermann Michael; Pres. and CEO Conrad Kloh; Music Dir James Sedares.

**Pittsburgh Symphony Orchestra:** Heinz Hall, 600 Penn Avenue, Pittsburgh, PA 15222-3259; tel. (412) 392-4900; fax (412) 392-4909; e-mail ldonnermeyer@pittsburghsymphony.org; website www.pittsburghsymphony.org; Music Dir: Mariss Jansons; Pres. and CEO: Lawrence Tamburri.

**Portland Symphony Orchestra:** 477 Congress Street, Mezzanine, Portland, ME 04104; tel. 1 207 773 6128; fax 1 207 773 6089; e-mail psobox@portlandsymphony.com; website www.portlandsymphony.com; Music Dir Toshiyuki Shimada; Exec. Dir Jane E. Hunter.

**Puerto Rico Symphony Orchestra:** PO Box 41227, San Juan, PR 00940; tel. 787 721 7727; fax 787 726 4009; website www.sinfonicapr.gobierno.pr; Music Dir Eugene Kohn; Gen. Dir Félix Rosas Crespo.

**Rhode Island Philharmonic Orchestra:** 222 Richmond Street, Providence, RI 02903; tel. 1 401 831 3123; fax 1 401 831 4577; e-mail information@ri-philharmonic.org; website www.ri-philharmonic.org; Music Dir Larry Rachleff; Exec. Dir David M. Wax.

**Richmond Symphony Orchestra:** The Berkshire, 300 W Franklin Street, Richmond, VA 23220; tel. 1 804 788 4717; fax 1 804 788 1541; website www.richmondsymphony.com; Music Dir Mark Russell Smith; Exec. Dir David Fisk.

**Rochester Philharmonic Orchestra:** 108 East Avenue, Rochester, NY 14604; tel. (585) 454-7311; fax (585) 423-2256; e-mail rpo@rpo.org; website www.rpo.org; Music Dir: Christopher Seaman; Pres. and CEO: Richard Nowlin.

**Sacramento Symphony Orchestra:** 77 Cadillac Drive, Suite 101, Sacramento, CA 95825; Music Dir Geoffrey Simon.

**San Antonio Symphony Orchestra:** 222 E Houston Street, Suite 200, San Antonio, TX 78205; tel. 1 210 554 1000; fax 1 210 554 1008; website www.sasymphony.org; Music Dir Larry Rachleff; Exec. Dir David Schillhammer.

**San Francisco Symphony:** Louise M. Davies Symphony Hall, 201 Van Ness Avenue, San Francisco, CA 94102; tel. 1 415 552 8000; fax 1 415 431 6857; website www.sfsymphony.org; Music Dir Michael Tilson Thomas; Exec. Dir Peter Pastreich.

**San Jose Symphony Orchestra:** 99 Almaden Blvd, Suite 400, San Jose, CA 95113; tel. 1 408 287 7383; fax 1 408 286 6391; Music Dir Leonid Grin.

**Santa Barbara Symphony Orchestra:** 1900 State Street, Suite G, Santa Barbara, CA 93101; tel. 1 805 898 9626; fax 1 805 898 9326; e-mail info@thesymphony.org; website www.thesymphony.org; Music Dir Gisèle Ben-Dor; Gen. Man. James L. Wright.

**Savannah Symphony Orchestra:** PO Box 9505, Savannah, GA 31412; website www.savannahsymphony.org; Music Dir Philip Greenberg; Gen. Man. Gregg W. Gustafson.

**Seattle Symphony Orchestra:** 200 University Street, Seattle, WA 98111; tel. 1 206 215 4700; fax 1 206 215 4701; e-mail info@seattlesymphony.org; website www.seattlesymphony.org; Music Dir Gerard Schwarz; Exec. Dir Deborah Card.

**South Dakota Symphony Orchestra:** 300 N Dakota Avenue, Suite 116, Sioux Falls, SD 57104; tel. 1 605 335 7933; fax 1 605 335 1958; e-mail sdsymphony@sdsymphony.org; website www.sdsymphony.org; Music Dir Henry Charles Smith; Exec. Dir Tom Bennett.

**Spokane Symphony Orchestra:** 818 W Riverside, Suite 100, Spokane, WA 99201; tel. 1 509 624 1200; website www.spokanesymphony.org; Music Dir Fabio Mechetti; Exec. Dir Richard Early.

**St Louis Symphony Orchestra:** Powell Symphony Hall, 718 N Grand Blvd, St Louis, MO 63103; tel. 1 314 533 2500; fax 1 314 286 4142; website www.slso.org; Music Dir David Robertson; Exec. Dir Bruce Coppock.

**The Saint Paul Chamber Orchestra:** 408 Saint Peter Street, Third Floor, Saint Paul, MN 55102-1497; tel. (651) 292-3248; fax (651) 292-3281; e-mail info@spcomail.org; website www.thespco.org; Pres. and Man. Dir Bruce Coppock.

**Stockton Symphony Orchestra:** 46 W Fremont Street, Stockton, CA 95202; tel. 1 209 951 0196; fax 1 209 951 1050; e-mail admin@stocktonsymphony.org; website www.stocktonsymphony.org; Music Dir Peter Jaffe; Exec. Dir George A. Sinclair.

**Syracuse Symphony Orchestra:** 411 Montgomery Street, Suite 40, Syracuse, NY 13202; tel. 1 315 424 8222; fax 1 315 424 1131; website www.syracusesymphony.org; Music Dir Daniel Hege; Exec. Dir Jeffry Comanici.

**Theater Chamber Players of Kennedy Center:** John F. Kennedy Center for the Performing Arts, Washington, DC 20566; Dirs Leon Fleisher, Dina Koston.

**Toledo Symphony Orchestra:** 1838 Parkwood Avenue, Suite 310, Toledo, OH 43624; tel. 1 419 246 8000; fax 1 419 321 0890; website www.toledosymphony.com; Principal Conductor Stefan Sanderling; Man. Dir Robert Bell.

**Tucson Symphony Orchestra:** Tucson Symphony Center, 2175 N Sixth Avenue, Tucson, AZ 85705; tel. 1 520 792 9155; website www.tucsonsymphony.org; Music Dir George Hanson; Exec. Dir Susan Franano.

**Utah Symphony Orchestra:** 123 W South Temple, Salt Lake City, UT 84101; tel. 1 801 533 5626; fax 1 801 521 6634; Music Dir Keith Lockhart; Artistic Admin. Cecil Cole.

**Virginia Symphony Orchestra:** 861 Glenrock Road, Suite 200, Norfolk, VA 23502; tel. 1 757 466 3060; fax 1 757 466 3046; website www.virginiasymphony.org; Music Dir JoAnn Falletta; Exec. Dir John Morison.

**West Virginia Symphony Orchestra:** PO Box 2292, Charleston, WV 24328; e-mail info@wvsymphony.org; website www.wvsymphony.org; Music Dir Thomas Conlin; Exec. Dir Paul A. Helfrich.

**Wichita Symphony Orchestra:** 225 W Douglas, Suite 207, Wichita, KS 67202; tel. 1 316 267 5259; fax 1 316 267 1937; e-mail symphony@wso.org; website www.wso.org; Music Dir Andrew Sewell; Gen. Man. Mitchell A. Berman.

**The Women's Philharmonic:** 44 Page Street, Suite 604D, San Francisco, CA 94102; tel. 1 415 437 0123; fax 1 415 437 0121; e-mail info@womensphil.org; website www.womensphil.org; Exec. Dir Shira Cion.

## Uruguay

**Orquesta Sinfónia del SODRE:** Calle Sarandi 450, Montevideo 1100; Music Dir Roberto Montenegro; Pres. Escribano Ramiro Llana.

## Venezuela

**Orquesta Sinfónica Municipal de Caracas:** PO Box 17390, Parque Central, Caracas 1015-A; Dir Carlos Riazuelo.

**Simón Bolivar Symphony Orchestra of Venezuela:** Torre Oeste, 1°, Parque Central, Caracas; Music Dir José Antonio Abreu.

# APPENDIX B: OPERA COMPANIES

## Argentina

**Teatro Colón:** Cerrito 618, 1010 Buenos Aires; tel. 54 1 382 8924; fax 54 1 111232; website www.teatrocolon.org.ar; Gen. and Artistic Dir Gabriel Senanes.

## Australia

**Opera Australia:** PO Box 291, Strawberry Hills, NSW 2012; tel. 61 2 9699 1099; fax 61 2 9699 3184; e-mail online@opera-australia.org.au; website www .opera-australia.org.au; Gen. Man. Donald McDonald; Artistic Dir Moffat Oxenbould.

**Opera Australia:** PO Box 389, South Melbourne, Vic. 3205; tel. 61 3 9685 3777; fax 61 3 9686 1441; e-mail online@opera-australia.org.au; website www .opera-australia.org.au; Public Affairs Man. Sonja Chambers.

**Opera Queensland:** Queensland Conservatorium, 16 Russell Street, South Bank, Qld 4101; tel. 61 7 3875 3030; fax 61 7 3844 5352; e-mail info@ operaqueensland.com.au; website www.operaqueensland.org.au; Gen. Dir: Chris J. Mangin; Gen. Man. Suzannah Conway.

**State Opera of South Australia:** 216 Marion Road, Netley, SA 5037; tel. 61 8 226 4790; fax 61 8 226 4791; e-mail info@saopera.sa.gov.au; website www .saopera.sa.gov.au; Artistic Dir Bill Gillespie; Gen. Dir Stephen Phillips.

**Victoria State Opera:** 77 Southbank Blvd, Melbourne, Vic. 3205; Gen. Man. Ken Mackenzie-Forbes; Artistic Admin. Kate Stevenson.

**West Australian Opera:** His Majesty's Theatre, 825 Hay Street, Perth, WA 6850; tel. 08 9321 5869; fax 08 9324 1134; website www.waopera.asn.au; Gen. Man. Carolyn Chard; Artistic Dir Richard Mills; Head of Music Marilyn Phillips.

## Austria

**Landestheater:** Promenade 39, 4010 Linz; tel. 43 732 761 1100; fax 43 732 761 1105; Dir Roman Zeilinger.

**Landestheater:** Schwarstrasse 22, 5020 Salzburg; tel. 43 662 871512; fax 43 662 87151213; Dir Lutz Hochstraate.

**Raimund Theater:** Wallgasse 18–20, 1060 Vienna.

**Sommertheater:** Wiesingerstrasse 7, 4820 Bad Ischl; Music Dir Eduard Macku; Man. Silvia Müller.

**Stadttheater:** Rathausplatz 11, 3100 St Pölten; Dir Perter Wolsdorff.

**Stadttheater:** Theaterplatz 4, 9020 Klagenfurt; Dir Dietmar Pflegerl.

**Stadttheater:** Theaterplatz 7, 2500 Baden bei Wien; Dir Helmuth Brand-stätter.

**Tiroler Landestheater:** Rennweg 2, 6020 Innsbruck; tel. 43 512 520744; fax 43 512 52074333; Dir Dominique Mentha.

**Vereinigte Bühnen Wien GmbH:** Linke Wienzeile 6, 1060 Vienna; tel. 43 1 588 30 200; fax 43 1 588 30 33; e-mail info@vbw.at; website www .musicalvienna.at; CEO: Franz Häussler; consists of three theatres: Theater an der Wien, Raimund Theater and Etablissement Ronacher.

**Vereinigte Bühnen:** Kaiser Josef Platz 10, 8010 Graz; tel. 43 316 8000; fax 43 316 8565; website www.theater-graz.com; Dir Gerhard Brunner.

**Volksoper:** Währingerstrasse 78, 1090 Vienna; tel. 43 1 514 443318; website www.volksoper.at; Dir Ioan Holender.

**Wiener Kammeroper:** Fleischmarkt 24, 1010 Vienna; tel. 43 1 512 0100; fax 43 1 512 010010; e-mail information@wienerkammeroper.at; website www .wienerkammeroper.at; Music Dir Daniel Hoyem-Cavazza; Gen. Mans Isabella Gabor, Holger Bleck.

**Wiener Staatsoper:** Opernring 2, 1010 Vienna; tel. and fax 43 1 51444; e-mail information@wiener-staatsoper.at; website www.wiener-staatsoper.at; Dir Ioan Holender.

## Belgium

**Opéra Royal de Wallonie:** 1 rue des Dominicains, 4000 Liège; tel. 32 4 221 4720; fax 32 4 221 0201.

**Opera voor Vlaanderen:** Schouwburgstraat 3, 9000 Ghent; tel. 32 9 225 2425; Music Dir Marc Minkowski; Gen. Man. Marc Clémeur.

**Théâtre Royal de la Monnaie:** 4 rue Léopold, 1000 Brussels; tel. 32 2 229 1200; fax 32 2 229 1330; website www.demunt.be; Dir Bernard Foccroulle.

**Vlaamse Opera:** Van Ertbornstraat 8, 2018 Antwerp; tel. 32 3 202 1011; fax 32 3 232 2661; website www.vlaamseopera.be.

## Bosnia and Herzegovina

**National Theater Opera:** Obala 9, 71000 Sarajevo.

## Bulgaria

**Bourgas State Opera:** K1, Ohridski St 2, 8000 Bourgas.

**Plovdiv State Opera:** 4000 Plovdiv.

**Sofia National Opera:** 30 Dondoukov Blvd, 1000 Sofia; tel. 359 2 988 5869; fax 3592 987 7998; Chief Conductor Gueorgui Notev; Gen. Man. Plamen Kartaloff.

**Stara Zagora State Opera:** 6000 Stara Zagora.

**Stefan Makedonski Musical Theater:** 3P Volov Street, 1500 Sofia.

**Varna State Opera:** 1 Nezavisimost Square, 9000 Varna; tel. 35952 602086; fax 35952 602088; e-mail opera.varna@mbox.actbg.bg; Gen. Dir Hristo Ignatov.

## Canada

**Calgary Opera:** 601 237-8 Avenue SE, Calgary, AB T2G 5C3; tel. 1 403 262 7286; fax 1 403 263 5428; website www.calgaryopera.com; Gen. Dir/CEO W. R. McPhee.

**Canadian Opera Company:** 227 Front Street E, Toronto, ON M5A 1E8; tel. 1 416 363 6671; fax 1 416 363 5584; e-mail info@coc.ca; website www.coc.ca; Gen. Dir Richard Bradshaw.

**Edmonton Opera:** Winspear Centre, 9720 102nd Avenue NW, Edmonton, AB T5J 4B2; tel. 1 780 424 4040; fax 1 780 429 0600; e-mail edmopera@ edmontonopera.com; website www.edmontonopera.com.

**Edmonton Opera Association:** 320-10232 112th Street, Edmonton, AB T5K 1M4; tel. 1 403 423 424 4040/1000; fax 1 403 423 429 0600; Gen. Dir Richard Mantle.

**Manitoba Opera:** 380 Graham Avenue, Winnipeg, MB RC3 4K2; tel. 1 204 942 7479; fax 1 204 949 0377; e-mail mbopera@manitobaopera.mb.ca; website www.manitobaopera.mb.ca; Dir Larry Desrochers.

**Opéra de Montréal:** 260 Blvd de Maisonneuve W, Montréal, QC H2X 1V9; tel. 1 514 985 2222; fax 1 514 985 2219; e-mail info@operademontreal.com; website www.operademontreal.com; Artistic and Gen. Dir David Moss.

**Opéra de Québec:** 1220 Avenue Taché, Québec, QC G1R 3B4; tel. 1 418 529 4142; fax 1 418 529 3735; e-mail operaqc@mediom.qc.ca; website www .operadequebec.qc.ca; Gen. and Artistic Dir Grégoire Legendre.

**Opera Mississauga:** Living Arts Centre, 4141 Living Arts Drive, Mississauga, ON L5B 4B8; tel. 1 905 306 0060; fax 1 905 306 9976; e-mail info@ royaloperacanada.com; website www.royaloperacanada.com; Gen. and Artistic Dir Dwight Bennett.

**Opera Ontario:** 110 King Street W, Second Floor, Hamilton, ON L8P 4S6; Artistic Dir Daniel Lipton.

**Pacific Opera Victoria:** 1316b Government Street, Victoria, BC V8W 1Y8; tel. 1 250 382 1641; fax 1 250 382 4944; website www.pov.bc.ca; Artistic Dir Timothy Vernon; Gen. Man. David Devan.

**Royal Opera Canada:** Toronto Centre for the Arts, 5040 Yonge Street, Toronto, ON M2N 6R8; tel. 1 416 322 0456; fax 1 416 482 7044; e-mail info@ royaloperacanada.com; website www.royaloperacanada.com; Gen. and Artistic Dir Dwight Bennett.

**Vancouver Opera:** 835 Cambie Street, Vancouver, BC V6B 2P4; tel. 1 604 682 2871; fax 1 604 682 3981; website www.vanopera.bc.ca; Music/Artistic Admin. Jonathan Darlington; Gen. Dir James W. Wright.

## Chile

**Opera del Teatro Municipal:** San Antonio 149, Santiago Centro; tel. 56 2 4631002; fax 56 2 6337214; e-mail giesen@ctcreuna.cl; website www .municipal.cl; Gen. Dir Cristobal Giesen.

## People's Republic of China

**Central Opera Theater:** Dongzhimenwai, Zuojiazhuang, Beijing 100028; tel. 86 465 2317; Dir Wang Shi-guang.

**China Peking Opera Theater:** Beijing; Pres. Zhang Dong-Chuan.

**Shanghai Opera House:** Lane 100, Changshu Road, Shanghai 200040; tel. 86 216 248 5359; fax 86 216 249 8127.

## Colombia

**Compañia Nacional de Opera:** Teatro Colón, Calle 10, No. 5-32, Bogotá.

## Costa Rica

**Compañía Lirica Nacional:** PO Box 1035, San José 1000; Dir Gloria Waissbluth.

## Czech Republic

**Moravian State Theatre:** Tr Svobdy 33, 771 07 Olomouc; tel. 420 68 522 5727; fax 420 68 522 5781.

**National Theatre:** Dvo ákova 11, 657 70 Brno; tel. 420 5 4232 1285; fax 420 5 4221 3746.

**National Theatre:** PO Box 865, 112 30 Prague 1; tel. 420 2 24 910312/901227; fax 420 2 24 911524.

**Ostrava State Theatre:** Pabla Nerudy 14, 701 04 Ostrava.

**Silesian Theatre:** Horní nám sti 13, 74669 Opava.

**State Opera:** Legerova 75, CRIII 21 Prague; tel. 420 22 4 227 6396; fax 420 22 423 0410/29437.

**Stavovske Divadlo (Theatre of the Estates):** Ostrovni, PO Box 865, 11230 Prague 1; tel. 44 2 24 215001/26 7797/901520; fax 44 2 24 91 1530.

**J. K. Tyl Theatre:** Prokopova 14, 304 11 Pize.

**Z nejedlý State Theatre:** Kralova Vý ina 10, 400 00 Ustí nad Labem.

## Denmark

**Den Jyske Opera (Danish National Opera):** Musikhuset Århus, Thomas Jensens Alle, 8000 Århus; tel. 45 89 409110; fax 45 86 133710; e-mail post@ jyske-opera.dk; website www.jyske-opera.dk; Gen. Dir Troels Kold; Admin. Tony Borup Mortenson.

**Det Kongelige Teater (Royal Danish Opera):** PO Box 2185, 1017 Copenhagen K; tel. 45 33 696933; fax 45 33 696767; website www.kgl-teater .dk; performs at the Copenhagen Opera House (address: Ekvipagemestervej 10, Copenhagen).

**Musikdramatisk Teater:** Ernst Meyersgade 8, 1772 Copenhagen V.

## Estonia

**Estonian National Opera:** Estonia Blvd 4, 10148 Tallinn; tel. 372 6831 201; fax 372 6313 080; e-mail info@opera.ee; website www.ooper.ee; Artistic Dir: Arvo Volmer.

## Finland

**Finnish National Opera:** PO Box 176, Helsingkatu 58, 00251 Helsinki; tel. 358 9 403021; fax 358 9 40302305; website www.operafin.fi; Gen. Dir Erkki Korhonen.

## France

**Angers Nantes Opéra:** Théâtre Graslin, 1 rue Molière, 44000 Nantes; tel. 2 40 89 84 00; fax 2 40 41 90 77; e-mail angers@angers-nantes-opera.com; website www.angers-nantes-opera.com.

**Atelier du Rhin:** 6 Route d'Ingersheim, PO Box 593, 68008 Colmar; tel. 33 3 89 41 71 92; fax 33 3 89 41 33 26; e-mail info@atelierdurhin.com; website www .atelierdurhin.com; Dir Matthew Jocelyn.

**Atelier Lyrique de Tourcoing:** 82 Blvd Gambetta, 59200 Tourcoing; tel. 33 3 20 26 66 03; fax 33 3 20 27 91 19; e-mail atelierlyriquedetourcoing@nordnet .fr; Gen. Dir Jean-Claude Malgoire; Gen. Admin. Catherine Noel.

**Châtelet Théâtre Musical:** 2 rue Edouard Colonne, 75001 Paris; tel. 33 1 40 28 28 28; fax 33 1 42 36 89 75; website www.chatelet-theatre.com; Gen. Dir Jean-Pierre Brossmann.

**Chorégies d'Orange:** PO Box 205, 84107 Orange Cedex; tel. 33 90 51 83 83; fax 33 90 34 87 67; e-mail info@choregies.asso.fr; website www.choregies.asso .fr.

**Ecole Art Lyrique de l'Opéra:** 5 rue Favart, 75009 Paris; Dir Michel Sénéchal; Admin. Francis Meunier.

**Grand Théâtre de Reims:** 13 rue Chanzy, 51100 Reims; tel. 33 3 26 50 31 00; fax 33 3 26 84 90 02.

**L'Opéra Comique:** 5 rue Favart, 75002 Paris; tel. 33 1 42 44 45 40/5; fax 33 1 49 26 05 93; website www.opera-comique.com; Dir Jérôme Savary.

**L'Opéra de Dijon:** Service Location, 2 rue Longpierre, 21000 Dijon; tel. 33 80 67 23 23; Dir Pierre Filippi.

**Opéra d'Avignon:** Regie Municipale, PO Box 111, 84007 Avignon; tel. 33 90 82 42 42; fax 33 90 85 04 23.

**Opéra de La Bastille:** 120 rue de Lyon, 75012 Paris; tel. 33 1 40 01 17 89; fax 33 1 44 73 13 00; website www.opera-de-paris.fr; Conductor James Conlon; Gen. Admin. Hugues Gall.

**Opéra de Lille:** Théâtre de l'Opéra, 2 rue des Bons Enfants, 59800 Lille; tel. 33 3 20 14 99 20; fax 33 3 20 14 99 27; website www.opera-lille.fr; Artistic Dir Ricardo Szwarcer; Admin. Michel Default.

**Opéra de Lyon:** 1 Place de la Comedie, 69001 Lyon; tel. 334 72 00 45 00; fax 334 72 00 45 01; website www.opera-lyon.com; Gen. Dir Serge Dorny; Deputy Dir Patrice Armengau.

**Opéra de Marseille:** 2 rue Molière, 1321 Marseille Cédex 01; tel. 33 4 91 55 21 12.

**Opéra de Nancy et de Lorraine:** 1 rue Ste Catherine, 54000 Nancy; tel. 33 83 85 33 20; fax 33 83 85 30 66; Dir Antoine Bourseiller; Admin. Christophe Bezzone.

**Opéra de Tours:** Grand Théâtre, 34 rue de la Scellerie, 37000 Tours; tel. 33 247 60 20 00; fax 33 247 60 20 40; e-mail theatre@ville-tours.fr; Dir: Jean-Yves Ossonce; Admin.: Luc Cavalier.

**Opéra du Rhin:** 19 Place Broglie, 67008 Strasbourg Cédex; tel. 33 3 88 75 48 23; fax 33 3 88 24 09 34; website www.opera-national-du-rhin.com; Gen. Dir Laurent Spielmann; Admin. Lucien Colinet.

**Opéra National de Bordeaux:** Grand Théâtre, place de la Comédie, BP 95, 33025 Bordeaux Cédex; tel. 33(0)5 56 00 85 20; fax 33(0)5 56 81 93 66; website www.opera-bordeaux.com; Dir Thierry Fouquet.

**Opéra National de Montpellier:** 11 Blvd Victor Hugo, 34967 Montpellier, Cédex 2; tel. 04 67 60 19 80; fax 04 67 60 19 90; website www.opera -montpellier.com; Gen. Dir Henri Maier; Admin. Renée Panabière.

**Opéra Théâtre de Metz:** 4–5 Place de la Comédie, 57000 Metz; tel. 03 87 55 51 71; fax 03 87 31 32 37; e-mail smtp.theatre@maine-metz.fr; Admin. Daniel Lucas.

**Opera de Rouen:** 7 rue du Docteur Rambert, 76000 Rouen; tel. 33 2 35 98 50 98; fax 33 2 35 15 33 49; website www.operaderouen.com; Dir Laurent Langlois; Musical Dir Oswald Sallaberger.

**Théâtre de Caen/Atelier Lyrique de Caen:** PO Box 217, 14007 Caen Cédex; Dir Jean Malraye.

**Théâtre de l'Opéra de Nice:** 4/6 rue St François de Paule, 06300 Nice; tel. 33 492 17 40 62; fax 33 492 17 40 65; e-mail olivier-cautres@ville-nice.fr; Music Dir: Marco Guidarini; Man. Paul-Emile Fourny.

**Théâtre des Arts:** 76177 Rouen Cédex; Dir Marc Adam.

**Théâtre des Champs-Elysées:** 15 Avenue Montaigne, 75008 Paris; tel. 33 1 49 52 50 00; fax 33 1 49 52 07 41; website www.theatrechampselysses.fr; Gen. Dir Alain Durel; Admin. Francis Lepigeon.

**Théâtre du Capitole:** Place du Capitole, 31000 Toulouse; tel. 33 61 23 21 35; website www.theatre-du-capitole.org; Artistic Dir Nicolas Joel; Admin. Robert Gouaze.

**Théâtre National de l'Opéra de Paris:** 8 rue Scribe, 75009 Paris.

## Germany

**Bühnen der Hansestadt Lübeck:** Fischergrube 5-21, 2400 Lübeck; Gen. Music Dir Erich Wächter; Gen. Man. Dietrich von Oertsen.

**Bühnen der Stadt Bielefeld:** Brunhenstrasse 3–9, Pf 220, 4800 Bielefeld; tel. 49 521512502; fax 49 521 513430; Gen. Music Dir Rainer Koch; Man. Heiner Bruns.

**Bühnen der Stadt Gera:** Küchengartenalle 2, 6500 Gera; Music Dir Wolfgang Wappler; Man. Eberhard Kneipel.

**Badisches Staatstheater Karlsruhe:** Baumeisterstrasse 11, Pf 1449, 7500 Karlsruhe; Gen. Music Dir Günter Neuhold; Gen. Man. Günter Könemann.

**Bayerische Kammeroper:** Rathaus, Gemeinde Veitshöchheim, 8707 Veit-shöchheim; Music Dir Siegfried Köhler; Man. Blagoy Apostolov.

**Bayerische Staatsoper-Nationaltheater:** Max-Joseph-Platz, 80539 Munich; tel. 49 89 2185 1000; fax 49 89 2185 1003; website www .staatstheater.bayern.de; Gen. and Artistic Dir: Sir Peter Jonas; Man. Dir: Dr Roland Felber.

**Berliner Kammeroper eV:** Kottbusser Damm 79, 10967 Berlin; tel. 49 30 693 1054; fax 49 30 692 5201; Music Dir Brynmor Llewelyn Jones; Artistic Dir Henry Akina.

**Big Bang Theater München:** Dachauer Strasse 192, 8000 Munich 50; Music Dir Walter Waidosch.

**Brandenburg Theater:** Grabenstrasse 14, 1800 Brandenburg; Music Dir Heiko Mathias Förster; Man. Ekkehard Phophet.

**Bremen Theater:** Pf 101046, 2800 Bremen.

**Comédia Opera Instabile:** Holzstrasse 11, 8000 Munich 5.

**Das Meininger Theater:** Bernhardstrasse 5, 6100 Meiningen; Music Dir Wolfgang Hocke; Man. Ulrich Burkhard.

**Deutsche Oper am Rhein:** Theatergemeinschaft Düsseldorf-Duisburg, Opernhaus; website www.deutsche-oper-am-rhein.de.

**Deutsche Oper Berlin:** Richard Wagner Str 10, 10585 Berlin; tel. 49 30 343 8401; fax 49 30 343 84232; website www.deutscheoperberlin.de; Gen. Music Dir Christian Thielemann.

**Deutsche Staatsoper Berlin:** Unter den Linden 7, 1060 Berlin; tel. 49 30 20 354555; fax 49 30 20 354481; Gen. Music Dir Daniel Barenboim; Man. Georg Quander.

**Deutsch-Sorbisches Volkstheater Bautzen:** Seminarstrasse 12, 8600 Bautzen; Music Dir Dieter Kempe; Man. Michael Grosse.

**Düsseldorf Heinrich-Heine-Alle 16a, 40213 Düsseldorf; tel. 49 211 89080; fax 49 211 890 8389 Gen. Music Dir Zoltan Pesko; Gen. Man. Kurt Horres.**

**Eduard-von-Winterstein-Theater:** Buchholzer Strasse 67, 9300 Annaberg-Buchholz; Music Dir Ulrich Sprenger; Man. Hans-Hermann Krug.

**Elbe-Saale-Bühnen Wittenberg-Bernburg:** Thomas-Müntzer-Strasse 14–15, 4600 Wittenberg; Music Dir Klaus Hofmann; Man. Helmut Blass.

**Hamburgische Staatsoper:** Grosse Theaterstrasse 34, 20354 Hamberg, Germany; tel. tel. 040 3568-0; website www.hamburgische-staatsoper.de.

**Hans Otto Theater Potsdam:** Berliner Strasse 27a (Schiffbauergasse), 14467 Potsdam; tel. 49 331 9811 0; fax 49 331 9811 280; e-mail hansottotheater@t-online.de; website www.hot.potsdam.de; Man. Dir Volkmar Raback; Art Dir Ralf-Günter Krolkiewicz.

**Hessisches Staatstheater:** Christian-Zais-Strasse 3–5, Pf 3247, 6200 Wiesbaden; Gen. Music Dir Oleg Caetani; Man. Claus Leininger.

**Kammeroper Frankfurt:** Nordenstrasse 60, 6000 Frankfurt am Main; tel. and fax 49 69 55 6189; Music Dir Martin Krähe; Artistic Dir Rainer Pudenz.

**Kammeroper-Niedersachsen:** Eibenstrasse 5c, 3012 Langenhagen; Music Dir Wolfgang M. Sieben; Man. Helmut M. Erlwein.

**Kleist-Theater:** Gerhart-Hauptmann-Strasse, 1200 Frankfurt an der Oder; Gen. Music Dir Nikos Athinäos; Maria-Luise Preuss.

**Komische Oper Berlin:** Behrenstrasse 55–57, 10117 Berlin; tel. 49 30 20 2600; fax 49 30 20 260405; Gen. Music Dir: Kirill Petrenko; Man.: Andreas Homoki.

**Landesbühne Sachsen-Anhalt Lutherstadt Eisleben:** An der Landwehr 5, 4250 Eisleben; Music Dir Paul Sergiou; Man. Frank Hofmann.

**Landesbühnen Sachsen:** Meissner Strasse 152, 01445 Dresden; tel. 49 351 704; fax 49 351 704201; Music Dir Joachim Widlak; Man. Christian Schmidt.

**Landestheater Altenburg:** Theaterplatz 19, 7400 Altenburg; Man. Georg Mittendrein.

**Landestheater Coburg:** Schlossplatz 6, 8630 Coburg; Gen. Music Dir Christian Fröhlich; Man. Ernö Weil.

**Landestheater Dessau:** Fritz-Hesse-Platz 1, 4500 Dessau; Man. Johannes Felsenstein.

**Landestheater Detmold:** Theaterplatz 1, 4930 Detmold; Man. Ulf Reiher.

**Landestheater Mecklenburg:** Friedrich-Ludwig-Jahn-Strasse, 2080 Neustrelitz; Music Dir Golo Berg; Man. Manfred Straube.

**Landestheater und Landeskapelle Eisenach:** Theaterplatz 4–7, 5900 Eisenach; Gen. Music Dir Harke de Roos; Man. Jürgen Fabritius.

**Münchner Opernbühne (Deutsches-Tourneetheater):** Damborstrasse 11, 8900 Augsburg; Conductors Paul Popescu, Tams Sulyok; Man. Kurt Rösler.

**Mecklenburgisches Staatstheater Schwerin:** Alter Garten, 2751 Schwerin.

**Minipolitan-Eschweges Kleine Schaubühne e V:** Niederhoner Strasse 2, 3440 Eschwege; Conductors Andreas Paetzold, Andreas Worm.

**Musiktheater im Revier:** Kennedyplatz, Pf 101854, 4650 Gelsenkirchen; tel. 49 209 4097-138; fax 49 209 4097-262; website www.musiktheater-im-revier.de; Gen. Music Dir Neil Varon; Gen. Man. Ludwig Baum.

**Musiktheater Oberlausitz/Niederschlesien GmbH:** Demianiplatz 2, 02826 Görlitz; tel. 49 3581-47 47 21; e-mail info@theater-goerlitz.de; website www.theater-goerlitz.de; Music Dir Eckehard Stier; Man. Dr Michael Wieler.

**Nationaltheater Mannheim:** Mozartstrasse 9, 68161 Mannheim; tel. 49 621 16800; fax 49 621 21540; Chief Conductor Jun Märkl; Man. Klaus Schultz.

**Neuburger Kammeroper:** Willstätter Strasse 18, 8070 Ingolstadt.

**Neue Flora:** Stresemannstrasse 159a, 2000 Hamburg 50; Music Dir David Caddick.

**Niedersächsische Staatstheater Hannover:** Opernhaus, Opernplatz 1, 30159 Hannover; tel. 49 511168 6161; fax 49 511 368 1768/363; Gen. Music Dir Christof Prick; Man. Hans-Peter Lehmann.

**Offenbach-Theater Köln:** Vietorstrasse 70, 5000 Cologne 91; Dir Karl-Wolfgang Saalmann.

**Oldenburgisches Staatstheater:** Theaterwall 18, 2900 Oldenburg; Gen. Music Dir Knut Mahike; Gen. Man.; Hans Häckermann.

**Oper der Stadt Bonn:** Am Boeselagerhof 1, Pf 2440, 53111 Bonn; tel. 49 228 7281; fax 49 228 728371; Man. Gian-Carlo del Monaco.

**Oper der Stadt Köln:** Offenbachplatz, Pf 180241, 50505 Cologne; tel. 49 221 221 8282/8400; Gen. Music Dir James Conlon; Man. Michael Hampe.

**Oper Frankfurt:** Untermainanlage 11, 6000 Frankfurt; tel. 49 69 37 333; fax 49 69 237 330; website www.oper-frankfurt.de; Gen. Music Dir Sylvain Cambreling; Press and Information Brigitta Mazamec.

**Oper Leipzig-Musikalische Komödie:** Dreilindenstrasse 30, 04109 Leipzig; tel. 49 341 12610; fax 49 341 12 61387; Music Dir Roland Seiffarth; Man. Udo Zimmermann.

**Oper Leipzig-Opernhaus:** Augustusplatz 12, 7010 Leipzig; website www.oper-leipzig.de; Man. Udo Zimmermann.

**Operettenhaus Hamburg:** Spielbudenplatz 1, 2000 Hamburg 36; Music Dir Koen Schoots.

**Opernhaus Halle:** Universitätsring 24, 4020 Halle an der Saale; Music Dir Wolfgang Balzer; Man. Klaus Froboese.

**Pfalztheater Kaiserslautern:** Willy Brandt-Platz 4–5, 67657 Kaiserslautern; tel. 631-36750; e-mail info@pfalztheater.bv-pfalz.de; website www.pfalztheater.de; Gen. Music Dir Francesco Corti; Man. Johannes Reitmeier; opera, operetta, musical, ballet.

**Pocket Opera Company Nürnberg:** Gertrudstrasse 21, 90429 Nürnberg; tel. 49 911 329047; fax 49 911 314606; e-mail info@pocket-opera.com; website www.pocket-opera.com; Artistic Dir Peter B. Wyrsch.

**Sächsische Staatsoper Dresden (Semperoper):** Theaterplatz 2, 01067 Dresden; tel. 49 351 49110; fax 49 351 491 1691; Music Dir Giuseppe Sinopoli; Man. Christoph Albrecht.

**Süddeutsche Kammeroper:** Am Eselsberg 10–12, 7900 Ulm.

**Südostbayerisches Städtetheater (Fürstbischöfliches Opernhaus):** Gottfried-Schäffer-Strasse 2, 8390 Passau; Music Dir Jeanpierre Faber; Man. Klaus Schlette.

**Saarländisches Staatstheater:** Schillerplatz, 66111 Saarbrücken; tel. 49 681 30920; fax 49 681 309 2325.

**Schleswig-Holsteinisches Landestheater und Sinfonieorchester:** Rathausstrasse 22, 2390 Flensburg; Gen. Music Dir Gerhard Schneider; Gen. Man. Dr Horst Mesalla.

**Sorbisches National-Ensemble Bautzen:** Aussere Lauenstrasse 2, 8600 Bautzen; Music Dir Jan Bulank; Man. Detlef Kobjela.

**Städtebundtheater:** Schützenstrasse 8, 8670 Hof an der Saale; Music Dir Klaus Straube; Man. Reinhold Röttger.

**Städtische Bühnen Dortmund:** Kuhstrasse 12, 4600 Dortmund; tel. 00 49 231 5027222; Gen. Music Dir Moshe Atzmon; Gen. Man. Horst Fechner; Artistic Dir John Dew.

**Städtische Bühnen Freiburg:** Bertoldstrasse 46, 79098 Freiburg im Breisgau; tel. 49 761 2012807; Music Dir Kwamé Ryan.

**Städtische Bühnen Münster:** Neubrückenstrasse 63, 4400 Münster; Gen. Music Dir Will Humburg; Gen. Man. Achim Thorwald.

**Städtische Bühnen Nürnberg:** Richard-Wagner-Platz 2–10, 90443 Nürnberg; tel. 49 911 231 3500; fax 49 911 231 3571; Gen. Man. Lew Bogdan.

**Städtische Bühnen Osnabrück GmbH:** Domhof 110-1, 4500 Osnabrück; Gen. Music Dir Jean-François Monnard; Man. Norbert Kleine-Borgmann.

**Städtische Bühnen Regensburg:** Bismarckplatz 7, 93047 Regensburg; tel. 49 941 507 1422; fax 49 941 507 4429; Gen. Music Dir Hilary Griffiths; Man. Marietheres List.

**Städtische Theater Chemnitz:** Theaterplatz 2, 9001 Chemnitz; Gen. Music Dir Dieter-Gerhardt Worm; Gen. Man. Jörg Liljeberg.

**Städttheater Würzburg:** Theaterstrasse 21, 8700 Würzburg; Gen. Music Dir Jonathan Seers; Man. Dr Tebbe Harms Kleen.

**Staatsoperette Dresden:** Pirnaer Landstrasse 131, 8045 Dresden; Music Dir Volker Münch; Man. Elke Schneider.

**Staatstheater am Gärtnerplatz 3:** 80469 Munich; tel. 089 20241 1; fax 089 20241-237; website www.staatstheater-am-gaertmerplatz.de; Music Dir: David Stahl; Man.: Prof. Klaus Schultz.

**Staatstheater Braunschweig:** PO Box 4539, 38100 Braunschweig; tel. 49 531 484 2700; fax 49 531 484 2727; Gen. Music Dir Jonas Alber; Gen. Man. Jürgen Flügge.

**Staatstheater Cottbus:** Karl-Liebknecht-Strasse 136, 7500 Cottbus; Gen. Music Dir Frank Morgenstern; Man. Johannes Steurich.

**Staatstheater Darmstadt:** PO Box 111432, 64229 Darmstadt; tel. 49 6151 28111; fax 49 6151 281 1226; Man. Peter Girth.

**Staatstheater Mainz:** Gutenbergplatz 7, 55116 Mainz; Gen. Music Dir Catherine Rückhardt; Man. Georges Delnon.

**Staatstheater Stuttgart:** Oberer Schlossgarten 6, 70173 Stuttgart; tel. 49 711 203 2520; fax 49 711 203 2514; website www.staatstheater.stuttgart.de; Music Dir Lothar Zagrosek; Gen. Dir Klaus Zehlein.

**Stadttheater Aachen:** Theaterplatz, 5100 Aachen; Music Dir Marcus R. Bosch; Gen. Man. Dr Paul Esterhazy.

**Stadttheater Bremerhaven:** Theodor-Heuss-Platz, Pf 120541, 27519 Bremerhaven; tel. 49 471 482 0645; fax 49 471 482 0682; Gen. Music Dir Leo Plettner; Man. Dirk Böttger.

**Stadttheater Döbein:** Theaterstrasse, 7300 Döbein; Music Dir Harald Weigel; Man. Wolfram Jacobi.

**Stadttheater Freiberg:** Borngasse 1, 9200 Freiberg; Music Dir Jany Renz; Man. Rüdiger Bloch.

**Stadttheater Giessen GmbH:** Berliner Platz, 65390 Giessen; tel. 0641 79 57 12; fax 0641 79 57 26; e-mail stadttheater-giessen.intendanz@t-online.de; website www.stadttheatergiessen.de; Gen. Music Dir Carlos Spierer; Man. Cathérine Miville.

**Stadttheater Hildesheim GmbH:** Theaterstrasse 6, 3200 Hildesheim; Music Dir Werner Seitzer; Man. Klaus Engeroff.

**Stadttheater Lüneburg:** An den Reeperbahnen 3, 2120 Lüneburg; Music Dir Michael Dixon; Man. Jan Aust.

**Stadttheater Pforzheim:** Am Waisenhausplatz 5, 75217 Pforzheim; tel. 7231 391488; fax 7231 391485; e-mail theater@stadt-pforzheim.de; website www.theater-pforzheim.de; Gen. Music Dir and Artistic Dir: Jari Hämäläinen.

**Starlighttheater Bochum:** Stadionring 24, 4630 Bochum; Music Dir Phil Edwards.

**Thüringer Landestheater:** Anger 1, 6820 Rudolstadt; Music Dir Konrad Bach; Man. Peter P. Pachl.

**Theater an der Rott:** Pfarrkirchener Strasse 70, 8330 Eggenfelden; Music Dir Lutz Teschendorf; Man. Adi Fischer.

**Theater Augsburg:** Kasernstrasse 4–6, 86152 Augsburg; tel. 49 821 32449; fax 49 821 3244544; e-mail theater@augsburg.de; website www.theater .augsburg.de; Gen. Music Dir: Rudolf Piehlmayer; Man.: Dr Ulrich Peters.

**Theater der Hansestadt Stralsund:** Olof-Palmer-Platz, 2300 Stralsund; Music Dir Daniel Kleiner; Man. Thomas Bayer.

**Theater der Landeshauptstadt Magdeburg:** Pf 1240, 39002 Magdeburg; tel. 49 391 540 6500; fax 49 391 540 6599; Gen. Music Dir Mathias Husmann; Gen. Man. Max K. Hoffmann.

**Theater der Stadt Gummersbach:** Reininghause Strasse, 5270 Gummersbach; Music Dir and Man. Gus Anton.

**Theater der Stadt Heidelberg:** Friedrichstrasse 5, 69117 Heidelberg; tel. 49 6221 583502; fax 49 6221 583599; Gen. Music Dir: Thomas Kalb; Man.: Günther Beelitz.

**Theater der Stadt Koblenz:** Clemensstrasse 1, 5400 Koblenz 1; Gen. Music Dir Christian Klutting; Man. Hannes Houska.

**Theater der Stadt Trier:** Am Augustinerhof, 5500 Trier; Gen. Music Dir Reinhard Petersen.

**Theater des Westens Berlin:** Kantstrasse 12, 1000 Berlin; Music Dir Peter Keuschnig; Man. Helmut Baumann.

**Theater Greifswald:** Anklamer Strasse 106, 2200 Greifswald; Chief Conductor Ekkehard Klemm; Man. Dieter Wagner.

**Theater Hagen:** Elberfelder Strasse 65, 58095 Hagen; Artistic Dir: Rainer Friedemann; Music Dir: Antony Hermus.

**Theater Halberstadt:** Spiegelstrasse 20a, 3600 Halberstadt; Music Dir Christian Hammer; Man. Gero Hammer.

**Theater-Hof:** Kulmbacherstrasse 5, 95030 Hof; e-mail info@theater-hof.com; website www.theater-hof.com.

**Theater Kiel:** Rathausplatz 4, 24103 Kiel; tel. 49 431 901 2880; fax 49 431 901 2838; e-mail info@theater-kiel.de; website www.kiel.de/buehnen; Artistic Dir (Opera): Anette Berg; Gen. Music Dir: Georg Fritesch.

**Theater Nordhausen:** Käthe-Kollwitz-Strasse 15, Pf 109, 5500 Nordhausen; Man. Hubert Kross.

**Theater und Philharmonie Essen:** Rolandstrasse 10, 4300 Essen 1; Gen. Music Dir Wolf-Dieter Hauschild.

**Theater Zeitz:** August-Bebel-Strasse 2, 4900 Zeitz; Music Dir Hans-Frieder Liebmann; Man. Wolfgang Eysold.

**Theater Zwickau:** Gewandhausstrasse 7, Pf 308, 9541 Zwickau; Music Dir Albrecht Hofmann; Man. Horst-Dieter Brand.

**Ulmer Theater:** Olgastrasse 73, 7900 Ulm; Gen. Music Dir Alicja Mounk; Man. Dr Bernd Wilms.

**Vereinigte Städtische Bühnen Krefeld und Mönchengladbach:** Theater Mönchengladbach, Odenkirchener Strasse 78, 41236 Mönchengladbach; tel. 2166-6151; fax 2166-420110; website www.theater-krefeld -moenchengladbach.de; Gen. Dir Jens Pesel.

**Vogtland-Theater Plauen:** Theaterstrasse 1–3, 9900 Plauen; Music Dir Paul Theissen; Man. Dieter Roth.

**Volkstheater Rostock:** Patriotischer Weg 33, 2500 Rostock; Gen. Music Dir Michael Zilm; Gen. Man. Berndt Renne.

**Wuppertaler Bühnen:** Bundesallee 260, 42103 Wuppertal; tel. 49 202 563 4261; fax 49 202 563 8078; Gen. Music Dir George Hanson; Gen. Man. Gerd Leo Kuck.

## Greece

**Greek National Opera:** 18-A Harilaou Trikoupi St, 106 79 Athens; tel. 30 1 363 3105; fax 30 1 360 0224; e-mail info@nationalopera.gr; website www .nationalopera.gr; Chief Conductor L. Karytinos.

## Hungary

**Csokonai Szinház (Csokonai Theatre):** PO Box 79, 4001 Debrecen.

**Magyar Állami Operaház (Hungarian State Opera House):** Andrássy út 22, 1061 Budapest; tel. (1) 312-4642; fax (1) 332-7331; e-mail opera@opera.hu; website www.opera.hu; Gen. Dir Miklós Szinetár; Music Dir Emil Petrovics.

**Pécsi Nemzeti Szinhás (Pécs National Theatre):** PO Box 126, 7601 Pécs.

**Szegedi Nemzeti Szinház (Szeged National Theatre):** PO Box 69, 6701 Szeged.

## Iceland

**The Icelandic Opera:** Ingolfsstraeti, PO Box 1416, 121 Reykjavík; tel. 354 511 6400; fax 354 552 7384; e-mail opera@opera.is; website www.opera.is; Gen. Dir: Bjarni Danielsson; Music Dir: Kurt Kopecky.

## Ireland

**Opera Ireland:** The Schoolhouse, 1 Grantham Street, Dublin 8; tel. 353 1 478 6041; fax 353 1 478 6046; e-mail info@opera-ireland.ie; website www .operaireland.com; Exec. Dir David Collopy; Artistic Dir Dieter Kaegi.

**Opera Theatre Company:** Temple Bar Music Centre, Curve Street, Dublin 2; tel. 353 1 679 4962; fax 353 1 679 4963; e-mail info@opera.ie; website www .opera.ie; Dir James Conway.

## Israel

**New Israeli Opera:** 28 Leonardo da Vinci St, PO Box 33321, Tel-Aviv 61332; tel. 972 3 6927803; fax 972 3 6954886; e-mail opera@mail.israel-opera.co.il; website www.israel-opera.co.il; Music Dir Asher Fisch.

## Italy

**Arena di Verona:** Piazza Bra 28, 37121 Verona; tel. 390 45 590109; fax 390 45 590201/8011566; website www.arena.it.

**Teatro Alighieri:** Piazza Garibaldi 5, 48100 Ravenna; website www .teatroalighieri.org.

**Teatro alla Scala di Milano:** Via Filodrammatici 2, 20121 Milan; tel. 39 2 88 791; fax 39 2 887 9331; website www.lascala.milano.it; Artistic Dir Roman Vlad; Musical Dir Riccardo Muti.

**Teatro Arena Sferisterio:** Piazza Mazzini 10, 62100 Macerata; tel. 39 733 26 1335; fax 39 733 26 1449.

**Teatro Coccia:** Via Fratelli Resselli 4, 28100 Novara; website www .teatrococcia.it; Artistic Dir Carlo Pesta.

**Teatro Comunale del Giglio:** Piazza del Giglio, 55100 Lucca; tel. 39 583 44 2101.

**Teatro Comunale dell'Opera de Genoa:** Passo al Teatro 4, 16121 Genoa; tel. 39 10 53811.

**Teatro Comunale di Bologna:** Largo Respighi 1, 40126 Bologna; tel. 390 51 52 9901; fax 390 51 52 9934/9905; website www.bolognacomunale.it; Chief Conductor Danielle Gatti.

**Teatro Comunale di Firenze:** Via Solferino 15, 50123 Florence; tel. 390 55 27791; fax 390 55 239 6954; Principal Conductor Zubin Mehta.

**Teatro Comunale G. B. Pergolesi:** Piazza della Repubblica, 60035 Jesi; tel. 39 731 59788; website www.teatropergolesi.org.

**Teatro Comunale G. Verdi:** Via Palestro 40, 56200 Pisa; website www .teatrodipisa.pi.it.

**Teatro Comunale:** TEATRI spa, Piazza San Leonardo 1, 31100 Treviso; tel. 0422 513 300; fax 0422 513 306; e-mail teatrispa@fondazionecassamarca.it; website www.teatrispa.it.

**Teatro Comunale:** Corso Vittorio Emanuele 52, 26100 Cremona; tel. 39 372 407273.

**Teatro Comunale:** G. Verdi di Trieste, Riva Novembre 1, 34121 Trieste; tel. 39 40 6722111; fax 39 40 6722 249.

**Teatro Comunale:** Corso Giovecca 12, 44100 Ferrara; website www .teatrocomunaleferrara.it.

**Teatro Comunale:** Via del Teatro 8, 41100 Modena; tel. 39 059 225 443; website www.teatrocomunalemodena.it.

**Teatro dell'Opera di Roma:** Piazza B. Gigli 8, 00184 Rome; tel. 39 648 81601; fax 39 6 488 1253.

**Teatro Donizetti:** Piazza Cavour 14, 24100 Bergamo.

**Teatro Grande:** Via Paganora 19, 25121 Brescia; tel. 39 030 29 79 311.

**Teatro La Fenice di Venezia:** Campo S. Fantin 2519, 30100 Venice; website www.teatrolafenice.it.

**Teatro Lirico G. Pierluigi da Palestrina di Cagliari:** Viale Regina Margherita 6, 09100 Cagliari.

**Teatro Massimo Bellini:** Via Perrotta 12, 95131 Catania; website www .teatromassimobellini.it.

**Teatro Massimo di Palermo:** Via R. Wagner 2, 90139 Palermo; tel. 39 91 605 3111; fax 39 91 605 3324/5.

**Teatro Municipale Romolo Valli:** Piazza Martiri 7 Luglio, 42100 Reggio Emilia; tel. 39 052 245 8811; fax 39 052 245 8922.

**Teatro Municipale:** Via Verdi 41, 29100 Piacenza; tel. 39 523 49 2254.

**Teatro Petruzzelli:** Via Cognetti 26, 70100 Bari.

**Teatro Politearna Greco:** Via XXV Luglio 30, 73100 Lecce.

**Teatro Regio di Torino:** Piazza Castello 215, 10124 Turin; tel. 39 011 88151; fax 39 011 881 5214.

**Teatro Regio:** Via Garibaldi 16, 43100 Parma; tel. 39 521 218912; fax 39 521 206156.

**Teatro San Carlo di Napoli:** Via San Carlo, 80132 Naples; tel. 39 81 797 2111; fax 39 81 797 2309; Artistic Dir Carlos Mayer.

**Teatro Sociale:** Piazza Cavollotti, 46100 Mantua; tel. 39 037 632 3860; fax 39 037 636 2739.

**Teatro Sociale:** Piazza Garibaldi 14, 45100 Rovigo.

**Teatro Sociale:** Via Bellini 3, 22100 Como; website www.teatrosocialecomo .it.

## Japan

**Kansai Nikkai Opera Company:** 3-3-9 Bingo-cho, Chyno-ku, Osaka; Dir Makoto Kikawada.

**Kansai Opera Group:** 3-57 Kyobashi, Higashi-ku, Osaka; Dir Takashi Asahina.

**Nihon Opera Shinkokai (Japanese Opera Foundation):** Nishiazabu 28, Mori Building, 4-16-13 Nishiazabu, Minato-ku, Tokyo 106; tel. 81 3 5466 3181; fax 813 5466 3186; Chair. Seiya Matsumoto.

## Republic of Korea

**National Opera Group:** c/o The National Theatre, Jangchoong-dong, Choong-ku, Seoul.

## Latvia

**Latvian National Opera:** Aspazijas Blvd 3, 1050 Riga; tel. 371 707 3715; fax 371 722 8930; e-mail info@opera.lv; website www.opera.lv; Gen. Dir: Andrejs Zagars; Principal Conductor: Andris Nelsons.

## Lithuania

**Lithuanian State Opera and Ballet Theatre:** Vienuolio 1, 232600 Vilnius; tel. 370 2 620093; fax 370 2 623503; Chief Conductor Rimas Geniuas; Admin. Zigmas Pieaitis.

## Luxembourg

**Théâtre Municipal:** 2525 Luxembourg; Dir Jeannot Comes.

## Malaysia

**Lyric Opera Malaysia:** in Kuala Lumpur; Dir: Mr Leow Siak Fah; (contact address: c/o Citystate Management Group Holdings Pte Ltd, 1B Club Street, 069400 Singapore).

## Mexico

**Compañía Nacional de Opera Palacio de Bellas Artes:** Avda Hidalgo 1, 3°, Centro, Mexico City, DF 06050; tel. 525 521 3668; fax 525 521 6776; Gen. Dir Gerardo Kleinburg.

## Monaco

**Opera de Monte Carlo:** Place du Casino, 98000 Monte Carlo; tel. 377 92 162318; fax 377 92 16 37 77; website www.opera.mc; Dir John Mordler.

## Netherlands

**De Nederlandse Opera:** Waterlooplein 22, 1011 PG, Amsterdam; tel. 31 20 551 8922; fax 3120 551 8311; e-mail info@nederlandse-opera.nl; website www .dno.nl; Artistic Dir Pierre Audi; Man. Dir Truze Lodder.

**Nationale Reisopera:** PO Box 1321, 7500 GH, Enschede; tel. 3153 4878500; fax 31 53 4321882; website www.reisopera.nl.

## New Zealand

**Auckland Opera Company:** PO Box 77066, Mount Albert, Auckland 1; tel. 64 9 846 7433; fax 64 9846 7141; Gen. Man. Stephen Morrison.

**Canterbury Regional Opera Trust:** PO Box 176, Christchurch 1; Chair. Lewis Brown.

**Dunedin Opera Company:** PO Box 533, Dunedin; Chair. Ian Page.

**National Opera:** State Opera House, PO Box 6588, Te Aro, Wellington; tel. 64 4 384 4434; fax 64 4 384 3333; Man. Patricia Hurley.

**NBR New Zealand Opera:** PO Box 6478, Wellesley Street, Auckland; tel. 64 9 379 4068; fax 64 9 3794066; website www.nzopera.com; Gen. Dir Alex Reedijk.

## Norway

**Den Norske Opera:** PO Box 8800 Youngstorget, 0028 Oslo; tel. 47 22 42 9475; fax 47 22 33 4027; website www.operaen.no; Artistic Dir Sven Olaf Eliasson.

**Opera Bergen:** Komediebakken 9, 5010 Bergen; tel. 47 55 32 3856; fax 47 55 32 24 35; e-mail vno@cdi.net; Artistic Dir Anne Randine Øverby.

**Operaen i Kristiansund:** PO Box 401, 6501 Kristiansund N; tel. 47 71 677733; fax 47 71 676657.

**Trondheim Opera:** Kongsgårdsgt 2, 7013 Trondheim; tel. 47 73 52 56 65.

## Poland

**Baltic Opera:** Al Zwyciêstwa 15, 80-219 Gdańsk; tel. 48 58 763 4912; fax 48 58 763 4914; website www.operabaltycka.pl.

**Kraków Music Theatre:** Senacka 6, 31-002 Kraków.

**Łódz Grand Theatre:** Plac Dâbrowskiego, 90-249 Łódz.

**Opera Nova:** 20 Gdanska St, 85-006 Bydgoszcz; tel. 0048 52 322 4985; fax 0048 52 3225950; e-mail promacja@opera.bydgoszcz.pl; website www.opera .bydgoszcz.pl; Artistic and Gen. Dir Maciej Figas.

**Poznán Grand Theatre:** Fredry 9, 60-967 Poznán.

**Silesian Opera:** Moniuszki 21, 41-902 Bytom; tel. 48 32 281 3431; fax 48 32 281 4335.

**The National Opera:** Grand Theatre, Plac Teatrainy 1, 00-950 Warsaw; tel. 48 22 826 3289; fax 48 22 826 0423.

**Warsaw Chamber Opera:** Nowogrodzka 49, 00-695 Warsaw; tel. 48 22 628-30-96; fax 48 22 629-32-33; e-mail artmgmt@wok.pol.pl; website www.wok.pol .pl; Man. and Artistic Dir Stefan Sutkowski; Deputy Man. and Artistic Dir Edward Pallasz; repertoire spans wide range of musical styles and genres; also holds annual festivals and numerous concerts.

**Wroclaw State Opera:** Swidnicka 35, 50-066 Wroclaw.

## Portugal

**Companhia de Opera do Teatro Nacional Sao Carlos:** Rua Serpa Pinto 9, 1200 Lisbon; tel. 35 1 346 8408.

**Teatro Nacional de Sao Carlos:** Rua Serpa Panto noG, 1200 442 Lisbon; tel. 3 51 21 34 68 408; fax 3 51 21 34 71 738; website www2.saocarlos.pt.

## Romania

**Bucharest State Operetta:** Str Operetei 4, Bucharest.

**Cluj-Napoca Hungarian Opera:** Str 1 Mai 26-28, Cluj-Napoca.

**Cluj-Napoca Romanian Opera:** Piata Stefan cel Mare 24, 3400 Cluj-Napoca.

**Iasi Musical Theatre:** Str 9 Mai nr 18, 6600 Iasi.

**Romanian State Opera:** Blvd Mihail Kogainiceanu 70–72, 70609 Bucharest.

**Timisoara State Opera:** Str M r sesti 2, Timisoara.

## Russia

**Bolshoi Theatre:** 1 Teatralnaya Square, Moscow; tel. 7 095 292 9986; website www.bolshoi.ru; Music Dir Mark Ermler.

**Kirov Opera:** 1 Theatre Square, St Petersburg; tel. 7 812 314 9083; Chief Conductor Valery Gergiev.

**Maly Opera:** St Petersburg; Artistic Dir N. Boyarchicov.

## Serbia and Montenegro

**Narodno Pozoriste (National Theatre Opera Company):** Francuska 3, 11000 Belgrade; tel. 381 11 624565; fax 381 11 622560; e-mail npozor@eunet.yu; Gen. Man. and Principal Conductor Dejan Saviá.

## Slovakia

**Bratislava Chamber Opera:** Fuikova 3, 816 01 Bratislava; Musical Dir Marián Vach.

**Kosice State Theatre Opera:** robárova 14, PO Box E-47, 042 77 Kosice; Musical Dir Igor Dohovic.

**Slovak National Theatre Opera:** Gorkého 4, 815 06 Bratislava; tel. 00421 7 544 35085; fax 00421 7 544 35072; Artistic Dir Ondrej Lenard; Dir of the Opera Juraj Hrubant.

## Slovenia

**Slovenian National Theatre Opera:** Zupanciceva 1, 61000 Ljubljana; website www.sngdrama-lj.si.

## South Africa

**Johannesburg Operatic and Dramatic Society:** PO Box 7010, Johannesburg 2000.

**Opera of the Cape Performing Arts Board:** PO Box 4107, Cape Town 8000; tel. 27 21 215470; fax 27 21 215.448.

**Opera of the Natal Performing Arts Council:** PO Box 5353, Durban 4000, Natal.

**Opera of the Orange Free State Performing Arts Council:** PO Box 1292, Bloemfontein 9300; Gen. Dir Fred Sharp.

**Opera of the Performing Arts Council, Transvaal:** PO Box 566, Pretoria 0001; tel. 2712 322 1665; fax 2712 322 3913; Gen. Man. Johan Maré.

## Spain

**Gran Teatre del Liceu:** La Rambla 51–59, 08002 Barcelona; tel. 34 93 4859900; fax 34 93 4859918; website www.liceubarcelona.com; Artistic Dir Joan Matabosch; Music Dir Bertrand de Billy.

**Madrid Opera:** Teatro Real, Plaza de Oriente s/n, 28013 Madrid; tel. 34 91 5160600; fax 34 91 5160651; e-mail info@teatro-real.com; website www.teatro-real.com; Gen. Dir Inés Argüelles; Artistic Dir Emilio Sag.

**Teatro de la Zarzuela:** Jovellanos, 28014, Madrid; tel. 34 1 429 8225; fax 34 1 429 7157; website www.teatrodelazarzuela.mcu.es.

## Sweden

**Drottningholms Slottsteater:** PO Box 15417, 10465 Stockholm; tel. 46 8 556 931 00; fax 46 8 556 931 01; website www.drottningholmsslottsteater.dtm.se; Artistic Dir Per Erik Ohrn.

**Folkoperan:** Hornsgatan 72, 118 21 Stockholm; tel. 46 8 616 0750/0700; fax 46 8 44146; website www.folkoperan.se; Music Dir Kerstin Nerbe.

**Göteborgs Operan:** Christina Nilssons Gatan, 411 04 Göteborg; tel. 46 31 1080; fax 46 31 1080 30; Man. Dir Dag Hallberg.

**Kungliga Operan AB (Royal Swedish Opera):** PO Box 16094, 103 22 Stockholm; tel. 46 8 791 4300; fax 46 8 791 4444; website www.operan.se; Gen. Man. Bengt Hall.

**Malmö Stadsteater:** PO Box 17520, 200 10 Malmö; Dir Lars Rudolfsson.

**Norriandsoperan:** PO Box 360, 901 08 Umea; tel. 46 0 90154300; fax 46 0 90126845; Artistic Dir Jonas Forsell.

## Switzerland

**Grand Théâtre de Genève:** 11 Blvd du Théâtre, 1211 Geneva 11; tel. 41 22 418 3000; fax 41 22 418 3001; website www.geneveopera.ch; Gen. Dir Renée Auphan.

**Opéra de Lausanne:** PO Box 3972, 1002 Lausanne; tel. 41 21 310 1616; fax 41 21 310 1690; e-mail opera@lausanne.ch; website www.opera-lausanne.ch.

**Opernhaus Zürich:** Falkenstrasse 1, 8008 Zürich; tel. 41 1 268 6400/6666; fax 41 1 268 6401/6555; website www.opernhaus.ch; Chief Conductor Franz Welser-Möst.

**Stadttheater Bern:** Nägeligasse 1, 3011 Bern; tel. 41 31 329 5111; fax 41 31 329 5100; website www.staadtheaterbern.ch; Admin. Ernst Gosteli.

**Stadttheater Biel:** Burggasse 19, 2502 Biel; tel. 41 32 328 8970; fax 41 32 328 8967; website www.ensemble-theater.ch; Admin. Mario Bettoli.

**Stadttheater Lucerne:** Theaterstrasse 2, 6002 Lucerne; tel. 4141 210 6618/9; fax 4141 210 3367; Music Dir Jonathan Nott.

**Stadttheater St Gallen:** Museumstrasse 24, 9000 St Gallen; tel. 41 71 242 0505; fax 41 71 242 0506; website www.theatersg.ch; Dir Werner Signer.

**Theater Basel:** Elisabethenstrasse 16, 4010 Basel; tel. 41 61 295 1460; fax 41 61 295 1590; website www.theater-basel.ch; Chief Conductor Julia Jones.

## Turkey

**Istanbul State Opera and Ballet:** Atatürk Merkezi, Taksim, 80090 Istanbul; tel. 90 212 245 16 36.

**Izmir State Opera and Ballet:** Izmir; website www.izdob.gov.tr.

**Turkish State Opera and Ballet:** Opera Binasi, Ankara.

## Ukraine

**Lviv S. Krushelnytskyi State Academic Opera:** 79000 Lviv, pr. Svobody; tel. (322) 72-85-62; internet www.lvivopera.org; f. 1900; Dir Tadei O. Eder; Artistic Dir Myron Yusypovych.

**Odesa State Academic Opera:** 65026 Odesa, prov. Chaikovskoho 1; e-mail opera-ballet@tm.odessa.ua; website www.opera-ballet.tm.odessa.ua.

**Ukrainian National Opera:** 01034 Kiev, vul. Volodymrska 50.

## United Kingdom

**Abbey Opera:** 68 Queens Gardens, London W2 3AH; tel. 020 7262 9023; Conductor Antony Shelley; Artistic Dir Mary Hill.

**Birmingham Opera Company:** 205 The Argent Centre, 60 Frederick Street, Birmingham B1 3HS; tel. (121) 2466644; fax (121) 2466633; Gen. Man.: Jean Nicholson; Artistic Dir: Graham Vick.

**Buxton Festival Opera:** 5 The Square, Buxton, Derbyshire SK17 6AZ; tel. 01298 70395; e-mail info@buxtonfestival.co.uk; website www.buxtonfestival.co.uk; Gen. Man. Glyn Foley.

**Dorset Opera:** 26 Central Acre, Yeovil, Somerset BA20 1NU; tel. 01935 479297; fax 01935 412210; e-mail info@dorsetopera.com; website www.dorsetopera.com; Music Dir Patrick Shelley; Admin. Joy Liddiard.

**D'Oyly Carte Opera Company:** The Power House, 6 Sancroft Street, London SE11 5UD; tel. 020 7793 7100; fax 020 7793 7300; website www.doylycarte.org.uk.

**Early Opera Project:** 112b High Street, Hungerford, Berkshire RG17 0NB; Musical Dirs Roger Norrington, Kay Lawrence.

**English National Opera—ENO:** London Coliseum, St Martin's Lane, London WC2N 4ES; tel. 020 7836 0111; fax 020 7845 9277; website www.eno.org; Music Dir Paul Daniel.

**Glyndebourne Festival Opera:** Glyndebourne, PO Box 2624, Lewes, East Sussex BN8 5UW; tel. (1273) 813813; fax (1273) 814686; website www.glyndebourne.com; Chair.: Gus Christie; Gen. Dir: David Pickard; Music Dir: Vladimir Jurowski.

**Glyndebourne on Tour:** Glyndebourne, Lewes, East Sussex BN8 5UU; tel. 01273 812321; fax 01273 812783; website www.glyndebourne.com; Music Dir: Edward Gardner; Admin.: Helen McCarthy.

**London Chamber Opera:** 82 Redcliffe Gardens, London SW10 9HE; tel. 020 7373 8535; Music Dir David Wordsworth.

**Midsummer Opera:** 90 Grange Road, London W5 3PJ; tel. 020 8579 7477/8840 9560; Music Dir David Roblou; Producer Alan Privett; Chair. David Skewes.

**Music Theatre Wales:** 5 Llandaff Road, Cardiff CF11 9NF; tel. 029 2023 0833; fax 029 2034 2046; e-mail enquiries@musictheatrewales.org.uk; website www.musictheatrewales.org.uk; Music Dir Abigail Pogson.

**Musica nel Chiostro:** 377 Liverpool Road, London N1; Dir Adam Pollock.

**New Sadler's Wells Opera:** Sadler's Wells Theatre, Roseberry Avenue, London EC1R 4TN; Dir Joseph Karaviotis.

**New Sussex Opera:** 22 Bradford Road, Lewes, East Sussex BN7 1RB; tel. and fax 01273 471851; e-mail mail@newsussexopera.com; website www.jjj.eurobell.co.uk; Gen. Dir David James.

**Nexus Opera:** 16 Kennington Park Road, London SE11 4AS; tel. 020 7582 0980; fax 020 7582 1444; website www.nexusopera.com; Artistic Dir Delia Lindon.

**Opera Anglia:** 3–5 Bridge Street, Hadleigh, Suffolk, IP7 6BY; tel. 01473 822596; fax 01473 824175; e-mail thomas.mcintosh@minstrelmusic.demon.co.uk; Artistic Dir Thomas McIntosh.

**Opera Brava Ltd:** Morley House, 67 Franklynn Road, Haywards Heath, West Sussex, RH16 4DT; tel. 01444 443060; fax 01444 443060; e-mail admin@operabrava.co.uk; website www.operabrava.co.uk; Artistic Dir Bronek Pomorski.

**Opera Holland Park:** Central Library, Phillimore Walk, London, W8 7RX; tel. 0845 230 9769 (box office); e-mail production@operahollandpark.com; boxoffice@operahollandpark.com; website www.operahollandpark.com; Prod.: James Clutton (tel. 20 7361-3364); Asst Prod.: Katharine Camiller (tel. 20

7631-2049); Marketing Man.: Michael Volpe (tel. 20 7631-2295); season runs from June–August.

**Opera Italiana:** 10a Radipole Road, Fulham, London SW6 5DL; tel. 020 7736 3821; fax 020 8447 1664; Artistic Dir Alexander Bryett.

**Opera North:** Grand Theatre, 46 New Briggate, Leeds, Yorkshire LS1 6NU; tel. (113) 243-9999; fax (113) 244-0418; e-mail info@operanorth.co.uk; website www.operanorth.co.uk; Gen. Dir Richard Mantle; Chair. Michael Beverly; Music Dir Richard Farnes.

**Opera Northern Ireland:** 35 Talbot Street, Belfast, Northern Ireland BT1 2LD; tel. 01232 322538; fax 01232 32291; Artistic Dir Stephen Barlow; Gen. Man. Tim Kerr.

**Opera on the Move:** 47 Queen's Drive, London N4 2SZ; Dirs Odaline de la Martinez, Linda Hirst.

**Opera Rara Ltd:** 134–146 Curtain Road, London EC2A 3AR; tel. 020 7613 2858; fax 020 7613 2261; website www.opera-rara.com; Artistic Dir Patric Schmid.

**Opera Restor'd:** 54 Astonville Street, London SW18 5AJ; tel. (20) 8870-7649; fax (20) 8516-6313; e-mail info@operarestord.co.uk; website www.operarestord.co.uk; Man.: Caroline Anderson; Music Dir: Peter Holman; Stage Dir: Jack Edwards.

**Pavilion Opera Company:** Thorpe Tilney Hall, Thorpe Tilney, nr Lincoln LN4 3SL; tel. 01526 378231; fax 01526 378315; Music Dir Peter Bailey; Gen. Man. Freddie Stockdale.

**Pisa Opera Group:** Flat 2, 79 Linden Gardens, London W2 4EU; tel. 020 7229 7060; Dir Stella J. Wright.

**Scottish Opera:** 39 Elmbank Crescent, Glasgow G2 4PT; tel. 0141 248 4567; fax 0141 221 8812; e-mail info@scottishopera.org.uk; website www.scottishopera.org.uk; Chief Exec. Chris Barron.

**Telemann Opera:** 1a Warwick Chambers, Pater Street, London W8 6EN; Artistic Dir Jill Watt.

**Thameside Opera:** 11 Arden Mhor, Pinner, Middlesex HA5 2HR; tel. 020 8866 3272; fax 020 8429 1179; e-mail thameside.opera@virgin.net; Gen. Man. Maurice F. Maggs; Musical Dir George Badacsonyi.

**The Royal Opera:** Royal Opera House, Covent Garden, London WC2E 9DD; tel. 020 7212 9502; fax 020 7212 9501; website www.royalopera.org; Music Dir Antonio Pappano; Chair. Colin Southgate; Exec. Chief Tony Hall; Opera Dir Elaine Padmore.

**Travelling Opera:** 114 St Mary's Road, Market Harborough, Leicestershire LE16 7DT; tel. 01858 434677; fax 01858 463617.

**Welsh National Opera:** Wales Millennium Centre, Bay Chambers, West Bute Street, Cardiff, CF10 5GG; tel. (29) 2040 2000; fax (29) 2040 2001; e-mail info@wmc.org.uk; website www.wno.org.uk, www.wmc.org.uk; Music Dir Carlo Rizzi; Gen. Dir Anthony Freud.

**Wessex Opera:** 11 Luccombe Hill, Redland, Bristol BS6 6SN; Music Dir Paul Webster; Gen. Man. Richard Evans.

## United States of America

**Abilene Opera Association:** PO Box 6611, Abilene, TX 79608; tel. 1 915 676 7372; fax 1 915 690 6660.

**Albuquerque Civic Light Opera Association:** 4201 Ellison NE, Albuquerque, NM 87109; Exec. Dir Linda E. McVey.

**American Chamber Opera:** PO Box 909, New York, NY 10023; Exec. Dir Doug Anderson.

**Anchorage Opera Company Inc:** 1507 Spar Avenue, Anchorage, AK 99501; tel. 1 907 279 2557; fax 1 907 279 7798; website www.anchorageopera.org; Dir Peter H. Brown.

**Arizona Opera Company:** 3501 N Mountain Avenue, Tucson, AZ 85719; tel. 1 520 293 4336; fax 1 520 293 5097; website www.azopera.com; Gen. Dir Clynn Ross; Artistic Dir Joel Revzen.

**Ash Lawn-Highland Opera Company:** Route 6, PO Box 37, Charlottesville, VA 22901; Gen. Man. Judith H. Walker.

**Aspen Music Festival:** PO Box AA, Aspen, CO 81612; tel. 1 970 925 3254; fax 1 970 925 3802; Music Dir Lawrence Foster; Pres. and CEO Robert Harth.

**Atlanta Opera:** 728 Peachtree Street NW, Atlanta, GA 30308; tel. 1 404 881 8801; fax 1 404 881 1711; website www.atlantaopera.org; Artistic Dir William Fred Scott; Gen. Man. Alfred D. Kennedy.

**Augusta Opera Company:** PO Box 3865, Hill Station, Augusta, GA 30904; Gen. Dir Edward Bradberry.

**Austin Lyric Opera:** PO Box 984, Austin, TX 78767; tel. 1 512 472 5927; fax 1 512 472 4143; website www.austinlyricopera.org; Artistic Dir Richard Buckley; Man. Dir Tamara Hale.

**Baltimore Opera Company Inc:** 110 W Mt Royal Avenue, Suite 306, Baltimore, MD 21201; tel. 1 410 625 1600; fax 1 410 625 6474; website www.baltimoreopera.com; Gen. Dir Michael Harrison; Music Dir William Yannuzzi.

**Baton Rouge Opera Inc:** PO Box 2269, Baton Rouge, LA 70821; Artistic Dir Marioara Trifan.

**Beaumont Civic Opera:** 1030 Harriot Street, Beaumont, TX 77705; Conductor L. Randolph Babin; Business Man. Delores Black.

**Berkeley Opera:** 715 Arlington, Berkeley, CA 94707; website www.berkeleyopera.org; Artistic Dir Jonathan Khuner.

**Berkshire Opera Company:** PO Box 598, 17 Main St, Lee, MA 01238; Artistic Dir Joel Revzen.

**Boise Opera Inc:** 516 S Ninth Street, Suite B, Boise, ID 83702.

**Boston Lyric Opera Company:** 45 Franklin Street, Fourth Floor, Boston, MA 02110; tel. 1 617 542 4912; fax 1 617 542 4913; website www.blo.org; Gen. Dir Janice DelSesto; Artistic Dir Leon Major; Music Dir Stephen Lord.

**Bronx Opera Company:** 5 Minerva Place, Bronx, NY 10468; website www.bronxopera.org; Artistic Dir Michael Spierman.

**Casa Italiana Opera Company:** 5959 Franklin Avenue, Suite 212, Hollywood, CA 90028; website www.casaitaliana.org; Gen. Dir Mario E. Leonetti.

**CCM Opera/Musical Theater:** University of Cincinnati College, Conservatory of Music, Cincinnati, OH 45221; Artistic Dir Malcolm Fraser.

**Central City Opera:** 400 S Colorado Blvd, Suite 530, Denver, CO 80246; tel. (303) 292-6500; fax (303) 292-4958; e-mail admin@centralcityopera.org; website www.centralcityopera.org.

**Chattanooga Opera:** 630 Chestnut Street, Chattanooga, TN 37402; tel. 1 423 267 8583; fax 1 423 265 6520; website www.chattanoogasymphony.org; Artistic Dir Robert Bernhardt; Man. Dir Donal L. Andrews.

**Chautauqua Opera:** Chautauqua Institution, Chautauqua, NY 14722; tel. 1 716 357 6200; fax 1 716 357 9014; website opera.ciweb.org; Artistic and Gen. Dir Jay Lesenger.

**Chicago Opera Theater:** 70 E Lake Street, Suite 540, Chicago, IL 60601; tel. 1 312 704 8420; fax 1 312 704 8421; website www.chicagooperatheater.org; Gen. Dir Brian Dickie.

**Cincinnati Opera:** Corbett Opera Center, Music Hall, 1243 Elm Street, Cincinnati, OH 45202; tel. (513) 768-5500; fax (513) 768-5552; e-mail info@cincinnatiopera.org; website www.cincinnatiopera.com.

**Cleveland Opera:** 1422 Euclid Avenue, Suite 1052, Cleveland, OH 44115; tel. (216) 575-0903; fax (216) 575-1918; e-mail mail@clevelandopera.org; website www.clevelandopera.org; Gen. Dir Robert Chumbley.

**Connecticut Grand Opera:** 61 Atlantic Street, Stamford, CT 06901; Artistic Dir Laurence Gilgore.

**Connecticut Opera Association:** 226 Farmington Avenue, Hartford, CT 06105; tel. 1 860 527 0713; fax 1 860 293 1715; website www.connecticutopera.org; Gen. and Artistic Dir Willie Anthony Waters.

**Dallas Opera:** The Centrum, 3102 Oak Lawn Avenue, Suite 450, LB-130, Dallas, TX 75219; website www.dallasopera.org; Music Dir Graeme Jenkins; Gen. Dir Plato Karayanis.

**Dayton Opera Association:** 138 N Main Street, Dayton, OH 45402; tel. 1 937 228 7591; fax 1 937 449 5068; e-mail info@daytonopera.org; website www.daytonopera.org; Artistic Dir Thomas Bankston; Gen. Dir Jane Nelson.

**Des Moines Metro Opera Inc:** 106 W Boston Avenue, Indianola, IA 50125; tel. 1 515 961 6221; fax 1 515 961 8175; e-mail dmmo@dmmo.org; website www.dmmo.org; Artistic Dir Robert L. Larsen.

**Eugene Opera:** PO Box 11200, Eugene, OR 97440; tel. 1 541 485 3895; fax 1 541 683 3783; website www.eugeneopera.com; Artistic Dir Robert Ashens.

**Fargo-Moorhead Civic Opera Company:** 1104 Second Avenue S, Fargo, ND 58103; tel. 1 701 239 4558; Artistic Dir David F. Martin.

**Florentine Opera Company:** 700 N Water Street, Suite 950, Milwaukee, WI 53202; tel. 1 414 291 5700; fax 1 414 291 5706; website www.florentineopera.org; Gen. Dir Dennis Hanthorn.

**Florida Grand Opera:** 1200 Coral Way, Miami, FL 33145; tel. 1 305 854 1643; fax 1 305 856 1042; website www.fgo.org; Music Dir Stewart Robertson; Gen. Man. Robert M. Heuer.

**Florida Lyric Opera Association/Lyric Opera Theater:** 1183 85 Terrace N, Suite D, St Petersburg, FL 33702-3333; tel. 1 727 578 1657; Gen. Man. Rosalia Maresca.

**Fort Worth Opera:** 3505 W Lancaster, Fort Worth, TX 76107; website www.fwopera.org; Gen. Dir William Walker.

**Fullerton Civic Light Opera:** 218 W Commonwealth, Fullerton, CA 92632; website www.fclo.com; Gen. Man. Griff Duncan.

**Glimmerglass Opera:** PO Box 191, Cooperstown, NY 13326; tel. (607) 547-5704; fax (607) 547-6030; e-mail info@glimmerglass.org; website www.glimmerglass.org; Dir of Artistic Operations: Nicholas G. Russell.

**Greensboro Opera Company:** PO Box 29031, Greensboro, NC 27429; website www.greensboroopera.org; Conductor Norman Johnson.

**Gulf Coast Opera Theatre Inc:** PO Box 118, Biloxi, MS 39552; tel. 1 228 436 6514; Pres. Dr Laurence M. Oden.

**Hawaii Opera Theater:** 987 Waimanu Street, Honolulu, HI 96814; tel. 1 808 596 7372; fax 1 808 596 0379; website www.hawaiiopera.org; Gen. Dir J. Mario Ramos.

**Houston Grand Opera Association:** 510 Preston Avenue, Houston, TX 77002; Gen. Dir R. David Gockley.

**Indiana Opera Theater:** 7515 E 30th Street, Indianapolis, IN 46219; Exec./ Artistic Dir Elaine Morgan Bookwalter.

**Indiana University Opera Theater:** School of Music, Indiana University, Bloomington, IN 47405.

**Indianapolis Opera:** 250 E 38th Street, Indianapolis, IN 46205; tel. 1 317 283 3531; fax 1 317 923 5611; e-mail info@indyopera.org; website www .indyopera.org; Artistic Dir James Caraher.

**Ithaca Opera:** 116 N Cayuga Street, Ithaca, NY 14850; tel. 1 607 272 0168.

**Juilliard Opera Center:** The Juilliard School, Lincoln Center for the Performing Arts, New York, NY 10023; Artistic Dir Frank Corsaro.

**Kentucky Opera:** 101 S Eighth Street, Louisville, KY 40202; tel. 1 502 584 4500; fax 1 502 584 7484; e-mail info@kyopera.org; website www.kyopera.org; Gen. Dir Deborah Sandler; Music Dir Robin Stamper.

**Knoxville Opera Company:** PO Box 16, Knoxville, TN 37901; tel. 1 865 524 0795; fax 1 865 524 7384; website www.knoxvilleopera.com; Gen. Dir Francis Graffeo.

**Lake George Opera Festival:** PO Box 2172, Glens Falls, NY 12801; website www.lakegeorgeopera.org; Artistic Dir Joseph Illick.

**Lancaster Opera Company:** PO Box 8382, Lancaster, PA 17604; tel. 1 717 392 0885; website www.lancasteropera.com; Artistic Dir Dorothy Rose Smith.

**Light Opera Works:** 927 Noyes Street, Evanston, IL 60201; tel. 1 847 869 6300; fax 1 847 869 6388; website www.light-opera-works.org; Artistic Dir Philip A. Kraus.

**Lincoln Opera:** 2456 N Surrey Court, Chicago, IL 60614; Artistic Dir Norma M. Williams.

**Long Beach Civic Light Opera:** PO Box 20280, Long Beach, CA 90801; Exec. Dir J. Phillip Keene III.

**Long Beach Opera:** PO Box 14895, Long Beach, CA 90853; tel. 1 562 439 2580; fax 1 562 439 2109; website www.longbeachopera.org; Gen. Dir Andreas Mitisek.

**Los Angeles Concert Opera:** 2250 Gloaming Way, Beverly Hills, CA 90210; Gen. Dir Loren L. Zachary.

**Los Angeles Music Center Opera:** 135 N Grand Avenue, Los Angeles, CA 90012; tel. 1 213 972 7219; fax 1 213 687 3490; website www.losangelesopera .com; Artistic Dir Placido Domingo.

**Lyric Opera Cleveland:** PO Box 93046, Cleveland, OH 44101; tel. 1 216 685 5976; website www.lyricoperacleveland.org; Exec. Dir Michael McConnell.

**Lyric Opera of Chicago:** 20 N Wacker Drive, Chicago, IL 60606; tel. 1 312 332 2244; fax 1 312 419 8345; website www.lyricopera.org/inc; Gen. Dir William Mason; Artistic Dir Matthew Epstein; Music Dir Andrew Davis.

**Lyric Opera of Dallas:** 8111 Preston Blvd, No. 818, Dallas, TX 75225; Gen. Dir Charles Kuba.

**Lyric Opera of Kansas City:** 1029 Central, Kansas City, MO 64105; tel. 1 816 471 7344; fax 1 816 471 0602; website kc-opera.org; Gen. Artistic Dir Russell Patterson.

**Lyric Theater of Oklahoma:** 1727 NW 16th Street, Oklahoma City, OK 73106; tel. 1 405 524 9310; fax 1 405 524 9316; website www.lyrictheatreokc .com; Artistic Dir Nick Dermos.

**Madison Opera:** 333 Glenway Street, Madison, WI 53705; tel. 1 608 238 8085; fax 1 608 233 3431; e-mail info@madisonopera.org; website www .madisonopera.org; Music Dir Roland Johnson; Man. Ann Stanke.

**Manhattan Opera Association:** PO Box 475, Planetarium Station, New York, NY 10024; Artistic Dir and Pres. Barbara Norcia.

**Metro Lyric Opera:** 40 Ocean Avenue, Allenhurst, NJ 07711; tel. 1 732 531 2378; website www.metrolyricopera.org; Gen. and Artistic Dir Erq M. Tognoli.

**Metropolitan Opera:** Lincoln Center for the Performing Arts, New York, NY 10023; tel. 1 212 799 3100/362 6000; fax 1 212 874 2569; website www .metopera.org; Artistic Dir James Levine; Gen. Dir Joseph Volpe.

**Michigan Opera Theater:** Detroit Opera House, 1526 Broadway, Detroit, MI 48226; tel. 1 313 961 3500; fax 1 313 237 3412; website www.metopera.org; Gen. Dir David DiChiera.

**Milwaukee Opera Company:** 820 E Knapp Street, Milwaukee, WI 53202; Exec. Dir Josephine Busalacchi.

**Minnesota Opera:** 620 N First Street, Minneapolis, MN 55401; tel. (612) 333-2700; fax (612) 333-0869; e-mail staff@mnopera.org; website www .mnopera.org; Pres. and CEO Kevin Smith.

**Mississippi Opera:** PO Box 1551, Jackson, MS 39215; tel. 1 601 960 2300; fax 1 601 960 1526; website www.msopera.org; Artistic Dir Carroll Freeman.

**Mobile Opera Inc:** 257 Dauphin Street, Mobile, AL 36602; tel. 1 251 432 6772; e-mail info@mobileopera.org; website www.mobileopera.org; Artistic Dir Jerome Shannon; Gen. Man. Pelham G. Pearce Jr.

**National Lyric Opera Company:** 5332 Sherrier Place NW, Washington, DC 20016; Gen. Man. Nikita Wells.

**National Opera Company:** PO Box 12800, Raleigh, NC 27605; Artistic Dir Don Wilder.

**Nevada Opera Association:** PO Box 3256, Reno, NV 89505; tel. 1 702 786 4046; fax 1 702 786 4063; Artistic Dir Ted Puffer.

**New England Lyric Operetta Inc:** PO Box 1007, Darien, CT 06820; tel. 203 655 0566; fax 203 655 8066; Pres. William H. Edgerton.

**New Jersey State Opera:** 50 Park Place, 10th Floor, Newark, NJ 07102; tel. 1 973 539 8970; Gen. Dir Alfredo Silipigni.

**New Orleans Opera Association:** 305 Baronne Street, Suite 500, New Orleans, LA 70112; tel. 1 504 529 2278; fax 1 504 529 7668; website www .neworleansopera.org; Gen. Dir Robert Tannebaum.

**New York City Opera:** New York State Theater, Lincoln Center for the Performing Arts, New York, NY 10023; tel. 1 212 870 5633/5600; website www .nycopera.com; Music Dir George Manahan.

**New York Gilbert and Sullivan Players Inc:** 251 W 91st Street, No. 4c, New York, NY 10024; website www.nygasp.org; Artistic Dir Albert Bergeret.

**New York Grand Opera:** 154 W 57th Street, Suite 125, New York, NY 10019; website www.newyorkgrandopera.org; Artistic Dir Vincent LaSelva.

**North Miami Beach Opera:** 5225 La Gorce Drive, Miami Beach, FL 33140; Music Dir Laurence Siegal.

**North Star Opera:** 75 W Fifth Street, Suite 414, St Paul, MN 55102; website www.northstaropera.org; Artistic Dir Steve Stucki; Admin. Dir Irma Wachtler.

**Oakland Lyric Opera:** PO Box 20709, Oakland, CA 94620; website www .oaklandlyricopera.org; Gen. Dir Marilyn Kosinski.

**Opera Carolina:** 345 N College Street, Suite 409, Charlotte, NC 28202; tel. 1 704 332 7177/372 1000; fax 1 704 332 6448/1154; website www.operacarolina .org; Gen. Dir and Principal Conductor James Meena.

**Opera Colorado:** 695 S Colorado Blvd, Suite 20, Denver, CO 80222; tel. 1 303 778 1500; fax 1 303 778 6533; website www.operacolorado.org; Gen. Dir Peter Russell.

**Opera Columbus:** 177 E Naghten Street, Columbus, OH 43215; tel. 1 614 461 8101; website www.operacols.org; Artistic Dir William Boggs; Gen. Dir Philip M. Dobard.

**Opera Company of Boston Inc:** PO Box 50, Boston, MA 02112; Artistic Dir Sarah Caldwell.

**Opera Company of Mid-Michigan:** 215 Washington Square, Suite 135, Lansing, MI 48933; Exec. Dir Theresa Weller.

**Opera Company of Philadelphia:** 1420 Locust Street, Suite 210, Philadelphia, PA 19102; tel. 1 215 893 3600; fax 1 215 893 7801; website www.operaphilly.com; Gen. Dir Robert Driver.

**Opera Delaware Inc:** 4 S Poplar Street, Wilmington, DE 19801; tel. 1 302 658 8063; fax 1 302 658 4991; website www.operade.org; Gen. Dir Leland Kimball, III.

**Opera Grand Rapids:** 161 Ottawa NW, Suite 205-B, Grand Rapids, MI 49503; tel. 1 616 451 2741; website www.operagr.org; Gen. Dir Robert Lyall.

**Opera Memphis:** 6745 Wolf River Parkway, Memphis, TN 38120; website www.operamemphis.org; Artistic Dir Michael Ching.

**Opera Northeast:** 530 E 89th Street, New York, NY 10128; Artistic Dir Donald Westwood.

**Opera Orchestra of New York:** 239 W 72nd Street, No. 2r, New York, NY 10023; tel. 1 212 799 1982; fax 1 212 721 9170; website www.oony.org; Music Dir Eve Queler; Man. Alix Barthelmes.

**Opera Pacific:** 9 Executive Circle, Suite 190, Irvine, CA 92714; website www .operapacific.org; Gen. Dir David DiChiera.

**Opera Roanoke:** 541 Luck Avenue, Suite 209, Roanoke, VA 24016; tel. 1 540 982 2742; fax 1 540 982 3601; website www.operaroanoke.org; Exec. Dir Judith Clark.

**Opera San JosÕ:** 2149 Paragon Drive, San JosÕ, CA 95131; tel. (408) 437-4450; fax (408) 437-4455; e-mail spielberger@operasj.org ; website www.operasj.org; performances at the California Theatre on 345 S First Street.

**Opera Southwest:** 515 15th Street NW, Albuquerque, NM 87104; tel. 1 505 243 0591; Artistic and Music Dir Richard Boldrey.

**Opera Theater of Connecticut:** PO Box 733, Clinton, CT 06413; website www.operatheater-ct.org; Admin. Dir Kate A. Ford.

**Opera Theater of Pittsburgh:** PO Box 110108, Pittsburgh, PA 15232; tel. 1 412 624 3500; fax 1 412 624 3525; website www.operatheaterpittsburgh.org; Artistic Dir Gary Race.

**Opera Theater of Saint Louis:** PO Box 191910, 539 Garden Avenue, St Louis, MO 63119; tel. 314 961 0171; fax 314 961 7463; e-mail info@opera.stl.org; website www.opera-stl.org; Gen. Dir Charles MacKay.

**Opera Theatre at Wildwood:** PO Box 25202, Little Rock, AR 72221; Artistic Dir Ann Chotard.

**Opera Theatre of Northern Virginia:** 2700 S Lang Street, Arlington, VA 22206; Artistic Dir John Edward Niles.

**Opera/Omaha Inc:** 1613 Farnam, Suite 200, Omaha, NE 68101; tel. 1 402 346 4398/0357; fax 1 402 346 7323; website www.operaomaha.org; Gen. Dir Mary Robert.

**Operaworks Ltd:** 170 W 73rd Street, New York, NY 10023; Dir Joel P. Casey.

**Orlando Opera Company Inc:** c/o Dr Phillips Center for Performing Arts, 1111 N Orange Avenue, Orlando, FL 32804; Gen. Dir Robert Swedberg.

**Palm Beach Opera Inc:** 415 S Olive Avenue, West Palm Beach, FL 33401; tel. 1 407 833 7888; fax 1 561 833 8294; website www.pbopera.org; Artistic Dir Anton Guadagno; Gen. Dir Herbert P. Benn.

**Pamiro Opera Company:** 115 S Jefferson Street, No. 301-A, Green Bay, WI 54301; website www.pamiro.org; Artistic and Music Dir Miroslav Pansky.

**Pittsburgh Opera Inc:** 711 Penn Avenue, Eighth Floor, Pittsburgh, PA 15222; website www.pbhopera.org; Gen. Dir Tito Capobianco.

**Portland Opera Association:** 1515 SW Morrison Street, Portland, OR 97205; tel. 503 241 1407; fax 503 241 4212; e-mail aom@portlandopera.org; Gen. Dir Robert Bailey.

**Potomac Valley Opera Company:** 2218 N Kensington Street, Arlington, VA 22205; Dir Richard Wilmer.

**Rimrock Opera Company:** PO Box 11, Billings, MT 59103; website www.rimrockopera.org; Artistic Dir Douglas Nagel; Exec. Dir John Baber.

**Sacramento Opera Company:** PO Box 161027, Sacramento, CA 95816; tel. (916) 264-5181; fax (916) 737-1032; e-mail info@sacopera.org; website www.sacopera.org; Exec. Dir: Rod Gideons.

**Salt Lake Opera Theatre:** 44 W 3000 South American Towers, No. 8075, Salt Lake City, UT 84101; Gen. Dir Robert Zabriskie.

**San Barnardino Civic Light Opera Association:** PO Box 606, San Bernardino, CA 92402; Gen. Man. Keith Stava.

**San Diego Civic Light Opera Association:** Starlight, PO Box 3519, San Diego, CA 92103; Exec. Dir Leon Drew.

**San Diego Comic Opera Company:** 545 Market Street, PO Box 1726, San Diego, CA 92101; Man. Dir Kathleen Switzer.

**San Diego Opera:** 18th Floor, Civic Center Plaza, 1200 Third Avenue, San Diego, CA 92101-4112; tel. 619 232 7636; fax 619 231 6915; e-mail sdostaff@sdopera.com; website www.sdopera.net; Gen. Dir Ian D. Campbell.

**San Francisco Opera:** War Memorial Opera House, San Francisco, CA 94102; tel. 1 415 565 6431/864 3300; fax 1 415 621 7508; website www.sfopera.com; Music Dir Donald Runnicles.

**San Jose Civic Light Opera:** 4 N Second, No. 100, San Jose, CA 95113; Artistic Dir Dianna Shuster.

**Santa Fe Opera:** PO Box 2408, Santa Fe, NM 87504; tel. 1 505 986 5955; fax 1 505 986 5999; Gen. Dir John Crosby.

**Sarasota Opera Association:** 61 N Pineapple Drive, Sarasota, FL 34236; tel. 1 941 366 8450; fax 1 941 955 5571; Artistic Dir Victor De Renzi; Exec. Dir Deane C. Allyn.

**Seattle Opera Association:** PO Box 9248, Seattle, WA 98109; tel. 1 206 389 7600; fax 1 206 389 7651; website www.seattleopera.org; Gen. Dir Speight Jenkins.

**Shreveport Opera:** 212 Texas Street, Suite 101, Shreveport, LA 71101; tel. 1 318 227 9503; fax 1 318 227 9518; Gen. Dir Gayle Norton; Artistic Dir Joseph Illick.

**Skylight Opera Theatre:** 158 N Broadway, Milwaukee, WI 53202; tel. 1 414 291 7811; website www.skylightopera.com.

**Sorg Opera Company:** 65 South Main Street, Middletown, OH 45044; tel. (513) 425-0180; fax (513) 425-0181; e-mail sorgopera@core.com; website www.sorgopera.org; Gen. Dir Curtis Tucker; professional opera productions.

**Spanish Lyric Theatre:** 1032 Coral Street, Tampa, FL 33602; Artistic Dir Rene Gonzalez.

**Springfield Regional Opera:** 109 Park Central Square, Springfield, MO 65806; Man. Artistic Dir James Billings.

**Stockton Opera:** PO Box 7883, Stockton, CA 95267; Artistic Dir George Buckbee.

**Summer Opera Theatre Company:** c/o Benjamin T. Rome School of Music, 620 Michigan; Gen. Man. Elaine R. Walter.

**Syracuse Opera Company:** PO Box 1223, Syracuse, NY 13202; tel. 1 315 475 5915; fax 1 315 475 6319; Artistic Dir Richard McKee.

**Tacoma Opera:** PO Box 7468, Tacoma, WA 98406; tel. 1 253 627 7789; fax 1 253 627 1620; website www.tacomaopera.com; Exec. Dir Kathryn Smith.

**Tampa Bay Opera:** 2035 Arbor Drive, Clearwater, FL 34620; Artistic Dir Mario Laurenti; Gen. Man. Cynthia Youkon.

**Teatro de la Opera Inc:** PO Box 40734, Minillas Station, Santurce, PR 09940; Artistic Dir Alberto Esteves.

**Tennessee Opera Theatre:** 5924 Sedberry Road, Nashville, TN 37205; Artistic Dir Daniel Killman.

**Toledo Opera Association:** 425 Jefferson Avenue, Suite 415, Toledo, OH 43604; tel. 1 419 255 7464; website www.toledo-opera.com; Principal Conductor and Gen. Dir James Meena.

**Triangle Opera Theater Association:** 120 Morris Street, Durham, NC 27701; Gen. Man. Rebecca Siegel.

**Tri Cities Opera Co Inc:** 315 Clinton Street, Binghamton, NY 13905; tel. (607) 729-3444; fax (607) 797-6344; e-mail info@tricitiesopera.com; website www.tricitiesopera.com; Artistic Dir Duane Skrabalak; Exec. Dir Reed W. Smith.

**Tulsa Opera:** 1610 S Boulder Avenue, Tulsa, OH 74119; Exec. Dir Gayle Pearson.

**Utah Symphony & Opera:** Abravanel Hall, 123 West South Temple, Salt Lake City, UT 84101; tel. (801) 533-5626; fax (801) 521-6634; website www.utahopera.org; Gen. Dir Anne Ewers.

**Virginia Opera:** PO Box 2580, Norfolk, VA 23501; Gen. Dir Peter Mark.

**Washington Concert Opera:** 1690 36th Street NW, Suite 411, Washington, DC 20007; Gen. Man. Stephen Crout.

**Washington Opera:** John F. Kennedy Center for the Performing Arts, Washington, DC 20566; tel. 1 202 416 7890; fax 1 202 298 6008; Artistic Dir Placido Domingo; Gen. Dir Martin Feinstein; Music Dir Heinz Fricke.

**West Bay Opera:** PO Box 1714, Palo Alto, CA 94302; Gen. Dir Maria Holt.

**West Coast Opera Theatre:** PO Box 166, Palm Desert, CA 92661; Gen. Dir Josephine Lombardo.

**Western Opera Theater:** War Memorial Opera House, San Francisco, CA 94102; Dir Christopher Hahn.

**Wolf Trap Opera Company:** 1624 Trap Road, Vienna, VA 22182; tel. 1 703 255 1935; fax 1 703 255 1924; Admin. Dir Peter Russell.

## Venezuela

**Opera de Caracas:** Museo del Teclado, Parque Central, Edif, Tacaqua, Mezzanina, Caracas 1010; Dir José Ignacio Cabrujas.

# APPENDIX C: FESTIVALS

## Argentina

**Festival Internacional de Música de San Juan:** 25 de Mayo y Urquiza, 5400 San Juan.

## Australia

**Adelaide Festival of Arts:** PO Box 8116, Station Arcade, Adelaide, SA 5000; tel. 61 8 8216 4444; fax 61 8 8216 4455; e-mail afa@adelaidefestival.net.au; website www.adelaidefestival.com.au; biennial festival held in Feb.–March.

**Australian Festival of Chamber Music:** PO Box 5871, Townsville, Qld 4810; tel. 61 7 4771 4144; fax 61 7 4771 4122; e-mail afcm@afcm.com.au; website www.afcm.com.au; July.

**Brisbane Warana Festival:** PO Box 3611, South Brisbane, Qld 4101; tel. 61 7 3852 2323; Sept.–Oct.

**Melbourne International Festival of Organ and Harpsichord:** PO Box 92, Parkville, Vic. 3052; tel. 61 3 9347 0447; Easter Week.

**Melbourne International Festival of the Arts:** 35 City Road, Melbourne, Vic. 3205; tel. 61 3 9662 4242; Oct.

**Musica Nova:** PO Box 9994, Brisbane, Qld 4001; Aug.

**Sydney Festival:** Level 2, 18 Hickson Road, The Rocks, Sydney, NSW 2000; tel. 61 2 8248 6500; fax 61 2 8248 6599; e-mail mail@sydneyfestival.org.au; website www.sydneyfestival.org.au; Jan.

**UWA Perth International Arts Festival:** UWA Festival Centre, 3 Crawley Avenue, Crawley, WA 6009; tel. 61 8 9380 2000; fax 61 8 9380 8555; e-mail festival@perthfestival.com.au; website www.perthfestival.com.au; Feb.–March.

## Austria

**Ars Electonica:** Museumsgesellschaft mbH, Haupstrasse 2, 4040 Linz; tel. 43 732 7272 75; fax 43 732 7272 77; e-mail festival@aec.at; website www.aec .at; June.

**Aspekte Salzburg:** Lasserstrasse 6, 5020 Salzburg; tel. 43 662 881547; fax 43 662 882143; e-mail office@aspekte-salzburg.at; website www.aspekte -salzburg.at; contemporary music festival held in Feb.–March; also monthly concerts.

**Bregenz Festival:** Platz der Wiener Symphoniker 1, 6900 Bregenz; tel. 43 5574 407224; fax 43 5574 407223; e-mail info@bregenzerfestspiele.com; website www.bregenzerfestspiele.com; July–Aug.

**Carinthian Summer:** Stift Ossiach, 9570 Ossiach; tel. 43 4243 2510; fax 43 4243 2353; website www.carinthischersommer.at; June–Aug.

**Chamber Music Festival Austria:** Germergasse 16, 2500 Baden; Aug.–Sept.

**Easter Festival Salzburg:** Herbert von Karajan Platz 9, 5020 Salzburg; tel. 43 662 8045-361; fax 43 662 8045-790; website www.osterfestspiele-salzburg .at.

**Festival Wien Modern:** PO Box 140, Lothringerstrasse 20, 1037 Vienna; tel. 43 1 242 00; e-mail office@wienmodern.at; website www.wienmodern.at; Oct.–Nov.

**Festival Wiener Klassik:** Preindlgasse 1, 1130 Vienna; April, July and Dec.

**Haydnfestival:** Schloss Esterhazy, 7000 Eisenstadt; tel. 43 2682 61 866; fax 43 2682 61 805; e-mail office@haydnfestival.at; website www.haydnfestival.at; Sept.

**Innsbruck Festival of Early Music:** Haspingerstrasse 1, 6020 Innsbruck; June–Sept.

**International Competition of Choral Singing:** Burgplatz 1, 9800 Spittal an der Drau; July.

**International Cultural Days and Symposium:** PO Box 18, 8692 Neuberg an der Mürz; July–Aug.

**International Youth and Music Festival:** Kongresszentrum, 1014 Vienna; July.

**Internationale Brucknerfest Linz:** Untere Donaulände 7, 4010 Linz; Sept.–Oct.

**Internationale Musikwochen Millstatt:** PO Box 27, 9872 Millstatt/See; May–Oct.

**Kitzbüheler Sommerkonzerte:** Stadtgemeinde, 6730 Kitzbühel; July–Aug.

**Mozart Festival Week:** Getreidegasse 14/2, 5020 Salzburg; Jan.

**Büro des Lehár Festival:** Kurhausstrasse 8, 4820 Bad Ischl; tel. (6132) 23839; fax (6132) 23839 39; e-mail info@leharfestival.at; website www .leharfestival.at; July–Aug.

**Salzburg Palace Concerts:** Makartplatz 9, 5020 Salzburg; Jan.–Dec.

**Salzburger Kulturtage:** PO Box 42, Waagplatz 1a, 5010 Salzburg; tel. 43 662 845346; fax 43 662 842665; e-mail kulturvereinigung@salzburg.com; held in Oct.

**Salzburger Operetten Konzerte:** Lerchenstrasse 33, 5023 Salzburg; May–Oct.

**Schubertiade Feldkirch:** Schubertplatz 1, PO Box 625, 6803 Feldkirch; June–July.

**Seefestspiele Mörbisch:** Schloss Esterhazy, 7000 Eisenstadt; June–Aug.

**Steirische Kulturveranstaltungen:** Palais Attems, Sackstrasse 17, 8010 Graz; tel. 43 316 812941; fax 43 316 82500015; e-mail info@styriarte.com; website www.styriarte.com; held in June–July.

**Styrian Autumn:** Sackstrasse 17/1, 8010 Graz; Oct.

**Szene:** International Theatre and Dance Festival: Anton Neumayr-Platz 2, 5020 Salzburg.

**Vienna Festival:** Lehargasse 11, 1060 Vienna; website www.festwochen.at; May–June.

**Vienna Music Summer:** Laudongasse 29, 1080 Vienna; June–Sept.

## Belgium

**Ars Musica:** The Spring of Contemporary Music: 18 Pl Eugène Flageyplein 18, Rm 245, 1050 Brussels; website www.arsmusica.be; March–April.

**Europalia:** 10 rue Royale, 1000 Brussels; website www.europalia.be; Sept.–Dec. of odd-numbered years.

**Festival de Wallonie:** 29 rue du Jardin Botanique, 4000 Liège; website www .festivaledewallonie.be; June–Nov.

**Festival Van Vlaanderen, Antwerpen:** Kortrijksesteenweg 90 h, 9830 Sint-Martens-Latem; Stadhuis, website www.festivale-van-vlaanderen.be; Aug.–Sept.

**Festival Van Vlaanderen, Brugge:** Collaert Mansionstraat 30, 8000 Bruges; tel. 050 33 22 83; fax 050 34 52 04; e-mail musica-antiqua@unicall .be; website www.musica-antiqua.com; held in July–Aug; includes annual competition.

**Week of Contemporary Music:** Muzikon vzw, Hoogpoort 64, 9000 Ghent; tel. 32 9 225 15 15; Feb.

## Bermuda

**Bermuda Festival:** PO Box HM 297, Hamilton, HM AX; tel. 441 295 1291; e-mail bdafest@ibl.bm; website www.bermudafestival.com; Jan.–Feb.

## Brazil

**Bienal de Música Contemporânes Brasileira:** Sala Cecilia Meireles, Largo da Lapa 47, Lapa, 20021 Rio de Janeiro; Nov.

**Festival Amazonas de Ópera (Amazonas Opera Festival):** Praça São Sebastião s/n, Manaus; tel. (92) 232-1768; website: www.operaamazonas.-com.br; f. 1997; April–May at the Teatro Amazonas.

**Festival Música Nova de Santos:** Sociedade Ars Viva, Rua Barâo de Paranapiacaba 31, 11050 Santos.

**Festival Villa-Lobos:** Rua Sorocaba 200, 22271 Rio de Janeiro; Nov.

**Petrópolis Summer Festival:** Rua Franio Peixoto 134, Bingen, 25600; Jan.–Feb.

**Petrópolis Winter Festival:** Petrópolis; June–Aug.

## Bulgaria

**Apollonia:** 54/B Korab Planina St, 1125 Sofia; April, Sept. and Oct.

**Chamber Music Festival:** PO Box 387, 1090 Sofia; June.

**March Music Days, Sofia Music Weeks:** PO Box 387, 1090 Sofia; May–June.

**Varna Summer:** Municipal Council BG, 9000 Varna; website www.varna.bg/kult/v_summer/lmf.htm; June–July.

## Canada

**Banff Festival of the Arts:** Box 1020, Station 28, Banff, Alta, T0L 0C0; June–Aug.

**Charlottetown Festival:** PO Box 848, Charlottetown, PE C1A 7L9; June–Oct.

**Festival International de Lanaudière:** 1500 Base-de-Roc Blvd, Joliette, QC J6E 3Z1; June–Aug.

**Festival International de Musique Baroque:** PO Box 644, Lameque, NB E0B 1V0; July.

**Festival of the Sound:** PO Box 750, Parry Sound, ON P2A 2Z1; July–Aug.

**Guelph Spring Festival:** PO Box 1718, Guelph, ON N1H 6Z9; May.

**Scotia Festival of Music:** 1541 Barrington St, Suite 317, Halifax, NS B3J 1Z5; May–June.

**Shaw Festival:** PO Box 774, Niagara-on-the-Lake, ON L0S 1J0; April–Nov.

**Vancouver Early Music Summer Festival:** 1254 W Seventh Avenue, Vancouver, BC V6H 1B6; July–Aug.

## Croatia

**Zagreb Musical Biennale Festival of Contemporary Music:** HD Skladatelja, Berislaviceva, 1000 Zagreb.

## Czech Republic

**Brno International Music Festival:** Uvoz 39, 602 00 Brno; tel. 420 543 233 116; fax 420 543 233 358; e-mail mhfb@arskoncert.cz; website www.mhfb.cz; Sept.–Oct.

**Prague Autumn Festival:** Sekaninova 26, 120 00 Prague 2.

**Prague Cultural Summer:** nam Republiky 5, 110 00 Prague 1; June–Sept.

**Prague Easter Festival:** Sonus Pod Smuký kou 1049, 150 00 Prague 5.

**Prague Festival:** Sonus Pod Smuký kou 1049, 150 00 Prague 5; Sept.–Oct.

**Prague Spring International Music Festival:** Hellichova 18, 118 00 Prague 1; tel. 420 257 320 468; fax 420 257 313 725; e-mail info@festival.cz; website www.festival.cz; held in May–June.

## Denmark

**Århus Festival:** Vester Allé 3, 8000 Århus; website www.aarhusfestuge.dk; Aug.–Sept.

**Fanø Music Festival:** Toftestein 21, Sønderho, 6720 Fanø; June, July and Aug.

**Lerchenborg Music Days:** Tuborgvej 99, 2900 Hellerup; July–Aug.

**Royal Danish Ballet and Opera Festival:** PO Box 2185, 1017 Copenhagen.

## Estonia

**Tallinn International Organ Festival:** Niguliste Str, 13, 0001 Tallinn; tel. 372 614 7737; fax 372 614 7709; July–Aug.

## Finland

**Finland Festivals:** PO Box 56, 00101 Helsinki; website www.festivals.fi; year-round.

**Helsinki Festival:** Lasipalatsi, Mannerheimintie 22–24, 00100 Helsinki; tel. 358 9 6126 5100; fax 358 9 6126 5161; e-mail info@helsinkifestival.fi; website www.helsinkifestival.fi; Aug.–Sept.

**Joensuu Song Festival:** Koskikatu 1, 80100 Joensuu; June.

**Jyväskylä Arts Festival:** Asemakatu 6, 40100 Jyväskylä; website www.jyvaskyla.fi/kesa/info; July.

**Kangasniemi Music Festival:** Kulttuuritoimisto, 51200 Kangasniemi; June–July.

**Karjaa Music Festival:** Rantatie 1, 10300 Karjaa; June–July.

**Korsholm Music Festival:** Festival Office, 65610 Korsholm; tel. 358 6 322 2390; fax 358 6 322 2393; e-mail music.festival@korsholm.fi; website www.korsholm.fi/music; June–July.

**Kuhmo Chamber Music Festival:** Torikatu 39, 88900 Kuhmo; tel. 358 8 652 0936; fax 358 8 652 1961; e-mail kuhmo.festival@kuhmofestival.fi; website www.kuhmofestival.fi; July–Aug.

**Lahti Organ Festival:** Kirkkokatu 5, 15110 Lahti; tel. 358 3 782 3184; fax 358 3 783 2190; e-mail lof@pp.phnet.fi; website www.lahtiorgan.net; held in Aug.

**Oulu Music Festival:** Lintulammentie 1 K, 90140 Oulu; Jan.–May.

**Naantali Music Festival:** PO Box 46, 21101 Naantali; tel. 358 2 4345363; fax 358 2 4345425; e-mail tiina.tunturi@naantali.fi; website www.naantalimusic.com; held in June.

**Savonlinna Opera Festival:** Olavinkatu 27, 57130 Savonlinna; tel. 358 15 476750; fax 358 15 4767540; e-mail info@operafestival.fi; website www.operafestival.fi; held in June–July.

**Suvisoitto-Porvoo Summer Sounds:** Erottajankatu 19 D 21, 00130 Helsinki; June–July.

**Tampere Biennale:** Tullikamarinaukio 2, 33100 Tampere; tel. 358 3 3146 6136; fax 358 3 223 0121; e-mail music@tampere.fi; website www.tampere.fi/biennale; held in 5–9 April 2006.

**Time of Music:** Kunnantalo, 44500 Vitasaari; July.

**Turku Music Festival:** Uudenmaankatu 1 A 20500 Turku; tel. 358 2 251 1162; fax 358 2 231 3316; e-mail info@turkumusicfestival.fi; website www.turkumusicfestival.fi; Aug.

## France

**Academie Internationale d'Art Musicale, Tours:** 17 rue des Ursulines, 37000 Tours; July.

**Avignon Festival:** 8 bis rue de Mons, 84000 Avignon; website www.festival-avignon.com; July–Aug.

**Biennale de la Musique Française:** Maison de Lyon, Place Bellecour, 69002 Lyon; Sept. of odd-numbered years.

**Chorégies d'Orange:** 18 Place Silvain, PO Box 205, 84107 Orange Cédex; July–Aug.

**Festival d'Aix:** Palais de l'Ancien Archevêché, 13100 Aix-en-Provence; tel. 33 442 17 34 00; fax 33 442 96 12 61; website www.festival-aix.com; f. 1948; June–July.

**Festival d'Art Sacré de la Ville de Paris:** 17 rue de l'Arbe Sec, 75001 Paris.

**Festival d'Automné à Paris:** 156 rue de Rivoli, 75001 Paris; website www.festival-automne.com; Sept.–Dec.

**Festival de Chartres/Grandes Orgues de Chartres:** 75 rue de Grenelle, 75007 Paris; July and Sept.

**Festival de Colmar:** 4 rue des Unterlinden, 68000 Colmar; tel. 33 389 20 68 97; fax 33 389 413 413; e-mail infofestival@ot-colmar.fr; website www.colmar-festival.com; July–Aug.

**Festival de la Rochelle:** 26 rue Washington, 75008 Paris; June–July.

**Festival de L'Ile de France:** 26 rue de Gramont, 75002 Paris; Sept.–Oct.

**Festival de Paris:** 2 rue Edouard Colonne, 75001 Paris; May–June.

**Festival de Prades:** rue Victor Hugo, 66500 Prades; July–Aug.

**Festival de Versailles:** Maire de Versailles, RP 144, 78011 Versailles; May–June.

**Festival de Ville d'Avray:** 10 rue de Marnes, 92410 Ville d'Avray; May–June.

**Festival des Instruments Anciens:** 58 rue Viollet-la-Duc, 94210 St Maur La Varenne; March–April.

**Festival des Nations Europeennes:** PO Box 60, 68140 Munster; July.

**Festival du Comminges:** Academie Internationale, 31260 Mazeres-sur-Salat; website www.festival-du-comminges.com; July–Aug.

**Festival Estival de Paris:** 20 rue Geoffroy l'Asnier, 75004 Paris; July–Sept.

**Festival International Atlantique:** 7 quai de Versailles, 44000 Nantes Cédex; June–Aug.

**Festival International d'Art Lyrique et de Musique:** Palais de l'Ancien Archevêché, 13100 Aix-en-Provence; July–Aug.

**Festival International d'Eté de Nantes:** Porte St Pierre, rue de l'Evêché, 44000 Nantes; July.

**Festival International de Besançon et Franche-Comte:** 2d rue Isenbart, 25000 Besançon; Aug.–Sept.

**Festival International de Carpentras:** La Charité, rue Cottier, PO Box 113, 84204 Carpentras Cédex; July–Aug.

**Festival International de Chant Choral de Nancy:** PO Box 3335, 54000 Nancy; tel. 33 383 27 56 56; fax 33 383 27 55 66; website www.fest.chantchoral.free.fr; May.

**Festival International de Musique Sacrée de Lourdes:** Place du Champ Commun, 65100 Lourdes; Easter.

**Festival International de Musique de Toulon:** Palais de la Bourse, Avenue Jean-Moulin, 83000 Toulon; tel. 33 494 93 52 84; June–July.

**Festival International des Musiques d'Aujourd'hui:** 9 rue de Général Frère, 67000 Strasbourg; Sept.–Oct.

**Festival J. S. Bach:** Palais Delphinal, 26260 Saint-Donat-sur-Berbasse; July–Aug.

**Festival Mediterranéen:** PO Box 4, 13129 Salin de Giraud; June–Aug.

**Festival Musique en Sorbonne:** 2 rue Francis de Croisset, 75018 Paris; June–July.

**Festival Radio France Montpellier:** Le Corum 9214, 34043 Montpellier Cédex 01.

**Festival 'Synthèse', International Festival of Electronic Music and Creations, Bourges:** place André Malraux, PO Box 39, 18000 Bourges; tel. 33(0)2 20 41 87; fax 33(0)2 48 20 45 51; e-mail administration@ime-bourges .org; website www.imeb.net. Festival programme of 30 concerts, presenting music from 24 countries, masterclasses, demonstrations of electronic art.

**Fêtes Musicales en Touraine:** Hôtel de Ville, 37032 Tours Cédex; June.

**Lille Festival:** 64 Avenue President J. F. Kennedy, 59800 Lille; Oct.–Dec.

**Nuits de la Fondation Maeght:** Fondation Maeght, 06570 St Paul-de-Vence; July.

**Recontres d'Eté de la Chartruese:** La Chartreuse, PO Box 30, 30400 Villeneuve-les-Avignon; July.

**Recontres internationales de la Guitare:** Hôtel de Ville, PO Box 114, 65013 Tarbes Cédex; July.

**Rencontres Musicales d'Evian:** Château de Blonay, 74500 Evain les Bains; May.

**Strasbourg International Festival:** Wolf Musique, 24 rue de la Mésange, 67000 Strasbourg; June–July.

## Germany

**Augsburger Mozart-Sommer:** Kulturamt, Maximilianstrasse 36, 8900 Augsburg; tel. 49 821 324 2727; Aug.–Sept.

**Bach Festival Berlin:** Rathaus, 2120 Lüneburg; June.

**Bachwoche Ansbach:** PO Box 1741, 8800 Ansbach; website www .bachwocheansbach.de; July–Aug. of odd-numbered years.

**Bad Hersfeld Festival Concerts and Opera:** Nachtigallenstrasse 9, 6430 Bad Hersfeld; tel. 49 6621 2109; June–Aug.

**Bayreuth Festival:** PO Box 100262, 95402 Bayreuth; tel. 49 9217 8780; website www.bayreuther-festspiele.de; July–Aug.

**Berliner Festwochen/Berliner Festspiele GmbH:** PO Box 301648, 10748 Berlin; tel. 49 30 254 890; fax 49 30 254 89111; e-mail info@berlinerfestspiele .de; website www.festwochen.de; Sept.–Nov.

**Bodensee Festival:** Olgastrasse 21, 88045 Friedrichshafen; tel. 49 75 4120 33300; fax 49 75 4120 33310; website www.bodfest.de; April–May.

**Bonner Herbst:** Wachsbleiche 21, 5300 Bonn 1; tel. 49 228 77 45 33; Oct.–Nov.

**Brühler Schlosskonzerte eV:** Schlosstrasse 2, 5040 Brühl; May–Sept.

**Cloister Concerts:** Kurverwaltung Alpirsbach, 7297 Alpirsbach; June–Aug.

**Collegium Musicum Schloss Pommersfelden:** Austrasse 10, 90559 Burgthann; tel. 49 9183 8245; fax 49 9183 7814; July–Aug.

**Corveyer Musikwochen:** Stadtverwaltung/Stadthaus am Petritor, 3470 Höxter 1; May–June.

**Dollart Festival:** PO Box 1580, 26585 Aurich; tel. 49 41 179 967; fax 49 41 179 975; website www.dollart-festival.de.

**Donaueschingen Festival of Contemporary Music:** Südwestfunk Baden-Baden, PO Box 820, 7570 Baden-Baden; Oct.

**Dresdner Musikfestspiele:** PO Box 202723, 01193 Dresden; tel. 49 351 478560; fax 49 351 website www.musikfestspiele.de; May–June.

**Dresdner Tage der Zeitgenössischen Musik:** Schevenstrasse 17/150-05, 8054 Dresden; Oct.

**Ettingen Schloss-Festspiele:** PO Box 0762, 7505 Ettingen; June–Aug.

**European Festival:** Dr Hans Kaptingerstrasse 22, 94032 Passau; June–July.

**Festliche Sommer in der Wies:** Bahnhofstrasse 44, 8920 Schongau; June–Aug.

**Festspiele am Roten Tor:** Kasernstrasse 4-6, 8900 Augsburg; July.

**Feuchtwangen Kreuzgangspiele:** Marktplatz, 91555 Feuchtwangen; tel. 9852 904 44; fax 9852 904 260; e-mail kulturamt@feuchtwangen.de; held in May–Aug.

**Gandersheimer Donfestspiele:** Barfüsserkloster 15, 3353 Bad Gandersheim; June–Aug.

**Gewandhaus-Festtage Leipzig:** Augusplatz 8, 7010 Leipzig; tel. 49 341 12700; June.

**Göttingen Handel Festival:** Hainholzweg 3–5, 3400 Göttingen; May–June.

**Händelfestspiele in Halle:** Gorsse Nikolaistrasse 5, 06108 Halle; tel. 49 345 5009 0222; June.

**Heidelberg Castle Festival:** Friedrichstrasse 5, 6900 Heidelberg; tel. 49 6221 583 521; July–Aug.

**Herbstliche Musiktage Bad Urach:** PO Box 1240, 7432 Bad Urach; tel. 49 7125 15 61 51; Sept.–Oct.

**Hitzacker Summer Music Festival:** Barkhausenweg 12, 2000 Hamburg; July–Aug.

**International Castle Concerts:** Schloss, 8851 Leitheim bei Donauwörth; April–Oct.

**Internationale Fasch-Festtage Zerbst:** Wikhaus Breiteskin, PO Box 1113, 39251, Zerbst.

**International May Festival:** PO Box 3247, 6200 Wiesbaden; tel. 49 611 1321; May.

**International Organ Festival:** Jacobikirchof 3, 3400 Göttingen; Oct. of odd-numbered years.

**Internationale Bachakademie Stuttgart:** Johann-Sebastian-Bach-Platz, 70178 Stuttgart; tel. 0711 6192132; fax 0711 6192130; e-mail office@ bachakademie.de; website www.bachakademie.de; organizes the annual Stuttgarter Bachwoche festival in Feb.–March.

**Internationale Festspiele Baden-Württemberg:** Marstallstrasse 5, 71634 Ludwigsburg; tel. 49 7141 9396-0; fax 49 7141 9396-77; e-mail info@ schlossfestspiele.de; website www.schlossfestspiele.de; held in June–Sept.

**Internationale Orgelwoche Nürnberg-Music Sacra:** Bismarckstrasse 46, 8500 Nürnberg; tel. 49 911 231 3528; June–July.

**Internationales Beethovenfest Bonn:** Wachsbleiche 21, 5300 Bonn; triennial.

**Kissinger Summer Music Festival:** PO Box 2260, 8730 Bad Kissingen; June–July.

**Leitheim Schloss Concerts:** Schloss Leitheim, 8851 Kaisheim; May–Oct.

**Limburger Organ Vespers:** Städtisches Verkehrsamt, 6250 Limburg an der Lahn; April–Aug.

**Ludwigsburger Schlossfestspiele:** Marstallstrasse 5, 71634 Ludwigsburg; tel. 49 7141 9396-0; fax 49 7141 9396-77; e-mail info@schlossfestspiele.de; website www.schlossfestspiele.de; held in June–Sept.

**Münchener Biennale:** Rindermarkt 3–4, 8000 Munich 2; tel. 49 89 290 41 83; April.

**Munich Opera Festival:** Bayerische Staatsoper, Max Jospeh Platz 2, 80539 Munich; July–Aug.

**Music in the 20th Century:** PO Box 1050, 6600 Saarbrücken; tel. 49 681 602 2210; May.

**Musica Bayreuth:** Ludwigstrasse 26, 8580 Bayreuth; tel. and fax 49 921 67367; website www.musica-bayreuth.de; held in May.

**Musikfest Hamburg:** Grosse Theaterstrasse 34, 2000 Hamburg 36; Sept.

**Musiksommer Obermain:** Bambergerstrasse 25, 8623 Staffelstein; May–Dec.

**Neue Bachgesellschaft e V:** Postfach 10 07 27, 04007 Leipzig; tel. 0341 9601463; fax 0341 2248182; e-mail info@neue-bachgesellschaft.de; website www.neue-bachgesellschaft.de; holds the annual Bach festival in June–July.

**Opera Festival Eutiner Sommerspiele GmbH:** PO Box 112, 2420 Eutin/ Holstein; tel. 49 4521 2161; July–Aug.

**Palace Courtyard Serenade Concerts:** Friedrichstrasse 5, 6900 Heidelberg; June–July.

**Pro Musica Nova:** Heinrich-Hertzstrasse 13, 2800 Bremen; May.

**Ruhrfestival-Europäisches Festival:** Otto Burrmeister Alle 1, 4350 Recklinghausen; tel. 49 2361 9180; May–June.

**Schleswig-Holstein Music Festival:** PO Box 2655, 23514 Lubeck; June–Aug.

**Schloss Elmau:** Schloss Elmau, 8101 Klais/Oberbayern.

**Schwetzingen Festival:** SWR Funkhaus Baden-Baden, Hans-Bredow-Strasse, 76530 Baden-Baden; held in April–June.

**Tage Alter Musik:** PO Box 100903, 93009 Regensburg; tel. 49 941 507 4410/ 11/12; fax 49 941 507 4419; website www.tage-alter-musik.allmusic.de; June.

**Tage für Neue Musik:** Kornbergstrasse 32, 7000 Stuttgart 1; Oct.–Nov.

**Tage Neuer Kammermusik Braunschweig:** Steintorwall 3, 3300 Braunschweig; Nov.–Dec.

**Telemann-Festtage:** Liebigstrasse 10, 3010 Magdeburg; website www .musikfeste.de; March.

**Witten Festival of Contemporary Chamber Music:** Bergerstrasse 25, 5810 Witten; tel. 49 2302 581 2424; April.

**Würzburg Bach Festival:** Hofstallstrasse 5, 8700 Würzburg; Nov.

**Würzburg Mozart Festival:** Haus zum Falken, 8700 Würzburg; June.

## Greece

**Athens Festival:** 23 Hadjichristou and Makriyianni, 11742 Athens; tel. 30 1 92 82 900; fax 30 1 92 82 941; website www.hellenicfestival.gr; May–Oct.

**Iraklion Summer Festival:** 71202 Iraklion, Crete; tel. 30 81 282 221.

**Patras International Festival:** PO Box 1184, 26110 Patras; tel. 30 61 278 730; June–Aug.

## Hong Kong

**Hong Kong Arts Festival:** 12/F Hong Kong Arts Centre, 2 Harbour Road, Wanchai, Hong Kong; tel. 852 2824 3555; fax 852 2824 3798/3722; website www.hk.artsfestival.org; Jan.–Feb.

## Hungary

**Beethoven Concerts:** Vörösmarty tér 1, 1364 Budapest; tel. 36 1 176 222; June–Aug.

**Budapest Autumn Festival:** PO Box 95, Rákóczi u. 65, VI 66, 1081 Budapest; tel. 36 1 210 2795; Oct.–Nov.

**Esztergom International Guitar Festival:** PO Box 38, 2501 Esztergom; tel. 36 33 313 808; July–Aug.

**Open Air Theatre-Summer Festival:** PO Box 95, 1525 Budapest; tel. 36 1175 5922; June–Aug.

**Sopron Early Music Days:** PO Box 80, 1366 Budapest; tel. 36 1 117 9838; June–July.

## Iceland

**Dark Music Days:** Laufásvegur 40, 101 Reykjavík; Jan.–Feb.

**Reykjavík Arts Festival:** PO Box 88, 121 Reykjavík; website www.artsfest.is; June.

## Ireland

**Adare Festival:** Adare Manor, Adare, County Limerick; July.

**Cork International Choral Festival:** PO Box 68, Cork; tel. 353 21 484 7277; fax 353 21 484 7278; e-mail chorfest@iol.ie; website www.corkchoral.ie; April–May.

**Dublin International Organ and Choral Festival:** 18 Eustace Street, Dublin 2; tel. 353 1 633 7392; e-mail organs@diocf.iol.ie; website www.dublinorganfestival.com; Sept.

**Galway Arts Festival:** Black Box Theatre, Dyke Road, Galway; tel. 353 91 509 700; fax 353 91 562 655; e-mail info@galwayartsfestival.ie; website www.galwayartsfestival.ie; July.

**Kilkenny Arts Week:** 92 High Street, Kilkenny; tel. 353 56 776 3663; fax 353 56 775 1704; e-mail info@kilkennyarts.ie; website www.kilkennyarts.ie; Aug.

**Waterford International Festival of Light Opera:** George's Street, Waterford; tel. 353 51 872639; fax 353 51 876002; website www.waterfordfestival.com; Sept.–Oct.

**Wexford Festival Opera:** Theatre Royal, High Street, Wexford; tel. 353 53 22400; fax 353 53 24289; e-mail info@wexfordopera.com; website www.wexfordopera.com; Oct.

## Israel

**Ein Gev Music Festival:** Ein Gev, 14940 Kibbutz Ein Gev; Passover.

**Israel Festival:** Jerusalem Theatre, PO Box 4409, 91040 Jerusalem; tel. 972 2 561 1438; May–June.

**Kol-Israel, Upper Galilee Chamber Music Days:** Hakirya, 61070 Tel-Aviv; July–Aug.

**Vocalisa 90:** PO Box 515, 20101 Carmiel; April.

## Italy

**Antidogma Musica Festival:** Via Alberto Nota 3, 10122 Turin; Sept.–Oct.

**Aterforum:** Piazetta Santa Anna 3, Int 8, 44100 Ferrara; June–July.

**Autunno Musicale a Como:** Via Cantoni 1, 22100 Como; Sept.–Oct.

**Batignano Musica nel Chiostro:** Santa Croce, Comune di Grosseto, 58041 Batignano; tel. 39 564 33 80 96; fax 39 564 33 80 85; July–Aug.

**Biennale di Venezia, Festival Internazionale di Musica Contemporanea:** Ca'Giustinian, S Marco, 30100 Venice; website www.labiennale.com; Sept.–Oct.

**Canto delle Pietro-Musiche Sacre e Spiritual:** Via Cantoni 1, 22100 Como; April–June.

**Ente Autonomo Spettacoli Lirici Arena di Verona:** Piazza Bra 28, 37121 Verona; tel. 39 045 805 18 11; July–Aug.

**Estate Maceratese:** Arena Sferisterio, 62100 Macerata; July.

**Festa Musica Pro Mundo Uno:** Via di Villa Maggiorani 20, 00168 Rome; July–Aug.

**Festival Barocco:** Corso Massimo d'Azeglio, 10126 Turin; May and Sept.

**Festival dell'Opera Siciliana e Taormina:** Via Cavour 117, 90133 Palermo; Oct.

**Festival di Musica Antica:** Via Zeffirino Re 2, 47023 Cesena; July.

**Festival di Musica Sacra:** Villa Igea, 90142 Palermo.

**Festival de Opera Barga:** Via della Fornacetta 11, 55051 Barga Lucca; July–Aug.

**Festival Internazionale di Musica Antica:** Via Confalonieri 5, 00195 Rome; July.

**Festival Internazionale di Musica Classica e Contemporanea:** PO Box N95, 16038 Santa Margherita Ligure; June–July.

**Festival Mozart in Lombardia:** Via Cantoni 1, 22100 Como; Sept.–Nov.

**Festival of Contemporary Music Nuovi Spazi Musicali:** Via Divisione Torino 139, 00143 Rome; tel. and fax 39 6 5021208; e-mail ada.gentile@tin.it; held annually in the autumn, with five or six concerts dedicated to performers and composers from all over the world.

**Festival of Two Worlds:** Via Cesare Beccaria 18, 00196 Rome; June–July.

**Festival Pontino:** Viale le Corbusier 379, 04100 Latina; tel. 0773 605551; fax 0773 628498; e-mail campus.musica@panservice.it; website www.campusmusica.it; held in June–July.

**Festival Romaeuropa:** Via Sistina 48, 00187 Rome; May–July.

**Festival Spaziomusica:** Via Liguria 60, 09127 Cagliari; tel. 39 070 400844; fax 39 070 485439; e-mail info@festivalspaziomusica.it; website www.festivalspaziomusica.it; held in Oct.–Nov.

**Gli Incontri Musicale Romani:** Largo Nazzareno 8, 00187 Rome.

**Gubbio Festival:** Corso Garibaldi 88, 06024 Gubbio; Sept.

**Incontri con La Nuova Musica:** PO Box 196, 25100 Brescia; Nov.–Dec.

**International Chamber Music Festival of Asolo:** Via Browning 141, 31011 Asolo; Aug.–Sept.

**Lucca in Villa Festival:** Via Turati 31, 55049 Viareggio, Lucca; Aug.

**Maggio Musicale Fiorentino:** Via Solferino 15, 50123 Florence; tel. 39 055 27791; fax 39 055 2396954; e-mail protocollo@maggiofiorentino.com; website www.maggiofiorentino.com; held in April–July.

**Musica 2000 Festival:** 8 Via Alpi, 60131 Ancona; April.

**Musica Verticale Festival:** Via Lamarmora 18, 00185 Rome; Oct.–Nov.

**Puccini Festival:** Piazza Belvedere Puccini 4, 55048 Lucca; tel. 39 584 350567; fax 39 584 341657; e-mail fpuccini@nodalisfree.it; website www.puccinifestival.it; July–Aug.

**Rassegna di Nuova Musica:** Arena Sferisterio, CP 92, 62100 Macerata; May–June.

**Ravenna Festival:** Via Dante Alighieri 1, 48100 Ravenna; tel. 39 544 249211; fax 39 544 36303; website www.ravennafestival.org; June–July.

**Rome Festival:** Via Francesco Duodo 49, 00136 Rome; tel. 39 328 411 7977; May–Aug. and Oct.–Nov.

**Rossini Opera Festival:** Via Rossini 37, 61100 Pesaro; tel. 39 721 380 0291; fax 39 721 380 0220; website www.rossinioperafestival.it; Aug.

**Sagra Musicale al Tempio Maiatestiano:** 47037 Rimini; Sept.

**Sagra Musicale Umbra:** PO Box 341, 06100 Perugia; website www.sagramusicaleumbra.com; Sept.

**Settembre Musica:** Piazza S Carlo 161, 10123 Turin; Aug.–Sept.

**Settimane Musicali di Stresa:** Via Carducci 38, 28838 Stresa; tel. 39 0323 31095; fax 39 0323 33006; e-mail info@settimanemusicali.net; website www.settimanemusicali.net; held in Aug.–Sept.

**Settimane Musicali Senese:** Via di Città 89, 53100 Siena; July.

**I Suoni del Tempo:** Via Zeffirino Re 2, 47023 Cesena; July.

**Taormina Arte:** Via Pirandello 31, 98039 Taormina; July–Sept.

**Triest Prima, Incontri internazionali:** Via Settefontane 30, 34141 Trieste; Sept.

**Veneto Festival:** Piazzale Pontecorvo 4a, 35100 Padua; May–July.

**Verdi Festival:** Via Farini 34, 43100 Parma; Sept.

**Verona Festival:** Piazza Brà 28, 37121 Verona; July–Sept.

## Japan

**Kusatsu International Summer Music Academy and Festival:** Wako Bldg 2f, 14-3 Motoyoyogi-cho, Shibuya-ku, Tokyo 151-0062; tel. 81 3 5790-

5561; fax 81 3 5790-5562; e-mail info@kusa2.jp; website www.kusa2.jp; held annually in the last two weeks of Aug.

**Min-On Contemporary Music Festival:** 1-32-13 Kita-Shinjuku, Shinjuku-ku, Tokyo 169; website www.min-on.org; June.

**National Arts Festival:** Ministry of Education, Tokyo 100; Oct.–Nov.

**Osaka International Festival Society:** New Asahi Building, Nakanoshima 2-3-18, Kita-ku, Osaka 530; April.

**Pacific Music Festival:** c/o Sapporo Concert Hall, 1-15 Nakajima-Koen, Chuo-ku, Sapporo 064; July–Aug.

**Tokyo City Arts Festival:** 3–5 Marunouchi, Chiyoda-ku, Tokyo; Jan.–March.

**Tokyo International Chamber Music Festival:** 32-11-411 Kamikitazawa 4-chome, Setagaya-ku, Tokyo; April–May.

**Tokyo Summer Festival:** Copacabana Building, 5F, 3-6-4 Akasaka, Minato-ku, Tokyo 107; July.

### Republic of Korea

**Autumn Music Festival in Seoul:** Dong-Hwa Building, Suite 210, 43-1, Pil-Dong 1-Ga, Choong-gu, Seoul 100-271; Oct.–Nov.

**Seoul International Music Festival:** Korean Broadcasting System, 18 Yoido-dong, Youngdungpo-gu, Seoul 150-790; Oct.–Nov.

### Lithuania

**Baltic Music Festival:** Mickevi iaus 29, 2600 Vilnius; tel. 370 2 220939; Oct.

### Luxembourg

**Festival Européen de Wiltz-Luxembourg:** Château de Wiltz, 9516 Wiltz; July.

**Festival International Echternach, Luxembourg:** Parvis de la Basilique 9, 6486 Echternach; May–June.

### Macao

**International Music Festival of Macao:** Avda Aviso Goncalves Zarco, s/n, First Floor, Macao; Oct.

### Mexico

**Festival de Música de Cámara de San Miguel de Allende:** Calle Hernández Macias 75, San Miguel de Allende; July–Aug.

**Festival de San Miguel de Allende:** Hospicio 48, San Miguel de Allende; tel. 52 415 2 5911; Dec.

**Festival Internacional Cervantino:** Alvaro Obregón 273, 06700 Mexico, DF; Oct.

**Gran Festival Ciudad de México:** Alvaro Obregón 73, 06700 Mexico, DF; July.

### Monaco

**Printemps des Arts de Monte Carlo:** rue Louis Notari, MC 98000 Monaco; April–May.

### The Netherlands

**Festival Amsterdam Chamber Music Society:** Ceintuurbaan 376, 1073 EM Amsterdam; tel. 31 20 626 9069; March and Nov.

**Festival Nieuwe Muziek:** PO Box 15, 4330 AA Middleburg; tel. 31 118 623650; fax 31 118 624754; June–July.

**Haarlem Organ Festival:** PO Box 3333, 2011 Haarlem; July.

**Holland Festival:** Antwoordnummer 10584, 1000 RA Amsterdam; website www.hollandfestival.nl; June.

**Holland Festival Early Music Utrecht:** PO Box 734, 3500 AS Utrecht; tel. 31 (0)30 2303838; fax 31 (0)30 2303839; e-mail info@oudemuziek.nl; website www.oudemuziek.nl; held in Aug.–Sept.

**International Choir Festival:** Plompetorengracht 3, 3512 CA Utrecht; tel. 31 30 233 56 00; fax 31 30 233 56 80; e-mail unisono@amateurmuziek.nl; website www.amateurmuziek.nl; held in June.

**International Gaudeamus Music Week:** Swammerdamstr 38, 1090 RV Amsterdam; Sept.

**New Music Festival Maastricht:** St Maartenspoort 23, 6221 BA Maastricht; tel. 31 43 25 0511; Sept.

### New Zealand

**New Zealand International Arts Festival:** PO Box 10113, Wellington 6036; tel. 64 4 473 0149; fax 64 4 471 1164; e-mail nzfestival@festival.co.nz; website www.nzfestival.telecom.co.nz; Feb.–March.

### Norway

**Bergen International Festival:** Strandgt 18, PO Box 183, 5001 Bergen; website www.fib.no; May.

**Elverum Festival:** PO Box 313, 2401 Elverum; Aug.

**Northern Norway Festival:** PO Box 901, 9401 Harstad; June.

**Oslo Sommeropera:** Grev Wedels Plass 2, 0151 Oslo; June.

**St Olav Festival:** PO Box 2045, 7410 Trondheim; tel. 47 73 84 14 50; fax 47 73 84 14 51; e-mail per.uddu@olavsfestdagene.no; held in July--Aug.

**Stord International Choir Festival:** PO Box 433, 5401 Stord; June.

### Philippines

**Philippine Music Festival:** NAMCYA-FAT, CCP Complex, Roxas Blvd, Manila; Oct.–Nov.

### Poland

**Festival of Early Music of Central and Eastern Europe:** Libelta 16, 85-080 Bydgoszcz; Sept.

**Henryk Wieniawski Days:** Tadeusza Ko ciuszki nr 19, 58-310 Szczawno-Zdrój; June.

**International Music and Arts Festival:** Rynek-Ratusz 24, 50-1010 Wroc-law; Sept.

**Music in Old Kraków:** ul. Zwierzyniecka 1, 31-103 Kraków; tel. 48 12 4214566; fax 48 12 4294328; e-mail amadeusz@capellacracoviensis.art.pl; website www.capellacracoviensis.art.pl; held in Aug.

**Polish and International Music Festival:** Chopina 30, 35-055 Rzeszów; May.

**Warsaw Autumn International Festival of Contemporary Music:** Rynek Starego Miasta 27, 00-272 Warsaw; tel. 48 22 8311634; fax 48 22 6359138; e-mail festival@warsaw-autumn.art.pl; website www.warsaw-autumn.art.pl; held in Sept.

### Romania

**Cluj-Napoca Musical Autumn:** Str E de Martonne 1, 3400 Cluj-Napoca; Oct.

**George Enescu International Festival:** Artexim, Calea Victoriei 155, Bl D1, Sc 8 et 2, 71012 Bucharest; website www.festivalenescu.ro; Sept.

**Tirgu Mures Musical Days:** 2 Enescu Str, 4300 Tirgu Mures; May.

### Russia

**December Nights:** Volkhona 12, 121019 Moscow; Dec.

**Festival Moscow:** Ul Kalantchovskaya 15, Moscow; July–Aug.

**International Music Festival St Petersburg Spring:** Herzena 45, 190000 St Petersburg; April.

**Moscow International Music Festival:** RosInterFest, 12 Sadovaya Triumfalnaya Str, 103006 Moscow; May.

**St Petersburg Palaces International Chamber Music Festival:** c/o M & N Artists Ltd, 400 W 43rd Street 19A, New York, NY 10036, USA; June.

**White Nights:** Fontanki 41, St Petersburg; June.

### Serbia and Montenegro

**Belgrade Music Festival:** Terazije 41, 11000 Belgrade; Oct.

### Singapore

**Singapore Festival of Arts:** PSA Building, 35th Storey, 460 Alexandria Road, Singapore 0511; June of even-numbered years.

### Slovakia

**Bratislava Cultural Summer:** Suché Mýto 17, 812 93 Bratislava; July–Aug.

**Evenings of New Music:** Fucikova 29, 811 02 Bratislava; June.

### Slovenia

**Ljubljana Festival:** Trg Francoske Revolucije 1–2, 1000 Ljubljana; tel. 386 1 241 60 00; fax 386 1 241 60 37; e-mail info@festival-lj.si; website www.festival-lj.si; held in July--Aug.

### Spain

**Curso de Música Barroca y Rococo:** Acuerdo 17-1 A, 28015 Madrid; Aug.

**Festival de Música de Canarias:** Leon y Castillo 427-3, 35007 Las Palmas de Gran Canaria; tel. 34 928 24 74 42; fax 34 928 27 60 42; website socaem.com; Jan.–Feb.

**Festival Internacional de Guitarra Andres Segovia:** Ramon Llull 2, 07001 Palma de Mallorca; Nov.

**Festival Internacional de Música y Danza de Granada:** PO Box 64, 18080 Granada; June–July.

**Festival Internacional de Música Castell de Peralada:** Pere de Moncada 1, 08034 Barcelona; tel. 34 935 03 86 46; website www.festivalperalada.com; July--Aug.

**Festival Internacional de Música Contemporánea de Alicante:** Santa Isabel 52, 28012 Madrid; Sept.

**Festival Internacional de Música de Barcelona:** Via Laietana, 41 pral, 08003 Barcelona.

**Festival Internacional de Organo:** Calle La Paloma 7, 24003 Leon; tel. 34 87 25 78 37; Sept.–Oct.

**Festival Internacional de Santander:** Avda Calvo Sotelo 15, 5°, 39004 Santander; website www.festival-int-santander.org; July--Sept.

**Semana de Música de Cámara Festival internacional de Segovia:** San Facundo 5, Segovia; July.

**Serenatas Musicales de Valencia:** Avellanas 603a, 46003 Valencia; tel. 34 6 391 90 48; July.

## Sweden

**Drottningholm Court Theatre Festival:** Drottningholms Slottsteater, Box 15417, 104 65 Stockholm; held in May–Sept.

**Electro-Acoustic Music Festival:** PO Box 101, 739 22 Skinnskatteberg; June.

**Helsingborg Summerfestival:** Konserthuset, 252 21 Helsingborg; Aug.

**Royal Palace Music Festival:** Royal Palace, 111 30 Stockholm; July–Aug.

**Stockholm New Music:** PO Box 1225, 111 82 Stockholm; March.

**Umeå International Festival of Chamber Music:** 901 78 Umeå; June.

**Visby Festival:** Tranhusgatan 47, 621 55 Visby; July–Aug.

## Switzerland

**Estate Musicale internazionale de Lugano:** Via Losanna, 6900 Lugano; Aug.

**European International Festival:** 10 rue des Eaux-Vives, 1207 Geneva; May–July.

**Festival de Musique Sacrée de Fribourg:** PO Box 292, 1701 Fribourg; July.

**Festival d'Eté, A Swiss Summer:** PO Box 10, 1211 Geneva; July–Aug.

**Festival de Sion Tibor Varga:** PO Box 1429, 1951 Sion; tel. 0041 27 323 4317; fax 0041 27 323 4662; July–Sept.

**Interlakner Festwochen:** PO Box, 3800 Interlaken; Aug.

**International Bach Festival:** Stadthaus, 8201 Schaffhausen; tel. 41 52 632 52 11; May.

**International Festival of Music, Lucerne:** Hirschmattstrasse 13, PO Box, 6002 Lucerne; Aug.–Sept.

**International Festival of Organ Music:** Ente Turistico del Gambarogno, 6574 Vira; tel. 41 91 795 12 14; June–July.

**Montreux Choral Festival:** CP 1526, 1820 Montreux; tel. 41 21 966 55 50; fax 41 21 966 55 69; e-mail montreuxchoralfestival@bluewin.ch; website www .choralfestival.ch; held in April; choirs from around the world sing classical, popular and folk repertoires.

**Montreux-Vevey Music Festival:** rue du Théâtre 5, PO Box 162, 1820 Montreux; Aug.–Oct.

**Settimane Musicale d'Ascona:** Via Lido 24, 6612 Ascona; tel. 41 91 791 00 90; Aug.–Oct.

**Tage für Neue Musik Zürich:** Hegibachstrasse 38, 8032 Zürich; Nov.

## Taiwan

**Taipei Music Festival:** 25 Pa Teh Road, Sec 3, 10560 Taipei; Sept.–Oct.

## Turkey

**Ankara International Festival:** Tunali Hilmi Cad 114/43, 06700 Kavakli-dere/Ankara; April.

**Istanbul International Festival:** Istiklal Caddesi 146, Luvr Apt, Beyoglu, 80070 Istanbul; website www.istfest.org; June–July.

**Izmire International Festival:** 1442 Sok No. 4/6, 35220 Alsancak, Izmir; June–July.

## United Kingdom

**Aberdeen International Youth Festival:** Linksfield Community Centre, 520 King Street, Aberdeen, Scotland AB24 5SS; tel. (1224) 494400; fax (1224) 494114; e-mail admin@aiyf.org; website www.aiyf.org; Aug.

**Aldeburgh/Almeida Opera:** Almeida Theatre, Almeida Street, London, NW1 1TA; tel. (20) 7359-4404; website www.almeida.co.uk.

**Aldeburgh Britten Festival:** Aldeburgh Productions, Snape Maltings Concert Hall, Snape, Suffolk IP17 1SP; tel. (1728) 687110; fax (1728) 687120; e-mail enquiries@aldeburgh.co.uk; website www.aldeburgh.co.uk; Oct.

**Aldeburgh Easter Festival:** Aldeburgh Productions, Snape Maltings Concert Hall, Snape, Suffolk IP17 1SP; tel. (1728) 687110; fax (1728) 687120; e-mail enquiries@aldeburgh.co.uk; website www.aldeburgh.co.uk; Easter Week.

**Aldeburgh Festival of Music and the Arts:** Aldeburgh Productions, Snape Maltings Concert Hall, Snape, Saxmundham, Suffolk IP17 1SP; tel. (1728) 687110; fax (1728) 687120; e-mail enquiries@aldeburgh.co.uk; website www .aldeburgh.co.uk; June.

**Arundel Festival:** 3 Castle Mews, Arundel, Sussex, BN19 9DG; website www.arundelfestival.co.uk; Aug.

**Bampton Opera:** tel. (20) 7222-1173; e-mail mail@bamptonopera.org; website www.bamptonopera.org; July--August.

**Bath International Festival of Music and the Arts:** Bath Festivals Trust, 2 Church Street, Abbey Green, Bath, Avon BA1 1NL; tel. (1225) 463362; website www.bathmusicfest.org.uk; May–June.

**Bath Mozartfest:** 110 Gloucester Avenue, London, NW1 8JA; Nov.

**BBC Henry Wood Promenade Concerts:** 16 Langham Street, Room 425, London, W1A 1AA; website www.bbc.co.uk/proms; July--Sept.

**Belfast Festival at Queen's:** 25 College Gardens, Belfast, Northern Ireland BT9 6BS; tel. (28) 9027 2600; website www.belfastfestival.com; Nov.

**Birmingham Early Music Festival:** 42 Beech Avenue, Worcester WR3 8PY; July.

**Bournemouth Live! Music Festival:** Visitor Information Bureau, Westover Road, Bournemouth BH1 2BU; tel. (1202) 451700; website www.bournemouth .co.uk; held in June--July.

**Bournemouth Musicmakers Festival:** Westover Road, Bournemouth BH1 2BU; held in June--July.

**Brighton Festival:** 54 Old Steine, Brighton, Sussex BN1 1EQ; website www .brighton-festival.org.uk; May.

**Bromsgrove Festival:** Festival Office, Bromsgrove Museum and Tourist Information Centre, 26 Birmingham Road, Bromsgrove B61 8AB; tel. (1527) 876504; fax (1527) 575366; April–May.

**Buxton Festival:** 5 The Square, Buxton, Derbyshire SK17 6AZ; tel. (1298) 70395; e-mail info@buxtonfestival.co.uk; website www.buxtonfestival.co.uk; July--Aug.

**Cambridge Summer Music Festival:** Cambridge Arts Theatre, 6 St Edward's Passage, Cambridge, CB2 3PJ; tel. (1223) 503333; website www .cambridgesummermusic.com; July--Aug.

**Canterbury Festival:** Festival Office, Christ Church Gate, The Precincts, Canterbury, Kent CT1 2EE; tel. (1227) 452853; e-mail info@ canterburyfestival.co.uk; website www.canterburyfestival.co.uk; Oct.

**Cardiff Festival of Music:** St David's Hall, The Hayes, Cardiff, Wales CF1 2SH; Sept.–Oct.

**Cheltenham International Festival of Music:** Town Hall, Imperial Square, Cheltenham, Gloucestershire GL50 1QA; tel. (1242) 227979; fax (1242) 573902; website www.cheltenhamfestivals.co.uk; July.

**Chester Summer Music Festival:** 8 Abbey Square, Chester, CH1 2HU; July.

**Chichester Festivities:** Canon Gate House, South Street, Chichester, Sussex PO19 1PU; e-mail info@chifest.org.uk; website www.chifest.org.uk; July.

**City of Leeds College of Music Festival:** Cookridge Street, Leeds, Yorkshire LS2 8B; Feb.–March.

**City of London Festival:** Bishopsgate Hall, 230 Bishopsgate, London, EC2M 4QH; tel. (20) 7377-0540; fax (20) 7377-1972; e-mail admin@colf.org; website www.colf.org; June--July.

**Dartington International Summer School:** The Barn, Dartington Hall, Totnes, Devon TQ9 6DE; tel. (1803) 847080; fax (1803) 847087; e-mail info@ dartingtonsummerschool.org.uk; website www.dartingtonsummerschool.org .uk; offers some 50 courses spanning western musical repertoire and music of other cultures; masterclasses, workshops, exhibitions and concerts

**East Anglia Summer Music Festival:** The Old School, Bridge Street, Hadleigh, Suffolk IP7 6BY; July–Aug.

**Edinburgh International Festival:** The Hub, Castlehill, Edinburgh, Scotland EH1 2NE; tel. (131) 473 2001; website www.eif.co.uk; Aug.

**Evening Standard Holland Park Theatre Festival:** Central Library, Phillimore Walk, Kensington, London, W8 7RX.

**Exeter Festival:** Exeter City Council, Civic Centre, Paris Street, Exeter EX1 1JN; tel. (1392) 265205; fax (1392) 265366; e-mail festival@exeter.gov.uk; website www.exeter.gov.uk/festival; July.

**Fishguard International Music Festival:** Festival Office, Fishguard, Pembrokeshire, Wales SA65 9BJ; tel. and fax (1348) 873612; e-mail fishguard-imf@cwcom.net; July.

**Garsington Opera Festival:** Garsington Opera, Garsington, Oxfordshire, OX44 9DH; tel. (1865) 361636; e-mail office@garsingtonopera.org; website www.garsingtonopera.org; June–July.

**Glyndebourne Festival Opera:** Glyndebourne, PO Box 2624, Lewes, East Sussex BN8 5UW; tel. (1273) 813813; fax (1273) 814686; website www.glyndebourne.com.

**Grange Park Opera:** tel. (1962) 868888; fax (1962) 868968; e-mail box@grangeparkopera.co.uk; website www.grangeparkopera.co.uk; June–July.

**Harrogate International Festival:** 1 Victoria Avenue, Harrogate, Yorkshire HG1 1EQ; tel. (1423) 562303; fax (1423) 521264; e-mail info@harrogate-festival.org.uk; website www.harrogate-festival.org.uk; July–Aug.

**Haslemere Festival:** Jesses, Grayswood Road, Haslemere, Surrey GU27 2BS; July.

**Henley Festival of Music and the Arts:** 14 Friday Street, Henley-on-Thames, RG9 1AH; tel. (1491) 843400; fax (1491) 410482; e-mail info@henley-festival.co.uk; website www.henley-festival.co.uk; July.

**Huddersfield Contemporary Music Festival:** University of Huddersfield, Queensgate, Huddersfield HD1 3DH; tel. (1484) 425082; fax (1484) 472957; e-mail info@hcmf.co.uk; website www.hcmf.co.uk; Nov.

**Iford Arts:** Theatre Royal, Bath, BA1 1ET; tel. (1225) 448844; fax (1225) 444080; e-mail info@ifordarts.co.uk; website www.ifordarts.co.uk.

**International East Anglian Summer Music Festival:** 3–5 Bridge Street, Hadleigh, Suffolk, IB7 6BY; tel. (1473) 822596; fax (1473) 824175.

**International Organ Festival:** PO Box 80, St Albans, AL3 4HR; July.

**King's Lynn Festival:** 29 King Street, King's Lynn, Norfolk PE30 1HA; July.

**Lake District Summer Music:** 92 Stricklandgate, Kendal, Cumbria LA9 4PU; tel. (1539) 724441; fax (1539) 741882; e-mail info@ldsm.org.uk; website www.ldsm.org.uk; July–Aug.

**Leamington Festival:** Pageant House, 2 Jury Street, Warwick, CV34 4EW; tel. (1926) 410747; fax (1926) 409050; e-mail admin@warwickarts.org.uk; website www.warwickarts.org.uk; held in May; includes chamber music concerts, Leamington Jazz Weekend, New Music Day, world music, puppets and literary events.

**Lichfield Festival:** 7 The Close, Lichfield, Staffordshire WS13 7LD; tel. (1543) 306270; e-mail lichfield.fest@lichfield-arts.org.uk; website www.lichfieldfestival.org; July.

**Llandaff Summer Festival:** 1 St Mary's, Cardiff, Wales CF5 2EB; May–July.

**Llangollen International Musical Eisteddfod:** Royal International Pavilion, Abbey Road, Llangollen, LL20 8SW; tel. (1978) 862000; fax (1978) 862002; e-mail info@ international-eisteddfod.co.uk; website www.international-eisteddfod.co.uk; July.

**London New Wind Festival:** 119 Woolstone Road, Forest Hill, London SE23 2TQ; tel. (20) 8699-1101; fax (20) 8699-2219.

**Longborough Festival Opera:** Longborough, Moreton-in-Marsh, Gloucestershire GL56 0QE; tel. (1451) 830292; website www.longboroughopera.com.

**Lufthansa Festival of Baroque Music:** 71 Priory Road, Kew Gardens, Surrey TW9 3DH; website www.lufthansa-festival.org.uk; June.

**Malvern Festival:** Rockliffe House, 40 Church Street, Malvern, Worcestershire WR14 2AZ; May–June.

**Manchester-Hallé Proms Festival:** Hallé Concerts Society, Heron House, Albert Square, Manchester, M2 5HD; June–July.

**Mayfest:** 18 Albion Street, Glasgow, Scotland G1 1LH; April–May.

**Musicfest Aberystwyth:** Aberystwyth Arts Centre, Penglais Campus, Aberystwyth, Ceredigion SY23 3DE; website www.musicfest-aberystwyth.org; July–Aug.

**Newbury Spring Festival:** 1 Bridge Street, Newbury, Berkshire RG14 5BE; tel. (1635) 32421; fax (1635) 528690; website www.newburyspringfestival.org.uk; May.

**Norfolk and Norwich Festival:** 42–58 St George's Street, Norwich, NR3 1AB; tel. (1603) 614921; fax (1603) 632303; e-mail info@n-joy.org.uk; website www.nnfest.demon.co.uk; Oct.

**North Wales Music Festival:** High Street, St Asaph, Clwyd, North Wales LL17 0RD; Sept.

**Opera Holland Park:** Central Library, Phillimore Walk, London, W8 7RX; tel. (845) 230 9769; e-mail production@operahollandpark.com; boxoffice@operahollandpark.com; website www.operahollandpark.com; season runs from June–August.

**Perkshore Festival:** Manor House Barn, Fladbury, Perkshore, Worcestershire WR10 2QN; June–July.

**Perth Festival of the Arts:** 2 High Street, Perth, Scotland; May.

**Peterborough Cathedral Festival:** The Cathedral Shop, 24 Minster Precincts, Peterborough PE1 1XZ; July.

**Presteigne Festival of Music and the Arts:** 17 Parliament Hill, London, NW3 2TA.

**Royal National Eisteddfod of Wales:** 40 Parc Ty Glas, Llansihen, Cardiff, Wales CF4 5WU; Aug.

**St Albans International Organ Festival:** PO Box 80, St Albans, Hertfordshire AL3 AHR; July (odd numbered years).

**St Endellion Easter and Summer Festivals of Music:** Churchtown Farmhouse, Michaelstow, Bodmin, Cornwall PL30 3PD; April and Aug.

**Salisbury Festival:** 75 New Street, Salisbury, SP1 2PH; tel. (1722) 332977; fax (1722) 410552; website www.salisburyfestival.co.uk; May–June.

**Sheffield Chamber Music Festival:** 65 Rawcliffe Lane, Clifton, York, YO3 6SJ; May.

**Spitalfields Festival:** 75 Brushfield Street, London, E1 6AA; tel. (20) 7377-0287; fax (20) 7247-0494; e-mail info@spitalfieldsfestival.org.uk; website www.spitalfieldsfestival.org.uk; held in June.

**Stratford-upon-Avon Music Festival:** Pageant House, 2 Jury Street, Warwick, CV34 4EW; tel. (1926) 410747; fax (1926) 409050; e-mail admin@warwickarts.org.uk; website www.warwickarts.org.uk; held in Oct.; includes chamber music concerts, early music, and other types of music.

**Swansea Festival of Music and the Arts:** The Guildhall, Swansea, SA1 4PE; Sept.–Nov.

**Three Choirs Festival:** The Festival Box Office, 3 Choirs Festival, Cathedral Plaza, 5 High Street, Worcester, WR1 2QW; tel. (1905) 610538; fax (1905) 610559; e-mail info.worcester@3choirs.org; website www.3choirs.org; Aug.

**Tilford Bach Festival:** Fairlawne, Kiln Way, Grayshott, GU26 6JF; tel. (1428) 713338; e-mail sa.greaves@tiscali.co.uk; website www.tilford-bach.org.uk; held in May–June.

**Vale of Glamorgan Festival:** St Donat's Castle, Llantwit Major, Wales CF6 9WF; Aug.

**Walsingham Variations:** The Grove, 61 Bracondale, Norwich, Norfolk NR1 2AT; Aug.

**Warwick Festival:** Pageant House, 2 Jury Street, Warwick, CV34 4EW; tel. (1926) 410747; fax (1926) 409050; e-mail admin@warwickarts.org.uk; website www.warwickarts.org.uk; held in June–July; includes orchestral, choral and chamber music concerts.

**Windsor Festival:** Dial House, Englefield Green, Egham, Surrey TW20 0DU; Sept.–Oct.

**York Early Music Festival:** National Centre For Early Music, St Margaret's Church, Walmgate, York YO1 9TL; tel. (1904) 632220; fax (1904) 612631; e-mail info@ncem.co.uk; website www.ncem.co.uk; July.

## United States of America

**American Music Festival:** National Gallery of Art, Sixth Street and Constitution Avenue NW, Washington, DC 20565; April–May.

**Ames Festival:** PO Box 1243, Ames, IA 50010.

**An Appalachian Summer:** ASU Office of Cultural Affairs, PO Box 32045, Boone, NC 28608; tel. (828) 262-4046; fax (828) 262-2848; website www.appsummer.com; July.

**Ann Arbor May Festival:** Burton Memorial Tower, Suite 100, Ann Arbor, MI 48109; May.

**Artpark:** 450 S Fourth Street, Lewiston, NY 14092; tel. (716) 754-9000; fax (716) 754-2741; website www.artpark.net; May–Sept.

**Arts Festival of Atlanta:** 999 Peachtree Street, Suite 140, Atlanta, GA 30309; Sept.

**Art Song Festival:** Cleveland Institute of Music, 11021 East Blvd, Cleveland, OH 44106; tel. (216) 791-5000; fax (216) 791-3063; website www.cim.edu; May.

**Aspen Music Festival:** 2 Music School Road, Aspen, CO 81611; tel. (970) 925-9042; fax (970) 925-8077; e-mail festival@aspenmusic.org; website www .aspenmusicfestival.com; June–Aug.

**Aston Magna Festival:** PO Box 28, Great Barrington, MA 01230; tel. (413) 528-3595; e-mail info@astonmagna.org; website www.astonmagna.org; held in July–Aug.

**Atlanta Symphony Orchestra:** Summer Concerts: 1293 Peachtree Street, NE, Suite 300, Atlanta, GA 30309; June–Aug.

**Bay Chamber Concerts:** PO Box 228, Rockport, ME 04856-0228; tel. (207) 236-2823; website www.baychamberconcerts.org; summer festival held in July–Aug.; performing arts series held in Oct.–June.

**Baltimore Symphony Orchestra Summerfest and Oregon Ridge Concert Series:** 1212 Cathedral Street, Baltimore, MD 21201; June–Aug.

**Bard Music Festival:** PO Box 5000, Bard College, Annandale-on-Hudson, NY 12504; tel. (845) 758-7410; e-mail bm@bard.edu; Aug.

**Berkeley Festival and Exhibition:** 101 Zellerbach Hall, University of California at Berkeley, Berkeley, CA 94720; website www.bfx.berkeley.edu/ bfx; June.

**Berkshire Choral Festival:** 245 N Undermountain Road, Sheffield, MA 01257; tel. (413) 229-8526; fax (413) 229-0109; e-mail bcf@choralfest.org; website www.chorusfest.org; held in July–Aug.

**Bethlehem Musikfest Association:** 22 Bethlehem Plaza, Bethlehem, PA 18018; website www.musikfest.org; Aug.

**Big Sky Arts Festival:** PO Box 160308, Big Sky, MT 59716; July.

**Binghamton Summer Music Festival:** PO Box 112, Binghamton, NY 13903; tel. (607) 777-4777; fax (607) 777-6780; e-mail bsmf1@yahoo.com; website summermusic.binghamton.edu; July–Aug.

**Boston Early Music Festival and Exhibition:** PO Box 1286, Cambridge, MA 02238; tel. (617) 424-7232; fax (617) 267-6539; e-mail bemf@bemf.org; website www.bemf.org; June.

**Boston Pops:** Symphony Hall, 301 Massachusetts Avenue, Boston, MA 02115; website www.bso.org; May–June.

**Boston Symphony Orchestra Tanglewood Festival:** Symphony Hall, 301 Massachusetts Avenue, Boston, MA 02115; tel. (617) 266-1492; fax (617) 638-9367; website www.bso.org; held in June–Aug.

**Bravo! Colorado Music Festival at Vail, Beaver Creek:** 953 South Frontage Road, Suite 104, Vail, CO 81657; tel. (970) 949-1999; July–Aug.

**Brevard Music Festival:** PO Box 312, 10000 Probart Street, Brevard, NC 28712; tel. (828) 862-2100; fax (828) 884-2036; e-mail bmc@brevardmusic.org; website www.brevardmusic.org; June–Aug.

**Britt Festivals, Music and Performing Arts Festivals:** PO Box 1124, Medford, OR 97501; tel. (541) 779-0847; fax (541) 776-3712; website www .brittfest.org; June–Sept.

**Cabrillo Music Festival:** 104 Walnut Lane, Suite 206, Santa Cruz, CA 95060; tel. (831) 426-6966; e-mail info@cabrillomusic.org; website www .cabrillomusic.org; Aug.

**Cape May Music Festival:** PO Box 340, Cape May, NJ 08204; May–June.

**Caramoor International Music Festival:** PO Box R, Katonah, NY 10536; June–Aug.

**Carmel Bach Festival:** PO Box 575, Carmel-by-the-Sea, CA 93921; tel. (831) 625-1521; fax (831) 624-2788; e-mail info@bachfestival.org; website www .bachfestival.org; 23 days of concerts and recitals in July–Aug.; Baroque and classical repertoire.

**Castle Hill Festival:** PO Box 563, Ipswich, MA 01938; July–Sept.

**Chamber Music Northwest:** 522 SW Fifth Avenue, Suite 725, Portland, OR 97204; tel. (503) 223-3202; fax (503) 294-1690; e-mail info@cmnw.org; website www.cmnw.org; June–July.

**Chautauqua Institution:** PO Box 28, Chautauqua, NY 14722; tel. (716) 357-6200; fax (716) 357-9014; website www.ciweb.org; June–Aug.

**Cincinnati May Festival:** Music Hall, 1241 Elm Street, Cincinnati, OH 45202; tel. (513) 621-1919; fax (513) 744-3535; website www.mayfestival.com; May–June.

**Cincinnati Opera Association Summer Festival:** 1241 Elm Street, Cincinnati, OH 45202; tel. (513) 241-2742; fax (513) 744-3530; website www .cincinnatiopera.org; June–July.

**Cincinnati Symphony and Pops Orchestras at Riverbend:** 1241 Elm Street, Cincinnati, OH 45202; website www.cincinnatisymphony.org; June–Aug.

**Cleveland Orchestra at the Blossom Music Center:** PO Box 1000, Cuyahoga Falls, OH 44223; May–Sept.

**Colorado Music Festival:** 1035 Pearl Street, Suite 303, Boulder, CO 80302; website www.coloradomusicfest.com; June–Aug.

**Columbia Festival of the Arts:** 5575 Sterrett Place, Suite 280, Columbia, MD 21044; tel. (410) 715-3044; fax (410) 715-3056; e-mail info@ columbiafestival.com; website www.columbiafestival.com; June.

**Connecticut Early Music Festival:** PO Box 329, New London, CT 06320; tel. (860) 444-2419; website www.ctearlymusic.org; June.

**Dallas Symphony Orchestra EDS International Summer Music Festival:** 2301 Flora Street, Dallas, TX 75201; tel. (214) 692-0203; website www.dallassymphony.com; June–July.

**Des Moines Metropolitan Opera:** 106 W Boston Avenue, Indianola, IA 50125; tel. (515) 961-6221; fax (515) 961-8175; website www.dmmo.org; June–July.

**Eastern Music Festival:** PO Box 22026, Greensboro, NC 27420; tel. (336) 333-7450 ext. 21; fax (336) 333-7454 ext. 21; e-mail emfinfo@bellsouth.net; website www.easternmusicfestival.com; June–July.

**Fanfare:** Southeastern Louisiana University, PO Box 797, Hammond, LA 70402; Oct.

**Festival at Sandpoint:** PO Box 695, Sandpoint, Idaho 83864; website www .festivalatsandpoint.com; July–Aug.

**Festival Casals:** PO Box 41227, Minillas Station, Santurce, Puerto Rico 09940; tel. (787) 721-7727; fax (787) 723-5843; website www.festcasalspr .gobierno.pr; June.

**Festival Miami:** University of Miami School of Music, PO Box 248165, Coral Gables, FL 33124; tel. (305) 284-4940; website www.music.miami.edu/ festivalmiami; Sept.–Oct.

**Festival Music Society of Indiana:** 6471 Central Avenue, Indianapolis, IN 46220; tel. (317) 251-5190; e-mail merfms@msn.com; website www.emindy .org; June–July.

**Festival of Young Orchestras of the Americas:** PO Box 41227, Minillas Station, Santurce, Puerto Rico 00940; June.

**Firefly Festival for the Performing Arts:** 202 S Michigan Street, Suite 845, South Bend, IN 46601; website www.fireflyfestival.com; June–Aug.

**Flagstaff Festival of the Arts:** PO Box 1607, Flagstaff, AZ 86002; July–Aug.

**Flathead Music Festival:** PO Box 1780, Whitefish, MT 59937; tel. (406) 257-0787; July.

**Florida International Festival:** PO Box 1310, Daytona Beach, FL 32115-1310; tel. (386) 681-2410; fax (386) 238-1663; website www.fif.lso.org; Aug. (odd-numbered years.

**Garden State Arts Center:** PO Box 116, Holmdel, NJ 0733; June–Sept.

**Gina Bachauer International Piano Festival:** 138 W Broadway, Suite 220, Salt Lake City, UT 84101; tel. (801) 297-4250; fax (801) 521-9202; e-mail gina@bachauer.com; website www.bachauer.com; held in June, rotating annually between four age groups (11–13, 14–18, 19–32 and 33–100).

**Glimmerglass Opera:** PO Box 191, Cooperstown, NY 13326; tel. (607) 547-5704; website www.glimmerglass.org; July–Aug.

**Grand Canyon Chamber Music Festival:** PO Box 1332, Grand Canyon, AZ 86023; tel. (928) 638-9215; e-mail gcmf@infomagic.net; website grandcanyonmusicfest.org; Sept.

**Grand Teton Music Festival:** 4015 W Lake Creek Drive, Suite 1, Wilson, WY 83014; tel. (307) 733-3050; fax (307) 739-9043; e-mail gtmf@gtmf.org; website www.gtmf.org; held in June–Aug.

**Grant Park Music Festival:** Chicago Park District Administration Bldg, 425 E McFetridge Drive, Chicago, IL 60605; June–Aug.

**Hartwood Music and Dance Festival:** 1520 Pennsylvania Avenue, Pittsburgh, PA 15222; May–Sept.

**Hollywood Bowl Summer Festival:** PO Box 1951, 2301 N Highlands Avenue, Hollywood, CA 90078; tel. (323) 850-2000; July–Sept.

**Houston International Festival:** 7413-B Westview Drive, Houston, TX 77055; tel. (713) 654-8808; fax (713) 654-1719; e-mail contactus@iFest.org; website www.iFest.org; April.

**Huntington Summer Arts Festival:** 213 Main Street, Huntington, NY 11743; tel. (516) 271-8442; June–Aug.

**Indiana University School of Music Summer Festival:** Indiana University School of Music, Bloomington, IN 47405; tel. (812) 855-1583; website www.music.indiana.edu; June–Aug.

**Indianapolis Symphony Orchestra, Marsh Symphony on the Prairie:** 32 E Washington Street, Suite 600, Indianapolis, IN 46204; tel. (317) 236-2040; fax (317) 236-2038; website www.indianapolissymphony.org; June–Aug.

**Inter-American Festival of the Arts:** PO Box 41227, Minillas Station, Santurce, Puerto Rico 00940; Sept.–Oct.

**Interlochen Arts Festival:** PO Box 199, Interlochen, MI 49643; tel. (231) 276-7200; fax (231) 276-6321; website www.michiweb.com/interlochen; June--Aug.

**Irving S. Gilmore International Keyboard Festival:** The Epic Center, 359 S Kalamazoo Mall, Suite 101, Kalamazoo, MI 49007; website www.gilmore.org; April--May (even-numbered years).

**Kent/Blossom Music:** Kent State University, E101 M&S, PO Box 5190, Kent, OH 44242; tel. (330) 672-2613; fax (330) 672-7837; e-mail jlacorte@kent.edu; website dept.kent.edu/blossom; f. 1968; professional training ground for young musicians embarking on professional careers; emphasis on chamber music and orchestral audition preparation; held in June--Aug.

**La Jolla Chamber Music Society:** 7946 Ivanhoe Avenue, Suite 309, La Jolla, CA 92037; tel. (858) 459-3724; fax (858) 459-3727; website www.ljcms.org; Aug.

**Lake George Opera Festival:** 480 Broadway, Suite 336, Saratoga Springs, NY 12866; tel. (518) 584-6018; fax (518) 584-6775; e-mail lgopera@aol.com; website www.lakegeorgeopera.org; July--Aug.

**Lakeside Summer Festival:** 236 Walnut Avenue, Lakeside, OH 43440; tel. (419) 798-4461; website www.lakesideohio.com; June--Sept.

**Lancaster Festival:** PO Box 1452, Lancaster, OH 43130; tel. (740) 687-4808; fax (740) 687-1980; e-mail lanfest@lanfest.org; website www.lanfest.org; held in July.

**Library of Congress Summer Chamber Festival:** Library of Congress, Washington, DC 20540; June.

**Lincoln Center Out-of-Doors:** 70 Lincoln Center Plaza, Ninth Floor, New York, NY 10023; website www.lincolncenter.org; Aug.

**Los Angeles Festival:** PO Box 5210, Los Angeles, CA 90055; Sept.

**Manchester Music Festival:** PO Box 33, Manchester, VT 05254; tel. (802) 362-1956; e-mail info@mmfvt.org; website www.mmfvt.org; July--Aug.

**Mann Music Center:** 1617 J. F. Kennedy Blvd, Philadelphia, PA 19103; website www.manncenter.org; June--Sept.

**Marlboro Music Festival:** Box K, Marlboro, VT 05344; tel. (802) 254-2394; fax (802) 254-4307; e-mail info@marlboromusic.org; website www.marlboromusic.org; July--Aug.

**Mendocino Music Festival:** PO Box 1808, Mendocino, CA 95460; tel. (707) 937-2044; fax (707) 937-1045; e-mail music@mendocinomusic.com; website www.mendocinomusic.com; held in July.

**Michigan Bach Festival:** 400 Town Center Drive, Suite 300, Dearbon, MI 48126; March--April.

**Midsummer Mozart Festival:** 3661 Buchanan Street, Suite 200, San Francisco, CA 94123; tel. (415) 292-9620; fax (415) 292-9622; e-mail amadeus@midsummermozart.org; website www.midsummermozart.org; July--Aug.

**Minnesota Orchestra Viennese Sommerfest:** 1111 Nicollet Mall, Minneapolis, MN 55403; tel. (612) 371-5656; July--Aug.

**Missouri River Festival of the Arts:** PO Box 1776, Boonville, MO 65233; Aug.

**Monadnock Music:** PO Box 255, Peterborough, NH 03458; tel. (603) 924-7610; fax (603) 924-9403; e-mail mm@monadnockmusic.org; website www.monadnockmusic.org; July--Aug.

**Mostly Mozart Festival:** 70 Lincoln Center Plaza, Ninth Floor, New York, NY 10023; July--Aug.

**Music Academy of the West Summer Concert Season:** 1070 Fairway Road, Santa Barbara, CA 93108; tel. (805) 969-4726; fax (805) 969-0686; website www.musicacademy.org; held in June--Aug.

**Music Festival of Arkansas:** PO Box 1243, Fayetteville, AR 72702; June.

**Music From Angel Fire:** PO Box 502, Angel Fire, NM 87710; website www.musicfromangelfire.org; Aug.--Sept.

**Music in the Mountains:** 530 Searls Avenue, Nevada City, CA 95959; tel. (530) 265-6173; fax (530) 265-6810; e-mail mim@musicinthemountains.org; website www.musicinthemountains.org; June--July.

**National Symphony Orchestra:** Concerts at the Capitol: John F. Kennedy Center for the Performing Arts, Washington, DC 20566; Memorial Day and Labor Day weekends, and Fourth of July.

**New England Bach Festival:** 38 Walnut Street, Brattleboro, VT 05301; website www.bmcvt.org/nebf; Sept.--Oct.

**New Hampshire Music Festival:** Festival House, 52 Symphony Lane, Center Harbour, NH 03226; tel. (603) 279-3300; e-mail info@nhmf.org; website www.nhmf.org.

**New Jersey Festival of American Music Theatre:** 1650 Broadway, New York, NY 10019; June--Aug.

**Newport Music Festival:** PO Box 3300, Newport, RI 02840; tel. (401) 846-1133; fax (401) 849-1857; e-mail staff@newportmusic.org; website www.newportmusic.org; 17 days with 64 concerts, festival of little-known chamber music, debuts of works by international artists.

**New York Festival of American Music Theatre:** 1650 Broadway, New York, NY 10019; July--Aug.

**Norfolk Chamber Music Festival:** 165 Elm Street, Suite 101, PO Box 208246, New Haven, CT 06520; tel. (203) 432-1966; fax (203) 432-2136; e-mail norfolk@yale.edu; website www.yale.edu/norfolk; June--Aug.

**North County Chamber Players Summer Festival:** PO Box 904, Littleton, NH 03561; tel. (603) 444-0309; e-mail nccp@ncia.net; July--Aug.

**Ohio Light Opera:** College of Wooster, Wooster, OH 44691; tel. (330) 263-2336; fax (330) 263-2272; e-mail OH_LT_OPERA@wooster.edu; website www.wooster.edu/ohiolightopera; June--Aug.

**Ojai Festival:** PO Box 185, Ojai, CA 93024; tel. (805) 646-2094; website www.ojaifestival.com; June.

**Oklahoma Mozart International Festival:** PO Box 2344, Bartlesville, OK 74005; June.

**Opera Theatre of St Louis:** PO Box 191910, St Louis, MO 63119; website www.opera-stl.org; May--June.

**Oregon Bach Festival:** University of Oregon School of Music, Eugene, OR 97403; tel. (800) 457-1486; fax (541) 346-5669; e-mail bachfest@darkwing.uoregon.edu; website bachfest.uoregon.edu; June--July.

**Ravinia Festival:** 1575 Oakwood Avenue, Highland Park, IL 60035; website www.ravinia.org; June--Sept.

**Redlands Bowl Summer Music Festival:** PO Box 466, Redlands, CA 92373; June--Aug.

**Rio Grande Valley International Music Festival:** PO Box 2315, McAllen, TX 78502; Feb.

**Riverbend Festival:** PO Box 886, Chattanooga, TN 37401; website www.riverbendfestival.com; June.

**Rockport Chamber Music Festival:** PO Box 312, Rockport, MA 01966; tel. (978) 546-7391; fax (978) 546-7391; e-mail rcmf.info@verizon.net; website www.rcmf.org; held in June.

**Round Top Festival:** PO Box 89, Round Top, TX 78954-0089; tel. (979) 249-3129; fax (979) 249-5078; e-mail info@festivalhill.org; June--July.

**Rutgers SummerFest:** Rutgers Arts Center, New Brunswick, NJ 08903; June--July.

**Saint Louis Symphony Orchestra Queeny Pops:** 718 N Grand Blvd, St Louis, MO 63103; July--Aug.

**St Petersburg Palaces International Chamber Music Festival:** c/o M & N Artists Ltd, 400 W 43rd Street 19A, New York, NY 10036; June.

**San Luis Obispo Mozart Festival:** PO Box 311, San Luis Obispo, CA 93406; tel. (805) 781-3008; fax (805) 781-3011; website www.mozartfestival.com; Aug.

**Santa Fe Chamber Music Festival:** PO Box 2227, Santa Fe, NM 87504-2227; tel. (505) 983-2075; fax (505) 986-0251; e-mail info@sfcmf.org; website www.sfcmf.org; held over six weeks in July--Aug.

**Santa Fe Opera Festival:** PO Box 2227, Santa Fe, NM 87504-2408; website www.santafeopera.org; July--Aug.

**Sarasota Music Festival:** 709 N Tamiami Trail, Sarasota, FL 34236; tel. (941) 952-9634; website www.fwcs.org/sarasota; May--June.

**Saratoga Performing Arts Center:** 108 Avenue of the Pines, Saratoga Springs, NY 12866; tel. (518) 584-9330; fax (518) 584-0809; e-mail elinehan@spac.org; website www.spac.org; f. 1966; numerous festivals and events held throughout the year.

**Seattle Chamber Music Festival:** 10 Harrison Street, Suite 306, Seattle, WA 98109; tel. (206) 283-8710; fax (206) 283-8826; e-mail info@seattlechambermusic.org; website www.scmf.org; June--July.

**Seattle Opera Summer Festival:** PO Box 9248, Seattle, WA 98109; July--Aug.

**SMU Conservatory Summer Music Festival:** Southern Methodist University, Dallas, TX 75275; June.

**Southeastern Music Center:** PO Box 8348, Columbus, GA 31908; tel. and fax (706) 568-2465; July.

**Spoleto Festival USA:** PO Box 157, Charleston, SC 29402; website www.spoletousa.com; May--June.

**Stern Grove Midsummer Music Festival:** 44 Page Street, Suite 604-D, San Francisco, CA 94102; June--Aug.

**Summer Music at Harkness Park:** 300 State Street, Suite 400, New London, CT 06320; tel. (860) 442-9199; fax (860) 442-9290; e-mail info@summer-music.org; website www.summer-music.org; July--Aug.

**Sun Valley Music Festival:** PO Box 656, Sun Valley, ID 83353; July--Aug.

**Texas Music Festival:** University of Houston School of Music, Houston, TX 77204; website www.texasmusicfestival.org; June--July.

**Three Rivers Arts Festival:** 707 Penn Avenue, Pittsburgh, PA 15222; tel. (412) 281-8723; fax (412) 281-8722; website www.artsfestival.net; June.

**Tweeter Center for the Performing Arts:** PO Box 810, Mansfield, MA 02048; tel. (508) 339-2331; website www.tweetercenter.com; June--Sept.

**Vermont Music Festival:** PO Box 512, Burlington, VT 05402; July–Aug.

**Waterloo Festival:** Village of Waterloo, Stanhope, NJ 07874; July–Aug.

**Winter Park Bach Festival:** Rollins College, PO Box 2763, Winter Park, FL 32789; tel. (407) 646-2182; website www.bachfestivalflorida.org; Feb.–March.

**Wolf Trap Foundation:** 1645 Trap Road, Vienna, VA 22182; website www .wolf-trap.org; May--Sept.

**Woodstock Mozart Festival:** PO Box 734, Woodstock, IL 60098; e-mail contactus@mozartfest.org; website www.mozartfest.org; July--Aug.

**Worcester Music Festival:** Memorial Auditorium, Worcester, MA 01608.

# APPENDIX D: MUSIC ORGANIZATIONS

## Albania

**Albanian National Music Committee:** Lidya e Shrkrimtare de Artistere, R. Kavojes Nr4, Tirana; tel. and fax 355 42 27471; Contact Dr Vasil S. Tob.

## Argentina

**Asociación Argentina de Interpretes (SADEM):** Avda Belgrano 3655, 1210 Buenos Aires; tel. 54 11 4957 4062/4932 5769.

**Consejo Argentino de la Música:** PO Box 5532, Correo Central, 1000 Buenos Aires.

**Fundación Encuentros Internacionales de Música Contemporánea:** PO Box 1008, Correo Central, 100 Buenos Aires; tel. 54 11 4822 1383.

**Sociedad Argentina de Autores y Compositores de Música (SADAIC):** Lavalle 1547, 1048 Buenos Aires; tel. 54 11 4379 8600; fax 54 11 4379 8633; website www.sadaic.org.ar.

## Australia

**Australasian Mechanical Copyright Owners Society Ltd (AMCOS):** Locked Bag 3665, St Leonards, NSW 2065; tel. 61 2 9935 7900; fax 61 2 9935 7999; website www.amcos.com.au.

**Australasian Performing Right Association (APRA):** Locked Bag 3665, St Leonards, NSW 2065; tel. 61 2 9935 7900; fax 61 2 9935 7999; website www.apra.com.au.

**Australia Council for the Arts:** 372 Elizabeth Street, Surry Hills, NSW 2010; tel. 61 2 9215 9302; e-mail mail@ozco.gov.au; website www.ozco.gov.au.

**Australian Copyright Council (ACC):** 245 Chalmers Street, Redfern, NSW 2016; tel. 61 2 9318 1788; fax 61 2 9698 3247; e-mail info@copyright.com.au ; website www.copyright.com.au.

**Australian Music Centre Ltd:** Level 4, The Arts Exchange, 18 Hickson Road, The Rocks, Sydney, NSW 2000; tel. 61 2 9247 4677; fax 61 2 9241 2873; e-mail info@amcoz.com.au; website www.amcoz.com.au.

**Australian Music Publishers Association Ltd (AMPAL):** Locked Bag 3665, St Leonards, NSW 2065; tel. 61 2 9935 7900; fax 61 2 9935 7999; website www.apra.com.au.

**Australian Record Industry Association Ltd—ARIA:** PO Box Q20, QVB Post Office, Sydney, NSW 1230; tel. 61 2 9267 7996; fax 61 2 9264 5589; e-mail aria@aria.com.au; website www.aria.com.au.

**Australian Society for Keyboard Music:** 42/35 Orchard Street, Chatswood, NSW 2067; tel. 61 2 9406 5131.

**Confederation of Australasian Performing Arts Presenters:** PO Box 4274, Sydney, NSW 2001.

**International Society for Contemporary Music (Australian Section)—ISCM:** c/o University of Sydney Music Department, Sydney, NSW 2006.

**Musica Viva Australia:** PO Box 1687, Strawberry Hills, NSW 2012; tel. 61 2 8394 6666; fax 61 2 9698 3878; e-mail musicaviva@mva.org.au; website www.mva.org.au.

**Phonographic Performance Company of Australia Ltd—PPCA:** PO Box Q20, QVB Post Office, Sydney, NSW 1320; tel. 61 2 8569 1100; fax 61 2 8569 1183; e-mail ppca@ppca.com.au; website www.ppca.com.au.

**Youth Music Australia:** PO Box Q186, QVB Postshop, NSW 1230; tel. 61 2 9283 7216; fax 61 2 9283 7217; e-mail youthmusic@yma.com.au.

## Austria

**Arnold Schöenberg Center Privatstiftung:** Schwarzenbergplatz 6, 1030 Vienna; tel. 431 712 18 88; fax 431 712 18 88-88; e-mail direktion@schoenberg.at; website www.schoenberg.at; Dir: Dr Christian Meyer; houses the legacy of Arnold Schönberg, including archive and library; organizes concerts, symposia and exhibitions.

**Gesellschaft der Musikfreunde in Wien:** Bösendorferstrasse 12, 101 Vienna; tel. 43 1 505 8190; website www.musikverein.at; Sec.-Gen.: Dr Thomas Angyan; promotes classical concerts.

**Gesellschaft für Forschungen zur Aufführungspraxis:** Zuckerkanlg 14 A, 1190 Vienna.

**Gewerkschaft Kunst:** Medien, Freie Berufe, Sektion Musiker, Maria Theresienstrasse 11, 1090 Vienna; website www.kmsfb.at.

**Herbert von Karajan Stiftung:** Prof. Peter Csobádi, Seestrasse 13, 5322 Hof bei Salzburg.

**IFDI Landesgruppe Österreich:** Habsburgergasse 6–8/18, 1010 Vienna.

**International Music Centre Vienna (IMZ):** Filmstadt Wien, Speisinger Strasse 121-127, 1230 Vienna; tel. 43 1 889 03 15; fax 43 1 889 03 15 77; e-mail office@imz.at; website www.imz.at.

**Internationale Bruckner Gesellschaft:** Rathausplatz 3, 1010 Vienna.

**Internationale Gesellschaft für Neue Musik:** Ungargasse 9/3, 1030 Vienna.

**Internationale Gustav Mahler Gesellschaft:** Wiedner Guertel 6, 1040 Vienna; tel. and fax 43 1 505 7330; website www.gustav-mahler.org.

**Internationale Hugo Wolf Gesellschaft:** Latschkagasse 4, 1090 Vienna.

**Internationale Schönberg Gesellschaft:** Bernhardgasse 6, 2340 Mödling.

**Literar-Mechana (Wahrnemungsgesellschaft für Urheberrechte):** Linke Wienzelle 18, 1060 Vienna; tel. 43 1 587 21 61; fax 43 1 587 21 619; website www.literar.at.

**Musikalische Jugend Österreichs—Jeunesse:** Administration Office, Lothringerstrasse 20, 1030 Vienna; tel. 7103616; fax 7103617; e-mail mail@jeunesse.at; website www.jeunesse.at; Sec.-Gen. Angelika Möser; f. 1949, mem. of Jeunesse Musicale International; organizes about 700 concerts a year for young people, contemporary music, world music, classical chamber music, orchestral concerts and jazz; organizes music camps and a Jeunesse Festival.

**Musikverleger Union Österreich:** Baumannstrasse 10, 1030 Vienna.

**Österreichischer Komponistenbund (OKB):** Ungargasse 9/3, 1030 Vienna.

**Staatlich Gesellschaft der Autoren Komponisten und Musikverleger:** Baumannstrasse 8-10, 1030 Vienna.

## Belgium

**Association des Arts et de la Culture:** rue royale 10, 1000 Brussels; website www.adac.be.

**Association des Artistes Professionnels de Belgique:** rue Paul Lauters 1, 1050 Brussels.

**Association Internationale du Théâtre Lyrique:** rue des Dominicains 1, 4000 Liège.

**Association pour la Diffusion de la musique Belge:** rue d'Arlon 75–77, 1040 Brussels.

**Atelier Créatif de Musique Électroacoustique—ACME:** PO Box 19, 1170 Brussels; website www.cahiersacme.org.

**Centre Belge de Documentation Musicale:** rue d'Arlon 75–77, 1040 Brussels; tel. 02 230 9430; fax 02 230 9437; e-mail info@cebedem.be; website www.cebedem.be; Dir Alain Van Kerikhoven.

**Centre International d'Echanges Musicaux:** rue des Patriotes 60, 1040 Brussels.

**Chambre Syndicale des Agents Artistiques et Impresario de Belgique:** rue Rogier 3, 6040 Charleroi.

**Confédération musicale de Belgique:** rue du Loncin 22, 4430 Alleur; Pres. S. Coucke.

**Conseil de la Musique de la Communauté française de Belgique:** Blvd Reyers 52, 1044 Brussels; Pres. Dr Robert Wangermée.

**Fondation pour la Promotion des Arts:** rue aux Choux 47, 1000 Brussels.

**Jeunesses musicales de la Communaute française de Belgique:** rue Royale 10, 1000 Brussels.

**Royale Union Artistique et Littéraire:** rue du Tombeux 52A, 1801 Stembert.

**Sociéte Belge de Musicologie:** rue de la Régence 30, 1000 Brussels; Contact Dr Robert Wangermée.

**Société Belge des Auteurs, Compositeurs et Editeurs—SABAM:** rue d'Arlon 75–77, 1040 Brussels; website www.sabam.be.

**Société Cesar Franck de Belgique:** rue des Foulons 11, 400 Liège.

**Sociéte Culturel des Arts Dramatiques et Musicaux:** rue F. Ferrer 37, 1360 Tubize.

**Société des Auteurs et Compositeurs Dramatiques:** Avenue Jeanne 29, 1050 Brussels.

**Société Liégoise de Musicologie:** Les Enclos 13, 4080 Werbomont.

**Union de la Presse Musicale Belge:** Avenue C. Woeste 140, 1090 Brussels.

**Union des Artistes:** rue du Marché aux Herbes 105, 1000 Brussels.

**Union des Compositeurs Belges—UCB:** rue d'Arlon 75–77, 1040 Brussels; tel. and fax 00322 2868381; Pres. Jacques Leduc.

**Union Royale Belge des Éditeurs de Musique:** rue F. Neuray 8, 1060 Brussels.

**Union Wallonne des Organistes:** rue Romainville 25a, 5228 Bas-Oha/Wanze.

## Bolivia

**Sociedad Boliviana de Autores and Compositores de Música:** Figueroa 788, Departamento 1, 2nd Floor, La Paz.

## Brazil

**Associacao Brasileira dos Produtores de Discos—ABPD:** Rua Marques de Sao Vicente 99-1, Gavea, 22451 Rio de Janeiro, RJ; tel. 55 21 2512 9908; fax 55 21 2259 4145; e-mail abpd@abpd.org.br; website www.abpd.org.br.

**Associacao de Canto Coral:** Rua das Marrecas 40, 9th Floor, 20080-010 Rio de Janeiro, RJ.

**Fundaçao de Educaçao Artistica:** Rua Gonçalves Dias 320, 30000 Belo Horizonte, MG.

**Instituto Brasileiro de Arte e Cultura:** Rua de Imprensa 16, 20030 Rio de Janeiro, RJ.

**Juventude Musical do Brasil:** PO Box 62626, 22257 Rio de Janeiro, RJ.

**Sindicato dos Músicos Profissionals do Estado de Sao Paulo:** Largo Paissandu, Sao Paulo.

**Sindicato dos Músicos Profissionals do Estado de Rio de Janeiro:** Rua Alvaro Alvim 24, Grupo 401, 20031 Rio de Janeiro, RJ.

**Sociedada Brasileira de Autores Teatrais:** Avda Almirante Barroso 97, 3rd Floor, PO Box 1503, 20031-002 Rio de Janeiro, RJ.

**Sociedada Brasileira de Música Contemporânea:** SQS 105, Bloco B, PO Box 506, 70344-020 Brasilia, DF.

**Sociedada Brasileira de Realizçoes Artistico-Culturais:** Avda Franklin Roosevelt 23, Room 310, 20021 Rio de Janeiro, RJ.

**Sociedad de Cultura Artistica:** Rua Nestor Pestana 196, CEP 01303 Sao Paulo.

**Sociedada Independente de Compositores and Autores Musicals:** Largo Paissandú 51, 10th, 11th, 16th Floors, 01034 Sao Paulo.

**Uniao Brasileira de Compositores:** Rua Visconde de Inhaúma-Centro, 20091-000 Rio de Janeiro; Chief Exec. Dr Vanisa Santiago.

**Uniao dos Músicos do Brasil:** Avda Rio Branco 185, Rio de Janeiro, RJ.

## Bulgaria

**Bulgarian Association of Music Producers—BAMP:** 7 Reznyovete Str, bl 128, entr B, app 27, Sofia Lozenets 1421; tel. 359 2 866 8120/0104; fax 359 2 963 2757; e-mail office@bamp-bg.org

**Union of Bulgarian Composers:** 2 Ivan Vazoz Str, 1000 Sofia.

## Canada

**Alliance for Canadian New Music Projects—ACNMP:** 20 St Joseph Street, Toronto, ON M4Y 1J9; tel. 1 416 963 5937; fax 1 416 961 7198; website www.acnmp.ca; Pres. Janet Fothergill.

**American Federation of Musicians of the United States and Canada:** 75 The Donway W, Suite 1010, Don Mills, ON M3C 2E9; Vice-Pres. (Canada) Ray Petch.

**Association of Canadian Women Composers—ACWC:** 20 St Joseph Street, Toronto, ON M4Y 1J9; tel. 1 416 239 5195; Chair. Lorraine Johnson.

**Association of Cultural Executives:** 720 Bathurst Street, Suite 503, Toronto, ON M5S 2R4.

**Canadian Amateur Musicians/Musiciens Amateurs du Canada—CAMMAC:** 85 Cammac Road, Harrington, QC J8G 2T2; tel. 1 819 687 3938; website www.cammac.ca; Dir-Gen. Barry Crago.

**Canada Council/Conseil des Arts du Canada:** PO Box 1047, 350 Albert Street, Ottawa, ON K1P 5V8; tel. 1 613 566 4414; fax 1 613 566 4390; website www.canadacouncil.ca; Dir Roch Carrier.

**Canadian Association of Artists Managers:** 117 Ava Road, Toronto, ON M6C 1W2.

**Canadian Association of Arts Administration Educators:** Simon Fraser University, 515 W Hastings Street, Vancouver, BC V6B 5K3; Pres. Letia Richardson.

**Canadian Bureau for the Advancement of Music:** Exhibition Place, Toronto, ON M6K 3C3.

**Canadian League of Composers:** Chalmers House, 20 St Joseph Street, Toronto, ON, M4Y 1J9; Pres. Patrick Cardy.

**Canadian Music Centre/Centre de Musique Canadienne:** 20 St Joseph Street, Toronto, ON M4Y 1J9; tel. 1 416 961 6601; fax 1 416 961 7198; e-mail info@musiccentre.ca; website www.musiccentre.ca; Exec. Dir Simone Auger.

**Canadian Music Educators' Association/L'Association canadienne des éducateurs de musique—CMEA:** 1207 Staffordshire Road, London, ON N6H 5R1; tel. (519) 474-6877; website www.musiceducationonline.org/cmea.index.html; Pres.: Gregg Bereznick; membership enquiries to: Betty Hanley, Faculty of Education, Box 3010, University of Victoria, Victoria, BC V8W 3N4.

**Canadian Music Publishers Association—CMPA:** 56 Wellesley Street W, Suite 320, Toronto, ON M5S 2S3; tel. 1 416 926 1966; fax 1 416 926 7521; e-mail dbaskin@cmpa.ca; website www.cmmra.ca; Pres. Mark Altman.

**Canadian Musical Reproduction Rights Agency Ltd—CMRRA:** 56 Wellesley Street W, Suite 320, Toronto, ON M5S 2S3; tel. 1 416 926 1966; fax 1 416 926 7521; website www.cmmra.ca; Gen. Man. David A. Basskin.

**Canadian Recording Industry Association—CRIA:** 890 Yonge Street, Suite 1200, Toronto, ON M4W 3P4; tel. 1 416 967 7272; fax 1 416 967 9415; e-mail info@cria.ca; website www.cria.ca; Pres. Brian Robertson.

**Canadian Resource Centre for Career Performing Artists:** PO Box 188, Station A, Toronto, ON M5W 1B2; Pres. Ann Summers.

**Canadian University Music Society—CUMS:** PO Box 507, Station Q, Toronto, ON M4T 2M5; tel. 1 416 483 7282; fax 1 416 489 1713; website www.cums/smuc.ca; Pres. Dr Eugene Cramer.

**Jeunesses Musicales du Canada:** 305 Avenue Mont-Royal E, Montréal, H2T 1P8; tel. 1 514 845 4108; fax 1 514 845 8241; website www.jeunessesmusicales.com; Gen. Dir Nicolas Desjardins; Artistic Dir Jacques Marquis.

**Ontario Choral Federation:** 20 St Joseph Street, Toronto, ON M4Y 1J9; Exec. Dir Bev Jahnke.

**Orchestras Canada:** 56 The Esplanade, Suite 203, Toronto, ON M5E 1A7; tel. (416) 366-8834; fax (416) 366-1780; e-mail info@oc.ca; website www.oc.ca; Exec. Dir Daniel Donaldson.

**Organization of Canadian Symphony Musicians—OCSM:** 455 Gérard Morisset, No. 6, Québec, QC G1S 4V5; Chair. Evelyne Robitaille.

**Saskatoon Symphony Society:** 703-601, Spading Crescent E, Saskatoon, SK S7K 3G8; tel. 306 6656414; fax 306 6523364; Gen. Man. Catherine McKeenan.

**Society of Composers, Authors and Music Publishers of Canada—SOCAN:** 41 Valleybrook Drive, Don Mills, Toronto, ON M3B 2S6; tel. 1 416 445 8700; fax 1 416 445 7108; website www.socan.ca; Gen. Man. Michael Rock.

## Chile

**Asociación Nacional de Compositores—ANC:** Almirante Moritt 453, Santiago; website www.anc.scd.cl.

**Instituto de Música:** Universidad Católica de Chile, Jaime Guzman E 3 300, Santiago.

**Juventudes Musicales:** Universidad de Chile, Facultad de Artes, Compañía 1264, 4°, Santiago.

**Sociedad Chilena del Derecho de Autor—SCD:** Condell 346, Providencia, Santiago; website www.musica.cl.

**Sociedad de Autores Teatrales de Chile:** San Diego 246, Santiago.

## People's Republic of China

**Association of Chinese Musicians:** Nong zhanguan Nan Li, No 10, Beijing 100026; tel. 86 10 65389265; fax 86 10 65004524.

## Colombia

**Asociación Colombiana de Músicos Profesionales:** Calle 17, No. 10–16, Oficina 607, Bogotá, DE.

**Asociación Colombiana de Productores de Fonogramas:** Avenida 15 No. 123–29, Torre C, Jorge Baron Oficina 208, AA 101540, Santa Fe de Bogota, DC; tel. 57 1 612 0350/0390; fax 57 1 612 0310.

**Asociación de Artistas de Colombia:** Calle 13, No. 9-63, Interior 104, PO Box 24627, Bogotá, DE.

**Centro de Documentación Musical, Instituto Colombiano de Cultura:** Calle 11, No. 5-51, 2°, Bogotá, DE.

**Instituto Colombiano de Cultura-Colcultura:** Calle 11, No. 5-51, 2°, Santafé de Bogotá, DC.

**Juventudes Musicales de Colombia:** PO Box 089436, Carrera 16A No. 202, Bogotá 8.

**Sociedad de Autores y Compositores de Colombia:** Carrera 19, No. 40-72, PO Box 6482, Santafé de Bogotá, DC ZP1.

## Costa Rica

**Juventudes Musicales de Costa Rica:** PO Box 1035, San José 1000.

## Croatia

**Croatian Composers' Society—HDS:** Berislaviceva 9, 41000 Zagreb, Croatia; tel. 385 1 423 463; fax 385 1 422 850.

## Cuba

**Centro de Información y Promoción de la Música Cubana Odilio Urfé:** Calle 17 esq. E, Vedado, Havana.

**Centro de Investigación y Desarrollo de la Música Cubana:** Calle G, No. 505 esq. 21 y 23, Vedado, Havana.

**Centro Nacional de Derecho de Autor—CENDA:** Calle Línea No. 365 (altos), esq. G, Vedado, Havana; website www.cenda.cu.

**Centro Nacional de Música de Concierto:** Calle Línea No. 365, esq. G, Vedado, Havana.

**Centro Nacional de Música Popular:** Avda 1a, esq. 10 y 12, Playa, Havana.

**Editora Musical de Cuba:** San Rafael No. 104, esq. Consulado, Centro Habana, Havana.

**Empresa de Grabaciones y Ediciones Musicales—EGREM:** Calle 3ra 1008 e, 10 y 12, Miramar, Havana; tel. 1 537 209 0687; fax 1 537 209 0688; website www.egrem.com.cu.

**Instituto Cubano de la Música:** Calle 15 No. 452, esq. F, Vedado, Havana.

**Unión de Escritores y Artistas de Cuba (Music Section)—UNEAC:** Calle 17 No. 351, esq. H, Vedado, Havana; website www.uneac.com.

## Czech Republic

**Authors' Association of Protection for Rights on Musical Works:** Armády 20, 160 56 Prague 6.

**Confederation of Arts and Culture:** Senovázné nám. 23, 110 00 Prague 1; tel. 420 224 142 555; fax 420 224 142 512; e-mail odborykuk@volny.cz; Pres.: Adriena Jirková.

**Czech Music Fund:** Besední 3, 118 00 Prague 1; tel. 420 2 57320008; fax 420 2 57312834; e-mail nchf@gts.cz; website www.nchf.cz; Dir Miroslav Drozd.

**Czech Music Information Centre:** Besední 3, 118 00 Prague 1; tel. 420 2-5731 2422; fax 420 2-5731 7424; e-mail his@vol.cz; website www.musica.cz; Dir: Miroslav Pudlak; documentation and information centre for Czech contemporary composers and events; funded principally by the Czech Music Fund; publications include Czech Music, Musical Events, HIS VOICE.

**Czech Music Society:** Radlická 99, 150 00 Prague 5; tel. 420 2 51552382; 420 2 51552453; e-mail czechmusiksoc@hotmail.com; Pres. Míla Smetácková.

**Czech Society for Chamber Music:** Korunní 98, 101 00 Prague 10.

**International Federation of Phonogram and Videogram Producers:** Gorkého nam. 23, 112 82 Prague 1.

**International Music Council (National Committee):** Valdstejnske nám. 1, Prague 1.

## Denmark

**Choir Conductors' Society:** Astrugårdsvej 12, 2650 Hvidovre.

**Danish Choral Association:** Slagelsegade 9, 2100 Copenhagen O.

**Danish Composers' Society:** Gråbrødretorv 16, 1154 Copenhagen K; tel. 45 33 13 54 05; fax 45 33 14 32 19; website www.komponistforeningen.dk.

**Danish Cultural Institute:** Kultorvet 2, 1175 Copenhagen K; tel. 45 33 13 54 48; fax 45 33 15 10 91; e-mail dankultur@dankultur.dk; website www.dankultur.dk.

**Danish Jazz Center:** Boripvej 66, 4683 Rønnede.

**Danish Music Information Centre:** 48 Vimmelskaftet, 1161 Copenhagen K; website www.mic.dk.

**Danish Musicians' Union:** Vendersgade 25, 1363 Copenhagen K.

**Danish Musicological Society:** Department of Musicology, University of Copenhagen, Klerkegade 2, 1308 Copenhagen K; Chair: Best Morten Michelsen.

**Danish Organists' and Precentors' Society:** Flegmade 14, 7100 Vejle.

**Danish Society of Composers, Authors and Editors:** Maltegårdsvej 24, 2820 Gentofte.

**Danish Society of Jazz, Rock, and Folk Composers:** Klerkegade 19, 1308 Copenhagen K.

**Danish Soloists' Association:** Sundholmsvej 49, 2300 Copenhagen S.

**Dansk Arbeider Sanger-og Musikforbund:** Skovgade 6, 5500 Middelfart.

**Dansk kapelmesterforening:** Rosenvangsvej 47, 2670 Greve Strand.

**Det dansk orgelselskab (Danish Organ Society):** Willemoesgade 85, 1.th., 2100 Copenhagen; website www.detdanskeorgelselskab.dk.

**International Society for Contemporary Music (Danish Section):** Valkendorfsgade 3, 1151 Copenhagen K.

**Samrået for Musikundervisning:** Vallerod-skolen, Stadion Allé, 2960 Rungsted Kyst.

**Society of Danish Church Singing:** Hoyrups Allé 7, 2900 Hellerup.

**State Music Council:** Vesterbrodgade 24, 1620 Copenhagen V.

**Union of Danish Singers:** Norre Sovej 26 A, 8800 Viborg.

## Ecuador

**Juventudes Musicales:** Casilla Correo, 8162, Sucursal 8, Quito.

## El Salvador

**Centro Nacional de Artes:** 2a Avda Norte Pje. Contreras, No. 145, San Salvador.

## Estonia

**Jeunesses Musicales Eestis:** Estonia pst 4 tuba 410, 200105 Tallinn.

## Finland

**Association of Finnish Conservatories:** Fredrikinkati 34 B, 00100 Helsinki.

**Association of Finnish Music Schools—SML:** Fredrikinkatu 25 B 26, 00120 Helsinki; tel. 358 9 646 122/646 116; fax 358 9 6843 8910; e-mail smlfmf@smlfmf.fi; website www.kolumbus.fi/smlfmf.

**Association of Finnish Operas:** Iso-Roobertinkatu 20-22 A 76, 00120 Helsinki.

**Association of Finnish Soloists:** Museokatu 3 B 12, 00100 Helsinki.

**Association of Finnish Symphony Orchestras:** Aninkaistenkatu 3 B, 20110 Turku.

**Association of Military Conductors:** Helsingin varuskuntasoittokunta, PL 13, 00251 Helsinki.

**Association of Music Libraries in Finland:** PO Box 148, 01301 Vantaa.

**Association of Swedish Speaking Church Musicians:** 10210 Ingå.

**Concert Centre:** Urho Kekkosen katu 8 C 30, 00100 Helsinki.

**Federation for Church Music in Finland:** Tollinpolku 1 C, 00410 Helsinki.

**Federation for Finnish Traditional Music:** Raumantie 1, 00350 Helsinki.

**Federation of Music Teachers in Finland:** Asemamiehenkatu 4, 00520 Helsinki.

**Finland Festivals:** PO Box 56, 00100 Helsinki.

**Finlands svenska sång-och musikförbund r.f.:** Handelsespladen 23 B, 65100 Vasa.

**Finnish Composers' Copyright Society—TEOSTO:** Lauttasaarentie 1, 00200 Helsinki; tel. 358 9 681011; fax 358 9 677134; e-mail teosto@teosto.fi; website www.teosto.fi; Man. Kalle Jamsen.

**Finnish Jazz Federation:** Arabiankatu 2, 00560 Helsinki; tel. 358 9 757 2077; fax 358 9 757 2067; Exec. Man. Timo Vahasilta.

**Finnish Music Information Centre:** Runeberginkatu 15 A, 00100 Helsinki.

**Finnish Music Publishers' Association:** Runeberginkatu 15 A 12, 00100 Helsinki; website www.musiikkikustantajat.fi.

**Finnish Musicians' Union:** Pieni Roobertinkatu 16, 00120 Helsinki.

**Finnish Performing Music Promotion Centre:** Pieni Roobertinkatu 16, 00100 Helsinki; tel. 358 9 6803 4040; fax 358 9 6803 4033; e-mail esek@gramex.fi.

**Finnish Society for Ethnomusicology:** Mannerheimintie 40 C 69, 00100 Helsinki.

**Folk Music Institute:** 69600 Kaustinen.

**Foundation for the Promotion of Finnish Music:** Runeberginkatu 15 A 6, 00100 Helsinki.

**Guild of Light Music Composers and Authors in Finland:** Runeberginkatu 15 A 11, 00100 Helsinki.

**Head Organization of Finnish Traditional Music:** 39170 Jumesniemi.

**IFPI (Finnish National Group):** Yrjonkatu 3, 00120 Helsinki.

**International Music Council (Finnish Section):** Ukonkivenpolku 4 D 28, 01610 Vantaa.

**Institute of Accordion Music in Finland:** Kvrösselänkatu 3, 39599 Ikaalinen.

**Korvat Aukiry (Society for Young Contemporary Composers):** Kurkisuontie 12 D 35, 00940 Helsinki.

**Music Artists Organization:** Kuususaarenkuia 9, 00340 Helsinki.

**Musicological Society of Finland:** Töölönkatu 28, 00260 Helsinki.

**Sibelius Museum:** Biskopsgatan 17, 20500 Åbo; tel. 358 2 2154494; fax 358 2 2518528; e-mail jbrusila@abo.fi; Curator Johannes Brusila.

**Society of Finnish Composers:** Runeberginkatu 15 A 11, 00100 Helsinki; tel. 358 9 445589; fax 358 9 440181; e-mail saveltajat@compose.pp.fi; Exec. Dir Annu Mikkonen.

**SULASOL (Federation of Amateur Musicians in Finland):** Fredrikinkatu 51–53B, 00100 Helsinki; tel. 358 9 41361100; fax 358 9 41361122; e-mail info@sulasol.fi; website www.sulasol.fi.

**Workers' Institute of Music:** Mannerheimintie 40 C 74, 00100 Helsinki.

**Workers' Musical Organization in Finland:** Hämeenpuisto 33 B 25, 33200 Tampere.

## France

**Académie du Disque Français et du Film musical:** 68 Blvd de Courcelles, 75017 Paris.

**American Center:** 51 rue de Bercy, 75592 Paris Cédex 12; tel. 33 1 44 73 77 77; fax 33 1 44 73 77 55.

**Association des Festivals Internationaux de France:** 16 Place du Havre, 75009 Paris.

**Association Nationale de Diffusion Culturelle:** 5 rue Bellart, 75015 Paris.

**Association pour le Developpement des Echanges Artistique et Culturels—ADEAC:** 101 Blvd Raspail, 75006 Paris.

**Bibliothèque Bozidar Kantuser, Centre International d'Information de Musique Contemporaine:** Conservatoire Supérieur de Paris—, 14 rue de Madrid, 75008 Paris; tel. 33 1 44 70 64 21; Pres.: Didier Duclos; fmrly the Bibliothèque Internationale de Musique Contemporaine.

**Bibliothèque-Musée de l'Opera de Paris:** 8 rue Scribe, 75009 Paris; tel. 33 1 47 42 07 02; fax 33 1 42 65 10 16.

**Bureau International d'Enregistrement et de Reproduction Méchanique—BIEM:** 14 rue Lincoln, 75008 Paris; tel. 33 1 53 93 67 00; fax 33 1 45 63 06 11; e-mail info@biem.org.

**Centre de Documentation de la Musique Contemporaine—CDMC:** 225 Avenue Charles de Gaulle, 92521 Neuilly-sur-Seine Cédeamerican center parisx; website www.cdmc.asso.fr; Dir Marianne Lyon.

**Centre de Documentation de Musique Internationale:** 116 Avenue du Président Kennedy, 75016 Paris.

**Chambre Syndicale de l'Edition Musicale—CSDEM:** 62 rue Blanche, 75009 Paris; Pres. Jean Devoust.

**Chambre Syndicale de la Facture Instrumentale:** 62 rue Blanche, 75009 Paris; Pres. Bernard Maillot.

**Chambre Syndicale des Editeurs de Musique:** Editions Choudens, 38 rue Jean Mermoz, 75008 Paris.

**Comite National de la Musique—CNM:** 252 rue de Faubourg St Honoré, Salle Pleyel, 75008 Paris; Gen. Man. Jacques Masson-Forestier.

**Commission d'Attribution de la Carte de Critique:** 6 bis rue Gabriel Laumain, 75010 Paris.

**Confédération Internationale des Sociétés d'Auteurs et Compositeurs—CISAC:** 11 rue Keppler, 75116 Paris.

**Fédération Nationale de la Musique:** 62 rue Blanche, 75009 Paris; Pres. Pierre Henry.

**Groupe de l'Edition Audiovisuelle et Electronique—HAVE:** 35 rue Gregoire de Tours, 75006 Paris.

**Groupment des Industries Electroniques—GIEL:** 11 rue Hamelin, 75783 Paris Cédex 16.

**Institut de Recherche et Coordination Acoustique/Musique:** 31 rue Saint-Merri, 75004 Paris; Dir Laurent Bayle; Hon. Dir Pierre Boulez.

**International Music Council (UNESCO):** 1 rue Miollis, 75732 Paris Cédex 15; tel. 33 1 45 68 25 50; fax 33 1 43 06 87 98; Sec.-Gen. Guy Huot.

**International Music Critics Association:** 11 Avenue de Lena, 75016 Paris.

**Jeunesses Musicales de France:** 20 rue Geoffroy l'Asnier, 75004 Paris; website www.lesjmf.org; Dir Robert Berthier.

**Médiathèque Musicale Gustav Mahler:** 11 bis rue de Vézelay, 75008 Paris; tel. 1 53 89 09 10; fax 1 43 59 70 22; website www.mediathequemahler.org.

**Musicora:** Salon de la Musique, 62 rue de Miromesnil, 75008 Paris.

**Société Alkan:** 9bis Avenue Médicis, 94100 St Maur de Fosses; e-mail alkan.association@voila.fr; Chief Officer Laurent Martin; Sec. François Luguenot.

**Société des Auteurs et Compositeurs Dramatiques—SACD:** 11 bis rue Ballu, 75009 Paris; tel. 33 1 40 23 44 44; fax 33 1 45 26 74 28; website www.sacd.fr; Chief Officer Jean-Jacques Plantin.

**Société des Auteurs, Compositeurs et Editeurs—SACE:** 62 rue Blanche, 75009 Paris; Pres. Wladimir Walberg.

**Société des Auteurs, Compositeurs et Editeurs de Musqiue—SACEM:** 225 Avenue Charles de Gaulle, 92521 Neuilly-sur-Seine Cédex; tel. 33 1 47 15 47 15; fax 33 1 47 45 12 94; Dir-Gen. Jean-Loup Tournier.

**Société pour l'Administration de Droit de Reproduction Méchanique des Auteurs, Compositeurs et Editeurs—SDRM:** 225 Avenue de Charles de Gaulle, 92521 Neuilly-sur-Seine Cédex.

**Syndicat des Artistes de Variétés-Syndicat des Artistes Lyriques:** 29 rue Jean Jacques Rousseau, 75001 Paris.

**Syndicat des Artistes Musiciens Professionnels de Paris—SAMUP:** 14–16 rue des Lilas, 75019 Paris; Sec.-Gen. François Nowak.

**Syndicat des Industries de Materiels Audiovisuels Electroniques—SIMAVELEC:** 11 rue Hamelin, 75783 Paris Cédex 16.

**Syndicat Francais des Artistes Interprétes—SFA:** 21 bis rue Victor Massé, 75009 Paris.

**Syndicat National des Artistes Musiciens de France—SNAM:** 14–16 rue des Lilas, 75019 Paris; Sec.-Gen. François Nowak.

**Syndicat National des Auteurs et des Compositeurs de Musique:** 80 rue Taitbout, 75442 Paris Cédex 09.

**Syndicat National des Chefs d'Orchestre:** 3 rue Chateau d'Eau, 75010 Paris.

**Union des Artistes:** 21 bis rue Victor Massé, 75009 Paris.

## Germany

**AG Song-Arbeitsgemeinschaft Der Liedermacher:** Mailaender Strasse 14/92, 60598, Frankfurt Am Main; tel. 069 686269.

**Akademie der Künste Berlin:** Hanseatenweg 10, 1000 Berlin 21; website www.adk.de; Pres. Prof. Dr Walter Jens.

**Allgemeiner Cäcilien-Verband für Deutschland (ACV Deutschland):** Andreasstrasse 9, 93059 Regensburg; tel. and fax 49 941 84339; Pres. Dr Wolfgang Bretschneider.

**Arbeitsgemeinschaft der Leiter Musikpädagogischer Studiengänge:** Hochschule der Künste Berlin, Fachbereich 8/KWE 2, Fasanenstrasse 1, 10623 Berlin; tel. 49 303 185 2399; Speaker Prof. Dr Ulrich Mahlert.

**Arbeitsgemeinschaft der Musikakademien, Konservatorien und Hochschulinstitute:** Ludwigshöhstrasse 120, 64285 Darmstadt; tel. 49 6151 96640; fax 49 6151 966413; Chair. Hartmut Gerhold.

**Arbeitsgemeinschaft Deutsche Saxophonisten e V (ARDESA):** Rötenäcktstrasse 2, 8500 Nürnberg 90; Chair. Günter Priesner.

**Arbeitsgemeinschaft Deutscher Chorverbände (ADC):** Adersheimer Strasse 60, 38304 Wolfenbüttel; tel. 49 5331 46018; fax 49 5331 43723; Chair. Lore Auerbach; Man. Rolf Pasdzierny.

**Arbeitsgemeinschaft Deutscher Musikakademien und Konservatorien:** Richard-Strauss-Konservatorium, Kellerstrasse 6, 81667 Munich; tel. 89 48098415; fax 89 48098417; e-mail sekretariat@rsk.musin.de; Pres. Martin Maria Krüger.

**Arbeitsgemeinschaft Deutscher Studentenorchester:** Wilhelmstrasse 30, 7400 Tübingen; Chair. Helmut Calgéer.

**Arbeitsgemeinschaft Deutscher Zupfinstrumenten-Verbände (AZV):** Rissweg 22, 7507 Pfinztal 2; Chair. Adolf Mössner.

**Arbeitsgemeinschaft Freikirchlicher Chorwerke in Europa (AFC):** Westfalenweg 207, 5600 Wuppertal 1; Chair. Pastoe Frieder Ringeis.

**Arbeitsgemeinschaft für Mittelrheinische Musikgeschichte e V:** Musikwissenschaftliches Institut der Universität Mainz, Arbeitsstelle für landeskundliche Musikforschung, Welderweg 18, PO Box 3980, 6500 Mainz; Chair. Prof. Dr Christoph-Hellmut Mahling.

**Arbeitsgemeinschaft für rheinische Musikgeschichte e V:** Musikwissenschaftliches Institut der Universität Köln, Albertus-Magnus-Platz, 5000 Cologne; Chair. Prof. Dr Siegfried Kross.

**Arbeitsgemeinschaft Musik in der Evangelischen Jugend e V (AG Musik):** Dorfstrasse 4, 24250 Löptin; tel. 49 4302 96780; fax 49 4302 967820; Chair. Carl-Walter Petersen.

**Arbeitsgemeinschaft Schulmusik an den Hochschulen für Musik:** Musikhochschule Lübeck, Grosse Peters-grube 17-29, 2400 Lübeck; Chair. Prof. Dr Wilfried Ribke.

**Arbeitskreis der Musikbildungsstatten in der Bundesrepublik Deutschland:** Landesakademie für die musikierende Jugend in Baden-Württemberg, Dr Hans-Bruno Ernst, Schlossbezirk 6, PO Box 1180, 7955, Ochsenhausen.

**Arbeitskreis der Orgelsachverständigen:** Hohenstrasse 19, 7541 Straubenhardt 6 (Langenalb); Chair. Heinrich R. Trötschel.

**Arbeitskreis für Schulmusik und allgemeine Musikpädagogik e V (AFS):** Gründgensstrasse 16, 2000 Hamburg 60; Chair. Prof. Dr Volker Schütz.

**Arbeitskreis Musik in der Jugend e V (AMJ):** Adersheimer Strasse 60, 38304 Wolfenbüttel; tel. 5331-46016; fax 5331-43723; e-mail amjmuiskinderjugend@t-online.de; website www.amj-musik.de; Chair. Helmut Steger; Gen. Sec. Martin Koch.

**Arbeitskreis Musikpädagogische Forschung e V (AMPF):** Nycolaystrasse, 4790 Paderborn-Dahl; Chair. Dr Georg Maas.

**Bayerische Akademie der Schönen Künste:** Max-Joseph-Platz, 8000 Munich 22; Pres. Heinz Friedrich.

**Bayerischer Landesverein für Heimatpflege e V:** Beratungsstelle für Volksmusik, Ludwigstrasse 23, Rgb., 8000 Munich 22; Chair. Max Streibl.

**Bayerischer Musiklehrer-Verband e V:** Willibaldstrasse 49, 8000 Munich 21; Chair. Roland Sieber.

**Berufverband der Musiktherapeuten Deutschlands e V (BMD):** Waldhüterofad 38, 1999 Berlin 37; Chair. Herbert Lunkenheimer.

**Berusfverband für Kunst-, Musik-und Tanztherapie:** Grüner Hang 16, 4400 Münster; Chair. Prof. Dr Georg Hörmann.

**Berufsverband Klinischer Musiktherapeuten in der Bundesrepublik Deutschland e V:** Stader Weg 31, 2800 Bremen; Chair. Ilse Wolfram.

**Bildungswerk Rhythmik eV (BWR):** Kalscheurer Weg S Nr. 12, 5000 Cologne 1; Chair. Christine Humpert.

**Bogenforschungsgesellscaft:** Ankerstrasse 34, 5205 Sankt Augustin; Chair. Rudolf Gahler.

**Brahmsgesellschaft Baden-Baden e V:** PO Box 1609, 7560 Gaggenau; Chair. Dr Werner Hoppe.

**Brandenburgisches Colloquiem für Neue Musik e V:** Clara-Zetkin-Strasse 1, 1276 Buckow.

**Bruder-Busch-Gesellschaft e V:** Untere Wiesenstrasse 33, 5912 Hilchenbach; Business Man. Wolfgang Burbcah.

**Bund der Theatergemeinden e V:** Bonner Talweg 10, 5300 Bonn 1; Pres. Friedrich von Kekulé.

**Bund Deutscher Blasmusikverbände e V (BDB):** Am Märzengraben 6, 7800 Freiburg im Breisgau; Pres. Dr Norbert Nothhelfer.

**Bund Deutscher Liebhaberorchester e V (BDLO):** Schlegelstrasse 14, 8500 Nürnberg; Chair. Dr Joachim Conradi.

**Bund Deutscher Orgelbaumeister e V (BDO):** Frankfurter Ring 243, 8000 Munich 40; Chair. Hans-Gerd Klais.

**Bund Deutscher Zupfmusiker e V (BDZ):** Huulkamp 26, 22397 Hamburg; tel. 49 40 6088 9013; fax 49 40 6088 9014; Chair. Rüdiger Grambow.

**Bundes-Eltern-Vertretung e V der Musikschulen des VdM:** Ossietzkyring 55, 3000 Hanover 91; Chair. Dieter Fröhling.

**Bundesinnungverband für das Musikinstrumenten-Handwerk (BIV):** Kreishandwerkerschaft Köln, Frankenwerft 35, Cologne; Chair. Johann Scholtz.

**Bundesverband der Deutschen Musikinstrumenten-Hersteller e V (BdMH):** Tennelbachstrasse 25, 65193 Wiesbaden; tel. 49 611 954 5885; fax 49 611 954 5886; Man. Dir Winfried Baumbach.

**Bundesverband der deutschen Volksbühnen-Vereine e V:** Am Handelshof 9, 4300 Essen 1; Chair. Axel Wolters.

**Bundesverband der Phonographischen Wirtschaft e V (Bundesverband Phono):** Oranienburger Strasse 67–68, 10117 Berlin; tel. 030 590038; fax 030 590038; Chair. Gerd Gebhardt; Gen. Man. Peter Zombik.

**Bundesverband Deutscher Gesangspädagogen e V (BDG):** Waldeck 7, 4930 Detmold; Pres. Prof. Helmut Kretschmar.

**Bundesverband für Tanztherapie Deutschland e V:** Hostrasse 16, Marienburg, 4019 Monheim; Chair. Wally Kaechele.

**Bundesverband Rhythmische Erziehung e V (BRE):** Akademie Remscheid, Küppelstein 34, 5630 Remscheid 1; Chair. Prof. Brigitte Steinmann.

**Bundesverband Studentische Kulturarbeit e V (BSK):** Kaiserstrasse 32, 5300 Bonn 1.

**Bundesvereinigung der Musikveranstalter e V:** Kronprinzenstrasse 46, 5300 Bonn 2; Pres. Leo Imhoff.

**Bundesvereinigung Deutscher Blas-und Volksmusikverbände e V (BDBV):** König-Karl-Strasse 13, 70372 Stuttgart; tel. 49 711 568397; fax 49 711 552523; Pres. Minister Gerhard Weiser.

**Bundesvereinigung Deutscher Orchesterverbände eV (BDO):** Rudolf-Maschke-Platz 6, 78647 Trossingen; tel. 49 7425 8312; fax 49 7425 21519; Pres. Ernst Burgbacher MdB; Dir Erik Hörenberg.

**Bundesvereinigung Kulturelle Jugendbildung e V (BKJ):** Küppelstein 34, 5630 Remscheid; Chair. Prof. Bruno Tetzner.

**Carl-Orff-Stiftung:** Königinstrasse 25, 8000 Munich 22; Chair. Liselotte Orff.

**Chopin-Gesellschaft in der Bundesrepublik Deutschland e V:** Kasinostrasse 3 (J. F. Kenedy-Haus), 6100 Darmstadt 11; Pres. Maciej Lukasz.

**Christlicher Sängerbund e V (CS):** Westfalenweg 207, 5600 Wuppertal 1.

**Club Deutscher Drehorgelfreunde e V:** Wilfried Hömmerich, Brusseler Strasse 20, PO Box 170103, 5300 Bonn 1; Chair. Wilfried Hömmerich.

**Deutsche Angestellten-Gewerkschaft (DAG):** Karl-Marx-Platz 1, PO Box 301230, Hamburg.

**Deutsche Arbeitsgemeinschaft für Akustik (DAGA):** Hauptstrasse 5, 5340 Bad Honnef 1; Chair. Prof. Dr H. Kuttruff.

**Deutsche Disc-Jockey-Organization (DDO):** Kaiser-Friedrich-Alle 1–3, 5100 Aachen; Contact Klaus Quirini.

**Deutsche Forschungsgemeinschaft e V (DFG):** Kennedyalle 40 PO Box 205004, 5300 Bonn 2; Pres. Prof. Dr Wolfgang Fruhwald.

**Deutsche Frank-Martin-Gesellschaft e V:** Hochschule für Musik Köln, Dagobertstrasse 38, 5000 Cologne 1; Pres. Dirk Schortemeier.

**Deutsche Gesellschaft für Flote e V:** Eschenheimer Anlage 30, 6000 Frankfurt am Main 1; Pres. András Adorján.

**Deutsche Gesellschaft für Musik bei Behinderten e V (DGMB):** Frangenheimstrasse 4, 5000 Cologne 41; Chair. Prof. Dr Helmut Moog.

**Deutsche Gesellschaft für Musikpsychologie e V (DGfM):** Meisenweg 7, 3008 Garbsen 1; Chair. Prof. Dr Klaus-Ernst Behne.

**Deutsche Gesellschaft für Musiktherapie e V (DGMT):** Libauerstrasse 17, 10245 Berlin; e-mail info@musiktherapie.de; website www.musiktherapie.de; Chair. Franz Mecklenbeck.

**Deutsche Gesellschaft für Volkstanz e V (DGV):** Anni Herrmann, Paul-Lincke-Ufer 25, 1000 Berlin 36; Chair. Gerhard Palmer.

**Deutsche Glockenspiel-Vereinigung e V:** Pfortenstr. 30, 07318 Saalfeld; Chair. Knut Schieferdecker.

**Deutsche Johann-Strauss-Gesellschaft e V:** Untere Anlage 2, 8630 Coburg; Chair. Arthur Kulling.

**Deutsche Mozart-Gesellschaft e V (DMG):** Karlstrasse 6, 8900 Augsburg.

**Deutsche Musikinstrumentenstiftung:** Emil-Nolde-Weg 29, 37085 Göttingen; tel. 0049 551 72198; Chair. Prof. Dr Jürgen Costede.

**Deutsche Orchestervereinigung e V in der DAG (DOV):** Heimhuder Strasse 5, 2000 Hamburg 13; Chair. Dr Rolf Dünnwald.

**Deutsche Phono-Akademie e V (DPhA):** Grelckstrasse 36, 22529 Hamburg; tel. 49 40 581935; fax 49 40 580533; Chair. Gerd Gebhardt.

**Deutsche Richard-Wagner-Gesellschaft e V:** Schlosstrasse 9a, 1000 Berlin 28; Chair. Prof. Uwe Faerber.

**Deutsche Rossini-Gesellschaft e V:** Hohenheimerstrasse 84, 7000 Stuttgart 1; Chair. Gustav Kuhn.

**Deutsche Sängerschaft (Weimarer CC):** Cranachweg 9, 7320 Göppingen; Chair. Franz Jedlitschka.

**Deutsche Schubert-Gesellschaft e V (DSG):** Handelstrasse 6, 4100 Duisburg 14 (Rheinhausen); Chair. Günter Berns.

**Deutsche Sektion der Gesellschaft für Elektroakustische Musik:** Treuchtlinger Strasse 8, Berlin; Chair. Folkmar Hein.

**Deutsche Stiftung Musikleben (DSM):** Herrengraben 3, 2000 Hamburg 11; Pres. Erhard Bouillons.

**Deutsche Suzuki Gesellschaft e V:** Ankerstrasse 34, 5205 Sankt Augustin 1; Chair. Rudolf Gahler.

**Deutscher Akkordeonlehrer-Verband e V (DALV):** PO Box 11 35, 78635 Trossingen; tel. 49 7425 20249; fax 49 7425 20448; Chair. Wolfgang Eschenbacher; Man. Matthias Keller.

**Deutscher Allgemeiner Sängerbund e V (DAS):** Barbarastrasse 7, 44357 Dortmund; tel. 49 231 336558; fax 49 231 333352; Pres. Fritz Neuhaus.

**Deutscher Berufsverband für Tanzpadagogik e V:** Hollestrasse 1g, 4300 Essen 1; Chair. Ulrich Roehm.

**Deutscher Bühnenverein-Bundesverband deutscher Theater e V (DBV):** Quatermarkt 5, 5000 Cologne 1; Contact Rolf Golwin.

**Deutscher Bundesverband Tanz e V (DBT):** Küppelstein 34, 5630 Remscheid; Chair. Annmargret Pretz.

**Deutscher Chorverband Pueri Cantores:** Zwölfling 12, 4300 Essen 1; Pres. Georg Sump.

**Deutscher Feuerwehrverband e V:** Fachgebiet Musik, Koblenzer Strasse 133, 5300 Bonn 2; Pres. Heinrich Struve.

**Deutscher Harmonika-Verband e V (DHV):** Rudolf-Maschke-Platz 6, PO Box 1150, 7218 Trossingen 1; Pres. Ernst Pfister.

**Deutscher Hotel-und Gaststättenverband (DEHOGA):** Fachabteilung musikveranstaltende Betriebe, Kronprinzenstr. 46, Bonn; Chair. Otto Manfred Lamm.

**Deutscher Komponisten-Verband e V (DKV):** Kadettenweg 80b, 12205 Berlin; tel. 49 30 8431 0580; fax 49 30 8431 0582; Pres. Karl Heinz Wahren.

**Deutscher Kulturrat:** Adenaueralle 7, 5300 Bonn 1.

**Deutscher Musikrat e V (DMR):** Nationalkomitee der Bundesrepublik Deutschland im Internationalen Musikrat, Am Michaelshof 4a, 5300 Bonn 2; Pres. Prof. Dr Franz Müller-Heuser.

**Deutscher Musikverleger-Verband e V (DMV):** Friedrich-Wilhelm-Strasse 31, 53113 Bonn; Gen. Man. Dr H. H. Wittgen.

**Deutscher Rockmusiker-Verband e V:** Kolbergerstrasse 30, 2120 Lüneburg; Chair. Ole Seelenmeyer.

**Deutscher Sängerbund e V (DSB):** Bernhardstrasse 166, 50968 Koln; Pres. Dr Heinz Eyrich.

**Deutscher Schützenbund e V:** Fachgruppe Musik, Niedersächsischer Sportschützenverband, Wunstorfer Landstrasse 57, 3000 Hannover 91.

**Deutscher Tanzrat/Deutscher ballettrat e V:** Bonner Künstlerhaus, Graurheindorfer Strasse 23, 5300 Bonn 1; Chair. Iskra Zankova.

**Deutscher Textdichter-Verband e V:** Dohlenweg 5, 5020 Frechen; Pres. Heinz Korn.

**Deutscher Zithermusik-bund e V (DZB):** Ulrich Oesterle, Steigäcker 4, 7140 Ludwigsburg.

**Deutsches High-Fidelity Institut e V (DHFI):** Karlstrasse 19–21, 6000 Frankfurt am Main 1; Chair. Karl Breh.

**Deutsches Tubaforum e V:** Saarbrückener Stasse 26, 3000 Hannover 71; Chair. Prof. Klemens Propper.

**Die Kunstlergilde e V:** Hafenmarkt 2, 73725 Esslingen; tel. 49 711 3969 0123; fax 49 711 3969 010; Chair. Albrecht Baehr.

**Dr Hanns-Simon-Stiftung:** Bedaplatz, 5520 Bitburg.

**Dramatiker-Union e V (DU):** Bismarckstrasse 107, 1000 Berlin 12; Pres. Prof. Giselher Klebe.

**Dramaturgische Gesellschaft e V:** Tempelhofer Ufer 22, 1000 Berlin 61; Chair. Dr Klaus Pierwoss.

**Dresdner Zentrum für zeitgenössischen Musik:** Schevenstrasse 17/150-05, 8054 Dresden; Dir Prof. Udo Zimmermann.

**Emil-Berliner-Stiftung in der Deutschen Phono-Akademie e V:** Grelckstrasse 36, 2000 Hamburg 54; Chair. Richard Busch.

**EPTA-Gesellschaft der Padagogik für Tasteninstrumente e V:** Bult 6, 4590 Cloppenburg; Chair. Prof. Edith Picht-Axenfeld.

**Ernst-Pepping-Gesellschaft e V:** Jebensstrasse 3, 1000 Berlin 12; Chair. Prof. Dr Heinrich Poos.

**Ernst-von-Siemens-Stiftung:** Zug (Schweiz), Wittelsbacherplatz 2, 8000 Munich 2.

**Eugen-Jochum-Gesellschaft e V:** Marktplatz 14, Kulturamt, 8942 Ottobeuren; Pres. Dr Georg Simnacher.

**Europa Cantat-Europäische Föderation Junger Chöre e V (EC-EFJC):** Grosser Hillen 38, 3000 Hannover 71; Sec.-Gen. Hans Dieter Reinecke.

**Europäische Arbeitsgemeinschaft Schulmusik—EAS (European Association for Music in Schools):** c/o Prof. Dr Franz Niermann, University of Music and Performing Arts Vienna, Institute for Music Education, Metternichgasse 8, 1030 Vienna; tel. (1) 71155-3700; fax (1) 71155-3799; e-mail niermann@mdw.ac.at; website www.musiceducation.at.

**Europäische Union der Musikwettbewerbe für die Jugend:** Herzog-Johann-Strasse 10, 8000 Munich 60; Contact Dr Eckart Rohlfs.

**European Guitar Teachers Association (EGTA):** Marblicksweg 55, 59555 Lippstadt; tel. 49 2941 60445; fax 49 2941 658029; Chair. Reinhard Froese, Michael Koch.

**European String Teachers Association (ESTA):** Dagmar klevenhusen, Friedenweg 6, 2807 Achim.

**Evangelischer Sängerbund e V (ESB):** Bremer Strasse 2, 5600 Wuppertal 1; Chair. Rudolf Steege.

**Fachverband Deutsche Klavierindustrie e V (FDK):** Friedrich-Wilhelm-Strasse 31, 53113 Bonn; tel. 49 228 539700; fax 49 228 539 7070; Gen. Man. Dr Hans-Henning Wittgen.

**Fachverbad Deutscher Berufscholeiter e V (FDB):** Unkenweg 19, 4330 Müllheim/Ruhr.

**Fachverband Historische Tasteninstrumente e V (FHT):** Untermarkt 40, 8190 Wolfratshausen; Chair. Reinhard Hoppe.

**Ferenc-Fricsay Gesellschaft e V (FFG):** Heerstrasse 70, 1000 Berlin 19; Chair. Prof. Dr Wolfgang Geisler.

**Förderkreis Hugo Herrmann e V:** Ringinger Tal 26, 7453 Burladingen; Chair. Werner Zintgraf.

**Förderkreis Instrumentales Musizieren e V:** Friedrich-Wilhelm-Strasse 31, 5300 Bonn 1; Chair. Alfred Döll.

**Förderkreis Unterhaltungsmusik e V (FKU):** Ringstrasse 4, 46562 Voerde; tel. 49 2855 2112; fax 49 2855 4514; Chair. Kurt Althans.

**Förderverein der Klassischen Gesangskunst in Deutschland e V:** PO Box 101516, 7000 Stuttgart 10; Chair. Prof. Sylvia Geszty.

**Fonds Darstellende Künste e V:** Am Handelshof 9, 4300 Essen 1; Chair. Prof. Dr Jürgen-Dieter Waidelich.

**Fonds Soziokultur e V:** Stirnband 10, 5800 Hagen 1; Chair. Dr Olaf Schwencke.

**Franz-Grothe-Stiftung:** Rosenheimer Strasse 11, 8000 Munich 80; Chair. Hans Schröpf.

**Franz-Liszt-Gesellschaft e V Weimar:** Platz der Demokratie 2–3, 5300 Weimar; Pres. Prof. Dr Detlef Altenburg.

**Frau und Musik-Internationaler Arbeitkreis e V Geschäftsstelle:** Adelheid Klammt, Vogesort 8 F, 3000 Hannover 91; Chair. Prof. Siegrid Ernst.

**Freie Akademie der Künste Hamburg:** Ferdinandstor la, 2000 Hamburg; Pres. Prof. Armin Sandig.

**Freunde der Querflöte:** Körnerstrasse 51, 5820 Gevelsberg; Chair. Elli Edler-Busch.

**Freunde der Tonkunst und Musikerziehung e V:** Landsberger Strasse 425, 8000 Munich 60; Chair. Dr Rüdiger von Canal.

**Friedrich-Kiel-Gesellschaft e V:** Ithstrasse 20, 31863 Coppenbrügge; tel. 49 5156 1637; fax 49 5156 1637; Chair. Dr Hartmut Wecker.

**Fritz-Büchtger-Kuratorium:** Musica Sacra Viva, PO Box 750202, 8000 Munich 75; Chair. Andreas Weymann.

**GEMA-Stiftung:** Rosenheimer Strasse 11, 8000 Munich 80; Chair. Prof. Dr Reinhold Kreile.

**Genossenschaft Deutscher Bühnenangehöriger (GDBA) in der DAG:** Feldbrunnenstrasse 74, 20148 Hamburg; tel. 49 40 443870; fax 49 40 459352; Pres. Hans Herdlein.

**Georg Hesse Stiftung:** Am Brühl 13, 7825 Lenzkirch 3 (Kappel); Chair. Hannelore Hesse-Mange.

**Georg-Friedrich-Händel-Gesellschaft-Internationale Vereinigung e V:** Grosse Nikolaistrasse 5, 06108 Halle an der Saale; Pres. Prof. Dr Wolfgang Ruf.

**Gesamtverband Deutscher Musikfachgeschäfte e V (GDM):** Friedrich-Wilhelm-Strasse 31, 53113 Bonn; tel. 49 228 539700; fax 49 228 539 7070; Gen. Man. Dr H. H. Wittgen.

**Gesellschaft der Orgelfreunde e V (GdO):** Josestrasse 6, 6642 Mettlach 1; Chair. Prof. Alfred Reichling.

**Gesellschaft für Alte Musik e V (GAM):** Birkenstrasse 18, 7218 Trossingen; Chair. Prof. Dr Ludger Lohmann.

**Gesellschaft für Bayerische Musikgeschichte e V:** PO Box 100611, 8000 Munich 1; Chair. Prof. Dr Theodor Göllner.

**Gesellschaft für Musikforschung (GfM):** Heinrich-Schütz-Allee 35, 34131 Kassel; tel. 49 561 310 5240; fax 49 561 31050; Pres. Prof. Dr Klaus W. Niemöller.

**Gesellschaft für Musikpädagogik e V (GMP):** Von-der-Tann-Strasse 38, 8400 Regensburg; Chair. Prof. Dr Reinhard Schneider.

**Gesellschaft für Neue Musik e V:** (GNM)-Sektion Bundesrepublik Deutschland der Internationalen Gesellschaft für Neue Musik (IGNM), Schwedlerstrasse 2–4, 6000 Frankfurt am Main 1; Pres. Friedrich Goldmann.

**Gesellschaft für Selbstspielende Musikinstrumente e V:** Heiligenstock 46, 5060 Bergisch Gladbach 2; Chair. Dr Jürgen Hocker.

**Gesellschaft für Theatergeschichte e V:** Mecklenburgische Strasse 56, 1000 Berlin 33; Chair. Prof. Dr Peter Spengel.

**Gesellschaft zur Förderung der Berufsbildung junger Künstler e V (GFBK):** Eichkatzweg 25, 3107 Hambuhren.

**Gesellschaft zur Förderung der Westfalischen Kulturarbeit e V:** Landschaftverband Westfalen-Lippe, Warendorfer Str 14, Münster; Chair. Reinhold Brauner.

**Gotthard-Schierse-Stiftung:** Bundesallee 1-12, 1000 Berlin 15; Chair. Horst Göbel.

**Günter Henle Stiftung München:** G Henle Verlag, Forstenrieder Allee 122, PO Box 710466, 8000 Munich 71; Chair. Anne Liese Henle.

**Hamburger, Internationaler Verën für die Musik der Bach-Sohne (HBG):** Durchschnitt 25, Hamburg; Chair. Prof. Edith Picht-Axenfeld.

**Hamburger Telemann-Gesellschaft e V:** Haus der Patriotischen Gesellschaft, Trostbrücke 4, 2000 Hamburg 11; Chair. Eckart Klessmann.

**Hamburgische Kulturstiftung:** Chilehaus C, 20095 Hamburg; tel. 49 040 33 90 99; fax 49 040 32 69 58.

**Hans-Breuer-Stiftung zur Pflege und Förderung des deutschen Liedgutes e V:** Hochschule für Musik and Theater, Harvestehuder Weg 10–12, 2000 Hamburg 13; Chair. Prof. Dr Hermann Rauhe.

**Hans-Pfitzner-Gesellschaft e V:** Mauerkircher Strasse 8, 8000 Munich 80; Chair. Gen. Music Dir Prof. Rolf Reuter.

**Heinrich-Heine-Gesellschaft e V (HHG):** Bolkerstrasse 53, PO Box 1120, 4000 Düsseldorf 1; Chair. Gerd Högener.

**Heinrich-Kaminski-Gesellschaft e V:** Storchen-Apotheke, Hauptstrasse 20, 7890 Waldshut-Tiengen 2; Chair. Jürgen Klein.

**Industriegewerkschaft Medien-Druck und Papier, Publizistik und Kunst (IG Medien):** Friedrichstrasse 15, 70174 Stuttgart; Man. Heinrich Bletcher.

**Institut für Bildung und Kultur e V (IBK):** Küppelstein 34, 5630 Remscheid; Chair. Prof. Bruno Tetzner.

**Institut fur Musiktherapie:** Waldhuterpfad 38, 14169 Berlin; tel. 030 8135080; fax 030 8135080.

**Institut für Neue Musik und Musikerziehung e V:** Grafenstrasse 35, 6100 Darmstadt; Chair. Dr Susanne Liegler.

**Institut für Studien der Musikkultur des Portugiesischen Sprachraumes:** An Der Münze 1, 50668 Cologne; Contact Dr Harald Hülskath.

**Interessenverband Deutscher Komponisten e V (IDK):** Willinghusener Landstrasse 70, 2000 Barsbüttel; Chair. Gustav Kneip.

**Interessenverband Deutscher Konzertveranstalter und Künstlervermittler e V (IDKV):** Lenhartstrasse 15, 20249 Hamburg; tel. 49 40 460 5028; fax 49 40 484443; website www.idkv.com; Pres. Jens Michow.

**International Association of the Wagner Societies:** Sonnhalde 123, 79104 Frieburg; tel. 49 761 53756; fax 49 761 53756; Pres. Josef Lienhart.

**International Association of Music and Education:** Heinrich-Schutz Allee 33, 34131, Kassel; tel. 49 561 93 51 70; fax 49 561 313772.

**International Federation of the Phonographic Industry (IFPI)-Deutsche Landesgruppe:** Grelckstrasse 36, 2000 Hamburg 54; Chair. Helmut Fest.

**Internationale Andreas-Werckmeister-Gesellschaft e V:** Kulturamt der Stadt Halberstadt, Dominikanerstrasse 16, Halberstad; Pres. Dr Rüdiger Pfeiffer.

**Internationale Arbeitsgemeinschaft der Theaterbesucher organisationen (IATO):** Am Handelshof 9, Essen; Pres. Prof. Dr Jurgen-Dieter Waidelich.

**International Carl-Maria-von-Weber-Gesellschaft e V:** Staatsbibliothek zu Berlin (Preussischer Kulturbesitz), Musikabteilung, Unter den Linden 8, PO Box 1312, 1086 Berlin; Chair. Dr Ute Schwab.

**Internationale Discotheken Organisationen:** Deutsche Diskotheken-Unternehmer, Kaiser-Friedrich-Allee 1–3, 5100 Aachen; Contact Halga Quirini.

**Internationale Draeseke-Gesellschaft e V:** Matthias-Grünewald-Strasse 5, 6720 Speyer; Chair. Dr Helmut Loos.

**Internationale Fasch-Gesellschaft e V:** Wiekhaus Breitestein, PO Box 1113, 39251 Zerbst; Pres. Dr Konstanze Musketa.

**Internationale Föderation für Chormusik-International Federation for Choral Music (IFCM):** Burgstrasse 33, Bonn; Pres. Dr H. Royce Saltzmann.

**Internationale Gesellschaft für Musik in der Medizin e V (ISFMIM):** Paulmannshöher Strasse 17, 5880 Ludenscheid; Chair. Dr Roland Droh.

**Internationale Gesellschaft für Musikerziehung (ISME):** Deutsche Sektion, Deutscher Musikrat/AGMM, Am Michaelsahof 4 a, 5300 Bonn 2.

**Internationale Gesellschaft für musikpädagogische Fortbildung e V (IGMF):** Johannes-Hummel-Weg 1, 57392 Schmallenberg; tel. 49 2974 9110; fax 49 2974 911100; Chair. Prof. Dr Hans-Walter Berg.

**Internationale Gesellschaft für Urheberrecht e V (INTERGU):** Rosenheimer Strasse 11, 8000 Munich 80.

**Internationale Gitarristische Vereinigung Freiburg e V (IGVF):** Lessingstrasse 4, 7800 Freiburg im Breisgau; Chair. Jörg Sommermeyer.

**Internationale Heinrich-Schütz-Gesellschaft e V (ISG):** Heinrich-Schütz-Allee 35, 5300 Kassel; Chair. Prof. Dr Arno Forchert.

**Internationale Hugo-Wolf-Akademie für Gesang-Dichtung-Liedkunst e V:** Neckarstrasse 86, 7000 Stuttgart 1; Chair. Dr Rainer Wilhelm.

**Internationale Johann-Nepomuk-David-Gesellschaft E V (IDG):** Fichenstrasse 19, 7336 Uhingen; Chair. Wolfgang Dallmann.

**Internationale Joseph Martin Kraus-Gesellschaft e V:** PO Box 1422, 74713 Buchen (Odenwald); tel. 49 6281 8898; fax 49 6281 556898; e-mail info@ kraus-gesellschaft.de; website www.kraus-gesellschaft.de; Chair.: Prof. Dr Reinhard Wiesend.

**Internationale Louis Spohr Gesellschaft e V:** Schöne Aussicht 2, 3500 Kassel; Pres. Wolfgang Windführ.

**Internationale Meyerbeer-Gesellschaft e V:** Tristanstrasse 10, 8034 Germering; Chair. Karl Zelenka.

**Internationale Posaunenvereinigung (IPV)-Sektion Deutschland:** Launhardt, Hahnenstrasse 18, 5024 Pulheim; Pres. Prof. Johannes Doms.

**Internationale vereinigung der Musikbibliotheken und:** Dr Bettina Seyfried, Gärtnerstrasse 25-32, PO Box 450229, 12207 Berlin; Pres. Dr Joachim Jaenecke.

**Internationale Viola-Gesellschaft:** c/o Dr Ronald Schmidt, Gechtemer Weg 52, 53332 Bornheim; fax 221 400 75283.

**Internationaler Arbeitskreis für Musik e V (IAM):** Am Kloster 1a, 49565 Bramsche-Halgarten; tel. 49(0) 5461 9963-0; Exec. Dir Peter Koch.

**Internationaler Verein Freund behinderter Tonkünstler e V:** Melchiorstrasse 74, 8000 Munich 71; Chair. Elisabeth Stöcklein-Weiss.

**Internationales Forum Junge Chormusik Rotenburg (Wümme) e V:** Rathaus, Grosse Strasse 1, Rotenburg/Wümme; Pres. Prof. Dr Guy Maneveau.

**Jacques-Offenbach-Gesellschaft e V Bad Ems (JOG):** Waldstrasse 3, 5427 Bad Ems; Contact Dr Günther Obst.

**Jean Sibelius Gesellschaft Deutschland e V:** Trivstrasse 19, 8000 Munich 19; Pres. Prof. August Everding.

**Jeunesses Musicales Deutschland:** Marktplatz 12, 97990 Weikersheim; tel. 49 7934 280; fax 49 7934 8526; website www.JeunessesMusicales.de; Gen. Sec. Thomas Rietschel.

**Johann Adolph Hasse-Gesellschaft München e V:** Ursula Biehl, Landsberger Strasse 55, 8080 Fürstenfeldbruck; Chair. Ursula Biehl.

**Johannes-Brahms-Gesellschaft Internationale e V:** Trostbrücke 4, 2000 Hamburg 11; Pres. Detlef Kraus.

**Jospeh-Haas-Gesellschaft e V (JHG):** Veroneserstrasse 4, 8000 Munich 90; Pres. Prof. Dr Siegfried Gmeinwieser.

**Jospeh-Suder-Gesellschaft e V:** Grünwalderstrasse 250, 8000 Munich 90; Chair. Reinhold Pfandzelter.

**Jürgen Ponto-Stiftung zur Förderung junger Künstler:** Jürgen-Ponto-Platz 1, 60301 Frankfurt am Main; tel. 49 69 263 52 396; fax 49 69 263 54 732; e-mail ponto-stiftung@dresdner-bank.com; website juergen-ponto-stiftung.de; Principal Man.: Karin Heyl.

**Karg-Elert-Gesellschaft e V (KEG):** Lortzingstrasse 11, 7980 Ravensburg; Chair. Prof. Dr Wolfgang Stockmeier, Johannes Michel.

**Karl-Klingler-Stiftung e V:** Siemens AG, Dr Rüdiger v Canal, Wittelsbacherplatz 2, 8000 Munich 2.

**Kodály-Gesellschaft e V:** Conrad W. Mayer, Grabenstrasse 22, 7812 Bad Krozingen.

**Körber-Stiftung:** Kampchaussee 10, PO Box 800660, 2050 Hamburg 80; Chair. Ulrich Voswinckel.

**Kulturinstitut Komponistinnen gestern-heute e V:** Theaterstrasse 11, 69117 Heidelberg; tel. 49 6221 166861; fax 49 6221 182072; Chair. Roswitha Sperber.

**Kulturkreis im Bundesverband der Deutschen Industrie e V:** Gustav-Heinemann-Ufer 84–88, 5000 Cologne 51; Chair. Dr Arend Oetker.

**Kulturpolitische Gesellschaft e V:** Stirnband 8–10, 5800 Hagen 1; Pres. Dr Olaf Schwencke.

**Kulturstiftung des Landes Schleswig-Holstein:** Ministerium für Bildung, Wissenschaft, Jugend und Kultur, Gartenstrasse 6, 2300 Kiel 1; Chair. Dr Peter Joachim Kreyenberg.

**Kunststiftung Baden-Württemberg GmbH:** Gerokstrasse 37, 7000 Stuttgart 1; Chair. Dr Christof Müller-Wirth.

**Kurt-Weill-Vereinigung Dessau:** Stadtverwaltung Dessau, Dezernat IV, Kulturamt, Zerbster Strasse 1, 4500 Dessau; Chair. Dr Jürgen Schebera.

**Landgraf-Moritz-Stiftung (LMST):** Heinrich-Schütz-Allee 35, PO Box 100329, 3500 Kassel; Chair. Walter Olbrich.

**Lohmann-Stiftung Wiesbaden e V:** Prinz-Nikolas-Strasse 26, 6200 Wiesbaden; Chair. Prof. Hildegund Lohmann-Becker.

**Medizinische Gesellschaft für Kunstschaffende-Musikkorthopädie und Kunstmedizine V:** Universität Ulm, Am Hochstrasse 8, PO Box 4066, Ulm. Dr A. Lahme.

**Mendelssohn-Gesellschaft e V:** Zerbster Strasse 59, 1000 Berlin 45; Chair. Ernst Thamm.

**Musica Reanimata:** Förderverein zur Wiederentdeckung NS-verfolgter Komponisten, Heidi Tamar Hoffmann, Johannisberger Strasse 12A, 1000 Berlin 33; Chair. Dr Albrecht Dümling.

**Musik + Tanz + Erziehung:** Orff-Schulwerk-Gesellschaft Deutschland e V, Hermann-Hummel-Strasse 25, 82166 Lochham; tel. 49 89 854 2953; fax 49 89 854 2851; Chair. Gerhard Kuhn.

**Musikalische Jugend Deutschlands e V (MJD):** Marktplatz 12, 6992 Weikersheim; Chair. Dr Michael Jenne.

**Musikfonds für Musikurheber e V:** Adenauerallee 134, 5300 Bonn 1; Chair. Prof. Dr Peter Ruzicka.

**Musiktherapie e V:** Von-Esmarch Strasse 111, 4400 Münster; Chair. Prof. Dr Karl Hörmann.

**Neue Bachgesellschaft e V (NBG):** Internationale Vereinigung, Thomaskirchhof 16, PO Box 727, Leipzig; Chair. Prof. Dr H. C. Helmuth Rilling.

**Neue Deutsche Händel-Gesellschaft e V:** Im Brögen 4 b, 5204 Lohmar 21; Pres. Prof. Dr Albert Scheibler.

**Neue Zentralstelle der Bühnenautoren und Bühnenverleger GmbH:** Bismarckstrasse 107, 1000 Berlin 12; Chair. Dr Maria Müller-Sommer.

**NRW Zentrum für Popularmusik und Kommunikationstechnologie:** Rottscheidter Strasse 6, PO Box 201414, 5600 Wupppertal 11; Contact Dieter Gorny.

**ORPLID internationale Gesellschaft für Musiktheater und Architektur e V:** Hohenheimer Strasse 84, 7000 Stuttgart; Chair. Wilhelm Keitel.

**Oscar-und-Vera-Ritter-Stiftung:** Bundesstrasse 4, 2000 Hamburg 13; Chair. Jürgen Wittekind.

**PE-Förderkreis für Studierende der Musik e V:** Dr Ralph Landsittel, Otto-Back-Strasse 46, 6800 Mannheim 1; Chair. Angelika Milos-Engelhorn.

**Percussion Creativ e V:** Hastverstr. 31, 90408 Nurnberg; tel. and fax 49 911 365 9768; Chair. Prof. Werner Thärichen.

**Posaunenwerk in der Evangelischen Kirche in Deutschland e V:** Hinter der Grambker Kirche 5, 2820 Bremen 77; Chair. Günther Schulz.

**Pro Musica Viva-Maria Strecker-Daelen-Stiftung (PMV):** PO Box 3146, 55021 Mainz; fax 06131-366432; e-mail Pro.MusicaViva@t-online.de.

**ProFolk, Dachverband für Folkmusik e V:** Brigitte Kempe, Oberachernerstrasse 93, 7590 Achern 2; Chair. Jens Peter Müller.

**Rachmaninoff-Gesellschaft e V Wiesbaden:** PO Box 4853, 6200 Wiesbaden; Pres. Richard Henger.

**Ralph-Vaughan-Williams-Gesellschaft e V:** Jugendmusik-u Kunstschule, Elberfelder Strasse 20, 5630 Remscheid; Chair. Dr Lutz-Werner Hesse.

**Rektorenkonferenz der Musikhochschulen in der BRD:** Hochschule für Musik Köln, Dagobertstr 38, 50668 Cologne; fax 49 221 131204; Contact Isabel Pfeiffer-Poensgen.

**Richard-Strauss-Gesellschaft München e V:** Viktualienmarkt 3, 8000 Munich 2; Chair. Prof. Wolfgang Sawallisch.

**Richard-Wagner-Verband International e V—RWVI (International Association of Wagner Societies):** Sonnhalde 123, 79098 Freiburg im Breisgau; Chair. Josef Lienhart; 136 societies; with some 37,000 members.

**Robert-Schumann-Gesellschaft e V:** Bilker Strasse 4–6, 4000 Düsseldorf 1; Chair. Dr Herbert Zapp.

**Robert-Schumann-Gesellschaft Zwickau e V:** Robert-Schumann-Haus, Hauptmarkt 5, 8540 Zwickau; Chair. Dr Martin Schoppe.

**Robert-Stolz-Stiftung e V:** Steinhauser-Strasse 3, 8000 Munich 80; Chair. Thomas M. Stein.

**Rudolf-Eberle-Stiftung:** c/o Akademie Schloss Solitude, Solitude 3, 70197 Stuttgart; tel. 711 99 6 19 471; Chair. Michael Russ.

**Sängerbund der Deutschen Polizei e V (SbdDP):** Rosenfelder Strasse 20, 2300 Kiel 14; Chair. Werner Busche.

**Schostakowitsch-Gesellschaft e V:** Klaustalerstrasse 2, 1100 Berlin; Chair. Hilmar Schmalenberg.

**Schütz-Akademie e V:** Heinrich-Schütz-Strasse 1, PO Box 22, 07586 Bad Kostritz; tel. 036605 36198; fax 036605 36199; e-mail heinrich-schutz-haus@t-online.de; Dir Friederike Böcher.

**Sinfonima-Stiftung:** Mannheimer Versicherung AG, Augstaanlage 66, PO Box 102161, 6800 Mannheim 1.

**Sonderhauser Verband akademisch-musikalischer Verbindungen (SV):** Hilger Schallen, Bahnweg 85, 6500 Mainz 42; Chair. Gerhard Seher.

**Spitzenverband Deutsche Musik e V (SPIDEM):** Adenauerallee 134, 5300 Bonn 1; Pres. Prof. Dr H. C. Erich Schulze.

**Stiftung Bayerischer Musikfonds:** Salvatorstrasse 2, 8000 Munich 2.

**Stiftung 100 Jahre Yamaha e V—Verein zur Popularisierung der Musik:** Siemensstrasse 22–34, 25462 Rellingen; Chair. Masahito Kato.

**Stiftung fur Kutturell Weiterbildung und Kulturberatung:** Jägerstrasse 51m, 1080 Berlin; Chair. Prof. Dr Hermann Glaser.

**Stiftung Kulturfonds:** Molkenmarkt 1–3, PO Box 240, 1020 Berlin.

**Stiftung Kunst und Kultur des landes Nordrhein-Westfalen:** Haus der Stiftungen in NRW, Rosstrasse 133, 4000 Düsseldorf 30; Chair. Johannes Rau

**Stiftung Ostdeutscher Kulturrat (OKR):** Kaiserstrasse 113, 5300 Bonn 1; Pres. Dr Herbert Hupka.

**Stiftung Preussischer Kulturbesitz:** Von-der-Heydt-Strasse 16–18, 10785 Berlin; tel. 49 (0)30 25463-0; fax 49 (0)30 25463-268; e-mail info@hv.spk-berlin.de; website www.preussischer-kulturbesitz.de; Pres. Prof. Dr hc Klaus-Dieter Lehmann; cultural organization with museums, the State Library, State Archive, research institutes, and various collections; administers various annual awards.

**Stiftung Rheinland-Pfalz für Kultur:** Ministerium für Wissenschaft, Weiterbildung, Forschung und Kulter, Mittlere Bleiche, 55116 Mainz; Chair. Minister Pres. Kurt Beck.

**Stiftung Volkslied (STV):** Heinrich-Shütz-Allee 33, 3500 Kassel; Chair. Alfred Peters.

**Sudetendeutscher Sängerbund e V (SDS):** Hans-Schitzer-Weg 19, 8960 Kempten; Chair. Gunther Wohlrab.

**Telemann-Gesellschaft e V Internationale Vereinigung:** Liebigstrasse 10, 3010 Magdeburg; Pres. Prof. Dr Martin Ruhnke.

**Union Deutscher Jazz-Musiker e V (UDJ):** Am Michaelshof 4a, 5300 Bonn 2; Chair. Prof. Joe Viera.

**Verband der Deutschen Konzertdirektionen e V:** Liebigstrasse 39, 8000 Munich 22; Pres. Michael Russ.

**Verband der deutschen Kritiker e V:** Andreas Richter, Prinz-Fr-Leopold Strasse 34a, 1000 Berlin 38; Chair. Hartmut Krug.

**Verband der Musikpädagogen e V (VMP):** Von-der-Tann-Strasse 38, 8400 Regensburg; Chair. Dr Lothar Schubert.

**Verband der Vertriebe von Musikinstrumenten und Musikelektronik:** Heinstrasse 169, Stuttgart; Chair. Werner Sonderwald.

**Verband Deutscher Bühnenverleger e V:** Bismarckstrasse 107, 1000 Berlin 12; Chair. Stefani Cremer-Hunzinger.

**Verband Deutscher Geigenbauer e V (VDG):** Oho-Devrient-Str 14, 07743 Jena; tel. 0049 3641 447804; fax 0049 3641 824884; Chair. Hieronymus Köstler.

**Verband Deutscher Komponisten:** An der Kolonnade 15, 1080 Berlin; Chair. Hans J. Wenzel.

**Verband Deutscher KonzertChöre e V (VDKC):** Kempener Strasse 5, 41749 Viersen; tel. 49 2162 67058; Pres. Hans-Heinrich Grosse-Brockhoff.

**Verband Deutscher Musikschaffender (VDM):** Kaiser-Friedrich-Allee 1–3, 5100 Aachen; Pres. Klaus Quirini.

**Verband Deutscher Musikschulen e V (VDM):** Plittersdorfer Strasse 93, 53173 Bonn; tel. 49 228 957060; website www.musikschulen.de; Chair. Reinhart von Gutzeit.

**Verband Deutscher Schulmusiker (VDS):** Weihergarten 5, PO Box 3640, 55116 Mainz; tel. 49 6131 234049; fax 49 6131 246823; website www.vds -musik.de; Chair. Prof. Dr Dieter Zimmerzchied.

**Verband Deutscher Tonmeister e V (VDT):** Masurenallee 8–14, 1000 Berlin 19; website www.tonmeister.de; Pres. Günter Griewisch.

**Verband evangelischer Kirchenchöre Deutschlands e V (VEK):** Hasenburger Weg 67, 2120 Lüneburg; Pres. Dr Hans-Christian Drömann.

**Verband evangelischer Kirchenmusiker Deutschlands (VeM):** Domplatz 5, 6720 Speyer; Pres. KMD Prof. Hermann Rau.

**Verein zur Förderung der Nordoff/Robbins Musiktherapie e V:** Dorfstrasse 22, 58099 Hagen; tel. 2304 642104; e-mail nordoff.robbins .verein@freenet.de.

**Verein zur Förderung Historischer Harfen e V:** Rainer m Thurau, Helenenstrasse 10, 6200 Wiesbaden; Chair. Elena Polonska.

**Vereinigung deutscher Harfenisten e V:** Vera Munkel-Remann, Goldammerweg 183, 5000 Cologne 30; Chair. Therese Reichling.

**Vereinigung Deutscher Musik-Bearbeiter e V:** Kiesstrasse 44a, 12209 Berlin; tel. and fax 030 772 6241.

**Vereinigung Deutscher Opernchöre und Buhnentanzer:** Bismarckstrasse 14–16, 5000 Cologne 1; Chair. Heinz Mersch.

**Villa Musica:** Stiftung zur Förderung der Musik, Auf der Bastei, 6500 Mainz; Chair. Mindirig Ernst Maurer.

**Walcker-Stiftung für orgelwissenschaftliche Forschung:** PO Box 1128, 6601 Kleinblittersdorf 2; Chair. Klaus Walcker.

**Walter Kaminsky-Stiftung:** Kösener Strasse 4, 1000 Berlin 33.

**Walther-Hensel-Gesellschaft e V:** Ob dem Staeffele 2, 71364 Winnenden; tel. 7195 2631; fax 7195 1397300; e-mail post@walther-hensel-gesellschaft.de; website www.walther-hensel-gesellschaft.de; Chair. Herbert Preisenhammer.

**Werkgemeinschaft Musik e V:** Carl-Mosterts-Platz 1, 40477 Düsseldorf; tel. 49 211 4693 191; fax 49 211 4693 159; website www.werkgemeinschaft -musik.de; Chair. Prof. Karl Berg.

**Wilhelm-Furtwängler-Gesellschaft e V:** Schwelmer Strasse 4, 1000 Berlin 45; Chair. Dr Friedhelm Schöning.

**Wilhelm-Petersen-Gesellschaft e V:** Brahmsweg 4, 6100 Darmstadt.

**Wissenschaftliche Sozietät Musikpädagogik e V (WSMP):** Fachbereich Erziehungswissenschaft, Insitut für Musikpadagogik, Von-Melle-Park 8, 2000 Hamburg 13; Chair. Prof. Dr Hermann J. Kaiser.

**Xaver and Philipp Scharwenka-Gesellschaft e V:** Prassekstrasse 5, 23566 Lübeck; tel. 49 (0)451 6 4264; fax 49 (0)451 6 5098; e-mail ETrenkner@ aol.com; website www.scharwenka.de; Chair. Prof. Evelinde Trenkner.

**Zentralverband Katholischer Kirchenangestellter Deutschlands e V (ZKD):** Am Kielshof 2, PO Box 990125, 5000 Cologne 91; Chair. Franz Kopecky.

**Zentrum Bundesrepublik Deutschland des Internationalen Theaterinstituts:** Bismarckstrasse 107, 100 Berlin 12; Pres. Prof. August Everding.

**Zentrum für Kunst und Medientechnologie Karlsruhe (ZKM):** Institut für Musik und Akustik, Ritterstrasse 42, Karlsruhe; Dir Prof. Dr Heinrich Klotz.

## Greece

**International Music Council (Greek Section):** 38 Mitropleos St, 105 63 Athens; Gen. Sec. Apostolos Kositios.

**Jeunesses Musicales de Grece/Musique Pour l'Enfant:** Stratigou Kallari 52, Psychico, 154 52 Athens; Pres. Domini Sarris.

**Société Hellenique pour la Protection de la Proprieté intellectuelle:** 14 Delighianni Street, 106 83 Athens; Man. Dir George Galanakis.

**Tsakalof Cultural Centre:** Platia G, Stavrou 5, 45444 Ioannina; Pres. Aspasia Zerva.

## Guatemala

**Asociación Guatemalteca de Autores y Compositores (AGAYC):** 14 Calle 11-42, Zona 1, 01001 Guatemala City.

**Juventudes Musicales de Guatemala:** Diagonal 6, Calle Real de la Villa 13-46, Zona 10, Guatemala City; Pres. Francisco Saravia.

## Hong Kong

**Hong Kong Arts Administrators Association Ltd:** c/o ARIC, Room 301, 3/ F Hong Kong Arts Centre, 2 Harbour Road, Wanchai.

**Hong Kong Government Music Office:** 25/F Wanchai Tower One, 12 Harbour Road, Wanchai; website www.usd.gov.hk/musicoffice.

## Hungary

**Artisjus Hungarian Bureau for the Protection of Authors' Rights:** PO Box 593, 1539 Budapest; tel. 36 1 212 1543; website www.artisjus.com; Pres. János Bródy; Gen. Dir Dr Péter Gyertyánfy.

**F. Liszt Society:** Vörösmarty u. 35, 1064 Budapest; tel. 36 1 342 15 73; Pres.: Prof. Istvan Lantos; Sec.-Gen.: Klara Hamburger.

**Hungarian Arts Foundation, Music Department:** Báthori-utca 10, 1054 Budapest; Dir of the Music Dept Kálmán Strém.

**Hungarian Composers Union:** 1051 Budapest, Vorosmarty Ter 1; tel. 36 1 338 4139; fax 36 1 338 4139; Pres. Maie Hoilos.

**International Kodály Society:** PO Box 8, 1502 Budapest.

**Jeunesses Musicales of Hungary:** PO Box 80, 1366 Budapest, Vörösmarty tér 1, 1051 Budapest; Sec.-Gen. Beáta Schanda.

**Magyar Tudományos Akadémia Zenetudományi Intézet (Institute for Musicology of the Hungarian Academy of Sciences):** PO Box 28, 1250 Budapest; Táncsics Mihály u. 7., 1014 Budapest; tel. 361 214 6770; fax 361 375 9282; e-mail info@zti.hu; website www.zti.hu; Dir Dr Tibor Tallián; research in music history, folk music and dance; holds the Bartók archives, Dohnányi archives, and publishes the Studia Musicologica, Musicalia Danubiana, CAO-ECE and Cantus Planus.

**Magyar Zenei Tanacs (Hungarian Music Council):** PO Box 47, 1364, Budapest; tel. 36 1 318 4243; fax 36 1 317 8267; e-mail hmc@holdon.hu; Pres.: Adrienne Csengery; Exec. Sec. Agnes Paldy.

**Music Information Centre of Hungary:** Lónyay u. 54, fsz.3., 1097 Budapest.

**National Centre of International Music Competitions and Festivals:** PO Box 80, 1366 Budapest, Vörösmarty tér 1, 1051 Budapest; Dir Tamás Klenjánszky.

**Trade Union of Hungarian Musicians:** Gorkij Fasor 38, 1068 Budapest.

## Iceland

**Association of Icelandic Composers:** Laufásvegi 40, Reykjavík.

**Association of Light Composers and Songwriters:** Háteigsvegur 28, 105 Reykjavík.

**Association of Music School Directors:** Kennarasamband Islands, Grettisgata 89, 105 Reykjavík.

**Association of Music School Teachers:** Kennarasamband Islands, Grettisgata 89, 105 Reykjavík.

**Iceland Music Information Centre:** Sidumuli 34, 108 Reykjavík; Dir Bergljót Jónsdóttir.

**Icelandic Musicians' Union:** Raudagerdi 27, 108 Reykjavík.

**International Society for Contemporary Music, Icelandic Section:** Tonskaldafelag Islands, Laufásvegur 40, Reykjavík.

**Reykjavík Music Society:** Garoastraeti 17, 101 Reykjavík.

**Society of Icelandic Musicians:** Laufásvegur 40, 101 Reykjavík.

**Union of Authors and Copyright Owners:** Laufásvegur 40, 101 Reykjavík.

## India

**Delhi Symphony Society:** 2 Humanyum Road, New Delhi 110003; tel. 11 6512091; fax 11 24361918.

**Inter-National Cultural Centre:** 205 Tansen Marg, New Delhi 1.

**National Centre for the Performing Arts:** Nariman Point, Mumbai 400021; tel. 11 22 285 4309; fax 11 22 283 3737.

## Ireland

**Arts Council (An Chomhairle Ealaion):** 70 Merrion Square, Dublin 2; tel. 353 1 618 0200; fax 353 1 676 1302/661 0349; website www.artscouncil.ie.

**Contemporary Music Centre:** 19 Fishamble Street, Temple Bar, Dublin 8; tel. 353 1 6731922; fax 353 1 6489100; e-mail info@cmc.ie; website www.cmc .ie; Promotion Man. Karen Hennessy.

**International Songwriters Association Ltd:** Raheen, Limerick City.

**Irish Composers Centre:** Liberty Hall, Room 804, Dublin 1.

**Irish Federation of Musicians and Associated Professions:** 63 Lower Gardiner Street, Dublin 1; tel. and fax 353 1 874 4645.

**Irish Music Rights Organization (IMRO):** Copyright House, Pembroke Row, Lower Baggot Street, Dublin 2; tel. 353 1 661 4844; fax 353 1 676 3125; website www.imro.ie.

**Mechanical Copyright Society Ltd (MCPS):** Copyright House, Pembroke Row, Lower Baggot Street, Dublin 2; tel. 353 1 676 6940; fax 353 1 661 1316.

## Israel

**Independent Musicians Union:** 6 Rabin Square, 64591 Tel-Aviv; Chair. Dany Gottfried.

**International Music Council (Israeli Section):** Ministry of Education and Culture, Devora Hanaviah Street 2, 91911 Jerusalem; Chief Officer Raaya Zimran.

**International Society for Contemporary Music (Israeli Section):** c/o Israel Composers' League, PO Box 45068, 61450 Tel-Aviv.

**Israel Composers' League:** PO Box 45068, 61450 Tel-Aviv; Chair. Manachem Zur.

**Israel Music Institute (IMI):** 144 Hayarkon Street, 63451 Tel-Aviv; tel. 972 3 527 0219; fax 972 3 524 5276; Dir Paul Landau.

**Israeli Musicians' Union:** 6 Rabin Square, Tel-Aviv 64951; tel. 972 3 695 9355; fax 972 3 696 3528; Pres.: Dan Gottfried.

**Jerusalem Music Centre:** PO Box 4568 Mishkanot Sha'ananim, Jerusalem 91045; Dir Benny Gal-Ed; Chair. Issac Stern.

**Jeunesses Musicales d'Israel:** 8 Sderot Chen, 64071 Tel-Aviv.

**Music Information Centre of Israel:** 144 Hayarkon Street, PO Box 3004, 63451 Tel-Aviv; tel. 972 3 524 6475; fax 972 3 524 5276; Dir Paul Landau.

**National Council for Culture and Arts:** 16 Hanatziv Street, 67018 Tel-Aviv; Chief Officer David Sinai.

**Society of Authors, Composers, and Music Publishers in Israel—ACUM:** 9 Tyval Street, Ramat-Gan 52117; Chair. Hana Goldberg.

## Italy

**Accademia Luigi Boccherini:** Piazza Insurrezione 10, 35129 Padua.

**Accademia Tartiniana:** Piazzale Pontecorvo 4/A, 35121 Padua.

**Associazione Antiquae Musicae Italicae Studiosi:** Via Remorsella 5/A, 40125 Bologna.

**Associazione Centro Studi Carusiani:** Via Omboni 1, 20129 Milan.

**Associazione dei Fonografici Italiani (AFI):** Via Vittor Pisani 10, 20124 Milan.

**Associazione dei Rappresentanti Italiani di Artisti di Concerti e Spettacoli:** Via Cappuccio 11, 20123 Milan.

**Associazione di Informatica Musicale Italiana (AIMI):** c/o La Biennale di Venezia, Settore Musica, San Marco, Ca Giustinian, 30124 Venice; website aimi.dist.unige.it.

**Associazione Festival Teatrali:** Musicali e Cinematografici (Federfestival), c/o AGIS, via di Villa Patrizi 10, 00161 Rome.

**Associazione Generale Italiana dello Spettacolo (AGIS):** Via di Villa Patrizi 10, 00161 Rome.

**Associazione Internazionale Biblioteche Musicali (AIBM):** Italian Section, c/o Conservatorio Giuseppe Verdi, via Conservatorio 12, 20111 Milan.

**Associazione Internazionale Studi di Canto Gregoriano:** Via Battaglione 58, 26100 Cremona.

**Associazione Italiana Archivi Sonori e Audiovisivi:** c/o Istituto di Ricerca per il Teatro Musicale, via Francesco Tamagno 65, 00168 Rome; tel. 39 066147277; fax 39 066144371; e-mail irtem@mclink.it; website www.irtem.it.

**Associazione Italiana Biblioteche (AIB):** c/o Biblioteca Nazionale, via le Castro Pretorio 105, 00186 Rome.

**Associazione Italiana Degli Editori di Musica (AIDEM):** Via Enrico Tito 4, 20123 Milan.

**Associazione Italiana delle Scuole di Musica:** Villa La Torraccia, via delle Fontanelle 24, 50016 San Domenico di Fiesole (FI).

**Associazione Italiana di Acustica (AIA):** Via Cassia 1216, 00189 Rome.

**Associazione Italiana Operatori Musicali (ASSIOM):** c/o Centro di Ricerca e Sperimentazione per la Didattica Musicale, Villa La Torraccia, via delle Fontanelle 24, 50016 San Domenico di Fiesolo (FI).

**Associazione Italiana per la Musica Sacra S. Cecilia (AISC):** Piazza S. Apollinare 49, 00186 Rome.

**Associazione Italiana Studi di Musicoterapia (AISMt):** Via Brignole De Ferrari 6, 16122 Genoa.

**Associazione Liutariana Italiana (ALI):** Piazza Cavour 5, 26100 Cremona.

**Associazione Nazionale Agenti Teatrali (ANAT):** Via Assietta, 00141 Rome.

**Associazione Nazionale Artisti Lirici Primarii Italiani (ANALPI):** Corso Venezia 61, 20121 Milan.

**Associazione Nazionale Bande Italiane Musicali (AMBIMA):** Via Marianna Dionigi 43, 00193 Rome.

**Associazione Nazionale Critici Musicali:** Via Cardinale Mimmi 32, 70124 Bari.

**Associazione Nazionale delle Cooperative Culturali:** Via dei Alpi 32, 00198 Rome.

**Associazione Nazionale Insegnanti di Danza (ANID):** Via A. Gramsci 36, 00197 Rome.

**Associazione Nazionale Liuteria Artistica Italiana (ANLAI):** Piazza Venezia 11, 00187 Rome.

**Associazione Nazionale Musicisti di Jazz (AMJ):** Via Vallerozzi 77, 53100 Siena.

**Associazione Pro Musica Studium:** Via Ferdinando Martini 23/8, 00137 Rome.

**Centre International de Recherche sur la Presse Musicale (CIRPEM):** Via del Conservatorio 31/B, 43100 Parma.

**Centro di Sonologia Computazionale:** c/o Università di Padova, via San Francesco 11, 35121 Padua.

**Centro di Studi Donizettiani:** c/o Ateneo di Scienze, Lettre ed Arti, via Torquato Tasso 4, 24121 Bergamo.

**Centro di Studi Musicali Ferruccio Busoni:** Piazza della Vittoria 16, 50053 Empoli (F1).

**Centro Internazionale per la Divulgazione della Musica Italiana:** Via Sistina 48, 00187 Rome.

**Centro Internazionale per la Ricerca Strumentale:** Cannaregio 3099, 30121 Venice.

**Centro Studi Giovanni Paisiello:** Via Euclide 15, 74100 Taranto.

**Centro Studi Rinascimento Musicale:** Villa Medicea La Ferdinanda, 50040 Artimino (F1).

**Centro di Studi Spontiniani:** c/o Comune, via Spontini, 60030 Maiolati Spontini (AN).

**CIDIM-National Music Committee of Italy (IMC-UNESCO):** Via Vittoria Colonna 18, 00193 Rome.

**Civico Instituto di Studi Paganiani:** c/o Comune di Genova, Settore Promozione della Città, Via Sottoripa 5, 16124 Genoa; tel. 39 0105574349; fax 39 0105574326; e-mail violinopaganini@comune.genova.it; website www .comune.genova.it.

**Editori Muscali Associati (EMA):** Piazza Liberty 2, 20121 Milan.

**Ente Nazionale Previdenza e Assistenza per i Lavoratori dello Spettacolo:** Viale Regina Margherita 206, 00198 Rome.

**Federazione Industria Musicale Italiana (FIMI):** Via Vittor Pisani 10, 20124 Milan.

**Federazione Informazione Spettacolo (FIS)CISL):** Via Boncompagni 19, 00187 Rome.

**Federazione Italiana dei Compositori de Musica Contemporanea:** Via Cavalieri di Vittorio Veneto 34, 56121 Cascina (PI).

**Federazione Italiana della Musica (FEDERMUSICA):** Via Vittor Piasni 10, 20124 Milan.

**Federazione Italiana Lavoratori informazione e Spettacolo (FILISC-GIL):** Piazza Sallustio 24, 00187 Rome.

**Federazione Italiana Lavoratori Stampa:** Spettacolo, Informazione e Cultura (FILSIC-UIL), via Belisario 7, 00187 Rome.

**Federazione Italiana Tradizioni Popolari (FITP):** Via E. Gattamelata 25, 00176 Rome.

**Federazione Nazionale delle Cooperative Culturali:** Piazza della Libertà, 00192 Rome.

**Federazione Nazionale Italiana delle Associazioni Regionali Corali:** Via Castellana 44, 30174 Venezia Mestre.

**Federazione Nazionale Lavoratori Spettacolo (CISNAL):** Via Principe Amedeo 42, 00185 Rome.

**Fondazione Claudio Monteverdi:** Via Pallavicino 7, 26100 Cremona.

**Fondazione Giacomo Puccini:** c/o Teatro del Giglio, corte San Lorenzo 9, 55100 Lucca.

**Fondazione Giorgio Cini:** Instituti per la Musica, Isola di San Giorgio Maggiore, 30124 Venice.

**Fondazione Giovanni Pierluigi da Palestrina:** Vicolo Pierluigi 3, 0036 Palestrina, Rome.

**Fondazione Rossini:** Piazza Olivieri 5, 61100 Pesaro.

**Fondazione Ugo e Olga Levi:** Centro di Cultura Musicale Superiore, Palazzo Giustinian-Lolin, San Marco 2893, 30124 Venice.

**Fondazione Vincenzo Bellini:** c/o Università degli Studi di Catania, via Biblioteca 13, 95124 Catania.

**Fondo Ottorino Respighi:** c/o Fondazione Giorgio Cini, Isola San Giorgio Maggiore, 30124 Venice.

**International Center of New Musical Sources:** Via Alberto Nota 3, 10122 Turin.

**International Dance Organization (IDO):** Via Bronzino 117, 50142 Florence.

**Istituto di Bibliografia Musicale:** c/o Biblioteca Nazionale, viale Casteo Pretoria 105, 00185 Rome.

**Istituto di Paleografia Musicale:** circonvallazione Casilini 122, 00176 Rome.

**Istituto di Ricerca per il Teatro Musicale:** Via Francesco Tamagno 65, 00168 Rome; tel. 39 066147277; fax 39 066144371; e-mail irtem@mclink.it; website www.irtem.it; Pres.: Carlo Marinelli; f. 1984; non-profit, publicly-financed institute sponsoring research into the fields of musical theatre, 20th century music, ethnomusicology and music-media relations; organizes annual international conference, and adminsters archives.

**Istituto di Studi Organologici:** Via monte Zebio 33, 00195 Rome.

**Istituto di Studi Rinascimentali:** Palazzo Paradiso, via delle Scienze 17, 44100 Ferrrara.

**Istituto Internazionale Luigi Cherubini:** Via Giovanni Secchi 3, 00136 Rome.

**Istituto Italiano Antonio Vivaldi:** c/o Fondazione Giorgio Cini, Isola di San Giorgio Maggiore, 30124 Venice; tel. 041 2710220; fax 041 5238540; e-mail vivaldi@cini.it; Dir Dr Francesco Fanna.

**Istituto Italiano per la Storia della Musica:** Via Vittoria 6, 00187 Rome.

**Istituto Mutualistico tra Artisti Interpreti Esecutori (IMAIE):** Via Piave 66, 00187 Rome.

**Istituto Nazionale di Studi Verdiani:** Strada della Repubblica 56, 43100 Parma.

**Istituto di Studi Pucciniani:** Piazza Buonarroti 29, 20149 Milan.

**Pontificio Instituto Ambrosiano di Musica Sacra:** Viala Gorizia 5, 20144 Milan.

**Pontificio Instituto di Musica Sacra:** Via di Torre Rossa 21, 001165 Rome.

**Sindacato Musicisti Italiani (SMI):** Via Goito 39, 00185 Rome.

**Sindacato Nazionale Instruzione Artistica:** Via Antonio Pio 40, 00145 Rome.

**Sindacato Nazionale Musicisti (SNM):** Via Pinelli 100, 10144 Turin.

**Società Italiana degli Autori ed Editori (SIAE):** Via le della Letteratura 30, 00144 Rome; website www.siae.it.

**Società Italiana della Viola da Gamba:** Via dei Servi 51, 50122 Florence.

**Società Italiana di Etnomusicologia (SIE):** c/o Centro Flog Tradizioni Popolari, via Maestri del Lavoro 1, 50134 Florence.

**Società Italiana di Musicologia (SldM):** Via Galliera 3, 40125 Bologna.

**Società Italiana Musica Contemporanea (SIMC):** Via F. Juvara 11, 21029 Milan.

**Società Italiana per l'Educazione Musicale (SIEM):** Via Guerrazzi 20, 40125 Bologna.

**UNION-Operatori Indipendenti:** c/o I Soluzionisti, via Trionfale 85, 00136 Rome.

**Unione Folclorica Italiana (UFI):** Via Mazzini 22, 33081 Aviano (PN).

**Unione Nazionale Arte Musica Spettacolo (UNAMS):** Viale delle Provincie 18, 00162 Rome.

**Unione Nazionale Editori di Musica Italiani (UNEMI):** Via Teulada 52, 00195 Rome.

## Japan

**Concert Managers Association of Japan:** Mitoko Building, 6-2-4 Akasaka, Minato-ku, Tokyo 107; Chair. Naoyasu Kajimoto.

**Electronic Industries Association of Japan:** Tokyo Shoko Kaigisho Building, 3-2-2 Marunouchi, Chiyoda-ku, Tokyo 100; Chair. Dr Tadahiro Sekimoto.

**Japan Audio Society:** Mori Building, 1-14-34 Jingumae, Tokyo 150; Sec.-Gen. Sho Nagasawa.

**Japan Conductors Association:** 4-18-20 Ogikubo Suginami-ku, Tokyo 167; Pres. Takashi Asahina.

**Japan International League of Artists:** 2-3-16-607 Shinjuku, Shinjuku-ku, Tokyo 160; Chief Officer Kazuhiko Hattori.

**Japanese Composers Society:** Ogawa Building, 3-7-15 Akasaka, Mina-toku, Tokyo 107.

**Japanese Society for Rights of Authors, Composers and Publishers:** 1-7-13 Nishishimbashi, Minato-ku, Tokyo 105.

**Music for Youth Inc:** Kowa Building, No. 24, 3-1-1 Roppongi, Minato-ku, Tokyo 106; Pres. Eloise Cunningham.

**Recording Industry Association of Japan:** 2-8-9 Tsukiji, Chuo-ku, Tokyo 104.

## Republic of Korea

**Asian Composers League (Korean Committee):** PO Box 874, Seoul 110-062; Dir Sung-Jae Lee.

**Federation of Artistic and Cultural Organizations of Korea:** 1-117 Dongsoong-dong, Chongro-ku, Seoul.

**Jeunesses Musicales of Korea:** PO Box 10980, Seoul.

**Korean Cultural Foundation Inc:** 25 Neung-Dong, Sung-ku, Seoul 133-180; Dir No Hi Pak.

**Music Association of Korea:** 1-117 Dongsoong-dong, Chongro-ku, Seoul; Pres. Sang-Hyun Cho.

## Luxembourg

**Luxemburger Gesellschaft für Neue Musik:** PO Box 828, 2018 Luxembourg; Pres. Marcel Wengler.

**Union Grand-Duc Adolphe:** 2 rue Sosthène Weis, 2722 Luxembourg.

## Macao

**Instituto Cultural de Macao:** Rua Pedro Coutinho 27, Third Floor, Macao.

## Mexico

**Asociación Mexicana de Productores de Fonogramas y Videogramas AC:** Francisco Petrarca 223-503, Chapultepec Morales, 11560 México.

**Juventudes Musicales de México:** Santisimo 25, San Angel, 01000 México 20, DF.

**Sociedad de Autores y Compositores de Música SA (SACM):** San Felipe 143, Col. General Anaya, 03330 México, DF.

## Netherlands

**BUMA (Composers Rights Society):** Prof. E. M. Meijerslaan 3, 1183 AV Amsterdam; website www.bumastemra.nl; Chief Officer: G. P. Willemsen.

**CNM (Center for Netherlands Music):** PO Box 1634, 1200 PB Hilversum; Chief Officer: J W ten Broeke.

**Foundation Gaudeamus (Center of Contemporary Music):** Swammer-damstraast 38, 1091 RV Amsterdam; Dir Henk Heuvelmans.

**Gentootschap van Nederlandse (Society of Netherlands Composers):** Prof. E. M. Meijerslaan 3, 1183 AV Amsterdam; Pres. Gilius van Bergejik.

**International Society for Contemporary Music (Netherlands Section):** Swammerdamstraat 38, 1091 RV Amsterdam; Pres. H. Reiziger.

**Jeugd en Musiek Nederland:** Roemer Visscherstraat 42, 1054 EZ Amsterdam; Pres. Jur Naessens.

**Katholieke Dirigenten en Organisten Vereniging—KDOV:** Donkere Begijnhof 5, 2011 HG Haarlem; e-mail gemcoe@cs.com; Sec.: Gemma Coebergh.

**Koninklijke Nederlandse Toonkunstenaars Vereniging:** Keizersgracht 480, 1017 EG Amsterdam; Chief Officer H. Luif.

**KNTV:** Keizersgracht 480, 1017 EG Amsterdam; tel. 31 020 5221020; fax 31 20 6200229.

**Muziek Groep Nederland:** Paulus Potterstraat 14, 1071 CZ Amsterdam; tel. 31 20 3058900; fax 31 20 6733588; e-mail info@muziekgroep.nl; website www.muziekgroep.nl.

**NTB (Nederlandse Toonkunstenaars Bond):** Herengracht 272, 1016 BW Amsterdam.

**Nederlandse Vereniging van Grammofoondetallhandelaren:** Die Noord 3, 1452 PS Ilpendam; Chair. J. F. T. Hotzenbosch.

**Netherlands Committee of the International Music Council:** Ruben-slaan 200, 3582 JJ Utrecht.

**Netherlands Theater Institute:** PO Box 19304, 1000 GH Amsterdam; Chief Officer Ton Offerman.

**STEMRA (Mechanical Rights Society):** Prof. E. M. Meijerslaan 3, 1183 AV Amsterdam; website www.bumastemra.nl; Chief Officer: G. P. Willemsem.

**Stichting Contactorgaan Electronische Muziek:** Swammerdamstraat 38, 1091 RV Amsterdam; Chief Officer Henk Heuvelmans.

**Stichting voor Kamermuziek:** Sijzenlaan 6, 2566 WG The Hague.

**Vereniging voor Nederlandse Muziekgeschiedenis:** PO Box 1514, 3500 BM Utrecht.

## New Zealand

**Australasian Performing Right Association Ltd (APRA):** PO Box 6315, 92 Parnell Road, Auckland 1; website www.apra.co.nz; Gen. Man. Bernie Darby.

**Composers Association of New Zealand:** PO Box 4065, Wellington; Pres. Denise Hulford.

**Music for Youth:** 26 Patanga Crescent, Wellington 6001; Chair. Beverley Wakem.

**Music Trades Association (NZ) Inc:** PO Box 386, Auckland; Exec. Officer Dean Reynolds.

**New Zealand Composers Foundation:** PO Box 633, Wellington; Chair. Ashley Heenan.

**New Zealand Music Centre Ltd:** SOUNZ New Zealand, PO Box 102, The Terrace, Wellington; Exec. Dir Nicholas McBryde.

**New Zealand Musicians Union:** 35–39 George Street, Kingsland, Auckland; tel. 09 375 2680; fax 09 375 2681; Sec. Peter Shannon.

**Phonographic Performances (New Zealand) Ltd:** PO Box 9241, Wellington; Gen. Man. Tony Chance.

**Queen Elizabeth II Arts Council of New Zealand:** PO Box 3806, Wellington; Dir Peter Quin.

**Recording Industry Association of New Zealand Inc:** 11 York Street, PO Box 37442 Parnell, Auckland; tel. 64 9 3080510; fax 64 9 3064977; website www.rianz.org.nz; Chief Exec. Terence O'Neill.

**Service Workers Union:** Musicians Division, Private Bag 68-914, Newton, Auckland; Sec. Peter Shannon.

## Norway

**International Music Council (National Committee):** c/o Statens Musikk-rad, Toftesgate 69, 0552 Oslo.

**International Society for Contemporary Music (Norwegian Section):** c/o Ny Musikk, Toftesgate 69, 0552 Oslo.

**Jeunesses Musicales (Norwegian Section):** c/o Landslaget Musikk i Skolen, Toftesgate 69, 0552 Oslo.

**Landslaget Musikk i Skolen (Youth and Music):** Toftesgate 69, 0552 Oslo.

**New Music (Ny Musikk):** Toftesgate 69, 0552 Oslo.

**NASOL (Norwegian Association of Symphony Orchestras):** Toftesgate 69, 0552 Oslo.

**Norsk Tonekunstnersamfund (Norwegian Association of Musical Artists):** Bogstadvn 66, 0366 Oslo.

**Norwegian Archives for Folk and Popular Songs:** Toftesgate 69, 0552 Oslo.

**Norwegian Cultural Council:** Militaerhospitalet, PO Box 101, Sentrum, 0102 Oslo.

**Norwegian Music Information Centre:** Toftesgate 69, 0552 Oslo; Man. Jostein Simble.

**Norwegian Musicians' Union:** Youngsgate 11, 0181 Oslo; Pres. Tore Nordvik.

**Norwegian Society of Composers:** PO Box 9171, Grønland, 0134 Oslo; tel. 47 22 05 72 00; fax 47 22 05 72 50; e-mail tono@tono.no; website www.tono.no.

**Norwegian Song and Music Council:** Toftesgate 69, 0552 Oslo.

**Rikskonsertene (Norwegian State Travelling Concerts Organization):** PO Box 7613, Skillebekk, 0205, Oslo.

## Paraguay

**Juventudes Musicales:** c/o Saul Gaona, RI 3 Corrales 516, Asunción.

**Sociedad Filarmónica de Asunción:** Mexico 145 (Estación del Ferrocarril), Asunción; Chair. Luis Szaran.

## Peru

**Asociación Peruana de Autores y Compositores (APDAYC):** Avda Petit Thouars No. 5038, Miraflores, Lima 18; website www.apdayc.pe; Chair. Armando Masse.

**Juventudes Musicales:** Garcilaso de la Vega 1746, Lima 14; Pres. Oscar Zamora.

## Philippines

**Andres Bobifacio Music Foundation:** Union Village, Tandang Sora, Quezon City.

**Choral Conductors Association of the Philippines:** c/o University of the Philippines, College of Music, Quezon City.

**Eliseo Pajaro Foundation Inc:** c/o Cultural Center of the Philippines, Roxas Blvd, Manila.

**Filipino Society of Composers, Authors and Publishers (FILSCAP):** 308 RCBC Building, Buendia Extension, Makati, Metro Manila.

**Kodály Society of the Philippines:** c/o St Paul's College, Herran Street, Manila.

**League of Filipino Composers:** c/o Cultural Center of the Philippines, Roxas Blvd, Manila.

**Music Theater Foundation:** c/o University of the Philippines, College of Music, Diliman, Quezon City.

**Musika:** 9-A Manga Road, New Manila, Quezon City.

**National Music Council of the Philippines:** c/o University of the Philippines, College of Music, Diliman, Quezon City.

**Organisasyon ng Pilipinong Mang-aawit (OPM):** Zeta Building, Suite 65, 191 Salcedo Street, Legaspi Village, Makati, Metro Manila.

**Piano Teachers' Guild of the Philippines:** c/o St Scholasticas's College, Leon Guinto, Malate, Manila.

**Philippine Musicians Guild:** 409 Unlad Condominium, Taft Avenue and General Malvar Street, Malate, Manila.

**Philippine Society for Music Education:** c/o Philippine Normal College, Music and Arts Department, Taft Avenue, Manila.

**Samahan ng mga Manunuri at Manunulat ng Musika sa Pilipinas (SAMMPI):** Aurora Pijuan Street, Blvd 5, Lot 1, BF Resort Village, Pamplona, Las Pinas, Metro Manila.

**University of the Philippines Musical Arts and Research Management Inc:** University of the Philippines, College of Music, Abelardo Hall, Diliman, Quezon City.

## Poland

**Association of Polish Violin Makers:** Krakowskie Przedmie cie 16/18, 00-325 Warsaw.

**Chopin Society of Music:** Okólnik 1, 00-368 Warsaw.

**Jeunesses Musicales de Pologne:** ul. Hoza 50–51, 00-682 Warsaw; tel. 48 22 6254984; fax 48 22 6255810.

**Karol Szymanowski Music Association:** 34-500 Zakopane, Willa Atma, ul. Kasprusie 1; tel. and fax 48 18 2014554.

**Polish Composers' Union:** Rynek Starego Miasta 27, 00-272 Warsaw; tel. and fax 48 22 8311741; e-mail zkp@zkp.org.pl; website www.zkp.org.pl; Pres.: Jerzy Kornowicz.

**Polish Composers' Union, Musicological Section:** Rynek Starego Miasta 27, 00-272 Warsaw; tel. and fax 48 22 8311741; e-mail zkp@zkp.org.pl; website www.zkp.org.pl; Pres.: Katarzyna Dadak-Kozicka.

**Polish Music Information Centre:** Rynek Starego Miasta 27, 00-272 Warsaw; tel. 48 22 8311634; fax 48 22 8310607; e-mail polmic@polmic.pl; website www.polmic.pl; Dir: Mieczyslaw Kominek.

**Polish Union of Artist Violin Makers:** ul. Krakowskie Przedm. 16–18, 00-325 Warsaw; tel. and fax 48 22 826 71 52; Dir Anna Kucharska.

**Society of Authors ZAIKS:** Hipoteczna 2, 00-092 Warsaw; Gen. Man. Witold Kolodziejski.

**Society of Music Education:** Koszykowa 24/7a, 00-553 Warsaw; Pres. Adrianna Poniecka-Piekutowska.

**Society of Polish Librarians:** Music Libraries Section, c/o Warszawskie Towarzystwo Muzyczne, Bibliotéka Zakroczymska 2, 00-225 Warsaw.

**Society of Polish Musicians:** Krucza 24–26, 00-526 Warsaw.

**Szymanowski Society of Music:** Kasprusie 19, willa Atma, 34-500 Zakopane.

**Union of Polish Lyric Writers and Composers of Light Music ZAKR:** Hipoteczna 2, 00-092 Warsaw.

**Warsaw Music Society:** Morskie Oko 2, 02-511 Warsaw.

**Wieniawski Society of Music:** Sweitos awska 7, 61-840 Poznań.

## Portugal

**Fundaçâo Calouste Gulbenkian:** Serviço de Música, Avda de Berna 45a, 1067-001 Lisbon; tel. 351 21 782 3000; fax 351 21 782 3041; e-mail musica@gulbenkian.pt; Dir of Music Dept: Luis Pereira Leal.

**Juventude Musical Portuguesa:** Rua Rosa Araujo 6, Third Floor, 1200 Lisbon; Pres. Miguel Henriques.

**Sindicato dos Músicos:** Avda D. Carlos I 72, Second Floor, 1200 Lisbon.

**Sociedade Portuguesa de Autores (SPA):** Avda Dugue de Louié 31, 1098 Lisbon Codex; Pres. Luis Francisco Rebelo.

## Romania

**Jeunesses Musicales:** Str Lipscani 53, Bucharest.

**Union of Romanian Composers and Musicologists:** Calea Victoriei 141, Sector 1, 70149 Bucharest; tel. 40 21 2127966; fax 40 21 2107211; e-mail ucmr@itcnet.ro; Pres.: Prof. Dr Adrian Iorgucescu.

## Russia

**Intercultcentre (International Center for Festivals and Competitions):** Arbat Str 35, 121835 Moscow; Dir Gen. Suren Shaumian.

**International Union of Musicians:** ul Gertsena 14/2, 103009 Moscow; Pres. Irina Arkhipova.

**State Academic Mariinsky Theatre:** Teatralnaya Square 1, 190000, St Petersburg; tel. 812 1143039; fax 812 2141744; Artistic and Gen. Dir Katia Sirakanian.

**Union of Composers of Russia:** Brusov Pereulok 8–10, 103009 Moscow; Chair. V Kazenin.

**VAAP (Russian Copyright Agency):** ul Bolshaia Bronnaia 6A, GSP K 104, 103670 Moscow.

## Serbia and Montenegro

**International Society for Contemporary Music (Yugoslav section):** PO Box 213, 11000 Belgrade.

**Union of Yugoslav Composers:** Misarska 12–14, 11000 Belgrade.

**Yugoslav Music Information Center of Sokoj:** Misarska 12–14, 11 000 Belgrade; tel. and fax 381 11 3245 192; Dir Ana Koievska.

## Singapore

**Musicians and Singers Association:** Block 3, 03-628, Rochor Centre, Rochor Road, Singapore 0718; Chief Officer Stephen Gomez.

**National Arts Council:** PSA Building, 35th Storey, 460 Alexandria Road, Singapore 0511.

## Slovakia

**Music Centre Slovakia:** Michalská 10, 815 36 Bratislava 1; tel. (2) 5920-4811; fax (2) 5443-0379; e-mail hc@hc.sk; website www.hc.sk; Dir Olga Smetanová.

**Slovak Music Association:** Afárikova nám 4, 811 02 Bratislava.

**Slovak Music Fund:** Fucikova 29, 811 02 Bratislava.

**Slovak Music Union:** Michalská 10, 815 36 Bratislava.

**Slovkoncert (Slovak Artistic and Publicity Agency):** Michalská 10, 815 36 Bratislava.

## South Africa

**Association of the South African Music Industry:** 150 Hendrils Verwoerb Drive, Frn Republic Road, Johannesburg; Chief Exec. Des Dubery; Gen. Man. Nhlamhla Sibisi.

**Dramatic, Artistic, and Literary Rights Organization Ltd (DALRO):** PO Box 9292, Johannesburg; Man. Dir Gideon Ross.

**Foundation for the Creative Arts:** PO Box 91122, Auckland Park 2006; Exec. Man. Herman Van Niekerk.

**Recording Industry of South Africa:** PO Box 367, Randburg 2194; tel. 27 11 886 1342; fax 27 11 886 4169; website www.risa.org.za

**South African Music Rights Organization Ltd (SAMRO):** 73 Juta Street, Braamfontein, Johannesburg 2001; tel. 011 489 5000; fax 011 403 1934; Man. Dir Gideon Ross; CEO Rob Hooijer.

**South African Recording Rights Association Ltd (SARRAL):** PO Box 4378, Johannesburg 2000; Chief Officer George Hardie.

**South African Society of Music Teachers:** PO Box 5318, Walmer 6065.

## Spain

**Asociación Cultural Laboratorio de Interpretación Musical (LIM):** Seco 12, 28007 Madrid; Pres. Jesús Villa Rojo.

**Asociación de Música en Compostela:** Pablo Aranda 6, 28006 Madrid; Pres. Margarita Pastor Zacharias.

**Centro Para la Difusión de la Música Contemporánea:** Santa Isabel 52, 28012 Madrid; Dir Tomas Marco.

**Direccion General de Música y Teatro:** Ministerio de Cultura, Paso del Rey 1, 28071 Madrid.

**International Society for Contemporary Music (Spanish Section):** Avda de America 58-5, 28028 Madrid; Sec.-Gen. José Maria Franco Gil.

**Instituto de Bibliografica Musical:** penulas 12, 12p 28071 Madrid; Pres. Jacinto Torres Mulas.

**Joventuts Musical de Barcelona:** Pau Claris 139, Fourth Floor, 1a, 08009 Barcelona.

**Juventudes Musicales:** Girona 10, 3, Barcelona.

**Sociedad de Conciertos:** Altamira 3, 03002 Alicante; Dir Margarita Berenger.

**Sociedad Española de Musicologia (SEM):** Canos del Peral 7, 28013 Madrid; Pres. Ismael Fernández de la Cuesta.

**Sociedad General de Autores de España (SGAE):** Fernando VI 4, 28004 Madrid; tel. 34 913 499 550; fax 34 913 499 500; website www.sgae.es; Pres. Manuel Gutierrez Aragón

## Sweden

**International Society for Contemporary Music (Swedish Section):** c/o FST, PO Box 27327, 102 54 Stockholm.

**Society of Music Teachers in Sweden:** c/o Nordstedt, Otroftagatan 37, 216 20 Malmö.

**Society of Swedish Church Musicians:** c/o S. Henriksson, Storgatan 36, 520 40 Floby.

**Society of Swedish Composers:** PO Box 27327, 102 54 Stockholm; Chair. Sten Melin.

**Sveriges Orkesterförbund (Association of Swedish Orchestras):** Stockholm; website www.orkester.nu; f. 1999; represents some 327 orchestras; Gen. Man.: Magnus Eriksson

**Swedish Artists and Musicians Interest Organization:** Mosebacke Torg 16, 116 20 Stockholm.

**Swedish Choral Association:** PO Box 38014, 100 64 Stockholm.

**Swedish Music Information Center:** PO Box 27327, 102 54 Stockholm; Dir Roland Sandberg.

**Swedish Musicians' Union:** PO Box 49144, 100 29 Stockholm; Chair. Roland Almlén.

**Swedish Performing Rights Society:** PO Box 27327, 102 54 Stockholm; tel. 46 8 783 88 00; fax 46 8 662 62 75; website www.stim.se; Dir Gunnar Petri.

**Swedish Piano Teachers Association:** Solbacken 9, 131 42 Nacka.

**Swedish Society for Musicology:** c/o Statens Musiksamlingar, PO Box 16326, 103 26 Stockholm.

**Swedish Society of Light Music Composers:** PO Box 27327, 102 54 Stockholm.

**Swedish Union of Professional Musicians:** Drottninggatan 55, 111 21 Stockholm.

## Switzerland

**Association of Concert Giving Societies of Switzerland:** Münsterplatz 18, 4051 Basel.

**Association of Swiss Musicians:** Avenue du Grammont 11 bis, PO Box 177, 1000 Lausanne 13; Gen. Sec. Hélène Petitpierre.

**European Association of Amateur Orchestras:** Heimstrasse 24, 3018 Berne; tel. and fax 0041 319912270; Vice-Pres.: Kathi Engel Pignolo.

**European Association of Music Festivals:** 120B, rue de Lausanne, 1202 Geneva; Sec. Dr Henry Siegwart.

**Federation of International Music Competitions:** 104 rue de Carouge, 1205 Geneva.

**Gesellschaft der Freunde alter Musikinstrumente:** Mühlebachstrasse 174, 8008 Zürich.

**Goethe Foundation of Arts and Sciences:** Münstergasse 9, 8001 Zürich.

**International Federation of Musicians:** Hofackerstrasse 7, 8032 Zürich.

**International Music Council (National Committee):** Bahnhofstrasse 78, 5000 Aarau.

**International Musicological Society:** PO Box 1561, 4001 Basel.

**International Society for Contemporary Music:** Association of Swiss Musicians, Avenue du Grammont 11 bis, PO Box 177, 1000 Lausanne 13.

**Jeunesses Musicales de Suisse:** rue Merle d'Aubigné 25, 1207 Geneva.

**National Association of Orchestras:** Wattenwylweg 30, 3006 Bern.

**National Association of Singers:** Burgstrasse 1, 4143 Dornach.

**National Music Association:** 3946 Turtmann.

**Performing Right Society of Switzerland (SUISA):** Bellariastrasse 82, 8038 Zürich.

**Romand Centre of Sacred Music:** PO Box 204, Champel, 1211 Geneva.

**Schweiz Chorvereinigung:** Scheuchzerstrasse 14, 8006 Zürich.

**SUISA Music Foundation (Music Information Centre):** Passage Maxmililien-de-Meuron 4, PO Box 409, 2001 Neuchâtel; website www.suisa.se; Man. Dir P. Liechti.

**SUISA Swiss Society for Rights of Authors of Musical Works:** Bellariastrasse 82, PO Box 782, 8038, Zurich; tel. 41 1 4856666; fax 41 1 4824333; website www.suisa.se.

**Swiss Association for Concert Managers:** 7 rue de la Fontaine, 1204 Geneva; Sec. and Pres. Jack Yfar.

**Swiss Association for Church Singing:** Hirschengraben 50, PO Box, 8025 Zürich.

**Swiss Association of Mixed Choirs:** Rainallee 68, 4125 Riehen.

**Swiss Association of Professional Conductors:** Stutzstrasse 9, 8834 Schindellegi.

**Swiss Association of Professional Musicians:** Elisabethenstrasse 2, 4051 Basel.

**Swiss Music Council:** Haus der Musik, Gönhardweg 32, 5000 A A RAU; tel. 41 62 822 9423; fax 41 62 822 9407.

**Swiss Music Education Association:** Forchstrasse 376, 8008 Zürich.

**Swiss Music Interpreters Society:** Mittelstrasse 49, 8008 Zürich.

**Swiss Music Teachers Association:** Forchstrasse 376, 8008 Zürich.

**Swiss Society of Music Teachers:** Alpstrasse 34, 6020 Emmenbrücke.

**Swiss Society for Musical Research:** PO Box 231, 4020 Basel.

**Swiss Society for Popular Music:** c/o SUISA, Bellariastrasse 82, 8038 Zürich.

**Swiss Workers' Music Association:** PO Box 29, 3000 Bern 9.

**World Federation of International Music Competitions:** rue de Carouge 104, 1205 Geneva; tel. 41 22 321 36 20; fax 41 22 781 14 18.

## United Kingdom

**Alkan Society:** 21 Heronswood, Salisbury, Wiltshire SP2 8DH; website www .alkansociety.org; Hon. Sec. Peter Grove.

**Amateur Music Association:** Medlock School, Wadeson Road, Manchester M13 9UR; Gen. Sec. Ian Clarke.

**Arts Council of Great Britain:** 2 Pear Tree Court, London EC1R 0DS; tel. 020 7608 6100; fax 020 7608 4100; e-mail enquiries@artscouncil.co.uk; website www.artscouncil.org.uk; Sec.-Gen. Anthony Everitt.

**Association for the Advancement of Teacher Education in Music:** 16 Ullswater Ave, Cardiff CF2 5PT; Chair. Dr William Salaman.

**Association of British Choral Directors:** 15 Granville Way, Sherborne, Dorset DT9 4AS; tel. 01935 389482; fax 0870 128 4085; website www.abcd.org .uk; Gen. Sec. Rachel Greaves.

**Association for British Music:** 2 Union Place, Boston, Lincolnshire PE21 6PS; Hon. Sec. Estelle Stiles.

**Association of British Orchestras:** 8 Gerrard Street, London W1D 5PJ; tel. 020 7287 0333; fax 020 7287 0444; e-mail info@abo.org.uk; website www.abo .org.uk; Dir Russell Jones.

**Association for Business Support of the Arts:** 2 Chester Street, London SW1X 7BB; Dir Colin Tweedy.

**Association of Entertainment and Arts Management:** 3a–5a Stanley Street, Southport, Merseyside PR9 0BY; Gen. Sec. J. B. A. Sharples.

**Association of Teachers of Singing:** Weir House, 108 Newton Road, Burton-on-Trent, Staffs DE15 0TT; tel. and fax 01283 542198; website www .aotos.co.uk; Membership Sec. Coral Gould.

**Association of Woodwind Teachers:** Hilltop, Gravel Hill, Chartham Hatch, Canterbury, Kent CT4 7NH; tel. 01227 730923; website www.awt .org.uk; Sec. Sheila Wyver.

**Audio Engineering Society Ltd (British Section):** PO Box 645, Slough SL1 8BJ; tel. (1628) 663725; fax (1628) 667002; website www.aes.org.

**Bantock Society:** 48 Ravenswood Road, Redland, Bristol BS6 6BT; tel. 0117 924 0506; website www.musicweb.uk.net/bantock; Chair. Ron Bleach.

**Barbirolli Society:** 2 Cedar Close, Uttoxeter, Staffs ST14 7NP; Chair. Pauline Pickering.

**Benslow Instrument Loan Scheme:** Little Benslow Hills, Benslow Lane, Hitchin, Hertfordshire SG4 9RB; tel. (1462) 420748; fax (1462) 440171; e-mail loanscheme@benslow.org; website www.benslow.org; Man. Liz Clark; Development Co-ordinator Clare Talbot; high quality string/woodwind instruments loaned to talented young players and students who cannot afford the calibre of instrument needed for further development.

**Benslow Music Trust:** Little Benslow Hills, Benslow Lane, Hitchin, Hertfordshire SG4 9RB; tel. (1462) 459446; fax (1462) 440171; e-mail info@ benslow.org; website www.benslow.org; Chief Exec. Lisa J. Railton; Dir of Music David Matthews; year-round residential and day music courses for adult amateur musicians of all ages and standards; also puts on concerts and has facilities for hire.

**Boughton Trust:** 14–15 Craven Street, London WC2N 5AD; tel. 020 7925 0303.

**Bowen Society:** Cairnbield, Gordon, Berwickshire; Chair. John Lindsay.

**Brighton and Hove Philharmonic Society:** 50 Grand Parade, Brighton, BN2 2QA; tel. 01273 622900; fax 01273 697887; website www.brightonphil.org .uk.

**British-American Arts Association:** Third Floor, 116–118 Commercial Street, London E1 6NF; tel. 020 7247 5385; Dir Jennifer Williams.

**British Arts Festivals Association:** Third Floor, Whitechapel Library, 77 Whitechapel High Street, London E1 7QX; Co-ordinator Gwyn Rhydderch.

**British Association of Symphonic Bands and Wind Ensembles (BASBWE):** 12 Wilshaw House, Creekside, Deptford, London SE8 4SF; website www.basbwe.org; Sec. Samuel Becker.

**British Broadcasting Corporation (BBC):** Broadcasting House, London W1A 1AA; website www.bbc.co.uk.

**British Copyright Council:** 29–33 Berners Street, London W1T 3AB; website www.britishcopyright.org.uk; Sec. Geoffrey Adams.

**British Council:** Arts Group, 10 Spring Gardens, London SW1A 2BN; tel. 020 7389 3194; fax 020 7389 3199; e-mail artweb@britishcouncil.org; website www2.britishcouncil.org; Dept of Music Dir John Acton.

**British Federation of Audio (BFA) Ltd:** PO Box 365, Farnham, Surrey GU10 2BD; tel. 01428 714616; fax 01428 717599.

**British Federation of Brass Bands (BFBB):** Unit 12, Maple Estate, Stocks Lane, Barnsley S75 2BL; tel. 01226 771015; website www.bfbb.co.uk; Registry and Office Man. Colin Johnson.

**British Federation of Music Festivals:** Festivals House, 198 Park Lane, Macclesfield, Cheshire SK11 6UD; tel. 01625 428297; fax 01625 503229; Sec. Eileen Craine.

**British Flute Society:** 41 Devon Avenue, Twickenham, Middlesex TW2 6PN; tel. 020 8241 7572; e-mail secretary@bfs.org.uk; website www.bfs.org .uk; Contact Julie Wright.

**British Horn Society:** c/o Paxman Ltd, 116 Long Acre, London WC2E 9PA; website www.british-horn.org; Contact Mike Fage.

**British Institute of Organ Studies:** 39 Church Street, Haslingfield, Cambridge, CB3 7JE; tel. 01223 872190; website www.bios.org.uk; Sec. Jose Hopkins.

**British Kodály Society:** 31 Woodlands Road, London SW13 0JZ.

**British Music Information Centre (BMIC):** 10 Stratford Place, London W1C 1BA; tel. 020 7499 8567; fax 020 7499 4795; e-mail info@bmic.co.uk; website www.bmic.co.uk; Man. Elizabeth Yeoman.

**British Music Society:** 8b Melton Drive, Hunstanton, PE36 5DD; tel. (1485) 534282; e-mail david.burnett@btinternet.com; Hon. Sec.: David Burnett.

**British Phonographic Industry (BPI) Ltd:** Riverside Building, County Hall, Westminster Bridge Road, London SE1 7JA; tel. 020 7803 1300; fax 020 7803 1310; e-mail general@bpi.co.uk; website www.bpi.co.uk; Dir-Gen. John Deacon.

**British Society for Electronic Music:** 277 Putney Bridge Road, London SW15 2PT; Sec. Dr Peter Zinovieff.

**British Suzuki Institute:** 39 High Street, Wheathampstead, St Albans, Herts AL4 8BB; tel. (1582) 832424; fax (1582) 834488; e-mail bsi@suzukimusic .force9.co.uk; website www.britishsuzuki.com; CEO: Landa Melrose.

**Cathedral Organists' Association:** Cleveland Lodge, Westhumble, Dorking, Surrey, RH5 6BW; tel. 01306 872800; fax 01306 887260; e-mail coa@rscm .com; Hon. Sec. Prof. John Harper.

**Celfyddydau Cymru (Arts Council of Wales):** 9 Museum Place, Cardiff CF10 3NX; tel. 02920 376500; fax 02920 221447; website www.artswales.org; Senior Arts Development Officer, Music Simon Lovell-Jones.

**Choir Schools' Association:** Westminster Cathedral Choir School, Ambros- den Avenue, London SW1P 1QH; website www.choirschools.org.uk; Hon. Sec. P. Hannigan.

**City of London Society of Organists:** Hill House, 17 Hans Place, London SW1X 0EP; Chair. and Sec. Richard Townend.

**Clarinet and Saxophone Society of Great Britain:** 15 Springwell, Ingleton, Co Durham, DL2 3JJ; Membership Sec. Susan Moss.

**Concert Artistes' Association:** 20 Bedford Street, London WC2E 9HP; tel. 020 7836 3172; Sec. Jo Palmer.

**Critics' Circle:** 51 Vartry Road, London N15 6PS; e-mail info@criticscircle .org.uk; website www.criticscircle.org.uk; Sec. Peter Hepple.

**Crotch Society:** 74 Pembroke Road, London W8 6NX; Sec. Jonathan Rennert.

**Dalcroze Society (UK) Inc:** 100 Elborough Street, London SW18 5DL; tel. 020 8870 1986; e-mail admin@dalcroze.org.uk; Chair. Ruth Stewart.

**Delius Society:** 21 Woodlands Drive, Brooklands, Sale, Cheshire M33 3PQ; tel. (161) 2823654; website www.delius.org.uk; Sec.: Ann Dixon.

**Delius Trust:** 16 Ogle Street, London W1W 6JA; tel. (20) 7436-4816; fax (20) 7637-4307; website www.delius.org.uk; Chair. David Lloyd-Jones; Sec. Marjorie Dickinson.

**Dolmetsch Concertante:** Lower Flat, 6 Junction Place, Haslemere, Surrey GU27 1LE; Sec. Pat Dutton.

**Donizetti Society:** 56 Harbut Road, London SW11 2RB; website www .donizettisociety.com; Hon. Sec. J. R. Carter.

**Dvořák Society:** 32 Glebe Way, Burnham-on-Crouch, Essex CM0 8QJ; Sec. Shawn Pullman.

**Early Music Centre Ltd:** Charles Clore House, 17 Russell Square, London WC1B 5DR; Admin. Frederik Martin.

**Electro-Acoustic Music Association of Great Britain:** 10 Stratford Place, London W1N 9AE; Admin. Charol Butler.

**Elgar Society:** 20 Geraldine Road, Malvern, Worcs WR14 3PA; website www .elgar.org.

**English Folk Dance and Song Society (EFDSS):** 2 Regents Park Road, London NW1 7AY; tel. 020 7485 2206; website www.efdss.org; Man. Dir Brenda Godrich.

**European Piano Teachers' Association (UK) Ltd:** Archpool House, High Street, Handcross, Haywards Heath, W Sussex, RH17 6BJ; tel. 01444 400852; fax 01444 401443; Chair. Frank Martin.

**European String Teachers' Association (ESTA):** 10 Swanns Meadow, Bookham, Leatherhead, Surrey KT23 4JX; website www.estaweb.org.uk; Sec. Leonie Anderson.

**Federation of Master Organ Builders:** Petersfield GU32 3AT; Sec. D. M. van Heck.

**Federation of Recorded Music Societies Ltd:** c/o The Secretary, 67 Galleys Bank, Whitehill, Kidsgrove, Staffs ST7 4DE; Sec. M. Williamson.

**Fellowship of Makers and Researchers of Historical Instruments:** London Guildhall University, 41–71 Commercial Road, London E1 1LA; tel. 020 7320 1841; fax 020 7320 1830; e-mail ljones@lgu.ac.uk; Hon. Sec. Lewis Jones.

**Galpin Society:** 37 Townsend Drive, St Albans, Herts AL3 5RF; Admin. Maggie Kilbey.

**Gilbert and Sullivan Society:** 273 Northfield Avenue, London W5 4UA.

**Percy Grainger Society:** 6 Fairfax Crescent, Aylesbury, Bucks HP20 2ES; tel. and fax 01296 428609/581185; website www.percygrainger.org.uk; Sec. Barry P. Ould.

**Guild of Professional Musicians:** 48 Chalcot Road, London NW1 8LS; Admin. Ian Bonner.

**Haydn Society of Great Britain:** c/o University of Lancaster, Department of Music, Lancaster LA1 4YW; e-mail d.mccaldin@lancaster.ac.uk; website www.haydnsocietyofgb.netfirms.com; Dir Denis McCaldin.

**Hazard Chase Ltd:** Norman House, Cambridge Place, Cambridge CB2 1NS; tel. 01223 312400; fax 01223 460827; website www.hazardchase.co.uk.

**Hymn Society of Great Britain and Ireland:** The Vicarage, 7 Paganel Road, Minehead, Somerset, TA24 5ET; website www.dsg.freeispshares.co.uk/ Hsoc; Sec. Rev. Geoffrey Wrayford.

**Incorporated Association of Organists:** 17 Woodland Road, Northfield, Birmingham B31 2HU; tel. and fax (121) 475-4408; e-mail w.j.stormont@ btinternet.com; website www.iao.org.uk; Gen. Sec.: John Stormont.

**Incorporated Society of Musicians:** 10 Stratford Place, London W1C 1AA; tel. (20) 7629-4413; fax (20) 7408-1538; e-mail membership@ism.org; website www.ism.org; CEO Neil Hoyle; professional body for all musicians: perfor- mers, composers, teachers, conductors, organists, etc.; represents musicians' interests, raise professional standards, and provide services (insurance, legal advice, etc.) to members.

**Incorporated Society of Organ Builders (ISOB):** Smithy Steads, Cragg Vale, Hebden Bridge, W Yorkshire, HX7 5SQ; tel. and fax 0870 139 3645; website www.isob.co.uk.

**Institute of Musical Instrument Technology (IMIT):** Northfield House, 11 Kendal Avenue South, Sanderstead, Croydon, Surrey CR2 0QR; website www.imit.org.uk; Hon. Sec. Malcolm Dalton.

**International Artist Managers' Asscn—IAMA:** 23 Garrick Street, Covent Garden, London WC2E 9BN; tel. (20) 7379-7336; fax (20) 7379-7338; e-mail info@iamaworld.com; websites www.iamaworld.com, www.classicalmusicar- tists.com.

**International Association of Music Libraries, Archives and Docu- mentation Centres (United Kingdom and Ireland Branch):** c/o Music Library, Edinburgh City Libraries, 9 George IV Bridge, Edinburgh EH1 1EG; website www.iaml.info; Gen. Sec. Peter Baxter.

**International Council for Traditional Music:** Flat 1, 30 Holland Park, London W11 3TA; Sec. Philippa Heale.

**International Federation of Musicians:** 29 Catherine Place, Buckingham Gate, London SW1E 6EH.

**International Federation of Phonogram and Videogram Producers:** 54 Regent Street, London W1R 5PJ.

**International Society for Contemporary Music:** British Section, c/o West Heath Studios 174 Mill Lane, London NW6 1TB; Admin. Richard Steele.

**Ireland Trust:** 35 St Mary's Mansions, St Mary's Terrace, London W2 1SQ; tel. 20 7723-6376; fax 20 7724-8362; website www.musicweb.uk.net/ireland/ trust.htm; Hon. Sec.: M. Taylor.

**Kempe Society:** 135 Stevenage Road, London SW6 6PB; Treasurer-Sec. J. Audrey Ellison.

**Korngold Society:** 12 Townhead Terrace, Paisley, Renfrewshire PA1 2AX; Sec. Konrad Hopkins.

**Liszt Society Ltd:** 135 Stevenage Road, London SW6 6PB; Sec. Audrey Ellison.

**London Artfest:** PO Box 34904, London SW6 6GX; tel. and fax 020 7736 4717; Artistic Dir Lana Bezanov.

**Lute Society:** Southside Cottage, Brook Hill, Albury, Guildford GU5 9DJ; tel. 01483 202159; fax 01483 203088; e-mail lutesoc@aol.com; website www .lutesoc.co.uk; Sec. Christopher Goodwin.

**Making Music (The National Federation of Music Societies):** 7–15 Rosebery Avenue, London EC1R 4SP; tel. 0870 903 3780; fax 0870 903 3785; e-mail info@makingmusic.org.uk; website www.makingmusic.org.uk; Chief Exec. Robin Osterley.

**Massenet Society:** Flat 2, 79 Linden Gardens, London W2 4EU; tel. 020 7229 7060; Dir Stella J. Wright.

**Mechanical Copyright Protection Society/Performing Rights Society (MCPS/PRS) Alliance:** 29–33 Berners Street, London W1T 3AB; tel. 020 7306 4777; fax 020 7631 8957; website www.mcps-prs-alliance.co.uk; Chief Exec. John Hutchinson.

**Music Advisers' National Association:** Education Department, Avon House North, St James Barton, Bristol BS99 7EB; Sec. Carl Sidgreaves.

**Music Industries Association (MIA):** Ivy Cottage Offices, Finch's Yard, Eastwick Road, Great Bookham, Surrey KT23 4BA; tel. 01372 750600; fax 01372 750515; e-mail office@mia.org.uk; website www.mia.org.uk.

**Music Masters' and Mistresses' Association (MMA):** Steepcot, Bedales School, Petersfield, Hants GU32 2DG; website www.mma-online.org.uk; Hon. Sec. Jonathan Willcocks.

**Music Publishers Asscn—MPA:** Third Floor, Strandgate, 20 York Bldgs, London WC2 6JU; tel. (20) 7839-7779; fax (20) 7839-7776; e-mail info@ mpaonline.org.uk; website www.mpaonline.org.uk; CEO Sarah Faulder; Asst Chief Exec. Jenny Goodwin; trade organization representing music publishers in the UK, advising or assisting members in the promotion and protection of music copyright.

**Music Retailers Association:** PO Box 249, London W4 5EX; Sec. Arthur Spencer-Bolland.

**Music for Youth:** 102 Point Pleasant, London SW18 1PP; tel. 020 8870 9624; fax 020 8870 9935; e-mail mfy@mfy.org.uk; website www.mfy.org.uk; Exec. Dir Larry Westland.

**Musicians' Union:** 60–62 Clapham Road, London SW9 0JJ; tel. 020 7582 5566; fax 020 7582 9805; website www.musiciansunion.org.uk; Gen. Sec. John Smith.

**National Association of Art Centres:** The Arts Centre, Room 110, Vane Terrace, Darlington DL3 7AX.

**National Association for Education in the Arts:** c/o University of Exeter, School of Education, St Luke's, Exeter EX1 2LU; Sec. Beryl Phillips.

**National Association of Teachers in Further and Higher Education:** 27 Britannia Street, London WC1X 9JP; tel. 020 7837 3636; fax 020 7837 4403; website www.natfhe.org.uk; Gen. Sec. Paul Mackney.

**National Association of Youth Orchestras:** Central Hall, West Tollcross, Edinburgh EH3 9BP; tel. 0131 221 1927; fax 0131 229 2921; website www .nayo.org.uk; Hon. Sec. John Clarkson.

**National Campaign for the Arts:** Pegasus House, 37–43 Sackville Street, London W1S 3EH; tel. 020 7333 0375; fax 020 7333 0660; e-mail nca@ artscampaign.org.uk; website www.artscampaign.org.uk; Dir Victoria Todd.

**National Early Music Association (NEMA):** 137 Preston Road, Wembley, Middx HA9 8NW; website www.nema-uk.org; Sec. Jane Beeson.

**National Federation of Gramophone Societies:** Withyfeld, 192c Woodrow Forest, Melksham, Wilts SN12 7RF; Chair. J. R. Shaw.

**National Operatic and Dramatic Association (NODA):** 58–60 Lincoln Road, Peterborough PE1 2RZ; tel. 0870 770 2480; fax 0870 770 2490; website www.noda.org.uk; Chief Exec. Mark Pemberton.

**National School Band Association (NSBA):** 52 Hall Orchard Lane, Frisby on the Wreake, Melton Mowbray, Leicestershire, LE14 2NH; Chair. Alan Winwood.

**Northern Sinfonia Concert Ltd:** The Sinfonia Centre, 41 Jejmundvale, Newcastle Upon Tyne, NE2 1PG; tel. 0191 240 1812; fax 0191 240 2668.

**Open University Arts Faculty:** Walton Hall, Milton Keynes MK7 6AA; tel. 01908 653280; website www.open.ac.uk; Contacts: Prof. D. Burrows, Prof. T. Herbert.

**Orff Society:** 7 Rothesay Avenue, Richmond, Surrey TW10 5EB; website www.orff.co.uk; Sec. Margaret Murray.

**Organ Club:** 10 Roxburgh Court, 69 Melrose Road, London SW18 1PG; Gen. Sec. Adrian Mumford.

**Personal Managers' Association:** c/o Rooke Holt and Co, 83 Elbury Street, London SW1; Chair. Peter Dunlop.

**Plainsong and Mediaeval Music Society:** c/o RSCM, Cleveland Lodge, Westhumble, Dorking, Surrey RH5 6BW; tel. 01306 872800; fax 01306 887260; e-mail pmms@rscm.com.

**Pro Corda:** Leiston Abbey House, Leiston, Suffolk IP16 4TB; tel. 01728 831354; fax 01728 832500; website www.procorda.com; Music Dir: Dr Ioan Davies; Admin. Mererid Crump.

**The Rawsthorne Trust:** The Alpines, Main Street, Hemingbrough, Selby YO8 6QF; tel. and fax (1757) 630256; website www.musicweb.uk.net/rawsth/index.htm; Chair.: John M. Belcher.

**Robert Farnon Society:** Stone Gables, Upton Lane, Seavington St Michael, Ilminster, Somerset TA19 0PZ; website www.rfsoc.org.uk; Sec.: David Ades.

**Royal College of Organists:** Kensington Gore, London SW7 2QS; website www.rco.org.uk; Hon. Sec. Stephen Cleobury.

**Royal Musical Association:** St Aldates, Faculty of Music, Oxford OX1 1DB; website www.rma.ac.uk; Sec. Dr Ewan West.

**Royal Philharmonic Society:** 10 Stratford Place, London W1C 1BA; tel. (20) 7491 8110; fax (20) 7493 7463; e-mail admin@royalphilharmonicsociety .org.uk; website www.royalphilharmonicsociety.org.uk; Chair.: Tony Fell; Admin.: Rosemary Johnson.

**Royal School of Church Music (RSCM):** Cleveland Lodge, Westhumble, Dorking, Surrey RH5 6BW; tel. 01306 872800; fax 01306 887260; website www.rscm.com; Dir Dr Lionel Dakers.

**The Royal Society of Musicians of Great Britain:** 10 Stratford Place, London, W1C 1BA; tel. and fax 020 7629 6137; Sec. Maggie Gibb.

**Schools Music Association:** 71 Margaret Road, New Barnet, Herts EN4 9NT; tel. and fax 020 8440 6919; website www.schoolsmusic.org.uk; Hon. Sec. Maxwell Pryce.

**Schubert Society of Great Britain:** Garden Flat, 125 Grosvenor Avenue, London N5 2NL; Sec. Alan Tabelin.

**Scottish Arts Council:** 12 Manor Place, Edinburgh EH3 7DD; tel. (131) 226-6051; fax (131) 225-9833; website www.sac.org.uk; Head of Music: Nod Knowles.

**Scottish Music Information Centre:** 1 Bowmont Gardens, Glasgow G12 9LR; tel. (141) 334-6393; fax (141) 337-1161; e-mail info@scottishmusiccentre .com; website www.scottishmusiccentre.com.

**Simpson Society:** 3 Engle Park, London NW7 2HE; Secs John Brooks, Sylvia Brooks.

**Society for the Promotion of New Music (SPNM):** Fourth Floor, 18–20 Southwark Street, London SE1 1TJ; tel. 020 7407 1640; website www.spnm .org.uk; Admin. Richard Steele.

**Society for the Research in the Psychology of Music:** Westminster College, N Hinksey, Oxford OX2 9AT; Sec. Dr Janet Mills.

**Spohr Society of Great Britain:** 123 Mount View Road, Sheffield S8 8PJ; Sec. Chris Tutt.

**Stokowski Society:** 7 Priestfields, Rochester, Kent ME1 3AG; Sec. Andrew Barker.

**United Kingdom Harpists Association:** 4 Fairlawn Park, Sydenham, London SE26 5RU; tel. 39 Villiers Close, Surbiton, Surrey KT5 8DN; website www.ukha.org.

**Viola da Gamba Society:** 93A Sutton Road, London N10 1HH; website www .vdgs.demon.co.uk; Admin. Caroline Wood.

**Wagner Society:** 15 David Avenue, Wickford, Essex SS11 7BG; website www .wagnersociety.org; Sec. Jeremy D. Rowe.

**Peter Warlock Society:** 32a Chipperfield House, Cale Street, London SW3 3SA; tel. 020 7589 9595; website www.peterwarlock.org; Sec. Malcolm Rudland.

**Welsh Amateur Music Federation:** Ty Cerdd, 15 Mount Stuart Square, Docks, Cardiff, CF10 5DP; tel. 029 2046 5700; fax 029 2046 2733; Dir Keith Griffin.

**Welsh Music Guild:** Bronyfelin, 17 Penyrheol Drive, Heol Felinfoel, Llanelli, Carmarthenshire, SA15 3NX; website www.welshmusic.org.uk.

**Welsh Music Information Centre:** Ty Cerdd, 15 Mount Stuart Square, Cardiff, CF10 5DP; tel. 02920 465700/462855; fax 02920 462733; Dir A. J. Howard Rees.

**Workers' Music Association:** 17 Prideaux House, Prideaux Place, London WC1; Sec. Anne Gilman.

**Worshipful Company of Musicians:** Sixth Floor, 2 London Wall Buildings, London Wall, London EC2M 5PP; tel. 020 7496 8990; fax 020 7588 3633; website www.wcom.org.uk; Clerk W. R. I. Crewdson.

## United States of America

**Amateur Chamber Music Players Inc:** 1123 Broadway, Room 304, New York, NY 10010-2007; tel. 1 212 645 7424; fax 1 212 741 2678; website www .amcp.net; Chair. Susan M. Lloyd.

**American Academy and Institute of Arts and Letters:** 633 W 155th Street, New York, NY 10032; Exec. Dir Virginia Dajani.

**American Academy of Teachers of Singing:** Hotel Ansonia, Studio No. 5-517, 2109 Broadway, New York, NY 10023; website www .voiceteachersacademy.org; Chair. Donald Read.

**American Accordionists' Association Inc:** 580 Kearny Avenue, Kearny, NJ 07032; tel. 1 201 991 2233; fax 1 201 991 1944; website www.ameraccord .com; Pres. Dr. Carmelo Pino.

**American Arts Aliance:** 1156 15th Street NW, Suite 820, Washington, DC 20005-1726; tel. 1 202 387 8300; fax 1 202 833 2686; website www .americanartsalliance.org.

**American Music Therapy Association Inc. (AMTA):** 8455 Colesville Road, Suite 1000, Silver Spring, MD 20910; tel. 1 301 589 3300; fax 1 301 589 5175; e-mail info@musictherapy.org; website www.musictherapy.org.

**American Beethoven Society:** San Jose State University, 1 Washington Square, Ira F. Brilliant Center for Beethoven Studies, San Jose, CA 95192; Contact William Meredith.

**American Berlin Opera Foundation Inc:** 6 87th Street, New York, NY 10128; tel. and fax 1 212 534 5383; e-mail gala@operafoundation.org; website www.operafoundation.org; Chief Officer Christa Drechsler.

**American Brahms Society:** University of Washington, School of Music, PO Box 353450, Seattle, WA 98195-3450; tel. 1 206 543 0400; fax 1 206 284 0111; e-mail brahms@u.washington.edu; website brahms.unh.edu; Exec. Dir George S. Bozarth.

**American Cello Council Inc:** 340 W 55th Street, New York, NY 10019; tel. 1 212 586 7137; Admin. and Treasurer Esther Prince.

**American Choral Directors' Association (ACDA):** 502 SW 38th Street, Lawton, OK 73505; tel. 1 580 355 8161; fax 1 580 248 1465; website www .acdaonline.org; Exec. Dir Gene Brooks.

**American College of Musicians:** PO Box 1807, 808 Rio Grande Street, Austin, TX 78701; tel. 1 512 478 5775; Pres. Richard Allison.

**American Composes Alliance and Edition:** 170 W 74th Street, New York, NY 10023; Pres. Richard Brooks.

**American Federation of Musicians:** 1501 Broadway, Suite 600, New York, NY 10036; tel. 1 212 869 1330; fax 1 212 764 6134; website www.afm.org; Pres. Mark Tully Massagli.

**American Federation of Television and Radio Artists (AFTRA):** 260 Madison Avenue, New York, NY 10016; tel. 1 212 532 0800; website www.aftra.org; National Exec. Dir Gregory Hessinger.

**American Federation of Violin and Bow Makers Inc (AFVBM):** 33 North B Street, No. 8, San Mateo, CA 94401; website www.afvbm.com; Sec. John Montgomery.

**American Guild of Music:** PO Box 599, Warren, MI 48090; tel. 1 248 336 9388; e-mail agm@americanguild.org; website www.americanguild.org; Registered Agent E. D. Herrick.

**American Guild of Musical Artists (AGMA):** 1430 Broadway, 14th Floor, New York, NY 10018; tel. 1 212 265 3687; fax 1 212 262 9088; e-mail AGMA@MusicalArtists.org; website www.musicalartists.org; National Exec. Dir Alan S. Gordon.

**American Guild of Organists:** 475 Riverside Drive, Suite 1260, New York, NY 10115; tel. 1 212 870 2310; fax 1 212 870 2163; e-mail info@agohq.org; website www.agohq.org; Exec. Dir Daniel N. Colburn.

**American Harp Society Inc:** 6331 Quebec Drive, Los Angeles, CA 90068; website www.harpsociety.org; Pres. Molly Hahn.

**American Liszt Society Inc:** 210 Devonshire Drive, Rochester, NY 14625; website www.americanlisztsociety.org; Pres. Fernando Laires.

**American Matthay Association:** 46 Popular Street, Pittsburgh, PA 15205; website www.matthay.org; Pres. Thomas C. Davis.

**American Mechanical Rights Agency Inc (AMRA):** 150 S Barrington Avenue, Suite 1, Los Angeles, CA 90049; tel. 1 310 440 8778; fax 1 310 440 0059; website www.amermecrights.com; Chief Officer Patricia Bente.

**American Music Center Inc:** 30 W 26th Street, Suite 1001, New York, NY 10010; tel. 1 212 366 5260; fax 1 212 366 5265; website www.amc.net; Exec. Dir Nancy C. Clarke.

**American Music Conference:** 5790 Armada Drive, Carlsbad, CA 92008; tel. 1 760 431 9124; fax 1 760 438 7327; website www.amc-music.com; Exec. Dir Robert Morrison; Contact Sharon McLaughlin.

**American Musical Instrument Society:** c/o Shrine to Music Museum, 414 E Clark Street, Vermilliom, SD 57069; website www.amis.org.

**American Musicians Union:** 8 Tobin Court, Dumont, NJ 07628; tel. 1 201 384 5378; Pres. Ben Intorre.

**American Musicological Society:** 201 S 34th Street, Philadelphia, PA 19104; tel. 1 215 898 8698; fax 1 215 573 3673; website www.ams-net.org; Exec. Dir Ruth Steiner.

**American New Music Consortium:** 87-27 Santiago Street, Holliswood, NY 11423; Exec. Dir Dinu Ghezzo.

**American Orff-Schulwerk Association:** PO Box 391089, Cleveland, OH 44139; tel. 1 440 543 5366; website www.aosa.org.

**American Society of Composers, Authors and Publishers (ASCAP):** 1 Lincoln Plaza, New York, NY 10023; tel. 1 212 621 6000; fax 1 212 724 9064; website www.ascap.com; Pres. Marilyn Bergman.

**American String Teachers Association Inc:** 4153 Chain Bridge Road, Fairfax, VA 22030; tel. 1 703 279 2113; fax 1 703 279 2114; website www.astaweb.com; Exec. Admin. Galen Wixson.

**American Symphony Orchestra League:** 910 17th Street NW, Washington, DC 20006; tel. 1 202 776 0215; fax 1 202 776 0224; website www.symphony.org; CEO Catherine French.

**American Viola Society:** 13140 Coit Road, Suite 320, LB 120, Dallas, TX 75240-5737; tel. 1 972 233 9107 ext 204; website www.americanviolasociety.org; Pres. Alan de Veritch.

**American Women Composers Inc:** George Washington University, Washington, DC 20052; Pres. Stephania de Kenessey.

**Americans for the Arts:** 1000 Vermont Avenue NW, Sixth Floor, Washington DC 20005; tel. 1 202 371 2830; fax 1 202 371 0424.

**Arts International Program:** Institute of International Education, 809 UN Plaza, New York, NY 10017; Dir Jane M. Gullong.

**The Asia Society:** 725 Park Avenue, New York, NY 10021; tel. 1 212 288 6400; fax 1 212 517 8315; e-mail info@asiasoc.org; website www.asiasociety.org; Dir Rhoda Grauer.

**Associated Male Choruses of America Inc:** PO Pox 771, Brainerd, MN 56401; website www.amcachorus.org; Exec. Sec. John Fleming.

**Association for Recorded Sound Collections Inc:** PO Box 543, Annapolis, MD 21404; website www.asrc-audio.org; Exec. Dir Peter Shambarger.

**Association of Arts Administration Educators (AAAE) Inc:** c/o American Council for the Arts, 1 E 53rd Street, New York, NY 10022; Pres. J. Dennis Rich.

**Association of Performing Arts Presenters:** 1112 16th Street NW, Suite 400, Washington, DC 20036; Exec. Dir Susan Farr.

**Audio Engineering Society Inc:** 60 E 42nd Street, Lincoln Building, Room 2520, New York, NY 10165; Exec. Dir Donald J. Plunkett.

**Broadcast Music Inc:** 320 W 57th Street, New York, NY 10019; tel. 1 212 586 2000; website www.bmi.com; Pres. and CEO Frances W. Preston.

**Bruckner Society of America Inc:** 2150 Dubuque Road, Iowa City, IA 52240; Pres. Charles L. Eble.

**Business Committee for the Arts Inc:** 29-27 Queens Plaza N, Fourth Floor, Long Island City, New York, NY 10001; tel. 1 718 482 9900; fax 1 718 482 9911; e-mail info@bcainc.org; website www.bcainc.org; Pres. Judith A. Jedlicka.

**Chamber Music America:** 305 Seventh Avenue, Fifth Floor, New York, NY 10001; tel. 1 212 242 2022; fax 1 212 242 7955; website www.chamber-music.org; Pres. Bonnie Hampton.

**Chopin Foundation of the United States:** 1440 79th Street Causeway, Suite 117, Miami, FL 33141; tel. 1 305 868 0624; fax 1 305 868 5150; e-mail info@chopin.org; website www.chopin.org.

**Choristers' Guild:** 2834 W Kingsley Road, Garland, TX 75041; tel. 1 972 271 1521; fax 1 972 840 3113; website www.choristersguild.org; Exec. Dir Jim Rindelaub.

**Chorus America:** Association of Professional Vocal Ensembles, 1156 15th Street NW, Suite 310, Washington, DC 20005; tel. 1 202 331 7577; website chorus.america.org; Exec. Dir Kenneth Garner.

**College Band Directors National Association:** University of Texas, PO Box 8028, Austin, TX 78713; website www.cbdna.org; Sec.-Treasurer Richard L. Floyd.

**The College Music Society Inc:** 312 E Pine Street, Missoula, MT 59802; tel. 1 406 721 9616; fax 1 406 721 9419; e-mail cms@music.org; website www.music.org; Exec. Dir Robby D. Gunstream.

**Composers' Forum Inc:** 73 Spring Street, Suite 506, New York, NY 10012.

**Composers Guild:** PO Box 586, Farmington, UT 84025; Pres. Ruth Gatrell.

**Composers' Resources Inc:** PO Box 19935, Atlanta, GA 30325; Pres. Howard Weshil.

**Concert Music Broadcasters Association:** Hotel St Francis, 335 Powell Street, San Francisco, CA 94102.

**Conductors' Guild Inc:** 5300 Glenside Drive, Suite 2207, Richmond, VA 23228; tel. 1 804 553 1378; fax 1 804 553 1876; website www.conductorsguild.org; Exec. Sec. Judy Ann Voois.

**Creative Audio and Music Electronics Organization:** 7753 State Blvd Ext, Meridan, MS 39305; Pres. Larry Blakely.

**Delta Omicron (International Music Fraternity):** 841 W Cherokee Drive, Jefferson City, TN 37760; website www.delta-omicron.org.

**Early Music America (EMA):** 2366 Eastlake Avenue E, Suite 429, Seattle, WA 98102; tel. 1 206 720 6270; website www.earlymusic.org.

**George Enescu Society of the United States Inc:** 4 Barrett Place, Northampton, MA 01060.

**Guitar Foundation of America:** PO Box 1240, Claremont, CA 91711; website www.guitarfoundation.org; Gen. Man. Gunnar Eisel.

**Gustav Mahler Society USA:** 1616 N Sierra Bonita Avenue, Los Angeles, CA 90046.

**The Hymn Society in the United States and Canada:** 745 Commonwealth Avenue, Boston, MA 02215; fax 1 617 353 7322; website www.hymnsociety.org; Exec. Dir W. Thomas Smith.

**Independent Composers Association:** PO Box 45134, Los Angeles, CA 90045; Pres. Burt Goldstein.

**Institute for Music, Health and Education:** PO Box 4179, Boulder, CO 80306; Dir Don G. Campbell.

**Institute of Audio Research:** School of Audio and Video Technology, 64 University Place, Greenwich Village, New York, NY 10003; tel. 1 212 777 8550; fax 1 212 677 6549; e-mail contact@audioschool.com; website www.audioschool.com; Dir Miriam Friedman.

**International Association of Auditorium Managers:** 4425 West Airport Freeway, Suite 590, Irving, TX 75062; Exec. Dir John S. Swinburn.

**International Computer Music Association:** 2040 Polk Street, Suite 330, San Francisco, CA 94109; website www.computermusic.org; Pres. Allen Strang.

**International Double Reed Society:** University of North Texas, School of Music, Denton, TX 76203; website www.idrs.org; Pres. Charles Veazey.

**International Federation of Festival Organizations:** 4230 Stansbury Avenue, No. 105 Sherman Oaks, CA 91423; Sec.-Gen. Armando Moreno.

**International Horn Society:** 2220 N 1400 E, Provo, UT 84604; website www.hornsociety.org; Exec. Sec. Ellen Powley.

**International Society of Bassists:** 4020 McEwen, Suite 105, Dallas, TX 75244; tel. 1 972 233 9107; website www.isbworldoffice.com; Gen. Man. Madeleine Crouch.

**International Society of Performing Arts Administrators:** 2920 Fuller Avenue, NE, Suite 205, Grand Rapids, MI 49505; Exec. Dir Michael C. Hardy.

**International Teleproduction Society Inc:** 350 Fifth Avenue, Suite 2400, New York, NY 10118; Exec. Dir Janet Luhrs.

**International Ticketing Association (INTIX):** 330 W 38th Street, Suite 605, New York, NY 10018; tel. 1 212 629 4036; fax 1 212 629 8532; e-mail info@intix.org; website www.intix.org.

**Jeunesses Musicales of the USA:** c/o Trinity University, 715 Stadium Drive, San Antonio, TX 78284; Dir Gerald Benjamin.

**Keyboard Teachers Association International Inc:** 361 Pin Oak Lane, Westbury, NY 11590; Pres. Albert DeVito.

**League of Composers:** International Society of Contemporary Music, PO Box 1205, New York, NY 10276; tel. 1 718 442 5225; e-mail league-iscm@league-iscm.org; website www.league-iscm.org; Exec. Dir Geoffrey Kidde.

**Leschetizky Association:** 105 W 72nd Street, New York, NY 10023; website www.leschetizky.org; Pres. Genia Robinor.

**Lincoln Center for the Performing Arts:** 70 Lincoln Center Plaza, New York, NY 10023; tel. 212 875 5000; fax 212 875 5745; website www.lincolncenter.org.

**Lute Society of America:** PO Box 1328, Lexington, VA 24450.

**The Masterwork Music and Art Foundation Inc:** Morristown, NJ 07962; tel. 1 909 781 5669; Exec. Dir Shirley S. May.

**Moravian Music Foundation Inc:** 457 S Church Street, Box L, Winston-Salem, NC 27108; tel. 1 336 725 0651; fax 1 336 725 4514; website www.moravianmusic.org; Pres. M. Keith Kapp.

**Mu Phi Epsilon:** 2212 Mary Hills Drive, Minneapolis, MN 55422; website home.muphiepsilon.org; Pres. Katherine Doepke.

**Music Association of America:** 224 King Street, Englewood, NJ 07631; Exec. Dir George Sturm.

**Music Critics Association Inc:** 7 Pine Court, Westfield, NJ 07090; website www.mcana.org; Man. Albert H. Cohen.

**Music Educators National Conference:** 1806 Robert Fulton Drive, Reston, VA 22091.

**Music Library Association Inc:** 8551 Research Way, Suite 180, Middleton, WI 53562; tel. 1 608 836 5825; fax 1 608 831 8200; website www.musiclibraryassoc.org.

**Music Publishers' Association of the United States:** 711 Third Avenue, New York, NY 10017; website www.mpa.org.

**Music Teachers National Association Inc:** 441 Vine Street, Suite 505, Cincinnati, OH 45202; tel. (513) 421-1420; fax (513) 421-2503; e-mail mtnanet@mtna.org; website www.mtna.org; Exec. Dir Gary L. Ingle.

**National Academy of Recording Arts and Sciences Inc:** 3402 Pico Blvd, Santa Monica, CA 90405; Pres. Michael Greene.

**National Assembly of State Arts Agencies:** 1010 Vermont Avenue NW, Suite 920, Washington, DC 20005; Exec. Dir Jonathan Katz.

**National Association for Music Therapy Inc:** 8455 Colesville Road, Suite 930, Silver Spring, MD 20910; tel. 1 301 589 3300; website www.musictherapy.org.

**National Association of Broadcasters:** 1771 N Street NW, Washington, DC 20036; tel. 1 202 429 5300; fax 1 202 429 4199; website www.nab.org; Pres. and CEO Edward Fritts.

**National Association of Negro Musicians:** 11551 S Laflin Street, Chicago, IL 60643; Exec. Sec. Ona Campbell.

**National Association of Pastoral Musicians:** 962 Wayne Avenue, Suite 210, Silver Spring, MD 20910; tel. 1 240 247 3000; fax 1 240 247 3001; website www.npm.org; Pres. Virgil C. Funk.

**National Association of Performing Arts Managers and Agents (NAPAMA) Inc:** 459 Columbus Avenue, Suite 133, New York, NY 10024; e-mail info@napama.org; website www.napama.org.

**National Association of Recording Merchandisers Inc:** 9 Eves Drive, Suite 120, Marlton, NJ 08053; tel. 1 856 596 2221; fax 1 856 596 3268; website www.narm.org; Exec. Vice-Pres. Pam Horovitz.

**National Association of Schools of Music:** 11250 Roger Bacon Drive, Suite 21, Reston, VA 22090; Exec. Dir Samuel Hope.

**National Association of Teachers of Singing Inc:** 2800 University Blvd N, Jacksonville, FL 32211; website www.nats.org.

**National Choral Council:** 1650 Broadway, New York, NY 10019; tel. 1 212 333 5333; fax 1 212 315 2420; website www.nationalchorale.org; Exec. Dir Martin Josman.

**National Council of Acoustical Consultants:** 66 Morris Avenue, Suite 1a, Springfield, NJ 07081; tel. 1 973 564 5859; fax 1 973 564 7480; e-mail info@ncac.com; website www.ncac.com; Exec. Sec. Virginia Marguire.

**National Federation of Music Clubs:** 1336 N Delaware Street, Indianapolis, IN 46202; website www.nfmc-music.org; Chief Officer D. Clifford Allison.

**National Foundation for Advancement in the Arts:** 800 Brickell Avenue, Suite 500, Miami, FL 33131; website www.nfaa.org; Pres. William H. Banchs.

**National Guild of Community Schools of the Arts Inc:** PO Box 8018, Englewood, NJ 07631; website www.nationalguild.com; Exec. Dir Lolita Mayadas.

**National Music Council:** 711 Third Avenue, Eighth Floor, New York, NY 10017; website www.musiccouncil.org.

**National Music Publishers' Association (NMPA) Inc:** 475 Park Avenue S, 29th Floor, New York, NY 10016; tel. 1 646 742 1651; fax 1 646 742 1779; e-mail pr@nmpa.org; website www.nmpa.org; Pres. Edward P. Murphy.

**National Opera Association:** Northwestern University, School of Music, 711 Elgin Road, Evanston, IL 60208; website www.noa.org.

**National Orchestral Association:** 245 Park Avenue, 15th Floor, New York, NY 10167.

**National School Orchestra Association:** PO Box 1087, Mill Valley, CA 94942.

**National Women Composers Resource Center:** 330 Townsend Street, Suite 218, San Francisco, CA 94107.

**Network for New Music:** PO Box 27556, Philadelphia, PA 19118; tel. 1 215 848 7647; e-mail info@networkfornewmusic.org; website www.networkfornewmusic.org; Artistic Dir Linda Reichert.

**New Music Alliance:** 508 Woodland Terrace, Philadelphia, PA 19104; Pres. Tina Davidson.

**New York Consortium for New Music:** 215 W 90th Street, New York, NY 10024; Pres. Patricia Spencer.

**OPERA America Inc:** 1156 15th Street NW, Suite 810, Washington DC 20005; tel. 1 202 293 4466; fax 1 202 393 0735; website www.operaam.org; Exec. Vice-Pres. and CEO Marc A. Scorca.

**Percussive Arts Society:** 701 NW Ferris Avenue, Lawton, OK 73507; tel. 1 580 353 1455; fax 1 580 353 1456; e-mail percarts@pas.org; website www.pas.org; Admin. Man. Steve Beck.

**Piano Manufacturers Association International:** National Piano Foundation, 4020 McEwen, Suite 105, Dallas, TX 75244; tel. 1 214 233 9107; fax 1 214 240 4219; Exec. Dir Donald W. Dillon.

**Piano Technicians Guild Inc:** 3930 Washington, Kansas City, MO 64111; Exec. Dir Larry Goldsmith.

**Recording Industry Association of America (RIAA):** 1330 Connecticut Avenue NW, Suite 300, Washington, DC 20036; tel. 1 202 775 0101; fax 1 202 775 7253; website www.riaa.com; Pres. Jason S. Berman.

**SESAC Inc:** 55 Music Square E, Nashville, TN 37203; tel. 1 615 320 0055; fax 1 615 329 9627; website www.sesac.com.

**Society for Ethnomusicology Inc:** Indiana University, Morrison Hall 005, Bloomington, IN 47405.

**Society of Composers Inc:** PO Box 450, Old Chelsea Station, New York, NY 10113; website www.societyofcomposers.org.

**Songwriters Guild of America:** 1500 Harbor Blvd, Weehawken, NJ 07087; website www.songwriters.org; Pres. George David Weiss.

**Sonneck Society for American Music:** PO Box 476, Canton, MA 02021.

**Suzuki Association of the Americas Inc:** PO Box 17310, Boulder, CO 80308; tel. 1 303 444 0948; e-mail info@suzukiassociation.org; website www.suzukiassociation.org; Pres. Jeffrey Cox.

**Theatre Communications Group Inc:** 355 Lexington Avenue, New York, NY 10017; tel. 1 212 697 5230; website www.tcg.org; Dir Peter Zeisler.

**Tubists Universal Brotherhood Association:** University of Texas at Austin, Austin, TX 78712.

**United States Information Agency, Arts America Program:** 301 Fourth Street SW, Washington, DC 20547.

**Viola da Gamba Society of America:** University of Colorado, Dept of Music, Boulder, CO 80302; website vdgsa.org; Pres. Gordon Sandford.

**Violin Society of America:** 48 Academy Street, Poughkeepsie, NY 12601; tel. 1 845 452 7557; website www.vsa.to; Pres. Hans E. Tausig.

**Violoncello Society Inc:** 127 W 72nd Street, No. 2R, New York, NY 10023; Exec. Admin. Esther Prince.

**Kurt Weill Foundation for Music Inc:** 7 E 20th Street, Third Floor, New York, NY 10003; website www.kwf.org; Pres. Kim H. Kowalke.

**Young Audiences Inc:** 115 E 92nd Street, New York, NY 10128; tel. 1 212 831 8110; fax 1 212 289 1202; website www.youngaudiences.org; Exec. Dir Richard Bell.

# Uruguay

**Asociación General de Autores del Uruguay:** Canelones 1122, PZ 11100 Montevideo; Pres. Antonio Italiano.

**Asociación, Uruguay de Musicos:** Calle Maldonado 983, PO Box 11100 Montevideo; Pres. Alfonson Coronel.

**Centro Cultural de la Música:** PO Box 5, Avda 18 de Julio 1006, 6°, Montevideo; Dir Jorge Calvetti.

**Juventudes Musicales del Uruguay:** Sarandi 444, 1°, Edificio SODRE, Montevideo; Pres. Maria Tania Siver.

**Sociedad Uruguay de Interpretes:** Canelones 1090, Montevideo; Pres. José Maria Lorenzo.

**Sociedad Uruguay de Música Contemporánea:** Casilla de Correo 1328, 11000 Montevideo; Pres. Diego Legrand.

# Venezuela

**Sociedad de Autores y Compositores de Venezuela:** Avda Andres Bello, Ede, Vam Torre Oeste, 10°, Caracas; Pres. Guillermo Carrasco.

# APPENDIX E: MAJOR COMPETITIONS AND AWARDS

Value of awards, restrictions on entrants, dates, etc. may vary from year to year and interested readers are advised to contact the sponsoring organizations directly for complete information. It should also be noted that many institutions listed in Appendix F also maintain competitions, awards and scholarship programmes.

## Australia

**Australian Broadcasting Corporation Young Performers' Awards:** PO Box 9994, Sydney, NSW 2001. Annual awards for singers and instrumentalists to the age of 30 who have been in continuous residence in Australia for one year. Must compete in state of residence. Award of $A 19,500 plus concert engagements.

**Australian Singing Competition:** PO Box A2325, Sydney South, NSW 1235; tel. 61 2 9231 4293; fax 61 2 9221 8201; e-mail asc@aussing.com.au; website www.aussing.com.au; Annual awards for operatic and classical singers. Must be an Australian or New Zealand citizen under the age of 26 for classical singers and under the age of 35 for operatic singers. Mathy and opera awards totalling $A 100,000.

**Sydney International Piano Competition of Australia:** PO Box 420, Double Bay, Sydney, NSW 1360; tel. 61 2 9326 2405; fax 61 2 9326 2604; e-mail info@sipca.com.au; website www.sipca.com.au. Quadrennial competition open to pianists of all nationalities between the ages of 17 and 30. Prizes include 1st prize of $A 25,000 and various other prizes totalling $120,000.

## Austria

**Ludwig van Beethoven International Piano Competition:** Anton-von-Webern-Platz 1, 1030 Vienna; tel. 43 1 71155 6050; fax 43 1 71155 6059; e-mail info@beethoven-comp.at; website www.beethoven-comp.at. Quadrennial competition open to pianists of all nationalities between the ages of 17 and 32. Prizes include: 1st prize of 80,000 Schillings, a Bösendorfer piano, and concert engagements; 2nd prize of 60,000 Schillings; 3rd prize of 50,000 Schillings; and three further prizes of 20,000 Schillings.

**International Anton Bruckner Organ Competition:** Untere Donaulande 7, 4010 Linz. Quadrennial competition open to organists of all nationalities to the age of 35. Prizes include 1st prize of 50,000 Schillings, 2nd prize of 40,000 Schillings and 3rd prize of 30,000 Schillings.

**International Belvedere Competition for Opera Singers:** Fleischmarkt 24, 1010 Vienna. Annual competition for singers to the age of 35. Prizes totalling 50,000 Schillings.

**International Fritz Kreisler Competition:** PO Box 76, 1030 Vienna; tel. 43 1 711 55 6021; fax 43 1 711 55 6029; e-mail office@fritz-kreisler.music.at; website www.fritz-kreisler.music.at. Quadrennial competition for violin and viola. Prizes include 1st prize of 150,000 Schillings, 2nd prize of 125,000 Schillings and 3rd prize of 100,000 Schillings.

**International Mozart Competition of the Universität Mozarteum:** Universität Mozarteum Salzburg, Alpenstrasse 48, 5020 Salzburg; tel. 43 662 6198; fax 43 662 6198-3033; website www.moz.ac.at. Quadrennial competition open to musicians of all nationalities. Prizes include the Mozart Prize from the Austrian Ministry of Science and Research, as well as other prizes and concert engagements. Next competition (for voice) in 2006.

**Internationaler Chorwettberwerb:** Kulturreferat der Stadtgemeinde, 9800 Spittal. Annual competition for Choirs. Prizes include money and documents.

**Prix Ars Electronica:** Museumsgesellschaft mbH, Hauptstrasse 2, 4040 Linz; tel. 43 732 72720; fax 43 732 72722; e-mail info@aec.at; website www.aec.at. Annual competition for the computer arts open to individuals, groups, and organizations. Prizes include money and awards.

**Nancy Van de Vate International Composition Prize for Opera:** Margaretenstrasse 125/15, 1050 Vienna. Annual competition open to all female composers of opera and music theatre.

**Vienna International Competition for Composers:** Casinos Austria, Dr Karl-Lueger Ring 14, 1015 Vienna. Annual competition open to composers to the age of 40, who submit a composition not previously accepted for performance, or performed in public, or awarded a prize in another competition.

## Belgium

**Concours International de Chant de Verviers:** Rue des Dominicains 1, 4000 Liège. Biennial competition open to singers of all nationalities.

**Concours International de Guitare:** c/o Le Printemps de la Guitare asbl, Place du Chef Lieu 9, 6040 Charleroi; tel. and fax 32-71 35 5320; e-mail info@printemps-guitare.be; website www.printemps-guitare.be. Biennial competition open to solo classical guitarists of all nationalities to the age of 32. Prizes

include 1st prize of 5,000 euros, 2nd prize of 3,700 euros, 3rd prize of 2,500 euros, 4th prize of 1,500 euros, 5th prize of 800 euros, and 6th prize of 500 euros.

**Festival Van Vlaanderen, Brugge:** Collaert Mansionstraat 30, 8000 Bruges; tel. 050 33 22 83; fax 050 34 52 04; e-mail musica-antiqua@unicall.be; website www.musica-antiqua.com; Annual competition, instrumentalist categories rotating annually on a triennial schedule. Prizes total 30,000 euros.

**Queen Elizabeth International Music Competition of Belgium:** 20 rue Aux Laines, 1000 Brussels.

## Bulgaria

**Boris Christoff International Competition for Young Opera Singers:** 56 rue Alabin, 1000 Sofia. Quadrennial competition open to men up to the age of 35 and to women up to the age of 33. Prizes include a Grand Prize, 1st prize, 2nd prize, 3rd prize, medals and diplomas.

## Canada

**Banff International String Quartet Competition:** c/o Banff Centre School of Fine Arts, PO Box 1020, Banff, AB T1L 1H5; tel. 1 403 762 6180; e-mail bisqc@banffcentre.ca; website www.banffcentre.ca/bisqc. Triennial competition open to quartets whose members are under 35 years of age at the time of the competition. Prizes include C $20,000, $12,000, $8,000, $5,000, $500, set of bows, Canadian tour, and Banff Centre residency.

**Canada Council/Conseil des Arts du Canada Grants and Awards:** PO Box 1047, 350 Albert Street, Ottawa, ON K1P 5V8; tel. 1 613 566 4414; fax 1 613 566 4390; website www.canadacouncil.ca; Grants and awards to artists of Canadian citizenship and to non-profit arts organizations.

**Canadian Music Competition:** 1450 City Councillors Street, Suite 220, Montréal, QC H3A 2E6; tel. 1 514 284 5398; fax 1 514 284 6828; e-mail mus@cmcnational.com; website www.cmcnational.com. Annual competition for pianists, string players, wind players and singers. Open to Canadian citizens or those holding a Landed Immigrant Certificate or those studying with a Canadian teacher for the last three years, between the age of seven and 31.

**Concours Orchestre Symphonique de Montréal:** 85 St Catherine West, Montréal, QC H2X 3P4. Annual competition open to Canadian citizens or those holding a Landed Immigrant Certificate featuring piano and voice one year and strings and wind the following year; piano: category A for between the ages of 18 and 25 and category B for those under 18; voice: for those between the ages of 18 and 30; strings: category A for those between the ages of 18 and 25 and category B for those under 18; wind: for those between the ages of 16 and 25. Prizes totalling C $15,500 and an appearance on the regular subscriptions series of the Orchestre Symphonique de Montréal.

**Eckhardt-Gramatté National Music Competition:** Queen Elizabeth II Music Building, Brandon University, 270 18th Street, Brandon, MB R7A 6A9; tel. (204) 728-8212; fax (204) 729-9085; e-mail eckhardt@brandonu.ca; website www.brandonu.ca/egre; Admin. Officer: Nancy Nehring. Annual competition open to Canadian citizens or Canadian residents, alternating annually between voice, strings and piano. Prizes include 1st prize of C $5,000 and a concert tour, 2nd prize of $3,000 and 3rd prize of $2,000.

**Glenn Gould Prize:** The Glenn Gould Foundation, PO Box 190, 260 Adelaide Street E, Toronto, ON M5A 1N1. Triennial honour to individuals of all nationalities who have made an exceptional contribution to music and its communication through the use of any communication technology. Previous laureates include R. Murray Schafer, Lord Menuhin, Toru Takemitsu, Yo-Yo Ma and Pierre Boulez. Any person may nominate a potential laureate by sending a complete rationale, in writing, to the Foundation office.

**Kamloops Symphony Orchestra New Celebrity Competition:** PO Box 57, Kamloops, BC V2C 5K3; tel. 1 250 372 5000; fax 1 250 372 5089; e-mail info@kamloopssymphony.com; website www.kamloopssymphony.com. Annual competition open to Canadian citizens or those holding a Landed Immigrant Certificate. Prizes include 1st prize of C $1,000 and 2nd prize of $500, with the two finalists appearing in concert with the Kamloops Symphony Orchestra.

**Montréal International Music Competition:** Place des Arts, 1501 Jeanne-Mance Street, Montréal QC H2X 1Z9.

## Czech Republic

**Prague Spring International Music Competition:** Hellichova 18, 118 00 Prague 1; tel. 42 2 533474; fax 42 2 536040. Annual competition open to performers of all nationalities with categories changing annually in five-year cycles. Prizes include money and an appearance at the Prague Spring International Music Festival.

## Denmark

**Carl Nielsen International Music Competitions:** Claus Bergs Gade 9, 5000 Odense C; tel. 45 66 12 00 57; fax 45 65 91 00 47; e-mail carlnielsencompetition@odensesymfoni.dk; website www.odensesymfoni.dk/ cncomp. Quadrennial competitions open to instrumentalists of all nationalities to the age of 30. Prizes include a minimum of 340,000 kroner.

**International Organ Competition, Odense:** Kultursekretariatet, Vindegade 18, 5000 Odense C; tel. and fax 45 65914318; e-mail kultur.ksf@odense .dk; website home13.inet.tele.dk/organcmp. Biennial competition open to organists of all nationalities to the age of 34. Prizes include 1st prize of 40,000 kroner, 2nd prize of 15,000 kroner, 3rd prize of 10,000 kroner, 4th prize of 5,000 kroner, and a special prize of 5,000 kroner.

**Nicolai Malko International Competition for Young Conductors:** c/o Danmarks Radio, Rosenoerns Alle 22, 1999 Frederiksberg C. Triennial competition open to conductors between the ages of 20 and 31. Prizes include money.

## Finland

**Jean Sibelius International Violin Competition:** PO Box 31, 00101 Helsinki; tel. 358 9 4114-3443; fax 358 10 850-4760; e-mail violin .competition@kolumbus.fi. Quinquennial competition for violinists born in or after 1975. Prizes totalling about 48,000 euros.

**Mirjam Helin International Singing Competition:** c/o Finnish Cultural Foundation, PO Box 203, Bulevardi 5 A, 00121 Helsinki; tel. 358 9 6128 1248; fax 358 9 640 474; e-mail mh@skr.fi; website www.skr.fi. Quinquennial competition open to singers of all nationalities, women born in or after 1973 and men born in or after 1971. Prizes separate for men and women, including four prizes totalling 100,000 euros.

**Paulo Cello Competition:** PO Box 1105, 00101 Helsinki; tel. 358 40 528 4876; fax 358 9 2243 2879; e-mail cello@paulo.fi; website www .cellocompetitionpaulo.org; Quinquennial competition for young cellists of all nationalities. Prizes include money.

## France

**Concours International d'Ensembles de Musique de Chambre de Colmar:** c/o Service des Activités Culturelles, Hôtel de Ville, 68000 Colmar. Triennial competition for chamber music ensembles for performers to the age of 35. Prizes include 30,000 French francs, 15,000 francs and 10,000 francs.

**Concours International d'Orgue Grand Prix de Chartres:** 75 rue de Grenelle, 75007 Paris; tel. 33 145 48 31 74; fax 33 145 46 14 34; e-mail orgues .chartres@free.fr; website orgues.chartres.free.fr. Biennial competition open to all organists born after 1 Jan 1961. Prizes include two grand prizes of 20,000 French francs each, one for interpretation and one for improvisation, and two 2nd prizes of 5,000 francs each, one for interpretation and one for improvisation.

**Concours International de Chant de La Ville de Toulouse:** c/o Théâtre du Capitole, 31000 Toulouse; tel. 33 61 23 21 35; fax 33 61 22 24 34. Annual competition open to singers between the ages of 18 and 33. Prizes totalling 135,000 French francs.

**Concours International de Chant de Paris:** 8 rue du Dôme, 75116; tel. 33 147 04 76 38; fax 33 147 27 35 03. Biennial competition open to singers, women to the age of 32 and men to the age of 34. Prizes include 120,000 French francs and concert engagements.

**Concours International de Chant Offenbach:** 79 rue Jouffroy, 75017 Paris. Biennial competition open to singers of all nationalities and all ages. Prizes include appearances in European theatres and festivals.

**Concours International de Clavecin:** c/o Festival Estival de Paris, 20 rue Geoffroy l'Asnier, 75004 Paris. Biennial competition open to harpsichordists to the age of 32. Prizes include money.

**Concours International de Flute Jean-Pierre Rampal:** 5 rue Bellart, 75015; Open to flautists up to the age of 30.

**Concours International de Guitare:** c/o Radio France, 116 Ave du President Kennedy, 75786 Paris Cédex 16. Annual competition open to classical guitarists of all nationalities to the ages of 30 and biennial competition open to composers of all nationalities. Prizes include money, concerts and recitals.

**Concours International de Jeunes Chefs d'Orchestre:** Square Saint Amour 3 bis, rue Léonel de Moustier, 25000 Besançon; tel. 33 381 25 05 85; fax 33 381 81 52 15. Annual competition open to conductors under the age of 35. Prizes include Emile Vuillermoz Prize.

**Concours International de Musique de Chambre:** Rue de Dôme 10, 75116 Paris. Biennial competition open to instrumentalists and singers to the age of 35. Prizes include 62,500 French francs.

**Concours International de Trompette Maurice André:** 5 rue Bellart, 75015 Paris. Competition for young trumpeters. Prizes include four grand prizes.

**Concours International de Violon Yehudi Menuhin:** 5 rue Bellart, 75015 Paris; tel. 33 1 47 83 33 58; fax 33 143 06 68 79. Competition for young violinists. Prizes include a grand prize and three other prizes.

**Concours International de Violoncelle Rostropovich:** 146 rue de Rennes, 75006 Paris. Competition for cellists of all nationalities to the age of 33. Prizes include money and public performances.

**Concours International du Festival de Musique de Toulon:** 117 avenue Lazare Carnot, 83000 Toulon. Annual competition open to instrumentalists between the ages of 18 and 30 with categories rotating annually. Prizes include 1st prize of 20,000 French francs, 2nd prize of 12,000 francs and 3rd prize of 8,000 francs.

**Concours International Marguerite Long-Jacques Thibaud:** 32 Ave Matignon, 75008 Paris; tel. 33 1 42 66 66 80; fax 33 1 42 66 06 43; website www .concours-long-thibaud.org. Triennial competition open to pianists and violinists between the ages of 16 and 30. Prizes include 250,000 French francs for winners in each category.

**Florilège Vocal de Tours:** PO Box 1452, 37014 Tours Cédex; tel. 33 2 47 21 65 26. Annual competition open to choral and vocal performers and composers. Prizes include 18 prizes totalling 100,000 French francs.

**Fondation des Etats-Unis Harriet Hale Woolley Scholarships:** 15 Blvd Jourdan, 75690 Paris Cédex 14. Annual scholarships open to single American instrumentalists or artists between the ages of 21 and 30 for study in Paris. Scholarships include from four to five US $8,500 awards.

**International Rostropovich Cello Competition:** c/o Association pour la Création et la Diffusion Artistique, 3 rue des Couronnes, 75020 Paris; tel. 1 40 33 45 35; fax 1 40 33 45 38; e-mail rostro@civp.com; website www.civp.com.

**Yvonne Lefébure International Piano Competition:** 131–135 boulevard Carnot, BP 23, 78110 Le Vesinet; tel. 33 1 39 76 76 44; fax 33 1 39 76 27 31. Biennial competition open to pianists of all nationalities to the age of 35. Prizes include money and public performances.

**Prix Musical International Arthur Honegger:** c/o Fondation de France, 40 Avenue Hoche, 75008 Paris; tel. 33 1 44 21 31 00; fax 33 1 44 21 31 01. Biennial competition open to all composers. Prizes include 50,000 French francs.

**Rencontres Musicales d'Evian International String Quartet Competition:** 6 rue Téhéran, 75008 Paris or Château de Blonay, 74500 Evian les Bains. Biennial competition open to string quartets of all nationalities whose average age does not exceed 33 years of age. Prizes total over 500,000 French francs.

**World Music Masters International Piano Competition:** Salle Gaveau, 45 rue La Boétie, 75008 Paris. Annual competition open only to pianists who have been finalists in other international competitions. Prizes include US $30,000 and concert engagements.

## Germany

**Hannover International Violin Competition:** Stiftung Niedersachsen, Ferdinandstrasse 4, 30175 Hannover. Triennial competition open to violinists of all nationalities between the ages of 16 and 30. Next competition in 2006. Prizes include money, a recording, and concert engagements.

**International Johann Sebastian Bach Competition:** Thomaskirchhof 16, 04109 Leipzig. Quadrennial competition open to pianists, organists, violinists, harpsichordists and singers of all nationalities. Age limitations: 16–34. Prizes include money.

**International Kuhlau Wettbewerb für Flotisten:** Herzogenplatz 5, PO Box 2061, 29525 Uelzen; tel. 49 581 800 227; fax 49 581 800 108. Triennial competition for solo flute and flute with piano, two flutes or two flutes with piano, or three or four flutes. Age limit: up to 32.

**International Music Competition of the Broadcasting Corporations of Germany:** c/o Bayerischer Rundfunk, Rundfunkplatz 1, 80300 Munich. Annual competition open to solo instrumentalists, string quartets, and singers with categories changing annually.

**International Piano Competition of Cologne:** c/o Foundation Tomassoni, Dagobertstrasse 38, 50668 Cologne. Triennial competition open to pianists of all nationalities between the ages of 18 and 29. Prizes include 1st prize of 15,000 Deutsche Marks, 2nd prize of 10,000 DM and 3rd prize of 5,000 DM.

**International Robert Schumann Contest:** Muenzstrasse 12, 08056 Zwickau; tel. 49 375 21 26 36; fax 49 375 83 41 30. Quadrennial competition open to pianists to the age of 25 and to singers to the age of 32. Prizes include money.

**International Violin Competition Louis Spohr:** Burgunderstrasse 4, 79104 Freiburg. Triennial competition open to violinists of all nationalities to the age of 32. Prizes include 1st prize of 12,000 Deutsche Marks, 2nd prize of 8,000 DM and 3rd prize of 5,000 DM.

**Internationaler Wettbewerb für Junge Pianisten Ettlingen:** Pforzheimerstrasse 25a, 76275 Ettlingen; tel. 7243 101-311; fax 7243 101-436; e-mail info@pianocompetition.org; website www.pianocompetition.org; Dir Frank Reich. Biennial competition open to pianists of all nationalities; category A for those born on or after 7 August 1988, or category B for those born on or after 7 August 1983.

**Internationaler Wettbewerb für Komponistinnen:** Elisabethstrasse 5, Mannheim. Quadrennial competition open to female composers of all nationalities. Prizes include money.

**Karl Klingler Wettbewerb:** c/o Internationaler Musikwettbewerb, z.Hd. Frau Ingeborg Krause, Bayerischer Rundfunk, 80300 München. Triennial competition open to string quartets whose total age is at least 128 years with no members over the age of 37. Prizes include money.

### Greece

**Dmitris Mitropoulos International Competition:** 18 Alex Soutaou, 10671 Athens; tel. 30 210 36 27 412; fax 30 210 36 21 477; website www.mitropouloscompetition.gr. Annual competition.

**International Maria Callas Music Competition:** Amerikis Street 8, 10671 Athens. Biennial competition open to singers (opera, oratorio, lieder) and pianists with the categories alternating annually. Prizes include money.

### Hungary

**Budapest International Music Competition:** c/o InterArt Festivalcenter, Vorosmarty ter 1, 1051 Budapest; tel. 36 1 117 9838; fax 36 1 317 9910. Annual competition with categories changing annually.

**International Conductors' Competition of Hungarian Television:** Vorasmarty tér 1, 1051 Budapest. Triennial competition open to conductors of all nationalities under the age of 35.

### Ireland

**AXA Dublin International Piano Competition Ltd:** AXA Insurance, Dublin Road, Bray, Co. Wicklow; tel. 353 1 272 1523; fax 353 1 252 1508; website www.axadipc.ie. Triennial competition open to pianists between the ages of 17 and 30. Prizes include 1st prize of 12,000 euros, debut recitals in London, Vienna, Paris and New York, and concert engagements with major international orchestras, 2nd prize of 9,000 euros, 3rd prize of 6,000 euros, and other prizes; next competition in 2006.

### Israel

**International Harp Contest in Israel:** 4 Aharonowitz Street, 63566 Tel-Aviv; tel. 972 3 528 0233; fax 972 3 629 9524; website www.harpa.com/israel-harp-contest.htm. Triennial competition open to harpists of all nationalities. Prizes include 1st prize of a Lyon & Healy concert harp, 2nd prize of US $6,000, 3rd prize of $4,000; next contest in 2006.

**Arthur Rubinstein International Piano Master Competition:** PO Box 6018, 61060 Tel-Aviv; tel. 972 3 685 6684; fax 972 3 685 4924; website www.arims.org.il. Triennial competition open to pianists of all nationalities between the ages of 18 and 32. Prizes include 1st prize of the Arthur Rubinstein Award Gold Medal and US $10,000, 2nd prize of the Silver Medal and $5,000, 3rd prize of the Bronze Medal and $3,000, and 4th, 5th, and 6th prizes of $1,000 each.

### Italy

**Associazione Concorisi & Rassegno Musicali (ACERM):** Borgo Albizi, 50122 Florence; tel. and fax 39 55 240672. Annual competition open to chamber music instrumentalists to the age of 32. Prizes totalling some 30,000,000 Italian lire.

**Valentino Bucchi Competition:** Via Ubaldino Peruzzi 20, 00139 Rome. Annual competition open to performers and composers. Prizes totalling some 100,000,000 Italian lire.

**Enrico Caruso International Competition for Young Tenors:** c/o Associazione Enrico Caruso, Via Degli Omenoni 2, 20121 Milan. Biennial competition open to tenors between the ages of 18 and 28.

**Alessandro Casagrande Concorso Pianistico Internazionale:** Comune de Terni, Vico S. Lorenzo 1, 05100 Terni. Biennial competition open to pianists born after 1 January 1970. Prizes include 1st prize of 12,000,000 Italian lire, 2nd prize of 8,000,000 lire and 3rd prize of 5,000,000 lire.

**Gaspar Cassadó International Cello Competition:** Via Solferino 15, 50123 Florence. Biennial competition open to cellists.

**Concorso Internazionale di Chitarra Classica Città di Alessandria:** Piazza Garibaldi 16, 15100 Alessandria. Annual competition open to solo classical guitarists of all nationalities. Prizes include money.

**Concorso Internazionale di Composizione 2 Agosto:** c/o Studio Colliva e Nannucci, Via Savioli 24, 40137 Bologna.

**Concorso Internazionale di Composizione Camilo Togni:** c/o Associazione Nuovi Spazi Sonori, PO Box 196, 25100 Brescia. Biennial competition open to composers of all nationalities born after 31 December 1960. Prizes include 1st prize of 10,000,000 Italian lire, plus publication and performance of winning composition.

**Concorso Internazionale di Composizione Goffredo Petrassi:** Fondazione Arturo Toscanini, Palazzo Marchi, Strada della Repubblica 57, 43100 Parma; tel. 39 521 391322; fax 1 39 521 391321; website www.fondazione-toscanini.org. Biennial competition open to composers of all nationalities born after 6 Nov. 1964 for an unpublished symphonic composition not exceeding 30 minutes in length. Prizes include 1st prize of 15,000,000 Italian lire.

**Concorso Internazionale di Composizione Guido d'Arezzo Fondazione:** Corso Italia 102, 52100 Arezzo. Annual competition for polyvocal composition not previously published or performed, of at least five minutes' duration.

**Concorso Internazionale di Direzione d'Orchestra Arturo Toscanini:** Fondazione Arturo Toscanini, Palazzo Marchi, Strada della Repubblica 57, 43100 Parma; tel. 39 521 391322; fax 1 39 521 391321; website www.fondazione-toscanini.org. Triennial competition open to conductors of all nationalities to the age of 32. Prizes include 1st prize of 15,000,000 Italian lire, 2nd prize of 10,000,000 lire and 3rd prize of 6,000,000 lire.

**Concorso Internazionale di Violino Alberto Curci:** Fondazione Alberto Curci, Via Santa Brigida 68, 80132 Naples; tel. 39 81 5513030/7649370; fax 39 81 7649370; e-mail curcicompetition@libero.it. Competition open to violinists to the age of 32.

**Concorso Internazionale di Violino Premino N. Paganini:** Via Sottoripa 5, 16124 Genoa; tel. 39 10 5574215.

**Concorso Internazionale Luigi Russolo per Giovani Compositori:** c/o Fondazione Russolo-Pratella, Via G Bagaini 6, 21100 Varese. Annual competition open to composers of all nationalities to the age of 35, for electroacoustic, analogue and digital music compositions.

**Concorso Internazionale per Contrabasso Giovanni Bottesini:** c/o Conservatorio di Musica Arrigo Boito, Via del Conservatorio 27, 43100 Parma. Triennial competition open to double bass players of all nationalities between the ages of 16 and 32. Prizes include 1st prize of 10,000,000 Italian lire, 2nd prize of 6,000,000 lire and 3rd prize of 4,000,000 lire.

**Concorso Internazionale per La Conquista Della Chitarra Classica:** CP 10673, 20125 Milan. Annual competition open to classical guitarists of all ages. Prizes include money, gold medals and guitars.

**Concorso Internazionale per Quartetto d'Archi Premio Paolo Borciani:** c/o Teatro Municipale Valli, Piazza Martiri del 7 luglio, 42100 Reggio Emilia; tel. (39) 0522 458811; fax (39) 0522 458822; e-mail premioborciani@iteatri.re.it; website www.premioborciani.iteatri.re.it. Triennial competition open to string quartets of all nations whose members' total age does not exceed 128 years on 12 June 2005. Prizes include 1st prize of 19,000 euros, 2nd prize of 13,800 euros, 3rd prize of 6,600 euros, and a special prize for the best performance of a new quartet, awarded by Sir Peter Maxwell Davies, of 2,500 euros.

**Concorso Internazionale per Voci Verdiane:** Fondazione Arturo Toscanini, Palazzo Marchi, Strada della Repubblica 57, 43100 Parma; tel. 39 521 391322; fax 1 39 521 391321; website www.fondazione-toscanini.org.

**Concorso Internazionale Pianistico Liszt Premio Mario Zanfi:** c/o Conservatorio di Musica Arrigo Boito, Via del Conservatorio 27, 43100 Parma. Triennial competition open to pianists of all nationalities between the ages of 16 and 32. Prizes include 1st prize of 10,000,000 Italian lire, 2nd prize of 6,000,000 lire and 3rd prize of 4,000,000 lire.

**Concorso Pianistico Internazionale Alfredo Casella:** Via del Parco Margherita 49, pal 5, 80121 Naples. Biennial competition open to pianists of all nationalities.

**Concorso Pianistico Internazionale Ettore Pozzoli:** Segreteria, Via Paradiso 6, 20038 Seregno; tel. and fax 39 0362 222 914; e-mail info@concorsopozzoli.it; website www.concorsopozzoli.it. Biennial competition open to pianists of all nationalities born on or after 1 Jan. 1973. Prizes include 1st prize of 10,000 euros and recording and release of a CD, 2nd prize of 5,000 euros, 3rd prize of 2,500 euros, two special prizes of 1,000 euros and two special prizes of 500 euros.

**Fondazione Concorso Pianistico Internazionale Ferruccio Busoni:** Piazza Domenicani 25, 39100 Bolzano. Biennial competition open to pianists of all nationalities between the ages of 15 and 28. Prizes include 1st prize of 22,000 euros and concert engagements, 2nd prize of 10,000 euros, 3rd prize of 5,000 euros, 4th prize of 4,000 euros, 5th prize of 3,000 euros, and 6th prize of 2,500 euros.

**International Competition of the Teatro Alla Scala:** Dino Ciani Prize: c/o Teatro alla Scala, Fondazione di Diritto Privato, Ufficio Assunzioni, PO Box 1611, 20101 Milan. Triennial competition open to pianists of all nationalities born after 31 December 1975. Prizes include 1st prize of 20,000,000 Italian lire, 2nd prize of 8,000,000 lire and 3rd prize of 3,000,000 lire, with medals and performances for each.

**Rodolfo Lipizer International Violin Contest:** Via Don Giovanni Bosco 91, 34170 Gorizia; tel. 39 481 34775/532551/533264; fax 39 481 536710; e-mail lipizer@lipizer.it; website www.lipizer.it. Annual competition open to violinists of all nationalities born after 17 Sept. 1966. Prizes include money and concert appearances.

**Niccolò Paganini Premio Internazionale di Violino:** Palazzo Doria, Via Garibaldi 9, 16124 Genoa. Annual competition open to violinists of all nationalities under the age of 35. Prizes include 1st prize of 20,000,000 Italian lire, 2nd prize of 10,000,000 lire, 3rd prize of 6,000,000 lire, 4th prize of 4,000,000 lire, 5th prize of 3,000,000 lire, and 6th prize of 2,000,000 lire.

**Antonio Pedrotti International Competition for Orchestra Conductors:** Via San Croce 67, 38100 Trento; tel. 39 461 231223; fax 39 461 232592. Biennial competition open to conductors between the ages of 18 and 33. Prizes include 1st prize of 10,000,000 Italian lire and engagements with Italian Orchestras, 2nd prize of 7,000,000 lire and 3rd prize of 5,000,000 lire.

**Premio Musicale Città di Trieste:** Concorso Internazionale di Composizione Sinfonica: Palazzo Municipale, Piazza dell'Unità d'Italia 4, 34121 Trieste. Biennial competition open to composers of all nationalities. Prizes include 1st prize of 5,000,000 Italian lire and performance of composition, 2nd prize of 2,500,000 lire and 3rd prize of 1,500,000 lire.

**Rassegna della Canzone d'Autore-Premio Tenco:** Via Meridiana 7, 18038 San Remo. Annual competition open to singers who are lyricists and composers, by invitation only.

**Toti dal Monte International Singing Competition:** Ente Teatro Comunale, Corso del Popolo 31, Via Diaz 7, 31100 Treviso.

**G. B. Viotti Concorso Internazionale di Musicale:** PO Box 127, 13100 Vercelli; tel. 39 0161 252667; fax 39 0161 255575; e-mail info@concorsoviotti .it; website www.concorsoviotti.it. Annual competition for singers and pianists.

**Vittorio Gui International Chamber Music Competition:** ACRM, Borgo degli Albizi 15, 50122 Florence; tel. and fax 39 55 240672; e-mail acerm@ frenze.net.

## Japan

**International Music Competition of Japan:** West Park Building 4F, 1-10-16, Ebisunhishi, Sibuya-ku, Tokyo 150. Triennial competition open to instrumentalists of all nationalities between the ages of 17 and 32. Prizes include money, medals, and concert appearances.

**Reiko Takahashi IRINO (Irino Prize Foundation):** c/o JML Seminar Yoshiro Irino Institute of Music, 5-22-2 Matsubara, Setagaya-ku, Tokyo 156-0043; tel. 3 3323-0646; fax 3 3325-5468; e-mail jml-irinopz@nyc.odn.ne.jp; website www.jml-irino.jp/IrinoPrize/index.html. Annual prize open to composers of all nationalities under the age of 40, rotating annually between an orchestral and a chamber music composition. Prizes include 650,00 yen for an orchestral composition and 200,000 yen for a chamber music composition.

**Tokyo International Competition for Chamber Music Composition:** c/o Japan International Artists, 2-3-16-607 Shinjuku, Shinjuku, Tokyo. Competition open to composers of chamber music of all ages and nationalities. Prizes include 1st prize of 300,000 yen, 2nd prize of 150,000 yen and 3rd prize of 100,000 yen.

**Tokyo International Music Competition:** 1-32-13 Kita-Shinjuku, Shinjuku-ku, Tokyo 169; website www.min-on.or.jp. Annual competition open to performers of all nationalities with categories changing annually. Prizes include 1st prize of 1,000,000 yen and a medal, 2nd prize of 700,000 yen and a medal, 3rd prize of 500,000 yen, a medal and a certificate of honourable mention, and 4th prize of 200,000 yen and a medal.

## Monaco

**Prix de Composition Musicale Prince Pierre de Monaco:** Centre Administratif, rue Louis Notari, 098000 Monaco. Annual prize awarded to the best musical composition of the year prize of 50,000 French francs.

## Netherlands

**BG S-Hertogenbosch International Singing Competition:** PO Box 1225, 5200 BG's-Hertogenbosch; tel. 31 736 900999. Annual competition open to singers. Prizes include money.

**César Franck Organ Competition:** Leeghwaterstraat 14, 2012 GD Haarlem; tel. 31 235 327070.

**Delft Chamber Music Festival:** 0.2. Voorburgwal 72, 1012 GE Amsterdam; tel. 31 20 643 2043; fax 31 20 640 3961; e-mail mbrinks@xs4all.nl; website www.delftmusicfestival.nl.

**I K F International Choir Festival:** Plomepetorengracht 3, 3512 CA Utrecht; tel. 31 302 313174; fax 31 302 318137. Quadrennial prizes awarded to choirs.

**International Competition for Early Music Ensembles:** Singel 308-sous, 1016 AE Amsterdam; tel. 31 206 391390; fax 31 206 227118. Annual competition open to young professional early music ensembles consisting of two to eight performers.

**International Competition for Organ Improvisation:** PO Box 3333, 2001 DH Haarlem; tel. 31 231 60574; fax 31 231 60576. Annual competition open to concert organists experienced in improvisation. Prizes include money.

**International Franz Liszt Piano Competition:** Muziekcentrum Vredenburg, PO Box 550, 3500 AN Utrecht; tel. 31 302 330233; fax 31 302 316522. Triennial competition open to pianists of all nationalities between the ages of 16 and 30. Prizes include money and engagements for the 1st prize winner.

**International Gaudeamus Composers' Competition:** Gaudeamus Foundation, Swammerdamstraat 38, 1091 RV Amsterdam; tel. 31 206 947349; fax 31 206 947258. Annual competition open to composers to the age of 30. Prizes include money.

**International Gaudeamus Interpreters' Competition:** Gaudeamus Foundation, Swammerdamstraat 38, 1091 RV Amsterdam; tel. 31 206 947349; fax 31 206 947258. Annual competition open to instrumentalists and singers of contemporary music. Prizes include money, with a 1st prize of 10,000 florins.

**International Kirill Kondrashin Competition for Young Conductors:** c/o NOS, PO Box 26444, 1202 JJ Hilversum; tel. 31 357 75453; fax 31 357 74311. Quinquennial competition open to conductors to the age of 36. Prizes include guest conducting engagements with major orchestras.

**Scheveningen International Music Competition:** Gevers Deynootweg 970 Z, 2586 BW Scheveningen; tel. 31 20 6947349; fax 31 20 6947258. Annual competition open to instrumentalists to the age of 30. Prizes include money.

## New Zealand

**Lexus New Zealand International Violin Competition:** PO Box 10-113, Wellington. Quadrennial competition open to violinists of all nationalities between the ages of 18 and 28. Prizes include money.

## Norway

**Queen Sonja International Music Competition:** PO Box 5190, Majorstua, 0302 Oslo 1; tel. 47 22 464055; fax 47 22 463630. Triennial competition open to instrumentalists or singers. Prizes include money and concert engagements.

## Poland

**Fryderyk Chopin International Piano Competition:** ul Okólnik 1, 00-368 Warsaw. Quinquennial competition open to pianists of all nationalities born between 1977 and 1988. Prizes include 1st prize of US $25,000 and a gold medal, 2nd prize of $20,000 and a silver medal, 3rd prize of $15,000 and a bronze medal, and three other money prizes.

**Grzegorz Fitelberg International Competition for Conductors:** Sokolska 2, 40-084 Katowice; tel. and fax 48 32 596074. Quadrenial competition open to conductors to the age of 35. Prizes include money and medals.

**International Composers' Competition Kasimierz Serocki:** ul Mazowiecka 11, 00-052 Warsaw. Triennial competition open to composers of all nationalities. Prizes include money.

**International Henryk Wieniawski Competition for Violinists, Composers, and Violin Makers:** Swietoslawska St 7, 61-840 Poznan; tel. 48 61 522642; fax 48 61 528991. Quinquennial competition open to violinists of all nationalities to the age of 30. Prizes include money.

**International Stanislaw Moniuszko Competition for Young Vocalists:** c/o Warsaw Philharmonic Orchestra, ul. Jasna 5, 00 950 Warsaw; tel. 48 22 5517101; fax 48 22 5517200; e-mail filharmonia@filharmonia.pl; website www .filharmonia.pl. Triennial competition open to young vocalists. Prizes include money.

**International Witold Lutoslawski Composers' Competition:** c/o Warsaw Philharmonic Orchestra, ul. Jasna 5, 00 950 Warsaw; tel. 48 22 5517101; fax 48 22 5517200; e-mail filharmonia@filharmonia.pl; website www .filharmonia.pl. Biennial competition open to composers of all nationalities and all ages. Prizes include money and performances by the Warsaw Philharmonic.

## Portugal

**Porto International Music Competition:** Rua Azevedo Coutinho 195, 4100 Porto; tel. 35 126 095099; fax 35 126 004307. Annual competition.

## Romania

**George Enescu International Piano, Violin and Singing Competition:** Calea Victoriei 155, Blvd D1, sc.8, et.2, 71012 Bucharest.

## Russia

**International Tchaikovsky Competition:** 15 Neglinnaya St, Moscow. Quadrennial competition open to pianists, violinists, cellists and singers of all nationalities. Prizes include money and medals.

## Singapore

**Rolex Music Performance Awards:** The Rolex Centre, 302 Orchard Road, 01-01 Tong Building, Singapore 0923. Biennial competition open to pianists and violinists who are citizens or permanent residents of Singapore, Malaysia,

Brunei, Indonesia, Thailand, the Philippines or Hong Kong. Prizes include money.

## Spain

**Concurso Internacional de Canto Julián Gayarre:** Calle Santo Domingo 6, 31001 Pamplona; tel. 34 48 106072; fax 34 48 223906. Biennial competition open to singers of all nationalities, women between the ages of 18 and 32, and men between the ages of 20 and 35. Prizes include money.

**Concurso Internacional de Ejecución Musical Maria Canals de Barcelona:** Gran Via de les Corts Catalanes 654, 08010 Barcelona; tel. and fax 34 33 187731. Annual competition open to instrumentalists between the ages of 18 and 32. Prizes include money.

**Concurso Internacional de Piano Frederic Chopin:** Conservatorio Professional de Música de Baleares, Calle Hospital 4, 07012 Palma de Mallorca; tel. 34 71 711157. Biennial competition open to pianists of all nationalities to the age of 35. Prizes include 1st prize of 1,000,000 pesetas and recitals, 2nd prize of 500,000 pesetas, and 3rd prize of 250,000 pesetas.

**Concurso Internacional de Piano José Iturbi:** Plaza de Manises 4, 46003 Valencia; tel. 34 63 882500; fax 34 63 882775. Biennial competition open to pianists of all nationalities under the age of 31 on the date of the competition. Prizes include 1st prize of 18,100 euros, 2nd prize of 12,100 euros, 3rd prize of 6,100 euros, with recitals for each category.

**Concurso Internacional de Piano Premio Jaén:** c/o Instituto de Estudios Giennenses, 23002 Jaén. Annual competition open to pianists of all nationalities, except winners of the Jaén Prize. Prizes include 1st prize of 2,000,000 pesetas, a gold medal and concert engagements, 2nd prize of 1,000,000 pesetas, 3rd prize of 400,000 pesetas, and the Rose Sabater Prize of 500,000 pesetas for the best interpreter of Spanish music.

**Palpma O'Shea Santander International Piano Competition:** Calle Hernán Cortés 3, 39009 Santander; fax 34 42 314816. Triennial competition open to pianists of all nationalities between the ages of 17 and 30. Prizes include money totalling 15,000,000 pesetas, recordings, concerts and travel grants.

**Premio Internacional de Canto Fundación Guerrero:** Gran Via 78, 28013 Madrid. Biennial competition open to singers of all nationalities and ages. Prizes include 1st prize of 2,500,000 pesetas and a prize of 600,000 pesetas for the best interpreter of the music of Jacinto e Inocencio Guerrero.

**Premio Internacional de Piano Fundación Guerrero:** Gran Via 78, 28013 Madrid. Biennial competition open to pianists of all nationalities and ages. Prizes include 1st prize of 2,500,000 pesetas.

**Pablo Sarasata International Violin Competition:** Calle Santo Domingo 6, 31001 Pamplona; tel. 34 48 106072/106500; fax 34 48 223906. Biennial competition open to violinists.

**Francisco Viñas International Singing Contest:** Bruc 125, 08037 Barcelona. Annual competition open to singers, women between the ages of 18 and 32 and men between the ages of 20 and 35. Prizes for both include 1st prize of 8,000 euros, 2nd prize of 5,000 euros, 3rd prize of 4,000 euros, and medals and special prizes.

## Sweden

**Jussi Björling Tenor Competition:** Borlänge Kommun 781, 81 Borlänge, Höbergstatan 76B, 11856 Stockholm; tel. 46 8 243 7400; fax 46 8 243 66208.

## Switzerland

**Concours Géza Anda:** Bleicherweg 18, 8002 Zürich; tel. 0041 1 205 14 23; fax 0041 1 205 14 29; e-mail info@gezaanda.ch; website www.gezaanda.ch. Triennial competition open to pianists to the age of 32. Prizes include money and major concert engagements. Next competition in June 2006.

**Concours International d'Execution Musicale:** 104 rue de Carouge, 1205 Geneva. Annual competition open to performers of all nationalities with categories changing annually. Prizes totalling 130,000 Swiss francs.

**Concours Suisse de l'Orgue:** Place du Prieur, 1323 Romainmôtier. Annual competition open to organists of all nationalities and ages.

**Clara Haskil Piano Competition:** 40 rue du Simplon, PO Box 234, 1800 Vevey; tel. 41 21 922 6704; fax 41 21 922 6734. Biennial competition open to pianists to the age of 30. Prizes include 20,000 Swiss francs and concert engagements.

**International Competition in Composition of Sacred Music:** PO Box 292, 1701 Fribourg. Biennial competition open to composers of all nationalities and ages. Prizes include 10,000 Swiss francs and the premiere of the winning work at the Fribourg Festival of Sacred Music.

**International Violin Competition Sion-Valais:** PO Box 1429, 1951 Sion; tel. 41 27 323 43 61; fax 41 27 323 46 62; e-mail info@sion.festival.ch; website www.sion.festival.ch. Annual competition open to violinists between the ages of 15 and 32. Prizes totalling 30,000 Swiss francs.

**Musical Prize Contest Queen Marie-José:** PO Box 19, 1252 Meinier, Geneva. Biennial competition open to composers of all nationalities and ages who submit an unpublished composition. Prizes include 10,000 Swiss francs.

**Swiss Organ Competition:** Place du Prieur, 1323 Romainmôtier; tel. 41 24 531718; fax 41 24 531150.

## United Kingdom

**BBC Television Young Musician of the Year Competition:** c/o BBC TV, Kensington House, Richmond Way, London W14 0AX; website www.bbc.co.uk. Biennial televised competition open to British resident performers to age 18 and composers to age 21. Prizes totalling £32,000.

**Cardiff Singer of the World Competition:** c/o BBC Wales, Music Department, Broadcasting House, Llandaff, Cardiff, Wales CF5 2YQ; website www.bbc.co.uk. Biennial competition open to singers 18 years of age or older. Prizes include £5,000 and concert engagements.

**City of London Carl Flesch International Violin Competition:** c/o City Arts Trust, Bishopsgate Hall, 230 Bishopsgate, London EC2M 4QH. Biennial competition open to violinists of all nationalities under the age of 28. Prizes include 1st prize of £6,000, 2nd prize of £4,000, 3rd prize of £3,000, 4th prize of £1,750, 5th prize of £1,250, and 6th prize of £750, with five additional prizes of £500 each.

**City of London Walter Gruner International Lieder Competition:** c/o City Arts Trust, Bishopsgate Hall, 230 Bishopsgate, London EC2M 4QH. Biennial competition open to singers to the age of 28. Prizes include 1st prize of £3,500 and a debut recital in London, 2nd prize of £2,250, 3rd prize of £1,250, and 4th prize of £750, with an accompanists' prize of £1,250.

**Donatella Flick Conducting Competition:** PO Box 34227, London NW5 1XP; fax 020 7482 1353; website www.conducting.org. Biennial competition open to European Community nationals under 35.

**Folkestone Menuhin International Violin Competition:** 72 Leopold Road, London SW19 7JQ. Biennial competition open to violinists. Prizes totalling £15,700.

**Great Grimsby International Competition for Singers:** 23 Enfield Ave, New Waltham, Great Grimsby, South Humberside DN36 5RD. Triennial competition open to singers between the ages of 20 and 30 with accompanists to age 26. Prizes include 1st prize of £2,000, 2nd prize of £1,000 and 3rd prize of £500, with an accompanists' prize of £500.

**Kathleen Ferrier Awards:** Kathleen Ferrier Memorial Scholarship Fund, Courtyard House, Neopardy, Crediton, Devon EX17 5EP; tel. 01363 777844; fax 01363 777845; e-mail info@ferrierawards.org.uk; website www.ferrierawards.org.uk. Annual competition open to British and Commonwealth singers aged 21-28. 1st prize £10,000 and Wigmore Hall recital.

**Leeds Conductors' Competition:** Music Department, Leeds Leisure Service, Town Hall, The Headrow, Leeds, LS1 3AD; tel. 0113 247 8336; website www.leedsconductors.com.

**Leeds International Pianoforte Competition:** Piano Competition Office, University of Leeds, Leeds LS2 9JT; tel. 0113 244 6586; website www.leedspiano.com. Triennial competition open to professional pianists under the age of 30. Prizes include money totalling £60,000 and concert engagements worldwide; next competition in Sept. 2006.

**London International Piano Competition:** 28 Wallace Road, London N1 2PG; tel. (20) 7354-1087; fax (20) 7704-1053; e-mail ldn-ipc@dircon.co.uk; website www.ldn-ipc.dircon.co.uk. Triennial competition open to pianists of all nationalities to the age of 29. Prizes include money totalling £30,000, concert engagements and scholarships.

**London International String Quartet Competition:** 62 High St, Fareham, Hampshire PO16 7BG. Triennial competition open to string quartets whose aggregate ages do not exceed 120 years. Prizes include 1st prize of £8,000 and the Amadeus Trophy, 2nd prize of £4,800, 3rd prize of £3,200, 4th prize of £2,400, and 5th prize of £1,600, with the Menuhin Prize of £750 and the Audience Prize of £500.

**Newport International Competition for Young Pianists:** Civic Centre, Newport, Gwent NP20 4UR; tel. 01633 662666; website www.newport.gov.uk/piano. Triennial competition open to pianists to the age of 25. Prizes include money and concerts; next competition in 2006.

**Performing Right Society Electroacoustic Composition Prize:** c/o Electroacoustic Music Association of Great Britain, 10 Stratford Place, London W1N 9AE. Biennial competition open to composers.

**The Queen's Medal for Music:** c/o Public Information Office, Buckingham Palace, London, SW1A 1AA; annual award, f. 2005, to raise the profile of music within the UK; winners may be of any nationality but they must have had a major influence on the musical life of the nation; decisions on eligibility for the Medal are made by the Music Committee, Chaired by the current Master of The Queen's Music; the winner is announced on 22 November, the day of the patron saint of music, St Cecilia.

**Royal Over-Seas League of Music Competition:** Over-Seas House, Park Place, St James's St, London SW1A 1LR. Annual competition open to

Commonwealth and former Commonwealth citizens, for instrumentalists to the age of 28 and for singers to the age of 30. Various prizes.

**Scottish International Piano Competition:** c/o SIPC Office, The Mitchell Library, 201 North Street, Glasgow G3 7DN; tel. 0141 287 2857; fax 0141 287 2858; website www.sipc2004.org. Triennial competition open to pianists of all nationalities to the age of 32. Prizes include £8,000.

**Tunbridge Wells International Young Concert Artists (TWIYCA) Competition:** Paddock Wood, Kent TN12 6PA. Biennial competition open to performers to the age of 25. Prizes totalling £9,000.

**Wigmore Hall International Song Competition:** Room 616a, Langham House, 308 Regent Street, London W1B 3AT; e-mail whisc@wigmore-hall.org.uk; website www.wigmore-hall.org.uk

**Yehudi Menuhin International Competition for Young Violinists:** c/o Royal Academy of Music, Marylebone Road, London, NW1 5HT; website www.geniusoftheviolin.org. Biennial competition open to violinists of any nationality under the age of 22. Prizes totalling £20,000. The competition forms part of the Genius of the Violin Festival.

## United States of America

**ALEA III International Composition Prize:** c/o Boston University School of Music, 855 Commonwealth Ave, Boston, MA 02215; tel. 1 617 353 3340; website www.aleaiii.com. Annual competition open to composers of all nationalities under the age of 40. Submitted composition must not have been published, publicly performed, or awarded any prize.

**ASCAP Foundation Grants to Young Composers:** 1 Lincoln Plaza, New York, NY 10023; tel. 1 212 621 6219; website www.ascap.com. Annual grants to composers who are citizens or permanent residents of the USA and have not reached their 30th birthday by 15 March.

**American Academy and Institute of Arts and Letters:** 633 W 155th St, New York, NY 10032. Various awards are given in the field of music.

**American Academy in Rome:** 7 E 60th Street, New York, NY 10022; tel. 1 212 751 7200; fax 1 212 751 7220; e-mail info@aarome.org; website www.aarome.org. Annual residents' programme to support distinguished artists and scholars as residents at the academy for a year and annual Rome Prize Fellowships for American composers to study at the academy.

**American Berlin Opera Foundation Inc:** 6 E 87th Street, New York, NY 10128; tel. 1 212 534 5383; e-mail ABOF@operafoundation.org; website www.operafoundation.org. Annual scholarships for American singers who are citizens or permanent residents between the ages of 18 and 32, to study at the Deutsche Oper Berlin. Prizes include a scholarship of US $15,000 and a round trip flight.

**American Guild of Organists (AGO)/National Young Artists Competition in Organ Performance:** 475 Riverside Drive, Suite 1260, New York, NY 10115; tel. 1 212 870 2310; fax 1 212 870 2163; e-mail info@agohq.org; website www.agohq.org. Biennial competition open to organists between the ages of 22 and 32.

**American Musicological Society Inc:** 201 South 34th St, Philadelphia, PA 19104. Noah Greenberg Award of up to US $2,000 for a distinguished contribution to the study and/or performance of music prior to 1700. Otto Kinkeldey Award of $400 and a scroll to a US or Canadian writer of the most notable full-length study in musicology. Alfred Einstein Award of $400 to a young scholar who has published an article on a musicological subject in the preceding year.

**American Pianists' Association National Fellowship Piano Auditions:** Clowes Memorial Hall, Butler University, 4600 Sunset Ave, Indianapolis, IN 46208; e-mail apainfo@americanpianists.org; website www.americanpianists.org. Biennial fellowships open to American classical pianists between the ages of 18 and 30. Prizes include three-year fellowship, US $10,000, sponsorship at an international competition, and US concert engagements.

**Artists International's Annual New York Debut Award Auditions:** 521 Fifth Ave, Suite 1700, New York, NY 10017; tel. 1 212 292 4257. Annual auditions open to performers of all nationalities who have not given a New York recital debut or who have not received a New York review for a solo recital. Prizes include New York recital debut at Carnegie Recital Hall, Merkin Concert Hall or Alice Tully Hall at the Lincoln Center.

**Artists International's Distinguished Artists Award Auditions:** 521 Fifth Ave, Suite 1700, New York, NY 10017; tel. 1 212 292 4257. Annual auditions open to soloists or chamber groups who have received at least one review from a major New York publication and have no management. Prizes include recital engagement in New York.

**Broadcast Music Inc (BMI) Student Composers Awards:** 320 W 57th St, New York, NY 10019; website www.bmi.com. Annual awards open to student composers who are citizens or permanent residents of a country in the western hemisphere, to the age of 25. Prizes totalling US $16,000.

**Johann Sebastian Bach International Competition:** 1211 Potomac St NW, Washington, DC 20007. Competition open to performers of the works of J S Bach between the ages of 20 and 40. Prizes include money and concert engagements.

**Gina Bachauer International Piano Competition:** 138 W Broadway, Suite 220, Salt Lake City, UT 84101; website www.bachauer.com. Triennial competition open to pianists between the ages of 19 and 32. Prizes include 1st prize of a grand piano and New York and Los Angeles debut concerts; other prizes include Gold, Silver, and Bronze medals, money prizes, concerts and recitals, with finalists appearing with the Utah Symphony Orchestra. Also a junior section for pianists between the ages of 8 and 18.

**Baltimore Opera Vocal Competition for American Operatic Artists:** 101 W Read St, Suite 605, Baltimore, MD 21201. Annual competition open to operatic singers between the ages of 20 and 35. Prizes include 1st prize of US $10,000, 2nd prize of $8,000, 3rd prize of $4,500, 4th prize of $2,500, 5th prize of $2,000, 6th prize of $1,200, and 7th prize of $1,000, with an additional prize of $1,000 awarded by the audience.

**Barlow International Competition:** c/o Brigham Young University, Harris Fine Arts Center, Provo, UT 84602. Annual competition open to composers of all nationalities; composition must not have won any other competition. Prizes totalling US $10,000.

**Joseph H Bearns Prize in Music:** c/o Columbia University, Department of Music, 703 Dodge Hall, New York, NY 10027; tel. 1 212 854 3825. Annual competition open to American composers between the ages of 18 and 25. Prizes include money.

**Frank Huntington Beebe Fund for Musicians:** 290 Huntington Ave, Boston, MA 02115; tel. 1 617 262 1120. Annual scholarships open to American post-graduate music students for study abroad.

**Simone Belsky Music Award Competition:** 153 North St, PO Box 1112, Litchfield, CT 06759; tel. 1 860 567 4162; fax 1 860 567 3592. Biennial competition open to pianists over 30 years old. Prizes include 1st prize of US $1,500 and concert engagements.

**Boston Classical Orchestra Youth Competition:** 551 Tremont St, Boston, MA 02116; tel. 1 617 423 3883. Annual competition open to high school seniors in New England and New York who wish to pursue a career as an instrumentalist. Prizes include a four-year merit scholarship to the Boston University School of Music and an appearance as soloist with the Boston Classical Orchestra at a youth concert.

**Brandeis University Creative Arts Awards:** Brandeis University, PO Box 549110, Waltham, MA 02254; tel. 1 781 736 2027; fax 1 781 736 3457; e-mail arts50@brandeis.edu. Annual prizes open to established artists in various fields, including music. Prizes include a medal and an honorarium.

**Benjamin Britten Memorial Fund:** 135 E 83rd St, Suite 4/5-C, New York, NY 10028. Annual scholarships open to American students for study at the Britten-Pears School for Advanced Musical Studies in Aldeburgh, Suffolk, England.

**Bryan International String Competition:** North Carolina Symphony Orchestra, PO Box 28026, Raleigh, NC 27611. Quadrennial competition open to violinists, violists, and cellists between the ages of 18 and 30. Prizes include 1st prize of US $12,000, 2nd prize of $6,000 and 3rd prize of $3,000.

**Grace Bumbry Student Assistance Award:** c/o AGMA Relief Fund, 1727 Broadway, New York, NY 10019. Study grant for American classical singers between the ages of 18 and 25. Prizes include 1st prize of US $2,000.

**William C Byrd Young Artist Competition:** c/o Flint Institute of Music, 1025 E Kearsley St, Flint, MI 48503; website www.byrdartists.com. Annual competition open to performers with categories changing annually. Prizes include 1st prize of US $2,500 and an appearance with the Flint Symphony Orchestra.

**CRS National Festival for the Performing Arts:** 724 Winchester Road, Broomall, PA 19008. Annual competition with prizes including fellowships, recording contracts, national appearances and artist representation.

**Carmel Chamber Music Competition:** PO Box 221458, Carmel, CA 93922; tel. 1 831 625 2212. Annual competition open to non-professional chamber groups of three to six players averaging under the age of 26. Prizes include money.

**Carmel Music Society Competition:** PO Box 1144, Carmel, CA 93921; tel. 1 831 625 9938; fax 1 831 625 6823; e-mail carmelmusic@sbcglobal.net; website www.carmelmusic.org. Annual competition open to musicians who are residents or full-time students in California. Prizes include money and an appearance at a Carmel Chamber Music concert.

**Center for Contemporary Opera International Opera Singers Competition:** PO Box 1350, Gracie Station, New York, NY 10028; tel. 1 212 308 6728; fax 1 212 308 6744. Annual competition open to singers who have not attained a major operatic career. Prizes include money.

**Chamber Music America:** Commissioning Program, 305 Seventh Ave, 5th Floor, New York, NY 10001-6008; tel. 1 212 242 2022; fax 1 212 242 7955. Annual ASCAP Awards for various activities devoted to the performance and promotion of chamber music.

**Chopin Foundation of the National Chopin Piano Competition of the United States:** 1440 79th St Causeway, Suite 117, Miami, FL 33141; tel. 1 305 868 0624; fax 1 305 868 5150; e-mail info@chopin.org; website www.chopin

.org. Quinquennial competition open to American pianists between the ages of 16 and 18, to enable them to participate in the International Chopin Piano Competition in Warsaw. Prizes include 1st prize of US $15,000, 2nd prize of $9,000, 3rd prize of $6,000, 4th prize of $3,500, 5th prize of $2,500, and 6th prize of $2,000.

**Civic Orchestra of Chicago Soloist Competition:** 220 S Michigan Ave, Chicago, IL 60604. Annual competition open to soloists between the ages of 19 and 30. Prizes include US $1,000 and concert engagements.

**Cleveland International Piano Competition:** 1988 Ford Drive, Cleveland, OH 44106; tel. 1 216 707 5397; fax 1 216 707 0224; e-mail ClevePiano@aol.com; website piano.wclv.com. Biennial competition open to pianists between the ages of 17 and 32. Prizes include money and concert engagements.

**Van Cliburn International Piano Competition:** 2525 Ridgmar Blvd, Suite 307, Fort Worth, TX 76116; tel. 1 817 738 6536; fax 1 817 738 6534; website www.cliburn.org. Quadrennial piano competition open to pianists between the ages 18 and 30. Prizes include 1st prize of US $15,000, Carnegie Hall recital and orchestral debuts, US recital and orchestral tour, and European recital and orchestral tour, 2nd prize of $10,000, New York debut, and US tour, 3rd prize of $7,500 and US tour, 4th prize of $5,000, 5th prize of $3,500, and 6th prize of $2,000.

**Coleman Chamber Ensemble Competition:** Coleman Chamber Music Association, 202 S Lake Avenue, Suite 201, Pasadena, CA 91101; tel. (626) 793-4191; fax (818) 787-1294; e-mail krfccma@aol.com; website coleman .caltech.edu/2004comp.pdf. Annual competition open to non-professional chamber ensembles whose members' average age is under 26, and prepared by a coach.

**Composers Guild Annual Competition Contest:** 40 North 100 West, PO Box 586, Farmington, UT 84025; tel. 1 801 451 2275. Annual competition open to composers. Prizes include money.

**Concert Artists Guild International New York Competition:** 850 Seventh Ave, Suite 1205, New York, NY 10019. Annual competition open to instrumentalists, chamber ensembles and singers. Prizes include money, concert engagements, recordings and free management services.

**Concerto Competition of the Rome Festival Orchestra:** Empire State Building, Suite 3304, New York, NY 10118; tel. 1 212 971 9702. Annual competition open to North American performers of violin, viola, cello, double bass, oboe and horn. Prizes include five tuition fellowships and solo appearance in Rome.

**Corporation of Yaddo:** PO Box 395, Union Ave, Saratoga Springs, NY 12866; tel. 1 518 584 0746; fax 1 518 584 1312; website www.yaddo.org. Room, board and studio for professional composers of all nationalities. Residency up to two months.

**Council for International Exchange for Scholars-Fulbright Scholar Program:** 3007 Tilden St NW, Suite 5M, Washington, DC 20008; tel. 1 202 686 4000; fax 1 202 362 3442; website www.cies.org. Annual grants for university lecturing and/or advanced research abroad by Americans, including several in the field of music.

**D'Angelo Young Artist Competition:** c/o Mercyhurst College, 501 E 38th St, Erie, PA 16546; tel. 1 814 824 2394. Annual competition open to performers under the age of 35 with categories rotating annually. Prizes include 1st prize of US $10,000 and concert engagements, 2nd prize of $5,000 and 3rd prize of $3,000, with $1,000 to all finalists.

**Kenneth Davenport National Competition for Orchestral Works:** c/o State University of New York, College of New Paltz, New Paltz, NY 12561; tel. 1 814 257 3860; fax 1 814 257 3859. Annual competition open to composers who are American citizens or permanent residents. Prizes include US $1,500 and performance of composition.

**Delius Composition Contest:** c/o Jacksonville University, College of Fine Arts, Jacksonville, FL 32211; tel. 1 904 745 7370; fax 1 904 745 7375. Annual competition open to composers. Prizes include 1st prize of US $500, $100 for the best vocal, keyboard, and instrumental composition, and high school composition category of 1st prize of $200 and 2nd prize of $100.

**Delta Omicron International Music Fraternity Triennial Composition Competition:** 8009 Volk Dr., Dayton, OH 45415; website www.delta -omicron.org. Triennial competition open to American composers of college age or older. Prizes include US $500 and premiere of composition.

**Detroit Symphony Orchestra Fellowship Program:** 400 Buhl Building, 535 Griswold St, Detroit, MI 48226; website www.detroitsymphony.com. One-year residency for African-American orchestral players with the Detroit Symphony Orchestra.

**Murray Dranoff International Two Piano Competition:** 180 NE 39th Street, Suite 207, Miami, FL 33137; tel. 1 305 572 9900; fax 1 305 572 9922; e-mail mail@dranoff2piano.org; website www.dranoff2piano.org. Biennial competition open to duo pianists between the ages of 18 and 35. Prizes include 1st prize of US $10,000, 2nd prize of $5,000 and 3rd prize of $2,000, plus concert engagements.

**East and West Artists International Auditions for New York Debut:** 310 Riverside Dr., Suite 313, New York, NY 10025; tel. 1 212 222 2433. Annual competition open to performers who have not given a New York debut recital. Prizes include debut at Weill Recital Hall at Carnegie Hall, money, radio and concert engagements.

**Fischoff National Chamber Music Competition:** 303 Brownson Hall, University of Notre Dame, Notre Dame, IN 46556; fax 1 574 631 2903; e-mail info@fischoff.org; website www.fischoff.org. Annual competition open to instrumental ensembles of three to five members to the age of 18. Prizes include money.

**Avery Fisher Artist Program:** Lincoln Center, 140 W 65th St, New York, NY 10023; tel. 1 212 875 5540; fax 1 212 875 5539. Career grants open to American instrumental soloists by a recommendation board and chosen by the executive committee. No applications accepted. Prizes include Avery Fisher Career Grant of US $10,000 and Avery Fisher Prize of $25,000.

**Fort Collins Symphony Association Young Artists Competition:** PO Box 1963, Fort Collins, CO 80522; tel. 1 970 482 4823; fax 1 970 482 4858; website www.fcsymphony.org. Annual competition open to instrumentalists. Prizes include US $2,000 Adeline Rosenberg Memorial Prize.

**Fort Smith Symphony Association Young Artist Competition:** PO Box 3151, Fort Smith, AR 72913; tel. 1 479 452 7575; website www .fortsmithsymphony.org. Annual competition open to string, brass and woodwind players to the age of 18. Prizes include 1st prize of US $1,000 and an apppearance with the Fort Smith Symphony Orchestra.

**Fromm Music Foundation:** Harvard University, Department of Music, Cambridge, MA 02138; tel. 1 617 495 2791; fax 1 617 496 8081. Sponsorship of composers, performers and concerts of contemporary music.

**Harvey Gaul Composition Contest:** c/o Duquesne University, School of Music, Pittsburgh, PA 15282. Biennial competition open to American composers of unpublished and unperformed compositions. Prizes include US $3,000 and performance of composition.

**Florida Grand Opera Young Artist/Technical/Apprentice Programs:** 1200 Coral Way, Miami, FL 33145; tel. 1 305 854 1643; fax 1 305 856 1042; website www.fgo.org. Annual seven-month programme (October-April) open to singers to work with the Greater Miami Opera.

**Charles Tomlinson Griffes American Music Composers Competition:** 5 Joseph Wallace Dr., Croton-on-Hudson, NY 10521. Annual competition open to American or permanent resident composers between the ages of 12 and 18 whose submitted composition has not won any other competition. Prizes include money and performance of composition.

**John Simon Guggenheim Memorial Foundation:** 90 Park Ave, New York, NY 10016; tel. 1 212 687 4470; fax 1 212 697 3248; e-mail fellowships@gf .org; website www.gf.org. Annual fellowships in music open to composers and scholars who have demonstrated previous outstanding ability. Fellowships in two categories: For citizens or permanent residents of the USA and Canada, and for citizens or permanent residents of Latin America and the Caribbean.

**Haddonfield Symphony Young Instrumentalists Solo Competition:** PO Box 212, Haddonfield, NJ 08033; tel. 1 856 429 1880; fax 1 856 428 5634; e-mail symphony@haddonfield-symphony.org; website www.haddonfield -symphony.org. Annual competition open to solo instrumentalists resident in one of the 11 northeastern states or the District of Columbia between the ages of 16 and 25. Prizes include 1st prize of US $2,500 and an appearance with the Haddonfield Symphony, and 2nd prize of $750.

**Hobin Harp Competition:** c/o Greater Trenton Symphony Orchestra Foundation, 28 W State St, Suite 201, Trenton, NJ 08608. Annual competition open to American harpists who are college students. Prizes include 1st prize of US $1,600.

**Joanna Hodges International Piano Competition:** see Virginia Waring International Piano Competition.

**Ima Hogg National Young Artist Audition:** c/o Houston Symphony Orchestra, 615 Louisiana St, Houston, TX 77002. Annual competition open to instrumentalists between the ages of 19 and 27. Prizes include 1st prize of US $5,000 and an appearance with the Houston Symphony, 2nd prize of $2,500 and an appearance with the Houston Symphony, and 3rd prize of $1,000.

**Henry Holt Memorial Scholarship:** PO Box 1714, Palo Alto, CA 94302. Annual scholarship open to singers between the ages of 18 and 26. Prizes include 1st prize of US $1,000 and 2nd prize of $500.

**Holtkamp/American Guild of Organists Award in Organ Composition:** 475 Riverside Dr., Suite 1260, New York, NY 10115. Biennial competition open to composers of organ compositions. Prizes include US $2,000 and publication and performance of composition.

**Houston Opera Studio Auditions:** c/o Houston Grand Opera, 510 Preston, Houston, TX 77002; website www.houstongrandopera.org. Annual auditions to work with the Houston Opera Studio.

**Indiana State University Contemporary Music Festival Competition:** c/o Louisville Orchestra, 609 W Main St, Louisville, KY 40202. Annual competition open to composers who have not won the competition within the previous five years.

**Institute of International Education/Fulbright and Other Graduate Study Scholarships:** 809 United Nations Plaza, New York, NY 10017; website www.iie.org. Annual scholarships open to Americans with a BA or equivalent, for graduate study abroad.

**International Horn Society Composition Contest:** c/o University of Missouri at Kansas City, Conservatory of Music, 4949 Cherry, Kansas City, MO 64110. Annual competition open to composers. Prizes include money.

**International Trombone Association Ensemble Composition Contest:** c/o University of North Texas, School of Music, Denton, TX 76203. Biennial competition open to composers. Prizes include $1,000.

**International Violin Competition of Indianapolis:** 32 E Washington Street, Suite 1320, Indianapolis, IN 46204; tel. 1 317 637 4574; fax 1 317 637 1302; e-mail ivci@violin.org; website www.violin.org. Quadrennial competition open to violinists of all nationalities between the ages of 18 and 30. Prizes include money totalling more than US $200,000, medals, concert engagements in North America and Europe, and recordings.

**Ivo Pogorelich International Solo Piano Competition (USA):** c/o Kantor Concert Management, 67 Teignmouth Road, London NW2 4EA, England. Open to prizewinners and finalists in any previous international competition. 1st prize US $100,000.

**Kennedy Center Friedheim Awards:** John F Kennedy Center for the Performing Arts, Washington, DC 20577. Annual award to a living American composer of orchestral or chamber music. Prizes include 1st prize of US $5,000, 2nd prize of $2,500, 3rd prize of $1,000 and 4th prize of $500.

**Kingsville International Young Performers' Competition:** PO Box 2873, Kingsville, TX 78363; tel. 1 361 592 2374; website www.kingsvillemusic.com. Annual competition open to pianists and orchestral instrumentalists to the age of 26. Prizes totalling more than US $20,000, with highest ranking winner receiving a minimum of $5,000 and an appearance with the Corpus Christi Symphony.

**Kate Neal Kinley Memorial Fellowship:** c/o University of Illinois, 110 Architecture Building, 608 E Lorado Taft Dr., Champaign, IL 61820; tel. 1 217 333 1661; website www.faa.uiuc.edu. Annual fellowship open to graduates under the age of 25 for advanced study in the USA or abroad. Fellowship of US $7,000.

**Irving M. Klein International String Competition:** California Music Center, 3260 Harrison Street, San Francisco, CA 94110; tel. 1 415 282 7160; e-mail info@kleincompetition.org; website www.kleincompetition.org. Annual competition open to string players between the ages of 15 and 23. Prizes include 1st prize of US $10,000 and appearances with the Peninsula and Santa Cruz Symphony Orchestras.

**Kosciuszko Foundation Chopin Piano Competition:** 15 E 65th St, New York, NY 10021; tel. 1 212 734 2130; fax 1 212 628 4552; e-mail info@thekf.org; website www.kosciuszkofoundation.org. Annual competition open to pianists who are American citizens or permanent residents of the USA or full-time foreign students with valid visa, between the ages of 17 and 23. Prizes include US $2,500, $1,500 and $1,000.

**Olga Koussevitsky Young Artist Awards Competition:** 165 W 66th St, New York, NY 10023. Annual competition open to performers between the ages of 16 and 26 with categories rotating annually. Prizes totalling US $3,500, concert engagements and auditions.

**Eleanor Lieber Awards for Young Singers:** 1516 SW Alder, Portland, OR 97205. Biennial awards open to singers who are residents of Oregon, Washington, Idaho, Montana or Alaska, between the ages of 20 and 31. Prizes include money.

**Liederkranz Foundation Scholarship Awards:** 6 E 87th St, New York, NY 10128. Annual awards open to singers and pianists. Prizes totalling some US $35,000.

**Luciano Pavarotti International Voice Competition:** 1616 Walnut St, Suite 2115, Philadelphia, PA 19103. Triennial competition.

**Macallister Award for Opera Singers:** c/o Indiana Opera Theatre, 7515 E 30th St, Indianapolis, IN 46206. Annual audition open to opera singers. Prizes include 1st prize of US $10,000, 2nd prize of $5,000, 3rd prize of $3,000, 4th prize of $1,500, and 5th prize of $1,000.

**MacDowell Colony Inc:** 100 High St, Peterborough, NH 03458; tel. 1 603 924 3886; fax 1 603 924 9142; e-mail info@macdowellcolony.org; website www.macdowellcolony.org. Awards residency fellowships for composers and other creative artists.

**Quinto Maganini Award in Composition:** 37 Valley View Road, Norwalk, CT 06851. Biennial competition open to American composers of orchestral music not publicly performed. Prizes include US $2,500 and premiere by the Norwalk Symphony Orchestra.

**Marguerite McCammon Voice Competition:** 422 Coombs Creek Dr., Dallas, TX 75211. Biennial competition open to singers between the ages of 21 and 32. Prizes include 1st prize of US $3,000 and operatic engagements.

**Louise D McMahon International Music Competition:** c/o School of Fine Arts, Cameron University, 2800 W Gore Blvd, Lawton, OK 73505. Competition open to instrumentalists and singers over 25 years old. Prizes include money and solo performance with orchestra.

**Marian Anderson Award:** The Ives Center, PO Box 2957, Danbury, CT; e-mail info@mariananandersonaward.org; website www.mariananandersonaward.org. A significant financial award to an American singer of concert and opera, by recommendation.

**Meadows Foundation Young Artists Auditions Competition:** 8 Drake Road, Somerset, NJ 08873; website www.mfi.org. Annual competition open to performers in three divisions: Junior Division (Junior High School), High School Division and Senior Division (to the age of 35). Prizes include money, recitals, concert and chamber music engagements.

**Metropolitan Opera National Council Auditions:** Lincoln Center, New York, NY 10023; tel. 1 212 870 4515; fax 1 212 870 7606; e-mail ncouncil@mail.metopera.org; website www.metopera.org. Annual competitive auditions open to singers between 20 and 30 years of age. Prizes include money and study grants.

**Midland-Odessa Symphony and Chorale Inc, National Young Artist Competition:** PO Box 60658, Midland, TX 79711; tel. 1 432 563 0921; e-mail symphony@mosc.org; website www.mosc.org. Biennial competition open to performers. Prizes include money and appearances with the Midland-Odessa Symphony and Chorale.

**Missouri Southern International Piano Competition:** Missouri Southern State University, 3950 E Newman Road, Joplin, MO 64801; tel. (417) 625-9755; fax (417) 625-9798; e-mail msipc@mssu.edu; website www.mssc.edu/msipc. Biennial competition open to pianists of all nationalities to the age of 30. Prizes include 1st prize of US $10,000 and appearance at Carnegie Recital Hall.

**Mu Phi Epsilon International Competition:** 4858 Stallcup Dr., Mesquite, TX 75150; website home.muphiepsilon.org. Triennial competition open to members of Mu Phi Epsilon who have appeared in recital and/or as soloist with orchestra, but are not under contract to professional management. Prizes include two-year concert engagements.

**Museum in the Community Composer's Award:** PO Box 251, Scott Depot, WV 25560. Biennial competition open to American composers of a composition for string quartet not previously performed in public. Prizes include US $5,000 and performance of composition.

**Music Teachers National Association-CCP/ Belwin Student Composition Competition:** c/o Eastman School of Music, 26 Gibbs St, Rochester, NY 14604; website www.mtna.org. Annual competition open to American composers who are in college, high school, junior high school or elementary school, who are studying with an active member of the Music Teachers National Association. Prizes include money.

**Naftzger Young Artists Auditions and Music Awards:** c/o Wichita Symphony Society, 225 W Douglas, Suite 207, Wichita, KS 67202; tel. (316) 267-5259; fax (316) 267-1937. Annual competition open to instrumentalists between the ages of 18 and 26 and to singers between the ages of 20 and 28. Entrants must be residents of/attend a university or college in Missouri, Oklahoma or Kansas. Prizes include US $5,000 Naftzger Young Artist Award and $2,000 in each of various categories.

**National Association of Teachers of Singing Artist Award Competition:** 4745 Sutton Park Court, Suite 201, Jacksonville, FL 32224; tel. 1 904 992 9101; fax 1 904 992 9326; e-mail info@nats.org; website www.nats.org. Competition held every 18 months. Open to singers between the ages of 21 and 35 whose most recent teacher has been a member of the National Association of Teachers of Singing. Prizes include 1st prize of US $10,000, Carnegie Hall concert and AIMS scholarship, and 2nd prize of $2,500.

**National Competition for Performing Artists:** c/o Contemporary Recording Society, 724 Winchester Road, Broomall, PA 19008. Annual competition open to performers. Prizes include recording.

**National Endowment for the Arts, Music Program Office:** 1100 Pennsylvania Ave NW, Washington, DC 20506; tel. 1 202 682 5400; website www.nea.gov. Lends organizational assistance to professional music organizations and gives fellowships to composers and performers.

**National Endowment for the Humanities:** 1100 Pennsylvania Ave NW, Washington, DC 20506; website www.neh.fed.us. Awards fellowships and grants for various projects in the field of music.

**National Federation of Music Clubs:** 1336 N Delaware St, Indianapolis, IN 46202; tel. 1 317 638 4003; fax 1 317 638 0503; e-mail info@nfmc-music.org; website www.nfmc-music.org. Provides various annual awards and fellowships.

**National Symphony Orchestra Young Soloists' Competition, College Division:** 5931 Oakdale Road, McLean, VA 22101. Annual competition open to high school graduates studying music in the Washington metropolitan area or Washington residents studying elsewhere. Prizes include money and appearances with the National Symphony Orchestra.

**Walter W Naumburg Foundation International Competition:** 60 Lincoln Center Plaza, New York, NY 10023. Annual competition open to performers of all nationalities with categories rotating annually. Prizes include 1st prize of US $5,000, concert engagements and a recording, 2nd prize of $2,500, and 3rd prize of $1,000.

**New Jersey Symphony Orchestra Young Artists Auditions:** Robert Treat Center, 2 Central Ave, Newark, NJ 07102. Annual competition open to instrumentalists under the age of 20, resident in New Jersey. Prizes include 1st prize of an appearance with the New Jersey Symphony Orchestra; prizes range from US $3,000 to $500.

**New York Foundation for the Arts Artists' Fellowship Program:** 155 Ave of the Americas, New York, NY 10013. Biennial fellowships for non-students of two or more years' residency in New York State. Prizes include grants.

**Omaha Symphony Guild New Music Competition:** 8723 N 57th St, Omaha, NE 68152; website www.omahasymphony.org. Annual competition open to composers of chamber orchestra compositions. Prizes include US $2,000.

**Opera at Florham Guild Vocal Competition:** PO Box 343, Convent Station, NJ 07961. Competition open to all singers between the ages of 18 and 35. Prizes include 1st prize of US $3,000 and a recital.

**Opera/Columbus Vocal Competition:** 177 E Naghten Street, Columbus, OH 43215; tel. 1 614 469 0939; e-mail info@operacolumbus.org; website www .operacols.org. Competition open to singers who are residents of Ohio. Prizes for senior level (ages 24 to 35) include 1st prize of US $2,000 and a scholarship to the American Institute of Musical Studies in Graz, Austria.

**Oratorio Society of New York Solo Competition:** Carnegie Hall, Suite 504, 881 Seventh Ave, New York, NY 10019; website www.oratoriosocietyofny .org. Annual competition open to solo oratorio singers under the age of 40. Prizes include US $10,000.

**Palm Beach Invitational International Piano Competition:** PO Box 3094, Palm Beach, FL 33480; tel. 1 561 833 8817; fax 1 561 833 6735. Annual competition open to 25 young pianists, each from a different nation and each the winner of an international competition. Prizes totalling US $50,000, including 1st prize of $15,000 and a concert at Alice Tully Hall in New York.

**Palm Beach Opera Vocal Competition:** 415 S Olive Ave, West Palm Beach, FL 33401; tel. 1 561 833 8924; fax 1 561 833 8294. Annual competition open to singers with Junior Division between the ages of 18 and 23 and Senior Division between the ages of 24 and 30. Prizes include money totalling US $43,000 and performances.

**Performing Arts Assistance Corporation:** PO Box 1296, Ansonia Station, New York, NY 10023. Gives seminars for performers.

**Gregor Piatigorsky Seminar for Cello:** c/o University of Southern California School of Music, Los Angeles, CA 90089. Seminar open to cellists.

**Rosa Ponselle International Vocal Competition for the Vocal Arts:** Windsor, Stevenson, MD 21153. Biennial competition open to singers to the age of 25. Prizes include study grants between US $20,000 and $25,000, medallions and training in Italy and France.

**Pro Musicis International Award:** 140 W 79th St, No 9F, New York, NY 10024. Annual career development award. Prizes include major recitals in New York, Los Angeles, Washington, DC, Boston, Paris and Rome.

**Pulitzer Prize in Music:** c/o Columbia University, 702 Journalism Building, New York, NY 10027. Annual prize of US $3,000 to an American composer for a major composition premiered in the USA during the year.

**Queens Opera Vocal Competition:** 313 Bay 14 St, Brooklyn, NY 11214. Annual competition open to singers who have appeared in one opera performance. Prizes include 1st prize of money and an appearance in a full opera performance.

**Rome Prize Fellowships of the American Academy in Rome:** 41 E 65th St, New York, NY 10021; website www.aarome.org/prize.htm. Annual fellowships for American composers with a BA or equivalent degree. Fellowships include one year residency at the American Academy in Rome, stipend, and travel allowance.

**San Antonio International Keyboard Competition:** PO Box 39636, San Antonio, TX 78218; tel. 1 210 655 0766; fax 1 210 822 6056. Triennial competition open to pianists between the ages of 20 and 32. Prizes include 1st prize of US $5,000 and gold medal, 2nd prize of $2,500 and silver medal, 3rd prize of $1,000 and bronze medal, and 4th prize of $500.

**San Francisco Opera Center National Auditions:** c/o War Memorial Opera House, San Francisco, CA 94102. Annual competitive auditions for singers, sopranos between the ages of 20 and 30 and all other singers between 20 and 34. Prizes include awards given in the Merola Opera Program totalling US $28,000. Participants may also apply for the Adler Fellowship Program.

**San Jose Symphony Young Pianist Concerto Competition:** 99 Almaden Blvd, Suite 400, San Jose, CA 95113. Annual competition open to pianists to the age of 30. Prizes include grand prize of US $5,000 and an appearance with the San Jose Symphony.

**Santa Barbara Symphony and the Esperia Foundation Young Artists' Competition:** 214 E Victoria St, Santa Barbara, CA 93101. Competition open to string players and pianist alternating between instruments annually. Prizes include money and an appearance with the Santa Barbara Symphony.

**Friedrich Schorr Memorial Performance Prize in Voice:** 110 S Madison St, Adrian, MI 49221. Annual competition open to all professional singers. Prizes include US $10,000 in performance awards/stipends.

**Sewanee Music Festival International Scholarships:** 735 University Ave, Sewanee, TN 37375. Annual scholarships for musicians of all nationalities between the ages of 16 and 25.

**Shreveport Symphony/Nena Plant Wideman Annual Piano Competition:** PO Box 205, Shreveport, LA 71162. Annual competition open to pianists between the ages of 18 and 28. Prizes include 1st prize of US $2,500, 2nd prize of $1,000 and 3rd prize of $500.

**Sinfonia Foundation:** c/o Phi Mus Alpha Sinfonia Fraternity, 10600 Old State Road, Evansville, IN 47711. Commissions to composers and annual research grants for scholarly research on music in America or American music.

**Sorantin Young Artists Award:** PO Box 5922, San Angelo, TX 76902.

**Sound Research Residencies:** c/o Yellow Springs Institute for Contemporary Studies and the Arts, 1645 Art School Road, Chester Springs, PA 19425. Annual 10-day residency for composers with at least three years of professional experience.

**Southwestern Youth Music Festival Competition:** PO Box 41104, Los Angeles, CA 90041; website www.symf.org. Annual competition open to pianists to the age of 18, whose teacher must become a member of the festival. Prizes include US $10,000 and orchestral appearances.

**James Spencer Memorial Performance Prize in Composition:** 110 S Madison St, Adrian, MI 49221. Open to American composers. Prizes include travel and housing allowance, lecture stipend, and performance and recording by the Adrian Symphony Orchestra.

**Spivey International Performance Competition:** Clayton State College, Morrow, GA 30260. Annual competition for performers. Prizes include 1st prize of US $5,000.

**Stewart Awards National Operatic Voice Competition:** PO Box 18321, Oklahoma City, OK 73154. Biennial competition open to American singers between the ages of 20 and 32. Prizes include money totalling US $14,000.

**Stravinsky Awards International Piano Competition for Children Aged 18 and Under:** 1003 W Church Street, Champaign, IL 61821; tel. (217) 352-0688; fax (217) 352-8707; Exec. Dir: Roger Shields. Biennial competition open to pianists of all nationalities in age divisions ranging from small children to 22.

**Julius Stulberg International String Competition:** PO Box 107, Kalamazoo, MI 49005; tel. 1 616 372 6237; fax 1 616 372 7513. Annual competition open to string players to the age of 19. Prizes include money and performances.

**Louis and Virginia Sudler International Wind Band Composition Contest:** c/o US Marine Bane, Eighth and First Sts SE, Washington, DC 20390. Biennial competition open to composers of wind music. Prizes include 1st prize of US $12,000.

**William Matheus Sullivan Musical Foundation Inc:** PO Box 189, Kent, CT 06757; tel. 1 860 927 3572; fax 1 860 927 1680; e-mail info@ sullivanfoundation.org; website www.sullivanfoundation.org. Annual assistance programme for professional young singers.

**Trebas Institute Scholarships:** 6464 Sunset Blvd, No. 1180, Hollywood, CA 90028. Annual scholarships for educational opportunities in the music business, and the recording arts and sciences.

**Richard Tucker Music Foundation:** 1790 Broadway, Suite 715, New York, NY 10019; tel. 1 212 757 2218; fax 1 212 757 2347; website www.richardtucker .org. Annual awards to American singers by recommendation. Prizes include the Richard Tucker Award of US $30,000, four career grants of $6,500, and other grants.

**USA International Harp Competition:** PO Box 5157, Bloomington, IN 47407. Triennial competition open to harpists of all nationalities, born between 1969 and 1985. Prizes include eight awards.

**Unisys African-American Composers Forum and Symposium:** DSOH Education Department, 400 Buhl Building, 535 Griswold St, Detroit, MI 48226. Encourages performances of orchestral compositions by African-American composers by major professional symphony orchestras.

**United States Information Agency Artistic Ambassador Program:** 301 Fourth St SW, Room 216, Washington, DC 20547. Annual programme for American musicians at least 21 years old, to serve as artistic ambassadors abroad at government expense, for four to six weeks.

**University of Louisville Grawemeyer Award for Music Composition:** c/o University of Louisville, School of Music, Grawemeyer Music Award Committee, Louisville, KY 40292. Annual award for outstanding achievement by a composer. Compositions may not be submitted by the composer but must be sponsored by a professional music organization or individual. Award totalling US $150,000, paid in five annual instalments of $30,000.

**University of Maryland International Competitions:** c/o University of Maryland, College Park, MD 20742. Annual competition open to pianists, cellists and singers of all nationalities. Prizes include 1st prize of US $20,000 and concert engagements, 2nd prize of $10,000 and 3rd prize of $5,000.

**Elizabeth Harper Vaughan Concerto Competition:** 1200 E Center St, Kingsport, TN 37660; tel. 1 423 392 8423; fax 1 423 392 8428. Annual competition open to performers of classical music to the age of 26. Prizes include US $1,000 and an appearance with the Kingsport Symphony Orchestra.

**Women's Association of the Minnesota Orchestra (WAMSO) Young Artist Competition:** c/o Minnesota Orchestra, 1111 Nicollet Mall, Minneapolis, MN 55403; tel. 1 612 371 5654; fax 1 612 371 7176; website www.wamso .org. Annual competition open to instrumentalists to the age of 25. Various prizes.

**Virginia Waring International Piano Competition:** College of the Desert, 43500 Monterey Avenue, Palm Desert, CA 92260; tel. (760)
773-2575; fax (760) 776-0168; website www.vwipc.org; Admin. Dir: Terri Fleck. Fmrly the Joanna Hodges International Piano Competition. Quadrennial competition. No minimum age, maximum age 35. Performance prizes include solo
and orchestral performances, including Carnegie Hall, Rome and Vienna.

**Washington International Competition:** 4530 Connecticut Ave, PO Box 704, Washington, DC 20008. Annual competition open to performers between the ages of 18 and 32 with categories rotating annually. Prizes include money.

**Abby Whiteside Foundation Inc:** 8 E 83rd Street, New York, NY 10028; website www.abbywhiteside.org; purpose to make the teaching principles of piano teacher Abby Whiteside better known; sponsors a series of piano recitals at Weill Hall, Carnegie Hall; Pres. Sophia Rosoff.

**Andrew Wolf Chamber Music Award:** PO Box 191, Camden, ME 04843; Newton Music School, 321 Chestnut St, West Newton, MA 02165. Biennial award given to an American chamber music pianist under the age of 40. Award includes US $10,000 and concert appearances.

**Young Concert Artists Inc:** 250 W 57th Street, Suite 1222, New York, NY 10107; tel. (212) 307-6655; e-mail yca@yca.org; website www.yca.org; Dir Susan Wadsworth. Annual auditions for solo performers and string quartets.

**Loren L Zachary Society Opera Awards National Vocal Competition:** 2250 Gloaming Way, Beverly Hills, CA 90210; tel. 1 310 276 2731; fax 1 310 275 8245; Pres. and Dir Nedra Zachary. Annual competition open to professional opera singers seeking contracts for leading roles in European opera houses; for women between the ages of 21 and 33 and for men between the ages of 21 and 35. Prizes totalling about US $25,000 and a round trip flight to Europe for auditioning purposes.

# Uruguay

**Concurso Internacional de Piano Ciudad de Montevideo:** Santiago Vásquez, Montevideo. Triennial competition open to pianists to the age of 32.

# APPENDIX F: MUSIC LIBRARIES

## Afghanistan

**Kabul Public Library:** Kabul.

## Albania

**Biblioteka Kombetare (National Library):** Tirana.

## Algeria

**Bibliothèque Nationale:** Avenue Frantz Fanon, Algiers.

**Bibliothèque Universitaire:** Rue Didouche Mourad, Algiers.

## Argentina

**Academia Nacional de Bellas Artes:** Biblioteca, Sanchez de Bustamante 2663, 1425 Buenos Aires.

**Biblioteca Nacional:** México 564, 1097 Buenos Aires.

**Fondo Nacional de las Artes:** Biblioteca, Alsina 673, 1087 Buenos Aires.

## Australia

**Australia Music Centre Ltd Library:** First Floor, Argyle Centre, 18 Argyle Street, The Rocks, NSW 2000.

**City of Sydney Public Library:** Town Hall House, Level 3, 456 Kent Street, Sydney, NSW 2000; tel. 61 2 9265 9470; fax 61 2 9265 9157; e-mail library@cityofsydney.nsw.gov.au.

**National Library of Australia:** Music and Dance Division, Parkes Place, Canberra, ACT 2600; tel. (2) 6262-1111; fax (2) 6273-5081; e-mail infoserv@nla.gov.au; website www.nla.gov.au.

**National Music Library:** Australian Broadcasting Corporation, PO Box 9994, Sydney, NSW 2001; tel. 61 2 8333 1627; fax 61 2 8333 1684.

**State Library of New South Wales:** Music Division, Macquarie Street, Sydney, NSW 2000; tel. 61 2 9273 1414; website www.sl.nsw.gov.au; Music Archivist: Meredith Lawn.

**State Library of Queensland:** Music Division, PO Box 3488, South Brisbane, Qld 4000; tel. 61 7 3840 7666; fax 61 7 3846 2421; website www.slq.qld.gov.au.

**State Library of South Australia:** Music Division, North Terrace, PO Box 419, Adelaide, SA 5001; tel. 61 8 8207 7200; fax 61 8 8207 7247; website www.slsa.sa.gov.au.

**State Library of Tasmania:** Music Division, 91 Murray Street, Hobart, TAS 7000; tel. 61 3 6233 7511; fax 61 3 6231 0927; website www.statel.ibrary.tas.gov.au.

**State Library of Victoria:** Music Division, 328 Swanston Street, Melbourne, Vic. 3000; tel. 61 3 8864 7000; website www.state.library.vic.gov.au.

**State Library of Western Australia:** Music Division, Alexander Library Building, Perth Cultural Centre, Perth, WA 6000; tel. 61 8 9427 3111; website www.liswa.wa.gov.au.

## Austria

**Büchereien der Stadt Linz:** Zentrale und Hauptbücherei, Museumstrasse 15, 4020 Linz.

**Burgenländische Landesbibliothek:** Landhaus Freiheitsplatz 1, 7001 Eisenstadt.

**Gesellschaft der Musikfreunde in Wien:** Archiv und Bibliothek, Bösendorferstrasse 12, 1010 Vienna; tel. 43 1 505 81 90; fax 43 1 505 81 90 94; website www.musikverein.at.

**Haus des Buches:** Hauptbücherei, Skodagasse 20, 1080 Vienna; tel. 43 1 400 08 45 00.

**Kammer für Arbeiter und Angestel.lte:** Volksbüchereien, Bahnhofplatz 3, 9021 Klagenfurt.

**Musik Informations Zentrum Österreich:** Stiftgasse 29, 1070 Vienna.

**Österreichische Akademie der Wissenschaften:** Bibliothek, Dr Ignaz Seipelplatz 2, 1010 Vienna 1.

**Österreichische Gesellschaft für Musik:** Bibliothek, Hanuschgasse 3, 1010 Vienna.

**Österreichische Nationalbibliothek:** Josefplatz 1, PO Box 308, 1015 Vienna; e-mail onb@onb.ac.at; website www.onb.ac.at.

**Österreichische Gewerkschaftsbund:** Bibliothek, Grillparzerstrasse 14, 1010 Vienna.

**Stadtbücherei:** Schloss Mirabell, 5020 Salzburg.

**Stadbücherei:** Herzog Leopoldstrasse 21, 2700 Wiener Neustadt.

**Stadbücherein:** Landhausgasse 2, 8010 Graz.

**Universitätsbibliothek der Universität für Musik und darstellende Kunst Wien:** Lothringerstrasse 18, 1030 Vienna; tel. (1) 71155-8101; website www.mdw.ac.at; Dir: Dr Susanne Eschwé.

**Wiener Stadt-und Landesbibliothek:** Rathaus, 1082 Vienna; tel. 43 1 400 08 49 20; website www.stadtbibliothek.wien.at.

## Belgium

**Academie royale des sciences, des lettres et des beaux arts de Belgique, Bibliothèque:** Palais des Académies, 1 rue Ducale, 1000 Brussels; tel. 32 2 550 22 55; fax 32 2 550 22 65; website www.armb.be.

**Bibliothèque Centrale:** En Hors Chateau 31, 4000 Liège.

**Bibliothèque Provinciale du Degré Moyen:** rue des Croisiers 15, 4000 Liège.

**Bibliothèque Royale Albert ler:** Blvd de l'Empereur 4, 1000 Brussels.

**Centre Belge de Documentation Musicale ASBL:** rue d'Arlon 75–77, 1040 Brussels.

**Koninklijke Academie voor Wetenschappen:** Defacqzstraat 1 bus 3, 1000 Brussels; tel. 32 2 538 02 11; fax 32 2 539 23 53.

**Stadsbibliotheek:** Hendrik Conscienceplein 4, 2000 Antwerp; website www.stadsbibliotheek.antwerpen.be.

## Bolivia

**Biblioteca y Archivo Nacional de Bolivia:** Calle España 25, PO Box 338, Sucre; tel. 591 64 1481.

## Brazil

**Biblioteca Nacional:** Fundaçao Nacional Pro-Memoria, Avda Rio Branco 219–239, 20040 Rio de Janeiro; tel. 21 2220 9367; fax 21 2220 4173; website www.bn.br.

## Bulgaria

**Nacionalna Biblioteka:** Kiril i Metodij, F. Tolbuhin 11, 1504 Sofia.

**Union of Bulgarian Composers:** lv Vazov 2, 1000 Sofia; website www.ubc-bg.com.

## Cambodia

**Bibliothèque Nationale:** 4, Phnom Penh.

## Canada

**Bibliothèque Municipale de Montréal:** 1210 Sheerbrooke Street East, Montréal, QC H2L 1L9.

**Bibliothèque Municipale de Québec:** 37 rue Sainte-Angéle, Québec, QC G1R 4G5.

**Bibliothèque Nationale du Québec (BNQ):** 2275 Holt, Montréal, QC H2G 3H1; tel. 1 514 873 1100; fax 1 514 873 7510; website www.bnquebec.ca.

**Calgary Public Library, Music Division:** 616 Macleod Trail SE, Calgary, AB T2G 2M2; website www.calgarypubliclibrary.com.

**Canadian Music Centre:** 20 St Joseph Street, Toronto, ON M4Y 1J9; tel. 1 416 961 6601; website www.musiccentre.ca.

**Edmonton Public Library, Music Division:** 7 Sir Winston Churchill Square, Edmonton, AB T5J 2V4; tel. 1 780 496 7000; website www.epl.ca.

**Greater Victoria Public Library, Music Division:** 735 Broughton Street, Victoria, BC V8W 3H2; tel. 1 250 382 7241; fax 1 250 382 7125; website www.gvpl.ca.

**Guelph Public Library, Music Division:** 100 Norfolk Street, Guelph, ON N1H 4J6; tel. 1 519 824 6220; website www.library.guelph.on.ca.

**Halifax City Regional Library, Music Division:** 5381 Spring Garden Road, Halifax, NS B3J 1E9; tel. 1 902 421 6980.

**Hamilton Public Library, Music Division:** 55 York Blvd, Hamilton, ON L8R 3K1; tel. 1 905 546 3200; website www.hpl.hamilton.on.ca.

**Kingston Frontenac Public Library, Music Division:** 130 Johnson Street E, Kingston, ON K7L 1X8; website www.kfpl.ca.

**Kitchener Public Library, Music Division:** 85 Queen Street N, Kitchener, ON N2H 2H1; tel. 1 519 743 0271; website www.kpl.org.

**National Library of Canada, Music Division:** 395 Wellington Street, Ottawa, ON K1A 0N4; tel. 1 613 995 9481; website www.nlc-bnc.ca.

**Ottawa Public Library:** 120 Metcalfe Street, Ottawa, ON K1P 5M2; website www.opl.ottawa.on.ca.

**Regina Public Library, Music Division:** 2311 12th Avenue, PO Box 2311, Regina, SK S4P 3Z5; website www.reginalibrary.ca.

**Saskatoon Public Library, Music Division:** 311 23rd Street E, Saskatoon, SK S7K 0J6; website www.publib.saskatoon.sk.ca.

**Toronto Public Library, Music Division:** 789 Yonge Street, Toronto, ON M4W 2G8; tel. 1 416 393 7131; website www.tpl.toronto.on.ca.

**Vancouver Public Library, Music Division:** 350 W Georgia Street, Vancouver, BC V6B 6B1; tel. 1 604 331 3603; website www.vpl.vancouver.bc.ca.

**Windsor Public Library, Music Division:** 850 Ouellette Avenue, Windsor, ON N9A 4M9; tel. 1 519 255 6770; website www.windsorpubliclibrary.com.

**Winnipeg Public Library, Music Division:** 251 Donald Street, Winnipeg, MB R3C 3P5; website www.wpl.winnipeg.ca.

## Chile

**Biblioteca Nacional:** Avda Bernardo O'Higgins 651, Santiago.

## People's Republic of China

**National Library of China:** 39 Baishiqiao Road, Haidian District, Beijing 100 081.

## Colombia

**Biblioteca Nacional de Colombia:** C24, 5-60, PO Box 27600, Bogotá.

## Costa Rica

**Biblioteca Nacional:** C 15-17, Avda 3Y 3b, PO Box 10008, San José.

## Cuba

**Biblioteca Nacional José Marti:** PO Box 3, Avda de Independencia 3, 20 de Mayo y Arangusen, Plaza de la Revolución José Marti, Havana.

## Czech Republic

**Mstská knihovna v Praze (City Library of Prague):** Knihovna Bedricha Smetany, Dr V. Vacka 1, 115 72 Prague.

**Music Information Centre:** Besední 3, 118 00 Prague 1.

**Státni knihovna (State Library):** Klementinum 190, 110 01 Prague 1.

## Denmark

**Danish Music Information Centre:** 48 Vimmelskaftet, 1161 Copenhagen K.

**Det Kongelige Bibliotek (Royal Library):** Christians Brygge 8, PO Box 2149, 1219 Copenhagen K; tel. 1 33 93 01 11.

**Musikhistorisk Museum and Carl Claudius' Samling:** Åbenrå 30, 1124 Copenhagen K; tel. 45 33 11 27 26; fax 45 33 11 60 44; e-mail info@musikhistoriskmuseum.dk; website www.musikhistoriskmuseum.dk.

## Dominican Republic

**Biblioteca Nacional:** César Nicolás Penson 91, Plaza de la Cultura, Santo Domingo.

## Ecuador

**Biblioteca Nacional de Ecuador:** 12 de Octubre 555, PO Box 67, Quito.

## Egypt

**Egyptian National Library:** Sharia Corniche El-Nil, Bulaq, Cairo.

## El Salvador

**Biblioteca Nacional:** 8A Avda Norte y Calle Delgado, San Salvador.

## Ethiopia

**National Library and Archives of Ethiopia:** PO Box 1907, Addis Ababa.

## Finland

**Finnish Music Information Centre:** Lauttasaarenti 1, 00120 Helsinki; tel. 358 9 6810 1313; website www.fimic.fi.

## France

**Bibliothèque centrale de prêt du Doubs et du Territoire de Belfort:** 24 Avenue de l'Observatoire, 25000 Besançon.

**Bibliothèque centrale de prêt du Pas-de-Calais:** 13 Place Guy Mollet, 62000 Arras.

**Bibliothèque de la ville de Caen:** Place Guillouard, 14027 Caen Cédex.

**Bibliothèque de la ville et du musée Fabre:** 37 Blvd Bonnes-Nouvelles, 34000 Montpellier.

**Bibliothèque municipale:** 32–34 rue Edouard-Delesalle, 59043 Lille Cédex; tel. 03 20 15 97 25; fax 03 20 63 94 59; e-mail dqueneutte@mairie-lille.fr.

**Bibliothèque municipale:** 30 Blvd Vivier-Merle, 69431 Lyon Cédex 03; website www.bm-lyon.fr.

**Bibliothèque municipale:** 38 rue du 141 Ria, 13001 Marseille Cédex 3.

**Bibliothèque municipale:** 1 Cour Elie Fleur, 57000 Metz; tel. 03 87 55 53 33.

**Bibliothèque municipale:** 19 Grand rue, 68090 Mulhouse Cédex.

**Bibliothèque municipale:** 43 rue Stanislas, 54000 Nancy; tel. 03 83 37 38 83.

**Bibliothèque municipale:** 37 rue Gambetta, 44041 Nantes Cédex.

**Bibliothèque municipale:** 1 rue Dupanloup, 45043 Orléans Cédex.

**Bibliothèque municipale:** 1 rue de La Borderie, 35042 Rennes Cédex; tel. 02 99 87 98 88.

**Bibliothèque municipale:** rue Jacques Villon, 76043 Rouen Cédex.

**Bibliothèque municipale:** 3 rue Kuhn, 67000 Strasbourg Cédex.

**Bibliothèque municipale:** 1 rue de Périgord, 31070 Toulouse; tel. 05 61 22 21 78.

**Bibliothèque municipale:** 2 bis Quai d'Orléans, 37042 Tours Cédex; tel. 02 47 05 47 33.

**Bibliothèque municipale:** 5 rue de l'Indépendance Américaine, 78000 Versailles.

**Bibliothèque municipale classée:** 3 rue Mably, 33075 Bordeaux, Cédex.

**Bibliothèque municipale classée:** 43 Place Charles-de-Gaulle, 86000 Poitiers.

**Bibliothèque municipale classée:** 2 Place Carnegie, 51100 Reims Cédex; website www.bm-reins.fr.

**Bibliothèque municipale d'étude et d'information:** Blvd Maréchal-Lyautey, PO Box 1095 RP, 38021 Grenoble Cédex.

**Bibliothèque municipale d'études:** 21 bis Blvd Dubouchage, 06047 Nice Cédex.

**Bibliothèque-Musée de l'Opéra:** rue Scribe, 75009 Paris; tel. 1 40 01 23 39; fax 1 42 65 10 16; e-mail pierre.vidal@bnf.fr; Dir Pierre Vidal; library located in Place de l'Opéra, Paris.

**Bibliothèque Musicale Gustav Mahler:** 11 bis rue Vézelay, 75008 Paris.

**Bibliothèque Nationale:** Department de la Musique, 2 rue Louvois, 75084 Paris.

**Institut de France, Acádemie des Beaux-Arts:** 23 Quai de Conti, 75006 Paris.

## Germany

**Akademie der Künste:** Robert-Koch-Platz 7, Berlin; website www.adk.de.

**Bayerische Staatsbibliothek:** Ludwigstrasse 16, 80539 Munich; tel. 49 89 286 38 23 22; website www.bsb-muenchen.de.

**Bibliothek der Hansestadt Lübeck:** Hundestrasse 5-17, Lübeck.

**Bibliothek des Handel-Houses Halle:** Grosse Nikolaiste 5, 06108, Halle.

**Bischöfliche Zentralbibliothek:** Proskesche Musikabteilung, Dr Raymond Dittrich, St Petersweg 11–13, 93047 Regensburg; tel. 0941 59532-2510; fax 0941 59532-2521; e-mail rdittrich.biblio@bistum-regensburg.de; website www.bistum-regensburg.de/bibliothek.

**Deutsche Bibliothek:** Frankfurt am Main, Adickesallee 1, 60322 Frankfurt am Main; website www.ddb.de.

**Deutsche Bücherei:** Deutscher Platz, Leipzig.

**Hamburger Öffentliche Bücherhallen:** Grosse Bleichen 23–27, 20354 Hamburg; tel. 040 35 60 61 23.

**Hessische Landes-und Hochschulbibliothek:** Schloss 6, 64283 Darmstadt; tel. 06151 16 58 50.

**Hochschule fur Musik 'Franz Liszt' Hochschulbibliothek:** Platz der Demokratie 2–3, 99423 Weimar.

**Kreisbibliothek:** Leipzig-Land, Karl-Rothe-Strasse 13, Leipzig.

**Kreisbibliothek Schwerin-Land:** Wismarsche Strasse 144, Schwerin.

**Landesbibliothek:** Schlossplatz 1, Schloss Ehrenburg, Coburg; tel. 09561 76757/8; fax 09561 99622; website www.bib-bvb.de/Landesbibliothek/home.htm.

**Lippische Landesbibliothek:** Hornschestrasse 41, 32756; Detmold; tel. 49 5231 92 6600; website www.lib-detmold.de.

**Münchner Städtische Bibliotheken:** Rosenheimerstrasse 5, Munich.

**Musikbibliothek de Stadt Leipzig:** Ferdinand-Lassale-Strasse 21, Leipzig.

**Öffentliche Bibliothek der Stadt Aachen:** Couvenstrasse 15, Pf 1210, Aachen.

**Offentliche Bücherei:** Hintern Brudern 23, Braunschweig.

**Ratsbücherei:** Am Marienplatz 3, PO Box 2540, Lüneburg.

**Sächsische Landesbibliothek:** Marienalle 12, Dresden.

**Staatsbibliothek:** Neue Residenz, Domplatz 8, 96049 Bamberg; tel. 49 951 955 030; website www.staatsbibliothek-bamberg.de.

**Staatsbibliothek:** Luitpoldplatz 7, PO Box 2840, Bayreuth.

**Staatsbibliothek zu Berlin Preussischer Kulturbesitz (Berlin State Library):** Haus Unter den Linden 8, 10117 Berlin; tel. 49 (0)30 266 1700; fax 49 (0)30 266 1751; e-mail generaldir@sbb.spk-berlin.de; website www .staatsbibliothek-berlin.de; Head: Barbara Schneider-Kempf; Head of Music Dept: Dr Helmut Hell.

**Staatsbibliothek:** 24 Berlin-Preussischen Kulturbesitz, Musikabteilung, Pf 1312 Berlin.

**Staats-und Stadtbibliothek:** Schaezlerstrasse 25, PO Box 111909, Augusburg.

**Staats-und Universitätsbibliothek:** Bibliothekstrasse, PO Box 330160, Bremen.

**Stadtarchiv und Stadtbibliothek:** Am Steine 7, Hildesheim.

**Stadtarchiv und Wissenschaftliche Stadtbibliothek:** Berliner Platz 2, Bonn.

**Stadtbibliothek:** Langestrasse 43, 76530 Baden-Baden; website www.baden -baden.de.

**Stadtbibliothek:** Wilhelmstrasse 3, PO Box 181, Bielefeld; website www .stadtbibliothek-bielfeld.de.

**Stadtbibliothek:** Schusterstrasse 7, Brandenburg.

**Stadtbibliothek:** Steintorwall 15, PO Box 3309, Braunschweig.

**Stadtbibliothek:** Schwachhauser Heerstrasse 30, Bremen; website www .stadtbibliothek-bremen.de.

**Stadtbibliothek:** Zerbsterstrasse 10, 06844 Dessau; tel. 0340 213264.

**Stadtbibliothek:** Düsseldorfer Strasse 5–7, 47049 Duisburg; website www .stadtbibliothek.duisburg.de.

**Stadtbibliothek:** Hollestrasse 3, 45127 Essen; tel. 0201 88 42001; website www.stadtbibliothek.essen.de.

**Stadtbibliothek:** Münsterplatz 17, 79098 Freiburg; tel. 0761 201 2207; fax 0761 201 2299; website www.stadtbibliothek.freiburg.de.

**Stadtbibliothek:** Jochmannstrasse 2–3, Görlitz.

**Stadtbibliothek:** Gotmarstrasse 8, PO Box 3842, Göttingen.

**Stadtbibliothek:** Hildesheimer Strasse 12, PO Box 125, 30169 Hannover; tel. 0511 168 42169; website www.stadtbibliothek.hannover.de.

**Stadtbibliothek:** Im Weiterbuldungszentrum, Klosterstrasse 8, 67655 Kaiserslautern; tel. 0631 365 1421; fax 0631 365 1429.

**Stadtbibliothek:** Ständehausstrasse 2, 76133 Karlsruhe; website www .karlsruhe.de/Bildung/Bib.

**Stadtbibliothek:** Rathaus, 34117 Kassel; tel. 49 561 787 4013.

**Stadtbibliothek:** Kornpforstrasse 15, PO Box 2064, Koblenz.

**Stadtbibliothek:** Bismarckstrasse 44–48, PO Box 212125, Ludwigshafen; tel. 0621 504 2601.

**Stadtbibliothek:** Rheinalle 3b, 55116 Mainz; tel. 06131 122649; fax 06131 04187 648.

**Stadtbibliothek:** Blücherstrasse 6, PO Box 85, Mönchengladbach.

**Stadtbibliothek:** Zentralbibliothek, Egidienplatz 23, 90403 Nuremberg; tel. 49 911 231 2790; fax 49 911 231 5476; website www.stadtbibliothek.nuernberg .de.

**Stadtbibliothek:** Nauwieser Strasse 5, Saarbrücken.

**Stadtbibliothek:** Weinhof 12, 89073 Ulm; tel. 49 731 161 4100; fax 49 731 161 1633; website www.stadtbibliothek.ulm.de.

**Stadtbibliothek:** Steubenstrasse 1, Weimer.

**Stadtbibliothek:** Rathauspassage, Wiesbaden.

**Stadtbibliothek:** Kolpingstrasse 8, 42103 Wuppertal; tel. 49 202 563 2162; fax 49 202 306 594; website www.wuppertal.de/stadtbib/welcome.htm.

**Stadtbibliothek:** Dr Friedrichs-Ring 19, 08056 Zwickau; tel. and fax 49 375 241 651.

**Stadtbücherei:** Gutenbergstrasse 2, 86150 Augsburg; tel. 49 821 324 2754; fax 49 821 324 2707.

**Stadtbücherei:** Friedrichstrasse 2, Bamberg.

**Stadtbücherei:** Rathausplatz 2–6, PO Box 102269-2270, Bochum.

**Stadtbücherei Bonn:** Bottlerplatz 1, Bonn.

**Stadtbücherei Köln:** Zentralbibliothek, Josef-Haubrich-Hof 1, Pf 108020, 50676 Cologne; tel. 49 221 221 3894; fax 49 221 221 3933; website www.stbib -koeln.de.

**Stadtbücherei:** Markt 12, PO Box 907, Dortmund.

**Stadtbücherei:** Marktplatz 1, PO Box 3160, Erlangen.

**Stadtbücherei:** Zentralbibliothek, Zeil 17–19, PO Box 102113, 60313 Frankfurt am Main; tel. 49 692 123 4482; fax 49 692 123 7949.

**Stadtbücherei:** Ebertstrasse 19, Gelsenkirchen.

**Stadtbücherei:** Deutschordenshof, Kirchbrunnenstrasse 12, 74072 Heilbronn; tel. 49 713 156 2663; fax 49 713 196 2931; website www.stadtbuecherei .stadt-heilbronn.de.

**Stadtbücherei:** Hallstrasse 2–4, 85049 Ingolstadt; tel. 49 841 305 1830; fax 49 841 305 1849.

**Stadtbücherei:** Holstenbrücke 1, PO Box 4140, 24103 Kiel; tel. 49 431 901 3434; fax 49 431 901 3450; website www.kiel.de/stadtbuecherei.

**Stadtbücherei:** N 3, 4 (Dalberghaus), PO Box 5868, 68161 Mannheim; tel. 49 621 293 8930; fax 49 621 239 8908; website www.stadtbuecherei.mannheim .de.

**Stadtbücherei:** Friedrich-Ebert-Strasse 47, PO Box 011620, 45468 Mülheim; tel. 49 208 455 4189; fax 49 208 455 4125.

**Stadtbücherei:** Alter Steinweg 7, PO Box 5909, Münster.

**Stadtbücherei:** Langemarkstrasse 19–21, Oberhausen.

**Stadtbücherei:** Haidplatz 8, 93047 Regensburg; tel. 49 941 507 2473; fax 49 941 507 4479.

**Stadtbücherei:** Konrad-Adenauer-Strasse 2, Stuttgart.

**Stadtbücherei:** Brunnenstrasse 3, Tübingen.

**Städtbucherei:** Max-Heim-Bücherei, Marktplatz 9, Haus zum Falken, 97070 Würzburg; tel. 49 931 372 444; fax 49 931 373 638.

**Stadtbüchereien:** Berliner Alle 59, PO Box 1120, Düsseldorf.

**Stadt-und Bezirksbibliothek:** Haus am Schillerplatz, Chemnitz.

**Stadt-und Bezirksbibliothek:** Salzgrafenstrasse 2, Halle.

**Stadt-und Bezirksbibliothek:** Mozartstrasse 1, Leipzig.

**Stadt-und Bezirksbibliothek:** Weitlingstrasse 1a, Magdeburg.

**Stadt-und Berzirksbibliothek:** Kröpeliner Strasse 82, Rostock.

**Stadt-und Kreisbibliothek Heinrich Heine:** Orangerie, Gotha.

**Stadt-und Kreisbibliothek:** Strasse d DSF 8, Ludwigslust.

**Stadt-und Kreisbibliothek:** Strasse des Friedens 54, Oranienburg.

**Stadt-und Kreisbibliothek:** August-Wolf-Strasse 10, Quedlinburg.

**Stadt-und Kreisbibliothek:** Ernestiner Strasse 38, Meiningen.

**Stadt-und Kreisbibliothek:** Mühlhausen.

**Stadt-und Kreisbibliothek:** Schulplatz 13, Rudolstadt.

**Stadt-und Kreisbibliothek:** Schloss Sondershausen.

**Stadt-und Landesbibliothek:** Königswall 18, 44137 Dortmund; tel. 49 231 502 3225; fax 49 231 502 3199; website www.dortmund.de/bibliotheken.

**Stadt-und Universitätsbibliothek:** Bockenheimer Landstrasse 134–138, 60325 Frankfurt; tel. 49 692 123 9244; fax 49 692 123 7398; website www.stub .uni-frankfurt.de/musik.htm.

## Ghana

**Central Reference and Research Library:** PO Box 1633, Accra; tel. 233 21 21 162.

## Greece

**Ethnike Bibliotheke tes Hellados:** Odos Venizelou 32, 10679 Athens; tel. 30 1 361 4413.

## Guatemala

**Biblioteca Nacional de Guatemala:** 5a Avda 7-26, Guatemala City; tel. 502 2 539 071; fax 502 2 322 443.

## Haiti

**Bibliothèque Nationale d'Haiti:** 193 rue du Centre, Port-au-Prince; tel. 509 223 2148; fax 509 223 2029.

## Honduras

**Biblioteca Nacional de Honduras:** 6a Avda Salvador Mendieta, Tegucigalpa; tel. 504 228 577.

## Hungary

**Állami Gorkij Könyvtar (Gorky State Library):** Molnár u 11, 1056 Budapest.

**Institute for Musicology of Hungarian Academy of Sciences:** PO Box 28, 1250, Budapest.

**Magyar Tudományos Akadémia Zenetudományi Intézete:** Táncsis M u 7, 1014 Budapest.

**Music Information Centre of the Hungarian Council:** POB 47, 1367 Budapest.

**Országos Széchémyi Könyvtar (National Széchémyi Library):** 1 Budavári Palota Fépület, 1827 Budapest; tel. 36 1 375 7533; fax 36 1 375 6167; website www.ozhk.hu.

## Iceland

**Landsbokasafn Islands (National Library of Iceland):** Arngrimsgötu 3, IS-107 Reykjavik; tel. 354 1 563 5600; fax 354 1 563 5615; website saga.bok.hi.is.

## India

**National Library:** Belvedere, Kolkata, West Bengal 700027; tel. 91 33 455 381.

## Indonesia

**Perpustakaan Nasional (National Library of Indonesia):** J1 Salemba Raya 28, PO Box 3624, Jakarta 10002; tel. 62 21 310 1411.

## Iran

**National Library of Iran:** Niavaran Street, Tehran; tel. 98 21 228 0937.

## Iraq

**National Library:** Bab-el-Muaddum, Baghdad.

## Ireland

**National Library of Ireland:** Kildare Street, Dublin 2; tel. 353 1 603 0200; fax 353 1 661 2523; website www.nli.ie.

**Royal Irish Academy of Music:** 36–38 Westland Row, Dublin 2.

## Israel

**AMLI Library of Music:** 23 Arlosoroff Street, Haifa.

**The Felicja Blumental Music Center & Library:** PO Box 4882, 26 Bialik Street, 61048 Tel-Aviv; tel. 972 3 5250499; fax 972 3 5281032; e-mail ryna_k@tzion.tel-aviv.gov.il; Dir: Irit Schoenhorn.

**Jewish National and University Library:** PO Box 503, 91004 Jerusalem.

## Italy

**Archivio di Stato di Ancona:** Via Maggini 80, 60127 Ancona.

**Archivio di Stato de Bari:** Via Pasubio 137, 70124 Bari.

**Archivio di Stato di Bologna:** Piazza dei Celestini 4, 40123 Bologna.

**Archivio di Stato di Cagliari:** Via Gallura 2, 09125 Cagliari.

**Archivio di Stato di Catania:** Via Vittorio Emanuele 156, 95131 Catania.

**Archivio di Stato di Firenze:** Loggiato degli Riffizi, 50100 Florence.

**Archivio di Stato di Genova:** Via Tommaso Reggio 14, 16123 Genoa; tel. 39 010 246 8373; fax 39 010 246 8992; website archivi.beniculturali.it/ASGE.

**Archivio de Stato di Milano:** Via Senato 10, 20121 Milan; tel. 39 02 774 2161; fax 39 02 7742 16230.

**Archivio di Stato di Napoli:** Via Grande Archivio 5, 80138 Naples; tel. 39 081 563 8111; fax 39 081 563 8300; website archivi.beniculturali.it/ASNA/index.htm.

**Archivio di Stato di Palermo:** Corso Vittorio Emanuele 31, 90133 Palermo.

**Archivio Centrale dello Stato:** Piazzale degli Archivi, 00144 Rome.

**Archivio di Stato di Trieste:** Via Lamarmora 17, 34139 Trieste; tel. 39 040 390 020; fax 39 040 394 461.

**Archivio de Stato di Torino:** Sezioni Riunite, Via Piave 21, 10122 Turin; tel. 39 011 540 382 / 460 4111; fax 39 011 546 176 / 436 4795; website www.multix.it/asto.

**Associazione Culturale Archivi del Sud:** Via Giovanni Spano 5, 07041 Alghero.

**Biblioteca Augusta del Domune di Perugia:** Palazzo Conestabile della Staffa, Via delle Prome 15, 06100 Perugia.

**Biblioteca Centrale della Regione Siciliana:** Corso Vittorio Emanuele 431, 90134 Palermo; tel. 39 091 581 602; fax 39 091 696 7644.

**Biblioteca Civica:** Via Tripoli 16, 15100 Alessandria.

**Biblioteca Civica:** Via Arte Botanico 5, 35123 Padua.

**Biblioteca Civica:** Piazza, Petrarca 2, 27100 Pavia.

**Biblioteca Civica:** Via Cappello 43, 37121 Verona; tel. 39 045 807 9710; fax 39 045 800 5701; website www.comune.verona.it/internet/Bibliotecaciv.

**Biblioteca Civica Angelo Mai:** Piazza Vecchia 15, 24100 Bergamo; tel. 39 035 399 111; fax 39 035 240 555; website www.bibliotecamai.org.

**Biblioteca Civica Bertoliana:** Via Riale 5–13, 36100 Vicenza.

**Biblioteca Civica Gambalunga:** Via Gambalunga 27, 47037 Rimini; tel. 39 0541 704 311.

**Biblioteca Civiche e Raccolte Storiche:** Via Cittadella 5, 10122 Turin; tel. 39 011 57 651; fax 39 011 442 9830.

**Biblioteca Comunale:** Via Independenza 87, 22100 Como.

**Biblioteca Comunale:** Via Roberto Ardigò 13, 46100 Mantua.

**Biblioteca Comunale Sormani:** Palazzo Sormani, Corso di Porta Vittoria 6, 20133 Milan; tel. 39 02 8846 3350; fax 39 02 8846 3353; website www.comune.milano.it/biblioteche/sub_sorman.

**Biblioteca Comunale:** Piazza Brunaccini, 90134 Palermo; tel. 39 091 331 274.

**Biblioteca Comunale:** Via Madruzzo 26, 38100 Trento; tel. 39 0461 2321 7123; fax 39 0461 985 166.

**Biblioteca Comunale:** Borgo Cavour 18, 31100 Treviso.

**Biblioteca Comunale A Saffi:** Corso della Repubblica 72, 47100 Forli.

**Biblioteca Comunale Arisotea:** Via delle Scienze 17, 44100 Ferrara; tel. 39 0532 418 200; fax 39 0532 204 296; website www.comune.fe.it/biblio.

**Biblioteca Comunale Classense:** Via Baccarini 3, 48100 Ravenna.

**Biblioteca Comunale degli Intronati:** Via della Sapienza 5, 53100 Sienna; tel. 39 0577 280 704.

**Biblioteca Comunale Forteguerriana:** Piazza della Sapienza 1, PO Box 177, Pistoia.

**Biblioteca Comunale Joppi:** Piazza Marconi 8, 33100 Udine.

**Biblioteca Comunale Labronica F. D. Guerrazzi:** Viale del Forte San Pietro 15, 57100 Livorno; tel. 39 0586 219 265; fax 39 0586 219 151; website www.comune.livorno.it/txt/labronica.html.

**Biblioteca Comunale Luciano Benincasa:** Via Bernabei 32, 60121 Ancona; tel. 39 071 222 5020-2; fax 39 071 222 2109.

**Biblioteca Comunale Passerini Landi:** Via Neve 3, 29100 Piacenza.

**Biblioteca del Civico Museo Correr:** Piazza San Marco 52, Procuratie Nuove, 30100 Venice.

**Biblioteca dell'Archivio di Stato di Trento:** Via Rome 51, Trento.

**Biblioteca della Città di Arezzo:** Via dei Pileati-Palazzo Pretorio, 52100 Arezzo.

**Biblioteca Durazzo Giustiniani:** Via Balbi 1, 16126 Genoa.

**Biblioteca Estense:** Palazzo dei Musei, Piazzo San Agostino 309, 41100 Modena.

**Biblioteca Medicea-Laurenziana:** Piazza San Lorenzo 9, 50123 Florence; tel. 39 055 210 760; fax 39 055 230 2992.

**Biblioteca Municipale A. Panizzi:** Via Farini 3, 42100 Reggio Emilia; tel. 39 0522 456 078; fax 39 0522 456 081.

**Biblioteca Nazionale Centrale:** Piazza Cavalleggeri 1B, 50122 Florence; tel. 39 055 249 191; fax 39 055 234 2482; website www.bncf.firenze.sbn.it.

**Biblioteca Nazionale Marciana:** Palazzi della libreria Vecchia e della Zecca, San Marco 7, 30124 Venice; tel. 39 041 520 8788.

**Biblioteca Nazionale Sagarriga-Visconti-Volpi:** Palazzo Ateneo, Piazza Umberto, 70122 Bari; tel. 39 080 521 1298; fax 39 080 521 1298.

**Biblioteca Nazionale Vittorio Emanuele III:** Palazzo Reale, 80132 Naples; tel. 39 081 407 921; fax 39 081 403 820.

**Biblioteca Palatina:** Via del Conservatorio 27, 43100 Parma; tel. 39 0521 289 429; fax 39 0521 235 662.

**Biblioteca Reale:** Piazzo Castel.lo 191, 10100 Turin; tel. 39 011 545 305; fax 39 011 543 855.

**Biblioteca Regionale Universitaria:** Via dei Verdi 73, 98100 Messina; tel. 39 090 771 908.

**Biblioteca Regionale Universitaria:** Piazza Università 2, 95124 Catania; tel. 39 095 321 725; fax 39 095 326 862.

**Biblioteca Riunita Civica e A Ursino Recupero:** Via Biblioteca 13, 95124 Catania.

**Biblioteca Statale e Libreria Civica:** Via Ugolani Dati 4, 26100 Cremona; tel. 39 0732 413 543; fax 39 0732 413 544.

**Biblioteca Statale di Lucca:** Via San Maria Corteorlandini 12, 55100 Lucca; tel. 39 0583 491 271; fax 39 0583 46 770; website www.bslu.librari .beniculturali.it.

**Biblioteca Universitaria:** Via Università 32A, 09100 Cagliari.

**Biblioteca Universitaria:** Palazzo dell'Università, 27100 Pavia.

**Biblioteca Universitaria:** Via Curtatone e Montanara 15, 56100 Pisa; tel. 39 050 24 506.

**Biblioteca Universitaria:** Via Aurelio Saffi 2, 61029 Urbino.

**Civica Biblioteca Queriniana:** Via Mazzini 1, 25100 Brescia.

**Istituto di Ricerca per il Teatro Musicale:** Via Francesco Tamagno 65, 00168 Rome; tel. 39 066147277; fax 39 066144371; e-mail irtem@mclink.it; website www.irtem.it; Pres.: Carlo Marinelli; f. 1984; non-profit, publicly-financed institute sponsoring research into the fields of musical theatre, 20th century music, ethnomusicology and music-media relations; organizes annual international conference, and adminsters archives.

**Istituto Nazionale di Studi Verdiani:** Strada della Repubblica 56, 43100 Parma.

**Istituto Storia Musica:** Via Vittoria 6, 00187 Roma.

**Raccolte storiche del Comune di Milano:** Biblioteca e Archivio, Palazzo De Marchi, Via Borgonuovo 23, 20121 Milan.

**Universitaria di Bologna Biblioteca:** Via Zamboni 35, 40126 Bologna; tel. 39 051 243 420; fax 39 051 252 110; website www.bub.unibo.it.

## Jamaica

**Institute of Jamaica Library:** 12–16 East Street, Kingston; tel. 1 876 9220 6207; fax 1 876 922 1147.

## Japan

**Documentation Centre of Modern Japanese Music:** 4-19-6 Nishi Azabu, Minato-ku, Tokyo 106; tel. 81 3 400 0079.

**Hiroshima Prefectural:** 2020 Kami-Nobori-machi, Hiroshima.

**Kyoto Prefectural Library:** Okazaki Park, Kyoto Shi, Kyoto.

**National Diet (Parliament) Library:** 10-1 Nagatacho 1-chome, Chiyoda-ku, Tokyo 100.

**Osaka Prefectural Nakanoshima Library:** 1-2-10 Nakanoshima, Kita-ku, Osaka 530; tel. 81 6 203 0474.

**Tokyo Metropolitan Central Library:** 5-7-13 Minami-Azabu, Monato-ku, Tokyo 106; tel. 81 3 3442 8451; fax 81 3 3447 8924.

## Jordan

**Greater Amman Public Library:** PO Box 182181, Amman; tel. 962 6 637 111.

## Kenya

**Central Government Archives:** PO Box 30050, Nairobi.

**Kenya National Archives:** PO Box 49210, Moi Ave, Nairobi.

## Democratic Republic of Korea

**Grand People's Study House (National Library):** PO Box 200, Pyongyang.

## Republic of Korea

**National Central Library:** 60-1, Panpo-Dong, Seocho-Gu, Seoul; tel. 82 2 535 4142; fax 82 2 599 6942.

## Laos

**Bibliothèque Nationale:** PO Box 122, Vientiane; tel. 856 21 212 452; fax 856 21 213 029.

## Lebanon

**Bibliothèque Nationale du Liban:** Place de l'Etoile, Beirut; tel. 961 1 486 374; fax 961 1 374 079.

## Libya

**National Library of Libya:** PO Box 9127, Benghazi.

## Luxembourg

**Bibliothèque Nationale:** 37 Blvd F. D. Roosevelt, 2450 Luxembourg; tel. 352 229 755; fax 352 475 672; website www.etat.lu/BNL.

## Malaysia

**Perpustakaan Negara Malaysia (National Library of Malaysia):** Lot G1 8 G2, Block A, Exchange Square, 50572 Kuala Lumpur; tel. 60 3 255 3144; fax 60 3 291 7436.

## Mexico

**Asociación Musical Manuel M. Ponce:** AC, Bucareli No. 12, Desp 411, Mexico City.

**Biblioteca Nacional de México:** Insurgentes Sur s/n, Centro Cultural, Ciudad Universitaria, Coyoacán, 04510.

## Monaco

**Bibliothèque Louis Notari:** 8 rue Louis Notari, 98000 Monte Carlo; tel. 377 9315 2940; fax 377 9315 2941.

## Morocco

**Bibliothèque Générale et Archives:** PO Box 1003, Avenue ibn Battouta, Rabat; tel. 212 7 771 890; fax 212 7 776 062.

## Myanmar

**National Library:** Six Storeyed Building, Strand Road, Yangon; tel. 95 1 72 058.

## Netherlands

**Gemeenschappelijke Openbare Bibliotheek:** Piazza 201, 5611 AG Eindhoven.

**Gemeenschappelijke Openbare Bibliotheek:** Ridderstraat 29, 6511 TM Nijmegen.

**Gemeentebibliothek:** Hoogstraat 110, 3011 PV Rotterdam.

**Gemeentel.ijke Utrechtse Openbare Bibliotheek:** Oude Gracht 167, 3511 AL Utrecht.

**Koninklijke Bibliotheek (Royal Library):** PO Box 90407, Prins Willem-Alexanderhof 5, 2509 LK, The Hague; tel. 31 70 314 0911; fax 31 70 314 0450; website www.kb.nl.

**Maatschappij tot Bevordering der Toonkunst:** le jac Van Campenstraat 59, 1072 BD Amsterdam.

**Openbare Bibliotheek:** Brink 70, 7411 BW Deventer.

**Openbare Bibliotheek:** H. B. Blijdensteinstichting, Pijpennstraat 15, 7511 GM Enschede.

**Openbare Bibliotheek:** Doelenplein 1, 2011 XR Haarlem; tel. 31 23 157 600; fax 31 23 157 669.

**Openbare Bibliotheek:** Bilderdijkstraat 103, 2513 CM The Hague.

**Openbare Bibliotheek:** Koningsplein 1, 5038 WG Tilburg.

**Openbare Bibliotheken (Public Library):** Centraale Bibliotheek, Prinsengracht 587, 1016 HT Amsterdam.

**Rotterdamsch Leeskabinet, Bibliotheek:** Burg Oudlaan 50 (16), PO Box 1738, 3000 DR Rotterdam.

**Stadsbibliotheek:** Nieuwenhofstraat 1, 6211 KG Maastricht; tel. 31 43 329 3259; fax 31 43 329 2795.

**Stichting Arnhemse Openbare en Gelderse Wetenschappelijke Bibliotheek:** Koningstaat 26, 6801 DG Arnhem.

**Stichting Centrale Bibliotheekdienst voor Friesland:** Zuiderkruisweg 2, PO Box 530, 8901 BH Leeuwarden.

**Stichting Openbare Bibliotheek:** PO Box 30004, 9700 RE Groningen.

**Stichting Openbare Bibliotheek:** Hinthamerstraat 72, 5211 MR Hertogenbosch.

**Stichting Openbare Bibliotheken:** Gravelandseweg 55, 1217 EH Hilversum.

**Stichting Samenwerkende Openbare Bibliotheken:** Kruissstraat 71, 2611 ML Delft.

## New Zealand

**Auckland City Libraries:** Lorne Street, PO Box 4138, Auckland 1; tel. 64 9 377 0209; fax 64 9 307 7741.

**Canterbury Public Library:** Orford Terrace and Gloucester Street, PO Box 1466, Christchurch 1.

**Centre for New Zealand Music Ltd (SOUNZ New Zealand):** PO Box 10 042, Level 3, 15 Brandon Street, Wellington.

**Dunedin Public Library:** 230 Moray Place, PO Box 5542, Dunedin; tel. 64 3 474 3690; fax 64 3 474 3660.

**National Library of New Zealand, Music Room:** PO Box 1467, Wellington; tel. 4 474 3000; fax 4 474 3035; website www.natlib.govt.nz; located at 70 Molesworth Street, Wellington.

**Wellington Public Library:** 65 Victoria Street, PO Box 1992, Wellington 1; tel. 64 4 801 4040; fax 64 4 801 4047.

## Nicaragua

**Biblioteca Nacional:** Calle del Triunfo 302, PO Box 101, Managua.

## Nigeria

**National Library of Nigeria:** 4 Wesley Street, Private Mail Bag 12626, Lagos; tel. 234 1 656 590.

## Norway

**Bergen offentlige bibliotek:** Hordaland fylkesbibliotek, Strømgaten 6, 5015 Bergen; tel. 47 5556 8560.

**Deichmanske Bibliotek:** Henrik Ibsensgate 1, 0179 Oslo; tel. 47 2220 4335; fax 47 2211 3389.

**Drammen folkebibliotek:** Gamle Kirke Plass 7, PO Box 1136, 3001 Drammen.

**Kristiansands folkebibliotek:** Radhusgate 11, PO Box 476, 4601 Kristiansand.

**Norsk Musikksamling (National Music Collection), Nasjonalbiblioteket (National Library of Norway):** PO Box 2674 Solli, 0203 Oslo; tel. 47 23 27 60 43; fax 47 23 27 60 49; e-mail musikk-nbo@nb.no; website www.nb.no; collection of Norwegian printed music, manuscript music, sound recordings, books and papers; library located at Observatoriegt 2, Oslo.

**Norsk Visearkiv (Norwegian Folk and Popular Song Archives):** Tollbugt 28, 0157 Oslo.

**Norwegian Music Information Centre:** 28 Tollbugate, 10157 Oslo; tel. 47 2242 9090; fax 47 2242 9095; website www.notam.uio.no/nmi.

**Rogaland folkebibliotek:** Haakon VII's gate 11, PO Box 310/320, 4001 Stavanger.

**Sør-Trøndelag folkebibliotek:** Søndregate 5 og Kongensgate 2, PO Box 926, 7001 Trondheim.

## Pakistan

**National Library of Pakistan:** H 558, Street 83, Sector G-6/4, Islamabad; tel. 92 51 822 449.

**Punjab Public Library:** Library Road, Lahore 1884.

## Panama

**Biblioteca Nacional:** PO Box 2444, Panama City 1892; website www.binal.ac.pa.

## Paraguay

**Biblioteca y Archivo Nacionales:** Mariscal Estigarriba 95, Asunción.

## Peru

**Biblioteca Nacional del Perú:** Avda Abancay s/n, PO Box 2335, Lima; tel. 51 1 428 7690; fax 51 1 427 7331.

## Philippines

**National Library:** Ermita, T. M. Kalaw Street, Ermita, Manila 1000; tel. 63 2 582 511.

## Poland

**Biblioteka Narodowa:** ul Niepodległości 213, PO Box 36, 00973 Warsaw; tel. 48 22 259 271; fax 48 22 255 251.

**Biblioteka Publiczna m st Warszawy:** ul Koszykowa 26, 00950 Warsaw; tel. 48 22 628 2001; fax 48 22 621 1968.

**Biblioteka Slaska (Silesian Library):** ul Francuska 12, 529, 40956 Katowice; tel. 48 3 155 4305; fax 48 3 156 4953.

**Biblioteka Uniwersytecka w Warszawie, Gabinet Zbiorów Muzycznych:** ul Dobra 56–66, 00312 Warsaw.

**Biblioteka w Krakowie PAN (Library of the Polish Academy of Sciences):** ul Slawkowska 17, 31016 Kraków.

**Library of the Polish Composers' Union:** Rynek Starego Miasta 27, 00-272 Warsaw; tel. 48 22 8311634; fax 48 22 8310607; e-mail polmic@polmic.pl; website www.polmic.pl.

**Miejska Biblioteka Publiczna (City Library):** ul Franciskanska 1, 31004 Kraków.

**Miejska Biblioteka Publiczna im Edwards Rqaczynskiego:** Pl Wolnosci 19, 60967 Poznań.

**Miejska Biblioteka Publiczna im L. Warynskiego:** 90508 ód, Gdańsk 102.

**Towarzystwo im Fryderyka Chopina (Frederic Chopin Society):** Ostrogski Castle, 1 Okolnik Street, 00-368 Warsaw; tel. (48 22) 826-59-35; fax (48 22) 827-95-99; e-mail info@chopin.pl; website www.chopin.pl; Chair.: Kazimierz Gierzod; houses the Chopin Museum, Library, and archive of historical data and recordings.

**Wojewódzka Biblioteka Publiczna i Ksiaeznica miejska:** ul J Slowackiego 8, 87100 Torun.

**Wojewódzka i Miejska Biblioteka Publiczna:** ul Warszawska 45, 40010 Katowice.

**Wojewódzka i Miejska Biblioteka Publiczna im H. Lopacinskiego:** ul Narutowicza 4, 20950 Lublin.

**Wojewódzka i Miejska Biblioteka Publiczna im St Staszica:** ul Podgórna 15, 70952 Szczecin.

**Wojewódzka i Miejska Biblioteka Publiczna im T. Mikulskiego:** Rynek 58, 50116 Wrocław.

## Portugal

**Biblioteca Municipal Central:** Largo do Campo Pequeno, Palácio Galveias, 1000 Lisbon.

**Biblioteca Nacional:** Rua Ocidental do Campo Grande 83, 1751 Lisbon; tel. 351 21 798 2000; fax 351 21 798 2140; website www.ibl.pt.

## Romania

**Academia România Library:** Calea Victoriei 196, 71104 Bucharest; tel. 40 21 650 5680.

**Biblioteca central de stat:** Str Ion Ghica 4, Bucharest.

## Russia

**Moscow State Library:** Vozdvizhenka 3, 101000 Moscow.

**St Petersburg State Library:** St Petersburg.

## Singapore

**National Library:** c/o National Library Board, 1 Temasek Avenue, Suite 06-00 Millenia Tower, Singapore 039192; tel. (65) 6332 3133; fax (65) 6332 3611; website www.nlb.gov.sg.

## Slovakia

**Matica slovenska Kni ica (Slovak National Library):** ulice Ladislava Novomeského 32, 03652 Martin; tel. 421 43 31 371.

## South Africa

**Cape Town City Libraries:** Mayor's Garden, Longmarket Street, PO Box 4728, Cape Town 8000.

**Durban Municipal Library:** Smith Street, City Hall, PO Box 917, Durban 4000; tel. 27 31 309 4405; fax 27 31 309 6033.

**Performing Arts Library:** Central Johannesburg Library, Private Bag X 93, Marshalltown, Johannesburg 2107; tel. 27 011 870 1247; fax 27 11 870 1252; e-mail kalieB@joburg.org.za; Performing Arts Librarian: P. J. Burger.

**Pretoria Public Library:** 159 Andries Street, Pretoria 0002.

**South African Library:** Queen Victoria Street, PO Box 496, Cape Town 8001; tel. 27 21 246 320; fax 27 21 244 848.

**State Library:** 239 Vermeulen Street, PO Box 397, Pretoria 0001; tel. 27 12 218 931; fax 27 12 325 5984.

## Spain

**Biblioteca de Menéndez Pelayo:** Rubio 6, Santander.

**Biblioteca del Ministerio de Cultura:** Calle San Marcos 40, 5A, 28004 Madrid; tel. 34 9142 924 44; website www.mec.es/mec/publicaciones/p_public.html.

**Biblioteca Municipal del Ayuntamiento:** Fuencarral 78, Madrid 4.

**Biblioteca Nacional:** Avda Calvo Sotelo, 28022 Madrid; website www.bne.es.

**Biblioteca Provincial:** Paseo del Misadero, Toledo.

**Biblioteca Pública:** F. Bonnemaison de Verdaguer i Callis, Baja de San Pedro 7, Barcelona.

**Biblioteca Pública:** Ramón Llull 3, Palma de Mallorca.

**Biblioteca Pública de la Ciudad:** Plaza de los Sitios 5, Zaragoza.

**Biblioteca Pública del Estado:** Jardines del Salón, s/n, Apdo Oficial, Granada.

**Biblioteca Pública del Estado:** Santa Nonia 5, Casa de Cultura, León.

**Biblioteca Pública del Estado:** Alfonso XII 19, 41001 Seville.

**Biblioteca Pública e Archivo Distrital de Ponta Delgada:** Rua Ernest do Canto, Ponta Delgada, San Miguel.

**Biblioteca Pública Provincial:** Plaza de San Juan, Burgos.

**Biblioteca Pública Provincial:** Avda Ramón Carranza 16, Cádiz.

**Biblioteca Pública Provincial:** Paseo de la Florida 9, Victoria.

**Centro de Documentación Música y de la Danza:** Torregalindo 10, 28016 Madrid; tel. 34 91 353 14 80; fax 34 91 353 13 73; e-mail cdmyd@inaem.mcu.es; website cdmyd.mcu.es.

**Real Academia de Bellas Artes de San Fernando:** Biblioteca, Alcala 13, 28014 Madrid; tel. 34 9153 190 53; website rabasf.onsde.es.

## Sri Lanka

**National Museum Library:** Sr Marcus Fernando Mawatha, PO Box 854, Colombo 7.

## Sweden

**Gävle stadsbibliotek:** Södra Strandgatan 6, Box 801, 80130 Gävle.

**Göteborgs stadsbibliotek:** Box 5404, 40229 Göteborg.

**Helsingborgs stadsbibliotek:** Bolbrogatan, 25225 Helsingborg.

**Kungliga Biblioteket (Royal Library):** Humlegården, PO Box 5039, 10241 Stockholm; tel. 46 8 679 5040; fax 46 8 611 6956; website www.kb.se.

**Malmö stadsbibliotek:** Regementsgatan 3, 21142 Malmö.

**Norrköpings stadsbibliotek:** Södra Promenaden 105, 60181 Norrköping.

**Örebros stadsbibliotek:** Nabbtorgsgatan 12, 70114 Örebro.

**Swedish Music Information Centre:** PO Box 27327, 79 Sandhamnsgatan, 10254 Stockholm; tel. 46 8 783 8800; fax 46 8 783 9510; website www.mic.stim.se.

**Uppsala stadsbibliotek:** Östra Ågatan 19, PO Box 643, 75127 Uppsala.

**Västerås stadsbibliotek:** Biskopsgatan 2, PO Box 717, 72187 Västerås; tel. 46 21 390000; fax 46 21 394680; e-mail musikinfo@vasteras.se; website www.bibliotek.vasteras.se; extensive media collection.

## Switzerland

**Allgemeine Bibliotheken der GGG:** Gerbergasse 24, 4001 Basel; tel. 41 61 264 1111; fax 41 61 264 1190.

**Berner Volksbücherie:** Monbijoustrasse 45a, PO Box 2267, 3001 Bern.

**Bibliothèque municipale:** 11 Place Chauderon, 1003 Lausanne.

**Bibliothèque publique et universitarie:** 3 Place Numa-Droz, 2000 Neuchâtel.; tel. 41 38 207 300; fax 41 38 207 309.

**Bibliothèques municipales:** 16 Place de la Madeleine, 1204 Geneva.

**Pestalozzi-Bibliothek:** Zahingerstrasse 17, 8001 Zürich.

**Stadtbibliothek:** Dufourstrasse 26, 2502 Biel.

**Stadtbibliothek:** Hauptgasse 12, 4600 Olten.

**Stadtbibliothek:** Kauffmannweg 4, 6003 Lucerne.

**Stadtbibliothek:** Goldsteinstrasse 15, PO Box 91, 82025 Schaffhausen.

**Stadtbibliothek:** Museumstrasse 52, 8401 Winterthur; tel. 41 52 267 5145; fax 41 52 267 5140.

## Syria

**Al Maktabah Al Wataniah (National Library):** Bab El-Faradj, Aleppo.

**Al Zahiriah National Library:** Bab el Barid, Damascus.

## Thailand

**Ho Samut Haeng Chat (National Library of Thailand):** Samsen Road, Bangkok 10300; tel. 66 2 281 5212; fax 66 2 281 0263; website www.natlib.moe.go.th.

## Tunisia

**Dar al-Katub Al-Watanlyya/Bibliothèque Nationale:** Ministere des Affaires Culturelles, 20 souk El Attarine, 1008 Tunis.

## Turkey

**Beyazit Deviet Kütüyshanesi (Beyazit State Library):** Imaret Sok 18, Istanbul; tel. 90 212 522 2488; fax 90 212 526 1133.

**Milli Kütüphane (National Library):** Bahçelievier, 06490 Ankara; tel. 90 312 222 3812; fax 90 312 223 0451; website www.mkutup.gov.tr.

## United Kingdom

**Aberdeen Central Library:** Rosemount Viaduct, Aberdeen, AB25 1GW, Scotland; tel. 01224 652511.

**Belfast Public Library:** Royal Ave, Belfast, BT1 1EK, Northern Ireland; tel. 028 9024 323.

**Birmingham Central Library:** Chamberlain Square, Birmingham B3 3HQ; tel. 0121 303 4511; fax 0121 233 4458.

**Bristol Central Library:** College Green, Bristol BS1 5TL; tel. 0117 903 7202.

**British Library Music Collections:** 96 Euston Road, London NW1 2DB; tel. (20) 7412-7772; e-mail music-collections@bl.uk; website www.bl.uk; Head of Music Collections: Chris Banks.

**British Library Sound Archive:** 96 Euston Road, London NW1 2DB; tel. 020 7412 7676; fax 020 7412 7441; website www.bl.uk.

**British Music Information Centre:** 10 Stratford Place, London W1C 1BA; tel. 020 7499 8567; fax 020 7499 4795; website www.bmic.co.uk.

**Cardiff Central Library:** Frederick Street, Cardiff, CF10 2DU, Wales; tel. (29) 2038-2116; Music Librarian: Sheila Basford.

**Carmarthen Public Library:** St Peter's Street, Carmarthen, SA31 1LN, Wales; tel. 01267 224830.

**Dundee Central Library:** The Wellgate, Dundee, DD1 1DB, Scotland; tel. 01382 431500; fax 01382 431558.

**Edinburgh Central Library:** George IV Bridge, Edinburgh, EG1 1EG, Scotland; tel. 0131 242 8000.

**English Folk Dance and Song Society:** Cecil Sharp House, Library, 2 Regent's Park Road, London NW1 7AY; tel. 020 7485 2206; website www.efdss.org.

**Leeds Central Library:** Calverley Street, Municipal Building, Leeds LS1 3AB; tel. 0113 247 8911.

**Liverpool Central Library:** William Brown Street, Liverpool L3 8EW; tel. 0151 225 5463; fax 0151 207 1342.

**Llyfrgell Genedlaethol Cymru (National Library of Wales):** Aberystwyth, Ceredigion, SY23 3BU, Wales; tel. (1970) 632800; fax (1970) 615709; e-mail holi@llgc.org.uk; website www.llgc.org.uk.

**Manchester Central Library:** St Peter's Square, Manchester M2 5PD; tel. (161) 2341976; fax (161) 2341961; e-mail music@libraries.manchester.gov.uk.

**Mitchell Library:** North Street, Glasgow, G3 7DN, Scotland; tel. 0141 248 7030; fax 0141 305 2815; website www.mitchelllibrary.org.

**National Library of Scotland:** George IV Bridge, Edinburgh, EH1 1EW, Scotland; tel. (131) 226-4531; fax (131) 622-4803; e-mail music@nls.uk; website www.nls.uk/collections/music/index.html; Head of Music: Almut Boehme.

**Newcastle upon Tyne City Library:** Princess Square, Newcastle upon Tyne NE99 1DX; tel. 0191 261 0691.

**University of Birmingham:** Department of Music, Barber Institute, Edgbaston, Birmingham B15 2TT; website www.bham.ac.uk.

## United States of America

**American Music Center:** 30 W 26th Street, Suite 1001, New York, NY 10010-2011; tel. 1 212 366 5260; fax 1 212 366 5265; website www.amc.net.

**Atlanta-Fulton Public Library:** 1 Margaret Mitchell Square NW, Atlanta, GA 30303; website www.af.public.lib.ga.us.

**Austin Public Library:** 800 Guadalupe Street, PO Box 2287, Austin, TX 78768; website www.cityofaustin.org/library.

**Birmingham Public Library:** 2100 Park Place, Birmingham, AL 35203; tel. 1 205 226 3610; website www.bplonline.org.

**Boston Public Library:** 700 Boylston Street, Boston, MA 02116; tel. 1 617 536 5400; website www.bpl.org.

**Buffalo and Erie County Public Library:** 1 Lafayette Square, Buffalo, NY 14203; tel. 1 716 858 8900; fax 1 716 858 6211; website www.buffalolib.org.

**California State Library:** PO Box 942837, Sacramento, CA 94237; website www.library.ca.gov.

**Carnegie Library of Pittsburgh:** 4400 Forbes Avenue, Pittsburgh, PA 15213; tel. 1 412 622 3114; website www.clpgh.org.

**Chicago Public Library:** 400 S State Street, Chicago, IL 60605; tel. 1 312 747 4882; fax 1 312 747 4887; website www.chipublib.org.

**City of Phoenix Public Library:** 1221 N Central Avenue, Phoenix, AZ 85004; tel. 1 602 261 8836; website www.ci.phoenix.az.us.

**Cleveland Public Library:** 325 Superior Avenue, Cleveland, OH 44114-1271; tel. 1 216 623 2881; fax 1 216 623 2935; website www.cpl.org.

**Columbus Metropolitan Library:** 28 S Hamilton Road, Columbus, OH 43213.

**Connecticut State Library:** 231 Capitol Avenue, Hartford, CT 06106.

**Dallas Public Library:** 1515 Young Street, Dallas, TX 75201.

**Denver Public Library:** 1357 Broadway, Denver, CO 80203; tel. 1 303 640 8880; fax 1 303 595 3034; website www.denver.lib.co.us.

**Detroit Public Library:** 5201 Woodward Avenue, Detroit, MI 48202; tel. 1 313 833 1460; fax 1 313 833 5039; website www.detroit.lib.mi.us.

**Enoch Pratt Free Library:** 400 Cathedral Street, Baltimore, MD 21201.

**Free Library of Philadelphia:** Logan Square, Philadelphia, PA 19103; tel. 1 215 686 5322; fax 1 215 563 3628; website www.library.phila.gov.

**Houston Public Library:** 500 McKinney Avenue, Houston, TX 77002.

**Illinois State Library:** Springfield, IL 62756.

**Indiana State Library:** 140 N Senate Avenue, Indianapolis, IN 46204.

**Indianapolis-Marion County Public Library:** 40 E St Clair Street, PO Box 211, Indianapolis, IN 46406.

**Kansas City Public Library:** 311 E 12th Street, Kansas City, MO 64106.

**Library of Congress, Music Division:** James Madison Building, LM 113, Washington, DC 20540; tel. 1 202 287 5507; website www.loc.gov.

**Library of Michigan:** 702 W Kalamazoo Street, PO Box 30740, Lansing, MI 48909; tel. 1 517 373 1300.

**Library of Virginia:** 800 E Broad Street, Richmond, VA 23219.

**Los Angeles Public Library:** 630 W Fifth Street, Los Angeles, CA 90071; tel. 1 213 612 3263; fax 1 213 612 0536.

**Louisville Free Public Library:** 301 York Street, Louisville, KY 40203.

**Memphis and Shelby County Public Library:** 1850 Peabody Avenue, Memphis, TN 38104.

**Miami-Dade Public Library:** 101 W Flagler Street, Miami, FL 33130; tel. 1 305 375 1505; fax 1 305 375 4436.

**Milwaukee Public Library:** 814 W Wisconsin Avenue, Milwaukee, WI 53233; tel. 1 414 286 3000; fax 1 414 286 2794; website www.mpl.org.

**Minneapolis Public Library:** 300 Nicollet Mall, Minneapolis, MN 55401; tel. 1 612 630 6000; fax 1 612 630 6210; website mpls.lib.mn.us.

**Missouri State Library:** 2002 Missouri Blvd, Jefferson City, MI 65102.

**New Hampshire State Library:** 20 Park Street, Concord, NH 03301.

**New Jersey State Library:** 185 W State Street, Trenton, NJ 08625.

**New Mexico State Library:** 325 Don Gaspar, Santa Fe, NM 87503.

**New Orleans Public Library:** 219 Loyola Avenue, New Orleans, LA 70140; tel. 1 504 596 2500.

**New York Public Library:** 40 Lincoln Center Plaza, New York, NY 10023-7498; tel. 1 212 870 1639; fax 1 212 787 3852; website www.nypl.org.

**New York State Library:** Cultural Education Center, Empire State Plaza, Albany, NY 12230; tel. 1 518 474 5930; fax 1 518 474 5786; website www.nysl.nysed.gov.

**Newark Public Library:** 5 Washington Street, PO Box 630, Newark, NJ 07101; tel. 1 973 733 7840; fax 1 973 733 5648; website www.npl.org.

**Oregon State Library:** State Library Building, Salem, OR 97310.

**Providence Public Library:** 225 Washington Street, Providence, RI 02903; tel. 1 401 455 8000; fax 1 401 455 8080; website www.provlib.org.

**Public Library of Cincinnati and Hamilton County:** 800 Vine Street, Library Square, Cincinnati, OH 45202; tel. 1 513 369 6955; fax 1 513 369 6067.

**Richmond Public Library:** 101 E Franklin Street, Richmond, VA 23219.

**Rochester Public Library:** 115 South Avenue, Rochester, NY 14604.

**Sacramento Public Library:** 1010 Eighth Street, Sacramento, CA 95814.

**St Louis Public Library:** 1301 Olive Street, St Louis, MI 63103; tel. 1 314 241 2288; fax 1 314 241 3840.

**St Paul Public Library:** 90 W Fourth Street, St Paul, MN 55102.

**San Diego Public Library:** 820 East Street, San Diego, CA 92101.

**San Francisco Public Library, Art and Music Center:** Civic Center, San Francisco, CA 94102; tel. 1 415 557 4400; fax 1 415 557 4524.

**Seattle Public Library:** 1000 Fourth Avenue, Seattle, WA 98104.

**State Library of Massachusetts:** 341 State House, Boston, MA 02133.

**State Library of Ohio:** 65 S Front Street, Columbus, OH 43215.

**State Library of Pennsylvania:** 333 Market Street, Harrisburg, PA 17105-1745.

**United States Information Agency:** Arts America Program, 301 Fourth Street, Room 568, Washington, DC 20547.

**Washington State Library:** Olympia, WA 98504.

## Uruguay

**Biblioteca Nacional del Uruguay:** 18 de Julio 1790, Casilla 452, Montevideo; tel. 598 2 496 011.

## Venezuela

**Biblioteca Nacional:** Bolsa a San Francisco, PO Box 68350, Caracas 106.

## Viet Nam

**National Library of Viet Nam:** 31 Trang-Thi, 10000 Hanoi.

**National Library II:** 69 Gia-Long St, Ho Chi Minh City 1976.

# APPENDIX G: MUSIC CONSERVATOIRES

## Argentina

**Conservatorio Provincial de Música de Bahia Blanca:** Belgrano 446, 800 Bahia Blanca, Provincia de Buenos Aires.

**Conservatorio de Música Julián Aguirre:** Gral Rodríguez 7672, Banfield, Provincia de Buenos Aires.

**Conservatorio Municipal de Música Manuel de Falla:** Sarmiento 1551, 1042 Buenos Aires.

**Conservatorio Nacional de Música:** Carlos López Buchardo, Calle 1521, 1024 Buenos Aires.

**Pontificia Universidad Católica Argentin Santa Maria de los Buenos Aires:** Faculty of Arts and Music, Juncal 1912, Buenos Aires 1116.

## Australia

**Canberra School of Music:** National Institute of the Arts, Australian National University, Building 105B, Canberra, ACT 0200; tel. 61 2 6125 5700; fax 61 2 6248 0997; website www.anu.edu.au/ITA/music.

**New South Wales State Conservatorium of Music:** Macquarie St, Sydney, NSW 2000.

**Newcastle Conservatorium of Music:** Auckland Street, Newcastle, NSW 2300; tel. 61 2 4921 8900; fax 61 2 4921 8958; e-mail conservatorium@ newcastle.edu.au; website www.newcastle.edu.au.

**Queensland Conservatorium of Music:** Griffith University, PO Box 3428, South Brisbane, Qld 4101; website www.gu.edu.au.

**Tasmanian Conservatorium of Music:** University of Tasmania, PO Box 63, Hobart, TAS 7001; tel. 61 3 6226 7314; fax 61 3 6266 7333; website www .utas.edu.au/music.

**University of Adelaide:** Elder Conservatorium of Music, PO Box 498, Adelaide, SA 5001; website www.adelaide.edu.au.

**University of Melbourne:** Faculty of Music, Parkville, Vic. 3010; tel. 61 3 8344 5256; fax 61 3 8344 5346; e-mail enquiries@music.unimelb.edu.au; website www.music.unimelb.edu.au.

**University of Queensland:** Faculty of Music, Qld 4072; website www.uq .edu.au.

**University of Sydney, Department of Music:** Sydney, NSW 2006; tel. 61 2 9351 2222; website www.usyd.edu.au.

**University of Western Australia:** School of Music, 35 Stirling Highway, Crawley, WA 6009; website www.uwa.edu.au.

**Victorian College of the Arts:** 234 St Kilda Road, Southbank, Melbourne, Vic. 3006; tel. 61 3 9685 9300; fax 61 3 9682 1841; website www.vca.unimelb .edu.au.

**Wollongong Conservatorium:** Gleniffer Brae: Murphys Avenue, PO Box 62, Keiraville, NSW 2500; tel. 61 2 4228 1122; fax 61 2 4226 6942; website www.wollconmusic.nsw.edu.au.

## Austria

**Bruckner-Konservatorium des Landes Oberösterreich:** Wildbergstrase 18, 4040 Linz; tel. 43 70 70 10000; fax 43 70 70 1000 30; website www.bk-linz .at.

**Hochschule für Musik und Darstellande Kunst:** Leonhardstrasse 15, 8010 Graz; tel. 43 316 389.

**Hochschule für Musik und Darstellende Kunst:** Universität für Musik und darstellende Kunst Wien, Anton-von-Webern-Platz 1, 1030 Vienna; tel. (1) 71155; website www.mdw.ac.at.

**Horak-Konservatorium für Musik und Darstellende Kunst:** Hegelgasse 3, 1010 Vienna.

**Kärntner Landeskonservatorium:** Miesstalerstrasse 8, 9021 Klagenfurt.

**Konservatorium der Stadt Innsbruck:** Museumstrasse 17a, 6020 Innsbruck.

**Konservatorium der Stadt Wien:** Johannesgasse 4a, 1010 Vienna 1.

**Konservatorium für Musik und Dramatische Kunst:** Mühlgasse 28–30, 1040 Vienna.

**Universitat Mozarteum Salzburg:** Alpenstrasse 48, 5020 Salzburg; tel. 43 662 6198; fax 43 662 6198-3033; website www.moz.ac.at.

## Belgium

**Chapelle Musicale Reine Elisabeth:** Chaussée de Tervuren 445, 1410 Argenteuil-Waterloo; tel. 32 2 352 0110; fax 32 2 351 1024; e-mail info@cmre .be; website www.cmre.be.

**Conservatoire de Musique de Charleroi:** 1 rue Adolphe Biarrent, 6000 Charleroi.

**Conservatoire de Musique de Grand:** 54 rue de la Hoogpoort, 9000 Ghent.

**Conservatoire de Musique de Huy:** 11-13 rue du Palais de Justice, 5200 Huy.

**Conservatoire de Musique de Ostende:** 36 rue de Rome, 8400 Ostend.

**Conservatoire de Musique de Tournai:** 2 Place Reine Astrid, 7500 Tournai.

**Conservatoire de Musique de Verviers:** 6 rue Chapuis, 4800 Verviers; website users.skynet.be/conservatoire/.

**Conservatoire de Musique:** Chaussée de Louvain 121, 5000 Namur.

**Conservatoire Royal de Musique de Bruxelles:** 30 rue de la Régence, 1000 Brussels; tel. 32 2 511 0427; website www.conservatoire.be.

**Conservatoire Royal de Musique de Liège:** 14 rue Forgeur, 4000 Liège; tel. 32 4 222 0306.

**Conservatoire Royal de Musique de Mons:** 7 rue de Nimy, 7000 Mons.

**Institut de Musique Sacrée:** 28 rue Juppin, 5000 Namur.

**Koninklijke Beiaardschool Jef Denyn:** Fredrik de Mersdestraat 63, 2800 Mechelen; tel. 32 15 20 47 92; fax 32 15 203176; e-mail beiaardschool@yucom .be; website www.beiaardschool.be.

**Koninklijk Musiekconservatorium van Gent:** Hoogpoort 64, 9000 Ghent.

**Koninklijk Muziekconservatorium van Brussel:** Regentschapstraat 30, 1000 Brussels.

**Koninklijk Vlaams Conservatorium van Antwerpen:** Desguinler 25, 2018 Antwerp.

**Stedelijk Conservatorium:** Dirk Boutslaan 60–62, 3000 Leuven; tel. 016 22 21 21; fax 016 31 08 28; e-mail conservatorium@leuven.be; website www .leuven.be; Contact: Cathérine Legaey.

**Stedelijk Muziekconservatorium:** Melaan 3–5, 2800 Mechelen; tel. 015 28-29-80; fax 015 28-29-89; e-mail conservatorium.mechelen@skynet.be; Dir Jan de Maeyer.

**Stedelijk Muziekconservatorium:** Sint-Jacobsstratt 23, 8000 Bruges.

## Bolivia

**Academia de Música Hohner:** Calle Goitia 162, La Paz.

**Conservatorio Nacional de Música:** Avda 6 de Agosto, No. 2092, La Paz.

**Escuela Superior de Bellas Artes:** Calle Rosendo Gutiérrez 323, La Paz.

## Brazil

**Conservatorio Brasileiro de Música:** Avda Graça Aranha 57, No. 12, 20030 Rio de Janeiro; website www.cbm-musica.org.br.

**Conservatorio Dramático e Musical de Sao Paulo:** Avda Sao Joao 269, São Paulo.

**Escola de Música e Belas Artes do Paraná:** rue Emilian Perneta 179, 80000 Curitiba, Paraná.

**Escola de Música-Minas Gerais:** rue Santa Catarina 466, 30000 Belo Horizonte, Mina Gerais.

**Faculdade de Música Mae de Deus:** Avda Sao Paulo 651, CP106, 86100 Londrina, Paraná.

**Faculdade de Música Sagrado Coracao de Jesus:** Rua Caraibas 882, CP 8383, Villa Pompéia, São Paulo.

**Faculdade Santa Marcelina:** Rua Dr Emilio Ribas 89, 05006 São Paulo; tel. 11 3824 5800; e-mail fasm@fasm.edu.br; website www.fasm.com.br.

**Fundaçao Universidade de Brasília:** Institute of Arts and Communication, Campus Universitário, Asa Norte, 70910 Brasilia, DF.

**Instituto de Letras a Artes:** Rua Marechal Floriano 179, 96100 Pelotas, RS.

**Instituto de Música de Bahia:** Universidade Catolica de Salvador, Rua Carlos Gomes 400, Centro, 4000 Salvador, Bahia.

**UNESP-Universidade Estadual Júlio de Mesquita Filho:** Instituto do Artes do Planalto, Dept of Music, Rua Dom Luis Lasagna 400, São Paulo.

**Universidade de Sao Paulo (USP):** Department of Music, Cidade Universitaria, Butanta, 05508 São Paulo; website www.usp.br.

**Universidade do Rio de Janeiro:** Letters and Arts Center, Avda Pasteur 296, 22290 Rio de Janeiro; website www.uerj.br.

**Universidade Federal de Bahia:** Escola de Música, Parque Universitario Edgard Santos, Canela, 40140, Salvador, Bahia; website www.ufba.br.

**Universidade Federal de Minas Gerais:** Escola de Música, Avda Antônio Carlos 6627, Pampulha, 3000 Belo Horizonte, Minas Gerais; website www .ufmg.br.

**Universidade Federal de Paraiba:** Department of Music, Cidade Universitária, 5800 Joao Pessôa, Paraiba; website www.ufpb.br.

**Universidade Federal do Rio de Janeiro:** Escola de Música, Rua do Passeio 98, Rio de Janeiro; website www.ufrj.br.

## Bulgaria

**Academy of Music and Dance:** Ul. Todor Samodumov 2, PO Box 117, 4025 Plovidiv; tel. (32) 601-441; fax (32) 631-668; e-mail amti_sekretar@evrocom .net; Rector Prof. Anastas Slavchev; faculties of Music Pedagogy, Music Folklore and Choreography, and Language and Special Training.

**Conservatoire Bulgare d'Etat:** Sofia 1505.

## Canada

**Acadia University, School of Music:** Wolfville, NS B0P 2R6; tel. 1 902 585 2001; website www.acadiau.ca.

**Banff Centre, School of Fine Arts:** PO Box 1020, Banff, AB T1L 1H5; tel. 1 403 762 6100; website www.banffcentre.ca.

**Brandon University, School of Music:** 270-18 Street, Brandon, MB R7A 6A9; website www.brandonu.ca.

**Carleton University, School for Studies in Art and Culture, Music Programme:** 1125 Colonel By Drive, Ottawa, ON K1S 5B6; tel. (613) 520-5770; fax (613) 520-3905; website www.carleton.ca.

**Concordia University, Department of Music:** 1455 de Maisonneuve Blvd W, Montréal, QC H3G 1M8; tel. 1 514 848 2424; website www.concordia.ca.

**Conservatoire de Musique de Québec:** 270 St Amable, QC G1R 5G1.

**Dalhousie University, Department of Music:** Arts Centre, Room 514, Halifax, NS B3H 4R2; tel. 1 902 494 2211; website www.dal.ca.

**Maritime Conservatory of Music:** 6199 Chebucto Road, Halifax, NS B3H 1X8; tel. 1 902 423 6995.

**McGill University, Faculty of Music:** 555 Sherbrooke Street W, Montréal, QC H3A 1E3; tel. 1 514 398 4455; website www.mcgill.ca.

**McMaster University, Department of Music:** 1280 Main Street W, Hamilton, ON L8S 4M2; website www.mcmaster.ca.

**Mount Allison University, Department of Music:** Sackville, NB E4L 1A6; website www.mta.ca.

**Queen's University, School of Music:** Kingston, ON K7L 3N6; website www.queensu.ca.

**Royal Conservatory of Music:** 273 Bloor Street W, Toronto, ON M5S 1W2; tel. (416) 408-2824; fax (416) 408-3096; website www.rcmusic.ca; Pres.: Dr Peter Simon. f. 1886. Largest and oldest independent arts educator in Canada, serving more than 500,000 active participants each year. Offers opportunities for learning and development through music and the arts, in all Canadian provinces and in a number of international locations.

**Simon Fraser University, School for the Contemporary Arts:** 8888 University Drive, Burnaby, BC V5A 1S6; tel. (604) 291-3363; fax (604) 291-5907; e-mail ca@sfu.ca; website www.sfu.ca/sca.

**St Francis Xavier University, Department of Music:** PO Box 108, Antigonish, NS B2G 1C0; website www.stfx.ca.

**Université de Moncton, Department of Music:** Moncton, NB E1A 3E9; website www.umoncton.ca.

**Université de Montréal, Faculty of Music:** 2900 Blvd Edouard-Montpetit, Montréal, QC H3C 3J7; website www.umontreal.ca.

**Université Laval, Faculté de musique:** Pavillon Louis-Jacques-Casault, Cité Universitaire, Québec, QC G1K 7P4; tel. 1 418 656 2131; fax 1 418 656 2809; website www.ulaval.ca.

**University of Alberta, Department of Music:** Edmonton, AB T6G 2C9; website www.ualberta.ca.

**University of British Columbia (UBC), School of Music:** 6361 Memorial Road, Vancouver, BC V6T 1W5; website www.ubc.ca.

**University of Calgary, Department of Music:** 2500 University Dr., NW Calgary, AB T2N 1N4; tel. 1 403 220 5110; website www.ucalgary.ca.

**University of Guelph College of Arts, Department of Music:** Room 207, Guelph, ON N1G 2W1; website www.uogelph.ca.

**University of Lethbridge, Department of Music:** 4401 University Dr., Lethbridge, AB T1K 3M4; website www.uleth.ca.

**University of Manitoba, School of Music:** 65 Dafoe Road, Winnipeg, MB R3T 2N2; tel. 1 204 474 8880; website www.umanitoba.ca.

**University of Ottawa, Department of Music:** 550 Cumberland, Ottawa, ON K1N 6N5; tel. 1 613 562 5700; website www.music.uottawa.ca.

**University of Regina, Department of Music:** 3737 Wascana Pkwy, Regina, SK S4S 0A2; website www.uregina.ca.

**University of Saskatchewan, Department of Music:** Saskatoon, SK S7N 0W0; tel. 1 306 966 4343; website www.usask.ca.

**University of Toronto, Faculty of Music:** Edward Johnson Building, Room 238, 80 Queen's Park Circle, Toronto, ON M5S 1A1; tel. 1 416 978 2011; website www.utoronto.ca.

**University of Victoria, School of Music:** PO Box 1700, Victoria, BC V8W 2Y2; website www.uvic.ca.

**University of Western Ontario, Don Wright Faculty of Music:** London, ON N6A 3K7; tel. (519) 661-2043; fax (519) 661-3531; e-mail music@uwo.ca; website www.uwo.ca; Dean: Dr Robert Wood.

**University of Windsor, School of Music:** 401 Sunset Ave, Windsor, ON N9B 3P4; tel. 1 519 253 4232.

**Vancouver Academy of Music:** Music Centre, Vanier Park, 1270 Chestnut Street, Vancouver, BC V6J 4R9; tel. 1 604 734 2301; fax 1 604 731 1920; website www.vam.bc.ca.

**Victoria Conservatory of Music:** 901 Pandora Ave, Victoria, BC V8V 3P4; tel. 1 250 386 5311; fax 1 250 386 6602; website www.vcm.bc.ca.

**Wilfrid Laurier University, Faculty of Music:** 75 University Ave W, Waterloo, ON N2L 3C5; tel. 1 519 884 1970; fax 1 519 886 9351; website www .wlu.ca.

**York University, Department of Music:** 4700 Keele Street, North York, ON M3J 1P3; tel. 1 416 736 2100; website www.yorku.ca.

## Chile

**Conservatorio Nacional de Música:** Compañia, 1264, Santiago.

**Pontificia Universidad Católica de Chile:** Faculty of Architecture and Fine Arts, Avda Alameda 340, PO Box 114-D, Santiago; website www.puc.cl.

**Universidad Católica de Valparaiso, Conservatorio de Música:** Avda Brasil 2950, Valparaiso; website www.ucv.cl.

**Universidad de Chile, Faculty of Fine Arts:** Avda Bernardo O'Higgins 1058, Casilla 10-D, Santiago; website www.uchile.cl.

## People's Republic of China

**Central Conservatory of Music:** 43 Baojiajie, Beijing; website www.ccom .edu.cn.

**Conservatory of Chinese Music:** 17 Qianhaixijie, Beijing.

**Guangzhou Xinghai Conservatory of Music:** 48 Xianliedonghenglu, Guangzhou.

**Harbin Normal University, Department of Music:** Harbin.

**Nanjing Arts College:** 15 Hujubeilu, Nanjing.

**Northwest Teacher's College, Department of Music:** Lanzhou.

**Shandong Academy of Arts, Music Division:** Shandong.

**Shanghai Conservatory of Music:** 20 Fen Yang Road, Shanghai 200031.

**Shengyang Conservatory of Music:** No. 1, Section 2, San Hao Street, Peace District, Shengyang.

**Sichuan Conservatory of Music:** Xinnanmenwai, Chengdu.

**Tianjin Conservatory of Music:** 5, 11th Meridian Road, Tianjin.

**Wuhan Conservatory of Music:** 255 Jiefanglu, Wuchang District, Wuhan.

**Xian Conservatory of Music:** 118 Changanzhonglu, Xian 710061.

## Colombia

**Conservatorio Nacional de Música:** Departmento de Música, Facultad de Artes, Universidad Nacional, Bogotá.

**Universidad del Atlántico, Conservatorio de Música:** Carrera 43, Nos 50–53, Apdo Nacional 148, Aéreo 1890, Barranquilla.

## Costa Rica

**Universidad de Costa Rica (UCR), School of Fine Arts:** San José website www.ucr.ac.cr.

## Cuba

**Instituto Superior de Arte, Facultad de Música:** Calle 120, No. 1110, Havana.

## Czech Republic

**Janá kova Akademie Mûzick ch Umeni (Janá ek Academy of Music and Dramatic Arts):** Komenskeho nam 6, 662 15 Brno.

**Konservato v Brne (Brno Conservatory):** Trida Kpt Jarose 43–45, Brno.

**Konservato v Otrave (Ostrava Conservatory):** Hrabakova 1, Ostrava.

**Prazska Konservator (Prague Conservatoire):** Na Rejdisti 1, 110 00 Prague 1; tel. 420 222 319 102; fax 420 222 326 406; e-mail conserv@prgcons .cz; website www.prgcons.cz; Dir: Veroslav Neumann.

**Vysoká Skola Mûzick ch Umeni v Praha (Academy of Music and Dramatic Arts Prague):** D m um lc, Alsovo náb e í 12, 1101 00 Prague 1.

## Denmark

**Carl Nielsen Academy of Music Odense:** Islandsgade 2, 5000 Odense C; tel. 45 66 11 06 63; fax 45 66 17 77 63; e-mail dfm@adm.dfm.dk; website www .dfm.dk.

**Det Fynske Musikkonservatorium (The Funen Conservatory of Music):** Islandsgade 2, 5000 Odense C; tel. 45 66 11 06 63; fax 45 66 17 77 63; e-mail dfm@adm.dfm.dk; website www.dfm.dk.

**Det Jyske Musikkonservatorium (Royal Academy of Music, Århus):** Fuglesangs Allé 26, PO Box 1300, 8210 Århus V; tel. 45 8948 3388; fax 45 8948 3322; website www.musik-kons.dk.

**Det Kongelige Danske Musikkonservatorium (The Royal Danish Conservatory of Music):** Niels Brocksgade 7, 1574 Copenhagen V; tel. 45 33 69 22 69; fax 45 33 69 22 79; e-mail dkdm@dkdm.dk; website www.dkdm .dk.

**Nordjysk Musikkonservatorium (North Jutland Conservatory of Music):** Ryesgade 52, 9000 Ålborg; tel. 45 98 12 77 44; fax 45 98 11 37 63; website www.nordkons.dk.

**University of Copenhagen, Department of Music:** Frue Plads, 1168 Copenhagen K; website www.ku.dk.

**Vestjysk Musikkonservatorium (West Jutland Conservatory of Music):** Islandsgade 50, 6700 Esbjerg; website www.vmk.dk.

## Dominican Republic

**Conservatorio Nacional de Música:** Cesar Nicolas Penson, Santo Domingo.

## Ecuador

**Conservatorio Nacional de Música, Quito:** Madrid 11-59, Quito.

## Egypt

**Cairo Conservatoire of Music:** Academy of Arts, Japan Street, Al Giza, Cairo; tel. 202 5613451; fax 202 561-1034; e-mail caiconserv@idsc.net.eg; Dean: Dr Rageh Daoud; part of the Academy of Arts; studies at all levels.

## El Salvador

**Centro Nacional de Artes CENAR, Department of Music:** 6A Avda Norte 319, San Salvador.

## Estonia

**Tallinn State Conservatory:** Vabaduse Pst 130, 200015 Tallinn.

## Finland

**Helsinki Conservatory of Music:** Ruoholahdentori 6, 00180 Helsinki; tel. 358 5860580; fax 358 58605868; e-mail rea.warme@stadia.fi; Rector: Rea Warme.

**Jyväskylä Polytechnic, School of Music:** Pitkäkatu 18–22, 40700 Jyväskylä; tel. 358 14 444 7371; fax 358 14 444 7399; e-mail music@jypoly .fi; website www.jypoly.fi.

**Kuopion Konservatorio:** Kuopionlahdenkatu 23 C, 70200 Kuopio; tel. 358 17 262 3617; website www.kuopionkonservatorio.net.

**Oulun Kaupungin Konservatorio:** Lintulammentie 1 K, 90140 Oulu; tel. 358 8 314 1951.

**Paijat-Hameen Konservatorio:** Sibeliuksenkatu 8, 15110 Lahti; tel. 358 3 752 0161.

**Sibelius Academy of Music:** Töölönkatu 28, 00260 Helsinki; website www .siba.fi.

**Sibeliusmuseum Misikvetenskapliga Institutionen vid Åbo Akademi (Sibelius Museum, Musicological Institution at Åbo Academy):** Biskopsgatan 17 20500, Åbo 50.

**Tampereen Konservatorio:** F. E. Sillanpään Katu 9, 33230 Tampere; tel. 358 3 245 2500; fax 358 3 245 2501; website www.tampereenkonservatorio .net.

## France

**Conservatoire de Caen:** 1 rue du Carel, 14027 Caen Cédex.

**Conservatoire National de Région:** Bordeaux, 22 Quai Saint Croix, 33800 Bordeaux; tel. 33 5 56 92 96 96; fax 33 5 56 92 22 30.

**Conservatoire National de Région, Dijon:** 24 Blvd Clemenceau, 21000 Dijon; tel. 33 3 80 73 22 43.

**Conservatoire National de Région, Grenoble:** 6 Chemin de Gordes, 38100 Grenoble; tel. 33 4 76 46 48 44.

**Conservatoire National de Région, Lille:** 48 Place du Concert, 59800 Lille; tel. 33 3 20 74 57 50.

**Conservatoire National de Région, Limoges:** 9 rue Fritz-James, 87000 Limoges; tel. 33 5 55 79 71 81.

**Conservatoire National de Région, Marseille:** 2 Place Carli, 13001 Marseille; tel. 33 4 91 55 35 72.

**Conservatoire National de Région, Metz:** 2 rue Paradis, 57036 Metz; tel. 33 3 87 55 54 56; fax 33 3 87 61 51 08.

**Conservatoire National de Région, Montpellier:** 14 rue Eugene Lisbonne, 34000 Montpellier; tel. 33 4 67 60 79 33.

**Conservatoire National de Région, Nancy:** 3 rue Michel Ney, 54000 Nancy; tel. 33 3 83 25 27 95; fax 33 3 83 36 47 85.

**Conservatoire National de Région, Nantes:** rue Gaëtan Rondeau Ile Beaulieu, 44200 Nantes; tel. 33 2 51 25 00 02.

**Conservatoire National de Région, Nice:** 24 Blvd de Cimiez, 06000 Nice; tel. 33 4 93 53 01 17.

**Conservatoire National de Région, Poitiers:** 5 rue Franklin, 86000 Poitiers; tel. 33 5 49 01 83 67; fax 33 5 49 01 19 94.

**Conservatoire National de Région, Reims:** 14 rue Carnot, 51100 Reims; tel. 33 3 26 86 77 00.

**Conservatoire National de Région, Rennes:** 26 rue Hoche, 35000 Rennes; tel. 33 2 99 28 55 72.

**Conservatoire National de Région, Rouen:** 50 Ave de la Porte des Champs, 76000 Rouen; tel. 33 2 32 08 13 50; fax 33 2 32 08 13 59.

**Conservatoire National de Région, Rueil-Malmaison:** 182 Ave Paul Doumer, 92500 Rueil-Malmaison; tel. 33 1 47 49 74 45.

**Conservatoire National de Région, Strasbourg:** 10 rue du Hohwald, 67000 Strasbourg; tel. 33 3 88 15 08 88.

**Conservatoire National de Région, Toulouse:** 3 rue Labéda, 31000 Toulouse; tel. 33 5 61 22 28 62.

**Conservatoire National de Région, Tours:** 17 rue des Ursulines, 37000 Tours; tel. 33 2 47 05 57 64.

**Conservatoire National de Région, Versailles:** 24 rue de la Chancellerie, 78000 Versailles; tel. 33 1 39 50 24 53.

**Conservatoire National Supérieur de Musique de Lyon:** 3 rue de l'Angile, 69005 Lyon.

**Conservatoire National Supérieur de Musique:** 209 avenue Jean Jaurès, 75019 Paris; tel. 33 1 40 40 46 46/47; fax 33 1 40 40 47 27; website www .cnsmdp.fr.

**École Normale de Musique:** 114 bis Blvd Malesherbes, 75017 Paris.

**Institut International de Musique Electroacoustique de Bourges— IMEB:** place André Malraux, PO Box 39, 18000 Bourges; tel. 33(0)2 20 41 87; fax 33(0)2 48 20 45 51; e-mail administration@ime-bourges.org; website www .imeb.net. f. 1970 (as GMEB until 1994); composition, research, diffusion, training, bibliographic and phonographic editions, archives, studies of electroacoustic music.

**Schola Cantorum, École Supérieure de Musique de Danse et d'Art Dramatique:** 269 rue St Jacques, Paris.

## Georgia

**Tbilisi State Conservatoire:** Tbilisi; e-mail tbil_conservatory@hotmail .com; Rector: Prof. Manana Doijashvili.

## Germany

**Bayerisches Staatskonservatorium für Musik:** Mergentheimerstrasse 76, Würzburg.

**Hochschule der Künste, Berlin:** Ernst-Feuter-Platz 10, 10587 Berlin; website www.hdk-berlin.de.

**Hochschule für Musik Carl Maria von Weber:** Wettiner Platz 13, 01067 Dresden; tel. 49 351 492 3600; website www.hfmdd.de.

**Hochschule für Musik Detmold:** Willi-Hofmann-Strasse 5, 32756 Detmold; tel. 5231 9755; fax 5231 975972; e-mail info@hfm-detmold.de; website www.hfm-detmold.de.

**Hochschule für Musik Felix Mendelssohn-Bartholdy:** Grassistrasse 8, 04107 Leipzig; tel. 49 341 214 455; fax 49 341 21 44 503; website www.hmt-leipzig.de.

**Hochschule für Musik Franz Liszt:** Platz der Demokratie 2–3, 99423 Weimar; tel. 49 3643 5550; fax 49 3643 555 117; website www.hfm-weimar.de.

**Hochschule für Musik Hanns Eisler:** Charlottenstrasse 55, 10117 Berlin; tel. 49 30 90269700; fax 49 30 90269701; e-mail rektorat.hfm@berlin.de; website www.hfm-berlin.de; Dir Prof. Christhard Gössling; Vice-Dir Prof. Michael Vogler.

**Hochschule für Musik und Darstellende Kunst, Frankfurt am Main:** Eschersheimer Landstrasse 29–39, 60322 Frankfurt am Main; tel. 49 69 154 007-0; fax 49 69 154 007-108; website www.jfmdk-frankfurt.de.

**Hochschule für Musik und Darstellende Kunst, Hamburg:** Harvestehuder Weg 12, 20148 Hamburg.

**Hochschule für Musik und Theater, Hannover:** Emmichplatz 1, 30175 Hannover; website www.hmt-hannover.de.

**Hochschule für Musik und Theater, München:** Arcisstrasse 12, 80333 Munich; tel. 49 89 28903; fax 49 89 28927419; e-mail verwaltung@musikhochschule-muenchen.de; website www.musikhochschule-muenchen.de; Rector: Prof. Dr Siegfried Mauser.

**Konservatorium der Stadt Nürnberg, Fachakademie für Musik:** Am Katharinenkloster 6, 90403 Nürnberg.

**Leopold-Mozart-Konservatorium, Augsburg:** Maximilianstrasse 59, 86150 Augsburg.

**Musikhochschule des Saarlandes:** Bismarckstrasse 1, 66111 Saarbrücken; tel. 49 681 967 310; fax 49 681 967 3130; website www.hmt.saarland.de.

**Musikhochschule, Lübeck:** Grosse Petersgrube 17–29, 23552 Lübeck.

**Richard-Strauss-Konservatorium:** Ismaningerstrasse 29, 81667 Munich.

**Staatliche Hochschule Düsseldorf:** Robert-Schumann-Institut, Fischerstrasse 110, 40416 Düsseldorf; tel. 49 211 49 180; fax 49 211 49 11 618; e-mail rsh@rsh-duesseldorf.de; website www.rsh-duesseldorf.de.

**Staatliche Hochschule für Musik Köln, Aachen:** Grenzland-Institut, Aachen, Theaterstrasse 2–4, 52062, Aachen; tel. 49 241 455 03; fax 49 241 455 499; website www.mhs-aachen.de.

**Staatliche Hochschule für Musik Köln:** Abteilung Wuppertal: Institut Wuppertal, Friedrich-Ebert-Strasse 141, 42117 Wuppertal; tel. 49 202 371 500; fax 49 202 371 5040; website www.mhs-wuppertal.de.

**Staatliche Hochschule für Musik Köln:** Dagobertstrasse 38, 50668 Cologne; website www.mhs-koeln.de.

**Staatliche Hochschule für Musik und Darstellende Kunst:** Urbanstrasse 25, 70182 Stuttgart; tel. 49 711 212 4620; website www.mh-stuttgart.de.

**Staatliche Hochschule für Musik, Freiburg im Breisgau:** Schwarzwaldstrasse 141, 79102 Freiburg im Breisgau.

**Staatliche Hochschule für Musik, Heidelberg-Mannheim:** Friedrich-Ebert-Anlage 62, Heidelberg.

**Staatliche Hochschule für Musik, Trossingen:** Schultheiss-Koch-Platz 3, 78647 Trossingen.

**Staatliche Hochschule für Musik:** PO Box 6040, 76040 Karlsruhe.

**Staatliches Institut für Musikforschung Preussischer Kulturbesitz (State Institute for Music Research):** Tiergartenstrasse 1, 10785 Berlin; tel. 49 (0)30 25481-0; fax 49 (0)30 25481-172; e-mail sim@sim.spk-berlin.de; website www.sim.spk-berlin.de; Head: Dr Thomas Ertelt; Head of Museum of Musical Instruments: Prof. Dr Conny Restle.

**Theater Erfurt:** Generalintendant, Dietrich Taube, PSF 244, 99005 Erfurt.

**Wiesbadener Musikakademie:** Bodenstedtstrasse 2, 65189 Wiesbaden.

## Greece

**Epirotic Conservatory Tsakalof:** Platia G, Stavrou 5, 45444 Ioannina.

**Kratikon Odeion Thessaloniki:** Leondos Sofou 16, 54625 Thessaloniki.

**Odeion Athenon:** Odos Rigillis and Vassileos Georgiou 17–19, Athens.

**Odeion Ethnikon:** Odos Maizonos 8, 108 Athens.

**Odeion Hellenikon:** Odos Phidiou 3, Athens.

**Skalkotas Conservatory:** Agias Lavras 78, Ano Patisia, 11141 Athens.

## Guatemala

**Conservatorio Nacional de Música:** 3a Avda 4-61, Zona 1, Guatemala City.

## Honduras

**Escuela Nacional de Música:** 2a Avda, 307, Tegucigalpa.

## Hong Kong

**Hong Kong Academy for Performing Arts, School of Music:** 1 Gloucester Road, Wanchai, Hong Kong; website www.hkapa.edu.

**University of Hong Kong, Faculty of Music:** Pokfulam Road, Hong Kong; tel. 852 2859 2111; fax 852 2858 2549; website www.hku.hk.

## Hungary

**Liszt Ferenc Zenemüves-zeti Föiskola (Franz Liszt Academy of Music):** PO Box 206, Liszt Ference tér 8, 1391 Budapest VI; website www.liszt.hu.

## Iceland

**Tónlistarskólinn i Rekyavík (Reykjavík College of Music):** Skipholt 33, 105 Reykjavík.

## India

**Bhavan's Bharatiya Sangeet and Nartan Skikshapeeth (Academy of Music and Drama):** Cahupatty Road, Mumbai 4000007.

**Delhi School of Music:** 8 Nyaya Marg, New Delhi 110021.

**Indira Kala Sangit Vishwavidyalaya (University of Music and Fine Arts):** Khairagarth, Madhya Pradesh 491881.

**Kalakshetra:** Tiruvanmiyur, Chennai 600041.

**Music Academy:** Teachers' College of Music, 306 TTK Road, Chennai 600041.

**Rabindra Bharati University, Department of Music:** 6–4 Dwarakanath Tagore Lane, Kolkata 700007; website www.rabindrabharatiuniversity.net.

**Sangeet Natak Akademi (National Academy of Music, Dance and Drama):** Rabindra Bhavan, Feroze Shah Road, New Delhi 11001.

**University of Madras, Department of Indian Music:** University Centenary Building, Chepauk, Triplicane, Tamil Nadu, Chennai 600005; website www.unom.ac.in.

## Indonesia

**Academi Seni Tari Indonesia:** Jl Buahbatu 212, Bandung.

**Institute Kesenian Jakarta:** Taman Ismial Marzuki, Jalan Cikini, Jakarta.

## Ireland

**Conservatory of Music and Drama:** Dublin Institute of Technology, Rathmines Road, Dublin 2; e-mail conservatory@dit.ie.

**Royal Irish Academy of Music:** 36–38 Westland Row, Dublin 2; tel. 353 1 676 4412/3; fax 353 1 662 2798; website www.riam.ie.

## Israel

**Israel Conservatory of Music:** 19 Shtriker St, Tel-Aviv.

**Jerusalem Academy of Music and Dance:** Givat-Ram Campus, 91904 Jerusalem; tel. 972 2 675 9911; fax 972 2 652 7713; website www.jmd.ac.il.

**Levinsky Teachers College, Music Teachers Seminary:** 15 Shoshana Persitz St N, PO Box 48130, Tel-Aviv.

**Rubin Academy of Music:** University of Tel-Aviv, Faculty of Fine Arts, PO Box 39040, Ramat Aviv, Tel-Aviv.

**Samuel Rubin Conservatory of Music:** 9 Haparsim St, Haifa; tel. 972 4 8521530; fax 972 4 8514405; e-mail ns_sigiw@bezegint.net; Contact: Stella Wenkert.

## Italy

**Accademia Musicale Chigiana:** Via di Città 89, 53100 Siena; tel. 0577 22091; fax 0577 288124; e-mail accademia.chigiana@chigiana.it.

**Accademia Musicale di Milano:** Viale dei Mille 17, Milan.

**Accademia Musicale Napoletana:** Via del Parco Margherita 49, pal 5, 80121 Naples.

**Accademia Nazionale di Santa Cecilia:** Via Vittoria 6, 00187 Rome.

**Conservatorio Statale di Musica Antonio Vivaldi:** Via Parma 1, Alessandria; website www.conservatoriovivaldi.it.

**Conservatorio Statale di Musica Arcangelo Corelli:** Via Bonino 1, 98100 Messina.

**Conservatorio Statale di Musica Arrigo Boito:** Via del Conservatorio 27, 43100 Parma; website www.conservatorio.pr.it.

**Conservatorio Statale di Musica Benedetto Marcello:** Palazzo Pisani, San Marco 2809, 30124 Venice.

**Conservatorio Statale di Musica Cesare Pollini:** Via Eremitani 6, 35121 Padua.

**Conservatorio Statale di Musica Claudio Monteverdi:** Piazza Domenicani 19, 39100 Bolzano.

**Conservatorio Statale di Musica Francesco Morlacchi:** Piazza Mariotti 2, 06100 Perugia; website www.conservatorio.pg.it.

**Conservatorio Statale di Musica Gioachino Rossini:** Piazza Olivieri 5, 61100 Pesaro.

**Conservatorio Statale di Musica Giovanni Battista Martini:** Piazza Rossini 2, 40126 Bologna.

**Conservatorio Statale di Musica Giovanni Pierluigi da Palestrina:** Via Bacaredda, 09100 Cagliari; website www.conservatorioca.it.

**Conservatorio Statale di Musica Girolamo Frescobaldi:** Via Previati 22, 44100; website www.commune.ferrara.it/conservatorio

**Conservatorio Statale di Musica Giuseppe Tartini:** Via Carlo Ghega 12, 34132 Trieste; website www.conservatorio.trieste.it.

**Conservatorio Statale di Musica Giuseppe Verdi:** Via del Conservatorio 12, 20122 Milan.

**Conservatorio Statale di Musica Giuseppe Verdi:** Via Mazzini 11, Piazza Bodoni, 10123 Turin; website www.arpnet.it/conservatorio.

**Conservatorio Statale di Musica Luigi Cherubini:** Piazza delle Belle Arti 2, 50122 Florence; tel. 39 055 292-180; fax 39 055 239-6785; e-mail direttore@conservatorio.firenze.it; website www.conservatorio.firenze.it; Dir: Mario Pazzaglia.

**Conservatorio Statale di Musica Niccòlo Paganini:** Via Albaro 38, 16145 Genoa.

**Conservatorio Statale di Musica Niccolo Piccinni:** Via Brigata Bari 26, 70124 Bari; website www.conservatoriopiccinni.it.

**Conservatorio Statale di Musica San Pietro a Majella:** Via San Pietro a Majella 35, 80138 Naples.

**Conservatorio Statale di Musica Santa Cecilia:** Via del Greci 18, 00187 Rome.

**Conservatorio Statale di Musica Vincenzo Bellini:** Via Squarcialupo 45, 90133 Palermo.

**Istituto Musicale Pareggiato Luigi Boccherini:** Piazza S. Ponziano, 55100 Lucca.

**Liceo Musicale Giovanni Battista Viotti:** Casella Postale 127, 13100 Vercelli.

**Pontificio Istituto di Musica Sacra:** Via di Torre Rossa 21, 00165 Rome.

## Japan

**Elizabeth University of Music:** 4-15 Nobori-cho, Naka-ku, Hiroshima 730.

**Kunitachi College of Music:** 5-5-1 Kashiwa-cho, Tachikawa-shi, Tokyo 190; website www.kunitachi.ac.jp.

**Kyoto City University of Fine Arts and Music:** 13-6 Ohe Kutsukake-cho, Nishikyo-ku, Kyoto 610-11; website www.kcua.ac.jp.

**Musashino Ongaku Daigaku (Musashino College of Music):** 1-13-1 Hazawa, Nerima-ku, Tokyo 176.

**Osaka College of Arts:** 469 Higashiyama, Kanan-cho, Minamilawachi-gun, Osaka 561.

**Osaka Ongaku Daigaku (Osaka College of Music):** 1-1-8 Saiwaimachi, Shonai, Toyonaka, Osaka 561.

**Toho Gakuen School of Music:** 1-41-1 Wakaba-cho, Chofu-shi, Tokyo 182-8510.

**Tokyo College of Music:** 3-4-5 Minami-Ikebukuro, Toshima-ku, Tokyo 171.

**Tokyo Daigaku (University of Tokyo) Faculty of Musicology:** 7-3-1 Hongo, Bungyo-ku, Tokyo 113; website www.u-tokyo.ac.jp.

**Tokyo Geijutsu Daigaku (Tokyo National University of Fine Arts and Music):** 12-8 Ueno-koen, Taito-ku, Tokyo 110-8714.

**Ueno Gakuen College, Department of Music:** 4-24-12 Higashiueno, Taito-ku, Tokyo 110.

## Republic of Korea

**Korean Union College, Department of Music:** Cheongryang, PO Box 18, Seoul.

**Korea University:** 1 5-KA, Anamdong, Sungbukku, Seoul 136-701; website www.korea.ac.kr.

**Kyung Hee University, College of Music:** 1 Hoegi-dong, Tongadaemun-gu Seoul 131; website www.kyunghee.ac.kr.

**National Academy of Arts, Department of Music:** 1 Sejongno, Chongno-gu, Seoul.

**Seoul National University, College of Music:** San 56-1, Shinrim-dong, Kwanak-gu, Seoul 151; website www.snu.ac.kr.

**Yonsei University, College of Music:** 134 Shinchon-dong, Sodaemun-gu, Seoul 120; website www.yonsei.ac.kr.

## Latvia

**Latvian Y Vitol State Conservatory:** Ul Krisyana Barona 1, 226050 Riga.

## Lithuania

**Lithuanian State Conservatory:** 232001 Vilnius.

## Luxembourg

**Conservatoire de Musique d'Esch-sur-Alzette:** 10 rue de l'Eglise, PO Box 145, 4002 Esch-sur-Alzette.

**Conservatoire de Musique de la Ville de Luxembourg:** 33 rue Charles Martel, 2134 Luxembourg.

## Mexico

**Conservatorio Nacional de Música de México:** Avda Presidente Masaryk 582, Mexico City 5, DF.

**Facultad de Música:** Universidad Veracruzana, Barragán No. 32, Xalapa Veracruz CP 91000.

**Universidad Nacional Autónoma de México:** Escuela Nacional de Música, Xicotencat 126, Coyoacán, Mexico City 04100, DF.

## Monaco

**Académie de Musique Prince Rainier III de Monaco:** 1 Blvd Albert, 98000 Monte Carlo.

## Morocco

**Conservatoire de Tangier:** Tangier.

**Conservatoire National de Musique:** de Danse, et d'Art Dramatique, Rabat.

**Conservatorie de Musique:** Marrakesh.

**Ecole Nationale de Musique:** 133 Ave Ziraoui, Casablanca.

**Ecole Nationale de Musique:** 22 rue Marrakchia, Kaa Ouarda, Meknes.

## Netherlands

**Akademie voor Muziek:** Koninginneweg 25, 1217 KR Hilversum.

**Amsterdamse Hogeschool voor de Kunsten:** Afdeling Conservatorium van Amsterdam, PO Box 78022, 1070 LP Amsterdam; tel. 020-5277550; fax 020-6761505; e-mail info@cva.ahk.nl; website www.cva.ahk.nl; Dir: Lucas Vis.

**Brabants Conservatorium voor Muziek en Dans:** Kempenbaan 27, 5022 KC Tilburg; website www.fontys.nl/bc.

**Christelijke Hogeschool voor de Kunsten Constantijn Huygens:** Aan de Stadsmuur 88, 8011 VD Zwolle.

**Hilversums Conservatorium:** Snelliuslaan 10, 1222 TE Hilversum.

**Hogeschool Enschede sector Conservatorium:** Van Essengaarde 10, 7511 PN Enschede.

**Hogeschool voor de Kunsten Arnhem:** Fakulteit Muziek, Weverstraat 40, 6811 EM Arnhem.

**Hogeschool voor Muziek en Dans Rotterdam:** Kruisplein 26, 3012 CC Rotterdam; tel. 10-217 11 00; fax 10-217 11 01; e-mail hmd@hmd.nl; website www.hmd.nl.

**Koninklijk Conservatorium voor Muziek en Dans:** Juliana van Stolberglaan 1, 2595 CA The Hague.

**Rijkshgeschool Maastricht:** Subfaculteit Conservatorium, Bonnefanten 15, 6211 KL Maastricht.

**Rijkshogeschool Groningen sector Kunstvakopleidingen afdeling Conservatorium:** Veemarktstraat 76, 9724 GA Groningen.

**Stedelijke Muziekpedagogische Akademie:** Eewal 56–58, Leeuwarden.

**Toonkunst Conservatorium:** Mathenesserlaan 219, Rotterdam.

**Utrechts Conservatorium:** Mariaplaats 28, 3511 LL Utrecht.

## New Zealand

**University of Auckland, Faculty of Music:** Private Bag 92019, Auckland 1020; tel. 64 9 373 7999; website www.auckland.ac.nz.

**University of Canterbury, Faculty of Music:** Private Bag 4800, Christchurch 8020; tel. 64 3 366 7001; fax 64 3 264 2999; website www.canterbury.ac.nz.

**University of Otago, School of Language, Literature and Performing Arts, Division of Humanities:** PO Box 56, Dunedin; website www.otago.ac.nz.

**Victoria University of Wellington, Faculty of Music:** PO Box 600 Wellington; website www.vuw.ac.nz.

## Nicaragua

**Escuela Nacional de Musica:** Antigua Hacienda el Retiro, Managua.

## Norway

**Bergen Musikkonservatorium:** Lars Hilles Gate 3, 5015 Bergen; tel. 47 5532 4950; fax 47 5532 3033.

**Kunsthøgakolen i Oslo (Oslo National College of the Arts):** Department of Operatic Art, PO Box 6853, St Olavs plass, 0130 Oslo; tel. 47 2299 55 00; fax 47 2299 55 02; e-mail khio@khio.no.

**Østlandets Musikkonservatorium:** Vetlandsveien 45, 0685 Oslo 6.

**Rogaland Musikkonservatorium:** Bjergsted, 4007 Stavanger.

**Trondelag Musikkonservatorium:** Homebergvn 1, 7038 Trondheim.

## Panama

**Escuela Nacional de Música:** PO Box 1414, Panama City.

## Paraguay

**Conservatorio Municipal de Música:** Mcal Estigarribia, E-Pai Perez y Curupayty, Asunción.

**Escuela Municipal de Canto:** Dr Eduardo Victor Haedo 682, Asunción.

## Peru

**Conservatorio Nacional de Música:** Emancipación 180, Lima 1.

## Philippines

**St Paul College, College of Music:** 680 Pedro Gil Street, Malate, Manila; website www.spcm.edu.ph.

**St Scholastica's College, School of Music:** 2560 Leon Guinto Sr Street, Malate, Manila.

**University of San Augustin:** Conservatory of Music, General Luna Street, Iloilo City 5901; website www.usa.edu.ph.

**University of Santo Tomas, Conservatory of Music:** Espana, Manila; website www.ust.edu.ph.

## Poland

**Akademia Muzyczna im Feliksa Nowowiejskiego w Bydgoszczy:** Ul J Slowackiego 7, 85-008 Bydgoszcz; website www.amuz.bydgoszczy.pl.

**Akademia Muzyczna im Fryderyka Chopina w Warzawie:** Ul Okólnik 2, 00-368 Warsaw.

**Akademia Muzyczna im Karola Szymanowskiego w Katowice:** UL Zacisze 3, Katowice; website www.am.katowice.pl.

**Akademia Muzyczna im Stanislaw Moniuszko w Gdansku:** Lagiewniki 3, 80-847 Gdańsk; website www.amuz.gda.pl.

**Akademia Muzyczna Poznań iu:** Ul Czerwonej Armii 87, 61-808 Poznań.website www.amuz.poznan.pl

**Akademia Muzyczna w Krakówie:** Ul Bohaterów Stalingradu 3, 31-038 Kraków; website www.amuz.krakow.pl.

**Akademia Muzyczna w Łódz:** Ul Gdanska 32, 90-716 Łódz.

**Akademia Muzyczna Wroclawiu:** Ul Powstancow Laskich 204, 53-140 Wroclaw.

## Portugal

**Academia de Amadores de Musica:** R. Nova da Trindade 18, 2°, E, 1200 Lisbon.

**Conservatório de Musica:** Rua de Maternidade 13, 4000 Oporto.

**Conservatório Regional de Coimbra:** Rua do Brasil, 3000 Coimbra.

**Escola Superior de Musica:** Conservatório Nacional, Rua dos Caetanos 29, 1200 Lisbon.

## Romania

**Conservatorul de Muzic Ciprian Porumbescu:** Str Stirbei Voda 33, 70732 Bucharest.

**Conservatorul de Muzic Georges Enescu:** Str Closca 9, 6600 Iasi.

**Conservatorul de Muzic Gheorghe Dima:** Str 23 August 25, 3400 Cluj-Napoca.

## Russia

**Moscow Conservatory:** Ul. B. Nikitinskaya 13, 103009 Moscow; website www.mosconsv.ru.

**St Petersburg Conservatory:** Teatralnaya Pl 3, 192041 St Petersburg.

## Singapore

**School of Arts and Language:** 469 Bukit Gimah Road, Singapore 1025.

## Slovakia

**Bratislava Konzervatorium:** Tolstého 11, 811 06 Bratislava.

**Vysoká Skola Mûzick ch Umeni v Bratisaave (Academy of Music and Dramatic Arts Bratislava):** Jiráskova 3, 81301 Bratislava.

## South Africa

**University of Cape Town, College of Music:** Private bag, Rondebosch 7700, Cape Town; website www.uct.ac.za.

**University of KwaZulu-Natal, School of Music:** Durban 4041; tel. 27 31 2603351; fax 27 31 2601048; e-mail hodges@nu.ac.za; website www.nu.ac.za/und/music.

**University of Pretoria, Department of Music:** Pretoria 0002; website www.up.ac.za.

**University of South Africa, Department of Music:** PO Box 392, Pretoria 0001; website www.unisa.ac.za.

**University of Stellenbosch, Department of Music:** Stellenbosch 7600; website www.sun.ac.za.

**University of the South Africa Free State, Department of Music:** PO Box 339, Bloemfontein 9300; tel. 51 401 28 10; fax 51 448 44 02; e-mail lampregp.hum@mail.uovs.ac.za; website www.uovs.ac.za; Head of Dept: Prof. Deon Lamprecht.

**University of the Witwatersrand, Wits School of Music:** Jan Smuts Ave, Johannesburg 2001; website www.wits.ac.za.

## Spain

**Conservatorio de Música Manuel de Falla:** Calle del Tinte 1, Cadiz.

**Conservatorio Superior de Música de Barcelona:** Calle Bruche 112, Barcelona 9.

**Conservatorio Superior de Música y Escuela de Arte Dramatico y Danza:** Calle Angel de Saavedra 1, 14003 Cordoba.

**Conservatorio Superior de Música y Escuela de Arte Dramatico:** Calle Jesús del Gran Poder 49, Seville 41002.

**Conservatorio Superior de Música y Escuela de Arte Dramatico y Danza:** Plaza San Esteban 3, Valencia.

**Conservatorio Superior de Música:** Easo 39, San Sebastian 20006.

**Escuela Superior de Música Sagrada y de Pedagogia Musical Escolar:** Victor Pradera 65 bis, Madrid 8.

**Real Conservatorio Nacional de Música y Declamacion:** San Bernardo 44, Madrid.

**Real Conservatorio Superior de Música:** Plaza de Isabell II s/n, Madrid 28013.

## Sri Lanka

**Institute of Aesthetic Studies:** 21 Albert Crescent, Colombo 7.

## Sweden

**Göteborgs Universitet, Musikhögskolan:** PO Box 3174, 400 10 Göteborg; website www.gu.se.

**Kungliga Musikaliska Academien (Royal Swedish Academy of Music):** Blasieholmstorg 8, 11148 Stockholm; tel. 46 8 407 1800; fax 46 8 611 8718; e-mail adm@musakad.se; website www.musakad.se.

**Musikhögskolan och teaterhögskolan:** PO Box 135 15, Ystadvägen 25, S-200 44 Malmö.

**Musikhögskolan:** Valhallavägen 103-109, 115 31 Stockholm.

# Switzerland

**Conservatoire de Musique de Genève:** Place Neuve, 1204 Geneva.

**Conservatoire de Musique de La Chaux-de-Fonds-Le Locie:** Ave Léopold-Robert 34, 2300 La Chaux-de-Fonds.

**Conservatoire de Musique de Lausanne:** rue de la Grotte 2, PO Box 2427, 1002 Lausanne; tel. 41 21 321 3535; fax 41 21 321 3536; website www.regart .ch/cml

**Conservatoire de Musique de Neuchâtel:** 106 Faubourg de l'Hopital, 2000 Neuchâtel.

**Conservatoire de Musique de Vevey:** 4 rue des Communaux, 1800 Vevey.

**Conservatoire et Académie de Musique:** 228-A rue Pierre Aeby, 1700 Friboug.

**Institute Jaques-Dalcroze:** 11 rue Sillem, 1207 Geneva; website www .dalcroze.ch.

**Konservatorium für Musik und Theater:** Kramgasse 36, 3011 Bern.

**Konservatorium Luzern:** Dreilindenstrasse 93, 6006 Lucern.

**Konservatorium und Musikhochschule Zürich:** Birchstrasse 95, 8050 Zürich.

**Musik-Akademie der Stadt Basel:** Leonhardsstrasse 6, 4501 Basel.

**Musikakademie Zürich:** Florastrasse 52, 8008 Zürich.

**Musikschule und Konservatorium Schaffhausen:** Rosengasse 16, 8200 Schaffhausen.

**Musikschule und Konservatorium Winterthur:** Tössertobelstrasse 1, 8400 Winterthur.

**Stadtische Musikschule und Konservatorium:** Ring 12, 2500 Biel.

**Stadtische Musikschule:** 4600 Olten.

# Taiwan

**National Institute of the Arts, Music Department:** 172 Chung Cheng Road, Ru Chow, Taipei.

**National Taiwan Academy of Arts:** 59, Section 1, Ta Kuan Road, Pan-Chiao Park, Taipei.

# Tunisia

**Institut Superieure de Musique:** 20 Ave de Paris, Tunis.

# Turkey

**Ankara State Conservatory:** Hacettepe Üniversitesi, Hacetlepe Parki, Ankara.

**Istanbul State Conservatory of Music:** Mimar Sinan Üniversitesi, Findikli, Istanbul.

**Turkish Conservatory of Music:** Istanbul Teknik Üniversitesi, Ayazaga, Istanbul.

# United Kingdom

**Birmingham Conservatoire:** UCE Birmingham, Paradise Place, Birmingham B3 3HG; tel. (121) 331-5901; fax (121) 331-5906; e-mail conservatoire@ uce.ac.uk; website www.conversatoire.uce.ac.uk; Principal: Prof. George Caird; f. over 100 years ago, national college of music performance and composition.

**Chetham's School of Music:** Long Millgate, Manchester M3 1SB; tel. 0161 834 9644; fax 0161 839 3609; e-mail chets@chethams.com; website www .chethams.com.

**City of Belfast School of Music—CBSM:** 99 Donegal Pass, Belfast, Northern Ireland BT7 1DR; tel. (28) 9032-2435; fax (28) 9032-9201; e-mail music.belb@btinternet.com; website www.cbsm.org.uk; Principal: Dr Joe McKee.

**Dartington College of Arts, Department of Music:** Totnes, Devon TQ9 6EJ; tel. (1803) 862224; fax (1803) 863569; e-mail registry@dartington.ac.uk; website www.dartington.ac.uk; Dir of Music: Dr Trevor Wiggins; specialises in contemporary music and arts.

**Department of Music, King's College London:** Strand, London WC2R 2LS; tel. 020 7836 5454; website www.kcl.ac.uk.

**Guildhall School of Music and Drama:** Silk Street, Barbican, London EC2Y 8DT; tel. 020 7628 2571; fax 020 7256 9438; website www.gsmd.ac.uk.

**Leeds College of Music:** 3 Quarry Hill, Leeds LS2 7PD; tel. (113) 222-3416; e-mail enquiries@lcm.ac.uk; website www.lcm.ac.uk. The UK's largest music college. Courses range from post-16 education to undergraduate and postgraduate degrees.

**London College of Music and Media:** St Mary's Road, London W5 5RF; tel. 020 8231 2304; fax 020 8231 2546; website www.tvu.ac.uk.

**London-City University, Department of Music:** Northampton Square, London EC1V 0HB; tel. (20) 7040-8284; fax (20) 7040-8576; e-mail music@city .ac.uk; website www.city.ac.uk/music.

**Middlesex University School of Arts 'Music':** Trent Park Campus, Bramley Road, London N14 4YZ; tel. (20) 8411-5684; fax (20) 8411-5684; website www.mdx.ac.uk.

**Purcell School:** Aldenham Road, Bushey, Herts, WD23 2TS; tel. 01923 331100; fax 01923 331166; website www.purcell-school.org.

**Queen's University of Belfast, School of Music:** University Road, Belfast, Northern Ireland BT7 1NN; website www.qub.ac.uk.

**Royal Academy of Music:** Marylebone Road, London NW1 5HT; tel. (20) 7873-7373; fax (20) 7873-7374; e-mail go@ram.ac.uk; website www.ram.ac.uk; Principal: Prof. Curtis Price; Vice-Principal and Dir of Studies: Prof. Jonathan Freeman-Attwood; Britain's foremost conservatoire, a college of the University of London.

**Royal College of Music:** Prince Consort Road, London SW7 2BS; tel. 020 7589 3643; fax 020 7589 7740; e-mail info@rcm.ac.uk; website www.rcm.ac.uk.

**Royal Holloway and Bedford College, Department of Music:** University of London, Egham, Surrey TW20 0EX; tel. 01784 443532; fax 01784 439441; e-mail music@rhul.ac.uk; website www.rhul.ac.uk/music.

**Royal Military School of Music:** Kneller Hall, Twickenham, Middlesex TW2 7DU; tel. 020 8744 8628.

**Royal Northern College of Music:** 124 Oxford Road, Manchester M13 9RD; tel. 0161 907 5200; website www.mcm.ac.uk.

**Royal School of Church Music:** Cleveland Lodge, Westhumble, Dorking, Surrey RH5 6BW; tel. 01306 872800; fax 01306 887260; e-mail enquiries@ rscm.com; website www.rscm.com.

**Royal Scottish Academy of Music and Drama—RSAMD:** 100 Renfrew Street, Glasgow G2 3DB; tel. 0141 332 4101; fax 0141 332 8901; website www .rsamd.ac.uk.

**Royal Welsh College of Music and Drama:** Castle Grounds, Cathays Park, Cardiff, Wales CF10 3ER; tel. 029 2034 2854; fax 029 2039 1304; website www .rwcmd.ac.uk.

**Salford College of Technology:** Adelphi, Peru Street, Salford, Manchester M3 6EQ.

**St Mary's Music School:** Coates Hall, 25 Grosvenor Crescent, Edinburgh, EH12 5EL, Scotland; tel. (131) 538-7766; fax (131) 467-7289; e-mail info@st -marys-music-school.co.uk; website www.st-marys-music-school.co.uk; Headteacher: Jennifer Rimer; Dir of Music: John Grundy.

**Trinity College of Music:** King Charles Court, Old Royal Naval College, Greenwich, London SE10 9JF; tel. 020 8305 4444; fax 020 8305 9444; e-mail info@tcm.ac.uk; website www.tcm.ac.uk.

**University of Birmingham, Department of Music:** Barber Institute, Edgbaston, Birmingham B15 2TT; tel. 0121 414 3344; fax 0121 414 3971; website www.bham.ac.uk.

**University of Cambridge, School of Music:** 11 West Road, Cambridge CB3 9DP; website www.mus.cam.ac.uk.

**University of Edinburgh, Faculty of Music:** Old College, South Bridge, Edinburgh, Scotland EH8 9YL; tel. 0131 650 1000; fax 0131 650 2147; website www.ed.ac.uk.

**University of Exeter, Department of Music:** Northcote House, The Queen's Drive, Exeter EX4 4QJ; website www.ex.ac.uk.

**University of Glasgow, Department of Music:** Glasgow, Scotland G12 8QQ; tel. 0141 330 2000; website www.gla.ac.uk.

**University of Hull, Department of Drama and Music:** Cottingham Road, Hull HU6 7RX; tel. (1482) 346311; fax (1482) 465998; e-mail p.a.muse@hull.ac .uk; website www.hull.ac.uk/music; Dir of Studies: Dr Alastair Borthwick.

**University of Lancaster, Department of Music:** Bailrigg, Lancaster LA1 4YW; tel. 01524 65201; website www.lancs.ac.uk.

**University of Leeds, Department of Music:** Leeds LS2 9JT; tel. 0113 243 1751; fax 0113 244 3923; website www.leeds.ac.uk.

**University of Leicester, Department of Music:** University Road, Leicester LE1 7RH; tel. 0116 252 2522; fax 0116 252 2200; website www.le .ac.uk.

**University of Liverpool, School of Music:** 80 Bedford Street S, Liverpool L69 7WW; tel. 0151 794 2000; website www.liv.ac.uk; Head of School: Prof. J. G. Williamson.

**University of London, Department of Music:** Senate House, London WC1E 7AU.

**University of Manchester, School of Music and Drama:** Department of Music, Coupland Street, Manchester M13 9PL; tel. (161) 275-4982; fax (161) 275-4994; website www.art.man.ac.uk/music.

**University of Oxford, Faculty of Music:** St Aldate's, Oxford OX1 1DB; tel. 01865 276125; website www.music.ox.ac.uk.

**University of Reading, Department of Music:** 35 Upper Redlands Road, Reading RG1 5JE; website www.rdg.ac.uk.

**University of Southampton, School for Humanities, Music:** Highfield, Southampton SO17 1BJ; tel. 023 8059 5000; fax 023 8059 3939; website www.soton.ac.uk.

**University of Sussex, Department of Music:** Arts Building, Falmer, Brighton, East Sussex BN1 9QN; tel. 01273 606755; fax 01273 678335; website www.susx.ac.uk.

**University of Wales, Bangor, School of Music:** College Road, Bangor, Gwynedd LL57 2DG, Wales; tel. (1248) 382181; fax (1248) 370297; e-mail r.ley@bangor.ac.uk; website www.bangor.ac.uk/music.

**University of Wales, Cardiff, School of Music:** 31 Corbett Road, Cardiff, CF10 3EB, Wales; tel. 029 2087 4816; fax 029 2087 4379; e-mail music@cardiff.ac.uk; website www.cf.ac.uk/music; Head of School: Prof. Robin Stowell.

**University of York, Department of Music:** Heslington, York YO10 5DD; website www.music.york.ac.uk.

**Yehudi Menuhin School:** Stoke D'Abernon, Cobham, Surrey KT11 3QQ; fax 01932 864633; website www.yehudimenuhinschool.co.uk.

## United States of America

**92nd St Y School of Music:** 1395 Lexington Ave, New York, NY 10128; tel. 1 212 415 5500; website www.92ndsty.org.

**Aaron Copland School of Music:** Queens College, City University of New York, 65-30 Kissena Blvd, Flushing, NY 11367; tel. 1 718 997 3800; fax 1 718 997 3849; website qcpages.qc.edu/music.

**Abilene Christian University, Department of Music:** PO Box 8274, Abilene, TX 79699; website www.acu.edu.

**Academy of Vocal Arts:** 1920 Spruce Street, Philadelphia, PA 19103; tel. (215) 735-1685; fax (215) 732-2189; website www.avaopera.org.

**Adelphi University, Department of Music:** Post Hall, Garden City, NY 11530; website www.adelphi.edu.

**Alabama State University, School of Music:** 915 S Jackson Street, Montgomery, AL 36101; website www.alasu.edu.

**Albion College, Department of Music:** Albion, MI 49224; website www.albion.edu.

**Alcorn State University, Fine Arts Department:** PO Box 29, Lorman, MS 39096; tel. 1 601 877 6100; website www.alcorn.edu.

**Alderson-Broaddus College:** Department of Music, PO Box 2126, Philippi, WV 26416; tel. (304) 457-1700; fax (304) 457-6239; website www.ab.edu.

**Allegheny College, Department of Music:** 520 N Main Street, Meadville, PA 16335; tel. 1 814 332 3100; website www.allegheny.edu.

**Alverno College, Department of Music:** 3400 S 43rd Street, Milwaukee, WI 53234; tel. 1 414 382 6000; website www.alverno.edu.

**Amarillo College, Department of Music:** PO Box 447, Amarillo, TX 79178; tel. 1 806 371 5000; website www.actx.edu.

**American Conservatory of Music:** 252 Wildwood Road, Hammond, IN 46324; tel. 1 219 931 6000; website www.americanconservatory.edu.

**American University, Department of Performing Arts:** Kreeger Building, 4400 Massachusetts Ave NW, Washington, DC 20016; tel. 1 202 885 3420; fax 1 202 885 1092; website www.american.edu.

**Amherst College, Department of Music:** Amherst, MA 01002; tel. 1 413 542 2000; website www.amherst.edu.

**Anderson College, Department of Music:** 316 Blvd, Anderson, SC 29621; tel. 1 864 231 2000; website www.anderson-college.edu.

**Anderson University, Department of Music:** 1100 E Fifth Street, Anderson, IN 46012; website www.anderson.edu.

**Andrews University, Department of Music:** Berrien Springs, MI 49104; tel. 1 269 471 7771; fax 1 269 471 6900; website www.andrews.edu.

**Angelo State University, Department of Music:** 2601 W Ave N, San Angelo, TX 76909; website www.angelo.edu.

**Appalachian State University, Hayes School of Music:** Broyhill Music Center, Boone, NC 28608; tel. (828) 262-3020; fax (828) 262-6446; website www.music.appstate.edu; Dean: Dr William G. Harbinson.

**Arizona State University, Interdisciplinary Fine Arts Department:** 4701 W Thunderbird Road, Phoenix, AZ 85069.

**Arizona State University, School of Music:** Tempe, AZ 85287; tel. 1 480 965 9011; website www.asu.edu.

**Arkansas State University, Department of Music:** PO Box 779, State University, AR 72467; website www.astate.edu.

**Arkansas Tech University, Department of Music:** 1509 N Boulder Ave, Russellville, AR 72801; tel. 1 479 968 0389; website www.atu.edu.

**Ashland University, Department of Music:** 401 College Ave, Ashland, OH 44805; website www.ashland.edu.

**Aspen Music School:** PO Box AA, Aspen, CO 81612.

**Aston Magna Performance Practice Institute:** PO Box 28, Great Barrington, MA 01230.

**Atlantic Christian College, Fine Arts Department:** Wilson, NC 27893.

**Auburn University, Department of Music:** Auburn, AL 36849; tel. 1 334 844 4000; website www.auburn.edu.

**Augsburg College, Department of Music:** 2211 Riverside Ave S, Minneapolis, MN 55454; tel. 1 612 330 1000; website www.augsburg.edu.

**Augustana College, Department of Music:** 639 38th Street, Rock Island, IL 61201; tel. 1 309 794 7000; website www.augustana.edu.

**Austin College, Department of Music:** 900 N Grand Ave, PO Box 1177, Sherman, TX 75090; website www.austincollege.edu.

**Austin Peay State University, Department of Music:** PO Box 4625, Clarksville, TN 37044; tel. 1 931 221 7011; website www.absu.edu.

**Azusa Pacific University, School of Music:** PO Box 7000, Azusa, CA 91702; website www.apu.edu.

**Baldwin-Wallace College, Conservatory of Music:** 275 Eastland Road, Berea, OH 44017; tel. (440) 826-2362; fax (440) 826-3239; e-mail thecon@bw.edu; website www.bw.edu/academics/conservatory.

**Ball State University, School of Music:** 2000 University Avenue, Muncie, IN 47306-0410; tel. (765) 285-5400; fax (765) 285-5401; website www.bsu.edu/music; Dir: Dr Peter A. McAllister.

**Baptist College at Charleston, Department of Music:** PO Box 10087, Charleston, SC 29411.

**Baruch College, City University of New York, Department of Music:** 1 Bernard Baruch Way, New York, NY 10010; tel. 1 646 312 1000; website www.baruch.cuny.edu.

**Bates College, Department of Music:** Lewiston, ME 04240; tel. 1 207 786 6255; website www.bates.edu.

**Baylor University, School of Music:** PO Box 7408, Waco, TX 76798; website www.baylor.edu.

**Belmont College, School of Music:** 1900 Belmont Blvd, Nashville, TN 37212; tel. 1 615 460 6785; website www.belmont.edu.

**Beloit College, Department of Music:** 700 College Street, Beloit, WI 53511; tel. 1 608 363 2000; website www.beloit.edu.

**Bemidji State University, Department of Music:** PO Box 53, 1500 Birchmont Dr. NE, No 53, Bemidji, MN 56601; tel. 1 218 755 2000; fax 1 218 755 4048; website www.bemidjistate.edu.

**Benjamin T. Rome School of Music:** The Catholic University of America, 620 Michigan Ave NE, Washington, DC 20064; tel. (202) 319-5414; fax (202) 319-6280; website music.cua.edu.

**Bennington College, Department of Music:** Jennings Hall, Bennington, VT 05201; website www.bennington.edu.

**Berea College, Department of Music:** CPO 1127, Berea, KY 40404; website www.berea.edu.

**Berklee College of Music:** 1140 Boylston St, Boston, MA 02215; website www.berklee.edu.

**Bethany College, Department of Music:** 421 N First St, Lindsborg, KS 67456.

**Bethel College, Department of Music:** 3900 Bethel Dr., St Paul, MN 55112; tel. 1 651 638 6400; website www.bethel.edu.

**Bethel College, Department of Music:** Drawer A, North Newton, KS 67117; website www.bethelks.edu.

**Biola University, Department of Music:** 13800 Biola Ave, La Mirada, CA 90639; tel. 1 562 903 6000; website www.biola.edu.

**Black Hills State University, School of Arts and Humanities:** PO Box 9003, Spearfish, SD 57783; website www.bhsu.edu.

**Bluffton College, Department of Music:** 280 W College Ave, Suite 1, Bluffton, OH 45817; tel. 1 419 358 3000; website www.bluffton.edu.

**Bob Jones University, Music Division:** PO Box 34533, Greenville, SC 29614; website www.bju.edu.

**Boise State University, Department of Music:** 1910 University Dr., Boise, ID 83725; tel. 1 208 426 1000; website www.boisestate.edu.

**Boston Conservatory:** Music Division, 8 The Fenway, Boston, MA 02215; tel. 1 617 536 6340; fax 1 617 536 3176; website www.bostonconservatory.edu.

**Boston University, School of Music:** 855 Commonwealth Ave, Boston, MA 02215; tel. 1 617 353 3350; website www.bu.edu/cfa/music.

**Bowdoin College, Department of Music:** Gibson Hall, Brunswick, ME 04011; website www.bowdoin.edu.

**Bowling Green State University, College of Musical Arts:** Bowling Green, OH 43403; tel. 1 419 372 2531; website www.bgsu.edu.

**Bradley University, Department of Music and Theatre Arts:** 1501 W Bradley Ave, Peoria, IL 61625; tel. (309) 677-2660; fax (309) 677-3505; website www.bradley.edu/theatre.

**Brandeis University, Department of Music:** South St, Waltham, MA 02254; website www.brandeis.edu.

**Brevard College, Fine Arts Division:** N Broad St, Brevard, NC 28712; website www.brevard.edu.

**Brigham Young University, Department of Music:** C-550 Harris Fine Arts Center, Provo, UT 84602; website www.byu.edu.

**Brooklyn College, Conservatory of Music:** Bedford Ave and Ave H, Brooklyn, NY 11210; tel. 1 718 951 5000; website www.brooklyn.cuny.edu.

**Brooklyn Conservatory of Music:** 58 Seventh Ave, Brooklyn, NY 11217; tel. 1 718 622 3300; website www.brooklynconservatory.com.

**Brown University, Department of Music:** PO Box 1924, 1 Young Orchard Ave, Providence, RI 02912; tel. 1 401 863 1000; website www.brown.edu.

**Bucknell University, Department of Music:** Moore Ave, Lewisburg, PA 17837; tel. 1 570 577 2000; website www.bucknell.edu.

**Butler University, Jordan College of Fine Arts:** 4600 Sunset Ave, Indianapolis, IN 46208; tel. 1 800 368 6852; fax 1 317 940 9930; e-mail info@butler.edu; website www.butler.edu.

**California Institute of the Arts, School of Music:** 24700 McBean Parkway, Valencia, CA 91355; tel. 1 661 255 1050; website www.calarts.edu.

**California State Polytechnic University, Department of Music:** 3801 W Temple Ave, Pomona, CA 91768; tel. 1 909 869 7659; website www.csupomona.edu.

**California State University, Bakersfield, Fine Arts Department:** 9001 Stockdale Highway, Bakersfield, CA 93311; tel. 1 661 664 2011; website www.csubak.edu.

**California State University, Chico, Department of Music:** 400 W 1st St, Chico, CA 95929; website www.csuchico.edu.

**California State University, Dominguez Hills, Department of Music:** 1000 E Victoria, Carson, CA 90747; tel. 1 310 243 3696; website www.csudh.edu.

**California State University, Fresno, Department of Music:** 5241 N Maple Ave, Fresno, CA 93740; tel. 1 559 278 4240; website www.csufresno.edu.

**California State University, Fullerton, Department of Music:** 800 N State College Blvd, Fullerton, CA 92834-6850; tel. (714) 278-2011; website www.fullerton.edu/arts/music.

**California State University, Hayward, Department of Music:** Hayward, CA 94542; tel. 1 510 885 3000; website www.csuhayward.edu.

**California State University, Long Beach, Department of Music:** 1250 Bellflower Blvd, Long Beach, CA 90840; tel. 1 562 985 4111; website www.csulb.edu.

**California State University, Los Angeles, Department of Music:** 5151 State University Dr., Los Angeles, CA 90032; tel. 1 323 343 3000; website www.calstatela.edu.

**California State University, Northridge, Department of Music:** 18111 Nordhoff St, Northridge, CA 91330; tel. 1 818 677 1200; website www.csun.edu.

**California State University, Stanislaus, Department of Music:** 801 Monte Vista Ave, Turlock, CA 95382; website www.csustan.edu.

**Calvin College, Department of Music:** Fine Arts Center, 1795 Knollcrest Circle SE, Grand Rapids, MI 49546-4404; tel. 1 616 526 6000; website www.calvin.edu.

**Cameron University, Department of Music:** Lawton, OK 73505; tel. 1 580 581 2200; website www.cameron.edu.

**Campbell University, Fine Arts Division:** PO Box 488, Buies Creek, NC 27506; tel. 1 800 334 4111; website www.campbell.edu.

**Cantors Institute-Seminary College of Jewish Music of the Jewish Theological Seminary of America:** 3080 Broadway, New York, NY 10027; tel. 1 212 678 8037.

**Capital University, Conservatory of Music:** 2199 E Main St, Columbus, OH 43209; tel. 1 614 236 6011; website www.capital.edu.

**Carleton College, Department of Music:** 1 N College St, Northfield, MN 55057; tel. 1 507 646 4000; website www.carleton.edu.

**Carnegie Mellon University, School of Music:** 5000 Forbes Avenue, Pittsburgh, PA 15213; tel. (412) 268-2372; website www.cmu.edu/cfa/music.

**Carroll College, Department of Music:** 100 NE Ave, Waukesha, WI 53186; website www.cc.edu.

**Carson-Newman College, Music Division:** PO Box 1839, Jefferson City, TN 37760; tel. 1 865 471 2000; website www.cn.edu.

**Carthage College, Department of Music:** 2001 Alford Park Drive, Kenosha, WI 53140; tel. 1 262 551 8500; website www.carthage.edu.

**Case Western Reserve University, Department of Music:** Haydn Hall, Cleveland, OH 44106; tel. 1 216 368 2000; website www.cwru.edu.

**Catawba College, Department of Music:** 2300 W Innes St, Salisbury, NC 28144; website www.catawba.edu.

**Centenary College of Louisiana, Hurley School of Music:** Shreveport, LA 71134; tel. 1 800 234 4448; website www.centenary.edu.

**Center for Creative Studies:** 200 E Kirby, Detroit, MI 48202; tel. 1 313 664 7400; fax 1 313 872 2739; website www.ccscad.edu.

**Central Methodist College, Swinney Conservatory of Music:** 411 CMC Sq., Fayette, MO 65248; website www.cmc.edu.

**Central Michigan University, Department of Music:** Powers Music Building, No 102, Mount Pleasant, MI 48859; tel. 1 989 774 4000; website www.cmich.edu.

**Central Missouri State University, Department of Music:** PO Box 800, Warrensburg, MO 64093; website www.cmsu.edu.

**Central State University, Department of Music:** 100 N University Dr., Edmond, OK 73034.

**Central State University, Department of Music:** Paul Robeson Cultural and Performing Arts Center, Room 218, Wilberforce, OH 45384; tel. 1 937 376 6011; website www.centralstate.edu.

**Central Washington University, Department of Music:** 400 E University Way, Ellensburg, WA 98926; website www.cwu.edu.

**Chautauqua Institution Summer School of Music:** PO Box 28, Chautauqua, NY 14722; website www.chautauqua-inst.org.

**Chicago Musical College of Roosevelt University:** 430 S Michigan Ave, Chicago, IL 60605; website www.roosevelt.edu.

**Chicago State University:** 95 State and King Dr., Chicago, IL 60628; website www.csu.edu.

**Christopher Newport University, Department of Music:** 1 University Place, Newport News, VA 23606; tel. 1 757 594 7000; website www.cnu.edu.

**City College of New York, Department of Music:** W 138th St and Convent Ave, New York, NY 10031; tel. 1 212 650 7000; website www.ccny.cuny.edu.

**Claremont Graduate University, Department of Music:** 150 E 20th St, Claremont, CA 91711; website www.cgu.edu.

**Clemson University, Performing Arts Department:** Clemson, SC 29634; tel. 1 864 656 3311; website www.clemson.edu.

**Cleveland Institute of Music:** 11021 East Blvd, Cleveland, OH 44106; tel. 1 216 791 5000; fax 1 216 791 3063; website www.cim.edu.

**Cleveland Music School Settlement:** 11125 Magnolia Dr., Cleveland, OH 44106; website www.thecmss.org.

**Cleveland State University, Department of Music:** 2121 Euclid Ave, Cleveland, OH 44115; tel. 1 216 687 2000; website www.csuohio.edu.

**Coe College, Department of Music:** 1220 First Ave NE, Cedar Rapids, IA 52402; tel. 1 319 399 8500; website www.coe.edu.

**Coker College, Department of Music:** 300 E College Ave, Hartsville, SC 29550; tel. 1 843 383 8000; website www.coker.edu.

**Colgate University, Department of Music:** Dana Arts Center, Hamilton, NY 13346; website www.colgate.edu.

**College of Mount St Joseph, Department of Music:** Delhi and Neeb Rds, Mount St Joseph, Cincinnati OH 45051; tel. 1 800 654 9314; website www.msj.edu.

**College of St Benedict, Department of Music:** 37 S College Ave, St Joseph, MN 56374; tel. 1 320 363 5011; website www.csbsju.edu.

**College of St Catherine, Department of Music:** 2004 Randolph Ave, St Paul, MN 55105; tel. 1 651 690 6000; website www.stkate.edu.

**College of Staten Island, City University of New York, Department of Music:** 130 Stuyvesant Place, Staten Island, NY 10301; tel. 1 718 982 2000; website www.csi.cuny.edu.

**College of William and Mary, Department of Music:** Williamsburg, VA 23185; website www.wm.edu.

**College of Wooster, Department of Music:** 1189 Beall Ave, Wooster, OH 44691; tel. 1 330 263 2000; website www.wooster.edu.

**Colorado College, Department of Music:** Packard Hall, Colorado Springs, CO 80903; tel. 1 719 389 6000; website www.coloradocollege.edu.

**Colorado State University, Pueblo, Department of Music:** 2200 Bonforte Blvd, Pueblo, CO 81001; tel. (719) 549-2552; fax (719) 549-2969.

**Colorado State University, Department of Music:** Fort Collins, CO 80523; website welcome.colostate.edu.

**Columbia College, Department of Music:** 1301 Columbia College Drive, Columbia, SC 29203; tel. 1 803 786 3871; website www.columbiacollegesc.edu.

**Columbia University, Department of Music:** 703 Dodge, New York, NY 10027; website www.columbia.edu.

**Columbus College, Schwob Music Department:** Columbus, GA 31993.

**Community School of the Arts:** 345 N College St, Suite 413, Charlotte, NC 28202; tel. 1 704 377 4187; website www.csarts.org.

**Concordia College, Department of Music:** Moorhead, MN 56560; website www.cord.edu.

**Concordia University, Nebraska, Department of Music:** 800 N Columbia Avenue, Seward, NE 68434; tel. (402) 643-7282; fax (402) 643-4073; e-mail music@cune.edu; website www.cune.edu; Chair, Dept of Music: Dr William Kuhn; institutional mem. of National Asscn of Schools of Music.

**Conservatory of Central Illinois:** 312 West Green, Urbana, IL 61801.

**Conservatory of Music of Puerto Rico:** PO Box 41227, Minillas Station, Santurce, PR 00940; tel. 1 787 751 0160.

**Converse College, Petrie School of Music:** 580 E Main Street, Spartanburg, SC 29301; website www.converse.edu.

**Cornell College, Department of Music:** Mount Vernon, IA 52314; website www.cornellcollege.edu.

**Cornell University, Department of Music:** Lincoln Hall, Ithaca, NY 14853; website www.cornell.edu.

**Cornish College of Arts, Department of Music:** 1000 Lenora St, Seattle, WA 98121; website www.cornish.edu.

**Corpus Christi State University, Visual and Performing Arts Department:** 6300 Ocean Dr., Corpus Christi, TX 78412.

**Cumberland College, Department of Music:** PO Box 7525, Williamsburg, KY 40769; tel. (606) 539-4332; e-mail jsmoak@cumberlandcollege.edu; website www.cumber.edu; Chair, Music Dept: Dr Jeff Smoak.

**Curtis Institute of Music:** 1726 Locust St, Philadelphia, PA 19103; tel. 1 215 893 5252; fax 1 215 893 9065; website www.curtis.edu.

**Dalcroze School of Music:** 161 E 73rd St, New York, NY 10021; website www.dalcroze.com.

**Darlington School of Music, Arts, Dance & Drama:** 977 Shavertown Road, Boothwyn, PA 19061; tel. 1 610 358 3632; website www.darlingtonarts.org.

**Dartmouth College, Department of Music:** Hopkins Center, Hanover, NH 03755; website www.dartmouth.edu.

**Davidson College, Department of Music:** PO Box 358, Davidson, NC 28036; website www.davidson.edu.

**De Paul University, School of Music:** 804 West Belden, Chicago, IL 60614; website www.depaul.edu.

**Delaware Music School:** PO Box 422, Milford, DE 19963; tel. 1 302 422 2043; website www.lewestoday.com/dms.

**Delta State University, Department of Music:** PO Box 3256, Cleveland, MS 38733; website www.deltastate.edu.

**Denison University, Department of Music:** Granville, OH 43023; website www.denison.edu.

**DePauw University, School of Music:** Performing Arts Center, Greencastle, IN 46135; tel. 1 765 658 4800; website www.depauw.edu.

**Diller-Quaile School of Music Inc:** 24 E 95th St, New York, NY 10128; tel. 1 212 369 1484; website www.diller-quaile.org.

**Drake University, School of Fine Arts:** Des Moines, IA 50311; tel. 1 515 271 2011; website www.drake.edu.

**Drexel University, Performing Arts Department:** 32 and Chestnut Sts, Philadelphia, PA 19104; website www.drexel.edu.

**Duke University, Department of Music:** Box 90665, Durham, NC 27708-0665; tel. (919) 660-3300; fax (919) 660-3301; e-mail duke-music@duke.edu; website www.duke.edu/music; Chair.: Scott Lindroth.

**Duquesne University, School of Music:** 600 Forbes Ave, Pittsburgh, PA 15282; tel. 1 412 396 6000; website www.duq.edu.

**East Tennessee State University, Department of Music:** PO Box 70267, Johnson City, TN 37614; tel. 1 423 439 1000; website www.etsu.edu.

**East Texas Baptist University, Department of Music:** 1209 North Grove, Marshall, TX 75670; tel. 1 903 935 7963; website www.etbu.edu.

**Eastern Illinois University, Department of Music:** Charleston, IL 61920; website www.eiu.edu.

**Eastern Kentucky University, Department of Music:** Richmond, NY 40475; website www.eku.edu.

**Eastern Michigan University, Department of Music:** N101 Alexander Music Building, Ypsilanti, MI 48197; website www.emich.edu.

**Eastern Montana College, Department of Music:** 1500 N 30th, Billings, MT 59101.

**Eastern New Mexico University, School of Music:** Station 16, Portales, NM 88130; tel. 1 505 562 1011; website www.enmu.edu.

**Eastern Washington University, Department of Music:** Cheney, WA 99004; website www.ewu.edu.

**Eastman School of Music:** University of Rochester, 26 Gibbs St, Rochester, NY 14604; website www.rochester.edu/ureastman.html.

**Edinboro University of Pennsylvania, Department of Music:** Heather Hall Music Building, Edinboro, PA 16444; tel. 1 814 732 2000; website www.edinboro.edu.

**Elizabeth City State University, Department of Music:** PO Box 820, Elizabeth City, NC 27909; website www.ecsu.edu.

**Elizabethtown College, Fine and Performing Arts Department:** Rider Hall, 1 Alpha Dr., Elizabethtown, PA 17022; website www.etown.edu.

**Emory University, Department of Music:** Humanities Building, Room 101, Atlanta, GA 30322; website www.emory.edu.

**Emporia State University, Division of Music:** 1200 Commercial St, Emporia, KS 66801; website www.emporia.edu.

**Esther Boyer College of Music:** Temple University, 13th and Norris Sts, Philadelphia, PA 19122; website www.temple.edu/boyer.

**Evangel College, Department of Music:** 1111 N Glenstone, Springfield, MO 65802; website www.evangel.edu.

**Fairleigh Dickinson University, Fine Arts Department:** 223 Montross Ave, Rutherford, NJ 07070; website www.fdu.edu.

**Fairmont State College, Fine Arts Division:** Fairmont, WV 26554; website www.fscwv.edu.

**Fisk University, Music Department:** 1000 17th Ave N, Nashville, TN 37208; tel. (615) 329-8702; fax (615) 329-8850; e-mail pautry@fisk.edu; website www.fisk.edu; Chair, Music Dept: Dr Philip E. Autry.

**Flint School of Performing Arts, Dort Music Center:** 1025 E Kearsley, Flint, MI 48503; website www.thefim.com/fspa.

**Florida Agricultural and Mechanical University, Department of Music:** Tallahassee, FL 32307; website www.famu.edu.

**Florida Atlantic University, Conservatory of Music:** College of Liberal Arts, 2912 College Ave, Boca Raton, FL 33314; website www.fau.edu.

**Florida International University, Department of Music:** University Park Campus, Miami, FL 33199; website www.fiu.edu.

**Florida State University, School of Music:** Tallahassee, FL 32306; website www.fsu.edu.

**Fort Hays State University, Department of Music:** 600 Park St, Hays, KS 67601; tel. 1 785 628 4000; website www.fhsu.edu.

**Friends University, Fine Arts Division:** 2100 University, Wichita, KS 67213; website www.friends.edu.

**Furman University, Department of Music:** Greenville, SC 29613; website www.furman.edu.

**Garden State Academy of Music:** 120 Jackson Ave, Rutherford, NJ 07070; tel. 1 201 933 5454; website www.gsamusic.org.

**Gardner-Webb College, Fine Arts Department:** Boiling Springs, NC 28017; website www.gardner-webb.edu.

**George Mason University, Department of Music:** 4400 University Dr., Fairfax, VA 22030; website www.gmu.edu.

**George Washington University, Department of Music:** B-144 Academic Center, Washington, DC 20052; website www.gwu.edu.

**Georgia Southern University, Department of Music:** PO Box 8052, Statesboro, GA 30460-8052; tel. (912) 681-5396; fax (912) 871-1295; e-mail music@georgiasouthern.edu; website www.gasou.edu.

**Georgia State University, School of Music:** University Plaza, Atlanta, GA 30303; website www.gsu.edu.

**Gettysburg College, Department of Music:** Gettysburg, PA 17325; website www.gettysburg.edu.

**Goucher College, Department of Music:** 1021 Dulaney Valley Road, Towson, MD 21204; website www.goucher.edu.

**Grambling State University, Department of Music:** Grambling, LA 71245; website www.gram.edu.

**Grand Valley State University, Department of Music:** Allendale, MI 49401; website www.gvsu.edu.

**Gustavus Adolphus College, Department of Music:** St Peter, MN 56082; website www.gac.edu.

**Guy Fraser Harrison Academy for the Performing Arts:** PO Box 60408, Oklahoma City, OK 73146; website www.harrisonacademy.org.

**Haddonfield School of Creative and Performing Arts:** PO Box 383, Haddonfield, NJ 08033; website www.haddonarts.org.

**Hamline University, Department of Music:** Hewitt Ave at Snelling, St Paul, MN 55104; website www.hamline.edu.

**Hampton University, Department of Music:** Hampton, VA 23668; website www.hamptonu.edu.

**Hanover College, Department of Music:** Hanover, IN 47243; website www.hanover.edu.

**Hardin-Simmons University, School of Music:** Drawer J Abilene, TX 79698; website www.hsutx.edu.

**Harlem School of the Arts Inc:** 645 St Nicholas Ave, New York, NY 10030; tel. 1 212 926 4100; website www.harlemschoolofthearts.org.

**Harvard University, Department of Music:** Music Building, Cambridge, MA 02138; website www.harvard.edu.

**Hastings College, Department of Music:** Seventh and Turner, Hastings, NE 68901; website www.hastings.edu.

**Hebrew Union College, Jewish Institute of Religion, School of Sacred Music:** 1 W Fourth St, New York, NY 10012; website www.huc.edu.

**Henderson State University, Department of Music:** 1100 Henderson St, Arkadelphia, AR 71923; website www.hsu.edu.

**Herbert H Lehman College, City University of New York, Department of Music:** Bedford Park Blvd W, Bronx, NY 10468; website www.lehman.cuny.edu.

**Hiram College, Department of Music:** Hiram, OH 44234; website www.hiram.edu.

**Hochstein Memorial Music School:** 50 N Plymouth Avenue, Rochester, NY 14614; tel. (585) 454-4596; fax (585) 454-4393; e-mail music@hochstein.org; website www.hochstein.org; Pres.: Margaret Quackenbush.

**Hoff-Barthelson Music School:** 25 School Lane, Scarsdale, NY 10583; tel. (914) 723-1169; fax (914) 723-0036; website www.hbms.org; Exec. Dir: Joan Behrens Bergman.

**Hofstra University, Department of Music:** 1000 Fulton Ave, Hempstead, NY 11550; website www.hofstra.edu.

**Hollins College, Department of Music:** PO Box 9642, Roanoke, VA 24020; website www.hollins.edu.

**Hope College, Department of Music:** Holland, MI 49423; website www.hope.edu.

**Houghton College, School of Music:** Houghton, NY 14744; website www.houghton.edu.

**Houston Baptist University, College of Fine Arts:** 7502 Fondren Road, Houston, TX 77074; website www.hbu.edu.

**Howard Payne University, School of Music:** 1000 Fisk St, Brownwood, TX 76801; tel. 1 325 649 8020; website www.hputx.edu.

**Howard University, College of Fine Arts:** Sixth and Fairmont Sts NW, Washington, DC 20059; website www.howard.edu.

**Hunter College, City University of New York, Department of Music:** 695 Park Ave, New York, NY 10021; tel. 1 212 772 4000; website www.hunter.cuny.edu.

**Idaho State University, Department of Music:** PO Box 8099, Pocatello, ID 83209; website www.isu.edu.

**Illinois State University, Department of Music:** Normal, IL 61761; website www.ilstu.edu.

**Illinois Wesleyan University, School of Music:** Presser Hall, Bloomington, IL 61702; website www.iwu.edu.

**Immaculate College, Department of Music:** Immaculate, PA 19345.

**Incarnate Word College, Department of Music:** 4301 Broadway, San Antonio, TX 78209; website www.uiw.edu.

**Indiana State University, Department of Music:** 217 N Sixth St, Terre Haute, IN 47809; website www.indstate.edu.

**Indiana University of Pennsylvania, Department of Music:** 101 Cogswell Hall, Indiana, PA 15705; website www.iup.edu.

**Indiana University, School of Music:** Music Building, Bloomington, IN 47405-2200; tel. 812 855 1583; website www.music.indiana.edu.

**Indiana University-Purdue University at Indianapolis, Department of Music:** 525 N Blackford St, Room 010, Indianapolis, IN 46202.

**Interamerican University of Puerto Rico, Department of Music:** Goodyear, PO Box 5100, San Germán, PR 00735.

**Interlochen Center for the Arts, Department of Music:** PO Box 199, Interlochen, MI 49643-0199; tel. 231 276 7200; fax 231 276 6321; e-mail ica@interlochen.k12.mi.us; website www.interlochen.org.

**Iowa State University, Department of Music:** 149 Music Hall, Ames, IA 50011; website www.iastate.edu.

**Ithaca College, School of Music:** Ithaca, NY 14850; website www.ithaca.edu.

**Jackson State University, Department of Music:** PO Box 17055, Jackson, MS 39217; website www.jsums.edu.

**Jacksonville State University, Department of Music:** Mason Hall, Jacksonville, AL 36265; website www.jsu.edu.

**Jacksonville University, College of Fine Arts, Division of Music:** Jacksonville, FL 32211; tel. 1 904 256 8000; website www.ju.edu.

**James Madison University, School of Music:** MSC 7301, Harrisonburg, VA 22807; tel. (540) 568-6714; website www.jmu.edu/music.

**Jersey City State College, Music, Dance and Theatre Department:** 2039 Kennedy Blvd, Jersey City, NJ 07305.

**Juilliard School:** 60 Lincoln Center Plaza, New York, NY 10023; tel. 1 212 799 5000; website www.juilliard.edu.

**Kalamazoo College, Department of Music:** 1200 Academy St, Kalamazoo, MI 49007; website www.kzoo.edu.

**Kansas State University, Department of Music:** McCain Auditorium, Room 109, Manhattan, KS 66506; tel. 1 785 532 6011; website www.ksu.edu.

**Kearney State College, Department of Music:** Kearney, NE 68847.

**Kent State University, School of Music:** Kent, OH 44242; website www.kent.edu.

**Kentucky State University, Fine Arts Division:** Frankfort, KY 40601; tel. 1 502 597 6000; website www.kysu.edu.

**La Salle University, Fine Arts Department:** Philadelphia, PA 19141; website www.lasalle.edu.

**Lamar University, Department of Music:** PO Box 10044, Beaumont, TX 77710; website www.lamar.edu.

**Lawrence University, Conservatory of Music:** PO Box 599, Appleton WI 54912; tel. 1 920 832 7000; website www.lawrence.edu.

**Lebanon Valley College, Department of Music:** Blair Music Center, Annville, PA 17003; website www.lvc.edu.

**Lenoir-Rhyne College, Department of Music:** PO Box 7355, Hickory, NC 28603; tel. 1 828 328 1741; website www.lrc.edu.

**Levine School of Music:** 1690 36th St NW, Washington, DC 20007; website www.levineschool.org.

**Lewis and Clark College, Department of Music:** 0615 SW Palatine Hill Road, Portland, OR 97219; website www.lclark.edu.

**Liberty University, Department of Music:** PO Box 20000, Lynchburg, VA 24506; website www.liberty.edu.

**Limestone College, Fine Arts Division:** 115 College Dr., Gaffney, SC 29340; website www.limestone.edu.

**Lionel Hampton School of Music:** University of Idaho, Moscow, ID 83843; website www.uidaho.edu/LS/Music.

**Longwood University, Department of Music:** 201 High St, Farmville, VA 23909; tel. 1 434 395 2000; website www.longwood.edu.

**Longy School of Music Inc:** 1 Follen St, Cambridge, MA 02138; website www.longy.edu.

**Los Angeles City College, Department of Music:** 855 N Vermont Ave, Los Angeles, CA 90029; tel. (323) 953-4000; fax (323) 953-4013; website www .lacitycollege.edu.

**Louisiana College, Department of Music:** 1140 College Drive, College Station, Pineville, LA 71360; tel. 1 318 487 7011; website www.lacollege.edu.

**Louisiana State University, School of Music:** Baton Rouge, LA 70803; website www.lsu.edu.

**Louisiana Tech University, School of Performing Arts:** PO Box 8608, Ruston, LA 71272; website www.latech.edu.

**Loyola University, College of Music:** 6363 St Charles Ave, New Orleans, LA 70118; website www.luc.edu.

**Luther College, Department of Music:** Decorah, IA 52101; website www .luther.edu.

**Macalester College, Department of Music:** 1600 Grand Ave, St Paul, MN 55105; website www.macalester.edu.

**Malone College, Fine Arts Department:** 515 25th St NW, Canton, OH 44709; website www.malone.edu.

**Manchester College, Department of Music:** College Ave, North Manchester, IN 46962; website www.manchester.edu.

**Manhattan School of Music:** 120 Claremont Ave, New York, NY 10027; tel. 1 212 749 2802; website www.mcmnyc.edu.

**Manhattanville College, Department of Music:** Purchase, NY 10577; website www.mville.edu.

**Mannes College of Music:** 150 W 85th St, New York, NY 10024; website www.mannes.edu.

**Mansfield University, Department of Music:** Butler Music Center, Mansfield, PA 16933; website www.mnsfld.edu.

**Marietta College, Edward E MacTaggart Department of Music:** Marietta, OH 45750; website www.marietta.edu.

**Mars Hill College, Fine Arts Division:** PO Box 530, Mars Hill, NC 28754; website www.mhc.edu.

**Marshall University, Department of Music:** Huntington, WV 25701; website www.marshall.edu.

**Mary Washington College, Department of Music:** Fredericksburg, VA 22401; website www.mwc.edu.

**Marylhurst University, Music Department:** PO Box 261, Marylhurst, OR 97036-0261; tel. (503) 699-6263; e-mail music@marylhurst.edu; website www .marylhurst.edu; Music Dept Chair: John Paul.

**Maryville College, Fine Arts Department:** PO Box 2805, Maryville, TN 37801; website www.maryvillecollege.edu.

**Marywood College, Department of Music:** 2300 Adams Ave, Scranton, PA 18509; website www.marywood.edu.

**Mason Gross School of the Arts of Rutgers University:** Marryott Music Building, Douglass Campus, 81 George Street, New Brunswick, NJ 08901; website www.masongross.rutgers.edu.

**Mayville State University, Humanities and Social Science Division:** Mayville, ND 58257; website www.masu.nodak.edu.

**Memphis State University, Department of Music:** Memphis, TN 38152.

**Mercyhurst College, D'Angelo School of Music:** Glenwood Hills, Erie, PA 16546; website www.mercyhurst.edu.

**Meredith College:** 3800 Hillsborough St, Raleigh, NC 27607; tel. 1 919 760 8600; website www.meredith.edu.

**Messiah College, Department of Music:** Grantham, PA 17027; website www.messiah.edu.

**Metropolitan State College, Department of Music:** 1006 11th St, PO Box 58, Denver, CO 80204; website www.mscd.edu.

**Miami University, Department of Music:** 121 Center for Performing Arts, Oxford, OH 45056; website www.muohio.edu.

**Michigan State University, School of Music:** Music Building, East Lansing, MI 48824; tel. 1 517 355 2308; fax 1 517 355 6473; website www .msu.edu.

**Middle Tennessee State University, Department of Music:** PO Box 47, Murfreesboro, TN 37132; website www.mtsu.edu.

**Middlebury College, Department of Music:** 326 Johnson Building, Middlebury, VT 05753; website www.middlebury.edu.

**Midwestern State University, Department of Music:** 3400 Taft, Wichita Falls, TX 76308; website www.mwsu.edu.

**Millersville University of Pennsylvania, Department of Music:** Northumberland House, Millersville, PA 17551.

**Millikin University, School of Music:** 1184 W Main St, Decatur, IL 62522; website www.millikin.edu.

**Mills College, Music Department:** 5000 MacArthur Blvd, Oakland, CA 94613; website www.mills.edu.

**Minnesota State University Mankato, Department of Music:** 202 Performing Arts Center, Mankato, MN 56001; tel. (507) 389-2118; fax (507) 389-2992; e-mail music@mnsu.edu; website www.mnsu.edu.

**Minnesota State University Moorhead, Department of Music:** 1104 Seventh Ave S, Moorhead, MN 56563; tel. (218) 477-2101; fax (218) 477-4097; e-mail music@mnstate.edu; website www.mnstate.edu/music.

**Minot State University, Music Division:** 500 Ninth Ave NW, Minot, ND 58701.

**Mississippi College, Department of Music:** PO Box 4206, Clinton, MS 39058; tel. 1 601 925 3000; website www.mc.edu.

**Mississippi State University, Department of Music Education:** Drawer F, Mississippi State, MS 39762; website www.msstate.edu.

**Missouri Southern State University, Department of Music:** 3950 E Newman Road, Joplin, MO 64801; tel. (417) 625-9755; fax (417) 625-9798; website www.mssc.edu.

**Missouri Western State College, Department of Music:** 4525 Downs Dr., St Joseph, MO 64507; website www.mwsc.edu.

**Montana State University, Department of Music:** Bozeman, MT 59717; website www.montana.edu.

**Montclair State University, School of Fine and Performing Arts:** Valley Road, Upper Montclair, NJ 07043; website www.montclair.edu.

**Montgomery College, Department of Music:** 51 Mannakee St, Rockville, MD 20850; website www.montgomerycollege.edu.

**Moody Bible Institute, Sacred Music Department:** 820 N LaSalle Drive, Chicago, IL 60610; tel. (312) 329-4082; fax (312) 329-4098; e-mail smdinfo@ moody.edu; website www.moody.edu.

**Morehead State University, Department of Music:** Baird Music Hall, Room 106, Morehead, KY 40351; website www.morehead-st.edu.

**Morgan State University, Department of Music:** 1700 E Cold Spring Lane, Baltimore, MD 21251; tel. 1 443 885 3333; website www.morgan.edu.

**Morningside College:** 1501 Morningside Ave, Sioux City, IA 51106; website www.morningside.edu.

**Mount Union College, Department of Music:** 1972 Clark Ave, Alliance, OH 44601; website www.muc.edu.

**Murray State University, Department of Music:** University Station, Murray, KY 42071; website www.murraystate.edu.

**Music Academy of the West:** 1070 Fairway Road, Santa Barbara, CA 93108; tel. (805) 969-4726; fax (805) 969-0686; website www.musicacademy.org; Pres. David L.Kuehn; Vice-Pres. and Dean W. Harold Laster; organizes a summer school and festival.

**Music and Arts Institute of San Francisco:** 2622 Jackson St, San Francisco, CA 94115.

**Music School of Brattleboro Music Center:** 15 Walnut St, Brattleboro, VT 05301; tel. 1 802 257 4523.

**Music/Arts Institute:** 1010 South Pearl, PO Box 1141, Independence, MO 64051.

**Musicians Institute:** 1655 McCadden Place, Hollywood, CA 90028; website www.mi.edu.

**Music School:** 75 John St, Providence, RI 02906.

**Muskingum College, Department of Music:** New Concord, OH 43762; website www.muskingum.edu.

**NcNeese State University, College of Liberal Arts, Department of Music:** Ryan St, Lake Charles, LA 70609.

**Nebraska Wesleyan University, Department of Music:** 50 and St Paul St, Lincoln, NE 68504; website www.nebrweslyan.edu.

**New England Conservatory of Music:** 290 Huntington Ave, Boston, MA 02115; tel. 1 617 585 1100; website www.newenglandconservatory.edu.

**New Mexico Highlands University, Creative and Performing Arts Department:** Las Vegas, NM 87701; website www.nmhu.edu.

**New Mexico State University, Department of Music:** PO Box 30001, Las Cruces, NM 88003; website www.nmsu.edu.

**New Orleans Baptist Theological Seminary, Church Music Ministries Division:** 3939 Gentilly Blvd, New Orleans, LA 70126; website www.nobts .edu.

**New School for Social Research, Department of Music:** 66 W 12th St, New York, NY 10011.

**New School of Music:** 25 Lowell St, Cambridge, MA 02138; tel. 1 617 492 8105; fax 1 617 864 7318; website www.cambridgemusic.org.

**New York University, Tisch School of the Arts:** 721 Broadway, 4th Floor, New York, NY 10003; website www.nyu.edu.

**Newberry College, Department of Music:** 2100 College Street, Newberry, SC 29108; tel. (803) 321-5174; fax (803) 321-5175; e-mail scherrington@ newberry.edu; website www.newberry.edu; Dept Chair: Dr Sally Cherrington.

**Norfolk State University, Department of Music:** 2401 Corprew Ave, Norfolk, VA 23504; website www.nsu.edu.

**North Carolina Agricultural and Technological State University, Department of Music:** 1601 E Market St, Greensboro, NC 27411; website www.ncat.edu.

**North Carolina Central University, Department of Music:** PO Box 19405, Durham, NC 27707; website www.nccu.edu.

**North Carolina School of the Arts, School of Music:** 200 Waughtown St, Winston-Salem, NC 27117; website www.ncarts.edu.

**North Dakota State University, Music and Visual Arts Department:** PO Box 5691, Fargo, ND 58105; website www.ndsu.nodak.edu.

**North Park College, Department of Music:** 3225 West Foster, Chicago, IL 60625; website www.northpark.edu.

**Northeast Louisiana University, School of Music:** 700 University, Monroe, LA 71209.

**Northeastern State University, College of Arts and Letters:** Tahlequah, OK 74464; tel. 1 918 456 5511; website www.nsuok.edu.

**Northeastern University, Department of Music:** 360 Huntington Ave, Boston, MA 02115; website www.northeastern.edu.

**Northern Arizona University, Music Department:** PO Box 6040, Flagstaff, AZ 86011; website www.nau.edu.

**Northern Illinois University, School of Music:** Music Building 140, DeKalb, IL 60115; website www.niu.edu.

**Northern Michigan University, Department of Music:** Fine Arts Building, C-130, Marquette, MI 49855; website www.nmu.edu.

**Northern State University, School of Fine Arts:** Aberdeen, SD 57401; website www.northern.edu.

**Northwest Missouri State University, Department of Music:** DeLuce Fine Arts Building, Maryville, MO 64468; tel. 1 800 633 1175; website www .nwmissouri.edu.

**Northwestern State University of Louisiana, Department of Music:** College Ave, Natchitoches, LA 71497; website www.nsula.edu.

**Northwestern University, School of Music:** 711 Elgin Road, Evanston, IL 60208; website www.northwestern.edu.

**Nyack College, Music and Fine Arts Department:** Nyack, NY 10960; website www.nyackcollege.edu.

**Oakland University, Music, Theatre and Dance Department:** Rochester, MI 48309; website www.oakland.edu.

**Oberlin College Conservatory of Music:** Oberlin, OH 44074; website www .oberlin.edu.

**Odessa College, Department of Music:** 201 W University Blvd, Odesa, TX 79764; website www.odessa.edu.

**Ohio Northern University, Department of Music:** 525 S Main Street, Ada, OH 45810; e-mail e-williams@onu.edu; website www.onu.edu; Chair, Dept of Music: Dr Edwin Williams.

**Ohio State University, School of Music:** 1866 College Road, Columbus, OH 43210; website www.osu.edu.

**Ohio University, School of Music:** Athens, OH 45701; website www.ohiou .edu.

**Ohio Wesleyan University, Department of Music:** Delaware, OH 43015; website www.owu.edu.

**Oklahoma City University, School of Music and Performing Arts:** 2501 North Blackwelder, Oklahoma City, OK 73106; tel. 1 405 521 5000; website www.okcu.edu.

**Oklahoma State University, Department of Music:** 132 Seretean Center, Stillwater, OK 74078; tel. 1 405 744 5000; website www.okstate.edu.

**Old Dominion University, Department of Music:** Norfolk, VA 23508; tel. 1 787 683 4154; website www.odu.edu.

**Oral Roberts University, Fine Arts Department:** Tulsa, OK 74171; website www.oru.edu.

**Oregon State University, Department of Music:** Benton 101, Corvallis, OR 97331; website www.oregonstate.edu.

**Otterbein College, Department of Music:** Battelle Fine Arts Center, Westerville, OH 43081; website www.otterbein.edu.

**Pacific Lutheran University, Department of Music:** Tacoma, WA 98447; website www.plu.edu.

**Pacific University, Department of Music:** Forest Grove, OR 97116; website www.pacificu.edu.

**Pan American University, Department of Music:** Edinburg, TX 78539; website www.panam.edu.

**Park College, Department of Music:** Parkville, Kansas City, MO 64152.

**Pasadena Conservatory of Music:** PO Box 91533, 1815 Queensberry Road, Pasadena, CA 91109; tel. 1 626 683 3355; website www.pasadenaconservatory .org.

**Peabody Institute of the Johns Hopkins University:** 1 E Mount Vernon Place, Baltimore, MD 21202; website www.peabody.jhu.edu.

**Pembroke State University, Department of Music:** Pembroke, NC 28372,

**Pennsylvania State University, School of Music:** 232 Music Building, University Park, PA 16802; website www.psu.edu.

**People's Music School:** 4750 N Sheridan, Suite 340, Chicago, IL 60640.

**Pfeiffer University, Fine Arts Department:** Misenheimer, NC 28109; website www.pfeiffer.edu.

**Philadelphia College of Performing Arts:** The University of the Arts, The School of Music, 250 S Broad St, Philadelphia, PA 19102.

**Philips University, Department of Music:** Division of Fine Arts, PO Box 2000, University Station, Enid, OK 73702.

**Pittsburg State University, Department of Music:** 1701 South Broadway, Pittsburg, KS 66762; tel. 1 620 231 7000; website www.pittstate.edu.

**Plymouth State University, Department of Music:** Plymouth, NH 03264; website www.plymouth.edu.

**Pomona College, Department of Music:** Thatcher Music Building, Claremont, CA 91711; website www.pomona.edu.

**Portland State University, Department of Music:** PO Box 751, Portland, OR 97207; website www.psx.edu.

**Preucil School of Music:** 524 N Johnson, Iowa City, IA 52245; website www .preucil.org.

**Princeton University, Department of Music:** Woolworth Center, Princeton, NJ 08544; website www.princeton.edu.

**Providence College, Department of Music:** River Ave and Easton St, Providence, RI 02918; website www.providence.edu.

**Purdue University, Department of Music:** 135 Hall of Music, W Lafayette, IN 47907; website www.purdue.edu.

**Quachita Baptist University, School of Music:** PO Box 37771, Arkadelphia, AR 71923; website www.obu.edu.

**Queens College, Fine Arts Division and Music Department:** 1900 Selwyn Ave, Charlotte, NC 28274; website www.queens.edu.

**Radford University, Department of Music:** E Norwood St, Radford, VA 24142; website www.radford.edu.

**Rhode Island College, Department of Music:** 600 Mount Pleasant Ave, Providence, RI 02908; website www.ric.edu.

**Rhodes College, Department of Music:** 2000 N Parkway, Memphis, TN 38112; tel. 1 901 843 3000; website www.rhodes.edu.

**Rice University, Shepherd School of Music:** PO Box 1892, Houston, TX 77251; tel. 1 713 348 0000; website www.rice.edu.

**Richland College, Humanities Division:** 12800 Abrams Road, Dallas, TX 75243; website www.rlc.dcccd.edu.

**Ricks College, Department of Music:** Rexburg, ID 83440.

**Ripon College, Department of Music:** 300 Seward St, PO Box 248, Ripon, WI 54971; website www.ripon.edu.

**Roanoke College, Fine Arts Department:** Olin Hall Center for Arts and Humanities, Salem, VA 24153; website www.roanoke.edu.

**Roberts Wesleyan College, Fine Arts Division:** 2301 Westside Dr., Rochester, NY 14624; website www.roberts.edu.

**Rowan University, Department of Music:** 201 Mullica Hill Road, Glassboro, NJ 08028; tel. 1 856 256 4000; website www.rowan.edu.

**Rutgers University, Faculty of Arts and Sciences, Department of Music:** Newark, NJ 07102; website www.rutgers.edu.

**SacraCalifornia State University, Sacramento, Department of Music:** 6000 Jay Ave, Sacramento, CA 95819.

**Saint Louis Conservatory and Schools for the Arts:** 560 Trinity at Delmar, St Louis, MO 63130.

**Saint Louis University, Department of Music:** 221 N Grand Blvd, St Louis, MO 63103; website www.slu.edu.

**Saint Mary-of-the-Woods College, Department of Music:** Saint Mary-of-the-Woods, IN 47876.

**Saint Mary's College of Maryland, Arts and Letters Division:** Saint Mary's City, MD 20686.

**Saint Mary's College, Department of Music:** Notre Dame, IN 46556.

**Salem College, School of Music:** Winston-Salem, NC 27108; website www.salem.edu.

**Sam Houston State University, Department of Music:** Huntsville, TX 77341; website www.shsu.edu.

**Samford University, School of Music:** 800 S Lakeshore Dr., Birmingham, AL 35229; tel. (205) 726-2778; fax (205) 726-2165; website www.samford.edu/schools/performingarts.

**San Diego State University, Department of Music:** 5300 Campanile Dr., San Diego, CA 92182; website www.sdsu.edu.

**San Francisco Conservatory of Music:** 1201 Ortega St, San Francisco, CA 94122; website www.sfcm.edu.

**San Francisco State University, Department of Music:** 1600 Holloway Ave, San Francisco, CA 94132; website www.sfsu.edu.

**San Jacinto College North, Fine Arts Division:** 5800 Uvalde Road, Houston, TX 77049.

**San Jose State University, Department of Music:** 1 Washington Sq., San Jose, CA 95192; website www.sjsu.edu.

**Sarah Lawrence College, Department of Music:** 1 Meadway, Bronxville, NY 10708; website www.slc.edu.

**Seattle Pacific University, School of Fine and Performing Arts:** 3307 Third Ave W, Seattle, WA 98119; website www.spu.edu.

**Seton Hill College, Department of Music:** Greensburg, PA 15601; website www.setonhill.edu.

**Settlement Music School:** 416 Queen St, Philadelphia, PA 19147; website www.smsmusic.org.

**Shenandoah College and Conservatory:** Winchester, VA 22601.

**Sherwood Conservatory of Music:** 1312 S Michigan Ave, Chicago, IL 60605; tel. 1 312 427 6267; website www.sherwoodmusic.org.

**Shorter College, Fine Arts Division:** PO Box 8, Rome, GA 30161; website www.shorter.edu.

**Silver Lake College, Department of Music:** 2406 S Alverno Road, Manitowoc, WI 54220; tel. (920) 686-6183; fax (920) 684-7082; e-mail mwagner@silver.sl.edu; website www.sl.edu/music; Chair: S. Marella Wagner.

**Simpson College, Amy Robertson Music Centre:** 701 North C Street, Indianola, IA 50125; tel. (515) 961-1637; e-mail dipalma@storm.simpson.edu; website www.simpson.edu; Chair, Dept of Music: Dr Maria DiPalma.

**Sioux Falls College, Fine Arts Division:** 1501 S Prairie Ave, Sioux Falls, SD 57105.

**Skidmore College, Department of Music:** Saratoga Springs, NY 12866; website www.skidmore.edu.

**Slippery Rock University, Department of Music:** Slippery Rock, PA 16057; website www.sru.edu.

**Smith College, Department of Music:** Northampton, MA 01063; website www.smith.edu.

**South Carolina State College, Department of Music:** PO Box 1917, Orangeburg, SC 29117; website www.scsu.edu.

**South Dakota State University, Department of Music:** Brookings, SD 57007.

**Southeast Missouri State University, Department of Music:** Brandt Music Hall, Cape Girardeau, MO 63701; website www.semo.edu.

**Southeastern Louisiana University, Department of Music:** PO Box 815, University Station, Hammond, LA 70402; website www.selu.edu.

**Southeastern Oklahoma State University, Department of Music:** PO Box 4173, Station A, Durant, OK 74701; website www.sosu.edu.

**Southern Baptist Theological Seminary, School of Church Music:** 2825 Lexington Road, Louisville, KY 40280.

**Southern Illinois University at Carbondale, School of Music:** Carbondale, IL 62901.

**Southern Illinois University at Edwardsville, Department of Music:** PO Box 1771, Edwardsville, IL 62026.

**Southern Methodist University, Meadows School of the Arts:** Owen Arts Center, Dallas, TX 75275; website www.smu.edu.

**Southern Nazarene University, School of Music:** 6729 NW 39 Expressway, Bethany, OK 73008; website www.snu.edu.

**Southern Oregon State College, Department of Music:** 1250 Siskiyou Blvd, Ashland, OR 97520; website www.sou.edu.

**Southern University, Department of Music:** PO Box 10215, Baton Rouge, LA 70813.

**Southwest Baptist University, School of Fine Arts:** 1601 S Springfield St, Bolivar, MO 65613.

**Southwest Missouri State University, Department of Music:** 901 South National, Springfield, MO 65804.

**Southwestern Baptist Theological Seminary, School of Church Music:** PO Box 22000, Fort Worth, TX 76122.

**Southwestern University, School of Fine Arts:** Georgetown, TX 78626.

**Spelman College, Department of Music:** 350 Spelman Lane SW, Atlanta, GA 30314; website www.spelman.edu.

**St Cloud State University, Department of Music:** Performing Arts Center, Room 240, St Cloud, MN 56301.

**St John's University, Department of Music:** Collegeville, MN 56321.

**St Mary's University of San Antonio, Department of Music:** 1 Camino Santa Maria, San Antonio, TX 78284; website www.stmarytx.edu.

**St Michael's College, Fine Arts Department:** 56 College Farkway, Winooski, VT 05404.

**St Norbert College, Department of Music:** De Pere, WI 54115.

**St Olaf College, Department of Music:** Northfield, MN 55057.

**Stanford University, Department of Music:** Stanford, CA 94305; website www.stanford.edu.

**State University of New York at Albany, Department of Music:** 1400 Washington Ave, Albany, NY 12222; website www.albany.edu.

**State University of New York at Binghamton, Department of Music:** Vestal Parkway, Binghamton, NY 13901; website www.binghamton.edu.

**State University of New York at Buffalo, Department of Music:** Baird Hall, Room 226, Amherst Campus, Buffalo, NY 14260; website www.buffalo.edu.

**State University of New York at Stony Brook, Department of Music:** Stony Brook, L I, NY 11794; website www.sunysb.edu.

**State University of New York, College at Brockport, Music and Theatre Department:** Tower Fine Arts Center, Holley St, Brockport, NY 14420; website www.brockport.edu.

**State University of New York, College at Buffalo, Performing Arts Department:** 1300 Elmwood Ave, Buffalo, NY 14222.

**State University of New York, College at Cortland, Department of Music:** PO Box 2000, Cortland, NY 13045; website www.cortland.edu.

**State University of New York, College at Fredonia, School of Music:** Mason Hall, Fredonia, NY 14063; website www.fredonia.edu.

**State University of New York, College at Geneseo, Department of Music:** Geneseo, NY 14454; website www.geneseo.edu.

**State University of New York, College at New Paltz, Department of Music:** New Paltz, NY 12561; website www.newpaltz.edu.

**State University of New York, College at Oneonta, Fine Arts Center:** Oneonta, NY 13820; website www.oneonta.edu.

**State University of New York, College at Oswego, Department of Music:** Tyler Hall, Oswego, NY 13126; website www.oswego.edu.

**State University of New York, College at Potsdam, Crane School of Music:** Pierrepont Ave, Potsdam, NY 13676; website www.potsdam.edu.

**State University of New York, College at Purchase, Music Division:** Purchase, NY 10577; website www.purchase.edu.

**Stephen F. Austin State University, Department of Music:** PO Box 13043, Nacogdoches, TX 75962; tel. (936) 468-4602; fax (936) 468-5810; e-mail randerson@sfasu.edu; website www.music.sfasu.edu; Chair, Dept of Music: Ronald E. Anderson.

**Stetson University, School of Music:** De Land, FL 32720; website www.stetson.edu.

**Sul Ross State University, Department of Music:** Alpine, TX 79832; website www.sulross.edu.

**Susquehanna University, Department of Music:** Selinsgrove, PA 17870; website www.susqu.edu.

**Sweet Briar College, Department of Music:** Sweet Briar, VA 24595; website www.sbc.edu.

**Syracuse University, School of Music:** 215 Crouse College, Syracuse, NY 13244; website www.syr.edu.

**Tanglewood Music Center:** c/o Boston Symphony Orchestra, 301 Massachusetts Avenue, Boston, MA 02115; tel. (617) 638-9230; fax (617) 638-9342; e-mail tmc@bso.org; website www.bso.org.

**Taylor University, Department of Music:** Upland, IN 46989.

**Tennessee State University, Department of Music:** 3500 John A Merritt Blvd, Nashville, TN 37203; website www.tnstate.edu.

**Tennessee Technological University, Department of Music:** PO Box 5045, Cookeville, TN 38505; website www.tntech.edu.

**Tennessee Temple University, Department of Music:** 1815 Union Ave, Chattanooga, TN 37404; website www.tntemple.edu.

**Tennessee Wesleyan College, Department of Music:** PO Box 40, Athens, TN 37303; website www.tnwcnet.edu.

**Texarkana College, Department of Music:** Texarkana, TX 75501.

**Texas A & I University, Department of Music:** PO Box 174, Kingsville, TX 78363.

**Texas A & M University, Department of Music:** Commerce, TX 75428; website www.tamu-commerce.edu.

**Texas Christian University, School of Music:** PO Box 297500, Fort Worth, TX 76129.

**Texas State University at San Marcos, School of Music:** San Marcos, TX 78666; website www.swt.edu.

**Texas Technical University, School of Music:** PO Box 4239, Lubbock, TX 79409; website www.ttu.edu.

**Texas Wesleyan University, School of Fine Arts:** Fort Worth, TX 76105.

**Texas Woman's University, Performing Arts Department:** PO Box 23865, Denton, TX 76204; website www.twu.edu.

**Towson State University, Department of Music:** Baltimore, MD 21204.

**Trenton State College, Department of Music:** Hillwood Lakes, CN4700, Trenton, NJ 08650.

**Trinity University, Department of Music:** 715 Stadium Dr., San Antonio, TX 78284.

**Troy State University, School of Fine Arts:** Music Department, Long Hall, Troy, AL 36082.

**Truman State University, Fine Arts Division:** Kirksville, MO 63501; tel. 1 660 785 4000; website www.truman.edu.

**Tufts University, Department of Music:** 20 Professors Row, Medford, MA 02155.

**Tulane University-Newcomb College, Department of Music:** Dixon Hall, New Orleans, LA 70118; website www.tulane.edu.

**Union University, Department of Music:** 2447 Highway 45 Bypass, Jackson, TN 38305.

**University of Akron, School of Music:** 302 E Buchtel, Akron, OH 44325; website www.uakron.edu.

**University of Alabama at Birmingham, Department of Music:** 401 Humanities Building, Birmingham, AL 35294; website www.uab.edu.

**University of Alabama, School of Music:** PO Box 2876, Tuscaloosa, AL 35487; tel. 1 205 348 6010; website www.ua.edu.

**University of Alaska, Anchorage, Music Department:** 3211 Providence Dr., Anchorage, AK 99508; tel. 1 907 786 1800; website www.uaa.alaska.edu.

**University of Alaska, Fairbanks, Music Department:** 301 Fine Arts Complex, Fairbanks, AK 99775; website www.alaska.edu.

**University of Arizona, School of Music:** Tucson, AZ 85721; tel. 1 520 621 2211; website www.arizona.edu.

**University of Arkansas at Little Rock, Department of Music:** 2801 South University, Little Rock, AR 72204; website www.ualr.edu.

**University of Arkansas, Department of Music:** 201A Music Building, Fayetteville, AR 72701; website www.uark.edu.

**University of Bridgeport, Department of Music:** Arnold Bernhard Arts-Humanities Center, Bridgeport, CT 06602; tel. 1 203 576 4000; website www.bridgeport.edu.

**University of California, Berkeley, Department of Music:** Morrison Hall, Berkeley, CA 94720; website www.berkeley.edu.

**University of California, Davis, Department of Music:** 112 Music Building, Davis, CA 95616; website www.ucdavis.edu.

**University of California, Irvine, School of Fine Arts, Department of Music:** Irvine, CA 92717; website www.uci.edu.

**University of California, Los Angeles (UCLA), Department of Music:** 405 Hilgard Ave, Los Angeles, CA 90024; website www.ucla.edu.

**University of California, Riverside, Department of Music:** 900 University Ave, Riverside, CA 92521; website www.ucr.edu.

**University of California, San Diego (UCSD), Department of Music:** B-026, La Jolla, CA 92093; website www.ucsd.edu.

**University of California, Santa Barbara, Department of Music:** Santa Barbara, CA 93106; website www.ucsb.edu.

**University of California, Santa Cruz, Department of Music:** Porter College, Santa Cruz, CA 95064; website www.ucsc.edu.

**University of Central Arkansas, Department of Music:** PO Box 1726, Conway, AR 72032; tel. (501) 450-3163; fax (501) 450-5773; e-mail jshowell@uca.edu; website www.uca.edu/cfac/music.

**University of Central Florida, Department of Music:** Orlando, FL 32816; website www.ucf.edu.

**University of Chicago, Department of Music:** 5845 S Ellis Ave, Chicago, IL 60637; website www.uchicago.edu.

**University of Cincinnati, College-Conservatory of Music:** Cincinnati, OH 45221; website www.uc.edu.

**University of Colorado, College of Music:** PO Box 301, Boulder, CO 80309; website www.colorado.edu.

**University of Connecticut, Department of Music:** PO Box U-12, Room 228, 876 Coventry Road, Storrs, CT 06269; website www.uconn.edu.

**University of Dayton, Music Division:** 300 College Park Dr., Dayton, OH 45469; website www.udayton.edu.

**University of Delaware, Department of Music:** Newark, DE 19716; website www.udel.edu.

**University of Denver, Lamont School of Music:** 7111 Mountview, Denver, CO 80220; website www.du.edu.

**University of Evansville, Department of Music:** 1800 Lincoln Ave, Evansville, IN 47722; website www.evansville.edu.

**University of Florida, Department of Music:** 130 MUB, Gainesville, FL 32611; website www.ufl.edu.

**University of Georgia, School of Music:** 203 Fine Arts Building, Athens, GA 30602; website www.uga.edu.

**University of The Hartt School:** University of Hartford, 200 Bloomfield Avenue, West Hartford, CT 06117; tel. (860) 768-4454; fax (860) 768-4441; e-mail Harttadm@hartford.edu; website www.hartford.edu/hartt; f. 1920 as Julius Hartt, Moshe Paranov and Associated Teachers; one of three founding institutions of the University of Hartford in 1957; performing arts conservatory with degree programmes in music, dance and theatre; also a community arts school.

**University of Hawaii, Department of Music:** 2411 Dole St, Honolulu, HI 96822; website www.hawaii.edu.

**University of Houston, School of Music:** 4800 Calhoun, Houston, TX 77204; website www.uh.edu.

**University of Illinois at Chicago, Department of Music:** PO Box 4348, Chicago, IL 60680; website www.uic.edu.

**University of Illinois, School of Music:** 1114 W Nevada Street, Urbana, IL 60801; website www.music.uiuc.edu.

**University of Indianapolis:** 1400 E Hanna, Indianapolis, IN 46227; website www.uindy.edu.

**University of Iowa, School of Music:** Iowa City, IA 52242; website www.uiowa.edu.

**University of Kansas, School of Fine Arts:** 452 Murphy St, Lawrence, KS 66045; website www.ku.edu.

**University of Kentucky, School of Music:** 105 Fine Arts Building, Lexington, KY 40506; website www.uky.edu.

**University of Louisville, School of Music:** Louisville, KY 40292; website www.louisville.edu.

**University of Lowell, College of Music:** 1 University Ave, Lowell, MA 01854; website www.uml.edu.

**University of Maine, Department of Music:** 123 Lord Hall, Orono, ME 04469; website www.umaine.edu.

**University of Maryland Eastern Shore, Fine Arts Department, Music Division:** Princess Anne, MD 21853.

**University of Maryland, Department of Music:** Tawes Fine Arts Building, College Park, MD 20742; website www.umd.edu.

**University of Massachusetts at Boston, Department of Music:** Harbor Campus, Boston, MA 02125; website www.umb.edu.

**University of Massachusetts, Music and Dance Department:** Fine Arts Center, Amherst, MA 01003; website www.umass.edu.

**University of Miami, School of Music:** PO Box 248165, Coral Gables, FL 33124; website www.miami.edu.

**University of Michigan, School of Music:** Ann Arbor, MI 48109; website www.umich.edu.

**University of Minnesota, Duluth, Department of Music:** 10 University Dr., Duluth, MN 55812; website www.d.umn.edu.

**University of Minnesota, Minneapolis, School of Music:** 2106 Fourth St S, Minneapolis, MN 55455; website www.umn.edu.

**University of Mississippi, Department of Music:** 132 Meek Hall, University, MS 38677; website www.olemiss.edu.

**University of Missouri at Columbia, Department of Music:** 140 Fine Arts Center, Columbia, MO 65211; website www.missouri.edu.

**University of Missouri at Kansas City (UMKC), Conservatory of Music:** 4949 Cherry, Kansas City, MO 64110; website www.umkc.edu.

**University of Missouri at St Louis, Department of Music:** 8001 Natural Bridge, St Louis, MO 63121; tel. 1 314 516 5000; website www.umsl.edu.

**University of Montana, Department of Music:** Missoula, MT 59812; website www.umt.edu.

**University of Montevallo, College of Fine Arts:** Station 6670, Montevallo, AL 35115; website www.montevallo.edu.

**University of Nebraska at Lincoln, School of Music:** Westbrook Music Building 120, Lincoln, NE 68588; website www.unl.edu.

**University of Nebraska at Omaha, Department of Music:** College of Fine Arts, 60 and Dodge St, Omaha, NE 68182; website www.unomaha.edu.

**University of Nevada, Las Vegas, Department of Music:** 4505 S Maryland Parkway, Las Vegas, NV 89154; website www.unlv.edu.

**University of Nevada, Reno, Department of Music:** Reno, NV 89557; website www.unr.edu.

**University of New Hampshire, Department of Music:** Paul Creative Arts Center, 30 College Road, Durham, NH 03824; tel. (603) 862-2404; fax (603) 862-3155; e-mail music.info@unh.edu; website www.unh.edu/music; Dept Chair: Mark DeTurk.

**University of New Mexico, Department of Music:** College of Fine Arts, Albuquerque, NM 87131; website www.unm.edu.

**University of New Orleans, Department of Music:** Lakefront, New Orleans, LA 70148; website www.uno.edu.

**University of North Carolina at Chapel Hill, Department of Music:** Hill Hall CB3320, Chapel Hill, NC 27599; tel. 1 919 962 2211; website www.unc.edu.

**University of North Carolina at Charlotte, Performing Arts Department:** Charlotte, NC 28223; website www.uncc.edu.

**University of North Carolina at Greensboro, School of Music:** Greensboro, NC 27412; website www.uncg.edu.

**University of North Carolina at Wilmington, Creative Arts Department:** 601 S College Road, Wilmington, NC 28403; website www.uncwil.edu.

**University of North Dakota, Department of Music:** PO Box 8124, Grand Forks, ND 58202; website www.und.edu.

**University of North Texas, School of Music:** PO Box 13887, Denton, TX 76203; website www.unt.edu.

**University of Northern Colorado, School of Music:** Greeley, CO 80639; website www.unco.edu.

**University of Northern Iowa, School of Music:** Cedar Falls, IA 50614; website www.uni.edu.

**University of Notre Dame, Department of Music:** Crowley Hall of Music, Notre Dame, IN 46556; website www.nd.edu.

**University of Oklahoma, School of Music:** 560 Parrington Oval, No 109A, Norman, OK 73019; website www.ou.edu.

**University of Oregon, School of Music:** Eugene, OR 97403-1225; tel. (541) 346-3761; fax (541) 376-0723; e-mail mushelp@oregon.uoregon.edu; website www.uoregon.edu.

**University of Pennsylvania, Department of Music:** 201 S 34th St, Philadelphia, PA 19104; website www.upenn.edu.

**University of Pittsburgh, Department of Music:** 110 Music Building, Pittsburgh, PA 15260; website www.pitt.edu.

**University of Portland, Performing and Fine Arts Department:** 5000 N Williamette Blvd, Portland, OR 97203; website www.up.edu.

**University of Puerto Rico, Department of Music:** PO Box 23335, Rio Piedras, PR 00931; website www.upr.clu.edu.

**University of Puget Sound, School of Music:** 1500 North Warner, Tacoma, WA 98416; website www.ups.edu.

**University of Redlands, School of Music:** PO Box 3080, Redlands, CA 92373; website www.redlands.edu.

**University of Rhode Island, Department of Music:** Fine Arts Center, Kingston, RI 02881; website www.uri.edu.

**University of Richmond, Department of Music:** Richmond, VA 23173; website www.urich.edu.

**University of St Thomas, Department of Music:** 2115 Summit Ave, St Paul, NB 55105; tel. 1 651 962 5000; website www.stthomas.edu.

**University of Sciences and Arts of Oklahoma:** PO Box 3388, Chickasha, OK 73018.

**University of South Alabama, Department of Music:** 9 Faculty Court E, Mobile, AL 36688; website www.southalabama.edu.

**University of South Carolina, School of Music:** Columbia, SC 29208; website www.sc.edu.

**University of South Dakota, Department of Music:** Vermillion, SD 57069; tel. (605) 677-5274; fax (605) 677-5988; e-mail lschon@usd.edu; website www.usd.edu/cfa/music; Chair: Dr Larry B. Schon.

**University of South Florida, Department of Music:** Tampa, FL 33620; website www.usf.edu.

**University of Southern California (USC), School of Music:** University Park, Los Angeles, CA 90089; website www.usc.edu.

**University of Southern Maine, Department of Music:** College Ave, 102A Corthell Hall, Gorham, ME 04038; website www.usm.maine.edu.

**University of Southern Mississippi, School of Music:** PO Box 5081, Southern Station, Hattiesburg, MS 39406; website www.usm.edu.

**University of Southwestern Louisiana, School of Music:** PO Box 41207, Lafayette, LA 70505.

**University of Tampa, Music Division:** 401 W J F Kennedy Blvd, Tampa, FL 33606; website www.utampa.edu.

**University of Tennessee at Chattanooga, Cadek Department of Music-1451:** 308 Fine Arts Center, 615 McCallie Avenue, Chattanooga, TN 37403-2598; tel. (423) 425-4601; fax (423) 425-4603; website www.utc.edu/music.

**University of Tennessee at Knoxville, Department of Music:** 1741 Volunteer Blvd, Knoxville, TN 37996; website www.utk.edu.

**University of Tennessee at Martin, Department of Music:** 232 Fine Arts Building, Martin, TN 38238; website www.utm.edu.

**University of Texas at Arlington, Department of Music:** PO Box 19105, Arlington, TX 76019; website www.uta.edu.

**University of Texas at Austin, Department of Music:** Austin, TX 78712; website www.utexas.edu.

**University of Texas at El Paso, Department of Music:** University Ave at Hawthorne, El Paso, TX 79968; website www.utep.edu.

**University of Texas at San Antonio, Music Division:** San Antonio, TX 78285; website www.utsa.edu.

**University of the Pacific, Conservatory of Music:** 3601 Pacific Ave, Stockton, CA 95211; website www.uop.edu.

**University of Toledo, Department of Music:** 2801 W Bancroft St, Toledo, OH 43606; website www.utoledo.edu.

**University of Tulsa, Department of Music:** 600 South College, Tulsa, OK 74104; website www.utulsa.edu.

**University of Utah, Department of Music:** 204 Gardner Hall, Salt Lake City, UT 84112; website www.utah.edu.

**University of Vermont, Department of Music:** Music Building, Redstone Campus, Bulington, VT 05405; website www.uvm.edu.

**University of Virginia, Department of Music:** 112 Old Cabell Hall, Charlottesville, VA 22903; website www.virginia.edu.

**University of Washington, School of Music:** DN-10, Seattle, WA 98195; website www.washington.edu.

**University of West Florida, Department of Music:** Pensacola, FL 32514; website www.uwf.edu.

**University of Wisconsin, Eau Claire, Department of Music:** Fine Arts Center, Eau Claire, WI 54701; website www.uwec.edu.

**University of Wisconsin, Green Bay, Department of Music:** Green Bay, WI 54301; website www.uwgb.edu.

**University of Wisconsin, La Crosse, Department of Music:** 234 Fine Arts Building, La Crosse, WI 54601; website www.uwlax.edu.

**University of Wisconsin, Madison, School of Music:** 455 Park St, Madison, WI 53706; website www.wisc.edu.

**University of Wisconsin, Milwaukee, Department of Music:** PO Box 413, Milwaukee, WI 53201; website www.uwm.edu.

**University of Wisconsin, Oshkosh, Department of Music:** Arts and Communication Center, 800 Algoma Blvd, Oshkosh, WI 54901; website www.uwosh.edu.

**University of Wisconsin, Parkside, Department of Music:** 285 Communication Arts Building, Kenosha, WI 53141; website www.uwp.edu.

**University of Wisconsin, Platteville, Department of Music:** 1 University Plaza, Platteville, WI 53818; website www.uwplatt.edu.

**University of Wisconsin, River Falls, Department of Music:** River Falls, WI 54022; website www.uwrf.edu.

**University of Wisconsin, Stevens Point, Department of Music:** Stevens Point, WI 54481; website www.uwsp.edu.

**University of Wisconsin, Superior, Department of Music:** Superior, WI 54880; website www.uwsuper.edu.

**University of Wisconsin, Whitewater, Department of Music:** 800 W Main St, Whitewater, WI 53190; website www.uww.edu.

**University of Wyoming, Department of Music:** PO Box 3037, University Station, Laramie, WY 82071; tel. 307 766 1121; website www.uwyo.edu.

**Utah State University, Department of Music:** Logan, UT 84322; website www.usu.edu.

**Valdosta State University, Department of Music:** N Patterson St, Valdosta, GA 31698; website www.valdosta.edu.

**Valley City State University, Department of Music:** Valley City, ND 58072; website www.vcsu.edu.

**Valparaiso University, Department of Music:** Valparaiso, IN 46383; website www.valpo.edu.

**Vanderbilt University, Blair School of Music:** 2400 Blakemore Ave, Nashville, TN 37212; website www.vanderbilt.edu.

**VanderCook College of Music:** 3209 S Michigan Ave, Chicago, IL 60616; website www.vandercook.edu.

**Vassar College, Department of Music:** Raymond Ave, Poughkeepsie, NY 12601; website www.vassar.edu.

**Virginia Commonwealth University, Department of Music:** 922 Park Ave, Richmond, VA 23284; website www.vcu.edu.

**Virginia Polytechnic Institute and State University, Department of Music:** 256 Lane, Blacksburg, VA 24061; website www.vt.edu.

**Virginia School of the Arts, Department of Music:** 2240 Rivermont Ave, Lynchburg, VA 24503.

**Virginia State University, Department of Music:** PO Box 7, Petersburg, VA 23803.

**Viterbo University, Department of Music:** 815 S Ninth St, La Crosse, WI 54601; website www.viterbo.edu.

**Wagner College, Department of Music:** 631 Howard Ave, Staten Island, NY 10301; website www.wagner.edu.

**Wake Forest University, Department of Music:** 7345 Reynolds Station, Winston-Salem, NC 27109; website www.wfu.edu.

**Walla Walla College, Department of Music:** College Place, WA 99324; website www.wwc.edu.

**Warren M Angell College of Fine Arts:** Oklahoma Baptist University, 500 West University, Shawnee, OK 74801.

**Wartburg College, Department of Music:** PO Box 1003, 222 Ninth St NW, Waverly, IA 50677; tel. 1 800 772 2085; website www.wartburg.edu.

**Washburn University, Department of Music:** 17 and College, Topeka, KS 66621; website www.washburn.edu.

**Washington State University, School of Music:** Kimbrough Music Building, Pullman, WA 99164; website www.wsu.edu.

**Washington University, Department of Music:** Campus Box 1032, 1 Brookings Dr., St Louis, MO 63130; website www.wustl.edu.

**Wausau Conservatory of Music:** 404 Seymour St, PO Box 606, Wausau, WI 54402; tel. 1 715 845 6279; fax 1 715 842 3527; website www.wausauconservatory.org.

**Wayne State University, Department of Music:** 5451 Cass Ave, Room 105 Music, Detroit, MI 48202; website www.wayne.edu.

**Weber State University, Performing Arts Department:** 1905 University Circle, Odgen, UT 84408-1905; tel. (801) 626-6991; fax (801) 626-6811; e-mail mpalumbo@weber.edu; website www.weber.edu; Chair, Dept for Performing Arts: Michael A. Palumbo.

**Webster University, Department of Music:** 470 E Lockwoof, St Louis, MO 63119; website www.webster.edu.

**Wesleyan University, Department of Music:** Middletown, CT 06457; website www.wesleyan.edu.

**West Georgia College, Department of Music:** Carrolton, GA 30118.

**West Liberty State College, Department of Music:** Hall of Fine Arts, West Liberty, WV 26074; website www.wlsc.edu.

**West Texas A & M University, Music and Dance Department:** PO Box 870, Canyon, TX 79016; website www.wtamu.edu.

**West Virginia State College, Department of Music:** PO Box 4, Institute, WV 25112; website www.wvsc.edu.

**West Virginia University, Department of Music:** Creative Arts Center, Morgantown, WV 26506; website www.wvu.edu.

**West Virginia Wesleyan College, Department of Music:** PO Box 40, Buckhannon, WV 26201; website www.wvwc.edu.

**Westchester Conservatory of Music:** 20 Soundview Ave, White Plains, NY 10606; website www.musicconservatory.org.

**Western Carolina University, Department of Music:** Cullowhee, NC 28723; website www.wcu.edu.

**Western Connecticut State University, Department of Music:** 181 White St, Danbury, CT 06810; website www.wcsu.edu.

**Western Illinois University, Department of Music:** 122 Browne Hall, Macomb, IL 61455; website www.wiu.edu.

**Western Kentucky University, Department of Music:** 351 Fine Arts Center, Bowling Green, KY 42101; website www.wku.edu.

**Western Michigan University, School of Music:** Kalamazoo, MI 49008; website www.wmich.edu.

**Western Oregon University, Creative Arts Division:** Monmouth, OR 97361; website www.wou.edu.

**Western Washington University, Department of Music:** PA 273, Bellingham, WA 98225; website www.wwu.edu.

**Westminster Choir College:** Rider University, 101 Walnut Lane, Princeton, NJ 08540; website www.rider.edu/westminster.

**Westminster College, Department of Music:** New Wilmington, PA 16172; website www.westminster.edu.

**Wheaton College, Conservatory of Music:** 501 College Avenue, Wheaton, IL 60187; tel. (630) 752-5099; fax (630) 752-5341; e-mail music@wheaton.edu; website www.wheaton.edu/conservatory.

**Whitman College, School of Music:** 345 Boyer Ave, Walla Walla, WA 99362; website www.whitman.edu.

**Whitworth College, Department of Music:** Spokane, WA 99251; website www.whitworth.edu.

**Wichita State University, School of Music:** 1845 Fairmont, Wichita, KS 67260-0053; tel. (316) 978-3500; fax (316) 978-3625; website www.wichita.edu/music/index.asp.

**Willamette University, Department of Music:** 900 State St, Salem, OR 97301; website www.williamette.edu.

**William Carey College, Winters School of Music:** Tuscan Ave, Hattiesburg, MS 39401; website www.wmcarey.edu.

**William Jewell College, Department of Music:** Liberty, MO 64068; website www.jewell.edu.

**William Paterson College of New Jersey, Department of Music:** 300 Pompton Road, Wayne, NJ 07470.

**Williams College, Department of Music:** Bernhard Music Center, Williamstown, MA 01267.

**Wilmington Music School:** 4101 Washington St, Wilmington, DE 19802; website www.wilmingtonmusic.org.

**Wingate University, Fine Arts Department:** Wingate, NC 28174; website www.wingate.edu.

**Winona State University, Department of Music:** 145 Performing Arts Center, Winona, MN 55987; website www.winona.msus.edu.

**Winston-Salem State University, Department of Music:** PO Box 13176, Winston-Salem, NC 27101; website www.wssu.edu.

**Winthrop University, Department of Music:** 112 Conservatory of Music, Rock Hill, SC 29733.

**Wisconsin Conservatory of Music:** 1584 N Prospect Ave, Milwaukee, WI 53202; tel. 1 414 276 5760; fax 1 414 276 6076; website www.wcmusic.org.

**Wittenberg University, Department of Music:** Springfield, OH 45501; website www.wittenberg.edu.

**Wright State University, Department of Music:** Dayton, OH 45435; website www.wright.edu.

**Xavier University of Louisiana, Department of Music:** 7352 Palmetto St, New Orleans, LA 70125; website www.xula.edu.

**Xavier University, Department of Music:** 3800 Victory Parkway, Cincinnati, OH 45207; website www.xu.edu.

**Yale University, School of Music:** PO Box 2104A, Yale Station, New Haven, CT 06520; website www.yale.edu.

**Youngstown State University, Dana School of Music:** 1 University Plaza, Youngstown, OH 44555-3636; tel. (330) 941-3636; website www.ysu .edu; Dir: Dr Michael R. Crist.

## Uruguay

**Conservatorio Falleri-Balzo:** Avda Uruguay 994, Montevideo.

**Conservatorio Nacional de Música:** 25 De Mayo 692, Montevideo.

**Escuela Universitaria de Música:** Paysandu 843, Montevideo.

## Venezuela

**Academia de Música Fischer:** Edificio Léon de San Marco, Avda Ciencias y Calle Risques, Los Chaguaramos, Caracas.

**Academia de Música Padre Sojo:** 4A Avda Trans, 8AY9A, PO Box 60479 Este, Caracas.

**Conservatorio Nacional de Música:** Juan José Landeata, Urbanización Campo Alegre, 4A Avda, Caracas.

**Conservatorio Italiano de Música:** Calle Montesacro, Colinas de Bello Monte, Caracas.

**Escuela de Música Lino Gallardo:** Avda Principal de la Castellana, Entre 21 y 3a Transversales, Quinta Yudith, Caracas.

**Escuela Nacional de Música Jose Angel Lamas:** Veroes a Santa Capilla, Avda Urdaneta, Caracas.

**Escuela Nacional de Opera:** Este 2 con Sur 25, El Conde, Los Caobos, Caracas.

## Viet Nam

**Vietnamese Institute for Musicology:** 32 Nguyen Thai Hoc, Ha Noi; tel. (84-4) 845-7368; fax (84-4) 843-4953; e-mail musicology@hn.vnn.vn; website www.vn-style.com/vim.

# The Europa World of Learning ONLINE

## www.worldoflearning.com

## Available Now

Locate academic institutions of every type, world-wide

- Universities and Colleges
- Schools of Art, Music and Architecture
- Learned Societies
- Research Institutes
- Libraries and Archives
- Museums and Art Galleries

Instant access to educational contacts around the globe

- Professors
- University Chancellors and Rectors
- Deans
- Librarians
- Curators
- Directors

Additional features of The Europa World of Learning online

- Multiple-user facility available
- A full range of sophisticated search and browse functions
- Regularly updated

Free 30-day trial available
For further information e-mail: info.europa@tandf.co.uk